THE AUTHORITY SINCE 1868

THE WORLD ALMANAC
AND BOOK OF FACTS
1991

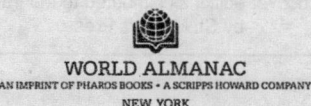

WORLD ALMANAC
AN IMPRINT OF PHAROS BOOKS · A SCRIPPS HOWARD COMPANY
NEW YORK

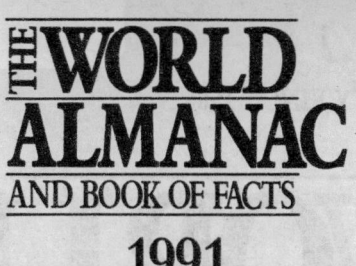

THE WORLD ALMANAC
AND BOOK OF FACTS
1991

Editor: Mark S. Hoffman
Associate Editor: June Foley **Senior Assistant Editor:** Thomas McGuire
Chronology & Special Features: Donald Young **Index:** Deborah G. Felder
Editorial Assistant: Aris Georgiadis

Pharos Books
Senior Vice President & Publisher: David Hendin
Vice President & Associate Publisher: Phyllis Henrici
Editor-in-Chief: Hana Umlauf Lane **Sales Manager:** Kevin McDonough
Publicity Manager: Martha Clarke **Director of Manufacturing:** Randy Lang

The editors acknowledge with thanks the many letters of helpful comment and criticism from readers of THE WORLD ALMANAC, and invite further suggestions and observations. Because of the volume of mail directed to the editorial offices, it is not possible to reply to each letter writer. However, every communication is read by the editors and all comments and suggestions receive careful attention. Inquiries regarding contents should be sent to: Editor, The World Almanac, 200 Park Avenue, New York, NY 10166.

THE WORLD ALMANAC is published annually in November.

THE WORLD ALMANAC does not decide wagers.

The first edition of THE WORLD ALMANAC, a 120-page volume with 12 pages of advertising, was published by the New York World in 1868, 123 years ago. Annual publication was suspended in 1876. Joseph Pulitzer, publisher of the New York World, revived THE WORLD ALMANAC in 1886 with the goal of making it a "compendium of universal knowledge." It has been published annually since then. In 1931, it was acquired by the Scripps Howard Newspapers; until 1951, it bore the imprint of the New York World-Telegram and thereafter, until 1967, that of the New York World-Telegram and Sun. It is now published in paper and clothbound editions by Pharos Books, a Scripps Howard company.

THE WORLD ALMANAC & BOOK OF FACTS 1991
Copyright© Pharos Books 1990
Library of Congress Catalog Card Number 4-3781
International Standard Serial Number (ISSN) 0084-1382
Pharos Books (softcover) ISBN 0-88687-578-1
Pharos Books (hardcover) ISBN 0-88687-580-3
Microform Edition since 1868: University Microfilms Intl.
Printed in the United States of America
The softcover and hardcover editions distributed to the trade in the United States
by St. Martin's Press.

WORLD ALMANAC
An Imprint of Pharos Books
A Scripps Howard Company
200 Park Avenue, New York, NY 10166

1991 HIGHLIGHTS

GENERAL INDEX

Addenda, Late News, Changes

Aerospace (p. 175)

The space shuttle *Discovery* had a successful 4-day mission, Oct. 6-10.

Awards

Broadcasting and Theater (p. 330)

Emmy Awards, by Academy of Television Arts and Sciences, for nighttime programs, 1989-90: Dramatic series: *L.A. Law,* NBC; actress: Patricia Wettig, *Thirtysomething,* ABC; actor: Peter Falk, *Columbo,* ABC; supporting actress: Marg Helgenberger, *China Beach,* ABC; actor: Jimmy Smits, *L.A. Law.* Comedy series: *Murphy Brown,* CBS; actress: Candice Bergen, *Murphy Brown;* actor: Ted Danson, *Cheers,* NBC; supporting actress: Bebe Neuwirth, *Cheers;* supporting actor: Alex Rocco, *The Famous Teddy Z,* CBS. Mini-series: *Drug Wars: The Camarena Story,* NBC; actress: Barbara Hershey, *A Killing in a Small Town,* CBS; actor: Hume Cronyn, *Age Old Friends,* HBO. Music-variety: *In*

Living Color, Fox; performer: Tracey Ullman, *The Tracey Ullman Show,* Fox. Special recognition: Jim Henson.

Miscellaneous (p. 331)

Country Music Awards, Entertainer: George Strait; single: "When I Call Your Name," Vince Gill; album: "Pickin' on Nashville," The Kentucky Headhunters; song (songwriters): "Where've You Been," Jon Vezner/Don Henry; female vocalist: Kathy Mattea; male vocalist: Clint Black; vocal group: The Kentucky Headhunters; Vocal duo: The Judds; vocal event: Keith Whitley and Lorrie Morgan; musician: Johnny Gimble, fiddle; horizon award: Garth Brooks; music video: "The Dance," Garth Brooks; Hall of Fame: Tennessee Ernie Ford.

Nobel Prizes (pp. 320-322)

(Each 1990 Nobel Prize included a cash award of around $710,000.)

Physiology or Medicine: Joseph E. Murray, a surgeon at the Brigham and Women's Hospital in Boston, who performed the first kidney transplants, and E. Donnall Thomas, of the Fred Hutchinson Cancer Research Center in Seattle, who transplanted bone marrow from one person to another, shared the award.

Physics: Richard E. Taylor, a Canadian professor at Stanford Univ., and Jerome I. Friedman and Henry W. Kendall, both of the Massachusetts Institute of Technology, shared the award for their "breakthrough in our understanding of matter" achieved by a series of experiments that confirmed the reality of quarks.

Chemistry: Elias James Corey, a Harvard Univ. professor, received the chemistry prize for developing new ways to synthesize complex molecules ordinarily found only in nature.

Peace: Pres. Mikhail S. Gorbachev of the Soviet Union won, in recognition of his initiatives in promoting international peace, including championing political change in Eastern Europe and helping to end the Cold War.

Literature: Octavio Paz became the first Mexican to win the Nobel Prize in Literature, for his poetry and essays, "impassioned writing with wide horizons, characterized by sensuous intelligence and humanistic integrity."

Memorial Prize in Economics: Three Americans, Harry M. Markowitz, of Baruch College, The City Univ. of New York; William F. Sharpe, Stanford Univ., and Merton H. Miller, The Univ. of Chicago, shared the prize for their pioneering theoretical insights into the economics of finance.

Miss America (p. 332)

Marjorie Judith Vincent, Miss Illinois, was named Miss America 1991.

Boxing (p. 920)

Evander Holyfield knocked out James (Buster) Douglas in the 3rd round to win the world heavyweight championship in Las Vegas, Oct. 25.

Census, 1990 (p. 34)

Early spot-checks by Census Bureau workers have found that some cities, including New York and Boston, have made the same kinds of mistakes (putting houses where they do not exist) that the bureau has been accused of making. The bureau said it would recanvass nearly 150,000 blocks containing more than 5.4 million housing units in response to local governments' challenges.

International Organizations (p. 781)

The Arab League voted to move its headquarters from Tunis back to Cairo.

Portugal is no longer a member of the European Free Trade Association. Liechtenstein is a member of the European Free Trade Association.

Nations of the World (pp. 698, 711, 718, 727, 728, 737, 740)

China: The newest census established that the nation's population is a bit more than 1.13 billion.

Germany: As of the closing date for this section, reunification had not yet taken place.

India: The post WWI history was mistakenly dropped; for details see *Index.*

Lebanon: Some 750 people were killed in a Syrian-lead offensive that toppled Michel Aoun, the Christian militia chief.

Liberia: Pres. Samuel K. Doe was killed by rebel forces, Sept. 10.

New Zealand: Prime Minister Geoffrey Palmer resigned, Sept. 4.

Pakistan: Prime Minister Benazir Bhutto was ousted, Aug. 6.

U.S. Government (p. 87)

Elizabeth Dole resigned as Sec. of Labor, Oct. 24.

U.S. Population (pp. 581, 591)

The correct figures for Greece, N.Y. are 75,136 (1970) and 81,367 (1980).

Census and Areas of Counties and States: The 1980 census was conducted on Apr. 1, 1980, not 1990.

Zip Codes (p.591)

The correct zip code for Green River, Wyoming is 82935.

Heroes of Young America: The Eleventh Annual Poll

Paula Abdul, the dancer, singer, and choreographer of pop music, was named the "Top Heroine" of Young America in *The World Almanac's* eleventh annual poll of high school students. The students in grades 8 through 12 were asked to select those individuals in public life they admired most. The schools chosen to participate represented a geographic cross-section of the United States. In addition to choosing a top hero/heroine, the teenagers were asked to make selections in 8 other categories as well as answering 10 general questions on entertainment and current events and leaders.

The Top Heroine/Hero

The selection of the 27-year-old Paula Abdul marks

the first time in the history of the poll that a woman was named as the person most admired. Ms. Abdul grew up in California's San Fernando Valley, where she was an A-student at Van Nuys High School. While attending California State Univ. at Northridge, Abdul became a cheerleader for the Los Angeles Lakers and quickly became their choreographer. She went on to become a choreographer and dance teacher for such notables as Janet Jackson, Aretha Franklin, and George Michael. Her debut album produced four number one singles—"Straight Up," "Forever Your Girl," "Cold Hearted," and "Opposites Attract." Ms. Abdul has received many entertainment awards and has also produced many hit videos.

The second place finisher was the write-in vote for

"Mom," while the write-in for "Dad" finished in fourth place. The third place winner was last year's top hero, Michael Jordan, the basketball star of the Chicago Bulls. In a tie for fifth place were first lady Barbara Bush and television talk show host Oprah Winfrey. For the first time, a political leader of a nation other than the U.S. finished in the top ten as South African Nelson Mandela placed sixth in the poll. Headline-grabbing real estate tycoon Donald Trump, who was the leading vote getter in the newsmaker category, placed seventh, and President George Bush was the eighth-place winner. Former top hero Tom Cruise finished ninth, followed by Janet Jackson in tenth place. Others who received support for top hero/heroine included Soviet leader Mikhail Gorbachev, Supreme Court Justice Sandra Day O'Connor, British Prime Minister Margaret Thatcher, Mother Theresa, and 13-year-old tennis player Jennifer Capriati.

Issues and Influential Individuals

According to the poll, the "most important public issue" facing 8th-12th graders is drug abuse, which received more than double the number of votes as the second and third choices of AIDS and environmental issues. The quality of education, racism, and teen pregnancy also received substantial consideration.

When asked to name the "foreign political leader you most admire," the teens narrowly chose Nelson Mandela over Mikhail Gorbachev. Others receiving support included Margaret Thatcher, Corazon Aquino, and Lech Walesa.

Best Friends and teachers were named as the "person most directly influential in your life" (other than parents).

Books, Sports, Songs, and TV Shows

The students chose S.E. Hinton's The Outsiders as their "all-time favorite book," followed by Stephen King's Pet Semetary, Harper Lee's To Kill a Mockingbird, and J.D. Salinger's The Catcher in the Rye.

The overwhelming choice for "favorite participation sport" was basketball, followed by volleyball, football, softball, baseball, and tennis.

When it came to "viewing sports events," the students' clear favorites were football and basketball, with baseball finishing a distant third.

The "favorite song of 1990" was M.C. Hammer's "U Can't Touch This." A close second was "Nothing Compares 2 U" by Sinead O'Connor. The "least favorite song of 1990" was "Hangin' Tough" by New Kids on the Block.

The runaway winner in the "favorite TV show of 1990" was "The Simpsons," which received 4-times as many votes as the second place finisher, "The Wonder Years." Finishing in third place was "The Cosby Show." The "least favorite TV show of 1990" was "Roseanne" with "Married With Children" coming in a close second.

Listed below are the top male and female vote-getters in each category. The winner is listed first.

Top Hero

Paula Abdul, singer, dancer, choreographer
Michael Jordan, basketball player, Chicago Bulls

Politicians and Newsmakers
Donald Trump, businessman
Sandra Day O'Connor, Supreme Court Justice
Artists, Writers, Filmmakers
Matt Groenig, "The Simpsons"
Judy Blume, Tiger Eyes
News and Sports Media
Barbara Walters, "20/20"
Tom Brokaw, NBC News
Sports
Michael Jordan, Chicago Bulls
Jennifer Capriati, tennis player

Music and Dance
Paula Abdul, singer/dancer
M.C. Hammer, rap singer
Comedy
Eddie Murphy, Harlem Nights
Roseanne Barr, "Roseanne"
Television Performers/Non-Comedy
Johnny Depp, "21 Jump Street"
Oprah Winfrey, "The Oprah Winfrey Show"
Movie Performers/Non-Comedy
Mel Gibson, "Lethal Weapon" series
Whoopi Goldberg, Ghost

Public Opinion Poll of Older Americans

A phone survey conducted for The World Almanac and Maturity News Service between Oct. 17-28, 1990 polled nearly 1,000 respondents aged 50 years and older concerning various public issues, individuals and historic events. A summary of the results follows:

1. Who do you consider to be the most influential political figure of your lifetime?—While John F. Kennedy received 25.8 percent of the total, Franklin D. Roosevelt was a close second with 21.4 percent. FDR received 30.3 percent of the vote from those aged 65 and over, and JFK totalled 41.8 percent from those between age 50-55.

2. What would you consider to be the most important political event of your lifetime?—JFK's assassination (13.3%) edged out the end of World War II (11.8%), and the tearing down of the Berlin Wall received a surprisingly low 3.5 percent.

3. What do you feel would be the most effective resolution to the current Middle East crisis?—Over 30 percent of the respondents said that the U.S. should continue to pressure allies for tougher sanctions against Iraq, while 22.2 percent said the U.S. should use military power to force Iraq out of Kuwait. Over 23 percent of the women polled said the U.S. should

gradually withdraw its troops and hope Iraq has learned its lesson.

4. Which living ex-president has conducted himself most appropriately and effectively since leaving office?—The overwhelming winner was Jimmy Carter (45.1%). Ronald Reagan (18.5%), Gerald Ford (14.5%), and Richard Nixon (9.0%) trailed Carter, whose approval rating is much higher since leaving office.

5. Which living ex-first lady has conducted herself most graciously and effectively since leaving office?—Like their husbands, Rosalynn Carter received the most votes (26.0%), with Nancy Reagan and Betty Ford placing second and third.

6. What is the best way to combat the growing problem of drug abuse and crime?—Almost half of the respondents (44.3%) said that the U.S. should offer more education and job training programs for youth; 22.6 percent said the military should be used to wipe out international drug supplies. A small percentage of those polled said the U.S. should offer more rehabilitation programs and build more and better prisons and hire more police.

1990 Census: Preliminary Results

The preliminary count for the nation's 1990 population, released in late August 1990, was about 245.8 million, based on the mail return of census forms and follow-up door-to-door head counts. The Census Bureau said that efforts to count people missed in those initial surveys would add at least 3 million people, bringing the total closer to the 250 million it had estimated earlier in the year.

The data showed that at least 55 percent of Americans now live in the South and West, up from 52 percent in 1980, and that 20 percent live in the Northeast, a 1.7 percent decrease from 1980. The Midwest also showed a decrease by approximately 2 percent with 24 percent of Americans now residing there.

The growth in the 1980s centered around metropolitan areas, with nearly 80 percent of the U.S. population now residing in or near a large city. While metropolitan areas were growing in population, rural areas lost more than 1 million people during the past decade. Reasons for the rural decline included the agricultural crises and general economic recession, particularly in the early 80s, which had a prolonged impact in states such as Iowa, North Dakota, Wyoming, and Louisiana.

Immigration

Almost 40 percent of the nation's population increase (23 million) was due to immigration, both legal and illegal, with 7-9 million immigrants (largely from Asia, Latin America, and the Caribbean) arriving between 1980-1990. This marked the largest impact on U.S. population by immigration since World War I. In California, as much as 30 percent of the state's growth was due to immigration. In New York, the estimated 1 million immigrants offset the out-migration and were responsible for its limited growth.

States

The preliminary 1990 census results showed that Nevada (49.1), Alaska (35.8), Arizona (33.1), and Florida (31.1) had the largest percentage increases in population since 1980. California, with an increase of 23.7 percent from 1980, and a population of 29,279,000, is the largest state with almost 12 percent of the total U.S. population. The state's growth of 5.6 million people nearly equaled the entire population of Massachusetts, as California now has more people than Canada or Australia. The second largest state remains New York with 17,627,000 (0.4% increase since 1980),

while Texas with a 1980-1990 increase of 18.3 percent is the third largest state with a population of 16,625,000. Almost 40 percent of the nation's population now resides in these three states.

The states that showed the largest percentage decreases in population from 1980 to 1990 were West Virginia (-8.6), Iowa (-5.1), and Wyoming (-4.3), while Washington D.C. showed a drop of 9.9 percent, losing 63,000 residents.

Cities

Among the 12 largest cities in 1990, New York (-0.5) Chicago (-9.3), Philadelphia (-8.6), and Detroit (-19.4) showed percentage decreases in 1980-1990 population. Los Angeles (15.3), Houston (0.9), San Diego (25.0), Dallas (9.6), Phoenix (23.0), San Antonio (17.9), San Jose (21.6), and Indianapolis (5.1) grew in population in the 1980s. During the decade, Los Angeles passed Chicago and became the country's second-largest city, and San Diego moved past Detroit and Dallas to become the sixth-largest. New York City is still the nation's largest city with 7,033,000 people, more than twice as many as Los Angeles (3,420,000).

Challenges to Preliminary Results

In mid-September 1990, New York City officials challenged the Census Bureau's counts, claiming that they had found 254,534 housing units that were not counted. They said that this finding solidified their claim that almost 1 million New York City residents had not been counted. In a formal challenge to the 1990 count, the city officials, using city records, aerial photographs, and data from utility companies, said the Census Bureau had missed five or more residences on nearly 12,000 of the more than 28,000 residential blocks in the city.

All of the 51 largest cities, plus one-seventh of the towns, counties, and cities in the U.S., challenged the Census Bureau's counts of their housing units. As many as 500,000 housing units, half of them in New York City, may have been overlooked, according to figures provided by the 15 largest cities. Census Bureau officials stated that they expect the preliminary results to rise as a result of some of the challenges. Census Bureau director, Barbara Everitt Bryant, appearing before a congressional committee in Sept. 1990, said that dwellings in 500,000 census blocks might be rechecked. The Bureau also stated that it had set aside money to recheck up to 2.1 million individual housing units.

1990 Census: Preliminary State Totals

Source: U.S. Bureau of the Census

Rank	State	1990	% change 1980-90	Rank	State	1990	% change 1980-90	Rank	State	1990	% change 1980-90
1	Cal.	29,279,000	23.7	19	Md.	4,733,000	12.2	36	Ut.	1,711,000	17.1
2	N.Y.	17,627,000	0.4	20	Minn.	4,359,000	6.9	37	Neb.	1,573,000	0.2
3	Tex.	16,825,000	18.3	21	La.	4,181,000	-0.6	38	N.M.	1,490,000	14.4
4	Fla.	12,775,000	31.1	22	Ala.	3,984,000	2.3	39	Me.	1,218,000	8.3
5	Pa.	11,764,000	-0.8	23	Ky.	3,665,000	0.1	40	Nev.	1,193,000	49.1
6	Ill.	11,325,000	-0.9	24	Az.	3,619,000	33.1	41	N.H.	1,103,000	19.8
7	Oh.	10,778,000	-0.2	25	P.R.	3,599,000	12.6	42	Ha.	1,095,000	13.5
8	Mich.	9,179,000	-0.9	26	S.C.	3,407,000	9.1	43	Id.	1,004,000	6.4
9	N.J.	7,617,000	3.4	27	Col.	3,272,000	13.2	44	R.I.	989,000	4.4
10	N.C.	6,553,000	11.4	28	Conn.	3,227,000	3.8	45	Mont.	794,000	0.9
11	Ga.	6,387,000	16.9	29	Okla.	3,124,000	3.3	46	S.D.	693,000	0.3
12	Va.	6,128,000	14.6	30	Ore.	2,828,000	7.4	47	Del.	658,000	10.8
13	Mass.	5,928,000	3.3	31	Ia.	2,767,000	-5.1	48	N.D.	634,000	-2.9
14	Ind.	5,499,000	0.2	32	Miss.	2,535,000	0.6	49	D.C.	575,000	-9.9
15	Mo.	5,079,000	3.3	33	Kan.	2,467,000	4.4	50	Vt.	560,000	9.6
16	Wis.	4,870,000	3.5	34	Ark.	2,337,000	2.2	51	Alas.	546,000	35.8
17	Wash.	4,827,000	16.8	35	W.V.	1,783,000	-8.6	52	Wy.	450,000	-4.3
18	Tenn.	4,822,000	5.0								

Projected Changes in Congressional Apportionment

Based on the Census Bureau's preliminary figures for 1990, these states will have changes in their congressional representation: Calif. (+7); Fla. (+4); Tex. (+3); Wash., Ariz., Ga., N.C., and Va. (+1 each); N.Y. (−3); Mich., Pa., Oh., and Ill. (−2 each); and W. Va., Ky., La., Kan., Ia., and Mon. (−1 each).

The World Almanac

and Book of Facts for 1991

The Top 10 News Stories

After a 45-year division into Communist and non-Communist states, the reunification of Germany was formalized on Oct. 3; 1990 also brought dramatic movements towards democratization in other Warsaw Pact nations.

Leaving Kuwait in ruins, Saddam Hussein's forces overran and annexed the oil-rich nation, which led to UN-backed economic sanctions against Iraq and U.S. military intervention to protect Saudi Arabia and American interests in the Persian Gulf.

Economic hardships, calls for independence among Soviet republics, and political dissent marked a year of domestic conflict; Pres. Mikhail Gorbachev, winner of the 1990 Nobel Peace Prize, attempted to move the USSR from a long history of Communist authoritarian rule to democracy and capitalism.

Xhosa, Zulu, and other South African tribes continued to clash in the wake of Nelson Mandela's release from prison and Pres. de Klerk's attempts to unify the nation and eliminate apartheid.

As economists predicted another recession and oil prices rose, the U.S. Congress worked out a budget that tried to deal with the growing deficit, taxation changes, unemployment, health care, and other domestic problems including the huge costs of the S&L crisis.

Navy, Army, Air Force, and Marine troops invaded Panama in Dec. 1989, as the U.S. overthrew the government of Manuel Noriega and arrested him on drug-trafficking charges.

Drug abuse, crime, racial tensions, and financial difficulties plagued large U.S. cities, while the 1990 Census reported an increase in homelessness and a decline in cities' population.

Exhibitions of Robert Mapplethorpe's photographs, 2 Live Crew's obscenity trial, NEA grants, and the new NC-17 movie rating were some of the particulars that exemplified the continuing debate over censorship and defining obscenity in the U.S.

Retiring after almost 34 years on the bench, Supreme Court Justice William Brennan was replaced by David Souter; abortion and civil rights issues were the focus of the Senate confirmation hearings.

HIV-2, a second strain of the AIDS virus originally found in West Africa, was found to be spreading; a report by the Centers for Disease Control estimated that 179,000-208,000 new cases of AIDS would be reported through the end of 1992.

The Decline of Communism

From the time of Karl Marx and Friedrich Engels in the 19th century, advocates of communism had written many books on the techniques that revolutionaries could utilize to overthrow capitalism and install a socialist economic system. In fact, a rather detailed blueprint was offered by the founders of communism and by Vladimir Lenin and others that included such evolutionary stages as the dictatorship of the proletariat, the withering away of the state, and so forth.

In 1990, the American writer George Will pointed out, however, that no one had ever written a book on the transfer of power in society from Communist authoritarian rule to a democracy. Nor had anyone ever offered a guide to the transition from a centrally planned economy to one driven by the demands of the marketplace.

The leaders of the nations of Eastern Europe and of the Soviet Union itself—still the putative mecca of world communism—could have benefitted from such a textbook in 1990, a year of surprise and shock in the shrinking Communist sphere, from Germany to Mongolia. In its absence, the leaders and street demonstrators in many countries proceeded to write the history of their times in a somewhat haphazard way. In Eastern Europe, only the elderly had much recollection of the meaning and implementation of democracy and a free-market economy. In the Soviet Union, with no relevant history at all, these concepts had no meaning. Therefore, despite some individual demonstrations of real statesmanship, the whole process of change seemed to some degree to be an exercise in which the blind were leading the blind.

In the now-discredited world of communist ideology, a comparative liberal was one so bold as to suggest that there was more than one road to socialism. It became apparent in 1990 that there were also several roads away from it, including a few cluttered with rough rocks and with branching byways that threatened to lead to dead ends.

The Soviet Union

The first Communist government had been established in Russia in 1917. Since then, leaders or would-be leaders of Marxist-Leninist states around the world had looked to the Soviet Union for guidance, and indeed the USSR, from Joseph Stalin to Nikita Khrushchev to Leonid Brezhnev, had exercised a form of command and control over governments in Eastern Europe, Asia, Latin America, and Africa that exceeded even the reach of the colonial empires of the 19th century. Even the schism with China in the 1960s had not jeopardized the Soviet Union's paramount role as the fountainhead of Communist thought and practice, backed up with nuclear muscle.

Hence, the inability of the Soviet system by 1990 to so much as put enough bread and meat on the tables of its citizens or cigarettes in their pockets exposed the ultimate bankruptcy of applied communism in the starkest way possible. But the travails of the Soviet Union went beyond the paralysis of industrial production and of agricultural planting and harvesting. The country, a jigsaw puzzle of 100 ethnic pieces, was at the point of falling apart. Almost all of the USSR's 15 constituent republics were demanding full independence or some degree of autonomy.

Whatever their grievances, the long-suffering people of the Soviet Union were prepared to make use of tools of resistance as diverse as rifles and the ballot box. A student of the Kremlin had once observed, "Nothing ever happens by accident in the Soviet Union." But in 1990, the process of "reform," whatever that meant, appeared to be out of anyone's control.

Pres. Mikhail Gorbachev, lionized in the West for allowing former Soviet satellites to choose their future course and for closing the books on the 40-year-old Cold War, lost popularity at home when he demonstrated a less sure hand in his efforts to create a better life for his people. A brilliant tactician in the arcane world of Kremlin politics, he survived many predictions that he would be overthrown, and it was instead many of his adversaries who disappeared from the upper echelons of the government and the Communist Party. But in the larger processes of governing, he was swept along by events, yielding to pressure when he had to, somehow conveying the impression that the crowd of citizens to his rear were following him, not chasing him.

Measured by his offical status in the party and the government, Gorbachev seemed firmly in control. As general secretary of the Communist Party, he held the post always recognized as the source of ultimate authority in the Soviet Union, and being president and chairman of the Defense Council made him perhaps less vulnerable to swift overthrow.

Apparently confident that his grip on the reins of power was secure, and equally confident that the country would not reject the party that had led it for 73 years, Gorbachev supported repeal of the provision in the Soviet Constitution granting the Communist Party a monopoly of political power. The party's Central Committee agreed to this change in February, and the Soviet Congress of People's Deputies followed suit in March. Yegor Ligachev, leader of the conservatives within the ruling party Politburo who resisted this and other Gorbachev reforms, protested in vain against the party being reduced to what he called a "shapeless organization, a political club."

No other political group seemed remotely ready to contest the Communist Party in nationwide elections, but it quickly became apparent that the party itself might break into factions. Liberals, working within the party, constantly pressing Gorbachev for more radical reform, had formed the Democratic Platform. They mobilized street demonstrations, and in March they scored some stunning upset victories in local elections, winning control of city councils in Moscow, Leningrad, and Kiev.

May began with an embarrassing (to the leadership) demonstration by thousands of marchers in Moscow's May Day Parade, who jeered those on the reviewing stand and called for radical reform. The month ended with the election of Boris Yeltsin as president of the Russian Republic, by far the largest of the 15 republics. Yeltsin, a radical gadfly whose career Gorbachev had sought to suppress, thus reemerged as a formidable threat to Gorbachev's leadership. The president's attacks on him had helped make Yeltsin a hero, a role he exploited. Neither an intellectual nor an ideologue, Yeltsin was a man of action who attacked Gorbachev as being timid and a lover of the perks of office. As a delegate from Moscow to the national legislature, Yeltsin had become an idol of the masses, and the presidency of Russia provided the platform to put his ideas into action. He favored a loose confederation for the USSR.

Yeltsin spoiled an otherwise successful—for Gorbachev—Congress of the Communist Party in July. Ligachev had denounced the draft platform for the 28th Congress with its references to the rights of the individual and the right to earned private property. Gorbachev was reelected general secretary and Ligachev was defeated for the second position in the party. A new Politburo was approved with the exclusion of most of its previous members—Gorbachev a notable exception—and the thrust of these changes was to strengthen the government at the expense of the party. But then Yeltsin renounced the party and walked out of the congress, and was joined by the mayors of Moscow and Leningrad.

In a curious footnote to the May summit meeting in the United States between Gorbachev and Pres. George Bush, White House Chief of Staff John Sununu agreed to go to Moscow to instruct the Soviets on the operation of a presidential office. Sununu, during his trip, dealt with such matters as scheduling, the flow of documents through the bureaucracy, and the techniques of decision-making and implementation of policy.

Unrest in the Republics

Paradoxically, as Gorbachev tightened his control at the top, the nation he governed began to crumble. Movements arose in almost all of the republics for some form of autonomy or even outright independence. During World War II, the formerly independent Baltic states of Estonia, Latvia, and Lithuania had been absorbed by the Soviet Union and these, the youngest "republics" of the USSR, were the most aggressive in seeking to exploit the loosening of the Communist Party's grip on the country. Citizens of the Baltics generally seemed more optimistic than the citizens elsewhere in the USSR that their agriculture and industry would revive once the burden of central planning imposed on them 50 years earlier was removed.

Gorbachev's trip in January to Vilnius, the capital of Lithuania, in an attempt to dissuade the Lithuania Communist Party from breaking with the mother party, was not a success. Candidates favoring independence for Lithuania ran strongly in elections to the Lithuanian parliament, and in March parliament voted unanimously for independence and then formed a noncommunist government. After Lithuania ignored a deadline to rescind the declaration, Gorbachev banned the sale or possession of firearms there, and a Soviet military convoy entered the capital. No shots were fired, but Soviet troops seized the headquarters of the Lithuanian Communist Party and Gorbachev stepped up the economic pressure, cutting off the flow of crude oil into Lithuania and shutting down 3 of 4 natural gas pipelines into the republic. Lithuania suspended enforcement of its declaration of independence in May, and talks with Moscow began. In June, the Lithuanian parliament agreed to suspend the declaration, and Moscow lifted the oil embargo.

Estonia and Latvia proceeded more cautiously, principally because their populations had been diluted by a substantial settlement of ethnic Russians who opposed secession. Estonia's parliament abolished the drafting of Estonians into the Soviet army and in May declared the birth of the Estonian Republic (dropping "Soviet Socialist" from the title). Latvia's parliament voted for secession in May, but it set no timetable for attaining that goal and avoided the brunt of Moscow's wrath.

Elsewhere, the Moldavian Republic, populated mostly by persons of Romanian descent, seemed eager to break away and join Romania. The Ukraine, the so-called breadbasket of the Soviet Union, and crucial to the economic well-being of the USSR, was divided on its future course, and was also split between adherents of the Roman Catholic and Russian Orthodox churches.

Unrest in other republics was punctuated by bursts of violence. Georgia, where a number of citizens demonstrating for independence were killed by soldiers in

1989, was quieter in 1990. But two neighboring republics, **Armenia** and **Azerbaijan**, fought each other openly. At issue was the region of Nagorno-Karabakh, and enclave populated by Armenians within Azerbaijan. In January, the Armenian parliament sought to integrate the economy of Nagorno-Karabakh into its own economy. Armenias are mostly Christian, the Azerbaijanis mostly Islamic. After Azerbaijanis attacked Armenians in Baku, the capital of Azerbaijan, and with guerrillas fighting each other in other locations, the Soviet government sent troops into Baku in January. The Azerbaijanis responded with a blockade, and 93 were reported killed in the ensuing fighting. The army prevailed, but at a price of profound hostility for Azerbaijan.

Blood was spilled in two other Central Asian republics. Party and government leaders resigned in **Tadzhikistan** after 18 people were killed in riots in February. In **Kirghizia**, 148 were reportedly killed in June in clashes between Uzbeks and Kirghiz citizens. Again, Soviet troops intervened.

The Red Army itself was wounded by the regional upheaval. Recruits from ethnic minorities had long been subjected to brutal hazing, and many soldiers had no stomach for firing on other Soviet citizens. Desertions and resistance to the draft became commonplace in some republics throughout the country.

Soviet Economy

Ironically, even as nationalist ties threatened to pull the Soviet Union apart, its diverse citizenry seemed united only in the common frustration at the system's failure to provide basic goods and services. Gorbachev had studied law, but had no training in economics. In the economic sphere as elsewhere, he had proved to be a rather cautious revolutionary, taking half steps that

disappointed some of his advisers. His objective was to reform the economic system, not scrap it. Five years into his era of *perestroika*, or the restructuring of Soviet institutions, the system of central planning was still in place. By early 1990, however, reforms were being drafted that would privatize most Soviet industry, sell small businesses to entrepreneurs, and lease large companies to their workers.

By late summer, shortages in stores were getting worse. Bread riots had played a part in bringing the Bolsheviks to power in 1917. In 1990, long bread lines were forming throughout Moscow, and the price of bread, when available, rose sharply. Elsewhere, crowds rioted and stormed through stores looking for scarce foodstuffs. Meanwhile, tons of grain were rotting in the fields because collective farms lacked equipment, fuel, and means of transportation. Gorbachev said farmers were withholding grain and ordered local officials to take it from them by force. Medicine, coal, and soap were also scarce.

The **Russian Republic**, under Yeltsin's leadership, responded to these circumstances with a 500-day plan that would see private property legalized, government subsidies abolished, price controls lifted, and the institution of private banks and a stock market. Meanwhile, Soviet Prime Minister Nikolai Ryzhkov had drawn up a more cautious plan that would preserve much of the central planning apparatus. But Gorbachev, in a candid statement to the Supreme Soviet in September, said, "The system is no longer there; it's gone." He supported an economic plan that would be a compromise between the Ryzkhov concept and the 500-day plan. Late in September, the Supreme Soviet agreed to work out the compromise, and at Gorbachev's request, it also granted the president emergency powers to put into effect new policies on wages, prices, finances, and the budget.

Reunification of Germany

The reunification of Germany, after a 45-year division of the German people into Communist and non-Communist states, was 1990's biggest headline from Eastern Europe. Political union came far more swiftly than most had expected, but full economic integration would clearly take longer.

In October 1989, Erich Honecker stepped down as leader of the Socialist Unity (Communist) Party in East Germany. His successor, Egon Krenz, who had declared, "Without the Communist Party, there is no German Democratic Republic," was unable to head off massive public demands for reform or removal of the regime. After East Germany opened its border with Czechoslovakia, thousands of East Germans sought permission to leave, and on Nov. 9 the East German government agreed to issue exit visas to those who asked for them. This was the day the **Berlin Wall** symbolically "came down," with young citizens of both east and west sitting atop it in celebration. Throngs of East Berliners flocked into the western sectors of the city to taste freedom and enjoy such Western pleasures as fast food and shopping.

The East German government collapsed, and the new premier, Hans Modrow, surpassed Krenz in popularity by calling for free elections and a multiparty system. The party was shaken up again, with Krenz departing, and parliament revoking the constitutional clause assuring the Communists a "leading role" in society. West German Chancellor Helmut Kohl called for confederation of the two Germanys. Public sentiment in East Germany soon rallied to this possibility, though a minority opposed any union with West Germany, preferring the security of the status quo and job guarantees available under communism.

The obstacles to reunion seemed massive, but with the cooperation of the U.S., England, France and the USSR, negotiations moved swiftly and agreement on the future of one German state became a shocking reality. Strong impetus for reunion came in March when Conservatives supported by Kohl won the East German parliamentary election. Modrow had favored a united nation that would be neutral militarily, but the West German government insisted that the new Germany be a part of NATO—as West Germany already was. In April, a noncommunist government was installed under Lothar de Maiziere, leader of the Christian Democratic Union. At a July meeting with Kohl, Gorbachev dropped his objection to a united Germany in NATO. At the same time, Kohl agreed to the continued presence of Soviet troops in East Germany for up to four years, and the promised limitations on Germany weaponry. West Germany and the USSR later signed a pact of "friendship and cooperation," and Bonn promised Moscow $10 billion in economic aid.

In still another breakthrough in July, the two Germanys and the four major allied powers of World War II guaranteed Poland's border with a united Germany. Thus, Poland would keep the former German territory awarded to it after World War II.

The details of economic union were troublesome but not insurmountable. In a treaty signed in May, the two Germanys established a unified monetary system using the West German mark as the sole official currency. The treaty, ratified by both parliaments, took effect July 1. East German marks were exchanged with the Deutsche Mark at rates of 1-1 or 2-1. The West German Bundesbank took control over East German monetary policy. East Germany was plugged into West

Germany's tax, pension, and unemployment-compensation systems.

For all the euphoria and fireworks that accompanied formal reunification on Oct. 3, the two parts of the new Germany remained quite different. East Germans had no experience with free democratic and economic institutions, and their economy, once perceived as the strongest in East Europe, was, in fact, in bad shape.

Manufactured goods were generally of poor quality, and East Germans, given a choice, spent their money on Western products. Unemployment in the East soared from almost nothing to 350,000 during the first eight months of 1990. Factories in the East were in disrepair and too few people had competent business skills.

Eastern Europe

In the other Warsaw Pact countries of Eastern Europe, new leaders were thrust to the fore and had to work out their destiny with far less outside assistance.

Romania's path to the future was the only one stained with bloodshed, and its route by late 1990 led only a short distance from standard Marxism-Leninism. Pres. Nicolae Ceausescu, in power for 24 years, was unanimously reelected Communist Party secretary in November 1989, but his days were numbered. The self-styled "Genius of the Carpathians" and "Danube of Thought" had squandered Romania's resources on grandiose public buildings and had sold off basic necessities of life, including textiles and chickens, to pay foreign debts. Ceausescu exercised ruthless control through the Securitate, 60,000 well-armed police who had better weapons than the army and who were fiercely loyal to the president. In a country where it was said that half of the people were spying on the other half, even typewriters were illegal.

News of the ferment in neighboring countries could not be kept out of Romania, and in December an incident occurred that quickly brought Romania into the maelstrom. A crowd in Timisoara, in Transylvania, protested the deportation of a Protestant minister who had supported the rights of ethnic Hungarians in the area. A demonstration for democracy emerged from this, and the army and Securitate moved in. A large number of civilians, later put at 95, were killed, and the spark fired up the whole country. Within days, Ceausescu was shouted down when he attempted to speak at a rally in Bucharest. He and his wife, Elena, also a powerful figure in the government, fled by helicopter and car, but were captured, tried in an unidentified location, and executed on Christmas day on charges of genocide, abuse of power, and theft. A mixed bag of former Communists, military officers, and students sought to form a government, the National Salvation Front, and Ion Iliescu, a former party official, was made interim president. The Securitate fought on for days, but eventually was subdued.

Amid the ensuing chaos, some reforms were introduced. Typewriters were back, food appeared on shelves, political prisoners were freed, and birth control was permitted again. Many citizens became convinced, however, that little had really changed, and some contended that the events of December had been nothing more than a coup by the Communist establishment against Ceausescu and his immediate circle, some of whom were later convicted of various charges. Large street protests were not matched by votes at the ballot box, however, and in the May election, the National Salvation Front turned back the challenge of a large number of parties, retaining about two thirds of the seats in parliament. Iliescu won about 85 percent of the vote for president.

In a scene reminiscent of the old regime, riot police attacked demonstrators in June, the protestors fought back, and four were killed and 200 injured. Then, 10,000 miners poured into Bucharest on Iliescu's appeal to save Romania from a "fascist rebellion," and sacked the headquarters of opposition parties.

Czechoslovakia's transition was accomplished virtually without violence, and its rejection of the past was more clear-cut. Here, a genuine popular hero emerged in Vaclav Havel, a dissident playwright who had been imprisoned by the Communists despite an international reputation based on plays that depicted misery under totalitarian rule. Havel organized an opposition group, Civic Forum, that began talks with the government in November 1989. Public protests in Prague grew swiftly, involving hundreds of thousands of people. Police brutality stirred the opposition. Confronted with the option of widespread repression, the party and the government backed down. Milos Jakes, the party leader, and 12 other members of the ruling Politburo resigned. General strikes and the power of Havel's moral leadership brought down the government as well, and by early December, Pres. Gustav Husak was out and the cabinet had a noncommunist majority.

Another popular figure, Alexander Dubcek, who had led the 1968 reform movement known as the Prague Spring, also came to the fore. His attempt to introduce "socialism with a human face" had been crushed by Soviet tanks. Both he and Havel aspired to lead the new Czechoslovakia, but Dubcek was, after all, still a Communist, and the majority of the population appeared to want a more thorough break with the past. Dubcek agreed to serve as chairman of parliament, and on December 29, Havel was elected president. Havel had said, "We want democracy, we want to rejoin the European Community, we want social justice and a free-market economy. We may be socialists, but without these things there can be no socialism."

Havel moved slowly in dealing with the entrenched bureaucracy, calling for forgiveness and saying he did not want a witch hunt. As the government explored options in moving to a market economy, and as the economy failed to respond to the desires of the people, Havel joined in blaming the Communists. In deference to the wishes of 5 million Slovaks, the country was formally renamed the Czech and Slovak Federal Republic. In June, Havel's party, Civic Forum, and its allied party easily won national parliamentary elections.

Poland had led the way to a new day in Eastern Europe with ten years of ferment created by the Solidarity labor movement, and a noncommunist government was in place by mid-1989. Poland also made bold moves in the economic sphere. In a country where food shortages had become the norm, the new government adopted a free-market economy in one leap. Price controls were lifted, and costs of basic commodities skyrocketed. The cost of gasoline doubled, and coal was up 600 percent. The government announced a timetable for "privatizing" state enterprises. This demonstration of commitment to radical reform produced an outpouring of economic aid from the United States and West Germany. As prices of food found their proper market level and the economy stabilized, a poll put the popularity of the government at 85 percent.

The pace was not fast enough, however, for Lech Walesa, the hero of the Solidarity movement, who announced in September that he would run for president. Tadeusz Mazowiecki, whom he had helped install as prime minister, also declared his candidacy for president. Pres. Wojciech Jarulzelski, a Communist who had run Poland until 1989, said he would not seek re-election.

In **Hungary,** another country in which Communist control had collapsed during 1989, elections to a national parliament were completed in April 1990. The center-right Democratic Forum and its allied parties captured almost 60 percent of the seats, while the Socialist (formerly Communist) party won only 8.5 percent of the seats.

Bulgaria also broke with its Stalinist past, but found both its government and economy in a state of uncertain transition. Pres. Todor Zhivkov, who as head of the Communist Party had run Bulgaria since 1954, resigned his presidency and party post in November 1989. In April, parliament approved free multiparty elections, which the Socialist (formerly Communist) Party won, but its margin over the opposition coalition was not overwhelming. Zhivkov's successor as president, Petar Mladenov, resigned in July after a videotape revealed that he had called for tanks to put down a pro-democracy demonstration the previous December. Parliament, in August, chose Zhelyu Zhelov, the opposition leader, who had been expelled from the Communist Party for questioning Lenin's theories, as president.

Bulgaria's economy suffered a setback when Iraq and the Soviet Union cut oil supplies. The economy was in decline in late 1990, with the rationing of electricity, gasoline, and some food. Bread was short in some areas, industrial production fell sharply, and drought reduced the grain harvests.

Albania, the smallest and by far most isolated of the East European countries, had long remained aloof even from its neighboring Communist "comrades," and yet it also made at least a cosmetic gesture toward reform in May. The courts were reorganized, the number of capital offenses reduced, restrictions on worship were relaxed (in the only nation in the world that had banned religion outright), and citizens were granted the right to obtain passports.

In July, police battled thousands of demonstrators in the capital, and, in apparent reaction, the regime removed hard-liners from the Workers' (Communist) Party Politburo. Albanians demanding the right to leave the country were granted their wish, and several thousand left for Italy and elsewhere.

Yugoslavia had broken away from Moscow's domination shortly after World War II, but had remained both Communist and authoritarian. In 1990, too, Yugoslavia began exploring the path toward democracy, but was plagued by the polyglot nature of its citizenry. A "nation" containing a number of ethnic groups, languages, and religions, Yugoslavia was in danger of fragmenting. To complicate matters, the 1974 constitution gave each of Yugoslavia's 6 republics virtual veto power over the Federal decision-making process. In Serbia, Croatia, and Slovenia, parliaments were drafting new constitutions, and the weakening of central authority made any forecast of the future difficult.

The turmoil in Eastern Europe contained several common features and trends. Despite the show of force in Lithuania, the days of Red Army tanks rolling through the streets of Budapest and Prague were over, and the change of commands occurred without Soviet intervention. Indeed, Gorbachev repeatedly made it explicitly clear that hard-liners who had previously enjoyed Moscow's support could not count on a rescue from Big Brother. The Soviet News Agency called Romania's Ceausescu "one of the most odious dictators of the 20th century."

When forced to leave Czechoslovakia on an early timetable, the soldiers of the Red Army were also obliged to take with them soil that they had contaminated with toxic chemicals and oil spills. In the Soviet Union, the soldiers faced a homecoming literally without homes, given the extent of the housing shortage. The East German army nearly fell apart, losing motivation and shrinking from 173,000 to 90,000 between November 1989 and March 1990, in large part through desertion. Some soldiers were assigned to civilian duty to replace refugees.

Communism Elsewhere

China was quiet in 1990, at least on the surface, with public protests a thing of the past after the tanks of the People's Army crushed the student-led demonstrations in Beijing in June 1989. China's elderly leaders did not relax their iron grip on the country, and no reforms were introduced. Martial law was lifted in January, but the adoption of other laws kept a lid on the population.

The **Mongolian People's Republic,** a vast and nearly empty land lying between the Soviet Union and China, stirred a bit in 1990. Jambyn Batmunh, general secretary of the Communist Party, announced in March that the party would work with others to seek political reform, and the party voted to drop its constitutional monopoly on power. Largely ignored by the world press, Mongolia pursued modest change in a communications vacuum.

Cuba was not swept up in the winds of change, after 31 years of tight Communist control under Fidel Castro. The economy was a shambles, and the regime was

forced to tighten food rations, but the availability of subsidized medical care, housing, and education apparently was enough to satisfy a large portion of the population. An annual $5 billion subsidy from the Soviet Union was put at risk by Castro's resistance to Gorbachev-style reform and by his patron's own economic woes.

Under the leadership of the Sandinistas since 1979, **Nicaragua** had taken on many characteristics of a Marxist state, but Pres. Daniel Ortega was defeated by Violeta Barrios de Chamorro in an election in February. The Soviet Union had indicated to Ortega's government that it was no longer going to prop up Nicaragua's revolution. Nonetheless, the Sandinistas retained a large following, and Chamorro, faced with rehabilitating Nicaragua after many years of civil war, reappointed Ortega's brother, Humberto, as chief of the armed forces and developed a close working relationship with him.

Present and Future Problems

The new governments of Eastern Europe faced the task of recovery under arduous circumstances. Addressing the situation in Romania, the dissident writer Norman Manea observed, "The dictator destroyed the entire political, economic and moral structure and it will be very difficult to reconstruct."

From country to country, **decay and deterioration of**

equipment and infrastructure were visible everywhere. Some bridges and roads had not been repaired since the Communists took over. Machines broke down and stood idle. In some cases, the workers who had operated them had disappeared in the night, across an international border.

Businesspeople faced a new world of risk. They were

unaccustomed to dealing with consumer demand. Almost no one had had the opportunity to acquire entrepreneurial skills. **Unemployment grew.** In several countries, the bureaucracies still groaned under the weight of Communist functionaries.

The **environment** was in bad shape. The land was scarred for miles by deep holes dug to extract coal, and dirt was piled high. Towns were ringed by smokestacks, their citizens under an umbrella of brown air. Incidence of cancer and respiratory disease was high. Factories were often too obsolete to be upgraded to meet any environmental requirements.

A Soviet offical said, "Crime is like a thermometer of social disintegration," and **crime** was up in the Soviet Union and elsewhere. So, too, was **antisemitism.** In the Soviet Union, where public antisemitism was one of the first results of new-found freedom of speech, Jews took advantage of relaxed emigration policies, as thousands left the country to resettle in Israel. The skinheads in East Germany, the newly jobless elsewhere, and others frustrated with an era of change all too often found familiar scapegoats. The Jews, only a few hundred in East Germany, and those in Poland, only a few thousand—compared with 3.3 million in 1939, at times were blamed for having introduced communism in the first place, and then, improbably, as planning to force capitalism on the East.

Although political unrest and divisions within society were still a fact of life in Eastern Europe, none of this conflict made communism appear any better. In January 1990, in his New Year's Day address to the people of Czechoslovakia, Pres. Vaclav Havel looked back:

"Notions such as love, friendship, compassion, humility and forgiveness have lost their depth and dimension ... The previous regime, armed with its arrogant and intolerant ideology, denigrated man into a production lever and nature into a production tool ... It made talented people who were capable of managing their own affairs ... into cogs in some kind of monstrous, ramshackle, smelly machine whose purpose no one can understand."

(See Oct. 90 Chronology for additional details.)

Don Young, Special Features Editor

Democrats Score Small Gains in 1990 Elections

Democrats added to their majorities in both houses of Congress in elections held on Nov. 6, and in races for governor they also maintained their control of a majority of the nation's statehouses.

Public-opinion polls had shown that voters were unhappy, and often angry, because of the decline of the economy, and because of a prolonged fight over the adoption of a federal budget that had ended just 10 days before the election. However, only one incumbent senator was defeated and about 96 percent of the incumbents seeking reelection to the House won.

In the contests for governor, the Democrats, who held a 29-21 advantage before the voting, emerged with about the same margin. Displeasure with high state taxes seemed to be a common thread in gubernatorial elections in which the statehouse shifted from one party to the other.

The results of these races was especially important because governors would play an influential role in the redistricting of Congressional and state legislative seats that would take place as a result of the 1990 census. Democrats captured statehouses in Florida and Texas, where several Congressional districts will be added. In Florida, former Sen. Lawton Chiles ousted Bob Martinez, whose popularity had plunged in 1989 after he sought unsuccessfully to get the legislature to approve curbs on abortion.

In Texas, State Treasurer Ann Richards defeated a wealthy rancher and oil man, Clayton Williams, who spent $8 million of his own money in pursuit of the governorship.

In California, though, Sen. Pete Wilson held the governorship for the Republicans, as he turned back former San Francisco Mayor Dianne Feinstein. Wilson opposed, and Feinstein supported, a ballot proposition known as "Big Green," which would have imposed a number of strict environmental controls. The proposition was defeated.

Gov. Mario Cuomo, a Democrat, easily won a third term in New York against Pierre Rinfret. The surprise here was Herbert London, the Conservative Party candidate, who got about 20 percent of the vote.

However, Republicans kept the governorships in Illinois and captured the statehouses in Ohio and (apparently) Michigan. In Massachusetts, the governorship went to William Weld, a former assistant U.S. attorney general. He defeated John Silber, the outspoken president of Boston University.

In Minnesota, the Republican candidate for governor, Jon Grunseth, withdrew from the race 2 weeks before the election following sexual misconduct charges. His replacement, Arne Carlson, defeated the incumbent, Rudy Perpich, in a very close race. Two independents, Lowell Weicker in Connecticut and Walter Hickel in Alaska, won governorships—both in political comebacks.

Minnesota was also the only state to see a change in a U.S. Senate seat. Rudy Boschwitz, a Republican, lost narrowly to Paul Wellstone, a college professor with strong liberal views. This gave the Democrats a 56-44 advantage in the new Senate.

Sen. Jesse Helms of North Carolina swept to victory over Harvey Gantt, the former mayor of Charlotte, who was seeking to become the first black senator from the South since the Reconstruction era. Helms, the most conservative member of the Senate, took a strong stand against quotas in hiring.

Abortion was the key issue in Iowa, where Sen. Tom Harkin, a Democrat, who was "pro-choice," turned back an opponent of abortion, Rep. Tom Tauke. Sen. Bill Bradley of New Jersey, a Democrat and strong vote-getter in the past, narrowly squeaked through to reelection, apparently because voters were angered by a package of state tax increases pushed through by Gov. Jim Florio, a Democrat.

In the House of Representatives, the Democrats had held a 257-176 advantage before the election, with 2 vacancies. Late returns showed that they would control the new House by about 267-167. One Socialist, Bernie Sanders, the former mayor of Burlington, who ran as an independent, won in Vermont.

Newt Gingrich of Georgia, the assistant Republican leader in the House, barely survived by a thousand votes. Gary Franks of Connecticut became the first black Republican elected to the House in more than 50 years.

Sharon Pratt Dixon was elected mayor of Washington, D.C., succeeding Marion Barry, who did not seek reelection. She became the first black woman mayor of a major city. Barry sought election at-large to the City Council but was defeated. The Rev. Jesse Jackson won elective office for the first time, becoming the "shadow senator" from the District of Columbia, which gave him a voice in Congress but not a vote.

CHRONOLOGY OF THE YEAR'S EVENTS

Reported Month by Month in 3 Categories: National, International, and General Oct. 15, 1989 to Oct. 31, 1990

OCTOBER

National

Severe Quake Hits Northern California — One of the strongest earthquakes ever recorded in California struck along the San Andreas fault in the northern part of the state, Oct. 17. More than 60 people were killed and several thousand injured. Some 100,000 houses were reported damaged. The worst damage was in San Francisco and Oakland, 75 miles north of the epicenter of the quake. Most of the deaths, more than 40, occurred when the upper level of the double-decker Nimitz Freeway (Interstate Highway 880) in Oakland collapsed. The freeway was packed with rush-hour traffic at 5:04 p.m., when the 15-second quake hit. In San Francisco, several fires broke out with the worst being in the Marina district, where a number of buildings were destroyed. Other cities that suffered heavily included Santa Cruz, where much of the downtown shopping district was leveled; San Jose; and Los Gatos. The tragedy struck just minutes before the start of the 3d game of baseball's World Series between the Oakland Athletics and the San Francisco Giants at San Francisco's Candlestick Park. The game was canceled and the crowd of 58,000 evacuated safely. The last survivor to be found, Buck Helm, a longshoreman, was pulled from the wreckage of the Nimitz Freeway, Oct. 21. The U.S. Geological Survey said, Oct. 24, that its estimate of the quake's intensity had been put at 7.1 on the Richter Scale, the 5th strongest of the century, though well below the impact of San Francisco's great earthquake of 1906. Congress, Oct. 25, approved an aid package totaling $4.15 billion. The World Series resumed, Oct. 27, at Candlestick Park, and Oakland completed a 4-game sweep of the Giants, Oct. 28.

Trade Gap Widens Again — The Commerce Dept. reported, Oct. 17, that the U.S. merchandise trade deficit had risen to $10.77 billion in August. The gap, the largest in 8 months, was attributed to the stronger U.S. dollar, which had made imports cheaper and exports more expensive. The Census Bureau said, Oct. 18, that the median U.S. family income stood at $32,191 in 1988, a slight decline from the $32,251 in 1987. The figures were adjusted for inflation. The Labor Dept. said, Oct. 19, that consumer prices rose 0.2 percent in September. The Commerce Dept. reported, Oct. 26, that the gross national product had grown at a 2.5 percent annual rate in the third quarter. The department said, Oct. 31, that its leading economic indicators had risen 0.2 percent in September.

Flag Amendment Fails in Senate — On Oct. 19, a week after Congress had completed action on a bill to outlaw desecration of the American flag, the Senate failed to approve an amendment to the U.S. Constitution that had the same purpose. The vote was 51-48, well below the two-thirds required for approval of amendments. Pres. George Bush, who feared that the law could be declared unconstitutional, had supported the amendment.

Senate Removes Federal Judge — U.S. District Judge Alcee Hastings of Florida was convicted of 8 articles of impeachment, Oct. 20, by the U.S. Senate. The convictions had the effect of removing him from the bench. Hastings, the 6th federal judge to be so removed, had been acquitted in 1983 of accepting a bribe in a case before him. However, a federal judicial panel found "clear and convincing evidence" in 1987 that Hastings had conspired to accept the bribe.

Congressman Convicted in Wedtech Scandal — In the last major trial to grow out of the Wedtech investigation, Rep. Robert Garcia (D, N.Y.) and his wife, Jane Lee, were found guilty of extortion and conspiracy, Oct. 20. Prosecutors charged that Garcia, who represented the Bronx district in which the company had been located, had demanded payoffs from Wedtech. Mrs. Garcia had been accused of receiving payoffs from the company totaling more than $75,000. More than 20 prominent persons had been convicted in the scandal. Federal Judge Leonard Sand Jan. 19 sentenced the Garcias to 3 years in prison. On June 29, 1990, a federal appeals court overturned the convictions of the Garcias.

Funding for Abortion Vetoed — The Senate and House approved a spending bill for the departments of Education, Labor, and Health and Human Services that reinstated funding for Medicaid abortions in instances of rape or incest. Pres. George Bush vetoed the bill, Oct. 21. The House, Oct. 25, voted 231-191 to override the veto, but this fell far short of the two-thirds vote needed, and the veto was sustained. Bush had supported federal funding only if the mother's life was in danger. Those who had supported the bill said the burden of the veto would fall most heavily on poor women who could not afford to pay for an abortion.

International

German Communists Remove Honecker — The 18-year rule of Erich Honecker in East Germany came to an end, Oct. 18, when he stepped down as head of the Socialist Unity (Communist) Party, chairman of the National Defense Council, and head of state. The Central Committee of the Party had clearly forced him out, though a statement said he had retired because of ill health. Honecker was succeeded by Egon Krenz, a member of the ruling Politburo. On Oct. 23 and 30, 300,000 persons in Leipzig demonstrated on behalf of political reform.

Hungary Proclaimed a Free Republic — The Hungarian National Assembly amended the constitution, Oct. 18, to prepare for multiparty free elections in 1990 when a new constitution was to be drafted. The Assembly ended the ruling party's monopoly on power, removed references to the "leading role" for the Communists, and renamed the country the Republic of Hungary, without reference to a "People's Republic." Acting Pres. Matyas Szuros, Oct. 23, proclaimed Hungary a free republic. The Assembly voted, Oct. 31, to conduct a national referendum on how to choose a president.

Soviets Admit Afghanistan Invasion was Illegal — Foreign Minister Eduard Shevardnadze, in a speech to the Soviet legislature, Oct. 23, said his country's invasion of Afghanistan in 1979 was illegal. Saying that the intervention "violated the norms of proper behavior," he blamed it on then-Pres. Leonid Brezhnev and some others in the inner circle. He also acknowledged that the Soviet radar complex at Krasnoyarsk violated the 1972 ABM treaty. The foreign minister said that historic changes in Poland and Hungary were acceptable to the Kremlin, and that the Soviet Union looked toward the eventual dissolution of the Warsaw Pact and NATO. Pres. George Bush said, Oct. 31, that he and Soviet Pres. Mikhail Gorbachev would hold an informal summit on ships in the Mediterranean Sea, Dec. 2-3.

Police Break Up Prague Demonstration — On Oct. 25, with political unrest in Czechoslovakia on the rise, Premier Ladislav Adamec rejected any dialogue between the government and those "who act for the liquidation of the socialist system ... and the Communist Party." On Oct. 27, several prominent dissidents were placed under detention. On Oct. 28, some 10,000 persons gathered in Wenceslas Square in Prague to observe the 71st anniversary of the founding of the republic. The demonstration was broken up by club-swinging police.

Ortega Announces End to Truce — On Oct. 27, on the first day of a 2-day summit meeting of heads of state of Western Hemisphere countries in San José, Costa Rica, Pres. Daniel Ortega of Nicaragua said he would end his regime's unilateral cease-fire against contra rebels. He claimed the contras had repeatedly violated the truce, leaving more than 3,000 Nicaraguans dead, wounded, or missing. Pres. George Bush, who attended the summit, Oct. 28, attacked Ortega as a "little man" and as "an animal at a garden party." Ortega announced, Nov. 1, that the cease-fire had ended, and the contras reported that the army had resumed operations.

General

Spacecraft Begins Journey to Jupiter — The space shuttle *Atlantis* was launched with a crew of 5 from Cape Canaveral, Fla., on Oct. 18. It carried the spacecraft Galileo, which separated from the shuttle on its 5th orbit and began a 6-year journey to the planet Jupiter. After arrival in the vicinity of Jupiter in 1995, the craft would explore that planet's atmosphere and moons. The shuttle landed at Edwards Air Force Base in California on Oct. 23.

Evangelist Jim Bakker Sentenced — Television evangelist Jim Bakker, who had been convicted of fraud and conspiracy, was sentenced, Oct. 24, to 45 years in prison and fined $500,000. He would be eligible for parole in 10 years.

Disasters — The crash into the Caspian Sea, Oct. 18, of a Soviet military transport plane carrying paratroopers resulted in the death of all 57 aboard. ... The crash, Oct. 21, of a Honduran jetliner into the side of a mountain in Honduras took the lives of 131 of the 146 persons aboard. ... More than 50 people burned to death, Oct. 21, in the Sudan after 2 buses collided. ... A China Airlines Boeing 737 crashed into a mountain after taking off from Hualien, in eastern Taiwan, Oct. 26, killing all 54 people aboard.

NOVEMBER

National

Minimum Wage Compromise Approved — Congress approved a compromise worked out with the White House on the minimum wage. The agreement provided that the current minimum of $3.35 an hour be increased to $4.25 an hour by 1991. A training wage of $3.35 would be permitted for workers 16 to 19 years old during their first 3 months on a job. The House approved the bill, Nov. 1, and the Senate followed on Nov. 8.

Flurry of Activity as Congress Adjourns — With concern shifting toward the economies of Eastern Europe, the Senate and House, Nov. 20, approved a foreign aid bill that contained $532.8 million for Poland and Hungary. The House voted, Nov. 21, 352-63, to repeal the Medicare Catastrophic Coverage Act of 1988. Many elderly Americans had complained that they had to finance it even though it duplicated other coverage. Also on Nov. 21, the House approved a deficit-reduction bill aimed at producing $14.6 billion in savings and new revenues. By voice vote, Nov. 22, the Senate gave its assent to the insurance repeal and the deficit-reduction bill. Congress adjourned, Nov. 22.

Cut in Capital Gains Dropped — Pres. George Bush and Republican leaders in Congress, Nov. 2, shelved their effort, for the time being, to win approval for a reduction in the capital gains tax. The House, in September, had attached a reduction to a deficit-reduction bill, but the Senate had not included the capital gains issue in its version of the bill.

Jobless Rate Steady — The nation's unemployment rate held at 5.2 percent in October, the Labor Dept. said, Nov. 3. The department reported, Nov. 9, that producer prices had risen 0.4 percent in October. The Commerce Dept., Nov. 16, put the merchandise trade deficit in September at $7.94 billion, the lowest since 1984. The Labor Dept. said, Nov. 21, that consumer prices had risen 0.5 percent in October.

Another Judge Removed by Senate — On Nov. 3, for the second time in 2 weeks, the U.S. Senate convicted a federal judge on impeachment charges and removed him from the bench. The charges involving U.S. District Judge Walter Nixon Jr. of Biloxi, Miss. related to his conviction in 1986 for lying to a grand jury about intervening in a drug case on behalf of the son of a contractor with whom Nixon had had financial dealings. Nixon asserted that he had been "unjustly and wrongfully convicted."

Quake Damage Put at $5.6 Billion — As Californians continued to repair the damage from the October earthquake, Gov. George Deukmejian, Nov. 7, signed a bill raising the sales tax temporarily by one-quarter percent as a means of obtaining money for earthquake relief. State officials estimated property damage, Nov. 11, at $5.6 billion. The insurance industry estimated that only $2 billion was covered by insurance. Repair work was completed, Nov. 16, on the San Francisco-Oakland Bay Bridge. Buck Helm, a longshoreman who had been trapped in the wreckage of a freeway for 89 hours before being rescued, died, Nov. 19. California officials placed the death toll at 62 on Nov. 19.

Democrats Strong in Off-Year Voting — Democrats won most of the top offices at stake in off-year elections, Nov. 7. Black candidates also scored some major breakthroughs. In a very close race for governor of Virginia, Lt. Gov. L. Douglas Wilder, a black, appeared to be the winner by a few thousand votes over J. Marshall Coleman, the Republican nominee. No state had had a black governor since the Reconstruction era after the Civil War. Wilder appeared to have benefitted from his support of abortion rights for women. Abortion was also a major issue in the New Jersey gubernatorial campaign. U.S. Rep. James Florio, the Democratic candidate, who favored the right of a woman to choose an abortion, won in a landslide over the Republican, U.S. Rep. Jim Courter. Manhattan Borough Pres. David Dinkins, a Democrat, became the first black to be elected mayor of New York City. He defeated former U.S. Attorney Rudolph Giuliani, stressing the themes of unity and harmony. Seattle, New Haven, Conn., and Durham, N.C. all elected their first black mayors. Coleman Young of Detroit and Kathy Whitmire of Houston, both Democrats, were among the mayors who were re-elected. On Nov. 27, the Virginia Board of Elections certified Wilder as the winner of the governorship.

Guilt Admitted in Arms Scandal — Air Force Maj. Gen. Richard Secord (ret.) pleaded guilty, Nov. 8, to making a false statement to Congress regarding the Iran-contra scandal. He admitted that he lied in June 1987 when he said he did not know that Lt. Col. Oliver North had benefitted financially from the sale of arms to Iran or from the diversion of profits to contra rebels in Nicaragua. Eleven other charges against Secord were dropped as part of a plea bargain agreement. He was sentenced, **Jan. 24, 1990,** to 2 years' probation.

Pennsylvania Acts on Abortion — The Pennsylvania legislature approved a bill restricting abortions, and Gov. Robert Casey signed it into law, **Nov. 18.** Pennsylvania became the first state to restrict abortions after the U.S. Supreme Court gave states the right to do so in July. Most abortions at public hospitals were banned, as were almost all abortions after 24 weeks of gestation. For abortions that were permitted, prior notification of the spouse and a 24-hour waiting period were required.

Congress Votes Itself a Raise — Congress approved increases in salaries for its own members and for federal judges and top officials in the executive branch. At present, members of both the Senate and House received $89,500. Under the bill, House salaries would go to $124,400 by 1991, and members would be barred from accepting speaking fees. Senators' pay would rise to $98,400 in 1990, with limits on speaking fees reduced by a like amount. The House and Senate gave their approval on **Nov. 16** and **17,** respectively. Apparently mindful of the storm of criticism that had averted approval of a pay increase earlier in the year, Congressional leaders unveiled the new plan only a day before the House voted. Pres. George Bush signed the bill, **Nov. 30.**

International

East Germany Opens Berlin Wall — A year of dramatic upheaval in Eastern Europe reached a climax in November when the East German Communist regime lifted its restrictions on travel and emigration to the West. On **Nov. 1,** East Germany opened its border with Czechoslovakia, prompting a sharp increase in East German emigration to West Germany through Czech territory. In 9 days, some 50,000 joined 110,000 who had previously gone west in 1989. On **Nov. 3,** 5 Politburo members resigned, and East German leader Egon Krenz promised economic and political reforms. More than 500,000 joined a peaceful pro-democracy rally in East Berlin, **Nov. 4.** Premier Willi Stoph and the entire Council of Ministers resigned, **Nov. 7,** and were joined by more Politburo members, **Nov. 8.** The Party's Central Committee, **Nov. 8,** nominated Hans Modrow, a reformist, for premier. A spokesman for the Soviet foreign ministry said, **Nov. 9,** that the changes were welcome. The government lifted travel and emigration restrictions, **Nov. 9,** and exit visas were issued to those who asked for them. Within hours, thousands of Germans from East and West massed at the Berlin wall, many of them sitting atop the barrier that had separated the 2 Germanys since 1961. On **Nov. 10,** East Germany opened more crossing points and East Germans by the hundreds of thousands poured into the West to shop, look around, and be reunited with family and friends. The migration was repeated in subsequent days. Although some East Germans remained in the West, most returned home. By **Nov. 15,** the East German government had issued 7.7 million travel visas. On **Nov. 28,** West German Chancellor Helmut Kohl proposed a plan for the confederation of the 2 Germanys.

Salvadoran Rebels Open Offensive — The Farabundo Martí National Liberation Front (FMLN) began a major offensive against the government of El Salvador in November. The leftist rebels pulled out of peace talks, **Nov. 2,** after 10 were killed in the bombing of a labor federation headquarters. The FMLN began its attack in San Salvador, the capital, and in other cities, **Nov. 11** and **12.** Hundreds of combatants and civilians died in the worst urban fighting of the 10-year civil war, and the government, **Nov. 12,** declared a state of siege. By **Nov. 15,** the rebels had been driven from some of their strongholds in the capital. Six Jesuit priests as well as a cook and her daughter were shot to death by uniformed gunmen at José Simeón Cañas University of Central America in San Salvador, **Nov. 16.** Democrats in the U.S. Congress warned, **Nov. 17,** that aid to El Salvador would be halted if the government failed to bring the killers to justice and end human rights abuses by the army and security forces. Rebels seized a hotel in San Salvador, **Nov. 21,** trapping 12 members of the U.S. Special Forces, or Green Berets. After being threatened with death, the soldiers were allowed to leave, **Nov. 22.** The rebels resumed their offensive in the capital, **Nov. 27,** and the homes of several U.S. diplomats were seized. On **Nov. 30,** the United States flew 282 embassy officials and dependents out of the country.

New Lebanese President Killed — René Moawad, a moderate Christian who enjoyed the support of Syria, was elected president of Lebanon, **Nov. 5,** but he was assassinated 17 days later. When electing Moawad, the Lebanese parliament also approved a plan supported by the Arab League to end Lebanon's civil war. The plan called for a balancing of political offices among the religious factions and would require militias to disband and Syrian troops to withdraw within 2 years. Gen. Michel Aoun, the Christian army commander, rejected the plan because Syrian troops would not leave at once. Moawad was assassinated, **Nov. 22,** when a bomb exploded along the route of his motorcade. It killed 23 other people. Parliament, **Nov. 24,** elected as president Elias Hrawi, like Moawad a moderate Maronite Catholic friendly to Syria.

U.S. to Return Iranian Assets — It was announced, **Nov. 6,** that the U.S. would unfreeze $567 million in Iranian assets that had been held since 1979. Pres. Bush said, **Nov. 7,** that he hoped Iran would use its influence to help free U.S. hostages in the Middle East. An Iranian newspaper said, **Nov. 9,** that the unfreezing of assets was an insufficient gesture of U.S. good will.

Bulgarian Communist Leader Resigns — Todor Zhivkov, who had been president of Bulgaria since 1971 and leader of the ruling Communist Party since 1954, resigned both posts, **Nov. 10.** The resignations came amid the first stirrings of the pro-democracy movement that was flourishing elsewhere in Eastern Europe. Zhivkov, 78, had ruled Bulgaria for a longer time than any other Eastern European leader. He was regarded as a hard-line Communist and loyal supporter of the Soviet Union. Zhivkov resigned at a meeting of the party's Central Committee, which named Foreign Minister Petar Mladenov to succeed him as the party's general secretary.

Czech Communist Leadership Replaced — The tide of political reform sweeping Eastern Europe engulfed Czechoslovakia in November. Unrest began to build, **Nov. 17,** when police used clubs, tear gas, and dogs to break up a demonstration by university students in Prague. More than 200,000 people marched in Prague, **Nov. 20,** calling for free elections. Czech Premier Ladislav Adamec met, **Nov. 21,** with playwright Vaclav Havel and other dissidents who had just formed a new opposition group, Civic Forum. Havel, addressing 150,000 afterward, said the regime had promised some reforms, but Communist Party leader Milos Jakes said on television that evening, "There are boundaries that should not be crossed." Alexander Dubcek, leader of the short-lived reform movement of 1968 that was crushed by Soviet tanks, spoke to pro-democracy crowds in Bratislava, **Nov. 23**, and Prague, **Nov. 24**. On **Nov. 24**, at an emergency meeting of the Communist Party Central Committee, Jakes and the other 12 members of the policy-making Presidium (politburo) resigned. Jakes, an opponent of reform, had been in power since 1987. A new Presidium, including 6 holdovers, was named, with Karel Urbanek as general secretary of the party. Havel, addressing 800,000 people in Prague, **Nov. 25**, dismissed the personnel shifts as a trick. Millions of workers joined a 2-hour general strike, **Nov. 27**. Adamec opened power-sharing talks with Civic Forum, **Nov. 28**. Parliament, **Nov. 29**, deleted from the Constitution a provision guaranteeing the Communist Party the "leading role" in society.

Communist Leader of Romania Re-Elected — Seemingly unaffected by turmoil elsewhere in Eastern Europe, the Romanian Communist Party opened its 14th Congress in Bucharest, **Nov. 20**. In a 5-hour keynote address, Pres. Nicolae Ceausescu proclaimed the party to be the "vital center" of life in Romania. Ceausescu, who had been in power since 1965, was unanimously re-elected party secretary, **Nov. 24**.

Prime Minister Gandhi Resigns — Prime Minister Rajiv Gandhi of India resigned after his Congress (I) Party did poorly in parliamentary elections. His popularity had been declining for some time amid accusations that his government was corrupt and inefficient. In elections to parliament, **Nov. 22-26**, his party lost more than half its seats. Opposition parties won more than half the seats. Gandhi announced his resignation, **Nov. 29**, subject to the selection of a new prime minister.

Hungarians Vote on President — In a national referendum, **Nov. 26**, Hungarians voted in favor of letting their next parliament choose the president of the country. Opposition groups had favored this approach, rather than the direct election of the president. Parliamentary elections would take place in 1990.

General

Conference Acts on Global Warming — Representatives of 68 countries met in the Netherlands to consider the threat posed by the warming of the atmosphere—the so-called greenhouse effect. This was the first ministerial-level meeting held on the problem. A compromise resolution, adopted unanimously, **Nov. 7**, committed the signers to stabilizing levels of carbon dioxide emissions by 2000. A stronger resolution that would have set specific goals did not get a consensus, meeting resistance from the United States and Japan.

Tornadoes Take 29 Lives — Violent weather, including tornadoes, struck the eastern United States in mid-November and claimed 29 lives. A tornado cut through downtown Huntsville, Ala., **Nov. 15**, killing 18 people and injuring 500. Outside Newburgh, N.Y. on **Nov. 16**, a tornado struck the East Coldenham Elementary School and knocked down a wall in the cafeteria. Nine students were killed and 16 injured.

Vitamin Pills Reduce Birth Defects — The *Journal of the American Medical Association* reported, **Nov. 24**, that women who take nonprescription multivitamin pills early in pregnancy reduce the risk of having a baby with certain neurological defects. These neural tube defects include anencephaly, or the absence of nearly all the brain, and spina bifida, in which part of the spinal cord protrudes from the spinal column. These defects may cause death or paralysis, and affect 1 to 2 babies in every 1,000 born. Mothers who took multivitamin pills containing folic acid during the first 6 weeks of pregnancy had only one fourth as many babies with these defects as women who did not take

such pills. Some 23,000 women participated in the study.

Disasters — A typhoon that stuck Thailand in the first week of November took at least 365 lives. ... A Colombian jetliner exploded in midair, **Nov. 27**, shortly after it took off from Bogotá, killing all 107 aboard.

DECEMBER

National

Stocks Score Big Gains in 1989 — The value of stocks on the major exchanges increased in 1989, even though economic data issued by the government continued to show no consistent pattern. The Commerce Dept. said, **Dec. 1**, that its leading economic indicators declined 0.4 percent in October. The Labor Dept. reported, **Dec. 8**, that the unemployment rate had edged upward to 5.3 percent in November. The department said, **Dec. 15**, that producer prices fell 0.1 percent in November. On **Dec. 15**, the Commerce Dept. reported that the U.S. merchandise trade deficit had jumped to $10.20 billion in October. Consumer prices rose 0.4 percent in November, the Labor Dept. reported, **Dec. 19**. The leading economic indicators edged upward 0.1 percent in November, the Commerce Dept. said, **Dec. 29**. When the stock exchanges closed on **Dec. 29**, their last trading day of 1989, the Dow Jones industrial average stood at 2753.20, up 27 percent for the year. Standard & Poor's index of 500 stocks was also up 27 percent for the year. The American Stock Exchange index was up 23 percent, and the Nasdaq over-the-counter market composite index posted a 19 percent gain for 1989.

U.S. Official Resigns S&L Position — M. Danny Wall, head of the federal Office of Thrift Supervision, resigned, **Dec. 4**. As the official in charge of overseeing the thrift industry, Wall had been criticized by members of Congress and other regulators for having overlooked signs that the Lincoln Savings and Loan Association of Irvine, Calif. was in financial trouble. The collapse of Lincoln and many other S&Ls was about to cost taxpayers many billions of dollars. Wall said he was being made a "scapegoat for the entire thrift crisis."

Bombs Kill Judge, Lawyer — Judge Robert Vance of the U.S. Court of Appeals for the 11th Circuit was killed, **Dec. 16**, in his home in a suburb of Birmingham, Ala., when he opened a package that contained a bomb. The explosion of the pipe bomb killed him instantly. Recent rulings by the court had angered white supremacists. In Savannah, Ga., **Dec. 18**, Robert Robinson, a lawyer and alderman, was killed by a similar bomb, sent to his office. Robinson, a black, had performed legal work for the National Association for the Advancement of Colored People. Two more bombs were seized at the federal court building in Atlanta, **Dec. 18**, and at the Jacksonville, Fla., office of the NAACP, **Dec. 19**, before they exploded. Federal investigators said, **Dec. 19**, that "hard forensic evidence" linked the 4 bombs.

International

Bush, Gorbachev Hold First Summit — Pres. George Bush and Soviet Pres. Mikhail Gorbachev held their first summit meeting in December. The shipboard summit took place in Marsaxlokk Bay at the Mediterranean island republic of Malta. Bush arrived in Valletta, the capital of Malta, **Dec. 1**, and met with Maltese leaders before boarding the *U.S.S. Belknap* in the bay. A heavy storm, **Dec. 2**, forced the 2 leaders to hold their talks aboard the large Soviet cruise ship

Maxim Gorky, rather than on a smaller cruiser. Bush proposed that bilateral treaties on strategic arms and conventional arms in Europe be completed during 1990. He offered to waive trade restrictions if the Soviets liberalized their emigration laws. The Soviet leader made no major proposals then or on the second day of their talks on the same ship, **Dec. 3.** After their second meeting, the 2 leaders held a joint press conference, another first for a superpower summit. They both seemed to agree that the Cold War was virtually a thing of the past and that the world, in Bush's words, was on the "threshold of a brand new era of U.S.-Soviet relations." Meeting with NATO leaders in Brussels, **Dec. 4,** Bush reported on the summit, pledged a continued U.S. military presence in Europe, and discussed the question of German reunification.

East German Party Shaken Up Again — December was another month of turmoil for the ruling Socialist Unity (Communist) Party in East Germany. On **Dec. 1,** parliament revoked a clause in the constitution guaranteeing the Communists a "leading role" in society. On **Dec. 2,** a committee reported to parliament that former party leader Erich Honecker and his associates had lived in luxury while they ran the country, and the committee said it had evidence that they had hidden $54 billion in Swiss bank accounts. These revelations led, **Dec. 3,** to the resignation of the entire leadership of the party, including General Secretary Egon Krenz, Premier Hans Modrow, the rest of the Politburo, and the entire Central Committee. Krenz remained head of state and Modrow head of government. Honecker and some former aides were put under house arrest, **Dec. 5.** Krenz resigned as head of state, **Dec. 6,** and was replaced by Manfred Gerlach, head of the small Liberal Democratic Party. Honecker and former Premier Willi Stoph were among 6 former officials charged, **Dec. 8,** with corruption and abuse of power. The party, **Dec. 9,** elected Gregor Gysi, a lawyer, to succeed Krenz. In Leipzig, **Dec. 11,** 200,000 persons demonstrated for German reunification. U.S. Sec. of State James Baker 3d delivered a speech in East Berlin, **Dec. 12,** and then met in Potsdam with Modrow. West German Chancellor Helmut Kohl met with Modrow, **Dec. 19.**

Another Coup Fails in Philippines — Rebel elements within the Philippines army launched another coup attempt, the 6th during the presidency of Corazon Aquino. Like its predecessors, the coup failed. Rebels attacked military positions in suburban Manilla, **Dec. 1,** and planes dropped a few bombs. One struck the presidential palace, but Aquino was unhurt. Responding to a request from Aquino, Pres. George Bush authorized 2 U.S. F-4 jet fighters from Clark Air Force Base to provide air support for the government. There were no reports that the U.S. planes fired any shots. Vice Pres. Salvador Laurel, **Dec. 3,** backed the coup attempt and urged Aquino to resign. Within a few days, most rebels had surrendered to regular army troops, and the fall of a key airport, **Dec. 9,** ended the uprising. The official casualty toll for both sides was reported as 119 killed and 418 wounded.

Pope and Gorbachev Meet — In an historic first, **Dec. 1,** the leader of the Soviet Union, Pres. Mikhail Gorbachev, met with the head of the Roman Catholic Church at the Vatican. Pope John Paul II endorsed Gorbachev's reforms in the Soviet Union, and the 2 agreed to work toward establishing diplomatic relations. In a statement, Gorbachev called the meeting "extraordinary" and promised a law that would guarantee to Soviet citizens the right to "satisfy their spiritual needs."

New Indian Prime Minister Named — Vishwanath Pratap Singh, a former minister in the cabinet of outgoing Pres. Rajiv Gandhi, was chosen as leader of the National Front coalition on **Dec. 1,** and on **Dec. 2** he was sworn in as prime minister of India. Gandhi had announced that he would step down after his Congress (I) Party did badly in the November elections. Singh's coalition would include both right- and left-wing groups.

Communists Lose Grip on Czechoslovakia — Communist domination of Czechoslovakia ended in December. In the wake of November's massive demonstrations, Premier Ladislav Adamec unveiled a new cabinet, **Dec. 3,** but the opposition Civic Forum rejected it because 16 of the 21 positions were still to be filled by Communists. Adamec resigned, **Dec. 7,** and Pres. Gustav Husak named Marian Calfa to replace him. The new cabinet, announced **Dec. 7,** had only 10 (of 21) Communists. In conversations with Civic Forum, **Dec. 8,** the Communists agreed to relinquish power. Husak, who had run the country for more than 20 years as Communist leader and president, resigned as president, **Dec. 10.** A hard-liner, he had come to power after Russian tanks crushed a reform movement in 1968. Vaclav Havel, a dissident playwright, and Alexander Dubcek, who had headed the 1968 reform movement, both declared their candidacies for president. The Communist Party, **Dec. 20,** replaced Karel Urbanek as its leader with Adamec. Parliament, **Dec. 28,** elected Dubcek as its speaker and on **Dec. 29,** it elected Havel president without opposition.

Bombings Linked to Drug Cartel — The government of Colombia said, **Dec. 5,** that it believed that the destruction of an Avianca Airlines jetliner, **Nov. 27,** was caused by the explosion of a bomb. The death toll, possibly including several persons on the ground struck by the falling wreckage, was put at 110. More than 60 people were killed and more than 1,000 wounded when a bomb exploded in front of the Dept. of Administrative Security in Bogotá, **Dec. 6.** The bomb contained half a ton of dynamite. Authorities believed both bombings represented acts of terrorism by drug dealers who were defying government efforts to eradicate their operations. On **Dec. 15,** some 300 commandos and soldiers attacked a ranch near Tolu, where they killed José Gonzalo Rodríguez Gacha, the number two man in the Medellín drug cartel. His son and 15 bodyguards were also killed. Rodríguez Gacha was one of those believed responsible for acts of terrorism and the killing of several prominent Colombians.

Lithuania Looks Toward Independence — The Baltic republic of Lithuania gave strong signals of its eagerness to break free from the Soviet Union. The Lithuanian parliament voted overwhelmingly, **Dec. 7,** to adopt a multiparty political system, the first time any republic in the USSR had taken such a step. The vote was to remove Article 6 of the republic's constitution guaranteeing the Communist Party a monopoly on power. At the federal level, at the opening of the Congress of People's Deputies, **Dec. 12,** in Moscow, Pres. Mikhail Gorbachev averted a similar effort to debate the leading role of the party in the Soviet Union. Among those opposing Gorbachev and calling for a debate was Andrei Sakharov, the nuclear physicist and political dissident. Sakharov, an admired figure around the world for his efforts in behalf of human rights and a recipient of the Nobel Peace Prize, died, **Dec. 14.** In another unprecedented move, the Lithuanian Communist Party declared itself independent of the national party, **Dec. 20.** The party further asserted that its goal was creation of an "independent democratic Lithuanian state." Gorbachev, **Dec. 26,** called this action "illegitimate" and ruled out secession by any of the nation's 15 republics.

Bush Envoys Meet Chinese Leaders — Two top Bush administration officials, National Security Adviser Brent Scowcroft and Deputy Sec. of State Lawrence Eagleburger, met with Chinese party and government leaders in Beijing, **Dec. 9** and **10.** Although it was announced that the purpose of the meeting was for the U.S. representatives to brief the Chinese on the Malta summit, it was widely assumed that an attempt to improve relations between China and the United States was the principal focus. The administration announced, **Dec. 18,** that Scowcroft and Eagleburger had also made a secret trip to China in July, a month after the Chinese regime had brutally crushed a pro-democracy demonstration in the capital.

Central American Leaders Sign Accord — The presidents of Costa Rica, El Salvador, Guatamala, Honduras, and Nicaragua, meeting in San José, Costa Rica, **Dec. 12,** signed a new peace agreement for the Central American region. The agreement declared that all support for the 10,000 rebels fighting against the Nicaraguan regime should be channeled through an international commission set up to disband the rebels. The accord included a strong endorsement of the government of Pres. Alfredo Cristiani of El Salvador, which was also under attack from a rebel force.

Pinochet Era Ending in Chile — On **Dec. 14,** Chile held its first presidential election since 1970. The result was a victory for opposition leader Patricio Aylwin, who received 55 percent of the vote. A more conservative candidate, Hernan Buchi, got 29 percent of the vote. Buchi, a former finance minister under Gen. Augusto Pinochet, was handicapped by his identification with Pinochet's authoritarian rule. Pinochet had come to power in a bloody coup in 1973, and the election results appeared to signal the end of his domination of the country, although he would remain chief of the armed forces.

U.S. Invades Panama, Pursues Noriega — Pres. George Bush sent U.S. military forces into Panama, and they engaged in a brief but bloody conflict with troops supporting the Panamanian dictator, Gen. Manuel Noriega. Panama's National Assembly of Representatives formally named Noriega head of government on **Dec. 15,** and also proclaimed that Panama "is declared to be in a state of war" with the United States. On **Dec. 16,** 4 off-duty U.S. servicemen were confronted at a roadblock by civilians and troops, and when they attempted to leave one was killed. U.S. troops stationed in Panama were placed on a high alert, **Dec. 17.** Some 12,000 U.S. military personnel were already in Panama, with the primary duty to safeguard the Panama Canal. On **Dec. 20,** in the early morning hours, 12,000 more Army, Navy, Air Force, and Marine troops landed. U.S. forces were divided into 5 task forces which attacked selected targets. One seized the headquarters of the Panama Defense Forces. Other targets included military and strategic locations in and around Panama City. An alternative government, headed by Guillermo Endara as president, was sworn in by a Panamanian judge at a U.S. military base. Endara claimed he had won a presidential election in May, but Noriega had annulled the vote. To protect shipping, U.S. troops closed the Panama Canal, **Dec. 20,** but reopened it, **Dec. 21.** Announcing the invasion, **Dec. 20,** Bush said he had the obligation to safeguard the lives of American citizens. Sec. of State James Baker 3d said, **Dec. 20,** that Noriega reportedly had planned to attack U.S. citizens in Panama. Most members of Congress supported the invasion, but the Organization of American States deplored it, **Dec. 22.** The U.S. Defense Department said, **Dec. 23,** that the secret radar-evading F-117A Stealth bombers had been used in combat for the first time, and had dropped 2 bombs near a barracks. On **Dec. 24,** Noriega took refuge in the Vatican's diplomatic mission in Panama

City. When this news came, most remaining resistance to the U.S. invasion collapsed. The mission had the right to grant Noriega asylum, and negotiations began among U.S., Vatican, and Panamanian diplomats as to his future. U.S. officials argued that because he had been indicted in the United States for drug trafficking he was not eligible for asylum. Casualty figures issued by U.S. military officials, **Dec. 27,** were: 23 U.S. soldiers, 3 American civilians, 297 Panamanian soldiers, and at least 400 Panamanian civilians killed; 322 U.S. soldiers, 1 American civilian, 123 Panamanian soldiers, and 2,000 Panamanian civilians wounded or injured. The U.N. Security Council, **Dec. 29,** voted 75-20, with 39 abstentions, to "strongly deplore" the U.S. invasion. On **Mar. 26,** U.S. officials confirmed it had lowered its tally of casualties suffered by Panamanians. It said about 50 members of the Panama military had been killed, and that the civilian death toll had been put at 202.

Gen. Manuel Noriega surrendered to U.S. authorities and agreed to give himself up after being assured that he would not face the death penalty. After leaving the mission, **Jan. 3,** Noriega was taken to a U.S. military base in Panama City and arrested on drug-trafficking indictments by U.S. Drug Enforcement Administration agents. He was flown to Florida and arraigned, **Jan. 4,** in federal district court in Miami. Noriega's lawyer refused to enter a plea, contending he was a political prisoner, and the court entered a plea of not guilty. Crowds in Panama City celebrated Noriega's capture. The chairman of the U.S. Joint Chiefs of Staff, Gen. Colin Powell, said, **Jan. 5,** that with Noriega in custody U.S. troops could be withdrawn from Panama within a few weeks. Pres. George Bush, **Jan. 25,** announced his support of a $1 billion package of cash, loans, and other types of aid to help rebuild the devastated economy of Panama. U.S. District Judge William Hoeveler, **Jan. 26,** ordered Noriega held without bail. U.S. Vice Pres. Dan Quayle visited Panama, Honduras, and Jamaica, **Jan. 27-29,** to explain administration policy on Latin America.

Romanian Leader Overthrown, Executed — Pres. Nicolae Ceausescu of Romania was overthrown in a popular uprising, and he and his wife Elena were executed. As first secretary of the Communist Party since 1965, Nicolae Ceausescu had ruled Romania for nearly a quarter century. For months, Romania had appeared untouched by the political unrest sweeping other Communist nations in Eastern Europe. Then, on **Dec. 15,** in Timisoara, in Transylvania, a crowd formed to protest the arrest and deportation of a Protestant minister who had been advocating the rights of ethnic Hungarians who lived in the region. The protest evolved into a pro-democracy demonstration, **Dec. 16,** and Army and Securitate (internal-security) troops moved in. A large number of citizens were shot to death, **Dec. 17,** during a demonstration. Protests spread to 2 other cities, **Dec. 19.** Ceausescu returned from an official visit to Iran, **Dec. 20,** denounced the demonstrators, and then addressed a rally in Bucharest, **Dec. 21.** He was jeered by many in the crowd, an unprecedented event considering how tightly he held power. Securitate troops, known for their fierce loyalty to Ceausescu, fired on the crowd, drove them elsewhere, and eventually killed up to 40. On **Dec. 22,** as up to 150,000 persons massed to defy Securitate forces, it was reported that the defense minister had committed suicide, though it was later determined that he had been shot for refusing to order the army to fire on the demonstrators. Military units joined the rebels. Pres. Ceausescu and Elena, his chief deputy in the government, fled the capital by helicopter. They landed and seized a car, but were in turn captured by insurgents near Tirgoviste. On **Dec. 25,**

after a brief trial by a military tribunal on charges of genocide, abuse of power, and theft, they were both shot at an undisclosed location. Meanwhile, on **Dec. 22,** a coalition of former Communist officials, military officers, students, and others formed a National Salvation Front to run the country. On **Dec. 26,** Ion Iliescu, a former party official, was named interim president. By the end of the month, the rebels were in control, but only after bloody fighting. Reports of the number of people killed in the 2 weeks of upheaval varied widely, but ran as high as tens of thousands.

General

Gunman in Montreal Kills 14 Women — A man armed with a hunting rifle shot 14 women to death on the campus of the University of Montreal, **Dec. 6.** He also wounded 13 others, mostly women, before killing himself. Six of the women were killed in one classroom. Police, **Dec. 7** identified the gunman as Marc Lepine, and said he had left a note in which he had said that women had ruined his life. The rampage was the worst mass shooting ever in Canada.

Driver Who Caused 27 Deaths Convicted — Larry Mahoney, the driver of a pickup truck that collided with a church bus near Carrollton, Ky. in May 1988 was convicted of 27 counts of manslaughter, **Dec. 21.** Mahoney's lawyers acknowledged that he had been drunk and driving in the wrong direction on an interstate highway at the time of the crash, but blamed a faulty gas tank on the bus for the fire that took the heavy toll of life, including 24 children and 3 adults. Twelve other persons were burned in the crash. The defendant was found not guilty of 27 counts of murder. On **Feb. 23,** Mahoney was sentenced to 16 years in prison.

JANUARY

National

Economic Growth Slowed in 1989 — Figures released in January showed that the U.S. economy slowed down in 1989, compared with 1988. The Dow Jones industrial average closed, **Jan. 2,** at 2810.15, an all-time high, before beginning a month-long decline. The Labor Dept. said, **Jan. 5,** that the unemployment rate had held steady in December at 5.3 percent. In the first shift downward in 6 months, major banks, **Jan. 8,** lowered their prime lending rate by 0.5 percent to 10 percent. The Labor Dept. said, **Jan. 12,** that for all of 1989 producer prices had risen 4.8 percent, the highest annual increase since a 7.1 jump in 1981. The Commerce Dept. reported, **Jan. 17,** that the merchandise trade deficit for November was $10.5 billion, the largest for any month in 1989. Consumer prices rose 4.6 percent in 1989, the highest rate since 1981, the Labor Dept. reported, **Jan. 18.** The Commerce Dept. said, **Jan. 26,** that the gross national product grew at 2.9 percent (later revised to 3.0 percent) for 1989. Thus, economic growth had slowed considerably from 1988, when it was 4.4 percent. The department said, **Jan. 31,** that the leading economic indicators had risen 0.8 percent in December.

Marketing of Cigarette to Blacks Deplored — Sec. of Health and Human Services Louis Sullivan, **Jan. 18,** sharply criticized a plan to market a cigarette to black Americans. R.J. Reynolds Tobacco Co. planned to test-market the new brand, *Uptown,* to blacks in Philadelphia. Sullivan, speaking to medical students at the University of Pennsylvania, said, "At a time when our people desperately need the message of health promotion, *Uptown's* message is more disease, more suffering and more death. ..." Surveys had found that smok-

ing was more common among blacks than whites. Reynolds, **Jan. 19,** canceled its test of the brand, saying that "the unfair and biased attention the brand had received" would invalidate the results of the test.

Washington, D.C. Mayor Arrested — City police and FBI agents, **Jan. 18,** arrested Washington, D.C. Mayor Marion Barry on a drug charge. Rumors, which Barry denied, had circulated for years that he used drugs. According to reports, law enforcement officials utilized a former model and friend of Barry's to lure him to the Vista International Hotel in downtown Washington. There, according to the FBI, Barry bought a small amount of crack cocaine from an undercover agent, put it in a pipe, and smoked it. This incident was reportedly videotaped, and Barry was arrested. He was arraigned, **Jan. 19,** in U.S. District Court on one charge of willfully possessing cocaine, a misdemeanor.

Agent Pleads Guilty in HUD Inquiry — Marilyn Louise Harrell, a private escrow agent, pleaded guilty in federal court in Baltimore, **Jan. 29,** to embezzling $4.5 million that was to go to the U.S. Dept. of Housing and Urban Development. She also admitted underreporting income on her tax return for 1987. She had previously claimed that she had given much of the money to charities and the poor, and had been nicknamed "Robin HUD." Prosecutors said that Harrell had been "her own biggest charity." On **June 22,** Harrell was sentenced to 46 months in prison and ordered to pay $600,000 in restitution.

Bush Budget Calls for No Tax Increases — Adhering to his pledge while running for president, George Bush submitted a budget for the 1991 fiscal year to Congress, **Jan. 29,** that called for no increase in taxes. The $1.23 trillion budget included a small cut in real spending for defense—a 1.9 percent increase in outlays that was below the rate of inflation. Larger cuts were proposed for some domestic programs, but not for environmental programs, the war on drugs, and space projects. Overall, the budget adhered to the deficit limitation of the Gramm-Rudman law, but the Congressional Budget Office and some economists said the deficit projections were based on economic forecasts that were far too optimistic.

International

Toll High in Sudanese Massacre — A rebel radio in Sudan reported, **Jan. 4,** that a pro-government Arab militia had killed 2,000 black villagers at the end of December. Reportedly, 2 members of the Shilok tribe killed their Moslem employer in a dispute, and local militiamen armed with machine guns then destroyed the entire village. Western diplomats and relief officials put the death toll at 300 to 1,500. The Moslem central government was in a sustained war against black Christians and animists.

New Romanian Leadership Assailed — The National Salvation Front, the new leadership group in Romania, became a target of much criticism. By **Jan. 5,** a deadline set by the government, many parties had declared their intention to run candidates in elections scheduled for April. During a visit to Romania, **Jan. 6,** Soviet Foreign Minister Eduard Shevardnadze said Moscow would support any form of political system that emerged. Thousands of Romanians demonstrated nationwide, **Jan. 7,** protesting the prominence of ex-Communists in the provisional regime. A large crowd gathered at Bucharest, **Jan. 12,** to protest the perceived influence of Communists in the leadership. Ion Iliescu, chairman of the front and interim president, managed to calm the crowd somewhat by announcing that the Communist Party had been outlawed. However, the government then lifted the ban on the party, **Jan. 17**, and canceled a referendum that was to decide its fate. Facing growing public unrest, the government, **Jan. 24**, outlawed unauthorized demonstrations. Vice Pres. Dumitru Mazilu resigned, **Jan. 26**, and accused the regime of using "Stalinist practices." A judge investigating the violence in Timisoara in December said, **Jan. 29**, that only 95 civilian deaths had been verified, against earlier reports that there had been thousands of victims.

Soldiers Held in Killing of Priests — Pres. Alfredo Cristiani of El Salvador said, **Jan. 7**, that the military had been involved in the murder of 6 Jesuit priests and 2 other people in San Salvador in November. The Jesuits had criticized human rights abuses by the government and had supported a negotiated settlement of the civil war with leftist guerrillas. Cristiani announced, **Jan. 13**, that a colonel, 2 lieutenants, and 5 other soldiers had been arrested in the killings. The 8 soldiers plus a 9th still being sought were indicted, **Jan. 19**. The soldiers in custody pleaded not guilty.

East Germans Sack Police HQ — An official of the East German government disclosed, **Jan. 8**, that 60,000 (of an original 85,000) secret-police personnel were still on the government payroll despite a promise in December that they would be disbanded. A party in the ruling coalition confirmed, **Jan. 10**, that the government was forming a new secret security agency. Premier Hans Modrow said, **Jan. 12**, that no new security force would be formed before national elections, and admitted that secret police had continued to spy on the political opposition. On **Jan. 15**, 100,000 persons gathered outside the East German headquarters of the state security service, and the peaceful rally soon turned violent. Many in the crowd stormed the headquarters, generally tore up the interior and destroyed or threw out thousands of documents. Pres. Mikhail Gorbachev of the Soviet Union, after meeting with Modrow, **Jan. 30**, indicated that German reunification was to be expected, adding "No one casts any doubt upon it."

Crises in Soviet Republics Continue — On **Jan. 9**, the parliament of the republic of Armenia voted to integrate the economy of the region of Nagorno-Karabakh into the economy of Armenia. The region, occupied predominantly by Armenians, lay within Azerbaijan. After the presidium of the national Supreme Soviet declared that step unconstitutional, Armenia's parliament, **Jan. 11**, asserted Armenia's right to override national laws that affected the republic. Soviet Pres. Mikhail Gorbachev arrived in Lithuania, **Jan. 11**, in an attempt to persuade the Lithuanian Communist Party to rescind its break with the national party. Some 250,000 persons demonstrated, **Jan. 11**, in Vilnius, the capital of the republic, on behalf of independence. In a walk through the streets of the city, Gorbachev denounced independence as a dead end and said the Soviet Union could not afford to lose its Baltic ports. Before leaving Lithuania, **Jan. 13**, Gorbachev expressed a willingness to accept a multiparty system in the USSR. In Baku, the capital of Azerbaijan, Azerbaijani youths, **Jan. 13**, went on a rampage through the Armenian section of town, and some 30 people, mostly Armenians, were reported killed. With guerrillas fighting elsewhere in the 2 republics in what had virtually become an ethnic civil war, the Soviet government sent troops into the area, **Jan. 15**. The Azerbaijanis resisted, destroying or blockading bridges, roads, and rail lines. Some troops were killed. Soviet troops led by tanks forced their way into central Baku, **Jan. 20**. The Azerbaijani parliament, **Jan. 22**, threatened to secede from the Soviet Union. By **Jan. 23**, the death toll in the fighting stood at 93.

Martial Law Ended in Beijing — Premier Li Peng of China announced, **Jan. 10**, that martial law would be lifted in Beijing. In a televised speech, he said that order had been restored and "a great victory has been won in checking the turmoil and quelling the counter-revolutionary rebellion." The end of martial law, which took effect, **Jan. 11**, had little practical effect because other laws introduced since the June 1989 protests had curtailed unauthorized political activity.

Bulgaria Ends Communist Monopoly — The Bulgarian National Assembly, though controlled by Communists, voted unanimously, **Jan. 15**, to repeal paragraphs in the constitution guaranteeing a dominant role for the Communist Party. It was reported, **Jan. 18**, that Todor Zhivkov, the former Communist Party leader, had been put under house arrest on charges of malfeasance in office and misuse of government property and money. It was announced, **Jan. 29**, that he had been transferred to a prison.

Polish Communists Form New Party — A congress of the United Workers' (Communist) Party opened in Warsaw, **Jan. 27**. Some 1,600 delegates attended. On **Jan. 29**, the party voted overwhelmingly to disband and create at once a new Social Democracy Party. But some former Communist Party members bolted and formed yet another new group, the Social Democratic Union.

Bush Proposes Troop Cuts in Europe — In his State of the Union address, **Jan. 31**, Pres. George Bush proposed a ceiling of 225,000 on the number of U.S. and Soviet troops that could be deployed in Europe. Under his plan, no more than 195,000 could be deployed by each side in the central zone of Europe. At present, the United States had 300,000 troops in Europe and the Soviet Union 565,000.

General

Suicide Adds Bizarre Turn to Murder Case — A murder case in Boston that had gained nationwide attention took an unexpected turn, **Jan. 4**, when the husband of the murder victim leaped to his death from a bridge in Boston harbor. The man, Charles Stuart, had learned that he had become the prime suspect in the case. In October 1989, Stuart had called from a phone in his car to report that his pregnant wife, Carol, had been shot and that he had been shot. The tapes of his pleas for help had been played on radio and television and had engendered widespread sympathy. Charles Stuart recovered from a serious wound but Carol Stuart died at the hospital. Her baby, delivered prematurely, also died. Stuart said a black man was their assailant. The Stuarts were white. On **Jan. 3**, Charles Stuart's brother Matthew told investigators that he had driven to the neighborhood where the shooting occurred and that Charles had given him his wife's bag and a gun, which Matthew threw into the Pines River. Matthew said he had decided to come forward after his brother had identified a black man in a police line-up as resembling the gunman. Based on Matthew's information, police divers recovered both the handbag and a .38 caliber revolver from the river. It was reported that Charles Stuart had taken out large insurance policies on his wife. Some black leaders objected to the intensity with which police had conducted investigations in black neighborhoods when it was believed that a black was the culprit.

Long Child Abuse Trial Ends — Peggy McMartin Buckey and her son, Raymond Buckey, were found not guilty on 52 counts of child molestation and conspiracy in Los Angeles, **Jan. 18**. The jury was deadlocked on one remaining count against Mrs. Buckey and on 13 counts against her son. The trial was the longest and costliest in U.S. history. It lasted 33 months, filled 60,000 pages of transcript, and cost the state of California about $15 million. Based on accounts by young children, 7 people had originally been indicted on child molestation charges—incidents that had allegedly occurred at the McMartin Pre-School in Manhattan Beach. Charges against the other 5 defendants had been dropped for insufficient evidence. Raymond Buckey had spent 5 years in jail and his mother 22 months in jail. Some jurors who were interviewed after the verdict said they had reservations about the technique used to interview children who may have been molested, especially the practice of asking them leading questions. The remaining count against Mrs. Buckey was dismissed. A mistrial was declared on the remaining counts against Raymond Buckey. He was then retried on 8 of the counts, but on July 27, the jury declared that it was deadlocked on all charges. On Aug. 1, Superior Court Judge Stanley Weisberg dismissed all charges against Buckey.

Value of Oat Bran Questioned — Researchers from Harvard University reported in the Jan. 18 New England Journal of Medicine that a study they had conducted failed to show that oat bran had any special ability to lower blood serum cholesterol levels. Based on the study of 20 adults, the researchers concluded that bran or any other starchy carbohydrate was beneficial primarily because people who ate it tended to eat less high-fat food. The oat bran fad had caught on after a previous study had shown that it lowered cholesterol. Manufacturers of oat bran products said the Harvard study was too small to be accepted.

Jet Crash on Long Island Kills 73 — A Colombian jetliner apparently ran out of fuel over Long Island in New York, Jan. 25, and crashed into a wooded area in the community of Cove Neck. Of the 161 persons aboard, 73 were killed and dozens of the rest were injured. The plane, en route from Bogotá via Medellin, Colombia, was to have landed at Kennedy International Airport. The landing was delayed more than an hour because of bad weather. The pilot had told controllers about 50 minutes before the crash that he needed a priority landing because of low fuel.

Disasters — A passenger train crashed into a stopped freight train in a station in Sangi, Pakistan, Jan. 4, causing the death of 307 people and injury to 700 others. . . . About 100 people were killed, Jan. 14, when a ferry collided with another vessel in a river near Dhaka, Bangladesh.

FEBRUARY

National

Reagan Testifies in Iran-Contra Trial — Former Pres. Ronald Reagan provided videotaped testimony for use in the trial of Adm. John Poindexter (ret.), his former national security adviser. Albert Hakim, who had pleaded guilty in November in one of the previous trials in the Iran-Contra case, was sentenced, Feb. 1, to 2-years' probation and fined $5,000. He had illegally supplemented the salary of former National Security Council staff member Oliver North. Poindexter's attorneys had asked Reagan to provide excerpts from his diaries, and Judge Harold Greene had directed Reagan to do so, but the former president declined, Feb. 5, asserting, in the words of his attorneys, a claim "to the constitutionally protected privacy of his diaries." Greene, Feb. 5, ordered Reagan to give videotaped testimony, agreeing with Poindexter that he possessed evidence unavailable from any other source. Reagan, Feb. 9, agreed to comply. In a closed Los Angeles courtroom, Feb. 16 and 17, Reagan provided 8 hours

of testimony. A transcript was made public, Feb. 22. Reagan testified that he had authorized, in general, the policies of selling arms to Iran and aiding the Nicaraguan contras. But he said he had repeatedly told subordinates to obey the law, and he said he had not known that North had been coordinating supply missions for the contras and otherwise assisting the contras at a time when Congress had banned U.S. support for them. Reagan often testified that he was unable to remember key meetings or conversations.

Special Prosecutor Asked in HUD Case — U.S. Attorney Gen. Richard Thornburgh recommended, Feb. 1, that a special prosecutor, or independent counsel, be appointed to investigate Samuel Pierce, Jr. and other former high officials in the Dept. of Housing and Urban Development. In compliance with procedures established by law, Thornburgh made his recommendations to a special 3-judge panel. He said the prosecutor would investigate charges that Pierce, a former secretary of HUD, and other officials had awarded grants to developers backed by well-known Republicans. The 3-judge panel, Mar. 2, named Arlin Adams, a retired federal judge from Philadelphia, as special prosecutor.

1989 Trade Gap Lowest in 5 Years — The Labor Dept. reported, Feb. 2, that the unemployment rate fell to 5.2 percent in January. The department reported, Feb. 9, that producer prices for finished goods had risen 1.8 percent in January, the largest monthly increase since November 1974. The sharp rise was primarily the result of a jump in heating oil prices during very cold weather. The Commerce Dept. said, Feb. 16, that the merchandise trade deficit, which stood at $108.58 billion for all of 1989, was the lowest since 1984. Exports rose 13 percent in 1989, imports only 7.3 percent.

ABA Supports Right to Abortion — At its meeting in Los Angeles, Feb. 13, the American Bar Assn. declared its support for a constitutional right to abortion. The vote by the ABA's house of delegates was 238-106. The resolution opposed legislation or other governmental action "that interferes with the confidential relationship between a pregnant woman and her physician or with the decision to terminate the pregnancy at any time before the fetus is capable of independent life."

Washington, D.C. Mayor Indicted — Mayor Marion Barry Jr. of Washington, D.C., who had been arrested in January, was indicted, Feb. 15, by a federal grand jury on 5 counts of cocaine possession and 3 counts of perjury. The perjury counts related to testimony he had given to a grand jury in January 1989. Barry, meanwhile, had entered an alcohol treatment program in Florida. He had denied having a drug problem, and called the indictments "a continuation of the political lynching and excesses of the Justice Department."

International

Reunified Germany Is Nearer to Reality — Addressing a press conference in East Berlin, Feb. 1, East German Premier Hans Modrow outlined a plan for reunifying East and West Germany. He described an approach for integrating economic and governmental institutions into a country that would become militarily neutral. West German Chancellor Helmut Kohl said, Feb. 1, he would not begin any negotiations until after East German elections in March. After meeting with Soviet Pres. Mikhail Gorbachev in Moscow, Feb. 10, Kohl said that the Soviet leaders supported "the right of the German people alone" to choose their form of relationship. Meeting in Bonn, Feb. 13, Kohl and Modrow agreed to talks on uniting their 2 monetary systems under the West German deutsche mark. At a first-ever meeting of foreign ministers of NATO and Warsaw Pact countries, in Ottawa, **Feb. 13**, a formula for reunification talks was established. The 2 Germanys would discuss internal and domestic issues relating to reunification. External issues, such as "security of the neighboring states," would be expanded to include the "Big 4" allies of World War II: the U.S., USSR, Great Britain, and France. In another tentative breakthrough at Ottawa, the Soviets agreed to limit their troops in Europe to 195,000 and to a larger limit—225,000—for U.S. troops in Europe. Kohl met with Pres. George Bush, **Feb. 24** and **25**. At a press conference, **Feb. 25**, they endorsed the concept of a united Germany within NATO. Bush said that the United States formally recognized the current German-Polish border. Some Poles were concerned that a united Germany might want to regain territory ceded to Poland after World War II.

Bulgarian Communists Elect New Leader — Alexander Lilov became chairman of the Communist Party in Bulgaria, and the party, **Feb. 1**, ratified a manifesto that endorsed democratic ideals but kept its Marxist-Leninist ideology. Premier Georgi Atanasov and his cabinet resigned, **Feb. 1**. Lilov, elected **Feb. 2**, to succeed Petar Mladenov, was seen as a compromise candidate, who was not identified with the ousted hard-line regime of Todor Zhivkov, and who could better lead the party in upcoming elections. Parliament, **Feb. 3**, confirmed Andrei Lukanov as premier.

Opposition Gains Ground in Romania — The National Salvation Front agreed, **Feb. 1**, to a power-sharing arrangement prior to elections in Romania. It was agreed that the interim legislative body would be increased in size and would include representatives of 30 registered political parties. On **Feb. 2**, a military court convicted 4 former top aides to the deposed Pres. Nicolae Ceasescu of complicity to commit genocide. The defendants included Emil Bobu, 3d-ranking figure in the government. The men were sentenced to life imprisonment.

South Africa Frees Mandela — South African Pres. F. W. de Klerk announced, **Feb. 2**, that black nationalist leader Nelson Mandela, who had been in prison for treason for 27 years, would soon be freed. In a surprising speech, de Klerk also said his government was lifting its ban on the African National Congress, the principal black organization opposing white minority rule. He also announced legalization of the South African Communist Party and the Pan-African Congress, and the lifting of restrictions on 33 groups and 374 individuals. He said news censorship would end, executions would be suspended, nonviolent political prisoners would be freed, and power-sharing talks with black leaders were on the horizon. Mandela, 71, was released from prison, **Feb. 11**. His release was hailed around the world. In his first speech, in Cape Town, **Feb. 11**, he urged that pressure be kept on the white government until the apartheid system of racial segregation was destroyed. More than 100,000 people welcomed him home to Soweto, **Feb. 13**. Up to 20,000 conservative whites protested in Pretoria, **Feb. 15**, against the legalization of ANC and the freeing of Mandela. In his first trip outside of South Africa since being released, Mandela went to Zambia, **Feb. 27**, to meet with ANC leaders. He was greeted by official delegations from many countries. Meeting with Pres. George Bush in Washington, D.C., **Feb. 28**, Zulu Chief Mangosuthu Gatsha Buthelezi called on the president to lift economic sanctions against South Africa.

Noriega Ordered to Stand Trial — The U.S. Justice Dept. announced, **Feb. 2**, that the government would treat ousted Panamanian dictator Manuel Noriega and one of his co-defendants as prisoners of war. The department noted, however, that the Geneva Convention provides that "prisoners of war may be prosecuted in the civilian courts of the detaining country." Congress, **Feb. 7**, approved $42 million in emergency aid to Panama and lifted economic sanctions against Panama. U.S. District Court Judge William Hoeveler ruled, **Feb. 8**, that Noriega must stand trial in Miami on drug-trafficking charges.

Multiparty System in Sight in USSR — The Central Committee of the Communist Party of the Soviet Union voted to end the party's monopoly on power, as guaranteed in the constitution. In Moscow, **Feb. 4**, 100,000 persons demonstrated on behalf of democracy. Pres. Mikhail Gorbachev, who favored the constitutional change, told the Central Committee, **Feb. 3**, that "We should abandon the ideological dogmatism that became ingrained during the past decades." Premier Nikolai Ryzhkov said, **Feb. 6**, that a multiparty system, in effect, already existed. Conservatives on the committee warned that any moves toward a multiparty system or free enterprise could lead to the disintegration of the Soviet Union. But the Central Committee endorsed Gorbachev's proposal, **Feb. 7**. Parliament and the standing legislature would still have to act. The KGB said, **Feb. 13**, that 786,098 persons had been shot to death as enemies of the state during the rule of Joseph Stalin. Tadzhikistan, in central Asia, became the latest Soviet republic to experience ethnic violence. On **Feb. 15**, after 18 people had been killed in rioting, party and governmental leaders there resigned. In multiparty elections to the Supreme Soviet (parliament) of Lithuania, **Feb. 24**, candidates favoring independence ran very well. Runoff elections would determine the final outcome. Hundreds of thousands of pro-democracy demonstrators turned out in more than 30 cities in the Soviet Union, **Feb. 25**. The Supreme Soviet, the standing Parliament, gave its approval, **Feb. 27**, to Gorbachev's proposal for a popularly elected president having broad executive powers.

Bush at Drug Summit in Colombia — The presidents of Bolivia, Colombia, Peru, and the United States signed an accord in Cartagena, Colombia, **Feb. 15**, to work together in the fight against illegal drug traffic. Most coca grown for the production of cocaine is found in Bolivia and Peru, and three-fourths of the world's cocaine supply is produced in Colombia. The presidents agreed to the need for encouraging trade and investment in the 3 South American countries. The presidents also recognized that reducing demand (in the U.S.) was as important as reducing supply. The meeting was held under tight security. Pres. George Bush had come under some pressure not to attend because of the danger of violence from the drug traffickers.

Japan's Ruling Party Wins Election — The Liberal Democratic Party won a clear-cut victory, **Feb. 18**, in elections to the lower house of the Diet, the parliament of Japan. The long rule of the Liberal Democrats had appeared threatened by the Recruit Co. scandal, in which the conglomerate had given millions of dollars in cash and stocks to leading political figures. However, the party lost only a few seats and held a majority in the lower house. The Socialist Party, the principal opposition, gained ground, but mostly at the expense of smaller parties. The results seemed to strengthen the position of Premier Toshiki Kaifu.

Czech President Addresses Congress — Czechoslovak Pres. Vaclav Havel began a trip to North America, **Feb. 18**, in Ottawa, where he conferred with Canadian Prime Minister Brian Mulroney. On his arrival in Washington, D.C., **Feb. 20**, he became the first head of state of his country to visit the United States. Havel, a leader of the nearly bloodless revolution that had ended Communist rule in Czechoslovakia in 1989, received an enthusiastic reception during an address to Congress, **Feb. 21.** He said he saw the rise of democracy in the Soviet bloc as a "historically irreversible process" and he foresaw "an era in which all of us, large and small, former slaves and former masters, will be able to create what your great President Lincoln called the 'family of man.' "

Sandinistas Lose Nicaraguan Election — The Sandinista National Liberation Front (FSLN), which had held power for 10 years in Nicaragua, was defeated in national elections, **Feb. 25.** Pres. Daniel Ortega lost, 55 percent to 41 percent, to Violeta Barrios de Chamorro of the National Opposition Union (UNO), and the UNO also won more seats in the National Assembly. Chamorro belonged to no party, and the UNO was a loose coalition. The assassination of her husband, an editor, in 1978, helped provoke the overthrow of the Somoza dictatorship by the Sandinistas, whom Mrs. Chamorro initially supported and then abandoned with their shift toward Marxist thinking. Dissatisfaction with the economy was regarded as the prime factor in the defeat of the Sandinistas. The election was monitored by some 2,000 foreign observers. Ortega conceded defeat, **Feb. 26.** However, he said, **Feb. 27,** that the contra rebels would have to demobilize before the Sandinistas yielded control of the army and the police. Chamorro, **Feb. 27,** called on the contras to disband to help speed the transfer of power.

General

Securities Firm Files for Bankruptcy — Drexel Burnham Lambert Group Inc., which made financial history on Wall Street in the 1980s, filed for Chapter 11 bankruptcy, **Feb. 13.** The firm had become highly profitable for a time through the utilization of so-called junk bonds, securities that paid high interest rates and had high risk. The use of these bonds facilitated the corporate takeover boom of the 1980s. Michael Milken, the firm's leading junk-bond trader, orchestrated many takeovers. Drexel's slide began after it agreed in 1988 to pay the government $650 million to settle insider-trading charges; Milken was indicted in 1989 on a variety of charges. Drexel was hurt further by the decline in the market value of junk bonds. Company officials said that the bankruptcy filing would lead to the liquidation of Drexel.

FDA Approves Fat Substitute — For the first time, **Feb. 22,** the U.S. Food and Drug Administration approved a low-calorie substitute for fat. Nutrasweet Company had developed the substance, Simplesse, a blend of proteins from egg white and milk. The FDA said Simplesse was safe for use in frozen dessert products, and the company said it could be used in other foods having a high fat content. Other food manufacturers were reported working on fat substitutes in response to concerns about nutrition.

Disasters — An Indian Airlines passenger jet crashed, **Feb. 14,** while preparing to land at Bangalore, killing 91 of the 146 persons aboard.

MARCH

National

Economic Indicators Show No Trend — The Commerce Dept. reported, **Mar. 2,** that the leading economic indicators were unchanged in January. The Labor Dept. reported, **Mar. 9,** that unemployment stood at 5.3 percent in February. The department said, **Mar. 16,** that the index of producer prices for unfinished goods was unchanged in February. The department

reported, **Mar. 20,** that consumer prices had jumped 0.5 percent in February, following an even sharper 1.1 percent runup in January. A record rise in oil imports caused the merchandise trade deficit to grow to $9.25 billion in January, the Commerce Dept. announced, **Mar. 20.**

North, Meese Testify in Poindexter Trial — The trial of John Poindexter, former national security adviser for Pres. Ronald Reagan, got under way in federal district court in Washington, D.C. Poindexter was charged with obstructing Congress and making false statements to Congress in connection with its investigation of the Iran-contra affair. Oliver North, a former aide to Poindexter who had been convicted on Iran-contra charges, was called as a witness for the prosecution. North sought to resist implicating Poindexter in a coverup, and said, **Mar. 9,** "No one told me to lie to Congress." He admitted, **Mar. 12,** that he had seen Poindexter destroy an order signed by Reagan authorizing U.S. participation in arms sales to Iran. Judge Harold Greene ruled, **Mar. 21,** that Reagan would not be required to provide his presidential diaries to Poindexter's defense. Former Attorney Gen. Edwin Meese 3d, who had led a Justice Dept. investigation of the Iran arms sales, testified for the defense, **Mar. 22,** that Poindexter had not tried to conceal details of the arms scandal from Congress.

Exxon Valdez **Captain Guilty of Negligence** — Joseph Hazelwood, who was captain of the oil tanker *Exxon Valdez* on Mar. 24, 1989, when it dumped nearly 11 million gallons of oil into Prince William Sound in Alaska, was found guilty of negligent discharge of oil in a state court in Anchorage, **Mar. 22.** He was acquitted of criminal mischief and 2 other charges. The spill contaminated more than 1,000 miles of coastline and claimed a heavy toll of wildlife. Hazelwood, **Mar. 23,** was sentenced to serve 1,000 hours of community service and ordered to make a "token restitution" of $50,000 over time.

Idaho Anti-Abortion Bill Vetoed — Gov. Cecil Andrus of Idaho vetoed, **Mar. 30,** a bill that would have banned most abortions. Under its provisions, an abortion in the case of rape would have been allowed only if the rape was reported within 7 days, and abortion in the case of incest would be allowed only if the victim was under 18. Andrus complained that anti-abortion activists had designed the bill for "the sole purpose of getting this issue back before the Supreme Court." Andrus said he had not been influenced by threats to abortion-rights groups to boycott Idaho potatoes.

International

Unrest Grows in South Africa — In the month after black nationalist leader Nelson Mandela was freed from prison, unrest among blacks in South Africa increased. On **Mar. 2,** at a meeting in Zambia, the executive committee of the African National Congress named Mandela the ANC's deputy president. Because Pres. Oliver Tambo was ill, Mandela in effect became the ANC leader. Mandela traveled to Zimbabwe, Tanzania, and Ethiopia, where he received enthusiastic welcomes, then met with Tambo in Sweden, **Mar. 12,** their first visit in 28 years. Meanwhile, tensions overflowed in several of the black "homelands" created by the minority white government of South Africa. These 10 tribal homelands were to become self-governing, but only 4 had been formally established. Black nationalists believed to be sympathetic to the ANC overthrew the president of one homeland, Ciskei, **Mar. 4.** After looting and arson became widespread, and 27 people were killed, South Africa sent soldiers and police into Ciskei, **Mar. 5.** By **Mar. 6,** protests had spread to 4 other homelands, led by pro-ANC activists, who, in turn, clashed with security forces in the homelands. In Bophuthatswana, **Mar. 7**, seven people were killed and 450 persons injured when local police opened fire on a crowd of 50,000 that had marched on a government office. On **Mar. 26**, in the black township of Sebokeng, 11 people were killed and hundreds wounded when police fired on a large crowd of demonstrators. In Natal Province, **Mar. 27** and **28**, fighting among black factions resulted in 25 fatalities.

Mystery Fire Strikes Libyan Plant — The United States said, **Mar. 6** and **7**, that poison gas was being produced at a plant at Rabta, Libya, about 50 miles southwest of Tripoli. White House spokesman Marlin Fitzwater said, **Mar. 7**, that evidence indicated that the plant was producing chemical weapons and called on the "international community" to "step up its efforts to deny Libya the ability to continue operating the plant." Libya claimed the plant was a pharmaceutical factory. A fire broke out at the plant, **Mar. 14**, and Pres. George Bush denied "absolutely" that the United States was responsible. Libyan and U.S. officials said, **Mar. 15**, that the plant had been damaged extensively and would be out of operation indefinitely. Libya's official news agency said at least 2 persons had been killed in the fire.

Britons Protest New Poll Tax — A new community charge, or poll tax, stirred protests across Great Britain. The community charge was to replace the previous system of property taxes. Prime Minister Margaret Thatcher contended that the new system was fairer, and she blamed local councils for overspending when they set charges at higher levels than the government had estimated. Left-wing groups led the protests. Violence occurred in Bristol, Southampton, and in several boroughs of London, including Hackney, where 29 police officers were hurt and 60 people were arrested, **Mar. 8**. A riot involving several thousand people occurred in London on **Mar. 31**, the day before the new rates were to go into effect. More than 400 were injured, including 331 police officers, and 341 arrests were made.

Lithuania Declares Independence — Lithuania, a republic of the Soviet Union, declared its independence, **Mar. 11**. Lithuania and its Baltic neighbors, Latvia and Estonia, had been annexed by the USSR in 1940. The vote in the Lithuanian Supreme Soviet (parliament) was 124-0, with 6 abstentions. The deputies then elected Vytautas Landsbergis, a professor of music history, as president. The U.S. State Dept., **Mar. 12**, declined to extend diplomatic recognition. Soviet Politburo member Yegor Ligachev, **Mar. 12**, called for a peaceful solution, adding, "Tanks will not help in this matter." Soviet Pres. Mikhail Gorbachev, **Mar. 13**, called Lithuania's step "illegitimate and invalid." On **Mar. 17**, the Lithuanian parliament formed a noncommunist government. Soviet forces began military maneuvers in Lithuania, **Mar. 18**. The Lithuanian government ignored the **Mar. 19** deadline set by Gorbachev for rescinding the declaration. On **Mar. 21**, Gorbachev banned all sale of firearms in Lithuania and ordered Lithuanians to surrender all their firearms to Soviet officials. A Soviet military convoy entered Vilnius, the capital of Lithuania, **Mar. 22**. The Soviet government, **Mar. 23**, ordered Western diplomats to leave the republic and restricted entry of foreigners into Lithuania. Soviet paratroopers, **Mar. 25**, seized the headquarters and other property of the rebellious Communist Party of Lithuania. Ethnic Lithuanians who had deserted the army were rounded up. All foreigners were ordered to leave, **Mar. 27**. Landsbergis, **Mar. 28**, called for talks with Moscow. Soviet troops, **Mar. 30**, seized the state prosecutor's office in the capi-

tal and the printing plant of a pro-independence newspaper. Estonia's parliament proclaimed, **Mar. 30**, that it was occupied and that it was entering a "transitional period" that would lead to independence. Gorbachev warned Lithuania, **Mar. 31**, of "grave consequences" if it did not annul its declaration of independence.

Disbanding of Contras Debated — Pres.-elect Violeta Barrios de Chamorro met with Pres. Oscar Arias in Costa Rica, **Mar. 6**, to discuss repatriation of the contras. She said after the meeting that she would solve the contra problem by declaring an amnesty. She called for demilitarization of Central America and said she would reduce Nicaragua's army to a small police force. Meeting with Vice Pres. Dan Quayle in Santiago, Chile, **Mar. 12**, Pres. Daniel Ortega gave assurances that his government would surrender control of the military and the security police to the new government. Pres. George Bush, **Mar. 13**, lifted economic sanctions against Nicaragua and asked Congress for $300 million in economic aid. The contras, **Mar. 23**, agreed to dismantle their camps in Honduras, and those in Nicaragua would gather in U.N.-supervised security zones until absorbed into civilian life. Contra leaders said, **Mar. 25**, that those gathering in the enclaves would remain there for months, and would keep their arms. The Sandinista government, **Mar. 27**, signed an agreement recognizing Chamorro's right to have full authority over the army and security forces.

Mongolian Communists Relax Grip — Jambyn Batmunh, general secretary of the Communist Party of Mongolia, said, **Mar. 12**, that the Communists would work with opposition forces to make needed political changes. The Central Committee of the People's Revolutionary (Communist) Party voted, **Mar. 14**, to drop its monopoly on power as guaranteed by the constitution. Gombojavyn Ochirbat, a reformist leader who had been living in Czechoslovakia, was selected to replace Batmunh, and an all-new Politburo was chosen.

Communist Monopoly in USSR Ended — The Soviet Congress of People's Deputies voted overwhelmingly (1,771 to 24, with 74 abstentions), **Mar. 13**, to repeal Article 6 of the Soviet constitution that gave the Communist Party a political monopoly. The historic change had been included in a platform approved by the party's Central Committee in February. Pres. Mikhail Gorbachev, who had pressed for the change, also won a victory with the approval by the deputies, **Mar. 13**, of a more powerful presidency with broad executive authority. He believed that a strong president could rise above partisan politics in the new multiparty system, but many deputies feared that his plan would lead to a dictatorship. The congress voted, **Mar. 14**, to begin popular elections for the presidency beginning in 1995. Gorbachev, as expected, was chosen president **Mar. 15**, but barely got the required two-thirds vote. Gorbachev already held the title of president. In local election results reported **Mar. 19**, opposition groups scored many victories over the Communists. It was reported that insurgents won 281 of 498 seats on the Moscow City Council, and the Communists also lost control of city councils in Kiev and Leningrad. Nationalist opposition movements continued to gain in Estonia, Latvia, and the Ukraine in voting for various local and republic offices.

Conservatives Win East German Election — Conservatives supported by West German Chancellor Helmut Kohl won big in East German elections held in March. Earlier, on **Mar. 14**, diplomatic representatives from both Germanys, France, Great Britain, the Soviet Union, and the U.S. began talks on German reunification in Bonn. The pace of reunification was apparently the key issue in the voting for the East German parliament, **Mar. 18**. Three conservative parties, who had joined together as the Alliance for Germany, and who favored rapid reunification, piled up 48 percent of the vote and earned an equivalent percentage of the seats in parliament. The Social Democratic Party ran a distant second with 22 percent of the vote. The Party of Democratic Socialism, the successor to the Communist Party, received 16 percent.

Shamir Government Falls in Israel — Israel's coalition government led by Prime Minister Yitzhak Shamir of the Likud Party fell, **Mar. 15,** when it was defeated in a 60-55 no-confidence vote in the Knesset (parliament). The vote came after Shamir refused to accept a U.S. plan for peace talks between Israel and the Palestinians. Likud's coalition partner, the Labor Party, voted against the government, but the key votes were held by the small religious parties. Five members of the Shas party withheld their support for Shamir after he refused to compromise on the U.S. proposal, and that allowed the no-confidence vote to carry.

Namibia Becomes Independent — Namibia, once known as South-West Africa, became independent, **Mar 21.** Once a German colony, the country was controlled from World War I by South Africa, which was granted a League of Nations mandate in 1920. The United Nations opposed South Africa's request to annex Namibia, and an armed independence struggle ensued. U.N.-supported negotiations began in 1978, and culminated in an accord on independence. Pres. Sam Nujoma, a former guerrilla leader, took a moderate stance at the independence celebration, saying he welcomed "inflows of capital and know-how from abroad."

General

AIDS Epidemic Seen at Its Peak — Two medical researchers concluded, **Mar. 16,** in an article in the *Journal of the American Medical Association* that the AIDS epidemic had reached its peak in the U.S. Dennis Bregman of the University of Southern California and Alexander Langmuir, former chief epidemiologist at the Centers for Disease Control, foresaw that new cases of AIDS, which had been increasing each year, would level off within a few years. They cited a theory of epidemiology which says that epidemics fade quickly after the disease spreads from highly susceptible members of the population to less susceptible members. However, other AIDS specialists were less optimistic, noting that hundreds of thousands of persons infected with the AIDS virus were expected to show symptoms of the condition in the future. The number of new AIDS cases in the U.S. rose by 9 percent in 1989, according to the Centers for Disease Control, the lowest rate of increase since the CDC began keeping records.

$100 Million in Art Stolen — Twelve works of art valued at $100 million or more were stolen from the Isabella Stewart Gardner Museum in Boston, **Mar. 18.** The robbery, in terms of value of the works, was the largest in the history of art. Two Rembrandt paintings, including his only seascape, were taken. Several works by Degas and one painting each by Vermeer and Manet were also seized. The museum said, **Mar. 19,** that the works were not insured because the premiums would have exceeded the museum's annual budget.

Aspirin Found Effective Against Strokes — Researchers reported in the *New England Journal of Medicine,* **Mar. 22,** that taking aspirin daily cut the risk of stroke from 50 percent to 80 percent among patients suffering from a common heartbeat irregularity, atrial fibrillation. Warfarin, a prescription drug that like aspirin thinned the blood, had a similar benefit. Some 70,000 Americans suffered a stroke each year connected with atrial fibrillation. Aspirin had previously been found to be effective against heart attacks and another kind of stroke caused by clots in the blood vessels of the brain.

87 Die in Fire at Bronx Club — Eighty-seven people died in a fire at a social club in the Bronx borough of New York City, **Mar. 25.** The fire, which police said was deliberately set, spread rapidly through the 2-story structure, and the victims died within minutes from burning or asphyxiation. Only a few persons escaped. The club had been ordered closed in 1988. Officials said it had no sprinklers, fire exits, emergency lights, or exit signs at the time of the tragedy. The club was popular with immigrants from Central America, and the majority of those who died were from Honduras. The police, **Mar. 25,** arrested Julio Gonzalez and charged him with arson and murder. They said he had had an argument with a former girl friend who worked at the club.

APRIL

National

Consumers Prices Jump Again — Another sharp increase in consumer prices highlighted statistics on the economy released in April. The Commerce Dept. reported, **Apr. 3,** that the leading economic indicators had fallen 1 percent in February. The Labor Dept. said, **Apr. 6,** that unemployment had stood at 5.2 percent in March. The department reported, **Apr. 13,** that the index of producer prices for finished goods had declined 0.2 percent in March. The department said, **Apr. 17,** that consumer prices had risen 0.5 percent in March, equaling the advance reported for February. The inflation rate for the first quarter of 1990, 8.5 percent, was the highest annual rate for any quarter since 1982. The Commerce Dept. said, **Apr. 18,** that the U.S. merchandise trade deficit had fallen to $6.49 billion in February, the smallest monthly gap since 1983. The department said, **Apr. 27,** that the gross national product had grown at an annual rate of 2.1 percent during the first quarter.

Poindexter Convicted on Iran-Contra Charges — John Poindexter, a former national security adviser for Pres. Ronald Reagan, was convicted, **Apr. 7,** on all 5 felony counts facing him at his trial in a federal district court in Washington, D.C. These included 2 counts of obstructing Congress, 2 of making false statements to Congress, and one of conspiracy to obstruct Congress. In one case, for example, he was found guilty of reporting falsely that no U.S. officials had known until January 1986 of a November 1985 shipment of Hawk anti-aircraft missiles to Iran by Israel. Poindexter was the highest-ranking official to be convicted in the Iran-contra affair. On **June 11,** he was sentenced to 6 months in prison, becoming the first defendant in the case to be sentenced to jail.

U.S. to Keep Records on "Hate" Crimes — Under a bill signed into law, **Apr. 23,** by Pres. George Bush, the federal government would keep records of crimes committed by persons motivated by racial, ethnic, or sexual prejudice. Under the Hate Crimes Statistics Act, data would be kept on incidents of murder, rape, assault, arson, vandalism, and intimidation. Some conservatives in Congress had opposed including "sexual orientation" in the bill along with race and religion. Homosexual-rights leaders said that this was the first federal law to include the classification of sexual orientation.

Foes of Abortion Demonstrate in Capital — Opponents of abortion came to Washington, D.C., **Apr. 28,** to demonstrate for their cause. The number of participants was officially put at 200,000, but organizers claimed the figure was closer to 700,000. After the Supreme Court in 1989 had granted states wide authority to restrict abortions, supporters of a woman's right to choose an abortion had become more active, and the latest rally was aimed at countering that sentiment. Pres. George Bush, addressing the rally by phone, said that the "widespread prevalence of abortion is a tragedy." Vice Pres. Dan Quayle, who attended the rally, said, "The pro-life movement is the humanitarian movement of our time."

HUD Described as 'Political Machine'— DuBois Gilliam, a deputy assistant secretary at the Dept. of Housing and Urban Development from 1984 to 1987, began testifying before the House Government Operations subcommittee, **Apr. 30.** Gilliam was serving a prison term for accepting payoffs from developers. Gilliam told the subcommittee, which was investigating other allegations of wrongdoing, that the department "was the best domestic political machine I've ever seen. We dealt strictly in politics." Gilliam admitted he had accepted about $100,000 in payoffs from developers and consultants who wanted to do business with HUD. He disputed testimony by Samuel Pierce, a former HUD secretary, who had asserted that he had played no role in awarding HUD grants. "I know for a fact that the secretary made decisions," Gilliam said. "We were not allowed to spend any discretionary funds without clearing it with him." Gilliam said Pierce transferred an employee who became suspicious about a link between politics and the awarding of grants. An attorney for Pierce denied the allegations against his client, **Apr. 30.**

International

USSR Increases Pressure on Lithuania — Tensions between the Soviet Union and its rebellious Baltic republics remained high in April. The Supreme Soviet, the national standing legislature, passed a law, **Apr. 2,** establishing the rules for secession. One would require a two-thirds approval in a referendum, and if this majority was not obtained a republic would have to wait 10 years before trying again. The parliament of Estonia declared, **Apr. 2,** that the law did not apply to Estonia. Pres. Vytautas Landsbergis said, **Apr. 2,** that the timing of Lithuania's declaration of independence was open to discussion, and he called for talks with the Soviet leadership. The Latvian Communist Party broke into pro- and anti-independence factions, **Apr. 7.** The Estonian parliament, **Apr. 11,** abolished the drafting of Estonians into the Soviet military. Soviet Pres. Mikhail Gorbachev, **Apr. 13,** threatened to impose an economic embargo on Lithuania. Pres. George Bush warned, **Apr. 17,** that if that happened the United States would consider "appropriate responses." On **Apr. 18,** the Soviet government cut off the flow of crude oil into Lithuania, and on **Apr. 19,** it shut down 3 or 4 natural gas pipelines serving Lithuania. On **Apr. 24,** Bush announced an indefinite delay in imposing sanctions on the Soviet Union, saying he did not want to add fuel to "an already volatile situation." Landsbergis, **Apr. 24,** called this a modern Munich, a reference to the attempt by France and Great Britain to appease Hitler in 1938.

Bulgaria Schedules Elections — The Bulgarian parliament gave its approval, **Apr. 3,** to free, multiparty national elections that would be held in June. Parliament also amended the constitution to create an executive presidency and delete the words communist and socialist from the document. Also on **Apr. 3,** parliament elected former Communist Party General Secretary Petar Mladenov as executive president. The Communist Party, **Apr. 3,** changed its name to the Bulgarian Socialist Party.

Chamorro Inaugurated in Nicaragua — Violeta Barrios de Chamorro began her term as president of Nicaragua in April. Meeting in Montelimar, Nicaragua, **Apr. 3,** 5 Central American presidents set a deadline 3 weeks hence for the demobilization of the Nicaraguan contras. On **Apr. 19,** representatives of the contras, the outgoing Sandinista regime, and the new government agreed to a cease-fire, which took effect that day. The contras agreed to move into 5 security zones by inauguration day, **Apr. 25.** Mrs. Chamorro's inauguration at a baseball stadium was an emotional occasion, with the stands filled with supporters of her and of the Sandinista government that she had defeated in the campaign. She surprised many by announcing that she would retain Gen. Humberto Ortega Saavedra as chief of the armed forces. He was the brother of the outgoing president, Daniel Ortega. A contra leader declared, **Apr. 25,** that the contras would not demobilize so long as Ortega stayed in power.

Mandela Meets With Pres. de Klerk — Pres. F. W. de Klerk of South Africa and Nelson Mandela, the black nationalist leader whom he had freed, met in Cape Town, **Apr. 5.** They agreed that formal talks would be held soon between the government and the African National Congress. Speaking to Parliament, **Apr. 18,** de Klerk rejected the concept of majority rule, which he said would result in black domination, but he endorsed the sharing of power between the races. This would include "the requirement of consensus on controversial matters." He said the ANC would have to renounce violence before participating in negotiations on a new constitution.

Conservatives Win Hungarian Election — The second round, or runoff, elections to the Hungarian parliament were completed, **Apr. 8.** The center-right Hungarian Democratic Forum captured 43 percent of the seats, and this party, in alliance with 2 smaller conservative parties, would control almost 60 percent of all the seats. The liberal Free Democrats won 24 percent of the seats. The ruling Socialist (formerly Communist) Party captured only 8.5 percent of the seats.

East Germany Installs New Government — Lothar de Maizière, leader of the Christian Democratic Union, a conservative party, became premier of East Germany, **Apr. 12.** In coalition with the Social Democratic Party, he headed East Germany's first freely chosen government. The Party of Democratic Socialism, the successor to the Communist Party, was not included in the coalition government. De Maizière, a lawyer, had formerly been a professional viola player. Meeting under its new leadership, **Apr. 12,** parliament asked for forgiveness from Jews and the Soviet Union for the policy of genocide practiced by the Nazis in World War II. Parliament also acknowledged that East Germany shared the guilt for invading Czechoslovakia in 1968, and it pledged "unequivocal recognition" of Poland's current border.

2 U.S. Hostages Freed in Lebanon — Kidnapers in Lebanon freed 2 U.S. hostages in April. The first, Robert Polhill, was freed, **Apr. 22,** after more than 3 years in captivity. Polhill, a diabetic who had received insulin injections from his captors, said he had never seen the sun during the time that he was held. He had been held with 2 other hostages. President George Bush said, **Apr. 22,** that if Iran wanted better relations with the United States it would have to use its influence with its Shiite allies in Lebanon to free the remaining hostages. Bush, **Apr. 23,** thanked Pres. Hafez al-Assad of Syria for his role in the release. A 2d U.S. hostage, Frank Reed, was freed, **Apr. 30.** He had disappeared in September 1986. Bush thanked the government of Iran for having used its influence to free Reed. Reed said, May 2, he had spent his time in captivity with 4 other Western hostages. Altogether, some 15 westerners were believed being held in Lebanon.

3d Candidate Slain in Colombia — Another presidential candidate was assassinated in Colombia, **Apr. 26.** Carlos Pizarro Leongomez, the candidate of the leftist movement known as M-19, was the third presidential aspirant to be killed during the current campaign. He was shot while traveling aboard an Avianca Airlines flight that had just left Bogotá. The gunman was immediately killed by Pizarro's bodyguards. An anonymous caller to a radio network claimed that the assassination was carried out by leaders of the drug cartel, but drug leaders, **Apr. 27,** issued a statement condemning the slaying.

General

Museum Indicted for Showing Photos — An exhibit of photographs by the late Robert Mapplethorpe opened at the Contemporary Arts Center in Cincinnati, **Apr. 7,** and on that day the museum and its director, Dennis Barrie, were indicted by a grand jury on obscenity charges—pandering and illegal use of a minor. Prosecutors had concentrated their charges on 7 (of 175) photographs in the exhibit that depicted naked children or homosexual acts. The Corcoran Gallery of Art in Washington, D.C. had canceled the same exhibit in 1989 after some members of Congress objected to the subject matter and threatened to restrict funding for the arts. On **Apr. 8,** U.S. District Judge Carl Rubin forbade law enforcement officials from closing the exhibit. The exhibit broke records for attendance at the museum.

Fire on Danish Ferry Takes Heavy Toll — A fire broke out on the Danish ferry *Scandinavian Star* while it was en route, **Apr. 7,** from Oslo, Norway to Frederikshavn, Denmark. Up to 176 persons died, mostly from smoke inhalation. About 360 persons escaped in life-boats.

Tuna Canners Act to Protect Dolphins — Three companies announced, **Apr. 12,** that they would no longer buy tuna that had been caught in nets that also trapped dolphins. H. J. Heinz Company, Van Camp Seafood Company, and Bumble Bee Seafoods Inc., which produced 70 percent of the canned tuna fish sold in the United States, acted in response to protests from enviromentalists. Tuna fisherman often used huge nets to capture tuna, and from 80,000 to 100,000 dolphins also perished each year when caught in the nets.

Pete Rose Pleads Guilty on Taxes — Pete Rose, one of baseball's greatest players, pleaded guilty, **Apr. 20,** to 2 counts of filing false tax returns. The admission, in U.S. District Court in Cincinnati, followed a long investigation into his gambling habit. Rose had been banned from baseball for life in 1989. In the court settlement, Rose agreed to pay $366,000 in back taxes, penalties, and interest. He remained subject to a possible prison sentence. On **July 19,** he was sentenced to 5 months in jail, fined $50,000, and ordered to perform 1,000 hours of community service.

200 Million Celebrate Earth Day — In what was believed to be the biggest grass-roots celebration ever, some 200 million people in Europe, Asia, Africa, and the Western Hemisphere participated in Earth Day activities, **Apr. 22.** Events were planned in some 3,600 cities and towns in 140 countries. The day marked the 20th anniversary of the original Earth Day in 1970. The intent was to focus on growing environmental problems that were threatening the quality of life everywhere. Concerts, street fairs, festivals, marches, and exhibits stressed such issues as recycling, global warming, endangered species of animals, and air and water quality. About 750,000 persons attended a rally and concert in Central Park in New York City.

Space Telescope Deployed by Shuttle — The shuttle *Discovery* lifted off from Cape Canaveral, Fla., **Apr. 24,** with a crew of 5. On **Apr. 25,** it deployed its 12.5-ton cargo, the Hubble Space Telescope. The $1.5-billion telescope, which had a 94.5-inch mirror, was put into orbit 381 miles above earth. It was anticipated that the telescope, which would be far above any atmospheric interference associated with the surface of the planet, would be able to see deeper into space than any other telescope, and with unprecedented clarity.

Milken Fined $600 Million in Fraud Case — Michael Milken, the former "junk bond king" at the securities firm of Drexel Burnham Lambert Inc., pleaded guilty, **Apr. 24,** to 6 counts relating to securities fraud, and agreed to pay a record total of $600 million in fines and restitution. Under the agreement, in U.S. District Court in New York, more serious charges against Milken were dropped, and a case against his brother, Lowell Milken, was also dropped. Michael Milken had helped spur the corporate takeover boom of the 1980s through the use of high-yield, high-risk junk bonds. Counts to which Milken pleaded guilty included conspiracy, aiding and abetting the filing of a false statement with the Securities and Exchange Commission, and assisting the filing of a false tax return. Milken still faced the possibility of being sentenced to prison.

Disasters — An explosion caused by a leaking gas cylinder killed at least 80 persons on a commuter train traveling near Kumrahar, Hihar state, India, **Apr. 16.** . . . An earthquake in central China, in Qinghai province, **Apr. 26,** killed 115 people.

MAY

National

More Testimony Heard in HUD Inquiry — DuBois Gilliam, a former deputy assistant secretary at the Dept. of Housing and Urban Development, continued his testimony before a House subcommittee. He said on **May 2,** that an assistant to then-Vice Pres. George Bush had once intervened on behalf of a Bush supporter, Hector Barreto. A developer in Kansas City, Barreto was granted $500,000 for a trade center project even though it had initially been rejected for HUD funds. Gilliam testified, **May 4,** that on several occasions former HUD Secretary Samuel Pierce had used discretionary funds to fund projects supported by friends or Republican figures. Pierce's attorney, **May 4,** said that nothing illegal had occurred. The Justice Dept. said, **May 29,** that Attorney Gen. Richard Thornburgh had asked that the independent counsel investigating the HUD allegations expand his inquiry to pursue assertions made by Gilliam.

Inflation Fears Ease a Bit — Figures on consumer and producer prices released during May indicated a lessening of inflation pressures. The Commerce Dept. reported, **May 2,** that leading economic indicators had risen 0.9 percent in March. The Labor Dept. reported, **May 4,** that the unemployment rate had edged upward to 5.4 percent in April, the highest level in more than a year. The department said, **May 11,** that producer prices for finished goods had declined 0.3 percent in April. It said, **May 16,** that consumer prices had risen just 0.2 percent in April, the smallest advance since September 1989. The Commerce Dept. reported, **May 17,** that the U.S. merchandise trade deficit had risen to $8.45 billion in March, propelled by a 10 percent surge in imports. The department, **May 24,** revised its estimate of the growth of the gross national product in the first quarter, putting the annual rate at a lower figure of 1.3 percent. It reported, **May 30,** that the leading economic indicators had fallen 0.2 percent in April. Stock prices advanced throughout May, with the Dow Jones industrial average setting a string of all-time highs. The highest point during the month was reached, **May 30,** when the Dow closed at 2878.56.

Budget 'Summit' Held at White House — Pres. George Bush, leaders of his administration, and Congressional leaders began a budget "summit" at the White House, **May 15,** amid concern about the growing national budget deficit. Administration estimates for the 1991 fiscal budget deficit had jumped from $101 billion to at least $123 billion. The administration attributed the growing gap to higher interest rates, a falloff in tax receipts, more spending on commercial bank failures, and, most of all, the size of the savings and loan bailout—although it was not officially a part of administration figures. At a news conference, **May 16,** Bush said, "when you take a look at the most recent estimates, the problem is of such a magnitude that we have to address it." He said the problem should be addressed now while the economy was reasonably strong. Those attending the summit, **May 17,** heard a Congressional Budget Office report putting the 1991 deficit projection as high as $159 billion. No agreements on the budget were reported from the talks.

S & L Bailout Cost Estimate Rises — Treasury Secretary Nicholas Brady told the Senate Banking Committee, **May 23,** that the cost of bailing out the savings and loan industry could run as high as $130 billion, nearly twice previous projections. He said the higher figure could become a reality if real-estate prices continued to fall and if thrifts continued to fail at an accelerating rate. Interest payments, furthermore, could help send the cost over the next 10 years toward $300 billion. Neil Bush, the son of the president, testified before the House Banking Committee, **May 23.** He was asked about his role as a director of Silverado Banking, an S & L in Colorado, which had been taken over by the government in 1988 at a cost to taxpayers of perhaps $1 billion. Questioned about possible conflicts of interest related to loans Silverado had made to 2 of his business partners, Bush denied any wrong-doing.

Navy Reopens Inquiry in Blast Fatal to 47 — The Navy said, **May 24,** that it was reopening its investigation into the explosion aboard the battleship *Iowa* in April 1989 that took the lives of 47 members of its crew. The explosion had occurred in a gun turret during a training exercise. The Navy later issued a report stating that it was "most likely" that the explosion had been caused by a suicidal crewman, Clayton Hartwig, who, according to the theory, had placed some sort of detonating device in the mechanism. Hartwig died in the explosion. Hartwig's family had fought to clear his name. At the request of the General Accounting Office, the Sandia National Laboratories in Albuquerque, N. M. examined 3 battleships and found traces of foreign chemical elements in all, undercutting a conclusion by the Navy that the presence of such materials on the *Iowa* suggested that an explosive device had been planted. On **May 24,** the Navy tested Sandia's suggestion that the explosion could have been caused because gunpowder was rammed too fast into the turret's center gun. The bags of gunpowder exploded on the 18th test.

International

Soviet Referendum on Economy Scheduled — On **May 1,** the annual May Day parade in Moscow's Red Square came to a surprising climax. As in years past, official delegations marched along the parade route, displaying their socialist unity. But, for the first time, independent and unofficial organizations were permitted to march, and thousands of persons jeered Pres. Mikhail Gorbachev and other national leaders as they passed the reviewing area atop Lenin's Mausoleum. These marchers, who included ethnic nationalists, human-rights and religious activists, and students and intellectuals, carried banners of protest, with such slogans as "Down with the Cult of Lenin" and "Seventy-two Years on the Road to Nowhere." No May Day celebrations were held at all in the capitals of 5 of the restive republics. On **May 24,** Premier Nikolai Ryzhkov presented to the Supreme Soviet, the standing national legislature, an economic-reform program that included an easing of price controls. Bread prices would triple, and the cost of some goods and services would go up 30 percent. Government subsidies had kept many prices artificially low. The program also included unemployment benefits and tax-indexing to assist workers. It also would set in motion a transformation of state enterprises into joint stock companies. The program would be subject to approval in a national referendum. Unrest flared anew in Armenia, **May 27,** and by **May 29,** the official death toll was put at 24. On **May 29,** on the third ballot, Boris Yeltsin was elected president of the Russian Republic, the largest and most important of the 15 republics of the Soviet Union. An advocate of radical reforms, Yeltsin had called for economic and political sovereignty for Russia, and said he favored turning the USSR into a loose confederation of republics.

Debate Over Baltic Republics Continues — Pres. Vytautas Landsbergis of Lithuania said, **May 2,** in a letter to French and West German leaders that Lithuania would consider suspending some pro-independence laws if that would get talks with the Kremlin underway. Premier Kasimiera Prunskiene met with Pres. George Bush in the White House, **May 3.** This was a private visit inasmuch as the United States did not recognize Lithuania as an independent nation. Bush declined to declare for Lithuanian independence but reiterated his support for the republic's "self-determination." Prunskiene indicated a willingness to suspend full implementation of Lithuania's declaration of independence to get negotiations started. On **May 4,** the parliament of Latvia voted 138-0 to declare its independence from the USSR, thus joining Lithuania and Estonia in that move. An unspecified period of transition was approved. Pres. Mikhail Gorbachev condemned this move, **May 5,** and on **May 7,** a column of Soviet tanks entered the Latvian capital of Riga. On **May 8,** the Estonian parliament declared the birth of the "Estonian Republic" and dropped the words "Soviet Socialist" from the republic's name. Gorbachev asserted, **May 14,** that the attempts by Latvia and Estonia to break from the Soviet Union had no legal basis. Demonstrators supporting unity with the Soviet Union, believed to be mostly ethnic Russians, stormed the parliament buildings in Estonia and Latvia, **May 15.** The Lithuanian government suspended enforcement of its independence laws, **May 16,** and on **May 17,** Gorbachev met with Premier Prunskiene in Moscow. She later said that the discussions were a big step forward. Gorbachev told Lithuanian leaders in Moscow, **May 24,** that the republic could be independent in 2 years if it suspended its declaration of independence.

Unified German Monetary System Approved — A treaty signed in May cleared the way for the unification of the economies of the 2 Germanys. Earlier, on **May 5,** foreign ministers of the 2 Germanys and of the

4 Allied powers in World War II met in Bonn to discuss reunification. Foreign Minister Eduard Shevardnadze of the Soviet Union reiterated his country's position that a united Germany in NATO was not acceptable. On May 18, the finance ministers of East and West Germany signed a treaty establishing a unified monetary system under the West German mark. The treaty would require approval of parliaments of both countries, and would take effect July 1. Under its terms, East Germans could exchange up to 4,000 East German marks for West German Deutsche marks, one for one. Wages and pensions would also be calculated in Deutsche marks at a one-to-one rate. East Germans would pay West German federal taxes and would be covered by West German laws on pensions and unemployment.

Albanian Parliament Approves Reforms — The parliament of Albania approved a package of legislation, May 8, that appeared to set the isolated Marxist nation on the path toward liberalization. Pres. Ramiz Alia, who was also first secretary of the Albanian Workers' (Communist) Party, provided the impetus for the legislation. Under the new laws, the court system was reorganized, the number of capital offenses was reduced from 34 to 11, restrictions on the right to worship were apparently relaxed, and citizens were guaranteed the right to obtain foreign passports.

Ruling Party Wins Romanian Election — Romania's National Salvation Front retained power in elections held in May. The front had led the country on an interim basis since the December 1989 revolution. Dozens of other parties competed in the election, but the front was better financed and better organized. The campaign was marked by violence, and the 2 major opposition parties complained that the front was responsible for beatings and harassment of hundreds of its supporters. The U.S. ambassador was withdrawn temporarily, May 10, and the State Dept. said it was concerned about "irregularities . . .which raise questions about whether those elections will be free and fair." In the voting, May 20, the front won about two-thirds of the seats in both houses of parliament. Interim Pres. Ion Iliescu also retained office, winning about 85 percent of the presidential vote.

2 U.S. Airmen Killed in Philippines — Two U.S. airmen were shot to death near Clark Air Force Base, a U.S. base in the Philippines, on May 13. The killings came at a critical time, because negotiations between the U.S. and the Philippines on the future of U.S. bases on the islands began in Manila, May 14. Many Filipinos wanted the U.S. to give up the bases. On May 15, communist rebels claimed responsibility for the deaths of the airmen.

Report Issued on Pan Am Bombing — A U.S. presidential commission issued a report, May 15, on the bombing in December 1988 that destroyed a Pan American airliner. All 259 persons aboard the plane and 11 on the ground at Lockerbie, Scotland died in the disaster. The commission said it was not certain how the bomb was smuggled aboard the plane but cited evidence that it was in an unaccompanied suitcase loaded in Frankfurt, West Germany. The report said that the security system for U.S. civil aviation "is seriously flawed and has failed to provide the proper level of protection to the traveling public." The commission called for greatly increased security at U.S. airports, the creation of the post of assistant secretary of transportation for security and intelligence, and establishment of a national system for warning passengers of credible threats against airlines or flights.

Bush, Gorbachev Open Summit Talks — Pres. Mikhail Gorbachev of the Soviet Union arrived in Washington, D.C. at the end of May to begin summit discussions with Pres. George Bush. Earlier in the month, Secretary of State James Baker 3d had visited the USSR, and on May 19, he reported progress on several issues. He said all major obstacles had been cleared away on strategic arms, opening the way to a treaty that would reduce nuclear missile arsenals by 30 percent. The agreement included limitations on both air- and sea-launched cruise missiles. The 2 superpowers also agreed to begin eliminating their arsenals of chemical weapons in 1992. However, no break-through was reported on reducing conventional arms in Europe. Bush said, May 24, that he opposed normalizing trade relations with the Soviet Union because of the impasse over Lithuanian independence and because the Soviet leadership had not pushed for more liberal emigration policies. Gorbachev met in Ottawa, May 29 and 30, with Prime Minister Brian Mulroney of Canada. Canadian officials announced they would extend a line of credit to the Soviet Union to facilitate purchase of Canadian goods and services by the USSR. Gorbachev and his entourage, including his wife, Raisa, flew to Washington, May 30, and on May 31, they were welcomed to the White House by President and Mrs. Bush. The 2 leaders and their aides met twice, May 31, focusing on German reunification, but failed to resolve the question of a united Germany's membership in NATO, which Gorbachev opposed. A number of leaders in the arts, entertainment, and politics attended a reception hosted by the Gorbachevs at the Soviet Embassy, May 31, and Mrs. Gorbachev helped open an exhibit of Russian religious texts at the Library of Congress, May 31.

Gorbachev met U.S. congressional leaders for breakfast at the Soviet Embassy, June 1, and the Soviet leader also met, June 1, with Vice Pres. Dan Quayle.

Bush and Gorbachev signed more than a dozen documents at the White House, June 1. One agreement, spelling out broad goals to be incorporated in a treaty, would reduce long-range nuclear weapons arsenals. As worked out in May during Sec. of State Baker's trip to Moscow, the agreement set a limit of 1,600 strategic delivery vehicles per side, with a total of 6,000 warheads per side for these long-range vehicles. Another agreement called for an immediate end to chemical weapons production by both superpowers.

A third agreement was something of a surprise. Bush signed the trade treaty Gorbachev wanted so much, even though the Soviet Union had not met the condition previously stated—liberalizing emigration laws. Apparently, Bush also put aside concerns over Lithuania in signing the treaty. The treaty, requiring approval by Congress, would be a step toward granting the Soviet Union most-favored-nation status.

Mrs. Gorbachev and Mrs. Bush addressed the graduating class of Wellesley College, Wellesley, Mass., June 1. Mrs. Gorbachev spoke on the role of women in Soviet society, and Mrs. Bush emphasized the importance of family and friends even for career women.

The 2 presidents conducted informal talks at Camp David, in Maryland, June 2. At a joint press conference in Washington, June 3, both leaders called the summit a success while acknowledging that agreement on German reunification had not been reached. Gorbachev said the Soviet Union might curb emigration of Soviet Jews to Israel unless Israel gave assurances that they would not settle in the occupied territories.

Gorbachev flew to Minnesota, June 3, met with Gov. Rudy Perpich, and visited the headquarters of Control Data Corp., a leading company in computer technology.

The Gorbachev party then flew to California, and on June 4, the Gorbachevs visited with former Pres.

Ronald Reagan and Mrs. Reagan. Speaking to 1,700 students at Stanford University, Gorbachev said, "The cold war is now behind us. Let us not wrangle over who won it."

Gorbachev met, **June 4**, in San Francisco with South Korean Pres. Roh Tae Woo, and Roh later said the 2 countries would normalize relations.

New Israeli-Palestinian Violence Flares — More acts of violence involving Israelis and Palestinians added to growing tensions in the region in May. On **May 20**, a former Israeli soldier opened fire on Palestinian workers with an automatic rifle. Seven were killed and at least 10 were wounded. The army said the gunman had a record of disciplinary problems. Israeli leaders condemned the massacre. Riots broke out in the occupied Gaza Strip and the West Bank. The army cracked down, sending in reinforcements and imposing curfews. By **May 22**, 15 Palestinians had been killed by Israeli forces. On **May 30**, Palestinian guerillas in speedboats sought to attack the coast of Israel. Israeli security forces captured one boat and its 5-man crew, which surrendered. Eleven men landed in a second boat, but 4 were killed and the rest captured. A radical faction of the Palestine Liberation Organization claimed responsibility for the raid, saying it was intended to avenge the 7 Palestinians killed, **May 20**. PLO Chairman Yasir Arafat denied, **May 31**, that the PLO had any "official" connection with the raid. Israeli leaders called on the United States to end its diplomatic contacts with the PLO.

Foe of Drug Lords Elected in Colombia — An opponent of the drug cartels, César Gaviria Trujillo, was elected president of Colombia. The campaign had cost the lives of some 2,000 persons, mostly as a result of violent acts by the drug cartels. Three presidential candidates had been killed. Threats of more violence kept the turnout for the **May 27** voting to 46 percent. Gaviria, the nominee of the ruling Liberal Party, received 48 percent of the vote. Alone among the 4 main candidates, he had supported extraditing drug traffickers to the U.S. Other candidates had advocated negotiating with the traffickers. Gaviria had served as minister of finance and as minister of government. In his victory speech, **May 27**, he vowed to put an end to terrorism, and he criticized industrialized countries for not doing enough to reduce consumption of drugs.

General

AIDS Drug Approved for Children — The Food and Drug Administration, **May 3**, approved the drug AZT for treating children 3 months to 12 years who had symptoms of AIDS or who were infected with the AIDS virus. Government officials estimated that up to 20,000 children in the U.S. were infected with the virus. In approving AZT, the FDA waived its rule requiring separate testing of drugs for children

Van Gogh Painting Sells for $82.5 Million — A record price for a painting sold at auction was set, **May 15**, at Christie's auction house in New York City. Vincent van Gogh's "Portrait of Dr. Gachet" was sold for $82.5 million (including Christie's commission) to a Japanese businessman, Ryoei Saito. On **May 17**, at Sotheby's in New York City, Saito was the successful bidder for Pierre Auguste Renoir's "Au Moulin de la Galette." The total cost of that transaction, $78.1 million, was the second highest for any painting.

Scientists Forecast Global Warming — A U.N. report issued **May 25**, by scientists from many countries, warned that global temperatures could rise by 2 degrees Fahrenheit within 35 years. They foresaw a 6 degrees F increase by the end of the next century, with serious consequences that could not be forecast now.

The report had received nearly unanimous approval from scientists representing 39 countries. The authors concluded that emissions of carbon dioxide, methane, and chlorofluorocarbons would have to be reduced by 60 percent in order to just stabilize atmospheric concentrations at current levels. Prime Minister Margaret Thatcher, **May 25**, set a target for Great Britain of a 30 percent reduction in projected emissions of carbon dioxide. In doing so, she broke away from the position of the Bush administration, which called for more research on the problem.

Disasters — A cyclone swept through Andhra Pradesh state, in India, **May 9-11**, killing at least 220 persons and leaving about 3 million homeless . . . At least 101 persons died in an earthquake that struck northern Peru, **May 30**.

JUNE

National

Jobless Rate Edges Downward — The Labor Dept. reported, **June 1**, that unemployment edged downward 0.1 percentage point in May to 5.3 percent. The department said, **June 14**, that producer prices for finished goods rose 0.3 percent in May, following 3 consecutive monthly drops. It reported, **June 15**, that consumer prices had edged upward 0.2 percent in May. The Dow Jones industrial average posted another all-time high, **June 15**, of 2935.89. The Commerce Dept. said, **June 15**, that the merchandise trade deficit had narrowed to $6.94 billion in April. The department reported, **June 21**, that the estimate of the growth in the gross national product, on an annual basis, for the first quarter of 1990 had been revised upward from 1.3 percent to 1.9 percent. This was the second lowest growth rate reported in the past 30 months. It reported, **June 27**, that the leading economic indicators had risen 0.8 percent in May.

D.C. Mayor's Drug Trial Opens — The trial of Marion Barry, the mayor of Washington, D.C., on drug charges got underway, **June 4**. He faced 11 misdemeanor counts relating to cocaine and 3 felony counts of lying to a grand jury. On **June 13**, Barry announced that he would not seek a 4th term, saying that his struggle to overcome dependency on drugs and alcohol was more important to him than another campaign. Opening arguments in the trial were presented, **June 19**. The defense attorney said that FBI agents had sought to entrap Barry when they videotaped him using cocaine in January. On **June 28**, the prosecution presented its key piece of evidence—the videotape apparently showing Barry smoking crack in a hotel room in the Vista International Hotel in Washington, D.C. The defense contended that the tape supported the entrapment defense.

Flag Amendment Fails in Congress — A proposed Constitutional amendment to permit the federal government or the states to prosecute those who desecrated the American flag failed to win approval in both houses of Congress. The U.S. Supreme Court, **June 11**, struck down a 1989 federal law barring desecration of the flag. Pres. George Bush renewed his call for an amendment to protect the flag. Many other political leaders, mostly Republicans, joined him. Democrats generally opposed an amendment, arguing that it would represent a compromise of the First Amendment's protection of free speech. On **June 21**, members of the House voted 254-177 in favor of the amendment, but this was well short of the two-thirds majority needed for the approval of an amendment. The Senate, **June 26**, voted 58-42 for the amendment, again well below the required majority.

Cardinal Issues Warning on Abortion — Cardinal John J. O'Connor, the Roman Catholic archbishop of New York City, said, **June 14,** that Catholic political leaders who supported the right of women to have an abortion "must be warned that they are at risk of excommunication." In an article in the archdiocese's newspaper, he said that the warning applied to women who obtained an abortion, to doctors who performed the procedure, and to officeholders who supported abortion or made funds available for it.

International

Violence Flares in Soviet Kirghizia — Violent clashes began, **June 4,** in the city of Osh, in the Soviet republic of Kirghizia, between Uzbeks and Kirghiz citizens. The dispute was over a proposed allocation of a large plot of land for housing for the Kirghiz. Thousands of Uzbeks rioted, and Soviet troops were sent to the area. By **June 7,** the death toll was reported as 48. On **June 8,** British Prime Minister Margaret Thatcher, at a joint press conference with Gorbachev during a visit to the Soviet Union, praised the president's reform programs as "the most exciting, the biggest, the most historic in Europe for a very long time." Tass reported, **June 13,** that the death toll in Kirghizia stood at 148. The Supreme Soviet (standing national legislature), **June 14,** approved the country's first corporate income tax, setting a basic rate of 45 percent. The Supreme Soviet, **June 14,** also rejected the government's proposal to triple the price of bread. Although parliament's approval was not required, its opposition appeared likely to force a revision of the price structure.

State of Emergency Eased in South Africa — Pres. F. W. de Klerk announced, **June 7,** that he would lift the 4-year-old state of emergency in 3 of South Africa's 4 provinces. He made an exception in Natal Province, where more than 3,000 blacks had been killed in 3 years of fighting between conservative and radical Zulu factions. Nelson Mandela, deputy president of the African National Congress, praised the action but urged the West to maintain sanctions against the government.

Shamir Forms Cabinet in Israel — The leadership paralysis in Israel ended, **June 8,** when Prime Minister Yitzhak Shamir announced that he had succeeded in forming a cabinet. This was to be no "national unity" government similar to the one that had fallen, but was composed of Shamir's Likud Party and several small nationalist and religious parties. It appeared likely that the new government would resist any concessions to reach a peace with the Palestinians. Ariel Sharon, an outspoken hardliner, was named housing minister and overseer of the influx of Jews from the Soviet Union. The new government went on record as favoring expansion of Jewish settlements in the occupied territories. The Knesset approved the new government 62-57 on **June 11.** Testifying before a U.S. House committee **June 13,** Sec. of State James Baker expressed his irritation with a statement by Israeli officials that the U.S. peace plan was irrelevant. He said, "When you're serious about peace, call us," and gave the White House phone number.

Czechoslovak Elections Held — On **June 8** and **9,** in the first free voting in Czechoslovakia in more than 4 decades, the Civic Forum and its sister party in Slovakia, Public Against Violence, won 46 percent of the vote for parliament and captured 170 of 300 seats in the bicameral body. Civic Forum was the party of Pres. Vaclav Havel. The Communist Party finished a distant second with 14 percent of the vote and 47 seats in the Federal Assembly. The allied parties also ran well ahead in voting for the legislatures of the Czech and Slovak republics. Havel, **June 12,** reappointed Marian Calfa as premier and asked him to form a new government.

Mandela Gets Big U.S. Welcome — Nelson Mandela, the black nationalist leader from South Africa, toured Europe and North America and received an enthusiastic welcome, most notably in the United States. Mandela, deputy president of the African National Congress, had been freed in February after 27 years in prison. He sought during his tour to raise money for the ANC and to encourage Western governments to maintain sanctions against the South African government. Between **June 9** and **June 16,** he met with officials and leaders in Switzerland, West Germany, France, Italy, and the Netherlands, including West German Chancellor Helmut Kohl and Pope John Paul II. In Canada, Mandela addressed parliament, **June 19,** and met with Prime Minister Brian Mulroney. Mandela and his wife, Winnie, arrived in New York City, **June 20,** to begin an extended U.S. tour that proved to be especially inspiring to blacks, who acclaimed him as a hero. The Mandelas were given a ticker-tape parade up Broadway to City Hall, the scene of a big rally. On **June 21,** events included a rally in Harlem and a rock concert and speech by Mandela in Yankee Stadium. On **June 22,** he met with corporate executives and spoke at the United Nations. In Boston, **June 23,** Mandela spoke at the John F. Kennedy Memorial Library at the Univ. of Massachusetts and attended a 6-hour pop concert and rally. Mandela met with Pres. George Bush in the White House, **June 25.** The president urged all parties in South Africa to renounce violence, but Mandela declined to make that commitment at that time. He addressed Congress, **June 26,** thanking the United States for imposing sanctions against the South African government and urging that they be maintained until "irreversible" reforms were established. Some members stayed away from the speech, objecting, in part, to Mandela's refusal to criticize Yasir Arafat, Fidel Castro, and Muammer el-Qaddafi, all of whom supported his cause. Before ending his tour of the U.S., **June 30,** Mandela visited Atlanta, Miami, Detroit, Los Angeles, and Oakland.

Miners Rout Students in Bucharest — On **June 13,** riot police attacked a tent city in downtown Bucharest, the capital that had been set up by anti-government demonstrators, most of them students. The police drove out some 200 persons, including some hunger strikers. Thousands of students then protested, rioting and burning the central police headquarters. Security forces killed 4 people, and more than 200 were injured. Pres.-elect Ion Illiescu appealed to the working class to save the country from a "fascist rebellion." Some 10,000 miners poured into Bucharest, **June 14,** routed the students, set up barricades, ransacked the headquarters of 2 opposition parties, and wrecked the offices of an independent newspaper. Members of the foreign press were also attacked. The U.S. State Dept. said, **June 15,** it would withhold U.S. economic aid from Romania. Illiescu was sworn in as president, **June 20.**

Most Nicaraguan Contras Disarm — Pres. Violeta Barrios de Chamorro of Nicaragua announced, **June 15,** that more than 14,000 contra rebels had disarmed under an agreement that she had reached with them. Their total force had been put at about 16,000. Chamorro also announced, **June 15,** that the Sandinista-trained armed forces would be cut to about 41,000 from its estimated strength of 55,000 to 60,000. She also said that an all-volunteer army would be created.

Bulgarian Socialists Win Parliament Election — The Bulgarian Socialist Party won parliamentary elections in the nation's first free election since the tide of change swept Eastern Europe. The first round of voting was held, **June 10**, and the run-offs were held, **June 17**. The Socialists were a Marxist party, though much reformed from the hard-line party that had run the country since World War II. The Socialists captured 211 of the 400 seats in the Grand National Assembly, or parliament. The opposition coalition, the Union of Democratic Forces, won 144 seats. Other parties ran far behind, with one representing ethnic Turks picking up 23 seats.

Bush Breaks Off PLO Talks — Pres. George Bush announced, **June 20**, that he was breaking off the diplomatic dialogue with the Palestine Liberation Organization. The talks, aimed at enhancing the prospects for a Middle East peace settlement, had begun in December 1988 after PLO chairman Yasir Arafat renounced terrorism. But Arafat and the PLO had failed to condemn an unsuccessful speedboat raid on Israel in May that had apparently been the work of a radical PLO faction. Israel hailed Bush's decision, **June 20**. But the PLO executive committee complained, **June 21**, that the U.S. had not responded in a similiar way to "Israeli crimes against Palestinians."

Canada Faces Constitutional Crisis — The failure of 2 provinces to ratify a series of constitutional amendments left the future of Canada in doubt. The deadline for adoption of the amendments, known as the Meech Lake Accord, passed without any approval from the legislatures of Newfoundland and Manitoba. The 2 holdout provinces feared that a clause in the accord designating Quebec as a "distinct society" within Canada would make Quebec too powerful. Prime Minister Brian Mulroney had led the fight for the amendments in the hopes of persuading Quebec to ratify Canada's 1982 constitution. Speaking to the nation, **June 23**, Mulroney urged Canadians to "mend the divisions and heal the wounds" caused by the failure of the accord. Quebec's premier Robert Bourassa, in a **June 23** speech, said he was willing to consider all possible options for Quebec. One plan supported by separatists in Quebec would give Quebec political independence while economic ties to Canada would be maintained.

Chinese Allow Dissidents to Leave — After living for more than a year in the U.S. Embassy in Beijing, a dissident Chinese couple left China, **June 25**, and flew to London on a U.S. Air Force plane. Fang Lizhi, a physicist, and his wife, Li Shuxian, had entered the embassy in 1989 to avoid being seized by Chinese authorities in the wake of the aborted uprising against the regime. The government accused the couple of helping incite the pro-democracy movement. In a statement issued as they left, they admitted opposing elements of the Chinese constitution and agreed not to participate in "activities whose motive lies in opposing China." Fang was to become affiliated with Cambridge University.

Bush Backs Tax Revenue Increases — Pres. George Bush issued a statement, **June 26**, in which he listed "tax revenue increases" as one of the necessary components of any plan to reduce the nation's budget deficits. In 1988, Bush had run successfully for president while saying repeatedly, "Read my lips. No new taxes." But he indicated in his statement that a compromise with Congress on the budget was not possible without agreeing to some sort of revenue increase. Democratic congressional leaders praised Bush for reversing his stand, but many Republicans were incensed. One letter, signed by more than half of the Republicans in the House, called a tax increase "unacceptable."

Oil Pipeline to Lithuania Reopened — Tensions between the Soviet Union and its rebellious republic of Lithuania eased in June. On **June 29**, the Lithuanian parliament agreed to suspend its declaration of independence for 100 days in exchange for an agreement by Moscow to negotiate on the issue and end economic sanctions. On **June 30**, the Soviet Union reopened the oil pipeline to Lithuania. During the oil embargo, tens of thousands of workers had been laid off and many factories had closed. On **July 2**, the Soviet government announced a complete lifting of its economic embargo on Lithuania.

General

'Suicide Machine' Used by Ill Woman — A woman from Oregon, assisted by a retired pathologist, committed suicide in Michigan, **June 4**, triggering a medical and ethical debate. Janet Adkins of Portland, Ore. had come to the Detroit area to meet with Dr. Jack Kevorkian, who had been promoting a suicide machine. Adkins, who was suffering from Alzheimer's Disease, had decided to take her own life. Her husband supported the decision. Kevorkian told police that he drove Mrs. Adkins to a park in his van and inserted an intravenous needle into her arm. She then pushed a button that fed a fatal combination of drugs into her bloodstream. Unlike many states, Michigan had no law prohibiting doctor-assisted suicide, but the American Medical Association's code of ethics prohibited doctors from helping patients to die.

33 Believed Dead in Ohio Flood — Heavy thunderstorms created a flash flood, **June 14**, that tore through a valley and into the town of Shadyside, Ohio, on the Ohio River, 10 miles south of Wheeling, W. Va. Almost 200 homes and trailers were destroyed, and part of a tavern was swept away with customers inside. As of **June 23**, there were 23 confirmed deaths and 10 others were missing.

Protestors Disrupt AIDS Conference — More than 10,000 specialists and public health officials attended the 6th International AIDS Conference in San Francisco, and heard 3,000 reports on the disease. Protests, which began on **June 19**, the eve of the conference, were organized in large part by the AIDS Coalition to Unleash Power (ACT-UP). Demonstrators, who numbered about 500 during the week, were primarily concerned about the slow pace of testing of anti-AIDS drugs and by the shortage of money for research and treatment. Luc Montagnier of France, co-discoverer of the virus that caused AIDS, said, **June 20**, he believed that a second microbe was also responsible, and that patients would not become ill until they had become infected with it as well. It was reported, **June 20**, that AIDS was continuing to spread in the U.S., especially among teen-agers, women whose sexual partners used intravenous drugs, and users of crack cocaine. According to a report, **June 23**, some 30 possible vaccines were being tested around the world. Protestors in the audience, **June 24**, disrupted an address by U.S. Sec. of Health and Human Services Louis Sullivan.

Iran Earthquake Kills 40,000 — An earthquake recorded as high as 7.7 on the Richter scale struck Iran, **June 21**. The epicenter was in the Caspian Sea a few miles north of the port city of Rasht. More than 100 communities were destroyed or badly damaged. Offers of help came from many countries, including the U.S., whose offer was accepted by Pres. Ali Akbar Hashemi Rafsanjani even though the 2 countries had no diplomatic relations. Iran estimated, **June 27**, that 40,000 people had been killed and 60,000 injured.

Flaw Found in Space Telescope — The Hubble Space Telescope, launched in April, was found to be suffering from a serious design flaw that would spoil many of its experiments. The National Aeronautics and Space Administration said, **June 27**, that an improper curvature in one or both mirrors in the $1.5 billion instrument prevented rays of light from meeting at a sharp focus at the cameras. The defect appeared to preclude any search for black holes and distant quasars, and might also jeopardize a calculation of the size of the universe. A camera could be sent up in 3 years to correct for the flaw, but the mirrors could not be replaced. The mirrors had not been tested together on the ground for reasons of cost, NASA said.

JULY

National

Governor Vetoes 2 Abortion Bills—Gov. Buddy Roemer of Louisiana vetoed a strong anti-abortion bill, **July 6.** The bill banned all abortions except to save the mother's life. Roemer, who described himself as pro-life, objected to the bill because it made no exceptions for victims of rape or incest. Both houses of the legislature, **July 8,** passed a second bill that made exceptions for incest and for rape—providing that the rape was reported to the police within 7 days. Roemer also vetoed this bill, **July 27,** saying he found the 7-day requirement too restrictive.

Dow Jones Average at 3,000 Level—The Dow Jones industrial average pushed to an all-time high on Wall Street even though most new economic data were not too encouraging. The Labor Dept. reported, **July 6,** that the unemployment rate had edged downward to 5.2 percent in May, but added that few new jobs had been created and that the labor force was increasing only slowly. The department said, **July 13,** that producer prices had risen 0.2 percent in June. On 2 consecutive days, **July 16** and **17,** the Dow Jones average closed at the identical figure of 2,999.75, an all-time high. On both days, the average was above 3,000 during the course of the day. Thereafter, the average began to decline. The Commerce Dept. reported, **July 17,** that the U.S. merchandise trade deficit had widened to $7.73 billion in May. The Labor Dept. said, **July 18,** that consumer prices had jumped 0.5 percent in June. The Commerce Dept. reported, **July 27,** that the gross national product had slowed to a 1.2 percent annual growth rate during the second quarter of 1990, a signal to some economists that the country was moving toward recession.

Law Protects Rights of Disabled—The House, **July 12,** and the Senate, **July 13,** gave overwhelming approval to a bill that would bar discrimination against people with physical or mental disabilities. The Americans with Disabilities Act defined disability as a condition that "substantially limits" an important activity such as walking or seeing. The bill covered people with AIDS as well as alcoholics and drug users undergoing treatment. Under the bill's provisions, all except small businesses were required to hire and promote employees without regard to any disability. Transportation systems were required to purchase new vehicles accessible to the disabled. Pres. George Bush signed the bill, **July 26.**

Congress Rebukes 2 of Its Members—The Senate Ethics Committee, **July 18,** recommended that the full Senate denounce Sen. David Durenberger (R, Minn.) for a number of ethical violations. The Committee said Durenberger had knowingly violated Senate rules and had "brought the Senate into dishonor and disrepute." The charges against him included accepting improper reimbursement for travel and housing from the Senate and conspiring to evade limits on speaking fees. The Committee advised the Senate to ask Durenberger to repay $29,050 in reimbursements and ask him to donate $95,000 to charity to compensate for excess fees. The House Ethics Committee, **July 19,** voted to reprimand Rep. Barney Frank (D, Mass.) for using his office improperly to assist a male prostitute. The committee found that Frank had used his influence to fix parking tickets for the man, Steven Gobie, and that he had attempted to influence parole officers to end Gobie's probation on felony charges. The Senate, **July 25,** accepting its committee recommendation, voted 96-0 to denounce Durenberger, who apologized for his behavior. The House, **July 26,** took up Frank's case. It rejected, 390-38, a move, supported largely by Republicans, that Frank be expelled from the House. A more severe penalty, censure, was rejected 287-141. Frank was then reprimanded, 408-18. Frank apologized for his conduct, attributing it in part to his efforts prior to 1987 to conceal his homosexuality.

Oliver North's Convictions Suspended—A 3-judge panel of the U.S. Court of Appeals in Washington, D.C. suspended Oliver North's 3 felony convictions in the Iran-contra, **July 20.** One was overturned outright. North, before being tried, had testified before Congress in 1987 under a grant of immunity from prosecution. The Appeals Court panel held that the trial judge, Gerhard Gesell, had failed to insure that witnesses testifying at North's trial had not used North's Congressional testimony to refresh their memories. In its decision, the panel was split 2-1. The majority held that if the case were to proceed Gesell must demonstrate that North's testimony was not used by witnesses or by the office of the prosecutor, Lawrence Walsh. The panel set aside convictions for deceiving Congress and for receiving an illegal gratuity, and overturned North's conviction for destroying government documents.

Brennan Retires From Supreme Court—Justice William Brennan, Jr. announced, **July 20,** that he was resigning from the U.S. Supreme Court, effective immediately. Brennan, 84, had served on the court for almost 34 years, and was recognized as the leader of the liberal bloc and as one of the court's most influential members. Major decisions that he had written included the ruling that established the "one person, one vote" principle in reapportionment cases and the ruling protecting the press in libel cases. His belief that the court must interpret the law in the light of present-day circumstances underlay the process by which he reached his conclusions. Brennan, who had suffered a mild stroke earlier in July, had incurred the opposition of conservatives, who believed that his approach represented an intrusion by the judicial branch into lawmaking. With the court closely divided on the legality of abortion and on other key issues, Pres. George Bush's nomination of a successor to Brennan was awaited with great interest. On July 23, he announced his choice, Judge David Souter of the U.S. Court of Appeals for the First Circuit in Boston. Souter, was a graduate of Harvard College and Harvard Law School. He had served as New Hampshire's attorney general and as a state Supreme Court judge before being named to the circuit court earlier in 1990.

More Money Asked for S&L Bailout—In testimony before a House committee, **July 30,** Resolution Trust Corp. Chairman William Seidman and Treasury Undersecretary Robert Glauber said that the RTC would need up to $100 billion in fiscal 1991 to continue the savings and loan bailout effort. This was twice the amount of money previously allocated for the rescue operation. A slump in real-estate values and a higher failure rate among thrift institutions were blamed for the need for more money.

International

Economy of 2 Germanys Unified—A treaty ratified in June that established a unified economic and monetary system for East and West Germany became effective, **July 1.** The West German deutsche mark became the sole legal tender for all of Germany. The West German Bundesbank (central bank) was given control over monetary policy for East Germany. East Germany also became wedded to West Germany's market economy, social security and tax systems, and labor and banking laws. East Germans were allowed to exchange from 2,000 to 6,000 East marks for deutsche marks at a 1-to-1 rate and the rest of their holdings at a rate of 2 East marks for one deutsche mark. The East German government, **July 2,** agreed to all-German elections in December. In mid-July, 2 more bold steps were taken toward German reunification. Meeting in the southern Russian town of Zhelezonovodsk, **July 16,** Soviet Pres. Mikhail Gorbachev and West German Chancellor Helmut Kohl announced that they had reached an agreement that would allow a unified Germany to join the North Atlantic Treaty Organization. Kohl called the agreement, which had not been anticipated so soon, "fantastic," and Gorbachev said it foreshadowed an era of "strong, prolonged peace." Kohl agreed to a limitation on German weaponry and military manpower and to a continuing presence of Soviet troops on East German soil for up to 4 years. Pres. George Bush and other Western leaders hailed the agreement. On July 17, in Paris, the 2 Germanys and the 4 Allied powers of World War II approved a plan to guarantee Poland's border with a united Germany. Poland had sought assurances that Germany would not seek to reclaim onetime German territory awarded to Poland after World War II.

Gorbachev Survives Party Congress—Pres. Mikhail Gorbachev appeared to have strengthened his hand during the tumultuous 28th Congress of the Communist Party of the Soviet Union. As the congress opened in Moscow, **July 2,** conservatives were concerned about a draft platform that did not refer directly to Marxism-Leninism and supported the right to "earned private property" and the "interests and requirements of the individual." Gorbachev, speaking **July 2,** admitted that the party leadership had made mistakes but that his program of restructuring was the nation's only hope. He reaffirmed the need for a regulated market economy. Foreign Minister Eduard Shevardnadze, **July 3,** criticized defense spending as too high and warned against military influence in shaping foreign policy. Yegor Ligachev, a conservative, got a positive response from the audience, **July 3,** when he denounced reform as "thoughtless radicalism" and opposed the draft platform. Gorbachev said, **July 4,** he would quit in 2 years if restructuring failed to produce positive results. By a 3-1 margin, **July 10,** the Congress approved Gorbachev's reelection as the party's general secretary. By an even greater margin, **July 11,** the congress chose Gorbachev's candidate, Vladimir Ivashko, over Ligachev for the number 2 position in the party. In a surprise, Boris Yelstin, the president of the Russian republic who had criticized the pace of reform as too slow, announced, **July 12,** that he was quitting the party. The mayors of Moscow and Leningrad also left the party, **July 13.** In accord with a plan approved at the congress, the party's central committee, **July 14,** approved a new, expanded, 24-member Politburo that included the party leader in each of the 15 republics. Ten of the 12 previous members of the Politburo (all but Gorbachev and Ivashko) were dropped. The changes appeared to have the effect of weakening the party's influence over the government.

Mrs. Marcos Not Guilty of Fraud—Mrs. Imelda Marcos, the widow of former Philippine's Pres. Ferdinand Marcos, was found not guilty of charges of racketeering, fraud, and obstruction of justice, **July 2,** in Federal Court in New York City. Her codefendant, Saudi Arabian financier Adnan Khashoggi, was found not guilty of mail fraud and obstruction of justice. The prosecution alleged that Mrs. Marcos had stolen $200 million from the Philippines treasury and spent most of it on herself. Khashoggi was said to have helped her buy office buildings in the U.S. The defense argued that Mrs. Marcos was unaware of any illegal activities on the part of her late husband. Jurors were reported to have found this assertion persuasive, and some said they did not understand why the trial was being conducted in the U.S.

Bulgaria's Socialist President Resigns—Although Bulgaria's Socialist (formerly Communist) Party had won parliamentary elections (in June), hundreds of students erected a tent city in Sofia, the capital, and demanded the resignation of Pres. Petar Mladenov and the prosecution of his predecessor, the longtime leader Todor Zhivkov. Mladenov's cause was undercut when a videotape showed that he had called for military tanks to quell a pro-democracy demonstration in December 1989. Mladenov resigned, **July 6.** After a 3-week impasse, Parliament, **Aug. 1,** chose Zhelyu Zhelev, leader of the 16-party opposition coalition, as the new president. A philosopher, he had been expelled from the party in 1965 for questioning the theories of Lenin.

Albanians Seek Refuge in Embassies—Thousands of Albanians sought refuge in foreign embassies in Tirana, the capital of Albania, in late June and early July. Their ranks swelled after pro-democracy demonstrators clashed with police several times. On **July 6,** riot police closed off the embassy district and attacked some 10,000 people who were demonstrating in the capital. The regime of Pres. Ramiz Alia dismissed hard-liners from the Workers' (Communist) Party Politburo, **July 7.** On **July 8,** the authorities agreed to permit the refugees to emigrate. The evacuation got under way, **July 9,** as 51 refugees were flown to Prague. Several thousand arrived in Italy, **July 13.**

NATO Modifies Its Strategy—Leaders of the North Atlantic Treaty Organization, meeting in London, **July 5 and 6,** approved some shifts in strategy that reflected the easing of tensions in Europe. Pres. George Bush was among the heads of government attending the meeting. The leaders agreed to scale back the number of troops in a front-line position. Essentially renouncing the possibility of using nuclear weapons in response to an attack by conventional forces, NATO's leaders declared that their nuclear arms were "truly weapons of the last resort." The U.S. said it would be willing to withdraw all of its nuclear-tipped artillery shells if the Soviet Union did the same. The leaders invited Pres. Mikhail Gorbachev and other leaders of the dissolving Soviet bloc to address NATO.

Leaders of Democracies Meet in Houston—The heads of government of the 7 major industrial democracies met in Houston, **July 9-11,** for their 16th annual summit on international economic issues. The leaders commissioned a study of the Soviet economy to determine if economic aid would be useful and what forms it might take. Pres. George Bush opposed direct aid to the Soviet Union until it made further moves toward a free-market economy. West German Chancellor Helmut Kohl had warned other summit leaders before they met that the prospect of global warming was "a threat to all mankind." But the U.S. position was that imposing strict goals for reducing emissions of carbon dioxide and some other gases would hurt the U.S.

economy and that scientific evidence of global warming was not conclusive in any case. Any commitment to cut back emissions was postponed until 1992. The leaders did, however, pledge to develop strategies for worldwide reforestation and to help Brazil save its imperiled rain forests.

U.S. Shifts Policy on Cambodia—U.S. Sec. of State James Baker announced in Paris, **July 18**, that the U.S. would no longer recognize the Cambodian rebel coalition and would instead open talks with Vietnam in an effort to end the civil war in Cambodia. He had met with Soviet Foreign Minister Eduard Shevardnadze, whose government was a backer of Vietnam and who endorsed Baker's shift in policy. The U.S. had become concerned because of the growing success on the battlefield of the Khmer Rouge, the brutal rulers of Cambodia from 1975 to 1979 who may have caused the deaths of 2 million Cambodians. Baker said it was "very important" to prevent the return to power of the Khmer Rouge. Vietnam was a supporter of the current Cambodian government.

Adviser to Thatcher Killed by Bomb—Violence attributed to the Provisional Irish Republican Army flared anew in Great Britain when the explosion of a land mine, **July 24**, apparently detonated from a nearby house, killed 3 Northern Ireland policemen in a car near Armagh in Ulster. A Roman Catholic nun, traveling in another car, was also killed by the blast. On **July 30**, Ian Gow, a member of Parliament and a close friend and adviser to British Prime Minister Margaret Thatcher, who had been a frequent critic of the IRA, was killed at his home in Hankham, East Sussex, when a bomb blew up his car.

Coup Fails in Trinidad & Tobago—A group of black Moslem rebels, complaining that the government had impoverished the country, launched a coup attempt in Trinidad and Tobago, **July 27**. The Caribbean island nation, a producer of oil, had suffered a recession in recent years as the price of oil had declined. The rebels seized the parliament building, **July 27**, and took Prime Minister Arthur Robinson hostage, along with cabinet members and other officials. Other hostages were seized at a television station. Robinson was shot in the leg. Negotiations began, **July 28**, and Robinson and the other hostages were released. The coup ended, **Aug. 1**, when 113 rebels surrendered. The government, **Aug. 2**, put the death toll in the coup attempt at 30.

General

Stampede Kills 1,426 in Mecca Tunnel—The government of Saudi Arabia said, **July 3**, that 1,426 Moslem pilgrims had been killed when a stampede occurred in a tunnel leading from a nearby tent city to the holy sites in Mecca. Some 50,000 people were crowded into the tunnel, which was 500 yards long and 20 yards wide. The crowd panicked after 7 people fell from a bridge at the entrance to the tunnel. The victims, including many from Indonesia, Pakistan, Egypt, and Malaysia, were suffocated or trampled to death.

Yankees' Owner Is Disciplined—Fay Vincent, the commissioner of major league baseball, ordered George Steinbrenner, principal owner of the New York Yankees, on **July 30**, to give up day-to-day control of the team. In addition to resigning as the team's general partner, Steinbrenner was required to reduce his holdings in the Yankees, then at 55 percent, to less than 50 percent. Vincent said Steinbrenner's relationship with Howard Spira, a "known gambler,"prompted his ruling. Spira said Steinbrenner paid him $40,000 after Spira provided information on Dave Winfield, a former

Yankee with whom Steinbrenner was feuding. Steinbrenner said he paid the money to Spira because he was afraid of him and wanted to be rid of him. Vincent also said that he had observed in Steinbrenner "a pattern of behavior that borders on the bizarre." Under Steinbrenner's stormy rule since 1973, the Yankees had won 2 World Series in 1977 and 1978, but had faded in recent years and had the worst record in baseball when Vincent made his decision. Steinbrenner had changed managers 18 times.

Disasters—An earthquake whose epicenter was 55 miles north of Manila struck the Philippines, **July 16**, killing more than 600 people and leaving 2,600 homeless.

AUGUST

National

Unemployment Rate Up Sharply — The Labor Dept. reported, **Aug. 3**, that the unemployment rate had increased in July to 5.5 percent from 5.2 percent. The 0.3 percent monthly increase, largest in more than 4 years, was taken as a sign the country might already be in a recession. The department reported, **Aug. 10**, that producer prices had declined 0.1 percent in July. It reported, **Aug. 16**, that consumer prices had jumped 0.4 percent in July, and that prices had risen at an annual rate of 5.8 percent during the first 7 months of the year. The Commerce Dept. said, **Aug. 17**, that the merchandise trade deficit had fallen to $5.07 billion in June, the lowest level in 7 years. The department reported, **Aug. 29**, that the index of leading economic indicators had not changed in July.

Price of Gasoline Rises in U.S. — Within a few days of Iraq's invasion of Kuwait, the price of fuel rose sharply. On **Aug. 6**, Pan Am Corp. announced that it was raising air fares 10 percent to cover the increase in fuel costs. Other air carriers made similar announcements. Executives of oil companies, testifying before Congress, **Aug. 7**, said that the cost of fuel had jumped quickly because their companies paid for oil when it was delivered to U.S. refineries, rather than when it was contracted for in the Middle East, so the worldwide rise in the cost of oil per barrel was reflected almost immediately. The American Automobile Association reported, **Aug. 9**, that the retail price for self-service unleaded gasoline had risen 18 cents per gallon in the week since the Iraqi invasion. As the price of oil fluctuated widely on world markets, the cost of gasoline leveled off. A number of economists expressed concern that the Mideast conflict, including its great cost to the U.S. Treasury, could hasten a slide into a recession. Such fears appeared to be reflected on Wall Street, where the Dow Jones industrial average slumped 14 percent in 3 weeks, closing **Aug. 23** at 2483.42. Concern over the status of the U.S. economy also appeared to be a factor in the decline of the dollar against other currencies. On **Aug. 23**, the dollar was trading at 1.56 German marks, the lowest since the mark was introduced in 1948.

D.C. Mayor Convicted on One Count — The trial of Marion Barry Jr., the mayor of Washington, D.C., on drug charges ended in August with a split verdict. Ten witnesses had testified during the trial that they had seen Barry use illegal drugs, and others had told of delivering drugs to him or obtaining drugs from him. A video tape had shown him inhaling from a crack pipe. The prosecution contended that evidence had been presented of more than 200 separate uses of illegal drugs by Barry. The defense conceded that the mayor had occasionally used drugs, but contended that there was reasonable doubt about each charge of cocaine possession. On **Aug. 10**, the jury found Barry guilty of one count of possession of crack and acquitted him on a second count. On 12 other misdemeanor and felony charges, the jury was unable to reach a verdict, and Judge Thomas Jackson declared a mistrial on those counts. Barry saw himself as largely vindicated, and on **Aug. 14**, he said he would seek an at-large seat on the City Council, running as an independent.

International

Gorbachev, Rival Unite on Economy — Soviet Pres. Mikhail Gorbachev and Boris Yeltsin, president of the Russian Federation, agreed, **Aug. 1**, to work together to transform the Soviet economy from central planning to a market system. The 2 men, who had frequently quarreled over the pace of reform, with Yeltsin pushing a more radical approach, signed a unity agreement. They set up a commission to draft proposals, and it was reported that a 500-day plan developed by Russia would be the basis for the commission's plan. Under the Russian Republic's 500-day plan, it would legalize private property, abolish government subsidies, lift price controls, and take other as yet unspecified steps to stabilize its economy. In the republic of Armenia, the Communist-dominated government resigned, **Aug. 13**, under pressure from parliament. On **Aug. 23**, in a 183-2 vote, the Armenian parliament declared the republic's independence from the Soviet Union. It also claimed control over the disputed area Nagorno-Karabakh, situated within the republic of Azerbaijan. Following the shooting deaths of 5 people, including a member of parliament, the Armenian parliament, **Aug. 29**, declared a state of emergency and outlawed the republic's largest paramilitary group.

U.S. Mariners Land in Liberia — U.S. Marines flew to Liberia to rescue American citizens endangered by the bloody civil war in the West African country. The war had raged since late 1989 when guerrillas led by Charles Taylor launched an effort to overthrow the government of Pres. Samuel Doe. The rebels reached the capital of Monrovia in July, but they also split into 2 factions, the other led by Prince Johnson, and fought each other as well as the government forces. There were many instances of brutality toward civilians, and at least 200, possibly many more, were killed when government troops stormed a Luthern church in Monrovia, **July 30**. Johnson said, **Aug. 4**, that he would begin to round up foreigners. Pres. George Bush authorized a rescue mission, and on **Aug. 5**, 230 Marines were flown to Monrovia from ships off the coast. Without firing a shot or suffering any casualties, the Marines evacuated 125 persons by **Aug. 8**. The Marines remained at the embassy in Monrovia.

Cease-Fire Approved in South Africa — The African National Congress and government officials began talks in South Africa, **Aug. 6**, and on **Aug. 7**, the ANC announced that it was suspending its 30-year armed struggle against the white regime. The cease-fire began immediately. Pres. F.W. deKlerk's government agreed to free political prisoners, allow exiled dissidents to return, and repeal the nation's security laws. Both sides agreed to seek an end to the violence in Natal Province, where some 3,000 persons had been killed in fighting among factions of the Zulu tribe. Fighting had also occurred in Transvaal Province between Zulus and other blacks.

3 Hostages Freed in Mideast — On **Aug. 8** and **14**, 2 Swiss Red Cross workers were freed in Damascus after being held in Lebanon for 10 months. On **Aug. 24**, a group called the Organization of Islamic Dawn turned another hostage, Brian Keenan, over to Syrian military officers and he was freed in Damascus. Keenan, who held both Irish and British citizenship, flew to Dublin, **Aug. 25**. A teacher, he had been held more than 4 years. It was believed that 13 more Western hostages were being held by Shiite Moslems.

Bhutto Removed as Pakistan's Leader — Prime Minister Benazir Bhutto of Pakistan was dismissed, **Aug. 6**, by Pres. Ghulam Ishaq Khan. He named Ghulam Mustafa Jatoi as interim prime minister, and declared a state of emergency. The president said that corruption in the Bhutto government had been widespread, and the press had reported a number of allegations. Ishaq Khan also cited a nationwide increase in crime and violence. Bhutto called her removal illegal and unconstitutional.

East Germany Sets Unity Date — The parliament of East Germany voted 294-62 on **Aug. 23**, to set Oct. 3 as the date for unification with West Germany. Under the West German constitution, any former German territory could declare its wish to unify, and the West German parliament was not required to take any action. The October date would fall about 2 months before the scheduled all-German elections.

General

3 Convicted in Attack on Jogger — Three teen-age boys were convicted in New York City, **Aug. 18**, of charges related to a crime that had shocked the public because of its brutality. In April 1989, a 28-year-old investment banker, who was jogging in Central Park in Manhattan, was attacked by a gang of young men. She was beaten severely and left unconscious. Alleged members of the gang, which reportedly numbered as many as 30, were seized by police and charged with a variety of crimes involving the attack on the jogger and attacks on others in the park. The first 3 defendants, aged 16, 16, and 15, were convicted of rape, assault, and other charges. Videotaped confessions were key evidence inasmuch as no hard physical evidence placed the accused at the scene of the crime. The jogger, who was not publicly identified by most members of the news media, testified briefly at the trial. More than a year after the attack, she had no memory of it, and she had lost her sense of smell, suffered from double vision, and had difficulty walking.

Tornado Kills 27 in Illinois — Without warning from the National Weather Service, which was taken by surprise, a tornado, **Aug. 28**, cut a 700-foot-wide swath across towns and cornfields 35 miles southwest of Chicago. Following an 8-mile course through Plainfield, Crest Hill, and Joliet, the tornado killed 27 persons and injured more than 350. Fifty houses and 500 apartments were destroyed. Some victims died when the tornado's vacuum lifted them into the sky and dropped them into nearby fields.

Disasters — An explosion, probably caused by coal dust or methane gas, tore through a coal mine 90 miles west of Belgrade, Yugoslavia, **Aug. 26**, killing more than 170 miners.

SEPTEMBER

National

Consumer Prices Jump — Fueled by an increase in energy costs because of the Persian Gulf crisis, consumer prices rose sharply in August. The Labor Dept. reported, **Sept. 7**, that the unemployment rate continued to edge up in August, to 5.6 percent. The department said, **Sept. 14**, that producer prices for finished goods jumped 1.3 percent in August. It released its report on consumer prices, **Sept. 18**, that showed a 0.8 percent increase in August. The Commerce Dept. reported, **Sept. 18**, that the merchandise trade deficit rose to $9.33 billion in July, 75 percent above the June figure. An increase in oil imports was a major factor. Alan Greenspan, chairman of the Federal Reserve Board, said, **Sept. 19,** that the Gulf crisis would likely slow economic growth and stimulate inflation. The Commerce Dept. reported, **Sept. 25,** that it had lowered its estimate of economic growth during the second quarter to just 0.4 percent on an annual basis from 1.2 percent. The department reported, **Sept. 28,** that the index of leading economic indicators had dropped 1.2 percent in August, the biggest monthly decline since 1987.

Negotiators on Budget Agree to Plan — Pres. George Bush and Congressional negotiators reached a tentative agreement on a controversial plan to reduce the Federal deficit. It was feared that the deficit in the 1991 fiscal year might reach $250 billion, with the bailout of the savings and loan industry being a major factor. Under the Gramm-Rudman deficit reduction law, the deficit would have to be pared to $64 billion or mandatory spending cuts would become automatic. Talks began, **Sept. 7,** between White House representatives and congressional leaders. Bush supported a cut in the capital-gains tax rate, but Democrats insisted that any such reduction be balanced by an increase in income-tax rates for Americans with high incomes. The talks broke down in disagreement, **Sept. 17,** and resumed, **Sept. 19,** with fewer negotiators. The way to a compromise seemed open, **Sept. 29,** when Bush dropped his position on capital gains. An agreement was announced, **Sept. 30.** It included big increases in taxes on gasoline, tobacco, and alcohol. Deductions available to Americans earning more than $100,000 a year would be limited, and an excise tax would be imposed on luxury items. Medicare taxes would rise. Spending on Medicare and other domestic programs would be cut. Members of Congress from both parties quickly announced that they would oppose the plan. In a new projection, **Sept. 30,** the 1991 deficit was put at $293.7 billion.

Primary Elections Include Surprises — Sharon Pratt Dixon, a former treasurer of the Democratic National Committee, who was seeking public office for the first time, was nominated by the Democratic Party for mayor of Washington, D.C. on **Sept. 11.** Of the 5 candidates, she had been the most outspoken in her criticism of the incumbent mayor, Marion Barry Jr., who had been convicted in August on a drug charge. In Massachusetts, **Sept. 18,** both gubernatorial primaries were won by candidates who had run poorly in the polls. John Silber, president of Boston University, won on the Democratic side. More conservative than most Democratic leaders in the state, he had criticized the state welfare system as too generous, and had made remarks that ethnic groups found offensive. His victory was believed to reflect a voter backlash against economic problems of the incumbent governor, Michael Dukakis, a liberal Democrat. On the Republican ballot, William Weld, a former U.S. attorney who supported abortion rights, prevailed over a more conservative opponent. Also, on **Sept. 18,** Oklahoma voters supported a concept that was being considered elsewhere—by approving a limitation of 12 years of service in the state legislature.

Hearings Held on Court Nominee — Judge David Souter appeared before the Senate Judiciary Committee, which was considering his nomination by Pres. George Bush to serve on the U.S. Supreme Court. On **Sept. 4,** the American Bar Association gave Souter its highest rating of "well qualified" for the Supreme Court. Appearing before the committee, **Sept. 13,** Souter declined to give his views on abortion, but he said,

"I believe that the due process clause of the 14th Amendment does recognize and does protect an unenumerated right of privacy." The right of privacy was the basis for Roe. v. Wade, a 1973 decision by the court establishing a woman's right to an abortion. Asked, **Sept. 14,** about his views on judges who "invented" rights, Souter said there was a difference between inventing rights and searching the text of the Constitution in order to recognize those that are implicitly stated. Several abortion-rights and women's-rights groups testified, **Sept. 18,** against the nomination, but other organizations dropped their opposition. The National Association for the Advancement of Colored People, **Sept. 21,** opposed the nomination, saying Souter had failed to articulate a sufficient level of concern "for fairness, equality, and justice for all citizens." The Senate committee voted, **Sept. 27,** to endorse Souter, 13-1.

Former Owner of S&L Indicted — Charles Keating, one of the most prominent figures in the investigation of the savings and loan financial crisis, was indicted, **Sept. 18,** on 42 charges of criminal fraud by a state grand jury in Los Angeles. He formerly owned Lincoln Savings & Loan Association. Three executives of American Continental, Lincoln's parent company, were also indicted. The charges involved an alleged scheme to defraud older persons by enticing them to invest in uninsured high-risk bonds. After American Continental filed for bankruptcy, the money—$250 million—could not be recovered. Keating was unable to pay the $5 million bail, and was put in jail. On **Sept. 22,** the Federal Deposit Insurance Corporation sued Neil Bush, the son of the president, and other officials of the defunct Silverado Banking, Savings and Loan Association for "gross negligence" that the FDIC said could cost taxpayers more than $1 billion.

International

USSR Moves Toward Economic Reform — The Soviet Union appeared to be well on its way toward embracing radical economic reform. The economic crisis was underscored, **Sept. 3,** when bread virtually disappeared from the shelves of food stores in Moscow. On **Sept. 5,** the government newspaper *Izvestia* published details of a plan on which aides to Pres. Mikhail Gorbachev and Russian Pres. Boris Yeltsin had been working. What had emerged was the "Shatalin plan," named for Stanislav Shatalin, an adviser to Gorbachev, and the plan was based on the 500-day plan already adopted by the Russian Republic. It would dismantle most central economic planning and stress private property and economic freedom. On **Sept. 11,** Premier Nikolai Ryzhkov addressed the Supreme Soviet, warning that the Shatalin plan, if implemented, would lead to high unemployment and a decline in the standard of living. But then, Gorbachev spoke and endorsed it. On **Sept. 14,** he submitted a modified version of the plan to the Supreme Soviet that would retain central authority over financial matters. The parliament of Russia, **Sept. 19,** called on Ryzhkov to resign. Gorbachev, **Sept. 21,** asked the Supreme Soviet for sweeping new powers to govern during the transition to a market economy. Ryzhkov said, **Sept. 23,** that the country faced a potato shortage because of a lack of success in collecting the harvest. The Supreme Soviet, **Sept. 24,** granted Gorbachev emergency economic powers, and agreed to accept a compromise plan for the economy at Gorbachev's request, heading off a showdown between him and the premier. The details of the compromise were yet to be worked out.

Rebels Kill President of Liberia — Pres. Samuel Doe was killed while in the hands of rebels in Liberia.

A multinational force from black Africa had entered Liberia in August in an attempt to help restore order between government forces and rebel armies. On **Sept. 9,** Doe and an entourage of bodyguards arrived at the headquarters of the multinational force. Rebels led by Prince Johnson arrived, gunfire broke out, and 78 were killed, mostly Doe's bodyguards. Doe was wounded and died the next day, under circumstances that were not clear. On **Sept. 21,** Charles Taylor, leader of another rebel faction, declared a unilateral cease-fire. But the cease-fire soon broke down, and on **Sept. 30,** Johnson's faction declared a renewal of the war against the Taylor rebels and the remnants of Doe's army.

Treaty signed on Germany — The Allied powers of World War II gave up their responsibilities over Germany, and on **Sept. 10,** West Germany and the Soviet Union agreed in principle on maintenance and repatriation of Soviet forces in East Germany. West Germany agreed to spend $8.2 billion to build 36,000 houses in the Soviet Union, cover continued cost of soldiers still stationed in East Germany, transport the soldiers home, and retrain them. On **Sept. 12,** in Moscow, West Germany, East Germany, France, Great Britain, the Soviet Union, and the United States signed the *Treaty on the Final Settlement with Respect to Germany.* The wartime allies pledged to "terminate their rights and responsibilities relating to Berlin and to Germany as a whole." The united Germany was thus granted full sovereignty over its internal and external affairs. On **Sept. 13,** with formal reunification still 3 weeks away, the foreign ministers of West Germany and the USSR signed a friendship pact in which the 2 nations pledged not to attack each other and to consult each other in time of crisis.

Cambodia Rivals Accept U.N. Plan — Four factions fighting for control of Cambodia agreed, **Sept. 10,** to accept a U.N. proposal to end their civil war. Meeting in Jakarta, Indonesia, they appointed a 12-member Supreme National Council that would run Cambodia until free elections could be held under U.N. supervision. The government named 6 to the council, 2 each from the 3 rebel groups.

S. Africa Leader Meets With Bush — Pres. F. W. de Klerk of South Africa met with Pres. George Bush in Washington, **Sept. 24.** De Klerk, who had freed black nationalist leader Nelson Mandela and taken other steps to ease South Africa's system of racial separation, was cordially received. Bush said that if South Africa continued its efforts to meet certain conditions set by Congress, he would seek to modify or suspend sanctions imposed on South Africa by Congress. De Klerk told members of Congress, **Sept. 25,** that he supported the principle of one man, one vote in elections, but that its application must include guarantees to protect the white minority in South Africa.

U.N. Summit Seeks to Help Children — Leaders of more than 70 nations, including the largest gathering ever of heads of state at the United Nations, met in New York City, **Sept. 30,** at the World Summit for Children. The primary goal of the summit was to improve the lives of children everywhere, and especially to reduce the number of children—put at 14 million—who died each year before the age of 5. The leaders also discussed ways to reduce malnutrition among children, reduce the number of mothers dying in childbirth, and provide clean water and education for all.

General

New Rating Applied to Adult Films — The Motion Picture Association of America announced, **Sept. 26,** that it had created a new "NC-17" rating that would be applied to films that had adult themes and perhaps scenes of sex and violence. The rating meant that no children under 17 would be admitted. The purpose was to permit "serious" movies to avoid the X rating that was also applied to pornographic movies. Many theaters refused to show X-rated films, and distributors were complaining that some important films thus failed to reach a large audience.

Disasters — As many as 160 people may have drowned, **Sept. 11,** when a crowded boat capsized in the Mahava River in Uttar Pradesh state in India . . . . Some 82,000 persons were homeless and more than 77 persons died after heavy rainfall in the vicinity of Seoul, South Korea, **Sept. 11,** resulted in massive flooding.

OCTOBER

National

Congress Approves Deficit-Reduction Plan — Congress approved a deficit-reduction bill that Pres. George Bush could accept, after an earlier plan, announced, **Sept. 30,** by Bush and endorsed by congressional negotiators, ran into trouble. Rep. Newt Gingrich (Ga.), the Republican whip in the House, rejected it, **Oct. 1,** saying it would "kill jobs, weaken the economy." He and many other conservatives objected to the inclusion of tax increases in the proposal, and many Democrats were concerned that these taxes would fall more heavily on the middle class than on wealthier Americans. An intense lobbying effort by the president and by congressional leaders of both parties failed. The House, **Oct. 5,** rejected the bill 254-179, with a majority from both parties in opposition. Congress passed a stopgap spending bill, but Bush vetoed it, **Oct. 6,** and this had the effect of shutting down the government. Congress passed and Bush signed new stopgap legislation, **Oct. 9,** which extended government's borrowing and spending power for 10 days. Bush said, **Oct. 9,** that a higher tax rate for the wealthy, perhaps in exchange for a cut in the capital-gains tax, was "on the table." Later that day, after meeting with 17 Republican senators, Bush pulled back any commitment to raising income taxes. In another shift, the White House said, **Oct. 10,** that it was up to Congress to decide whether to couple an increase in rates with a cut in the capital-gains tax. The House, **Oct. 16,** approved a new budget compromise that would increase taxes on wealthy Americans. This passed 238-192, with only 10 Republicans supporting it. The Senate passed its budget package, **Oct. 19,** 54-46. This version had more of an impact on the middle class through a doubling of the gasoline tax and a cut in Medicare benefits. As the House and Senate bills went to conference committee, Bush, **Oct. 19,** signed another stopgap bill to keep the government going 5 more days. The president signaled a willingness to accept a small increase in the tax rate for the wealthy. On **Oct. 27,** both the Senate (54-45) and the House (228-200) approved the conference committee report, but with a majority of House and Senate Republicans in opposition. Bush said he would sign the bill, which was designed to reduce deficits by nearly $500 billion over 5 years. Under the law, the top tax rate would rise from 28 percent to 31 percent, and exemptions for upper-income Americans would be phased out. The gasoline tax would jump 5 cents a gallon to 14 cents, and the cigarette tax would rise by 8 cents a pack to 24 cents. The tax on a 6-pack of beer would double to 32 cents. A luxury tax would be imposed on top-of-the-line aircraft, cars, boats, furs, and jewelry. The increase in Medicare premiums was less than elderly Americans had feared.

Ex-Klansman Loses Bid for Senate — David Duke, a former grand wizard in the Ku Klux Klan, made a strong but unsuccessful showing in an election for the U.S. Senate in Louisiana. He was contesting the re-election bid of Sen. J. Bennett Johnston, a Democrat. State Sen. Ben Bagert was the official Republican candidate, but Duke, a Republican member of the State House of Representatives, also entered the race. Duke gained wide support by appealing for "equal rights for whites" and focusing on the state's economic troubles. Fearing they would be embarrassed by a Duke victory, 8 Republican U.S. senators endorsed Johnston, **Oct. 2.** Bagert dropped out of the race, **Oct. 4.** On **Oct. 6,** Johnston defeated Duke by 54 percent to 44 percent.

Souter Confirmed for Supreme Court — The U.S. Senate, **Oct. 2,** confirmed Judge David Souter for a seat on the U.S. Supreme Court. The vote was 90-9, with all those in opposition being Democrats. Souter was sworn in as the nation's 105th justice on **Oct. 8.**

Unemployment Rises Again — The Labor Dept. reported, **Oct. 5,** that unemployment in September had edged upward to 5.7 percent, the third consecutive monthly increase. The jobless rate stood at its highest level since the spring of 1988. The department said, **Oct. 18,** that in September, for the second straight month, consumer prices had risen by 0.8 percent. Oil prices, affected by the Persian Gulf crisis, accounted for more than half of the increase. The Commerce Dept. reported, **Oct. 30,** that the gross national product grew at an annual rate of 1.8 percent during the third quarter, a sharp improvement over the 0.4 rate reported during the second quarter. On **Oct. 31,** General Motors reported its greatest quarterly loss ever, $1.98 billion. It announced that it would close 4 assembly plants permanently and said that 5 other plants might be closed.

Bush Vetoes Civil Rights Bill — Pres. George Bush vetoed a civil rights bill, which sought in effect to reverse 6 recent Supreme Court decisions that civil rights organizations contended had weakened anti-discrimination laws on hiring and promoting. Bush said, **Oct. 20,** that the bill "will have the effect of coercing businesses to adopt quotas in hiring and promotion." Bush, who opposed the concept of quotas, said businesses would have to adopt quotas to avoid expensive litigation. He vetoed the bill, **Oct. 22.** The Senate voted 66-34, on **Oct. 24,** to override the veto, but this was one vote short of the required two-thirds.

Mayor Receives Prison Term — Mayor Marion Barry, Jr. of Washington, D.C. was sentenced, **Oct. 20,** to 6 months in prison and fined $5,000 and costs on his conviction on a misdemeanor charge of possessing cocaine. Federal District Judge Thomas Penfield Jackson said that an example should be set for other public officials and said that Barry had "given aid, comfort and encouragement to the drug culture at large."

Dole Resigns as Labor Secretary — Elizabeth Dole, the highest-ranking woman in the administration of Pres. George Bush, resigned, **Oct. 24,** as Secretary of Labor. She was the first member of the Bush cabinet to step down. Dole planned to accept the presidency of the American Red Cross.

Sweeping Clean Air Act Approved — Congress, **Oct. 27,** completed action on the 1990 Clean Air Act, a comprehensive updating of the original Clean Air Act adopted in 1970. The bill, which Pres. George Bush said he would sign, set an overall annual level of emissions of sulfer dioxide from power plants at less than one-half of current emissions, with a target date of 2000. In another effort to eliminate acid rain, nitrogen oxide emissions would be cut by one-third. Oil companies would be required to develop new types of gasoline that burn more cleanly, and cities would have to reduce concentration of ozone, a component of smog. The bill would halt production of chemicals that threatened the earth's ozone sheild.

International

Germany United After 45 Years — The reunification of Germany was completed at midnight, **Oct. 2-3.** Since the end of World War II in 1945 there had been 2 Germanys, but the rush to unification had been swift since the collapse of the hard-line Communist regime in East Germany late in 1989. The new nation, having a population of 78 million, would be known formally as the Federal Republic of Germany, previously the official designation of West Germany.

Arabs Are Killed Near Holy Shrines — From 17 to 21 Palestinians were shot fatally by Israeli police in Jerusalem's Old City, **Oct. 8,** and more than 100 were wounded. The shootings took place at a site sacred to both Islam and Judaism, where the Western Wall, or Wailing Wall, stands near 2 mosques, Al Aksa and Dome of the Rock. A Jewish religious group, the Temple Mount Faithful, had declared their intention to raze the mosques and build a new temple to replace one destroyed by the Romans. Members of this group came to the site, **Oct. 8,** and thousands of Palestinians came to confront them. Israeli authorities barred the Jewish group, but the Palestinians threw stones at Jews worshipping at the Western Wall. Some 2 dozen policemen and Jewish civilians were reportedly struck. Police fired on the protestors. Apparently motivated in part by a desire to retain Arab support in the Persian Gulf crisis, the U.S., **Oct. 9,** asked the U.N. Security Council to condemn Israel for the shootings. Israeli Prime Minister Yitzhak Shamir, **Oct. 10,** appointed a commission to investigate the shootings. The Security Council, **Oct. 12,** voted 15-0 to condemn Israel and to support sending a U.N. mission to investigate. Shamir said, **Oct. 13,** that the U.N. delegation would receive no help from Israel, and the Israeli cabinet, **Oct. 14,** denounced the mission on the basis that the investigation would call into question asserted Israeli sovereignty over East Jerusalem. The Security Council, **Oct. 24,** voted unanimously to deplore Israel's refusal to cooperate with the investigation. An aide to Shamir declared, **Oct. 25,** that the U.S. in supporting the U.N. resolutions, was playing into the hands of Saddam Hussein, the ruler of Iraq. A report published, **Oct. 26,** by the Israeli commission criticized Israeli commanders for not having prepared for the possibility of trouble. The commission placed the blame for the tragedy on the Palestinians even though it also acknowledged that the Jewish worshippers had long since fled from the scene before the police had opened fire.

Bhutto Fails to Regain Power — Pakistan's deposed prime minister, Benazir Bhutto, failed in an effort to regain power. Her husband, Asif Ali Zandari, was arrested, **Oct. 10,** and charged with extortion and the kidnapping in 1989 of a British businessman. Bhutto called the investigation a witch hunt. In elections to the lower house of parliament, **Oct. 24,** Bhutto's party was defeated, losing more than half of its seats. An opposing party, the Islamic Democratic Alliance, won a clear majority of seats.

Lebanese Christian Militia Leader Surrenders — Gen. Michel Aoun, who led a Christian force that fought the government of Lebanon for 11 months, surrendered, **Oct. 13,** after entering the French embassy to seek refuge from Syrian air and ground attacks. It was reported, **Oct. 18**, that at least 750 people were killed in the final Syrian-led offensive that brought down Aoun.

Soviet Parliament Approves Economic Reforms — On **Oct. 16**, Soviet Pres. Mikhail Gorbachev revealed the details of his economic reform package and presented the proposal to the Soviet Parliament. The proposal generally reflected the radical views of economists who had presented their plan in broad outline in September. It included the selling of state property to private individuals, the lifting of price controls, and the transferring of many economic decisions to the 15 republics. But some sectors, including transportation, communications, defense industries, energy, banking, and foreign trade would remain under control of the central government. Futhermore, Gorbachev dropped the 500-day timetable for accomplishing the goals of the plan that the economists had originally advocated. Parliament, **Oct. 19**, gave its approval to the plan, 333 to 12, with 34 abstentions. Boris Yeltsin, president of the Russian Republic, criticized the plan for not placing more authority in the hands of the republics.

General

132 Killed in Plane Hijack Attempt — An attempt to hijack a plane in China, **Oct. 2**, ended in tragedy. One or more hijackers demanded that the Boeing 737 be flown to Taiwan or Hong Kong, according to reports. As the plane attempted to land in Guangzhou (Canton), a struggle for control of the plane reportedly occurred, and the plane struck 2 other passenger liners on the ground, one empty and another filled with passengers. Chinese officials reported that 132 people on the 2 planes were killed and that 95 survived, including 50 who were injured.

Juries Decide Obscenity Cases — A jury in Broward County Court in Fort Lauderdale, Fla., **Oct. 3**, found a record store owner, Charles Freeman, guilty of obscenity charges. At issue was the sale of an album, *As Nasty as They Wanna Be*, by the rap group 2 Live Crew. The lyrics contained many references to sexual intercourse and oral and anal sex, as well as unflattering references to woman. On **Oct. 5**, in Cincinnati, a jury found Cincinnati's Contemporary Arts Center and its director, Dennis Barrie, not guilty of obscenity charges. The museum had exhibited 175 photographs by the late Robert Mapplethorpe. Five of these depicted sadomasochistic or homoerotic acts, and 2 others showed children with exposed genitals. The jury agreed that the photos showed serious artistic merit and hence did not meet the Supreme Court's definition of obscenity. Another jury in Fort Lauderdale concluded on **Oct. 20**, that the music of 2 Live Crew was art and found members of the band not guilty of obscenity charges filed after they performed at a nightclub in June.

Iraq Overruns and Annexes Kuwait—
United States and Other Nations Send Military Forces

Iraq invaded and quickly conquered its small but oil rich neighbor Kuwait in early August. An Iraqi assault on Saudi Arabia, which could bring nearly one half of the world's known oil reserves under its control, appeared possible. The United States sent a strong military force to defend Saudi Arabia, and some other nations sent smaller contingents. A wide spectrum of nations deplored the Iraqi aggression, and Iraq soon found itself virtually isolated from the world community.

In a televised speech, **July 17**, Pres. Saddam Hussein charged that some rulers of Persian Gulf states had been "inspired by America" to keep oil prices low through over-production. In a letter made public **July 18**, Iraq charged that Kuwait and the United Arab Emirates had participated in an "imperialist-Zionist plan" to depress oil prices. It accused Kuwait of having stolen $2.4 billion worth of oil from an Iraqi oilfield. Iraq had claimed sovereignty over Kuwait in 1961.

Pres. Hosni Mubarak of Egypt, **July 25**, said that Hussein had assured him that he had no intention of invading Kuwait. Oil ministers of the OPEC nations, meeting in Geneva **July 27**, agreed to an increase in the price of oil per barrel, from $18 to $21, less than what Iraq had demanded.

Talks between Iraq and Kuwait over oil and border disputes broke off **Aug. 1**. Meanwhile, Iraq had massed 100,000 soldiers on its border with Kuwait. Kuwait's entire army contained only 20,000 men, and it was overmatched by Iraq in all categories of weaponry.

Iraqi tanks and infantry invaded Kuwait before dawn, **Aug. 2**, and Iraq announced it was responding to a call from Kuwaiti revolutionaries who had overthrown the monarchy. Despite resistance from the Kuwaitis, Iraqi forces quickly seized key roads and buildings, and soon claimed effective control of the country. The emir of Kuwait escaped from the presidential palace by helicopter.

Pres. George Bush, **Aug. 2**, denounced Iraq's action as "naked aggression," and he signed executive orders banning most trade with Iraq and freezing Iraq's and Kuwait's assets in the U.S. An aircarft carrier battle group was dispatched to the Persian Gulf.

Voting 14-0, the U.N. Security Council, **Aug. 2**, condemned the invasion and demanded the withdrawal of Iraqi troops. The Soviet Union, Iraq's biggest arms supplier, **Aug. 2**, suspended sales of military equipment to Baghdad, and on **Aug. 3**, Soviet Foreign Minister Eduard Shevardnadze and U.S. Sec. of State James Baker issued a joint statement condemning the invasion.

Reflecting fears that petroleum supplies from the Mideast would be disrupted, oil prices began to rise worldwide.

By **Aug. 3**, Iraqi forces were massing along the Saudi Arabian border. The Arab League opposed, **Aug. 3**, the "aggression" against Kuwait, but the resolution was supported by only 14 of the league's 21 members. The 12 nations of the European Community, **Aug. 4**, banned oil imports from Iraq and Kuwait, embargoed arms, and suspended most trade with Iraq. Most nations in the West, as well as Japan, had already frozen Kuwaiti assets, estimated at $100 billion.

Kuwaiti radio, controlled by Iraq, announced, **Aug. 4**, that Kuwait's "provisional government" had formed a 9-man military cabinet.

In a 13-0 vote, the U.N. Security Council, **Aug. 6**, asked all 159 U.N. members to end all trade, financial and commercial dealings, and transportation links with Iraq and Kuwait. Turkey said it would cut off the flow of Iraqi oil from the pipeline that ran from Iraq through Turkey to the Red Sea.

U.S. Defense Secretary Richard Cheney met with King Fahd of Saudi Arabia, **Aug. 6**. The king gave permission for the U.S. to deploy a military defense force on Saudi soil. Bush ordered such a deployment, and the first U.S. forces left for Saudi Arabia **Aug. 7**. The elements of the U.S. deployment, in an operation named Desert Shield, included F-15 fighters, 2,300 paratroopers, B-52 bombers, F-111 fighter-bombers, and AWACS radar planes. On the seas, 2 more carrier groups were bound for the gulf. On **Aug. 8**, Prime Minister Margaret Thatcher ordered British air and naval forces to the gulf at King Fahd's request.

Bush, addressing the American people, **Aug. 8**, said he sought the withdrawal of Iraq from Kuwait, restoration of the Kuwaiti government, stability in the Persian Gulf region, and protection of Americans living in the region.

Iraq declared, **Aug. 8**, that it had annexed Kuwait, and the U.N. Security Council declared that action "null and void" in an unanimous 15-0 vote, **Aug. 9**.

Throughout August, the U.S. forces on the ground in Saudi Arabia continued to build toward a projected total of perhaps 100,000 soldiers.

On **Aug. 9**, Iraq sealed its borders and said that only foreign diplomats would be allowed to leave. Concern rose over the status of thousands of foreigners in Iraq and Kuwait.

Pres. Hosni Mubarak of Egypt called for an emergency meeting of the Arab League and declared that Egypt would be willing to provide troops for a joint Arab force to oppose Iraq and allow Western forces to withdraw. The league, **Aug. 10**, voted to send troops to Saudi Arabia. In a 12-3 vote, only Iraq, Libya, and the Palestine Liberation Organization opposed the unprecedented decision. Saddam Hussein, **Aug. 10**, called on "Moslem masses" to launch a "holy war" against foreign troops and "corrupt" Arab rulers. Troops from Egypt and Morocco began arriving in Saudi Arabia, **Aug. 11**, and Syrian troops followed, **Aug. 14**.

Hussein, **Aug. 12**, offered to link an Iraqi withdrawal from Kuwait to an Israeli withdrawal from occupied territories and other conditions.

It was reported, **Aug. 12**, that Bush had ordered the Navy fleet in the Mideast to be prepared to use force to prevent any ships from breaking the economic embargo of Iraq.

In an apparent effort to mend its relations on another border, Iraq, **Aug. 15**, offered to meet demands made by Iran during the Persian Gulf war of the 1980's. Saddam Hussein offered to accept a 1975 agreement giving each country sovereignty over half of a waterway dividing the 2 countries. He also offered to withdraw Iraqi troops from Iranian territory and to begin an exchange of prisoners.

In a speech, **Aug. 15**, Bush stressed "access to energy resources" and "Our jobs, our way of life" as factors related to the intervention in the gulf.

Iraq ordered all foreign embassies in Kuwait to be shut down, and on **Aug. 16**, it ordered 6,500 Americans and Britons in Kuwait to assemble in 2 hotels. Few of the Westerners responded. On **Aug. 17**, the speaker of Iran's parliament said that Iraq had decided to "play host" to citizens of "aggressive nations" as long as Iraq remained threatened. He said they would be given "appropriate accommodations" at industrial and military installations—potential targets if a war broke out. Bush, **Aug. 18**, denounced this plan as "totally unacceptable" and "contrary to all accepted norms of international conduct." France, **Aug. 18**, warned of "grave consequences" if its 560 citizens in Iraq and Kuwait were harmed.

U.S. naval warships fired warning shots, **Aug. 18**, past 2 outbound Iraqi oil tankers, which kept moving despite the shots. At the Yemeni port of Aden, **Aug. 21**, Yemen refused to unload the oil. Bush, **Aug. 22**, ordered a limited mobilization of U.S. military reserves. Most would fill noncombat support roles.

On **Aug. 23**, a barrel of a benchmark grade of U.S. crude oil stood at almost $32, an increase of $14 since early July.

Saddam Hussein met, **Aug. 23**, with a group of Britons being detained in Iraq and assured them in an encounter that was shown on television that they were "guests" and not hostages. Several young British children seemed frightened, and the British Foreign Office called the broadcast a "repulsive charade." Iraqi troops surrounded some foreign embassies in Kuwait, **Aug. 24**, after they refused to shut down. Iraq said women and children dependents of U.S. diplomats could leave, but that the men would have to stay. Britain reported that hundreds of its citizens were being held hostage in Kuwait and Iraq.

The U.N. Security Council, **Aug. 25**, authorized the naval armada in the Persian Gulf to use force if necessary to prevent violations of U.N. economic sanctions imposed on Iraq. The support of the Soviet Union had proved crucial in the adoption of the unprecedented resolution—the first time the United Nations had approved the use of military force not under the U.N. flag or command.

Saddam Hussein, **Aug. 28**, ordered the release, as a humanitarian gesture, of all foreign women and children who were being detained.

On **Aug. 29**, the Organization of Petroleum Exporting Countries authorized its members to increase oil production to maintain normal supplies during the crisis.

In resolutions adopted **Sept. 1**, 12 members of the Arab League called on Iraq to leave Kuwait, pay reparations, and free all foreign nationals. Libya opposed the resolutions, and 8 members boycotted the meeting.

Beginning **Sept. 1**, Iraq began freeing hundreds of foreigners from a number of countries, but many more were still held as hostages. Some 2,500 Americans, including many women and children, were believed still stranded in Iraq and Kuwait. By early September, some 600,000 refugees had streamed through Jordan, and 100,000 still remained there, often going hungry in desert camps.

Bush announced, **Sept. 4**, that, subject to congressional approval, he was forgiving Egypt's $7 billion military debt to the U.S. for supporting American policy in the Persian Gulf.

Sec. of State James Baker, during a Middle East trip, received large pledges of financial support, **Sept. 6**, from King Fahd of Saudi Arabia and, **Sept. 7**, from the exiled emir of Kuwait.

Bush and Soviet Pres. Mikhail Gorbachev met at a summit conference in Helsinki, Finland, **Sept. 9**, to discuss the Gulf crisis. The summit was held to demonstrate superpower unity on the issue, and an outgrowth was a clear U.S. recognition that the Soviet Union had a role to play in the Middle East. At a joint press conference, Bush said that no military options had been discussed. Gorbachev said that Soviet participation in the area would be limited to 2 naval vessels.

Baker, at a NATO foreign ministers meeting in Brussels, **Sept. 10**, called the Soviets reliable partners in the crisis. He said that Saudi Arabia, Kuwait, and the United Arab Emirates had made pledges of support totaling $12 billion for the rest of 1990. Half of this would go to cover U.S. military costs, and the rest would assist the economies of Egypt, Jordan, and Turkey, which had been damaged by the trade embargo of Iraq.

Bush, addressing a joint session of Congress, **Sept. 11**, said the U.S. could not allow the oil resource to be controlled by anyone as ruthless as Saddam Hussein. He said that in any future action he would not be deterred by Iraq's policy of using Western hostages as shields.

After a meeting of the foreign ministers of Iraq and Iran, during which they agreed to resume diplomatic relations, Iran's supreme religious leader, Ayatollah Ali Khamenei, said, **Sept. 12,** that a jihad, or holy war, was justified in combatting the U.S. military buildup.

After an Iraqi tanker in the Gulf of Oman refused to stop, **Sept. 14,** U.S. and Australian ships fired warning shots at it. The ship stopped, was inspected by U.S. and Australian sailors, and then allowed to proceed. U.S. forces were boarding several ships a day, mainly in the Red Sea.

Iraqi troops raided several Western embassies in Kuwait City, **Sept. 14.** Four French citizens were seized, then released. French Pres. Francois Mitterrand denounced the incident, **Sept. 14,** and Britain announced, **Sept. 14,** it was sending an armored brigade of 8,000 troops and 120 tanks to Saudi Arabia. West Germany, **Sept. 15,** announced a $2 billion package of aid for the Gulf effort, and Mitterrand ordered 4,000 soldiers, as well as planes, helicopters, and tanks, sent to Saudi Arabia.

Iraq, **Sept. 15,** opened the border between Kuwait and Saudi Arabia and allowed thousands of Kuwaitis to flee into exile. But the refugee flow dwindled when Iraqis began seizing military-age Kuwaiti men. The refugees reported widespread incidences of torture and execution by Iraqi troops.

A video tape recorded by Bush was played on Iraqi TV, **Sept. 16.** Iraq had offered the time after Bush complained that Hussein was getting too much exposure on American television. In the 8-minute tape, Bush warned the Iraqi people that Hussein had brought them to the brink of war and that ultimately Iraq would have to withdraw from Kuwait.

Defense Secretary Cheney, **Sept. 17,** removed Gen. Michael Dugan as Air Force chief of staff after Dugan had discussed details of the gulf operation that were later published. He had also referred to a contingency plan to kill Hussein.

Hussein warned, **Sept. 23,** that Iraq might attack oilfields in Saudi Arabia, other Arab countries, and Israel if economic sanctions "strangled" Iraq.

Shevardnadze warned the U.N. General Assembly, **Sept. 25,** that war was close in the Gulf unless Iraq withdrew from Kuwait. The U.N. Security Council voted 14-1 to impose an embargo on air traffic on Iraq.

Bush, addressing the U.N. General Assembly, **Oct. 1,** said he hoped for a diplomatic solution to the crisis. On **Oct. 1,** the House adopted a resolution endorsing Bush's actions in the gulf, 380-29. The Senate did the same, **Oct. 2,** 96-3. Hussein, visiting Kuwait, **Oct. 3,** said there would be "no compromise" and vowed not to give up "one inch" of what was now called province 19.

On **Oct. 10,** Iraq allowed about 360 people, mostly American men of Arab descent, to leave Kuwait.

Secretary of State James Baker said, **Oct. 16,** that a reported compromise offer from Iraq was unacceptable. It involved Iraq's withdrawal from Kuwait if it could retain a strategic island.

The Iraqi government announced, **Oct. 19,** that it would introduce gasoline rationing because of a lack of the chemicals needed to refine oil.

Cheney announced, **Oct. 25,** that the number of American troops in the Persian Gulf area would be increased by up to 100,000, which could bring the total to 340,000 and give the U.S. forces an offensive capability.

Hussein, **Oct. 28,** canceled the rationing of gasoline and fired his oil minister, saying he had made a miscalculation. Some observers thought that the original announcement was a ruse to make it appear that sanctions were working so that a military attack on Iraq would not be necessary.

The U.N. Security Council, **Oct. 29,** passed a resolution, 13-0 with 2 abstentions, warning Iraq that "further measures" might be taken under the U.N. Charter—by implication, including military action. In separate statements, **Oct. 29,** Bush and Baker warned that in light of barbarous acts by the Iraqis in Kuwait, the use of force remained a possibility.

Major Actions of the 101st Congress, 1990

(As of Oct. 28, 1990. For further information, see *Congress, Chronology,* and *Addenda.*)
The 101st Congress reconvened Jan. 23.

Legislation Passed by Congress and Signed or Vetoed by Pres. Bush

Chinese Exchange Student Deportation. The Senate voted, Jan. 25, 62-37, to uphold Pres. Bush's veto of a 1989 bill that would have barred the deportation of Chinese exchange students from the U.S. The House had voted, Jan. 24, 390-25, to override the veto. Pres. Bush cited his earlier executive order that would protect Chinese students who feared persecution if forced to return to their homeland when their visas expired. If the bill became law, the pres. said, China would cut off all student exchange programs with the U.S.

"Hate Crime" Statistics. Pres. Bush signed into law, Apr. 23, a bill requiring the federal government to keep records of crimes motivated by ethnic, racial, or sexual prejudice. The Hate Crimes Statistics Act had been passed by the House, Apr. 4, 408-18; and by the Senate, Feb. 8, 92-4. The law required the Justice Dept. to compile and publish data for the next five years on crimes including murder, rape, assault, arson, vandalism and intimidation. Several states already required such monitoring, but the new bill marked the first time the federal government would collect data nationwade as to the motivation behind such crimes, in order to monitor their extent, determine law enforcement priorities, and suggest possible legal changes.

Supplemental Spending. Congress cleared, and Pres. Bush signed, May 25, a bill providing $4.3 billion in fiscal 1990 supplemental appropriations, including $720 million in economic aid for Panama and Nicaragua. The House had approved the bill, May 24, 308-108; the Senate, May 25, by voice vote. A House-Senate conference committee had approved the legislation, May 22, after deleting controversial amendments on the death penalty and abortion rights, May 17. The final measure was partially financed via $2 billion in defense cuts.

Amtrak Fund Authorization. Pres. Bush vetoed a bill, May 24, that would authorize funds for Amtrak, the national passenger rail system, for the next 2 fiscal years. Pres. Bush cited a provision authorizing the Interstate Commerce Commission to review freight-railroad takeovers by nonrail companies as "an unwarranted regulatory roadblock to financial restructuring of the industry." The bill would have authorized $684 million for Amtrak for fiscal 1991, beginning Oct. 1, and $712 million for fiscal 1992. The measure had been approved by the House, May 9, 322-93; and by a Senate voice vote, May 10. The Senate, June 12, upheld the veto by 2 votes, after the House had voted, June 7,
(continued)

294-123, to override the veto.

Family Emergency "Time Off." Pres. Bush vetoed a bill, June 29, that would have required workers to be allowed unpaid time off for births, adoptions, and major medical emergencies at home. The president cited strong objections to the government's dictating such a policy to employers. The bill would have required businesses with 50 or more employees to grant workers up to 12 weeks of unpaid leave to care for newborn or adopted children or seriously ill family members. The House failed to override the veto, July 25, 232-195.

Discrimination Against Disabilities Banned. Pres. Bush signed into law, July 26, The Americans with Disabilities Act, which prohibited discrimination in employment, public accomodations, telecommunications, and transportation against people with a physical or mental condition that "substantially limited" a major life activity, such as seeing or walking. The definition of disabled would include AIDS victims, and drugs addicts and alcoholics undergoing treatment. Some 43 million Americans were expected to be affected. The Senate had approved, 91-6, July 13; the House, July 12, 377-28.

Emergency Federal Funds for AIDS. Pres. Bush signed into law, Aug. 18, a bill authorizing emergency federal aid to help cities and states deal with the rising costs of treating and preventing AIDS. The Senate had passed the bill, 95-4, May 16; the House, 408-14, June 13. The measure provided a total of $4 billion over the next five years, mostly toward testing, counseling, and early drug treatment for those found infected with the virus causing AIDS.

Civil Rights. Pres. Bush vetoed, Oct. 20, the Civil Rights Act of 1990. The measure would have allowed women and members of minority groups to collect damages if they could prove intentional discrimination. Workers accusing their employers of discrimination would have had to cite the specific practices that excluded women, blacks, or other minorities, however, and could not have won damages if employers could show that the practice was not intended to discriminate. The pres. contended that the legislation would have led to the widespread use of quotas in hiring and promotion. The Senate, Oct. 24, failed by one vote to override the veto.

Other Legislation

Constitutional Amendment. The Senate rejected, 58-42, a proposed constitutional amendment, June 26, that would have permitted states to prosecute those who destroyed or desecrated the American flag. The House had rejected the amendment, June 21, 254-177. (See Chronology.)

Puerto Rico Status Decision. The House passed a bill, Oct. 10, by voice vote, calling for a referendum in 1991 under which the people of Puerto Rico could choose statehood, independence, or continuation of their commonwealth status, the first time either house of Congress had voted to hold such a referendum.

Ads on Children's TV Restricted. Pres. Bush allowed a bill that limited TV commercials on children's programming to become law without his signature, Oct. 17. The law imposed a limit of 10½ minutes of TV commercials an hour for children's programming on weekends and 12 minutes an hour on weekends. Both House and Senate approved by voice vote, July 23 and July 19, respectively.

Budget. Congress approved a budget bill, Oct. 27, The House, 228-200, and the Senate, 54-45. The measure would raise taxes by more than $140 billion over the next five years, the core of a plan to reduce the federal deficit by $40 billion this year and $500 billion over five years. The measure included higher taxes, with the top income tax rate increased to 31 percent from 28 percent, a phaseout of exemptions for upper-income taxpayers, and the top capital gains rate set at 28 percent; an increase in excise taxes on gasoline, gas-guzzling cars, cigarettes, and alcohol; increased passenger airline ticket tax and domestic air cargo tax; and a new "luxury tax" on such items as expensive cars, airplanes, yachts, and furs. The measure also included spending cuts in Medicaid, Medicare, federal pensions, student loans, federal housing, and military spending. Pres. Bush said that he would sign the bill.

Immigration. The House approved, 264-118, a major revision of the country's immigration law, Oct. 27. The bill would permit 700,000 people to immigrate each year from 1992 to 1994, compared with 500,000 under current law. The bill also would reduce the severity and scope of restrictions on new citizens and other immigrants. The Senate had approved the measure, Oct. 26. Pres. Bush indicated that he would sign it.

As of Oct. 29, 1990, Congress was continuing to work on bills concerning several major issues, including crime, clean air, housing, foreign aid, and the financing of the National Endowment for the Arts.

Major Decisions of the U.S. Supreme Court, 1989-90

(For further information, see Supreme Court, Chronology, and Addenda.)

The Supreme Court began its 1989-90 term on Oct. 2. Summaries of notable actions follow. The Court:

Ruled, unanimously, that universities accused of discriminating in faculty tenure decisions had no special status under the First Amendment right of academic freedom that would allow them to withhold peer-review materials from federal investigators. (Jan. 9)

Ruled, 5-4, to reaffirm its exclusion of illegally obtained evidence in a criminal trial, except for the specific purpose of contradicting testimony in court by a defendant. (Jan. 10)

Ruled, unanimously, that state taxes on religious materials sold by religious organizations failed to violate the First Amendment's guarantee of religious freedom. (Jan. 17)

Ruled, 5-4, that the Sixth Amendment required not a "representative" jury reflecting a cross-section of the community, but an "impartial" jury. (Jan. 22)

Ruled, 7-2, that a parent under court supervision for having previously abused a child could not cite his or her Fifth Amendment rights as justification for evading court orders to reveal the child's whereabouts.

Declined to review, thus let stand, a federal appeals court prohibition against biographers' or historians' use of quotations from unpublished materials without permission. (Feb. 20)

Declined to review, thus let stand, the military's policy of barring homosexuals from service. (Feb. 26)

Ruled, 7-2, that police arresting a suspect in his home could make a warrantless search of the premises to make certain that they were not in danger, and that evidence seized at this time could be used against the defendant. (Feb. 28)

Ruled, 5-4, that Pennsylvania's death penalty, which required a death sentence if a jury found that a murder

(continued)

was committed with at least one "aggravating" circumstance and no "mitigating" circumstances, was constitutional. The law was similar to those in at least 12 other states. (Feb. 28)

Ruled, 5-4, in two cases, that federal judges, in deciding habeas corpus petitions, could not give retroactive application to court decisions that came after the date of an inmate's conviction, even if a later decision indicated that the inmate might have been tried or sentenced unconstitutionally. (Mar. 5)

Ruled, 6-3, that a state death penalty law could not require the jury's unanimous consent for the consideration of "mitigating" circumstances. (Mar. 5)

Ruled, unanimously, that the First Amendment guarantee of freedom of speech disallowed the prohibition of grand jury witnesses from discussing the "content, gist, or import" of their testimony following the completion of the investigation. (Mar. 21)

Ruled, unanimously, that migrant farm workers injured on the job were not restricted to what they could recover under state workers' compensation laws, but were entitled to sue their employers for damages under the Migrant and Seasonal Agricultural Workers' Protection Act. (Mar. 21)

Ruled, 5-4, that state appeals courts were permitted to weigh "aggravating" factors against "mitigating" factors of a crime and decide whether to impose the death penalty, if a jury had considered factors that were improper. (Mar. 28)

Declined to review, thus let stand, a ban on school dances allegedly derived from a Christian fundamentalist belief that social dance was sinful. (Apr. 16)

Ruled, 9-0, that Title VII of the Civil Rights Act of 1964, barring employment discrimination on the basis of sex, did not prohibit the filing of such discrimination suits in state as well as federal courts. (Apr. 17)

Ruled, 6-3, that a state may ban the use of the drug peyote, containing the hallucinogenic substance mescaline, in Native American religious rituals. The sacramental use of peyote was exempted from criminal penalties by federal law and the laws of 23 states. (Apr. 17)

Ruled, 6-3, that states could make unlawful the possession of pornographic photos of children even in private homes, the first time the court banned the private possession of pornography, already prohibited by 19 states. (Apr. 18)

Declined to review, thus let stand, a decision permitting a lawsuit for parental rights by a man who had donated sperm for the artificial insemination of a woman to whom he was not married. (Apr. 23)

Ruled, 5-4, that the prosecution of a drunk driver for homicide, after he had pleaded guilty to two misdemeanors in a fatal traffic accident, would constitute double jeopardy. (May 29)

Ruled, 8-1, that the 1984 Equal Access Act, requiring public high schools to give student religious and political groups the same access to facilities as other student organizations, did not violate the Constitution's requirement of separation between church and state. (June 4)

Ruled, 8-1, that police need not have provided the Miranda warning as to rights against self-incrimination in the case of a jailed suspect who confessed to an undercover police officer posing as a fellow inmate, since this involved "strategic deception" and not "coercion." (June 4)

Ruled, 5-4, that a 1989 federal law making it a crime to burn or deface the American flag was unconstitutional, since it violated the First Amendment's guarantee of free speech. (June 11)

Ruled, 6-3, that an anonymous tip was sufficient grounds for suspicion to permit police legally to stop and question a suspect. (June 11)

Ruled, 6-3, that police checkpoints to examine drivers for evidence of intoxication, although resulting in a "seizure," were nevertheless "reasonable" in view of the merely "slight" intrusion on motorists, combined with the state's interest in decreasing drunken driving. (June 14)

Ruled, 5-4, that hospitals and nursing homes could sue states for higher Medicaid Reimbursement rates. (June 14)

Ruled, 6-2, that an exemption from patent infringement for drugs, to permit testing, also could be applied to medical devices, both of which were regulated under the Food, Drug, and Cosmetic Act. (June 16)

Ruled, 8-1, that the police could videotape drunk-driving suspects and use evidence of their slurred speech against them at a trial, without having advised the drivers first of their constitutional rights. However, in a separate decision, the court ruled, 5-4, against the use of a defendant's videotaped response to a police request to name the year in which he had turned six years old. (June 18)

Ruled, 7-2, that editorial statements of opinion were not automatically exempted by the First Amendment from libel lawsuits. (June 21)

Ruled, 5-4, that it was unconstitutional to use partisan political considerations as the basis for hiring, promoting, or transferring public employees in non-policy-making positions. (June 21)

Ruled, 5-4, that a person whose wishes were clearly known had a constitutional right to refuse life-sustaining medical treatment. However, in this first ruling on a "right to die" case, the court also ruled that there was no such "clear and convincing evidence" as to the wishes of the individual in question. (June 25)

Ruled, 5-4, that states could require a teenage girl to notify both parents before having an abortion, if the law offered the alternative of a court hearing for those who did not want their parents involved. The court also held, 5-4, that a state law requiring notification of both parents was constitutional only because it provided the alternative of a court hearing. Further, the court upheld a provision that the states could require minors to wait 48 hours for an abortion after parental notification. In a separate decision, the court ruled, 6-3, that states could require a minor either to notify one parent or to seek permission from a court because she believed she was mature enough to make her own decision or because notifying a parent would not be in her best interest. (June 25)

Ruled, 5-4, that states could permit alleged victims of child abuse to testify on closed-circuit TV or via other indirect methods, in order to avoid confronting the defendant in court, if this was absolutely necessary to prevent emotional trauma to a child and if the defendant's attorney had an opportunity to cross-examine the child. In a separate ruling, 5-4, the court barred a physician's testimony about statements made to him by an alleged child-abuse victim who was considered incapable of testifying in person, unless prosecutors explained why the child could not testify and why the third-party testimony should be considered reliable. (June 27)

Ruled, 5-4, that affirmative action policies created to increase the number of broadcast licenses held by minorities and women could be adopted by Congress, the first court approval of an affirmative action program for a reason other than simply correcting the effects of past discrimination. (June 27)

(continued)

The court concluded the 1989 session June 28, having issued 129 signed majority opinions, the smallest number in a decade. Justice William J. Brennan resigned from the Court, July 20, after nearly 34 years of service, citing his age of 84 and a stroke suffered that month. On July 23, Pres. Bush named David H. Sou-ter, 50, of New Hampshire, and on Oct. 3. the Senate voted, 90-9, to confirm him as Justice Brennan's successor. Issues facing the court in the 1990-91 session included school desegregation, sex discrimination, and the authority of federal judges and agencies.

Historical Anniversaries
1941—50 Years Ago

World War II becomes a worldwide conflict as German troops invade Soviet Russia and Japanese forces attack Pearl Harbor. A Lend-Lease program to aid the Allies is recommended by U.S. Pres. Franklin D. Roosevelt, despite widespread isolationism. German troops lay seige to Leningrad in June, confidently carrying no winter clothing, but in December are still fighting. Pearl Harbor, on the Hawaiian island of Oahu is attacked Dec. 7 (Dec. 8, Tokyo time) from 360-carrier based Japanese planes, which sink the battle ships U.S.S. Arizona, Oklahoma, California, Nevada, and West Virginia; damage 3 others as well as 3 cruisers and 3 destroyers, destroy 200 U.S. planes, and kill 2,344 men. The attack precedes Japan's declaration of war. FDR calls Dec. 7 "a date that will live in infamy," and declares war on Japan. Germany declares war on the U.S., Dec. 11, Italy follows; the U.S. declares war on Germany and Italy; Romania declares war on the U.S., Dec. 12; Bulgaria, Dec. 13. The Japanese invade the Philippines Dec. 22; Wake Island falls Dec. 23, Hong Kong, Dec. 25. In the Soviet Union, German SS units machine-gun some 3,000 Jewish men, women and children, and from 50,000-96,000 Ukrainians, at least 60% Jews. In Estonia, Galicia, Latvia, Lithuania, Poland, and Russia, Jews flee from advancing German troops; those caught are forced into labor gangs, ghettos, military brothels, machine-gunned, or shipped in freight cars to detention camps where many are found dead on arrival. Jewish stores, factories, libraries, synagogues, and cemeteries are damaged or destroyed. FDR calls for a world with Four Freedoms protected: freedom of speech, freedom of religion, freedom from want, and freedom from fear. The U.S. Treasury issues war bonds. U.S. tax rates are increased sharply to raise billions for war-related expenditures.

Grand Coulee Dam, the world's largest hydroelectric installation, begins generating power on the Columbia River in Washington.

A U.S. Fair Employment Practice Committee is created by FDR, after a march of 50,000 blacks on Washington is threatened by A. Philip Randolph, pres. of the Brotherhood of Sleeping Car Porters, to protest unfair employment practices in the war industry and the government.

The first U.S. diesel freight locomotives go into service for the Atchinson, Topeka and Santa Fe.

The Lincoln Continental is introduced by Ford.

Mount Rushmore sculptor John Gutzon Borglum dies, his son continues, but leaves the work incomplete.

Dacron is introduced.

Quality Inns motel company is established.

Cheerios cereal is introduced.

Casserole Cookery by Marian Tracy is published, and will become the war bride's favorite.

Le Pavillon opens in New York.

Stan Musial begins playing for the St. Louis Cardinals.

The National Gallery of Art opens in Washington, D.C.

Books: nonfiction: Let Us Now Praise Famous Men, James Agee and Walker Evans; Escape from Freedom, Erich Fromm; fiction: The Last Tycoon, F. Scott Fitzgerald (posthumously); Mildred Pierce, James M. Cain; The Keys of the Kingdom, A.J. Cronin; What Makes Sammy Run?, Budd Shulberg; juvenile: Curious George, H.A. Rey and Margaret Rey.

Movies: Orson Welles's "Citizen Kane," John Huston's "The Maltese Falcon," Chaplin's "The Great Dictator," Alfred Hitchcock's "Rebecca"; "Sergeant York," "How Green Was My Valley," "The Sea Wolf," "The Little Foxes," "Penny Serenade," "Never Give a Sucker an Even Break," "The Lady Eve," Walt Disney's "Dumbo."

Theater: "Arsenic and Old Lace," Joseph Kesselring; "Native Son," Richard Wright and Paul Green; "Watch on the Rhine," Lillian Hellman; "Mother Courage," Bertolt Brecht; "Blithe Spirit," Noel Coward; musicals: "Lady in the Dark."

Radio: "Duffy's Tavern" begins.

Music: "Lili Marlene," "Blues in the Night," "(There'll Be Bluebirds Over) The White Cliffs of Dover," "I Don't Want to Walk Without You," "Take the A Train," "I'll Remember April," "Deep in the Heart of Texas," "Jersey Bounce," "Cow-Cow Boogie," "Chattanooga Choo-Choo," "Boogie-Woogie Bugle Boy," "Anniversary Waltz."

1791—200 Years Ago

Louis XVI accepts the French constitution, France annexes Avignon and Venaissin, and the National Assembly dissolves.

British orator Edmund Burke criticizes the French Revolution; America's Thomas Paine replies with the pamphlet "The Rights of Man."

The Society of United Irishmen is founded to agitate for independence from Great Britain.

The Canada Act of the British Parliament divides Canada at the Ottawa River into Upper, mainly English, and Lower, mainly French.

Odessa is established by Russian pioneers on the Black Sea.

Blacks born of free parents in the French West Indies gain the vote and the same privileges of all French citizens, but Saint Domingue's white colonists threaten to cecede; the blacks and mulattoes revolt, and in several months some 2,000 whites, 10,000 blacks and mulattoes are killed.

More humane treatment of the insane is proposed by French physician Philippe Pinel.

The waltz becomes fashionable in England.

Vermont is admitted to the Union as the 14th state.

The Bill of Rights becomes law as Virginia ratifies the first 10 Amendments to the Constitution.

The first U.S. crop report is prepared by Pres. George Washington.

Books: biography: The Life of Samuel Johnson, James Boswell; poetry: "Tam O'Shanter," Robert Burns.

Music: opera: "Cosi Fan Tutte," and "The Magic Flute," Mozart.

CONGRESS

The One Hundred and Second Congress
With 1990 Election Results

The Senate

Terms are for 6 years and end Jan. 3 of the year preceding name. Annual salary $98,400, with a cost-of-living increase scheduled for Jan. 1, 1991; President Pro Tempore, Majority Leader, and Minority Leader $109,500, with a cost-of-living increase scheduled for Jan. 1, 1991. To be eligible for the U.S. Senate a person must be at least 30 years of age, a citizen of the United States for at least 9 years, and a resident of the state from which he is chosen. The Congress must meet annually on Jan. 3, unless it has, by law, appointed a different day.

Senate officials (101st Congress): President Pro Tempore Robert Byrd; Majority Leader George Mitchell; Majority Whip Alan Cranston; Minority Leader Bob Dole; Minority Whip Alan Simpson.

Dem., 56; Rep., 44; Total, 100. *Incumbent. Bold face denotes winner.

Preliminary Totals (Source: News Election Service)

Term ends	Senator (Party)/Service from[1]	1990 Election	Term ends	Senator (Party)/Service from[1]	1990 Election
	Alabama			**Indiana**	
1997	**Howell Heflin*** (D)/1979	708,982	1997	**Dan Coats*** (R)/1989	799,410
	Bill Cabaniss (R)	461,421		Baron P. Hill (D)	692,246
1993	Richard C. Shelby (D)/1987		1995	Richard G. Lugar* (R)/1977	
	Alaska			**Iowa**	
1997	**Ted Stevens*** (R)/12/24/68	106,465	1997	**Tom Harkin*** (D)/1985	525,098
	Michael Beasley (D)	51,966		Tom Tauke (R)	446,892
1993	Frank Murkowski (R)/1981		1993	Charles E. Grassley (R)/1981	
	Arizona			**Kansas**	
1993	John S. McCain (R)/1987		1997	**Nancy L. Kassebaum*** (R)/12/23/78	575,231
1995	Dennis DeConcini* (D)/1977			Dick Williams (D)	206,428
			1993	Robert J. Dole (R)/1969	
	Arkansas			**Kentucky**	
1997	**David Pryor*** (D)/1979	Unopposed	1997	**Mitch McConnell*** (R)/1985	476,812
1993	Dale Bumpers (D)/1975			G. Harvey I. Sloane (D)	436,542
			1993	Wendell H. Ford (D)/12/28/74	
	California			**Louisiana**	
1993	Alan Cranston (D)/1969		1997	**J. Bennett Johnston*** (D)/11/14/72	
1995	Pete Wilson* (R)/1983		1993	John B. Breaux (D)/1987	
	Colorado			**Maine**	
1997	**Hank Brown** (R)	568,095	1997	**William S. Cohen*** (R)/1979	308,783
	Josie Heath (D)	425,543		Neil Rolde (D)	194,932
1993	Timothy E. Wirth (D)/1987		1995	George J. Mitchell* (D)/5/17/80	
	Connecticut			**Maryland**	
1993	Christopher J. Dodd (D)/1981		1993	Barbara A. Mikulski (D)/1987	
1995	Joe Lieberman (D)/1989		1995	Paul S. Sarbanes* (D)/1977	
	Delaware			**Massachusetts**	
1997	**Joseph R. Biden Jr.*** (D)/1973	112,128	1997	**John F. Kerry*** (D)/1/2/85	1,180,209
	M. Jane Brady (R)	64,682		Jim Rappaport (R)	892,624
1995	William V. Roth Jr.* (R)/1/1/71		1995	Edward M. Kennedy* (D)/11/7/62	
	Florida			**Michigan**	
1993	Bob Graham (D)/1987		1997	**Carl Levin*** (D)/1979	1,450,319
1995	Connie Mack (R)/1989			Bill Schuette (R)	1,036,169
			1995	Donald W. Riegle Jr.* (D)/12/30/76	
	Georgia			**Minnesota**	
1997	**Sam Nunn*** (D)/1972	Unopposed	1997	**Paul David Wellstone** (D)	862,525
1993	Wyche Fowler Jr. (D)/1987			Rudy Boschwitz* (R)/12/30/78	802,407
			1995	David Durenberger* (R)/11/8/78	
	Hawaii			**Mississippi**	
1993	Daniel K. Inouye (D)/1963		1997	**Thad Cochran*** (R)/12/27/78	
1995	**Daniel K. Akaka*** (D)/5/16/90	188,900	1995	Trent Lott (R)/3/3/89	
	Patricia Saiki (R)	155,978			
	Ken Schoolland (B)	4,787		**Missouri**	
			1993	Christopher S. Bond (R)/1987	
	Idaho		1995	John C. Danforth* (R)/12/27/76	
1997	**Larry E. Craig*** (R)	178,653			
	Ron J. Twilegar (D)	112,752		**Montana**	
1993	Steven D. Symms (R)/1981		1997	**Max Baucus*** (D)/12/15/78	217,451
				Allen Kolstad (R)	93,984
	Illinois		1995	Conrad Burns (R)/1989	
1997	**Paul Simon*** (D)/1985	2,075,493			
	Lynn Martin (R)	1,120,179			
1993	Alan J. Dixon (D)/1981				

Term ends	Senator (Party)/Service from[1]	1990 Election	Term ends	Senator (Party)/Service from[1]	1990 Election
	Nebraska			**Rhode Island**	
1997	**J. James Exon*** (D)/1979	342,642	1997	**Claiborne Pell** (D)/1961	216,253
	Hal Daub (R)	237,244		Claudine Schneider (R)	133,552
1995	J. Robert Kerrey (D)/1989		1995	John H. Chafee* (R)/12/29/76	
	Nevada			**South Carolina**	
1993	Harry M. Reid (D)/1987		1997	**Strom Thurmond*** (R)/11/7/56	475,510
1995	Richard H. Bryan (D)/1989			Bob Cunningham (D)	241,847
	New Hampshire		1993	Ernest Fritz Hollings* (D)/11/9/66	
1997	**Robert Smith** (R)	188,854		**South Dakota**	
	John Durkin (D)	91,786	1997	**Larry Pressler*** (R)/1979	135,443
1993	Warren Rudman (R)/12/31/80			Ted Muenster (D)	116,431
	New Jersey			Dean L. Sinclair (I)	6,548
1997	**Bill Bradley*** (D)/1979	969,363	1993	Thomas A. Daschle (D)/1987	
	Christine Todd Whitman (R)	911,247		**Tennessee**	
1995	Frank R. Lautenberg* (D)/12/27/82		1997	**Albert Gore Jr.*** (D)/1985	526,869
	New Mexico			William R. Hawkins (R)	229,714
1997	**Pete V. Domenici*** (R)/1973	294,226	1995	James R. Sasser* (D)/1977	
	Tom R. Benavides (D)	109,375		**Texas**	
1995	Jeff Bingaman* (D)/1983		1997	**Phil Gramm*** (R)/1985	2,293,144
	New York			Hugh Parmer (D)	1,425,395
1993	Alfonse M. D'Amato (R)/1981		1995	Lloyd Bentsen* (D)/1971	
1995	Daniel Patrick Moynihan* (D)/1977			**Utah**	
	North Carolina		1993	Jake Garn (R)/12/21/74	
1997	**Jesse Helms*** (R)/1973	1,071,332	1995	Orrin G. Hatch* (R)/1977	
	Harvey Gantt (D)	969,620		**Vermont**	
1993	Terry Sanford (D)	11/5/86	1993	Patrick J. Leahy (D)/1975	
	North Dakota		1995	James M. Jeffords (R)/1989	
1993	Kent Conrad (D)/1987			**Virginia**	
1995	Quentin N. Burdick* (D)/8/8/60		1997	**John W. Warner*** (R)/1/2/79	872,764
	Ohio			Nancy Spanaus (I)	196,258
1993	John Glenn (D)/12/24/74		1995	Charles S. Robb (D)/1989	
1995	Howard M. Metzenbaum* (D)/12/29/76			**Washington**	
	Oklahoma		1993	Brock Adams (D)/1987	
1997	**David L. Boren** (D)/1979	735,644	1995	Slade Gorton (R)/1981	
	Stephen Jones (R)	148,814		**West Virginia**	
1993	Don Nickles (R)/1981		1997	**John D. Rockefeller IV*** (D)/1/15/85	274,614
	Oregon			John Yoder (R)	126,035
1997	**Mark O. Hatfield*** (R)/1/10/67	541,035	1995	Robert C. Byrd* (D)/1959	
	Harry Lonsdale (D)	463,438		**Wisconsin**	
1993	Bob Packwood (R)/1969		1993	Robert W. Kasten Jr. (R)/1981	
	Pennsylvania		1995	Herbert H. Kohl (D)/1989	
1993	Arlen Specter (R)/1981			**Wyoming**	
1995	John Heinz* (R)/1977		1997	**Alan K. Simpson*** (R)/1979	100,800
				Kathy Helling (D)	56,692
			1995	Malcolm Wallop* (R)/1977	

(1) Jan. 3, unless otherwise noted. (2) Elected governor; seat to be filled.

The House of Representatives

Members' terms to Jan. 3, 1993. Annual salary $96,600 increasing to at least $120,800 on Jan. 1, 1991; Speaker of the House, $124,000, increasing to $155,000 on Jan. 1, 1991; Majority Leader and Minority Leader $107,300, increasing to $134,100 on Jan. 1, 1991. To be eligible for membership, a person must be at least 25, a U.S. citizen for at least 7 years, and a resident of the state from which he or she is chosen.

House Officials (101st Congress): Speaker Thomas S. Foley; Majority Leader Richard A. Gephardt; Majority Whip William H. Gray 3d; Minority Leader Robert H. Michel; Minority Whip Newt Gingrich.

D-Democrat; R-Republican; AI-American Independent; ASI-Amer. System Independent; B-Libertarian; C-Conservative; I-Independent; IC-Ind. Conservative; IS-Illinois Solidarity; JW-Jim Wham; L-Liberal; LP-Liberty Party; LU-Liberty Union; NA-New Alliance; PO-Populist; PF-Peace & Freedom; T-Right to Life; TB-Tax Break; TC-Tax Cut.

Dem., 267, Rep., 167, Ind., 1. Total 435. *Incumbent. Bold face denotes winner.

Preliminary Totals, write-ins not included. (Source: News Election Service)

Dist.	Representative (Party)	1990 Election	Dist.	Representative (Party)	1990 Election
	Alabama			Faye Baggiano (D)	82,883
1.	**H.L."Sonny" Callahan*** (R)	Unopposed	3.	**Glen Browder*** (D)	100,408
2.	**William L. Dickinson*** (R)	87,277			

Dist.	Representative (Party)	1990 Election
	Don Sledge (R)	35,857
4.	Tom Bevill* (D)	Unopposed
5.	Bud Cremer (D)	112,065
	Albert McDonald (R)	55,081
6.	Ben Erdreich* (D)	134,412
	David A. Alvarez (I)	8,640
	Nathaniel Ivory (NA)	1,745
7.	Claude Harris Jr.* (D)	125,549
	Michael D. Barker (R)	52,391

Alaska At Large

Dist.	Representative (Party)	1990 Election
	Don Young* (R)	82,549
	John C. Devens (D)	79,086

Arizona

Dist.	Representative (Party)	1990 Election
1.	John J. Rhodes III (R)	Unopposed
2.	Morris K. Udall* (D)	75,642
	Joseph D. Sweeney (R)	38,763
3.	Bob Stump* (R)	132,004
	Roger Hartstone (D)	101,219
4.	John Kyl* (R)	139,569
	Mark Ivey Jr. (D)	87,767
5.	Jim Kolbe* (R)	138,500
	Chuck Phillips (D)	75,398

Arkansas

Dist.	Representative (Party)	1990 Election
1.	Bill Alexander* (D)	91,393
	Terry Hayes (R)	51,774
2.	Ray Thornton (D)	102,790
	Jim Keet (R)	68,312
3.	John Paul Hammerschmidt* (R)	129,285
	Dan Ivy (D)	54,013
4.	Beryl Anthony Jr.* (D)	102,862
	Roy Rood (R)	40,079

California

Dist.	Representative (Party)	1990 Election
1.	Frank Riggs (R)	91,891
	Douglas H. Bosco* (D)	89,918
	Darlene G. Comingore (PF)	31,505
2.	Wally Herger* (R)	128,943
	Erwin E. "Bill" Rush (D)	63,720
	Ross Crain (B)	10,473
3.	Robert T. Matsui* (D)	122,412
	Lowell Patrick Landowski (R)	70,075
	David M. McCann (B)	10,033
4.	Vic Fazio* (D)	108,113
	Mark Baughman (R)	77,328
	Bryce Bigwood (B)	11,965
5.	Nancy Pelosi* (D)	112,738
	Alan Nichols (R)	32,460
6.	Barbara Boxer* (D)	128,446
	Bill Boerum (R)	59,973
7.	George Miller* (D)	114,872
	Roger A. Payton (R)	73,588
8.	Ronald V. Dellums* (D)	111,526
	Barbara Galewski (R)	68,575
9.	Fortney H. "Pete" Stark* (D)	89,572
	Victor Romero (R)	62,689
10.	Don Edwards* (D)	77,184
	Mark Patrosso (R)	45,228
11.	Tom Lantos* (D)	93,992
	G.M. "Bill" Quraishi (R)	40,025
	June R. Genis (B)	7,962
12.	Tom Campbell* (R)	114,238
	Robert Palmer (D)	64,474
	Chuck Olson (B)	10,412
13.	Norman Y. Mineta* (D)	92,255
	David E. Smith (R)	56,131
	John H. Webster (B)	10,025
14.	John T. Doolittle (R)	110,808
	Patricia Malberg (D)	105,730
15.	Gary A. Condit* (D)	82,883
	Cliff Burris (R)	42,873
16.	Leon E. Panetta* (D)	122,667
	Jerry M. Reiss (R)	36,085
	Brian H. Tucker (B)	6,276
17.	Calvin Dooley (D)	77,092

Dist.	Representative (Party)	1990 Election
	Charles "Chip" Pashayan* (R)	63,894
18.	Richard H. Lehman* (D)	Unopposed
19.	Robert J. "Bob" Lagomarsino* (R)	82,053
	Anita Perez Ferguson (D)	68,655
20.	Bill Thomas* (R)	100,046
	Michael A. Thomas (D)	58,710
	William H. Dilbeck (B)	9,489
21.	Elton Gallegly* (R)	107,531
	Richard D. Freiman (D)	64,043
	Peggy Christensen (B)	14,249
22.	Carlos J. Moorhead* (R)	97,495
	David Bayer (D)	57,012
	William H. Wilson (B)	6,139
	Jan B. Tucker (PF)	3,643
23.	Anthony C. Beilenson* (D)	94,688
	Jim Salomon (R)	51,399
	John Honigsfeld (PF)	6,304
24.	Henry A. Waxman* (D)	66,103
	John N. Cowles (R)	23,953
	Maggie Phair (PF)	5,277
25.	Edward R. Roybal* (D)	44,657
	Steven J. Renshaw (R)	15,166
	Robert H. Scott (B)	3,300
26.	Howard L. Berman* (D)	72,529
	Roy Dahlson (R)	40,833
	Bernard Zimring (B)	4,920
27.	Mel Levine* (D)	84,556
	David Barrett Cohen (R)	53,090
	Edward E. Ferrer (PF)	6,618
28.	Julian C. Dixon* (D)	64,849
	George Zandivar Adams (R)	19,339
	William R. Williams (PF)	2,539
	Bob Weber (B)	1,993
29.	Maxine Waters (D)	48,769
	Bill De Witt (R)	11,186
	Waheed R. Boctor (B)	1,194
30.	Matthew G. Martinez* (D)	42,263
	Reuben D. Franco (R)	26,279
	G. Curtis Feger (B)	3,437
31.	Mervyn M. Dymally* (D)	53,239
	Eunice N. Sato (R)	25,488
32.	Glenn M. Anderson* (D)	63,536
	Sanford W. Kahn (R)	39,093
33.	David Dreier* (R)	93,094
	Georgia Houston Webb (D)	46,619
	Gail Lightfoot (B)	7,338
34.	Esteban E. Torres* (D)	51,840
	John Eastman (R)	33,334
35.	Jerry Lewis* (R)	117,302
	Barry Norton (D)	64,379
	Jerry Johnson (B)	12,606
36.	George E. Brown Jr.* (D)	68,956
	Bob Hammock (R)	60,779
37.	Al McCandless* (R)	104,407
	Ralph Waite (D)	95,226
	Gary R. Odom (AI)	5,874
	Bonnie Flickinger (B)	5,569
38.	Robert K. "Bob" Dornan* (R)	53,745
	Barbara Jackson (D)	38,669
39.	William E. "Bill" Dannemeyer* (R)	99,402
	Francis X. "Frank" Hoffman (D)	47,985
	Maxine B. Quirk (PF)	5,947
40.	Christopher Cox (R)	121,828
	Eugene C. Gratz (D)	59,674
41.	Bill Lowery* (R)	93,897
	Dan Kripke (D)	85,022
	Karen S.R. Works (PF)	14,021
42.	Dana Rohrabacher* (R)	99,239
	Guy C. Kimbrough (D)	62,206
	Richard Gibb Martin (B)	7,118
43.	Ron Packard* (R)	133,424
	Doug Hansen (PF)	36,069
	Richard L. "Rick" Arnold (B)	27,684
44.	Randy "Duke" Cunningham (R)	46,171
	Jim Bates* (D)	45,189
	Donna White (PF)	4,796
	John Wallner (B)	3,961
45.	Duncan Hunter* (R)	111,274
	Joe Shea (B)	41,769

Dist.	Representative (Party)	1990 Election
	Colorado	
1.	**Patricia Schroeder*** (D)	**81,859**
	Gloria Gonzales Roemer (R)	46,780
2.	**David E. Skaggs*** (D)	**105,245**
	Jason Lewis (R)	68,220
3.	**Ben Nighthorse Campbell*** (D)	**127,137**
	Bob Ellis (R)	49,801
4.	**Wayne Allard*** (R)	**88,911**
	Richard R. "Dick" Bond (D)	75,720
5.	**Joel Hefley*** (R)	**127,736**
	Cal Johnston (D)	57,771
6.	**Daniel Schaefer*** (R)	**104,969**
	Don Jarrett (D)	57,771
	Connecticut	
1.	**Barbara Bailey Kennelly*** (D)	**126,343**
	James P. Garvey (R)	50,644
2.	**Samuel Gejdenson*** (D)	**103,945**
	John M. Ragsdale (R)	70,642
3.	**Rosa L. De Lauro*** (D)	**89,702**
	Thomas Scott (R)	82,135
4.	**Christopher Shays*** (R)	**106,396**
	Al Smith (D)	32,963
5.	**Gary A. Franks** (R)	**93,041**
	Anthony "Toby" Moffett (D)	84,746
	William G. Hare (LP)	1,914
6.	**Nancy L. Johnson*** (R)	**138,758**
	Paul Kulas (D)	48,604
	Delaware At Large	
	Thomas R. Carper* (D)	**116,423**
	Ralph O. Williams (R)	57,552
	Florida	
1.	**Earl Hutto*** (D)	**83,899**
	Terry Ketchel (R)	76,833
2.	**Pete Peterson** (D)	**101,615**
	Bill Grant* (R)	76,518
3.	**Charles E. Bennett*** (D)	**80,983**
	Rod Sullivan (R)	30,011
4.	**Craig T. James*** (R)	**89,637**
	Reid Hughes (D)	70,457
5.	**Bill McCollum*** (R)	**93,627**
	Bob Fletcher (D)	62,956
6.	**Cliff Stearns*** (R)	**136,675**
	Art Johnson (D)	94,403
7.	**Sam M. Gibbons*** (D)	**96,248**
	Charles D. Prout (R)	45,426
8.	**C. W. Bill Young*** (R)	**Unopposed**
9.	**Michael Bilirakis*** (R)	**140,837**
	Cheryl Davis Knapp (D)	101,670
10.	**Andy Ireland*** (R)	**Unopposed**
11.	**Jim Bacchus** (D)	**121,013**
	Bill Tolley (R)	111,950
12.	**Tom Lewis*** (R)	**Unopposed**
13.	**Porter J. Goss*** (R)	**Unopposed**
14.	**Harry A. Johnston*** (D)	**156,025**
	Scott Shore (R)	80,182
15.	**E. Clay Shaw Jr.*** (R)	**Unopposed**
16.	**Larry Smith*** (D)	**Unopposed**
17.	**William Lehman*** (D)	**73,759**
	Earl Rodney (R)	21,290
18.	**Ileana Ros-Lehtinen*** (R)	**55,780**
	Bernard "Bernie" Anscher (D)	34,394
19.	**Dante B. Fascell*** (D)	**87,221**
	Bob Allen (R)	53,436
	Georgia	
1.	**Lindsay Thomas*** (D)	**82,056**
	Chris Meredith (R)	32,278
2.	**Charles Hatcher*** (D)	**73,546**
	Jonathan Perry Waters (R)	27,443
3.	**Richard Ray*** (D)	**71,752**
	Paul Broun (R)	41,702
4.	**Ben Jones*** (D)	**96,525**
	John Linder (R)	87,569

Dist.	Representative (Party)	1990 Election
5.	**John Lewis*** (D)	**86,037**
	J. W. Tibbs Jr. (R)	27,781
6.	**Newt Gingrich*** (R)	**78,463**
	Dave Worley (D)	77,480
7.	**George "Buddy" Darden*** (D)	**95,767**
	Al Beverly (R)	63,563
8.	**J. Roy Rowland*** (D)	**80,428**
	Robert F. "Bob" Cunningham (R)	36,474
9.	**Ed Jenkins*** (D)	**95,156**
	Joe Hoffman (R)	75,000
10.	**Doug Barnard Jr.*** (D)	**88,829**
	Sam Jones (R)	63,099
	Hawaii	
1.	**Neil Abercrombie** (D)	**97,622**
	Mike Liu (R)	62,982
2.	**Patsy Takemoto Mink*** (D)	**118,155**
	Andy Poepoe (R)	54,625
	Idaho	
1.	**Larry LaRocco** (D)	**76,987**
	C.A. "Skip" Smyser (R)	67,991
2.	**Richard Stallings*** (D)	**91,751**
	Sean McDevitt (R)	53,402
	Illinois	
1.	**Charles A. Hayes*** (D)	**93,804**
	Babette Peyton (R)	6,152
2.	**Gus Savage*** (D)	**75,182**
	William T. Hespel (R)	21,219
3.	**Martin A. Russo*** (D)	**106,294**
	Carl L. Klein (R)	44,109
4.	**George E. Sangmeister*** (D)	**76,796**
	Manny Hoffman (R)	52,824
5.	**William O. Lipinski*** (D)	**70,832**
	David J. Shestokas (R)	33,621
6.	**Henry J. Hyde*** (R)	**96,042**
	Robert J. Cassidy (D)	48,059
7.	**Cardiss Collins*** (D)	**77,175**
	Michael Dooley (R)	19,742
8.	**Dan Rostenkowski*** (D)	**66,932**
	Robert Marshall (B)	17,894
9.	**Sidney R. Yates*** (D)	**92,015**
	Herbert Sohn (R)	37,470
10.	**John E. Porter*** (R)	**103,281**
	Peg McNamara (D)	47,057
11.	**Frank Annunzio*** (D)	**78,838**
	Walter W. Dudycz (R)	66,223
12.	**Philip M. Crane*** (R)	**111,950**
	Steve Pedersen (IS)	24,273
13.	**Harris W. Fawell*** (R)	**115,307**
	Steven K. Thomas (D)	59,976
14.	**J. Dennis Hastert*** (R)	**112,355**
	Donald J. Westphal (D)	55,580
15.	**Edward R. Madigan*** (R)	**Unopposed**
16.	**John W. Cox Jr.*** (D)	**83,061**
	John W. Hallock Jr. (R)	69,105
17.	**Lane Evans*** (D)	**102,003**
	Dan Lee (R)	51,341
18.	**Robert H. Michel*** (R)	**Unopposed**
19.	**Terry L. Bruce*** (D)	**113,958**
	Robert F. Kerans (R)	55,680
	Brian James O'Neill II (IS)	2,250
20.	**Richard J. Durbin*** (D)	**130,023**
	Paul Jurgens (R)	66,389
21.	**Jerry F. Costello*** (D)	**93,536**
	Robert H. Gaffner (R)	48,365
22.	**Glenn Poshard*** (D)	**137,792**
	Jim Wham (JW)	26,790
	Indiana	
1.	**Peter J. Visclosky*** (D)	**68,920**
	William "Bill" Costas (R)	35,524
2.	**Philip R. Sharp*** (D)	**92,653**
	Mike Pence (R)	63,408
3.	**Timothy J. Roemer** (D)	**80,422**
	John Hiler* (R)	77,613
4.	**Jill L. Long*** (D)	**97,179**
	Richard Walter Hawks (R)	63,514

Dist.	Representative (Party)	1990 Election
5.	**James Jontz*** (D)	81,204
	John Johnson (R)	71,632
6.	**Dan Burton*** (R)	114,796
	James Philip Fadely (D)	66,363
7.	**John T. Myers*** (R)	88,589
	John William Riley Sr. (D)	65,239
8.	**Francis X. McCloskey*** (D)	97,980
	Richard E. Mourdock (R)	80,811
9.	**Lee H. Hamilton*** (D)	107,175
	Floyd Coates (R)	48,315
10.	**Andrew Jacobs Jr.*** (D)	66,519
	Janos Horvath (R)	33,626

Iowa

Dist.	Representative (Party)	1990 Election
1.	**Jim Leach*** (R)	Unopposed
2.	**Jim Nussle** (R)	80,829
	Eric Tabor (D)	79,349
3.	**David R. Nagle*** (D)	Unopposed
4.	**Neal Smith*** (D)	Unopposed
5.	**Jim Ross Lightfoot*** (R)	99,534
	Rod Powell (D)	47,966
6.	**Fred Grandy*** (R)	111,878
	Mike D. Earll (D)	43,935

Kansas

Dist.	Representative (Party)	1990 Election
1.	**Pat Roberts*** (R)	102,224
	Duane E. West (D)	61,340
2.	**Jim Slattery*** (D)	98,949
	Scott Morgan (R)	58,570
3.	**Jan Meyers*** (R)	88,679
	Leroy Jones (D)	58,876
4.	**Dan Glickman*** (D)	109,607
	Roger M. Grund Sr. (R)	45,512
5.	**Dick Nichols** (R)	90,476
	George D. Wingert (D)	62,162

Kentucky

Dist.	Representative (Party)	1990 Election
1.	**Carroll Hubbard Jr.*** (D)	85,323
	Marvin Seat (PO)	12,954
2.	**William H. Natcher*** (D)	77,023
	Martin A. Tori (R)	39,721
3.	**Romano L. Mazzoli*** (D)	84,205
	Al Brown (R)	54,811
4.	**Jim Bunning*** (R)	101,598
	Galen Martin (D)	44,866
5.	**Harold Rogers*** (R)	Unopposed
6.	**Larry J. Hopkins*** (R)	Unopposed
7.	**Carl C. Perkins*** (D)	60,933
	William T. "Will" Scott (R)	58,878

Louisiana

Dist.	Representative (Party)	1990 Election
1.	**Bob Livingston*** (R)	Declared Elected
2.	**William J. Jefferson** (D)	55,371
	Marc H. Morial (D)	50,197
3.	**Billy Tauzin*** (D)	Declared Elected
4.	**Jim McCrery*** (R)	Declared Elected
5.	**Jerry Huckaby*** (D)	Declared Elected
6.	**Richard Baker*** (R)	Unopposed
7.	**James A. "Jimmy" Hayes*** (D)	Declared Elected
8.	**Clyde C. Holloway*** (R)	Declared Elected

In Louisiana, all candidates of all parties run against each other in an open primary, unless they are unopposed incumbents in which case they are declared elected. All candidates who receive more than 50 percent of the primary vote are also declared elected, and do not appear on the General Election ballot.

Maine

Dist.	Representative (Party)	1990 Election
1.	**Thomas H. Andrews** (D)	162,686
	David F. Emery (R)	105,830
2.	**Olympia J. Snowe*** (R)	119,131
	Patrick K. McGowan (D)	115,125

Dist.	Representative (Party)	1990 Election

Maryland

1.	**Wayne T. Gilchrest** (R)	85,576
	Roy Dyson* (D)	65,272
2.	**Helen Delich Bentley*** (R)	112,477
	Ronald P. Bowers (D)	38,918
3.	**Benjamin L. Cardin*** (D)	79,915
	Harwood Nichols (R)	34,911
4.	**Thomas McMillen*** (D)	83,539
	Robert P. Duckworth (R)	58,204
5.	**Steny H. Hoyer*** (D)	83,079
	Lee F. Breuer (R)	19,817
6.	**Beverly B. Byron*** (D)	103,497
	Christopher P. Fiotes Jr. (R)	54,933
7.	**Kweisi Mfume*** (D)	58,092
	Kenneth Kondner (R)	10,341
8.	**Constance A. Morella** (R)	125,626
	James Walker Jr. (D)	38,197

Massachusetts

1.	**Silvio O. Conte*** (R)	129,137
	John R. Arden (D)	36,857
2.	**Richard E. Neal*** (D)	Unopposed
3.	**Joseph D. Early*** (D)	Unopposed
4.	**Barney Frank*** (D)	137,420
	John R. Soto (R)	70,848
5.	**Chester G. Atkins*** (D)	104,369
	John F. MacGovern (R)	96,529
6.	**Nicholas Mavroules*** (D)	138,456
	Edgar L. Kelley (R)	71,378
7.	**Edward J. Markey*** (D)	Unopposed
8.	**Joseph P. Kennedy II** (D)	94,470
	Glenn W. Fiscus (R)	31,063
9.	**John Joseph Moakley*** (D)	115,598
	Robert Horan (I)	48,101
10.	**Gerry E. Studds*** (D)	110,616
	Jon L. Bryan (R)	101,794
11.	**Brian J. Donnelly*** (D)	Unopposed

Michigan

1.	**John Conyers Jr.*** (D)	76,510
	Ray Shoulders (R)	7,290
2.	**Carl D. Pursell*** (R)	76,831
	Elmer White (D)	43,147
3.	**Howard Wolpe*** (D)	82,409
	Brad Haskins (R)	60,060
4.	**Fred Upton*** (R)	75,877
	JoAnne McFarland (D)	55,230
5.	**Paul B. Henry*** (R)	126,092
	Thomas Trzybinski (D)	41,109
6.	**Bob Carr*** (D)	Unopposed
7.	**Dale E. Kildee*** (D)	90,298
	David J. Morrill (R)	41,749
8.	**Bob Traxler*** (D)	98,369
	James White (R)	45,229
9.	**Guy Vander Jagt*** (R)	89,107
	Geraldine Greene (D)	73,638
10.	**Dave Camp** (R)	99,605
	Joan Louise Dennison (D)	51,022
11.	**Robert W. Davis*** (R)	94,599
	Marcia Gould (D)	59,753
12.	**David E. Bonior*** (D)	97,990
	Jim Dingeman (R)	50,962
13.	**Barbara-Rose Collins** (D)	53,321
	Carl R. Edwards Sr. (R)	7,590
14.	**Dennis M. Hertel*** (D)	72,185
	Kenneth C. McNealy (R)	36,819
15.	**William D. Ford*** (D)	55,930
	Burl C. Adkins (R)	32,589
16.	**John D. Dingell*** (D)	87,599
	Frank Beaumont (R)	42,976
17.	**Sander Levin*** (D)	76,910
	Blaine L. Lankford (R)	36,487
18.	**William S. Broomfield*** (R)	126,627
	Walter O. Briggs IV (D)	64,189

Minnesota

1.	**Timothy J. "Tim" Penny*** (D)	137,656
	Doug Anderson (R)	38,182
2.	**Vin Weber*** (R)	121,828
	Jim Stone (D)	73,625

Dist.	Representative (Party)	1990 Election
3.	**Jim Ramstad** (R)	**165,140**
	Lou Demars (D)	84,429
4.	**Bruce F. Vento*** (D)	**142,249**
	Ian Maitland (R)	76,996
5.	**Martin Olav Sabo*** (D)	**137,833**
	Raymond C. "Buzz" Gilbertson (R)	51,487
6.	**Gerry Sikorski*** (D)	**153,009**
	Bruce D. Anderson (R)	84,250
7.	**Collin C. Peterson** (D)	**102,275**
	Arlan Strangeland* (R)	88,811
8.	**James L. Oberstar*** (D)	**148,090**
	Jerry Shuster (R)	55,123

Mississippi

1.	**Jamie L. Whitten*** (D)	**43,567**
	Bill Bowlin (R)	23,594
2.	**Mike Espy*** (D)	**58,352**
	Dorothy Benford (R)	11,026
3.	**G. V. "Sonny" Montgomery*** (D)	**Unopposed**
4.	**Mike Parker*** (D)	**56,939**
	Jerry "Rev" Parks (R)	13,665
5.	**Gene Taylor*** (D)	**89,566**
	Sheila Smith (R)	20,563

Missouri

1.	**William "Bill" Clay*** (D)	**62,547**
	Wayne G. Piotrowski (R)	40,157
2.	**Joan Kelly Horn** (D)	**94,300**
	Jack Buechner* (R)	94,248
3.	**Richard A. Gephardt*** (D)	**88,892**
	Malcolm L. "Mack" Holekamp (R)	67,656
4.	**Ike Skelton*** (D)	**105,541**
	David Eyerly (R)	65,093
5.	**Alan Wheat*** (D)	**71,957**
	Robert H. Gardner (R)	43,980
6.	**E. Thomas Coleman*** (R)	**79,028**
	Bob McClure (D)	72,937
7.	**Melton D. "Mel" Hancock*** (R)	**83,605**
	Thomas Patrick "Pat" Deaton (D)	76,918
8.	**Bill Emerson*** (R)	**81,020**
	Russ Carnahan (D)	60,490
9.	**Harold L. Volkmer*** (D)	**94,060**
	Don Curtis (R)	70,187

Montana

1.	**Pat Williams*** (D)	**100,371**
	Brad Johnson (R)	63,794
2.	**Ron Marlenee*** (R)	**96,451**
	Don Burris (D)	56,644

Nebraska

1.	**Douglas K. Bereuter*** (R)	**127,330**
	Larry Hall (D)	69,565
2.	**Peter Hoagland*** (D)	**109,955**
	Ally Milder (R)	79,258
3.	**Bill Barrett** (R)	**95,361**
	Sandra K. Scofield (D)	91,478

Nevada

1.	**James H. Bilbray*** (D)	**84,519**
	Bob Dickinson (R)	47,293
2.	**Barbara F. Vucanovich*** (R)	**103,133**
	Jane Wisdom (D)	59,365

New Hampshire

1.	**"Bill" Zeliff*** (R)	**81,239**
	Joseph F. Keefe (D)	65,409
2.	**"Dick" Swett** (D)	**75,802**
	Chuck Douglas* (R)	66,764

New Jersey

1.	**Robert E. Andrews** (D)	**72,391**
	Daniel J. Mangini (R)	57,188
2.	**William J. Hughes*** (D)	**97,625**
	William A. Kanengiser (PO)	13,128
3.	**Frank Pallone Jr.*** (D)	**77,866**
	Paul A. Kapalko (R)	73,696
4.	**Christopher H. Smith*** (R)	**100,089**
	Mark Setaro (D)	55,073

Dist.	Representative (Party)	1990 Election
5.	**Marge Roukema*** (R)	**118,101**
	Lawrence Wayne Olsen (D)	35,010
6.	**Bernard J. Dwyer*** (D)	**61,383**
	Paul "Daniels" Danielczyk (R)	56,531
7.	**Matthew J. Rinaldo*** (R)	**98,156**
	Bruce H. Bergen (D)	30,856
8.	**Robert A. Roe*** (D)	**55,797**
	Stephen Sibilia (IC)	13,180
	Bruce Eden (PO)	3,563
9.	**Robert G. Torricelli*** (D)	**82,535**
	Peter J. Russo (R)	59,658
10.	**Donald M. Payne*** (D)	**42,313**
	Howard E. Berkeley (R)	8,872
11.	**Dean A. Gallo*** (R)	**91,786**
	Michael Gordon (D)	47,414
12.	**Dick Zimmer** (R)	**107,851**
	Marguerite Chandler (D)	52,256
13.	**H. James Saxton*** (R)	**99,688**
	John H. Adler (D)	67,587
14.	**Frank J. Guarini*** (D)	**56,455**
	Fred J. Theemling Jr. (R)	24,870

New Mexico

1.	**Steven H. Schiff*** (R)	**97,270**
	Rebecca Vigil-Giron (D)	41,258
2.	**Joe Skeen*** (R)	**Unopposed**
3.	**Bill Richardson*** (D)	**102,194**
	Phil T. Archuletta (R)	35,054

New York

1.	**George J. Hochbrueckner*** (D,TB)	**73,709**
	Francis W. Creighton (R)	45,431
	Clayton Baldwin Jr. (C)	6,997
	Peter J. O'Hara (T)	5,178
2.	**Thomas J. Downey*** (D)	**55,307**
	John W. Bugler (R,T,TC)	36,820
	Dominic A. Curcio (C)	8,186
3.	**Robert J. Mrazek*** (D,L)	**71,844**
	Robert Previdi (R,C)	58,550
	Francis A. Dreger (T)	5,083
4.	**Norman F. Lent*** (R,C)	**79,015**
	Francis T. Goban (D)	41,065
	John J. Dunkle (T)	6,718
	Ben-Zion J. Heyman (L)	2,420
5.	**Raymond J. McGrath*** (R,C)	**72,086**
	Mark S. Edstein (D,L)	53,823
	Edward K. Kitt (T)	6,185
6.	**Floyd H. Flake*** (D,L)	**43,665**
	William Sampol (R)	13,788
	John Cronin (T)	3,062
7.	**Gary L. Ackerman*** (D,L)	**Unopposed**
8.	**James H. Scheuer*** (D,L)	**55,126**
	Gustave Reifenkugel (R,C)	21,202
9.	**Thomas J. Manton*** (D)	**34,902**
	Ann Pfoser Darby (R)	12,974
	Thomas V. Ognibene (C)	6,190
10.	**Charles E. Schumer*** (D,L)	**59,587**
	Patrick J. Kinsella (R,C)	14,808
11.	**Edolphus Towns*** (D,L)	**35,484**
	Ernest Johnson (C)	1,629
	Lorraine Stevens (NA)	1,002
12.	**Major R. Owens*** (D,L)	**39,494**
	Joseph N.O. Caesar (C)	1,090
	Mamie Moore (NA)	944
13.	**Stephen J. Solarz*** (D,L)	**46,983**
	Edwin Ramos (R,C)	11,874
14.	**Susan Molinari*** (R,C)	**56,605**
	Anthony J. Pocchia (D,L)	33,549
	Christine Sacchi (T)	4,457
15.	**Bill Green*** (R,IN)	**50,845**
	Frances L. Reiter (D,L)	32,581
	Michael T. Berns (C)	3,879
16.	**Charles B. Rangel*** (D,R,L)	**53,896**
	Alvaader Frazier (NA)	1,514
17.	**Ted Weiss*** (D,L)	**76,430**
	William W. Koeppel Jr. (R)	14,576
	Mark Goret (C)	2,947
	John Patterson (NA)	1,231

Dist.	Representative (Party)	1990 Election
18.	**Jose Serrano*** (D,L)	**36,694**
	Joseph Chiavaro (R)	1,181
19.	**Eliot L. Engel*** (D,L)	**44,249**
	William J. Gouldman (R)	16,483
	Kevin Brawley (C,T)	11,602
20.	**Nita M. Lowey*** (D)	**73,740**
	Glenn D. Bellitto (R)	32,979
	John M. Schafer (C,T)	12,524
21.	**Hamilton Fish Jr.*** (R,C)	**89,315**
	Richard L. Barbuto (D)	30,763
	Richard S. Curtin (T)	5,829
22.	**Benjamin A. Gilman*** (R)	**91,548**
	John G. Dow (D)	35,803
	Margaret M. Beirne (T).	6,594
23.	**Michael R. McNulty*** (D,C)	**114,555**
	Margaret B. Burhmaster (R)	64,765
24.	**Gerald B. Solomon*** (R,C,T)	**118,335**
	Bob Lawrence (D)	55,603
25.	**Sherwood L. Boehlert*** (R)	**83,964**
	William L. Griffin (L)	16,172
26.	**David O'B. Martin*** (R,C)	**Unopposed**
27.	**James T. Walsh*** (R,C)	**95,267**
	Peggy L. Murray (D,L)	51,992
	Stephen K. Hoff (T)	3,152
28.	**Matthew F. McHugh*** (D)	**88,147**
	Seymour Krieger (R)	48,219
29.	**Frank Horton*** (R)	**85,857**
	Alton F. Eber (D)	33,750
	Peter DeMauro (C)	12,256
	Donald M. Peters (T)	4,780
30.	**Louise M. Slaughter*** (D)	**95,144**
	John M. Regan Jr. (R,C,T)	65,877
31.	**William Paxon*** (R,C,T)	**88,922**
	Kevin P. Gaughan (D,L)	68,607
32.	**John J. LaFalce*** (D,L)	**67,015**
	Michael T. Waring (R)	39,287
	Kenneth J. Kowalski (C,T)	16,731
33.	**Henry J. Nowak*** (D,L)	**83,951**
	Thomas K. Kepfer (R)	18,165
	Louis P. Corrigan Jr. (C)	6,563
34.	**Amory Houghton Jr.*** (R,C)	**87,591**
	Joseph P. Leahey (D)	37,492
	Nevin K. Eklund (L)	1,764

North Carolina

Dist.	Representative (Party)	1990 Election
1.	**Walter B. Jones*** (D)	**106,380**
	Howard D. Moye (R)	57,349
2.	**I.T. "Tim" Valentine Jr.*** (D)	**127,617**
	Hal C. Sharpe (R)	43,620
3.	**Martin Lancaster*** (D)	**83,585**
	Don Davis (R)	57,105
4.	**David E. Price*** (D)	**139,189**
	John Carrington (R)	100,420
5.	**Stephen Neal*** (D)	**110,725**
	Ken Bell (R)	73,633
6.	**Howard Coble*** (R)	**125,817**
	Helen R. Allegrone (D)	62,995
7.	**Charles G. Rose III*** (D)	**94,077**
	Robert C. Anderson (R)	49,644
8.	**W. G. "Bill" Hefner*** (D)	**98,264**
	Ted Blanton (R)	80,752
9.	**J. Alex McMillan*** (R)	**131,298**
	David P. McKnight (D)	80,476
10.	**T. Cass Ballenger*** (R)	**105,676**
	Daniel R. Green Jr. (D)	65,278
11.	**Charles H. Taylor*** (R)	**102,248**
	James McClure Clarke* (D)	98,923

North Dakota At Large

	Byron L. Dorgan* (D)	**149,241**
	Edward T. Schafer (R)	79,623

Ohio

Dist.	Representative (Party)	1990 Election
1.	**Charles Luken** (D)	**82,992**
	J. Kenneth Blackwell (R)	79,807
2.	**Willis D. Gradison Jr.*** (R)	**103,245**
	Tyrone K. Yates (D)	56,974

Dist.	Representative (Party)	1990 Election
3.	**Tony P. Hall*** (D)	**Unopposed**
4.	**Michael G. Oxley*** (R)	**102,510**
	Thomas E. Burkhart (D)	63,682
5.	**Paul E. Gillmor*** (R)	**113,880**
	P. Scott Mange (D)	41,913
6.	**Bob McEwen*** (R)	**116,276**
	Ray Mitchell (D)	47,221
7.	**David L. Hobson** (R)	**96,239**
	Jack Schira (D)	58,746
8.	**John A. Boehner** (R)	**99,174**
	Gregory V. Jolivette (D)	63,044
9.	**Marcy Kaptur*** (D)	**116,652**
	Jerry D. Lammers (R)	33,621
10.	**Clarence E. Miller*** (R)	**104,954**
	John M. Buchanan (D)	61,197
11.	**Dennis E. Eckart*** (D)	**111,260**
	Margaret R. Mueller (R)	58,163
12.	**John R. Kasich*** (R)	**129,623**
	Mike Gelpi (D)	50,699
13.	**Donald J. Pease*** (D)	**92,349**
	William D. Nielsen (R)	60,387
14.	**Thomas C. Sawyer*** (D)	**97,365**
	Jean E. Bender (R)	66,103
15.	**Chalmers P. Wylie*** (R)	**98,331**
	Thomas V. Erney (D)	68,064
16.	**Ralph Regula*** (R)	**100,425**
	Warner D. Mendenhall (D)	70,081
17.	**James A. Traficant Jr.*** (D)	**132,446**
	Robert R. DeJulio Jr. (R)	37,949
18.	**Douglas Applegate*** (D)	**119,694**
	John A. Hales (R)	41,634
19.	**Edward F. Feighan*** (D)	**132,038**
	Susan M. Lawko (R)	71,755
20.	**Mary Rose Oakar*** (D)	**108,697**
	Bill Smith (R)	39,609
21.	**Louis Stokes*** (D)	**102,076**
	Franklin H. Roski (R)	25,698

Oklahoma

Dist.	Representative (Party)	1990 Election
1.	**James M. Inhofe*** (R)	**75,714**
	Kurt G. Glassco (D)	59,521
2.	**Mike Synar*** (D)	**90,820**
	Terry M. Gorham (R)	57,337
3.	**Bill Brewster** (D)	**107,406**
	Patrick K. Miller (R)	26,497
4.	**Dave McCurdy*** (D)	**100,879**
	Howard Bell (R)	36,232
5.	**Mickey Edwards*** (R)	**114,608**
	Bryce Baggett (D)	50,086
6.	**Glenn English*** (D)	**110,120**
	Robert Burns (R)	27,540

Oregon

Dist.	Representative (Party)	1990 Election
1.	**Les AuCoin*** (D)	**135,143**
	Earl Molander (R)	62,703
	Rick Livingston (I)	13,934
2.	**Bob Smith*** (R)	**123,351**
	Jim Smiley (D)	58,339
3.	**Ron Wyden*** (D)	**154,779**
	Phil Mooney (R)	36,038
4.	**Peter A. DeFazio*** (D)	**151,839**
	Tonie Nathan (B)	24,283
5.	**Mike Kopetski** (D)	**110,543**
	Denny Smith* (R)	89,904

Pennsylvania

Dist.	Representative (Party)	1990 Election
1.	**Thomas M. Foglietta*** (D)	**69,385**
	James Love Jackson (R)	18,491
2.	**William H. Gray III*** (D)	**90,977**
	Donald Bakove (R)	8,266
3.	**Robert A. Borski*** (D)	**84,285**
	Joseph Marc McColgan (R)	58,106
4.	**Joseph P. Kolter*** (D)	**73,992**
	Gordon R. Johnson (R)	58,429
5.	**Richard T. Schulze*** (R)	**74,988**
	Samuel C. Stretton (D)	50,548
	Lewis duPont Smith (ASI)	5,789
6.	**Gus Yatron*** (D)	**72,928**
	John F. Hicks (R)	54,736

Dist.	Representative (Party)	1990 Election
7.	**Curt Weldon*** (R)	**105,469**
	John Innelli (D)	56,209
8.	**Peter H. Kostmayer*** (D)	**84,872**
	Audrie Zettick Schaller (R)	64,925
9.	**Bud Shuster*** (R, D)	**Unopposed**
10.	**Joseph M. McDade*** (R,D)	**Unopposed**
11.	**Paul E. Kanjorski*** (D)	**Unopposed**
12.	**John P. Murtha*** (D)	**80,485**
	Willeam A. Choby (R)	50,005
13.	**Lawrence Coughlin*** (R)	**87,741**
	Bernard Tomkin (D)	58,266
14.	**William J. Coyne*** (D)	**76,605**
	Richard E. Caligiuri (R)	30,363
15.	**Don Ritter*** (R)	**76,431**
	Richard J. Orloski (D)	50,497
16.	**Robert S. Walker*** (R)	**85,382**
	Ernest Eric Guyll (D)	43,837
17.	**George W. Gekas*** (R, D)	**Unopposed**
18.	**Rick Santorum*** (R)	**85,251**
	Doug Walgren* (D)	80,764
19.	**William F. Goodling*** (R)	**Unopposed**
20.	**Joseph M. Gaydos*** (D)	**82,040**
	Robert C. Lee (R)	43,034
21.	**Thomas J. Ridge*** (R)	**Unopposed**
22.	**Austin J. Murphy*** (D)	**78,234**
	Suzanne Hayden (R)	45,387
23.	**William F. Clinger Jr.*** (R)	**78,130**
	Daniel J. Shannon (D)	53,352

Rhode Island

Dist.	Representative (Party)	1990 Election
1.	**Ronald K. Machtley*** (R)	**86,793**
	J. Scott Wolf (D)	70,566
2.	**John F. Reed** (D)	**103,968**
	Gertrude M. Coxe (R)	71,537

South Carolina

Dist.	Representative (Party)	1990 Election
1.	**Arthur Ravenel Jr.*** (R)	**78,763**
	Eugene Platt (D)	41,880
2.	**Floyd D. Spence*** (R)	**90,970**
	Geb Sommer (B)	11,095
3.	**Butler Derrick*** (D)	**72,316**
	Ray Haskett (R)	52,215
4.	**Liz J. Patterson*** (D)	**81,129**
	Terry E. Haskins (R)	51,068
5.	**John Spratt*** (D)	**Unopposed**
6.	**Robin Tallon*** (D)	**Unopposed**

South Dakota At Large

Dist.	Representative (Party)	1990 Election
	Tim Johnson* (D)	**173,429**
	Donald Frankenfeld (R)	83,474

Tennessee

Dist.	Representative (Party)	1990 Election
1.	**James H. "Jimmy" Quillen*** (R)	**Unopposed**
2.	**John J. Duncan Jr.*** (R)	**61,993**
	Peter Hebert (I)	14,892
3.	**Marilyn Lloyd*** (D)	**49,700**
	Grady L. Rhoden (R)	36,835
4.	**Jim Cooper*** (D)	**52,057**
	Claiborne "Clay" Sanders (R)	22,948
5.	**Bob Clement*** (D)	**55,387**
	Tom Stone (I)	13,539
	Al Borgman (I)	5,365
	Maurice C. Kuttab (I)	2,182
6.	**Bart Gordon*** (D)	**60,381**
	Gregory Cochran (R)	26,323
7.	**Don Sundquist*** (R)	**65,694**
	Ken Bloodworth (D)	40,587
8.	**John Tanner*** (D)	**Unopposed**
9.	**Harold E. Ford*** (D)	**48,620**
	Aaron C. Davis (R)	25,727

Texas

Dist.	Representative (Party)	1990 Election
1.	**Jim Chapman*** (D)	**88,505**
	Hamp Hodges (R)	57,709
2.	**Charles Wilson*** (D)	**76,463**
	Donna Peterson (R)	61,365

Dist.	Representative (Party)	1990 Election
3.	**Steve Bartlett*** (R)	**Unopposed**
4.	**Ralph M. Hall*** (D)	**Unopposed**
5.	**John Bryant*** (D)	**65,151**
	Jerry Rucker (R)	41,205
6.	**Joe Barton*** (R)	**126,913**
	John E. Welch (D)	63,299
7.	**Bill Archer*** (R)	**Unopposed**
8.	**Jack Fields*** (R)	**Unopposed**
9.	**Jack Brooks*** (D)	**79,739**
	Maury Meyers (R)	58,320
10.	**J. J. "Jake" Pickle*** (D)	**152,642**
	David Beilharz (R)	73,754
11.	**Chet Edwards** (D)	**73,699**
	Hugh D. Shine (R)	63,329
12.	**Pete Geren*** (D)	**98,026**
	Mike McGinn (R)	39,438
13.	**Bill Sarpalius*** (D)	**81,459**
	Dick Waterfield (R)	62,982
14.	**Greg Laughlin*** (D)	**89,211**
	Joe Dial (R)	75,151
15.	**E. "Kika" de la Garza*** (D)	**Unopposed**
16.	**Ronald Coleman*** (D)	**Unopposed**
17.	**Charles W. Stenholm*** (D)	**Unopposed**
18.	**Craig A. Washington*** (D)	**Unopposed**
19.	**Larry Combest*** (R)	**Unopposed**
20.	**Henry B. Gonzalez*** (D)	**Unopposed**
21.	**Lamar Smith*** (R)	**141,906**
	Kirby J. Roberts (D)	47,543
22.	**Tom DeLay*** (R)	**93,130**
	Bruce Director (D)	37,612
23.	**Albert G. Bustamente*** (D)	**71,104**
	Jerome L. "Jerry" Gonzales (R)	40,833
24.	**Martin Frost*** (D)	**Unopposed**
25.	**Mike Andrews*** (D)	**Unopposed**
26.	**Dick Armey*** (R)	**147,609**
	John Wayne Caton (D)	62,040
27.	**Solomon P. Ortiz*** (D)	**Unopposed**

Utah

Dist.	Representative (Party)	1990 Election
1.	**James V. Hansen*** (R)	**82,315**
	Kenley Brunsdale (D)	69,210
2.	**Wayne Owens*** (D)	**85,080**
	Genevieve Atwood (R)	58,830
3.	**Bill Orton** (D)	**79,102**
	Karl Snow (R)	49,369

Vermont At Large

Dist.	Representative (Party)	1990 Election
	Bernie Sanders (I)	**117,374**
	Peter Smith* (R)	82,774
	Dolores Sandoval (D)	6,290
	Peter Diamondstone (LU)	1,980

Virginia

Dist.	Representative (Party)	1990 Election
1.	**Herbert H. "Herb" Bateman*** (R)	**71,790**
	Fox (D)	69,233
2.	**Owen B. Pickett*** (D)	**54,895**
	Broskie (I)	15,741
3.	**Thomas J. "Tom" Bliley Jr.*** (R)	**77,124**
	Starke (D)	36,254
	Simpson (I)	4,317
4.	**Norman Sisisky*** (D)	**71,371**
	McReynolds (I)	12,217
	Chandler (I)	7,487
5.	**L. F. Payne Jr.*** (D)	**Unopposed**
6.	**James R. "Jim" Olin*** (D)	**91,446**
	Berg (I)	17,932
7.	**D. French Slaughter*** (R)	**81,200**
	Smith (D)	58,675
8.	**Moran** (D)	**88,470**
	Stan Parris* (R)	76,391
	Murphy (I)	5,962
9.	**Frederick C. "Rick" Boucher*** (D)	**Unopposed**
10.	**Frank R. Wolf*** (R)	**103,705**
	Canter (D)	56,970
	Minnich (I)	5,282
	LaRouche (I)	2,290

Washington

Dist.	Representative (Party)	1990 Election
1.	**John Miller*** (R)	**87,998**
	Cynthia Sullivan (D)	83,358

Dist.	Representative (Party)	1990 Election
2.	Al Swift* (D)	84,282
	Doug Smith (R)	67,642
3.	Jolene Unsoeld* (D)	87,062
	Bob Williams (R)	74,205
4.	Sid Morrison* (R)	93,748
	Ole H. Hougen (D)	38,494
5.	Thomas S. Foley* (D)	102,453
	Marlyn Derby (R)	46,114
6.	Norman D. Dicks* (D)	64,096
	Norbert "Bert" Mueller (R)	38,774
7.	Jim McDermott* (D)	96,434
	Larry Penberthy (R)	30,807
8.	Rod Chandler* (R)	82,705
	David Giles (D)	65,497

West Virginia

Dist.	Representative (Party)	1990 Election
1.	Alan B. Mollohan* (D)	72,562
	Howard K. Tuck (R)	35,387
2.	Harley O. Staggers Jr.* (D)	62,846
	Oliver Luck (R)	50,409

Dist.	Representative (Party)	1990 Election
3.	Bob Wise* (D)	Unopposed
4.	Nick J. Rahall II * (D)	39,696
	Marianne R. Brewster (R)	36,723

Wisconsin

Dist.	Representative (Party)	1990 Election
1.	Les Aspin* (D)	Unopposed
2.	Scott L. Klug (R)	96,603
	Robert W. Kastenmeier* (D)	85,011
3.	Steven C. Gunderson* (R)	94,581
	James L. Ziegeweid (D)	60,385
4.	Gerald D. Kleczka* (D)	95,893
	Joseph L. Cook (R)	43,003
5.	Jim Moody* (D)	77,552
	Donalda Arnell Hammersmith (R)	31,245
6.	Thomas E. Petri* (R)	Unopposed
7.	David R. Obey* (D)	100,093
	John L. McEwen (R)	60,893
8.	Toby Roth* (R)	96,051
	Jerome Van Sistine (D)	83,413
9.	F. James Senstenbrenner Jr.* (R)	Unopposed

Wyoming At Large

Craig Thomas* (R)		87,010
Pete Maxfield (D)		70,903

Resident Commissioner (Non-Voting)

Puerto Rico
Jaime B. Fuster* (PDP)

Non-Voting Delegates

District of Columbia	Guam	American Samoa
Eleanor Holmes Norton (D)	Ben G. Blaz* (R)	Eni F.H. Faleomavaega* (D)
	Virgin Islands	
	Ron de Lugo* (D)	

Political Divisions of the U.S. Senate and House of Representatives From 1927 (70th Cong.) to 1993 (102nd Cong.)

Source: Clerk of the House of Representatives; Secretary of the Senate

		Senate				House of Representatives				
Congress	Years	Number of Senators	Democrats	Republicans	Other parties	Vacant	Number of Representatives	Democrats	Republicans	Other parties	Vacant
70th	1927-29	96	47	48	1		435	195	237	3	
71st	1929-31	96	39	56	1		435	163	267	1	4
72d	1931-33	96	47	48	1		435	²216	218	1	
73d	1933-35	96	59	36	1		435	313	117	5	
74th	1935-37	96	69	25	2		435	322	103	10	
75th	1937-39	96	75	17	4		435	333	89	13	
76th	1939-41	96	69	23	4		435	262	169	4	
77th	1941-43	96	66	28	2		435	267	162	6	
78th	1943-45	96	57	38	1		435	222	209	4	
79th	1945-47	96	57	38	1		435	243	190	2	
80th	1947-49	96	45	51			435	188	246	1	
81st	1949-51	96	54	42			435	263	171	1	
82d	1951-53	96	48	47	1		435	234	199	2	
83d	1953-55	96	46	48	2		435	213	221	1	
84th	1955-57	96	48	47	1		435	232	203		
85th	1957-59	96	49	47			435	234	201		
86th	1959-61	98	64	34			³436	283	153		
87th	1961-63	100	64	36			⁴437	262	175		
88th	1963-65	100	67	33			435	258	176		1
89th	1965-67	100	68	32			435	295	140		
90th	1967-69	100	64	36			435	248	187		
91st	1969-71	100	58	42			435	243	192		
92d	1971-73	100	54	44	2		435	255	180		
93d	1973-75	100	56	42	2		435	242	192	1	
94th	1975-77	100	61	37	2		435	291	144		
95th	1977-79	100	61	38	1		435	292	143		
96th	1979-81	100	58	41	1		435	277	158		
97th	1981-83	100	46	53	1		435	242	190		3
98th	1983-85	100	46	54			435	269	166		
99th	1985-87	100	47	53			435	253	182		
100th	1987-89	100	54	46			435	258	177		
101st	1989-91	100	57	43			435	262	173		
102nd	1991-93	100	56	44			435	267	167	1	

(2) Democrats organized House due to Republican deaths. (3) Proclamation declaring Alaska a State issued Jan. 3, 1959. (4) Proclamation declaring Hawaii a State issued Aug. 21, 1959.

Congressional Committees

Senate Standing Committees
(As of June 12, 1990)

Agriculture, Nutrition, and Forestry
Chairman: Patrick J. Leahy, Vt.
Ranking Rep.: Richard G. Lugar, Ind.

Appropriations
Chairman: Robert C. Byrd, W.V.
Ranking Rep.: Mark O. Hatfield, Ore.

Armed Services
Chairman: Sam Nunn, Ga.
Ranking Rep.: John W. Warner, Va.

Banking, Housing, and Urban Affairs
Chairman: Donald W. Riegle Jr., Mich.
Ranking Rep.: Jake Garn, Utah

Budget
Chairman: Jim Sasser, Tenn.
Ranking Rep.: Pete V. Dominici, N.M.

Commerce, Science, and Transportation
Chairman: Ernest F. Hollings, S.C.
Ranking Rep.: John C. Danforth, Mo.

Energy and Natural Resources
Chairman: J. Bennett Johnston, La.
Ranking Rep.: James A. McClure, Ida.

Environment and Public Works
Chairman: Quentin N. Burdick, N.D.
Ranking Rep.: John H. Chafee, R.I.

Finance
Chairman: Lloyd Bentsen, Tex.
Ranking Rep.: Bob Packwood, Ore.

Foreign Relations
Chairman: Claiborne Pell, R.I.
Ranking Rep.: Jesse Helms, N.C.

Governmental Affairs
Chairman: John Glenn, Ohio
Ranking Rep.: William V. Roth Jr., Del.

Judiciary
Chairman: Joseph R. Biden Jr., Del.
Ranking Rep.: Strom Thurmond, S.C.

Labor and Human Resources
Chairman: Edward M. Kennedy, Mass.
Ranking Rep.: Orrin G. Hatch, Utah

Rules and Administration
Chairman: Wendell H. Ford, Ky.
Ranking Rep.: Ted Stevens, Alas.

Small Business
Chairman: Dale Bumpers, Ark.
Ranking Rep.: Rudy Boschwitz, Minn.

Veterans' Affairs
Chairman: Alan Cranston, Cal.
Ranking Rep.: Frank H. Murkowski, Alas.

Senate Select and Special Committees
(As of June 12, 1990)

Aging
Chairman: David H. Pryor, Ark.
Ranking Rep.: John Heinz, Pa.

Ethics
Chairman: Howell Heflin, Ala.
Ranking Rep.: Warren Rudman, N.H.

Indian Affairs
Chairman: Daniel K. Inouye, Ha.
Ranking Rep.: John McCain, Ariz.

Intelligence
Chairman: David L. Boren, Okla.
V. Chairman: William S. Cohen, Me.

Joint Committees of Congress

Economic
Chairman: Rep. Lee H. Hamilton (D), Ind.
V. Chairman: Sen. Paul S. Sarbanes (D), Md.

Library
Chairman: Rep. Frank Annunzio (D), Ill.
V. Chairman: Sen. Claiborne Pell (D), R.I.

Printing
Chairman: Sen. Wendell H. Ford (D), Ky.
V. Chairman: Rep. Frank Annunzio (D), Ill.

Taxation
Chairman: Rep. Dan Rostenkowski (D), Ill.
V. Chairman: Sen. Lloyd Bentsen (D), Tex.

House Standing Committees
(As of June 14, 1990)

Agriculture
Chairman: E de la Garza, Tex.
Ranking Rep.: Edward R. Madigan, Ill.

Appropriations
Chairman: Jamie L. Whitten, Miss.
Ranking Rep.: Silvio O. Conte, Mass.

Armed Services
Chairman: Les Aspin, Wis.
Ranking Rep.: William L. Dickinson, Ala.

Banking, Finance, and Urban Affairs
Chairman: Henry B. Gonzalez, Tex.
Ranking Rep.: Chalmers P. Wylie, Ohio

Budget
Chairman: Leon E. Panetta, Cal.
Ranking Rep.: Bill Frenzel, Mich.

District of Columbia
Chairman: Ronald V. Dellums, Cal.
Ranking Rep.: Stan Parris, Va.

Education and Labor
Chairman: Augustus F. Hawkins, Cal.
Ranking Rep.: William F. Goodling, Pa.

Energy and Commerce
Chairman: John D. Dingell, Mich.
Ranking Rep.: Norman F. Lent, N.Y.

Foreign Affairs
Chairman: Dante B. Fascell, Fla.
Ranking Rep.: William S. Broomfield, Mich.

Government Operations
Chairman: John Conyers Jr., Mich.
Ranking Rep.: Frank Horton, N.Y.

House Administration
Chairman: Frank Annunzio, Ill.
Ranking Rep.: William M. Thomas, Cal.

Interior and Insular Affairs
Chairman: Morris K. Udall, Ariz.
Ranking Rep.: Don Young, Alas.

Judiciary
Chairman: Jack Brooks, Tex.
Ranking Rep.: Hamilton Fish Jr., N.Y.

Merchant Marine and Fisheries
Chairman: Walter B. Jones, N.C.
Ranking Rep.: Robert W. Davis, Mich.

Post Office and Civil Service
Chairman: William D. Ford, Mich.
Ranking Rep.: Benjamin A. Gilman, N.Y.

Public Works and Transportation
Chairman: Glenn M. Anderson, Cal.
Ranking Rep.: John Paul Hammerschmidt, Ark.

Rules
Chairman: John Moakley, Mass.
Ranking Rep.: James H. Quillen, Tenn.

Science, Space, and Technology
Chairman: Robert A. Roe, N.J.
Ranking Rep.: Robert S. Walker, Pa.

Small Business
Chairman: John J. LaFalce, N.Y.
Ranking Rep.: Joseph M. McDade, Pa.

Standards of Official Conduct
Chairman: Julian C. Dixon, Cal.
Ranking Rep.: John T. Myers, Ind.

Veterans' Affairs
Chairman: G.V. Montgomery, Miss.
Ranking Rep.: Bob Stump, Ariz.

Ways and Means
Chairman: Dan Rostenkowski, Ill.
Ranking Rep.: Bill Archer, Tex.

House Select Committees

Aging
Chairman: Edward R. Roybal, Cal.
Ranking Rep.: Matthew J. Rinaldo, N.J.

Children, Youth, and Families
Chairman: George Miller, Cal.
Ranking Rep.: Thomas J. Bliley Jr., Va.
Hunger
Chairman: Tony P. Hall, Ohio
Ranking Rep.: Bill Emerson, Mo.

Intelligence
Chairman: Anthony C. Beilenson, Cal.
Ranking Rep.: Henry J. Hyde, Ill.
Narcotics Abuse and Control
Chairman: Charles B. Rangel, N.Y.
Ranking Rep.: Lawrence Coughlin, Pa.

Congress: Selected Characteristics, 1975-1989

Source: *Congressional Quarterly, Congressional Directory*

(As of beginning of first session of each Congress. Figures for Representatives exclude vacancies.)

	Male	Female	Black	Under 40	40-49	50-59	60-69	70-79	80 and over	Less than 2 years	2-9 years	10-19 years	20-29 years	30 years or more
				Age						**Seniority[1]**				
Representatives														
94th Cong., 1975	416	19	15	69	138	137	75	14	2	96	162	125	42	10
95th Cong., 1977	417	18	16	81	121	147	71	15	—	71	207	116	33	8
96th Cong., 1979	417	16	16	86	125	145	63	14	—	80	206	105	32	10
97th Cong., 1981	416	19	17	94	142	132	54	12	1	77	231	96	23	8
98th Cong., 1983	413	21	21	86	145	132	57	13	1	83	224	88	28	11
99th Cong., 1985	412	22	20	71	154	131	59	17	2	49	237	104	34	10
100th Cong., 1987	412	23	23	63	153	137	56	24	2	51	221	114	37	12
101st Cong., 1989	410	25	24	41	163	133	74	20	2	39	207	139	35	13
Senators														
94th Cong., 1975[2]	100	—	1	5	21	35	24	15	—	11	41	34	10	4
95th Cong., 1977	100	—	1	6	26	35	21	10	2	18	41	24	12	5
96th Cong., 1979	99	1	—	10	31	33	17	8	1	20	41	23	12	4
97th Cong., 1981	98	2	—	9	35	36	14	6	—	19	51	17	11	2
98th Cong., 1983	98	2	—	7	28	39	20	3	3	5	61	21	10	3
99th Cong., 1985	98	2	—	4	27	38	25	4	2	8	56	27	7	2
100th Cong., 1987	98	2	—	5	30	36	22	5	2	14	41	36	7	2
101st Cong., 1989	98	2	—	—	30	40	22	6	2	23	22	43	10	2

(-) Represents zero. NA=Not available. (1) Represents consecutive years of service. (2) Includes Senator Durkin, NH., seated Sept. 1975.

Congress: Measures Introduced and Enacted, and Time in Session, 1971-1988

Source: *Calendars of the U.S. House of Representatives and History of Legislation; Vital Statistics on Congress, 1987-89.*

(excludes simple and concurrent resolutions)

	92nd Cong., 1971-72	93d Cong., 1973-74	94th Cong., 1975-76	95th Cong., 1977-78	96th Cong., 1979-80	97th Cong., 1981-82	98th Cong., 1983-84	99th Cong., 1985-86	100th Cong., 1987-88
Measures introduced	22,969	23,396	21,096	19,387	12,583	11,490	11,156	9,885	9,588
Bills	21,363	21,950	19,762	18,045	11,722	10,582	10,134	8,697	8,515
Joint resolutions	1,606	1,446	1,334	1,342	861	908	1,022	1,188	1,073
Measures enacted	768	774	729	803	736	529	677	483	767
Public	607	651	588	633	613	473	623	466	713
Private	161	123	141	170	123	56	54	17	48
House of Representatives									
Number of days	298	318	311	323	326	303	266	281	298
Number of hours	1,429	1,487	1,788	1,898	1,876	1,420	1,705	1,794	1,659
Number of hours per day	4.8	4.7	5.7	5.9	5.8	4.7	6.4	6.4	5.6
Senate									
Number of days	348	334	320	337	333	312	281	313	307
Number of hours	2,294	2,028	2,210	2,510	2,324	2,158	1,951	2,531	2,341
Number of hours per day	6.6	6.1	6.9	7.4	7.0	6.9	6.9	8.1	7.6

NA=Not available.

Congressional Bills Vetoed, 1789-1990

Source: Senate Library

	Regular vetoes	Pocket vetoes	Total vetoes	Vetoes overridden		Regular vetoes	Pocket vetoes	Total vetoes	Vetoes overridden
Washington	2	—	2	—	Cleveland	304	110	414	2
John Adams	—	—	—	—	Benjamin Harrison	19	25	44	1
Jefferson	—	—	—	—	Cleveland	42	128	170	5
Madison	5	2	7	—	McKinley	6	36	42	—
Monroe	1	—	1	—	Theodore Roosevelt	42	40	82	1
John Q. Adams	—	—	—	—	Taft	30	9	39	1
Jackson	5	7	12	—	Wilson	33	11	44	6
Van Buren	—	1	1	—	Harding	5	1	6	—
William Harrison	—	—	—	—	Coolidge	20	30	50	4
Tyler	6	4	10	1	Hoover	21	16	37	3
Polk	2	1	3	—	Franklin Roosevelt	372	263	635	9
Taylor	—	—	—	—	Truman	180	70	250	12
Fillmore	—	—	—	—	Eisenhower	73	108	181	2
Pierce	9	—	9	5	Kennedy	12	9	21	—
Buchanan	4	3	7	—	Lyndon Johnson	16	14	30	—
Lincoln	2	5	7	—	Nixon	26	17	43	7
Andrew Johnson	21	8	29	15	Ford	48	18	66	12
Grant	45	48	93	4	Carter	13	18	31	2
Hayes	12	1	13	1	Reagan	39	39	78	9
Garfield	—	—	—	—	Bush[1]	14	1	15	0
Arthur	4	8	12	1	**Total**	**1,452**	**1,052**	**2,485**	**103**

(1) As of Oct. 11 1990.

UNITED STATES GOVERNMENT

LEGISLATIVE BRANCH	EXECUTIVE BRANCH	JUDICIAL BRANCH
CONGRESS Senate House Architect of the Capitol U.S. Botanic Garden General Accounting Office Government Printing Office Library of Congress Office of Technology Assessment Congressional Budget Office Copyright Royalty Tribunal U.S. Tax Court	**PRESIDENT** Vice President Cabinet **Executive Office of the President** White House Office Office of Management and Budget Council of Economic Advisors National Security Council Office of Policy Development Office of the U.S. Trade Representative Council on Environmental Quality Office of Science and Technology Policy Office of Administration Office of National Drug Control Policy	**Supreme Court of the United States** Courts Of Appeals District Courts Claims Court Court of Appeals for the Federal Circuit Court of International Trade Territorial Courts Court of Military Appeals Administrative Office of the Courts Federal Judicial Center

The Bush Administration

As of mid-1990

Terms of office of the president and vice president, from Jan. 20, 1989 to Jan. 20, 1993. No person may be elected president of the United States for more than two 4-year terms.

President — George Bush of Texas receives salary of $200,000 a year taxable; in addition an expense allowance of $50,000 to assist in defraying expenses resulting from his official duties. Also there may be expended not exceeding $100,000, nontaxable, a year for travel expenses and $20,000 for official entertainment available for allocation within the Executive Office of the President. Congress has provided lifetime pensions of $69,630 a year, free mailing privileges, free office space, and up to $96,000 a year for office help for former Presidents except for the first 30 month period during which a former President is entitled to staff assistance for which an amount up to $150,000 a year may be paid, and $20,000 annually for their widows.

Vice President — Dan Quayle of Indiana receives salary of $115,000 a year and $10,000 for expenses, all of which is taxable.

For succession to presidency, see Succession in Index.

The Cabinet

(Salary: $99,500 per annum)

Secretary of State — James A. Baker 3d, Tex.
Secretary of Treasury — Nicholas F. Brady, N.J.
Secretary of Defense — Richard B. Cheney, Wyo.
Attorney General — Richard "Dick" Thornburgh, Pa.
Secretary of Interior — Manuel Lujan, N.M.
Secretary of Agriculture — Clayton K. Yeutter, Neb.
Secretary of Commerce — Robert A. Mosbacher, Tex.
Secretary of Labor — Elizabeth Hanford Dole, N.C.
Secretary of Health and Human Services — Louis W. Sullivan, Ga.
Secretary of Housing and Urban Development — Jack F. Kemp, N.Y.
Secretary of Transportation — Samuel K. Skinner, Ill.
Secretary of Energy — James D. Watkins, Cal.
Secretary of Education — Lauro F. Cavazos, Tex.
Secretary of Veterans Affairs — Edward J. Derwinski, Ill.

The White House Staff

1600 Pennsylvania Ave. NW 20500

Chief of Staff — John H. Sununu.
Asst. to the President & Deputy to the Chief of Staff — Andrew Card Jr., James W. Cicconi.
Assistants to the President
  Counsel to the President — C. Boyden Gray.

Presidential Personnel — Charles G. Untermeyer.
Public Events & Initiatives — Sigmund A. Rogich.
Science & Technology — Allan Bromley.
Press Secretary — Max Marlin Fitzwater.
Legislative Affairs — Frederick D. McClure.
Communications — David Demarest Jr.
Economic & Domestic Affairs — Roger B. Porter.
Management & Admin. — J. Bonnie Newman.
Cabinet Secy. — Edith Holiday.
National Security — Brent Scowcroft.

Executive Agencies

Council of Economic Advisers — Michael J. Boskin.
Central Intelligence Agency — William H. Webster, dir.
Office of National Drug Control Policy — William J. Bennett.
Office of Management and Budget — Richard G. Darman.
U.S. Trade Representative — Carla Hills.
Council on Environmental Quality — Michael Deland, chmn.

Department of State

2201 C St. NW 20520

Secretary of State — James A. Baker 3d.
Deputy Secretary — Lawrence S. Eagleburger.
Under Sec. for Political Affairs — Robert M. Kimmitt.
Under Sec. for Security Assistance, Science and Technology — Reginald Bartholomew.
Under Sec. for Economic Agricultural Affairs — Richard T. McCormack.
Under Secretary for Management — Ivan Selin.
Legal Advisor — vacant.
Assistant Secretaries for:
  Administration — Arthur W. Forte.
  African Affairs — Herman J. Cohen.
  East Asian & Pacific Affairs — Richard H. Solomon.
  Consular Affairs — Elizabeth Tamposi.
  Diplomatic Security — Sheldon Krys.
  Economic & Business Affairs — Eugene J. McAllister.
  European & Canadian Affairs — Richard Seitz.
  Human Rights & Humanitarian Affairs — Richard Schifter.
  Intelligence & Research — Douglas P. Mulholland.
  Legislative Affairs — Janet Mullins.
  Inter-American Affairs — Bernard Aronson.

International Narcotics Matters — Melvin Levitsky.
International Organizations — John R. Bolton.
Near-Eastern & S. Asian Affairs — John H. Kelly.
Political-Military Affairs — Richard Clarke.
Public Affairs & Spokesman — Margaret DeB. Tutwiler.
Oceans, International Environmental & Scientific Affairs — Frederick M. Bernthal.
Dir. General, Foreign Service & Dir. of Personnel — Edward J. Perkins.
Management Policy — C. Edward Dillery, dir.
Inspector General — Sherman M. Funk.
Policy Planning Staff — Dennis Rose.
Refugee Programs — Princeton Lyman.

Treasury Department

1500 Pennsylvania Ave. NW 20220
Secretary of the Treasury — Nicholas F. Brady.
Deputy Sec. of the Treasury — John E. Robson.
Under Sec. for Finance — Robert R. Glauber.
Under Sec. for International Affairs — David C. Mulford.
General Counsel — Jeanne Archibald, act.
Assistant Secretaries: — Roger Bolton (Public Affairs & Public Liaison); Charles H. Dallara (Intl. Affairs); Michael Basham, act. (Domestic Finance); Peter Nunez (Enforcement); Gerald Murphy (Fiscal); Kenneth W. Gideon (Tax Policy); Bryce Larry Harlow (Legislative Affairs); Sidney Jones (Economic Policy); Hollis S. McLoughlin (Policy Management).
Bureaus:
Alcohol, Tobacco & Firearms — Stephen E. Higgins, dir.
Comptroller of the Currency — Robert Clarke.
Customs — Carol Hallett, comm.
Engraving & Printing — Peter H. Daley, dir.
Federal Law Enforcement Training Center — Charles F. Rinkevich, dir.
Financial Management Service — William E. Douglas, comm.
Internal Revenue Service — Fred T. Goldberg, comm.
Mint — Donna Pope, dir.
Public Debt — Richard L. Gregg, comm.
Treasurer of the U.S. — Catalina Villalpando.
U.S. Savings Bond Division — Jerrold B. Speers, dir.
U.S. Secret Service — John R. Simpson, dir.

Department of Defense

The Pentagon 20301
Secretary of Defense — Richard B. Cheney.
Deputy Secretary — Donald J. Atwood Jr.
Special Assistant — David S. Addington.
Under Secy. for Acquisition — John A. Betti.
Under Secy. for Policy — Paul Wolfowitz.
Asst. Secretaries:
Atomic Energy — Robert B. Barker.
Command Control Communications & Intelligence — Duane P. Andrews.
Force Management & Personnel — Christopher Jehn.
Health Affairs — Enrique Mendez Jr.
International Security Affairs — Henry S. Rowen.
International Security Policy — Stephen J. Hadley.
Legislative Affairs — David Gribbin 3d.
Products & Logistics — Colin R. McMillan.
Program Analysis & Evaluation — David S.C. Chu.
Public Affairs — Pete Williams.
Reserve Affairs — Stephen M. Duncan.
Chairman, Joint Chiefs of Staff — Gen. Colin L. Powell, USA.
General Counsel — Terrance O'Donnell.
Admin. & Management — David O. Cooke, dir.
Operational Test & Evaluation — Robert C. Duncan, dir.

Department of the Army

The Pentagon 20310
Secretary of the Army — Michael P.W. Stone.

Under Secretary — John W. Shannon.
Assistant Secretaries for:
Civil Works — Robert W. Page.
Installations & Logistics — Susan Livingstone.
Financial Management — Douglas A. Brook.
Research, Development and Acquisition — Stephen Conver.
Manpower & Reserve Affairs — G. Kim Wincup.
Chief of Public Affairs — Brig. Gen. Charles W. McClain.
Chief of Staff — Gen. Carl E. Vuono.
Inspector General — Lt. Gen. J.H. Corns.
Deputy Chiefs of Staff:
Logistics — Lt. Gen. Jimmy D. Ross.
Operations & Plans — Lt. Gen. Dennis J. Reymer.
Personnel — Maj. Gen. William H. Reno.
Intelligence — Lt. Gen. Charles B. Eichelberger.
Commanders:
U.S. Army Materiel Command — Gen. William G.T. Tuttle Jr.
U.S. Army Forces Command — Gen. Edwin Burba.
U.S. Army Training and Doctrine Command — Gen. John W. Foss.
First U.S. Army — Lt. Gen. James E. Thompson.
Second U.S. Army — Lt. Gen. James W. Crysel.
Third U.S. Army — Lt. Gen. John J. Yeosock.
Fourth U.S. Army — Lt. Gen. James R. Hall.
Fifth U.S. Army — Lt. Gen. George R. Stotser.
Sixth U.S. Army — Lt. Gen. William H. Harrison.

Department of the Navy

The Pentagon 20350
Secretary of the Navy — H. Lawrence Garrett 3d.
Under Secretary — J. Daniel Howard.
Assistant Secretaries for:
Financial Management — Robert C. McCormack.
Installations & Environment — Jacqueline Schafer.
Manpower, Reserve Affairs — Barbara Spyridon Pope.
Research, Development & Acquisition — Gerald Cann.
Judge Advocate General — RADM E. D. Stumbaugh.
Chief of Naval Operations — ADM Frank B. Kelso 2d.
Chief of Information — RADM Brent Baker.
Military Sealift Command — VADM Francis R. Donovan.
Chief of Naval Personnel — VADM Jeremy M. Boorda.

U.S. Marine Corps:
(Arlington Annex 20380)

Commandant — Gen. A.M. Gray.
Asst. Commandant — Gen. John R. Dailey.
Chief of Staff — Lt. Gen. L.H. Buehl.

Department of the Air Force

The Pentagon 20330
Secretary of the Air Force — Donald B. Rice.
Under Secretary — Anne N. Foreman.
Assistant Secretaries for:
Financial Management — Michael B. Donley.
Space — Martin C. Faga.
Manpower & Reserve Affairs — Jerome G. Cooper.
Acquisition — John J. Welch Jr.
Public Affairs — Brig. Gen. Hallie E. Robertson.
Office of Space Systems — Brig. Gen. Donald R. Walker.
Chief of Staff — vacant.
Inspector General — Lt. Gen. Bradley C. Hosmer.
Deputy Chiefs of Staff:
Logistics & Engineering — Lt. Gen. Henry Viccellio Jr.
Programs & Resources — Lt. Gen. Robert L. Rutherford.
Personnel — Lt. Gen. Thomas J. Hickey.
Plans & Operations — Lt. Gen. Jimmie V. Adams.
Major Air Commands:
AF Logistics Command — Gen. Charles C. McDonald.
AF Systems Command — Gen. Bernard P. Randolph.

Strategic Air Command — Gen. John T. Chain.
Tactical Air Command — Gen. Robert D. Russ.
Alaskan Air Command — Lt. Gen. Thomas G. McInerney.
Pacific Air Forces — Gen. Merrill A. McPeak.
USAF Europe — Gen. Robert C. Oaks.
Electronic Security Command — Maj. Gen. Gary W. O'Shaughnessy.
AF Communications Command — Maj. Robert H. Ludwig.
Air Training Command — Lt. Gen. Joseph W. Ashy.
Military Airlift Command — Gen. Duane H. Cassidy.
AF Space Command — Lt. Gen. Donald J. Kutyna.

Department of Justice

Constitution Ave. & 10th St. NW 20530
Attorney General — Richard "Dick" Thornburgh.
Deputy Attorney General — William P. Barr.
Solicitor General — Kenneth W. Starr.
Liaison Services —William Lucas.
Intelligence Policy & Review — Mary Lawton.
Professional Responsibility —Michael E. Shaheen Jr.
Assistants:
Antitrust Division — James F. Rill.
Civil Division — Stuart M. Gerson.
Civil Rights Division — John R. Dunne.
Criminal Division — vacant.
Justice Programs —Richard Abell.
Justice Management Division — Harry H. Flickinger.
Environment & Natural Resources Division — Richard B. Stewart.
Policy Development — Thomas M. Boyd.
Legal Counsel — William B. Bark.
Legislative Affairs — Bruce Navarro, act.
Tax Division — Shirley D. Peterson.
Fed. Bureau of Investigation — William S. Sessions, dir.
Exec. Off. for Immigration Review — David L. Milhollan, dir.
Bureau of Prisons — J. Michael Quinlan.
Comm. Relations Service — Grace F. Hughes.
Office of Inspector General — Richard J. Hankinson.
Office of Special Counsel for Immigration Related Unfair Employment Practices — Andrew Strotny, act.
Exec. Off. for U.S. Trustees — John Logan, act. dir.
Exec. Off. for U.S. Attorneys — Laurence S. McWhorter.
Public Affairs — David R. Runkel, dir.
Immigration and Naturalization Service — Gene McNary.
Pardon Attorney — David C. Stephenson.
U.S. Parole Commission — Benjamin F. Baer, chmn.
U.S. Marshals Service — K. Michael Moore, dir.
Foreign Claims Settlement Comm. — Stanley J. Glod.
Interpol, U.S. Natl. Central Bureau — Richard C. Stiener, chief.

Department of the Interior

C St. between 18th & 19th Sts. NW 20240
Secretary of the Interior — Manuel Lujan.
Under Secretary — Frank A. Bracken.
Assistant Secretaries for:
Fish, Wildlife and Parks — Constance Harriman.
Policy, Budget, and Administration — Lou Gallegos.
Indian Affairs — Eddie Frank Brown.
Territorial & Intl. Affairs — Stella Guerra.
Bureau of Land Management — Cy Jamison, dir.
Bureau of Mines — T.S. Ary, dir.
Bureau of Reclamation — Dennis C. Underwood.
Fish & Wildlife Service — John F. Turner, dir.
Geological Survey — Dallas L. Peck, dir.
National Park Service — James M. Ridenour.
Public Affairs — I. Stephen Goldstein, dir.
Office of Congressional and Legislative Affairs — James F. Spagnole.
Solicitor — Thomas L. Sansonetti.

Department of Agriculture

The Mall, 12th & 14th Sts. 20250
Secretary of Agriculture — Clayton Yeutter.
Deputy Secretary — Jack C. Parnell.
Administration — Adis Vila.
Internatl. Affairs & Commodity Programs — Richard T. Crowder.
Food & Consumer Services — Catherine A. Bertini.
Marketing & Inspection Services — Jo Ann Smith.
Small Community & Rural Development — Roland Vautour.
Economics — Bruce L. Gardner.
Congressional Relations — Franklin E. Bailey.
Natural Resources & Environment — Patricia Kearney, act.
General Counsel — Alan Raul.
Science & Education — Charles Hess.
Inspector General — Leon Snead.
Public Affairs — Paul E. Kindinger.

Department of Commerce

14th St. between Constitution & E St. NW 20230
Secretary of Commerce — Robert Mosbacher.
Deputy Secretary — Thomas Murrin.
General Counsel — Wendell Willkie.
Assistant Secretaries:
Administration — Thomas Collamore.
Economic Development Adm. — L. Joyce Hampers.
Intl. Economic Policy — Thomas Duesterberg.
Import Administration — Eric I. Garfinkel.
Legislative Affairs — vacant.
Natl. Telecommunications Information Adm. — Janice Obuchowski.
Patent & Trademark Office — Harry F. Manbeck.
Trade Development — Michael Skarzynski.
Bureau of the Census — Dr. Barbara E. Bryant, dir.
Bureau of Economic Analysis — Allan H. Young, dir.
Under Secy. for International Trade — J. Michael Farren.
Under Secy. for Econ. Affairs — Michael Darby.
Under Secy. for Technology — Robert M. White.
Natl. Oceanic & Atmospheric Admin. — John A. Knauss.
Natl. Technical Info. Service — Joseph F. Caponio, dir.
Natl. Institute For Standards & Technology — John W. Lyons.
Minority Business Development Agency — Kenneth Bolton.
Public Affairs — Marion Blakey, dir.
Consumer Affairs — John Gibbons.

Department of Labor

200 Constitution Ave. NW 20210
Secretary of Labor — Elizabeth Dole.
Deputy Secretary — Roderick A. DeArment.
Assistant Secretaries for:
Administration and Management — Thomas C. Komarek.
Congressional Affairs — Kathleen M. Harrington.
Employment & Training — Roberts Jones.
Employment Standards — William C. Brooks.
Labor-Management Standards — William C. White.
Mine Safety & Health — William Tattersall.
Occupational Safety & Health — Gerard F. Scannell.
Pension & Welfare Benefit Programs — David Ball.
Policy — Jennifer Lynn Dorn.
Public and Intergovernmental Affairs — Dale Triber Tate.
Veterans Employment — Thomas E. Collins 3d.
Solicitor of Labor — Robert P. Davis.
Dep. Under Secy. for International Affairs — Shellyn Gae McCaffrey.
Dep. Under Secy. for Labor-Management Relations & Co-operative Programs — John R. Stepp.
Office of Information & Public Affairs — Johanna Schneider, dir.

Women's Bureau — Jean Curtis, act. dir.
Inspector General — vacant.
Comm. of Labor Statistics — Janet L. Norwood.

Department of Health and Human Services

200 Independence Ave. SW 20201

Secretary of HHS — Louis W. Sullivan.
Under Secretary — Constance Horner.
Assistant Secretaries for:
 Management and Budget — Kevin E. Moley.
 Public Affairs — Kay C. James.
 Health — James Mason.
 Planning and Evaluation — Martin Gerry.
 Human Development Services — Mary Sheila Gall.
 Legislation — vacant.
 Personnel Administration — Thomas McFee.
General Counsel — Michael Astrue.
Inspector General — Richard P. Kusserow.
Civil Rights — Edward Mercado.
Surgeon General — Antonia C. Novello.
Social Security Adm. — Gwendolyn S. King.
Consumer Affairs — Bonnie Guiton.

Department of Housing and Urban Development

451 7th St. SW 20410

Secretary of Housing & Urban Development — Jack Kemp.
Under Secretary — Alfred A. DelliBovi.
 Deputies — Edwin I. Gardner, Stephen A. Glaude.
Assistant Secretaries for:
 Administration — vacant.
 Community Planning & Development — S. Anna Kondratas.
 Housing & Federal Housing Commissioner — C. Austin Fitts.
 Legislation & Congressional Relations — Timothy L. Coyle.
 Policy Development & Research — John Weicher.
 Public Affairs — vacant.
 Public & Indian Housing — Joseph G. Schiff.
 Fair Housing & Equal Opportunity — Gordon H. Mansfield.
President, Govt. Natl. Mortgage Assn. — Arthur J. Hill.
International Affairs — Theodore Britton Jr.
General Counsel — Francis A. Keating 2d.
Inspector General — Paul A. Adams.
Indian & Alaska Native Programs — Elaine Dudley.
Board of Contract Appeals — David T. Anderson.
Chief Administrative Law Judge — Alan W. Heifetz.

Department of Transportation

400 7th St. SW 20590

Secretary of Transportation — Samuel K. Skinner.
Deputy Secretary — Elaine Chao.
Assistant Secretaries — Jeffrey Shane (Policy and International Affairs); Kate Moore (Budget and Programs); John H. Seymour (Administration); vacant (Public Affairs); Galen Reser (Governmental Affairs).

National Highway Traffic Safety Admin. — Jerry Curry.
U. S. Coast Guard Commandant — Adm. Paul A. Yost Jr.
Federal Aviation Admin. — James Busey.
Federal Highway Admin. — Thomas Larson.
Federal Railroad Admin. — Gilbert Carmichael.
Maritime Admin. — Capt. Warren LeBack.
Urban Mass Transportation Admin. — Brian Clymer.
Research & Special Programs Admin. — Travis Dungan.
Saint Lawrence Seaway Development Corp. — James L. Emery.

Department of Energy

1000 Independence Ave. SW 20585
Secretary of Energy — James D. Watkins.
Deputy Secy. — W. Henson Moore.
Under Secretary — John C. Tuck.
General Counsel — Stephen A. Wakefield.
Inspector General — John C. Layton.
Assistant Secretaries — Jacqueline Knox Brown (Congressional, Intergovernmental & Public Affairs); John C. Tuck (Defense Programs); James J. Easton Jr. (International Affairs & Energy Emergencies); William A. Young (Nuclear Energy); Robert H. Gentile (Fossil Energy); J. Michael Davis (Conservation & Renewable Energy); Peter N. Brush (Environment, Safety & Health).
Energy Information Adm. — Helmut A. Merklein.
Economic Regulatory Adm. — C. L. Van Orman, adm.
Federal Energy Regulatory Comm. — Martin L. Allday, chmn.
Hearings & Appeals — George B. Breznay, dir.
Energy Research — James F. Decker.
Civilian Radioactive Waste Management — John W. Bartlett.
Minority Economic Impact — Melva G. Wray, dir.
Board of Contract Appeals — E. Barclay van Doren, chmn.
Public Affairs — M.J. Jameson, dir.

Department of Education

400 Maryland Ave. SW 20202
Secretary of Education — Lauro F. Cavazos.
Under Secretary — John Theodore Sanders.
Chief of Staff — Chino Chapa.
Deputy Under Secretaries — George Pieler, Michelle Easton, Thomas E. Anfinson.
General Counsel — Edward C. Stringer.
Assistant Secretaries:
 Legislation — Nancy Mohr Kennedy.
 Elementary and Secondary Education — John T. MacDonald.
 Postsecondary Education — Leonard L. Haynes 3d.
 Educational Research and Improvement — Christopher T. Cross.
 Adult & Vocational Education — Betsy Brand.
 Special Education and Rehabilitative Services — Robert Davila.
 Civil Rights — William Smith, act.
 Bilingual & Minority Languages — Rita Esquivel.

Department of Veterans Affairs

810 Vermont Ave. NW 20420
Secretary of Veterans Affairs — Edward J. Derwinski.
Deputy — Anthony J. Principi.
Inspector General — Dean Trodden.
Veterans Benefits Adm. — D'Wayne Gray.
Veterans Health Services & Research Adm. — James W. Holsinger Jr.
General Counsel — Raoul L. Carroll.

Judiciary of the U.S.

Data as of July 23, 1990

Justices of the United States Supreme Court

The Supreme Court comprises the chief justice of the United States and 8 associate justices, all appointed by the president with advice and consent of the Senate. Salaries: chief justice $124,000 annually, associate justice $118,600.

Chief Justices in italics

Name; appptd from	Service Term	Yrs.	Born	Died
John Jay, N.Y.	1789-1795	5	1745	1829
John Rutledge, S.C.	1789-1791	1	1739	1800
William Cushing, Mass.	1789-1810	20	1732	1810
James Wilson, Pa.	1789-1798	8	1742	1798
John Blair, Va.	1789-1796	6	1732	1800
James Iredell, N.C.	1790-1799	9	1751	1799
Thomas Johnson, Md.	1791-1793	1	1732	1819
William Paterson, N.J.	1793-1806	13	1745	1806
John Rutledge, S.C.	1795(a)	—	1739	1800
Samuel Chase, Md.	1796-1811	15	1741	1811
Oliver Ellsworth, Conn.	1796-1800	4	1745	1807
Bushrod Washington, Va.	1798-1829	31	1762	1829
Alfred Moore, N.C.	1799-1804	4	1755	1810
John Marshall, Va.	1801-1835	34	1755	1835
William Johnson, S.C.	1804-1834	30	1771	1834
Henry B. Livingston, N.Y.	1806-1823	16	1757	1823
Thomas Todd, Ky.	1807-1826	18	1765	1826
Joseph Story, Mass.	1811-1845	33	1779	1845
Gabriel Duval, Md.	1811-1835	22	1752	1844
Smith Thompson, N.Y.	1823-1843	20	1768	1843
Robert Trimble, Ky.	1826-1828	2	1777	1828
John McLean, Oh.	1829-1861	32	1785	1861
Henry Baldwin, Pa.	1830-1844	14	1780	1844
James M. Wayne, Ga.	1835-1867	32	1790	1867
Roger B. Taney, Md.	1836-1864	28	1777	1864
Philip P. Barbour, Va.	1836-1841	4	1783	1841
John Catron, Tenn.	1837-1865	28	1786	1865
John McKinley, Ala.	1837-1852	15	1780	1852
Peter V. Daniel, Va.	1841-1860	19	1784	1860
Samuel Nelson, N.Y.	1845-1872	27	1792	1873
Levi Woodbury, N.H.	1845-1851	5	1789	1851
Robert C. Grier, Pa.	1846-1870	23	1794	1870
Benjamin R. Curtis, Mass.	1851-1857	6	1809	1874
John A. Campbell, Ala.	1853-1861	8	1811	1889
Nathan Clifford, Me.	1858-1881	23	1803	1881
Noah H. Swayne, Oh.	1862-1881	18	1804	1884
Samuel F. Miller, Ia.	1862-1890	28	1816	1890
David Davis, Ill.	1862-1877	14	1815	1886
Stephen J. Field, Cal.	1863-1897	34	1816	1899
Salmon P. Chase, Oh.	1864-1873	8	1808	1873
William Strong, Pa.	1870-1880	10	1808	1895
Joseph P. Bradley, N.J.	1870-1892	21	1813	1892
Ward Hunt, N.Y.	1872-1882	9	1810	1886
Morrison R. Waite, Oh.	1874-1888	14	1816	1888
John M. Harlan, Ky.	1877-1911	34	1833	1911
William B. Woods, Ga.	1880-1887	6	1824	1887
Stanley Matthews, Oh.	1881-1889	7	1824	1889
Horace Gray, Mass.	1881-1902	20	1828	1902
Samuel Blatchford, N.Y.	1882-1893	11	1820	1893
Lucius Q. C. Lamar, Miss.	1888-1893	5	1825	1893
Melville W. Fuller, Ill.	1888-1910	21	1833	1910
David J. Brewer, Kan.	1889-1910	20	1837	1910
Henry B. Brown, Mich.	1890-1906	15	1836	1913
George Shiras Jr., Pa.	1892-1903	10	1832	1924
Howell E. Jackson, Tenn.	1893-1895	2	1832	1895
Edward D. White, La.	1894-1910	16	1845	1921
Rufus W. Peckham, N.Y.	1895-1909	13	1838	1909
Joseph McKenna, Cal.	1898-1925	26	1843	1926
Oliver W. Holmes, Mass.	1902-1932	29	1841	1935
William R. Day, Oh.	1903-1922	19	1849	1923
William H. Moody, Mass.	1906-1910	3	1853	1917
Horace H. Lurton, Tenn.	1909-1914	4	1844	1914
Charles E. Hughes, N.Y.	1910-1916	5	1862	1948
Willis Van Devanter, Wy.	1910-1937	26	1859	1941
Joseph R. Lamar, Ga.	1910-1916	5	1857	1916
Edward D. White, La.	1910-1921	10	1845	1921
Mahlon Pitney, N.J.	1912-1922	10	1858	1924
James C. McReynolds, Tenn.	1914-1941	26	1862	1946
Louis D. Brandeis, Mass.	1916-1939	22	1856	1941
John H. Clarke, Oh.	1916-1922	5	1857	1945
William H. Taft, Conn.	1921-1930	8	1857	1930
George Sutherland, Ut.	1922-1938	15	1862	1942
Pierce Butler, Minn.	1922-1939	16	1866	1939
Edward T. Sanford, Tenn.	1923-1930	7	1865	1930
Harlan F. Stone, N.Y.	1925-1941	16	1872	1946
Charles E. Hughes, N.Y.	1930-1941	11	1862	1948
Owen J. Roberts, Pa.	1930-1945	15	1875	1955
Benjamin N. Cardozo, N.Y.	1932-1938	6	1870	1938
Hugo L. Black, Ala.	1937-1971	34	1886	1971
Stanley F. Reed, Ky.	1938-1957	19	1884	1980
Felix Frankfurter, Mass.	1939-1962	23	1882	1965
William O. Douglas, Conn.	1939-1975	36	1898	1980
Frank Murphy, Mich.	1940-1949	9	1890	1949
Harlan F. Stone, N.Y.	1941-1946	5	1872	1946
James F. Byrnes, S.C.	1941-1942	1	1879	1972
Robert H. Jackson, N.Y.	1941-1954	12	1892	1954
Wiley B. Rutledge, Ia.	1943-1949	6	1894	1949
Harold H. Burton, Oh.	1945-1958	13	1888	1964
Fred M. Vinson, Ky.	1946-1953	7	1890	1953
Tom C. Clark, Tex.	1949-1967	18	1899	1977
Sherman Minton, Ind.	1949-1956	7	1890	1965
Earl Warren, Cal.	1953-1969	16	1891	1974
John Marshall Harlan, N.Y.	1955-1971	16	1899	1971
William J. Brennan Jr., N.J.	1956-1990	33	1906	—
Charles E. Whittaker, Mo.	1957-1962	5	1901	1973
Potter Stewart, Oh.	1958-1981	23	1915	1985
Byron R. White, Col.	1962 —		1917	—
Arthur J. Goldberg, Ill.	1962-1965	3	1908	—
Abe Fortas, Tenn.	1965-1969	4	1910	1982
Thurgood Marshall, N.Y.	1967 —		1908	—
Warren E. Burger, Va.	1969-1986	17	1907	—
Harry A. Blackmun, Minn.	1970 —		1908	—
Lewis F. Powell Jr., Va.	1972-1987	15	1907	—
William H. Rehnquist, Ariz.	1972-1986	14	1924	—
John Paul Stevens, Ill.	1975 —		1920	—
Sandra Day O'Connor, Ariz.	1981 —		1930	—
William H. Rehnquist, Ariz.	1986 —		1924	—
Antonin Scalia, Va.	1986 —		1936	—
Anthony M. Kennedy, Cal.	1988 —		1936	—
David H. Souter	1990 —		1939	—

(a) Rejected Dec. 15, 1795.

U.S. Court of International Trade

New York, NY 10007 (Salaries, $96,600)

Chief Judge — Edward D. Re.

Judges — James L. Watson, Gregory W. Carman, Jane A. Restani, Dominick L. DiCarlo, Thomas J. Aquilino Jr., Nicholas Tsoucalas, R. Kenton Musgrave.

U.S. Claims Court

Washington, D.C. 20005 (Salaries, $96,600)

Chief Judge — Loren A. Smith.

Judges — James F. Merow, John P. Wiese, Robert J. Yock, Reginald W. Gibson, Lawrence S. Margolis, Christine C. Nettesheim, Moody R. Tidwell 3d, Marian Blank Horn, Eric G. Bruggink, Bohdan A. Futey, Wilkes C. Robinson, Roger B. Andewelt, James T. Turner, Randall R. Rader.

U.S. Tax Court

Washington DC 20217 (Salaries, $96,600)

Chief Judge — Arthur L. Nims 3d.

Judges — Herbert L. Chabot, Edna G. Parker, Jules J. Korner 3d, Meade Whitaker, Mary Ann Cohen, John O. Colvin, Perry Shields, Charles E. Clapp 2d, Lapsley W. Hamblen Jr., Stephen J. Swift, Joel Gerber, Julien I. Jacobs, Lawrence A. Wright, Carolyn Miller Parr, Robert P. Ruwe, Thomas B. Wells, Laurence J. Whalen, B. John Williams Jr.

U.S. Courts of Appeals

(Salaries, $102,500. CJ means Chief Judge)

Federal Circuit — Howard T. Markey, CJ; Giles S. Rich, Helen W. Nies; Pauline Newman, Glenn L. Archer Jr., H. Robert Mayer, Paul R. Michel, S. Jay Plager; Clerk's Office, Washington, DC 20439.

District of Columbia — Patricia M. Wald, CJ; Abner J. Mikva, Harry T. Edwards, Ruth Bader Ginsburg, Laurence H. Silberman; James L. Buckley, Stephen F. Williams, Douglas Ginsburg, David B. Sentelle; Clerk's Office, Washington, DC 20001.

First Circuit (Me., Mass., N.H., R.I., Puerto Rico) — Stephen Breyer, CJ; Levin H. Campbell, Hugh H. Bownes, Juan R. Torruella, Bruce M. Selya, Conrad K. Cyr; Clerk's Office, Boston, MA 02109.

Second Circuit (Conn., N.Y., Vt.) — James L. Oakes, CJ; Wilfred Freiberg, Thomas J. Meskill, Jon O. Newman, Amalya Lyle Kearse, Richard J. Cardamone, Ralph K. Winter Jr., George C. Pratt, Roger J. Miner, Frank X. Altimari, J. Daniel Mahoney, John M. Walker; Clerk's Office, New York, NY 10007.

Third Circuit (Del., N.J., Pa., Virgin Is.) — A. Leon Higginbotham Jr., CJ; Dolores K. Sloviter, Edward R. Becker, Carol Los Mansmann, Walter K. Stapleton, Morton I. Ginsberg, Anthony J. Scirica, William D. Hutchinson, Robert E. Cowen, Richard L. Nygaard; Clerk's Office, Philadelphia, PA 19106.

Fourth Circuit (Md., N.C., S.C., Va., W.Va.) — Sam J. Ervin 3d, CJ; Kenneth K. Hall, Donald Stuart Russell, H. Emory Widener Jr., James D. Phillips Jr., Francis D. Murnaghan Jr., James M. Sprouse, Robert F. Chapman, J. Harvie Wilkinson 3d, William W. Wilkins Jr.; Clerk's Office, Richmond, VA 23219.

Fifth Circuit (La., Miss., Tex.) — Charles Clark, CJ; Thomas G. Gee, Alvin B. Rubin, Thomas M. Reavley, Henry A. Politz, Carolyn D. King, Samuel D. Johnson, Jerre S. Williams, William L. Garwood, E. Grady Jolly, Patrick E. Higginbotham, W. Eugene Davis, Jerry E. Smith, Edith Hollan Jones, John M. Duhe Jr.; Clerk's Office, New Orleans, LA 70130.

Sixth Circuit (Ky., Mich., Ohio, Tenn.) — Gilbert S. Merritt, CJ; Damon J. Keith, Boyce F. Martin Jr., Nathaniel R. Jones, Robert B. Krupansky, Harry W. Wellford, Cornelia G. Kennedy, H. Ted Milburn, Ralph B. Guy Jr., David A. Nelson, James L. Ryan, Danny J. Boggs, Alan E. Norris; Clerk's Office, Cincinnati, OH 45202.

Seventh Circuit (Ill., Ind., Wis.) — William J. Bauer, CJ; Walter J. Cummings, Harlington Wood Jr., Richard D. Cudahy, Richard A. Posner, John L. Coffey, Joel M. Flaum, Frank H. Easterbrook, Kenneth F. Ripple, Daniel A. Manion, Michael S. Kanne; Clerk's Office, Chicago, IL 60604.

Eighth Circuit (Ark., Ia., Minn., Mo., Neb., N.D., S.D.) — Donald P. Lay, CJ; Theodore McMillian, Richard S. Arnold, John R. Gibson, George C. Fagg, Pasco M. Bowman 2d, Roger L. Wollman, Frank J. Magill, C. Arlen Beam; Clerk's Office, St. Louis, MO 63101.

Ninth Circuit (Alaska, Ariz., Cal., Ha., Ida., Mont., Nev., Ore., Wash., Guam, N. Mariana Islands) — Albert T. Goodwin, CJ; James R. Browning, J. Clifford Wallace, Procter Hug Jr., Thomas Tang, Jerome Farris, Betty B. Fletcher, Mary M. Schroeder, Harry Pregerson, Arthur L. Alarcon, Cecil F. Poole, Dorothy W. Nelson, William C. Canby Jr., William A. Norris, Stephen Reinhardt, Robert R. Beezer, Cynthia M. Hall, Charles E. Wiggins, Melvin Brunetti, Alex Kozinski, David R. Thompson, John T. Noonan, Diarmuid F. O'Scannlain, Edward Leavy, Stephen S. Trout, Ferdinand F. Fernandez; Clerk's Office, San Francisco, CA 94101.

Tenth Circuit (Col., Kan., N.M., Okla., Ut., Wy.) — William J. Holloway Jr., CJ; Monroe G. McKay, James K. Logan, Stephanie K. Seymour, John P. Moore, Stephen H. Anderson, Deanell R. Tacha, Bobby R. Baldock, Wade Brorby, David M. Ebel; Clerk's Office, Denver, CO 80294.

Eleventh Circuit (Ala. Fla., Ga.)— Gerald B. Tjoflat, CJ; Peter T. Fay, Robert S. Vance, Phyllis A. Kravitch, Frank M. Johnson Jr., Joseph W. Hatchett, R. Lanier Anderson 3d, Thomas A. Clark, J.L. Edmondson, Emmett R. Cox; Clerk's Office, Atlanta GA 30303.

Temporary Emergency Court of Appeals — Reynaldo G. Garza, CJ; Clerk's Office, Washington, DC 20001 .

U.S. District Courts

(Salaries, $96,600. CJ means Chief Judge)

Alabama — Northern: Sam C. Pointer Jr., CJ; James Hughes Hancock, Robert B. Propst, E. B. Haltom Jr., U. W. Clemon, William M. Acker Jr., Edwin L. Nelson; Clerk's Office, Birmingham 35203. **Middle:** Truman M. Hobbs, CJ; Myron H. Thompson, Joel F. Dubina; Clerk's Office, Montgomery 36101. **Southern:** Alex T. Howard Jr., CJ; Charles R. Butler Jr.; Clerk's Office, Mobile 36602.

Alaska — H. Russel Holland, CJ; Andrew J. Kleinfeld; Clerk's Office, Anchorage 99513.

Arizona — Richard M. Bilby, CJ; Charles L. Hardy, Alfredo C. Marquez, Earl H. Carroll, William D. Browning, Paul G. Rosenblat, Robert C. Bloomfield, Roger G. Strand; Clerk's Office, Phoenix 85025.

Arkansas — Eastern: Garnett Thomas Eisele, CJ; Henry Woods, George Howard Jr., Stephen M. Reasoner; Clerk's Office, Little Rock 72203. **Western:** H. Franklin Waters, CJ; George Howard Jr., Morris S. Arnold; Clerk's Office, Fort Smith 72902.

California — Northern: William A. Ingram, CJ; William W. Schwarzer, Robert P. Aguilar, Thelton E. Henderson, Marilyn H. Patel, Eugene F. Lynch, John P. Vukasin Jr., Charles A. Legge, D. Lowell Jensen, Fern M. Smith, Vaughn R. Walker; Clerk's Office, San Francisco 94102. **Eastern:** Robert E. Coyle, CJ; Lawrence K. Karlton, Edward J. Garcia; Clerk's Office, Sacramento 95814. **Central:** Manuel L. Real, CJ; Wm. Matthew Byrne Jr., Robert M. Takasugi, Mariana R. Pfaelzer, Terry J. Hatter Jr., A. Wallace Tashima, Consuelo Bland Marshall, David V. Kenyon, Richard A. Gadbois, Edward Rafeedie, Harry L. Hupp, Alicemarie H. Stotler, James M. Ideman, William J. Rea, William D. Keller, Stephen V. Wilson, J. Spencer Letts, Dickran M. Tevrizian Jr., John G. Davies, Ronald S.W. Lew, Robert C. Bonner; Clerk's Office, Los Angeles 90012. **Southern:** Gordon Thompson Jr., CJ; William B. Enright, Judith N. Keep, Earl B. Gilliam, J. Lawrence Irving, Rudi M. Brewster, John S. Rhoades Sr.; Clerk's Office, San Diego 92189.

Colorado — Sherman G. Finesilver, CJ; Richard P. Matsch, Jim R. Carrigan, Zita L. Weinshienk, Lewis T. Babcock, Edward W. Nottingham; Clerk's Office, Denver 80294.

Connecticut — Ellen B. Burns, CJ; T.F. Gilroy Daly, Warren W. Eginton, Jose A. Cabranes, Peter C. Dorsey, Alan H. Nevas; Clerk's Office, New Haven 06510.

Delaware — Joseph J. Longobardi, CJ; Joseph J. Farnan Jr., Jane R. Roth; Clerk's Office, Wilmington 19801.

District of Columbia — Aubrey E. Robinson Jr., CJ; Gerhard A. Gesell, Charles R. Richey, Louis F. Oberdorfer, Harold H. Greene, John Garrett Penn, Joyce Hens Green, Norma H. Johnson, Thomas P. Jackson, Thomas F. Hogan, Stanley S. Harris, George H. Revercomb, Stanley Sporkin, Royce C. Lamberth; Clerk's Office, Washington DC 20001.

Florida — Northern: William H. Stafford Jr. CJ; Maurice M. Paul, C. Roger Vinson; Clerk's Office, Tallahassee 32301. **Middle:** Susan H. Black, CJ; William Terrell Hodges, Howell W. Melton, William J. Castagna; John H. Moore 2d, Elizabeth A. Kovachevich, George K. Sharp, Patricia C. Fawsett; Clerk's Office, Jacksonville 32201. **Southern:** James Lawrence King, CJ; Norman C. Roetiger Jr.; William H. Hoeveler, Jose A. Gonzalez Jr., James C. Paine, James W. Kehoe, Eugene P. Spellman, Edward B. Davis, Lenore C. Nesbitt, Stanley Marcus, Thomas E. Scott, William J. Zloch, Kenneth L. Ryskamp; Clerk's Office, Miami 33128.

Georgia — Northern: William C. O'Kelley, CJ; Richard C. Freeman, Harold L. Murphy, Marvin H. Shoob, G. Ernest Tidwell, Orinda Dale Evans, Robert L. Vining Jr., Robert H. Hall, Harold T. Ward, J. Owen Forrester, Jack T. Camp; Clerk's Office, Atlanta 30335. **Middle:** Wilbur D. Owens Jr., CJ; J. Robert Elliott, Duross Fitzpatrick; Clerk's Office, Macon 31202. **Southern:** B. Avant Edenfield, CJ; Anthony A. Alaimo, Dudley H. Bowen Jr.; Clerk's Office, Savannah 31412.

Hawaii — Harold M. Fong, CJ, Alan C. Kay, David A. Ezra; Clerk's Office, Honolulu 96850.

Idaho — Harold L. Ryan, CJ; Edward J. Lodge; Clerk's Office, Boise, 83724.

Illinois — Northern: John F. Grady, CJ; Nicholas J. Bua, Stanley J. Roszkowski, James B. Moran, Marvin E. Aspen, Milton I. Shadur, Charles P. Kocoras, John A. Nordberg, William T. Hart, Paul E. Plunkett, Ilana Diamond Rovner, Charles R. Norgle Sr., James F. Holderman Jr., Ann C. Williams, Brian Barnett Duff, Harry D. Lienenweber, James B. Zagel, James H. Alesia, Suzanne B. Conlon, George M. Marovich, George W. Lindberg; Clerk's Office, Chicago 60604. **Central:** Harold Albert Baker, CJ; Michael M. Mihm, Richard Mills; Clerk's Office. Springfield 62705. **Southern:** James L. Foreman, CJ; William L. Beatty, William D. Stiehl; Clerk's Office, E. St. Louis 62202.

Indiana — Northern: Allen Sharp, CJ; William C. Lee, James T. Moody, Robert L. Miller Jr., Rudy Lozano; Clerk's Office, South Bend 46601. **Southern:** Gene E. Brooks, CJ; S. Hugh Dillin, Sarah E. Barker, Larry J. McKinney, John D. Tinder; Clerk's Office, Indianapolis 46204.

Iowa — Northern: Donald E. O'Brien, CJ, David R. Hansen; Clerk's Office, Cedar Rapids 52401. **Southern:** Harold D. Vietor, CJ; Charles R. Wolle; Clerk's Office, Des Moines 50309.

Kansas — Earl E. O'Connor, CJ; Dale E. Saffels, Patrick F. Kelly, Sam A. Crow, C. Thomas Van Bebber; Clerk's Office, Wichita 67202.

Kentucky — Eastern: Eugene E. Siler Jr., CJ; William Bertelsman, Henry R. Wilhoit Jr., Karl S. Forester; Clerk's Office, Lexington 40586. **Western:** Edward H. Johnstone, CJ; Thomas A. Ballantine, Ronald E. Meredith, Charles R. Simpson 3d; Clerk's Office, Louisville 40202.

Louisiana — Eastern: Frederick J. R. Heebe, CJ; Charles Schwartz Jr., Morley L. Sear, Adrian A. Duplantier, Robert F. Collins, George Arceneaux Jr., Veronica D. Wicker, Patrick E. Carr, Peter Beer, A J. McNamara, Henry A. Mentz Jr., Martin L. C. Feldman, Marcel Livaudais Jr.; Clerk's Office, New Orleans 70130. **Middle:** John V. Parker, CJ; Frank J. Polozola; Clerk's Office, Baton Rouge 70821. **Western:** Tom Stagg, CJ; Earl Ernest Veron, John M. Shaw, F. A. Little Jr., Donald E. Walter; Clerk's Office, Shreveport 71101.

Maine — Conrad K. Cyr, CJ; Gene Carter; Clerk's Office, Portland 04112.

Maryland — Alexander Harvey 2d, CJ; Joseph C. Howard, Norman P. Ramsey, William E. Black Jr., John R. Hargrove, J. Frederick Motz, Frederic N. Smalkin, Paul V. Niemeyer, Marvin J. Garbis; Clerk's Office, Baltimore 21201.

Massachusetts — Frank H. Freedman, CJ; Joseph L. Tauro, Walter Jay Skinner, A. David Mazzone, Robert E. Keeton, John J. McNaught, Rya W. Zobel, David S. Nelson, William G. Young, Mark L. Wolf, Douglas P. Woodlock, Edward F. Harrington; Clerk's Office, Boston 02109.

Michigan — Eastern: Julian A. Cook Jr., CJ; Stewart A. Newblatt, Avern Cohn, Anna Diggs Taylor, Horace W. Gilmore, George E. Woods, Richard F. Suhrheinrich, George La Plata, Barbara K. Hackett, Lawrence P. Zatkoff, Patrick J. Duggan, Bernard A. Friedman, Paul V. Gadola; Clerk's Office, Detroit 48226. **Western:** Douglas W. Hillman, CJ; Benjamin F. Gibson, Richard A. Enslen, Robert H. Bell; Clerk's Office, Grand Rapids 49503.

Minnesota — Donald D. Alsop, CJ; Harry H. MacLaughlin, Robert G. Renner, Diana E. Murphy, Paul A. Magnuson, James M. Rosenbaum, David S. Doty; Clerk's Office, St. Paul 55101.

Mississippi — Northern: L. T. Senter Jr., CJ; Neal Biggers, Glen H. Davidson; Clerk's Office, Oxford 38655. **Southern:** William H. Barbour Jr.; Harry T. Wingate, Tom S. Lee, Walter J. Gex 3d; Clerk's Office, Jackson 39201.

Missouri — Eastern: John F. Nangle, CJ; Edward D. Filippine; William L. Hungate, Clyde S. Cahill Jr., Stephen N. Limbaugh, George F. Gunn Jr.; Clerk's Office, St. Louis 63101. **Western:** Scott O. Wright, CJ; Russell G. Clark, Howard F. Sachs, Joseph E. Stevens Jr., D. Brook Bartlett, Dean Whipple; Clerk's Office, Kansas City 64106.

Montana — Paul G. Hatfield, CJ; Charles C. Lovell; Clerk's Office, Billings 59101.

Nebraska — Lyle E. Strom, CJ; Warren K. Urbom, William G. Cambridge; Clerk's Office, Omaha 68101.

Nevada — Edward C. Reed Jr., CJ; Lloyd D. George, Howard D. McKibben, Philip M. Pro; Clerk's Office, Las Vegas 89101.

New Hampshire — Shane Devine, CJ; Martin F. Loughlin; Clerk's Office, Concord 03301.

New Jersey — John F. Gerry, CJ; Stanley S. Brotman, Anne E. Thompson, D. R. Debevoise, H. Lee Sarokin, Harold A. Ackerman, John W. Bissell, Maryanne Trump Barry, Joseph H. Rodriguez, Garrett E. Brown Jr., Alfred J. Lechner Jr., Nicholas H. Politan, Alfred M. Wolin, John C. Lifland; Clerk's Office, Newark 07102.

New Mexico — Juan G. Burciaga, CJ; Santiago E. Campos, John E. Conway, James A. Parker; Clerk's Office, Albuquerque 87103.

New York — Northern: Neal P. McCurn, CJ; Howard G. Munson, Thomas J. McAvoy, Con G. Cholakis; Clerk's Office, Albany 12201. **Eastern:** Thomas C. Platt Jr., CJ; Jack B. Weinstein, Charles P. Sifton, Eugene H. Nickerson, Joseph M. McLaughlin, Israel Leo Glasser, Raymond J. Dearie, Leonard D. Wexler, Edward R. Korman, Reena Raggi; Clerk's Office, Brooklyn 11201. **Southern:** Charles L. Brieant, CJ; David N. Edelstein, Thomas P. Griesa, Robert J. Ward, Kevin Thomas Duffy, Leonard B. Sand, Mary Johnson Lowe, Gerard L. Goettel, Charles S. Haight Jr., Pierre N. Leval, Robert W. Sweet, John E. Sprizzo, Shirley Wohl Kram, John F. Keenan, Peter K. Leisure, John M. Walker, Louis L. Stanton, Miriam G. Cedarbaum, Michael B. Mukasey, Kenneth Conboy, Kimba Wood, Robert P. Patterson Jr.; Clerk's Office N. Y. City 10007. **Western:** Michael A. Telesca, CJ; Richard J. Arcara, David G. Larimer; Clerk's Office, Buffalo 14202.

North Carolina — Eastern: W. Earl Britt, CJ; James C. Fox, Terrence W. Boyle, Malcolm J. Howard; Clerk's Office, Raleigh 27611. **Middle:** Richard C. Erwin, CJ; Frank W. Bullock, N. Carlton Tilley Jr.; Clerk's Office, Greensboro 27402. **Western:** Robert D. Potter, CJ; Richard L. Woorhees; Clerk's Office Asheville 28801.

North Dakota — Patrick A. Conmy, CJ; Rodney S. Webb; Clerk's Office, Bismarck 58502.

Ohio — Northern: Thomas D. Lambros, CJ; Frank J. Battisti, John M. Manos, George W. White, Ann Aldrich, Alvin I. Krenzler, John W. Potter, David D. Dowd Jr., Sam H. Bell, Alice M. Batchelder; Clerk's Office, Cleveland 44114. **Southern:** John D. Holschuh, CJ; Carl B. Rubin, Walter H. Rice, S. Arthur Spiegel, Herman J. Weber, James L. Graham, George C. Smith; Clerk's Office, Columbus 43215.

Oklahoma — Northern: H. Dale Cook, CJ; James O. Ellison, Thomas R. Brett, Clerk's Office, Tulsa 74103. **Eastern:** Frank H. Shey, CJ; Clerk's Office, Muskogee 74401. **Western:** Ralph G. Thompson, CJ; Wayne Alley, Lee R. West, Layn R. Phillips; Clerk's Office, Oklahoma City 73102.

Oregon — Owen M. Panner, CJ; James A. Redden, Helen J. Frye, Malcolm F. Marsh; Clerk's Office, Portland 97205.

Pennsylvania — Eastern: Louis Charles Bechtle, CJ; Joseph L. McGlynn Jr., Edward N. Cahn, Louis H. Pollak, Norma L. Shapiro, James T. Giles, James McGirr Kelly, Thomas N. O'Neill Jr., Marvin Katz, Edmund V. Ludwig, Robert F. Kelly, Franklin S. Van Antwerpen, Robert S. Gawthrop, Lowell A. Reed Jr., Jan E. Dubois, Herbert J. Hutton; Clerk's Office, Philadelphia 19106. **Middle:** Richard P. Conaboy, CJ; Sylvia H. Rambo, William W. Caldwell, Edward M. Kosik; Clerk's Office Scranton 18501. **Western:** Maurice B. Cohill Jr., CJ; Paul A. Simmons, Gustave Diamond, Donald E. Ziegler, Alan N. Bloch, Glenn E. Mencer, William L. Standish, D. Brooks Smith, Donald J. Lee; Clerk's Office, Pittsburgh 15230.

Rhode Island — Francis J. Boyle, CJ; Ronald R. Lagueux, Ernest C. Torres; Clerk's Office, Providence 02903.

South Carolina — Solomon Blatt Jr., CJ; C. Weston Houck, Falcon B. Hawkins, Matthew J. Perry Jr., George R. Anderson Jr.; Clyde H. Hamilton, Karen L. Henderson, Joseph F. Anderson Jr.; Clerk's Office, Columbia 29202.

South Dakota — Donald J. Porter, CJ; Richard H. Battey, John Bailey Jones; Clerk's Office, Sioux Falls 57102.

Tennessee — Eastern: Thomas G. Hull, CJ; James H. Jarvis, R. Allan Edgar, Leon Jordan; Clerk's Office, Knoxville 37901. **Middle:** Thomas A. Wiseman Jr., CJ; Thomas A. Higgins, John T. Nixon; Clerk's Office, Nashville 37203. **Western:** Odell Horton, CJ; Julia S. Gibbons, James D. Todd, Jerome Turner; Clerk's Office, Memphis 38103.

Texas — Northern: Barefoot Sanders, CJ; Robert W. Porter, Mary Lou Robinson, David O. Belew Jr., Jerry Buchmeyer, A. Joe Fish, Robert B. Maloney, Sidney A. Fitzwater, Samuel R. Cummings; Clerk's Office, Dallas 75242. **Southern:** James De Anda, CJ; Norman W. Black, George P. Kazen, Filemon B. Vela, Hayden W. Head Jr., Ricardo H. Hinojosa, Lynn N. Hughes, David Hittner, Kenneth M. Hoyt, Simeon T. Lake 3d, Melinda Harmon; Clerk's Office, Houston 77208. **Eastern:** William Wayne Justice, CJ; Robert M. Parker, Howell Cobb, Sam B. Hall Jr., Paul N. Brown, Richard A. Schell; Clerk's Office, Tyler 75702. **Western:** Lucius D. Bunton 3d, CJ; Harry Lee Hudspeth, Hipolito F. Garcia, James R. Nowlin, Edward C. Prado, Walter S. Smith Jr., Emilio M. Garza; Clerk's Office, San Antonio 78206.

Utah — Bruce S. Jenkins, CJ; J. Thomas Greene, David Sam, David K. Winder; Clerk's Office, Salt Lake City 84101.

Vermont — Franklin S. Billings Jr., CJ; Clerk's Office, Burlington 05402.

Virginia — Eastern: Albert V. Bryan Jr., CJ; J. Calvitt Clarke, Richard L. Williams, James C. Cacheris, Robert G. Doumar, Claude M. Hilton, James R. Spencer, Thomas S. Ellis 3d, Rebecca Beach Smith; Clerk's Office, Alexandria 22320. **Western:** James C. Turk, CJ; James H. Michael Jr., Jackson L. Kiser; Clerk's Office, Roanoke 24006.

Washington — Eastern: Justin L. Quackenbush, CJ; Robert J. McNichols, Alan A. McDonald; Clerk's Office, Spokane 99210. **Western:** Barbara J. Rothstein, CJ; Jack E. Tanner, John C. Coughenour, Carolyn R. Dimmick, Robert J. Bryan, William L. Dwyer, Thomas Zilly; Clerk's Office, Seattle 98104.

West Virginia — Northern: Robert Earl Maxwell, CJ; Clerk's Office, Elkins 26241. **Southern:** Charles H. Haden 2d, CJ; Robert J. Staker, John T. Copenhaver Jr., Elizabeth V. Hallanan; Clerk's Office, Charleston 25329.

Wisconsin — Eastern: Robert W. Warren, CJ; Terence T. Evans, Thomas J. Curran, J.P. Stadtmueller; Clerk's Office, Milwaukee 53202. **Western:** Barbara B. Crabb, CJ; John C. Shabaz; Clerk's Office, Madison 53701.

Wyoming — Clarence A. Brimmer, CJ; Alan B. Johnson; Clerk's Office, Cheyenne 82001.

U.S. Territorial District Courts

Guam — Cristobal C. Duenas; Clerk's Office, Agana 96910.

Puerto Rico — Juan M. Perez-Gimenez, CJ; Gilberto Gierbolini, Carmen Consuelo Cerezo, Jaime Pieras Jr., Raymond L. Acosta, Hector M. Laffitte, Jose Antonio Fuste; Clerk's Office, San Juan 00904.

Virgin Islands — vacancy CJ; Clerk's Office, Charlotte Amalie, St. Thomas 00801.

U.S. Court of Veterans Appeals

(established by Congress in 1989)

State Officials, Salaries, Party Membership

Governors reflect results of Nov. 6, 1990 elections; other officials are as of mid-1990; † Ind. or other party.

Alabama

Governor — Guy Hunt, R., $70,222.
Lt. Gov. — Jim Folsom Jr., D., $40 per legislative day, plus annual salary of $1,900 per month plus $1,500 per month for expenses.
Sec. of State — Perry Hand, R., $36,234.
Atty. Gen. — Don Siegelman, D., $77,420.
Treasurer — George Wallace Jr., D., $49,500.
Legislature: meets annually the 3d Tuesday in Apr. (first year of term of office, first Tuesday in Feb. (2d and 3d years), 2d Tuesday in Jan. (4th year) at Montgomery. Members receive $10 a day salary, plus $1,900 per month expenses, plus $40 per day expenses during legislative sessions, and mileage of 10c per mile.
Senate — Dem., 27; Rep., 8. Total, 35.
House — Dem., 83; Rep., 22. Total, 105.

Alaska

Governor — Walter Hickel, † $81,648.
Lt. Gov. — Stephen McAlpine, D., $76,188.
Atty. General — Douglas Baily, D., $77,304.
Legislature: meets annually in January at Juneau, for 120 days with a 10-day extension possible upon ⅔ vote. First session in odd years. Members receive $22,140 per year plus $80 a day per diem.
Senate — Dem., 8; Rep., 12. Total, 20.
House — Dem., 24; Rep., 16. Total, 40.

Arizona

Governor — Fife Symington, R., $75,000.
Sec. of State — Jim Shumway, D., $50,000.
Atty. Gen. — Bob Corbin, R., $70,000.
Treasurer — Ray Rottas, R., $50,000.
Legislature: meets annually in January at Phoenix. Each member receives an annual salary of $15,000.
Senate — Dem., 13; Rep., 17. Total, 30.
House — Dem., 26; Rep., 34. Total, 60.

Arkansas

Governor — Bill Clinton, D., $35,000.
Lt. Gov. — Winston Bryant, D., $14,000.
Sec. of State — W. J. "Bill" McCuen, D., $22,500.
Atty. Gen. — Steve Clark, D., $26,500.
Treasurer — Jimmie Lou Fisher, D., $22,500.
General Assembly: meets odd years in January at Little Rock. Members receive $7,500 per year, $74 a day while in regular session, plus 21 cents a mile travel expense.
Senate — Dem., 31; Rep., 4. Total, 35.
House — Dem., 88; Rep. 11; 1 ind. Total, 100.

California

Governor — Pete Wilson, R., $102,079.
Lt. Gov. — Leo T. McCarthy, D., $87,068.
Sec. of State — March Fong Eu, D., $87,068.
Controller — Gray Davis, D., $87,068.
Atty. Gen. — John Van de Kamp, D., $93,073.
Legislature: meets at Sacramento; regular sessions commence on the first Monday in Dec. of every even-numbered year; each session lasts 2 years. Members receive $44,898 per year plus mileage and $65 per diem.
Senate — Dem., 24; Rep., 14, 1 ind., 1 vac.; Total, 40.
Assembly — Dem., 46; Rep., 33, 1 vac.; Total, 80.

Colorado

Governor — Roy Romer, D., $70,000.
Lt. Gov. — Mike Callihan, D., $48,500.
Secy. of State — Natalie Meyer, R., $48,500.
Atty. Gen. — Duane Woodard, D., $60,000.
Treasurer — Gail Schoettler, D., $48,500.
General Assembly: meets annually in January at Denver. Members receive $17,500 annually.
Senate — Dem., 11; Rep., 24. Total, 35.
House — Dem., 26; Rep., 39. Total, 65.

Connecticut

Governor — Lowell Weicker, † $78,000.
Lt. Gov. — Joseph J. Fauliso, D., $55,000.
Sec. of State — Julia H. Tashjian, D., $50,000.
Treasurer — Francisco Borges, D., $50,000.
Comptroller — J. Edward Caldwell, D., $50,000.
Atty. Gen. — Clarine Nardi Riddle, Act., $60,000.
General Assembly: meets annually odd years in January and even years in February at Hartford. Salary $15,200 per year plus $4,500 (senator), $3,500 (representative) per year for expenses, plus travel allowance.
Senate — Dem., 23; Rep., 13. Total, 36.
House — Dem., 86; Rep., 65. Total, 151.

Delaware

Governor — Michael N. Castle, R., $80,000.
Lt. Gov. — Dale E. Wolf, R., $35,000.
Sec. of State — Michael Harkins, R., $69,900.
Atty. Gen. — Charles Oberly 3d, D., $81,400.
Treasurer — Janet C. Rzewnicki, R., $63,000.
General Assembly: 55 day session beginning the 2d Tuesday in January until June 30. Members receive $23,000 base salary, plus $5,500 expense account.
Senate — Dem., 13; Rep., 8. Total, 21.
House — Dem., 18; Rep., 23. Total, 41.

Florida

Governor — Lawton Chiles, D., $100,883.
Lt. Gov. — Bobby Brantley, R., $91,301.
Sec. of State — Jim Smith, R., $91,301.
Comptroller — Gerald Lewis, D., $91,301.
Atty. Gen. — Robert Butterworth, D., $91,301.
Treasurer — Tim Gallagher, R., $81,967.
Legislature: meets annually at Tallahassee. Members receive $21,648 per year plus expense allowance while on official business.
Senate — Dem., 23; Rep., 17. Total, 40.
House — Dem., 72; Rep., 48. Total, 120.

Georgia

Governor — Zell Miller, D., $88,872.
Lt. Gov. — vacant, $56,293.
Sec. of State — Max Cleland, D., $71,186.
Insurance Comm. — Warren Evans, D., $71,174.
Atty. Gen. — Michael J. Bowers, $72,824.
General Assembly: meets annually at Atlanta. Members receive $10,000 per year, $59 per diem, and $4,800 expense reimbursement. During session $59 per day for expenses.
Senate — Dem., 45; Rep., 11. Total, 56.
House — Dem., 144; Rep., 36. Total, 180.

Hawaii

Governor — John Waihee, D., $80,000.
Lt. Gov. — Benjamin Cayetano, D., $76,000.
Atty. Gen. — Warren Price, $68,400.
Comptroller — Russel Nagata, $68,400.
Dir. of Budget & Finance — Yukio Takemoto, $68,400.
Legislature: meets annually on 3d Wednesday in January at Honolulu. Members receive $27,000 per year plus expenses.
Senate — Dem., 22. Rep., 3. Total, 25.
House — Dem., 45. Rep., 6. Total, 51.

Idaho

Governor — Cecil D. Andrus, D., $55,000.
Lt. Gov. — C. L. "Butch" Otter, R., $15,000.
Sec. of State — Pete T. Cenarrusa, R., $45,000.
Treasurer — Lydia Justice Edwards, R., $45,000.
Atty. Gen. — Jim Jones, R., $48,000.
Legislature: meets annually the Monday on or nearest the 9th of January at Boise. Members receive $30 per day during session, $15 per day when not in session, plus certain travel and living allowances.
Senate — Dem., 19; Rep., 23. Total, 42.
House — Dem., 20; Rep., 64. Total, 84.

Illinois

Governor — Jim Edgar, R., $93,266.
Lt. Gov. — George H. Ryan, R., $65,835.
Sec. of State — Jim Edgar, R., $82,294.
Comptroller — Roland W. Burris, D., $71,321.
Atty. Gen. — Neil F. Hartigan, D., $82,294.
Treasurer — Jerry Costentino, D., $71,321.
General Assembly: meets annually in January at Springfield. Members receive $35,661 per annum.
Senate — Dem., 31; Rep., 28. Total, 59.
House — Dem., 67; Rep., 51. Total, 118.

Indiana

Governor — Evan Bayh, D., $77,000 plus discretionary expenses.
Lt. Gov. — Frank O'Bannon, D., $64,000 plus discretionary expenses.
Sec. of State — Joseph Hogsett D., $46,000.
Atty. Gen. — Linley E. Pearson, R., $51,000.
Treasurer — Marjorie O'Laughlin, R., $46,000.
Auditor — Ann G. Devore, R., $46,000.
General Assembly: meets annually in January. Members receive $11,600 per year plus $75 per day while in session, $15 per day while not in session.
Senate — Dem., 24; Rep., 26. Total, 50.
House — Dem., 50; Rep., 50. Total, 100.

Iowa

Governor — Terry E. Branstad, R., $72,500.
Lt. Gov. — Jo Ann Zimmerman, D., $25,100.
Sec. of State — Elaine Baxter, D., $55,700.
Atty. Gen. — Tom Miller, D., $69,700.
Treasurer — Michael L. Fitzgerald, D., $55,700.
Auditor — Richard D. Johnson, R., $55,700.
Secy. of Agriculture — Dale M. Cochran, D., $53,000.
General Assembly: meets annually in January at Des Moines. Members receive $16,600 annually plus maximum expense allowance of $40 per day for first 110 days of first session, and first 100 days of 2d session; mileage expenses at 21c a mile.
Senate — Dem., 30; Rep., 20. Total, 50.
House — Dem., 61; Rep., 39. Total, 100.

Kansas

Governor — Joan Finney, D., $73,138.
Lt. Gov. — Jack Walker, R., $20,688.
Sec. of State — Bill Graves, R., $56,400.
Atty. Gen. — Robert T. Stephan, R., $65,345.
Treasurer — Joan Finney, D., $56,816.
Legislature: meets annually in January at Topeka. Members receive $59 a day plus $69 a day expenses while in session, plus $600 per month while not in session.
Senate — Dem., 18; Rep., 22. Total, 40.
House — Dem., 57; Rep., 68. Total, 125.

Kentucky

Governor — Wallace G. Wilkinson, D., $69,730.
Lt. Gov. — Brereton Jones, D., $59,262.
Sec. of State — Bremer Ehrler, D., $59,262.
Atty. Gen. — Fred Cowan, D., $59,262.
Treasurer — Robert Meade, D., $59,262.
Auditor — Bob Babbage, D., $59,262.
General Assembly: meets even years in January at Frankfort. Members receive $100 per day and $100 per day during session and $950 per month for expenses for interim.
Senate — Dem., 30; Rep., 8. Total, 38.
House — Dem., 71; Rep., 29. Total, 100.

Louisiana

Governor — Charles "Buddy" Roemer, D., $73,440.
Lt. Gov. — Paul Hardy, R., $63,367.
Sec. of State — Fox McKeithen, D., $60,169.
Atty. Gen. — William J. Guste Jr., D., $60,169.
Treasurer — Mary Landrieu, D., $60,169.
Legislature: meets annually for 60 legislative days commencing on 3d Monday in April. Members receive $75 per day and mileage plus annual salary of $16,800.
Senate — Dem., 33; Rep., 6. Total, 39.
House — Dem., 87; Rep., 18. Total, 105.

Maine

Governor — John R. McKernan Jr., R., $70,000.
Sec. of State — G. William Diamond D., $37,523.
Atty. Gen. — James Tierney, D., $58,073.
Treasurer — Samuel Shapiro, D., $50,044.
Legislature: meets annually in December at Augusta. Members receive $9,000 for first regular sessions, $6,000 for second regular session plus expenses; presiding officers receive 50% more.
Senate — Dem., 20; Rep., 15. Total, 35.
House — Dem., 97; Rep., 54. Total, 151.

Maryland

Governor — William Donald Schaefer, D., $85,000.
Lt. Gov. — Melvin Steinberg, D., $72,500.
Comptroller — Louis L. Goldstein, D., $72,500.
Atty. Gen. — J. Joseph Curran Jr., D., $72,500.
Sec. of State — Winfield M. Kelly Jr., D., $45,000.
Treasurer — Lucille Maurer, D., $72,500.
General Assembly: meets 90 consecutive days annually beginning on the 2d Wednesday in January at Annapolis. Members receive $25,000 per year plus expenses.
Senate — Dem., 40; Rep., 7. Total, 47.
House — Dem., 125; Rep., 16. Total, 141.

Massachusetts

Governor — William Weld, R., $75,000.
Lt. Gov. — Evelyn Murphy, $60,000.
Sec. of State — Michael Joseph Connolly, D., $60,000.
Atty. Gen. — James M. Shannon, D., $65,000.
Treasurer — Robert Q. Crane, D., $60,000.
Auditor — A. Joseph DeNucci, D., $60,000.
General Court (Legislature): meets each January in Boston. Salaries $30,000 per annum.
Senate — Dem., 32; Rep., 8. Total, 40.
House — Dem., 129; Rep., 31. Total, 160.

Michigan

Governor — John Engler, R., $100,100.
Lt. Gov. — Martha W. Griffiths, D., $67,400.
Sec. of State — Richard H. Austin, D., $89,000.
Atty. Gen. — Frank J. Kelley, D., $89,000.
Treasurer — Robert A. Bowman, N-P, $80,300.
Legislature: meets annually in January at Lansing. Members receive $42,670 per year, plus $8,100 expense allowance.
Senate — Dem., 18; Rep. 20. Total, 38.
House — Dem., 61; Rep., 49. Total, 110.

Minnesota

Governor — Arne Carlson, R., $103,860.
Lt. Gov. — Marlene Johnson, DFL, $57,125.
Sec. of State — Joan Anderson Growe, DFL, $57,125.
Atty. Gen. — Hubert H. Humphrey 3d, DFL, $81,138.
Treasurer — Michael McGrath, DFL, $54,042.
Auditor — Arnie Carlson, IR, $62,320.
Legislature: meets for a total of 120 days within every 2 years at St. Paul. Members receive $26,395 per year, plus expense allowance during session.
Senate — DFL., 44; IR, 23. Total, 67.
House — DFL., 80; IR, 54. Total, 134.
(DFL means Democratic-Farmer-Labor. IR means Independent Republican.)

Mississippi

Governor — Ray Mabus, D., $63,000.
Lt. Gov. — Brad Dye, D., $40,800.
Sec. of State — Dick Molpus, D., $54,000.
Atty. Gen. — Mike Moore, D., $61,200.
Treasurer — Marshall Bennett, D., $54,000.
Legislature: meets annually in January at Jackson. Members receive $10,100 per regular session plus travel allowance, and $500 per month while not in session.
Senate — Dem., 45; Rep., 7. Total, 52.
House — Dem., 115; Rep., 7. Total, 122.

Missouri

Governor — John D. Ashcroft, R., $88,851.
Lt. Gov. — Mel Carnahan, D., $53,277.
Sec. of State — Roy D. Blunt, R., $70,909.
Atty. Gen. — William L. Webster, R., $76,786.
Treasurer — Wendell Bailey, R., $70,909.
State Auditor — Margaret Kelly, R., $70,909.
General Assembly: meets annually in Jefferson City on the first Wednesday after first Monday in January. Members receive $22,414 annually.
Senate — Dem., 22; Rep., 12. Total, 34.
House — Dem., 104; Rep., 59. Total, 163.

Montana

Governor — Stan Stephens, R., $50,452.
Lt. Gov. — Alan Kolstad, R., $36,141.
Sec. of State — Mike Cooney, D., $33,342.
Atty. Gen. — Marc Racicot, R., $46,016.
Legislative Assembly: meets odd years in January at Helena. Members receive $59.12 per legislative day plus $50 per day for expenses while in session.
Senate — Dem., 27; Rep., 23. Total, 50.
House — Dem., 52; Rep., 48. Total, 100.

Nebraska

Governor — Ben Nelson, D., $58,000.
Lt. Gov. — William Nichol, R., $40,000.
Sec. of State — Allen J. Beermann, R., $40,000.
Atty. Gen. — Robert Spire, R., $57,500.
Treasurer — Frank Marsh, R., $35,000.
Legislature: meets annually in January at Lincoln. Members receive salary of $12,000 annually plus travelling expenses.
Unicameral body composed of 49 members who are elected on a nonpartisan ballot and are classed as senators.

Nevada

Governor — Robert Miller, D., $77,500.
Lt. Gov. — vacant, $12,500.
Sec. of State — Frankie Sue Del Papa, D., $50,500.
Comptroller — Darrel Daines, R., $49,000.
Atty. Gen. — Brian McKay, R., $62,500.
Treasurer — Ken Santor, R., $49,000.
Legislature: meets odd years in January at Carson City. Members receive $130 per day for 60 days (20 days for special sessions).
Senate — Dem., 8; Rep., 13. Total, 21.
Assembly — Rep., 12; Dem., 30. Total, 42.

New Hampshire

Governor — Judd Gregg, R., $72,146.
Sec. of State — William M. Gardner, D., $50,675.
Atty. Gen. — Stephen E. Merrill, $58,940.
Treasurer — Georgie A. Thomas, R., $50,675.
General Court (Legislature): meets ev.. y year in January at Concord. Members receive $200; presiding officers $250.
Senate — Dem., 8; Rep., 16. Total, 24.
House — Rep., 281; Dem., 119. Total, 400.

New Jersey

Governor — James J. Florio, D., $85,000.
Sec. of State — Joan Haberle, D., $95,000.
Atty. Gen. — Robert J. Del Tuso, D., $95,000.
Treasurer — Douglas C. Berman, D., $95,000.
Legislature: meets throughout the year at Trenton. Members receive $25,000 per year, except president of Senate and speaker of Assembly who receive 1/3 more.
Senate — Dem., 23; Rep., 17. Total, 40.
Assembly — Dem., 43; Rep. 36, 1 vacancy; Total, 80.

New Mexico

Governor — Bruce King, D., $90,000.
Lt. Gov. — Jack Stahl, R., $65,000.
Sec. of State — Rebecca Vigil-Giron, D., $65,000.
Atty. Gen. — Hal Stratton, R., $72,500.
Treasurer — James Lewis, D., $65,000.
Legislature: meets on the 3d Tuesday in January at Santa Fe; odd years for 60 days, even years for 30 days. Members receive $75 per day while in session.
Senate — Dem., 26; Rep., 16. Total, 42.
House — Dem., 45; Rep., 25. Total, 70.

New York

Governor — Mario M. Cuomo, D., $130,000.
Lt. Gov. — Stan Lundine, D., $95,000.
Sec. of State — Gail S. Shaffer, D., $87,338.
Comptroller — Edward V. Regan, R., $110,000.
Atty. Gen. — Robert Abrams, D., $110,000.
Legislature: meets annually in January at Albany. Members receive $57,500 per year.

Senate — Dem., 27; Rep., 34. Total, 61.
Assembly — Dem., 93; Rep., 57. Total, 150.

North Carolina

Governor — James G. Martin, R., $109,728 plus $11,500 per year expenses.
Lt. Gov. — James C. Gardner, R., $66,972 per year, plus $11,500 per year expense allowance.
Sec. of State — Rufus L. Edmisten, D., $66,972.
Atty. Gen. — Lacy Thornberg, D., $66,972.
Treasurer — Harlan E. Boyles, D., $66,972.
General Assembly: meets odd years in January at Raleigh. Members receive $11,124 annual salary and $5,500 annual expense allowance, plus $81 per diem subsistence and travel allowance while in session.
Senate — Dem., 37; Rep., 13. Total, 50.
House — Dem., 74; Rep., 46. Total, 120.

North Dakota

Governor — George A. Sinner, D., $65,200.
Lt. Gov. — Lloyd B. Omdahl, D., $53,500.
Sec. of State — Jim Kusler, D., $49,300.
Atty. Gen. — Nicholas Spaeth, D., $55,700.
Treasurer — Robert Hanson, D., $49,300.
Legislative Assembly: meets odd years in January at Bismarck. Members receive $90 per day expenses during session and $180 per month when not in session.
Senate — Dem., 32; Rep., 21. Total, 53.
House — Dem., 45; Rep., 61. Total, 106.

Ohio

Governor — George Voinovich, R., $65,000.
Lt. Gov. — Paul R. Leonard, $44,903.
Sec. of State — Sherrod Brown, D., $67,005.
Atty. Gen. — Anthony J. Celebrezze Jr., D., $67,005.
Treasurer — Mary Ellen Withrow, D., $67,005.
Auditor — Thomas E. Ferguson, D., $67,005.
General Assembly: meets odd years at Columbus on first Monday in January; no limit on session. Members receive $34,905 per annum.
Senate — Dem., 14; Rep., 19. Total, 33.
House — Dem., 59; Rep., 40. Total, 99.

Oklahoma

Governor — David Walters, D., $70,000.
Lt. Gov. — Robert S. Kerr 3d, D., $40,000.
Sec. of State — Hannah Diggs Atkins, D., $37,500.
Atty. Gen. — Robert H. Henry, D., $55,000.
Treasurer — Ellis Edwards, D., $50,000.
Legislature: meets annually in January at Oklahoma City. Members receive $32,000 annually.
Senate — Dem., 33; Rep., 15. Total, 48.
House — Dem., 69; Rep., 32. Total, 101.

Oregon

Governor — Barbara Roberts, D., $80,000, plus $500 monthly expenses.
Sec. of State — Barbara Roberts, D., $61,500.
Atty. Gen. — David B. Frohnmayer, R., $66,000.
Treasurer — Tony Meeker, R., $61,500.
Legislative Assembly: meets odd years in January at Salem. Members receive $989 monthly and $66 expenses per day both during & out of session.
Senate — Dem., 19; Rep., 11. Total, 30.
House — Dem., 32; Rep., 28. Total, 60.

Pennsylvania

Governor — Robert Casey, D., $85,000.
Lt. Gov. — Mark S. Singel, D., $67,500.
Sec. of the Commonwealth — James J. Haggerty, D., $58,000.
Atty. Gen. — Ernest R. Preate, R., $84,000.
Treasurer — Catherine Baker Knoll, D., $84,000.
General Assembly — convenes annually in January at Harrisburg. Members receive $35,000 per year plus expenses.
Senate — Dem., 23; Rep., 27. Total, 50.
House — Dem., 103; Rep., 99; 1 vacancy. Total, 203.

Rhode Island

Governor — Bruce Sundlun, D., $69,000.
Lt. Gov. — Roger N. Begin, D., $52,000.
Sec. of State — Kathleen S. Connell, D., $52,000.
Atty. Gen. — James E. O'Neil, D., $55,000.
Treasurer — Anthony J. Solomon, D., $52,000.
General Assembly: meets annually in January at Providence. Members receive $5 per day for 60 days, and travel allowance of 8c per mile.
Senate — Dem., 41; Rep., 9. Total, 50.
House — Dem., 83; Rep., 17. Total, 100.

South Carolina

Governor — Carroll A. Campbell Jr., R., $83,232.
Lt. Gov. — Nick Theodore, D., $36,414.
Sec. of State — John T. Campbell, D., $70,447.
Comptroller Gen. — Earle E. Morris Jr., D., $70,447.
Atty. Gen. — T.T. Medlock, D., $70,447.
Treasurer — G.L. Patterson Jr., D., $70,447.
General Assembly: meets annually in January at Columbia.
Members receive $10,000 per year and expense allowance of $74
per day, plus travel and postage allowance.
Senate — Dem., 35; Rep., 11. Total, 46.
House — Dem. 83; Rep., 40; 1 vacancy. Total, 124.

South Dakota

Governor — George S. Mickelson, R., $60,819.
Lt. Gov. — Walter Miller, R., $52,915.
Sec. of State — Joyce Hazeltine, R., $41,308.
Treasurer — David Volk, R., $41,308.
Atty. Gen. — Roger Tellinghuisen, R., $51,625.
Auditor — Vernon Larson, R., $41,308.
Legislature: meets annually in January at Pierre. Members receive $4,267 for 40-day session in odd-numbered years, and $3,733 for 35-day session in even-numbered years, plus $75 per legislative day.
Senate — Dem., 15; Rep., 20. Total, 35.
House — Dem., 24. Rep., 46. Total, 70.

Tennessee

Governor — Ned Ray McWherter, D., $85,000.
Lt. Gov. — John S. Wilder, D., $49,500.
Sec. of State — Bryant Millsaps, D., $65,500.
Comptroller — William Snodgrass, D., $65,000.
Atty. Gen. — Charles W. Burson, D., $65,650.
General Assembly: meets annually in January at Nashville.
Members receive $16,500 yearly plus $78.00 per diem plus office expenses.
Senate — Dem., 22; Rep., 11. Total, 33.
House — Dem., 58; Rep., 41. Total, 99.

Texas

Governor — Ann Richards, D., $93,342.
Lt. Gov. — Bill Hobby, D., $7,200.
Sec. of State — George S. Bayoud Jr., R., $64,890.
Comptroller — Bob Bullock, D., $74,698.
Atty. Gen. — Jim Mattox, D., $74,698.
Treasurer — Ann W. Richards, D., $74,698.
Legislature: meets odd years in January at Austin. Members receive annual salary not exceeding $7,200, per diem while in session, and travel allowance.
Senate — Dem., 23; Rep., 8. Total, 31.
House — Dem., 93; Rep., 57. Total, 150.

Utah

Governor — Norman Bangerter, R., $70,000.
Lt. Gov. — W. Val Oveson, R., $52,500.
Atty. Gen. — R. Paul Van Dam, R., $56,000.
Treasurer — Edward T. Alter, D., $53,000.
Legislature: convenes for 45 days on 2d Monday in January each year; members receive $25 per day, $15 daily expenses, and mileage.
Senate — Dem., 7; Rep., 22. Total, 29.
House — Dem., 28; Rep., 47. Total, 75.

Vermont

Governor — Peter Snelling, R., $75,800.
Lt. Gov. — Howard Dean, D., $31,600.
Sec. of State — James H. Douglas, R., $47,700.
Atty. Gen. — Jeffrey Amestoy, R., $57,300.
Treasurer — Paul W. Ruse Jr., D., $47,700.
Auditor of Accounts — Alexander V. Acebo, R., $47,700.
General Assembly: meets odd years in January at Montpelier.
Members receive $6,750 plus $90 per day for special session, plus specified expenses.
Senate — Dem., 16; Rep., 14. Total, 30.
House — Dem., 75; Rep., 75. Total, 150.

Virginia

Governor — L. Douglas Wilder, D., $85,000.
Lt. Gov. — Donald S. Beyer Jr., $28,000.
Atty. Gen. — Mary Sue Terry, D., $75,000.
Sec. of the Commonwealth — Pamela Womack, D., $53,085.
Treasurer — Eddie N. Moore Jr., $65,000.
General Assembly: meets annually in January at Richmond.
Members receive $18,000 annually plus expense and mileage allowances.
Senate — Dem., 30; Rep., 10. Total, 40.
House — Dem., 59; Rep., 39; Ind., 2. Total, 100.

Washington

Governor — Booth Gardner, D., $96,700.
Lt. Gov. — Joel Pritchard, D., $51,100.
Sec. of State — Ralph Munro, R., $52,600.
Atty. Gen. — Ken Eikenberry, R., $75,700.
Treasurer — Daniel K. Grimm, D., $65,000.
Legislature: meets annually in January at Olympia. Members
receive $17,900 annually plus per diem of $66 per diem and 24¢ per
mile while in session, and $66 per diem for attending meetings during interim.
Senate — Dem., 24; Rep., 25. Total, 49.
House — Dem., 63; Rep., 35. Total, 98.

West Virginia

Governor — Gaston Caperton, D., $72,000.
Sec. of State — Ken Hechler, D., $43,200.
Atty. Gen. — Roger W. Tompkins, D., $50,400.
Treasurer — Tom Loehr, D., $50,400.
Comm. of Agric. — Cleve Benedict, R., $46,800.
Auditor — Glen B. Gainer Jr., D., $46,800.
Legislature: meets annually in January at Charleston. Members
receive $6,500.
Senate — Dem., 29; Rep., 5. Total, 34.
House — Dem., 79; Rep., 21. Total, 100.

Wisconsin

Governor — Tommy G. Thompson, R., $86,149.
Lt. Gov. — Scott McCallum, R., $46,360.
Sec. of State — Douglas La Follette, D., $42,089.
Treasurer — Charles P. Smith, D., $42,089.
Atty. Gen. — Donald Hanaway, R., $73,930.
Superintendent of Public Instruction — Herbert J. Grover, $66,536.
Legislature: meets in January at Madison. Members receive
$31,236 annually plus $55 per day expenses.
Senate — Dem., 19; Rep., 14. Total, 33.
Assembly — Dem., 55; Rep., 42.; 2 vacancies. Total, 99.

Wyoming

Governor — Mike Sullivan, D., $70,000.
Sec. of State — Kathy Karpan, D., $52,500.
Atty. Gen. — Joseph Meyer, $52,500.
Treasurer — Stan Smith, R., $52,500.
Auditor — Jack Sidi, R., $52,500.
Legislature: meets odd years in January, even years in February,
at Cheyenne. Members receive $75 per day while in session, plus
$60 per day for expenses.
Senate — Dem., 11; Rep., 19. Total, 30.
House — Dem., 23; Rep. 41. Total, 64.

Puerto Rico

Governor — Rafael Hernández-Colón.
Secretary of State — Antonio J. Colorado-Laguna.
Secy. of Justice — Héctor Rivera-Cruz.
These officials belong to the Popular Democratic Party.
Legislature: composed of a Senate of 27 members and a House
of Representatives of 53 members. Majority of the members of
both chambers belongs to the Popular Democratic Party. They
meet annually on the 2d Monday in January at San Juan.

U.S. Government Independent Agencies

Source: National Archives & Records Administration

Address: Washington, DC. Location and ZIP codes of agencies in parentheses; as of mid-1990.

ACTION — Jane A. Kenny, dir. (1100 Vermont Ave., NW, 20525).
Administrative Conference of the United States — Marshall J. Breger, chmn. (2120 L St. NW, 20037).

African Development Foundation — Leonard H. Robinson Jr., pres. (1625 Massachusetts Ave. NW, 20036).

(continued)

American Battle Monuments Commission — Gen. Andrew J. Goodpaster, chmn. (2020 Massachusetts Ave. NW, 20314).

Appalachian Regional Commission — Winifred A. Pizzano, federal co-chmn.; Gov. Carroll A. Campbell Jr. of South Carolina, states' co-chmn. (1666 Connecticut Ave. NW, 20235).

Board for International Broadcasting — Malcolm S. Forbes Jr., chmn. (1201 Connecticut Ave. NW. 20036).

Central Intelligence Agency — William H. Webster, dir. (Wash., DC 20505).

Commission of Fine Arts — J. Carter Brown, chmn. (708 Jackson Pl. NW, 20006).

Commission on Civil Rights — Arthur A. Fletcher, chmn. (1121 Vermont Ave. NW, 20425).

Commodity Futures Trading Commission — Wendy L. Gramm, chmn. (2033 K St. NW, 20581).

Consumer Product Safety Commission — Jacquline Jones-Smith, chmn. (5401 Westbard Ave., Bethesda, MD 20207).

Environmental Protection Agency — William K. Reilly, adm. (401 M St., SW, 20460).

Equal Employment Opportunity Commission — Evan J. Kemp, Jr., chmn. (1801 L St. NW., 20507).

Export-Import Bank of the United States — John D. Macomber, pres. and chmn. (811 Vermont Ave. NW 20571).

Farm Credit Administration — Harold B. Steele, chmn., Federal Farm Credit Board (1501 Farm Credit Drive, McLean, VA 22102).

Federal Communications Commission — Alfred C. Sikes, chmn. (1919 M St. NW, 20554).

Federal Deposit Insurance Corporation — L. William Seidman, chmn. (550 17th St. NW, 20429).

Federal Election Commission — Lee Ann Elliott, chmn. (999 E. St. NW, 20463).

Federal Emergency Management Agency — Robert H. Morris, act. dir. (500 C St. SW, 20472).

Federal Housing Finance Board — Jack Kemp, act. chmn. (777 F St. NW., 20006).

Federal Labor Relations Authority — Jean McKee, chmn. (500 C St. SW, 20424).

Federal Maritime Commission — James J. Carey, act. chmn. (1100 L St. NW 20573).

Federal Mediation and Conciliation Service — Bernard E. DeLury, dir. (2100 K St. NW, 20427).

Federal Reserve System — Chairman, board of governors: Alan Greenspan. (20th St. & Constitution Ave. NW, 20551).

Federal Trade Commission — Janet D. Steiger, chmn. (Pennsylvania Ave. at 6th St. NW, 20580).

General Accounting Office — Comptroller General of the U.S.; Charles A. Bowsher (441 G St. NW, 20548).

General Services Administration — Richard G. Austin, act. adm. (18th & F Sts. NW, 20405).

Government Printing Office — Public printer: Robert W. Houk. (North Capitol and H Sts. NW, 20401).

Inter-American Foundation — Victor Blanco, chmn. (1515 Wilson Blvd., Rosslyn, VA 22209).

Interstate Commerce Commission — Edward J. Philbin, chmn. (12th St. & Constitution Ave. NW, 20423).

Library of Congress — James H. Billington, librarian

(101 Independence Ave. SE, 20540).

Merit Systems Protection Board — Daniel R. Levinson, chmn. (1120 Vermont Ave. NW, 20419).

National Aeronautics and Space Administration — Richard H. Truly, adm. (600 Independence Ave., SW 20546).

National Archives & Records Administration — Don W. Wilson archivist (7th & Pennsylvania Ave. NW, 20408)

National Credit Union Administration — Roger W Jepsen, chmn. (1776 G St. NW, 20456).

National Foundation on the Arts and the Humanities — John E. Frohnmayer, (arts) 1100 Pennsylvania Ave. NW, 20506; Lynne V. Cheney, chmn. (humanities), same address. Institute of Museum Services: Daphne W. Murray, dir., same address.

National Labor Relations Board — James M. Stephens, chmn. (1717 Pennsylvania Ave. NW, 20570).

National Mediation Board — Joshua M. Javits, chmn (1425 K St. NW, 20572).

National Science Foundation — Mary L. Good, chmn., National Science Board (1800 G St. NW, 20550).

National Transportation Safety Board — James L. Kolstad, chmn. (800 Independence Ave. SW, 20594).

Nuclear Regulatory Commission — Kenneth M. Carr, chmn. (1717 H St. NW, 20555).

Occupational Safety and Health Review Commission — Edwin G. Foulke Jr., chmn. (1825 K St. NW, 20006).

Office of Personnel Management — Constance B. Newman, dir., (1900 E St. NW, 20415).

Peace Corps — Paul D. Coverdell, dir. (1990 K St. NW, 20526).

Postal Rate Commission — George W. Haley, chmn. (1333 H. St. NW, 20268-0001).

Railroad Retirement Board — Glen L. Bower, chmn. (2000 L. St. NW, 20036), Main Office (844 Rush St., Chicago, IL 60611).

Securities and Exchange Commission — Richard C. Breeden, chmn. (450 5th St. NW, 20549).

Selective Service System — Samuel K. Lessey Jr., dir. (1023 31st St. NW, 20435).

Small Business Administration — Susan S. Engeleiter, adm. (1441 L St. NW, 20416).

Smithsonian Institution — Robert McC. Adams, secy. (1000 Jefferson Dr. SW, 20560).

Tennessee Valley Authority — Chairman, board of directors: Marvin Runyon. (400 W. Summit Hill Dr., Knoxville, TN 37902 and Capitol Hill Office Bldg., Room 300, 412 1st St. SE, Washington, DC 20444).

United States Arms Control & Disarmament Agency — Ronald F. Lehman 2d, dir. (320 21st St. NW 20451).

United States Information Agency — Bruce S. Gelb, dir. (301 4th St. SW, 20547).

United States International Development Cooperation Agency — Mark Edelman, act. dir. (320 21st St. NW 20523).

United States International Trade Commission — Anne E. Brunsdale, chmn. (500 E St. NW, 20436).

United States Postal Service — Anthony M. Frank, postmaster general (475 L'Enfant Plaza West SW, 20260).

Governors of States and Possessions

(Reflecting Preliminary Results of Nov. 6, 1990 Elections)

State	Capital	Governor	Party	Term years	Term expires	Annual salary
Alabama	Montgomery	Guy Hunt	Rep.	4	Jan. 1995	$70,222
Alaska	Juneau	Walter Hickel	Ind.	4	Dec. 1994	81,648
Arizona	Phoenix	Fife Symington	Rep.	4	Jan. 1995	75,000
Arkansas	Little Rock	Bill Clinton	Dem.	4	Jan. 1995	35,000
California	Sacramento	Pete Wilson	Rep.	4	Jan. 1995	102,079
Colorado	Denver	Roy Romer	Dem.	4	Jan. 1995	70,000
Connecticut	Hartford	Lowell Weicker	Ind.	4	Jan. 1995	78,000
Delaware	Dover	Michael N. Castle	Rep.	4	Jan. 1993	80,000
Florida	Tallahassee	Lawton Chiles	Dem.	4	Jan. 1995	100,883
Georgia	Atlanta	Zell Miller	Dem.	4	Jan. 1995	88,872
Hawaii	Honolulu	John Waihee	Dem.	4	Dec. 1994	80,000
Idaho	Boise	Cecil D. Andrus	Dem.	4	Jan. 1995	55,000

(continued)

State	Capital	Governor	Party	Term years	Term expires	Annual salary
Illinois	Springfield	Jim Edgar	Rep.	4	Jan. 1995	93,266
Indiana	Indianapolis	Evan Bayh	Dem.	4	Jan. 1993	77,000
Iowa	Des Moines	Terry E. Branstad	Rep.	4	Jan. 1995	72,500
Kansas	Topeka	Joan Finney	Dem.	4	Jan. 1995	73,138
Kentucky	Frankfort	Wallace G. Wilkinson	Dem.	4	Dec. 1991	69,730
Louisiana	Baton Rouge	Charles "Buddy" Roemer	Dem.	4	May 1992	73,440
Maine	Augusta	John McKernan Jr.	Rep.	4	Jan. 1995	70,000
Maryland	Annapolis	William Donald Schaefer	Dem.	4	Jan. 1995	85,000
Massachusetts	Boston	William Weld	Rep.	4	Jan. 1995	75,000
Michigan	Lansing	John Engler	Rep.	4	Jan. 1995	100,100
Minnesota	St. Paul	Arne Carlson	Rep.	4	Jan. 1995	103,860
Mississippi	Jackson	Ray Mabus	Dem.	4	Jan. 1992	63,000
Missouri	Jefferson City	John D. Ashcroft	Rep.	4	Jan. 1993	88,851
Montana	Helena	Stan Stephens	Rep.	4	Jan. 1993	50,452
Nebraska	Lincoln	Ben Nelson	Dem.	4	Jan. 1995	58,000
Nevada	Carson City	Robert Miller	Dem.	4	Jan. 1995	77,500
New Hampshire	Concord	Judd Gregg	Rep.	2	Jan. 1993	72,146
New Jersey	Trenton	James Florio	Dem.	4	Jan. 1994	85,000
New Mexico	Santa Fe	Bruce King	Dem.	4	Jan. 1995	90,000
New York	Albany	Mario M. Cuomo	Dem.	4	Jan. 1995	130,000
North Carolina	Raleigh	James G. Martin	Rep.	4	Jan. 1993	109,728
North Dakota	Bismarck	George A. Sinner	Dem.	4	Jan. 1993	65,200
Ohio	Columbus	George Voinovich	Rep.	4	Jan. 1995	65,000
Oklahoma	Oklahoma City	David Walters	Dem.	4	Jan. 1995	70,000
Oregon	Salem	Barbara Roberts	Dem.	4	Jan. 1995	80,000
Pennsylvania	Harrisburg	Robert Casey	Dem.	4	Jan. 1995	85,000
Rhode Island	Providence	Bruce Sundlun	Dem.	2	Jan. 1993	69,000
South Carolina	Columbia	Carroll A. Campbell Jr.	Rep.	4	Jan. 1995	83,232
South Dakota	Pierre	George S. Mickelson	Rep.	4	Jan. 1995	60,819
Tennessee	Nashville	Ned Ray McWherter	Dem.	4	Jan. 1995	85,000
Texas	Austin	Ann Richards	Dem.	4	Jan. 1995	93,342
Utah	Salt Lake City	Norman Bangerter	Rep.	4	Jan. 1993	70,000
Vermont	Montpelier	Peter Snelling	Rep.	2	Jan. 1993	78,800
Virginia	Richmond	L. Douglas Wilder	Dem.	4	Jan. 1994	85,000
Washington	Olympia	Booth Gardner	Dem.	4	Jan. 1993	96,700
West Virginia	Charleston	Gaston Caperton	Dem.	4	Jan. 1993	72,000
Wisconsin	Madison	Tommy G. Thompson	Rep.	4	Jan. 1995	86,149
Wyoming	Cheyenne	Mike Sullivan	Dem.	4	Jan. 1995	70,000
Amer. Samoa	Pago Pago	Peter T. Coleman	Rep.	4	Jan. 1993	—
Guam	Agana	Joseph Ada	Dem.	4	Jan. 1991	—
Puerto Rico	San Juan	Rafael Hernandez Colón	P.D.	4	Jan. 1993	—
Virgin Islands	Charlotte Amalie	Alexander Farreley	Dem.	4	Jan. 1991	—

The Race for Governor: 1990
Source: News Election Service (preliminary returns)
(bold face denotes winner)

State	Republican	Vote	Democrat	Vote
Alabama	**Guy Hunt***	**629,554**	Paul R. Hubbert	583,444
Alaska	Arliss Sturgelwski (R) 44,156	**Walter Hickel (I)** **63,558** Tony Knowles (D)	**50,775**		
Arizona	**Fife Symington**	**519,558**	Terry Goddard	515,999
Arkansas	Sheffield Nelson	285,324	**Bill Clinton***	**380,924**
California	**Pete Wilson**	**3,435,145**	Dianne Feinstein	3,256,858
Colorado	John Andrews	362,670	**Roy Romer***	**624,775**
Connecticut	John G. Rowland (R) 426,448	**Lowell Weicker (I)** **459,818** Bruce Morrison (D)	**232,901**		
Florida	Bob Martinez*	1,487,302	**Lawton Chiles**	**1,938,174**
Georgia	Johnny Isakson	638,573	**Zell Miller**	**758,664**
Hawaii	Fred Hemmings	131,310	**John Waihee***	**203,491**
Idaho	Roger Fairchild	96,069	**Cecil Andrus***	**199,467**
Illinois	**Jim Edgar**	**1,633,706**	Neil Hartigan	1,536,711
Iowa	**Terry Branstad***	**583,897**	Donald Avenson	375,839
Kansas	Mike Hayden*	332,351	**Joan Finney**	**379,974**
Maine	**John McKernan Jr.***	**235,736**	Joseph Brennan	222,519
Maryland	William Shepard	435,361	**William Donald Schaefer***	**644,528**
Massachusetts	**William Weld**	**1,056,971**	John Silber	993,159
Michigan	**John Engler**	**1,253,525**	James J. Blanchard*	1,240,702
Minnesota	**Arne Carlson**	**753,265**	Rudy Perpich*	732,866
Nebraska	Kay Orr*	281,827	**Ben Nelson**	**286,608**
Nevada	Jim Gallaway	95,445	**Bob Miller***	**207,053**
New Hampshire	**Judd Gregg***	**176,560**	J. Joseph Grandmaison	101,496
New Mexico	Frank M. Bond	187,549	**Bruce King**	**223,526**
New York	Pierre Rinfret	851,482	**Mario Cuomo***	**2,098,784**
Ohio	**George Voinovich**	**1,924,198**	Anthony Celebrezze Jr.	1,527,150
Oklahoma	Bill Price	296,588	**David Walters**	**525,511**
Oregon	Dave Frohnmayer	402,384	**Barbara Roberts**	**469,802**
Pennsylvania	Barbara Hafer	986,010	**Bob Casey***	**2,057,377**
Rhode Island	Edward DiPrete*	87,961	**Bruce Sundlun**	**255,495**
South Carolina	**Carroll A. Campbell Jr.***	**520,493**	Theo Mitchell	209,878
South Dakota	**George Mickelson***	**150,953**	Bob Samuelson	105,298
Tennessee	Dwight Henry	286,668	**Ned McWherter***	**476,996**

(continued)

State	Republican	Vote	Democrat	Vote
Texas	Clayton Williams	1,816,856	Anne Richards	1,913,882
Vermont	**Richard Snelling**	108,208	Peter Welch	96,259
Wisconsin	**Tommy G. Thompson***	801,426	Thomas Loftus	575,669
Wyoming	Mary Mead	55,426	**Mike Sullivan***	104,500
*Incumbent.				

Mayors and City Managers of Selected U.S. Cities

Reflecting Nov. 6, 1990 elections

*Asterisk before name denotes city manager. All others are mayors. For mayors, dates are those of next election; for city managers, they are dates of appointment.

D, Democrat; R, Republican; N-P, Non-Partisan

City	Name	Term
Abilene, Tex.	Gary McCaleb, N-P	1993, May.
Abington, Pa.	*Albert Herrmann	1978, May
Akron, Oh.	D.L. Plusquellic, D	1991, Nov.
Alameda, Cal.	Chuck Corica, N-P	1991, Apr.
Albany, Ga.	*Nicholas M. Meiszer	1985, Sept.
Albany, N.Y.	Thomas M. Whalen,3d,D	1993, Nov.
Albuquerque, N.M.	Louis Saavedra, N-P	1993, Nov.
Alexandria, La.	Edward Randolph Jr., D	1994, Oct.
Alexandria, Va.	*Vola Lawson	1985, Sept.
Alhambra, Cal.	*Kevin J. Murphy	1983, May
Allentown, Pa.	Joseph S. Daddona, D	1993, Nov.
Altoona, Pa.	Alan Mikula, D	1991, Nov.
Amarillo, Tex.	*John Ward	1983, June
Ames, Ia.	*Steven L. Schainker	1982, Oct.
Anaheim, Cal.	*James Roth	1990, May
Anchorage, Alas.	Tom Fink, N-P	1991, Nov.
Anderson, Ind.	J. Mark Lawler, D	1991, Nov.
Anderson, S.C.	*Richard Burnette	1976, Sept.
Ann Arbor, Mich.	*Del Borgsdorf.	1988, Aug.
Appleton, Wis.	Dorothy Johnson, N-P	1992, Apr.
Arcadia, Cal.	*George J. Watts	1981, Feb.
Arlington, Mass.	*Donald R. Marquis	1966, Nov.
Arlington, Tex.	*William Kirchhoff	1985, Oct.
Arlington Hts., Ill.	William Maki, N-P	1993, Apr.
Arvada, Col.	*Neal G. Berlin	1986, Mar.
Asheville, N.C.	*Douglas Bean	1986, Apr.
Athens, Ga.	Dwain Chambers, D	1991, Nov.
Atlanta, Ga.	Maynard Jackson, D	1993, Oct.
Atlantic City, N.J.	Jim Whelan, N-P	1994, May
Auburn, N.Y.	*Bruce Clifford.	1966, Aug.
Augusta, Ga.	Charles Devaney, D.	1993, Nov.
Aurora, Col.	*James Griesemer	1984, Jan.
Aurora, Ill.	David L. Pierce, N-P.	1993, Apr.
Austin, Tex.	*Camille Barnett.	1989, Mar.
Bakersfield, Cal.	*J. Dale Hawley	1988, Jan.
Baldwin Park, Cal.	*Donald Penman	1990, Jan.
Baltimore, Md.	Kurt Schmoke, D	1991, Nov.
Bangor, Me.	*John W. Flynn	1977, Feb.
Baton Rouge, La.	Tom Ed McHugh, D	1992, Oct.
Battle Creek, Mich.	*Rance L. Leaders	1988, June
Bay City, Mich.	*David D. Barnes	1979, May
Bayonne, N.J.	Richard Rutkowski, N-P	1994, May
Baytown, Tex.	*Bobby Rountree	1989, May
Beaumont, Tex.	*Ray A. Riley	1989, Feb.
Belleville, Ill.	Terry Lukens, N-P	1991, Nov.
Bellevue, Wash.	*Phillip Kushlan	1985, Feb.
Bellflower, Cal.	*Jack Simpson	1980, July
Beloit, Wis.	*David Wilcox	1986, Feb.
Berkeley, Cal.	*Hal Cronkite	1986, Apr.
Bessemer, Ala.	Quittman Mitchell, N-P	1994, July
Bethlehem, Pa.	Kenneth Smith, R.	1993, Nov.
Beverly Hills, Cal.	*Edward Kreins	1979, Oct.
Billings, Mont.	*Alan Tandy	1985, May
Biloxi, Miss.	Peter Halat, D	1993, May
Binghamton, N.Y.	Juanita M. Crabb, D.	1993, Nov.
Birmingham, Ala.	Richard Arrington Jr., D.	1991, Oct.
Bismarck, N.D.	Bill Sorensen, N-P	1994, Apr.
Bloomfield, N.J.	James Gasparini, D	1993, Nov.
Bloomington, Ill.	Jesse Smart, D	1993, Apr.
Bloomington, Ind.	Tomilea Allison, D	1991, Nov.
Bloomington, Minn.	*John Pidgeon	1967, Dec.
Boca Raton, Fla.	Emil Danciu, N-P	1991, Mar.
Boise, Ida.	Dirk Kempthorne, N-P	1993, Nov.
Boston, Mass.	Raymond L. Flynn, D	1991 Nov.
Boulder, Col.	*Joseph deRaines.	1989, Apr.
Bowie, Md.	*Charles Moore	1976, Mar.
Bowling Green, Ky.	*Charles W. Coates.	1977, Feb.
Bridgeport, Conn.	Mary Moran, R.	1991, Nov.
Bristol, Conn.	John Leone, D.	1991, Nov.
Brockton, Mass.	Carl Pitaro, D	1991, Nov.
Brooklyn Center, Minn.	*Gerald G. Splinter	1977, Oct.
Brownsville, Tex.	*Steve Fitzgibbons	1987, Jan.
Bryan, Tex.	*Ernest R. Clark	1979, Feb.
Buena Park, Cal.	*Kevin O'Rourke	1985, Nov.
Buffalo, N.Y.	James D. Griffin, D	1993, Nov.
Burbank, Cal.	*Bud Ovrom	1984, June
Burlington, Vt.	Peter Clavelle, N-P	1991, Mar.
Calumet City, Ill.	Robert C. Stefaniak, D	1993, Apr.
Cambridge, Mass.	*Robert Healy,	1981, July
Camden, N.J.	Melvin Primas Jr., D.	1993, May
Canton, Oh.	Sam Purses, D.	1991, Nov.
Cape Girardeau, Mo.	*J. Ronald Fischer	1988, Feb.
Carson, Cal.	*Jack Smith	1988, Dec.
Casper, Wyo.	*Thomas Forslund	1988, June
Cedar Rapids, Ia.	Jon Crews, N-P	1991, Nov.
Champaign, Ill.	*Steven C. Carter.	1985, Feb.
Charleston, S.C.	Joseph P. Riley Jr., D.	1991, Nov.
Charleston, W. Va.	Charles Gardner, R .	1991, Apr.
Charlotte, N.C.	Sue Myrick, R	1991, Nov.
Charlottesville, Va.	*Cole Hendrix	1970, Jan.
Chattanooga, Tenn.	Gene Roberts, R	1991, Apr.
Chesapeake, Va.	*James W. Rein.	1987, Mar.
Chester, Pa.	Willie Mae James Leake, R	1991, Nov.
Cheyenne, Wyo.	Gary Schaeffer, R.	1992, Nov.
Chicago, Ill.	Richard M. Daley, D.	1991, Apr.
Chicago Hts., Ill.	Charles Panici, R	1991, Apr.
Chicopee, Mass.	Joseph Chessey, D	1991, Nov.
Chino, Cal.	*Richard Rowe	1985, Feb.
Chula Vista, Cal.	*John Goss	1983, Jan.
Cincinnati, Oh.	*Gerald Newfarmer.	1990, Sept.
Clearwater, Fla.	*Ronald H. Rabun.	1988, Apr.
Cleveland, Oh.	Michael Wright, N-P	1993, Nov.
Cleveland Hgts., Oh.	*Robert Downey.	1985, Jan.
Col. Spgs., Col.	*Roy Pederson	1989, Jan.
Columbia, Mo.	*Raymond A. Beck	1985, Aug.
Columbia, S.C.	*Miles Hadley	1989, Dec.
Columbus, Ga.	Frank Martin, D	1994, Nov.
Columbus, Oh.	Dana Rinehart, R	1991, Nov.
Commerce, Cal.	*Robert Hinderliter	1973, Aug.
Compton, Cal.	*Howard Caldwell.	1989, June
Concord, Cal.	*Michael Uberuaga	1986, May
Coon Rapids., Minn.	*Richard Thistle	1979, July
Coral Gables, Fla.	*H.C. Eads Jr.	1988, May
Corpus Christi, Tex.	*Juan Garza	1988, Apr.
Corvallis, Ore.	*Gerald Seals	1988, Feb.
Costa Mesa, Cal.	*Allan L. Roeder.	1985, Oct.
Council Bluffs, Ia.	Tom Hanafan, N-P	1993, Nov.
Covington, Ky.	*Arnold Simpson	1986, Nov.
Cranston, R.I.	Michael Traficante, D	1994, Nov.
Crystal, Minn.	*John Irving	1963, Jan.
Culver City, Cal.	*Dale Jones	1967, Sept.
Cuyahoga Falls, Oh.	Don L. Robart, R	1993, Nov.
Dallas, Tex.	*Richard Knight	1986, Dec.
Daly City, Cal.	*David R. Rowe	1969, Sept.
Danbury, Conn.	Gene Eriquez, N-P	1991, Nov.
Danville, Va.	*Charles Church	1981, June
Davenport, Ia.	Thomas W. Hart, R	1991, Nov.
Dayton, Oh.	Richard Clay Dixon, D.	1993, Nov.
Daytona Bch., Fla.	*Howard D. Tipton	1978, Oct.
Dearborn, Mich.	Michael Guido, N-P	1993, Nov.
Dearborn Hts., Mich.	Lyle Van Houton, R.	1993, Nov.
Decatur, Ill.	*James Bacon Jr..	1988, Oct.
Denton, Tex.	*Larry Harrell	1986, Feb.
Denver, Col.	Federico Pena, D	1991, May
Des Moines, Ia.	John Dorrian, D .	1991, Nov.
Des Plaines, Ill.	Michael Albrecht, N-P.	1993, Apr.
Detroit, Mich.	Coleman A. Young, N-P	1993, Nov.
Dotham, Ala.	*Don J. Marnon	1987, May
Dover, Del.	*vacant	
Downers Grove, Ill.	*James R. Griesemer.	1972, Sept.
Downey, Cal.	*Gerald Caton	1989, Oct.
Dubuque, Ia.	*W. Kenneth Gearhart	1979, Aug.
Duluth, Minn.	John Fedo, N-P	1991, Nov.
Durham, N.C.	*Orville Powell	1983, Mar.

City	Name	Term
E. Chicago, Ind.	Robert A. Pastrick, D	1991, Nov.
E. Hartford, Conn.	Susan Kniep, R.	1991, Nov.
E. Lansing, Mich.	Liz Schweitzer, N-P	1991, Nov.
E. Orange, N.J.	Cardell Cooper, D	1993, Nov.
Eau Claire, Wis.	*Eric Anderson	1984, Jan.
Edina, Minn.	*Kenneth Rosland.	1977, Nov.
Edison, N.J.	Thomas Paterniti, D	1993, Nov.
El Cajon, Cal.	Joan Shoemaker, R.	1994, June
El Monte, Cal.	Don McMillen, N-P	1994, Apr.
El Paso, Tex.	Suzie Azar, N-P	1991, May
Elgin, Ill.	*Larry L. Rice	1989, Oct.
Elizabeth, N.J.	Thomas G. Dunn, D	1992, Nov.
Elkhart, Ind.	James Perron, D	1992, Nov.
Elmhurst, Ill.	Charles Garrigues, N-P	1991, Apr.
Elmira, N.Y.	*W. Gregg LaMar	1987, July
Elyria, Oh.	Michael Keys, D.	1991, Nov.
Enfield, Conn.	*Robert J. Mulready.	1983, Feb.
Enid, Okla.	*Jim Ferree	1990, May
Erie, Pa.	Joyce Savocchio, D.	1994, Nov.
Escondido, Cal.	Jerry Harmon, D.	1992, June
Euclid, Oh.	David Lynch, R	1991, Nov.
Eugene, Ore.	*Michael Gleason	1981, Jan.
Evanston, Ill.	*Joel Asprooth.	1982, May
Evansville, Ind.	Frank McDonald, D	1991, Nov.
Everett, Mass.	John McCarthy, D.	1991, Nov.
Everett, Wash.	Pete Kinch, N-P	1993, Nov.
Fairborn, Oh.	*Michael Hammond.	1985, Dec.
Fairfield, Cal.	*Charles Long	1988, Sept.
Fair Lawn, N.J.	*Joseph Garger	1979, Oct.
Fall River, Mass.	Carlton Viveiros, N-P	1991, Nov.
Fargo, N.D.	Jon Lindgren, D	1994, Apr.
Farmington Hills, Mich.	*William M. Costick	1981, Jan.
Fayetteville, Ark.	*Scott Linebaugh	1990, May
Fayetteville, N.C.	*John P. Smith.	1981, Jan.
Fitchburg, Mass.	Jeffrey Bean, D	1991, Nov.
Flagstaff, Ariz.	*Frank Abeyta	1981, Jan.
Flint, Mich.	Matthew Collier, N-P	1991, Nov.
Florissant, Mo.	James J. Eagan, N-P	1991, Apr.
Fond du Lac, Wis.	*Jack Howley	1989, Aug.
Ft. Collins, Col.	*Steven Burkett	1986, Apr.
Ft. Lauderdale, Fla.	*George Hanbury 2d	1990, Apr.
Ft. Lee, N.J.	Nicholas Corbiscello, R.	1991, Nov.
Ft. Smith, Ark.	*William Vines, N-P	1990, Nov.
Ft. Wayne, Ind.	Paul Helmke, R	1991, Nov.
Ft. Worth, Tex.	*David Ivory	1989, Sept.
Fountain Valley, Cal.	*Judy Kelsey.	1984, May
Fremont, Cal.	*Charles Kent McClain	1981, May
Fresno, Cal.	*vacant . .	
Fullerton, Cal.	*William C. Winter	1979, Oct.
Gadsden, Ala.	David Nolen, D.	1994, July
Gainesville, Fla.	*W.D. Higginbotham Jr.	1984, Sept.
Galesburg, Ill.	*Robert Knabel	1989, Feb.
Galveston, Tex.	*Douglas W. Matthews	1985, Mar.
Gardena, Cal.	*Kenneth Landau	1985, Apr.
Garden Grove, Cal.	*Delbert L. Powers	1980, July
Garfield Hts., Oh.	Thomas Longo, D.	1993, Nov.
Garland, Tex.	*James K. Spore	1985, Mar.
Gary, Ind.	Thomas Barnes, D	1991, Nov.
Gastonia, N.C.	*Gary Hicks	1973, Dec.
Glendale, Ariz.	*Martin Vanacour	1985, Mar.
Glendale, Cal.	*David Ramsay	1988, May
Grand Forks, N.D.	Michael Polovitz, D	1992, Apr.
Grand Island, Neb.	Ernie Dobesh, N-P	1994, Nov.
Gr. Prairie, Tex.	*Wendel Hulse	1987, Apr.
Gr. Rapids, Mich.	*Kurt Kimball.	1987, Apr.
Great Falls, Mont.	*G. Allen Johnson	1981, Jan.
Greeley, Col.	*Sam Sasaki.	1987, Mar.
Green Bay, Wis.	Samuel Halloin, N-P	1991, Nov.
Greensboro, N.C.	*W.H. Carstarphen	1984, June
Greenville, S.C.	*John Dullea	1971, Oct.
Greenwich, Conn.	John Margenot, D, first selectman	1991, Nov.
Groton, Conn.	Catherine Kolnaski, D.	1991, May
Gulfport, Miss.	Ken Combs, R.	1993, June
Hackensack, N.J.	*James Lacava	1990, Feb.
Hagerstown, Md.	Stephen Sager	1993, May
Hamden, Conn.	John L. Carusone, D	1991, Nov.
Hamilton, Oh.	*Hal Shepherd.	1989, Apr.
Hammond, Ind.	Thomas McDermott, R	1991, Nov.
Hampton, Va.	James Eason, D.	1992, May
Harlingen, Tex.	*Mike Perez	1989, July
Harrisburg, Pa.	Stephen Reed, D	1993, Nov.
Hartford, Conn.	Carrie Saxon Perry, D	1991, Nov.
Hattiesburg, Miss.	Ed Morgan, D	1993, June
Haverhill, Mass.	Theodore Pelosi, R	1991, Nov.
Hawthorne, Cal.	*James Mitsch.	1990, Dec.
Hayward, Cal.	*Louis Garcia	1989, Jan.
Hialeah, Fla.	Raul Martinez, D.	1993, Nov.
High Point, N.C.	*H. Lewis Price	1983, July
Hollywood, Fla.	*Irving Rosenbaum	1988, Aug.
Holyoke, Mass.	Michael Dunn, D.	1991, Nov.
Honolulu, Ha.	Frank Fasi, R	1992, Nov.
Hot Springs, Ark.	*Gus Pappas.	1989, Mar.
Houston, Tex.	Kathryn Whitmire, N-P	1991, Nov.
Huntington, W. Va.	Robert Nelson, D	1993, June
Huntington Beach, Cal.	*Michael Ubervaga	1990, Feb.
Huntsville, Ala.	Steve Hettinger, N-P	1992, Aug.
Hutchinson, Kan.	*Joe Palacioc	1989, Jan.
Idaho Falls, Ida.	Thomas Campbell, N-P.	1993, Nov.
Independence, Mo.	*L.C. Kaufman.	1990, Aug.
Indianapolis, Ind.	William Hudnut, R	1991, Nov.
Inglewood, Cal.	*Paul Eckles	1975, Nov.
Inkster, Mich.	*S. Thomas White.	1990, Feb.
Iowa City, Ia.	*Stephen Atkins	1986, July
Irving, Tex.	*Jack Huffman.	1974, Jan.
Irvington, N.J.	Michael Steele, D.	1994, May
Jackson, Mich.	*William P. Buchanan.	1985, Nov.
Jackson, Miss.	Kane Ditto, D.	1993, May
Jackson, Tenn.	Charles Farmer, D	1991, May
Jacksonville, Fla.	Tommy Hazouri, D	1991, May
Janesville, Wis.	*Steven Sheiffer.	1987, May
Jersey City, N.J.	Gerald McCann, N-P	1993, May
Johnson City, Tenn.	*John G. Campbell	1984, June
Johnstown, Pa.	Herbert Pfuhl Jr., R	1993, Nov.
Joliet, Ill.	*John M. Mezera	1987, Jan.
Joplin, Mo.	*Leonard A. Martin	1986, Sept.
Kalamazoo, Mich.	*James Holgersson	1989, June
Kansas City, Kan.	*David Isabell	1985, June
Kansas City, Mo.	Richard Berkley, R	1991, Apr.
Kenner, La.	Aaron Broussard, N-P	1994, June
Kenosha, Wis.	Patrick Moran, N-P	1992, Apr.
Kettering, Oh.	Richard Hartmann, R.	1993, Nov.
Key West, Fla.	*G. Felix Cooper	1990, May
Killeen, Tex.	*Daniel Hobbs	1990, Jan.
Knoxville, Tenn.	Victor Ashe, R	1991, Nov.
Kokomo, Ind.	Robert Sargent, D.	1991, Nov.
LaCrosse, Wis.	Patrick Zielke, N-P	1993, Apr.
La Habra, Cal.	*Lee Risner	1970, Nov.
La Mesa, Cal.	*David Wear	1990, Apr.
La Mirada, Cal.	*Gary K. Sloan	1961, Apr.
Lafayette, Ind.	James Riehle, D.	1991, Nov.
Lafayette, La.	Dud Lastrapes, R	1992, Mar.
Lake Charles, La.	James Sudduth, D.	1993, Apr.
Lakeland, Fla.	*E.S. Strickland	1986, Feb.
Lakewood, Cal.	*Howard L. Chambers	1976, June
Lakewood, Col.	*Larry Rice.	1986, May
Lakewood, Oh.	Anthony Sinagra, R	1991, Nov.
Lancaster, Pa.	Janice Stork, D.	1993, Nov.
Lansing, Mich.	Terry John McKane, N-P	1993, Nov.
Laredo, Tex.	*Marvin Townsend	1982, June
Largo, Fla.	George McGough, R	1991, Apr.
Las Cruces, N.M.	*Dana Miller	1983, Feb.
Las Vegas, Nev.	Ron Lurie, D	1991, June
Lawrence, Kan.	*Buford M. Watson Jr.	1970, Jan.
Lawrence, Mass.	Kevin Sullivan, N-P	1991, Nov.
Lawton, Okla.	*Robert Hopkins.	1990, Jan.
Lewiston, Me.	James Howaniec, D.	1991, Nov.
Lexington, Ky.	Scotty Baesler, N-P	1991, Nov.
Lima, Oh.	David Berger, N-P.	1993, Nov.
Lincoln, Neb.	Bill Harris, D	1991, May
Little Rock, Ark.	*Thomas Dalton.	1986, June
Livermore, Cal.	*Leland Horner	1978, Oct.
Livonia, Mich.	Robert Bennett, N-P	1991, Nov.
Lombard, Ill.	*William Lichter	1985, Jan.
Long Beach, Cal.	*James Hankla	1987, Mar.
Long Beach, N.Y.	*Edwin Eaton	1979, June
Longmont, Col.	*Geoff Dolan	1987, Jan.
Longview, Tex.	*C. Ray Jackson	1980, Apr.
Lorain, Oh.	Alex Olejko, D.	1991, Nov.
Los Angeles, Cal.	Thomas Bradley, N-P	1993, June
Louisville, Ky.	Jerry Abramson, D	1993, Nov.
Lowell, Mass.	*James Campbell	1987, Jan.
L. Merion, Pa.	*Thomas B. Fulweiler	1968, Jan.
Lubbock, Tex.	*Larry Cunningham	1976, Sept.
Lynchburg, Va.	*E. Allen Culverhouse	1979, June
Lynn, Mass.	Albert DiVirgilio, D	1991, Nov.
Lynwood, Cal.	*Charles Gomez	1982, Mar.
Macon, Ga.	William L. Robinson, D	1991, Nov.
Madison, Wis.	Paul Soglin, D	1991, Apr.
Malden, Mass.	James S. Conway, D	1991, Nov.
Manchester, N.H.	Ray Wiecvorek, R	1991, Nov.
Manitowoc, Wis.	Kevin Crawford, N-P	1991, Apr.
Mansfield, Oh.	Edward Meehan, D	1991, Nov.
Marion, Ind.	Robert Mitchell, D.	1991, Nov.
Marion, Oh.	Robert S. Brown, R	1991, Nov.

City	Name	Term
McAllen, Tex.	Othal Brand, R.	1993, Apr.
McKeesport, Pa.	Lou Washowich, D	1991, Nov.
Medford, Mass.	Michael McGlynn, N-P	1991, Nov.
Melbourne, Fla.	*Samuel Halter	1978, July
Memphis, Tenn.	Richard C. Hackett, N-P	1991, Oct.
Mentor, Oh.	*Julian Suso	1990, Mar.
Meriden, Conn.	*Michael Aldi.	1988, Mar.
Meridian, Miss.	Jimmy Kemp, R	1993, June
Mesa, Ariz.	*C.K. Luster	1979, June
Mesquite, Tex.	*James Prugel.	1987, Dec.
Miami, Fla.	*Cesar H. Odio	1985, Dec.
Miami Beach, Fla.	*Rob Parkins.	1982, Apr.
Middletown, Oh.	*William Klosterman	1988, July
Midland, Tex.	Carroll M. Thomas, N-P	1992, May
Midwest City, Okla.	*Charles Johnson	1984, Nov.
Milford, Conn.	Frederick Lisman, R.	1991, Nov.
Milwaukee, Wis.	John Norquist, D.	1992, Apr.
Minneapolis, Minn.	Donald Fraser, D	1993, Nov.
Minnetonka, Minn.	*James F. Miller.	1980, Jan.
Minot, N.D.	*Robert Schempp, R	1977, Nov.
Mobile, Ala.	Michael Dow, N-P	1993, Aug.
Modesto, Cal.	*Garth Lipsky	1974, Jan.
Monroe, La.	Robert Powell, D	1992, Apr.
Montclair, N.J.	*Bertrand Kendall	1980, Sept.
Montebello, Cal.	*Richard Torres	1989, May
Monterey Park, Cal.	*Mark Lewis	1988, July
Montgomery, Ala.	Emory Folmar, R	1991, Nov.
Mt. Lebanon, Pa.	*James Cain	1982, Apr.
Mt. Prospect, Ill.	*John F. Dixon.	1987, Mar.
Mt. Vernon, N.Y.	Roland Blackwood, D.	1991, Nov.
Mountain View, Cal.	*Bruce Liedstrand.	1976, June
Muncie, Ind.	James Carey, D.	1991, Nov.
Muskegon, Mich.	Norman Kruse, R.	1991, Nov.
Muskogee, Okla.	*Walter Beckham	1984, Feb.
Napa, Cal.	*Patricia Thompson	1989, Oct.
Naperville, Ill.	*Ralph DeSantis.	1986, June
Nashua, N.H.	James Donchess, N-P	1991, Nov.
Nashville, Tenn.	Bill Boner, D	1991, Aug.
National City, Cal.	*Tom McCabe	1979, Mar.
New Bedford, Mass.	John Bullard, D	1991, Nov.
New Britain, Conn.	Donald DeFronzo, D	1991, Nov.
New Castle, Pa.	Richard Christofer, D	1991, Nov.
New Haven, Conn.	John Daniels, D	1991, Nov.
New London, Conn.	*C.F. Driscoll.	1969, May
New Orleans, La.	Sidney Barthelemy, D.	1994, Mar.
New Rochelle, N.Y.	*C. Samuel Kissinger	1975, Apr.
New York, N.Y.	David Dinkins, D.	1990, Nov.
Newark, N.J.	Sharpe James, D	1994, May
Newark, Oh.	William Moore, R	1991, Nov.
Newport, R.I.	*Francis Edwards	1987, Jan.
Newport Beach, Cal.	*Robert L. Wynn.	1971, Aug.
Newport News, Va.	*Ed Maroney.	1987, Jan.
Newton, Mass.	Theodore Mann, R	1993, Nov.
Niagara Falls, N.Y.	Michael O'Laughlin, D	1991, Nov.
Norfolk, Va.	*James B. Oliver Jr.	1987, Jan.
Norman, Okla.	*Ron Wood	1989, May
Norristown, Pa.	William DeAngelis, D..	1993, Nov.
North Charleston, S.C.	John Bourne Jr., R	1994, May
North Las Vegas	*Michael Dyal	1982, May
No. Little Rock, Ark.	Patrick Hayes, D	1992, Nov.
Norwalk, Cal.	*Ray Gibbs.	1984, Feb.
Norwalk, Conn.	Frank Esposito, R.	1991, Nov.
Norwich, Conn.	*Ernest Zmyslinski.	1988, July
Novato, Cal.	*Phillip J. Brown.	1975, May
Oak Park, Ill.	*J.N. Nielsen.	1986, July
Oak Ridge, Tenn.	*Jeffrey J. Broughton.	1986, Sept.
Oakland, Cal.	*Henry L. Gardner	1981, June
Oceanside, Cal.	*James Turner.	1990, Aug.
Odessa, Tex.	*William Brown Jr.	1987, Nov.
Ogden, Ut.	Scott Sneddon, N-P.	1991, Nov.
Oklahoma City, Okla.	*Paula Hearn	1989, Oct.
Omaha, Neb.	P.J. Morgan, D.	1993, May
Ontario, Cal.	*Roger Hughbanks, N-P	1975, May
Orange, Cal.	*J. William Little	1984, Jan.
Orange, N.J.	Robert L. Brown, D	1992, May
Orlando, Fla.	Bill Frederick, N-P	1992, Sept.
Oshkosh, Wis.	*W. O. Frueh.	1976, Aug.
Overland Park, Kan.	*Donald Pipes	1977, June
Owensboro, Ky.	*Max Rhoads	1959, Sept.
Oxnard, Cal.	*Vernon Hazen	1990, Aug.
Pacifica, Cal.	*Daniel Pincetich	1985, Dec.
Palm Springs, Cal.	*Dallas Flicek	1990, Aug.
Palo Alto, Cal.	*William Zaner.	1979, Sept.
Park Ridge, Ill.	*Martin Butler, N-P	1993, Apr.
Parkersburg, W. Va.	Helen Albright, R	1993, Nov.
Parma, Oh.	Michael Ries, D	1991, Nov.
Pasadena, Cal.	Jeff Hughston, N-P	1992, May
Pasadena, Tex.	John Ray Harrison	1993, May
Paterson, N.J.	William Pascrell, D	1994, May
Pawtucket, R.I.	Brian Sarault, D.	1991, Nov.
Peabody, Mass.	Peter Torigian, D	1991, Nov.
Pekin, Ill.	Larry Homerin, D	1991, Apr.
Pensacola, Fla.	*Steve Garman	1986, June
Peoria, Ill.	*Thomas Mikulecky.	1987, July
Perth Amboy, N.J..	George J. Otlowski, D	1992, May
Petersburg, Va.	*Richard M. Brown	1984, Oct.
Philadelphia, Pa.	W. Wilson Goode, D	1991, Nov.
Phoenix, Ariz.	Terry Goddard, N-P	1991, Oct.
Pico Rivera, Cal..	*Dennis Courtemarche	1984, Nov.
Pine Bluff, Ark	Carolyn Robinson, D	1992, Nov.
Pittsburgh, Pa..	Sophie Masloff, D	1993, Nov.
Pittsfield, Mass.	Anne E. Wojtkowski, D.	1991, Nov.
Plainfield, N.J.	Harold Mitchell, D.	1993, Nov.
Plano, Tex.	*Thomas Muehlenbeck.	1987, Dec.
Pocatello, Ut.	Peter Angstadt, N-P.	1993, Nov.
Pomona, Cal.	*Julio Fuentes	1989, Dec.
Pompano Beach, Fla.	*Roy Stype.	1989, Oct.
Pontiac, Mich.	Wallace Holland, N-P	1993, Nov.
Port Arthur, Tex..	*Cornelius Boganey.	1990, Apr.
Port Huron, Mich.	*Gerald R. Bouchard	1965, June
Portland, Me..	*Robert Ganley	1986, Sept.
Portland, Ore.	Bud Clark, N-P	1992, Nov.
Portsmouth, Oh.	Franklin Gerlach, N-P	1993, Nov.
Portsmouth, Va.	*George Hanbury.	1982, June
Poughkeepsie, N.Y.	*William J. Theysohn	1982, Mar.
Prichard, Ala.	Margie M. Wilson D..	1992, Aug.
Providence, R.I.	Undecided	1994, Nov.
Provo, Ut.	Joseph Jenkins, R.	1993, Nov.
Pueblo, Col.	*Lewis A. Quigley	1987, Jan.
Quincy, Ill.	Verne Hagstorm, D.	1993, Apr.
Quincy, Mass.	James Sheets, N-P	1991, Nov.
Racine, Wis.	N. Owen Davies, N-P	1991, Apr.
Raleigh, N.C.	*Dempsey Benton.	1983, Dec.
Rapid City, S.D.	Keith Carlyle, N-P	1991, Apr.
Reading, Pa.	William Haggerty Jr., D.	1991, Nov.
Redding, Cal.	*Robert Christofferson	1987, Jan.
Redlands, Cal.	*vacant	
Redondo Beach, Cal.	*R.H. Griest	1990, July
Redwood City, Cal.	*James M. Smith	1982, Feb.
Reno, Nev.	*Harold Schilling.	1986, Mar.
Revere, Mass.	George V. Colella, D.	1992, Nov.
Richardson, Tex.	*Bob Hughey	1974, Jan.
Richfield, Minn..	*James Prosser.	1986, Sept.
Richmond, Cal.	*Larry Moore	1987, Aug.
Richmond, Ind.	Frank Waltermann, D.	1991, Nov.
Richmond, Va.	*Robert C. Bobb.	1986, July
Riverside, Cal.	*John E. Holmes	1990, Oct.
Roanoke, Va.	*W.R. Herbert	1985, Nov.
Rochester, Minn.	*Steven Kvenvold	1979, June
Rochester, N.Y.	Thomas Ryan Jr., D.	1993, Nov.
Rock Hill, S.C.	*Joe Lanford	1979, July
Rock Island, Ill.	*John Phillips	1986, Nov.
Rockford, Ill.	Charles Box, D	1993, Apr.
Rockville, Md.	*Bruce Romer	1988, Sept.
Rome, N.Y.	Carl Eilenberg, R	1991, Nov.
Roseville, Mich.	Jeanne Riesterer, N-P	1993, Nov.
Roswell, N.M.	*Ralph Fresquez	1986, Jan.
Royal Oak, Mich.	*William Baldridge.	1975, Sept.
Sacramento, Cal.	*Walter Slipe.	1976, Mar.
Saginaw, Mich.	*Vernon E. Stoner.	1987, Feb.
St. Clair Shores, Mich.	*Mark Wollenweber.	1990, Jan.
St. Cloud, Minn.	Charles Winkleman, N-P	1993, Nov.
St. Joseph, Mo.	Glenda Kelly, N-P	1994, Apr.
St. Louis, Mo.	Vincent Schoemehl, D	1993, Apr.
St. Louis Park, Minn.	*William C. Dixon	1988, Oct.
St. Paul, Minn.	James Scheibel, N-P	1993, Nov.
St. Petersburg, Fla.	*Robert Obering.	1985, Oct.
Salem, Mass.	Neil Harrington, N-P.	1991, Nov.
Salem, Ore.	*Gary Eide.	1988, Jan.
Salina, Kan.	*Dennis Kissinger	1988, Jan.
Salinas, Cal.	*Roy Herte.	1988, Sept.
Salt Lake City, Ut.	Palmer DePaulis, D	1991, Nov.
San Angelo, Tex.	*Stephen Brown.	1982, May
San Antonio, Tex.	Lila Cockrell, D	1991, Apr.
San Bernardino, Cal.	Bob Holcomb, D.	1993, May
San Bruno, Cal.	*Lew Pond	1990, May
San Diego, Cal.	Maureen O'Connor, N-P	1992, Nov.
San Francisco, Cal.	Art Agnos, D.	1991, Nov.
San Jose, Cal.	*Leslie White.	1989, May
San Leandro, Cal.	*Richard H. Randall.	1986, July
San Mateo, Cal.	*Richard Delong.	1976, Sept.
San Rafael, Cal.	*Pamela Nicolai.	1985, Dec.
Sandusky, Oh.	*Frank Link.	1972, Jan.
Sandy City, Ut.	Larry Smith, N-P.	1991, Nov.
Santa Ana, Cal.	*David Ream	1986, July
Santa Barbara, Cal.	*Richard Thomas.	1977, Jan.

City	Name	Term	City	Name	Term
Santa Clara, Cal.	*Jennifer Sparacino	1987, Mar.	Tucson, Ariz.	*Thomas Wilson	1990, July
Santa Cruz, Cal.	*Richard Wilson	1981, June	Tulsa, Okla.	Rodger Randle, D	1994, Apr.
Santa Fe, N.M.	Sam Pick, D	1994, Mar.	Tuscaloosa, Ala.	Alvin DuPont, D	1993, Oct.
Santa Maria, Cal.	*Wayne Schwammel	1989, June	Tyler, Tex.	*Gary Gwyn	1982, Nov.
Santa Monica, Cal.	*John Jalili	1984, Dec.	Union City, N.J.	Robert Menendez, D	1994, May
Santa Rosa, Cal.	*Kenneth Blackman	1970, July	Univ. City, Mo.	*Frank Ollendorff	1980, Mar.
Sarasota, Fla.	*David Sollenberger	1987, Mar.	Upland, Cal.	*Ray Silver	1988, Dec.
Savannah, Ga.	*Arthur A. Mendonsa	1962, July	Upper Arlington, Oh.	*Richard King	1984, Aug.
Schenectady, N.Y.	Karen Johnson, D	1991, Nov.	Utica, N.Y.	Louis La Polla, R	1991, Nov.
Scottsdale, Ariz.	*Jorge Carrasco	1988, Oct.	Vallejo, Cal.	*Edward Wohlenberg	1989, Apr.
Scranton, Pa.	James Connors, R	1992, Nov.	Vancouver, Wash.	*Paul Grattet	1980, Aug.
Seattle, Wash.	Norman Rice, N-P	1993, Nov.	Ventura, Cal.	*John Baker	1986, Nov.
Shaker Heights, Oh.	Stephen Alfred, N-P	1991, Nov.	Victoria, Tex.	*James J. Miller	1980, June
Sheboygan, Wis.	Richard Schneider, N-P	1993, Apr.	Vineland, N.J.	Harry Curley, N-P	1992, May
Shreveport, La.	*Judy Purgerson	1988, Aug.	Virginia Beach, Va.	Meyera Oberndorf, N-P	1992, May
Simi Valley, Cal.	*M.L. Koester	1979, Sept.	Waco, Tex.	*John Harrison	1977, Sept.
Sioux City, Ia.	Robert Scott, N-P	1991, Nov.	Walnut Creek, Cal.	*Donald Blubaugh	1988, Apr.
Sioux Falls, S.D.	Jack White, R	1991, June	Waltham, Mass.	William Stanley, D	1991, Nov.
Skokie, Ill.	*Albert Rigoni	1987, Jan.	Warren, Mich.	Ronald Bonkowski, N-P	1991, Nov.
Somerville, Mass.	Michael Capuano, D	1991, Nov.	Warren, Oh.	Daniel Sferra, D	1991, Nov.
South Bend, Ind.	Joseph Kernan, D	1991, Nov.	Warwick, R.I.	Charles Donovan, N-P	1994, Nov.
South Gate, Cal.	*vacant		Wash, D.C.	Sharon Dixon, D	1994, Nov.
Southfield, Mich.	*Robert Block	1985, Jan.	Waterbury, Conn.	Joseph Santopietro, R	1991, Nov.
Sparks, Nev.	*Patricia Thompson	1983, Sept.	Waterloo, Ia.	Bernard L. McKinley, N-P	1991, Nov.
Spartanburg, S.C.	*Wayne Bowers	1984, Sept.	Waukegan, Ill.	Haig Paravonian, R	1993, Apr.
Spokane, Wash.	*Terry Novak	1978, July	Waukesha, Wis.	Paul Vrakas, N-P	1994, Apr.
Springfield, Ill.	Ossie Langfelder, D	1991, Apr.	Wausau, Wis.	John Robinson, D	1992, Apr.
Springfield, Mass	Mary Hurley, N-P	1991, Nov.	Wauwatosa, Wis.	James Brundahl, N-P	1992, Apr.
Springfield, Mo.	*Thomas Tinnie	1990, Apr.	W. Allis, Wis.	Fred Cashmore, N-P	1992, Apr.
Springfield, Oh.	*Matthew Kridler	1988, Oct.	W. Covina, Cal.	*Herman Fast	1976, Aug.
Springfield, Ore.	*Michael Kelly	1989, Jan.	W. New York, N.J.	Anthony DeFino, D	1991, May
Stamford, Conn.	Thom Serrani, D	1991, Nov.	W. Orange, N.J.	Samuel Spina, D	1994, May
Sterling Hts., Mich.	*Steve Duchane	1987, Nov.	W. Palm Beach, Fla.	*Paul Steinbrenner	1986, Jan.
Stillwater, Okla.	*Carl Weinaug	1983, Apr.	Westland, Mich.	Robert Thomas, D	1993, Nov.
Stockton, Cal.	*Alan N. Harvey	1988, Aug.	Westminster, Cal.	*Jerry Kenny	1989, Jan.
Stratford, Conn.	*Ronald Owens	1984, July	Westminster, Col.	*William Christopher	1978, June
Sunnyvale, Cal.	*Thomas Lewcock	1980, Apr.	Wheaton, Ill.	*Donald Rose	1980, Nov.
Syracuse, N.Y.	Thomas G. Young, D	1993, Nov.	Wheeling, W. Va.	*Jimmy Curnes	1990, May
Tacoma, Wash.	*Ray Corpuz Jr.	1990, Jan.	White Plains, N.Y.	Alfred Del Vecchio, R	1993, Nov.
Tallahassee, Fla.	*Daniel A. Kleman.	1974, Aug.	Whittier, Cal.	Thomas Sawyer, N-P	1992, Apr.
Tampa, Fla.	Sandra Friedman, N-P	1991, Mar.	Wichita, Kan.	*Chris Cherches	1985, Oct.
Taunton, Mass.	Richard Johnson, D	1991, Nov.	Wichita Falls, Tex.	*James Berzina	1983, June
Taylor, Mich.	Cameron Priebe, D	1993, Nov.	Wilkes-Barre, Pa.	Lee Namey, D	1991, Nov.
Teaneck, N.J.	*Werner H. Schmid	1959, Mar.	Williamsport, Pa.	Jessie Bloom, D	1991, Nov.
Tempe, Ariz.	Harry E. Mitchell, D	1992, Mar.	Wilmington, Del.	Daniel Frawley, D	1992, Nov.
Temple, Tex.	*Jack Parker	1985, Apr.	Wilmington, N.C.	*William B. Farris	1983, May
Terre Haute, Ind.	P. Pete Chalos, D	1991, Nov.	Winston-Salem, N.C.	*Bryce A. Stuart	1980, Jan.
Thousand Oaks, Cal.	*Grant Brimhall	1978, Jan.	Woonsocket, R.I.	Francis Lanctot, D	1991, Nov.
Titusville, Fla.	*Norman Hickey	1974, June	Worcester, Mass.	Jordan Levy, D	1991, Nov.
Toledo, Oh.	*Thomas Hoover	1990, Sept.	Wyandotte, Mich.	James R. DeSana, D	1991, Apr.
Topeka, Kan.	Butch Felker, N-P	1993, Apr.	Wyoming, Mich.	*James Sheeran	1976, Nov.
Torrance, Cal.	*Leroy J. Jackson	1983, Jan.	Yakima, Wash.	*Richard Zais Jr.	1979, Jan.
Trenton, N.J.	Douglas Palmer, N-P	1994, May	Yonkers, N.Y.	*Neil De Luca	1988, Jan.
Troy, Mich.	*Frank Gerstenecker	1970, Feb	York, Pa.	William Althaus, R	1993, Nov.
Troy, N.Y.	*Steven Dworsky	1986, July	Youngstown, Oh.	Patrick Ungaro, D	1993, Nov.
			Yuma, Ariz.	*Doug Lowe, R	1984, Jan.
			Zanesville, Oh.	Donald Lewis Mason, R	1991, Nov.

How a Bill Becomes a Law

1. A Senator or Representative introduces a bill by sending it to the clerk of the House, who assigns it a number and title. This procedure is termed the *first reading*. The clerk then refers the bill to the appropriate Senate or House committee.

2. If the committee opposes the bill, they immediately *table*, or kill it. Otherwise, the committee holds hearings to listen to opinions and facts offered by members and other interested parties. The committee then debates the bill and possibly offers amendments. A vote is taken, and if favorable, the bill is sent back to the clerk of the House.

3. The clerk reads the bill to the House. This is termed the *second reading*. Members may then debate the bill and suggest amendments.

4. *The third reading* is simply by title, and the bill is put to a voice or roll call vote.

5. The bill then goes to the other house, where it may be defeated, or passed with or without amendments. If defeated, the bill dies. If passed with amendments, a joint Congressional committee works out the differences and arrives at a compromise.

6. After its final passage by both houses, the bill is sent to the President. If he signs it, the bill becomes a law. However, he may *veto* the bill by refusing to sign it and sending it back to the house where it originated, with his reasons for the veto.

7. The President's objections are then read and debated, and a roll-call vote taken. If the bill receives less than a two-thirds vote, it is defeated. If it receives at least two-thirds, it is sent to the other house. If that house also passes it by at least two-thirds, the President's veto is *overridden*, and the bill becomes a law.

8. If the President wishes neither to sign nor to veto the bill, he may retain it for 10 days—not including Sunday—after which it automatically becomes a law even without his signature. However, if Congress has adjourned within those 10 days, the bill is automatically killed; this indirect rejection is termed a *pocket veto*.

ECONOMICS

U.S. Budget Receipts and Outlays—1986-1989

Source: U.S. Treasury Department. Financial Management Service
(Fiscal years end Sept. 30)
(millions of dollars)

Classification	Fiscal 1986	Fiscal 1987	Fiscal 1988	Fiscal 1989
Net Receipts				
Individual income taxes	$348,959	$392,557	$401,181	$445,690
Corporation income taxes	63,143	83,926	94,195	103,291
Social insurance taxes and contributions:				
Federal old-age and survivors insurance	182,518	194,541	220,337	240,595
Federal disability insurance	17,711	18,861	21,154	23,071
Federal hospital insurance	51,335	55,992	59,859	65,396
Railroad retirement fund	2,103	3,634	3,743	3,798
Total employment taxes and contributions . .	255,062	273,028	305,093	332,859
Other insurance and retirement:				
Unemployment.	24,098	25,575	24,584	22,011
Federal employees retirement	4,645	4,613	4,537	4,428
Civil service retirement and disability	96	102	122	119
Total social insurance taxes and				
contributions	283,901	303,318	334,335	359,416
Excise taxes . . . . : .	32,919	32,457	35,540	34,386
Estate and gift taxes	6,958	7,493	7,594	8,745
Customs duties	13,323	15,085	15,411	16,334
Deposits of earnings-Federal Reserve Banks	18,374	16,817	17,163	19,604
All other miscellaneous receipts.	1,514	2,490	2,746	3,323
Net Budget Receipts	$769,091	$854,143	$908,166	990,789
Net Outlays				
Legislative Branch.	$1,665	$1,812	$1,852	$2,094
The Judiciary.	1,069	1,178	1,337	1,493
Executive Office of the President:				
The White House Office.	23	25	26	27
Office of Management and Budget.	37	37	41	42
Total Executive Office	107	109	121	124
Funds appropriated to the President:				
International security assistance	10,371	6,820	4,273	1,012
Multinational assistance	1,838	1,306	1,498	1,492
Agency for International Development.	1,220	1,294	1,404	1,225
International Development Assistance.	3,121	2,673	2,980	2,790
Total funds appropriated to the President. . .	11,379	10,406	7,252	4,302
Agriculture Department:				
Food stamp program	12,443	12,405	13,145	13,725
Farmer's Home Admin.	8,001	3,748	7,277	7,608
Forest service	2,284	2,221	2,688	2,944
Total Agriculture Department.	58,666	49,593	44,003	48,414
Commerce Department	2,083	2,156	2,279	2,571
Bureau of the Census	—	217	333	557
Defense Department:				
Military personnel	71,511	72,020	76,337	80,676
Operation and maintenance	75,259	76,178	84,475	87,001
Procurement	76,517	80,744	77,166	81,620
Research, development, test, evaluation	32,283	33,596	34,792	37,002
Military construction	5,067	5,853	5,874	5,275
Total Defense Department (military)	265,636	273,938	281,935	294,876
Defense Department (civil)	20,243	20,659	22,047	23,427
Education Department	17,673	16,800	18,246	21,608
Energy Department	11,025	10,688	11,166	11,387
Health and Human Services Department:				
Food and Drug Administration	417	422	463	510
National Institutes of Health.	5,115	5,222	6,334	6,992
Public Health Service	9,504	9,886	11,408	12,250
Health Care Financing Adm.	119,307	130,472	144,654	163,028
Human Development Services	5,412	5,448	5,886	6,850
Total Health and Human Services Dept.	143,252	148,893	158,991	172,301
Social Security	190,684	202,422	214,178	227,473
Housing and Urban Development Department. . . .	14,139	15,464	18,956	19,772
Interior Department	4,791	5,045	5,147	5,308
Justice Department:				
Federal Bureau of Investigation	1,183	1,216	1,384	1,528
Total Justice Department	3,768	4,333	5,426	6,232
Labor Department:				
Unemployment Trust Fund	21,819	20,527	18,598	18,730
Total Labor Department	24,141	23,453	21,870	22,657
State Department	2,865	2,788	3,421	3,722
Transportation Department.	27,365	25,431	26,404	26,689
Federal Aviation Adm	4,673	4,895	5,192	5,822
Treasury Department:				
Internal Revenue Service	7,188	7,513	9,363	11,049
Interest on the public debt.	190,151	195,390	214,145	240,863
Total Treasury Department	179,189	180,345	201,644	230,573
Veterans Affairs Dept.	—	—	18,528	18,794
Environmental Protection Agency	4,869	4,903	4,872	4,906
General Services Administration.	286	74	−281	−462

(continued)

Classification **Net Receipts**	Fiscal 1986	Fiscal 1987	Fiscal 1988	Fiscal 1989
National Aeronautics and Space Administration . . .	7,403	7,591	9,092	11,036
Office of Personnel Management	23,955	26,966	29,191	29,073
Small Business Administration	490	−72	−54	83
Independent agencies:				
Action	154	159	153	163
Board for International Broadcasting	127	156	194	199
Corporation for Public Broadcasting	160	200	214	228
District of Columbia	530	560	550	538
Equal Employment Opportunity Commission . .	159	158	176	182
Export-Import Bank of the United States	−1,167	−2,300	−894	47
Federal Communications Commission	92	79	52	49
Federal Deposit Insurance Corporation	705	−1,438	2,146	2,784
Federal Trade Commission	62	66	69	65
Interstate Commerce Comm.	—	—	43	44
Intragovernmental Agencies	218	203	200	165
Legal Services Corporation	305	309	306	307
National Archives & Record Adm.	96	96	102	126
National Foundation on the Arts and Humanities	320	310	322	331
National Labor Relations Board	132	127	132	136
National Science Foundation	1,550	1,562	1,665	1,752
Nuclear Regulatory Commission	421	393	232	189
Railroad Retirement Board	3,980	4,196	4,147	4,315
Securities and Exchange Commission.	104	108	126	140
Smithsonian Institution.	224	242	260	288
Tennessee Valley Authority	906	1,091	1,089	348
U.S. Information Agency	780	830	843	888
Total independent agencies	11,865	14,266	23,446	32,323
Undistributed offsetting receipts	−64,914	−72,400	−78,474	−89,155
Net Budget Outlays.	990,231	1,003,804	1,063,318	1,142,869
Less net receipts.	769,091	854,143	908,166	990,789
Deficit	−221,140	−149,661	−155,151	−152,080

U.S. Net Receipts and Outlays

Source: U.S. Treasury Department; annual statements for year ending June 30 (thousands of dollars)

Yearly average	Receipts	Outlays	Yearly average	Receipts	Outlays	Yearly average	Receipts	Outlays
1789-1800[1]	5,717	5,776	1866-1870	447,301	377,642	1901-1905	559,481	535,559
1801-1810[2]	13,056	9,086	1871-1875	336,830	287,460	1906-1910	628,507	639,178
1811-1820[2]	21,032	23,943	1876-1880	288,124	255,598	1911-1915	710,227	720,252
1821-1830[2]	21,928	16,162	1881-1885	366,961	257,691	1916-1920	3,483,652	8,065,333
1831-1840[2]	30,461	24,495	1886-1890	375,448	279,134	1921-1925	4,306,673	3,578,989
1841-1850[2]	28,545	34,097	1891-1895	352,891	363,599	1926-1930	4,069,138	3,182,807
1851-1860	60,237	60,163	1896-1900	434,877	457,451	1931-1935[3]	2,770,973	5,214,874
1861-1865	160,907	683,785						

(1) Average for period March 4, 1789, to Dec. 31, 1800. (2) Years ended Dec. 31, 1801 to 1842; average for 1841-1850 is for the period Jan. 1, 1841, to June 30, 1850. (3) Expenditures for years 1932 through 1935 have been revised to include Government corps. (wholly owned) etc. (net).

Summary of Receipts, Outlays, and Surpluses or Deficits (—); 1934-1985

(In millions of dollars)

Source: U.S. Treasury Department, Financial Management Service

Year	Total Receipts	Total Outlays	Surplus or Deficit (−)	Year	Total Receipts	Total Outlays	Surplus or Deficit (−)
1934	2,955	6,541	−3,586	1961	94,388	97,723	−3,335
1935	3,609	6,412	−2,803	1962	99,676	106,821	−7,146
1936	3,923	8,228	−4,304	1963	106,560	111,316	−4,756
1937	5,387	7,580	−2,193	1964	112,613	118,528	−5,915
1938	6,751	6,840	−89	1965	116,817	118,228	−1,411
1939	6,295	9,141	−2,846	1966	130,835	134,532	−3,698
1940	6,548	9,468	−2,920	1967	148,822	157,464	−8,643
1941	8,712	13,653	−4,941	1968	152,973	178,134	−25,161
1942	14,634	35,137	−20,503	1969	186,882	183,640	3,242
1943	24,001	78,555	−54,554	1970	192,807	195,649	−2,842
1944	43,747	91,304	−47,557	1971	187,139	210,172	−23,033
1945	45,159	92,712	−47,553	1972	207,309	230,681	−23,373
1946	39,296	55,232	−15,936	1973	230,799	245,707	−14,908
1947	38,514	34,496	4,018	1974	263,224	269,359	−6,135
1948	41,560	29,764	11,796	1975	279,090	332,332	−53,242
1949	39,415	38,835	580	1976	298,060	371,779	−73,719
1950	39,443	42,562	−3,119	Transition quarter[1] . .	81,232	95,973	−14,741
1951	51,646	45,514	6,102	1977	355,559	409,203	−53,644
1952	66,167	67,686	−1,519	1978	399,561	458,729	−59,168
1953	69,608	76,101	−6,493	1979	463,302	503,464	−40,162
1954	69,701	70,855	−1,154	1980	517,112	590,920	−73,808
1955	65,451	68,444	−2,993	1981	599,272	678,209	−78,936
1956	74,587	70,640	3,947	1982	617,766	745,706	−127,940
1957	79,990	76,578	3,412	1983	600,562	808,327	−207,764
1958	79,636	82,405	−2,769	1984	666,457	851,781	−185,324
1959	79,249	92,098	−12,849	1985	734,057	946,316	−212,260
1960	92,492	92,191	301				

(1) Effective fiscal year 1977, fiscal year is reckoned Oct. 1-Sept. 30; Transition Quarter covers July 1, 1976-Sept. 30, 1976.

The Federal Budget Process

Source: Executive Office of the President, Office of Management and Budget.

Executive budget process	Timing	Congressional budget process
Agencies subject to executive branch review submit initial budget request materials.	Sept. 1	
Fiscal year begins. President's initial GRH sequester order takes effect (amounts are withheld from obligation pending issuance of final order).	Oct. 1	Fiscal year begins.
	Oct. 10	CBO issues revised GRH report to OMB and Congress.
OMB reports on changes in initial GRH estimates and determinations resulting from legislation enacted and regulations promulgated after its initial report to Congress. President issues final GRH sequester order, which is effective immediately, and transmits message to Congress within 15 days of final order. Agencies not subject to executive branch review submit budget request materials.	Oct. 15	
Legislative branch and the judiciary submit budget request materials.	Nov. 15 Nov.- Dec.	Comptroller General issues GRH compliance report.
President transmits the budget to Congress.	1st Mon. after Jan. 3	Congress receives the President's budget.
OMB sends allowance letters to agencies.	Jan.-Feb.	
	Feb. 15	CBO reports to the Budget Committees on the President's budget.
	Feb. 25	Committees submit views and estimates to Budget Committee in their own house.
OMB and the President conduct reviews to establish presidential policy to guide agencies in developing the next budget.	Apr.- June	
	Apr. 1	Senate Budget Committee reports concurrent resoluion on the budget.
	Apr. 15	Congress completes action on concurrent resolution.
	May 15	House may consider appropriations bills in the absence of a concurrent resolution on the budget.
	June 10	House Appropriations Committee reports last appropriations bill.
	June 15	Congress completes action on reconciliation legislation.
	June 30	House completes action on annual appropriations bills.
President transmits the mid-session review, updating the budget estimates.	July 15	Congress receives mid-session review of the budget.
OMB provides agencies with policy guidance for the upcoming budget.	July- Aug.	
Date of "snapshot" of projected deficits for the upcoming fiscal year for initial OMB and CBO GRH reports.	Aug. 15	
	Aug. 20	CBO issues its initial GRH report to OMB and Congress.
OMB issues its initial GRH report providing estimates and determinations to the President and Congress. President issues initial GRH sequester order and sends message to Congress within 15 days.	Aug. 25	

CBO = Congressional Budget Office; GRH = Gramm-Rudman-Hollings (*Balanced Budget and Emergency Deficit Control Act of 1985*); OMB = Office of Management and Budget.

Public Debt of the U.S.

Source: U.S. Treasury Department, Bureau of Public Debt

Fiscal year	Debt (billions)	Per. cap. (dollars)	Interest paid (billions)	Pct. of federal outlays	Fiscal year	Debt (billions)	Per. cap. (dollars)	Interest paid (billions)	Pct. of federal outlays
1870	$2.4	$61.06	—	—	1975	$533.2	$2,475	$32.7	9.8
1880	2.0	41.60	—	—	1976	620.4	2,852	37.1	10.0
1890	1.1	17.80	—	—	1977	698.8	3,170	41.9	10.2
1900	1.2	16.60	—	—	1978	771.5	3,463	48.7	10.6
1910	1.1	12.41	—	—	1979	826.5	3,669	59.8	11.9
1920	24.2	228	—	—	1980	907.7	3,985	74.9	12.7
1930	16.1	131	—	—	1981	997.9	4,338	95.6	14.1
1940	43.0	325	$1.0	10.5	1982	1,142.0	4,913	117.4	15.7
1945	258.7	1,849	3.8	4.1	1983	1,377.2	5,870	128.8	15.9
1950	256.1	1,688	5.7	13.4	1984	1,572.3	6,640	153.8	18.1
1955	272.8	1,651	6.4	9.4	1985	1,823.1	7,598	178.9	18.9
1960	284.1	1,572	9.2	10.0	1986	2,125.3	8,774	190.2	19.2
1965	313.8	1,613	11.3	9.6	1987	2,350.3	9,615	195.4	19.5
1970	370.1	1,814	19.3	9.9	1988	2,602.3	10,534	214.1	20.1
					1989	2,857.4	11,545	240.8	25.0

Note: Through 1976 the fiscal year ended June 30. From 1977 on, fiscal year ends Sept. 30.

U.S. International Transactions

Source: Bureau of Economic Analysis, U.S. Commerce Department

(millions of dollars)

	1960	1965	1970	1975	1980	1985	1988	1989
Exports of goods services and income[1]	30,556	42,722	68,387	157,936	343,241	366,049	533,438	603,169
Merchandise, adjusted, excluding military[2]	19,650	26,461	42,469	107,088	224,269	215,935	320,337	360,465
Transfers under U.S. military agency sales contracts	2,030	2,465	4,214	6,256	9,029	8,699	9,520	8,331
Travel	919	1,380	2,331	4,697	10,588	17,663	28,935	34,432
Passenger fares	175	271	544	1,039	2,591	4,323	8,771	10,101
Other transportation	1,607	2,175	3,125	5,840	11,618	14,674	18,939	20,416
Royalties and license fees[3]	837	1,534	2,331	4,300	7,085	5,995	10,858	11,815
Other private services	570	714	1,294	2,920	6,276	15,601	25,359	29,461
U.S. Government miscellaneous services	153	285	332	446	398	878	672	613
Income receipts on U.S. assets abroad:	4,616	7,437	11,748	25,351	71,388	82,282	110,048	127,536
Direct investment	3,621	5,506	8,169	16,595	37,146	28,295	49,819	53,617
Other private receipts	646	1,421	2,671	7,644	31,680	48,487	53,530	68,377
U.S. Government receipts	349	510	907	1,112	2,562	5,499	6,699	5,542
Imports of goods, services and income	-23,670	-32,708	-59,901	-33,745	-333,774	-473,998	-647,295	-696,483
Merchandise, adjusted, excluding military[2]	-14,758	-21,510	-39,866	-98,185	-249,750	-338,083	-447,323	-475,329
Direct defense expenditures	-3,087	-2,952	-4,855	-4,795	-10,851	-12,795	-14,972	-14,651
Travel	-1,750	-2,438	-3,980	-6,417	-10,397	-25,155	-33,098	-34,977
Passenger fares	-513	-717	-1,215	-2,263	-3,607	-6,650	-7,932	-8,522
Other transportation	-1,402	-1,951	-2,843	-5,708	-11,790	-15,643	-19,675	-20,791
Royalties and license fees[3]	-74	-135	-244	-472	-724	-891	-2,054	-2,245
Other private services	-593	-461	-827	-1,551	-2,909	-5,840	-11,843	-11,481
U.S. Government miscellaneous services	-254	-457	-576	-789	-1,214	-1,735	-1,960	-2,040
Income payments on foreign assets in the U.S.								
Direct investment	-394	-657	-875	-2,234	-8,635	-6,079	-16,748	-14,004
Other private payments	-511	-942	-3,617	-5,788	-21,214	-37,064	-61,526	-78,489
U.S. Government payments	-332	-489	-1,024	-4,542	-12,684	-22,972	-30,164	-35,955
Unilateral transfers, net	-4,062	-4,583	-6,156	-7,075	-8,349	-15,473	-15,005	-14,720
U.S. Government grants	-3,367	-3,444	-4,449	-5,101	-5,486	-11,268	-10,744	-10,963
U.S. Government pensions and other transfers	-273	-463	-611	-1,068	-1,818	-2,138	-2,491	-2,432
Private remittances and other transfers	-423	-677	-1,096	-906	-1,044	-2,068	-1,770	-1,326
U.S. assets abroad, net (increase/capital outflow (-))	-4,099	-5,716	-9,337	-39,703	-86,118	-27,721	-84,176	-127,061
U.S. official reserve assets, net	2,145	1,225	2,481	-849	-8,155	-3,858	3,912	-25,293
U.S. Government assets, other than official reserve assets, net	-1,100	-1,605	-1,589	-3,474	-5,162	-2,821	2,969	1,185
U.S. private assets, net	-5,144	-5,336	-10,229	-35,380	-72,802	-21,043	-83,232	-102,953
Foreign assets in U.S., net (increase/capital inflow (+))	2,294	742	6,359	15,670	58,112	130,012	221,442	214,652
Statistical discrepancy (sum of above items with sign reversed)	-1,019	-457	-219	5,917	25,736	20,041	-8,404	22,443
Memoranda:								
Balance on merchandise trade								
Balance on services	4,892	4,951	2,603	8,903	-25,481	-122,148	-126,986	-114,864
Balance on investment income	3,379	5,350	6,233	12,707	28,856	16,166	1,610	913
Balance on goods, services, and income	-1,385	-287	-349	3,501	6,093	-877	11,519	20,463
Balance on current account	2,824	5,431	2,331	18,116	1,119	-122,332	-128,862	-110,034

(1) Excludes transfers of goods and services under U.S. military grant programs. (2) Excludes exports of goods under U.S. military agency sales contracts identified in Census export documents, excludes imports of goods under direct defense expenditures identified in Census import documents, and reflects various other adjustments. (3) Redefined in 1982.

U.S. Direct Investment Abroad in Selected Countries

Source: Bureau of Economic Analysis, U.S. Commerce Department

(millions of dollars)

	1987	1988	1989		1987	1988	1989
All countries	314,307	333,501	373,436	Luxembourg	660	850	904
Africa	5,869	5,468	5,024	Netherlands	14,842	16,047	17,168
Egypt	1,669	1,670	1,802	Portugal	495	546	612
Libya	310	315	311	Spain	4,076	4,979	6,002
Nigeria	894	660	461	United Kingdom	44,512	49,274	60,810
S. Africa	1,497	1,269	714	Non E.E.C.	31,010	31,342	33,375
Asia and Pacific (excl. Japan)	17,010	18,515	20,991	Austria	619	688	688
Hong Kong	4,389	5,244	5,853	Finland	389	408	484
India	439	436	549	Norway	3,843	4,371	3,640
Indonesia	3,070	2,925	3,696	Sweden	1,139	1,119	1,102
Malaysia	952	1,135	1,098	Switzerland	19,665	18,357	19,952
Philippines	1,396	1,511	1,682	Turkey	207	246	312
Singapore	2,384	2,290	2,213	Japan	15,684	17,927	19,341
South Korea	1,178	1,501	1,889	South America	21,227	21,690	23,557
Taiwan	1,372	1,622	1,949	Argentina	2,744	2,597	2,624
Thailand	1,274	1,132	1,279	Brazil	10,951	12,460	14,687
Australia	11,363	13,186	14,495	Chile	348	691	1,018
Bermuda	19,215	19,040	17,849	Colombia	3,104	2,248	1,900
Canada	57,783	62,610	66,856	Ecuador	466	431	395
Europe	150,439	156,932	176,736	Peru	1,022	986	912
European Communities	119,428	125,590	143,360	Venezuela	2,095	1,897	1,537
Belgium	7,267	7,448	8,290	Central America	12,218	13,119	15,880
Denmark	1,070	1,163	1,246	Mexico	4,913	5,694	7,079
France	11,868	♦3,150	14,747	Panama	6,622	6,632	7,906
Germany, West	24,388	21,742	23,059	Middle East	4,084	3,806	3,886
Greece	132	195	265	Israel	635	700	770
Ireland	5,425	6,212	6,237	Saudi Arabia	2,092	1,782	1,812
Italy	9,264	9,540	10,634	United Arab Emirates	694	672	674

National Income by Industry

Source: Bureau of Economic Analysis, U.S. Commerce Department

(billions of dollars)

	1960	1965	1970	1975	1980	1988	1989
National income without capital consumption adjustment	428.6	583.6	835.1	1,315.0	2,263.9	3,957.2	4,228.5
Domestic industries	425.1	577.8	827.8	1,297.4	2,216.3	3,923.7	4,190.9
Private industries	371.6	500.8	695.4	1,088.3	1,894.5	3,357.5	3,584.9
Agriculture, forestry, fisheries	17.8	21.0	25.9	46.5	61.4	94.7	101.0
Mining	5.6	6.1	8.4	21.2	43.8	35.2	36.4
Construction	22.5	32.3	47.4	69.9	126.6	215.8	225.1
Manufacturing	125.3	171.6	215.6	317.5	532.1	782.2	803.8
Durable goods	73.4	105.6	127.7	185.0	313.7	453.7	465.6
Nondurable goods	52.0	66.1	87.9	132.5	218.4	328.6	338.2
Transportation, public utilities	35.8	47.0	64.4	101.1	177.3	298.2	314.2
Transportation	18.5	23.7	31.5	48.0	85.8	131.2	136.6
Communication	8.2	11.5	17.6	26.8	48.1	80.3	87.4
Electric, gas, and sanitary services	9.1	11.7	86.8	90.2	43.4	86.8	90.2
Wholesale trade	25.0	32.5	47.5	83.0	143.3	228.6	247.4
Retail trade	41.3	55.1	79.9	123.1	189.4	340.9	360.1
Finance, insurance, and real estate	51.3	67.4	96.4	143.9	279.5	562.0	613.8
Services	46.9	67.9	109.8	182.1	341.0	799.9	883.0
Government, government enterprises	53.5	76.9	132.4	209.1	321.8	566.2	606.9
Rest of the world	3.5	5.8	7.2	17.5	47.6	33.5	37.6

National Income by Type of Income

Source: Bureau of Economic Analysis, U.S. Commerce Department

(billions of dollars)

	1960	1965	1970	1975	1980	1988	1989
National income[1]	424.9	585.2	832.6	1,289.1	2,203.5	3,984.9	4,223.3
Compensation of employees	296.7	399.8	618.3	948.7	1,638.2	2,905.1	3,079.0
Wages and salaries	272.8	363.7	551.5	814.7	1,372.0	2,431.1	2,573.2
Government	49.2	69.9	117.1	176.1	260.1	446.6	476.6
Other	223.7	293.8	434.3	638.6	1,111.8	1,984.5	2,096.6
Supplements to wages, salary	23.8	36.1	66.8	134.0	266.3	474.0	505.8
Employer contrib. for social ins.	12.6	18.3	34.3	68.0	127.9	248.5	263.9
Other labor income	11.2	17.8	32.5	65.9	138.4	225.5	241.9
Proprietors' income	52.1	65.1	80.2	125.4	180.7	354.2	379.3
Farm	11.6	13.0	14.7	25.4	20.5	43.7	48.6
Nonfarm	40.5	52.1	65.4	100.0	160.1	310.5	330.7
Rental income of persons with capital consump. adjust.	15.3	18.1	18.2	13.5	6.6	16.3	8.2
Corp. prof., with inv. adjust.	49.8	76.2	69.5	123.9	194.0	289.8	286.1
Corp. profits before tax	49.9	77.4	76.0	134.8	237.1	316.7	307.7
Corp. profits tax liability	22.7	30.9	34.4	50.9	84.8	136.2	135.1
Corp. profits after tax	27.2	46.5	41.7	83.9	152.3	180.5	172.6
Dividends	12.9	19.1	22.5	29.6	54.7	110.0	123.5
Undistributed profits	14.3	27.4	19.2	54.3	97.6	70.5	49.1
Inventory valuation adjustment	-.2	-1.2	-6.6	-11.0	-43.1	-27.0	-21.7
Net interest	11.3	20.9	41.2	83.8	200.9	371.8	445.1

(1) *National income* is the aggregate of labor and property earnings which arises in the current production of goods and services. It is the sum of employee compensation, proprietors' income, rental income, corporate profits, and net interest. It measures the total factor costs of the goods and services produced by the economy. Income is measured before deduction of taxes on income.

Gross National Product, Net National Product, National Income, and Personal Income

Source: Bureau of Economic Analysis, U.S. Commerce Department
(billions of dollars)

	1960	1970	1975	1980	1988	1989
Gross national product[1]	515.3	1,015.5	1,598.4	2,732.0	4,873.7	5,200.8
Less: Capital consumption allowances	46.4	88.8	161.8	303.8	514.3	554.4
Equals: Net national product	468.9	926.6	1,436.6	2,428.1	4,359.4	4,646.4
Less: Indirect business tax and nontax liability	45.3	94.0	140.0	213.3	388.7	414.0
Business transfer payments	2.0	4.1	7.4	12.1	30.3	32.4
Statistical discrepancy	−2.8	−1.1	2.5	4.9	−28.2	−17.0
Plus: Subsidies less current surplus of government enterprises	.4	2.9	2.4	5.7	16.2	6.3
Equals: National income	424.9	832.6	1,289.1	2,203.5	3,984.9	4,223.3
Less: Corporate profits with inventory valuation and capital consumption adjustment	49.5	74.7	117.6	177.2	337.6	311.6
Net interest	11.3	41.2	83.8	200.9	371.8	445.1
Contributions for social insurance	21.9	62.2	118.5	216.5	442.6	476.8
Wage accruals less disbursement	.0	.0	.1	.0	0	0
Plus: Government transfer payment to persons	27.5	81.8	185.7	312.6	557.4	604.5
Personal interest income	24.9	69.3	122.5	271.9	547.9	643.2
Personal dividend income	12.9	22.2	28.7	52.9	102.2	114.4
Business transfer payments	2.0	4.1	7.4	12.1	30.3	32.4
Equals: Personal income	409.4	831.8	1,313.4	2,258.5	4,070.8	4,384.3

(1) Gross National Product is the market value of all goods and services that have been bought for final use during a year. The GNP is considered the most comprehensive measure of a nation's economic activity.

Stock Exchanges
N.Y. Stock Exchange Transactions

Year	Yearly volume Stock shares	Yearly volume Bonds par values	Year	Yearly volume Stock shares	Yearly volume Bonds par values
1900	138,981,000	$579,293,000	1970	2,937,359,448	$4,494,864,600
1905	260,569,000	1,026,254,000	1975	4,693,427,000	5,178,300,000
1910	163,705,000	634,863,000	1980	11,352,294,000	5,190,304,000
1915	172,497,000	961,700,000	1981	11,853,740,659	5,733,071,000
1920	227,636,000	3,868,422,000	1982	16,458,036,768	7,155,443,000
1925	459,717,623	3,427,042,210	1983	21,589,576,997	7,572,315,000
1929	1,124,800,410	2,996,398,000	1984	23,071,031,447	6,982,291,000
1930	810,632,546	2,720,301,800	1985	27,510,706,353	9,046,453,000
1935	381,635,752	3,339,458,000	1986	35,680,016,341	10,475,399,000
1940	207,599,749	1,669,438,000	1987	47,801,308,660	9,726,244,000
1950	524,799,621	1,112,425,170	1988	40,438,346,358	7,594,644,000
1960	766,693,818	1,346,419,750	1989	41,698,538,270	8,836,374,000

American Stock Exchange Transactions

Year	Yearly volume Stock shares	Bonds[1] princ. amts.	Year	Yearly volume Stock shares	Bonds[1] princ. amts.	Year	Yearly volume Stock shares	Bonds[1] princ. amts.
1929	476,140,375	$513,551,000	1970	843,116,260	$641,270,000	1985	2,100,860,000	$645,182,000
1930	222,270,065	863,541,000	1980	1,626,072,625	355,723,000	1986	2,978,540,000	810,264,000
1940	42,928,337	303,902,000	1981	1,343,400,220	301,226,000	1987	3,505,950,000	684,965,000
1945	143,309,392	167,333,000	1982	1,485,831,536	325,240,000	1988	2,515,210,000	604,950,000
1950	107,792,340	47,549,000	1983	2,081,270,000	395,190,000	1989	3,125,030,000	708,836,000
1960	286,039,982	32,670,000	1984	1,545,010,000	371,990,000			

(1) Corporate

Components of Dow Jones Industrial Average

Allied-Signal
Aluminum Co. of Amer.
American Express
AT&T
Bethlehem Steel
Boeing
Chevron
Coca-Cola
DuPont
Eastman Kodak
Exxon

General Electric
General Motors
Goodyear
IBM
International Paper
McDonald's
Merck
Minn. Mining & Manuf.
Navistar
Philip Morris

Primerica
Procter & Gamble
Sears, Roebuck
Texaco
Union Carbide
United Technologies
USX Corp.
Westinghouse
Woolworth

Components of Dow Jones Transportation Average

AMR Corp.
Airborne Freight
Alaska Air
American President
Burlington Northern
CSX
Carolina Freight

Consolidated Freightways
Consolidated Rail
Delta Air Lines
Federal Express
Norfolk Southern
Pan Am
Ryder System

Santa Fe Pacific
Southwest Air Lines
UAL
Union Pacific
USAir Group
XTRA Corp

Components of Dow Jones Utility Average

American Electric Power
Centerior Energy
Columbia Gas System
Commonwealth Edison
Consolidated Edison

Consolidated Natural Gas
Detroit Edison
Houston Industries
Niagara Mohawk Power
Pacific Gas & Electric

Panhandle Eastern
Peoples Energy
Philadelphia Electric
Public Service Enterprises
SCE

Dow Jones Industrial Average Since 1954

High	Year	Low	High	Year	Low
Dec. 31 404.39	1954	Jan. 11 279.87	Jan. 11 1051.70	1973	Dec. 5 788.31
Dec. 30 488.40	1955	Jan. 17 388.20	Mar. 13 891.66	1974	Dec. 6 577.60
Apr. 6 521.05	1956	Jan. 23 462.35	July 15 881.81	1975	Jan. 2 632.04
July 12 520.77	1957	Oct. 22 419.79	Sept. 21 1014.79	1976	Jan. 2 858.71
Dec. 31 583.65	1958	Feb. 25 436.89	Jan. 3 999.75	1977	Nov. 2 800.85
Dec. 31 679.36	1959	Feb. 9 574.46	Sept. 8 907.74	1978	Feb. 28 742.12
Jan. 5 685.47	1960	Oct. 25 566.05	Oct. 5 897.61	1979	Nov. 7 796.67
Dec. 13 734.91	1961	Jan. 3 610.25	Nov. 20 1000.17	1980	Apr. 21 759.13
Jan. 3 726.01	1962	June 26 535.76	Apr. 27 1024.05	1981	Sept. 25 824.01
Dec. 18 767.21	1963	Jan. 2 646.79	Dec. 27 1070.55	1982	Aug. 12 776.92
Nov. 18 891.71	1964	Jan. 2 766.08	Nov. 29 1287.20	1983	Jan. 3 1027.04
Dec. 31 969.26	1965	June 28 840.59	Jan. 6 1286.64	1984	July 24 1086.57
Feb. 9 995.15	1966	Oct. 7 744.32	Dec. 16 1553.10	1985	Jan. 4 1184.96
Sept. 25 943.08	1967	Jan. 3 786.41	Dec. 2 1955.57	1986	Jan. 22 1502.29
Dec. 3 985.21	1968	Mar. 21 825.13	Aug. 25 2722.42	1987	Oct. 19 1738.74
May 14 968.85	1969	Dec. 17 769.93	Oct. 21 2183.50	1988	Jan. 20 1879.14
Dec. 29 842.00	1970	May 6 631.16	Oct. 9 2791.41	1989	Jan. 3 2144.64
Apr. 28 950.82	1971	Nov. 23 797.97	July 16 2999.75	1990*	Oct. 11 2365.10
Dec. 11 1036.27	1972	Jan. 26 889.15			*As of 10/15/90

Most Active Common Stocks in 1989

New York Exchange	Volume (millions of shares)	American Exchange	Volume (millions of shares)	NASDAQ	Volume (millions of shares)
AT&T	462.1	BAT Industries	173.7	MCI	485.4
IBM	402.3	Wang Labs "B"	123.6	Apple Computer	454.6
General Electric	357.6	Texas Air	119.1	Intel	384.3
Exxon	336.2	Amdahl	99.0	Sun Microsystems	295.8
Union Carbide	316.9	Echo Bay Mines	84.4	Seagate Technology	199.2
Texaco	297.3	Fruit of the Loom	82.3	Jaguar	196.7
USX	286.6	DWG	64.4	Tele-Comm. "A"	184.9
Eastman Kodak	281.9	ENSCO	56.9	Oracle Systems	182.2
Philip Morris	280.3	Diasonics	50.3	First Executive	168.0
Ford Motor	263.9	Bolar Pharm	43.5	Liz Claiborne	154.2
Warner Comm.	256.1	Hasbro	40.0	Microsoft	135.4
General Motors	252.3	New York Times	35.9	Laidlaw Transpt "B"	131.9
Citicorp	238.8	Home Shopping	35.1	Lin Broadcasting	130.0
American Express	236.7	Atari	34.5	Lotus Development	129.8
Texas Utilities	230.8	Western Digital	34.1	Reuters Holdings	122.9
BankAmerica	225.8	Magma Copper	33.5	Micron Technology	122.4
Bristol-Myers	224.5	OMI	32.0	McCaw Technology	116.9
		Carnival Cruise	31.6	3 Com	116.6

Top Mutual Funds

Source: Lipper Analytical Services Inc.

Ten Years 12/31/79 To 12/31/89	Percent	Five Years 12/31/84 To 12/31/89	Percent	1989 12/31/88 To 12/31/89	Percent
Fidelity Magellan	1123.85	New England Zenith Cap Growth	497.61	Alger: Small Capital	65.08
Merrill Lynch Pacific A	940.74	Fidelity Overseas	353.21	United Services Gold Shrs	64.73
Japan Fund	663.90	Merrill Lynch Pacific A	328.87	Strategic Investments	61.21
Loomis-Sayles Capital	624.22	Japan Fund	314.44	GT Global Growth: Japan	60.73
Phoenix: Growth	620.91	Trustees Commingled Intl	292.02	Financial Port: Health	59.72
Lindner Fund	592.25	Alliance International	285.43	Fidelity Sel Energy Ser	59.44
New England: Growth	569.91	Vanguard World: Intl Growth	285.22	Fidelity Sel Medical	58.02
Janus Fund	558.51	Kleinwort Benson: Intl Eq	282.49	Vista: Growth & Inc	56.85
Phoenix: Stock	555.17	GAM International	278.01	GT Global Growth: America	54.77
Lindner Dividend	553.83	T Rowe Price Intl Stock	268.97	SLH Amer Telecom: Income	52.22
AIM: Weingarten Equity	545.90	20th Century: Giftrust	261.33	20th Century: Vista Inv	52.20
20th Century: Select	542.24	GT Global Growth: Pacific	258.40	Eagle Growth Shares	52.09
GT Global Growth: Pacific	540.00	Financial Port: Pacific	256.53	International Investors	51.27
IDS New Dimensions	536.16	Intl Fd for Institutions	255.00	Fidelity Sel Telecom	50.88
New York Venture	535.48	Oppenheimer Global	250.21	Janus Twenty	50.85
Amev Capital	526.48	FT International	249.64	20th Century: Giftrust	50.21
Windsor Fund	524.81	PaineWebber Classic: Atlas	246.79	Delaware: Trend	49.69
Amev Growth	524.67	Scudder International	241.92	Flag Inv Telephone Inc	48.86
SteinRoe Special	523.27	Bailard, Biehl&Kaiser Intl	240.06	One Hundred	48.31
Fidelity Destiny I	520.47	Financial Port: Health	239.20	GT Global Growth: Pacific	48.12
Vanguard High Yield Stock	515.11	Putnam Intl Equities	234.70	Sherman, Dean	47.27
United Vanguard	513.98	Kemper International	232.68	Kaufmann Fund	46.85
SoGen International	513.53	First Inv Global	231.79	Janus Fund	46.32
Washington Mutual Inv	512.88	Oppenheimer Gld & Sp Min	227.01	Medical Research Inv	45.51
Sequoia Fund	499.46	Templeton Foreign	224.52	Amev Advntge: Capital App	45.02

NASDAQ in 1989

NASDAQ, The National Association of Securities Dealers Automated Quotations reported turnover volume of 33.3 billion shares in 1989. This was an increase of 7.9% over 1988. The number of companies with shares traded in this market was 4,963 at the start of 1990, making NASDAQ the third-largest market in the world, after the New York and Tokyo exchanges.

Employee Stock Ownership Plans

Source: National Center for Employee Ownership

One of the fastest growing forms of employee compensation is the employee stock ownership plan (ESOP). The following table shows how ESOPs have grown during the 1980s.

Year	Number of plans	Employees in ESOPs (millions)	Year	Number of plans	Employees in ESOPs (millions)	Year	Number of plans	Employees in ESOPs (millions)
1980	5,009	4.048	1984	6,904	6.576	1987	8,777	8.860
1981	5,680	4.537	1985	7,402	7.353	1988	9,700	9.700
1982	6,082	4.745	1986	8,046	7.860	1989	10,000[1]	10,000[2]
1983	6,456	5.397						

(1) Estimated. (2) As of May 25, 1989.

Foreign Stock Markets

The following shows how the world's stock market indexes performed for the first 9 months of 1990

Index	Close 9/28/90	Pct. change year-to-date	Index	Close 9/28/90	Pct. change year-to-date
Sydney (All Ordinaries)	1398.3	−15.20	Zurich (Swiss index)	894.5	−21.39
Toronto (300 comp.)	3159.4	−20.41	Paris (CAC 40)	1491.8	−25.45
Dow Jones industrials	2452.48	−10.92	Singapore (Str. Times)	1098.7	−25.83
Amsterdam (CBS-all sh.)	167.6	−17.36	Frankfurt (DAX avg.)	1334.9	−25.44
Hong Kong (Hng. Sng.)	2760.8	−2.67	Tokyo (Nikkei average)	20,983.5	−46.08
London (FTSE 100)	1990.2	−17.85			

Leading U.S. Businesses in 1989

Source: FORTUNE Magazine; World Almanac Research

(millions of sales, unless otherwise noted)

Aerospace
Boeing	$20,276
United Technologies	19,766
McDonnell Douglas	14,995
Rockwell International	12,633
Allied-Signal	12,021
General Dynamics	10,053
Lockheed	9,932
Textron	7,440
Martin Marietta	5,814
Northrop	5,200

Apparel
Levi Strauss	$3,628
VF	2,540
Claiborne (Liz)	1,411
Fruit of the Loom	1,321
Hartmarx	1,312
Crystal Brands	857
Leslie Fay	786
Kellwood	754
Russell	688
Phillips-Van Heusen	642

Beverages
Pepsico	$15,420
Anheuser-Busch	9,481
Coca-Cola	9,171
Seagold Vineyards Hldg.	3,005
Coors (Adolph)	1,770
Brown-Forman	1,012

Building Materials
Owens-Illinois	$3,692
American Standard	3,631
Owens-Corning Fiber.	3,021
Corning	2,469
Manville	2,228
USG	2,201
Norton	1,535
Lafarge	1,497
Certainteed	1,365
National Gypsum	1,364

Chemicals
Du Pont (E.I.) De Nemours	$35,209
Dow Chemical	17,730
Union Carbide	8,744
Monsanto	8,681
Grace (W.R.)	6,115
Hoechst Celanese	6,016
Hanson Ind. NA	5,933
PPG Industries	5,825
Bayer USA	5,425
BASF	5,422

Computers (incl. office equip.)
IBM	$63,438
Digital Equipment	12,866
Hewlett-Packard	11,899
Unisys	10,097
NCR	5,956
Apple Computer	5,284
Wang Laboratories	3,078
Pitney Bowes	2,959
Control Data	2,952
Compaq Computer	2,876

Electronics
General Electric	$55,264
Westinghouse Electric	12,844
Motorola	9,620
Raytheon	8,796
TRW	7,408
Honeywell	7,242
Emerson Electric	7,071
Texas Instruments	6,592
Whirlpool	6,289
North American Philips	6,203

Food
Philip Morris	$39,069
RJR Nabisco	15,224
Sara Lee	11,738
Conagra	11,340
Archer Daniels	8,057
Borden	7,593
Ralston Purina	6,712
Heinz (H.J.)	5,832
General Mills	5,798
Quaker Oats	5,724

Forest Products
International Paper	$11,378
Georgia-Pacific	10,171
Weyerhaeuser	10,106
James River	5,902
Kimberly-Clark	5,777
Stone Container	5,361
Champion International	5,254
Scott Paper	5,066
Mead	4,647
Boise Cascade	4,338

Furniture
Johnson Controls	$3,690
Interco	3,278
Lear Siegler Seating	1,015
Leggett & Platt	992
Miller (Herman)	799
Ohio Mattress Hldg.	706
Hon Industries	608
Kimball International	597
La-Z-Boy Chair	556

Industrial and Farm Equip.
Tenneco	$14,439
Caterpillar	11,126
Deere	7,221
Dresser Industries	4,023
Cummins Engine	3,511
Ingersoll-Rand	3,447
Black & Decker	3,221
Parker Hannifin	2,520
Baker Hughes	2,328
Dover	2,136

Life Insurance[1]
Prudential of America	$129,118
Metropolitan Life	98,740
Equitable Life Assurance	52,512
Aetna Life	52,023
Teachers Insurance & Annuity	44,374
New York Life	37,302
Connecticut General Life	33,991
Travelers	32,088
John Hancock Mutual Life	30,925
Northwestern Mutual Life	28,500

(continued)

Metal Products

Gillette	$3,850
Masco	3,151
Illinois Tool Works	2,173
McDermott	2,121
Stanley Works	1,981
Crown Cork & Seal	1,910
Harsco	1,351
Ball	1,222
Hillenbrand Ind.	1,144
Newell	1,123

Metals

Aluminum Co. of Amer.	$11,162
LTV	6,362
Reynolds Metals	6,201
Bethlehem Steel	5,306
Inland Steel Inc	4,147
Amax	3,915
Phelps Dodge	2,726
National Steel	2,577
Armco	2,494
Maxxam	2,423

Motor Vehicles and Parts

General Motors	$126,974
Ford Motor	96,933
Chrysler	36,156
Dana	5,157
Navistar	4,296
Eaton	4,249
Paccar	3,373
Mack Trucks	1,958
Masco Industries	1,687
Fleetwood Enterprises	1,632

Petroleum Refining

Exxon	$86,656
Mobil	50,976
Texaco	32,416
Chevron	29,443
Amoco	24,214
Shell Oil	21,703
USX	17,755
Atlantic Richfield	15,905
Phillips Petroleum	12,492
Unocal	10,417

Pharmaceuticals

Johnson & Johnson	$9,844
Bristol-Myers Squibb	9,422
American Home Products	6,747
Merck	6,698
Pfizer	5,904
Abbott Laboratories	5,454
Warner-Lambert	4,272
Lilly (Eli)	4,176
Schering-Plough	3,243
Upjohn	2,916

Publishing & Printing

Time Warner	$7,642
Gannett	3,523
Times Mirror	3,517
Donnelly (R.R.)	3,128
Berkshire Hathaway	2,484
Tribune	2,455
Knight-Ridder	2,343
Reader's Digest	1,871
New York Times	1,807
McGraw-Hill	1,789

Retail[2]

Sears Roebuck	$53,913
K Mart	29,557
Wal-Mart Stores	25,922
American Stores	22,004
Kroger	19,088
J.C. Penney	16,405
Safeway Stores	14,325
Dayton Hudson	13,645
May Department Stores	12,043
Great Atlantic & Pacific Tea	10,073

Rubber and Plastics Products

Goodyear Tire	$11,045
Premark	2,601
Uniroyal Goodrich	2,267
Rubbermaid	1,349
Raychem	1,104
Cooper Tire & Rubber	870
Tredegar Ind.	638
Schulman	626
Standard Products	560
Carlisle	558

Scientific and Photographic Equip.

Eastman Kodak	$18,398
Xerox	17,635
Minnesota Mining	11,990
Baxter International	7,399
Polaroid	1,942
Becton Dickinson	1,921
EG&G	1,655
Tektronix	1,439
Bausch & Lomb	1,231
Perkin-Elmer	1,105

Soaps, Cosmetics

Procter & Gamble	$21,689
Unilever U.S.	8,114
Colgate-Palmolive	5,110
Avon Products	3,396
Revlon Group	2,739
Clorox	1,471
International Flavors	870
Alberto-Culver	717
Helene Curtis Ind.	629
Chemed	594

Textiles

Wickes	$4,802
Armstrong World Ind.	2,864
West Point-Pepperell	2,568
Burlington Holdings	2,198
Springs Industries	1,909
Amoskeag	1,402
DWG	1,185
Shaw Industries	1,176
JPS Textile Group	821
Cone Mills	715

Tobacco

American Brands	$7,265
Universal	2,920
Lorillard	1,475
Standard Commercial	951
Dibrell Brothers	689
UST	670

Transportation[3]

United Parcel Service	$12,380
AMR	10,590
UAL	9,915
Delta Air Lines	8,090
CSX	7,821
Texas Air	6,769
Union Pacific	6,590
NWA	6,554
USAir Group	6,257
Federal Express	5,183

Utilities[1]

GTE	$31,987
BellSouth	30,050
Bell Atlantic	26,220
NYNEX	25,909
US West	25,426
Pacific Gas & Electric	21,352
Pacific Telesis Group	21,194
Southwestern Bell	21,161
Southern	20,086
American Information Tech.	19,833

(1) Millions of assets as of Dec. 31, 1989; (2) Includes revenues from nonretailing activities; (3) Includes revenues from non-transportation activities.

U.S. Industrial Corporations with Largest Sales in 1989

Source: *FORTUNE Magazine*

Company (1988 rank)	Sales[1] (billions)	Income[1] (or loss) (millions)	Company (1988 rank)	Sales[1] (billions)	Income[1] (or loss) (millions)
General Motors (1)	$127.0	$4,224	Digital Equipment (30)	12.9	1,072
Ford Motor (2)	96.9	3,835	Westinghouse Electric (27)	12.8	922
Exxon (3)	86.6	3,510	Rockwell International (28)	12.6	734
IBM (4)	63.4	3,758	Phillips Petroleum (31)	12.5	219
General Electric (5)	55.3	3,939	Allied-Signal (29)	12.0	528
Mobil (6)	60.0	1,809	Minnesota Mining & Manufacturing (34)	12.0	1,244
Philip Morris (10)	39.1	2,946	Hewlett-Packard (39)	11.9	829
Chrysler (7)	36.1	359	Sara Lee (36)	11.7	410
Du Pont (9)	35.2	2,480	International Paper (42)	11.4	864
Texaco (8)	32.4	2,413	ConAgra (44)	11.3	197
Chevron (11)	29.4	251	ALCOA (40)	11.2	944
Amoco (12)	24.2	1,610	Caterpillar (35)	11.1	497
Shell Oil (13)	21.7	1,405	Goodyear (32)	11.0	206
Procter & Gamble (15)	21.7	1,206	Unocal (47)	10.4	260
Boeing (19)	20.3	973	Georgia Pacific (43)	10.2	661
Occidental Petroleum (14)	20.1	285	Weyerhaeuser (37)	10.1	341
United Technologies (16)	19.8	702	Unisys (38)	10.1	(639)
Eastman Kodak (18)	18.4	529	General Dynamics (41)	10.0	293
USX (23)	17.7	965	Lockheed (33)	9.9	2
Dow Chemical (21)	17.7	2,487	Sun (48)	9.9	98
Xerox (22)	17.6	704	Johnson & Johnson (45)	9.8	1,082
Atlantic Richfield (17)	15.9	1,953	Motorola (52)	9.6	498
Pepsico (26)	15.4	901	Anheuser-Busch (46)	9.5	767
RJR Nabisco (20)	15.2	(1,149)	Bristol-Myers Squibb (73)	9.4	747
McDonnell Douglas (25)	15.0	219	(1) Fiscal year.		
Tenneco (24)	14.4	584			

Largest Corporate Mergers or Acquisitions in U.S.

(as of mid-1990)

Company	Acquirer	Dollars	Year	Company	Acquirer	Dollars	Year
RJR Nabisco	Kohlberg Kravis Roberts	24.9 bln.	1988	Cities Service	Occidental Petroleum	4.0 bln.	1982
				Dome Petroleum	Amoco	3.8 bln.	1987
Warner Communications	Time	13.9 bln.	1989	R.H. Macy	various investors	3.7 bln.	1986
Gulf Oil	Chevron	13.3 bln.	1984	American Hospital	Baxter Travenol	3.7 bln.	1986
Kraft	Philip Morris	11.5 bln.	1988	Owens-Illinois	Kohlberg Kravis Roberts	3.6 bln.	1987
Squibb	Bristol-Myers	11.5 bln.	1989				
Getty Oil	Texaco	10.1 bln.	1984	Belridge Oil	Shell Oil	3.6 bln.	1979
Conoco	DuPont	8.0 bln.	1981	NWA	Checchi Group	3.6 bln.	1988
Standard Oil	British Petroleum	7.9 bln.*	1987	Allied Stores	Campeau	3.5 bln.	1986
Federated Dept. Stores	Campeau	7.4 bln.	1988	Fort Howard Paper	Morgan Stanley Group	3.5 bln.	1988
Marathon Oil	U.S. Steel	6.5 bln.	1981	ABC Broadcasting	Capital Cities Comm.	3.5 bln.	1985
Contel	GTE	6.2 bln.	1990	Columbia Pictures	Sony	3.4 bln.	1989
Beatrice	Kohlberg Kravis Roberts	6.2 bln.	1986	Viacom	National Amusements	3.4 bln.	1987
				McCaw Cellular	LIN Broadcasting	3.3 bln.	1989
RCA	General Electric	6.2 bln.	1986	Panhandle Eastern	Texas Eastern	3.2 bln.	1989
Superior Oil	Mobil Oil	5.7 bln.	1984	Chesebrough-Pond's	Unilever N.V.	3.1 bln.	1987
Pillsbury	Grand Metropolitan	5.7 bln.	1988	MidCon	Occidental Petroleum	3.0 bln.	1986
General Foods	Philip Morris	5.6 bln.	1986	American Medical Intl.	IMA Holdings	3.0 bln.	1989
Safeway Stores	Kohlberg Kravis Roberts	5.3 bln.	1986	Texas Oil and Gas	USX Corp.	3.0 bln.	1986
				Emhart	Black & Decker	2.8 bln.	1989
Farmers Group	B.A.T. Industries	5.2 bln.	1988	Carnation	Nestle	2.8 bln.	1984
Southern Pacific	Santa Fe Railroad	5.2 bln.	1983	Celanese	American Hoechst	2.7 bln.	1987
Southland	J.T. Acquisition	5.1 bln.	1987	Esmark	Beatrice Foods	2.7 bln.	1984
Hughes Aircraft	General Motors	5.0 bln.	1985	G.D. Searle	Monsanto	2.7 bln.	1986
Nabisco	R.J. Reynolds	4.9 bln.	1985	Continental Group	Kiewit-Murdock	2.7 bln.	1984
Signal Cos.	Allied Corp.	4.9 bln.	1986	St. Joe Minerals	Fluor	2.6 bln.	1981
Sperry	Burroughs	4.8 bln.	1986	Electronic Data Systems	General Motors	2.6 bln.	1984
Connecticut General	INA	4.3 bln.	1981	Firestone Tire	Bridgestone	2.6 bln.	1988
Borg-Warner	AV Holdings	4.2 bln.	1987	Macmillan	Maxwell Comm.	2.6 bln.	1988
Texasgulf	Elf Aquitaine	4.2 bln.	1981	Associated Dry Goods	May Dept. Stores	2.5 bln.	1986

*For the 45% of Standard Oil that British Petroleum did not already own.

Highest Paid Business Executives in 1989

Source: *Business Week*

The annual compensation survey of Business Week Magazine showed that U.S. chief executive officers make more than 3 times as much as Japanese CEOs and 33 percent more than their European counterparts. Compensation includes stock options and other performance bonuses.

Executive, Company	1989 Compensation (in millions)	Executive, Company	1989 Compensation (in millions)
Craig O. McCaw, McCaw Cellular	$53.9	William G. McGowan, MCI	$8.7
Steven J. Ross, Time Warner	34.2	James R. Moffett, Freeport-McMoRan	7.3
Donald A. Pels, Lin Broadcasting	22.8	Donald E. Petersen, Ford Motor	7.1
Jim P. Manzi, Lotus Development	16.4	P. Roy Vagelos, Merck	6.8
Paul Fireman, Reebok International	14.6	W. Michael Blumenthal, Unisys	6.5
Ronald K. Richey, Torchmark	12.7	S. Parker Gilbert, Morgan Stanley	5.5
Martin S. Davis, Paramount	11.6	Harry A. Merlo, Louisiana-Pacific	5.3
Roberto C. Goizueta, Coca-Cola	10.7	Reuben Mark, Colgate-Palmolive	5.0
Michael D. Eisner, Walt Disney	9.6	Robert J. Pfeiffer, Alexander & Baldwin	5.0
August A. Busch III, Anheuser-Busch	8.9	William P. Stiritz, Ralston Purina	4.9

Distribution of Total Personal Income

Source: Bureau of Economic Analysis; U.S. Commerce Department

(in billions)

Year	Personal income	Personal taxes	Disposable Personal income	Personal outlays	Personal Savings Amount	As a pct. of disposable income
1960	$ 402.3	$ 50.4	$ 352.0	$ 332.3	$ 19.7	5.6%
1965	540.7	64.9	475.8	442.1	33.7	7.1
1970	811.1	115.8	695.3	639.5	55.8	8.0
1974	1,168.6	170.2	998.3	913.2	85.1	8.5
1975	1,265.0	168.9	1,096.1	1,001.8	94.3	8.6
1976	1,391.2	196.8	1,194.4	1,111.9	82.5	6.9
1977	1,540.4	226.4	1,314.0	1,236.0	78.0	5.9
1978	1,732.7	258.7	1,474.0	1,384.6	89.4	6.1
1979	1,951.2	301.0	1,650.2	1,553.5	96.7	5.9
1980	2,165.3	336.5	1,828.9	1,718.7	110.2	6.0
1981	2,429.5	387.7	2,041.7	1,904.3	137.4	6.7
1982	2,584.6	404.1	2,180.5	2,044.5	136.0	6.2
1983	2,838.6	410.5	2,428.1	2,297.4	130.6	5.4
1984	3,108.7	440.2	2,668.6	2,504.5	164.1	6.1
1985	3,325.3	486.6	2,838.7	2,713.3	125.4	4.4
1986	3,526.2	512.9	3,013.3	2,888.5	124.9	4.1
1987	3,776.6	571.7	3,205.9	3,104.1	101.8	3.2
1988	4,070.8	591.6	3,479.2	3,333.6	145.6	4.2
1989	4,384.3	658.8	3,725.5	3,553.7	171.8	4.6

Consumer Price Index

The Consumer Price Index (CPI) is a measure of the average change in prices over time of basic consumer goods and services. From Jan. 1978, the Bureau of Labor Statistics began publishing CPI's for two population groups: (1) a CPI for All Urban Consumers (CPI-U) which covers about 80% of the total population; and (2) a CPI for Urban Wage Earners and Clerical Workers (CPI-W) which covers about 32% of the total population. The CPI-U includes, in addition to wage earners and clerical workers, groups such as professional, managerial, and technical workers, the self-employed, short-term workers, the unemployed, retirees and others not in the labor force.

The CPI is based on prices of food, clothing, shelter, fuels, transportation fares, charges for doctors' and dentists' services, drugs, and the other goods and services bought for day-to-day living. The index had been measuring price changes from a designated reference date—1967—which equaled 100.0.

Beginning with the release of data for January 1988, the standard reference base period for the Consumer Price Index is 1982-84. The rebasing is in keeping with the government's policy that index bases should be updated periodically. The 1982-84 period was chosen to coincide with the time period of the updated CPI's expenditure weights, which are based upon the Consumer Expenditure Surveys for 1982, 1983, and 1984. All of the CPI figures in the following tables have been changed to reflect the new reference base.

Consumer Price Indexes, 1990

Source: Bureau of Labor Statistics, U.S. Labor Department

(1982-84 = 100)	Unadjusted indexes June 1990	CPI-U Unadjusted percent change to June 1990 from— June 1989	May 1990	Seasonally adjusted percent change from— May to June	Unadjusted indexes June 1990	CPI-W Unadjusted percent change to June 1990 from— June 1989	May 1990	Seasonally adjusted percent change from— May to June
Food, beverages	131.7	5.4	0.5	0.7	131.5	5.5	0.6	0.7
Housing	128.3	4.4	0.9	0.6	126.2	4.2	0.9	0.6
Apparel, upkeep	123.3	4.7	−1.8	−0.1	122.4	4.7	−1.8	0
Transportation	118.2	2.0	0.4	0.4	117.7	1.5	0.5	0.4
Medical care	161.9	9.0	0.7	0.7	161.8	8.7	0.6	0.6
Entertainment[1]	131.9	4.5	0.2	0.2	131.0	4.4	0.2	0.2
Other goods, services	157.8	7.9	0.8	0.9	157.8	7.9	1.0	1.1
Services	138.8	5.5	0.9	0.7	137.4	5.2	0.9	0.6
Special Indexes								
All items less food	129.4	4.4	0.5	0.5	127.4	4.2	0.6	0.5
Commodities less food	115.8	2.7	−0.1	0.3	115.4	2.6	0.1	0.4
Nondurables[1]	124.6	4.7	0.3	0.3	124.4	4.7	0.4	0.4
Energy	99.5	0.5	2.9	0.6	99.2	0.3	3.0	0.8
All items less energy	134.2	5.1	0.4	0.6	132.5	4.8	0.4	0.5

Consumer Price Indexes for Selected Items and Groups

Source: Bureau of Labor Statistics, U.S. Labor Dept.

(all urban consumers = CPI-U)

(1982-84 = 100. Annual averages of monthly figures)

	1970	1975	1980	1985	1986	1987	1988	1989
All Items	38.8	53.8	82.4	107.6	109.6	113.6	118.3	124.0
Food and beverages	40.1	60.2	86.7	105.6	109.1	113.5	118.2	124.9
Food	39.2	59.8	86.8	105.6	109.0	113.5	118.2	125.1
Food at home	39.9	61.8	88.4	104.3	107.3	111.9	116.6	124.2
Cereals, bakery prods.	37.1	62.9	83.9	107.9	110.9	114.8	122.1	132.4
Meats, poultry, fish, eggs	44.6	67.0	92.0	100.1	104.5	110.5	114.3	121.3
Dairy prods.	44.7	62.6	90.9	103.2	103.3	105.9	108.4	115.6
Fruits, vegetables	37.8	56.9	82.1	106.4	109.4	119.1	128.1	138.0
Sugar, sweets	30.5	65.3	90.5	105.8	109.0	111.0	114.0	119.4
Fats, oils	39.2	73.5	89.3	106.9	106.5	108.1	113.1	121.2
Nonalcoholic beverages	27.1	41.3	91.4	104.3	110.4	107.5	107.5	111.3
Other prepared foods	39.6	58.9	83.6	106.4	109.2	113.8	118.0	125.5
Food away from home	37.5	54.5	83.4	108.3	112.5	117.0	121.8	127.4
Alcoholic beverages	52.1	65.9	86.4	106.4	111.1	114.1	118.6	123.5
Housing	36.4	50.7	81.1	107.7	110.9	114.2	118.5	123.0
Shelter	35.5	48.8	81.0	109.8	115.8	121.3	127.1	132.8
Rent	46.5	58.0	80.9	111.8	118.3	123.1	127.8	132.8
Maintenance, repairs	35.8	54.1	82.4	106.5	107.9	111.8	114.7	118.0
Fuel, other utilities	29.1	45.4	75.4	106.5	104.1	103.0	104.4	107.8
Electricity	31.8	50.0	75.8	106.9	110.4	110.0	111.5	114.7
Household furnishings & operation	46.8	63.4	86.3	103.8	105.2	107.1	109.4	111.2
House furnishings	55.5	69.8	88.5	101.7	102.2	103.6	105.1	105.5
Apparel & upkeep	59.2	72.5	90.9	105.0	105.9	110.6	115.4	118.6
Apparel commodities	63.3	76.7	92.9	104.0	104.2	108.9	113.7	116.7
Men's & boys'	62.2	75.5	89.4	105.0	106.2	109.1	113.4	117.0
Women's & girls'	71.8	85.5	96.0	104.9	104.0	110.4	114.9	116.4
Footwear	56.8	69.6	91.8	102.3	101.9	105.1	109.9	114.4
Transportation	37.5	50.1	83.1	106.4	102.3	105.4	108.7	114.1
Private	37.5	50.6	84.2	106.2	101.2	104.2	107.6	112.9
New cars	53.0	62.9	88.4	106.1	110.6	114.6	116.9	119.2
Used cars	31.2	43.8	62.3	113.7	108.8	113.1	118.0	120.4
Gasoline	27.9	45.1	97.5	98.6	77.0	80.1	80.8	88.5
Auto insurance	42.0	48.4	82.0	119.2	135.0	146.2	156.6	166.6
Public	35.2	43.5	69.0	110.5	117.0	121.1	123.3	129.5
Airline fares	28.3	38.0	68.0	112.5	117.1	122.8	124.2	131.6
Medical care	34.0	47.5	74.9	113.5	122.0	130.1	138.6	149.3

(continued)

Prescription drugs	47.4	51.2	72.5	120.1	130.4	140.8	152.0	165.2
Physicians' services	34.5	48.1	76.5	113.3	121.5	130.4	139.8	150.1
Dental services.	39.2	53.2	78.9	114.2	120.6	128.8	137.5	146.1
Hospital room	23.6	38.3	68.0	115.4	122.3	131.1	143.3	158.1
Entertainment	47.5	62.0	83.6	107.9	111.6	115.3	120.3	126.5
Other goods & services	40.9	53.9	75.2	114.5	121.4	128.5	137.0	147.7
Tobacco products	43.1	54.7	72.0	116.7	124.7	133.6	145.8	164.4
Personal care	43.5	57.9	81.9	106.3	111.9	115.1	119.4	125.0
Toilet goods	42.7	58.0	79.6	107.6	111.3	113.9	118.1	123.2
Personal care services	44.2	57.7	83.7	108.9	112.5	116.2	120.7	126.8
Personal, educational expenses	35.5	48.7	70.9	119.1	128.6	138.5	147.9	158.1

Consumer Price Indexes Annual Percent Change

Source: Bureau of Labor Statistics. U.S. Labor Department

The Consumer Price Index (CPI-U) measures the average change in prices of goods and services purchased by all urban consumers.

	1977[1]	1978	1979	1980	1981	1982	1983	1985	1986	1987	1988	1989
All items	6.5	7.6	11.3	13.5	10.3	6.2	3.2	3.6	1.9	3.6	4.1	4.8
Food	6.3	9.9	11.0	8.6	7.8	4.1	2.1	2.3	3.2	4.1	4.1	5.8
Shelter	6.6	10.2	13.9	17.6	11.7	7.1	2.3	5.6	5.5	4.7	4.8	4.5
Rent, residential	6.1	6.9	7.2	8.9	8.7	7.6	5.8	6.2	5.8	4.1	3.8	3.9
Fuel & other utilities . .	10.7	6.9	10.8	16.4	14.6	9.8	5.6	1.6	−2.3	−1.1	−1.4	3.3
Apparel and upkeep . .	4.5	3.6	4.3	7.1	4.8	2.6	2.5	2.8	0.9	4.4	4.3	2.8
Private transportation .	7.4	4.7	14.7	17.4	11.4	3.5	2.3	2.5	−4.7	−3.0	3.3	4.9
New cars	5.2	7.7	7.9	8.1	6.0	3.9	2.6	3.2	4.2	3.6	2.0	2.0
Gasoline.	5.7	4.2	35.5	38.9	11.3	−5.3	−3.3	.8	−21.9	−4.0	0.9	9.5
Public transportation . .	4.6	3.0	6.6	25.7	24.1	10.9	4.8	4.5	5.9	3.5	1.8	5.0
Medical care	9.6	8.4	9.2	11.0	10.7	11.6	8.8	6.3	7.5	6.6	6.5	7.7
Entertainment	4.9	5.3	6.7	9.0	7.8	6.5	4.3	3.9	3.4	3.3	4.3	5.2
Commodities	5.8	7.2	11.3	12.3	8.4	4.1	2.9	2.1	−0.9	3.2	3.5	4.7

(1) Change from 1976.

Consumer Price Index by Region and Selected Cities

Source: Bureau of Labor Statistics. U.S. Labor Department

	CPI-U Indexes			Percent change to June 1990 from—	CPI-W Indexes			Percent change to June 1990 from—
Area (1982-84 = 100)	Apr. 1990	May 1990	June 1990	June 1989	Apr. 1990	May 1990	June 1990	June 1989
U.S. city average	128.9	129.2	129.9	4.7	127.3	127.5	128.3	4.5
Northeast urban	134.5	134.7	134.9	5.0	133.1	133.3	133.6	4.9
More than 1,200,000.	135.4	135.4	135.4	4.9	133.1	133.1	133.3	4.9
500,000 to 1,200,000	133.5	133.6	134.4	5.8	132.0	132.1	132.9	5.6
50,000 to 500,000	132.0	132.5	133.4	4.5	134.4	134.9	135.7	4.1
North Central urban.	125.8	126.0	126.9	4.2	123.7	123.9	124.8	4.1
More than 1,200,000.	127.3	127.4	128.6	4.6	124.4	124.4	125.6	4.4
360,000 to 1,200,000	124.8	125.3	125.6	3.9	122.3	122.8	123.1	3.9
50,000 to 360,000	125.6	125.9	126.5	3.6	124.4	124.6	125.2	3.5
Less than 50,000	121.1	121.4	122.3	4.2	120.8	121.1	122.0	4.1
South urban	126.1	126.5	127.3	4.6	125.3	125.6	126.4	4.2
More than 1,200,000.	126.8	127.1	127.8	4.4	125.6	125.9	126.7	4.1
450,000 to 1,200,000	127.4	128.0	128.2	4.2	124.8	125.4	125.7	3.9
50,000 to 450,000	124.6	124.5	125.3	4.1	125.0	124.9	125.7	3.8
Less than 50,000	125.3	125.8	128.2	6.5	126.0	126.4	128.5	5.9
West urban	129.6	130.0	130.8	5.0	128.0	128.3	129.1	4.7
More than 1,250,000.	131.5	132.0	132.6	5.0	128.4	128.8	129.4	4.7
50,000 to 330,000	126.2	126.4	127.7	4.3	125.5	125.7	126.8	4.2
Selected areas								
Chicago, Ill.–Gary-Lake County, Ill., Ind., Wis.	130.4	130.4	131.7	4.8	126.5	126.5	127.9	5.0
L.A.–Anaheim, Riverside, Cal. .	134.2	134.6	135.0	4.9	130.2	130.7	131.1	4.6
New York, N.Y.–Northern N.J., Long Island, N.Y.	137.3	137.2	137.1	5.1	135.0	134.9	135.0	4.9
Philadelphia, Wilmington, Trenton, Pa., Del., N.J.	134.3	134.6	135.1	4.9	134.4	134.9	135.5	5.1
San Francisco–Oakland, San Jose, Cal.	130.7	130.8	131.6	4.3	129.8	129.9	130.7	4.1
Baltimore, Md.	—	129.0	—	—	—	128.3	—	—
Boston, Lawrence, Salem, Mass., N.H.	—	137.0	—	—	—	137.3	—	—
Cleveland, Akron, Lorain Oh. .	—	128.1	—	—	—	122.1	—	—
Miami, Ft. Lauderdale, Fla. . .	—	126.4	—	—	—	124.6	—	—
St. Louis, E. St. Louis, Mo.–Ill. .	—	126.7	—	—	—	126.0	—	—
Washington, D.C.–Md.–Va. . . .	—	134.0	—	—	—	132.8	—	—
Dallas–Fort Worth, Tex.	122.9	—	123.8	3.2	122.2	—	123.2	2.7
Detroit, Ann Arbor, Mich.	126.9	—	127.7	4.6	123.9	—	124.7	4.5
Houston, Galveston, Brazoria, Tex.	118.3	—	119.7	4.9	118.6	—	120.0	4.8
Pittsburgh, Beaver Valley, Pa. .	124.9	—	125.0	3.8	120.1	—	120.3	3.8

Personal Consumption Expenditures in the U.S.

Source: Bureau of Economic Analysis, U.S. Commerce Department

(billions of dollars)

	1985	1986	1987	1988	1989	Average Annual % change 1980-1985	1985-1989
Personal consumption expenditures	2,629.0	2,797.4	3,009.4	3,238.2	3,450.1	8.7	6.2
Food & Tobacco	503.8	533.7	566.4	599.6	636.9	6.4	5.3
Food purchased for off-premise consumption	322.7	339.1	353.7	372.6	395.4	5.9	4.5
Purchased meals and beverages	139.9	151.6	165.5	176.6	188.8	6.9	6.9
Tobacco products	32.2	33.6	35.6	36.9	41.7	9.1	5.9
Clothing, accessories, jewelry	193.3	207.5	222.3	240.0	257.8	7.4	6.7
Shoes	22.9	24.3	25.9	27.5	29.8	6.3	6.0
Clothing and accessories less shoes	133.4	142.4	152.5	163.4	174.7	7.7	6.2
Jewelry and watches	20.5	22.8	24.7	26.4	27.4	5.9	6.7
Personal care	38.8	41.4	44.4	48.5	52.3	7.4	7.0
Toilet articles, preparations	23.1	24.6	26.3	27.9	29.7	—	5.7
Barbershops, beauty parlors, baths, health clubs	15.7	16.8	18.2	20.4	22.6	—	8.8
Housing	403.0	434.2	468.9	502.3	533.9	9.0	6.5
Owner-occupied nonfarm dwellings space rent	272.7	293.7	316.9	339.2	361.7	8.9	6.5
Tenant-occupied nonfarm dwellings rent	103.8	114.3	123.6	132.9	141.2	10.9	7.2
Rental value of farm dwellings	10.9	9.7	10.3	10.4	10.3	-.2	-1.1
Household operation	334.1	347.5	363.3	386.1	404.9	7.5	4.2
Furniture, incl. bedding	28.0	30.4	31.8	32.9	33.6	6.0	3.3
Kitchen, other household appliances	23.7	25.5	26.7	28.4	29.4	—	4.8
China, glassware, tableware, utensils	13.0	14.3	15.3	16.5	18.0	—	7.7
Other durable house furnishings	28.2	30.6	33.5	37.0	39.2	—	7.8
Semidurable house furnishings	14.0	15.2	16.0	17.3	18.7	7.0	6.7
Cleaning, household supplies, paper products	26.4	27.8	29.1	30.8	32.8	5.6	4.8
Household utilities	124.2	122.4	125.8	132.6	139.3	8.2	2.4
Telephone, telegraph	40.4	42.7	44.1	47.2	48.7	7.8	4.1
Medical care	327.5	357.6	399.0	444.0	483.5	11.8	9.5
Drug preparations, sundries	28.1	30.2	32.3	34.3	36.4	8.4	5.9
Physicians	73.5	80.6	94.0	106.1	113.0	11.8	10.7
Dentists	21.5	22.8	25.0	27.1	29.0	9.4	7.0
Privately controlled hospitals and sanitariums	140.2	152.4	166.3	182.9	201.1	11.3	8.7
Health insurance	21.6	22.4	25.3	27.7	29.6	11.9	7.4
Personal business	169.9	192.5	215.4	227.1	243.1	11.9	8.6
Brokerage charges, investment counseling	14.8	19.7	20.5	17.6	19.2	—	5.9
Bank service charges, trust services, safe deposit box rental	11.7	13.0	14.6	15.6	17.5	—	9.9
Legal services	28.0	30.9	35.0	39.6	42.9	15.2	10.6
Funeral, burial expenses	6.3	6.6	7.0	7.5	7.9	7.4	5.1
Transportation	359.5	366.3	379.7	407.5	425.7	8.6	3.7
User-operated transportation	330.1	335.9	346.3	371.0	387.6	8.8	3.5
New autos	87.4	101.3	93.5	101.1	99.7	13.5	2.8
Used autos	35.1	33.6	38.5	40.9	41.6	18.7	3.7
Repair, greasing, washing, parking, storage, rental	49.1	52.0	55.9	63.2	69.6	8.7	8.4
Gasoline and oil	90.6	73.5	75.3	77.3	83.8	1.6	-1.5
Tolls	1.4	1.7	1.9	1.7	1.7	—	4.3
Insurance premiums less claims paid	9.9	12.6	15.4	16.7	17.0	—	14.3
Purchased local transportation	7.2	7.8	8.2	8.7	8.9	4.4	4.7
Transit systems	3.6	3.8	4.0	4.2	4.3	8.4	3.8
Taxicab	3.1	3.3	3.5	3.8	3.9	—	5.2
Railway (commutation)	.5	.6	.7	.7	.7	10.8	8.0
Purchased intercity transportation	22.2	22.6	25.5	27.7	29.2	6.9	6.3
Railway (excl. commutation)	.6	.7	.7	.8	.9	—	10.0
Bus	1.2	1.1	1.4	1.6	1.3	—	1.6
Airline	18.5	18.8	20.8	22.8	24.2	6.7	6.2
Recreation	185.7	201.2	223.2	245.1	264.4	10.1	8.5
Books, maps	8.1	8.6	9.5	10.5	11.4	—	8.1
Magazines, newspapers, sheet music	13.2	13.9	15.4	17.0	18.5	4.9	8.0
Nondurable toys and sport supplies	21.1	23.1	26.2	28.0	30.2	7.6	8.6
Wheel goods, durable toys, sports equipment, boats, pleasure aircraft	26.7	29.7	33.2	35.4	36.2	—	7.1
Radio and TV receivers, records, musical instruments	37.0	38.8	41.6	47.1	51.1	13.2	7.6
Flowers, seeds, potted plants	5.5	5.8	7.0	7.5	8.1	—	9.5
Admissions to specified spectator amusements	9.5	10.2	11.3	12.1	13.4	—	8.2
Motion picture theaters	3.6	3.9	4.2	4.4	5.0	—	7.8
Legitimate theater, opera	3.0	3.3	4.0	4.5	4.9	—	12.7
Spectator sports	2.9	2.9	3.0	3.2	3.5	—	4.1
Clubs, fraternal organizations	4.8	5.0	5.5	5.9	6.3	—	6.3
Commerical amusements	15.1	16.0	17.1	18.7	20.2	—	6.8
Private education, research	43.3	46.6	50.9	57.7	64.3	9.7	9.7
Higher education	15.7	16.9	17.7	19.3	20.9	—	6.6
Elementary and secondary schools	13.8	14.5	15.5	17.0	18.6	—	7.0
Religious and welfare activities	57.1	62.9	68.1	75.9	82.9	9.2	9.0

Percent Change in Consumer Prices in Selected Countries

Source: International Monetary Fund

Country	1970-1975, avg.	1975-1980, avg.	1980-1985, avg.	1986-1987 avg.	Country	1970-1975, avg.	1975-1980, avg.	1980-1985, avg.	1986-1987 avg.
United States	6.7	8.9	5.5	3.7	Japan	11.5	6.5	2.7	0
Australia	10.2	10.6	8.3	8.5	Netherlands	8.6	6.0	4.2	−0.5
Austria	7.3	5.3	4.9	1.4	Norway	8.4	8.4	9.0	8.7
Belgium	8.4	6.4	7.0	1.6	Portugal	15.4	21.8	23.2	9.3
Canada	7.3	8.7	7.4	4.4	Spain	12.1	18.6	12.2	5.3
France	8.8	10.5	9.6	3.3	Sweden	8.0	10.5	9.0	4.2
Germany, W.	6.1	4.1	3.9	0.3	Switzerland	7.7	2.3	4.3	1.4
Greece	12.3	16.3	20.7	16.4	Turkey	18.6	50.1	37.8	38.8
Italy	11.3	16.3	13.7	4.7	United Kingdom	13.0	14.4	7.2	4.2

Inflation

Source: Bureau of Labor Statistics

Inflation started the 1980s in double digits but sank to as low as 1.1 percent in 1986. For the decade, prices rose 64.4 percent from the start of 1980 through December 1989. This was a marked improvement over the 1970s when inflation exploded 103.0 percent, mostly as the result of soaring oil prices. The 1960s saw inflation rise 28.2 percent, and the 1950s 24.6 percent.

Inflation In The 1980s

12.5% '80   8.9% '81   3.8% '82   3.8% '83   3.9% '84   3.8% '85   1.1% '86   4.4% '87   4.4% '88   4.6% '89

Index of Leading Economic Indicators

Source: Bureau of Economic Analysis, U.S. Department of Commerce

The index of leading economic indicators, which is issued to project the economy's performance six months or a year ahead, was unchanged in July 1990. Analysts said that the increase suggests that the economy may be on the verge of a recession.

The index is made up of eleven measurements of economic activity that tend to change direction long before the overall economy does. The volatility of the index, caused in part by the fact that many of the statistics covered do not reach the Commerce Department until weeks after the initial report, usually results in at least one revision after the initial reporting.

Leading Indicators: Component Analysis

Components	Contribution to change June to July 1990	Components	Contribution to change June to July 1990
Average workweek of production workers in manufacturing	−0.07	adjusted for inflation	+0.21
Average weekly claims for state unemployment insurance[1]	−0.01	New building permits issued	−0.07
New orders for consumer goods and materials, adjusted for inflation	−0.00	Change in manufactureres unfilled orders, durable goods	−0.08
Vendor performance (companies receiving slower deliveries from suppliers)	−0.17	Change in sensitive materials prices	+0.12
Contracts and orders for plant and equipment,		Index of stock prices	−0.01
		Money supply: M-2, adjusted for inflation	−0.08
		Index of consumer expectations	+0.03
		Leading indicators index, percent change	**0.00**

(1) Series is inverted in computing index; that is, a decrease in the series is considered upward movement.

State Finances
Revenues, Expenditures, Debts, Taxes, and U.S. Aid
(fiscal year 1989)
Source: Census Bureau, U.S. Commerce Dept.

State, bond rating[1]	Revenue (millions)	Expenditures (millions)	Debt (millions)	Per cap. debt	Per cap. taxes	Per cap. U.S. aid
Alabama, AA	$8,278	$7,401	$4,078	$990	$889	$428
Alaska, AA−	5,112	4,448	5,611	10,647	2,674	1,142
Arizona, NR	7,578	7,157	2,069	581	1,141	290
Arkansas, AA	4,300	3,840	1,767	734	902	426
California, AAA . . .	81,708	72,583	26,207	901	1,418	493
Colorado, NR	6,967	5,878	2,171	654	875	380
Connecticut, AA+ .	9,045	8,972	9,573	2,955	1,484	489
Delaware, AA+ . .	2,257	1,929	2,831	4,206	1,679	460
Florida, AA	22,160	19,977	8,967	707	983	279
Georgia, AA+ . . .	11,898	10,835	3,039	472	986	415
Hawaii, AA	4,041	3,184	3,063	2,754	1,993	453
Idaho, NR	2,195	1,858	834	822	996	465
Illinois, AA+	22,243	20,346	14,158	1,214	1,008	360
Indiana, NR	10,733	9,668	3,587	641	1,055	362
Iowa, NR	6,441	5,892	1,618	569	1,112	431
Kansas, NR	4,630	4,206	344	136	993	350
Kentucky, AA	8,028	7,401	5,136	1,378	1,083	459
Louisiana, BBB+ . .	9,558	8,734	12,160	2,775	905	477
Maine, AAA	3,164	2,837	2,032	1,662	1,301	547
Maryland, AAA . . .	11,501	10,117	5,834	1,242	1,319	406
Massachusetts, BBB	16,000	17,320	16,336	2,762	1,534	500
Michigan, AA	22,707	20,881	8,198	884	1,199	456
Minnesota, AA+ . .	12,390	10,584	3,601	827	1,469	478
Mississippi, AA− . .	5,055	4,528	1,346	513	882	496
Missouri, AAA. . . .	8,703	7,738	4,893	948	908	314
Montana, AA− . . .	2,087	1,880	1,347	1,670	903	647
Nebraska, NR . . .	2,864	2,559	1,411	875	900	385
Nevada, AA	2,784	2,532	1,423	1,280	1,206	302
New Hampshire, AA+	1,840	1,851	2,946	2,661	553	318
New Jersey, AAA . .	21,869	20,812	17,393	2,248	1,357	430
New Mexico, AA . .	4,596	3,962	1,896	1,240	1,237	494
New York, A	60,678	54,073	43,306	2,412	1,480	654
North Carolina, AAA	13,533	12,366	2,950	448	1,121	380
North Dakota, AA−	1,756	1,725	927	1,404	1,007	663
Ohio, AA.	27,478	22,975	10,513	963	991	386
Oklahoma, AA . . .	7,011	6,212	3,577	1,109	1,027	446
Oregon, AA−	6,767	5,686	6,737	2,388	917	525
Pennsylvania, AA−	25,681	22,987	10,540	875	1,048	413
Rhode Island, AA. .	2,960	2,744	3,343	3,349	1,161	612
South Carolina, AAA	8,061	6,958	3,775	1,074	1,058	418
South Dakota, NR .	1,407	1,253	1,860	2,601	654	596
Tennessee, AA+. . .	8,325	7,742	2,574	520	823	454
Texas, AA.	29,389	24,226	6,665	392	822	329
Utah, AAA.	3,693	3,513	1,694	992	831	536
Vermont, AA	1,530	1,434	1,108	1,953	1,118	666
Virginia, AAA	13,096	11,724	5,510	903	1,085	338
Washington, AA . .	13,507	11,650	5,364	1,126	1,367	458
West Virginia, AA−	3,985	3,820	2,452	1,320	1,030	445
Wisconsin, AA . . .	13,132	10,514	5,931	1,218	1,316	462
Wyoming, NR. . . .	1,843	1,566	926	1,950	1,225	1,023
United States . . .	**$586,560**	**$525,077**	**$295,618**	**$1,193.76**	**$1,147.02**	**$437**

(1) Standard & Poor's long-term bond ratings for the states. The assessments range from AAA to BBB depending on the credit agency's estimate of their ability to pay principal and interest and their susceptibility to adverse economic conditions. Ratings as of Mar. 1990. NR = States that have no outstanding debt or have never applied for a rating. Totals do not add up due to rounding.

Federal Aid to State and Local Governments
Source: U.S. Office of Management and Budget
(million of dollars)

Type of aid, function, and major program	1970	1975	1980	1985	1988	1989[1]
Grant-in-aid shared revenue	24,065	49,791	91,451	105,897	115,294	123,563
National defense.	37	74	93	157	188	232
Natural resources & environment	411	2,437	5,363	4,069	3,747	3,736
Energy	25	43	499	529	475	437
Agriculture	604	404	569	2,420	2,069	1,715
Transportation[2].	4,599	5,864	13,087	17,055	18,083	18,188
Airports	83	292	590	789	825	1,123
Highways	4,395	4,702	9,209	12,841	926	13,509
Railroads.	—	(z)	54	35	22	25
Urban mass transit	105	689	3,129	2,797	3,227	3,434
Commerce & housing credit	4	2	3	2	1	

(continued)

Type of aid, function, and major program	1970	1975	1980	1985	1988	1989[1]
Community & regional development[2] . . .	1,780	2,842	6,486	5,221	4,267	4,316
Education, employment, training, social services[2]	6,393	12,133	21,862	17,817	19,882	22,359
Health[2]	3,849	8,810	15,758	24,451	586	36,615
Alcohol, drug abuse, & mental health[3] .	146	590	679	501	720	927
Medicaid[3]	2,727	6,840	13,957	22,655	462	34,292
Income security[2]	5,819	9,352	18,495	27,153	620	33,389
Assistance payment program[3]	4,142	5,121	6,888	8,592	764	11,322
Food stamps, administration	559	136	413	886	113	1,373
Child nutrition & special milk programs[3]	379	1,565	3,388	3,480	158	4,491
Housing assistance[3]	436	1,326	3,435	6,407	618	9,166
Veterans benefits & services	18	33	90	91	106	128
Administration of justice	42	725	529	95	338	359
General government[4]	49	101	138	182	1,950	2,090

(1) Estimate. (2) Includes items not shown separately. (3) Incl. grants for payments to individuals. (4) Incl. general purpose fiscal assistance.

Percent Change in Federal Aid to State and Local Governments

Source: U.S. Office of Management and Budget

Type of aid, function, and major program	1970-1975	1975-1980	1980-1985	1985-1989
Grant-in-aid shared revenue	106%	83%	15%	16%
National defense	100	25	68	47
Natural resources & environment	492	120	-24	-8
Energy	72	1,060	6	-17
Agriculture	-33	40	325	-29
Transportation[2]	27	123	30	6
Commerce & housing credit	-50	50	-33	—
Community & regional development[2]	59	128	-19	-17
Education, employment, training, social services[2]	89	80	-18	25
Health[2]	128	78	55	49
Income security[2]	60	97	46	22
Veterans benefits & services	83	172	1	40
Administration of justice	1,626	-27	-82	277
General government[4]	106	36	31	1,048

Foreign Direct Investment in the U.S.

Source: Bureau of Economic Analysis; U.S. Commerce Department

(billions of dollars)

Five countries accounted for 77 percent of the $401 billion worth of foreign direct investment in the U.S. at the end of 1989.

	1970	1975	1980	1985	1987	1988	1989
All Countries	13.2	27.6	83.0	184.6	271.7	328.8	401.0
Canada	3.1	5.3	12.1	17.1	24.0	27.3	32.0
Netherlands	2.1	5.3	19.1	37.0	49.1	48.9	60.0
Switzerland	1.5	2.1	5.0	10.5	14.6	15.8	—
United Kingdom	4.1	6.3	14.1	43.5	79.6	101.9	119.0
W. Germany	0.680	1.4	7.5	14.8	20.3	23.8	28.0
Japan	0.229	0.591	4.7	19.3	35.1	53.3	70.0

Consumer Credit Outstanding, 1970 to 1988

Source: Federal Reserve System

(billions of dollars)
Estimated amounts of credit outstanding as of end of year. Seasonally adjusted.

Type of Credit	1970	1975	1980	1982	1983	1984	1985	1986	1987	1988
Credit outstanding .	131.6	204.9	349.4	381.1	430.4	511.8	592.4	647.2	679.2	728.9
Ratio to disposable personal income[1] (percent)	18.3	17.9	18.2	16.9	17.7	19.1	20.8	21.4	21.2	21.0
Installment	103.9	167.0	297.6	323.5	367.9	442.5	517.8	572.0	607.7	659.5
Automobile paper .	36.3	56.9	111.9	124.2	143.7	173.7	209.6	247.3	266.0	281.2
Revolving	4.9	14.5	54.8	66.2	78.6	100.2	122.0	137.0	153.9	174.8
Mobile home paper .	2.4	15.3	18.6	22.8	23.7	25.7	26.8	27.4	26.4	25.7
All other loans . . .	60.2	80.1	112.1	110.2	121.6	142.8	159.2	160.4	161.5	177.8
Commercial banks	48.6	82.9	145.5	149.1	169.3	209.1	241.6	263.0	282.9	318.9
Finance companies	27.2	32.7	61.9	74.9	82.9	89.5	111.0	133.9	140.3	145.2
Credit unions	12.8	25.4	43.6	46.8	52.9	65.5	71.9	76.2	80.1	86.1
Retailers[2]	12.9	16.6	26.1	29.4	34.1	37.2	39.1	39.4	41.0	43.5
Other[3]	2.3	9.2	20.3	23.2	28.4	41.1	53.9	59.4	63.5	65.8
Noninstallment . . .	27.7	37.9	51.8	57.6	62.5	69.2	74.7	75.1	71.4	69.4
Single-payment loans	18.9	26.8	39.6	45.5	48.8	54.6	59.1	58.4	53.0	49.0
Charge accounts .	8.7	11.0	12.1	12.0	13.6	14.6	15.6	16.7	18.5	20.4

(1) Based on fourth quarter seasonally adjusted disposable personal income at annual rates as published by the U.S. Bureau of Economic Analysis. (2) Excludes 30-day charge credit held by travel and entertainment companies. (3) Comprises savings institutions and gasoline companies.

Philanthropy in the U.S.

Source: Giving USA, 1989; a publication of the American Association of Fund-Raising Counsel Trust for Philanthropy

(billions of dollars)

Sources of Contributors

Corporations		Foundations		Bequests		Individuals		Total Amount	
1970	.797	1970	1.90	1970	2.13	1970	16.19	1970	21.02
1975	1.202	1975	1.65	1975	2.23	1975	23.53	1975	28.61
1980	2.359	1980	2.81	1980	2.86	1980	40.71	1980	48.74
1985	4.472	1985	4.90	1985	4.77	1985	66.17	1985	80.31
1988	4.800	1988	6.15	1988	6.57	1988	86.35	1988	103.87
1989	5.000	1989	6.70	1989	6.70	1989	6.57	1989	96.43

Uses of Contributions

	Religion	Education	Health	Human service	Arts, culture & humanities	Public/ society benefit	Other
1970	9.34	2.60	3.44	2.92	.663	.455	2.64
1975	12.81	2.83	3.61	2.94	1.56	.790	4.40
1980	22.23	4.96	5.34	4.91	3.15	1.46	6.68
1985	37.46	8.17	7.72	8.50	5.08	2.22	11.16
1988	48.09	10.23	9.58	10.49	6.79	3.21	15.47
1989	54.32	10.69	10.04	11.39	7.49	3.62	17.15

Federal Reserve System

(as of Aug. 1990)

The Federal Reserve System is the central bank for the United States. The system was established on December 23, 1913, originally to give the country an elastic currency, to provide facilities for discounting commercial paper, and to improve the supervision of banking. Since then, the System's responsibilities have been broadened. Over the years, stability and growth of the economy, a high level of employment, stability in the purchasing power of the dollar, and reasonable balance in transactions with foreign countries have come to be recognized as primary objectives of governmental economic policy.

The Federal Reserve System consists of the Board of Governors, the 12 District Reserve Banks and their branch offices, and the Federal Open Market Committee. Several advisory councils help the Board meet its varied responsibilities.

The hub of the System is the seven member Board of Governors in Washington. The members of the Board are appointed by the President and confirmed by the Senate, to serve 14-year terms. The President also appoints the Chairman and Vice-Chairman of the Board from among the board members for 4-year terms that may be renewed. Currently, the board members are: Alan Greenspan, Chairman; Edward W. Kelley, Jr.; Martha R. Seger; Wayne D. Angell; John P. La Ware.

The Board is the policy-making body. In addition to its policy making responsibilities, it supervises the budget and operations of the Reserve Banks, approves the appointments of their presidents and appoints 3 of each District Bank's directors, including the chairman and vice chairman of each Reserve Bank's board.

The 12 Reserve Banks and their branch offices serve as the decentralized portion of the System, carrying out day-to-day operations such as circulating currency and coin, providing fiscal agency functions and payments mechanism services. The District Banks are located in Boston, New York, Philadelphia, Cleveland, Richmond, Atlanta, Chicago, St. Louis, Minneapolis, Kansas City, Dallas and San Francisco.

The System's principal function is monetary policy, which it controls using three tools: reserve requirements, the discount rate and open market operations. Uniform reserve requirements, set by the Board, are applied to the transaction accounts and nonpersonal time deposits of all depository institutions. Responsibility for setting the discount rate (the interest rate at which depository institutions can borrow money from the Reserve Banks) is shared by the Board of Governors and the Reserve Banks. Changes in the discount rate are recommended by the individual Boards of Directors of the Reserve Banks and are subject to approval by the Board of Governors. The most important tool of monetary policy is open market operations (the purchase and sale of government securities). Responsibility for influencing the cost and availability of money and credit through the purchase and sale of government securities lies with the Federal Open Market Committee (FOMC). This committee is composed of the 7 members of the Board of Governors, the president of the Federal Reserve Bank of New York, and 4 other Federal Reserve Bank presidents, who serve one-year terms on a rotating basis. The committee bases its decisions on current economic and financial developments and outlook, setting yearly growth objectives for key measures of money supply and credit. The decisions of the committee are carried out by the Domestic Trading Desk of the Federal Reserve Bank of New York.

The Federal Reserve Act prescribes a Federal Advisory Council, consisting of one member from each Federal Reserve District, elected annually by the Board of Directors of each of the 12 Federal Reserve Banks. They meet with the Federal Reserve Board four times a year to discuss business and financial conditions and to make advisory recommendations.

The Consumer Advisory Council is a statutory body, including both consumer and creditor representatives, which advises the Board of Governors on its implementation of consumer regulations and other consumer-related matters.

Following the passage of the Monetary Control Act of 1980, the Board of Governors established the Thrift Institutions Advisory Council to provide information and views on the special needs and problems of thrift institutions. The group is comprised of representatives of mutual savings banks, savings and loan associations, and credit unions.

Federal Reserve Board Discount Rate

The discount rate is the rate of interest set by the Federal Reserve that member banks are charged when borrowing money through the Federal Reserve System.

Effective Date	Rate		Effective Date	Rate		Effective Date	Rate		Effective Date	Rate
1980: Feb. 15	13	1981:	May 5	14		Oct. 12	9½	1986:	March 7	7
May 30	12		Nov. 2	13		Nov. 22	9		April 21	6½
June 13	11		Dec. 4	12		Dec. 15	8½		July 11	6
July 28	10	1982:	July 20	11½	1984:	April 9	9		Aug. 21	5½
Sept. 26	11		Aug. 2	11		Nov. 21	8½	1987:	Sept. 4	6
Nov. 17	12		Aug. 16	10½		Dec. 24	8	1988:	Aug. 9	6½
Dec. 5	13		Aug. 27	10	1985:	May 20	7½	1989:	Feb. 24	7
									In effect Aug. 30, 1990 .	7

Gold Reserves of Central Banks and Governments

Source: IMF, *International Financial Statistics*
(Million fine troy ounces)

Year end	All countries[1]	United States	Canada	Japan	Belgium	France	West Germany	Italy	Nether-lands	Switzer-land	United Kingdom
1973	1,022.24	275.97	21.95	21.11	42.17	100.91	117.61	82.48	54.33	83.20	21.01
1974	1,020.24	275.97	21.95	21.11	42.17	100.93	117.61	82.48	54.33	83.20	21.03
1975	1,018.71	274.71	21.95	21.11	42.17	100.93	117.61	82.48	54.33	83.28	21.03
1976	1,014.23	274.68	21.62	21.11	42.17	101.02	117.61	82.48	54.33	83.28	21.03
1977	1,029.19	277.55	22.01	21.62	42.45	101.67	118.30	82.91	54.63	83.28	22.23
1978	1,036.82	276.41	22.13	23.97	42.59	101.99	118.64	83.12	54.78	83.28	22.83
1979	944.44	264.60	22.18	24.23	34.21	81.92	95.25	66.71	43.97	83.28	18.25
1980	952.99	264.32	20.98	24.23	34.18	81.85	95.18	66.67	43.94	83.28	18.84
1981	953.72	264.11	20.46	24.23	34.18	81.85	95.18	66.67	43.94	83.28	19.03
1982	949.16	264.03	20.26	24.23	34.18	81.85	95.18	66.67	43.94	83.28	19.01
1983	947.84	263.39	20.17	24.23	34.18	81.85	95.18	66.67	43.94	83.28	19.01
1984	946.79	262.79	20.14	24.23	34.18	81.85	95.18	66.67	43.94	83.28	19.03
1985	949.39	262.65	20.11	24.33	34.18	81.85	95.18	66.67	43.94	83.28	19.03
1986	949.11	262.04	19.72	24.23	34.18	81.85	95.18	66.67	43.94	83.28	19.01
1987	944.49	262.38	18.52	24.23	33.63	81.85	95.18	66.67	43.94	83.28	19.01
1988	944.92	261.87	17.14	24.23	33.67	81.85	95.18	66.67	43.94	83.28	19.00
1989	938.95	261.93	16.10	24.23	30.23	81.85	95.18	66.67	43.94	83.28	18.99

(1) Covers IMF members with reported gold holdings. For countries not listed above, see *International Financial Statistics*, a monthly publication of the International Monetary Fund.

The Savings and Loan Crisis

The savings and loan industry had its worst year ever in 1989 as losses soared to $19.2 billion. This exceeded the previous biggest shortfall, which came in 1988, when savings and loans lost $13.4 billion. There is no way to forecast how much the U.S. government will eventually pay to save the troubled industry. The following is the General Accounting Office estimate of the cost of the bailout as of June 1990. (*See Chronology for additional information.*)

Estimates of Major Costs through the Year 2029

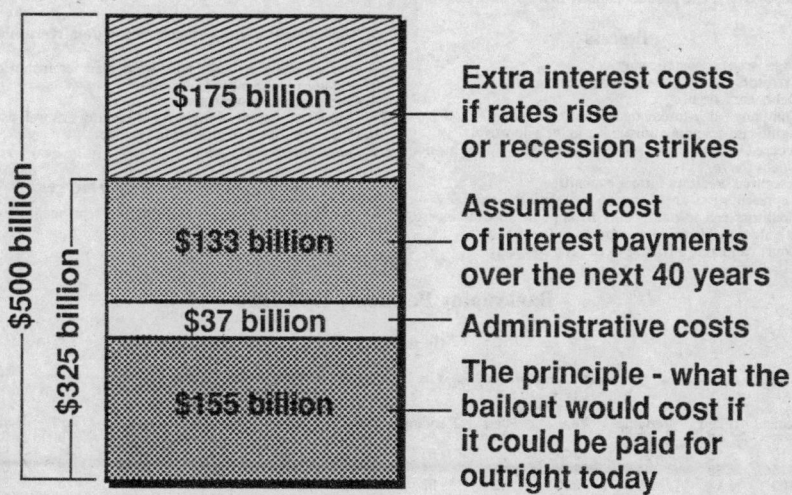

$175 billion	Extra interest costs if rates rise or recession strikes
$133 billion	Assumed cost of interest payments over the next 40 years
$37 billion	Administrative costs
$155 billion	The principle - what the bailout would cost if it could be paid for outright today

$500 billion
$325 billion

In June 1990, The Resolution Trust Corporation, the government organization created in 1989 to handle the savings & loan industry bailout, released its list of real estate for sale. It included 35,908 properties with a book value of $14.9 billion. The properties had been owned by 148 failed savings and loans in liquidation.

Type of Property

Nearly 84 percent of the property for sale was residential property, mainly in Texas. The remaining 16 percent was commercial property; less than 1 percent was undeveloped land.

Properties by State and Type

	Commercial	Land	Residential		Commercial	Land	Residential
Alabama	102	11	314	Missouri	11	1	150
Alaska	21	0	331	Montana	0	1	1
Arizona	349	6	1,576	Nebraska	12	0	67
Arkansas	60	2	303	Nevada	4	0	38
California	81	4	222	New Jersey	2	0	7
Colorado	444	10	1,384	New Mexico	148	6	649
Connecticut	0	0	7	New York	0	0	18
Delaware	1	0	1	North Carolina	13	0	47
District of Columbia	0	0	3	North Dakota	15	0	59
Florida	276	6	1,174	Ohio	10	0	113
Georgia	34	5	622	Oklahoma	153	3	1,770
Hawaii	1	0	1	Oregon	10	1	156
Idaho	2	0	12	Pennsylvania	15	1	263
Illinois	30	3	334	South Carolina	19	0	113
Indiana	7	1	16	Tennessee	34	21	298
Iowa	20	1	77	Texas	3,063	127	15,156
Kansas	65	2	410	Utah	45	2	440
Kentucky	0	0	35	Virginia	11	0	140
Louisiana	395	9	2,486	Washington	21	0	65
Maine	1	0	1	West Virginia	1	0	3
Maryland	3	0	14	Wisconsin	23	3	20
Massachusetts	0	0	3	Wyoming	13	0	43
Michigan	2	0	9	State not known	86	4	631
Minnesota	20	1	131	Puerto Rico	0	0	1
Mississippi	76	1	263	**Total**	**5,699**	**232**	**29,977**

Capital Gains Tax

Source: U.S. Chamber of Commerce

The following shows how the top effective tax rate on capital gains has changed since 1960.

Year	Effective rate (percent)	Year	Effective rate (percent)	Year	Effective rate (percent)	Year	Effective rate (percent)
1960	25.0	1970	32.2	1976	49.1	1987	28.0
1968	26.9	1971	34.4	1979	28.0	1988	33.0
1969	27.5	1972	45.5	1981	20.0		

Chapter 11

Chapter 11 refers to the provisions in the Federal Bankruptcy Act for court-supervised reorganization of debtor companies. A company files for Chapter 11 protection when it can no longer pay its creditors or when it expects future liabilities it cannot hope to pay, like product liability damage awards.

Process

1. Judge issues automatic stay
- Creditors cannot press suits for repayment.
- Debts are frozen.
- Company's day-to-day operations continue.
- Significant spending must have judge's approval.
- Secured creditors can ask court for hardship exemption from debt freeze.

2. Unsecured creditors form a committee
- Representatives are chosen to deal with the company.
- Creditors can ask the court to appoint an examiner to investigate possible fraud or mismanagement.
- Court can name a trustee to run the company.

3. The committee and company negotiate a reorganization plan.
- Parties hammer out a repayment plan for frozen debts. This step can take months or years.

4. Creditors approve the plan
- Must have assent of majority of creditors as well as creditors who are owed two-thirds of the debt.

5. Judge approves the plan

Reorganized Company Emerges

- It must meet the terms of the agreed repayment plan.
- It operates as a normal company.

Bankruptcy Petitions, 1905-1988

(In thousands)

Source: Administrative Office of the U.S. Courts, Annual Report of the Director

Year	Filed	Pending	Year	Filed	Pending	Year	Filed	Pending	Year	Filed	Pending
1905	17	28	1935	69	65	1965	180	162	1983	375	537
1910	18	28	1940	53	55	1970	194	191	1984	344	578
1915	28	44	1945	13	21	1975	254	202	1985	365	609
1920	14	30	1950	33	38	1980	278	346	1986	478	729
1925	46	60	1955	59	56	1981	360	362	1987	561	809
1930	63	61	1960	110	95	1982	368	461	1988	594	815

For fiscal years ending in year shown. Covers all U.S. bankruptcy courts. Bankruptcy petitions "Filed" means the commencement of a proceeding through the presentation of a petition to the clerk of the bankruptcy court; "Pending" is a proceeding in which the administration has not been completed.

Notable Bankruptcy Filings

Company	Year	Assets (billions)	Company	Year	Assets (billions)
Texaco	1987	$35.89	Lomas Financial	1989	6.64
Financial Corp. of America	1988	33.86	LTV Corp.	1986	6.31
MCorp.	1989	20.23	American Continental	1989	5.10
Baldwin-United	1983	9.38	Drexel Burnham Lambert	1990	3.60
Southmark	1989	9.16	Manville	1982	2.00
Allied/Federated	1990	9.13	Wheeling-Pittsburgh Steel	1985	1.00
Penn Central	1970	6.85			

All Banks in U.S.—Number, Deposits

Source: Federal Reserve System

Comprises all national banks in the United States and all state commercial banks, trust companies, mutual stock savings banks, private and industrial banks, and special types of institutions that are treated as banks by the federal bank supervisory agencies. Data as of June 30 prior to 1975.

Year	Total all banks	F.R.S. members Total	Nat'l	State	Nonmembers Mutual savings	Other	Total all banks	F.R.S. members Total	Nat'l	State	Nonmembers Mutual savings	Other
1925	26,479	9,538	8,066	1,472	621	18,320	$51,641	$32,457	$19,912	$12,546	$7,089	$12,095
1930	23,855	8,315	7,247	1,068	604	14,936	59,828	38,069	23,235	14,834	9,117	12,642
1935	16,047	6,410	5,425	985	569	9,068	51,149	34,938	22,477	12,461	9,830	6,381
1940	14,955	6,398	5,164	1,234	551	8,008	70,770	51,729	33,014	18,715	10,631	8,410
1945	14,542	6,840	5,015	1,825	539	7,163	151,033	118,378	76,534	41,844	14,413	18,242
1950	14,674	6,885	4,971	1,914	527	7,262	163,770	122,707	82,430	40,277	19,927	21,137
1955	14,309	6,611	4,744	1,867	525	7,173	208,850	154,670	98,636	56,034	27,310	26,870
1960	14,006	6,217	4,542	1,675	513	7,276	249,163	179,519	116,178	63,341	35,316	34,328
1965	14,295	6,235	4,803	1,432	504	7,556	362,611	259,743	171,528	88,215	50,980	51,889
1970	14,167	5,805	4,638	1,167	496	7,866	502,542	346,289	254,322	91,967	69,285	86,968
1975	15,108	5,787	4,741	1,046	475	8,846	896,879	590,999	447,590	143,409	110,569	195,311
1980	15,145	5,422	4,425	997	460	9,263	1,333,399	843,030	651,848	191,182	150,000	340,369
1985	14,713	6,044	4,964	1,080	344	8,325	1,973,816	1,285,562	1,033,631	251,931	137,535	500,179
1987	14,068	5,736	4,630	1,106	371	7,961	2,150,569	1,415,436	1,139,441	275,995	168,320	566,813
1988	13,500	5,435	4,363	1,072	376	7,689	2,287,274	1,510,695	1,223,410	287,285	183,045	593,533
1989	13,102	5,245	4,198	1,047	375	7482	2,412,373	1,606,860	1,307,953	298,907	188,628	616,885

Federal Deposit Insurance Corporation (FDIC)

The primary purpose of the Federal Deposit Insurance Corporation (FDIC) is to insure deposits in all banks approved for insurance coverage benefits under the Federal Deposit Insurance Act. The major functions of the FDIC are to pay off depositors of insured banks closed without adequate provision having been made to pay depositors' claims, to act as receiver for all national banks placed in receivership and for state banks placed in receivership when appointed receiver by state authorities, and to prevent the continuance or development of unsafe and unsound banking practices. The FDIC's entire income consists of assessments on insured banks and income from investments; it receives no appropriations from Congress. It may borrow from the U.S. Treasury not to exceed $3 billion outstanding, but has made no such borrowings since it was organized in 1933. The FDIC surplus (Deposit Insurance Fund) as of Jan. 1, 1990 was $13.2 billion.

Assets and Liabilities of Individuals in the U.S.[1]

Source: Federal Reserve System

(billions of dollars)

	1960	1965	1970	1975	1980	1985	1988	1989
Total financial assets	1010.1	1501.9	1963.5	2625.6	4680.0	8057.1	10391.7	11700.1
Checkable deposits & currency	91.4	107.0	136.9	186.2	298.8	447.9	574.7	586.8
Time & savings deposits	164.8	289.7	427.4	766.3	1276.8	2025.6	2394.8	2529.0
Money market fund shares	—	—	—	3.7	64.9	214.5	287.0	371.9
Securities	513.3	763.6	923.2	906.7	1604.8	2817.6	3551.5	4149.1
U.S. savings bonds	45.6	49.7	52.1	67.4	72.5	79.8	109.6	117.7
Other U.S. Treasury securities	27.3	26.5	33.5	50.6	150.6	409.3	479.0	498.3
U.S. Govt. agency securities	1.0	1.1	15.9	8.0	45.4	98.0	218.4	326.1
Tax-exempt obligations	31.0	36.5	47.1	67.2	78.2	219.2	282.0	298.8
Corporate & foreign bonds	10.9	9.0	33.8	68.2	53.2	38.0	93.9	147.5
Open-market paper	2.0	5.8	13.6	8.0	41.4	85.7	143.9	157.2
Mutual fund shares	17.0	34.4	44.5	38.7	52.1	203.0	415.9	463.1
Other corporate equities	378.4	600.5	682.7	598.6	1111.3	1684.7	1809.0	2140.4
Private life insurance res.	78.8	98.9	123.3	158.5	207.4	246.5	314.4	342.0
Private insured pension res.	18.9	27.3	41.0	72.3	172.0	400.0	627.7	735.9
Private noninsured pension res.	38.1	74.4	112.0	225.0	469.6	848.1	1116.7	1250.4
Govt. insurance & pension res.	40.2	60.8	95.2	154.7	283.6	563.7	825.3	966.6
Miscellaneous financial assets	64.5	80.3	104.4	152.1	302.3	493.1	699.5	768.5
Total liabilities	287.1	448.7	650.3	1127.2	2180.0	3642.9	4809.3	5182.4
Mtg. debt on nonfarm homes	139.1	216.3	292.2	473.3	950.3	1485.4	2166.2	2383.4
Other mortgage debt[2]	34.0	63.3	117.4	223.4	413.8	768.1	994.7	1045.6
Consumer credit	61.3	97.5	134.0	207.6	355.4	601.8	743.7	790.6
Security credit	5.4	9.1	10.4	12.1	28.5	56.8	53.5	54.3
Policy loans	5.7	8.3	17.0	25.5	42.6	55.5	56.4	59.8
Other liabilities[2]	41.7	54.2	79.2	185.3	389.4	675.3	794.7	848.7

(1) Combined statement for households, farm business, and nonfarm noncorporate business. (2) Includes corporate farms.

Largest U.S. Commercial Banks

Source: American Banker; based on deposits Dec. 31, 1989.

(thousands)

Rank	Deposits	Rank	Deposits
Citibank NA, New York	$111,487,000	Meridian Bank, Reading, Pa.	$8,394,187
Bank of America NT&SA, San Francisco . . .	73,295,000	Valley National Bank, Phoenix	8,370,893
Chase Manhattan Bank NA, New York	61,720,245	Connecticut National Bank, Hartford	8,196,372
Manufacturers Hanover Trust Co., New York.	42,736,000	Michigan National Bank, Farmington Hills . . .	7,888,735
Morgan Guaranty Trust Co., New York	40,953,451	Midlantic National Bank, Newark, N.J. . . .	7,791,480
Security Pacific National Bank, Los Angeles .	40,597,338	Boston Safe Deposit & Trust Co..	7,782,273
Wells Fargo Bank NA, San Francisco	36,462,605	Crestar Bank, Richmond	7,631,619
Bank of New York	34,411,451	Comerica Bank-Detroit	7,561,148
Chemical Bank, New York	32,312,000	Philadephia National Bank	7,261,814
Bankers Trust Co., New York.	27,879,571	First Union National Bank of Florida, Jackson-	
First National Bank, Chicago	26,403,340	ville	7,090,935
NCNB Texas National Bank, Dallas	25,623,428	AmeriTrust Co. NA, Cleveland	7,072,134
First National Bank, Boston	22,061,157	United States National Bank, Portland, Ore. .	6,994,001
Continental Bank NA, Chicago	18,178,226	Manufacturers National Bank, Detroit	6,946,034
Marine Midland Bank NA, Buffalo, N.Y.	18,021,665	Bank of Hawaii, Honolulu	6,940,435
First Interstate Bank of California, Los Angeles	17,849,795	Fidelity Bank NA, Philadelphia	6,919,305
Mellon Bank NA, Pittsburgh	15,022,808	Harris Trust & Savings Bank, Chicago. . . .	6,854,159
Republic National Bank, New York	14,250,340	Maryland National Bank, Baltimore	6,631,568
National Westminster Bank USA, New York .	12,740,471	Huntington National Bank, Columbus, Oh. . .	6,566,863
Southeast Bank NA, Miami	12,715,951	Security Pacific Bank Washington, Seattle . .	6,439,119
National Bank of Detroit	12,288,133	Texas Commerce Bank NA, Houston	6,416,672
Union Bank, San Francisco	11,637,088	Society National Bank, Cleveland	6,280,633
Wachovia Bank & Trust Co. NA, Winston-Sa-		First National Bank, Atlanta	6,139,163
lem, N.C.	11,344,443	State Street Bank & Trust Co., Boston	6,137,917
NCNB National Bank of North Carolina, Char-		Fleet National Bank, Providence, R.I.	6,111,457
lotte	10,585,048	First Interstate Bank of Arizona NA, Phoenix .	6,105,115
First Union National Bank, Charlotte, N.C.. . .	10,507,659	Florida National Bank, Jacksonville	6,055,322
Pittsburgh National Bank	10,263,540	First Interstate Bank of Texas NA, Houston. .	5,881,038
Sovran Bank NA, Richmond	10,193,846	Bank of Tokyo Trust Co., New York	5,805,020
Seattle-First National Bank	9,660,669	AmSouth Bank NA, Birmingham, Ala.	5,787,896
NCNB National Bank of Florida, Tampa	9,637,057	Riggs National Bank, Washington, D.C. . . .	5,702,593
Citizens & Southern National Bank, Atlanta . .	9,468,585	Provident National Bank, Philadelphia	5,692,972
Bank of New England NA, Boston	9,208,787	Norwest Bank Minnesota NA, Minneapolis . .	5,654,443
First Bank NA, Minneapolis	9,104,370	Hibernia National Bank, New Orleans	5,604,612
First Fidelity Bank NA, Newark, N.J.	8,615,504	Sanwa Bank California, San Francisco	5,564,162
Banc One, Texas NA, Dallas	8,525,136	National City Bank, Cleveland	5,528,397
Connecticut Bank & Trust Co. NA, Hartford. .	8,450,053		

Largest Foreign Banks

Source: American Banker; based on deposits Dec. 31, 1989, or nearest fiscal year-end.

(thousands of U.S. dollars)

Bank, country	Deposits	Bank, country	Deposits
Dai-Ichi Kangyo Bank Ltd., Tokyo, Japan	$314,780,128	Taiyo Kobe Bank, Ltd., Kobe, Japan	$136,538,177
Sumitomo Bank Ltd., Osaka, Japan	288,242,189	Dresdner Bank, Frankfurt, Germany	135,670,068
Mitsubishi Bank Ltd., Tokyo, Japan.	278,806,753	Yasuda Trust & Banking Co., Ltd., Tokyo, Japan .	135,105,776
Fuji Bank Ltd., Tokyo, Japan.	278,642,535	Daiwa Bank, Ltd., Osaka, Japan	131,680,308
Sanwa Bank Ltd., Osaka, Japan	275,972,496	Hongkong and Shanghai Banking Corp., Hong	
Industrial Bank of Japan, Ltd., Tokyo, Japan	213,287,599	Kong	118,504,960
Banque Nationale de Paris, France	192,525,992	Commerzbank, Frankfurt, Germany	106,668,460
Mitsubishi Trust & Banking Corp., Tokyo, Japan . .	192,294,268	Swiss Bank Corp., Basle, Switzerland	100,865,736
Deutsche Bank, Frankfurt, Germany	184,378,643	Toyo Trust & Banking Co. Ltd., Tokyo, Japan. . . .	100,172,771
Tokai Bank Ltd., Nagoya, Japan	179,030,994	Union Bank of Switzerland, Zurich, Switzerland. . .	96,977,909
Norinchukin Bank, Tokyo, Japan.	176,329,604	Westdeutsche Landesbank Girozentrale, Duessel-	
Credit Lyonnais, Paris, France	176,099,988	dorf, Germany	96,532,850
Sumitomo Trust & Banking Co., Ltd., Osaka, Ja-		Bayerische Vereinsbank, Munich, Germany	95,993,000
pan	171,664,091	Nippon Credit Bank, Ltd., Tokyo, Japan	88,179,792
Credit Agricole Mutuel, Paris, France	169,711,546	Midland Bank Plc, London, U.K.	88,034,800
Barclays Bank Plc, London, U.K..	167,127,661	Banca Nazionale del Lavoro, Rome, Italy	84,811,188
National Westminster Bank Plc, London, U.K. . . .	163,014,110	Lloyds Bank Plc, London, U.K.	84,355,950
Mitsui Trust & Banking Co., Ltd., Tokyo, Japan . .	159,219,084	Bayerische Hypotheken-und Wechsel-Bank, Mu-	
Mitsui Bank, Ltd., Tokyo, Japan.	157,894,949	nich, Germany	83,191,003
Bank of Tokyo, Ltd., Japan	152,933,845	Istituto Bancario San Paolo di Torino, Turin, Italy .	79,614,718
Long-Term Credit Bank of Japan Ltd., Tokyo, Ja-		Kyowa Bank, Ltd, Tokyo, Japan.	78,919,007
pan	148,398,357	Banca Commerciale Italiana, Milan, Italy	77,865,384
Societe Generale, Paris, France	141,977,467		

Bank Failures

Source: Federal Deposit Insurance Corp

Year	Closed	Year	Closed	Year	Closed	Year	Closed
1934	61	1960	2	1971	6	1982	42
1935	32	1961	9	1972	3	1983	48
1936	72	1963	2	1973	6	1984	79
1937	84	1964	8	1975	14	1985	120
1938	81	1965	9	1976	17	1986	138
1939	72	1966	8	1978	7	1987	184
1940	48	1967	4	1979	10	1988	200
1955	5	1969	9	1980	10	1989	206
1959	3	1970	8	1981	10		

United States Mint

Source: United States Mint, U.S. Treasury Department

The United States Mint was created by Act of Congress April 2, 1792, which established the U.S. national coinage system. Initially, operations were conducted at Philadelphia, then the nation's capital. Supervision of the Mint was a function of the secretary of state, but in 1799, it became an independent agency reporting directly to the president. The Mint was made a statutory bureau of the Treasury Department in 1873, with a director appointed by the president to oversee its operations from headquarters offices in the Treasury Department in Washington, D.C.

The Mint manufactures all U.S. coins and distributes them through the Federal Reserve banks and branches. The Mint also maintains physical custody of the treasury's monetary stocks of gold and silver, moving, storing and releasing from custody as authorized. There are 6 field facilities. Mints are located in Philadelphia and Denver; the San Francisco Mint and San Francisco Old Mint perform coinage operations and numismatic functions; two depositories, one at Fort Knox, Ky., for the storage of gold, and the other at West Point, N.Y., where gold and silver are stored and coinage is produced by congressional authorization. A museum is maintained at the San Francisco Old Mint.

The traditional 90% silver coinage was phased out and cupronickel clad coinage introduced when the Coinage Act of 1965 removed all silver from the dime and quarter and reduced the silver content of the half dollar to 40%. In 1970, legislative action removed the remaining silver from the half dollar and in providing for the resumption of dollar coinage, directed that both denominations produced for circulation also be cupronickel clad metal. Changes in the design, weight and size of the standard silver dollar were approved by Congress in 1978, and beginning in 1979, a smaller cupronickel dollar coin bearing the likeness of Susan B. Anthony and the Apollo 11 moon landing was released.

A change in the composition of the cent was effected in 1982, when the current copper-plated zinc cent was introduced to replace the traditional 95% copper cent.

The Mint manufactures and sells bronze medals of a national character, produces numismatic coins and coin sets. Special government-sponsored numismatic coinage includes congressionally authorized 90% silver half dollars produced in 1982 to mark the 250th anniversary of George Washington's birth, and 90% gold $10 coins dated 1984 and two 90% silver dollars dated 1983 and 1984, respectively, commemorating the 1984 Olympic games, and a 90% gold $5 coin, a 90% silver dollar coin and a cupronickel half dollar for the Statue of Liberty Centennial in 1986. The Mint issued a 1987 dated 90% gold $5 coin and a 1987 dated 90% silver dollar coin honoring the 200th Anniversary of the U.S. Constitution. Other Congressionally authorized commeroratives include the 1990 Eisenhower silver dollar and the 1991 Mt. Rushmore gold, silver and lead coin series. Congress has also directed the U.S. Mint to commence the production and sale of legal tender gold and silver bullion coins designated as "American Eagle Bullion Coins" by the mint. The coins in the series contain .9167 fine gold, and have a face value of $50 (1 oz.), $25 (¹/₂ oz.), $10 (¹/₄ oz.), and $5 (¹/₁₀ oz.). The American Eagle silver bullion coin has a face value of $1 and contains 1 troy ounce of .999 fine silver. Information concerning these and other Mint coin programs and coin availability, may be secured from the United States Mint, 10001 Aerospace Road, Lanham, MD 20706.

Domestic Coin Production

	Cents	Nickels	Dimes	Quarters	Halves	Total¹
1980	12,554,803,660	1,095,327,448	1,454,524,321	1,154,159,487	77,590,449	16,426,066,073
1981	12,864,985,677	1,022,305,843	1,388,934,143	1,177,438,833	57,383,533	16,520,790,029
1982	16,725,504,368	666,081,544	1,062,188,584	980,973,788	23,959,102	19,458,707,386
1983	14,219,554,428	1,098,341,276	1,377,154,224	1,291,341,446	66,611,244	18,053,002,618
1984	13,720,317,906	1,264,444,146	1,561,472,976	1,223,028,064	52,291,158	17,821,554,250
1985	10,935,889,813	1,106,862,408	1,293,180,932	1,295,781,850	38,520,996	14,670,235,999
1986	8,934,262,191	898,702,633	1,155,976,667	1,055,497,993	28,473,778	12,072,913,262
1987	9,561,856,445	782,090,085	1,415,912,883	1,238,094,177	99,481	12,998,053,071
1988	11,346,550,443	1,435,131,652	1,992,935,488	1,158,862,687	25,626,096	15,959,106,366
1989	12,837,140,268	1,497,523,652	2,240,355,488	1,417,290,422	41,196,188	18,033,506,018

Portraits on U.S. Treasury Bills, Bonds, Notes and Savings Bonds

Denomination	Savings bonds	Treas. bills	Treas. bonds	Treas. notes
50	Washington		Jefferson	
75	Adams			
100	Jefferson		Jackson	
200	Madison			
500	Hamilton		Washington	
1,000	Franklin	H. McCulloch	Lincoln	Lincoln
5,000	Revere	J.G. Carlisle	Monroe	Monroe
10,000	Wilson	J. Sherman	Cleveland	Cleveland
50,000		C. Glass		
100,000		A. Gallatin	Grant	Grant
1,000,000		O. Wolcott	T. Roosevelt	T. Roosevelt
100,000,000				Madison
500,000,000				McKinley

Large Denominations of U.S. Currency Discontinued

The largest denomination of United States currency now being issued is the $100 bill. Issuance of currency in denominations larger than $100 was discontinued in 1969.

As large denomination bills reach the Federal Reserve Bank they are removed from circulation.

Because some of the discontinued currency is expected to be in the hands of holders for many years, the description of the various denominations below is continued:

Amt.	Portrait	Embellishment on back	Amt.	Portrait	Embellishment on back
$ 1	Washington	Great Seal of U.S.	$ 100	Franklin	Independence Hall
2	Jefferson	Signers of Declaration	500	McKinley	Ornate denominational marking
5	Lincoln	Lincoln Memorial	1,000	Cleveland	Ornate denominational marking
10	Hamilton	U.S. Treasury	5,000	Madison	Ornate denominational marking
20	Jackson	White House	10,000	Chase	Ornate denominational marking
50	Grant	U.S. Capitol	100,000*	Wilson	Ornate denominational marking

*For use only in transactions between Federal Reserve System and Treasury Department.

U.S. Currency and Coin

Source: U.S. Treasury Department; Financial Management Service (Mar. 31, 1990)

Amounts Outstanding and in Circulation

Currency	Amounts outstanding	Less amounts held by: United States Treasury	Less amounts held by: Federal Reserve Banks[1]	Amounts in circulation
Federal Reserve notes[1]	$278,708,725,606	$6,901,702	$39,764,853,750	$238,936,970,154
United States notes	325,520,966	32,563,039	213	292,957,714
Currency no longer issued.	266,409,785	224,029	13,282	266,172,474
Total	$279,300,656,357	$39,688,770	$39,764,867,245	$239,496,100,342
Coin[2]				
Dollars[3]	$2,024,703,898	$332,383,689	$105,494,856	$1,596,825,353
Fractional coin	17,224,335,000	190,490,530	462,405,815	16,571,438,655
Total	$19,249,038,898	$512,874,219	$567,900,671	$18,168,264,008
Total currency and coin.	$298,549,695,255	$552,562,989	$40,332,767,916	$257,664,364,350

Currency in Circulation by Denominations

Denomination	Total currency in circulation	Federal Reserve Notes[1]	U.S. Notes	Currency no longer issued
1 Dollar	$4,637,138,793	$4,485,760,535	$143,481	$151,234,777
2 Dollars	813,797,428	680,965,674	132,818,858	12,896
5 Dollars	5,772,195,480	5,624,058,815	111,783,055	36,353,610
10 Dollars	11,657,610,095	11,633,396,500	5,950	24,207,645
20 Dollars	63,607,774,344	63,587,626,680	3,380	20,144,284
50 Dollars	31,156,036,500	31,144,482,950	—	11,553,550
100 Dollars	121,523,382,100	121,453,055,000	48,202,900	22,124,200
500 Dollars	149,620,000	149,431,000	—	189,000
1,000 Dollars	173,305,000	173,098,000	—	207,000
5,000 Dollars	1,790,000	1,745,000	—	45,000
10,000 Dollars	3,450,000	3,350,000	—	100,000
Fractional parts	487	—	—	487
Partial notes[4]	115	—	90	25
Total currency	$239,496,100,342	$238,936,970,154	$292,957,714	$266,172,474

Comparative Totals of Money in Circulation — Selected Dates

Date	Dollars (in millions)	Per capita[5]	Date	Dollars (in millions)	Per capita[5]	Date	Dollars (in millions)	Per capita[5]
Mar. 31, 1990	257,664.4	1,028.71	June 30, 1975	81,196.4	380.08	June 30, 1940	7,847.5	59.40
June 30, 1989	249,182.7	1,002.54	June 30, 1970	54,351.0	265.39	June 30, 1935	5,567.1	43.75
June 30, 1988	235,415.9	956.57	June 30, 1965	39,719.8	204.14	June 30, 1930	4,522.0	36.74
June 30, 1987	215,158.6	883.45	June 30, 1960	32,064.6	177.47	June 30, 1925	4,815.2	41.56
June 30, 1986	199,309.2	883.45	June 30, 1955	30,229.3	182.90	June 30, 1920	5,467.6	51.36
June 30, 1985	185,890.7	778.58	June 30, 1950	27,156.3	179.03	June 30, 1915	3,319.6	33.01
June 30, 1984	175,059.6	739.64	June 30, 1945	26,746.4	191.14	June 30, 1910	3,148.7	34.07
June 30, 1983	127,097.2	558.28						

(1) Issued on and after July 1, 1929. (2) Excludes coin sold to collectors at premium prices. (3) Includes $481,781,898 in standard silver dollars. (4) Represents value of certain partial denominations not presented for redemption. (5) Based on Bureau of the Census estimates of population.

The requirement for a gold reserve against U.S. notes was repealed by Public Law 90-269 approved Mar. 18, 1968. Silver certificates issued on and after July 1, 1929 became redeemable from the general fund on June 24, 1968. The amount of security after those dates has been reduced accordingly.

Seigniorage on Coin and Silver Bullion

Source: U.S. Treasury Department, Financial Management Service

Seigniorage is the profit from coining money; it is the difference between the monetary value of coins and their cost, including the manufacturing expense.

Fiscal year	Dollars	Fiscal year	Dollars
Jan. 1, 1935–June 30, 1965, cumulative	2,525,927,763.84	1983	477,479,387.58
1968	383,141,339.00[1]	1984	498,371,724.09
1970	274,217,884.01	1985	515,906,969.31
1972	580,586,683.00	1986	392,445,674.57
1974	320,706,638.49	1987	458,070,694.43
1975	660,898,070.69	1988	470,409,480.20
1980	662,814,791.48	Cumulative Jan. 1, 1935–Sept. 30, 1988	13,727,374,271.32

(1) Revised to include seigniorage on clad coins.

AGRICULTURE
U.S. Farms

Source: U.S. Department of Agriculture

The Department of Agriculture estimated the number of U.S. farms in June, 1989 at 2.17 million, a drop of 1.1 percent from June, 1988, when there were 2.19 million farms. The decline continued a slide that began in 1982, when there were 2.4 million farms. The size of the average U.S. farm increased in 1989 to 456 acres, from 453 acres in 1988. Overall, about 991 million U.S. acres were devoted to agriculture, as of June 1989.

State	Number of Farms	% Change	State	Number of Farms	% Change	State	Number of Farms	% Change
Alabama	47,000	-2.1	Louisiana	35,000	6.1	Ohio	87,000	2.4
Alaska	600	-3.2	Maine	7,300	0.0	Oklahoma	69,000	-1.4
Arizona	8,100	0.0	Maryland	15,600	-2.5	Oregon	37,000	1.4
Arkansas	49,000	0.0	Mass.	6,900	0.0	Pennsylvania	54,000	-1.8
California	84,000	0.0	Michigan	55,000	-1.8	Rhode Island	770	0.0
Colorado	27,300	0.0	Minnesota	90,000	-2.2	S. Carolina	25,500	-1.9
Connecticut	4,000	0.0	Mississippi	41,000	-2.4	S. Dakota	35,000	0.0
Delaware	3,000	0.0	Missouri	108,000	-1.8	Tennessee	91,000	0.0
Florida	41,000	0.0	Montana	24,700	0.4	Texas	186,000	-0.5
Georgia	48,000	-2.0	Nebraska	57,000	-1.7	Utah	13,000	-2.3
Hawaii	4,650	0.0	Nevada	2,500	-3.8	Vermont	7,100	0.0
Idaho	22,300	-0.9	New Hampshire	3,200	0.0	Virginia	47,000	-2.1
Illinois	86,000	-2.3	New Jersey	8,300	0.0	Washington	38,000	0.0
Indiana	71,000	-4.1	New Mexico	14,000	0.0	West Virginia	21,000	0.0
Iowa	105,000	-1.9	New York	39,000	-4.9	Wisconsin	81,000	-1.2
Kansas	69,000	0.0	N. Carolina	65,000	-4.4	Wyoming	8,900	0.0
Kentucky	96,000	-1.0	N. Dakota	33,500	0.0	Total	2,173,220	-1.1

Farm Income—Marketings and Goverment Payments

Source: Economic Research Service, U.S. Department of Agriculture

(1,000 dollars)

State	1988 Farm marketings Total	Crops	Livestock and products	1989 Farm marketings Total	Crops	Livestock and products	Government payments
AL	2,422,328	727,686	1,694,642	2,627,670	695,506	1,932,164	120,859
AK	30,128	20,198	9,930	28,632	19,817	8,815	1,143
AZ	1,968,560	1,176,873	791,687	1,902,460	1,158,261	744,199	85,106
AR	3,831,380	1,551,698	2,279,682	4,131,042	1,470,176	2,660,866	439,675
CA	16,651,568	11,969,628	4,681,940	17,514,795	12,422,046	5,092,749	372,090
CO	3,699,885	1,034,111	2,665,774	3,898,614	1,249,557	2,649,057	183,442
CT	397,741	214,465	183,276	404,360	218,060	186,300	2,200
DE	595,191	151,654	443,537	622,568	159,619	502,949	4,818
FL	5,819,668	4,687,549	1,132,119	6,202,954	4,982,354	1,220,600	38,323
GA	3,569,538	1,553,763	2,015,775	3,868,531	1,598,141	2,270,390	173,058
HI	578,897	490,277	88,620	586,934	494,982	91,952	267
ID	2,324,460	1,285,380	1,039,080	2,715,312	1,669,802	1,045,510	99,089
IL	6,182,225	3,927,100	2,255,125	6,710,436	4,458,464	2,251,972	725,941
IN	4,036,261	2,320,256	1,716,005	4,318,493	2,501,584	1,816,909	333,691
IA	8,774,969	3,787,193	4,987,776	9,119,202	3,910,522	5,208,680	981,206
KS	6,319,703	2,195,389	4,124,314	6,324,292	2,078,981	4,245,311	588,446
KY	2,509,516	979,590	1,529,926	2,928,062	1,257,742	1,670,320	118,423
LA	1,876,454	1,294,525	581,929	1,661,437	1,047,694	613,743	249,758
ME	414,176	197,489	216,687	447,383	232,742	214,641	7,143
MD	1,224,339	456,736	767,603	1,346,228	476,367	869,861	23,735
MA	409,928	305,295	104,633	428,892	316,779	112,113	3,863
MI	2,739,381	1,534,589	1,204,792	2,940,387	1,627,449	1,312,938	261,971
MN	6,066,701	2,649,046	3,417,655	6,525,541	2,809,080	3,716,461	599,852
MS	2,304,852	1,132,802	1,172,050	2,291,761	1,000,023	1,291,738	325,161
MO	3,757,664	1,746,152	2,011,512	3,900,434	1,732,009	2,168,425	356,391
MT	1,432,966	616,704	816,262	1,609,736	710,482	899,254	289,382
NE	7,799,582	2,409,260	5,390,322	8,521,087	2,878,449	5,642,638	542,306
NV	237,998	78,872	159,126	235,109	94,055	141,054	6,301
NH	136,120	77,436	58,684	142,085	78,748	63,337	2,302
NJ	644,581	452,040	192,541	660,078	462,769	197,309	21,483
NM	1,283,132	374,528	908,604	1,423,759	449,663	974,096	64,675
NY	2,668,132	865,499	1,802,633	2,856,650	911,132	1,945,518	76,025
NC	4,037,795	1,850,167	2,187,628	4,550,587	2,046,063	2,504,524	93,917
ND	2,358,232	1,507,398	850,834	2,107,575	1,465,427	642,148	474,846
OH	3,563,523	1,979,660	1,583,863	3,812,118	2,114,380	1,697,738	274,003
OK	3,354,415	1,111,886	2,242,529	3,594,261	1,185,277	2,408,984	234,817
OR	2,181,559	1,508,477	673,082	2,297,095	1,557,620	739,475	60,384
PA	3,295,551	963,662	2,331,889	3,581,168	985,791	2,595,377	68,396
RI	79,072	65,732	13,340	79,022	66,150	12,872	90
SC	1,106,007	615,714	490,293	1,225,491	674,571	550,920	72,696
SD	2,944,782	895,056	2,049,726	2,992,072	883,954	2,108,118	340,262
TN	1,932,702	876,954	1,055,748	1,920,550	860,628	1,059,922	141,049
TX	10,251,368	3,689,338	6,562,030	10,760,414	3,897,010	6,863,404	1,248,713
UT	701,250	173,025	528,225	748,188	173,933	574,255	34,536
VT	401,222	50,603	350,619	425,541	51,005	374,536	7,064
VA	1,913,993	614,333	1,299,660	2,057,820	685,423	1,372,397	38,599
WA	3,336,153	2,196,242	1,139,911	3,638,971	2,437,817	1,201,154	131,132
WV	285,930	68,179	217,751	313,961	64,115	249,846	11,599
WI	4,979,643	764,405	4,215,238	5,277,971	940,548	4,337,423	522,332
WY	761,204	176,995	584,209	855,570	186,353	669,217	34,142
U.S.	150,192,425	71,371,609	78,820,816	159,173,299	75,449,120	83,724,179	10,886,702

Farms—Number and Acreage by State, 1980 and 1990

Source: Natl. Agricultural Statistics Service: U.S. Agriculture Department

State	Farms (1,000) 1980	1990	Acreage (mil.) 1980	1990	Acreage per Farm 1980	1990	State	Farms (1,000) 1980	1990	Acreage (mil.) 1980	1990	Acreage per Farm 1980	1990
U.S....	2,437	2,143	1,039	988	426	461	Nebraska..	65	57	48	47	734	826
Alabama	59	47	12	10	207	219	Nevada..	3	3	9	9	3,100	3,560
Alaska...	(z)	1	2	1	3,378	1,724	New Hampshire.....	3	3	1	(z)	160	163
Arizona ...	7	8	38	36	5,080	4,615	New Jersey.	10	8	1	1	109	107
Arkansas ..	58	47	17	16	280	330	New Mexico	13	14	47	45	3,467	3,296
California ..	79	85	34	31	417	362	New York..	48	39	9	8	200	218
Colorado ..	26	27	36	33	1,358	1,249	North Carolina..	92	62	12	10	126	156
Connecticut.	4	4	(z)	(z)	117	108	North Dakota	41	34	42	41	1,043	1,191
Delaware .	4	3	1	1	186	197	Ohio.....	96	84	16	16	171	187
Florida....	38	41	13	11	344	266	Oklahoma..	72	70	35	33	481	471
Georgia ...	59	49	15	13	254	255	Oregon ...	34	37	18	18	517	488
Hawaii	4	5	2	2	458	372	Pennsylvania	61	53	9	8	145	153
Idaho	24	22	15	14	623	628	Rhode Island	1	1	(z)	(z)	87	92
Illinois ...	108	83	29	29	269	343	South Carolina......	35	25	6	5	188	212
Indiana ...	88	68	17	16	193	240	South Dakota	39	35	45	44	1,169	1,266
Iowa	121	104	34	34	284	322	Tennessee ..	96	89	14	12	142	139
Kansas ...	75	69	48	48	644	694	Texas	192	186	138	132	715	710
Kentucky ..	103	93	15	14	143	152	Utah.....	13	13	12	11	919	856
Louisiana ..	37	34	10	9	273	265	Vermont...	7	7	2	2	226	215
Maine	8	7	2	1	195	199	Virginia ...	59	46	10	9	169	198
Maryland ..	17	15	3	2	157	148	Washington.	37	37	16	16	429	432
Massachusetts.	6	7	1	1	116	99	West Virginia	20	21	4	4	191	180
Michigan..	66	54	11	11	175	200	Wisconsin..	94	80	19	18	200	220
Minnesota..	104	89	30	30	291	337	Wyoming ..	9	10	35	35	3,846	3,910
Mississippi ..	56	40	15	13	265	325							
Missouri...	121	108	31	30	261	281							
Montana...	24	25	62	61	2,601	2,449							

(z) Less than 500 farms or 500,000 acres

Livestock on Farms in the U.S.

Source: Natl. Agricultural Statistics Service: U.S. Agriculture Department (thousands)

Year (On Jan. 1)	All cattle	Milk cows	All sheep	Hogs[3]	Year (On Jan. 1)	All cattle	Milk cows	All sheep	Hogs[3]
1890	60,014	15,000	44,518	48,130	1955	96,592	23,462	31,582	50,474
1900	59,739	16,544	48,105	51,055	1960	96,236	19,527	33,170	59,026
1910	58,993	19,450	50,239	48,072	1965	109,000	16,981[2]	25,127	56,106
1920	70,400	21,455	40,743	60,159	1970	112,369	13,303	20,423	57,046
1925	63,373	22,575	38,543	55,770	1975	132,028	11,220	14,515	54,693
1930	61,003	23,032	51,565	55,705	1980	111,242	10,758	10,716	67,318
1935	68,846	26,082	51,808	39,066	1985	109,749	10,805	10,145	54,073
1940	68,309	24,940	52,107	61,165	1988	99,622	10,311	10,945	54,384
1945	85,573	27,770	46,520	59,373	1989	99,180	10,212	10,858	55,469
1950	77,963	23,853	29,826	58,937	1990	99,337	10,149	11,368	53,652

(1) Total estimated value on farms as of Jan. 1, 1990, was (avg. value per head in parentheses): cattle & calves $63,627,207 ($641); sheep & lambs $997,809,000 ($87.80); hogs & pigs $4,258,285,000 ($79.10). (2) New series, milk cows & heifers that have calved, from 1965. (3) As of Dec. 1 of preceding year.

U.S. Meat and Lard Production and Consumption

Source: Economic Research Service, U.S. Agriculture Department (million lbs.)

Year	Beef Production	Beef Consumption[1]	Veal Production	Veal Consumption[1]	Lamb and mutton Production	Consumption[1]	Pork (exclud. lard) Production	Consumption[1]	All meats[3] Production	Consumption[1]	Lard Production	Consumption[2]
1940	7,175	7,257	981	981	876	873	10,044	9,701	19,076	18,812	2,288	1,901
1950	9,534	9,529	1,230	1,206	597	596	10,714	10,390	22,075	21,721	2,631	1,891
1960	14,728	15,465	1,109	1,118	769	857	13,905	14,057	30,511	31,497	2,562	1,358
1970	21,685	23,391	588	610	551	663	14,699	14,871	37,523	39,535	1,913	939
1980	21,643	23,513	400	418	318	349	16,617	16,690	38,978	40,953	1,207	588
1985	23,728	25,472	515	533	359	386	14,807	15,733	39,409	42,125	927	425
1989	23,082	24,326	355	356	342	406	15,813	16,576	39,592	41,664	(4)	(4)

(1) Includes shipments. (2) Direct use. Excludes lard used in indirect food use such as table spreads and shortenings. (3) Meats may not add to total. (4) Discontinued series.

Selected Indexes of Farm Inputs: 1960 to 1988

Source: Economic Research Service, U.S. Agriculture Department

(1977 = 100. Inputs based on physical quantities of resources used in production.)

Input	1960	1965	1970	1975	1980	1981	1982	1983	1985	1986	1987	1988[1]
Total	99	97	96	97	103	102	99	97	92	87	86	85
Farm labor	177	144	112	106	96	96	93	97	85	80	78	75
Farm real estate[2] ...	103	103	105	97	103	104	102	101	95	93	92	91
Mechanical power and machinery	83	80	85	96	101	98	92	88	80	75	72	71
Agricultural chemicals[3] ..	32	49	75	83	123	129	118	105	123	110	111	113
Feed, seed, and livestock purchases[4] ..	77	86	96	93	114	108	108	110	106	103	111	107
Taxes and interest ..	95	101	102	100	100	99	92	97	91	93	92	86

(1) Preliminary. (2) Includes service buildings, improvements. (3) Includes fertilizer, lime, and pesticides. (4) Nonfarm portion.

Residence of the Population, 1988

Source: Economic Research Service, U.S. Department of Agriculture; and Bureau of the Census, U.S. Department of Commerce, 1988.

(Numbers in thousands)

Residence	Total	Metro-politan	Nonmet-ropolitan	Residence	Total	Metro-politan	Nonmet-ropolitan
Total.	240,887[1]	187,106	53,781	**Percent distribution**			
Urban	176,089	157,392	18,697	Total.	100.0	77.7	22.3
Rural	64,798	29,714	35,084	Urban	100.0	89.4	10.6
Rural nonfarm	59,847	28,415	31,432	Rural	100.0	45.9	54.1
Rural farm.	4,951	1,299	3,652	Rural nonfarm	100.0	47.5	52.5
				Rural farm.	100.0	26.2	73.8

(1) Refers only to civilian noninstitutionalized population.

Source: U.S. Agriculture Department

Age and Sex of the Farm and Nonfarm Population, 1988

Source: Economic Research Service, U.S. Department of Agriculture; and Bureau of the Census, U.S. Department of Commerce, 1988.

(Numbers in thousands)

Age	Farm — Both sexes	Farm — Male	Farm — Female	Nonfarm — Both sexes	Nonfarm — Male	Nonfarm — Female
All ages	4,951	2,586	2,366	235,936	114,060	121,875
Under 15 years	1,000	519	481	51,945	26,575	25,371
15 to 19	421	219	202	17,435	8,788	8,647
20 to 24	279	161	117	18,155	8,769	9,387
25 to 29	268	149	119	21,023	10,299	10,724
30 to 34	316	162	154	21,003	10,324	10,680
35 to 39	321	170	151	18,535	9,073	9,461
40 to 44	344	175	169	15,585	7,588	7,997
45 to 49	337	166	171	12,584	6,107	6,477
50 to 54	304	158	146	10,778	5,192	5,586
55 to 59	343	171	172	10,495	4,996	5,499
60 to 64	321	165	156	10,482	4,861	5,620
65 to 69	276	149	126	9,557	4,313	5,243
70 to 74	199	105	94	7,484	3,205	4,280
75 years and over	222	115	107	10,874	3,970	6,904
Median age (years)	38.0	37.4	38.6	32.2	31.3	33.2
Percent Distribution						
All ages	100.0	100.0	100.0	100.0	100.0	100.0
Under 15 years	20.2	20.1	20.3	22.0	23.3	20.8
15 to 19	8.5	8.5	8.5	7.4	7.7	7.1
20 to 24	5.6	6.2	4.9	7.7	7.7	7.7
25 to 29	5.4	5.8	5.0	8.9	9.0	8.8
30 to 34	6.4	6.3	6.5	8.9	9.1	8.8
35 to 39	6.5	6.6	6.4	7.9	8.0	7.8
40 to 44	6.9	6.8	7.1	6.6	6.7	6.6
45 to 49	6.8	6.4	7.2	5.3	5.4	5.3
50 to 54	6.1	6.1	6.2	4.6	4.6	4.6
55 to 59	6.9	6.6	7.3	4.4	4.4	4.5
60 to 64	6.5	6.4	6.6	4.4	4.3	4.6
65 to 69	5.6	5.8	5.3	4.1	3.8	4.3
70 to 74	4.0	4.1	4.0	3.2	2.8	3.5
75 years and over	4.5	4.4	4.5	4.6	3.5	5.7

Persons in Farm Occupations, 1820-1988

Source: Economic Research Service. U.S. Department of Agriculture; and Bureau of the Census. U.S. Department of Commerce. 1988.

(Numbers in thousands)

Year	Total workers[1]	Farm occupations Number	Farm occupations % of total	Year	Total workers[1]	Farm occupations Number	Farm occupations % of total
1820	2,881	2,069	71.8	1950	59,230	6,858	11.6
1850	7,697	4,902	63.7	1960	67,990	4,132	6.1
1870	12,925	6,850	53.0	1970	79,802	2,881	3.6
1900	29,030	10,888	37.5	1980	104,058	2,818	2.7
1920	42,206	11,390	27.0	1985 (March)	106,214	2,949	2.8
1930	48,686	10,321	21.2	1988 (March)	113,299	2,891	2.6
1940	51,742	8,995	17.4				

(1) Total workers for 1985 to 1988 are employed workers 15 years and over; total workers for 1970 and 1980 are members of the experienced civilian labor force 16 years and over; total workers for 1900 to 1960 are members of the experienced civilian labor forced 14 years and over; and total workers for 1820 to 1890 are gainful workers 10 years and over.

Grain, Hay, Potato, Cotton, Soybean, Tobacco Production

Source: Economic Research Service. U.S. Agriculture Department

1989 State	Barley 1,000 bushels	Corn, grain 1,000 bushels	Cotton lint 1,000 bales	All Hay 1,000 tons	Oats 1,000 bushels	Potatos 1,000 cwt.	Soybeans 1,000 bushels	Tobacco 1,000 pounds	All Wheat 1,000 bushels
Alabama	—	14,580	390	1,540	1,375	2,571	11,970	—	6,600
Alaska	—	—	—	—	—	—	—	—	—
Arizona	1,236	1,885	1,115	1,280	—	1,827	—	—	10,722
Arkansas	—	7,076	850	2,228	3,796	—	76,800	—	52,800
California	13,440	27,200	2,688	8,524	3,150	17,991	—	—	52,605
Colorado	12,160	134,850	—	3,450	3,025	22,587	—	—	62,100
Connecticut	—	—	—	171	—	66	—	2,793	—
Delaware	2,200	13,300	—	73	—	1,152	7,250	—	3,108
Florida	—	5,920	34	598	—	8,304	2,640	17,755	1,885
Georgia	—	52,250	350	1,620	4,130	—	28,600	87,200	22,400
Hawaii	—	—	—	—	—	—	—	—	—
Idaho	59,500	6,250	—	4,043	4,080	102,475	—	—	91,420
Illinois	—	1,322,250	—	3,526	17,000	858	354,000	—	105,020
Indiana	—	691,600	—	2,365	6,840	960	168,350	13,327	51,920
Iowa	—	1,445,500	—	6,650	54,000	270	322,920	—	3,290
Kansas	576	155,000	1	5,620	9,000	—	49,950	—	213,600
Kentucky	1,139	136,880	—	5,501	480	—	36,855	366,551	22,500
Louisiana	—	12,540	875	781	—	27	33,600	—	10,850
Maine	—	—	—	420	2,590	22,000	—	—	—
Maryland	4,000	44,000	—	629	1,320	315	16,500	8,103	8,600
Massachusetts	—	—	—	237	—	600	—	746	—
Michigan	2,320	222,610	—	5,205	20,100	9,200	38,880	—	33,920
Minnesota	44,000	700,000	—	6,400	46,750	15,750	185,000	—	102,504
Mississippi	—	9,800	1,560	1,560	—	—	40,000	—	15,300
Missouri	—	219,840	269	6,764	3,600	—	123,975	5,450	86,950
Montana	68,800	320	—	4,470	6,670	2,228	—	—	145,030
Nebraska	650	852,000	—	5,800	8,640	3,126	81,920	—	55,350
Nevada	990	—	—	1,463	—	2,600	—	—	1,200
New Hampshire	—	—	—	167	—	—	—	—	—
New Jersey	472	7,242	—	241	264	888	3,616	—	1,365
New Mexico	375	9,765	122	1,260	—	4,025	—	—	3,200
New York	—	53,010	—	4,538	9,145	6,628	—	—	5,850
North Carolina	2,064	88,350	140	1,161	3,135	2,310	41,850	541,056	21,420
North Dakota	98,050	34,875	—	3,020	20,150	15,070	13,860	—	242,320
Ohio	—	342,200	—	4,553	15,750	1,462	127,360	15,925	62,730
Oklahoma	900	9,204	180	5,025	2,040	—	6,840	—	153,900
Oregon	12,060	3,520	—	2,890	6,860	23,308	—	—	53,835
Pennsylvania	5,015	98,880	—	4,709	13,770	4,175	10,370	17,925	7,955
Rhode Island	—	—	—	17	—	300	—	—	—
South Carolina	560	30,940	155	564	2,360	—	20,160	103,680	17,835
South Dakota	19,250	190,800	—	4,290	44,000	1,980	48,880	—	83,080
Tennessee	—	56,710	473	3,499	—	60	29,760	79,820	18,900
Texas	480	148,400	3,028	9,582	6,600	3,408	12,450	—	60,000
Utah	9,006	2,640	—	1,986	1,258	1,495	—	—	5,950
Vermont	—	—	—	754	—	—	—	—	—
Virginia	4,875	40,150	3	2,565	495	1,440	17,280	93,184	12,650
Washington	28,420	15,750	—	2,814	2,835	64,310	—	—	110,610
West Virginia	—	4,370	—	1,036	300	—	—	1,885	516
Wisconsin	3,705	310,800	—	8,080	46,860	23,460	15,170	11,391	9,320
Wyoming	7,200	3,895	—	1,776	1,410	578	—	—	4,708
Total U.S.	403,443	7,527,152	12,233	145,445	373,778	370,497	1,926,806	1,367,331	2,035,818

Production of Chief U.S. Crops

Source: National Agricultural Statistics Service: U.S. Agriculture Department

Year	Corn for grain 1,000 bushels	Oats 1,000 bushels	Barley 1,000 bushels	Sorghum for grain 1,000 bushels	All Wheat 1,000 bushels	Rye 1,000 bushels	Flax- seed 1,000 bushels	Cotton lint 1,000 bales	Cotton seed 1,000 tons
1970..	4,152,243	915,236	416,091	683,179	1,351,558	36,840	29,416	10,192	4,068
1975..	5,828,961	638,960	379,162	754,354	2,126,927	15,924	15,553	8,302	3,218
1980..	6,639,396	458,792	361,135	579,343	2,380,934	15,958	7,728	11,122	4,470
1982..	8,235,101	592,630	515,935	835,083	2,764,967	19,533	10,278	11,963	4,744
1984..	7,672,130	473,661	598,034	866,241	2,594,777	32,407	7,022	12,982	5,149
1985..	8,875,453	518,490	590,213	1,120,271	2,424,115	20,337	8,293	13,432	5,279
1986..	8,249,864	386,356	610,522	938,124	2,091,635	19,522	11,538	9,731	3,801
1987..	7,131,300	373,713	521,499	730,809	2,107,685	19,526	7,444	14,760	5,769
1988..	4,928,681	217,600	289,994	576,686	1,812,201	14,689	1,615	15,412	6,062
1989..	7,527,152	373,778	403,443	617,860	2,035,818	13,482	1,355	12,233	4,766

Year	Tobacco 1,000 lbs.	All Hay 1,000 tons	Beans dry edible 1,000 cwt.	Peas dry edible 1,000 cwt.	Peanuts 1,000 lbs.	Soy- beans 1,000 bushels	Pota- toes 1,000 cwt.	Sweet pota- toes 1,000 cwt.
1970.....	1,906,453	126,969	17,399	3,315	2,983,121	1,127,100	325,716	13,164
1975.....	2,182,304	132,397	17,442	2,731	3,846,722	1,548,344	321,978	12,891
1980.....	1,786,225	130,740	26,729	3,285	2,302,762	1,797,543	303,905	10,953
1982.....	1,994,494	149,241	25,563	NA	3,440,255	2,190,297	355,131	14,833
1984.....	1,727,962	150,582	21,070	NA	4,405,945	1,860,863	362,039	12,902
1985.....	1,511,638	148,719	22,298	NA	4,122,787	2,099,056	406,609	14,573
1986.....	1,163,940	155,529	22,886	3,196	3,700,745	1,940,101	361,511	12,674
1987.....	1,188,868	147,457	26,031	3,385	3,616,010	1,937,722	389,320	11,611
1988.....	1,369,500	126,010	19,253	3,868	3,980,917	1,548,841	356,438	10,945
1989.....	1,414,179	145,445	24,333	3,883	4,030,050	1,926,806	370,344	11,997

Year	Rice 1,000 cwt.	Sugar- cane 1,000 tons	Sugar beets 1,000 tons	Pecans 1,000 tons	Al- monds 1,000 tons	Wal- nuts 1,000 tons	Fil- berts 1,000 tons	Oranges* 1,000 boxes	Grape- fruit* 1,000 boxes
1970	NA	23,996	26,378	NA	NA	111.8	9.3	185,770	53,910
1975	NA	28,344	29,704	NA	NA	199.3	12.1	237,810	61,610
1980	146,150	26,963	23,502	91.8	264.4	197.0	15.4	273,630	73,200
1982	153,637	29,770	20,894	109.3	283.5	234.0	18.8	176,690	70,550
1984	138,810	27,340	22,134	116.2	467.2	213.0	13.4	169,440	53,840
1985	134,913	28,213	22,529	122.2	375.6	219.0	24.6	158,350	56,150
1986	133,356	30,311	25,167	136.4	201.3	180.0	15.1	175,710	57,470
1987	129,603	29,218	28,072	131.1	519.0	247.0	21.8	181,175	63,775
1988	159,897	29,904	24,810	154.0	451.9	209.0	16.5	200,250	68,700
1989	154,487	29,570	25,553	108.8	367.6	215.0	13.0	208,950	69,500

NA=Not available. *Crop year ending in year cited.

Harvested Acreage of Principal U.S. Crops

Source: National Agricultural Statistics Service: U.S. Department of Agriculture (thousands of acres)

State	1987	1988	1989p	State	1987	1988	1989p
Alabama	2,358	2,389	2,356	Nebraska	15,932	16,765	17,641
Arizona	723	784	830	Nevada	558	549	554
Arkansas	7,132	7,538	7,595	New Hampshire	102	99	93
California	4,950	5,107	4,891	New Jersey	381	368	380
Colorado	5,634	5,609	5,677	New Mexico	953	936	926
Connecticut.	132	124	128	New York.	3,628	3,439	3,560
Delaware	514	504	537	North Carolina	4,155	4,104	4,526
Florida	1,108	1,115	1,137	North Dakota.	19,415	16,216	20,660
Georgia	3,601	3,754	4,210	Ohio	9,698	9,731	10,259
Hawaii.	87	86	80	Oklahoma	8,353	8,482	9,380
Idaho	4,141	4,018	4,333	Oregon	2,257	2,168	2,339
Illinois	20,335	21,581	22,977	Pennsylvania	4,257	4,199	4,199
Indiana	10,781	11,082	11,631	Rhode Island	13	11	10
Iowa.	20,956	23,092	24,097	South Carolina	1,925	2,022	2,283
Kansas	19,924	19,191	18,795	South Dakota	14,601	13,508	15,294
Kentucky	4,975	4,968	5,491	Tennessee	4,463	4,548	4,564
Louisiana	3,905	4,308	3,933	Texas	16,267	16,527	16,644
Maine	356	346	364	Utah	1,080	1,026	983
Maryland	1,493	1,493	1,603	Vermont.	465	453	442
Massachusetts.	158	143	136	Virginia	2,732	2,708	2,767
Michigan	6,124	6,401	6,390	Washington	3,902	3,890	4,045
Minnesota	17,397	18,767	18,661	West Virginia	657	644	664
Mississippi	5,020	5,149	4,613	Wisconsin	8,351	8,430	8,614
Missouri.	12,436	12,684	13,249	Wyoming	1,796	1,674	1,628
Montana	9,242	7,118	9,475	*Total U.S.	289,422	289,846	305,641

P = Preliminary. * States may not add due to rounding.

Average Prices Received by U.S. Farmers

Source: Natl. Agricultural Statistics Service, U.S. Agriculture Department

The figures represent dollars per 100 lbs. for hogs, beef cattle, veal calves, sheep, lamb, and milk (wholesale), dollars per head for milk cows; cents per lb. for milk fat (in cream), chickens, broilers, turkeys, and wool; cents for eggs per dozen.

Weighted calendar year prices for livestock and livestock products other than wool. 1943 through 1963, wool prices are weighted on marketing year basis. The marketing year has been changed (1964) from a calendar year to a Dec.-Nov. basis for hogs, chickens, broilers and eggs.

Year	Hogs	Cattle (beef)	Calves (veal)	Sheep	Lambs	Cows (milk)	Chickens All milk	Chickens (excl. broilers)	Broilers	Turkeys	Eggs	Wool
1930	8.84	7.71	9.68	4.74	7.76	74	2.21	...	...	20.2	23.7	19.5
1940	5.39	7.56	8.83	3.95	8.10	61	1.82	13.0	17.3	15.2	18.0	28.4
1950	18.00	23.30	26.30	11.60	25.10	198	3.89	22.2	27.4	32.8	36.3	62.1
1960	15.30	20.40	22.90	5.61	17.90	223	4.21	12.2	16.9	25.4	36.1	42.0
1970	22.70	27.10	34.50	7.51	26.40	332	5.71	9.1	13.6	22.6	39.1	35.4
1975	46.10	32.20	27.20	11.30	42.10	412	8.75	9.9	26.3	34.8	54.5	44.8
1979	41.80	66.10	88.80	26.30	66.70	1,040	12.00	14.4	25.9	41.3	58.3	86.3
1980	38.00	62.40	76.80	21.30	63.60	1,190	13.05	11.0	27.7	41.3	56.3	88.1
1984	47.10	57.30	59.90	16.40	60.10	895	13.46	15.9	33.7	48.9	72.3	79.5
1985	44.00	53.70	62.10	23.90	67.70	860	12.76	14.8	30.1	49.1	57.2	63.3
1986	49.30	52.60	61.10	25.60	69.00	820	12.51	12.5	34.5	47.0	61.5	66.8
1987	51.20	61.10	78.50	29.50	77.60	920	12.54	11.0	28.7	34.8	54.7	91.7
1988	42.30	66.60	89.20	25.60	69.10	990	12.26	9.2	33.1	38.6	52.8	1.38
1989	42.50	69.50	90.80	24.40	66.10	10.30	13.56	14.9	36.6	40.9	68.9	1.22

The figures represent cents per lb. for cotton, apples, and peanuts; dollars per bushel for oats, wheat, corn, barley, and soybeans; dollars per 100 lbs. for rice, sorghum, and potatoes; dollars per ton for cottonseed and baled hay.

Weighted crop year prices. Crop years are as follows: apples, June-May; wheat, oats, barley, hay and potatoes, July-June; cotton, rice, peanuts and cottonseed, August-July; soybeans, September-August; and corn and sorghum grain, October-September.

	Corn	Wheat	Upland cotton[1]	Oats	Barley	Rice	Soybeans	Sorghum	Peanuts	Cottonseed	Hay	Potatoes	Apples
1930	.598	.663	9.46	0.311	.420	1.74	1.34	1.02	5.01	22.00	11.00	1.47	...
1940	.618	.674	9.83	0.298	.393	1.80	.892	.873	3.72	21.70	9.78	.850	...
1950	1.52	2.00	39.90	0.788	1.19	5.09	2.47	1.88	10.9	86.60	21.10	1.50	...
1960	13.00	1.74	30.08	0.599	.840	4.55	2.13	1.49	10.0	42.50	21.70	2.00	2.72
1970	1.33	1.33	21.86	0.623	.973	5.17	2.85	2.04	12.8	56.40	26.10	2.21	6.52
1975	2.54	3.55	51.10	1.45	2.42	8.35	4.92	4.21	19.6	97.00	52.10	4.48	8.80
1979	2.52	3.78	62.3	1.36	2.29	10.50	6.28	4.18	20.6	121.00	59.50	3.43	15.40
1980	3.11	3.91	74.4	1.79	2.86	12.80	7.57	5.25	25.1	129.00	71.00	6.55	12.1
1984	2.63	3.39	58.7	1.67	2.29	8.04	5.84	4.15	27.9	99.50	72.70	5.69	15.5
1985	2.23	3.08	56.8	1.23	1.98	6.53	5.05	3.45	24.4	66.00	67.60	3.92	17.3
1986	1.50	2.42	51.5	1.21	1.61	3.75	4.78	2.45	29.2	80.00	59.70	5.03	19.1
1987	1.94	2.57	63.7	1.56	1.81	7.27	5.88	3.04	27.7	82.50	65.10	4.35	12.7
1988	2.55	3.72	54.8	2.61	2.79	6.70	7.55	4.07	26.9	119.00	87.10	5.49	10.8
1989	2.33	3.72	63.3	1.49	2.42	7.53	5.60	3.66	2.79	105.00	86.00	6.85	13.4

(1) Beginning 1964, 480 lb. net weight bales.

Grain Storage Capacity at Principal Grain Centers in U.S.

Source: Chicago Board of Trade Market Information Department, Aug. 1990

(bushels)

Cities	Capacity	Cities	Capacity
Atlantic Coast	31,700,000	Fort Worth	68,600,000
Great Lakes		Texas High Plains	79,500,000
Toledo	53,600,000	Enid	79,700,000
Buffalo	15,200,000	Gulf Points	
Chicago	52,400,000	South Mississippi	44,700,000
Milwaukee	6,600,000	North Texas Gulf	24,200,000
Duluth	64,300,000	South Texas Gulf	15,300,000
River Points		Plains	
Minneapolis	105,800,000	Wichita	37,400,000
Peoria	3,300,000	Topeka	54,100,000
St. Louis	17,700,000	Salina	49,500,000
Sioux City	7,800,000	Hutchinson	42,000,000
Omaha-Council Bluffs	23,100,000	Hastings-Grand Island	25,300,000
Atchison	16,500,000	Lincoln	33,700,000
St. Joseph	22,300,000	Pacific N.W.	
Kansas City, Mo.	92,200,000	Puget Sound (incl. Portland)	35,100,000
Southwest		California ports	NA

Atlantic Coast — Albany, N.Y., Philadelphia, Pa., Baltimore, Md., Norfolk, Va. **Gulf Points** — New Orleans, Baton Rouge, Ama. Belle Chase, La., Mobile, Ala. **North Texas Gulf** — Houston, Galveston, Beaumont, Port Arthur, Texas. **South Texas Gulf** — Corpus Christi, Brownsville, Texas. **Pacific N.W.** — Seattle, Tacoma, Wash., Portland, Oreg., Columbia River. **Texas High Plains** — Amarillo, Lubbock, Hereford, Plainview, Texas. NA = Not available.

Consumption of Major Food Commodities per Person

Source: Economic Research Service: U.S. Agriculture Department

Commodity[1]	1987	1988	1989p	Commodity[1]	1987	1988	1989p
Red Meats[2,3]	113.3	115.1	111.3	Fresh[7]	96.9	94.4	NA
Beef[2]	69.2	68.2	65.0	Citrus[7]	24.7	25.6	NA
Veal[2]	1.3	1.1	1.0	Noncitrus[7]	72.2	68.8	NA
Lamb and mutton[2]	1.0	1.0	1.1	Processed:			
Pork[2]	41.8	44.7	44.3	Canned fruit	8.8	8.8	NA
Poultry[2,3]	55.3	57.1	60.5	Frozen fruit	3.9	3.8	NA
Chicken[2]	43.2	44.5	47.0	Dried Fruit	2.7	2.9	NA
Turkey[2]	12.0	12.6	13.5	Vegetables:			
Fish[2]	15.5	15.0	15.7	Fresh[7,8]	95.4	98.7	101.9
Eggs	32.1	31.0	29.7	For canning[7]	87.1	83.1	NA
Dairy products:				For freezing[7]	16.8	17.9	16.9
Cheese (natural equivalent)	24.0	23.6	23.7	Potatoes[7]	125.4	123.5	123.3
Condensed and evaporated milk	3.4	3.5	3.0	Grains:			
Fluid milk and cream	237.4	233.4	230.5	Wheat flour	129.3	129.3	122.7
Whole milk	111.1	105.2	95.3	Rice	13.5	14.3	15.7
Lowfat milk[4]	100.1	100.0	103.6	Pasta (excl. fresh)	11.9	12.2	12.8
Skim milk	14.0	16.0	19.7	Caloric and noncaloric sweeteners[9]	151.4	153.0	NA
Cream[5]	4.6	4.6	4.7	Caloric sweeteners	132.4	133.0	133.3
Yogurt	4.4	4.6	4.3	Refined cane and beet sugar	62.4	62.0	62.2
Specialty cream products[6]	2.9	3.0	3.0	Corn sweeteners	68.6	69.6	69.7
Ice cream	18.3	17.2	16.0	High fructose	47.1	48.0	47.8
Fats and Oils—Total fat content	62.7	62.7	60.7	Low-calorie sweeteners[10]	19.0	20.0	NA
Butter	4.6	4.5	4.3	Other:			
Margarine	10.5	10.2	10.1	Coffee (beans)	10.2	10.2	10.2
Lard (direct use)	1.8	1.7	1.8	Tea	0.7	0.7	0.7
Edible tallow (direct use)	1.0	0.8	0.9	Cocoa (beans)	4.8	4.9	5.0
Shortening	21.3	21.2	21.2	Peanuts (shelled)	6.4	6.8	7.1
Salad and cooking oils	24.7	24.8	23.6	Tree nuts	2.2	2.2	2.5
Other edible fats and oils	1.3	1.3	1.3	Dry edible beans	5.0	5.7	NA
Fruits:							

(1) Quantity in pounds, retail weight unless otherwise shown. Data on calendar year basis except for dried fruits, fresh citrus fruits, and peanuts which are on a crop-year basis, and rice and eggs which are on a marketing year basis. Data as of August 1990. (2) Boneless, trimmed weight. (3) Total may not add due to rounding. (4) Includes plain lowfat, flavored, and buttermilk. (5) Includes heavy cream, light cream, and half and half. (6) Includes eggnog and sour cream and dip. (7) Farm weight. (8) Commercial production for sale as fresh produce. (9) Dry weight. (10) Sugar-sweetness equivalent. P = Preliminary. NA = not available.

U.S. Egg Production

Source: Economic Research Service. U.S. Agriculture Department (millions of eggs)

State	1986	1987	1988	1989	State	1986	1987	1988	1989	State	1986	1987	1988	1989
Ala.	2,723	2,605	2,596	2,184	La.	336	323	311	299	Oh.	3,873	4,351	4,477	4,353
Alas.	12.8	6.6	0.7	0.7	Me.	1,239	1,827	1,300	1,138	Okla.	809	805	863	885
Ariz.	121	98	86	79	Md.	890	926	932	965	Ore.	659	638	617	678
Ark.	3,731	3,874	3,784	3,352	Mass.	315	273	262	238	Pa.	4,692	4,853	5,317	5,232
Cal.	7,850	8,023	7,718	7,317	Mich.	1,644	1,656	1,553	1,454	R.I.	58	55	52	46
Col.	575	641	784	824	Minn.	2,312	2,263	2,250	2,236	S.C.	1,615	1,604	1,432	1,342
Conn.	1,281	1,200	1,121	935	Miss.	1,274	1,259	1,251	1,289	S.D.	395	358	348	373
Del.	135	144	146	147	Mo.	1,351	1,397	1,526	1,485	Tenn.	663	670	532	318
Fla.	2,683	2,568	2,758	2,602	Mont.	201	205	194	180	Tex.	3,355	3,424	3,363	3,304
Ga.	4,318	4,476	4,294	4,233	Neb.	829	869	902	1,037	Ut.	457	496	490	460
Ha.	227	223	224.4	226.5	Nev.	2.2	2.2	2.2	2.3	Vt.	57	60	54	36
Ida.	230	238	217	217	N.H.	95	76	51	53	Va.	914	937	911	894
Ill.	663	709	780	794	N.J.	501	475	486	437	Wash.	1,295	1,303	1,327	1,299
Ind.	5,561	5,750	5,644	5,529	N.M.	280	302	287	294	W. Va.	109	128	126	121
Ia.	1,441	1,534	2,140	2,140	N.Y.	1,523	1,115	1,013	1,036	Wis.	830	877	881	852
Kan.	463	486	387	387	N.C.	3,400	3,251	3,396	3,312	Wyo.	4.5	4.3	3.6	2.3
Ky.	420	466	407	407	N.D.	118	61	59	47	Total*	68,407	68,398	69,655	67,100

Note: The egg and chicken production year runs from Dec. 1 of the previous year through Nov. 30. (1) Included are eggs destroyed because of possible PCB contamination. * States may not add to total.

Farm-Real Estate Debt Outstanding by Lender Groups[1]

Source: Economic Research Service. U.S. Agriculture Department

Dec. 31	Total farm-real estate debt[2] $1,000	Federal land banks[2] $1,000	Amounts held by principal lender groups — Farmers Home Administration[3] $1,000	Life insurance companies[4] $1,000	All commercial banks $1,000	Other[5] $1,000
1955	9,048,676	1,480,000	413,000	2,272,000	1,275,000	3,609,000
1960	12,867,524	2,539,000	723,000	2,975,000	1,592,000	5,039,000
1965	21,220,912	4,240,000	1,497,000	4,802,000	2,607,000	8,070,000
1970	30,492,357	7,145,363	2,440,043	5,610,300	3,772,377	11,524,000
1975	49,852,888	16,029,468	3,368,747	6,726,000	6,296,286	17,432,000
1980	97,486,996	36,196,103	8,163,270	12,927,800	8,563,457	31,636,000
1982	111,312,036	47,821,589	9,169,874	12,801,546	8,391,800	33,127,000
1985	105,739,201	44,583,842	10,426,971	11,830,400	11,384,920	27,507,000
1986	95,879,799	37,757,626	10,348,597	10,940,200	12,710,650	24,123,000
1987	87,717,601	32,637,687	10,083,239	9,895,800	14,455,162	20,646,000
1988	82,952,518	30,326,707	9,606,796	9,581,700	15,416,700	18,020,000
1989	80,476,478	28,501,000	8,719,822	9,597,900	16,646,179	17,011,577

(1) Includes opertator households. (2) Includes data for joint stock land banks and real estate loans by Agricultural Credit Assn. (3) Includes loans made directly by FmHA for farm ownership, soil and water loans to individuals, Indian tribe land acquisition, grazing associations, and half of economic emergency loans. Also includes loans for rural housing on farm tracts and labor housing. (4) American Council of Life Insurance. (5) Estimated by ERS, USDA. Includes CCC storage and drying facility loans.

Government Payments by Programs and State[1]

Source: Economic Research Service, U.S. Agriculture Department (thousands)

1989 State	Feed Grain	Wheat	Rice	Cotton	Wool Act	Conservation[2]	Miscellaneous[3]	Total
Alabama	$8,573	$2,132	0	$44,156	$6	$28,951	$37,041	$120,859
Alaska	23	0	0	0	4	1,075	41	1,143
Arizona	2,527	1,176	0	73,089	1,179	2,031	5,104	85,106
Arkansas	12,708	11,195	$275,616	70,957	72	16,157	52,970	439,675
California	10,331	10,426	124,811	148,324	3,203	13,684	61,311	372,090
Colorado	45,314	22,761	0	0	2,517	87,262	25,588	183,442
Connecticut	624	0	0	0	10	326	1,240	2,200
Delaware	2,057	58	0	0	2	281	2,420	4,818
Florida	4,546	499	38	3,166	6	9,578	20,490	38,323
Georgia	27,331	7,937	0	33,427	9	33,032	71,322	173,058
Hawaii	0	0	0	0	0	267	0	267
Idaho	4,862	18,721	0	0	1,216	38,555	35,735	99,089
Illinois	437,335	9,610	0	0	247	50,585	228,164	725,941
Indiana	204,923	5,045	0	0	114	28,084	95,525	333,691
Iowa	578,178	248	0	0	784	154,809	247,187	981,206
Kansas	166,126	103,644	0	37	593	160,417	157,629	588,446
Kentucky	41,522	2,493	0	0	61	28,335	46,012	118,423
Louisiana	6,608	2,225	105,932	90,576	12	8,769	35,636	249,758
Maine	651	0	0	0	30	4,376	2,086	7,143
Maryland	9,918	285	0	0	33	2,042	11,457	23,735
Massachusetts	256	0	0	0	13	478	3,116	3,863
Michigan	98,903	6,385	0	0	569	15,433	140,681	261,971
Minnesota	257,740	28,691	0	0	505	101,057	211,859	599,852
Mississippi	7,370	3,801	53,764	171,377	8	34,187	54,654	325,161
Missouri	94,961	14,846	18,702	23,238	357	101,412	102,875	356,391
Montana	11,344	48,614	0	0	2,589	105,442	121,393	289,382
Nebraska	377,604	24,256	0	0	478	76,744	63,224	542,306
Nevada	92	268	0	0	292	1,167	4,482	6,301
New Hampshire	193	0	0	0	9	671	1,429	2,302
New Jersey	2,870	177	0	0	11	633	17,792	21,483
New Mexico	10,596	2,950	0	8,802	3,416	21,588	17,323	64,675
New York	27,879	1,626	0	0	118	7,962	38,440	76,025
North Carolina	41,464	2,584	0	11,513	25	10,590	27,741	93,917
North Dakota	38,688	86,525	0	0	568	101,104	247,961	474,846
Ohio	120,695	7,194	0	0	533	18,336	127,245	274,003
Oklahoma	10,968	48,418	129	31,399	1,840	53,630	88,433	234,817
Oregon	2,699	12,633	0	0	945	29,968	14,139	60,384
Pennsylvania	17,083	434	0	0	193	9,392	41,294	68,396
Rhode Island	1	0	0	0	2	65	22	90
South Carolina	17,698	3,487	0	16,578	1	14,434	20,498	72,696
South Dakota	101,989	28,893	0	0	2,362	63,749	143,269	340,262
Tennessee	18,730	3,405	69	40,826	18	26,178	51,823	141,049
Texas	165,919	38,589	91,921	416,170	50,131	177,398	308,585	1,248,713
Utah	1,368	1,523	0	0	2,069	12,176	17,400	34,536
Vermont	525	3	0	0	34	1,882	4,620	7,064
Virginia	14,514	1,277	0	181	275	7,358	14,994	38,599
Washington	8,077	35,241	0	0	198	54,270	33,346	131,132
West Virginia	1,806	36	0	0	142	2,447	7,168	11,599
Wisconsin	122,410	961	0	0	176	39,967	358,818	522,332
Wyoming	2,197	1,725	0	0	3,428	12,330	14,462	34,142
Total U.S.	$3,140,796	$602,997	$670,982	$1,183,816	$81,403	$1,770,664	$3,436,044	$10,886,702

(1) Includes both cash payments and payment-in-kind (PIK). (2) Includes amount paid under agriculture and conservation programs (Conservation Bonus, Conservation Reserve, Agriculture Conservation, Emergency Conservation, and Great Plains Program). (3) The programs included: Rural Clean Water, Clean Lakes, Animal Waste Management, Forest Incentive, Water Bank, Milk Indemnity, Dairy Termination, Emergency Feed, Extended Warehouse Storage, Extended Farm Storage, Milk Diversion, Disaster Program Crops, Disaster Program Non-Crops, Colorado River Salinity, Warehouse Storage Deduction, Livestock Emergency Assistance, Interest Penalty Payments, Disaster, and Loan Deficiency.

Federal Food Assistance Programs[1]

Source: Food and Nutrition Service, U.S. Agriculture Department (millions of dollars)

	1981	1982	1983	1984	1985	1986	1987	1988	1989	1990
Food Stamp Pgm.[2,5]	10,328	10,159	11,863	11,595	11,721	11,694	11,644	12,356	12,908	15,518
P.R. Nutrition Asstnce. Grant[3]	908	898	825	825	824	824	853	879	908	937
Natl. School Lunch Pgm.[4]	3,276	2,942	3,203	3,335	3,380	3,537	3,685	3,730	3,772	4,342
School Breakfast Pgm.	332	317	344	364	379	406	447	482	513	537
Special Supp. Food Pgm. for Women, Infants, Children[5]	872	949	1,126	1,388	1,489	1,583	1,680	1,798	1,909	2,128
Summer Food Service Pgm. [4]	106	87	93	96	112	115	129	133	147	164
Child and Adult Care Food Pgm.[4]	340	324	356	407	452	496	506	623	697	879
Special Milk Pgm.	101	18	17	16	16	16	15	19	19	21
Nutrition Pgm. for the Elderly[4]	94	102	120	127	134	137	139	146	144	144
Needy Family Pgm.[4]	37	41	44	51	60	60	63	62	66	60
Commodity Supp. Food Pgm.[4,7]	28	28	41	48	48	48	56	62	73	78
Food Distribution to Charities Inst.[4,8]	78	117	154	190	170	240	158	159	136	141
Other Costs[9]	56	233	1,079	1,126	1,080	952	904	697	364	417
Total[10]	16,556	16,216	19,264	19,568	19,865	20,107	20,279	21,146	21,656	25,366

(1) Data are for Fiscal (not Calendar) years. 1989 and prior years are updated per current reports; 1990 data represent the program level under current law in the 1991 budget. (2) Excludes Puerto Rico. (3) Grant was initiated in June 1982; prior data are Food Stamp Costs. (4) Includes the value of commodities (entitlement, bonus and cash-in-lieu). (5) Includes program studies; excludes Farmers Market Demo. Projects. (6) Includes SAE, other program costs, and transfers. (7) Includes Elderly Feeding Projects. (8) Includes Summer Camps. (9) Includes Child Nutrition State Admin. Expenses, CN Nutrition Studies & Education, Temporary Emergency Food Assist. Program (commodity and admin. costs), and the costs of entitlement foods distributed to Soup Kitchens/Food Banks. (10) Excludes food program administration (FPA) costs, Northern Marianas Nutrition Assistance Grant, and Disaster Relief. The Northern Marianas Grant was $0.9 million in FY 1982, and $3.7 million for subsequent years.

World Wheat, Rice and Corn Production, 1988

Source: U.N. Food and Agriculture Organization

(thousands of metric tons)

Country	Wheat	Rice	Corn	Country	Wheat	Rice	Corn
World, total	509,952	483,466	405,460	Kampuchea	N/A	2,000	100
Afghanistan	2,900	490	839	Korea (DPR)	880	6,350	2,950
Argentina	7,769	383	9,200	Korean Republic	3	8,400	130
Australia	14,102	740	208	Laos	N/A	1,003	40
Austria	1,430	N/A	1,640	Madagascar	N/A	2,100	150
Bangladesh	1,048	21,900	3	Malaysia	N/A	1,669	31
Belgium[1]	1,327	N/A	40	Mexico	3,700	420	11,800
Brazil	5,436	11,804	24,709	Myanmar	241	14,000	300
Bulgaria	4,713	60	1,625	Nepal	745	2,787	890
Canada	15,655	N/A	5,369	Netherlands	816	N/A	5
Chile	1,734	162	661	New Zealand	235	N/A	190
China	87,505	172,365	73,820	Pakistan	12,675	4,577	1,150
Colombia	63	1,775	908	Panama	N/A	166	97
Cuba	N/A	488	95	Peru	134	1,080	880
Czechoslovakia	6,547	N/A	996	Philippines	N/A	8,971	4,428
Denmark	2,080	N/A	N/A	Poland	7,582	N/A	204
Ecuador	31	420	387	Portugal	401	151	663
Egypt	2,839	1,900	4,088	Romania	9,000	150	19,500
Ethiopia	825	N/A	1,650	South Africa	3,400	3	6,900
Finland	285	N/A	N/A	Soviet Union	84,500	2,900	16,000
France	29,677	65	13,996	Spain	6,514	499	3,577
Germany (GDR)	3,697	N/A	1	Sri Lanka	N/A	2,466	43
Germany (FDR)	12,044	N/A	1,435	Sweden	1,357	N/A	N/A
Greece	2,550	116	2,116	Switzerland	553	N/A	237
Hungary	6,962	52	6,027	Syria	2,067	N/A	61
India	45,096	101,950	7,500	Thailand	N/A	20,813	5,166
Indonesia	N/A	41,769	6,668	Turkey	20,500	263	2,100
Iran	8,200	1,757	60	United Kingdom	11,605	N/A	1
Iraq	1,200	250	62	United States	49,295	7,237	125,003
Ireland	418	N/A	N/A	Uruguay	390	381	118
Israel	211	N/A	25	Venezuela	1	385	1,400
Italy	7,945	1,094	6,318	Vietnam	N/A	15,200	580
Japan	1,021	12,419	1	Yugoslavia	6,303	36	7,697

(1) Includes Luxembourg. Note: Some figures are FAO estimates. NA = Not available.

Wheat, Rice and Corn—Exports and Imports of 10 Leading Countries

Source: Economic Research Service, U.S. Agriculture Department

(thousands of metric tons)

Leading Exporters	Exports[1]			Leading Importers	Imports[1]		
	1980	1988	1989[p]		1980	1988	1989[p]
Wheat				**Wheat**			
United States	41,204	38,619	33,557	USSR	16,000	15,500	14,000
France	13,423	18,843	19,100	China	13,789	15,500	13,000
Canada	16,262	12,420	17,500	Egypt	5,423	7,000	7,000
Australia	9,577	11,375	11,000	Japan	5,840	5,405	5,400
Argentina	3,845	4,034	5,900	Italy	3,028	5,500	5,100
United Kingdom	1,100	2,200	4,500	Iran	1,896	3,200	5,100
Germany, Fed Rep	1,502	3,700	2,800	Algeria	2,294	4,200	4,300
Italy	1,620	3,600	2,400	Iraq	1,366	2,800	3,400
Saudi Arabia	0	2,000	1,900	Turkey	0	300	3,000
Hungary	700	1,900	1,500	South Korea	2,095	2,822	2,200
Rice				**Rice**			
Thailand	3,049	6,037	4,000	Iran	583	1,000	900
United States	3,028	2,786	2,497	USSR	1,283	600	640
Vietnam	5	1,400	2,000	Philippines	0	195	575
Pakistan	1,163	792	850	Saudi Arabia	356	525	525
Italy	475	443	525	Iraq	350	570	500
Australia	468	500	461	Indonesia	2,040	33	412
India	900	400	400	China	110	1,400	400
China	580	320	300	Hong Kong	362	380	400
Uruguay	184	209	290	Senegal	340	410	385
Burma	674	456	200	Malaysia	167	350	360
Corn				**Corn**			
United States	60,737	51,525	59,693	USSR	11,800	18,600	18,100
France	2,380	6,685	7,470	Japan	13,989	15,900	16,300
China	125	3,700	2,500	South Korea	2,355	5,700	6,800
Argentina	9,098	1,800	2,400	Taiwan	2,703	4,100	5,000
Thailand	2,142	1,560	1,250	Mexico	3,833	3,120	4,700
South Africa	4,955	4,400	1,200	Netherlands	2,638	1,996	2,020
Zimbabwe	305	400	400	United Kingdom	2,349	1,400	1,535
Indonesia	15	225	350	Malaysia	717	1,375	1,500
Kenya	0	125	260	Spain	4,251	2,150	1,500
Hungary	300	152	170	Brazil	0	100	1,500

(1) Marketing years; (p) Preliminary.

EMPLOYMENT

U.S. Labor Force, Employment and Unemployment

Source: Bureau of Labor Statistics. U.S. Labor Department

(numbers in thousands)

Employment status	Annual averages			1990			
	1987	1988	1989	Jan.	March	May	July
Civilian labor force	119,865	121,669	123,869	124,397	124,829	125,004	124,767
Employed	112,440	114,968	117,342	117,863	118,334	118,350	117,953
Unemployed	7,425	6,701	6,528	6,535	6,495	6,653	6,814
Unemployment rate	6.2	5.5	5.3	5.3	5.2	5.3	5.5

Selected Unemployment Indicators

(quarterly averages, seasonally adjusted)

Category Characteristic	1987			1988				1989				1990	
	II	III	IV	I	II	III	IV	I	II	III	IV	I	II
Total (all civilian workers) . . .	6.3	6.0	5.8	5.7	5.5	5.5	5.3	5.2	5.3	5.3	5.3	5.2	5.3
Men, 20 years and over. . .	5.6	5.3	5.0	4.9	4.8	4.7	4.6	4.4	4.4	4.6	4.6	4.6	4.8
Women, 20 years and over.	5.4	5.3	5.2	5.1	4.9	4.9	4.7	4.6	4.8	4.7	4.8	4.7	4.6
Both sexes, 16 to 19 years .	17.0	16.2	16.6	16.0	15.1	15.5	14.5	15.0	15.0	15.0	15.2	14.5	14.8
White	5.4	5.1	5.0	4.9	4.7	4.8	4.6	4.4	4.5	4.5	4.5	4.6	4.6
Black and other	11.7	11.4	11.0	11.0	10.6	10.0	9.9	10.2	9.8	9.8	10.3	9.6	9.3
Black	13.1	12.7	12.3	12.3	12.0	11.4	11.3	11.5	11.3	11.3	11.8	10.8	10.4
Hispanic origin	8.7	8.1	8.5	8.1	8.8	7.9	7.8	7.3	8.0	8.6	8.1	7.5	7.6
Married men, spouse present	4.1	3.8	3.5	3.4	3.2	3.2	3.1	3.0	3.0	3.1	3.0	3.2	3.3
Married women, spouse present.	4.3	4.2	4.2	4.1	3.8	3.9	3.7	3.5	3.9	3.8	3.9	3.7	3.6
Women who maintain families	9.5	9.1	8.6	8.2	8.3	8.0	7.9	8.0	8.0	8.1	8.0	7.8	7.6
Full-time workers	5.9	5.6	5.5	5.3	5.1	5.1	5.0	4.9	4.9	5.0	5.0	4.9	5.0
Part-time workers	8.2	8.2	8.2	8.0	7.6	7.7	7.1	7.1	7.3	7.2	7.4	7.2	7.4
Unemployed 15 weeks and over[1]	1.7	1.6	1.5	1.4	1.3	1.3	1.2	1.1	1.1	1.1	1.1	1.1	1.1
Labor force time lost[2]	7.2	6.9	6.7	6.6	6.3	6.4	6.2	6.0	6.0	6.0	5.9	5.9	6.0
Industry													
Nonagricultural private wage and salary workers	6.3	6.0	5.8	5.7	5.5	5.5	5.4	5.3	5.3	5.4	5.4	5.5	5.5
Goods-producing industries.	7.5	7.0	6.6	6.8	6.4	6.5	6.4	6.1	6.0	6.3	6.3	6.6	6.5
Mining.	11.1	8.2	7.5	7.8	8.4	7.1	8.1	6.9	4.8	6.8	5.2	5.9	3.8
Construction	12.0	11.4	10.9	11.2	10.6	10.1	10.4	10.0	9.8	10.2	9.6	9.4	10.6
Manufacturing	6.1	5.7	5.4	5.4	5.2	5.4	5.1	5.0	5.0	5.2	5.4	5.8	5.4
Durable goods	6.0	5.7	5.0	5.4	4.8	5.1	4.9	4.7	4.6	4.8	5.3	5.6	5.3
Nondurable goods	6.3	5.8	6.0	5.6	5.7	5.8	5.5	5.4	5.5	5.6	5.6	6.1	5.5
Service-producing industries	5.7	5.5	5.3	5.2	5.0	5.0	4.9	5.0	5.0	5.0	4.9	5.0	5.0
Transportation and public utilities	4.5	4.3	4.5	3.9	4.0	3.7	3.9	3.9	4.0	4.1	3.6	3.9	3.5
Wholesale and retail trade	7.1	6.7	6.4	6.5	6.1	6.2	6.0	5.9	5.8	6.0	6.2	6.1	6.2
Finance and service industries	4.9	4.9	4.7	4.6	4.5	4.4	4.4	4.4	4.5	4.4	4.3	4.4	4.5
Government workers.	3.4	3.4	3.3	3.0	2.9	2.9	2.6	2.7	2.8	2.8	2.7	2.4	2.5
Agricultural wage and salary workers	8.9	10.2	11.3	11.1	10.6	11.2	9.5	9.2	10.0	8.6	10.6	9.6	9.6

(1) Unemployment as a percent of the civilian labor force. (2) Aggregate hours lost by the unemployed and persons on part time for economic reasons as a percent of potentially available labor force hours.

Employed Persons by Occupation, Sex, and Age

Source: Bureau of Labor Statistics

(in thousands)

Occupation	Total 16 years and over		Men 16 years and over		Women 16 years and over	
	1988	1989	1988	1989	1988	1989
Total.	114,968	117,342	63,273	64,315	51,696	53,027
Managerial and professional specialty	29,190	30,398	16,139	16,652	13,050	13,746
Executive, administrative and managerial.	14,216	14,848	8,626	8,944	5,590	5,904
Professional specialty	14,974	15,550	7,513	7,708	7,460	7,842
Technical, sales and administrative support	35,532	36,127	12,494	12,687	23,038	23,440
Technicians and related support	3,521	3,645	1,833	1,887	1,688	1,759
Sales occupations	13,747	14,065	7,025	7,124	6,722	6,941
Administrative support, including clerical.	18,264	18,416	3,636	3,676	14,628	14,741
Service occupations.	15,332	15,556	6,056	6,164	9,275	9,391
Private household	909	872	34	36	875	836
Protective service	1,944	1,960	1,664	1,654	279	305
Service, except private household and protective	12,479	12,724	4,358	4,474	8,121	8,250
Precision production, craft, and repair.	13,664	13,818	12,474	12,627	1,190	1,190
Mechanics and repairers	4,454	4,550	4,307	4,397	147	153
Construction trades	5,098	5,142	4,991	5,034	107	108
Other precision production, craft, and repair	4,112	4,126	3,176	3,196	936	929
Operators, fabricators, and laborers	17,814	18,022	13,234	13,327	4,580	4,695
Machine operators, assemblers, and inspectors	8,117	8,248	4,806	4,878	3,311	3,370
Transportation and material moving occupations	4,831	4,886	4,397	4,436	434	450
Handlers, equipment cleaners, helpers, and laborers	4,866	4,888	4,031	4,013	835	875

Selected Unemployment Insurance Data by State

Calendar year 1989, state programs only.

	Insured claimants[1]	Beneficiaries[2]	Exhaustions[3]	Initial claims[4]	Benefits paid[5]	Avg. weekly benefit for total unemployment	Employers subject to state law
AL.	172,035	151,376	27,858	64,267	$155,821,512	$108.78	79,183
AK	36,364	33,093	13,972	354,277	72,743,596	157.17	13,552
AZ	108,583	73,524	19,738	213,522	125,151,023	116.97	78,119
AR	117,317	83,388	20,339	171,548	126,156,831	131.14	48,862
CA	1,258,789	1,023,682	287,428	2,559,133	1,704,985,041	120.51	756,039
CO	96,996	74,111	25,133	139,383	148,021,233	160.94	88,829
CT	126,385	119,473	22,904	219,229	271,438,639	191.12	94,990
DE	27,564	22,049	2,213	34,381	33,564,096	163.31	17,839
DC	26,793	19,462	10,208	46,935	71,896,747	200.32	21,198
FL	254,036	186,715	63,265	388,179	339,811,769	145.39	306,721
GA	285,901	209,516	50,190	401,529	253,551,957	136.24	140,240
HI	26,250	19,098	3,395	46,581	38,779,522	176.59	25,758
ID	41,997	36,539	10,069	138,358	54,827,684	139.30	24,951
IL	291,363	302,991	95,294	98,592	767,866,371	159.73	243,162
IN	171,622	115,811	22,511	688,648	121,397,965	104.88	107,022
IA	89,264	73,393	15,970	323,160	130,014,218	155.75	61,425
KS	86,072	69,306	19,550	161,241	153,437,954	167.22	58,716
KY	143,125	113,154	19,744	286,997	159,210,022	125.70	70,799
LA	126,097	99,250	32,900	249,293	164,542,924	105.42	80,597
ME	55,431	44,387	8,677	486,565	68,194,923	149.12	33,432
MD	146,689	88,861	19,697	212,442	199,349,371	167.15	110,801
MA	151,987	260,788	69,468	119,044	819,279,901	211.73	152,071
MI	304,853	393,128	101,631	941,068	938,913,234	189.86	185,924
MN	146,184	122,906	34,140	239,919	321,214,321	185.32	98,727
MS	97,717	71,642	18,034	431,059	93,474,660	109.27	45,954
MO	201,464	160,747	42,282	208,775	244,231,722	127.09	125,077
MT	27,608	21,827	7,296	45,476	35,246,124	131.54	23,616
NE	36,720	27,469	6,988	703,263	35,986,902	259.41	39,326
NV	50,095	35,647	7,741	31,898	65,279,320	153.24	27,164
NH	43,145	32,041	923	57,377	26,376,311	127.22	33,728
NJ	326,645	267,941	88,531	55,776	757,055,702	192.45	203,033
NM	35,501	28,267	9,850	511,566	57,245,958	125.34	32,923
NY	594,845	544,073	160,305	59,284	1,401,610,242	165.68	441,844
NC	312,000	210,837	27,817	74,910	223,396,524	146.20	131,776
ND	17,231	15,217	6,447	1,098,028	26,884,963	134.42	17,954
OH	385,419	305,056	64,506	673,746	479,446,349	129.05	205,964
OK	67,790	49,749	16,470	123,224	95,386,044	145.01	64,705
OR	126,707	105,684	22,757	270,060	206,562,095	154.57	75,140
PA	501,204	406,243	88,757	1,043,877	993,924,350	182.31	230,947
PR	100,087	107,584	47,055	216,432	111,076,342	75.90	51,117
RI	61,359	46,217	12,058	98,955	109,602,344	181.81	28,112
SC	151,554	96,588	16,227	305,966	104,026,053	120.67	68,749
SD	10,590	8,284	925	21,620	10,545,939	119.46	18,626
TN	218,317	164,170	39,543	450,229	196,655,235	109.18	92,485
TX	458,543	340,411	133,002	711,368	751,510,465	160.31	312,596
UT	46,980	31,371	8,890	56,247	58,424,474	160.28	31,831
VT	24,171	19,300	2,102	316,479	29,853,017	140.95	18,804
VA	176,453	130,971	18,567	5,324	135,932,901	141.12	126,919
VI	4,965	1,267	404	38,439	3,328,724	124.24	3,175
WA	219,574	168,682	44,690	456,679	371,652,302	155.89	122,699
WV	54,157	52,999	10,961	382,559	95,504,918	141.50	34,540
WI	213,505	172,008	37,757	90,401	317,879,374	156.39	101,611
WY	15,237	10,407	3,024	30,206	23,631,317	159.55	15,267
Total...	8,871,280	7,368,700	1,940,203	17,153,514	14,301,901,725	152.08	5,624,639

(1) Claimants whose base-period earnings or whose employment, covered by the unemployment insurance program, was sufficient to make them eligible for unemployment insurance benefits as provided by state law. (2) First payments. (3) Final payments. Claimants who exhaust their benefit rights in one benefit year may be entitled to further benefits in the following benefit year. (4) Excludes intrastate transitional claims. (5) Adjusted for voided benefit checks and transfers under interstate combined wage plan.

Employment and Unemployment in the U.S.

Source: Bureau of Labor Statistics

Civilian labor force, persons 16 years of age and over (in thousands)

Year*	Employed	Unemployed	Unemployment Rate	Year*	Employed	Unemployed	Unemployment Rate
1940[1]	47,520	8,120	14.6%	1982*	99,526	10,678	9.7
1950	58,918	3,288	5.0	1983	100,834	10,717	9.6
1960	65,778	3,852	5.5	1984	105,005	8,539	7.5
1970	78,678	4,093	4.9	1985	107,150	8,312	7.2
1975	85,846	7,929	8.5	1986[2]	109,597	8,237	7.0
1978	96,048	6,202	6.1	1987	112,440	7,425	6.2
1980	99,303	7,637	7.1	1988	114,988	6,701	5.5
1981	100,397	8,273	7.6	1989	117,342	6,528	5.3

(1) Persons 14 years of age and over; (2) Not strictly comparable with prior years.
*Early unemployment rates: 1915, 9.7; 1916, 4.8; 1917, 4.8; 1918, 1.4; 1919, 2.3; 1920, 4.0; 1921, 11.9; 1922, 7.6; 1923, 3.2; 1924, 5.5; 1925, 4.0; 1926, 1.9; 1927, 4.1; 1928, 4.4; 1929, 3.2; 1930, 8.7; 1931, 15.9; 1932, 23.6; 1933, 24.9; 1934, 21.7; 1935, 20.1; 1936, 16.9; 1937, 14.3; 1938, 19.0; 1939, 17.2.

Employment and Training Services and Unemployment Insurance

Source: Employment and Training Administration, U.S. Department of Labor

Employment Service

The Federal-State Employment Service consists of the United States Employment Service and affiliated state employment services which make up the nation's public employment service system. During program year 1987, the public employment service listed 7.2 million job openings and placed more than 3.8 million people in jobs.

The employment service refers employable applicants to job openings that use their highest skills and helps the unemployed obtain services or training to make them employable. It also provides special attention to handicapped workers, migrants and seasonal farmworkers, workers who lose their jobs because of foreign trade competition, and other worker groups. Veterans receive priority services including referral to jobs and training. During program year 1987, 455,813 veterans were placed in jobs.

Job Training

The Job Training Partnership Act (JTPA), which became fully operational on October 1, 1983, provides job training and employment services for economically disadvantaged youth and adults, dislocated workers, and others who face significant employment barriers. The goal of the Act is to move as many jobless workers as possible into permanent, unsubsidized, self-sustaining employment.

Since its inception, JTPA has provided approximately four and a half million Americans with training and employment services. Its placement rate is 68 percent, making it one of the most successful job and training efforts ever undertaken.

Title I of the Act's five titles basically establishes an administrative structure for the delivery of job and training services. Generally, state governors receive bloc grants from the Labor Department, and the funds are then distributed to Service Delivery Areas — areas of 200,000 population or more where local elected officials work with Private Industry Councils to plan and conduct local training projects.

Title II is in two parts, with Title II-A spelling out the Act's provision of employment and training projects for the economically disadvantaged. In program year 1987 (July 1, 1987 to June 30, 1988), these projects served more than 1.3 million people.

Title II-A outlines a summer youth program offering basic and remedial education, institutional and on-the-job training, work experience, and supportive services. This program had nearly 640,000 participants in program year 1987.

Title III, Economic Dislocation and Worker Adjustment Assistance, provides for job and training help for dislocated workers — workers who lose jobs and are unlikely to return to their previous industries or occupations. This includes workers who lose their jobs because of plant closings or mass layoffs; long-term unemployed persons with limited local opportunities for jobs in their fields; farmers, ranchers, and other self-employed persons who become jobless due to general economic conditions or natural disasters; and, under certain circumstances, displaced homemakers. Such assistance benefitted nearly 183,000 workers in program year 1987.

Title IV authorizes programs to address the employment and training needs of specific groups facing significant barriers to productive employment, including Native Americans, migrant and seasonal farmworkers, and the disabled. In program year 1987, these programs served 33,000 Native Americans; 46,800 migrant and seasonal farmworkers; and 8,550 disabled persons.

In addition, Title IV includes the Job Corps, which each year enrolls approximately 100,000 young people between the ages of 16 and 21 in 107 residential job training centers throughout the United States; the National Commission for Employment Policy; and nationally administered programs for technical assistance, labor market information, research and evaluation, and pilots and demonstrations.

Title V contains miscellaneous provisions, including amendments to the Wagner-Peyser Act of 1933 — the legislation authorizing the federal-state Employment Service.

Trade Ajustment Assistance for Workers

The Trade Adjustment Assistance (TAA) is available to workers who lose their jobs or whose hours of work and wages are reduced as a result of increased imports. TAA includes a variety of benefits and reemployment services to help unemployed workers prepare for and obtain suitable employment. Workers may be eligible for training, job search, relocation and other reemployment services. Additionally, weekly trade readjustment allowances (TRA) may be payable to eligible workers following their exhaustion of unemployment insurance benefits. In fiscal year 1989, about 23,700 workers received $186 million in TRA payments; about 15,200 workers entered training; about 900 workers were involved in job search visits; and about 1,000 workers relocated in order to obtain long term jobs.

The TAA program is administered by the Employment and Training Administration's Office of Trade Adjustment Assistance. State employment security agencies serve as agents of the U.S., under an agreement with the Secretary of Labor, for administering the TAA benefit provisions in the Trade Act of 1974.

Unemployment Insurance

Unlike old-age and survivors insurance, entirely a federal program, the unemployment insurance program is a Federal-State system that provides insured wage earners with partial replacement of wages lost during involuntary unemployment. The program protects most workers. During calendar year 1989, an estimated 104.8 million workers in commerce, industry, agriculture, and government, including the armed forces, were covered under the Federal-State system. In addition, an estimated 308,000 railroad workers were insured against unemployment by the Railroad Retirement Board.

Each state, as well as the District of Columbia, Puerto Rico, and the Virgin Islands, has its own law and operates its own program. The amount and duration of the weekly benefits are determined by state laws, based on prior wages and length of employment. States are required to extend the duration of benefits when unemployment rises to and remains above specified state levels; costs of extended benefits are shared by the state and federal governments.

Under the Federal Unemployment Tax Act, as amended in 1985, the tax rate is 6.2% on the first $7,000 paid to each employee of employers with one or more employees in 20 weeks of the year or a quarterly payroll of $1,500. A credit of up to 5.4% is allowed for taxes paid under state unemployment insurance laws that meet certain criteria, leaving the federal share at 0.8% of taxable wages.

Social Security Requirement

The Social Security Act requires, as a condition of such grants, prompt payment of due benefits. The Federal Unemployment Tax Act provides safeguards for workers' right to benefits if they refuse jobs that fail to meet certain labor standards. Through the Unemployment Insurance Service of the Employment and Training Administration, the Secretary of Labor determines whether states qualify for grants and for tax offset credit from employers.

Benefits are financed solely by employer contributions, except in Alaska, Pennsylvania and New Jersey where employees also contribute. Benefits are paid through the states' public employment offices, at which unemployed workers must register for work and to which they must report regularly for referral to a possible job during the time when they are drawing weekly benefit payments. During the fiscal year 1989, $14.30 billion in benefits was paid under state unemployment insurance programs to 7 million beneficiaries. They received an average weekly payment of $152.08 for total unemployment for an average of 13.3 weeks.

Average Annual Pay, by State

Source: Bureau of Labor Statistics

State	Average annual pay[1] 1988[2]	1989[2]	% Change 1988-89[3]	State	Average annual pay[1] 1988[2]	1989[2]	% Change 1988-89[3]
U.S.	$21,872	$22,567	3.2	Missouri	$20,295	$20,899	3.0
Alabama	19,003	19,593	3.1	Montana	16,957	17,224	1.6
Alaska	28,033	29,704	6.0	Nebraska	17,190	17,694	2.9
Arizona	20,383	20,808	2.1	Nevada	20,548	21,342	3.9
Arkansas	17,023	17,418	2.3	New Hampshire	20,749	21,551	3.9
California	24,126	24,921	3.3	New Jersey	25,748	26,780	4.0
Colorado[4]	21,472	21,940	2.2	New Mexico	18,259	18,667	2.2
Connecticut	26,234	27,500	4.8	New York	26,347	27,303	3.6
Delaware	21,977	23,268	5.9	North Carolina	18,636	19,320	3.7
District of Columbia	30,253	32,106	6.1	North Dakota	16,508	16,932	2.6
Florida	19,523	20,072	2.8	Ohio	21,501	21,986	2.3
Georgia	20,504	21,071	2.8	Oklahoma	19,098	19,530	2.3
Hawaii	20,444	21,624	5.8	Oregon	19,637	20,303	3.4
Idaho	17,648	18,146	2.8	Pennsylvania	21,485	22,312	3.8
Illinois	23,608	24,211	2.6	Rhode Island	20,206	21,128	4.6
Indiana	20,437	20,931	2.4	South Carolina	18,009	18,797	4.4
Iowa	17,928	18,420	2.7	South Dakota	15,424	15,810	2.5
Kansas	19,030	19,474	2.3	Tennessee	19,209	19,712	2.6
Kentucky	18,545	19,001	2.5	Texas	21,130	21,740	2.9
Louisiana	19,330	19,750	2.2	Utah	18,910	19,362	2.4
Maine	18,347	19,202	4.7	Vermont	18,640	19,497	4.6
Maryland	22,515	23,466	4.2	Virginia	21,053	21,879	3.9
Massachusetts	24,143	25,233	4.5	Washington	20,806	21,617	3.9
Michigan	24,193	24,853	2.7	West Virginia	19,341	19,789	2.3
Minnesota	21,481	22,155	3.1	Wisconsin	19,743	20,204	2.3
Mississippi	16,522	17,047	3.2	Wyoming	19,097	19,230	.7

(1) Includes workers covered by Unemployment Insurance (UI) and Unemployment Compensation for Federal Employees (UCFE) programs. (2) Data are preliminary. (3) Percent changes were computed from unrounded average annual pay data and may differ from those computed using data rounded to the nearest dollar.

Employment Growth, By State, 1979-1987

Source: Bureau of Labor Statistics

	State	'87-'89 % chg.	'79-'87 rank		State	'87-'89 % chg.	'79-'87 rank
1.	Nevada	17.1	5	26.	Tennessee	5.3	21
2.	Idaho	11.5	45	27.	Georgia	5.2	4
3.	Washington	10.5	18	28.	Delaware	4.9	9
4.	Hawaii	8.8	15	29.	Nebraska	4.8	35
5.	Oregon	8.7	37	30.	Arizona	4.7	2
6.	Utah	8.7	20	31.	Vermont	4.6	8
7.	Florida	8.4	1	32.	Ohio	4.5	40
8.	Alaska	8.4	7	33.	Maryland	4.4	13
9.	Maine	7.5	10	34.	Missouri	4.2	30
10.	S. Carolina	7.4	14	35.	Texas	4.2	23
11.	Iowa	7.2	46	36.	Oklahoma	4.0	44
12.	Montana	6.9	47	37.	Alabama	4.0	28
13.	California	6.6	12	38.	Illinois	3.9	43
14.	N. Carolina	6.5	11	39.	Colorado	3.7	22
15.	Kentucky	6.4	31	40.	Michigan	3.7	38
16.	Indiana	6.2	34	41.	New Jersey	3.2	16
17.	Minnesota	6.0	29	42.	Pennsylvania	2.9	41
18.	New Mexico	6.0	24	43.	N. Dakota	2.5	42
19.	Wisconsin	5.9	33	44.	W. Virginia	2.1	49
20.	Virginia	5.9	6	45.	New York	1.9	27
21.	S. Dakota	5.8	32	46.	Louisiana	1.2	48
22.	Kansas	5.8	36	47.	Connecticut	0.7	19
23.	Arkansas	5.8	26	48.	Rhode Island	0.3	25
24.	Wyoming	5.7	50	49.	Massachusetts	0.2	17
25.	Mississippi	5.3	39	50.	New Hampshire	0.9	3

Employment Status of Women 16 Years and Over By Presence and Age of Own Children, March 1988

Source: Bureau of Labor Statistics

(Numbers in thousands)

	Total	Total With Own Children Under 18	With Children Under 6	With Children Under 3
Total	96,516	33,098	15,812	9,451
In Labor Force	53,987	21,528	8,865	4,959
Labor Force Participation Rate	55.9	65.0	56.1	52.5
Employed	51,027	20,132	8,104	4,492
Full time	37,448	14,682	5,628	3,067
Part time	13,579	5,450	2,476	1,425
Unemployed	2,960	1,396	761	467
Unemployment Rate	5.5	6.5	8.6	9.4

Earnings by Occupation and Sex

Source: Bureau of Labor Statistics

(Median usual weekly earnings of full-time wage and salary workers by occupation and sex, annual averages)

Occupation	Number of Workers (in thousands) 1989	1990	Median weekly earnings 1989	1990
Men				
Managerial and professional specialty	12,125	12,588	$675	$726
Executive, administrative, and managerial	6,324	6,534	670	743
Professional specialty	5,801	6,054	678	712
Technical, sales, and administrative support	9,109	9,472	482	496
Technicians and related support	1,645	1,729	543	563
Sales occupations	4,467	4,701	484	506
Administrative support, including clerical	2,996	3,041	435	432
Service occupations	4,086	4,229	305	323
Private household	11	0	(1)	(1)
Protective service	1,389	1,518	458	481
Service, except private household and protective	2,686	2,712	266	270
Precision production, craft, and repair	10,142	10,109	467	486
Mechanics and repairers	3,777	3,693	452	480
Construction trades	3,369	3,524	448	468
Other precision production, craft, and repair	2,997	2,892	494	511
Operators, fabricators, and laborers	11,025	10,758	361	382
Machine operators, assemblers, and inspectors	4,525	4,449	369	396
Transportation and material moving occupations	3,584	3,502	403	416
Handlers, equipment cleaners, helpers, and laborers	2,915	2,807	294	314
Farming, forestry, and fishing	1,037	1,020	$249	$261
Women				
Managerial and professional specialty	10,261	10,501	487	506
Executive, administrative, and managerial	4,681	4,651	456	467
Professional specialty	5,580	5,851	505	533
Technical, sales, and administrative support	15,180	16,239	314	326
Technicians and related support	1,330	1,443	394	419
Sales occupations	3,046	3,560	281	287
Administrative support, including clerical	10,804	11,236	313	326
Service occupations	4,405	4,350	213	232
Private household	334	292	179	186
Protective service	172	189	386	388
Service, except private household and protective	3,899	3,870	214	233
Precision production, craft, and repair	1,003	921	302	310
Mechanics and repairers	149	149	366	429
Construction trades	52	56	(1)	(1)
Other precision production, craft, and repair	802	716	293	295
Operators, fabricators, and laborers	3,752	3,493	241	261
Machine operators, assemblers, and inspectors	2,944	2,691	240	260
Transportation and material moving occupations	253	238	317	318
Handlers, equipment cleaners, helpers, and laborers	554	565	217	236
Farming, forestry, and fishing	152	124	203	206

(1) Data not shown where base is less than 100,000.

Occupations with Projected Largest Job Growth, 1988-2000

Source: Bureau of Labor Statistics; May, 1990

(Numbers in thousands)

Occupation	Employment 1988	2000	Numerical change	% change
Paralegals	83	145	62	75.3
Medical assistants	149	253	104	70.0
Radiologic technologists and technicians	132	218	87	66.0
Homemaker-home health aides	327	537	207	63.3
Data processing equipment repairers	71	115	44	61.2
Medical record technicians	47	75	28	59.9
Medical secretaries	207	327	120	58.0
Physical therapists	68	107	39	57.0
Surgical technicians	35	55	20	56.4
Operations research analysts	55	85	30	55.4
Securities and financial services sales workers	200	309	109	54.8
Travel agents	142	219	77	54.1
Actuaries	16	24	8	53.6
Computer systems analysts	403	617	214	53.3
Physical and corrective therapy assistants	39	60	21	52.5
Subway and streetcar operators	8	13	4	52.0
EEG technologists	6	10	3	50.4
Occupational therapists	33	48	16	48.8
Computer programmers	519	769	250	48.1
Human services workers	118	171	53	44.9
Occupational therapy assistants and aides	8	13	4	44.7
Respiratory therapists	56	79	23	41.3
Correction officers	186	262	76	40.8
Employment interviewers	81	113	33	40.5
Electrical and electronics engineers	439	615	176	40.1
Receptionists	833	1,164	331	39.8
Registered nurses	1,577	2,190	613	38.9
Flight attendants	88	123	34	38.7
Electromedical and biomedical equipment repairers	7	10	3	37.2
Recreational therapists	26	35	10	36.9
Licensed practical nurses	626	855	229	36.6
Guards	795	1,050	256	32.2
Nursing aides, orderlies, and attendants	1,184	1,562	378	31.9
Lawyers	582	763	180	31.0
Waiters and waitresses	1,786	2,338	551	30.9
Food service and lodging managers	560	721	161	28.8
Child care workers	670	856	186	27.8
Cooks, restaurant	572	728	155	27.2

Women Employed as Executives, Administrators, and Managers, by Industry

(1988 annual averages)

Source: Bureau of Labor Statistics

Industry (in thousands)	Employed Women Managers (in thousands)	Women as % of Total	% of Employed Women Managers	Industry (in thousands)	Employed Women Managers (in thousands)	Women as % of Total	% of Employed Women Managers
Total	**5,590**	**39.3**	**100.0**	Wholesale and Retail			
Agriculture	23	*	*	Trade	865	42.5	15.5
Mining	28	*	*	Wholesale Trade	167	32.5	3.0
Construction	129	12.9	2.3	Retail Trade	698	45.9	12.5
Manufacturing	647	26.3	11.6	Finance, Insurance, and			
Durable Goods	365	24.3	6.5	Real Estate	1,014	50.7	18.1
Nondurable Goods	282	29.4	5.0	Services**	2,114	47.4	37.8
Transportation and Public				Professional Services	1,336	54.7	23.9
Utilities	274	29.9	4.9	Public Administration	496	42.8	8.9

*Percentage not shown where base is less than 35,000. **Includes business and repair services; personal services, except private household; entertainment and recreation services; professional and related services; and forestry and fisheries.

Multiple Jobholding

Source: Bureau of Labor Statistics

Percentage of working people holding more than one job

MEN: '70 = 7.0, '79 = 5.9, '89 = 6.4

WOMEN: '70 = 2.2, '79 = 3.5, '89 = 5.9

Percent of People, Age 16-64, with a Work Disability

Source: Bureau of the Census; 1988 figures

Characteristics	Both sexes Total	Both sexes Severe	Males Total	Males Severe	Females Total	Females Severe
Total	8.6	4.8	8.7	4.9	8.4	4.6
Age						
16 to 24 years.	3.8	1.7	4.1	1.9	3.6	1.6
25 to 34 years.	5.6	2.7	5.9	3.1	5.4	2.4
35 to 44 years.	7.1	3.6	7.7	4.3	6.5	3.0
45 to 54 years.	10.3	6.0	10.3	6.0	10.2	6.0
55 to 64 years.	22.3	14.0	22.4	13.7	22.2	14.2
Years of School Completed[1]						
Less than 8 years.	29.7	23.4	29.1	23.2	30.2	23.7
8	24.6	16.8	23.9	15.8	25.2	17.8
9 to 11	17.7	11.6	17.5	11.7	17.9	11.4
12	8.8	4.5	9.3	5.1	8.4	4.1
13 to 15	7.5	3.2	8.4	3.4	6.7	3.0
16 or more	3.8	1.3	3.8	1.4	3.8	1.2
Income to Poverty Ratio						
Less than 1.00	21.9	15.5	24.4	17.9	20.3	13.8
1.00 to 1.24	17.8	12.4	19.0	14.6	16.8	10.5
1.25 to 1.49	13.4	8.3	13.4	8.6	13.4	8.1
1.50 to 1.99	11.3	6.9	12.8	8.4	9.9	5.6
2.00 and over	5.6	2.4	5.8	2.4	5.3	2.3
Race and Hispanic Origin[2]						
White	7.9	4.1	8.2	4.3	7.7	3.9
Black	13.7	9.9	13.7	10.3	13.8	9.5
Hispanic Origin	8.2	5.6	8.4	5.9	7.9	5.2

(1) Persons 25-64 years old. (2) Persons of Hispanic origin may be of any race.

Full-Time Employees Participating in Selected Employee Benefit Programs

Source: Bureau of Labor Statistics
(In percent; medium and large firms. 1989)

Employee benefit program	All employees	Professional and administrative employees	Technical and clerical employees	Production and service employees	Employee benefit program	All employees	Professional and administrative employees	Technical and clerical employees	Production and service employees
Paid:					Long-term disability insurance	45	65	57	27
Holidays. . . .	97	97	96	97	Medical care . .	92	93	91	93
Vacations . . .	97	98	99	95	Dental care . . .	66	69	66	65
Personal leave	22	28	30	14	Life insurance. .	94	95	94	93
Lunch period .	10	4	4	16	Defined benefit pension	63	64	63	63
Rest period . .	71	57	69	80	Defined contribution	48	59	52	40
Funeral leave .	84	87	86	80	Retirement[2]. .	36	43	39	31
Jury duty leave	90	95	92	87	Capital accumulation[3] . .	14	18	14	11
Military leave .	53	61	57	45	All retirement[4]. .	81	85	81	80
Sick leave. . .	68	93	87	44	Flexible benefits plans	9	14	15	3
Maternity leave	3	4	2	3	Reimbursement accounts . . .	23	36	31	11
Paternity leave	1	2	1	1					
Unpaid:									
Maternity leave	37	39	37	35					
Paternity leave	18	20	17	17					
Sickness and accident insurance.	43	29	29	58					

(1) Survey coverage excludes executives and employees in constant travel status, such as airline pilots, as well as data for Alaska and Hawaii. Except for maternity and paternity leave and reimbursement accounts, benefits paid for entirely by the employee were excluded from the tabulations. Professional-administrative and technical-clerical workers are often discussed jointly as white-collar workers. Production-service workers are often called blue-collar workers. (2) Includes money purchase pension, profit sharing, savings and thrift, stock bonus, and employee stock ownership plans in which employer contributions must remain in the participant's account until retirement age, death, disability, separation from service, age 59½, or hardship. (3) Includes plans in which participants may withdraw employer contributions from their accounts without regard to the conditions listed in footnote 2. (4) Includes defined benefit pension plans and defined contribution retirement plans. Many employees participated in both types of plans.

Injuries and Illnesses in Industry

Source: Bureau of Labor Statistics

(in thousands)

Industry division	Total cases[1]		Lost workday cases		Nonfatal cases without lost workdays		Lost workdays	
	1987	1988	1987	1988	1987	1988	1987	1988
Injuries and illnesses[2]	6,035.9	6,438.6	2,801.6	2,975.9	3,230.6	3,458.8	50,941.4	56,942.9
Agriculture, forestry, and fishing[2].	99.6	101.9	50.8	52.7	48.8	49.0	837.7	952.1
Mining[3]	61.5	64.4	35.1	37.7	26.2	26.3	1,039.5	1,113.2
Construction	638.3	656.5	295.0	307.8	342.3	347.8	5,895.3	6,396.8
Manufacturing	2,212.6	2,464.8	976.5	1,079.2	1,235.2	1,384.8	17,689.9	20,254.7
Durable goods.	1,385.6	1,601.7	597.0	671.2	788.1	930.0	10,699.2	12,538.9
Nondurable goods	827.0	863.1	379.5	408.0	447.1	454.8	6,990.7	7,715.8
Transportation and public utilities	429.2	464.8	250.6	264.6	178.1	199.5	5,497.2	6,165.6
Wholesale and retail trade	1,470.5	1,534.8	654.8	684.0	815.1	850.2	10,725.2	11,933.3
Wholesale trade.	408.7	432.9	205.4	216.9	202.9	215.7	3,525.7	3,915.8
Retail trade	1,061.8	1,101.9	449.4	467.1	612.2	634.5	7,199.4	8,017.5
Finance, insurance, and real estate . . .	115.3	119.4	51.2	55.6	63.9	63.8	832.9	1,022.6
Services	1,009.0	1,031.9	487.5	494.3	521.0	537.4	8,423.6	9,104.6
Injuries.	5,845.5	6,197.7	2,721.3	2,878.4	3,120.8	3,315.7	49,069.6	54,286.8
Illnesses	190.4	240.9	80.3	97.5	109.8	143.1	1,871.7	2,656.1

(1) Includes fatalities; (2) Excludes farms with fewer than 11 employees; (3) Excludes independent mining contractors. Note: Because of rounding, components may not add to totals.

Projected Job Growth in Metropolitan Areas: 1985-2000

Source: National Planning Association

Following are the top 30 metro area for employment growth:

City	Year 2000 job totals	1985-2000 increase	City	Year 2000 job Totals	1985-2000 increase
			Denver	1,283,700	354,800
Los Angeles	5,306,000	1,032,000	Minneapolis-St. Paul	1,652,800	352,000
Boston	3,056,800	754,700	Detroit	2,177,300	328,500
Anaheim	1,849,900	701,500	Nassau-Suffolk, NY.	1,498,500	318,500
San Jose	1,453,600	539,200	Orlando	773,700	308,600
Phoenix.	1,453,700	537,000	Fort Lauderdale	796,400	299,400
Washington	2,622,100	509,000	Miami	1,198,400	284,100
Houston	2,191,500	497,700	Oakland	1,149,000	277,700
Chicago	3,627,700	493,500	Seattle	1,202,500	268,400
Dallas.	1,853,700	485,000	Baltimore	1,445,800	249,000
Atlanta	1,875,900	462,700	Middlesex Cty., NJ	736,000	206,100
San Diego	1,438,400	422,400	Riverside, CA	816,500	200,500
Tampa	1,245,400	421,500	West Palm Beach	534,200	196,400
Philadelphia	2,700,000	406,100	Newark	1,232,300	195,300
New York	4,700,800	383,600	Hartford	844,800	190,200
San Francisco	1,435,700	360,400	**United States . . . .**	**140.1 mil.**	**26.1 mil.**

Unpaid Volunteer Workers, May 1989

Source: Bureau of Labor Statistics

(Numbers in thousands)

Characteristic	Total both sexes Civilian noninstitutional population	Volunteer workers Number	% of population	Men Civilian noninstitutional population	Volunteer workers Number	% of population	Women Civilian noninstitutional population	Volunteer workers Number	% of population
Total									
Total, 16 years and over	186,181	38,042	20.4	88,656	16,681	18.8	97,525	21,361	21.9
16-19 years	14,231	1,902	13.4	7,133	879	12.3	7,098	1,023	14.4
20-24 years	18,114	2,064	11.4	8,784	935	10.6	9,330	1,129	12.1
25-34 years	42,868	8,680	20.2	21,110	3,678	17.4	21,758	5,002	23.0
35-44 years	35,775	10,337	28.9	17,483	4,683	26.8	18,292	5,655	30.9
45-54 years	24,668	5,670	23.0	11,957	2,601	21.8	12,711	3,069	24.1
55-64 years	21,373	4,455	20.8	10,053	1,987	19.8	11,320	2,468	21.8
65 years and over	29,153	4,934	16.9	12,135	1,917	15.8	17,017	3,106	17.7
Race and Hispanic Origin									
White	159,200	34,823	21.9	76,395	15,273	20.0	82,805	19,550	23.6
Black	20,985	2,505	11.9	9,422	1,082	11.5	11,563	1,423	12.3
Hispanic origin	13,728	1,289	9.4	6,793	587	8.6	6,935	702	10.1
Marital Status									
Single, never married	46,071	6,327	13.7	24,976	3,102	12.4	21,095	3,225	15.3
Married, spouse present	106,117	26,344	24.8	53,234	12,131	22.8	52,883	14,213	26.9
Married, spouse absent	5,772	765	13.2	2,276	275	12.1	3,496	489	14.0
Divorced	14,551	2,510	17.3	5,942	908	15.3	8,609	1,602	18.6
Widowed	13,671	2,096	15.3	2,227	266	11.9	11,444	1,831	16.0
Educational Attainment									
Less than 4 years of high school	35,240	2,939	8.3	16,594	1,295	7.8	18,646	1,644	8.8
4 years of high school	59,156	11,105	18.8	25,671	4,120	16.0	33,485	6,985	20.9
1 to 3 years of college	26,992	7,572	28.1	12,649	3,042	24.0	14,343	4,531	31.6
4 years of college or more	32,448	12,459	38.4	17,823	6,410	36.0	14,624	6,049	41.4

Data relate to persons 25 years and over.

Note: Data on volunteer workers relate to persons who performed unpaid work for an organization or institution during the year ended May 1989. Detail for race and Hispanic-origin groups do not add to totals because data for the "other races" group are not presented and Hispanics are included in both the white and black population groups.

Employed Wage and Salary Workers Paid at or Below Minimum Hourly Wage Rate, 1989

Source: Bureau of Labor Statistics

Characteristic	Number of Workers[1](1,000) Total paid hourly rates	At $3.35	Below $3.35	Percent Distribution Total paid Hourly rates	At $3.35	Below $3.35	Percent of all Workers Paid Hourly Rates At $3.35	Below $3.35
Total, 16 years and over[2]	62,389	1,790	1,372	100.0	100.0	100.0	2.9	2.2
16 to 24 years	15,635	1,050	673	25.1	58.7	49.1	6.7	4.3
16 to 19 years	6,077	710	369	9.7	39.7	26.9	11.7	6.1
25 years and over	46,754	739	699	74.9	41.3	50.9	1.6	1.5
Male, 16 years and over	31,687	733	379	50.8	40.9	27.6	2.3	1.2
16 to 24 years	8,135	497	220	13.0	27.8	16.0	6.1	2.7
16 to 19 years	3,066	343	118	4.9	19.2	8.6	11.2	3.8
25 years and over	23,552	237	159	37.8	13.2	11.6	1.0	0.7
Women, 16 years and over	30,702	1,056	994	49.2	59.0	72.4	3.4	3.2
16 to 24 years	7,500	553	453	12.0	30.9	33.0	7.4	6.0
16 to 19 years	3,011	367	251	4.8	20.5	18.3	12.2	8.3
25 years and over	23,203	503	540	37.2	28.1	39.4	2.2	2.3
White	52,249	1,380	1,213	83.7	77.1	88.4	2.6	2.3
Black	8,152	372	119	13.1	20.8	8.7	4.6	1.5
Hispanic origin[3]	5,692	192	85	9.1	10.7	6.2	3.4	1.5
Full-time workers	47,059	585	455	75.4	32.7	33.2	1.2	1.0
Part-time workers[4]	15,330	1,204	918	24.6	67.3	66.9	7.9	6.0
Private sector	54,540	1,590	1,305	87.4	88.8	95.1	2.9	2.4
Goods-producing industries[5]	19,468	234	89	31.2	13.1	6.5	1.2	0.5
Service-producing industries[6]	35,072	1,356	1,215	56.2	75.8	88.6	3.9	3.5
Retail trade	13,314	868	847	21.3	48.5	61.7	6.5	6.4
Services	14,133	413	328	22.7	23.1	23.9	2.9	2.3
Public sector	7,849	199	68	12.6	11.1	5.0	2.5	0.9

(1) Excludes the incorporated self-employed. (2) Includes races not shown separately. (3) Persons of Hispanic origin may be of any race. (4) Working fewer than 35 hours per week. (5) Includes agriculture, mining, construction, and manufacturing. (6) Includes transportation and public utilities; wholesale trade; finance, insurance, and real estate; private households; and other service industries, not shown separately.

Federal Minimum Hourly Wage Rates Since 1950

Source: U.S. Department of Labor.

(Employee estimates as of September 1984, except as indicated. The Fair Labor Standards Act of 1938 and subsequent amendments provide for minimum wage coverage applicable to specified nonsupervisory employment categories. Exempt from coverage are executives and administrators or professionals).

| | Minimum Rates for Nonfarm Workers | | | | | Minimum Rates for Nonfarm Workers | | |
Effective date	Laws prior to 1966[1]	Percent, avg earnings[2]	1966 and later[3]	Minimum rates for farm workers[4]	Effective date	Laws prior to 1966[1]	Percent, avg earnings[2]	1966 and later[3]	Minimum rates for farm workers[4]
Jan. 25, 1950 . .	$.75	54	(X)	(X)	Jan. 1, 1975 . .	2.10	45	2.00	1.80
Mar. 1, 1956 . . .	1.00	52	(X)	(X)	Jan. 1, 1976 . . .	2.30	46	2.20	2.00
Sept. 3, 1961 . .	1.15	50	(X)	(X)	Jan. 1, 1977 . . .	(5)	(5)	2.30	2.20
Sept. 3, 1963 . .	1.25	51	(X)	(X)	Jan. 1, 1978 . . .	2.65	44	2.65	2.65
Feb. 1, 1967 . . .	1.40	50	$1.00	$1.00	Jan. 1, 1979 . . .	2.90	45	2.90	2.90
Feb. 1, 1968 . . .	1.60	54	1.15	1.15	Jan. 1, 1980 . . .	3.10	45	3.10	3.10
Feb. 1, 1969 . . .	(5)	(5)	1.30	1.30	Jan. 1, 1981 . . .	3.35	43	3.35	3.35
Feb. 1, 1970 . . .	(5)	(5)	1.45	(5)	Apr. 1, 1990 . . .	3.80[6]			3.80[6]
Feb. 1, 1971 . . .	(5)	(5)	1.60	1.60	Apr. 1, 1991 . . .	4.25[6]			4.25[6]
May 1, 1974 . . .	2.00	46	1.90	1.60					

(X) Not applicable. (1) Applies to workers covered prior to 1961 Amendments and, after Sept. 1965, to workers covered by 1961 Amendments. Rates set by 1961 Amendments were: Sept. 1961, $1.00; Sept. 1964, $1.15; and Sept. 1965, $1.25. (2) Percent of gross average hourly earnings of production workers in manufacturing. (3) Applies to workers newly covered by Amendments of 1966, 1974, and 1977, and Title IX of Education Amendments of 1972. (4) Included in coverage as of 1966, 1974, and 1977 Amendments. (5) No change in rate. (6) Training wage for workers age 16-19 in first six months of first job: 1990, $3.35; 1991, $3.61.

Average Weekly Earnings of Production Workers[1] by Major Industry, 1966-1989

Source: Bureau of Labor Statistics

(annual averages)

Year	Mining	Construction	Manufacturing	Transportation and public utilities	Wholesale trade
1966	$130.24	$146.26	$112.19	$128.13	$111.11
1967	135.89	154.95	114.49	130.82	116.06
1968	142.71	164.49	122.51	138.85	122.31
1969	154.80	181.54	129.51	147.74	129.85
1970	164.40	195.45	133.33	155.93	137.26
1971	172.14	211.67	142.44	168.82	144.18
1972	189.14	221.19	154.71	187.86	151.69
1973	201.40	235.89	166.46	203.31	160.34
1974	219.14	249.25	176.80	217.48	170.33
1975	249.31	266.08	190.79	233.44	183.05
1976	273.90	283.73	209.32	256.71	194.66
1977	301.20	295.65	228.90	278.90	209.13
1978	332.88	318.69	249.27	302.80	228.14
1979	365.07	342.99	269.34	325.58	247.93
1980	397.06	367.78	288.62	351.25	267.96
1981	438.75	399.26	318.00	382.18	291.06
1982	459.88	426.82	330.26	402.48	309.85
1983	479.40	442.97	354.08	420.81	329.18
1984	503.58	458.51	374.03	438.13	342.27
1985	519.93	464.46	386.37	450.30	351.74
1986	525.81	466.75	396.01	458.64	358.11
1987	531.70	480.44	406.31	471.58	365.76
1988	541.44	495.73	418.81	475.69	380.24
1989	569.75	512.41	430.09	490.53	394.82

(1) Production or nonsupervisory workers or private nonagriculture payrolls

Work Stoppages (Strikes) in the U.S.

Source: Bureau of Labor Statistics

(involving 1,000 workers or more)

Year	Number stoppages[1]	Workers involved[1] (thousands)	Work days idle[1] (thousands)		Number stoppages[1]	Workers involved[1] (thousands)	Work days idle[1] (thousands)
1955	363	2,055	21,100	1977	298	1,212	21,258
1960	222	896	13,260	1978	219	1,006	23,774
1965	268	999	15,140	1979	235	1,021	20,409
1966	321	1,300	16,000	1980	187	795	20,844
1967	381	2,192	31,320	1981	145	729	16,908
1968	392	1,855	35,567	1982	96	656	9,061
1969	412	1,576	29,397	1983	81	909	17,461
1970	381	2,468	52,761	1984	62	376	8,499
1971	298	2,516	35,538	1985	54	324	7,079
1972	250	975	16,764	1986	69	533	11,861
1973	317	1,400	16,260	1987	46	174	4,481
1974	424	1,796	31,809	1988	40	118	4,364
1975	235	965	17,563	1989	51	452	16,996
1976	231	1,519	23,962				

(1) The number of stoppages and workers relate to stoppages that began in the year. Days of idleness include all stoppages in effect. Workers are counted more than once if they were involved in more than one stoppage during the year.

Civilian Employment of the Federal Government

Source: Workforce Analysis and Statistics Division, U.S. Office of Personnel Management as of May 1990
(Payroll in thousands of dollars)

Agency	All Areas Employment	All Areas Payroll	United States Employment	United States Payroll	Wash., D.C. MSA Employment	Wash., D.C. MSA Payroll	Overseas Employment	Overseas Payroll
Total, all agencies[1]	3,496,573	8,178,282	3,354,214	7,836,373	359,177	1,105,910	142,359	341,909
Legislative branch	38,149	113,984	38,094	113,793	35,810	106,341	55	191
Congress.	20,000	54,306	20,000	54,306	20,000	54,306	—	—
U.S. Senate	7,581	20,690	7,581	20,690	7,581	20,690	—	—
House of Rep Summary . . .	12,404	33,575	12,404	33,575	12,404	33,575	—	—
Comm. on Scty & Coop in Eur	15	41	15	41	15	41	—	—
Architect of the Capitol	2,246	5,080	2,246	5,080	2,246	5,080	—	—
Botanic Garden	66	150	66	150	66	150	—	—
Committee on Agricltl. Workers .	5	11	5	11	5	11	—	—
Comm Int Mig&Coop Econ Dev .	9	33	9	33	9	33	—	—
Congressional Budget Ofc. . . .	218	1,033	218	1,033	218	1,033	—	—
Copyright Royalty Tribunal. . . .	9	36	9	36	9	36	—	—
General Accounting Ofc	5,309	17,486	5,260	17,682	3,460	11,857	49	164
Government Printing Ofc.	5,017	21,142	5,017	21,142	4,539	19,534	—	—
Library of Congress.	4,722	12,647	4,716	12,620	4,716	12,620	6	27
Nat Comm on AIDS Syndrome .	8	30	8	30	7	28	—	—
Nat Comm Prev Infant Mort . . .	10	20	10	20	10	20	—	—
Ofc Technology Assessment . .	193	458	193	458	193	458	—	—
Physician Payment Rev Comm .	1	1	1	1	1	1	—	—
Prosptv Paymt Assessmt Com .	5	5	5	5	5	5	—	—
U.S. Tax Court.	331	1,186	331	1,186	326	1,169	—	—
Judicial Branch	22,903	63,012	22,644	62,296	1,965	5,925	259	716
Supreme Court	346	869	346	869	346	869	—	—
U.S. Courts	22,525	62,042	22,266	61,326	1,587	4,955	259	716
U.S. Court of Vets Appeals . .	32	101	32	101	32	101	—	—
Executive Branch	3,435,521	8,001,286	3,293,476	7,660,284	321,402	993,644	12,045	341,002
Exec Ofc of the President	1,682	5,777	1,673	5,729	1,673	5,729	9	48
White House Office	386	1,156	386	1,156	386	1,156	—	—
Ofc of Vice President	21	75	21	75	21	75	—	—
Ofc of Mgt & Budget	536	2,047	536	2,047	536	2,047	—	—
Office of Administration	217	567	217	567	217	567	—	—
Council Economic Advisors . .	27	112	27	112	27	112	—	—
Council on Environ Qual	17	63	17	63	17	63	—	—
Ofc of Policy Development . .	37	103	37	103	37	103	—	—
Exec Residence at WH	90	338	90	338	90	338	—	—
Natl Crit Materials Coun . . .	1	6	1	6	1	6	—	—
National Security Council . . .	65	235	65	235	65	235	—	—
National Space Council	3	13	3	13	3	13	—	—
Ofc of Natl Drug Control. . . .	91	325	91	325	91	325	—	—
Ofc of Sci and Tech Policy . .	21	113	21	113	21	113	—	—
Ofc of U.S. Trade Rep.	170	624	161	576	161	576	9	48
Executive Departments	2,432,594	5,491,012	2,310,965	5,199,228	242,178	748,516	121,629	291,784
State	25,222	70,568	9,366	28,622	8,345	25,339	15,856	41,946
Treasury.	164,753	381,585	163,692	378,159	21,540	68,096	1,061	3,426
Defense, Total	1,054,279	2,755,549	958,099	2,531,493	89,247	267,633	96,180	224,056
Dept of the Army.	374,930	879,961	329,530	788,687	28,087	59,698	45,400	91,274
Dept of the Navy.	338,790	949,715	315,454	916,225	37,824	131,434	23,336	33,490
Dept of the Air Force	247,124	66,757	232,862	613,781	6,624	17,783	14,262	52,976
Defense Log Agcy	51,480	118,038	51,074	116,603	3,306	11,774	406	1,435
Other Defense Activities . .	41,955	141,078	29,179	96,197	13,406	46,944	12,776	44,881
Justice	81,690	241,111	80,266	236,321	19,511	59,321	1,424	4,790
Interior	76,301	176,868	75,917	175,809	9,131	26,639	384	1,059
Agriculture.	118,959	258,484	117,430	255,734	12,542	36,792	1,529	2,750
Commerce	421,153	277,521	420,252	274,441	19,362	57,736	901	3,080
Labor	17,844	54,963	17,807	54,817	6,135	19,959	37	146
Health and Human Services .	122,514	315,915	121,825	314,149	27,905	84,816	689	1,766
Housing & Urban Dev	13,313	36,628	13,194	36,285	3,353	11,243	119	343
Transportation	66,617	242,413	66,097	240,370	9,512	35,565	520	2,043
Energy	17,473	57,717	17,468	57,685	6,180	22,262	5	32
Education	4,831	14,461	4,826	14,446	3,289	10,313	5	15
Veterans Affairs	247,645	607,229	244,726	600,897	6,126	22,802	2,919	6,332
Independent agencies[1]	1,001,245	2,504,497	980,838	2,455,327	77,551	239,399	20,407	49,170
Environmtl Protect Agcy	16,625	47,767	16,608	47,705	5,583	17,998	17	62
Equal Employ Opp Comm	2,795	7,803	2,795	7,803	686	2,202	—	—
Federal Deposit Ins Corp. . . .	14,415	44,483	14,401	44,433	2,049	7,652	14	50
Fed Emergency Mgmt Agcy . . .	3,479	9,098	3,263	8,794	1,545	4,703	216	304
General Svcs Admin.	20,258	51,367	20,177	51,139	6,802	19,979	81	228
Natl Archives & Recds, Admin. .	3,032	5,015	3,032	5,015	1,183	2,706	—	—
Natl Aero Space Admin	24,561	96,262	24,553	96,202	5,339	21,540	8	60
Nuclear Regulatory Comm. . . .	3,318	14,908	3,318	14,908	2,172	10,048	—	—
Office of Personnel Mgmt	6,705	13,574	6,680	13,538	2,697	6,937	25	36
Panama Canal Commission . . .	8,289	15,713	18	47	7	24	8,271	15,666
Small Business Admin	5,376	14,642	5,057	13,834	993	3,135	319	808
Smithsonian, Summary.	5,060	11,810	4,912	11,500	4,656	10,732	148	310
Tennessee Valley Auth.	26,769	89,533	26,767	89,529	10	28	2	4
U.S. Information Agency	8,635	28,146	4,283	16,930	4,041	15,529	4,352	11,216
U.S. Intnatl Dev Coop Agcy . . .	4,826	16,439	2,452	8,169	2,442	8,123	2,374	8,270
U.S. Postal Service	823,314	1,964,407	819,677	1,954,148	22,367	59,967	3,637	10,259

(1) Included in Total are other independent agencies with fewer than 2,500 employees.

Labor Union Directory

Source: Bureau of Labor Statistics; World Almanac questionnaire
(*) Independent union; all others affiliated with AFL-CIO.

American Federation of Labor & Congress of Industrial Organizations (AFL-CIO), 815 16th St. NW, Washington, DC 20006; 14.5 mln. members.

Actors and Artistes of America, Associated (AAAA), 165 W. 46th St., New York, NY 10036; founded 1919; Theodore Bikel, Pres.; no individual members, 9 National Performing Arts Unions are affiliates; approx. 220,000 combined membership.

Actors' Equity Association, 165 W. 46th St., New York, NY 10036; founded 1913; Colleen Dewhurst, Pres.; 39,000 active members.

Air Line Pilots Association, 1625 Massachusetts Ave. NW, Washington, DC 20036. Henry A. Duffy, Pres.; 41,000 members.

Aluminum Brick & Glass Workers International Union (ABG-WIU), 3362 Hollenberg Drive, Bridgeton, MO 63044; founded 1953; Ernie Labaff, Pres. (since 1985); 51,800 members, 390 locals.

Automobile, Aerospace & Agricultural Implement Workers of America, International Union, United (UAW), 8000 E. Jefferson Ave., Detroit, MI 48214; founded 1935; Owen Bieber, Pres. (since 1983); 1,000,000 members, 1,194 locals.

Bakery, Confectionery & Tobacco Workers International Union (BC&T), 10401 Connecticut Ave., Kensington, MD 20895; founded 1886; John DeConcini, Pres. (since 1978); 139,000 members, 139 locals.

Boilermakers, Iron Shipbuilders, Blacksmiths, Forgers and Helpers, International Brotherhood of (IBBISB/BF&H), 570 New Brotherhood Bldg., 753 State Ave., Kansas City, KS 66101; founded 1880; Charles W. Jones, Pres. (since 1983) 95,000 members, 375 locals.

Bricklayers and Allied Craftsmen, International Union of, 815 15th St. NW, Washington, DC 20005; John T. Joyce, Pres.; 106,000 members, 525 locals.

Carpenters and Joiners of America, United Brotherhood of, 101 Constitution Ave. NW, Washington, DC 20001; founded 1881; Sigurd Lucassen, Gen. Pres.; 595,000 members, 1,500 locals.

Chemical Workers Union, International (ICWU), 1655 West Market St., Akron, OH 44313; founded 1944; Frank D. Martino, Pres. (since 1975); 50,000 members, 350 locals.

Clothing and Textile Workers Union, Amalgamated (ACTWU), 15 Union Square, New York, NY 10003; founded 1976; union founded 1914; Jack Sheinkman, Pres. (since 1987); 272,669 members, 1,400 locals.

Communications Workers of America, (AFL-CIO, CLC) 1925 K St. NW, Washington, DC 20006; Morton Bahr, Pres.; 700,000 members, 1,200 locals.

Distillery, Wine & Allied Workers International Union (DWU), 66 Grand Ave., Englewood, NJ 07631; founded 1940; George J. Orlando, Pres. (since 1984); 15,500 members, 57 locals.

***Education Association, National,** 1201 16th St. NW, Washington, DC 20036; Keith Geiger, Pres. (since 1989); 2,000,000 members, 12,000 affiliates.

Electrical Workers, International Brotherhood of (IBEW), 1125 15th St., NW, Washington, DC 20005; founded 1891; J.J. Barry, Int'l Pres.; 1,000,000 members, 1,400 locals.

Electronic, Electrical, Salaried, Machine and Furniture Workers, International Union of (IUE), 1126 16th St. NW, Washington, DC 20036; founded 1949; William H. Bywater, Pres. (since 1982); 190,000 members, 530 locals.

Farm Workers of America, United (UFW), P.O. Box 62, Keene, CA 93531; founded 1962; Cesar E. Chavez, Pres. (since 1962); 100,000 members.

***Federal Employees, National Federation of (NFFE),** 1016 16th St. NW, Washington, DC 20036; founded 1917; James M. Peirce Jr., Pres. (since 1976); 60,000+ members, 487 locals.

Fire Fighters, International Association of, 1750 New York Ave. NW, Washington, DC 20006; John A. Gannon, Pres.; 172,401 members, 1,943 locals.

Firemen and Oilers, International Brotherhood of, 1100 Circle 75 Parkway, Suite 350, Atlanta, GA 30339; Jimmy L. Walker, Pres.; 30,000 members.

Food and Commercial Workers International Union, United, (UFCW) 1775 K St., NW, Washington, DC 20006; founded 1979 following merger; William H. Wynn, Int'l Pres. (since 1977); 1.3 million members, 600 locals.

Garment Workers of America, United (UGWA), 4207 Lebanon Rd., Hermitage, TN 37076; founded 1891; Earl W. Carroll, Gen. Pres. (since 1987); 25,000 members, 125 locals.

Glass, Molders, Pottery, Plastics & Allied Workers Intl. Union (GMP), 608 E. Baltimore Pike, P.O. Box 607, Media, PA 19063; founded 1842; James E. Hatfield, Int'l Pres. (since 1977); 90,000 members, 435 locals.

Government Employees, American Federation of (AFGE) AFL-CIO, 80 F St., NW, Washington, DC 20001; founded 1932; John N. Sturdivant, Natl. Pres. (since 1988); 210,000 members, 1,300 locals.

Grain Millers, American Federation of (AFGM), 4949 Olson Memorial Hwy., Minneapolis, MN 55422; founded 1948; Robert W. Willis, Gen. Pres.; 30,000 members, 210 locals.

Graphic Communications International Union (GCIU), 1900 L St., NW, Washington, DC 20036; founded 1983; James J. Norton, Pres. (since 1985); 182,706 members, 520 locals.

Hotel Employees and Restaurant Employees International Union, 1219-28th St., NW, Washington, DC 20007; Edward T. Henley, Gen. Pres.; 330,000 members, 190 locals.

Industrial Workers of America, International Union, Allied (AIW), 3520 W. Oklahoma Ave., Milwaukee, WI 53215; founded 1935; Dominick D'Ambrosio, Intl. Pres. (since 1975); 61,000 members, 330 locals.

Iron Workers, International Association of Bridge Structural and Ornamental, 1750 New York Ave. NW, Washington, DC 20006; Jake West, Gen. Pres.; 145,000 members, 300 locals.

Laborers' International Union of North America (LIUNA), 905 16th St. NW, Washington, DC 20006; founded 1903; Angelo Fosco, Gen. Pres. (since 1976); 450,000 members, 696 locals.

Ladies Garment Workers Union, International (ILGWU), 1710 Broadway, New York, NY 10019; founded 1900; Jay Mazur, Pres. (since 1986); 175,000 members, 340 locals.

Leather Goods, Plastic and Novelty Workers' Union, International, 265 W. 14th St., New York, NY 10011; Domenic DiPaolo, Gen. Pres.; 20,000 members, 85 locals.

Letter Carriers, National Association of (NALC), 100 Indiana Ave. NW, Washington, DC 20001; founded 1889; Vincent R. Sombrotto, Pres. (since 1978); 315,281 members, 3,622 locals.

***Locomotive Engineers, Brotherhood of (BLE),** The Standard Bldg., Cleveland, OH 44113; founded 1863; Larry McFather, Pres. (since 1987); 56,000 members, 650 divisions.

Longshoremen's Association, International, 17 Battery Pl., New York, NY 10004; Thomas W. Gleason, Pres.; 76,579 members, 367 locals.

***Longshoremen's & Warehousemen's Union, International (ILWU),** 1188 Franklin St., San Francisco, CA 94109; founded 1937; James R. Herman, Pres. (since 1977); 55,000 members, 58 locals.

Machinists and Aerospace Workers, International Association of (IAM), 1300 Connecticut Ave. NW, Washington, DC 20036; founded 1888; George J. Kourpias , Int'l Pres.; 826,875 members, 1,700 locals.

Maintenance of Way Employes, Brotherhood of (BMWE), 12050 Woodward Ave., Detroit, MI 48203; founded 1887; Geoffrey N. Zeh, Pres. (since 1986); 75,000 members, 910 locals.

Marine & Shipbuilding Workers of America, Industrial Union of (IUMSWA), 5101 River Rd., #110, Bethesda, MD 20816; founded 1934; (merged with Machinists and Aerospace Workers, effective Dec. 1, 1990).

Marine Engineer Beneficial Assn./National Maritime Union (MEBA/NMU), 444 N. Capitol St. NW, Suite 800, Washington, D.C. 20001; C.E. DeFries, Pres.; 50,000 members.

***Mine Workers of America, United (UMWA),** 900 15th St. NW, Washington, DC 20005; founded 1890; Richard Trumka, Int'l Pres. (since 1982); 186,000 members, 800 locals.

Musicians of the United States and Canada, American Federation of (AF of M), 1501 Broadway, Suite 600, New York, NY 10036; founded 1896; J. Martin Emerson, Pres. (since 1987); 206,000 members, 480 locals.

Newspaper Guild, The (TNG), 8611 Second Ave., Silver Spring, MD 20910; founded 1933; Charles Dale, Pres. (since 1987); 33,000 members, 80 locals.

Novelty & Production Workers, Intl. Union of Allied, 1815 Franklin Ave., Valley Stream, NY 11581; Julius Isaacson, Pres. 30,000 members, 18 locals.

*Nurses Association, American, 2420 Pershing Rd., Kansas City, MO 64108; Lucille A. Joel, Ed.D, R.N., F.A.A.N., Pres.; 53 constituent state assns.

Office and Professional Employees International Union (OPEIU), 265 W. 14th St., New York, NY 10011; founded 1945 (AFL Charter); John Kelly, Int'l Pres. (since 1979); 135,000 members, 300 locals.

Oil, Chemical and Atomic Workers International Union (OCAW), PO Box 2812, Denver, CO 80201; Joseph M. Misbrener, Pres. (since 1983); 100,000 members, 400 locals.

Operating Engineers, International Union of (IUOE), 1125 17th St. NW, Washington, DC 20036; founded 1896; Larry Dugan, Jr., Gen. Pres. (since 1985); 375,000 members, 200 locals.

Painters and Allied Trades, International Brotherhood of (IBPAT), 1750 New York Ave. NW, Washington, DC 20006; founded 1887; William A. Duval, Gen. Pres. (since 1984); 156,597 members, 640 locals.

Paperworkers International Union, United (UPIU), 3340 Perimeter Hill Dr., Nashville, TN 37202; founded 1884; Wayne E. Glenn, Pres. (since 1978); 230,000 members, 1,100 locals.

*Plant Guard Workers of America, International Union, United (UPGWA), 25510 Kelly Rd., Roseville, MI 48066; founded 1948; Gene McConville, Pres.; 28,000 members, 176 locals.

Plasterers' and Cement Mason's International Association of the United States & Canada; Operative, 1125 17th St. NW, Washington, DC 20036; Robert J. Holton, Pres.; Vincent J. Panepinto, Secy.-Treas.; 65,000 members, 365 locals.

Plumbing and Pipe Fitting Industry of the United States and Canada, United Association of Journeymen and Apprentices of the, 901 Massachusetts Ave. NW, Washington, DC 20001; Marvin J. Boede, Pres.; 325,000 members.

*Police, Fraternal Order of, 2100 Gardiner Lane, Louisville, KY 40205; Dewey R. Stokes, Natl. Pres. and Charles R. Orms, Natl. Secy.; 212,000 members, 1,843 affiliates.

*Postal Supervisors, National Association of, 490 L'Enfant Plaza SW, Suite 3200, Washington, DC 20024-2120; Rubin Handelman, Pres.; 44,000 members, 443 locals.

Postal Workers Union, American (APWU), 1300 L St. NW, Washington, DC 20005; founded 1971; Moe Biller, Pres. (since 1980); 365,000 members, 2,000 locals.

Railway Carmen Division of Transportation Communications Int'l. Union (BRC Division/TCU), 4929 Main St., Kansas City, MO 64112; founded 1888; W.G. Fairchild, Gen. Pres. (since 1989); 50,000 members, 310 locals.

Retail, Wholesale and Department Store Union, 30 E. 29th St., New York, NY 10016; Lenore Miller, Pres.; 200,000 members, 250 locals.

Roofers, Waterproofers & Allied Workers, United Union of, 1125 17th St. NW, Washington, DC 20036; Earl J. Kruse, Pres.; 27,000 members, 138 locals.

Rubber, Cork, Linoleum and Plastic Workers of America, United (URW), 87 South High St., Akron, OH 44308; founded 1935; Milan Stone; Int'l Pres. (since 1981); 109,000 members, 411 locals.

*Rural Letter Carriers' Association, National, Suite 100, 1448 Duke St., Alexandria, VA 22314; founded 1903; Vernon H. Meier, Pres. (since 1989); 80,000 members; 47 state organizations.

Seafarers International Union of North America (SIUNA), 5201 Auth Way, Camp Springs, MD 20746; founded 1938; Michael Sacco, Pres.; 90,000 members.

Service Employees International Union (SEIU), 1313 L St. NW, Washington, DC 20005; founded 1921; John J. Sweeney, Pres. (since 1980); 850,000 members, 300 locals.

Sheet Metal Workers' International Association (SMWIA), 1750 New York Ave. NW, Washington, DC 20006; founded 1888; Edward J. Carlough, Gen. Pres. (since 1970); 150,000 members, 245 locals.

State, County and Municipal Employees, American Federation of, 1625 L St. NW, Washington, DC 20036; Gerald McEntee, Pres.; 1,200,000 members, 2,991 locals.

Steelworkers of America, United (USWA), 5 Gateway Center, Pittsburgh, PA 15222; founded 1936; Lynn Williams, Int'l Pres. (since 1984); 750,000 members, 3,500 locals.

Teachers, American Federation of (AFT), 555 New Jersey Ave. NW, Washington, DC 20001; founded 1916; Albert Shanker, Pres. (since 1974); 750,000 members, 2,400 locals.

Teamsters, Chauffeurs, Warehousemen and Helpers of America, International Brotherhood of (IBT), 25 Louisiana Ave. NW, Washington, DC 20001; founded 1903; William J. McCarthy, Gen. Pres.; 1,600,000 members, 700 locals.

Television and Radio Artists, American Federation of, 260 Madison Ave., New York, NY 10016; founded 1937; Reed Farrell, Pres.; 67,000 members, 38 locals.

Textile Workers of America, United (UTWA), 2 Echelon Plaza, Laurel Rd., P.O. Box 749, Voorhees, NJ 08043-0749; founded 1901; Vernon Mustard, Intl. Pres. (since 1986); 26,000 members, 180 locals.

Theatrical Stage Employes and Moving Picture Machine Operators of the United States and Canada, International Alliance of, 1515 Broadway, New York, NY 10036; Alfred W. Di Tolla, Pres.; 61,471 members, 750 locals.

Transit Union, Amalgamated (ATU), 5025 Wisconsin Ave. NW, Washington, DC 20016; founded 1892; James La Sala, Intl. Pres. (since 1986); 165,000 members, 275 locals.

Transport Workers Union of America, 80 West End Ave., New York, NY 10023; founded 1934; George Leitz, Int'l Pres. (since 1985); 100,000 members, 94 locals.

Transportation Communications International Union (TCU), 3 Research Place, Rockville, MD 20850; Richard I. Kilroy, Int'l Pres. (since 1981); 160,000 members, 750 locals.

*Transportation Union, United (UTU), 14600 Detroit Ave., Cleveland, OH 44107; founded 1969; Fred A. Hardin, Pres. (since 1979); 100,000 members; 769 locals.

*Treasury Employees Union, National (NTEU), 1730 K St. NW, Suite 1101, Washington, DC 20006; founded 1938; Robert M. Tobias, Natl. Pres. (since 1983); 120,000 represented, 250 chapters.

*University Professors, American Association of (AAUP), 1012-14th St., Washington, DC 20005; founded 1915; Carol Simpson Stern, Pres.; 40,000 members, 600 chapters.

Upholsterers' International Union of North America (UIU), 25 N. 4th St., Philadelphia, PA 19106; founded 1882; John Serembus, Pres.; 31,827 members, 133 locals.

Utility Workers Union of America (UWUA), 815 16th St. NW, Washington, DC 20006; founded 1945; James Joy Jr., Natl. Pres. (since 1980); 60,000 members, 220 locals.

International Woodworkers of America —U.S. (IWA—U.S.), 25 Cornell, Gladstone, OR 97027; founded 1987; Wilson (Bill) Hubbell, Natl. Pres.; 28,000 members, 100 locals.

U.S. Union Membership, 1930-1989

Source: Bureau of Labor Statistics

Year	Labor[1] Force (thousands)	Union[2] Members (thousands)	Percent	Year	Labor[1] Force (thousands)	Union[2] Members (thousands)	Percent
1930	29,424	3,401	11.6	1975	76,945	19,611	25.5
1935	27,053	3,584	13.2	1980	90,564	19,843	21.9
1940	32,376	8,717	26.9	1983	88,290	17,717	20.1
1945	40,394	14,322	35.5	1984	92,194	17,340	18.8
1950	45,222	14,267	31.5	1985	94,521	16,996	18.0
1955	50,675	16,802	33.2	1986	96,903	16,975	17.5
1960	54,234	17,049	31.4	1987	99,303	16,913	17.0
1965	60,815	17,299	28.4	1988	101,407	17,002	16.8
1970	70,920	19,381	27.3	1989	103,480	16,960	16.4

(1) Does not include agricultural employment; from 1983 data do not include self-employed or unemployed persons. (2) From 1930 to 1980 data are the number of dues paying members of traditional trade unions with members counted regardless of employment status; from 1983 members include employee associations that engage in collective bargaining with employers.

TAXES

Federal Income Tax

Source: George W. Smith III, CPA, *Cut Your Own Taxes and Save*, Pharos Books.

During the past decade, Congress enacted the most dramatic changes in our tax law in over fifty years. Its purpose was to create a more equitable income tax system for all taxpayers. Many of the provisions resulting from these massive changes in legislation will affect all taxpayers filing their 1990 income tax return.

History of the United States Income Tax

The history of taxation in the United States centers primarily around the income tax and is consistent with the pattern of taxation in almost every highly developed country. Although the Massachusetts Bay Colony enacted an income tax in 1643, the first U.S. income tax was not created until the Civil War. However, this infant income tax had little vitality and it expired soon after the war.

In 1894, another income tax act was passed by Congress. By this time, income tax had become a very important political issue, but in the following year, the Supreme Court held that the income tax law was unconstitutional and invalidated the entire statute.

Congress did not give up and passed the Sixteenth Amendment to the United States Constitution. This amendment was passed by Congress on July 12, 1909 and laid the foundation for the basic framework of our modern income tax system. It was ratified by the required number of state legislatures early in 1913 and states broadly and explicitly:

"The Congress shall have the power to lay and collect taxes on incomes, from whatever source derived, without apportionment among the several States, and without regard to any census or enumeration."

Congress quickly expanded on this newly sanctioned source of revenue. Corporations as well as individuals became subject to the new income tax. Since then various revenue acts have been passed. One of the most important of these acts was the Current Tax Payment Act of 1943. This act instituted for the first time the "pay-as-you go" system. This system, which requires the regular withholding of tax from each employee's paycheck and the filing of estimated tax payments, remains the basic method for the collection of our income taxes today.

During the past few decades, Congress enacted several major tax acts. However, the Tax Reform Act of 1986 represents the most extensive overhaul of the tax code since 1954. This Act contains approximately 1,850 separate Code amendments. Because of the scope and magnitude of these amendments Congress decided to redesignate the 1954 Code as the Internal Revenue Code of 1986.

Tax Law Changes
and
Recent Developments

- Interest earned on Series EE bonds issued in 1990 or later may be exempt from federal income tax if used to pay tuition and fees for a taxpayer, spouse or dependents to attend a college, university or qualified technical school during the year the bonds are redeemed. This exclusion is subject to an income phaseout.

- Parents may elect to include on their income tax return the unearned income of a dependent child under age 14 whose income is more than $500 but less than $5,000. The income must consist solely of interest, dividends or Alaska Permanent Fund dividends. This election is not available if estimated tax payments were made in the child's name. Form 8814, Parent's Election to Report Child's Interest and Dividends, is required to report this income.

- For individuals age 55 or over, the 3 out of 5 year home use rule for the sale of a principal residence has been expanded. Certain incapacitated individuals who reside in state licensed facilities may exclude from gross income up to $125,000 of gain resulting from the sale of their house if the house was used as their principal residence for at least one year out of the last 5 years.

- For a taxpayer to be eligible for the child and dependent care credit, the dependent must be under age 13. The taxpayer must also report the name, address, and identification number of the child care provider on their income tax return or the taxpayer will not be entitled to the credit.

- An individual may not claim an exemption for a dependent child for 1990 who qualifies as a full time student and is over age 23 at the end of the year unless the child's gross income is less than $2,050.

- A taxpayer must list the social security number of any dependent claimed on his income tax return who is at least 2 years old by the end of the tax year. The penalty for noncompliance can be $50 per omitted number.

- A business deduction is not allowed for the base rate on the first telephone line into a personal residence. This disallowance does not affect the deductibility of long distance calls or optional services such as call waiting, call forwarding, three-way calling or extra directory listings as long as they are business related.

- IRA investments are allowed for certain gold and silver coins issued by the U.S. Government. Investments also may include coins issued by a state government. However, only certain state coins issued after November 10, 1988 qualify.

- Jury duty pay surrendered by an employee to an employer in return for his normal salary is deductible as an adjustment to income—not as an itemized deduction.

- Starting with 1990, the IRS does not require the filing of Form 4562, Depreciation and Amortization, for individuals claiming a deduction for depreciation on nonlisted property placed in service in a previous year.

- For 1990, the standard mileage rate for business use of an automobile has been increased to 26 cents per mile. This rate applies to all business miles driven and not just for the first 15,000 miles as in prior years.

- Starting with 1990, the business use of a cellular phone must be for the convenience of the employer and a condition of employment to be an allowable business deduction for employees.

- For 1990, self-employed persons will be entitled to an income tax deduction up to one-half of the social security self-employment (SE) tax liability. The SE tax rate for 1990 is 15.3 percent of the first $51,300 of net earnings from self-employment or a maximum tax of $7,848.90. The deduction is also taken into account when computing SE net income and may reduce the SE tax liability.

1990 Individual Tax Rates

There will be only two rates for 1990 — 15% and 28%. The dollar bracket amounts have been adjusted for inflation.

Single

Tax Rates	Bracket
15%	$0 to $19,450
28%	Over $19,450

Married Filing Jointly or Qualifying Widow(er)

Tax Rates	Bracket
15%	$0 to $32,450
28%	Over $32,450

(continued)

Married Filing Separately

Tax Rate	Bracket
15%	$0 to $16,225
28%	Over $16,225

Head of Household

Tax Rate	Bracket
15%	$0 to $26,050
28%	Over $26,050

Certain higher incomes will be subject to an additional 5% tax. This 5% rate adjustment phases out the benefit of the lower 15% tax rate. For married taxpayers filing jointly, the 5% phaseout begins with taxable income of $78,400 and is fully phased out at $162,770.

Heads of household with taxable income over $67,200 but not exceeding $134,930 will be subject to the 5% adjustment as will single individuals with taxable income over $47,050 but not exceeding $97,620. The phaseout for married taxpayers filing separately will apply when taxable income is over $39,200 but not exceeding $123,570.

Standard Deduction

The standard deduction is a flat amount that is subtracted from adjusted gross income for taxpayers who do not itemize their deductions. The amount of the basic standard deduction depends upon the taxpayer's filing status and is adjusted annually for inflation.

Taxpayers with itemized deductions such as medical expenses, charitable contributions, interest, taxes, etc., totaling more than the standard deduction amount should not use the standard deduction. Instead, they should itemize their deductions.

1990 Basic Standard Deduction

Single	$3,250
Married filing jointly or Qualifying widow(er)	$5,450
Married filing separately	$2,725
Head of household	$4,750

An individual claimed as a dependent on another person's income tax return may claim on their return the larger of $500, or the amount of earned income up to the amount of the standard deduction which the taxpayer would normally be allowed. Earned income includes wages, salaries, commissions, tips, net profit from self-employment—any money received as compensation for personal services rendered. It also includes any part of a scholarship or fellowship grant that must be included in gross income.

Example: A dependent parent, age 60, had unearned income (interest and dividends) of $1,700 during 1990. He had no earned income. His basic standard deduction would be $500. He would have taxable income of $1,200

Example: A dependent son had $10,000 of unearned income and $100 of earned income. He is entitled to a $500 standard deduction. He is limited to this amount because he is a dependent and his earned income is less than $500. The taxpayer would, therefore, have $9,600 in taxable income.

Example: A dependent daughter with $4,000 of earned income and $600 of unearned income would claim a maximum $3,250 standard deduction because her earned income of $4,000 is greater than the standard deduction. She would have taxable income of $1,350.

Additional Standard Deduction for Age and Blindness

Elderly or blind taxpayers may also claim an additional standard deduction. Taxpayers who are age 65 or over or blind at the end of 1990, qualify for the additional standard deduction for age and/or blindness. Taxpayers who claim the additional standard deduction for blindness must attach a doctor's statement to their income tax return. Taxpayers who itemize their deductions will lose the additional standard deduction. This standard deduction is adjusted each year for inflation.

1990 Additional Standard Deduction

Single or Head of household, age 65 or over or blind $ 800
Single or Head of household, age 65 or over and blind $1,600
Married filing jointly, or Qualifying widow(er), age 65 or over or blind (per person) $650
Married filing jointly or Qualifying widow(er), age 65 or over and blind (per person) $1,300

Example: A single, sixty-five year old individual would have a standard deduction of $4,050 computed as follows:

Basic standard deduction for a single person	$3,250
Additional standard deduction for age	800
Total	$4,050

Example: A seventy year old husband and a fifty-eight year old blind wife filing jointly would be entitled to a standard deduction totaling $6,750 computed as follows.

Basic standard deduction for married filing jointly	$5,450
Additional standard deduction for (husband's) age	650
Additional standard deduction for (wife's) blindness	650
Total	$6,750

Exemptions

The 1990 personal exemption amount is $2,050 and is adjusted each year for inflation.

Adjustments to Income

Individual Retirement Accounts (IRAs)

Taxpayers with earned income may still make contributions to their IRAs; however, there may be limits as to the amount that can be deducted on their income tax return if they are covered by a qualified retirement plan by their employer. Income earned from IRAs will remain tax-free until the taxpayer withdraws it.

For 1990, married taxpayers filing jointly with adjusted gross income of $40,000 or less may take an IRA deduction whether or not they are active participants in a qualified retirement plan. Single taxpayers in qualified retirement plans may also deduct IRAs if their adjusted gross income is $25,000 or less. The IRA deduction phases out over the next $10,000 of adjusted gross income if taxpayers are active participants in a qualified retirement plan. Consequently, married couples filing jointly with adjusted gross income over $50,000 or single filers with adjusted gross income over $35,000 may not deduct any contributions to their IRAs.

Taxpayers who do not have a qualified retirement plan where they are employed may take an IRA deduction up to the lesser of $2,000, or the amount of their earned income, regardless of their total income.

Taxpayers who are eligible to participate in their employers' qualified plans are considered to belong to the plan even if they choose not to participate.

A qualified retirement plan generally includes: (1) a qualified pension, profit-sharing or stock bonus plan; (2) a qualified annuity plan; (3) a simplified employee pension plan; or (4) a plan established for its employees by the federal, state or other political subdivision or by an agency of these entities.

(continued)

Itemized Deductions

- Medical expenses are deductible, but only for the amount that exceeds 7.5 percent of adjusted gross income.
- 1990 is the final year for the consumer interest deduction such as finance charges on personal credit cards and installment interest on personal automobile loans. Only 10% of this interest is deductible in 1990. Beginning in 1991, there will be no consumer interest deduction.
- Investment interest for 1990 is deductible to the extent of net investment income plus up to 10% of the next $10,000 of investment interest expense ($5,000 for a married person filing separately).
- Mortgage interest on a taxpayer's first and second homes remains fully deductible. However, there are limitations.
- Home equity loans are deductible up to the first $100,000 in equity debt.
- Charitable contributions by an individual to qualified charities for business purposes are deductible but only if the taxpayer itemizes deductions.
- State and local income taxes, real estate taxes, and personal property taxes remain fully deductible.
- Casualty and theft losses are deductible subject to the 10% and $100 limitations.
- Miscellaneous deductions, such as union and professional dues, tax preparation fees, safe deposit box rental and employee business expenses are deductible, but only for the amount that exceeds 2 percent of adjusted gross income.

Moving Expenses

Taxpayers who change jobs during the year can usually deduct some of their moving expenses. These expenses include the cost of moving household goods, travel to the new home, househunting trips, temporary living quarters, and other related expenses. To qualify, the move must be job-related and it must meet several other requirements including a distance and time test. The expenses for moving household goods and traveling to a new home have some limitations. All other deductible moving expenses, such as househunting trips or temporary living quarters, are subject to a $3,000 ceiling. Meal expenses are only 80% deductible. Moving expenses are deductible only if the taxpayer itemizes deductions on Schedule A of Form 1040. Moves within the U.S. are reported on Form 3903.

Employee Business Expense

All employee business expenses including travel, automobile, and entertainment are allowed only as itemized miscellaneous deductions. Only 80% of the cost of customer meals and entertainment is deductible. These expenses are then subject to the 2% of adjusted gross income limitation for miscellaneous deductions.

Earned Income Credit

Low income workers who have dependent children and maintain a household are eligible for a refundable earned income credit. The credit for 1990 is calculated on earned income with a maximum credit of $953. When income is more than $10,730, the credit begins to phase out until it is completely phased out at $20,264.

If an individual qualifies, the credit is refundable even if the taxpayer is not required to file an income tax return. However, a tax return must be filed in order to receive the credit. To assist individuals, the IRS publishes a table showing the earned income credit at various levels of income.

Taxing Children's Income

A child who may be claimed as a dependent by another taxpayer may not claim their own exemption on their tax return. Further, children under age 14 with at least one living parent may use up to $500 of their standard deduction against unearned income. Unearned income includes dividends and interest income. If the child's unearned income is more than $1,000, that income will be taxed at the child's tax rate, or the parent's rate, whichever is higher.

The effect of this is to charge a higher tax rate on children's unearned income by taxing it at the parent's rate when that rate is higher. The parent has the option of including the child's unearned income on their tax return. However, if the unearned income is reported on the child's tax return, only the amount over $1,000 is subject to this treatment. Therefore, the child does get the benefit of a lower tax rate on the first $1,000.

For example, assuming the child has $3,000 of interest income, the child's taxable income would be $2,500, allowing for the $500 standard deduction. Assuming that the parent's rate is 28%, the child's tax would be $637 ($77 from the tax table plus 28% of $2,000).

Who Must File

Whether U.S. citizens or resident aliens living in the United States must file an income tax return depends on their gross income, filing status, and age.

Generally, U.S. citizens or resident aliens will have to file an income tax return if their gross income for the year is at least as much as the amount shown in the following table.

Filing Status	1990 Gross Income
Single	
• Under 65	$5,300
• 65 or older	$6,100
Married filing jointly	
• Both spouses under 65	$9,550
• One spouse 65 or older	$10,200
• Both spouses 65 or older	$10,850
Married filing separately	$2,050
Head of household	
• Under 65	$6,800
• 65 or older	$7,600
Qualifying widow(er)	
• Under 65	$7,500
• 65 or older	$8,150

Example: John and Mary Smith intend to file a joint return for 1990. John's income is all from wages. Mary receives no income subject to tax. Neither John nor Mary is blind. John is 67 years old but Mary will not be 65 until next year. For 1990, their combined gross income subject to tax will be $10,750. They will have to file a tax return because their gross income will be at least $10,200.

If Mary were age 65, they would not have to file a 1990 tax return because their gross income would be less than $10,850 as shown in the table.

Some Exceptions to Filing Requirements. An individual must file a tax return if:

- Net earnings from self employment for the year are $400 or more.
- Advance earned income credit payments were received during the year from their employer.
- Qualifications for the earned income credit are met.
- An income tax refund is due.
- Gross income is less than the filing requirement amount

but additional taxes are owed for:
- Social security tax on unreported tips;
- Alternative minimum tax;
- Recapture of investment credit;
- Tax attributable to qualified retirement plans (including IRAs), annuities, and modified endowment contracts.

When to File

For 1990, U.S. individual income tax returns are required to be filed with the Internal Revenue Service no later than Monday, April 15, 1991.

If an income tax return cannot be completed by the due date, file Form 4868, Application for Automatic Extension of Time to File U.S. Individual Income Tax Return, to receive an automatic four-month extension.

The automatic extension does not extend time for paying the tax liability. If a return is filed late, it may be subject to penalties and interest on any unpaid tax liability. Form 4868 must be filed on or before April 15, 1991.

Which Form to File

You may be able to use the short Form 1040EZ if:
• You are single and do not claim any dependents.
• You are not 65 or older or blind.
• You have income only from wages, salaries, tips, taxable scholarships or fellowships, and not more than $400 of interest income.
• Your taxable income is less than $50,000.
• You do not itemize deductions or claim any adjustments to income or tax credits.
• You did not make estimated tax payments.

You may be able to use Form 1040A if:
• You have income from wages, salaries, tips, taxable scholarships or fellowships, interest, and dividends.
• You have income from Individual Retirement Account (IRA) distributions, pensions, annuities, unemployment compensation, and social security benefits.
• Your taxable income is less than $50,000.
• You do not itemize deductions.
• You claim a deduction for qualified contributions to an IRA.
• You claim a credit for child and dependent care expenses, credit for the elderly or the disabled, or the earned income credit.
• You have made estimated tax payments.
• You filed for an extension of time to file.
Either use Form 1040EZ or Form 1040A unless filing Form 1040 allows you to pay a lower tax. Forms 1040EZ

and 1040A are easier to complete than the longer Form 1040. Even if you do meet the above tests, you will have to file Form 1040 if any of the following situations apply.

You must use Form 1040 if:
• Your taxable income is $50,000 or more.
• You itemize deductions.
• You receive any nontaxable dividends or capital gain distributions.
• You have foreign accounts and/or foreign trusts.
• You have taxable refunds of state and local income taxes.
• You have business, farm or rental income.
• You have miscellaneous income not allowed on Form 1040EZ or 1040A such as alimony or lottery winnings.
• You have certain adjustments to income such as alimony paid.
• You can claim a foreign tax credit or certain other credits to which you are entitled.
• You have other taxes such as self-employment tax or the alternative minimum tax.
• You file any of these forms:

Form 2555, Foreign Earned Income.
Form 3903, Moving Expense.
Form 8814, Parent's Election To Report Child's Interest and Dividends.

Electronic Filing

Electronic filing is a process of transmitting completed personal income tax returns to the Internal Revenue Service. Originating as a pilot program in 1986, almost 4,000,000 returns were filed electronically during 1990.

If a refund is due on your 1990 income tax return, you may be able to have your return filed electronically. Electronic filing shortens the average time for processing returns to within 3 weeks. Refunds may also be deposited directly into your savings or checking account. Since electronic filing automates most of the manual steps needed to process standard paper returns, processing is faster, less expensive, and more accurate.

The electronic filing method can be used by many tax return preparers. These preparers are equipped to send tax return information over telephone lines to an Internal Revenue Service Center. The preparer will ask you to sign a declaration form, Form 8453, U.S. Individual Income Tax Declaration for Electronic Filing. This form is not a power of attorney and it does not authorize your tax preparer to receive information from the IRS about your account.

Frequently Used Tax Forms

706
U.S. Estate (and Generation-Skipping Transfer) Tax Return
Used for the estate of a deceased United States resident or citizen.
709—A
U.S. Short Form Gift Tax Return
Used by married couples to report nontaxable gifts of more than $10,000 but less than $20,000.

1040
U.S. Individual Income Tax Return
Used by citizens and residents of the United States to report income tax.

1040-ES
Estimated Tax for individuals
Used to make estimated tax payments as a means for paying currently any income tax (including self-employment tax and the alternative minimum tax) due in excess of the tax withheld from wages, salaries, and other payments for personal services. It is not required unless the total tax exceeds withholding (if any) and applicable tax credits by $500 or more.

1040NR
U.S. Nonresident Alien Income Tax Return
Used by all nonresident alien individuals who file a U.S. tax return, whether or not engaged in a trade or business within the United States. Also used as required for filing nonresident alien fiduciary (estate and trust) returns.
1040X
Amended U.S. Individual Income Tax Return
Used to correct Form 1040, Form 1040A or 1040EZ that you have already filed.
1041
U.S. Fiduciary Income Tax Return
Used by a fiduciary for domestic estate or domestic trust.
1065
U.S. Partnership Return of Income
Used by partnerships as an information return.
1116
Computation of Foreign Tax Credit—Individual, Fiduciary, or Nonresident Alien Individual

Used to figure and support the foreign tax credit claimed for the amount of any income, war profits, and excess profits taxes paid or accrued during the tax year to any foreign country or U.S. possession.

1120
U.S. Corporation Income Tax Return
Used by a corporation to report income tax.
1120S
U.S. Income Tax Return for an S Corporation
Used by S corporations to report taxes under Subchapter S of the IRC and as an information return.
1139
Corporation Application for Tentative Refund
Used by corporations that have certain carrybacks and desire a quick refund of taxes.
1310
Statement of Person Claiming Refund Due a Deceased Taxpayer
Used by a claimant to secure payment of refund on behalf of a deceased taxpayer.

2106
Employee Business Expenses
For use by employee and outside salespersons to support deductions from income for travel, transportation, and expenses (except moving expenses).

2119
Sale of Your Home
For use by individuals who sold their principal residence. Also used by those individuals 55 or older who elect to exclude gain on the sale of their principal residence.

2120
Multiple Support Declaration
Used as a statement to disclaim as an income tax exemption an individual to whose support the taxpayer and others have contributed.

2441
Child and Dependent Care Expenses
Used to figure the credit for child and dependent care expenses.

2688
Application for Additional Extension of Time To File U.S. Individual Income Tax Return
Used to apply for an additional extension of time to file Form 1040.

2848
Power of Attorney and Declaration of Representative
Used as an authorization for one person to act for another in any tax matter (except alcohol and tobacco taxes and firearms activities).

3903
Moving Expenses
For optional use to support deductions from income for expenses of travel, transportation (including meals and lodging), and certain expenses of selling an old residence and buying a new residence for employees or self-employed individuals moving to a new job location in the U.S. or its possessions.

4562
Depreciation and Amortization
For use by: individuals, estates and trusts, partnerships, and corporations claiming depreciation, amortization, and section 179 expense deduction. Also used to provide required information for automobiles and all other "listed property."

4684
Casualties and Thefts
For use by all taxpayers for reporting gains and losses from casualties and thefts.

4868
Application for Automatic Extension of Time To File U.S. Individual Income Tax Return
Used to apply for an automatic 4-month extension of time to file Form 1040.

5329
Return for Additional Taxes Attributable to Qualified Retirement Plans (Including IRAs), Annuities, and Modified Endowment Contracts
Used to report tax on excess contributions, premature distributions, excess distributions and excess accumulations.

5500EZ
Annual Return of One-Participant (Owners and Their Spouses) Pension Benefit Plan
Used to report on a pension, profit-sharing, etc., plan covering an individual, partner or an individual and spouse or partners and spouses who wholly own a business.

6251
Alternative Minimum Tax—Individuals
Used by individuals to report tax preference items and to figure their alternative minimum tax liability.

7004
Application for Automatic Extension of Time To File Corporation Income Tax Return
Used by corporations and certain exempt organizations to request an automatic extension of 6 months to file their income tax returns.

8283
Noncash Charitable Contributions
Used by taxpayers to report contributions of property in which the total claimed fair market value of all property contributed exceeds $500.

8582
Passive Activity Loss Limitations
Used to determine limitations on passive activity losses.

8606
Nondeductible IRA Contributions, IRA Basis, and Nontaxable IRA Distributions
Used to report the nondeductible amount of IRA, contributions and distributions. It is also used to determine IRA basis.

8615
Computation of Tax for Children Under Age 14 Who Have Investment Income of More Than $1,000
Used to figure the tax on unearned income of more than $1,000 belonging to a child under age 14.

Internal Revenue Service Audit

There are two important facts that should be remembered regarding the IRS audit program. First, fewer than one out of every hundred individual tax returns will be audited in 1991. Second, the IRS is good at selecting returns for audit that will yield additional income taxes.

Returns to be audited are chosen by one of the following six methods and also by random selection:
• The Discriminate Function System (DIF)
• Taxpayer Compliance Measurement Program (TCMP)
• Matching Information Documents
• Targeted Group Projects
• Discrepancies in Your Return
• Tips from Informants

If your return is audited and you feel you are not being treated fairly, or that proper attention is not being paid to your statements, you have a right to ask for a hearing at the IRS appellate level. If you are still dissatisfied, you can take your case to the United States Tax Court. If the total amount in question is less than $10,000, your case can be handled under the Small Tax Case procedures. If you are still dissatisfied, your next move would be the United States Circuit Court of Appeals.

Your Rights As a Taxpayer

Congress responded to complaints that taxpayers were not being treated fairly by the IRS and passed a comprehensive law to force the IRS to explain, in easy to understand language, the actions it proposes to take against a taxpayer and to relax some of its audit and collection procedures. This law is called "The Taxpayer Bill of Rights."

Some of the features of this bill of rights are:
• Plain English statements
• Allowing recordings of audit conferences
• Not requiring taxpayers to attend the examination
• New audit location rules
• Guidelines for installment payment of taxes
• Acting on wrong IRS advice
• Hardship relief
• Specific basis of IRS decision
• Levies on property
• Suing the IRS for damages
You can obtain the IRS Publication, "Your Rights As a Taxpayer," free by calling 1-800-424-FORM. Ask for Publication 1.

Federal Death Taxes and the State "Pick-Up" Credit

Source: Advisory Commission on Intergovernmental Relations, 1990

Federal death taxes are made up of two components—gift taxes and estate taxes. Gift taxes are levied on the donor, *while the donor is alive*, on transfers above $10,000 ($20,000 for joint gifts), *per donee*, for a single year. Estate taxes are levied on the entire taxable estate (gross estate less administrative expenses, bequests to spouse, debts, charitable contributions, and funeral expenses) *after the death of the donor*. Gift taxes paid during the donor's lifetime are credited dollar for dollar against estate taxes due at time of death.

Although estate and gift tax rates begin at the first dollar of taxable estate, there is a unified credit of $192,800 against transfer tax liability. This is equivalent to a $600,000 exemption. In addition to the unified credit, a credit for state death taxes is also allowed; see the table below for maximum state death tax credit (Pick-Up").

(continued)

| Unified Transfer Tax Rates[1] | | | | Maximum State Death Tax Credit | | |
Taxable Estate	Tax on Lower Amount	Rate on Excess		Adjusted Taxable Estate[2]	Federal Credit	Rate on Excess
$10,000 or less	$0	18%		$40,000-89,999	$0	0.8%
10,000-19,999	1,800	20		90,000-139,999	400	1.6
20,000-39,999	3,800	22		140,000-239,999	1,200	2.4
40,000-59,999	8,200	24		240,000-439,999	3,600	3.2
60,000-79,999	13,000	26		440,000-639,999	10,000	4.0
80,000-99,999	18,200	28		640,000-839,999	18,000	4.8
100,000-149,999	23,800	30		840,000-1,039,999	27,600	5.6
150,000-249,999	38,800	32		1,040,000-1,539,999	38,800	6.4
250,000-499,999	70,800	34		1,540,000-2,039,999	70,800	7.2
500,000-749,999	155,800	37		2,040,000-2,539,999	106,800	8.0
750,000-999,999	248,300	39		2,540,000-3,039,999	146,800	8.8
1,000,000-1,249,999	345,800	41		3,040,000-3,539,999	190,800	9.6
1,250,000-1,499,999	448,300	43		3,540,000-4,039,999	238,800	10.4
1,500,000-1,999,999	555,800	45		4,040,000-5,039,999	290,800	11.2
2,000,000-2,499,999	780,800	49		5,040,000-6,039,999	402,800	12.0
2,500,000-2,999,999	1,025,800	53		6,040,000-7,039,999	522,800	12.8
over 3,000,000[3]	1,290,800	55		7,040,000-8,039,999	650,800	13.6
				8,040,000-9,039,999	786,800	14.4
				9,040,000-10,039,999	930,800	15.2
				over 10,040,000	1,082,800	16.0

(1) For decedents dying from 1984 through 1992. (2) Taxable estate less $60,000. (3) On taxable estates between $10,000,000 and $21,040,000, an additional tax of 5% of the transfer above $10,000,000 is imposed.

Federal Tax Filing Dates, 1991

January 15

Individuals. File an estimated tax payment for 1990 if you did not pay your income tax for the year through withholding (or did not pay in enough tax that way). Use Form 1040-ES. This is the final installment date for 1990 estimated tax. However, you do not have to make this payment if you file your 1990 return (Form 1040) and pay any tax due by January 31, 1991.

Farmers and fishermen. Pay your estimated tax for 1990 using Form 1040-ES. You can then file your 1990 income tax return (Form 1040) by April 15. If you do not pay at this time, file your 1990 return by March 1.

January 31

All employers. Give your employees their Form W-2 for 1990. In addition, furnish Notice 797, *You May Be Eligible for a Refund on Your Federal Income Tax Return Because of the Earned Income Credit (EIC)*, to each employee you employed during 1990 who did not have any tax withheld during 1990.

Individuals. File your income tax return (Form 1040) for 1990 if you did not pay your last installment of estimated tax by January 15. Filing your return now prevents any penalty for late payment of the last installment.

February 15

Individuals. If you claimed exemption from income tax withholding last year on Form W-4, you must file a new Form W-4 by this date to continue your exemption for another year with your employer.

March 1

Farmers and fishermen. File your 1990 income tax return (Form 1040) to avoid an underpayment penalty if you owe estimated tax. However, you have until April 15 if you paid your 1990 estimated tax by January 15, 1991.

March 15

Corporations. File a 1990 calendar year income tax return (Form 1120 or 1120-A) and pay any tax due. If you want an automatic 6-month extension, file Form 7004 and deposit what you estimate you owe.

S Corporations. File a 1990 calendar year income tax return (Form 1120S) and pay any tax due. If you want an automatic 6-month extension, file Form 7004 and deposit what you estimate you owe.

Corporations. File Form 2553 to choose to be treated as an S corporation, beginning with calendar year 1991. If Form 2553 is filed late, S treatment will begin with calendar year 1992.

April 15

Individuals. File an income tax return for 1990 (Form 1040, 1040A, or 1040EZ) and pay any tax due. If you want an automatic 4-month extension, file Form 4868 and pay any tax you estimate will be due. Then file Form 1040 or 1040A by August 15. If you want an additional extension, file Form 2688 as soon as possible so that your application can be acted on before August 15.

Individuals. If you are not paying your 1991 income tax through withholding (or will not pay in enough tax during the year that way), pay the first installment of your 1991 estimated tax by this date. Use Form 1040-ES.

Partnerships. File a 1990 calendar year return (Form 1065).

C and S Corporations. Deposit the 1st installment of your estimated income tax for 1991.

June 17

Individuals. Make a payment of your 1991 estimated tax by this date if you are not paying your income tax for the year through withholding (or will not pay in enough tax that way). Use Form 1040-ES. This is the 2nd installment date for estimated tax in 1991.

C and S Corporations. Deposit the 2nd installment of your estimated income tax for 1991.

August 15

Individuals. If you were given an automatic 4-month extension to file your income tax return for 1990, file Form 1040 and pay any tax, interest, and penalties due.

September 16

Individuals. Make a payment of your 1991 estimated tax by this date, if you are not paying your income tax for the year through withholding (or will not pay in enough tax that way). Use Form 1040-ES. This is the 3rd installment date for estimated tax in 1991.

Corporations. File a 1990 income tax return (Form 1120 or 1120A) and pay any tax due. This due date applies only if you were given an automatic 6-month extension from March 15.

S Corporations. File a 1990 income tax return (Form 1120S) and pay any tax due. This due date applies only if you were given an automatic 6-month extension from March 15.

C and S Corporations. Deposit the 3rd installment of your estimated income tax for 1991.

December 16

C and S Corporations. Deposit the 4th installment of your estimated income tax for 1991.

Free IRS Tax Services

IRS Information and Assistance

The Internal Revenue Service provides over 100 publications on various topics to help taxpayers understand the complex tax laws. Most of these publications are revised annually.

Most taxpayers should be able to meet the requirements of the tax laws by using information such as tax package instructions, publications, taxpayer education programs, films, and library programs.

Toll-free telephone numbers and walk-in assistance are available to answer questions on a taxpayer's account, IRS procedures, or technical inquiries on tax-related matters.

• **Telephone Service**

Toll-free telephone assistance is available in all 50 states, the District of Columbia, Puerto Rico, and the Virgin Islands. Through the toll-free system, taxpayers may obtain assistance on their questions.

During periods of peak demand for telephone assistance, it may be difficult to get through. Generally, early in the morning and later in the week are the best times to call the IRS.

Telephone service for deaf taxpayers. Toll-free telephone assistance for deaf taxpayers is available for those who have access to TV/Telephone-TTY equipment. The hours of operation for this service are 8:00 a.m. to 6:45 p.m. Eastern Standard Time for January thru April 15 and 8:00 a.m. to 4:30 p.m. for April 16 thru December. Residents of Indiana may call 1-800-382-4059. Residents elsewhere in the U.S.

including Alaska, Hawaii, Puerto Rico, and the Virgin Islands may call 1-800-428-4732.

• **Information for the Blind**

Braille materials are available at Regional Libraries for the Blind and Physically Handicapped in conjunction with the Library of Congress. These materials include Publications 17 and 334, Forms 1040, 1040A, and 1040EZ, and Schedules A and B, and instructions.

• **Walk-In Service**

While the Internal Revenue Service will not prepare tax returns, assistors are available in most IRS offices throughout the country to help taxpayers prepare their own returns. Taxpayers will be expected to help themselves to the maximum extent possible. However, they will be provided assistance and, at the same time, provided the opportunity of learning how to research and prepare their own tax returns. An assistor will "walk-through" a return with a number of taxpayers in a group setting.

In many IRS offices a walk-in counter is available to help with inquiries that do not involve preparation of a return, such as receipt of an IRS notice or bill. Certain technical information or publications may also be obtained at most IRS offices.

Taxpayers who wish assistance with their tax returns should bring in their tax packages, Forms W-2 and 1099, and any other information (such as a copy of last year's return) which will enable the IRS to help.

Taxpayer Education Programs

The Internal Revenue Service has a number of programs designed to educate the public about our nation's voluntary compliance tax system and each citizen's share in it so that the system works as smoothly as possible. The more that citizens understand about their role in this tax system, the better they will be able to carry out their responsibilities with the minimum amount of confusion. Most of these taxpayer education programs offer opportunity for citizen involvement through service as a volunteer.

• **Understanding Taxes**

This is a tax education program that begins in the schools, where young people are taught about their tax rights and responsibilities under our voluntary compliance tax system. They also learn how to fill out basic tax returns. Since many of them already are working, often at their first job, this learning has immediate practical value. They also learn about the history of taxes and current issues in taxation, such as tax reform. All materials a teacher may need are available free of charge, including a series of video programs. These films were produced in cooperation with the states. Workshops are conducted during the year to help prepare teachers for course instruction.

• **Small Business Workshops**

These workshops help people start small businesses by providing them with the information they need to carry out their tax responsibilities, including tax withholding, making correct and timely tax deposits, and filing a business return.

Some sessions focus on the needs of the self-employed, minority entrepreneurs, and specialized business groups. Active or retired businesspersons often volunteer their services and provide invaluable information.

• **Volunteer Income Tax Assistance**

The Volunteer Income Tax Assistance program (VITA) provides free tax assistance to elderly, non-English-speaking, handicapped people, and also to members of the military. Generally, those who receive these services can't afford professional tax assistance. After completing the IRS training, volunteers provide free help at special locations.

• **Tax Counseling for the Elderly**

Tax Counseling for the Elderly (TCE) provides free tax assistance to people 60 or older, especially those who are disabled or have other special needs. Non-profit organizations under cooperative agreements with the IRS provide local assistance.

Both VITA and TCE sites are usually located in neighborhood centers, libraries, churches, and other places in the community.

• **Community Outreach Tax Assistance**

This is a year-round program of assistance to groups who need help understanding the tax laws, especially as they apply to members of their profession or group, such as teaching, business, or farming. Seminars are conducted at times and locations in the community that are convenient for members of the group.

State Government Individual Income Taxes

Source: Advisory Commission on Intergovernmental Relations

(As of October 1989. Only basic rates, brackets, and exemptions are shown. Local income tax rates, even those mandated by the state, are not included. Taxable income rates and brackets listed below apply to single taxpayers and married taxpayers filing "combined separate" returns in states where this is permitted.)

State	Taxable Income Brackets Tax Rates (range in percent)	Lowest: Amount Under	Highest: Amount Over	Personal Exemptions Single	Married-Joint Return	Dependents	Standard Deduction Percent	Single	Married-Joint Return	Federal Income Tax Deductible[b]
AL·*	2.0-5.0%	$500	$3,000	$1,500	$3,000	$300	20%	$2,000	$4,000	yes
AK	No state income tax									
AZ[c]	2.0-8.0	1,290	7,740	2,229	4,458	1,337	22.29	1,115	2,229	yes
AR	1.0-7.0	3,000	25,000	20	40	20	10	1,000	1,000	no
CA[c]	1.0-9.3	4,020	26,380	55[d]	110[d]	55[d]	NA	2,070	4,140	no
CO	5 percent of modified federal taxable income									
CT·	Limited income tax									
DE·	3.2-7.7	1,000	40,000	1,250	2,500	1,250	10	1,300	1,600	no
DC	6.0-9.5	10,000	20,000	1,160	2,320	1,160	NA	2,000	2,000	no
FL	No state income tax									
GA	1.0-6.0	750	7,000	1,500	3,000	1,500	NA	2,300	3,000	no
HI*	2.0-10.0	1,500	20,500	1,040	2,080	1,040	NA	1,500	1,900	no
ID	2.0-8.2	1,000	20,000	Same as federal[e]						no
IL	3.0	Flat rate		1,000	2,000	1,000	NA	NA	NA	no
IN·	3.4	Flat rate		1,000	2,000	1,000	NA	NA	NA	no
IA·*	0.4-9.98	1,016	45,720	20[d]	40[d]	15[d]	NA	1,230	3,030	yes
KS*	4.5-5.95	27,500	27,500	2,000	4,000	2,000	NA	3,000	5,000	yes
KY·	2.0-6.0	3,000	8,000	20	40	20	NA	650	650	yes
LA	2.0-6.0	10,000	50,000	4,500	9,000	1,000	Combined with exemptions			yes
ME	2.0-8.5	4,000	16,000	2,000	4,000	2,000	NA	3,100	5,200	no
MD·*	2.0-5.0	1,000	3,000	1,100	2,200	1,100	15	2,000	4,000	no
MA*	5.0-10.0	Flat rate		2,200	4,400	1,000	NA	NA	NA	no
MI·	4.6	Flat rate		2,000	4,000	2,000	NA	NA	NA	no
MN*	6.0-8.0	13,000	13,000	Same as federal[e]						no
MS	3.0-5.0	5,000	10,000	6,000	9,500	1,500	15	2,300	3,400	no
MO·*	1.5-6.0	1,000	9,000	1,200	2,400	400	NA	Same as federal		yes
MT[c]	2.0-11.0	1,500	52,500	1,200	2,400	1,200	20	2,250	4,500	yes
NE	2.0-5.9	1,800	27,000	1,180	2,360	1,180	NA	Same as federal		no
NV	No state income tax									
NH*	Limited income tax									
NJ*	2.0-3.5	20,000	50,000	1,000	2,000	1,000	NA	NA	NA	no
NM	1.8-8.5	5,200	64,000	2,000	4,000	2,000	NA	3,000	5,000	no
NY·*	4.0-7.5	5,500	13,000	0	0	1,000	NA	6,000	9,500	no
NC*	6.0-7.0	12,750	12,750	2,000	4,000	2,000	NA	3,000	5,000	no
ND*	2.6-12.0	3,000	50,000	Same as federal						yes
OH·*	0.743-6.9	5,000	100,000	650	1,300	650	NA	NA	NA	no
OK*	0.5-6.0	1,000	7,500	1,000	2,000	1,000	15	2,000	2,000	yes
OR*[c]	5.0-9.0	2,000	5,000	94[d]	188[d]	94[d]	NA	1,800	3,000	yes
PA·	2.1	Flat rate		NA	NA	NA	NA	NA	NA	no
RI	22.96 percent of federal income tax liability									no
SC[c]	3.0-7.0	4,000	10,000	Same as federal[e]						no
SD	No state income tax									
TN*	Limited income tax									
TX	No state income tax									
UT*	2.55-7.2	750	3,750	75 percent of federal exemptions			Same as federal			yes
VT*	25 percent of federal income tax liablity									no
VA*	2.0-5.75	3,000	16,000	800	1,600	800	NA	3,000	5,000	no
WA	No state income tax									
WV*	3.0-6.5	10,000	60,000	2,000	4,000	2,000	NA	NA	NA	no
WI*	4.9-6.93	7,500	15,000	0	0	50[d]	NA	5,200	8,900	no
WY	No state income tax									

Notes: (NA) = not applicable. (+) = states in which one or more local governments levy a local income tax. (a) The lesser of (1) the percentage indicated, multiplied by adjusted gross income, or (2) the dollar value listed. In some states, when a standard deduction computed using a percentage of AGI is less than the fixed amount shown above, a minimum dollar deduction is allowed. Maryland and Utah have a minimum deduction as well. (b) A state provision that allows the taxpayer to deduct fully the federal income tax reduces the effective marginal tax rate for persons in the highest state and federal tax brackets by approximately 30% of the nominal tax rate—the deduction is of a lesser benefit to other taxpayers with lower federal and state top tax brackets. (c) Indexed by an inflation factor. (d) Tax credit per dependent. Taxpayers 65 or older receive a $25 credit.

*State Notes:

Alabama: Social Security taxes are included in itemized deductions. Taxable income brackets for married filing joint over $6,000, taxed at highest rate.

Arizona: Federal income taxes are deducted from taxable income. An additional deduction from income is allowed in the amount of 65% of federal tax liability or $600, whichever is greater, but not to exceed $10,000 for married filing joint or $5,000 for all other filers.

Arkansas: Tax credit per dependent. Taxpayers 65 or older receive a $20 credit.

Colorado: Modifications for federal interest income, non-Colorado state and local interest income, and Colorado pension exclusion.

Connecticut: There is an income tax on interest, capital gains, and dividend income only. The rate of this tax ranges from 1% of interest and dividend income for taxpayers with an AGI of $54,000-$57,999 to 12% of such income of taxpayers with an AGI over $100,000. Capital gains are taxed at 7% after an exemption of $100 is applied.

District of Columbia: Exemption will increase to $1,370 by 1991.

Hawaii: A refundable tax credit of $45 per exemption is granted; credit of $1.25 per exemption is granted for 1989; a refund-

(continued)

Idaho: Idaho allows a refundable $15/exemption credit.

Illinois: Effective 1/1/90 an additional $1,000 exemption for persons 65 years of age or older. An additional $1,000 exemption for persons who are blind.

Indiana: Additional $1,000 exemption if taxpayer or spouse is over 65 or blind.

Iowa: Tax may not reduce after-tax income of taxpayer below $5,000 (single) or $7,500 (married filing joint, head-of-household, surviving spouse). Only limitation for the standard deduction is that the deduction otherwise allowable of $1,230 or $3,030 may not exceed the amount of income remaining after the federal tax deduction.

Kansas: A child care credit equal to 25% of the federal child care credit is allowed to taxpayers claiming the federal credit. These rates and brackets apply to single persons not deducting federal income tax. For individuals deducting the tax, rates range from 4.75% of the first $2,000 to 8.5% on income over $30,000.

Kentucky: Tax credit per dependent. Taxpayers 65 or older receive a $60 credit.

Maryland: All counties have a local income tax surcharge of at least 20% of the state tax liability; most counties have a surcharge of 50%. Personal exemption increases to $1,200 in 1990. Blind and elderly get an additional exemption of $1,000 beginning with 1989.

Massachusetts: 10% (flat rate) imposed on net capital gains, interest, and dividends of residents, and Massachusetts business income of nonresidents. All other net income taxed at 5%. No tax is imposed on a single person whose gross income is $8,000 or less ($12,000 married). Social Security taxes are deducted from taxable income up to $2,000 per taxpayer.

Missouri: For taxpayers itemizing deductions, Social Security taxes are deductible.

Minnesota: Additional rate of 0.5% on certain income classes to reflect federal phaseout of personal exemptions and the 15% federal rate bracket. Total rate on brackets of higher income is 8.5%.

Montana: Taxable income brackets, personal exemption level, and standard deduction levels are indexed annually for inflation.

New Hampshire: There is a 5% tax on interest and dividends (excluding income from savings bank deposits) in excess of $1,200 ($2,400 married). There is no filing requirement for an individual whose total interest and dividend income, after deducting all interest from U.S. obligations, New Hampshire and Vermont banks or credit unions; and dividends from New Hampshire non-holding company bonds is less than $1,200 ($2,400 for joint filers) for a taxable period.

New Jersey: No taxpayer is subject to tax if gross income is $3,000 or less ($1,500 married, filing separately).

New Mexico: Several rebates are available for lower income taxpayers.

New York: Rates are scheduled to be reduced further in 1990, when the top rate will be 7%.

North Carolina: Breaking point for higher marginal tax rate varies according to filing status. Taxable income brackets shown are for single taxpayers.

North Dakota: Information in table applies to the long form method. As an alternative, taxpayers may use the short form method where the tax is 14% of the adjusted federal income tax liability.

Ohio: Taxpayers take a $20 tax credit per exemption.

Oklahoma: These rates and brackets apply to single persons not deducting federal income tax. For individuals deducting the tax, rates range from 0.5% of the first $1,000 to 10% on income over $23,000.

Oregon: Federal tax deduction limited to $3,000 ($1,500 if married filing separately).

Tennessee: Interest and dividends taxed at 6%. Persons over 65 having total annual gross income derived from any and all sources of $9,000 or less are exempt. Blindness is a basis for total exemption.

Utah: One-half of federal tax liability is deductible.

Vermont: Refundable state earned income tax credit (25% of federal credit, maximum $227.50).

Virginia: Top tax bracket is increased to $17,000 in 1990.

West Virginia: Eliminated standard deduction; all itemized deductions prohibited and replaced with larger personal exemptions.

Wisconsin: The standard deduction is gradually phased out as income increases; deduction is completely phased out at $50,830 of AGI for single filers and $55,000 of AGI for joint filers.

Estimated State and Local Taxes Paid by a Family of Four in Selected Large Cities, by Income Level: 1988

Source: Government of the District of Columbia, Department of Finance and Revenue

(Preliminary. Data based on average family of four, two wage earners and two school age children, owning their own home and living in a city where taxes apply. Comprises state and local sales, income, auto, and real estate taxes.

City	Total Taxes Paid by Gross Family Income Level (dol.)				Percent of Income by Income Level			
	$25,000	$50,000	$75,000	$100,000	$25,000	$50,000	$75,000	$100,000
Albuquerque, NM	1,898	3,944	6,296	8,796	7.6	7.9	8.4	8.8
Atlanta, GA	2,107	4,403	7,014	9,208	8.4	8.8	9.4	9.2
Baltimore, MD	2,809	5,712	8,594	11,374	11.2	11.4	11.5	11.4
Bridgeport, CT	2,188	3,653	6,033	7,622	8.8	7.3	8.0	7.6
Burlington, VT	2,015	4,055	6,653	9,031	8.1	8.1	8.9	9.0
Charleston, WV	2,097	4,134	7,166	9,623	8.4	8.3	9.6	9.6
Charlotte, NC	2,255	4,539	6,815	9,440	9.0	9.1	9.1	9.4
Chicago, IL	2,031	3,913	5,762	7,468	8.1	7.8	7.7	7.5
Cleveland, OH	2,508	5,256	8,148	11,219	10.0	10.5	10.9	11.2
Columbia, SC	2,131	4,540	7,394	9,718	8.5	9.1	9.9	9.7
Des Moines, IA	2,640	5,444	8,451	11,183	10.6	10.9	11.3	11.2
Detroit, MI	3,002	6,068	9,236	12,864	12.0	12.1	12.3	12.9
Honolulu, HI	2,522	5,299	8,054	10,949	10.1	10.6	10.7	10.9
Indianapolis, IN	2,239	3,943	6,299	8,059	9.0	7.9	8.4	8.1
Jackson, MS	1,921	3,863	6,556	8,553	7.7	7.7	8.7	8.6

(continued)

City	Total Taxes Paid by Gross Family Income Level (dol.)				Percent of Income by Income Level			
	$25,000	$50,000	$75,000	$100,000	$25,000	$50,000	$75,000	$100,000
Louisville, KY	2,193	4,417	6,586	8,614	8.8	8.8	8.8	8.6
Memphis, TN.	1,890	3,163	4,522	5,733	7.6	6.3	6.0	5.7
Milwaukee, WI.	3,425	7,299	11,044	14,564	13.7	14.6	14.7	14.6
Newark, NJ	2,751	5,572	8,542	11,249	11.0	11.1	11.4	11.2
New York City, NY	2,465	6,393	10,151	13,797	9.9	12.8	13.5	13.8
Norfolk, VA.	2,327	4,444	7,258	9,399	9.3	8.9	9.7	9.4
Omaha, NE	2,241	4,257	7,002	9,324	9.0	8.5	9.3	9.3
Philadelphia, PA.	3,073	5,781	8,356	10,949	12.3	11.6	11.1	10.9
Portland, ME.	1,966	4,890	8,482	11,270	7.9	9.8	11.3	11.3
Portland, OR.	3,332	7,018	10,973	14,574	13.3	14.0	14.6	14.6
Providence, RI.	2,614	4,986	8,297	11,006	10.5	10.0	11.1	11.0
St. Louis, MO	2,076	3,969	6,090	7,848	8.3	7.9	8.1	7.8
Salt Lake City, UT.	2,285	4,771	7,254	9,538	9.1	9.5	9.7	9.5
Sioux Falls, SD	2,337	4,052	5,724	7,181	9.3	8.1	7.6	7.2
Washington, DC.	2,514	5,427	8,557	11,662	10.1	10.9	11.4	11.7
Median[1].	2,031	4,001	6,574	8,936	8.1	8.0	8.8	8.9

(1) Median of all 51 cities.

Residential Property Tax Rates in Selected Large Cities: 1988

Source: Government of the District of Columbia, Department of Finance and Revenue.

City	Effective tax rate per $100 Rank	Rate	Assess-ment level (percent)	Nominal rate per $100	City	Effective tax rate per $100 Rank	Rate	Assess-ment level (percent)	Nominal rate per $100
Detroit, MI	1	4.10	49.5	8.28	Anchorage, AK.	26	1.48	90.3	1.64
Milwaukee, WI.	2	3.69	99.4	3.71	New Orleans, LA	27	1.39	10.0	14.63
Newark, NJ	3	3.20	22.2	14.46	Jackson, MS.	28	1.39	10.0	13.92
Portland, OR.	4	3.10	100.0	3.10	Louisville, KY.	29	1.33	100.0	1.33
Des Moines, IA.	5	2.97	80.0	3.71	Billings, MT.	30	1.30	3.9	33.65
Baltimore, MD.	6	2.64	42.5	6.21	Charlotte, NC	31	1.25	100.0	1.25
Sioux Falls, IA	7	2.47	46.0	5.37	Seattle, WA	32	1.24	92.5	1.34
Providence, RI.	8	2.39	100.0	2.39	Norfolk, VA.	33	1.22	90.6	1.35
Philadelphia, PA.	9	2.38	30.2	7.87	Wichita, KS.	34	1.17	7.8	14.97
Omaha, NE.	10	2.29	88.0	2.61	St. Louis, MO	35	1.16	19.0	6.13
Minneapolis, MN.	11	2.15	17.9	12.02	Columbia, SC	36	1.13	4.0	28.25
Cleveland, OH.	12	2.10	35.0	6.00	Washington, DC.	37	1.13	92.4	1.22
Jacksonville, FL.	13	1.97	97.3	2.02	New York City, NY	38	1.13	12.1	9.27
Boise City, ID	14	1.93	100.0	1.93	Salt Lake City, UT.	39	1.11	100.0	1.11
Memphis, TN.	15	1.77	25.0	7.09	Boston, MA.	40	1.08	100.0	1.08
Burlington, VT.	16	1.76	81.0	2.17	Charleston, WV	41	1.07	62.0	1.73
Manchester, NH.	17	1.71	17.0	10.07	Little Rock, AR.	42	1.02	20.0	5.10
Fargo, ND	18	1.62	4.5	36.11	Albuquerque, NM	43	1.01	33.3	3.03
Portland, ME.	19	1.57	48.0	3.28	Denver, CO	44	.94	16.0	5.89
Indianapolis, IN.	20	1.57	15.0	10.48	Las Vegas, NV.	45	.88	32.5	2.71
Wilmington, DE.	21	1.56	100.0	1.56	Oklahoma City, OK	46	.81	11.0	7.35
Bridgeport, CT.	22	1.55	27.0	5.74	Casper, WY	47	.70	9.1	7.74
Chicago, IL.	23	1.55	16.0	9.66	Birmingham, AL.	48	.70	10.0	6.95
Houston, TX	24	1.53	100.0	1.53	Phoenix, AZ	49	.68	5.4	12.53
Atlanta, GA.	25	1.50	28.9	5.20	Los Angeles, CA.	50	.64	61.2	1.04
					Honolulu, HI	51	.59	89.0	.66

Tax Revenues—Selected Countries: 1975 to 1987

Source: Organization for Economic Cooperation and Development

(Covers national and local taxes and Social Security contributions.)

Country	Tax Revenues, 1987 Total (bil. dol.)	Per capita (dol.)	Tax Revenues as Percent of Gross Domestic Product 1975	1980	1985	1987	Percent Change in Total Tax Revenue as Expressed in National Currency 1975-1980	1980-1985	1986-1987
United States	$1,316.1	$5,396	29.0	29.5	29.2	30.0	76.7	46.5	10.1
Australia	64.6	3,975	27.9	29.2	30.3	31.3	88.9	80.4	13.8
Austria	49.6	6,550	38.6	41.2	42.5	42.3	61.5	41.8	2.8
Belgium	65.8	6,665	41.1	43.6	46.9	46.1	61.5	47.2	4.9
Canada	146.5	5,710	32.4	31.6	33.1	34.5	75.5	59.1	12.8
Denmark	52.6	10,257	41.4	45.5	49.2	52.0	90.1	77.6	6.4
Finland	32.1	6,515	35.3	33.3	37.3	35.9	73.7	95.1	3.0
France	394.9	7,099	37.4	42.5	45.6	44.8	116.2	78.2	6.5
Greece	17.6	1,764	24.6	28.6	35.1	37.4	195.7	231.9	17.1
Italy	273.9	4,778	25.1	30.0	34.7	36.2	222.0	139.2	9.7
Japan	727.5	5,959	20.9	25.5	28.0	30.2	5.7	43.5	9.4
Netherlands	102.9	7,012	43.7	45.8	45.0	48.0	60.6	21.7	5.7
New Zealand	13.5	4,076	31.3	33.0	34.3	38.6	120.1	99.7	23.3
Norway	39.9	9,546	44.8	47.1	47.8	48.3	101.1	77.3	4.8
Portugal	11.6	1,185	24.7	28.7	31.1	31.4	286.4	208.1	10.3
Spain	95.5	2,459	19.6	24.1	28.8	33.0	210.3	119.8	19.1
Sweden	89.9	10,707	43.9	49.4	50.5	56.7	96.4	68.0	13.9
Switzerland	54.7	8,267	29.6	30.8	32.1	32.0	26.3	39.2	3.1
United Kingdom.	253.4	4,451	35.4	35.3	38.1	37.5	116.6	64.5	6.7
West Germany	420.7	6,880	35.7	38.0	37.8	37.6	53.2	23.6	4.0

MANUFACTURES AND MINERALS

Industrial Production Indexes, by Industry

Source: Federal Reserve System

Major Industry Group	1970	1975	1980	1985	1986	1987	1988
Industrial production	79	85	109	124	125	134	137
Manufacturing.	77	83	100	126	129	135	143
Durable goods.	78	83	109	127	128	133	142
Lumber and products	81	81	93	113	124	130	137
Furniture and fixtures	75	80	109	140	144	153	162
Clay, glass, and stone products	76	83	102	116	118	119	123
Primary metals	95	88	90	81	75	81	89
Fabricated metal products . .	82	83	102	107	108	111	121
Nonelectrical machinery . . .	73	85	123	145	145	153	171
Electrical machinery	69	77	130	168	166	172	181
Transportation equipment. . .	75	81	97	121	128	129	132
Instruments.	60	81	122	139	140	144	154
Nondurable goods	76	85	107	125	130	137	144
Food.	82	90	111	130	134	138	143
Tobacco products	92	100	106	100	97	104	105
Textile mill products	81	85	101	103	109	116	116
Paper and products	81	85	111	128	137	144	150
Printing and publishing. . . .	82	84	115	154	161	172	184
Chemicals and products . . .	67	83	106	127	132	140	152
Petroleum products	80	87	94	87	93	94	96
Rubber and plastic products .	58	73	108	147	151	164	174
Leather and products	117	102	93	69	61	60	60
Mining	99	97	112	109	100	101	103
Utilities	81	94	107	112	109	110	114

1977 = 100.

Manufacturing Production Worker Statistics

Source: Bureau of Labor Statistics, U.S. Labor Department (p — preliminary)

Year	All employees	Production workers	Constant Dollars[1]	Avg. weekly earnings	Avg. hourly earnings	Avg. hrs. per wk.
1955	16,882,000	13,288,000	—	$75.30	$1.85	40.7
1960	16,796,000	12,586,000	183.5	89.72	2.26	39.7
1965	18,062,000	13,434,000	206.4	107.53	2.61	41.2
1970	19,367,000	14,044,000	208.0	133.33	3.35	39.8
1975	18,323,000	13,043,000	214.9	190.79	4.83	39.5
1980	20,285,000	14,214,000	212.0	288.62	7.27	39.7
1985	19,260,000	13,092,000	220.15	386.37	9.54	40.5
1987	19,024,000	12,970,000	220.10	406.31	9.91	41.0
1988	19,403,000	13,254,000	217.80	418.40	10.18	41.1
1989	19,612,000	13,375,000	—	429.27	10.47	41.0
1990[p] Jan.	19,231,000	13,018,000	—	429.95	10.59	40.6
July	19,289,000	13,068,000	—	440.64	10.88	40.5

(1) Earnings in current dollars divided by the Consumer Price Index on a 1977 basis.

International Manufacturing Productivity and Labor Costs

Source: Bureau of Labor Statistics, U.S. Labor Department (1982=100)

Output per hour

Country	1960	1965	1970	1975	1980	1985	1987	1988	1989
United States	56.9	70.2	75.2	86.9	95.3	115.9	124.7	127.6	130.1
Canada	51.6	66.1	76.9	90.1	99.9	119.8	119.2	121.2	123.8
Japan	17.2	25.9	48.0	65.0	90.9	119.4	130.7	136.9	144.8
France	30.7	41.4	58.5	72.7	90.6	108.8	113.8	119.6	125.1
West Germany	36.9	49.4	65.2	82.5	97.8	112.4	109.5	114.4	119.6
Italy	28.9	40.0	54.3	67.1	95.1	122.1	126.5	130.1	133.8
Norway	47.8	58.0	74.5	88.6	96.3	116.0	120.4	123.9	131.7
Sweden	36.5	50.4	69.6	86.4	96.4	112.6	115.7	117.4	119.3
United Kingdom	49.4	58.4	70.8	83.7	89.9	118.0	130.1	137.1	144.1

Unit Labor Costs in U.S. dollars

Country	1960	1965	1970	1975	1980	1985	1987	1988	1989
United States	39.5	37.5	47.7	61.6	87.8	95.9	95.6	96.8	99.0
Canada	40.6	34.4	44.1	63.6	83.1	88.2	98.6	109.7	121.6
Japan	26.2	32.5	36.2	79.6	107.3	97.0	156.9	172.7	161.8
France	32.2	37.4	36.2	78.8	125.2	87.7	137.2	137.3	128.2
West Germany	21.7	27.2	35.8	74.1	123.6	84.5	154.1	157.1	146.8
Italy	29.6	37.6	46.2	90.2	116.8	87.7	137.6	140.3	143.4
Norway	18.7	23.2	29.8	69.2	110.2	85.7	131.8	140.5	130.0
Sweden	31.0	36.6	42.5	86.9	130.2	84.9	129.7	142.1	147.4
United Kingdom	23.4	27.0	28.7	54.9	118.1	77.1	101.3	110.9	106.9

NOTE: The data relate to all employed persons (wage & salary, the self-employed, and unpaid family workers) in the U.S. and Canada, and all employees (wage & salary earners) in the other countries.

Sales and Profits of Manufacturing Corporations by Industry Group

Source: Bureau of the Census—Economic Surveys Division

(millions of dollars)

Industry group	Sales 1Q 1989	Sales 4Q 1989	Sales 1Q 1990	Income after taxes 1Q 1989	Income after taxes 4Q 1989	Income after taxes 1Q 1990
All manufacturing corporations	665,974	690,248	667,193	37,851	28,645	27,766
Nondurable manufacturing corporations	334,317	350,541	343,382	21,911	19,821	16,100
Food and kindred products.	93,573	101,259	95,179	3,865	5,406	3,493
Textile mill products.	13,686	13,883	13,345	340	158	(47)
Paper and allied products	27,594	28,661	28,534	1,998	1,160	1,389
Printing and publishing	32,220	36,537	34,233	1,605	2,774	1,026
Chemicals and allied products	69,490	67,523	68,960	6,960	4,510	5,467
Industrial chemicals and synthetics.	28,892	25,978	26,592	3,006	1,120	1,687
Drugs	12,458	13,552	14,075	2,102	2,043	2,107
Petroleum and coal products	61,325	68,000	70,386	5,679	5,262	4,071
Rubber and miscellaneous plastics products. . . .	19,217	18,819	18,649	786	326	430
Other nondurable manufacturing corporations. . .	17,213	15,770	14,096	679	226	271
Durable manufacturing corporations	331,656	339,706	323,811	15,940	8,824	11,666
Stone, clay, and glass products	12,765	13,961	12,933	(26)	282	(6)
Primary metal industries	29,475	26,497	27,451	1,704	441	1,035
Iron and steel	14,306	12,821	13,356	475	163	316
Nonferrous metals	15,169	13,677	14,095	1,228	278	720
Fabricated metal products	36,960	34,836	34,617	1,629	781	1,369
Machinery, except electrical	59,524	65,674	61,672	2,550	2,505	2,378
Electrical and electronic equipment	53,447	57,605	51,961	2,364	2,508	2,053
Transportation equipment	87,991	87,110	82,397	5,221	370	2,684
Motor vehicles and equipment	58,637	52,186	48,855	3,950	(249)	1,345
Aircraft, guided missiles, and parts.	26,490	31,625	30,435	1,237	610	1,222
Instruments and related products	23,974	25,505	24,782	1,574	1,330	1,472
Other durable manufacturing corporations	27,520	28,518	27,998	925	607	681
All mining corporations*	8,603	9,929	9,822	486	314	693
All retail trade corporations*	132,746	173,025	NA	2,365	4,603	NA
All wholesale trade corporations*	165,367	183,743	187,513	1,857	1,260	1,530

*With assets over $50 million.

Annual Percent Change in Productivity and Related Data, 1979-1989

Source: Bureau of Labor Statistics. U.S. Labor Department

Item	1979	1980	1981	1982	1983	1984	1985	1986	1987	1988	1989
Business sector:											
Output per hour of all persons	1.1	−0.3	1.5	−0.7	2.4	2.6	2.0	2.3	1.2	1.7	1.1
Real compensation per hour[1]	−1.4	−2.6	−0.9	1.2	0.6	−0.2	0.8	3.3	0.2	0.6	0.6
Unit labor cost	11.1	10.9	7.7	8.3	1.4	1.5	2.3	2.8	2.6	3.0	4.4
Unit nonlabor payments. . . .	5.3	5.4	13.5	1.4	7.3	7.0	2.8	0.7	2.6	2.9	2.9
Implicit price deflator[2]	9.0	9.0	9.6	5.9	3.3	3.3	2.5	2.1	2.6	2.9	3.9
Nonfarm business sector:											
Output per hour of all persons	−1.5	−0.4	1.1	−0.9	3.0	2.1	1.3	2.0	1.1	2.0	0.9
Real compensation per hour[1]	−1.6	−2.6	−0.7	1.1	0.7	−0.4	0.5	3.2	−0.1	0.5	0.6
Unit labor cost	11.2	11.0	8.3	8.4	1.0	1.8	2.8	3.0	2.6	2.7	4.5
Unit nonlabor payments. . . .	4.5	7.1	12.7	2.2	8.7	5.5	3.6	0.9	2.7	2.7	2.5
Implicit price deflator[2]	8.9	9.7	9.7	6.3	3.5	3.0	3.0	2.3	2.6	2.7	3.8
Manufacturing:											
Output per hour of all persons	0.0	0.0	2.3	2.5	5.2	5.4	4.5	3.8	3.7	2.7	2.8
Real compensation per hour . .	−1.4	−1.6	−0.5	2.6	−0.7	−0.9	1.2	2.6	−1.0	−0.5	−0.5
Unit labor cost	9.7	11.7	7.3	6.2	−2.5	−1.9	0.3	0.7	−1.0	0.9	1.5

(1) Adjusted for changes in the CPI for all urban consumers; (2) Current dollar gross product divided by constant dollar gross product.

U.S. Reliance on Foreign Supplies of Minerals

Source: Bureau of Mines. U.S. Interior Department

Mineral	Percent imported in 1989	Major sources (1985-88)	Major uses
Columbium	100%	Brazil, Canada, Thailand	Steelmaking and aerospace alloys
Graphite	100	Mexico, China, Brazil, Madagascar	Metallurgical processes
Manganese	100	Gabon, S. Africa	Steelmaking
Mica (sheet)	100	India, Belgium, France, Japan	Electronic and electrical equipment
Strontium (Celestite)	100	Mexico, Spain, China	Television picture tubes, pyrotechnics
Bauxite and alumina	97	Australia, Guinea, Jamaica, Suriname	Aluminum production
Platinum group	95	South Africa, Britain, USSR	Catalytic converters for autos, electrical and electronic equipment
Fluorspar	91	Mexico, South Africa	Raw material for metallurgical and chemical industries
Diamonds (industrial)	90	South Africa, Britain, Ireland, Zaire	Machinery for grinding and cutting
Cobalt	86	Zaire, Zambia, Canada, Norway	Aerospace alloys
Tantalum	85	Thailand, Brazil, Australia, Canada	Electronic components
Chromium	79	South Africa, Zimbabwe, Turkey, Yugoslavia	Stainless steel
Tungsten	73	China, Bolivia, Germany, Canada	Lamp filaments
Tin	73	Brazil, Indonesia, Bolivia	Cans, electrical construction
Barite	71	China, Morocco, India	Oil drilling fluids
Potash	70	Canada, Israel, East Germany, USSR	Fertilizer
Zinc	69	Canada, Mexico, Peru, Spain	Construction and transportation materials
Nickel	65	Canada, Australia, Norway	Stainless steel and other alloys
Cadmium	62	Canada, Australia, Mexico, West Germany	Batteries, plating and coating of metals
Silver	NA	Canada, Mexico, Britain, Peru	Photography, electrical and electronic prods.

Minerals

Source: Bureau of Mines, U.S. Interior Department, as of mid-1990

Aluminum: the most abundant metal element in the Earth's crust. Bauxite is the main source of aluminum; convert to aluminum equivalent by multiplying by 0.211. Guinea and Australia have 46 percent of the world's reserves. Aluminum is used in the U.S. in packaging 31%, transportation 22% and building 19%.

Chromium: some 99 percent of the world's chromite is found in South Africa and Zimbabwe. The chemical and metallurgical industries use about 85% of the chromite consumed in the U.S.

Cobalt: used in superalloys for jet engines; chemicals (paint driers, catalysts, magnetic coatings); permanent magnets; and cemented carbides for cutting tools. Principal cobalt producing countries include Zaire, Zambia, and the USSR. The U.S. uses about one-third of total world consumption. Although its resources are relatively large, the U.S. has produced no cobalt since 1971; cobalt resources are low grade and production from these deposits is not economically feasible.

Columbium: used mostly as an additive in steel making and in superalloys. Brazil and Canada are the world's leading producers. There is no U.S. columbium mining industry.

Copper: main uses of copper in the U.S. are in nonelectrical building construction 15%, electrical and electronic products 72%, industrial machinery and equipment 6%, transportation 3%. The leading producer is Chile, followed by the U.S., USSR, Canada, Zambia, and Zaire. Principal mining states are Arizona, New Mexico, and Utah.

Gold: used in the U.S. in jewelry and arts 56%, industrial (mainly electronic) 36%, dental 8%. South Africa has about half of the world's resources; significant quantities are also present in the U.S., Canada, USSR, and Brazil. Gold mining in the U.S. takes place in nearly all of the western states and Alaska.

Iron ore: the source of primary iron for the world's iron and steel industries. Major iron ore producers include the USSR, Brazil, Australia, and China.

Lead: the U.S. is the world's largest producer and consumer of lead metal. Transportation accounted for the major end use in the U.S. with 71% used in batteries, gasoline additives, and other applications. Other uses include emergency power supply batteries, construction sheeting, sporting am-

munition and TV tubes. Other major mine producers include the USSR, Australia, and Canada.

Manganese: essential to iron and steel production. The U.S., Japan, and Western Europe are all nearly deficient in economically minable manganese. South Africa and the USSR have over 70% of the world's reserves.

Nickel: vital to stainless steel industry and played a key role in the development of the chemical and aerospace industries. Leading producers include the USSR, Canada, Japan and Australia.

Platinum-Group Metals: the platinum group comprises 6 closely related metals: platinum, palladium, rhodium, ruthenium, iridium, and osmium. They commonly occur together in nature and are among the scarcest of the metallic elements. They are consumed in the U.S. by the following industries: automotive 37%, electrical and electronic 25%, and chemical 11%. The USSR and South Africa have nearly all the world's reserves.

Silver: used in the following U.S. industries: photography; electrical and electronic products; sterlingware, electroplated ware, and jewelry. Silver is mined in more than 56 countries. Nevada produces over 30% of the U.S. silver.

Tantalum: a refractory metal with unique electrical, chemical, and physical properties used mostly in the U.S to produce electronic components tantalum capacitors. Thailand, Australia, Brazil and Canada are the leading producers. There is no U.S. tantalum mining industry.

Titanium: a metal which is mostly used in jet engines, airframes, and space and missile applications. It is produced in the USSR, Japan, and the western and central U.S., the United Kingdom, and China.

Vanadium: used as an alloying element in steel, as an alloying agent in aerospace titanium alloys, and as a catalyst in the production of sulfuric acid and maleic anhydride. The USSR and South Africa are the world's largest producers.

Zinc: used as protective coating on steel, as diecastings, as an alloying metal with copper to make brass, and as chemical compounds in rubber and paints. It is mined in over 50 countries with Canada the leading producer, followed by the USSR, Australia, Peru and China. In the U.S., mine production comes mostly from Tennessee, Missouri, New York and Alaska.

World Mineral Reserve Base

Source: Bureau of Mines, U.S. Interior Department

Mineral	Reserve Base[1]	Mineral	Reserve Base[1]
Aluminum	25,000 mln. metric tons[2]	Nickel	121,000 thousand short tons
Chromium	6,800 mln. metric tons	Platinum—	
Cobalt	8,340 thou. metric tons.	Group Metals	2,140 mln. troy oz.
Columbium	9,100 mln. lbs.	Silver	420,000 metric tons
Copper	570 mln. metric tons	Tantalum	76 mln. lbs.
Gold	1,510 mln. troy oz.	Titanium	320 mln. metric tons
Iron	210,000 mln. metric tons[3]	Vanadium	18,300 thousand short tons
Lead	125 mln. metric tons	Zinc	295 mln. metric tons
Manganese	3,900,000 thousand short tons		

(1) Includes demonstrated resources that are currently economic (reserves), marginally economic (marginal reserves), and some of those that are currently subeconomic. (2) Bauxite. (3) Crude ore.

U.S. Nonfuel Mineral Production—Leading States in 1988

Source: Bureau of Mines, U.S. Interior Department

State	Value (thousands)	Principal minerals
Arizona	$2,733,411	Copper, gold, sand and gravel.
California	2,708,768	Cement, boron minerals, sand and gravel (construction), stone (crushed).
Nevada	1,944,566	Gold, sand & gravel (construction), silver.
Michigan	1,587,561	Cement, sand & gravel, stone.
Texas	1,468,818	Cement, stone (crushed), sand and gravel (construction), salt.
Florida	1,391,881	Stone (crushed), cement, phosphate rock.
Georgia	1,373,825	Clays, stone (crushed).
Minnesota	1,267,499	Iron ore, sand and gravel (construction), stone (crushed).
Pennsylvania	1,042,493	Cement, stone (crushed), lime, sand and gravel (construction).
New Mexico	1,022,072	Potassium salts, copper.
Utah	1,014,847	Cement, lime, sand and gravel.
Missouri	967,949	Cement, lead, stone (crushed).
Ohio	737,252	Stone (crushed), sand and gravel (construction), salt, lime.

U.S. Nonfuel Mineral Production

Source: Bureau of Mines, U.S. Interior Department

Production as measured by mine shipments, sales, or marketable production (including consumption by producers)

Metals		1987 Quantity	1987 Value (thousands)	1988 Quantity	1988 Value (thousands)
Antimony (ore and concentrate)	short tons	W	W	W	W
Bauxite	metric tons, dried equivalent	576	$10,916	587,889	$10,566
Beryllium concentrates	short tons	—	—	5,851	6
Copper (recoverable content of ores, etc.)	metric tons	1,243,638	2,261,833	1,419,645	3,771,570
Gold (recoverable content of ores, etc.)	troy ounces	947,040	216,027	6,459,539	2,831,281
Iron ore, usable (includes byproduct material)	thousand metric tons	47,983	1,503,087	57,113	1,716,661
Iron oxide pigments, crude	short tons	42,773	3,598	43,774	3,815
Lead (recoverable content of ores, etc.)	metric tons	311,381	246,720	384,983	315,222
Magnesium metal	short tons	137,123	381,914	156,509	469,767
Manganiferous ore (5% to 35% Mn)	short tons, gross weight	W	W	W	W
Molybdenum (content of ore and concentrate)	thousand pounds	69,868	179,286	99,738	266,899
Nickel (content of ore and concentrate)	short tons	—	—	—	—
Silver (recoverable content of ores, etc.)	troy ounces	39,896	279,675	53,415,677	349,339
Tungsten ore and concentrate	metric tons	W	W	W	W
Zinc (recoverable content of ores, etc.)	metric tons	216,327	199,924	244,314	324,249
Combined value of antimony, mercury, platinum-group metals, rare-earth metal concentrates, tin, titanium concentrates (ilmenite and rutile), valadium zircon concentrate, and values indicated by symbol W		XX	139,596	XX	159,409
Total metals		XX	7,423,000	XX	10,219,000
Industrial Minerals (except fuels)					
Abrasive stones[1]	short tons	12,773	957	14,675	1,183
Asbestos	metric tons	50,600	17,198	W	W
Barite	thousand short tons	448	15,810	445	15,512
Boron minerals	do	1,385	475,092	1,267	429,667
Bromine	thousand pounds	335,000	107,000	360,000	144,000
Cement: Masonry	thousand short tons	3,680	259,926	3,574	243,941
Portland	do	74,868	3,646,561	74,074	3,575,906
Clays	short tons	47,657	1,202,284	49,069,375	1,400,820
Diatomite	thousand short tons	658	134,239	693	143,774
Emory	short tons	1,945	W	W	W
Feldspar	do	720,000	26,100	715,484	28,082
Fluorspar	do	68,839	11,725	W	W
Garnet (abrasive)	do	42,277	4,350	46,855	4,707
Gem stones		NA	21,389	NA	43,508
Gypsum	thousand short tons	15,612	106,977	16,390	109,205
Helium (crude)	million cubic feet	730	16,068	W	W
Helium (Grade A)	do	2,230	82,540	2,574	95,238
Iodine	lbs.	W	W	2,238,152	W
Lime	thousand short tons	15,733	786,125	17,293	828,007
Mica (scrap)	do	161	8,201	143	6,793
Peat	do	958	26,170	929	19,933
Perlite	do	533	16,494	576	17,652
Phosphate rock	metric tons	40,954	793,280	45,389,000	887,809
Potassium salts K²O equivalent	thousand metric tons,	1,485	195,700	1,427	240,300
Pumice	thousand short tons	392	4,493	389	4,129
Salt	do	36,493	684,170	37,997	680,174
Sand and gravel (construction)	do	895,200	3,002,500	923,400	3,126,000
Sand and gravel (industrial)	do	28,010	364,100	28,480	388,000
Sodium sulfate (natural)	do	382	33,086	398	31,377
Stone² (crushed)	do	1,200,100	5,248,600	1,247,800	5,558,000
Stone² (dimension)	short tons	1,183,849	190,153	1,189,333	196,289
Sulfur, Frasch process	thousand metric tons	3,610	386,834	4,341	430,814
Talc and pyrophyllite	short tons	1,281,789	28,782	1,376,560	29,444
Tripoli	do	114,926	975	110,152	864
Vermiculite	do	302,926	33,105	303,544	33,948
Combined value of aplite, asphalt (native), graphite, kyanite, lithium minerals, magnesite, marl (greensand), olivine, staurolite, wollastonite, calcium chloride (natural), and values indicated by symbol W		XX	374,832	XX	442,620
Total nonmetals		XX	18,894,000	XX	19,803,000
Grand total		XX	26,317,000	XX	30,022,000

(W) Withheld to avoid disclosing company proprietary data; included in "Combined value" figures. (XX) Not applicable. (NA) Not available.
(1) Grindstones, pulpstones, sharpening stones, excludes mill liners & grinding pebbles.
(2) Excludes abrasive stone, bituminous limestone and sandstone; all included elsewhere in table.

U.S. Pig Iron and Raw Steel Output

Source: American Iron and Steel Institute (net tons)

Year	Total pig iron	Raw steel	Year	Total pig iron	Raw steel
1940	46,071,666	66,982,686	1980	68,721,000	111,835,000
1945	53,223,169	79,701,648	1984	51,904,000	92,528,000
1950	64,586,907	96,836,075	1985	50,446,000	88,259,000
1955	76,857,417	117,036,085	1986	43,952,000	81,606,000
1960	66,480,648	99,281,601	1987	48,410,000	89,151,000
1965	88,184,901	131,461,601	1988	55,745,000	99,924,000
1970	91,435,000	131,514,000	1989	55,873,000	97,943,000
1975	101,208,000	116,642,000			

Steel figures include only that portion of the capacity and production of steel for castings used by foundries which were operated by companies producing steel ingots.

U.S. Copper, Lead, and Zinc Production

Source: Bureau of Mines. U.S. Interior Department

Year	Copper Quantity (metric tons)	Copper Value ($1,000)	Lead Quantity (metric tons)	Lead Value ($1,000)	Zinc Quantity (metric tons)	Zinc Value ($1,000)	Year	Copper Quantity (metric tons)	Copper Value ($1,000)	Lead Quantity (metric tons)	Lead Value ($1,000)	Zinc Quantity (metric tons)	Zinc Value ($1,000)
1950	827	379,122	390,839	113,078	565,516	167,000	1983	1,038	1,751,476	449,295	214,745	275,294	251,204
1960	1,037	733,706	223,774	57,722	395,013	112,365	1984	1,103	1,625,000	322,677	181,745	252,768	270,833
1965	1,226	957,028	273,196	93,959	554,429	178,284	1985	1,105	1,631,000	413,955	174,008	226,545	201,607
1970	1,560	1,984,484	518,698	178,609	484,560	163,650	1986	1,144	1,666,000	339,793	165,150	202,983	170,050
1975	1,282	1,814,763	563,783	267,230	425,792	366,097	1987	1,244	2,262,000	311,381	246,720	216,281	200,529
1980	1,181	2,666,931	550,366	515,189	317,103	261,671	1988	1,420	3,772,000	384,983	315,222	244,314	324,249

World Gold Production

(Troy Ounces)

Year	World prod.	South Africa	Africa Ghana	Africa Zaire	United States	North and South America Canada	North and South America Mexico	North and South America Colombia	Australia	China	Other Philippines	USSR
1972	44,843,374	29,245,273	724,051	140,724	1,449,943	2,078,567	146,061	188,137	754,866	—	606,730	—
1975	38,476,371	22,937,820	523,889	103,217	1,052,252	1,653,611	144,710	308,864	526,821	—	502,577	—
1977	38,906,145	22,501,886	480,884	80,418	1,100,347	1,733,609	212,709	257,070	624,270	—	558,554	—
1978	38,983,019	22,648,558	402,034	76,077	998,832	1,735,077	202,003	246,446	647,579	—	586,531	—
1979	38,768,978	22,617,179	362,000	69,992	964,390	1,644,265	190,364	269,369	596,910	—	535,166	—
1980	39,197,315	21,669,468	353,000	39,963	969,782	1,627,477	195,991	510,439	547,591	—	753,452	8,425,000
1982	43,082,814	21,355,111	331,000	62,233	1,465,686	2,081,230	214,349	472,674	866,815	1,800,000	834,439	8,550,000
1983	45,163,364	21,847,310	276,000	192,930	2,002,526	2,363,411	198,177	426,517	983,522	1,850,000	816,536	8,600,000
1984	46,929,444	21,860,933	287,000	117,115	2,084,615	2,682,786	270,998	736,670	1,295,963	1,900,000	827,149	8,650,000
1985	49,283,691	21,565,230	299,363	63,022	2,427,232	2,815,118	265,693	1,142,385	1,881,491	1,950,000	1,062,997	8,700,000
1986	51,534,056	20,513,665	287,127	167,827	3,739,015	3,364,700	250,615	1,285,878	2,413,842	2,100,000	1,296,400	8,850,000
1987	53,033,614	19,176,500	327,598	140,561	4,947,040	3,724,000	256,822	853,600	3,558,954	2,300,000	1,048,081	8,850,000
1988[e]	58,453,814	19,881,126	372,979	140,000	6,459,539	4,110,000	296,689	933,000	4,887,000	2,500,000	1,134,920	9,000,000
1989[p]	63,369,158	19,386,892	429,469	112,528	8,537,329	5,093,957	266,851	870,963	6,523,377	2,550,000	1,125,275	9,150,000

(e) estimated (p) preliminary

U.S. and World Silver Production

Source: Bureau of Mines. U.S. Interior Department

(metric tons)

Largest production of silver in the United States in 1915—2,332 metric tons.

Year	United States	World	Year	United States	World	Year	United States	World
1930 ..	1,578	7,736	1960 ..	1,120	7,505	1985 ..	1,227	13,051
1935 ..	1,428	6,865	1965 ..	1,238	8,007	1986 ..	1,074	12,970
1940 ..	2,164	8,565	1970 ..	1,400	9,670	1987 ..	1,241	13,757
1945 ..	904	5,039	1975 ..	1,087	9,428	1988[p] ..	1,661	14,167
1950 ..	1,347	6,323	1980 ..	1,006	10,556	1989[e] ..	2,007	14,452
1955 ..	1,134	6,967						

(p) preliminary. (e) estimate.

Aluminum Summary, 1980 to 1988

Source: Bureau of Mines. U.S. Interior Department

Item	Unit	1980	1983	1984	1985	1986	1987	1988
U.S. production	1,000 metric ton . .	5,914	4,917	5,859	5,262	4,810	5,329	6,066
Primary aluminum	1,000 metric ton . .	4,654	3,353	4,099	3,500	3,037	3,343	3,944
Plant capacity, U.S.	1,000 metric ton . .	(NA)	5,001	(NA)	4,706	4,038	3,895	3,960
Secondary aluminum[1]	1,000 metric ton . .	1,260	1,564	1,760	1,762	1,773	1,986	2,122
Primary aluminum	Bil. dol	7.3	5.8	7.3	6.3	5.4	5.3	9.6
Price (Primary alum.)[2]	Cents/lb	71.6	77.8	81.0	81.0	81.0[5]	72.3[6]	110.1[6]
Imports for consumption[3] . . .	1,000 metric ton . .	647	1,091	1,477	1,420	1,967	1,850	1,620
Exports[3]	1,000 metric ton . .	1,346	776	734	908	753	917	1,247
World production, est.	1,000 metric ton . .	15,383	13,904	15,705	15,398	15,354	16,378	17,304
World plant capacity	1,000 metric ton . .	16,978	17,737	18,215	18,010	17,855	17,968	18,480

(1) Recoverable aluminum content from scrap, old and new; (2) Average prices for primary aluminum, quoted by *Metals Week*; (3) Crude and semicrude (including metal and alloys, plates, bars, etc., and scrap).

TRADE AND TRANSPORTATION

U.S. Foreign Trade with Leading Countries

Source: Office of Industry and Trade Information. U.S. Commerce Department
(millions of dollars)

Exports from the U.S. to the following areas and countries and imports into the U.S. from those areas and countries:	Exports 1980	Exports 1988	Exports 1989	Imports 1980	Imports 1988	Imports 1989
Total	220,705	320,385	363,812	240,834	459,925	473,211
Western Hemisphere	74,114	113,155	NA	78,489	135,135	NA
Canada	35,395	69,233	78,809	41,455	81,434	87,953
20 Latin American Republics	36,030	40,077	44,396	29,851	51,194	54,816
Central American Common Market	1,951	2,254	2,580	1,849	2,154	2,277
Dominican Republic	795	1,362	1,645	786	1,479	1,646
Panama	699	633	724	330	297	268
Bahamas	396	741	772	1,382	426	462
Jamaica	305	758	1,006	383	472	509
Netherlands Antilles	448	432	412	2,564	440	383
Trinidad and Tobago	680	328	563	2,378	773	768
Western Europe	71,372	87,995	100,165	47,849	105,035	101,764
OECD countries (excludes depend. and Yugo.)	66,654	87,236	99,456	45,952	103,996	100,859
European Economic Community	53,679	75,926	86,331	35,958	88,748	85,153
Belgium and Luxembourg	6,661	7,405	8,522	1,914	4,719	4,555
Denmark	863	970	1,051	725	1,756	1,535
France	7,485	10,086	11,579	5,247	12,689	13,014
Germany, Federal Republic of	10,960	14,331	16,862	11,681	27,421	24,833
Greece	922	649	697	292	569	473
Ireland	836	2,182	2,483	411	1,425	1,566
Italy	5,511	6,782	7,215	4,313	12,277	11,933
Netherlands	8,669	10,095	11,364	1,910	4,874	4,810
Portugal	911	752	925	256	738	800
Spain	3,179	4,217	4,796	1,209	3,470	3,317
United Kingdom	12,694	18,404	20,837	9,755	18,740	18,319
Austria	448	748	873	388	1,137	1,136
Finland	505	763	969	439	1,297	1,370
Iceland	79	98	179	200	200	208
Norway	843	932	1,037	2,632	1,561	1,991
Sweden	1,767	2,705	3,139	1,617	5,217	4,892
Switzerland	3,781	4,207	4,911	2,787	4,745	4,714
Turkey	540	1,843	2,003	175	1,071	1,372
Yugoslavia	756	534	499	446	925	799
Eastern Europe	3,860	3,650	5,307	1,433	2,385	2,064
USSR	1,513	2,768	4,284	453	649	709
Asia	60,168	99,705	NA	78,848	200,360	NA
Near East	11,900	10,857	11,126	17,280	12,483	15,120
Iran	23	73	55	339	9	9
Iraq	724	1,156	1,169	352	1,605	2,415
Israel	2,045	3,248	2,827	943	3,068	3,239
Jordan	407	373	380	3	13	8
Kuwait	886	690	853	472	507	973
Lebanon	303	123	94	33	42	30
Saudi Arabia	5,769	3,799	3,574	12,509	6,237	7,157
Syria	239	89	91	26	42	98
Japan	20,790	37,732	44,493	30,701	93,168	93,553
East and South Asia	27,478	46,061	NA	30,867	85,438	NA
Bangladesh	292	258	282	85	413	428
China, People's Republic of	3,755	5,039	5,755	1,054	9,270	11,990
China (Taiwan)	4,337	12,131	11,335	6,850	26,256	24,313
Hong Kong	2,686	5,691	6,291	4,736	10,810	9,722
India	1,689	2,498	2,458	1,098	3,167	3,315
Indonesia	1,545	1,056	1,248	5,183	3,494	3,529
Korea, Republic of	4,685	11,290	13,459	4,147	21,209	19,737
Malaysia	1,337	2,139	2,870	2,577	3,853	4,744
Pakistan	642	1,093	1,134	733	498	523
Philippines	1,999	1,880	2,202	1,730	2,906	3,068
Singapore	3,033	5,770	7,345	1,920	8,226	9,003
Thailand	1,263	1,964	2,288	816	3,424	4,380
Oceania	4,876	8,242	NA	3,392	5,299	NA
Australia	4,093	6,981	8,331	2,509	3,856	3,873
New Zealand and Samoa	599	946	1,121	703	1,306	1,212
Africa	9,060	7,431	6,044	32,251	11,710	12,626
Algeria	542	733	756	6,577	1,972	1,829
Botswana	...	41	30	...	9	17
Egypt	1,874	2,340	2,612	458	243	227
Gabon	48	56	46	278	199	437
Ghana	127	117	121	206	210	127
Ivory Coast	185	75	79	288	313	234
Kenya	141	92	133	54	69	68
Liberia	113	68	98	128	116	106
Libya	509	(z)	(2)	7,124	.1	.1
Morocco	344	428	394	35	102	98
Nigeria	1,150	356	490	10,905	3,536	5,284
South Africa, Rep. of	2,464	1,690	1,659	3,321	1,589	1,531
Sudan	143	109	81	17	24	20
Tunisia	174	185	160	60	46	55
Zaire	155	125	122	361	384	330

(z) = Less than one-half of rounded unit. NA = not available.

U.S. Exports and Imports of Leading Commodities

Source: Office of Industry and Trade Information. U.S. Commerce Department (millions of dollars)

Commodity	Exports 1980	Exports 1987	Exports 1988	Imports 1980	Imports 1987	Imports 1988
Food and live animals	27,744	19,179	26,415	15,763	20,547	20,107
Cattle, except for breeding	...	...	...	228	417	595
Meat and preparations	1,293	1,768	2,430	2,346	2,786	2,738
Dairy products and eggs	255	385	496	318	442	402
Fish	915	1,588	2,177	2,612	4,788	5,327
Grains and preparations	18,079	8,058	12,281	...	...	...
Wheat, including flour	6,586	3,248	5,080	...	...	...
Rice	1,285	576	802	...	...	...
Grains and Animal feed	2,878	3,907	6,064	331	815	1,011
Vegetables and Fruit	...	2,956	3,488	1,188	4,476	4,662
Sugar	...	...	...	1,988	438	436
Coffee, crude	...	...	...	3,872	2,706	2,289
Cocoa or cacao beans	...	...	...	395	504	405
Tea	...	...	...	131	106	130
Beverages and tobacco	2,663	3,667	4,548	2,772	4,105	4,139
Alcoholic beverages	...	...	...	2,220	3,268	3,414
Tobacco, unmanufactured	2,390	1,091	1,252	422	588	448
Crude materials, inedible, except fuels	23,791	20,416	25,135	10,496	11,528	13,398
Hides and skins	694	1,450	1,639	88	82	102
Oilseeds, oil nuts, oil kernels	5,883	4,343	4,816	...	58	94
Synthetic rubber and rubber latex	695	761	858	...	...	...
Lumber and rough wood	2,675	3,007	4,086	2,134	3,341	3,179
Wood pulp and pulpwood	2,454	3,084	4,002	1,725	2,110	2,663
Textile fibers and wastes	2,864	1,631	1,975	242	438	524
Ores and metal scrap	4,518	3,018	4,279	3,696	2,446	3,264
Mineral fuels and related materials	7,982	7,713	8,186	9,058	44,220	41,088
Coal	4,523	6,740	8,054	...	...	...
Petroleum and products	2,833	3,922	3,679	73,771	41,529	38,175
Natural gas	...	...	...	5,155	2,504	2,577
Animal and vegetable oils and fats	1,946	981	945	533	568	849
Chemicals	20,740	26,381	32,300	8,583	16,213	19,876
Medicines and pharmaceuticals	1,932	3,782	3,941	508	1,456	1,859
Fertilizers, manufactured	2,265	2,259	2,497	1,104	795	1,021
Plastic materials and resins	3,884	5,493	7,277	...	...	...
Machinery and transport equip.	84,629	108,596	135,135	60,546	177,809	197,053
Machinery	55,790	69,637	88,432	31,904	99,433	117,281
Aircraft engines and parts	1,915	4,390	5,502	...	4,475	5,168
Auto engines and parts	1,688	2,406	3,812	...	...	...
Agricultural machinery	3,104	1,493	1,956	682	1,836	2,123
Tractors and parts	1,809	625	885	...	391	1,189
Office machines and computers	8,709	18,692	23,128	2,929	18,462	22,601
Transport equipment	28,839	38,959	46,703	28,642	57,024	79,772
Road motor vehicles and parts	14,590	20,879	8,312	24,134	61,598	71,346
Aircraft and parts except engines	12,816	16,903	20,004	1,885	4,475	5,168
Other manufactured goods	42,714	19,409	22,885	55,900	118,539	132,101
Tires and tubes	511	514	772	1,143	2,271	2,448
Wood and manufactures, exc. furniture	2,675	...	...	632	...	...
Paper and manufactures	2,831	3,180	313	3,587	7,310	8,336
Glassware and pottery	...	...	...	1,224	2,871	2,975
Diamonds, excl. industrial	...	...	...	2,252	3,423	4,306
Nonmetallic mineral manuf.	2,209	2,289	2,861	...	...	...
Metal manufactures	4,205	3,534	...	8,053	...	11,415
Pig iron and ferroalloys	3,123	...	2,173	...	...	...
Iron and steel-mill products	2,998	1,229	2,017	6,686	8,490	10,274
Nonferrous base metals	2,964	1,853	...	7,623	7,991	10,302
Textiles, other than clothing	3,632	677	709	2,493	6,511	6,373
Clothing	1,203	1,156	1,574	6,427	20,491	21,518
Footwear	...	...	...	2,808	7,237	8,041
Furniture	521	624	837	...	...	...
Professional, scientific, controlling instruments	6,763	7,388	8,890	...	4,509	5,173
Printed matter	1,097	1,562	1,918	613	1,494	1,581
Clocks and watches	133	93	125	1,097	1,702	1,909
Toys, games, sporting goods	1,012	885	1,272	1,914	5,987	6,719
Artworks and antiques	...	...	...	2,672	1,925	2,044
Other transactions	8,496	20,381	27,483	7,183	12,672	12,672
Total	220,705	252,856	306,014	240,834	405,901	441,282

U.S. Exports and General Imports by Principal Commodity Groupings, 1989

Source: Office of Industry and Trade Information, U.S. Commerce Department

(in millions of dollars, not seasonally adjusted)

Item	Exports	Imports	Item	Exports	Imports
Total	363,811.5	473,210.8	Paper/paperboard/ and articles	4,585.5	8,491.8
Agricultural commodities	41,319.4	22,035.3	Photographic apparatus/supplies	2,535.0	3,435.6
Animal feeds	3,081.1	279.0	Power generating machinery	15,348.7	14,257.1
Cereal flour; and flour preparations	694.5	558.1	Printed matter	3,002.2	1,617.8
Cocoa	22.0	732.0	Plastic articles, n.e.s.	1,700.0	2,998.6
Coffee	12.7	2,273.5	Rubber articles, n.e.s.	670.5	912.5
Corn	6,734.2	55.1	Scientific instruments and parts	11,488.6	5,848.9
Cotton, raw	2,244.1	3.3	Specialized industrial machinery	14,351.9	12,839.4
Dairy products; eggs	446.5	440.9	Telecommunications apparatus; equipment; and parts	8,131.7	23,233.8
Grain sorghum; rye; oats	1,045.2	162.6	Textile yarns, fabrics, and articles	4,301.7	6,087.1
Hides and skins, undressed	1,576.6	97.9	Tires and tubes—automotive	819.1	2,383.8
Meat and preparations	2,963.8	2,560.0	Toys/games/sporting goods	1,630.9	8,396.1
Oils/fats, vegetable	739.6	655.5	Travel goods	114.0	2,127.6
Rice	981.4	61.9	Vehicles and parts:		
Soybeans	4,011.5	23.9	Cars, new Canadian	6,823.7	12,870.6
Sugar	3.3	605.3	Cars, new Japanese	326.8	19,912.2
Tobacco, unmanufactured	1,339.9	667.6	Cars, new other countries	2,274.2	11,370.7
Vegetables and fruit	4,530.4	4,908.6	Trucks	2,842.8	8,807.2
Wheat	5,907.1	57.5	Chassis/bodies	207.3	1,095.0
Other agricultural	41,319.4	22,035.3	Parts	13,224.8	15,248.3
Manufactured goods	272,166.4	379,425.4	Vessels/floating structures/parts	1,050.2	578.7
ADP equipment; office machinery	23,992.2	25,714.5	Watches/clocks/parts	177.3	907.7
Airplanes	14,432.6	2,947.8	Wood manufacturers	1,064.9	2,028.7
Airplane parts	8,791.6	2,929.1	Other manufactured goods	18,187.7	28,202.8
Aluminum	2,988.2	3,143.5	Petroleum and petroleum products	5,021.1	49,704.2
Artwork/antiques	1,653.0	2,172.2	Crude petroleum	205.4	35,529.2
Chemicals-dyeing tanning	1,248.9	1,131.0	Other petroleum products	4,185.6	14,175.0
Chemicals-fertilizers	2,707.8	1,003.2	Mineral fuels, excluding petroleum products	4,658.9	2,553.5
Chemicals-medicinal pharmaceutical	3,692.5	2,087.6	Coal	4,087.1	84.1
Chemicals-organic/inorganic	14,710.4	10,248.3	Natural gas	215.5	1,849.7
Chemicals-perfume materials; polishing and cleaning preparations	1,553.5	1,157.6	Crude materials excluding agricultural and fuels	16,390.6	11,562.1
Chemicals-plastic	8,559.1	3,308.9	Cork, wood, lumber	5,203.5	3,499.4
Chemicals-turpentine; waxes and products, n.s.p.f.	4,884.3	1,777.1	Pulp & waste paper	4,394.5	3,050.4
Clothing and footwear	2,530.5	32,931.2	Metal ores; scrap	5,520.9	3,866.4
Electrical machinery	25,409.3	32,373.0	Other crude material	1,271.6	1,145.8
Fixtures-plumbing, heating/lighting	623.7	1,159.5	Fish and preparations	3,296.2	5,388.8
Furniture and parts	1,294.8	4,907.9	Fish—fresh; chilled; frozen	1,436.8	2,132.2
Gem diamonds	1,097.6	4,347.3	Beverages; tobacco excl. agricultural	3,954.9	1,906.1
General industrial machinery	15,034.5	14,486.9	Cigarettes	3,362.4	49.3
Glass	979.0	788.8	Distilled alcoholic beverages	222.4	1,587.7
Iron and steel mill products	3,599.2	9,392.7	Other beverages; tobacco excluding agricultural	370.1	269.1
Metal manufacturers, n.s.p.f.	4,494.4	6,371.6	All other domestic exports and general imports	1,429.9	114.2
Metalworking machinery	2,738.5	3,867.9			
Motorcycles/parts, bicycles/trailers	729.2	1,552.5			
Musical instruments/recording media	2,957.2	2,446.5			

Note: Details may not equal totals due to rounding and other statistical procedures.

Value of U.S. Exports, Imports, and Merchandise Balance

Source: Office of Trade and Investment Analysis, U.S. Dept. of Commerce

(millions of dollars)

Year	Principal Census trade totals					Other Census totals		
	U.S. exports and reexports excluding military grant-aid	U.S. general imports f.a.s. transaction values[1]	U.S. merchandise balance f.a.s.[1]	U.S. general imports c.i.f.	U.S. balance exports f.a.s. imports c.i.f.	Military grant-aid shipments	Exports of domestic merchandise	Re-exports
1950	9,997	8,954	1,043	—	—	282	10,146	133
1955	14,298	11,566	2,732	—	—	1,256	15,426	128
1960	19,659	15,073	4,586	—	—	949	20,408	201
1965	26,742	21,520	5,222	—	—	779	27,178	343
1970	42,681	40,356	2,325	42,833	-152	565	42,612	634
1975	107,652	98,503	9,149	105,935	1,716	461	106,622	1,490
1980	220,626	244,871	-24,245	256,984	-36,358	156	216,668	4,115
1985	213,133	345,276[2]	-132,143	361,626	-148,493	13	206,925	6,221
1987	252,853[3]	405,910[2]	-153,035	424,082	-171,223	13	243,859	9,007
1988	322,418	440,952	-118,534	459,542	-137,124	8	310,049	12,377
1989	363,805	473,211	-109,405	493,196	-129,391	6	347,527	16,285

Note: Export values include both commercially-financed shipments and shipments under government-financed programs such as AID and PL-480. (1) Prior to 1974, imports are customs values, i.e. generally at prices in principal foreign markets. (2) In 1981 import value changes back to customs value. (3) Includes undocumented exports to Canada.

Major Merchant Fleets of the World

Source: Maritime Administration. U.S. Commerce Department

Fleets of oceangoing steam and motor ships totalling 1 million gross tons and over as of Jan. 1, 1990. Excludes ships operating exclusively on the Great Lakes and inland waterways and special types such as channel ships, icebreakers, cable ships, etc., and merchant ships owned by any military force. Gross tonnage is a volume measurement; each cargo gross ton represents 100 cubic ft. of enclosed space. Deadweight tonnage is the carrying capacity of a ship in long tons (2,240 lbs.). Tonnage figures may not add, due to rounding.

(tonnage in thousands)

	Total			Type of Vessel Freighters			Bulk Carriers			Tankers		
	Number	Gross Tons	Dwt. Tons	Number	Gross Tons	Dwt. Tons	Number	Gross Tons	Dwt. Tons	Number	Gross Tons	Dwt. Tons
All Countries[1]	22,983	366,764	604,489	12,195	94,780	118,060	5,335	131,135	233,139	5,133	137,129	251,923
United States[2]	655	16,265	24,417	371	6,643	7,237	26	739	1,270	239	8,604	15,754
Privately owned	407	13,096	20,439	171	4,360	4,439	26	739	1,270	206	7,903	14,693
Government owned	248	3,169	3,978	200	2,283	2,798	—	—	—	33	701	1,061
Brazil	293	5,766	9,755	114	827	1,127	94	2,930	5,071	83	2,007	3,555
British Colonies	545	14,046	24,810	252	1,913	2,444	176	5,548	9,810	111	6,551	12,542
* China	1,281	12,747	19,611	860	6,140	8,664	240	4,735	8,098	168	1,745	2,778
Cyprus	1,054	16,580	29,729	537	3,326	5,082	410	8,750	15,742	104	4,482	8,899
Denmark	199	4,100	6,288	136	1,683	1,799	9	281	505	54	2,136	3,984
Germany (Fed. Rep.)	310	3,125	3,954	244	2,409	2,918	10	242	356	50	408	646
Greece	914	19,799	36,537	238	1,902	2,781	442	9,941	18,365	203	7,722	15,285
India	296	5,885	9,843	112	1,138	1,705	118	2,977	5,101	63	1,755	3,030
Indonesia	323	1,394	2,219	217	703	1,098	13	144	213	86	540	897
Italy	479	6,437	10,514	181	1,134	1,381	67	2,418	4,334	222	2,704	4,737
Japan	1,007	23,285	36,237	411	4,459	3,575	287	10,063	18,468	295	8,635	14,144
Korea (Rep. of)	429	7,244	11,909	211	1,677	1,883	154	4,673	8,415	64	694	1,611
Liberia	1,409	47,711	88,275	311	4,236	4,843	511	14,867	27,989	574	28,299	55,366
Malta	293	3,601	6,257	144	754	1,196	79	1,398	2,441	68	1,430	2,614
Nassau, Bahamas	530	11,723	19,719	225	1,680	2,233	114	2,934	5,020	159	6,532	12,322
Netherlands	326	2,697	3,638	256	1,663	2,149	13	263	436	53	662	1,035
Norway	587	15,991	28,800	138	1,148	1,441	177	5,494	10,299	261	9,117	17,009
Panama	3,189	44,051	70,537	1,707	13,858	17,164	854	18,151	31,817	590	11,565	21,340
Philippines	558	8,891	14,948	225	1,394	1,753	285	7,102	12,479	38	352	691
Poland	245	3,020	4,258	143	1,248	1,408	92	1,607	2,593	7	145	247
* Romania	304	3,698	5,789	220	1,241	1,647	70	1,807	2,993	14	650	1,149
Singapore	407	7,048	11,494	216	2,345	2,997	70	1,891	3,391	121	2,812	5,106
Spain	301	2,885	5,492	178	438	694	43	799	1,477	80	1,648	3,321
Sweden	162	1,824	2,246	80	921	904	17	327	522	61	509	800
Taiwan	226	5,274	7,985	147	2,375	2,804	63	2,352	4,212	15	545	969
Turkey	317	2,904	5,061	202	715	1,099	58	1,416	2,553	53	754	1,402
United Kingdom	198	3,761	4,708	89	1,569	1,578	29	684	1,200	68	1,243	1,854
* U.S.S.R.	2,428	18,917	25,735	1,732	9,621	11,543	244	4,395	7,060	420	4,625	7,061
Yugoslavia	272	3,704	5,943	167	1,380	1,954	90	1,990	3,451	12	317	533

(1) Includes Combination Passenger & Cargo Ships; (2) Excludes non-merchant type and/or Navy-owned vessels that are currently in the Nat. Reserve Fleet. *Source material limited.

Top 50 U.S. Industrial Exporters

Source: FORTUNE Magazine. July 16, 1990

Rank 1989	1988	Company	Export sales $ Millions	% change 1988-89	Exports as % of Sales
1	3	Boeing	11,021.0	40.4	54.4
2	1	General Motors	10,185.1	8.4	8.0
3	2	Ford Motor	8,602.0	-2.5	8.9
4	4	General Electric	7,268.0	26.5	13.2
5	5	Int'l Business Machines	5,476.0	10.6	8.6
6	7	E.I. Du Pont De Nemours	4,844.0	15.4	13.8
7	6	Chrysler	4,649.0	7.0	12.9
8	10	United Technologies	3,307.4	16.1	16.7
9	9	Caterpillar	3,291.0	12.3	29.6
10	8	McDonnell Douglas	2,896.0	-16.6	19.3
11	11	Eastman Kodak	2,874.0	3.7	15.6
12	13	Hewlett-Packard	2,634.0	27.6	22.1
13	14	Unisys	2,400.1	2.0	23.8
14	16	Motorola	2,319.0	33.1	24.1
15	15	Philip Morris	2,288.0	22.8	5.9
16	12	Digital Equipment	2,103.3	4.2	16.3
17	17	Occidental Petroleum	1,995.0	18.5	9.9
18	19	Allied-Signal	1,692.0	15.6	14.1
19	20	Weyerhaeuser	1,574.0	12.6	15.6
20	21	Union Carbide	1,561.0	12.5	17.9
21	18	General Dynamics	1,522.1	-4.7	15.1
22	22	Raytheon	1,340.0	2.5	15.2
23	23	Textron	1,210.0	7.4	16.3
24	26	Archer Daniels Midland	1,208.5	11.1	15.0
25	25	Dow Chemical	1,157.0	4.3	6.5
26	24	Westinghouse Electric	1,131.0	1.4	8.8
27	28	International Paper	1,100.0	10.0	9.7
28	27	Monsanto	1,070.0	-1.2	12.3
29	29	Hoechst Celanese	1,039.0	7.4	17.3
30	40	Merck	1,038.6	39.3	15.5
31	32	Minnesota Mining & Mfg.	1,019.0	21.9	8.5
32	30	Exxon	1,019.0	8.8	1.2
33	31	Intel	997.9	7.8	30.4
34	43	Aluminum Co. of America	935.0	20.8	8.4
35	41	Compaq Computer	896.1	46.5	31.2
36	39	Rockwell International	800.0	29.0	6.3
37	•	Xerox	770.0	93.0	4.4
38	33	Bayer USA	759.5	7.3	14.0
39	34	Lockheed	754.0	9.9	7.6
40	•	Sun Microsystems	751.0	99.3	42.4
41	38	Deere	742.0	19.3	10.3
42	42	Honeywell	718.0	17.7	9.9
43	44	North American Philips	693.6	17.9	11.2
44	48	Abbott Laboratories	685.0	25.2	12.6
45	46	Amoco	668.0	15.6	2.8
46	•	Tenneco	644.0	28.8	4.5
47	•	Bristol-Myers Squibb	638.0	N.A.	6.8
48	37	FMC	631.4	-2.5	18.2
49	49	Ethyl	592.7	9.2	21.5
50	•	Cooper Industries	571.5	27.8	11.1
		Total	$110,081.7		

Notable Ocean Passages by Ships
Compiled by N.R.P. Bonsor

Sailing Vessels

Date	Ship	From	To	Nautical miles	Time D. H. M	Speed (knots)
1846	Yorkshire	Liverpool	New York	3150	16. 0. 0	8.46†
1853	Northern Light	San Francisco	Boston	—	76. 6. 0	—
1854	James Baines	Boston Light	Light Rock	—	12. 6. 0	—
1854	Flying Cloud	New York	San Francisco	15091	89. 0. 0	7.07†
1868-9	Thermopylae	Liverpool	Melbourne	—	63.18.15	—
—	Red Jacket	New York	Liverpool	3150	13. 1.25	10.05†
—	Starr King	50 S. Lat	Golden Gate	—	36. 0. 0	—
—	Golden Fleece	Equator	San Francisco	—	12.12. 0	—
1905	Atlantic	Sandy Hook	England	3013	12. 4. 0	10.32

Atlantic Crossing by Passenger Steamships

Date	Ship		From	To	Nautical miles	Time D. H. M	Speed (knots)
1819 (5/22 - 6/20)	Savannah (a)	US	Savannah	Liverpool	—	29. 4. 0	—
1838 (5/7 - 5/22)	Great Western	Br	New York	Avonmouth	3218	14.15.59	9.14
1840 (8/4 - 8/14)	Britannia (b)	Br	Halifax	Liverpool	2610	9.21.44	10.98†
1854 (6/28 - 7/7)	Baltic	US	Liverpool	New York	3037	9.16.52	13.04
1856 (8/6 - 8/15)	Persia	Br	Sandy Hook	Liverpool	3046	8.23.19	14.15†
1876 (12/16-12/24)	Britannic	Br	Sandy Hook	Queenstown	2882	7.12.41	15.94
1895 (5/18 - 5/24)	Lucania	Br	Sandy Hook	Queenstown	2897	5.11.40	22.00
1898 (3/30 - 4/5)	Kaiser Wilhelm der Grosse	Ger	Needles	Sandy Hook	3120	5.20. 0	22.29
1901 (7/10 - 7/17)	Deutschland	Ger	Sandy Hook	Eddystone	3082	5.11. 5	23.51
1907 (10/6 - 10/10)	Lusitania	Br	Queenstown	Sandy Hook	2780	4.19.52	23.99
1924 (8/20 - 8/25)	Mauretania	Br	Ambrose	Cherbourg	3198	5. 1.49	26.25
1929 (7/17 - 7/22)	Bremen*	Ger	Cherbourg	Ambrose	3164	4.17.42	27.83
1933 (6/27 - 7/2)	Europa	Ger	Cherbourg	Ambrose	3149	4.16.48	27.92
1933 (8/11 - 8/16)	Rex	It	Gibraltar	Ambrose	3181	4.13.58	28.92
1935 (5/30 - 6/3)	Normandie*	Fr	Bishop Rock	Ambrose	2971	4. 3. 2	29.98
1938 (8/10 - 8/14)	Queen Mary	Br	Ambrose	Bishop Rock	2938	3.20.42	31.69
1952 (7/11 - 7/15)	United States	US	Bishop Rock	Ambrose	2906	3.12.12	34.51
1952 (7/3 - 7/7)	United States* (e)	US	Ambrose	Bishop Rock	2942	3.10.40	35.59

Other Ocean Passages

Date	Ship	From	To	Nautical miles	Time D. H. M	Speed (knots)
1928 (June)	USS Lexington	San Pedro	Honolulu	2226	3. 0.36	30.66
1944 (Jul-Sep)	St. Roch (c) (Can)	Halifax	Vancouver	7295	86. 0. 0	—
1945 (7/16-7/19)	USS Indianapolis (d)	San Francisco	Oahu, Hawaii	2091	3. 2.20	28.07
1945 (11/26)	USS Lake Champlain	Gibraltar	Newport News	3360	4. 8.51	32.04
1950 (Jul-Aug)	USS Boxer	Japan	San Francisco	5000	7.18.36	26.80†
1951 (6/1-6/9)	USS Philippine Sea	Yokohama	Alameda	5000	7.13. 0	27.62†
1958 (2/25-3/4)	USS Skate (f)	Nantucket	Portland, Eng	3161	8.11. 0	15.57
1958 (3/23-3/29)	USS Skate (f)	Lizard, Eng	Nantucket	—	7. 5. 0	—
1958 (7/23-8/7)	USS Nautilus (g)	Pearl Harbor	Iceland (via N. Pole)	—	15. 0. 0	—
1960 (2/16-5/10)	USS Triton (h)	New London	Rehobeth, Del	41500	84. 0. 0	20.59†
1960 (8/15-8/20)	USS Seadragon (i)	Baffin Bay	NW Passage, Pac	850	6. 0. 0	—
1962 (10/30-11/11)	African Comet* (U.S.)	New York	Cape Town	6786	12.16.22	22.03
1973 (8/20)	Sea-Land Exchange (k) (U.S.)	Bishop Rock	Ambrose	2912	3.11.24	34.92
1973 (8/24)	Sea-Land Trade (U.S.)	Kobe	Race Rock, BC	4126	5. 6. 0	32.75

† The time taken and/or distance covered is approximate and so, therefore, is the average speed.
* Maiden voyage. (a) The Savannah, a fully rigged sailing vessel with steam auxiliary (over 300 tons, 98.5 ft. long, beam 25.8 ft., depth 12.9 ft.) was launched in the East River in 1818. It was the first ship to use steam in crossing any ocean. It was supplied with engines and detachable iron paddle wheels. On its famous voyage it used steam 105 hours. (b) First Cunard liner. (c) First ship to complete NW Passage in one season. (d) Carried Hiroshima atomic bomb in World War II. (e) Set world speed record; average speed eastbound on maiden voyage 35.59 knots (about 41 m.p.h.). (f) First atomic submarine to cross Atlantic both ways submerged. (g) World's first atomic submarine also first to make undersea voyage under polar ice cap, 1,830 mi. from Point Barrow, Alaska, to Atlantic Ocean, Aug. 1-4, 1958, reaching North Pole Aug. 3. Second undersea transit of the North Pole made by submarine USS Skate Aug. 11, 1958, during trip from New London, Conn., and return. (h) World's largest submarine. Nuclear-powered Triton was submerged during nearly all its voyage around the globe. It duplicated the route of Ferdinand Magellan's circuit (1519-1522) 30,708 mi., starting from St. Paul Rocks off the NE coast of Brazil, Feb. 24-Apr. 25, 1960, then sailed to Cadiz, Spain, before returning home. (i) First underwater transit of Northwest Passage. (k) Fastest freighter crossing of Atlantic.

Commerce at Principal U.S. Ports
Source: Corps of Engineers, Department of the Army (by tonnage, 1990)

	Total	Foreign		Total	Foreign
New Orleans, La.	175,500,858	67,596,175	St. Louis, Metro., Mo.	29,011,497	0
New York, N.Y.	155,061,763	55,644,950	Pascagoula, Miss.	28,527,726	16,873,038
Houston, Tex.	124,886,883	64,617,686	Port Arthur, Tex.	23,801,409	15,091,001
Valdez Harbor, Ak.	107,144,515	7,357	Chicago, Il.	22,893,740	2,978,802
Baton Rouge, La.	78,857,473	27,995,133	Paulsboro, NJ.	22,004,472	12,498,533
Corpus Christi, Tex.	57,931,945	34,212,215	Newport News, Va.	21,391,195	19,041,729
Tampa Harbor, Fla.	50,252,299	20,823,125	Tacoma Harbor., Wa.	20,667,517	15,067,865
Norfolk Harbor, Va.	46,872,002	36,164,879	Boston, Ma., Port of	20,641,073	12,476,648
Long Beach, Calif.	46,559,885	21,496,646	Richmond, Calif.	18,912,900	4,801,797
Los Angeles, Calif.	45,213,855	22,021,515	Seattle, Wa.	18,645,664	11,376,322
Texas City, Tex.	42,746,698	23,026,869	Huntington, WVa.	17,700,717	0
Baltimore Hrbr., Md.	41,925,745	28,732,108	Lorain Harbor, Oh.	17,475,549	31,822
Duluth-Supr., Minn.	40,002,268	7,059,821	Indiana Harbor, In.	16,643,362	488,722
Philadelphia, Pa.	37,826,999	23,321,765	Jacksonville, Fla.	15,805,551	7,155,320
Lake Charles, La.	37,311,924	17,837,502	Detroit, Mi.	15,331,351	3,189,250
Mobile, Ala.	36,476,377	16,781,670	Freeport, Tex.	15,137,891	6,314,920
Pittsburgh, Pa.	34,373,364	0	Toledo Harbor, Oh.	14,741,752	5,978,700
Portland, Ore.	31,970,940	19,339,492	Cleveland, Oh.	14,550,876	2,543,005
Beaumont, Tex.	31,947,319	9,740,115	Port Everglades, Fla.	14,207,239	4,699,919
Marcus Hook, Pa.	29,815,233	16,371,785	Savannah, Ga.	13,980,978	11,079,180

Commerce on U.S. Inland Waterways

Source: Corps of Engineers, Department of the Army, 1990

Mississippi River System and Gulf Intracoastal Waterway

Waterway	Tons
Mississippi River, Minneapolis to the Gulf	441,546,399
Mississippi River, Minneapolis to St. Louis	82,016,213
Mississippi River, St. Louis to Cairo	106,068,681
Mississippi River, Cairo to Baton Rouge	169,016,176
Mississippi River, Baton Rouge to New Orleans. .	305,874,107
Mississippi River, New Orleans to Gulf	266,707,139
Gulf Intracoastal Waterway	117,712,086
Mississippi River System.	601,625,327

Ton-Mileage of Freight Carried on Inland Waterways

System	Ton-miles
Atlantic Coast Waterways	28,122,048
Gulf Coast Waterways	44,638,479
Pacific Coast Waterways	24,538,563
Mississippi River System, including Ohio River and Tributaries.	257,806,540
Great Lakes System, U.S. Commerce only . . .	83,078,874
Total:	**438,184,504**

Important Waterways and Canals

The St. Lawrence & Great Lakes Waterway, the largest inland navigation system on the continent, extends from the Atlantic Ocean to Duluth at the western end of Lake Superior, a distance of 2,342 miles. With the deepening of channels and locks to 27 ft., ocean carriers are able to penetrate to ports in the Canadian interior and the American midwest.

The major canals are those of the St. Lawrence Great Lakes waterway — the 3 new canals of the St. Lawrence Seaway, with their 7 locks, providing navigation for vessels of 26-foot draught from Montreal to Lake Ontario; the Welland Ship Canal by-passing the Niagara River between Lake Ontario and Lake Erie with its 8 locks, and the Sault Ste. Marie Canal and lock between Lake Huron and Lake Superior. These 16 locks overcome a drop of 580 ft. from the head of the lakes to Montreal. From Montreal to Lake Ontario the former bottleneck of narrow, shallow canals and of slow passage through 22 locks has been overcome, giving faster and safer movement for larger vessels. The new locks and linking channels now accommodate all but the largest ocean-going vessels and the upper St. Lawrence and Great

Lakes are open to 80% of the world's saltwater fleet.

Subsidiary Canadian canals or branches include the St. Peters Canal between Bras d'Or Lakes and the Atlantic Ocean in Nova Scotia; the St. Ours and Chambly Canals on the Richelieu River, Quebec; the Ste. Anne and Carillon Canals on the Ottawa River; the Rideau Canal between the Ottawa River and Lake Ontario, the Trent and Murrary Canals between Lake Ontario and Georgian Bay in Ontario and the St. Andrew's Canal on the Red River. The commercial value of these canals is not great but they are maintained to control water levels and permit the passage of small vessels and pleasure craft. The Canso Canal, completed 1957, permits shipping to pass through the causeway connecting Cape Breton Island with the Nova Scotia mainland.

The Welland Canal overcomes the 326-ft. drop of Niagara Falls and the rapids of the Niagara River. It has 8 locks, each 859 ft. long, 80 ft. wide and 30 ft. deep. Regulations permit ships of 730-ft. length and 75-ft. beam to transit.

Shortest Navigable Distances Between Ports

Source: Distances Between Ports. (Pub. 151 5th Edition 1985) Defense Mapping Agency Hydrographic/Topographic Center
Distances shown are in nautical miles (1,852 meters or about 6,076.115 feet). To get statute miles, multiply by 1.15.

TO	FROM New York	Montreal	Colon[1]
Algiers, Algeria	3,617	3,592	4,745
Amsterdam, Netherlands	3,418	3,162	4,825
Baltimore, Md.	410	1,820	1,901
Barcelona, Spain	3,710	3,695	4,842
Boston, Mass.	378	1,309	2,157
Buenos Aires, Argentina	5,871	6,455	5,346
Cape Town, S. Africa[2]	6,766	7,115	6,429
Cherbourg, France	3,127	2,878	4,541
Cobh, Ireland	2,879	2,603	4,308
Copenhagen, Denmark	3,720	3,241	5,129
Dakar, Senegal	3,335	3,562	3,694
Galveston, Tex.	1,895	3,165	1,492
Gibraltar[3]	3,204	3,184	4,329
Glasgow, Scotland	3,065	2,691	4,746
Halifax, N.S.	600	958	2,295
Hamburg, W. Germany	3,636	3,398	5,054
Hamilton, Bermuda	697	1,621	1,659
Havana, Cuba	1,199	2,473	998
Helsinki, Finland	4,208	3,778	5,902
Istanbul, Turkey	5,001	4,981	6,129
Kingston, Jamaica	1,474	2,690	551
Lagos, Nigeria	4,883	5,130	5,033
Lisbon, Portugal	2,980	2,941	4,155
Marseille, France	3,891	3,870	5,019
Montreal, Quebec	1,516		3,126
Naples, Italy	4,181	4,159	5,309
Nassau, Bahamas	962	2,274	1,166
New Orleans, La.	1,761	2,991	1,389
New York, N.Y.		1,516	1,974
Norfolk, Va.	287	1,697	1,779
Oslo, Norway	3,701	3,222	5,306
Piraeus, Greece	4,687	4,661	5,806
Port Said, Egypt	5,123	5,093	6,238
Rio de Janeiro, Brazil	4,770	5,342	4,367
St. John's, Nfld.	1,093	1,038	2,345
San Juan, Puerto Rico	1,399	2,445	993
Southampton, England	3,156	3,063	4,514

TO	FROM San. Fran.	Vancouver	Panama
Acapulco, Mexico	1,833	2,645	1,426
Anchorage, Alas.	1,872	1,347	5,117
Bombay, India	9,791	9,519	9,248
Calcutta, India	9,006	8,728	10,929
Colon, Panama[1]	3,289	4,076	44
Jakarta, Indonesia	7,642	7,413	10,570
Haiphong, Vietnam	6,657	6,358	9,806
Hong Kong	6,044	5,756	9,195
Honolulu, Hawaii	2,091	2,423	4,685
Los Angeles, Cal.	369	1,162	2,913
Manila, Philippines	6,221	5,756	9,347
Melbourne, Australia	6,970	7,342	7,928
Pusan, S. Korea	4,914	4,623	8,074
Ho Chi Min City, Vietnam	6,878	6,606	10,017
San Francisco, Cal.		812	3,245
Seattle, Wash.	796	126	4,020
Shanghai, China	5,398	5,110	8,566
Singapore	7,353	7,078	10,505
Suva, Fiji	4,749	5,199	6,325
Valparaiso, Chile	5,140	5,915	2,616
Vancouver, B.C.	812		4,032
Vladivostok, USSR	4,563	4,262	7,739
Yokohama, Japan	4,536	4,262	7,682

TO	FROM Port Said	Cape Town[2]	Singapore
Bombay, India	3,046	4,616	2,441
Calcutta, India	4,691	5,638	1,649
Dar es Salaam, Tanzania	3,238	2,365	4,042
Jakarta, Indonesia	5,293	5,212	526
Hong Kong	6,472	7,006	1,454
Kuwait	3,306	5,169	3,845
Manila, Philippines	6,348	6,777	1,330
Melbourne, Australia	7,837	6,104	3,844
Ho Chi Min City, Vietnam	5,667	6,263	649
Singapore	5,018	5,611	
Yokohama, Japan	7,907	8,503	2,889

(1) Colon on the Atlantic is 44 nautical miles from Panama (port) on the Pacific. (2) Cape Town is 35 nautical miles northwest of the Cape of Good Hope. (3) Gibraltar (port) is 24 nautical miles east of the Strait of Gibraltar.

Fastest Scheduled Passenger Train Runs in U.S. and Canada

Source: Darrell J. Smith, figures are based on 1990 timetables

Railroad	Train	From	To	Dis. miles	Time min.	Speed mph.
Amtrak	20 Metroliner Service trains	Baltimore[1]	Wilmington	68.4	43	95.0
Amtrak	Express Metroliner Service train 203	Metropark	Washington	201.0	129	93.5
Amtrak	Express Metroliner Service train 223	New York	New Carrollton	216.0	143	90.8
Amtrak	Express Metroliner Service train 202	New Carrollton	New York	216.0	145	89.3
Amtrak	Express Metroliner Service train 222	Washington	Metropark	201.0	137	88.2
Amtrak	Four Metroliner Service trains	Newark	Philadelphia	80.7	56	86.8
Amtrak	Six Metroliner Service trains	Newark	Philadelphia	80.7	57	84.9
VIA	Renaissance	Dorval	Kingston	165.0	118	83.8
Amtrak	Nine Metroliner Service trains	Philadelphia	Newark	80.7	58	83.2
VIA	York	Cornwall	Kingston	108.0	78	83.1
VIA	Renaissance	Kingston	Dorval	165.0	120	82.5
VIA	York	Kingston	Cornwall	108.0	79	81.8

Fastest Scheduled Passenger Train Runs in Foreign Countries

Source: Donald M. Steffee, figures based on 1989 time tables

Country	Train	From	To	Dis. miles	Time min.	Speed mph.
France	TGV trains (2 runs)	Paris	Macon	225.7	100	135.4
Japan	Yamabiko trains (6 runs)	Morica	Sendi	106.3	50	127.6
Great Britain	High Speed Trains (3 runs)	Swindon	Reading	41.5	23	108.3
West Germany	Intercity trains (7 runs)	Celle	Uelzen	32.5	19	102.6
Italy	IC501	Milan	Bologna	135.8	86	94.7
Soviet Union	High Speed Train[2]	Leningrad[1]	Moscow[3]	403.6	270	89.7
Sweden	Seven trains	Skvode	Hallsberg	70.8	48	88.5
Spain	Talgos 120 and 121	Alcazar[1]	Albacete	80.7	57	84.9
Australia	Riverina XPT	Culcairn	Wagga Wagga	47.0	35	80.6

(1) Runs listed in both directions. (2) Once weekly: Thursday from Leningrad, Fri. from Moscow. (3) Probable operating stop at Ologuye; times unavailable

Ownership of Motor Vehicles by Household, 1988

Source: Motor Vehicle Manufacturers Association

Characteristic	Number of Households (Million)	Average Per Household			Characteristic	Number of Households (Million)	Average Per Household		
		Number of Vehicles	Vehicle Miles Traveled	Fuel Consumption (Gallons)			Number of Vehicles	Vehicle Miles Traveled	Fuel Consumption (Gallons)
Average Number of Vehicles Per Household:					Outside Central City	39.0	1.9	20,385	1,083
Fewer than 1	3.9	.6	5,271	316	Nonmetropolitan	18.3	1.8	18,627	1,081
1	24.5	1.0	10,170	526	Household Size:				
Between 1 and 2	9.1	1.5	17,049	936	1 Person	16.9	1.2	10,813	586
2	24.3	2.0	20,251	1,100	2 Persons	28.6	1.8	16,817	928
Between 2 and 3	8.2	2.4	25,456	1,386	3 Persons	14.2	2.0	22,679	1,209
3	5.9	3.0	28,995	1,614	4 Persons	12.6	2.1	23,323	1,257
Between 3 and 4	2.8	3.4	36,820	2,078	5 or More Persons	8.9	2.3	25,930	1,449
4 or more	2.7	4.3	42,332	2,407	1987 Family Income:				
Census Region:					Less than $10,000	10.2	1.3	10,932	652
Northeast	15.2	1.7	17,997	917	$10,000-$14,999	11.8	1.4	12,978	762
Midwest	20.4	1.8	18,518	1,016	$15,000-$19,999	8.3	1.6	15,837	879
South	28.3	1.8	18,859	1,046	$20,000-$24,999	8.6	1.7	17,813	980
West	17.3	1.9	18,783	1,046	$25,000-$34,999	16.0	1.8	18,617	1,025
Metropolitan Status:					$35,000-$49,999	12.9	2.2	24,170	1,275
Metropolitan	63.0	1.8	18,586	995	$50,000-$74,999	8.8	2.3	25,555	1,330
Central city	24.0	1.6	15,669	852	$75,000 or More	4.5	2.4	27,428	1,391
					U.S. Total	81.3	1.8	18,595	1,014

Personal Consumption Expenditures for Transportation

Source: Motor Vehicle Manufacturers Association

(in millions)

	1978	1980	1982	1984	1987	1988	1989
User-Operated Transportation							
New Autos	$48,521	$46,395	$53,336	$77,560	$93,497	$101,157	$100,378
Net Purchases of Used Autos	13,704	14,905	19,648	30,151	38,155	43,047	43,051
Other Motor Vehicles[1]	19,150	12,298	15,637	26,412	35,128	36,122	38,020
Tires, Tubes and Accessories and Parts	13,706	16,684	20,234	23,319	28,693	31,294	32,420
Repair, Greasing, Washing, Parking, Storage and Rental	28,016	32,327	35,441	42,838	55,501	62,476	69,754
Gasoline and Oil	51,301	83,721	89,090	90,006	75,162	76,786	83,952
Bridge, Tunnel, Ferry and Road Tolls	955	1,061	1,224	1,300	1,878	1,986	2,142
Insurance Premiums, Less Claims Paid	8,340	9,383	9,054	9,993	15,379	16,809	16,625
Total User-Operated Transportation	$183,693	$216,774	$243,664	$301,579	$343,393	$369,677	$386,342
Purchased Local Transportation							
Transit Systems	$2,243	$2,431	$3,038	$3,428	$3,967	$4,110	$4,158
Taxicabs	2,617	3,082	2,953	3,042	3,530	3,802	3,916
Railway Commutation	242	300	395	458	658	518	485
Total Purchased Local Transportation	$5,102	$5,813	$6,386	$6,928	$8,155	$8,430	$8,559
Purchased Intercity Transportation							
Railway Excluding Commutation	$261	$362	$445	$582	$714	$825	$946
Bus	847	1,171	1,252	1,227	1,413	1,640	1,781
Airline	9,331	13,425	14,653	17,536	21,190	23,292	23,969
Other	639	939	1,236	1,640	2,231	2,490	2,762
Total Purchased Intercity Transportation	$11,078	$15,897	$17,586	$20,985	$25,548	$28,247	$29,458
Total Transportation	$199,873	$238,484	$267,636	$329,492	$377,096	$406,354	$424,359
Total Personal Consumption Expenditures	$1,403,501	$1,732,559	$2,050,661	$2,430,455	$3,010,821	$3,235,095	$3,471,089

(1) New and used trucks, recreation vehicles, etc.

Delays at U.S. Airports

Source: U.S. Department of Transportation

The following is the percentage of flights that left within 15 minutes of their scheduled departure time at 30 major U.S. airports from January through April, 1990. Delays caused by mechanical problems are not counted.

City	Departures on time (overall)	Worst hours to fly	Departures on time (at worst hours)	City	Departures on time (overall)	Worst hours to fly	Departures on time (at worst hours)
Philadelphia	76	5 to 6 P.M.	67.3	San Diego	82.1	7 to 8 P.M.	72.9
Chicago (O'Hare)	76.4	8 to 9 P.M.	62.2	Orlando	82.2	7 to 8 P.M.	62.6
New York (La Guardia)	76.6	6 to 7 P.M.	65	Tampa	83.2	11 P.M. to 6 A.M.	71
Denver	77	10 to 11 P.M.	67.4	Charlotte, N.C.	82.3	8 to 9 P.M.	73.3
New York (Kennedy)	78.4	5 to 6 P.M.	73	Kansas City	83.6	11 P.M. to 6 A.M.	66.9
Boston	78.5	5 to 6 P.M.	65	Miami	83.9	7 to 8 P.M.	74.3
Pittsburgh	78.9	9 to 10 A.M.	71.5	Minneapolis-St. Paul	84	9 to 10 P.M.	73
Dallas-Fort Worth	78.9	6 to 7 P.M.	68.5	St. Louis	84.2	10 to 11 P.M.	79.7
Atlanta	79.3	8 to 9 P.M.	70.6	Washington (National)	84.3	3 to 4 P.M.	78
Newark	79.7	10 to 11 P.M.	67.9	Baltimore	84.3	9 to 10 P.M.	78.7
Seattle	80.2	9 to 10 P.M.	79.7	Washington (Dulles)	85.7	7 to 8 P.M.	76
Houston	80.3	8 to 9 P.M.	70.9	Los Angeles	85.9	5 to 6 P.M.	78
Phoenix	81.2	8 to 9 P.M.	70.5	Salt Lake City	85.4	8 to 9 P.M.	63
San Francisco	81.2	1 to 2 P.M.	72	Las Vegas	85.9	noon to 1 P.M.	81.9
Detroit	82	10 to 11 A.M.	74.5	Memphis	87.4	10 to 11 P.M.	74.5

Motorcycles, 1970-1988

Source: Federal Highway Administration

Year	Number of registered vehicles (1,000)	Travel (mil. veh. miles)	Average travel per vehicle (miles)	Fuel Consumption Total (mil. gal.)	Fuel Consumption Average per vehicle (gal.)	Average miles per gallon consumed
1970	2,824	2,979	1,055	59.6	21	50
1975	4,964	5,629	1,134	112.6	23	50
1980	5,694	10,214	1,794	204.3	36	50
1985	5,444	9,086	1,669	181.7	33	50
1986	5,262	9,414	1,789	188.3	36	50
1987	4,917	9,506	1,933	190.1	39	50
1988	4,584	10,022	2,186	200.4	44	50

Motor Vehicle Production, by Country, 1989

Source: Motor Vehicle Manufacturers Association

Country	Passenger Cars	Trucks and Buses	Total	Country	Passenger Cars	Trucks and Buses	Total
Argentina	107,597	20,227	127,824	Japan	9,052,406	3,973,272	13,025,678
Australia	330,492	27,772	358,264	Korea, South	871,898	257,572	1,129,470
Austria	6,638	5,026	11,664	Mexico	439,538	202,241	641,779
Belgium	304,055	84,524	388,579	The Netherlands	130,000	33,330	163,330
Brazil	731,013	280,970	1,011,983	Poland	285,600	53,000	338,600
Canada	1,001,588	937,914	1,939,502	Spain	1,638,615	406,942	2,045,557
China	21,568	467,907	489,475	Sweden	384,206	81,670	465,876
Czechoslovakia	188,611	50,570	239,181	United Kingdom	1,299,082	326,590	1,625,672
France	3,409,017	510,759	3,919,776	United States	6,823,097	4,028,958	10,852,055
Germany, East	215,000	42,000	257,000	U.S.S.R.	1,200,000	900,000	2,100,000
Germany, West	4,563,673	287,974	4,851,647	Yugoslavia	302,985	39,949	342,934
Hungary	—	11,930	11,930				
India	117,190	155,325	332,515	Total	35,455,838	13,435,227	48,891,065
Italy	1,971,969	248,805	2,220,774				

Passenger Car Production, U.S. Plants

Source: Motor Vehicle Manufacturers Association

	1987	1988	1989		1987	1988	1989
Renault Alliance	16,004	—	—	Camaro	121,550	99,820	100,613
Total Eagle	16,004	—	—	Beretta—Corsica	348,806	434,313	370,741
Horizon	45,663	78,794	32,937	Celebrity	285,111	189,912	70,365
Reliant	136,109	100,462	—	Monte Carlo	72,745	—	—
Sundance	89,678	104,310	100,618	Chevrolet	200,583	203,494	162,792
Acclaim	—	7,241	125,292	Corvette	28,514	22,878	25,256
Caravelle	42,955	9,834		Total Chevrolet	1,515,571	1,381,967	1,196,953
Gran Fury	7,180	13,059		Sunbird	89,470	113,736	151,177
Total Plymouth	321,585	313,700	258,847	Fiero	33,935	13,296	—
LeBaron	64,089	7,912	10	Firebird	77,731	66,456	56,441
LeBaron GTS	37,508	9,539	2,946	Grand Am	247,701	242,121	226,882
Le Baron J	113,858	90,449	93,670	6000	67,943	94,663	78,910
Fifth Avenue	65,675	33,280	32,623	Bonneville H	125,014	121,914	90,886
New Yorker (C)	18,916	106,832	74,375	Total Pontiac	657,281	806,356	732,177
New Yorker (E)	57,102	—		Firenza	17,978	5,230	—
Total Chrysler-Plymouth	678,733	561,712	462,471	Calais	115,085	119,690	87,747
Omni	40,039	77,332	34,621	Ciera	108,766	38,053	87,908
Shadow	96,073	103,190	104,145	Cutlass Supreme	76,751	140,513	115,084
Daytona	64,054	79,657	75,452	Delta 88	193,737	167,785	148,411
Aries	127,948	91,998		Oldsmobile 98	73,004	76,341	71,497
Spirit	—	8,090	108,046	Toronado	16,453	15,308	10,334
Dodge 600	39,773	8,549	—	Total Oldsmobile	601,774	562,920	520,981
Lancer	23,123	9,365	1,528	Skyhawk	34,517	28,037	6,913
Dynasty	8,486	114,156	132,636	Somerset and Skylark	63,612	55,343	68,464
Diplomat	15,188	18,796	—	Century	152,892	142,454	122,766
Total Dodge	414,684	511,133	453,428	Regal	40,425	—	—
Total Chrysler Corp.	1,109,421	1,072,845	915,899	LeSabre	152,836	144,924	164,856
				Electra	94,485	92,099	80,049
Thunderbird	157,507	111,533	137,326	Riviera	13,468	13,631	20,626
Taurus	405,640	395,512	362,144	Realta	332	8,363	6,378
Tempo	145,812	183,124	146,928	Total Buick	552,567	484,851	470,052
Escort	394,699	414,596	347,271	Cimarron	10,404	3,693	—
Mustang	214,128	200,054	172,217	Cadillac	218,741	200,118	236,877
Total Ford	1,317,786	1,304,819	1,165,886	Eldorado	20,538	35,385	29,161
Cougar	138,464	87,765	114,250	Seville	21,395	23,514	24,319
Sable	121,641	135,436	116,874	Allante	4,803	2,320	3,232
Topaz	46,975	70,565	66,554	Total Cadillac	275,881	265,030	293,589
Lynx	21,352	—		Total General Motors	3,603,074	3,501,124	3,213,752
Town Car	142,017	123,110	127,486	Diamond Star	—	—	90,727
Mark	28,546	28,734	21,544	Honda	324,065	366,354	362,274
Continental	13,595	55,312	64,487	Mazda	4,200	163,289	216,501
Total Lincoln—Mercury	512,590	500,922	511,195	Nissan	117,334	109,897	115,584
Total Ford Motor Co.	1,830,376	1,805,741	1,677,081	Toyota	43,744	55,480	231,279
Geo, Prizm	142,934	73,743	112,111	Volkswagen of America	66,696	35,998	—
Cavalier	315,328	357,807	355,075	Total Passenger Cars	7,098,910	7,110,728	6,823,097

Best-Selling Cars in the U.S., 1978 and 1989

Source: Ward's Automotive Reports

1978	1978	1989	1989
Chevrolet (full-size model)	Ford LTD	Honda Accord	Toyota Camry
Oldsmobile Cutlass Supreme	Ford Thunderbird	Ford Taurus	Ford Tempo
Ford Fairmont	Oldsmobile 88	Ford Escort	Nissan Sentra
Chevrolet Malibu	Chevrolet Camaro	Chevrolet Corsica/Beretta	Pontiac Grand Am
Chevrolet Monte Carlo	Cadillac	Chevrolet Cavalier	Toyota Corolla

Selected Motor Vehicle Statistics

Source: Federal Highway Adm.; National Transportation Safety Board; Insurance Institute for Highway Safety

State	Driver's age Jan. 1, 1990 (1) Regular	(2) Juvenile	1989 Licensed drivers[3] (mlns.)	1989 Registered autos, buses & trucks[3] (mlns.)	State gas tax gal. cents (April 1, 1990)	1988 Vehicle-Miles of Travel (mlns.)	1989 Motorfuel consumption[3] Highway (mln) gallons	Non-Highway (mln) gallons	Safety belt use law[4] (Aug. 1, 1990)
Alabama	16	—	2.1	4.1	13	39,684	2,605	59	No
Alaska	16	—	.3	.4	8	3,841	241	30	S
Arizona	16	—	2.4	2.8	17	34,247	1,966	43	S*
Arkansas	16	—	1.7	1.4	13.5	19,219	1,624	43	No
California	16/18	14	19.3	21.7	9	241,575	14,708	349	S
Colorado	18	16	2.2	2.9	20	27,665	1,654	39	S
Connecticut	16/18	—	2.4	2.7	20	26,062	1,556	32	P
Delaware	16/18	—	.5	.5	16	6,404	395	13	No
Dist. of Col.	18	16	.4	.3	18	3,405	202	4	S
Florida	16	—	9.0	11.4	9.7	105,319	6,582	287	S
Georgia	16	—	4.5	5.4	7.5	62,262	4,399	110	S
Hawaii	15	—	.6	.7	11	7,419	390	21	S
Idaho	16	14	.7	1.0	18	8,127	557	40	P
Illinois	16/18	—	7.3	8.1	19	78,483	5,560	113	S
Indiana	16/18	—	3.8	4.3	15	51,124	3,306	83	S
Iowa	16/18	—	1.9	2.6	20	21,907	1,666	95	P
Kansas	16	14	1.7	2.2	15	21,161	1,525	55	S
Kentucky	16	—	2.4	2.8	15	31,614	2,377	63	No
Louisiana	15/17	15	2.6	3.0	20	34,682	2,377	102	S
Maine	16/17	16	.9	1.0	17	11,401	743	29	No
Maryland	16/18	16	3.2	3.5	18.5	37,498	2,401	70	S
Massachusetts	17/18	16½	4.3	3.8	11	43,334	2,680	67	No
Michigan	16/18	14	6.4	7.3	15	77,899	4,750	144	S
Minnesota	16/18	15	2.5	3.3	20	36,447	2,342	132	S
Mississippi	15	—	1.8	1.8	18	22,043	1,508	56	P
Missouri	16	—	3.6	3.9	11	45,570	3,254	74	S
Montana	15/16	13	.5	.7	20	8,138	521	33	S
Nebraska	16	14	1.1	1.3	22	13,407	937	59	No
Nevada	16	14	.8	.8	16.25	8,989	727	17	S
New Hampshire	16/18	16	.8	1.0	14	9,507	571	11	No
New Jersey	17	16	5.5	5.9	10.5	58,671	3,963	89	S
New Mexico	15/16	—	1.1	1.2	16.2	15,283	1,008	23	P
New York	17/18	16	10.3	10.2	8	103,692	6,347	160	P
North Carolina	16/18	—	4.5	5.2	21.7	57,943	3,864	111	P
North Dakota	16	14	.4	.7	17	5,765	407	43	No
Ohio	16/18	14	7.4	8.8	18	81,990	5,618	209	S
Oklahoma	16	—	2.3	2.6	16	32,388	1,962	72	S
Oregon	16	14	2.2	2.4	18	25,204	1,612	45	No
Pennsylvania	17/18	16	7.8	7.9	12	81,238	5,519	106	S
Rhode Island	16/18	—	.7	.7	20	5,853	422	14	No
South Carolina	16	15	2.3	2.5	16	31,759	1,769	82	No
South Dakota	16	14	.5	.7	18	6,634	452	34	No
Tennessee	16	14	3.2	4.4	21	44,193	3,152	78	S
Texas	16/18	15	11.1	12.6	15	156,458	9,626	377	P
Utah	16/18	—	1.0	1.2	19	13,263	875	21	S
Vermont	18	16	.4	.5	16	5,553	327	10	No
Virginia	16/19	—	4.2	4.7	17.7	57,453	3,604	80	S
Washington	16/18	—	3.2	4.1	18	41,813	2,542	70	S
West Virginia	16/18	16	1.3	1.3	15.5	13,884	1,022	29	No
Wisconsin	16/18	14	3.2	4.0	20.8	42,458	2,423	86	S
Wyoming	16	14	.4	.5	9	5,658	434	25	S
Total[5]			164.9	183.7		2,025,586	131,072	4,037	

(1) Unrestricted operation of private passenger car. When 2 ages are shown, license is issued at lower age upon completion of approved driver education course. (2) Juvenile license issued with consent of parent or guardian. (3) Estimated, 1989. (4) P = an officer may stop a vehicle for a violation (primary); S = an officer may only issue a seat belt citation when the vehicle is stopped for another moving violation (secondary); (5) Figures may not add, due to rounding. *Law goes into effect 12/31/90.

Automobile Factory Sales

Source: Motor Vehicle Manufacturers Association

Year	Passenger cars Number	Motor trucks, buses Number	Total Number	Year	Passenger cars Number	Motor trucks, buses Number	Total Number
1900	4,192	—	4,190	1981	6,255,340	1,700,908	7,956,248
1910	181,000	6,000	187,000	1982	5,049,184	1,906,455	6,955,639
1920	1,905,560	321,789	2,227,349	1983	6,739,223	2,413,897	9,153,120
1930	2,787,456	575,364	3,362,820	1985	8,002,259	3,356,905	11,359,164
1940	3,717,385	754,901	4,472,286	1986	7,516,189	3,392,885	10,909,074
1950	6,665,863	1,337,193	8,003,056	1987	7,085,147	3,821,410	10,906,557
1960	6,665,863	1,194,475	7,869,271	1988	7,104,617	4,120,574	11,225,191
1970	6,546,817	1,692,440	8,239,257	1989	6,807,416	4,061,950	10,869,366

After July 1, 1964 all tactical vehicles are excluded. Federal excise taxes are excluded in all years.

Road Mileage Between Selected U.S. Cities

	Atlanta	Boston	Chicago	Cincinnati	Cleveland	Dallas	Denver	Des Moines	Detroit	Houston
Atlanta, Ga.	...	1,037	674	440	672	795	1,398	870	699	789
Boston, Mass. . .	1,037	...	963	840	628	1,748	1,949	1,280	695	1,804
Chicago, Ill. . .	674	963	...	287	335	917	996	327	266	1,067
Cincinnati, Oh. . .	440	840	287	...	244	920	1,164	571	259	1,029
Cleveland, Oh. . .	672	628	335	244	...	1,159	1,321	652	170	1,273
Dallas Tex.	795	1,748	917	920	1,159	...	781	684	1,143	243
Denver, Col. . . .	1,398	1,949	996	1,164	1,321	781	...	669	1,253	1,019
Detroit, Mich. . .	699	695	266	259	170	1,143	1,253	584	...	1,265
Houston, Tex. . .	789	1,804	1,067	1,029	1,273	243	1,019	905	1,265	...
Indianapolis, Ind. .	493	906	181	106	294	865	1,058	465	278	987
Kansas City, Mo..	798	1,391	499	591	779	489	600	195	743	710
Los Angeles, Cal.	2,182	2,979	2,054	2,179	2,367	1,387	1,059	1,727	2,311	1,538
Memphis, Tenn. .	371	1,296	530	468	712	452	1,040	599	713	561
Milwaukee, Wis. .	761	1,050	87	374	422	991	1,029	361	353	1,142
Minneapolis, Minn.	1,068	1,368	405	692	740	936	841	252	671	1,157
New Orleans, La..	479	1,507	912	786	1,030	496	1,273	978	1,045	356
New York, N.Y..	841	206	802	647	473	1,552	1,771	1,119	637	1,608
Omaha, Neb. ..	986	1,412	459	693	784	644	537	132	716	865
Philadelphia, Pa. .	741	296	738	567	413	1,452	1,691	1,051	573	1,508
Pittsburgh, Pa. ..	687	561	452	287	129	1,204	1,411	763	287	1,313
Portland Ore....	2,601	3,046	2,083	2,333	2,418	2,009	1,238	1,786	2,349	2,205
St. Louis, Mo...	541	1,141	289	340	529	630	857	333	513	779
San Francisco . .	2,496	3,095	2,142	2,362	2,467	1,753	1,235	1,815	2,399	1,912
Seattle, Wash. . .	2,618	2,976	2,013	2,300	2,348	2,078	1,307	1,749	2,279	2,274
Tulsa, Okla. . . .	772	1,537	683	736	925	257	681	443	909	478
Washington, D.C..	608	429	671	481	346	1,319	1,616	984	506	1,375

	Indianapolis	Kansas City	Los Angeles	Louisville	Memphis	Milwaukee	Minneapolis	New Orleans	New York	Omaha
Atlanta, Ga.	493	798	2,182	382	371	761	1,068	479	841	986
Boston, Mass. . .	906	1,391	2,979	941	1,296	1,050	1,368	1,507	206	1,412
Chicago, Ill. . .	181	499	2,054	292	530	87	405	912	802	459
Cincinnati, Oh. . .	106	591	2,179	101	468	374	692	786	647	693
Cleveland Oh. . .	294	779	2,367	345	712	422	740	1,030	473	784
Dallas, Tex.	865	489	1,387	819	452	991	936	496	1,552	644
Denver, Col. . . .	1,058	600	1,059	1,120	1,040	1,029	841	1,273	1,771	537
Detroit, Mich. . . .	278	743	2,311	360	713	353	671	1,045	637	716
Houston, Tex. . .	987	710	1,538	928	561	1,142	1,157	356	1,608	865
Indianapolis, Ind. .	...	485	2,073	111	435	268	586	796	713	587
Kansas City, Mo..	485	...	1,589	520	451	537	447	806	1,198	201
Los Angeles, Cal.	2,073	1,589	...	2,108	1,817	2,087	1,889	1,883	2,786	1,595
Memphis, Tenn. .	435	451	1,817	367	...	612	826	390	1,100	652
Milwaukee, Wis. .	268	537	2,087	379	612	...	332	994	889	493
Minneapolis, Minn.	586	447	1,889	697	826	332	...	1,214	1,207	357
New Orleans, La..	796	806	1,883	685	390	994	1,214	...	1,311	1,007
New York, N.Y...	713	1,198	2,786	748	1,100	889	1,207	1,311	...	1,251
Omaha, Neb. ..	587	201	1,595	687	652	493	357	1,007	1,251	...
Philadelphia, Pa. .	633	1,118	2,706	668	1,000	825	1,143	1,211	100	1,183
Pittsburgh, Pa. ..	353	838	2,426	388	752	539	857	1,070	368	895
Portland, Ore.. . .	1,227	1,809	959	2,320	2,259	2,010	1,678	2,505	2,885	1,654
St. Louis, Mo....	235	257	1,845	263	285	363	552	673	948	449
San Francisco . .	2,256	1,835	379	2,349	2,125	2,175	1,940	2,249	2,934	1,663
Seattle, Wash. . .	2,194	1,839	1,131	2,305	2,290	1,940	1,608	2,574	2,815	1,638
Tulsa, Okla.	631	248	1,452	659	401	757	695	647	1,344	387
Washington, D.C..	558	1,043	2,631	582	867	758	1,076	1,078	233	1,116

	Philadelphia	Pittsburgh	Portland	St. Louis	Salt Lake City	San Francisco	Seattle	Toledo	Tulsa	Washington
Atlanta, Ga.	741	687	2,601	541	1,878	2,496	2,618	640	772	608
Boston, Mass. . .	296	561	3,046	1,141	2,343	3,095	2,976	739	1,537	429
Chicago, Ill.	738	452	2,083	289	1,390	2,142	2,013	232	683	671
Cincinnati, Oh. . .	567	287	2,333	340	1,610	2,362	2,300	200	736	481
Cleveland Oh. . .	413	129	2,418	529	1,715	2,467	2,348	111	925	346
Dallas, Tex.	1,452	1,204	2,009	630	1,242	1,753	2,078	1,084	257	1,319
Denver, Col. . . .	1,691	1,411	1,238	857	504	1,235	1,307	1,218	681	1,616
Detroit, Mich. . . .	576	287	2,349	513	1,647	2,399	2,279	59	909	506
Houston, Tex. . . .	1,508	1,313	2,205	779	1,438	1,912	2,274	1,206	478	1,375
Indianapolis, Ind. .	633	353	2,227	235	1,504	2,256	2,194	219	631	558
Kansas City, Mo..	1,118	838	1,809	257	1,086	1,839	687	248	1,043	
Los Angeles, Cal.	2,706	2,426	959	1,845	715	379	1,131	2,276	1,452	2,631
Memphis, Tenn. .	1,000	752	2,259	285	1,535	2,125	2,290	654	401	867
Milwaukee, Wis. .	825	539	2,010	363	1,423	2,175	1,940	319	757	758
Minneapolis, Minn.	1,143	857	1,678	552	1,186	1,940	1,608	637	695	1,076
New Orleans, La..	1,211	1,070	2,505	673	1,738	2,249	2,574	986	647	1,078
New York, N.Y...	100	368	2,885	948	2,182	2,934	2,815	578	1,344	233
Omaha, Neb. ..	1,183	895	1,654	449	931	1,683	1,638	681	387	1,116
Philadelphia, Pa. .	...	288	2,821	868	2,114	2,866	2,751	514	1,264	133
Pittsburgh, Pa. ..	288	...	2,535	588	1,826	2,578	2,465	228	984	221
Portland, Ore.. . .	2,821	2,535	...	2,060	767	636	172	2,315	1,913	2,754
St. Louis, Mo. . .	868	588	2,060	...	1,337	2,089	2,081	454	396	793
San Francisco . .	2,866	2,578	636	2,089	752	...	808	2,364	1,760	2,799
Seattle, Wash. . .	2,751	2,465	172	2,081	836	808	...	2,245	1,982	2,684
Tulsa, Okla.	1,264	984	1,913	396	1,172	1,760	1,982	850	...	1,189
Washington, D.C..	133	221	2,754	793	2,047	2,799	2,684	447	1,189	...

Air Distances Between Selected World Cities in Statute Miles

Point-to-point measurements are usually from City Hall

	Bangkok	Beijing	Berlin	Cairo	Cape Town	Caracas	Chicago	Hong Kong	Hono-lulu	Lima
Bangkok	...	2,046	5,352	4,523	6,300	10,555	8,570	1,077	6,609	12,244
Bejing	2,046	...	4,584	4,698	8,044	8,950	6,604	1,217	5,077	10,349
Berlin	5,352	4,584	...	1,797	5,961	5,238	4,414	5,443	7,320	6,896
Cairo	4,523	4,698	1,797	...	4,480	6,342	6,141	5,066	8,848	7,726
Cape Town	6,300	8,044	5,961	4,480	...	6,366	8,491	7,376	11,535	6,072
Caracas	10,555	8,950	5,238	6,342	6,366	...	2,495	10,165	6,021	1,707
Chicago	8,570	6,604	4,414	6,141	8,491	2,495	...	7,797	4,256	3,775
Hong Kong	1,077	1,217	5,443	5,066	7,376	10,165	7,797	...	5,556	11,418
Honolulu	6,609	5,077	7,320	8,848	11,535	6,021	4,256	5,556	...	5,947
London	5,944	5,074	583	2,185	5,989	4,655	3,958	5,990	7,240	6,316
Los Angeles	7,637	6,250	5,782	7,520	9,969	3,632	1,745	7,240	2,557	4,171
Madrid	6,337	5,745	1,165	2,087	5,308	4,346	4,189	6,558	7,872	5,907
Melbourne	4,568	5,643	9,918	8,675	6,425	9,717	9,673	4,595	5,505	8,059
Mexico City	9,793	7,753	6,056	7,700	8,519	2,234	1,690	8,788	3,789	2,639
Montreal	8,338	6,519	3,740	5,427	7,922	2,438	745	7,736	4,918	3,970
Moscow	4,389	3,607	1,006	1,803	6,279	6,177	4,987	4,437	7,047	7,862
New York	8,669	6,844	3,979	5,619	7,803	2,120	714	8,060	4,969	3,639
Paris	5,877	5,120	548	1,998	5,786	4,732	4,143	5,990	7,449	6,370
Rio de Janeiro	9,994	10,768	6,209	6,143	3,781	2,804	5,282	11,009	8,288	2,342
Rome	5,494	5,063	737	1,326	5,231	5,195	4,824	5,774	8,040	6,750
San Francisco	7,931	5,918	5,672	7,466	10,248	3,902	1,859	6,905	2,398	4,518
Singapore	883	2,771	6,164	5,137	6,008	11,402	9,372	1,605	6,726	11,689
Stockholm	5,089	4,133	528	2,096	6,423	5,471	4,331	5,063	6,875	7,166
Tokyo	2,865	1,307	5,557	5,958	9,154	8,808	6,314	1,791	3,859	9,631
Warsaw	5,033	4,325	322	1,619	5,935	5,559	4,679	5,147	7,366	7,215
Washington, D.C.	8,807	6,942	4,181	5,822	7,895	2,047	596	8,155	4,838	3,509

	London	Los Angeles	Madrid	Mel-bourne	Mexico City	Mon-treal	Mos-cow	New Delhi	New York	Paris
Bangkok	5,944	7,637	6,337	4,568	9,793	8,338	4,389	1,813	8,669	5,877
Bejing	5,074	6,250	5,745	5,643	7,753	6,519	3,607	2,353	6,844	5,120
Berlin	583	5,782	1,165	9,918	6,056	3,740	1,006	3,598	3,979	548
Cairo	2,185	7,520	2,087	8,675	7,700	5,427	1,803	2,758	5,619	1,998
Cape Town	5,989	9,969	5,308	6,425	8,519	7,922	6,279	5,769	7,803	5,786
Caracas	4,655	3,632	4,346	9,717	2,234	2,438	6,177	8,833	2,120	4,732
Chicago	3,958	1,745	4,189	9,673	1,690	745	4,987	7,486	714	4,143
Hong Kong	5,990	7,240	6,558	4,595	8,788	7,736	4,437	2,339	8,060	5,990
Honolulu	7,240	2,557	7,872	5,505	3,789	4,918	7,047	7,412	4,969	7,449
London	...	5,439	785	10,500	5,558	3,254	1,564	4,181	3,469	214
Los Angeles	5,439	...	5,848	7,931	1,542	2,427	6,068	7,011	2,451	5,601
Madrid	785	5,848	...	10,758	5,643	3,448	2,147	4,530	3,593	655
Melbourne	10,500	7,931	10,758	...	8,426	10,395	8,950	6,329	10,359	10,430
Mexico City	5,558	1,542	5,643	8,426	...	2,317	6,676	9,120	2,090	5,725
Montreal	3,254	2,427	3,448	10,395	2,317	...	4,401	7,012	331	3,432
Moscow	1,564	6,068	2,147	8,950	6,676	4,401	...	2,698	4,683	1,554
New York	3,469	2,451	3,593	10,359	2,090	331	4,683	7,318	...	3,636
Paris	214	5,601	655	10,430	5,725	3,432	1,554	4,102	3,636	...
Rio de Janeiro	5,750	6,330	5,045	8,226	4,764	5,078	7,170	8,753	4,801	5,684
Rome	895	6,326	851	9,929	6,377	4,104	1,483	3,684	4,293	690
San Francisco	5,367	347	5,803	7,856	1,887	2,543	5,885	7,691	2,572	5,577
Singapore	6,747	8,767	7,080	3,759	10,327	9,203	5,228	2,571	9,534	6,673
Stockholm	942	5,454	1,653	9,630	6,012	3,714	716	3,414	3,986	1,003
Tokyo	5,959	5,470	6,706	5,062	7,035	6,471	4,660	3,638	6,757	6,053
Warsaw	905	5,922	1,427	9,598	6,337	4,022	721	3,277	4,270	852
Washington, D.C.	3,674	2,300	3,792	10,180	1,885	489	4,876	7,500	205	3,840

	Rio de Janiero	Rome	San Fran-cisco	Singa-pore	Stock-holm	Teheran	Tokyo	Vienna	Warsaw	Wash., D.C.
Bangkok	9,994	5,494	7,931	883	5,089	3,391	2,865	5,252	5,033	8,807
Bejing	10,768	5,063	5,918	2,771	4,133	3,490	1,307	4,648	4,325	6,942
Berlin	6,209	737	5,672	6,164	528	2,185	5,557	326	322	4,181
Cairo	6,143	1,326	7,466	5,137	2,096	1,234	5,958	1,481	1,619	5,822
Cape Town	3,781	5,231	10,248	6,008	6,423	5,241	9,154	5,656	5,935	7,895
Caracas	2,804	5,195	3,902	11,402	5,471	7,320	8,808	5,372	5,559	2,047
Chicago	5,282	4,824	1,859	9,372	4,331	6,502	6,314	4,698	4,679	596
Hong Kong	11,009	5,774	6,905	1,605	5,063	3,843	1,791	5,431	5,147	8,155
Honolulu	8,288	8,040	2,398	6,726	6,875	8,070	3,859	7,632	7,366	4,838
London	5,750	895	5,367	6,747	942	2,743	5,959	771	905	3,674
Los Angeles	6,330	6,326	347	8,767	5,454	7,682	5,470	6,108	5,922	2,300
Madrid	5,045	851	5,803	7,080	1,653	2,978	6,706	1,128	1,427	3,792
Melbourne	8,226	9,929	7,856	3,759	9,630	7,826	5,062	9,790	9,598	10,180
Mexico City	4,764	6,377	1,887	10,327	6,012	8,184	7,035	6,320	6,337	1,885
Montreal	5,078	4,104	2,543	9,203	3,714	5,880	6,471	4,009	4,022	489
Moscow	7,170	1,483	5,885	5,228	716	1,532	4,660	1,043	721	4,876
New York	4,801	4,293	2,572	9,534	3,986	6,141	6,757	4,234	4,270	205
Paris	5,684	690	5,577	6,673	1,003	2,625	6,053	645	852	3,840
Rio de Janeiro	...	5,707	6,613	9,785	6,683	7,374	11,532	6,127	6,455	4,779
Rome	5,707	...	6,259	6,229	1,245	2,127	6,142	477	820	4,497
San Francisco	6,613	6,259	...	8,448	5,399	7,362	5,150	5,994	5,854	2,441
Singapore	9,785	6,229	8,448	...	5,936	4,103	3,300	6,035	5,843	9,662
Stockholm	6,683	1,245	5,399	5,936	...	2,173	5,053	780	494	4,183
Tokyo	11,532	6,142	5,150	3,300	5,053	4,775	...	5,689	5,347	6,791
Warsaw	6,455	820	5,854	5,843	494	1,879	5,689	347	...	4,472
Washington, D.C.	4,779	4,497	2,441	9,662	4,183	6,341	6,791	4,438	4,472	...

AEROSPACE
Memorable Manned Space Flights

Sources: National Aeronautics and Space Administration and The World Almanac.

Crew, date	Mission name	Orbits[1]	Duration	Remarks
Yuri A. Gagarin (4/12/61)	Vostok 1	1	1h 48m	First manned orbital flight.
Alan B. Shepard Jr. (5/5/61)	Mercury-Redstone 3	(2)	15m 22s	First American in space.
Virgil I. Grissom (7/21/61)	Mercury-Redstone 4	(2)	15m 37s	Spacecraft sank. Grissom rescued.
Gherman S. Titov (8/6-7/61)	Vostok 2	16	25h 18m	First space flight of more than 24 hrs.
John H. Glenn Jr. (2/20/62)	Mercury-Atlas 6	3	4h 55m 23s	First American in orbit.
M. Scott Carpenter (5/24/62)	Mercury-Atlas 7	3	4h 56m 05s	Manual retrofire error caused 250 mi. landing overshoot.
Andrian G. Nikolayev (8/11-15/62)	Vostok 3	64	94h 22m	Vostok 3 and 4 made first group flight.
Pavel R. Popovich (8/12-15/62)	Vostok 4	48	70h 57m	On first orbit it came within 3 miles of Vostok 3.
Walter M. Schirra Jr. (10/3/62)	Mercury-Atlas 8	6	9h 13m 11s	Closest splashdown to target to date (4.5 mi.).
L. Gordon Cooper (5/15-16/63)	Mercury-Atlas 9	22	34h 19m 49s	First U.S. evaluation of effects on man of one day in space.
Valery F. Bykovsky (6/14-6/19/63)	Vostok 5	81	119h 06m	Vostok 5 and 6 made 2d group flight.
Valentina V. Tereshkova (6/16-19/63)	Vostok 6	48	70h 50m	First woman in space.
Vladimir M. Komarov, Konstantin P. Feoktistov, Boris B. Yegorov (10/12/64)	Voskhod 1	16	24h 17m	First 3-man orbital flight; first without space suits.
Pavel I. Belyayev, Aleksei A. Leonov (3/18/65)	Voskhod 2	17	26h 02m	Leonov made first "space walk" (10 min.)
Virgil I. Grissom, John W. Young (3/23/65)	Gemini-Titan 3	3	4h 53m 00s	First manned spacecraft to change its orbital path.
James A. McDivitt, Edward H. White 2d, (6/3-7/65)	Gemini-Titan 4	62	97h 56m 11s	White was first American to "walk in space" (20 min.).
L. Gordon Cooper Jr., Charles Conrad Jr. (8/21-29/65)	Gemini-Titan 5	120	190h 55m 14s	First use of fuel cells for electric power; evaluated guidance and navigation system.
Frank Borman, James A. Lovell Jr. (12/4-18/65)	Gemini-Titan 7	206	330h 35m 31s	Longest duration Gemini flight
Walter M. Schirra Jr., Thomas P. Stafford (12/15-16/65)	Gemini-Titan 6-A	16	25h 51m 24s	Completed world's first space rendezvous with Gemini 7.
Neil A. Armstrong, David R. Scott (3/16-17/66)	Gemini-Titan 8	6.5	10h 41m 26s	First docking of one space vehicle with another; mission aborted, control malfunction.
John W. Young, Michael Collins (7/18-21/66)	Gemini-Titan 10	43	70h 46m 39s	First use of Agena target vehicle's propulsion systems.
Charles Conrad Jr., Richard F. Gordon Jr. (9/12-15/66)	Gemini-Titan 11	44	71h 17m 08s	Docked, made 2 revolutions of earth tethered; set Gemini altitude record (739.2 mi.).
James A. Lovell Jr., Edwin E. Aldrin Jr. (11/11-15/66)	Gemini-Titan 12	59	94h 34m 31s	Final Gemini mission; record 5½ hrs. of extravehicular activity.
Vladimir M. Komarov (4/23/67)	Soyuz 1	17	26h 40m	Crashed after re-entry killing Komarov.
Walter M. Schirra Jr., Donn F. Eisele, R. Walter Cunningham (10/11-22/68)	Apollo-Saturn 7	163	260h 09m 03s	First manned flight of Apollo spacecraft command-service module only.
Georgi T. Beregovoi (10/26-30/68)	Soyuz 3	64	94h 51m	Made rendezvous with unmanned Soyuz 2.
Frank Borman, James A. Lovell Jr., William A. Anders (12/21-27/68)	Apollo-Saturn 8	10[3]	147h 00m 42s	First flight to moon (command-service module only); views of lunar surface televised to earth.
Vladimir A. Shatalov (1/14-17/69)	Soyuz 4	45	71h 14m	Docked with Soyuz 5.
Boris V. Volyanov, Aleksei S. Yeliseyev, Yevgeny V. Khrunov (1/15-18/69)	Soyuz 5	46	72h 46m	Docked with Soyuz 4; Yeliseyev and Khrunov transferred to Soyuz 4.
James A. McDivitt, David R. Scott, Russell L. Schweickart (3/3-13/69)	Apollo-Saturn 9	151	241h 00m 54s	First manned flight of lunar module.

(continued)

Crew, date	Mission name	Orbits[1]	Duration	Remarks
Thomas P. Stafford, Eugene A. Cernan, John W. Young (5/18-26/69)....	Apollo-Saturn 10	31[4]	192h 03m 23s	First lunar module orbit of moon.
Neil A. Armstrong, Edwin E. Aldrin Jr., Michael Collins (7/16-24/69)......	Apollo-Saturn 11	30[3]	195h 18m 35s	First lunar landing made by Armstrong and Aldrin; collected 48.5 lbs. of soil, rock samples; lunar stay time 21 h, 36m, 21 s.
Georgi S. Shonin, Vaiery N. Kubasov (10/11-16/69)	Soyuz 6	79	118h 42m.	First welding of metals in space. Space lab construction tests made; Soyuz 6, 7 and 8 — first time 3 spacecraft 7 crew orbited earth at once.
Anatoly V. Filipchenko, Vladislav N. Volkov, Viktor V. Gorbatko (10/12-17/69).....	Soyuz 7	79	118h 41m.	
Charles Conrad Jr., Richard F. Gordon, Alan L. Bean (11/14-24/69).....	Apollo-Saturn 12	45[3]	244h 36m 25s	Conrad and Bean made 2d moon landing; collected 74.7 lbs. of samples, lunar stay time 31 h, 31 m.
James A. Lovell Jr., Fred W. Haise Jr., John L. Swigart Jr. (4/11-17/70)......	Apollo-Saturn 13	...	142h 54m 41s	Aborted after service module oxygen tank ruptured; crew returned safely using lunar module oxygen and power.
Alan B. Shepard Jr., Stuart A. Roosa, Edgar D. Mitchell (1/31-2/9/71)......	Apollo-Saturn 14	34[3]	216h 01m 57s	Shepard and Mitchell made 3d moon landing, collected 96 lbs. of lunar samples; lunar stay 33 h, 31 m.
Georgi T. Dobrovolsky, Vladislav N. Volkov, Viktor I. Patsayev (6/6-30/71).......	Soyuz 11	360	569h 40m.	Docked with Salyut space station; and orbited in Salyut for 23 days; crew died during re-entry from loss of pressurization.
David R. Scott, Alfred M. Worden, James B. Irwin (7/26-8/7/71)......	Apollo-Saturn 15	74[3]	295h 11m 53s	Scott and Irwin made 4th moon landing; first lunar rover use; first deep space walk; 170 lbs. of samples; 66 h, 55 m, stay.
Charles M. Duke Jr., Thomas K. Mattingly, John W. Young (4/16-27/72)......	Apollo-Saturn 16	64[3]	265h 51m 05s	Young and Duke made 5th moon landing; collected 213 lbs. of lunar samples; lunar stay line 71 h, 2 m.
Eugene A. Cernan, Ronald E. Evans, Harrison H. Schmitt (12/7-19/72)......	Apollo-Saturn 17	75[3]	301h 51m 59s	Cernan and Schmitt made 6th manned lunar landing; collected 243 lbs. of samples; record lunar stay of 75 h.
Charles Conrad Jr., Joseph P. Kerwin, Paul J. Weitz (5/25-6/22/73).....	Skylab 2	...	672h 49m 49s	First American manned orbiting space station; made long-flights tests, crew repaired damage caused during boost.
Alan L. Bean, Jack R. Lousma, Owen K. Garriott (7/28-9/25/73).....	Skylab 3	...	1,427h 09m 04s	Crew systems and operational tests, exceeded pre-mission plans for scientific activities; space walk total 13h, 44 m.
Gerald P. Carr, Edward G. Gibson, William Pogue (11/16/73-2/8/74)...	Skylab 4	...	2,017h 16m 30s	Final Skylab mission; record space walk of 7 h, 1 m., record space walks total for a mission 22 h, 21 m.
Alexi Leonov, Valeri Kubasov (7/15-7/21/75)	Soyuz 19	96	143h 31m	
Vance Brand, Thomas P. Stafford, Donald K. Slayton (7/15-7/24/75).....	Apollo 18	136	217h 30m.	U.S.-USSR joint flight. Crews linked-up in space, conducted experiments, shared meals, and held a joint news conference.
Leonid Kizim, Vladmir Solovyov, Oleg Atkov (2/8-10/2/84)......	Salyut 7	...	237 days	Set space endurance record. (since broken)

(1) The U.S. measures orbital flights in revolutions while the Soviets use "orbits." (2) Suborbital. (3) Moon orbits in command module. (4) Moon orbits.
Fire aboard spacecraft Apollo I on the ground at Cape Kennedy, Fla. killed Virgil I. Grissom, Edward H. White and Roger B. Chaffee on Jan. 27, 1967. They were the only U.S. astronauts killed in space tests.

U.S. Space Shuttles

Name, date	Crew	Name, date	Crew
Columbia (4/12-14/81) ...	Robert L. Crippen, John W. Young.	Challenger (4/4-9/83)	Paul Weitz, Karol Bobko, Story Musgrave, Donald Peterson.
Columbia (11/12-14/81) ..	Joe Engle, Richard Truly.		
Columbia (3/22-30/82) ...	Jack Lousma, C. Gordon Fullerton.	Challenger (6/18-24/83) ..	Robert L. Crippen, Norman Thagard, John Fabian, Frederick Hauck, Sally K. Ride (1st U.S. woman in space).
Columbia (6-27/7-4/82) ...	Thomas Mattingly 2d, Henry Hartsfield Jr.		
Columbia (11/11-16/82) ..	Vance Brand, Robert Overmyer, William Lenoir, Joseph Allen.		

(continued

Name, date	Crew	Name, date	Crew
			C. Stewart.
Challenger (8/30-9/5/83) . .	Richard Truly, Daniel Brand-enstein, William Thornton, Guion Bluford (1st U.S. black in space), Dale Gardner.	Challenger (10/30-11/6/85)	Henry W. Hartsfield Jr., Steven R. Nagel, Bonnie J. Dunbar, James F. Buchli, Guion S. Bluford Jr., Ernst Messerschmid,
Columbia (11/28-12/8/83) .	John Young, Brewster Shaw Jr., Robert Parker, Owen Garriott, Byron Lichtenberg, Ulf Merbold.	Atlantis (11/26-12/3/85) . .	Reinhard Furrer, Wubbo J. Ockels. Brewster H. Shaw Jr., Bryan D. O'Connor, Charles
Challenger (2/3-11/84) . .	Vance Brand, Robert Gibson, Ronald McNair, Bruce McCandless, Robert Stewart.		Walker, Rodolfo Neri (first Mexican), Jerry L. Ross, Sherwood C. Spring, Mary L. Cleave.
Challenger (4/6-13/84) . .	Robert L. Crippen, Francis R. Scobee, George D. Nelson, Terry J. Hart, James D. Van Hoften.	Columbia (1/12-1/18/86) . .	Robert L. Gibson, Charles F. Bolden Jr., George D. Nelson, Bill Nelson (first congressman), Franklin R. Chang-Diaz, Steven A.
Discovery (8/30-9/5/84) . .	Henry W. Hartsfield Jr., Michael L. Coats, Steven A. Hawley, Judith A. Resnik, Richard M. Mullane, Charles D. Walker.	Challenger (1/28/86- exploded after takeoff)	Hawley, Robert J. Cenker. Francis R. Scobee, Michael J. Smith, Ronald E. McNair, Ellison S. Onizuka, Judith A. Resnik,
Challenger (10/5-13/84) . .	Robert L. Crippen, Jon A. McBride, Kathryn D. Sullivan, Sally K. Ride, Marc Garneau (first Canadian), David C. Leestma, Paul D. Scully-Power.	Discovery (9/29-10/3/88) . .	Gregory B. Jarvis, Sharon Christa McAuliffe. Frederick H. Hauck, Richard O. Covey, David C. Hilmers, George D. Nelson, John M. Lounge.
Discovery (11/8-16/84) . . .	Frederick H. Hauck, David M. Walker, Dr. Anna L. Fisher, Joseph P. Allen, Dale A. Gardner.	Atlantis (12/3-12/6/88) . .	Robert L. Gibson, Guy S. Gardner, Richard M. Mullane, Jerry L. Ross, William M. Shepherd.
Discovery (1/24-27/85) . . .	Thomas K. Mattingly, Loren J. Shriver, James F. Buchli, Ellison S. Onizuka, Gary E. Payton.	Discovery (3/13-3/18/89) . .	Michael L. Coats, John E. Blaha, James F. Buchli, Robert C. Springer, James P. Bagian.
Discovery (4/12-19/85) . . .	Karol J. Bobko, Donald E. Williams, Sen. Jake Garn, Charles D. Walker, Jeffrey A. Hoffman, S. David Griggs, M. Rhea Seddon.	Atlantis (5/4-5/8/89)	David M. Walker, Ronald J. Grabe, Mary L. Cleave, Norman E. Thagard, Mark C. Lee.
Challenger (4/29-5/6/85) . .	Robert F. Overrmyer, Frederick D. Gregory, Don L. Lind, Taylor G. Wang, Lodewijk van den Berg, Norman Thagard, William Thornton.	Columbia (8/8-8/13/89) . . .	Brewster H. Shaw Jr., Richard N. Richards, David C. Leestma, James C. Adamson, Mark N. Brown.
Discovery (6/17-6/24/85) . .	John O. Creighton, Shannon W. Lucid, Steven R. Nagel, Daniel C. Brandenstein, John W. Fabian, Prince Sultan Salman al-Saud (first Arab), Patrick Baudry.	Atlantis (10/18-10/23/89) . .	Donald E. Williams, Michael J. McCulley, Shannon W. Lucid, Ellen S. Baker, Franklin R. Chang-Diaz. Frederick D. Gregory, John E. Blaha, Manley L. Carter, F. Story Musgrave, Katherine C.
Challenger (7/29-8/6/85) . .	Roy D. Bridges Jr., Anthony W. England, Karl G. Henize, F. Story Musgrave, C. Gordon Fullerton, Loren W. Acton, John-David F. Bartoe.	Discovery (11/22-11/27/89) Colombia (1/9-1/20/90) . .	Thornton. Daniel C. Brandenstein, Bonnie J. Dunbar, James D. Wetherbee, Marsha S. Ivins, G. David Low.
Discovery (8/27-9/3/85) . .	John M. Lounge, James D. van Hoften, William F. Fisher, Joe H. Engle, Richard O. Covey.	Atlantis (2/28-3/4/90)	John O. Creighton, John H. Casper, David C. Hilmers, Richard M. Mullane, Pierre J. Thuot.
Atlantis (10/4-10/7/85) . . .	Karol J. Bobko, Ronald J. Grabe, David C. Hilmers, William A. Pailes, Robert	Discovery (4/24-4/29/90) . .	Bruce McCandless 2d, Kathryn D. Sullivan, Loren J. Shriver, Charles F. Bolden Jr., Steven A. Hawley.

International Space Projects

Source: *Omni Space Almanac.* Pharos Books

Date	Event	Date	Event
1991	Eureca, Europe's first free-flying, retrievable space platform, launched.	1995	station module launched. Europe's Ariane 5 heavy-lift launch vehicle becomes operational.
1992	Japan's H-2 launch rocket operational.		
1995	Europe's Columbus module and Japan's space	1997	Europe's spaceplane, Hermes, built by France.

Notable U.S. Unmanned and Planetary Missions

Spacecraft	Launch date (GMT)	Mission	Remarks
Mariner 2	Aug. 27, 1962	Venus	Passed within 22,000 miles from Venus 12/14/62; contact lost 1/3/63 at 54 million miles
Ranger 7	July 28, 1964	Moon	Yielded over 4,000 photos
Mariner 4	Nov. 28, 1964	Mars	Passed behind Mars 7/14/65; took 22 photos from 6,000 miles
Ranger 8	Feb. 17, 1965	Moon	Yielded over 7,000 photos
Surveyor 3	Apr. 17, 1967	Moon	Scooped and tested lunar soil
Mariner 5	June 14, 1967	Venus	In solar orbit; closest Venus fly-by 10/19/67
Mariner 6	Feb. 25, 1969	Mars	Came within 2,000 miles of Mars 7/31/69; sent back data, photos
Mariner 7	Mar. 27, 1969	Mars	Came within 2,000 miles of Mars 8/5/69
Mariner 9	May 30, 1971	Mars	First craft to orbit Mars 11/13/71; sent back over 7,000 photos
Pioneer 10	Mar. 3, 1972	Jupiter	Passed Jupiter 12/3/73; exited the solar system 6/14/83
Mariner 10	Nov. 3, 1973	Venus, Mercury	Passed Venus 2/5/74; arrived Mercury 3/29/74. First time gravity of one planet (Venus) used to whip spacecraft toward another (Mercury)
Viking 1	Aug. 20, 1975	Mars	Landed on Mars 7/20/76; did scientific research, sent photos; functioned 6 1/2 years
Viking 2	Sept. 9, 1975	Mars	Landed on Mars 9/3/76; functioned 3 1/2 years
Voyager 1	Sept. 5, 1977	Jupiter, Saturn	Encountered Jupiter 3/5/79; Saturn 11/13/80
Voyager 2	Aug. 20, 1977	Jupiter, Saturn, Uranus, Neptune	Encountered Jupiter 7/9/79; Saturn 8/26/81; Uranus 1/8 and 1/27/86; Neptune 8/24/89
Pioneer 12	May 20, 1978	Venus	Entered Venus orbit 12/4/78
Pioneer 13	Aug. 8, 1978	Venus	Encountered Venus 12/9/78
Titan 4	June 14, 1989	Orbit Earth	First of 41 such rockets whose primary purpose is defense

Successful Space Launches: 1957 to 1988

(Criterion of success is attainment of Earth orbit or Earth escape)

Year	Total[1]	USSR	United States	Japan	European Space Agency	India	China
Total	2,976	2,016	875	34	16	3	19
1957-1959	21	6	15	—	—	—	—
1960-1964	268	76	192	—	—	—	—
1965-1969	586	302	279	—	—	—	—
1970-1974	555	405	139	5	—	—	2
1975-1979	607	461	126	10	1	—	6
1980-1984	605	483	93	12	8	3	6
1985	121	98	17	2	3	—	1
1986	103	91	6	2	2	—	2
1987	110	95	8	3	2	—	2
1988	116	90	12	2	7	—	4

(1) Incl. launches in countries not shown.

Notable Proposed U.S. Space Missions

Source: National Aeronautics and Space Administration

Year, Month		Mission	Purpose
1991	Jan.	Tethered Satellite System (c)	Study gas clouds and electrical fields in space
	Feb.	International Microgravity Lab (c)	Establish system for life-science studies
	May	Atmospheric Lab for Applications & Science (c)	Study variations in solar spectrum and Earth's atmosphere
	July	Spacelab (c)	Low-gravity experiments
	Aug.	Extreme Ultraviolet Explorer (a)	Catalog ultraviolet spectrum of stars and galaxies
	Oct.	Upper Atmosphere Research Satellite (c)	Study physical processes of upper atmosphere
	Nov.	Doppler Imaging Interferometer (c)	Study upper-atmospheric winds
		Small Explorer-1 (a)	First of a series to study space physics and atmospheric science
1992	May	Space Radar Lab (c)	Acquire radar images of Earth's surface
	June	TOPEX/Poseidon (a)	Study relationship of ocean systems to climate
	Sept.	Mars Observer (a)	Study climate and surface of Mars
		Shuttle High-energy Astrophysics Lab (c)	Study X-ray sources and spectrum in space
1993	June	Gravity Probe (b)	Prototype of mission to test Einstein's theory of relativity
		Polar (a)	Study physical properties of the aurora borealis
	Nov.	Waves in Space Plasmas (c)	Study gaslike particles in space with radio-signal experiments
1994		X-ray Timing Explorer (a)	Study compact X-ray sources such as neutron stars and black holes
1995		Advanced X-ray Astronomy Facility (b)	Observatory with high-resolution telescope; to be in orbit 15 years
1996		Comet Rendezvous Asteroid Flyby (a)	Study origin and evolution of solar system
1997		Earth Observing System (a)	Orbit and study Earth
1998		Cassini (a)	Study Saturn
1999		Space Infrared Telescope Facility (b)	Measure infrared emissions from Milky Way to get clearer picture of galaxy
2000		Mars Rover Sample Return (d)	Collect Martian-soil samples and return to Earth for observation

(a) Launched by expendable rocket. (b) Launched by shuttle. (c) Carried aboard shuttle. (d) To be determined.

Notable Around the World and Intercontinental Trips

	From/To	Miles	Time	Date
Nellie Bly	New York/New York		72d 06h 11m	1889
George Francis Train	New York/New York		67d 12h 03m	1890
Charles Fitzmorris	Chicago/Chicago		60d 13h 29m	1901
J. W. Willis Sayre	Seattle/Seattle		54d 09h 42m	1903
J. Alcock-A.W. Brown (1)	Newfoundland/Ireland	1,960	16h 12m	June 14-15, 1919
Two U.S. Army airplanes	Seattle/Seattle	26,103	35d 01h 11m	1924
Richard E. Byrd (2)	Spitsbergen/N. Pole	1,545	15h 30m	May 9, 1926
Amundsen-Ellsworth-Nobile Expedition	Spitsbergen/Teller, Alaska		80h	May 11-14,1926
E.S. Evans and L. Wells (N. Y.World) (3)	New York/New York	18,400	28d 14h 36m 05s	June 16-July 14, 1926
Charles Lindbergh (4)	New York/Paris	3,610	33h 29m 30s	May 20-21, 1927
Amelia Earhart, W. Stultz, L. Gordon	Newfoundland/Wales		20h 40m	June 17-18, 1928
Graf Zeppelin	Friedrichshafen, Ger./Lakehurst, N.J.	6,630	4d 15h 46m	Oct. 11-15, 1928
Graf Zeppelin	Friedrichshafen, Ger./Lakehurst, N.J.	21,700	20d 04h	Aug. 14-Sept. 4, 1929
Wiley Post and Harold Gatty (Monoplane Winnie Mae)	New York/New York	15,474	8d 15h 51m	July 1, 1931
C. Pangborn-H. Herndon Jr. (5)	Misawa, Japan/Wenatchee, Wash.	4,458	41h 34m	Oct. 3-5, 1931
Amelia Earhart (6)	Newfoundland/Ireland	2,026	14h 56m	May 20-21, 1932
Wiley Post (Monoplane Winnie Mae) (7)	New York/New York	15,596	115h 36m 30s	July 15-22, 1933
Hindenburg Zeppelin	Lakehurst, N.J./Frankfort, Ger.		42h 53m	Aug. 9-11, 1936
H. R. Ekins (Scripps-Howard Newspapers in race) (Zeppelin Hindenburg to Germany air planes from Frankfurt)	Lakehurst, N.J./Lakehurst, N.J.	25,654	18d 11h 14m 33s	Sept, 30-Oct. 19, 1936
Howard Hughes and 4 assistants	New York/New York	14,824	3d 19h 08m 10s	July 10-13, 1938
Douglas Corrigan	New York/Dublin		28h 13m	July 17-18, 1938
Mrs. Clara Adams (Pan American Clipper)	Port Washington, N.Y./ Newark, N.J.		16d 19h 04m	June 28-July 15, 1939
Globester, U.S. Air Transport Command	Wash., D.C./Wash., D.C.	23,279	149h 44m	Oct. 4, 1945
Capt. William P. Odom (A-26 Reynolds Bombshell)	New York/New York	20,000	78h 55m 12s	Apr. 12-16, 1947
America, Pan American 4-engine Lockheed Constellation (8)	New York/New York	22,219	101h 32m	June 17-30, 1947
Col. Edward Eagan	New York/New York	20,559	147h 15m	Dec. 13, 1948
USAF B-50 Lucky Lady II (Capt. James Gallagher) (9)	Ft. Worth, Tex./Ft. Worth, Tex.	23,452	94h 01m	Feb. 26-Mar. 2, 1949
Col. D. Schilling, USAF (10)	England/Limestone, Me.	3,300	10h 01m	Sept. 22, 1950
C.F. Blair Jr.	Norway/Alaska	3,300	10h 29m	May 29, 1951
Two U.S. S-55	Massachusetts/Scotland	3,410	42h 30m	July 15-31, 1952
Canberra Bomber (11)	N. Ireland/Newfoundland	2,073	04h 34m	Aug. 26, 1952
	Newfoundland/N. Ireland	2,073	03h 25m	Aug. 26, 1952
Three USAF B-52 Stratofortresses (12)	Merced, Cal./Cal.	24,325	45h 19m	Jan. 15-18, 1957
Max Conrad	Chicago/Rome	5,000	34h 03m	Mar. 5-6, 1959
USSR TU-114 (13)	Moscow/New York	5,092	11h 06m	June 28, 1959
Boeing 707-320	New York/Moscow	c.5090	08h 54m	July 23, 1959
Peter Gluckmann (solo)	San Francisco/San Francisco	22,800	29d	Aug. 22-Sept. 20, 1959
Sue Snyder	Chicago/Chicago	21,219	62h 59m	June 22-24, 1960
Max Conrad (solo)	Miami/Miami	25,946	8d 18h 35m 57s	Feb. 28-Mar. 8, 1961
Sam Miller & Louis Fodor	New York/New York		46h 28m	Aug. 3-4, 1963
Robert & Joan Wallick	Manila/Manila	23,129	05d 06h 17m 10s	June 2-7, 1966
Arthur Godfrey, Richard Merrill Fred Austin, Karl Keller	New York/New York	23,333	86h 9m 01s	June 4-7, 1966
Trevor K. Brougham	Darwin, Australia/Darwin	24,800	5d 05h 57m	Aug. 5-10, 1972
Walter H. Mullikin, Albert Frink, Lyman Watt, Frank Cassaniti, Edward Shields	New York/New York	23,137	1d 22h 50m	May 1-3,1976
David Kunst (15)	Waseca, Minn./Waseca, Minn.	14,500	4yrs 3mos 16d	June 10, 1970-Oct. 5, 1974
Arnold Palmer	Denver/Denver	22,985	57h 25m 42s	May 17-19, 1976
Boeing 747 (14)	San Francisco/San Francisco	26,382	54h 7m 12s	Oct. 28-31, 1977
Concorde	London/Wash., D.C.	1,023 mph	03h 34m 48s	May 29, 1976
Concorde	Paris/New York	1,037.50 mph	03h 30m 11s	Aug. 22, 1978
Richard Rutan & Jeana Yeager (16)	Edwards AFB, Cal.	24,986	09d 03m 44s	Dec. 14-23, 1986

(1) Non-stop transtlantic flight. (2) Polar flight. (3) Mileage by train and auto, 4,110; by plane, 6,300; by steamship, 8,000. (4) Solo transatlantic flight in the Ryan monoplane the "Spirit of St. Louis". (5) Non-stop Pacific flight. (6) Woman's trans-oceanic solo flight. (7) First to fly solo around northern circumference of the world, also first to fly twice around the world. (8) Inception of regular commercial global air service. (9) First non-stop round-the-world flight, refueled 4 times in flight. (10) Non-stop jet transatlantic flight. (11) Transatlantic round trip on same day. (12) First non-stop global flight by jet planes; refueled in flight by KC-97 aerial tankers; average speed approx. 525 mph. (13) Non-stop between Moscow and New York. (14) Speed record around the world over both the earth's poles. (15) First to circle the earth on foot. (16) Circled the earth nonstop without refueling.

International Aeronautical Records

Source: The National Aeronautic Association, 1763 R St. NW, Washington, DC 20009, representative in the United States of the Federation Aeronautique Internationale, certifying agency for world aviation and space records. The International Aeronautical Federation was formed in 1905 by representatives from Belgium, France, Germany, Great Britain, Spain, Italy, Switzerland, and the United States, with headquarters in Paris. Regulations for the control of official records were signed Oct. 14, 1905. World records are defined as maximum performance, regardless of class or type of aircraft used. Records to mid-1990.

World Absolute Records—Maximum Performance in Any Class

Speed over a straight course — 2,193.16 mph — Capt. Elden W. Joersz, USAF, Lockheed SR-71; Beale AFB, Cal., July 28, 1976.
Speed over a closed circuit — 2,092.294 mph — Maj. Adolphus H. Bledsoe Jr., USAF, Lockheed SR-71; Beale AFB, Cal., July 27, 1976.
Speed around the world, non-stop, nonrefueled — 115.65 mph — Richard Rutan & Jeana Yeager, U.S., Voyager, Edwards AFB, Cal. Dec. 14-23, 1986.
Altitude — (123,523.58 feet) — Alexander Fedotov, USSR, E-266M; Podmoskovnoye, USSR, Aug. 31, 1977.
Altitude in horizontal flight — 85,068.997 ft. — Capt. Robert C. Helt, USAF, Lockheed SR-71; Beale AFB, Cal., July 28, 1976.

Class K Spacecraft

Duration — 326 days, 11 hours, 15 minutes — Col. Yuri V. Romanenko, USSR, space station *MIR*; Feb. 5 —Dec. 29, 1987.
Altitude — 234,672.5 mi. — Frank Borman, James A. Lovell Jr., William Anders, Apollo 8; Dec. 21-27, 1968.
Greatest mass lifted — 282,197 lbs. — Frank Borman, James A. Lovell Jr., William Anders, Apollo 8; Dec. 21-27, 1968.
Distance — 87,436.800 mi. — Anatoly Beresovoy & Valentin Lebedev, USSR, Salyut 7, Soyuz T5, Soyuz T7; May 13-Dec. 10, 1982.

World "Class" Records

All other records, international in scope, are termed World "Class" records and are divided into classes: airships, free balloons, airplanes, seaplanes, amphibians, gliders, and rotorplanes. Airplanes (Class C) are sub-divided into four groups: Group I — piston engine aircraft, Group II — turboprop aircraft, Group III — jet aircraft, Group IV — rocket powered aircraft. A partial listing of world records follows:

Airplanes (Class C-I, Group I—piston engine)

Distance, closed circuit — 24,986.727 mi. — Richard Rutan & Jeana Yeager, U.S., Voyager; Edwards AFB, Cal., Dec. 14-23, 1986.
Speed for 100 kilometers (62.137 miles) without payload — 469.549 mph — Jacqueline Cochran, U.S.; North American P-51; Coachella Valley, Cal., Dec. 10, 1947.
Speed for 1,000 kilometers (621.369 miles) without payload — 431.09 mph — Jacqueline Cochran, U.S.; North American P-51; Santa Rosasummit, Cal. — Flagstaff, Ariz. course, May 24, 1948.
Speed for 5,000 kilometers (3,106.849 miles) without payload — 338.39 mph — Capt. James Bauer, USAF, Boeing B-29; Dayton, Oh., June 28, 1946.
Speed around the world — 203.64 mph — D.N. Dalton, Australia; Beechcraft Duke; Brisbane, Aust., July 20-25, 1975. Time: 5 days, 2 hours, 19 min., 57 sec.

Light Airplanes—(Class C-1.d)

Great Circle distance without landing — 7,929.71 mi. — Peter Wilkins, Australia, Piper Malibu, Sydney, Aust. to Phoenix, Ariz., Mar. 30-Apr. 1, 1987.
Speed for 100 kilometers — (62,137 miles) in a closed circuit — 322.780 mph — Ms. R. M. Sharpe, Great Britain; Vickers Supermarine Spitfire 5-B; Wolverhampton, June 17, 1950.

Helicopters (Class E-1)

Great Circle distance without landing — 2,213.04 mi. — Robert G. Ferry, U.S.; Hughes YOH-6A helicopter; Culver City, Cal., to Ormond Beach, Fla., Apr. 6-7, 1966.
Speed around the world —35.40 mph — H. Ross Perot Jr.; Bell 206 L-11 Long Ranger N39112; Dallas, Tex.–Dallas, Tex.; Sept. 1-30, 1982; 29 days, 3 hrs., 8 min., 13 sec.

Gliders (Class D-I—single seater)

Distance, straight line — 907.7 mi. — Hans Werner Grosse, West Germany; ASK 12 sailplane; Luebeck to Biarritz, Apr. 25, 1972.
Distance to a goal & return — 1,023.25 mi. — Thomas Knauff, U.S. Nimbus III; Williamsport, Pa., Apr. 25, 1983.

Airplanes (Class C-I, Group II—Turboprop)

Great Circle distance without landing — 8,732.09 mi.— Lt. Col. Edgar L. Allison Jr., USAF, Lockheed HC-130 Hercules aircraft; Taiwan to Scott AFB, Ill.; Feb. 20, 1972.
Altitude — (51,014 ft.) — Donald R. Wilson, U.S.; LTV L450F aircraft; Greenville, Tex., Mar. 27, 1972.
Speed for 1,000 kilometers (621.369 miles) without payload — 541.449 mph — Ivan Soukhomline, USSR; TU-114 aircraft; Sternberg, USSR; Apr. 24, 1960.
Speed for 5,000 kilometers (3,106.849 miles) without payload — 545.072 mph — Ivan Soukhomline, USSR; TU-114 aircraft, Sternberg, USSR; Apr. 9, 1960.
Speed around the world —304.80 mph — Joe Harnish, U.S., Gulfstream Commander 695A, Elkhart, Ind., Mar. 21-24, 1983.

Airplanes (Class C-1, Group III—Engine)

Great Circle distance without landing — 12,532.28 mi. — Maj. Clyde P. Evely, USAF, Boeing B-52-H, Kadena, Okinawa to Madrid, Spain, Jan. 10-11, 1962.
Distance in a closed circuit — 12,521.78 mi. — Vladimir Tersky, USSR, AN-124, Podmoskovnoye, USSR, May 6-7, 1987.
Altitude — 123,523.58 ft. — Alexander Fedotov, USSR; E-226M airplane; Podmoskovnoye, USSR, Aug. 31, 1977.
Speed for 100 kilometers in a closed circuit — 1,618.7 mph — Alexander Fedotov, USSR; E-266 airplane, Apr. 8, 1973.
Speed for 500 kilometers in a closed circuit — 1,852.61 mph — Mikhail Komarov, USSR; E-266 airplane, Oct. 5, 1967.
Speed for 1,000 kilometers in a closed circuit — 2,092.294 mph — Maj. Adolphus H. Bledsoe Jr., USAF; Lockheed SR-71; Beale AFB, Cal., July 27, 1976.
Speed for 2,000 kilometers without payload — 1,250.42 mph — S. Agapov, USSR; Podmoscovnde, USSR; July 20, 1983.
Speed around the world — 637.71 mph — Allen E. Paulson, U.S., Gulfstream IV, Houston, Tex., Feb. 26-28, 1988.

Balloons-Class A

Altitude — (113,739.9 ft.) — Cmdr. Malcolm D. Ross, USNR; Lee Lewis Memorial Winzen Research Balloon; Gulf of Mexico, May 4, 1961.
Distance —(5,208.67 mi.) — Ben Abruzzo; Raven Experimental; Nagashima, Japan to Covello, Cal., Nov. 9-12, 1981.

Duration —137 hr., 5 min., 50 sec. — Ben Abruzzo and Maxie Anderson; Double Eagle II; Presque Isle, Maine to Miserey, France (3,107.61 mi.); Aug. 12-17, 1978.

FAI Course Records

Los Angeles to New York — 1,214.65 mph — Capt. Robert G. Sowers, USAF; Convair B-58 Hustler; elapsed time: 2 hrs. 58.71 sec., Mar. 5, 1962.
New York to Los Angeles — 1,081.80 mph — Capt. Robert G. Sowers, USAF; Convair B-58 Hustler; elapsed time: 2 hrs. 15 min. 50.08 sec., Mar. 5, 1962.
New York to Paris — 1,089.36 mph — Maj. W. R. Payne, U.S.; Convair B-58 Hustler; elapsed time: 3 hrs 19 min. 44 sec., May 26, 1961.
London to New York — 587.457 mph — Maj. Burl Davenport, USAF; Boeing KC-135; elapsed time: 5 hrs. 53 min. 12.77 sec.; June 27, 1958.
Baltimore to Moscow, USSR — 563.36 mph — Col. James B. Swindal, USAF; Boeing VC-137 (707); elapsed time: 8 hrs. 33 min. 45.4 sec., May 19, 1963.
New York to London — 1,806.964 mph — Maj. James V. Sullivan, USAF; Lockheed SR-71; elapsed time 1 hr. 54 min. 56.4 sec., Sept. 1, 1974.
London to Los Angeles — 1,435.587 mph — Capt. Harold B. Adams, USAF; Lockheed SR-71; elapsed time: 3 hrs. 47 min. 39 sec., Sept. 13, 1974.

The Busiest U.S. Airports in 1989

Source: Air Transport Association of America (Passengers arriving & departing)

Chicago O'Hare	59,130,007	Boston	23,272,690
Dallas/Ft. Worth	47,579,046	Detroit	21,495,159
Los Angeles	44,967,221	Newark	20,927,946
Atlanta	43,312,285	Phoenix	20,710,790
New York (JFK)	30,323,077	St. Louis	20,015,015
San Francisco	29,939,835	Minneapolis/St. Paul	19,400,815
Denver	27,568,033	Orlando	17,232,351
Miami	23,385,010	Pittsburgh	17,145,272
New York (LGA)	23,158,317	Las Vegas	16,684,036
Honolulu	22,617,340	Houston	16,007,355

Busiest Foreign Airports in 1989*

Source: Airport Operators Council International (passengers arriving & departing)

London, UK, Heathrow	39,905,200	Rome, Italy, Fiumicino	16,117,277
Tokyo, Japan, Haneda	36,567,738	Amsterdam, Netherlands, Schiphol	15,998,174
Frankfurt, W. Germany	26,006,900	Stockholm, Sweden, Arlanda	14,278,156
Paris, France, Orly	24,288,440	Singapore, Changi	12,973,237
Osaka, Japan	21,873,831	Bangkok	12,669,102
London, UK, Gatwick	21,293,200	Copenhagen, Denmark	12,436,654
Paris, France, Charles De Gaulle	20,669,542	Zurich, Switzerland	12,150,558
Toronto, Canada, Lester B. Pearson	20,418,094	Athens	10,514,367
Hong Kong	17,431,124	Munich-Riem, W. Germany	10,100,858
New Tokyo-Narita	16,982,055		

*Does not include airports that did not respond to the AOCI survey.

U.S. Scheduled Airline Traffic

Source: Air Transport Association of America (thousands)

	1987	1988	1989
Passenger traffic			
Revenue passengers enplaned	447,678	454,614	453,692
Revenue passenger miles	404,471,484	423,301,559	432,714,309
Available seat miles	648,720,938	676,802,328	684,375,876
Revenue passenger load factor(%)	62.3	62.5	63.2
Cargo traffic (ton miles)	10,016,111	11,469,193	12,185,968
Freight and express	8,260,278	9,632,219	10,274,534
U.S. Mail	1,721,263	1,836,974	1,911,434
Overall traffic and service			
Total revenue ton miles—charter service	4,448,871	4,597,536	5,616,380
Total revenue ton miles—all services	54,917,632	58,397,186	61,073,778
Total available ton miles—all services	99,152,795	105,372,555	109,360,431

U.S. Airline Safety

Source: National Transportation Safety Board

	Departures (millions)	Fatal accidents	Fatalities	Fatal accidents per 100,000 departures		Departures (millions)	Fatal accidents	Fatalities	Fatal accidents per 100,000 departures
1976	4.8	2	38	0.041	1983	5.0	4	15	0.079
1977	4.9	3	78	0.061	1984	5.4	1	4	0.018
1978	5.0	5	160	0.100	1985	5.8	4	197	0.069
1979	5.4	4	351	0.074	1986	6.4	2	5	0.016
1980	5.4	0	0	0.000	1987	6.6	4[1]	231	0.046[1]
1981	5.2	4	4	0.077	1988	6.7	3[1]	285	0.030[1]
1982	5.0	4	233	0.060	1989	6.6	11	278	0.167

(1) Sabotage-caused accidents are incl. in the Accidents but not in the Accident rates.

Leading Passenger Airlines in 1989

(In thousands)

Airline	Passengers	Airline	Passengers	Airline	Passengers
American	72,359	Southwest	20,241	Midway	4,681
Delta	68,200	Pan American	17,174	Braniff	4,316
United	54,919	Piedmont	16,657	Aloha	4,002
USAir	44,495	Eastern	14,517	Air Wisconsin	2,195
Northwest	38,627	America West	13,300	West Air	1,819
Continental	34,957	Hawaiian	5,277	Horizon Air	1,587
Trans World	25,150	Alaska	4,963		

Aircraft in Operation and Aircraft Age: 1983 to 1989

Source: AVMARK, Arlington, VA.

(As of January 1. For U.S. domestic major and national services. Major carriers have operating revenues of $1 billion of more; national carriers have operating revenues of $75 million to $1 billion)

Type of Aircraft	Aircraft in Operation				Mean Age (years)			
	1983	1985	1987	1989	1983	1985	1987	1989
Industry total	2,360	2,790	2,816	3,190	10.5	10.8	11.8	12.0
Boeing 727[1]	1,001	996	993	956	10.5	12.0	13.9	15.5
Boeing 737	270	365	547	698	8.9	9.1	8.8	8.2
Boeing 747	130	136	124	136	10.9	11.8	15.0	15.8
Boeing 757	2	23	73	107	1.0	2.0	2.4	3.6
Boeing 767	14	54	61	111	1.0	2.6	3.9	4.3
Airbus A300/A310	30	134	59	76	3.4	1.9	5.7	5.3
Lockheed L-1011[1]	119	164	107	111	7.3	7.5	11.0	13.0
McDonnell Douglas DC-8[1]	98	72	52	40	15.8	17.2	18.8	20.9
McDonnell Douglas DC-9[1]	541	658	433	455	11.9	9.9	16.7	18.5
McDonnell Douglas DC-10[1]	155	168	161	159	9.1	9.8	12.5	14.6
McDonnell Douglas MD-80	X	X	206	341	X	X	3.1	3.9

(X) Not applicable. (1) No longer in production.

NASA Outlays for Operations & Research and Development

Source: U.S. Office of Management and Budget

(millions of dollars)

Year	Total outlays	Percent change[1]	Performance				Facilities			
			Total	Space flight	Space science applications	Air transport and other	Total	Space flight	Space science applications	Air transport and other
1970	$3,753	−11.7	$3,699	$2,195	$963	$541	$54	$14	$21	$19
1975	3,266	.3	3,181	1,500	1,076	606	85	35	9	42
1980	4,850	15.8	4,710	2,556	1,341	482	140	38	5	97
1985	7,251	2.9	7,004	3,852	1,834	594	247	70	23	154
1988	9,092	19.8	8,693	4,882	1,777	1,018	399	130	48	221

(1) Change from immediate prior year.

National Aviation Hall of Fame

The National Aviation Hall of Fame at Dayton, Oh., is dedicated to honoring the outstanding pioneers of air and space.

Allen, William M.
Andrews, Frank M.
Armstrong, Neil A.
Arnold, Henry H. "Hap"
Atwood, John Leland
Balchen, Bernt
Baldwin, Thomas S.
Beachey, Lincoln
Beech, Olive A.
Beech, Walter H.
Bell, Alexander Graham
Bell, Lawrence D.
Boeing, William E.
Bong, Richard I.
Borman, Frank
Boyd, Albert
Brown, George "Scratchley"
Byrd, Richard E.
Cessna, Clyde V.
Chamberlin, Clarence D.
Chanute, Octave
Chennault, Claire L.
Cochran (Odlum), Jacqueline
Collins, Michael
Conrad Jr., Charles
Crossfield, A. Scott
Cunningham, Alfred A.
Curtiss, Glenn H.
deSeversky, Alexander P.
Doolittle, James H.
Douglas, Donald W.
Draper, Charles S.
Eaker, Ira C.

Earhart, (Putnam), Amelia
Eielson, C. Benjamin
Ellyson, Theodore G.
Ely, Eugene B.
Everest, Frank K.
Fairchild, Sherman M.
Fleet, Reuben H.
Fokker, Anthony H.G.
Ford, Henry
Foss, Joseph
Foulois, Benjamin D.
Gabreski, Francis S.
Glenn Jr., John H.
Goddard, George W.
Goddard, Robert H.
Godfrey, Arthur
Goldwater, Barry M.
Grissom, Virgil I.
Gross, Robert E.
Grumman, Leroy R.
Guggenheim, Harry F.
Haughton, Daniel J.
Hegenberger, Albert F.
Heinemann, Edward H.
Hoover, Robert A.
Hughes, Howard R.
Ingalls, David S.
Jeppesen, Elrey B.
Johnson, Clarence L.
Kenney, George C.
Kettering, Charles F.
Kindelberger, James H.
Knabenshue, A. Roy

Knight, William J.
Lahm, Frank P.
Langley, Samuel P.
Lear, William P. Sr.
LeMay, Curtis E.
LeVier, Anthony W.
Lindbergh, Anne M.
Lindbergh, Charles A.
Link, Edwin A.
Lockheed, Allan H.
Loening, Grover
Luke Jr., Frank
Macready, John A.
Martin, Glenn L.
McDonnell, James S.
Mitscher, Marc A.
Meyer, John C.
Mitchell, William "Billy"
Montgomery, John J.
Moorer, Thomas H.
Moss, Sanford A.
Neumann, Gerhard
Northrop, John K.
Patterson, William A.
Piper Sr., William T.
Post, Wiley H.
Read, Albert C.
Reeve, Robert C.
Rentschler, Frederick B.
Richardson, Holden C.
Rickenbacker, Edward V.
Rodgers, Calbraith P.
Rogers, Will

Rushworth, Robert A.
Ryan, T. Claude
Schirra, Walter M.
Schriever, Bernard A.
Selfridge, Thomas E.
Shepard Jr., Alan B.
Sikorsky, Igor I.
Six, Robert F.
Smith, C.R.
Spaatz, Carl A.
Sperry Sr., Elmer A.
Sperry Sr., Lawrence B.
Stanley, Robert M.
Stapp, John P.
Stearmann, Lloyd C.
Taylor, Charles E.
Towers, John H.
Trippe, Juan T.
Turner, Roscoe
Twining, Nathan F.
von Braun, Wernher
von Karman, Theodore
von Ohain, Hans P.
Vought, Chance M.
Wade, Leigh
Walden, Henry W.
Wilson, Thornton A.
Wright, Orville
Wright, Wilbur
Yeager, Charles E.
Young, John W.

ENERGY

Major Energy Developments

Source: Energy Information Administration. *Annual Energy Review 1989*

U.S. total energy consumption in 1989 reached a record high of 81 quadrillion Btu (3)—an increase of 1.3 percent from 1988—as growth in the economy promoted an increase in energy demand. The inability of members of the Organization of Petroleum Exporting Countries (OPEC) to restrain production played a role in keeping oil prices low during the post-1986 period. Domestic production of crude oil continued to suffer from the effects of four years of low oil prices. Because of close ties between the price of crude oil and market conditions, in 1989 three key oil exploration indicators fell to their lowest level in at least 41 years. In contrast, the domestic refinery industry benefited from market conditions in 1989, when low crude oil prices and strong product demand tended to increase profit margins in the refining industry. Record energy demand coupled with a slight decline in energy production led to continued growth in net energy imports—up 7 percent from the 1988 level to 14 quadrillion Btu—a level that continued to fuel concerns about U.S. dependence on foreign sources of supply.

(See *Chronology and Index* for 1990 information.)

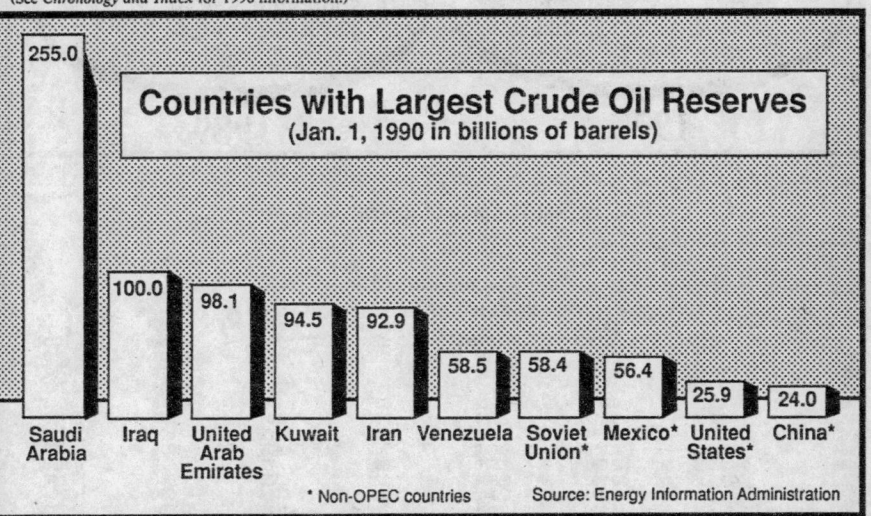

Countries with Largest Crude Oil Reserves
(Jan. 1, 1990 in billions of barrels)

Saudi Arabia	Iraq	United Arab Emirates	Kuwait	Iran	Venezuela	Soviet Union*	Mexico*	United States*	China*
255.0	100.0	98.1	94.5	92.9	58.5	58.4	56.4	25.9	24.0

* Non-OPEC countries   Source: Energy Information Administration

World Production of Crude Oil¹, 1960-1990

Source: Energy Information Administration. Annual Energy Review, 1989 (millions of barrels per day)

Year	Total² OPEC	Canada	China	Mexico	U.K.	U.S.	USSR	Other	Total World
1960	8.70	0.52	0.10	0.27	(³)	7.04	2.91	1.42	20.96
1965	14.34	0.81	0.23	0.32	(³)	7.80	4.79	2.01	30.30
1970	23.41	1.26	0.60	0.49	(³)	9.64	6.97	3.50	45.87
1971	25.33	1.35	0.78	0.49	(³)	9.46	7.44	3.64	48.48
1972	27.09	1.53	0.90	0.51	(³)	9.44	7.88	3.77	51.13
1973	30.99	1.80	1.09	0.47	(³)	9.21	8.33	3.80	55.68
1974	30.73	1.55	1.32	0.57	(³)	8.77	8.86	3.86	55.66
1975	27.15	1.43	1.49	0.71	0.01	8.38	9.47	4.14	52.78
1976	30.74	1.31	1.67	0.83	0.25	8.13	9.99	4.36	57.27
1977	31.30	1.32	1.87	0.98	0.77	8.25	10.49	4.62	59.59
1978	29.88	1.32	2.08	1.21	1.08	8.71	10.95	4.78	60.00
1979	31.00	1.50	2.12	1.46	1.57	8.55	11.19	5.09	62.48
1980	26.99	1.44	2.11	1.94	1.62	8.60	11.46	5.20	59.35
1981	22.84	1.29	2.01	2.31	1.81	8.57	11.55	5.39	55.78
1982	19.15	1.27	2.05	2.75	2.07	8.65	11.62	5.65	53.18
1983	17.89	1.36	2.12	2.69	2.29	8.69	11.68	6.25	52.97
1984	17.86	1.44	2.30	2.78	2.48	8.88	11.58	6.90	54.20
1985	16.63	1.47	2.51	2.75	2.53	8.97	11.25	7.54	53.65
1986	18.75	1.47	2.62	2.44	2.55	8.68	11.54	7.85	55.89
1987	18.58	1.53	2.69	2.54	2.48	8.35	11.69	8.23	56.10
1988	20.90	1.61	2.73	2.51	2.23	8.14	11.68	8.66	58.46
1989	22.63	1.56	2.76	2.51	1.79	7.61	11.36	9.24	59.46
1990 (Jan.-Mar. Avg.)	24.17	1.51	2.78	2.51	1.90	7.46	11.21	9.62	61.16

(1) Includes lease condensate, excludes natural gas plant liquids; (2) Current membership of the Organization of the Petroleum Exporting Countries consist of Algeria, Ecuador, Gabon, Indonesia, Iran, Iraq, Kuwait, Libya, Nigeria, Qatar, Saudi Arabia, United Arab Emirates, and Venezuela; production from the Neutral Zone between Kuwait and Saudi Arabia is included in "Total OPEC" production. (3) Less than 5,000 barrels per day.

U.S. Oil Use 1970 and 1989

Source: Energy Information Administration

U.S. Net Imports[1] of Energy by Source

Source: Energy Information Administration. *Monthly Energy Review, March 1990*

(Quadrillion Btu)

Annual Total	Coal	Crude Oil[2]	Petroleum Products[3]	Natural Gas	Electricity[4]	Coal Coke	Total
1973	−1.422	6.883	6.097	0.981	0.148	−0.007	12.680
1975	−1.738	8.708	3.800	.904	.064	.014	11.752
1980	−2.391	10.586	2.912	.957	.217	−.035	12.247
1981	−2.918	8.854	2.522	.857	.347	−.016	9.646
1982	−2.768	6.917	2.128	.898	.306	−.022	7.460
1983	−2.013	6.731	2.351	.887	.372	−.016	8.311
1984	−2.119	6.918	2.970	.792	.409	−.011	8.959
1985	−2.389	6.381	2.570	.896	.423	−.013	7.868
1988	−2.446	10.698	3.308	1.221	.325	.040	13.146
1989	−2.581	12.286[R]	3.046[R]	1.309	.114[E]	.030	14.204[R]
1990 (Jan.-Mar.)	−.571	3.159	.861	.368	−.28[E]	−.001	3.789

(1) Net imports equals imports minus exports. Minus sign indicates exports are greater than imports. (2) Includes crude oil, lease condensate, and imports of crude oil for the Strategic Petroleum Reserve. (3) Includes petroleum products, unfinished oils, pentanes plus, and gasoline blending components. (4) Assumed to be hydroelectricity and estimated at the average input heat rate for fossil fuel steam-electric power plant generation, which has ranged from 10.3 to 10.5 thousand Btu per kilowatthour since 1973. E = Estimate; R = Revised.

Notes: Geographic coverage is the 50 States and the District of Columbia. Totals may not equal sum of components due to independent rounding.

U.S Dependence on Petroleum Net Imports[1]

Source: Energy Information Administration. *Monthly Energy Review, March 1990*

Annual Average Rate	Net Imports[2]				Net Imports as % of U.S. Petroleum Products Supplied		
	From Arab OPEC[3]	From OPEC[4]	From All Countries	Petroleum Products Supplied	From Arab OPEC[3]	From OPEC[4]	From All Countries
	Thousand Barrels per Day				Percent		
1973	914	2,991	6,025	17,308	5.3	17.3	34.8
1975	1,382	3,599	5,846	16,322	8.5	22.0	35.8
1980	2,549	4,293	6,365	17,056	14.9	25.2	37.3
1981	1,844	3,315	5,401	16,058	11.5	20.6	33.6
1982	852	2,136	4,298	15,296	5.6	14.0	28.1
1983	630	1,843	4,312	15,231	4.1	12.1	28.3
1984	817	2,037	4,715	15,726	5.2	13.0	30.0
1985	470	1,821	4,286	15,726	3.0	11.6	27.3
1988	1,837	3,513	6,587	17,283	10.6	20.3	38.1
1989	2,128[R]	4,124[R]	7,202[R]	17,325[R]	12.3	23.8	41.6[R]
1990 (Jan.-Mar.)	2,399	4,578	7,661	17,025	14.1	26.9	45.0

(1) Beginning in October 1977, Strategic Petroleum Reserves are included. (2) Net imports equals imports minus exports. Imports from members of the Organization of Petroleum Exporting Countries (OPEC) exclude indirect imports, which are petroleum products imported primarily from Caribbean and West European areas and refined from crude oil produced by OPEC. (3) The Arab members of OPEC are Algeria, Iraq, Kuwait, Libya, Qatar, Saudi Arabia, and the United Arab Emirates. Net imports from the Neutral Zone between Kuwait and Saudi Arabia are included in net imports from "Arab OPEC." (4) OPEC consists of Ecuador, Gabon, Indonesia, Iran, Nigeria, and Venezuela, as well as the Arab members. R = Revised data.

Notes: Geographic coverage is the 50 States and the District of Columbia. Annual averages may not equal average of quarters due to independent rounding.

U.S. Total Energy Production by Source, 1960-1990

Source: Energy Information Administration. *Annual Energy Review, 1989* (quadrillion Btu, except as noted)

Year	Coal	Natural Gas[1]	Crude Oil[2]	Natural Gas Plant Liquids	Hydroelectric Power[3]	Nuclear Electric Power[4]	Geothermal[4]	Total	Percent Change[5]
1960	10.82	12.66	14.93	1.46	1.61	0.01	0	41.49	2.2
1965	13.06	15.78	16.52	1.88	2.06	0.04	(6)	49.34	3.4
1970	14.61	21.67	20.40	2.51	2.63	0.24	0.01	62.07	5.0
1975	14.99	19.64	17.73	2.37	3.15	1.90	0.07	59.86	−1.6
1978	14.91	19.49	18.43	2.25	2.94	3.02	0.06	61.10	1.5
1979	17.54	20.08	18.10	2.29	2.93	2.78	0.08	63.80	4.4
1980	18.60	19.91	18.25	2.25	2.90	2.74	0.11	64.76	1.5
1981	18.38	19.70	18.15	2.31	2.76	3.01	0.12	64.42	−0.5
1982	18.64	18.25	18.31	2.19	3.26	3.13	0.10	63.89	−0.8
1983	17.25	16.53	18.39	2.18	3.50	3.20	0.13	61.19	−4.2
1984	19.72	17.93	18.85	2.27	3.31	3.55	0.16	65.81	7.6
1985	19.33	16.92	18.99	2.24	2.94	4.15	0.20	64.78	−1.6
1986	19.51	16.47	18.38	2.15	3.03	4.47	0.22	64.25	−0.8
1987	20.14	17.05	17.67	2.22	2.59	4.91	0.23	64.82	0.9
1988	20.74	17.49	17.28	2.26	2.31	5.66	0.24	65.97	1.6
1989	21.33	17.61	16.12	2.16	2.75	5.69	0.22	65.87	NA
1990 (Jan.-Mar.)	5.74	4.60	3.89	.53	.78	1.62	0.05	17.22	NA

(1) Dry natural gas; (2) Includes lease condensate; (3) Electric utility and industrial generation of hydroelectric power; (4) Generated by electric utilities; (5) Percent change from previous year calculated from data prior to rounding; (6) Less than 0.005 quadrillion Btu; NA = Not Available.

U.S. Total Energy Consumption by Source, 1960-1990

Source: Energy Information Administration. *Annual Energy Review, 1989* (quadrillion Btu, except as noted)

Year	Coal	Natural Gas	Petroleum[1]	Hydroelectric Power[2]	Nuclear Electric Power[3]	Geothermal[3]	Total	Percent Change[4]
1960	9.84	12.39	19.92	1.66	0.01	(5)	43.80	3.9
1965	11.58	15.77	23.25	2.06	0.04	(5)	52.68	4.3
1970	12.26	21.79	29.52	2.65	0.24	0.01	66.43	3.5
1975	12.66	19.95	32.73	3.22	1.90	0.07	70.55	−2.8
1978	13.77	20.00	37.97	3.14	3.02	0.06	78.09	2.4
1979	15.04	20.67	37.12	3.14	2.78	0.08	78.90	1.0
1980	15.42	20.39	34.20	3.12	2.74	0.11	75.96	−3.7
1981	15.91	19.93	31.93	3.11	3.01	0.12	73.99	−2.6
1982	15.32	18.51	30.23	3.56	3.13	0.10	70.84	−4.3
1983	15.90	17.36	30.05	3.87	3.20	0.13	70.50	−0.5
1984	17.07	18.51	31.05	3.72	3.55	0.16	74.06	5.1
1985	17.48	17.85	30.92	3.36	4.15	0.20	73.96	−0.1
1986	17.26	16.71	32.20	3.40	4.47	0.22	74.26	0.4
1987	18.01	17.67	32.87	3.07	4.91	0.23	76.77	3.4
1988	18.85	18.55	34.23	2.64	5.66	0.27	80.20	4.1
1989	18.92	19.36	34.21	2.86	5.67	0.25	81.28	1.3
1990 (Jan.-Mar.)	4.59	5.89	8.29	.75	1.62	0.05	21.20	NA

(1) Petroleum products supplied including natural gas plant liquids and crude oil burned as fuel; (2) Electric utility and industrial generation of hydroelectric power and net electricity imports; (3) Generated by electric utilities; (4) Percent change from previous year calculated from data prior to rounding; (5) Less than 0.005 quadrillion Btu; NA = Not Available.

Oil Consumption 1989
(In millions of barrels)

United States	6,323.6
Japan	1,818.1
West Germany	831.5
Italy	708.1
France	677.4
Canada	643.1
Britain	634.0

Source: Energy Information Administration

U.S. Coal Production and Consumption, 1965-1989

Source: Energy Information Administration. *Annual Energy Review 1989* (million short tons)

	Production					Consumption				
Year	Bituminous Coal	Sub- bituminous Coal	Lignite	Anthracite	Total	Electric Utilities	Coke Plants	Trans- portation	Residential & Com- mercial	Total
1965	512.1	(¹)	(¹)	14.9	527.0	244.8	95.3	0.7	25.7	472.0
1970	578.5	16.4	8.0	9.7	612.7	320.2	96.5	0.3	16.1	523.2
1975	577.5	51.1	19.8	6.2	654.6	406.0	83.6	(²)	9.4	562.6
1976	588.4	64.8	25.5	6.2	684.9	448.4	84.7	(²)	8.9	603.8
1977	581.0	82.1	28.2	5.9	697.2	477.1	77.7	(²)	9.0	625.3
1978	534.0	96.8	34.4	5.0	670.2	481.2	71.4	(²)	9.5	625.2
1979	612.3	121.5	42.5	4.8	781.1	527.1	77.4	(²)	8.4	680.5
1980	628.8	147.7	47.2	6.1	829.7	569.3	66.7	(²)	6.5	702.7
1981	608.0	159.7	50.7	5.4	823.8	596.8	61.0	(²)	7.4	732.6
1982	620.2	160.9	52.4	4.6	838.1	593.7	40.9	(²)	8.2	706.9
1983	568.6	151.0	58.3	4.1	782.1	625.2	37.0	(²)	8.4	736.7
1984	649.5	179.2	63.1	4.2	895.9	664.4	44.0	(²)	9.1	791.3
1985	613.9	192.7	72.4	4.7	883.6	693.8	41.1	(²)	7.8	818.0
1986	620.1	189.6	76.4	4.3	890.3	685.1	36.0	(²)	7.7	804.3
1987	636.6	200.2	78.4	3.6	918.8	717.9	37.0	(²)	6.9	836.9
1988	638.1	223.5	85.1	3.6	950.3	758.4	41.9	(²)	7.1	889.6
1989	656.3	227.2	89.6	3.5	974.7	765.6	40.7	(²)	6.2	889.6

(1) Included in bituminous; (2) Less than 0.05 million short tons; (p) = preliminary.

Major U.S. Dams and Reservoirs

Source: Committee on Register of Dams, Corps of Engineers, U.S. Army; September, 1989

Highest Dams

Order	Dam Name	River	State	Type	Feet	Meters	Year Complete
1	Oroville	Feather	Cal.	E	754	230	1968
2	Hoover	Colorado	Nev.	A	725	221	1936
3	Dworshak	N Fork Clearwater	Id.	G	718	219	1973
4	Glen Canyon	Colorado	Ariz.	A	708	216	1966
5	New Bullards Bar	North Yuba	Cal.	A	636	194	1970
6	New Melones	Stanislaus	Cal.	R	626	191	1979
7	Swift	Lewis	Wash.	E	610	186	1958
8	Mossyrock	Cowlitz	Wash.	A	607	185	1968
9	Shasta	Sacramento	Cal.	G	600	183	1945
10	Hungry Horse	S Fork Flathead	Mon.	A	564	172	1953
11	Grand Coulee	Columbia	Wash.	G	551	168	1942
12	Ross	Skagit	Wash.	A	541	165	1949

E = Embankment, Earthfill; R = Embankment, Rockfill; G = Gravity; A = Arch.

Largest Embankment Dams

					Volume		
Order	Dam Name	River	State	Type	Cubic yards X 1000	Cubic Meters X 1000	Year Complete
1	Fort Peck	Missouri	Mon.	E	125,624	96,050	1937
2	Oahe	Missouri	S.D.	E	91,996	70,339	1958
3	Oroville	Feather	Cal.	E	77,997	59,635	1968
4	San Luis	San Luis Creek	Cal.	E	77,897	59,559	1967
5	Garrison	Missouri	N.D.	E	66,498	50,843	1953
6	Cochiti	Rio Grande	N.M.	E	65,693	50,228	1975
7	Earthquake Lake	Madison	Mon.	E-G	49,998	38,228	1959
8	Fort Randall	Missouri	S.D.	E	49,962	38,200	1952
9	Castaic	Castaic Creek	Cal.	E	43,998	33,640	1973
10	Ludington P/S	Lake Michigan	Mich.	E	37,699	28,824	1973
11	Kingsley	N. Platte	Neb.	E	31,999	24,466	1941
12	Warm Springs	Dry Creek	Cal.	E	29,977	22,920	1982

E = Embankment, Earthfill; R = Embankment, Rockfill; E-R = Embankment, Earth & Rockfill; G = Gravity; A = Arch.

Largest Man-Made Reservoirs

				Reservoir Capacity		
Order	Dam Name	Reservoir	Location	Acre-Feet	Cubic Meters x 1000	Year Completed
1	Hoover	Lake Mead	Nev.	28,253,000	34,850,000	1936
2	Glen Canyon	Lake Powell	Ariz.	26,997,000	33,300,000	1966
3	Garrison	Lake Sakakawea	N.D.	22,635,000	27,920,000	1953
4	Oahe	Lake Oahe	S.D.	22,238,000	27,430,000	1958
5	Fort Peck	Fort Peck Lake	Mon.	17,933,000	22,120,000	1937
6	Grand Coulee	F D Roosevelt Lake	Wash.	9,558,000	11,790,000	1942
7	Libby	Lake Koocanusa	Mon.	5,813,000	7,170,000	1973
8	Fort Randall	Lake Francis Case	S.D.	4,621,000	5,700,000	1952
9	Shasta	Lake Shasta	Cal.	4,548,000	5,610,000	1945
10	Toledo Bend	Toledo Bend Lake	La.	4,475,000	5,520,000	1968
11	Wolf Creek	Cumberland Lake	Ky.	3,997,000	4,930,000	1951
12	Flaming Gorge	Flaming Gorge Reservoir	Ut.	3,786,000	4,670,000	1964

† acre foot = 1 acre of water, 1 foot deep

World's Largest Capacity Hydro Plants

Source: U.S. Committee on Large Dams, of the Intl. Commission on Large Dams, Aug. 1990

Rank order	Name	Country	Rated capacity now (MW)	Rated capacity planned (MW)	Rank order	Name	Country	Rated capacity now (MW)	Rated capacity planned (MW)
1	Turukhansk (Lower Tunguska)*	USSR		20,000	13=	Bratsk	USSR	4,500	4,500
					13=	Ust-Ilim	USSR	3,675	4,500
2	Itaipu	Brazil/Paraguay	7,400	13,320	15	Cabora Bassa	Mozambique	2,425	4,150
3	Grand Coulee	USA	9,070	10,830	16	Boguchany	USSR		4,000
4	Guri (Raúl Leoni)	Venezuela	10,300	10,300	17=	Rogun*	USSR		3,600
5	Tucuruí	Brazil	2,640	7,260	17=	Oak Creek	USA	3,600	3,600
6	Sayano Shushensk*	USSR	6,400	6,400	19	Paulo Afonso I	Brazil	1,524	3,409
7=	Corpus Posadas	Argentina/Paraguay	4,700	6,000	20	Pati*	Argentina		3,300
7=	Krasnoyarsk	USSR	6,000	6,000	21=	Ilha Solteira	Brazil	3,200	3,200
9	La Grande 2	Canada	5,328	5,328	21=	Brumley Gap*	USA	3,200	3,200
10	Churchill Falls	Canada	5,225	5,225	23	Chapetôn*	Argentina		3,000
11	Xingo	Brazil	3,012	5,020	24	Gezhouba	China	2,715	2,715
12	Tarbela	Pakistan	1,750	4,678	25	John Day	USA	2,160	2,700
					25	Nurek	USSR	900	2,700
					25=	Yacyreta*	Argentina/Paraguay		2,700

*Planned or under construction.

Major Dams of the World

Source: U.S. Committee on Large Dams, of the Intl. Commission of Large Dams; Aug. 1990

World's Highest Dams

Rank order	Name	Country	Height above lowest formation (m)	Rank order	Name	Country	Height above lowest formation (m)
1	Rogun*	USSR	335	11	Mica	Canada	242
2	Nurek	USSR	300	12	Mauvoisin	Switzerland	237
3	Grand Dixence	Switzerland	285	13	Chivor	Colombia	237
4	Inguri	USSR	272	14	El Cajón	Honduras	234
5	Chicoasèn	Mexico	261	15	Chirkei	USSR	233
6	Tehri*	India	261	16	Oroville	USA	230
7	Kishau*	India	253	17	Bhakra	India	226
8=	Ertan	China	245	18	Hoover	USA	221
9=	Sayano-Shushensk*	USSR	245	19	Contra	Switzerland	220
10	Guavio*	Colombia	243	20	Mratinje	Yugoslavia	220

*Under construction.

World's Largest Volume Embankment Dams

Rank order	Name	Country	Volume cubic meters × 1000	Rank Order	Name	Country	Volume cubic meters × 1000
1	Tarbela	Pakistan	148,500	11	Gardiner	Canada	65,000
2	Fort Peck	USA	96,050	12	Afsluitdijk	Netherlands	63,400
3	Tucuruí	Brazil	85,200	13	Mangla	Pakistan	63,379
4	Ataturk*	Turkey	85,000	14	Oroville	USA	59,635
5	Yacireta*	Argentina	81,000	15	San Luis	USA	59,559
6	Rogun*	USSR	75,500	16	Nurek	USSR	58,000
7	Oahe	USA	70,339	17	Tanda	Pakistan	57,250
8	Guri	Venezuela	70,000	18	Garrison	USA	50,843
9	Parambikulam	India	69,165	19	Chochiti	USA	50,228
10	High Island West	Hong Kong	67,000	20	Oosterschelde	Netherlands	50,000

*Under construction.

World's Largest Capacity Manmade Reservoirs

Rank order	Name	Country	Capacity cubic meters × 1000	Rank Order	Name	Country	Capacity cubic meters × 1000
1	Owen Falls	Uganda	204,800	11	Cabora Bassa	Mozambique	63,000
2	Bratsk	USSR	169,000	12	La Grande 2	Canada	61,715
3	Aswan (High)	Egypt	162,000	13	La Grande 3	Canada	60,020
4	Kariba	Zimbabwe/Zambia	160,368	14	Ust-Ilim	USSR	59,300
5	Akosombo	Ghana	147,960	15	Boguchany*	USSR	58,200
6	Daniel Johnson	Canada	141,851	16	Kuibyshev	USSR	58,000
7	Guri	Venezuela	135,000	17	Serra de Mesa	Brazil	54,400
8	Krasnoyarsk	USSR	73,300	18	Caniapiscau Barrage KA 3	Canada	53,790
9	W A C Bennett (Portage Mt.)	Canada	70,309	19	Bukhtarma	USSR	49,800
10	Zeya	USSR	68,400	20	Ataturk	Turkey	48,700

*Under construction

Net Electricity Generation at Electric Utilities by Energy Source

Source: Energy Information Administration. *Annual Energy Review 1989* (billion kilowatthours)

	Coal	Petroleum	Natural Gas	Nuclear Electric Power	Hydro-electric Power	Other[1]	Total
1975	853	289	300	173	300	3	1,918
1980	1,162	246	346	251	276	6	2,286
1981	1,203	206	346	273	261	6	2,295
1982	1,192	147	305	283	309	5	2,241
1983	1,259	144	274	294	332	6	2,310
1984	1,342	120	297	328	321	9	2,416
1985	1,402	100	292	384	281	11	2,470
1986	1,386	137	249	414	291	12	2,487
1987	1,464	118	273	455	250	12	2,572
1988	1,541	149	253	527	223	12	2,704
1989[p]	1,551	158	264	529	264	11	2,779

(1) Electricity produced from geothermal, wood, waste, wind, photovoltaic, and solar thermal energy sources connected to electric utility distribution systems; p = preliminary.

U.S. Passenger Car Efficiency, 1966-1988

Source: Energy Information Administration. *Annual Energy Review 1989*

	Mileage		Fuel Consumption		Fuel Rate	
Year	Thousand Miles per Car	Index 1973 = 100.0	Gallons per Car	Index 1973 = 100.0	Miles per Gallon	Index 1973 = 100.0
1966	9.92	96.7	703	91.2	14.1	106.0
1968	10.14	98.8	731	94.8	13.9	104.5
1970	10.27	100.0	760	98.6	13.5	101.5
1975	9.69	94.4	716	93.9	13.5	101.5
1977	9.88	96.3	716	93.9	13.8	103.8
1980	9.14	89.1	591	76.7	15.5	116.5
1981	9.19	89.6	576	74.7	15.9	119.6
1982	9.43	91.9	566	73.4	16.7	125.6
1983	9.48	92.4	553	71.7	17.1	128.6
1984	9.56	93.2	536	69.5	17.8	133.8
1985	9.56	93.2	525	68.1	18.2	136.8
1986	9.61	93.7	526	68.2	18.3	137.6
1987	9.88	96.3	514	66.7	19.2	144.4
1988[p]	10.12	98.7	507	65.8	20.0	150.0

(p) = preliminary

Household Energy Consumption and Expenditures by Application and Fuel Source, 1978-1987

Source: Energy Information Administration. *Annual Energy Review 1989*

Application/Fuel Source	Consumption (Quadrillion Btu)				Expenditures (Billion Dollars)			
	1978	1980	1984	1987	1978	1980	1984	1987
Space Heating								
Natural Gas.	4.26	3.32	3.51	3.38	$11.49	$12.80	$20.66	$18.05
Electricity[1].	0.41	0.28	0.30	0.28	3.53	3.71	5.71	5.53
Distillate Fuel Oil and Kerosene	2.05	1.32	1.10	1.05	8.06	10.59	8.51	6.25
Liquefied Petrol. Gases .	0.23	0.25	0.21	0.22	1.05	1.90	2.00	1.85
Total	6.95	5.17	5.13	4.94	24.14	29.00	36.85	31.68
Air Conditioning[2]								
Electricity[1].	0.31	0.32	0.36	0.44	3.97	5.07	7.51	9.77
Water Heating								
Natural Gas.	1.04	1.24	1.10	1.10	2.88	4.79	6.63	6.02
Electricity[1].	0.29	0.31	0.32	0.31	3.15	4.54	6.44	6.45
Distillate Fuel Oil and Kerosene	0.14	0.24	0.15	0.17	0.56	1.89	1.09	0.94
Liquefied Petrol. Gases .	0.06	0.07	0.06	0.06	0.36	0.59	0.58	0.50
Total	1.53	1.86	1.62	1.64	6.94	11.80	14.76	13.91
Appliances								
Natural Gas.	0.28	0.38	0.35	0.34	0.93	1.71	2.31	2.02
Electricity[1].	1.46	1.55	1.53	1.72	19.24	26.82	34.95	39.83
Liquefied Petrol. Gases .	0.03	0.04	0.04	0.04	0.25	0.41	0.54	0.46
Total	1.77	1.97	1.92	2.10	20.42	28.94	37.81	42.33
Total[2]	10.56	9.32	9.04	9.13	55.47	74.81	97.00	97.75
Natural Gas[2]	5.58	4.94	4.98	4.83	15.30	19.30	29.80	26.15
Electricity[1]	2.47	2.46	2.48	2.76	29.89	40.14	54.50	61.58
Distillate Fuel Oil and Kerosene	2.19	1.55	1.26	1.22	8.62	12.48	9.60	7.21
Liquefied Petrol. Gases .	0.33	0.36	0.31	0.32	1.66	2.89	3.10	2.81

(1) Includes electricity generated for distribution from wood, waste, geothermal, wind, photovoltaic, and solar thermal electricity. (2) A small amount of natural gas used for air conditioning is included in "Total" and "Natural Gas" under "Total."

Note: Sum of components may not equal total due to independent rounding.

World Nuclear Power

Source: International Atomic Energy Agency, Dec. 31, 1989

Country	Reactors in Operation # of Units	Total MW(e)[1]	Reactors under Construction # of Units	Total MW(e)[1]	Nuclear Electricity Supplied, 1989 TW(e).h[1]	% of Total	Total Operating Experience to December 31, 1989 Years	Months
Argentina	2	935	1	692	4.6	11.4	22	7
Belgium	7	5,500	—	—	38.8	60.8	93	7
Brazil	1	626	1	1,245	1.7	0.7	7	9
Bulgaria	5	2,585	2	1,906	14.6	35.6	48	8
Canada	18	12,185	4	3,524	75.4	15.6	224	0
China	—	—	3	2,148	—	—	—	—
Cuba	—	—	2	816	—	—	—	—
Czechoslovakia	8	3,264	8	5,120	22.9	27.6	52	1
Finland	4	2,310	—	—	18.0	35.4	43	4
France	55	52,588	9	12,245	289.0	74.6	543	1
East Germany	6	2,102	5	3,024	11.1	10.9	78	2
West Germany	24	22,716	1	295	141.2	34.3	303	3
Hungary	4	1,645	—	—	13.0	49.8	18	2
India	7	1,374	7	1,540	3.4	1.6	79	2
Iran	—	—	2	2,392	—	—	—	—
Italy	2	1,120	—	—	—	—	79	10
Japan	39	29,300	12	10,629	185.8	27.8	432	4
South Korea	9	7,220	2	1,900	45.0	50.2	45	1
Mexico	1	654	1	654	—	—	—	9
Netherlands	2	508	—	—	3.8	5.4	37	9
Pakistan	1	125	—	—	0.1	0.2	18	3
Romania	—	—	5	3,125	—	—	—	—
South Africa	2	1,842	—	—	11.1	7.4	10	3
Spain	10	7,544	—	—	53.7	38.4	92	7
Sweden	12	9,817	—	—	62.8	45.1	147	2
Switzerland	5	2,952	—	—	21.5	41.6	73	10
United Kingdom	39	11,242	1	1,188	63.4	21.7	850	10
United States	110	98,331	4	4,284	529.4	19.1	1,371	4
Soviet Union	46	34,230	26	22,180	212.6	12.3	468	11
Yugoslavia	1	632	—	—	4.5	5.9	8	3
Total*	426	318,271	96	78,907	1,854.5	—	5,201	1

1 terawatt-hour (TW(e).h) = 10⁶ megawatt-hour (MW(e).h). For an average power plant, 1 TW(e).h = 0.39 megatonnes of coal equivalent (input) and 0.23 megatonnes of oil equivalent (input). * Total includes data from Taiwan, China: 6 units, 4924 MW(e) in operation; 27.1 TW.h of nuclear electricity generation, or 35.2% of total electricity generated there; 50 yrs., 1 month of experience.

U.S. Nuclear Power Plant Operations

Source: Energy Information Administration. *Monthly Energy Review. March 1990*

	Operable Reactors Number	Nuclear-Based Electricity Generation Million Net Kilowatthours	Nuclear Portion of Domestic Electricity Generation Percent		Operable Reactors Number	Nuclear-Based Electricity Generation Million Net Kilowatthours	Nuclear Portion of Domestic Electricity Generation Percent
1976	61	191,104	9.4	1984	86	327,634	13.6
1977	65	250,883	11.8	1985	95	383,691	15.5
1978	70	276,403	12.5	1986	100	414,038	16.6
1979	68	255,155	11.4	1987	107	455,270	17.7
1980	70	251,116	11.0	1988	108	526,973	19.5
1981	74	272,674	11.9	1989	110	529,355	19.0
1982	77	282,773	12.6	1990 Jan.-Mar.	111	151,169	22.4
1983	80	293,677	12.7				

Status of U.S. Nuclear Reactor Units

Source: Energy Information Administration. *Monthly Energy Review. March 1990*

	Licensed for Operation Operable	In Startup	Construction Permits Granted	Pending	On Order	Announced	Total	Total Design Capacity Million Net Kilowatts
			Number of Reactor Units					
1978	70	0	90	32	9	4	205	204
1979	68	0	91	21	3	0	183	179
1980	70	2	82	12	3	0	169	163
1981	74	0	75	11	3	0	163	157
1982	77	2	60	3	2	0	144	135
1983	80	3	53	0	2	0	138	129
1984	86	6	38	0	2	0	132	123
1985	95	3	30	0	2	0	130	121
1986	100	7	19	0	2	0	128	119
1987	107	4	14	0	2	0	127	119
1988	108	3	12	0	0	0	123	115
1989	110	1	10	0	0	0	121	114
1990 March	111	1	9	0	0	0	121	114

SCIENCE AND TECHNOLOGY

Scientific Achievements and Discoveries: 1990

Origins of Life on Earth

For the first time, researchers demonstrated outside the lab that a species changed its reproductive behavior over a period of years as predicted by the tenets of **natural selection**, the cornerstone of evolutionary theory. The change occurred over 11 years in a group of guppies in Trinidad that was moved to a site where it was subject to different predators. The study was the first to demonstrate the change in an experiment in the natural world. David. A. Reznick and Heather Bryga of the Univ. of Calif. at Riverside, and John A. Endler of the Univ. af Calif. at Santa Barbara used the guppies to test a mathematical theory that explains why some species have many offspring and invest little in their care, while others have very few offspring and devote their lives to caring for their young. The theory states that animals that are preyed on as adults will have as many babies as possible during their short life span, starting at an early age. Therefore, they will have shorter lives, having invested all their energy in reproducing.

Fossil fragments found in northern Colorado by a team led by Robert T. Bakker, one of the leading paleontologists in the world, showed that a dinosaur named **Epanterias amplexus**, equal in size to Tyrannosaurus rex, flourished 30 million years before tyrannosaurus roamed the earth. Epanterias was about 50 feet long and had jaws that could expand like those of a snake. It could have eaten an animal the size of a 1,400 lb. cow with a single gulp. While epanterias must have looked like the tyrannosaur, it differed in its large powerful forelimbs, each tipped with three claws (tyrannosaur had two). Epanterias also probably moved with a crouching gait, with its head much closer to the ground than that of a tyrannosaur.

Scientists at Yale Univ. identified a tiny fossilized plant, barely one inch tall and resembling today's black pepper plant, as the **oldest known flower**. It lived 120 million years ago, and its flower was probably a drab green or beige. Due to its similarities to two major branches of modern flowering plants, the plant could be their common ancestor and represent a kind of "missing link" needed to understand plant evolution. About a half million species, nearly all the world's plants that bear seed, are likely descendants of the small plant. The scientists said the plant grew in scraggly underbrush on the edge of a pond in the Koonwarra area of Australia. The earliest flowering plants may date back to 130 or 140 million years ago.

A "**golden calf**" was unearthed by Harvard Univ. archeologists near the Israeli port city of Ashkelon that is believed to be an object of worship dating from the second millennium B.C. Recovered almost intact, the calf, about $4\frac{1}{2}$ inches long and $4\frac{1}{4}$ inches tall and weighing less than one pound, is made of bronze and other metals. The temple in which it was housed was destroyed during a conquest of Ashkelon in about 1550 B.C., midway through the Bronze Age. In the *Bible*, golden calves similiar in form but much larger are referred to in the story of Aaron during the Exodus, in ancient Jerusalem's rivalry with northern, calf-worshipping Hebrew king Jeroboam, and in other Old Testament accounts.

At the Lamont-Doherty Geological Laboratory of Columbia Univ. at Palisades, N.Y., scientists have theorized that large errors in **carbon dating**, some by as much as 3,500 years, are the result of fluctuations in the amount of carbon 14 in the air. They arrived at this conclusion by comparing age estimates obtained using two different methods—analysis of radioactive carbon in a sample and determination of the ratio of uranium to thorium in the sample. They said that **uranium-thorium dating** not only is more precise than carbon dating in some cases, but also can be used to date much older objects. While carbon dating is unreliable for objects older than about 30,000 years, uranium-thorium dating may be possible for objects up to 500,000 years old. Since 1947, scientists have estimated the ages of many objects by measuring the amounts of radioactive carbon they contain.

Hubble Telescope

Launched by the space shuttle *Discovery* on Apr. 25, 1990, the $1.5 billion Hubble Space Telescope was found to have a major flaw in the main light-gathering mirrors, which will severely limit its ability to view the depths of the universe for several years. A distortion in one of the two mirrors means that the path of light between the mirrors is out of alignment, resulting in less than clearly focused images when it reaches other instruments and cameras. The wide-field and planetary camera that was to perform 40 percent of the Hubble's work will not be usable, and the camera for making extremely precise images of faint objects will not function as scientists had planned. It was hoped that Hubble would be able to collect light coming from near the edge of the universe and thus near the beginning of time. The 25,000 lb. telescope is 43 feet long and 14 feet in diameter at its widest point, and is circling the Earth every 97 minutes at an altitude of 381 miles. The craft is designed to be visited and serviced periodically by astronauts from a space shuttle. NASA officials announced that a space shuttle mission is scheduled for 1993 during which the telescope will hopefully be repaired.

Despite its flawed mirror, the Hubble telescope should produce a more detailed view of the skies than has been possible from any ground telescope. The first of these views was received in August showing an unexpected concentration of stars, attracted by some mysterious force around what once appeared to be an ordinary galaxy, and a glowing ring of gaseous matter around the remnant of a star seen to explode three years ago.

Astronomical Findings

Evidence of an early universe devoid of disturbances and irregularities that could explain the origin of the galaxy clusters, expansive voids, and other large structures common to space were revealed by the unmanned *Cosmic Background Explorer* (COBE). Presented at the annual meeting of the American Astronomical Society, early data appeared to confirm the **Big Bang theory** of the origin of the universe. The theory holds that all existence sprang from the explosion of a fist-sized ball of unknown primordial material 15 billion years ago. "We can see no deviation from a simple Big Bang theory," John Mather, the chief project scientist for COBE, said in January. "But it's hard to understand that with all the large features we see in the universe, we have no evidence of their origin." New understanding of the origin of the universe and the early formation of matter is expected from studying measurements of radiation, supposedly released in the Big Bang explosion, recorded by COBE.

Scientists whose goal it is to scan the sky with dish-shaped antennas listening for faint signals from advanced civilizations received federal funding for their

0-year project. The **search for extraterrestrial intelligence (SETI)** will address one of mankind's ultimate questions: Are we alone? Skeptics say there is no evidence of other beings in the galaxy, and that if there were such beings, earth would have heard from them by now. The receiving apparatus is scheduled to be switched on in Oct. 1992, the 500th anniversary of Columbus's discovery of America, and is to run until the turn of the century.

Initial **images of Venus** sent by the *Magellan* space probe show a fractured, rubbled surface scarred by what appeared to be volcanic action, quakes, and shifting land. The images showed a more disrupted surface than some scientists had expected. The images were constructed from radar beams penetrating the thick atmosphere that obscures the planet from ordinary pictures. The *Magellan* sent back two image strips based on one-and-a-half orbits, both showing 12-mile-wide areas of surface, one 7,000 miles long and the other 5,000 miles long.

Medicine and Genetics

In a clinical trial of 21 healthy men ranging in age from 61 to 81, researchers found that after six months of injections of a genetically engineered version of the **natural growth hormone**, the men emerged with bodies that had many characteristics of bodies 20 years younger than their actual age. "This is not a fountain of youth," said Daniel Rudman of the Medical College of Wisconsin in Milwaukee, as researchers cautioned that the results were highly preliminary and that the long-term side effects of growth hormone remain unknown. Although the weight of the men remained the same, they lost almost 15 percent body fat and gained almost 9 percent in lean body mass. The men's skin regained a youthful thickness, and the level of an important growth-stimulating hormone in the blood returned to that of those under the age of 40. The bones of the spine also gained in mass, although other parts of the skeleton did not. Researchers speculated that careful administration of human growth hormone could prove beneficial for those elderly people whose muscles are wasting away or who need greater strength to help them recover from a hip fracture, stroke, or other debilitating illness. Dr. Rudman said that while his study used men only, the same impact could be expected with women.

Scientists at Johns Hopkins Univ. School of Medicine in Baltimore, led by Solomon Snyder, a neuroscientist, have for the first time grown an important type of **human brain cell** in the laboratory. The cells are neurons from the most highly evolved part of the brain, the cerebral cortex, the place of human thought, memory, and creativity. This development will allow for the study of the human brain in greater biochemical and genetic detail. The cells also offer a valuable tool for testing new drugs to treat Alzheimer's disease, epilepsy, Parkinson's disease, drug addiction, and other brain disorders.

While doctors have treated fetuses with medications, probed the womb from the outside with needles and shunts, and removed fetuses for minor surgery on their bladders, for the first time, under the direction of Michael R. Harrison at the Univ. of Calif. in San Francisco, **livesaving surgery was performed on a fetus** and a healthy baby was delivered seven weeks later. The fetus, which was partly removed from the womb for the operation, had a hernia of the diaphragm, a fairly common and usually fatal congenital malformation. His stomach, spleen, and large and small intestines had migrated through a hole in the diaphragm, the wall of muscle and tendons between the abdomen and the chest, taking up so much space that his lungs could

not grow. Dr. Harrison emphasized that he did not expect many fetuses to be saved by such fetal surgery. He said too few fetuses had operable defects and too few doctors were trained in the procedure. Ways to correct the condition were first developed by using fetal lambs and monkeys.

For the first time, **a gene has been found that causes osteoarthritis**, the most common form of arthritis, according to a report in the *Proceedings of the National Academy of Sciences*. "This study strongly supports the idea that a single genetic flaw can cause at least one form of osteoarthritis and perhaps can cause others," said Lawrence E. Shulman, a leading rheumatologist and the director of the Natl. Inst. of Arthritis and Musculoskeletal and Skin Diseases. The family members studies showed early expression (as early as 16 years of age) of clinical symptoms of primary generalized osteoarthritis. The cause of this disease has remained unknown; it can affect many parts of the body, including the hands, feet, hips, and knees. Individuals with the disease suffer pain, stiffness, and often limitations in mobility that get worse over time. Osteoarthritis, which affects about 16 million Americans, is a major reason for the over 150,000 total joint replacement procedures performed each year in the U.S.

A widely used antiviral drug, **acyclovir, was found to shorten the course and severity of chicken pox** infections in normal children. Chicken pox is the only remaining childhood disease that is not prevented by routine vaccination. As many as 3.5 million Americans get chicken pox each year, and 4,000 are hospitalized with complications. According to the Centers for Disease Control, about 100 to 200 people die from the disease each year. About 95 percent of Americans get chicken pox by the time they are 18 years old. The disease confers a lifelong immunity so that no one gets it twice. Acyclovir is already available for the treatment of diseases caused by the chicken pox virus, such as genital herpes infections in adults, and herpes zoster, or shingles, a viral infection of the sensory nerves.

The first effort to **insert foreign genes into human cancer patients** was successful, as the experiment sought to test the premise that new genes can be plugged into white blood cells and those cells transfused into people. In some cases, the patients' cancer went into remission, offering hope that the new therapy may someday prove extremely valuable in treating advanced tumors. The experiment was led by Steven A. Rosenberg of the Natl. Cancer Inst. in Bethesda, Md. Two other gene therapy proposals are nearing final approval by the Food and Drug Admin. One would treat children suffering from a severe immune deficiency disorder by supplying them with a critical gene they lack. In the second proposal, Dr. Rosenberg plans to insert into the tumor-infiltrating cells a gene for an enzyme known as tumor necrosis factor, which could lend the cells extra tumor-fighting strength. Other researchers hope to use gene therapy to fight cystic fibrosis, hereditary globin disorders, metabolic diseases, and a broad range of human ailments.

There were many other **discoveries in the field of genetics** including: a defective gene that results in one form of retinitis pigmentosa, an inherited disorder that is a leading cause of blindness; a gene that puts people at risk of becoming alcoholics; the gene that causes the disfiguring and sometimes fatal condition known as Elephant Man's disease; two defective genes that cause thickening of the heart; a key gene on the Y chromosome that seems to act as a master switch for maleness, transforming a growing human fetus that otherwise would become a girl into a baby boy; and a gene that is responsible for producing a key receptor that responds to marijuana in parts of the brain. Scientists also extracted strands of DNA, the genetic code of life, from a **17 million year old magnolia leaf** that was still green when it was found embedded in sediment in an ancient lake bed in Idaho. The oldest DNA previously analyzed came from a woolly mammoth that lived 40,000 years ago.

Additionally, the U.S.'s **first genetically engineered calves** were born on a farm near Marquez, Texas. The 4 calves have genes from other species, including humans. Also, the F.D.A. approved the **first genetically engineered food product** for humans, an enzyme used in making cheese.

AIDS

At the **Sixth International AIDS Conference**, researchers reported substantial progress in learning about AIDS, but also a sense that the disease continues to outrun gains in knowledge as the epidemic continues to spread. Early treatment with the antiviral drug AZT was shown to slow the progress of AIDS, and AZT also appears to make people with the AIDS virus less infectious to their sex partners. Among other findings reported were: a study of a brothel in Nevada where prostitution is legal found that latex condoms were effective in preventing the spread of sexually transmitted disease; a study of diabetics who are also intravenous drug users suggested that access to clean needles curtails AIDS transmission; a study of 1,000 homosexual men found that smokers infected with the AIDS virus became ill more quickly and had higher deathrates than was the case for nonsmokers; HIV-2, a second strain of the AIDS virus originally found in West Africa, is spreading in Portugal; and abnormalities in mental development have been found in children born to women infected with the AIDS virus, even when the children themselves were not infected.

A report by the Centers for Disease Control estimated that 179,000 to 208,000 new cases of AIDS will be reported through the end of 1992. The number of new cases reported each year will continue to rise, and more infants will get AIDS in 1990 than in any year since the epidemic began. The report estimates the current (Jan. 1990) number of people infected with the virus, with or without symptoms, at 800,000 to 1.3 million. Based on these estimates, projections of the number of people who will be reported as AIDS cases are: 53,000-60,000 in 1990; 60,000-68,000 in 1991; 66,000-80,000 in 1992; and 67,000-90,000 in 1993.

A **new AIDS therapy** that involves giving a drug, withdrawing some of the patient's blood, shining ultraviolet light on it, and returning it to the body has shown promising preliminary results in a limited study of five patients. In a report in Aug. 1990 in *The Annals of Internal Medicine*, researchers said the treatment appeared to stimulate the immune system in ways that were not clear. The therapy is called photopheresis and was conducted by researchers from Morristown Memorial Hospital in N.J. and the Columbia Univ. College of Physicians and Surgeons in N.Y.

Virtual Reality

Virtual or artificial reality is a concept wherein a person puts on special clothing that is wired to a computer, including gloves that transmit and receive data,

and goggles that include two tiny video screens. The computer generates images, either of the real world or an imaginary one, that appear to the viewer in three dimensions. A user can be sitting in the driver's seat of a racing car or hitting a tennis ball in an imaginary game. The user can pick up an object, or fly, or do just about anything. Software programs exist, or soon will, to allow people to see the world from many vantage points (from that of another person or animal). They can also interact with real people connected to the same virtual world. Virtual reality is a concept with serious purposes, like teaching a surgeon how to handle a scapel without using real patients, or creating a workplace for employees separated by great distances. Scientists at universities, at small companies, and at NASA are just beginning to create the first usable systems.

Patents

In 1989, for the first time in 26 years, Americans received a larger share of the patents issued in the U.S. than they had in the previous year. The Patent and Trademark Office reported that inventors based in the U.S. obtained 54,762 patents, or 53.3 percent of the total, a rise of six-tenths of 1 percent, in the fiscal year ended Sept. 30. Hitachi Ltd. of Japan (1,053 patents) heads the top 10 companies obtaining patents in the U.S., while the three leading American companies were IBM, G.E., and Eastman Kodak. The university with the most patents was the Massachusetts Inst. of Technology, with 101.

Inventors of the Year

Three inventors at the Chrysler Corp., Maurice B. Leising, Howard L. Benford, and Gerald L. Holbrook, who patented the first fully electronic force-feed automatic transmission, shared the award for Inventor of the Year issued by Intellectual Property Owners Inc., a trade association representing corporate and individual inventors. The Ultradrive transmission uses a computer processor to make shifting decisions and was introduced in 1989 in most Chrysler V-6 models.

Inventions of 1990

Some of the more "interesting" inventions issued patents during 1990 were: a crib that soothes infants by stimulating movements of the womb; an experimental test to predict whether a person infected with the AIDS virus will quickly develop symptoms; a laser system to remove tooth and gum decay without the need for drills, scrapers, or Novocain; a golf putter featuring a built-in level indicator to estimate the slope of a putting green; heated automobile windshield wipers; a quiet alarm clock that sets off vibrations in pillows; a garbage collector in space to protect spacecraft from collisions with orbiting debris; and a device that uses echoes to help blind people find their way by judging the distance of surrounding objects.

Also, Adobe Systems Inc. received the first copyright registration issued by the U.S. Copyright Office for a computer program that generates a particular style of type. The decision gave protection only for the computer programs that draw the letters, not for the designs of the letters themselves.

First Human Receives Engineered Genes

On Sept. 14, 1990, a 4-year-old girl became the first person to receive human gene therapy. The new method is an approach for treating disease by giving patients copies of critical genes they lack. The young girl suffers from a rare and severe immune deficiency

resulting from the lack of a gene that regulates production of an enzyme needed to keep the body's immune cells alive. During a 30-minute procedure, the patient was infused with about one billion white blood cells that had been outfitted through recombinant DNA technology with copies of the gene she lacked. If the procedure is successful, the genetically engineered blood cells will pump out normal levels of the crucial enzyme and restore the girl's immune system to full health.

The specific disorder the girl suffers from is adenosine deaminase (ADA) deficiency, which results from a lack of the ADA gene, which makes an enzyme needed to clean up dangerous metabolic byproducts in the body.

The experimental procedure was developed by Dr. R. Michael Blaese of the Natl. Cancer Inst., Dr. W. French Anderson of the Natl. Heart, Lung and Blood Inst., and Dr. Kenneth W. Culver.

Inventions and Discoveries

Invention	Date	Inventor	Nation.
Adding machine	1642	Pascal	French
Adding machine	1885	Burroughs	U.S.
Aerosol spray	1926	Rotheim	Norwegian
Air brake	1868	Westinghouse	U.S.
Air conditioning	1911	Carrier	U.S.
Air pump	1654	Guericke	German
Airplane, automatic pilot	1912	Sperry	U.S.
Airplane, experimental	1896	Langley	U.S.
Airplane jet engine	1939	Ohain	German
Airplane with motor	1903	Wright bros.	U.S.
Airplane, hydro	1911	Curtiss	U.S.
Airship	1852	Giffard	French
Airship, rigid dirigible	1900	Zeppelin	German
Arc welder	1919	Thomson	U.S.
Autogyro	1920	de la Cierva	Spanish
Automobile, differential gear	1885	Benz	German
Automobile, electric	1892	Morrison	U.S.
Automobile, exp'mtl	1864	Marcus	Austrian
Automobile, gasoline	1889	Daimler	German
Automobile, gasoline	1892	Duryea	U.S.
Automobile magneto	1897	Bosch	German
Automobile muffler	...	Maxim, H.P.	U.S.
Automobile self-starter	1911	Kettering	U.S.
Babbitt metal	1839	Babbitt	U.S.
Bakelite	1907	Baekeland	Belg., U.S.
Balloon	1783	Montgolfier	French
Barometer	1643	Torricelli	Italian
Bicycle, modern	1885	Starley	English
Bifocal lens	1780	Franklin	U.S.
Block signals, railway	1867	Hall	U.S.
Bomb, depth	1916	Tait	U.S.
Bottle machine	1895	Owens	U.S.
Braille printing	1829	Braille	French
Burner, gas	1855	Bunsen	German
Calculating machine	1833	Babbage	English
Camera—see also Photography			
Camera, Kodak	1888	Eastman, Walker	U.S.
Camera, Polaroid Land	1948	Land	U.S.
Car coupler	1873	Janney	U.S.
Carburetor, gasoline	1893	Maybach	German
Card time recorder	1894	Cooper	U.S.
Carding machine	1797	Whittemore	U.S.
Carpet sweeper	1876	Bissell	U.S.
Cassette, audio	1963	Philips Co.	Dutch
Cassette, videotape	1969	Sony	Japanese
Cash register	1879	Ritty	U.S.
Cathode ray oscilloscope	1897	Braun	German
Cathode ray tube	1878	Crookes	English
CAT scan (computerized tomography)	1973	Hounsfield	English
Cellophane	1908	Brandenberger	Swiss
Celluloid	1870	Hyatt	U.S.
Cement, Portland	1824	Aspdin	English
Chronometer	1761	Harrison	English
Circuit breaker	1925	Hilliard	U.S.
Circuit, integrated	1959	Kilby, Noyce, Texas Instr.	U.S
Clock, pendulum	1657	Huygens	Dutch
Coaxial cable system	1929	Affel, Espensched	U.S.
Coke oven	1893	Hoffman	Austrian
Compressed air rock drill	1871	Ingersoll	U.S.
Comptometer	1887	Felt	U.S.
Computer, automatic sequence	1944	Aiken et al.	U.S.
Computer, mini	1960	Digital Corp.	U.S.
Condenser microphone (telephone)	1916	Wente	U.S.
Contraceptive, oral	1954	Pincus, Rock	U.S.
Corn, hybrid	1917	Jones	U.S.
Cotton gin	1793	Whitney	U.S.
Cream separator	1878	DeLaval	Swedish
Cultivator, disc	1878	Mallon	U.S.
Cystoscope	1878	Nitze	German
Diesel engine	1895	Diesel	German
Disk, compact	1972	RCA	U.S.
Disk, floppy	1970	IBM	U.S.
Disk player, compact	1979	Sony, Philips Co	Japan., Dutch
Disk, video	1972	Philips Co.	Dutch
Dynamite	1866	Nobel	Swedish
Dynamo, continuous current	1871	Gramme	Belgian
Dynamo, hydrogen cooled	1915	Schuler	U.S.
Electric battery	1800	Volta	Italian
Electric fan	1882	Wheeler	U.S.
Electrocardiograph	1903	Einthoven	Dutch
Electroencephalograph	1929	Berger	German
Electromagnet	1824	Sturgeon	English
Electron spectrometer	1944	Deutsch, Elliott, Evans	U.S.
Electron tube multigrid	1913	Langmuir	U.S.
Electroplating	1805	Brugnatelli	Italian
Electrostatic generator	1929	Van de Graaff	U.S.
Elevator brake	1852	Otis	U.S.
Elevator, push button	1922	Larson	U.S.
Engine, automatic transmission	1910	Fottinger	German
Engine, coal-gas 4-cycle	1876	Otto	German
Engine, compression ignition	1883	Daimler	German
Engine, electric ignition	1883	Benz	German
Engine, gas, compound	1926	Eickemeyer	U.S.
Engine, gasoline	1872	Brayton, Geo.	U.S.
Engine, gasoline	1889	Daimler	German
Engine, steam, piston	1705	Newcomen	English
Engine, steam, piston	1769	Watt	Scottish
Engraving, half-tone	1852	Talbot	U.S.
Fiberglass	1938	Owens-Corning	U.S.
Fiber optics	1955	Kapany	English
Filament, tungsten	1913	Coolidge	U.S.
Flanged rail	1831	Stevens	U.S.
Flatiron, electric	1882	Seely	U.S.
Food, frozen	1924	Birdseye	U.S.
Furnace (for steel)	1858	Siemens	German
Galvanometer	1820	Sweigger	German
Gas discharge tube	1922	Hull	U.S.
Gas lighting	1792	Murdoch	Scottish
Gas mantle	1885	Welsbach	Austrian
Gasoline (lead ethyl)	1922	Midgley	U.S.
Gasoline, cracked	1913	Burton	U.S.
Gasoline, high octane	1930	Ipatieff	Russian
Geiger counter	1913	Geiger	German
Glass, laminated safety	1909	Benedictus	French
Glider	1853	Cayley	English
Gun, breechloader	1811	Thornton	U.S.
Gun, Browning	1897	Browning	U.S.
Gun, magazine	1875	Hotchkiss	U.S.
Gun, silencer	1908	Maxim, H.P.	U.S.
Guncotton	1847	Schoenbein	German
Gyrocompass	1911	Sperry	U.S.
Gyroscope	1852	Foucault	French
Harvester-thresher	1818	Lane	U.S.
Heart, artificial	1982	Jarvik	U.S.
Helicopter	1939	Sikorsky	U.S.
Hydrometer	1768	Baume	French
Ice-making machine	1851	Gorrie	U.S.
Iron lung	1928	Drinker, Shaw	U.S.
Kaleidoscope	1817	Brewster	Scottish
Kinetoscope	1889	Edison	U.S.
Lacquer, nitrocellulose	1921	Flaherty	U.S.
Lamp, arc	1847	Staite	English

(continued)

Invention	Date	Inventor	Nation.
Lamp, flourescent	1938	General Electric, Westinghouse	U.S.
Lamp, incandescent	1879	Edison	U.S.
Lamp, incand., frosted	1924	Pipkin	U.S.
Lamp, incand., gas	1913	Langmuir	U.S.
Lamp, Klieg	1911	Kliegl, A.&J.	U.S.
Lamp, mercury vapor	1912	Hewitt	U.S.
Lamp, miner's safety	1816	Davy	English
Lamp, neon	1909	Claude	French
Lathe, turret	1845	Fitch	U.S.
Launderette	1934	Cantrell	U.S.
Lens, achromatic	1758	Dollond	English
Lens, fused bifocal	1908	Borsch	U.S.
Leydenjar (condenser)	1745	von Kleist	German
Lightning rod	1752	Franklin	U.S.
Linoleum	1860	Walton	English
Linotype	1884	Mergenthaler	U.S.
Lock, cylinder	1851	Yale	U.S.
Locomotive, electric	1851	Vail	U.S.
Locomotive, exp'mtl	1802	Trevithick	English
Locomotive, exp'mtl	1812	Fenton et al.	English
Locomotive, exp'mtl	1813	Hedley	English
Locomotive, exp'mtl	1814	Stephenson	English
Locomotive practical	1829	Stephenson	English
Locomotive, 1st U.S.	1830	Cooper, P.	U.S.
Loom, power	1785	Cartwright	English
Loudspeaker, dynamic	1924	Rice, Kellogg	U.S.
Machine gun	1861	Gatling	U.S.
Machine gun, improved	1872	Hotchkiss	U.S.
Machine gun (Maxim)	1883	Maxim, H.S.U.S.	Eng.
Magnet, electro	1826	Henry	U.S.
Mantle, gas	1885	Welsbach	Austrian
Mason jar	1858	Mason, J.	U.S.
Match, friction	1827	John Walker	English
Mercerized textiles	1843	Mercer, J.	English
Meter, induction	1888	Shallenberg	U.S.
Metronome	1816	Malezel	German
Micrometer	1636	Gascoigne	English
Microphone	1877	Berliner	U.S.
Microscope, compound	1590	Janssen	Dutch
Microscope, electronic	1931	Knoll, Ruska	German
Microscope, field ion.	1951	Mueller	German
Monitor, warship	1861	Ericsson	U.S.
Monotype	1887	Lanston	U.S.
Motor, AC	1892	Tesla	U.S.
Motor, DC	1837	Davenport	U.S.
Motor, induction	1887	Tesla	U.S.
Motorcycle	1885	Daimler	German
Movie machine	1894	Jenkins	U.S.
Movie, panoramic	1952	Waller	U.S.
Movie, talking	1927	Warner Bros.	U.S.
Mower, lawn	1831	Budding, Ferrabee	English
Mowing machine	1822	Bailey	U.S.
Neoprene	1930	Carothers	U.S.
Nylon synthetic	1930	Carothers	U.S.
Nyion	1937	Du Pont lab.	U.S.
Oil cracking furnace	1891	Gavrilov	Russian
Oil filled power cable	1921	Emanueli	Italian
Oleomargarine	1869	Mege-Mouries	French
Ophthalmoscope	1851	Helmholtz	German
Paper machine	1809	Dickinson	U.S.
Parachute	1785	Blanchard	French
Pen, ballpoint	1838	Biro	Hungarian
Pen, fountain	1884	Waterman	U.S.
Pen, steel	1780	Harrison	English
Pendulum	1583	Galileo	Italian
Percussion cap	1807	Forsythe	Scottish
Phonograph	1877	Edison	U.S.
Photo, color	1892	Ives	U.S.
Photo film, celluloid	1893	Reichenbach	U.S.
Photo film, transparent	1884	Eastman, Goodwin	U.S.
Photoelectric cell	1895	Elster	German
Photographic paper	1835	Talbot	U.S.
Photography	1835	Talbot	English
Photography	1835	Daguerre	French
Photography	1816	Niepce	French
Photophone	1880	Bell	U.S.-Scot.
Phototelegraphy	1925	Bell Labs	U.S.
Piano	1709	Cristofori	Italian
Piano, player	1863	Fourneaux	French
Pin, safety	1849	Hunt	U.S.
Pistol (revolver)	1836	Colt	U.S.
Plow, cast iron	1785	Ransome	English
Plow, disc	1896	Hardy	U.S.
Pneumatic hammer	1890	King	U.S.
Powder, smokeless	1884	Vieille	French
Printing press, rotary	1845	Hoe	U.S.
Printing press, web	1865	Bullock	U.S.
Propeller, screw	1804	Stevens	U.S.
Propeller, screw	1837	Ericsson	Swedish
Pulsars	1967	Bell	English
Punch card accounting	1889	Hollerith	U.S.
Quasars	1963	Schmidt	U.S.
Radar	1940	Watson-Watt	Scottish
Radio amplifier	1906	De Forest	U.S.
Radio beacon	1928	Donovan	U.S.
Radio crystal oscillator	1918	Nicolson	U.S.
Radio receiver, cascade tuning	1913	Alexanderson	U.S.
Radio receiver, heterodyne	1913	Fessenden	U.S.
Radio transmitter triode modulation	1914	Alexanderson	U.S.
Radio tube-diode	1905	Fleming	English
Radio tube oscillator	1915	De Forest	U.S.
Radio tube triode	1906	De Forest	U.S.
Radio, signals	1895	Marconi	Italian
Radio, magnetic detector	1902	Marconi	Italian
Radio FM 2-path	1933	Armstrong	U.S.
Rayon	1883	Swan	English
Razor, electric	1917	Schick	U.S.
Razor, safety	1895	Gillette	U.S.
Reaper	1834	McCormick	U.S.
Record, cylinder	1887	Bell, Tainter	U.S.
Record, disc	1887	Berliner	U.S.
Record, long playing	1947	Goldmark	U.S.
Record, wax cylinder	1888	Edison	U.S.
Refrigerants, low-boiling fluorine compound1930		Midgely and co-workers	U.S.
Refrigerator car	1868	David	U.S.
Resin, synthetic	1931	Hill	English
Richter scale	1935	Richter	U.S.
Rifle, repeating	1860	Spencer	U.S.
Rocket engine	1926	Goddard	U.S.
Rubber, vulcanized	1839	Goodyear	U.S.
Saw, band	1808	Newberry	English
Saw, circular	1777	Miller	English
Searchlight, arc	1915	Sperry	U.S.
Sewing machine	1846	Howe	U.S.
Shoe-sewing machine	1860	McKay	U.S.
Shrapnel shell	1784	Shrapnel	English
Shuttle, flying	1733	Kay	English
Sleeping-car	1865	Pullman	U.S.
Slide rule	1620	Oughtred	English
Soap, hardwater	1928	Bertsch	German
Spectroscope	1859	Kirchoff, Bunsen	German
Spectroscope (mass)	1918	Dempster	U.S.
Spinning jenny	1767	Hargreaves	English
Spinning mule	1779	Crompton	English
Steamboat, exp'mtl	1778	Jouffroy	French
Steamboat, exp'mtl	1785	Fitch	U.S.
Steamboat, exp'mtl	1787	Rumsey	U.S.
Steamboat, exp'mtl	1788	Miller	Scottish
Steamboat, exp'mtl	1803	Fulton	U.S.
Steamboat, exp'mtl	1804	Stevens	U.S.
Steamboat, practical	1802	Symington	Scottish
Steamboat, practical	1807	Fulton	U.S.
Steam car	1770	Cugnot	French
Steam turbine	1884	Parsons	English
Steel (converter)	1856	Bessemer	English
Steel alloy	1891	Harvey	U.S.
Steel alloy, high-speed	1901	Taylor, White	U.S.
Steel, electric	1900	Heroult	French
Steel, manganese	1884	Hadfield	English
Steel, stainless	1916	Brearley	English
Stereoscope	1838	Wheatstone	English
Stethoscope	1819	Laennec	French
Stethoscope, binaural	1840	Cammann	U.S.
Stock ticker	1870	Edison	U.S.
Storage battery, rechargeable	1859	Plante	French
Stove, electric	1896	Hadaway	U.S.
Submarine	1891	Holland	U.S.
Submarine, even keel	1894	Lake	U.S.

Invention	Date	Inventor	Nation.
Submarine, torpedo	1776	Bushnell	U.S.
Superconductivity (BCS theory)	1957	Bardeen, Cooper, Schreiffer	U.S.
Tank, military	1914	Swinton	English
Tape recorder, magnetic	1899	Poulsen	Danish
Teflon	1938	Du Pont	U.S.
Telegraph, magnetic	1837	Morse	U.S.
Telegraph, quadruplex	1864	Edison	U.S.
Telegraph, railroad	1887	Woods	U.S.
Telegraph, wireless high frequency	1895	Marconi	Italian
Telephone	1876	Bell	U.S.-Scot.
Telephone amplifier	1912	De Forest	U.S.
Telephone, automatic	1891	Stowger	U.S.
Telephone, radio	1900	Poulsen, Fessenden	Danish
Telephone, radio	1906	De Forest	U.S.
Telephone, radio, l. d	1915	AT&T	U.S.
Telephone, recording	1898	Poulsen	Danish
Telephone, wireless	1899	Collins	U.S.
Telescope	1608	Lippershey	Neth.
Telescope	1609	Galileo	Italian
Telescope, astronomical	1611	Kepler	German
Teletype	1928	Morkrum, Kleinschmidt	U.S.
Television, iconoscope	1923	Zworykin	U.S.
Television, electronic	1927	Farnsworth	U.S.
Television, (mech. scanner)	1923	Baird	Scottish
Thermometer	1593	Galileo	Italian
Thermometer	1730	Reaumur	French
Thermometer, mercury	1714	Fahrenheit	German
Time recorder	1890	Bundy	U.S.
Time, self-regulator	1918	Bryce	U.S.
Tire, double-tube	1845	Thomson	Scottish
Tire, pneumatic	1888	Dunlop	Scottish
Toaster, automatic	1918	Strite	U.S.
Tool, pneumatic	1865	Law	English
Torpedo, marine	1804	Fulton	U.S.
Tractor, crawler	1904	Holt	U.S.
Transformer A.C.	1885	Stanley	U.S.
Transistor	1947	Shockley, Brattain, Bardeen	U.S.
Trolley car, electric	1884 -87	Van DePoele, Sprague	U.S.
Tungsten, ductile	1912	Coolidge	U.S.
Tupperware	1945	Tupper	U.S.
Turbine, gas	1849	Bourdin	French
Turbine, hydraulic	1849	Francis	U.S.
Turbine, steam	1884	Parsons	English
Type, movable	1447	Gutenberg	German
Typewriter	1867	Sholes, Soule, Glidden	U.S.
Vacuum cleaner, electric	1907	Spangler	U.S.
Velcro	1948	de Mestral	Swiss
Video game ("Pong")	1972	Buschnel	U.S.
Video home system (VHS)	1975	Matsushita, JVC	Japanese
Washer, electric	1901	Fisher	U.S.
Welding, atomic hydrogen	1924	Langmuir, Palmer	U.S.
Welding, electric	1877	Thomson	U.S.
Wind tunnel	1912	Eiffel	French
Wire, barbed	1874	Glidden	U.S.
Wire, barbed	1875	Haisn	U.S.
Wrench, double-acting	1913	Owen	U.S.
X-ray tube	1913	Coolidge	U.S.
Zipper	1891	Judson	U.S.

Discoveries and Innovations: Chemistry, Physics, Biology, Medicine

	Date	Discoverer	Nation.
Acetylene gas	1892	Wilson	U.S.
ACTH	1949	Armour & Co.	U.S.
Adrenalin	1901	Takamine	Japanese
Aluminum, electrolytic process	1886	Hall	U.S.
Aluminum, isolated	1825	Oersted	Danish
Analine dye	1856	Perkin	English
Anesthesia, ether	1842	Long	U.S.
Anesthesia, local	1885	Koller	Austrian
Anesthesia, spinal	1898	Bier	German
Anti-rabies	1885	Pasteur	French
Antiseptic surgery	1867	Lister	English
Antitoxin, diphtheria	1891	Von Behring	German
Argyrol	1901	Barnes	U.S.
Arsphenamine	1910	Ehrlich	German
Aspirin	1889	Dresser	German
Atabrine		Mietzsch, et al.	German
Atomic numbers	1913	Moseley	English
Atomic theory	1803	Dalton	English
Atomic time clock	1947	Libby	U.S.
Atom-smashing theory	1919	Rutherford	English
Aureomycin	1948	Duggar	U.S.
Bacitracin	1945	Johnson, et al.	U.S.
Bacteria (described)	1676	Leeuwenhoek	Dutch
Barbital	1903	Fischer	German
Bleaching powder	1798	Tennant	English
Blood, circulation	1628	Harvey	English
Bordeaux mixture	1885	Millardet	French
Bromine from sea	1924	Edgar Kramer	U.S.
Calcium carbide	1888	Wilson	U.S.
Calculus	1670	Newton	English
Camphor synthetic	1896	Haller	French
Canning (food)	1804	Appert	French
Carbomycin	1952	Tanner	U.S.
Carbon oxides	1925	Fisher	German
Chlorine	1774	Scheele	Swedish
Chloroform	1831	Guthrie, S.	U.S.
Chloromycetin	1947	Burkholder	U.S.
Classification of plants and animals	1735	Linnaeus	Swedish
Cocaine	1860	Niermann	German
Combustion explained	1777	Lavoisier	French
Conditioned reflex	1914	Pavlov	Russian
Conteben	1950	Belmisch, Mietzsch, Domagk	German
Cortisone	1936	Kendall	U.S.
Cortisone, synthesis	1946	Sarett	U.S.
Cosmic rays	1910	Gockel	Swiss
Cyanimide	1905	Frank, Caro	German
Cyclotron	1930	Lawrence	U.S.
DDT (not applied as insecticide until 1939)	1874	Zeidler	German
Deuterium	1932	Urey, Brickwedde, Murphy	U.S.
DNA (structure)	1951	Crick	English
		Watson	U.S.
		Wilkins	English
Electric resistance (law)	1827	Ohm	German
Electric waves	1888	Hertz	German
Electrolysis	1852	Faraday	English
Electromagnetism	1819	Oersted	Danish
Electron	1897	Thomson, J.	English
Electron diffraction	1936	Thomson, G.	English
		Davisson	U.S.
Electroshock treatment	1938	Cerletti, Bini	Italian
Erythromycin	1952	McGuire	U.S.
Evolution, natural selection	1858	Darwin	English
Falling bodies, law	1590	Galileo	Italian
Gases, law of combining volumes	1808	Gay-Lussac	French
Geometry, analytic	1619	Descartes	French
Gold (cyanide process for extraction)	1887	MacArthur, Forest	British
Gravitation, law	1687	Newton	English
Holograph	1948	Gabor	British
Human heart transplant	1967	Barnard	S. African

	Date	Discoverer	Nation.
Indigo, synthesis of	1880	Baeyer	German
Induction, electric	1830	Henry	U.S.
Insulin	1922	Banting, Best, Macleod	Canadian, Scottish
Intelligence testing	1905	Binet, Simon	French
Isinazid	1952	Hoffman-La-Roche	U.S.
		Domagk	German
Isotopes, theory	1912	Soddy	English
Laser (light amplification by stimulated emission of radiation)	1958	Townes, Schawlow	U.S.
Light, velocity	1675	Roemer	Danish
Light, wave theory	1690	Huygens	Dutch
Lithography	1796	Senefelder	Bohemian
Lobotomy	1935	Egas Moniz	Portuguese
LSD-25	1943	Hoffman	Swiss
Mendelian laws	1866	Mendel	Austrian
Mercator projection (map)	1568	Mercator (Kremer)	Flemish
Methanol	1925	Patard	French
Milk condensation	1853	Borden	U.S.
Molecular hypothesis	1811	Avogadro	Italian
Motion, laws of	1687	Newton	English
Neomycin	1949	Waksman, Lechevalier	U.S.
Neutron	1932	Chadwick	English
Nitric acid	1648	Glauber	German
Nitric oxide	1772	Priestley	English
Nitroglycerin	1846	Sobrero	Italian
Oil cracking process	1891	Dewar	U.S.
Oxygen	1774	Priestley	English
Ozone	1840	Schonbein	German
Paper, sulfite process	1867	Tilghman	U.S.
Paper, wood pulp, sulfate process	1884	Dahl	German
Penicillin	1929	Fleming	Scottish
practical use	1941	Florey, Chain	English
Periodic law and table of elements	1869	Mendeleyev	Russian
Planetary motion, laws	1609	Kepler	German
Plutonium fission	1940	Kennedy, Wahl, Seaborg, Segre	U.S.
Polymixin	1947	Ainsworth	English
Positron	1932	Anderson	U.S.
Proton	1919	Rutherford	N. Zealand
Psychoanalysis	1900	Freud	Austrian
Quantum theory	1900	Planck	German
Quasars	1963	Matthews, Sandage	U.S.
Quinine synthetic	1918	Rabe	German
Radioactivity	1896	Becquerel	French
Radium	1898	Curie, Pierre	French
		Curie, Marie	Pol.-Fr.
Relativity theory	1905	Einstein	German
Reserpine	1949	Jal Vaikl	Indian
Salvarsan (606)	1910	Ehrlich	German
Schick test	1913	Schick	U.S.
Silicon	1823	Berzelius	Swedish
Streptomycin	1945	Waksman	U.S.
Sulfadiazine	1940	Roblin	U.S.
Sulfanilamide	1934	Domagk	German
Sulfanilamide theory	1908	Gelmo	German
Sulfapyridine	1938	Ewins, Phelps	English
Sulfathiazole	...	Fosbinder, Walter	U.S.
Sulfuric acid	1831	Phillips	English
Sulfuric acid, lead	1746	Roebuck	English
Terramycin	1950	Finlay, et al.	U.S.
Tuberculin	1890	Koch	German
Uranium fission (theory)	1939	Hahn, Meitner, Strassmann	German
		Bohr	Danish
		Fermi	Italian
		Einstein, Pegram, Wheeler	U.S.
Uranium fission, atomic reactor	1942	Fermi, Szilard	U.S.
Vaccine, measles	1954	Enders, Peebles	U.S.
Vaccine, polio	1953	Salk	U.S.
Vaccine, polio, oral	1955	Sabin	U.S.
Vaccine, rabies	1885	Pasteur	French
Vaccine, smallpox	1796	Jenner	English
Vaccine, typhus	1909	Nicolle	French
Van Allen belts, radiation	1958	Van Allen	U.S.
Vitamin A	1913	McCollum, Davis	U.S.
Vitamin B	1916	McCollum	U.S.
Vitamin C	1912	Holst, Froelich	Norwegian
Vitamin D	1922	McCollum	U.S.
Wassermann test	1906	Wassermann	German
Xerography	1938	Carlson	U.S.
X-ray	1895	Roentgen	German

Chemical Elements, Discoverers, Atomic Weights

Atomic weights, based on the exact number 12 as the assigned atomic mass of the principal isotope of carbon, carbon 12, are provided through the courtesy of the International Union of Pure and Applied Chemistry and Butterworth Scientific Publications.

For the radioactive elements, with the exception of uranium and thorium, the mass number of either the isotope of longest half-life (*) or the better known isotope (**) is given.

Chemical element	Symbol	Atomic number	Atomic weight	Year discov.	Discoverer
Actinium	Ac	89	227*	1899	Debierne
Aluminum	Al	13	26.9815	1825	Oersted
Americium	Am	95	243*	1944	Seaborg, et al.
Antimony	Sb	51	121.75	1450	Valentine
Argon	Ar	18	39.948	1894	Rayleigh, Ramsay
Arsenic	As	33	74.9216	13th c.	Albertus Magnus
Astatine	At	85	210*	1940	Corson, et al.
Barium	Ba	56	137.34	1808	Davy
Berkelium	Bk	97	249**	1949	Thompson, Ghiorso, Seaborg
Beryllium	Be	4	9.0122	1798	Vauquelin
Bismuth	Bi	83	208.980	15th c.	Valentine
Boron	B	5	10.811a	1808	Gay-Lussac, Thenard
Bromine	Br	35	79.904b	1826	Balard
Cadmium	Cd	48	112.40	1817	Stromeyer
Calcium	Ca	20	40.08	1808	Davy
Californium	Cf	98	251*	1950	Thompson, et al.
Carbon	C	6	12.01115a	B.C.	
Cerium	Ce	58	140.12	1803	Klaproth
Cesium	Cs	55	132.905	1860	Bunsen, Kirchhoff
Chlorine	Cl	17	35.453b	1774	Scheele
Chromium	Cr	24	51.996b	1797	Vauquelin
Cobalt	Co	27	58.9332	1735	Brandt
Copper	Cu	29	63.546b	B.C.	

Chemical element	Symbol	Atomic number	Atomic weight	Year discov.	Discoverer
Curium	Cm	96	247*	1944	Seaborg, James, Ghiorso
Dysprosium	Dy	66	162.50	1886	Boisbaudran
Einsteinium	Es	99	254*	1952	Ghiorso, et al.
Erbium	Er	68	167.26	1843	Mosander
Europium	Eu	63	151.96	1901	Demarcay
Fermium	Fm	100	257*	1953	Ghiorso, et al.
Fluorine	F	9	18.9984	1771	Scheele
Francium	Fr	87	223*	1939	Perey
Gadolinium	Gd	64	157.25	1886	Marignac
Gallium	Ga	31	69.72	1875	Boisbaudran
Germanium	Ge	32	72.59	1886	Winkler
Gold	Au	79	196.967	B.C.	
Hafnium	Hf	72	178.49	1923	Coster, Hevesy
Hahnium	Ha	105	262*	1970	Ghiorso, et al.
Helium	He	2	4.0026	1868	Janssen, Lockyer
Holmium	Ho	67	164.930	1878	Soret, Delafontaine
Hydrogen	H	1	1.00797a	1766	Cavendish
Indium	In	49	114.82	1863	Reich, Richter
Iodine	I	53	126.9044	1811	Courtois
Iridium	Ir	77	192.2	1804	Tennant
Iron	Fe	26	55.847b	B.C.	
Krypton	Kr	36	83.80	1898	Ramsay, Travers
Lanthanum	La	57	138.91	1839	Mosander
Lawrencium	Lr	103	262*	1961	Ghiorso, T. Sikkeland, A.E. Larsh, and R.M. Latimer
Lead	Pb	82	207.19	B.C.	
Lithium	Li	3	6.939	1817	Arfvedson
Lutetium	Lu	71	174.97	1907	Welsbach, Urbain
Magnesium	Mg	12	24.312	1829	Bussy
Manganese	Mn	25	54.9380	1774	Gahn
Mendelevium	Md	101	258*	1955	Ghiorso, et al.
Mercury	Hg	80	200.59	B.C.	
Molybdenum	Mo	42	95.94	1782	Hjelm
Neodymium	Nd	60	144.24	1885	Welsbach
Neon	Ne	10	20.183	1898	Ramsay, Travers
Neptunium	Np	93	237*	1940	McMillan, Abelson
Nickel	Ni	28	58.71	1751	Cronstedt
Niobium[1]	Nb	41	92.906	1801	Hatchett
Nitrogen	N	7	14.0067	1772	Rutherford
Nobelium	No	102	259*	1958	Ghiorso, et al.
Osmium	Os	76	190.2	1804	Tennant
Oxygen	O	8	15.9994a	1774	Priestley, Scheele
Palladium	Pd	46	106.4	1803	Wollaston
Phosphorus	P	15	30.9738	1669	Brand
Platinum	Pt	78	195.09	1735	Ulloa
Plutonium	Pu	94	242**	1940	Seaborg, et al.
Polonium	Po	84	210**	1898	P. and M. Curie
Potassium	K	19	39.102	1807	Davy
Praseodymium	Pr	59	140.907	1885	Welsbach
Promethium	Pm	61	147**	1945	Glendenin, Marinsky, Coryell
Protactinium	Pa	91	231*	1917	Hahn, Meitner
Radium	Ra	88	226*	1898	P. & M. Curie, Bemont
Radon	Rn	86	222*	1900	Dorn
Rhenium	Re	75	186.2	1925	Noddack, Tacke, Berg
Rhodium	Rh	45	102.905	1803	Wollaston
Rubidium	Rb	37	85.47	1861	Bunsen, Kirchhoff
Ruthenium	Ru	44	101.07	1845	Klaus
Rutherfordium	Rf	104	261*	1969	Ghiorso, et al.
Samarium	Sm	62	150.35	1879	Boisbaudran
Scandium	Sc	21	44.956	1879	Nilson
Selenium	Se	34	78.96	1817	Berzelius
Silicon	Si	14	28.086a	1823	Berzelius
Silver	Ag	47	107.868b	B.C.	
Sodium	Na	11	22.9898	1807	Davy
Strontium	Sr	38	87.62	1790	Crawford
Sulfur	S	16	32.064a	B.C.	
Tantalum	Ta	73	180.948	1802	Ekeberg
Technetium	Tc	43	99**	1937	Perrier and Segre
Tellurium	Te	52	127.60	1782	Von Reichenstein
Terbium	Tb	65	158.924	1843	Mosander
Thallium	Tl	81	204.37	1861	Crookes
Thorium	Th	90	232.038	1828	Berzelius
Thulium	Tm	69	168.934	1879	Cleve
Tin	Sn	50	118.69	B.C.	
Titanium	Ti	22	47.90	1791	Gregor
Tungsten (Wolfram)	W	74	183.85	1783	d'Elhujar
Uranium	U	92	238.03	1789	Klaproth
Vanadium	V	23	50.942	1830	Sefstrom
Xenon	Xe	54	131.30	1898	Ramsay, Travers
Ytterbium	Yb	70	173.04	1878	Marignac
Yttrium	Y	39	88.905	1794	Gadolin
Zinc	Zn	30	65.37	B.C.	
Zirconium	Zr	40	91.22	1789	Klaproth

(1) Formerly Columbium. (a) Atomic weights so designated are known to be variable because of natural variations in isotopic composition. The observed ranges are: hydrogen ± 0.0001; boron ± 0.003; carbon ± 0.005; oxygen ± 0.0001; silicon ± 0.001; sulfur ± 0.003. (b) Atomic weights so designated are believed to have the following experimental uncertainties: chlorine ± 0.001; chromium ± 0.001; iron ± 0.003; bromine ± 0.001; silver ± 0.001; copper ± 0.001.

HEALTH
Ethics on Care of the Terminally Ill

The Supreme Court heard its first ever "right-to-die" case on Dec. 6, 1989. *Cruzan v. Missouri Dept. of Health* concerned Nancy Beth Cruzan, 32, who had been unconscious since Jan. 1983, after a car accident. Her parents and a guardian appointed to represent her sought to stop the medical treatment sustaining her in a "persistent vegetative state." On June 25, 1990, the Supreme Court ruled, 5-4, that a person whose wishes were clearly known had a constitutional right to refuse life-sustaining medical treatment. However, the court held that "clear and convincing" evidence as to her wishes was absent in the case of Nancy Cruzan.

As of January, 1988, hospitals are required by the Joint Commission on Accreditation of Health Care Organizations to have formal policies specifying when doctors and nurses can refrain from trying to resuscitate terminally ill patients. The policy must be developed in consultation with the medical staff and the nursing staff, adopted by the medical staff and then approved by the hospital's governing body. The policy must define the roles of physicians, nursing personnel, and members of the patient's family in any decision to withhold resuscitation. It must also include "provisions designed to assure that a patient's rights are respected."

In March 1986, the American Medical Association announced that it would be ethical for doctors to withhold "all means of life prolonging medical treatment," including food and water, from permanently unconscious patients even if death was not imminent. The withholding of such therapy should occur only when a patient's unconscious state "is beyond doubt irreversible and there are adequate safeguards to confirm the accuracy of the diagnosis," the association's judicial council said.

In June 1989, the Council on Ethical and Judicial Affairs of the AMA published a revised opinion on "Withholding or Withdrawing Life-Prolonging Medical Treatment," which stated that: "In deciding whether the administration of potentially life-prolonging medical treatment is in the best interest of the patient who is incompetent to act in his own behalf, the surrogate decisionmaker and physician should consider several factors, including: the possibility for extending life under humane and comfortable conditions; the patient's values about life and the way it should be lived; and the patient's attitude toward sickness, suffering, medical procedures, and death." The opinion also stated that, "In treating a terminally ill or permanently unconsious patient, the dignity of the patient should be maintained at all times."

Many states have tried to clear the issue of treating the comatose who are terminally ill by acting to define brain death. In at least 37 states, legislatures or courts have worked out a definition modeled along the lines of a recommendation previously released by the A.M.A. that said a person is brain dead when he has suffered "irreversible cessation of the functions of the entire brain, including the brain stem."

A number of states have "living will" statutes that set out a procedure for a mentally competent person to declare that he or she does not wish to be subjected to a "death-prolonging" procedure.

Information on living wills and health-care powers of attorney can be obtained from the American Bar Association's Commission on Legal Problems of the Ederly.

Immunization Schedule for Children

Source: American Academy of Pediatrics (AAP)

Childhood immunization means protection against eight major diseases: polio, measles, mumps, rubella (German measles), whooping cough (pertussis), diphtheria, tetanus, and Haemophilus influenczae type b (Hib) infections. Check the table and ask your pediatrician if your child is up to date on vaccines. It could save a life or prevent disability. Measles, mumps, rubella, polio, pertussis, diphtheria, Haemophilus infections and tetanus are not just harmless childhood illnesses. All of them can cripple or kill.

All are preventable. In order to be completely protected against diphtheria, tetanus and pertussis, your child needs a shot of the combination diphtheria-tetanus-pertussis (DPT) vaccine at 2, 4, 6, 15 and 18 months, and a booster prior to school entry (4-6 years). At 15 months your child should have a shot for measles, mumps and rubella (MMR). A second MMR, primarily to boost measles and mumps immunity, should be given to children 11 years or older who have not had measles. In the event of measles outbreaks in the community, this MMR booster may be given on entry to kindergarten or at an earlier age. Children in high risk populations should be tested for tuberculosis in the first year. Hib conjugate vaccine is due at 15 months. At 14 to 16 years a tetanus-diphtheria booster shot should be given.

If you don't have a pediatrician or family physician, call your local public health department. It usually has supplies of vaccine and may give shots free.

*Note: The American College of Physicians recommends that adolescents and adults consult with their physicians about further vaccinations. Those without natural infection or proper immunization against childhood diseases like measles, mumps, rubella, and polio may be at increased risk for such disease and their complications as adults; in addition, tetanus and diphtheria should be boosted periodically; and various ages, occupations, lifestyles, environmental risks, and outbreaks of disease may call for adult immunization.

	DTP	Polio	TB Test*	Measles	Mumps	Rubella	Hib/Conjugate	Tetanus-Diphtheria
2 months	✓	✓						
4 months	✓	✓						
6 months	✓							
12-15 mos.			✓					
15 months				✓	✓	✓	✓	
15-18 months	✓	✓						
4-6 years	✓	✓						
5-21 years				✓	✓	✓		
14-16 years								✓

*Only in high-prevalence populations.

Cancer's 7 Warning Signals*

Source: American Cancer Society

1. A change in bowel or bladder habits.
2. A sore that does not heal.
3. Unusual bleeding or discharge.
4. Thickening or lump in breast or elsewhere.
5. Indigestion or difficulty in swallowing.
6. Obvious change in wart or mole.
7. Nagging cough or hoarseness.
*If you have a warning signal, see your doctor.

Cancer Prevention

Source: American Cancer Society, 1990

PRIMARY PREVENTION: steps that might be taken to avoid those factors that might lead to the development of cancer.

Smoking

Cigarette smoking is responsible for 85% of lung cancer cases among men, 75% among women—about 83% overall. Smoking accounts for about 30% of all cancer deaths. Those who smoke two or more packs of cigarettes a day have lung cancer mortality rates 15-25 times greater than nonsmokers.

Nutrition

Risk for colon, breast and uterine cancers increases in obese people. High-fat diets may contribute to the development of certain cancers such as breast, colon and prostate. High-fiber foods may help reduce risk of colon cancer. A varied diet containing plenty of vegetables and fruits rich in vitamins A and C may reduce risk for cancers of larynx, esophagus, stomach, and lung. Salt-cured, smoked and nitrite-cured foods have been linked to esophageal and stomach cancer. The heavy use of alcohol, especially when accompanied by cigarette smoking or chewing tobacco, increases risk of cancers of the mouth, larynx, throat, esophagus, and liver.

Sunlight

Almost all of the more than 600,000 cases of non-melanoma skin cancer developed each year in the U.S. are considered to be sun-related. Such exposure is a major factor in the development of melanoma, and the incidence increases for those living near the equator.

Alcohol

Oral cancer and cancers of the larynx, throat, esophagus, and liver occur more frequently among heavy drinkers of alcohol.

Smokeless Tobacco

Use of chewing tobacco or snuff increases risk for cancers of the mouth, larynx, throat, and esophagus.

Estrogen

For mature women, estrogen treatment to control menopausal symptoms, increases risk of endometrial cancer. Use of estrogen needs careful discussion by the menopausal woman and her physician.

Radiation

Excessive exposure to ionizing radiation can increase cancer risk. Most medical and dental X rays are adjusted to deliver the lowest dose possible without sacrificing image quality. Excessive radon exposure in the home may increase lung cancer, especially in cigarette smokers. If levels are found to be too high, remedial actions should be taken.

Occupational hazards

Exposure to a number of industrial agents (nickel, chromate, asbestos, vinyl chloride, etc.) increases risk of various cancers. Risk from asbestos is greatly increased when combined with smoking.

SECONDARY PREVENTION: steps to be taken to diagnose a cancer or precursor as early as possible after it has developed.

Colorectal tests

The ACS recommends 3 tests for the early detection of colon and rectum cancer in people without symptoms: The digital rectal examination performed by a physician during an office visit, every year after the age of 40; the stool blood test every year after 50; and the proctosigmoidoscopy examination every 3 to 5 years, based on the advice of a physician.

Pap test

For cervical cancer, women who are or have been sexually active, or have reached 18 years, should have an annual Pap test and pelvic examination. After a woman has had 3 or more consecutive satisfactory normal exams, the Pap test may be performed less frequently at the discretion of her physician.

Breast cancer detection

The ACS recommends the monthly practice of breast self-examination by women 20 years and older. Physical examination of the breast should be done every 3 years from ages 20-40 and then every year. The ACS recommends a mammogram every year for asymptomatic women age 50 and over, and a baseline mammogram between ages 35-39. Women 40-49 should have mammography every 1-2 years, depending on physical and mammographic findings.

Estimated New Cancer Cases and Deaths By Sex for Selected Sites, 1990*

Source: American Cancer Society

	Estimated New Cases			Estimated Deaths		
	Total	Male	Female	Total	Male	Female
All Sites	1,040,000	520,000[1]	520,000[1]	502,000	266,000	236,000
Oral	30,500	20,400	10,100	8,350	5,575	2,775
Colon-Rectum	110,000	52,000	58,000	53,300	26,000	27,300
Lung	157,000	102,000	55,000	142,000	92,000	50,000
Skin	27,600+[2]	14,800+[2]	12,800+[2]	8,800[3]	5,700	3,100
Breast	150,900[4]	900[4]	150,000[4]	44,300	300	44,000
Uterus	13,500[4]	—	13,500[4]	6,000		6,000

*Note: The estimates of new cancer cases are offered as a rough guide and should not be regarded as definitive. (1) Carcinoma in situ and non-melanoma skin cancers are not included in totals. Carcinoma in situ of the uterine cervix accounts for more than 50,000 new cases annually, and carcinoma in situ of the female breast accounts for about 15,000 new cases annually. Non-melanoma skin cancer accounts for more than 600,000 new cases annually. (2) Melanoma only. (3) Melanoma 6,300; other skin 2,500. (4) Invasive cancer only.

Heart and Blood Vessel Disease

Warning Signs

Source: American Heart Association, Dallas

Of Heart Attack
• Uncomfortable pressure, fullness, squeezing or pain in the center of the chest lasting two minutes or longer
• Pain may radiate to the shoulder, arm, neck or jaw
• Sweating may accompany pain or discomfort
• Nausea and vomiting may also occur
• Shortness of breath, dizziness, or fainting may accompany other signs

The American Heart Association advises immediate action at the onset of these symptoms. The Association points out that more than half of heart attack victims die before they reach the hospital and that the average victim waits 2 hours before seeking help.

Of Stroke
• Sudden temporary weakness or numbness of face or limbs on one side of the body
• Temporary loss of speech, or trouble speaking or understanding speech
• Temporary dimness or loss of vision, particularly in one eye
• Unexplained dizziness, unsteadiness, or sudden falls

Major Risk Factors

Blood pressure—High blood pressure increases the risk of stroke, heart attack, kidney failure and congestive heart failure.

Cholesterol—A cholesteral concentration over 240 mg/dl approximately doubles the risk of coronary heart disease; about 25% of the U.S. adult population falls into this category. Blood cholesterol values between 200 and 240 mg/dl are in a zone of moderate and increasing risk.

Cigarettes—Cigarette smokers have more than twice the risk of heart attack and 2 to 4 times the risk of sudden cardiac death than nonsmokers. Young smokers have a higher risk for early death due to stroke.

Cardiovascular Diseases Statistical Summary

1988
Prevalence — 68,090,000 Americans have one or more forms of heart and blood vessel disease.
• hypertension — 61,870,000.
• coronary heart disease — 6,080,000
• rheumatic heart disease — 1,290,000.
• stroke — 2,930,000.

Mortality — 982,574 in 1988 (45.3% of all deaths).
• nearly one-fifth of all persons killed by CVD are under age 65.
Congenital or inborn heart defects —
• post-natal mortality from heart defects was estimated at more than 5,600 in 1988.

Heart attack — caused 511,050 deaths in 1988.
• 6,080,000 alive today have history of heart attack and/or angina pectoris.
• As many as 1,500,000 Americans will have a heart attack this year and over 500,000 of them will die.

Stroke — killed an estimated 150,300 in 1988; afflicts 2,930,000.

Hypertension (high blood pressure) — 61,870,000 Americans age 6 and above—nearly one in 3 adults.
Rheumatic heart disease — afflicts 1,290,000.
• killed about 6,520 in 1988.
Note: 1988 mortality data are estimates based on 1988 provisional data as published by the National Center for Health Statistics.

U.S. Metropolitan Areas with AIDS Rates of 25% or More, 1989-1990, and Cumulative Totals

Source: *HIV/AIDS Surveilliance Report.* Department of Health and Human Services

Metropolitan area of residence	Aug. 1988-July 1989 No.	Rate (per 100,000 pop.)	Aug. 1989-July 1990 No.	Rate (per 100,000 pop.)	Cumulative Totals Adults/Adolescents	Children Under 13 Yrs.	Total
Atlanta, Ga.	781	27.6	922	31.7	2,825	25	2,850
Austin, Tex.	155	19.6	245	29.9	627	5	632
Baltimore, Md.	408	17.4	594	25.2	1,586	46	1,632
Dallas, Tex.	583	22.4	711	26.6	2,474	12	2,486
Ft. Lauderdale, Fla.	471	39.3	910	74.7	2,239	46	2,285
Houston, Tex.	881	26.6	1,245	36.9	4,231	31	4,262
Jacksonville, Fla.	158	17.2	240	25.5	622	12	634
Jersey City, N.J.	410	75.5	326	60.2	1,561	36	1,597
Miami, Fla.	907	49.7	1,082	58.9	3,600	150	- 3,750
New Orleans, La.	285	21.3	401	29.8	1,280	18	1,298
New York, N.Y.	5,437	63.4	6,565	76.3	26,581	655	27,236
Newark, N.J.	988	52.0	994	52.2	3,875	114	3,989
San Diego, Calif.	461	19.1	682	27.6	2,067	17	2,084
San Francisco, Calif.	1,676	104.0	1,935	119.1	8,500	17	8,517
San Juan, P.R.	861	55.1	947	60.4	2,481	92	2,573
Seattle, Wash.	323	17.5	437	23.3	1,446	10	1,456
Washington, D.C.	876	23.3	1,059	27.7	4,006	60	4,006
West Palm Beach, Fla.	303	35.8	353	40.3	1,198	52	1,250
Metropolitan Area Subtotal[1]	**28,040**	**19.2**	**33,997**	**23.0**	**120,732**	**2,073**	**122,805**
All other areas	5,207	5.1	6,963	6.7	20,090	391	20,481
Total.	**33,247**	**13.3**	**40,960**	**16.3**	**140,822**	**2,464**	**143,286**

(1) Includes data from metropolitan areas with populations of 500,000 or more.

Drug Usage: America's High School Students

Source: National Institute on Drug Abuse/Univ. of Michigan Inst. for Social Research

Reporting on the 15th annual national survey of American high school seniors, and the 10th annual survey of American college students, researchers at the Univ. of Michigan concluded that the longer-term trend away from the use of marijuana, cocaine and other drugs continued in 1989. The likelihood of a high school or college student actively using illicit drugs is only about half of what it was a decade ago. However, in 1989 some 51 percent of the high school seniors and 56 percent of the college students in the survey reported having at least tried an illicit drug during their lifetime.

Concerning **high school dropouts,** the report acknowledged that those who fail to complete high school are at a higher-than-average risk for drug involvement.

In reporting the usage of **crack,** the researchers stated that "we know we are not going to capture many heavy crack users in these surveys, and it is clear from other types of information that there are plenty of heavy users out there. What may be more significant here is the fact that crack has not heavily penetrated these mainstream populations of American young people and that the initiation rates among them appear to be on the decline."

Results are based on large, representative sample surveys of 135 graduating classes enrolled in public and private high schools across the United States.

	Class of 1975	Class of 1978	Class of 1980	Class of 1983	Class of 1984	Class of 1985	Class of 1986	Class of 1987	Class of 1988	Class of 1989	'88-'89 change
				Percent ever used							
Marijuana/Hashish	47.3	59.2	60.3	57.0	54.9	54.2	50.9	50.2	47.2	43.7	−3.5ss
Inhalants	NA	12.0	11.9	13.6	14.4	15.4	15.9	17.0	16.7	17.6	+0.9
Inhalants Adjusted[1]	NA	NA	17.6	18.8	19.0	18.1	20.1	18.6	17.5	18.6	+1.1
Amyl & Butyl Nitrites	NA	NA	11.1	8.4	8.1	7.9	8.6	4.7	3.2	3.3	+0.1
Hallucinogens	16.3	14.3	13.3	11.9	10.7	10.3	9.7	10.3	8.9	9.4	+0.5
Hallucinogens Adjusted[2]	NA	NA	15.7	14.7	13.3	12.1	11.9	10.6	9.2	9.9	+0.7
LSD	11.3	9.7	9.3	8.9	8.0	7.5	7.2	8.4	7.7	8.3	+0.6
PCP	NA	NA	9.6	5.6	5.0	4.9	4.8	3.0	2.9	3.9	+1.0
Cocaine	9.0	12.9	15.7	16.2	16.1	17.3	16.9[5]	15.2	12.1	10.3	−1.8ss
"Crack"	NA	NA	NA	NA	NA	NA	NA	5.6	4.8	4.7	−0.1
Heroin	2.2	1.6	1.1	1.2	1.3	1.2	1.1	1.2	1.1	1.3	+0.2
Other opiates[3]	9.0	9.9	9.8	9.4	9.7	10.2	9.0	9.2	8.6	8.3	−0.3
Stimulants[3]	22.3	22.9	26.4	35.4	NA	NA	NA	NA	NA	NA	NA
Stimulants Adjusted[3,4]	NA	NA	NA	26.9	27.9	26.2	23.4	21.6	19.8	19.1	−0.7
Sedatives[3]	18.2	16.0	14.9	14.4	13.3	11.8	10.4	8.7	7.8	7.4	−0.4
Barbiturates[3]	16.9	13.7	11.0	9.9	9.9	9.2	8.4	7.4	6.7	6.5	−0.2
Methaqualone[3]	8.1	7.9	9.5	10.1	8.3	6.7	5.2	4.0	3.3	2.7	−0.6
Tranquilizers[3]	17.0	17.0	15.2	13.3	12.4	11.9	10.9	10.9	9.4	7.6	−1.8ss
Alcohol	90.4	93.1	93.2	92.6	92.6	92.2	91.3	92.2	92.0	90.7	−1.3
Cigarettes	73.6	75.3	71.0	70.6	69.7	68.8	67.6	67.2	66.4	65.7	−0.7

NA = Not available. Level of significance between the two most recent classes: s = .05, ss = .01, sss = .001.
(1) Adjusted for underreporting of amyl and butyl nitrites. (2) Adjusted for underreporting of PCP. (3) Only drug use which was not under a doctor's orders. (4) Adjusted for overreporting of the non-prescription stimulants. (5) In 1986, 12.6 percent of those who used cocaine used it in powder form, while 4.1 percent used the "crack" form.

Drug Usage: America's College Students

Source: National Institute on Drug Abuse/University of Michigan Institute for Social Research

Percent who used in last twelve months

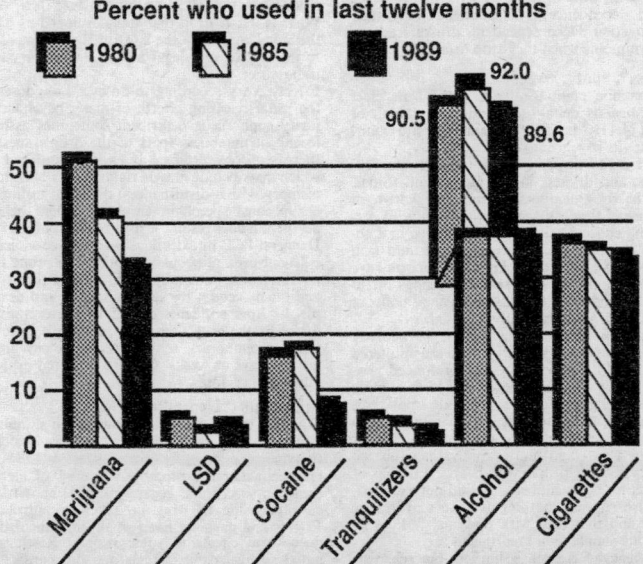

1980   1985   1989

Marijuana   LSD   Cocaine   Tranquilizers   Alcohol   Cigarettes

Effects of Commonly Abused Drugs

Source: National Institute on Drug Abuse

Tobacco

Effects and dangers: Nicotine, the active ingredient in tobacco, acts as a stimulant on the heart and nervous system. When tobacco smoke is inhaled the immediate effects on the body are a faster heart beat and elevated blood pressure. These effects, however, are quickly dissipated. Tar (in the smoke) contains many carcinogens. These compounds, many of which are in polluted air but are found in vastly greater quantities in cigarette smoke, have been identified as major causes of cancer and respiratory difficulties. Even relatively young smokers can have shortness of breath, nagging cough, or develop cardiovascular and respiratory difficulties. A third principal component of cigarette smoke, carbon monoxide, is also a cause of some of the more serious health effects of smoking. Carbon monoxide can reduce the blood's ability to carry oxygen to body tissues and can promote the development of arteriosclerosis (hardening of the arteries). Long-term effects of smoking cigarettes are emphysema, chronic bronchitis, heart disease, lung cancer, and cancer in other parts of the body.

Risks during pregnancy: Women who smoke during pregnancy are more likely to have babies that weigh less.

Alcohol

Effects: Like sedatives, it is a central nervous system depressant. In small doses, it has a tranquilizing effect on most people, although it appears to stimulate others. Alcohol first acts on those parts of the brain which affect self-control and other learned behaviors, which often leads to the aggressive behavior associated with some people who drink.

Dangers: In large doses, alcohol can dull sensation and impair muscular coordination, memory, and judgment. Taken in larger quantities over a long period time, alcohol can damage the liver and heart and can cause permanent brain damage. A large dose of alcohol can interfere with the part of the brain that controls breathing. The respiratory failure which results can bring death. Delirium tremens, the most extreme manifestation of alcohol withdrawal, can also cause death.

Risks during pregnancy: Women who drink heavily during pregnancy (more than 3 ounces of alcohol per day or about 2 mixed drinks) run a higher risk of delivering babies with physical, mental and behavioral abnormalities.

Dependence: Repeated drinking produces tolerance to the drug's effects and dependence. The drinker's body then needs alcohol to function. Once dependent, drinkers experience withdrawal symptoms when they stop drinking.

Marijuana ("grass", "pot", "weed")

What is it?: A common plant (*Cannabis sativa*), its chief psychoactive ingredient is delta-9-tetrahydrocannabinol, or THC. The amount of THC in the marijuana cigarette (joint) primarily determines its psychoactive potential.

Effects: Most users experience an increase in heart rate, reddening of the eyes, and dryness in the mouth and throat. Studies indicate the drug temporarily impairs short-term memory, alters sense of time, and reduces the ability to perform tasks requiring concentration, swift reactions, and coordination. Many feel that their hearing, vision, and skin sensitivity are enhanced by the drug, but these reports have not been objectively confirmed by research. Feelings of euphoria, relaxation, altered sense of body image, and bouts of exaggerated laughter are also commonly reported.

Dangers: Scientists believe marijuana can be particularly harmful to lungs because users typically inhale the unfiltered smoke deeply and hold it in their lungs for prolonged periods of time. Marijuana smoke has been found to have more cancer-causing agents than are found in cigarette smoke (see above). Because marijuana use increases heart rate as much as 50% and brings on chest pain in people who have a poor blood supply to the heart (and more rapidly than tobacco smoke does), doctors believe people with heart conditions or who are at high risk for heart ailments, should not use marijuana. Findings also suggest that regular use may reduce fertility in women and that men with marginal fertility or endocrine functioning should avoid marijuana use.

Risks during pregnancy: Research is limited, but scientists believe marijuana which crosses the placental barrier, may have a toxic effect on embryos and fetuses.

Dependence: Tolerance to marijuana, the need to take more and more of the drug over time to get the original effect, has been proven in humans and animals. Physical dependence has been demonstrated in research subjects who ingested an amount equal to smoking 10 to 20 joints a day. When the drug was discontinued, subjects experienced withdrawal symptoms—irritability, sleep disturbances, loss of appetite and weight, sweating, and stomach upset.

Bad reactions: Most commonly reported immediate adverse reaction to marijuana use is the "acute panic anxiety reaction," usually described as an exaggeration of normal marijuana effects in which intense fears of losing control accompany severe anxiety. The symptoms often disappear in a few hours when the acute drug effects have worn off.

Hallucinogens ("psychedelics")

What are they?: Drugs which affect perception, sensation, thinking, self-awareness, and emotion.

(1) **LSD (lysergic acid diethylamide),** a synthetic, is converted from lysergic acid which comes from fungus (ergot).

Effects: Vary greatly according to dosage, personality of the user, and conditions under which the drug is used. Basically, it causes changes in sensation. Vision alters; users describe changes in depth perception and in the meaning of the perceived object. Illusions and hallucinations often occur. Physical reactions range from minor changes such as dilated pupils, a rise in temperature and heartbeat, or a slight increase in blood pressure, to tremors. High doses can greatly alter the state of consciousness. Heavy use of the drug may produce flashbacks, recurrences of some features of a previous LSD experience days or months after the last dose.

Dangers: After taking LSD, a person loses control over normal thought processes. Although many perceptions are pleasant, others may cause panic or may make a person believe that he or she cannot be harmed. Longer-term harmful reactions include anxiety and depression, or "breaks from reality" which may last from a few days to months. Heavy users sometimes develop signs of organic brain damage, such as impaired memory and attention span, mental confusion, and difficulty with abstract thinking. It is not known yet whether such mental changes are permanent.

(2) **Mescaline:** Comes from peyote cactus and its effects are similar to those of LSD.

Phencyclidine (PCP or "angel dust")

What is it?: A drug that was developed as a surgical anesthetic for humans in the late 1950s. PCP was soon restricted to its only current legal use as a veterinary anesthetic and tranquilizer.

Effects: Vary according to dosage. Low doses may provide the usual releasing effects of many psychoactive drugs. A floaty euphoria is described, sometimes associated with a feeling of numbness (part of the drug's anesthetic effects). Increased doses produce an excited, confused intoxication, which may include muscle rigidity, loss of concentration and memory, visual disturbances, delirium, feelings of isolation, convulsions, speech impairment, violent behavior, fear of death, and changes in the user's perceptions of their bodies.

Dangers: PCP intoxication can produce violent and bizarre behavior even in people not otherwise prone to such behavior. Violent actions may be directed at themselves or others and often account for serious injuries and death. More people die from accidents caused by the erratic behavior produced by the drug than from the drug's direct effect on the body. A temporary, schizophrenic-like psychosis, which can last for days or weeks, has also occurred in users of moderate or higher doses.

Stimulants ("Uppers")

What are they?: A class of drugs which stimulate the central nervous system and produce an increase in alertness and activity.

(1) **Amphetamines** promote a feeling of alertness and increase in speech and general physical activity. Under medical supervision, the drugs are taken to control appetite.

Effects and dangers: Even small, infrequent doses can produce toxic effects in some people. Restlessness, anxiety, mood swings, panic, circulatory and cardiac disturbances, paranoid thoughts, hallucinations, convulsions, and coma have all been reported. Heavy, frequent doses can produce brain damage which results in speed disturbances and difficulty in turning thoughts into words. Death can result from injected amphetamine overdose. Long-term users often have acne resembling a measles rash; trouble with teeth, gums and nails, and dry lifeless hair. As heavy users who inject amphetamines accumulate larger amounts of the drug in their bodies, the resulting toxicity can produce amphetamine psychosis. People in this extremely suspicious, paranoid state, frequently exhibit bizarre, sometimes violent behavior.

Dependence: People with a history of sustained low-dose use quite often become dependent and feel they need the drug to get by.

(2) **Cocaine** is a stimulant extracted from the leaves of the coca plant. It is available in many forms, the most available of which is cocaine hydrochloride. Cocaine hydrochloride is often used medically as a local anesthetic, but is also sold illegally on the street in large pieces called rocks. Street cocaine is a white, crystal-like powder that is most commonly inhaled or snorted, though some users ingest, inject, or smoke a form of the drug called freebase or crack.

Freebase and crack are formed by chemically converting street cocaine to a purified substance that is more suitable for smoking. Smoking freebase or crack produces a shorter, but more intense high than other ways of using the drug. It is the most direct and rapid means of getting the drug to the brain, and because larger amounts are reaching the brain more quickly, the effects of the drug are more intense and the dangers associated with its use are greater.

Ice, or crystal methamphetamine, is another stimulant that can be smoked and which has many of the same euphoric and adverse effects as crack.

Effects: The drug's usual effects are dilated pupils and increased blood pressure, heart rate, breathing rate, and body temperature. Even small doses may elicit feelings of euphoria; illusions of increased mental and physical strength and sensory awareness; and a decrease in hunger, pain, and the perceived need for sleep. Large doses significantly magnify these effects, sometimes causing irrational behavior and confusion.

Dangers: Paranoia is not an uncommon response to heavy doses. Psychosis may be triggered in users prone to mental instability. Repeated inhalation often results in nostril and nasal membrane irritation. Some regular users have reported feelings of restlessness, irritability, and anxiety. Others have experienced hallucinations of touch, sight, taste, or smell. When people stop using cocaine after taking it for a long time, they frequently become depressed. They tend to fight off this depression by taking more cocaine, just as in the up/down amphetamine cycle.

Cocaine is toxic. Although few people realize it, overdose deaths, though rare, have occurred as a result of injecting, ingesting and even snorting cocaine. The deaths are a result of seizures followed by respiratory arrest and coma, or sometimes by cardiac arrest. Other dangers associated with cocaine include the risk of infection, such as hepatitis, resulting from the use of unsterile needles and the risk of fire or explosion resulting from the use of volatile substances necessary for freebase preparation.

Dependence: Cocaine is not a narcotic; no evidence suggests that it produces a physical dependence. However, cocaine is psychologically a very dangerous, dependence-producing drug. Smoking freebase or crack increases this risk of dependence.

(3) **Caffeine** may be the world's most popular drug. It is primarily consumed in coffee and tea, but is also found in cocoa, cola and other soft drinks, as well as in many over-the-counter medicines.

Effects: Two to four cups of coffee increase heart rate, body temperature, urine production, and gastric juice secretion. Caffeine can also raise sugar levels and cause tremors, loss of coordination, decreased appetite, and postponement of fatigue. It can interfere with the depth of sleep and the amount of dream sleep by causing more rapid eye movement (REM) sleep at first, but less than average over an entire night. Extremely high doses may cause diarrhea, sleeplessness, trembling, severe headache, and nervousness.

Dependence: A form of physical dependence may result with regular consumption. In such cases, withdrawal symptoms may occur if caffeine use is stopped or interrupted. These symptoms include headache, irritability, and fatigue. Toler-

ance may develop with the use of six to eight cups or more a day. A regular user of caffeine who has developed a tolerance may also develop a craving for the drug's effects.

Dangers: Poisonous doses of caffeine have occurred occasionally and have resulted in convulsions, breathing failure, and even death. However, it is almost impossible to die from drinking too much coffee or tea. The deaths that have been reported have resulted from the misuse of tablets containing caffeine.

Sedatives (Tranquilizers, sleeping pills)

What are they?: Drugs which depress the central nervous system, more appropriately called sedative-hypnotics because they include drugs which calm the nerves (the sedation effect) and produce sleep (the hypnotic effect). Of drugs in this class, barbiturates ("barbs," "downers," "reds") have the highest rate of abuse and misuse. The most commonly abused barbiturates include pentobarbital (Nembutal), secobarbital (Seconal), and amobarbital (Amytal). These all have legitimate use as sedatives or sleeping aids. Among the most commonly abused nonbarbiturate drugs are glutethimide (Doriden), meprobamate (Miltown), methyprylon (Noludar), ethchlorvynol (Placidyl), and methaqualone (Sopor, Quaalude). These are prescribed to help people sleep. Benzodiazepines, especially diazepam (Valium), prescribed to relieve anxiety, are commonly abused, and their rate of abuse and misuse is increasing.

Dangers: These can kill. Barbiturate overdose is implicated in nearly one-third of all reported drug-induced deaths. Accidental deaths may occur when a user takes an unintended larger or repeated dose of sedatives because of confusion or impairment in judgment caused by initial intake of the drug. With lesser, but still large doses, users can go into coma. Moderately large doses often produce an intoxicated stupor. Users' speech is often slurred, memory vague, and judgment impaired. Taken along with alcohol, the combination can be fatal. Tranquilizers act somewhat differently from other sedatives and are considered less hazardous. But even by themselves, or in combination with other drugs (especially alcohol and other sedatives) they can be quite dangerous.

Dependence: Potential for dependence is greatest with barbiturates, but all sedatives, tranquilizers, can be addictive. Barbiturate withdrawal is often more severe than heroin withdrawal.

Narcotics

What they are?: Drugs that relieve pain and often induce sleep. The opiates, which are narcotics, include opium and drugs derived from opium, such as morphine, codeine, and heroin. Narcotics also include certain synthetic chemicals that have a morphine-like action, such as methadone.

Which are abused?: Heroin ("junk," "smack") accounts for 90% of narcotic abuse in the U.S. Sometimes medicinal narcotics are also abused, including paregoric containing codeine and methadone, meperidine, and morphine.

Dependence: Anyone can become heroin dependent if he or she takes the drug regularly. Although environmental stress and problems of coping have often been considered as factors that lead to heroin addiction, physicians or psychologists do not agree that some people just have an "addictive personality" and are prone to dependence. All we know for certain is that continued use of heroin causes dependence.

Dangers: Physical dangers depend on the specific drug, its source, and the way it is used. Most medical problems are caused by the uncertain dosage level, use of unsterile needles and other paraphernalia, contamination of the drug, or combination of a narcotic with other drugs, rather than by the effects of the heroin (or another narcotic) itself. The life expectancy of a heroin addict who injects the drug intravenously is significantly lower than that of one who does not. An overdose can result in death. If, for example, an addict obtains pure heroin and is not tolerant of the dose, he or she may die minutes after injecting it. Infections from unsterile needles, solutions, syringes, cause many diseases. Serum hepatitis is common. Skin abscesses, inflammation of the veins and congestion of the lungs also occur.

Withdrawal: When a heroin-dependent person stops taking the drug, withdrawal begins within 4-6 hours after the last injection. Full-blown withdrawal symptoms—which include shaking, sweating, vomiting, a running nose and eyes, muscle aches, chills, abdominal pains, and diarrhea—begin some 12-16 hours after the last injection. The intensity of symptoms depends on the degree of dependence.

Basic First Aid

First aid experts stress that knowing what to do for an injured person until a doctor or trained person gets to an accident scene can save a life, especially in cases of stoppage of breath, severe bleeding, and shock.

People with special medical problems, such as diabetes, cardiovascular disease, epilepsy, or allergy, are also urged to wear some sort of emblem identifying it, as a safeguard against use of medication that might be injurious or fatal in an emergency. Emblems may be obtained from Medic Alert Foundation, Turlock, CA 95380.

Most accidents occur in homes. National Safety Council figures show that home accidents exceed those in other locations, such as in cars, at work, or in public places.

In all cases, get medical assistance as soon as possible.

Animal bite — Wound should be washed with soap under running water and animal should be caught alive for rabies test.

Asphyxiation — Start mouth-to-mouth resuscitation immediately after getting patient to fresh air.

Bleeding — Elevate the wound above the heart if possible. Press hard on wound with sterile compress until bleeding stops. Send for doctor if it is severe.

Burn — If mild, with skin unbroken and no blisters, plunge into ice water until pain subsides. Apply a dry dressing if necessary. Send for physician if burn is severe. Apply sterile compresses and keep patient quiet and comfortably warm until doctor's arrival. Do not try to clean burn, or to break blisters.

Chemical in eye — With patient lying down, pour cupsful of water immediately into corner of eye, letting it run to other side to remove chemicals thoroughly. Cover with sterile compress. Get medical attention immediately .

Choking — Do not use back slaps to dislodge obstruction. (See Abdominal Thrust)

Convulsions — Place person on back on bed or rug. Loosen clothing. Turn head to side. Do not place a blunt object between the victim's teeth. If convulsions do not stop, get medical attention immediately.

Cut (minor) — Apply mild antiseptic and sterile compress after washing with soap under warm running water.

Drowning — (See Mouth-to-Mouth Resuscitation) Artificial breathing must be started at once, before victim is out of the water, if possible. If the victim's stomach is bloated with water, put victim on stomach, place hands under stomach, and lift. If no pulse is felt, begin cardio-pulmonary resuscitation. This should only be done by those professionally trained. If necessary, treat for shock. (See Shock)

Electric shock — If possible, turn off power. Don't touch victim until contact is broken; pull him from contact with electrical source using rope, wooden pole, or loop of dry cloth. Start mouth-to-mouth resuscitation if breathing has stopped.

Foreign body in eye — Touch object with moistened corner of handkerchief if it can be seen. If it cannot be seen or does not come out after a few attempts, take patient to doctor. Do not rub eye.

Fainting — If victim feels faint, lower head to knees. Lay him down with head turned to side if he becomes unconscious. Loosen clothing and open windows. Keep patient lying quietly for at least 15 minutes after he regains consciousness. Call doctor if faint lasts for more than a few minutes.

Fall — Send for physician if patient has continued pain. Cover wound with sterile dressing and stop any severe bleeding. Do not move patient unless absolutely necessary — as in case of fire — if broken bone is suspected. Keep patient warm and comfortable.

Loss of Limb — If a limb is severed, it is important to properly protect the limb so that it can possibly be reattached to the victim. After the victim is cared for, the limb should be placed in a clean plastic bag, garbage can or other suitable container. Pack ice around the limb on the OUTSIDE of the bag to keep the limb cold. Call ahead to the hospital to alert them of the situation.

Poisoning — Call doctor. Use antidote listed on label if container is found. Call local Poison Control Center if possible. Except for lye, other caustics, and petroleum products, induce vomiting unless victim is unconscious. Give milk if poison or antidote is unknown.

Shock (injury-related) — Keep the victim lying down; if uncertain as to his injuries, keep him flat on his back. Maintain the victim's normal body temperature; if the weather is cold or damp, place blankets or extra clothing over and under the victim; if weather is hot, provide shade.

Snakebite — Immediately get victim to a hospital. If there is mild swelling or pain, apply a constricting band 2 to 4 inches above the bite.

Sting from insect — If possible, remove stinger and apply solution of ammonia and water, or paste of baking soda. Call physician immediately if body swells or patient collapses.

Unconsciousness — Send for doctor and place person on his back. Start resuscitation if he stops breathing. Never give food or liquids to an unconscious person.

Abdominal Thrust

The American Red Cross and the American Heart Association both agree that the recommended first aid for choking victims is the abdominal thrust, also known as the Heimlich maneuver, after its creator, Dr. Henry Heimlich. Slaps on the back are no longer advised and may even prove detrimental in an attempt to assist a choking victim.

- Get behind the victim and wrap your arms around him above his waist.
- Make a fist with one hand and place it, with the thumb knuckle pressing inward, just below the point of the "v" of the rib cage.
- Grasp the wrist with the other hand and give one or more upward thrusts or hugs.
- Start mouth-to-mouth resuscitation if breathing stops.

Mouth-to-Mouth Resuscitation

Stressing that your breath can save a life, the American Red Cross gives the following directions for mouth-to-mouth resuscitation if the victim is not breathing:

- Determine consciousness by tapping the victim on the shoulder and asking loudly, "Are you okay?"
- Tilt the victim's head back so that his chin is pointing upward. Do not press on the soft tissue under the chin, as this might obstruct the airway. If you suspect that an accident victim might have neck or back injuries, open the airway by placing the tips of your index and middle fingers on the corners of the victim's jaw to lift it forward without tilting the head.
- Place your cheek and ear close to the victim's mouth and nose. Look at the victim's chest to see if it rises and falls. Listen and feel for air to be exhaled for about 5 seconds.
- If there is no breathing, pinch the victim's nostrils shut with the thumb and index finger of your hand that is pressing on the victim's forehead. Another way to prevent leakage of air when the lungs are inflated is to press your cheek against the victim's nose.
- Blow air into victim's mouth by taking a deep breath and then sealing your mouth tightly around the victim's mouth. Initially, give two, quick (approx. 1.5 seconds each), full breaths without allowing the lungs to deflate completely between each breath.
- Watch the victim's chest to see if it rises.
- Stop blowing when the victim's chest is expanded. Raise your mouth; turn your head to the side and listen for exhalation.
- Watch the chest to see if it falls.
- Repeat the blowing cycle until the victim starts breathing.

    Note: Infants (up to one year) and children (1 to 8 years) should be administered mouth-to-mouth resuscitation as described above, except for the following:

- Do not tilt the head as far back as an adult's head.
- Both the mouth and nose of the infant should be sealed by the mouth.
- Give breaths to a child once every four seconds.
- Blow into the infant's mouth and nose once every three seconds with less pressure and volume than for a child.

Stress: How Much Can Affect Your Health?

Source: Reprinted with permission from the *Journal of Psychosomatic Research*, Vol. 11, pp. 213-218, T.H. Holmes, M.D., R.H. Rahe, M.D.; The Social Readjustment Rating Scale © 1967, Pergamon Press, Ltd.

Change, both good and bad, can create stress and stress, if sufficiently severe, can lead to illness. Drs. Thomas Holmes and Richard Rahe, psychiatrists at the University of Washington in Seattle, developed the Social Readjustment Rating Scale. In their study, they gave a point value to stressful events. The psychiatrists discovered that in 79 percent of the persons studied, major illness followed the accumulation of stress-related changes totaling over 300 points in one year.

The Social Readjustment Rating Scale

Life Event	Value	Life Event	Value
Death of Spouse	100	In-law troubles	29
Divorce	73	Outstanding personal achievement	28
Marital separation from mate	65	Wife beginning or ceasing work outside the home	26
Detention in jail or other institution	63	Beginning or ceasing formal schooling	26
Death of a close family member	63	Major change in living conditions (e.g., building a new	
Major personal injury or illness	53	home, remodeling, deterioration of home or neighborhood)	25
Marriage	47		
Being fired at work	47	Revision of personal habits (dress, manners, association, etc.)	24
Marital reconciliation with mate	45	Troubles with the boss	23
Retirement from work	45	Major change in working hours or conditions	20
Major change in the health or behavior of a family member	44	Change in residence	20
Pregnancy	40	Changing to a new school	20
Sexual difficulties	39	Major change in usual type and/or amount of recreation	19
Gaining a new family member (e.g., through birth, adoption, moving in, etc.)	39	Major change in church activities (e.g., a lot more or a lot less than usual)	19
Major business readjustment (e.g., merger, reorganization, bankruptcy, etc.)	39	Major change in social activities (e.g., clubs, dancing, movies, visiting, etc.)	18
Major change in financial state (e.g., a lot worse off or a lot better off than usual)	38	Taking out a mortgage or loan for a lesser purchase (e.g., for a car, TV, freezer, etc.)	17
Death of a close friend	37	Major change in sleeping habits (a lot more or a lot less sleep, or change in part of day when asleep)	16
Changing to a different line of work	36		
Major change in the number of arguments with spouse (e.g., either a lot more or a lot less than usual regarding child-rearing, personal habits, etc.)	35	Major change in number of family get-togethers (e.g., a lot more or a lot less than usual)	15
Taking out a mortgage or loan for a major purchase (e.g. for a home, business, etc.)	31	Major change in eating habits (a lot more or a lot less food intake, or very different meal hours or surroundings)	15
Foreclosure on a mortgage or loan	30	Vacation	13
Major change in responsibilities at work (e.g., promotion, demotion, lateral transfer)	29	Christmas	12
Son or daughter leaving home (e.g., marriage, attending college, etc.)	29	Minor violations of the law (e.g., traffic tickets, jaywalking, disturbing the peace, etc.)	11

A Patient's Bill of Rights

Source: American Hospital Association, © copyright 1972.

Often, as a hospital patient, you feel you have little control over your circumstances. You do, however, have some important rights. They have been enumerated by the American Hospital Association.

1. The patient has the right to considerate and respectful care.

2. The patient has the right to obtain from his physician complete current information concerning his diagnosis, treatment, and prognosis in terms the patient can be expected to understand. When it is not medically advisable to give such information to the patient, the information should be made available to an appropriate person in his behalf. He has the right to know, by name, the physician responsible for coordinating his care.

3. The patient has the right to receive from his physician information necessary to give informed consent prior to the start of any procedure and/or treatment. Except in emergencies, such information for informed consent should include but not necessarily be limited to the specific procedure and/or treatment, the medically significant risks involved, and the probable duration of incapacitation. Where medically significant alternatives for care or treatment exist, or when the patient requests information concerning medical alternatives, the patient has the right to such information. The patient also has the right to know the name of the person responsible for the procedures and/or treatment.

4. The patient has the right to refuse treatment to the extent permitted by law and to be informed of the medical consequences of his action.

5. The patient has the right to every consideration of his privacy concerning his own medical care program. Case discussion, consultation, examination, and treatment are confidential and should be conducted discreetly. Those not directly involved in his care must have the permission of the patient to be present.

6. The patient has the right to expect that all communications and records pertaining to his care should be treated as confidential.

7. The patient has the right to expect that within its capacity a hospital must make reasonable response to the request of a patient for services. The hospital must provide evaluation, service, and/or referral as indicated by the urgency of the case. When medically permissable, a patient may be transferred to another facility only after he has received complete information and explanation concerning the need for and alternatives to such a transfer. The receiving institution must first have accepted the patient for transfer.

8. The patient has the right to obtain information as to any relationship of his hospital to other health care and education institutions insofar as this care is concerned. The patient has the right to obtain information as to the existence of any professional relationships among individuals, by name, who are treating him.

9. The patient has the right to be advised if the hospital proposes to engage in or perform human experimentation affecting his care or treatment. The patient has the right to refuse to participate in such research projects.

10. The patient has the right to expect reasonable continuity of care. He has the right to know in advance what appointment times and physicians are available and where. The patient has the right to expect that the hospital will provide a mechanism whereby he is informed by his physician of the patient's continuing health care requirements following discharge.

11. The patient has the right to examine and receive an explanation of his bill, regardless of the source of payment.

12. The patient has the right to know what hospital rules and regulations apply to his conduct as a patient.

Nutritive Value of Food (Calories, Proteins, etc.)

Source: Home and Garden Bulletin No. 72; available from Supt. of Documents, U. S. Government Printing Office, Washington, DC 20402

Food	Measure	Grams	Food Energy (calories)	Protein (grams)	Fat (grams)	Saturated fats (grams)	Carbohydrate (grams)	Calcium (milligrams)	Iron (milligrams)	Vitamin A (I.U.)	Thiamin (milligrams)	Riboflavin (milligrams)
Dairy products												
Cheese, cheddar	1 oz.	28	115	7	9	6.1	T	204	.2	300	.01	.11
Cheese, cottage, small curd	1 cup	210	220	26	9	6.0	6	126	.3	340	.04	.34
Cheese, cream	1 oz.	28	100	2	10	6.2	1	23	.3	400	T	.06
Cheese, Swiss	1 oz.	28	105	8	8	5.0	1	272	T	240	.01	.10
Half-and-Half	1 tbsp.	15	20	T	2	1.1	1	16	T	20	.01	.02
Cream, sour	1 tbsp.	15	25	T	3	1.6	1	14	T	90	T	.02
Milk, whole	1 cup	244	150	8	8	5.1	11	291	.1	310	.09	.40
Milk, nonfat (skim)	1 cup	244	85	8	T	.3	12	302	.1	500	.09	.37
Milkshake, chocolate	10.6 oz.	300	355	9	8	5.0	63	396	.9	260	.14	.67
Ice Cream, hardened	1 cup	133	270	5	14	8.9	32	176	.1	540	.05	.33
Sherbet	1 cup	193	270	2	4	2.4	59	103	.3	190	.03	.09
Yogurt, fruit-flavored	8 oz.	227	230	10	3	1.8	42	343	.2	120	.08	.40
Eggs												
Fried in butter	1	46	85	5	6	2.4	1	26	.9	290	.03	.13
Hard-cooked	1	50	80	6	6	1.7	1	28	1.0	260	.04	.14
Scrambled in butter (milk added)	1	64	95	6	7	2.8	1	47	.9	310	.04	.16
Fats & oils												
Butter	1 tbsp.	14	100	T	12	7.2	T	3	T	430	T	T
Margarine	1 tbsp.	14	100	T	12	2.1	T	3	T	470	T	T
Salad dressing, blue cheese	1 tbsp.	15	75	1	8	1.6	1	12	T	30	T	.02
Salad dressing, French	1 tbsp.	16	65	T	6	1.1	3	2	1	—	—	—
Salad dressing, Italian	1 tbsp.	15	85	T	9	1.6	1	2	T	T	T	T
Mayonnaise	1 tbsp.	14	100	T	11	2.0	T	3	.1	40	T	.01
Meat, poultry, fish												
Bluefish, baked with butter or margarine	3 oz.	85	135	22	4	—	0	25	0.6	40	.09	.08
Clams, raw, meat only	3 oz.	85	65	11	1	—	2	59	5.2	90	.08	.15
Crabmeat, white or king, canned	1 cup	135	135	24	3	.6	1	61	1.1	—	.11	.11
Fish sticks, breaded, cooked, frozen	1 oz.	28	50	5	3	—	2	3	.1	0	.01	.02
Salmon, pink, canned	3 oz.	85	120	17	5	.9	0	167	.7	60	.03	.16
Sardines, Atlantic, canned in oil	3 oz.	85	175	20	9	3.0	0	372	2.5	190	.02	.17
Shrimp, French fried	3 oz.	85	190	17	9	2.3	9	61	1.7	—	.03	.07
Tuna, canned in oil	3 oz.	85	170	24	7	1.7	0	7	1.6	70	.04	.10
Bacon, broiled or fried crisp	2 slices	15	85	4	8	2.5	T	2	.5	0	.08	.05
Ground beef, broiled, 10% fat	3 oz.	85	185	23	10	4.0	0	10	3.0	20	.08	.20
Roast beef, relatively lean	3 oz.	85	165	25	7	2.8	0	11	3.2	10	.06	.19
Beef steak, lean and fat	3 oz.	85	330	20	27	11.3	0	9	2.5	50	.05	.15
Beef & vegetable stew	1 cup	245	220	16	11	4.9	15	29	2.9	2,400	.15	.17
Lamb, chop, lean and fat	3.1 oz.	89	360	18	32	14.8	0	8	1.0	—	.11	.19
Liver, beef	3 oz.	85	195	22	9	2.5	5	9	7.5	45,390	.22	3.56
Ham, light cure, lean and fat	3 oz.	85	245	18	19	6.8	0	8	2.2	0	.40	.15
Pork, chop, lean and fat	2.7 oz.	78	305	19	25	8.9	0	9	2.7	0	.75	.22
Bologna	1 slice	28	85	3	8	3.0	T	2	.5	—	.05	.06
Frankfurter, cooked	1	56	170	7	15	5.6	1	3	.8	—	.08	.11
Sausage, pork link, cooked	1 link	13	60	2	6	2.1	T	1	.3	0	.10	.04
Veal, cutlet, braised or boiled	3 oz.	85	185	23	9	4.0	0	9	2.7	—	.06	.21
Chicken, drumstick, fried, bones removed	1.3 oz.	38	90	12	4	1.1	T	6	.9	50	.03	.15
Chicken, half broiler, broiled, bones removed	6.2 oz.	176	240	42	7	2.2	0	16	3.0	160	.09	.34
Fruits & products												
Apple, raw, 2-3/4 in. diam.	1	138	80	T	1	—	20	10	.4	120	.04	.03
Applejuice	1 cup	248	120	T	T	—	30	15	1.5	—	.02	.05
Apricots, raw	3	107	55	1	T	—	14	18	.5	2,890	.03	.04
Banana, raw	1	119	100	1	T	—	26	10	.8	230	.06	.07
Cherries, sweet, raw	10	68	45	1	T	—	12	15	.3	70	.03	.04
Fruit cocktail, canned in heavy syrup	1 cup	255	195	1	T	—	50	23	1.0	360	.05	.03
Grapefruit, raw, medium, white	1/2	241	45	1	T	—	12	19	.5	10	.05	.02
Grapes, Thompson seedless	10	50	35	T	T	—	9	6	.2	50	.03	.02
Lemonade, frozen, diluted	1 cup	248	105	T	T	—	28	2	.1	10	.01	.02
Cantaloupe, 5-in. diam.	1/2	477	80	2	T	—	20	38	1.1	9,240	.11	.08
Orange, 2-5/8 in. diam.	1	131	65	1	T	—	16	54	.5	260	.13	.05
Orange juice, diluted	1 cup	249	120	2	T	—	29	25	.2	540	.23	.03
Peach, raw, 2-1/2 in. diam.	1	100	40	1	T	—	10	9	.5	1,330	.02	.05
Raisins, seedless	1 cup	145	420	4	T	—	112	90	5.1	30	.16	.12
Strawberries, whole	1 cup	149	55	1	1	—	13	31	1.5	90	.04	.10
Watermelon, 4 by 8 in. wedge	1 wedge	926	110	2	1	—	27	30	2.1	2,510	.13	.13
Grain products												
Bagel, egg	1	55	165	6	2	.5	28	9	1.2	30	.14	.10
Biscuit, 2 in. diam., from home recipe	1	28	105	2	5	1.2	13	34	.4	T	.08	.08
Bread, enriched, soft-crumb	1 slice	25	70	2	1	.2	13	21	.6	T	.10	.06
Bread, whole wheat, soft-crumb	1 slice	28	65	3	1	.1	14	24	.8	T	.09	.03
Oatmeal or rolled oats	1 cup	240	130	5	2	.4	23	22	1.4	0	.19	.05
Bran flakes (40% bran), added sugar, salt, iron, vitamins	1 cup	35	105	4	1	—	28	19	12.4	1,650	.41	.49
Corn flakes, added sugar, salt, iron, vitamins	1 cup	25	95	2	T	—	21	*	0.6	1,180	.29	.35
Rice, puffed, added iron, thiamin, niacin	1 cup	15	60	1	T	—	13	3	.3	0	.07	.01
Wheat, shredded, plain, 1 biscuit or 1/2 cup	1 serving	25	90	2	1	—	20	11	.9	0	.06	.03
Cake, angel food, 1/12 of cake	1	53	135	3	T	—	32	50	.2	0	.03	.08
Cupcake, 2-1/2 in. diam., with chocolate icing	1	36	130	2	5	2.0	21	47	.4	60	.05	.06
Boston cream pie with custard filling, 1/12 of cake	1	69	210	3	6	1.9	34	46	.7	140	.09	.11
Fruitcake, dark, 1/30 of loaf	1	15	55	1	2	.5	9	11	.4	20	.02	.02
Cake, pound, 1/17 of loaf	1	33	160	2	10	2.5	16	6	.5	80	.05	.06
Brownies, with nuts, from commercial recipe	1	20	85	1	4	.9	13	9	.4	20	.03	.02
Cookies, chocolate chip, from home recipe	4	40	205	2	12	3.5	24	14	.8	40	.06	.06
Crackers, graham	2	14	55	1	1	.3	10	6	.5	0	.02	.08

Food	Measure	Grams	Food Energy (calories)	Protein (grams)	Fat (grams)	Saturated fats (grams)	Carbohydrate (grams)	Calcium (milligrams)	Iron (milligrams)	Vitamin A (I.U.)	Thiamin (milligrams)	Riboflavin (milligrams)
Crackers, saltines	4	11	50	1	1	.3	8	2	.5	0	.05	.05
Danish pastry, round piece	1	65	275	5	15	4.7	30	33	1.2	200	.18	.19
Doughnut, cake type	1	25	100	1	5	1.2	13	10	.4	20	.05	.05
Macaroni and cheese, from home recipe	1 cup	200	430	17	22	8.9	40	362	1.8	860	.20	.40
Muffin, corn	1	40	125	3	4	1.2	19	42	.7	120	.10	.10
Noodles, enriched, cooked	1 cup	160	200	7	2	—	37	16	1.4	110	.22	.13
Pie, apple, 1/7 of pie	1	135	345	3	15	3.9	51	11	.9	40	.15	.11
Pie, cherry, 1/7 of pie	1	135	350	4	15	4.0	52	19	.9	590	.16	.12
Pie, lemon meringue, 1/7 of pie	1	120	305	4	12	3.7	45	17	1.0	200	.09	.12
Pie, pecan, 1/7 of pie	1	118	495	6	27	4.0	61	55	3.7	190	.26	.14
Pizza, cheese, 1/8 of 12 in. diam. pie	1	60	145	6	4	1.7	22	86	1.1	230	.16	.18
Popcorn, popped, plain	1 cup	6	25	1	T	T	5	1	.2	—	—	.01
Pretzels, stick	10	3	10	T	T	—	2	1	T	0	.01	.01
Rolls, enriched, brown & serve	1	26	85	2	2	.4	14	20	.5	T	.10	.06
Rolls, frankfurter & hamburger	1	40	120	3	2	.5	21	30	.8	T	.16	.10
Spaghetti with meat balls & tomato sauce	1 cup	248	330	19	12	3.3	39	124	3.7	1,590	.25	.30
Legumes, nuts, seeds												
Beans, Great Northern, cooked	1 cup	180	210	14	1	—	38	90	4.9	0	.25	.13
Peanuts, roasted in oil, salted	1 cup	144	840	37	72	13.7	27	107	3.0	—	.46	.19
Peanut butter	1 tbsp.	16	95	4	8	1.5	3	9	.3	—	.02	.02
Sunflower seeds	1 cup	145	810	35	69	8.2	29	174	10.3	70	2.84	.33
Sugars & sweets												
Candy, caramels	1 oz.	28	115	1	3	1.6	22	42	.4	T	.01	.05
Candy, milk chocolate	1 oz.	28	145	2	9	5.5	16	65	.3	80	.02	.10
Fudge, chocolate	1 oz.	28	115	1	3	1.3	21	22	.3	T	.01	.03
Candy, hard	1 oz.	28	110	0	T	0	28	6	.5	0	0	0
Honey	1 tbsp.	21	65	T	0	0	17	1	.1	0	T	.01
Jams & Preserves	1 tbsp.	20	55	T	T	T	14	4	.2	T	T	.01
Sugar, white, granulated	1 tbsp.	12	45	0	0	0	12	0	T	0	0	0
Vegetables												
Asparagus, canned, spears	4 spears	80	15	2	T	—	3	15	1.5	640	.05	.08
Beans, green, from frozen, cuts	1 cup	135	35	2	T	—	8	54	.9	780	.09	.12
Broccoli, cooked	1 stalk	180	45	6	1	—	8	158	1.4	4,500	.16	.36
Cabbage, raw, coarsely shredded or sliced	1 cup	70	15	1	T	—	4	34	.3	90	.04	.04
Carrots, raw, 7-1/2 by 1-1/8 in.	1	72	30	1	T	—	7	27	.5	7,930	.04	.04
Celery, raw	1 stalk	40	5	T	T	—	2	16	.1	110	.01	.01
Collards, cooked	1 cup	190	65	7	1	—	10	357	1.5	14,820	.21	.38
Corn, sweet, cooked	1 ear	140	70	2	1	—	16	2	.5	310	.09	.08
Lettuce, iceberg, chopped	1 cup	55	5	T	T	—	2	11	.3	180	.03	.03
Mushrooms, raw	1 cup	70	20	2	T	—	3	4	.6	T	.07	.32
Onions, raw, chopped	1 cup	170	65	3	T	—	15	46	.9	T	.05	.07
Peas, frozen, cooked	1 cup	160	110	8	T	—	19	30	3.0	960	.43	.14
Potatoes, baked, peeled	1	156	145	4	T	—	33	14	1.1	T	.15	.07
Potatoes, frozen, French fried	10	50	110	2	4	1.1	17	5	.9	T	.07	.01
Potatoes, mashed, milk added	1 cup	210	135	4	2	.7	27	50	.8	40	.17	.11
Potato chips	10	20	115	1	8	2.1	10	8	.4	T	.04	.01
Potato salad	1 cup	250	250	7	7	2.0	41	80	1.5	350	.20	.18
Spinach, chopped, from frozen	1 cup	205	45	6	1	—	8	232	4.3	16,200	.14	.31
Sweet potatoes, baked in skin, peeled	1	114	160	2	1	—	37	46	1.0	9,230	.10	.08
Tomatoes, raw	1	135	25	1	T	—	6	16	.6	1,110	.07	.05
Miscellaneous												
Beer	12 fl. oz.	360	150	1	0	0	14	18	T	—	.01	.11
Gin, rum, vodka, whisky, 86 proof	1-1/2 fl. oz.	42	105	—	0	0	T	—	—	—	—	—
Wine, table	3-1/2 fl. oz.	102	85	T	0	0	4	9	.4	—	T	.01
Cola-type beverage	12 fl. oz.	369	145	0	0	0	37	—	—	0	0	0
Ginger ale	12 fl. oz	366	115	0	0	0	29	—	—	0	0	0
Gelatin dessert	1 cup	240	140	4	0	0	34	—	—	—	—	—
Olives, pickled, green	4 medium	16	15	T	2	.2	T	8	.2	40	—	—
Pickles, dill, whole	1	65	5	T	T	—	1	17	.7	70	T	.01
Popsicle, 3 fl. oz.	1	95	70	0	0	0	18	0	T	0	0	0
Soup, tomato, prepared with water	1 cup	245	90	2	3	.5	16	15	.7	1,000	.05	.05

T — Indicates trace   * — Varies by brand

Calories Used Per Minute According to Body Weight

Activity	Weight in Pounds					
	100	120	150	170	200	220
Volleyball (moderate)	2.3	2.7	3.4	3.9	4.6	5.0
Walking (3 mph)	2.7	3.2	4.0	4.6	5.4	5.9
Table tennis	2.7	3.2	4.0	4.6	5.4	5.9
Bicycling (5.5 mph)	3.1	3.8	4.7	5.3	6.3	6.9
Calisthenics	3.3	3.9	4.9	5.6	6.6	7.2
Skating (moderate)	3.6	4.3	5.4	6.1	7.2	7.9
Golf	3.6	4.3	5.4	6.1	7.2	7.9
Walking (4 mph)	3.9	4.6	5.8	6.6	7.8	8.5
Tennis	4.5	5.4	6.8	7.7	9.1	10.0
Canoeing (4 mph)	4.6	5.6	7.0	7.9	9.3	10.2
Swimming (breaststroke)	4.8	5.7	7.2	8.1	9.6	10.5
Bicycling (10 mph)	5.4	6.5	8.1	9.2	10.8	11.9
Swimming (crawl)	5.8	6.9	8.7	9.8	11.6	12.7
Jogging (11-min. mile)	6.1	7.3	9.1	10.4	12.2	13.4
Handball	6.3	7.6	9.5	10.7	12.7	13.9
Racquetball	6.3	7.6	9.5	10.7	12.7	13.9
Skiing (downhill)	6.3	7.6	9.5	10.7	12.7	13.9
Mountain climbing	6.6	8.0	10.0	11.3	13.3	14.6
Squash	6.8	8.1	10.2	11.5	13.6	14.9
Skiing (cross-country)	7.2	8.7	10.8	12.3	14.5	15.9
Running (8-min. mile)	9.4	11.3	14.1	16.0	18.8	20.7

Note: Many other factors, including air temperature, clothing, and the vigor with which a person exercises, can mean an increase or decrease in the number of calories used.

Food and Nutrition

Food contains proteins, carbohydrates, fats, water, vitamins and minerals. Nutrition is the way your body takes in and uses these ingredients to maintain proper functioning.

Federal health officials recommended, Feb. 1990, that all Americans, not just those with high cholesterol levels, reduce the fat content of their diets by an average of 10%, to lower their risk of heart disease. In March 1989, the Natl. Research Council reported on the role of diet in cardiovascular diseases, cancer, chronic liver and kidney diseases, diabetes, osteoporosis, obesity, and dental cavities. Major recommendations included: reducing fat intake to 30% or less of total calories, reducing saturated fat to less than 10% of calories, and reducing cholesterol to less than 300 milligrams daily; eating 5 or more half-cup servings per day of vegetables and fruits, especially green and yellow vegetables and citrus fruits; eating 6 or more servings daily of bread, cereals, and legumes, for a total of more than 55% of calories; eating no more than twice the recommended daily allowance of protein, and no more than 1.6 grams per day per kilogram of body weight; eating less than 6 grams a day of salt, limiting its use in cooking, avoiding it at the table, and consuming salty foods sparingly; and maintaining an adequate intake of calcium.

Protein

Proteins, composed of amino acids, are indispensable in the diet. They build, maintain, and repair the body. Best sources: eggs, milk, fish, meat, poultry, soybeans, nuts. High quality proteins such as eggs, meat, or fish supply all 8 amino acids needed in the diet.

Fats

Fats provide energy by furnishing calories to the body, and by carrying vitamins A, D, E, and K. They are the most concentrated source of energy in the diet. Best sources: butter, margarine, salad oils, nuts, cream, egg yolks, most cheeses, lard, meat.

Carbohydrates

Carbohydrates provide energy for body function and activity by supplying immediate calories. The carbohydrate group includes sugars, starches, fiber, and starchy vegetables. Best sources: grains, legumes, nuts, potatoes, fruits.

Water

Water dissolves and transports other nutrients throughout the body, aiding the processes of digestion, absorption, circulation, and excretion. It helps regulate body temperature.

Vitamins

Vitamin A—promotes good eyesight and helps keep the skin and mucous membranes resistant to infection. Best sources: liver, carrots, sweet potatoes, kale, collard greens, turnips, fortified milk.

Vitamin B1 (thiamine)—prevents beriberi. Essential to carbohydrate metabolism and health of nervous system.

Vitamin B2 (riboflavin)—protects skin, mouth, eye, eyelids, and mucous membranes. Essential to protein and energy metabolism. Best sources: liver, milk, meat, poultry, broccoli, mushrooms.

Vitamin B6 (pyridoxine)—important in the regulation of the central nervous system and in protein metabolism. Best sources: whole grains, meats, nuts, brewers' yeast.

Vitamin B12 (cobalamin)—needed to form red blood cells. Best sources: liver, meat, fish, eggs, soybeans.

Niacin—maintains the health of skin, tongue, and digestive system. Best sources: poultry, peanuts, fish, organ meats, enriched flour and bread.

Other B vitamins—biotin, choline, folic acid (folacin), inositol, PABA (para-aminobenzoic acid), pantothenic acid.

Vitamin C (ascorbic acid)—maintains collagen, a protein necessary for the formation of skin, ligaments, and bones. It helps heal wounds and mend fractures, and aids in resisting some types of virus and bacterial infections. Best sources: citrus fruits and juices, turnips, broccoli, Brussels sprouts, potatoes and sweet potatoes, tomatoes, cabbage.

Vitamin D—important for bone development. Best sources: sunlight, fortified milk and milk products, fish-liver oils, egg yolks, organ meats.

Vitamin E (tocopherol)—helps protect red blood cells. Best sources: vegetable oils, wheat germ, whole grains, eggs, peanuts, organ meats, margarine, green leafy vegetables.

Vitamin K—necessary for formation of prothrombin, which helps blood to clot. Also made by intestinal bacteria. Best dietary sources: green leafy vegetables, tomatoes.

Minerals

Calcium—the most abundant mineral in the body, works with phosphorus in building and maintaining bones and teeth. Best sources: milk and milk products, cheese, and blackstrap molasses.

Phosphorus—the 2d most abundant mineral, performs more functions than any other mineral, and plays a part in nearly every chemical reaction in the body. Best source: whole grains, cheese, milk.

Iron—Necessary for the formation of myoglobin, which transports oxygen to muscle tissue, and hemoglobin, which transports oxygen in the blood. Best sources: organ meats, beans, green leafy vegetables, and shellfish.

Other minerals—chromium, cobalt, copper, fluorine, iodine, magnesium, manganese, molybdenum, potassium, selenium, sodium, sulfur, and zinc.

Recommended Daily Dietary Allowances

Source: Food and Nutrition Board, Natl. Academy of Sciences—Natl. Research Council; 1989

Age (years) and sex group	Weight (lbs.)	Protein (grams)	Fat soluble vitamins					Water soluble vitamins						Minerals						
			Vitamin A[1]	Vitamin D[2]	Vitamin E[3]	Vitamin K	Vitamin C	Thiamin (mg.)	Riboflavin (mg.)	Niacin (mg.)[4]	Vitamin B6 (mg.)	Folate (micrograms)	Vitamin B12 (micrograms)	Calcium (mg.)	Phosphorus (mg.)	Magnesium (mg.)	Iron (mg.)	Zinc (mg.)	Iodine (micrograms)	Selenium (micrograms)
Infants . . . to 5 mos.	13	13	375	7.5	3	5	30	0.3	0.4	5	0.3	25	0.3	400	300	40	6	5	40	10
to 1 yr.	20	14	375	10	4	10	35	0.4	0.5	6	0.6	35	0.5	600	500	60	10	5	50	15
Children . . 1-3	29	16	400	10	6	15	40	0.7	0.8	9	1.0	50	0.7	800	800	80	10	10	70	20
4-6	44	24	500	10	7	20	45	0.9	1.1	12	1.1	75	1.0	800	800	120	10	10	90	20
7-10	62	28	700	10	7	30	45	1.0	1.2	13	1.4	100	1.4	800	800	170	10	10	120	30
Males . . . 11-14	99	45	1000	10	10	45	50	1.3	1.5	17	1.7	150	2.0	1200	1200	270	12	15	150	40
15-18	145	59	1000	10	10	65	60	1.5	1.8	20	2.0	200	2.0	1200	1200	400	12	15	150	50
19-24	160	58	1000	10	10	70	60	1.5	1.7	19	2.0	200	2.0	1200	1200	350	10	15	150	70
25-50	174	63	1000	5	10	80	60	1.5	1.7	19	2.0	200	2.0	800	800	350	10	15	150	70
51+	170	63	1000	5	10	80	60	1.2	1.4	15	2.0	200	2.0	800	800	350	10	15	150	70
Females . 11-14	101	46	800	10	8	45	50	1.1	1.3	15	1.4	150	2.0	1200	1200	280	15	12	150	45
15-18	120	44	800	10	8	55	60	1.1	1.3	15	1.5	180	2.0	1200	1200	300	15	12	150	50
19-24	128	46	800	10	8	60	60	1.1	1.3	15	1.6	180	2.0	1200	1200	280	15	12	150	55
25-50	138	50	800	5	8	65	60	1.1	1.3	15	1.6	180	2.0	800	800	280	15	12	150	55
51+	143	50	800	5	8	65	60	1.0	1.2	13	1.6	180	2.0	800	800	280	10	12	150	55

(1) Retinol equivalents. (2) Micrograms of cholecalciferol. (3) Milligrams alpha-tocopherol equivalents. (4) Niacin equivalents.

EDUCATION

Educational Attainment by Age, Race, and Sex

Source: U.S. Bureau of the Census unpublished data as of March, 1988 (Number of persons in thousands)

Race, age, and sex	Years of school completed					Percent			
	All persons	Less than high school, 4 years	High school, 4 years	College, 1 to 3 years	College, 4 years or more	Less than high school, 4 years	High school, 4 years	College, 1 to 3 years	College, 4 years or more
March 1988									
All races									
18 to 24 years	26,060	5,627	11,254	7,148	2,029	21.6	43.2	27.4	7.8
25 years and over	151,616	36,114	58,940	25,783	30,779	38.9	38.9	17.0	20.3
25 to 34 years	42,970	5,836	17,889	9,069	10,174	13.6	41.6	21.1	23.7
35 to 44 years	34,682	4,841	13,200	7,309	9,332	14.0	38.1	21.1	26.9
45 to 54 years	23,795	5,230	9,860	3,698	5,008	22.0	41.4	15.5	21.0
55 to 64 years	21,642	7,024	8,580	2,793	3,246	32.5	39.6	12.9	15.0
65 years and over	28,527	13,183	9,412	2,915	3,018	46.2	33.0	10.2	10.6
Male, 25 years and over . .	71,941	16,944	25,674	12,052	17,269	23.6	35.7	16.8	24.0
Female, 25 years and over . .	79,676	19,171	33,266	13,730	13,510	24.1	41.8	17.2	17.0
White									
18 to 24 years	21,552	4,400	9,295	6,041	1,819	20.4	43.1	28.0	8.4
25 years and over	131,092	29,282	51,795	22,599	27,416	22.3	39.5	17.2	20.9
25 to 34 years	36,148	4,613	15,052	7,621	8,861	12.8	41.6	21.1	24.5
35 to 44 years	29,783	3,804	11,339	6,351	8,290	12.8	38.1	21.3	27.8
45 to 54 years	20,448	4,099	8,645	3,281	4,424	20.0	42.3	16.0	21.6
55 to 64 years	19,074	5,672	7,854	2,562	2,985	29.7	41.2	13.4	15.6
65 years and over	25,639	11,095	8,905	2,784	2,857	43.3	34.7	10.9	11.1
Male, 25 years and over . .	62,679	13,959	22,541	10,572	15,608	22.3	36.0	16.9	24.9
Female, 25 years and over . .	68,414	15,323	29,255	12,027	11,808	22.4	42.8	17.6	17.3
Black									
18 to 24 years	3,619	1,065	1,627	791	134	29.4	45.0	21.9	3.7
25 years and over	15,929	5,838	5,914	2,382	1,796	36.7	37.1	15.0	11.3
25 to 34 years	5,272	1,029	2,446	1,104	693	19.5	46.4	20.9	13.1
35 to 44 years	3,700	841	1,563	724	571	22.7	42.2	19.6	15.4
45 to 54 years	2,501	969	969	290	274	38.7	38.7	11.6	11.0
55 to 64 years	2,074	1,175	580	172	146	56.7	28.0	8.3	7.0
65 years and over	2,383	1,824	357	91	111	76.5	15.0	3.8	4.7
Male, 25 years and over . . .	7,067	2,571	2,612	1,091	792	36.4	37.0	15.4	11.2
Female, 25 years and over . .	8,863	3,267	3,302	1,291	1,003	36.9	37.3	14.6	11.3
Hispanic Origin[1]									
18 to 24 years	2,665	1,106	1,040	438	80	41.5	39.0	16.4	3.0
25 years and over	9,940	4,874	2,815	1,257	995	49.0	28.3	12.6	10.0
25 to 34 years	3,785	1,449	1,239	647	450	38.3	32.7	17.1	11.9
35 to 44 years	2,624	1,157	823	363	282	44.1	31.4	13.8	10.7
45 to 54 years	1,488	820	386	126	155	55.1	25.9	8.5	10.4
55 to 64 years	1,142	749	240	82	71	65.6	21.0	7.2	6.2
65 years and over	903	701	126	39	37	77.6	14.0	4.3	4.1
Male, 25 years and over . .	4,889	2,346	1,332	625	585	48.0	27.2	12.8	12.0
Female, 25 years and over . .	5,051	2,528	1,482	632	410	50.0	29.3	12.5	8.1

(1) Persons of Hispanic origin may be of any race.

Historical Summary of Public Elementary and Secondary Schools

Source: National Center for Education Statistics, U.S. Dept. of Education

	1899-1900	1909-10	1919-20	1929-30	1939-40	1949-50	1959-60	1969-70	1979-80	1987-88
Pupils and teachers (thousands) .										
Total U.S. population	75,995	90,492	104,512	121,770	130,880	148,665	179,323	203,212	224,567	243,419
Population 5-17 years of age	21,573	24,009	27,556	31,417	30,150	30,168	43,881	52,490	48,040	45,291
Percent aged 5-17 years.	28.4	26.5	26.4	25.8	23.0	20.3	24.5	25.8	21.4	18.6
Enrollment (thousands)										
Elementary and secondary	15,503	17,814	21,578	25,678	25,434	25,111	36,087	45,619	41,645	40,008
Percent pop. 5-17 enrolled	71.9	74.2	78.3	81.7	84.4	83.2	82.2	86.9	86.7	88.3
Percent in high schools	3.3	5.1	10.2	17.1	26.0	22.7	23.5	28.5	32.9	30.2
High school graduates.	62	111	231	592	1,143	1,063	1,627	2,589	2,748	2,497
Average school term (in days). . . .	144.3	157.5	161.9	172.7	175.0	177.9	178.0	178.9	178.5	. . .
Total instructional staff	. . .	. . .	678	880	912	962	1,464	2,253	2,441	. . .
Teachers, librarians: Men	127	110	93	140	195	195	402	691	782[4]	. . .
Women	296	413	565	703	681	719	985	1,440	1,518[4]	. . .
Percent men	29.9	21.1	14.1	16.6	22.2	21.3	29.0	33.4	34.0[4]	. . .
Revenue & expenditures (millions)										
Total revenue	$219	$433	$970	$2,088	$2,260	$5,437	$14,746	$40,267	$96,881	$169,651
Total expenditures	214	426	1,036	2,316	2,344	5,837	15,613	40,683	95,962	172,000[4]
Current elem. and secondary . . .	179	356	861	1,843	1,941	4,687	12,329	34,218	86,984[4]	157,222
Capital outlay	35	69	153	370	257	1,014	2,661	4,659	6,506	. . .
Interest on school debt	. . .	. . .	18	92	130	100	489	1,171	1,874	. . .
Other	. . .	. . .	3	9	13	35	132	636	598	. . .
Salaries and pupil cost	(Data in unadjusted dollars)									
Average annual teacher salary[2]. . .	$325	$485	$871	$1,420	$1,441	$3,010	$5,174	$8,840	$16,715	$29,177
Expenditure per capita total pop. . .	2.83	4.71	9.91	19.03	17.91	39	87	200	424	707[4]
Current expenditure per pupil ADA[3].	16.67	27.85	53.32	86.70	88.09	209	375	816	2,272	4,243

(1) Because of a modification of the scope, "current expenditures for elementary and secondary schools" data for 1959-60 and later years are not entirely comparable with data for prior years. (2) Includes supervisors, principals, teachers and other non-supervisory instructional staff. (3) "ADA" means average daily attendance in elementary and secondary day schools. (4) Estimated.

Fall Enrollment and Teachers in Full-time Day Schools
Elementary and Secondary Day Schools, Fall 1988
Source: National Center for Education Statistics, U.S. Dept. of Education; National Education Assn.

	Local school districts Total	Total enrollment	Pupils per teacher	Classroom teachers	Teacher's average pay (1988-1989)	Instructional aides	Expenditure per pupil
United States	15,376	40,192,386	17.4	2,316,428	$31,304	355,660	$4,243
Alabama	129	724,751	18.7	38,845	25,500	4,106	2,718
Alaska	55	106,481	17.0	6,272	43,153	1,537	7,971
Arizona	238	574,890	18.2	31,617	29,600	4,584	3,744
Arkansas	329	436,387	15.7	27,730	22,009	3,456	2,989
California	1,077	4,618,120	22.7	203,342	38,996	51,468	3,840
Colorado	176	560,081	17.8	31,398	30,700	4,040	4,462
Connecticut.	166	463,488	13.1	35,502	40,496	—	6,230
Delaware	19	96,678	16.4	5,898	33,480	719	5,017
District of Columbia . . .	1	84,792	13.3	6,394	36,450	639	6,132
Florida	67	1,720,930	17.1	100,370	28,525	19,113	4,092
Georgia	186	1,107,994	18.5	59,916	27,892	14,094	3,434
Hawaii.	1	167,488	21.1	7,950	32,047	1,800	3,919
Idaho	115	214,615	20.6	10,425	23,494	994	2,667
Illinois	972	1,794,916	17.1	105,097	33,014	12,340	4,369
Indiana	303	960,994	17.8	54,029	30,493	10,327	3,794
Iowa.	433	478,200	15.8	30,226	26,747	3,243	4,124
Kansas	304	426,596	15.2	28,122	28,671	2,708	4,076
Kentucky	177	637,627	17.8	35,788	26,275	5,609	3,011
Louisiana	66	786,683	18.2	43,203	22,993	7,101	3,138
Maine	210	212,902	14.6	14,593	26,881	2,895	4,258
Maryland	24	688,947	16.8	40,899	36,092	5,480	5,201
Massachusetts.	359	823,428	13.7	60,068	34,225	9,511	5,471
Michigan	561	1,582,785	19.8	79,847	36,010	10,783	4,692
Minnesota	436	726,950	17.0	42,750	32,190	7,556	4,386
Mississippi	152	503,326	18.4	27,283	24,363	7,946	2,548
Missouri.	544	806,639	15.9	50,693	27,229	3,930	3,786
Montana	549	152,191	15.8	9,626	25,081	1,033	4,246
Nebraska	862	269,434	15.0	18,003	24,751	2,454	3,943
Nevada	17	176,474	20.3	8,699	30,587	—	3,623
New Hampshire	170	169,413	16.2	10,442	28,939	1,981	4,457
New Jersey	602	1,080,871	13.6	79,698	36,030	8,789	6,564
New Mexico	88	292,425	18.5	15,770	25,120	3,067	3,691
New York.	721	2,573,715	14.9	172,807	38,800	24,430	7,151
North Carolina	140	1,083,156	17.5	61,933	27,814	18,016	3,368
North Dakota.	296	118,809	15.4	7,731	23,016	965	3,519
Ohio.	613	1,778,544	17.6	101,105	31,170	8,031	3,998
Oklahoma	609	580,426	16.5	35,116	23,070	3,680	3,093
Oregon	304	461,752	18.4	25,147	30,563	4,048	4,789
Pennsylvania	501	1,659,714	15.9	104,379	32,809	10,624	4,989
Rhode Island	37	134,347	14.6	9,192	36,057	1,009	5,329
South Carolina	91	615,774	17.2	35,877	27,076	4,731	3,408
South Dakota	191	126,910	15.4	8,260	21,300	1,138	3,249
Tennessee	141	821,580	19.3	42,657	27,052	7,437	3,068
Texas	1,062	3,283,707	—	—	27,502	—	3,608
Utah.	40	431,119	24.5	17,590	23,652	2,778	2,454
Vermont	276	93,464	13.6	6,852	28,798	1,128	5,207
Virginia	136	982,393	16.1	60,883	30,926	8,942	4,149
Washington	296	790,918	20.4	38,780	30,475	5,502	4,164
West Virginia	55	335,912	15.1	22,177	22,842	2,838	3,858
Wisconsin.	430	774,857	16.0	48,541	32,320	6,232	4,747
Wyoming	49	97,793	14.6	6,693	28,184	1,247	5,051

Programs for the Handicapped
Source: Office of Special Educ. and Rehabilitative Services, U.S. Dept. of Education

Number of children 3 to 21 years old served annually in educational programs for the handicapped and percent of total public school enrollment.

Type of Handicapped	1981-82	1982-83	1983-84	1984-85	1985-86	1986-87	1987-88	1988-89
	Number Served, in Thousands							
All conditions.	4,198	4,255	4,298	4,315	4,317	4,374	4,446	4,544
Learning disabled	1,622	1,741	1,806	1,832	1,862	1,914	1,928	1,987
Speech impaired.	1,135	1,131	1,128	1,126	1,125	1,136	953	967
Mentally retarded	786	757	727	694	660	643	582	564
Seriously emotionally disturbed . .	339	352	361	372	375	383	373	376
Hard of hearing and deaf	75	73	72	69	66	65	56	56
Orthopedically handicapped	58	57	56	56	57	57	47	47
Visually handicapped	29	28	29	28	27	26	22	23
Deaf-blind.	2	2	2	2	2	2	1	2
	As Percent of Total Enrollment							
All conditions.	10.47	10.73	10.92	10.98	10.93	10.97	11.10	11.30
Learning disabled	4.05	4.39	4.59	4.66	4.71	4.80	4.82	4.94
Speech impaired.	2.83	2.85	2.87	2.87	2.85	2.85	2.38	2.41
Mentally retarded	1.96	1.91	1.85	1.77	1.67	1.61	1.45	1.40
Seriously emotionally disturbed . .	.85	.89	.92	.95	.95	.96	0.94	0.94
Hard of hearing and deaf	.19	.18	.18	.17	.17	.16	.14	0.14
Orthopedically handicapped	.14	.14	.14	.14	.14	.14	.12	0.12
Visually handicapped	.07	.07	.07	.07	.07	.07	.06	0.06
Deaf-blind.	.01	.01	.01	.01	.01	.01	.01	(1)

Note: Counts are based on reports from the 50 States, District of Columbia and Puerto Rico (i.e., figures from U.S. territories are not included). Percentages of total enrollment are based on the total annual enrollment of U.S. public schools, preprimary through 12th grade. Details may not add to totals because of rounding. (1) Less than .005.

Federal Funds for Education, 1980-1990

Source: U.S. Office of Management and Budget

Federal funds obligated for programs administered by the Department of Education: Fiscal years 1980 to 1990
(In thousands of dollars)

	1980	1982	1984	1988	1989	1990[1]
Total.................	$14,102,165	$15,069,598	$17,072,698	$20,697,311	$24,473,634	$25,700,889
Elementary and secondary						
education..............	4,239,022	3,802,234	4,294,269	5,682,997	5,997,160	7,171,545
Grants for the disadvantaged....	3,204,664	3,063,651	3,501,383	4,357,970	4,600,444	5,372,571
Special programs..........	788,918	524,730	549,117	1,067,213	1,129,444	1,536,651
Bilingual education..........	169,540	136,292	173,051	191,470	196,309	188,674
Indian education..........	75,900	77,561	70,718	66,344	70,963	73,649
School assistance in federally						
affected areas............	812,873	457,227	608,791	731,241	731,768	773,632
Maintenance and operations	690,000	438,498	555,300	685,498	708,396	717,354
Construction..............	110,873	15,951	28,491	35,640	18,400	37,748
Disaster assistance..........	12,000	2,778	25,000	10,103	4,972	18,530
Other.................	—	—	—	—	—	—
Education for the handicapped ...	1,555,253	2,023,536	2,416,799	3,075,456	3,814,846	4,204,099
State grant programs	815,805	933,657	1,082,180	1,115,333	1,642,647	1,809,207
Early childhood education[2]......	38,745	40,673	53,164	210,752	319,012	430,164
Special centers, projects, and						
research	55,075	35,057	54,871	78,600	102,141	96,889
Captioned films and media						
services	17,778	11,438	14,000	13,026	13,346	15,192
Personnel training	55,375	48,911	55,540	66,153	67,023	71,000
Handicapped rehabilitation						
Service and research	572,475	953,800	1,157,044	1,591,592	1,670,677	1,781,647
Vocational education and adult						
programs	1,153,743	751,118	954,320	1,000,055	1,052,470	1,202,736
Basic programs[3]	744,653	530,669	689,324	823,299	859,239	925,024
Consumer and homemaking	63,169	29,363	36,792	32,752	32,816	34,517
Program improvement and						
supportive services	162,512	91,650	117,249	—	—	—
State planning and advisory						
councils	13,423	8,800	11,200	7,681	7,945	8,268
Adult education, grants to States ..	153,724	90,636	99,755	129,183	139,771	217,392
Other.................	16,262	—	—	7,140	12,699	17,535
Postsecondary student financial						
assistance	5,108,534	6,584,012	7,478,401	8,807,929	11,482,608	10,801,185
Educational opportunity grants[4]...	2,534378	2,546,167	3,565,209	4,620,133	5,379,725	5,318,006
Work-study	596,065	523,910	561,322	604,445	620,644	606,362
Direct student loans	322,749	193,686	191,962	216,963	202,904	182,471
Guaranteed student loans......	1,597,877	3,297,776	3,130,939	3,297,305	5,203,843	4,615,022
Other student assistance						
programs	57,465	22,473	28,969	69,083	75,492	79,324
Direct aid to postsecondary						
institutions	277,068	284,467	311,221	341,063	398,318	457,769
Aid to minority and developing						
institutions.............	114,680	119,829	132,081	135,222	179,062	215,947
Special programs for the						
disadvantaged	147,389	150,238	164,740	205,841	219,256	241,822
Cooperative education........	14,999	14,400	14,400	—	—	—
Higher education facilities	268,493	449,191	216,893	162,528	77,362	94,223
Construction loans and						
insurance	35,362	38,690	54,105	89,820	37,109	45,083
Interest subsidy grants........	24,626	23,759	23,925	24,466	22,524	31,059
College housing loans	208,505	386,742	138,863	48,242	17,729	18,081
Other higher education						
programs	34,927	38,226	82,410	79,305	73,574	89,717
International education and						
foreign languages	19,977	23,923	30,800	—	—	—
Fund for Improvement of						
Postsecondary Education.....	12,000	11,503	11,710	65,813	67,236	86,755
Other.................	2,950	2,800	39,900	13,492	6,338	2,962
Public Library services........	101,218	80,074	107,895	135,731	141,884	145,367
Public Library services	66,451	60,000	65,000	78,922	80,944	82,505
Interlibrary cooperation	—	11,520	15,000	18,395	18,826	19,551
Public Library construction.......	—	—	21,015	23,577	27,289	27,621
Research Libraries	5,992	5,760	6,000	5,744	5,675	5,738
Other.................	28,775	2,794	880	9,093	9,150	9,952
Payments to special institutions ..	273,860	251,570	249,610	271,658	284,056	293,212
American Printing House for the						
Blind................	4,349	5,000	5,000	5,266	5,335	5,663
National Technical Institute for						
the Deaf..............	19,799	26,300	28,000	31,594	33,326	36,070
Gallaudet College	49,409	64,815	56,288	62,195	65,998	67,643
Howard University	200,303	155,455	160,322	172,603	179,397	183,836

(continued)

	1980	1982	1984	1988	1989	1990[1]
Departmental accounts	277,174	347,943	352,089	409,348	419,588	467,404
Educational research and improvement	51,415	61,550	57,165	68,147	78,263	95,241
Departmental management account	223,857	283,906	293,351	341,171	341,286	371,543
Other	1,875	2,290	1,401	—	—	—
Trust funds	27	197	172	30	39	620

(1) Estimated. (2) Includes preschool incentive grants. (3) Includes programs of national significance and special programs for the disadvantaged. (4) Includes Pell Grants, Supplemental Education Opportunity Grants and State Student Incentive Grants, and Income Contingent Loans. (—) Data are not available or not applicable.
NOTE: Because of rounding, details may not add to totals.

Public Libraries

Source: World Almanac questionnaire (1990)

City	No. bound Volumes	Circulation	Annual Acquisitions Expend.	City	No. bound Volumes	Circulation	Annual Acquisitions Expend.
Akron, Oh.[a] (18)	1,200,677	1,953,376	NA	Mesa, Ariz. (2)	517,012	2,301,346	$ 954,245
Albuquerque, N.M.[a] (11)	610,502	2,283,512	$1,168,447	Miami, Fla.[a] (28)	2,386,204	4,200,000	2,200,000
Anaheim, Cal.[a] (4)	383,000	1,361,538	611,212	Milwaukee, Wis.[a] (12)	2,051,114	3,382,982	1,360,814
Anchorage, Alas. (5)	395,700	1,099,780	662,790	Minneapolis, Minn. (14)	1,888,934	3,012,111	1,771,400
Arlington, Tex. (5)	321,487	1,238,631	307,336	Mobile, Ala.[a] (5)	363,511	949,993	460,513
Atlanta, Ga. (33)	1,678,750	2,303,681	3,011,362	Nashville, Tenn.[a] (16)	608,346	1,945,454	871,515
Baltimore, Md. (30)	2,289,857	1,532,279	2,418,089	New Orleans, La. (15)	1,039,264	1,159,303	750,063
Baton Rouge, La.[a] (10)	640,385	1,733,200	1,028,000	New York, N.Y. (research)	9,189,489	—	—
Birmingham, Ala.[a] (19)	1,092,285	2,072,444	916,174	Branches (58)	3,180,866	9,669,316	14,931,000
Boston, Mass.[a] (25)	4,916,277	1,454,414	NA	Brooklyn (58)	4,637,167	8,610,459	5,133,434
Buffalo, N.Y.[a] (53)	3,602,478	6,237,516	2,023,551	Queens (61)	5,500,000	11,320,000	5,500,000
Charlotte, N.C. (19)	1,200,000	2,700,000	1,400,000	Norfolk, Va. (11)	880,564	823,908	540,747
Cincinnati, Oh.[a] (39)	3,700,000	7,179,389	4,205,140	Oklahoma City, Okla. (11)	933,241	4,184,437	1,346,726
Cleveland, Oh. (29)	2,261,043	4,550,994	4,588,427	Oakland, Cal.[a] (16)	907,082	1,627,320	806,836
Colorado Springs, Col. (13)	743,898	1,649,441	7,945,110	Omaha, Neb.[a] (10)	588,013	1,860,728	892,109
Columbus, Oh. (20)	1,600,000	4,100,000	4,475,615	Philadelphia, Pa. (53)	3,458,700	4,800,000	6,200,000
Corpus Christi, Tex.[a](4)	293,452	750,138	284,750	Phoenix, Az. (10)	1,683,458	4,529,337	2,500,000
Dallas, Tex. (19)	2,409,864	4,364,027	17,201,527	Pittsburgh, Pa. (18)	1,880,241	2,841,120	13,764,737
Dayton, Oh. (19)	1,500,000	5,239,231	11,000,000	Portland, Ore. (15)	4,000,000	2,000,000	1,400,000
Denver, Col. (21)	2,239,106	3,396,268	1,856,485	Richmond, Va. (10)	780,000	858,213	450,000
Des Moines, Ia. (5)	487,444	1,246,350	292,163	Rochester, N.Y. (11)	500,000	1,587,691	7,200,000
Detroit, Mich. (25)	2,746,021	1,743,314	1,900,000	Sacramento, Cal. (24)	1,663,893	3,977,515	2,045,262
District of Columbia[a] (25)	1,507,556	1,843,098	1,530,000	St. Louis, Mo. (18)	1,903,218	7,915,559	2,700,000
El Paso, Tex. (10)	600,000	1,300,000	3,500,000	St. Paul, Minn. (12)	740,171	2,414,263	949,246
Fairfax, Va. (22)	1,761,264	8,454,714	3,387,721	San Diego, Cal.[a] (31)	1,561,232	4,568,116	1,862,547
Ft. Worth, Tex. (10)	1,126,931	3,356,148	1,157,965	San Francisco, Cal.[a] (26)	1,749,129	2,470,091	NA
Fresno, Cal. (33)	1,007,199	1,930,588	449,265	Shreveport, La.[a] (19)	376,069	956,907	394,686
Honolulu, Ha. (49)	2,310,843	6,454,824	2,886,133	Syracuse, N.Y.[a] (8)	509,386	1,189,319	NA
Indianapolis, Ind. (21)	1,500,000	5,376,388	2,170,167	Tampa, Fla. (17)	1,100,600	3,200,000	1,800,000
Jersey City, N.J.[a] (11)	744,383	395,266	447,465	Toledo, Oh.[a] (18)	1,500,000	4,400,000	NA
Kansas City, Mo.[a] (14)	1,346,364	875,040	NA	Tucson, Ariz.[a] (15)	760,000	3,900,000	NA
Los Angeles, Cal.[a] (62)	5,663,240	10,382,321	4,469,364	Tulsa, Okla. (20)	825,000	3,236,081	1,419,000
Louisville, Ky.[a] (14)	903,084	3,084,620	979,836	Wichita, Kan.[a] (12)	894,942	1,396,667	400,000
Memphis, Tenn. (23)	1,700,000	2,700,000	3,228,007	Yonkers, N.Y. (3)	233,532	865,901	481,286

(a) Has not provided up-to-date information. Figure in parentheses denotes number of branches. (NA) Not available.

Preprimary School Enrollment of Children 3 to 5 Years Old: 1970 to 1989

Source: U.S. Bureau of the Census

Civilian noninstitutional population. Includes public and non-public nursery school and kindergarten programs. Excludes 5 year olds enrolled in elementary school.

	Number of children (1,000)						Enrollment rate				
	1970	1980	1985	1987	1988	1989	1970	1985	1987	1988	1989
Population, 3–5 years old .	10,877	9,284	10,733	10,872	10,994	11,038					
Total Enrolled[1]	4,075	4,878	5,865	5,932	5,977	6,026	37.5	54.6	54.6	54.4	54.6
Nursery	1,093	1,982	2,477	2,555	2,621	2,825	10.0	23.1	23.5	23.8	25.6
Kindergarten	2,982	2,896	3,388	3,377	3,356	3,201	27.4	31.6	31.1	30.5	29.0
White	3,414	3,994	4,757	4,748	4,891	4,911	37.8	54.7	54.1	55.4	55.0
Black	585	725	919	893	814	872	34.9	55.8	54.2	48.2	54.2
Hispanic origin[3]	NA	370	496	587	544	520	NA	43.3	45.5	44.2	41.6
3 years old	454	857	1,035	1,022	1,028	1,005	13.0	28.8	28.6	27.6	27.1
4 years old	1,003	1,423	1,765	1,717	1,768	1,882	27.9	49.1	47.7	49.1	51.0
5 years old	2,617	2,598	3,065	3,192	3,183	3,139	69.2	86.5	86.1	86.6	86.4
Labor Force Status of Mother											
All races:[2] With mother in labor force[4]	1,345	2,480	3,306	3,422	3,478	3,488	38.8	58.1	58.2	57.4	57.0
3 and 4 years old . . .	526	1,252	1,656	1,568	1,619	1,708	23.5	43.6	41.6	41.1	41.8
5 years old	818	1,229	1,649	1,854	1,859	1,780	66.6	87.2	87.9	87.5	88.0
Employed	1,246	2,256	2,999	3,180	3,258	3,236	39.3	59.1	58.9	57.8	57.4
Full-time	770	1,445	1,969	2,085	2,140	2,152	38.6	57.4	57.9	57.6	55.3
Mother not in labor force .	2,694	2,266	2,372	2,250	2,197	2,201	37.0	50.4	50.1	50.6	51.7

(NA) Not available. (1) Includes children with mothers whose labor force status is unknown and children with no mother present in household, not shown separately. (2) Includes other races not shown separately. (3) Person of Hispanic origin may be of any race. (4) Includes children with mothers who are unemployed, not shown separately.

Average Starting Salary of Public School Teachers Compared with Salaries in Private Industry: 1975-1988

Source: Northwestern Univ. Placement Center. *The Northwestern Lindquist-Endicott Report*

Salaries represent what corporations plan to offer graduates graduating in the year shown with bachelor's degrees. Based on survey of approximately 200 companies.

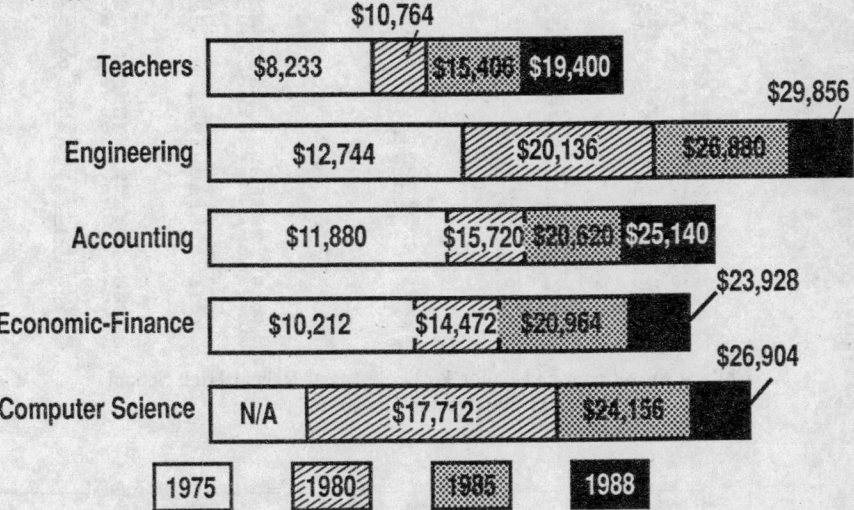

NA=not available. For teachers, estimate based on minimum mean salary according to National Education Assn.

Characteristics of Private Elementary and Secondary Schools: 1986

Source: National Center for Education Statistics. U.S. Dept. of Education.

Item	Total	Level of School				Religious Affiliation		
		Elementary	Secondary	Combined	Other	Catholic	Other	None
Number of schools	25,616	15,303	2,438	4,949	2,926	9,911	10,771	4,934
Percent Distribution								
Minority enrollment:								
Less than 5 percent	38.9	45.1	27.8	37.1	18.7	45.8	40.5	21.6
5 to 14 percent	22.4	19.8	36.1	23.4	22.9	20.4	20.9	29.4
15 to 24 percent	10.6	7.7	14.4	11.6	21.1	8.9	12.7	9.8
25 to 49 percent	10.0	7.8	11.8	5.1	28.6	7.2	8.4	19.3
50 to 89 percent	9.9	9.2	4.4	18.2	4.6	6.3	12.1	12.7
90 percent or more	8.1	10.4	5.4	4.6	4.1	11.5	5.4	7.1
Annual tuition:								
Less than $500	13.0	18.8	4.8	5.4	1.1	25.6	6.3	1.1
$500 to $1,000	27.9	35.1	4.4	29.6	5.0	37.1	30.8	1.0
$1,001 to $1,500	26.4	29.1	34.4	22.7	9.3	25.7	30.7	17.6
$1,501 to $2,500	14.6	8.3	28.7	18.0	31.8	7.7	20.4	16.0
More than $2,500	18.2	8.8	27.8	24.4	52.9	3.9	11.9	64.3
Mean enrollment	234	218	541	211	94	363	142	174

Tuition and College Costs 1990-91

Based on the Peterson's Guides Annual Survey of Undergraduate Institutions, the average cost of tuition, mandatory fees, and college room and board at four-year private colleges is $11,269. The average cost at four-year public colleges is $4,711 for state residents and $7,582 for nonresidents. Two-year public colleges are the least expensive group of institutions; tuition and fees average $924 for state residents and $3,036 for nonresidents. Tuition and fees at two-year private colleges average $4,877.

The most expensive four-year institutions, including tuition, mandatory fees, and college room and board, are Bennington College ($21,550); Sarah Lawrence College ($21,490); Barnard College ($21,344); Brandeis University ($21,289); Boston University ($21,105); Columbia University, School of Engineering and Applied Science ($21,062); Tufts University ($20,987); Bard College ($20,870); Brown University ($20,851); and Yale University ($20,820). Bennington College has the highest tuition of all four-year undergraduate institutions ($17,790). The least expensive are the U.S. service academies, which are all free.

Public High School Graduation and Dropout Rates, 1988

Source: National Center for Education Statistics, U.S. Dept. of Education

	Graduation rate, rank		Dropout rate, rank			Graduation rate, rank		Dropout rate rank	
U.S.	72.6%		27.4%		Mo.	75.5%	(27)	24.5%	(25)
Ala.	74.1	(29)	25.9	(23)	Mont.	84.7	(6)	15.3	(46)
Alaska	69.8	(38)	31.2	(14)	Neb.	85.9	(5)	14.1	(47)
Ariz.	66.6	(44)	33.4	(8)	Nev.	73.0	(32)	27.0	(20)
Ark.	78.7	(15)	21.3	(37)	N.H.	77.2	(21)	22.8	(31)
Calif.	68.5	(41)	31.5	(11)	N.J.	80.4	(14)	19.6	(38)
Colo.	76.5	(24)	23.5	(28)	N.M.	73.4	(31)	26.6	(21)
Conn.	82.2	(9)	17.8	(43)	N.Y.	66.3	(45)	33.7	(7)
Del.	69.8	(37)	30.2	(15)	N.C.	68.0	(42)	32.0	(10)
D.C.	60.2	(51)	39.8	(1)	N.D.	88.3	(2)	11.7	(50)
Fla.	63.0	(49)	27.0	(3)	Ohio	76.4	(25)	23.6	(27)
Ga.	63.4	(48)	26.6	(4)	Okla.	74.0	(30)	26.0	(22)
Hawaii.	81.7	(10)	28.3	(42)	Ore.	71.7	(34)	28.3	(18)
Idaho	76.8	(23)	23.2	(29)	Penn.	81.1	(13)	18.9	(39)
Ill.	78.2	(16)	21.8	(36)	R.I.	70.5	(35)	29.5	(17)
Ind.	78.1	(17)	21.9	(35)	S.C.	65.2	(46)	34.8	(6)
Iowa	86.9	(3)	13.1	(49)	S.D.	86.7	(4)	13.3	(48)
Kan.	82.7	(8)	17.3	(44)	Tenn.	68.6	(40)	31.4	(12)
Ky.	69.1	(39)	30.9	(13)	Tex.	64.9	(47)	35.1	(5)
La.	61.6	(50)	38.4	(2)	Utah	81.3	(11)	18.7	(41)
Me.	77.7	(19)	22.3	(33)	Vt.	81.2	(12)	18.8	(40)
Md.	76.1	(26)	23.9	(26)	Va.	74.6	(28)	25.4	(24)
Mass.	69.9	(36)	30.1	(16)	Wash.	78.0	(18)	22.0	(34)
Mich.	72.9	(33)	27.1	(19)	W.V.	76.8	(22)	23.2	(30)
Minn.	89.5	(1)	10.5	(51)	Wis.	83.3	(7)	16.7	(45)
Miss.	67.5	(43)	22.5	(9)	Wyo.	77.5	(20)	22.5	(32)

College Enrollment and Labor Force Status of Recent High School Graduates and Dropouts

Source: Bureau of Labor Statistics

School enrollment status	Total			Men			Women		
	Civilian noninsti- tutional population (1,000)	Labor force partici- pation rate	Unemploy- ment rate	Civilian noninsti- tutional population (1,000)	Labor force partici- pation rate	Unemploy- ment rate	Civilian noninsti- tutional population (1,000)	Labor force partici- pation rate	Unemploy- ment rate
1978									
High school graduates.	3,178	64.5	13.8	1,500	67.9	11.2	1,679	61.5	16.3
Enrolled in college .	1,593	42.9	13.0	767	45.0	11.3	827	41.0	14.7
Not enrolled in col- lege	1,585	86.3	14.0	733	91.8	11.2	852	81.3	17.0
High school dropouts .	839	68.8	27.6	479	80.2	24.0	360	53.4	34.4
1988									
High school graduates.	2,673	62.7	13.5	1,334	65.1	13.4	1,339	60.3	13.7
Enrolled in college .	1,575	47.4	11.6	761	47.6	9.5	814	47.3	13.6
Not enrolled in col- lege	1,098	84.7	15.1	572	88.5	16.2	526	80.6	13.7
High school dropouts .	552	59.2	26.7	307	74.4	28.5	245	40.1	22.4

A record 59 percent of high school graduates in 1988 were enrolled in college by October 1988.

The percentage of high school graduates going on to college has risen nearly 10 percent over the past decade. The college enrollment rate of black high school graduates (45 percent) has remained below that of whites (61 percent) and hispanics (57 percent).

About 100,000 graduates not in college were enrolled in at least one vocational education course. These courses include secretarial, trade, or technical classes.

Institutions of Higher Education—Charges: 1970 to 1990

Source: National Center for Education Statistics, U.S. Dept. of Education.

Data are for the entire academic year ending in year shown. Figures for 1970 are average charges for full-time resident degree-credit students; figures for later years are average charges per full-time equivalent student. Room and board are based on full-time students.

Academic Control and year	Tuition and Required Fees			Board Rates			Dormitory Charges		
	All institu- tions	2-yr. colleges	4-yr. univer- sities	All institu- tions	2-yr. colleges	4-yr. univer- sities	All institu- tions	2-yr. colleges	4-yr. univer- sities
Public:									
1970	$323	$178	$427	$511	$465	$540	$369	$308	$395
1975	432	277	599	625	638	634	506	424	527
1980	583	355	840	867	894	898	715	572	749
1985	971	584	1,386	1,241	1,302	1,276	1,196	921	1,237
1989	1,285	730	1,846	1,533	1,488	1,576	1,457	965	1,483
1990 est. . . .	1,367	758	2,006	1,638	1,609	1,720	1,516	958	1,563
Private:									
1970	1,533	1,034	1,809	561	546	608	436	413	503
1975	2,117	1,367	2,614	700	660	771	586	564	691
1980	3,130	2,062	3,811	955	924	1,078	827	769	999
1985	5,314	3,485	6,843	1,462	1,294	1,647	1,426	1,424	1,753
1989	7,461	4,817	9,451	1,880	1,609	2,269	1,849	1,540	2,353
1990 est. . . .	8,174	5,324	10,400	1,951	1,800	2,345	1,931	1,648	2,420

Scholastic Aptitude Test (SAT) Mean Scores and Characteristics of College Bound Seniors: 1970 to 1989

Source: College Entrance Examination Board

(For school year ending in year shown)

Type of Test and Characteristic Test Scores[1]	Unit	1970	1975	1980	1981	1982	1984	1985	1986	1987	1988	1989
Verbal, total[1]	Point	460	434	424	424	426	426	431	431	430	428	427
Male	Point	459	437	428	430	431	433	437	437	435	435	434
Female	Point	461	431	420	418	421	420	425	426	425	422	421
Math, total[2]	Point	488	472	466	466	467	471	475	475	476	476	476
Male	Point	509	495	491	492	493	495	499	501	500	498	500
Female	Point	465	449	443	443	443	449	452	451	453	455	454
Participants												
Total	NA	NA	996	992	994	989	965	977	1,001	1,080	1,134	1,088
Male	Percent	NA	49.9	48.2	48.0	48.1	48.2	48.3	48.1	48.0	48.0	48.0
White	Percent	NA	86.0	82.1	81.9	81.7	80.3	80.0	NA	78.0	77.0	75.0
Black	Percent	NA	7.9	9.1	9.0	8.9	9.1	8.9	NA	9.0	9.0	10.0
Obtaining scores[1] of—600 or above:												
Verbal	Percent	NA	7.9	7.2	7.0	7.1	7.0	7.0	8.0	8.0	7.0	7.8
Math	Percent	NA	15.6	15.1	14.4	15.3	17.0	17.0	17.0	18.0	17.0	18.0
Below 400:												
Verbal	Percent	NA	37.8	41.8	41.6	40.2	40.0	40.0	38.0	40.0	42.0	40.5
Math	Percent	NA	28.5	30.2	29.5	29.5	29.0	28.0	28.0	29.0	27.0	28.0

(NA) Not available. (1) Minimum score, 200; maximum score, 800. (2) 1967 and 1970 are estimates based on total number of persons taking SAT.

American College Testing (ACT) Program Mean Scores and Characteristics of College-Bound Students: 1970 to 1989

Source: The American College Testing Program

Data for academic year ending in year shown.

Type of Test and Mean Test Scores[1]	Unit	1970	1975	1980	1982	1984	1985	1986	1987	1988	1989
Composite	Point	19.9	18.6	18.5	18.4	18.5	18.6	18.8	18.7	18.8	18.6
Male	Point	20.3	19.5	19.3	19.2	19.3	19.4	19.6	19.5	19.6	19.3
Female	Point	19.4	17.8	17.9	17.8	17.9	17.9	18.1	18.1	18.1	18.0
English	Point	18.5	17.7	17.9	17.9	18.1	18.1	18.5	18.4	18.5	18.4
Male	Point	17.6	17.1	17.3	17.3	17.5	17.6	17.9	17.9	18.0	17.8
Female	Point	19.4	18.3	18.3	18.4	18.6	18.6	18.9	18.9	19.0	18.9
Math	Point	20.0	17.6	17.4	17.2	17.3	17.2	17.3	17.2	17.2	17.1
Male	Point	21.1	19.3	18.9	18.6	18.6	18.6	18.8	18.6	18.4	18.3
Female	Point	18.8	16.2	16.2	16.0	16.1	16.0	16.0	16.1	16.1	16.1
Social Studies	Point	19.7	17.4	17.2	17.3	17.3	17.4	17.6	17.5	17.4	17.2
Male	Point	20.3	18.7	18.2	18.1	18.1	18.3	18.6	18.4	18.4	18.1
Female	Point	19.0	16.4	16.4	16.6	16.5	16.6	16.9	16.7	16.6	16.4
Natural Science	Point	20.8	21.1	21.1	20.8	21.0	21.2	21.4	21.4	21.4	21.2
Male	Point	21.6	22.4	22.4	22.2	22.4	22.6	22.7	22.9	22.8	22.6
Female	Point	20.0	20.0	20.0	19.7	19.9	20.0	20.2	20.1	20.2	20.0
Participants											
Total	1,000	788	714	822	805	849	739	730	777	842	855
Male	Percent	52	46	45	45	46	46	46	46	46	46
White	Percent	(NA)	77	83	83	82	82	82	81	81	80
Black	Percent	4	7	8	8	9	8	8	8	9	9
Obtaining composite scores of—											
26 or above	Percent	14	14	13	13	13	14	14	14	14	14
15 or below	Pecent	21	33	33	34	34	32	31	31	31	32

(NA) Not available. (1) Minimum score, 1; maximum score, 36. (2) Test scores and characteristics of college-bound students based on a 10% sample through 1984. Begining in 1985, these data are now based on the performance of all ACT-tested students who graduated in the spring of a given school year and who took the ACT Assessment during junior or senior year of high school.

College Faculty Salaries and Benefits: 1970-1989

Source: Annual Report on the Economic Status of the Profession. American Assn. of University Professors

(thousands of dollars)

[For academic year ending in year shown. Figures are for 9 months teaching for full-time faculty members in four-year colleges and universities.]

Type of control and academic rank Average Salaries	1970	1975	1980	1981	1982	1983	1984	1985	1986	1987	1988	1989
Public: All ranks	13.1	16.6	22.1	23.9	26.2	28.6	29.4	31.2	33.4	35.8	37.2	39.6
Professor	17.3	21.7	28.8	31.0	33.7	36.0	37.1	39.6	42.3	45.3	47.2	50.1
Associate professor	13.2	16.7	21.9	23.4	25.7	27.5	28.4	30.2	32.2	34.2	35.6	37.9
Assistant professor	10.9	13.7	18.0	19.2	21.2	22.6	23.5	25.0	26.7	28.5	29.6	31.7
Instructor	9.1	11.2	14.8	15.1	16.7	17.7	19.1	19.5	20.9	21.8	22.2	23.9
Private[1]: All ranks	13.1	16.6	22.1	24.4	26.8	29.2	31.1	33.0	35.4	37.8	39.7	42.4
Professor	17.8	22.4	30.1	32.7	35.8	38.8	41.5	44.1	47.0	50.3	52.2	55.9
Associate professor	12.6	16.0	21.0	23.1	25.4	27.5	29.4	30.9	32.9	34.9	36.6	38.8
Assistant professor	10.3	13.0	17.0	18.4	20.4	22.1	23.7	25.0	26.8	28.3	30.1	31.9
Instructor	8.6	10.9	13.3	14.4	15.9	17.6	18.4	19.0	19.8	20.4	22.7	24.1
Average fringe benefits												
All ranks combined:												
Public	1.9	2.5	3.9	4.7	5.1	5.4	6.0	7.0	7.3	7.8	8.2	9.0
Private[1]	2.2	2.8	4.1	4.9	5.4	5.7	6.4	7.2	8.0	8.6	9.2	10.0

(1) Excludes church-related colleges and universities.

American Colleges and Universities
General Information for the 1989–90 Academic Year
Source: Peterson's Guides

These listings include all accredited undergraduate degree-granting institutions in the United States and U.S. territories that are classified as either four-year colleges with total institutional enrollments of 750 or more or two-year colleges with total institutional enrollments of 1,000 or more. Four-year colleges (those that award a bachelor's as their highest undergraduate degree) are listed first, followed by two-year colleges (those that award an associate as their highest or primary undergraduate degree).

All institutions are coeducational except those where the zip code is followed by: (1)–men only, (2)–primarily men, (3)–women only, (4)–primarily women.

Year is that of founding.

Governing official is the chief executive officer.

Institutional control: 1–independent (nonprofit), 2–independent-religious, 3–proprietary (profit making), 4–federal, 5–state, 7–commonwealth (Puerto Rico), 8–territory (U.S. territories), 9–county, 10–district, 11–city, 12–state and local, 13–state related.

Highest degree offered: B–bachelor's, M–master's, D–doctorate (includes first professional degrees).

Enrollment is the total number of matriculated undergraduate and (if applicable) graduate students.

Faculty is the total number of faculty members teaching undergraduate courses.

Any data not reported are indicated as NR.

Four-Year Colleges

Name, address	Year	Governing official, control, and highest degree offered		Enroll-ment	Faculty
Abilene Christian U, Abilene, TX 79699	1906	Dr. William J. Teague	2-D	4,186	244
Acad of Art Coll, San Francisco, CA 94108	1929	Dr. Andrew Jameson	3-M	2,153	140
Adams State Coll, Alamosa, CO 81102	1921	Dr. William M. Fulkerson, Jr.	5-M	2,507	121
Adelphi U, Garden City, NY 11530	1896	Dr. Peter Diamandopoulos	1-D	8,739	820
Adrian Coll, Adrian, MI 49221	1859	Dr. Stanley P. Caine	2-B	1,207	134
Alabama Agricultural and Mechanical U, Normal, AL 35762	1875	Dr. Carl Marbury	5-D	4,500	314
Alabama State U, Montgomery, AL 36195	1874	Dr. Leon Howard	6-M	4,456	270
Alaska Pacific U, Anchorage, AK 99508	1959	Dr. F. Thomas Trotter	2-D	809	58
Albany State Coll, Albany, GA 31705	1903	Dr. Billy C. Black	5-M	2,306	151
Albion Coll, Albion, MI 49224	1835	Dr. Melvin L. Vulgamore	2-B	1,700	122
Albright Coll, Reading, PA 19612	1856	Dr. David G. Ruffer	2-B	1,306	128
Alcorn State U, Lorman, MS 39096	1871	Dr. Walter Washington	5-M	2,847	183
Alderson-Broaddus Coll, Philippi, WV 26416	1871	Dr. W. Christian Sizemore	2-B	759	74
Alfred U, Alfred, NY 14802	1836	Dr. Edward G. Coll, Jr.	1-D	2,341	175
Allegheny Coll, Meadville, PA 16335	1815	Dr. Daniel F. Sullivan	2-M	1,956	205
Allentown Coll of St Francis de Sales, Center Valley, PA 18034	1962	Very Rev. Daniel Gambet	2-M	1,700	90
Alma Coll, Alma, MI 48801	1886	Dr. Alan J. Stone	2-B	1,241	103
Alvernia Coll, Reading, PA 19607	1958	Sr. M. Dolorey	2-B	1,011	93
Alverno Coll, Milwaukee, WI 53215 (3)	1887	Joel Read	1-B	2,310	166
American International Coll, Springfield, MA 01109	1885	Dr. Harry J. Courniotes	1-D	1,790	120
American U, Washington, DC 20016	1893	NR	2-D	10,153	1,060
American U of Puerto Rico, Bayamón, PR 00621	1963	Juan B. Nazario-Negron	1-B	4,295	250
Amherst Coll, Amherst, MA 01002	1821	Peter R. Pouncey	1-B	1,585	183
Anderson U, Anderson, IN 46012	1917	Dr. James L. Edwards	2-M	2,115	194
Andrews U, Berrien Springs, MI 49104	1874	Dr. W. Richard Lesher	2-D	2,907	282
Angelo State U, San Angelo, TX 76909	1928	Dr. Lloyd Drexell Vincent	5-M	6,408	222
Anna Maria Coll, Paxton, MA 01612	1946	Sr. Bernadette Madore	2-M	1,395	85
Appalachian State U, Boone, NC 28608	1899	Dr. John E. Thomas	5-M	11,501	660
Aquinas Coll, Grand Rapids, MI 49506	1886	Mr. R. Paul Nelson	2-M	2,625	164
Arizona State U, Tempe, AZ 85287	1885	Dr. Lattie F. Coor	5-D	43,546	1,756
Arkansas Coll, Batesville, AR 72503	1872	Dr. John V. Griffith	2-B	831	69
Arkansas State U, State University, AR 72467	1909	Dr. Eugene W. Smith	5-M	9,181	360
Arkansas Tech U, Russellville, AR 72801	1909	Dr. Kenneth G. Kersh	5-M	3,837	205
Armstrong State Coll, Savannah, GA 31419	1935	Dr. Robert A. Burnett	5-M	3,702	172
Art Ctr Coll of Design, Pasadena, CA 91103	1930	Mr. David R. Brown	1-M	1,185	208
Art Inst of Fort Lauderdale, Fort Lauderdale, FL 33316	1968	NR	3-B	2,000	100
Asbury Coll, Wilmore, KY 40390	1890	Dr. Dennis F. Kinlaw	2-B	1,082	97
Ashland U, Ashland, OH 44805	1878	Dr. Joseph Shultz	2-M	4,391	177
Assumption Coll, Worcester, MA 01615	1904	Joseph H. Hagan	2-M	2,173	175
Athens State Coll, Athens, AL 35611	1822	Dr. James R. Chasteen	5-B	2,417	140
Atlantic Christian Coll, Wilson, NC 27893	1902	Dr. James B. Hemby	2-B	1,434	108
Atlantic Union Coll, South Lancaster, MA 01561	1882	Dr. Lawrence T. Geraty	2-B	1,029	73
Auburn U, Auburn University, AL 36849	1856	Dr. James E. Martin	5-D	21,701	1,201
Auburn U at Montgomery, Montgomery, AL 36193	1967	Dr. James O. Williams	5-D	6,027	250
Augsburg Coll, Minneapolis, MN 55454	1869	Dr. Charles S. Anderson	2-M	2,702	123
Augusta Coll, Augusta, GA 30910	1925	Dr. Richard S. Wallace	5-M	4,709	190
Augustana Coll, Rock Island, IL 61201	1860	Dr. Thomas Tredway	2-B	2,267	165
Augustana Coll, Sioux Falls, SD 57197	1860	Dr. Lloyd Svendsbye	2-M	2,004	171
Aurora U, Aurora, IL 60506	1893	Thomas H. Zarle	1-M	2,045	225
Austin Coll, Sherman, TX 75091	1849	Dr. Harry E. Smith	2-M	1,227	88
Austin Peay State U, Clarksville, TN 37044	1927	Dr. Oscar Page	5-M	6,292	328
Averett Coll, Danville, VA 24541	1859	Dr. Frank R. Campbell	2-M	1,216	95
Avila Coll, Kansas City, MO 64145	1916	Dr. Larry Kramer	2-M	1,307	152
Azusa Pacific U, Azusa, CA 91702	1899	Dr. Ted W. Engstrom	2-M	2,933	180
Babson Coll, Babson Park, MA 02157	1919	Mr. William F. Glavin	1-M	3,000	152
Baker Coll, Flint, MI 48507	1911	Mr. Edward J. Kurtz	1-B	3,234	123
Baker Coll of Owosso, Owosso, MI 48867	1984	Mr. Edward Kurtz	1-B	943	37
Baker U, Baldwin City, KS 66006	1858	Dr. Daniel M. Lambert	2-B	1,121	78
Baldwin-Wallace Coll, Berea, OH 44017	1845	Dr. Neal Malicky	2-M	4,713	286
Ball State U, Muncie, IN 47306	1918	Dr. John E. Worthen	5-D	18,993	915
Baptist Bible Coll, Springfield, MO 65803	1950	NR	2-M	815	37
Baptist Coll at Charleston, Charleston, SC 29411	1964	Dr. Jairy C. Hunter, Jr.	2-M	2,051	95
Bard Coll, Annandale-on-Hudson, NY 12504	1860	Dr. Leon Botstein	1-M	1,050	109
Barnard Coll, New York, NY 10027 (3)	1889	Mrs. Barbara S. Schmitter	1-B	2,200	256

Name, address	Year	Governing official, control, and highest degree offered		Enrollment	Faculty
Barry U, Miami Shores, FL 33161	1940	Sr. Jeanne O'Laughlin	2-D	5,900	NR
Baruch Coll of the City U of New York, New York, NY 10010	1968	Dr. Joel Segall	12-M	18,100	975
Bates Coll, Lewiston, ME 04240	1855	Dr. Donald W. Harward	1-B	1,500	150
Bayamón Central U, Bayamón, PR 00621	1970	Rev. Vincent A. M. Van Rooij, OP	2-M	2,917	135
Baylor U, Waco, TX 76798	1845	Dr. Herbert H. Reynolds	2-D	11,774	580
Beaver Coll, Glenside, PA 19038	1853	Dr. Bette E. Landman	2-M	2,294	131
Bellarmine Coll, Louisville, KY 40205	1950	Dr. Joseph J. McGowan	2-M	2,584	196
Bellevue Coll, Bellevue, NE 68005	1965	Dr. John B. Muller	1-B	1,956	66
Belmont Abbey Coll, Belmont, NC 28012	1876	Dr. Joseph Brosnan	2-B	1,031	90
Belmont Coll, Nashville, TN 37212	1951	Dr. William E. Troutt	2-M	2,706	261
Beloit Coll, Beloit, WI 53511	1846	Dr. Roger H. Hull	1-M	1,066	117
Bemidji State U, Bemidji, MN 56601	1919	Dr. Leslie C. Duly	5-M	5,150	250
Benedict Coll, Columbia, SC 29204	1870	Dr. Marshall C. Grigsby	2-B	1,616	118
Benedictine Coll, Atchison, KS 66002	1859	Thomas O. James	2-B	803	88
Bentley Coll, Waltham, MA 02154	1917	Dr. Gregory H. Adamian	1-M	7,254	362
Berea Coll, Berea, KY 40404	1855	Dr. John B. Stephenson	1-B	1,550	130
Berklee Coll of Music, Boston, MA 02215	1945	Mr. Lee Eliot Berk	1-B	2,784	300
Berry Coll, Rome, GA 30149	1902	Dr. Gloria M. Shatto	1-M	1,824	149
Bethany Coll, Bethany, WV 26032	1840	Dr. D. Duane Cummins	2-B	825	71
Bethel Coll, St Paul, MN 55112	1871	Dr. George K. Brushaber	2-B	1,832	151
Bethune-Cookman Coll, Daytona Beach, FL 32115	1904	Dr. Oswald P. Bronson, Sr.	2-M	2,145	174
Biola U, La Mirada, CA 90639	1908	Dr. Clyde Cook	2-D	2,566	222
Birmingham-Southern Coll, Birmingham, AL 35254	1856	Dr. Neal R. Berte	2-M	1,937	145
Black Hills State U, Spearfish, SD 57783	1883	Dr. Clifford M. Trump	5-M	2,412	106
Bloomfield Coll, Bloomfield, NJ 07003	1868	Dr. John F. Noonan	2-B	1,605	124
Bloomsburg U of Pennsylvania, Bloomsburg, PA 17815	1839	Dr. Harry Ausprich	5-M	7,143	385
Bluefield State Coll, Bluefield, WV 24701	1895	Dr. Gregory D. Adkins	5-B	2,558	160
Bob Jones U, Greenville, SC 29614	1927	Dr. Bob Jones, III	2-D	4,367	348
Boise State U, Boise, ID 83725	1932	Dr. John H. Keiser	5-M	12,000	851
Boston Coll, Chestnut Hill, MA 02167	1863	Rev. J. Donald Monan, SJ	2-D	14,449	939
Boston U, Boston, MA 02215	1839	Jon Westling	1-D	28,454	2,391
Bowdoin Coll, Brunswick, ME 04011	1794	Mr. Robert H. Edwards	1-B	1,350	133
Bowie State U, Bowie, MD 20715	1865	Dr. James E. Lyons, Sr.	5-M	3,748	155
Bowling Green State U, Bowling Green, OH 43403	1910	Dr. Paul J. Olscamp	5-D	18,043	943
Bradley U, Peoria, IL 61625	1897	Dr. Martin G. Abegg	1-M	5,658	383
Brandeis U, Waltham, MA 02254	1948	Dr. Evelyn E. Handler	1-D	3,523	470
Brenau Professional Coll, Gainesville, GA 30501	1878	Dr. John S. Burd	1-M	1,222	150
Brescia Coll, Owensboro, KY 42301	1950	Dr. Ruth Gehres	2-B	814	66
Brewton-Parker Coll, Mt Vernon, GA 30445	1904	Dr. Y. Lynn Holmes	2-B	1,804	81
Briar Cliff Coll, Sioux City, IA 51104	1930	Sr. Margaret Wick	2-B	1,120	84
Bridgewater Coll, Bridgewater, VA 22812	1880	Dr. Wayne F. Geisert	2-B	985	81
Bridgewater State Coll, Bridgewater, MA 02324	1840	Dr. Adrian Tinsley	5-M	5,406	341
Brigham Young U, Provo, UT 84602	1875	Dr. Rex E. Lee	2-D	27,973	1,591
Brigham Young U–Hawaii Cmps, Laie, Oahu, HI 96762	1955	Dr. Alton L. Wade	2-B	2,040	138
Brooklyn Coll of the City U of New York, Brooklyn, NY 11210	1930	Dr. Robert Hess	12-M	16,689	993
Brown U, Providence, RI 02912	1764	Vartan Gregorian	1-D	7,643	548
Bryant Coll, Smithfield, RI 02917	1863	Dr. William Trueheart	1-M	5,495	204
Bryn Mawr Coll, Bryn Mawr, PA 19010 (4)	1885	Mary Patterson McPherson	1-D	1,839	238
Bucknell U, Lewisburg, PA 17837	1846	Dr. Gary A. Sojka	1-M	3,598	249
Buena Vista Coll, Storm Lake, IA 50588	1891	Dr. Keith G. Briscoe	2-B	1,045	87
Butler U, Indianapolis, IN 46208	1855	Dr. Geoffrey Bannister	1-M	4,187	370
Cabrini Coll, Radnor, PA 19087	1957	Sr. Eileen Currie, MSC	2-M	1,375	118
Caldwell Coll, Caldwell, NJ 07006	1939	Sr. Vivien Jennings	2-B	1,089	84
California Coll of Arts and Crafts, Oakland, CA 94618	1907	Mr. Neil J. Hoffman	1-M	1,058	167
California Inst of Tech, Pasadena, CA 91125	1891	Dr. Thomas E. Everhart	1-D	1,841	270
California Inst of the Arts, Valencia, CA 91355	1961	Dr. Steven D. Lavine	1-M	955	186
California Lutheran U, Thousand Oaks, CA 91360	1959	Dr. Jerry H. Miller	2-M	2,853	180
California Polytechnic State U, San Luis Obispo, San Luis Obispo, CA 93407	1901	Dr. Warren J. Baker	5-M	17,564	1,000
California State Polytechnic U, Pomona, Pomona, CA 91768	1938	Dr. Hugh O. La Bounty	5-M	19,579	1,137
California State U, Bakersfield, Bakersfield, CA 93311	1970	Dr. Tomas A. Arciniega	5-M	5,215	337
California State U, Chico, Chico, CA 95929	1887	Dr. Robin Wilson	5-M	16,569	1,051
California State U, Dominguez Hills, Carson, CA 90747	1960	Dr. Robert Detweiler	5-M	8,819	844
California State U, Fresno, Fresno, CA 93740	1911	Dr. Harold H. Haak	5-M	19,124	1,171
California State U, Fullerton, Fullerton, CA 92634	1957	Dr. Jewel Plummer Cobb	5-M	24,961	1,431
California State U, Hayward, Hayward, CA 94542	1957	Dr. Ellis E. McCune	5-M	12,825	666
California State U, Long Beach, Long Beach, CA 90840	1949	Dr. Curtis L. McCray	5-M	32,875	1,940
California State U, Los Angeles, Los Angeles, CA 90032	1947	Dr. James M. Rosser	5-D	20,804	1,361
California State U, Northridge, Northridge, CA 91330	1958	Dr. James Cleary	5-M	30,657	1,753
California State U, Sacramento, Sacramento, CA 95819	1947	Dr. Donald R. Gerth	5-M	25,559	1,378
California State U, San Bernardino, San Bernardino, CA 92407	1965	Dr. Anthony H. Evans	5-M	10,873	450
California U of Pennsylvania, California, PA 15419	1852	Dr. John Pierce Watkins	5-M	6,748	378
Calumet Coll of Saint Joseph, Whiting, IN 46394	1951	Dr. Dennis C. Rittenmeyer	2-B	1,000	63
Calvin Coll, Grand Rapids, MI 49546	1876	Dr. Anthony J. Diekema	2-M	4,325	308
Cameron U, Lawton, OK 73505	1908	Dr. Don Davis	5-M	5,465	221
Campbell U, Buies Creek, NC 27506	1887	Dr. Norman A. Wiggins	2-D	4,820	243
Canisius Coll, Buffalo, NY 14208	1870	Rev. James M. Demske, SJ	1-M	4,504	336
Capital U, Columbus, OH 43209	1830	Josiah H. Blackmore	2-D	3,008	146
Cardinal Stritch Coll, Milwaukee, WI 53217	1937	Sr. M. Camille Kliebhan	2-M	3,376	141
Carleton Coll, Northfield, MN 55057	1866	Dr. Stephen R. Lewis, Jr.	1-B	1,850	157
Carlow Coll, Pittsburgh, PA 15213 (4)	1929	Grace Ann Geibel, RSM	2-M	1,044	124
Carnegie Mellon U, Pittsburgh, PA 15213	1900	Dr. Robert Mehrabian	1-D	6,997	740
Carroll Coll, Helena, MT 59625	1909	Dr. Matthew Quinn	2-B	1,333	117
Carroll Coll, Waukesha, WI 53186	1846	Dr. Dan C. West	2-B	1,478	133
Carson-Newman Coll, Jefferson City, TN 37760	1851	Dr. J. Cordell Maddox	2-M	2,017	122
Carthage Coll, Kenosha, WI 53140	1847	Dr. F. Gregory Campbell	2-M	2,002	115
Case Western Reserve U, Cleveland, OH 44106	1826	Dr. Agnar Pytte	1-D	8,386	1,771
Castleton State Coll, Castleton, VT 05735	1787	Dr. Lyle A. Gray	5-M	1,655	136
Catawba Coll, Salisbury, NC 28144	1851	Dr. Stephen H. Wurster	2-B	1,044	87
Catholic U of America, Washington, DC 20064	1887	Rev. William J. Byron, SJ	2-D	6,670	570
Catholic U of Puerto Rico, Ponce, PR 00732	1948	Rev. F. Toselló Giangiacomo	2-M	12,507	474
Cedar Crest Coll, Allentown, PA 18104 (4)	1867	Dr. Dorothy G. Blaney	2-B	962	101

Name, address	Year	Governing official, control, and highest degree offered		Enroll-ment	Faculty
Cedarville Coll, Cedarville, OH 45314	1887	Dr. Paul H. Dixon	2-B	1,942	145
Centenary Coll, Hackettstown, NJ 07840 (4)	1867	Dr. Stephanie M. Bennett	2-B	820	88
Centenary Coll of Louisiana, Shreveport, LA 71134	1825	Dr. Donald A. Webb	2-M	1,033	102
Ctr for Creative Studies—Coll of Art and Design, Detroit, MI 48202	1926	Jerome Grove	1-B	948	231
Central Bible Coll, Springfield, MO 65803	1922	H. Maurice Lednicky	2-B	972	53
Central Connecticut State U, New Britain, CT 06050	1849	Dr. John W. Shumaker	5-M	14,463	708
Central Methodist Coll, Fayette, MO 65248	1854	Dr. Joe A. Howell	2-B	754	70
Central Michigan U, Mount Pleasant, MI 48859	1892	Dr. Edward B. Jakubauskas	5-D	17,229	776
Central Missouri State U, Warrensburg, MO 64093	1871	Dr. Ed Elliott	5-M	10,813	481
Central State U, Wilberforce, OH 45384	1887	Dr. Arthur E. Thomas	5-B	2,550	140
Central State U, Edmond, OK 73034	1890	Dr. Bill J. Lillard	5-M	14,214	542
Central U of Iowa, Pella, IA 50219	1853	Dr. William M. Wiebenga	2-B	1,751	118
Central Washington U, Ellensburg, WA 98926	1891	Dr. Donald L. Garrity	5-M	7,109	312
Centre Coll, Danville, KY 40422	1819	Dr. Michael F. Adams	2-B	855	87
Chadron State Coll, Chadron, NE 69337	1911	Dr. Samuel H. Rankin	5-M	2,850	96
Chaminade U of Honolulu, Honolulu, HI 96816	1955	Mr. Kent M. Keith	2-M	2,610	195
Chapman Coll, Orange, CA 92666	1861	Dr. Allen E. Koenig	2-M	2,221	138
Charter Oak Coll, Farmington, CT 06032	1973	Dr. Merle W. Harris	5-B	940	NR
Chestnut Hill Coll, Philadelphia, PA 19118 (4)	1924	Sr. Matthew Anita MacDonald	2-M	1,149	98
Cheyney U of Pennsylvania, Cheyney, PA 19319	1837	Dr. LeVerne McCummings	5-M	1,646	107
Chicago State U, Chicago, IL 60628	1867	Dr. Harold Delaney	5-M	6,034	397
Christian Brothers U, Memphis, TN 38104	1871	Br. Theodore Drahmann, FSC	2-M	1,772	136
Christopher Newport Coll, Newport News, VA 23606	1961	Dr. Anthony Santoro	5-B	4,832	171
The Citadel, The Military Coll of South Carolina, Charleston, SC 29409 (1)	1842	Maj. Gen. James A. Grimsley, Jr.	5-M	3,670	152
City Coll of the City U of New York, New York, NY 10031	1847	Bernard W. Harleston	12-D	13,563	1,352
Claflin Coll, Orangeburg, SC 29115	1869	Oscar A. Rogers	2-B	850	59
Claremont McKenna Coll, Claremont, CA 91711	1946	Mr. Jack L. Stark	1-B	851	106
Clarion U of Pennsylvania, Clarion, PA 16214	1867	Dr. Diane L. Reinhard	5-M	6,434	408
Clark Atlanta U, Atlanta, GA 30314	1869	Dr. Thomas Cale, Jr.	1-D	3,339	208
Clarke Coll, Dubuque, IA 52001	1843	Dr. Catherine Dunn, BVM	2-M	854	56
Clarkson U, Potsdam, NY 13676	1896	Dr. Richard H. Gallagher	1-D	3,569	231
Clark U, Worcester, MA 01610	1887	Dr. Richard P. Traina	1-D	2,879	214
Clayton State Coll, Morrow, GA 30260	1969	NR	5-B	3,863	98
Cleary Coll, Ypsilanti, MI 48197	1883	Mr. Thomas Sullivan	1-B	1,200	67
Clemson U, Clemson, SC 29634	1889	Dr. Max Lennon	5-D	16,072	1,050
Cleveland State U, Cleveland, OH 44115	1964	Dr. John A. Flower	5-D	18,534	770
Clinch Valley Coll of the U of Virginia, Wise, VA 24293	1954	Dr. Jimmy A. Knight	5-B	1,594	111
Coe Coll, Cedar Rapids, IA 52402	1851	Dr. John E. Brown	2-B	1,217	106
Colby Coll, Waterville, ME 04901	1813	William R. Cotter	1-B	1,734	164
Coleman Coll, La Mesa, CA 92041	1963	Dr. Bob Wall	1-M	988	75
Colgate U, Hamilton, NY 13346	1819	Dr. Neil R. Grabois	1-M	2,716	254
Coll for Human Services, New York, NY 10014	1964	Audrey C. Cohen	1-M	910	41
Coll Misericordia, Dallas, PA 18612	1924	Dr. Pasquale DiPasquale	2-M	1,125	120
Coll of Aeronautics, Flushing, NY 11371 (2)	1932	Dr. Sam Frank	1-B	1,300	70
Coll of Boca Raton, Boca Raton, FL 33431	1962	Dr. Donald E. Ross	1-M	1,150	75
Coll of Charleston, Charleston, SC 29424	1770	Dr. Harry M. Lightsey, Jr.	5-M	6,778	399
Coll of Great Falls, Great Falls, MT 59405	1932	Dr. William A. Shields	2-M	1,200	80
Coll of Idaho, Caldwell, ID 83605	1891	Mr. Robert L. Hendren, Jr.	2-M	1,189	85
Coll of Insurance, New York, NY 10007	1962	Dr. Ellen Thrower	1-M	1,339	96
Coll of Mount St Joseph, Cincinnati, OH 45051	1920	Francis Marie Thrailkill, OSU	2-M	2,566	175
Coll of Mount Saint Vincent, Riverdale, NY 10471 (4)	1847	Sr. Doris Smith	1-M	985	84
Coll of New Rochelle, New Rochelle, NY 10805 (4)	1904	Sr. Dorothy A. Kelly	1-M	2,345	92
Coll of New Rochelle, New Resources Division, New Rochelle, NY 10805	1972	NR	1-B	2,751	408
Coll of Notre Dame, Belmont, CA 94002	1851	Sr. Veronica Skillin	2-M	1,066	98
Coll of Saint Benedict, Saint Joseph, MN 56374 (3)	1887	Sr. Colman O'Connell, OSB	2-B	1,872	153
Coll of St Catherine, St Paul, MN 55105 (3)	1905	Dr. Anita Pampusch	2-M	2,585	218
Coll of Saint Elizabeth, Convent Station, NJ 07961 (4)	1899	Sr. Jacqueline Burns	2-M	1,074	103
Coll of St Francis, Joliet, IL 60435	1920	Dr. John C. Orr	2-M	1,804	93
Coll of St Mary, Omaha, NE 68124 (4)	1923	Dr. Kenneth Nielsen	2-M	1,127	139
Coll of Saint Rose, Albany, NY 12203	1920	Dr. Louis C. Vaccaro	1-M	3,624	216
Coll of St Scholastica, Duluth, MN 55811	1906	Dr. Daniel H. Pilon	2-M	1,900	142
Coll of St Thomas, St Paul, MN 55105	1885	Msgr. Terrence J. Murphy	2-D	9,120	483
Coll of Santa Fe, Santa Fe, NM 87501	1947	Dr. James A. Fries	2-M	1,208	78
Coll of Staten Island of the City U of New York, Staten Island, NY 10301	1955	Dr. Edmond L. Volpe	12-M	11,388	678
Coll of the Holy Cross, Worcester, MA 01610	1843	Rev. John E. Brooks, SJ	2-B	2,684	244
Coll of William and Mary, Williamsburg, VA 23185	1693	Dr. Paul R. Verkuil	5-D	7,542	716
Coll of Wooster, Wooster, OH 44691	1866	Dr. Henry J. Copeland	2-B	1,787	164
Colorado Christian U, Lakewood, CO 80226	1914	Dr. Joe L. Wall	2-M	781	57
Colorado Coll, Colorado Springs, CO 80903	1874	Dr. Gresham Riley	1-M	1,906	235
Colorado Sch of Mines, Golden, CO 80401	1874	Dr. George S. Ansell	5-D	2,412	225
Colorado State U, Fort Collins, CO 80523	1862	Dr. Albert C. Yates	5-D	20,149	NR
Colorado Tech Coll, Colorado Springs, CO 80907	1965	Mr. David D. O'Donnell	3-M	1,182	89
Columbia Bible Coll and Sem, Columbia, SC 29230	1923	Mr. J. Robertson McQuilkin	2-D	938	32
Columbia Coll, Chicago, IL 60605	1890	Mr. Mirron Alexandroff	1-M	6,498	691
Columbia Coll, New York, NY 10027	1754	Dr. Jack Greenberg	1-B	3,114	420
Columbia Coll, Columbia, SC 29203 (3)	1854	Dr. Peter T. Mitchell	2-M	1,173	79
Columbia Union Coll, Takoma Park, MD 20912	1904	Dr. William A. Loveless	2-B	1,173	61
Columbia U, Sch of Engineering & Applied Sci, New York, NY 10027	1864	Dr. Robert Gross	1-D	1,940	156
Columbia U, Sch of General Studies, New York, NY 10027	1754	Ward H. Dennis	1-M	1,320	450
Columbia U, Sch of Nursing, New York, NY 10032 (4)	1935	Dr. Mary O. Mundinger	1-M	101	41
Columbus Coll, Columbus, GA 31993	1958	Dr. Frank D. Brown	5-M	3,904	NR
Columbus Coll of Art and Design, Columbus, OH 43215	1879	Mr. Joseph V. Canzani	1-B	1,600	92
Concord Coll, Athens, WV 24712	1872	Dr. Jerry L. Beasley	5-B	2,560	153
Concordia Coll, Moorhead, MN 56560	1891	Dr. Paul J. Dovre	2-B	2,884	234
Concordia Coll, St Paul, MN 55104	1893	Dr. John Johson	2-B	1,128	89
Concordia Teachers Coll, Seward, NE 68434	1894	Orville C. Walz	2-M	830	75
Concordia U, River Forest, IL 60305	1864	Dr. Eugene L. Krentz	2-D	1,275	135
Concordia U Wisconsin, Mequon, WI 53092	1881	Dr. R. John Buuck	2-M	1,480	75
Connecticut Coll, New London, CT 06320	1911	Claire L. Gaudiani	1-M	2,017	230
Converse Coll, Spartanburg, SC 29301 (3)	1889	Dr. Ellen Wood Hall	1-M	1,199	90

Name, address	Year	Governing official, control, and highest degree offered		Enroll-ment	Faculty
Cooper Union for the Advancement of Science & Art, New York, NY 10003	1859	Mr. John Jay Iselin	1-M	1,027	167
Coppin State Coll, Baltimore, MD 21216	1900	Dr. Calvin W. Burnett	5-M	2,229	158
Cornell Coll, Mount Vernon, IA 52314	1853	Dr. David G. Marker	2-B	1,147	115
Cornell U, Ithaca, NY 14853	1865	Dr. Frank H. T. Rhodes	1-D	18,240	1,617
Creighton U, Omaha, NE 68178	1878	Rev. Michael G. Morrison, SJ	2-D	6,068	719
Culver-Stockton Coll, Canton, MO 63435	1853	Dr. Walter S. Reuling	2-B	1,067	65
Cumberland Coll, Williamsburg, KY 40769	1889	Dr. James Taylor	2-M	1,881	110
Curry Coll, Milton, MA 02186	1879	Dr. William L. Boyle, Jr.	1-M	1,031	167
Daemen Coll, Amherst, NY 14226	1947	Dr. Robert S. Marshall	1-B	1,707	120
Dakota State U, Madison, SD 57042	1881	Dr. Jerald Tunheim	5-B	1,224	69
Dallas Baptist U, Dallas, TX 75211	1898	Dr. Gary R. Cook	2-M	2,269	115
Dartmouth Coll, Hanover, NH 03755	1769	Dr. James O. Freedman	1-D	5,400	316
Davenport Coll of Business, Grand Rapids, MI 49503	1866	Donald W. Maine	1-B	3,529	113
Davenport Coll of Business, Lansing Cmps, Lansing, MI 48933	1979	Don Colizzi	1-B	1,413	86
David Lipscomb U, Nashville, TN 37204	1891	Dr. Harold Hazelip	2-M	2,518	166
Davidson Coll, Davidson, NC 28036	1837	Dr. John W. Kuykendall	2-B	1,400	NR
Davis & Elkins Coll, Elkins, WV 26241	1904	Dr. Dorothy I. MacConkey	2-B	856	77
The Defiance Coll, Defiance, OH 43512	1850	Dr. Marvin J. Ludwig	2-B	1,006	63
Delaware State Coll, Dover, DE 19901	1891	Dr. William B. DeLauder	5-M	2,610	122
Delaware Valley Coll, Doylestown, PA 18901	1896	Mr. William H. Rorer, III	1-B	1,100	80
Delta State U, Cleveland, MS 38733	1925	Dr. F. Kent Wyatt	5-D	3,820	241
Denison U, Granville, OH 43023	1831	Michele T. Myers	1-B	2,027	170
DePaul U, Chicago, IL 60604	1898	Rev. John T. Richardson, CM	2-D	15,387	734
DePauw U, Greencastle, IN 46135	1837	Dr. Robert Bottoms	2-B	2,415	237
Detroit Coll of Business, Dearborn, MI 48126	1962	Dr. James Mendola	1-B	2,625	82
Detroit Coll of Business, Warren Cmps, Warren, MI 48092	1975	Janet Guggenheim	1-B	852	59
DeVry Inst of Tech, Phoenix, AZ 85021	1967	James A. Dugan	3-B	2,699	60
DeVry Inst of Tech, City of Industry, CA 91746	1983	Paul R. McGuirk	3-B	1,965	56
DeVry Inst of Tech, Decatur, GA 30030	1969	William N. Weaver	3-B	2,872	NR
DeVry Inst of Tech, Chicago, IL 60618	1931	Dr. E. Arthur Stunnard	3-M	3,417	51
DeVry Inst of Tech, Lombard, IL 60148	1982	Jerry R. Dill	3-M	2,482	44
DeVry Inst of Tech, Kansas City, MO 64131	1931	Mr. Charles R. Levalley	3-B	1,817	48
DeVry Inst of Tech, Columbus, OH 43209	1952	Mr. Richard A. Czerniak	3-B	2,394	85
DeVry Inst of Tech, Irving, TX 75038	1969	Mr. Thomas E. Colvin	3-B	2,317	NR
Dickinson Coll, Carlisle, PA 17013	1773	Dr. A. Lee Fritschler	1-B	1,977	151
Dickinson State U, Dickinson, ND 58601	1918	Dr. Albert A. Watrel	5-B	1,402	98
Dillard U, New Orleans, LA 70122	1869	Dr. Samuel DuBois Cook	2-B	1,668	NR
Dominican Coll of Blauvelt, Orangeburg, NY 10962	1952	Sr. Kathleen Sullivan	1-B	1,479	162
Dordt Coll, Sioux Center, IA 51250	1955	Dr. John B. Hulst	2-B	1,038	82
Dowling Coll, Oakdale, NY 11769	1959	Dr. Victor P. Meskill	1-M	4,206	274
Drake U, Des Moines, IA 50311	1881	Dr. Michael R. Ferrari	1-D	7,778	295
Drew U, Madison, NJ 07940	1866	Dr. Thomas H. Kean	2-D	2,289	167
Drexel U, Philadelphia, PA 19104	1891	Dr. Richard D. Breslin	1-D	11,959	905
Drury Coll, Springfield, MO 65802	1873	Dr. John E. Moore, Jr.	2-M	1,395	111
Duke U, Durham, NC 27706	1838	Dr. H. Keith H. Brodie	2-D	10,376	3,193
Duquesne U, Pittsburgh, PA 15282	1878	John E. Murray, Jr.	2-D	6,846	501
Dyke Coll, Cleveland, OH 44115	1848	Dr. John C. Corfias	1-B	1,261	130
D'Youville Coll, Buffalo, NY 14201	1908	Dr. Denise A. Roche, GNSH	1-M	1,200	97
Earlham Coll, Richmond, IN 47374	1847	Dr. Richard J. Wood	2-M	1,267	122
East Carolina U, Greenville, NC 27858	1907	Dr. Richard Eakin	5-D	16,029	1,063
East Central U, Ada, OK 74820	1909	Dr. Bill S. Cole	5-M	4,140	200
Eastern Coll, Saint Davids, PA 19087	1932	Dr. Roberta Hestenes	2-M	1,282	108
Eastern Connecticut State U, Willimantic, CT 06226	1889	David G. Carter	5-M	4,450	195
Eastern Illinois U, Charleston, IL 61920	1895	Dr. Stanley Rives	5-M	10,427	638
Eastern Mennonite Coll, Harrisonburg, VA 22801	1917	Dr. Joseph L. Lapp	2-B	969	85
Eastern Michigan U, Ypsilanti, MI 48197	1849	Dr. William E. Shelton	5-M	24,807	1,033
Eastern Montana Coll, Billings, MT 59101	1927	Dr. Bruce H. Carpenter	5-M	4,055	242
Eastern Nazarene Coll, Quincy, MA 02170	1918	Dr. Stephen W. Nease	2-M	912	62
Eastern New Mexico U, Portales, NM 88130	1934	Dr. Thomas Bond	5-M	3,655	200
Eastern Oregon State Coll, La Grande, OR 97850	1929	David E. Gilbert	5-M	1,812	NR
Eastern Washington U, Cheney, WA 99004	1882	Dr. B. Dell Felder	5-M	8,098	469
East Stroudsburg U of Pennsylvania, East Stroudsburg, PA 18301	1893	Dr. James Gilbert	5-M	5,431	277
East Tennessee State U, Johnson City, TN 37614	1911	Dr. Ronald E. Beller	5-D	11,590	563
East Texas Baptist U, Marshall, TX 75670	1912	Dr. Robert E. Craig	2-B	811	68
East Texas State U, Commerce, TX 75428	1889	Dr. Jerry D. Morris	5-D	7,811	201
East Texas State U at Texarkana, Texarkana, TX 75505	1971	Dr. John F. Moss	5-M	1,336	55
Eckerd Coll, St Petersburg, FL 33733	1958	Dr. Peter H. Armacost	2-B	1,351	109
Edgewood Coll, Madison, WI 53711	1927	Dr. James A. Ebben	2-M	1,252	96
Edinboro U of Pennsylvania, Edinboro, PA 16444	1857	Foster F. Diebold	5-M	7,466	417
Electronic Data Processing Coll of Puerto Rico, Hato Rey, PR 00918	1968	Jesus Ramos	3-B	992	46
Elizabeth City State U, Elizabeth City, NC 27909	1891	Dr. Jimmy R. Jenkins	5-B	1,694	133
Elizabethtown Coll, Elizabethtown, PA 17022	1899	Dr. Gerhard E. Spiegler	2-B	1,878	156
Elmhurst Coll, Elmhurst, IL 60126	1871	Dr. Ivan E. Frick	2-B	3,007	138
Elmira Coll, Elmira, NY 14901	1855	Dr. Thomas K. Meier	1-B	867	95
Elon Coll, Elon College, NC 27244	1889	Dr. J. Fred Young	2-M	3,368	173
Embry-Riddle Aeronautical U, Daytona Beach, FL 32114	1926	Kenneth Tallman	1-M	5,337	213
Embry-Riddle Aeronautical U, Coll of Continuing Ed, Daytona Beach, FL 32114	1926	NR	1-M	3,808	NR
Embry-Riddle Aeronautical U, Prescott Cmps, Prescott, AZ 86301	1978	Paul S. Daly	1-B	1,771	NR
Emerson Coll, Boston, MA 02116	1880	Dr. John Zacharis	1-M	2,483	238
Emmanuel Coll, Boston, MA 02115 (3)	1919	Dr. Janet Eisner	2-M	964	89
Emory & Henry Coll, Emory, VA 24327	1836	Dr. Charles W. Sydnor, Jr.	2-B	853	61
Emory U, Atlanta, GA 30322	1836	Dr. James T. Laney	2-D	9,398	496
Emporia State U, Emporia, KS 66801	1863	Dr. Robert E. Glennen	5-M	6,021	294
ETI Tech Coll, Cleveland, OH 44103	1929	A. Jablonski	3-B	1,000	38
Eugene Lang Coll, New Sch for Social Research, New York, NY 10011	1985	Donald Scott	1-B	328	59
Evangel Coll, Springfield, MO 65802	1955	Dr. Robert H. Spence	2-B	1,525	122
Evergreen State Coll, Olympia, WA 98505	1967	Dr. Joseph D. Olander	5-M	3,237	210
Fairfield U, Fairfield, CT 06430	1942	Rev. Aloysius P. Kelley	2-M	4,895	353

Name, address	Year	Governing official, control, and highest degree offered	Enrollment	Faculty
Fairleigh Dickinson U, Florham-Madison Cmps, Madison, NJ 07940	1958	Dr. Robert H. Donaldson 1-M	3,800	187
Fairleigh Dickinson U, Rutherford Cmps, Rutherford, NJ 07070	1942	Dr. Francis J. Mertz 1-M	2,635	137
Fairleigh Dickinson U, Teaneck-Hackensack Cmps, Teaneck, NJ 07666	1954	Dr. Robert H. Donaldson . . . 1-D	5,841	539
Fairmont State Coll, Fairmont, WV 26554	1865	Dr. Robert Dillman 5-B	6,129	317
Fashion Inst of Tech, New York, NY 10001	1944	Dr. Marvin J. Feldman . . . 12-M	11,944	803
Faulkner U, Montgomery, AL 36193	1942	Dr. Billy D. Hilyer 2-D	1,027	37
Fayetteville State U, Fayetteville, NC 28301	1867	Dr. Lloyd V. Hackley 5-M	3,034	192
Ferris State U, Big Rapids, MI 49307	1884	Dr. J. William Wenrich 5-D	11,847	638
Ferrum Coll, Ferrum, VA 24088	1913	Dr. Jerry M. Boone 2-B	1,238	103
Fisk U, Nashville, TN 37208	1866	Dr. Henry Ponder 2-M	891	81
Fitchburg State Coll, Fitchburg, MA 01420	1894	Dr. Vincent J. Mara 5-M	6,224	274
Flagler Coll, St Augustine, FL 32085	1968	Dr. William L. Proctor 1-B	1,159	93
Florida Agricultural and Mechanical U, Tallahassee, FL 32307	1887	Dr. Frederick Humphries . . 5-D	7,469	670
Florida Atlantic U, Boca Raton, FL 33431	1961	Dr. Anthony James Catanese 5-D	11,481	690
Florida Inst of Tech, Melbourne, FL 32901	1958	Dr. Lynn E. Weaver 1-D	4,117	683
Florida International U, Miami, FL 33199	1965	Dr. Modesto A. Maidique . . 5-D	19,529	878
Florida Southern Coll, Lakeland, FL 33801	1885	Dr. Robert A. Davis 2-M	1,955	154
Florida State U, Tallahassee, FL 32306	1857	Dr. Bernard F. Sliger 5-D	28,000	1,434
Fontbonne Coll, St Louis, MO 63105	1917	Dr. Meneve Dunham 2-M	1,108	140
Fordham U, New York, NY 10458	1841	Rev. Joseph A. O'Hare, SJ . 2-D	13,036	933
Fort Hays State U, Hays, KS 67601	1902	Dr. Edward H. Hammond . . 5-M	4,997	229
Fort Lewis Coll, Durango, CO 81301	1911	Joel M. Jones 5-B	3,984	180
Fort Valley State Coll, Fort Valley, GA 31030	1895	Dr. Melvin E. Walker, Jr. . . 5-M	2,097	160
Framingham State Coll, Framingham, MA 01701	1839	Dr. Paul F. Weller 5-M	4,042	234
Franciscan U of Steubenville, Steubenville, OH 43952	1946	Rev. Michael Scanlan 2-M	1,523	84
Francis Marion Coll, Florence, SC 29501	1970	Dr. Thomas C. Stanton . . . 5-M	3,883	210
Franklin and Marshall Coll, Lancaster, PA 17604	1787	Dr. A. Richard Kneedler . . . 1-B	1,850	174
Franklin Coll of Indiana, Franklin, IN 46131	1834	Mr. William Bryan Martin . . 2-B	801	81
Franklin Pierce Coll, Rindge, NH 03461	1962	Dr. Walter Peterson 1-B	1,300	105
Franklin U, Columbus, OH 43215	1902	Dr. Paul J. Otte 1-B	3,946	195
Freed-Hardeman U, Henderson, TN 38340	1869	Dr. E. Claude Gardner 2-M	1,174	82
Fresno Pacific Coll, Fresno, CA 93702	1944	Dr. Richard Kriegbaum . . . 2-M	1,364	43
Friends U, Wichita, KS 67213	1898	Dr. Richard Felix 2-M	1,287	110
Frostburg State U, Frostburg, MD 21532	1898	Dr. Herb F. Reinhard, Jr. . . 5-M	4,800	287
Furman U, Greenville, SC 29613	1826	Dr. John E. Johns 2-M	2,794	206
Gallaudet U, Washington, DC 20002	1856	Dr. I. King Jordan 1-D	2,373	330
Gannon U, Erie, PA 16541	1925	Dr. M. Daniel Henry 2-M	4,578	342
Gardner-Webb Coll, Boiling Springs, NC 28017	1905	Dr. M. Christopher White . . 2-M	2,189	151
Geneva Coll, Beaver Falls, PA 15010	1848	Dr. Joseph McFarland 2-M	1,308	79
George Fox Coll, Newberg, OR 97132	1891	Dr. Edward F. Stevens 2-B	944	74
George Mason U, Fairfax, VA 22030	1957	Dr. George W. Johnson . . . 5-D	19,747	1,003
Georgetown Coll, Georgetown, KY 40324	1829	Dr. W. Morgan Patterson . . 2-M	1,562	93
Georgetown U, Washington, DC 20057	1789	Rev. Leo J. O'Donovan, SJ . 1-D	11,449	650
George Washington U, Washington, DC 20052	1821	Mr. Stephen J. Trachtenberg 1-D	16,947	1,142
Georgia Coll, Milledgeville, GA 31061	1889	Dr. Edwin G. Speir 5-M	4,820	168
Georgia Inst of Tech, Atlanta, GA 30332	1885	Dr. John P. Crecine 5-D	12,090	559
Georgian Court Coll, Lakewood, NJ 08701 (4)	1908	Sr. Barbara Williams 2-M	2,151	142
Georgia Southern U, Statesboro, GA 30460	1906	Dr. Nicholas Henry 5-M	11,238	543
Georgia Southwestern Coll, Americus, GA 31709	1906	Dr. William H. Capitan 5-M	2,251	155
Georgia State U, Atlanta, GA 30303	1913	Dr. John M. Palms 5-D	23,039	931
Gettysburg Coll, Gettysburg, PA 17325	1832	Mr. Charles E. Anderson . . 2-B	1,950	150
Glassboro State Coll, Glassboro, NJ 08028	1923	Dr. Herman D. James 5-M	9,500	445
Glenville State Coll, Glenville, WV 26351	1872	Dr. William K. Simmons . . . 5-B	2,204	100
GMI Engineering & Management Inst, Flint, MI 48504	1919	Dr. William B. Cottingham . . 1-M	3,148	125
Golden Gate U, San Francisco, CA 94105	1901	Dr. Otto W. Butz 1-D	8,729	766
Goldey-Beacom Coll, Wilmington, DE 19808	1886	Mr. William R. Baldt 1-B	1,920	65
Gonzaga U, Spokane, WA 99258	1887	Rev. Bernard J. Coughlin, SJ 2-D	3,840	288
Gordon Coll, Wenham, MA 01984	1889	Dr. Richard F. Gross 2-B	1,216	94
Goshen Coll, Goshen, IN 46526	1894	Dr. Victor Stoltzfus 2-B	1,152	112
Goucher Coll, Baltimore, MD 21204	1885	Dr. Rhoda M. Dorsey 1-M	968	143
Governors State U, University Park, IL 60466	1969	Dr. Leo Goodman-Malamuth, II 5-M	5,314	270
Graceland Coll, Lamoni, IA 50140	1895	Dr. Barbara J. Higdon 2-B	898	70
Grambling State U, Grambling, LA 71245	1901	Dr. Joseph B. Johnson . . . 5-M	6,205	275
Grand Canyon U, Phoenix, AZ 85061	1949	Dr. Bill Williams 2-M	1,842	161
Grand Rapids Baptist Coll and Sem, Grand Rapids, MI 49505	1941	Dr. Charles Wagner 2-M	902	48
Grand Valley State U, Allendale, MI 49401	1960	Mr. Arend D. Lubbers 5-M	10,914	408
Grand View Coll, Des Moines, IA 50316	1896	Dr. Arthur E. Puotinen 2-B	1,407	106
Greensboro Coll, Greensboro, NC 27401	1838	Dr. William H. Likins 2-B	1,078	80
Griffin Coll, Seattle, WA 98121	1909	Wayne P. Wilson 3-B	2,000	72
Grinnell Coll, Grinnell, IA 50112	1846	Dr. George A. Drake 1-B	1,233	135
Grove City Coll, Grove City, PA 16127	1876	Dr. Charles S. MacKenzie . . 2-B	2,125	124
Guilford Coll, Greensboro, NC 27410	1837	Dr. William R. Rogers 2-B	1,155	114
Gustavus Adolphus Coll, St Peter, MN 56082	1862	Dr. John S. Kendall 2-B	2,349	194
Gwynedd-Mercy Coll, Gwynedd Valley, PA 19437 (4)	1948	Sr. Isabelle Keiss, RSM . . . 2-M	1,934	166
Hahnemann U, Philadelphia, PA 19102	1848	Mr. Iqbal F. Paroo 1-D	1,326	430
Hamilton Coll, Clinton, NY 13323	1812	Dr. Harry C. Payne 1-B	1,673	178
Hamline U, St Paul, MN 55104	1854	Dr. Larry G. Osnes 2-M	2,235	143
Hampden-Sydney Coll, Hampden-Sydney, VA 23943 (1)	1776	Dr. James R. Leutze 2-B	944	90
Hampshire Coll, Amherst, MA 01002	1965	Mr. Gregory S. Prince, Jr. . . 1-B	1,282	100
Hampton U, Hampton, VA 23668	1868	Dr. William R. Harvey 1-M	5,342	380
Hannibal-LaGrange Coll, Hannibal, MO 63401	1858	Dr. Paul Brown 2-B	995	66
Hanover Coll, Hanover, IN 47243	1827	Dr. Russell L. Nichols 2-B	1,072	92
Harding U, Searcy, AR 72143	1924	Dr. David B. Burks, Jr. 2-M	3,284	185
Hardin-Simmons U, Abilene, TX 79698	1891	Dr. Jesse C. Fletcher 2-M	1,863	138
Harris-Stowe State Coll, St Louis, MO 63103	1857	Dr. Henry Givens, Jr. 5-B	1,881	110
Hartwick Coll, Oneonta, NY 13820	1797	Dr. Philip S. Wilder, Jr. . . . 1-B	1,534	145
Harvard U, Cambridge, MA 02138	1636	Mr. Derek Bok 1-D	17,856	800
Hastings Coll, Hastings, NE 68902	1882	Dr. Thomas J. Reeves 2-M	953	84
Haverford Coll, Haverford, PA 19041	1833	Tom G. Kessinger 1-B	1,159	128
Hawaii Pacific U, Honolulu, HI 96813	1965	Mr. Chatt Wright 1-M	4,962	228

Name, address	Year	Governing official, control, and highest degree offered	Enrollment	Faculty
Heidelberg Coll, Tiffin, OH 44883	1850	Dr. William C. Cassell ... 2-M	1,303	NR
Henderson State U, Arkadelphia, AR 71923	1890	Dr. Charles D. Dunn ... 5-M	3,369	163
Hendrix Coll, Conway, AR 72032	1876	Dr. Joe B. Hatcher ... 2-B	1,029	78
High Point Coll, High Point, NC 27261	1924	Dr. Jacob C. Martinson, Jr. ... 2-B	2,023	114
Hillsdale Coll, Hillsdale, MI 49242	1844	Dr. George C. Roche, III ... 1-B	1,102	102
Hiram Coll, Hiram, OH 44234	1850	Dr. G. Benjamin Oliver ... 2-B	930	86
Hobart Coll, Geneva, NY 14456 (1)	1822	Mr. Carroll Brewster ... 2-B	1,105	178
Hofstra U, Hempstead, NY 11550	1935	Dr. James M. Shuart ... 1-D	12,225	856
Hollins Coll, Roanoke, VA 24020 (3)	1842	Dr. Paula P. Brownlee ... 1-M	1,108	96
Holy Family Coll, Philadelphia, PA 19114	1954	Sr. M. Francesca Onley ... 2-B	1,859	176
Holy Names Coll, Oakland, CA 94619	1868	Sr. Lois MacGillivray, SNJM ... 2-M	812	81
Hood Coll, Frederick, MD 21701 (4)	1893	Dr. Martha E. Church ... 2-M	1,976	93
Hope Coll, Holland, MI 49423	1862	Dr. John Jacobson, Jr. ... 2-B	2,770	231
Houghton Coll, Houghton, NY 14744	1883	Dr. Daniel R. Chamberlain ... 2-B	1,164	104
Houston Baptist U, Houston, TX 77074	1960	Dr. E. Douglas Hodo ... 2-M	2,243	145
Howard Payne U, Brownwood, TX 76801	1889	Dr. Don Newbury ... 2-B	1,283	88
Howard U, Washington, DC 20059	1867	Franklyn G. Jenifer ... 1-D	11,452	1,100
Humboldt State U, Arcata, CA 95521	1913	Dr. Alistair W. McCrone ... 5-M	7,301	529
Hunter Coll of the City U of New York, New York, NY 10021	1870	Dr. Paul Le Clerc ... 12-M	20,038	NR
Huntingdon Coll, Montgomery, AL 36194	1854	Dr. Allen K. Jackson ... 2-B	838	68
Husson Coll, Bangor, ME 04401	1898	Dr. William H. Beardsley ... 1-M	1,722	57
Idaho State U, Pocatello, ID 83209	1901	Dr. Richard Bowen ... 5-D	8,700	459
Illinois Benedictine Coll, Lisle, IL 60532	1887	Dr. Richard C. Becker ... 2-M	2,662	195
Illinois Coll, Jacksonville, IL 62650	1829	Dr. Donald C. Mundinger ... 2-B	813	85
Illinois Inst of Tech, Chicago, IL 60616	1892	Dr. Henry Linden ... 1-D	6,300	510
Illinois State U, Normal, IL 61761	1857	Thomas P. Wallace ... 5-D	23,108	1,059
Illinois Wesleyan U, Bloomington, IL 61702	1850	Dr. Minor Myers, Jr. ... 2-B	1,749	172
Immaculata Coll, immaculata, PA 19345 (4)	1920	Sr. Marian William ... 2-M	2,200	152
Incarnate Word Coll, San Antonio, TX 78209	1881	Dr. Louis J. Agnese, Jr. ... 2-M	2,429	156
Indiana Inst of Tech, Fort Wayne, IN 46803	1930	Donald J. Andorfer ... 1-B	902	42
Indiana State U, Terre Haute, IN 47809	1865	Dr. Richard G. Landini ... 5-D	12,005	778
Indiana U at Kokomo, Kokomo, IN 46904	1945	Dr. Hugh L. Thompson ... 5-M	3,438	195
Indiana U at South Bend, South Bend, IN 46634	1922	H. Daniel Cohen ... 5-M	6,981	463
Indiana U Bloomington, Bloomington, IN 47405	1820	Kenneth R. R. Gros Louis ... 5-D	34,863	1,640
Indiana U East, Richmond, IN 47374	1971	Dr. Charlie Nelms ... 5-B	1,921	126
Indiana U Northwest, Gary, IN 46408	1959	Dr. Peggy G. Elliott ... 5-M	4,813	310
Indiana U of Pennsylvania, Indiana, PA 15705	1875	Dr. John D. Welty ... 5-D	13,861	805
Indiana U–Purdue U at Fort Wayne, Fort Wayne, IN 46805	1917	Dr. Joanne B. Lantz ... 5-M	11,422	667
Indiana U–Purdue U at Indianapolis, Indianapolis, IN 46202	1969	Gerald L. Bepko, Jr. ... 5-D	26,649	1,922
Indiana U Southeast, New Albany, IN 47150	1941	Dr. Leon Rand ... 5-M	5,452	304
Indiana Wesleyan U, Marion, IN 46953	1920	Dr. James Barnes ... 2-M	1,068	100
Inter American U of PR, Aguadilla Regional Coll, Aguadilla, PR 00605	1957	Ms. Hilda Baco ... 1-B	3,629	163
Inter American U of PR, San Germán Cmps, San Germán, PR 00753	1912	Dr. Federico Matheu ... 1-M	5,553	277
Iona Coll, New Rochelle, NY 10801	1940	Dr. John G. Driscoll, CFC ... 1-M	6,090	375
Iowa State U of Science and Tech, Ames, IA 50011	1858	Dr. Gordon P. Eaton ... 5-D	25,489	2,006
Iowa Wesleyan Coll, Mount Pleasant, IA 52641	1842	Robert J. Prins ... 2-B	803	52
Ithaca Coll, Ithaca, NY 14850	1892	Dr. James J. Whalen ... 1-M	6,389	536
ITT Tech Inst, Fort Wayne, IN 46825	1967	Jack B. Cozad ... 3-B	1,027	31
ITT Tech Inst, Indianapolis, IN 46268	1966	Alan Crews ... 3-B	1,215	45
Jackson State U, Jackson, MS 39217	1877	Dr. James A. Hefner ... 5-D	7,152	395
Jacksonville State U, Jacksonville, AL 36265	1883	Dr. Harold J. McGee ... 5-M	8,260	367
Jacksonville U, Jacksonville, FL 32211	1934	Dr. James J. Brady ... 1-M	2,445	NR
James Madison U, Harrisonburg, VA 22807	1908	Dr. Ronald E. Carrier ... 5-M	10,709	651
Jamestown Coll, Jamestown, ND 58401	1883	Dr. James Walker ... 2-B	841	51
Jersey City State Coll, Jersey City, NJ 07305	1927	Dr. William J. Maxwell ... 5-M	6,972	420
John Brown U, Siloam Springs, AR 72761	1919	Dr. John E. Brown, III ... 2-B	930	80
John Carroll U, University Heights, OH 44118	1886	Rev. Michael J. Lavelle, SJ ... 2-M	4,407	271
John Jay Coll of Criminal Justice of City U of NY, New York, NY 10019	1964	Dr. Gerald Lynch ... 12-D	8,300	507
Johns Hopkins U, Baltimore, MD 21218	1876	Dr. Steven Muller ... 1-D	4,147	716
Johnson & Wales U, Providence, RI 02903	1914	Dr. John A. Yena ... 1-M	7,085	312
Johnson C Smith U, Charlotte, NC 28216	1867	Dr. Robert L. Albright ... 1-B	1,310	97
Johnson State Coll, Johnson, VT 05656	1828	Mr. Eric R. Gilbertson ... 5-M	1,652	104
Jones Coll, Jacksonville, FL 32211	1918	James M. Patch ... 1-B	1,500	57
Juilliard Sch, New York, NY 10023	1905	Dr. Joseph W. Polisi ... 1-D	815	220
Juniata Coll, Huntingdon, PA 16652	1876	Dr. Robert W. Neff ... 1-B	1,125	89
Kalamazoo Coll, Kalamazoo, MI 49007	1833	Dr. Timothy Light ... 1-B	1,255	106
Kansas Newman Coll, Wichita, KS 67213	1933	Dr. Timothy J. Duszynski ... 2-B	851	43
Kansas State U, Manhattan, KS 66506	1863	Dr. Jon Wefald ... 5-D	20,110	1,843
Kansas Wesleyan U, Salina, KS 67401	1886	Dr. Marshall P. Stanton ... 2-B	761	48
Kean Coll of New Jersey, Union, NJ 07083	1855	Dr. Elsa Gomez ... 5-M	12,891	756
Keene State Coll, Keene, NH 03431	1909	Dr. Judith A. Sturnick ... 5-M	3,403	250
Kennesaw State Coll, Marietta, GA 30061	1966	Dr. Betty L. Siegel ... 5-M	9,140	359
Kent State U, Kent, OH 44242	1910	Dr. Michael Schwartz ... 5-D	23,727	1,238
Kentucky State U, Frankfort, KY 40601	1886	Dr. Mary L. Smith ... 13-M	2,190	158
Kentucky Wesleyan Coll, Owensboro, KY 42302	1858	Dr. Paul W. Hartman ... 2-B	850	80
Kenyon Coll, Gambier, OH 43022	1824	Dr. Philip H. Jordan, Jr. ... 1-B	1,524	166
King's Coll, Wilkes-Barre, PA 18711	1946	Rev. James Lackenmier, CSC ... 2-B	2,324	165
Knox Coll, Galesburg, IL 61401	1837	Dr. John P. McCall ... 1-B	1,029	88
Knoxville Coll, Knoxville, TN 37921	1875	Mr. John B. Turner ... 2-B	1,225	95
Kutztown U of Pennsylvania, Kutztown, PA 19530	1866	Dr. David E. McFarland ... 5-M	7,609	358
Lafayette Coll, Easton, PA 18042	1826	Dr. David W. Ellis ... 2-B	1,993	195
LaGrange Coll, LaGrange, GA 30240	1831	Dr. Walter Y. Murphy ... 2-M	964	74
Lake Erie Coll, Painesville, OH 44077	1856	Dr. Clodus R. Smith ... 1-M	844	62
Lake Forest Coll, Lake Forest, IL 60045	1857	Dr. Eugene Hotchkiss, III ... 1-M	1,124	106
Lakeland Coll, Sheboygan, WI 53082	1862	Dr. David R. Black ... 2-B	1,766	42
Lake Superior State U, Sault Sainte Marie, MI 49783	1946	Dr. H. Erik Shaar ... 5-M	3,432	155
Lamar U, Beaumont, TX 77710	1923	Dr. Bill J. Franklin ... 5-D	11,848	725
Lambuth Coll, Jackson, TN 38301	1843	Dr. Thomas F. Boyd ... 2-B	804	53
Lander Coll, Greenwood, SC 29649	1872	Dr. Larry A. Jackson ... 5-M	2,334	156

Name, address	Year	Governing official, control, and highest degree offered	Enroll-ment	Faculty
Laredo State U, Laredo, TX 78040	1969	Dr. Leo Sayavedra 5-M	1,123	57
La Roche Coll, Pittsburgh, PA 15237	1963	Sr. Margaret Huber 2-M	1,868	128
La Salle U, Philadelphia, PA 19141	1863	Br. Patrick Ellis 2-M	6,640	326
Lawrence Tech U, Southfield, MI 48075	1932	Dr. Richard E. Marburger . 1-M	5,509	301
Lawrence U, Appleton, WI 54912	1847	Dr. Richard Warch 1-B	1,228	121
Lebanon Valley Coll, Annville, PA 17003	1866	Mr. John A. Synodinos . . . 2-M	1,303	121
Lee Coll, Cleveland, TN 37311	1918	Dr. Paul Conn 2-B	1,535	118
Lees-McRae Coll, Banner Elk, NC 28604	1900	Dr. Bradford L. Crain . . . 2-B	833	59
Lehigh U, Bethlehem, PA 18015	1865	Dr. Peter Likins 1-D	6,569	487
Lehman Coll of the City U of New York, Bronx, NY 10468	1931	Dr. Leonard Lief 12-M	9,851	628
Le Moyne Coll, Syracuse, NY 13214	1946	Rev. Kevin G. O'Connell, SJ 2-B	1,974	191
Lenoir-Rhyne Coll, Hickory, NC 28603	1891	Dr. John E. Trainer, Jr. . . 2-M	1,853	135
Lesley Coll, Cambridge, MA 02138 (3)	1909	Margaret A. McKenna . . . 1-D	4,747	34
LeTourneau U, Longview, TX 75607	1946	Dr. Alvin O. Austin 2-B	773	59
Lewis and Clark Coll, Portland, OR 97219	1867	Dr. Michael J. Mooney . . . 1-D	2,721	151
Lewis-Clark State Coll, Lewiston, ID 83501	1894	Dr. Lee A. Vickers 5-B	2,164	107
Lewis U, Romeoville, IL 60441	1932	Br. James Gaffney, FSC . . 2-M	3,500	160
Liberty U, Lynchburg, VA 24506	1971	Dr. A. Pierre Guillermin . . 2-M	16,805	275
Limestone Coll, Gaffney, SC 29340	1845	Dr. G. Frederick Payne . . 1-B	940	77
Lincoln Memorial U, Harrogate, TN 37752	1897	Dr. Gary J. Burchett 1-M	1,785	109
Lincoln U, Jefferson City, MO 65101	1866	Dr. Wendell G. Rayburn . . 5-M	3,063	160
Lincoln U, Lincoln University, PA 19352	1854	Dr. Niara Sudarkasa 13-M	1,304	131
Lindenwood Coll, St Charles, MO 63301	1827	Dr. Dennis Spellmann . . . 2-M	2,105	108
Lindsey Wilson Coll, Columbia, KY 42728	1903	Dr. John B. Begley 2-B	1,153	53
Linfield Coll, McMinnville, OR 97128	1849	Dr. Charles U. Walker . . . 2-M	1,312	115
Livingston U, Livingston, AL 35470	1835	Dr. Asa N. Green 5-M	1,761	98
Lock Haven U of Pennsylvania, Lock Haven, PA 17745	1870	Dr. Craig Dean Willis . . . 5-M	3,012	188
Lockyear Coll, Evansville Cmps, Evansville, IN 47706	1893	Tony A. Payne 3-B	801	59
Loma Linda U, Riverside, CA 92515	1915	Dr. R. Dale McCune 2-D	4,243	NR
Long Island U, Brooklyn Cmps, Brooklyn, NY 11201	1926	Dr. David J. Steinberg . . . 1-D	4,600	400
Long Island U, C W Post Cmps, Brookville, NY 11548	1954	Dr. David J. Steinberg . . . 1-M	8,964	685
Long Island U, Southampton Cmps, Southampton, NY 11968	1963	Dr. David J. Steinberg . . . 1-M	1,230	119
Longwood Coll, Farmville, VA 23901	1839	Dr. William F. Dorrill . . . 5-M	3,142	181
Loras Coll, Dubuque, IA 52001	1839	Rev. Msgr. James Barta . . 2-M	2,054	156
Los Angeles Coll of Chiropractic, Whittier, CA 90609	1911	Dr. E. Maylon Drake 1-D	1,003	81
Louisiana Coll, Pineville, LA 71359	1906	Dr. Robert L. Lynn 2-B	1,242	80
Louisiana State U and A&M Coll, Baton Rouge, LA 70803	1860	Dr. E. Grady Bogue 5-D	25,977	1,279
Louisiana State U in Shreveport, Shreveport, LA 71115	1965	Dr. E. Grady Bogue 5-M	4,110	218
Louisiana Tech U, Ruston, LA 71272	1894	Dr. Daniel D. Reneau . . . 5-D	10,018	421
Lourdes Coll, Sylvania, OH 43560	1958	Sr. Ann Francis Klimkowski, OSF 2-B	886	108
Loyola Coll, Baltimore, MD 21210	1852	Rev. Joseph A. Sellinger, SJ 2-D	6,136	404
Loyola Marymount U, Los Angeles, CA 90045	1911	Rev. James N. Loughran, SJ 2-D	5,347	411
Loyola U Chicago, Chicago, IL 60611	1870	Rev. Raymond C. Baumhart, SJ 2-D	14,343	746
Loyola U, New Orleans, New Orleans, LA 70118	1912	Rev. James C. Carter, SJ . 2-D	4,916	360
Lubbock Christian U, Lubbock, TX 79407	1957	Dr. Steven S. Lemley . . . 2-M	1,075	110
Luther Coll, Decorah, IA 52101	1861	Dr. H. George Anderson . . 2-B	2,299	191
Lycoming Coll, Williamsport, PA 17701	1812	Dr. James E. Douthat . . . 2-B	1,204	98
Lynchburg Coll, Lynchburg, VA 24501	1903	Dr. George N. Rainsford . . 2-M	2,559	173
Lyndon State Coll, Lyndonville, VT 05851	1911	Dr. Margaret R. Williams . 5-M	1,034	85
Macalester Coll, St Paul, MN 55105	1874	Dr. Robert M. Gavin, Jr. . . 2-B	1,855	211
Madonna Coll, Livonia, MI 48150	1947	Sr. Mary Francilene 2-M	4,064	223
Malone Coll, Canton, OH 44709	1892	Dr. E. Arthur Self 2-M	1,457	90
Manchester Coll, North Manchester, IN 46962	1889	Dr. William P. Robinson . . 2-M	1,100	93
Manhattan Coll, Riverdale, NY 10471	1853	Br. Thomas J. Scanlan . . . 1-M	3,836	316
Manhattan Sch of Music, New York, NY 10027	1917	Dr. Peter C. Simon 1-D	838	214
Manhattanville Coll, Purchase, NY 10577	1841	Dr. Marcia Savage 1-M	1,500	130
Mankato State U, Mankato, MN 56001	1867	Dr. Margaret R. Preska . . 5-M	16,185	680
Mannes Coll of Music, New York, NY 10024	1916	Dr. Charles Kaufman 1-M	120	216
Mansfield U of Pennsylvania, Mansfield, PA 16933	1857	Mr. Rod C. Kelchner 5-M	3,233	176
Marian Coll, Indianapolis, IN 46222	1851	Dr. Daniel A. Felicetti . . . 2-B	1,228	123
Marian Coll of Fond du Lac, Fond du Lac, WI 54935	1936	Matthew G. Flanigan 2-M	1,000	81
Marietta Coll, Marietta, OH 45750	1835	Dr. Patrick D. McDonough . 1-M	1,365	109
Marist Coll, Poughkeepsie, NY 12601	1929	Dr. Dennis J. Murray 1-M	4,479	302
Marquette U, Milwaukee, WI 53233	1881	Rev. John P. Raynor, SJ . . 2-D	12,025	985
Marshall U, Huntington, WV 25755	1837	Dr. Dale F. Nitzschke . . . 5-D	12,580	573
Mars Hill Coll, Mars Hill, NC 28754	1856	Dr. Fred B. Bentley 2-B	1,344	137
Marycrest Coll, Davenport, IA 52804	1939	Dr. Wanda D. Bigham . . . 2-M	2,357	79
Marygrove Coll, Detroit, MI 48221	1910	Dr. John E. Shay, Jr. . . . 2-M	1,230	67
Maryland Inst Coll of Art, Baltimore, MD 21217	1826	Mr. Fred Lazarus 1-M	923	126
Marylhurst Coll, Marylhurst, OR 97036	1893	Nancy A. Wilgenbusch . . . 2-M	1,031	274
Marymount Coll, Tarrytown, NY 10591 (4)	1907	Sr. Brigid Driscoll 1-B	1,122	145
Marymount Manhattan Coll, New York, NY 10021 (4)	1936	Sr. Raymunde McKay . . . 1-B	1,200	155
Marymount U, Arlington, VA 22207	1950	Sr. M. Majella Berg, RSHM 2-M	2,934	218
Maryville Coll, Maryville, TN 37801	1819	Dr. Richard I. Ferrin 2-B	787	58
Maryville Coll–Saint Louis, St Louis, MO 63141	1872	Dr. Claudius Pritchard . . . 1-M	3,143	205
Mary Washington Coll, Fredericksburg, VA 22401	1908	Dr. William M. Anderson, Jr. 5-M	3,533	197
Marywood Coll, Scranton, PA 18509	1915	Sr. Mary Reap, IHM 2-M	2,929	211
Massachusetts Coll of Art, Boston, MA 02115	1873	Dr. William F. O'Neil 5-M	1,154	96
Mass Coll of Pharmacy and Allied Health Sciences, Boston, MA 02115	1823	Dr. Louis P. Jeffrey 1-D	1,128	122
Massachusetts Inst of Tech, Cambridge, MA 02139	1861	Dr. Paul E. Gray 1-D	9,500	985
Master's Coll, Newhall, CA 91322	1927	Dr. John F. MacArthur, Jr. . 2-M	1,008	75
Mayville State U, Mayville, ND 58257	1889	Dr. James A. Schobel . . . 5-B	764	50
McKendree Coll, Lebanon, IL 62254	1828	Dr. Gerrit J. TenBrink . . . 2-B	1,098	72
McMurry U, Abilene, TX 79697	1923	Dr. Thomas K. Kim 2-B	1,720	118
McNeese State U, Lake Charles, LA 70609	1939	Dr. Robert D. Hebert . . . 5-M	7,579	342
Medaille Coll, Buffalo, NY 14214	1875	Kevin I. Sullivan 1-B	1,021	70
Medgar Evers Coll of the City U of New York, Brooklyn, NY 11225	1969	Dr. Leo A. Corbie 12-B	2,733	272
Medical Coll of Georgia, Augusta, GA 30912	1828	Dr. Francis J. Tedesco . . . 5-D	1,946	127
Medical U of South Carolina, Charleston, SC 29425	1824	Dr. James B. Edwards . . . 5-D	2,194	1,804
Memphis State U, Memphis, TN 38152	1912	Dr. Thomas G. Carpenter . 5-D	20,728	1,013
Mercer U, Macon, GA 31207	1833	Dr. R. Kirby Godsey 2-D	3,985	165
Mercer U Atlanta, Atlanta, GA 30341	1968	Dr. R. Kirby Godsey 2-D	1,300	126

Name, address	Year	Governing official, control, and highest degree offered		Enrollment	Faculty
Mercy Coll, Dobbs Ferry, NY 10522	1951	Dr. Wilbert J. LeMelle	1-M	5,548	640
Mercy Coll of Detroit, Detroit, MI 48219	1941	Maureen A. Fay, OP	2-M	2,218	210
Mercyhurst Coll, Erie, PA 16546	1926	Dr. William P. Garvey	2-M	2,145	117
Meredith Coll, Raleigh, NC 27607 (3)	1891	Dr. John E. Weems	2-M	2,212	183
Merrimack Coll, North Andover, MA 01845	1947	Rev. John E. Deegan, OSA	2-B	2,480	176
Mesa State Coll, Grand Junction, CO 81502	1925	Dr. Ray N. Kieft	5-B	3,958	146
Messiah Coll, Grantham, PA 17027	1909	Dr. D. Ray Hostetter	2-B	2,280	203
Methodist Coll, Fayetteville, NC 28311	1956	Dr. M. Elton Hendricks	2-B	1,447	82
Metropolitan State Coll, Denver, CO 80204	1965	Dr. Thomas Brewer, Jr.	5-B	16,278	853
Metropolitan State U, St Paul, MN 55101	1971	Dr. Charles J. Graham	5-M	6,602	678
Miami U, Oxford, OH 45056	1809	Dr. Paul G. Pearson	5-D	16,157	873
Michigan State U, East Lansing, MI 48824	1855	Dr. John DiBiaggio	5-D	42,866	4,101
Michigan Tech U, Houghton, MI 49931	1885	Dr. Dale F. Stein	5-D	6,662	370
MidAmerica Nazarene Coll, Olathe, KS 66061	1966	Dr. Richard Spindle	2-M	1,189	81
Middlebury Coll, Middlebury, VT 05753	1800	Dr. Olin C. Robison	1-D	1,950	200
Middle Tennessee State U, Murfreesboro, TN 37132	1911	Dr. Wallace S. Prescott	5-D	14,136	653
Midland Lutheran Coll, Fremont, NE 68025	1883	Dr. Carl L. Hansen	2-B	935	65
Midwestern State U, Wichita Falls, TX 76308	1922	Dr. Louis J. Rodriguez	5-M	5,512	208
Millersville U of Pennsylvania, Millersville, PA 17551	1854	Dr. Joseph A. Caputo	5-M	7,791	405
Milligan Coll, Milligan College, TN 37682	1866	Dr. Marshall J. Leggett	2-M	760	63
Millikin U, Decatur, IL 62522	1901	Dr. J. Roger Miller	2-B	1,805	172
Millsaps Coll, Jackson, MS 39210	1890	Dr. George M. Harmon	2-M	1,443	105
Mills Coll, Oakland, CA 94613 (3)	1852	Dr. Mary S. Metz	1-M	1,050	167
Milwaukee Sch of Engineering, Milwaukee, WI 53201	1903	Dr. Robert R. Spitzer	1-M	2,170	211
Minot State U, Minot, ND 58701	1913	Dr. Gordon B. Olson	5-M	3,304	171
Mississippi Coll, Clinton, MS 39058	1826	Dr. Lewis Nobles	2-D	4,221	176
Mississippi State U, Mississippi State, MS 39762	1878	Dr. Donald W. Zacharias	5-D	13,141	883
Mississippi U for Women, Columbus, MS 39701 (4)	1884	Dr. Clyda S. Rent	5-M	2,085	126
Mississippi Valley State U, Itta Bena, MS 38941	1946	Dr. William W. Sutton	5-M	1,691	136
Missouri Baptist Coll, St Louis, MO 63141	1968	Dr. Patrick O. Copley	2-M	1,032	60
Missouri Southern State Coll, Joplin, MO 64801	1937	Dr. Julio Leon	5-B	5,901	270
Missouri Valley Coll, Marshall, MO 65340	1889	Dr. Earl J. Reeves	2-B	1,177	60
Missouri Western State Coll, St Joseph, MO 64507	1915	Dr. Janet Gorman Murphy	5-B	4,338	251
Mobile Coll, Mobile, AL 36613	1961	Dr. Michael A. Magnoli	2-M	1,190	92
Molloy Coll, Rockville Centre, NY 11570	1955	Dr. Janet A. Fitzgerald, OP	1-M	1,534	158
Monmouth Coll, West Long Branch, NJ 07764	1933	Dr. Samuel H. Magill	1-M	4,273	320
Montana Coll of Mineral Science and Tech, Butte, MT 59701	1895	Dr. Lindsay D. Norman, Jr.	5-M	1,771	115
Montana State U, Bozeman, MT 59717	1893	Dr. William J. Tietz	5-D	10,251	550
Montclair State Coll, Upper Montclair, NJ 07043	1908	Dr. Irvin D. Reid	5-M	13,070	782
Moody Bible Inst, Chicago, IL 60610	1886	Dr. Joseph M. Stowell, III	2-M	1,507	106
Moorhead State U, Moorhead, MN 56560	1887	Dr. Roland Dille	5-M	8,793	417
Moravian Coll, Bethlehem, PA 18018	1742	Dr. Roger Harry Martin	2-M	1,785	135
Morehead State U, Morehead, KY 40351	1922	Dr. C. Nelson Grote	5-M	7,965	388
Morehouse Coll, Atlanta, GA 30314 (1)	1867	Dr. Leroy Keith, Jr.	1-B	2,620	150
Morgan State U, Baltimore, MD 21239	1867	Dr. Earl Richardson	5-D	4,399	NR
Morningside Coll, Sioux City, IA 51106	1894	Dr. Miles Tommeraasen	2-M	1,240	98
Morris Brown Coll, Atlanta, GA 30314	1881	Dr. Calvert H. Smith	2-B	1,805	NR
Morris Coll, Sumter, SC 29150	1908	Dr. Luns C. Richardson	2-B	796	55
Mount Holyoke Coll, South Hadley, MA 01075 (3)	1837	Mrs. Elizabeth T. Kennan	1-B	1,948	186
Mount Marty Coll, Yankton, SD 57078	1936	Sr. Jacquelyn Ernster	2-M	917	81
Mount Mary Coll, Milwaukee, WI 53222 (3)	1913	Sr. Ruth Hollenbach	2-M	1,420	135
Mount Mercy Coll, Cedar Rapids, IA 52402	1928	Dr. Thomas R. Feld	2-B	1,591	109
Mount Olive Coll, Mount Olive, NC 28365	1951	Dr. W. Burkette Raper	2-B	996	66
Mount Saint Mary Coll, Newburgh, NY 12550	1930	Sr. Ann Sakac	1-M	1,281	105
Mount St Mary's Coll, Los Angeles, CA 90049 (4)	1925	Sr. Karen Kennelly	2-M	1,152	141
Mount Saint Mary's Coll, Emmitsburg, MD 21727	1808	Dr. Robert J. Wickenheiser	2-M	1,866	132
Mount Senario Coll, Ladysmith, WI 54848	1962	Dr. John N. Cable	1-B	1,067	40
Mount Union Coll, Alliance, OH 44601	1846	Dr. Harold M. Kolenbrander	2-B	1,359	110
Mount Vernon Nazarene Coll, Mount Vernon, OH 43050	1964	Dr. E. LeBron	2-B	1,061	76
Muhlenberg Coll, Allentown, PA 18104	1848	Dr. Jonathan C. Messerli	2-B	1,630	132
Mundelein Coll, Chicago, IL 60660 (4)	1929	Sr. Mary Breslin, BVM	2-M	1,102	97
Murray State U, Murray, KY 42071	1922	Dr. Kala M. Stroup	5-M	8,044	371
Muskegon Coll, Muskegon, MI 49442	1888	Mr. Robert D. Jewell	1-B	1,741	60
Muskingum Coll, New Concord, OH 43762	1837	Dr. Samuel W. Speck, Jr.	2-B	1,122	95
National–Louis U, Evanston, IL 60201	1886	NR	1-D	7,436	193
National U, San Diego, CA 92108	1971	Dr. Jerry C. Lee	1-D	10,318	1,626
Nazareth Coll of Rochester, Rochester, NY 14610	1924	Dr. Rose Marie Beston	1-M	2,935	153
Nebraska Wesleyan U, Lincoln, NE 68504	1887	Dr. John W. White, Jr.	2-B	1,607	130
Neumann Coll, Aston, PA 19014	1965	Dr. Nan B. Hechenberger	2-M	1,093	73
New England Coll, Henniker, NH 03242	1946	William R. O'Connell, Jr.	1-M	1,296	117
New England Inst of Tech, Warwick, RI 02886 (2)	1940	Dr. Richard I. Gouse	1-B	1,941	125
New Hampshire Coll, Manchester, NH 03104	1932	Richard A. Gustafson	1-M	3,049	77
New Jersey Inst of Tech, Newark, NJ 07102	1881	Dr. Saul K. Fenster	13-D	7,801	528
New Mexico Highlands U, Las Vegas, NM 87701	1893	Dr. Gilbert Sanchez	5-M	2,234	105
New Mexico Inst of Mining and Tech, Socorro, NM 87801	1889	Dr. Laurence H. Lattman	5-D	1,345	98
New Mexico State U, Las Cruces, NM 88003	1888	Dr. James E. Halligan	5-D	14,300	780
New Sch Bach of Arts, New Sch for Social Research, New York, NY 10011	1919	Gerald A. Heeger	1-B	254	545
New York Inst of Tech, Old Westbury, NY 11568	1955	Dr. Alexander Schure	1-M	12,744	1,340
New York U, New York, NY 10011	1831	Dr. John Brademas	1-D	30,966	3,732
Niagara University, Niagara, NY 14109	1856	Rev. Brian J. O'Connell, CM	1-M	3,137	234
Nicholls State U, Thibodaux, LA 70310	1948	Dr. Donald J. Ayo	5-M	6,845	265
Nichols Coll, Dudley, MA 01570	1815	Dr. Lowell C. Smith	1-M	1,968	49
Norfolk State U, Norfolk, VA 23504	1935	Dr. Harrison B. Wilson	5-M	7,721	511
North Adams State Coll, North Adams, MA 01247	1894	Dr. Catherine Tisinger	5-M	2,341	127
North Carolina Agricultural and Tech State U, Greensboro, NC 27411	1891	Dr. Edward B. Fort	5-M	6,536	443
North Carolina Central U, Durham, NC 27707	1910	Dr. Tyronza R. Richmond	5-M	5,343	405
North Carolina State U, Raleigh, NC 27695	1887	Dr. Larry K. Monteith	5-D	26,209	1,442
North Carolina Wesleyan Coll, Rocky Mount, NC 27804	1956	Dr. Leslie H. Garner, Jr.	2-B	1,475	48
North Central Bible Coll, Minneapolis, MN 55404	1930	Dr. Don H. Argue	2-B	1,174	65
North Central Coll, Naperville, IL 60566	1861	Mr. Gael D. Swing	2-M	2,555	167
North Dakota State U, Fargo, ND 58105	1890	Dr. Jim Ozbun	5-D	9,432	420
Northeastern Illinois U, Chicago, IL 60625	1961	Dr. Gordon Lamb	5-M	10,293	539
Northeastern State U, Tahlequah, OK 74464	1846	Dr. W. Roger Webb	5-D	8,723	329
Northeastern U, Boston, MA 02115	1898	John A. Curry	1-D	32,809	2,442

Name, address	Year	Governing official, control, and highest degree offered	Enrollment	Faculty
Northeast Louisiana U, Monroe, LA 71209	1931	Dr. Dwight D. Vines ... 5-D	10,560	428
Northeast Missouri State U, Kirksville, MO 63501	1867	Dr. Charles J. McClain ... 5-M	6,158	404
Northern Arizona U, Flagstaff, AZ 86011	1899	Dr. Eugene M. Hughes ... 5-D	16,095	899
Northern Illinois U, De Kalb, IL 60115	1895	Dr. John E. LaTourette ... 5-D	24,443	1,283
Northern Kentucky U, Highland Heights, KY 41076	1968	Dr. Leon E. Boothe ... 5-M	9,555	579
Northern Michigan U, Marquette, MI 49855	1899	Dr. James B. Appleberry ... 5-M	8,375	368
Northern State Coll, Aberdeen, SD 57401	1901	Dr. Terence Brown ... 5-M	3,100	NR
North Georgia Coll, Dahlonega, GA 30597	1873	Dr. John H. Owen ... 5-M	2,353	111
North Park Coll, Chicago, IL 60625	1891	Dr. David G. Horner ... 2-B	1,098	70
Northrop U, Los Angeles, CA 90045	1942	Dr. John R. Beljan ... 1-D	1,057	157
Northwestern Coll, Orange City, IA 51041	1882	Dr. James E. Bultman ... 2-M	1,064	88
Northwestern Coll, St Paul, MN 55113	1902	Dr. Donald Ericksen ... 2-B	1,036	82
Northwestern Oklahoma State U, Alva, OK 73717	1897	Dr. Joe J. Struckle ... 5-M	1,816	96
Northwestern State U of Louisiana, Natchitoches, LA 71497	1884	Dr. Robert A. Alost ... 5-M	6,925	274
Northwestern U, Evanston, IL 60208	1851	Dr. Arnold R. Weber ... 1-D	11,554	870
Northwest Missouri State U, Maryville, MO 64468	1905	Dr. Dean L. Hubbard ... 5-M	5,901	274
Northwest Nazarene Coll, Nampa, ID 83686	1913	Dr. A. Gordon Wetmore ... 2-M	1,133	85
Northwood Inst, Midland, MI 48640	1959	Dr. David E. Fry ... 1-B	1,850	57
Norwich U, Northfield, VT 05663	1819	Lt. Gen. W. Russel Todd ... 1-M	2,308	218
Notre Dame Coll, Manchester, NH 03104	1950	Dr. Carol J. Descoteaux, CSC ... 2-M	1,095	80
Notre Dame Coll of Ohio, Cleveland, OH 44121 (3)	1922	Sr. Marla Loehr, SND ... 2-B	827	83
Nova U, Fort Lauderdale, FL 33314	1964	Dr. Abraham S. Fischler ... 1-D	14,308	239
Nyack Coll, Nyack, NY 10960	1882	Mr. Rexford A. Boda ... 2-M	814	77
Oakland U, Rochester, MI 48309	1957	Dr. Joseph E. Champagne ... 5-D	12,385	600
Oakwood Coll, Huntsville, AL 35896	1896	Dr. Benjamin F. Reaves ... 2-B	1,223	110
Oberlin Coll, Oberlin, OH 44074	1833	S. Frederick Starr ... 1-M	2,920	241
Occidental Coll, Los Angeles, CA 90041	1887	Dr. John B. Slaughter ... 1-M	1,697	147
Oglala Lakota Coll, Kyle, SD 57752	1970	Elgin Bad Wound ... 12-B	890	113
Oglethorpe U, Atlanta, GA 30319	1835	Dr. Donald S. Stanton ... 1-M	1,131	87
Ohio Dominican Coll, Columbus, OH 43219	1911	Sr. Mary Andrew Matesich ... 2-B	1,257	89
Ohio Northern U, Ada, OH 45810	1871	Dr. DeBow Freed ... 2-D	2,595	179
Ohio State U, Columbus, OH 43210	1870	Dr. Edward Jennings ... 5-D	52,895	3,796
Ohio State U–Lima Cmps, Lima, OH 45804	1960	Dr. James J. Countryman ... 5-B	1,313	NR
Ohio State U–Mansfield Cmps, Mansfield, OH 44906	1958	Dr. John O. Riedl, Jr. ... 5-B	1,336	NR
Ohio State U–Marion Cmps, Marion, OH 43302	1957	Francis E. Hazard ... 5-B	1,161	NR
Ohio State U–Newark Cmps, Newark, OH 43055	1957	Dr. Julius S. Greenstein ... 5-B	1,582	NR
Ohio U, Athens, OH 45701	1804	Dr. Charles J. Ping ... 5-D	16,500	950
Ohio U–Belmont, St Clairsville, OH 43950	1957	Dr. James W. Newton ... 5-B	1,080	45
Ohio U–Chillicothe, Chillicothe, OH 45601	1946	Dr. Delbert Meyer ... 5-B	1,501	67
Ohio U–Ironton, Ironton, OH 45638	1956	Mr. Bill Dingus ... 5-B	1,477	103
Ohio U–Lancaster, Lancaster, OH 43130	1968	Dr. Raymond Wilkes ... 5-M	1,369	114
Ohio U–Zanesville, Zanesville, OH 43701	1946	Dr. Craig D. Laubenthal ... 5-B	1,385	49
Ohio Wesleyan U, Delaware, OH 43015	1842	Dr. David L. Warren ... 2-B	1,966	160
Oklahoma Baptist U, Shawnee, OK 74801	1910	Dr. Bob R. Agee ... 2-B	2,173	128
Oklahoma Christian U of Science and Arts, Oklahoma City, OK 73136	1950	Dr. Terry Johnson ... 2-M	1,671	114
Oklahoma City U, Oklahoma City, OK 73106	1904	Dr. Jerald C. Walker ... 2-M	3,778	234
Oklahoma Panhandle State U, Goodwell, OK 73939	1909	Dr. Robert L. Griffin ... 5-B	1,250	71
Oklahoma State U, Stillwater, OK 74078	1890	Dr. John Campbell ... 5-D	20,110	733
Old Dominion U, Norfolk, VA 23529	1930	Hon. William B. Spong, Jr. ... 5-D	16,239	814
Olivet Coll, Olivet, MI 49076	1844	Dr. Donald A. Morris ... 2-B	766	63
Olivet Nazarene U, Kankakee, IL 60901	1907	Dr. Leslie Parrott ... 2-M	1,875	115
Oral Roberts U, Tulsa, OK 74171	1963	Mr. G. Oral Roberts ... 2-D	4,170	390
Oregon Health Sciences U, Portland, OR 97201	1974	Dr. Peter O. Kohler ... 5-D	1,317	162
Oregon Inst of Tech, Klamath Falls, OR 97601	1947	NR ... 5-B	3,023	144
Oregon State U, Corvallis, OR 97331	1868	Dr. John V. Byrne ... 5-D	15,958	2,362
Orlando Coll, Orlando, FL 32810	1918	Mrs. Ouida B. Kirby ... 3-M	1,220	44
Otis Art Inst Parsons Sch of Des, New Sch Soc Res, Los Angeles, CA 90057	1917	Roger Workman ... 1-M	794	193
Otterbein Coll, Westerville, OH 43081	1847	Dr. C. Brent DeVore ... 2-M	2,315	162
Ouachita Baptist U, Arkadelphia, AR 71923	1886	Dr. Ben M. Elrod ... 2-M	1,316	101
Our Lady of Holy Cross Coll, New Orleans, LA 70131	1916	Rev. Thomas E. Chambers, CSC ... 2-M	800	63
Our Lady of the Lake U of San Antonio, San Antonio, TX 78207	1911	Sr. Elizabeth Anne Sueltenfuss ... 2-D	2,381	144
Pace U, New York, NY 10038	1906	Dr. William G. Sharwell ... 1-D	9,194	1,222
Pace U, Pleasantville/Briarcliff Cmps, Pleasantville, NY 10570	1963	Dr. Richard Podgorski ... 1-M	4,028	1,222
Pace U, White Plains Cmps, White Plains, NY 10603	1923	Dr. Margaret R. Gotti ... 1-D	4,366	1,222
Pacific Lutheran U, Tacoma, WA 98447	1890	Dr. William O. Rieke ... 2-M	3,855	294
Pacific Union Coll, Angwin, CA 94508	1882	Dr. D. Malcolm Maxwell ... 2-M	1,678	116
Pacific U, Forest Grove, OR 97116	1849	Dr. Robert F. Duvall ... 1-D	1,398	111
Palm Beach Atlantic Coll, West Palm Beach, FL 33402	1968	Dr. Claude H. Rhea, Jr. ... 2-B	1,375	98
Palmer Coll of Chiropractic, Davenport, IA 52803	1895	Donald P. Kern ... 1-D	1,600	110
Parks Coll of Saint Louis U, Cahokia, IL 62206	1927	Dr. Paul A. Whelan ... 2-B	1,137	60
Parsons Sch of Design, New Sch for Social Research, New York, NY 10011	1896	Charles S. Olton ... 1-M	2,603	332
Pembroke State U, Pembroke, NC 28372	1887	Dr. Paul R. Givens ... 5-M	3,081	154
Penn State U at Erie, The Behrend Coll, Erie, PA 16563	1926	Dr. John M. Lilley ... 13-M	2,838	182
Penn State U at Harrisburg—The Capital Coll, Middletown, PA 17057	1966	Dr. Ruth Leventhal ... 13-D	3,276	173
Penn State U Univ Park Cmps, University Park, PA 16802	1855	Dr. Bryce Jordan ... 13-D	37,718	2,063
Pepperdine U, Culver City, CA 90230	1937	Dr. David Davenport ... 2-D	3,816	35
Pepperdine U, Malibu, CA 90265	1937	Dr. David Davenport ... 2-D	3,377	270
Peru State Coll, Peru, NE 68421	1867	Dr. Jerry L. Gallentine ... 5-M	1,835	82
Pfeiffer Coll, Misenheimer, NC 28109	1885	Dr. Zane E. Eargle ... 2-M	905	72
Philadelphia Coll of Pharmacy and Science, Philadelphia, PA 19104	1821	Dr. Allen Misher ... 1-D	1,621	161
Philadelphia Coll of Textiles and Science, Philadelphia, PA 19144	1884	Dr. James P. Gallagher ... 1-M	3,417	160
Phillips U, Enid, OK 73701	1906	Dr. Robert Peck ... 2-M	1,005	74
Pikeville Coll, Pikeville, KY 41501	1889	Mr. William H. Owens ... 2-B	915	64
Pittsburg State U, Pittsburg, KS 66762	1903	Dr. Donald W. Wilson ... 5-M	5,960	288
Pitzer Coll, Claremont, CA 91711	1963	Dr. Frank L. Ellsworth ... 1-B	770	88

Name, address	Year	Governing official, control, and highest degree offered		Enrollment	Faculty
Plymouth State Coll of the U System of NH, Plymouth, NH 03264	1871	Dr. William J. Farrell	5-M	4,000	200
Point Loma Nazarene Coll, San Diego, CA 92106	1902	Dr. Jim L. Bond	2-M	2,221	204
Point Park Coll, Pittsburgh, PA 15222	1960	Dr. J. Matthew Simon	1-M	3,035	194
Polytechnic U, Brooklyn Cmps, Brooklyn, NY 11201	1854	Dr. George Bugliarello	1-D	2,140	393
Polytechnic U, Farmingdale Cmps, Farmingdale, NY 11735	1854	Dr. James J. Conti	1-D	1,095	393
Pomona Coll, Claremont, CA 91711	1887	Dr. David Alexander	1-B	1,390	154
Portland State U, Portland, OR 97207	1946	Dr. Roger N. Edgington	5-D	14,838	697
Post Coll, Waterbury, CT 06708	1890	Dr. N. Patricia Yarborough	1-B	1,630	277
Prairie View A&M U, Prairie View, TX 77446	1878	Mr. Julius W. Becton	5-M	5,686	314
Pratt Inst, Brooklyn, NY 11205	1887	Mr. Richardson Pratt, Jr.	1-M	3,527	479
Presbyterian Coll, Clinton, SC 29325	1880	Dr. Kenneth B. Orr	2-B	1,146	97
Princeton U, Princeton, NJ 08544	1746	Harold T. Shapiro	1-D	6,294	822
Providence Coll, Providence, RI 02918	1917	Rev. John F. Cunningham, OP	2-D	5,771	289
Purdue U, West Lafayette, IN 47907	1869	Dr. Steven C. Beering	5-D	35,817	2,249
Purdue U Calumet, Hammond, IN 46323	1951	Mr. Richard J. Combs	5-M	7,789	404
Purdue U North Central, Westville, IN 46391	1967	Dr. Dale W. Alspaugh	5-M	3,351	200
Queens Coll, Charlotte, NC 28274	1857	Dr. Billy O. Wireman	2-M	1,573	109
Queens Coll of the City U of New York, Flushing, NY 11367	1937	Dr. Shirley Strum Kenny	12-M	17,708	1,134
Quincy Coll, Quincy, IL 62301	1860	Rev. James Toal, OFM	2-M	1,601	93
Quinnipiac Coll, Hamden, CT 06518	1929	Dr. John L. Lahey	1-M	3,126	150
Radford U, Radford, VA 24142	1910	Dr. Donald N. Dedmon	5-M	9,925	496
Ramapo Coll of New Jersey, Mahwah, NJ 07430	1969	Dr. Robert A. Scott	5-B	4,291	238
Randolph-Macon Coll, Ashland, VA 23005	1830	Dr. Ladell Payne	2-B	1,120	118
Randolph-Macon Woman's Coll, Lynchburg, VA 24503 (3)	1891	Ms. Linda Koch Lorimer	2-B	750	87
Reed Coll, Portland, OR 97202	1909	Dr. James L. Powell	1-M	1,286	117
Regis Coll, Denver, CO 80221	1877	Rev. David M. Clarke, SJ	2-M	5,100	90
Regis Coll, Weston, MA 02193 (3)	1927	Sr. Therese Higgins, CSJ	2-B	1,103	106
Rensselaer Polytechnic Inst, Troy, NY 12180	1824	Roland W. Schmitt	1-D	6,556	470
Rhode Island Coll, Providence, RI 02908	1854	Dr. John Nazarian	5-M	8,044	422
Rhode Island Sch of Design, Providence, RI 02903	1877	Dr. Thomas F. Schutte	1-M	1,900	250
Rhodes Coll, Memphis, TN 38112	1848	Dr. James H. Daughdrill, Jr.	2-B	1,386	154
Rice U, Houston, TX 77251	1912	Dr. George Rupp	1-D	4,027	454
Rider Coll, Lawrenceville, NJ 08648	1865	Dr. J. Barton Luedeke	1-M	5,510	275
Ripon Coll, Ripon, WI 54971	1851	Mr. William R. Stott, Jr.	1-B	829	103
Rivier Coll, Nashua, NH 03060 (3)	1933	Sr. Jeanne Perreault	2-M	2,500	53
Roanoke Coll, Salem, VA 24153	1842	Dr. David M. Gring	2-B	1,696	116
Robert Morris Coll, Coraopolis, PA 15108	1921	Dr. Edward A. Nicholson	1-M	5,420	211
Roberts Wesleyan Coll, Rochester, NY 14624	1866	Dr. William C. Crothers	2-B	824	66
Rochester Inst of Tech, Rochester, NY 14623	1829	Dr. M. Richard Rose	1-D	12,672	1,127
Rockford Coll, Rockford, IL 61108	1847	Dr. Gretchen Kreuter	1-M	1,372	126
Rockhurst Coll, Kansas City, MO 64110	1910	Rev. Thomas J. Savage, SJ	2-M	3,239	180
Roger Williams Coll, Bristol, RI 02809	1948	Dr. Natale A. Sicuro	1-B	2,060	208
Rollins Coll, Winter Park, FL 32789	1885	Dr. Rita Bornstein	1-M	2,070	131
Roosevelt U, Chicago, IL 60605	1945	Dr. Theodore L. Gross	1-M	6,374	508
Rosary Coll, River Forest, IL 60305	1848	Jean Murray, OP	2-M	1,767	79
Rose-Hulman Inst of Tech, Terre Haute, IN 47803 (1)	1874	Dr. Samuel F. Hulbert	1-M	1,420	97
Rush U, Chicago, IL 60612	1969	Dr. Leo M. Henikoff	1-D	1,112	170
Russell Sage Coll, Troy, NY 12180 (3)	1916	Dr. Sara Chapman	1-M	2,227	174
Rutgers, State U of NJ, Camden Coll of Arts & Scis, Camden, NJ 08102	1927	Walter K. Gordon	5-B	2,657	NR
Rutgers, State U of NJ, Coll of Engineering, Piscataway, NJ 08855	1864	Dr. Ellis H. Dill	5-B	2,561	NR
Rutgers, State U of NJ, Coll of Nursing, Newark, NJ 07102 (4)	1956	Dorothy J. DeMaio	5-B	410	NR
Rutgers, State U of NJ, Coll of Pharmacy, New Brunswick, NJ 08903	1927	Dr. John Louis Colaizzi	5-B	747	NR
Rutgers, State U of NJ, Cook Coll, New Brunswick, NJ 08903	1921	Daryl B. Lund	5-B	2,879	NR
Rutgers, State U of NJ, Douglass Coll, New Brunswick, NJ 08903 (3)	1918	Dr. Mary S. Hartman	5-B	3,380	NR
Rutgers, State U of NJ, Livingston Coll, New Brunswick, NJ 08903	1969	Walton Johnson	5-B	3,725	NR
Rutgers, State U of NJ, Mason Gross Sch of Arts, New Brunswick, NJ 08903	1976	Marilyn F. Somville	5-M	647	NR
Rutgers, State U of NJ, Newark Coll of Arts & Scis, Newark, NJ 07102	1946	David Hosford	5-B	3,541	NR
Rutgers, State U of NJ, Rutgers Coll, New Brunswick, NJ 08903	1766	James Reed	5-B	8,366	NR
Rutgers, State U of NJ, U Coll–Camden, Camden, NJ 08102	1950	Walter K. Gordon	5-B	908	NR
Rutgers, State U of NJ, U Coll–Newark, Newark, NJ 07102	1934	David Hosford	5-B	1,851	NR
Rutgers, State U of NJ, U Coll–New Brunswick, New Brunswick, NJ 08903	1934	Amy Cohen	5-B	3,178	NR
Sacred Heart U, Fairfield, CT 06432	1963	Dr. Anthony J. Cernera	2-M	4,191	293
Saginaw Valley State U, University Center, MI 48710	1963	Dr. Eric R. Gilbertson	5-M	5,915	331
St Ambrose U, Davenport, IA 52803	1882	Dr. Edward J. Rogalski	2-M	2,300	174
St Andrews Presbyterian Coll, Laurinburg, NC 28352	1958	Dr. Thomas L. Reuschling	2-B	794	77
Saint Anselm Coll, Manchester, NH 03102	1889	Br. Joachim W. Froehlich, OSB	2-B	1,830	157
Saint Augustine's Coll, Raleigh, NC 27610	1867	Dr. Prezell R. Robinson	2-B	1,885	112
St Bonaventure U, St Bonaventure, NY 14778	1854	Very Rev. Mathias Doyle, OFM	2-M	2,907	217
St Cloud State U, St Cloud, MN 56301	1869	Dr. Brendan McDonald	5-M	16,551	716
St Edward's U, Austin, TX 78704	1885	Dr. Patricia Hayes	2-M	2,974	175
Saint Francis Coll, Fort Wayne, IN 46808	1890	Sr. M. JoEllen Scheetz	2-M	1,012	80
St Francis Coll, Brooklyn Heights, NY 11201	1858	Br. Donald Sullivan, OSF	1-B	1,785	128
Saint Francis Coll, Loretto, PA 15940	1847	Rev. Christian R. Oravec	2-M	1,274	80
St John Fisher Coll, Rochester, NY 14618	1948	Dr. William L. Pickett	1-M	3,432	164
Saint John's U, Collegeville, MN 56321 (1)	1857	Fr. Hilary Thimmesh, OSB	2-M	2,003	164
St John's U, Jamaica, NY 11439	1870	Very Rev. Joseph T. Cahill, CM	2-D	18,969	951
Saint Joseph Coll, West Hartford, CT 06117 (3)	1932	Dr. M. Paton Ryan, RSM	2-M	905	124

Name, address	Year	Governing official, control, and highest degree offered	Enrollment	Faculty
Saint Joseph's Coll, Rensselaer, IN 47978	1889	Fr. Charles Banet 2-M	1,001	85
St Joseph's Coll, Brooklyn, NY 11205	1916	Sr. George A. O'Connor 1-B	821	91
St Joseph's Coll, Suffolk Cmps, Patchogue, NY 11772	1916	Sr. George Aquin O'Connor . 1-B	1,918	158
Saint Joseph's U, Philadelphia, PA 19131	1851	Rev. Nicholas S. Rashford, SJ 2-M	6,187	344
St Lawrence U, Canton, NY 13617	1856	Patti McGill Peterson 1-M	2,278	183
Saint Leo Coll, Saint Leo, FL 33574	1889	Msgr. Frank Mouch 2-M	1,068	77
St Louis Coll of Pharmacy, St Louis, MO 63110	1864	Dr. Sumner M. Robinson . . . 1-D	791	58
Saint Louis U, St Louis, MO 63103	1818	Rev. Lawrence Biondi, SJ . . 2-D	11,555	892
Saint Mary Coll, Leavenworth, KS 66048	1923	Br. Peter Clifford, FSC . . . 2-B	1,071	107
Saint Mary of the Plains Coll, Dodge City, KS 67801	1952	Dr. Francis J. Kerins 2-B	1,003	87
Saint Mary-of-the-Woods Coll, Saint Mary-of-the-Woods, IN 47876 (3)	1840	Barbara Doherty, SP 2-M	910	55
Saint Mary's Coll, Notre Dame, IN 46556 (3)	1844	Dr. William A. Hickey 2-B	1,794	183
Saint Mary's Coll of California, Moraga, CA 94575	1863	Br. Mel Anderson 2-M	3,605	180
St Mary's Coll of Maryland, St Mary's City, MD 20686	1840	Dr. Edward T. Lewis 5-B	1,333	136
Saint Mary's Coll of Minnesota, Winona, MN 55987	1912	Br. Louis DeThomasis, FSC . 2-M	3,273	117
St Mary's U of San Antonio, San Antonio, TX 78228	1852	Rev. John Moder, SM 2-D	3,932	179
Saint Michael's Coll, Colchester, VT 05439	1904	Dr. Paul J. Reiss 2-M	2,528	163
St Norbert Coll, De Pere, WI 54115	1898	Dr. Thomas A. Manion 2-M	1,950	146
St Olaf Coll, Northfield, MN 55057	1874	Dr. Melvin George 2-B	3,132	392
Saint Peter's Coll, Jersey City, NJ 07306	1872	Rev. Edward Glynn, SJ . . . 2-M	3,380	452
St Thomas Aquinas Coll, Sparkill, NY 10976	1958	Dr. Donald T. McNelis 1-M	2,075	115
St Thomas U, Miami, FL 33054	1961	Dr. Richard Greene 2-D	2,500	202
Saint Vincent Coll, Latrobe, PA 15650	1846	Rev. John F. Murtha, OSB . . 2-M	1,189	85
Saint Xavier Coll, Chicago, IL 60655	1847	Dr. Ronald Champagne . . . 2-M	2,653	195
Salem Coll, Winston-Salem, NC 27108 (3)	1772	Dr. Thomas V. Litzenburg, Jr. 2-M	886	75
Salem State Coll, Salem, MA 01970	1854	Mr. Kenneth J. McIlraith . . 5-M	8,654	323
Salisbury State U, Salisbury, MD 21801	1925	Dr. Thomas A. Bellavance . 5-M	5,446	308
Salve Regina Coll, Newport, RI 02840	1934	Dr. M. Lucille McKillop, RSM 2-M	2,252	212
Samford U, Birmingham, AL 35229	1841	Dr. Thomas E. Corts 2-D	4,159	293
Sam Houston State U, Huntsville, TX 77341	1879	Dr. Elliott T. Bowers 5-M	12,352	486
San Diego State U, San Diego, CA 92182	1897	Dr. Thomas B. Day 5-D	35,582	2,450
San Francisco State U, San Francisco, CA 94132	1899	Dr. Robert A. Corrigan . . . 5-D	28,120	1,913
Sangamon State U, Springfield, IL 62794	1969	Dr. Durward Long 5-M	3,971	231
San Jose State U, San Jose, CA 95192	1857	Dr. Gail Fullerton 5-M	29,847	1,850
Santa Clara U, Santa Clara, CA 95053	1851	Rev. Paul L. Locatelli, SJ . . 2-D	7,892	560
Sarah Lawrence Coll, Bronxville, NY 10708	1926	Dr. Alice Stone Ilchman . . . 1-M	1,150	157
Savannah Coll of Art and Design, Savannah, GA 31401	1978	Richard G. Rowan 1-M	1,700	88
Savannah State Coll, Savannah, GA 31404	1890	William E. Gardner, Jr. . . . 5-M	2,075	147
Sch of the Art Inst of Chicago, Chicago, IL 60603	1866	Mr. Anthony Jones 1-M	2,077	347
Sch of the Museum of Fine Arts, Boston, MA 02115	1876	Bruce K. MacDonald 1-M	760	66
Sch of the Ozarks, Point Lookout, MO 65726	1906	Dr. Jerry C. Davis 1-B	1,434	101
Sch of Visual Arts, New York, NY 10010	1947	David Rhodes 3-M	2,188	690
Seattle Pacific U, Seattle, WA 98119	1891	Dr. David Le Shana 2-M	3,435	240
Seattle U, Seattle, WA 98122	1891	Rev. William J. Sullivan, SJ . 2-D	4,510	230
Seton Hall U, South Orange, NJ 07079	1856	Msgr. Richard Liddy 2-D	8,248	470
Seton Hill Coll, Greensburg, PA 15601 (4)	1883	JoAnne W. Boyle 2-M	976	90
Shawnee State U, Portsmouth, OH 45662	1986	Dr. Clive Veri 5-B	2,952	247
Shenandoah Coll and Conservatory, Winchester, VA 22601	1875	Dr. James A. Davis 2-M	1,016	130
Shepherd Coll, Shepherdstown, WV 25443	1871	Dr. Michael P. Riccards . . . 5-B	3,600	172
Shippensburg U of Pennsylvania, Shippensburg, PA 17257	1871	Dr. Anthony F. Ceddia . . . 5-M	6,530	359
Shorter Coll, Rome, GA 30161	1873	Dr. James D. Jordan 2-B	883	90
Siena Coll, Loudonville, NY 12211	1937	Fr. William McConville 2-B	3,596	247
Siena Heights Coll, Adrian, MI 49221	1919	Sr. Cathleen Real, CMH . . . 2-M	1,572	110
Silver Lake Coll, Manitowoc, WI 54220	1869	Sr. Barbara Belinske 2-M	785	114
Simmons Coll, Boston, MA 02115 (3)	1899	William J. Holmes 1-D	2,876	279
Simpson Coll, Indianola, IA 50125	1860	Dr. Stephen G. Jennings . . 2-B	1,737	141
Sioux Falls Coll, Sioux Falls, SD 57105	1883	Dr. Thomas F. Johnson . . . 2-M	962	66
Skidmore Coll, Saratoga Springs, NY 12866	1903	Dr. David H. Porter 1-B	2,165	220
Slippery Rock U of Pennsylvania, Slippery Rock, PA 16057	1889	Dr. Robert Aebersold 5-M	7,484	404
Smith Coll, Northampton, MA 01063 (3)	1871	Mrs. Mary Maples Dunn . . . 1-D	2,750	290
Sonoma State U, Rohnert Park, CA 94928	1961	Dr. David W. Benson 5-M	8,759	449
South Dakota Sch of Mines and Tech, Rapid City, SD 57701	1885	Dr. Richard J. Gowen 5-D	2,156	140
South Dakota State U, Brookings, SD 57007	1881	Dr. Robert T. Wagner 5-D	7,080	518
Southeastern Coll of the Assemblies of God, Lakeland, FL 33801	1935	Dr. James Hennesy 2-B	1,130	80
Southeastern Louisiana U, Hammond, LA 70402	1925	Dr. G. Warren Smith 5-M	9,551	377
Southeastern Massachusetts U, North Dartmouth, MA 02747	1895	Dr. John R. Brazil 5-M	6,174	442
Southeastern Oklahoma State U, Durant, OK 74701	1909	Dr. Larry Williams 5-M	3,714	166
Southeastern U, Washington, DC 20024	1879	Dr. W. Robert Higgins 1-M	1,317	128
Southeast Missouri State U, Cape Girardeau, MO 63701	1873	Dr. Bill W. Stacy 5-M	8,520	450
Southern Arkansas U, Magnolia, AR 71753	1909	Dr. Harold T. Brinson 5-M	2,363	121
Southern California U, Costa Mesa, CA 92626	1920	Mr. Wayne E. Kraiss 2-M	898	81
Southern Coll of Seventh-Day Adventists, Collegedale, TN 37315	1892	Dr. Donald R. Sahly 2-B	1,526	126
Southern Coll of Tech, Marietta, GA 30060	1948	Dr. Stephen R. Cheshier . . 5-M	4,026	190
Southern Connecticut State U, New Haven, CT 06515	1893	Mr. Michael J. Adanti 5-M	13,182	671
Southern Illinois U at Carbondale, Carbondale, IL 62901	1869	Dr. John C. Guyon 5-D	24,596	1,473
Southern Illinois U at Edwardsville, Edwardsville, IL 62026	1957	Earl E. Lazerson 5-D	11,320	726
Southern Methodist U, Dallas, TX 75275	1911	Mr. A. Kenneth Pye 1-D	8,924	570
Southern Nazarene U, Bethany, OK 73008	1899	Dr. Loren P. Gresham . . . 2-M	1,402	103
Southern Oregon State Coll, Ashland, OR 97520	1926	Dr. Joseph Cox 5-M	4,801	311
Southern U and A&M Coll, Baton Rouge, LA 70813	1880	Dr. Dolores R. Spiks 5-D	9,811	NR
Southern U at New Orleans, New Orleans, LA 70126	1959	Dr. Robert B. Gex 5-M	3,650	235
Southern Utah State Coll, Cedar City, UT 84720	1897	Gerald R. Sherratt 5-M	3,629	145
Southwest Baptist U, Bolivar, MO 65613	1878	Dr. James L. Sells 2-M	2,920	195
Southwestern Adventist Coll, Keene, TX 76059	1894	Dr. Marvin E. Anderson . . 2-M	758	55
Southwestern Oklahoma State U, Weatherford, OK 73096	1903	Dr. Leonard G. Campbell . . 5-M	5,355	237
Southwestern U, Georgetown, TX 78626	1840	Dr. Roy B. Shilling, Jr. . . . 2-B	1,219	102
Southwest Missouri State U, Springfield, MO 65804	1905	Dr. Marshall Gordon 5-M	18,003	849
Southwest State U, Marshall, MN 56258	1963	Dr. Doug Treadway 5-B	2,814	117
Southwest Texas State U, San Marcos, TX 78666	1899	Dr. Jerome Supple 5-M	20,770	901
Spalding U, Louisville, KY 40203	1814	Dr. Eileen M. Egan 2-D	1,112	91
Spelman Coll, Atlanta, GA 30314 (3)	1881	Dr. Johnetta B. Cole 1-B	1,789	136
Spring Arbor Coll, Spring Arbor, MI 49283	1873	Dr. Dorsey W. Brause . . . 2-B	807	86

Name, address	Year	Governing official, control, and highest degree offered		Enrollment	Faculty
Springfield Coll, Springfield, MA 01109	1885	Dr. Frank S. Falcone	1-D	2,502	259
Spring Garden Coll, Philadelphia, PA 19119	1851	Dr. Daniel N. DeLucca	1-B	1,465	100
Spring Hill Coll, Mobile, AL 36608	1830	Very Rev. Donald I. MacLean, SJ	2-M	938	84
Stanford U, Stanford, CA 94305	1891	Dr. Donald Kennedy	1-D	13,354	1,325
State U of NY at Albany, Albany, NY 12222	1844	Vincent I. O'Leary	5-D	16,595	942
State U of NY at Binghamton, Binghamton, NY 13902	1946	Clifford D. Clark	5-D	12,218	741
State U of NY at Buffalo, Buffalo, NY 14260	1846	Dr. Steven B. Sample	5-D	24,489	2,068
State U of NY at Stony Brook, Stony Brook, NY 11794	1957	Dr. John H. Marburger, III	5-D	15,072	1,518
State U of NY Coll at Brockport, Brockport, NY 14420	1867	Dr. John E. Van de Wetering	5-M	7,717	520
State U of NY Coll at Buffalo, Buffalo, NY 14222	1867	Dr. F. C. Richardson	5-M	11,032	558
State U of NY Coll at Cortland, Cortland, NY 13045	1868	Dr. James M. Clark	5-M	6,170	390
State U of NY Coll at Fredonia, Fredonia, NY 14063	1826	Dr. Donald A. MacPhee	5-M	4,851	319
State U of NY Coll at Geneseo, Geneseo, NY 14454	1867	Dr. Carol C. Harter	5-M	4,900	300
State U of NY Coll at New Paltz, New Paltz, NY 12561	1828	Alice Chandler	5-M	8,256	455
State U of NY Coll at Old Westbury, Old Westbury, NY 11568	1965	Dr. L. Eudora Pettigrew	5-B	4,084	188
State U of NY Coll at Oneonta, Oneonta, NY 13820	1889	Dr. Alan B. Donovan	5-M	6,000	320
State U of NY Coll at Oswego, Oswego, NY 13126	1861	Dr. Stephen Weber	5-M	8,205	410
State U of NY Coll at Plattsburgh, Plattsburgh, NY 12901	1889	Dr. Charles Warren	5-M	6,444	404
State U of NY Coll at Potsdam, Potsdam, NY 13676	1816	Dr. William Merwin	5-M	4,531	263
State U of NY Coll at Purchase, Purchase, NY 10577	1967	Dr. Sheldon Grebstein	5-M	2,495	292
State U of NY Coll of Environ Sci and Forestry, Syracuse, NY 13210	1911	Dr. Ross S. Whaley	5-D	1,257	122
State U of NY Empire State Coll, Saratoga Springs, NY 12866	1971	Dr. James W. Hall	5-M	6,522	354
State U of NY Health Science Ctr at Brooklyn, Brooklyn, NY 11203	1858	Dr. Donald J. Scherl	5-D	1,631	144
State U of NY Health Science Ctr at Syracuse, Syracuse, NY 13210	1950	Dr. John Bernard Henry	5-D	1,032	45
State U of NY Inst of Tech at Utica/Rome, Utica, NY 13504	1966	Dr. Peter J. Cayan	5-M	2,510	149
State U of NY Maritime Coll, Throgs Neck, NY 10465	1874	Rear Adm. Floyd Miller	5-M	801	109
Stephen F Austin State U, Nacogdoches, TX 75962	1923	Dr. Donald E. Bowen	5-D	12,786	617
Stephens Coll, Columbia, MO 65215 (4)	1833	Dr. Patsy H. Sampson	1-B	1,166	82
Stetson U, DeLand, FL 32720	1883	Dr. H. Douglas Lee	2-D	3,090	187
Stevens Inst of Tech, Hoboken, NJ 07030	1870	Dr. Harold J. Raveche	1-D	3,600	250
Stockton State Coll, Pomona, NJ 08240	1971	Dr. Vera King Farris	5-B	5,297	243
Stonehill Coll, North Easton, MA 02357	1948	Rev. Bartley MacPhaidin	2-B	1,908	162
Strayer Coll, Washington, DC 20005	1892	Charles E. Palmer, Jr.	3-M	1,587	74
Suffolk U, Boston, MA 02108	1906	Dr. David J. Sargeant	1-D	5,551	250
Sul Ross State U, Alpine, TX 79832	1917	Dr. Jack W. Humphries	5-M	2,290	118
Susquehanna U, Selinsgrove, PA 17870	1858	Dr. Joel L. Cunningham	2-B	1,529	138
Swarthmore Coll, Swarthmore, PA 19081	1864	Dr. David W. Fraser	1-B	1,320	179
Syracuse U, Syracuse, NY 13244	1870	Dr. Melvin A. Eggers	1-D	17,098	1,611
Tampa Coll, Tampa, FL 33614	1890	Mr. David Zorn	3-M	985	36
Tarleton State U, Stephenville, TX 76402	1899	Dr. Barry B. Thompson	5-M	5,901	267
Taylor U, Upland, IN 46989	1846	Dr. Jay L. Kesler	1-B	1,708	132
Temple U, Philadelphia, PA 19122	1884	Mr. Peter J. Liacouras	13-D	31,181	2,591
Temple U, Ambler Cmps, Ambler, PA 19002	1910	Mr. James Blackhurst	13-D	5,212	375
Tennessee State U, Nashville, TN 37209	1912	Dr. Otis Floyd	5-D	8,270	444
Tennessee Tech U, Cookeville, TN 38505	1915	Dr. Angelo A. Volpe	5-D	8,063	517
Tennessee Temple U, Chattanooga, TN 37404	1946	Dr. J. Don Jennings	2-D	1,130	94
Texas A&I U, Kingsville, TX 78363	1925	Dr. Manuel L. Ibanez	5-D	5,872	242
Texas A&M U, College Station, TX 77843	1876	Dr. William H. Mobley	5-D	40,492	2,008
Texas A&M U at Galveston, Galveston, TX 77553	1962	Dr. William J. Merrell	5-B	936	80
Texas Christian U, Fort Worth, TX 76129	1873	Dr. William Tucker	2-D	6,725	371
Texas Lutheran Coll, Seguin, TX 78155	1891	Dr. Charles H. Oestreich	2-B	1,015	79
Texas Southern U, Houston, TX 77004	1947	Dr. William H. Harris	5-D	9,198	448
Texas Tech U, Lubbock, TX 79409	1923	Robert W. Lawless	5-D	25,027	1,689
Texas Wesleyan U, Fort Worth, TX 76105	1891	Dr. Jerry G. Bawcom	2-M	1,561	111
Texas Woman's U, Denton, TX 76204 (4)	1901	Dr. Shirley Sears Chater	5-D	9,412	505
Thiel Coll, Greenville, PA 16125	1866	Dr. C. Carlyle Haaland	2-B	918	92
Thomas A Edison State Coll, Trenton, NJ 08625	1972	Dr. George A. Pruitt	5-B	7,202	NR
Thomas Coll, Waterville, ME 04901	1894	Dr. George R. Spann	1-M	1,068	58
Thomas Jefferson U, Philadelphia, PA 19107	1824	Paul C. Brucker, MD	1-D	1,128	83
Thomas More Coll, Crestview Hills, KY 41017	1921	Dr. Charles J. Bensman	2-B	1,170	120
Tiffin U, Tiffin, OH 44883	1888	Dr. George Kidd, Jr.	1-M	815	47
Toccoa Falls Coll, Toccoa Falls, GA 30598	1907	Dr. Paul L. Alford	2-B	795	58
Tougaloo Coll, Tougaloo, MS 39174	1869	Dr. Adib A. Shakir	2-B	948	62
Touro Coll, New York, NY 10001	1971	Dr. Bernard Lander	1-D	4,958	316
Towson State U, Towson, MD 21204	1866	Dr. Hoke L. Smith	5-M	14,958	935
Transylvania U, Lexington, KY 40508	1780	Dr. Charles L. Shearer	2-B	1,076	102
Trenton State Coll, Trenton, NJ 08650	1855	Dr. Harold Eickhoff	5-M	7,352	512
Trevecca Nazarene Coll, Nashville, TN 37210	1901	Dr. Homer J. Adams	2-M	1,436	131
Trinity Coll, Hartford, CT 06106	1823	Tom Gerety, Jr.	1-M	2,074	194
Trinity Coll, Washington, DC 20017 (3)	1897	Patricia A. McGuire	2-M	1,095	101
Trinity Coll, Deerfield, IL 60015	1897	Dr. Kenneth M. Meyer	2-B	849	58
Trinity Coll of Vermont, Burlington, VT 05401 (4)	1925	Sr. Janice Ryan	2-B	1,074	115
Trinity U, San Antonio, TX 78212	1869	Dr. Ronald K. Calgaard	2-M	2,573	253
Tri-State U, Angola, IN 46703	1884	Dr. Richard A. Kenyon	1-B	1,185	67
Troy State U, Troy, AL 36082	1887	Dr. Jack Hawkins, Jr.	5-M	4,123	205
Troy State U at Dothan, Dothan, AL 36303	1962	Dr. Thomas Harrison	5-M	1,825	82
Troy State U in Montgomery, Montgomery, AL 36104	1957	Dr. Millard E. Elrod	5-M	2,834	132
Tufts U, Medford, MA 02155	1852	Dr. Jean Mayer	1-D	7,786	548
Tulane U, New Orleans, LA 70118	1834	Dr. Eamon M. Kelly	1-D	11,516	709
Tuskegee U, Tuskegee, AL 36088	1881	Dr. Benjamin F. Payton	1-D	3,510	318
Union Coll, Barbourville, KY 40906	1879	Dr. Jack C. Phillips	2-M	1,050	66
Union Coll, Schenectady, NY 12308	1795	Dr. John S. Morris	1-D	2,355	199
Union Inst, Cincinnati, OH 45202	1964	Robert T. Conley	1-D	1,180	129
Union U, Jackson, TN 38305	1823	Dr. Hyran E. Barefoot	2-B	1,730	112
United States Air Force Acad, Colorado Springs, CO 80840	1954	Lt. Gen. Charles Hamm	4-B	4,438	568
United States Coast Guard Acad, New London, CT 06320	1876	Rear Adm. Thomas T. Matteson	4-B	868	110
United States International U, San Diego, CA 92131	1952	Dr. Kenneth McLennan	1-D	3,530	236

Name, address	Year	Governing official, control, and highest degree offered	Enrollment	Faculty
United States Merchant Marine Acad, Kings Point, NY 11024	1943	Rear Adm. P. L. Krinsky ... 4-B	880	80
United States Military Acad, West Point, NY 10996	1802	Lt. Gen. Dave R. Palmer ... 4-B	4,458	545
United States Naval Acad, Annapolis, MD 21402 (2)	1845	Rear Adm. Virgil L. Hill, Jr. ... 4-B	4,525	600
Universidad Adventista de las Antillas, Mayagüez, PR 00709	1957	Mr. Moises Velazquez ... 2-B	788	58
Universidad Politécnica de Puerto Rico, Hato Rey, PR 00919	1974	Ernesto Vazquez-Torres ... 1-B	3,124	146
U of Akron, Akron, OH 44325	1870	William V. Muse ... 5-D	28,967	1,795
U of Alabama, Tuscaloosa, AL 35487	1831	Dr. E. Roger Sayers ... 5-D	19,432	1,002
U of Alabama at Birmingham, Birmingham, AL 35294	1969	Dr. Charles A. McCallum ... 5-D	15,508	NR
U of Alabama in Huntsville, Huntsville, AL 35899	1950	Dr. Louis Padulo ... 5-D	8,082	405
U of Alaska Anchorage, Anchorage, AK 99508	1954	Dr. Donald F. Behrend ... 5-M	12,860	851
U of Alaska Fairbanks, Fairbanks, AK 99775	1917	Dr. Patrick J. O'Rourke ... 5-M	8,290	583
U of Alaska Southeast, Juneau, AK 99801	1972	Dr. Marshall Lind ... 5-M	2,787	105
U of Arizona, Tucson, AZ 85721	1885	Dr. Henry Koffler ... 5-D	35,569	2,148
U of Arkansas, Fayetteville, AR 72701	1871	Dr. Daniel E. Ferritor ... 5-D	14,281	799
U of Arkansas at Little Rock, Little Rock, AR 72204	1927	Dr. James H. Young ... 5-D	10,842	836
U of Arkansas at Monticello, Monticello, AR 71655	1909	Dr. Fred J. Taylor ... 5-B	1,978	117
U of Arkansas at Pine Bluff, Pine Bluff, AR 71601	1873	Dr. Charles A. Walker ... 5-B	3,077	202
U of Arkansas for Medical Sciences, Little Rock, AR 72205	1879	Dr. Harry P. Ward ... 5-D	1,356	NR
U of Baltimore, Baltimore, MD 21201	1925	Dr. H. Mebane Turner ... 5-D	5,522	278
U of Bridgeport, Bridgeport, CT 06601	1927	Dr. Janet D. Greenwood ... 1-D	5,376	375
U of California at Berkeley, Berkeley, CA 94720	1868	Ira Michael Heyman ... 5-D	31,612	NR
U of California, Davis, Davis, CA 95616	1906	Dr. Theodore L. Hullar ... 5-D	22,571	1,527
U of California, Irvine, Irvine, CA 92717	1965	Jack W. Peltason ... 5-D	16,149	720
U of California, Los Angeles, Los Angeles, CA 90024	1919	Charles E. Young ... 5-D	36,378	3,150
U of California, Riverside, Riverside, CA 92521	1954	Dr. Rosemary S. J. Schraer ... 5-D	8,220	649
U of California, San Diego, La Jolla, CA 92093	1959	Dr. Richard C. Atkinson ... 5-D	17,595	1,226
U of California, Santa Barbara, Santa Barbara, CA 93106	1891	Dr. Barbara S. Uehling ... 5-D	19,082	700
U of California, Santa Cruz, Santa Cruz, CA 95064	1965	Dr. Robert B. Stevens ... 5-D	9,784	449
U of Central Arkansas, Conway, AR 72032	1907	Winfred L. Thompson ... 5-M	7,477	361
U of Central Florida, Orlando, FL 32816	1963	Dr. Steven Altman ... 5-D	20,057	823
U of Charleston, Charleston, WV 25304	1888	Mr. Lewis McManus ... 1-M	1,610	156
U of Chicago, Chicago, IL 60637	1891	Hanna Holborn Gray ... 1-D	9,300	598
U of Cincinnati, Cincinnati, OH 45221	1819	Dr. Joseph A. Steger ... 5-D	30,737	1,899
U of Colorado at Boulder, Boulder, CO 80309	1876	James N. Corbridge, Jr. ... 5-D	24,364	2,293
U of Colorado at Colorado Springs, Colorado Springs, CO 80933	1965	Dr. Dwayne C. Nuzum ...	4,699	383
U of Colorado at Denver, Denver, CO 80204	1912	John Buechner ... 5-D	8,802	516
U of Colorado Health Sciences Ctr, Denver, CO 80262	1883	Dr. Bernard W. Nelson ... 5-D	1,652	NR
U of Connecticut, Storrs, CT 06269	1881	Dr. John T. Casteen, III ... 5-D	17,936	1,250
U of Connecticut at Hartford, West Hartford, CT 06117	1946	Dr. Russell F. Farnen ... 5-B	1,514	91
U of Connecticut at Stamford, Stamford, CT 06903	1951	Dr. Karen Arms ... 5-M	1,175	93
U of Dallas, Irving, TX 75062	1956	Dr. Robert F. Sasseen ... 2-D	2,796	124
U of Dayton, Dayton, OH 45469	1850	Br. Raymond L. Fitz, SM ... 2-D	11,284	693
U of Delaware, Newark, DE 19716	1743	Dr. David P. Roselle ... 13-D	16,997	954
U of Denver, Denver, CO 80208	1864	Mr. Daniel Ritchie ... 1-D	7,266	548
U of Detroit, Detroit, MI 48221	1877	Rev. Robert A. Mitchell, SJ ... 2-D	5,832	436
U of Dubuque, Dubuque, IA 52001	1852	Dr. Walter F. Peterson ... 2-M	1,126	66
U of Evansville, Evansville, IN 47722	1854	Dr. James S. Vinson ... 2-M	3,290	162
U of Findlay, Findlay, OH 45840	1882	Dr. Kenneth E. Zirkle ... 2-M	1,799	165
U of Florida, Gainesville, FL 32611	1853	Dr. Robert A. Bryan ... 5-D	34,022	4,015
U of Georgia, Athens, GA 30602	1785	Dr. Charles B. Knapp ... 5-D	27,448	2,025
U of Guam, Mangilao, GU 96923	1952	Dr. Wilfred P. Leon Guerrezo ... 8-M	2,385	191
U of Hartford, West Hartford, CT 06117	1877	Humphrey Tonkin ... 1-D	6,431	636
U of Hawaii at Manoa, Honolulu, HI 96822	1907	Dr. Albert J. Simone ... 5-D	18,622	4,819
U of Health Sciences/Chicago Medical Sch, North Chicago, IL 60064	1912	Dr. Herman M. Finch ... 1-D	836	17
U of Houston, Houston, TX 77004	1927	Dr. Marguerite Ross Barnett ... 5-D	32,289	2,280
U of Houston–Clear Lake, Houston, TX 77058	1971	Dr. Thomas M. Stauffer ... 5-M	7,450	321
U of Houston–Downtown, Houston, TX 77002	1974	Manuel T. Pacheco ... 5-B	8,008	325
U of Houston–Victoria, Victoria, TX 77901	1973	Dr. Glenn A. Goerke ... 5-M	1,175	74
U of Idaho, Moscow, ID 83843	1889	Dr. Elisabeth Zinser ... 5-D	9,967	557
U of Illinois at Chicago, Chicago, IL 60680	1965	Dr. Donald N. Langenberg ... 5-D	24,195	2,037
U of Illinois at Urbana-Champaign, Urbana, IL 61801	1867	Dr. Morton W. Weir ... 5-D	35,032	2,967
U of Indianapolis, Indianapolis, IN 46227	1902	Dr. G. Benjamin Lantz, Jr. ... 2-M	3,119	239
U of Iowa, Iowa City, IA 52242	1847	Dr. Hunter R. Rawling, III ... 5-D	28,884	1,600
U of Kansas, Lawrence, KS 66045	1866	Gene A. Budig ... 5-D	26,320	1,277
U of Kansas Medical Ctr, Kansas City, KS 66103	1905	D. Kay Clawson, MD ... 5-D	2,453	122
U of Kentucky, Lexington, KY 40506	1865	Dr. Charles T. Wethington, Jr. ... 5-D	22,711	1,879
U of La Verne, La Verne, CA 91750	1891	Dr. Stephen Morgan ... 1-D	5,933	506
U of Louisville, Louisville, KY 40292	1798	Dr. Donald C. Swain ... 5-D	23,186	1,576
U of Lowell, Lowell, MA 01854	1894	Dr. William T. Hogan ... 5-D	11,179	620
U of Maine, Orono, ME 04469	1865	Dr. Dale W. Lick ... 5-D	11,645	934
U of Maine at Farmington, Farmington, ME 04938	1864	Dr. J. Michael Orenduff ... 5-B	2,737	162
U of Maine at Machias, Machias, ME 04654	1909	Mr. Frederic A. Reynolds ... 5-B	876	63
U of Maine at Presque Isle, Presque Isle, ME 04769	1903	Dr. James R. Roach ... 5-M	1,512	105
U of Mary, Bismarck, ND 58504	1959	Sr. Thomas Welder ... 2-M	1,431	87
U of Mary Hardin-Baylor, Belton, TX 76513	1845	Dr. Bobby E. Parker ... 2-M	1,762	75
U of Maryland Baltimore County, Baltimore, MD 21228	1966	Dr. Michael K. Hooker ... 5-D	9,740	626
U of Maryland Coll Park, College Park, MD 20742	1856	Dr. William E. Kirwan ... 5-D	35,825	1,769
U of Maryland Eastern Shore, Princess Anne, MD 21853	1886	Dr. William P. Hytche ... 5-D	1,828	148
U of Maryland U Coll, College Park, MD 20742	1947	Dr. T. Benjamin Massey ... 5-M	40,776	NR
U of Massachusetts at Amherst, Amherst, MA 01003	1863	Joseph Duffey ... 5-D	24,000	1,418
U of Massachusetts at Boston, Boston, MA 02125	1964	Dr. Sherry H. Penney ... 5-D	11,270	824
U of Miami, Coral Gables, FL 33124	1925	Dr. Edward T. Foote, II ... 1-D	13,790	1,168
U of Michigan, Ann Arbor, MI 48109	1817	Dr. James J. Duderstadt ... 5-D	36,338	3,619
U of Michigan–Dearborn, Dearborn, MI 48128	1959	Dr. Blenda Wilson ... 5-M	6,707	374
U of Michigan–Flint, Flint, MI 48502	1956	Dr. Clinton B. Jones ... 5-M	6,506	211
U of Minnesota, Morris, Morris, MN 56267	1959	Dr. John Q. Imholte ... 5-B	2,041	138
U of Minnesota, Twin Cities Cmps, Minneapolis, MN 55455	1851	Nils Hasselmo ... 5-D	41,016	5,012
U of Mississippi, University, MS 38677	1844	Dr. R. Gerald Turner ... 5-D	10,370	548
U of Missouri–Columbia, Columbia, MO 65211	1839	Dr. Haskell Monroe ... 5-D	24,220	1,549
U of Missouri–Kansas City, Kansas City, MO 64110	1933	Dr. George A. Russell ... 5-D	11,548	1,041
U of Missouri–Rolla, Rolla, MO 65401	1870	Dr. Martin Jischke ... 5-D	5,576	381
U of Missouri–St Louis, St Louis, MO 63121	1963	Dr. Marguerite Ross Barnett ... 5-D	12,872	635

Name, address	Year	Governing official, control, and highest degree offered	Enrollment	Faculty
U of Montana, Missoula, MT 59812	1893	Dr. James V. Koch ... 5-D	9,679	483
U of Montevallo, Montevallo, AL 35115	1896	Dr. John W. Stewart ... 5-M	3,175	182
U of Nebraska at Kearney, Kearney, NE 68849	1903	Dr. William R. Nester ... 5-M	9,745	379
U of Nebraska at Omaha, Omaha, NE 68182	1908	Dr. Del D. Weber ... 5-D	15,305	688
U of Nebraska–Lincoln, Lincoln, NE 68588	1869	Dr. Martin A. Massengale ... 5-D	23,926	1,504
U of Nebraska Medical Ctr, Omaha, NE 68105	1869	Dr. Charles E. Andrews ... 5-D	2,405	155
U of Nevada, Las Vegas, Las Vegas, NV 89154	1957	Dr. Robert Maxson ... 5-D	16,320	521
U of Nevada–Reno, Reno, NV 89557	1874	Dr. Joseph N. Crowley ... 5-D	10,093	445
U of New England, Biddeford, ME 04005	1939	Dr. Charles W. Ford ... 1-D	1,174	106
U of New Hampshire, Durham, NH 03824	1866	Dr. Gordon A. Haaland ... 5-D	11,566	778
U of New Haven, West Haven, CT 06516	1920	Dr. Phillip S. Kaplan ... 1-D	6,360	428
U of New Mexico, Albuquerque, NM 87131	1889	Gerald May ... 5-D	24,525	1,445
U of New Orleans, New Orleans, LA 70148	1958	Dr. Gregory M. O'Brien ... 5-D	15,559	633
U of North Alabama, Florence, AL 35632	1872	Mr. Robert L. Potts ... 5-M	5,581	228
U of North Carolina at Asheville, Asheville, NC 28804	1927	Dr. David G. Brown ... 5-M	3,291	229
U of North Carolina at Chapel Hill, Chapel Hill, NC 27599	1795	Paul Hardin, III ... 5-D	23,592	1,951
U of North Carolina at Charlotte, Charlotte, NC 28223	1946	Dr. James H. Woodward, Jr. ... 5-M	13,222	830
U of North Carolina at Greensboro, Greensboro, NC 27412	1891	Dr. William E. Moran ... 5-D	11,584	698
U of North Carolina at Wilmington, Wilmington, NC 28403	1947	Dr. William H. Wagoner ... 5-M	7,003	397
U of North Dakota, Grand Forks, ND 58202	1883	Dr. Thomas J. Clifford ... 5-D	12,210	639
U of Northern Colorado, Greeley, CO 80639	1890	Mr. Robert C. Dickeson ... 5-D	9,645	536
U of Northern Iowa, Cedar Falls, IA 50614	1876	Dr. Constantine W. Curris ... 5-D	11,837	789
U of North Florida, Jacksonville, FL 32216	1965	Dr. Adam W. Herbert ... 5-M	7,727	193
U of North Texas, Denton, TX 76203	1890	Dr. Alfred F. Hurley ... 5-D	26,519	921
U of Notre Dame, Notre Dame, IN 46556	1842	Rev. Edward A. Malloy, CSC ... 2-D	9,700	800
U of Oklahoma, Norman, OK 73019	1890	Dr. Richard L. Van Horn ... 5-D	19,250	966
U of Oklahoma Health Sciences Ctr, Oklahoma City, OK 73190	1890	Dr. Clayton Rich ... 5-D	3,366	NR
U of Oregon, Eugene, OR 97403	1872	Myles Brand ... 5-D	17,818	1,133
U of Osteopathic Medicine and Health Sciences, Des Moines, IA 50312	1898	Dr. J. Leonard Azneer ... 1-D	1,002	108
U of Pennsylvania, Philadelphia, PA 19104	1740	Dr. F. Sheldon Hackney ... 1-D	20,305	3,854
U of Phoenix, Phoenix, AZ 85040	1976	William Gibbs ... 3-M	5,714	1,000
U of Pittsburgh, Pittsburgh, PA 15260	1787	Dr. Wesley W. Posvar ... 13-D	28,362	3,042
U of Pittsburgh at Bradford, Bradford, PA 16701	1963	Dr. Richard E. McDowell ... 13-B	1,103	89
U of Pittsburgh at Greensburg, Greensburg, PA 15601	1963	Dr. George F. Chambers ... 13-B	1,675	94
U of Pittsburgh at Johnstown, Johnstown, PA 15904	1927	Dr. Frank H. Blackington, III ... 13-B	3,242	177
U of Portland, Portland, OR 97203	1901	Rev. Thomas C. Oddo, CSC ... 2-M	2,415	187
U of Puerto Rico at Arecibo, Arecibo, PR 00613	1967	Prof. Ana J. Babilonia ... 7-B	3,421	174
U of Puerto Rico at Bayamón, Bayamón, PR 00619	1971	Aida Canals de Bird ... 7-B	3,849	202
U of Puerto Rico at Ponce, Ponce, PR 00732	1970	Mr. Pedro E. Laboy ... 7-B	2,240	135
U of Puerto Rico, Cayey U Coll, Cayey, PR 00633	1967	Dr. Margarita Benítez ... 7-B	3,332	178
U of Puerto Rico, Humacao U Coll, Humacao, PR 00661	1962	Elsa I. Berríos de Santos ... 7-B	3,892	229
U of Puerto Rico, Mayagüez Cmps, Mayagüez, PR 00709	1911	Dr. Jose L. Martínez-Pico ... 7-D	9,432	676
U of Puerto Rico Medical Sciences Cmps, San Juan, PR 00936	1950	Dr. Jose M. Saldana ... 7-D	2,895	856
U of Puerto Rico, Rio Piedras, Rio Piedras, PR 00931	1903	Dr. Juan R. Fernández ... 7-D	22,210	1,504
U of Puget Sound, Tacoma, WA 98416	1888	Dr. Philip M. Phibbs ... 2-M	3,303	216
U of Redlands, Redlands, CA 92373	1907	Dr. James R. Appleton ... 1-M	2,300	134
U of Rhode Island, Kingston, RI 02881	1892	Dr. Edward D. Eddy ... 5-D	12,201	804
U of Richmond, Richmond, VA 23173	1830	Dr. Richard L. Morrill ... 2-M	4,909	314
U of Rio Grande, Rio Grande, OH 45674	1876	Dr. Paul C. Hayes ... 1-B	2,013	108
U of Rochester, Rochester, NY 14627	1850	G. Dennis O'Brien ... 1-D	7,959	655
U of San Diego, San Diego, CA 92110	1949	Dr. Author E. Hughes ... 2-D	5,921	398
U of San Francisco, San Francisco, CA 94117	1855	Rev. John J. Lo Schiavo, SJ ... 2-D	6,028	525
U of Science and Arts of Oklahoma, Chickasha, OK 73018	1908	Dr. Roy Troutt ... 5-B	1,451	75
U of Scranton, Scranton, PA 18510	1888	Rev. J. A. Panuska, SJ ... 2-M	5,111	358
U of South Alabama, Mobile, AL 36688	1963	Dr. Frederick P. Whiddon ... 5-D	11,329	737
U of South Carolina, Columbia, SC 29208	1801	Dr. James B. Holderman ... 5-D	25,692	1,443
U of South Carolina at Aiken, Aiken, SC 29801	1961	Dr. Robert E. Alexander ... 5-B	2,633	230
U of South Carolina at Spartanburg, Spartanburg, SC 29303	1967	Dr. Olin B. Sansbury, Jr. ... 5-B	3,422	218
U of South Carolina–Coastal Carolina Coll, Conway, SC 29526	1954	Dr. Ronald G. Eaglin ... 5-B	4,101	223
U of South Dakota, Vermillion, SD 57069	1862	Dr. Betty Turner Asher ... 5-D	6,397	401
U of Southern California, Los Angeles, CA 90089	1880	Dr. James H. Zumberge ... 1-D	29,021	3,506
U of Southern Colorado, Pueblo, CO 81001	1933	Dr. Robert Shirley ... 5-M	4,257	240
U of Southern Indiana, Evansville, IN 47712	1965	Dr. David L. Rice ... 5-M	5,713	290
U of Southern Maine, Portland, ME 04103	1878	Dr. Patricia Plante ... 5-D	10,545	458
U of Southern Mississippi, Hattiesburg, MS 39406	1910	Dr. Aubrey K. Lucas ... 5-D	11,544	676
U of South Florida, Tampa, FL 33620	1956	Dr. Francis T. Borkowski ... 5-D	31,638	1,422
U of Southwestern Louisiana, Lafayette, LA 70504	1898	Dr. Ray P. Authement ... 5-D	15,515	636
U of Tampa, Tampa, FL 33606	1931	Mr. Bruce A. Samson ... 1-M	2,476	189
U of Tennessee at Chattanooga, Chattanooga, TN 37403	1886	Dr. Frederick W. Obear ... 5-M	7,564	314
U of Tennessee at Martin, Martin, TN 38238	1927	Dr. Margaret N. Perry ... 5-M	4,800	NR
U of Tennessee, Knoxville, Knoxville, TN 37996	1794	Dr. Jack E. Reese ... 5-D	25,016	1,173
U of Tennessee, Memphis, Memphis, TN 38163	1911	Dr. James C. Hunt ... 5-D	1,747	920
U of Texas at Arlington, Arlington, TX 76019	1895	Dr. Wendell H. Nedderman ... 5-D	23,872	887
U of Texas at Austin, Austin, TX 78712	1883	Dr. William H. Cunningham ... 5-D	50,245	4,876
U of Texas at Dallas, Richardson, TX 75083	1969	Dr. Robert H. Rutford ... 5-D	8,101	250
U of Texas at El Paso, El Paso, TX 79968	1913	Dr. Diana Natalicio ... 5-D	15,707	672
U of Texas at San Antonio, San Antonio, TX 78285	1969	Samuel A. Kirkpatrick ... 5-M	14,031	657
U of Texas at Tyler, Tyler, TX 75701	1972	Dr. George F. Hamm ... 5-M	4,103	204
U of Texas Health Science Ctr at Houston, Houston, TX 77225	1943	Dr. M. David Low ... 5-D	2,894	79
U of Texas Health Science Ctr at San Antonio, San Antonio, TX 78284	1976	Dr. John P. Howe, III ... 5-D	2,362	120
U of Texas Medical Branch at Galveston, Galveston, TX 77550	1891	Dr. Thomas N. James ... 5-D	1,678	610
U of Texas of the Permian Basin, Odessa, TX 79762	1969	Dr. Duane M. Leach ... 5-M	2,111	105
U of Texas–Pan American, Edinburg, TX 78539	1927	Dr. Miguel A. Nevarez ... 5-M	12,100	450
U of Texas Southwestern Medical Ctr at Dallas, Dallas, TX 75235	1943	Dr. C. Kern Wildenthal ... 5-D	1,458	270
U of the Arts, Philadelphia, PA 19102	1876	Peter Solmssen ... 1-M	1,500	382
U of the District of Columbia, Washington, DC 20008	1976	Dr. Rafael L. Cortada ... 10-M	11,869	838
U of the Ozarks, Clarksville, AR 72830	1834	Dr. Fritz H. Ehren ... 2-M	796	56
U of the Pacific, Stockton, CA 95211	1851	Dr. Bill L. Atchley ... 1-D	5,800	324
U of the Sacred Heart, Santurce, PR 00914	1935	Jose Alberto Morales, Esq. ... 2-M	7,302	417

Name, address	Year	Governing official, control, and highest degree offered	Enrollment	Faculty
U of the South, Sewanee, TN 37375	1857	Dr. Samuel R. Williamson, Jr. 2-D	1,075	111
U of State of New York, Regents Coll Degrees, Albany, NY 12230	1971	C. Wayne Williams 13-B	14,600	NR
U of the Virgin Islands, Charlotte Amalie, St Thomas, VI 00802	1962	Dr. Arthur A. Richards 8-M	2,665	175
U of Toledo, Toledo, OH 43606	1872	Mr. Frank E. Horton 5-D	23,926	1,200
U of Tulsa, Tulsa, OK 74104	1894	Dr. E. Joseph Middlebrook 2-D	4,318	469
U of Utah, Salt Lake City, UT 84112	1850	Dr. Chase N. Peterson 5-D	23,626	924
U of Vermont, Burlington, VT 05405	1791	Dr. George H. Davis 5-D	9,554	955
U of Virginia, Charlottesville, VA 22906	1819	John T. Casteen, III 5-D	17,444	1,157
U of Washington, Seattle, WA 98195	1861	William P. Gerberding 5-D	33,238	3,230
U of West Florida, Pensacola, FL 32514	1963	Dr. Morris L. Marx 5-M	7,576	255
U of Wisconsin-Eau Claire, Eau Claire, WI 54701	1916	Dr. Larry Schnack 5-M	10,773	594
U of Wisconsin-Green Bay, Green Bay, WI 54311	1968	Dr. David L. Outcalt 5-M	4,776	208
U of Wisconsin-La Crosse, La Crosse, WI 54601	1909	Dr. Noel J. Richards 5-M	8,984	461
U of Wisconsin-Madison, Madison, WI 53706	1848	Dr. Donna E. Shalala 5-D	41,100	2,368
U of Wisconsin-Milwaukee, Milwaukee, WI 53201	1956	Dr. Clifford V. Smith, Jr. 5-D	24,857	1,263
U of Wisconsin-Oshkosh, Oshkosh, WI 54901	1871	NR 5-M	10,881	516
U of Wisconsin-Parkside, Kenosha, WI 53141	1968	Dr. Sheila Kaplan 5-M	5,265	290
U of Wisconsin-Platteville, Platteville, WI 53818	1866	Dr. William W. Chmurny 5-M	5,430	290
U of Wisconsin-River Falls, River Falls, WI 54022	1874	Dr. Gary A. Thibodeau 5-M	5,243	295
U of Wisconsin-Stevens Point, Stevens Point, WI 54481	1894	Dr. Keith R. Sanders 5-M	8,538	383
U of Wisconsin-Stout, Menomonie, WI 54751	1891	Dr. Charles Sorensen 5-M	7,322	494
U of Wisconsin-Superior, Superior, WI 54880	1893	Dr. Terrence MacTaggart 5-M	2,561	162
U of Wisconsin-Whitewater, Whitewater, WI 53190	1868	Dr. James R. Connor 5-M	10,270	476
U of Wyoming, Laramie, WY 82071	1886	Dr. Terry P. Roark 5-D	10,994	812
Upper Iowa U, Fayette, IA 52142	1857	Dr. James R. Rocheleau 1-B	1,439	NR
Upsala Coll, East Orange, NJ 07019	1893	Rev. Robert E. Karsten 2-M	990	114
Urbana U, Urbana, OH 43078	1850	Dr. Paul G. Bunnell 2-B	821	90
Ursinus Coll, Collegeville, PA 19426	1869	Dr. Richard P. Richter 2-B	1,100	117
Ursuline Coll, Pepper Pike, OH 44124 (4)	1871	Sr. Anne Marie Diederich, OSU 2-M	1,526	110
Utah State U, Logan, UT 84322	1888	Dr. Stanford Cazier 5-D	12,650	733
Utica Coll of Syracuse U, Utica, NY 13502	1946	Dr. Michael K. Simpson 1-B	1,600	140
Valdosta State Coll, Valdosta, GA 31698	1906	Dr. Hugh C. Bailey 5-M	7,300	390
Valley City State U, Valley City, ND 58072	1890	Dr. Charles B. House, Jr. 5-B	1,140	66
Valparaiso U, Valparaiso, IN 46383	1859	Dr. Alan F. Harre 2-D	3,858	331
Vanderbilt U, Nashville, TN 37240	1873	Mr. Joe B. Wyatt 1-D	9,059	691
Vassar Coll, Poughkeepsie, NY 12601	1861	Frances D. Fergusson 1-M	2,395	243
Villa Julie Coll, Stevenson, MD 21153	1952	Dr. Carolyn Manuszak 1-B	1,459	111
Villanova U, Villanova, PA 19085	1842	Rev. Edmund J. Dobbin, OSA 2-D	11,388	644
Virginia Commonwealth U, Richmond, VA 23298	1838	Dr. Edmund F. Ackell 5-D	21,391	2,195
Virginia Military Inst, Lexington, VA 24450 (1)	1839	Maj. Gen. John W. Knapp 5-B	1,310	92
Virginia Polytechnic Inst and State U, Blacksburg, VA 24061	1872	James D. McComas 5-D	22,611	1,607
Virginia State U, Petersburg, VA 23803	1882	Dr. Wesley C. McClure 5-M	4,073	239
Virginia Union U, Richmond, VA 23220	1865	Dr. S. Dallas Simmons 2-M	1,200	NR
Virginia Wesleyan Coll, Norfolk, VA 23502	1961	Dr. Lambuth M. Clarke 2-B	1,280	100
Viterbo Coll, La Crosse, WI 54601	1890	Dr. Robert E. Gibbons 2-M	1,147	89
Wabash Coll, Crawfordsville, IN 47933 (1)	1832	Dr. F. Sheldon Wettack 1-B	832	79
Wagner Coll, Staten Island, NY 10301	1883	Dr. Norman R. Smith 1-M	1,654	135
Wake Forest U, Winston-Salem, NC 27109	1834	Dr. Thomas K. Hearn, Jr. 2-D	5,337	349
Walla Walla Coll, College Place, WA 99324	1892	Dr. Neils-Eric Andreason 2-M	1,581	168
Walsh Coll, Canton, OH 44720	1958	Dr. Francis Blouin 2-M	1,444	104
Walsh Coll of Accountancy and Business Admin, Troy, MI 48007	1922	Dr. Jeffery W. Barry 1-M	2,997	124
Wartburg Coll, Waverly, IA 50677	1852	Dr. Robert Vogel 2-B	1,456	122
Washburn U of Topeka, Topeka, KS 66621	1865	Dr. Hugh Thompson 11-M	6,574	324
Washington and Jefferson Coll, Washington, PA 15301	1781	Dr. Howard J. Burnett 1-B	1,234	104
Washington and Lee U, Lexington, VA 24450	1749	Dr. John D. Wilson 1-D	2,023	128
Washington Coll, Chestertown, MD 21620	1782	Mr. Douglass Cater 1-M	1,016	81
Washington State U, Pullman, WA 99164	1892	Dr. Samuel H. Smith 5-D	17,138	886
Washington U, St Louis, MO 63130	1853	Dr. William H. Danforth 1-D	9,415	2,845
Wayland Baptist U, Plainview, TX 79072	1908	Dr. Lanny Hall 2-M	2,052	181
Waynesburg Coll, Waynesburg, PA 15370	1849	Dr. Timothy R. Thyreen 2-M	1,155	81
Wayne State Coll, Wayne, NE 68787	1910	Dr. Donald J. Mash 5-M	3,324	162
Wayne State U, Detroit, MI 48202	1868	Dr. David Adamany 5-D	32,477	2,257
Weber State Coll, Ogden, UT 84408	1889	Dr. Allen F. Simkins 5-M	12,920	417
Webster U, St Louis, MO 63119	1915	NR 1-D	9,061	358
Wellesley Coll, Wellesley, MA 02181 (3)	1870	Dr. Nannerl Keohane 1-B	2,323	316
Wentworth Inst of Tech, Boston, MA 02115	1904	Dr. Edward T. Kirkpatrick 1-B	3,034	154
Wesleyan U, Middletown, CT 06457	1831	Mr. William Chace 1-D	2,818	341
Wesley Coll, Dover, DE 19901	1873	Dr. Reed M. Stewart 2-B	1,200	98
West Chester U of Pennsylvania, West Chester, PA 19383	1871	Dr. Kenneth L. Perrin 5-M	11,615	633
West Coast U, Los Angeles, CA 90020	1909	Dr. Robert M. L. Baker, Jr. 1-M	1,600	250
Western Carolina U, Cullowhee, NC 28723	1889	Dr. Myron L. Coulter 5-M	6,134	381
Western Connecticut State U, Danbury, CT 06810	1903	Dr. Stephen Feldman 5-M	6,293	372
Western Illinois U, Macomb, IL 61455	1899	Dr. Ralph H. Wagoner 5-M	12,500	626
Western International U, Phoenix, AZ 85021	1978	Robert S. Webber 1-M	3,214	88
Western Kentucky U, Bowling Green, KY 42101	1906	Dr. Thomas C. Meredith 5-M	14,821	831
Western Maryland Coll, Westminster, MD 21157	1867	Dr. Robert H. Chambers 1-M	2,071	127
Western Michigan U, Kalamazoo, MI 49008	1903	Dr. Diether H. Haenicke 5-D	26,315	948
Western Montana Coll of the U of Montana, Dillon, MT 59725	1893	Dr. W. Michael Easton 5-B	889	42
Western New England Coll, Springfield, MA 01119	1919	Dr. Beverly W. Miller 1-D	4,489	236
Western New Mexico U, Silver City, NM 88061	1893	Dr. Rudolph Gomez 5-M	1,773	92
Western Oregon State Coll, Monmouth, OR 97361	1856	Dr. Richard S. Meyers 5-M	3,856	256
Western State Coll of Colorado, Gunnison, CO 81230	1911	Dr. William T. Hamilton 5-B	2,381	125
Western State U Coll of Law of Orange County, Fullerton, CA 92631	1966	NR 3-D	1,340	62
Western Washington U, Bellingham, WA 98225	1893	Dr. Kenneth P. Mortimer 5-M	9,322	509
Westfield State Coll, Westfield, MA 01086	1838	Dr. Ronald L. Applbaum 5-M	5,137	204
West Georgia Coll, Carrollton, GA 30118	1933	Dr. Maurice K. Townsend 5-M	7,252	321
West Liberty State Coll, West Liberty, WV 26074 (1)	1837	Dr. Clyde D. Campbell 5-B	2,467	138
Westminster Coll, New Wilmington, PA 16172	1852	Dr. Oscar E. Remick 2-M	1,554	112

Name, address	Year	Governing official, control, and highest degree offered		Enrollment	Faculty
Westminster Coll of Salt Lake City, Salt Lake City, UT 84105	1875	Dr. Charles H. Dick	1-M	1,977	71
Westmont Coll, Santa Barbara, CA 93108	1940	Dr. David K. Winter	2-B	1,256	109
West Texas State U, Canyon, TX 79016	1909	Dr. Ed Roach	5-M	5,718	306
West Virginia Inst of Tech, Montgomery, WV 25136	1895	Dr. Robert C. Gillespie	5-M	2,852	198
West Virginia State Coll, Institute, WV 25112	1891	Hazo W. Carter	5-B	4,635	221
West Virginia U, Morgantown, WV 26506	1867	Dr. Neil S. Bucklew	5-D	19,997	1,381
West Virginia Wesleyan Coll, Buckhannon, WV 26201	1890	Dr. Thomas B. Courtice	2-M	1,571	106
Wheaton Coll, Wheaton, IL 60187	1860	Dr. J. Richard Chase	2-M	2,548	246
Wheaton Coll, Norton, MA 02766	1834	Alice F. Emerson	1-B	1,219	114
Wheeling Jesuit Coll, Wheeling, WV 26003	1954	Fr. Thomas S. Acker, SJ	2-M	1,375	68
Wheelock Coll, Boston, MA 02215 (4)	1888	Dr. Daniel S. Cheever, Jr.	1-M	1,141	152
Whitman Coll, Walla Walla, WA 99362	1859	Dr. David E. Maxwell	1-B	1,268	151
Whittier Coll, Whittier, CA 90608	1887	Dr. James L. Ash, Jr.	1-D	1,579	90
Whitworth Coll, Spokane, WA 99251	1890	Dr. Arthur J. De Jong	2-M	1,788	92
Wichita State U, Wichita, KS 67208	1895	Dr. Warren B. Armstrong	5-D	17,419	852
Widener U, Chester, PA 19013	1821	Mr. Robert J. Bruce	1-D	8,516	299
Wilberforce U, Wilberforce, OH 45384	1856	John L. Henderson	2-B	779	66
Wilkes U, Wilkes-Barre, PA 18766	1933	Dr. Christopher N. Breiseth	1-M	3,097	NR
Willamette U, Salem, OR 97301	1842	Dr. Jerry E. Hudson	2-D	2,223	143
William Carey Coll, Hattiesburg, MS 39401	1906	Mr. James W. Edwards	2-M	1,600	NR
William Jewell Coll, Liberty, MO 64068	1849	Dr. J. Gordon Kingsley	2-B	1,400	142
William Paterson Coll of New Jersey, Wayne, NJ 07470	1855	Dr. Arnold Speert	5-M	8,116	643
Williams Coll, Williamstown, MA 01267	1793	Dr. Francis C. Oakley	1-M	2,112	274
William Smith Coll, Geneva, NY 14456 (3)	1908	Mr. Carroll W. Brewster	1-B	850	176
William Woods Coll, Fulton, MO 65251 (3)	1870	Dr. John M. Bartholomy	2-B	750	59
Wilmington Coll, New Castle, DE 19720	1967	Dr. Audrey K. Doberstein	1-M	1,698	135
Wilmington Coll, Wilmington, OH 45177	1870	Neil Thorburn	2-B	890	69
Wilson Coll, Chambersburg, PA 17201 (4)	1869	Dr. Mary-Linda Merriam	2-B	792	78
Wingate Coll, Wingate, NC 28174	1895	Dr. Paul R. Corts	2-B	1,690	92
Winona State U, Winona, MN 55987	1858	Dr. Darrell Krueger	5-M	7,500	400
Winston-Salem State U, Winston-Salem, NC 27110	1892	Dr. Cleon F. Thompson, Jr.	5-B	2,576	186
Winthrop Coll, Rock Hill, SC 29733	1886	Dr. Anthony DiGiorgio	5-M	5,388	424
Wittenberg U, Springfield, OH 45501	1845	Dr. William A. Kinnison	2-B	2,340	182
Wofford Coll, Spartanburg, SC 29301	1854	Dr. Joab M. Lesesne	2-B	1,121	83
Woodbury U, Burbank, CA 91510	1884	Dr. Wayne L. Miller	1-M	946	90
Worcester Polytechnic Inst, Worcester, MA 01609	1865	Dr. Jon C. Strauss	1-D	3,955	330
Worcester State Coll, Worcester, MA 01602	1874	Dr. Philip D. Vairo	5-M	4,800	199
Wright State U, Dayton, OH 45435	1964	Dr. Paige E. Mulhollan	5-D	17,423	950
Xavier U, Cincinnati, OH 45207	1831	NR	2-M	6,477	396
Xavier U of Louisiana, New Orleans, LA 70125	1925	Dr. Norman C. Francis	2-M	2,906	224
Yale U, New Haven, CT 06520	1701	Benno C. Schmidt, Jr.	1-D	10,967	723
Yeshiva U, New York, NY 10033	1886	Dr. Norman Lamm	1-D	4,602	164
York Coll of Pennsylvania, York, PA 17403	1787	Dr. Robert V. Iosue	1-M	4,954	260
York Coll of the City U of New York, Jamaica, NY 11451	1967	Mr. Milton G. Bassin	12-B	5,229	200
Youngstown State U, Youngstown, OH 44555	1908	Dr. Neil D. Humphrey	5-M	14,864	870

Two-Year Colleges

The highest undergraduate degree offered for all two-year colleges is the associate degree.

Name, address	Year	Governing official, control		Enrollment	Faculty
Abraham Baldwin Agricultural Coll, Tifton, GA 31794	1933	Dr. Harold J. Loyd	5	2,138	89
Adirondack Comm Coll, Queensbury, NY 12804	1960	Dr. Roger Andersen	12	3,200	140
Aiken Tech Coll, Aiken, SC 29802	1972	Dr. Paul L. Blowers	12	1,701	175
Aims Comm Coll, Greeley, CO 80632	1967	Dr. George R. Conger	10	8,018	420
Alamance Comm Coll, Haw River, NC 27258	1959	Dr. W. Ronald McCarter	5	3,259	145
Allan Hancock Coll, Santa Maria, CA 93454	1920	Dr. Gary R. Edelbrock	12	9,500	368
Allegany Comm Coll, Cumberland, MD 21502	1961	Dr. Donald L. Alexander	12	2,474	160
Allen County Comm Coll, Iola, KS 66749	1923	Dr. William A. Griffin, Jr.	12	1,345	125
Alpena Comm Coll, Alpena, MI 49707	1952	Dr. Donald L. Newport	12	2,238	122
Alvin Comm Coll, Alvin, TX 77511	1949	Dr. A. Rodney Allbright	12	3,906	209
Amarillo Coll, Amarillo, TX 79178	1929	Dr. George T. Miller	12	5,439	NR
American Inst of Business, Des Moines, IA 50321	1921	Keith Fenton	1	1,054	60
American River Coll, Sacramento, CA 95841	1955	Dr. Queen F. Randall	10	21,675	NR
Anderson Coll, Anderson, SC 29621	1911	Dr. Mark L. Hopkins	2	1,038	58
Angelina Coll, Lufkin, TX 75902	1968	Dr. Jack W. Hudgins	12	3,050	136
Anne Arundel Comm Coll, Arnold, MD 21012	1961	Dr. Thomas E. Florestano	12	12,000	590
Anoka-Ramsey Comm Coll, Coon Rapids, MN 55433	1965	Dr. Richard Carpenter	12	5,142	179
Antelope Valley Coll, Lancaster, CA 93536	1929	Dr. Allan W. Kurki	12	8,589	349
Arapahoe Comm Coll, Littleton, CO 80160	1965	Dr. James F. Weber	12	7,478	408
Arizona Western Coll, Yuma, AZ 85366	1962	Dr. James R. Carruthers	12	5,200	384
Arkansas State U-Beebe Branch, Beebe, AR 72012	1927	Mr. William H. Owen, Jr.	5	1,370	62
Art Inst of Atlanta, Atlanta, GA 30326	1949	John R. Knepper	3	1,480	108
Art Inst of Dallas, Dallas, TX 75231	1978	Ms. Deborah G. Wright	3	1,030	45
Art Inst of Philadelphia, Philadelphia, PA 19103	1966	William K. Bauer	3	1,100	90
Art Inst of Pittsburgh, Pittsburgh, PA 15222	1921	Saundra M. Van Dyke	3	2,208	94
Asheville-Buncombe Tech Comm Coll, Asheville, NC 28801	1959	Mr. Harvey L. Haynes	5	3,200	255
Asnuntuck Comm Coll, Enfield, CT 06082	1972	Dr. Harvey S. Irlen	5	1,850	79
Atlanta Metropolitan Coll, Atlanta, GA 30310	1974	Dr. Edwin A. Thompson	5	1,570	NR
Atlantic Comm Coll, Mays Landing, NJ 08330	1966	Dr. William Orth	9	4,165	215
Austin Comm Coll, Austin, MN 55912	1940	Mr. James Flannery	5	1,204	73
Austin Comm Coll, Austin, TX 78714	1972	Dr. Dan Angel	10	23,067	1,217
Bakersfield Coll, Bakersfield, CA 93305	1913	Dr. Richard Wright	12	12,473	448
Barton County Comm Coll, Great Bend, KS 67530	1969	Dr. Jimmie L. Downing	12	3,219	260
Bay de Noc Comm Coll, Escanaba, MI 49829	1963	Dr. Dwight E. Link	9	2,263	143
Beaufort County Comm Coll, Washington, NC 27889	1968	Mr. James P. Blanton	5	1,353	95
Beckley Coll, Beckley, WV 25802	1933	Dr. George D. Balsama	1	1,889	105
Bee County Coll, Beeville, TX 78102	1965	Dr. Norman Wallace	9	2,376	140
Belleville Area Coll, Belleville, IL 62221	1946	Dr. Joseph Cipfl	10	12,669	661
Bellevue Comm Coll, Bellevue, WA 98009	1966	B. Jean Floten	5	8,393	479
Belmont Tech Coll, St Clairsville, OH 43950	1971	Lewis C. Miller	5	1,699	138
Bergen Comm Coll, Paramus, NJ 07652	1965	Dr. Jose Lopez-Isa	9	7,302	493
Berkshire Comm Coll, Pittsfield, MA 01201	1960	Dr. Cathryn L. Addy	5	2,150	126
Bessemer State Tech Coll, Bessemer, AL 35021	1966	Dr. W. Michael Bailey	5	1,628	102

Name, address	Year	Governing official, control	Enrollment	Faculty
Big Bend Comm Coll, Moses Lake, WA 98837	1962	Dr. Greg Fitch 5	2,151	147
Bishop State Comm Coll, Mobile, AL 36690	1965	Dr. Yvonne Kennedy 5	1,857	60
Bismarck State Comm Coll, Bismarck, ND 58501	1939	Dr. Kermit Lidstrom 5	2,602	117
Black Hawk Coll–Quad-Cities Cmps, Moline, IL 61265	1946	Dr. Herbert C. Lyon 12	5,226	297
Blackhawk Tech Coll, Janesville, WI 53547	1968	Dr. James C. Catania 10	2,100	128
Blinn Coll, Brenham, TX 77833	1883	Walter C. Schwartz 12	6,472	205
Blue Mountain Comm Coll, Pendleton, OR 97801	1962	Mr. Ronald L. Daniels 9	3,552	189
Blue Ridge Comm Coll, Weyers Cave, VA 24486	1965	Dr. James R. Perkins 5	2,514	160
Blue Ridge Tech Coll, Flat Rock, NC 28731	1969	Dr. David W. Sink 12	1,313	82
Borough of Manhattan Comm Coll of City U of NY, New York, NY 10007	1963	Dr. Augusta Souza Kappner 12	13,845	1,108
Bossier Parish Comm Coll, Bossier City, LA 71111	1967	James M. Conerly 12	2,820	103
Bowling Green State U–Firelands Coll, Huron, OH 44839	1968	Dr. Robert DeBard 5	1,338	72
Brainerd Comm Coll, Brainerd, MN 56401	1938	Sally Jane Ihne 5	1,644	77
Brazosport Coll, Lake Jackson, TX 77566	1948	Dr. John R. Grable 12	3,729	135
Brevard Comm Coll, Cocoa, FL 32922	1960	Dr. Maxwell C. King 5	13,617	896
Bristol Comm Coll, Fall River, MA 02720	1965	Ms. Eileen Farley 5	2,802	177
Brookdale Comm Coll, Lincroft, NJ 07738	1967	Dr. Joshua L. Smith 9	11,308	443
Brookhaven Coll, Farmers Branch, TX 75244	1978	Dr. Patsy J. Fulton 9	8,246	385
Broome Comm Coll, Binghamton, NY 13902	1946	Dr. Donald A. Dellow 12	6,400	453
Broward Comm Coll, Fort Lauderdale, FL 33301	1960	Dr. Willis N. Holcombe 5	21,370	744
Brunswick Coll, Brunswick, GA 31523	1961	NR 5	1,332	65
Bryant and Stratton Business Inst, Buffalo, NY 14202	1854	Mr. James J. Pautler 3	1,408	92
Bryant and Stratton Business Inst, E Hills Cmps, Williamsville, NY 14221	1978	David J. Pauldine 3	1,154	64
Bucks County Comm Coll, Newtown, PA 18940	1964	Dr. William E. Vincent 9	11,042	375
Bunker Hill Comm Coll, Boston, MA 02129	1973	NR 5	6,074	155
Burlington County Coll, Pemberton, NJ 08068	1966	Dr. Robert Messina 5	6,843	150
Butler County Comm Coll, El Dorado, KS 67042	1927	Dr. Rodney Cox 12	4,393	294
Butler County Comm Coll, Butler, PA 16001	1965	Dr. William N. Price 9	2,930	120
Butte Coll, Oroville, CA 95965	1966	Dr. Wendell L. Reeder 10	12,838	575
Cabrillo Coll, Aptos, CA 95003	1959	Dr. Robert F. Agrella 10	13,113	492
Caldwell Comm Coll and Tech Inst, Hudson, NC 28638	1964	Dr. Eric B. McKeithan 5	2,600	183
California Coll for Health Sciences, National City, CA 92050	1977	Charles Sinks 3	3,000	4
Camden County Coll, Blackwood, NJ 08012	1967	Dr. Robert W. Ramsay 12	10,410	385
Cañada Coll, Redwood City, CA 94061	1968	NR 10	7,500	239
Cape Cod Comm Coll, West Barnstable, MA 02668	1961	Dr. Vernon Beuke 5	2,026	160
Cape Fear Comm Coll, Wilmington, NC 28401	1959	Dr. E. Thomas Satterfield, Jr. .5	2,700	77
Carl Albert Jr Coll, Poteau, OK 74953	1934	NR 5	1,655	160
Carl Sandburg Coll, Galesburg, IL 61401	1967	Jack W. Fuller 5	2,912	117
Carteret Comm Coll, Morehead City, NC 28557	1963	Dr. Donald W. Bryant 5	1,436	86
Casper Coll, Casper, WY 82601	1945	Dr. Lester Vierra 5	2,118	171
Catawba Valley Comm Coll, Hickory, NC 28602	1960	Dr. Cuyler A. Dunbar 12	3,200	150
Catonsville Comm Coll, Catonsville, MD 21228	1957	Dr. Mary Ellen Duncan 9	10,236	505
Cayuga County Comm Coll, Auburn, NY 13021	1953	Dr. Lawrence H. Poole 12	2,792	144
Cazenovia Coll, Cazenovia, NY 13035	1824	Dr. Stephen M. Schneeweiss .1	1,055	134
Cecil Comm Coll, North East, MD 21901	1968	Dr. Robert L. Gell 9	1,632	107
Cedar Valley Coll, Lancaster, TX 75134	1977	Dr. Floyd S. Elkins 5	3,281	130
Central Alabama Comm Coll–Alexander City Cmps, Alexander City, AL 35010	1965	Dr. James H. Cornell 5	1,863	81
Central Carolina Comm Coll, Sanford, NC 27330	1962	Dr. Marvin R. Joyner 12	2,658	177
Central Comm Coll–Grand Island Cmps, Grand Island, NE 68802	1976	Donald Nelson 12	3,897	75
Central Comm Coll–Hastings Cmps, Hastings, NE 68902	1966	Dr. Carl H. Rolf 12	2,730	116
Central Comm Coll–Platte Cmps, Columbus, NE 68602	1968	Dr. Peter Rush 12	3,243	97
Central Florida Comm Coll, Ocala, FL 32678	1957	Dr. William J. Campion 12	4,800	180
Centralia Coll, Centralia, WA 98531	1925	Dr. Henry P. Kirk 5	1,900	112
Central Ohio Tech Coll, Newark, OH 43055	1971	Dr. Julius S. Greenstein 5	1,545	106
Central Oregon Comm Coll, Bend, OR 97701	1949	Dr. Robert L. Barber 10	2,700	195
Central Piedmont Comm Coll, Charlotte, NC 28235	1963	Dr. Ruth Shaw 12	16,672	1,100
Central Virginia Comm Coll, Lynchburg, VA 24502	1966	Dr. J. E. Merritt 5	4,199	114
Central Wyoming Coll, Riverton, WY 82501	1966	Dr. JoAnne McFarland 12	1,429	72
Cerritos Coll, Norwalk, CA 90650	1956	Dr. Ernest Martinez 12	19,961	713
Cerro Coso Comm Coll, Ridgecrest, CA 93555	1973	Dr. Raymond A. McCue 5	3,865	131
Chabot Coll, Hayward, CA 94545	1961	Dr. Richard D. Yeo 5	19,686	1,075
Chaffey Coll, Rancho Cucamonga, CA 91701	1883	Dr. Jerry W. Young 10	13,372	500
Champlain Coll, Burlington, VT 05402	1878	Dr. Robert A. Skiff 1	1,590	114
Charles County Comm Coll, La Plata, MD 20646	1958	Dr. John Sine 12	5,143	247
Charles Stewart Mott Comm Coll, Flint, MI 48502	1923	Mr. David G. Moore 9	10,469	345
Chattahoochee Valley State Comm Coll, Phenix City, AL 36867	1974	Dr. James E. Owen 5	1,621	71
Chattanooga State Tech Comm Coll, Chattanooga, TN 37406	1965	Dr. Harry D. Wagner 5	7,412	NR
Chemeketa Comm Coll, Salem, OR 97309	1955	William Segura 12	8,997	685
Chesapeake Coll, Wye Mills, MD 21679	1965	Dr. Robert C. Schleiger 12	2,247	216
Chipola Jr Coll, Marianna, FL 32446	1947	Dr. Jerry W. Kandzer 5	2,128	110
Chippewa Valley Tech Coll, Eau Claire, WI 54701	1912	Mr. Norbert K. Wurtzel 10	3,750	400
Chowan Coll, Murfreesboro, NC 27855	1848	Dr. Jerry F. Jackson 2	1,015	66
Cincinnati Tech Coll, Cincinnati, OH 45223	1966	Dr. James P. Long 5	4,501	349
Cisco Jr Coll, Cisco, TX 76437	1940	Dr. Roger C. Schustereit 12	1,984	98
Citrus Coll, Glendora, CA 91740	1915	Dr. Louis F. Zellers 12	9,326	527
City Coll of San Francisco, San Francisco, CA 94112	1935	Dr. Willis R. Kirk 12	29,691	1,097
City Colls of Chicago, Chicago City-Wide Coll, Chicago, IL 60606	1975	Dr. Martha Bazik 12	3,145	306
City Colls of Chicago, Harold Washington Coll, Chicago, IL 60601	1962	Dr. Bernice Miller 12	7,238	187
City Colls of Chicago, Harry S Truman Coll, Chicago, IL 60640	1956	Dr. Wallace B. Appelson 12	4,925	170
City Colls of Chicago, Kennedy-King Coll, Chicago, IL 60621	1935	Dr. Harold Pates 12	3,001	163
City Colls of Chicago, Malcolm X Coll, Chicago, IL 60612	1911	Dr. Milton F. Brown 12	1,921	142
City Colls of Chicago, Olive-Harvey Coll, Chicago, IL 60628	1970	Mr. Homer D. Franklin 12	3,345	132
City Colls of Chicago, Richard J Daley Coll, Chicago, IL 60652	1960	Dr. William P. Conway 12	4,990	166
City Colls of Chicago, Wilbur Wright Coll, Chicago, IL 60634	1934	Mr. Raymond F. LeFevour 12	5,648	161

Name, address	Year	Governing official, control	Enrollment	Faculty
Clackamas Comm Coll, Oregon City, OR 97045	1966	Dr. John S. Keyser 9	5,990	577
Clarendon Coll, Clarendon, TX 79226	1898	Dr. Jerry Stockton 12	1,000	57
Clark Coll, Vancouver, WA 98663	1933	Dr. Earl P. Johnson 5	9,300	320
Clark County Comm Coll, North Las Vegas, NV 89030	1971	Dr. Paul E. Meacham 5	16,037	526
Clark State Comm Coll, Springfield, OH 45501	1962	Mr. Albert A. Salerno 5	2,381	121
Clatsop Comm Coll, Astoria, OR 97103	1958	Mr. Philip L. Bainer 9	2,630	169
Cleveland Comm Coll, Shelby, NC 28150	1965	Dr. James B. Petty 5	1,487	80
Cleveland Inst of Electronics, Cleveland, OH 44114 (2)	1934	John R. Drinko 3	3,100	6
Cleveland State Comm Coll, Cleveland, TN 37320	1967	Dr. James W. Ford 5	3,098	180
Clinton Comm Coll, Clinton, IA 52732	1946	Desna L. Wallin 5	1,173	64
Clinton Comm Coll, Plattsburgh, NY 12901	1969	Dr. Jay Fennell 12	2,007	156
Cloud County Comm Coll, Concordia, KS 66901	1965	Dr. James P. Ihrig 12	2,811	271
Coahoma Comm Coll, Clarksdale, MS 38614	1949	Dr. McKinley C. Martin 12	1,478	85
Coastal Carolina Comm Coll, Jacksonville, NC 28540	1964	Dr. Ronald K. Lingle, Jr. 12	3,737	165
Coastline Comm Coll, Fountain Valley, CA 92708	1976	Dr. William M. Vega 12	16,753	490
Cochise Coll, Douglas, AZ 85607	1962	Dr. Dan W. Rehurek 12	4,897	313
Coffeyville Comm Coll, Coffeyville, KS 67337	1923	Dr. Dan Kinney 12	2,106	86
Coll of Alameda, Alameda, CA 94501	1970	Ronald A. Kong 12	5,914	NR
Coll of DuPage, Glen Ellyn, IL 60137	1967	Dr. Harold D. McAninch 12	28,037	1,532
Coll of Eastern Utah, Price, UT 84501	1937	Dr. Michael A. Petersen 5	2,341	96
Coll of Lake County, Grayslake, IL 60030	1967	Dr. Daniel J. La Vista 10	13,930	615
Coll of San Mateo, San Mateo, CA 94402	1922	Dr. Lois A. Callahan 12	14,424	485
Coll of Southern Idaho, Twin Falls, ID 83303	1964	Mr. Gerald R. Meyerhoeffer . . 12	2,684	108
Coll of The Albemarle, Elizabeth City, NC 27906	1960	Dr. Parker Chesson, Jr. 5	1,696	110
Coll of the Canyons, Valencia, CA 91355	1969	Dr. Dianne G. Van Hook 12	5,667	228
Coll of the Desert, Palm Desert, CA 92260	1959	Dr. David A. George 12	12,000	315
Coll of the Mainland, Texas City, TX 77591	1967	Mr. Larry L. Stanley 12	3,527	180
Coll of the Redwoods, Eureka, CA 95501	1964	Dr. Cedric A. Sampson 12	7,724	NR
Coll of the Sequoias, Visalia, CA 93277	1925	Dr. Lincoln H. Hall 12	8,525	380
Coll of the Siskiyous, Weed, CA 96094	1957	Dr. Eugene Schumacher 12	2,505	158
Collin County Comm Coll, McKinney, TX 75070	1985	Dr. John H. Anthony 12	8,567	439
Colorado Inst of Art, Denver, CO 80203	1952	Cheryl Murphy 3	1,357	70
Columbia Basin Coll, Pasco, WA 99301	1955	Dr. Marv Weiss 5	5,940	350
Columbia Coll, Columbia, CA 95310	1968	Dr. Dean Cunningham 12	3,600	104
Columbia-Greene Comm Coll, Hudson, NY 12534	1969	Dr. Terry A. Cline 12	1,521	110
Columbia State Comm Coll, Columbia, TN 38401	1966	Dr. Paul Sands 5	3,053	95
Columbus State Comm Coll, Columbus, OH 43216	1963	Dr. Harold M. Nestor 5	11,094	778
Comm Coll of Allegheny County Allegheny Cmps, Pittsburgh, PA 15212	1966	NR 9	7,530	1,449
Comm Coll of Allegheny County Boyce Cmps, Monroeville, PA 15146	1966	Dr. Carl A. Di Sibio 9	4,316	779
Comm Coll of Allegheny County Coll Ctr–North, Pittsburgh, PA 15237	1972	Dr. Fred F. Bartok 9	3,395	1,394
Comm Coll of Allegheny County South Cmps, West Mifflin, PA 15122	1967	Dr. Thomas A. Juravich 9	5,294	760
Comm Coll of Aurora, Aurora, CO 80011	1983	Larry Carter 5	4,226	232
Comm Coll of Baltimore, Baltimore, MD 21215	1947	Dr. Joseph T. Durham 12	6,200	493
Comm Coll of Beaver County, Monaca, PA 15061	1966	Dr. Margaret J. Williams 5	2,704	150
Comm Coll of Denver, Denver, CO 80204	1970	Dr. Byron McClenney 5	5,098	186
Comm Coll of Philadelphia, Philadelphia, PA 19130	1964	Dr. B. A. Barringer 12	14,542	861
Comm Coll of Rhode Island, Warwick, RI 02886	1964	Edward Liston 5	9,299	543
Comm Coll of the Air Force, Maxwell Air Force Base, AL 36112	1972	Col. R. A. Gregory, Jr. 4	370,000	10,000
Comm Coll of the Finger Lakes, Canandaigua, NY 14424	1965	Dr. Charles J. Meder 12	3,669	209
Comm Coll of Vermont, Waterbury, VT 05676	1970	Mr. Kenneth G. Kalb 5	1,259	461
Compton Comm Coll, Compton, CA 90221	1927	Dr. Warren A. Washington . . . 12	5,248	347
Condie Jr Coll, Campbell, CA 95008	1968	Leslie E. Pritchard 3	1,000	45
Connors State Coll, Warner, OK 74469	1908	Dr. Carl O. Westbrook 5	1,963	78
Contra Costa Coll, San Pablo, CA 94806	1948	Dr. D. Candy Rose 12	8,214	281
Cooke County Coll, Gainesville, TX 76240	1924	Dr. Luther Bud Joyner 9	3,044	164
Copiah-Lincoln Comm Coll, Wesson, MS 39191	1928	Dr. Billy B. Thames 12	1,479	116
Corning Comm Coll, Corning, NY 14830	1956	Dr. Donald H. Hangen 12	2,853	129
Cosumnes River Coll, Sacramento, CA 95823	1970	Dr. Marc E. Hall 10	8,854	264
County Coll of Morris, Randolph, NJ 07869	1966	Dr. Edward J. Yaw 9	9,995	730
Cowley County Comm Coll and Voc-Tech Sch, Arkansas City, KS 67005	1922	Dr. Patrick J. McAtee 12	2,533	58
Crafton Hills Coll, Yucaipa, CA 92399	1972	Dr. Donald L. Singer 12	4,574	211
Craven Comm Coll, New Bern, NC 28560	1965	Dr. Thurman E. Brock 5	2,360	188
Crowder Coll, Neosho, MO 64850	1963	Dr. Kent A. Farnsworth 12	1,531	NR
Culinary Inst of America, Hyde Park, NY 12538	1946	Mr. Ferdinand E. Metz 1	1,833	100
Cumberland County Coll, Vineland, NJ 08360	1963	Dr. Roland J. Chapdelaine . . 12	2,416	97
Cuyahoga Comm Coll, Eastern Cmps, Warrensville Township, OH 44122	1971	Dr. Grace Carolyn Brown . . . 12	5,644	253
Cuyahoga Comm Coll, Metropolitan Cmps, Cleveland, OH 44115	1963	Dr. Ronald R. Zambetti 12	5,682	NR
Cuyahoga Comm Coll, Western Cmps, Parma, OH 44130	1966	Mr. Ronald M. Sobel 12	11,811	527
Cypress Coll, Cypress, CA 90630	1966	Dr. Kirk Avery 12	14,500	398
Dabney S Lancaster Comm Coll, Clifton Forge, VA 24422	1964	Dr. John F. Backels 5	1,510	NR
Dalton Coll, Dalton, GA 30720	1963	Dr. Derrell C. Roberts 5	2,160	61
Danville Comm Coll, Danville, VA 24541	1967	Dr. Arnold R. Oliver 5	3,050	141
Darton Coll, Albany, GA 31707	1965	Dr. Peter J. Sireno 5	1,934	84
Davenport Coll of Business, Kalamazoo Cmps, Kalamazoo, MI 49007 (4)	1866	C. Dexter Rohm 1	1,059	79
Davidson County Comm Coll, Lexington, NC 27293	1958	Dr. J. Bryan Brooks 12	2,721	153
Dean Jr Coll, Franklin, MA 02038	1865	Mr. Richard E. Crockford . . . 1	1,200	102
De Anza Coll, Cupertino, CA 95014	1967	Dr. A. Robert Dehart 12	25,959	897
DeKalb Coll, Decatur, GA 30034	1964	Dr. Marvin M. Cole 5	12,661	NR
Delaware County Comm Coll, Media, PA 19063	1967	Dr. Richard D. De Cosmo . . . 12	8,703	419
Delaware Tech & Comm Coll, Southern Cmps, Georgetown, DE 19947	1967	Mr. Jack F. Owens 5	2,738	364
Delaware Tech & Comm Coll, Stanton/Wilmington Cmps, Newark, DE 19702	1968	Orlando J. George 5	5,470	530
Delaware Tech & Comm Coll, Terry Cmps, Dover, DE 19901	1972	Dr. Linda C. Jolly 5	1,749	280
Delgado Comm Coll, New Orleans, LA 70119	1921	Dr. James Caillier 5	9,100	484
Del Mar Coll, Corpus Christi, TX 78404	1935	Mr. B. R. Venters 12	10,283	480
Delta Coll, University Center, MI 48710	1961	Mr. Donald J. Carlyon 10	10,923	431

Name, address	Year	Governing official, control	Enrollment	Faculty
Des Moines Area Comm Coll, Ankeny, IA 50021	1966	Dr. Joseph Borgen 12	10,338	217
Dixie Coll, St George, UT 84770	1911	Dr. Douglas Alder 5	2,350	106
Dodge City Comm Coll, Dodge City, KS 67801	1935	Dr. Thomas E. Gamble 12	2,414	84
Dundalk Comm Coll, Baltimore, MD 21222	1970	Dr. Martha A. Smith 9	3,336	191
Durham Tech Comm Coll, Durham, NC 27703	1961	Dr. Phail Wynn, Jr. 5	4,875	242
Dutchess Comm Coll, Poughkeepsie, NY 12601	1957	Dr. Jerry Lee 12	6,747	338
Dyersburg State Comm Coll, Dyersburg, TN 38025	1969	Dr. Karen A. Bowyer 5	1,207	136
East Central Coll, Union, MO 63084	1968	Fred E. Davis 10	2,753	120
East Central Comm Coll, Decatur, MS 39327	1928	Dr. Eddie M. Smith 12	1,199	53
Eastern Arizona Coll, Thatcher, AZ 85552	1888	Mr. Gherald L. Hoopes, Jr. . . 12	1,058	246
Eastern New Mexico U–Roswell, Roswell, NM 88202	1958	Dr. Loyd R. Hughes 5	1,842	85
Eastern Oklahoma State Coll, Wilburton, OK 74578	1907	NR 5	2,446	89
Eastern Wyoming Coll, Torrington, WY 82240	1948	Mr. Guido Smith 12	1,627	49
Eastfield Coll, Mesquite, TX 75150	1970	Dr. Justus D. Sundermann . . 12	9,125	399
East Los Angeles Coll, Monterey Park, CA 91754	1945	Dr. Omero Suarez 12	13,000	450
Edgecombe Comm Coll, Tarboro, NC 27886	1968	Mr. Charles B. McIntyre . . . 12	1,502	134
Edison Comm Coll, Fort Myers, FL 33906	1962	Dr. David G. Robinson 12	8,597	355
Edison State Comm Coll, Piqua, OH 45356	1973	Dr. Kenneth A. Yowell 5	2,797	157
Edmonds Comm Coll, Lynnwood, WA 98036	1967	Mr. Thomas C. Nielsen . . . 12	5,352	278
El Centro Coll, Dallas, TX 75202	1966	Dr. Wright L. Lassiter, Jr. . . .9	5,735	322
El Reno Jr Coll, El Reno, OK 73036	1938	Dr. Larry F. Devane 12	1,260	73
Enterprise State Jr Coll, Enterprise, AL 36331	1965	Dr. Joseph D. Talmadge 5	2,171	114
Erie Comm Coll, City Cmps, Buffalo, NY 14203	1971	Dr. Louis M. Ricci 12	3,272	170
Erie Comm Coll, North Cmps, Williamsville, NY 14221	1946	Dr. Louis M. Ricci 12	6,157	299
Erie Comm Coll, South Cmps, Orchard Park, NY 14127	1974	Dr. Louis M. Ricci 12	3,554	226
Essex Comm Coll, Baltimore, MD 21237	1957	Dr. John E. Ravekes 12	10,728	483
Essex County Coll, Newark, NJ 07102	1966	Dr. Zachary Yamba 9	6,284	156
Eugenio María de Hostos Comm Coll of City U of NY, Bronx, NY 10451	1968	Dr. I. Santiago 12	4,075	NR
Everett Comm Coll, Everett, WA 98201	1941	Mr. Robert Drewel 5	3,932	230
Evergreen Valley Coll, San Jose, CA 95135	1975	Dr. Gerald H. Strelitz 12	10,954	257
Fairleigh Dickinson U, Edward Williams Coll, Hackensack, NJ 07601	1964	Kenneth T. Vehrkens 1	1,501	67
Fashion Inst of Design & Merchandising, LA Cmps, Los Angeles, CA 90017	1969	Ms. Tonian Hohberg 3	3,052	160
Fayetteville Tech Comm Coll, Fayetteville, NC 28303	1961	Dr. Craig Allen 5	6,318	396
Feather River Coll, Quincy, CA 95971	1968	Dr. Donald Donato 12	1,202	83
Fiorello H LaGuardia Comm Coll of City U of NY, Long Island City, NY 11101	1971	Martin G. Moed 12	9,231	633
Flathead Valley Comm Coll, Kalispell, MT 59901	1967	Dr. Howard L. Fryett 12	1,758	119
Florence-Darlington Tech Coll, Florence, SC 29501	1963	Dr. Michael B. McCall 5	2,215	210
Floyd Coll, Rome, GA 30163	1970	Dr. David B. McCorkle 5	1,615	66
Foothill Coll, Los Altos Hills, CA 94022	1958	Dr. Thomas H. Clements . . . 12	18,191	500
Forsyth Tech Comm Coll, Winston-Salem, NC 27103	1964	Dr. Bob H. Greene 5	4,874	231
Fort Scott Comm Coll, Fort Scott, KS 66701	1919	Mr. Richard D. Hedges 12	1,900	131
Fox Valley Tech Coll, Appleton, WI 54915	1967	Dr. Stanley J. Spanbauer . . . 12	4,749	1,241
Frederick Comm Coll, Frederick, MD 21701	1957	Dr. Lee J. Betts 12	3,703	253
Fresno City Coll, Fresno, CA 93741	1910	Dr. Ernest R. Leach 10	17,122	534
Front Range Comm Coll, Westminster, CO 80030	1968	Dr. Cary Israel 5	8,761	450
Fullerton Coll, Fullerton, CA 92634	1913	Dr. Philip W. Borst 12	19,236	678
Fulton-Montgomery Comm Coll, Johnstown, NY 12095	1964	Mr. John G. Boshart 12	1,745	122
Gadsden State Comm Coll, Gadsden, AL 35999	1965	Dr. Victor Ficker 5	5,042	NR
Gainesville Coll, Gainesville, GA 30503	1964	Dr. J. Foster Watkins 12	2,347	93
Galveston Coll, Galveston, TX 77550	1967	John E. Pickelman 12	2,060	122
Garden City Comm Coll, Garden City, KS 67846	1919	Dr. James H. Tangeman . . . 10	2,021	100
Gaston Coll, Dallas, NC 28034	1963	Dr. W. Wayne Scott 12	3,652	256
Gateway Comm Coll, Phoenix, AZ 85034	1968	Phil Randolph 12	5,356	213
Gateway Tech Coll, Racine, WI 53403	1911	Dr. John R. Birkholz 12	7,973	759
Genesee Comm Coll, Batavia, NY 14020	1966	Dr. Stuart Steiner 12	3,124	187
George Corley Wallace State Comm Coll, Selma, AL 36702	1966	Dr. Julius Ray Brown 5	1,526	72
Georgia Military Coll, Milledgeville, GA 31061	1879	Maj. Gen. William Acker . . . 12	1,614	187
Germanna Comm Coll, Locust Grove, VA 22508	1970	Dr. Francis S. Turnage 5	2,500	83
Glendale Comm Coll, Glendale, AZ 85302	1965	Dr. John R. Waltrip 12	18,240	590
Glen Oaks Comm Coll, Centreville, MI 49032	1965	Dr. Philip G. Ward 12	1,467	81
Gloucester County Coll, Sewell, NJ 08080	1967	Dr. Richard N. Jones 12	4,114	151
Gogebic Comm Coll, Ironwood, MI 49938	1932	Dr. James R. Grote 12	1,148	79
Golden West Coll, Huntington Beach, CA 92647	1966	Ms. Judith Valles 5	14,900	430
Gordon Coll, Barnesville, GA 30204	1852	Dr. Jerry M. Williamson 5	1,428	80
Grays Harbor Coll, Aberdeen, WA 98520	1930	Dr. Jewell Manspeaker 5	1,471	115
Grayson County Coll, Denison, TX 75020	1964	Dr. Jim M. Williams 12	3,185	176
Greater Hartford Comm Coll, Hartford, CT 06105	1967	Dr. Conrad L. Mallett 5	2,991	NR
Great Lakes Jr Coll of Business, Saginaw, MI 48607	1907	Angelo Guerriero 1	1,941	133
Greenfield Comm Coll, Greenfield, MA 01301	1962	Katherine H. Sloan 5	1,682	81
Greenville Tech Coll, Greenville, SC 29606	1962	Dr. Thomas E. Barton, Jr. . . .5	9,015	493
Grossmont Coll, El Cajon, CA 92020	1961	Dr. Ivan L. Jones 12	16,207	609
Guam Comm Coll, Guam Main Facility, GU 96921	1977	Mr. John T. Cruz 8	1,965	253
Guilford Tech Comm Coll, Jamestown, NC 27282	1958	Dr. Ray Needham 12	7,346	539
Gulf Coast Comm Coll, Panama City, FL 32401	1957	Dr. Robert L. McSpadden 5	5,237	299
Hagerstown Jr Coll, Hagerstown, MD 21740	1946	Dr. Norman P. Shea 9	3,164	196
Harford Comm Coll, Bel Air, MD 21014	1957	Dr. Richard J. Pappas 12	4,875	276
Harrisburg Area Comm Coll, Harrisburg, PA 17110	1964	Dr. Kenneth B. Woodbury, Jr. . 12	8,123	375
Hartnell Coll, Salinas, CA 93901	1920	Dr. James R. Hardt 10	7,455	272
Hawkeye Inst of Tech, Waterloo, IA 50704	1967	Dr. John E. Hawse 12	2,054	165
Haywood Comm Coll, Clyde, NC 28721	1964	Dr. Dan W. Moore 12	1,161	86
Henry Ford Comm Coll, Dearborn, MI 48128	1938	Dr. Andrew A. Mazzara 10	16,119	1,005
Herkimer County Comm Coll, Herkimer, NY 13350	1966	Dr. Ronald F. Williams 12	2,444	86
Hesser Coll, Manchester, NH 03101	1900	Linwood W. Galeucia 3	2,200	60
Hibbing Comm Coll, Hibbing, MN 55746	1916	Dr. Andrew Kuznik 5	1,821	70
Highland Comm Coll, Freeport, IL 61032	1962	Dr. Joseph C. Piland 10	2,983	169
Highland Comm Coll, Highland, KS 66035	1858	Dr. Walter Browe 12	2,003	162
Highline Comm Coll, Des Moines, WA 98198	1961	Dr. Shirley B. Gordon 5	8,700	432
Hill Coll of the Hill Jr Coll District, Hillsboro, TX 76645	1923	Dr. W. R. Auvenshine 10	1,500	98
Hillsborough Comm Coll, Tampa, FL 33631	1968	Dr. Andreas A. Paloumpis 5	16,981	570

Name, address	Year	Governing official, control	Enrollment	Faculty
Hinds Comm Coll, Raymond, MS 39154	1917	NR . . . 12	8,107	656
Holmes Comm Coll, Goodman, MS 39079	1928	NR . . . 12	1,986	125
Holyoke Comm Coll, Holyoke, MA 01040	1946	Dr. David M. Bartley . . . 5	3,026	189
Horry-Georgetown Tech Coll, Conway, SC 29526	1965	Dr. D. Kent Sharples . . . 12	1,659	113
Housatonic Comm Coll, Bridgeport, CT 06608	1966	Dr. Vincent S. Darnowski . . . 5	2,568	92
Houston Comm Coll System, Houston, TX 77270	1971	Mr. J. B. Whiteley . . . 12	32,314	1,246
Howard Coll, Big Spring, TX 79720	1945	Dr. Bob E. Riley . . . 12	1,597	127
Howard Coll, Columbia, MD 21044	1966	Dr. Dwight A. Burrill . . . 12	4,198	255
Hudson County Comm Coll, Jersey City, NJ 07306	1974	Mark Oromaner . . . 12	2,708	NR
Hudson Valley Comm Coll, Troy, NY 12180	1953	Dr. Joseph J. Bulmer . . . 12	9,331	448
Hutchinson Comm Coll, Hutchinson, KS 67501	1928	Dr. James H. Stringer . . . 12	4,278	286
ICS Ctr for Degree Studies, Scranton, PA 18515	1975	Mr. Gary Keisling . . . 3	23,171	5
Illinois Central Coll, East Peoria, IL 61635	1967	Dr. Thomas K. Thomas . . . 12	12,960	526
Illinois Eastern Comm Colls, Frontier Comm Coll, Fairfield, IL 62837	1976	Richard Mason . . . 12	2,535	171
Illinois Eastern Comm Colls, Olney Central Coll, Olney, IL 62450	1960	Dr. Stephen J. Kridelbaugh . . 12	1,744	96
Illinois Eastern Comm Colls, Wabash Valley Coll, Mount Carmel, IL 62863	1960	Dr. Harry K. Benson . . . 12	3,358	90
Illinois Valley Comm Coll, Oglesby, IL 61348	1924	Dr. Alfred E. Wisgoski . . . 10	4,366	NR
Imperial Valley Coll, Imperial, CA 92251	1922	Dr. John A. DePaoli . . . 12	4,693	143
Independence Comm Coll, Independence, KS 67301	1925	Dr. Jo Ann C. McDowell . . . 10	1,948	153
Indiana Business Coll, Indianapolis, IN 46204	1902	Kenneth J. Konesco . . . 3	1,600	NR
Indiana Vocational Tech Coll—Central Indiana, Indianapolis, IN 46206	1963	Dr. Meredith L. Carter . . . 5	5,117	316
Indiana Vocational Tech Coll—Columbus, Columbus, IN 47203	1963	NR . . . 5	2,261	134
Indiana Vocational Tech Coll—Eastcentral, Muncie, IN 47302	1968	NR . . . 5	1,910	120
Indiana Vocational Tech Coll—Kokomo, Kokomo, IN 46901	1968	Dr. Ken Martin . . . 5	2,009	110
Indiana Vocational Tech Coll—Lafayette, Lafayette, IN 47903	1968	Dr. Elizabeth J. Doversberger . . 5	1,745	104
Indiana Vocational Tech Coll—Northcentral, South Bend, IN 46619	1968	Dr. Carl F. Lutz . . . 5	2,693	186
Indiana Vocational Tech Coll—Northeast, Fort Wayne, IN 46805	1969	Mr. Jon L. Rupright . . . 5	3,087	180
Indiana Vocational Tech Coll—Northwest, Gary, IN 46409	1963	Mrs. Della Burt-Bradley . . . 5	2,519	186
Indiana Vocational Tech Coll—Southcentral, Sellersburg, IN 47172	1968	Jonathan W. Thomas . . . 5	1,494	107
Indiana Vocational Tech Coll—Southwest, Evansville, IN 47710	1963	Dr. H. Victor Baldi . . . 5	2,202	148
Indiana Vocational Tech Coll—Wabash Valley, Terre Haute, IN 47802	1966	Mr. Sam E. Borden . . . 5	1,935	118
Indiana Vocational Tech Coll—Whitewater, Richmond, IN 47374	1963	Dr. Judith A. Redwine . . . 5	1,023	72
Indian Hills Comm Coll, Ottumwa, IA 52501	1966	Dr. Lyle A. Hellyer . . . 12	2,857	139
Indian River Comm Coll, Fort Pierce, FL 34954	1960	Dr. Edwin R. Massey . . . 5	5,000	720
Inver Hills Comm Coll, Inver Grove Heights, MN 55076	1969	Dr. Patrick A. Roche . . . 5	5,096	192
Iona Coll–Sch of Associate Degree Studies, Yonkers, NY 10701	1940	NR . . . 1	1,399	158
Iowa Central Comm Coll, Fort Dodge, IA 50501	1966	Dr. Jack L. Bottenfield . . . 12	2,500	155
Iowa Western Comm Coll, Council Bluffs, IA 51502	1966	Dr. Carl L. Heinrich . . . 10	3,013	166
Irvine Valley Coll, Irvine, CA 92720	1979	Anna L. McFarlin . . . 12	7,460	227
Isothermal Comm Coll, Spindale, NC 28160	1965	Dr. Willard L. Lewis . . . 5	1,483	92
Itasca Comm Coll, Grand Rapids, MN 55744	1922	Dr. Lawrence N. Dukes . . . 5	1,414	89
Itawamba Comm Coll, Fulton, MS 38843	1947	Dr. W. O. Benjamin . . . 12	3,250	102
Jackson Comm Coll, Jackson, MI 49201	1928	Dr. Clyde LeTarte . . . 9	7,000	440
Jackson State Comm Coll, Jackson, TN 38301	1967	Dr. Walter L. Nelms . . . 5	3,010	145
James H Faulkner State Jr Coll, Bay Minette, AL 36507	1965	Dr. Gary L. Branch . . . 5	2,923	117
Jamestown Comm Coll, Jamestown, NY 14701	1950	Mr. Paul A. Benke . . . 12	4,378	245
Jefferson Coll, Hillsboro, MO 63050	1963	Dr. Gery Hochanadel . . . 12	3,719	163
Jefferson Comm Coll, Watertown, NY 13601	1961	Mr. John T. Henderson . . . 12	1,903	180
Jefferson Davis State Jr Coll, Brewton, AL 36427	1965	Sandra K. McLeod . . . 5	1,085	75
Jefferson State Comm Coll, Birmingham, AL 35215	1965	Dr. Judy M. Merritt . . . 12	7,205	340
Jefferson Tech Coll, Steubenville, OH 43952	1966	Dr. Edward L. Florak . . . 12	1,528	98
John A Logan Coll, Carterville, IL 62918	1967	Dr. Ray Hancock . . . 12	4,145	202
John C Calhoun State Comm Coll, Decatur, AL 35609	1965	Dr. James R. Chasteen . . . 5	7,544	305
Johnson County Comm Coll, Overland Park, KS 66210	1967	Dr. Charles J. Carlsen . . . 12	12,163	530
Johnston Comm Coll, Smithfield, NC 27577	1969	Dr. John L. Tart . . . 5	2,222	145
John Tyler Comm Coll, Chester, VA 23831	1967	Dr. Freddie W. Nicholas, Sr. . . 12	5,366	215
John Wood Comm Coll, Quincy, IL 62301	1974	Dr. Robert C. Keys . . . 10	3,947	118
Joliet Jr Coll, Joliet, IL 60436	1901	Dr. Raymond A. Pietak . . . 12	9,567	476
Jones County Jr Coll, Ellisville, MS 39437	1928	Dr. T. Terrell Tisdale . . . 12	3,788	149
Jordan Coll, Cedar Springs, MI 49319	1967	Lexie K. Coxon . . . 2	2,140	176
J Sargeant Reynolds Comm Coll, Richmond, VA 23261	1972	Dr. S. A. Burnette . . . 5	2,220	493
Kalamazoo Valley Comm Coll, Kalamazoo, MI 49009	1966	Dr. Marilyn J. Schlack . . . 12	4,586	309
Kankakee Comm Coll, Kankakee, IL 60901	1966	Dr. Larry D. Huffman . . . 12	3,600	213
Kansas City Kansas Comm Coll, Kansas City, KS 66112	1923	Dr. Bill Spencer . . . 9	4,394	289
Kaskaskia Coll, Centralia, IL 62801	1956	Mr. Raymond D. Woods . . . 12	3,127	192
Kellogg Comm Coll, Battle Creek, MI 49017	1956	Dr. Paul R. Ohm . . . 12	5,471	250
Kent State U. Stark Cmps, Canton, OH 44720	1967	Dr. William G. Bittle . . . 5	2,043	75
Kent State U. Trumbull Cmps, Warren, OH 44483	1954	John N. Cable . . . 5	1,695	89
Kent State U. Tuscarawas Cmps, New Philadelphia, OH 44663	1962	Harold D. Shade . . . 5	1,130	72
Keystone Jr Coll, La Plume, PA 18440	1868	Robert E. Mooney, Jr. . . . 1	1,265	102
Kilgore Coll, Kilgore, TX 75662	1935	NR . . . 12	4,599	191
Kings River Comm Coll, Reedley, CA 93654	1926	Dr. Abel B. Sykes, Jr. . . . 12	4,424	221
Kirkwood Comm Coll, Cedar Rapids, IA 52406	1966	Dr. Norm Nielsen . . . 12	7,741	429
Kirtland Comm Coll, Roscommon, MI 48653	1966	Mr. Raymond D. Homer . . . 10	1,287	79
Kishwaukee Coll, Malta, IL 60150	1967	Dr. Norman L. Jenkins . . . 12	3,583	NR
Labette Comm Coll, Parsons, KS 67357	1923	Mrs. Jackie Vietti . . . 12	2,654	261
Lake City Comm Coll, Lake City, FL 32055	1962	Dr. Muriel Kay Heimer . . . 5	2,230	190
Lake Land Coll, Mattoon, IL 61938	1966	Dr. Robert K. Luther . . . 12	4,317	269
Lakeland Comm Coll, Mentor, OH 44060	1967	Dr. Ralph R. Doty . . . 12	8,580	416
Lake Michigan Coll, Benton Harbor, MI 49022	1946	Dr. Anne E. Mulder . . . 10	3,335	240
Lakeshore Tech Coll, Cleveland, WI 53015	1967	Dr. Dennis Ladwig . . . 12	3,627	344

234 Education—Colleges and Universities

Name, address	Year	Governing official, control	Enrollment	Faculty
Lake-Sumter Comm Coll, Leesburg, FL 34788	1961	Dr. Carl C. Andersen ... 12	2,223	90
Lake Tahoe Comm Coll, South Lake Tahoe, CA 95702	1975	Dr. Guy F. Lease ... 12	2,400	96
Lakewood Comm Coll, White Bear Lake, MN 55110	1967	Dr. Jerry Owens ... 5	5,721	165
Lamar U–Orange, Orange, TX 77630	1969	Dr. Andrew Johnson ... 5	1,250	63
Lamar U–Port Arthur, Port Arthur, TX 77641	1909	Dr. Sam Monroe ... 5	2,005	91
Lane Comm Coll, Eugene, OR 97405	1964	Mr. John Carter ... 12	8,002	383
Laney Coll, Oakland, CA 94607	1953	Mr. Odell Johnson ... 5	11,208	379
Lansing Comm Coll, Lansing, MI 48901	1957	Dr. Abel B. Sykes, Jr. ... 12	23,390	1,000
Laramie County Comm Coll, Cheyenne, WY 82007	1968	Dr. Timothy Davies ... 9	4,026	213
Laredo Jr Coll, Laredo, TX 78040	1946	Dr. Roger L. Worsley ... 12	4,981	283
Lawson State Comm Coll, Birmingham, AL 35221	1965	Dr. Perry W. Ward ... 5	1,470	54
Lee Coll, Baytown, TX 77520	1934	Dr. Vivian Bowling Blevins ... 10	5,039	231
Lehigh County Comm Coll, Schnecksville, PA 18078	1967	Dr. Robert L. Barthlow ... 12	3,770	130
Lenoir Comm Coll, Kinston, NC 28502	1960	Dr. Lonnie H. Blizzard ... 5	2,240	159
Lewis and Clark Comm Coll, Godfrey, IL 62035	1970	NR ... 10	5,450	284
Lima Tech Coll, Lima, OH 45804	1971	Dr. James J. Countryman ... 5	2,269	167
Lincoln Land Comm Coll, Springfield, IL 62708	1967	Dr. William D. Law, Jr. ... 10	7,877	401
Linn-Benton Comm Coll, Albany, OR 97321	1966	Mr. Jon Carnahan ... 12	12,867	640
Long Beach City Coll, Long Beach, CA 90808	1927	Dr. Beverly O'Neill ... 5	27,632	850
Longview Comm Coll, Lee's Summit, MO 64081	1969	Mr. Aldo W. Leker ... 10	8,892	391
Lorain County Comm Coll, Elyria, OH 44035	1963	Dr. Roy Church ... 12	6,616	312
Lord Fairfax Comm Coll, Middletown, VA 22645	1969	Dr. Marilyn C. Beck ... 12	2,724	110
Los Angeles City Coll, Los Angeles, CA 90029	1929	Dr. Stelle Feuers ... 12	16,500	700
Los Angeles Harbor Coll, Wilmington, CA 90744	1949	Dr. Robert S. Standen ... 12	8,990	310
Los Angeles Mission Coll, San Fernando, CA 91340	1974	Mr. Lowell J. Erickson ... 12	5,916	115
Los Angeles Pierce Coll, Woodland Hills, CA 91371	1947	Mr. Daniel Means ... 12	18,106	548
Los Angeles Southwest Coll, Los Angeles, CA 90047	1967	Dr. Thomas G. Lakin ... 12	5,063	228
Los Angeles Trade-Tech Coll, Los Angeles, CA 90015	1925	Dr. Evelyn C. Wong ... 12	13,392	250
Los Angeles Valley Coll, Van Nuys, CA 91401	1949	Dr. Mary E. Lee ... 12	18,692	260
Los Medanos Coll, Pittsburg, CA 94565	1974	Dr. Chester H. Case ... 10	7,369	216
Louisiana State U at Alexandria, Alexandria, LA 71302	1960	Dr. Ben F. Martin ... 5	2,300	109
Louisiana State U at Eunice, Eunice, LA 70535	1967	Dr. Michael Smith ... 5	1,886	79
Lower Columbia Coll, Longview, WA 98632	1934	Dr. Vernon R. Pickett ... 5	1,430	199
Lurleen B Wallace State Jr Coll, Andalusia, AL 36420	1969	Dr. William H. McWhorter ... 5	1,161	39
Luzerne County Comm Coll, Nanticoke, PA 18634	1966	Thomas J. Moran ... 9	6,250	249
Macomb Comm Coll, Warren, MI 48093	1954	Dr. Albert L. Lorenzo ... 10	28,003	841
Macon Coll, Macon, GA 31297	1968	Dr. S. Aaron Hyatt ... 5	3,915	126
Madison Area Tech Coll, Madison, WI 53704	1911	Dr. Beverly S. Simone ... 10	11,865	1,619
Manatee Comm Coll, Bradenton, FL 34207	1957	Dr. Stephen J. Korcheck ... 5	7,804	270
Manchester Comm Coll, Manchester, CT 06040	1963	Dr. Jonathan M. Daube ... 5	7,000	200
Maple Woods Comm Coll, Kansas City, MO 64156	1969	Dr. Stephen R. Brainard ... 12	4,146	180
Marin Comm Coll, Kentfield, CA 94904	1926	Ms. Myrna R. Miller ... 12	10,366	NR
Marion Tech Coll, Marion, OH 43302	1971	Dr. John Richard Bryson ... 13	1,465	105
Marshalltown Comm Coll, Marshalltown, IA 50158	1927	Dr. William Simpson ... 10	1,300	93
Marymount Coll, Palos Verdes, California, Rancho Palos Verdes, CA 90274	1932	Dr. Thomas D. Wood ... 2	1,070	70
Massachusetts Bay Comm Coll, Wellesley Hills, MA 02181	1961	Mr. Roger A. Van Winkle ... 5	4,390	171
Massasoit Comm Coll, Brockton, MA 02402	1968	Dr. Gerard F. Burke ... 5	6,868	330
Mattatuck Comm Coll, Waterbury, CT 06708	1967	Dr. Richard L. Sanders ... 5	4,167	54
McHenry County Coll, Crystal Lake, IL 60012	1967	Mr. Robert C. Bartlett ... 12	3,684	167
McLennan Comm Coll, Waco, TX 76708	1965	Dr. Dennis F. Michaelis ... 9	5,536	230
Mendocino Coll, Ukiah, CA 95482	1973	Dr. Leroy R. Lowery ... 12	4,550	165
Merced Coll, Merced, CA 95348	1962	Dr. Tom K. Harris, Jr. ... 12	7,422	368
Mercer County Comm Coll, Trenton, NJ 08690	1966	Mr. John P. Hanley ... 12	6,894	331
Meridian Comm Coll, Meridian, MS 39305	1937	Dr. William F. Scaggs ... 12	2,849	236
Merritt Coll, Oakland, CA 94619	1953	Mr. Donald Hongisto ... 12	6,683	NR
Mesabi Comm Coll, Virginia, MN 55792	1918	Richard Kohlase ... 5	1,097	50
Mesa Comm Coll, Mesa, AZ 85202	1965	Dr. Larry K. Christiansen ... 12	19,577	525
Metropolitan Comm Coll, Omaha, NE 68103	1974	Dr. J. Richard Gilliland ... 12	7,383	364
Miami-Dade Comm Coll, Miami, FL 33132	1960	Dr. Robert H. McCabe ... 12	49,145	1,837
Miami U–Hamilton Cmps, Hamilton, OH 45011	1968	Dr. Harriet Taylor ... 5	2,089	160
Miami U–Middletown Cmps, Middletown, OH 45042	1966	Dr. Michael P. Governanti ... 5	2,035	165
Middle Georgia Coll, Cochran, GA 31014	1884	Dr. Fretwell G. Crider ... 5	1,469	81
Middlesex Comm Coll, Middletown, CT 06457	1966	Dr. Leila Gonzalez Sullivan ... 5	3,400	130
Middlesex Comm Coll, Bedford, MA 01730	1970	Dr. Evan S. Dobelle, Jr. ... 5	3,200	195
Middlesex County Coll, Edison, NJ 08818	1964	Dr. Flora M. Edwards ... 9	11,218	329
Midland Coll, Midland, TX 79705	1969	Dr. Jess H. Parrish ... 12	3,789	192
Midlands Tech Coll, Columbia, SC 29202	1974	Dr. James L. Hudgins ... 12	6,954	NR
Mid Michigan Comm Coll, Harrison, MI 48625	1965	Dr. Eugene F. Schorzmann ... 12	2,178	198
Mid-Plains Comm Coll, North Platte, NE 69101	1965	Mr. Kenneth L. Aten ... 10	2,004	87
Mid-State Comm Coll, Wisconsin Rapids, WI 54494	1917	Dr. M. H. Schneeberg ... 12	2,219	86
Milwaukee Area Tech Coll, Milwaukee, WI 53233	1912	Dr. Rus F. Slicker ... 10	21,900	1,604
Mineral Area Coll, Flat River, MO 63601	1922	Dr. Dixie Kohn ... 10	2,584	75
Minneapolis Comm Coll, Minneapolis, MN 55403	1965	Earl W. Bowman ... 5	3,675	175
MiraCosta Coll, Oceanside, CA 92056	1934	Dr. H. Deon Holt ... 5	9,776	369
Mission Coll, Santa Clara, CA 95054	1977	Dr. Betty M. Dean ... 12	11,500	311
Mississippi County Comm Coll, Blytheville, AR 72316	1975	Dr. John P. Sullins ... 5	1,646	118
Mississippi Delta Jr Coll, Moorhead, MS 38761	1926	Dr. David W. Powe ... 10	1,867	128
Miss Gulf Coast Comm Coll, Jackson County Cmps, Gautier, MS 39553	1965	Mr. Curtis L. Davis ... 10	2,713	131
Miss Gulf Coast Comm Coll, Jefferson Davis Cmps, Gulfport, MS 39507	1965	Mr. Glen W. Cadle ... 12	3,745	188
Mitchell Comm Coll, Statesville, NC 28677	1852	Dr. Charles C. Poindexter ... 5	1,553	81
Moberly Area Jr Coll, Moberly, MO 65270	1927	Dr. Andrew Komar, Jr. ... 12	1,500	78
Modesto Jr Coll, Modesto, CA 95350	1921	Dr. Stanley L. Hodges ... 12	7,313	454
Mohave Comm Coll, Kingman, AZ 86401	1971	Dr. Charles W. Hall ... 5	3,959	294
Mohawk Valley Comm Coll, Utica, NY 13501	1946	Dr. Michael I. Schafer ... 12	6,500	343
Monroe Business Inst, Bronx, NY 10468	1933	Stephen J. Jerome ... 3	2,200	100
Monroe County Comm Coll, Monroe, MI 48161	1964	Mr. Gerald D. Welch ... 9	3,261	162
Montcalm Comm Coll, Sidney, MI 48885	1965	Dr. Donald C. Burns ... 12	2,711	111
Monterey Peninsula Coll, Monterey, CA 93940	1947	Dr. David W. Hopkins, Jr. ... 5	8,500	235
Montgomery Coll–Germantown Cmps, Germantown, MD 20874	1975	Dr. Robert E. Parilla ... 12	3,436	130
Montgomery Coll–Rockville Cmps, Rockville, MD 20850	1965	Dr. Robert E. Parilla ... 12	14,128	661
Montgomery Coll–Takoma Park Cmps, Takoma Park, MD 20912	1946	Dr. Robert E. Parilla ... 12	4,613	204
Montgomery County Comm Coll, Blue Bell, PA 19422	1964	Dr. Edward M. Sweitzer ... 9	7,504	274

Name, address	Year	Governing official, control	Enrollment	Faculty
Moorpark Coll, Moorpark, CA 93021	1967	Dr. Stanley L. Bowers 9	11,800	335
Moraine Park Tech Coll, Fond du Lac, WI 54936	1967	Dr. John J. Shanahan 12	5,513	284
Moraine Valley Comm Coll, Palos Hills, IL 60465	1967	Dr. Fred Gaskin 12	13,590	570
Morton Coll, Cicero, IL 60650	1924	Mr. Charles P. Ferro 12	4,277	239
Motlow State Comm Coll, Tullahoma, TN 37388	1969	Dr. A. Frank Glass 5	2,544	237
Mountain Empire Comm Coll, Big Stone Gap, VA 24219	1972	Dr. Ruth Mercedes Smith 5	3,200	138
Mountain View Coll, Dallas, TX 75211	1970	Dr. William H. Jordan 9	6,063	224
Mt Hood Comm Coll, Gresham, OR 97030	1966	Dr. Paul Kreider 12	7,961	501
Mount Ida Coll, Newton Centre, MA 02159	1899	Dr. Bryan E. Carlson 1	1,650	140
Mt San Antonio Coll, Walnut, CA 91789	1946	Dr. John D. Randall 10	22,272	1,257
Mt San Jacinto Coll, San Jacinto, CA 92383	1963	Dr. Richard H. Lowe 12	4,398	166
Mount Wachusett Comm Coll, Gardner, MA 01440	1963	Daniel M. Asquino 5	2,100	112
Murray State Coll, Tishomingo, OK 73460	1908	Dr. Clyde R. Kindell 5	1,390	NR
Muscatine Comm Coll, Muscatine, IA 52761	1929	Dr. Victor G. McAvoy 5	1,111	59
Muskegon Comm Coll, Muskegon, MI 49442	1926	Dr. James L. Stevenson 12	5,009	218
Muskingum Area Tech Coll, Zanesville, OH 43701	1969	Dr. Lynn H. Willett 12	2,109	104
Napa Valley Coll, Napa, CA 94558	1942	Dr. William H. Feddersen 12	6,451	307
Nash Comm Coll, Rocky Mount, NC 27804	1967	Dr. J. Reid Parrott, Jr. 5	1,483	92
Nashville State Tech Inst, Nashville, TN 37209	1970	Dr. Richard M. Turner, III 5	5,646	298
Nassau Comm Coll, Garden City, NY 11530	1959	Dr. Sean A. Fanelli 12	16,608	1,332
National Ed Ctr-Bauder Coll Cmps, Fort Lauderdale, FL 33334	1964	Mr. Dale Oakley 3	1,117	41
National Ed Ctr-Brown Inst Cmps, Minneapolis, MN 55407	1946	Ralph H. Vieau 3	1,600	65
National Ed Ctr-Spartan Sch of Aeronautics Cmps, Tulsa, OK 74158 (2)	1928	Frank D. Iacobucci 3	2,450	150
National Ed Ctr-Tampa Tech Inst Cmps, Tampa, FL 33610	1948	Lyle R. Groth 3	1,400	63
National Sch of Tech, Inc, North Miami Beach, FL 33162	1977	NR 3	1,100	30
Navajo Comm Coll, Tsaile, AZ 86556	1968	Mr. Laurence Gishey 4	1,496	136
Navarro Coll, Corsicana, TX 75110	1946	Dr. Gerald Burson 12	2,631	148
Neosho County Comm Coll, Chanute, KS 66720	1936	George H. VanAllen 12	1,500	117
New England Banking Inst, Boston, MA 02111	1909	NR 1	1,644	230
New Hampshire Tech Inst, Concord, NH 03302	1964	Dr. David E. Larrabee, Sr. 5	1,194	NR
New Mexico Jr Coll, Hobbs, NM 88240	1965	Dr. Charles D. Hays 12	2,345	96
New Mexico State U-Alamogordo, Alamogordo, NM 88310	1958	Dr. Charles R. Reidlinger 5	1,814	98
New Mexico State U-Carlsbad, Carlsbad, NM 88220	1950	Dr. Shelton W. Marlow 5	1,024	68
New Orleans Baptist Theological Sem, New Orleans, LA 70126	1917	Dr. Landrum P. Leavell, II 2	1,708	8
New River Comm Coll, Dublin, VA 24084	1969	Dr. Floyd M. Hogue 5	2,046	185
New York City Tech Coll of City U of NY, Brooklyn, NY 11201	1946	Dr. Charles W. Merideth 12	10,323	1,074
Niagara County Comm Coll, Sanborn, NY 14132	1962	Gerald L. Miller 12	5,151	319
Nicolet Area Tech Coll, Rhinelander, WI 54501	1968	Dr. Patricia A. Travis 5	1,111	64
Normandale Comm Coll, Bloomington, MN 55431	1968	Mr. Dale A. Lorenz 5	9,297	300
Northampton County Area Comm Coll, Bethlehem, PA 18017	1967	Dr. Robert J. Kopecek 12	5,146	335
North Arkansas Comm Coll, Harrison, AR 72601	1974	Dr. Bill Baker 12	1,072	75
North Central Tech Coll, Mansfield, OH 44906	1961	Dr. Byron E. Kee 5	1,924	130
Northcentral Tech Coll, Wausau, WI 54401	1912	Dr. Donald Hagen 10	2,200	210
North Country Comm Coll, Saranac Lake, NY 12983	1967	David W. Petty 12	1,575	150
North Dakota State Coll of Science, Wahpeton, ND 58076	1903	Dr. Jerry Olson 5	2,290	151
Northeast Alabama State Jr Coll, Rainsville, AL 35986	1963	Dr. Charles M. Pendley 5	1,360	47
Northeast Comm Coll, Norfolk, NE 68702	1973	Dr. Robert P. Cox 12	2,745	122
Northeastern Jr Coll, Sterling, CO 80751	1941	Dr. Henry M. Milander 12	2,040	72
Northeastern Oklahoma A&M Coll, Miami, OK 74354	1919	Dr. Bobby R. Wright 5	2,300	133
Northeast Mississippi Comm Coll, Booneville, MS 38829	1948	Joe M. Childers 12	2,750	NR
Northeast Texas Comm Coll, Mount Pleasant, TX 75455	1985	NR 12	1,679	83
Northeast Wisconsin Tech Coll, Green Bay, WI 54307	1913	Dr. Gerald D. Prindiville 12	5,816	190
Northern Essex Comm Coll, Haverhill, MA 01830	1960	Dr. John R. Dimitry 5	6,548	252
Northern Nevada Comm Coll, Elko, NV 89801	1967	Dr. Ronald K. Remington 5	2,209	124
Northern New Mexico Comm Coll, Española, NM 87532	1909	Connie A. Valdez 5	1,487	117
Northern Oklahoma Coll, Tonkawa, OK 74653	1901	Dr. Edwin E. Vineyard 5	1,993	73
Northern Virginia Comm Coll, Annandale, VA 22003	1965	Dr. Richard J. Ernst 5	34,539	1,420
North Harris County Coll District, Houston, TX 77060	1972	Dr. Joe A. Airola 12	14,040	609
North Hennepin Comm Coll, Minneapolis, MN 55445	1966	Dr. John Helling 5	9,200	350
North Idaho Coll, Coeur d'Alene, ID 83814	1933	Dr. Carl R. Bennett 12	2,660	148
North Iowa Area Comm Coll, Mason City, IA 50401	1918	Dr. David Buettner 12	2,657	85
North Lake Coll, Irving, TX 75038	1977	Dr. James F. Horton, Jr. 9	6,102	270
Northland Pioneer Coll, Holbrook, AZ 86025	1974	Dr. Marvin L. Vasher 12	6,255	400
North Seattle Comm Coll, Seattle, WA 98103	1970	Dr. Barbara Daum 5	8,575	232
North Shore Comm Coll, Beverly, MA 01915	1965	Dr. George Traicoff 5	3,126	200
Northwest Alabama Comm Coll, Phil Campbell, AL 35581	1961	Dr. Charles W. Britnell 5	1,600	83
Northwest Coll, Powell, WY 82435	1946	Dr. Phillip Kendall 12	1,739	166
Northwestern Business Coll-Tech Ctr, Lima, OH 45805	1920	Mr. Loren R. Jarvis 3	1,346	52
Northwestern Connecticut Comm Coll, Winsted, CT 06098	1965	Dr. Booker T. DeVaughn 5	2,418	68
Northwestern Michigan Coll, Traverse City, MI 49684	1951	Dr. Phillip E. Runkel 12	4,698	282
Northwest Tech Coll, Archbold, OH 43502	1968	Dr. James O. Miller 5	2,330	96
Norwalk Comm Coll, Norwalk, CT 06854	1961	Dr. William H. Schwab 5	3,633	151
Oakland Comm Coll, Bloomfield Hills, MI 48013	1964	Dr. R. Stephen Nicholson 12	27,756	583
Oakton Comm Coll, Des Plaines, IL 60016	1969	Dr. Thomas TenHoeve 10	10,400	495
Ocean County Coll, Toms River, NJ 08753	1964	Dr. Milton Shaw 5	6,214	261
Odessa Coll, Odessa, TX 79764	1946	Dr. Philip T. Speegle 12	4,700	225
Ohlone Coll, Fremont, CA 94539	1967	Dr. Peter Blomerley 12	8,743	413
Okaloosa-Walton Comm Coll, Niceville, FL 32578	1963	Dr. James R. Richburg 12	5,403	316
Oklahoma City Comm Coll, Oklahoma City, OK 73159	1969	Dr. Kenneth P. Walker 5	7,912	227
Oklahoma State U Tech Branch, Oklahoma City, Oklahoma City, OK 73107	1961	Dr. James Hooper 5	3,877	206
Oklahoma State U, Tech Branch, Okmulgee, Okmulgee, OK 74447	1946	Dr. Robert Klabenes 5	2,147	137
Olympic Coll, Bremerton, WA 98310	1946	Dr. Wallace A. Simpson 5	6,873	294
Onondaga Comm Coll, Syracuse, NY 13215	1962	Dr. Bruce H. Leslie 12	8,000	400
Orangeburg-Calhoun Tech Coll, Orangeburg, SC 29115	1968	Mr. M. Rudolph Groomes 12	1,437	65
Orange Coast Coll, Costa Mesa, CA 92628	1947	Dr. Donald R. Bronsard 12	22,900	868
Orange County Comm Coll, Middletown, NY 10940	1950	Dr. William F. Messner 12	5,460	310
Owens Tech Coll, Toledo, OH 43699	1966	NR 5	6,603	370
Oxnard Coll, Oxnard, CA 93033	1975	Dr. Elise D. Schneider 9	6,207	250

Name, address	Year	Governing official, control	Enrollment	Faculty
Palm Beach Comm Coll, Lake Worth, FL 33461	1933	Dr. Edward M. Eissey 5	14,688	650
Palo Alto Coll, San Antonio, TX 78224	1987	Dr. Terry Dicianna 12	3,958	221
Palomar Coll, San Marcos, CA 92069	1946	Dr. George R. Boggs 12	20,945	802
Panola Coll, Carthage, TX 75633	1947	Dr. Gary McDaniel 12	1,457	61
Paris Jr Coll, Paris, TX 75460	1924	Mr. Bobby R. Walters 12	2,221	121
Parkland Coll, Champaign, IL 61821	1967	Dr. Zelema M. Harris 10	8,455	457
Parks Jr Coll, Denver, CO 80229	1895	Dr. Morgan Landry 3	1,100	NR
Pasadena City Coll, Pasadena, CA 91106	1924	Dr. Jack A. Scott 10	21,242	900
Pasco-Hernando Comm Coll, Dade City, FL 33525	1972	Dr. Milton O. Jones 5	4,685	NR
Passaic County Comm Coll, Paterson, NJ 07509	1968	Kenneth E. Wright 9	3,158	207
Patrick Henry Comm Coll, Martinsville, VA 24115	1962	NR 5	1,048	80
Paul D Camp Comm Coll, Franklin, VA 23851	1971	Dr. Edwin L. Barnes 5	1,425	65
Pearl River Comm Coll, Poplarville, MS 39470	1909	Dr. Ted J. Alexander 12	2,455	134
Peirce Jr Coll, Philadelphia, PA 19102	1865	Dr. Raymond C. Lewin 1	1,133	74
Pellissippi State Tech Comm Coll, Knoxville, TN 37933	1974	Mr. J. L. Goins 5	4,702	137
Peninsula Coll, Port Angeles, WA 98362	1961	Dr. Paul G. Cornaby 5	1,001	126
Pennsylvania Coll of Tech, Williamsport, PA 17701	1965	Dr. Robert Breuder 13	3,776	278
Penn State U Altoona Cmps, Altoona, PA 16601	1929	Dr. James A. Duplass 13	2,615	128
Penn State U Beaver Cmps, Monaca, PA 15061	1964	David B. Otto 13	1,055	65
Penn State U Berks Cmps, Reading, PA 19610	1924	Dr. Frederick H. Gaige 13	1,489	84
Penn State U Delaware County Cmps, Media, PA 19063	1966	Edward S. J. Tomezsko 13	1,975	110
Penn State U Hazelton Cmps, Hazelton, PA 18201	1934	Dr. James J. Staudenmeier 13	1,262	68
Penn State U McKeesport Cmps, McKeesport, PA 15132	1947	Dr. Cash J. Kowalski 13	1,380	87
Penn State U New Kensington Cmps, New Kensington, PA 15068	1958	Dr. Robert D. Arbuckle 13	1,492	73
Penn State U Ogontz Cmps, Abington, PA 19001	1950	Dr. Robert A. Bernoff 13	3,330	166
Penn State U Schuylkill Cmps, Schuylkill Haven, PA 17972	1934	Dr. Wayne Lammie 13	1,230	61
Penn State U Shenango Cmps, Sharon, PA 16146	1965	Dr. Carolyn Prager 13	1,196	78
Penn State U Worthington Scranton Cmps, Dunmore, PA 18512	1923	Dr. James D. Gallagher 13	1,295	82
Penn State U York Cmps, York, PA 17403	1926	Dr. John J. Romano 13	1,946	98
Penn Valley Comm Coll, Kansas City, MO 64111	1969	Dr. Zelema Harris 10	6,621	350
Pensacola Jr Coll, Pensacola, FL 32504	1948	Dr. Horace E. Hartsell 5	8,955	938
Phillips County Comm Coll, Helena, AR 72342	1965	Dr. Steven Jones 12	1,662	107
Phoenix Coll, Phoenix, AZ 85013	1920	Ms. Myrna Harrison 12	13,146	770
Piedmont Comm Coll, Roxboro, NC 27573	1970	Dr. H. James Owen 5	1,073	51
Piedmont Tech Coll, Greenwood, SC 29648	1966	Dr. Lex D. Walters 5	2,066	92
Piedmont Virginia Comm Coll, Charlottesville, VA 22901	1972	Dr. Deborah M. DiCroce 5	4,350	262
Pierce Coll, Tacoma, WA 98498	1967	Dr. Frank Brouillet 5	10,400	402
Pikes Peak Comm Coll, Colorado Springs, CO 80906	1969	Dr. Marijane Axtell Paulsen 5	6,009	332
Pima Comm Coll, Tucson, AZ 85702	1966	Mr. Jonas R. Hockaday 5	26,747	1,291
Pitt Comm Coll, Greenville, NC 27835	1961	Dr. Charles E. Russell 12	3,888	207
Pittsburgh Inst of Aeronautics, Pittsburgh, PA 15236 (2)	1929	Ivan D. Livi 1	1,012	41
Polk Comm Coll, Winter Haven, FL 33881	1964	Dr. Maryly VanLeer Peck 5	5,600	NR
Porterville Coll, Porterville, CA 93257	1927	Dr. Paul D. Alcantra 5	2,883	132
Portland Comm Coll, Portland, OR 97219	1961	Dr. Daniel F. Moriarty 12	35,737	1,166
Potomac State Coll of West Virginia U, Keyser, WV 26726	1901	Dr. Joseph M. Gratto 5	1,206	83
Prairie State Coll, Chicago Heights, IL 60411	1958	Dr. W. Harold Garner 12	4,758	253
Pratt Comm Coll, Pratt, KS 67124	1938	Dr. William Wojciechowski 10	1,600	48
Prince George's Comm Coll, Largo, MD 20772	1958	Dr. Robert I. Bickford 9	13,810	591
Puerto Rico Jr Coll, Rio Piedras, PR 00928	1949	Ledo Alberto Maldonado Ruiz . . .1	4,405	105
Queensborough Comm Coll of City U of NY, Bayside, NY 11364	1958	Dr. Kurt R. Schmeller 12	11,715	628
Quincy Jr Coll, Quincy, MA 02169	1958	Dr. O. Clayton Johnson 11	1,667	69
Quinebaug Valley Comm Coll, Danielson, CT 06239	1971	Dr. Robert E. Miller 5	1,283	59
Quinsigamond Comm Coll, Worcester, MA 01606	1963	Dr. Clifford S. Peterson 5	4,593	185
Rancho Santiago Coll, Santa Ana, CA 92706	1915	Dr. Robert D. Jensen 5	21,757	1,302
Randolph Comm Coll, Asheboro, NC 27204	1962	Dr. Larry K. Linker 5	1,394	80
Rappahannock Comm Coll, Glenns, VA 23149	1970	Dr. John H. Upton 12	1,892	111
Raritan Valley Comm Coll, Somerville, NJ 08876	1965	Dr. S. Charles Irace 9	5,033	259
Reading Area Comm Coll, Reading, PA 19603	1971	Dr. Gust Zogas 10	2,075	136
Red Rocks Comm Coll, Lakewood, CO 80401	1967	Ms. Dorothy A. Horrell 5	5,522	220
Rend Lake Coll, Ina, IL 62846	1967	Dr. Jonathan Astroth 5	4,042	197
Richard Bland Coll, Petersburg, VA 23805	1961	Dr. Clarence Maze, Jr. 5	1,169	49
Richland Coll, Dallas, TX 75243	1972	Dr. Stephen Mittelstet 12	12,981	640
Richland Comm Coll, Decatur, IL 62521	1971	Dr. Charles R. Novak 5	4,323	195
Richmond Comm Coll, Hamlet, NC 28345	1964	Joseph W. Grimsley 5	1,026	100
Ricks Coll, Rexburg, ID 83460	1888	Dr. Steven D. Bennion 2	7,784	359
Rio Hondo Comm Coll, Whittier, CA 90608	1960	Alex A. Sanchez 12	12,921	710
Rio Salado Comm Coll, Phoenix, AZ 85003	1978	Dr. Charles A. Green 12	14,000	648
Riverside Comm Coll, Riverside, CA 92506	1916	Dr. Charles A. Kane 12	17,300	480
Roane State Comm Coll, Harriman, TN 37748	1971	Dr. Sherry L. Hoppe 5	4,319	234
Robert Morris Coll, Chicago Cmps, Chicago, IL 60601	1965	Richard D. Pickett 1	1,640	109
Robeson Comm Coll, Lumberton, NC 28359	1965	Fred W. Williams, Jr. 5	1,300	96
Rochester Comm Coll, Rochester, MN 55904	1915	Dr. Geraldine A. Evans 5	3,999	164
Rockingham Comm Coll, Wentworth, NC 27375	1964	Dr. N. J. Owens, Jr. 5	1,809	111
Rockland Comm Coll, Suffern, NY 10901	1959	Dr. F. Thomas Clark 12	7,515	769
Rock Valley Coll, Rockford, IL 61101	1964	Dr. Karl J. Jacobs 10	6,646	205
Rogers State Coll, Claremore, OK 74017	1909	Dr. Richard H. Mosier 5	3,411	157
Rogue Comm Coll, Grants Pass, OR 97527	1971	Dr. Harvey Bennett 12	3,740	315
Rose State Coll, Midwest City, OK 73110	1971	Dr. Larry Nutter 12	10,319	341
Rowan-Cabarrus Comm Coll, Salisbury, NC 28145	1963	Dr. Richard L. Brownell 5	3,062	130
Sacramento City Coll, Sacramento, CA 95822	1916	Dr. Robert M. Harris 12	16,513	420
Saddleback Coll, Mission Viejo, CA 92692	1967	NR 12	21,210	660
Saint Augustine Coll, Chicago, IL 60640	1980	Fr. Carlos A. Plazas 1	1,350	176
St Bernard Parish Comm Coll, Chalmette, LA 70043	1967	Dr. Daniel Daste 12	1,013	47
Saint Charles County Comm Coll, St Charles, MO 63301	1986	Donald D. Shook 5	2,947	130
St Clair County Comm Coll, Port Huron, MI 48061	1923	Dr. Richard L. Norris 9	4,321	284
St Johns River Comm Coll, Palatka, FL 32177	1958	Dr. R. L. McLendon, Jr. 5	2,937	148
St Louis Comm Coll at Florissant Valley, St Louis, MO 63135	1963	Dr. Michael T. Murphy 10	10,816	379
St Louis Comm Coll at Forest Park, St Louis, MO 63110	1962	Dr. Vernon O. Crawley 10	7,353	81
St Louis Comm Coll at Meramec, Kirkwood, MO 63122	1963	Dr. Gwendolyn W. Stephenson 10	14,429	481
St Paul Tech Coll, St Paul, MN 55102	1922	Dr. Harlan H. Sheely 12	1,900	675

Name, address	Year	Governing official, control	Enrollment	Faculty
St Petersburg Jr Coll, St Petersburg, FL 33733	1927	Dr. Carl M. Kuttler, Jr. 12	18,019	531
St Philip's Coll, San Antonio, TX 78203	1898	Dr. Stephen R. Mitchell . . . 10	5,632	387
Salem Comm Coll, Carneys Point, NJ 08069	1971	Dr. William Wenzel 9	1,250	NR
Salt Lake Comm Coll, Salt Lake City, UT 84130	1948	Dr. Orville D. Carnahan 5	11,279	NR
San Antonio Coll, San Antonio, TX 78284	1925	Dr. Max Castillo 12	20,653	854
San Bernardino Valley Coll, San Bernardino, CA 92410	1926	Dr. Donald L. Singer 12	12,000	375
Sandhills Comm Coll, Pinehurst, NC 28374	1963	Dr. John Dempsey 12	2,297	118
San Diego City Coll, San Diego, CA 92101	1914	Jeanne L. Atherton 12	15,728	NR
San Diego Mesa Coll, San Diego, CA 92111	1962	Dr. Allen Brooks 10	27,000	898
San Diego Miramar Coll, San Diego, CA 92126	1969	Dr. Jerome Hunter 12	8,513	213
San Jacinto Coll–North Cmps, Houston, TX 77049	1974	Dr. Edwin E. Lehr 12	3,336	193
San Jacinto Coll–South Cmps, Houston, TX 77089	1979	Dr. Parker Williams 12	4,583	201
San Joaquin Delta Coll, Stockton, CA 95207	1935	Dr. L. H. Horton, Jr. 10	16,307	610
San Jose City Coll, San Jose, CA 95128	1921	Dr. Byron R. Skinner 10	9,835	354
San Juan Coll, Farmington, NM 87401	1958	Dr. James C. Henderson 9	3,068	165
Santa Barbara City Coll, Santa Barbara, CA 93109	1908	Dr. Peter R. MacDougall . . . 10	11,602	501
Santa Fe Comm Coll, Gainesville, FL 32602	1966	Dr. Larry W. Tyree 12	10,261	417
Santa Fe Comm Coll, Santa Fe, NM 87502	1983	William C. Witter 12	2,935	175
Santa Monica Coll, Santa Monica, CA 90405	1929	Dr. Richard L. Moore 12	24,730	638
Santa Rosa Jr Coll, Santa Rosa, CA 95401	1918	Dr. Roy G. Mikalson 12	32,291	754
Sauk Valley Comm Coll, Dixon, IL 61021	1965	Dr. Richard L. Behrendt . . . 12	2,569	185
Schenectady County Comm Coll, Schenectady, NY 12305	1968	Dr. Peter F. Burnham 12	3,149	164
Schoolcraft Coll, Livonia, MI 48152	1961	Dr. Richard W. McDowell . . . 10	9,099	397
Scott Comm Coll, Bettendorf, IA 52722	1966	Lenny E. Stone 12	3,200	180
Scottsdale Comm Coll, Scottsdale, AZ 85256	1969	Dr. Arthur W. Decabooter . . 12	9,347	380
Seattle Central Comm Coll, Seattle, WA 98122	1966	Dr. Charles H. Mitchell 12	7,825	380
Seminole Comm Coll, Sanford, FL 32773	1966	Dr. Earl S. Weldon 12	6,796	487
Seminole Jr Coll, Seminole, OK 74868	1931	Gregory G. Fitch 5	1,493	71
Seward County Comm Coll, Liberal, KS 67905	1969	Dr. Theodore W. Wischropp . 12	1,800	147
Shasta Coll, Redding, CA 96049	1948	Kenneth B. Cerreta 12	12,096	392
Shawnee Comm Coll, Ullin, IL 62992	1967	NR 12	2,500	111
Shelby State Comm Coll, Memphis, TN 38174	1972	Dr. Douglas Covington 5	4,216	255
Shelton State Comm Coll, Tuscaloosa, AL 35405	1979	Dr. Tom Umphrey 5	3,435	NR
Sheridan Coll, Sheridan, WY 82801	1948	Dr. Stephen Maier 12	2,141	73
Shoreline Comm Coll, Seattle, WA 98133	1964	Dr. Ronald E. Bell 5	7,498	253
Sierra Coll, Rocklin, CA 95677	1936	Dr. Gerald C. Angove 5	12,859	499
Sinclair Comm Coll, Dayton, OH 45402	1887	Dr. David H. Ponitz 12	17,433	875
Skagit Valley Coll, Mount Vernon, WA 98273	1926	Dr. James M. Ford 5	2,494	296
Skyline Coll, San Bruno, CA 94066	1969	Ms. Linda Graef Salter 9	8,368	268
Snead State Jr Coll, Boaz, AL 35957	1935	Dr. William H. Osborn 5	1,490	66
South Central Comm Coll, New Haven, CT 06511	1968	Dr. Antonio Perez 5	3,537	174
Southeast Comm Coll, Lincoln Cmps, Lincoln, NE 68520	1973	NR 5	4,670	540
Southeastern Comm Coll, Whiteville, NC 28472	1964	Dr. Stephen C. Scott 5	1,420	110
Southeastern Comm Coll, North Cmps, West Burlington, IA 52655	1968	Dr. R. Gene Gardner 12	1,832	94
Southeastern Illinois Coll, Harrisburg, IL 62946	1960	Dr. Harry W. Abell 5	3,415	163
Southern Maine Tech Coll, South Portland, ME 04106	1946	Dr. Wayne H. Ross 5	1,610	148
Southern State Comm Coll, Hillsboro, OH 45133	1975	Dr. George R. McCormick . . .5	1,488	146
Southern Union State Jr Coll, Wadley, AL 36276	1922	Dr. Richard J. Federinko 5	2,786	138
Southern U, Shreveport–Bossier City Cmps, Shreveport, LA 71107	1964	Dr. Robert H. Smith 5	1,042	75
Southern West Virginia Comm Coll, Logan, WV 25601	1971	Dr. Harry J. Boyer 5	2,640	127
South Florida Comm Coll, Avon Park, FL 33825	1965	Dr. Catherine P. Cornelius . . .5	1,500	112
South Georgia Coll, Douglas, GA 31533	1906	Dr. Edward D. Jackson, Jr. . . .5	1,038	47
South Plains Coll, Levelland, TX 79336	1958	Dr. Marvin L. Baker 12	4,803	295
South Puget Sound Comm Coll, Olympia, WA 98502	1970	Dr. Kenneth Minnaert 5	4,420	178
South Seattle Comm Coll, Seattle, WA 98106	1970	Mr. Jerry M. Brockey 5	6,104	234
Southside Virginia Comm Coll, Alberta, VA 23821	1970	Dr. John J. Cavan 5	1,402	173
South Suburban Coll, South Holland, IL 60473	1927	Dr. Richard Fonte 5	8,029	429
Southwestern Baptist Theological Sem, Fort Worth, TX 76122	1908	Dr. Russell H. Dilday 2	3,814	183
Southwestern Coll, Chula Vista, CA 92010	1961	Joseph M. Conte 12	15,290	616
Southwestern Comm Coll, Creston, IA 50801	1966	Richard L. Byerly 5	1,047	65
Southwestern Comm Coll, Sylva, NC 28779	1964	Dr. Norman K. Myers 5	1,244	186
Southwestern Michigan Coll, Dowagiac, MI 49047	1964	Mr. David C. Briegel 12	3,200	172
Southwestern Oregon Comm Coll, Coos Bay, OR 97420	1961	Dr. Robert L. Barber 5	4,780	204
Southwest Mississippi Comm Coll, Summit, MS 39666	1918	NR 10	1,480	75
Southwest Texas Jr Coll, Uvalde, TX 78801	1946	Dr. Jimmy Goodson 12	2,397	177
Southwest Virginia Comm Coll, Richlands, VA 24641	1968	Dr. Charles R. King 12	7,021	273
Southwest Wisconsin Tech Coll, Fennimore, WI 53809	1967	Dr. Richard A. Rogers 12	1,102	117
Spartanburg Methodist Coll, Spartanburg, SC 29301	1911	Dr. George D. Fields 2	1,100	76
Spartanburg Tech Coll, Spartanburg, SC 29305	1961	Dr. Jack A. Powers 5	1,966	NR
Spokane Comm Coll, Spokane, WA 99207	1963	Dr. Donald Bressler 5	5,280	384
Spokane Falls Comm Coll, Spokane, WA 99204	1967	Dr. Vern Loland 5	5,293	599
Spoon River Coll, Canton, IL 61520	1959	Felix T. Haynes 5	2,100	133
Springfield Tech Comm Coll, Springfield, MA 01105	1967	Andrew M. Scibelli 5	3,291	200
Stanly Comm Coll, Albemarle, NC 28001	1971	Dr. Jan J. Crawford 5	1,353	107
Stark Tech Coll, Canton, OH 44720	1970	Dr. John J. McGrath 12	3,413	188
State Comm Coll of East St Louis, East St Louis, IL 62201	1969	Dr. Richard M. Bonner 5	1,032	83
State Fair Comm Coll, Sedalia, MO 65301	1966	Dr. Marvin Fielding 10	2,224	98
State Tech Inst at Memphis, Memphis, TN 38134	1967	Dr. Charles Temple 5	8,852	NR
State U of NY Coll of A&T at Cobleskill, Cobleskill, NY 12043	1916	Dr. Neal V. Robbins 5	2,769	164
State U of NY Coll of A&T at Morrisville, Morrisville, NY 13408	1908	Dr. Frederick W. Woodward . .5	3,491	192
State U of NY Coll of Tech at Alfred, Alfred, NY 14802	1908	Dr. John O. Hunter 5	3,789	211
State U of NY Coll of Tech at Canton, Canton, NY 13617	1906	Dr. Earl W. MacArthur 5	2,437	109
State U of NY Coll of Tech at Delhi, Delhi, NY 13753	1913	Mr. Seldon M. Kruger 5	2,415	135
State U of NY Coll of Tech at Farmingdale, Farmingdale, NY 11735	1912	Dr. Frank A. Cipriani 5	10,880	550
Suffolk County Comm Coll–Ammerman Cmps, Selden, NY 11784	1962	Mr. Robert T. Kreiling 12	11,857	471
Suffolk County Comm Coll–Eastern Cmps, Riverhead, NY 11901	1977	Steven T. Kenny 12	2,361	120
Suffolk County Comm Coll–Western Cmps, Brentwood, NY 11717	1974	Salvatore J. LaLima 12	5,039	275
Sullivan Coll, Louisville, KY 40232	1864	A. R. Sullivan 3	1,868	63
Sullivan County Comm Coll, Loch Sheldrake, NY 12759	1962	Dr. John F. Walter 12	1,779	NR

Name, address	Year	Governing official, control	Enroll-ment	Faculty
Sumter Area Tech Coll, Sumter, SC 29150	1963	Dr. Herbert C. Robbins 5	1,850	120
Surry Comm Coll, Dobson, NC 27017	1965	Dr. Swanson Richards 5	2,675	94
Tacoma Comm Coll, Tacoma, WA 98465	1965	Dr. Carleton Opgaard 5	4,758	287
Tallahassee Comm Coll, Tallahassee, FL 32304	1966	Dr. James H. Hinson, Jr. 12	8,848	352
Tarrant County Jr Coll, Fort Worth, TX 76102	1967	Mr. C. A. Roberson 9	27,559	890
Tech Career Institutes, New York, NY 10001	1974	Dr. David M. Goodman 3	2,200	86
Tech Coll of the Lowcountry, Beaufort, SC 29902	1972	Dr. Anne S. McNutt 5	1,112	65
Temple Jr Coll, Temple, TX 76504	1926	Dr. Marvin R. Felder 10	2,398	118
Terra Tech Coll, Fremont, OH 43420	1968	Dr. Richard M. Simon 5	2,603	148
Texarkana Coll, Texarkana, TX 75501	1927	Dr. Carl M. Nelson 12	3,759	182
Texas Southmost Coll, Brownsville, TX 78520	1926	Dr. Juliet V. Garcia 10	5,751	252
Texas State Tech Inst–Harlingen Cmps, Harlingen, TX 78551	1967	Dr. J. Gilbert Leal 5	2,312	180
Texas State Tech Inst–Waco Cmps, Waco, TX 76705	1965	Mr. Don E. Goodwin 5	3,956	362
Thomas Nelson Comm Coll, Hampton, VA 23670	1968	Dr. Robert G. Templin, Jr. 5	7,308	318
Three Rivers Comm Coll, Poplar Bluff, MO 63901	1966	Dr. Stephen M. Poort 5	1,932	67
Tidewater Comm Coll, Chesapeake Cmps, Chesapeake, VA 23320	1968	Dr. George B. Pass 5	2,963	88
Tidewater Comm Coll, Portsmouth Cmps, Portsmouth, VA 23703	1968	Dr. George B. Pass 5	4,208	203
Tidewater Comm Coll, Virginia Beach Cmps, Virginia Beach, VA 23456	1968	Dr. George B. Pass 5	11,178	413
Tompkins Cortland Comm Coll, Dryden, NY 13053	1968	Eduardo J. Marti 12	2,820	225
Treasure Valley Comm Coll, Ontario, OR 97914	1962	Dr. Glenn Mayle 12	2,177	121
Tri-Cities State Tech Inst, Blountville, TN 37617	1966	Dr. R. Wade Powers 5	1,820	90
Tri-County Tech Coll, Pendleton, SC 29670	1962	Dr. Don C. Garrison 5	2,705	NR
Trinity Valley Comm Coll, Athens, TX 75751	1946	Mr. Ron Baugh 12	3,893	NR
Triton Coll, River Grove, IL 60171	1964	Dr. James Catanzaro 5	13,540	1,454
Truckee Meadows Comm Coll, Reno, NV 89512	1971	Dr. John Gwaltney 5	9,131	496
Tulsa Jr Coll, Tulsa, OK 74135	1968	Dr. Dean P. Van Trease 5	18,600	700
Tunxis Comm Coll, Farmington, CT 06032	1969	Ms. Marilyn Menack 5	2,008	167
Tyler Jr Coll, Tyler, TX 75711	1926	Dr. Raymond M. Hawkins 12	7,984	364
Ulster County Comm Coll, Stone Ridge, NY 12484	1962	Mr. Robert T. Brown 12	2,898	170
Umpqua Comm Coll, Roseburg, OR 97470	1964	Dr. James Kraby 12	1,931	120
Union County Coll, Cranford, NJ 07016	1933	Mr. LeRoy W. Smith 12	8,772	382
U of Akron–Wayne Coll, Orrville, OH 44667	1972	Dr. William V. Muse 5	1,330	109
U of Alaska Anchorage, Kenai Peninsula Coll, Soldotna, AK 99669	1964	Ginger Steffy 5	1,364	65
U of Alaska Anchorage, Matanuska-Susitna Coll, Palmer, AK 99645	1958	Mr. Glenn F. Massay 5	1,432	96
U of Alaska Southeast, Sitka Cmps, Sitka, AK 99835	1962	Mr. Richard M. Griffin 5	1,119	32
U of Cincinnati Clermont Coll, Batavia, OH 45103	1972	Dr. Roger J. Barry 5	1,251	95
U of Cincinnati Raymond Walters Coll, Cincinnati, OH 45236	1967	Dr. Ernest G. Muntz 5	3,933	191
U of Hawaii–Honolulu Comm Coll, Honolulu, HI 96817	1920	Dr. Peter R. Kessinger 5	4,168	238
U of Hawaii–Kapiolani Comm Coll, Honolulu, HI 96816	1946	Dr. John F. Morton 5	5,717	239
U of Hawaii–Kauai Comm Coll, Lihue, HI 96766	1965	Mr. David Iha 5	1,299	101
U of Hawaii–Leeward Comm Coll, Pearl City, HI 96782	1968	Dr. Barbara. B. Polk 5	5,987	264
U of Hawaii–Maui Comm Coll, Kahului, HI 96732	1967	Ms. Alma Henderson 5	2,100	147
U of Hawaii–Windward Comm Coll, Kaneohe, HI 96744	1972	Dr. Peter T. Dyer 5	1,604	72
U of Kentucky, Ashland Comm Coll, Ashland, KY 41101	1937	Dr. Anthony Newberry 5	2,744	104
U of Kentucky, Elizabethtown Comm Coll, Elizabethtown, KY 42701	1964	Dr. Charles E. Stebbins 5	2,932	108
U of Kentucky, Hazard Comm Coll, Hazard, KY 41701	1968	Dr. G. Edward Hughes 5	1,227	64
U of Kentucky, Henderson Comm Coll, Henderson, KY 42420	1963	Dr. Patrick R. Lake 5	1,272	69
U of Kentucky, Hopkinsville Comm Coll, Hopkinsville, KY 42240	1965	Dr. Thomas L. Riley 5	1,877	87
U of Kentucky, Jefferson Comm Coll, Louisville, KY 40202	1968	Dr. Ronald J. Horvath 5	7,599	365
U of Kentucky, Lexington Comm Coll, Lexington, KY 40506	1965	Dr. Allen G. Edwards 5	3,920	183
U of Kentucky, Madisonville Comm Coll, Madisonville, KY 42431	1968	Dr. Arthur D. Stumpf 5	1,960	127
U of Kentucky, Maysville Comm Coll, Maysville, KY 41056	1967	Dr. James C. Shires 5	1,062	71
U of Kentucky, Owensboro Comm Coll, Owensboro, KY 42303	1986	NR 5	2,135	63
U of Kentucky, Paducah Comm Coll, Paducah, KY 42002	1932	Dr. Donald J. Clemens 5	2,565	106
U of Kentucky, Prestonsburg Comm Coll, Prestonsburg, KY 41653	1964	Dr. Henry A. Campbell, Jr. 5	2,260	89
U of Kentucky, Somerset Comm Coll, Somerset, KY 42501	1965	Dr. Rollin J. Watson 5	1,759	75
U of Kentucky, Southeast Comm Coll, Cumberland, KY 40823	1960	Dr. W. Bruce Ayers 5	1,703	97
U of Maine at Augusta, Augusta, ME 04330	1965	Dr. George P. Connick 5	4,342	196
U of Minnesota, Crookston, Crookston, MN 56716	1966	Dr. Donald G. Sargeant 5	1,287	75
U of New Mexico–Gallup Branch, Gallup, NM 87301	1968	Dr. John M. Phillips 5	1,422	113
U of New Mexico–Valencia Cmps, Los Lunas, NM 87031	1981	NR 5	1,060	81
U of Puerto Rico, Aguadilla Regional Coll, Ramey, PR 00604	1972	Ricardo E. Villalon 7	1,585	NR
U of South Carolina at Sumter, Sumter, SC 29150	1966	Mr. J. C. Anderson, Jr. 5	1,372	76
U of Wisconsin Ctr–Fox Valley, Menasha, WI 54952	1933	Dr. Robert E. Young 5	1,440	55
U of Wisconsin Ctr–Marathon County, Wausau, WI 54401	1933	NR 5	1,188	71
U of Wisconsin Ctr–Waukesha County, Waukesha, WI 53188	1966	Dr. Mary S. Knudten 5	2,164	89
Utah Valley Comm Coll, Orem, UT 84058	1941	Dr. Kerry D. Romesburg 5	7,758	331
Valencia Comm Coll, Orlando, FL 32802	1967	Dr. Paul C. Gianini, Jr. 5	17,632	674
Vance-Granville Comm Coll, Henderson, NC 27536	1969	Dr. Ben F. Currin 5	2,152	107
Ventura Coll, Ventura, CA 93003	1925	Dr. Robert W. Long 12	12,000	541
Vernon Regional Jr Coll, Vernon, TX 76384	1972	Dr. Joe Mills 12	1,708	112
Victoria Coll, Victoria, TX 77901	1925	Dr. Roland E. Bing 9	3,172	120
Victor Valley Coll, Victorville, CA 92392	1960	Dr. Ruth N. Johnson 5	5,500	347
Vincennes U, Vincennes, IN 47591	1801	Dr. Phillip M. Summers 5	6,139	400
Vincennes U–Jasper Ctr, Jasper, IN 47546	1970	Dr. Gerald J. Altstadt 5	1,111	60
Virginia Highlands Comm Coll, Abingdon, VA 24210	1967	Dr. N. DeWitt Moore, Jr. 5	2,180	102
Virginia Western Comm Coll, Roanoke, VA 24038	1966	Dr. Charles L. Downs 5	7,100	202
Vista Coll, Berkeley, CA 94704	1974	Dr. Barbara Beno 5	5,100	NR
Volunteer State Comm Coll, Gallatin, TN 37066	1970	Dr. Hal R. Ramer 5	3,670	237

Name, address	Year	Governing official, control		Enrollment	Faculty
Wake Tech Comm Coll, Raleigh, NC 27603	1958	Dr. Bruce I. Howell	12	5,905	589
Wallace State Comm Coll, Hanceville, AL 35077	1966	Dr. James C. Bailey	5	3,735	211
Walla Walla Comm Coll, Walla Walla, WA 99362	1967	Dr. Steven L. VanAusdle	5	5,355	120
Walters State Comm Coll, Morristown, TN 37813	1970	Dr. Jack E. Campbell	5	4,220	205
Washington Tech Coll, Marietta, OH 45750	1971	Dr. Carson K. Miller	5	1,407	79
Washtenaw Comm Coll, Ann Arbor, MI 48106	1965	Dr. Gunder A. Myran	12	10,045	677
Waterbury State Tech Coll, Waterbury, CT 06708	1964	Mr. Charles A. Ekstrom	5	1,378	45
Waubonsee Comm Coll, Sugar Grove, IL 60554	1966	Dr. John J. Swalec	10	6,615	401
Waukesha County Tech Coll, Pewaukee, WI 53072	1923	Dr. Richard T. Anderson	12	4,424	520
Wayne Comm Coll, Goldsboro, NC 27533	1957	Dr. G. Herman Porter	12	2,219	137
Wayne County Comm Coll, Detroit, MI 48226	1967	Dr. Ronald J. Temple	12	10,269	417
Weatherford Coll, Weatherford, TX 76086	1869	Dr. E. W. Mince	5	2,384	93
Wenatchee Valley Coll, Wenatchee, WA 98801	1939	Dr. Arnie Heuchert	12	3,387	168
Westark Comm Coll, Fort Smith, AR 72913	1928	Mr. Joel R. Stubblefield	12	5,009	230
Westchester Business Inst, White Plains, NY 10602	1915	Ernest H. Sutkowski	3	1,000	28
Westchester Comm Coll, Valhalla, NY 10595	1946	Dr. Joseph N. Hankin	12	9,069	536
Western Iowa Tech Comm Coll, Sioux City, IA 51102	1966	Dr. Robert H. Kiser	5	1,471	NR
Western Nebraska Comm Coll–Scottsbluff Cmps, Scottsbluff, NE 69361	1926	Dr. John N. Harms	12	1,702	51
Western Nevada Comm Coll, Carson City, NV 89703	1971	Dr. Anthony D. Calabro	5	5,036	272
Western Oklahoma State Coll, Altus, OK 73521	1926	Dr. Stephen R. Hensley	5	2,003	94
Western Piedmont Comm Coll, Morganton, NC 28655	1964	Dr. Jim A. Richardson	12	2,534	132
Western Texas Coll, Snyder, TX 79549	1969	Dr. Harry L. Krenek	12	1,144	55
Western Wisconsin Tech Coll, La Crosse, WI 54602	1911	Mr. James Lee Rasch	10	3,073	172
Western Wyoming Comm Coll, Rock Springs, WY 82901	1959	Dr. T. L. Boggs	12	2,506	103
West Hills Coll, Coalinga, CA 93210	1932	Stan R. Arterberry	5	2,870	148
West Los Angeles Coll, Culver City, CA 90230	1969	Dr. Linda M. Thor	12	6,436	NR
Westmoreland County Comm Coll, Youngwood, PA 15697	1970	Dr. Daniel C. Krezenski	9	5,027	307
West Shore Comm Coll, Scottville, MI 49454	1967	Dr. William M. Anderson	10	1,226	71
West Valley Coll, Saratoga, CA 95070	1963	Dr. Leo Chavez	12	13,941	882
West Virginia Northern Comm Coll, Wheeling, WV 26003	1972	Dr. Ron Hutkin	5	2,806	151
West Virginia U at Parkersburg, Parkersburg, WV 26101	1971	Dr. Eldon L. Miller	5	3,562	176
Wharton County Jr Coll, Wharton, TX 77488	1946	Dr. Elbert C. Hutchins	12	2,571	140
Whatcom Comm Coll, Bellingham, WA 98226	1970	Dr. Harold G. Heiner	5	1,537	104
Wilkes Comm Coll, Wilkesboro, NC 28697	1965	Dr. James R. Randolph	5	1,950	105
William Rainey Harper Coll, Palatine, IL 60067	1965	Dr. Paul N. Thompson	12	19,826	919
Willmar Comm Coll, Willmar, MN 56201	1961	Harold G. Conradi	5	1,351	78
Willmar Tech Coll, Willmar, MN 56201	1961	Ronald Erpelding	12	1,368	95
Wilson Tech Comm Coll, Wilson, NC 27893	1958	Dr. Frank L. Eagles	5	1,370	88
Wisconsin Indianhead Tech Coll, Rice Lake Cmps, Rice Lake, WI 54868	1941	Mary Ellen Filkins	10	1,150	80
Wor-Wic Tech Comm Coll, Salisbury, MD 21801	1976	Dr. Arnold H. Maner	12	1,247	69
Wytheville Comm Coll, Wytheville, VA 24382	1967	Dr. William F. Snyder	5	1,256	137
Yakima Valley Comm Coll, Yakima, WA 98907	1928	Dr. V. Philip Tullar	5	4,785	352
Yavapai Coll, Prescott, AZ 86301	1966	Dr. Paul Walker	12	6,824	361
York Tech Coll, Rock Hill, SC 29730	1961	Mr. Dennis F. Merrell	5	2,837	215
Yuba Coll, Marysville, CA 95901	1927	Dr. Patricia L. Wirth	12	12,979	267

College Freshmen Attitudes

Six out of every seven college freshmen believe that "the federal government is not doing enough to control environmental pollution," according to the 24th annual survey of entering college freshmen conducted jointly by the Univ. of California at Los Angeles's Higher Education Research Inst. and the American Council on Education. For the 5th consecutive year, student concern for the environment increased, with 86.3 percent of freshmen endorsing the statement in 1989, compared with 83.9 percent in 1988 and 80.9 percent in 1987.

Support for legalized abortion, which has remained fairly stable (between 53 and 59 percent) since 1977, jumped sharply between the 1988 and 1989 surveys, from 57.0 to 64.7 percent.

Survey results also suggest a growing tendency toward greater student activism. The share of freshmen who participated in organized demonstrations during the year prior to entering college reached a high of 36.7 percent, which is greater than the percentages observed during the late 1960s. At the same time, the percentage of freshmen who said that there is a "very good chance" that they will participate in student protests or demonstrations in college also reached an all-time high of 6.3 percent, up from 5.4 percent in 1988 and 4.7 percent in 1967. An all-time high of 44.1 percent of students reported that it is a "very important" goal for them to "influence social values." Almost one-fourth of the students cited participation in community action programs as a very important goal, up from

18.5 percent in 1986, while 35.3 percent cited "helping to promote racial understanding" as an important goal, up from 27.2 percent in 1986. A record high of 19.9 percent of freshmen reported "influencing the political structure" as a major goal.

Support for legislation prohibiting homosexual behavior dropped to 45.4 percent in 1989, down from 49.0 in 1988. Support for a national health care plan to cover health care costs increased sharply to 75.8 percent, compared to 60.5 percent in 1985. Considering a question asked for the first time, 78.2 percent of students endorsed greater governmental efforts to control the sale of handguns. Support for the abolition of the death penalty continued its sharp decline, with 21.3 percent opposing the penalty, compared to 23.0 in 1988 and 57.6 percent in 1971.

Students' aspirations for advanced degrees reached a record high of 59.6 percent in 1989, up from 48.8 percent in 1980. At the same time, the numbers of students who say that "to prepare for graduate or professional school" is a major reason for attending college reached an all-time high of 51.5 percent.

The 1989 national survey involves questionnaires completed by 295,966 new freshmen entering 587 two- and four-year colleges and universities. Of these, 216,362 questionnaires from 403 institutions were used to compute the 1989 national norms, which were statistically adjusted to represent the nation's total population of approximately 1.6 million first-time, full-time entering students.

METEOROLOGY

National Weather Service Watches and Warnings

Source: National Weather Service, NOAA, U.S. Commerce Department; Glossary of Meteorology, American Meteorological Society

National Weather Service forecasters issue a Tornado Watch for a specific area where tornadoes are most likely to occur during the valid time of the watch. A Watch alerts people to check for threatening weather, make plans for action, and listen for a Tornado Warning. A Tornado Warning means that a tornado has been sighted or indicated by radar, and that safety precautions should be taken at once. A Hurricane Watch means that an existing hurricane poses a threat to coastal and inland communities in the area specified by the Watch. A Hurricane Warning means hurricane force winds and/or dangerously high water and exceptionally high waves are expected in a specified coastal area within 24 hours.

Tornado—A violent rotating column of air in contact with the ground and pendant from a thundercloud, usually recognized as a funnel-shaped vortex accompanied by a loud roar. With rotating winds est. up to 300 mph., on a local scale, it is the most destructive storm. Tornado paths have varied in length from a few feet to nearly 300 miles (avg. 5 mi.); diameter from a few feet to over a mile (average 220 yards); average forward speed, 30 mph.

Cyclone—An atmospheric circulation of winds rotating counterclockwise in the northern hemisphere and clockwise in the southern hemisphere. Tornadoes, hurricanes, and the lows shown on weather maps are all examples of cyclones having various sizes and intensities. Cyclones are usually accompanied by precipitation or stormy weather.

Hurricane—A severe cyclone originating over tropical ocean waters and having winds 74 miles an hour or higher. (In the western Pacific, such storms are known as typhoons.) The area of strong winds takes the form of a circle or an oval, sometimes as much as 500 miles in diameter. In the lower latitudes hurricanes usually move toward the west or northwest at 10 to 15 mph. When the center approaches 25° to 30° North Latitude, direction of motion often changes to northeast, with increased forward speed.

Blizzard—A severe weather condition characterized by strong winds bearing a great amount of snow. The National Weather Service specifies a wind of 35 miles an hour or higher, and sufficient falling and/or blowing snow to reduce visibility to less than 1/4 of a mile for a duration of three hours or longer.

Severe Thunderstorm—A thunderstorm with winds of 58 mph. or greater and/or hail three-fourths of an inch or larger in diameter.

Flood—The condition that occurs when water overflows the natural or artificial confines of a stream or other body of water, or accumulates by drainage over low-lying areas.

National Weather Service Marine Warnings and Advisories

Small Craft Advisory: A Small Craft Advisory alerts mariners to sustained (exceeding two hours) weather and/or sea conditions either present or forecast, potentially hazardous to small boats. Hazardous conditions may include winds of 18 to 33 knots and/or dangerous wave or inlet conditions. It is the responsibility of the mariner, based on his experience and size or type of boat, to determine if the conditions are hazardous. When a mariner becomes aware of a Small Craft Advisory, he should immediately obtain the latest marine forecast to determine the reason for the Advisory.

Gale Warning indicates that winds within the range 34 to 47 knots are forecast for the area.

Tropical Storm Warning indicates that winds of 34 to 63 knots are forecast in a specified coastal area in 24 hours or less. Only issued for winds produced by tropical weather systems.

Storm Warning indicates that winds 48 knots and above, no matter how high the speed, are forecast for the area.

Hurricane Warning indicates that winds 64 knots and above are forecast for the area. Only issued for winds produced by tropical weather systems.

Special Marine Warning: A warning for potentially hazardous weather conditions, usually of short duration (2 hours or less) and producing wind speeds of 34 knots or more, not adequately covered by existing marine warnings.

Primary sources of dissemination are commercial radio, TV, U.S. Coast Guard Radio stations, and NOAA VHF-FM broadcasts. These broadcasts on 162.40 to 162.55 MHz can usually be received 20-40 miles from the transmitting antenna site, depending on terrain and quality of the receiver used. Where transmitting antennas are on high ground, the range is somewhat greater, reaching 60 miles or more.

Speed of Winds in the U.S.

Source: Natl. Climatic Data Center, NESDIS, NOAA, U.S. Department of Commerce
Miles per hour — average through 1989. High through 1989. Wind velocities in true values.

Station	Avg.	High	Station	Avg.	High	Station	Avg.	High
Albuquerque, N.M.	9.0	90	Helena, Mont.	7.7	73	Mt. Washington, N.H.	35.3	231
Anchorage, Alas.	6.9	75	Honolulu, Ha.	11.4	(b)67	New Orleans, La.	8.2	(b)98
Atlanta, Ga.	9.1	60	Houston, Tex.	7.9	51	New York, N.Y.(c)	9.4	70
Baltimore, Md.	9.2	80	Indianapolis, Ind.	9.6	46	Omaha, Neb.	10.6	109
Bismarck, N.D.	10.2	(b)72	Jacksonville, Fla.	8.0	(b)82	Philadelphia, Pa.	9.5	73
Boston, Mass.	12.5	61	Kansas City, Mo.	10.7	70	Phoenix, Ariz.	6.3	86
Buffalo, N.Y.	12.0	91	Lexington, Ky.	9.3	46	Pittsburgh, Pa.	9.1	58
Cape Hatteras, N.C.	11.2	(b)110	Little Rock, Ark.	7.9	65	Portland, Ore.	7.9	88
Casper, Wyo.	12.9	81	Los Angeles, Cal.	6.2	49	St. Louis, Mo.	9.7	(b)60
Chicago, Ill.	10.3	58	Louisville, Ky.	8.3	61	Salt Lake City, Ut.	8.8	71
Cleveland, Oh.	10.6	(b)74	Memphis, Tenn.	8.9	46	San Diego, Cal.	6.9	56
Dallas, Tex.	10.9	73	Miami, Fla.	9.3	(a)74	San Francisco, Cal.	8.7	47
Denver, Col.	8.7	(b)56	Milwaukee, Wis.	11.6	54	Seattle, Wash.	9.0	66
Detroit, Mich.	10.3	48	Minneapolis, Minn.	10.6	(b)92	Spokane, Wash.	8.9	59
Galveston, Tex.	11.0	(d)100	Mobile, Ala.	9.0	63	Washington, D.C.	9.3	78

(a) Highest velocity ever recorded in Miami area was 132 mph. at former station in Miami Beach in September, 1926.
(b) Previous location. (c) Data for Central Park, Battery Place data through 1960, avg. 14.5, high 113. (d) Recorded before anemometer blew away. Estimated high 120.

The Meaning of "One Inch of Rain"

An acre of ground contains 43,560 square feet. Consequently, a rainfall of 1 inch over 1 acre of ground would mean a total of 6,272,640 cubic inches of water. This is equivalent of 3,630 cubic feet.

As a cubic foot of pure water weights about 62.4 pounds, the exact amount varying with the density, it follows that the weight of a uniform coating of 1 inch of rain over 1 acre of surface would be 226,512 pounds, or about 113 short tons. The weight of 1 U.S. gallon of pure water is about 8.345 pounds. Consequently a rainfall of 1 inch over 1 acre of ground would mean 27,143 gallons of water.

Tides and Their Causes

Source: NOAA, National Ocean Service, U.S. Department of Commerce

The tides are a natural phenomenon involving the alternating rise and fall in the large fluid bodies of the earth caused by the combined gravitational attraction of the sun and moon. The combination of these two variable force influences produces the complex recurrent cycle of the tides. Tides may occur in both oceans and seas, to a limited extent in large lakes, the atmosphere, and, to a very minute degree, in the earth itself. The period between succeeding tides varies as the result of many factors and force influences.

The tide-generating force represents the difference between (1) the centrifugal force produced by the revolution of the earth around the common center-of-gravity of the earth-moon system and (2) the gravitational attraction of the moon acting upon the earth's overlying waters. Since, on the average, the moon is only 238,852 miles from the earth compared with the sun's much greater distance of 92,956,000 miles, this closer distance outranks the much smaller mass of the moon compared with that of the sun, and the moon's tide-raising force is, accordingly, $2^{1}/_{2}$ times that of the sun.

The effect of the tide-generating forces of the moon and sun acting tangentially to the earth's surface (the so-called "tractive force") tends to cause a maximum accumulation of the waters of the oceans at two diametrically opposite positions on the surface of the earth and to withdraw compensating amounts of water from all points 90° removed from the positions of these tidal bulges. As the earth rotates beneath the maxima and minima of these tide-generating forces, a sequence of two high tides, separated by two low tides, ideally is produced each day.

Twice in each lunar month, when the sun, moon, and earth are directly aligned, with the moon between the earth and the sun (at new moon) or on the opposite side of the earth from the sun (at full moon), the sun and the moon exert their gravitational force in a mutual or additive fashion. Higher high tides and lower low tides are produced. These are called spring tides. At two positions 90° in between, the gravitational forces of the moon and sun — imposed at right angles—tend to counteract each other to the greatest extent, and the range between high and low tides is reduced. These are called neap tides. This semi-monthly variation between the spring and neap tides is called the phase inequality.

The inclination of the moon's orbit to the equator also produces a difference in the height of succeeding high tides and in the extent of depression of succeeding low tides which is known as the diurnal inequality. In extreme cases, this phenomenon can result in only one high tide and one low tide each day.

The actual range of tide in the waters of the open ocean may amount to only one or two feet. However, as this tide approaches shoal waters and its effects are augmented the tidal range may be greatly increased. In Nova Scotia along the narrow channel of the Bay of Fundy, the range of tides or difference between high and low waters, may reach 43 1/2 feet or more (under spring tide conditions) due to resonant amplification.

At New Orleans, the periodic rise and fall of the tide varies with the state of the Mississippi, being about 10 inches at low stage and zero at high. The Canadian Tide Tables for 1972 gave a maximum range of nearly 50 feet at Leaf Basin, Ungava Bay, Quebec.

In every case, actual high or low tide can vary considerably from the average, due to weather conditions such as strong winds, abrupt barometric pressure changes, or prolonged periods of extreme high or low pressure.

The Average Rise and Fall of Tides

Places	Ft.	In.	Places	Ft.	In.	Places	Ft.	In.
Baltimore, Md.	1	1	Mobile, Ala.	1	6¹	San Diego, Cal.	5	9¹
Boston, Mass.	9	6	New London, Conn.	2	7	Sandy Hook, N.J.	4	8
Charleston, S.C.	5	3	Newport, R.I.	3	6	San Francisco, Cal.	5	10¹
Cristobal, Panama	1	1¹	New York, N.Y.	4	7	Savannah, Ga.	7	5
Eastport, Me.	18	4	Old Pt. Comfort, Va.	2	6	Seattle, Wash.	11	4¹
Galveston, Tex.	1	5¹	Philadelphia, Pa.	6	2	Tampa, Fla.	2	10¹
Halifax, N.S.	4	5	Portland, Me.	9	1	Vancouver, B.C.	10	6¹
Key West, Fla.	1	10¹	St. John's, Nfld.	2	7	Washington, D.C.	2	9

(1) Diurnal range.

Hurricane Names in 1991

U.S. government agencies responsible for weather and related communications have used girls' names to identify major tropical storms since 1953. A U.S. proposal that both male and female names be adopted for hurricanes, starting in 1979, was accepted by a committee of the World Meteorological Organization.

Names assigned to Atlantic hurricanes, 1991 — Ana, Bob, Claudette, Danny, Elena, Fabian, Gloria, Henri, Isabel, Juan, Kate, Larry, Mindy, Nicholas, Odette, Peter, Rose, Sam, Teresa, Victor, Wanda.

Names assigned to Eastern Pacific hurricanes, 1991 — Andres, Blanca, Carlos, Dolores, Enrique, Fefa, Guillermo, Hilda, Ignacio, Jimena, Kevin, Linda, Marty, Nora, Olaf, Pauline, Rick, Sandra, Terry, Vivian, Waldo.

Hurricane Hotlines

When tropical storms or hurricanes threaten, you will be able to get updates on the telephone from the National Oceanic and Atmospheric Administration. Recorded messages will identify areas under a hurricane watch or warning, the location of the storm, its forecast movement and wind speeds and tidal effects.

Two Hurricane Hotlines will be set up, one to be activated when hurricanes or tropical storms threaten the Eastern and Gulf Coast states, another for Hawaii. The number for the East Coast hot line is (900) 410-6622 (or NOAA). For Hawaii, the number is (900) 410-2263 (or CANE).

Callers will be billed 50 cents for the first minute and 45 cents for each additional minute. The average call is expected to cost about 85 cents.

Explanation of Normal Temperatures

Normal temperatures listed in the tables on pages 242 and 243 are based on records of the National Weather Service for the 30-year period from 1951-1980 inclusive. To obtain the average maximum or minimum temperature for any month, the daily temperatures are added; the total is then divided by the number of days in that month.

The normal maximum temperature for January, for example, is obtained by adding the average maximums for Jan., 1951, Jan., 1952, etc., through Jan., 1980. The total is then divided by 30. The normal minimum temperature is obtained in a similar manner by adding the average minimums for each January in the 30-year period and dividing by 30. The normal temperature for January is one half of the sum for the normal maximum and minimum temperatures for that month. The mean temperature for any one day is one-half the total of the maximum and minimum temperatures for that day.

Monthly Normal Temperature and Precipitation

Source: Natl. Climatic Data Center. NESDIS. NOAA. U.S. Department of Commerce

These normals are based on records for the 30-year period 1951 to 1980 inclusive. (See explanation on page 241.) For stations that did not have continuous records from the same instrument site for the entire 30 years, the means have been adjusted to the record at the present site.

Airport station; *city office stations. T, temperature in Fahrenheit; P, precipitation in inches; L, less than .05 inch.

Station	Jan. T	Jan. P	Feb. T	Feb. P	Mar. T	Mar. P	Apr. T	Apr. P	May T	May P	June T	June P	July T	July P	Aug. T	Aug. P	Sept. T	Sept. P	Oct. T	Oct. P	Nov. T	Nov. P	Dec. T	Dec. P
Albany, N.Y.	21	2.4	23	2.3	34	3.0	47	2.9	58	3.3	67	3.3	71	3.0	69	3.3	61	3.2	51	2.9	39	3.0	26	3.0
Albuquerque, N.M.	35	0.3	39	0.4	46	0.5	55	0.4	64	0.5	75	0.5	79	1.3	76	1.5	69	0.9	57	0.9	44	0.4	36	0.5
Anchorage, Alas.	13	0.8	18	0.7	25	0.7	35	0.7	46	0.6	54	1.1	58	2.0	56	2.1	48	2.5	35	1.7	22	1.1	14	1.1
Asheville, N.C.	37	3.5	39	3.6	46	5.1	55	3.8	63	4.2	70	4.2	73	4.4	73	4.8	70	4.0	56	3.3	46	3.3	39	3.5
Atlanta, Ga.	42	4.9	45	4.4	53	5.9	62	4.4	69	4.0	76	3.4	79	4.7	78	3.4	73	3.2	62	2.5	52	3.4	45	4.2
Atlantic City, N.J.	34	3.3	35	3.2	42	3.7	51	3.1	60	2.9	68	2.9	74	3.9	74	4.5	68	2.7	58	2.8	48	3.5	38	3.5
Baltimore, Md.	33	3.0	35	3.0	43	3.7	54	3.3	63	3.4	72	3.7	77	3.9	75	4.6	69	3.5	57	3.1	46	3.1	37	3.4
Barrow, Alas.	-14	0.2	-20	0.2	-16	0.2	-2	0.2	19	0.2	33	0.4	39	0.9	38	1.0	31	0.6	14	0.6	-1	0.3	-13	0.2
Birmingham, Ala.	42	5.2	46	4.7	54	6.6	63	5.0	70	4.5	77	3.7	80	5.4	80	3.9	74	4.3	62	2.7	52	3.6	45	5.0
Bismarck, N.D.	7	0.5	15	0.5	26	0.7	43	1.5	55	2.2	64	3.0	70	2.0	69	1.7	57	1.4	46	0.8	29	0.5	15	0.5
Boise, Ida.	30	1.6	36	1.1	41	1.0	49	1.2	57	1.2	66	1.0	75	0.3	72	0.4	63	0.6	52	0.8	40	1.3	32	1.3
Boston, Mass.	30	4.0	31	3.7	38	4.1	49	3.7	59	3.5	68	2.9	74	2.7	72	3.7	65	3.4	55	3.4	45	4.2	34	4.9
Buffalo, N.Y.	24	3.0	25	2.4	33	3.0	45	3.0	56	2.9	66	2.7	71	3.0	69	4.2	62	3.4	52	2.9	40	3.6	29	3.4
Burlington, Vt.	17	1.9	18	1.7	29	2.2	43	2.8	55	3.0	65	3.6	70	3.4	67	3.9	59	3.2	48	2.8	37	2.8	23	2.4
Caribou, Me.	11	2.4	13	2.1	24	2.4	37	2.6	50	2.9	60	3.5	65	4.0	63	4.0	54	3.5	43	3.1	31	3.2	16	3.1
Charleston, S.C.	49	3.3	51	3.4	57	4.4	66	2.6	73	4.4	79	6.5	82	7.3	81	6.5	77	4.9	68	2.9	59	2.2	52	3.1
Chicago, Ill.	21	1.6	26	1.3	36	2.6	49	3.7	59	3.2	69	4.1	73	3.6	72	3.5	65	3.4	54	2.3	40	2.1	28	2.1
Cleveland, Oh.	26	2.5	27	2.2	37	3.0	48	3.3	58	3.3	68	3.5	72	3.4	70	3.4	64	2.9	53	2.5	42	2.8	31	2.8
Columbus, Oh.	27	2.8	30	2.2	40	3.2	51	3.4	61	3.8	70	4.0	74	4.0	72	3.7	66	2.8	54	1.9	42	2.6	32	2.6
Dallas-Ft. Worth, Tex.	44	1.7	49	1.9	56	2.4	66	3.6	74	4.3	82	2.6	86	2.0	86	1.8	79	3.3	68	2.5	56	1.8	48	1.7
Denver, Col.	30	0.5	34	0.7	38	1.2	47	1.8	57	2.5	67	1.6	73	1.9	71	1.5	63	1.2	52	1.0	39	0.8	33	0.6
Des Moines, Ia.	19	1.0	25	1.1	35	2.2	51	3.2	62	4.0	72	4.2	76	3.2	74	4.1	65	3.1	54	2.2	39	1.5	26	1.5
Detroit, Mich.	23	1.9	26	1.7	35	2.5	47	3.2	58	2.8	68	3.4	72	3.1	71	3.2	63	2.3	52	2.1	40	2.3	29	2.5
Dodge City, Kan.	30	0.5	35	0.5	42	1.5	54	1.8	64	3.3	75	3.0	80	3.1	78	2.5	69	1.9	58	1.3	43	0.8	34	0.5
Duluth, Minn.	6	1.2	12	0.9	23	1.8	38	2.2	50	3.2	59	4.0	65	4.0	63	4.1	54	3.3	44	2.2	28	1.7	14	1.3
Eureka, Cal.*	47	7.0	49	5.2	48	5.1	49	2.9	52	1.6	55	0.6	56	0.1	57	0.4	57	0.9	54	2.7	51	5.9	48	6.2
Fairbanks, Alas.	-13	0.5	-4	0.5	9	0.4	30	0.3	48	0.6	59	1.3	62	1.8	57	1.9	45	1.1	25	0.7	4	0.7	-10	0.7
Fresno, Cal.	46	2.0	51	1.9	54	1.6	60	1.2	68	0.3	75	0.1	81	L	79	L	74	0.2	65	0.3	54	1.2	45	1.6
Galveston, Tex.*	54	3.0	56	2.3	62	2.1	69	2.6	76	3.3	81	3.5	83	3.8	83	4.4	80	5.8	73	2.6	63	3.2	57	3.6
Grand Junction, Col.	26	0.6	34	0.5	42	0.8	52	0.7	62	0.8	72	0.4	79	0.5	76	0.9	67	0.7	55	0.9	40	0.6	28	0.6
Gr. Rapids, Mich.	22	1.9	24	1.5	33	2.5	46	3.6	58	3.0	67	3.9	71	3.0	70	3.5	62	3.1	51	2.9	39	2.9	27	2.6
Hartford, Conn.	25	3.5	28	3.2	37	4.2	49	4.0	59	3.4	69	3.4	73	3.1	71	4.0	63	3.9	52	3.5	42	4.1	29	4.2
Helena, Mon.	18	0.7	26	0.4	32	0.7	42	1.0	52	1.7	60	2.0	68	1.0	66	1.2	56	0.8	45	0.7	31	0.5	23	0.6
Honolulu, Ha.	73	3.8	73	2.7	74	3.5	76	1.5	78	1.2	79	0.5	80	0.5	81	0.6	80	1.9	77	3.2	74	3.4	73	3.6
Houston, Tex.	51	3.2	55	3.3	61	2.7	69	4.2	75	4.7	81	4.0	83	3.3	83	3.7	78	4.9	70	3.7	60	3.4	54	3.7
Huron, S.D.	11	0.4	18	0.8	29	1.2	46	2.0	57	2.7	68	3.3	74	2.3	72	2.0	61	1.4	49	1.4	32	0.7	19	0.5
Indianapolis, Ind.	26	2.7	30	2.5	40	3.6	52	3.7	63	3.7	72	4.0	75	4.3	73	3.5	67	2.7	55	2.5	42	3.0	32	3.0
Jackson, Miss.	46	5.0	49	4.9	56	5.9	65	5.9	73	4.8	79	2.9	82	4.4	81	3.7	76	3.6	65	2.6	55	4.2	49	5.4
Jacksonville, Fla.	53	3.1	55	3.5	61	3.7	68	3.3	74	4.9	79	5.4	81	6.5	81	7.2	78	7.3	70	3.6	61	1.9	55	2.6
Juneau, Alas.	22	3.7	28	3.7	31	3.3	39	2.9	46	3.4	53	3.0	56	4.1	55	5.0	49	6.4	42	7.7	33	5.2	27	4.7
Kansas City, Mo.	26	1.0	32	1.0	42	2.1	55	2.7	65	3.4	76	4.1	79	3.5	77	3.2	68	3.3	58	2.5	43	1.2	32	1.1
Knoxville, Tenn.	38	4.7	42	4.2	50	5.5	60	3.9	67	3.7	74	4.0	78	4.3	77	3.0	72	3.0	60	2.7	49	3.8	41	4.6
Lander, Wyo.	20	0.5	26	0.6	32	1.1	42	2.2	53	2.7	62	1.5	71	0.7	69	0.5	58	0.9	47	1.2	31	0.6	23	0.5
Lexington, Ky.	32	3.6	35	3.3	44	4.8	55	4.0	64	4.4	72	4.3	76	5.0	75	4.0	69	3.3	57	2.3	45	3.3	36	3.8
Little Rock, Ark.	40	3.9	44	3.8	52	4.7	62	5.4	71	5.3	79	3.7	82	3.6	81	3.1	74	4.3	63	2.8	51	4.4	43	4.2
Los Angeles, Cal.*	57	3.7	59	3.0	60	2.4	62	1.2	65	0.2	69	L	74	L	75	0.1	73	0.3	69	0.2	63	1.9	58	2.0
Louisville, Ky.	33	3.4	36	3.2	45	4.7	57	4.1	65	4.2	74	3.6	78	4.1	76	3.3	70	3.6	58	2.6	46	3.5	37	3.5
Marquette, Mich.*	12	2.0	14	1.9	23	2.8	37	3.6	50	4.0	60	3.9	65	3.2	63	3.3	54	3.8	44	3.3	30	2.9	18	2.4
Memphis, Tenn.	40	4.6	44	4.3	52	5.4	63	5.8	71	5.1	79	3.6	82	4.0	81	3.7	74	3.4	62	2.4	51	4.2	43	4.9
Miami, Fla.	67	2.1	68	2.1	72	1.9	75	3.1	79	6.5	81	9.2	83	6.0	83	7.0	82	8.1	78	7.1	73	2.7	69	1.9
Milwaukee, Wis.	19	1.6	23	1.3	32	2.6	45	3.4	55	2.6	65	3.6	71	3.5	69	3.1	62	2.9	51	2.3	37	2.0	25	2.0
Minneapolis, Minn.	11	0.8	18	0.9	29	1.7	46	2.1	59	3.2	68	4.1	73	3.5	71	3.6	61	2.5	50	1.9	33	1.3	19	0.9
Mobile, Ala.	51	4.6	54	4.9	60	6.5	68	5.4	75	5.5	81	5.1	82	7.7	82	6.8	78	6.6	69	2.6	59	3.7	53	5.4
Moline, Ill.	20	1.6	25	1.3	36	2.8	50	4.0	61	4.2	71	4.3	75	4.9	73	3.8	65	3.7	54	2.7	39	2.6	26	1.9
Nashville, Tenn.	37	4.5	40	4.0	49	5.6	60	4.8	68	4.6	76	3.7	79	3.9	78	3.7	72	3.4	60	2.7	49	3.5	41	4.9
Newark, N.J.	31	3.1	33	3.1	41	4.2	52	3.6	62	3.6	71	3.9	76	4.3	74	4.3	68	3.7	57	3.1	47	3.6	36	3.4
New Orleans, La.	52	5.0	55	5.2	61	4.7	69	4.5	75	5.1	80	4.6	82	6.7	82	6.0	77	5.9	70	2.7	60	4.1	55	5.3
New York, N.Y.*	32	3.2	33	3.1	41	4.2	53	3.8	62	3.8	71	3.2	77	3.8	75	4.0	68	3.4	58	3.4	47	4.1	36	3.8
Nome, Alas.	9	0.8	3	0.5	7	0.6	18	0.6	36	0.5	45	1.2	51	2.2	50	3.2	42	2.3	28	1.3	16	0.9	4	0.7
Norfolk, Va.	40	3.7	41	3.3	49	3.9	58	2.9	67	3.8	76	3.5	78	5.2	78	5.3	72	4.4	61	3.4	52	2.9	44	3.2
Okla. City, Okla.	36	1.0	41	1.3	49	2.1	60	2.9	68	5.5	77	3.9	82	3.0	81	2.4	73	3.4	62	2.7	49	1.5	40	1.2
Omaha, Neb.	19	0.8	25	0.9	35	1.9	50	2.9	62	4.3	71	4.1	76	3.6	74	4.1	64	2.5	54	2.1	38	1.3	26	0.8
Pago Pago, Amer. Samoa.	81	13	81	13	81	11	81	11	80	11	80	8.6	79	6.5	79	7.1	79	6.7	80	11	80	11	81	14
Philadelphia, Pa.	31	3.2	33	2.8	42	3.9	53	3.6	63	3.2	72	3.9	77	3.9	75	4.1	68	3.4	57	2.8	46	3.3	36	3.5
Phoenix, Ariz.	52	0.7	56	0.6	61	0.8	68	0.3	77	0.1	87	0.2	92	0.7	90	1.0	85	0.6	73	0.6	61	0.5	53	0.8
Pittsburgh, Pa.	27	2.9	29	2.4	39	3.6	50	3.3	60	3.5	68	3.3	72	3.8	71	3.3	64	2.8	53	2.5	42	2.3	31	2.6
Portland, Me.	22	3.8	23	3.6	32	4.0	43	3.9	54	3.4	63	3.1	68	2.8	67	2.8	59	3.3	49	3.9	38	4.7	26	4.5
Portland, Ore.	39	6.2	43	3.9	46	3.6	50	2.3	57	2.1	63	1.5	68	0.5	67	1.1	63	1.6	54	3.1	46	5.2	41	6.4
Providence, R.I.	28	4.1	29	3.7	37	4.3	48	4.0	58	3.5	67	3.1	73	3.0	71	3.8	64	3.6	54	3.5	45	4.7	32	4.5
Raleigh, N.C.	40	3.6	42	3.4	49	3.7	59	2.9	67	3.7	74	3.8	78	4.4	77	4.4	71	3.0	60	2.7	50	2.9	42	3.1
Rapid City, S.D.	21	0.4	26	0.6	33	1.0	45	2.0	55	2.8	65	3.3	73	2.1	71	1.4	61	1.0	50	0.9	34	0.5	25	0.5
Reno, Nev.	32	1.2	37	1.0	41	0.7	46	0.5	53	0.7	61	0.4	69	0.3	67	0.3	59	0.3	50	0.4	41	0.5	33	1.2
Richmond, Va.	37	3.2	39	3.1	47	3.6	58	2.9	67	3.6	74	3.6	78	5.3	76	4.9	70	3.3	59	3.2	49	3.0	40	3.3
St. Louis, Mo.	29	1.7	34	2.1	43	3.3	56	3.6	66	3.5	75	3.8	79	3.7	78	2.6	70	2.7	58	2.3	45	2.5	34	2.2
Salt Lake City, Ut.	29	1.4	34	1.3	41	1.7	49	2.2	58	1.5	68	1.0	77	0.7	75	0.9	65	0.7	53	1.3	40	1.3	31	1.4
San Antonio, Tex.	50	1.6	54	1.9	62	1.3	70	2.7	76	3.7	82	3.0	85	1.9	84	2.7	79	3.2	70	2.9	60	2.3	53	1.5
San Diego, Cal.	57	2.1	58	1.4	59	1.6	61	0.8	63	0.2	66	0.1	70	L	72	0.1	70	0.2	67	0.3	62	1.1	57	1.4
San Francisco, Cal.*	49	4.7	52	3.2	53	2.6	55	1.5	58	0.3	61	0.1	63	0.1	64	0.2	61	0.1	59	1.1	55	2.4	49	3.6
San Juan, P.R.	77	3.0	77	2.0	78	2.3	80	3.6	79	5.6	80	4.7	82	4.9	82	5.5	81	5.9	81	5.3	80	5.6	78	4.7
Sault Ste. Marie, Mich.*	13	2.2	14	1.7	24	2.0	38	2.4	50	2.9	58	3.3	64	3.0	63	3.5	55	3.7	46	3.7	32	3.2	20	2.6
Savannah, Ga.	49	3.1	52	3.2	58	3.8	66	3.2	73	4.6	79	5.7	81	7.4	81	6.7	75	5.2	67	2.3	58	1.9	51	2.8
Seattle, Wash.	39	6.0	43	4.2	44	3.6	49	2.4	55	1.6	61	1.4	65	0.7	64	1.3	60	2.0	52	3.4	45	5.6	41	6.3
Spokane, Wash.	26	2.5	32	1.6	38	1.4	46	1.1	54	1.4	62	1.2	70	0.5	68	0.7	60	0.7	48	1.1	35	2.1	29	2.5
Springfield, Mo.	32	1.6	36	2.1	45	3.4	56	4.0	65	4.3	73	4.7	78	3.4	77	3.3	70	4.0	59	3.2	46	2.9	35	2.0
Syracuse, N.Y.	23	2.6	24	2.7	33	3.1	46	3.3	57	3.2	67	3.6	71	3.8	70	3.8	62	3.5	53	3.1	41	3.5	28	3.2
Tampa, Fla.	60	2.2	61	3.0	66	3.5	72	1.8	77	3.4	81	5.3	82	7.4	82	7.6	81	6.2	74	2.3	67	1.9	61	2.1
Washington, D.C.	31	2.8	34	2.6	42	3.2	53	2.9	63	3.7	72	3.4	77	4.2	74	4.2	68	3.3	55	3.0	45	3.0	35	3.3
Wilmington, Del.	31	3.1	33	3.0	42	3.9	52	3.4	62	3.2	71	3.5	76	3.9	75	4.0	68	3.6	56	2.9	46	3.3	36	3.5

Normal Temperatures, Highs, Lows, Precipitation

Source: Natl. Climatic Data Center, NESDIS, NOAA. U.S. Department of Commerce

These normals are based on records for the thirty-year period 1951-1980. (See explanation on page 241.) The extreme temperatures (through 1989) are listed for the stations shown and may not agree with the states records shown on page 245-246.

Airport stations; * designates city office stations. The minus (−) sign indicates temperatures below zero. Fahrenheit thermometer registration.

State	Station	Normal temperature January Max.	Jan. Min.	July Max.	July Min.	Extreme temperature Highest	Lowest	annual precipitation (inches)
Alabama	Mobile	61	41	91	73	104	3	64.64
Alabama	Montgomery	57	36	92	72	105	0	49.16
Alaska	Juneau	27	16	64	47	90	−22	53.15
Arizona	Phoenix	65	39	105	80	118	17	7.11
Arkansas	Little Rock	50	30	93	71	112	−5	49.20
California	Los Angeles*	67	48	84	64	110	28	14.85
California	San Francisco	55	42	71	53	106	20	19.71
Colorado	Denver	43	16	88	59	104	−30	15.31
Connecticut	Hartford	34	17	85	62	102	−26	44.39
Delaware	Wilmington	39	23	86	66	102	−14	41.38
Dist. of Col.	Washington	43	28	88	70	104	−5	39.00
Florida	Jacksonville	65	42	91	72	105	7	52.76
Florida	Key West	72	66	89	80	95	41	39.42
Florida	Miami	75	59	89	76	98	30	57.55
Georgia	Atlanta	51	33	88	69	105	−8	48.61
Hawaii	Honolulu	80	65	87	73	94	53	23.47
Idaho	Boise	37	23	91	59	111	−23	11.71
Illinois	Chicago	29	14	83	63	104	−27	33.34
Indiana	Indianapolis	34	18	85	65	104	−23	39.12
Iowa	Des Moines	27	10	86	66	108	−24	30.83
Iowa	Dubuque	24	7	82	62	101	−28	38.59
Kansas	Wichita	40	19	93	70	113	−21	28.61
Kentucky	Louisville	41	24	88	68	105	−20	43.56
Louisiana	New Orleans	62	43	91	74	102	11	59.74
Maine	Portland	31	12	79	57	103	−39	43.52
Maryland	Baltimore	41	24	87	67	105	−7	41.84
Massachusetts	Boston	36	23	82	65	102	−12	43.84
Michigan	Detroit	31	16	83	61	104	−21	30.97
Michigan	Sault Ste. Marie*	21	5	75	52	98	−36	33.48
Minnesota	Minn.-St. Paul	20	2	83	63	105	−34	26.36
Mississippi	Jackson	57	35	93	68	106	2	52.82
Missouri	St. Louis	38	20	89	69	107	−18	33.91
Montana	Helena	28	8	84	52	105	−42	11.37
Nebraska	Omaha	30	10	89	67	114	−23	30.34
Nevada	Las Vegas	45	33	105	76	116	8	4.19
New Hampshire	Concord	31	9	83	56	102	−37	36.53
New Jersey	Atlantic City	41	23	84	65	106	−11	41.93
New Mexico	Albuquerque	47	22	93	65	105	−17	8.12
New Mexico	Roswell	55	27	94	69	109	−9	9.70
New York	Albany	30	12	83	60	100	−28	35.74
New York	New York-La Guardia	37	26	84	69	107	−3	42.82
No. Carolina	Charlotte	50	31	88	69	104	−5	43.16
No. Carolina	Raleigh	50	29	88	67	105	−9	41.76
No. Dakota	Bismarck	18	−4	84	56	109	−44	15.36
Ohio	Cincinnati-Greater	37	20	86	65	102	−25	40.14
Ohio	Cleveland	33	19	82	61	104	−19	35.40
Oklahoma	Oklahoma City	47	25	94	71	110	−8	30.89
Oregon	Portland	44	34	80	56	107	−3	37.39
Pennsylvania	Harrisburg	37	22	86	65	107	−9	39.09
Pennsylvania	Philadelphia	39	24	86	67	104	−7	41.42
Rhode Island	Block Island	37	25	76	64	92	−4	41.91
So. Carolina	Charleston	59	37	89	72	104	6	51.59
So. Dakota	Huron	22	0	87	61	112	−39	18.66
So. Dakota	Rapid City	32	9	87	57	110	−29	16.27
Tennessee	Nashville	46	28	90	69	107	−17	48.49
Texas	Amarillo	49	22	91	66	108	−14	19.10
Texas	Galveston*	59	48	87	79	101	8	40.24
Texas	Houston	62	41	94	73	107	7	44.76
Utah	Salt Lake City	37	20	93	62	107	−30	15.31
Vermont	Burlington	25	8	81	59	101	−30	33.69
Virginia	Norfolk	48	32	90	70	104	−3	45.22
Washington	Seattle-Tacoma	44	34	75	54	99	0	38.60
Washington	Spokane	31	20	84	55	108	−25	16.71
West Virginia	Huntington	41	25	86	65	102	−16	40.74
Wisconsin	Madison	25	7	83	58	104	−37	30.84
Wisconsin	Milwaukee	26	11	80	61	103	−26	30.94
Wyoming	Cheyenne	37	15	83	55	100	−34	13.31
Puerto Rico	San Juan	83	70	88	75	98	60	53.99

Mean Annual Snowfall (inches) based on record through 1980: Boston, Mass. 42; Sault Ste. Marie, Mich., 113; Albany, N.Y. 65.2; Rochester, N.Y. 89.2; Burlington, Vt., 78.6; Cheyenne, Wyo., 53.3; Juneau, Alas. 105.8.

Wettest Spot: Mount Waialeale, Ha., on the island of Kauai, is the rainiest place in the world, according to the National Geographic Society, with an average annual rainfall of 460 inches.

Highest Temperature: A temperature of 136° F. observed at Azizia, Tripolitania in Northern Africa on Sept. 13, 1922, is generally accepted as the world's highest temperature recorded under standard conditions.

The record high in the United States was 134° in Death Valley, Cal., July 10, 1913.

Lowest Temperature: A record low temperature of −128.6° F. was recorded at the Soviet Antarctica station Vostok on July 21, 1983.

The record low in the United States was −80° at Prospect Creek, Alas., Jan. 23, 1971.

The lowest official temperature on the North American continent was recorded at 81 degrees below zero in February, 1947, at a lonely airport in the Yukon called Snag.

These are the meteorological champions—the official temperature extremes—but there are plenty of other claimants to thermometer fame. However, sun readings are unofficial records, since meteorological data to qualify officially must be taken on instruments in a sheltered and ventilated location.

Annual Climatological Data

Source: Natl. Climatic Data Center, NESDIS, NOAA, U.S. Department of Commerce

1989 Station	Elev. ft.	Temperature °F Highest	Date	Lowest	Date	Precipitation Total (in.)	Greatest in 24 hrs.	Date	Sleet or snow Total (in.)	Greatest in 24 hours	Date	Fastest Wind MPH	Date	No. of days Clear*	Cloudy*	Prec. .01 in. or more	Snow, sleet 1 in. or more
Albany, N.Y.	275	93	8/4	−15	12/24	39.67	2.26	10/19	21.1	4.5	12/15	35	11/20	65	175	147	6
Albuquerque, N.M.	5311	103	6/19	5	2/6	4.99	0.80	10/4	12.2	3.2	2/5	41	4/12	180	77	40	6
Anchorage, Alas.	114	82	7/2	−30	1/29	27.55	4.12	8/25	64.1	6.5	12/17	51	3/3	68	236	145	21
Asheville, N.C.	2140	90	8/5	1	12/23	60.63	2.49	7/30	11.2	3.9	2/18	33	2/23	85	164	147	5
Atlanta, Ga.	1010	95	7/29	6	12/23	63.31	5.41	10/1	2.0	1.1	12/9	56	6/14	96	162	127	1
Baltimore, Md.	148	94	7/23	4	12/23	51.88	2.60	8/28	21.4	4.1	12/8	52	11/16	84	176	133	8
Barrow, Alas.	31	—	—	—	—	—	—	—	—	—	—	55	2/25	81	196	—	—
Birmingham, Ala.	678	96	8/25	1	12/23	53.71	3.81	7/1	0.4	0.4	12/9	39	11/15	80	182	134	0
Bismarck, N.D.	1647	103	7/8	−35	12/19	11.33	1.33	7/28	42.9	6.5	1/6	40	5/29	115	161	93	16
Boise, Ida.	2838	108	7/7	−15	2/5	10.44	0.70	3/18	9.1	3.4	1/5	31	4/25	127	139	71	3
Boston, Mass.	15	96	7/26	4	12/23	42.42	2.22	8/12	22.5	4.4	11/23	38	11/21	94	177	134	7
Buffalo, N.Y.	705	90	7/25	−4	12/23	41.16	3.01	6/9	98.1	11.3	2/6	44	11/20	45	205	183	29
Burlington, Vt.	332	94	7/27	−18	12/24	36.03	2.11	8/4	53.4	11.4	12/16	38	1/26	61	184	157	20
Charleston, S.C.	40	98	8/6	14	12/25	55.72	5.58	9/21	8.9	6.6	12/22	52	9/22	87	170	130	2
Charleston, W. Va.	939	93	8/4	−12	12/23	57.97	2.39	9/15	24.4	3.5	12/8	28	3/18	66	198	164	10
Chicago, Ill.	658	101	7/10	−14	12/21	29.45	3.69	8/4	34.2	5.6	10/19	39	5/25	84	180	132	11
Cincinnati, Oh.	869	95	7/11	−20	12/22	49.61	2.23	3/28	23.3	7.0	12/15	35	3/15	83	177	142	6
Cleveland, Oh.	777	96	7/10	−15	12/22	43.90	2.58	5/25	68.3	8.9	12/15	31	11/5	60	207	169	23
Columbus, Oh.	812	94	7/11	−17	12/22	43.76	1.79	7/26	22.1	4.2	12/15	32	8/29	77	192	144	6
Concord, N.H.	342	95	7/27	−20	12/24	38.23	2.11	5/1	40.3	7.7	12/15	—	—	83	178	145	12
Dallas, Tex.	551	101	9/3	−1	12/23	39.95	5.34	5/16	1.8	0.8	3/4	41	6/2	130	140	74	0
Denver, Co.	5283	103	7/8	−24	2/5	15.47	1.49	6/2	58.5	8.8	1/27	38	4/16	129	117	88	17
Des Moines, Ia.	938	99	7/10	−22	12/23	29.14	3.11	8/25	26.5	7.4	2/12	41	4/27	120	148	108	8
Detroit, Mich.	633	92	7/10	−9	12/22	29.26	2.87	7/19	34.7	4.1	2/20	44	3/14	79	175	130	15
Dodge City, Kan.	2582	100	8/4	−21	12/22	20.95	2.17	9/12	13.8	5.7	3/9	53	4/2	130	120	66	3
Duluth, Minn.	1428	92	8/4	−30	2/3	26.29	2.14	9/20	97.0	11.6	1/7	39	5/24	99	173	125	24
Fairbanks, Alas.	436	87	7/8	−51	1/30	10.43	1.20	6/24	78.7	6.3	12/22	32	7/4	75	204	104	30
Fresno, Cal.	328	107	7/7	24	2/7	6.91	0.98	3/25	T		2/8	25	3/2	204	86	29	0
Galveston, Tex.	7	96	9/3	14	12/23	40.59	6.56	8/1	1.0	1.0	12/22	56	10/15	—	—	82	1
Grand Rapids, Mich.	784	91	8/3	−11	12/23	33.90	3.17	6/23	92.7	7.4	11/17	37	1/8	74	198	142	36
Hartford, Conn.	169	95	7/26	−9	12/24	54.61	4.90	5/23	26.3	6.8	12/15	40	11/16	76	186	138	8
Helena, Mont.	3828	96	7/20	−33	2/4	12.49	1.02	9/17	81.9	8.5	3/16	49	7/26	—	—	111	24
Honolulu, Ha.	7	92	8/11	56	12/16	27.52	5.56	10/3	0	0	—	30	12/9	85	100	82	0
Houston, Tex.	96	99	9/4	7	12/23	52.73	10.36	5/17	1.7	1.7	12/22	39	6/26	75	168	106	1
Huron, S.D.	1281	101	7/5	−28	12/22	14.50	1.62	6/25	52.4	8.6	3/16	43	5/24	112	134	91	15
Indianapolis, Ind.	792	94	6/25	−23	12/22	50.57	2.96	9/8	24.4	7.5	10/19	35	7/8	86	178	134	8
Jackson, Miss.	291	98	8/28	4	12/23	52.55	3.43	5/4	0.1	0.1	12/9	32	5/4	92	183	111	0
Jacksonville, Fla.	26	98	7/10	20	12/25	51.45	4.89	9/27	0.8	0.8	12/23	30	8/25	86	153	120	0
Kansas City, Mo.	1014	99	7/7	−23	12/23	37.64	4.51	9/8	13.5	3.7	12/18	38	3/14	128	135	89	4
Lander, Wyo.	5557	99	7/8	−24	2/3	15.50	1.82	5/29	62.5	11.2	10/28	72	1/31	107	135	76	19
Little Rock, Ark.	257	99	8/27	−1	12/23	49.25	2.71	3/28	3.0	2.0	1/8	—	—	—	—	115	2
Los Angeles, Cal.	97	102	4/6	35	2/6	4.19	0.98	2/8	0	0	—	—	—	169	81	20	0
Louisville, Ky.	−477	94	7/11	−15	12/22	50.97	3.12	7/19	8.5	3.5	12/14	29	5/26	97	173	134	3
Marquette, Mich.	1415	91	8/4	−22	3/2	29.53	2.80	6/7	246.3	19.8	3/14	—	—	—	—	163	59
Memphis, Tenn.	258	98	8/29	−4	12/22	58.89	4.24	2/13	0.7	0.4	12/17	38	3/18	101	166	116	0
Miami, Fla.	7	97	8/16	30	12/25	42.63	3.55	8/29	0	0	—	31	10/10	90	87	116	0
Milwaukee, Wis.	672	95	7/9	−15	12/21	30.30	2.68	7/19	55.4	9.1	11/21	44	8/4	85	169	129	13
Minneapolis, Minn.	834	97	7/5	−24	2/3	23.32	1.72	7/18	65.2	8.5	3/3	35	12/25	93	152	111	23
Mobile, Ala.	211	98	9/2	9	12/24	64.00	5.87	11/7	T	T	12/25	44	6/8	111	153	116	0
Moline, Ill.	582	100	7/10	−24	12/23	31.93	3.02	9/1	22.5	4.0	2/12	38	1/7	100	160	104	8
Nashville, Tenn.	590	96	7/26	−10	12/22	57.03	4.73	2/14	5.6	4.4	2/27	33	3/26	100	159	132	1
Newark, N.J.	7	99	8/27	11	12/23	53.99	2.53	5/16	13.6	5.7	11/22	46	11/20	76	174	125	3
New Orleans, La.	4	93	8/27	11	12/23	67.46	12.66	11/6	0.5	0.5	12/22	44	5/4	78	171	121	0
New York, N.Y.	132	96	7/26	6	12/23	65.11	3.50	8/11	13.9	5.0	1/6	29	11/21	—	—	124	3
Norfolk, Va.	24	99	7/11	11	12/25	56.63	2.68	8/11	25.4	14.2	2/17	40	11/15	80	173	147	3
Oklahoma City, Okla.	1285	100	9/1	−8	12/23	40.89	4.56	6/13	11.1	4.8	1/13	48	6/27	140	118	80	4
Omaha, Neb.	997	100	8/4	−23	12/22	23.80	2.71	9/8	23.0	4.0	2/12	40	4/27	109	146	92	7
Philadelphia, Pa.	5	94	9/10	6	12/22	48.66	4.49	7/4	20.7	5.1	1/6	56	3/18	79	173	131	7
Phoenix, Ariz.	1110	118	7/4	33	2/7	4.94	1.23	3/25	0	0	—	35	8/7	221	51	26	0
Pittsburgh, Pa.	1137	94	7/25	−12	12/22	42.51	1.99	6/20	30.7	6.8	12/15	39	11/20	43	216	154	6
Portland, Me.	43	95	7/26	−13	12/24	41.55	4.86	5/11	48.0	7.7	12/15	32	11/21	86	172	132	15
Portland, Ore.	21	93	6/24	9	2/5	30.05	1.11	12/3	3.2	2.0	3/1	41	2/3	62	222	129	1
Providence, R.I.	51	92	7/27	2	12/23	56.06	3.43	7/16	33.5	8.5	12/15	40	2/21	81	180	141	3
Raleigh, N.C.	434	96	7/11	7	12/25	54.15	2.65	8/17	14.6	5.8	2/18	35	3/31	79	191	147	4
Rapid City, S.D.	3162	101	7/8	−29	12/22	13.57	1.48	9/20	44.2	4.3	3/2	49	6/16	124	128	107	17
Reno, Nev.	4404	100	7/19	−1	2/7	7.34	0.76	8/7	19.6	6.6	2/3	—	—	185	85	47	6
Richmond, Va.	164	96	7/11	7	12/25	49.74	2.43	7/15	24.6	7.6	2/18	46	5/6	73	183	134	7
Rochester, N.Y.	547	94	7/25	−4	12/14	32.66	1.91	6/15	115.3	10.8	5/7	40	3/15	55	202	175	37
St. Louis, Mo.	535	98	7/10	−16	12/22	28.60	2.25	3/19	24.1	10.7	3/5	37	12/2	99	172	108	5
Salt Lake City, Ut.	4221	104	7/20	−14	2/6	10.87	1.20	10/25	45.8	11.9	2/1	52	8/17	120	146	80	14
San Antonio, Tex.	788	106	7/19	6	12/23	22.14	3.11	10/7	T	T	12/22	34	4/29	118	132	69	0
San Diego, Cal.	13	100	9/25	37	1/9	3.83	1.01	12/23	0	0	—	23	10/25	155	93	23	0
San Francisco, Cal.	8	98	6/22	31	2/6	11.35	1.28	11/25	T	T	2/8	46	1/5	181	101	52	0
Sault Ste. Marie, Mich.	721	92	7/23	−22	12/21	25.89	1.08	8/3	154.2	10.5	11/15	49	5/25	78	190	161	48
Savannah, Ga.	46	98	8/6	16	12/24	46.87	6.00	9/21	4.6	3.4	12/22	—	—	104	152	118	2
Seattle, Wash.	400	91	8/9	7	2/4	34.69	1.99	12/3	14.2	7.4	3/1	43	1/16	69	220	145	4
Shreveport, La.	254	98	8/28	5	12/23	60.90	5.07	5/4	T	T	12/22	38	5/16	111	162	108	0
Sioux City, Ia.	1095	102	7/9	−24	12/23	19.39	2.66	7.29	25.6	4.9	12/10	50	8/5	111	143	78	9
Spokane, Wash.	2356	97	8/7	−11	2/2	14.71	1.07	8/23	45.2	8.3	2/16	43	1/16	91	195	110	16
Springfield, Mo.	1268	94	8/27	−16	12/23	31.50	5.81	5/21	24.9	12.9	3/5	31	7/30	116	157	84	6
Syracuse, N.Y.	410	92	8/4	−14	12/24	36.93	2.39	9/19	135.0	16.7	12/16	38	11/28	64	210	193	35
Tampa, Fla.	19	97	5/31	24	12/24	43.63	1.97	7/21	T	T	12/23	30	7/13	148	71	101	0
Washington, D.C.	10	97	9/10	−4	12/25	44.34	2.61	5/5	22.7	5.0	12/8	55	6/14	67	192	136	6
Wilmington, Del.	74	96	7/26	4	12/23	49.77	6.83	7/4	25.3	5.6	11/22	40	11/16	79	186	124	9

*To get partly cloudy days deduct the total of clear and cloudy days from 365 (1 yr.). T—trace. (1) Date shown is the starting date of the storm (in some cases it lasted more than one day).

Record Temperatures by States Through 1989

Source: Natl. Climatic Data Center. NESDIS, NOAA. U.S. Commerce Department

State	Lowest °F	Highest	Latest date	Station	Approximate elevation in feet
Alabama	−27		Jan. 30, 1966	New Market	760
		112	Sept. 5, 1925	Centerville	345
Alaska	−80		Jan. 23, 1971	Prospect Creek Camp	1,100
		100	June 27, 1915	Fort Yukon	419
Arizona	−40		Jan. 7, 1971	Hawley Lake	8,180
		127	July 7, 1905¹	Parker	345
Arkansas	−29		Feb. 13, 1905	Pond	1,250
		120	Aug. 10, 1936	Ozark	396
California	−45		Jan. 20, 1937	Boca	5,532
		134	July 10, 1913	Greenland Ranch	−178
Colorado	−61		Feb. 1, 1985	Maybell	5,920
		118	July 11, 1888	Bennett	5,484
Connecticut	−32		Feb. 16, 1943	Falls Village	585
		105	July 22, 1926	Waterbury	400
Delaware	−17		Jan. 17, 1893	Millsboro	20
		110	July 21, 1930	Millsboro	20
Dist. of Col.	−15		Feb. 11, 1899	Washington	112
		106	July 20, 1930	Washington	112
Florida	−2		Feb. 13, 1899	Tallahassee	193
		109	June 29, 1931	Monticello	207
Georgia	−17		Jan. 27, 1940	CCC Camp F-16	1,000
		112	Jul. 24, 1952	Louisville	132
Hawaii	12		May 17, 1979	Mauna Kea	13,770
		100	Apr. 27, 1931	Pahala	850
Idaho	−60		Jan. 16, 1943	Island Park Dam	6,285
		118	July 28, 1934	Orofino	1,027
Illinois	−35		Jan. 22, 1930	Mount Carroll	817
		117	July 14, 1954	E. St. Louis	410
Indiana	−35		Feb. 2, 1951	Greensburg	954
		116	July 14, 1936	Collegeville	672
Iowa	−47		Jan. 12, 1912	Washta	1,157
		118	July 20, 1934	Keokuk	614
Kansas	−40		Feb. 13, 1905	Lebanon	1,812
		121	July 24, 1936¹	Alton (near)	1,651
Kentucky	−34		Jan. 28, 1963	Cynthiana	684
		114	July 28, 1930	Greensburg	581
Louisiana	−16		Feb. 13, 1899	Minden	194
		114	Aug. 10, 1936	Plain Dealing	268
Maine	−48		Jan. 19, 1925	Van Buren	510
		105	July 10, 1911¹	North Bridgton	450
Maryland	−40		Jan. 13, 1912	Oakland	2,461
		109	July 10, 1936¹	Cumberland and Frederick	623-325
Massachusetts	−35		Jan. 12, 1981	Chester	640
		107	Aug. 2, 1975	Chester and New Bedford	120-640
Michigan	−51		Feb. 9, 1934	Vanderbilt	785
		112	July 13, 1936	Mio	963
Minnesota	−59		Feb. 16, 1903¹	Pokegama Dam	1,280
		114	July 6, 1936¹	Moorhead	904
Mississippi	−19		Jan. 30, 1966	Corinth	420
		115	July 29, 1930	Holly Springs	600
Missouri	−40		Feb. 13, 1905	Warsaw	700
		118	July 14, 1954¹	Warsaw and Union	687-560
Montana	−70		Jan. 20, 1954	Rogers Pass	5,470
		117	July 5, 1937	Medicine Lake	1,950
Nebraska	−47		Feb. 12, 1899	Camp Clarke	3,700
		118	July 24, 1936¹	Minden	2,169
Nevada	−50		Jan. 8, 1937	San Jacinto	5,200
		122	June 23, 1954¹	Overton	1,240
New Hampshire	−46		Jan. 28 1925	Pittsburgh	1,575
		106	July 4, 1911	Nashua	125
New Jersey	−34		Jan. 5, 1904	River Vale	70
		110	July 10, 1936	Runyon	18
New Mexico	−50		Feb. 1, 1951	Gavilan	7,350
		116	July 14, 1934¹	Orogrande	4,171
New York	−52		Feb. 18, 1979	Old Forge	1,720
		108	July 22, 1926	Troy	35
North Carolina	−34		Jan. 21, 1985	Mt. Mitchell	6,525
		110	Aug. 21, 1983	Fayetteville	213
North Dakota	−60		Feb. 15, 1936	Parshall	1,929
		121	July 6, 1936	Steele	1,857
Ohio	−39		Feb. 10, 1899	Milligan	800
		113	July 21, 1934¹	Gallipolis (near)	673
Oklahoma	−27		Jan. 18, 1930	Watts	958
		120	July 26, 1943¹	Tishmoningo	670
Oregon	−54		Feb. 10, 1933¹	Seneca	4,700
		119	Aug. 10, 1938	Pendleton	1,074
Pennsylvania	−42		Jan. 5, 1904	Smethport	1,469
		111	July 10, 1936¹	Phoenixville	100
Rhode Island	−23		Jan. 11, 1942	Kingston	100
		104	Aug. 2, 1975	Providence	51
South Carolina	−19		Jan. 21, 1985	Caesar's Head	3,100
		111	June 28, 1954¹	Camden	170
South Dakota	−58		Feb. 17, 1936	McIntosh	2,277
		120	July 5, 1936	Gannvalley	1,750

State	Lowest °F	Highest	Latest date	Station	Approximate elevation in feet
Tennessee	−32		Dec. 30, 1917	Mountain City	2,471
		113	Aug. 9, 1930¹	Perryville	377
Texas	−23		Feb. 8, 1933	Seminole	3,275
		120	Aug. 12, 1936	Seymour	1,291
Utah	−69		Feb. 1, 1985	Peter's Sink	8,092
		117	Jul. 5, 1985	Saint George	2,880
Vermont	−50		Dec. 30, 1933	Bloomfield	915
		105	July 4, 1911	Vernon	310
Virginia	−30		Jan. 22, 1985	Mtn. Lake Bio. Stn.	3,870
		110	July 15, 1954	Balcony Falls	725
Washington	−48		Dec. 30, 1968	Mazama	2,120
	−48		Dec. 30, 1968	Winthrop	1,765
		118	Aug. 5, 1961¹	Ice Harbor Dam	475
West Virginia	−37		Dec. 30, 1917	Lewisburg	2,200
		112	July 10, 1936¹	Martinsburg	435
Wisconsin	−54		Jan. 24, 1922	Danbury	908
		114	July 13, 1936	Wisconsin Dells	900
Wyoming	−63		Feb. 9, 1933	Moran	6,770
		114	July 12, 1900	Basin	3,500

(1) Also on earlier dates at the same or other places.

International Temperature and Precipitation

Source: Environmental Data Service, U.S. Commerce Department

A standard period of 30 years has been used to obtain the average daily maximum and minimum temperatures and precipitation. The length of record of extreme maximum and minimum temperatures includes all available years of data for a given location and is usually for a longer period.

Station	Elev. Ft.	Temperature F° — Average Daily January Max.	Min.	July Max.	Min.	Extreme Max.	Min.	Average annual precipitation (inches)
Addis Ababa, Ethiopia	8,038	75	43	69	50	94	32	48.7
Algiers, Algeria	194	59	49	83	70	107	32	30.0
Amsterdam, Netherlands	5	40	34	69	59	95	3	25.6
Athens, Greece	351	54	42	90	72	109	20	15.8
Auckland, New Zealand	23	73	60	56	46	90	33	49.1
Bangkok, Thailand	53	89	67	90	76	104	50	57.8
Beirut, Lebanon	111	62	51	87	73	107	30	35.1
Belgrade, Yugoslavia	453	37	27	84	61	107	−14	24.6
Berlin, Germany	187	35	26	74	55	96	−15	23.1
Bogota, Colombia	8,355	67	48	64	50	75	30	41.8
Bombay, India	27	88	62	88	75	110	46	71.2
Bucharest, Romania	269	33	20	86	61	105	−18	22.8
Budapest, Hungary	394	35	26	82	61	103	−10	24.2
Buenos Aires, Argentina	89	85	63	57	42	104	22	37.4
Cairo, Egypt	381	65	47	96	70	117	34	1.1
Capetown, South Africa	56	78	60	63	45	103	28	20.0
Caracas, Venezuela	3,418	75	56	78	61	91	45	32.9
Casablanca, Morocco	164	63	45	79	65	110	31	15.9
Copenhagen, Denmark	43	36	29	72	55	91	−3	23.3
Damascus, Syria	2,362	53	36	96	64	113	21	8.6
Dublin, Ireland	155	47	35	67	51	86	8	29.7
Geneva, Switzerland	1,329	39	29	77	58	101	−1	33.9
Havana, Cuba	80	79	65	89	75	104	43	48.2
Hong Kong	109	64	56	87	78	97	32	85.1
Istanbul, Turkey	59	45	36	81	65	100	17	31.5
Jerusalem, Israel	2,654	55	41	87	63	107	26	19.7
Lagos, Nigeria	10	88	74	83	74	104	60	72.3
La Paz, Bolivia	12,001	63	43	62	33	80	26	22.6
Lima, Peru	394	82	66	67	57	93	49	1.6
London, England	149	44	35	73	55	99	9	22.9
Madrid, Spain	2,188	47	33	87	62	102	14	16.5
Manila, Philippines	49	86	69	88	75	101	58	82.0
Mexico City, Mexico	7,340	66	42	74	54	92	24	23.0
Moscow, U.S.S.R.	505	21	9	76	55	96	−27	24.8
Nairobi, Kenya	5,971	77	54	69	51	87	41	37.7
Oslo, Norway	308	30	20	73	56	93	−21	26.9
Paris, France	164	42	32	76	55	105	1	22.3
Prague, Czechoslovakia	662	34	25	74	58	98	−16	19.3
Reykjavik, Iceland	92	36	28	58	48	74	4	33.9
Rome, Italy	377	54	39	88	64	104	20	29.5
San Salvador, El Salvador	2,238	90	60	89	65	105	45	70.0
Santiago, Chile	1,706	85	53	59	37	99	24	14.2
Sao Paolo, Brazil	2,628	77	63	66	53	100	32	57.3
Shanghai, China	16	47	32	91	75	104	10	45.0
Singapore	33	86	73	88	75	97	66	95.0
Stockholm, Sweden	146	31	23	70	55	97	−26	22.4
Sydney, Australia	62	78	65	60	46	114	35	46.5
Teheran, Iran	3,937	45	27	99	72	109	−5	9.7
Tokyo, Japan	19	47	29	83	70	101	17	61.6
Tripoli, Libya	72	61	47	85	71	114	33	15.1
Vienna, Austria	664	34	26	75	59	98	−14	25.6
Warsaw, Poland	294	30	21	75	56	98	−22	22.0

Record Maximum 24-Hour Precipitation by State

(through 1989)

Source: Natl. Climatic Data Center, NESDIS, NOAA, U.S. Department of Commerce

State	Precip. (inches)	Date	Station	Elevation (feet)	State	Precip. (inches)	Date	Station	Elevation (feet)
Ala.	20.33	4/13/55	Axis	36	Mont.	11.50	6/20/21	Circle	2,440
Alas.	15.20	10/12/82	Angoon	15	Neb.	13.15	7/8-9/50	York	1,610
Ariz.	11.40	9/4-5/70	Workman Creek	6,970	Nev.	7.40	3/19/07	Lewer's Ranch	5,200
Ark.	14.06	12/3/82	Big Fork	1,100	N.H.	10.38	2/10-11/70	Mount Washington	6,260
Cal.	26.12	1/22-23/43	Hoegees Camp	2,760	N.J.	14.81	8/19/39	Tuckerton	20
Colo.	11.08	6/17/65	Holly	3,390	N.M.	11.28	5/18-19/55	Lake Maloya	7,400
Conn.	12.77	8/19/55	Burlington	460	N.Y.	11.17	10/9/03	NYC Central Park	130
Del.	8.50	7/13/75	Dover	30	N.C.	22.22	7/15-16/16	Altapass	2,600
Fla.	38.70	9/5/50	Yankeetown	5	N.D.	8.10	6/29/75	Litchville	1,470
Ga.	18.00	8/28/11	St. George	77	Ohio.	10.51	7/12/66	Sandusky	610
Ha.	38.00	1/24-25/56	Kilauea Plantation	180	Okla.	15.50	9/3-4/40	Sapulpa	740
Id.	7.17	11/23/09	Rattlesnake Creek	4,000	Ore.	10.17	12/21/15	Glenora	575
Ill.	16.54	6/14-15/57	East St. Louis	410	Pa.	34.50*	7/17/42	Smethport	1,510
Ind.	10.50	8/6/05	Princeton	480	R.I.	12.13	9/16-17/32	Westerly	40
Ia.	16.70	8/5-6/59	Decatur Co.	1,110	S.C.	13.25	7/14-15/16	Effingham	110
Kan.	12.59	5/31-6/1/41	Burlington	1,010	S.D.	8.00	9/10/00	Elk Point	1,127
Ky.	10.40	6/28/60	Dunmor	610	Tenn.	11.00	3/28/02	McMinnville	900
La.	22.00	8/28-29/62	Hackberry	10	Texas.	43.00*	7/25-26/79	Alvin	50
Me.	8.05	9/11/54	Brunswick	70	Utah.	6.00*	9/5/70	Bug Point	6,600
Md.	14.75	7/26-27/97	Jewell	152	Vt.	8.77	11/3-4/27	Somerset	2,080
Mass.	18.15	8/18-19/55	Westfield	220	Va.	27.00*	8/20/69	Nelson Co.	est. 500
Mich.	9.78	8/31-9/1/14	Bloomingdale	750	Wash.	12.00	1/21/35	Quinault R.S.	220
Minn.	10.84	7/21-22/72	Fort Ripley	1,140	W.Va.	19.00*	7/18/89	Rockport	700
Miss.	15.68	7/9/68	Columbus	190	Wis.	11.72	6/24/46	Mellen	1,150
Mo.	18.18	7/20/65	Edgarton	850	Wyo.	6.06	8/1/85	Cheyenne	6,126

*Estimated

Wind Chill Table

Source: National Weather Service, NOAA, U.S. Commerce Department

Both temperature and wind cause heat loss from body surfaces. A combination of cold and wind makes a body feel colder than the actual temperature. The table shows, for example, that a temperature of 20 degrees Fahrenheit, plus a wind of 20 miles per hour, causes a body heat loss equal to that in minus 10 degrees with no wind. In other words, the wind makes 20 degrees feel like minus 10.

Top line of figures shows actual temperatures in degrees Fahrenheit. Column at left shows wind speeds.

MPH	35	30	25	20	15	10	5	0	−5	−10	−15	−20	−25	−30	−35	−40	−45
5	33	27	21	16	12	7	0	−5	−10	−15	−21	−26	−31	−36	−42	−47	−52
10	22	16	10	3	−3	−9	−15	−22	−27	−34	−40	−46	−52	−58	−64	−71	−77
15	16	9	2	−5	−11	−18	−25	−31	−38	−45	−51	−58	−65	−72	−78	−85	−92
20	12	4	−3	−10	−17	−24	−31	−39	−46	−53	−60	−67	−74	−81	−88	−95	−103
25	8	1	−7	−15	−22	−29	−36	−44	−51	−59	−66	−74	−81	−88	−96	−103	−110
30	6	−2	−10	−18	−25	−33	−41	−49	−56	−64	−71	−79	−86	−93	−101	−109	−116
35	4	−4	−12	−20	−27	−35	−43	−52	−58	−67	−74	−82	−89	−97	−105	−113	−120
40	3	−5	−13	−21	−29	−37	−45	−53	−60	−69	−76	−84	−92	−100	−107	−115	−123
45	2	−6	−14	−22	−30	−38	−46	−54	−62	−70	−78	−85	−93	−102	−109	−117	−125

(Wind speeds greater than 45 mph have little additional chilling effect.)

Heat Index

The index is a measure of the contribution that high humidity makes with abnormally high temperatures in reducing the body's ability to cool itself. For example, the index shows that for an actual air temperature of 100 degrees Fahrenheit and a relative humidity of 50 percent, the effect on the human body would be same as 120 degrees. Sunstroke and heat exhaustion are likely when the heat index reaches 105. This index is a measure of what hot weather "feels like" to the average person for various temperatures and relative humidities.

Relative Humidity	Air Temperature* / Apparent Temperature* 70	75	80	85	90	95	100	105	110	115	120
0%	64	69	73	78	83	87	91	95	99	103	107
10%	65	70	75	80	85	90	95	100	105	111	116
20%	66	72	77	82	87	93	99	105	112	120	130
30%	67	73	78	84	90	96	104	113	123	135	148
40%	68	74	79	86	93	101	110	123	137	151	
50%	69	75	81	88	96	107	120	135	150		
60%	70	76	82	90	100	114	132	149			
70%	70	77	85	93	106	124	144				
80%	71	78	86	97	113	136					
90%	71	79	88	102	122						
100%	72	80	91	108							

*Degrees Fahrenheit.

Average Relative Humidity (%)

Source: Natl. Climatic Data Center, NESDIS, NOAA, U.S. Department of Commerce

(M-morning; A-afternoon; through 1989)

	Jan. M	Jan. A	Feb. M	Feb. A	Mar. M	Mar. A	Apr. M	Apr. A	May M	May A	June M	June A	July M	July A	Aug. M	Aug. A	Sept. M	Sept. A	Oct. M	Oct. A	Nov. M	Nov. A	Dec. M	Dec. A
Mobile, Ala.	81	60	81	56	84	55	87	52	87	54	87	55	89	60	91	61	89	60	86	53	86	57	83	61
Juneau, Alas.	79	76	83	74	82	67	81	63	79	63	80	65	83	70	87	74	91	77	89	79	85	80	84	82
Phoenix, Ariz.	67	32	60	27	56	24	43	16	35	13	31	11	45	20	51	23	49	23	52	23	58	27	67	34
Little Rock, Ark.	80	61	80	59	79	56	82	56	87	57	86	55	88	57	88	56	89	58	86	53	83	59	80	62
Los Angeles, Calif.	63	50	71	52	74	52	78	54	81	55	85	56	84	53	84	55	78	54	76	56	61	49	62	50
San Francisco, Calif.	81	63	83	63	81	61	82	61	89	68	89	72	92	74	93	73	87	66	81	60	82	63	80	63
Denver, Colo.	63	49	67	44	67	40	67	35	70	38	69	35	66	34	69	35	68	34	65	35	68	48	65	51
Hartford, Conn.	71	56	72	54	71	50	69	45	73	47	77	51	78	51	83	53	86	54	83	51	79	56	75	59
Wilmington, Del.	70	60	75	57	73	52	73	50	76	53	78	54	79	54	83	56	85	56	84	54	80	56	76	59
Dist. of Colo.	77	59	78	55	78	51	77	48	84	56	85	56	86	55	89	56	90	56	88	55	83	56	78	58
Jacksonville, Fla.	87	57	86	53	86	50	86	48	85	50	87	57	88	58	91	60	92	63	91	58	89	56	88	58
Miami, Fla.	84	59	83	57	82	56	80	53	81	59	85	65	84	63	86	65	88	66	86	63	85	62	83	59
Atlanta, Ga.	78	59	75	54	77	51	78	49	82	53	84	56	88	60	90	60	88	60	84	53	81	55	79	58
Columbus, Ga.	84	59	83	54	85	52	85	48	85	50	85	52	89	58	91	57	90	57	89	52	88	54	85	58
Honolulu, Ha.	81	62	79	59	73	57	70	56	67	54	66	52	67	51	68	53	68	52	70	55	75	58	79	61
Boise, Ida.	80	71	80	60	74	45	70	36	69	34	67	30	54	22	52	23	59	30	67	39	77	60	81	71
Chicago, Ill.	76	67	77	65	79	61	77	55	77	53	78	55	82	57	85	57	85	57	82	56	81	64	80	70
Indianapolis, Ind.	80	70	80	67	79	62	78	55	81	55	82	56	87	60	90	61	90	58	86	57	84	66	83	72
Des Moines, Ia.	75	67	78	65	78	60	77	55	77	54	79	55	82	57	84	58	85	59	79	56	79	63	79	69
Dubuque, Ia.	75	68	77	65	78	62	76	55	78	56	82	59	85	59	87	61	87	61	82	58	81	65	80	71
Wichita, Kan.	79	63	79	60	77	54	78	52	83	56	83	53	78	48	79	50	82	54	80	53	79	57	80	62
Louisville, Ky.	76	64	77	62	75	57	75	52	82	55	83	57	85	58	88	58	89	59	85	55	79	61	77	64
New Orleans, La.	85	66	84	63	84	60	88	59	89	60	89	63	91	66	91	66	89	65	87	59	86	62	86	66
Portland, Me.	76	61	76	58	75	58	73	55	75	58	78	60	80	59	83	59	85	60	84	59	83	63	79	61
Baltimore, Md.	71	57	71	54	71	50	71	49	77	53	79	53	81	53	84	55	85	55	83	54	78	55	74	57
Boston, Mass.	66	57	67	56	68	56	68	55	72	59	73	59	74	56	76	59	79	60	77	58	74	60	70	59
Detroit, Mich.	79	69	79	65	79	61	78	54	78	53	79	54	82	53	86	56	87	57	84	57	82	66	81	71
Minneapolis-St. Paul, Minn.	73	67	75	65	76	62	74	52	75	51	78	54	80	53	83	56	85	59	81	58	80	66	78	70
Jackson, Miss.	87	64	87	60	87	57	90	54	92	56	91	56	93	59	94	59	94	59	93	53	90	58	88	63
Kansas City, Mo.	75	63	77	64	78	59	77	55	82	58	84	58	84	56	86	59	86	59	80	56	79	62	78	65
St. Louis, Mo.	82	66	82	64	81	59	78	54	82	55	83	55	85	56	88	56	89	58	85	56	83	63	83	68
Helena, Mont.	70	63	72	55	72	46	70	38	71	38	72	37	66	29	67	30	72	36	73	42	74	58	72	66
Omaha, Neb.	77	65	79	63	78	57	76	52	79	54	82	55	84	57	86	59	87	60	82	55	81	62	80	68
Las Vegas, Nev.	55	30	50	26	44	21	35	16	32	13	24	10	29	15	35	17	34	17	38	19	46	27	55	32
Reno, Nev.	79	51	74	40	69	33	65	28	66	25	65	22	63	18	66	20	69	22	73	27	75	42	77	51
Concord, N.H.	75	58	76	55	76	53	75	46	77	48	82	53	84	52	88	53	90	55	87	53	83	60	80	62
Atlantic City, N.J.	77	58	78	56	77	54	76	52	79	56	81	56	83	57	86	58	87	58	87	56	84	58	78	58
Albuquerque, N.M.	70	40	65	32	56	24	49	18	48	18	46	18	60	27	66	30	62	31	62	30	65	35	70	43
Buffalo, N.Y.	79	72	80	70	80	65	77	57	75	56	77	56	78	55	83	58	84	60	82	60	81	69	81	73
New York-LaGuardia, N.Y.	65	57	65	55	66	53	66	50	71	53	72	54	73	53	75	55	76	57	74	55	71	58	68	59
Charlotte, N.C.	78	56	76	52	79	50	78	46	83	52	84	55	87	57	89	58	90	57	87	53	83	54	79	56
Bismarck, N.D.	74	68	77	68	80	63	79	51	78	48	83	52	83	47	83	46	83	50	79	51	80	64	78	70
Cleveland, Ohio	77	69	78	68	78	63	76	57	77	57	78	57	81	57	85	60	84	60	80	59	77	65	77	70
Oklahoma City, Okla.	78	59	78	58	75	52	76	51	83	57	83	56	80	49	80	50	83	55	79	52	79	55	77	58
Eugene, Ore.	92	80	92	72	91	64	90	57	91	54	90	49	87	38	88	39	89	43	94	63	93	79	93	84
Portland, Ore.	86	75	86	67	86	60	86	55	85	53	84	49	82	45	84	46	87	49	90	63	88	74	87	79
Philadelphia, Pa.	73	59	71	55	71	52	70	49	75	53	77	54	79	54	81	55	83	56	83	54	78	56	74	58
Pittsburgh, Pa.	75	65	74	62	74	57	72	50	76	52	79	52	82	53	85	56	86	56	81	54	78	62	77	67
Providence, R.I.	70	56	70	54	70	52	69	48	73	53	75	56	77	56	80	56	82	55	80	53	77	57	74	57
Charleston, S.C.	83	55	81	52	83	51	83	49	85	53	86	59	88	60	90	63	90	62	88	55	86	53	83	55
Huron, S.D.	74	67	79	69	83	66	83	55	84	54	86	56	86	52	88	52	87	54	82	54	82	64	78	69
Memphis, Tenn.	78	63	78	60	76	56	78	53	82	55	82	56	84	57	86	57	86	56	83	51	80	56	78	61
Nashville, Tenn.	79	63	79	60	78	53	80	51	86	55	87	55	90	57	90	58	91	59	86	54	82	59	80	63
Dallas-Ft. Worth, Tex.	79	60	79	59	79	56	82	56	87	60	85	55	80	48	80	49	85	56	82	55	81	57	79	59
Houston, Tex.	85	64	86	61	87	59	89	57	92	59	92	59	93	58	93	58	93	60	91	56	89	59	86	61
Salt Lake City, Ut.	79	69	77	59	70	47	66	39	65	33	59	26	52	22	54	23	61	29	69	41	74	59	79	71
Burlington, Vt.	71	63	73	62	74	58	74	53	74	51	77	55	78	53	83	57	86	61	81	61	78	66	76	68
Norfolk, Va.	74	59	74	57	74	54	73	50	77	55	79	56	82	59	84	61	83	61	62	59	79	56	75	58
Seattle-Tacoma, Wash.	81	74	80	67	82	62	83	57	82	54	81	52	81	49	83	51	86	57	87	67	83	74	82	77
Huntington, W.Va.	77	65	77	62	75	54	76	49	85	53	88	57	90	60	92	60	92	60	87	55	80	60	78	65
Milwaukee, Wis.	75	68	77	67	79	65	79	55	78	61	78	60	80	61	82	61	87	63	87	63	82	63	80	72
Cheyenne, Wyo.	57	50	61	48	65	46	61	41	71	43	71	41	69	38	69	38	66	38	61	41	60	50	59	53
San Juan, P.R.	81	64	80	62	77	60	75	62	77	66	78	66	79	67	80	66	79	67	80	66	81	67	81	66

Average Annual Snowfall

Source: Natl. Climatic Data Center, NESDIS, NOAA, U.S. Department of Commerce

(inches; through 1989)

The following are among the "snowiest" places in the U.S.:

Anchorage, Alas.	68.5	South Bend, Ind.	72.2	Mt. Washington, N.H.	254.8
Bettles, Alas.	78.8	Caribou, Me.	111.5	Albany, N.Y.	64.3
Cold Bay, Alas.	61.6	Portland, Me.	70.7	Binghamton, N.Y.	82.3
Fairbanks, Alas.	65.5	Blue Hill, Mass.	59.8	Buffalo, N.Y.	91.7
Homer, Alas.	57.9	Worcester, Mass.	68.6	Rochester, N.Y.	88.9
Juneau, Alas.	98.2	Alpena, Mich.	86.3	Syracuse, N.Y.	110.5
Kodiak, Alas.	76.5	Grand Rapids, Mich.	72.2	Youngstown, Ohio	56.2
McGrath, Alas.	90.6	Houghton Lake, Mich.	76.9	Sexton Summit, Ore.	97.8
Nome, Alas.	56.1	Marquette, Mich.	126.0	Erie, Pa.	85.8
St. Paul Is., Alas.	56.5	Muskegon, Mich.	98.4	Salt Lake City, Ut.	57.9
Talkeetna, Alas.	109.0	Sault St. Marie, Mich.	116.4	Burlington, Vt.	77.1
Valdez, Alas.	308.0	Duluth, Minn.	77.1	Stampede Pass, Wash.	432.4
Yakutat, Alas.	204.6	Intl. Falls, Minn.	61.5	Beckley, W.Va.	61.2
Flagstaff, Ariz.	96.4	Billings, Mont.	57.2	Elkins, W.Va.	74.3
Blue Canyon, Calif.	240.8	Great Falls, Mont.	59.7	Casper, Wyo.	80.1
Mt. Shasta, Calif.	104.9	Kalispell, Mont.	64.2	Lander, Wyo.	103.9
Denver, Colo.	59.8	Concord, N.H.	63.8	Sheridan, Wyo.	71.6

ENVIRONMENT

Environmental Quality Index

Source: Feb.-Mar. 1990 issue of *National Wildlife* magazine

In 1990, *National Wildlife* magazine published the twenty-second in its series of annual reports on the environment. For those concerned with the environment, 1989 was a year of disillusionment, symbolized by the worst oil-spill disaster in American history, the 11 million gallon spill into Alaska's Prince William Sound on March 24. The continuing environmental irresponsibility of 1989, according to the report, was heightened by a litany of broken laws and broken promises.

Wildlife: Though in many areas of the U.S. wildlife continued to suffer from lingering effects of the 1988 drought, many elk and deer herds in the West were unnaturally large, due to a succession of mild winters. In Yellowstone National Park, a needed boost for the grizzly population was expected as the bears could prey on the elk in the area, which would also help to cull the large herds. In coastal waters off New England, record low numbers of several fish species such as cod and haddock were attributed to overharvesting. Also near an all-time low was North America's waterfowl population. Though late spring rains replenished drought-ravaged wetlands, drainage of wetlands by farmers was the highest in 20 years, despite "Swampbuster" provisions in the 1985 U.S. Farm Act. The Alaskan oil spill brought about the deaths of tens of thousands of seabirds, and hundreds of eagles and sea otters. According to a General Accounting Office study of the National Wildlife Refuge System, areas intended as sanctuary for animals were threatened by pollution, development, military exercises, and recreational activity.

Air: The problems concerning the quality of air did not ease, although the summer of 1989 was milder than that of the previous year. It was reported that 2.6 billion pounds of poisons were released into the air by American industry. Of the 320 toxicants emitted, 60 of them were cancer-causing, enough to provide 10 pounds of poison for every person in the U.S. In 1989, 81 U.S. cities still failed to meet long-mandated standards for air quality, including the regulation of tiny bits of solid matter emitted into the air that remain dangerous to health. The EPA failed to enact and enforce progressively tougher standards for air quality, as required by the Clean Air Act. Some measures were being considered by Congress to place stringent national controls on auto emissions, similiar to those in effect in California.

Water: Coastal waters and beaches still faced trouble in 1989. Beaches in New Jersey and other Atlantic Coast states continued to report high bacteria counts from raw sewage and trash. Only 200 of 700 miles of shoreline coated with oil from the *Exxon Valdez* were treated by Exxon. Faced with water supply worries, East Coast officials initiated conservation tactics similar to those used in the arid West. The EPA reported that more than 15,600 wastewater treatment plants had water quality or public health problems. The agency estimated the cost for bringing the faulty systems up to standards at $83.5 billion. The EPA also reported in 1989 that 10% of the nation's lakes, rivers and coastal areas were contaminated by toxic chemicals and metals dangerous to aquatic life, increasing the risk of human cancer from eating such fish. A study of sport fish taken from the Great Lakes reported that nine out of ten fish were tainted with levels of toxic chemicals, while one in four contained levels regarded as harmful to humans. Surface waters continued to be polluted by toxic chemicals entering from the air or runoff from farms and city streets.

Forests: The controversy surrounding the preservation of the spotted owl at the expense of the logging industry was an indicator of the troubled state of woodlands. The threat to America's forests remained the ever-increasing appetite for wood products, causing the industry to cut more timber than could be grown. As supply ran low in the Pacific Northwest, causing mills to close, the logging industry wished to cut into publicly-owned old growth, among the last U.S. stands of virgin timber and an irreplaceable ecosystem and home of the spotted owl. To save ancient forests, environmentalists managed to obtain protection for the bird as a threatened species, which may help reduce by half the permissible harvest of old-growth trees. The Forest Service planned to increase harvesting in six Appalachian forests and to construct 3,000 miles of logging roads. Congress voted, however, to stop all timber sales in Alaska's 17-million-acre Tongass National Forest, the last intact rain forest in the U.S.

Energy: During the first half of 1989, America imported more oil than it produced, and consumption did not appear to be slowing down. While some officials in Washington favored domestic production, the Alaskan oil spill prompted Congress to shelve a plan that would have allowed drilling in the Arctic National Wildlife Refuge. A ban on oil or gas leases off the Californian and Mid-Atlantic Coasts was also approved. While it remained uncertain if wildlife would win out over oil rigs in Alaska, Congress began to seriously consider the use of renewable energy, such as photovoltaic cells and wind turbines. Critics of the Energy Department felt that more conservation was needed to curb America's troubled energy future.

Soil: The nation's soil took a terrible beating in 1988 and 1989. As the drought of 1988 eased up, wind erosion in early 1989 damaged 4.7 million acres of cropland. The loss of topsoil was 40% greater than in 1988, and the worst in over 30 years. Spring rains caused heavy flooding in some areas that washed away even more tons of topsoil. An additional burden that remained was the potential threat of agricultural chemicals that could affect topsoil chemistry and underground aquifers. A study by the National Academy of Sciences found that farmers who applied little or no chemicals to their crops were usually as productive as those landowners who did. Public lands were also in trouble, as the Federal government continued to open up many of these lands for mining, oil exploration, and logging. One concern was that the lands were not being cared for, despite legislative provisions that called for environmental stewardship and balanced, multiple uses. Moreover, ranchers used these lands for half the cost of using private rangelands to graze cattle. As a result, the U.S. Bureau of Land Management believed more than 94 million acres of public lands to be in trouble while it lost millions of dollars in uncollected range fees from ranchers. The result in Colorado, for example, was damage to 84% of the public range, affecting the food supplies and habitat for deer, elk and other wildlife.

Selected Air Pollutants in Certain U.S. Metropolitan Statistical Areas

Source: National Air Quality & Emissions Trend Report. 1988. U.S. Environmental Protection Agency

	Ozone (PPM)	CO (PPM)	SO$_2$ (PPM)	PM$_{10}$ (UGM)		Ozone (PPM)	CO (PPM)	SO$_2$ (PPM)	PM$_{10}$ (UGM)
Anaheim-Santa Ana, Cal.	0.24	10	0.018	43	Middlesex-Somerset-Hunterdon, N.J.	0.21	5	0.043	IN
Baltimore, Md.	0.19	10	0.043	43	Milwaukee, Wis.	0.19	6	0.042	36
Bergen, Passaic, N.J.	0.19	7	0.058	46	Philadelphia, Pa.-N.J.	0.20	8	0.068	47
Bridgeport-Milford, Ct.	0.22	7	0.064	31	Reno, Nev.	0.19	10	IN	IN
Chicago, Ill.	0.22	7	0.044	47	Riverside-San Bernardino, Cal.	0.28	7	0.019	95
Dallas, Tex.	0.20	NA	0.051	26	San Diego	0.19	10	0.022	40
Hartford, Ct.	0.19	10	0.076	30	Stamford, Ct.	0.22	7	0.062	28
Houston, Tex.	0.22	8	0.053	32	Trenton, N.J.	0.20	4	0.044	32
Jersey City, N.J.	0.20	8	0.065	36	Wilmington, Del.-N.J.-Md.	0.19	5	0.074	35
Los Angeles-Long Beach, Cal.	0.33	23	0.021	65					

PPM = Units are parts per million. UGM = Units are micrograms per cubic meter. CO = Carbon monoxide. SO$_2$ = Sulfur dioxide. PM$_{10}$ = Particulate matter. NA = Data not available. IN = Insufficient data.

Acid Rain Trouble Areas

Source: National Acid Precipitation Assessment Program

Area	No. of lakes over 10 acres	No. acidified	% acidified	Area	No. of lakes over 10 acres	No. acidified	% acidified
Adirondacks				Northeast Lakes	187	21	11
Southwest Lakes	450	171	38	Pine Barrens Streams	675	378	56
New England				Other Streams	7,452	745	10
Seaboard Lowlands Lakes	848	68	8	**Florida**			
Highland Lakes	3,574	71	2	Northern Highland Lakes	522	329	63
Appalachia				Northern Highland Streams	669	187	28
Forested Lakes	433	43	10	**Eastern Upper Midwest**			
Forested Streams	11,631	1,396	12	Low Silica Lakes	1,254	201	16
Atlantic Coastal Plain				High Silica Lakes	1,673	50	3

Hazardous Waste Sites

Source: Environmental Protection Agency, Natl. Priorities List Fact Book. Feb. 1990

State/Territory	Final Non-Fed.	Fed.	Proposed Non-Fed.	Fed.	Total	State/Territory	Final Non-Fed.	Fed.	Proposed Non-Fed.	Fed.	Total
New Jersey	100	4	3	2	109	Oklahoma	9	1	2	0	12
Pennsylvania	87	3	5	1	96	Utah	4	3	4	1	12
California	57	17	13	4	91	Arizona	6	2	2	1	11
New York	78	3	1	1	83	Arkansas	9	0	2	0	11
Michigan	75	0	4	0	79	Kansas	10	0	0	1	11
Florida	42	3	5	1	51	Louisiana	9	1	1	0	11
Washington	28	13	3	1	45	Rhode Island	9	2	0	0	11
Minnesota	39	2	1	0	42	Maryland	7	2	1	0	10
Wisconsin	37	0	3	0	40	Montana	8	0	2	0	10
Illinois	25	4	9	0	38	New Mexico	7	1	1	1	10
Indiana	32	0	3	0	35	Idaho	5	1	2	1	9
Ohio	29	3	1	0	33	Maine	7	2	0	0	9
Texas	24	1	2	2	29	Puerto Rico	8	1	0	0	9
Massachusetts	22	3	0	0	25	Oregon	6	1	1	0	8
Missouri	17	3	4	0	24	Vermont	8	0	0	0	8
South Carolina	21	1	1	0	23	Hawaii	0	0	6	1	7
North Carolina	20	1	1	0	22	Alaska	1	1	1	3	6
Iowa	11	0	9	1	21	Nebraska	3	1	2	0	6
Delaware	15	1	4	0	20	West Virginia	5	0	0	0	5
Virginia	18	1	1	0	20	Mississippi	2	0	1	0	3
Kentucky	14	0	3	0	17	South Dakota	1	0	1	1	3
Colorado	12	3	1	0	16	Wyoming	1	1	1	0	3
New Hampshire	15	1	0	0	16	North Dakota	2	0	0	0	2
Connecticut	13	0	1	1	15	Guam	1	0	0	0	1
Tennessee	11	2	1	0	14	Nevada	0	0	1	0	1
Georgia	9	2	2	0	13	**Total**	988	93	113	24	1218
Alabama	9	2	1	0	12						

National Ambient Water Quality in Rivers and Streams—Violation Rate: 1975 to 1988

Source: U.S. Geological Survey.

(in percent.)

Violation level based on U.S. Environmental Protection Agency water quality criteria. Violation rate represents the proportion of all measurements of a specific water quality pollutant which exceeds the "violation level" for that pollutant. "Violation" does not necessarily imply a legal violation. Data based on U.S. Geological Survey's National Stream Quality Accounting Network (NASQAN) data system. Years refer to water years. A water year begins in Oct. and ends in Sept. μg = micrograms. mg = milligrams.

Pollutant	Violation Level	1975	1980	1981	1982	1983	1984	1985	1986	1987	1988
Fecal coliform bacteria	Above 200 cells per 100 ml	36	31	30	33	34	30	28	24	23	22
Dissolved oxygen	Below 5 mg per liter	5	5	4	5	4	3	3	3	2	2
Phosphorus, total, as phosporous	Above 1.0 mg per liter	5	4	4	3	3	4	3	3	3	4
Lead, dissolved	Above 50 μg per liter	(B)	5	3	2	5	(Z)	(Z)	(Z)	(Z)	(Z)
Cadmium, dissolved	Above 10 μg per liter	(B)	1	1	1	1	(Z)	(Z)	(Z)	(Z)	(Z)

B = Base figure too small to meet statistical standards for reliability of derived figures. Z = Less than 1.

Endangered and Threatened Species and Recovery Plans

Source: U.S. Fish and Wildlife Service, U.S. Interior Department; June 6, 1989.

Group	Endangered U.S. only	Endangered U.S. & foreign	Endangered Foreign only	Threatened U.S. only	Threatened U.S. & foreign	Threatened Foreign only	Listed species total	Species with plans
Mammals	32	19	241	6	2	23	323	24
Birds	61	15	145	7	3	0	231	57
Reptiles	8	7	59	14	4	14	106	22
Amphibians	5	0	8	3	1	0	17	5
Fishes	45	2	11	24	.6	0	88	47
Snails	3	0	1	6	0	0	10	7
Clams	32	0	2	0	0	0	34	22
Crustaceans	8	0	0	1	0	0	9	4
Insects	10	0	0	7	0	0	17	12
Arachnids	3	0	0	0	0	0	3	0
Plants	153	6	1	40	6	2	208	85
Total	**360**	**49**	**468**	**108**	**22**	**39**	**1,046**	**285**

Total U.S. Endangered	409	Approved recovery plans	245
Total U.S. Threatened	130	Species/populations in above plans.	301
Total U.S. listed	**539**	Percentage of listed species covered by 1 or more plans.	52.9%

Note: Separate populations of a species, listed both as Endangered and Threatened, are tallied twice. Those 9 species are: grizzly bear (US=T & Mex=E), leopard, gray wolf, bald eagle, piping plover, roseate tern, Nile crocodile, green sea turtle, and olive Ridley sea turtle. Further, there are 9 species of lemurs; 9 gibbons; 2 each of musk deer, sifakas, and uakaris; and 29–41 species of Oahu tree snails; these are each counted as one species above.

Some Endangered Species in North America

Source: U.S. Fish and Wildlife Service, U.S. Interior Department; as of April 15, 1990

Common name	Scientific name	Range
Mammals		
Ozark big-eared bat	Plecotus townsendii ingens	U.S. (Mo., Okla., Ariz.)
Brown or grizzly bear	Ursus arctos horribilis	U.S. (48 conterminous states)
Eastern cougar.	Felis concolor cougar	Eastern N.A.
Columbian white-tailed deer	Odocoileus virginianus leucurus	U.S. (Wash., Ore.)
San Joaquin kit fox	Vulpes macrotis mutica.	U.S. (Cal.)
Southeastern beach mouse	Peromyscus polionotus phasma	U.S. (Fla.)
Ocelot	Felis pardalis	U.S. (Tex., Ariz.)
Southern sea otter	Enhydra lutris hereis	U.S. (Wash., Ore., Cal.)
Florida panther	Felis concolor coryi.	U.S. (La., Ark. east to S.C., Fla.)
Utah prairie dog.	Cynomys parvidens	U.S. (Ut.)
Morro Bay kangaroo rat	Dipodomys heermanni morroensis. . . .	U.S. (Cal.)
Carolina northern flying squirrel . . .	Glaucomys sabrinus coloratus	U.S. (N.C., Tenn.)
Hualapai Mexican vole	Microtus mexicanus hualpaiensis . . .	U.S. (Ariz.)
Red wolf	Canis rufus	U.S. (Southeast to central Tex.)
Birds		
Masked bobwhite (quail)	Colinus virginianus ridgwayi	U.S. (Ariz.)
California condor	Gymnogyps californianus	U.S. (Ore., Cal.)
Whooping crane.	Grus americana	U.S. (Rky. Mntns. east to Carolinas), Canada
Eskimo curlew.	Numenius borealis	Alaska and N. Canada
Bald eagle	Haliaeetus leucocephalus	U.S. (most states), Canada
American peregrine falcon	Falco peregrinus anatum	Canada to Mexico
Hawaiian hawk	Buteo solitarius	U.S. (Hi.)
Attwater's greater prairie-chicken . .	Tympanuchus cupido attwateri	U.S. (Tex.)
Bachman's warbler (wood)	Vermivora bachmanii	U.S. (Southeast), Cuba
Kirtland's warbler (wood)	Dendroica kirtlandii	U.S., Canada, Bahama Is.
Ivory-billed woodpecker	Campephilus principalis	U.S. (Southcentral and Southeast), Cuba
Reptiles		
American alligator	Alligator mississippiensis.	U.S (Southeastern)
American crocodile	Crocodylus acutus	U.S. (Fla.)
Atlantic salt marsh snake.	Nerodia fasciatia taeniata.	U.S. (Fla.)
Plymouth red-bellied turtle	Pseudemys rubiventris bangsi	U.S. (Mass.)
Fishes		
Yaqui catfish	Ictalupus pricei	U.S. (Ariz.)
Bonytail chub	Gila elegans	U.S. (Ariz., Cal., Col., Nev., Ut., Wyo.)
Gila trout	Salmo gilae	U.S. (Ariz., N.M.)

Some Endangered Species in the World

Source: U.S. Fish and Wildlife Service. U.S. Interior Department; as of April 15, 1990

Common name	Scientific name	Historic range
Mammals		
Asian wild ass	Equus hemianus	Southwestern & Central Asia
Bobcat	Felis rufus escuinapae	Central Mexico
Cheetah	Acinonyx jubatus	Africa to India
Chinese river dolphin	Lipotes vexillifer	China
Asian elephant	Elephas maximas	Southcentral, Southeast Asia
Bactrian camel	Camelus bactrianus	Mongolia, China
Gorilla	Gorilla gorilla	Central & W. Africa
Leopard	Panthera pardus	Africa, Asia
Asiatic lion	Panthera leo persica	Turkey to India
Howler monkey	Alouatta pigra	Mexico to S. America
Giant panda	Ailuropoda melanoleuca	China
Black rhinoceros	Diceros bicornis	Sub-Saharan Africa
Tiger	Panthera tigris	Asia
Gray whale	Eschrichtius robustus	N. Pacific Ocean
Wild yak	Bos grunniens	China (Tibet), India
Mountain zebra	Equus zebra zebra	South Africa
Birds		
Hooded crane	Grus monacha	Japan, USSR
Indigo macaw	Anodorhynchus leari	Brazil
West African ostrich	Struthio camelus spatzi	Spanish Sahara
Golden parakeet	Aratinga guarouba	Brazil
Australian parrot	Geopsittacus occidentalis	Australia

Speeds of Animals

Source: Natural History magazine, March 1974.
Copyright © The American Museum of Natural History, 1974.

Animal	Mph	Animal	Mph	Animal	Mph
Cheetah	70	Mongolian wild ass	40	Human	27.89
Pronghorn antelope	61	Greyhound	39.35	Elephant	25
Wildebeest	50	Whippet	35.50	Black mamba snake	20
Lion	50	Rabbit (domestic)	35	Six-lined race runner	18
Thomson's gazelle	50	Mule deer	35	Wild turkey	15
Quarterhorse	47.5	Jackal	35	Squirrel	12
Elk	45	Reindeer	32	Pig (domestic)	11
Cape hunting dog	45	Giraffe	32	Chicken	9
Coyote	43	White-tailed deer	30	Spider (Tegenaria atrica)	1.17
Gray fox	42	Wart hog	30	Giant tortoise	0.17
Hyena	40	Grizzly bear	30	Three-toed sloth	0.15
Zebra	40	Cat (domestic)	30	Garden snail	0.03

Most of these measurements are for maximum speeds over approximate quarter-mile distances. Exceptions are the lion and elephant, whose speeds were clocked in the act of charging; the whippet, which was timed over a 200-yard course; the cheetah over a 100-yard distance; man for a 15-yard segment of a 100-yard run (of 13.6 seconds); and the black mamba, six-lined race runner, spider, giant tortoise, three-toed sloth, and garden snail, which were measured over various small distances.

Gestation, Longevity, and Incubation of Animals

Longevity figures were supplied by Ronald T. Reuther. They refer to animals in captivity; the potential life span of animals is rarely attained in nature. Maximum longevity figures are from the Biology Data Book, 1972. Figures on gestation and incubation are averages based on estimates by leading authorities.

Animal		Gestation (day)	Average longevity (years)	Maximum longevity (yrs., mos.)	Animal	Gestation (day)	Average longevity (years)	Maximum longevity (yrs., mos.)
Ass		365	12	35-10	Leopard	98	12	19-4
Baboon		187	20	35-7	Lion	100	15	25-1
Bear:	Black	219	18	36-10	Monkey (rhesus)	164	15	—
	Grizzly	225	25	—	Moose	240	12	—
	Polar	240	20	34-8	Mouse (meadow)	21	3	—
Beaver		122	5	20-6	Mouse (dom. white)	19	3	3-6
Buffalo (American)		278	15	—	Opossum (American)	14-17	1	—
Bactrian camel		406	12	29-5	Pig (domestic)	112	10	27
Cat (domestic)		63	12	28	Puma	90	12	19
Chimpanzee		231	20	44-6	Rabbit (domestic)	31	5	13
Chipmunk		31	6	8	Rhinoceros (black)	450	15	—
Cow		284	15	30	Rhinoceros (white)	—	20	—
Deer (white-tailed)		201	8	17-6	Sea lion (California)	350	12	28
Dog (domestic)		61	12	20	Sheep (domestic)	154	12	20
Elephant (African)		—	35	60	Squirrel (gray)	44	10	—
Elephant (Asian)		645	40	70	Tiger	105	16	26-3
Elk		250	15	26-6	Wolf (maned)	63	5	—
Fox (red)		52	7	14	Zebra (Grant's)	365	15	—
Giraffe		425	10	33-7				
Goat (domestic)		151	8	18	**Incubation time (days)**			
Gorilla		257	20	39-4	Chicken			21
Guinea pig		68	4	7-6	Duck			30
Hippopotamus		238	25	—	Goose			30
Horse		330	20	46	Pigeon			18
Kangaroo		42	7	—	Turkey			26

Major Venomous Animals

Snakes

Coral snake - 2 to 4 ft. long, in Americas south of Canada; bite is nearly painless; very slow onset of paralysis, difficulty breathing; mortality high without antivenin.

Rattlesnake - 2 to 8 ft. long, throughout W. Hemisphere. Rapid onset of symptoms of severe pain, swelling; mortality low, but amputation of affected limb is sometimes necessary; antivenin. Probably higher mortality rate for Mojave rattler.

Cottonmouth water moccasin - up to 5 ft. long, wetlands of southern U.S. from Virginia to Texas. Rapid onset of symptoms of severe pain, swelling; mortality low, but tissue destruction can be extensive; antivenin.

Copperhead - less than 4 ft. long, from New England to Texas; pain and swelling; very seldom fatal; antivenin seldom needed.

Bushmaster - up to 12 ft. long, wet tropical forests of C. and S. America; few bites occur, but mortality rate is high.

Barba Amarilla or **Fer-de-lance** - up to 7 ft. long, from tropical Mexico to Brazil; severe tissue damage common; moderate mortality; antivenin.

Asian pit vipers - from 2 to 5 ft. long throughout Asia; reactions and mortality vary but most bites cause tissue damage and mortality is generally low.

Sharp-nosed pit viper or **One Hundred Pace Snake** - up to 5 ft. long, in southern Vietnam and Taiwan, China; the most toxic of Asian pit vipers; very rapid onset of swelling and tissue damage, internal bleeding; moderate mortality; antivenin.

Boomslang - under 6 ft. long, in African savannahs; rapid onset of nausea and dizziness, often followed by slight recovery and then sudden death from internal hemorrhaging; bites rare, mortality high; antivenin.

European vipers - from 1 to 3 ft. long; bleeding and tissue damage; mortality low; antivenins.

Puff adder - up to 5 ft. long, fat; south of the Sahara and throughout the Middle East; rapid large swelling, great pain, dizziness; moderate mortality often from internal bleeding; antivenin.

Gaboon viper - over 6 ft. long, fat; 2-inch fangs; south of the Sahara; massive tissue damage, internal bleeding; few recorded bites.

Saw-scaled or carpet viper - up to 2 ft. long, in dry areas from India to Africa; severe bleeding, fever; high mortality, causes more human fatalities than any other snake; antivenin.

Desert horned viper - in dry areas of Africa and western Asia; swelling and tissue damage; low mortality; antivenin.

Russell's viper or tic-palonga - over 5 ft. long, throughout Asia; internal bleeding; moderate mortality rate; bite reports common; antivenin.

Black mamba - up to 14 ft. long, fast-moving; S. and C. Africa; rapid onset of dizziness, difficulty breathing, erratic heart-beat; mortality high, nears 100% without antivenin.

Kraits - in S. Asia; rapid onset of sleepiness; numbness; up to 50% mortality even with antivenin treatment.

Common or Asian cobra - 4 to 8 ft. long, throughout S. Asia; considerable tissue damage, sometimes paralysis; mortality probably not more than 10%; antivenin.

King cobra - up to 16 ft. long, throughout S. Asia; rapid swelling, dizziness, loss of consciousness, difficulty breathing, erratic heart-beat; mortality varies sharply with amount of venom involved, most bites involve non-fatal amounts; antivenin.

Yellow or Cape cobra - 7 ft. long, in southern Africa; most toxic venom of any cobra; rapid onset of swelling, breathing and cardiac difficulties; mortality high without treatment; antivenin.

Ringhals, or spitting, cobra - 5 ft. and 7 ft. long; southern Africa; squirt venom through holes in front of fangs as a defense; venom is severely irritating and can cause blindness.

Australian brown snakes - very slow onset of symptoms of cardiac or respiratory distress; moderate mortality; antivenin.

Tiger snake - 2 to 6 ft. long, S. Australia; pain, numbness, mental disturbances with rapid onset of paralysis; may be the most deadly of all land snakes though antivenin is quite effective.

Death adder - less than 3 ft. long, Australia; rapid onset of faintness, cardiac and respiratory distress; at least 50% mortality without antivenin.

Taipan - up to 11 ft. long, in Australia and New Guinea; rapid paralysis with severe breathing difficulty; mortality nears 100% without antivenin.

Sea snakes - throughout Pacific, Indian oceans except NE Pacific; almost painless bite, variety of muscle pain, paralysis; mortality rate low, many bites are not envenomed; some antivenins.

Notes: Not all snake bites by venomous snakes are actually envenomed. Any animal bite, however, carries the danger of tetanus and anyone suffering a venomous snake bite should seek medical attention. Antivenins are not certain cures; they are only an aid in the treatment of bites. Mortality rates above are for envenomed bites; low mortality, up to 2% result in death; moderate, 2–5%; high, 5–15%. Even when the victim recovers fully, prolonged hospitalization and extensive medical procedures are usually required.

Lizards

Gila monster - up to 24 inches long with heavy body and tail, in high desert in southwest U.S. and N. Mexico; immediate severe pain followed by vomiting, thirst, difficulty swallowing, weakness approaching paralysis; no recent mortality.

Mexican beaded lizard - similar to Gila monster, Mexican west-coast; reaction and mortality rate similar to Gila monster.

Insects

Ants, bees, wasps, hornets, etc. Global distribution. Usual reaction is piercing pain in area of sting. Not directly fatal, except in cases of massive multiple stings. Many people suffer allergic reactions - swelling, rashes, partial paralysis –and a few may die within minutes from severe sensitivity to the venom (anaphylactic shock).

Spiders, scorpions

Black widow - small, round-bodied with hour-glass marking; the widow and its relatives are found around the world in tropical and temperate zones; sharp pain, weakness, clammy skin, muscular rigidity, breathing difficulty and, in small children, convulsions; low mortality; antivenin.

Recluse or fiddleback and brown spiders - small, oblong body; throughout U.S.; pain with later ulceration at place of bite; in severe cases fever, nausea, and stomach cramps; ulceration may last months; very low mortality.

Atrax spiders - several varieties, often large, in Australia; slow onset of breathing, circulation difficulties; low mortality.

Tarantulas - large, hairy spiders found around the world; American tarantulas, and probably all others, are harmless, though their bite may cause some pain and swelling.

Scorpions - crab-like body with stinger in tail, various sizes, many varieties throughout tropical and subtropical areas; various symptoms may include severe pain spreading from the wound, numbness, severe emotional agitation, cramps; severe reactions include vomiting, diarrhea, respiratory failure; low mortality, usually in children; antivenins.

Sea Life

Sea wasps - jellyfish, with tentacles up to 30 ft. long, in the S. Pacific; very rapid onset of circulatory problems; high mortality largely because of speed of toxic reaction; antivenin.

Portuguese man-of-war - jellyfish-like, with tentacles up to 70 ft. long, in most warm water areas; immediate severe pain; not fatal, though shock may cause death in a rare case.

Octopi - global distribution, usually in warm waters; all varieties produce venom but only a few can cause death; rapid onset of paralysis with breathing difficulty.

Stingrays - several varieties of differing sizes, found in tropical and temperate seas and some fresh water; severe pain, rapid onset of nausea, vomiting, breathing difficulties; wound area may ulcerate, gangrene may appear; seldom fatal.

Stonefish - brownish fish which lies motionless as a rock on bottom in shallow water; throughout S. Pacific and Indian oceans; extraordinary pain, rapid paralysis; low mortality.

Cone-shells - molluscs in small, beautiful shells in the S. Pacific and Indian oceans; shoot barbs into victims; paralysis; low mortality.

How Much Water Is Used . . .?

Source: American Water Works Assn.

1. In the average residence during a year? **107,000 gallons**
2. By an average person daily? **168 gallons**
3. To flush a toilet? **5-7 gallons**
4. To take a shower? **25-50 gallons**
5. To brush your teeth (water running)? **2 gallons**
6. To shave (water running)? **10-15 gallons**
7. To wash dishes by hand? **20 gallons**
8. To run a dishwasher? **10 gallons**

Major U.S. Public Zoological Parks

Source: World Almanac questionnaire. 1990; budget and attendance in millions. (*) park has not provided up-to-date data.

Zoo	Budget	Attend-ance	Acres	Species	Major attractions
Arizona-Sonora Desert Museum (Tucson)	$3.4	0.6	15	210	Mountain Habitat, Sonora Desert Exhibit
Audubon (New Orleans)*	9.0	1.0	58	372	Asian Domain, Louisiana Swamp, Australia Exhibit
Bronx (N.Y.C.)	24.6	2.2	265	657	Himalayan Highlands, African Plains, Wild Asia, Mouse House, endangered species
Buffalo	4.0	0.5	23	270	Habicat, Gorilla Habitat, Children's Zoo
Chicago (Brookfield)	25.0	2.0	204	434	7 Seas Panorama, Tropic World, Australian Walkabout, The Fragile Kingdom
Cincinnati*	10.0	1.5	67	735	Gorilla World, Insect World, white bengal tigers
Cleveland	5.7	0.8	165	470	African Plains, rhino/cheetah, Animals of China
Dallas	6.4	0.5	70	330	25-acre Wilds of Africa with monorail, nature trail, Gorilla Conservation Center
Denver	5.2	1.2	74	400	Bear Mountain, Wolf Pack Woods, Feline House
Detroit	11.4	1.0	125	300	Penguinarium, Chimps of Harambee
Houston*	2.6	2.0	55	649	Children's Zoo, Aquarium
Lincoln Park (Chicago)	8.8	4.5	35	382	Lion House, Birds of Prey, Children's Zoo
Los Angeles	1.7	2.0	111	500	Koalas, elephant & camel rides, Aviary
Louisville*	2.5	0.4	73	245	African Panorama, polar bear, Siberian tiger
Memphis	2.5	0.8	36	403	Cat Country, Primate World, The Forest
Miami Metrozoo	7.2	0.8	290	260	Koalas, Aviary, cageless exhibits, Asian River Life
Milwaukee	12.0	1.5	194	300	Sea Lion Exhibit, Predator Prey, Dairy Complex
Minnesota	10.0	1.0	485	311	Tropics Trail, Minnesota Trail, koalas, dolphins
National (Wash. D.C.)	13.0	3.0	163	509	Giant pandas, Komodo dragon lizards, gorillas
Oklahoma City	5.0	0.6	110	500	Aquaticus dolphin & sea lion shows
Philadelphia	12.0	1.3	42	550	World of Primates, Treehouse, Rare Animal House, African Plains, Small Mammals
Phoenix	7.0	1.0	125	300	African Veldt, Children's Zoo, Arizona exhibit
Rio Grande (Albuquerque)	2.2	0.5	60	289	Ape Country, Free-flying Bird Show, Rainforest
Riverbanks (Columbia, S.C.)	3.2	1.0	50	230	Aquarium Reptile Complex, Riverbanks Farm
St. Louis	11.3	2.8	83	720	Big Cat Country, Bear Pits, Jungle of the Apes
San Antonio	6.5	0.9	30	700	Children's Zoo, Australian Walkabout, Barrier Reef
San Diego*	40.0	3.5	100	800	Tiger River, Southeast Asian exhibit, koalas
San Diego (Wild Animal Park)*	15.0	1.3	1,800	260	Mixed-species enclosures; exotic species, monorail with 50-minute, narrated tour
San Francisco*	8.0	1.2	125	270	Primate Discovery Center, Koala Crossing, Gorilla World, Penguin Island
Toledo	7.5	0.8	33	400	Hippoquarium, African Savanna, Children's Zoo
Washington Pk (Portland)	12.6	1.1	66	153	Alaska Tundra, Penguinarium, 3-acre Africa exhibit
Woodland Pk (Seattle)	5.3	0.9	90	258	African Savanna, gorillas, Asian Elephant Forest

Top 50 American Kennel Club Registrations

Breed	Rank	1989	Rank	1988	Breed	Rank	1989	Rank	1988
Cocker Spaniels	1	111,636	1	108,720	Brittanys	26	14,557	26	14,439
Labrador Retrievers	2	91,107	2	86,446	Maltese	27	14,420	25	14,453
Poodles	3	78,600	3	82,600	West Highland White Terriers	28	12,189	29	11,565
Golden Retrievers	4	64,269	4	62,950	Pugs	29	11,204	28	11,659
German Shepherd Dogs	5	58,422	5	57,139	Bichons Frises	30	10,639	30	9,684
Rottweilers	6	51,291	7	42,748	Bulldogs	31	10,129	31	9,566
Chow Chows	7	50,150	6	50,781	German Shorthaired Pointers	32	9,975	32	9,111
Dachshunds	8	44,305	9	41,921	Great Danes	33	9,024	33	8,996
Beagles	9	43,314	8	41,983	Samoyeds	34	8,923	34	8,986
Miniature Schnauzers	10	42,175	10	41,558	Scottish Terriers	35	8,759	35	8,106
Shetland Sheepdogs	11	39,665	12	38,730	Keeshonden	36	7,569	36	7,431
Yorkshire Terriers	12	39,268	13	36,040	Akitas	37	7,531	38	6,518
Shih Tzu	13	38,131	11	38,829	Cairn Terriers	38	7,318	37	7,187
Pomeranians	14	32,109	14	30,516	Alaskan Malamutes	39	5,803	39	5,811
Lhasa Apsos	15	28,810	15	30,194	Miniature Pinschers	40	5,568	40	5,579
Chihuahuas	16	24,917	17	23,487	Pembroke Welsh Corgis	41	4,480	45	3,796
Pekingese	17	22,986	22	20,134	Chesapeake Bay Retrievers	42	4,427	42	4,315
Boxers	18	22,037	20	20,604	Airedale Terriers	43	4,412	41	4,687
Siberian Huskies	19	21,875	18	21,430	St. Bernards	44	4,099	44	3,827
Doberman Pinschers	20	21,782	16	23,928	Old English Sheepdogs	45	3,835	43	3,973
Basset Hounds	21	21,517	19	21,423	Weimaraners	46	3,679	46	3,653
English Springer Spaniels	22	20,911	21	20,238	Norwegian Elkhounds	47	3,520	47	3,416
Collies	23	18,227	23	18,931	Silky Terriers	48	3,329	49	2,862
Dalmatians	24	17,488	27	14,109	Wire Fox Terriers	49	3,293	48	3,095
Boston Terriers	25	15,355	24	14,988	Shipperkes	50	3,087	52	2,684

Cat Breeds

There are 27 cat breeds recognized: abyssinian, american shorthair, balinese, birman, bombay, burmese, colorpoint shorthair, egyptian mau, exotic shorthair, havana brown, himalayan, japanese bobtail, korat, leopard cat, lilac foreign shorthair, maine coon cat, manx, ocicat, oriental shorthair, persian, rex, russian blue, scottish fold, siamese, sphynx, turkish angora, wirehair shorthair.

Mammals: Orders and Major Families

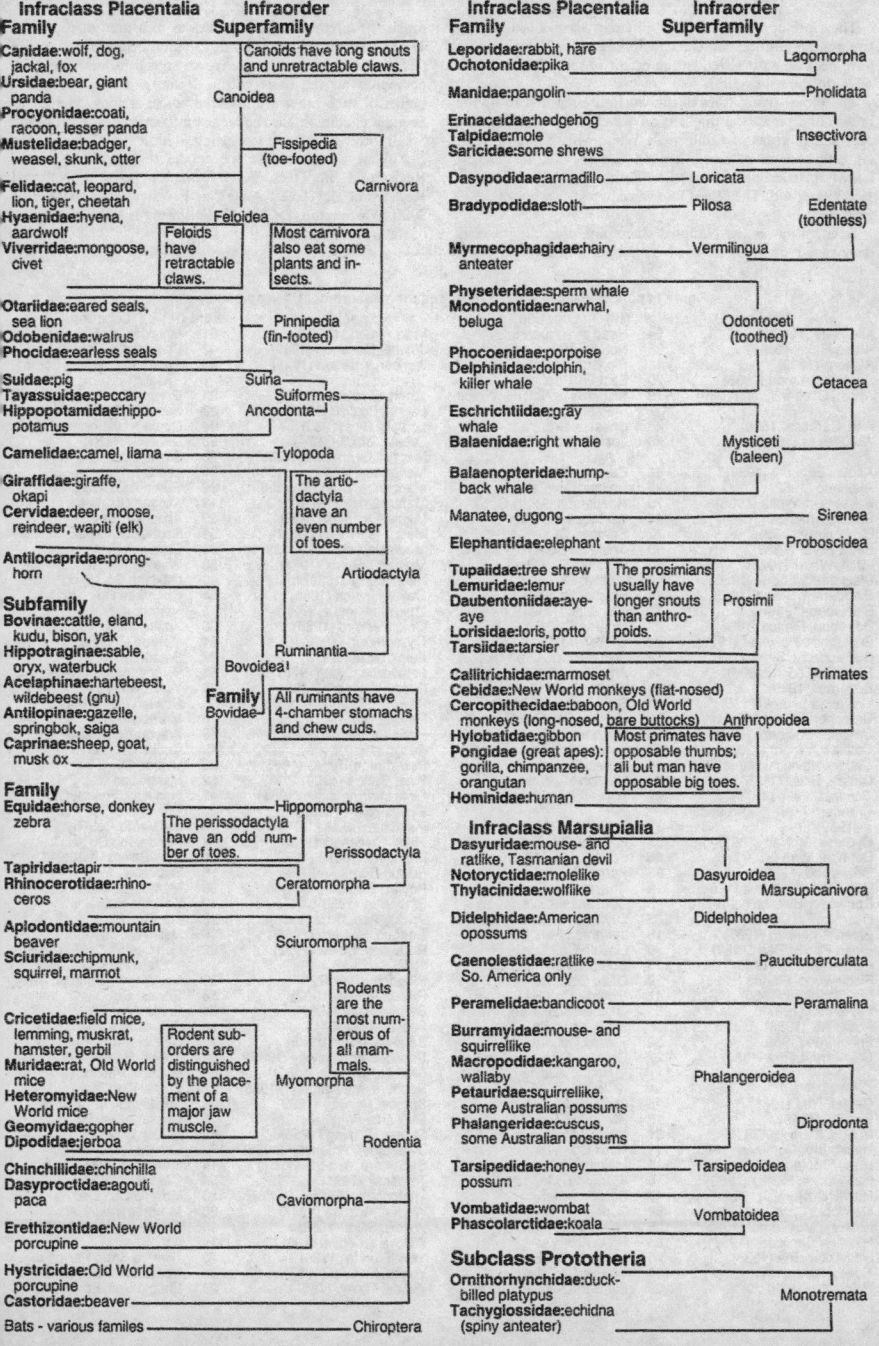

Subclass Theria — Infraclass Placentalia

Family | Suborder / Infraorder / Superfamily | Order

- **Canidae:** wolf, dog, jackal, fox
- **Ursidae:** bear, giant panda
- **Procyonidae:** coati, racoon, lesser panda
- **Mustelidae:** badger, weasel, skunk, otter
  - *Canoids have long snouts and unretractable claws.*
  - Canoidea — Fissipedia (toe-footed)
- **Felidae:** cat, leopard, lion, tiger, cheetah
- **Hyaenidae:** hyena, aardwolf
- **Viverridae:** mongoose, civet
  - Feloidea — *Feloids have retractable claws.*
  - *Most carnivora also eat some plants and insects.*
  - **Order: Carnivora**
- **Otariidae:** eared seals, sea lion
- **Odobenidae:** walrus
- **Phocidae:** earless seals
  - Pinnipedia (fin-footed)

- **Suidae:** pig
- **Tayassuidae:** peccary — Suina — Suiformes
- **Hippopotamidae:** hippopotamus — Ancodonta
- **Camelidae:** camel, llama — Tylopoda
- **Giraffidae:** giraffe, okapi
- **Cervidae:** deer, moose, reindeer, wapiti (elk)
  - *The artiodactyla have an even number of toes.*
  - **Order: Artiodactyla**
- **Antilocapridae:** pronghorn

Subfamily
- **Bovinae:** cattle, eland, kudu, bison, yak
- **Hippotraginae:** sable, oryx, waterbuck
- **Acelaphinae:** hartebeest, wildebeest (gnu)
- **Antilopinae:** gazelle, springbok, saiga
- **Caprinae:** sheep, goat, musk ox
  - Ruminantia — Bovoidea
  - **Family: Bovidae** — *All ruminants have 4-chamber stomachs and chew cuds.*

Family
- **Equidae:** horse, donkey, zebra — Hippomorpha
  - *The perissodactyla have an odd number of toes.*
  - **Order: Perissodactyla**
- **Tapiridae:** tapir
- **Rhinocerotidae:** rhinoceros — Ceratomorpha

- **Aplodontidae:** mountain beaver
- **Sciuridae:** chipmunk, squirrel, marmot — Sciuromorpha
  - *Rodents are the most numerous of all mammals.*
- **Cricetidae:** field mice, lemming, muskrat, hamster, gerbil
- **Muridae:** rat, Old World mice
- **Heteromyidae:** New World mice
- **Geomyidae:** gopher
- **Dipodidae:** jerboa
  - *Rodent suborders are distinguished by the placement of a major jaw muscle.*
  - Myomorpha — **Order: Rodentia**
- **Chinchillidae:** chinchilla
- **Dasyproctidae:** agouti, paca — Caviomorpha
- **Erethizontidae:** New World porcupine
- **Hystricidae:** Old World porcupine
- **Castoridae:** beaver

Bats - various families — Chiroptera

Subclass Theria — Infraclass Placentalia

Family | Suborder / Infraorder / Superfamily | Order

- **Leporidae:** rabbit, hare
- **Ochotonidae:** pika — Lagomorpha
- **Manidae:** pangolin — Pholidata
- **Erinaceidae:** hedgehog
- **Talpidae:** mole
- **Saricidae:** some shrews — Insectivora
- **Dasypodidae:** armadillo — Loricata
- **Bradypodidae:** sloth — Pilosa
  - **Edentate (toothless)**
- **Myrmecophagidae:** hairy anteater — Vermilingua
- **Physeteridae:** sperm whale
- **Monodontidae:** narwhal, beluga — Odontoceti (toothed)
- **Phocoenidae:** porpoise
- **Delphinidae:** dolphin, killer whale
  - **Order: Cetacea**
- **Eschrichtiidae:** gray whale
- **Balaenidae:** right whale — Mysticeti (baleen)
- **Balaenopteridae:** humpback whale
- **Manatee, dugong** — Sirenea
- **Elephantidae:** elephant — Proboscidea
- **Tupaiidae:** tree shrew
- **Lemuridae:** lemur
- **Daubentoniidae:** aye-aye
- **Lorisidae:** loris, potto
- **Tarsiidae:** tarsier
  - *The prosimians usually have longer snouts than anthropoids.*
  - Prosimii — **Order: Primates**
- **Callitrichidae:** marmoset
- **Cebidae:** New World monkeys (flat-nosed)
- **Cercopithecidae:** baboon, Old World monkeys (long-nosed, bare buttocks)
- **Hylobatidae:** gibbon
- **Pongidae (great apes):** gorilla, chimpanzee, orangutan
- **Hominidae:** human
  - *Most primates have opposable thumbs; all but man have opposable big toes.*
  - Anthropoidea

Infraclass Marsupialia
- **Dasyuridae:** mouse- and ratlike, Tasmanian devil
- **Notoryctidae:** molelike
- **Thylacinidae:** wolflike
  - Dasyuroidea — Marsupicarnivora
- **Didelphidae:** American opossums — Didelphoidea
- **Caenolestidae:** ratlike So. America only — Paucituberculata
- **Peramelidae:** bandicoot — Peramalina
- **Burramyidae:** mouse- and squirrellike
- **Macropodidae:** kangaroo, wallaby
- **Petauridae:** squirrellike, some Australian possums
- **Phalangeridae:** cuscus, some Australian possums
  - Phalangeroidea — Diprodonta
- **Tarsipedidae:** honey possum — Tarsipedoidea
- **Vombatidae:** wombat
- **Phascolarctidae:** koala — Vombatoidea

Subclass Prototheria
- **Ornithorhynchidae:** duck-billed platypus
- **Tachyglossidae:** echidna (spiny anteater)
  - Monotremata

Giant Trees of the U.S.

Source: The American Forestry Association, Washington, D.C.

There are approximately 748 different species of trees native to the continental U.S., including a few imports that have become naturalized to the extent of reproducing themselves in the wild state.

The oldest living trees in the world are reputed to be the bristlecone pines, the majority of which are found growing on the arid crags of California's White Mts. Some of them are estimated to be more than 4,600 years old. The largest known bristlecone pine is the "Patriarch," believed to be 1,500 years old. The oldest known redwoods are about 3,500 years old.

Recognition as the National Champion of each species is determined by total mass of each tree, based on this formula: the circumference in inches as measured at a point 4 1/2 feet above the ground plus the total height of the tree in feet plus 1/4 of the average crown spread in feet. Trees are compared on the basis of this formula. Trees within five points of each other are declared co-champions. The Giant Sequoia champion has the largest circumference, 83 ft. 2 in., Smallflower Paw Paw the smallest, 4 in.

Anyone can nominate the candidates for the National Register of Big Trees. For information, write to National Register of Big Trees, American Forestry Assn., P.O. Box 2000, Washington, DC 20013. Following is a small selection of the trees registered.

(Figure in parentheses is year of most recent measurement; * = co-champion)

Species	Height (ft.)	Location
Ailanthus (1952)	64	Head of Harbor, L.I.
Alder, Hazel (1989)	35	Norfolk, Va.
Allthorn (1989)*	11	Rio Grande City, Tex.
Apple, Common (1986)	70	East End, Va.
Apple, Oregon Crab (1989).	79	Nisqually Natl. Wildlife Refuge, Wash.
Ash, Carolina (1988)	48	Chesapeake, Va.
Ash, Texas (1989)	66	Lost Maples State Natl. Area, Tex.
Aspen, Bigtooth (1989)*	66	Caroline Co., Md.
Avocado (1982)	40	Hallandale, Fla.
Basswood, White (1986)	75	Henderson Co., N.C.
Beech, American (1984)	130	Ashtabula Co., Oh.
Birch, Gray (1989)	77	Somers, Ct.
Birch, River (1988)*	90	Appleton Comm., Tenn.
Birch, Water (1973)	53	Wallowa Co., Ore.
Blackbead, Ebony (1986).	40	Hidalgo Co., Tex.
Bladdernut, Sierra (1986).	28	Fresno, Co., Cal.
Bluewood (1989)	30	San Juan, Tex.
Boxwood, Florida (1986)	27	Monroe Co., Fla.
Buckthorn, Hollyleaf (1976).	22	Greenfield, Cal.
Buffaloberry, Silver (1975)	22	Malheur Co., Ore.
Burnelia, Tough (1987)	41	Amelia Is., Fla.
Butternut (1989)*	88	Eugene, Ore.
California Laurel (1978)	88	Siskiyou Natl. For., Ore.
Camphor-Tree (1977)	72	Hardee Co., Fla.
Catalpa, Southern (1981)	80	Henderson Co., Ill.
Catclaw, Wright (1986)	36	Uvalde Co., Tex.
Cedar, Atlantic white (1985)	88	Escambia Co., Ala.
Cherry, Bitter (1985).	104	Vashon Is., Wash.
Coconut, Palm (1979)	92	Hilo, Hi.
Cranberrybush, American (1989)*	25	Trenton, Mich.
Cypress, McNab (1981).	55	Amador Co., Cal.
Dahoon, Myrtle (1972)	46	Lawtey, Fla.
Devilwood (1989)	36	Perry, Fla.
Dogwood, Blackfruit (1986).	18	Shasta Co., Cal.
Dogwood, Swamp (1989)*.	23	Chesapeake, Va.
Douglas-Fir, Coast (1989)	298	Olympic Natl. Park, Wash.
Elder, American (1987)	16	Jefferson Natl. For., Va.
Elder, Pacific Red (1989)	30	Lincoln Co., Ore.
Elm, American (1985)	125	Southampton Co., Va.
Fiddlewood, Florida (1988)	39	Dade Co., Fla.
Fig, Shortleaf (1986).	41	Monroe Co., Fla.
Fir, Grand (1987)	251	Olympic Natl. Park, Wash.
Franklinia (1968)	36	Wyndmoor, Pa.
Fringetree (1989)*.	32	Fairfax Co., Va.
Gallberry, Large (1989)	27	Great Dismal Swamp Natl. Wildlife Refuge, Va.
Geiger Tree (1988)	25	Lee Co., Fla.
Guajillo (1989)	15	Starr Co., Tex.
Guiana Plum (1976)	31	Coral Gables, Fla.
Hackberry, Common (1989)	111	Rock Co., Wis.
Haw, Frosted (1989)	15	Maiden Springs, Va.
Hawthorne, Fleshy (1988)	8	Kirkwood, Mo.
Hazel, California (1984).	47	Seattle, Wash.
Hemlock, Carolina (1972).	88	Burke Co., N.C.
Hickory, Mockernut (1985)*	125	Monroe Co., Ala.
Hickory, Shellbark (1986).	105	Rixeyville, Va.
Holly, Carolina (1986).	25	Jacksonville, Fla.
Honeylocust (1972)	115	Wayne Co., Mich.
Huisache (1989)	33	Big Bend Natl. Park, Tex.
India Almond (1986).	61	Monroe Co., Fla.
Jujube, Common (1989)	43	Fort Worth, Tex.
Juniper, Western (1945)	86	Stanislaus Natl. Forest., Cal.
Larch, European (1989).	83	Greenwich, Ct.
Laurel, English (1985).	32	Seattle, Wash.
Loblolly Bay (1963)	94	Ocala Natl. Forest, Fla.
Locust, Black (1974)	96	Dansville, N.Y.
Magnolia, Umbrella (1969)	50	Bucks Co., Pa.
Mahogany, W. Indies (1988)	70	Lee Co., Fla.
Manzanita, Common (1989)	22	Guerneville, Cal.
Maple, Black (1976).	118	Allegan Co., Mich.
Maple, Douglas (1985)*.	65	Ahsahka, Ida.
Mesquite, Honey (1984).	52	Real County, Tex.
Mountain Ash, Sitka (1981).	50	Gardiner, Ore.
Mulberry, Black (1971)	68	Westminster, Md.
Nannyberry (1989)	40	Oakland Co., Mich.
Oak, Bluejack (1985)	64	Cherokee Co., Tex.
Oak, Chestnut (1972)	75	Northport, N.Y.
Oak, Harvard (1986)	30	Yoakum Co., Tex.
Oysterwood (1986)	24	Monroe Co., Fla.
Palm, Dwarf (1979)	27	Brazoria, Tex.
Paloverde, Blue (1976)	53	Riverside Co., Cal.
Paper-Mulberry (1989)	34	Yorktown, Va.
Pawpaw, Common (1986)	60	Newton Co., Miss.
Peach (1986).	18	Morrisville, Va.
Pear, Common (1985).	55	Wayne Co., Mich.
Pecan (1980).	143	Cocke Co., Tenn.
Persimmon, Texas (1965)	26	Uvalde Co., Tex.
Pine, Bishop (1986)	112	Mendocino Co., Cal.
Pine, Intermountain (1951) .	47	Inyo Natl. Forest, Cal.
Pine, Virginia (1989)	120	Chambers Co., Ala.
Pistache, Texas (1976)	39	Val Verde Co., Tex.
Plum, Chicasaw (1988)	32	Henderson Co., N.C.
Plum, Wildgoose (1989).	26	New Salem Village, Ill.
Poison-Sumac (1972)	16	Robins Is., N.Y.
Poplar, Balsam (1984)	138	Marquette, Mich.
Portiatree (1968).	42	Kekaha, Ha.
Prickly-Ash, Lime (1988)	25	Lee Co., Fla.
Redbud, Eastern (1989).	36	Nashville, Tenn.
Redwood, Coast (1972).	362	Humboldt Redwoods State Park, Cal.
Ribbonbush (1977)	23	No. Warner Springs, Cal.
Russian-Olive (1982)	58	Cortez, Col.
Saffron-Plum (1987).	31	Santa Ana, Tex.
Sassafras (1954)	76	Owensboro, Ky.
Sequoia, Giant (1975)	275	Sequoia Natl. Park, Cal.
Serviceberry, Downy (1986)	60	Burkes Garden, Va.
Silktree, Mimosa (1986)* .	54	Webster Parish, La.
Sophora, Mescalbean (1983)	27	Comal Co., Tex.
Spruce, Norway (1989)	94	Susquehanna City, Pa.
Stewartia, Virginia (1987) .	15	Chesapeake, Va.
Sumac, Shining (1986)	49	Marion Co., Tex.
Sweetgum, American (1986)	136	Craven Co., N.C.
Sycamore, Arizona (1981)	114	Sierra Co., N.M.
Tamarisk (1981)	34	Columbus, N.M.
Thatchpalm, Florida (1986).	23	Monroe Co., Fla.
Walnut, Arizona (1987)	85	Mimbres Valley, N.M.
Willow, Sitka (1988)	34	Coupeville, Wash.
Willow, Weeping (1982)* .	114	Asheville, N.C.
Yew, Florida (1986)	20	Torreya State Park, Fla.
Yucca, Mojave (1987).	24	Needles Res. Area, Cal.
Yucca, Torrey (1987)	23	Lincoln Natl. Forest, N.M.

ASTRONOMY AND CALENDAR

Edited by Dr. Kenneth L. Franklin, Astronomer Emeritus
American Museum-Hayden Planetarium

Celestial Events Highlights, 1991

(Greenwich Mean Time, or as indicated)

This late spring and early summer we will be able to witness a spectacular gathering of the Moon and planets in our evening sky. The suspense builds subtly even in January, as Mars begins to fade while Venus enters the scene from the western wings of evening twilight. Each month, the Moon passes Venus, Mars, and Jupiter in more rapid succession as the three planets slowly converge. By early June, it becomes obvious that they will meet about the same time, between June 14 to 16, with the four-day crescent Moon passing them on the 15th, in sight of the whole U.S., weather permitting. While we will not see Mars pass Jupiter on the 14th, we will be able to watch Venus pass Jupiter on the 17th, but we will again miss the Venus-Mars encounter on the 23rd. These and other encounters favor other parts of the Earth, except for the dawn close meeting of Mercury, Jupiter, and Regulus the morning of September 10, but only here our east coast is favored.

Antares is occulted by the Moon four times this year, the last for several years occurring in April. Uranus is occulted 12 times, Neptune 6, Saturn, Mars, and Mercury twice, each, and Venus once. Only part of southern Florida may have a chance of seeing the February occultation of Antares, all the other events being unobservable from the U.S.

All the United States except Alaska and most of New England will see a partial eclipse of the Sun on July 11. The path of totality will sweep over the island of Hawaii, the southern tip of Baja California, Guadalajara and Mexico City in Mexico, pass along the Pacific Coast of Central America, missing Panama, before ending in the jungles of Brazil. The maximum duration of totality will occur just east of the Baja in the Sea of Cortez, a few seconds short of 7 minutes, the longest eclipse on the North American continent in scores of years, and, according to one authority, "...the finest total eclipse for North Americans between the years 1806 and 2510..."

As always, use notice of close approaches as a guide to watch the night before and after the events to observe the relative motions of the bodies involved. The sky is a dynamic place.

January

Mercury is a morning object all month long, rising before the Sun in the southeast, at greatest elongation, 24° west of the Sun, on the 14th, and increasing in brightness into February; it is stationary on the 3rd, north of the Moon on the 13th, passes north of Uranus on the 23rd, and south of Neptune on the 26th.

Venus is low in the southwest after sunset this month, just emerging from the evening twilight, and passing south of Saturn on the 1st, and south of the very thin crescent Moon on the 17th.

Mars resumes its direct motion on the 1st at the western edge of Taurus, fading rapidly from minus 1st magnitude, passing south of the Moon on the 25th.

Jupiter, in Cancer, passes the fat, but waning, gibbous Moon on the 2nd, is at minus 2.5 magnitude or brighter in opposition to the Sun on the 29th, and passes the nearly full Moon on the 30th.

Saturn is lost to view this month as it is in conjunction with the Sun on the 18th.

Moon passes Jupiter on the 2nd, occults Antares on the 12th, passes Mercury on the 13th, eclipses the Sun on the 16th, passes Venus on the 17th, Mars on the 25th, and Jupiter again on the 30th.

Jan. 1—Venus passes 1°.2 south of Saturn; Mars stationary in Taurus.

Jan. 2—Moon passes 2° south of Jupiter.

Jan. 3—Earth at perihelion, 91.4 million miles from the sun, closest this year; Mercury stationary, resuming direct motion; Quadrantid meteor shower, ideally showing about 40 per hour, should be affected by the Moon.

Jan. 5—Neptune in conjunction.

Jan. 12—Antares is occulted by the waning crescent moon; see them quite close this morning in the southeast.

Jan. 13—Moon passes 4° south of Mercury.

Jan. 14—Mercury at greatest elongation, 24° west of the Sun in the dawn sky.

Jan. 16—Annular eclipse of the sun.

Jan. 17—Moon passes 3° north of Venus.

Jan. 18—Saturn in conjunction.

Jan. 19—Sun enters Capricornus.

Jan. 23—Mercury passes 0°.4 north of Uranus.

Jan. 25—Moon passes 2° north of Mars.

Jan. 26—Mercury passes 1°.1 south of Neptune.

Jan. 29—Jupiter at opposition in Cancer, rising at sunset and setting at sunrise.

Jan. 30—Moon passes 1°.8 south of Jupiter; penumbral lunar eclipse.

February

Mercury is lost from view after the first week as it heads for superior conjunction early next month.

Venus is increasingly prominent in the evening twilight, passing south of the crescent Moon on the 17th, and setting due west before month's end.

Mars remains in Taurus for another month as it obviously fades while picking up speed in its direct, eastern, motion against the background stars, passing Aldebaran and the Moon on the 22nd.

Jupiter continues to dominate the night sky, the background stars of Cancer demonstrating their normal obscurity, the giant planet letting the nearly full Moon pass to its south on the 26th.

Saturn finally leaves Sagittarius for Capricornus by mid-month after being occulted by the thin waning crescent Moon on the 12th.

Moon occults Antares on the 8th, occults Uranus and passes Neptune on the 11th, occults Saturn on the 12th, passes Venus on the 17th, Mars on the 22nd, and Jupiter on the 26th.

Feb. 5—Mercury is 1°.2 south of Saturn.

Feb. 8—Moon occults Antares, possibly visible from the southeastern part of North America.

Feb. 11—Moon occults Uranus and passes 1°.9 south of Neptune.

Feb. 12—Moon occults Saturn.

Feb. 16—Sun enters Aquarius.

Feb. 17—Moon passes 6° north of Venus.

Feb. 22—Mars passes 8° north of Aldebaran, and 1°.6 south of the Moon.

Feb. 25—Pluto stationary in Serpens Caput.

Feb. 26—Moon passes 1°.6 south of Jupiter.

257

March

Mercury, in superior conjunction beyond the Sun on the 2nd, remains in the twilight glow until the end of the month, a very difficult object to see.

Venus is still more prominent each week, as it moves east of the Sun and toward the north even while brightening.

Mars continues to fade as it moves eastward in Taurus.

Jupiter, with the Moon passing close to the south on the 25th, ends its retrograde motion on the 30th, still in Cancer.

Saturn, occulted by the Moon on the 12th, climbs steadily away from the dawn twilight, looking like a misplaced 1st magnitude star in faint Capricornus.

Moon occults Antares on the 7th, Uranus on the 10th, passes Neptune on the 10th, occults Saturn on the 12th, passes Mercury on the 17th, Venus on the 19th, occults Mars on the 22nd, passes Jupiter on the 25th, and occults the asteroid, Pallas, on the 28th.

Mar. 2—Mercury in superior conjunction.
Mar. 7—Moon occults Antares.
Mar. 10—Moon occults Uranus; passes 1°.8 south of Neptune.
Mar. 11—Sun enters Pisces.
Mar. 12—Moon occults Saturn.
Mar. 17—Moon passes 5° north of Mercury.
Mar. 19—Moon passes 5° north of Venus.
Mar. 21—Vernal equinox, 3:02 GMT (Mar. 20, 10:02 pm EST); spring begins in the northern hemisphere, fall in the southern, as the Sun crosses the Earth's equator from south to north.
Mar. 22—Moon occults Mars.
Mar. 25—Moon passes 1°.6 south of Jupiter.
Mar. 27—Mercury at greatest elongation, 29° east of the Sun.
Mar. 28—Moon occults asteroid Pallas.
Mar. 30—Jupiter stationary in Cancer, resuming direct motion.

April

Mercury, stationary on the 4th and the 27th, passes through inferior conjunction on the 14th, thus lost to view until the last few days of this month.

Venus and the Moon make an interesting tableau the evenings of the 16th and 17th, as the crescent Moon passes 2° north of the evening star before noon on the 17th.

Mars, passing into Gemini early this month, is occulted by the Moon on the 20th.

Jupiter outshines all the stars of Cancer as it moves ponderously toward Leo, being passed by the first quarter Moon on the 21st.

Saturn, in Capricornus, is passed by the fat waning crescent Moon on the 8th.

Moon occults Antares for the last time for many a year on the 4th, Uranus on the 7th, passes Neptune on the 7th, Saturn on the 8th, Venus on the 17th, occults Mars on the 20th, and passes Jupiter on the 21st.

Apr. 4—Moon occults Antares; Mercury stationary, beginning retrograde motion.
Apr. 7—Moon occults Uranus; passes 1°.5 south of Neptune.
Apr. 8—Moon occults Saturn.
Apr. 14—Mercury in inferior conjunction.
Apr. 17—Moon passes 2° north of Venus.
Apr. 18—Uranus and Neptune stationary in Sagittarius, each beginning retrograde motion; Sun enters Aries.
Apr. 20—Moon occults Mars.

Apr. 21—Moon passes 1°.9 south of Jupiter.
Apr. 22—Venus passes 7° north of Aldebaran.
Apr. 27—Mercury stationary, resuming direct motion.

May

Mercury is in the southeast sky before dawn getting brighter all month, at greatest elongation on the 12th, 26° west of the Sun.

Venus is approached by the waxing crescent Moon on the evening of the 16th, their separation only 1°.6 as they close with the horizon.

Mars, brighter than a 2nd magnitude star, after passing 5° south of Pollux on the 16th, joins Jupiter in Cancer near the end of the month.

Jupiter, considerably fainter than Venus, lower in the west, is still very much brighter than Mars or any star in the neighborhood called Cancer.

Saturn, in Capricornus, is stationary on the 17th, beginning its retrograde motion, and is passed by the nearly last quarter Moon on the 6th.

Moon occults Uranus on the 4th, passes Neptune on the 4th, Saturn on the 6th, Mercury on the 12th, Venus on the 17th, Mars on the 18th, Jupiter on the 19th, and occults Uranus and Neptune on the 31st.

May 4—Moon occults Uranus; passes 1°.2 south of Neptune.
May 6—Moon passes 1°.8 north of Saturn.
May 10—Pluto at opposition in Serpens Caput.
May 12—Moon 9° north of Mercury; Mercury at greatest elongation 26° west of the Sun.
May 13—Sun enters Taurus.
May 16—Mars 5° south of Pollux.
May 17—Moon passes 1°.6 south of Venus; Saturn stationary in Capricornus, beginning retrograde motion.
May 18—Moon passes 2° south of Mars.
May 19—Moon passes 2° south of Jupiter; with binoculars, watch Jupiter pass south of the stars of Praesepe, the Beehive cluster of stars in the constellation of Cancer.
May 31—Venus passes 4° south of Pollux; Moon occults Uranus and Neptune.

June

Mercury is effectively lost to our skies this month as it passes superior conjunction on the 17th, beyond the sun.

Venus, at greatest eastern elongation on the 13th, joins the fat crescent Moon, Jupiter, and Mars in a fantastic display of celestial summitry on the evening of the 15th, all in Cancer, the crab; Venus passes north of Jupiter on the 17th, and of Mars on the 23rd.

Mars, after transiting Praesepe on the 6th, passes Jupiter in Cancer on the 14th, north of the Moon on the 16th, and close to Venus on the 23rd, participating in a great meeting of the planets.

Jupiter, slogging toward Leo, is overtaken by faint but fleet Mars on the 14th, the inconstant Moon on the 15th, and dazzling Venus on the 17th.

Saturn, ever patient in Capricornus in the morning sky, is passed by the waning gibbous Moon on the 2nd and the 29th.

Jun. 2—Moon passes 2° north of Saturn.
Jun. 13—Venus at greatest elongation, 45° east of the Sun.
Jun. 14—Mars passes 0°.6 north of Jupiter.
Jun. 15—Moon passes 4° south of Venus, and 3° south of Jupiter.
Jun. 16—Moon passes 4° south of Mars.

Jun. 17—Mercury in superior conjunction, beyond the Sun; Venus passes 0°.3 north of Mars.

Jun. 20—Sun enters Gemini.

Jun. 21—Summer solstice at 21:19 GMT (4:19 pm EST) when the Sun is as far north as it can come; summer begins in the northern hemisphere, winter in the southern.

Jun. 23—Venus passes 0°.3 north of Mars.

Jun. 27—Penumbral lunar eclipse; Moon occults Uranus.

Jun. 28—Moon occults Neptune.

Jun. 29—Moon passes 2° north of Saturn.

Jun. 30—Mercury passes 5° south of Pollux.

July

Mercury, the messenger of the gods, is a bit late for last month's summit conference, but it rushes through Praesepe in Cancer on the 7th, passes the Moon on the 13th and almost seems to collide with Jupiter on the 15th before achieving its greatest eastern elongation from the Sun on the 25th in the northwest twilight, and passing south of Regulus on the 27th.

Venus passes south of Regulus on the 11th, north of the Moon on the 14th, is at greatest brilliancy on the 17th, passes Mars on the 22nd, and is stationary on the 30th, beginning its retrograde motion.

Mars, nearly as faint as a 2nd magnitude star, is busy again one day this month, passing both the Moon and Leo's Regulus on the 14th.

Jupiter, after a close encounter with Mercury on the 15th, descends into the evening twilight by the month's end to be lost to our evening sky until next spring.

Saturn is at opposition on the 27th, a few hours after the full Moon passes it following the Moon's own penumbral eclipse.

Moon totally eclipses the Sun on the 11th, passes Mercury and Jupiter on the 13th, Mars and Venus on the 14th, occults Uranus on the 24th, passes Neptune on the 25th, has a penumbral eclipse and passes Saturn on the 26th.

Jul. 4—Uranus at opposition in Sagittarius.

Jul. 6—Earth at aphelion, 94.4 million miles from the sun, the farthest this year.

Jul. 8—Neptune at opposition in Sagittarius.

Jul. 11—Venus 1°.0 south of Regulus; total solar eclipse.

Jul. 13—Moon passes 3° south of Mercury, and 3° south of Jupiter.

Jul. 14—Moon passes 5° south of Mars; Mars passes 0°.7 north of Regulus; Moon passes 3° south of Venus.

Jul. 15—Mercury passes 0°.08 south of Jupiter.

Jul. 17—Venus at greatest brilliancy.

Jul. 20—Sun enters Cancer.

Jul. 22—Venus passes 4° south of Mars.

Jul. 24—Moon occults Uranus.

Jul. 25—Mercury at greatest elongation, 27° east of the sun; Moon passes 1°.2 south of Neptune.

Jul. 26—Penumbral lunar eclipse; Moon passes 1°.9 north of Saturn.

Jul. 27—Saturn at opposition in Capricornus; Mercury 2° south of Regulus.

Jul. 30—Venus stationary, beginning its retrograde motion.

August

Mercury is stationary and passes Venus on the 7th looking like only a 1st magnitude star, low in the west-northwest evening twilight, lost in the sun's glare for the rest of the month, as it passes through inferior conjunction on the 21st, becoming stationary again on the 30th.

Venus is over 100 times brighter than Mercury when they pass on the 7th, low in the evening twilight, then it, too, is quickly caught up in the sun's brilliance as it passes through inferior conjunction on this side of the Sun on the 22nd.

Mars, only slightly brighter than a 2nd magnitude star, can easily be missed low in the west after sunset, as it moves into Virgo before the end of the month.

Jupiter, which has been so prominent all year, moves beyond the sun, in conjunction on the 17th, thus lost to view as it leaves the evening sky.

Saturn, god of time, has its patience rewarded by having the entire night sky virtually to itself for the rest of the year in Capricornus, now that Mars is so obscure.

Moon passes Venus on the 11th, and occults Mercury on the 11th, passes Mars on the 12th, occults Uranus on the 21st and passes Neptune on the 21st, and Saturn on the 22nd.

Aug. 2—Pluto stationary in Serpens Caput, resuming its direct motion.

Aug. 7—Mercury stationary, beginning its retrograde motion; Mercury 2° north of Venus.

Aug. 10—Sun enters Leo.

Aug. 11—Moon passes 3° north of Venus; Moon occults Mercury.

Aug. 12—Moon passes 6° south of Mars; Perseid meteor shower should be free of lunar interference after an early moonset.

Aug. 17—Venus 9° south of Regulus; Jupiter in conjunction.

Aug. 21—Moon occults Uranus; Moon passes 1°.2 south of Neptune; Mercury in inferior conjunction.

Aug. 22—Venus in inferior conjunction; Moon passes 1°.8 north of Saturn.

Aug. 29—Mercury passes 6° north of Venus.

Aug. 30—Mercury stationary, resuming direct motion.

September

Mercury briefly emerges a bit from the morning twilight for the first half of the month to be sought north of east before dawn, at greatest elongation on the 7th, and pointed out by Regulus and Jupiter on the 10th which are extremely close.

Venus becomes the glorious morning star, stationary on the 12th, achieving its greatest brilliancy on the 28th.

Mars may still be found as a 2nd magnitude star very low in the west after the end of twilight, until the end of the month.

Jupiter begins its inexorable climb out of the dawn twilight to a close encounter with Regulus on the 10th followed by another seeming collision with Mercury a couple of hours later.

Saturn is the sole planetary possessor of the evening sky, still in retrograde in Capricornus.

Moon passes Venus on the 6th, Mercury and Jupiter on the 7th, Mars on the 9th, occults Uranus and Neptune on the 17th, and passes Saturn on the 19th.

Sep. 6—Moon passes 5° north of Venus.

Sep. 7—Moon passes 3° south of Mercury; Moon passes 5° south of Jupiter; Mercury at greatest elongation, 18° west of the sun.

Sep. 10—Moon passes 6° south of Mars; Jupiter passes 0°.4 north of Regulus; Mercury passes 0°.07 south of Jupiter; Mercury passes 0°.3 north of Regulus.

Sep. 16—Sun enters Virgo.

Sep. 17—Moon occults Uranus and Neptune.

Sep. 19—Moon passes 1°.8 north of Saturn; Uranus stationary in Sagittarius.

Sep. 13—Autumnal equinox, 12:48 GMT (7:48 am EST); Autumn begins in the northern hemisphere, spring in the southern, as the Sun now crosses the Earth's equator from north to south.

Sep. 26—Neptune stationary in Sagittarius.

Sep. 28—Venus at greatest brilliancy.

October

Mercury is lost from view for northern hemisphere observers all month, passing through superior conjunction on the 3rd, and remaining far to the south.

Venus is occulted by the Moon on the 15th, passes south of Regulus on the 8th, and south of Jupiter on the 17th.

Mars is lost in the evening twilight all month.

Jupiter passes brilliant Venus on the 17th, then is the highest bright object in the morning sky for the rest of the year.

Saturn is stationary on the 5th at the end of its retrograde loop in Capricornus, having the evening sky all to itself for the rest of the year.

Moon occults Venus on the 4th, passes Jupiter on the 5th, occults Uranus on the 14th, and Neptune on the 15th, and passes Saturn on the 16th.

Oct. 3—Mercury in superior conjunction.

Oct. 4—Moon occults Venus.

Oct. 5—Saturn stationary in Capricornus, resuming its direct motion; Moon passes Jupiter.

Oct. 6—Mars passes 3° north of Spica.

Oct. 8—Venus passes 3° south of Regulus.

Oct. 14—Moon occults Uranus.

Oct. 15—Moon occults Neptune.

Oct. 16—Moon passes 2° north of Saturn.

Oct. 17—Venus passes 2° south of Jupiter.

Oct. 30—Sun enters Libra.

November

Mercury joins Saturn in the evening sky, but it is too far to the southwest after evening twilight to be easily seen by northern observers.

Venus is at greatest elongation in the morning sky on the 2nd, letting Jupiter continue its climb up the sky alone.

Mars is in conjunction, far beyond the sun, on the 8th, the reason it cannot be found in either the evening or the morning sky.

Jupiter is passed by the Moon on the 1st and the 29th, doing nothing else exciting all month.

Saturn, brighter than a 1st magnitude star in the faint background of Capricornus, is the attraction in the southwest after twilight all month.

Moon passes Jupiter on the 1st, Venus on the 2nd, occults Mercury on the 8th, Uranus and Neptune on the 11th, passes Saturn on the 12th, and Jupiter on the 29th.

Nov. 1—Moon passes 6° south of Jupiter.

Nov. 2—Venus at greatest elongation, 47° west of the sun; Moon passes 6° south of Venus.

Nov. 8—Moon occults Mercury; Mars in conjunction with the sun.

Nov. 11—Moon occults Uranus and Neptune; Mercury 2° north of Antares.

Nov. 12—Moon passes 2° north of Saturn.

Nov. 13—Pluto in conjunction with the Sun.

Nov. 17—The sometimes surprising Leonid meteor shower can be best seen after moonset tonight.

Nov. 19—Mercury at greatest elongation, 22° east of the Sun.

Nov. 22—Sun enters Scorpius.

Nov. 28—Mercury stationary, beginning its retrograde motion.

Nov. 29—Moon passes 6° south of Jupiter; Venus passes 8° north of Spica; Sun enters Ophiuchus.

December

Mercury, although passing through inferior conjunction on the 8th, may be visible in the southeast before dawn during the second half, after being stationary on the 18th, and at greatest elongation on the 27th.

Venus is very prominent in the southeast before dawn twilight.

Mars emerges from beyond the sun into the morning twilight, looking like another star in Ophiuchus, but one which moves.

Jupiter is in southeastern Leo becoming stationary on the last day of the year, so beginning its retrograde motion.

Saturn, still the only planet to be seen in the evening sky, is approaching the evening twilight in the southwest, looking brighter than a 1st magnitude star in Capricornus.

Moon passes Venus on the 2nd, occults Uranus and Neptune on the 8th, passes Saturn on the 10th, is partially eclipsed on the 21st, and passes Jupiter on the 26th.

Dec. 2—Moon passes 8° south of Venus.

Dec. 8—Moon occults Uranus and Neptune; Mercury in inferior conjunction.

Dec. 10—Moon passes 3° north of Saturn.

Dec. 11—Mars passes 4° north of Antares.

Dec. 13—Mercury passes 3° north of Mars.

Dec. 14—Geminid meteor shower may show its 50/hour tonight after the midnight moonset.

Dec. 15—Mercury passes 8° north of Antares.

Dec. 16—Sun enters Sagittarius.

Dec. 18—Mercury stationary, resuming direct motion.

Dec. 21—Mercury passes 7° north of Antares; partial lunar eclipse.

Dec. 22—Winter solstice, 8:54 GMT (3:54 am EST); winter begins in the northern hemisphere, summer in the southern; the Sun now being as far south as it can go, it begins its northward trek.

Dec. 26—Moon passes 7° south of Jupiter.

Dec. 27—Mercury at greatest elongation, 22° west of the Sun.

Dec. 31—Jupiter stationary, beginning its retrograde motion in Leo.

Planets and the Sun

The planets of the solar system, in order of their mean distance from the sun, are Mercury, Venus, Earth, Mars, Jupiter, Saturn, Uranus, Neptune and Pluto. Both Uranus and Neptune are visible through good field glasses, but Pluto is so distant and so small that only large telescopes or long exposure photographs can make it visible.

Since Mercury and Venus are nearer to the sun than is the earth, their motions about the sun are seen from the earth as wide swings first to one side of the sun and then to the other, although they are both passing continuously around the sun in orbits that are almost circular. When their passage takes them either between the earth and the sun, or beyond the sun as seen from the earth, they are invisible to us. Because of the laws which govern the motions of planets about the sun, both Mercury and Venus require much less time to pass between the earth and the sun than around the far side of the sun, so their periods of visibility and invisibility are unequal.

The planets that lie farther from the sun than does the earth may be seen for longer periods of time and are invisible only when they are so located in our sky that they rise and set about the same time as the sun when, of course, they are overwhelmed by the sun's great brilliance. None of the planets has any light of its own but each shines only by reflecting sunlight from its surface. Mercury and Venus, because they are between the earth and the sun, show phases very much as the moon does. The planets farther from the sun are always seen as full, although Mars does occasionally present a slightly gibbous phase — like the moon when not quite full.

The planets move rapidly among the stars because they are very much nearer to us. The stars are also in motion, some of them at tremendous speeds, but they are so far away that their motion does not change their apparent positions in the heavens sufficiently for anyone to perceive that change in a single lifetime. The very nearest star is about 7,000 times as far away as the most distant planet.

Planets of the Solar System

Mercury

Mercury, nearest planet to the sun, is the second smallest of the nine planets known to be orbiting the sun. Its diameter is 3,100 miles and its mean distance from the sun is 36,000,000 miles.

Mercury moves with great speed in its journey about the sun, averaging about 30 miles a second to complete its circuit in 88 of our days. Mercury rotates upon its axis over a period of nearly 59 days, thus exposing all of its surface periodically to the sun. It is believed that the surface passing before the sun may have a temperature of about 800° F., while the temperature on the side turned temporarily away from the sun does not fall as low as might be expected. This night temperature has been described by Russian astronomers as "room temperature" — possibly about 70°. This would contradict the former belief that Mercury did not possess an atmosphere, for some sort of atmosphere would be needed to retain the fierce solar radiation that strikes Mercury. A shallow but dense layer of carbon dioxide would produce the "greenhouse" effect, in which heat accumulated during exposure to the sun would not completely escape at night. The actual presence of a carbon dioxide atmosphere is in dispute. Other research, however, has indicated a nighttime temperature approaching −300°.

This uncertainty about conditions upon Mercury and its motion arise from its shorter angular distance from the sun as seen from the earth, for Mercury is always too much in line with the sun to be observed against a dark sky, but is always seen during either morning or evening twilight.

Mariner 10 made 3 passes by Mercury in 1974 and 1975. A large fraction of the surface was photographed from varying distances, revealing a degree of cratering similar to that of the moon. An atmosphere of hydrogen and helium may be made up of gases of the solar wind temporarily concentrated by the presence of Mercury. The discovery of a weak but permanent magnetic field was a surprise. It has been held that both a fluid core and rapid rotation were necessary for the generation of a planetary magnetic field. Mercury may demonstrate these conditions to be unnecessary, or the field may reveal something about the history of Mercury.

Venus

Venus, slightly smaller than the earth, moves about the sun at a mean distance of 67,000,000 miles in 225 of our days. Its synodical revolution — its return to the same relationship with the earth and the sun, which is a result of the combination of its own motion and that of the earth — is 584 days. Every 19 months, then, Venus will be nearer to the earth than any other planet of the solar system. The planet is covered with a dense, white, cloudy atmosphere that conceals whatever is below it. This same cloud reflects sunlight efficiently so that when Venus is favorably situated, it is the third brightest object in the sky, exceeded only by the sun and the moon.

Spectral analysis of sunlight reflected from Venus' cloud tops has shown features that can best be explained by identifying the material of the clouds as sulphuric acid (oil of vitriol). Infrared spectroscopy from a balloon-borne telescope nearly 20 miles above the earth's surface gave indications of a small amount of water vapor present in the same region of the atmosphere of Venus. In 1956, radio astronomers at the Naval Research Laboratories in Washington, D. C., found a temperature for Venus of about 600° F., in marked contrast to minus 125° F., previously found at the cloud tops. Subsequent radio work confirmed a high temperature and produced evidence for this temperature to be associated with the solid body of Venus. With this peculiarity in mind, space scientists devised experiments for the U.S. space probe Mariner 2 to perform when it flew by in 1962. Mariner 2 confirmed the high temperature and the fact that it pertained to the ground rather than to some special activity of the atmosphere. In addition, Mariner 2 was unable to detect any radiation belts similar to the earth's so-called Van Allen belts. Nor was it able to detect the existence of a magnetic field even as weak as 1/100,000 of that of the earth.

In 1967, a Russian space probe, Venera 4, and the American Mariner 5 arrived at Venus within a few hours of each other. Venera 4 was designed to allow an instrument package to land gently on the planet's surface via parachute. It ceased transmission of information in about 75 minutes when the temperature it read went above 500° F. After considerable controversy, it was agreed that it still had 20 miles to go to reach the surface. The U.S. probe, Mariner 5, went around the dark side of Venus at a distance of about 6,000 miles. Again, it detected no significant magnetic field but its radio signals passed to earth through Venus' atmosphere twice — once on the night side and once on the day side. The results are startling. Venus' atmosphere is nearly all carbon dioxide and must exert a pressure at the planet's surface of up to 100 times the earth's normal sea-level pressure of one atmosphere. Since the earth and Venus are about the same size, and were presumably formed at the same time by the same general process from the same mixture of chemical elements, one is faced with the question: which is the planet with the unusual history — earth or Venus?

Radar astronomers using powerful transmitters as well as sensitive receivers and computers have succeeded in determining the rotation period of Venus. It turns out to be 243 days clockwise — in other words, contrary to the spin of most of the other planets and to its own motion around the sun. If it were exactly

243.16 days, Venus would always present the same face toward the earth at every inferior conjunction. This rate and sense of rotation allows a "day" on Venus of 117.4 earth days. Any part of Venus will receive sunlight on its clouds for over 58 days and will be in darkness for 58 days. Recent radar observations have shown surface features below the clouds. Large craters, continent-sized highlands, and extensive, dry "ocean" basins have been identified.

Mariner 10 passed Venus before traveling on to Mercury in 1974. The carbon dioxide molecule found in such abundance in the atmosphere is rather opaque to certain ultraviolet wavelengths, enabling sensitive television cameras to take pictures of the Venusian cloud cover. Photos radioed to earth show a spiral pattern in the clouds from equator to the poles.

In December, 1978, two U. S. Pioneer probes arrived at Venus. One went into orbit about Venus, the other split into 5 separate probes targeted for widely-spaced entry points to sample different conditions. The instrumentation ensemble was selected on the basis of previous missions that had shown the range of conditions to be studied. The probes confirmed expected high surface temperatures and high winds aloft. Winds of about 200 miles per hour, there, may account for the transfer of heat into the night side in spite of the low rotation speed of the planet. Surface winds were light at the time, however. Atmosphere and cloud chemistries were examined in detail, providing much data for continued analysis. The probes detected 4 layers of clouds and more light on the surface than expected solely from sunlight. This light allowed Russian scientists to obtain at least two photos showing rocks on the surface. Sulphur seems to play a large role in the chemistry of Venus, and reactions involving sulphur may be responsible for the glow. To learn more about the weather and atmospheric circulation on Venus, the orbiter takes daily photos of the daylight side cloud cover. It confirms the cloud pattern and its circulation shown by Mariner 10. The ionosphere shows large variability. The orbiter's radar operates in 2 modes: one, for ground elevation variability, and the second for ground reflectivity in 2 dimensions, thus "imaging" the surface. Radar maps of the entire planet that show the features mentioned above have been produced.

Mars

Mars is the first planet beyond the earth, away from the sun. Mars' diameter is about 4,200 miles, although a determination of the radius and mass of Mars by the space-probe, Mariner 4, which flew by Mars on July 14, 1965 at a distance of less than 6,000 miles, indicated that these dimensions were slightly larger than had been previously estimated. While Mars' orbit is also nearly circular, it is somewhat more eccentric than the orbits of many of the other planets, and Mars is more than 30 million miles farther from the sun in some parts of its year than it is at others. Mars takes 687 of our days to make one circuit of the sun, traveling at about 15 miles a second. Mars rotates upon its axis in almost the same period of time that the earth does — 24 hours and 37 minutes. Mars' mean distance from the sun is 141 million miles, so that the temperature on Mars would be lower than that on the earth even if Mars' atmosphere were about the same as ours. The atmosphere is not, however, for Mariner 4 reported that atmospheric pressure on Mars is between 1% and 2% of the earth's atmospheric pressure. This thin atmosphere appears to be largely carbon dioxide. No evidence of free water was found.

There appears to be no magnetic field about Mars. This would eliminate the previous conception of a dangerous radiation belt around Mars. The same lack of a magnetic field would expose the surface of Mars to an influx of cosmic radiation about 100 times as intense as that on earth.

Deductions from years of telescopic observation indicate that 5/8ths of the surface of Mars is a desert of reddish rock, sand, and soil. The rest of Mars is covered by irregular patches that appear generally green in hues that change through the Martian year. These were formerly held to be some sort of primitive vegetation, but with the findings of Mariner 4 of a complete lack of water and oxygen, such growth does not appear possible. The nature of the green areas is now unknown. They may be regions covered with volcanic salts whose color changes with changing temperatures and atmospheric conditions, or they may be gray, rather than green. When large gray areas are placed beside large red areas, the gray areas will appear green to the eye.

Mars' axis of rotation is inclined from a vertical to the plane of its orbit about the sun by about 25° and therefore Mars has seasons as does the earth, except that the Martian seasons are longer because Mars' year is longer. White caps form about the winter pole of Mars, growing through the winter and shrinking in summer. These polar caps are now believed to be both water ice and carbon dioxide ice. It is the carbon dioxide that is seen to come and go with the seasons. The water ice is apparently in many layers with dust between them, indicating climatic cycles.

The canals of Mars have become more of a mystery than they were before the voyage of Mariner 4. Markings forming a network of fine lines crossing much of the surface of Mars have been seen there by men who have devoted much time to the study of the planet, but no canals have shown clearly enough in previous photographs to be universally accepted. A few of the 21 photographs sent back to earth by Mariner 4 covered areas crossed by canals. The pictures show faint, ill-defined, broad, dark markings, but no positive identification of the nature of the markings.

Mariners 6 & 7 in 1969 sent back many more photographs of higher quality than those of the pioneering Mariner 4. These pictures showed cratering similar to the earlier views, but in addition showed 2 other types of terrain. Some regions seemed featureless for many square miles, but others were chaotic, showing high relief without apparent organization into mountain chains or craters.

Mariner 9, the first artificial body to be placed in an orbit about Mars, has transmitted over 10,000 photographs covering 100% of the planet's surface. Preliminary study of these photos and other data shows that Mars resembles no other planet we know. Using terrestrial terms, however, scientists describe features that seem to be clearly of volcanic origin. One of these features is Nix Olympica, (now called Olympus Mons), apparently a shield volcano whose caldera is over 50 miles wide, and whose outer slopes are over 300 miles in diameter, and which stands about 90,000 feet above the surrounding plain. Some features may have been produced by cracking (faulting) of the surface and the sliding of one region over or past another. Many craters seem to have been produced by impacting bodies such as may have come from the nearby asteroid belt. Features near the south pole may have been produced by glaciers that are no longer present. Flowing water, non-existent on Mars at the present time, probably carved canyons, one 10 times longer and 3 times deeper than the Grand Canyon.

Although the Russians landed a probe on the Martian surface, it transmitted for only 20 seconds. In 1976, the U.S. landed 2 Viking spacecraft on the Martian surface. The landers had devices aboard to perform chemical analyses of the soil in search of evidence of life. The results have been inconclusive. The 2 Viking orbiters have returned the best pictures yet of Martian topographic features. Many features can be explained only if Mars once had large quantities of flowing water.

Mars' position in its orbit and its speed around that orbit in relation to the earth's position and speed bring Mars fairly close to the earth on occasions about two years apart and then move Mars and the earth too far apart for accurate observation and photography. Every 15-17 years, the close approaches are especially favorable to close observation.

Mars has 2 satellites, discovered in 1877 by Asaph Hall. The outer satellite, Deimos, revolves around Mars in about 31 hours. The inner satellite, Phobos, whips around Mars in a little more than 7 hours, making 3 trips around the planet each Martian day. Mariner and Viking photos show these bodies to be irregularly shaped and pitted with numerous craters. Phobos also shows a system of linear grooves, each about 1/3-mile across and roughly parallel. Phobos measures about 8 by 12 miles and Deimos about 5 by 7.5 miles in size.

Jupiter

Jupiter is the largest of the planets. Its equatorial diameter is 88,000 miles, 11 times the diameter of the earth. Its polar diameter is about 6,000 miles shorter. This is an equilibrium condition resulting from the liquidity of the planet and its extremely rapid rate of rotation: a Jupiter day is only 10 earth hours long. For a planet this size, this rotational speed is amazing, and it moves a point on Jupiter's equator at a speed of 22,000 miles an hour, as compared with 1,000 miles an hour for a point on the earth's equator. Jupiter is at an average distance of 480 million miles from the sun and takes almost 12 of our years to make one complete circuit of the sun.

The only directly observable chemical constituents of Jupiter's atmosphere are methane (CH_4) and ammonia (NH_3), but it is reasonable to assume the same mixture of elements available to make Jupiter as to make the sun. This would mean a large fraction of hydrogen and helium must be present also, as well as water (H_2O). The temperature at the tops of the clouds may be about minus 260° F. The clouds are probably ammonia ice crystals, becoming ammonia droplets lower down. There may be a space before water ice crystals show up as clouds: in turn, these become water droplets near the bottom of the entire cloud layer. The total atmosphere may be only a few hundred miles in depth, pulled down by the surface gravity (= 2.64 times earth's) to a relatively thin layer. Of course, the gases become denser with depth until they may turn into a slush or a slurry. Perhaps there is no surface — no real interface between the gaseous atmosphere and the body of Jupiter. Pioneers 10 and 11 provided evidence for considering Jupiter to be almost entirely liquid hydrogen. Long before a rocky core about the size of the earth is reached, hydrogen mixed with helium becomes a liquid metal at very high temperature and pressure. Jupiter's cloudy atmosphere is a fairly good reflector of sunlight and makes it appear far brighter than any of the stars.

Fourteen of Jupiter's 17 or more satellites have been found through earth-based observations. Four of the moons are large and bright, rivaling our own moon and the planet Mercury in diameter, and may be seen through a field glass. They move rapidly around Jupiter and their change of position from night to night is extremely interesting to watch. The other satellites are much smaller and in all but one instance much farther from Jupiter and cannot be seen except through powerful telescopes. The 4 outermost satellites are revolving around Jupiter clockwise as seen from the north, contrary to the motions of the great majority of the satellites in the solar system and to the direction of revolution of the planets around the sun. The reason for this retrograde motion is not known, but one theory is that Jupiter's tremendous gravitational power may have captured 4 of the minor planets or asteroids that move about the sun between Mars and Jupiter, and that these would necessarily revolve backward. At the great distance of these bodies from Jupiter — some 14 million miles — direct motion would result in decay of the orbits, while retrograde orbits would be stable. Jupiter's mass is more than twice the mass of all the other planets put together, and accounts for Jupiter's tremendous gravitational field and so, probably, for its numerous satellites and its dense atmosphere.

In December, 1973, Pioneer 10 passed about 80,000 miles from the equator of Jupiter and was whipped into a path taking it out of our solar system in about 50 years, and beyond the system of planets, on June 13, 1983. In December, 1974, Pioneer 11 passed within 30,000 miles of Jupiter, moving roughly from south to north, over the poles.

Photographs from both encounters were useful at the time but were far surpassed by those of Voyagers I and II. Thousands of high resolution multi-color pictures show rapid variations of features both large and small. The Great Red Spot exhibits internal counterclockwise rotation. Much turbulence is seen in adjacent material passing north or south of it. The satellites Amalthea, Io, Europa, Ganymede, and Callisto were photographed, some in great detail. Each is individual and unique, with no similarities to other known planets or satellites. Io has active volcanoes that probably have ejected material into a doughnut-shaped ring enveloping its orbit about Jupiter. This is not to be confused with the thin flat disk-like ring closer to Jupiter's surface. Now that such a ring has been seen by the Voyagers, older uncertain observations from Earth can be reinterpreted as early sightings of this structure.

Saturn

Saturn, last of the planets visible to the unaided eye, is almost twice as far from the sun as Jupiter, almost 900 million miles. It is second in size to Jupiter but its mass is much smaller. Saturn's specific gravity is less than that of water. Its diameter is about 71,000 miles at the equator; its rotational speed spins it completely around in a little more than 10 hours, and its atmosphere is much like that of Jupiter, except that its temperature at the top of its cloud layer is at least 100° lower. At about 300° F. below zero, the ammonia would be frozen out of Saturn's clouds. The theoretical construction of Saturn resembles that of Jupiter; it is either all gas, or it has a small dense center surrounded by a layer of liquid and a deep atmosphere.

Until Pioneer 11 passed Saturn in September 1979 only 10 satellites of Saturn were known. Since that time, the situation is quite confused. Added to data interpretations from the fly-by are earth-based observations using new techniques while the rings were edge-on and virtually invisible. It was hoped that the Voyager I and II fly-bys would help sort out the system. It is now believed that Saturn has at least 22 satellites, some sharing orbits. The Saturn satellite system is still confused.

Saturn's ring system begins about 7,000 miles above the visible disk of Saturn, lying above its equator and extending about 35,000 miles into space. The diameter of the ring system visible from Earth is about 170,000 miles; the rings are estimated to be no thicker than 10 miles. In 1973, radar observation showed the ring particles to be large chunks of material averaging a meter on a side.

Voyager I and II observations showed the rings to be considerably more complex than had been believed, so much so that interpretation will take much time. To the untrained eye, the Voyager photographs could be mistaken for pictures of a colorful phonograph record.

Uranus

Voyager II, after passing Saturn in August 1981, headed for a rendezvous with Uranus culminating in a fly-by January 24, 1986. This encounter answered many questions, and raised others.

Uranus, discovered by Sir William Herschel on Mar. 13, 1781, lies at a distance of 1.8 billion miles from the sun, taking 84 years to make its circuit around our star. Uranus has a diameter of about 32,000 miles and spins once in some 16.8 hours, according to fly-by data. One of the most fascinating features of Uranus is how far it is tipped over. Its north pole lies 98° from being directly up and down to its orbit plane. Thus, its seasons are extreme. When the sun rises at the north pole, it stays up for 42 years; then it sets and the north pole will be in darkness (and winter) for 42 years.

The satellite system of Uranus, consisting of at least 15 moons, (the 5 largest having been known before the fly-by) have orbits lying in the plane of the planet's equator. In that plane there is also a complex of rings, 9 of which were discovered in 1978. Invisible from Earth, the 9 original rings were found by observers watching Uranus pass before a star. As they waited, they saw their photoelectric equipment register several short eclipses of the star. Then the planet occulted the star as expected. After the star came out from behind Uranus, the star winked out several more times. Subsequent observations and analyses indicated the 9 narrow, nearly opaque rings circling Uranus. Evidence from the Voyager II fly-by has shown the ring particles to be predominantly a yard or so in diameter.

In addition to the 10 new, very small satellites, Voyager II returned detailed photos of the 5 large satellites. As in the case of other satellites newly observed in the Voyager program, these bodies proved to be entirely different from each other and any others. Miranda has grooved markings, reminiscent of Jupiter's Ganymede, but often arranged in a chevron pattern. Ariel shows rifts and channels. Umbriel is extremely dark, prompting some observers to regard its surface as among the oldest in the system. Titania has rifts and fractures, but not the evidence of flow found on Ariel. Oberon's main feature is its surface saturated with craters, unrelieved by other formations.

The structure of Uranus is subject to some debate. Basically, however, it may have a rocky core surrounded by a thick icy mantle on top of which is a crust of hydrogen and helium that gradually becomes an atmosphere. Perhaps continued analysis of the wealth of data returned by Voyager II will shed some light on this problem.

Neptune

Neptune, currently the most distant planet from the sun (until 1999), lies at an average distance of 2.8 billion miles. It was the last planet visited in Voyager II's epic 12 year trek from earth. While much new information was immediately perceived, much more must await further analysis of the tremendous amount of data returned from the spacecraft.

As with the other giant planets, there may be no solid surface to give real meaning to a measure of a diameter. However, a mean value of 30,600 miles may be as-

signed to a diameter between atmosphere levels where the pressure is about the same as sea level on earth, as determined by radio experimenters. A different radio observational technique gave evidence of a rotation period for the bulk of Neptune of 16.1 hours, a shorter value than the 18.2 hours given by the clouds seen in the blue atmosphere. Neptune orbits the sun in 164 years in nearly a circular orbit.

Voyager II, which passed 3000 miles from Neptune's north pole, found a magnetic field which is considerably asymmetric to the planet's structure, similar, but not so extreme, to that found at Uranus.

Neptune's atmosphere was seen to be quite blue, with quickly changing white clouds often suspended high above an apparent surface. In that apparent surface were found features, one of which was reminiscent of the Great Red Spot of Jupiter, even to the counterclockwise rotation expected in a high-pressure system in the southern hemisphere. Atmospheric constituents are mostly hydrocarbon compounds. Although lightning and auroras have been found on other giant planets, only the aurora phenomenon has been seen on Neptune.

Six new satellites were discerned around Neptune, one confirming a 1981 sighting that was then difficult to recover for proper identification. Five of these satellites orbit Neptune in a half day or less. Of the eight satellites of Neptune, the largest, Triton, is in a retrograde orbit suggesting that it was captured rather than being co-eval with Neptune. Triton is sufficiently large to raise significant tides on Neptune which will one day, say 100 million years from now, cause Triton to come close enough to Neptune for it to be torn apart. Nereid was found in 1949, and is in a long looping orbit suggesting it, too, was captured. Each of the satellites that has been photographed by the two Voyagers in the planetary encounters has been different from any of the other satellites, and certainly from any of the planets. Only about half of Triton has been observed, but its terrain shows cratering and a strange regional feature described as resembling the skin of a cantaloupe. Triton has a tenuous atmosphere of nitrogen with a trace of hydrocarbons, and evidence of active geysers injecting material into it. At minus 238 degrees Celsius, Triton is one of the coldest objects in the solar system observed by Voyager II.

In addition to the satellite system, Voyager II confirmed the existence of at least three rings composed of very fine particles. There may some clumpiness in their structure, but the known satellites may not contribute to the formation or maintenance of the rings, as they have in other systems.

As with the other giant planets, Neptune is emitting more energy than it receives from the sun, Voyager finding the excess to be 2.7 times the solar contribution. These excesses are thought to be cooling from internal heat sources and from the heat of formation of the planets.

Pluto

Although Pluto on the average stays about 3.6 billion miles from the sun, its orbit is so eccentric that it is now approaching its minimum distance of 2.7 billion miles, less than the current distance of Neptune. Thus Pluto, until 1999, is temporarily planet number 8 from the sun. At its mean distance, Pluto takes 247.7 years to circumnavigate the sun. Until recently that was about all that was known of Pluto.

About a century ago, a hypothetical planet was believed to lie beyond Neptune and Uranus. Little more than a guess, a mass of one Earth was assigned to the mysterious body and mathematical searches were begun. Amid some controversy about the validity of the predictive process, Pluto was found nearly where it was predicted to be. It was found by Clyde Tombaugh at the Lowell Observatory in Flagstaff, Ariz., in 1930.

At the U.S. Naval Observatory, also in Flagstaff, on July 2, 1978, James Christy obtained a photograph of Pluto that was distinctly elongated. Repeated observations of this shape and its variation were convincing evidence of the discovery of a satellite of Pluto. Now named Charon, it may be 500 miles across, at a distance of over 10,000 miles, and taking 6.4 days to

move around Pluto, the same length of time Pluto takes to rotate once. Gravitational laws allow these interactions to give us the mass of Pluto as 0.0017 of the Earth and a diameter of 1,500 miles. This makes the density about the same as that of water.

It is now clear that Pluto, the body found by Tombaugh, could not have influenced Neptune and Uranus to go astray. Theorists are again at work looking for a new planet X.

Greenwich Sidereal Time for 0ʰ GMT, 1991

(Add 12 hours to obtain Right Ascension of Mean Sun)

Date		h	m	Date		h	m	Date		h	m	Date		h	m
Jan.	1	06	40.6		11	13	14.8		20	19	49.1	Nov.	7	03	02.8
	11	07	20.0		21	13	54.3		30	20	28.5		17	03	42.2
	21	07	59.4	May	1	14	33.7	Aug.	9	21	07.9		27	04	21.6
	31	08	38.9		11	15	13.1		19	21	47.4	Dec.	7	05	01.1
Feb.	10	09	18.3		21	15	52.5		29	22	26.8		17	05	40.5
	20	09	57.7		31	16	32.0	Sept.	8	23	06.2		27	06	19.9
Mar.	2	10	37.1	June	10	17	11.4		18	23	45.7	1991 Jan. 6		06	59.3
	12	11	16.6		20	17	50.8		28	00	25.1				
	22	11	56.0		30	18	30.2	Oct.	8	01	04.5				
Apr.	1	12	35.4	July	10	19	09.7		18	01	43.9				

Astronomical Signs and Symbols

☉	The Sun	⊕	The Earth	♅	Uranus	□	Quadrature
☾	The Moon	♂	Mars	♆	Neptune	♊	Opposition
☿	Mercury	♃	Jupiter	♇	Pluto	☊	Ascending Node
♀	Venus	♄	Saturn	☌	Conjunction	☋	Descending Node

Two heavenly bodies are in "conjunction" (☌) when they are due north and south of each other, either in Right Ascension (with respect to the north celestial pole) or in Celestial Longitude (with respect to the north ecliptic pole). If the bodies are seen near each other, they will rise and set at nearly the same time. They are in "opposition" (☍) when their Right Ascensions differ by exactly 12 hours, or their Celestial Longitudes differ by 180°. One of the two objects in opposition will rise while the other is setting. "Quadrature" (□) refers to the arrangement when the coordinates of two bodies differ by exactly 90°. These terms may refer to the relative positions of any two bodies as seen from the earth, but one of the bodies is so fre-

quently the sun that mention of the sun is omitted; otherwise both bodies are named. The geocentric angular separation between sun and object is termed "elongation." Elongation is limited only for Mercury and Venus; the "greatest elongation" for each of these bodies is noted in the appropriate tables and is approximately the time for longest observation. When a planet is in its "ascending" (☊) or "descending" (☋) node, it is passing northward or southward, respectively, through the plane of the earth's orbit, across the celestial circle called the ecliptic. The term "perihelion" means nearest to the sun, and "aphelion," farthest from the sun. An "occultation" of a planet or star is an eclipse of it by some other body, usually the moon.

Planetary Configurations, 1991

Greenwich Mean Time (0 designates midnight; 12 designates noon; * = star; ☽ = moon)

Mo.	D.	h.	m.			
Jan.	1	15	-	☌ ♀ ♄		
	1	16	-		♂ Stationary
	2	23	-	☌ ♃ ☽	♃ 2°N
	3	03	-		⊕ Perihelion
	3	19	-		☿ Stationary
	5	03	-	☌ ♆ ☉	
	12	03	-	☌ ☽ *	Antares 0°.6 S Occultation
	13	20	-	☌ ☿ ☽	☿ 4° N
	14	09	-		☿ Gr Elong 24° W of ☉
	16	00	-	☌ ☽ ☉	Annular Solar Eclipse
	17	18	-	☌ ♀ ☽	♀ 3° S
	18	08	-	☌ ♄ ☉	
	23	17	-	☌ ☿ ♅	☿ 0°.4 N
	25	15	-	☌ ♂ ☉	♂ 2° S
	26	14	-	☌ ☿ ♆	☿ 1°.1 S
	29	00	-	☍ ♃ ☉	
	30	05	-	☌ ♃ ☽	♃ 1°.8 N
	30	06	-		Penumbral Lunar Eclipse
Feb.	5	16	-	☌ ☿ ☽	☿ 1°.2 S
	8	11	-	☌ ☽ *	Antares 0°.7 S Occ'n
	11	04	-	☌ ♅ ☽	♅ 1°.1 N Occ'n
	11	11	-	☌ ♆ ☽	♆ 1°.9 N
	12	18	-	☌ ♄ ☽	♄ 0°.5 S Occ'n

Mo.	D.	h.	m.			
	17	02	-	☌ ♀ ☽	♀ 6° S
	22	08	-	☌ ♂ *	♂ 8°N of Aldebaran
	22	13	-	☌ ♂ ☽	♂ 1°.6 S
	25	14	-		♇ Stationary
	26	09	-	☌ ♃ ☽	♃ 1°.6 N
Mar.	2	03	-	☌ ☿ ☉	Superior
	7	19	-	☌ ☽ *	Antares 0°.8 S Occ'n
	10	15	-	☌ ♅ ☽	♅ 0°.9 N Occ'n
	10	21	-	☌ ♆ ☽	♆ 1°.8 N Occ'n
	17	15	-	☌ ☿ ☽	☿ 5° S
	21	03	02		Vernal Equinox; Spring begins Northern Hemisphere
	22	17	-	☌ ♂ ☽	♂ 0°.7 S Occ'n
	25	13	-	☌ ♃ ☽	♃ 1°.6 N
	27	15	-		☿ Gr Elong 19°E of ☉
	30	14	-		♃ Stationary
Apr.	4	03	-	☌ ☽ *	Antares 1°.1 S Occ'n
	4	17	-		☿ Stationary
	7	00	-	☌ ♅ ☽	♅ 0°.6 N Occ'n
	7	06	-	☌ ♆ ☽	♆ 1°.5 N
	8	21	-	☌ ♄ ☽	♄ 1°.4 S
	14	21	-	☌ ☿ ☉	Inferior
	17	16	-	☌ ♀ ☽	♀ 2° S

Mo.	D. h. m.						
	18 12	-			♅ Stationary		
	18 23	-			♆ Stationary		
	20 00	-	☌	♂ ☽	♂ 0°.6 N Occ'n		
	21 19	-	☌	♃ ☽	♃ 1°.9 N		
	22 04	-	☌	♀ *	♀ 7° N of Aldebaran		
	27 06	-			☿ Stationary		
May	4 08	-	☌	♅ ☽	♅ 0°.3 N Occ'n		
	4 14	-	☌	♆ ☽	♆ 1°.2 N		
	6 07	-	☌	♄ ☽	♄ 1°.8 S		
	10 03	-	☍	♇ ☉			
	12 18	-			☿ Gr Elong 26° W of ☉		
	16 05	-	☌	♂ *	♂ 5° S of Pollux		
	17 07	-	☌	♀ ☽	♀ 1°.6 N		
	17 11	-			♄ Stationary		
	18 10	-	☌	♂ ☽	♂ 2° N		
	19 07	-	☌	♃ ☽	♃ 2° N		
	31 01	-	☌	♀ *	♀ 4° S of Pollux		
	31 13	-	☌	♅ ☽	♅ 0°.2 N Occ'n		
	31 20	-	☌	♆ ☽	♆ 1°.1 N Occ'n		
June	2 14	-	☌	♄ ☽	♄ 2° S		
	13 22	-			♀ Gr Elong 45° E of ☉		
	14 05	-	☌	♂ ♃	♂ 0°.6 N		
	15 20	-	☌	♀ ☽	♀ 4° N		
	15 22	-	☌	♃ ☽	♃ 3° N		
	16 00	-	☌	♂ ☽	♂ 4° N		
	17 05	-	☌	☿ ☉	Superior		
	17 23	-	☌	♀ ♃	♀ 1°.2 N		
	21 21 19				Summer Solstice; Summer begins, Northern Hemisphere		
	23 12	-	☌	♀ ♂	♀ 0°.3 N		
	27 03	-			Penumbral Lunar Eclipse		
	27 17	-	☌	♅ ☽	♅ 0°.3 N Occ'n		
	28 00	-	☌	♆ ☽	♆ 1°.1 N Occ'n		
	29 18	-	☌	♄ ☽	♄ 2° S		
	30 22	-	☌	☿ *	☿ 5° S of Pollux		
July	4 07	-	☍	♅ ☉			
	6 15	-			⊕ at Aphelion		
	8 00	-	☍	♆ ☉			
	11 08	-	☌	♀ *	♀ 1°.0 S of Regulus		
	11 19	-			Total Solar Eclipse		
	13 14	-	☌	☿ ☽	☿ 3° N		
	13 17	-	☌	♃ ☽	♃ 3° N		
	14 15	-	☌	♂ ☽	♂ 5° N		
	14 16	-	☌	♂ *	♂ 0°.7 N of Regulus		
	14 18	-	☌	♀ ☽	♀ 3° N		
	15 08	-	☌	☿ ♃	☿ 0°.08 S		
	17 05	-			♀ Gr Brillancy		
	22 06	-	☌	♀ ♂	♀ 4° S		
	24 21	-	☌	♅ ☽	♅ 0°.4 N Occ'n		
	25 02	-			☿ Gr Elong 27° E of ☉		
	25 05	-	☌	♆ ☽	♆ 1°.2 N		
	26 18	-			Penumbral Lunar Eclipse		
	26 20	-	☌	♄ ☽	♄ 1°.9 S		
	27 00	-	☍	♄ ☉			
	27 01	-	☌	☿ *	☿ 2° S of Regulus		
	30 04	-			♀ Stationary		
Aug.	2 19	-			♇ Stationary		
	7 04	-			☿ Stationary		
	7 06	-	☌	☿ ♀	☿ 2° N		
	11 07	-	☌	♀ ☽	♀ 3° S		
	11 08	-	☌	☿ ☽	☿ 0°.6 S Occ'n		
	12 08	-	☌	♂ ☽	♂ 6° N		
	17 00	-	☌	♀ *	♀ 9° S of Regulus		
	17 22	-	☌	♃ ☉			

Mo.	D. h. m.				
	21 02	-	☌	♅ ☽	♅ 0°.4 N Occ'n
	21 10	-	☌	♆ ☽	♆ 1°.2 N
	21 21	-	☌	☿ ☉	Inferior
	22 20	-	☌	♀ ☉	Inferior
	22 23	-	☌	♄ ☽	♄ 1°.8 S
	29 05	-	☌	☿ ♀	☿ 6° N
	30 20	-			☿ Stationary
Sept.	6 17	-	☌	♀ ☽	♀ 5° S
	7 05	-	☌	☿ ☽	☿ 3° N
	7 11	-	☌	♃ ☽	♃ 5° N
	7 18	-			☿ Gr Elong 18° W of ☉
	10 02	-	☌	♂ ☽	♂ 6° N
	10 08	-	☌	♃ *	♃ 0°.4 N of Regulus
	10 10	-	☌	♃ ♂	♂ 0°.07 S
	10 10	-	☌	☿ *	☿ 0°.3 N of Regulus
	12 02	-			♀ Stationary
	17 09	-	☌	♅ ☽	♅ 0°.2 N Occ'n
	17 17	-	☌	♆ ☽	♆ 1°.0 N Occ'n
	19 04	-	☌	♄ ☽	♄ 1°.8 S
	19 09	-			♅ Stationary
	23 12 48				Autumnal Equinox; Autumn begins, Northern Hemisphere
	26 05	-			♆ Stationary
	28 23	-			♀ Gr Brilliancy
Oct.	3 17	-	☌	☿ ☉	Superior
	4 15	-	☌	♀ ☽	♀ 0°.2 N; Occ'n
	5 02	-			♄ Stationary
	5 05	-	☌	♃ ☽	♃ 5° N
	6 00	-	☌	♂ *	♂ 3° N of Spica
	8 04	-	☌	♀ *	♀ 3° S of Regulus
	14 18	-	☌	♅ ☽	♅ 0°.06 S Occ'n
	15 02	-	☌	♆ ☽	♆ 0°.7 N Occ'n
	16 02	-	☌	♄ ☽	♄ 2° S
	17 03	-	☌	♀ ♃	♀ 2° S
Nov.	1 20	-	☌	♃ ☽	♃ 6° N
	2 09	-			♀ Gr Elong 47° W of ☉
	2 21	-	☌	♀ ☽	♀ 6° N
	8 05	-	☌	☿ ☽	☿ 0°.7 N Occ'n
	8 09	-	☌	♂ ☉	
	11 03	-	☌	♅ ☽	♅ 0°.4 S Occ'n
	11 07	-	☌	☿ *	☿ 2° N of Antares
	11 11	-	☌	♆ ☽	♆ 0°.4 N Occ'n
	12 22	-	☌	♄ ☽	♄ 2° S
	13 04	-	☍	♇ ☉	
	19 02	-			☿ Gr Elong 22° E of ☉
	28 18	-			♂ Stationary
	29 08	-	☌	♃ ☽	♃ 6° N
	29 09	-	☌	♀ *	♀ 4° N of Spica
Dec.	2 14	-	☌	♀ ☽	♀ 8° N
	8 14	-	☌	♅ ☽	♅ 0°.6 S Occ'n
	8 15	-	☌	☿ ☉	Inferior
	8 20	-	☌	♆ ☽	♆ 0°.2 N Occ'n
	10 10	-	☌	♄ ☽	♄ 3° S
	11 15	-	☌	♂ *	♂ 4° N of Antares
	13 16	-	☌	☿ ♂	☿ 3° N
	15 22	-	☌	☿ *	☿ 8° N of Antares
	18 12	-			☿ Stationary
	21 06	-	☌	☿ *	☿ 7° N of Antares
	21 10	-			Partial Lunar Eclipse
	22 08 54				Winter Solstice; Winter begins, Northern Hemisphere
	26 17	-	☌	♃ ☽	♃ 7° N
	27 21	-			☿ Gr Elong 22° W of ☉
	31 12	-			♃ Stationary

Rising and Setting of Planets, 1991

Greenwich Mean Time (0 designates midnight)

		20° N. Latitude		30° N. Latitude		40° N. Latitude		50° N. Latitude		60° N. Latitude	
		Rise	Set	Rise	Set	Rise	Set	Rise	Set	Rise	Set
						Venus, 1991					
Jan.	10	7:47	18:52	8:05	18:34	8:28	18:12	8:59	17:41	9:50	16:50
	20	7:53	19:09	8:08	18:55	8:26	18:37	8:50	18:12	9:30	17:33
	30	7:56	19:25	8:06	19:14	8:19	19:01	8:37	18:44	9:04	18:17
Feb.	9	7:56	19:39	8:02	19:33	8:10	19:25	8:20	19:15	8:36	19:00

		20° N. Latitude		30° N. Latitude		40° N. Latitude		50° N. Latitude		60° N. Latitude	
		Rise	Set	Rise	Set	Rise	Set	Rise	Set	Rise	Set
	19	7:54	19:52	7:56	19:51	7:59	19:48	8:02	19:46	8:06	19:42
Mar.	1	7:52	20:05	7:49	20:08	7:46	20:11	7:42	20:16	7:35	20:23
	11	7:50	20:18	7:43	20:25	7:34	20:34	7:22	20:46	7:04	21:05
	21	7:48	20:31	7:37	20:43	7:23	20:57	7:04	21:17	6:33	21:48
	31	7:48	20:45	7:33	21:01	7:14	21:20	6:47	21:47	6:03	22:32
Apr.	10	7:51	21:00	7:32	21:19	7:08	21:43	6:34	22:18	5:36	23:17
	20	7:56	21:14	7:34	21:36	7:06	22:05	6:26	22:45	5:12	24:00
	30	8:03	21:28	7:39	21:52	7:08	22:23	6:24	23:06	5:02	0:19
May	10	8:12	21:40	7:48	22:05	7:16	22:36	6:29	23:23	4:57	0:54
	20	8:23	21:48	7:58	22:13	7:27	22:43	6:42	23:29	5:13	0:57
	30	8:32	21:52	8:10	22:15	7:41	22:44	6:59	23:25	5:42	0:43
June	9	8:40	21:52	8:20	22:12	7:54	22:37	7:18	23:13	6:14	0:18
	19	8:44	21:45	8:27	22:02	8:06	22:23	7:36	22:53	6:45	23:43
	29	8:44	21:34	8:30	21:47	8:13	22:04	7:49	22:27	7:10	23:05
July	9	8:37	21:15	8:26	21:25	8:13	21:38	7:56	21:55	7:27	22:23
	19	8:21	20:49	8:14	20:56	8:05	21:05	7:52	21:17	7:33	21:36
	29	7:54	20:12	7:49	20:17	7:43	20:23	7:35	20:31	7:22	20:43
Aug.	8	7:11	19:24	7:08	19:27	7:03	19:31	6:58	19:37	6:49	19:46
	18	6:13	18:25	6:10	18:28	6:06	18:32	6:00	18:38	5:52	18:47
	28	5:08	17:25	5:04	17:29	4:58	17:35	4:51	17:42	4:39	17:54
Sept.	7	4:11	16:34	4:05	16:40	3:57	16:48	3:47	16:59	3:30	17:15
	17	3:29	15:58	3:22	16:05	3:12	16:15	3:00	16:28	2:40	16:48
	27	3:03	15:34	2:55	15:42	2:45	15:52	2:31	16:06	2:09	16:28
Oct.	7	2:49	15:18	2:41	15:26	2:31	15:36	2:18	15:49	1:57	16:09
	17	2:42	15:08	2:36	15:15	2:28	15:22	2:17	15:33	1:59	15:50
	27	2:41	15:01	2:37	15:05	2:31	15:11	2:24	15:18	2:12	15:30
Nov.	6	2:45	14:55	2:43	14:57	2:40	14:59	2:37	15:02	2:31	15:07
	16	2:50	14:50	2:51	14:49	2:53	14:48	2:54	14:46	2:56	14:43
	26	2:58	14:47	3:02	14:43	3:08	14:37	3:15	14:30	3:25	14:19
Dec.	6	3:08	14:45	3:15	14:37	3:25	14:28	3:38	14:15	3:57	13:55
	16	3:19	14:45	3:30	14:34	3:44	14:20	4:03	14:01	4:32	13:32
	26	3:32	14:48	3:46	14:33	4:04	14:16	4:28	13:51	5:08	13:12

Mars, 1991

		20° N. Latitude		30° N. Latitude		40° N. Latitude		50° N. Latitude		60° N. Latitude	
		Rise	Set	Rise	Set	Rise	Set	Rise	Set	Rise	Set
Jan.	10	13:47	3:02	13:26	3:22	13:00	3:48	12:23	4:25	11:18	5:30
	20	13:14	2:30	12:53	2:50	12:26	3:17	11:49	3:54	10:41	4:02
	30	12:44	2:02	12:23	2:23	11:56	2:50	11:17	3:29	10:07	4:39
Feb.	9	12:18	1:37	11:56	1:59	11:28	2:27	10:48	3:08	9:34	4:21
	19	11:54	1:16	11:32	1:38	11:03	2:07	10:21	2:49	9:04	4:06
Mar.	1	11:33	0:56	11:10	1:19	10:40	1:49	9:57	2:32	8:36	3:53
	11	11:13	0:38	10:49	1:01	10:19	1:31	9:35	2:16	8:11	3:40
	21	10:55	0:20	10:31	0:44	10:00	1:15	9:16	2:00	7:49	3:27
	31	10:38	0:04	10:14	0:28	9:43	0:59	8:58	1:44	7:31	3:11
Apr.	10	10:23	23:46	9:59	0:12	9:28	0:42	8:43	1:27	7:17	2:53
	20	10:08	23:30	9:44	23:54	9:14	0:25	8:31	1:09	7:07	2:33
	30	9:54	23:14	9:31	23:37	9:02	0:08	8:20	0:50	7:01	2:09
May	10	9:41	22:58	9:19	23:20	8:51	23:47	8:11	0:30	6:57	1:43
	20	9:28	22:41	9:07	23:02	8:41	23:28	8:03	0:08	6:56	1:15
	30	9:15	22:24	8:56	22:43	8:31	23:08	7:56	23:42	6:56	0:45
June	9	9:03	22:06	8:45	22:24	8:22	22:46	7:51	23:18	6:57	0:14
	19	8:50	21:48	8:34	22:04	8:14	22:24	7:45	22:52	6:58	23:39
	29	8:38	21:29	8:23	21:44	8:05	22:01	7:41	22:26	7:00	23:06
July	9	8:25	21:10	8:13	21:23	7:57	21:38	7:36	21:59	7:02	22:33
	19	8:13	20:51	8:02	21:01	7:49	21:14	7:32	21:31	7:04	21:59
	29	8:00	20:31	7:52	20:39	7:42	20:50	7:28	21:03	7:06	21:25
Aug.	8	7:48	20:11	7:42	20:17	7:34	20:25	7:24	20:35	7:07	20:51
	18	7:35	19:52	7:31	19:55	7:26	20:00	7:20	20:06	7:09	20:17
	28	7:23	19:32	7:21	19:33	7:19	19:35	7:16	19:38	7:11	19:42
Sept.	7	7:11	19:12	7:11	19:11	7:12	19:10	7:13	19:09	7:14	19:08
	17	6:59	18:52	7:02	18:49	7:05	18:46	7:10	18:41	7:17	18:34
	27	6:48	18:33	6:53	18:28	6:59	18:22	7:07	18:13	7:20	18:01
Oct.	7	6:37	18:15	6:44	18:07	6:53	17:58	7:05	17:46	7:24	17:27
	17	6:26	17:57	6:36	17:47	6:48	17:36	7:04	17:20	7:28	16:55
	27	6:17	17:40	6:29	17:28	6:43	17:14	7:03	16:54	7:34	16:23
Nov.	6	6:08	17:24	6:22	17:10	6:39	16:53	7:02	16:30	7:40	15:52
	16	5:59	17:10	6:15	16:54	6:35	16:34	7:02	16:07	7:46	15:22
	26	5:52	16:56	6:09	16:38	6:31	16:16	7:02	15:46	7:52	14:55
Dec.	6	5:44	16:44	6:04	16:25	6:28	16:01	7:01	15:27	7:58	14:30
	16	5:38	16:33	5:58	16:12	6:24	15:47	7:00	15:11	8:03	14:08
	26	5:31	16:23	5:53	16:02	6:19	15:35	6:57	14:57	8:05	13:50

Jupiter, 1991

		20° N. Latitude		30° N. Latitude		40° N. Latitude		50° N. Latitude		60° N. Latitude	
		Rise	Set	Rise	Set	Rise	Set	Rise	Set	Rise	Set
Jan.	10	19:05	8:07	18:49	8:24	18:28	8:44	17:59	9:13	17:11	10:01
	20	18:20	7:23	18:03	7:40	17:42	8:01	17:13	8:31	16:23	9:20
	30	17:35	6:39	17:18	6:57	16:56	7:18	16:26	7:48	15:35	8:39
Feb.	9	16:50	5:55	16:32	6:13	16:10	6:35	15:39	7:06	14:47	7:58
	19	16:05	5:12	15:47	5:29	15:25	5:52	14:53	6:23	13:59	7:17

		20° N. Latitude		30° N. Latitude		40° N. Latitude		50° N. Latitude		60° N. Latitude	
		Rise	Set	Rise	Set	Rise	Set	Rise	Set	Rise	Set
Mar.	1	15:21	4:29	15:03	4:47	14:40	5:09	14:08	5:42	13:13	6:36
	11	14:38	3:46	14:20	4:05	13:57	4:28	13:25	5:00	12:29	5:56
	21	13:57	3:05	13:39	3:24	13:16	3:47	12:43	4:20	11:47	5:16
	31	13:17	2:26	12:59	2:44	12:36	3:07	12:03	3:40	11:07	4:36
Apr.	10	12:39	1:47	12:20	2:05	11:57	2:28	11:25	3:01	10:29	3:57
	20	12:02	1:09	11:43	1:28	11:21	1:51	10:48	2:23	9:53	3:18
	30	11:26	0:33	11:08	0:51	10:45	1:14	10:13	1:46	9:19	2:40
May	10	10:51	23:54	10:33	0:15	10:11	0:37	9:40	1:09	8:46	2:02
	20	10:18	23:19	10:00	23:37	9:38	23:58	9:07	0:33	8:15	1:25
	30	9:45	22:45	9:28	23:02	9:06	23:24	8:36	23:54	7:46	0:48
June	9	9:13	22:12	8:56	22:28	8:35	22:49	8:06	23:18	7:17	0:11
	19	8:41	21:39	8:25	21:55	8:05	22:15	7:37	22:43	6:50	23:30
	29	8:11	21:06	7:55	21:22	7:35	21:41	7:08	22:09	6:23	22:54
July	9	7:40	20:34	7:25	20:49	7:06	21:08	6:40	21:34	5:57	22:17
	19	7:10	20:02	6:56	20:16	6:38	20:34	6:12	20:59	5:31	21:40
	29	6:40	19:30	6:26	19:44	6:09	20:01	5:45	20:25	5:06	21:03
Aug.	8	6:10	18:58	5:57	19:11	5:41	19:27	5:18	19:50	4:41	20:27
	18	5:41	18:26	5:28	18:38	5:13	18:54	4:51	19:15	4:16	19:50
	28	5:11	17:54	4:59	18:06	4:44	18:20	4:24	18:41	3:51	19:13
Sept.	7	4:41	17:22	4:30	17:33	4:16	17:47	3:57	18:06	3:26	18:36
	17	4:11	16:49	4:01	17:00	3:47	17:13	3:29	17:31	3:01	17:59
	27	3:41	16:17	3:31	16:27	3:19	16:39	3:02	16:56	2:35	17:22
Oct.	7	3:10	15:44	3:01	15:53	2:49	16:05	2:33	16:20	2:08	16:45
	17	2:39	15:11	2:30	15:19	2:19	15:30	2:04	15:45	1:41	16:08
	27	2:07	14:37	1:59	14:45	1:49	14:55	1:35	15:09	1:13	15:30
Nov.	6	1:34	14:03	1:27	14:10	1:17	14:20	1:04	14:33	0:44	14:53
	16	1:01	13:28	0:54	13:35	0:45	13:44	0:32	13:56	0:13	14:15
	26	0:26	12:52	0:20	12:59	0:11	13:07	23:56	13:19	23:38	13:37
Dec.	6	23:47	12:16	23:41	12:22	23:33	12:30	23:22	12:42	23:04	12:59
	16	23:11	11:38	23:04	11:45	22:56	11:53	22:45	12:04	22:28	12:21
	26	22:33	11:00	22:26	11:06	22:18	11:14	22:08	11:25	21:51	11:42

Saturn, 1991

		20° N. Latitude		30° N. Latitude		40° N. Latitude		50° N. Latitude		60° N. Latitude	
Jan.	10	7:07	18:07	7:26	17:48	7:50	17:25	8:22	16:52	9:18	15:57
	20	6:33	17:33	6:51	17:15	7:14	16:51	7:47	16:19	8:41	15:25
	30	5:58	16:59	6:16	16:41	6:39	16:18	7:11	15:46	8:04	14:53
Feb.	9	5:23	16:25	5:41	16:07	6:04	15:44	6:35	15:13	7:27	14:21
	19	4:48	15:51	5:06	15:33	5:28	15:11	5:59	14:40	6:50	13:48
Mar.	1	4:13	15:16	4:30	14:58	4:52	14:37	5:23	14:06	6:13	13:16
	11	3:37	14:41	3:55	14:24	4:16	14:02	4:46	13:32	5:36	12:42
	21	3:01	14:06	3:18	13:49	3:40	13:27	4:09	12:58	4:59	12:08
	31	2:25	13:30	2:42	13:13	3:03	12:52	3:32	12:22	4:21	11:34
Apr.	10	1:48	12:53	2:05	12:37	2:26	12:16	2:55	11:47	3:43	10:59
	20	1:11	12:16	1:27	12:00	1:48	11:39	2:17	11:10	3:05	10:22
	30	0:33	11:39	0:49	11:22	1:10	11:01	1:39	10:32	2:26	9:45
May	10	23:50	11:00	0:11	10:43	0:31	10:23	1:00	9:54	1:47	9:07
	20	23:11	10:21	23:28	10:04	23:48	9:44	0:21	9:15	1:08	8:28
	30	22:31	9:41	22:48	9:24	23:09	9:03	23:37	8:35	0:29	7:47
June	9	21:51	9:00	22:08	8:44	22:28	8:23	22:57	7:54	23:45	7:06
	19	21:10	8:19	21:27	8:02	21:46	7:41	22:17	7:12	23:05	6:24
	29	20:29	7:37	20:46	7:20	21:07	6:59	21:36	6:30	22:25	5:41
July	9	19:47	6:55	20:04	6:38	20:26	6:16	20:55	5:47	21:45	4:57
	19	19:05	6:13	19:22	5:55	19:44	5:33	20:14	5:03	21:04	4:13
	29	18:23	5:30	18:41	5:12	19:03	4:50	19:33	4:20	20:24	3:29
Aug.	8	17:41	4:47	17:59	4:29	18:21	4:07	18:52	3:36	19:43	2:45
	18	16:59	4:05	17:17	3:47	17:39	3:25	18:11	2:53	19:03	2:01
	28	16:17	3:23	16:36	3:05	16:58	2:42	17:30	2:11	18:23	1:18
Sept.	7	15:36	2:41	15:55	2:23	16:17	2:00	16:49	1:29	17:42	0:35
	17	14:56	2:00	15:14	1:42	15:37	1:19	16:09	0:47	17:02	23:49
	27	14:16	1:20	14:34	1:02	14:57	0:39	15:29	0:07	16:23	23:09
Oct.	7	13:36	0:40	13:55	0:22	14:17	23:55	14:50	23:23	15:43	22:29
	17	12:57	23:58	13:16	23:39	13:39	23:17	14:11	22:45	15:04	21:51
	27	12:19	23:20	12:37	23:01	13:00	22:39	13:32	22:07	14:26	21:13
Nov.	6	11:41	22:43	12:00	22:24	12:22	22:02	12:54	21:30	13:47	20:37
	16	11:04	22:06	11:23	21:48	11:45	21:25	12:17	20:54	13:09	20:01
	26	10:28	21:30	10:46	21:12	11:08	20:50	11:39	20:19	12:31	19:27
Dec.	6	9:52	20:55	10:10	20:37	10:32	20:15	11:02	19:44	11:54	18:53
	16	9:16	20:20	9:34	20:02	9:55	19:40	10:26	19:10	11:16	18:19
	26	8:41	19:45	8:58	19:28	9:19	19:06	9:49	18:36	10:39	17:47

Moonrise Tonight

The idea of estimating the time of moonrise tonight may have scared you off in the past because you assumed that it involved a difficult and mysterious series of calculations. The actual process is quite easy to do, however, especially with the little pocket calculators that seem ubiquitous today. The first major step involves finding three numbers for your city obtained from the latitude and longitude figures listed on pages 292–293 . If your city is not here, find the information from a map, atlas or other source. These answers are permanent and never need to be determined for that city again. You can write these numbers down and use them every year you stay in that city. The second step involves taking the correct four figures from the tables of moonrise and moonset for the date you want. The third major step involves adjusting this answer to standard time.

Let us determine the time of rise for the full moon of July 26, 1991, for Tucson, Arizona.

First, to determine the 3 constant numbers for Tucson, find the latitude and longitude from the table on page 293.

I. Latitude: 32° 13′ 15″
   Longitude: 110° 58′ 08″

IA. Convert these values to decimals: Latitude
   15″/60 = .25′
   13′ + .25′ = 13.25′
   13.25′/60 = .2208°
   32° .2208 = 32.22°
   Longitude:
   8″/60 = .133
   58′ + .133 = 58.133′
   58.133/60 = .969°
   110° + .969 = 110.97°
   Thus, 32.22 for latitude and 110.97 for longitude.

IB. Fraction between 30° and 40° that Tucson lies:
   40 − 30 = 10
   32.22 − 30 = 2.22
   2.22/10 = .222.

IC. Fraction of the world that Tucson lies west of Greenwich (home of GMT): 110.97/360 = .308.

ID. Correction from local to standard time: (Mountain Time meridian is 105° .0) 110.97 − 105 = 5.97° west of the standard time meridian. Events in Tucson happen 4 minutes per degree after they happen for the standard time meridian. Thus, 5.97 × 4 = 23.88, or 24 minutes later.

IE. These three numbers, IB, IC, and ID, never have to be calculated for Tucson again.

II. Find the time of moonrise for Tucson's latitude at Greenwich.

IIA. From the calendar page 285, find the moonrise

data for the latitudes north and south of Tucson, 40° and 30°, and for the times before and after the time wanted, 26th and 27th.

	30°	40°
June 26	18:50	19:11
June 27	19:23	19:39

IIB. We want to find the Greenwich meridian time of moonrise for Tucson's latitude for both the 26th and 27th. This time lies .222 (Ans. IB) times the difference between the rise times on each date for 30° and 40° added to the earlier times:
   For the 26th:
   19:11 − 18:59 = 12
   12 × .222 = 2.7 or 3 minutes
   18:59 + 3 = 19:02
   For the 27th:
   19:39 − 19:23 = 17
   17 × .222 = 3.8 or 4 minutes
   19:23 + 4 = 19:27.

IIC. Since the moon moves at Greenwich from the 26th to the 27th, take the proportion of the change in time between 19:02 on the 26th at Greenwich and 19:27 on the 27th that Tucson lies west of Greenwich (Ans. IC) added to the earlier time:
   19:27 − 19:02 = 25 minutes
   25 × .308 = 7.7 or 8 minutes
   19:02 + 8 = 19:10 local time

IID. Next correct for the standard meridian (Ans. ID):
   19:10 + 24 = 19:34 Mountain Standard Time.
   Note: Arizona does not observe Daylight Time.

Star Tables

These tables include stars of visual magnitude 2.5 and brighter. Co-ordinates are for mid-1991. Where no parallax figures are given, the trigonometric parallax figure is smaller than the margin for error and the distance given is obtained by indirect methods. Stars of variable magnitude designated by v.

To find the time when the star is on meridian, subtract R.A.M.S. of the sun table on page 238 from the star's right ascension, first adding 24h to the latter, if necessary. Mark this result P.M., if less than 12h; but if greater than 12, subtract 12h and mark the remainder A.M.

Star	Magnitude	Parallax ″	Light yrs.	Right ascen. h. m.	Declination ° ′
α Andromedae (Alpheratz)	2.06	0.02	90	0 08.0	29 03
β Cassiopeiae	2.27v	0.07	45	0 08.7	59 06
α Phoenicis	2.39	0.04	93	0 25.9	−42 21
α Cassiopeiae (Schedir)	2.23	0.01	150	0 40.0	56 29
β Ceti	2.04	0.06	57	0 43.2	−18 02
γ Cassiopeiae	2.47v	0.03	96	0 56.2	60 40
β Andromedae	2.06	0.04	76	1 09.3	35 34
α Eridani (Achernar)	0.46	0.02	118	1 37.4	−57 16
γ Andromedae	2.26		260	2 03.4	42 17
α Arietis	2.00	0.04	76	2 06.7	23 25
o Ceti	2.00v	0.01	103	2 18.9	−3 02
α Ursae Min. (Pole Star)	2.02v		680	2 22.1	89 13
β Persei (Algol)	2.12v	0.03	105	3 07.6	40 55
α Persei	1.80	0.03	570	3 23.7	49 50
α Tauri (Aldebaran)	0.85v	0.05	68	4 35.4	16 30
β Orionis (Rigel)	0.12v		900	5 14.1	−8 13
α Aurigae (Capella)	0.08	0.07	45	5 16.1	45 59
γ Orionis (Bellatrix)	1.64	0.03	470	5 24.7	6 20
β Tauri (El Nath)	1.65	0.02	300	5 25.7	28 36
δ Orionis	2.23v		1500	5 31.6	0 18
ε Orionis	1.70		1600	5 35.8	−1 12
ζ Orionis	2.05	0.02	1600	5 40.3	−1 57
κ Orionis	2.06	0.01	2100	5 47.3	−9 40
α Orionis (Betelgeuse)	0.50v		520	5 54.7	7 24
β Aurigae	1.90	0.04	88	5 58.9	44 57
β Canis Majoris	1.98	0.01	750	6 22.3	−17 57
α Carinae (Canopus)	−0.72	0.02	98	6 23.7	−52 41
γ Geminorum	1.93	0.03	105	6 37.2	16 24
α Canis Majoris (Sirius)	−1.46	0.38	8.7	6 44.8	−16 42
ε Canis Majoris	1.50		680	6 58.3	−28 58
δ Canis Majoris	1.86		2100	7 08.0	−26 23
η Canis Majoris	2.44		2700	7 23.7	−29 17
α Geminorum (Castor)	1.99	0.07	45	7 34.1	31 55
α Canis Minoris (Procyon)	0.38	0.29	11.3	7 38.9	5 15
β Geminorum (Pollux)	1.14	0.09	35	7 44.8	28 03
ζ Puppis	2.25		2400	8 03.3	−39 59
γ Velorum	1.82		520	8 09.2	−47 19
ε Carinae	1.86		340	8 22.3	−59 29
δ Velorum	1.96	0.04	76	8 44.4	−54 40
λ Velorum	2.21	0.02	750	9 07.7	−43 24
β Carinae	1.68	0.04	86	9 13.1	−69 41
ι Carinae	2.25		750	9 16.8	−59 15
κ Velorum	2.50	0.01	470	9 21.8	−54 59
α Hydrae	1.98	0.02	94	9 27.2	−8 37
α Leonis (Regulus)	1.35	0.04	84	10 07.9	12 01
γ Leonis	1.90	0.02	90	10 19.5	19 54
β Ursae Majoris (Merak)	2.37	0.04	78	11 01.3	56 26

(continued)

Star	Magnitude	Parallax "	Light yrs.	Right ascen. h. m.	Declination ° '
α Ursae Majoris (Dubhe)	1.79	0.03	105	11 03.2	61 48
β Leonis (Denebola)	2.14	0.08	43	11 48.6	14 37
γ Ursae Majoris (Phecda)	2.44	0.02	90	11 53.4	53 45
α Crucis	1.58		370	12 26.1	−63 04
γ Crucis	1.63		220	12 30.7	−57 04
γ Centauri	2.17		160	12 41.0	−48 54
β Crucis	1.25v		490	12 47.2	−59 39
ε Ursae Majoris (Alioth)	1.77v	0.01	68	12 53.7	57 01
ζ Ursae Majoris (Mizar)	2.05	0.04	88	13 23.6	54 58
α Virginis (Spica)	0.97v	0.02	220	13 24.8	−11 07
ε Centauri	2.30v		570	13 39.4	−53 26
η Ursae Majoris (Alkaid)	1.86		210	13 47.2	49 21
β Centauri	0.61v	0.02	490	14 03.3	−60 20
θ Centauri	2.06	0.06	55	14 06.2	−36 20
α Bootis (Arcturus)	−0.04	0.09	36	14 15.3	19 14
η Centauri	2.31v		390	14 35.0	−42 08
α Centauri	−0.01	0.75	4.3	14 39.1	−60 48
α Lupi	2.30v		430	14 41.3	−47 21
ε Bootis	2.40	0.01	103	14 44.5	27 07
β Ursae Minoris	2.08	0.03	105	14 50.8	74 12
α Coronae Borealis	2.23v	0.04	76	15 34.4	26 45
δ Scorpii	2.32		590	15 59.9	−22 36
α Scorpii (Antares)	0.96v	0.02	520	16 28.9	−26 25
α Trianguli Australis	1.92	0.02	82	16 47.8	−69 01
ε Scorpii	2.29	0.05	66	16 49.7	−34 17
η Ophiuchi	2.43	0.05	69	17 09.9	−15 43
λ Scorpii	1.63v		310	17 33.1	−37 06
α Ophiuchi	2.08	0.06	58	17 34.6	12 34
θ Scorpii	1.87	0.02	650	17 36.8	−43 00
κ Scorpii	2.41v		470	17 41.9	−39 02
γ Draconis	2.23	0.02	108	17 56.5	51 29
ε Sagittarii	1.85	0.02	124	18 23.7	−34 23
α Lyrae (Vega)	0.03	0.12	26.5	18 36.7	38 47
σ Sagittarii	2.02		300	18 54.8	−26 18
α Aquilae (Altair)	0.77	0.20	16.5	19 50.4	8 51
γ Cygni	2.20		750	20 22.0	40 14
α Pavonis	1.94		310	20 25.0	−56 46
α Cygni (Deneb)	1.25		1600	20 41.2	45 15
ε Cygni	2.46	0.04	74	20 45.9	33 56
α Cephei	2.44	0.06	52	21 18.4	62 33
ε Pegasi	2.39		780	21 43.8	9 50
α Gruis	1.74	0.05	64	22 07.7	−47 00
β Gruis	2.11v		280	22 42.2	−46 55
α Piscis Austrinis (Fomalhaut)	1.16	0.14	22.6	22 57.2	−29 40
β Pegasi	2.42v	0.02	210	23 03.4	28 02
α Pegasi	2.49	0.03	109	23 04.4	15 10

Constellations

Culturally, constellations are imagined patterns among the stars that, in some cases, have been recognized through millenia of tradition. In the early days of astronomy, knowledge of the constellations was necessary in order to function as an astronomer. For today's astronomers, constellations are simply areas on the entire sky in which interesting objects await observation and interpretation.

Because western culture has prevailed in establishing modern science, equally viable and interesting constellations and celestial traditions of other cultures (of Asia or Africa, for example) are not well known outside of their regions of origin. Even the patterns with which we are most familiar today have undergone considerable change over the centuries, because the western heritage embraces teachings of cultures disparate in time as well as place.

Today, students of the sky the world over recognize 88 constellations that cover the entire celestial sphere. Many of these have their origins in ancient days; many are "modern," contrived out of unformed stars by astronomers a few centuries ago. Unformed stars were those usually too faint or inconveniently placed to be included in depicting the more prominent constellations. When astronomers began to travel to South Africa in the 16th and 17th centuries, they found a sky that itself was unformed, and showing numerous brilliant stars. Thus, we find constellations in the southern hemisphere like the "air pump," the "microscope," the "furnace," and other technological marvels of the time, as well as some arguably traditional forms, such as the "fly."

Many of the commonly recognized constellations had their origins in ancient Asia Minor—Syria, Babylon, etc. These were adopted by the Greeks and Romans who translated their names and stories into their own languages, some details being modified in the process. After the declines of these cultures, most such knowledge entered oral tradition, or remained hidden in monastic libraries. Beginning in the 8th century, the Moslem explosion spread through the Mediterranean world. Wherever possible, everything was translated into Arabic to be taught in the universities the Moslems established all over their new-found world.

In the 13th century, Alphonsus XX of Spain, an avid student of astronomy, succeeded in having Claudius Ptolemy's *Almagest*, as its Arabian title was known, translated into Latin. It thus became widely available to European scholars. In the process, the constellation names were translated, but the star names were retained in their Arabic forms. Transliterating Arabic into the Roman alphabet has never been an exact art, so many of the star names we use today only "seem" Arabic to all but scholars.

Names of stars often indicated what parts of the traditional figures they represented: Deneb, the tail of the swan; Betelgeuse, the armpit of the giant. Thus, the names were an indication of the position in the sky of a particular star, provided one recognized the traditional form of the mythic figure.

In English, usage of the Latin names for the constellations couples often inconceivable creatures, represented in unimaginable configurations, with names that often seem unintelligible. Avoiding traditional names, astronomers may designate the brighter stars in a constellation with Greek letters, usually in order of brightness. Thus, the "alpha star" is often the brightest star of that constellation. The "of" implies possession, so the genetive (possessive) form of the constellation name is used, as in Alpha Orionis, the first star of Orion (Betelgeuse). Astronomers usually use a 3-letter form for the constellation name, understanding it to be read as either the nominative or genitive case of the name.

Until the 1920's, astronomers used curved boundaries for the constellation areas. As these were rather arbitrary at best, the International Astronomical Union adopted boundaries that ran due north-south and east-west, filling the sky much as the contiguous states fill up the area of the "lower 48" United States.

Within these boundaries, and occasionally crossing them, popular "asterisms" are recognized: the Big Dipper is a small part of Ursa Major, the big bear; the Sickle is the traditional head and mane of Leo, the lion; one of the horntips of Taurus, the bull, properly belongs to Auriga, the charioteer; the northeast star of the Great Square of Pegasus is Alpha Andromedae.

It is unlikely that further change will occur in the realm of the celestial constellations.

Name	Genitive	Abbreviation	Meaning
Andromeda	Andromedae	And	Chained Maiden
Antlia	Antliae	Ant	Air Pump
Apus	Apodis	Aps	Bird of Paradise
Aquarius	Aquarii	Aqr	Water Bearer
Aquila	Aquilae	Aql	Eagle
Ara	Arae	Ara	Altar
Aries	Arietis	Ari	Ram
Auriga	Aurigae	Aur	Charioteer
Bootes	Bootis	Boo	Herdsmen
Caelum	Caeli	Cae	Chisel
Camelopardalis	Camelopardalis	Cam	Giraffe
Cancer	Cancri	Cnc	Crab
Canes Venatici	Canum Venaticorum	CVn	Hunting Dogs
Canis Major	Canis Majoris	CMa	Great Dog
Canis Minor	Canis Minoris	CMi	Little Dog
Capricornus	Capricorni	Cap	Sea-goat
Carina	Carinae	Car	Keel
Cassiopeia	Cassiopeiae	Cas	Queen
Centaurus	Centauri	Cen	Centaur
Cepheus	Cephei	Cep	King
Cetus	Ceti	Cet	Whale
Chamaeleon	Chamaeleontis	Cha	Chameleon
Circinus	Circini	Cir	Compasses (art)
Columba	Columbae	Col	Dove
Coma Berenices	Comae Berenices	Com	Berenice's Hair
Corona Australis	Coronae Australis	CrA	Southern Crown
Corona Borealis	Coronae Borealis	CrB	Northern Crown
Corvus	Corvi	Crv	Crow
Crater	Crateris	Crt	Cup
Crux	Crucis	Cru	Cross (southern)
Cygnus	Cygni	Cyg	Swan
Delphinus	Delphini	Del	Dolphin
Dorado	Doradus	Dor	Goldfish
Draco	Draconis	Dra	Dragon
Equuleus	Equulei	Equ	Little Horse
Eridanus	Eridani	Eri	River
Fornax	Fornacis	For	Furnace
Gemini	Geminorum	Gem	Twins
Grus	Gruis	Gru	Crane (bird)
Hercules	Herculis	Her	Hercules
Horologium	Horologii	Hor	Clock
Hydra	Hydrae	Hya	Water Snake (female)
Hydrus	Hydri	Hyi	Water Snake (male)

Name	Genitive	Abbreviation	Meaning
Indus	Indi	Ind	Indian
Lacerta	Lacertae	Lac	Lizard
Leo	Leonis	Leo	Lion
Leo Minor	Leonis Minoris	LMi	Little Lion
Lepus	Leporis	Lep	Hare
Libra	Librae	Lib	Balance
Lupus	Lupi	Lup	Wolf
Lynx	Lyncis	Lyn	Lynx
Lyra	Lyrae	Lyr	Lyre
Mensa	Mensae	Men	Table Mountain
Microscopium	Microscopii	Mic	Microscope
Monoceros	Monocerotis	Mon	Unicorn
Musca	Muscae	Mus	Fly
Norma	Normae	Nor	Square (rule)
Octans	Octantis	Oct	Octant
Ophiuchus	Ophiuchi	Oph	Serpent Bearer
Orion	Orionis	Ori	Hunter
Pavo	Pavonis	Pav	Peacock
Pegasus	Pegasi	Peg	Flying Horse
Perseus	Persei	Per	Hero
Phoenix	Phoenicis	Phe	Phoenix
Pictor	Pictoris	Pic	Painter
Pisces	Piscium	Psc	Fishes
Piscis Austrinius	Piscis Austrini	PsA	Southern Fish
Puppis	Puppis	Pup	Stern (deck)
Pyxis	Pyxidis	Pyx	Compass (sea)
Reticulum	Reticuli	Ret	Reticle
Sagitta	Sagittae	Sge	Arrow
Sagittarius	Sagittarii	Sgr	Archer
Scorpius	Scorpii	Sco	Scorpion
Sculptor	Sculptoris	Scl	Sculptor
Scutum	Scuti	Sct	Shield
Serpens	Serpentis	Ser	Serpent
Sextans	Sextantis	Sex	Sextant
Taurus	Tauri	Tau	Bull
Telescopium	Telescopii	Tel	Telescope
Triangulum	Trianguli	Tri	Triangle
Triangulum Australe	Trianguli Australis	TrA	Southern Triangle
Tucana	Tucanae	Tuc	Toucan
Ursa Major	Ursae Majoris	UMa	Great Bear
Ursa Minor	Ursae Minoris	UMi	Little Bear
Vela	Velorum	Vel	Sail
Virgo	Virginis	Vir	Maiden
Volans	Volantis	Vol	Flying Fish
Vulpecula	Vulpeculae	Vul	Fox

Aurora Borealis and Aurora Australis

The Aurora Borealis, also called the Northern Lights, is a broad display of rather faint light in the northern skies at night. The Aurora Australis, a similar phenomenon, appears at the same time in southern skies. The aurora appears in a wide variety of forms. Sometimes it is seen as a quiet glow, almost foglike in character; sometimes as vertical streamers in which there may be considerable motion; sometimes as a series of luminous expanding arcs. There are many colors, with white, yellow, and red predominating.

The auroras are most vivid and most frequently seen at about 20 degrees from the magnetic poles, along the northern coast of the North American continent and the eastern part of the northern coast of Europe. They have been seen as far south as Key West and as far north as Australia and New Zealand, but rarely.

While the cause of the auroras is not known beyond question, there does seem to be a definite correlation between auroral displays and sun-spot activity. It is thought that atomic particles expelled from the sun by the forces that cause solar flares speed through space at velocities of 400 to 600 miles per second. These particles are entrapped by the earth's magnetic field, forming what are termed the Van Allen belts. The encounter of these clouds of the solar wind with the earth's magnetic field weakens the field so that previously trapped particles are allowed to impact the upper atmosphere. The collisions between solar and terrestrial atoms result in the glow in the upper atmosphere called the aurora. The glow may be vivid where the lines of magnetic force converge near the magnetic poles.

The auroral displays appear at heights ranging from 50 to about 600 miles and have given us a means of estimating the extent of the earth's atmosphere.

The auroras are often accompanied by magnetic storms whose forces, also guided by the lines of force of the earth's magnetic field, disrupt electrical communication.

Eclipses, 1991
(Greenwich Mean Time)

There are six eclipses in 1991, two of the sun and four of the moon.

I. Annular eclipse of the sun, January 15-16.

Partial phases are visible throughout most of the South Pacific Ocean, part of Antarctica south of Australia, eastern Australia, and New Zealand. The path of annularity begins west of the southwestern tip of Australia, passes over that tip into the Great Australian Bight, grazes the southeastern tip of Australia, passes over all but the southern tip of Tasmania, touches both islands of New Zealand, ending in the Pacific Ocean on the equator due south of Yuma, Arizona.

Circumstances of the Eclipse

Event	Date		h	m
Eclipse begins	Jan.	15	20	51
Central eclipse begins		15	22	0
Central eclipse at local noon		15	23	44
Central eclipse ends		16	1	46
Eclipse ends		16	2	55

Maximum duration of annularity: 7:49.4.

II. Penumbral eclipse of the moon, January 30.

The beginning of the penumbral phase is visible in extreme eastern Asia, North America, Central America, South America, Greenland, Europe, most of Africa, the Palmer Peninsula of Antarctica, the Artic regions, the eastern Pacific Ocean, and the Atlantic Ocean; the end is visible in extreme eastern Asia, most of New Zealand, North America, Central America, South America, Greenland, the Arctic regions, the Pacific Ocean, and the northern Atlantic Ocean.

Circumstances of the Eclipse

Event	Date		h	m
Moon enters penumbra	Jan.	30	3	58
Middle of eclipse		30	5	59
Moon leaves penumbra		30	7	59

Penumbral magnitude of the eclipse: 0.906.

III. Penumbral eclipse of the moon, June 27.

The beginning the penumbral phase is visible in eastern North America, Central America, South America, Antarctica, Africa, Europe south of Scandinavia, the western Indian Ocean, the Atlantic Ocean, and the southeastern Pacific Ocean; the end is visible in North America except for Alaska and northwestern Canada, Central America, South America, Antarctica, the western half of Africa, the western Iberian Peninsula of Europe, the Atlantic Ocean, and the southeastern Pacific Ocean.

Circumstances of the Eclipse

Event	Date		h	m
Moon enters penumbra	June	27	1	46
Middle of eclipse		27	3	15
Moon leaves penumbra		27	4	43

Penumbral magnitude of eclipse: 0.339.

IV. Total eclipse of the sun, July 11.

Partial phases visible in the northeastern Pacific Ocean south of the Aleutian Islands, southwestern to south central Canada, all of the United States except Alaska, Central America, the Caribbean Region, South America except south of latitude 36 degrees. The path of totality begins southwest of Hawaii, crosses the island of Hawaii, the southern tip of Baja California Sur, Southern Mexico, the west coast of Central America, and ends in the jungles of Brazil.

Circumstances of the Eclipse

Event	Date		h	m
Eclipse begins	July	11	16	29
Central eclipse begins		11	17	23
Central eclipse at local moon		11	19	6
Central eclipse ends		11	20	49
Eclipse ends		11	21	43

Maximum duration of totality: 6:58.1.

V. Penumbral eclipse of the moon, June 26.

The beginning of the penumbral phase is visible in southern and eastern Africa, most of Asia, Australia, New Zealand, most of Antarctica, the western Pacific Ocean, and the Indian Ocean; the end visible in most of Europe, most of Africa, most of Asia, Australia, southern New Zealand, Antarctica, the eastern South Atlantic Ocean, and the Indian Ocean.

Circumstances of the Eclipse

Event	Date		h	m
Moon enters the penumbra	July	26	16	48
Middle of eclipse		26	18	8
Moon leaves the penumbra		26	19	28

Penumbral magnitude of the eclipse: 0.280.

VI. Partial eclipse of the moon, December 21.

The beginning of the umbral phase is visible in eastern Australia, New Zealand, northern and eastern Asia, North America, Central America, northwestern South America, Greenland, northern Scandinavia, the Arctic regions, the Pacific Ocean, and the northwestern Atlantic Ocean; the end visible in northern and eastern Asia, Australia, New Zealand, North America, Central America, Greenland, northern Scandinavia, the Artic regions, and the Pacific Ocean.

Circumstances of the Eclipse

Event	Date		h	m
Moon enters the penumbra	Dec.	21	8	25
Moon enters the umbra		21	10	0
Middle of eclipse		21	10	33
Moon leaves umbra		21	11	6
Moon leaves the penumbra		21	12	41

Magnitude of the eclipse: 0.093.

The Planets and the Solar System

Planet	Mean daily motion "	Orbital velocity miles per sec.	Sidereal revolution days	Synodical revolution days	Dist. from sun in millions of mi. Max.	Min.	Dist. from Earth in millions of mi. Max.	Min.	Light at[1] perihelion	aphelion
Mercury . .	14732	29.75	88.0	115.9	43.4	28.6	136	50	10.58	4.59
Venus . . .	5768	21.76	224.7	583.9	67.7	66.8	161	25	1.94	1.89
Earth. . . .	3548	18.51	365.3	—	94.6	91.4	—	—	1.03	0.97
Mars	1886	14.99	687.0	779.9	155.0	128.5	248	35	0.524	0.360
Jupiter . . .	299	8.12	4332.1	398.9	507.0	460.6	600	368	0.0408	0.0336
Saturn . . .	120	5.99	10825.9	378.1	937.5	838.4	1031	745	0.01230	0.00984
Uranus . . .	42	4.23	30676.1	369.7	1859.7	1669.3	1953	1606	0.00300	0.00250
Neptune . .	21	3.38	59911.1	367.5	2821.7	2760.4	2915	2667	0.00114	0.00109
Pluto	14	2.95	90824.2	366.7	4551.4	2756.4	4644	2663	0.00114	0.00042

1. Light at perihelion and aphelion is solar illumination in units of mean illumination at Earth.

Planet	Mean longitude of:* ascending node ° ' "	perihelion ° ' "	Inclination* of orbit to ecliptic ° ' "	Mean* distance**	Eccentricity* of orbit	Mean longitude at the epoch* ° ' "
Mercury. . . .	48 12 58	77 18 25	- 7 00 25	0.387098	0.205635	146 49 38
Venus.	76 35 35	131 11 24	3 23 40	0.723330	0.006761	263 5 28
Earth	— — —	102 47 31	— — —	0.999998	0.016678	206 50 19
Mars	49 29 33	335 48 25	1 50 59	1.523736	0.093455	297 52 24
Jupiter	100 23 13	15 31 41	1 18 18	5.20317	0.048207	99 44 26
Saturn	113 34 9	91 49 19	2 29 16	9.51632	0.055328	241 15 50
Uranus	73 58 1	169 47 35	0 46 19	19.1573	0.047694	271 31 4
Neptune . . .	131 39 54	56 14 24	1 46 19	30.0022	0.010034	283 33 52
Pluto	110 05 49	223 35 53	17 09 44	39.4698	0.248646	224 33 30

*Consistent for the standard Epoch: 1990 Apr. 19 Ephemeris Time **Astronomical units

Sun and planets	Semi-diameter at unit distance ' "	at mean least dist. ' "	in miles mean s.d.	Volume ⊕=1.	Mass. ⊕=1.	Density ⊕=1.	Sidereal period of rotation d.	h.	m.	s.	Gravity at surface ⊕=1.	Reflecting power Pct.	Probable temperature °F.
Sun	959.62	___	432560	1303730	332830	0.26	24	16	48		27.9		+ 10,000
Mercury . . .	3.37	5.5	1515	0.0559	0.0553	0.99	58	21	58		0.37	0.06	+ 620
Venus	8.34	30.1	3760	0.8541	0.8150	0.95	243			R	0.88	0.72	+ 900
Earth	___	___	3963	1.000	1.000	1.00		23	56	4.1		0.39	+ 72
Moon	2.40	932.4	1080	0.020	0.0123	0.62	27	7	43		0.17	0.07	— 10
Mars	4.69	8.95	2108.4	0.1506	0.1074	0.71		24	37	23	0.38	0.16	— 10
Jupiter	98.35	23.4	44362	1403	317.83	0.23		9	3	30	2.64	0.70	— 240
Saturn	82.83	9.7	37280	832	95.16	0.11		10	30		1.15	0.75	— 300
Uranus	35.4	1.9	15800	63	14.50	0.23		15	36	R	1.15	0.90	— 340
Neptune . . .	33.4	1.2	15300	55	17.20	0.31		16	7		1.12	0.82	— 370
Pluto*	1.9	0.05	930	0.01	0.0025	0.25	6	9	17		0.04	?	?

*Observers at the U.S. Naval Observatory have derived values similar to these after having discovered that Pluto has a satellite. It apparently revolves about Pluto in a period equal to Pluto's rotation period. (R) retrograde of Venus and Uranus.

Telescopes

Most of the world's major astronomical installations are in the northern hemisphere, while many of astronomy's major problems are found in the southern sky. This imbalance has long been recognized and is being remedied.

In the northern hemisphere the largest reflector is the 236-inch mirror at the Special Astrophysical Observatory in the Caucasus in the Soviet Union. The largest reflectors in the U.S. include 3 in California: at Palomar Mtn., 200 inches; at Lick Observatory, Mt. Hamilton, 120 inches; and at Mt. Wilson Observatory, 100 inches. Also in the U.S. are the Multiple Mirror Telescope (MMT) at Mt. Hopkins Observatory in Amado, AZ, which is a 176-inch single mirror reflector, a 158-inch reflector at Kitt Peak, Arizona, dedicated in June 1973, and a 107-inch telescope at the McDonald Observatory in Mt. Locke in Texas. A telescope at the Crimean Astrophysical Observatory in the Soviet Union has a 104-inch mirror.

Placed in service in 1975 were three large reflectors for the southern hemisphere. Associated Universities for Research in Astronomy (AURA), the operating organization of Kitt Peak National Observatory, dedicated the 158-inch reflector (twin of the telescope on Kitt Peak) at Cerro Tololo International Observatory, Chile; the European Southern Observatory has a 141-inch reflector at La Silla, Chile; and the Anglo-Australian telescope, 152 inches in diameter, is at Siding Spring Observatory in Australia.

Optical Telescopes

Optical astronomical telescopes are of two kinds, refracting and reflecting. In the first, light passes through a lens which brings the light rays into focus, where the image may be examined after being magnified by a second lens, the eye-piece, or directly photographed.

The reflector consists of a concave parabolic mirror, generally of Pyrex or now of a relatively heat insensitive material, cervit, coated with silver or aluminum, which reflects the light rays back toward the upper end of the telescope, where they are either magnified and observed by the eye-piece or, as in the case of the refractors, photographed. In most reflecting telescopes, the light is reflected again by a secondary mirror and comes to a focus after passing through a hole in the side of the telescope, where the eye-piece or camera is located, or after passing through a hole in the center of the primary mirror.

The Sun

The sun, the controlling body of our solar system, is a star whose dimensions cause it to be classified among stars as average in size, temperature, and brightness. Its proximity to the earth makes it appear to us as tremendously large and bright. A series of thermo-nuclear reactions involving the atoms of the elements of which it is composed produces the heat and light that make life possible on earth.

The sun has a diameter of 864,000 miles and is distant, on the average, 92,900,000 miles from the earth. It is 1.41 times as dense as water. The light of the sun reaches the earth in 499.012 seconds or slightly more than 8 minutes. The average solar surface temperature has been measured by several indirect methods which agree closely on a value of 6,000° Kelvin or about 10,000° F. The interior temperature of the sun is about 35,000,000 F.°.

When sunlight is analyzed with a spectroscope, it is found to consist of a continuous spectrum composed of all the colors of the rainbow in order, crossed by many dark lines. The "absorption lines" are produced by gaseous materials in the atmosphere of the sun. More than 60 of the natural terrestrial elements have been identified in the sun, all in gaseous form because of the intense heat of the sun.

Spheres and Corona

The radiating surface of the sun is called the **photosphere,** and just above it is the **chromosphere.** The chromosphere is visible to the naked eye only at times of total solar eclipses, appearing then to be a pinkish-violet layer with occasional great prominences projecting above its general level. With proper instruments the chromosphere can be seen or photographed whenever the sun is visible without waiting for a total eclipse. Above the chromosphere is the **corona,** also visible to the naked eye only at times of total eclipse. Instruments also permit the brighter portions of the corona to be studied whenever conditions are favorable. The pearly light of the corona surges millions of miles from the sun. Iron, nickel, and calcium are believed to be principal contributors to the composition of the corona, all in a state of extreme attenuation and high ionization that indicates temperatures on the order of a million degrees Fahrenheit.

Sunspots

There is an intimate connection between sunspots and the corona. At times of low sunspot activity, the fine streamers of the corona will be much longer above the sun's equator than over the polar regions of the sun, while during high sunspot activity, the corona extends fairly evenly outward from all regions of the sun, but to a much greater distance in space. Sunspots are dark, irregularly-shaped regions whose diameters may reach tens of thousands of miles. The average life of a sunspot group is from two to three weeks, but there have been groups that have lasted for more than a year, being carried repeatedly around as the sun rotated upon its axis. The record for the duration of a sunspot is 18 months. Sunspots reach a low point every 11.3 years, with a peak of activity occurring irregularly between two successive minima.

The sun is 400,000 times as bright as the full moon and gives the earth 6 million times as much light as do all the other stars put together. Actually, most of the stars that can be easily seen on any clear night are brighter than the sun.

The Zodiac

The sun's apparent yearly path among the stars is known as the **ecliptic.** The zone 16° wide, 8° on each side of the ecliptic, is known as the **zodiac.** Inside of this zone are the apparent paths of the sun, moon, earth, and major planets. Beginning at the point on the ecliptic which marks the position of the sun at the vernal equinox, and thence proceeding eastward, the zodiac is divided into twelve signs of 30° each, as shown herewith.

These signs are named from the twelve constellations of the zodiac with which the signs coincided in the time of the astronomer Hipparchus, about 2,000 years ago. Owing to the precession of the equinoxes, that is to say, to the retrograde motion of the equinoxes along the ecliptic, each sign in the zodiac has, in the course of 2,000 years, moved backward 30° into the constellation west of it; so that the sign Aries is now in the constellation Pisces, and so on. The vernal equinox will move from Pisces into Aquarius about the middle of the 26th century. The signs of the zodiac with their Latin and English names are as follows:

Spring	1.	♈ Aries.	The Ram.
	2.	♉ Taurus.	The Bull.
	3.	♊ Gemini.	The Twins.
Summer	4.	♋ Cancer.	The Crab.
	5.	♌ Leo.	The Lion.
	6.	♍ Virgo.	The Virgin.
Autumn	7.	♎ Libra.	The Balance.
	8.	♏ Scorpius.	The Scorpion.
	9.	♐ Sagittarius.	The Archer.
Winter	10.	♑ Capricorn.	The Goat.
	11.	♒ Aquarius.	The Water Bearer.
	12.	♓ Pisces.	The Fishes.

Moon's Perigee and Apogee, 1991

			Perigee						Apogee		
Date	GMT	EST	Date	GMT	EST	Date	GMT	EST	Date	GMT	EST
			Perigee						**Apogee**		
Date	**GMT**	**EST**	**Date**	**GMT**	**EST**	**Date**	**GMT**	**EST**	**Date**	**GMT**	**EST**
Jan. . . .	28	09	04	Aug. . .	8	18	13	Jan. . . .	12	11	06	July . . .	24	11	06
Feb. . . .	25	01	20*	Sept. . .	5	19	14	Feb. . . .	9	04	23*	Aug. . .	20	23	18
Mar. . .	22	05	00	Oct. . . .	2	18	15	Mar. . .	9	01	20*	Sept. . .	17	15	10
Apr. . . .	17	17	12	Oct. . . .	27	16	11	Apr. . . .	5	21	16	Oct. . . .	15	11	06
May . .	15	17	12	Nov. . .	24	09	04	May . .	3	15	10	Nov. . .	12	08	03
June . .	13	00	19*	Dec. . .	22	09	04	May . .	31	03	22*	Dec. . .	10	02	21*
July . . .	11	10	05					June . .	27	07	02				

*Previous day

Astronomical Constants; Speed of Light

The following were adopted in 1968, in accordance with the resolutions and recommendations of the International Astronomical Union (Hamburg 1964): Speed of light, 299,792.5 kilometers per second, or about 186,282.3976 statute miles per second; solar parallax, 8".794; constant of nutation, 9".210; and constant of aberration, 20".496.

The Moon

The moon completes a circuit around the earth in a period whose mean or average duration is 27 days 7 hours 43.2 minutes. This is the moon's sidereal period. Because of the motion of the moon in common with the earth around the sun, the mean duration of the lunar month — the period from one new moon to the next new moon — is 29 days 12 hours 44.05 minutes. This is the moon's synodical period.

The mean distance of the moon from the earth according to the American Ephemeris is 238,857 miles. Because the orbit of the moon about the earth is not circular but elliptical, however, the maximum distance from the earth that the moon may reach is 252,710 miles and the least distance is 221,463 miles. All distances are from the center of one object to the center of the other.

The moon's diameter is 2,160 miles. If we deduct the radius of the moon, 1,080 miles, and the radius of the earth, 3,963 miles from the minimum distance or perigee, given above, we shall have for the nearest approach of the bodies' surfaces 216,420 miles.

The moon rotates on its axis in a period of time exactly equal to its sidereal revolution about the earth — 27.321666 days. The moon's revolution about the earth is irregular because of its elliptical orbit. The moon's rotation, however, is regular and this, together with the irregular revolution, produces what is called "libration in longitude" which permits us to see first farther around the east side and then farther around the west side of the moon. The moon's variation north or south of the ecliptic permits us to see farther over first one pole and then the other of the moon and this is "libration in latitude." These two libration effects permit us to see a total of about 60% of the moon's surface over a period of time. The hidden side of the moon was photographed in 1959 by the Soviet space vehicle Lunik III. Since then many excellent pictures of nearly all of the moon's surface have been transmitted to earth by Lunar Orbiters launched by the U.S.

The tides are caused mainly by the moon, because of its proximity to the earth. The ratio of the tide-raising power of the moon to that of the sun is 11 to 5.

Harvest Moon and Hunter's Moon

The Harvest Moon, the full moon nearest the Autumnal Equinox, ushers in a period of several successive days when the moon rises soon after sunset. This phenomenon gives farmers in temperate latitudes extra hours of light in which to harvest their crops before frost and winter come. The 1991 Harvest Moon falls on Sept. 23 GMT. Harvest moon in the south temperate latitudes falls on Mar. 30.

The next full moon after Harvest Moon is called the Hunter's Moon, accompanied by a similar phenomenon but less marked; — Oct. 23, northern hemisphere; Apr. 28, southern hemisphere.

The Earth: Size, Computation of Time, Seasons

Size and Dimensions

The earth is the fifth largest planet and the third from the sun. Its mass is 6 sextillion, 588 quintillion short tons. Using the parameters of an ellipsoid adopted by the International Astronomical Union in 1964 and recognized by the International Union of Geodesy and Geophysics in 1967, the length of the equator is 24,901.55 miles, the length of a meridian is 24,859.82 miles, the equatorial diameter is 7,926.41 miles, and the area of this reference ellipsoid is approximately 196,938,800 square miles.

The earth is considered a solid, rigid mass with a dense core of magnetic, probably metallic material. The outer part of the core is probably liquid. Around the core is a thick shell or mantle of heavy crystalline rock which in turn is covered by a thin crust forming the solid granite and basalt base of the continents and ocean basins. Over broad areas of the earth's surface the crust has a thin cover of sedimentary rock such as sandstone, shale, and limestone formed by weathering of the earth's surface and deposition of sands, clays, and plant and animal remains.

The temperature in the earth increases about 1°F. with every 100 to 200 feet in depth, in the upper 100 kilometers of the earth, and the temperature near the core is believed to be near the melting point of the core materials under the conditions at that depth. The heat of the earth is believed to be derived from radioactivity in the rocks, pressures developed within the earth, and original heat (if the earth in fact was formed at high temperatures).

Atmosphere of the Earth

The earth's atmosphere is a blanket composed of nitrogen, oxygen, and argon, in amounts of about 78, 21, and 1% by volume. Also present in minute quantities are carbon dioxide, hydrogen, neon, helium, krypton, and xenon.

Water vapor displaces other gases and varies from nearly zero to about 4% by volume. The height of the ozone layer varies from approximately 12 to 21 miles above the earth. Traces exist as low as 6 miles and as high as 35 miles. Traces of methane have been found.

The atmosphere rests on the earth's surface with the weight equivalent to a layer of water 34 ft. deep. For about 300,000 ft. upward the gases remain in the proportions stated. Gravity holds the gases to the earth. The weight of the air compresses it at the bottom, so that the greatest density is at the earth's surface. Pressure, as well as density, decreases as height increases because the weight pressing upon any layer is always less than that pressing upon the layers below.

The temperature of the air drops with increased height until the tropopause is reached. This may vary from 25,000 to 60,000 ft. The atmosphere below the tropopause is the troposphere; the atmosphere for about twenty miles above the tropopause is the stratosphere, where the temperature generally increases with height except at high latitudes in winter. A temperature maximum near the 30-mile level is called the stratopause. Above this boundary is the mesosphere where the temperature decreases with height to a minimum, the **mesopause**, at a height of 50 miles. Extending above the mesosphere to the outer fringes of the atmosphere is the **thermosphere**, a region where temperature increases with height to a value measured in thousands of degrees Fahrenheit. The lower portion of this region, extending from 50 to about 400 miles in altitude, is characterized by a high ion density, and is thus called the **ionosphere**. The outer region is called **exosphere**; this is the region where gas molecules traveling at high speed may escape into outer space, above 600 miles.

Latitude, Longitude

Position on the globe is measured by means of meridians and parallels. Meridians, which are imaginary lines drawn around the earth through the poles, determine **longitude**. The meridian running through Greenwich, England, is the **prime meridian of longitude**, and all others are either east or west. Parallels, which are imaginary circles parallel with the equator, determine **latitude**. The length of a degree of longitude varies as the cosine of the latitude. At the equator a degree is 69.171 statute miles; this is gradually reduced toward the poles. Value of a longitude degree at the poles is zero.

Latitude is reckoned by the number of degrees north or south of the equator, an imaginary circle on the earth's surface everywhere equidistant between the two poles. According to the IAU Ellipsoid of 1964, the length of a degree of latitude is 68.708 statute miles at the equator and varies slightly north and south because of the oblate form of the globe; at the poles it is 69.403 statute miles.

Computation of Time

The earth rotates on its axis and follows an elliptical orbit around the sun. The rotation makes the sun appear to move across the sky from East to West. It determines day and night and the complete rotation, in relation to the sun, is called the **apparent** or **true solar day**. This varies but an average determines the **mean solar day** of 24 hours.

The mean solar day is in universal use for civil purposes. It may be obtained from apparent solar time by correcting observations of the sun for the equation of time, but when high precision is required, the mean solar time is calculated from its relation to sidereal time. These relations are extremely complicated, but for most practical uses, they may be considered as follows:

Sidereal time is the measure of time defined by the diurnal motion of the vernal equinox, and is determined from observation of the meridian transits of stars. One complete rotation of the earth relative to the equinox is called the **sidereal day**. The **mean sidereal day** is 23 hours, 56 minutes, 4.091 seconds of mean solar time.

The **Calendar Year** begins at 12 o'clock midnight precisely local clock time, on the night of Dec. 31-Jan. 1. The day and the calendar month also begin at midnight by the clock. The interval required for the earth to make one absolute revolution around the sun is a **sidereal year**; it consisted of 365 days, 6 hours, 9 minutes, and 9.5 seconds of mean solar time (approximately 24 hours per day) in 1900, and is increasing at the rate of 0.0001-second annually.

The **Tropical Year**, on which the return of the seasons depends, is the interval between two consecutive returns of the sun to the vernal equinox. The tropical year consists of 365 days, 5 hours, 48 minutes, and 46 seconds in 1900. It is decreasing at the rate of 0.530 seconds per century.

In 1956 the unit of time interval was defined to be identical with the second of **Ephemeris Time**, 1/31,556,925.9747 of the tropical year for 1900 January Od 12th hour E.T. A physical definition of the second based on a quantum transition of cesium (atomic second) was adopted in 1964. The atomic second is equal to 9,192,631,770 cycles of the emitted radiation. In 1967 this atomic second was adopted as the unit of time interval for the Intern'l System of Units.

The Zones and Seasons

The five zones of the earth's surface are Torrid, lying between the Tropics of Cancer and Capricorn; North Temperate, between Cancer and the Arctic Circle; South Temperate, between Capricorn and the Antarctic Circle; The Frigid Zones, between the polar Circles and the Poles.

The inclination or tilt of the earth's axis with respect to the sun determines the seasons. These are commonly marked in the North Temperate Zone, where spring begins at the vernal equinox, summer at the summer solstice, autumn at the autumnal equinox and winter at the winter solstice.

In the South Temperate Zone, the seasons are reversed. Spring begins at the autumnal equinox, summer at the winter solstice, etc.

If the earth's axis were perpendicular to the plane of the earth's orbit around the sun there would be no change of seasons. Day and night would be of nearly constant length and there would be equable conditions of temperature. But the axis is tilted 23° 27' away from a perpendicular to the orbit and only in March and September is the axis at right angles to the sun.

The points at which the sun crosses the equator are the equinoxes, when day and night are most nearly equal. The points at which the sun is at a maximum distance from the equator are the solstices. Days and nights are then most unequal.

In June the North Pole is tilted 23° 27' toward the sun and the days in the northern hemisphere are longer than the nights, while the days in the southern hemisphere are shorter than the nights. In December the North Pole is tilted 23° 27' away from the sun and the situation is reversed.

The Seasons in 1991

In 1991 the 4 seasons will begin as follows: add one hour to EST for Atlantic Time; subtract one hour for Central, two hours for Mountain, 3 hours for Pacific, 4 hours for Yukon, 5 hours for Alaska-Hawaii and six hours for Bering Time. Also shown in Greenwich Mean Time.

		Date	GMT	EST
Vernal Equinox	Spring	Mar. 21	3:02	22:02*
Summer Solstice	Summer	June 21	21:19	16:19
Autumnal Equinox	Autumn	Sept. 23	12:48	7:48
Winter Solstice	Winter	Dec. 22	8:54	3:54

*Previous Day

Poles of The Earth

The geographic (rotation) poles, or points where the earth's axis of rotation cuts the surface, are not absolutely fixed in the body of the earth. The pole of rotation describes an irregular curve about its mean position.

Two periods have been detected in this motion: (1) an annual period due to seasonal changes in barometric pressure, load of ice and snow on the surface and to other phenomena of seasonal character; (2) a period of about 14 months due to the shape and constitution of the earth.

In addition there are small but as yet unpredictable irregularities. The whole motion is so small that the actual pole at any time remains within a circle of 30 or 40 feet in radius centered at the mean position of the pole.

The pole of rotation for the time being is of course the pole having a latitude of 90° and an indeterminate longitude.

Magnetic Poles

The **north magnetic pole** of the earth is that region where the magnetic force is vertically downward and the **south magnetic pole** that region where the magnetic force is vertically upward. A compass placed at the magnetic poles experiences no directive force in azimuth.

There are slow changes in the distribution of the earth's magnetic field. These changes were at one time attributed in part to a periodic movement of the magnetic poles around the geographical poles, but later evidence refutes this theory and points, rather, to a slow migration of "disturbance" foci over the earth.

There appear shifts in position of the magnetic poles due to the changes in the earth's magnetic field. The center of the area designated as the north magnetic pole was estimated to be in about latitude 70.5° N and longitude 96° W in 1905; from recent nearby measurements and studies of the secular changes, the position in 1970 is estimated as latitude 76.2° N and longitude 101° W. Improved data rather than actual motion account for at least part of the change.

The position of the south magnetic pole in 1912 was near 71° S and longitude 150° E; the position in 1970 is estimated at latitude 66° S and longitude 139.1° E.

The direction of the horizontal components of the magnetic field at any point is known as magnetic north at that point, and the angle by which it deviates east or west of true north is known as the magnetic declination, or in the mariner's terminology, the **variation of the compass.**

A compass without error points in the direction of magnetic north. (In general this is *not* the direction of the magnetic north pole.) If one follows the direction indicated by the north end of the compass, he will travel along a rather irregular curve which eventually reaches the north magnetic pole (though not usually by a great-circle route). However, the action of the compass should not be thought of as due to any influence of the distant pole, but simply as an indication of the distribution of the earth's magnetism at the place of observation.

Rotation of The Earth

The **speed** of rotation of the earth about its axis has been found to be slightly variable. The variations may be classified as:

(A) **Secular.** Tidal friction acts as a brake on the rotation and causes a slow secular increase in the length of the day, about 1 millisecond per century.

(B) **Irregular.** The speed of rotation may increase for a number of years, about 5 to 10, and then start decreasing. The maximum difference from the mean in the length of the day during a century is about 5 milliseconds. The accumulated difference in time has amounted to approximately 44 seconds since 1900. The cause is probably motion in the interior of the earth.

(C) **Periodic.** Seasonal variations exist with periods of one year and six months. The cumulative effect is such that each year the earth is late about 30 milliseconds near June 1 and is ahead about 30 milliseconds near Oct. 1. The maximum seasonal variation in the length of the day is about 0.5 millisecond. It is believed that the principal cause of the annual variation is the seasonal change in the wind patterns of the Northern and Southern Hemispheres. The semiannual variation is due chiefly to tidal action of the sun, which distorts the shape of the earth slightly.

The secular and irregular variations were discovered by comparing time based on the rotation of the earth with time based on the orbital motion of the moon about the earth and of the planets about the sun. The periodic variation was determined largely with the aid of quartz-crystal clocks. The introduction of the cesium-beam atomic clock in 1955 made it possible to determine in greater detail than before the nature of the irregular and periodic variations.

Morning and Evening Stars, 1991

(GMT)

	Morning	Evening		Morning	Evening
Jan.	Mercury from Jan. 9	Mercury Jan. 1 to Jan. 9	**Apr.**	Venus	Mercury
	Venus from Jan. 18	Venus Jan. 1 to Jan. 18		Mars	Jupiter
	Mars Jan. 1	Jupiter Jan. 1		Saturn	
	Uranus Jan. 1	Saturn Jan. 1 to Jan. 6		Uranus	
	Neptune from Jan. 2	Neptune to Jan. 2		Neptune	
	Pluto Jan. 1			Pluto	
Feb.	Mercury		**May**	Mercury from May 3	Mercury to May 3
	Venus			Venus	Jupiter
	Mars			Mars	Pluto from May 7
	Saturn	Jupiter		Saturn	
	Uranus			Uranus	
	Neptune			Neptune	
	Pluto			Pluto to May 7	
Mar.	Mercury to Mar. 20	Mercury from Mar. 20	**June**	Mercury	Jupiter
	Venus	Jupiter		Venus	Uranus from June 29
	Mars			Mars	Pluto
	Saturn			Saturn	
	Uranus			Uranus to June 29	
	Neptune			Neptune	
	Pluto				

	Morning	Evening		Morning	Evening
July	Mercury to July 2	Mercury from July 2	Oct.	Mercury to Oct. 21	Mercury from Oct. 21
	Venus	Jupiter to July 15		Venus	Saturn
	Mars	Saturn from July 14		Mars	Uranus
	Jupiter from July 15	Uranus		Jupiter	Neptune
	Saturn to July 14	Neptune from July 5			Pluto
	Neptune to July 5	Pluto	Nov.	Venus to Nov. 1	Mercury
Aug.	Venus	Mercury		Mars to Nov. 27	Venus from Nov. 1
	Mars	Saturn		Jupiter	Mars from Nov. 27
	Jupiter	Uranus		Pluto from Nov. 10	Uranus
		Neptune			Neptune
		Pluto			Pluto to Nov. 10
Sept.	Mercury from Sept. 8	Mercury to Sept. 8	Dec.	Mercury from Dec. 24	Mercury to Dec. 24
	Venus	Saturn		Jupiter	Venus
	Mars	Uranus		Uranus from Dec. 31	Mars
	Jupiter	Neptune		Pluto	Saturn
		Pluto			Uranus to Dec. 31
					Neptune

Astronomical Twilight—Meridian of Greenwich

Date 1991		20° Begin h m	End h m	30° Begin h m	End h m	40° Begin h m	End h m	50° Begin h m	End h m	60° Begin h m	End h m
Jan.	1	5 16	6 50	5 30	6 35	5 45	6 21	6 00	6 07	6 18	5 49
	11	5 19	6 56	5 33	6 43	5 46	6 30	6 00	6 17	6 15	6 01
	21	5 21	7 01	5 32	6 51	5 43	6 40	5 55	6 30	6 06	6 18
Feb.	1	5 21	7 07	5 29	6 58	5 38	6 51	5 45	6 44	5 51	6 38
	11	5 18	7 11	5 24	7 05	5 29	7 01	5 32	6 59	5 32	7 01
	21	5 13	7 15	5 17	7 12	5 17	7 12	5 16	7 14	5 09	7 23
Mar.	1	5 08	7 18	5 08	7 19	5 06	7 21	4 59	7 29	4 44	7 45
	11	5 00	7 21	4 58	7 24	4 50	7 32	4 38	7 46	4 12	8 12
	21	4 52	7 24	4 45	7 32	4 33	7 44	4 14	8 04	3 37	8 43
Apr.	1	4 42	7 28	4 31	7 39	4 14	7 57	3 47	8 25	2 53	9 21
	11	4 32	7 32	4 18	7 47	3 56	8 09	3 20	8 47	2 03	10 10
	21	4 23	7 36	4 04	7 54	3 37	8 23	2 52	9 11	0 37	11 47
May	1	4 14	7 41	3 52	8 04	3 19	8 37	2 22	9 39		
	11	4 08	7 46	3 41	8 13	3 03	8 53	1 49	10 09		
	21	4 02	7 52	3 32	8 22	2 48	9 07	1 13	10 46		
June	1	3 58	7 58	3 26	8 30	2 36	9 20	0 21	11 52		
	11	3 56	8 03	3 22	8 36	2 29	9 30				
	21	3 57	8 06	3 22	8 40	2 28	9 35				
July	1	3 59	8 07	3 25	8 41	2 30	9 35				
	11	4 03	8 06	3 30	8 39	2 40	9 30				
	21	4 08	8 03	3 39	8 33	2 52	9 18	1 12	11 23		
Aug.	1	4 15	7 56	3 48	8 23	3 09	9 01	1 49	10 20		
	11	4 20	7 50	3 56	8 13	3 22	8 46	2 21	9 46		
	21	4 24	7 41	4 05	8 01	3 34	8 27	2 47	9 15		
Sept.	1	4 29	7 31	4 14	7 46	3 51	8 08	3 13	8 43	1 40	10 02
	11	4 32	7 20	4 20	7 33	4 02	7 50	3 33	8 16	2 36	9 12
	21	4 35	7 11	4 26	7 19	4 14	7 31	3 52	7 52	3 11	8 31
Oct.	1	4 38	7 02	4 33	7 05	4 25	7 13	4 10	7 28	3 41	7 54
	11	4 40	6 53	4 40	6 53	4 35	6 58	4 26	7 05	4 07	7 23
	21	4 43	6 47	4 45	6 44	4 45	6 43	4 41	6 46	4 32	6 55
Nov.	1	4 46	6 41	4 52	6 34	4 56	6 30	4 58	6 27	4 56	6 27
	11	4 50	6 38	4 59	6 28	5 06	6 21	5 13	6 14	5 17	6 08
	21	4 55	6 36	5 06	6 25	5 16	6 15	5 26	6 04	5 37	5 52
Dec.	1	5 00	6 37	5 13	6 24	5 25	6 11	5 38	5 58	5 53	5 42
	11	5 06	6 40	5 20	6 26	5 34	6 12	5 48	5 57	6 06	5 38
	21	5 11	6 45	5 25	6 30	5 39	6 16	5 55	6 00	6 15	5 40
	31	5 15	6 50	5 30	6 35	5 44	6 21	6 00	6 06	6 18	5 48

Chronological Eras, 1991

The year 1991 of the Christian Era comprises the latter part of the 215th and the beginning of the 216th year of the independence of the United States of America.

Era	Year	Begins in 1991		Era	Year	Begins in 1991	
				Japanese	2651	Jan.	1
Byzantine	7500	Sept.	14	Grecian	2303	Sept.	14
Jewish	5752	Sept.	8	(Seleucidae)		or Oct.	14
		(sunset)		Diocletian	1708	Sept.	12
Roman (Ab Urbe Condita)	2744	Jan.	14	Indian (Saka)	1913	Mar.	22
Nabonassar (Babylonian)	2740	Apr.	26	Mohammedan (Hegira)	1412	July	22

Chronological Cycles, 1991

Dominical Letter	F	Golden Number (Lunar Cycle)	XVI	Roman Indiction	14
Epact	14	Solar Cycle	12	Julian Period (year of)	6704

1st Month   January, 1991   31 days

Greenwich Mean Time

NOTE: Light numbers indicate Sun. Dark numbers indicate **Moon.** *Degrees are North Latitude.*

FM = full moon; LQ = last quarter; NM = new moon; FQ = first quarter.

CAUTION: Must be converted to local time. For instructions see page 268.

Day of month / week / year	Sun on Meridian / Moon phase (h m s)	Sun's Declination (° ')	20° Rise Sun/Moon (h m)	20° Set Sun/Moon (h m)	30° Rise Sun/Moon (h m)	30° Set Sun/Moon (h m)	40° Rise Sun/Moon (h m)	40° Set Sun/Moon (h m)	50° Rise Sun/Moon (h m)	50° Set Sun/Moon (h m)	60° Rise Sun/Moon (h m)	60° Set Sun/Moon (h m)
1 Tu	12 3 24	− 23 4	6 35	17 32	6 56	17 11	7 22	16 45	7 59	16 08	9 03	15 04
1			18 31	7 11	18 11	7 33	17 45	8 00	17 08	8 39	16 04	9 47
2 We	12 3 52	− 22 59	6 35	17 32	6 56	17 12	7 22	16 46	7 59	16 09	9 02	15 06
2			19 37	8 04	19 22	8 21	19 03	8 43	18 36	9 12	17 52	10 00
3 Th	12 4 20	− 22 53	6 36	17 33	6 56	17 12	7 22	16 47	7 58	16 10	9 01	15 07
3			20 39	8 50	20 29	9 02	20 17	9 17	20 01	9 37	19 34	10 08
4 Fr	12 4 47	− 22 48	6 36	17 34	6 56	17 13	7 22	16 48	7 58	16 12	9 01	15 09
4			21 37	9 31	21 33	9 37	21 28	9 46	21 21	9 57	21 10	10 13
5 Sa	12 5 14	− 22 42	6 36	17 34	6 57	17 14	7 22	16 49	7 58	16 13	9 00	15 11
5			22 32	10 08	22 33	10 10	22 35	10 11	22 37	10 13	22 40	10 16
6 Su	12 5 41	− 22 35	6 36	17 35	6 57	17 15	7 22	16 49	7 58	16 14	8 59	15 12
6			23 24	10 44	23 31	10 40	23 39	10 35	23 50	10 29	– –	10 19
7 Mo	12 6 7	− 22 28	6 37	17 36	6 57	17 16	7 22	16 50	7 57	16 15	8 58	15 14
7	18 35 LQ		– –	11 19	– –	11 10	– –	11 00	– –	10 45	0 08	10 23
8 Tu	12 6 33	− 22 20	6 37	17 36	6 57	17 16	7 22	16 51	7 57	16 16	8 57	15 16
8			0 16	11 55	0 28	11 42	0 42	11 25	1 02	11 02	1 34	10 27
9 We	12 6 58	− 22 12	6 37	17 37	6 57	17 17	7 22	16 52	7 57	16 18	8 56	15 18
9			1 08	12 33	1 24	12 15	1 44	11 53	2 13	11 23	3 00	10 32
10 Th	12 7 23	− 22 4	6 37	17 38	6 57	17 18	7 22	16 53	7 56	16 19	8 55	15 20
10			2 01	13 14	2 21	12 52	2 46	12 25	3 22	11 48	4 26	10 42
11 Fr	12 7 47	− 21 55	6 37	17 38	6 57	17 19	7 21	16 54	7 56	16 20	8 54	15 22
11			2 53	13 58	3 17	13 34	3 46	13 03	4 29	12 19	5 49	10 58
12 Sa	12 8 11	− 21 46	6 37	17 39	6 57	17 20	7 21	16 55	7 55	16 22	8 53	15 24
12			3 46	14 45	4 11	14 20	4 43	13 47	5 30	12 59	7 03	11 27
13 Su	12 8 34	− 21 36	6 38	17 40	6 57	17 20	7 21	16 56	7 54	16 23	8 51	15 26
13			4 37	15 36	5 03	15 10	5 36	14 38	6 24	13 50	7 59	12 15
14 Mo	12 8 56	− 21 26	6 38	17 40	6 57	17 21	7 21	16 58	7 54	16 24	8 50	15 28
14			5 26	16 29	5 51	16 05	6 22	15 34	7 08	14 50	8 34	13 25
15 Tu	12 9 18	− 21 15	6 38	17 41	6 57	17 22	7 20	16 59	7 53	16 26	8 48	15 31
15	23 50 NM		6 12	17 23	6 34	17 01	7 03	16 35	7 43	15 56	8 53	14 48
16 We	12 9 39	− 21 4	6 38	17 42	6 57	17 23	7 20	17 00	7 52	16 27	8 47	15 33
16			6 55	18 16	7 14	17 59	7 37	17 37	8 10	17 07	9 05	16 15
17 Th	12 9 59	− 20 53	6 38	17 42	6 56	17 24	7 19	17 01	7 52	16 29	8 45	15 35
17			7 34	19 09	7 49	18 56	8 07	18 40	8 32	18 18	9 11	17 42
18 Fr	12 10 19	− 20 41	6 38	17 43	6 56	17 25	7 19	17 02	7 51	16 30	8 44	15 38
18			8 11	20 01	8 21	19 54	8 33	19 44	8 50	19 30	9 16	19 09
19 Sa	12 10 38	− 20 29	6 38	17 44	6 56	17 25	7 19	17 03	7 50	16 32	8 42	15 40
19			8 46	20 53	8 51	20 51	8 58	20 47	9 06	20 43	9 19	20 35
20 Su	12 10 56	− 20 17	6 38	17 44	6 56	17 26	7 18	17 04	7 49	16 34	8 40	15 42
20			9 21	21 46	9 21	21 49	9 21	21 52	9 21	21 56	9 22	22 02
21 Mo	12 11 14	− 20 4	6 38	17 45	6 55	17 27	7 17	17 05	7 48	16 35	8 38	15 45
21			9 56	22 40	9 51	22 48	9 45	22 58	9 37	23 11	9 25	23 32
22 Tu	12 11 30	− 19 50	6 38	17 45	6 55	17 28	7 17	17 07	7 47	16 37	8 36	15 47
22			10 34	23 37	10 24	23 50	10 11	– –	9 54	– –	9 29	– –
23 We	12 11 46	− 19 37	6 38	17 46	6 55	17 29	7 16	17 08	7 46	16 38	8 34	15 50
23	14 21 FQ		11 15	– –	11 00	– –	10 41	0 06	10 15	0 29	9 34	1 06
24 Th	12 12 1	− 19 23	6 37	17 47	6 54	17 30	7 16	17 09	7 45	16 40	8 33	15 52
24			12 01	0 37	11 41	0 55	11 16	1 18	10 42	1 50	9 44	2 45
25 Fr	12 12 16	− 19 8	6 37	17 47	6 54	17 31	7 15	17 10	7 43	16 42	8 30	15 55
25			12 54	1 40	12 30	2 03	12 01	2 31	11 18	3 12	10 01	4 27
26 Sa	12 12 29	− 18 54	6 37	17 48	6 54	17 31	7 14	17 11	7 42	16 43	8 28	15 57
26			13 54	2 46	13 28	3 11	12 55	3 43	12 08	4 30	10 36	6 01
27 Su	12 12 42	− 18 38	6 37	17 49	6 53	17 32	7 13	17 12	7 41	16 45	8 26	16 00
27			14 59	3 51	14 34	4 17	14 01	4 49	13 14	5 37	11 42	7 09
28 Mo	12 12 53	− 18 23	6 37	17 49	6 53	17 33	7 13	17 14	7 40	16 47	8 24	16 02
28			16 07	4 52	15 44	5 16	15 15	5 46	14 34	6 29	13 18	7 47
29 Tu	12 13 4	− 18 7	6 37	17 50	6 52	17 34	7 12	17 15	7 38	16 48	8 22	16 05
29			17 14	5 48	16 56	6 08	16 33	6 33	16 01	7 08	15 06	8 06
30 We	12 13 15	− 17 51	6 36	17 50	6 52	17 35	7 11	17 16	7 37	16 50	8 20	16 08
30	6 10 FM		18 18	6 37	18 05	6 52	17 50	7 11	17 28	7 36	16 52	8 16
31 Th	12 13 24	− 17 35	6 36	17 51	6 51	17 36	7 10	17 17	7 36	16 52	8 17	16 10
31			19 19	7 21	19 12	7 31	19 03	7 43	18 51	7 58	18 33	8 22

2nd Month   February, 1991   28 days

Greenwich Mean Time

NOTE: Light numbers indicate Sun. **Dark** numbers indicate **Moon**. *Degrees are North Latitude.*

FM = full moon; LQ = last quarter; NM = new moon; FQ = first quarter.

CAUTION: Must be converted to local time. For instructions see page 268.

Day of month week year	Sun on Meridian / Moon phase (h m s)	Sun's Declination (° ')	20° Rise Sun/Moon	20° Set Sun/Moon	30° Rise Sun/Moon	30° Set Sun/Moon	40° Rise Sun/Moon	40° Set Sun/Moon	50° Rise Sun/Moon	50° Set Sun/Moon	60° Rise Sun/Moon	60° Set Sun/Moon
1 Fr 32	12 13 33	−17 18	6 36	17 52	6 51	17 37	7 09	17 18	7 34	16 53	8 15	16 13
			20 17	8 01	20 15	8 05	20 14	8 10	20 11	8 17	20 08	8 27
2 Sa 33	12 13 40	−17 1	6 35	17 52	6 50	17 38	7 08	17 20	7 33	16 55	8 13	16 15
			21 12	8 39	21 16	8 37	21 21	8 36	21 28	8 33	21 39	8 30
3 Su 34	12 13 47	−16 44	6 35	17 53	6 49	17 38	7 07	17 21	7 31	16 57	8 10	16 18
			22 06	9 15	22 15	9 09	22 27	9 01	22 43	8 50	23 08	8 33
4 Mo 35	12 13 54	−16 26	6 35	17 53	6 49	17 39	7 06	17 22	7 30	16 58	8 08	16 21
			22 59	9 52	23 13	9 40	23 31	9 26	23 56	9 07	− −	8 37
5 Tu 36	12 13 59	−16 8	6 34	17 54	6 48	17 40	7 05	17 23	7 28	17 00	8 05	16 23
			23 52	10 30	− −	10 14	− −	9 54	− −	9 26	0 37	8 42
6 We 37	12 14 3 / 13 52 LQ	−15 50	6 34	17 54	6 47	17 41	7 04	17 24	7 27	17 02	8 03	16 26
			− −	11 10	0 11	10 50	0 34	10 25	1 07	9 50	2 04	8 50
7 Th 38	12 14 7	−15 32	6 33	17 55	6 47	17 42	7 03	17 26	7 25	17 04	8 01	16 29
			0 46	11 53	1 08	11 30	1 36	11 01	2 16	10 19	3 30	9 03
8 Fr 39	12 14 10	−15 13	6 33	17 56	6 46	17 43	7 02	17 27	7 24	17 05	7 58	16 31
			1 39	12 40	2 03	12 14	2 35	11 42	3 20	10 56	4 49	9 26
9 Sa 40	12 14 12	−14 54	6 33	17 56	6 45	17 43	7 01	17 28	7 22	17 07	7 55	16 34
			2 30	13 29	2 56	13 03	3 29	12 30	4 17	11 42	5 52	10 07
10 Su 41	12 14 14	−14 35	6 32	17 57	6 45	17 44	7 00	17 29	7 20	17 09	7 53	16 37
			3 20	14 21	3 46	13 56	4 18	13 25	5 05	12 39	6 35	11 09
11 Mo 42	12 14 15	−14 16	6 32	17 57	6 44	17 45	6 59	17 30	7 19	17 11	7 50	16 39
			4 07	15 15	4 31	14 52	5 00	14 24	5 43	13 43	6 59	12 28
12 Tu 43	12 14 15	−13 56	6 31	17 58	6 43	17 46	6 57	17 32	7 17	17 12	7 48	16 42
			4 51	16 09	5 12	15 50	5 37	15 26	6 13	14 52	7 13	13 54
13 We 44	12 14 14	−13 36	6 31	17 58	6 42	17 47	6 56	17 33	7 15	17 14	7 45	16 44
			5 32	17 02	5 48	16 48	6 09	16 30	6 37	16 04	7 22	15 23
14 Th 45	12 14 12 / 17 32 NM	−13 16	6 30	17 59	6 41	17 48	6 55	17 34	7 13	17 16	7 42	16 47
			6 10	17 55	6 22	17 46	6 37	17 34	6 56	17 17	7 27	16 51
15 Fr 46	12 14 10	−12 55	6 30	17 59	6 40	17 48	6 54	17 35	7 12	17 17	7 40	16 50
			6 47	18 48	6 53	18 44	7 02	18 38	7 13	18 30	7 31	18 18
16 Sa 47	12 14 7	−12 35	6 29	18 00	6 40	17 49	6 52	17 36	7 10	17 19	7 37	16 52
			7 22	19 42	7 24	19 42	7 26	19 43	7 29	19 44	7 34	19 46
17 Su 48	12 14 3	−12 14	6 28	18 00	6 39	17 50	6 51	17 38	7 08	17 21	7 34	16 55
			7 58	20 36	7 54	20 42	7 50	20 50	7 45	21 00	7 37	21 16
18 Mo 49	12 13 59	−11 53	6 28	18 00	6 38	17 51	6 50	17 39	7 06	17 23	7 31	16 58
			8 35	21 32	8 26	21 44	8 16	21 58	8 02	22 18	7 41	22 49
19 Tu 50	12 13 53	−11 32	6 27	18 01	6 37	17 51	6 48	17 40	7 04	17 24	7 29	17 00
			9 15	22 31	9 01	22 48	8 45	23 09	8 22	23 38	7 46	− −
20 We 51	12 13 48	−11 11	6 27	18 01	6 36	17 52	6 47	17 41	7 02	17 26	7 26	17 03
			9 59	23 33	9 41	23 54	9 18	− −	8 46	− −	7 54	0 27
21 Th 52	12 13 41 / 22 58 FQ	−10 49	6 26	18 02	6 35	17 53	6 46	17 42	7 00	17 28	7 23	17 05
			10 49	− −	10 27	− −	9 58	0 21	9 18	0 59	8 08	2 07
22 Fr 53	12 13 34	−10 27	6 25	18 02	6 34	17 54	6 44	17 43	6 58	17 29	7 20	17 08
			11 45	0 36	11 20	1 01	10 48	1 32	10 02	2 17	8 35	3 42
23 Sa 54	12 13 26	−10 6	6 25	18 03	6 33	17 54	6 43	17 44	6 57	17 31	7 17	17 11
			12 46	1 40	12 21	2 05	11 48	2 38	11 00	3 26	9 27	4 59
24 Su 55	12 13 18	−9 44	6 24	18 03	6 32	17 55	6 42	17 46	6 55	17 33	7 15	17 13
			13 51	2 40	13 27	3 05	12 57	3 37	12 12	4 22	10 50	5 46
25 Mo 56	12 13 8	−9 21	6 23	18 03	6 31	17 56	6 40	17 47	6 53	17 34	7 12	17 16
			14 56	3 37	14 36	3 58	14 10	4 26	13 34	5 04	12 30	6 11
26 Tu 57	12 12 59	−8 59	6 22	18 04	6 30	17 57	6 39	17 48	6 51	17 36	7 09	17 18
			16 00	4 27	15 45	4 45	15 26	5 06	14 59	5 36	14 15	6 24
27 We 58	12 12 49	−8 37	6 22	18 04	6 29	17 57	6 37	17 49	6 49	17 38	7 06	17 21
			17 01	5 12	16 52	5 25	16 39	5 40	16 22	6 00	15 56	6 32
28 Th 59	12 12 38 / 16 25 FM	−8 14	6 21	18 05	6 28	17 58	6 36	17 50	6 47	17 40	7 03	17 23
			18 00	5 54	17 56	6 01	17 51	6 09	17 44	6 20	17 33	6 37

3rd Month   March, 1991   31 days

Greenwich Mean Time

NOTE: Light numbers indicate Sun. **Dark** numbers indicate **Moon.** *Degrees are North Latitude.*

FM = full moon; LQ = last quarter; NM = new moon; FQ = first quarter.

CAUTION: Must be converted to local time. For instructions see page 268.

Day of month / week / year	Sun on Meridian / Moon phase (h m s)	Sun's Declina-tion (° ')	20° Rise Sun/Moon (h m)	20° Set Sun/Moon (h m)	30° Rise Sun/Moon (h m)	30° Set Sun/Moon (h m)	40° Rise Sun/Moon (h m)	40° Set Sun/Moon (h m)	50° Rise Sun/Moon (h m)	50° Set Sun/Moon (h m)	60° Rise Sun/Moon (h m)	60° Set Sun/Moon (h m)
1 Fr	12 12 26	− 7 52	6 20	18 05	6 27	17 59	6 34	17 51	6 45	17 41	7 00	17 26
60			18 57	6 32	18 58	6 34	19 00	6 35	19 02	6 37	19 06	6 41
2 Sa	12 12 14	− 7 29	6 20	18 05	6 26	17 59	6 33	17 52	6 42	17 43	6 57	17 28
61			19 52	7 09	19 58	7 06	20 07	7 01	20 18	6 54	20 37	6 44
3 Su	12 12 2	− 7 6	6 19	18 06	6 24	18 00	6 31	17 53	6 40	17 44	6 54	17 31
62			20 46	7 47	20 58	7 37	21 13	7 26	21 33	7 11	22 07	6 48
4 Mo	12 11 49	− 6 43	6 18	18 06	6 23	18 01	6 30	17 54	6 38	17 46	6 51	17 34
63			21 40	8 25	21 57	8 11	22 18	7 53	22 47	7 30	23 36	6 53
5 Tu	12 11 36	− 6 20	6 17	18 06	6 22	18 01	6 28	17 56	6 36	17 48	6 48	17 36
64			22 35	9 04	22 55	8 46	23 21	8 23	23 59	7 52	– –	7 00
6 We	12 11 22	− 5 57	6 16	18 07	6 21	18 02	6 27	17 57	6 34	17 49	6 45	17 39
65			23 29	9 47	23 52	9 25	– –	8 58	– –	8 19	1 04	7 11
7 Th	12 11 8	− 5 33	6 16	18 07	6 20	18 03	6 25	17 58	6 32	17 51	6 42	17 41
66			– –	10 33	– –	10 08	0 22	9 37	1 06	8 53	2 27	7 30
8 Fr	12 10 54	− 5 10	6 15	18 07	6 19	18 03	6 24	17 59	6 30	17 53	6 39	17 44
67	10 32 LQ		0 21	11 21	0 47	10 56	1 19	10 23	2 06	9 36	3 38	8 03
9 Sa	12 10 39	− 4 47	6 14	18 08	6 18	18 04	6 22	18 00	6 28	17 54	6 37	17 46
68			1 12	12 12	1 38	11 47	2 10	11 15	2 58	10 28	4 30	8 56
10 Su	12 10 24	− 4 23	6 13	18 08	6 17	18 05	6 21	18 01	6 26	17 56	6 34	17 49
69			2 01	13 05	2 25	12 42	2 55	12 12	3 39	11 29	5 01	10 08
11 Mo	12 10 8	− 3 60	6 12	18 08	6 15	18 05	6 19	18 02	6 24	17 58	6 31	17 51
70			2 45	13 58	3 07	13 38	3 34	13 12	4 12	12 36	5 19	11 31
12 Tu	12 9 53	− 3 36	6 11	18 09	6 14	18 06	6 17	18 03	6 21	17 59	6 28	17 54
71			3 27	14 52	3 45	14 36	4 08	14 15	4 39	13 46	5 30	12 58
13 We	12 9 37	− 3 13	6 11	18 09	6 13	18 07	6 16	18 04	6 19	18 01	6 25	17 56
72			4 06	15 45	4 20	15 34	4 37	15 19	5 00	14 59	5 37	14 26
14 Th	12 9 20	− 2 49	6 10	18 09	6 12	18 07	6 14	18 05	6 17	18 02	6 22	17 58
73			4 44	16 39	4 53	16 32	5 04	16 24	5 18	16 12	5 41	15 54
15 Fr	12 9 4	− 2 25	6 09	18 09	6 11	18 08	6 13	18 06	6 15	18 04	6 19	18 01
74			5 20	17 32	5 24	17 31	5 29	17 29	5 35	17 27	5 45	17 23
16 Sa	12 8 47	− 2 2	6 08	18 10	6 09	18 09	6 11	18 07	6 13	18 06	6 16	18 03
75	8 10 NM		5 56	18 27	5 55	18 31	5 53	18 36	5 51	18 43	5 48	18 53
17 Su	12 8 30	− 1 38	6 07	18 10	6 08	18 09	6 09	18 08	6 11	18 07	6 13	18 06
76			6 34	19 24	6 27	19 34	6 19	19 45	6 08	20 02	5 52	20 27
18 Mo	12 8 12	− 1 14	6 06	18 10	6 07	18 10	6 08	18 09	6 09	18 09	6 09	18 08
77			7 14	20 24	7 02	20 38	6 47	20 57	6 28	21 23	5 57	22 05
19 Tu	12 7 55	− 0 50	6 06	18 11	6 06	18 10	6 06	18 10	6 06	18 10	6 06	18 11
78			7 58	21 26	7 41	21 45	7 20	22 10	6 51	22 45	6 05	23 46
20 We	12 7 37	− 0 27	6 05	18 11	6 05	18 11	6 05	18 11	6 04	18 12	6 03	18 13
79			8 47	22 29	8 25	22 53	7 59	23 23	7 22	– –	6 18	– –
21 Th	12 7 20	− 0 3	6 04	18 11	6 03	18 12	6 03	18 12	6 02	18 14	6 00	18 16
80			9 41	23 33	9 17	23 59	8 46	– –	8 02	0 05	6 41	1 25
22 Fr	12 7 2	0 21	6 03	18 11	6 02	18 12	6 01	18 13	6 00	18 15	5 57	18 18
81			10 41	– –	10 15	– –	9 43	0 31	8 56	1 18	7 25	2 48
23 Sa	12 6 44	0 44	6 02	18 12	6 01	18 13	6 00	18 14	5 58	18 17	5 54	18 21
82	6 3 FQ		11 44	0 35	11 19	1 00	10 48	1 32	10 03	2 18	8 37	3 44
24 Su	12 6 26	1 8	6 01	18 12	6 00	18 14	5 58	18 16	5 55	18 18	5 51	18 23
83			12 48	1 31	12 26	1 54	11 59	2 23	11 20	3 03	10 11	4 15
25 Mo	12 6 8	1 32	6 00	18 12	5 59	18 14	5 56	18 17	5 53	18 20	5 48	18 25
84			13 50	2 22	13 33	2 41	13 12	3 05	12 42	3 37	11 52	4 31
26 Tu	12 5 49	1 55	5 59	18 13	5 57	18 15	5 55	18 18	5 51	18 22	5 45	18 28
85			14 51	3 08	14 39	3 22	14 24	3 40	14 04	4 03	13 31	4 40
27 We	12 5 31	2 19	5 59	18 13	5 56	18 15	5 53	18 19	5 49	18 23	5 42	18 30
86			15 49	3 50	15 42	3 59	15 34	4 10	15 23	4 24	15 06	4 47
28 Th	12 5 13	2 42	5 58	18 13	5 55	18 16	5 52	18 20	5 47	18 25	5 39	18 33
87			16 45	4 29	16 44	4 32	16 42	4 37	16 41	4 42	16 38	4 51
29 Fr	12 4 55	3 6	5 57	18 13	5 54	18 17	5 50	18 21	5 45	18 27	5 36	18 35
88			17 40	5 06	17 44	5 04	17 49	5 02	17 57	4 59	18 09	4 55
30 Sa	12 4 36	3 29	5 56	18 14	5 53	18 17	5 48	18 22	5 42	18 28	5 33	18 38
89	7 17 FM		18 34	5 42	18 43	5 35	18 55	5 27	19 12	5 16	19 38	4 59
31 Su	12 4 18	3 52	5 55	18 14	5 51	18 18	5 47	18 23	5 40	18 29	5 30	18 40
90			19 28	6 20	19 43	6 08	20 01	5 54	20 26	5 34	21 08	5 03

4th Month   **April, 1991**   **30 days**

Greenwich Mean Time

NOTE: Light numbers indicate Sun. **Dark** numbers indicate **Moon.** *Degrees are North Latitude.*

FM = full moon; LQ = last quarter; NM = new moon; FQ = first quarter.

CAUTION: Must be converted to local time. For instructions see page 268.

Day of month / week / year	Sun on Meridian Moon phase h m s	Sun's Declination ° '	20° Rise Sun/Moon h m	20° Set Sun/Moon h m	30° Rise Sun/Moon h m	30° Set Sun/Moon h m	40° Rise Sun/Moon h m	40° Set Sun/Moon h m	50° Rise Sun/Moon h m	50° Set Sun/Moon h m	60° Rise Sun/Moon h m	60° Set Sun/Moon h m
1 Mo	12 4 0	4 16	5 54	18 14	5 50	18 18	5 45	18 24	5 38	18 31	5 27	18 42
91			20 23	6 59	20 42	6 43	21 05	6 23	21 39	5 55	22 37	5 10
2 Tu	12 3 42	4 39	5 53	18 14	5 49	18 19	5 43	18 25	5 36	18 33	5 24	18 45
92			21 18	7 41	21 40	7 21	22 08	6 55	22 49	6 20	- -	5 20
3 We	12 3 24	5 02	5 52	18 15	5 48	18 20	5 42	18 26	5 34	18 34	5 21	18 47
93			22 11	8 26	22 36	8 02	23 07	7 33	23 53	6 51	0 03	5 36
4 Th	12 3 7	5 25	5 52	18 15	5 47	18 20	5 40	18 27	5 32	18 36	5 18	18 50
94			23 03	9 13	23 29	8 48	- -	8 17	- -	7 31	1 19	6 03
5 Fr	12 2 49	5 48	5 51	18 15	5 45	18 21	5 39	18 28	5 29	18 37	5 15	18 52
95			23 53	10 04	- -	9 38	0 01	9 06	0 48	8 19	2 19	6 48
6 Sa	12 2 32	6 11	5 50	18 15	5 44	18 21	5 37	18 29	5 27	18 39	5 12	18 55
96			- -	10 56	0 17	10 32	0 49	10 01	1 34	9 17	2 59	7 53
7 Su	12 2 15 6 45 LQ	6 33	5 49	18 16	5 43	18 22	5 35	18 30	5 25	18 40	5 09	18 57
97			0 39	11 48	1 01	11 27	1 30	11 00	2 10	10 21	3 22	9 11
8 Mo	12 1 58	6 56	5 48	18 16	5 42	18 23	5 34	18 31	5 23	18 42	5 06	19 00
98			1 21	12 41	1 41	12 23	2 05	12 01	2 39	11 29	3 35	10 35
9 Tu	12 1 42	7 18	5 47	18 16	5 41	18 23	5 32	18 32	5 21	18 43	5 03	19 02
99			2 01	13 34	2 17	13 20	2 36	13 03	3 02	12 40	3 44	12 01
10 We	12 1 25	7 41	5 47	18 17	5 40	18 24	5 31	18 33	5 19	18 45	5 00	19 04
100			2 39	14 26	2 50	14 18	3 03	14 07	3 21	13 52	3 50	13 27
11 Th	12 1 9	8 3	5 46	18 17	5 38	18 24	5 29	18 34	5 17	18 47	4 57	19 07
101			3 15	15 20	3 21	15 16	3 29	15 11	3 39	15 05	3 54	14 55
12 Fr	12 0 54	8 25	5 45	18 17	5 37	18 25	5 28	18 35	5 15	18 48	4 54	19 09
102			3 51	16 14	3 52	16 15	3 53	16 17	3 55	16 20	3 58	16 24
13 Sa	12 0 38	8 47	5 44	18 17	5 36	18 26	5 26	18 36	5 13	18 50	4 51	19 12
103			4 28	17 10	4 24	17 17	4 19	17 26	4 12	17 38	4 02	17 56
14 Su	12 0 23 19 38 NM	9 09	5 43	18 18	5 35	18 26	5 25	18 37	5 10	18 51	4 48	19 14
104			5 08	18 09	4 58	18 22	4 47	18 38	4 31	18 59	4 07	19 34
15 Mo	12 0 8	9 30	5 43	18 18	5 34	18 27	5 23	18 38	5 08	18 53	4 45	19 17
105			5 51	19 12	5 36	19 30	5 18	19 52	4 53	20 23	4 14	21 16
16 Tu	11 59 54	9 52	5 42	18 18	5 33	18 27	5 22	18 39	5 06	18 54	4 42	19 19
106			6 39	20 17	6 20	20 39	5 55	21 07	5 22	21 47	4 26	22 58
17 We	11 59 40	10 13	5 41	18 19	5 32	18 28	5 20	18 40	5 04	18 56	4 39	19 22
107			7 33	21 23	7 10	21 48	6 41	22 19	5 59	23 05	4 46	- -
18 Th	11 59 26	10 34	5 40	18 19	5 31	18 29	5 19	18 41	5 02	18 58	4 36	19 24
108			8 33	22 27	8 08	22 52	7 36	23 24	6 50	- -	5 23	0 31
19 Fr	11 59 13	10 55	5 39	18 19	5 30	18 29	5 17	18 42	5 00	18 59	4 33	19 27
109			9 37	23 27	9 12	23 50	8 40	- -	7 55	0 11	6 28	1 38
20 Sa	11 58 60	11 16	5 39	18 20	5 28	18 30	5 16	18 43	4 58	19 01	4 31	19 29
110			10 41	- -	10 19	- -	9 51	0 19	9 10	1 01	7 57	2 16
21 Su	11 58 47 12 39 FQ	11 37	5 38	18 20	5 27	18 31	5 14	18 44	4 56	19 02	4 28	19 32
111			11 45	0 20	11 27	0 40	11 04	1 05	10 31	1 39	9 37	2 37
22 Mo	11 58 35	11 57	5 37	18 20	5 26	18 31	5 13	18 45	4 54	19 04	4 25	19 34
112			12 45	1 07	12 32	1 23	12 16	1 41	11 53	2 07	11 15	2 48
23 Tu	11 58 24	12 17	5 37	18 21	5 25	18 32	5 12	18 46	4 52	19 05	4 22	19 37
113			13 43	1 49	13 35	2 00	13 25	2 13	13 12	2 30	12 50	2 56
24 We	11 58 12	12 37	5 36	18 21	5 24	18 32	5 10	18 47	4 50	19 07	4 19	19 39
114			14 39	2 28	14 36	2 33	14 33	2 40	14 28	2 48	14 21	3 01
25 Th	11 58 2	12 57	5 35	18 21	5 23	18 33	5 09	18 48	4 49	19 09	4 16	19 42
115			15 33	3 05	15 35	3 05	15 38	3 05	15 43	3 05	15 50	3 05
26 Fr	11 57 51	13 17	5 34	18 22	5 22	18 34	5 07	18 49	4 47	19 10	4 13	19 44
116			16 26	3 41	16 34	3 36	16 43	3 30	16 57	3 22	17 18	3 09
27 Sa	11 57 41	13 36	5 34	18 22	5 21	18 34	5 06	18 50	4 45	19 12	4 11	19 47
117			17 20	4 18	17 32	4 08	17 48	3 56	18 10	3 39	18 45	3 14
28 Su	11 57 32 20 58 FM	13 55	5 33	18 22	5 20	18 35	5 05	18 51	4 43	19 13	4 08	19 49
118			18 14	4 56	18 31	4 41	18 52	4 23	19 23	3 59	20 14	3 20
29 Mo	11 57 23	14 14	5 32	18 23	5 20	18 36	5 03	18 52	4 41	19 15	4 05	19 51
119			19 08	5 37	19 29	5 18	19 55	4 55	20 33	4 22	21 40	3 28
30 Tu	11 57 15	14 33	5 32	18 23	5 19	18 36	5 02	18 53	4 39	19 16	4 02	19 54
120			20 02	6 20	20 26	5 58	20 56	5 30	21 39	4 51	23 01	3 42

5th Month   **May, 1991**   **31 days**

Greenwich Mean Time

NOTE: Light numbers indicate Sun. **Dark** numbers indicate **Moon**. *Degrees are North Latitude.*

FM = full moon; LQ = last quarter; NM = new moon; FQ = first quarter.

CAUTION: Must be converted to local time. For instructions see page 268.

Day of month / week / year	Sun on Meridian Moon phase h m s	Sun's Declina- tion ° '	20° Rise Sun / Moon h m	20° Set Sun / Moon h m	30° Rise Sun / Moon h m	30° Set Sun / Moon h m	40° Rise Sun / Moon h m	40° Set Sun / Moon h m	50° Rise Sun / Moon h m	50° Set Sun / Moon h m	60° Rise Sun / Moon h m	60° Set Sun / Moon h m
1 We	11 57 7	14 51	5 31	18 23	5 18	18 37	5 01	18 54	4 37	19 18	4 00	19 56
121			20 55	7 07	21 20	6 43	21 52	6 12	22 38	5 28	– –	4 05
2 Th	11 56 60	15 10	5 31	18 24	5 17	18 38	5 00	18 55	4 36	19 19	3 57	19 59
122			21 46	7 56	22 11	7 31	22 42	7 00	23 28	6 13	0 07	4 44
3 Fr	11 56 53	15 28	5 30	18 24	5 16	18 38	4 58	18 56	4 34	19 21	3 54	20 01
123			22 33	8 48	22 56	8 24	23 25	7 53	– –	7 07	0 54	5 41
4 Sa	11 56 47	15 45	5 29	18 24	5 15	18 39	4 57	18 57	4 32	19 22	3 51	20 04
124			23 17	9 40	23 37	9 18	– –	8 50	0 07	8 09	1 23	6 55
5 Su	11 56 42	16 3	5 29	18 25	5 14	18 40	4 56	18 58	4 30	19 24	3 49	20 06
125			23 57	10 33	– –	10 14	0 03	9 49	0 39	9 15	1 40	8 16
6 Mo	11 56 37	16 20	5 28	18 25	5 13	18 40	4 55	18 59	4 29	19 25	3 46	20 09
126			– –	11 25	0 14	11 09	0 35	10 50	1 04	10 24	1 51	9 40
7 Tu	11 56 32	16 37	5 28	18 26	5 13	18 41	4 54	19 00	4 27	19 27	3 44	20 11
127	0 46 LQ		0 35	12 16	0 47	12 05	1 03	11 52	1 24	11 34	1 57	11 04
8 We	11 56 28	16 53	5 27	18 26	5 12	18 41	4 53	19 01	4 26	19 28	3 41	20 14
128			1 11	13 08	1 19	13 02	1 29	12 55	1 42	12 45	2 02	12 29
9 Th	11 56 25	17 10	5 27	18 26	5 11	18 42	4 51	19 02	4 24	19 30	3 38	20 16
129			1 46	14 00	1 49	13 59	1 53	13 58	1 58	13 57	2 07	13 55
10 Fr	11 56 22	17 26	5 26	18 27	5 10	18 43	4 50	19 03	4 22	19 31	3 36	20 19
130			2 22	14 54	2 20	14 59	2 18	15 05	2 15	15 12	2 11	15 24
11 Sa	11 56 20	17 42	5 26	18 27	5 10	18 43	4 49	19 04	4 21	19 33	3 33	20 21
131			2 59	15 52	2 52	16 02	2 44	16 14	2 33	16 31	2 15	16 58
12 Su	11 56 19	17 57	5 25	18 27	5 09	18 44	4 48	19 05	4 19	19 34	3 31	20 23
132			3 41	16 53	3 28	17 08	3 13	17 27	2 53	17 53	2 22	18 37
13 Mo	11 56 18	18 12	5 25	18 28	5 08	18 45	4 47	19 06	4 18	19 36	3 28	20 26
133			4 27	17 57	4 09	18 17	3 48	18 43	3 19	19 19	2 31	20 21
14 Tu	11 56 18	18 27	5 25	18 28	5 08	18 45	4 46	19 07	4 16	19 37	3 26	20 28
134	4 36 NM		5 19	19 05	4 57	19 28	4 30	19 58	3 53	20 41	2 47	22 02
15 We	11 56 18	18 42	5 24	18 29	5 07	18 46	4 45	19 08	4 15	19 39	3 24	20 31
135			6 18	20 12	5 54	20 37	5 23	21 09	4 38	21 55	3 17	23 23
16 Th	11 56 19	18 56	5 24	18 29	5 06	18 47	4 44	19 09	4 14	19 40	3 21	20 33
136			7 22	21 15	6 57	21 40	6 25	22 10	5 39	22 54	4 11	– –
17 Fr	11 56 20	19 10	5 23	18 29	5 06	18 47	4 44	19 09	4 12	19 41	3 19	20 35
137			8 29	22 13	8 06	22 34	7 37	23 00	6 54	23 37	5 36	0 14
18 Sa	11 56 22	19 23	5 23	18 30	5 05	18 48	4 43	19 11	4 11	19 43	3 17	20 38
138			9 35	23 04	9 16	23 20	8 51	23 41	8 16	– –	7 16	0 40
19 Su	11 56 25	19 37	5 23	18 30	5 05	18 49	4 42	19 12	4 10	19 44	3 15	20 40
139			10 39	23 48	10 24	– –	10 06	– –	9 40	0 10	8 58	0 55
20 Mo	11 56 28	19 50	5 22	18 31	5 04	18 49	4 41	19 12	4 08	19 45	3 12	20 42
140	19 46 FQ		11 38	– –	11 29	0 00	11 17	0 15	11 01	0 34	10 36	1 04
21 Tu	11 56 31	20 2	5 22	18 31	5 04	18 50	4 40	19 13	4 07	19 47	3 10	20 44
141			12 35	0 29	12 31	0 35	12 26	0 43	12 19	0 54	12 08	1 10
22 We	11 56 35	20 15	5 22	18 32	5 03	18 50	4 39	19 14	4 06	19 48	3 08	20 47
142			13 29	1 06	13 30	1 08	13 32	1 09	13 34	1 12	13 37	1 15
23 Th	11 56 40	20 26	5 22	18 32	5 03	18 51	4 39	19 15	4 05	19 49	3 06	20 49
143			14 22	1 42	14 28	1 39	14 36	1 34	14 47	1 28	15 04	1 19
24 Fr	11 56 45	20 38	5 21	18 32	5 02	18 52	4 38	19 16	4 04	19 51	3 04	20 51
144			15 15	2 18	15 26	2 10	15 40	1 59	16 00	1 45	16 31	1 23
25 Sa	11 56 50	20 49	5 21	18 33	5 02	18 52	4 37	19 17	4 03	19 52	3 02	20 53
145			16 08	2 56	16 24	2 42	16 44	2 26	17 11	2 04	17 57	1 29
26 Su	11 56 56	21 00	5 21	18 33	5 01	18 53	4 37	19 18	4 02	19 53	3 00	20 55
146			17 02	3 35	17 22	3 17	17 47	2 56	18 22	2 26	19 24	1 37
27 Mo	11 57 3	21 10	5 21	18 34	5 01	18 53	4 36	19 18	4 01	19 54	2 58	20 57
147			17 56	4 17	18 19	3 56	18 48	3 30	19 29	2 53	20 46	1 49
28 Tu	11 57 10	21 21	5 21	18 34	5 01	18 54	4 35	19 19	4 00	19 55	2 57	20 59
148	11 37 FM		18 49	5 03	19 14	4 39	19 45	4 09	20 30	3 27	21 57	2 09
29 We	11 57 17	21 30	5 20	18 34	5 00	18 54	4 35	19 20	3 59	19 56	2 55	21 01
149			19 40	5 51	20 05	5 26	20 37	4 55	21 23	4 09	22 51	2 41
30 Th	11 57 25	21 40	5 20	18 35	5 00	18 55	4 34	19 21	3 58	19 58	2 53	21 03
150			20 29	6 42	20 52	6 17	21 23	5 46	22 06	5 00	23 25	3 33
31 Fr	11 57 33	21 49	5 20	18 35	5 00	18 56	4 34	19 22	3 57	19 59	2 52	21 05
151			21 13	7 34	21 35	7 11	22 02	6 42	22 40	6 00	23 45	4 42

6th Month · June, 1991 · 30 days

Greenwich Mean Time

NOTE: Light numbers indicate Sun. **Dark numbers indicate Moon.** *Degrees are North Latitude.*

FM = full moon; LQ = last quarter; NM = new moon; FQ = first quarter.

CAUTION: Must be converted to local time. For instruction see page 268.

Day of month / week / year	Sun on Meridian / Moon phase (h m s)	Sun's Declination (° ')	20° Rise	20° Set	30° Rise	30° Set	40° Rise	40° Set	50° Rise	50° Set	60° Rise	60° Set
1 Sa 152	11 57 42	21 57	5 20	18 36	4 59	18 56	4 33	19 22	3 56	20 00	2 50	21 07
			21 55	8 27	22 13	8 06	22 35	7 41	23 06	7 05	23 58	6 01
2 Su 153	11 57 51	22 6	5 20	18 36	4 59	18 57	4 33	19 23	3 56	20 01	2 49	21 08
			22 33	9 18	22 47	9 02	23 04	8 41	23 28	8 12	- -	7 24
3 Mo 154	11 58 1	22 13	5 20	18 36	4 59	18 57	4 33	19 24	3 55	20 02	2 47	21 10
			23 09	10 09	23 18	9 57	23 30	9 42	23 46	9 21	0 06	8 47
4 Tu 155	11 58 11	22 21	5 20	18 37	4 59	18 58	4 32	19 24	3 54	20 03	2 46	21 12
			23 43	11 00	23 49	10 52	23 55	10 43	- -	10 30	0 11	10 10
5 We 156	11 58 21 / 15 30 LQ	22 28	5 20	18 37	4 59	18 58	4 32	19 25	3 54	20 04	2 45	21 13
			- -	11 51	- -	11 48	- -	11 45	0 03	11 40	0 16	11 33
6 Th 157	11 58 32	22 35	5 20	18 37	4 59	18 59	4 32	19 26	3 53	20 04	2 43	21 15
			0 18	12 43	0 18	12 45	0 19	12 48	0 19	12 52	0 20	12 58
7 Fr 158	11 58 43	22 41	5 20	18 38	4 58	18 59	4 31	19 26	3 53	20 05	2 42	21 16
			0 54	13 37	0 49	13 44	0 43	13 54	0 35	14 07	0 24	14 26
8 Sa 159	11 58 54	22 47	5 20	18 38	4 58	19 00	4 31	19 27	3 52	20 06	2 41	21 17
			1 32	14 34	1 22	14 47	1 10	15 03	0 54	15 25	0 29	16 01
9 Su 160	11 59 6	22 52	5 20	18 38	4 58	19 00	4 31	19 27	3 52	20 07	2 40	21 19
			2 15	15 36	2 00	15 54	1 41	16 16	1 16	16 48	0 37	17 41
10 Mo 161	11 59 18	22 57	5 20	18 39	4 58	19 00	4 31	19 28	3 51	20 08	2 39	21 20
			3 03	16 42	2 43	17 04	2 19	17 32	1 45	18 11	0 49	19 23
11 Tu 162	11 59 30	23 2	5 20	18 39	4 58	19 01	4 31	19 28	3 51	20 08	2 39	21 21
			3 58	17 49	3 35	18 14	3 06	18 45	2 25	19 31	1 11	20 56
12 We 163	11 59 42 / 12 6 NM	23 6	5 20	18 39	4 58	19 01	4 31	19 29	3 51	20 09	2 38	21 22
			5 01	18 56	4 36	19 21	4 04	19 52	3 18	20 38	1 52	22 03
13 Th 164	11 59 54	23 10	5 20	18 40	4 58	19 02	4 31	19 29	3 51	20 10	2 37	21 23
			6 08	19 58	5 44	20 21	5 13	20 49	4 28	21 30	3 04	22 41
14 Fr 165	12 0 7	23 14	5 20	18 40	4 58	19 02	4 31	19 30	3 50	20 10	2 37	21 24
			7 17	20 54	6 56	21 12	6 29	21 36	5 50	22 08	4 42	23 00
15 Sa 166	12 0 20	23 17	5 20	18 40	4 58	19 02	4 31	19 30	3 50	20 11	2 36	21 25
			8 24	21 43	8 08	21 56	7 47	22 13	7 17	22 36	6 28	23 12
16 Su 167	12 0 33	23 19	5 20	18 41	4 59	19 03	4 31	19 31	3 50	20 11	2 36	21 25
			9 28	22 26	9 16	22 34	9 02	22 45	8 43	22 58	8 11	23 19
17 Mo 168	12 0 46	23 22	5 21	18 41	4 59	19 03	4 31	19 31	3 50	20 12	2 36	21 26
			10 27	23 05	10 21	23 08	10 14	23 12	10 04	23 17	9 49	23 24
18 Tu 169	12 0 59	23 23	5 21	18 41	4 59	19 03	4 31	19 31	3 50	20 12	2 36	21 27
			11 24	23 43	11 23	23 41	11 23	23 38	11 22	23 34	11 21	23 29
19 We 170	12 1 12 / 4 19 FQ	23 25	5 21	18 41	4 59	19 04	4 31	19 32	3 50	20 12	2 36	21 27
			12 18	- -	12 23	- -	12 29	- -	12 37	23 51	12 50	23 33
20 Th 171	12 1 25	23 26	5 21	18 42	4 59	19 04	4 31	19 32	3 50	20 13	2 36	21 28
			13 11	0 19	13 21	0 12	13 33	0 03	13 50	- -	14 17	23 39
21 Fr 172	12 1 38	23 26	5 21	18 42	4 59	19 04	4 31	19 32	3 51	20 13	2 36	21 28
			14 04	0 56	14 19	0 44	14 37	0 30	15 02	0 10	15 44	23 46
22 Sa 173	12 1 51	23 26	5 22	18 42	4 59	19 04	4 31	19 32	3 51	20 13	2 36	21 28
			14 58	1 35	15 16	1 18	15 40	0 58	16 13	0 31	17 10	23 56
23 Su 174	12 2 4	23 26	5 22	18 42	5 00	19 04	4 32	19 32	3 51	20 13	2 36	21 28
			15 51	2 16	16 13	1 56	16 41	1 31	17 21	0 56	18 34	- -
24 Mo 175	12 2 17	23 26	5 22	18 42	5 00	19 05	4 32	19 33	3 51	20 13	2 36	21 28
			16 45	3 00	17 09	2 37	17 40	2 08	18 24	1 27	19 49	0 13
25 Tu 176	12 2 30	23 24	5 22	18 43	5 00	19 05	4 32	19 33	3 52	20 13	2 37	21 28
			17 36	3 48	18 01	3 23	18 33	2 52	19 19	2 06	20 48	0 41
26 We 177	12 2 42	23 23	5 23	18 43	5 01	19 05	4 33	19 33	3 52	20 13	2 37	21 28
			18 26	4 38	18 50	4 13	19 21	3 41	20 05	2 55	21 28	1 26
27 Th 178	12 2 55 / 2 58 FM	23 21	5 23	18 43	5 01	19 05	4 33	19 33	3 52	20 13	2 38	21 27
			19 12	5 29	19 34	5 06	20 02	4 36	20 42	3 52	21 52	2 30
28 Fr 179	12 3 7	23 19	5 23	18 43	5 01	19 05	4 33	19 33	3 53	20 13	2 39	21 27
			19 54	6 22	20 13	6 01	20 37	5 34	21 10	4 56	22 06	3 47
29 Sa 180	12 3 19	23 16	5 23	18 43	5 01	19 05	4 34	19 33	3 53	20 13	2 40	21 26
			20 33	7 14	20 48	6 56	21 07	6 34	21 33	6 03	22 15	5 09
30 Su 181	12 3 31	23 13	5 24	18 43	5 02	19 05	4 34	19 33	3 54	20 13	2 41	21 26
			21 09	8 05	21 21	7 52	21 34	7 35	21 53	7 11	22 21	6 33

7th Month   July, 1991   31 days

Greenwich Mean Time

NOTE: Light numbers indicate Sun. **Dark** numbers indicate **Moon**. *Degrees are North Latitude.*

FM = full moon; LQ = last quarter; NM = new moon; FQ = first quarter.

CAUTION: Must be converted to local time. For instruction see page 268.

Day of month / week / year	Sun on Meridian / Moon phase (h m s)	Sun's Declination (° ')	20° Rise Sun / Moon (h m)	20° Set Sun / Moon (h m)	30° Rise Sun / Moon (h m)	30° Set Sun / Moon (h m)	40° Rise Sun / Moon (h m)	40° Set Sun / Moon (h m)	50° Rise Sun / Moon (h m)	50° Set Sun / Moon (h m)	60° Rise Sun / Moon (h m)	60° Set Sun / Moon (h m)
1 Mo / 182	12 3 43	23 9	5 24	18 43	5 02	19 05	4 35	19 33	3 55	20 13	2 42	21 25
			21 44	8 56	21 51	8 47	21 59	8 35	22 09	8 20	22 26	7 55
2 Tu / 183	12 3 54	23 5	5 24	18 43	5 03	19 05	4 35	19 33	3 55	20 12	2 43	21 25
			22 18	9 46	22 20	9 42	22 22	9 36	22 25	9 29	22 30	9 17
3 We / 184	12 4 6	23 1	5 25	18 43	5 03	19 05	4 36	19 32	3 56	20 12	2 44	21 24
			22 52	10 36	22 49	10 37	22 46	10 38	22 41	10 39	22 34	10 40
4 Th / 185	12 4 17	22 56	5 25	18 44	5 03	19 05	4 36	19 32	3 57	20 12	2 45	21 23
			23 29	11 28	23 21	11 34	23 11	11 41	22 58	11 50	22 38	12 05
5 Fr / 186	2 50 LQ	22 51	5 25	18 44	5 04	19 05	4 37	19 32	3 57	20 11	2 46	21 22
	12 4 27		- -	12 23	23 55	12 33	23 39	12 47	23 18	13 05	22 45	13 34
6 Sa / 187	12 4 38	22 46	5 26	18 44	5 04	19 05	4 37	19 32	3 58	20 11	2 48	21 21
			0 08	13 21	- -	13 36	- -	13 56	23 43	14 23	22 54	15 09
7 Su / 188	12 4 48	22 40	5 26	18 44	5 05	19 05	4 38	19 32	3 59	20 10	2 49	21 20
			0 52	14 22	0 34	14 43	0 13	15 08	- -	15 44	23 10	16 48
8 Mo / 189	12 4 57	22 33	5 26	18 43	5 05	19 04	4 38	19 31	4 00	20 10	2 50	21 18
			1 42	15 28	1 21	15 51	0 54	16 21	0 16	17 04	23 39	18 25
9 Tu / 190	12 5 7	22 27	5 27	18 43	5 06	19 04	4 39	19 31	4 01	20 09	2 52	21 17
			2 40	16 34	2 16	16 59	1 45	17 31	1 01	18 17	- -	19 45
10 We / 191	12 5 16	22 20	5 27	18 43	5 06	19 04	4 40	19 30	4 02	20 08	2 54	21 16
			3 45	17 38	3 20	18 02	2 48	18 33	2 02	19 16	0 34	20 36
11 Th / 192	19 6 NM	22 12	5 27	18 43	5 07	19 04	4 40	19 30	4 03	20 08	2 55	21 14
	12 5 24		4 53	18 37	4 30	18 58	4 00	19 25	3 18	20 01	2 00	21 03
12 Fr / 193	12 5 32	22 4	5 28	18 43	5 07	19 04	4 41	19 30	4 04	20 07	2 57	21 13
			6 02	19 31	5 43	19 47	5 19	20 07	4 44	20 34	3 45	21 18
13 Sa / 194	12 5 40	21 56	5 28	18 43	5 08	19 03	4 42	19 29	4 05	20 06	2 59	21 11
			7 09	20 18	6 55	20 29	6 37	20 42	6 13	21 00	5 33	21 28
14 Su / 195	12 5 47	21 47	5 29	18 43	5 08	19 03	4 43	19 29	4 06	20 05	3 01	21 10
			8 12	21 00	8 04	21 06	7 53	21 12	7 39	21 21	7 17	21 34
15 Mo / 196	12 5 53	21 38	5 29	18 43	5 09	19 03	4 43	19 28	4 07	20 04	3 02	21 08
			9 12	21 39	9 09	21 39	9 06	21 39	9 01	21 39	8 54	21 39
16 Tu / 197	12 5 59	21 29	5 29	18 43	5 09	19 02	4 44	19 28	4 08	20 03	3 04	21 06
			10 09	22 17	10 12	22 12	10 15	22 06	10 20	21 57	10 27	21 44
17 We / 198	12 6 5	21 19	5 30	18 42	5 10	19 02	4 45	19 27	4 09	20 02	3 06	21 04
			11 04	22 55	11 12	22 45	11 22	22 32	11 36	22 15	11 58	21 49
18 Th / 199	15 11 FQ	21 9	5 30	18 42	5 10	19 02	4 46	19 26	4 10	20 01	3 08	21 03
	12 6 10		11 58	23 34	12 11	23 19	12 28	23 00	12 50	22 35	13 27	21 55
19 Fr / 200	12 6 14	20 59	5 30	18 42	5 11	19 01	4 46	19 26	4 11	20 00	3 10	21 01
			12 53	- -	13 10	23 56	13 32	23 32	14 02	22 59	14 54	22 04
20 Sa / 201	12 6 18	20 48	5 31	18 42	5 12	19 01	4 47	19 25	4 13	19 59	3 12	20 59
			13 47	0 14	14 08	- -	14 34	- -	15 12	23 28	16 20	22 19
21 Su / 202	12 6 22	20 37	5 31	18 41	5 12	19 00	4 48	19 24	4 14	19 58	3 15	20 57
			14 40	0 58	15 04	0 36	15 34	0 08	16 17	- -	17 39	22 42
22 Mo / 203	12 6 24	20 25	5 32	18 41	5 13	19 00	4 49	19 23	4 15	19 57	3 17	20 55
			15 32	1 44	15 57	1 20	16 29	0 49	17 15	0 05	18 44	23 22
23 Tu / 204	12 6 27	20 13	5 32	18 41	5 13	18 59	4 50	19 23	4 16	19 56	3 19	20 52
			16 22	2 34	16 47	2 09	17 18	1 37	18 04	0 50	19 30	- -
24 We / 205	12 6 28	20 1	5 32	18 40	5 14	18 59	4 51	19 22	4 18	19 54	3 21	20 50
			17 09	3 25	17 32	3 01	18 02	2 30	18 43	1 45	19 58	0 20
25 Th / 206	12 6 29	19 49	5 33	18 40	5 14	18 58	4 51	19 21	4 19	19 53	3 23	20 48
			17 53	4 17	18 13	3 55	18 39	3 21	19 14	2 47	20 15	1 33
26 Fr / 207	18 24 FM	19 36	5 33	18 40	5 15	18 58	4 52	19 20	4 20	19 52	3 25	20 46
	12 6 29		18 33	5 10	18 50	4 51	19 11	4 27	19 39	3 53	20 25	2 55
27 Sa / 208	12 6 29	19 23	5 33	18 39	5 16	18 57	4 53	19 19	4 22	19 51	3 28	20 44
			19 11	6 01	19 23	5 46	19 39	5 28	23 00	5 02	20 32	4 18
28 Su / 209	12 6 28	19 9	5 34	18 39	5 16	18 56	4 54	19 18	4 23	19 49	3 30	20 41
			19 46	6 52	19 54	6 42	20 04	6 29	20 17	6 11	20 37	5 42
29 Mo / 210	12 6 27	18 55	5 34	18 39	5 17	18 56	4 55	19 17	4 24	19 48	3 32	20 39
			20 20	7 43	20 24	7 37	20 28	7 30	20 33	7 20	20 42	7 04
30 Tu / 211	12 6 25	18 41	5 34	18 38	5 17	18 55	4 56	19 16	4 26	19 46	3 35	20 37
			20 54	8 33	20 53	8 32	20 51	8 31	20 49	8 29	20 45	8 27
31 We / 212	12 6 22	18 27	5 35	18 38	5 18	18 54	4 57	19 15	4 27	19 45	3 37	20 34
			21 29	9 24	21 23	9 28	21 25	9 33	21 05	9 40	20 50	9 50

8th Month   August, 1991   31 days

Greenwich Mean Time

NOTE: Light numbers indicate Sun. **Dark** numbers indicate **Moon**. *Degrees are North Latitude.*

FM = full moon; LQ = last quarter; NM = new moon; FQ = first quarter.

CAUTION: Must be converted to local time. For instruction see page 268.

Light numbers = Sun; **Dark** numbers = **Moon**. Each day has two rows: the upper (Sun) and lower (Moon).

Day of month / week / year	Sun on Meridian / Moon phase (h m s)	Sun's Declination (° ')	20° Rise	20° Set	30° Rise	30° Set	40° Rise	40° Set	50° Rise	50° Set	60° Rise	60° Set
1 Th	12 6 19	18 12	5 35	18 37	5 19	18 54	4 58	19 14	4 28	19 43	3 39	20 32
213			22 07	10 17	21 56	10 26	21 42	10 37	21 24	10 53	20 55	11 17
2 Fr	12 6 15	17 57	5 36	18 37	5 19	18 53	4 59	19 13	4 30	19 42	3 42	20 29
214			22 48	11 13	22 32	11 27	22 13	11 44	21 46	12 08	21 03	12 47
3 Sa	12 6 11	17 42	5 36	18 36	5 20	18 52	5 00	19 12	4 31	19 40	3 44	20 27
215	11 25 LQ		23 34	12 11	23 14	12 30	22 49	12 53	22 14	13 26	21 15	14 22
4 Su	12 6 6	17 26	5 36	18 36	5 20	18 51	5 01	19 11	4 33	19 39	3 46	20 24
216			--	13 13	--	13 35	23 34	14 04	22 52	14 44	21 37	15 58
5 Mo	12 6 0	17 10	5 37	18 35	5 21	18 51	5 01	19 10	4 34	19 37	3 49	20 22
217			0 27	14 17	0 04	14 41	--	15 13	23 44	15 58	22 18	17 24
6 Tu	12 5 54	16 54	5 37	18 35	5 22	18 50	5 02	19 09	4 36	19 35	3 51	20 19
218			1 27	15 20	1 02	15 45	0 30	16 16	--	17 02	23 28	18 27
7 We	12 5 48	16 37	5 37	18 34	5 22	18 49	5 03	19 08	4 37	19 34	3 54	20 16
219			2 31	16 21	2 07	16 43	1 36	17 12	0 52	17 52	--	19 03
8 Th	12 5 40	16 21	5 38	18 33	5 23	18 48	5 04	19 06	4 38	19 32	3 56	20 14
220			3 39	17 16	3 18	17 35	2 51	17 58	2 12	18 30	1 03	19 23
9 Fr	12 5 32	16 4	5 38	18 33	5 23	18 47	5 05	19 05	4 40	19 30	3 58	20 11
221			4 47	18 06	4 30	18 20	4 09	18 36	3 39	18 59	2 50	19 35
10 Sa	12 5 24	15 46	5 38	18 32	5 24	18 46	5 06	19 04	4 41	19 28	4 01	20 08
222	2 28 NM		5 52	18 51	5 40	18 59	5 26	19 09	5 07	19 23	4 36	19 43
11 Su	12 5 15	15 29	5 39	18 32	5 25	18 45	5 07	19 03	4 43	19 27	4 03	20 06
223			6 54	19 32	6 49	19 35	6 42	19 38	6 32	19 42	6 17	19 49
12 Mo	12 5 5	15 11	5 39	18 31	5 25	18 45	5 08	19 01	4 44	19 25	4 06	20 03
224			7 54	20 12	7 54	20 09	7 54	20 06	7 54	20 01	7 55	19 54
13 Tu	12 4 55	14 53	5 39	18 30	5 26	18 44	5 09	19 00	4 46	19 23	4 08	20 00
225			8 51	20 51	8 57	20 43	9 04	20 33	9 14	20 19	9 29	19 59
14 We	12 4 44	14 35	5 40	18 30	5 26	18 43	5 10	18 59	4 47	19 21	4 10	19 57
226			9 48	21 30	9 58	21 17	10 12	21 01	10 31	20 39	11 01	20 05
15 Th	12 4 33	14 17	5 40	18 29	5 27	18 42	5 11	18 57	4 49	19 19	4 13	19 55
227			10 43	22 11	10 59	21 53	11 18	21 32	11 46	21 02	12 31	20 13
16 Fr	12 4 21	13 58	5 40	18 28	5 28	18 41	5 12	18 56	4 50	19 17	4 15	19 52
228			11 38	22 54	11 58	22 33	12 23	22 07	12 58	21 30	14 00	20 26
17 Sa	12 4 9	13 39	5 40	18 28	5 28	18 40	5 13	18 55	4 52	19 16	4 18	19 49
229	5 1 FQ		12 33	23 40	12 56	23 16	13 25	22 47	14 06	22 04	15 22	20 46
18 Su	12 3 56	13 20	5 41	18 27	5 29	18 39	5 14	18 53	4 53	19 14	4 20	19 46
230			13 26	--	13 51	--	14 22	23 32	15 07	22 46	16 34	21 19
19 Mo	12 3 42	13 1	5 41	18 26	5 29	18 38	5 15	18 52	4 55	19 12	4 22	19 43
231			14 17	0 28	14 42	0 04	15 14	--	16 00	23 38	17 27	22 11
20 Tu	12 3 28	12 41	5 41	18 25	5 30	18 37	5 16	18 51	4 56	19 10	4 25	19 40
232			15 06	1 19	15 29	0 55	15 59	0 23	16 42	--	18 01	23 19
21 We	12 3 14	12 21	5 42	18 25	5 30	18 36	5 17	18 49	4 58	19 08	4 27	19 38
233			15 50	2 11	16 12	1 48	16 38	1 19	17 16	0 37	18 22	--
22 Th	12 2 59	12 1	5 42	18 24	5 31	18 34	5 18	18 48	4 59	19 06	4 30	19 35
234			16 32	3 04	16 50	2 44	17 12	2 18	17 43	1 42	18 34	0 38
23 Fr	12 2 44	11 41	5 42	18 23	5 32	18 33	5 19	18 46	5 01	19 04	4 32	19 32
235			17 10	3 56	17 24	3 39	17 42	3 19	18 05	2 50	18 43	2 02
24 Sa	12 2 28	11 21	5 42	18 22	5 32	18 32	5 20	18 45	5 02	19 02	4 34	19 29
236			17 47	4 47	17 56	4 35	18 08	4 20	18 24	3 59	18 49	3 25
25 Su	12 2 12	11 0	5 43	18 22	5 33	18 31	5 20	18 43	5 04	19 00	4 37	19 26
237	9 7 FM		18 22	5 38	18 27	5 31	18 33	5 22	18 41	5 09	18 53	4 49
26 Mo	12 1 55	10 40	5 43	18 21	5 33	18 30	5 21	18 42	5 05	18 58	4 39	19 23
238			18 56	6 29	18 56	6 27	18 56	6 23	18 57	6 19	18 57	6 12
27 Tu	12 1 38	10 19	5 43	18 20	5 34	18 29	5 22	18 40	5 07	18 56	4 42	19 20
239			19 31	7 21	19 27	7 23	19 21	7 26	19 13	7 30	19 02	7 36
28 We	12 1 21	9 58	5 43	18 19	5 34	18 28	5 23	18 39	5 08	18 54	4 44	19 17
240			20 08	8 13	19 59	8 21	19 47	8 30	19 31	8 42	19 07	9 02
29 Th	12 1 3	9 37	5 44	18 18	5 35	18 27	5 24	18 37	5 10	18 51	4 46	19 14
241			20 48	9 08	20 34	9 21	20 16	9 36	19 52	9 57	19 14	10 31
30 Fr	12 0 45	9 16	5 44	18 17	5 36	18 25	5 25	18 36	5 11	18 49	4 49	19 11
242			21 32	10 06	21 14	10 23	20 50	10 44	20 18	11 14	19 25	12 04
31 Sa	12 0 26	8 54	5 44	18 17	5 36	18 24	5 26	18 34	5 13	18 47	4 51	19 08
243			22 22	11 06	22 00	11 27	21 32	11 53	20 52	12 31	19 43	13 39

9th Month   September, 1991   30 days

Greenwich Mean Time

NOTE: Light numbers indicate Sun. **Dark** numbers indicate **Moon**. *Degrees are North Latitude.*

FM = full moon; LQ = last quarter; NM = new moon; FQ = first quarter.

CAUTION: Must be converted to local time. For instruction see page 268.

The first (light) line of each day is Sun data; the second (dark) line is Moon data. For each latitude, the first value is Rise and the second is Set (h m).

Day of month / week / year	Sun on Meridian / Moon phase (h m s)	Sun's Declination (° ')	20° Rise	20° Set	30° Rise	30° Set	40° Rise	40° Set	50° Rise	50° Set	60° Rise	60° Set
1 Su	12 0 7	8 33	5 44	18 16	5 37	18 23	5 27	18 32	5 14	18 45	4 53	19 05
244	18 16 LQ		23 18	12 08	22 53	12 31	22 22	13 02	21 38	13 45	20 15	15 07
2 Mo	11 59 48	8 11	5 44	18 15	5 37	18 22	5 28	18 31	5 16	18 43	4 56	19 02
245			– –	13 09	23 54	13 34	23 23	14 06	22 38	14 51	21 12	16 17
3 Tu	11 59 29	7 49	5 45	18 14	5 38	18 21	5 29	18 29	5 17	18 41	4 58	18 59
246			0 19	14 09	– –	14 33	– –	15 02	23 51	15 45	22 35	17 02
4 We	11 59 10	7 27	5 45	18 13	5 38	18 20	5 30	18 28	5 19	18 39	5 01	18 56
247			1 23	15 05	1 01	15 25	0 32	15 51	– –	16 27	– –	17 27
5 Th	11 58 50	7 05	5 45	18 12	5 39	18 18	5 31	18 26	5 20	18 37	5 03	18 53
248			2 29	15 55	2 10	16 11	1 46	16 31	1 12	16 58	0 15	17 42
6 Fr	11 58 30	6 43	5 45	18 11	5 39	18 17	5 32	18 24	5 21	18 34	5 05	18 50
249			3 33	16 42	3 19	16 52	3 02	17 06	2 38	17 24	1 58	17 51
7 Sa	11 58 10	6 20	5 46	18 10	5 40	18 16	5 33	18 23	5 23	18 32	5 08	18 47
250			4 36	17 24	4 27	17 30	4 17	17 36	4 03	17 45	3 40	17 58
8 Su	11 57 49	5 58	5 46	18 10	5 40	18 15	5 34	18 21	5 24	18 30	5 10	18 44
251	11 1 NM		5 36	18 05	5 34	18 04	5 30	18 04	5 26	18 04	5 19	18 04
9 Mo	11 57 29	5 35	5 46	18 09	5 41	18 14	5 35	18 20	5 26	18 28	5 12	18 41
252			6 35	18 44	6 38	18 38	6 41	18 32	6 46	18 23	6 54	18 09
10 Tu	11 57 8	5 13	5 46	18 08	5 42	18 12	5 36	18 18	5 27	18 26	5 15	18 38
253			7 33	19 24	7 41	19 13	7 51	19 00	8 05	18 42	8 28	18 15
11 We	11 56 47	4 50	5 46	18 07	5 42	18 11	5 37	18 16	5 29	18 24	5 17	18 35
254			8 30	20 05	8 43	19 49	9 00	19 30	9 23	19 04	10 01	18 23
12 Th	11 56 26	4 27	5 47	18 06	5 43	18 10	5 38	18 15	5 30	18 21	5 19	18 32
255			9 26	20 48	9 44	20 28	10 06	20 04	10 38	19 31	11 32	18 34
13 Fr	11 56 5	4 04	5 47	18 05	5 43	18 09	5 38	18 13	5 32	18 19	5 22	18 29
256			10 22	21 33	10 44	21 11	11 11	20 43	11 49	20 03	12 59	18 51
14 Sa	11 55 44	3 41	5 47	18 04	5 44	18 07	5 39	18 11	5 33	18 17	5 24	18 26
257			11 17	22 22	11 41	21 57	12 11	21 27	12 55	20 42	14 16	19 19
15 Su	11 55 22	3 18	5 47	18 03	5 44	18 06	5 40	18 10	5 35	18 15	5 26	18 23
258	22 1 FQ		12 10	23 12	12 34	22 47	13 06	22 16	13 51	21 31	15 18	20 04
16 Mo	11 55 1	2 55	5 47	18 02	5 45	18 05	5 41	18 08	5 36	18 13	5 29	18 20
259			12 59	– –	13 23	23 40	13 54	23 10	14 38	22 27	15 59	21 06
17 Tu	11 54 40	2 32	5 48	18 01	5 45	18 04	5 42	18 06	5 38	18 10	5 31	18 17
260			13 45	0 04	14 08	– –	14 35	– –	15 15	23 30	16 25	22 22
18 We	11 54 18	2 9	5 48	18 00	5 46	18 02	5 43	18 05	5 39	18 08	5 33	18 14
261			14 28	0 56	14 47	0 35	15 11	0 08	15 45	– –	16 41	23 43
19 Th	11 53 57	1 46	5 48	18 00	5 46	18 01	5 44	18 03	5 41	18 06	5 36	18 11
262			15 08	1 48	15 23	1 30	15 42	1 08	16 09	0 36	16 51	– –
20 Fr	11 53 35	1 22	5 48	17 59	5 47	18 00	5 45	18 01	5 42	18 04	5 38	18 08
263			15 45	2 40	15 56	2 26	16 10	2 09	16 29	1 45	16 58	1 06
21 Sa	11 53 14	0 59	5 48	17 58	5 47	17 59	5 46	18 00	5 44	18 02	5 40	18 05
264			16 20	3 31	16 27	3 22	16 35	3 10	16 47	2 54	17 03	2 29
22 Su	11 52 53	0 36	5 49	17 57	5 48	17 58	5 47	17 58	5 45	17 59	5 43	18 02
265			16 55	3 22	16 57	4 18	17 00	4 12	17 03	4 04	17 08	3 52
23 Mo	11 52 32	0 12	5 49	17 56	5 49	17 56	5 48	17 56	5 47	17 56	5 45	17 58
266	22 40 FM		17 31	4 14	17 28	5 14	17 24	5 15	17 20	5 16	17 13	5 17
24 Tu	11 52 11	– 0 11	5 49	17 55	5 49	17 55	5 49	17 55	5 48	17 55	5 48	17 55
267			18 08	5 07	18 00	6 12	17 50	6 19	17 38	6 29	17 18	6 43
25 We	11 51 50	– 0 34	5 49	17 54	5 50	17 54	5 50	17 53	5 50	17 53	5 50	17 52
268			18 48	7 02	18 35	7 12	18 19	7 26	17 58	7 44	17 25	8 12
26 Th	11 51 29	– 0 58	5 50	17 53	5 50	17 52	5 51	17 52	5 51	17 51	5 52	17 49
269			19 31	7 59	19 14	8 15	18 53	8 34	18 23	9 01	17 35	9 46
27 Fr	11 51 8	– 1 21	5 50	17 52	5 51	17 51	5 52	17 50	5 53	17 48	5 55	17 46
270			20 20	9 00	19 59	9 19	19 32	9 44	18 55	10 19	17 52	11 21
28 Sa	11 50 48	– 1 44	5 50	17 51	5 51	17 50	5 53	17 48	5 54	17 46	5 57	17 43
271			21 14	10 01	20 50	10 24	20 20	10 53	19 37	11 35	18 20	12 52
29 Su	11 50 28	– 2 8	5 50	17 50	5 52	17 49	5 54	17 47	5 56	17 44	5 59	17 40
272			22 13	11 03	21 49	11 28	21 17	11 59	20 32	12 44	19 08	14 08
30 Mo	11 50 8	– 2 31	5 50	17 50	5 52	17 47	5 55	17 45	5 58	17 42	6 02	17 37
273			23 16	12 03	22 52	12 27	22 23	12 57	21 40	13 41	20 22	15 00

10th Month   October, 1991   31 days

Greenwich Mean Time

NOTE: Light numbers indicate Sun. Dark numbers indicate **Moon**. *Degrees are North Latitude.*

FM = full moon; LQ = last quarter; NM = new moon; FQ = first quarter.

CAUTION: Must be converted to local time. For instruction see page 268.

Day of month / week / year	Sun on Meridian Moon phase h m s	Sun's Declination ° ′	20° Rise Sun/Moon h m	20° Set Sun/Moon h m	30° Rise Sun/Moon h m	30° Set Sun/Moon h m	40° Rise Sun/Moon h m	40° Set Sun/Moon h m	50° Rise Sun/Moon h m	50° Set Sun/Moon h m	60° Rise Sun/Moon h m	60° Set Sun/Moon h m
1 Tu 274	11 49 48	− 2 54	5 51	17 49	5 53	17 46	5 56	17 43	5 59	17 40	6 04	17 34
	0 30 LQ		- -	12 59	23 59	13 20	23 34	13 47	22 58	14 25	21 55	15 30
2 We 275	11 49 29	− 3 18	5 51	17 48	5 54	17 45	5 57	17 42	6 01	17 38	6 06	17 31
			0 19	13 50	- -	14 07	- -	14 29	- -	14 59	23 24	15 48
3 Th 276	11 49 10	− 3 41	5 51	17 47	5 54	17 44	5 58	17 40	6 02	17 35	6 09	17 28
			1 22	14 36	1 07	14 49	0 47	15 05	0 20	15 26	- -	15 59
4 Fr 277	11 48 52	− 4 4	5 51	17 46	5 55	17 43	5 59	17 38	6 04	17 33	6 11	17 25
			2 24	15 19	2 13	15 26	2 00	15 36	1 42	15 48	1 13	16 07
5 Sa 278	11 48 33	− 4 27	5 52	17 45	5 55	17 41	6 00	17 37	6 05	17 31	6 14	17 22
			3 23	15 59	3 18	16 01	3 12	16 04	3 03	16 08	2 50	16 13
6 Su 279	11 48 16	− 4 50	5 52	17 44	5 56	17 40	6 01	17 35	6 07	17 29	6 16	17 19
			4 21	16 38	4 21	16 35	4 22	16 31	4 23	16 26	4 24	16 19
7 Mo 280	11 47 58	− 5 13	5 52	17 43	5 57	17 39	6 02	17 34	5 41	16 46	5 57	16 25
	21 39 NM		5 18	17 17	5 24	17 09	5 31	16 59	6 08	17 27	6 18	17 16
8 Tu 281	11 47 41	− 5 36	5 53	17 43	5 57	17 38	6 03	17 32	6 10	17 25	6 21	17 13
			6 15	17 58	6 26	17 45	6 40	17 29	6 59	17 07	7 29	16 32
9 We 282	11 47 24	− 5 59	5 53	17 42	5 58	17 37	6 04	17 31	6 11	17 23	6 23	17 10
			7 12	18 40	7 28	18 23	7 48	18 01	8 15	17 31	9 01	16 42
10 Th 283	11 47 8	− 6 22	5 53	17 41	5 58	17 36	6 05	17 29	6 13	17 20	6 26	17 07
			8 09	19 25	8 29	19 04	8 54	18 38	9 29	18 01	10 31	16 57
11 Fr 284	11 46 52	− 6 45	5 53	17 40	5 59	17 34	6 06	17 27	6 15	17 18	6 28	17 04
			9 05	20 13	9 28	19 50	9 56	19 20	10 38	18 38	11 54	17 21
12 Sa 285	11 46 37	− 7 8	5 54	17 39	6 00	17 33	6 07	17 26	6 16	17 16	6 31	17 01
			9 59	21 03	10 24	20 39	10 54	20 08	11 39	19 23	13 03	17 59
13 Su 286	11 46 22	− 7 30	5 54	17 38	6 00	17 32	6 08	17 24	6 18	17 14	6 33	16 59
			10 51	21 55	11 15	21 31	11 46	21 01	12 30	20 17	13 53	18 55
14 Mo 287	11 46 8	− 7 53	5 54	17 38	6 01	17 31	6 09	17 23	6 19	17 12	6 35	16 56
			11 39	22 47	12 01	22 25	12 30	21 57	13 11	21 17	14 25	20 05
15 Tu 288	11 45 54	− 8 15	5 55	17 37	6 01	17 30	6 10	17 21	6 21	17 10	6 38	16 53
	17 33 FQ		12 23	23 39	12 43	23 20	13 08	22 56	13 44	22 22	14 45	21 24
16 We 289	11 45 41	− 8 37	5 55	17 36	6 02	17 29	6 11	17 20	6 23	17 08	6 40	16 50
			13 03	- -	13 20	- -	13 41	23 56	14 10	23 30	14 57	22 45
17 Th 290	11 45 28	− 8 59	5 55	17 35	6 03	17 28	6 12	17 18	6 24	17 06	6 43	16 47
			13 41	0 31	13 54	0 15	14 10	- -	14 31	- -	15 06	- -
18 Fr 291	11 45 16	− 9 21	5 56	17 35	6 03	17 27	6 13	17 17	6 26	17 04	6 45	16 44
			14 17	1 22	14 26	1 10	14 36	0 57	14 50	0 38	15 12	0 07
19 Sa 292	11 45 5	− 9 43	5 56	17 34	6 04	17 26	6 14	17 16	6 27	17 02	6 48	16 41
			14 52	2 12	14 56	2 06	15 01	1 58	15 07	1 47	15 17	1 30
20 Su 293	11 44 54	− 10 5	5 56	17 33	6 05	17 25	6 15	17 14	6 29	17 00	6 50	16 38
			15 27	3 03	15 26	3 02	15 25	3 00	15 24	2 57	15 22	2 53
21 Mo 294	11 44 43	− 10 26	5 57	17 33	6 05	17 24	6 16	17 13	6 31	16 58	6 53	16 36
			16 04	3 56	15 58	3 59	15 51	4 03	15 42	4 09	15 28	4 18
22 Tu 295	11 44 34	− 10 48	5 57	17 32	6 06	17 23	6 17	17 11	6 32	16 56	6 55	16 33
			16 43	4 50	16 32	4 59	16 19	5 09	16 01	5 24	15 34	5 46
23 We 296	11 44 25	− 11 9	5 57	17 31	6 07	17 22	6 18	17 10	6 34	16 54	6 58	16 30
	11 8 FM		17 26	5 48	17 10	6 01	16 51	6 18	16 25	6 41	15 44	7 19
24 Th 297	11 44 17	− 11 30	5 58	17 30	6 08	17 21	6 19	17 09	6 35	16 52	7 00	16 27
			18 14	6 48	17 54	7 06	17 29	7 29	16 55	8 01	15 58	8 55
25 Fr 298	11 44 9	− 11 51	5 58	17 30	6 08	17 20	6 21	17 07	6 37	16 50	7 03	16 24
			19 07	7 51	18 45	8 13	18 16	8 41	17 35	9 20	16 23	10 31
26 Sa 299	11 44 2	− 12 12	5 59	17 29	6 09	17 19	6 22	17 06	6 39	16 49	7 05	16 22
			20 06	8 55	19 42	9 19	19 11	9 49	18 27	10 33	17 05	11 55
27 Su 300	11 43 56	− 12 32	5 59	17 29	6 10	17 17	6 24	17 04	6 40	16 47	7 08	16 19
			21 09	9 57	20 46	10 21	20 16	10 51	19 33	11 35	18 13	12 56
28 Mo 301	11 43 51	− 12 52	5 59	17 28	6 10	17 17	6 24	17 03	6 42	16 45	7 11	16 16
			22 13	10 55	21 52	11 17	21 26	11 45	20 48	12 24	19 42	13 32
29 Tu 302	11 43 46	− 13 13	6 00	17 27	6 11	17 16	6 25	17 02	6 44	16 43	7 13	16 13
			23 16	11 47	23 00	12 06	22 38	12 29	22 09	13 01	21 19	13 54
30 We 303	11 43 42	− 13 33	6 00	17 27	6 12	17 15	6 26	17 01	6 45	16 41	7 16	16 11
			- -	12 35	- -	12 49	23 51	13 06	23 30	13 30	22 57	14 07
31 Th 304	11 43 39	− 13 52	6 01	17 26	6 13	17 14	6 27	17 00	6 47	16 40	7 18	16 08
			0 18	13 18	0 06	13 27	- -	13 38	- -	13 53	- -	14 15

11th Month   November, 1991   30 days

Greenwich Mean Time

NOTE: Light numbers indicate Sun. **Dark** numbers indicate **Moon.** *Degrees are North Latitude.*

FM = full moon; LQ = last quarter; NM = new moon; FQ = first quarter.

CAUTION: Must be converted to local time. For instruction see page 268.

Day of month / week / year	Sun on Meridian Moon phase h m s	Sun's Declination ° '	20° Rise Sun/Moon h m	20° Set Sun/Moon h m	30° Rise Sun/Moon h m	30° Set Sun/Moon h m	40° Rise Sun/Moon h m	40° Set Sun/Moon h m	50° Rise Sun/Moon h m	50° Set Sun/Moon h m	60° Rise Sun/Moon h m	60° Set Sun/Moon h m
1 Fr 305	11 43 37	− 14 12	6 01	17 26	6 13	17 13	6 28	16 58	6 49	16 38	7 21	16 06
	0 30 LQ		1 16	13 58	1 10	14 02	1 01	14 06	0 50	14 13	0 32	14 22
2 Sa 306	11 43 36	− 14 31	6 02	17 25	6 14	17 13	6 30	16 57	6 50	16 36	7 23	16 03
			2 13	14 36	2 12	14 35	2 10	14 33	2 08	14 31	2 04	14 28
3 Su 307	11 43 35	− 14 50	6 02	17 25	6 15	17 12	6 31	16 56	6 52	16 34	7 26	16 00
			3 09	15 14	3 13	15 08	3 18	15 00	3 25	14 50	3 35	14 34
4 Mo 308	11 43 35	− 15 9	6 03	17 24	6 16	17 11	6 32	16 55	6 54	16 33	7 28	15 58
			4 05	15 53	4 14	15 42	4 25	15 28	4 41	15 10	5 05	14 41
5 Tu 309	11 43 36	− 15 27	6 03	17 24	6 17	17 10	6 33	16 54	6 55	16 31	7 31	15 55
			5 01	16 34	5 15	16 19	5 32	15 59	5 56	15 33	6 36	14 50
6 We 310	11 43 38	− 15 46	6 04	17 23	6 17	17 10	6 34	16 53	6 57	16 30	7 34	15 53
			5 57	17 18	6 15	16 59	6 38	16 34	7 10	16 00	8 05	15 03
7 Th 311	11 43 41	− 16 4	6 04	17 23	6 18	17 09	6 35	16 52	6 59	16 28	7 36	15 50
	21 39 NM		6 54	18 05	7 15	17 43	7 42	17 14	8 21	16 34	9 31	15 23
8 Fr 312	11 43 45	− 16 22	6 05	17 23	6 19	17 08	6 36	16 51	7 00	16 26	7 39	15 48
			7 49	18 55	8 12	18 31	8 42	18 00	9 25	17 16	10 46	15 55
9 Sa 313	11 43 49	− 16 39	6 05	17 22	6 20	17 08	6 38	16 50	7 02	16 25	7 41	15 45
			8 42	19 46	9 06	19 22	9 36	18 51	10 21	18 07	11 44	16 45
10 Su 314	11 43 54	− 16 56	6 06	17 22	6 20	17 07	6 39	16 49	7 04	16 24	7 44	15 43
			9 31	20 38	9 54	20 16	10 24	19 47	11 06	19 06	12 23	17 50
11 Mo 315	11 44 0	− 17 13	6 06	17 22	6 21	17 06	6 40	16 48	7 05	16 22	7 46	15 41
			10 17	21 31	10 38	21 11	11 05	20 45	11 42	20 09	12 47	19 06
12 Tu 316	11 44 7	− 17 30	6 07	17 21	6 22	17 06	6 41	16 47	7 07	16 21	7 49	15 38
			10 59	22 22	11 17	22 05	11 39	21 45	12 10	21 15	13 02	20 26
13 We 317	11 44 15	− 17 46	6 07	17 21	6 23	17 05	6 42	16 46	7 09	16 19	7 52	15 36
			11 37	23 13	11 52	23 00	12 09	22 44	12 34	22 22	13 12	21 47
14 Th 318	11 44 24	− 18 2	6 08	17 21	6 24	17 05	6 43	16 45	7 10	16 18	7 54	15 34
			12 13	– –	12 24	23 54	12 36	23 44	12 53	23 30	13 19	23 08
15 Fr 319	11 44 33	− 18 18	6 09	17 20	6 25	17 04	6 44	16 44	7 12	16 17	7 57	15 32
	17 33 FQ		12 48	0 02	12 54	– –	13 01	– –	13 10	– –	13 25	– –
16 Sa 320	11 44 43	− 18 33	6 09	17 20	6 25	17 04	6 46	16 43	7 14	16 15	7 59	15 30
			13 22	0 52	13 24	0 49	13 25	0 44	13 27	0 38	13 30	0 28
17 Su 321	11 44 54	− 18 48	6 10	17 20	6 26	17 03	6 47	16 43	7 15	16 14	8 02	15 27
			13 58	1 43	13 54	1 44	13 50	1 46	13 44	1 48	13 35	1 51
18 Mo 322	11 45 6	− 19 3	6 10	17 20	6 27	17 03	6 48	16 42	7 17	16 13	8 04	15 25
			14 35	2 36	14 27	2 42	14 16	2 49	14 03	3 00	13 42	3 16
19 Tu 323	11 45 19	− 19 17	6 11	17 20	6 28	17 02	6 49	16 41	7 18	16 12	8 07	15 23
			15 16	3 31	15 03	3 42	14 46	3 56	14 24	4 15	13 50	4 46
20 We 324	11 45 32	− 19 31	6 11	17 19	6 29	17 02	6 50	16 41	7 20	16 11	8 09	15 21
			16 02	4 30	15 44	4 46	15 22	5 06	14 52	5 34	14 02	6 20
21 Th 325	11 45 47	− 19 45	6 12	17 19	6 30	17 02	6 51	16 40	7 21	16 10	8 11	15 20
			16 54	5 33	16 32	5 53	16 05	6 19	15 27	6 55	14 22	7 58
22 Fr 326	11 46 2	− 19 58	6 13	17 19	6 30	17 01	6 52	16 39	7 23	16 09	8 14	15 18
			17 52	6 38	17 28	7 01	16 58	7 31	16 15	8 13	14 57	9 30
23 Sa 327	11 46 18	− 20 11	6 14	17 19	6 31	17 01	6 54	16 39	7 24	16 08	8 16	15 16
	11 8 FM		18 56	7 43	18 32	8 07	18 01	8 38	17 18	9 22	15 56	10 43
24 Su 328	11 46 34	− 20 24	6 14	17 19	6 32	17 01	6 55	16 38	7 26	16 07	8 18	15 15
			20 02	8 45	19 40	9 08	19 12	9 36	18 32	10 18	17 21	11 31
25 Mo 329	11 46 52	− 20 36	6 15	17 19	6 33	17 01	6 56	16 38	7 27	16 06	8 21	15 12
			21 08	9 41	20 49	10 01	20 27	10 26	19 55	11 00	19 00	11 57
26 Tu 330	11 47 10	− 20 48	6 15	17 19	6 34	17 00	6 57	16 37	7 29	16 05	8 23	15 11
			22 11	10 32	21 58	10 47	21 41	11 06	21 18	11 32	20 40	12 13
27 We 331	11 47 29	− 20 60	6 16	17 19	6 35	17 00	6 58	16 37	7 30	16 04	8 25	15 09
			23 11	11 17	23 03	11 27	22 53	11 40	22 39	11 57	22 18	12 24
28 Th 332	11 47 49	− 21 11	6 16	17 19	6 35	17 00	6 59	16 36	7 32	16 03	8 28	15 08
			– –	11 58	– –	12 03	– –	12 10	23 58	12 18	23 51	12 31
29 Fr 333	11 48 10	− 21 21	6 17	17 19	6 36	17 00	7 00	16 36	7 33	16 03	8 30	15 06
			0 09	12 37	0 06	12 37	0 03	12 37	– –	12 37	– –	12 37
30 Sa 334	11 48 31	− 21 31	6 18	17 19	6 37	17 00	7 01	16 36	7 35	16 02	8 32	15 05
	7 10 LQ		1 05	13 15	1 07	13 10	1 10	13 04	1 15	12 56	1 21	12 43

12th Month   December, 1991   31 days

Greenwich Mean Time

NOTE: Light numbers indicate Sun. **Dark** numbers indicate **Moon.** *Degrees are North Latitude.*

FM = full moon; LQ = last quarter; NM = new moon; FQ = first quarter.

CAUTION: Must be converted to local time. For instruction see page 268.

Day of month / week / year	Sun on Meridian Moon phase h m s	Sun's Declina- tion ° '	20° Rise Sun/Moon h m	20° Set Sun/Moon h m	30° Rise Sun/Moon h m	30° Set Sun/Moon h m	40° Rise Sun/Moon h m	40° Set Sun/Moon h m	50° Rise Sun/Moon h m	50° Set Sun/Moon h m	60° Rise Sun/Moon h m	60° Set Sun/Moon h m
1 Su 335	11 48 53	−21 41	6 18	17 19	6 38	17 00	7 02	16 35	7 36	16 01	8 34	15 03
			2 00	13 53	2 07	13 43	2 17	13 31	2 30	13 15	2 50	12 50
2 Mo 336	11 49 15	−21 51	6 19	17 19	6 39	17 00	7 03	16 35	7 37	16 01	8 36	15 02
			2 55	14 32	3 07	14 18	3 23	14 01	3 44	13 36	4 19	12 58
3 Tu 337	11 49 39	−21 60	6 20	17 20	6 39	17 00	7 04	16 35	7 39	16 00	8 38	15 01
			3 50	15 15	4 07	14 56	4 28	14 34	4 57	14 02	5 47	13 09
4 We 338	11 50 2	−22 8	6 20	17 20	6 40	17 00	7 05	16 35	7 40	16 00	8 40	15 00
			4 45	16 00	5 06	15 38	5 32	15 11	6 08	14 33	7 13	13 27
5 Th 339	11 50 27	−22 16	6 21	17 20	6 41	17 00	7 06	16 35	7 41	15 59	8 42	14 59
			5 41	16 48	6 03	16 24	6 33	15 55	7 14	15 12	8 31	13 54
6 Fr 340	11 50 52 11 11 NM	−22 24	6 21	17 20	6 42	17 00	7 07	16 35	7 42	15 59	8 43	14 58
			6 34	17 39	6 58	17 14	7 29	16 44	8 13	16 00	9 36	14 37
7 Sa 341	11 51 17	−22 31	6 22	17 20	6 42	17 00	7 08	16 35	7 44	15 59	8 45	14 57
			7 25	18 31	7 49	18 08	8 19	17 38	9 02	16 56	10 21	15 37
8 Su 342	11 51 43	−22 38	6 23	17 21	6 43	17 00	7 09	16 35	7 45	15 59	8 47	14 56
			8 12	19 23	8 34	19 02	9 02	18 36	9 41	17 58	10 50	16 50
9 Mo 343	11 52 10	−22 45	6 23	17 21	6 44	17 00	7 10	16 35	7 46	15 58	8 48	14 56
			8 55	20 15	9 14	19 57	9 38	19 35	10 12	19 03	11 08	18 09
10 Tu 344	11 52 37	−22 51	6 24	17 21	6 45	17 01	7 10	16 35	7 47	15 58	8 50	14 55
			9 35	21 06	9 51	20 52	10 10	20 34	10 37	20 10	11 20	19 30
11 We 345	11 53 4	−22 56	6 25	17 22	6 45	17 01	7 11	16 35	7 48	15 58	8 52	14 54
			10 12	21 55	10 23	21 46	10 38	21 33	10 57	21 16	11 28	20 50
12 Th 346	11 53 32	−23 1	6 25	17 22	6 46	17 01	7 12	16 35	7 49	15 58	8 53	14 54
			10 46	22 44	10 54	22 39	11 03	22 32	11 15	22 23	11 34	22 09
13 Fr 347	11 54 0	−23 6	6 26	17 22	6 47	17 01	7 13	16 35	7 50	15 58	8 54	14 54
			11 20	23 34	11 23	23 33	11 27	23 32	11 31	23 31	11 39	23 29
14 Sa 348	11 54 29 9 32 FQ	−23 10	6 26	17 23	6 47	17 02	7 14	16 35	7 51	15 58	8 55	14 53
			11 54	– –	11 52	– –	11 50	– –	11 48	– –	11 44	– –
15 Su 349	11 54 57	−23 14	6 27	17 23	6 48	17 02	7 14	16 36	7 52	15 58	8 57	14 53
			12 29	0 24	12 23	0 28	12 15	0 33	12 05	0 40	11 49	0 50
16 Mo 350	11 55 26	−23 17	6 27	17 23	6 49	17 02	7 15	16 36	7 52	15 58	8 58	14 53
			13 07	1 16	12 56	1 25	12 42	1 36	12 24	1 51	11 56	2 15
17 Tu 351	11 55 55	−23 20	6 28	17 24	6 49	17 03	7 16	16 36	7 53	15 59	8 59	14 53
			13 49	2 12	13 34	2 26	13 14	2 43	12 48	3 07	12 06	3 45
18 We 352	11 56 25	−23 22	6 29	17 24	6 50	17 03	7 16	16 36	7 54	15 59	9 00	14 53
			14 37	3 12	14 17	3 30	13 53	3 53	13 19	4 25	12 21	5 19
19 Th 353	11 56 54	−23 24	6 29	17 25	6 50	17 03	7 17	16 37	7 54	15 59	9 00	14 53
			15 32	4 15	15 09	4 37	14 40	5 04	14 00	5 44	12 47	6 55
20 Fr 354	11 57 24	−23 25	6 30	17 25	6 51	17 04	7 17	16 37	7 55	16 00	9 01	14 54
			16 34	5 20	16 09	5 44	15 39	6 15	14 55	6 58	13 33	8 20
21 Sa 355	11 57 53 10 23 FM	−23 26	6 30	17 26	6 51	17 04	7 18	16 38	7 56	16 00	9 02	14 54
			17 40	6 25	17 17	6 49	16 48	7 19	16 05	8 02	14 48	9 21
22 Su 356	11 58 23	−23 26	6 31	17 26	6 52	17 05	7 19	16 39	7 56	16 01	9 02	14 54
			18 49	7 26	18 29	7 47	18 03	8 14	17 27	8 52	16 25	9 57
23 Mo 357	11 58 53	−23 26	6 31	17 27	6 52	17 05	7 19	16 39	7 57	16 01	9 03	14 55
			19 56	8 21	19 40	8 39	19 21	9 00	18 54	9 30	18 09	10 18
24 Tu 358	11 59 23	−23 26	6 32	17 27	6 53	17 06	7 19	16 39	7 57	16 02	9 03	14 56
			21 00	9 10	20 50	9 23	20 37	9 38	20 20	9 59	19 52	10 31
25 We 359	11 59 52	−23 25	6 32	17 28	6 53	17 06	7 20	16 40	7 57	16 02	9 03	14 56
			22 01	9 55	21 56	10 02	21 51	10 11	21 43	10 22	21 31	10 40
26 Th 360	12 0 22	−23 23	6 33	17 28	6 54	17 07	7 20	16 41	7 58	16 03	9 04	14 57
			22 59	10 36	23 00	10 38	23 01	10 40	23 02	10 43	23 05	10 47
27 Fr 361	12 0 52	−23 21	6 33	17 29	6 54	17 08	7 21	16 41	7 58	16 04	9 04	14 58
			23 55	11 15	– –	11 11	– –	11 07	– –	11 02	– –	10 53
28 Sa 362	12 1 21 1 55 LQ	−23 19	6 33	17 29	6 55	17 08	7 21	16 42	7 58	16 05	9 04	14 59
			– –	11 53	0 01	11 45	0 09	11 35	0 19	11 21	0 36	11 00
29 Su 363	12 1 51	−23 16	6 34	17 30	6 55	17 09	7 21	16 43	7 58	16 05	9 03	15 00
			0 51	12 33	1 02	12 20	1 15	12 04	1 34	11 42	2 05	11 07
30 Mo 364	12 2 20	−23 13	6 34	17 31	6 55	17 10	7 21	16 43	7 59	16 06	9 03	15 02
			1 46	13 14	2 01	12 57	2 21	12 35	2 48	12 06	3 33	11 17
31 Tu 365	12 2 49	−23 9	6 35	17 31	6 56	17 10	7 22	16 44	7 59	16 07	9 03	15 03
			2 41	13 58	3 00	13 37	3 25	13 11	3 59	12 35	5 00	11 32

Julian and Gregorian Calendars; Leap Year; Century

Calendars based on the movements of sun and moon have been used since ancient times, but none has been perfect. The Julian calendar, under which western nations measured time until 1582 A.D., was authorized by Julius Caesar in 46 B.C., the year 709 of Rome. His expert was a Greek, Sosigenes. The Julian calendar, on the assumption that the true year was 365 1/4 days long, gave every fourth year 366 days. The Venerable Bede, an Anglo-Saxon monk, announced in 730 A.D. that the 365 1/4-day Julian year was 11 min., 14 sec. too long, making a cumulative error of about a day every 128 years, but nothing was done about it for over 800 years.

By 1582 the accumulated error was estimated to have amounted to 10 days. In that year Pope Gregory XIII decreed that the day following Oct. 4, 1582, should be called Oct. 15, thus dropping 10 days.

However, with common years 365 days and a 366-day leap year every fourth year, the error in the length of the year would have recurred at the rate of a little more than 3 days every 400 years. So 3 of every 4 centesimal years (ending in 00) were made common years, not leap years. Thus 1600 was a leap year, 1700, 1800 and 1900 were not, but 2000 will be. **Leap years** are those divisible by 4 except centesimal years, which are common unless divisible by 400.

The Gregorian calendar was adopted at once by France, Italy, Spain, Portugal and Luxembourg. Within 2 years most German Catholic states, Belgium and parts of Switzerland and the Netherlands were brought under the new calendar, and Hungary followed in 1587. The rest of the Netherlands, along with Denmark and the German Protestant states made the change in 1699-1700 (German Protestants retained the old reckoning of Easter until 1776).

The British Government imposed the Gregorian calendar on all its possessions, including the American colonies, in 1752. The British decreed that the day following Sept. 2, 1752, should be called Sept. 14, a loss of 11 days. All dates preceding were marked O.S., for Old Style. In addition New Year's Day was moved to Jan. 1 from Mar. 25. (e.g., under the old reckoning, Mar. 24, 1700 had been followed by Mar. 25, 1701.) George Washington's birth date, which was Feb. 11, 1731, O.S., became Feb. 22, 1732, N.S. In 1753 Sweden too went Gregorian, retaining the old Easter rules until 1844.

In 1793 the French Revolutionary Government adopted a calendar of 12 months of 30 days each with 5 extra days in September of each common year and a 6th extra day every 4th year. Napoleon reinstated the Gregorian calendar in 1806.

The Gregorian system later spread to non-European regions, first in the European colonies, then in the independent countries, replacing traditional calendars at least for official purposes. Japan in 1873, Egypt in 1875, China in 1912 and Turkey in 1917 made the change, usually in conjunction with political upheavals. In China, the republican government began reckoning years from its 1911 founding — e.g., 1948 was designated the year 37. After 1949, the Communists adopted the Common, or Christian Era year count, even for the traditional lunar calendar.

In 1918 the revolutionary government in Russia decreed that the day after Jan. 31, 1918, Old Style, would become Feb. 14, 1918, New Style. Greece followed in 1923. (In Russia the Orthodox Church has retained the Julian calendar, as have various Middle Eastern Christian sects.) For the first time in history, all major cultures have one calendar.

To change from the Julian to the Gregorian calendar, add 10 days to dates Oct. 5, 1582, through Feb. 28, 1700; after that date add 11 days through Feb. 28, 1800; 12 days through Feb. 28, 1900; and 13 days through Feb. 28, 2100.

A **century** consists of 100 consecutive calendar years. The 1st century consisted of the years 1 through 100. The 20th century consists of the years 1901 through 2000 and will end Dec. 31, 2000. The 21st century will begin Jan. 1, 2001.

Julian Calendar

To find which of the 14 calendars printed on pages 294-295 applies to any year, starting Jan. 1, under the Julian system, find the century for the desired year in the three left-hand columns below; read across. Then find the year in the four top rows; read down. The number in the intersection is the calendar designation for that year.

Century	**Year** (last two figures of desired year)							
	01 02 03 04	05 06 07 08	09 10 11 12	13 14 15 16	17 18 19 20	21 22 23 24	25 26 27 28	
	29 30 31 32	33 34 35 36	37 38 39 40	41 42 43 44	45 46 47 48	49 50 51 52	53 54 55 56	
	57 58 59 60	61 62 63 64	65 66 67 68	69 70 71 72	73 74 75 76	77 78 79 80	81 82 83 84	
	00 85 86 87 88	89 90 91 92	93 94 95 96	97 98 99				
0 700 1400	12 7 1 2	10 5 6 7	8 3 4 5	1 2 3 11	6 7 1 9	4 5 6 14	2 3 4 12	
100 800 1500	11 6 7 1	9 4 5 6	14 2 3 4	12 7 1 2	10 5 6 7	8 3 4 5 13	1 2 3 11	
200 900 1600	10 5 6 7	8 3 4 5	13 1 2 3	11 6 7 1	9 4 5 6 14	2 3 4 12	7 1 2 10	
300 1000 1700	9 4 5 6 14	2 3 4 12	7 1 2 10	5 6 7 8	3 4 5 13	1 2 3 11	6 7 1 9	
400 1100 1800	8 3 4 5 13	1 2 3 11	6 7 1 9	4 5 6 14	2 3 4 12	7 1 2 10	5 6 7 8	
500 1200 1900	2 3 4 12	7 1 2 10	5 6 7 8	3 4 5 13	1 2 3 11	6 7 1 9	4 5 6 14	
600 1300 2000	13 1 2 3 11	6 7 1 9	4 5 6 14	2 3 4 12	7 1 2 10	5 6 7 8	3 4 5 13	

Gregorian Calendar

Pick desired year from table below or on page 294 (for years 1800 to 2059). The number shown with each year shows which calendar to use for that year, as shown on pages 294-295. (The Gregorian calendar was inaugurated Oct. 15, 1582. From that date to Dec. 31, 1582, use calendar 6.)

1583-1802

1583. . 7	1603. . 4	1623. . 1	1643. . 5	1663. . 2	1683. . 6	1703. . 2	1723. . 6	1743. . 3	1763. . 7	1783. . 4
1584. . 8	1604. 12	1624. . 9	1644. 13	1664. 10	1684. 14	1704. 10	1724. 14	1744. 11	1764. . 8	1784. 12
1585. . 3	1605. . 7	1625. . 4	1645. . 1	1665. . 5	1685. . 2	1705. . 5	1725. . 2	1745. . 6	1765. . 3	1785. . 7
1586. . 4	1606. . 1	1626. . 2	1646. . 2	1666. . 6	1686. . 3	1706. . 6	1726. . 3	1746. . 7	1766. . 4	1786. . 1
1587. . 5	1607. . 2	1627. . 6	1647. . 3	1667. . 7	1687. . 4	1707. . 7	1727. . 4	1747. . 1	1767. . 5	1787. . 2
1588. 13	1608. 10	1628. 14	1648. 11	1668. . 8	1688. 12	1708. . 8	1728. 12	1748. . 9	1768. 13	1788. 10
1589. . 1	1609. . 5	1629. . 2	1649. . 6	1669. . 3	1689. . 7	1709. . 3	1729. . 7	1749. . 4	1769. . 1	1789. . 5
1590. . 2	1610. . 6	1630. . 3	1650. . 7	1670. . 4	1690. . 1	1710. . 4	1730. . 1	1750. . 5	1770. . 2	1790. . 6
1591. . 3	1611. . 7	1631. . 4	1651. . 1	1671. . 5	1691. . 2	1711. . 5	1731. . 2	1751. . 6	1771. . 3	1791. . 7
1592. 11	1612. . 8	1632. 12	1652. . 9	1672. 13	1692. 10	1712. 13	1732. 10	1752. 14	1772. 11	1792. . 8
1593. . 6	1613. . 3	1633. . 7	1653. . 4	1673. . 1	1693. . 5	1713. . 1	1733. . 5	1753. . 2	1773. . 6	1793. . 3
1594. . 7	1614. . 4	1634. . 1	1654. . 5	1674. . 2	1694. . 6	1714. . 2	1734. . 6	1754. . 3	1774. . 7	1794. . 4
1595. . 1	1615. . 5	1635. . 2	1655. . 6	1675. . 3	1695. . 7	1715. . 3	1735. . 7	1755. . 4	1775. . 1	1795. . 5
1596. . 9	1616. 13	1636. 10	1656. 14	1676. 11	1696. . 8	1716. 11	1736. . 8	1756. 12	1776. . 9	1796. 13
1597. . 4	1617. . 1	1637. . 5	1657. . 2	1677. . 6	1697. . 3	1717. . 6	1737. . 3	1757. . 7	1777. . 4	1797. . 1
1598. . 5	1618. . 2	1638. . 6	1658. . 3	1678. . 7	1698. . 4	1718. . 7	1738. . 4	1758. . 1	1778. . 5	1798. . 2
1599. . 6	1619. . 3	1639. . 7	1659. . 4	1679. . 1	1699. . 5	1719. . 1	1739. . 5	1759. . 2	1779. . 6	1799. . 3
1600. 14	1620. 11	1640. . 8	1660. 12	1680. . 9	1700. . 6	1720. . 9	1740. 13	1760. 10	1780. 14	1800. . 4
1601. . 2	1621. . 6	1641. . 3	1661. . 7	1681. . 4	1701. . 7	1721. . 4	1741. . 1	1761. . 5	1781. . 2	1801. . 5
1602. . 3	1622. . 7	1642. . 4	1662. . 1	1682. . 5	1702. . 1	1722. . 5	1742. . 2	1762. . 6	1782. . 3	1802. . 6

Latitude, Longitude, and Altitude of North American Cities

Source: National Oceanic and Atmospheric Administration, U.S. Commerce Department for geographic positions.
Source for Canadian cities: Geodetic Survey of Canada, Dept. of Energy, Mines, and Resources.
Altitudes U.S. Geological Survey and various sources. *Approx. altitude at downtown business area U.S.; in Canada at city hall except where (a) is at tower of major airport.

City	Lat. N °	′	″	Long. W °	′	″	Alt.* feet
Abilene, Tex.	32	27	05	99	43	51	1710
Akron, Oh.	41	05	00	81	30	44	874
Albany, N.Y.	42	39	01	73	45	01	20
Albuquerque, N.M.	35	05	01	106	39	05	4,945
Allentown, Pa.	40	36	11	75	28	06	255
Alert, N.W.T.	82	29	50	62	21	15	95
Altoona, Pa.	40	30	55	78	24	03	1,180
Amarillo, Tex.	35	12	27	101	50	04	3,685
Anchorage, Alas.	61	10	00	149	59	00	118
Ann Arbor, Mich.	42	16	59	83	44	52	880
Asheville, N.C.	35	35	42	82	33	26	1,985
Ashland, Ky.	38	28	36	82	38	23	536
Atlanta, Ga.	33	45	10	84	23	37	1,050
Atlantic City, N.J.	39	21	32	74	25	53	10
Augusta, Ga.	33	28	01	81	58	00	143
Augusta, Me.	44	18	53	69	46	29	45
Austin, Tex.	30	16	09	97	44	37	505
Bakersfield, Cal.	35	22	31	119	01	18	400
Baltimore, Md.	39	17	26	76	36	45	20
Bangor, Me.	44	48	13	68	46	18	20
Baton Rouge, La.	30	26	58	91	11	00	57
Battle Creek, Mich.	42	18	58	85	10	48	820
Bay City, Mich.	43	36	04	83	53	15	595
Beaumont, Tex.	30	05	20	94	06	09	20
Belleville, Ont.	44	09	42	77	23	11	257
Bellingham, Wash.	48	45	34	122	28	36	60
Berkeley, Cal.	37	52	10	122	16	17	40
Bethlehem, Pa.	40	37	16	75	22	34	235
Billings, Mon.	45	47	00	108	30	04	3,120
Biloxi, Miss.	30	23	48	88	53	00	20
Binghamton, N.Y.	42	06	03	75	54	47	865
Birmingham, Ala.	33	31	01	86	48	36	600
Bismarck, N.D.	46	48	23	100	47	17	1,674
Bloomington, Ill.	40	28	58	88	59	36	800
Boise, Ida.	43	37	07	116	11	58	2,704
Boston, Mass.	42	21	24	71	03	25	21
Bowling Green, Ky.	36	59	41	86	26	33	510
Brandon, Man.	49	51	00	99	57	00	1,265(a)
Brantford, Ont.	43	08	34	80	15	39	705(a)
Brattleboro, Vt.	42	51	06	72	33	48	300
Bridgeport, Conn.	41	10	49	73	11	22	10
Brockton, Mass.	42	05	02	71	01	25	130
Brownsville, Tex.	25	54	07	97	29	58	35
Buffalo, N.Y.	42	52	52	78	52	21	585
Burlington, Ont.	43	19	33	79	47	57	284
Burlington, Vt.	44	28	34	73	12	46	110
Butte, Mon.	46	01	06	112	32	11	5,765
Calgary, Alta.	51	02	46	114	03	24	3,427
Cambridge, Mass.	42	22	01	71	06	22	20
Camden, N.J.	39	56	41	75	07	14	30
Canton, Oh.	40	47	50	81	22	37	1,030
Carson City, Nev.	39	10	00	119	46	00	4,680
Cedar Rapids, Ia.	41	58	01	91	39	53	730
Central Islip, N.Y.	40	47	24	73	12	00	80
Champaign, Ill.	40	07	05	88	14	48	740
Charleston, S.C.	32	46	35	79	55	53	9
Charleston, W.Va.	38	21	01	81	37	52	601
Charlotte, N.C.	35	13	44	80	50	45	720
Charlottetown, P.E.I.	46	14	07	63	07	49	31
Chattanooga, Tenn.	35	02	41	85	18	32	675
Cheyenne, Wy.	41	08	09	104	49	07	6,100
Chicago, Ill.	41	52	28	87	38	22	595
Churchill, Man.	58	45	15	94	10	00	94(a)
Cincinnati, Oh.	39	06	07	84	30	35	550
Cleveland, Oh.	41	29	51	81	41	50	660
Colorado Springs	38	50	07	104	49	16	5,980
Columbia, Mo.	38	57	03	92	19	46	730
Columbia, S.C.	34	00	02	81	02	00	190
Columbus, Ga.	32	28	07	84	59	24	265
Columbus, Oh.	39	57	47	83	00	17	780
Concord, N.H.	43	12	22	71	32	25	290
Corpus Christi, Tex.	27	47	51	97	23	45	35
Dallas, Tex.	32	47	09	96	47	37	435
Dartmouth, N.S.	44	39	50	63	34	08	24
Davenport, Ia.	41	31	19	90	34	33	590
Dawson, Yukon	64	03	30	139	26	00	1,211(a)
Dayton, Oh.	39	45	32	84	11	43	574
Daytona Beach, Fla.	29	12	44	81	01	10	7
Decatur, Ill.	39	50	42	88	56	47	682
Denver, Col.	39	44	58	104	59	22	5,280
Des Moines, Ia.	41	35	14	93	37	00	803
Detroit, Mich.	42	19	48	83	02	57	585
Dodge City, Kan.	37	45	17	100	01	09	2,480
Dubuque, Ia.	42	29	55	90	40	08	620
Duluth, Minn.	46	46	56	92	06	24	610
Durham, N.C.	36	00	00	78	54	45	405
Eau Claire, Wis.	44	48	31	91	29	49	790
Edmonton, Alta.	53	32	43	113	29	21	2,186
El Paso, Tex.	31	45	36	106	29	11	3,695
Elizabeth, N.J.	40	39	43	74	12	59	21
Enid, Okla.	36	23	40	97	52	35	1,240
Erie, Pa.	42	07	15	80	04	57	685
Eugene, Ore.	44	03	16	123	05	30	422
Eureka, Cal.	40	48	08	124	09	46	45
Evansville, Ind.	37	58	20	87	34	21	385
Fairbanks, Alas.	64	48	00	147	51	00	448
Fall River, Mass.	41	42	06	71	09	18	40
Fargo, N.D.	46	52	30	96	47	18	900
Flagstaff, Ariz.	35	11	36	111	39	06	6,900
Flint, Mich.	43	00	50	83	41	33	750
Ft. Smith, Ark.	35	23	10	94	25	36	440
Fort Wayne, Ind.	41	04	21	85	08	26	790
Fort Worth, Tex.	32	44	55	97	19	44	670
Fredericton, N.B.	45	57	47	66	38	38	29
Fresno, Cal.	36	44	12	119	47	11	285
Gadsden, Ala.	34	00	57	86	00	41	555
Gainesville, Fla.	29	38	56	82	19	19	175
Gallup, N.M.	35	31	30	108	44	30	6,540
Galveston, Tex.	29	18	10	94	47	43	5
Gary, Ind.	41	36	12	87	20	19	590
Grand Junction, Col.	39	04	06	108	33	54	4,590
Grand Rapids, Mich.	42	58	03	85	40	13	610
Great Falls, Mon.	47	29	33	111	18	23	3,340
Green Bay, Wis.	44	30	48	88	00	50	590
Greensboro, N.C.	36	04	17	79	47	25	839
Greenville, S.C.	34	50	50	82	24	01	966
Guelph, Ont.	43	32	35	80	14	54	1,065
Gulfport, Miss.	30	22	04	89	05	36	20
Halifax, N.S.	44	38	54	63	34	30	60
Hamilton, Ont.	43	15	20	79	52	30	329
Hamilton, Oh.	39	23	59	84	33	47	600
Harrisburg, Pa.	40	15	43	76	52	59	365
Hartford, Conn.	41	46	12	72	40	49	40
Helena, Mon.	46	35	33	112	02	24	4,155
Hilo, Hawaii	19	43	30	155	05	24	40
Holyoke, Mass.	42	12	29	72	36	36	115
Honolulu, Ha.	21	18	22	157	51	35	21
Houston, Tex.	29	45	26	95	21	37	40
Hull, Que.	45	25	42	75	42	41	185
Huntington, W.Va.	38	25	12	82	26	33	565
Huntsville, Ala.	34	44	18	86	35	19	640
Indianapolis, Ind.	39	46	07	86	09	46	710
Iowa City, Ia.	41	39	37	91	31	53	685
Jackson, Mich.	42	14	43	84	24	22	940
Jackson, Miss.	32	17	56	90	11	06	298
Jacksonville, Fla.	30	19	44	81	39	42	20
Jersey City, N.J.	40	43	50	74	03	56	20
Johnstown, Pa.	40	19	35	78	55	03	1,185
Joplin, Mo.	37	05	26	94	30	00	990
Juneau, Alas.	58	18	12	134	24	30	50
Kalamazoo, Mich.	42	17	29	85	35	14	755
Kansas City, Kan.	39	07	04	94	38	24	750
Kansas City, Mo.	39	04	56	94	35	20	750
Kenosha, Wis.	42	35	43	87	50	11	610
Key West, Fla.	24	33	00	81	48	12	5
Kingston, Ont.	44	13	53	76	28	48	264
Kitchener, Ont.	43	26	58	80	29	12	1,100
Knoxville, Tenn.	35	57	39	83	55	07	890
Lafayette, Ind.	40	25	11	86	53	39	550
Lancaster, Pa.	40	02	25	76	18	29	355
Lansing, Mich.	42	44	01	84	33	15	830
Laredo, Tex.	27	30	22	99	30	30	440
La Salle, Que.	45	25	30	73	39	30	110
Las Vegas, Nev.	36	10	20	115	08	37	2,030
Laval, Que.	45	33	05	73	44	42	142
Lawrence, Mass.	42	42	16	71	10	08	65
Lethbridge, Alta.	49	41	38	112	49	58	2,985
Lexington, Ky.	38	02	50	84	29	46	955
Lihue, Ha.	21	58	48	159	22	30	210
Lima, Oh.	40	44	35	84	06	20	865
Lincoln, Neb.	40	48	59	96	42	15	1,150
Little Rock, Ark.	34	44	42	92	16	37	286
London, Ont.	42	59	17	81	14	03	822
Long Beach, Cal.	33	46	14	118	11	18	35
Lorain, Oh.	41	28	05	82	10	49	610
Los Angeles, Cal.	34	03	15	118	14	28	340
Louisville, Ky.	38	14	47	85	45	49	450
Lowell, Mass.	42	38	25	71	19	14	100
Lubbock, Tex.	33	35	05	101	50	33	3,195

City	Lat. N °	′	″	Long. W °	′	″	Alt.* feet
Macon, Ga.	32	50	12	83	37	36	335
Madison, Wis.	43	04	23	89	22	55	860
Manchester, N.H.	42	59	28	71	27	41	175
Marshall, Tex.	32	33	00	94	23	00	410
Memphis, Tenn.	35	08	46	90	03	13	275
Meriden, Conn.	41	32	06	72	47	30	190
Mexico City, Mexico.	19	25	45	99	07	00	7,347
Miami, Fla.	25	46	37	80	11	32	10
Milwaukee, Wis.	43	02	19	87	54	15	635
Minneapolis, Minn.	44	58	57	93	15	43	815
Minot, N.D.	48	14	09	101	17	38	1,550
Mississauga, Ont.	43	33	00	79	35	00	260(a)
Mobile, Ala.	30	41	36	88	02	33	5
Moline, Ill.	41	30	31	90	30	49	585
Moncton, N.B.	46	05	18	64	46	41	38
Montgomery, Ala.	32	22	33	86	18	31	160
Montpelier, Vt.	44	15	36	72	34	41	485
Montreal, Que.	45	30	33	73	33	14	90
Moose Jaw, Sask.	50	23	34	105	32	04	1,784
Muncie, Ind.	40	11	28	85	23	16	950
Nashville, Tenn.	36	09	33	86	46	55	450
Natchez, Miss.	31	33	48	91	23	30	210
Newark, N.J.	40	44	14	74	10	19	55
New Bedford, Mass.	41	38	13	70	55	41	15
New Britain, Conn.	41	40	08	72	46	59	200
New Haven, Conn.	41	18	25	72	55	30	40
New Orleans, La.	29	56	53	90	04	10	5
New York, N.Y.	40	45	06	73	59	39	55
Niagara Falls, N.Y.	43	05	34	79	03	26	570
Niagara Falls, Ont.	43	06	22	79	03	51	590
Nome, Alas.	64	30	00	165	25	00	25
Norfolk, Va.	36	51	10	76	17	21	10
North Bay, Ont.	46	18	35	79	27	45	670
Oakland, Cal.	37	48	03	122	15	54	25
Ogden, Ut.	41	13	31	111	58	21	4,295
Oklahoma City.	35	28	26	97	31	04	1,195
Omaha, Neb.	41	15	42	95	56	14	1,040
Orlando, Fla.	28	32	42	81	22	38	70
Oshawa, Ont.	43	53	46	78	51	57	350
Ottawa, Ont.	45	26	24	75	41	42	185
Paducah, Ky.	37	05	13	88	35	56	345
Pasadena, Cal.	34	08	44	118	08	41	830
Paterson, N.J.	40	55	01	74	10	21	100
Pensacola, Fla.	30	24	51	87	12	56	15
Peoria, Ill.	40	41	42	89	35	33	470
Peterborough, Ont.	44	18	32	78	19	13	673
Philadelphia, Pa.	39	56	58	75	09	21	100
Phoenix, Ariz.	33	27	12	112	04	28	1,090
Pierre, S.D.	44	22	18	100	20	54	1,480
Pittsburgh, Pa.	40	26	19	80	00	00	745
Pittsfield, Mass.	42	26	53	73	15	14	1,015
Pocatello, Ida.	42	51	38	112	27	01	4,460
Port Arthur, Tex.	29	52	30	93	56	15	10
Portland, Me.	43	39	33	70	15	19	25
Portland, Ore.	45	31	06	122	40	35	77
Portsmouth, N.H.	43	04	30	70	45	24	20
Portsmouth, Va.	36	50	07	76	18	14	10
Prince Rupert, B.C.	54	19	00	130	19	00	125(a)
Providence, R.I.	41	49	32	71	24	41	80
Provo, Ut.	40	14	06	111	39	24	4,550
Pueblo, Col.	38	16	17	104	36	33	4,690
Quebec City, Que.	46	48	51	71	12	30	163
Racine, Wis.	42	43	49	87	47	12	630
Rapid City, S.D.	44	04	52	103	13	11	3,230
Raleigh, N.C.	35	46	38	78	38	21	365
Reading, Pa.	40	20	09	75	55	40	265
Regina, Sask.	50	26	55	104	36	50	1,894(a)
Reno, Nev.	39	31	27	119	48	40	4,490
Richmond, Va.	37	32	15	77	26	09	160
Roanoke, Va.	37	16	13	79	56	44	905
Rochester, Minn.	44	01	21	92	28	03	990
Rochester, N.Y.	43	09	41	77	36	21	515
Rockford, Ill.	42	16	07	89	05	48	715
Sacramento, Cal.	38	34	57	121	29	41	30
Saginaw, Mich.	43	25	52	83	56	05	595
St. Catharines, Ont.	43	09	33	79	14	50	362(a)
St. Cloud, Minn.	45	34	00	94	10	24	1,040
Saint John, N.B.	45	16	22	66	03	48	27
St. John's, Nfld.	47	33	42	52	42	48	200(a)
St. Joseph, Mo.	39	45	57	94	51	02	850
St. Louis, Mo.	38	37	45	90	12	22	455
St. Paul, Minn.	44	57	19	93	06	07	780
St. Petersburg, Fla.	27	46	18	82	38	19	20
Salem, Ore.	44	56	24	123	01	59	155
Salina, Kan.	38	50	36	97	36	46	1,229
Salt Lake City, Ut.	40	45	23	111	53	26	4,390
San Angelo, Tex.	31	27	39	100	26	03	1,845
San Antonio, Tex.	29	25	37	98	29	06	650
San Bernardino, Cal.	34	06	30	117	17	28	1,080
San Diego, Cal.	32	42	53	117	09	21	20
San Francisco, Cal.	37	46	39	122	24	40	65
San Jose, Cal.	37	20	16	121	53	24	90
San Juan, P.R.	18	27	00	66	04	15	35
Santa Barbara, Cal.	34	25	18	119	41	55	100
Santa Cruz, Cal.	36	58	18	122	01	18	20
Santa Fe, N.M.	35	41	11	105	56	10	6,950
Sarasota, Fla.	27	20	05	82	32	30	20
Saskatoon, Sask.	52	07	49	106	39	35	1,587
Sault Ste. Marie, Ont.	46	30	24	84	20	04	589
Savannah, Ga.	32	04	42	81	05	37	20
Schenectady, N.Y.	42	48	42	73	55	42	245
Scranton, Pa.	41	24	32	75	39	46	725
Seattle, Wash.	47	36	32	122	20	12	10
Sheboygan, Wis.	43	45	03	87	42	52	630
Sherbrooke, Que.	45	24	24	71	51	07	535(a)
Sheridan, Wy.	44	47	55	106	57	10	3,740
Shreveport, La.	32	30	46	93	44	58	204
Sioux City, Ia.	42	29	46	96	24	30	1,110
Sioux Falls, S.D.	43	32	35	96	43	35	1,395
Somerville, Mass.	42	23	15	71	06	07	13
South Bend, Ind.	41	40	33	86	15	01	710
Spartanburg, S.C.	34	57	03	81	56	06	875
Spokane, Wash.	47	39	32	117	25	33	1,890
Springfield, Ill.	39	47	58	89	38	51	610
Springfield, Mass.	42	06	21	72	35	32	85
Springfield, Mo.	37	13	03	93	17	32	1,300
Springfield, Oh.	39	55	38	83	48	29	980
Stamford, Conn.	41	03	09	73	32	24	35
Steubenville, Oh.	40	21	42	80	36	53	660
Stockton, Cal.	37	57	30	121	17	16	20
Sudbury, Ont.	46	29	24	80	59	24	850(a)
Superior, Wis.	46	43	14	92	06	07	630
Sydney, N.S.	46	08	15	60	11	48	15
Syracuse, N.Y.	43	03	04	76	09	14	400
Tacoma, Wash.	47	14	59	122	26	15	110
Tallahassee, Fla.	30	26	30	84	16	56	150
Tampa, Fla.	27	56	58	82	27	25	15
Terre Haute, Ind.	39	28	03	87	24	26	495
Texarkana, Tex.	33	25	48	94	02	30	324
Thunder Bay, Ont.	48	22	54	89	14	42	616
Toledo, Oh.	41	39	14	83	32	39	585
Topeka, Kan.	39	03	16	95	40	23	930
Toronto, Ont.	43	39	10	79	23	00	300
Trenton, N.J.	40	13	14	74	46	13	35
Trois-Rivieres, Que.	46	20	36	72	32	37	115(a)
Troy, N.Y.	42	43	45	73	40	58	35
Tucson, Ariz.	32	13	15	110	58	08	2,390
Tulsa, Okla.	36	09	12	95	59	34	804
Urbana, Ill.	40	06	42	88	12	06	725
Utica, N.Y.	43	06	12	75	13	33	415
Vancouver, B.C.	49	18	56	123	04	44	141
Victoria, B.C.	48	25	43	123	21	49	57
Waco, Tex.	31	33	12	97	08	00	405
Walla Walla, Wash.	46	04	08	118	20	24	936
Washington, D.C.	38	53	51	77	00	33	25
Waterbury, Conn.	41	33	13	73	02	31	260
Waterloo, Ia.	42	29	40	92	20	20	850
West Palm Beach, Fla.	26	42	36	80	03	07	15
Wheeling, W. Va.	40	04	03	80	43	20	650
Whitehorse, Yukon	60	43	17	135	03	03	2,305(a)
White Plains, N.Y.	41	02	00	73	45	48	220
Wichita, Kan.	37	41	30	97	20	16	1,290
Wichita Falls, Tex.	33	54	34	98	29	28	945
Wilkes-Barre, Pa.	41	14	32	75	53	17	640
Wilmington, Del.	39	44	46	75	32	51	135
Wilmington, N.C.	34	14	44	77	56	58	35
Windsor, Ont.	42	18	56	83	02	10	603
Winnipeg, Man.	49	53	56	97	08	23	762
Winston-Salem, N.C.	36	05	52	80	14	42	860
Worcester, Mass.	42	15	37	71	48	17	475
Yakima, Wash.	46	36	09	120	30	39	1,060
Yellowknife, N.W.T.	62	27	16	114	22	33	674(a)
Yonkers, N.Y.	40	55	55	73	53	54	10
York, Pa.	39	57	35	76	43	36	370
Youngstown, Oh.	41	05	57	80	39	02	840
Yuma, Ariz.	32	42	54	114	37	24	160
Zanesville, Oh.	39	56	18	82	00	30	720

World Cities

City	Lat. N °	′	″	Long. W °	′	″	Alt.* feet
London, UK (Greenwich)	51	30	00N	0	0	0	245
Paris, France.	48	50	14N	2	20	14E	300
Berlin, Germany.	52	32	00N	13	25	00E	110
Rome, Italy.	41	53	00N	12	30	00E	95
Warsaw, Poland.	52	15	00N	21	00	00E	360
Moscow, USSR.	55	45	00N	37	42	00E	394
Athens, Greece.	37	58	00N	23	44	00E	300
Jerusalem, Israel.	31	47	00N	35	13	00E	2,500
Johannesburg, So. Afr.	26	10	00S	28	02	00E	5,740
New Delhi, India.	28	38	00N	77	12	00E	770
Peking, China.	39	54	00N	116	26	00E	600
Rio de Janeiro, Brazil.	22	53	43S	43	13	22W	30
Tokyo, Japan.	35	45	00N	139	45	00E	30
Sydney, Australia.	33	52	00S	151	12	00E	25

Perpetual Calendar

The number shown for each year indicates which Gregorian calendar to use. For 1583–1802, or for Julian calendar, see page 291. For years 1803–1820, use numbers for 1983–2000, respectively.

1990   **1991**

(Calendar grids for reference numbers 1–6 with monthly calendars, and a year-to-calendar-number lookup table covering years 1821–2079.)

Perpetual calendar grids numbered 7, 8, 9, 10, 11 (1992), 12, 13, 14, each showing the twelve months (JANUARY, FEBRUARY, MARCH, APRIL, MAY, JUNE, JULY, AUGUST, SEPTEMBER, OCTOBER, NOVEMBER, DECEMBER) with day columns S M T W T F S.

The Julian Period

How many days have you lived? To determine this, you must multiply your age by 365, add the number of days since your last birthday until today, and account for all leap years. Chances are your answer would be wrong. Astronomers, however, find it convenient to express dates and long time intervals in days rather than in years, months and days. This is done by placing events within the Julian period.

The Julian period was devised in 1582 by Joseph Scaliger and named after his father Julius (not after the Julian calendar). Scaliger had Julian Day (JD) #1 begin at noon, Jan. 1, 4713 B. C., the most recent time that three major chronological cycles began on the same day — 1) the 28-year solar cycle, after which dates in the Julian calendar (e.g., Feb. 11)

return to the same days of the week (e.g., Monday); 2) the 19-year lunar cycle, after which the phases of the moon return to the same dates of the year; and 3) the 15-year indiction cycle, used in ancient Rome to regulate taxes. It will take 7980 years to complete the period, the product of 28, 19, and 15.

Noon on Dec. 31, 1990, marks the beginning of JD 2,448,257; that many days will have passed since the start of the Julian period. The JD at noon of any date in 1991 may be found by adding to this figure the day of the year for that date, which is given in the left hand column in the chart below. Simple JD conversion tables are used by astronomers.

Days Between Two Dates

Table covers period of two ordinary years. Example—Days between Feb. 10, 1989 and Dec. 15, 1990; subtract 41 from 714; answer is 673 days. For leap year, such as 1992, one day must be added: final answer is 674.

Date	Jan.	Feb.	Mar.	April	May	June	July	Aug.	Sept.	Oct.	Nov.	Dec.	Date	Jan.	Feb.	Mar.	April	May	June	July	Aug.	Sept.	Oct.	Nov.	Dec.
1	1	32	60	91	121	152	182	213	244	274	305	335	1	366	397	425	456	486	517	547	578	609	639	670	700
2	2	33	61	92	122	153	183	214	245	275	306	336	2	367	398	426	457	487	518	548	579	610	640	671	701
3	3	34	62	93	123	154	184	215	246	276	307	337	3	368	399	427	458	488	519	549	580	611	641	672	702
4	4	35	63	94	124	155	185	216	247	277	308	338	4	369	400	428	459	489	520	550	581	612	642	673	703
5	5	36	64	95	125	156	186	217	248	278	309	339	5	370	401	429	460	490	521	551	582	613	643	674	704
6	6	37	65	96	126	157	187	218	249	279	310	340	6	371	402	430	461	491	522	552	583	614	644	675	705
7	7	38	66	97	127	158	188	219	250	280	311	341	7	372	403	431	462	492	523	553	584	615	645	676	706
8	8	39	67	98	128	159	189	220	251	281	312	342	8	373	404	432	463	493	524	554	585	616	646	677	707
9	9	40	68	99	129	160	190	221	252	282	313	343	9	374	405	433	464	494	525	555	586	617	647	678	708
10	10	41	69	100	130	161	191	222	253	283	314	344	10	375	406	434	465	495	526	556	587	618	648	679	709
11	11	42	70	101	131	162	192	223	254	284	315	345	11	376	407	435	466	496	527	557	588	619	649	680	710
12	12	43	71	102	132	163	193	224	255	285	316	346	12	377	408	436	467	497	528	558	589	620	650	681	711
13	13	44	72	103	133	164	194	225	256	286	317	347	13	378	409	437	468	498	529	559	590	621	651	682	712
14	14	45	73	104	134	165	195	226	257	287	318	348	14	379	410	438	469	499	530	560	591	622	652	683	713
15	15	46	74	105	135	166	196	227	258	288	319	349	15	380	411	439	470	500	531	561	592	623	653	684	714
16	16	47	75	106	136	167	197	228	259	289	320	350	16	381	412	440	471	501	532	562	593	624	654	685	715
17	17	48	76	107	137	168	198	229	260	290	321	351	17	382	413	441	472	502	533	563	594	625	655	686	716
18	18	49	77	108	138	169	199	230	261	291	322	352	18	383	414	442	473	503	534	564	595	626	656	687	717
19	19	50	78	109	139	170	200	231	262	292	323	353	19	384	415	443	474	504	535	565	596	627	657	688	718
20	20	51	79	110	140	171	201	232	263	293	324	354	20	385	416	444	475	505	536	566	597	628	658	689	719
21	21	52	80	111	141	172	202	233	264	294	325	355	21	386	417	445	476	506	537	567	598	629	659	690	720
22	22	53	81	112	142	173	203	234	265	295	326	356	22	387	418	446	477	507	538	568	599	630	660	691	721
23	23	54	82	113	143	174	204	235	266	296	327	357	23	388	419	447	478	508	539	569	600	631	661	692	722
24	24	55	83	114	144	175	205	236	267	297	328	358	24	389	420	448	479	509	540	570	601	632	662	693	723
25	25	56	84	115	145	176	206	237	268	298	329	359	25	390	421	449	480	510	541	571	602	633	663	694	724
26	26	57	85	116	146	177	207	238	269	299	330	360	26	391	422	450	481	511	542	572	603	634	664	695	725
27	27	58	86	117	147	178	208	239	270	300	331	361	27	392	423	451	482	512	543	573	604	635	665	696	726
28	28	59	87	118	148	179	209	240	271	301	332	362	28	393	424	452	483	513	544	574	605	636	666	697	727
29	29	—	88	119	149	180	210	241	272	302	333	363	29	394	—	453	484	514	545	575	606	637	667	698	728
30	30	—	89	120	150	181	211	242	273	303	334	364	30	395	—	454	485	515	546	576	607	638	668	699	729
31	31	—	90	—	151	—	212	243	—	304	—	365	31	396	—	455	—	516	—	577	608	—	669	—	730

Lunar Calendar, Chinese New Year, Vietnamese Tet

The ancient Chinese lunar calendar is divided into 12 months of either 29 or 30 days (compensating for the fact that the mean duration of the lunar month is 29 days, 12 hours, 44.05 minutes). The calendar is synchronized with the solar year by the addition of extra months at fixed intervals.

The Chinese calendar runs on a sexagenary cycle, i.e., 60 years. The cycles 1876-1935 and 1936-1995, with the years grouped under their twelve animal designations, are printed below. The Year 1991 (Lunar Year 4689) is found in the eighth column, under Sheep, and is known as a "Year of the Goat." Readers can find the animal name for the year of their birth, marriage, etc., in the same chart. (Note: the first 3-7 weeks of each of the western years belong to the previous Chinese year and animal designation.)

Both the western (Gregorian) and traditional lunar calendars are used publicly in China, and two New Year's celebrations are held. On Taiwan, in overseas Chinese communities, and in Vietnam, the lunar calendar has been used only to set the dates for traditional festivals, with the Gregorian system in general use.

The four-day Chinese New Year, Hsin Nien, and the three-day Vietnamese New Year festival, Tet, begin at the first new moon after the sun enters Aquarius. The day may fall, therefore, between Jan. 21 and Feb. 19 of the Gregorian calendar. Feb. 15, 1991 marks the start of the new Chinese year. The date is fixed according to the date of the new moon in the Far East. Since this is west of the International Date Line the date may be one day later than that of the new moon in the United States.

Rat	Ox	Tiger	Hare (Rabbit)	Dragon	Snake	Horse	Sheep (Goat)	Monkey	Rooster	Dog	Pig
1876	1877	1878	1879	1880	1881	1882	1883	1884	1885	1886	1887
1888	1889	1890	1891	1892	1893	1894	1895	1896	1897	1898	1899
1900	1901	1902	1903	1904	1905	1906	1907	1908	1909	1910	1911
1912	1913	1914	1915	1916	1917	1918	1919	1920	1921	1922	1923
1924	1925	1926	1927	1928	1929	1930	1931	1932	1933	1934	1935
1936	1937	1938	1939	1940	1941	1942	1943	1944	1945	1946	1947
1948	1949	1950	1951	1952	1953	1954	1955	1956	1957	1958	1959
1960	1961	1962	1963	1964	1965	1966	1967	1968	1969	1970	1971
1972	1973	1974	1975	1976	1977	1978	1979	1980	1981	1982	1983
1984	1985	1986	1987	1988	1989	1990	1991	1992	1993	1994	1995

Standard Time, Daylight Saving Time, and Others

Source: Defense Mapping Agency Hydrographic Center; Department of Transportation; National Inst. of Standards & Technology; U.S. Naval Observatory

Standard Time

Standard time is reckoned from Greenwich, England, recognized as the Prime Meridian of Longitude. The world is divided into 24 zones, each 15° of arc, or one hour in time apart. The Greenwich meridian (0°) extends through the center of the initial zone, and the zones to the east are numbered from 1 to 12 with the prefix "minus" indicating the number of hours to be subtracted to obtain Greenwich Time. Each zone extends 7¹/₂° on either side of its central meridian.

Westward zones are similarly numbered, but prefixed "plus" showing the number of hours that must be added to get Greenwich Time. While these zones apply generally to sea areas, it should be noted that the Standard Time maintained in many countries does not coincide with zone time. A graphical representation of the zones is shown on the Standard Time Zone Chart of the World published by the Defense Mapping Agency Combat Support Center, Attn: PMSR Washington, DC 20315-0020.

The United States and possessions are divided into eight Standard Time zones, as set forth by the Uniform Time Act of 1966, which also provides for the use of Daylight Saving Time therein. Each zone is approximately 15° of longitude in width. All places in each zone use, instead of their own local time, the time counted from the transit of the "mean sun" across the Standard Time meridian which passes near the middle of that zone.

These time zones are designated as Atlantic, Eastern, Central, Mountain, Pacific, Yukon, Alaska-Hawaii, and Bering (Samoa), and the time in these zones is basically reckoned from the 60th, 75th, 90th, 105th, 120th, 135th, 150th and 165th meridians west of Greenwich. The line wanders to conform to local geographical regions. The time in the various zones is earlier than Greenwich Time by 4, 5, 6, 7, 8, 9, 10, and 11 hours respectively.

24-Hour Time

24-hour time is widely used in scientific work throughout the world. In the United States it is used also in operations of the Armed Forces. In Europe it is frequently used by the transportation networks in preference to the 12-hour a.m. and p.m. system. With the 24-hour system the day begins at midnight and is designated 0000 through 2359.

International Date Line

The Date Line is a zig-zag line that approximately coincides with the 180th meridian, and it is where the calendar dates are separated. The date must be advanced one day when crossing in a westerly direction and set back one day when crossing in an easterly direction.

The line is deflected eastward through the Bering Strait and westward of the Aleutians to prevent separating these areas by date. The line is again deflected eastward of the Tonga and New Zealand Islands in the South Pacific for the same reason.

Daylight Saving Time

Daylight Saving Time is achieved by advancing the clock one hour. Under the Uniform Time Act, which became effective in 1967, all states, the District of Columbia, and U.S. possessions were to observe Daylight Saving Time beginning at 2 a.m. on the first Sunday in April and ending at 2 a.m. on the last Sunday in October. Any state could, by law, exempt itself; a 1972 amendment to the act authorized states split by time zones to take that into consideration in exempting themselves. Arizona, Hawaii, Puerto Rico, the Virgin Islands, American Samoa, and part of Indiana are now exempt. Some local zone boundaries in Kansas, Texas, Florida, Michigan, and Alaska have been modified in the last several years by the Dept. of Transportation, which oversees the act. To conserve energy Congress put most of the nation on year-round Daylight Saving Time for two years effective Jan. 6, 1974 though Oct. 26, 1975; but a further bill, signed in October, 1974, restored Standard Time from the last Sunday in that month to the last Sunday in February, 1975. At the end of 1975, Congress failed to renew this temporary legislation and the nation returned to the older end-of April to end-of October DST system.

On July 8, 1986, Pres. Ronald Reagan signed legislation moving up the start of daylight saving time to the first Sunday in April. Daylight Saving Time, which used to start the last Sunday in April, will still end the last Sunday in October. The Transportation Dept. estimated that the earlier starting date will help save more than $28 million in traffic accident costs and prevent more than 1,500 injuries and 20 deaths. The new law, opposed by some farm state lawmakers, took effect in 1987.

International

Adjusting clock time to be able to use the added daylight on summer evenings is common throughout the world.

Western Europe is on daylight saving time generally from the last Sunday in March to the last Sunday in September; however, the United Kingdom continues until the last Sunday in October.

The Soviet Union lies over 11 time zones, but maintains its standard time 1 hour fast of the zone designation. Additionally, it proclaims daylight saving time as does Europe.

China lies across 5 time zones, but has decreed that the entire country be placed on one zone time minus 8 hours with daylight saving time from April 12 to September 12.

Many of the countries in the Southern Hemisphere maintain daylight saving time generally from October to March; however, most countries near the equator do not deviate from standard time.

Standard Time Differences—World Cities

The time indicated in the table is fixed by law and is called the legal time, or, more generally, Standard Time. Use of Daylight Saving Time varies widely. *Indicates morning of the following day. At 12:00 noon, Eastern Standard Time, the standard time (in 24-hour time) in foreign cities is as follows:

City	Time	City	Time	City	Time	City	Time
Addis Ababa	20 00	Cape Town	19 00	Leningrad	20 00	Santiago (Chile)	13 00
Alexandria	19 00	Caracas	13 00	Lima	12 00	Seoul	2 00*
Amsterdam	18 00	Casablanca	17 00	Lisbon	17 00	Shanghai	1 00*
Athens	19 00	Copenhagen	18 00	Liverpool	17 00	Singapore	1 00*
Auckland	5 00*	Dacca	23 00	London	17 00	Stockholm	18 00
Baghdad	20 00	Delhi	22 30	Madrid	18 00	Sydney (Australia)	3 00*
Bangkok	0 00	Dublin	17 00	Manila	1 00*	Tashkent	23 00
Beijing	1 00*	Gdansk	18 00	Mecca (Saudi Arabia)	20 00	Teheran	20 30
Belfast	17 00	Geneva	18 00	Melbourne	3 00*	Tel Aviv	19 00
Berlin	18 00	Havana	12 00	Mexico City	11 00	Tokyo	2 00*
Bogota	12 00	Helsinki	19 00	Montevideo	14 00	Valparaiso	13 00
Bombay	22 30	Ho Chi Minh City	0 00	Moscow	20 00	Vladivostok	3 00*
Bremen	18 00	Hong Kong	1 00*	Nagasaki	2 00*	Vienna	18 00
Brussels	18 00	Istanbul	19 00	Oslo	18 00	Warsaw	18 00
Bucharest	19 00	Jakarta	0 00	Paris	18 00	Wellington (N.Z.)	5 00*
Budapest	18 00	Jerusalem	19 00	Prague	18 00	Yokohama	2 00*
Buenos Aires	14 00	Johannesburg	19 00	Rangoon	23 30	Zurich	18 00
Cairo	19 00	Karachi	22 00	Rio De Janeiro	14 00		
Calcutta	22 30	Le Havre	18 00	Rome	18 00		

Standard Time Differences — North American Cities

At 12 o'clock noon, Eastern Standard Time, the standard time in N.A. cities is as follows:

Akron, Oh.	12.00	Noon	Frankfort, Ky. . . .	12.00	Noon	*Phoenix, Ariz.	10.00	A.M.
Albuquerque, N.M. .	10.00	A.M.	Galveston, Tex. . . .	11.00	A.M.	Pierre, S.D.	11.00	A.M.
Atlanta, Ga.	12.00	Noon	Grand Rapids, Mich.	12.00	Noon	Pittsburgh, Pa. . . .	12.00	Noon
Austin, Tex.	11.00	A.M.	Halifax, N.S.	1.00	P.M.	Portland, Me.	12.00	Noon
Baltimore, Md. . . .	12.00	Noon	Hartford, Conn. . . .	12.00	Noon	Portland, Ore. . . .	9.00	A.M.
Birmingham, Ala. . .	11.00	A.M.	Helena, Mon.	10.00	A.M.	Providence, R.I. . . .	12.00	Noon
Bismarck, N.D.	11.00	A.M.	*Honolulu, Ha. . . .	7.00	A.M.	*Regina, Sask. . . .	11.00	A.M.
Boise, Ida.	10.00	A.M.	Houston, Tex.	11.00	A.M.	Reno, Nev.	9.00	A.M.
Boston, Mass.	12.00	Noon	*Indianapolis, Ind. . .	12.00	Noon	Richmond, Va. . . .	12.00	Noon
Buffalo, N.Y.	12.00	Noon	Jacksonville, Fla. . .	12.00	Noon	Rochester, N.Y. . . .	12.00	Noon
Butte, Mon.	10.00	A.M.	Juneau, Alas.	8.00	A.M.	Sacramento, Cal. . .	9.00	A.M.
Calgary, Alta.	10.00	A.M.	Kansas City, Mo. . .	11.00	A.M.	St. John's, Nfld. . . .	1.30	P.M.
Charleston, S.C. . . .	12.00	Noon	Knoxville, Tenn. . . .	12.00	Noon	St. Louis, Mo.	11.00	A.M.
Charleston, W.Va. . .	12.00	Noon	Lexington, Ky.	12.00	Noon	St. Paul, Minn. . . .	11.00	A.M.
Charlotte, N.C. . . .	12.00	Noon	Lincoln, Neb.	11.00	A.M.	Salt Lake City, Ut. . .	10.00	A.M.
Charlottetown, P.E.I.	1.00	P.M.	Little Rock, Ark. . . .	11.00	A.M.	San Antonio, Tex. . .	11.00	A.M.
Chattanooga, Tenn. .	12.00	Noon	Los Angeles, Cal. . .	9.00	A.M.	San Diego, Cal. . . .	9.00	A.M.
Cheyenne, Wy.	10.00	A.M.	Louisville, Ky.	12.00	Noon	San Francisco, Cal. .	9.00	A.M.
Chicago, Ill.	11.00	A.M.	*Mexico City	11.00	A.M.	Santa Fe, N.M. . . .	10.00	A.M.
Cleveland, Oh.	12.00	Noon	Memphis, Tenn. . . .	11.00	A.M.	Savannah, Ga.	12.00	Noon
Colorado Spr., Col. .	10.00	A.M.	Miami, Fla.	12.00	Noon	Seattle, Wash.	9.00	A.M.
Columbus, Oh. . . .	12.00	Noon	Milwaukee, Wis. . . .	11.00	A.M.	Shreveport, La. . . .	11.00	A.M.
Dallas, Tex.	11.00	A.M.	Minneapolis, Minn. .	11.00	A.M.	Sioux Falls, S.D. . . .	11.00	A.M.
*Dawson, Yuk.	9.00	A.M.	Mobile, Ala.	11.00	A.M.	Spokane, Wash. . . .	9.00	A.M.
Dayton, Oh.	12.00	Noon	Montreal, Que. . . .	12.00	Noon	Tampa, Fla.	12.00	Noon
Denver, Col.	10.00	A.M.	Nashville, Tenn. . . .	11.00	A.M.	Toledo, Oh.	12.00	Noon
Des Moines, Ia. . . .	11.00	A.M.	New Haven, Conn. . .	12.00	Noon	Topeka, Kan.	11.00	A.M.
Detroit, Mich.	12.00	Noon	New Orleans, La. . .	11.00	A.M.	Toronto, Ont.	12.00	Noon
Duluth, Minn.	11.00	A.M.	New York, N.Y. . . .	12.00	Noon	*Tucson, Ariz.	10.00	A.M.
El Paso, Tex.	10.00	A.M.	Nome, Alas.	8.00	A.M.	Tulsa, Okla.	11.00	A.M.
Erie, Pa.	12.00	Noon	Norfolk, Va.	12.00	Noon	Vancouver, B.C. . . .	9.00	A.M.
Evansville, Ind. . . .	11.00	A.M.	Okla. City, Okla. . . .	11.00	A.M.	Washington, D.C. . . .	12.00	Noon
Fairbanks, Alas. . . .	8.00	A.M.	Omaha, Neb.	11.00	A.M.	Wichita, Kan.	11.00	A.M.
Flint, Mich.	12.00	Noon	Peoria, Ill.	11.00	A.M.	Wilmington, Del. . . .	12.00	Noon
*Fort Wayne, Ind. . .	12.00	Noon	Philadelphia, Pa. . .	12.00	Noon	Winnipeg, Man. . . .	11.00	A.M.
Fort Worth, Tex. . . .	11.00	A.M.						

*Cities with an asterisk do not observe daylight saving time. During much of the year, it is necessary to add one hour to the cities which do observe daylight savings time to get the proper time relation.

Legal or Public Holidays, 1991

Technically there are no national holidays in the United States; each state has jurisdiction over its holidays, which are designated by legislative enactment or executive proclamation. In practice, however, most states observe the federal legal public holidays, even though the President and Congress can legally designate holidays only for the District of Columbia and for federal employees. Federal legal public holidays are New Year's Day, Martin Luther King Day, Washington's Birthday, Memorial Day, Independence Day, Labor Day, Columbus Day, Veterans' Day, Thanksgiving, and Christmas.

Chief Legal or Public Holidays

When a holiday falls on a Sunday or a Saturday it is usually observed on the following Monday or preceding Friday. For some holidays, government and business closing practices vary. In most states, the office of the Secretary of State can provide details of holiday closings. In most states, the following will be legal or public holidays in 1991:

Jan. 1 (Tuesday) — New Year's Day.

Jan. 21 (Monday) — Martin Luther King Day. In some states, combined with Robert E. Lee Day.

Feb. 12 (Tuesday) — Lincoln's Birthday.

Feb. 18 (3d Mon. in Feb.) — Washington's Birthday, or Presidents' Day, or Washington-Lincoln Day.

May 27 (last Mon. in May) — Memorial Day, or Decoration Day.

July 4 (Thursday) — Independence Day.

Sept. 2 (1st Mon. in Sept.) — Labor Day.

Oct. 14 (2d Mon. in Oct.) — Columbus Day, or Discoverers' Day, or Pioneers' Day.

Nov. 11 (Monday) — Veterans' Day.

Nov. 28 (4th Thurs. in Nov.) — Thanksgiving Day.

Dec. 25 (Wednesday) — Christmas Day.

In some states, the following will be legal or public holidays in 1991:

Mar. 29 (Friday) — Good Friday. In some states, observed for half or part of day.

Nov. 5 (1st Tues. after the 1st Mon. in Nov.) — Election Day.

Selected Foreign Holidays

Jan. 5 — Twelfth Night (Wassail Eve), England.

Jan. 14 — Vinegrower's Day, Bulgaria.

Feb. 3 — Hamstrom Day, Switzerland.

Feb. 3 — Setsubun (bean-throwing festival), Japan.

Feb. 11 — Youth Day, Cameroon.

Feb. 9-12 — Carnival, Brazil.

Apr. 7 — Ching Ming Festival, China.

Apr. 18 — Buddha's Birthday, Korea.

Apr. 22 — Independence Day, Israel.

Apr. 25 — ANZAC Day, Australia & New Zealand.

May 5 — Cinco de Mayo, Mexico.

May 9 — Victory over Fascism Day, USSR.

May 25 — African Freedom Day, Chad, Zambia.

June 22 — Midsummer Eve, Denmark.

July 14 — Bastille Day, France.

mid July — Feria de San Fermin, Spain.

July 24 — Simon Bolivar's Birthday, Venezuela.

Aug. 13 — Fox Hill Day, Bahamas.

Aug. 15 — Sour Herring Premiere, Sweden.

Sept. 19 — St. Gennaro, Italy.

Oct. 2 — Mahatma Gandhi's Birthday, India.

Oct. 6 — Ivy Day, Ireland.

Oct. 9 — Korean Alphabet Day.

Nov. 5 — Guy Fawkes Day, England.

Nov. 7-8 — October Revolution Anniversary, USSR.

Nov. 16 — Elephant Round-up, Thailand.

Nov. 17 — Volkstrauertag (Memorial Day), Germany.

Dec. 5 — Lover's Fair, Belgium.

Dec. 16-Jan. 6 — Christmas Observance, Phillipines.

WEIGHTS AND MEASURES

Source: National Institute of Standards and Technology, U.S. Commerce Department

The International System of Units

Two systems of weights and measures exist side by side in the United States today, with roughly equal but separate legislative sanction: the U.S. Customary System and the International (Metric) System. Throughout U.S. history, the Customary System (inherited from, but now different from, the British Imperial System) has been, as its name implies, customarily used; a plethora of federal and state legislation has given it, through implication, standing as our primary weights and measures system. However, the Metric System (incorporated in the scientists' new SI or Systeme International d'Unites) is the only system that has ever received specific legislative sanction by Congress. The "Law of 1866" reads:

It shall be lawful throughout the United States of America to employ the weights and measures of the metric system; and no contract or dealing, or pleading in any court, shall be deemed invalid or liable to objection because the weights or measures expressed or referred to therein are weights or measures of the metric system.

Over the last 100 years, the Metric System has seen slow, steadily increasing use in the United States. In science and also in the pharmaceutical industry, the use of metrics has for many years been predominant; today, the manufacturing industry is steadily increasing its use of the metric system largely motivated by the automotive industry, which is now predominantly metric.

On Feb. 10, 1964, the National Bureau of Standards issued the following bulletin:

Henceforth it shall be the policy of the National Bureau of Standards to use the units of the International System (SI), as adopted by the 11th General Conference on Weights and Measures (October 1960), except when the use of these units would obviously impair communication or reduce the usefulness of a report.

The Trade Act of 1988 calls for the federal government to adopt metric specifications by Dec. 31, 1992, and mandates the Commerce Dept. to oversee the program.

What had been the Metric System became the International System (SI), a more complete scientific system.

Seven units have been adopted to serve as the base for the International System as follows: length—meter; mass—kilogram; time—second; electric current—ampere; thermodynamic temperature—kelvin; amount of substance—mole; and luminous intensity—candela.

Prefixes

The following prefixes, in combination with the basic unit names, provide the multiples and submultiples in the International System. For example, the unit name "meter," with the prefix "kilo" added, produces "kilometer," meaning "1,000 meters."

Prefix	Symbol	Multiples	Equivalent	Prefix	Symbol	Submultiples	Equivalent
exa	E	10^{18}	quintillionfold	deci	d	10^{-1}	tenth part
peta	P	10^{15}	quadrillionfold	centi	c	10^{-2}	hundredth part
tera	T	10^{12}	trillionfold	milli	m	10^{-3}	thousandth part
giga	G	10^{9}	billionfold	micro	μ	10^{-6}	millionth part
mega	M	10^{6}	millionfold	nano	n	10^{-9}	billionth part
kilo	k	10^{3}	thousandfold	pico	p	10^{-12}	trillionth part
hecto	h	10^{2}	hundredfold	femto	f	10^{-15}	quadrillionth part
deka	da	10	tenfold	atto	a	10^{-18}	quintillionth part

Tables of Metric Weights and Measures

Linear Measure

10 millimeters (mm)	= 1 centimeter (cm)
10 centimeters	= 1 decimeter (dm) = 100 millimeters
10 decimeters	= 1 meter (m) = 1,000 millimeters
10 meters	= 1 dekameter (dam)
10 dekameters	= 1 hectometer (hm) = 100 meters
10 hectometers	= 1 kilometer (km) = 1,000 meters

Area Measure

100 square millimeters (mm²)	= 1 square centimeter (cm²)
10,000 square centimeters	= 1 square meter (m²) = 1,000,000 square millimeters
100 square meters	= 1 are (a)
100 ares	= 1 hectare (ha) = 10,000 square meters
100 hectares	= 1 square kilometer (km²) = 1,000,000 square meters

Fluid Volume Measure

10 milliliters (mL)	= 1 centiliter (cL)
10 centiliters	= 1 deciliter (dL) = 100 milliliters
10 deciliters	= 1 liter (L) = 1,000 milliliters
10 liters	= 1 dekaliter (daL)
10 dekaliters	= 1 hectoliter (hL) = 100 liters
10 hectoliters	= 1 kiloliter (kL) = 1,000 liters

Cubic Measure

1,000 cubic millimeters (mm³)	= 1 cubic centimeter (cm³)
1,000 cubic centimeters	= 1 cubic decimeter (dm³) = 1,000,000 cubic millimeters
1,000 cubic decimeters	= 1 cubic meter (m³) = 1 stere = 1,000,000 cubic centimeters = 1,000,000,000 cubic millimeters

Weight

10 milligrams (mg)	= 1 centigram (cg)
10 centigrams	= 1 decigram (dg) = 100 milligrams
10 decigrams	= 1 gram (g) = 1,000 milligrams
10 grams	= 1 dekagram (dag)
10 dekagrams	= 1 hectogram (hg) = 100 grams
10 hectograms	= 1 kilogram (kg) = 1,000 grams
1,000 kilograms	= 1 metric ton (t)

Table of U.S. Customary Weights and Measures

Linear Measure

12 inches (in)	= 1 foot (ft)
3 feet	= 1 yard (yd)
5 ½ yards	= 1 rod (rd), pole, or perch (16 ½ feet)
40 rods	= 1 furlong (fur) = 220 yards = 660 feet
8 furlongs	= 1 statute mile (mi) = 1,760 yards = 5,280 feet
3 miles	= 1 league = 5,280 yards = 15,840 feet
6076.11549 feet	= 1 International Nautical Mile

Liquid Measure

When necessary to distinguish the liquid pint or quart from the dry pint or quart, the word "liquid" or the abbreviation "liq" should be used in combination with the name or abbreviation of the liquid unit.

4 gills	= 1 pint (pt) = 28.875 cubic inches
2 pints	= 1 quart (qt) = 57.75 cubic inches
4 quarts	= 1 gallon (gal) = 231 cubic inches = 8 pints = 32 gills

Area Measure

Squares and cubes of units are sometimes abbreviated by using "superior" figures. For example. ft² means square foot, and ft³ means cubic foot.

144 square inches	= 1 square foot (ft²)
9 square feet	= 1 square yard (yd²) = 1,296 square inches
30 ¼ square yards	= 1 square rod (rd²) = 272 ¼ square feet
160 square rods	= 1 acre = 4,840 square yards = 43,560 square feet
640 acres	= 1 square mile (mi²)
1 mile square	= 1 section (of land)
6 miles square	= 1 township = 36 sections = 36 square miles

Cubic Measure

1 cubic foot (ft³)	= 1,728 cubic inches (in³)
27 cubic feet	= 1 cubic yard (yd³)

Gunter's or Surveyors' Chain Measure

7.92 inches (in)	= 1 link
100 links	= 1 chain (ch) = 4 rods = 66 feet
80 chains	= 1 survey mile (mi) = 320 rods = 5,280 feet

Troy Weight

24 grains	= 1 pennyweight (dwt)
20 pennyweights	= 1 ounce troy (oz t) = 480 grains
12 ounces troy	= 1 pound troy (lb t) = 240 pennyweights = 5,760 grains

Dry Measure

When necessary to distinguish the dry pint or quart from the liquid pint or quart, the word "dry" should be used in combination with the name or abbreviation of the dry unit.

2 pints (pt)	= 1 quart (qt) = 67.2006 cubic inches
8 quarts	= 1 peck (pk) = 537.605 cubic inches = 16 pints
4 pecks	= 1 bushel (bu) = 2,150.42 cubic inches = 32 quarts

Avoirdupois Weight

When necessary to distinguish the avoirdupois ounce or pound from the troy ounce or pound, the word "avoirdupois" or the abbreviation "avdp" should be used in combination with the name or abbreviation of the avoirdupois unit.

(The "grain" is the same in avoirdupois and troy weight.)

27 11/32 grains	= 1 dram (dr)
16 drams	= 1 ounce (oz) = 437 ½ grains
16 ounces	= 1 pound (lb) = 256 drams = 7,000 grains
100 pounds	= 1 hundredweight (cwt)*
20 hundredweights	= 1 ton = 2,000 pounds*

In "gross" or "long" measure, the following values are recognized.

112 pounds	= 1 gross or long hundredweight*
20 gross or long hundredweights	= 1 gross or long ton = 2,240 pounds*

*When the terms "hundredweight" and "ton" are used unmodified, they are commonly understood to mean the 100-pound hundredweight and the 2,000-pound ton, respectively; these units may be designated "net" or "short" when necessary to distinguish them from the corresponding units in gross or long measure.

Tables of Equivalents

In this table it is necessary to distinguish between the "international" and the "survey" foot. The international foot, defined in 1959 as exactly equal to 0.3048 meter, is shorter than the old survey foot by exactly 2 parts in one million. The survey foot is still used in data expressed in feet in geodetic surveys within the U.S. In this table the survey foot is italicized.

When the name of a unit is enclosed in brackets thus, [1 hand], this indicates (1) that the unit is not in general current use in the United States, or (2) that the unit is believed to be based on "custom and usage" rather than on formal definition.

Equivalents involving decimals are. in most instances, rounded off to the third decimal place except where they are exact, in which cases these exact equivalents are so designated.

Lengths

1 angstrom (A)	0.1 nanometer (exactly) 0.000 1 micrometer (exactly) 0.000 000 1 millimeter (exactly) 0.000 000 004 inch
1 cable's length	120 fathoms (exactly) 720 *feet* (exactly) 219 meters
1 centimeter (cm)	0.3937 inch
1 chain (ch) (Gunter's or surveyors)	66 *feet* (exactly) 20.1168 meters
1 chain (engineers)	100 feet 30.48 meters (exactly)
1 decimeter (dm)	3.937 inches
1 degree (geographical)	364,566.929 feet 69.047 miles (avg.) 111.123 kilometers (avg.)
-of latitude	68.708 miles at equator 69.403 miles at poles
-of longitude	69.171 miles at equator
1 dekameter (dam)	32.808 feet
1 fathom	6 *feet* (exactly) 1.8288 meters (exactly)
1 foot (ft)	0.3048 meters (exactly)
1 furlong (fur)	660 *feet* (exactly) 10 chains (surveyors) (exactly) ⅛ statute mile (exactly) 201.168 meters
[1 hand] (height measure for horses from ground to top of shoulders)	4 inches
1 inch (in)	2.54 centimeters (exactly)
1 kilometer (km)	0.621 mile 3,281.5 feet

1 league (land)	3 survey miles (exactly) 4.828 kilometers
1 link (Gunter's or surveyors)	7.92 inches (exactly) 0.201 meter
1 link engineers	1 foot 0.305 meter
1 meter (m)	39.37 inches 1.094 yards
1 micrometer (μm) [the Greek letter mu]	0.001 millimeter (exactly) 0.000 039 37 inch
1 mil	0.001 inch (exactly) 0.025 4 millimeter (exactly)
1 mile (mi) (statute or land)	5,280 feet (exactly) 1.609 kilometers
1 international nautical mile (nmi)	1.852 kilometers (exactly) 1.150779 survey miles 6,076.11549 feet
1 millimeter (mm)	0.039 37 inch
1 nanometer (nm)	0.001 micrometer (exactly) 0.000 000 039 37 inch
1 pica (typography)	12 points
1 point (typography)	0.013 837 inch (exactly) 0.351 millimeter
1 rod (rd), pole, or perch	16 ½ *feet* (exactly) 5.029 meters
1 yard (yd)	0.9144 meter (exactly)

Areas or Surfaces

1 acre	43,560 square *feet* (exactly) 4,840 square yards 0.405 hectare
1 are (a)	119.599 square yards 0.025 acre

1 bolt (cloth measure):
length . . . .   100 yards (on modern looms)
width . . . .   { 42 inches (usually, for cotton)
                                 { 60 inches (usually, for wool)
1 hectare (ha) . . . .   2.471 acres
[1 square (building)] . . . .   100 square feet
1 square centimeter (cm²) . . . .   0.155 square inch
1 square decimeter (dm²) . . . .   15.500 square inches
1 square foot (ft²) . . . .   929.030 square centimeters
1 square inch (in²) . . . .   6.4516 square centimeters (exactly)
1 square kilometer (km²) . . .   { 247.104 acres
                                 { 0.386 square mile
1 square meter (m²) . . . . . . { 1.196 square yards
                                 { 10.764 square feet
1 square mile (mi²) . . . .   258.999 hectares
1 square millimeter (mm²) . . . .   0.002 square inch
1 square rod (rd²) sq. pole, or
sq. perch . . . .   25.293 square meters
1 square yard (yd²) . . . .   0.836 square meter

Capacities or Volumes

1 barrel (bbl) liquid . . . .   31 to 42 gallons°
"There are a variety of "barrels," established by law or usage.
For example: federal taxes on fermented liquors are based on a barrel of 31 gallons: many state laws fix the "barrel for liquids" as 31 ½ gallons; one state fixes a 36-gallon barrel for cistern measurement; federal law recognizes a 40-gallon barrel for "proof spirits"; by custom, 42 gallons comprise a barrel of crude oil or petroleum products for statistical purposes, and this equivalent is recognized "for liquids" by 4 states.

1 barrel (bbl), standard,   { 7,056 cubic inches
for fruits, vegetables,   { 105 dry quarts
and other dry com-
modities except dry   { 3.281 bushels, struck
cranberries . . . . {   measure
                               { 5.826 cubic inches
1 barrel (bbl), standard,   { 86⁴⁵/₆₄ dry quarts
cranberry   { 2.709 bushels, struck
                               {   measure
1 board foot (lumber measure) . .   a foot-square board 1 inch thick
1 bushel (bu) (U.S.)   { 2,150.42 cubic inches
(struck measure)   {   (exactly)
                               { 35.239 liters
                               { 2,747.715 cubic inches
[1 bushel, heaped (U.S.)]   { 1.278 bushels, struck
                               {   measure°
°Frequently recognized as 1¼ bushels, struck measure.
[1 bushel (bu) (British   { 1.032 U.S. bushels
Imperial) (struck   {   struck measure
measure)]   { 2,219.36 cubic inches
1 cord (cd) firewood . . . .   128 cubic feet (exactly)
1 cubic centimeter (cm³) . . . .   0.061 cubic inch
1 cubic decimeter (dm³) . . . .   61.024 cubic inches
                               { 0.554 fluid ounce
1 cubic inch (in³) . . . . . . { 4.433 fluid drams
                               { 16.387 cubic centimeters
                               { 7.481 gallons
1 cubic foot (ft³) . . . . . . { 28.317 cubic decimeters
1 cubic meter (m³) . . . .   1.308 cubic yards
1 cubic yard (yd³) . . . .   0.765 cubic meter
1 cup, measuring . . . . { 8 fluid ounces (exactly)
                               { 1½ liquid pint (exactly)
[1 dram, fluid (fl dr)   { 0.961 U.S. fluid dram
(British)] . . . .   { 0.217 cubic inch
                               { 3.552 milliliters
1 dekaliter (daL) . . . . . . { 2.642 gallons
                               { 1.135 pecks
                               { 231 cubic inches (exactly)
1 gallon (gal) (U.S.) . . . . { 3.785 liters
                               { 0.833 British gallon
                               { 128 U.S. fluid ounces (exactly)
                               { 277.42 cubic inches
[1 gallon (gal)   { 1.201 U.S. gallons
British Imperial] . . . . .   { 4.546 liters
                               { 160 British fluid ounces (exactly)
                               { 7.219 cubic inches
1 gill (gi) . . . . { 4 fluid ounces (exactly)
                               { 0.118 liter
                               { 26.418 gallons
1 hectoliter (hL) . . . . . . { 2.838 bushels
                               { 1.057 liquid quarts
1 liter (L) (1 cubic decimeter exactly) . . . . { 0.908 dry quart
                               { 61.025 cubic inches

1 milliliter (mL) (1 cu cm exactly) . . . . . . { 0.271 fluid dram
                                                { 16.231 minims
                                                { 0.061 cubic inch
1 ounce, liquid   { 1.805 cubic inches
(U.S.) . . . .   { 29.573 milliliters
                               { 1.041 British fluid ounces
                               { 0.961 U.S. fluid ounce
[1 ounce, fluid (fl oz) (British)] { 1.734 cubic inches
                               { 28.412 milliliters
1 peck (pk) . . . .   8.810 liters
1 pint (pt), dry . . . . { 33.600 cubic inches
                               { 0.551 liter
1 pint (pt), liquid . . . . . { 28.875 cubic inches (exactly)
                               { 0.473 liter
                               { 67.201 cubic inches
1 quart (qt) dry (U.S.) . . . { 1.101 liters
                               { 0.969 British quart
                               { 57.75 cubic in (exactly)
1 quart (qt) liquid (U.S.) .   { 0.946 liter
                               { 0.833 British quart
                               { 69.354 cubic inches
[1 quart (qt) (British)] . . . { 1.032 U.S. dry quarts
                               { 1.201 U.S. liquid quarts
                               { 3 teaspoons (exactly)
1 tablespoon . . . . { 4 fluid drams
                               { ½ fluid ounce (exactly)
1 teaspoon . . . . { ⅓ tablespoon (exactly)
                               { 1⅓ fluid drams°
"The equivalent "1 teaspoon—1⅓ fluid drams" has been found by the bureau to correspond more closely with the actual capacities of "measuring" and silver teaspoons than the equivalent "1 teaspoon—1 fluid dram" which is given by many dictionaries.

Weights or Masses

1 assay ton°° (AT) . . . .   29.167 grams
°°Used in assaying. The assay ton bears the same relation to the milligram that a ton of 2,000 pounds avoirdupois bears to the ounce troy; hence the weight in milligrams of precious metal obtained from one assay ton of ore gives directly the number of troy ounces to the net ton.

1 bale (cotton measure) . . . { 500 pounds in U.S.
                               { 750 pounds in Egypt
1 carat (c) . . . . { 200 milligrams (exactly)
                               { 3.086 grains
1 dram avoirdupois (dr avdp)   { 27¹¹/₃₂ (= 27.344) grains
gamma, see microgram   { 1.772 grams
1 grain . . . .   64.799 milligrams
                               { 15.432 grains
1 gram . . . .   { 0.035 ounce, avoirdupois
1 hundredweight, gross or   { 112 pounds (exactly)
long°°° (gross cwt) . . . .   { 50.802 kilograms
1 hundredweight, net or short . . . . { 100 pounds (exactly)
(cwt. or net cwt.) . . . . { 45.359 kilograms
1 kilogram (kg) . . . .   2.205 pounds
1 microgram (μg [The Greek letter mu in
combination with the letter g]) . . .   0.000001 gram (exactly)
1 milligram (mg) . . . .   0.015 grain
1 ounce, avoirdupois   { 437.5 grains (exactly)
(oz avdp) . . . .   { 0.911 troy ounce
                               { 28.350 grams
                               { 480 grains (exactly)
1 ounce, troy (oz t) . . . .   { 1.097 avoirdupois ounces
                               { 31.103 grams
1 pennyweight (dwt) . . . . .   1.555 grams
1 pound, avoirdupois   { 7,000 grains (exactly)
(lb avdp) . . . .   { 1.215 troy pounds
                               { 453.592 37 grams (exactly)
                               { 5,760 grains (exactly)
1 pound, troy (lb t) . . . .   { 0.823 avoirdupois pound
                               { 373.242 grams
1 ton, gross or long°°°   { 2,240 pounds (exactly)
(gross ton) . . . .   { 1.12 net tons (exactly)
                               { 1.016 metric tons
°°°The gross or long ton and hundredweight are used commercially in the United States to only a limited extent, usually in restricted industrial fields. These units are the same as British "ton" and "hundredweight."

                               { 2,204.623 pounds
1 ton, metric (t) . . . . . . { 0.984 gross ton
                               { 1.102 net tons
1 ton, net or short (sh ton) . . { 2,000 pounds (exactly)
                               { 0.893 gross ton
                               { 0.907 metric ton

Tables of Interrelation of Units of Measurement

Units of length and area of the international and survey measures are included in the following tables. Units unique to the survey measure are italicized. See p. 300, Tables of Equivalents, 1st para.

1 international foot	= 0.999 998 survey foot (exactly)
1 survey foot	= 1200/3937 meter (exactly)
1 international foot	= 12 × 0.0254 meter (exactly)

Bold face type indicates exact values

Units of Length

Units	Inches	*Links*	Feet	Yards	*Rods*	*Chains*	Miles	cm	Meters
1 inch=	1	0.126 263	0.083 333	0.027 778	0.005 051	0.001 263	0.000 016	2.54	0.025 4
1 *link=*	7.92	1	0.66	0.22	0.04	0.01	0.000 125	20.117	0.201 168
1 foot=	12	1.515 152	1	0.333 333	0.060 606	0.015 152	0.000 189	30.48	0.304 8
1 yard=	36	4.545 45	3	1	0.181 818	0.045 455	0.000 568	91.44	0.914 4
1 *rod=*	198	25	16.5	5.5	1	0.25	0.003 125	502.92	5.029 2
1 *chain=*	792	100	66	22	4	1	0.012 5	2011.68	20.116 8
1 mile=	63 360	8000	5280	1760	320	80	1	160 934.4	1609.344
1 cm=	0.3937	0.049 710	0.032 808	0.010 936	0.001 988	0.000 497	0.000 006	100	0.01
1 meter=	39.37	4.970 960	3.280 840	1.093 613	0.198 838	0.049 710	0.000 621	100	1

Units of Area

Units	Sq. inches	*Sq. links*	Sq. feet	Sq. yards	*Sq. rods*	*Sq. chains*
1 sq. inch=	1	.015 942 3	0.006 944	0.000 771 605	0.000 025 5	0.000 001 594
1 sq. *link=*	62.726 4	1	0.435 6	0.0484	0.0016	0.000 1
1 sq. foot=	144	2.295 684	1	0.111 111 1	0.003 673 09	0.000 229 568
1 sq. yard=	1296	20.661 16	9	1	0.033 057 85	0.002 066 12
1 sq. *rod=*	39 204	625	272.25	30.25	1	0.062 5
1 sq. *chain=*	627 264	10 000	4 356	484	16	1
1 acre=	6 272 640	100 000	43 560	4 840	160	10
1 sq. mile=	4 014 489 600	64 000 000	27 878 400	3 097 600	102 400	6400
1 sq. cm=	0.155 000 3	0.002 471 05	0.001 076	0.000 119 599	0.000 003 954	0.000 000 247
1 sq. meter=	1550.003	24.710 44	10.763 91	1.195 990	0.039 536 70	0.002 471 044
1 *hectare=*	15 500 031	247 104	107 639.1	11 959.90	395.367 0	24.710 44

Units	*Acres*	*Sq. miles*	Sq. cm	Sq. meters	*Hectares*
1 sq. inch=	0.000 000 159 423	0.000 000 000 249 10	6.451 6	0.000 645 16	0.000 000 065
1 sq. *link=*	0.000 01	0.000 000 015 625	404.685 642 24	0.040 468 56	0.000 004 047
1 sq. foot=	0.000 022 956 84	0.000 000 035 870 06	929.034 1	0.092 903 41	0.000 009 290
1 sq. yard=	0.000 206 611 6	0.000 000 322 830 6	8 361.273 6	0.836 127 36	0.000 083 613
1 sq. *rod=*	0.006 25	0.000 009 765 625	252 929.5	25.292 95	0.002 529 295
1 sq. *chain=*	0.1	0.000 156 25	4 046 873	404.687 3	0.040 468 73
1 acre=	1	0.001 562 5	40 468 73	4 046.873	0.404 687 3
1 sq. mile=	640	1	25 899 881 103	2 589 988.11	258.998 811 034
1 sq. cm=	0.000 000 024 711	0.000 000 000 038 610	1	0.000 1	0.000 000 01
1 sq. meter=	0.000 247 104 4	0.000 000 386 102 2	10 000	1	0.0001
1 *hectare=*	2.471 044	0.003 861 006	100 000 000	10 000	1

Units of Mass Not Greater than Pounds and Kilograms

Units	Grains	Pennyweights	Avdp drams	Avdp ounces
1 grain=	1	0.041 666 67	0.036 571 43	0.002 285 71
1 pennyweight=	24	1	0.877 714 3	0.054 857 14
1 dram avdp=	27.343 75	1.139 323	1	0.062 5
1 ounce avdp=	437.5	18.229 17	16	1
1 ounce troy=	480	20	17.554 29	1.097 143
1 pound troy=	5760	240	210.651 4	13.165 71
1 pound avdp=	7000	291.666 7	256	16
1 milligram=	0.015 432	0.000 643 015	0.000 564 383	0.000 035 274
1 gram=	15.432 36	0.643 014 9	0.564 383 4	0.035 273 96
1 kilogram=	15 432.36	643.014 9	564.383 4	35.273 96

Units	Troy ounces	Troy pounds	Avdp pounds	Milligrams	Grams	Kilograms
1 grain=	0.002 083 33	0.000 173 611	0.000 142 857	64.798 91	0.064 798 91	0.000 064 799
1 pennyw't.=	0.05	0.004 166 667	0.003 428 571	1555.173 84	1.555 173 84	0.001 555 174
1 dram avdp=	0.056 966 15	0.004 747 179	0.003 906 25	1771.845 195	1.771 845 195	0.001 771 845
1 oz avdp=	0.911 458 3	0.075 954 86	0.062 5	28 349.523 125	28.349 523 125	0.028 349 52
1 oz troy=	1	0.083 333 333	0.068 571 43	31 103.476 8	31.103 476 8	0.031 103 48
1 lb troy=	12	1	0.822 857 1	373 241.721 6	373.241 721 6	0.373 241 722
1 lb avdp=	14.583 33	1.215 278	1	453 592.37	453.592 37	0.453 592 37
1 milligram=	0.000 032 151	0.000 002 679	0.000 002 205	1	0.001	0.000 000 1
1 gram=	0.032 150 75	0.002 679 229	0.002 204 623	1000	1	0.001
1 kilogram=	32.150 75	2.679 229	2.204 623	1 000 000	1000	1

Units of Mass Not Less than Avoirdupois Ounces

Units	Avdp oz	Avdp lb	Short cwt	Short tons	Long tons	Kilograms	Metric tons
1 oz av=	1	0.0625	0.000 625	0.000 031 25	0.000 027 902	0.028 349 523	0.000 028 350
1 lb av=	16	1	0.01	0.000 5	0.000 446 429	0.453 592 37	0.000 453 592
1 sh cwt=	1 600	100	1	0.05	0.044 642 86	45.359 237	0.045 359 237
1 sh ton=	32 000	2000	20	1	0.892 857 1	907.184 74	0.907 184 74
1 long ton=	35 840	2240	22.4	1.12	1	1016.046 908 8	1.016 046 909
1 kg=	35.273 96	2.204 623	0.022 046 23	0.001 102 311	0.000 984 207	1	0.001
1 metric ton=	35 273.96	2 204.623	22.046 23	1.102 311	0.984 206 5	1000	1

Units of Volume

Units	Cubic inches	Cubic feet	Cubic yards	Cubic cm	Cubic dm	Cubic meters
1 cubic inch=	1	0.000 578 704	0.000 021 433	16.387 064	0.016 387	0.000 016 387
1 cubic foot=	1728	1	0.037 037 04	28 316.846 592	28.316 847	0.028 316 847
1 cubic yard=	46 656	27	1	764 554.857 984	764.554 858	0.764 554 858
1 cubic cm=	0.061 023 74	0.000 035 315	0.000 001 308	1	0.001	0.000 001
1 cubic dm=	61.023 74	0.035 314 67	0.001 307 951	1 000	1	0.001
1 cubic meter	61 023.74	35.314 67	1.307 951	1 000 000	1000	1

Units of Capacity (Liquid Measure)

Units	Minims	Fluid drams	Fluid ounces	Gills	Liquid pt
1 minim=	1	0.016 666 7	0.002 083 33	0.000 520 833	0.000 130 208
1 fluid dram=	60	1	0.125	0.031 25	0.007 812 5
1 fluid ounce=	480	8	1	0.25	0.062 5
1 gill=	1920	32	4	1	0.25
1 liquid pint=	7680	128	16	4	1
1 liquid quart=	15 360	256	32	8	2
1 gallon=	61 440	1024	128	32	8
1 cubic inch=	265.974	4.432 900	0.554 112 6	0.138 528 1	0.034 632 03
1 cubic foot=	459 603.1	7 660.052	957.506 5	239.376 6	59.844 16
1 milliliter=	16.230 73	0.270 512 18	0.033 814 02	0.008 453 506	.002 113 376
1 liter=	16 230.73	270.512 18	33.814 02	8.453 506	2.113 376

Units	Liquid quarts	Gallons	Cubic inches	Cubic feet	Liters
1 minim=	0.000 065 104 17	0.000 016 276 04	0.003 759 766	0.000 002 175 790	0.000 061 611 52
1 flu. dram=	0.003 906 25	0.000 976 562 5	0.225 585 9	0.000 130 547 4	0.003 696 691
1 fluid oz=	0.031 25	0.007 812 5	1.804 687 5	0.001 044 379	0.029 573 53
1 gill=	0.125	0.031 25	7.218 75	0.004 177 517	0.118 294 118
1 liquid pt=	0.5	0.125	28.875	0.016 710 07	0.473 176 473
1 liquid qt=	1	0.25	57.75	0.033 420 14	0.946 352 946
1 gallon=	4	1	231	0.133 680 6	3.785 411 784
1 cubic in.=	0.017 316 02	0.004 329 004	1	0.000 578 703 7	0.016 387 064
1 cubic foot=	29.922 08	7.480 519	1728	1	28.316 846 592
1 liter=	1.056 688	0.264 172 05	61.023 74	0.035 314 67	1

Units of Capacity (Dry Measure)

Units	Dry pints	Dry quarts	Pecks	Bushels	Cubic in.	Liters
1 dry pint=	1	0.5	0.062 5	0.015 625	33.600 312 5	0.550 610 47
1 dry quart=	2	1	0.125	0.031 25	67.200 625	1.101 220 9
1 peck=	16	8	1	0.25	537.605	8.809 767 5
1 bushel=	64	32	4	1	2150.42	35.239 07
1 cubic inch=	0.029 761 6	0.014 880 8	0.001 860 10	0.000 465 025	1	0.016 387 06
1 liter=	1.816 166	0.908 083	0.113 510 37	0.028 377 59	61.023 74	1

Miscellaneous Measures

Caliber—the diameter of a gun bore. In the U.S., caliber is traditionally expressed in hundredths of inches, eg. .22 or .30. In Britain, caliber is often expressed in thousandths of inches, eg. .270 or .465. Now, it is commonly expressed in millimeters, eg. the 7.62 mm. M14 rifle and the 5.56 mm. M16 rifle. Heavier weapons' caliber has long been expressed in millimeters, eg. the 81 mm. mortar, the 105 mm. howitzer (light), the 155 mm. howitzer (medium or heavy).

Naval guns' caliber refers to the barrel length as a multiple of the bore diameter. A 5-inch, 50-caliber naval gun has a 5-inch bore and a barrel length of 250 inches.

Carat, karat—a measure of the amount of alloy per 24 parts in gold. Thus 24-carat gold is pure; 18-carat gold is one-fourth alloy.

Decibel (dB)—a measure of the relative loudness or intensity of sound. A 20-decibel sound is 10 times louder than a 10-decibel sound; 30 decibels is 100 times louder; 40 decibels is 1,000 times louder, etc. One decibel is the smallest difference between sounds detectable by the human ear. A 120-decibel sound is painful.

10 decibels	– a light whisper
20	– quiet conversation
30	– normal conversation
40	– light traffic
50	– typewriter, loud conversation
60	– noisy office
70	– normal traffic, quiet train
80	– rock music, subway
90	– heavy traffic, thunder
100	– jet plane at takeoff

Em—a printer's measure designating the square width of any given type size. Thus, an em of 10-point type is 10 points. An en is half an em.

Gauge—a measure of shotgun bore diameter. Gauge numbers originally referred to the number of lead balls of the gun barrel diameter in a pound. Thus, a 16 gauge shotgun's bore was smaller than a 12-gauge shotgun's. Today, an international agreement assigns millimeter measures to each gauge. eg:

Gauge	Bore diameter in mm
6	23.34
10	19.67
12	18.52
14	17.60
16	16.81
20	15.90

Horsepower—the power needed to lift 550 pounds one foot in one second, or to lift 33,000 pounds one foot in one minute. Equivalent to 746 watts or 2,546.0756 Btu/h.

Quire—25 sheets of paper

Ream—500 sheets of paper

Electrical Units

The watt is the unit of power (electrical, mechanical, thermal, etc.). Electrical power is given by the product of the voltage and the current.

Energy is sold by the joule, but in common practice the billing of electrical energy is expressed in terms of the kilowatt-hour, which is 3,600,000 joules or 3.6 megajoules.

The horsepower is a non-metric unit sometimes used in mechanics. It is equal to 746 watts.

The ohm is the unit of electrical resistance and represents the physical property of a conductor that offers a resistance to the flow of electricity, permitting just 1 ampere to flow at 1 volt of pressure.

Compound Interest

Compounded Annually

Principal $100	Period	4%	5%	6%	7%	8%	9%	10%	12%	14%	16%
	1 day	0.011	0.014	0.016	0.019	0.022	0.025	0.027	0.033	0.038	0.044
	1 week	0.077	0.096	0.115	0.134	0.153	0.173	0.192	0.230	0.268	0.307
	6 mos.	2.00	2.50	3.00	3.50	4.00	4.50	5.00	6.00	7.00	8.00
	1 year	4.00	5.00	6.00	7.00	8.00	9.00	10.00	12.00	14.00	16.00
	2 years	8.16	10.25	12.36	14.49	16.64	18.81	21.00	25.44	29.96	34.56
	3 years	12.49	15.76	19.10	22.50	25.97	29.50	33.10	40.49	48.15	56.09
	4 years	16.99	21.55	26.25	31.08	36.05	41.16	46.41	57.35	68.90	81.06
	5 years	21.67	27.63	33.82	40.26	46.93	53.86	61.05	76.23	92.54	110.03
	6 years	26.53	34.01	41.85	50.07	58.69	67.71	77.16	97.38	119.50	143.64
	7 years	31.59	40.71	50.36	60.58	71.38	82.80	94.87	121.07	150.23	182.62
	8 years	36.86	47.75	59.38	71.82	85.09	99.26	114.36	147.60	185.26	227.84
	9 years	42.33	55.13	68.95	83.85	99.90	117.19	135.79	177.31	225.19	280.30
	10 years	48.02	62.89	79.08	96.72	115.89	136.74	159.37	210.58	270.72	341.14
	12 years	60.10	79.59	101.22	125.22	151.82	181.27	213.84	289.60	381.79	493.60
	15 years	80.09	107.89	139.66	175.90	217.22	264.25	317.72	447.36	613.79	826.55
	20 years	119.11	165.33	220.71	286.97	366.10	460.44	572.75	864.63	1,274.35	1,846.08

Ancient Measures

Biblical
Cubit = 21.8 inches
Omer = 0.45 peck
  3.964 liters
Ephah = 10 omers
Shekel = 0.497 ounce
  14.1 grams

Greek
Cubit = 18.3 inches
Stadion = 607.2 or 622 feet
Obolos = 715.38 milligrams
Drachma = 4.2923 grams
Mina = 0.9463 pounds
Talent = 60 mina

Roman
Cubit = 17.5 inches
Stadium = 202 yards
As, libra, = 325.971 grams,
pondus .71864 pounds

Weight of Water

1	cubic inch	.0360 pound		1	imperial gallon	10.0 pounds
12	cubic inches	.433 pound		11.2	imperial gallons	112.0 pounds
1	cubic foot	62.4 pounds		224	imperial gallons	2240.0 pounds
1	cubic foot	7.48052 U.S. gal		1	U.S. gallon	8.33 pounds
1.8	cubic feet	112.0 pounds		13.45	U.S. gallons	112.0 pounds
35.96	cubic feet	2240.0 pounds		269.0	U.S. gallons	2240.0 pounds

Density of Gases and Vapors

at 0°C and 760 mmHg
Source: National Bureau of Standards (kilograms per cubic meter)

Gas	Wgt.	Gas	Wgt.	Gas	Wgt.
Acetylene	1.171	Ethylene	1.260	Methyl fluoride	1.545
Air	1.293	Fluorine	1.696	Mono methylamine	1.38
Ammonia	.759	Helium	.178	Neon	.900
Argon	1.784	Hydrogen	.090	Nitric oxide	1.341
Arsene	3.48	Hydrogen bromide	3.50	Nitrogen	1.250
Butane-iso.	2.60	Hydrogen chloride	1.639	Nitrosyl chloride	2.99
Butane-n	2.519	Hydrogen iodide	5.724	Nitrous oxide	1.997
Carbon dioxide	1.977	Hydrogen selenide	3.66	Oxygen	1.429
Carbon monoxide	1.250	Hydrogen sulfide	1.539	Phosphine	1.48
Carbon oxysulfide	2.72	Krypton	3.745	Propane	2.020
Chlorine	3.214	Methane	.717	Silicon tetrafluoride	4.67
Chlorine monoxide	3.89	Methyl chloride	2.25	Sulfur dioxide	2.927
Ethane	1.356	Methyl ether	2.091	Xenon	5.897

Temperature Conversion Table

The numbers in bold face type refer to the temperature either in degrees Celsius or Fahrenheit which are to be converted. If converting from degrees Fahrenheit to Celsius, the equivalent will be found in the column on the left, while if converting from degrees Celsius to Fahrenheit the answer will be found in the column on the right.

For temperatures not shown. To convert Fahrenheit to Celsius subtract 32 degrees and multiply by 5, divide by 9; to convert Celsius to Fahrenheit, multiply by 9, divide by 5 and add 32 degrees.

Celsius	Fahrenheit		Celsius		Fahrenheit	Celsius		Fahrenheit
− 273.2	− 459.7		− 17.8	0	32	35.0	95	203
− 184	− 300		− 12.2	10	50	36.7	98	208.4
− 169	− 273	− 459.4	− 6.67	20	68	37.8	100	212
− 157	− 250	− 418	− 1.11	30	86	43	110	230
− 129	− 200	− 328	4.44	40	104	49	120	248
− 101	− 150	− 238	10.0	50	122	54	130	266
− 73.3	− 100	− 148	15.6	60	140	60	140	284
− 45.6	− 50	− 58	21.1	70	158	66	150	302
− 40.0	− 40	− 40	23.9	75	167	93	200	392
− 34.4	− 30	− 22	26.7	80	176	121	250	482
− 28.9	− 20	− 4	29.4	85	185	149	300	572
− 23.3	− 10	14	32.2	90	194			

Boiling and Freezing Points of Water

Water boils at 212°F at sea level. For every 550 feet above sea level, boiling point of water is lower by about 1°F. Methyl alcohol boils at 148°F. Average human oral temperature, 98.6°F. Water freezes at 32°F. Although "Centigrade" is still frequently used, the International Committee on Weights and Measures and the National Bureau of Standards have recommended since 1948 that this scale be called "Celsius."

Breaking the Sound Barrier; Speed of Sound

The prefix Mach is used to describe supersonic speed. It derives from Ernst Mach, a Czech-born German physicist, who contributed to the study of sound. When a plane moves at the speed of sound it is Mach 1. When twice the speed of sound it is Mach 2. When it is near but below the speed of sound its speed can be designated at less than Mach 1, for example, Mach .90. Mach is defined as "in jet propulsion, the ratio of the velocity of a rocket or a jet to the velocity of sound in the medium being considered."

When a plane passes the sound barrier—flying faster than sound travels—listeners in the area hear thunderclaps, but pilots do not hear them.

Sound is produced by vibrations of an object and is transmitted by alternate increase and decrease in pressures that radiate outward through a material media of molecules —somewhat like waves spreading out on a pond after a rock has been tossed into it.

The frequency of sound is determined by the number of times the vibrating waves undulate per second, and is measured in cycles per second. The slower the cycle of waves, the lower the frequency. As frequencies increase, the sound is higher in pitch.

Sound is audible to human beings only if the frequency falls within a certain range. The human ear is usually not sensitive to frequencies of less than 20 vibrations per second, or more than about 20,000 vibrations per second—although this range varies among individuals. Anything at a pitch higher than the human ear can hear is termed ultrasonic.

Intensity or loudness is the strength of the pressure of these radiating waves, and is measured in decibels. The human ear responds to intensity in a range from zero to 120 decibels. Any sound with pressure over 120 decibels is painful.

The speed of sound is generally placed at 1,088 feet per second at sea level at 32°F. It varies in other temperatures and in different media. Sound travels faster in water than in air, and even faster in iron and steel. If in air it travels a mile in 5 seconds, it does a mile under water in 1 second, and through iron in ⅓ of a second. It travels through ice cold vapor at approximately 4,708 feet per second, ice-cold water, 4,938; granite, 12,960; hardwood, 12,620; brick, 11,960; glass, 16,410 to 19,690; silver, 8,658; gold, 5,717.

Colors of the Spectrum

Color, an electromagnetic wave phenomenon, is a sensation produced through the excitation of the retina of the eye by rays of light. The colors of the spectrum may be produced by viewing a light beam refracted by passage through a prism, which breaks the light into its varie lenghts.

Customarily, the primary colors of the spectrum are thought of as those 6 monochromatic colors that occupy relatively large areas of the spectrum: red, orange, yellow, green, blue, and violet. However, Sir Isaac Newton named a 7th, indigo, situated between blue and violet on the spectrum. Aubert estimated (1865) the solar spectrum to contain approximately 1,000 distinguishable hues of which according to Rood (1881) 2 million tints and shades can be distinguished; Luckiesh stated (1915) that 55 distinctly different hues have been seen in a single spectrum.

Many physicists recognize only 3 primary colors: red, yellow, and blue (Mayer, 1775); red, green, and violet (Thomas Young, 1801); red, green, and blue (Clerk Maxwell, 1860).

The color sensation of black is due to complete lack of stimulation of the retina, that of white to complete stimulation. The infra-red and ultra-violet rays, below the red (long) end of the spectrum and above the violet (short) end respectively, are invisible to the naked eye. Heat is the principal effect of the infra-red rays and chemical action that of the ultra-violet rays.

Common Fractions Reduced to Decimals

8ths	16ths	32ds	64ths		8ths	16ths	32ds	64ths		8ths	16ths	32ds	64ths	
			1	.015625				23	.359375				45	.703125
		1	2	.03125	3	6	12	24	.375			23	46	.71875
			3	.046875				25	.390625				47	.734375
	1	2	4	.0625			13	26	.40625	6	12	24	48	.75
			5	.078125				27	.421875				49	.765625
		3	6	.09375		7	14	28	.4375			25	50	.78125
			7	.109375				29	.453125				51	.796875
1	2	4	8	.125			15	30	.46875		13	26	52	.8125
			9	.140625				31	.484375				53	.828125
		5	10	.15625	4	8	16	32	.5			27	54	.84375
			11	.171875				33	.515625				55	.859375
	3	6	12	.1875			17	34	.53125	7	14	28	56	.875
			13	.203125				35	.546875				57	.890625
		7	14	.21875		9	18	36	.5625			29	58	.90625
			15	.234375				37	.578125				59	.921875
2	4	8	16	.25			19	38	.59375		15	30	60	.9375
			17	.265625				39	.609375				61	.953125
		9	18	.28125	5	10	20	40	.625			31	62	.96875
			19	.296875				41	.640625				63	.984375
	5	10	20	.3125			21	42	.65625	8	16	32	64	1.
			21	.328125				43	.671875					
		11	22	.34375		11	22	44	.6875					

Spirits Measures

Pony	0.5 jigger
Shot	{ 0.666 jigger / 1.0 ounce
Jigger	1.5 shot
Pint	{ 16 shots / 0.625 fifth
Fifth	{ 25.6 shots / 1.6 pints / 0.8 quart / 0.75706 liter

Quart	{ 32 shots / 1.25 fifth
Magnum	{ 2 quarts / 2.49797 bottles (wine)

For champagne and brandy only:

Jeroboam	{ 6.4 pints / 1.6 magnum / 0.8 gallon

For champagne only:

Rehoboam	3 magnums
Methuselah	4 magnums
Salmanazar	6 magnums
Balthazar	8 magnums
Nebuchadnezzar	10 magnums

Wine bottle (standard):

	{ 0.800633 quart / 0.7576778 liter

Mathematical Formulas

To find the CIRCUMFERENCE of a:

Circle — Multiply the diameter by 3.14159265 (usually 3.1416).

To find the AREA of a:

Circle — Multiply the square of the diameter by .785398 (usually .7854).

Rectangle — Multiply the length of the base by the height.

Sphere (surface) — Multiply the square of the radius by 3.1416 and multiply by 4.

Square — Square the length of one side.

Trapezoid — Add the two parallel sides, multiply by the height and divide by 2.

Triangle — Multiply the base by the height and divide by 2.

To find the VOLUME of a:

Cone — Multiply the square of the radius of the base by 3.1416, multiply by the height, and divide by 3.

Cube — Cube the length of one edge.

Cylinder — Multiply the square of the radius of the base by 3.1416 and multiply by the height.

Pyramid — Multiply the area of the base by the height and divide by 3.

Rectangular Prism — Multiply the length by the width by the height.

Sphere — Multiply the cube of the radius by 3.1416, multiply by 4 and divide by 3.

Playing Cards and Dice Chances

Poker Hands

Hand	Number possible	Odds against
Royal flush	4	649,739 to 1
Other straight flush	36	72,192 to 1
Four of a kind	624	4,164 to 1
Full house	3,744	693 to 1
Flush	5,108	508 to 1
Straight	10,200	254 to 1
Three of a kind	54,912	46 to 1
Two pairs	123,552	20 to 1
One pair	1,098,240	4 to 3 (1.37 to 1)
Nothing	1,302,540	1 to 1
Total	**2,598,960**	

Dice
(probabilities on 2 dice)

Total	Odds against (Single toss)	Total	Odds against (Single toss)
2	35 to 1	8	31 to 5
3	17 to 1	9	8 to 1
4	11 to 1	10	11 to 1
5	8 to 1	11	17 to 1
6	31 to 5	12	35 to 1
7	5 to 1		

Dice
(Probabilities of consecutive winning plays)

No. consecutive wins	By 7, 11 or point	No. consecutive wins	By 7, 11 or point
1	244 in 495	6	1 in 70
2	6 in 25	7	1 in 141
3	3 in 25	8	1 in 287
4	1 in 17	9	1 in 582
5	1 in 34		

Pinochle Auction
(Odds against finding in "widow" of 3 cards)

Open places	Odds against	Open places	Odds against
1	5 to 1	4	3 to 2 for
2	2 to 1	5	2 to 1 for
3	Even		

Bridge

The odds—against suit distribution in a hand of 4-4-3-2 are about 4 to 1, against 5-4-2-2 about 8 to 1, against 6-4-2-1 about 20 to 1, against 7-4-1-1 about 254 to 1, and against 8-4-1-0 about 2,211 to 1, and against 13-0-0-0 about 158,753,389,899 to 1.

Measures of Force and Pressure

Dyne = force necessary to accelerate a 1-gram mass 1 centimeter per second squared = 0.000072 poundal

Poundal = force necessary to accelerate a 1-pound mass 1 foot per second squared = 13,825.5 dynes = 0.138255 newtons

Newton = force needed to accelerate a 1-kilogram mass 1 meter per second squared

Pascal (pressure) = 1 newton per square meter = 0.020885 pound per square foot

Atmosphere (air pressure at sea level) = 2,116.102 pounds per square foot = 14.6952 pounds per square inch = 1.0332 kilograms per square centimeter = 101,323 newtons per square meter.

Large Numbers

U.S.	Number of zeros	French British, German	U.S.	Number of zeros	French British, German
million	6	million	sextillion	21	1,000 trillion
billion	9	milliard	septillion	24	quadrillion
trillion	12	billion	octillion	27	1,000 quadrillion
quadrillion	15	1,000 billion	nonillion	30	quintillion
quintillion	18	trillion	decillion	33	1,000 quintillion

Roman Numerals

I	–	1	VI	–	6	XI	–	11	L	–	50	CD	–	400	$\overline{X}$	–	10,000
II	–	2	VII	–	7	XIX	–	19	LX	–	60	D	–	500	$\overline{L}$	–	50,000
III	–	3	VIII	–	8	XX	–	20	XC	–	90	CM	–	900	$\overline{C}$	–	100,000
IV	–	4	IX	–	9	XXX	–	30	C	–	100	M	–	1,000	$\overline{D}$	–	500,000
V	–	5	X	–	10	XL	–	40	CC	–	200	$\overline{V}$	–	5,000	$\overline{M}$	–	1,000,000

ARTS AND MEDIA
Notable Movies of the Year (Aug. 1989 to July 1990)

Movie	Stars	Director
Always	Richard Dreyfuss, Holly Hunter, John Goodman	Steven Spielberg
Another 48 Hours	Nick Nolte, Eddie Murphy	Walter Hill
Arachnophobia	Jeff Daniels, John Goodman	Frank Marshall
Back to the Future, II	Michael J. Fox, Christopher Lloyd, Lea Thompson	Robert Zemeckis
Back to the Future, III	Michael J. Fox, Christopher Lloyd, Mary Steenburgen	Robert Zemeckis
Bird on a Wire	Mel Gibson, Goldie Hawn	John Badham
Black Rain	Michael Douglas, Andy Garcia	Ridley Scott
Blaze	Paul Newman, Lolita Davidovich	Ron Shelton
Blue Steel	Jamie Lee Curtis, Ron Silver	Kathryn Bigelow
Born on the Fourth of July	Tom Cruise	Oliver Stone
Cadillac Man	Robin Williams, Tim Robbins	Roger Donaldson
Casualties of War	Michael J. Fox, Sean Penn	Brian DePalma
Crimes and Misdemeanors	Woody Allen, Martin Landau, Alan Alda, Mia Farrow	Woody Allen
Dad	Jack Lemmon, Ted Danson, Kathy Baker, Olympia Dukakis	Gary David Goldberg
Days of Thunder	Tom Cruise, Robert Duvall, Randy Quaid, Nicole Kidman	Tony Scott
Dick Tracy	Warren Beatty, Madonna, Glenne Headly, Al Pacino	Warren Beatty
Die Hard 2	Bruce Willis, Bonnie Bedelia	Renny Harlin
Driving Miss Daisy	Jessica Tandy, Morgan Freeman, Dan Aykroyd	Bruce Beresford
Drugstore Cowboy	Matt Dillon, Kelly Lynch	Gus Van Sant
Enemies, A Love Story	Ron Silver, Anjelica Huston, Lena Olin	Paul Mazursky
Family Business	Sean Connery, Dustin Hoffman, Matthew Broderick	Sidney Lumet
Glory	Matthew Broderick, Denzel Washington, Morgan Freeman	Edward Zwick
Harlem Nights	Eddie Murphy, Richard Pryor, Redd Foxx, Danny Aiello	Eddie Murphy
In Country	Bruce Willis, Emily Lloyd, Joan Allen	Norman Jewison
Joe Versus the Volcano	Tom Hanks, Meg Ryan	John Patrick Shanley
Mo' Better Blues	Denzel Washington, Spike Lee	Spike Lee
Parenthood	Steve Martin, Mary Steenburgen, Rick Moranis, Tom Hulce	Ron Howard
Presumed Innocent	Harrison Ford, Brian Dennehy, Bonnie Bedelia	Alan J. Pakula
Pretty Woman	Richard Gere, Julia Roberts	Garry Marshall
Quick Change	Bill Murray, Geena Davis, Randy Quaid	H. Franklin, B. Murray
Revenge	Kevin Costner, Anthony Quinn	Tony Scott
Sea of Love	Al Pacino, Ellen Barkin, John Goodman	Harold Becker
She-Devil	Meryl Streep, Roseanne Barr, Ed Begley Jr.	Susan Seidelman
Steel Magnolias	Sally Field, Dolly Parton, Daryl Hannah, Shirley MacLaine	Herbert Ross
Tango and Cash	Sylvester Stallone, Kurt Russell	Andrei Konchalovsky
The Fabulous Baker Boys	Michelle Pfeiffer, Jeff Bridges, Beau Bridges	Steve Kloves
The Freshman	Marlon Brando, Matthew Broderick	Andrew Bergman
The Handmaid's Tale	Natasha Richardson, Elizabeth McGovern, Robert Duvall	Volker Schlondorff
The Hunt for Red October	Sean Connery, Alec Baldwin, Scott Glenn, James Earl Jones	John McTiernan
The War of The Roses	Michael Douglas, Kathleen Turner, Danny DeVito	Danny DeVito
Total Recall	Arnold Schwarzenegger, Ronny Cox	Paul Verhoeven
Uncle Buck	John Candy	John Hughes
We're No Angels	Robert DeNiro, Sean Penn	Neil Jordan

Notable New York Theater Openings, 1989-90 Season

A Few Good Men, play by Aaron Sorkin; with Tom Hulce, Stephen Lang, Megan Gallagher, and Mark Nelson.

Accomplice, play by Rupert Holmes; with Jason Alexander, Michael McKean, Natalia Nogulich, and Pamela Brull.

Artist Descending a Staircase, play by Tom Stoppard; with Paxton Whitehead, John McMartin, Harold Gould, and Stephanie Roth.

Aspects of Love, musical by Andrew Lloyd Webber, Don Black, and Charles Hart; with Michael Ball, Kevin Colson, Ann Crumb, and Kathleen Rowe McAllen.

Bad Habits, revival of Terrence McNally's 1974 comedy; with Kate Nelligan and Nathan Lane.

Cat On a Hot Tin Roof, revival of Tennessee Williams' 1955 drama; with Kathleen Turner, Charles Durning, Daniel Hugh Kelly, and Polly Holliday.

City of Angels, musical by Cy Coleman, David Zippel, and Larry Gelbart; with James Naughton, Gregg Edelman, Randy Graff, and Rene Auberjonois.

Grand Hotel, musical by Robert Wright, George Forrest, and Maury Yeston based on the Vicki Baum novel; directed and choreographed by Tommy Tune; with Liliane Montevecchi, David Carroll, Jane Krakowski, and Michael Jeter.

Gypsy, revival of the Jule Styne, Stephen Sondheim 1959 musical; with Tyne Daly, Crista Moore, Tracy Venner, and Jonathan Hadary.

Lettuce and Lovage, comedy by Peter Shaffer; with Maggie Smith and Margaret Tyzack.

Meet Me in St. Louis, musical based on the Hugh Martin, Ralph Blane 1943 film musical; with Milo O'Shea, Donna Kane, Betty Garrett and George Hearn.

Miss Margarida's Way, revival of Roberto Athayde's 1978 drama; with Estelle Parsons.

My Children! My Africa! play by Athol Fugard; with Courtney B. Vance, John Kani, and Lisa Fugard.

Prelude to A Kiss, play by Craig Lucas; with Timothy Hutton, Mary-Louise Parker, and Barnard Hughes.

Sex, Drugs, Rock & Roll, social sketches by Eric Bogosian; with Eric Bogosian.

Six Degrees of Separation, play by John Guare; with Stockard Channing, James McDaniel, and John Cunningham.

Some Americans Abroad, comedy by Richard Nelson; with Nathan Lane, Kate Burton, Colin Stinton, John Bedford Lloyd.

The Art of Success, play by Nick Dear; with Tim Curry, Suzanne Bertish, and Mary-Louise Parker.

The Circle, revival of W. Somerset Maugham's 1921 comedy; with Rex Harrison, Stewart Granger, and Glynis Johns.

The Crucible, revival of Arthur Miller's 1953 drama; with Harriet Harris, Randle Mell, and Justine Bateman.

The Grapes of Wrath, Frank Galati's adaption of the John Steinbeck novel; with Gary Sinise, Lois Smith, and Terry Kinney.

The Merchant of Venice, the Shakespeare play directed by Peter Hall; with Dustin Hoffman, Geraldine James, Michael Siberry, and Leigh Lawson.

The Piano Lesson, play by August Wilson; with Charles S. Dutton, S. Epatha Merkerson, Carl Gordon, Lou Myers, and Rocky Carroll.

The Sound of Music, revival of the Rodgers and Hammerstein 1959 musical; with Debby Boone, Laurence Guittard, and Werner Klemperer.

The 10th Man, revival of Paddy Chayefsky's 1959 play; with Bob Dishy, Jack Weston, Phoebe Cates, Peter Friedman, and Joseph Wiseman.

Threepenny Opera, revival of the Kurt Weill, Bertold Brecht 1928 classic; with Sting, Suzzanne Douglas, and Georgia Brown.

Tru, play by Jay Presson Allan based on the work of Truman Capote; with Robert Morse.

When She Danced, play by Martin Sherman about the final years of Isadora Duncan; with Elizabeth Ashley.

National Film Registry

In accordance with the National Film Preservation Act passed by Congress in 1988, these 25 films were placed on the National Film Registry in September 1989 as "culturally, historically, or esthetically significant." Another 25 will be chosen in 1990, and 25 more in 1991.

Film	Year	Director	Stars
The Best Years of Our Lives	1946	William Wyler	Frederic March, Myrna Loy, Dana Andrews
Casablanca	1942	Michael Curtiz	Humphrey Bogart, Ingrid Bergman, Claude Rains
Citizen Kane	1941	Orson Welles	Orson Welles, Joseph Cotton, Everett Sloane
The Crowd	1928	King Vidor	James Murray, Eleanor Boardman
Dr. Strangelove (or, How I Learned to Stop Worrying and Love the Bomb)	1964	Stanley Kubrick	Peter Sellers, George C. Scott, Sterling Hayden
The General	1927	Buster Keaton	Buster Keaton
Gone With the Wind	1939	Victor Fleming	Vivien Leigh, Clark Gable, Leslie Howard, Olivia de Havilland
The Grapes of Wrath	1940	John Ford	Henry Fonda, Jane Darwell
High Noon	1952	Fred Zinnemann	Gary Cooper, Grace Kelly
Intolerance	1916	D.W. Griffith	Lillian Gish, Robert Harron, Mae Marsh
The Learning Tree	1969	Gordon Parks	Kyle Johnson, Alex Clarke
The Maltese Falcon	1941	John Huston	Humphrey Bogart, Mary Astor, Sydney Greenstreet, Peter Lorre
Mr. Smith Goes to Washington	1939	Frank Capra	James Stewart, Jean Arthur, Claude Rains
Modern Times	1936	Charlie Chaplin	Charlie Chaplin, Paulette Goddard
Nanook of the North	1921	Robert Flaherty	documentary
On the Waterfront	1954	Elia Kazan	Marlon Brando, Eva Marie Saint, Karl Malden, Lee J. Cobb, Rod Steiger
The Searchers	1956	John Ford	John Wayne, Jeffrey Hunter, Vera Miles, Natalie Wood
Singin' in the Rain	1952	Gene Kelly/ Stanley Donen	Gene Kelly, Debbie Reynolds, Donald O'Connor, Jean Hagen
Snow White and the Seven Dwarfs	1937	Walt Disney	animated
Some Like It Hot	1959	Billy Wilder	Jack Lemmon, Marilyn Monroe, Tony Curtis
Star Wars	1977	George Lucas	Mark Hamill, Harrison Ford, Carrie Fisher
Sunrise	1927	F.W. Murnau	George O'Brien, Janet Gaynor
Sunset Boulevard	1950	Billy Wilder	Gloria Swanson, William Holden, Erich von Stroheim
Vertigo	1958	Alfred Hitchcock	James Stewart, Kim Novak
The Wizard of Oz	1939	Victor Fleming	Judy Garland, Ray Bolger, Bert Lahr, Jack Haley

Top Video Rentals, 1989

Source: *Variety*, January 1990

Rank	Title	Release date (1st Monday)	'89 national boxoffice ($ millions)	Rank	Title	Release date (1st Monday)	'89 national boxoffice ($ millions)
1	A Fish Called Wanda	Feb. 27	60.0	27	The Naked Gun	Aug. 21	78.0
2	Die Hard	Jan. 30	79.6	28	Married To The Mob	Feb. 27	21.3
3	Rain Man	Sept. 4	168.8	29	Midnight Run	Feb. 27	37.4
4	Coming To America	Mar. 22	128.1	30	Major League	Oct. 9	49.4
5	Big	Mar. 27	113.3	31	Child's Play	May 1	32.8
6	Twins	June 19	106.4	32	Mystic Pizza	Apr. 10	12.4
7	The Accused	Mar. 15	29.6	33	Alien Nation	June 19	24.9
8	Beaches	Aug. 28	55.2	34	Three Men And A Baby	Nov. 21 '88	167.7
9	Tequila Sunrise	Aug. 7	39.7	35	Bill & Ted's Excellent Adventure	Sept. 4	39.5
10	Cocktail	Apr. 24	77.1	36	Pet Sematary	Oct. 16	56.6
11	Dirty Rotten Scoundrels	June 26	41.4	37	The Best Of Eddie Murphy	Aug. 28	NA
12	Mississippi Burning	July 31	34.5	38	The 'Burbs	Aug. 14	35.2
13	Bull Durham	Jan. 30	50.3	39	Crocodile Dundee II	Mar. 20	109.2
14	Tucker: The Man And His Dream	Apr. 17	19.6	40	Big Business	Mar. 6	39.6
15	Gorillas In The Mist	Apr. 17	23.0	41	Short Circuit 2	Dec. 19 '88	20.7
16	Young Guns	Jan. 9	43.4	42	The Great Outdoors	Jan. 16	38.0
17	Red Heat	Jan. 2	35.0				
18	Dangerous Liaisons	July 17	32.2	43	The Unbearable Lightness Of Being	Jan. 2	10.0
19	Working Girl	Oct. 9	63.7				
20	The Dead Pool	Jan. 30	37.8	44	Bat 21	Apr. 10	3.8
21	Who Framed Roger Rabbit	Oct. 16	154.1	45	True Believer	July 24	8.7
				46	Scrooged	Nov. 13	60.3
22	My Stepmother Is An Alien	June 12	12.9	47	Three Fugitives	Nov. 6	41.0
23	The Presidio	Jan. 30	20.0	48	Batman	Nov. 20	241.0
24	Betrayed	Mar. 27	25.7	49	K-9	Nov. 20	39.0
25	The Accidental Tourist	July 3	30.2	50	Ghostbusters II	Nov. 27	111.0
26	Bloodsport	Dec. 26 '88	11.7				

Note: Some videos are ranked low because they were released late in the year, e.g., "Batman." No. 48, was released Nov. 20.

Record Long Run Broadway Plays[1]

Source: *Variety*

Chorus Line	6,137	Hair	1,750	*Les Miserables	1,319
Oh, Calcutta (revival)	5,959	The Wiz	1,672	Oh! Calcutta! (original)	1,314
42d Street	3,486	Born Yesterday	1,642	Brighton Beach Memoirs	1,299
Grease	3,388	Ain't Misbehavin'	1,604	Angel Street	1,295
Fiddler on the Roof	3,242	Best Little Whorehouse in Texas	1,584	Lightnin'	1,291
*Cats	3,237	Mary, Mary	1,572	Promises, Promises	1,281
Life With Father	3,224	Evita	1,567	The King and I	1,246
Tobacco Road	3,182	Voice of the Turtle	1,557	Cactus Flower	1,234
Hello Dolly	2,844	Barefoot in the Park	1,530	Sleuth	1,222
My Fair Lady	2,717	Dreamgirls	1,521	Torch Song Trilogy	1,222
Annie	2,377	Mame	1,508	"1776"	1,217
Man of La Mancha	2,328	Same Time, Next Year	1,453	Equus	1,209
Abie's Irish Rose	2,327	Arsenic and Old Lace	1,444	Sugar Babies	1,208
Oklahoma!	2,212	The Sound of Music	1,443	Guys and Dolls	1,200
Pippin	1,944	How To Succeed in Business		Amadeus	1,181
South Pacific	1,925	Without Really Trying	1,417	Cabaret	1,165
Magic Show	1,920	Me and My Girl	1,412	Mister Roberts	1,157
Deathtrap	1,792	Hellzapoppin	1,404	Annie Get Your Gun	1,147
Gemini	1,788	The Music Man	1,375	Seven Year Itch	1,141
Harvey	1,775	Funny Girl	1,348	Butterflies Are Free	1,128
Dancin'	1,774	Murnenschanz	1,326	Pins and Needles	1,108
La Cage aux Folles	1,761				

(1) Number of performances through July 2, 1990. *Still running July 2, 1990.

All-Time Top 50 Movies

Source: *Variety*, January, 1990

Rental figures are in absolute dollars, reflecting actual amounts received by the distributors (estimated for movies in current release). Ticket price inflation favors recent films, but older films have the advantage of numerous reissues adding to their totals.

Title	Total Rentals	Title	Total Rentals	Title	Total Rentals
1. E.T. the Extra-Terrestrial; 1982	$228,618,939	19. Close Encounters of the Third Kind; 1977/1980	82,750,000	1987	70,000,000
2. Star Wars; 1977	193,500,000	20. Three Men and a Baby; 1987	81,313,000	35. Platoon; 1986	69,742,143
3. Return of the Jedi; 1983	168,002,414	21. Who Framed Roger Rabbit; 1988	81,244,000	36. Rocky III; 1982	66,262,796
4. Batman; 1989	150,500,000	22. Beverly Hills Cop II; 1987	80,857,776	37. Superman II; 1981	65,100,000
5. The Empire Strikes Back; 1980	141,600,000	23. The Sound of Music; 1965	79,748,000	38. Coming to America; 1988	65,000,000
6. Ghostbusters; 1984	130,211,324	24. Gremlins; 1984	79,500,000	39. Back to the Future II; 1989	63,000,000
7. Jaws; 1975	129,549,325	25. Top Gun; 1986	79,400,000	40. Snow White and the Seven Dwarfs; 1937	61,752,000
8. Raiders of the Lost Ark; 1981	115,598,000	26. Gone With the Wind; 1939	79,375,077	41. Ghostbusters II; 1989	61,649,019
9. Indiana Jones and the Last Crusade; 1989	115,500,000	27. Rambo: First Blood Part II; 1985	78,919,250	42. On Golden Pond; 1981	61,174,744
10. Indiana Jones and the Temple of Doom	109,000,000	28. The Sting; 1973	78,212,000	43. Kramer Vs. Kramer; 1979	59,986,335
11. Beverly Hills Cop; 1984	108,000,000	29. Rocky IV; 1985	76,023,246	44. One Flew Over the Cuckoo's Nest; 1975	59,939,701
12. Back to the Future; 1985	104,408,738	30. Saturday Night Fever; 1977	74,100,000	45. 9 to 5; 1980	59,100,000
13. Grease; 1978	96,300,000	31. Honey, I Shrunk the Kids; 1989	71,097,000	46. Smokey And the Bandit; 1977	58,949,938
14. Tootsie; 1982	96,292,736	32. National Lampoon's Animal House; 1978	70,826,000	47. Stir Crazy; 1980	58,364,420
15. The Exorcist; 1973	89,000,000	33. Crocodile Dundee; 1986	70,227,000	48. The Karate Kid Part II; 1986	58,362,026
16. The Godfather; 1972	86,275,000	34. Fatal Attraction;		49. Twins; 1988	57,237,170
17. Superman; 1978	82,800,000			50. Look Who's Talking; 1989	55,000,000
18. Rain Man; 1989	86,000,000				

Top Movie Grosses, 1989

Source: *Variety*, January, 1990

Figures represent U.S. and Canadian rentals accruing to distributors, not total ticket sales receipts taken in at theaters.

Title/Month Released	Total Rentals	Title/Month Released	Total Rentals	Title/Month Released	Total Rentals
1. Batman; June	$150,500,000	8. Look Who's Talking; Oct.	55,000,000	15. The War Of The Roses; Dec.	33,000,000
2. Indiana Jones And The Temple Of Doom; May	115,500,000	9. Parenthood; Aug.	48,600,000	16. Field Of Dreams; Apr.	30,309,587
3. Lethal Weapon 2; July	79,500,000	10. Dead Poets Society; June	47,596,000	17. The Little Mermaid; Nov.	30,000,000
4. Honey, I Shrunk The Kids; June	71,097,000	11. National Lampoon's Christmas Vacation; Dec.	42,000,000	18. Uncle Buck; Aug.	29,190,348
5. Rain Man; continuing 1989 run	65,000,000	12. When Harry Met Sally; July	41,976,751	19. The Abyss; Aug.	28,700,000
6. Back To The Future, Part II; Nov.	63,000,000	13. Harlem Nights; Nov.	35,000,000	20. Sea Of Love; Sept.	27,500,000
7. Ghostbusters II; June	61,649,019	14. Turner & Hooch; July	34,263,000	21. Star Trek V: The Final Frontier; June	27,100,000
				22. Pet Sematary; Apr.	26,400,000

(continued)

Title/Month Released	Total Rentals	Title/Month Released	Total Rentals	Title/Month Released	Total Rentals
23. Steel Magnolias; Nov.	26,000,000	33. The 'Burbs; Feb.	17,318,125	41. Lean On Me; Mar.	14,400,000
24. Twins; continuing 1989 run	25,237,000	34. Tango & Cash; Dec.	17,000,000	42. The Dream Team; Apr.	14,384,108
25. Beaches; Dec. 1986	24,882,000	35. Bill & Ted's Excellent Adventure; Feb.	16,800,000	43. Weekend At Bernie's; July.	14,000,000
26. Black Rain; Sept.	22,500,000	36. Licence To Kill; July.	16,662,000	44. Peter Pan (reissue)	13,052,000
27. Major League; Apr.	21,500,000	37. Working Girl; continuing 1989 run	16,600,000	45. Do The Right Thing; June	13,043,257
28. See No Evil, Hear No Evil; May	20,147,000	38. The Accidental Tourist; Dec. 1988	15,900,000	46. Road House; May.	12,412,000
29. The Karate Kid Part III; June	19,225,899	39. Dangerous Liaisons; Dec. 1988	15,500,000	47. All Dogs Go To Heaven; Nov.	11,000,000
30. Three Fugitives; Jan.	18,567,000	40. Mississippi Burning; Dec. 1988	14,700,000	48. Always; Dec.	11,000,000
31. K-9; Apr.	18,402,231			49. The Bear; Oct.	11,000,000
32. Fletch Lives; Mar.	17,818,173			50. Oliver & Company; continuing 1989 run	10,268,000

Notable Books of 1989

Source: American Library Association

Fiction

Cat's Eye, Margaret Atwood
Mr. Field's Daughter, Richard Bausch
If the River Was Whiskey, T. Coraghessan Boyle
Any Old Iron, Anthony Burgess
Absent Friends, Frederick Busch
Spartina, John Casey
Baumgartner's Bombay, Anita Desai
The Other Side, Mary Gordon
Loving Women, Pete Hamill

A Prayer for Owen Meany, John Irving
The Remains of the Day, Ishiguro Kazuo
Homeland, Barbara Kingsolver
The Shawl, Cynthia Ozick
Buffalo Afternoon, Susan Fromberg Schaeffer
The Joy Luck Club, Amy Tan
Terrible Kisses, Robley Wilson
Five Seasons, A.B. Yehoshua

Poetry

A New Path to the Waterfall, Raymond Carver
An Ear to the Ground: An Anthology of Contemporary American Poetry, ed. Marie Harris and Kathleen Aguero

Poets for Life: Seventy-Six Poets Respond to AIDS, ed. Michael Klein

Nonfiction

Maasai Days, Cheryl Bentsen
Parting the Waters, Branch Taylor
The Road from Coorain, Jill Ker Conway
The Broken Cord, Michael Dorris
Paul Robeson, Martin Bauml Duberman
From Beirut to Jerusalem, Thomas L. Friedman

Songs from the Alley, Kathleen Hirsch
Among Schoolchildren, Tracy Kidder
Ki Ki's Paris, Billy Kluver and Julie Martin
Strangers from a Different Shore, Ronald Takaki

Bestselling Children's Books of 1989

Source: Publisher's Weekly

(All books are hardcover.)

1. The Way Things Work, David Macaulay; 561,452
2. The Great Waldo Search, Martin Handford; 304,230
3. Find Waldo Now, Martin Handford; 268,706
4. International Children's Bible; 251,124
5. The Eleventh Hour, Graeme Base; 250,000
6. Swan Lake, Mark Helprin, illus. Chris Van Allsburg; 242,127
7. Macmillan Dictionary for Children; 195,416
8. Carl Goes Shopping, Alexandra Day; 167,481
9. The Magic Locket, Elizabeth Koda-Callan; 161,583
10. The Book of the Sandman, Rien Poortvliet, text by Wil Huygen; 150,000
11. Disney Babies A to Z, Margo Lundell, illus. Darrell Baker; 142,792
12. Baby Donald's Busy Play Group, illus. Darrell Baker; 124,383
13. Glow-in-the-Dark Night Sky Book, Clint Hatchett, illus. Stephen Marchesi; 122,558
14. The Market Square Dog, James Herriot, illus. Ruth Brown; 109,587
15. The Silver Slippers, Elizabeth Koda-Callan; 103,804
16. Baby's Animal Friends, Phoebe Dunn; 98,173
17. The Very Busy Spider, Eric Carle; 97,735
18. The Big Golden Book of Dinosaurs, Mary Elting, illus. Christopher Santoro; 95,343
19. Sesame Street Hide-and-Seek Safari, illus. Tom Cooke; 94,738
20. Joyful Noise: Poems for Two Voices, Paul Fleischman, illus. Eric Beddows; 93,872
21. Amy the Dancing Bear, Carl Simon, illus. Margo Datz; 87,869
22. Nothing to Do, Liza Alexandra, illus. Tom Cooke; 83,917
23. Song and Dance Man, Karen Ackerman, illus. Stephen Gammell; 81,912
24. When Is My Birthday?, Ray Shepherd, illus. Tom Cooke; 81,807
25. Bedtime Hugs for Little Ones, Debby Boone, illus. Gabriel Ferrer; 77,213

All-Time Bestselling Children's Books

Source: *Publishers Weekly*

(The number of copies sold is from the date of original publication through 1988, as estimated by each publisher, and does not include book club or international sales.)

Hardcover

1. *The Tale of Peter Rabbit,* Beatrix Potter, 1902; 9,000,000
2. *Pat the Bunny,* Dorothy Kunhardt, 1940; 4,857,417
3. *The Littlest Angel,* Charles Tazewell, 1946; 4,665,209
4. *The Cat in the Hat,* Dr. Seuss, 1957; 3,693,197
5. *Green Eggs and Ham,* Dr. Seuss, 1960; 3,683,097
6. *The Children's Bible,* 1965; 3,683,097
7. *The Real Mother Goose,* illus. Blanche F. Wright, 1916; 3,600,000
8. *Richard Scarry's Best Word Book Ever,* 1963; 3,303,583
9. *One Fish, Two Fish, Red Fish, Blue Fish,* Dr. Seuss, 1960; 2,970,833
10. *Hop on Pop,* Dr. Seuss, 1963; 2,953,324
11. *Where the Sidewalk Ends,* Shel Silverstein, 1974; 2,851,477
12. *Dr. Seuss's ABC,* 1963; 2,753,823
13. *The Cat in the Hat Comes Back,* Dr. Seuss, 1958; 2,470,305
14. *The Giving Tree,* Shel Silverstein, 1964; 2,453,679
15. *Winnie-the-Pooh,* A.A. Milne, illus. Ernest H. Shepard, 1926; 2,445,398

Paperback

1. *The Outsiders,* S.E. Hinton, 1968; 5,855,085
2. *Are You There, God? It's Me, Margaret,* Judy Blume, 1974; 5,278,412
3. *Charlotte's Web,* E.B. White, illus. Garth Williams, 1973; 4,607,131
4. *Tales of a Fourth Grade Nothing,* Judy Blume, 1976; 4,582,039
5. *Little House on the Prairie,* Laura Ingalls Wilder, illus. Garth Williams, 1971; 3,803,209
6. *The Little Prince,* Antoine de Saint-Exupery, 1968; 3,667,861
7. *Little House in the Big Woods,* Laura Ingalls Wilder, illus. Garth Williams, 1971; 3,495,079
8. *That Was Then, This Is Now,* S.E. Hinton, 1972; 3,351,194
9. *Where the Red Fern Grows,* Wilson Rawls, 1974; 3,347,000
10. *Superfudge,* Judy Blume, 1981; 3,243,442
11. *Freckle Juice,* Judy Blume, 1978; 2,835,052
12. *Blubber,* Judy Blume, 1976; 2,745,782
13. *Little House on the Prairie,* Laura Ingalls Wilder, illus. Garth Williams, 1971; 2,559,486
14. *On the Banks of Plum Creek,* Laura Ingalls Wilder, illus Garth Williams, 1971; 2,559,265
15. *Farmer Boy,* Laura Ingalls Wilder, illus. Garth Williams, 1971; 2,533,801

Best-Selling Books of 1989

Source: *Publishers Weekly,* March 9, 1990

Hardcover Fiction

1. *Clear and Present Danger,* Tom Clancy
2. *The Dark Half,* Stephen King
3. *Daddy,* Danielle Steel
4. *Star,* Danielle Steel
5. *Caribbean,* James A. Michener
6. *The Satanic Verses,* Salman Rushdie
7. *The Russia House,* John le Carre
8. *The Pillars of the Earth,* Ken Follett
9. *California Gold,* John Jakes
10. *While My Pretty One Sleeps,* Mary Higgins Clark

Hardcover Nonfiction

1. *All I Really Need to Know I Learned in Kindergarten,* Robert Fulghum
2. *Wealth Without Risk,* Charles J. Givens
3. *A Woman Named Jackie,* C. David Heymann
4. *It Was on Fire When I Lay Down on It,* Robert Fulghum
5. *Better Homes and Gardens New Cook Book*
6. *The Way Things Work,* David Macaulay
7. *It's Always Something,* Gilda Radner
8. *Roseanne,* Roseanne Barr
9. *The Frugal Gourmet Cooks Three Ancient Cuisines,* Jeff Smith
10. *My Turn,* Nancy Reagan

Trade Paperbacks

1. *So Worthy My Love,* Kathleen Woodiwiss
2. *Yukon, Ho!,* Bill Watterson
3. *The Calvin and Hobbes Lazy Sunday Book,* Bill Watterson
4. *Drawing of the Three,* Stephen King

5. *The PreHistory of the Far Side,* Gary Larson
6. *Wildlife Preserves,* Gary Larson
7. *The Night of the Mary Kay Commandos,* Berke Breathed
8. *The Closing of the American Mind,* Allan Bloom
9. *Garfield Chews the Fat,* Jim Davis
10. *Love in the Time of Cholera,* Gabriel Garcia Marquez

Mass Market Paperbacks

1. *Fine Things,* Danielle Steel
2. *Presumed Innocent,* Scott Turow
3. *Kaleidoscope,* Danielle Steel
4. *Zoya,* Danielle Steel
5. *Patriot Games,* Tom Clancy
6. *Fallen Hearts,* V.C. Andrews
7. *Sands of Time,* Sidney Sheldon
8. *Misery,* Stephen King
9. *Tommyknockers,* Stephen King
10. *Cardinal of the Kremlin,* Tom Clancy

Atlases, Annuals, and Almanacs

1. *The World Almanac & Book of Facts 1990,* Mark Hoffman, ed.
2. *J.K. Lasser, Your Income Tax 1989*
3. *The Arthur Young Tax Guide 1990,* Peter W. Bernstein, ed.
4. *Information Please Almanac 1990*
5. *OPG Baseball Cards 1990,* James Beckett
6. *Mobil Road Atlas 1989*
7. *The 1989 What Color is Your Parachute?,* Richard Nelson Bolles
8. *Steve Birnbaum's Guide to Disneyworld 1990*
9. *1989 Buying Guide Issue,* Consumer Reports
10. *The Universal Almanac 1990,* John Wright, ed.

100 Bestselling U.S. Magazines

Source: Audit Bureau of Circulations, Schaumburg, Ill.

General magazines, exclusive of groups and comics; also exclusive of magazines that failed to file reports to ABC by press time. Based on total average paid circulation during the 6 months prior to Dec. 31, 1989.

Magazine	Circulation	Magazine	Circulation	Magazine	Circulation
1. Modern Maturity	21,430,990	34. Country Living	1,801,414	69. Health	1,088,696
2. NRTA/AARP Bulletin	21,092,794	35. Ebony	1,791,976	70. Discover	1,053,034
3. Reader's Digest	16,343,599	36. Home & Away	1,791,728	71. Organic Gardening	1,037,214
4. National Geographic	10,890,660	37. Seventeen	1,766,161	72. Michigan Living	1,026,085
5. Better Homes and		38. Parents	1,752,697	73. Golf	1,019,379
Gardens	8,005,311	39. Life	1,749,723	74. Weight Watchers	1,007,755
6. Family Circle	5,461,786	40. Popular Mechanics	1,650,693	75. Yankee	1,002,781
7. Good Housekeeping	5,152,245	41. Discovery	1,607,574	76. American Health	1,000,689
8. McCall's	5,088,686	42. 1,001 Home Ideas	1,603,099	77. Business Week, World	
9. Ladies' Home Journal	5,038,297	43. Woman's World	1,560,496	Wide	992,820
10. Woman's Day	4,705,288	44. Outdoor Life	1,507,529	78. YM	967,249
11. Time	4,339,029	45. The Elks	1,501,652	79. Country Home	963,081
12. Guideposts	4,203,934	46. Adventure Road	1,479,616	80. Scouting	949,405
13. National Enquirer	4,100,740	47. Soap Opera Digest	1,466,104	81. House Beautiful	939,735
14. Star	3,588,753	48. The American Rifleman	1,442,317	82. Car and Driver	934,377
15. First for Women	3,509,688	49. Sunset	1,393,015	83. Omni	925,436
16. Sports Illustrated	3,424,393	50. New Woman	1,390,830	84. Home	925,335
17. Playboy	3,421,203	51. The Family Handyman	1,382,547	85. Popular Photography	923,388
18. People	3,270,835	52. The American Hunter	1,380,230	86. Hot Rod	911,667
19. Newsweek	3,180,011	53. US	1,365,892	87. Working Women	909,201
20. Prevention	3,134,914	54. Golf Digest	1,363,907	88. Workbench	909,119
21. The American Legion	2,828,238	55. Bon Appetit	1,355,404	89. National Examiner	893,956
22. Cosmopolitan	2,702,125	56. Boys' Life	1,334,659	90. Business Week, North	
23. Smithsonian	2,342,443	57. Globe	1,329,413	America	889,535
24. Southern Living	2,318,841	58. Changing Times	1,300,153	91. Psychology Today	887,770
25. Glamour	2,224,135	59. The Workbasket	1,295,578	92. Jet	860,671
26. U.S. News & World		60. Vogue	1,247,920	93. Nation's Business	858,228
Report	2,209,996	61. Sesame Street	1,235,842	94. Essence	851,034
27. Field & Stream	2,015,577	62. Rolling Stone	1,216,781	95. Elle	826,336
28. VFW	1,979,899	63. Self	1,213,314	96. Food & Wine	823,530
29. NEA Today	1,919,340	64. Home Mechanix	1,209,395	97. Motor Trend	818,021
30. Motorland	1,866,430	65. Mademoiselle	1,162,206	98. Consumers Digest	813,373
31. Money	1,834,618	66. True Story	1,150,844	99. Gourmet	807,377
32. Penthouse	1,830,823	67. Leisure & Travel	1,115,328	100. Victoria	793,790
33. Popular Science	1,818,403	68. 'Teen	1,100,237		

Selected U.S. Daily Newspaper Circulation

Source: Audit Bureau of Circulations report of average paid circulation for 6 months to Mar. 31, 1990.

Newspaper	Daily	Newspaper	Daily	Newspaper	Daily
Akron Beacon Journal(m)	153,683	Daytona Beach		Madison (Wis.) State	
Albuquerque Journal(m)	†121,396	News-Journal(m)	97,214	Journal(m)	*82,412
Albuquerque Tribune(e)	†40,987	Dubuque Telegraph-Herald(e)	34,312	Middletown (N.Y.) Times	
Amarillo News(m)	42,809	El Paso Herald-Post(e)	†29,205	Herald Record(m)	†83,356
Amarillo Globe-Times(e)	*22,153	Erie (Pa.) News(m)	*30,782	Mobile Press(e)	*†43,380
Anchorage Times(e)	*32,777	Erie (Pa.) Times(e)	*40,842	Mobile Register(m)	*†58,603
Ann Arbor News(e)	49,828	Evansville (Ind.) Courier(m)	63,245	Modesto (Cal.) Bee(m)	†81,522
Athens (Ga.) News(m)	*13,848	Evansville (Ind.) Press(e)	35,825	Montgomery Advertiser(m)	*50,200
Athens (Ga.) Banner-Herald(e)	*13,808	Everett (Wash.) Herald(e)	54,517	Montgomery Journal(e)	*15,090
Augusta (Ga.) Chronicle(m)	*67,656	Fargo (N.D.) Forum(m)	55,020	Nashville Banner(e)	61,684
Augusta (Ga.) Herald(e)	*12,436	Ft. Lauderdale News(e)	*14,483	Newport News (Va.) Press(m)	*†79,077
Bakersfield Californian(m)	†83,423	Ft. Myers (Fla.)		Newport News (Va.) Times	
Bangor (Me.) News(m)	*78,222	News-Press(m)	97,560	Herald(e)	*†26,367
Baton Rouge Advocate(m)	67,635	Ft. Wayne Journal-Gazette(m)	63,200	Pensacola News-Journal(m)	†61,285
Baton Rouge State-Times(e)	27,442	Gary Post-Tribune(m)	74,365	Peoria Journal Star(a)	*91,532
Bergen Co. (N.J.) Record(e)	*161,546	Greenville (S.C.) News(m)	*88,088	Phoenix Gazette(e)	†95,911
Billings (Mont.) Gazette(m)	54,677	Greenville (S.C.) Piedmont(e)	*25,726	Portland (Me.) Press	
Binghamton (N.Y.) Press &		Honolulu Advertiser(m)	*†102,515	Herald(m)	*52,864
Sun Bulletin(m)	70,413	Honolulu Star-Bulletin(e)	†91,658	Reno Gazette Journal(m)	64,942
Birmingham Post-Herald(m)	*64,532	Huntington (W.Va.)		Roanoke Times & World	
Bismark (N.D.) Tribune(m)	30,825	Herald-Dispatch(m)	†43,209	News(m&e)	*123,018
Bridgeport (Conn.) Post(e)	55,977	Hyannis: Cape Cod Times(m)	41,108	Rockford (Ill.) Register-Star(m)	72,976
Bristol (Va.) Herald-Courier		Jackson (Miss.)		Salem (Ore.)	
Tennessean(a)	44,868	Clarion-Ledger(m)	*102,124	Statesman-Journal(m)	59,298
Camden (N.J.) Courier-Post(e)	†103,295	Jacksonville Times-Union(m)	*179,009	Salt Lake City Tribune(m)	112,630
Casper (Wyo.) Star Tribune(m)	34,691	Kalamazoo Gazette(e)	66,531	San Bernardino Sun(m)	88,817
Charleston (W.Va.) Gazette(m)	55,172	Knoxville News-Sentinel(m)	103,722	Sarasota Herald-Tribune(m)	†139,036
Chattanooga News-Free		Lansing (Mich.) State		Savannah News(m)	*53,456
Press(e)	55,428	Journal(m)	70,083	Savannah Press(e)	*18,374
Cincinnati Post(e)	106,440	Las Vegas Review-Journal(a)	*134,371	Scranton Times(m)	*51,876
Columbia (S.C.) State(m)	144,995	Lynchburg (Va.) News &		Scrantonian Tribune(m)	*37,234
Columbus (Ga.)		Advance(a)	†41,773	Sioux City Journal(m)	*50,458
Ledger-Enquirer(m)	57,843	Macon (Ga.) Telegraph &		Spokane Chronicle(e)	*24,829
Corpus Christi Caller-Times(m)	†68,136	News(m)	73,983	(continued)	

(continued)

Newspaper	Daily	Newspaper	Daily	Newspaper	Daily
Springfield (Ill.) State Journal Register(m).	69,260	Tallahassee Democrat(m) . .	60,637	Wilmington (N.C.) Star(m). . .	49,093
Springfield (Mass.) Union News(a)	112,180	Terre Haute Tribune Star(m) .	35,621	Winston-Salem Journal(m) . .	95,110
		Toledo Blade(e)	154,365	Worcester Telegram	
Syracuse Herald-Journal(e) .	92,661	Topeka Capital-Journal(m) . .	67,818	Gazette(a)	*†117,339
Syracuse Post-Standard(m) .	85,189	Tucson Star(m).	†94,565	Yakima (Wash.)	
Tacoma News Tribune(m). . .	†118,152	Tulsa Tribune(e)	†67,704	Herald-Republic(a)	†41,023
		Wilmington News Journal(a) .	†119,315	Youngstown Vindicator(e). . .	†89,541

(m) morning; (e) evening; (a) all day; *Mon.-Fri. average; †3 months.

Top 100 U.S. Daily Newspapers

Source: *Editor & Publisher Yearbook.*

During the six-month period ending Sept. 30, 1989, average daily newspaper circulation stayed relatively steady. When compared with the same period in 1988, there was a drop of less than one-tenth of 1%, from 62,694,816 to 62,649,218. The number of morning newspapers, increasing steadily in recent years, increased by one-from 529 to 530; the number of evening newspapers continued to drop, from 1,141 to 1,125.

		Circulation			Circulation
New York (NY) Wall Street Journal.	(m)	1,835,713	Des Moines (IA) Register	(m)	209,765
Arlington (VA) USA Today	(m)	1,325,507	Memphis (TN) Commercial Appeal	(m)	209,205
New York (NY) Daily News. . . .	(m)	1,194,237	Providence (RI) Journal	(all day)	204,196
Los Angeles (CA) Times	(m)	1,107,623	Seattle (WA) Post-Intelligencer .	(m)	203,560
New York (NY) Times.	(m)	1,068,217	St. Paul (MN) Pioneer Press Dispatch	(all day)	200,508
Washington (DC) Post	(m)	772,749	Cincinnati (OH) Enquirer	(m)	196,290
Chicago (IL) Tribune.	(m)	720,155	Los Angeles (CA) Daily News . .	(m)	185,736
Long Island (NY) Newsday . . .	(all day)	700,174	Atlanta (GA) Journal.	(e)	181,440
Detroit (MI) News	(all day)	690,422	San Antonio (TX) Express-News.	(all day)	179,590
Detroit (MI) Free Press	(m)	626,434	Dayton (OH) Daily News	(m)	178,615
San Francisco (CA) Chronicle . .	(m)	560,640	Milwaukee (WI) Sentinel	(m)	178,364
Chicago (IL) Sun-Times.	(m)	535,864	Jacksonville (FL) Times-Union . .	(m)	173,528
Boston (MA) Globe	(m)	516,031	Austin (TX) American-Statesman	(m)	172,518
New York (NY) Post.	(m)	507,568	Kansas City (MO) City Star. . .	(e)	170,801
Philadelphia (PA) Inquirer. . . .	(m)	504,903	San Antonio (TX) Light	(all day)	170,800
Newark (NJ) Star-Ledger.	(m)	463,738	Baltimore (MD) Evening Sun . .	(e)	170,750
Houston (TX) Chronicle	(all day)	437,481	Birmingham (AL) News	(e)	170,327
Cleveland (OH) Plain Dealer. . .	(m)	433,615	West Palm Beach (FL) Post . . .	(m)	169,360
Miami (FL) Herald	(m)	427,954	Pittsburgh (PA) Post-Gazette. . .	(m)	164,309
Minneapolis (MN) Star-Tribune. .	(m)	406,292	Hackensack (NJ) Record.	(m)	156,019
St. Louis (MO) Post-Dispatch . .	(m)	376,888	Toledo (OH) Blade	(e)	155,579
Dallas (TX) Morning News	(m)	371,537	Little Rock (AR) Gazette	(m)	154,001
Boston (MA) Herald	(m)	358,218	Akron (OH) Beacon Journal . . .	(m)	153,550
Denver (CO) Rocky Mountain News	(m)	345,943	Norfolk (VA) Virginian-Pilot	(m)	150,958
Orange County-Santa Ana (CA) Register.	(all day)	343,899	Asbury Park (NJ) Press.	(e)	150,590
St. Petersburg (FL) Times	(m)	349,460	Fort Worth (TX) Star-Telegram .	(m)	150,190
Houston (TX) Post	(m)	325,407	Riverside (CA) Press-Enterprise .	(m)	147,424
Phoenix (AZ) Arizona Republic. .	(m)	322,534	Fresno (CA) Bee.	(m)	146,723
Buffalo (NY) News.	(all day)	312,246	Grand Rapids (MI) Press	(e)	143,101
Portland (OR) Oregonian	(all day)	310,446	Richmond (VA) Times-Dispatch .	(m)	142,151
Atlanta (GA) Constitution	(m)	284,015	Raleigh (NC) News & Observer .	(m)	141,800
New Orleans (LA) Times-Picayune	(all day)	276,195	Columbia (SC) State	(m)	141,742
Kansas City (MO) Times	(m)	275,844	San Francisco (CA) Examiner . .	(e)	137,969
Milwaukee (WI) Journal.	(e)	275,632	Allentown (PA) Morning Call . . .	(m)	137,228
San Jose (CA) Mercury News . .	(all day)	274,484	Boston (MA) Christian Science Monitor	(m)	137,161
Tampa (FL) Tribune	(m)	268,681	Oakland (CA) Tribune.	(m)	134,504
San Diego (CA) Union.	(m)	268,450	Las Vegas (NV) Review-Journal .	(all day)	132,903
Orlando (FL) Sentinel	(all day)	266,549	Rochester (NY) Democrat and Chronicle	(m)	129,394
Sacramento (CA) Bee.	(m)	259,497	Nashville (TN) Tennessean . . .	(m)	126,092
Columbus (OH) Dispatch	(m)	252,206	Tulsa (OK) World	(m)	123,510
Denver (CO) Post	(m)	240,162	Long Beach (CA) Press-Telegram	(m)	123,371
Baltimore (MD) Sun	(m)	238,533	Lexington (KY) Herald-Leader . .	(m)	122,673
Charlotte (NC) Observer	(m)	236,496	Omaha (NE) World-Herald	(m)	121,985
Indianapolis (IN) Star	(m)	234,888	San Diego (CA) Tribune.	(e)	121,835
Seattle (WA) Times	(e)	233,106	Worcester (MA) Telegram & Gazette.	(all day)	120,568
Pittsburgh (PA) Press	(e)	232,282	Wilmington (DE) News Journal. .	(all day)	120,143
Philadelphia (PA) Daily News. . .	(e)	232,129	Wichita (KS) Eagle.	(m)	119,013
Louisville (KY) Courier-Journal. .	(m)	231,042	Tacoma (WA) Morning News-Tribune.	(m)	118,807
Hartford (CT) Courant.	(m)	227,763			
Dallas (TX) Times Herald.	(all day)	225,691			
Fort Lauderdale (FL) Sun-Sentinel	(m)	224,208			
Oklahoma City (OK) Daily Oklahoman.	(m)	220,183			

m = morning; e = evening

U.S. Opera Companies with Budgets of $500,000 or More

Source: Central Opera Service, Lincoln Center, New York, N.Y. 10023; July 1990

Anchorage Opera; William Russell, gen. dir.

Arizona Opera Co. (Tucson); Glynn Ross, gen. dir.

Fullerton Civic Light Opera (Calif.); R. G. Duncan, gen. mgr.

Long Beach Opera (Calif.); Micheal Milenski, gen. dir.

Long Beach Civic Light Opera (Calif.); P. Logefeil, mng. dir.

Los Angeles Music Center Opera Assn.; Peter Hemmings, exec. dir.

Opera Pacific (Costa Mesa, Calif.); David DiChiera, gen. dir.

Sacramento Opera Assn. (Calif.); Yuriko Ishii, gen. dir.

San Diego Civic Light Opera; Harris Goldman, gen mgr.

San Diego Opera Assn.; Ian Campbell, gen. mgr.

San Francisco Opera; Lotfi Mansouri, gen. dir.

San Francisco Opera Center (inc. Western Opera Theater); Christine Bullin, mgr.

Opera San José (Calif.); Irene Dalis, art. dir.

San José Civic Light Opera (Calif.); Stewart Slater, dir.

Central City Opera (Denver); Daniel Rule, gen. mgr.

Opera Colorado (Denver); Nathaniel Merrill, art. dir.

Connecticut Opera (Hartford); George Osborne, gen. dir.

Goodspeed Opera House (E. Haddam, Conn.); Michael Price, exec. dir.

Washington Opera (D.C.); Martin Feinstein, gen. dir.

Greater Miami Opera Assn.; Robert Heuer, gen. mgr.

Orlando Opera Co. (Fla.); vacant, gen. dir.

Palm Beach Opera; H. P. Benn, gen. dir.

Sarasota Opera Assn. (Fla.); Deane Allyn, exec. dir.

Atlanta Opera (Ga.); Alfred Kennedy, gen. mgr.

Hawaii Opera Theatre; Marshall Turkins, gen. dir.

Chicago Opera Theater; Alan Stone, art. dir.

Lyric Opera of Chicago; Ardis Krainik, gen. mgr.

Indianapolis Opera; Robert Driver, art. dir.

Des Moines Metro Opera (Indianola); Robert Larsen, art. dir.

Music Theatre of Wichita; Wayne Bryan, prod. dir.

Kentucky Opera Assn. (Louisville); Thomson Smillie, gen. dir.

New Orleans Opera Assn.; Arthur Cosenza, gen. dir.

Baltimore Opera Co.; Michael Harrison, gen. dir.

Opera Company of Boston; Sarah Caldwell, art. dir.

Michigan Opera Theatre (Detroit); David DiChiera, gen. dir.

Minnesota Opera Co. (St. Paul); Kevin Smith, gen. dir.

Lyric Opera of Kansas City (Missouri); Russell Patterson, gen. dir. & art. dir.

Opera Theatre of St. Louis (Missouri); Charles MacKay, gen. dir.

Opera/Omaha (Neb.); Mary Robert, gen. dir.

Nevada Opera (Reno); Ted Puffer, gen. dir.

New Jersey State Opera (Newark); Alfredo Silipigni, art. dir.

Santa Fe Opera (New Mexico); John Crosby, gen. dir.

Tri-Cities Opera (Binghamton, N.Y.); P. Hibbitt & C. Savoca, art. dirs.

Chautauqua Opera (N.Y.); Linda Jackson, gen. mgr.

Glimmerglass Opera (Cooperstown, N.Y.); Paul Kellogg, gen. mgr.

Syracuse Opera; Robert Swedberg, gen. dir.

Metropolitan Opera Assn. (New York City); vacant, gen. mgr.

New York City Opera; Christopher Keene, gen. dir.

New York City Opera Natl. Co.; Nancy Kelly, adm. dir.

Opera Orchestra of N.Y. (N.Y.C.); Eve Queler, art dir.

Opera Carolina (Charlotte, N.C.); James Wright, gen. dir.

Cincinnati Opera Assn.; James deBlasis, art. dir.

Cleveland Opera; David Bamberger, gen. dir.

Opera/Columbus (Oh.); John Gage, gen. dir.

Dayton Opera Assn. (Oh.); Jane Nelson, mng. dir.

Tulsa Opera (Oklahoma); Myrna S. Ruffner, gen. mgr.

Portland Opera Assn. (Oregon); Robert Bailey, exec. dir.

American Music Theater Festival (Phila.); Marjorie Samoff, prod. dir.

Opera Company of Philadelphia; vacant, gen. dir.

Pennsylvania Opera Theater (Phila.); Barbara Silverstein, art dir. & gen. mgr.

Pittsburgh Civic Light Opera; Charles Gray, exec. dir.

Pittsburgh Opera; Tito Capobianco, gen. dir.

Opera Memphis (Tenn.); Robert Driver, gen. & art. dir.

Austin Lyric Opera (Tex.) Walter Ducloux, art. dir.

Dallas Opera; Plato Karayanis, gen. dir.

Lyric Opera of Dallas (Tex.); John Burrows, art. dir.

Fort Worth Opera; J. Mario Ramos, mng. dir.

Houston Grand Opera Assn.; R. David Gockley, gen. dir.

Texas Opera Theater (Houston); Ann Tomfohrde, dir.

Theatre Under the Stars (Houston); Frank Young, exec. dir.

Utah Opera (Salt Lake City); vacant, gen. dir.

Virginia Opera (Norfolk); Peter Mark, gen. dir.

Seattle Opera Assn.; Speight Jenkins, gen. dir.

Florentine Opera of Milwaukee; Dennis Hanthorn, gen. mgr.

Skylight Comic Opera (Milwaukee); Jane Keegan, mng. dir.

Some Notable U.S. Dance Companies

Source: Dance/USA, July 13, 1990

African-American Dance Ensemble, Durham, NC

Aman Folk Ensemble, Los Angeles, CA

American Ballet Theatre, New York, NY

Armitage Ballet, New York, NY

Ballet Arizona, Pheonix, AZ

Ballet Hispanico of New York, New York, NY

Ballet Metropolitan, Columbus, OH

Ballet West, Salt Lake City, UT

Bebe Miller and Company, New York, NY

Bill T. Jones/Arnie Zane Company, New York, NY

Boston Ballet, Newton, MA

Caribbean Dance Company, St. Croix, VI

Carlota Santana Spanish Dance Arts Co., New York, NY

Chen & Dancers, New York, NY

Cincinnati/New Orleans City Ballet, Cincinnati, OH

Cleveland/San Jose Ballet, Cleveland, OH

Cunningham Dance Foundation, New York, NY

Dan Wagoner and Dancers, New York, NY

Dance Alloy, Pittsburgh, PA

Dance Exchange, Washington, DC

Dance Theatre of Harlem, New York, NY

Danceteller, Philadelphia, PA

David Gordon Pick Up Co., New York, NY

David Parsons Company, New York, NY

Dayton Ballet Association, Dayton, OH

Dayton Contemporary Dance Company, Dayton, OH

Donald Byrd/The Group, New York, NY

Elisa Monte Dance Company, New York, NY

Feld Ballets, New York, NY

Fort Worth Ballet, Fort Worth, TX

Garth Fagan's Bucket Dance Theatre, Rochester, NY

HARRY, New York, NY

Hartford Ballet, Hartford, CT

Houston Ballet, Houston, TX

Hubbard Street Dance Company, Chicago, IL

Jazz Tap Ensemble, Los Angeles, CA

Jennifer Muller and the Works, New York, NY

Jose Limon Dance Company, New York, NY

Joseph Holmes Dance Theater, Chicago, IL

Joyce Trisler Danscompany, New York, NY

KHADRA International Folk Ballet, San Francisco, CA

Lar Lubovitch Dance Company, New York, NY

Laura Dean Dancers and Musicians, New York, NY

(continued)

Lewitzky Dance Foundation, Los Angeles, CA
Louisville Ballet, Louisville, KY
Lucinda Childs Dance Company, New York, NY
Margaret Jenkins Dance Company, San Francisco, CA
Miami City Ballet, Miami Beach, FL
Milwaukee Ballet, Milwaukee, WI
Mordine & Company, Chicago, IL
New Dance Ensemble, Minneapolis, MN
New York City Ballet, New York, NY
Nicholas Rodriguez and Dance-Compass, Montclair, NJ
Nina Wiener Dance Company, New York, NY
North Carolina Dance Theater, Winston Salem, NC
Oakland Ballet, Oakland, CA
ODC/San Francisco, San Francisco, CA
Ohio Ballet, Akron, OH
Pacific Northwest Ballet, Seattle, WA
Paul Taylor Dance Company, New York, NY
Pennsylvania Ballet, Philadelphia, PA
Philadanco, Philadelphia, PA
Pilobolus, Washington, CT

Pittsburgh Ballet Theatre, Pittsburgh, PA
Pittsburgh Dance Alloy, Pittsburgh, PA
Princeton Ballet, New Brunswick, NJ
Rebecca Kelly Dance Company, New York, NY
Repertory Dance Theatre, Salt Lake City, UT
Richmond Ballet, Richmond, VA
Ririe-Woodbury Dance Company, Salt Lake City, UT
Rosalind Newman and Dancers, New York, NY
San Francisco Ballet, San Francisco, CA
Solomons Company/Dance, New York, NY
State Ballet of Missouri, Kansas City, MO
Stuart Pimsler Dance & Theater, Columbus, OH
Tandy Beal and Company, Santa Cruz, CA
Trisha Brown Company, New York, NY
Tulsa Ballet Theatre, Tulsa, OK
Washington Ballet, Washington, DC
Zenon Dance Company, Minneapolis, MN
ZeroMoving Dance Company, Philadelphia, PA
Zivili Kolo Ensemble, Granville, OH

Symphony Orchestras of the U.S.

Source: American Symphony Orchestra League, 777 14th St., N.W., Washington, DC 20005

(All orchestras listed had budgets in excess of $1 million in fiscal 1989.)

Symphony Orchestra[1]	Music Director[2]
Alabama (Birmingham)	Paul Polivnick
American (N.Y.C.)	Catherine Comet
Atlanta (Ga.)	Yoel Levi
Austin (Tex.)	Sung Kwak
Baltimore (Md.)	David Zinman
Boston (Mass.)	Seiji Ozawa
Brooklyn Philharmonic (N.Y.)	Dennis Russell Davies
Buffalo Philharmonic (N.Y.)	Maximiano Valdez
Cedar Rapids (Mich.)	Christian Tiemeyer
Charleston (S.C.)	David Stahl
Charlotte (N.C.)	Leo B. Driehuys
Chattanooga, & Opera Assn. (Tenn.)	Vakhtang Jordania
Chicago (Ill.)	Georg Solti
Cincinnati (Oh.)	Jesus Lopez-Cobos
Cleveland (Oh.)	Christoph von Dohnanyi
Colorado Springs (Col.)	Christopher P. Wilkins
Columbus (Oh.)	Christian Badea
Concerto Soloists Chamber Or. (Philadelphia, Pa.)	Marc S. Mostovoy
Dallas (Tex.)	Eduardo Mata
Dayton Philharmonic (Oh.)	Isaiah Jackson
Delaware (Wilmington)	Stephen Gunzenhauser
Detroit (Mich.)	Vacant[3]
Eastern Philharmonic (Greensboro, N.C.)	Sheldon Morgenstern
Fairfax (Annandale, Va.)	William L. Hudson
Flint (Mich.)	Enrique Arturo Diemecke
Philharmonic Orchestra of Florida (Fort Lauderdale)	James Judd
The Florida Orchestra (Tampa)	Jahja Ling
Florida (Orlando)	Kenneth Jean
Florida Symphonic Pops (Boca Raton)	Mark S. Azzolina
Fort Wayne Philharmonic (Ind.)	Ronald Ondrejka
Fort Worth (Tex.)	John Giordano
Grand Rapids (Mich.)	Catherine Comet
Grant Park (Chicago, Ill.)	Zdenek Macal
Handel and Haydn Soc. (Boston, Mass.)	Christopher Hogwood
Hartford (Conn.)	Michael Lankester
Honolulu (Ha.)	Donald Johanos
Houston (Tex.)	Christoph Eschenbach
Hudson Valley Philharmonic (Poughkeepsie, N.Y.)	Imre Pallo
Indianapolis (Ind.)	Raymond Leppard
Jacksonville (Fla.)	Roger Nierenberg
Kansas City (Mo.)	William McGlaughlin
Knoxville (Tenn.)	Kirk Trevor
Little Orchestra Soc. of N.Y. (N.Y.C.)	Dino Anagnost
Long Beach (Cal.)	JoAnn Falletta
Long Island Philharmonic (N.Y.)	Marin Alsop
Los Angeles Chamber Or. (Cal.)	Iona Brown
Los Angeles Philharmonic (Cal.)	Esa-Pekka Salonen
The Louisville Orchestra (Ky.)	Lawrence Leighton Smith
Madison (Wis.)	Roland A. Johnson
Memphis (Tenn.)	Alan Balter
Milwaukee (Wis.)	Zdenek Macal

Symphony Orchestra[1]	Music Director[2]
The Minnesota Orchestra (Minneapolis)	Edo de Waart
Music of the Baroque (Chicago, Ill.)	Thomas S. Wikman
The Nashville Symphony (Tenn.)	Kenneth S. Schermerhorn
National (Washington, D.C.)	Mstislav Rostropovich
New Haven (Conn.)	Michael Palmer
New Jersey (Newark)	Hugh Wolff
New Mexico (Albuquerque)	Neal H. Stulberg
New Orleans (La.)	Maxim Shostakovich
New World Symphony (Miami Beach, Fla.)	Michael Tilson Thomas
New York Philharmonic (N.Y.C.)	Zubin Mehta
North Carolina (Raleigh)	Gerhardt Zimmermann
Northeastern Pennsylvania Philharmonic (Avoca, Pa.)	Hugh Keelan
Oklahoma City Philharmonic (Okla.)	Vacant[3]
Omaha (Neb.)	Bruce B. Hangen
Oregon (Portland)	James DePreist
Orpheus Chamber Or. (N.Y.C., N.Y.)	None
Pacific Symphony (Irvine, Cal.)	Carl St. Clair
The Philadelphia Orchestra (Pa.)	Riccardo Muti
Philharmonia Virtuosi (Dobbs Ferry, N.Y.)	Richard P. Kapp
Phoenix (Ariz.)	James L. Sedares
Pittsburgh (Pa.)	Lorin Maazel
Portland (Me.)	Toshi Shimada
Puerto Rico (Santurce)	Odo Alonso
Rhode Island Philharmonic Or. (Providence)	Andrew Massey
The Richmond Symphony (Va.)	George Manahan
Rochester Philharmonic Or. (N.Y.)	Darryl One
Sacramento (Cal.)	Carter Nice
St. Louis (Mo.)	Leonard Slatkin
St. Paul Chamber Or. (Minn.)	Christopher Hogwood
San Antonio (Tex.)	Zdenek Macal
San Diego (Cal.)	Yoav Talmi
San Francisco (Cal.)	Herbert Blomstedt
San Jose (Cal.)	George Cleve
Savannah (Ga.)	Philip B. Greenberg
Seattle (Wash.)	Vacant[3]
Spokane (Wash.)	Bruce Ferden
Springfield (Mass.)	Raymond C. Hervey
Syracuse (N.Y.)	Kazuyoshi Akiyama
Toledo (Oh.)	Andrew Massey
Tucson (Ariz.)	Robert E. Bernhardt
Tulsa Philharmonic Or. (Okla.)	Bernard Rubenstein
Utah (Salt Lake City)	Joseph Silverstein
The Virginia Symphony (Norfolk)	Vacant[3]
West Virginia (Charleston)	Thomas B. Conlin
Wichita (Kan.)	Michael Palmer
Winston-Salem Symphony Assn. (N.C.)	Peter J. Perret

(1) Orchestra name=place name + Symphony Orchestra, unless otherwise noted; (2) General title; listed is highest-ranking member of conducting personnel; (3) As of mid-1990.

Recordings & Music Videos

The Recording Industry of America, Inc. confers Gold Awards on single records that sell 1 million units, albums and their tape equivalents that sell 500,000 units, and music videos that sell 25,000 units. Platinum Awards go to single records that sell 2 million units, to albums and tapes that sell 1 million, and to music videos that sell 50,000. Multi-Platinum Awards are conferred on single records that sell 3 million units or more, albums and tapes that sell 2 million or more, and music videos that sell 100,000 units or more. 1989 Multi-Platinum and Platinum Awards for music released in 1989 follow.

Artists, Recording Titles

Albums, Multi-Platinum
(Number in parentheses-millions of albums sold)
Fine Young Cannibals; The Raw and the Cooked (2)
Debbie Gibson; Electric Youth (2)
Great White; Twice Shy (2)
Janet Jackson; Rhythm Nation 1814 (2)
Billy Joel; Storm Front (2)
Madonna; Like a Prayer (2)
Richard Marx; Repeat Offender (3)
Milli Vanilli; Girl You Know It's True (5)
Motley Crue; Dr. Feelgood (2)
New Kids on the Block; Merry, Merry Christmas (2)
Tom Petty; Fool Moon Fever (2)
Prince; Batman Soundtrack (2)
Skid Row; Skid Row (2)
Tone Loc; Loc'd After Dark (2)

Albums, Platinum
Aerosmith; Pump
B-52's; Cosmic Thing
Baby Face; Tender Lover
Tracy Chapman; Crossroads
Cher; Heart of Stone
John Cougar Mellencamp; Big Daddy
The Cure; Disintegration
Gloria Estefan & Miami Sound Machine; Cuts Both Ways
Heavy D and the Boyz; Big Tyme
Don Henley; The End of the Innocence
L.L Cool J; Walking with a Panther
N.W.A.; Straight Outta Compton
Roy Orbison; Mystery Girl
The Rolling Stones; Steel Wheels
Linda Ronstadt; Cry Like a Rainstorm,
   Howl Like the Wind
Ricky Van Shelton; Loving Proof
Soul II Soul; Keep on Movin'
Tears for Fears; The Seeds of Love
Tesla; The Great Radio Controversy
The 2 Live Crew; As Nasty As They Wanna Be
Too Short; Life Is . . .Too Short
Warrant; Dirty Rotten Filthy Stinking Rich

Hank Williams Jr., Greatest Hits III
M.C. Young; Stone Cold Rhymin'

Singles, Platinum
Bobby Brown; On Our Own
Janet Jackson; Miss You Much
Madonna; Like a Prayer
Richard Marx; Right Here Waiting
New Kids on the Block; Hangin' Tough
Prince; Batdance
Soul II Soul; Back to Life
Soul II Soul; Keep on Movin'
Technotronic; Pump Up the Jam
Tone Loc; Funky Cold Medina

Music Videos, Multi-Platinum
Paula Abdul; Straight Up
California Raisins; Meet the Raisins
Def Leppard; Hysteria
Def Leppard; In the Round in Your Face Live
Michael Jackson; Moonwalker
Metallica; Cliff 'Em All
Milli Vanilli; In Motion
Motley Crue; Uncensored
Raffi; Raffi in Concert with Rise & Shine Band
Bruce Springsteen; Video Anthology, 1978-1988

Music Videos, Platinum
Phil Collins; No Jacket Required
The Cure; Staring at the Sea—The Images
The Doors; The Doors Live at the Hollywood Bowl
The Doors; Dance on Fire
Gloria Estefan & Miami Sound Machine; Homecoming
   Concert
Debbie Gibson; Live in Concert—The Out of the Blue Tour
Inxs; Kick the Video Flick
Metallica; 2 of One
Prince; Sign o' the Times
Queensryche; Video Mindcrime
Ratt: Ratt: The Video
Rush; A Show of Hands
George Strait; George Strait Live
Stryper; Live in Japan
Various; Natural States

Top Ten Singles and Albums of 1989

Source: Billboard

Albums
1. Bobby Brown; Don't Be Cruel
2. New Kids on the Block; Hangin' Tough
3. Paula Abdul; Forever Your Girl
4. Bon Jovi; New Jersey
5. Guns 'N' Roses; Appetite for Destruction
6. Fine Young Cannibals; The Raw and the Cooked
7. Guns 'N' Roses; G 'N' R Lies
8. Traveling Wilburys; Traveling Wilburys
9. Def Leppard; Hysteria
10. Milli Vanilli; Girl You Know It's True

Singles
1. Chicago; Look Away
2. Bobby Brown; My Prerogative
3. Poison; Every Rose Has Its Thorns
4. Paula Abdul; Straight Up
5. Janet Jackson; Miss You Much
6. Paula Abdul; Cold Hearted
7. Bette Midler; Wind Beneath My Wings
8. Milli Vanilli; Girl You Know It's True
9. Will to Power; Baby, I Love Your Way/Freebird Medley
10. Anita Baker; Giving You the Best That I Got

America's Favorite Television Programs: 1989

Source: Nielsen Media Research
(Percent of TV households and persons in TV households)

Regularly Scheduled Network Programs (February 1990)

(Nielsen People Meter Average Audience Estimates)

Program	TV House-holds	Women	Men	Teens	Children	Program	TV House-holds	Women	Men	Teens	Children
Bill Cosby Show	23.2	17.1	11.8	18.8	20.1	ABC Sunday Movie		11.2		11.8	
Cheers	23.1	17.1	13.8	14.9		Coach				11.4	
Roseanne	22.1	16.9	11.9	18.6	12.5	Full House				12.2	16.9
A Different World	21.6	15.9	10.6	19.0	19.4	Growing Pains				13.3	11.0
America's Funniest Home Videos	20.8	15.9	14.7	20.1	19.5	Family Matters				11.3	16.0
Golden Girls	20.7	17.9	10.7			Hogan Family				11.2	12.5
Wonder Years	19.7	13.9		19.2	14.6	Head of the Class				11.9	
Empty Nest	19.6	16.8				Doogie Howser, M.D.				15.4	
60 Minutes	18.9	14.7	13.5			Alf					14.3
Unsolved Mysteries	18.2	14.5	11.7			Perfect Strangers					14.3
L.A. Law	18.2	14.0	11.6			Just the Ten of Us					13.2
Who's the Boss?	18.0			15.5	12.5	Magical World of Disney					14.4
Grand	17.8	13.4	10.1			Slimer & Real Ghosts.II					12.0
Murder, She Wrote	18.5	15.5	10.2								
NBC Sunday Night Movie	17.2		11.5								
Matlock		14.2	10.5								
In The Heat Of The Night		13.7	10.8								

Favorite Syndicated Programs

Source: Nielsen Media Research. February, 1990

(Ratings based on Designated Market Area coverage as reported by Nielsen's Cassandra Report)

Program	TV house-holds	Women	Men	Teens	Children	Program	TV house-holds	Women	Men	Teens	Children
Wheel of Fortune	15.9	13.4	9.3	4.1	4.3	Entertainment Tonight	9.4	7.3	5.3	2.9	1.7
Jeopardy	14.2	11.6	7.9	4.0	2.8	Inside Edition	7.5	5.6	4.3	1.7	0.9
Oprah Winfrey Show	11.0	9.2	3.3	3.7	1.3	Cheers	7.3	4.9	5.0	3.8	2.1
Star Trek Next Generation	10.5	6.4	8.6	6.1	5.5	Family Feud	7.3	5.8	3.6	4.0	3.3
Cosby Show	10.2	7.3	5.1	10.1	9.5	Night Court	7.3	4.6	4.8	6.1	3.9
PM Magazine	9.5	7.3	5.6	2.3	1.9	Who's The Boss?	7.3	4.8	3.4	8.3	6.2
Current Affair	9.5	7.2	5.8	3.0	1.9	Jeopardy Two	7.0	5.9	3.8	1.0	0.9
						Donahue	6.7	5.2	2.5	0.9	0.4

Average Television Viewing Time

Source: Nielsen Media Research. Feb. 1990 (hours: minutes, per week)

		Mon.-Fri. 10am-4:30pm	Mon.-Fri. 4:30pm-7:30pm	Mon.-Sun. 8-11pm	Sat. 7am-1pm	Mon.-Fri. 11:30pm-1am
Total Persons	age 2+	4:29	4:13	8:47	:49	1:08
Total Women	age 18+	5:55	4:44	9:49	:38	1:18
	18-24	4:55	3:18	6:43	:32	:57
	25-54	5:06	3:52	9:18	:39	1:20
	55+	7:52	6:55	12:06	:38	1:22
Total Men	age 18+	3:31	3:46	9:05	:40	1:20
	18-24	2:56	2:35	5:55	:33	1:14
	25-54	2:56	3:05	8:46	:41	1:20
	55+	5:37	6:07	11:46	:41	1:23
Female Teens	12-17	2:40	3:30	6:27	:46	:36
Male Teens	12-17	2:20	3:35	7:16	:55	:49
Children	2-5	6:30	4:38	6:04	1:41	:25
Children	6-11	2:34	4:10	6:32	1:35	:23

All-time Top Television Programs

Source: A.C. Nielsen estimates. Jan. 30. 1960 through Apr. 17. 1989, excluding unsponsored or joint network telecasts or programs under 30 minutes long. Ranked by percent of average audience.

	Program	Date	Network	Households (000)		Program	Date	Network	Households (000)
1	M*A*S*H Special	2/28/83	CBS	50,150		Day After)	11/20/83	ABC	38,550
2	Dallas	11/21/80	CBS	41,470	16	Roots Pt. VI	1/28/77	ABC	32,680
3	Roots Pt. VIII	1/30/77	ABC	36,380	16	The Fugitive	8/29/67	ABC	25,700
4	Super Bowl XVI	1/24/82	CBS	40,020	18	Super Bowl XXI	1/25/87	CBS	40,030
5	Super Bowl XVII	1/30/83	NBC	40,480	19	Roots Pt. V	1/27/77	ABC	32,540
6	Super Bowl XX	1/26/86	NBC	41,490	20	Ed Sullivan	2/9/64	CBS	23,240
7	Gone With The Wind-Pt. 1	11/7/76	NBC	33,960	21	Bob Hope Christmas Special	1/14/71	NBC	27,050
8	Gone With The Wind-Pt. 2	11/8/76	NBC	33,750	22	Roots Pt. III	1/25/77	ABC	31,900
9	Super Bowl XII	1/15/78	CBS	34,410	23	Super Bowl XI	1/9/77	NBC	31,610
10	Super Bowl XIII	1/21/79	NBC	35,090	23	Super Bowl XV	1/25/81	NBC	34,540
11	Bob Hope Christmas Show	1/15/70	NBC	27,260	25	Super Bowl VI	1/16/72	CBS	27,450
					26	Roots Pt. II	1/24/77	ABC	31,400
12	Super Bowl XVIII	1/22/84	CBS	38,800	27	Beverly Hillbillies	1/8/64	CBS	22,570
12	Super Bowl XIX	1/20/85	ABC	39,390	28	Roots Pt. IV	1/26/77	ABC	31,190
14	Super Bowl XIV	1/20/80	CBS	35,330	28	Ed Sullivan	2/16/64	CBS	22,445
15	ABC Theater (The				30	Super Bowl XXIII	1/22/89	NBC	39,320

Top-Rated TV Shows of the Past

Source: A.C. Nielsen

1950s			1960s			1970s		
Program	Network	Avg. rating over decade	Program	Network	Avg. rating over decade	Program	Network	Avg. rating over decade
1. A. Godfrey's Talent Scouts	CBS	32.9	1. Bonanza	NBC	29.6	1. All in the Family	CBS	23.1
2. I Love Lucy	CBS	31.6	2. The Red Skelton Show	CBS	26.4	2. M*A*S*H	CBS	17.6
3. You Bet Your Life	NBC	30.1	3. The Andy Griffith Show	CBS	22.4	3. Hawaii Five-O	CBS	16.5
4. Dragnet	NBC	24.6	4. The Beverly Hillbillies	CBS	21.9	4. Happy Days	ABC	15.9
5. The Jack Benny Show	CBS	22.3	5. The Ed Sullivan Show	CBS	21.7	5. The Waltons	CBS	14.0
6. A. Godfrey and Friends	CBS	19.5	6. The Lucy Show/Here's Lucy	CBS	21.3	6. The Mary Tyler Moore Show	CBS	13.7
7. Gunsmoke	CBS	15.6				7. Sanford & Son	NBC	13.4
8. The Red Skelton Show	NBC	15.2	7. The Jackie Gleason Show	CBS	16.5	8. One Day at a Time	CBS	11.4
9. December Bride	CBS	13.8	8. Bewitched	ABC	14.8	9. Three's Company	ABC	10.8
10. I've Got a Secret	CBS	12.9	9. Gomer Pyle	CBS	13.4	10. 60 Minutes	CBS	10.0
11. $64,000 Question	CBS	11.2	10. Candid Camera	CBS	11.2	11. Maude	CBS	9.8
12. Disneyland	ABC	10.8	11. The Dick Van Dyke Show	CBS	11.1	12. Gunsmoke	CBS	9.7
13. The Ed Sullivan Show	CBS	10.6	12. The Danny Thomas Show	CBS	10.7	13. Charlie's Angels	ABC	9.6
14. Have Gun—Will Travel			13. Family Affair	CBS	9.8	14. The Jeffersons	CBS	9.4
15. The Danny Thomas Show	CBS	10.3	14. Laugh-In	NBC	7.9	15. Laverne & Shirley	ABC	9.3
	CBS	9.9	15. Rawhide	CBS	7.5			

U.S. Television Sets and Stations Received

Set Ownership

(Nielsen est. as of Jan. 1, 1990)
Total TV Households   92,100,000
(98% of U.S. households own at least one TV set)
Homes with:

Color TV sets	90,100,000	98%
B&W only	2,000,000	2%
2 or more sets	59,865,000	65%
One set	32,235,000	35%
Cable (May 1990)	53,970,600	58.6%

Total TV Households:	92,100,000
Total Persons 2+:	235,230,000
Total Women 18+:	94,600,000
Total Men 18+:	85,570,000
Total Teens 12-17:	19,570,000
Total Children 2-11:	35,490,000

Stations Receivable
(Nielsen, September 1989)
% of TV homes receiving:

1-6	8%
7-10	33%
11-14	33%
15-19	19%
20-29	7%
30+	IFR

IFR = Less than 1%

100 Leading U.S. Advertisers, 1988

Source: *Advertising Age*, Sept. 27, 1989 © Crain Communications Inc. 1989

Rank	Advertiser	Ad spending (millions)	Rank	Advertiser	Ad spending (millions)	Rank	Advertiser	Ad spending (millions)
1	Philip Morris	$2,058.2	34	Walt Disney	$300.6	69	Kroger	$144.1
2	Procter & Gamble	1,506.9	35	Hershey Foods	298.6	70	Seagram	143.1
3	General Motors	1,294.0	36	U.S. Government	295.1	71	Volkswagen	140.3
4	Sears, Roebuck	1,045.2	37	General Electric	276.6	72	Paramount	139.2
5	RJR Nabisco	814.5	38	Toyota Motor	272.9	73	News	139.1
6	Grand Metropolitan	773.9	39	SmithKline Beecham	264.2	74	CPC	134.4
7	Eastman Kodak	735.9	40	Schering-Plough	262.2	75	Wm. Wrigley Jr.	134.2
8	McDonald's	728.3	41	Campeau	260.5	76	Bayer	132.2
9	PepsiCo	712.3	42	American Cyanamid	256.2	77	E.I. du Pont de Nemours	131.4
10	Kellogg	683.1	43	American Stores	250.5	78	Texas Air	128.8
11	Anheuser-Busch	634.5	44	American Express	247.2	79	Noxell	126.7
12	K mart	632.0	45	Honda Motor	243.3	80	American Dairy Farmers	126.6
13	Warner-Lambert	609.2	46	Tandy	232.0	81	Sony	125.9
14	Unilever	607.5	47	Dayton Hudson	230.2	82	Goodyear Tire & Rubber	124.6
15	Nestle	573.8	48	Pfizer	230.1	83	Loews	123.8
16	Ford Motor	569.8	49	Nissan Motor	224.9	84	Levi Strauss	123.1
17	American Telephone & Telegraph	547.5	50	IBM	214.4	85	Columbia Pictures	122.4
18	Chrysler	474.0	51	Hyundai	204.5	86	Dr Pepper/Seven-Up	121.9
19	General Mills	470.1	52	Campbell Soup	202.5	87	AMR	120.7
20	Johnson & Johnson	468.8	53	Adolph Coors	200.8	88	Marriott	120.2
21	Bristol-Myers Squibb	430.7	54	B.A.T.	184.1	89	UAL	120.2
22	J.C. Penney	426.6	55	BCI	180.2	90	Hallmark Cards	119.8
23	Quaker Oats	423.4	56	Revlon	177.3	91	Citicorp	118.4
24	Ralston Purina	421.0	57	American Brands	168.7	92	ITT	115.9
25	Time Warner	409.7	58	Hasbro	164.5	93	Franklin Mint	114.8
26	May Department Stores	399.7	59	Gillette	160.5	94	Wendy's	114.2
27	American Home Products	393.2	60	Nynex	160.4	95	Bell Atlantic	113.2
28	Coca-Cola	385.1	61	Carter Hawley Hale	159.8	96	Delta Air Lines	112.6
29	H.J. Heinz	340.1	62	Dow Chemical	156.7	97	Whitman	111.7
30	Mars	339.7	63	Mobil	155.9	98	S.C. Johnson & Son	111.6
31	Sara Lee	326.9	64	Montgomery Ward & Co.	155.3	99	Borden	110.5
32	Macy	308.9	65	MCA	153.7	100	Subaru	108.0
33	Colgate-Palmolive	306.6	66	Clorox	148.3			
			67	Mazda Motor	146.7			
			68	Philips	144.3			

Media Spending by 35 Leading Advertisers

Source: *Advertising Age*, Sept. 27, 1989; copyright © Crain Communications Inc., 1989

(In thousands)

Rank '88	Rank '87	Advertiser	'88-'87 % chg	Estimated unmeasured	Subtotal measured	Measured print	Measured TV	Measured radio	Measured outdoor
1	1	Philip Morris	7.2	926,200	1,132,023	363,961	657,847	48,791	61,425
2	2	Procter & Gamble	2.8	678,100	828,791	102,640	684,158	41,311	682
3	3	General Motors	34.0	345,105	948,895	293,515	573,943	78,440	2,997
4	4	Sears, Roebuck	4.4	627,100	418,085	195,943	128,295	93,043	804
5	5	RJR Nabisco	-3.4	356,100	458,437	173,320	222,307	5,443	57,366
6	40	Grand Metropolitan	-2.0	410,800	363,114	75,730	258,498	21,090	7,796
7	7	Eastman Kodak	8.5	491,900	244,045	42,615	194,323	6,551	557
8	8	McDonald's	10.7	322,159	406,161	6,899	387,798	5,158	6,306
9	6	PepsiCo	1.4	252,900	459,447	9,425	414,802	32,140	3,080
10	17	Kellogg	21.8	281,200	401,889	23,335	378,411	73	70
11	10	Anheuser-Busch	4.4	222,100	412,431	21,720	325,917	58,087	6,708
12	11	K mart	0.0	422,050	209,950	98,842	92,597	18,388	123
13	15	Warner-Lambert	3.3	398,500	210,656	23,963	168,474	18,015	204
14	12	Unilever	-4.0	243,000	364,469	75,585	274,833	13,337	715
15	28	Nestle	12.4	269,600	304,220	83,159	210,315	9,957	789
16	9	Ford Motor	3.0	132,800	436,983	155,574	255,383	23,870	2,157
17	16	American Telephone & Telegraph	3.1	200,000	347,504	104,021	224,627	18,494	361
18	14	Chrysler	0.1	104,300	369,709	119,017	219,147	30,605	940
19	13	General Mills	3.0	110,000	360,058	43,623	309,120	7,020	295
20	26	Johnson & Johnson	5.8	233,700	235,135	38,393	195,263	1,402	77
21	26	Bristol-Myers Squibb	1.6	202,800	227,893	50,984	172,151	4,758	0
22	18	J.C. Penney	-5.5	273,000	153,580	87,587	54,442	11,503	49
23	27	Quaker Oats	12.6	204,300	219,120	45,592	170,100	2,971	456
24	24	Ralston Purina	-8.5	264,200	156,773	40,616	106,842	7,155	160
25	NA	Time Warner	17.1	152,400	257,315	108,943	138,673	8,851	848
26	120	May Department Stores	-4.5	139,900	259,787	228,661	29,982	1,024	120
27	23	American Home Products	-0.3	168,300	224,921	21,589	197,981	5,350	0
28	25	Coca-Cola	15.2	154,100	230,985	13,993	198,758	15,696	2,538
29	38	H.J. Heinz	22.1	190,000	150,089	31,506	118,222	337	24
30	24	Mars	-14.0	151,800	187,857	15,731	163,430	8,673	23
31	31	Sara Lee	19.6	170,500	156,444	49,038	105,756	1,586	64
32	NA	Macy	2.8	108,100	200,779	184,463	15,651	289	376
33	30	Colgate-Palmolive	4.9	194,100	112,524	18,876	90,794	1,509	1,344
34	36	Walt Disney	26.6	144,300	156,281	44,865	103,050	7,823	543
35	69	Hershey Foods	17.5	200,100	98,531	19,362	69,137	10,001	32

AWARDS — MEDALS — PRIZES

The Alfred B. Nobel Prize Winners

Alfred B. Nobel, inventor of dynamite, bequeathed $9,000,000, the interest to be distributed yearly to those who had most benefited mankind in physics, chemistry, medicine-physiology, literature, and peace. The first Nobel Memorial Prize in Economics was awarded in 1969. No awards given for years omitted. In 1989, each prize was worth approximately $455,000 to $470,000. (For 1990, see *Addenda*.)

Physics

1989 Norman F. Ramsey, U.S.; Hans G. Dehmelt, German-U.S. & Wolfgang Paul, German
1988 Leon M. Lederman, Melvin Schwartz, Jack Steinberger, all U.S.
1987 K. Alex Muller, Swiss; J. Georg Bednorz, W. German
1986 Ernst Ruska, German, Gerd Binnig, W. German, Heinrich Rohrer, Swiss
1985 Klaus von Klitzing, W. German
1984 Carlo Rubbia, Italian, Simon van der Meere, Dutch
1983 Subrahmanyan Chandrasekhar, William A. Fowler, both U.S.
1982 Kenneth G. Wilson, U.S.
1981 Nicolass Bloembergen, Arthur Schaalow, both U.S.; Kai M. Siegbahn, Swedish
1980 James W. Cronin, Val L. Fitch, U.S.
1979 Steven Weinberg, Sheldon L. Glashow, both U.S.; Abdus Salam, Pakistani
1978 Pyotr Kapitsa, USSR; Arno Penzias, Robert Wilson, both U.S.
1977 John H. Van Vleck, Philip W. Anderson, both U.S.; Nevill F. Mott, British
1976 Burton Richter, U.S. Samuel C.C. Ting, U.S.
1975 James Rainwater, U.S. Ben Mottelson, U.S.-Danish, Aage Bohr, Danish
1974 Martin Ryle, British Antony Hewish, British
1973 Ivar Giaever, U.S. Leo Esaki, Japan Brian D. Josephson, British
1972 John Bardeen, U.S. Leon N. Cooper, U.S. John R. Schrieffer, U.S.
1971 Dennis Gabor, British
1970 Louis Neel, French Hannes Alfven, Swedish
1969 Murray Gell-Mann, U.S.

1968 Luis W. Alvarez, U.S.
1967 Hans A. Bethe, U.S.
1966 Alfred Kastler, French
1965 Richard P. Feynman, U.S. Julian S. Schwinger, U.S. Shinichiro Tomonaga, Japanese
1964 Nikolai G. Basov, USSR Aleksander M. Prochorov, USSR Charles H. Townes, U.S.
1963 Maria Goeppert-Mayer, U.S. J. Hans D. Jensen, German Eugene P. Wigner, U.S.
1962 Lev. D. Landau, USSR
1961 Robert Hofstadter, U.S. Rudolf L. Mossbauer, German
1960 Donald A. Glaser, U.S.
1959 Owen Chamberlain, U.S. Emilio G. Segre, U.S.
1958 Pavel Cherenkov, Ilya Frank, Igor Y. Tamm, all USSR
1957 Tsung-dao Lee, Chen Ning Yang, both U.S.
1956 John Bardeen, U.S. Walter H. Brattain, U.S. William Shockley, U.S.
1955 Polykarp Kusch, U.S. Willis E. Lamb, U.S.
1954 Max Born, British Walter Bothe, German
1953 Frits Zernike, Dutch
1952 Felix Bloch, U.S. Edward M. Purcell, U.S.
1951 Sir John D. Cockroft, British Ernest T. S. Walton, Irish
1950 Cecil F. Powell, British
1949 Hideki Yukawa, Japanese
1948 Patrick M. S. Blackett, British
1947 Sir Edward V. Appleton, British
1946 Percy Williams Bridgman, U.S.
1945 Wolfgang Pauli, U.S.
1944 Isidor Isaac Rabi, U.S.
1943 Otto Stern, U.S.
1939 Ernest O. Lawrence, U.S.
1938 Enrico Fermi, U.S.
1937 Clinton J. Davisson, U.S. Sir George P. Thomson, British

1936 Carl D. Anderson, U.S. Victor F. Hess, Austrian
1935 Sir James Chadwick, British
1933 Paul A. M. Dirac, British Erwin Schrodinger, Austrian
1932 Werner Heisenberg, German
1930 Sir Chandrasekhara V. Raman, Indian
1929 Prince Louis-Victor de Broglie, French
1928 Owen W. Richardson, British
1927 Arthur H. Compton, U.S. Charles T. R. Wilson, British
1926 Jean B. Perrin, French
1925 James Franck, Gustav Hertz, both German
1924 Karl M. G. Siegbahn, Swedish
1923 Robert A. Millikan, U.S.
1922 Niels Bohr, Danish
1921 Albert Einstein, Ger.-U.S.
1920 Charles E. Guillaume, French
1919 Johannes Stark, German
1918 Max K. E. L. Planck, German
1917 Charles G. Barkla, British
1915 Sir William H. Bragg, British Sir William L. Bragg, British
1914 Max von Laue, German
1913 Heike Kamerlingh-Onnes, Dutch
1912 Nils G. Dalen, Swedish
1911 Wilhelm Wien, German
1910 Johannes D. van der Waals, Dutch
1909 Carl F. Braun, German Guglielmo Marconi, Italian
1908 Gabriel Lippmann, French
1907 Albert A. Michelson, U.S.
1906 Sir Joseph J. Thomson, British
1905 Philipp E. A. von Lenard, Ger.
1904 John W. Strutt, Lord Rayleigh, British
1903 Antoine Henri Becquerel, French Marie Curie, Polish-French Pierre Curie, French
1902 Hendrik A. Lorentz, Pieter Zeeman, both Dutch
1901 Wilhelm C. Roentgen, German

Chemistry

1989 Thomas R. Cech, Sidney Altman, both U.S.
1988 Johann Deisenhofer, Robert Huber, Hartmut Michel, all W. German
1987 Donald J. Cram, Charles J. Pederson, both U.S.; Jean-Marie Lehn, French
1986 Dudley Herschbach, Yuan T. Lee, both U.S.; John C. Polanyi, Canadian
1985 Herbert A. Hauptman, Jerome Karle, both U.S.
1984 Bruce Merrifield, U.S.
1983 Henry Taube, Canadian
1982 Aaron Klug, S. African
1981 Kenichi Fukui, Japan., Roald Hoffmann, U.S.
1980 Paul Berg, U.S.; Walter Gilbert, U.S., Frederick Sanger, U.K.
1979 Herbert C. Brown, U.S. George Wittig, German
1978 Peter Mitchell, British
1977 Ilya Prigogine, Belgian
1976 William N. Lipscomb, U.S.
1975 John Cornforth, Austral.-Brit., Vladimir Prelog, Yugo.-Switz.
1974 Paul J. Flory, U.S.
1973 Ernst Otto Fischer, W. German Geoffrey Wilkinson, British

1972 Christian B. Anfinsen, U.S. Stanford Moore, U.S. William H. Stein, U.S.
1971 Gerhard Herzberg, Canadian
1970 Luis F. Leloir, Arg.
1969 Derek H. R. Barton, British Odd Hassel, Norwegian
1968 Lars Onsager, U.S.
1967 Manfred Eigen, German Ronald G. W. Norrish, British George Porter, British
1966 Robert S. Mulliken, U.S.
1965 Robert B. Woodward, U.S.
1964 Dorothy C. Hodgkin, British
1963 Giulio Natta, Italian Karl Ziegler, German
1962 John C. Kendrew, British Max F. Perutz, British
1961 Melvin Calvin, U.S.
1960 Willard F. Libby, U.S.
1959 Jaroslav Heyrovsky, Czech
1958 Frederick Sanger, British
1957 Sir Alexander R. Todd, British
1956 Sir Cyril N. Hinshelwood, British Nikolai N. Semenov, USSR
1955 Vincent du Vigneaud, U.S.
1954 Linus C. Pauling, U.S.
1953 Hermann Staudinger, German
1952 Archer J. P. Martin, British Richard L. M. Synge, British

1951 Edwin M. McMillan, U.S. Glenn T. Seaborg, U.S.
1950 Kurt Alder, German Otto P. H. Diels, German
1949 William F. Giauque, U.S.
1948 Arne W. K. Tiselius, Swedish
1947 Sir Robert Robinson, British
1946 James B. Sumner, John H. Northrop, Wendell M. Stanley, U.S.
1945 Artturi I. Virtanen, Finnish
1944 Otto Hahn, German
1943 Georg de Hevesy, Hungarian
1939 Adolf F. J. Butenandt, German Leopold Ruzicka, Swiss
1938 Richard Kuhn, German
1937 Walter N. Haworth, British Paul Karrer, Swiss
1936 Peter J. W. Debye, Dutch
1935 Frederic Joliot-Curie, French Irene Joliot-Curie, French
1934 Harold C. Urey, U.S.
1932 Irving Langmuir, U.S.
1931 Friedrich Bergius, German Karl Bosch, German
1930 Hans Fischer, German
1929 Sir Arthur Harden, British Hans von Euler-Chelpin, Swed.
1928 Adolf O. R. Windaus, German
1927 Heinrich O. Wieland, German
1926 Theodor Svedberg, Swedish

1925 Richard A. Zsigmondy, German
1923 Fritz Pregl, Austrian
1922 Francis W. Aston, British
1921 Frederick Soddy, British
1920 Walther H. Nernst, German
1918 Fritz Haber, German
1915 Richard M. Willstatter, German
1914 Theodore W. Richards, U.S.

1913 Alfred Werner, Swiss
1912 Victor Grignard, French
     Paul Sabatier, French
1911 Marie Curie, Polish-French
1910 Otto Wallach, German
1909 Wilhelm Ostwald, German
1908 Ernest Rutherford, British

1907 Eduard Buchner, German
1906 Henri Moissan, French
1905 Adolf von Baeyer, German
1904 Sir William Ramsay, British
1903 Svante A. Arrhenius, Swedish
1902 Emil Fischer, German
1901 Jacobus H. van't Hoff, Dutch

Physiology or Medicine

1989 J. Michael Bishop, Harold E.
     Varmus, both U.S.
1988 Gertrude B. Elion, George H.
     Hitchings, both U.S; Sir James
     Black, Brit.
1987 Susumu Tonegawa, Japanese
1986 Rita Levi-Montalcini, It.-U.S.,
     Stanley Cohen, U.S.
1985 Michael S. Brown, Joseph L.
     Goldstein, both U.S.
1984 Cesar Milstein, Brit.-Argentina;
     Georges J. F. Koehler, German;
     Niels K. Jerne, Brit.-Danish
1983 Barbara McClintock, U.S.
1982 Sune Bergstrom, Bengt
     Samuelsson, both Swedish;
     John R. Vane, British.
1981 Roger W. Sperry,
     David H. Hubel, Tosten N. Wiesel,
     all U.S.
1980 Baruj Benacerraf, George Snell,
     both U.S.; Jean Dausset, France
1979 Alian M. Cormack, U.S.
     Geoffrey N. Hounsfield, British
1978 Daniel Nathans, Hamilton O. Smith,
     both U.S.; Werner Arber, Swiss
1977 Rosalyn S. Yalow, Roger C.L.
     Guillemin, Andrew V. Schally, U.S.
1976 Baruch S. Blumberg, U.S.
     Daniel Carleton Gajdusek, U.S.
1975 David Baltimore, Howard Temin,
     both U.S.; Renato Dulbecco,
     Ital.-U.S.
1974 Albert Claude, Lux.-U.S.; George
     Emil Palade, Rom.-U.S.; Christian
     Rene de Duve, Belg.
1973 Karl von Frisch, Ger.; Konrad
     Lorenz, Ger.-Austrian; Nikolaas
     Tinbergen, Brit.
1972 Gerald M. Edelman, U.S.
     Rodney R. Porter, British
1971 Earl W. Sutherland Jr., U.S.
1970 Julius Axelrod, U.S.
     Sir Bernard Katz, British
     Ulf von Euler, Swedish
1969 Max Delbruck,
     Alfred D. Hershey,
     Salvador Luria, all U.S.
1968 Robert W. Holley,

     H. Gobind Khorana,
     Marshall W. Nirenberg, all U.S.
1967 Ragnar Granit, Swedish
     Haldan Keffer Hartline, U.S.
     George Wald, U.S.
1966 Charles B. Huggins,
     Francis Peyton Rous, both U.S.
1965 Francois Jacob, Andre Lwoff,
     Jacques Monod, all French
1964 Konrad E. Bloch, U.S.
     Feodor Lynen, German
1963 Sir John C. Eccles, Australian
     Alan L. Hodgkin, British
     Andrew F. Huxley, British
1962 Francis H. C. Crick, British
     James D. Watson, U.S.
     Maurice H. F. Wilkins, British
1961 Georg von Bekesy, U.S.
1960 Sir F. MacFarlane Bumet,
     Australian
     Peter B. Medawar, British
1959 Arthur Kornberg,
     Severo Ochoa, U.S.
1958 George W. Beadle, U.S.
     Edward L. Tatum, U.S.
     Joshua Lederberg, U.S.
1957 Daniel Bovet, Italian
1956 Andre F. Cournand, U.S.
     Werner Forssmann, German
     Dickinson W. Richards, Jr., U.S.
1955 Alex H. T. Theorell, Swedish
1954 John F. Enders,
     Frederick C. Robbins,
     Thomas H. Weller, all U.S.
1953 Hans A. Krebs, British
     Fritz A. Lipmann, U.S.
1952 Selman A. Waksman, U.S.
1951 Max Theiler, U.S.
1950 Philip S. Hench,
     Edward C. Kendall, both U.S.
     Tadeus Reichstein, Swiss
1949 Walter R. Hess, Swiss
     Antonio Moniz, Portuguese
1948 Paul H. Müller, Swiss
1947 Carl F. Cori,
     Gerty T. Cori, both U.S.
     Bernardo A. Houssay, Arg.
1946 Hermann J. Muller, U.S.

1945 Ernst B. Chain, British
     Sir Alexander Fleming, British
     Sir Howard W. Florey, British
1944 Joseph Erlanger,
     Herbert S. Gasser, U.S.
1943 Henrik C. P. Dam, Danish
     Edward A. Doisy, U.S.
1939 Gerhard Domagk, German
1938 Corneille J. F. Heymans, Belg.
1937 Albert Szent-Gyorgyi, Hung.-U.S.
1936 Sir Henry H. Dale, British
     Otto Loewi, U.S.
1935 Hans Spemann, German
1934 George R. Minot, Wm. P. Murphy,
     G. H. Whipple, all U.S.
1933 Thomas H. Morgan, U.S.
1932 Edgar D. Adrian, British
     Sir Charles S. Sherrington, Brit.
1931 Otto H. Warburg, German
1930 Karl Landsteiner, U.S.
1929 Christiaan Eijkman, Dutch
     Sir Frederick G. Hopkins, British
1928 Charles J. H. Nicolle, French
1927 Julius Wagner-Jauregg, Aus.
1926 Johannes A. G. Fibiger, Danish
1924 Willem Einthoven, Dutch
1923 Frederick G. Banting, Canadian
     John J. R. Macleod, Scottish
1922 Archibald V. Hill, British
     Otto F. Meyerhof, German
1920 Schack A. S. Krogh, Danish
1919 Jules Bordet, Belgian
1914 Robert Barany, Austrian
1913 Charles R. Richet, French
1912 Alexis Carrel, French
1911 Allvar Gullstrand, Swedish
1910 Albrecht Kossel, German
1909 Emil T. Kocher, Swiss
1908 Paul Ehrlich, German
     Elie Metchnikoff, French
1907 Charles L. A. Laveran, French
1906 Camillo Golgi, Italian
     Santiago Ramon y Cajal, Sp.
1905 Robert Koch, German
1904 Ivan P. Pavlov, Russian
1903 Niels R. Finsen, Danish
1902 Sir Ronald Ross, British
1901 Emil A. von Behring, German

Literature

1989 Camilo José Cela, Spanish
1988 Naguib Mahfouz, Egyptian
1987 Joseph Brodsky, USSR-U.S.
1986 Wole Soyinka, Nigerian
1985 Claude Simon, French
1984 Jaroslav Siefert, Czech.
1983 William Golding, British
1982 Gabriel Garcia Marquez,
     Colombian-Mex.
1981 Elias Canetti, Bulgarian-British
1980 Czeslaw Milosz, Polish-U.S.
1979 Odysseus Elytis, Greek
1978 Isaac Bashevis Singer, U.S.
     (Yiddish)
1977 Vicente Aleixandre, Spanish
1976 Saul Bellow, U.S.
1975 Eugenio Montale, Ital.
1974 Eyvind Johnson, Harry Edmund
     Martinson, both Swedish
1973 Patrick White, Australian
1972 Heinrich Boll, W. German
1971 Pablo Neruda, Chilean
1970 Aleksandr I. Solzhenitsyn, Russ.
1969 Samuel Beckett, Irish
1968 Yasunari Kawabata, Japanese
1967 Miguel Angel Asturias, Guate.

1966 Samuel Joseph Agnon, Israeli
     Nelly Sachs, Swedish
1965 Mikhail Sholokhov, Russian
1964 Jean Paul Sartre, French
     (Prize declined)
1963 Giorgos Seferis, Greek
1962 John Steinbeck, U.S.
1961 Ivo Andric, Yugoslavian
1960 Saint-John Perse, French
1959 Salvatore Quasimodo, Italian
1958 Boris L. Pasternak, Russian
     (Prize declined)
1957 Albert Camus, French
1956 Juan Ramon Jimenez,
     Span.
1955 Halldor K. Laxness, Icelandic
1954 Ernest Hemingway, U.S.
1953 Sir Winston Churchill, British
1952 Francois Mauriac, French
1951 Par F. Lagerkvist, Swedish
1950 Bertrand Russell, British
1949 William Faulkner, U.S.
1948 T.S. Eliot, British
1947 Andre Gide, French
1946 Hermann Hesse, Swiss
1945 Gabriela Mistral, Chilean

1944 Johannes V. Jensen, Danish
1939 Frans E. Sillanpaa, Finnish
1938 Pearl S. Buck, U.S.
1937 Roger Martin du Gard, French
1936 Eugene O'Neill, U.S.
1934 Luigi Pirandello, Italian
1933 Ivan A. Bunin, French
1932 John Galsworthy, British
1931 Erik A. Karlfeldt, Swedish
1930 Sinclair Lewis, U.S.
1929 Thomas Mann, German
1928 Sigrid Undset, Norwegian
1927 Henri Bergson, French
1926 Grazia Deledda, Italian
1925 George Bernard Shaw, British
1924 Wladyslaw S. Reymont, Polish
1923 William Butler Yeats, Irish
1922 Jacinto Benavente, Spanish
1921 Anatole France, French
1920 Knut Hamsun, Norwegian
1919 Carl F. G. Spitteler, Swiss
1917 Karl A. Gjellerup, Danish
     Henrik Pontoppidan, Danish
1916 Verner von Heidenstam, Swed.
1915 Romain Rolland, French
1913 Rabindranath Tagore, Indian

1912 Gerhart Hauptmann, German
1911 Maurice Maeterlinck, Belgian
1910 Paul J. L. Heyse, German
1909 Selma Lagerlof, Swedish
1908 Rudolf C. Eucken, German

1907 Rudyard Kipling, British
1906 Giosue Carducci, Italian
1905 Henryk Sienkiewicz, Polish
1904 Frederic Mistral, French
     Jose Echegaray, Spanish

1903 Bjornsterne Bjornson, Norw.
1902 Theodor Mommsen, German
1901 Rene F. A Sully Prudhomme,
     French

Nobel Memorial Prize in Economics

1989 Trygve Haavelmo, Norwegian
1988 Maurice Allais, French
1987 Robert M. Solow, U.S.
1986 James M. Buchanan, U.S.
1985 Franco Modigliani, It.-U.S.
1984 Richard Stone, British
1983 Gerard Debreu, Fr.-U.S.
1982 George J. Stigler, U.S.
1981 James Tobin, U.S.

1980 Lawrence R. Klein, U.S.
1979 Theodore W. Schultz, U.S.,
     Sir Arthur Lewis, British
1978 Herbert A. Simon, U.S.
1977 Bertil Ohlin, Swedish
     James E. Meade, British
1976 Milton Friedman, U.S.
1975 Tjalling Koopmans, Dutch-U.S.,
     Leonid Kantorovich, USSR

1974 Gunnar Myrdal, Swed.,
     Friedrich A. von Hayek, Austrian
1973 Wassily Leontief, U.S.
1972 Kenneth J. Arrow, U.S.
     John R. Hicks, British
1971 Simon Kuznets, U.S.
1970 Paul A. Samuelson, U.S.
1969 Ragnar Frisch, Norwegian
     Jan Tinbergen, Dutch

Peace

1989 Dalai Lama, Tibet
1988 United Nations Peacekeeping
     Forces
1987 Oscar Arias Sanchez, Costa Rican
1986 Elie Wiesel, Romania-U.S.
1985 Intl. Physicians for the Prevention of
     Nuclear War, U.S.
1984 Bishop Desmond Tutu, So. African
1983 Lech Walesa, Polish
1982 Alva Myrdal, Swedish; Alfonso
     Garcia Robles, Mexican
1981 Office of U.N. High Commissioner
     for Refugees
1980 Adolfo Perez Esquivel, Argentine
1979 Mother Teresa of Calcutta,
     Albanian-Indian
1978 Anwar Sadat, Egyptian
     Menachem Begin, Israeli
1977 Amnesty International
1976 Mairead Corrigan, Betty Williams,
     N. Irish
1975 Andrei Sakharov, USSR
1974 Eisaku Sato, Japanese, Sean
     MacBride, Irish
1973 Henry Kissinger, U.S.
     Le Duc Tho, N. Vietnamese
     (Tho declined)
1971 Willy Brandt, W. German
1970 Norman E. Borlaug, U.S.
1969 Intl. Labor Organization
1968 Rene Cassin, French
1965 U.N. Children's Fund (UNICEF)
1964 Martin Luther King Jr., U.S.

1963 International Red Cross,
     League of Red Cross Societies
1962 Linus C. Pauling, U.S.
1961 Dag Hammarskjold, Swedish
1960 Albert J. Luthuli, South African
1959 Philip J. Noel-Baker, British
1958 Georges Pire, Belgian
1957 Lester B. Pearson, Canadian
1954 Office of the UN High
     Commissioner for Refugees
1953 George C. Marshall, U.S.
1952 Albert Schweitzer, French
1951 Leon Jouhaux, French
1950 Ralph J. Bunche, U.S.
1949 Lord John Boyd Orr of Brechin
     Mearns, British
1947 Friends Service Council, Brit.
     Amer. Friends Service Com.
1946 Emily G. Balch,
     John R. Mott, both U.S.
1945 Cordell Hull, U.S.
1944 International Red Cross
1938 Nansen International Office
     for Refugees
1937 Viscount Cecil of Chelwood, Brit.
1936 Carlos de Saavedra Lamas, Arg.
1935 Carl von Ossietzky, German
1934 Arthur Henderson, British
1933 Sir Norman Angell, British
1931 Jane Addams, U.S.
     Nicholas Murray Butler, U.S.
1930 Nathan Soderblom, Swedish
1929 Frank B. Kellogg, U.S.

1927 Ferdinand E. Buisson, French
     Ludwig Quidde, German
1926 Aristide Briand, French
     Gustav Stresemann, German
1925 Sir J. Austen Chamberlain, Brit.
     Charles G. Dawes, U.S.
1922 Fridtjof Nansen, Norwegian
1921 Karl H. Branting, Swedish
     Christian L. Lange, Norwegian
1920 Leon V.A. Bourgeois, French
1919 Woodrow Wilson, U.S.
1917 International Red Cross
1913 Henri La Fontaine, Belgian
1912 Elihu Root, U.S.
1911 Tobias M.C. Asser, Dutch
     Alfred H. Fried, Austrian
1910 Permanent Intl. Peace Bureau
1909 Auguste M. F. Beernaert, Belg.
     Paul H. B. B. d'Estournelles de
     Constant, French
1908 Klas P. Arnoldson, Swedish
     Fredrik Bajer, Danish
1907 Ernesto T. Moneta, Italian
     Louis Renault, French
1906 Theodore Roosevelt, U.S.
1905 Baroness Bertha von Suttner,
     Austrian
1904 Institute of International Law
1903 Sir William R. Cremer, British
1902 Elie Ducommun,
     Charles A. Gobat, both Swiss
1901 Jean H. Dunant, Swiss
     Frederic Passy, French

Pulitzer Prizes in Journalism, Letters, and Music

The Pulitzer Prizes were endowed by Joseph Pulitzer (1847-1911), publisher of The World, New York, N.Y., in a bequest to Columbia University, and are awarded annually by the president of the university on recommendation of the Pulitzer Prize Board for work done during the preceding year. The administrator is Robert C. Christopher of Columbia Univ. All prizes are $3,000 (originally $500) in each category, except Meritorious Public Service for which a gold medal is given.

Journalism

Meritorious Public Service

For distinguished and meritorious public service by a United States newspaper.

1918—New York Times. Also special award to Minna Lewinson and Henry Beetle Hough.
1919—Milwaukee Journal.
1921—Boston Post.
1922—New York World.
1923—Memphis (Tenn.) Commercial Appeal.
1924—New York World.
1926—Enquirer-Sun, Columbus, Ga.
1927—Canton (Oh.) Daily News.
1928—Indianapolis Times.
1929—Evening World, New York.
1931—Atlanta (Ga.) Constitution.
1932—Indianapolis (Ind.) News.
1933—New York World-Telegram.
1934—Medford (Ore.) Mail-Tribune.
1935—Sacramento (Cal.) Bee.
1936—Cedar Rapids (Ia.) Gazette.
1937—St.Louis Post-Dispatch.

1938—Bismarck (N.D.) Tribune.
1939—Miami (Fla.) Daily News.
1940—Waterbury (Conn.) Republican and American.
1941—St.Louis Post-Dispatch.
1942—Los Angeles Times.
1943—Omaha World Herald.
1944—New York Times.
1945—Detroit Free Press.
1946—Scranton (Pa.) Times.
1947—Baltimore Sun.
1948—St. Louis Post-Dispatch.
1949—Nebraska State Journal.
1950—Chicago Daily News; St. Louis Post-Dispatch.
1951—Miami (Fla.) Herald and Brooklyn Eagle.
1952—St. Louis Post-Dispatch.
1953—Whiteville (N.C.) News Reporter; Tabor City (N.C.) Tribune.
1954—Newsday (Long Island, N.Y.)
1955—Columbus (Ga.) Ledger and Sunday Ledger-Enquirer.
1956—Watsonville (Cal.) Register-Pajaronian.
1957—Chicago Daily News.
1958—Arkansas Gazette, Little Rock.
1959—Utica (N.Y.) Observer-Dispatch and Utica Daily Press.

1960—Los Angeles Times.
1961—Amarillo (Tex.) Globe-Times.
1962—Panama City (Fla.) News-Herald.
1963—Chicago Daily News.
1964—St.Petersburg (Fla.) Times.
1965—Hutchinson (Kan.) News.
1966—Boston Globe.
1967—The Louisville Courier-Journal; The Milwaukee Journal.
1968—Riverside (Cal.) Press-Enterprise.
1969—Los Angeles Times.
1970—Newsday (Long Island, N.Y.).
1971—Winston Salem (N.C.) Journal & Sentinel.
1972—New York Times.
1973—Washington Post.
1974—Newsday (Long Island, N.Y.).
1975—Boston Globe.
1976—Anchorage Daily News.
1977—Lufkin (Tex.) News.
1978—Philadelphia Inquirer.
1979—Point Reyes (Cal.) Light.
1980—Gannett News Service.
1981—Charlotte (N.C.) Observer.
1982—Detroit News.
1983—Jackson (Miss.) Clarion-Ledger.
1984—Los Angeles Times.
1985—Ft. Worth (Tex.) Star-Telegram.
1986—Denver Post.
1987—Pittsburgh Press.
1988—Charlotte Observer.
1989—Anchorage Daily News.
1990—The Philadelphia Inquirer for reporting by Gilbert M. Gaul; Washington (N.C.) Daily News.

Reporting

This category originally embraced all fields, local, national, and international. Later separate categories were created for the different fields of reporting.

1917—Herbert Bayard Swope, New York World.
1918—Harold A. Littledale, New York Evening Post.
1920—John J. Leary, Jr., New York World.
1921—Louis Seibold, New York World.
1922—Kirke L. Simpson, Associated Press.
1923—Alva Johnston, New York Times.
1924—Magner White, San Diego Sun.
1925—James W. Mulroy and Alvin H. Goldstein, Chicago Daily News.
1926—William Burke Miller, Louisville Courier-Journal.
1927—John T. Rogers, St. Louis Post-Dispatch.
1929—Paul Y. Anderson, St. Louis Post-Dispatch.
1930—Russell D. Owens, New York Times. Also $500 to W.O. Dapping, Auburn (N.Y.) Citizen.
1931—A.B. MacDonald, Kansas City (Mo.) Star.
1932—W.C. Richards, D.D. Martin, J.S. Pooler, F.D. Webb, J.N.W. Sloan, Detroit Free Press.
1933—Francis A. Jamieson, Associated Press.
1934—Royce Brier, San Francisco Chronicle.
1935—William H.Taylor, New York Herald Tribune.
1936—Lauren D.Lyman, New York Times.
1937—John J. O'Neill, N.Y.Herald Tribune; William L. Laurence, N.Y Times; Howard W. Blakeslee, A.P.; Gobind Behari Lal, Universal Service; and David Dietz, Scripps-Howard Newspapers.
1938—Raymond Sprigle, Pittsburgh Post-Gazette.
1939—Thomas L. Stokes, Scripps-Howard Newspaper Alliance.
1940—S.Burton Heath, New York World-Telegram.
1941—Westbrook Pegler, New York World-Telegram.
1942—Stanton Delaplane, San Francisco Chronicle.
1943—George Weller, Chicago Daily News.
1944—Paul Schoenstein, New York Journal-American.
1945—Jack S. McDowell, San Francisco Call-Bulletin.
1946—William L. Laurence, New York Times.
1947—Frederick Woltman, New York World-Telegram.
1948—George E. Goodwin, Atlanta Journal.
1949—Malcolm Johnson, New York Sun.
1950—Meyer Berger, New York Times.
1951—Edward S. Montgomery, San Francisco Examiner.
1952—Geo. de Carvalho, San Francisco Chronicle.

(1) General or Spot; (2) Special or Investigative

1953—(1) Providence (R.I.) Journal and Evening Bulletin; (2) Edward J. Mowery, New York World-Telegram & Sun.
1954—(1) Vicksburg (Miss.) Sunday Post-Herald; (2) Alvin Scott McCoy, Kansas City (Mo.) Star.
1955—(1) Mrs. Caro Brown, Alice (Tex.) Daily Echo; (2) Roland K. Towery, Cuero (Tex.) Record.
1956—(1) Lee Hills, Detroit Free Press; (2) Arthur Daley, New York Times.
1957—(1) Salt Lake Tribune, Salt Lake City, Ut.; (2) Wallace Turner and William Lambert, Portland Oregonian.

1958—(1) Fargo, (N.D.) Forum; (2) George Beveridge, Evening Star, Washington, D.C.
1959—(1) Mary Lou Werner, Washington Evening Star; (2) John Harold Brislin, Scranton (Pa.) Tribune, and The Scrantonian.
1960—(1) Jack Nelson, Atlanta Constitution; (2) Miriam Ottenberg, Washington Evening Star.
1961—(1) Sanche de Gramont, New York Herald Tribune; (2) Edgar May, Buffalo Evening News.
1962—(1) Robert D.Mullins, Deseret News, Salt Lake City; (2) George Bliss, Chicago Tribune.
1963—(1) Shared by Sylvan Fox, William Longgood, and Anthony Shannon, New York World-Telegram & Sun; (2) Oscar Griffin, Jr., Pecos (Tex.) Independent and Enterprise.
1964—(1) Norman C.Miller, Wall Street Journal; (2) Shared by James V. Magee, Albert V. Gaudiosi, and Frederick A. Meyer, Philadelphia Bulletin.
1965—(1) Melvin H.Ruder, Hungry Horse News (Columbia Falls, Mon.); (2) Gene Goltz, Houston Post.
1966—(1) Los Angeles Times Staff; (2) John A. Frasca, Tampa (Fla.) Tribune.
1967—(1) Robert V.Cox, Chambersburg (Pa.) Public Opinion; (2) Gene Miller, Miami Herald.
1968—Detroit Free Press Staff; (2) J. Anthony Lukas, New York Times.
1969—(1) John Fetterman, Louisville Courier-Journal and Times; (2) Albert L.Delugach, St. Louis Globe Democrat, and Denny Walsh, Life.
1970—(1) Thomas Fitzpatrick, Chicago Sun-Times; (2) Harold Eugene Martin, Montgomery Advertiser & Alabama Journal.
1971—(1) Akron Beacon Journal Staff, (2) William Hugh Jones, Chicago Tribune.
1972—(1) Richard Cooper and John Machacek, Rochester Times-Union; (2) Timothy Leland, Gerard M. O'Neill, Stephen A. Kurkjian and Anne De Santis, Boston Globe.
1973—(1) Chicago Tribune; (2) Sun Newspapers of Omaha.
1974—(1) Hugh F. Hough, Arthur M. Petacque, Chicago Sun-Times; (2) William Sherman, New York Daily News.
1975—(1) Xenia (Oh.) Daily Gazette; (2) Indianapolis Star.
1976—(1) Gene Miller, Miami Herald; (2) Chicago Tribune.
1977—(1) Margo Huston, Milwaukee Journal; (2) Acel Moore, Wendell Rawls Jr., Philadelphia Inquirer.
1978—(1) Richard Whitt, Louisville Courier-Journal; (2) Anthony R. Dolan, Stamford (Conn.) Advocate.
1979—(1) San Diego (Cal.) Evening Tribune; (2) Gilbert M. Gaul, Elliot G.Jaspin, Pottsville (Pa.) Republican.
1980—(1) Philadelphia Inquirer; (2) Stephen A. Kurkjian, Alexander B.Hawes Jr., Nils Bruzelius, Joan Vennochi, Robert M. Porterfield, Boston Globe.
1981—(1) Longview (Wash.) Daily News staff; (2) Clark Hallas and Robert B. Lowe, Arizona Daily Star.
1982—(1) Kansas City Star, Kansas City Times; (2) Paul Henderson, Seattle Times.
1983—(1) Fort Wayne (Ind.) News-Sentinel; (2) Loretta Tofani, Washington Post.
1984—(1) Newsday (N.Y.); (2) Boston Globe.
1985—(1) Thomas Turcol, Virginian-Pilot and Ledger-Star, Norfolk, Va.; (2) William K.Marimow, Philadelphia Inquirer; Lucy Morgan & Jack Reed, St. Petersburg (Fla.) Times.
1986—(1) Edna Buchanan, Miami Herald; (2) Jeffrey A. Marx & Michael M. York, Lexington (Ky.) Herald-Leader.
1987—(1) Akron Beacon Journal; (2) Daniel R. Biddle, H.G. Bissinger, Fredric N. Tulsky, Philadelphia Inquirer; John Woestendiek, Philadelphia Inquirer.
1988—(1) Alabama Journal; Lawrence (Mass.) Eagle-Tribune; (2) Walt Bogdanich, Wall Street Journal.
1989—(1) Louisville Courier-Journal; (2) Bill Dedman, Atlanta Journal and Constitution.
1990—(1) San Jose Mercury News; (2) Lon Kilzer, Chris Ison, Star Tribune, Minneapolis-St. Paul.

Criticism or Commentary

(1) Criticism; (2) Commentary

1970—(1) Ada Louise Huxtable, New York Times; (2) Marquis W. Childs, St.Louis Post-Dispatch.
1971—(1) Harold C.Schonberg, New York Times; (2) William A. Caldwell, The Record, Hackensack, N.J.
1972—(1) Frank Peters Jr., St. Louis Post-Dispatch; (2) Mike Royko, Chicago Daily News.
1973—(1) Ronald Powers, Chicago Sun-Times; (2) David S. Broder, Washington Post.
1974—(1) Emily Genauer, Newsday, (N.Y.); (2) Edwin A. Roberts, Jr., National Observer.
1975—(1) Roger Ebert, Chicago Sun Times; (2) Mary McGrory, Washington Star.
1976—(1) Alan M.Kriegsman, Washington Post; (2) Walter W. (Red) Smith, New York Times.
1977—(1) William McPherson, Washington Post; (2) George F. Will, Wash. Post Writers Group.

1978—(1) Walter Kerr, New York Times; (2) William Safire, New York Times.
1979—(1) Paul Gapp, Chicago Tribune; (2) Russell Baker, New York Times.
1980—(1) William A. Henry III, Boston Globe; (2) Ellen Goodman, Boston Globe.
1981—(1) Jonathan Yardley, Washington Star; (2) Dave Anderson, New York Times.
1982—(1) Martin Bernheimer, Los Angeles Times; (2) Art Buchwald, Los Angeles Times Syndicate.
1983—(1) Manuela Hoelterhoff, Wall St. Journal; (2) Claude Sitton, Raleigh (N.C.) News & Observer.
1984—(1) Paul Goldberger, New York Times; (2) Vermont Royster, Wall St. Journal
1985—(1) Howard Rosenberg, Los Angeles Times; (2) Murray Kempton, Newsday (N.Y.).
1986—(1) Donal J. Henahan, New York Times; (2) Jimmy Breslin, New York Daily News.
1987—(1) Richard Eder, Los Angeles Times; (2) Charles Krauthammer, Washington Post.
1988—(1) Tom Shales, Washington Post; (2) Dave Barry, Miami Herald.
1989—(1) Michael Skube, News and Observer, Raleigh, N.C.; (2) Clarence Page, Chicago Tribune.
1990—(1) Allan Temko, San Francisco Chronicle; (2) Jim Murray, Los Angeles Times

National Reporting

1942—Louis Stark, New York Times.
1944—Dewey L. Fleming, Baltimore Sun.
1945—James B. Reston, New York Times.
1946—Edward A. Harris, St. Louis Post-Dispatch.
1947—Edward T. Folliard, Washington Post.
1948—Bert Andrews, New York Herald Tribune; Nat S. Finney, Minneapolis Tribune.
1949—Charles P. Trussell, New York Times.
1950—Edwin O. Guthman, Seattle Times.
1952—Anthony Leviero, New York Times.
1953—Don Whitehead, Associated Press.
1954—Richard Wilson, Des Moines Register.
1955—Anthony Lewis, Washington Daily News.
1956—Charles L. Bartlett, Chattanooga Times.
1957—James Reston, New York Times.
1958—Relman Morin, AP; Clark Mollenhoff, Des Moines Register & Tribune.
1959—Howard Van Smith, Miami (Fla.) News.
1960—Vance Trimble, Scripps-Howard, Washington, D.C.
1961—Edward R. Cony, Wall Street Journal.
1962—Nathan G. Caldwell and Gene S. Graham, Nashville Tennessean.
1963—Anthony Lewis, New York Times.
1964—Merriman Smith, UPI.
1965—Louis M. Kohlmeier, Wall Street Journal.
1966—Haynes Johnson, Washington Evening Star.
1967—Monroe Karmin and Stanley Penn, Wall Street Journal.
1968—Howard James, Christian Science Monitor; Nathan K. Kotz, Des Moines Register.
1969—Robert Cahn, Christian Science Monitor.
1970—William J. Eaton, Chicago Daily News.
1971—Lucinda Franks & Thomas Powers, UPI.
1972—Jack Anderson, United Feature Syndicate.
1973—Robert Boyd and Clark Hoyt, Knight Newspapers.
1974—James R. Polk, Washington Star-News; Jack White, Providence Journal-Bulletin.
1975—Donald L. Barlett and James B. Steele, Philadelphia Inquirer.
1976—James Risser, Des Moines Register.
1977—Walter Mears, Associated Press.
1978—Gaylord D. Shaw, Los Angeles Times.
1979—James Risser, Des Moines Register.
1980—Charles Stafford, Bette Swenson Orsini, St. Petersburg (Fla.) Times.
1981—John M. Crewdson, New York Times.
1982—Rick Atkinson, Kansas City Times.
1983—Boston Globe.
1984—John Noble Wilford, New York Times.
1985—Thomas J. Knudson, Des Moines (Ia.) Register.
1986—Craig Flournoy & George Rodrigue, Dallas Morning News; Arthur Howe, Philadelphia Inquirer.
1987—Miami Herald; and New York Times.
1988—Tim Weiner, Philadelphia Inquirer.
1989—Donald L. Barlett & James B. Steele, Philadelphia Inquirer.
1990—Ross Anderson, Bill Dietrich, Mary Ann Gwinn, Eric Nalder, The Seattle Times.

International Reporting

1942—Laurence Edmund Allen, Associated Press.
1943—Ira Wolfert, No. Am. Newspaper Alliance.
1944—Daniel DeLuce, Associated Press.
1945—Mark S. Watson, Baltimore Sun.
1946—Homer W. Bigart, New York Herald Tribune.
1947—Eddy Gilmore, Associated Press.
1948—Paul W. Ward, Baltimore Sun.
1949—Price Day, Baltimore Sun.
1950—Edmund Stevens, Christian Science Monitor.
1951—Keyes Beech and Fred Sparks, Chicago Daily News; Homer Bigart and Marguerite Higgins, New York Herald Tribune; Relman Morin and Don Whitehead, AP.
1952—John M. Hightower, Associated Press.
1953—Austin C. Wehrwein, Milwaukee Journal.
1954—Jim G. Lucas, Scripps-Howard Newspapers.
1955—Harrison Salisbury, New York Times.
1956—William Randolph Hearst, Jr., Frank Conniff, Hearst Newspapers; Kingsbury Smith, INS.
1957—Russell Jones, United Press.
1958—New York Times.
1959—Joseph Martin and Philip Santora, New York News.
1960—A.M. Rosenthal, New York Times.
1961—Lynn Heinzerling, Associated Press.
1962—Walter Lippmann, New York Herald Tribune Synd.
1963—Hal Hendrix, Miami (Fla.) News.
1964—Malcolm W. Browne, AP; David Halberstam, New York Times.
1965—J.A. Livingston, Philadelphia Bulletin.
1966—Peter Arnett, AP.
1967—R. John Hughes, Christian Science Monitor.
1968—Alfred Friendly, Washington Post.
1969—William Tuohy, Los Angeles Times.
1970—Seymour M. Hersh, Dispatch News Service.
1971—Jimmie Lee Hoagland, Washington Post.
1972—Peter R. Kann, Wall Street Journal.
1973—Max Frankel, New York Times.
1974—Hedrick Smith, New York Times.
1975—William Mullen and Ovie Carter, Chicago Tribune.
1976—Sydney H. Schanberg, New York Times.
1978—Henry Kamm, New York Times.
1979—Richard Ben Cramer, Philadelphia Inquirer.
1980—Joel Brinkley, Jay Mather, Louisville (Ky.) Courier-Journal.
1981—Shirley Christian, Miami Herald.
1982—John Darnton, New York Times.
1983—Thomas L. Friedman, New York Times; Loren Jenkins, Washington Post.
1984—Karen Elliot House, Wall St. Journal
1985—Josh Friedman, Dennis Bell, Ozler Muhammad, Newsday (N.Y.).
1986—Lewis M. Simons, Pete Carey, Katherine Ellison, San Jose (Calif.) Mercury News.
1987—Michael Parks, Los Angeles Times.
1988—Thomas L. Friedman, New York Times.
1989—Glenn Frankel, Washington Post; Bill Keller, New York Times.
1990—Nicholas D. Kirstof, Sheryl WuDunn, New York Times.

Correspondence

For Washington or foreign correspondence. Category was merged with those in national and international reporting in 1948.
1929—Paul Scott Mowrer, Chicago Daily News.
1930—Leland Stowe, New York Herald Tribune.
1931—H.R. Knickerbocker, Philadelphia Public Ledger and New York Evening Post.
1932—Walter Duranty, New York Times, and Charles G. Ross, St. Louis Post-Dispatch.
1933—Edgar Ansel Mowrer, Chicago Daily News.
1934—Frederick T. Birchall, New York Times.
1935—Arthur Krock, New York Times.
1936—Wilfred C. Barber, Chicago Tribune.
1937—Anne O'Hare McCormick, New York Times.
1938—Arthur Krock, New York Times.
1939—Louis P. Lochner, Associated Press.
1940—Otto D. Tolischus, New York Times.
1941—Bronze plaque to commemorate work of American correspondents on war fronts.
1942—Carlos P. Romulo, Philippines Herald.
1943—Hanson W. Baldwin, New York Times.
1944—Ernest Taylor Pyle, Scripps-Howard Newspaper Alliance.
1945—Harold V. (Hal) Boyle, Associated Press.
1946—Arnaldo Cortesi, New York Times.
1947—Brooks Atkinson, New York Times.

Editorial Writing

1917—New York Tribune.
1918—Louisville (Ky.) Courier-Journal.
1920—Harvey E. Newbranch, Omaha Evening World-Herald.
1922—Frank M. O'Brien, New York Herald.
1923—William Allen White, Emporia Gazette.
1924—Frank Buxton, Boston Herald, Special Prize. Frank I. Cobb, New York World.
1925—Robert Lathan, Charleston (S.C.) News and Courier.
1926—Edward M. Kingsbury, New York Times.
1927—F. Lauriston Bullard, Boston Herald.
1928—Grover C. Hall, Montgomery Advertiser.
1929—Louis Isaac Jaffe, Norfolk Virginian-Pilot.
1931—Chas. Ryckman, Fremont (Neb.) Tribune.
1933—Kansas City (Mo.) Star.
1934—E. P. Chase, Atlantic (Ia.) News Telegraph.
1936—Felix Morley, Washington Post. George B. Parker, Scripps-Howard Newspapers.
1937—John W. Owens, Baltimore Sun.
1938—W.W. Waymack, Des Moines (Ia.) Register and Tribune.
1939—Ronald G. Callvert, Portland Oregonian.
1940—Bart Howard, St. Louis Post-Dispatch.
1941—Reuben Maury, Daily News, N.Y.
1942—Geoffrey Parsons, New York Herald Tribune.
1943—Forrest W. Seymour, Des Moines (Ia.) Register and Tribune.
1944—Henry J. Haskell, Kansas City (Mo.) Star.
1945—George W. Potter, Providence (R.I.) Journal-Bulletin.
1946—Hodding Carter, Greenville (Miss.) Delta Democrat-Times.
1947—William H. Grimes, Wall Street Journal.
1948—Virginius Dabney, Richmond (Va.) Times-Dispatch.
1949—John H. Crider, Boston (Mass.) Herald, Herbert Elliston, Washington Post.
1950—Carl M. Saunders, Jackson (Mich.) Citizen-Patriot.
1951—William H. Fitzpatrick, New Orleans States.
1952—Louis LaCoss, St. Louis Globe Democrat.
1953—Vermont C. Royster, Wall Street Journal.
1954—Don Murray, Boston Herald.
1955—Royce Howes, Detroit Free Press.
1956—Lauren K. Soth, Des Moines (Ia.) Register and Tribune.
1957—Buford Boone, Tuscaloosa (Ala.) News.
1958—Harry S. Ashmore, Arkansas Gazette.
1959—Ralph McGill, Atlanta Constitution.
1960—Lenoir Chambers, Norfolk Virginian-Pilot.
1961—William J. Dorvillier, San Juan (Puerto Rico) Star.
1962—Thomas M. Storke, Santa Barbara (Cal.) News-Press.
1963—Ira B. Harkey, Jr., Pascagoula (Miss.) Chronicle.
1964—Hazel Brannon Smith, Lexington (Miss.) Advertiser.
1965—John R. Harrison, The Gainesville (Fla.) Sun.
1966—Robert Lasch, St. Louis Post-Dispatch.
1967—Eugene C. Patterson, Atlanta Constitution.
1968—John S. Knight, Knight Newspapers.
1969—Paul Greenberg, Pine Bluff (Ark.) Commercial.
1970—Philip L. Geyelin, Washington Post.
1971—Horance G. Davis, Jr., Gainesville (Fla.) Sun.
1972—John Strohmeyer, Bethlehem (Pa.) Globe-Times.
1973—Roger B. Linscott, Berkshire Eagle, Pittsfield, Mass.
1974—F. Gilman Spencer, Trenton (N.J.) Trentonian.
1975—John D. Maurice, Charleston (W. Va.) Daily Mail.
1976—Philip Kerby, Los Angeles Times.
1977—Warren L. Lerude, Foster Church, and Norman F. Cardoza, Reno (Nev.) Evening Gazette and Nevada State Journal.
1978—Meg Greenfield, Washington Post.
1979—Edwin M. Yoder, Washington Star.
1980—Robert L. Bartley, Wall Street Journal.
1982—Jack Rosenthal, New York Times.
1983—Editorial board, Miami Herald.
1984—Albert Scardino, Georgia Gazette.
1985—Richard Aregood, Philadelphia Daily News.
1986—Jack Fuller, Chicago Tribune.
1987—Jonathan Freedman, The Tribune (San Diego).
1988—Jane Healy, Orlando Sentinel.
1989—Lois Wille, Chicago Tribune.
1990—Thomas J. Hylton, The Pottstown (Pa.) Mercury.

Editorial Cartooning

1922—Rollin Kirby, New York World.
1924—Jay N. Darling, Des Moines Register.
1925—Rollin Kirby, New York World.
1926—D. R. Fitzpatrick, St. Louis Post-Dispatch.
1927—Nelson Harding, Brooklyn Eagle.
1928—Nelson Harding, Brooklyn Eagle.
1929—Rollin Kirby, New York World.
1930—Charles Macauley, Brooklyn Eagle.
1931—Edmund Duffy, Baltimore Sun.

1932—John T. McCutcheon, Chicago Tribune.
1933—H. M. Talburt, Washington Daily News.
1934—Edmund Duffy, Baltimore Sun.
1935—Ross A. Lewis, Milwaukee Journal.
1937—C. D. Batchelor, New York Daily News.
1938—Vaughn Shoemaker, Chicago Daily News.
1939—Charles G. Werner, Daily Oklahoman.
1940—Edmund Duffy, Baltimore Sun.
1941—Jacob Burck, Chicago Times.
1942—Herbert L. Block, Newspaper Enterprise Assn.
1943—Jay N. Darling, Des Moines Register.
1944—Clifford K. Berryman, Washington Star.
1945—Bill Mauldin, United Feature Syndicate.
1946—Bruce Alexander Russell, Los Angeles Times.
1947—Vaughn Shoemaker, Chicago Daily News.
1948—Reuben L. (Rube) Goldberg, N. Y. Sun.
1949—Lute Pease, Newark (N.J.) Evening News.
1950—James T. Berryman, Washington Star.
1951—Reginald W. Manning, Arizona Republic.
1952—Fred L. Packer, New York Mirror.
1953—Edward D. Kuekes, Cleveland Plain Dealer.
1954—Herbert L. Block, Washington Post & Times-Herald.
1955—Daniel R. Fitzpatrick, St. Louis Post-Dispatch.
1956—Robert York, Louisville (Ky.) Times.
1957—Tom Little, Nashville Tennessean.
1958—Bruce M. Shanks, Buffalo Evening News.
1959—Bill Mauldin, St. Louis Post-Dispatch.
1961—Carey Orr, Chicago Tribune.
1962—Edmund S. Vaitman, Hartford Times.
1963—Frank Miller, Des Moines Register.
1964—Paul Conrad, Denver Post.
1966—Don Wright, Miami News.
1967—Patrick B. Oliphant, Denver Post.
1968—Eugene Gray Payne, Charlotte Observer.
1969—John Fischetti, Chicago Daily News.
1970—Thomas F. Darcy, Newsday.
1971—Paul Conrad, L. A. Times.
1972—Jeffrey K. MacNelly, Richmond News-Leader.
1974—Paul Szep, Boston Globe.
1975—Garry Trudeau, Universal Press Syndicate.
1976—Tony Auth, Philadelphia Inquirer.
1977—Paul Szep, Boston Globe.
1978—Jeffrey K. MacNelly, Richmond News Leader.
1979—Herbert L. Block, Washington Post.
1980—Don Wright, Miami (Fla.) News.
1981—Mike Peters, Dayton (Oh.) Daily News.
1982—Ben Sargent, Austin American-Statesman.
1983—Richard Lochner, Chicago Tribune.
1984—Paul Conrad, Los Angeles Times.
1985—Jeffrey K. MacNelly, Chicago Tribune.
1986—Jules Feiffer, Village Voice (N.Y. City)
1987—Berke Breathed, Washington Post.
1988—Doug Marlette, Atlanta Constitution, Charlotte Observer.
1989—Jack Higgins, Chicago Sun-Times.
1990—Tom Toles, The Buffalo News.

Spot News Photography

1942—Milton Brooks, Detroit News.
1943—Frank Noel, Associated Press.
1944—Frank Filan, AP; Earl L. Bunker, Omaha World-Herald.
1945—Joe Rosenthal, Associated Press, for photograph of planting American flag on Iwo Jima.
1947—Arnold Hardy, amateur, Atlanta, Ga.
1948—Frank Cushing, Boston Traveler.
1949—Nathaniel Fein, New York Herald Tribune.
1950—Bill Crouch, Oakland (Cal.) Tribune.
1951—Max Desfor, Associated Press.
1952—John Robinson and Don Ultang, Des Moines Register and Tribune.
1953—William M. Gallagher, Flint (Mich.) Journal.
1954—Mrs. Walter M. Schau, amateur.
1955—John L. Gaunt, Jr., Los Angeles Times.
1956—New York Daily News.
1957—Harry A. Trask, Boston Traveler.
1958—William C. Beall, Washington Daily News.
1959—William Seaman, Minneapolis Star.
1960—Andrew Lopez, UPI.
1961—Yasushi Nagao, Mainichi Newspapers, Tokyo.
1962—Paul Vathis, Associated Press.
1963—Hector Rondon, La Republica, Caracas, Venezuela.
1964—Robert H. Jackson, Dallas Times-Herald.
1965—Horst Faas, Associated Press.
1966—Kyoichi Sawada, UPI.
1967—Jack R. Thornell, Associated Press.
1968—Rocco Morabito, Jacksonville Journal.
1969—Edward Adams, AP.
1970—Steve Starr, AP.
1971—John Paul Filo, Valley Daily News & Daily Dispatch of

Tarentum & New Kensington, Pa.
1972—Horst Faas and Michel Laurent, AP.
1973—Huynh Cong Ut, AP.
1974—Anthony K. Roberts, AP.
1975—Gerald H. Gay, Seattle Times.
1976—Stanley Forman, Boston Herald American.
1977—Neal Ulevich, Associated Press; Stanley Forman, Boston Herald American.
1978—John H. Blair, UPI.
1979—Thomas J. Kelly III, Pottstown (Pa.) Mercury.
1980—UPI.
1981—Larry C. Price, Ft. Worth (Tex.) Star-Telegram.
1982—Ron Edmonds, Associated Press.
1983—Bill Foley, AP.
1984—Stan Grossfeld, Boston Globe.
1985—The Register, Santa Ana, Calif.
1986—Carol Guzy & Michel duCille, Miami Herald.
1987—Kim Komenich, San Francisco Examiner.
1988—Scott Shaw, Odessa (Tex.) American.
1989—Ron Olshwanger, St. Louis Post-Dispatch.
1990—The Oakland (Calif.) Tribune photo staff.

Feature Photography

1968—Toshio Sakai, UPI.
1969—Moneta Sleet Jr., Ebony.
1970—Dallas Kinney, Palm Beach Post.
1971—Jack Dykinga, Chicago Sun-Times.
1972—Dave Kennerly, UPI.
1973—Brian Lanker, Topeka Capitol-Journal.
1974—Slava Veder, AP.
1975—Matthew Lewis, Washington Post.
1976—Louisville Courier-Journal and Louisville Times.
1977—Robin Hood, Chattanooga News-Free Press.
1978—J. Ross Baughman, AP.
1979—Staff Photographers, Boston Herald American.
1980—Erwin H. Hagler, Dallas Times-Herald.
1981—Taro M. Yamasaki, Detroit Free Press.
1982—John H. White, Chicago Sun-Times.
1983—James B. Dickman, Dallas Times-Herald.
1984—Anthony Suad, Denver Post.
1985—Stan Grossfeld, Boston Globe; Larry C. Price, Philadelphia Inquirer.
1986—Tom Gralish, Philadelphia Inquirer.
1987—David Peterson, Des Moines Register.
1988—Michel duCille, Miami Herald.
1989—Manny Crisostomo, Detroit Free Press.
1990—David C. Turnley, Detroit Free Press.

Special Citation

1938—Edmonton (Alberta) Journal, bronze plaque.
1941—New York Times.
1944—Byron Price and Mrs. William Allen White. Also to Richard Rodgers and Oscar Hammerstein 2d, for musical, Oklahoma!
1945—Press cartographers for war maps.
1947—(Pulitzer centennial year.) Columbia Univ. and the Graduate School of Journalism, and St. Louis Post-Dispatch.
1948—Dr. Frank Diehl Fackenthal.
1951—Cyrus L. Sulzberger, New York Times.
1952—Max Kase, New York Journal-American, Kansas City Star.
1953—The New York Times; Lester Markel.
1957—Kenneth Roberts, for his historical novels.
1958—Walter Lippmann, New York Herald Tribune.
1960—Garrett Mattingly, for The Armada.
1961—American Heritage Picture History of the Civil War.
1964—The Gannett Newspapers.
1973—James T. Flexner, for biography of George Washington.
1976—John Hohenberg, for services to American journalism.
1977—Alex Haley, for Roots.
1978—Richard Lee Strout, Christian Science Monitor and New Republic.
   —E.B. White.
1984—Theodore Geisel ("Dr. Seuss").
1985—William Schuman, composer, educational leader.
1987—Joseph Pulitzer Jr.

Feature Writing

1979—Jon D. Franklin, Baltimore Evening Sun.
1980—Madeleine Blais, Miami Herald Tropic Magazine. Janet Cooke, Washington Post.
1981—Teresa Carpenter, Village Voice, New York City.
1982—Saul Pett, Associated Press.
1984—Peter M. Rinearson, Seattle Times.
1985—Alice Steinbach, Baltimore Sun.
1986—John Camp, St. Paul Pioneer Press & Dispatch
1987—Steve Twomey, Philadephia Inquirer.
1988—Jacqui Banaszynski, St. Paul Pioneer Press Dispatch.
1989—David Zucchino, Philadelphia Inquirer.
1990—Dave Curtin, Colorado Springs Gazette Telegraph.

Explanatory Journalism

1985—Jon Franklin, Baltimore Evening Sun.
1986—New York Times Staff.
1987—Jeff Lyon & Peter Gorner, Chicago Tribune.
1988—Daniel Hertzberg, James B. Stewart, Wall Street Journal.
1989—David Hanners, William Snyder, Karen Blessen, Dallas Morning News.
1990—David A. Vise, Steve Coll, The Washington Post.

Specialized Reporting

1985—Randall Savage, Jackie Crosby, Macon (Ga.) Telegraph and News.
1986—Andrew Schneider & Mary Pat Flaherty, Pittsburgh Press.
1987—Alex S. Jones, New York Times.
1988—Dean Baquet, William Gaines, Ann Marie Lipinski, Chicago Tribune.
1989—Edward Humes, Orange County (Calif.) Register.
1990—Tamar Stieber, Albuquerque Journal.

Letters

Fiction

For fiction in book form by an American author, preferably dealing with American life.
1918—Ernest Poole, His Family.
1919—Booth Tarkington, The Magnificent Ambersons.
1921—Edith Wharton, The Age of Innocence.
1922—Booth Tarkington, Alice Adams.
1923—Willa Cather, One of Ours.
1924—Margaret Wilson, The Able McLaughlins.
1925—Edna Ferber, So Big.
1926—Sinclair Lewis, Arrowsmith. (Refused prize.)
1927—Louis Bromfield, Early Autumn.
1928—Thornton Wilder, Bridge of San Luis Rey.
1929—Julia M. Peterkin, Scarlet Sister Mary.
1930—Oliver LaFarge, Laughing Boy.
1931—Margaret Ayer Barnes, Years of Grace.
1932—Pearl S. Buck, The Good Earth.
1933—T. S. Stribling, The Store.
1934—Caroline Miller, Lamb in His Bosom.
1935—Josephine W. Johnson, Now in November.
1936—Harold L. Davis, Honey in the Horn.
1937—Margaret Mitchell, Gone with the Wind.
1938—John P. Marquand, The Late George Apley.
1939—Marjorie Kinnan Rawlings, The Yearling.
1940—John Steinbeck, The Grapes of Wrath.
1942—Ellen Glasgow, In This Our Life.
1943—Upton Sinclair, Dragon's Teeth.
1944—Martin Flavin, Journey in the Dark.
1945—John Hersey, A Bell for Adano.
1947—Robert Penn Warren, All the King's Men.
1948—James A Michener, Tales of the South Pacific.
1949—James Gould Cozzens, Guard of Honor.
1950—A. B. Guthrie Jr., The Way West.
1951—Conrad Richter, The Town.
1952—Herman Wouk, The Caine Mutiny.
1953—Ernest Hemingway, The Old Man and the Sea.
1955—William Faulkner, A Fable.
1956—MacKinlay Kantor, Andersonville.
1958—James Agee, A Death in the Family.
1959—Robert Lewis Taylor, The Travels of Jaimie McPheeters.
1960—Allen Drury, Advise and Consent.
1961—Harper Lee, To Kill a Mockingbird.
1962—Edwin O'Connor, The Edge of Sadness.
1963—William Faulkner, The Reivers.
1965—Shirley Ann Grau, The Keepers of the House.
1966—Katherine Anne Porter, Collected Stories of Katherine Anne Porter.
1967—Bernard Malamud, The Fixer.
1968—William Styron, The Confessions of Nat Turner.
1969—N. Scott Momaday, House Made of Dawn.
1970—Jean Stafford, Collected Stories.
1972—Wallace Stegner, Angle of Repose.
1973—Eudora Welty, The Optimist's Daughter.

1975—Michael Shaara, The Killer Angels.
1976—Saul Bellow, Humboldt's Gift.
1978—James Alan McPherson, Elbow Room.
1979—John Cheever, The Stories of John Cheever.
1980—Norman Mailer, The Executioner's Song.
1981—John Kennedy Toole, A Confederacy of Dunces.
1982—John Updike, Rabbit is Rich.
1983—Alice Walker, The Color Purple.
1984—William Kennedy, Ironweed.
1985—Alison Lurie, Foreign Affairs.
1986—Larry McMurtry, Lonesome Dove.
1987—Peter Taylor, A Summons to Memphis.
1988—Toni Morrison, Beloved.
1989—Anne Tyler, Breathing Lessons.
1990—Oscar Hijuelos, The Mambo Kings Play Songs of Love.

Drama

For an American play, preferably original and dealing with American life.
1918—Jesse Lynch Williams, Why Marry?
1920—Eugene O'Neill, Beyond the Horizon.
1921—Zona Gale, Miss Lulu Bett.
1922—Eugene O'Neill, Anna Christie.
1923—Owen Davis, Icebound.
1924—Hatcher Hughes, Hell-Bent for Heaven.
1925—Sidney Howard, They Knew What They Wanted.
1926—George Kelly, Craig's Wife.
1927—Paul Green, In Abraham's Bosom.
1928—Eugene O'Neill, Strange Interlude.
1929—Elmer Rice, Street Scene.
1930—Marc Connelly, The Green Pastures.
1931—Susan Glaspell, Alison's House.
1932—George S. Kaufman, Morrie Ryskind and Ira Gershwin, Of Thee I Sing.
1933—Maxwell Anderson, Both Your Houses.
1934—Sidney Kingsley, Men in White.
1935—Zoe Akins, The Old Maid.
1936—Robert E. Sherwood, Idiot's Delight.
1937—George S. Kaufman and Moss Hart, You Can't Take It With You.
1938—Thornton Wilder, Our Town.
1939—Robert E. Sherwood, Abe Lincoln in Illinois.
1940—William Saroyan, The Time of Your Life.
1941—Robert E. Sherwood, There Shall Be No Night.
1943—Thornton Wilder, The Skin of Our Teeth.
1945—Mary Chase, Harvey.
1946—Russel Crouse and Howard Lindsay, State of the Union.
1948—Tennessee Williams, A Streetcar Named Desire.
1949—Arthur Miller, Death of a Salesman.
1950—Richard Rodgers, Oscar Hammerstein 2d, and Joshua Logan, South Pacific.
1952—Joseph Kramm, The Shrike.
1953—William Inge, Picnic.
1954—John Patrick, Teahouse of the August Moon.
1955—Tennessee Williams, Cat on a Hot Tin Roof.
1956—Frances Goodrich and Albert Hackett, The Diary of Anne Frank.
1957—Eugene O'Neill, Long Day's Journey Into Night.
1958—Ketti Frings, Look Homeward, Angel.
1959—Archibald MacLeish, J. B.
1960—George Abbott, Jerome Weidman, Sheldon Harnick and Jerry Bock, Fiorello.
1961—Tad Mosel, All the Way Home.
1962—Frank Loesser and Abe Burrows, How To Succeed in Business Without Really Trying.
1965—Frank D. Gilroy, The Subject Was Roses.
1967—Edward Albee, A Delicate Balance.
1969—Howard Sackler, The Great White Hope.
1970—Charles Gordone, No Place to Be Somebody.
1971—Paul Zindel, The Effect of Gamma Rays on Man-in-the-Moon Marigolds.
1973—Jason Miller, That Championship Season.
1975—Edward Albee, Seascape.
1976—Michael Bennett, James Kirkwood, Nicholas Dante, Marvin Hamlisch, Edward Kleban, A Chorus Line.
1977—Michael Cristofer, The Shadow Box.
1978—Donald L. Coburn, The Gin Game.
1979—Sam Shepard, Buried Child.
1980—Lanford Wilson, Talley's Folly.
1981—Beth Henley, Crimes of the Heart.
1982—Charles Fuller, A Soldier's Play.
1983—Marsha Norman, 'night, Mother.
1984—David Mamet, Glengarry Glen Ross.
1985—Stephen Sondheim, James Lapine, Sunday in the Park with George.
1987—August Wilson, Fences.
1988—Alfred Uhry, Driving Miss Daisy.

1989—Wendy Wasserstein, The Heidi Chronicles.
1990—August Wilson, The Piano Lesson.

History

For a book on the history of the United States.
1917—J. J. Jusserand, With Americans of Past and Present Days.
1918—James Ford Rhodes, History of the Civil War.
1920—Justin H. Smith, The War with Mexico.
1921—William Sowden Sims, The Victory at Sea.
1922—James Truslow Adams, The Founding of New England.
1923—Charles Warren, The Supreme Court in United States History.
1924—Charles Howard McIlwain, The American Revolution: A Constitutional Interpretation.
1925—Frederick L. Paxton, A History of the American Frontier.
1926—Edward Channing, A History of the U.S.
1927—Samuel Flagg Bemis, Pinckney's Treaty.
1928—Vernon Louis Parrington, Main Currents in American Thought.
1929—Fred A. Shannon, The Organization and Administration of the Union Army, 1861-65.
1930—Claude H. Van Tyne, The War of Independence.
1931—Bernadotte E. Schmitt, The Coming of the War, 1914.
1932—Gen. John J. Pershing, My Experiences in the World War.
1933—Frederick J. Turner, The Significance of Sections in American History.
1934—Herbert Agar, The People's Choice.
1935—Charles McLean Andrews, The Colonial Period of American History.
1936—Andrew C. McLaughlin, The Constitutional History of the United States.
1937—Van Wyck Brooks, The Flowering of New England.
1938—Paul Herman Buck, The Road to Reunion, 1865-1900.
1939—Frank Luther Mott, A History of American Magazines.
1940—Carl Sandburg, Abraham Lincoln: The War Years.
1941—Marcus Lee Hansen, The Atlantic Migration, 1607-1860.
1942—Margaret Leech, Reveille in Washington.
1943—Esther Forbes, Paul Revere and the World He Lived In.
1944—Merle Curti, The Growth of American Thought.
1945—Stephen Bonsal, Unfinished Business.
1946—Arthur M. Schlesinger Jr., The Age of Jackson.
1947—James Phinney Baxter 3d, Scientists Against Time.
1948—Bernard De Voto, Across the Wide Missouri.
1949—Roy F. Nichols, The Disruption of American Democracy.
1950—O. W. Larkin, Art and Life in America.
1951—R. Carlyle Buley, The Old Northwest: Pioneer Period 1815-1840.
1952—Oscar Handlin, The Uprooted.
1953—George Dangerfield, The Era of Good Feelings.
1954—Bruce Catton, A Stillness at Appomattox.
1955—Paul Horgan, Great River: The Rio Grande in North American History.
1956—Richard Hofstadter, The Age of Reform.
1957—George F. Kennan, Russia Leaves the War.
1958—Bray Hammond, Banks and Politics in America—From the Revolution to the Civil War.
1959—Leonard D. White and Jean Schneider, The Republican Era; 1869-1901.
1960—Margaret Leech, In the Days of McKinley.
1961—Herbert Feis, Between War and Peace: The Potsdam Conference.
1962—Lawrence H. Gibson, The Triumphant Empire: Thunderclouds Gather in the West.
1963—Constance McLaughlin Green, Washington: Village and Capital, 1800-1878.
1964—Sumner Chilton Powell, Puritan Village: The Formation of A New England Town.
1965—Irwin Unger, The Greenback Era.
1966—Perry Miller, Life of the Mind in America.
1967—William H. Goetzmann, Exploration and Empire: the Explorer and Scientist in the Winning of the American West.
1968—Bernard Bailyn, The Ideological Origins of the American Revolution.
1969—Leonard W. Levy, Origin of the Fifth Amendment.
1970—Dean Acheson, Present at the Creation: My Years in the State Department.
1971—James McGregor Burns, Roosevelt: The Soldier of Freedom.
1972—Carl N. Degler, Neither Black Nor White.
1973—Michael Kammen, People of Paradox: An Inquiry Concerning the Origins of American Civilization.
1974—Daniel J. Boorstin, The Americans: The Democratic Experience.
1975—Dumas Malone, Jefferson and His Time.
1976—Paul Horgan, Lamy of Santa Fe.
1977—David M. Potter, The Impending Crisis.
1978—Alfred D. Chandler, Jr., The Visible Hand: The Manage-

rial Revolution in American Business.
1979—Don E. Fehrenbacher, The Dred Scott Case: Its Significance in American Law and Politics.
1980—Leon F. Litwack, Been in the Storm So Long.
1981—Lawrence A. Cremin, American Education: The National Experience, 1783-1876.
1982—C. Vann Woodward, ed., Mary Chestnut's Civil War.
1983—Rhys L. Issac, The Transformation of Virginia, 1740-1790.
1985—Thomas K. McCraw, Prophets of Regulation.
1986—Walter A. McDougall, . . . The Heavens and the Earth.
1987—Bernard Bailyn, Voyagers to the West.
1988—Robert V. Bruce, The Launching of Modern American Science 1846-1876.
1989—Taylor Branch, Parting the Waters: America in the King Years, 1954-63; and James M. McPherson, Battle Cry of Freedom: The Civil War Era.
1990—Stanley Karnow, In Our Image: America's Empire in the Philippines.

Biography or Autobiography

For a distinguished biography or autobiography by an American author.
1917—Laura E. Richards and Maude Howe Elliott, assisted by Florence Howe Hall, Julia Ward Howe.
1918—William Cabell Bruce, Benjamin Franklin, Self-Revealed.
1919—Henry Adams, The Education of Henry Adams.
1920—Albert J. Beveridge, The Life of John Marshall.
1921—Edward Bok, The Americanization of Edward Bok.
1922—Hamlin Garland, A Daughter of the Middle Border.
1923—Burton J. Hendrick, The Life and Letters of Walter H. Page.
1924—Michael Pupin, From Immigrant to Inventor.
1925—M. A. DeWolfe Howe, Barrett Wendell and His Letters.
1926—Harvey Cushing, Life of Sir William Osler.
1927—Emory Holloway, Whitman: An Interpretation in Narrative.
1928—Charles Edward Russell, The American Orchestra and Theodore Thomas.
1929—Burton J. Hendrick, The Training of an American: The Earlier Life and Letters of Walter H. Page.
1930—Marquis James, The Raven (Sam Houston).
1931—Henry James, Charles W. Eliot.
1932—Henry F. Pringle, Theodore Roosevelt.
1933—Allan Nevins, Grover Cleveland.
1934—Tyler Dennett, John Hay.
1935—Douglas Southall Freeman, R. E. Lee
1936—Ralph Barton Perry, The Thought and Character of William James.
1937—Allan Nevins, Hamilton Fish: The Inner History of the Grant Administration.
1938—Divided between Odell Shepard, Pedlar's Progress; Marquis James, Andrew Jackson.
1939—Carl Van Doren, Benjamin Franklin.
1940—Ray Stannard Baker, Woodrow Wilson, Life and Letters.
1941—Ola Elizabeth Winslow, Jonathan Edwards.
1942—Forrest Wilson, Crusader in Crinoline.
1943—Samuel Eliot Morison, Admiral of the Ocean Sea (Columbus).
1944—Carleton Mabee, The American Leonardo: The Life of Samuel F. B. Morse.
1945—Russell Blaine Nye, George Bancroft; Brahmin Rebel.
1946—Linny Marsh Wolfe, Son of the Wilderness.
1947—William Allen White, The Autobiography of William Allen White.
1948—Margaret Clapp, Forgotten First Citizen: John Bigelow.
1949—Robert E. Sherwood, Roosevelt and Hopkins.
1950—Samuel Flag Bemis, John Quincy Adams and the Foundations of American Foreign Policy.
1951—Margaret Louise Coit, John C. Calhoun: American Portrait.
1952—Merlo J. Pusey, Charles Evans Hughes.
1953—David J. Mays, Edmund Pendleton, 1721-1803.
1954—Charles A. Lindbergh, The Spirit of St. Louis.
1955—William S. White, The Taft Story.
1956—Talbot F. Hamlin, Benjamin Henry Latrobe.
1957—John F. Kennedy, Profiles in Courage.
1958—Douglas Southall Freeman (decd. 1953), George Washington, Vols. I-VI: John Alexander Carroll and Mary Wells Ashworth, Vol. VII.
1959—Arthur Walworth, Woodrow Wilson: American Prophet.
1960—Samuel Eliot Morison, John Paul Jones.
1961—David Donald, Charles Sumner and The Coming of the Civil War.
1963—Leon Edel, Henry James: Vol. II. The Conquest of London, 1870-1881; Vol. III, The Middle Years, 1881-1895.
1964—Walter Jackson Bate, John Keats.
1965—Ernest Samuels, Henry Adams.
1966—Arthur M. Schlesinger Jr., A Thousand Days.

1967—Justin Kaplan, Mr. Clemens and Mark Twain.
1968—George F. Kennan, Memoirs (1925-1950).
1969—B. L. Reid, The Man from New York: John Quinn and his Friends.
1970—T. Harry Williams, Huey Long.
1971—Lawrence Thompson, Robert Frost: The Years of Triumph, 1915-1938.
1972—Joseph P. Lash, Eleanor and Franklin.
1973—W. A. Swanberg, Luce and His Empire.
1974—Louis Sheaffer, O'Neill, Son and Artist.
1975—Robert A. Caro, The Power Broker: Robert Moses and the Fall of New York.
1976—R.W.B. Lewis, Edith Wharton: A Biography.
1977—John E. Mack, A Prince of Our Disorder, The Life of T.E. Lawrence.
1978—Walter Jackson Bate, Samuel Johnson.
1979—Leonard Baker, Days of Sorrow and Pain: Leo Baeck and the Berlin Jews.
1980—Edmund Morris, The Rise of Theodore Roosevelt.
1981—Robert K. Massie, Peter the Great: His Life and World.
1982—William S. McFeely, Grant: A Biography.
1983—Russell Baker, Growing Up.
1984—Louis R. Harlan, Booker T. Washington.
1985—Kenneth Silverman, The Life and Times of Cotton Mather.
1986—Elizabeth Frank, Louise Bogan: A Portrait.
1987—David J. Garrow, Bearing the Cross: Martin Luther King Jr. and the Southern Christian Leadership Conference.
1988—David Herbert Donald, Look Homeward: A Life of Thomas Wolfe.
1989—Richard Ellmann, Oscar Wilde.
1990—Sebastian de Grazia, Machiavelli in Hell.

American Poetry

Before this prize was established in 1922, awards were made from gifts provided by the Poetry Society: 1918—Love Songs, by Sara Teasdale. 1919—Old Road to Paradise, by Margaret Widemer; Corn Huskers, by Carl Sandburg.
1922—Edwin Arlington Robinson, Collected Poems.
1923—Edna St. Vincent Millay, The Ballad of the Harp-Weaver; A Few Figs from Thistles; Eight Sonnets in American Poetry, 1922; A Miscellany.
1924—Robert Frost, New Hampshire: A Poem with Notes and Grace Notes.
1925—Edwin Arlington Robinson, The Man Who Died Twice.
1926—Amy Lowell, What's O'Clock.
1927—Leonora Speyer, Fiddler's Farewell.
1928—Edwin Arlington Robinson, Tristram.
1929—Stephen Vincent Benet, John Brown's Body.
1930—Conrad Aiken, Selected Poems.
1931—Robert Frost, Collected Poems.
1932—George Dillon, The Flowering Stone.
1933—Archibald MacLeish, Conquistador.
1934—Robert Hillyer, Collected Verse.
1935—Audrey Wurdemann, Bright Ambush.
1936—Robert P. Tristram Coffin, Strange Holiness.
1937—Robert Frost, A Further Range.
1938—Marya Zaturenska, Cold Morning Sky.
1939—John Gould Fletcher, Selected Poems.
1940—Mark Van Doren, Collected Poems.
1941—Leonard Bacon, Sunderland Capture.
1942—William Rose Benet, The Dust Which Is God.
1943—Robert Frost, A Witness Tree.
1944—Stephen Vincent Benet, Western Star.
1945—Karl Shapiro, V-Letter and Other Poems.
1947—Robert Lowell, Lord Weary's Castle.
1948—W. H. Auden, The Age of Anxiety.
1949—Peter Viereck, Terror and Decorum.
1950—Gwendolyn Brooks, Annie Allen.
1951—Carl Sandburg, Complete Poems.
1952—Marianne Moore, Collected Poems.
1953—Archibald MacLeish, Collected Poems.
1954—Theodore Roethke, The Waking.
1955—Wallace Stevens, Collected Poems.
1956—Elizabeth Bishop, Poems, North and South.
1957—Richard Wilbur, Things of This World.
1958—Robert Penn Warren, Promises: Poems 1954-1956.
1959—Stanley Kunitz, Selected Poems 1928-1958.
1960—W. D. Snodgrass, Heart's Needle.
1961—Phyllis McGinley, Times Three: Selected Verse from Three Decades.
1962—Alan Dugan, Poems.
1963—William Carlos Williams, Pictures From Breughel.
1964—Louis Simpson, At the End of the Open Road.
1965—John Berryman, 77 Dream Songs.
1966—Richard Eberhart, Selected Poems.
1967—Anne Sexton, Live or Die.
1968—Anthony Hecht, The Hard Hours.

1969—George Oppen, Of Being Numerous.
1970—Richard Howard, Untitled Subjects.
1971—William S. Merwin, The Carrier of Ladders.
1972—James Wright, Collected Poems.
1973—Maxine Winokur Kumin, Up Country.
1975—Gary Snyder, Turtle Island.
1976—John Ashbery, Self-Portrait in a Convex Mirror.
1977—James Merrill, Divine Comedies.
1978—Howard Nemerov, Collected Poems.
1979—Robert Penn Warren, Now and Then: Poems 1976-1978.
1980—Donald Justice, Selected Poems.
1981—James Schuyler, The Morning of the Poem.
1982—Sylvia Plath, The Collected Poems.
1983—Galway Kinnell, Selected Poems.
1984—Mary Oliver, American Primitive.
1985—Carolyn Kizer, Yin.
1986—Henry Taylor, The Flying Change.
1987—Rita Dove, Thomas and Beulah.
1988—William Meredith, Partial Accounts: New and Selected Poems.
1989—Richard Wilbur, New and Collected Poems.
1990—Charles Simic, The World Doesn't End

General Non-Fiction

1962—Theodore H. White, The Making of the President 1960.
1963—Barbara W. Tuchman, The Guns of August.
1964—Richard Hofstadter, Anti-Intellectualism in American Life.
1965—Howard Mumford Jones, O Strange New World.
1966—Edwin Way Teale, Wandering Through Winter.
1967—David Brion Davis, The Problem of Slavery in Western Culture.

1968—Will and Ariel Durant, Rousseau and Revolution.
1969—Norman Mailer, The Armies of the Night; and Rene Jules Dubos, So Human an Animal: How We Are Shaped by Surroundings and Events.
1970—Eric H. Erikson, Gandhi's Truth.
1971—John Toland, The Rising Sun.
1972—Barbara W. Tuchman, Stilwell and the American Experience in China, 1911-1945.
1973—Frances FitzGerald, Fire in the Lake: The Vietnamese and the Americans in Vietnam; Robert Coles, Children of Crisis, Volumes II & III.
1974—Ernest Becker, The Denial of Death.
1975—Annie Dillard, Pilgrim at Tinker Creek.
1976—Robert N. Butler, Why Survive? Being Old in America.
1977—William W. Warner, Beautiful Swimmers.
1978—Carl Sagan, The Dragons of Eden.
1979—Edward O. Wilson, On Human Nature.
1980—Douglas R. Hofstadter, Gödel, Escher, Bach: An Eternal Golden Braid.
1981—Carl E. Schorske, Fin-de-Siecle Vienna: Politics and Culture.
1982—Tracy Kidder, The Soul of a New Machine.
1983—Susan Sheehan, Is There No Place on Earth for Me?
1984—Paul Starr, Social Transformation of American Medicine.
1985—Studs Terkel, The Good War.
1986—Joseph Lelyveld, Move Your Shadow; J. Anthony Lukas, Common Ground.
1987—David K. Shipler, Arab and Jew.
1988—Richard Rhodes, The Making of the Atomic Bomb.
1989—Neil Sheehan, A Bright Shining Lie: John Paul Vann and America in Vietnam.
1990—Dale Maharidge, Michael Williamson, And Their Children After Them.

Music

For composition by an American (before 1977, by a composer resident in the U.S.), in the larger forms of chamber, orchestra or choral music or for an operatic work including ballet. A special posthumous award was granted in 1976 to Scott Joplin.
1943—William Schuman, Secular Cantata No. 2, A Free Song.
1944—Howard Hanson, Symphony No. 4, Op. 34.
1945—Aaron Copland, Appalachian Spring.
1946—Leo Sowerby, The Canticle of the Sun.
1947—Charles E. Ives, Symphony No. 3.
1948—Walter Piston, Symphony No. 3.
1949—Virgil Thomson, Louisiana Story.
1950—Gian-Carlo Menotti, The Consul.
1951—Douglas Moore, Giants in the Earth.
1952—Gail Kubik, Symphony Concertante.
1954—Quincy Porter, Concerto for Two Pianos and Orchestra.
1955—Gian-Carlo Menotti, The Saint of Bleecker Street.
1956—Ernest Toch, Symphony No. 3.
1957—Norman Dello Joio, Meditations on Ecclesiastes.
1958—Samuel Barber, Vanessa.
1959—John La Montaine, Concerto for Piano and Orchestra.
1960—Elliott Carter, Second String Quartet.
1961—Walter Piston, Symphony No. 7.
1962—Robert Ward, The Crucible.
1963—Samuel Barber, Piano Concerto No. 1.
1966—Leslie Bassett, Variations for Orchestra.
1967—Leon Kirchner, Quartet No. 3.

1968—George Crumb, Echoes of Time and The River.
1969—Karel Husa, String Quartet No. 3.
1970—Charles W. Wuorinen, Time's Encomium.
1971—Mario Davidovsky, Synchronisms No. 6.
1972—Jacob Druckman, Windows.
1973—Elliott Carter, String Quartet No. 3.
1974—Donald Martino, Notturno. (Special citation) Roger Sessions.
1975—Dominick Argento, From the Diary of Virginia Woolf.
1976—Ned Rorem, Air Music.
1977—Richard Wernick, Visions of Terror and Wonder.
1978—Michael Colgrass, Deja Vu for Percussion and Orchestra.

1979—Joseph Schwantner, Aftertones of Infinity.
1980—David Del Tredici, In Memory of a Summer Day.
1982—Roger Sessions, Concerto For Orchestra. (Special Citation) Milton Babbitt.
1983—Ellen T. Zwilich, Three Movements for Orchestra.
1984—Bernard Rands, Canti del Sole.
1985—Stephen Albert, Symphony, RiverRun.
1986—George Perle, Wind Quintet IV.
1987—John Harbison, The Flight Into Egypt.
1988—William Bolcom, 12 New Etudes for Piano.
1989—Roger Reynolds, Whispers Out of Time.
1990—Mel Powell, Duplicates: A Concerto For Two Pianos and Orchestra.

Special Awards

Awarded in 1989 or 1990

Books, Allied Arts

Academy of American Poets Fellowship for Distinguished Achievement, $20,000: William Meredith.

Booker Prize: The Remains of the Day, Kazuo Ishiguro.

Boston Globe-Horn Book Awards for Excellence in Children's Literature, $500 and engraved silver bowl: fiction: The Village by the Sea. Paula Fox; nonfiction: The Way Things Work, David Macaulay; picture book: Shy Charles, Rosemary Wells.

Caldecott Medal, for distinguished American picture book for children: Lon Po Po: A Red-Riding Hood Story from China, Ed Young.

Carey-Thomas Awards, by Publishers Weekly, for creative publishing: main prize: Thunder Mouth Press, alternative fiction and nonfiction; honor citations: Curbstone Press, for Latin American writers and issues & Seal Press, for feminist

issues; special citation: Eridanos Press, for translations of 20th-century classics.

Chicago Sun-Times Book of the Year Award: Noble Rot, Richard Stern.

Golden Kite Awards, for children's books, by Society of Children's Book Writers: fiction: Jenny of the Tetons. Kristiana Gregory; nonfiction: Panama Canal: Gateway to the World, Judith St. George; picture book illustration: Tom Thumb, Richard Jesse Watson.

National Arts Club Medal of Honor for Literature: Iris Murdoch.

National Book Awards, by National Book Foundation, $10,000: fiction: Spartina, John Casey; nonfiction: From Beirut to Jerusalem, Thomas L. Friedman; distinguished contribution to American letters: Daniel J. Boorstin.

National Book Critics Circle Awards: fiction: *Billy Bathgate,* E.L. Doctorow; general nonfiction: *The Broken Cord,* Michael Dorris; biography/autobiography: *A First-Class Temperament: The Emergence of Franklin Roosevelt,* Geoffrey C. Ward; poetry: *Transparent Gestures,* Rodney Jones; criticism: *Not by Facts Alone: Essays on the Writing and Reading of History,* John Clive; citation for excellence in book reviewing: Carol Anshaw, *Voice Literary Supplement;* contribution to book publishing: James Laughlin, New Directions.

Newbery Medal, for children's literature: *Number the Stars,* Lois Lowry.

O'Dell Award, for historical fiction, by Bulletin of the Center for Children's Books, $5,000: *Shades of Gray,* Carolyn Reeder.

Whiting Foundation Writers' Awards, $25,000 each: Timberlake Wertenbaker, Ellen Atkins, Tobias Wolff, Mary Karr, C.D. Wright, Natalie Kusz, Russell Edson, Ian Frazier, Luc Sante.

Journalism Awards

Bernstein Award for Excellence in Journalism, by New York Public Library, $15,000: Thomas L. Friedman, *From Beirut to Jerusalem.*

Catholic Press Assn. Awards: general excellence, national: *Our Sunday Visitor,* Huntington, Ind.; diocesan, circulation to 17,000: *The Florida Catholic,* Venice, Fla.; 17,001-40,000: *The Catholic Observer,* Springfield, Mass.; from 40,001: *The Catholic Sun,* Syracuse, N.Y.

Magazine Merit Awards, by Society of Children's Book Writers: fiction: Elaine Marie Alphin, *Young and Alive;* nonfiction: Elizabeth R. Hennefrund, *Ranger Rick;* illustrations: Bianca Lavies, *Ranger Rick.*

National Journalism Awards, by Scripps Howard Foundation, $41,000: college cartoonist: Nick Anderson, *Ohio State Lantern,* Columbus; editorial writing: Ann Daly Goodwin, *St. Paul* (Minn.) *Pioneer Press Dispatch;* environmental journalism: Sam Atwood, *The* (San Bernardino, Calif.) *Sun; The Boston Globe;* commitment to literacy: WFSB-TV, Hartford, Conn.; *The San Antonio Light;* human interest writing: Rose Post, *The Salisbury* (N.C.) *Post;* broadcast journalism: KWTO-TV, Springfield, Mo.; WSM Radio, Nashville, Tenn.; KARK-TV, Little Rock, Ark.; WCBS-TV, New York; First Amendment service: *The San Francisco Chronicle;* public service: *The Charleston* (W.Va.) *Gazette; The Fort Worth* (Tex.) *Star-Telegram.*

National Magazine Awards, by American Society of Magazine Editors, bronze plaque and reproduction of Calder sta-

bile each: general excellence, circulation of 1 million or more: *Sports Illustrated;* 400,000 to 1 million: *Metropolitan Home;* 100,000-400,000: *Texas Monthly;* less than 100,000: 7 *Days;* reporting: *The New Yorker;* fiction: *The New Yorker;* photography: *Texas Monthly;* essays and criticism: *Vanity Fair;* feature-writing: *The Washingtonian;* public interest: *Southern Exposure;* single-topic: *National Geographic;* personal service: *Consumer Reports;* special interests: *Art & Antiques;* design: *Esquire.*

Polk Awards in Journalism, by Long Island University: career: Fred M. Hechinger, *New York Times;* foreign: Nicholas D. Kristof, Sheryl WuDunn, *New York Times;* international: Stephen Engelberg, Michael R. Gordon, *New York Times;* national: Rick Atkinson, *Washington Post;* political: Andrew Melnykovych, *Casper* (Wyo.) *Star-Tribune;* regional: Miranda Ewell, David Schrieberg, *San Jose* (Calif.) *Mercury News;* local: *Hartford* (Conn.) *Courant;* medical: John M. Crewdson, *Chicago Tribune;* network TV: CBS News; local TV: WCSC-TV, Charleston, S.C.; TV investigative: Jonathan Kwitny, "The Kwitny Report," WNYC-TV; radio: Robert Knight, "Undercurrents," WBAI-FM.

Reuben Awards, by National Cartoonists Society: cartoonist of the year: Jim Davis, "Garfield," United Feature Syndicate; commercial: Roy Doty; electronic media: Chuck Jones; magazines and books: Sergio Aragones; editorial & sports: Pat Oliphant Universal Press Syndicate; strips & panels: Johnny Hart, "B.C.," Creators Syndicate.

Movie, Radio, TV, and Theater Awards

Audelco Recognition Awards, for black theater: outstanding pioneer: Cynthia Belgrave; play: "The Talented Tenth," Richard Wesley; musical: "Song of Sheba," Clarice Laverne Thompson, Elmo Terry Morgan; playwright: Richard Wesley; director: M. Neema Barnette; musical director: Clarice Laverne Thompson; actor: Alili Prince, "The Forbidden City;" actress: Marie Thomas, "The Talented Tenth;" musical actor: Anthony Cooper, "Song of Sheba;" musical actress: Johanna Daughtery, "Song of Sheba."

Directors Guild of America Awards: feature film director: Oliver Stone, "Born on the Fourth of July;" TV directors: comedy: Barnet Kellman, *Murphy Brown;* drama special: Dan Curtis, "War and Remembrance;" drama series: Eric Laneuville, *L.A. Law;* daytime drama series: Victoria Hochberg, *Wonderworks;* musical variety: Don Mischer, *Great Performances;* documentary: Peter Rosen, "The Eighth Van Cliburn Intl. Piano Competition;" sports: Bob Fishman, "U.S. Open Tennis Tournament;" commercial: David Cornell, A.T.&T.'s "Small Town."

du Pont-Columbia Univ. Awards, for broadcast journalism: gold baton: *Frontline,* PBS; silver batons: CBS News, CNN, ABC News & Koppel Communications; WETA, Washington, D.C.; radio silver baton: National Public Radio; independent TV production: Appalshop, Kentucky; silver batons, major market TV stations: WFAA-TV, Dallas, KCET, Los Angeles; medium-size-market: Maryland Public Television; small-market: WJXT, Jacksonville, Fla.; WBRZ, Baton Rouge, La.

Emmy Awards, by Academy of Television Arts and Sciences, for nighttime programs, 1988-89: Dramatic series: *L.A. Law,* NBC; actress, Dana Delany, *China Beach,* ABC; actor: Carroll O'Connor, *In the Heat of the Night,* NBC; supporting actress: Melanie Mayron, *thirtysomething,* ABC; supporting actor: Larry Drake, *L.A. Law,* NBC. Comedy series: *Cheers,* NBC; actress: Candice Bergen, *Murphy Brown,* CBS; actor: Richard Mulligan, *Empty Nest,* NBC;

supporting actress: Rhea Perlman, *Cheers,* NBC; supporting actor: Woody Harrelson, *Cheers,* NBC. Miniseries: *War and Remembrance,* ABC; actress: Holly Hunter, *Roe vs. Wade,* NBC; actor: James Woods, *Hallmark Hall of Fame: My Name Is Bill W.,* ABC; supporting actress: Colleen Dewhurst, *Those She Left Behind,* NBC; supporting actor: Derek Jacobi, *Hallmark Hall of Fame: The Tenth Man,* CBS. Drama-Comedy Special: (tie) *Day One,* CBS; *Roe vs. Wade,* NBC. Variety, Music or Comedy Program: *The Tracey Ullman Show,* Fox. Performance in a Variety or Musical Program: Linda Ronstadt, *Great Performances: Canciones de mi Padre,* PBS. Children's Program: *Free to Be . . . a Family,* ABC. Classical Program in Performing Arts: *Great Performances: Bernstein at 70!,* PBS; Governor's Award: Lucille Ball. (For 1989-90, see *Addenda.*)

Golden Globe Awards, by Hollywood Foreign Press Assn.: dramatic picture: "Born on the Fourth of July;" director: Oliver Stone, "Born on the Fourth of July;" actor: Tom Cruise, "Born on the Fourth of July;" actress: Michelle Pfeiffer, "The Fabulous Baker Boys;" musical or comic picture: "Driving Miss Daisy;" musical or comic actor: Morgan Freeman, "Driving Miss Daisy;" musical or comic actress: Jessica Tandy, "Driving Miss Daisy;" TV series, dramatic: *China Beach,* ABC; musical or comic: *Murphy Brown,* CBS; mini series: *Lonesome Dove.*

Kennedy Center for the Performing Arts Awards, for lifetime achievement in the arts, gold medallions: Harry Belafonte, Claudette Colbert, Mary Martin, Alexandra Danilova, William Schuman.

Kesserling Award for Playwrights, by National Arts Club, $10,000: Jo Carson, "Daytrips," Los Angeles Theater Center.

New York Drama Critics Circle Awards: new play: "The Piano Lesson," August Wilson; new musical: "City of Angels," Larry Gelbart, Cy Coleman, David Zippel; new foreign play: "Privates on Parade," Peter Nichols.

New York Film Critics Circle Awards: film: "My Left Foot;" actor: Daniel Day-Lewis, "My Left Foot;" actress: Michelle Pfeiffer, "The Fabulous Baker Boys;" director: Paul Mazursky, "Enemies, a Love Story;" supporting actor: Alan Alda, "Crimes and Misdemeanors;" supporting actress: Lena Olin, "Enemies, a Love Story;" foreign film: "Story of Women," Claude Chabrol; documentary: "Roger and Me," Michael Moore; new director: Kenneth Branagh, "Henry V;" cinematography: Ernest Dickerson, "Do the Right Thing;" screenplay: Daniel Yost, "Drugstore Cowboy."

Tony (Antoinette Perry) Awards: play: "The Grapes of Wrath;" musical: "City of Angels;" revival: "Gypsy;" actor: Robert Morse, "Tru;" actress: Maggie Smith, "Lettice and Lovage;" actor, musical: James Naughton, "City of Angels;" actress, musical: Tyne Daly, "Gypsy;" featured actor: Charles Durning, "Cat on a Hot Tin Roof;" featured actress: Margaret Tyzack, "Lettice and Lovage;" featured actor, musical: Michael Jeter, "Grand Hotel;" featured actress, musical: Randy Graff, "City of Angels;" direction: Frank Galati, "The Grapes of Wrath;" direction, musical: Tommy Tune, "Grand Hotel;" book, musical: Larry Gelbert, "City of Angels;" original musical score: Cy Coleman, David Zippel, "City of Angels;" scenic design: Robin Wagner, "City of Angels;" lighting design: Jules Fisher, "Grand Hotel;" costume design: Santo Loquasto, "Grand Hotel;" choreography: Tommy Tune, "Grand Hotel."

Miscellaneous Awards

American Choreographer Awards, by The National Corporate Fund for Dance and The General Electric Foundation, for talented emerging choreographers, $5,000 each: David Dorfman, Miriam Mahdaviani, Sara Pearson, Daniel Shapiro & Joanie Smith, Liz Lerman.

American Composers Alliance Awards, for contribution to American music: Frank Wigglesworth.

American Institute of Architects Gold Medal for Lifetime Achievement: Fay Jones.

Bard Awards, by City Club of New York, for architecture and urban design: Central Park Zoo, Kevin Roche, John Dinkeloo & Associates; Brooklyn Borough Hall, Conklin Rossant Architects; special awards: John Lindsay, Paul A. Crotty, Abraham Biderman.

Carnegie Hall International American Music Competition for Violinists, $10,000 cash award, $20,000 career grand, recital and concerto soloist appearances at Carnegie Hall, New World Records contract, music reference works: Michelle Makarski, Santa Barbara, Calif.

Candace Awards, by National Coalition of 100 Black Women, for leadership and achievement: Euzhan Palcy, film director; Judith Jamison, artistic director of Alvin Ailey Dance Theater; Maya Angelou, writer; Barbara Lamont, owner of WWCL TV in New Orleans; Hazel N. Dukes, pres. of NAACP board of directors; Sara Lawrence Lightfoot, professor, Harvard Graduate School of Education; Clara Hale, founder of Hale House for drug-addicted babies; Gay J. McDougall, director of Southern Africa Project Lawyers' Committee for Civil Rights; Vivian W. Pinn-Wiggins, chairwoman of pathology at Howard Univ. College of Medicine; distinguished service: Derrick A. Bell Jr., Weld Professor of Law, Harvard Law School.

Cleveland Prize, by Amer. Assn. for the Advancement of Science, $5,000 and bronze medal, to author of outstanding paper published in Science: William H. Landschulz, Peter F. Johnson, Steven L. McKnight, "The Leucine Zipper: A Hypothetical Structure Common to a New Class of DNA Binding Proteins," and "The DNA Binding Domain of the Rat Liver Nuclear Protein C/EBP Is Bipartite."

Draper Prize, by National Academy of Engineering, $350,000: Jack S. Kilby and Robert N. Noyce, for coinventing the monolithic integrated circuit.

Grawyemeyer Award, by University of Louisville, for original music composition, $150,000: "Silver Ladders," Joan Tower, Bard College, Annandale-on-Hudson, N.Y.

International Ballet Competition: Grand Prix City of Jackson Award, $10,000: Jose Manuel Carreno; gold medal, $7,000, senior female: Martha Butler; silver medal, $5,000 each: Luis Ortigoza, Pierre Quinn; Simona Noja, bronze medals, $3,000 each: Toomas Edue, Irma Nioradze.

Lasker Awards, for medical research, $15,000 each: Etienne-Emile Baulieu, for abortion drug, RU 486; Michael J. Berridge, Alfred G. Gilman, Edwin G. Krebs, Yasutomi Nishizuka, for research on how cells receive information from hormones, growth factors, and neurotransmitters; public service award: Lewis Thomas, Cornell Univ. Medical College, New York.

National Spelling Bee (See Language)

New York State Governor's Arts Awards, bronze sculptures: Vivienne Anderson, Agnes de Mille; Avery Fisher; Maria Irene Fornes; Kurt Vonnegut; Brooklyn Museum; New York Chinatown History Project; DeWitt Historical Society of Tompkins County; Jamaica Arts Center; M&T Bank of Buffalo; Rockland County and the Arts Council of Rockland, Visual AIDS.

Praemium Imperiale Award, by Japan Art Association, for lifetime achievement in the arts. $100,000 and medal each: composer Leonard Bernstein; film maker Federico Fellini; sculptor Arnaldo Pomodoro; architect James Stirling; painter Antoni Tapies.

Scripps American Dance Festival Award, for lifetime contribution by choreographer, $25,000: Twyla Tharp.

Songwriters Hall of Fame: Smokey Robinson, Michel Legrand, Jim Croce.

Tucker Award, by Richard Tucker Music Foundation, $25,000: Renee Fleming; career grants: Ruth Ann Swenson, Susan Graham, Emily Manhart, Alan J. Held; study grant: Camellia Johnson; Ruth Richards Grant for promising tenor: John T. Keys; Robert M. Jacobson Study Grants: Angela Randell, Denyce Graves, Mark Oswald.

Westinghouse Science Talent Search winners: first prize, $20,000 college scholarship: Matthew Peter Headrick, Chicago; second prize, $15,000: David Ruchien Liu, Riverside, Calif.; third prize, $15,000: David Michael Shull, Tacoma, Washington; fourth prize, $10,000: Soojin Ryu, New York City; fifth prize, $10,000: Joshua B. Fischman, Bethesda, Md.; sixth prize, $10,000: Royce Yung-Tze Peng, Rancho Palos Verdes, Calif.; seventh prize: $7,500: Laura Andrea Ascenzi, New York City; eighth prize, $7,500: Andrew M. Lines, Arlington, Va.; ninth prize, $7,500: Mina Kim Yu, Fairfax, Va.; tenth prize, $7,500: Bianca Denise Santomasso, New York City.

The Spingarn Medal

The Spingarn Medal has been awarded annually since 1914 by the National Association for the Advancement of Colored People for the highest achievement by a black American.

1946	Dr. Percy L. Julian	1956	Martin Luther King Jr.	1964	Leontyne Price
1947	Channing H. Tobias	1957	Mrs. Daisy Bates and the Little Rock Nine	1965	John H. Johnson
1948	Ralph J. Bunche			1966	Edward W. Brooke
1949	Charles Hamilton Houston	1958	Edward Kennedy (Duke) Ellington	1967	Sammy Davis Jr.
1950	Mabel Keaton Staupers			1968	Clarence M. Mitchell Jr.
1951	Harry T. Moore	1959	Langston Hughes	1969	Jacob Lawrence
1952	Paul R. Williams	1960	Kenneth B. Clark	1970	Leon Howard Sullivan
1953	Theodore K. Lawless	1961	Robert C. Weaver	1971	Gordon Parks
1954	Carl Murphy	1962	Medgar Wiley Evers	1972	Wilson C. Riles
1955	Jack Roosevelt Robinson	1963	Roy Wilkins		

(continued)

1973 Damon Keith	1979 Dr. Rayford W. Logan	1985 Dr. Benjamin L. Hooks
1974 Henry (Hank) Aaron	1980 Coleman Young	1986 Percy E. Sutton
1975 Alvin Ailey	1981 Dr. Benjamin Elijah Mays	1987 Frederick Douglass Patterson
1976 Alex Haley	1982 Lena Horne	1988 Jesse Jackson
1977 Andrew Young	1983 Thomas Bradley	1989 L. Douglas Wilder
1978 Mrs. Rosa L. Parks	1984 Bill Cosby	

Miss America Winners

1921 Margaret Gorman, Washington, D.C.	1961 Nancy Fleming, Montague, Michigan
1922-23 Mary Campbell, Columbus, Ohio	1962 Maria Fletcher, Asheville, North Carolina
1924 Ruth Malcolmson, Philadelphia, Pennsylvania	1963 Jacquelyn Mayer, Sandusky, Ohio
1925 Fay Lamphier, Oakland, California	1964 Donna Axum, El Dorado, Arkansas
1926 Norma Smallwood, Tulsa, Oklahoma	1965 Vonda Kay Van Dyke, Phoenix, Arizona
1927 Lois Delaner, Joliet, Illinois	1966 Deborah Irene Bryant, Overland Park, Kansas
1933 Marion Bergeron, West Haven, Connecticut	1967 Jane Anne Jayroe, Laverne, Oklahoma
1935 Henrietta Leaver, Pittsburgh, Pennsylvania	1968 Debra Dene Barnes, Moran, Kansas
1936 Rose Coyle, Philadelphia, Pennsylvania	1969 Judith Anne Ford, Belvidere, Illinois
1937 Bette Cooper, Bertrand Island, New Jersey	1970 Pamela Anne Eldred, Birmingham, Michigan
1938 Marilyn Meseke, Marion, Ohio	1971 Phyllis Ann George, Denton, Texas
1939 Patricia Donnelly, Detroit, Michigan	1972 Laurie Lea Schaefer, Columbus, Ohio
1940 Frances Marie Burke, Philadelphia, Pennsylvania	1973 Terry Anne Meeuwsen, DePere, Wisconsin
1941 Rosemary LaPlanche, Los Angeles, California	1974 Rebecca Ann King, Denver, Colorado
1942 Jo-Caroli Dennison, Tyler, Texas	1975 Shirley Cothran, Fort Worth, Texas
1943 Jean Bartel, Los Angeles, California	1976 Tawney Elaine Godin, Yonkers, N.Y.
1944 Venus Ramey, Washington, D.C.	1977 Dorothy Kathleen Benham, Edina, Minnesota
1945 Bess Myerson, New York City, N.Y.	1978 Susan Perkins, Columbus, Ohio
1946 Marilyn Buferd, Los Angeles, California	1979 Kylene Barker, Galax, Virginia
1947 Barbara Walker, Memphis, Tennessee	1980 Cheryl Prewitt, Ackerman, Mississippi
1948 BeBe Shopp, Hopkins, Minnesota	1981 Susan Powell, Elk City, Oklahoma
1949 Jacque Mercer, Litchfield, Arizona	1982 Elizabeth Ward, Russellville, Arkansas
1951 Yolande Betbeze, Mobile, Alabama	1983 Debra Maffett, Anaheim, California
1952 Coleen Kay Hutchins, Salt Lake City, Utah	1984 Vanessa Williams, Milwood, New York*
1953 Neva Jane Langley, Macon, Georgia	Suzette Charles, Mays Landing, New Jersey
1954 Evelyn Margaret Ay, Ephrata, Pennsylvania	1985 Sharlene Wells, Salt Lake City, Utah
1955 Lee Meriwether, San Francisco, California	1986 Susan Akin, Meridian, Mississippi
1956 Sharon Ritchie, Denver, Colorado	1987 Kellye Cash, Memphis, Tennessee
1957 Marian McKnight, Manning, South Carolina	1988 Kaye Lani Rae Rafko, Monroe, Michigan
1958 Marilyn Van Derbur, Denver, Colorado	1989 Gretchen Carlson, Anoka, Minnesota
1959 Mary Ann Mobley, Brandon, Mississippi	1990 Debbye Turner, Columbia, Missouri
1960 Lynda Lee Mead, Natchez, Mississippi	

*Resigned July 23, 1984.

Motion Picture Academy Awards (Oscars)

1927-28
Actor: Emil Jannings, *The Way of All Flesh.*
Actress: Janet Gaynor, *Seventh Heaven.*
Director: Frank Borzage, *Seventh Heaven;* Lewis Milestone, *Two Arabian Knights.*
Picture: *Wings,* Paramount.

1928-29
Actor: Warner Baxter, *In Old Arizona.*
Actress: Mary Pickford, *Coquette.*
Director: Frank Lloyd, *The Divine Lady.*
Picture: *Broadway Melody,* MGM.

1929-30
Actor: George Arliss, *Disraeli.*
Actress: Norma Shearer, *The Divorcee.*
Director: Lewis Milestone, *All Quiet on the Western Front.*
Picture: *All Quiet on the Western Front,* Univ.

1930-31
Actor: Lionel Barrymore, *Free Soul.*
Actress: Marie Dressler, *Min and Bill.*
Director: Norman Taurog, *Skippy.*
Picture: *Cimarron,* RKO.

1931-32
Actor: Fredric March, *Dr. Jekyll and Mr. Hyde;* Wallace Beery, *The Champ* (tie).
Actress: Helen Hayes, *Sin of Madelon Claudet.*
Director: Frank Borzage, *Bad Girl.*
Picture: *Grand Hotel,* MGM.
Special: Walt Disney, *Mickey Mouse.*

1932-33
Actor: Charles Laughton, *Private Life of Henry VIII.*
Actress: Katharine Hepburn, *Morning Glory.*
Director: Frank Lloyd, *Cavalcade.*
Picture: *Cavalcade,* Fox.

1934
Actor: Clark Gable, *It Happened One Night.*
Actress: Claudette Colbert, *It Happened One Night.*
Director: Frank Capra, *It Happened One Night.*
Picture: *It Happened One Night,* Columbia.

1935
Actor: Victor McLaglen, *The Informer.*
Actress: Bette Davis, *Dangerous.*
Director: John Ford, *The Informer.*
Picture: *Mutiny on the Bounty,* MGM.

1936
Actor: Paul Muni, *Story of Louis Pasteur.*
Actress: Luise Rainer, *The Great Ziegfeld.*
Sup. Actor: Walter Brennan, *Come and Get It.*
Sup. Actress: Gale Sondergaard, *Anthony Adverse.*
Director: Frank Capra, *Mr. Deeds Goes to Town.*
Picture: *The Great Ziegfeld,* MGM.

1937
Actor: Spencer Tracy, *Captains Courageous.*
Actress: Luise Rainer, *The Good Earth.*
Sup. Actor: Joseph Schildkraut, *Life of Emile Zola.*
Sup. Actress: Alice Brady, *In Old Chicago.*
Director: Leo McCarey, *The Awful Truth.*
Picture: *Life of Emile Zola,* Warner.

1938
Actor: Spencer Tracy, *Boys Town.*
Actress: Bette Davis, *Jezebel.*
Sup. Actor: Walter Brennan, *Kentucky.*
Sup. Actress: Fay Bainter, *Jezebel.*
Director: Frank Capra, *You Can't Take It With You.*
Picture: *You Can't Take It With You,* Columbia.

1939
Actor: Robert Donat, *Goodbye Mr. Chips.*
Actress: Vivien Leigh, *Gone With the Wind.*
Sup. Actor: Thomas Mitchell, *Stage Coach.*
Sup. Actress: Hattie McDaniel, *Gone With the Wind.*
Director: Victor Fleming, *Gone With the Wind.*
Picture: *Gone With the Wind,* Selznick International.

1940
Actor: James Stewart, *The Philadelphia Story.*
Actress: Ginger Rogers, *Kitty Foyle.*
Sup. Actor: Walter Brennan, *The Westerner.*
Sup. Actress: Jane Darwell, *The Grapes of Wrath.*
Director: John Ford, *The Grapes of Wrath.*
Picture: *Rebecca,* Selznick International.

1941
Actor: Gary Cooper, *Sergeant York.*
Actress: Joan Fontaine, *Suspicion.*
Sup. Actor: Donald Crisp, *How Green Was My Valley.*

Sup. Actress: Mary Astor, *The Great Lie.*
Director: John Ford, *How Green Was My Valley.*
Picture: *How Green Was My Valley,* 20th Cent.-Fox.
1942
Actor: James Cagney, *Yankee Doodle Dandy.*
Actress: Greer Garson, *Mrs. Miniver.*
Sup. Actor: Van Heflin, *Johnny Eager.*
Sup. Actress: Teresa Wright, *Mrs. Miniver.*
Director: William Wyler, *Mrs. Miniver.*
Picture: *Mrs. Miniver,* MGM.
1943
Actor: Paul Lukas, *Watch on the Rhine.*
Actress: Jennifer Jones, *The Song of Bernadette.*
Sup. Actor: Charles Coburn, *The More the Merrier.*
Sup. Actress: Katina Paxinou, *For Whom the Bell Tolls.*
Director: Michael Curtiz, *Casablanca.*
Picture: *Casablanca,* Warner.
1944
Actor: Bing Crosby, *Going My Way.*
Actress: Ingrid Bergman, *Gaslight.*
Sup. Actor: Barry Fitzgerald, *Going My Way.*
Sup. Actress: Ethel Barrymore, *None But the Lonely Heart.*
Director: Leo McCarey, *Going My Way.*
Picture: *Going My Way,* Paramount.
1945
Actor: Ray Milland, *The Lost Weekend.*
Actress: Joan Crawford, *Mildred Pierce.*
Sup. Actor: James Dunn, *A Tree Grows in Brooklyn.*
Sup. Actress: Anne Revere, *National Velvet.*
Director: Billy Wilder, *The Lost Weekend.*
Picture: *The Lost Weekend,* Paramount.
1946
Actor: Fredric March, *Best Years of Our Lives.*
Actress: Olivia de Havilland, *To Each His Own.*
Sup. Actor: Harold Russell, *The Best Years of Our Lives.*
Sup. Actress: Anne Baxter, *The Razor's Edge.*
Director: William Wyler, *The Best Years of Our Lives.*
Picture: *The Best Years of Our Lives,* Goldwyn, RKO.
1947
Actor: Ronald Colman, *A Double Life.*
Actress: Loretta Young, *The Farmer's Daughter.*
Sup. Actor: Edmund Gwenn, *Miracle on 34th Street.*
Sup. Actress: Celeste Holm, *Gentleman's Agreement.*
Director: Elia Kazan, *Gentleman's Agreement.*
Picture: *Gentleman's Agreement,* 20th Cent.-Fox.
1948
Actor: Laurence Olivier, *Hamlet.*
Actress: Jane Wyman, *Johnny Belinda.*
Sup. Actor: Walter Huston, *Treasure of Sierra Madre.*
Sup. Actress: Claire Trevor, *Key Largo.*
Director: John Huston, *Treasure of Sierra Madre.*
Picture: *Hamlet,* Two Cities Film, Universal International.
1949
Actor: Broderick Crawford, *All the King's Men.*
Actress: Olivia de Havilland, *The Heiress.*
Sup. Actor: Dean Jagger, *Twelve O'Clock High.*
Sup. Actress: Mercedes McCambridge, *All the King's Men.*
Director: Joseph L. Mankiewicz, *Letter to Three Wives.*
Picture: *All the King's Men,* Columbia.
1950
Actor: Jose Ferrer, *Cyrano de Bergerac.*
Actress: Judy Holliday, *Born Yesterday.*
Sup. Actor: George Sanders, *All About Eve.*
Sup. Actress: Josephine Hull, *Harvey.*
Director: Joseph L. Mankiewicz, *All About Eve.*
Picture: *All About Eve,* 20th Century-Fox.
1951
Actor: Humphrey Bogart, *The African Queen.*
Actress: Vivien Leigh, *A Streetcar Named Desire.*
Sup. Actor: Karl Malden, *A Streetcar Named Desire.*
Sup. Actress: Kim Hunter, *A Streetcar Named Desire.*
Director: George Stevens, *A Place in the Sun.*
Picture: *An American in Paris,* MGM.
1952
Actor: Gary Cooper, *High Noon.*
Actress: Shirley Booth, *Come Back, Little Sheba.*
Sup. Actor: Anthony Quinn, *Viva Zapata!*
Sup. Actress: Gloria Grahame, *The Bad and the Beautiful.*
Director: John Ford, *The Quiet Man.*
Picture: *Greatest Show on Earth,* C.B. DeMille, Paramount.
1953
Actor: William Holden, *Stalag 17.*
Actress: Audrey Hepburn, *Roman Holiday.*
Sup. Actor: Frank Sinatra, *From Here to Eternity.*
Sup. Actress: Donna Reed, *From Here to Eternity.*
Director: Fred Zinnemann, *From Here to Eternity.*
Picture: *From Here to Eternity,* Columbia.

1954
Actor: Marlon Brando, *On the Waterfront.*
Actress: Grace Kelly, *The Country Girl.*
Sup. Actor: Edmond O'Brien, *The Barefoot Contessa.*
Sup. Actress: Eva Marie Saint, *On the Waterfront.*
Director: Elia Kazan, *On the Waterfront.*
Picture: *On the Waterfront,* Horizon-American, Colum.
1955
Actor: Ernest Borgnine, *Marty.*
Actress: Anna Magnani, *The Rose Tattoo.*
Sup. Actor: Jack Lemmon, *Mister Roberts.*
Sup. Actress: Jo Van Fleet, *East of Eden.*
Director: Delbert Mann, *Marty.*
Picture: *Marty,* Hecht and Lancaster's Steven Prods., U.A.
1956
Actor: Yul Brynner, *The King and I.*
Actress: Ingrid Bergman, *Anastasia.*
Sup. Actor: Anthony Quinn, *Lust for Life.*
Sup. Actress: Dorothy Malone, *Written on the Wind.*
Director: George Stevens, *Giant.*
Picture: *Around the World in 80 Days,* Michael Todd, U.A.
1957
Actor: Alec Guinness, *The Bridge on the River Kwai.*
Actress: Joanne Woodward, *The Three Faces of Eve.*
Sup. Actor: Red Buttons, *Sayonara.*
Sup. Actress: Miyoshi Umeki, *Sayonara.*
Director: David Lean, *The Bridge on the River Kwai.*
Picture: *The Bridge on the River Kwai,* Columbia.
1958
Actor: David Niven, *Separate Tables.*
Actress: Susan Hayward, *I Want to Live.*
Sup. Actor: Burl Ives, *The Big Country.*
Sup. Actress: Wendy Hiller, *Separate Tables.*
Director: Vincente Minnelli, *Gigi.*
Picture: *Gigi,* Arthur Freed Production, MGM.
1959
Actor: Charlton Heston, *Ben-Hur.*
Actress: Simone Signoret, *Room at the Top.*
Sup. Actor: Hugh Griffith, *Ben-Hur.*
Sup. Actress: Shelley Winters, *Diary of Anne Frank.*
Director: William Wyler, *Ben-Hur.*
Picture: *Ben-Hur,* MGM.
1960
Actor: Burt Lancaster, *Elmer Gantry.*
Actress: Elizabeth Taylor, *Butterfield 8.*
Sup. Actor: Peter Ustinov, *Spartacus.*
Sup. Actress: Shirley Jones, *Elmer Gantry.*
Director: Billy Wilder, *The Apartment.*
Picture: *The Apartment,* Mirisch Co., U.A.
1961
Actor: Maximilian Schell, *Judgment at Nuremberg.*
Actress: Sophia Loren, *Two Women.*
Sup. Actor: George Chakiris, *West Side Story.*
Sup. Actress: Rita Moreno, *West Side Story.*
Director: Jerome Robbins, Robert Wise, *West Side Story.*
Picture: *West Side Story,* United Artists.
1962
Actor: Gregory Peck, *To Kill a Mockingbird.*
Actress: Anne Bancroft, *The Miracle Worker.*
Sup. Actor: Ed Begley, *Sweet Bird of Youth.*
Sup. Actress: Patty Duke, *The Miracle Worker.*
Director: David Lean, *Lawrence of Arabia.*
Picture: *Lawrence of Arabia,* Columbia.
1963
Actor: Sidney Poitier, *Lilies of the Field.*
Actress: Patricia Neal, *Hud.*
Sup. Actor: Melvyn Douglas, *Hud.*
Sup. Actress: Margaret Rutherford, *The V.I.P.s.*
Director: Tony Richardson, *Tom Jones.*
Picture: *Tom Jones,* Woodfall Prod., UA-Lopert Pictures.
1964
Actor: Rex Harrison, *My Fair Lady.*
Actress: Julie Andrews, *Mary Poppins.*
Sup. Actor: Peter Ustinov, *Topkapi.*
Sup. Actress: Lila Kedrova, *Zorba the Greek.*
Director: George Cukor, *My Fair Lady.*
Picture: *My Fair Lady,* Warner Bros.
1965
Actor: Lee Marvin, *Cat Ballou.*
Actress: Julie Christie, *Darling.*
Sup. Actor: Martin Balsam, *A Thousand Clowns.*
Sup. Actress: Shelley Winters, *A Patch of Blue.*
Director: Robert Wise, *The Sound of Music.*
Picture: *The Sound of Music,* 20th Century-Fox.
1966
Actor: Paul Scofield, *A Man for All Seasons.*
Actress: Elizabeth Taylor, *Who's Afraid of Virginia Woolf?*
Sup. Actor: Walter Matthau, *The Fortune Cookie.*

Sup. Actress: Sandy Dennis, *Who's Afraid of Virginia Woolf?*
Director: Fred Zinnemann, *A Man for All Seasons.*
Picture: *A Man for All Seasons,* Columbia.

1967

Actor: Rod Steiger, *In the Heat of the Night.*
Actress: Katharine Hepburn, *Guess Who's Coming to Dinner.*
Sup. Actor: George Kennedy, *Cool Hand Luke.*
Sup. Actress: Estelle Parsons, *Bonnie and Clyde.*
Director: Mike Nichols, *The Graduate.*
Picture: *In the Heat of the Night.*

1968

Actor: Cliff Robertson, *Charly.*
Actress: Katharine Hepburn, *The Lion in Winter;* Barbra Streisand, *Funny Girl* (tie).
Sup. Actor: Jack Albertson, *The Subject Was Roses.*
Sup. Actress: Ruth Gordon, *Rosemary's Baby.*
Director: Sir Carol Reed, *Oliver!*
Picture: *Oliver!*

1969

Actor: John Wayne, *True Grit.*
Actress: Maggie Smith, *The Prime of Miss Jean Brodie.*
Sup. Actor: Gig Young, *They Shoot Horses, Don't They?*
Sup. Actress: Goldie Hawn, *Cactus Flower.*
Director: John Schlesinger, *Midnight Cowboy.*
Picture: *Midnight Cowboy.*

1970

Actor: George C. Scott, *Patton* (refused).
Actress: Glenda Jackson, *Women in Love.*
Sup. Actor: John Mills, *Ryan's Daughter.*
Sup. Actress: Helen Hayes, *Airport.*
Director: Franklin Schaffner, *Patton.*
Picture: *Patton.*

1971

Actor: Gene Hackman, *The French Connection.*
Actress: Jane Fonda, *Klute.*
Sup. Actor: Ben Johnson, *The Last Picture Show.*
Sup. Actress: Cloris Leachman, *The Last Picture Show.*
Director: William Friedkin, *The French Connection.*
Picture: *The French Connection.*

1972

Actor: Marlon Brando, *The Godfather* (refused).
Actress: Liza Minnelli, *Cabaret.*
Sup. Actor: Joel Grey, *Cabaret.*
Sup. Actress: Eileen Heckart, *Butterflies are Free.*
Director: Bob Fosse, *Cabaret.*
Picture: *The Godfather.*

1973

Actor: Jack Lemmon, *Save the Tiger.*
Actress: Glenda Jackson, *A Touch of Class.*
Sup. Actor: John Houseman, *The Paper Chase.*
Sup. Actress: Tatum O'Neal, *Paper Moon.*
Director: George Roy Hill, *The Sting.*
Picture: *The Sting.*

1974

Actor: Art Carney, *Harry and Tonto.*
Actress: Ellen Burstyn, *Alice Doesn't Live Here Anymore.*
Sup. Actor: Robert DeNiro, *The Godfather, Part II.*
Sup. Actress: Ingrid Bergman, *Murder on the Orient Express.*
Director: Francis Ford Coppola, *The Godfather, Part II.*
Picture: *The Godfather, Part II.*

1975

Actor: Jack Nicholson, *One Flew Over the Cuckoo's Nest.*
Actress: Louise Fletcher, *One Flew Over the Cuckoo's Nest.*
Sup. Actor: George Burns, *The Sunshine Boys.*
Sup. Actress: Lee Grant, *Shampoo.*
Director: Milos Forman, *One Flew Over the Cuckoo's Nest.*
Picture: *One Flew Over the Cuckoo's Nest.*

1976

Actor: Peter Finch, *Network.*
Actress: Faye Dunaway, *Network.*
Sup. Actor: Jason Robards, *All the President's Men.*
Sup. Actress: Beatrice Straight, *Network.*
Director: John G. Avildsen, *Rocky.*
Picture: *Rocky.*

1977

Actor: Richard Dreyfuss, *The Goodbye Girl.*
Actress: Diane Keaton, *Annie Hall.*
Sup. Actor: Jason Robards, *Julia.*
Sup. Actress: Vanessa Redgrave, *Julia.*
Director: Woody Allen, *Annie Hall.*
Picture: *Annie Hall.*

1978

Actor: Jon Voight, *Coming Home.*
Actress: Jane Fonda, *Coming Home.*
Sup. Actor: Christopher Walken, *The Deer Hunter.*
Sup. Actress: Maggie Smith, *California Suite.*
Director: Michael Cimino, *The Deer Hunter.*
Picture: *The Deer Hunter.*

1979

Actor: Dustin Hoffman, *Kramer vs. Kramer.*
Actress: Sally Field, *Norma Rae.*
Sup. Actor: Melvyn Douglas, *Being There.*
Sup. Actress: Meryl Streep, *Kramer vs. Kramer.*
Director: Robert Benton, *Kramer vs. Kramer.*
Picture: *Kramer vs. Kramer.*

1980

Actor: Robert DeNiro, *Raging Bull.*
Actress: Sissy Spacek, *Coal Miner's Daughter.*
Sup. Actor: Timothy Hutton, *Ordinary People.*
Sup. Actress: Mary Steenburgen, *Melvin & Howard.*
Director: Robert Redford, *Ordinary People .*
Picture: *Ordinary People.*

1981

Actor: Henry Fonda, *On Golden Pond.*
Actress: Katharine Hepburn, *On Golden Pond.*
Sup. Actor: John Gielgud, *Arthur.*
Sup. Actress: Maureen Stapleton, *Reds.*
Director: Warren Beatty, *Reds.*
Picture: *Chariots of Fire.*

1982

Actor: Ben Kingsley, *Gandhi.*
Actress: Meryl Streep, *Sophie's Choice.*
Sup. Actor: Louis Gossett, Jr., *An Officer and a Gentleman.*
Sup. Actress: Jessica Lange, *Tootsie.*
Director: Richard Attenborough, *Gandhi.*
Picture: *Gandhi.*

1983

Actor: Robert Duvall, *Tender Mercies.*
Actress: Shirley MacLaine, *Terms of Endearment.*
Supporting Actor: Jack Nicholson, *Terms of Endearment.*
Supporting Actress: Linda Hunt, *The Year of Living Dangerously.*
Director: James L. Brooks, *Terms of Endearment.*
Picture: *Terms of Endearment.*

1984

Actor: F. Murray Abraham, *Amadeus.*
Actress: Sally Field, *Places in the Heart.*
Supporting Actor: Haing S. Ngor, *The Killing Fields.*
Supporting Actress: Peggy Ashcroft, *A Passage to India.*
Director: Milos Forman, *Amadeus.*
Picture: *Amadeus.*

1985

Actor: William Hurt, *Kiss of the Spider Woman.*
Actress: Geraldine Page, *The Trip to Bountiful.*
Supporting Actor: Don Ameche, *Cocoon.*
Supporting Actress: Anjelica Huston, *Prizzi's Honor.*
Director: Sydney Pollack, *Out of Africa.*
Picture: *Out of Africa.*

1986

Actor: Paul Newman, *The Color of Money.*
Actress: Marlee Matlin, *Children of a Lesser God.*
Supporting Actor: Michael Caine, *Hannah and Her Sisters.*
Supporting Actress: Dianne Wiest, *Hannah and Her Sisters.*
Director: Oliver Stone, *Platoon.*
Picture: *Platoon.*

1987

Actor: Michael Douglas, *Wall Street.*
Actress: Cher, *Moonstruck.*
Supporting Actor: Sean Connery, *The Untouchables.*
Supporting Actress: Olympia Dukakis, *Moonstruck.*
Director: Bernardo Bertolucci, *The Last Emperor.*
Picture: *The Last Emperor.*

1988

Actor: Dustin Hoffman, *Rain Man.*
Actress: Jodie Foster, *The Accused.*
Supporting Actor: Kevin Kline, *A Fish Called Wanda.*
Supporting Actress: Geena Davis, *The Accidental Tourist.*
Director: Barry Levinson, *Rain Man.*
Picture: *Rain Man.*

1989

Picture: *Driving Miss Daisy.*
Actor: Daniel Day-Lewis, *My Left Foot.*
Actress: Jessica Tandy, *Driving Miss Daisy.*
Supporting Actor: Denzel Washington, *Glory.*
Supporting Actress: Brenda Fricker, *My Left Foot.*
Director: Oliver Stone, *Born on the Fourth of July.*
Foreign-Language Film: *Cinema Paradiso,* Italy.
Original Screenplay: Tom Schulman, *Dead Poets Society.*
Screenplay Adaptation: Alfred Uhry, *Driving Miss Daisy.*
Cinematography: Freddie Francis, *Glory.*
Editing: David Brenner, Joe Hutshing, *Born on the Fourth of July.*
Original Score: Alan Menken, *The Little Mermaid.*
Original Song: Alan Menken and Howard Ashman, "Under the Sea," *The Little Mermaid.*
Art Direction: Anton Furst and Peter Young, *Batman.*
Costume Design: Phyllis Dalton, *Henry V.*
Sound: Donald O. Mitchell, Gregg C. Rudloff, Elliot Tyson, Russell Williams 2d, *Glory.*

Sound Editing: Ben Burtt, Richard Hymns, *Indiana Jones and the Last Crusade.*

Makeup: Manlio Rocchetti, *Driving Miss Daisy.*

Visual Effects: John Bruno, Dennis Muren, Hoyt Yeatman, Dennis Skotak, *The Abyss.*

Documentary Feature: *Common Threads: Stories from the Quilt.*

Documentary Short Subject: *The Johnstown Flood.*

Short Film, Animated: *Balance.*

Short Film, Live: *Work Experience.*

Honorary Award, for lifetime achievement: Akira Kurosawa.

Jean Hersholt Humanitarian Award: Howard W. Koch.

Gordon E. Sawyer Technical Award: Pierre Angenieux, for zoom lens invention.

Grammy Awards

Source: National Academy of Recording Arts & Sciences

1958
Record: Domenico Modugno, *Nel Blu Dipinto Di Blu (Volare).*
Album: Henry Mancini, *The Music from Peter Gunn.*

1959
Record: Bobby Darin, *Mack the Knife.*
Album: Frank Sinatra, *Come Dance With Me.*

1960
Record: Percy Faith, *Theme From A Summer Place.*
Album: Bob Newhart, *Button Down Mind.*

1961
Record: Henry Mancini, *Moon River.*
Album: Judy Garland, *Judy At Carnegie Hall.*

1962
Record: Tony Bennett, *I Left My Heart in San Francisco.*
Album: Vaughn Meader, *The First Family.*

1963
Record: Henry Mancini, *The Days of Wine and Roses.*
Album: *The Barbra Streisand Album.*

1964
Record: Stan Getz and Astrud Gilberto, *The Girl From Ipanema.*
Album: *Getz/Gilberto.*

1965
Record: Herb Alpert, *A Taste Of Honey.*
Album: Frank Sinatra, *September of My Years.*

1966
Record: Frank Sinatra, *Strangers in the Night.*
Album: Frank Sinatra, *A Man and His Music.*

1967
Record: 5th Dimension, *Up, Up and Away.*
Album: The Beatles, *Sgt. Pepper's Lonely Hearts Club Band.*

1968
Record: Simon & Garfunkel, *Mrs. Robinson.*
Album: Glen Campbell, *By the Time I Get to Phoenix.*

1969
Record: 5th Dimension, *Aquarius/Let the Sunshine In.*
Album: *Blood, Sweat and Tears.*

1970
Record: Simon & Garfunkel, *Bridge Over Troubled Water.*
Album: *Bridge Over Troubled Water.*

1971
Record: Carole King, *It's Too Late.*
Album: Carole King, *Tapestry.*

1972
Record: Roberta Flack, *The First Time Ever I Saw Your Face.*
Album: *The Concert For Bangla Desh.*

1973
Record: Roberta Flack, *Killing Me Softly with His Song.*
Album: Stevie Wonder, *Innervisions.*

1974
Record: Olivia Newton-John, *I Honestly Love You.*
Album: Stevie Wonder, *Fulfillingness' First Finale.*

1975
Record: Captain & Tennille, *Love Will Keep Us Together.*
Album: Paul Simon, *Still Crazy After All These Years.*

1976
Record: George Benson, *This Masquerade.*
Album: Stevie Wonder, *Songs in the Key of Life.*

1977
Record: Eagles, *Hotel California.*
Album: Fleetwood Mac, *Rumours.*

1978
Record: Billy Joel, *Just the Way You Are.*
Album: Bee Gees, *Saturday Night Fever.*

1979
Record: The Doobie Brothers, *What a Fool Believes.*
Album: Billy Joel, *52nd Street.*

1980
Record: Christopher Cross, *Sailing.*
Album: Christopher Cross, *Christopher Cross.*

1981
Record: Kim Carnes, *Bette Davis Eyes.*
Album: John Lennon, Yoko Ono, *Double Fantasy.*

1982
Record: Toto, *Rosanna.*
Album: Toto, *Toto IV.*

1983
Record: Michael Jackson, *Beat It.*
Album: Michael Jackson, *Thriller.*

1984
Record: Tina Turner, *What's Love Got to Do With It.*
Album: Lionel Richie, *Can't Slow Down.*

1985
Record: USA for Africa, *We Are the World.*
Album: Phil Collins, *No Jacket Required.*

1986
Record: Steve Winwood, *Higher Love.*
Album: Paul Simon, *Graceland.*

1987
Record: Paul Simon, *Graceland.*
Album: U2, *The Joshua Tree.*

1988
Record: Bobby McFerrin, *Don't Worry, Be Happy.*
Album: George Michael, *Faith.*

1989
Record: Bette Midler, *Wind Beneath My Wings.*
Album: Bonnie Raitt, *Nick of Time.*
Male Pop Vocal: Michael Bolton, *How Am I Supposed to Live Without You?*
Female Pop Vocal: Bonnie Raitt, *Nick of Time.*
Duo or Group Pop Vocal: Linda Ronstadt and Aaron Neville, *Don't Know Much.*
Pop Instrumental: Neville Brothers, *Healing Chant.*
New Artist: Milli Vanilli.
Male Rock Vocal: Don Henley, *The End of the Innocence.*
Female Rock Vocal: Bonnie Raitt, *Nick of Time.*
Duo or Group Rock Vocal: The Traveling Wilburys, *The Traveling Wilburys, Vol. 1.*
Rock Instrumental: Jeff Beck's Guitar Shop with Terry Bozzio and Tony Humas.
Rap: Young MC, *Bust a Move.*
Male Country Vocal: Lyle Lovett, *Lyle Lovett and His Large Band.*
Female Country Vocal: K.D. Laing, *Absolute Torch and Twang.*
Duo or Group Country Vocal: Nitty Gritty Dirt Band, *Will the Circle Be Unbroken? Vol. 2.*
Country Vocal Collaboration: Hank Williams Jr. and Hank Williams Sr., *There's a Tear in My Beer.*
Country Instrumental: Randy Scruggs, *Amazing Grace.*
Bluegrass: Bruce Hornsby and the Nitty Gritty Dirt Band, *The Valley Road.*
Male R&B Vocal: Bobby Brown, *Every Little Step.*
Female R&B Vocal: Anita Baker, *Giving You the Best That I Got.*
Duo or Group R&B: Soul II Soul, *Back to Life.*
R&B Instrumental: Soul II Soul, *African Dance.*
Male Jazz Vocal: Harry Connick Jr., *When Harry Met Sally . . .*
Female Jazz Vocal: Ruth Brown, *Blues on Broadway.*
Duo or Group Jazz Vocal: Dr. John and Rickie Lee Jones, *Makin' Whoopee.*
Solo Jazz Instrumental: Miles Davis, *Aura.*
Group Jazz Instrumental: Miles Davis, *Aura.*
Big Band Jazz Instrumental: Chick Corea, *Chick Corea Akoustic Band.*
New Age: Peter Gabriel, *Passion—Music for the Last Temptation of Christ.*
Classical Album: Emerson String Quartet, *Bartok: 6 String Quartets.*
Orchestral Recording: Leonard Bernstein, New York Philharmonic, *Mahler: Symphony No. 3 in D Minor.*
Chamber Music: Emerson String Quartet, *Bartok: 6 String Quartets.*
Solo Classical Vocalist: Dawn Upshaw, *Summer of 1915.*
Opera: James Levine, Metropolitan Opera Orchestra, *Wagner: Die Walküre.*
Musical Original Cast Album: *Jerome Robbins' Broadway.*
Comedy: Prof. Peter Schickele, The Greater Hoople Area Off-Season Philharmonic, *P.D.Q. Bach: 1712 Overture and Other Musical Assaults.*
Non-Musical Spoken Word: Gilda Radner, *It's Always Something.*
Children: Tanya Goodman, *The Rock-a-Bye Collection, Vol. 1.*

NOTED PERSONALITIES

Widely Known Americans of the Present

Statesmen, authors of nonfiction, military men, and other prominent persons not listed in other categories; as of mid-1990.

Name (Birthplace)	Birthdate	Name (Birthplace)	Birthdate
Arledge, Roone (Forest Hills, N.Y.)	7/8/31	Gephardt, Richard (St. Louis, Mo.)	1/31/41
Anderson, Jack (Long Beach, Cal.)	10/19/22	Gingrich, Newt (Harrisburg, Pa.)	6/17/43
Armstrong, Neil (Wapakoneta, Oh.)	8/5/30	Ginsberg, Allen (Paterson, N.J.)	6/3/21
Armstrong, William L. (Fremont, Neb.)	1937	Glenn, John (Cambridge, Oh.)	7/18/21
Ash, Mary Kay (Hot Wells, Tex.)	—	Goldwater, Barry M. (Phoenix, Ariz.)	1/1/09
Aspin, Les (Milwaukee, Wis.)	7/21/38	Goodman, Ellen (Newton, Mass.)	4/11/41
Baker, James A. (Houston, Tex.)	4/28/30	Gore, Albert Jr. (Washington, D.C.)	3/31/48
Baker, Russell (Loudoun Co., Va.)	8/14/25	Gottlieb, Robert A. (New York)	4/9/31
Barnes, Clive (London, England)	5/13/27	Gould, Stephen Jay (New York, N.Y.)	9/10/41
Barthelmy, Sidney K. (New Orleans, La.)	3/17/42	Graham, Billy (Charlotte, N.C.)	11/7/18
Bennett, William J. (Salem, Oh.)	5/4/44	Graham, Katharine (New York, N.Y.)	6/16/17
Bentsen, Lloyd (Mission, Tex.)	2/11/21	Gramm, Phil (Ft. Bennington, Ga.)	7/8/42
Biden, Joseph R. Jr. (Scranton, Pa.)	11/20/42	Gray, William H. 3d (Baton Rouge, La.)	8/20/41
Blackmun, Harry (Nashville, Ill.)	11/12/08	Greenfield, Meg (Seattle, Wash.)	12/27/30
Blass, Bill (Ft. Wayne, Ind.)	6/22/22	Greenspan, Alan (New York, N.Y.)	3/6/26
Bombeck, Erma (Dayton, Oh.)	2/21/27	Gumble, Bryant (New Orleans, La.)	9/29/48
Boorstin, Daniel (Atlanta, Ga.)	10/1/14	Halberstam, David (New York, N.Y.)	4/10/34
Bradlee, Ben (Boston, Mass.)	8/26/21	Hammer, Armand (New York, N.Y.)	5/21/98
Bradley, Bill (Crystal City, Mo.)	7/28/43	Harvey, Paul (Tulsa, Okla.)	9/4/18
Bradley, Ed (Philadelphia, Pa.)	6/22/41	Hatch, Orrin (Homestead, Pa.)	3/22/34
Bradley, Thomas (Calvert, Tex.)	12/29/17	Hatfield, Mark O. (Dallas, Ore.)	7/12/22
Brady, Nicholas (New York, N.Y.)	4/11/30	Heflin, Howell (Poulan, Ga.)	6/19/21
Brennan, William J. (Newark, N.J.)	4/25/06	Hefner, Hugh (Chicago, Ill.)	4/9/26
Breslin, Jimmy (Jamaica, N.Y.)	10/17/30	Helms, Jesse (Monroe, N.C.)	10/18/21
Brinkley, David (Wilmington, N.C.)	7/10/20	Heloise (Waco, Tex.)	4/15/51
Broder, David (Chicago Heights, Ill.)	9/11/29	Hills, Carla (Los Angeles, Cal.)	1/3/34
Brody, Jane (Brooklyn, N.Y.)	5/19/41	Hollings, Ernest (Charleston, S.C.)	1/1/22
Brokaw, Tom (Webster, S. Dak.)	2/6/40	Iacocca, Lee A. (Allentown, Pa.)	10/15/24
Brothers, Joyce (New York, N.Y.)	9/20/28	Icahn, Carl (New York, N.Y.)	1936
Brown, Helen Gurley (Green Forest, Ark.)	2/18/22	Inouye, Daniel K. (Honolulu, Ha.)	9/7/24
Buchanan, Pat (Washington, D.C.)	11/2/38	Jackson, Jesse (Greenville, S.C.)	10/8/41
Buchwald, Art (Mt. Vernon, N.Y.)	10/20/25	Jennings, Peter (Toronto, Ont.)	8/29/38
Buckley, William F. (New York, N.Y.)	11/24/25	Johnson, Lady Bird (Karnack, Tex.)	12/22/12
Bumpers, Dale (Charleston, Ark.)	8/12/25	Jordan, Barbara (Houston, Tex.)	2/21/36
Buscaglia, Leo (Los Angeles, Cal.)	3/31/24	Kael, Pauline (Petaluma, Calif.)	6/19/19
Bush, Barbara (Rye, N.Y.)	6/8/25	Karan, Donna (Forest Hills, N.Y.)	10/2/48
Byrd, Robert (N. Wilkesboro, N.C.)	11/20/17	Kassebaum, Nancy (Topeka, Kan.)	7/29/32
Canby, Vincent (Chicago, Ill.)	7/27/24	Keillor, Garrison (Anoka, Minn.)	8/7/42
Carter, Jimmy (Plains, Ga.)	10/1/24	Kemp, Jack (Los Angeles, Cal.)	7/13/35
Carter, Rosalynn (Plains, Ga.)	8/18/27	Kennedy, Anthony (Sacramento, Cal.)	7/23/36
Chancellor, John (Chicago, Ill.)	7/14/27	Kennedy, Edward M. (Brookline, Mass.)	2/22/32
Chavez, Cesar (Yuma, Ariz.)	3/31/27	Kennedy, Rose (Boston, Mass.)	7/22/90
Cheney, Richard B. (Lincoln, Neb.)	1/30/41	Kerr, Walter (Evanston, Ill.)	7/8/13
Child, Julia (Pasadena, Cal.)	8/15/12	King, Coretta Scott (Marion, Ala.)	4/27/27
Chisholm, Shirley (Brooklyn, N.Y.)	11/30/24	King, Larry (Brooklyn, N.Y.)	11/19/34
Chung, Connie (Washington, D.C.)	8/20/46	Kirkland, Lane (Camden, S.C.)	3/12/22
Claiborne, Craig (Sunflower, Miss.)	9/4/20	Kirkpatrick, Jeane (Duncan, Okla.)	11/19/26
Clark, William (Dallas, Tex.)	12/11/30	Kissinger, Henry (Fuerth, Germany)	5/27/23
Collins, Martha (Shelby Cty, Ky.)	12/7/36	Klein, Calvin (New York, N.Y.)	11/19/42
Commager, Henry Steele (Pittsburgh, Pa.)	10/25/02	Koch, Edward I. (New York, N.Y.)	12/12/24
Cooney, Joan Ganz (Phoenix, Ariz.)	10/30/29	Koop, C. Everett (Brooklyn, N.Y.)	10/14/16
Cosell, Howard (Winston-Salem, N.C.)	3/25/20	Koppel, Ted (Lancashire, Eng.)	2/8/40
Cousins, Norman (Union Hill, N.J.)	6/24/12	Kuhn, Maggie (Buffalo, N.Y.)	1905
Cranston, Alan (Palo Alto, Cal.)	6/19/14	Kunstler, William (New York, N.Y.)	7/7/19
Crist, Judith (New York, N.Y.)	5/22/22	Landers, Ann (Sioux City, Ia.)	7/4/18
Cronkite, Walter (St. Joseph, Mo.)	11/4/16	Lauder, Estee (New York, N.Y.)	—
Cuomo, Mario (Queens, N.Y.)	6/15/32	Lauren, Ralph (Bronx, N.Y.)	10/14/39
Daley, Richard M. (Chicago, Ill.)	4/24/42	Leahy, Patrick (Montpelier, Vt.)	3/31/40
Dellums, Ronald (Oakland, Cal.)	11/24/35	Lear, Norman (New Haven, Conn.)	7/27/22
Dingell, John D. Jr. (Colorado Spngs., Col.)	7/8/26	Lehrer, Jim (Wichita, Kan.)	5/19/34
Dinkins, David (Trenton, N.J.)	7/10/27	Lindbergh, Anne Morrow (Englewood, N.J.)	1906
Dodd, Christopher (Willimantic, Conn.)	5/27/44	Lorenzo, Frank (New York, N.Y.)	5/19/40
Dole, Elizabeth (Salisbury, N.C.)	7/29/36	Lott, Trent (Grenada, Miss.)	10/9/41
Dole, Robert (Russell, Kan.)	7/22/23	Lugar, Richard G. (Indianapolis, Ind.)	4/4/32
Domenici, Pete (Albuquerque, N.M.)	5/7/32	Lukas, J. Anthony (New York, N.Y.)	4/25/33
Donaldson, Sam (El Paso, Tex.)	3/11/34	MacNeil, Robert (Montreal, Que.)	1/19/31
Drew, Elizabeth (Cincinnati, Oh.)	11/16/35	Marshall, Thurgood (Baltimore, Md.)	7/2/08
Dukakis, Michael S. (Boston, Mass.)	11/3/33	Martinez, Bob (Tampa, Fla.)	12/25/34
Dymally, Mervyn (Trinidad, W.I.)	5/12/26	Metzenbaum, Howard (Cleveland, Oh.)	6/4/17
Eisner, Michael (New York, N.Y.)	3/7/42	Michel, Robert H. (Peoria, Ill.)	3/2/23
Ephron, Nora (New York, N.Y.)	5/19/41	Mikulski, Barbara (Baltimore, Md.)	7/20/36
Falwell, Jerry (Lynchburg, Va.)	8/11/33	Mitchell, George (Waterville, Me.)	8/20/33
Feinstein, Dianne (San Francisco, Cal.)	6/22/33	Mondale, Walter (Ceylon, Minn.)	1/5/28
Feldstein, Martin (New York, N.Y.)	11/25/39	Mosbacher, Robert (Mt. Vernon, N.Y.)	3/11/27
Ferraro, Geraldine (Newburgh, N.Y.)	8/26/35	Moyers, Bill (Hugo, Okla.)	6/5/34
Fitzwater, Marlin (Salina, Kan.)	11/24/42	Moynihan, Daniel P. (Tulsa, Okla.)	3/16/27
Florio, James J. (New York, N.Y.)	8/29/37	Mudd, Roger (Washington, D.C.)	2/9/28
Foley, Thomas S. (Spokane, Wash.)	3/6/29	Murdoch, Rupert (Melbourne, Austr.)	5/11/31
Ford, Betty (Chicago, Ill.)	4/8/18	Nader, Ralph (Winsted, Conn.)	2/27/34
Ford, Gerald R. (Omaha, Neb.)	7/14/13	Nidetch, Jean (Brooklyn, N.Y.)	10/12/23
Friedan, Betty (Peoria, Ill.)	2/4/21	Nixon, Pat (Ely, Nev.)	3/16/12
Friedman, Milton (Brooklyn, N.Y.)	7/31/12	Nixon, Richard (Yorba Linda, Cal.)	1/9/13
Galbraith, John Kenneth (Ontario, Can.)	10/15/08	North, Oliver (San Antonio, Tex.)	10/7/43

336

Norton, Eleanor Holmes (Washington, D.C.)	6/13/37
Nunn, Sam (Perry, Ga.)	9/8/38
O'Connor, Cardinal John (Phila., Pa.)	1/15/20
O'Connor, Sandra Day (nr. Duncan, Ariz.)	3/26/30
Onassis, Jacqueline (Southampton, N.Y.)	7/28/29
O'Neill, Thomas P. (Cambridge, Mass.)	12/9/12
Packwood, Bob (Portland, Ore.)	9/11/32
Paley, William S. (Chicago, Ill.)	9/28/01
Pauley, Jane (Indianapolis, Ind.)	10/31/50
Pauling, Linus (Portland, Ore.)	2/28/01
Perot, H. Ross ( )	1930
Pickens, T. Boone (Holdenville, Okla.)	5/22/28
Pickering, Thomas (Orange, N.J.)	11/5/31
Plimpton, George (New York, N.Y.)	3/18/27
Podhoretz, Norman (New York, N.Y.)	1/16/30
Porter, Sylvia (Patchogue, N.Y.)	6/18/13
Poussaint, Alvin F. (New York, N.Y.)	5/15/34
Powell, Colin (New York, N.Y.)	4/5/37
Quayle, Dan (Indianapolis, Ind.)	2/4/47
Quinn, Jane Bryant (Niagara Falls, N.Y.)	2/5/39
Rangel, Charles (New York, N.Y.)	6/11/30
Rather, Dan (Wharton, Tex.)	10/31/31
Reagan, Nancy (New York, N.Y.)	7/6/23
Reagan, Ronald (Tampico, Ill.)	2/6/11
Reasoner, Harry (Dakota City, Ia.)	4/17/23
Rehnquist, William (Milwaukee, Wis.)	10/1/24
Rich, Frank (Washington, D.C.)	6/2/49
Ride, Sally K. (Encino, Calif.)	1952
Roberts, Oral (nr. Ada, Okla.)	1/24/18
Robertson, Pat (Lexington, Va.)	3/22/30
Rockefeller, David (New York, N.Y.)	6/12/15
Rockefeller, John D. 4th "Jay" (New York, N.Y.)	6/18/37
Rockefeller, Laurance S. (New York, N.Y.)	5/26/10
Roemer, Charles E. "Buddy" (Shreveport, La.)	10/4/43
Rooney, Andy (Albany, N.Y.)	1/14/19
Rostenkowski, Dan (Chicago, Ill.)	1/2/28
Rozelle, Pete (S. Gate, Calif.)	3/1/26
Rukeyser, Louis (New York, N.Y.)	1/30/33
Safer, Morley (Toronto, Ontario)	11/8/31
Safire, William (New York, N.Y.)	12/17/29
Sagan, Carl (New York, N.Y.)	11/9/34
Salk, Jonas (New York, N.Y.)	10/28/14
Sawyer, Diane (Glasgow, Ky.)	12/22/45
Scalia, Antonin (Trenton, N.J.)	3/11/36
Schlesinger, Arthur Jr. (Columbus, Oh.)	10/15/17
Schroeder, Patricia (Portland, Ore.)	7/30/40
Schuller, Robert (Alton, Ia.)	9/16/26
Scowcroft, Brent (Ogden, Ut.)	3/19/25
Sculley, John (New York, N.Y.)	4/6/39
Seaborg, Glenn T. (Ishpeming, Mich.)	4/19/12
Shanker, Albert (New York, N.Y.)	9/14/28
Shriver, Maria (Chicago, Ill.)	11/6/55
Shultz, George P. (New York, N.Y.)	12/13/20
Silverstein, Shel (Chicago, Ill.)	1932
Simmons, Richard (New Orleans, La.)	7/12/48
Simon, Paul (Eugene, Ore.)	11/29/28
Simpson, Alan K. (Cody, Wyo.)	9/2/31
Smith, Liz (Ft. Worth, Tex.)	2/2/23
Solarz, Stephen J. (New York, N.Y.)	9/2/40
Spock, Benjamin (New Haven, Conn.)	5/2/03
Stahl, Lesley (Lynn, Mass.)	12/16/41
Steinbrenner, George (Rocky River, Oh.)	7/4/30
Steinem, Gloria (Toledo, Oh.)	3/25/34
Stern, David J. (New York, N.Y.)	9/22/42
Stevens, John Paul (Chicago, Ill.)	4/20/20
Sullivan, Louis (Atlanta, Ga.)	11/3/33
Sulzberger, Arthur Ochs (New York, N.Y.)	2/5/26
Sununu, John H. (Havana, Cuba)	7/2/39
Terkel, Studs (New York, N.Y.)	5/16/12
Thornburgh, Dick (Pittsburgh, Pa.)	7/16/32
Thurmond, J. Strom (Edgefield, S.C.)	12/5/02
Tinker, Grant (Stamford, Conn.)	1/11/26
Tisch, Laurence (New York, N.Y.)	3/15/23
Toland, John (LaCrosse, Wis.)	6/29/12
Trillin, Calvin (Kansas City, Mo.)	12/5/35
Truman, Margaret (Independence, Mo.)	2/17/24
Trump, Donald (New York, N.Y.)	1946
Turner, Ted (Cincinnati, Oh.)	1938
Udall, Morris K. (St. Johns, Ariz.)	6/15/22
Ueberroth, Peter (Chicago, Ill.)	9/2/37
Van Buren, Abigail (Sioux City, Ia.)	7/4/18
Wallace, George (Clio, Ala.)	8/25/19
Wallace, Mike (Brookline, Mass.)	5/9/18
Walters, Barbara (Boston, Mass.)	9/25/31
Walton, Sam (Kingfisher, Okla.)	1920
Webster, William H. (St. Louis, Mo.)	3/6/24
Weicker, Lowell (Paris, France)	5/16/31
Wenner, Jann (New York, N.Y.)	1/7/46
Westheimer, Ruth (Germany)	1928
White, Bill (Lakewood, Fla.)	1/28/34
White, Byron (Ft. Collins, Col.)	6/8/17
Wicker, Tom (Hamlet, N.C.)	6/18/26
Wiesel, Elie (Sighet, Transyl.)	9/30/28
Wilder, L. Douglas (Richmond, Va.)	1/17/31
Will, George (Champaign, Ill.)	1941
Wright, James C. Jr. (Ft. Worth, Tex.)	12/22/22
Yard, Molly (Shanghai, China)	
Young, Andrew (New Orleans, La.)	3/12/32
Young, Coleman (Tuscaloosa, Ala.)	5/24/18
Ziegler, John (Grosse Point, Mich.)	2/9/34

Noted Black Americans

Names of black athletes and entertainers are not included here as they are listed elsewhere in The World Almanac.

The Rev. Dr. Ralph David Abernathy, 1926-1990, organizer, 1957, and president, 1968, of the Southern Christian Leadership Conference.

Crispus Attucks, c. 1723-1770, agitator who led group that precipitated the "Boston Massacre," Mar. 5, 1770.

James Baldwin, 1924-1987, author, playwright; *The Fire Next Time, Blues for Mister Charlie, Just Above My Head.*

Benjamin Banneker, 1731-1806, inventor, astronomer, mathematician, and gazetteer; served on commission that surveyed and laid out Washington, D. C.

Imamu Amiri Baraka, b. LeRoi Jones, 1934, poet, playwright.

James P. Beckwourth, 1798-c. 1867, western fur-trader, scout, after whom Beckwourth Pass in northern California is named.

Dr. Mary McCleod Bethune, 1875-1955, adviser to presidents Roosevelt, Truman; division administrator, Natl. Youth Administration, 1935; founder, pres. Bethune-Cookman College.

Henry Blair, 19th century, obtained patents (believed the first issued to a black) for a corn-planter, 1834, and for a cotton-planter, 1836.

Julian Bond, b. 1940, civil rights leader first elected to the Georgia state legislature, 1965; helped found Student Nonviolent Coordinating Committee.

Edward Bouchet, 1852-1918, first black to earn a Ph.D., Yale, 1876, at a U. S. university; first black elected to Phi Beta Kappa.

Thomas Bradley, b. 1917, elected mayor of Los Angeles, 1973.

Andrew F. Brimmer, b. 1926, first black member, 1966, Federal Reserve Board.

Edward W. Brooke, b. 1919, attorney general, 1962, of Massachusetts; first black elected to U. S. Senate, 1967, since 19th century Reconstruction.

Gwendolyn Brooks, b. 1917, poet, novelist; first black to win a Pulitzer Prize, 1950, for *Annie Allen.*

Sterling A. Brown, 1901-1989, poet, literature professor; helped establish Afro-American literary criticism.

William Wells Brown, 1815-1884, novelist, dramatist; first American black to publish a novel.

Dr. Ralph Bunche, 1904-1971, first black to win the Nobel Peace Prize, 1950; undersecretary of the UN, 1950.

Sherian Grace Cadoria, b. 1940, brigadier general; highest ranking black woman in U.S. armed forces as of 1990.

Alexa Canady, b. 1950, first black woman neurosurgeon in U.S.

George E. Carruthers, b. 1940, physicist developed the Apollo 16 lunar surface ultraviolet camera/spectograph.

George Washington Carver, 1861-1943, botanist, chemurgist, and educator; his extensive experiments in soil building and plant diseases revolutionized the economy of the South.

Charles Waddell Chestnutt, 1858-1932, author known primarily for his short stories, including *The Conjure Woman.*

Shirley Chisholm, b. 1924, first black woman elected to House of Representatives, Brooklyn, N. Y., 1968.

Bishop Philip R. Cousin, b. 1933, Pres., Natl. Council of Churches of Christ in the USA, 1985-.

Countee Cullen, 1903-1946, poet; won many literary prizes.

Lt. Gen. Benjamin O. Davis Jr. b. 1912, West Point, 1936, first black Air Force general, 1954.

Brig. Gen. Benjamin O. Davis Sr., 1877-1970, first black general, 1940, in U. S. Army.

William L. Dawson, 1886-1970, Illinois congressman, first black chairman of a major House of Representatives committee.

David Dinkins, b. 1927, first black mayor of New York City, 1990-.

Isaiah Dorman, 19th century, U. S. Army interpreter, killed with Custer, 1876, at Battle of the Little Big Horn.

Aaron Douglas, 1900-1979, painter; called father of black American art.

Frederick Douglass, 1817-1895, author, editor, orator, diplomat; edited the abolitionist weekly, The North Star, in Rochester, N. Y.; U.S. minister and consul general to Haiti.

Dr. Charles Richard Drew, 1904-1950, pioneer in development of blood banks; director of American Red Cross blood donor project in World War II.

William Edward Burghardt Du Bois, 1868-1963, historian, sociologist; a founder of the National Association for the Advancement of Colored People (NAACP), 1909, and founder of its magazine The Crisis; author, The Souls of Black Folk.

Paul Laurence Dunbar, 1872-1906, poet, novelist; won fame with Lyrics of Lowly Life, 1896.

Jean Baptiste Point du Sable, c. 1750-1818, pioneer trader and first settler of Chicago, 1779.

Marian Wright Edelman, b. 1939, founder, pres. of Children's Defense Fund.

Ralph Ellison, b. 1914, novelist, essayist, Invisible Man.

James Farmer, b. 1920, a founder of the Congress of Racial Equality, 1942; asst. secretary, Dept. of HEW, 1969.

Henry O. Flipper, 1856-1940, first black to graduate, 1877, from West Point.

Charles Fuller, b. 1939, Pulitzer Prize-winning playwright; A Soldier's Play.

Mary Hatwood Futrell, b. 1940, president, Natl. Education Assn., 1983-.

Marcus Garvey, 1887-1940, founded Universal Negro Improvement Assn., 1911.

Kenneth Gibson, b. 1932, Newark, N.J., mayor, 1970-1986.

Charles Gordone, b. 1925, won 1970 Pulitzer Prize in Drama, with No Place to Be Somebody.

Vice Adm. Samuel L. Gravely Jr. b. 1922, first black admiral, 1971, served in World War II, Korea, and Vietnam; commander, Third Fleet.

William H. Gray 3d, b. 1941, U.S. representative from Pa., 1979—; chairman, Budget Committee, 1985-88; chairman, House Democratic Caucus, 1988-89; majority whip, 1989-.

Ewart Guinier, 1911-1990, trade unionist, first chairman of Harvard Univ.'s Department of Afro-American Studies.

Alex Haley, b. 1921, Pulitzer Prize-winning author; Roots, The Autobiography of Malcolm X.

Jupiter Hammon, c. 1720-1800, poet; the first black American to have his works published, 1761.

Lorraine Hansberry, 1930-1965, playwright; won New York Drama Critics Circle Award, 1959, with Raisin in the Sun.

Barbara Harris, b. 1931, first woman Episcopal bishop.

Patricia Roberts Harris, 1924-1985, U. S. ambassador to Luxembourg, 1965-67; secretary; Dept. of HUD, 1977-1979, Dept. of HHS, 1979-1981.

William H. Hastie, 1904-1976 first black federal judge, appointed 1937; governor of Virgin Islands, 1946-49; judge, U.S. Circuit Court of Appeals, 1949.

Chester Himes, 1909-1984, novelist, Cotton Comes to Harlem.

Matthew A. Henson, 1866-1955, member of Peary's 1909 expedition to the North Pole; placed U.S. flag at the Pole.

Dr. William A. Hinton, 1883-1959, developed the Hinton and Davies-Hinton tests for detection of syphilis; first black professor, 1949, at Harvard Medical School.

Benjamin L. Hooks, b. 1925, first black member, 1972-1979, Federal Communications Comm.; exec. dir., NAACP, 1977—.

Nathan I. Huggins, 1927-1989, historian, scholar; Harvard professor from 1980, director of that university's Institute for Afro-American Research from 1981.

Langston Hughes, 1902-1967, poet; story, song lyric author.

Charlayne Hunter-Gault, b. 1942, first black woman admitted to Univ. of Ga., 1961; ran N.Y. Times Harlem Bureau, 1968-1977; broadcast journalist, 1978—.

The Rev. Jesse Jackson, b. 1941, national director, Operation Bread Basket; campaigned for Democratic presidential nomination, 1984, 1988.

Maynard Jackson, b. 1938, elected mayor of Atlanta, 1973.

Gen. Daniel James Jr. 1920-1978, first black 4-star general, 1975; Commander, North American Air Defense Command.

Pvt. Henry Johnson, 1897-1929, the first American decorated by France in World War I with the Croix de Guerre.

James Weldon Johnson, 1871-1938, poet, lyricist, novelist; first black admitted to Florida bar; U.S. consul in Venezuela and Nicaragua.

John H. Johnson, b. 1918, publisher, editor of Ebony, Jet, Ebony Jr. magazines, from 1942.

Barbara Jordan, b. 1936, former congresswoman from Texas; member, House Judiciary Committee.

Vernon E. Jordan, b. 1935, exec. dir. Natl. Urban League, 1972.

Ernest E. Just, 1883-1941, marine biologist, studied egg development; author, Biology of Cell Surfaces, 1941.

Leontine T.C. Kelly, b. 1920, United Methodist bishop; first black woman bishop of a major American denomination, 1989.

The Rev. Dr. Martin Luther King Jr., 1929-1968, led 382-day Montgomery, Ala., boycott that brought 1956 U.S. Supreme Court decision holding segregation on buses unconstitutional; founder, president, Southern Christian Leadership Conference, 1957; won Nobel Peace Prize, 1964.

Lewis H. Latimer, 1848-1928, associate of Edison; supervised installation of first electric street lighting in N.Y.C.

Mickey Leland, 1944-1989, U.S. representative from Texas, 1978 until death; chairman of Congressional Black Caucus; guiding force behind House Select Committee on Hunger, which he chaired from its 1984 founding.

Malcolm X, 1925-1965, leading spokesman for black pride, founded, 1963, Organization of Afro-American Unity.

Thurgood Marshall, b. 1908, first black U.S. solicitor general 1965; first black justice of the U. S. Supreme Court, 1967; as a lawyer led the legal battery that won the historic decision from the Supreme Court declaring racial segregation of public schools unconstitutional, 1954.

Jan Matzeliger, 1852-1889, invented lasting machine, patented 1883, which revolutionized the shoe industry.

Benjamin Mays, 1895-1984, educator, civil rights leader; headed Morehouse College, 1940-1967.

Wade H. McCree Jr., 1920-1987, solicitor general of the U.S., 1977-1981.

Donald E. McHenry, b. 1936, U.S. ambassador to the United Nations, 1979-1981.

Ronald McNair, 1950-1986, physicist, first black astronaut; killed in Challenger explosion.

Dorie Miller, 1919-1943, Navy hero of Pearl Harbor attack; awarded the Navy Cross.

Ernest N. Morial, b. 1929, elected first black mayor of New Orleans, 1977.

Toni Morrison, novelist; Song of Solomon, Tar Baby; won 1988 Pulitzer prize for Beloved.

Willard Motley, 1912-1965, novelist; Knock on Any Door.

Elijah Muhammad, 1897-1975, founded Black Muslims, 1931.

Pedro Alonzo Nino, navigator of the Nina, one of Columbus' 3 ships on his first voyage of discovery to the New World, 1492.

Rosa Parks, b. 1913, Montgomery Ala. Citizen arrested for refusing to move to the back of the bus, Dec. 1, 1955, bringing a 382-day bus boycott led by Martin Luther King Jr.

Frederick D. Patterson, 1901-1988, founder of United Negro College Fund, 1944; Tuskegee Institute's third pres., 1935-1953.

Adam Clayton Powell, 1908-1972, early civil rights leader, congressman, 1945-1969; chairman, House Committee on Education and Labor, 1960-1967.

Colin Powell, b. 1937, first black Natl. Security Advisor, 1987-88; first black chairman of Joint Chiefs of Staff, 1989-.

Joseph H. Rainey, 1832-1887, first black elected to House of Representatives, 1869, from South Carolina.

A. Philip Randolph, 1889-1979, organized the Brotherhood of Sleeping Car Porters, 1925; organizer of 1941 and 1963 March on Washington movements; vice president, AFL-CIO.

Charles Rangel, b. 1930, congressman from N.Y.C. from 1970; member, Ways and Means Committee; chairman, Select Committee on Narcotics Abuse & Control.

Hiram R. Revels, 1822-1901, first black U.S. senator, elected in Mississippi, served 1870-1871.

Lloyd Richards, b. 1922(?), first black to direct a Broadway play, 1959; dean, Yale Univ. School of Drama & artistic director of Yale Repertory Theatre, 1979-1991.

Wilson C. Riles, b. 1917, elected, 1970, California State Superintendent of Public Instruction.

Norbert Rillieux, 1806-1894; invented a vacuum pan evaporator, 1846, revolutionizing the sugar-refining industry.

Paul Robeson, 1898-1976, actor and concert singer, graduated 1st in class at Rutgers, 1918, Phi Beta Kappa; grad. Columbia Univ. law school, 1923; associated with communist causes.

Max Robinson, 1939-1988, TV journalist, first black to anchor network news, 1978.

Carl T. Rowan, b. 1925, prize-winning journalist; director of the U.S. Information Agency, 1964, the first black to sit on the National Security Council; U. S. ambassador to Finland, 1963.

John B. Russwurm, 1799-1851, with Samuel E. Cornish, 1793-1858, founded, 1827, the nation's first black newspaper, Freedom's Journal, in N.Y.C.

Bayard Rustin, 1910-1987, organizer of the 1963 March on Washington; executive director, A. Philip Randolph Institute.

Peter Salem, at the Battle of Bunker Hill, June 17, 1775, shot and killed British commander Maj. John Pitcairn.

Ntozake Shange, b. 1948, writer, For Colored Girls Who Have Considered Suicide/When the Rainbow is Enuf.

Bishop Stephen Spottswood, 1897-1974, board chairman of NAACP, 1961-1974.

The Rev. Leon H. Sullivan, b. 1922, economic development planner, first black on General Motors Bd. of Directors.

Willard Townsend, 1895-1957, organized the United Transport Service Employees, 1935 (redcaps, etc.); vice pres. AFL-CIO.

Sojourner Truth, 1797-1883, born Isabella Baumfree; preacher, abolitionist; raised funds for Union in Civil War; worked for black educational opportunities.

Harriet Tubman, 1823-1913, Underground Railroad conductor served as nurse and spy for Union Army in the Civil War.

Nat Turner, 1800-1831, led the most significant of over 200 slave revolts in U.S., in Southampton, Va.; hanged.

Alice Walker, b. 1944, novelist, essayist, *The Color Purple.*

Booker T. Washington, 1856-1915, founder, 1881, and first president of Tuskegee Institute; author, *Up From Slavery.*

Harold Washington, 1922-1978, first black mayor of Chicago, from 1983 until death.

Dr. Robert C. Weaver, b. 1907, first black member of the U.S. Cabinet, secretary, Dept. of HUD, 1966.

Ida B. Wells (Barnett), 1862-1931, journalist who waged anti-lynching crusade.

Clifton R. Wharton Jr., b. 1926, first black pres. of major U.S. univ.; chancellor, nation's largest univ. system, 8 yrs.; chairman & CEO, country's largest pension fund, 1987—.

Phillis Wheatley, c. 1753-1784, poet; 2d American woman and first black woman to have her works published, 1770.

Bill White, b. 1934, first black baseball league president; named Natl. League head, 1989.

Walter White, 1893-1955, exec. secretary, NAACP, 1931-1955.

L. Douglas Wilder, first black governor, elected Virginia chief executive 1989.

Roy Wilkins, 1901-1981, exec. director, NAACP, 1955-1977.

Dr. Daniel Hale Williams, 1858-1931, performed one of first 2 open-heart operations, 1893; founded Provident, Chicago's first Negro hospital; first black elected a fellow of the American College of Surgeons.

August Wilson, b. 1945, playwright, won 1987 Pulitzer Prize for *Fences,* 1990 Pulitzer for *The Piano Lesson.*

Granville T. Woods, 1856-1910, invented the third-rail system now used in subways, a complex railway telegraph device that helped reduce train accidents, and an automatic air brake.

Dr. Carter G. Woodson, 1875-1950, historian; founded Assn. for the Study of Negro Life and History, 1915, and Journal of Negro History, 1916.

Richard Wright, 1908-1960, novelist; *Native Son, Black Boy.*

Frank Yerby, b. 1916, first best-selling American black novelist; *The Foxes of Harrow, Vixen.*

Andrew Young, b. 1932, civil rights leader, congressman from Georgia, U.S. ambassador to the United Nations, 1977-79; mayor of Atlanta, 1982-.

Whitney M. Young Jr., 1921-1971, exec. director, 1961, National Urban League; author, lecturer, newspaper columnist.

About 5,000 blacks served in the Continental Army during the **American Revolution,** mostly in integrated units, some in all-black combat units. Some 200,000 blacks served in the Union Army during the **Civil War;** 38,000 gave their lives; 22 won the Medal of Honor, the nation's highest award. Of 367,000 blacks in the armed forces during **World War I,** 100,000 served in France. More than 1,000,000 blacks served in the armed forces during **World War II;** all-black fighter and bomber AAF units and infantry divisions gave distinguished service. In 1954 the policy of all-black units was finally abolished. Of 274,937 blacks who served in the armed forces during the **Vietnam War** (1965-1974), 5,681 were killed in combat.

As of Jan., 1989, there were 299 black mayors, 2,882 members of municipal governing boards, 416 state legislators, and 24 U.S. representatives. There were then 7,226 blacks holding elected office in the U.S. and Virgin Islands, an increase of 5.8% over the previous year, according to a survey by the Joint Center for Political Studies, Washington, D.C..

Notable Living American Fiction Writers and Playwrights

Name (Birthplace)	Birthdate
Adams, Alice (Fredericksburg, Va.)	8/14/26
Albee, Edward (Washington, D.C.)	3/12/28
Asimov, Isaac (Petrovichi, Russia)	1/2/20
Auchincloss, Louis (Lawrence, N.Y.)	9/27/17
Barth, John (Cambridge, Md.)	5/27/30
Beattie, Ann (Washington, D.C.)	9/7/47
Bellow, Saul (Quebec, Canada)	7/10/15
Benchley, Peter (New York, N.Y.)	5/8/40
Berger, Thomas (Cincinnati, Oh.)	7/20/24
Blume, Judy (Elizabeth, N.J.)	2/12/38
Bradbury, Ray (Waukegan, Ill.)	8/22/20
Brooks, Gwendolyn (Topeka, Kan.)	6/7/17
Calisher, Hortense (New York, N.Y.)	12/20/11
Clark, Mary Higgins (New York, N.Y.)	12/24/31
Clavell, James (England)	10/10/24
Cleary, Beverly (McMinnville, Ore.)	1916
Connell, Evan S. (Kansas City, Mo.)	8/17/24
Conroy, Pat (Atlanta, Ga.)	10/26/45
Crews, Harry (Alma, Ga.)	6/6/35
Crichton, Michael (Chicago, Ill.)	10/23/42
Dailey, Janet (Storm Lake, Ia.)	5/21/44
De Vries, Peter (Chicago, Ill.)	2/27/10
Didion, Joan (Sacramento, Cal.)	12/5/34
Doctorow, E. L. (New York, N.Y.)	1/6/31
Dunne, John Gregory (Hartford, Conn.)	5/25/32
Elkin, Stanley (New York, N.Y.)	5/11/30
Ellison, Ralph (Oklahoma City, Okla.)	3/1/14
Fast, Howard (New York, N.Y.)	11/11/14
Fox, Paula (New York, N.Y.)	4/22/23
French, Marilyn (New York, N.Y.)	11/21/29
Fuller, Charles (Philadelphia, Pa.)	3/5/39
Gaddis, William (New York, N.Y.)	1922
Geisel, Theodore ("Dr. Seuss," Springfield, Mass.)	3/2/04
Gilroy, Frank (New York, N.Y.)	10/13/25
Godwin, Gail (Birmingham, Ala.)	6/18/37
Gold, Herbert (Cleveland, Oh.)	3/9/24
Goldman, William (Chicago, Ill.)	8/12/31
Gordon, Mary (Long Island, N.Y.)	12/8/49
Grau, Shirley Ann (New Orleans, La.)	7/8/29
Guare, John (New York, N.Y.)	2/5/38
Hailey, Arthur (Luton, England)	4/5/20
Haley, Alex (Ithaca, N.Y.)	8/11/21
Hawkes, John (Stamford, Conn.)	8/17/25
Heller, Joseph (Brooklyn, N.Y.)	5/1/23
Helprin, Mark (New York, N.Y.)	6/28/47
Hersey, John (Tientsin, China)	6/17/14
Hinton, S.E. (Tulsa, Okla.)	1948
Irving, John (Exeter, N.H.)	3/2/42
Jong, Erica (New York, N.Y.)	3/26/42
Kennedy, William (Albany, N.Y.)	1/16/28
Kerr, Jean (Scranton, Pa.)	7/10/23
King, Stephen (Portland, Me.)	9/21/47
Knowles, John (Fairmont, W. Va.)	9/16/26
Kosinski, Jerzy (Lódz, Poland)	6/14/33
Krantz, Judith (New York, N.Y.)	1/9/28
LeGuin, Ursula (Berkeley, Cal.)	10/21/29
L'Engle, Madeleine (New York, N.Y.)	11/29/18
Leonard, Elmore (New Orleans, La.)	10/11/25
Levin, Ira (New York, N.Y.)	8/27/29
Ludlum, Robert (New York, N.Y.)	5/25/27
Lurie, Alison (Chicago, Ill.)	9/3/26
Mailer, Norman (Long Branch, N.J.)	1/31/23
Mamet, David (Chicago, Ill.)	11/30/47
McGuane, Thomas (Wyandotte, Mich.)	12/11/39
McMurtry, Larry (Wichita Falls, Tex.)	6/3/36
Michener, James A. (New York, N.Y.)	2/3/07
Miller, Arthur (New York, N.Y.)	10/17/15
Morris, Wright (Central City, Neb.)	1/6/10
Morrison, Toni (Lorain, Oh.)	
Oates, Joyce Carol (Lockport, N.Y.)	6/16/38
Ozick, Cynthia (New York, N.Y.)	4/17/28
Paley, Grace (New York, N.Y.)	12/11/22
Percy, Walker (Birmingham, Ala.)	5/28/16
Piercy, Marge (Detroit, Mich.)	3/31/36
Potok, Chaim (New York, N.Y.)	2/17/29
Price, Reynolds (Macon, N.C.)	2/1/33
Puzo, Mario (New York, N.Y.)	10/15/20
Pynchon, Thomas (Glen Cove, N.Y.)	5/8/37
Rabe, David (Dubuque, Ia.)	3/10/40
Reed, Ishmael (Chattanooga, Tenn.)	2/22/38
Roth, Henry (Austria-Hungary)	2/8/06
Roth, Philip (Newark, N.J.)	3/19/33
Salinger, J. D. (New York, N.Y.)	1/1/19
Sanders, Lawrence (New York, N.Y.)	1920
Sendak, Maurice (New York, N.Y.)	6/10/28
Shepard, Sam (Ft. Sheridan, Ill.)	11/5/43
Simon, Neil (New York, N.Y.)	7/4/27
Singer, Isaac Bashevis (Radzymin, Poland)	7/14/04
Spillane, Mickey (Brooklyn, N.Y.)	3/9/18
Stegner, Wallace (Lake Mills, Ia.)	2/18/09
Stern, Richard (New York, N.Y.)	2/25/28
Stone, Irving (San Francisco, Cal.)	7/14/03
Stone, Robert (Brooklyn, N.Y.)	8/21/37
Taylor, Peter (Trenton, Tenn.)	1/8/17
Theroux, Paul (Medford, Mass.)	4/10/41
Tyler, Anne (Minneapolis, Minn.)	10/25/41

Name (Birthplace)	Birthdate
Updike, John (Shillington, Pa.)	3/18/32
Uris, Leon (Baltimore, Md.)	8/3/24
Vidal, Gore (West Point, N.Y.)	10/3/25
Vonnegut, Kurt Jr. (Indianapolis, Ind.)	11/11/22
Walker, Alice (Eatonton, Ga.)	1944
Wambaugh, Joseph (East Pittsburgh, Pa.)	1/22/37

Name (Birthplace)	Birthdate
Welty, Eudora (Jackson, Miss.)	4/13/09
Wilson, August (Pittsburgh, Pa.)	4/27/45
Wilson, Lanford (Lebanon, Mo.)	4/13/37
Wolfe, Tom (Richmond, Va.)	3/2/31
Wolff, Tobias (Birmingham, Ala.)	6/19/45
Wouk, Herman (New York, N.Y.)	5/27/15

American Architects and Some of Their Achievements

Max Abramovitz, b. 1908, Avery Fisher Hall, Lincoln Center, N.Y.C.

Henry Bacon, 1866-1924, Lincoln Memorial.

Pietro Belluschi, b. 1899, Juilliard School of Music, Lincoln Center, N.Y.C.

Marcel Breuer, 1902-1981, Whitney Museum of American Art, N.Y.C. (with Hamilton Smith).

Charles Bulfinch, 1763-1844, State House, Boston; Capitol, Wash. D.C.; (part).

Gordon Bunshaft, b. 1909, Lever House, Park Ave, N.Y.C.; Hirshhorn Museum, Wash., D.C.

Daniel H. Burnham, 1846-1912, Union Station, Wash. D.C.; Flatiron, N.Y.C.

Irwin Chanin, 1892-1988, New York City theaters, skyscrapers.

Ralph Adams Cram, 1863-1942, Cathedral of St. John the Divine, N.Y.C.; U.S. Military Academy (part).

R. Buckminster Fuller, 1895-1983, U.S. Pavilion, Expo 67, Montreal (geodesic domes).

Cass Gilbert, 1859-1934, Custom House, Woolworth Bldg., N.Y.C.; Supreme Court bldg., Wash., D.C.

Bertram G. Goodhue, 1869-1924, Capitol, Lincoln, Neb.; St. Thomas, St. Bartholomew, N.Y.C.

Walter Gropius, 1883-1969, Pan Am Building, N.Y.C. (with Pietro Belluschi).

Peter Harrison, 1716-1775, Touro Synagogue, Redwood Library, Newport, R.I.

Wallace K. Harrison, 1895-1981, Metropolitan Opera House, Lincoln Center, N.Y.C.

Thomas Hastings, 1860-1929, Public Library, Frick Mansion, N.Y.C.

James Hoban, 1762-1831, The White House.

Raymond Hood, 1881-1934, Rockefeller Center, N.Y.C. (part); Daily News, N.Y.C.; Tribune, Chicago.

Richard M. Hunt, 1827-1895, Metropolitan Museum, N.Y.C. (part); Natl. Observatory, Wash., D.C.

William Le Baron Jenney, 1832-1907, Home Insurance, Chicago (demolished 1931).

Philip C. Johnson, b. 1906, N.Y. State Theater, Lincoln Center, N.Y.C.

Albert Kahn, 1869-1942, Athletic Club Bldg., General Motors Bldg., Detroit.

Louis Kahn, 1901-1974, Salk Laboratory, La Jolla, Cal.; Yale Art Gallery.

Christopher Grant LaFarge, 1862-1938, Roman Catholic Chapel, West Point.

Benjamin H. Latrobe, 1764-1820, U.S. Capitol (part).

William Lescaze, 1896-1969, Philadelphia Savings Fund Society; Borg-Warner Bldg., Chicago.

Bernard R. Maybeck, 1862-1957, Hearst Hall, Chick House, Univ. of Cal., First Church of Christ Scientist, Berkeley.

Charles F. McKim, 1847-1909, Public Library, Boston, Columbia Univ., N.Y.C. (part).

Charles M. McKim, b. 1920, KUHT-TV Transmitter Building, Houston; Lutheran Church of the Redeemer, Houston.

Ludwig Mies van der Rohe, 1886-1969, Seagram Building, N.Y.C. (with Philip C. Johnson); National Gallery, Berlin.

Robert Mills, 1781-1855, Washington Monument.

Richard J. Neutra, 1892-1970, Mathematics Park, Princeton; Orange Co. Courthouse, Santa Ana, Cal.

Gyo Obata, b. 1923, Natl. Air & Space Mus., Smithsonian Institution; Dallas-Ft. Worth Airport.

Frederick L. Olmsted, 1822-1903, Central Park, N.Y.C.; Fairmount Park, Philadelphia.

I(eoh) M(ing) Pei, b. 1917, National Center for Atmospheric Research, Boulder, Col.; East Wing, Natl. Gallery of Art, Wash., D.C.; Pyramid, The Louvre, Paris.

William Pereira, 1909-1985, Cape Canaveral; Transamerica Bldg., San Francisco.

John Russell Pope, 1874-1937, National Gallery.

George Browne Post, 1837-1913, New York Stock Exchange, Wisconsin state capitol.

John Portman, b. 1924, Peachtree Center, Atlanta.

James Renwick Jr., 1818-1895, Grace Church, St. Patrick's Cathedral, N.Y.C.; Smithsonian, Corcoran Galleries, Wash., D.C.

Henry H. Richardson, 1838-1886, Trinity Church, Boston.

Kevin Roche, b. 1922, Oakland Cal. Museum; Fine Arts Center, U. of Mass.

James Gamble Rogers, 1867-1947, Columbia-Presbyterian Medical Center, N.Y.C.; Northwestern Univ., Chicago.

John Wellborn Root, 1887-1963, Palmolive Building, Chicago; Hotel Statler, Washington; Hotel Tamanaco, Caracas.

Paul Rudolph, b. 1918, Jewitt Art Center, Wellesley College; Art & Architecture Bldg., Yale.

Charles M. Russell, 1866-1926, Western life.

Eero Saarinen, 1910-1961, Gateway to the West Arch, St. Louis; Trans World Flight Center, N.Y.C.

Louis Skidmore, 1897-1962, AEC town site, Oak Ridge, Tenn.; Terrace Plaza Hotel, Cincinnati.

Clarence S. Stein, 1882-1975, Temple Emanu-El, N.Y.C.

Edward Durell Stone, 1902-1978, U.S. Embassy, New Delhi, India; (H. Hartford) Gallery of Modern Art, N.Y.C.

Louis H. Sullivan, 1856-1924, Auditorium, Chicago.

Richard Upjohn, 1802-1878, Trinity Church, N.Y.C.

Ralph T. Walker, 1889-1973, N.Y. Telephone Hdqrs., N.Y.C.; IBM Research Lab., Poughkeepsie, N.Y.

Roland A. Wank, 1898-1970, Cincinnati Union Terminal; head architect TVA, 1933-44.

Stanford White, 1853-1906, Washington Arch; first Madison Square Garden, N.Y.C.

Frank Lloyd Wright, 1867 (or 1869)-1959, Imperial Hotel, Tokyo; Guggenheim Museum, N.Y.C.; Unity Church, Oak Park, Ill; Robie House, Chicago; Taliesin, Wis.

William Wurster, 1895-1973, Ghirardelli Sq., San Francisco; Cowell College, U. Cal., Berkeley.

Minoru Yamasaki, 1912-1986, World Trade Center, N.Y.C.

Noted American Cartoonists

Charles Addams, 1912-1988, macabre cartoons.

Brad Anderson, b. 1924, Marmaduke.

Peter Arno, 1904-1968, urban characterizations.

Tex Avery, 1908-1980, **Friz Freleng**, b. 1905?, **Chuck Jones**, b. 1912, animators of Bugs Bunny, Porky Pig, Daffy Duck.

George Baker, 1915-1975, The Sad Sack.

C. C. Beck, b. 1910, Captain Marvel.

Jim Berry, b. 1932, Berry's World.

Herb Block (**Herblock**), b. 1909, leading political cartoonist.

George Booth, b. 1926, New Yorker cartoonist.

Berke Breathed, b. 1957, Bloom County.

Clare Briggs, 1875-1930, Mr. & Mrs.

Dik Browne, 1917-1989, Hi & Lois, Hagar the Horrible.

Ernie Bushmiller, 1905-1982, Nancy.

Milton Caniff, 1907-1988, Terry & the Pirates; Steve Canyon.

Al Capp, 1909-1979, Li'l Abner.

Paul Conrad, 1924, political cartoonist.

Roy Crane, 1901-1977, Captain Easy; Buz Sawyer.

Robert Crumb, b. 1943, "Underground" cartoonist.

Jay N. Darling (**Ding**), 1876-1962, political cartoonist.

Jim Davis, b. 1945, Garfield.

Billy DeBeck, 1890-1942, Barney Google.

Rudolph Dirks, 1877-1968, The Katzenjammer Kids.

Walt Disney, 1901-1966, producer of animated cartoons; created Mickey Mouse & Donald Duck.

Steve Ditko, b. 1927, Spider-Man.

Mort Drucker, b. 1929, Mad magazine.

Jules Feiffer, b. 1929, satirical Village Voice cartoonist.

Bud Fisher, 1884-1954, Mutt & Jeff.

Ham Fisher, 1900-1955, Joe Palooka.

James Montgomery Flagg, 1877-1960, illustrator; created the famous Uncle Sam recruiting poster during WWI.

Max Fleischer, 1883-1972, creator of Betty Boop, Popeye cartoons.

Hal Foster, 1892-1982, Tarzan; Prince Valiant.

Fontaine Fox, 1884-1964, Toonerville Folks.

Rube Goldberg, 1883-1970, Boob McNutt.

Chester Gould, 1900-1985, Dick Tracy.

Harold Gray, 1894-1968, Little Orphan Annie.

Matt Groenig, b. 1954, Life is Hell, The Simpsons.
Cathy Guisewite, b. 1950, Cathy.
Bill Hanna, b. 1910, **& Joe Barbera,** b. 1911, animators of Tom & Jerry, Huckleberry Hound, Yogi Bear, Flintstones.
Johnny Hart, b. 1931, BC, Wizard of Id.
Jimmy Hatlo, 1898-1963, Little Iodine.
John Held Jr., 1889-1958, "Jazz Age" cartoonist.
George Herriman, 1881-1944, Krazy Kat.
Harry Hershfield, 1885-1974, Abie the Agent.
Al Hirschfeld, b. 1903, N.Y. Times theater caricaturist.
Burne Hogarth, b. 1911, Tarzan.
Helen Hokinson, 1900-1949, satirized clubwomen.
Bil Keane, b. 1922, The Family Circus.
Walt Kelly, 1913-1973, Pogo.
Hank Ketcham, b. 1920, Dennis the Menace.
Ted Key, b. 1912, Hazel.
Frank King, 1883-1969, Gasoline Alley.
Jack Kirby, b. 1917, Fantastic Four.
Rollin Kirby, 1875-1952, political cartoonist.
B(ernard) Kliban, b. 1935, cat books.
Edward Koren, b. 1935, New Yorker woolly characters.
Walter Lantz, b. 1900, Woody Woodpecker.
Gary Larson, b. 1950, The Far Side.
Mell Lazarus, b. 1929, Momma, Miss Peach.
Stan Lee, b. 1922, Marvel Comics.
Don Martin, b. 1931, Mad magazine.
Bill Mauldin, b. 1921, depicted squalid life of the G.I. in WWII.
Jeff MacNelly, b. 1947, political cartoonist, and strip Shoe.
Winsor McCay, 1872-1934, Little Nemo.
John T. McCutcheon, 1870-1949, midwestern rural life.
George McManus, 1884-1954, Bringing Up Father.
Dale Messick, b. 1906, Brenda Starr.
Norman Mingo, 1896-1980, Alfred E. Neuman.
Bob Montana, 1920-1975, Archie.

Dick Moores, 1909-1986, Gasoline Alley.
Willard Mullin, 1902-1978, sports cartoonist; created Dodgers "Bum" and Mets "Kid".
Russell Myers, b. 1938, Broom Hilda.
Thomas Nast, 1840-1902, political cartoonist; created the Democratic donkey and Republican elephant.
Pat Oliphant, b. 1935, political cartoonist.
Frederick Burr Opper, 1857-1937, Happy Hooligan.
Richard Outcault, 1863-1928, Yellow Kid; Buster Brown.
Mike Peters, b. 1943, editorial cartoons; Mother Goose & Grimm.
George Price, b. 1901, New Yorker lower-class life.
Alex Raymond, 1909-1956, Flash Gordon; Jungle Jim.
Art Sansom, b. 1920, The Born Loser.
Charles Schulz, b. 1922, Peanuts.
Elzie C. Segar, 1894-1938, Popeye.
Jerry Siegel, b. 1914, **& Joe Shuster,** b. 1914, Superman.
Sydney Smith, 1887-1935, The Gumps.
Otto Soglow, 1900-1975, Little King; Canyon Kiddies.
William Steig, b. 1907, New Yorker cartoonist.
James Swinnerton, 1875-1974, Little Jimmy.
Paul Terry, 1887-1971, animator of Mighty Mouse.
Bob Thaves, b. 1924, Frank and Ernest.
James Thurber, 1894-1961, New Yorker cartoonist.
Garry Trudeau, b. 1948, Doonesbury.
Mort Walker, b. 1923, Beetle Bailey.
Bill Watterson, b. 1958, Calvin and Hobbes.
Russ Westover, 1887-1966, Tillie the Toiler.
Frank Willard, 1893-1958, Moon Mullins.
J. R. Williams, 1888-1957, The Willets Family; Out Our Way.
Gahan Wilson, b. 1930, cartoonist of the macabre.
Tom Wilson, b. 1931, Ziggy.
Art Young, 1866-1943, political radical and satirist.
Chic Young, 1901-1973, Blondie.

Noted Political Leaders of the Past

(U.S. presidents and most vice presidents, Supreme Court justices, signers of Declaration of Independence, listed elsewhere.)

Abu Bakr, 573-634, Mohammedan leader, first caliph, chosen successor to Mohammed.
Dean Acheson, 1893-1971, (U.S.) secretary of state, chief architect of cold war foreign policy.
Samuel Adams, 1722-1803, (U.S.) patriot, Boston Tea Party firebrand.
Konrad Adenauer, 1876-1967, (G.) West German chancellor.
Emilio Aguinaldo, 1869-1964, (Philip.) revolutionary, fought against Spain and the U.S.
Akbar, 1542-1605, greatest Mogul emperor of India.
Salvador Allende Gossens, 1908-1973, (Chil.) president, advocate of democratic socialism.
Herbert H. Asquith, 1852-1928, (Br.) Liberal prime minister, instituted an advanced program of social reform.
Atahualpa, ?-1533, Inca (ruling chief) of Peru.
Kemal Atatürk, 1881-1938, (Turk.) founded modern Turkey.
Clement Attlee, 1883-1967, (Br.) Labour party leader, prime minister, enacted national health, nationalized many industries.
Stephen F. Austin, 1793-1836, (U.S.) led Texas colonization.
Mikhail Bakunin, 1814-1876, (R.) revolutionary, leading exponent of anarchism.
Arthur J. Balfour, 1848-1930, (Br.) as foreign secretary under Lloyd George issued Balfour Declaration expressing official British approval of Zionism.
Bernard M. Baruch, 1870-1965, (U.S.) financier, gvt. adviser.
Fulgencio Batista y Zaldivar, 1901-1973, (Cub.) ruler overthrown by Castro.
Lord Beaverbrook, 1879-1964, (Br.) financier, statesman, newspaper owner.
Eduard Benes, 1884-1948, (Czech.) president during interwar and post-WW II eras.
David Ben-Gurion, 1886-1973, (Isr.) first premier of Israel.
Thomas Hart Benton, 1782-1858, (U.S.) Missouri senator, championed agrarian interests and westward expansion.
Lavrenti Beria, 1899-1953, (USSR) Communist leader prominent in political purges under Stalin.
Aneurin Bevan, 1897-1960, (Br.) Labour party leader.
Ernest Bevin, 1881-1951, (Br.) Labour party leader, foreign minister, helped lay foundation for NATO.
Otto von Bismarck, 1815-1898, (G.) statesman known as the Iron Chancellor, uniter of Germany, 1870.
James G. Blaine, 1830-1893, (U.S.) Republican politician, diplomat, influential in launching Pan-American movement.
Léon Blum, 1872-1950, (F.) socialist leader, writer, headed first Popular Front government.
Simón Bolívar, 1783-1830, (Venez.) South American revolutionary who liberated much of the continent from Spanish rule.

William E. Borah, 1865-1940, (U.S.) isolationist senator, instrumental in blocking U.S. membership in League of Nations and the World Court.
Cesare Borgia, 1476-1507, (It.) soldier, politician, an outstanding figure of the Italian Renaissance.
Leonid Brezhnev, 1906-1982, (USSR) leader of the Soviet Union, 1964-82.
Aristide Briand, 1862-1932, (F.) foreign minister, chief architect of Locarno Pact and anti-war Kellogg-Briand Pact.
William Jennings Bryan, 1860-1925, (U.S.) Democratic, populist leader, orator, 3 times lost race for presidency.
Nikolai Bukharin, 1888-1938, (USSR) communist leader.
William C. Bullitt, 1891-1967, (U.S.) diplomat, first ambassador to USSR, ambassador to France.
Ralph Bunche, 1904-1971, (U.S.) a founder and key diplomat of United Nations for more than 20 years.
John C. Calhoun, 1782-1850, (U.S.) political leader, champion of states' rights and a symbol of the Old South.
Robert Castlereagh, 1769-1822, (Br.) foreign secy, guided Grand Alliance against Napoleon.
Camillo Benso Cavour, 1810-1861, (It.) statesman, largely responsible for uniting Italy under the House of Savoy.
Nicolae Ceausescu, 1918-1989, Rumanian Communist leader, head of state from 1967-1989.
Austen Chamberlain, 1863-1937, (Br.) Conservative party leader, largely responsible for Locarno Pact of 1925.
Neville Chamberlain, 1869-1940, (Br.) Conservative prime minister whose appeasement of Hitler led to Munich Pact.
Salmon P. Chase, 1808-1873, (U.S.) public official, abolitionist, jurist, 6th Supreme Court chief justice.
Chiang Kai-shek, 1887-1975, (Chin.) Nationalist Chinese president whose govt. was driven from mainland to Taiwan.
Chou En-lai, 1898-1976, (Chin.) diplomat, prime minister, a leading figure of the Chinese Communist party.
Winston Churchill, 1874-1965, (Br.) prime minister, soldier, author, guided Britain through WW II.
Galeazzo Ciano, 1903-1944, (It.) fascist foreign minister, helped create Rome-Berlin Axis, executed by Mussolini.
Henry Clay, 1777-1852, (U.S.) "The Great Compromiser," one of most influential pre-Civil War political leaders.
Georges Clemenceau, 1841-1929, (F.) twice premier, Wilson's chief antagonist at Paris Peace Conference after WW I.
DeWitt Clinton, 1769-1828, (U.S.) political leader, responsible for promoting idea of the Erie Canal.
Robert Clive, 1725-1774, (Br.) first administrator of Bengal, laid foundation for British Empire in India.
Jean Baptiste Colbert, 1619-1683, (F.) statesman, influential under Louis XIV, created the French navy.

Oliver Cromwell, 1599-1658, (Br.) Lord Protector of England, led parliamentary forces during Civil War.

Curzon of Kedleston, 1859-1925, (Br.) viceroy of India, foreign secretary, major force in dealing with post-WW I problems in Europe and Far East.

Édouard Daladier, 1884-1970, (F.) radical socialist politician, arrested by Vichy, interned by Germans until liberation in 1945.

Georges Danton, 1759-1794, (F.) a leading figure in the French Revolution.

Jefferson Davis, 1808-1889, (U.S.) president of the Confederate States of America.

Charles G. Dawes, 1865-1951, (U.S.) statesman, banker, advanced Dawes Plan to stabilize post-WW I German finances.

Alcide De Gasperi, 1881-1954, (It.) premier, founder of the Christian Democratic party.

Charles DeGaulle, 1890-1970, (F.) general, statesman, and first president of the Fifth Republic.

Eamon De Valera, 1882-1975, (Ir.-U.S.) statesman, led fight for Irish independence.

Thomas E. Dewey, 1902-1971, (U.S.) New York governor, twice loser in try for presidency.

Ngo Dinh Diem, 1901-1963, (Viet.) South Vietnamese president, assassinated in government take-over.

Everett M. Dirksen, 1896-1969, (U.S.) Senate Republican minority leader, orator.

Benjamin Disraeli, 1804-1881, (Br.) prime minister, considered founder of modern Conservative party.

Engelbert Dollfuss, 1892-1934, (Aus.) chancellor, assassinated by Austrian Nazis.

Andrea Doria, 1466-1560, (It.) Genoese admiral, statesman, called "Father of Peace" and "Liberator of Genoa."

Stephen A. Douglas, 1813-1861, (U.S.) Democratic leader, orator, opposed Lincoln for the presidency.

John Foster Dulles, 1888-1959, (U.S.) secretary of state under Eisenhower, cold war policy maker.

Friedrich Ebert, 1871-1925, (G.) Social Democratic movement leader, instrumental in bringing about Weimar constitution.

Sir Anthony Eden, 1897-1977, (Br.) foreign secretary, prime minister during Suez invasion of 1956.

Ludwig Erhard, 1897-1977, (G.) economist, West German chancellor, led nation's economic rise after WW II.

Hamilton Fish, 1808-1893, (U.S.) secretary of state, successfully mediated disputes with Great Britain, Latin America.

James V. Forrestal, 1892-1949, (U.S.) secretary of navy, first secretary of defense.

Francisco Franco, 1892-1975, (Sp.) leader of rebel forces during Spanish Civil War and dictator of Spain.

Benjamin Franklin, 1706-1790, (U.S.) printer, publisher, author, inventor, scientist, diplomat.

Louis de Frontenac, 1620-1698, (F.) governor of New France (Canada); encouraged explorations, fought Iroquois.

Hugh Gaitskell, 1906-1963, (Br.) Labour party leader, major force in reversing its stand for unilateral disarmament.

Albert Gallatin, 1761-1849, (U.S.) secretary of treasury who was instrumental in negotiating end of War of 1812.

Léon Gambetta, 1838-1882, (F.) statesman, politician, one of the founders of the Third Republic.

Indira Gandhi, 1917-1984, (Ind.) succeeded father, Jawaharlal Nehru, as prime minister, assassinated.

Mohandas K. Gandhi, 1869-1948, (Ind.) political leader, ascetic, led nationalist movement against British rule.

Giuseppe Garibaldi, 1807-1882, (It.) patriot, soldier, a leading figure in the Risorgimento, the Italian unification movement.

Genghis Khan, c. 1167-1227, brilliant Mongol conqueror, ruler of vast Asian empire.

William E. Gladstone, 1809-1898, (Br.) prime minister 4 times, dominant force of Liberal party from 1868 to 1894.

Paul Joseph Goebbels, 1897-1945, (G.) Nazi propagandist, master of mass psychology.

Klement Gottwald, 1896-1953, (Czech.) communist leader ushered communism into his country.

Che (Ernesto) Guevara, 1928-1967, (Arg.) guerilla leader, prominent in Cuban revolution, killed in Bolivia.

Haile Selassie, 1891-1975, (Eth.) emperor, maintained monarchy through invasion, occupation, internal resistance.

Alexander Hamilton, 1755-1804, (U.S.) first treasury secretary, champion of strong central government.

Dag Hammarskjold, 1905-1961, (Swed.) statesman, UN secretary general.

John Hancock, 1737-1793, (U.S.) revolutionary leader, first signer of Declaration of Independence.

John Hay, 1838-1905, (U.S.) secretary of state, primarily associated with Open Door Policy toward China.

Patrick Henry, 1736-1799, (U.S.) major revolutionary figure, remarkable orator.

Édouard Herriot, 1872-1957, (F.) Radical Socialist leader, twice premier, president of National Assembly.

Theodor Herzl, 1860-1904, (Aus.) founder of modern Zionism.

Heinrich Himmler, 1900-1945, (G.) chief of Nazi SS and Gestapo, primarily responsible for the Holocaust.

Paul von Hindenburg, 1847-1934, (G.) field marshal, president.

Hirohito, 1902-1989; emperor of Japan from 1926.

Adolf Hitler, 1889-1945, (G.) dictator, founder of National Socialism.

Ho Chi Minh, 1890-1969, (Viet.) North Vietnamese president, Vietnamese Communist leader, national hero.

Harry L. Hopkins, 1890-1946, (U.S.) New Deal administrator, closest adviser to FDR during WW II.

Edward M. House, 1858-1938, (U.S.) diplomat, confidential adviser to Woodrow Wilson.

Samuel Houston, 1793-1863, (U.S.) leader of struggle to win control of Texas from Mexico.

Cordell Hull, 1871-1955, (U.S.) secretary of state, initiated reciprocal trade to lower tariffs, helped organize UN.

Hubert H. Humphrey, 1911-1978, (U.S.) Minnesota Democrat, senator, vice president, spent 32 years in public service.

Ibn Saud, c. 1888-1953, (S. Arab.) founder of Saudi Arabia and its first king.

Jacob Javits, 1904-1986 (U.S.) U.S. senator from New York for 24 years.

Jinnah, Muhammed Ali, 1876-1948, (Pak.) founder, first governor-general of Pakistan.

Benito Juarez, 1806-1872, (Mex.) rallied countrymen against foreign threats, sought to create democratic, federal republic.

Kamehameha I, c. 1758-1819, (Haw.) founder, first monarch of unified Hawaii.

Frank B. Kellogg, 1856-1937, (U.S.) secretary of state, negotiated Kellogg-Briand Pact to outlaw war.

Robert F. Kennedy, 1925-1968, (U.S.) attorney general, senator, assassinated while seeking presidential nomination.

Aleksandr Kerensky, 1881-1970, (R.) revolutionary, served as premier after Feb. 1917 revolution until Bolshevik overthrow.

Ruhollah Khomeini, 1900-1989, (Iran), religious leader with Islamic title "ayatollah," directed overthrow of shah, 1979, became source of political authority in succeeding governments.

Nikita Khrushchev, 1894-1971, (USSR) premier, first secretary of Communist party, initiated de-Stalinization.

Lajos Kossuth, 1802-1894, (Hung.) principal figure in 1848 Hungarian revolution.

Pyotr Kropotkin, 1842-1921, (R.) anarchist, championed the peasants but opposed Bolshevism.

Kublai Khan, c. 1215-1294, Mongol emperor, founder of Yüan dynasty in China.

Béla Kun, 1886-c.1939, (Hung.) communist, member of 3d International, tried to foment worldwide revolution.

Robert M. LaFollette, 1855-1925, (U.S.) Wisconsin public official, leader of progressive movement.

Pierre Laval, 1883-1945, (F.) politician, Vichy foreign minister, executed for treason.

Andrew Bonar Law, 1858-1923, (Br.) Conservative party politician, led opposition to Irish home rule.

Vladimir Ilyich Lenin (Ulyanov), 1870-1924, (USSR) revolutionary, founder of Bolshevism, Soviet leader 1917-1924.

Ferdinand de Lesseps, 1805-1894, (F.) diplomat, engineer, conceived idea of Suez Canal.

Rene Levesque, 1922-1987 (Can.) Premier of Quebec, 1976-85; led unsuccessful fight to separate from Canada.

Liu Shao-ch'i, c.1898-1974, (Chin.) communist leader, fell from grace during "cultural revolution."

Maxim Litvinov, 1876-1951, (USSR) revolutionary, commissar of foreign affairs, favored cooperation with Western powers.

David Lloyd George, 1863-1945, (Br.) Liberal party prime minister, laid foundations for modern welfare state.

Henry Cabot Lodge, 1850-1924, (U.S.) Republican senator, led opposition to participation in League of Nations.

Huey P. Long, 1893-1935, (U.S.) Louisiana political demagogue, governor, assassinated.

Rosa Luxemburg, 1871-1919, (G.) revolutionary, leader of the German Social Democratic party and Spartacus party.

J. Ramsay MacDonald, 1866-1937, (Br.) first Labour party prime minister of Great Britain.

Harold Macmillan, 1895-1987 (Br.) prime minister of Great Britain, 1957-63.

Joseph R. McCarthy, 1908-1957, (U.S.) senator notorious for his witch hunt for communists in the government.

Makarios III, 1913-1977, (Cypr.) Greek Orthodox archbishop, first president of Cyprus.

Malcolm X (Malcolm Little), 1925-1965, (U.S.) black separatist leader, assassinated.

Mao Tse-tung, 1893-1976, (Chin.) chief Chinese Marxist theorist, soldier, led Chinese revolution establishing his nation as an important communist state.

Jean Paul Marat, 1743-1793, (F.) revolutionary, politician, identified with radical Jacobins, assassinated.

José Marti, 1853-1895, (Cub.) patriot, poet, leader of Cuban struggle for independence.

Jan Masaryk, 1886-1948, (Czech.) foreign minister, died by mysterious suicide following communist coup.

Thomas G. Masaryk, 1850-1937, (Czech.) statesman, philosopher, first president of Czechoslovak Republic.

Jules Mazarin, 1602-1661, (F.) cardinal, statesman, prime minister under Louis XIII and queen regent Anne of Austria.

Giussepe Mazzini, 1805-1872, (It.), reformer dedicated to the Risorgimento, 19th-century movement for the political and social renewal of Italy.

Tom Mboya, 1930-1969, (Kenyan) political leader, instrumental in securing independence for his country.

Cosimo I de' Medici, 1519-1574, (It.) Duke of Florence, grand duke of Tuscany.

Lorenzo de' Medici, the Magnificent, 1449-1492, (It.) merchant prince, a towering figure in Italian Renaissance.

Catherine de Medicis, 1519-1589, (F.) queen consort of Henry II, regent of France, influential in Catholic-Huguenot wars.

Golda Meir, 1898-1979, (Isr.) prime minister, 1969-74.

Klemens W.N.L Metternich, 1773-1859, (Aus.) statesman, arbiter of post-Napoleonic Europe.

Anastas Mikoyan, 1895-1978, (USSR) prominent Soviet leader from 1917; president 1964-65.

Guy Mollet, 1905-1975, (F.) social politician, resistance leader.

Henry Morgenthau Jr., 1891-1967, (U.S.) secretary of treasury, raised funds to finance New Deal and U.S. WW II activities.

Gouverneur Morris, 1752-1816, (U.S.) statesman, diplomat, financial expert who helped plan decimal coinage system.

Wayne Morse, 1900-1974, (U.S.) senator, long-time critic of Vietnam War.

Muhammad Ali, 1769?-1849, (Egypt) pasha, founder of dynasty that encouraged emergence of modern Egyptian state.

Benito Mussolini, 1883-1945, (It.) dictator and leader of the Italian fascist state.

Imre Nagy, c. 1895-1958, (Hung.) communist premier, assassinated after Soviets crushed 1956 uprising.

Gamal Abdel Nasser, 1918-1970, (Egypt.) leader of Arab unification, second Egyptian president.

Jawaharlal Nehru, 1889-1964, (Ind.) prime minister, guided India through its early years of independence.

Kwame Nkrumah, 1909-1972, (Ghan.) dictatorial prime minister, deposed in 1966.

Frederick North, 1732-1792, (Br.) prime minister, his inept policies led to loss of American colonies.

Daniel O'Connell, 1775-1847, (Ir.) political leader, known as The Liberator.

Omar, c.581-644, Mohammedan leader, 2d caliph, led Islam to become an imperial power.

Ignace Paderewski, 1860-1941, (Pol.) statesman, pianist, composer, briefly prime minister, an ardent patriot.

Viscount Palmerston, 1784-1865, (Br.) Whig-Liberal prime minister, foreign minister, embodied British nationalism.

George Papandreou, 1888-1968, (Gk.) Republican politician, served three times as prime minister.

Franz von Papen, 1879-1969, (G.) politician, played major role in overthrow of Weimar Republic and rise of Hitler.

Charles Stewart Parnell, 1846-1891, (Ir.) nationalist leader, "uncrowned king of Ireland."

Lester Pearson, 1897-1972, (Can.) diplomat, Liberal party leader, prime minister.

Robert Peel, 1788-1850, (Br.) reformist prime minister, founder of Conservative party.

Juan Perón, 1895-1974, (Arg.) president, dictator.

Joseph Pilsudski, 1867-1935, (Pol.) statesman, instrumental in re-establishing Polish state in the 20th century.

Charles Pinckney, 1757-1824, (U.S.) founding father, his Pinckney plan was largely incorporated into constitution.

William Pitt, the Elder, 1708-1778, (Br.) statesman, called the "Great Commoner," transformed Britain into imperial power.

William Pitt, the Younger, 1759-1806, (Br.) prime minister during French Revolutionary wars.

Georgi Plekhanov, 1857-1918, (R.) revolutionary, social philosopher, called "father of Russian Marxism."

Raymond Poincaré, 1860-1934, (F.) 9th president of the Republic, advocated harsh punishment of Germany after WW I.

Georges Pompidou, 1911-1974, (F.) Gaullist political leader, president from 1969 to 1974.

Grigori Potemkin, 1739-1791, (R.) field marshal, favorite of Catherine II.

Edmund Randolph, 1753-1813, (U.S.) attorney, prominent in drafting, ratification of constitution.

John Randolph, 1773-1833, (U.S.) southern planter, strong advocate of states' rights.

Jeannette Rankin, 1880-1973, (U.S.) pacifist, first woman member of U.S. Congress.

Walter Rathenau, 1867-1922, (G.) industrialist, social theorist, statesman.

Sam Rayburn, 1882-1961, (U.S.) Democratic leader, representative for 47 years, House speaker for 17.

Paul Reynaud, 1878-1966, (F.) statesman, premier in 1940 at the time of France's defeat by Germany.

Syngman Rhee, 1875-1965, (Kor.) first president of the Republic of Korea.

Cecil Rhodes, 1853-1902, (Br.) imperialist, industrial magnate, established Rhodes scholarships in his will.

Cardinal de Richelieu, 1585-1642, (F.) statesman, known as "red eminence," chief minister to Louis XIII.

Maximilien Robespierre, 1758-1794, (F.) leading figure of French Revolution, responsible for much of Reign of Terror.

Nelson Rockefeller, 1908-1979, (U.S.) Republican gov. of N.Y., 1959-73; U.S. vice president, 1974-77.

Eleanor Roosevelt, 1884-1962, (U.S.) humanitarian, United Nations diplomat.

Elihu Root, 1845-1937, (U.S.) lawyer, statesman, diplomat, leading Republican supporter of the League of Nations.

John Russell, 1792-1878, (Br.) Liberal prime minister during the Irish potato famine.

Anwar el-Sadat, 1918-1981, (Egypt) president, 1970-1981, promoted peace with Israel.

Antônio de O. Salazar, 1899-1970, (Port.) statesman, longtime dictator.

José de San Martín, 1778-1850, South American revolutionary, protector of Peru.

Eisaku Sato, 1901-1975, (Jap.) prime minister, presided over Japan's post-WW II emergence as major world power.

Philipp Scheidemann, 1865-1939, (G.) Social Democratic leader, first chancellor of the German republic.

Robert Schuman, 1886-1963, (F.) statesman, founded European Coal and Steel Community.

Carl Schurz, 1829-1906, (U.S.) German-American political leader, journalist, orator, dedicated reformer.

Kurt Schuschnigg, 1897-1977, (Aus.) chancellor, unsuccessful in stopping his country's annexation by Germany.

William H. Seward, 1801-1872, (U.S.) anti-slavery activist, as Lincoln's secretary of state purchased Alaska.

Carlo Sforza, 1872-1952, (It.) foreign minister, anti-fascist.

Alfred E. Smith, 1873-1944, (U.S.) New York Democratic governor, first Roman Catholic to run for presidency.

Jan C. Smuts, 1870-1950, (S.Af.) statesman, philosopher, soldier, prime minister.

Paul Henri Spaak, 1899-1972, (Belg.) statesman, socialist leader.

Joseph Stalin, 1879-1953, (USSR) Soviet dictator, 1924-53.

Edwin M. Stanton, 1814-1869, (U.S.) Lincoln's secretary of war during the Civil War.

Edward R. Stettinius Jr., 1900-1949, (U.S.) industrialist, secretary of state who coordinated aid to WW II allies.

Adlai E. Stevenson, 1900-1965, (U.S.) Democratic leader, diplomat, Illinois governor, presidential candidate.

Henry L. Stimson, 1867-1950, (U.S.) statesman, served in 5 administrations, influenced foreign policy in 1930s and 1940s.

Gustav Stresemann, 1878-1929, (G.) chancellor, foreign minister, dedicated to regaining friendship for post-WW I Germany.

Sukarno, 1901-1970, (Indon.) dictatorial first president of the Indonesian republic.

Sun Yat-sen, 1866-1925, (Chin.) revolutionary, leader of Kuomintang, regarded as the father of modern China.

Robert A. Taft, 1889-1953, (U.S.) conservative Senate leader, called "Mr. Republican."

Charles de Talleyrand, 1754-1838, (F.) statesman, diplomat, the major force of the Congress of Vienna of 1814-15.

U Thant, 1909-1974 (Bur.) statesman, UN secretary-general.

Norman M. Thomas, 1884-1968, (U.S.) social reformer, 6 times unsuccessful Socialist party presidential candidate.

Josip Broz Tito, 1892-1980, (Yug.) president of Yugoslavia from 1953, World War II guerrilla chief, postwar rival of Stalin, leader of 3d world movement.

Palmiro Togliatti, 1893-1964, (It.) major leader of Italian Communist party.

Hideki Tojo, 1885-1948, (Jap.) statesman, soldier, prime minister during most of WW II.

François Toussaint L'Ouverture, c. 1744-1803, (Hait.) patriot, martyr, thwarted French colonial aims.

Leon Trotsky, 1879-1940, (USSR) revolutionary, founded Red Army, expelled from party in conflict with Stalin.

Rafael L. Trujillo Molina, 1891-1961, (Dom.) absolute dictator, assassinated.

Moise K. Tshombe, 1919-1969, (Cong.) politician, president of secessionist Katanga, premier of Republic of Congo (Zaire).

William M. Tweed, 1823-1878, (U.S.) politician, absolute leader of Tammany Hall, NYC's Democratic political machine.

Walter Ulbricht, 1893-1973, (G.) communist leader of German Democratic Republic.

Arthur H. Vandenberg, 1884-1951, (U.S.) senator, proponent of anti-communist bipartisan foreign policy after WW II.

Eleutherios Venizelos, 1864-1936, (Gk.) most prominent Greek statesman in early 20th century; expanded territory.

344 Noted Personalities — Political Leaders; Military Leaders

Hendrik F. Verwoerd, 1901-1966, (S.Af.) prime minister, rigorously applied apartheid policy despite protest.
Robert Walpole, 1676-1745, (Br.) statesman, generally considered Britain's first prime minister.
Daniel Webster, 1782-1852, (U.S.) orator, politician, advocate of business interests during Jacksonian agrarianism.

Chaim Weizmann, 1874-1952, Zionist leader, scientist, first Israeli president.
Wendell L. Willkie, 1892-1944, (U.S.) Republican who tried to unseat FDR when he ran for his 3d term.
Emiliano Zapata, c. 1879-1919, (Mex.) revolutionary, major influence on modern Mexico.

Notable Military and Naval Leaders of the Past

Creighton Abrams, 1914-1974, (U.S.) commanded forces in Vietnam, 1968-72.
Harold Alexander, 1891-1969, (Br.) led Allied invasion of Italy, 1943.
Ethan Allen, 1738-1789, (U.S.) headed Green Mountain Boys; captured Ft. Ticonderoga, 1775.
Edmund Allenby, 1861-1936, (Br.) in Boer War, WW1; led Egyptian expeditionary force, 1917-18.
Benedict Arnold, 1741-1801, (U.S.) victorious at Saratoga; tried to betray West Point to British.
Henry "Hap" Arnold, 1886-1950, (U.S.) commanded Army Air Force in WW2.
Petr Bagration, 1765-1812, (R.) hero of Napoleonic wars.
John Barry, 1745-1803, (U.S.) won numerous sea battles during revolution.
Pierre Beauregard, 1818-1893, (U.S.) Confederate general ordered bombardment of Ft. Sumter that began the Civil War.
Gebhard v. Blücher, 1742-1819, (G.) helped defeat Napoleon at Waterloo.
Napoleon Bonaparte, 1769-1821, (F.) defeated Russia and Austria at Austerlitz, 1805; invaded Russia, 1812; defeated at Waterloo, 1815.
Edward Braddock, 1695-1755, (Br.) commanded forces in French and Indian War.
Omar N. Bradley, 1893-1981, (U.S.) headed U.S. ground troops in Normandy invasion, 1944.
John Burgoyne, 1722-1792, (Br.) defeated at Saratoga.
Claire Chennault, 1890-1958, (U.S.) headed Flying Tigers in WW2.
Mark Clark, 1896-1984, (U.S.) led forces in WW2 and Korean War.
Karl v. Clausewitz, 1780-1831, (G.) wrote books on military theory.
Henry Clinton, 1738-1795, (Br.) commander of forces in America, 1778-81.
Lucius D. Clay, 1897-1978, (U.S.) led Berlin airlift, 1948-49.
Charles Cornwallis, 1738-1805, (Br.) victorious at Brandywine, 1777; surrendered at Yorktown.
Crazy Horse, 1849-1877, (U.S.) Sioux war chief victorious at Little Big Horn.
George A. Custer, 1839-1876, (U.S.) defeated and killed at Little Big Horn.
Moshe Dayan, 1915-1981, (Isr.) directed campaigns in the 1967, 1973 wars.
Stephen Decatur, 1779-1820, (U.S.) naval hero of Barbary wars, War of 1812.
Anton Denikin, 1872-1947, (R.) led White forces in Russian civil war.
George Dewey, 1837-1917, (U.S.) destroyed Spanish fleet at Manila, 1898.
Hugh C. Dowding, 1883-1970, (Br.) headed RAF, 1936-40.
Jubal Early, 1816-1894, (U.S.) Confederate general led raid on Washington, 1864.
Dwight D. Eisenhower, 1890-1969, (U.S.) commanded Allied forces in Europe, WW2.
David Farragut, 1801-1870, (U.S.) Union admiral captured New Orleans, Mobile Bay.
Ferdinand Foch, 1851-1929, (F.) headed victorious Allied armies, 1918.
Nathan Bedford Forrest, 1821-1877, (U.S.) Confederate general led cavalry raids against Union supply lines.
Frederick the Great, 1712-1786, (G.) led Prussia in The Seven Years War.
Nathanael Greene, 1742-1786, (U.S.) defeated British in Southern campaign, 1780-81.
Charles G. Gordon, 1833-1885, (Br.) led forces in China; killed at Khartoum.
Horatio Gates, 1728-1806, (U.S.) commanded army at Saratoga.
Ulysses S. Grant, 1822-1885, (U.S.) headed Union army, 1864-65; forced Lee's surrender, 1865.
Heinz Guderian, 1888-1953, (G.) tank theorist led panzer forces in Poland, France, Russia.
Douglas Haig, 1861-1928, (Br.) led British armies in France, 1915-18.
William F. Halsey, 1882-1959, (U.S.) defeated Japanese fleet at Leyte Gulf, 1944.
Sir Arthur Travers Harris, 1895-1984, (Br.) led Britain's WWII bomber command.

Richard Howe, 1726-1799, (Br.) commanded navy in America, 1776-78; first of June victory against French, 1794.
William Howe, 1729-1814, (Br.) commanded forces in America, 1776-78.
Isaac Hull, 1773-1843, (U.S.) sunk British frigate Guerriere, 1812.
Thomas (Stonewall) Jackson, 1824-1863, (U.S.) Confederate general led forces in the Shenandoah Valley campaign.
Joseph Joffre, 1852-1931, (F.) headed Allied armies, won Battle of the Marne, 1914.
John Paul Jones, 1747-1792, (U.S.) raided British coast; commanded Bonhomme Richard in victory over Serapis, 1779.
Stephen Kearny, 1794-1848, (U.S.) headed Army of the West in Mexican War.
Ernest J. King, 1878-1956, (U.S.) chief naval strategist in WW2.
Horatio H. Kitchener, 1850-1916, (Br.) led forces in Boer War; victorious at Khartoum; organized army in WW1.
Lavrenti Kornilov, 1870-1918, (R.) Commander-in-Chief, 1917; led counter-revolutionary march on Petrograd.
Thaddeus Kosciusko, 1746-1817, (P.) aided American cause in revolution.
Mikhail Kutuzov, 1745-1813, (R.) fought French at Borodino, 1812; abandoned Moscow; forced French retreat.
Marquis de Lafayette, 1757-1834, (F.) aided American cause in the revolution.
Thomas E. Lawrence (of Arabia), 1888-1935, (Br.) organized revolt of Arabs against Turks in WW1.
Henry (Light-Horse Harry) Lee, 1756-1818, (U.S.) cavalry officer in revolution.
Robert E. Lee, 1807-1870, (U.S.) Confederate general defeated at Gettysburg; surrendered to Grant, 1865.
Lyman Lemnitzer, 1899-1988, (U.S.) WWII hero, later general, chairman of Joint Chiefs of Staff.
James Longstreet, 1821-1904, (U.S.) aided Lee at Gettysburg.
Douglas MacArthur, 1880-1964, (U.S.) commanded forces in SW Pacific in WW2; headed occupation forces in Japan, 1945-51; UN commander in Korean War.
Francis Marion, 1733-1795, (U.S.) led guerrilla actions in S.C. during revolution.
Duke of Marlborough, 1650-1722, (Br.) led forces against Louis XIV in War of the Spanish Sucession.
George C. Marshall, 1880-1959, (U.S.) chief of staff in WW2; authored Marshall Plan.
George B. McClellan, 1826-1885, (U.S.) Union general commanded Army of the Potomac, 1861-62.
George Meade, 1815-1872, (U.S.) commanded Union forces at Gettysburg.
Billy Mitchell, 1879-1936, (U.S.) air-power advocate; court-martialed for insubordination, later vindicated.
Helmuth v. Moltke, 1800-1891, (G.) victorious in Austro-Prussian, Franco-Prussian wars.
Louis de Montcalm, 1712-1759, (F.) headed troops in Canada; defeated at Quebec, 1759.
Bernard Law Montgomery, 1887-1976, (Br.) stopped German offensive at Alamein, 1942; helped plan Normandy invasion.
Daniel Morgan, 1736-1802, (U.S.) victorious at Cowpens, 1781.
Louis Mountbatten, 1900-1979, (Br.) Supreme Allied Commander of SE Asia, 1943-46.
Joachim Murat, 1767-1815, (F.) leader of cavalry at Marengo, 1800; Austerlitz, 1805; and Jena, 1806.
Horatio Nelson, 1758-1805, (Br.) naval commander destroyed French fleet at Trafalgar.
Michel Ney, 1769-1815, (F.) commanded forces in Switzerland, Austria, Russia; defeated at Waterloo.
Chester Nimitz, 1885-1966, (U.S.) commander of naval forces in Pacific in WW2.
George S. Patton, 1885-1945, (U.S.) led assault on Sicily, 1943; headed 3d Army invasion of German-occupied Europe.
Oliver Perry, 1785-1819, (U.S.) won Battle of Lake Erie in War of 1812.
John Pershing, 1860-1948, (U.S.) commanded Mexican border campaign, 1916; American expeditionary forces in WW1.
Henri Philippe Pétain, 1856-1951, (F.) defended Verdun, 1916; headed Vichy government in WW2.
George E. Pickett, 1825-1875, (U.S.) Confederate general famed for "charge" at Gettysburg.

Hyman Rickover, 1900-1986 (U.S.) father of the nuclear navy.

Erwin Rommel, 1891-1944, (G.) headed Afrika Korps.

Karl v. Rundstedt, 1875-1953, (G.) supreme commander in West, 1943-45.

Aleksandr Samsonov, 1859-1914, (R.) led invasion of E. Prussia, defeated at Tannenberg, 1914.

Winfield Scott, 1786-1866, (U.S.) hero of War of 1812; headed forces in Mexican war, took Mexico City.

Philip Sheridan, 1831-1888, (U.S.) Union cavalry officer headed Army of the Shenandoah, 1864-65.

William T. Sherman, 1820-1891, (U.S.) Union general sacked Atlanta during "march to the sea," 1864.

Carl Spaatz, 1891-1974, (U.S.) directed strategic bombing against Germany, later Japan, in WW2.

Raymond Spruance, 1886-1969, (U.S.) victorious at Midway Island, 1942.

Joseph W. Stilwell, 1883-1946, (U.S.) headed forces in the China, Burma, India theater in WW2.

J.E.B. Stuart, 1833-1864, (U.S.) Confederate cavalry commander.

George H. Thomas, 1816-1870, (U.S.) saved Union army at Chattanooga, 1863; victorious at Nashville, 1864.

Semyon Timoshenko, 1895-1970, (USSR) defended Moscow, Stalingrad; led winter offensive, 1942-43.

Alfred v. Tirpitz, 1849-1930, (G.) responsible for submarine blockade in WW1.

Jonathan M. Wainwright, 1883-1953, (U.S.) forced to surrender on Corregidor, 1942.

George Washington, 1732-1799, (U.S.) led Continental army, 1775-83.

Archibald Wavell, 1883-1950, (Br.) commanded forces in N. and E. Africa, and SE Asia in WW2.

Anthony Wayne, 1745-1796, (U.S.) captured Stony Point, 1779; defeated Indians at Fallen Timbers, 1794.

Duke of Wellington, 1769-1852, (Br.) defeated Napoleon at Waterloo.

James Wolfe, 1727-1759, (Br.) captured Quebec from French, 1759.

Georgi Zhukov, 1895-1974, (USSR) defended Moscow, 1941; led assault on Berlin.

Poets Laureate of England

There is no authentic record of the origin of the office of Poet Laureate of England. According to Warton, there was a Versificator Regis, or King's Poet, in the reign of Henry III (1216-1272), and he was paid 100 shillings a year. Geoffrey Chaucer (1340-1400) assumed the title of Poet Laureate, and in 1389 got a royal grant of a yearly allowance of wine. In the reign of Edward IV (1461-1483), John Kay held the post. Under Henry VII (1485-1509), Andrew Bernard was the Poet Laureate, and was succeeded under Henry VIII (1509-1547) by John Skelton. Next came Edmund Spenser, who died in 1599; then Samuel Daniel, appointed 1599, and then Ben Jonson, 1619. Sir William D'Avenant was appointed in 1637. He was a godson of William Shakespeare.

Others were John Dryden, 1670; Thomas Shadwell, 1688; Nahum Tate, 1692; Nicholas Rowe, 1715; the Rev. Laurence Eusden, 1718; Colley Cibber, 1730; William Whitehead, 1757, on the refusal of Gray; Rev. Thomas Warton, 1785, on the refusal of Mason; Henry J. Pye, 1790; Robert Southey, 1813, on the refusal of Sir Walter Scott; William Wordsworth, 1843; Alfred, Lord Tennyson, 1850; Alfred Austin, 1896; Robert Bridges, 1913; John Masefield, 1930; Cecil Day Lewis, 1967; Sir John Betjeman, 1972; Ted Hughes, 1984.

U.S. Poet Laureate

Robert Penn Warren, the poet, novelist, and essayist, was named the country's first official Poet Laureate on Feb. 26, 1986. The only writer to have won the Pulitzer Prize for fiction and poetry (twice), Warren was chosen by Daniel J. Boorstin, the Librarian of Congress. The appointment began in September, 1986. On April 17, 1987, Richard Wilbur was named the second Poet Laureate. In May 1988, Howard Nemerov was named the third, and in May 1990 Mark Strand was named the fourth.

Noted Writers of the Past

Henry Adams, 1838-1918, (U.S.) historian, philosopher. *The Education of Henry Adams.*

George Ade, 1866-1944, (U.S.) humorist. *Fables in Slang.*

Conrad Aiken, 1889-1973, (U.S.) poet, critic.

Louisa May Alcott, 1832-1888, (U.S.) novelist. *Little Women.*

Sholom Aleichem, 1859-1916. (R.) Yiddish writer. *Tevye's Daughter, The Great Fair.*

Vicente Aleixandre, 1898-1984, (Sp.) poet. 1977 Nobel Prize winner.

Horatio Alger, 1832-1899, (U.S.) "rags-to-riches" books.

Hans Christian Andersen, 1805-1875, (Den.) author of fairy tales. *The Princess and the Pea, The Ugly Duckling.*

Maxwell Anderson, 1888-1959, (U.S.) playwright. *What Price Glory?, High Tor, Winterset, Key Largo.*

Sherwood Anderson, 1876-1941, (U.S.) author. *Winesburg, Ohio.*

Matthew Arnold, 1822-1888, (Br.) poet, critic. "Thrysis," "Dover Beach," "The Gypsy Scholar."

Jane Austen, 1775-1817, (Br.) novelist. *Pride and Prejudice, Sense and Sensibility, Emma, Mansfield Park, Persuasion.*

Isaac Babel, 1894-1941, (R.) short-story writer, playwright. *Odessa Tales, Red Cavalry.*

James M. Barrie, 1860-1937, (Br.) playwright, novelist. *Peter Pan, Dear Brutus, What Every Woman Knows.*

Honoré de Balzac, 1799-1850, (Fr.) novelist. *Le Père Goriot, Cousine Bette, Eugénie Grandet, The Human Comedy.*

Charles Baudelaire, 1821-1867, (Fr.) symbolist poet. *Les Fleurs du Mal.*

L. Frank Baum, 1856-1919, (U.S.) children's author. Wizard of Oz series.

Simone de Beauvoir, 1908-1986, (Fr.) novelist, essayist. *The Second Sex.*

Samuel Beckett, 1906-1989, (Ir.) novelist, playwright, in French and English. *Waiting for Godot, Endgame* (plays); *Murphy, Watt, Molloy* (novels).

Brendan Behan, 1923-1964, (Ir.) playwright. *The Quare Fellow, The Hostage, Borstal Boy.*

Robert Benchley, 1889-1945, (U.S.) humorist. *From Bed to Worse, My Ten Years in a Quandary.*

Stephen Vincent Benét, 1898-1943, (U.S.) poet, novelist. *John Brown's Body.*

John Berryman, 1914-1972, (U.S.) poet. *Homage to Mistress Bradstreet.*

Ambrose Bierce, 1842-1914, (U.S.) short-story writer, journalist. *In the Midst of Life, The Devil's Dictionary.*

William Blake, 1757-1827, (Br.) poet, artist. *Songs of Innocence, Songs of Experience.*

Giovanni Boccaccio, 1313-1375, (It.) poet, storyteller. *Decameron, Filostrato.*

Jorge Luis Borges, 1900-1986 (Arg.) short-story writer, poet, essayist. *Labyrinths.*

James Boswell, 1740-1795, (Sc.) author. *The Life of Samuel Johnson.*

Anne Bradstreet, c. 1612-1672, (U.S.) poet. *The Tenth Muse Lately Sprung Up in America.*

Bertolt Brecht, 1898-1956, (G.) dramatist, poet. *The Threepenny Opera, Mother Courage and Her Children.*

Charlotte Brontë, 1816-1855, (Br.) novelist. *Jane Eyre.*

Emily Brontë, 1818-1848, (Br.) novelist. *Wuthering Heights.*

Elizabeth Barrett Browning, 1806-1861, (Br.) poet. *Sonnets from the Portuguese, Aurora Leigh.*

Robert Browning, 1812-1889, (Br.) poet. "My Last Duchess," "Fra Lippo Lippi," *The Ring and The Book.*

Pearl Buck, 1892-1973, (U.S.) novelist. *The Good Earth.*

Mikhail Bulgakov, 1891-1940, (R.) novelist, playwright. *The Heart of a Dog, The Master and Margarita.*

John Bunyan, 1628-1688, (Br.) writer. *Pilgrim's Progress.*

Robert Burns, 1759-1796, (Sc.) poet. "Flow Gently, Sweet Afton," "My Heart's in the Highlands," "Auld Lang Syne."

Edgar Rice Burroughs, 1875-1950, (U.S.) novelist. *Tarzan of the Apes.*

George Gordon Lord Byron, 1788-1824, (Br.) poet. *Don Juan, Childe Harold.*

Itaio Calvino, 1923-1985 (It.) novelist, short story writer. *If on a Winter's Night a Traveler . . .*

Albert Camus, 1913-1960, (F.) novelist. *The Plague, The Stranger, Caligula, The Fall.*

Lewis Carroll, 1832-1898, (Br.) writer, mathematician. *Alice's Adventures in Wonderland, Through the Looking Glass.*

Karel Capek, 1890-1938, (Czech.) playwright, novelist, essayist. *R.U.R. (Rossum's Universal Robots).*

Giacomo Casanova, 1725-1798, (It.) Venetian adventurer, author, world famous for his memoirs.

Willa Cather, 1876-1947, (U.S.) novelist, essayist. *O Pioneers!, My Antonia.*

Miguel de Cervantes Saavedra, 1547-1616, (Sp.) novelist, dramatist, poet. *Don Quixote de la Mancha.*

Raymond Chandler, 1888-1959, (U.S.) writer of detective fiction. Philip Marlowe series.

Geoffrey Chaucer, c. 1340-1400, (Br.) poet. *The Canterbury Tales.*

John Cheever, 1912-1982, (U.S.) short story writer, novelist. *The Wapshot Scandal, "The Country Husband."*

Anton Chekhov, 1860-1904, (R.) short-story writer, dramatist. *Uncle Vanya, The Cherry Orchard, The Three Sisters.*

G.K. Chesterton, 1874-1936, (Br.) author, Fr. Brown series.

Agatha Christie, 1891-1976, (Br.) mystery writer. *And Then There Were None, Murder on the Orient Express.*

Jean Cocteau, 1889-1963, (F.) writer, visual artist, filmmaker. *The Beauty and the Beast, Enfants Terribles.*

Samuel Taylor Coleridge, 1772-1834, (Br.) poet, man of letters. *"Kubla Khan," "The Rime of the Ancient Mariner."*

(Sidonie) Colette, 1873-1954, (F.) novelist. *Claudine, Gigi.*

Joseph Conrad, 1857-1924, (Br.) novelist. *Lord Jim, Heart of Darkness, The Nigger of the Narcissus.*

James Fenimore Cooper, 1789-1851, (U.S.) novelist. *Leather-Stocking Tales.*

Pierre Corneille, 1606-1684, (F.) Dramatist. *Medeé, Le Cid, Horace, Cinna, Polyeucte.*

Hart Crane, 1899-1932, (U.S.) poet. *"The Bridge."*

Stephen Crane, 1871-1900, (U.S.) novelist. *The Red Badge of Courage.*

e.e. cummings, 1894-1962, (U.S.) poet. *Tulips and Chimneys.*

Gabriele D'Annunzio, 1863-1938, (It.) poet, novelist, dramatist. *The Child of Pleasure, The Intruder, The Victim.*

Dante Alighieri, 1265-1321, (It.) poet. *The Divine Comedy.*

Daniel Defoe, 1660-1731, (Br.) writer. *Robinson Crusoe, Moll Flanders, Journal of the Plague Year.*

Charles Dickens, 1812-1870, (Br.) novelist. *David Copperfield, Oliver Twist, Great Expectations, The Pickwick Papers.*

Emily Dickinson, 1830-1886, (U.S.) poet.

Isak Dinesen (Karen Blixen), 1885-1962, (Dan.) author. *Out of Africa, Seven Gothic Tales, Winter's Tales.*

John Donne, 1573-1631, (Br.) poet. *Songs and Sonnets, Holy Sonnets, "Death Be Not Proud."*

John Dos Passos, 1896-1970, (U.S.) author. *U.S.A.*

Fyodor Dostoyevsky, 1821-1881, (R.) author. *Crime and Punishment, The Brothers Karamazov, The Possessed.*

Arthur Conan Doyle, 1859-1930, (Br.) author, created Sherlock Holmes.

Theodore Dreiser, 1871-1945, (U.S.) novelist. *An American Tragedy, Sister Carrie.*

John Dryden, 1631-1700, (Br.) poet, dramatist, critic. *Fables, Ancient and Modern.*

Alexandre Dumas, 1802-1870, (F.) novelist, dramatist. *The Three Musketeers, The Count of Monte Cristo.*

Alexandre Dumas (fils), 1824-1895, (F.) dramatist, novelist. *La Dame aux camélias, Le Demi-Monde.*

Ilya G. Ehrenburg, 1891-1967, (R.) novelist, journalist. *The Thaw.*

George Eliot, 1819-1880, (Br.) novelist. *Adam Bede, Silas Marner, The Mill on the Floss, Middlemarch.*

T.S. Eliot, 1888-1965, (Br.) poet, critic. *The Waste Land, "The Love Song of J. Alfred Prufrock," Murder in the Cathedral.*

Ralph Waldo Emerson, 1803-1882, (U.S.) poet, essayist. *"The Concord Hymn," "Brahma," Nature.*

James T. Farrell, 1904-1979, (U.S.) novelist. Studs Lonigan trilogy.

William Faulkner, 1897-1962, (U.S.) novelist. *Sanctuary, Light in August, The Sound and the Fury, Absalom, Absalom!*

Edna Ferber, 1885-1968, (U.S.) novelist, dramatist. *Show Boat, Saratoga Trunk, Giant, Dinner at Eight.*

Henry Fielding, 1707-1754, (Br.) novelist. *Tom Jones.*

F. Scott Fitzgerald, 1896-1940, (U.S.) short-story writer, novelist. *The Great Gatsby, Tender is the Night.*

Gustave Flaubert, 1821-1880, (Fr.) novelist. *Madame Bovary.*

C.S. Forester, 1899-1966, (Br.) novelist. Horatio Hornblower series.

E.M. Forster, 1879-1970, (Br.) novelist. *A Passage to India.*

Anatole France, 1844-1924, (F.) writer. *Penguin Island, My Friend's Book, Le Crime de Sylvestre Bonnard.*

Robert Frost, 1874-1963, (U.S.) poet. *"Birches," "Fire and Ice," "Stopping by Woods on a Snowy Evening."*

John Galsworthy, 1867-1933, (Br.) novelist, dramatist. *The Forsyte Saga, A Modern Comedy.*

Erle Stanley Gardner, 1889-1970, (U.S.) author, lawyer. Perry Mason series.

Jean Genet, 1911-1986, (Fr.) playwright, novelist. *"The Blacks."*

André Gide, 1869-1951, (F.) writer. *The Immoralist, The Pastoral Symphony, Strait is the Gate.*

Jean Giraudoux, 1882-1944, (F.) novelist, dramatist. *Electra, The Madwoman of Chaillot, Ondine, Tiger at the Gate.*

Johann W. von Goethe, 1749-1832, (G.) poet, dramatist, novelist. *Faust.*

Nikolai Gogol, 1809-1852, (R.) short-story writer, dramatist, novelist. *Dead Souls, The Inspector General.*

Oliver Goldsmith, 1730?-1774, (Br.-Ir.) writer. *The Vicar of Wakefield, She Stoops to Conquer.*

Maxim Gorky, 1868-1936, (R.) writer, founder of Soviet realism. *Mother, The Lower Depths.*

Robert Graves, 1895-1985, (Br.) poet, classical scholar, novelist. *The White Goddess.*

Thomas Gray, 1716-1771, (Br.) poet. *"Elegy Written in a Country Churchyard."*

Zane Grey, 1875-1939, (U.S.) writer of western stories.

Jakob Grimm, 1785-1863, (G.) philologist, folklorist. *German Methodology, Grimm's Fairy Tales.*

Wilhelm Grimm, 1786-1859, (G.) philologist, folklorist. *Grimm's Fairy Tales.*

Edgar A. Guest, 1881-1959, (U.S.) poet. *A Heap of Livin!*

Dashiell Hammett, 1894-1961, (U.S.) writer of detective fiction, created Sam Spade.

Knute Hamsun, 1859-1952 (Nor.) novelist. *Hunger.*

Thomas Hardy, 1840-1928, (Br.) novelist, poet. *The Return of the Native, Tess of the D'Urbervilles, Jude the Obscure.*

Joel Chandler Harris, 1848-1908, (U.S.) short-story writer. Uncle Remus series.

Moss Hart, 1904-1961, (U.S.) playwright. *Once in a Lifetime, You Can't Take It With You, The Man Who Came to Dinner.*

Bret Harte, 1836-1902, (U.S.) short-story writer, poet. *The Luck of Roaring Camp.*

Jaroslav Hasek, 1883-1923, (Czech.) writer. *The Good Soldier Schweik.*

Nathaniel Hawthorne, 1804-1864, (U.S.) novelist, short story writer. *The Scarlet Letter, The House of the Seven Gables.*

Heinrich Heine, 1797-1856, (G.) poet. *Book of Songs.*

Lillian Hellman, 1905-1984, (U.S.) playwright, author of memoirs, *"The Little Foxes," An Unfinished Woman, Pentimento.*

Ernest Hemingway, 1899-1961, (U.S.) novelist, short-story writer. *A Farewell to Arms, For Whom the Bell Tolls.*

O. Henry (W.S. Porter), 1862-1910, (U.S.) short-story writer. *"The Gift of the Magi."*

Hermann Hesse, 1877-1962, (G.) novelist, poet. *Death and the Lover, Steppenwolf, Siddhartha.*

Oliver Wendell Holmes, 1809-1894, (U.S.) poet, novelist. *The Autocrat of the Breakfast-Table.*

Alfred E. Housman, 1859-1936, (Br.) poet. *A Shropshire Lad.*

William Dean Howells, 1837-1920, (U.S.) novelist, critic, dean of late 19th century American letters.

Langston Hughes, 1902-1967, (U.S.) poet, playwright. *The Weary Blues, One-Way Ticket, Shakespeare in Harlem.*

Victor Hugo, 1802-1885, (F.) poet, dramatist, novelist. *Notre Dame de Paris, Les Misérables.*

Aldous Huxley 1894-1963, (Br.) author. *Point Counter Point, Brave New World.*

Henrik Ibsen, 1828-1906, (Nor.) dramatist, poet. *A Doll's House, Ghosts, The Wild Duck, Hedda Gabler.*

William Inge, 1913-1973, (U.S.) playwright. *Come Back Little Sheba, Bus Stop, The Dark at the Top of the Stairs, Picnic.*

Washington Irving, 1783-1859, (U.S.) essayist, author. *"Rip Van Winkle," "The Legend of Sleepy Hollow."*

Shirley Jackson, 1919-1965, (U.S.) writer. *"The Lottery."*

Henry James, 1843-1916, (U.S.) novelist, critic. *Washington Square, Portrait of a Lady, The American, Daisy Miller.*

Robinson Jeffers, 1887-1962, (U.S.) poet, dramatist. *Tamar and Other Poems, Medea.*

Samuel Johnson, 1709-1784, (Br.) author, scholar, critic. *Dictionary of the English Language.*

Ben Jonson, 1572-1637, (Br.) dramatist, poet. *Volpone.*

James Joyce, 1882-1941, (Ir.) novelist. *Ulysses, A Portrait of the Artist as a Young Man, Finnegans Wake.*

Franz Kafka, 1883-1924, (G.) novelist, short-story writer. *The Trial, Amerika, The Castle, The Metamorphosis.*

George S. Kaufman, 1889-1961, (U.S.) playwright. *The Man Who Came to Dinner, You Can't Take It With You, Stage Door.*

Nikos Kazantzakis, 1883?-1957, (Gk.) novelist. *Zorba the Greek, A Greek Passion.*

John Keats, 1795-1821, (Br.) poet. *On a Grecian Urn, La Belle Dame Sans Merci.*

Joyce Kilmer, 1886-1918, (U.S.) poet, *"Trees."*

Rudyard Kipling, 1865-1936, (Br.) author, poet. "The White Man's Burden," "Gunga Din," *The Jungle Book*.

Jean de la Fontaine, 1621-1695, (F.) poet. *Fables choisies*.

Pär Lagerkvist, 1891-1974, (Swed.) poet, dramatist, novelist. *Barabbas, The Sybil*.

Selma Lagerlöf, 1858-1940, (Swed.) novelist. *Jerusalem, The Ring of the Lowenskolds*.

Alphonse de Lamartine, 1790-1869, (F.) poet, novelist, statesman. *Méditations poétiques*.

Charles Lamb, 1775-1834, (Br.) essayist. *Specimens of English Dramatic Poets, Essays of Elia*.

Giuseppe di Lampedusa, 1896-1957, (It.) novelist. *The Leopard*.

Ring Lardner, 1885-1933, (U.S.) short story writer, humorist. *You Know Me, Al*.

D. H. Lawrence, 1885-1930, (Br.) novelist. *Sons and Lovers, Women in Love, Lady Chatterley's Lover*.

Mikhail Lermontov, 1814-1841, (R.) novelist, poet. "Demon," *Hero of Our Time*.

Alain-René Lesage, 1668-1747, (F.) novelist. *Gil Blas de Santillane*.

Gotthold Lessing, 1729-1781, (G.) dramatist, philosopher, critic. *Miss Sara Sampson, Minna von Barnhelm*.

Sinclair Lewis, 1885-1951, (U.S.) novelist, playwright. *Babbitt, Arrowsmith, Dodsworth, Main Street*.

Vachel Lindsay, 1879-1931, (U.S.) poet. *General William Booth Enters into Heaven, The Congo*.

Hugh Lofting, 1886-1947, (Br.) Dr. Doolittle series.

Jack London, 1876-1916, (U.S.) novelist, journalist. *Call of the Wild, The Sea-Wolf*.

Henry Wadsworth Longfellow, 1807-1882, (U.S.) poet. *Evangeline, The Song of Hiawatha*.

Amy Lowell, 1874-1925, (U.S.) poet, critic. "Lilacs."

James Russell Lowell, 1819-1891, (U.S.) poet, editor. *Poems, The Bigelow Papers*.

Robert Lowell, 1917-1977, (U.S.) poet. "Lord Weary's Castle," "For the Union Dead."

Emil Ludwig, 1881-1948, (G.) biographer. *Goethe, Beethoven, Napoleon, Bismarck*.

Niccolò Machiavelli, 1469-1527, (It.) author, statesman. *The Prince, Discourses on Livy*.

Bernard Malamud, 1914-1986, (U.S.) short story writer, novelist. "The Magic Barrel," *The Assistant, The Fixer*.

Stéphane Mallarmé, 1842-1898, (F.) poet. *The Afternoon of a Faun*.

Thomas Malory, ?-1471, (Br.) writer. *Morte d'Arthur*.

Andre Malraux, 1901-1976, (F.) novelist. *Man's Fate*.

Osip Mandelstam, 1891-1938, (R.) Acmeist poet.

Thomas Mann, 1875-1955, (G.) novelist, essayist. *Buddenbrooks, Death in Venice, The Magic Mountain*.

Katherine Mansfield, 1888-1923, (Br.) short story writer. "Bliss," "The Garden Party."

Christopher Marlowe, 1564-1593, (Br.) dramatist, poet. *Tamburlaine the Great, Dr. Faustus, The Jew of Malta*.

John Masefield, 1878-1967, (Br.) poet. "Sea Fever," "Cargoes," *Salt Water Ballads*.

Edgar Lee Masters, 1869-1950, (U.S.) poet, biographer. *Spoon River Anthology*.

W. Somerset Maugham, 1874-1965, (Br.) author. *Of Human Bondage, The Razor's Edge, The Moon and Sixpence*.

Guy de Maupassant, 1850-1893, (F.) novelist, short-story writer. "A Life," "Bel-Ami," "The Necklace."

François Mauriac, 1885-1970, (F.) novelist, dramatist. *Viper's Tangle, The Kiss to the Leper*.

Vladimir Mayakovsky, 1893-1930, (R.) poet, playwright. *The Cloud in Trousers*.

Mary McCarthy, 1912-1989, (U.S.) critic, novelist. *Memories of a Catholic Girlhood*.

Carson McCullers, 1917-1967, (U.S.) novelist. *The Heart is a Lonely Hunter, Member of the Wedding*.

Herman Melville, 1819-1891, (U.S.) novelist, poet. *Moby Dick, Typee, Billy Budd, Omoo*.

H.L. Mencken, 1880-1956, (U.S.) author, critic, editor. *Prejudices, The American Language*.

George Meredith, 1828-1909, (Br.) novelist, poet. *The Ordeal of Richard Feverel, The Egoist*.

Prosper Mérimée, 1803-1870, (F.) author. *Carmen*.

Edna St. Vincent Millay, 1892-1950, (U.S.) poet. *The Harp Weaver and Other Poems, A Few Figs from Thistles*.

A.A. Milne, 1882-1956, (Br.) author. *Winnie-the-Pooh*.

John Milton, 1608-1674, (Br.) poet. *Paradise Lost*.

Gabriela Mistral, 1889-1957, (Chil.) poet. *Sonnets of Death, Desolación, Tala, Lagar*.

Margaret Mitchell, 1900-1949, (U.S.) novelist. *Gone With the Wind*.

Jean Baptiste Molière, 1622-1673, (F.) dramatist. *Le Tartuffe, Le Misanthrope, Le Bourgeois Gentilhomme*.

Ferenc Molnár, 1878-1952, (Hung.) dramatist, novelist. *Liliom, The Guardsman, The Swan*.

Michel de Montaigne, 1533-1592, (F.) essayist. *Essais*.

Eugenio Montale, 1896-1981, (It.) poet.

Clement C. Moore, 1779-1863, (U.S.) poet, educator. "A Visit from Saint Nicholas."

Marianne Moore, 1887-1972, (U.S.) poet. *O to Be a Dragon*.

Thomas More, 1478-1535, (Br.) author. *Utopia*.

H.H. Munro (Saki), 1870-1916, (Br.) author. *Reginald, The Chronicles of Clovis, Beasts and Super-Beasts*.

Alfred de Musset, 1810-1857, (F.) poet, dramatist. *Confession d'un enfant du siècle*.

Vladimir Nabokov, 1899-1977, (Rus.-U.S.) author. *Lolita*.

Ogden Nash, 1902-1971, (U.S.) poet. *Hard Lines, I'm a Stranger Here Myself, The Private Dining Room*.

Pablo Neruda, 1904-1973, (Chil.) poet. *Twenty Love Poems and One Song of Despair, Toward the Splendid City*.

Sean O'Casey, 1884-1964, (Ir.) dramatist. *Juno and the Paycock, The Plough and the Stars*.

Flannery O'Connor, 1925-1964, (U.S.) novelist, short story writer. *Wise Blood*, "A Good Man Is Hard to Find."

Clifford Odets, 1906-1963, (U.S.) playwright. *Waiting for Lefty, Awake and Sing, Golden Boy, The Country Girl*.

John O'Hara, 1905-1970, (U.S.) novelist. *From the Terrace, Appointment in Samarra*.

Omar Khayyam, c. 1028-1122, (Per.) poet. *Rubaiyat*.

Eugene O'Neill, 1888-1953, (U.S.) playwright. *Emperor Jones, Anna Christie, Long Day's Journey into Night*.

George Orwell, 1903-1950, (Br.) novelist, essayist. *Animal Farm, Nineteen Eighty-Four*.

Thomas (Tom) Paine, 1737-1809, (U.S.) author, political theorist. *Common Sense*.

Dorothy Parker, 1893-1967, (U.S.) poet, short-story writer. *Enough Rope, Laments for the Living*.

Boris Pasternak, 1890-1960, (R.) poet, novelist. *Doctor Zhivago, My Sister, Life*.

Samuel Pepys, 1633-1703, (Br.) public official, author of the greatest diary in the English language.

S. J. Perelman, 1904-1979, (U.S.) humorist. *The Road to Miltown, Under the Spreading Atrophy*.

Francesco Petrarca, 1304-1374, (It.) poet, humanist. *Africa, Trionfi, Canzoniere, On Solitude*.

Luigi Pirandello, 1867-1936, (It.) novelist, dramatist. *Six Characters in Search of an Author*.

Edgar Allan Poe, 1809-1849, (U.S.) poet, short-story writer, critic. "Annabel Lee," "The Raven," "The Purloined Letter."

Alexander Pope, 1688-1744, (Br.) poet. *The Rape of the Lock, An Essay on Man*.

Katherine Anne Porter, 1890-1980, (U.S.) novelist, short story writer. *Ship of Fools*.

Ezra Pound, 1885-1972, (U.S.) poet. *Cantos*.

Marcel Proust, 1871-1922, (F.) novelist. *A la recherche du temps perdu (Remembrance of Things Past)*.

Aleksandr Pushkin, 1799-1837, (R.) poet, prose writer. *Boris Godunov, Eugene Onegin, The Bronze Horseman*.

François Rabelais, 1495-1553, (F.) writer, physician. *Gargantua, Pantagruel*.

Jean Racine, 1639-1699, (F.) dramatist. *Andromaque, Phèdre, Bérénice, Britannicus*.

Ayn Rand, 1905-1982 (Rus.-U.S.) novelist, philosopher. *The Fountainhead, Atlas Shrugged*.

Erich Maria Remarque, 1898-1970, (Ger.-U.S.) novelist. *All Quiet on the Western Front*.

Samuel Richardson, 1689-1761, (Br.) novelist. *Clarissa Harlowe, Pamela; or, Virtue Rewarded*.

James Whitcomb Riley, 1849-1916, (U.S.) poet. "When the Frost is on the Pumpkin," "Little Orphant Annie."

Rainer Maria Rilke, 1875-1926, (G.) poet. *Life and Songs, Divine Elegies, Sonnets to Orpheus*.

Arthur Rimbaud, 1854-1891, (F.) *A Season in Hell*.

Edwin Arlington Robinson, 1869-1935, (U.S.) poet. "Richard Cory," "Miniver Cheevy."

Theodore Roethke, 1908-1963, (U.S.) poet. *Open House, The Waking, The Far Field*.

Romain Rolland, 1866-1944, (F.) novelist, biographer. *Jean-Christophe*.

Pierre de Ronsard, 1524-1585, (F.) poet. *Sonnets pour Hélène*.

Edmond Rostand, 1868-1918, (F.) poet, dramatist. *Cyrano de Bergerac*.

Damon Runyon, 1880-1946, (U.S.) short-story writer, journalist. *Guys and Dolls, Blue Plate Special*.

John Ruskin, 1819-1900, (Br.) critic, social theorist. *Modern Painters, The Seven Lamps of Architecture*.

Antoine de Saint-Exupery, 1900-1944, (F.) writer, aviator. *Wind, Sand and Stars, Le Petit Prince*.

George Sand, 1804-1876, (F.) novelist. *Consuelo, The Haunted Pool, Les Maitres sonneurs*.

Carl Sandburg, 1878-1967, (U.S.) poet. *Chicago Poems, Smoke and Steel, Harvest Poems*.

George Santayana, 1863-1952, (U.S.) poet, essayist, philosopher. *The Sense of Beauty, The Realms of Being.*

William Saroyan, 1908-1981, (U.S.) playwright, novelist. *The Time of Your Life, The Human Comedy.*

Jean-Paul Sartre, 1905-1980, (Fr.) philosopher, novelist, playwright, essayist. *Nausea, No Exit.*

Friedrich von Schiller, 1759-1805, (G.) dramatist, poet, historian. *Don Carlos, Maria Stuart, Wilhelm Tell.*

Sir Walter Scott, 1771-1832, (Sc.) novelist, poet. *Ivanhoe, Rob Roy, The Bride of Lammermoor.*

Jaroslav Seifert, 1902-1986, (Cz.) poet.

William Shakespeare, 1564-1616, (Br.) dramatist, poet. *Romeo and Juliet, Hamlet, King Lear, The Merchant of Venice.*

George Bernard Shaw, 1856-1950, (Ir.) playwright, critic. *St. Joan, Pygmalion, Major Barbara, Man and Superman.*

Mary Wollstonecraft Shelley, 1797-1851, (Br.) author. *Frankenstein.*

Percy Bysshe Shelley, 1792-1822, (Br.) poet. *Prometheus Unbound, Adonais,* "Ode to the West Wind," "To a Skylark."

Richard B. Sheridan, 1751-1816, (Br.) dramatist. *The Rivals, School for Scandal.*

Robert Sherwood, 1896-1955, (U.S.) playwright. *The Petrified Forest, Abe Lincoln in Illinois, Reunion in Vienna.*

Mikhail Sholokhov, 1906-1984 (U.S.S.R.) author, 1965 Nobel laureate. *And Quiet Flows the Don.*

Upton Sinclair, 1878-1968, (U.S.) novelist. *The Jungle.*

Edmund Spenser, 1552-1599, (Br.) poet. *The Faerie Queen.*

Christina Stead, 1903-1983 (Austral.) novelist, short-story writer. *The Man Who Loved Children.*

Richard Steele, 1672-1729, (Br.) essayist, playwright, began the Tatler and Spectator. *The Conscious Lovers.*

Lincoln Steffens, 1866-1936, (U.S.) editor, author. *The Shame of the Cities.*

Gertrude Stein, 1874-1946, (U.S.) author. *Three Lives.*

John Steinbeck, 1902-1968, (U.S.) novelist. *Grapes of Wrath, Of Mice and Men, Winter of Our Discontent.*

Stendhal (Marie Henri Beyle), 1783-1842, (F.) poet, novelist. *The Red and the Black, The Charterhouse of Parma.*

Laurence Sterne, 1713-1768, (Br.) novelist. *Tristram Shandy.*

Wallace Stevens, 1879-1955, (U.S.) poet. *Harmonium, The Man With the Blue Guitar, Transport to Summer.*

Robert Louis Stevenson, 1850-1894, (Br.) novelist, poet, essayist. *Treasure Island, A Child's Garden of Verses.*

Rex Stout, 1886-1975, (U.S.) novelist, created Nero Wolfe.

Harriet Beecher Stowe, 1811-1896, (U.S.) novelist. *Uncle Tom's Cabin.*

Lytton Strachey, 1880-1932, (Br.) biographer, critic. *Eminent Victorians, Queen Victoria, Elizabeth and Essex.*

August Strindberg, 1849-1912, (Swed.) dramatist, novelist. *The Father, Miss Julie, The Creditors.*

Jonathan Swift, 1667-1745, (Br.) author. *Gulliver's Travels.*

Algernon C. Swinburne, 1837-1909, (Br.) poet, critic. *Songs Before Sunrise.*

John M. Synge, 1871-1909, (Ir.) poet, dramatist. *Riders to the Sea, The Playboy of the Western World.*

Rabindranath Tagore, 1861-1941, (Ind.), author, poet. *Sadhana, The Realization of Life, Gitanjali.*

Booth Tarkington, 1869-1946, (U.S.) novelist. *Seventeen, Alice Adams, Penrod.*

Sara Teasdale, 1884-1933, (U.S.) poet. *Helen of Troy and Other Poems, Rivers to the Sea, Flame and Shadow.*

Alfred Lord Tennyson, 1809-1892, (Br.) poet. *Idylls of the King, In Memoriam,* "The Charge of the Light Brigade."

William Makepeace Thackeray, 1811-1863, (Br.) novelist. *Vanity Fair.*

Dylan Thomas, 1914-1953, (Welsh) poet. *Under Milk Wood, A Child's Christmas in Wales.*

Henry David Thoreau, 1817-1862, (U.S.) transcendentalist thinker, writer. *Walden.*

James Thurber, 1894-1961, (U.S.) humorist, artist. *The New Yorker, The Owl in the Attic, Thurber Carnival.*

J.R.R. Tolkien, 1892-1973, (Br.) author. *The Hobbit, Lord of the Rings.*

Leo Tolstoy, 1828-1910, (R.) novelist. *War and Peace, Anna Karenina.*

Anthony Trollope, 1815-1882, (Br.) novelist. *The Warden, Barchester Towers,* The Palliser novels.

Ivan Turgenev, 1818-1883, (R.) novelist, short-story writer. *Fathers and Sons, First Love, A Month in the Country.*

Mark Twain (Samuel Clemens), 1835-1910, (U.S.) novelist, humorist. *The Adventures of Huckleberry Finn, Tom Sawyer.*

Sigrid Undset, 1881-1949, (Nor.) novelist, poet. *Kristin Lavransdatter.*

Paul Valéry, 1871-1945, (F.) poet, critic. *La Jeune Parque, The Graveyard by the Sea.*

Jules Verne, 1828-1905, (F.) novelist, originator of modern science fiction. *Twenty Thousand Leagues Under the Sea.*

François Villon, 1431-1463?, (F.) poet. *Le petit et le Grand, Testament.*

Evelyn Waugh, 1903-1966, (Br.) satirist. *The Loved One.*

H.G. Wells, 1866-1946, (Br.) author. *The Time Machine, The Invisible Man, The War of the Worlds.*

Rebecca West, 1893-1983 (Br.) author. *Black Lamb and Grey Falcon.*

Edith Wharton, 1862-1937, (U.S.) novelist. *The Age of Innocence, The House of Mirth.*

E.B. White, 1899-1985 (U.S.), essayist, children's book author. *Here is New York, Charlotte's Web, Stuart Little.*

T.H. White, 1906-1964, (Br.) author. *The Once and Future King.*

Walt Whitman, 1819-1892, (U.S.) poet. *Leaves of Grass.*

John Greenleaf Whittier, 1807-1892, (U.S.) poet, journalist. *Snow-bound.*

Oscar Wilde, 1854-1900, (Ir.) author, wit. *The Picture of Dorian Gray, The Importance of Being Earnest.*

Laura Ingalls Wilder, 1867-1957, (U.S.) children's books. *Little House on the Prairie.*

Thornton Wilder, 1897-1975, (U.S.) playwright. *Our Town, The Skin of Our Teeth, The Matchmaker.*

Tennessee Williams, 1912-1983 (U.S.) playwright. *A Streetcar Named Desire, Cat on a Hot Tin Roof, The Glass Menagerie.*

William Carlos Williams, 1883-1963, (U.S.) poet, physician. *Tempers, Al Que Quiere!, Paterson.*

Edmund Wilson, 1895-1972, (U.S.) author, literary and social critic. *Axel's Castle, To the Finland Station.*

P.G. Wodehouse, 1881-1975, (U.S.) poet, dramatist. The "Jeeves" novels, *Anything Goes.*

Thomas Wolfe, 1900-1938, (U.S.) novelist. *Look Homeward, Angel, You Can't Go Home Again, Of Time and the River.*

Virginia Woolf, 1882-1941, (Br.) novelist, essayist. *Mrs. Dalloway, To the Lighthouse, The Waves.*

William Wordsworth, 1770-1850, (Br.) poet. "Tintern Abbey," "Ode: Intimations of Immortality."

William Butler Yeats, 1865-1939, (Ir.) poet, playwright. *The Wild Swans at Coole, The Tower, Last Poems.*

Émile Zola, 1840-1902, (F.) novelist. *Nana, The Dram Shop.*

Noted Artists and Sculptors of the Past

Artists are painters unless otherwise indicated.

Washington Allston, 1779-1843, (U.S.) landscapist. Belshazzar's Feast.

Albrecht Altdorfer, 1480-1538, (Ger.) landscapist. Battle of Alexander.

Andrea del Sarto, 1486-1530, frescoes. Madonna of the Harpies.

Fra Angelico, c. 1400-1455, (It.) Renaissance muralist. Madonna of the Linen Drapers' Guild.

Alexsandr Archipenko, 1887-1964, (U.S.) sculptor. Boxing Match, Medranos.

John James Audubon, 1785-1851, (U.S.) Birds of America.

Hans Baldung Grien, 1484-1545, (Ger.) Todentanz.

Ernst Barlach, 1870-1938, (Ger.) Expressionist sculptor. Man Drawing a Sword.

Frederic-Auguste Bartholdi, 1834-1904, (Fr.) Liberty Enlightening the World, Lion of Belfort.

Fra Bartolommeo, 1472-1517, (It.) Vision of St. Bernard.

Aubrey Beardsley, 1872-1898, (Br.) illustrator. Salome, Lysistrata.

Max Beckmann, 1884-1950, (Ger.) Expressionist. The Descent from the Cross.

Gentile Bellini, 1426-1507, (It.) Renaissance. Procession in St. Mark's Square.

Giovanni Bellini, 1428-1516, (It.) St. Francis in Ecstasy.

Jacopo Bellini, 1400-1470, (It.) Crucifixion.

George Wesley Bellows, 1882-1925, (U.S.) sports artist. Stag at Sharkey's.

Thomas Hart Benton, 1889-1975, (U.S.) American regionalist. Threshing Wheat, Arts of the West.

Gianlorenzo Bernini, 1598-1680, (It.) Baroque sculpture. The Assumption.

Albert Bierstadt, 1830-1902, (U.S.) landscapist. The Rocky Mountains, Mount Corcoran.

George Caleb Bingham, 1811-1879, (U.S.) Fur Traders Descending the Missouri.

William Blake, 1752-1827, (Br.) engraver. Book of Job, Songs of Innocence, Songs of Experience.

Rosa Bonheur, 1822-1899, (Fr.) The Horse Fair.

Pierre Bonnard, 1867-1947, (Fr.) Intimist. The Breakfast Room.

Gutzon Borglum, 1871-1941, (U.S.) sculptor. Mt. Rushmore Memorial.

Hieronymus Bosch, 1450-1516, (Flem.) religious allegories. The Crowning with Thorns.

Sandro Botticelli, 1444-1510, (It.) Renaissance. Birth of Venus.

Constantin Brancusi, 1876-1957, (Rum.) Nonobjective sculptor. Flying Turtle, The Kiss.

Georges Braque, 1882-1963, (Fr.) Cubist. Violin and Palette.

Pieter Bruegel the Elder, c. 1525-1569, (Flem.) The Peasant Dance.

Pieter Bruegel the Younger, 1564-1638, (Flem.) Village Fair, The Crucifixion.

Edward Burne-Jones, 1833-1898, (Br.) Pre-Raphaelite artist-craftsman. The Mirror of Venus.

Alexander Calder, 1898-1976, (U.S.) sculptor. Lobster Trap and Fish Tail.

Michelangelo Merisi da Caravaggio, 1573-1610, (It.) Baroque. The Supper at Emmaus.

Emily Carr, 1871-1945, (Can.) landscapist. Blunden Harbour, Big Raven.

Carlo Carra, 1881-1966, (It.) Metaphysical school. Lot's Daughters.

Mary Cassatt, 1845-1926, (U.S.) Impressionist. Woman Bathing.

George Catlin, 1796-1872, (U.S.) American Indian life. Gallery of Indians.

Benvenuto Cellini, 1500-1571, (It.) Mannerist sculptor, goldsmith. Perseus.

Paul Cezanne, 1839-1906, (Fr.) Card Players, Mont-Sainte-Victoire with Large Pine Trees.

Marc Chagall, 1887-1985, (Rus.) Jewish life and folklore. I and the Village.

Jean Simeon Chardin, 1699-1779, (Fr.) still lifes. The Kiss, The Grace.

Frederic Church, 1826-1900, (U.S.) Hudson River school. Niagara, Andes of Ecuador.

Giovanni Cimabue, 1240-1302, (It.) Byzantine mosaicist. Madonna Enthroned with St. Francis.

Claude Lorrain, 1600-1682, (Fr.) ideal-landscapist. The Enchanted Castle.

Thomas Cole, 1801-1848, (U.S.) Hudson River school. The Ox-Bow.

John Constable, 1776-1837, (Br.) landscapist. Salisbury Cathedral from the Bishop's Grounds.

John Singleton Copley, 1738-1815, (U.S.) portraitist. Samuel Adams, Watson and the Shark.

Lovis Corinth, 1858-1925, (Ger.) Expressionist. Apocalypse.

Jean-Baptiste-Camille Corot, 1796-1875, (Fr.) landscapist. Souvenir de Mortefontaine, Pastorale.

Correggio, 1494-1534, (It.) Renaissance muralist. Mystic Marriages of St. Catherine.

Gustave Courbet, 1819-1877, (Fr.) Realist. The Artist's Studio.

Lucas Cranach the Elder, 1472-1553, (Ger.) Protestant Reformation portraitist. Luther.

Nathaniel Currier, 1813-1888, and **James M. Ives,** 1824-1895, (both U.S.) lithographers. A Midnight Race on the Mississippi.

John Steuart Curry, 1897-1946, (U.S.) Americana, murals. Baptism in Kansas.

Salvador Dali, 1904-1989, (Sp.) Surrealist. Persistence of Memory.

Honore Daumier, 1808-1879, (Fr.) caricaturist. The Third-Class Carriage.

Jacques-Louis David, 1748-1825, (Fr.) Neoclassicist. The Oath of the Horatii.

Arthur Davies, 1862-1928, (U.S.) Romantic landscapist. Unicorns.

Edgar Degas, 1834-1917, (Fr.) The Ballet Class.

Eugene Delacroix, 1789-1863, (Fr.) Romantic. Massacre at Chios.

Paul Delaroche, 1797-1856, (Fr.) historical themes. Children of Edward IV.

Luca Della Robbia, 1400-1482, (It.) Renaissance terracotta artist. Cantoria (singing gallery), Florence cathedral.

Donatello, 1386-1466, (It.) Renaissance sculptor. David, Gattamelata.

Jean Dubuffet, 1902-1985, (Fr.) painter, sculptor, printmaker. Group of Four Trees.

Marcel Duchamp, 1887-1968, (Fr.) Nude Descending a Staircase.

Raoul Dufy, 1877-1953, (Fr.) Fauvist. Chateau and Horses.

Asher Brown Durand, 1796-1886, (U.S.) Hudson River school. Kindred Spirits.

Albrecht Durer, 1471-1528, (Ger.) Renaissance engraver, woodcuts. St. Jerome in His Study, Melancholia I, Apocalypse.

Anthony van Dyck, 1599-1641, (Flem.) Baroque portraitist. Portrait of Charles I Hunting.

Thomas Eakins, 1844-1916, (U.S.) Realist. The Gross Clinic.

Jacob Epstein, 1880-1959, (Br.) religious and allegorical sculptor. Genesis, Ecce Homo.

Jan van Eyck, 1380-1441, (Flem.) naturalistic panels. Adoration of the Lamb.

Anselm Feuerbach, 1829-1880, (Ger.) Romantic Classicism. Judgement of Paris, Iphigenia.

John Bernard Flannagan, 1895-1942, (U.S.) animal sculptor. Triumph of the Egg.

Jean-Honore Fragonard, 1732-1806, (Fr.) Rococo. The Swing.

Daniel Chester French, 1850-1931, (U.S.) The Minute Man of Concord; seated Lincoln, Lincoln Memorial, Washington, D.C.

Caspar David Friedrich, 1774-1840, (Ger.) Romantic landscapes. Man and Woman Gazing at the Moon.

Thomas Gainsborough, 1727-1788, (Br.) portraitist. The Blue Boy.

Paul Gauguin, 1848-1903, (Fr.) Post-impressionist. The Tahitians.

Lorenzo Ghiberti, 1378-1455, (It.) Renaissance sculptor. Gates of Paradise baptistry doors, Florence.

Alberto Giacometti, 1901-1966, (It.) attenuated sculptures of solitary figures. Man Pointing.

Giorgione, c. 1477-1510, (It.) Renaissance. The Tempest.

Giotto di Bondone, 1267-1337, (It.) Renaissance. Presentation of Christ in the Temple.

Francois Girardon, 1628-1715, (Fr.) Baroque sculptor of classical themes. Apollo Tended by the Nymphs.

Vincent van Gogh, 1853-1890, (Dutch) The Starry Night, L'Arlesienne.

Arshile Gorky, 1905-1948, (U.S.) Surrealist. The Liver Is the Cock's Comb.

Francisco de Goya y Lucientes, 1746-1828, (Sp.) The Naked Maja, The Disasters of War (etchings).

El Greco, 1541-1614, (Sp.) View of Toledo.

Horatio Greenough, 1805-1852, (U.S.) Neo-classical sculptor. George Washington.

Matthias Grünewald, 1480-1528, (Ger.) mystical religious themes. The Resurrection.

Frans Hals, c. 1580-1666, (Dutch) portraitist. Laughing Cavalier, Gypsy Girl.

Childe Hassam, 1859-1935, (U.S.) Impressionist. Southwest Wind.

Edward Hicks, 1780-1849, (U.S.) folk painter. The Peaceable Kingdom.

Hans Hofmann, 1880-1966, (U.S.) early Abstract Expressionist. Spring. The Gate.

William Hogarth, 1697-1764, (Br.) caricaturist. The Rake's Progress.

Katsushika Hokusai, 1760-1849, (Jap.) printmaker. Crabs.

Hans Holbein the Elder, 1460-1524, (Ger.) late Gothic. Presentation of Christ in the Temple.

Hans Holbein the Younger, 1497-1543, (Ger.) portraitist. Henry VIII.

Winslow Homer, 1836-1910, (U.S.) marine themes. Marine Coast, High Cliff.

Edward Hopper, 1882-1967, (U.S.) realistic urban scenes. Sunlight in a Cafeteria.

Jean-Auguste-Dominique Ingres, 1780-1867, (Fr.) Classicist. Valpincon Bather.

George Inness, 1825-1894, (U.S.) luminous landscapist. Delaware Water Gap.

Vasily Kandinsky, 1866-1944, (Rus.) Abstractionist. Capricious Forms.

Paul Klee, 1879-1940, (Swiss) Abstractionist. Twittering Machine.

Oscar Kokoschka, 1886-1980, (Aus.) Expressionist. View of Prague.

Kathe Kollwitz, 1867-1945, (Ger.) printmaker, social justice themes. The Peasant War.

Gaston Lachaise, 1882-1935, (U.S.) figurative sculptor. Standing Woman.

John La Farge, 1835-1910, (U.S.) muralist. Red and White Peonies.

Fernand Leger, 1881-1955, (Fr.) machine art. The Cyclists.

Leonardo da Vinci, 1452-1519, (It.) Mona Lisa, Last Supper, The Annunciation.

Emanuel Leutze, 1816-1868, (U.S.) historical themes. Washington Crossing the Delaware.

Jacques Lipchitz, 1891-1973, (Fr.) Cubist sculptor. Harpist.

Filippino Lippi, 1457-1504, (It.) Renaissance. The Vision of St. Bernard.

Fra Filippo Lippi, 1406-1469, (It.) Renaissance. Coronation of the Virgin.

Morris Louis, 1912-1962, (U.S.) Abstract Expressionist. Signa, Stripes.

Aristide Maillol, 1861-1944, (Fr.) sculptor. The Mediterranean.

Edouard Manet, 1832-1883, (Fr.) forerunner of Impressionism. Luncheon on the Grass, Olympia.

Andrea Mantegna, 1431-1506, (It.) Renaissance frescoes. Triumph of Caesar.

Franz Marc, 1880-1916, (Ger.) Expressionist. Blue Horses.

John Marin, 1870-1953, (U.S.) expressionist seascapes. Maine Island.

Reginald Marsh, 1898-1954, (U.S.) satirical artist. Tattoo and Haircut.

Masaccio, 1401-1428, (It.) Renaissance. The Tribute Money.

Henri Matisse, 1869-1954, (Fr.) Fauvist. Woman with the Hat.

Michelangelo Buonarroti, 1475-1564, (It.) Pieta, David, Moses, The Last Judgment, Sistine Ceiling.

Jean-Francois Millet, 1814-1875, (Fr.) painter of peasant subjects. The Gleaners, The Man with a Hoe.

Joan Miró, 1893-1983, (Sp.) Exuberant colors, playful images. Catalan landscape, Dutch Interior.

Amedeo Modigliani, 1884-1920, (It.) Reclining Nude.

Piet Mondrian, 1872-1944, (Dutch) Abstractionist. Composition.

Claude Monet, 1840-1926, (Fr.) Impressionist. The Bridge at Argenteuil, Haystacks.

Henry Moore, 1898-1986, (Br.) sculptor of large-scale, abstract works. Reclining Figure (several).

Gustave Moreau, 1826-1898, (Fr.) Symbolist. The Apparition, Dance of Salome.

James Wilson Morrice, 1865-1924, (Can.) landscapist. The Ferry, Quebec, Venice, Looking Over the Lagoon.

Grandma Moses, 1860-1961, (U.S.) folk painter. Out for the Christmas Trees.

Edvard Munch, 1863-1944, (Nor.) Expressionist. The Cry.

Bartolome Murillo, 1618-1682, (Sp.) Baroque religious artist. Vision of St. Anthony. The Two Trinities.

Barnett Newman, 1905-1970, (U.S.) Abstract Expressionist. Stations of the Cross.

Isamu Noguchi, 1904-1988, (U.S.) trad. Japanese art, modern techniques.

Georgia O'Keeffe, 1887-1986, (U.S.) Southwest motifs. Cow's Skull.

Jose Clemente Orozco, 1883-1949, (Mex.) frescoes. House of Tears.

Charles Willson Peale, 1741-1827, (U.S.) American Revolutionary portraitist. Washington, Franklin, Jefferson, John Adams.

Rembrandt Peale, 1778-1860, (U.S.) portraitist. Thomas Jefferson.

Pietro Perugino, 1446-1523, (It.) Renaissance. Delivery of the Keys to St. Peter.

Pablo Picasso, 1881-1973, (Sp.) Guernica, Dove, Head of a Woman.

Piero della Francesca, c. 1415-1492, (It.) Renaissance. Duke of Urbino, Flagellation of Christ.

Camille Pissarro, 1830-1903, (Fr.) Impressionist. Morning Sunlight.

Jackson Pollock, 1912-1956, (U.S.) Abstract Expressionist. Autumn Rhythm.

Nicolas Poussin, 1594-1665, (Fr.) Baroque pictorial classicism. St. John on Patmos.

Maurice B. Prendergast, c. 1860-1924, (U.S.) Post-impressionist water colorist. Umbrellas in the Rain.

Pierre-Paul Prud'hon, 1758-1823, (Fr.) Romanticist. Crime pursued by Vengeance and Justice.

Pierre Cecile Puvis de Chavannes, 1824-1898, (Fr.) muralist. The Poor Fisherman.

Raphael Sanzio, 1483-1520, (It.) Renaissance. Disputa, School of Athens, Sistine Madonna.

Man Ray, 1890-1976, (U.S.) Dadaist. Observing Time, The Lovers.

Odilon Redon, 1840-1916, (Fr.) Symbolist lithographer. In the Dream.

Rembrandt van Rijn, 1606-1669, (Dutch) The Bridal Couple, The Night Watch.

Frederic Remington, 1861-1909, (U.S.) painter, sculptor, portrayer of the American West. Bronco Buster.

Pierre-Auguste Renoir, 1841-1919, (Fr.) Impressionist. The Luncheon of the Boating Party.

Joshua Reynolds, 1723-1792, (Br.) portraitist. Mrs. Siddons as the Tragic Muse.

Diego Rivera, 1886-1957, (Mex.) frescoes. The Fecund Earth.

Norman Rockwell, 1894-1978, (U.S.) illustrator. Saturday Evening Post covers.

Auguste Rodin, 1840-1917, (Fr.) sculptor. The Thinker, The Burghers of Calais.

Mark Rothko, 1903-1970, (U.S.) Abstract Expressionist. Light, Earth and Blue.

Georges Rouault, 1871-1958, (Fr.) Expressionist. The Old King.

Henri Rousseau, 1844-1910, (Fr.) primitive exotic themes. The Snake Charmer.

Theodore Rousseau, 1812-1867, (Swiss-Fr.) landscapist. Under the Birches, Evening.

Peter Paul Rubens, 1577-1640, (Flem.) Baroque. Mystic Marriage of St. Catherine.

Jacob van Ruisdael, c. 1628-1682, (Dutch) landscapist. Jewish Cemetery.

Salomon van Ruysdael, c. 1600-1670, (Dutch) landscapist. River with Ferry-Boat.

Albert Pinkham Ryder, 1847-1917, (U.S.) seascapes and allegories. Toilers of the Sea.

Augustus Saint-Gaudens, 1848-1907, (U.S.) memorial statues. Farragut, Mrs. Henry Adams (Grief).

Andrea Sansovino, 1460-1529, (It.) Renaissance sculptor. Baptism of Christ.

Jacopo Sansovino, 1486-1570, (It.) Renaissance sculptor. St. John the Baptist.

John Singer Sargent, 1856-1925, (U.S.) Edwardian society portraitist. The Wyndham Sisters, Madam X.

Georges Seurat, 1859-1891, (Fr.) Pointillist. Sunday Afternoon on the Island of Grande Jatte.

Gino Severini, 1883-1966, (It.) Futurist and Cubist. Dynamic Hieroglyph of the Bal Tabarin.

Ben Shahn, 1898-1969, (U.S.) social and political themes. Sacco and Vanzetti series, Seurat's Lunch, Handball.

Charles Sheeler, 1883-1965, (U.S.) Abstractionist. Upper Deck.

David Alfaro Siqueiros, 1896-1974, (Mex.) political muralist. March of Humanity.

John F. Sloan, 1871-1951, (U.S.) depictions of New York City. Wake of the Ferry.

David Smith, 1906-1965, (U.S.) welded metal sculpture. Hudson River Landscape, Zig, Cubi series.

Gilbert Stuart, 1755-1828, (U.S.) portraitist. George Washington.

Thomas Sully, 1783-1872, (U.S.) portraitist. Col. Thomas Handasyd Perkins, The Passage of the Delaware.

Yves Tanguy, 1900-1955, (Fr.) Surrealist. Rose of the Four Winds.

Giovanni Battista Tiepolo, 1696-1770, (It.) Rococo frescoes. The Crucifixion.

Jacopo Tintoretto, 1518-1594, (It.) Mannerist. The Last Supper.

Titian, c. 1485-1576, (It.) Renaissance. Venus and the Lute Player, The Bacchanal.

Henri de Toulouse-Lautrec, 1864-1901, (Fr.) At the Moulin Rouge.

John Trumbull, 1756-1843, (U.S.) historical themes. The Declaration of Independence.

J(oseph) M(allord) W(illiam) Turner, 1775-1851, (Br.) Romantic landscapist. Snow Storm.

Paolo Uccello, 1397-1475, (It.) Gothic-Renaissance. The Rout of San Romano.

Maurice Utrillo, 1883-1955, (Fr.) Impressionist. Sacre-Coeur de Montmartre.

John Vanderlyn, 1775-1852, (U.S.) Neo-classicist. Ariadne Asleep on the Island of Naxos.

Diego Velazquez, 1599-1660, (Sp.) Baroque. Las Meninas, Portrait of Juan de Pareja.

Jan Vermeer, 1632-1675, (Dutch) interior genre subjects. Young Woman with a Water Jug.

Paolo Veronese, 1528-1588, (It.) devotional themes, vastly peopled canvases. The Temptation of St. Anthony.

Andrea del Verrocchio, 1435-1488, (It.) Florentine sculptor. Colleoni.

Maurice de Vlaminck, 1876-1958, (Fr.) Fauvist landscapist. The Storm.

Andy Warhol, 1928-1987 (U.S.) Pop Art, Campbell's Soup Cans.

Antoine Watteau, 1684-1721, (Fr.) Rococo painter of "scenes of gallantry". The Embarkation for Cythera.

George Frederic Watts, 1817-1904, (Br.) painter and sculptor of grandiose allegorical themes. Hope, Physical Energy.

Benjamin West, 1738-1820, realistic historical themes. Death of General Wolfe.

James Abbott McNeill Whistler, 1834-1903, (U.S.) Arrangement in Grey and Black, No. 1: The Artist's Mother.

Archibald M. Willard, 1836-1918, (U.S.) The Spirit of '76.

Grant Wood, 1891-1942, (U.S.) Midwestern regionalist. American Gothic, Daughters of Revolution.

Ossip Zadkine, 1890-1967, (Rus.) School of Paris sculptor. The Destroyed City, Musicians, Christ.

Noted Philosophers and Religionists of the Past

Lyman Abbott, 1835-1922, (U.S.) clergyman, reformer; advocate of Christian Socialism.
Pierre Abelard, 1079-1142, (F.) philosopher, theologian, and teacher, used dialectic method to support Christian dogma.
Felix Adler, 1851-1933, (U.S.) German-born founder of the Ethical Culture Society.
St. Augustine, 354-430, Latin bishop considered the founder of formalized Christian theology.
Averroes, 1126-1198, (Sp.) Islamic philosopher.
Roger Bacon, c.1214-1294, (Br.) philosopher and scientist.
Karl Barth, 1886-1968, (Sw.) theologian, a leading force in 20th-century Protestantism.
St. Benedict, c.480-547, (It.) founded the Benedictines.
Jeremy Bentham, 1748-1832, (Br.) philosopher, reformer, founder of Utilitarianism.
Henri Bergson, 1859-1941, (F.) philosopher of evolution.
George Berkeley, 1685-1753, (Ir.) philosopher, churchman.
John Biddle, 1615-1662, (Br.) founder of English Unitarianism.
Jakob Boehme, 1575-1624, (G.) theosophist and mystic.
William Brewster, 1567-1644, (Br.) headed Pilgrims, signed Mayflower Compact.
Emil Brunner, 1889-1966, (Sw.) theologian.
Giordano Bruno, 1548-1600, (It.) philosopher.
Martin Buber, 1878-1965, (G.) Jewish philosopher, theologian, wrote *I and Thou.*
Buddha (Siddhartha Gautama), c.563-c.483 BC, (Ind.) philosopher, founded Buddhism.
John Calvin, 1509-1564, (F.) theologian, a key figure in the Protestant Reformation.
Rudolph Carnap, 1891-1970, (U.S.) German-born philosopher, a founder of logical positivism.
William Ellery Channing, 1780-1842, (U.S.) clergyman, early spokesman for Unitarianism.
Auguste Comte, 1798-1857, (F.) philosopher, the founder of positivism.
Confucius, 551-479 BC, (Chin.) founder of Confucianism.
John Cotton, 1584-1652, (Br.) Puritan theologian.
Thomas Cranmer, 1489-1556, (Br.) churchman, wrote much of *Book of Common Prayer;* promoter of English Reformation.
René Descartes, 1596-1650, (F.) philosopher, mathematician.
John Dewey, 1859-1952, (U.S.) philosopher, educator; helped inaugurate the progressive education movement.
Denis Diderot, 1713-1784, (F.) philosopher, creator of first modern encyclopedia.
Mary Baker Eddy, 1821-1910, (U.S.) founder of Christian Science.
Jonathan Edwards, 1703-1758, (U.S.) preacher, theologian.
(Desiderius) Erasmus, c.1466-1536, (Du.) Renaissance humanist.
Johann Fichte, 1762-1814, (G.) philosopher, the first of the Transcendental Idealists.
George Fox, 1624-1691, (Br.) founder of Society of Friends.
St. Francis of Assisi, 1182-1226, (It.) founded Franciscans.
al Ghazali, 1058-1111, Islamic philosopher.
Georg W. Hegel, 1770-1831, (G.) Idealist philosopher.
Martin Heidegger, 1889-1976, (G.) existentialist philosopher, affected fields ranging from physics to literary criticism.
Johann G. Herder, 1744-1803, (G.) philosopher, cultural historian; a founder of German Romanticism.
David Hume, 1711-1776, (Sc.) philosopher, historian.
Jan Hus, 1369-1415, (Czech.) religious reformer.
Edmund Husserl, 1859-1938, (G.) philosopher, founded the Phenomenological movement.
Thomas Huxley, 1825-1895, (Br.) philosopher, educator.
Ignatius of Loyola, 1491-1556, (Sp.) founder of the Jesuits.
William Inge, 1860-1954, (Br.) theologian, explored the mystic aspects of Christianity.
William James, 1842-1910, (U.S.) philosopher, psychologist; advanced theory of the pragmatic nature of truth.
Karl Jaspers, 1883-1969, (G.) existentialist philosopher.

Immanuel Kant, 1724-1804, (G.) metaphysician, preeminent founder of modern critical philosophy.
Soren Kierkegaard, 1813-1855, (Den.) philosopher, considered the father of Existentialism.
John Knox, 1505-1572, (Sc.) leader of the Protestant Reformation in Scotland.
Lao-Tzu, 604-531 BC, (Chin.) philosopher, considered the founder of the Taoist religion.
Gottfried von Leibniz, 1646-1716, (G.) philosopher, mathematician.
Martin Luther, 1483-1546, (G.) leader of the Protestant Reformation, founded Lutheran church.
Maimonides, 1135-1204, (Sp.) Jewish philosopher.
Jacques Maritain, 1882-1973, (F.) Neo-Thomist philosopher.
Cotton Mather, 1663-1728, (U.S.) defender of orthodox Puritanism; founded Yale, 1701.
Philipp Melanchthon, 1497-1560, (G.) theologian, humanist; an important voice in the Reformation.
Thomas Merton, 1915-1968, (U.S.) Trappist monk, spiritual writer.
Mohammed, c.570-632, Arab prophet of the religion of Islam.
Dwight Moody, 1837-1899, (U.S.) evangelist.
George E. Moore, 1873-1958, (Br.) ethical theorist.
Elijah Muhammad, 1897-1975, (U.S.) leader of the Black Muslim sect.
Heinrich Muhlenberg, 1711-1787, (G.) organized the Lutheran Church in America.
John H. Newman, 1801-1890, (Br.) Roman Catholic cardinal, led Oxford Movement.
Reinhold Niebuhr, 1892-1971, (U.S.) Protestant theologian, social and political critic.
Friedrich Nietzsche, 1844-1900, (G.) moral philosopher.
Blaise Pascal, 1623-1662, (F.) philosopher and mathematician.
St. Patrick, c.389-c.461, brought Christianity to Ireland.
St. Paul, ?-c.67, a founder of the Christian religion.
Charles S. Peirce, 1839-1914, (U.S.) philosopher, logician; originated concept of Pragmatism, 1878.
Josiah Royce 1855-1916, (U.S.) Idealist philosopher.
Charles T. Russell, 1852-1916, (U.S.) founder of Jehovah's Witnesses.
Fredrich von Schelling, 1775-1854, (G.) philosopher.
Friedrich Schleiermacher, 1768-1834, (G.) theologian, a founder of modern Protestant theology.
Arthur Schopenhauer, 1788-1860, (G.) philosopher.
Joseph Smith, 1805-1844, (U.S.) founded Latter Day Saints (Mormon) movement, 1830.
Herbert Spencer, 1820-1903, (Br.) philosopher of evolution.
Baruch Spinoza, 1632-1677, (Du.) rationalist philosopher.
Billy Sunday, 1862-1935, (U.S.) evangelist.
Daisetz Teitaro Suzuki, 1870-1966, (Jap.) Buddhist scholar.
Emanuel Swedenborg, 1688-1722, (Swed.) philosopher, mystic.
Thomas à Becket, 1118-1170, (Br.) archbishop of Canterbury, opposed Henry II.
Thomas à Kempis, c.1380-1471, (G.) theologian probably wrote *Imitation of Christ.*
Thomas Aquinas, 1225-1274, (It.) theologian, philosopher.
Paul Tillich, 1886-1965, (U.S.) German-born philosopher and theologian.
John Wesley, 1703-1791, (Br.) theologian, evangelist; founded Methodism.
Alfred North Whitehead, 1861-1947, (Br.) philosopher, mathematician.
William of Occam, c.1285-c.1349 (Br.) philosopher.
Roger Williams, c.1603-1683, (U.S.) clergyman, championed religious freedom and separation of church and state.
Ludwig Wittgenstein, 1889-1951, (Aus.) philosopher.
John Wycliffe, 1320-1384, (Br.) theologian, reformer.
Brigham Young, 1801-1877, (U.S.) Mormon leader, colonized Utah.
Huldrych Zwingli, 1484-1531, (Sw.) theologian, led Swiss Protestant Reformation.

Noted Social Reformers and Educators of the Past

Jane Addams, 1860-1935, (U.S.) co-founder of Hull House; won Nobel Peace Prize, 1931.
Susan B. Anthony, 1820-1906, (U.S.) a leader in temperance, anti-slavery, and women's suffrage movements.
Henry Barnard, 1811-1900, (U.S.) public school reformer.
Thomas Barnardo, 1845-1905, (Br.) social reformer, pioneered in the care of destitute children.
Clara Barton, 1821-1912, (U.S.) organizer of the American Red Cross.

Henry Ward Beecher, 1813-1887, (U.S.) clergyman, abolitionist.
Sarah G. Blanding, 1899-1985, (U.S.), head of Vassar College, 1946-64.
Amelia Bloomer, 1818-1894, (U.S.) social reformer, women's rights advocate.
William Booth, 1829-1912, (Br.) founded the Salvation Army.
Nicholas Murray Butler, 1862-1947, (U.S.) educator headed Columbia Univ., 1902-45; won Nobel Peace Prize, 1931.

Frances X. (Mother) Cabrini, 1850-1917, (U.S.) Italian-born nun founded charitable institutions; first American canonized.

Carrie Chapman Catt, 1859-1947, (U.S.) suffragette, helped win passage of the 19th amendment.

Dorothy Day, 1897-1980, (U.S.) founder of Catholic Worker Movement.

Eugene V. Debs, 1855-1926, (U.S.) labor leader, led Pullman strike, 1894; 4-time Socialist presidential candidate.

Melvil Dewey, 1851-1931, (U.S.) devised decimal system of library-book classification.

Dorothea Dix, 1802-1887, (U.S.) crusader for humane care of mentally ill.

Frederick Douglass, 1817-1895, (U.S.) abolitionist.

W.E.B. DuBois, 1868-1963, (U.S.) Negro-rights leader, educator, and writer.

William Lloyd Garrison, 1805-1879, (U.S.) abolitionist, reformer.

Giovanni Gentile, 1875-1944, (It.) philosopher, educator; reformed Italian educational system.

Samuel Gompers, 1850-1924, (U.S.) labor leader; a founder and president of AFL.

William Green, 1873-1952, (U.S.) president of AFL, 1924-52.

Michael Harrington, 1928-1989, (U.S.) revealed poverty in affluent U.S. in *The Other America,* 1963.

Sidney Hillman, 1887-1946, (U.S.) labor leader, helped organize CIO.

John Holt, 1924-1985, (U.S.) educator and author, *How Children Fail.*

Samuel G. Howe, 1801-1876, (U.S.) social reformer, changed public attitudes toward the handicapped.

Helen Keller, 1880-1968, (U.S.) crusader for better treatment for the handicapped.

Martin Luther King Jr., 1929-1968, (U.S.) civil rights leader; won Nobel Peace Prize, 1964.

John L. Lewis, 1880-1969, (U.S.) labor leader, headed United Mine Workers, 1920-60.

Horace Mann, 1796-1859, (U.S.) pioneered modern public school system.

William H. McGuffey, 1800-1873, (U.S.) author of *Reader,* the mainstay of 19th century U.S. public education.

Alexander Meiklejohn, 1872-1964, (U.S.) British-born educator, championed academic freedom and experimental curricula.

Lucretia Mott, 1793-1880, (U.S.) reformer, pioneer feminist.

Philip Murray, 1886-1952, (U.S.) Scotch-born labor leader.

Florence Nightingale, 1820-1910, (Br.) founder of modern nursing.

Emmeline Pankhurst, 1858-1928, (Br.) woman suffragist.

Elizabeth P. Peabody, 1804-1894, (U.S.) education pioneer, founded 1st kindergarten in U.S., 1860.

Walter Reuther, 1907-1970, (U.S.) labor leader, headed UAW.

Jacob Riis, 1849-1914, (U.S.) crusader for urban reforms.

Margaret Sanger, 1883-1966, (U.S.) social reformer, pioneered the birth control movement.

Elizabeth Seton, 1774-1821, (U.S.) established parochial school education in U.S.

Earl of Shaftesbury (A.A. Cooper), 1801-1885, (Br.) social reformer.

Elizabeth Cady Stanton, 1815-1902, (U.S.) women's suffrage pioneer.

Lucy Stone, 1818-1893, (U.S.) feminist, abolitionist.

Harriet Tubman, c.1820-1913, (U.S.) abolitionist, ran Underground Railroad.

Booker T. Washington, 1856-1915, (U.S.) educator, reformer; championed vocational training for blacks.

Walter F. White, 1893-1955, (U.S.) headed NAACP, 1931-55.

William Wilberforce, 1759-1833, (Br.) social reformer, prominent in struggle to abolish the slave trade.

Emma Hart Willard, 1787-1870, (U.S.) pioneered higher education for women.

Frances E. Willard, 1839-1898, (U.S.) temperance, woman's rights leader.

Whitney M. Young Jr., 1921-1971, (U.S.) civil rights leader, headed National Urban League, 1961-71.

Noted Historians, Economists, and Social Scientists of the Past

Brooks Adams, 1848-1927, (U.S.) historian, political theoretician.

Francis Bacon, 1561-1626, (Br.) philosopher, essayist, and statesman.

George Bancroft, 1800-1891, (U.S.) historian, wrote 10-volume *History of the United States.*

Charles A. Beard, 1874-1948, (U.S.) historian, attacked motives of the Founding Fathers.

Bede (the Venerable), c.673-735, (Br.) scholar, historian.

Ruth Benedict, 1887-1948, (U.S.) anthropologist, studied Indian tribes of the Southwest.

Bruno Bettleheim, 1903-1990, (Aust.-U.S.) psychoanalyst specializing in autistic children; *The Uses of Enchantment.*

Louis Blanc, 1811-1882, (F.) Socialist leader and historian whose ideas were a link between utopian and Marxist socialism.

Leonard Bloomfield, 1887-1949, (U.S.) linguist. *Language.*

Franz Boas, 1858-1942, (U.S.) German-born anthropologist, studied American Indians.

Van Wyck Brooks, 1886-1963, (U.S.) cultural historian, critic.

Edmund Burke, 1729-1797, (Ir.) British parliamentarian and political philosopher; influenced many Federalists.

Joseph Campbell, 1904-1987, (U.S.) authored books on mythology, folklore.

Thomas Carlyle, 1795-1881, (Sc.) philosopher, historian, and critic.

Edward Channing, 1856-1931, (U.S.) historian, wrote 6-volume *A History of the United States.*

John R. Commons, 1862-1945, (U.S.) economist, labor historian.

Benedetto Croce, 1866-1952, (It.) philosopher, statesman, and historian.

Bernard A. De Voto, 1897-1955, (U.S.) historian, won Pulitzer prize in 1948 for *Across the Wide Missouri.*

Ariel Durant, 1898-1981, (U.S.) historian, collaborated with husband on 11-volume *The Story of Civilization.*

Will Durant, 1885-1981, (U.S.) historian. *The Story of Civilization, The Story of Philosophy.*

Emile Durkheim, 1858-1917, (F.) a founder of modern sociology.

Friedrich Engels, 1820-1895, (G.) political writer, with Marx wrote the *Communist Manifesto.*

Irving Fisher, 1867-1947, (U.S.) economist, contributed to the development of modern monetary theory.

John Fiske, 1842-1901, (U.S.) historian and lecturer, popularized Darwinian theory of evolution.

Charles Fourier, 1772-1837, (F.) utopian socialist.

Henry George, 1839-1897, (U.S.) economist, reformer, led single-tax movement.

Edward Gibbon, 1737-1794, (Br.) historian, wrote *The History of the Decline and Fall of the Roman Empire.*

Francesco Guicciardini, 1483-1540, (It.) historian, wrote *Storia d'Italia,* principal historical work of the 16th-century.

Alvin Hansen, 1887-1975, (U.S.) economist.

Thomas Hobbes, 1588-1679, (Br.) social philosopher.

Richard Hofstadter, 1916-1970, (U.S.) historian, wrote *The Age of Reform.*

John Maynard Keynes, 1883-1946, (Br.) economist, principal advocate of deficit spending.

Alfred L. Kroeber, 1876-1960, (U.S.) cultural anthropologist, studied Indians of North and South America.

James L. Laughlin, 1850-1933, (U.S.) economist, helped establish Federal Reserve System.

Lucien Lévy-Bruhl, 1857-1939, (F.) philosopher, studied the psychology of primitive societies.

Kurt Lewin, 1890-1947, (U.S.) German-born psychologist, studied human motivation and group dynamics.

John Locke, 1632-1704, (Br.) political philosopher.

Konrad Lorenz, 1904-1989, (Aus.) ethologist, pioneer in study of animal behavior.

Thomas B. Macauley, 1800-1859, (Br.) historian, statesman.

Bronislaw Malinowski, 1884-1942, (Pol.) anthropologist, considered the father of social anthropology.

Thomas R. Malthus, 1766-1834, (Br.) economist, famed for *Essay on the Principle of Population.*

Karl Mannheim, 1893-1947, (Hung.) sociologist, historian.

Karl Marx, 1818-1883, (G.) political philosopher, proponent of modern communism.

Giuseppe Mazzini, 1805-1872, (It.) political philosopher.

George H. Mead, 1863-1931, (U.S.) philosopher and social psychologist.

Margaret Mead, 1901-1978, (U.S.) cultural anthropologist, popularized field.

James Mill, 1773-1836, (Sc.) philosopher, historian, and economist; a proponent of Utilitarianism.

John Stuart Mill, 1806-1873, (Br.) philosopher, political economist.

Perry G. Miller, 1905-1963, (U.S.) historian, interpreted 17th-century New England.

Theodor Mommsen, 1817-1903, (G.) historian, wrote *The History of Rome.*

Charles-Louis Montesquieu, 1689-1755, (F.) social philosopher.

Samuel Eliot Morison, 1887-1976, (U.S.) historian, chronicled voyages of early explorers.

Lewis Mumford, 1895-1990, (U.S.) sociologist, critic, *The Culture of Cities.*

Gunnar Myrdal, 1898-1987 (Swe.) economist, social scientist.

Allan Nevins, 1890-1971, (U.S.) historian, biographer; twice won Pulitzer prize.

Jose Ortega y Gasset, 1883-1955, (Sp.) philosopher and humanist; advocated control by an elite.

Robert Owen, 1771-1858, (Br.) political philosopher, reformer.

Vilfredo Pareto, 1848-1923, (It.) economist, sociologist.

Francis Parkman, 1823-1893, (U.S.) historian, wrote 8-volume France and England in North America, 1851-92.

Marco Polo, c.1254-1324, (It.) narrated an account of his travels to China.

William Prescott, 1796-1859, (U.S.) early American historian.

Pierre Joseph Proudhon, 1809-1865, (F.) social theorist, regarded as the father of anarchism.

Francois Quesnay, 1694-1774, (F.) economic theorist, demonstrated circular flow of economic activity through society.

David Ricardo, 1772-1823, (Br.) economic theorist, advocated free international trade.

James H. Robinson, 1863-1936, (U.S.) historian, educator.

Carl Rogers, 1902-1987, (U.S.) psychotherapist, author.

Jean-Jacques Rousseau, 1712-1778, (F.) social philosopher, author.

Edward Sapir, 1884-1939 (Ger.-U.S.) anthropologist, studied ethnology and linguistics of some U.S. Indian groups.

Ferdinand de Saussure, 1857-1913, (Swiss) a founder of modern linguistics.

Hjalmar Schacht, 1877-1970, (G.) economist.

Joseph Schumpeter, 1883-1950, (U.S.) Czech.-born economist, championed big business, capitalism.

Albert Schweitzer, 1875-1965, (Alsatian) social philosopher, theologian, and humanitarian.

George Simmel, 1858-1918, (G.) sociologist, philosopher.

Adam Smith, 1723-1790, (Br.) economist, advocated laissez-faire economy and free trade.

Jared Sparks, 1789-1866, (U.S.) historian, among first to do research from original documents.

Oswald Spengler, 1880-1936, (G.) philosopher and historian, wrote The Decline of the West.

William G. Sumner, 1840-1910, (U.S.) social scientist, economist; championed laissez-faire economy, Social Darwinism.

Hippolyte Taine, 1828-1893, (F.) historian.

Frank W. Taussig, 1859-1940, (U.S.) economist, educator.

Nikolaas Tinbergen, 1907-1988, (Dutch-Br.) ethologist, pioneer in study of animal behavior.

Alexis de Tocqueville, 1805-1859, (F.) political scientist, historian.

Francis E. Townsend, 1867-1960, (U.S.) author of old-age pension plan.

Arnold Toynbee, 1889-1975, (Br.) historian, wrote 10-volume A Study of History.

Heinrich von Treitschke, 1834-1896, (G.) historian, political writer.

George Trevelyan, 1838-1928, (Br.) historian, statesman.

Barbara Tuchman, 1912-1989, (U.S.) author of Pulitzer Prize-winning history books, The Guns of August.

Frederick J. Turner, 1861-1932, (U.S.) historian, educator.

Thorstein B. Veblen, 1857-1929, (U.S.) economist, social philosopher.

Giovanni Vico, 1668-1744, (It.) historian, philosopher.

Voltaire (F.M. Arouet), 1694-1778, (F.) philosopher, historian, and poet.

Izaak Walton, 1593-1683, (Br.) author, wrote first biographical works in English literature.

Sidney J., 1859-1947, and wife Beatrice, 1858-1943, Webb (Br.) leading figures in Fabian Society and British Labour Party.

Walter P. Webb, 1888-1963, (U.S.) historian of the West.

Max Weber, 1864-1920, (G.) sociologist. The Protestant Ethic and the Spirit of Capitalism.

Noted Scientists of the Past

Howard H. Aiken, 1900-1973, (U.S.) mathematician, credited with designing forerunner of digital computer.

Albertus Magnus, 1193-1280, (G.) theologian, philosopher, scientist, established medieval Christian study of natural science.

Andre-Marie Ampère, 1775-1836, (F.) scientist known for contributions to electrodynamics.

Amedeo Avogadro, 1776-1856, (It.) chemist, physicist, advanced important theories on properties of gases.

A.C. Becquerel, 1788-1878, (F.) physicist, pioneer in electrochemical science.

A.H. Becquerel, 1852-1908, (F.) physicist, discovered radioactivity in uranium.

Alexander Graham Bell, 1847-1922, (U.S.) inventor, first to patent and commercially exploit the telephone, 1876.

Daniel Bernoulli, 1700-1782, (Swiss) mathematician, advanced kinetic theory of gases and fluids.

Jöns Jakob Berzelius, 1779-1848, (Swed.) chemist, developed modern chemical symbols and formulas.

Henry Bessemer, 1813-1898, (Br.) engineer, invented Bessemer steel-making process.

Louis Blériot, 1872-1936, (F.) engineer, pioneer aviator, invented and constructed monoplanes.

Niels Bohr, 1885-1962, (Dan.) physicist, leading figure in the development of quantum theory.

Max Born, 1882-1970, (G.) physicist known for research in quantum mechanics.

Satyendranath Bose, 1894-1974, (In.) physicist, chemist, mathematician known for Bose statistics, forerunner of modern quantum theory.

Walter Brattain, 1902-1987, (U.S.) inventor, worked on invention of transistor.

Louis de Broglie, 1893-1987, (F.) physicist, best known for wave theory.

Robert Bunsen, 1811-1899, (G.) chemist, invented Bunsen burner.

Luther Burbank, 1849-1926, (U.S.) plant breeder whose work developed plant breeding into a modern science.

Vannevar Bush, 1890-1974, (U.S.) electrical engineer, developed differential analyzer, first electronic analogue computer.

Alexis Carrel, 1873-1944, (F.) surgeon, biologist, developed methods of suturing blood vessels and transplanting organs.

George Washington Carver, 1860?-1943, (U.S.) agricultural chemist, experimenter, benefactor of South, a black hero.

Henry Cavendish, 1731-1810, (Br.) chemist, physicist, discovered hydrogen.

James Chadwick, 1891-1974, (Br.) physicist, discovered the neutron.

Jean M. Charcot, 1825-1893, (F.) neurologist known for work on hysteria, hypnotism, sclerosis.

Albert Claude, 1899-1983, (Belg.) a founder of modern cell biology.

John D. Cockcroft, 1897-1967, (Br.) nuclear physicist, constructed first atomic particle accelerator with E.T.S. Walton.

William Crookes, 1832-1919, (Br.) physicist, chemist, discovered thallium, invented a cathode-ray tube, radiometer.

Marie Curie, 1867-1934, (Pol.-F.) physical chemist known for work on radium and its compounds.

Pierre Curie, 1859-1906, (F.) physical chemist known for work with his wife on radioactivity.

Gottlieb Daimler, 1834-1900, (G.) engineer, inventor, pioneer automobile manufacturer.

John Dalton, 1766-1844, (Br.) chemist, physicist, formulated atomic theory, made first table of atomic weights.

Charles Darwin, 1809-1882, (Br.) naturalist, established theory of organic evolution.

Humphry Davy, 1778-1829, (Br.) chemist, research in electrochemistry led to isolation of potassium, sodium, calcium, barium, boron, magnesium, and strontium.

Lee De Forest, 1873-1961, (U.S.) inventor, pioneer in development of wireless telegraphy, sound pictures, television.

Max Delbruck, 1907-1981, (U.S.) pioneer in modern molecular genetics.

Rudolf Diesel, 1858-1913, (G.) mechanical engineer, patented Diesel engine.

Thomas Dooley, 1927-1961, (U.S.) "jungle doctor," noted for efforts to supply medical aid to underdeveloped countries.

Christian Doppler, 1803-1853, (Aus.) physicist, demonstrated Doppler effect (change in energy wavelengths caused by motion).

Thomas A. Edison, 1847-1931, (U.S.) inventor, held over 1,000 patents, including incandescent electric lamp, phonograph.

Paul Ehrlich, 1854-1915, (G.) bacteriologist, pioneer in modern immunology and bacteriology.

Albert Einstein, 1879-1955, (Ger.-U.S.) theoretical physicist, known for formulation of relativity theory.

John F. Enders, 1897-1985, (U.S.) virologist who helped discover vaccines against polio, measles, and mumps.

Leonhard Euler, 1707-1783, (Swiss) mathematician, physicist, authored first calculus book.

Gabriel Fahrenheit, 1686-1736, (G.) physicist, introduced Fahrenheit scale for thermometers.

Michael Faraday, 1791-1867, (Br.) chemist, physicist, known for work in field of electricity.

Pierre de Fermat, 1601-1665, (F.) mathematician, discovered analytic geometry, founded modern theory of numbers and calculus of probabilities.

Enrico Fermi, 1901-1954, (It.) physicist, one of chief architects of the nuclear age.

Galileo Ferraris, 1847-1897, (It.) physicist, electrical engineer, discovered principle of rotary magnetic field.

Richard Feynman, 1918-1988, (U.S.) a leading theoretical physicist of the postwar generation.

Camille Flammarion, 1842-1925, (F.) astronomer, popularized study of astronomy.

Alexander Fleming, 1881-1955, (Br.) bacteriologist, discovered penicillin.

Jean B.J. Fourier, 1768-1830, (F.) mathematician, discovered theorem governing periodic oscillation.

James Franck, 1882-1964, (G.) physicist, proved value of quantum theory.

Sigmund Freud, 1856-1939, (Aus.) psychiatrist, founder of psychoanalysis.

Galileo Galilei, 1564-1642, (It.) astronomer, physicist, a founder of the experimental method.

Luigi Galvani, 1737-1798, (It.) physician, physicist, known as founder of galvanism.

Carl Friedrich Gauss, 1777-1855, (G.) mathematician, astronomer, physicist, made important contributions to almost every field of physical science, founded a number of new fields.

Joseph Gay-Lussac, 1778-1850, (F.) chemist, physicist, investigated behavior of gases, discovered law of combining volumes.

Josiah W. Gibbs, 1839-1903, (U.S.) theoretical physicist, chemist, founded chemical thermodynamics.

Robert H. Goddard, 1882-1945 (U.S.) physicist, father of modern rocketry.

George W. Goethals, 1858-1928, (U.S.) army engineer, built the Panama Canal.

William C. Gorgas, 1854-1920, (U.S.) sanitarian, U.S. army surgeon-general, his work to prevent yellow fever, malaria helped insure construction of Panama Canal.

Ernest Haeckel, 1834-1919, (G.) zoologist, evolutionist, a strong proponent of Darwin.

Otto Hahn, 1879-1968, (G.) chemist, worked on atomic fission.

J.B.S. Haldane, 1892-1964, (Sc.) scientist, known for work as geneticist and application of mathematics to science.

James Hall, 1761-1832, (Br.) geologist, chemist, founded experimental geology, geochemistry.

Edmund Halley, 1656-1742, (Br.) astronomer, calculated the orbits of many planets.

William Harvey, 1578-1657, (Br.) physician, anatomist, discovered circulation of the blood.

Hermann v. Helmholtz, 1821-1894, (G.) physicist, anatomist, physiologist, made fundamental contributions to physiology, optics, electrodynamics, mathematics, meteorology.

William Herschel, 1738-1822, (Br.) astronomer, discovered Uranus.

Heinrich Hertz, 1857-1894, (G.) physicist, his discoveries led to wireless telegraphy.

David Hilbert, 1862-1943, (G.) mathematician, formulated first satisfactory set of axioms for modern Euclidean geometry.

Edwin P. Hubble, 1889-1953, (U.S.) astronomer, produced first observational evidence of expanding universe.

Alexander v. Humboldt, 1769-1859, (G.) explorer, naturalist, propagator of earth sciences, originated ecology, geophysics.

Julian Huxley, 1887-1975, (Br.) biologist, a gifted exponent and philosopher of science.

Edward Jenner, 1749-1823, (Br.) physician, discovered vaccination.

William Jenner, 1815-1898, (Br.) physician, pathological anatomist.

Frederic Joliot-Curie, 1900-1958, (F.) physicist, with his wife continued work of Curies on radioactivity.

Irene Joliot-Curie, 1897-1956, (F.) physicist, continued work of Curies in radioactivity.

James P. Joule, 1818-1889, (Br.) physicist, determined relationship between heat and mechanical energy (conservation of energy).

Carl Jung, 1875-1961, (Sw.) psychiatrist, founder of analytical psychology.

Wm. Thomson Kelvin, 1824-1907, (Br.) mathematician, physicist, known for work on heat and electricity.

Sister Elizabeth Kenny, 1886-1952, (Austral.) nurse, developed method of treatment for polio.

Johannes Kepler, 1571-1630, (G.) astronomer, discovered important laws of planetary motion.

Joseph Lagrange, 1736-1813, (F.) geometer, astronomer, worked in all fields of analysis, and number theory, and analytical and celestial mechanics.

Jean B. Lamarck, 1744-1829, (F.) naturalist, forerunner of Darwin in evolutionary theory.

Irving Langmuir, 1881-1957, (U.S.) physical chemist, his studies of molecular films on solid and liquid surfaces opened new fields in colloid research and biochemistry.

Pierre S. Laplace, 1749-1827, (F.) astronomer, physicist, put forth nebular hypothesis of origin of solar system.

Antoine Lavoisier, 1743-1794, (F.) chemist, founder of modern chemistry.

Ernest O. Lawrence, 1901-1958, (U.S.) physicist, invented the cyclotron.

Louis Leakey, 1903-1972, (Br.) anthropologist, discovered important fossils, remains of early hominids.

Anton van Leeuwenhoek, 1632-1723, (Du.) microscopist, father of microbiology.

Gottfried Wilhelm Leibniz, 1646-1716, (G.) mathematician, developed theories of differential and integral calculus.

Justus von Liebig, 1803-1873, (G.) chemist, established quantitative organic chemical analysis.

Joseph Lister, 1827-1912, (Br.) pioneer of antiseptic surgery.

Percival Lowell, 1855-1916, (U.S.) astronomer, predicted the existence of Pluto.

Guglielmo Marconi, 1874-1937, (It.) physicist, known for his development of wireless telegraphy.

James Clerk Maxwell, 1831-1879, (Sc.) physicist, known especially for his work in electricity and magnetism.

Maria Goeppert Mayer, 1906-1972, (G.-U.S.) physicist, independently developed theory of structure of atomic nuclei.

Lise Meitner, 1878-1968, (Aus.) physicist whose work contributed to the development of the atomic bomb.

Gregor J. Mendel, 1822-1884, (Aus.) botanist, known for his experimental work on heredity.

Franz Mesmer, 1734-1815, (G.) physician, developed theory of animal magnetism.

Albert A. Michelson, 1852-1931, (U.S.) physicist, established speed of light as a fundamental constant.

Robert A. Millikan, 1868-1953, (U.S.) physicist, noted for study of elementary electronic charge and photoelectric effect.

Thomas Hunt Morgan, 1866-1945, (U.S.) geneticist, embryologist, established chromosome theory of heredity.

Isaac Newton, 1642-1727, (Br.) natural philosopher, mathematician, discovered law of gravitation, laws of motion.

J. Robert Oppenheimer, 1904-1967, (U.S.) physicist, director of Los Alamos during development of the atomic bomb.

Wilhelm Ostwald, 1853-1932, (G.) physical chemist, philosopher, chief founder of physical chemistry.

Louis Pasteur, 1822-1895, (F.) chemist, originated process of pasteurization.

Max Planck, 1858-1947, (G.) physicist, originated and developed quantum theory.

Henri Poincaré, 1854-1912, (F.) mathematician, physicist, influenced cosmology, relativity, and topology.

Joseph Priestley, 1733-1804, (Br.) chemist, one of the discoverers of oxygen.

Rabi, Isidor Isaac, 1899-1988 (U.S.) physicist, pioneered atom exploration.

Walter S. Reed, 1851-1902, (U.S.) army pathologist, bacteriologist, proved mosquitos transmit yellow fever.

Bernhard Riemann, 1826-1866, (G.) mathematician, contributed to development of calculus, complex variable theory, and mathematical physics.

Wilhelm Roentgen, 1845-1923, (G.) physicist, discovered X-rays.

Bertrand Russell, 1872-1970, (Br.) logician, philosopher, one of the founders of modern logic, wrote *Principia Mathematica*.

Ernest Rutherford, 1871-1937, (Br.) physicist, discovered the atomic nucleus.

Giovanni Schiaparelli, 1835-1910, (It.) astronomer, hypothesized canals on the surface of Mars.

Angelo Secchi, 1818-1878, (It.) astronomer, pioneer in classifying stars by their spectra.

Harlow Shapley, 1885-1972, (U.S.) astronomer, noted for his studies of the galaxy.

Charles P. Steinmetz, 1865-1923, (G.-U.S.) electrical engineer, developed basic ideas on alternating current systems.

Leo Szilard, 1898-1964, (Hung.-U.S.) physicist, helped create first sustained nuclear reaction.

Nikola Tesla, 1856-1943, (Croatia-U.S.) electrical engineer, contributed to most developments in electronics.

Rudolf Virchow, 1821-1902, (G.) pathologist, a founder of cellular pathology.

Alessandro Volta, 1745-1827, (It.) physicist, pioneer in electricity.

Alfred Russell Wallace, 1823-1913, (Br.) naturalist, proposed concept of evolution similar to Darwin.

August v. Wasserman, 1866-1925, (G.) bacteriologist, discovered reaction used as test for syphilis.

James E. Watt, 1736-1819, (Sc.) mechanical engineer, inventor, invented modern steam condensing engine.

Alfred L. Wegener, 1880-1930, (G.) meteorologist, geophysicist, postulated theory of continental drift.

Norbert Wiener, 1894-1964, (U.S.) mathematician, founder of the science of cybernetics.

Sewall Wright, 1890-1988 (U.S.) a leading evolutionary theorist.

Ferdinand v. Zeppelin, 1838-1917 (G.) soldier, aeronaut, airship designer.

Noted Business Leaders, Industrialists, and Philanthropists of the Past

Elizabeth Arden (F.N. Graham), 1884-1966, (U.S.) Canadian-born businesswoman founded and headed cosmetics empire.

Philip D. Armour, 1832-1901, (U.S.) industrialist, streamlined meat packing.

John Jacob Astor, 1763-1848, (U.S.) German-born fur trader, banker, real estate magnate; at death, richest in U.S.

Francis W. Ayer, 1848-1923, (U.S.) ad industry pioneer.

August Belmont, 1816-1890, (U.S.) German-born financier.

James B. (Diamond Jim) Brady, 1856-1917, (U.S.) financier, philanthropist, legendary bon vivant.

Adolphus Busch, 1839-1913, (U.S.) German-born businessman, established brewery empire.

Asa Candler, 1851-1929, (U.S.) founded Coca-Cola Co.

Andrew Carnegie, 1835-1919, (U.S.) Scots-born industrialist, founded U.S. Steel; financed over 2,800 libraries.

William Colgate, 1783-1857, (U.S.) British-born businessman, philanthropist; founded soap-making empire.

Jay Cooke, 1821-1905, (U.S.) financier, sold $1 billion in Union bonds during Civil War.

Peter Cooper, 1791-1883, (U.S.) industrialist, inventor, philanthropist.

Ezra Cornell, 1807-1874, (U.S.) businessman, philanthropist; headed Western Union, established univ.

Erastus Corning, 1794-1872, (U.S.) financier, headed N.Y. Central.

Charles Crocker, 1822-1888, (U.S.) railroad builder, financier.

Samuel Cunard, 1787-1865, (Can.) pioneered trans-Atlantic steam navigation.

Marcus Daly, 1841-1900, (U.S.) Irish-born copper magnate.

Walt Disney, 1901-1966, (U.S.) pioneer in cinema animation, built entertainment empire.

Herbert H. Dow, 1866-1930, (U.S.) Canadian-born founder of chemical co.

James Duke, 1856-1925, (U.S.) founded American Tobacco, Duke Univ.

Eleuthere I. du Pont, 1771-1834, (U.S.) French-born gunpowder manufacturer; founded one of world's largest business empires.

Thomas C. Durant, 1820-1885, (U.S.) railroad official, financier.

William C. Durant, 1861-1947, (U.S.) industrialist, formed General Motors.

George Eastman, 1854-1932, (U.S.) inventor, manufacturer of photographic equipment.

Marshall Field, 1834-1906, (U.S.) merchant, founded Chicago's largest department store.

Harvey Firestone, 1868-1938, (U.S.) industrialist, founded tire co.

Henry M. Flagler, 1830-1913, (U.S.) financier, helped form Standard Oil; developed Florida as resort state.

Malcolm Forbes, 1919-1990, (U.S.) publisher of *Fortune* magazine.

Henry Ford, 1863-1947, (U.S.) auto maker, developed first popular low-priced car.

Henry Ford 2d, 1917-1987, (U.S.) headed auto company founded by grandfather.

Henry C. Frick, 1849-1919, (U.S.) industrialist, helped organize U.S. Steel.

Jakob Fugger (Jakob the Rich), 1459-1525, (G.) headed leading banking house, trading concern, in 16th-century Europe.

Alfred C. Fuller, 1885-1973, (U.S.) Canadian-born businessman, founded brush co.

Elbert H. Gary, 1846-1927, (U.S.) U.S. Steel head, 1903-27.

Amadeo P. Giannini, 1870-1949, (U.S.) founded Bank of America.

Stephen Girard, 1750-1831, (U.S.) French-born financier, philanthropist; richest man in U.S. at his death.

Jean Paul Getty, 1892-1976, (U.S.) founded oil empire.

Jay Gould, 1836-1892, (U.S.) railroad magnate, financier, speculator.

Hetty Green, 1834-1916, (U.S.) financier, the "witch of Wall St."; richest woman in U.S in her day.

William Gregg, 1800-1867, (U.S.) launched textile industry in the South.

Meyer Guggenheim, 1828-1905, (U.S.) Swiss-born merchant, philanthropist; built merchandising, mining empires.

Edward H. Harriman, 1848-1909, (U.S.) railroad financier, administrator; headed Union Pacific.

William Randolph Hearst, 1863-1951, (U.S.) a dominant figure in American journalism; built vast publishing empire.

Henry J. Heinz, 1844-1919, (U.S.) founded food empire.

James J. Hill, 1838-1916, (U.S.) Canadian-born railroad magnate, financier; founded Great Northern Railway.

Conrad N. Hilton, 1888-1979, (U.S.) intl. hotel chain founder.

Howard Hughes, 1905-1976, (U.S.) industrialist, financier, movie maker.

H.L. Hunt, 1889-1974, (U.S.) oil magnate.

Collis P. Huntington, 1821-1900, (U.S.) railroad magnate.

Henry E. Huntington, 1850-1927, (U.S.) railroad builder, philanthropist.

Walter L. Jacobs, 1898-1985, (U.S.) founder of the first rental car agency, which later became Hertz.

Howard Johnson, 1896-1972, (U.S.) founded restaurant chain.

Henry J. Kaiser, 1882-1967, (U.S.) industrialist, built empire in steel, aluminum.

Minor C. Keith, 1848-1929, (U.S.) railroad magnate; founded United Fruit Co.

Will K. Kellogg, 1860-1951, (U.S.) businessman, philanthropist, founded breakfast food co.

Richard King, 1825-1885, (U.S.) cattleman, founded half-million acre King Ranch in Texas.

William S. Knudsen, 1879-1948, (U.S.) Danish-born auto industry executive.

Samuel H. Kress, 1863-1955, (U.S.) businessman, art collector, philanthropist; founded "dime store" chain.

Ray A. Kroc, 1902-1984, (U.S.) builder of McDonald's fast food empire; owner, San Diego Padres baseball team.

Alfred Krupp, 1812-1887, (G.) armaments magnate.

Albert Lasker, 1880-1952, (U.S.) businessman, philanthropist.

Thomas Lipton, 1850-1931, (Scot.) merchant, built tea empire.

James McGill, 1744-1813, (Can.) Scots-born fur trader, founded univ.

Andrew W. Mellon, 1855-1937, (U.S.) financier, industrialist; benefactor of National Gallery of Art.

Charles E. Merrill, 1885-1956, (U.S.) financier, developed firm of Merrill Lynch.

John Pierpont Morgan, 1837-1913, (U.S.) most powerful figure in finance and industry at the turn-of-the-century.

Malcolm Muir, 1885-1979, (U.S.) created *Business Week* magazine; headed *Newsweek,* 1937-61.

Samuel Newhouse, 1895-1979, (U.S.) publishing and broadcasting magnate, built communications empire.

Aristotle Onassis, 1900-1975, (Gr.) shipping magnate.

George Peabody, 1795-1869, (U.S.) merchant, financier, philanthropist.

James C. Penney, 1875-1971, (U.S.) businessman, developed department store chain.

William C. Procter, 1862-1934, (U.S.) headed soap co.

John D. Rockefeller, 1839-1937, (U.S.) industrialist, established Standard Oil; became world's wealthiest person.

John D. Rockefeller Jr., 1874-1960, (U.S.) philanthropist, established foundation; provided land for United Nations.

Meyer A. Rothschild, 1743-1812, (G.) founded international banking house.

Thomas Fortune Ryan, 1851-1928, (U.S.) financier, dominated N.Y. City public transportation; helped found American Tobacco.

Russell Sage, 1816-1906, (U.S.) financier.

David Sarnoff, 1891-1971, (U.S.) broadcasting pioneer, established first radio network, NBC.

Richard W. Sears, 1863-1914, (U.S.) founded mail-order co.

(Ernst) Werner von Siemens, 1816-1892, (G.) industrialist, inventor.

Alfred P. Sloan, 1875-1966, (U.S.) industrialist, philanthropist; headed General Motors.

A. Leland Stanford, 1824-1893, (U.S.) railroad official, philanthropist; founded univ.

Nathan Strauss, 1848-1931, (U.S.) German-born merchant, philanthropist; headed Macy's.

Levi Strauss, c.1829-1902, (U.S.) pants manufacturer.

Clement Studebaker, 1831-1901, (U.S.) wagon, carriage manufacturer.

Gustavus Swift, 1839-1903, (U.S.) pioneer meat-packer; promoted refrigerated railroad cars.

Gerard Swope, 1872-1957, (U.S.) industrialist, economist; headed General Electric.

James Walter Thompson, 1847-1928, (U.S.) ad executive.

Theodore N. Vail, 1845-1920, (U.S.) organized Bell Telephone system, headed ATT.

Cornelius Vanderbilt, 1794-1877, (U.S.) financier, established steamship, railroad empires.

Henry Villard, 1835-1900, (U.S.) German-born railroad executive, financier.

Charles R. Walgreen, 1873-1939, (U.S.) founded drugstore chain.

DeWitt Wallace, 1890-1981, (U.S.) and **Lila Wallace,** 1890-1984, (U.S.) co-founders of *Reader's Digest* magazine, philanthropists.

John Wanamaker, 1838-1922, (U.S.) pioneered department-store merchandising.

Aaron Montgomery Ward, 1843-1913, (U.S.) established first mail-order firm.

Thomas J. Watson, 1874-1956, (U.S.) headed IBM, 1924-49.

John Hay Whitney, 1905-1982, (U.S.) publisher, sportsman, philanthropist.

Charles E. Wilson, 1890-1961, (U.S.) auto industry executive; public official.

Frank W. Woolworth, 1852-1919, (U.S.) created 5 & 10 chain.

William Wrigley Jr., 1861-1932, (U.S.) founded chewing gum co.

Composers of the Western World

Carl Philipp Emanuel Bach, 1714-1788, (G.) Prussian and Wurtembergian Sonatas.

Johann Christian Bach, 1735-1782, (G.) Concertos; sonatas.

Johann Sebastian Bach, 1685-1750, (G.) St. Matthew Passion, The Well-Tempered Clavichord.

Samuel Barber, 1910-1981, (U.S.) Adagio for Strings, Vanessa.

Bela Bartok, 1881-1945, (Hung.) Concerto for Orchestra, The Miraculous Mandarin.

Ludwig Van Beethoven, 1770-1827, (G.) Concertos (Emperor); sonatas (Moonlight, Pastorale, Pathetique); symphonies (Eroica).

Vincenzo Bellini, 1801-1835, (It.) La Sonnambula, Norma, I Puritani.

Alban Berg, 1885-1935, (Aus.) Wozzeck, Lulu.

Hector Berlioz, 1803-1869, (F.) Damnation of Faust, Symphonie Fantastique, Requiem.

Leonard Bernstein, b. 1918, (U.S.) Jeremiah, West Side Story.

Georges Bizet, 1838-1875, (F.) Carmen, Pearl Fishers.

Ernest Bloch, 1880-1959, (Swiss) Schelomo, Voice in the Wilderness, Sacred Service.

Luigi Boccherini, 1743-1805, (It.) Cello Concerto in B Flat, Symphony in D.

Alexander Borodin, 1833-1887, (R.) Prince Igor, In the Steppes of Central Asia.

Johannes Brahms, 1833-1897, (G.) Liebeslieder Waltzes, Rhapsody in E Flat Major, Opus 119 for Piano, Academic Festival Overture; symphonies; quartets.

Benjamin Britten, 1913-1976, (Br.) Peter Grimes, Turn of the Screw, Ceremony of Carols, War Requiem.

Anton Bruckner, 1824-1896, (Aus.) Symphonies (Romantic), Intermezzo for String Quintet.

Ferruccio Busoni, 1866-1924, (It.) Doctor Faust, Comedy Overture.

Dietrich Buxtehude, 1637-1707, (D.) Cantatas, trio sonatas.

William Byrd, 1543-1623, (Br.) Masses, sacred songs.

(Alexis-) Emmanuel Chabrier, 1841-1894, (Fr.) Le Roi Malgre Lui, Espana.

Gustave Charpentier, 1860-1956, (F.) Louise.

Frederic Chopin, 1810-1849, (P.) Polonaises, mazurkas, waltzes, etudes, nocturnes. Polonaise No. 6 in A Flat Major (Heroic); sonatas.

Aaron Copland, b. 1900, (U.S.) Appalachian Spring.

(Achille-) Claude Debussy, 1862-1918, (F.) Pelleas et Melisande, La Mer, Prelude to the Afternoon of a Faun.

C.P. Leo Delibes, 1836-1891, (F.) Lakme, Coppelia, Sylvia.

Norman Dello Joio, b. 1913, (U.S.), Triumph of St. Joan, Psalm of David.

Gaetano Donizetti, 1797-1848, (It.) Elixir of Love, Lucia Di Lammermoor, Daughter of the Regiment.

Paul Dukas, 1865-1935, (F.) Sorcerer's Apprentice.

Antonin Dvorak, 1841-1904, (C.) Symphony in E Minor (From the New World).

Edward Elgar, 1857-1934, (Br.) Pomp and Circumstance.

Manuel de Falla, 1876-1946, (Sp.) La Vide Breve, El Amor Brujo.

Gabriel Faure, 1845-1924, (Fr.) Requiem, Ballade.

Friedrich von Flotow, 1812-1883, (G.) Martha.

Cesar Franck, 1822-1890, (Belg.) D Minor Symphony.

George Gershwin, 1898-1937, (U.S.) Rhapsody in Blue, American in Paris, Porgy and Bess.

Umberto Giordano, 1867-1948, (It.) Andrea Chenier.

Alexander K. Glazunoff, 1865-1936, (R.) Symphonies, Stenka Razin.

Mikhail Glinka, 1804-1857, (R.) Ruslan and Ludmilla.

Christoph W. Gluck, 1714-1787, (G.) Alceste, Iphigenie en Tauride.

Charles Gounod, 1818-1893, (F.) Faust, Romeo and Juliet.

Edvard Grieg, 1843-1907, (Nor.) Peer Gynt Suite, Concerto in A Minor.

George Frederick Handel, 1685-1759, (G., Br.) Messiah, Xerxes, Berenice.

Howard Hanson, 1896-1981, (U.S.) Symphonies No. 1 (Nordic) and 2 (Romantic).

Roy Harris, 1898-1979, (U.S.) Symphonies, Amer. Portraits.

Joseph Haydn, 1732-1809, (Aus.) Symphonies (Clock); oratorios; chamber music.

Paul Hindemith, 1895-1963, (U.S.) Mathis Der Maler.

Gustav Holst, 1874-1934, (Br.) The Planets.

Arthur Honegger, 1892-1955, (Swiss) Judith, Le Roi David, Pacific 231.

Alan Hovhaness, b. 1911, (U.S.) Symphonies, Magnificat.

Engelbert Humperdinck, 1854-1921, (G.) Hansel and Gretel.

Charles Ives, 1874-1954, (U.S.) Third Symphony.

Aram Khachaturian, 1903-1978, (Armen.) Gayane (ballet), symphonies.

Zoltan Kodaly, 1882-1967, (Hung.) Hary Janos, Psalmus Hungaricus.

Fritz Kreisler, 1875-1962, (Aus.) Caprice Viennois, Tambourin Chinois.

Rodolphe Kreutzer, 1766-1831, (F.) 40 etudes for violin.

Edouard V.A. Lalo, 1823-1892, (F.) Symphonie Espagnole.

Ruggiero Leoncavallo, 1857-1919, (It.) Pagliacci.

Franz Liszt, 1811-1886, (Hung.) 20 Hungarian rhapsodies; symphonic poems.

Edward MacDowell, 1861-1908, (U.S.) To a Wild Rose.

Gustav Mahler, 1860-1911, (Aus.) Lied von der Erde.

Pietro Mascagni, 1863-1945, (It.) Cavalleria Rusticana.

Jules Massenet, 1842-1912, (F.) Manon, Le Cid, Thais.

Felix Mendelssohn, 1809-1847, (G.) Midsummer Night's Dream, Songs Without Words.

Gian-Carlo Menotti, b. 1911, (It.-U.S.) The Medium, The Consul, Amahl and the Night Visitors.

Giacomo Meyerbeer, 1791-1864, (G.) Robert le Diable, Les Huguenots.

Claudio Monteverdi, 1567-1643, (It.) Opera; masses; madrigals.

Wolfgang Amadeus Mozart, 1756-1791, (Aus.) Magic Flute, Marriage of Figaro; concertos; symphonies; etc.

Modest Moussorgsky, 1835-1881, (R.) Boris Godunov, Pictures at an Exhibition.

Jacques Offenbach, 1819-1880, (F.) Tales of Hoffmann.

Carl Orff, 1895-1982, (G.) Carmina Burana.

Ignace Paderewski, 1860-1941, (P.) Minuet in G.

Giovanni P. da Palestrina, c. 1525-1594, (It.) Masses; madrigals.

Amilcare Ponchielli, 1834-1886, (It.) La Gioconda.

Francis Poulenc, 1899-1963, (F.) Dialogues des Carmelites.

Serge Prokofiev, 1891-1953, (R.) Love for Three Oranges, Lt. Kije, Peter and the Wolf.

Giacomo Puccini, 1858-1924, (It.) La Boheme, Manon Lescaut, Tosca, Madame Butterfly.

Sergei Rachmaninov, 1873-1943, (R.) 24 preludes, E concerti, 4 symphonies. Prelude in C Sharp Minor.

Maurice Ravel, 1875-1937, (Fr.) Bolero, Daphnis et Chloe, Rapsodie Espagnole.

Nikolai Rimsky-Korsakov, 1844-1908, (R.) Golden Cockerel, Capriccio Espagnol, Scheherazade, Russian Easter Overture.

Gioacchino Rossini, 1792-1868, (It.) Barber of Seville, Semiramide, William Tell.

Chas. Camille Saint-Saens, 1835-1921, (F.) Samson and Delilah, Danse Macabre.

Alessandro Scarlatti, 1660-1725, (It.) Cantatas; concertos.

Domenico Scarlatti, 1685-1757, (It.) Harpsichord sonatas.

Arnold Schoenberg, 1874-1951, (Aus.) Pelleas and Melisande, Transfigured Night, De Profundis.

Franz Schubert, 1797-1828, (A.) Lieder; symphonies (Unfinished); overtures (Rosamunde).

William Schuman, b. 1910, (U.S.) Credendum, New England Triptych.

Robert Schumann, 1810-1856, (G.) Symphonies, songs.

Aleksandr Scriabin, 1872-1915, (R.) Prometheus.

Dimitri Shostakovich, 1906-1975, (R.) Symphonies, Lady Macbeth of Mzensk, The Nose.

Jean Sibelius, 1865-1957, (Finn.) Finlandia, Karelia.

Bedrich Smetana, 1824-1884, (Cz.). The Bartered Bride.

Karlheinz Stockhausen, b. 1928, (G.) Kontrapunkte, Kontakte.

Richard Strauss, 1864-1949, (G.) Salome, Elektra, Der Rosenkavalier, Thus Spake Zarathustra.

Igor F. Stravinsky, 1882-1971, (R.-U.S.) Oedipus Rex, Le Sacre du Printemps, Petrushka.

Peter I. Tchaikovsky, 1840-1893, (R.) Nutcracker Suite, Swan Lake, Eugene Onegin.

Ambroise Thomas, 1811-1896, (F.) Mignon.

Virgil Thomson, b. 1896, (U.S.) Opera, ballet; Four Saints in Three Acts.

Ralph Vaughan Williams, 1872-1958, (Br.) Job, London Symphony, Symphony No. 7 (Antartica).

Giuseppe Verdi, 1813-1901, (It.) Aida, Rigoletto, Don Carlo, Il Trovatore, La Traviata, Falstaff, Macbeth.

Heitor Villa-Lobos, 1887-1959, (Brazil) Choros.

Antonio Vivaldi, 1678-1741, (It.) Concerti, The Four Seasons.

Richard Wagner, 1813-1883, (G.) Rienzi, Tannhauser, Lohengrin, Tristan und Isolde.

Carl Maria von Weber, 1786-1826, (G.) Der Freischutz.

Composers of Operettas, Musicals, and Popular Music

Richard Adler, b. 1921, (U.S.) Pajama Game; Damn Yankees.

Milton Ager, 1893-1979, (U.S.) I Wonder What's Become of Sally; Hard Hearted Hannah; Ain't She Sweet?

Leroy Anderson, 1908-1975, (U.S.) Syncopated Clock.

Paul Anka, b. 1941, (Can.) My Way; She's a Lady; Tonight Show theme.

Harold Arlen, 1905-1986, (U.S.) Stormy Weather; Over the Rainbow; Blues in the Night; That Old Black Magic.

Burt Bacharach, b. 1928, (U.S.) Raindrops Keep Fallin' on My Head; Walk on By; What the World Needs Now is Love.

Ernest Ball, 1878-1927, (U.S.) Mother Machree; When Irish Eyes Are Smiling.

Irving Berlin, 1888-1989 (U.S.) This is the Army; Annie Get Your Gun; Call Me Madam; God Bless America; White Christmas.

Leonard Bernstein, b. 1918, (U.S.) On the Town; Wonderful Town; Candide; West Side Story.

Eubie Blake, 1883-1963, (U.S.) Shuffle Along; I'm Just Wild about Harry.

Jerry Bock, b. 1928, (U.S.) Mr. Wonderful; Fiorello; Fiddler on the Roof; The Rothschilds.

Carrie Jacobs Bond, 1862-1946, (U.S.) I Love You Truly.

Nacio Herb Brown, 1896-1964, (U.S.) Singing in the Rain; You Were Meant for Me; All I Do Is Dream of You.

Hoagy Carmichael, 1899-1981, (U.S.) Stardust; Georgia on My Mind; Old Buttermilk Sky.

George M. Cohan, 1878-1942, (U.S.) Give My Regards to Broadway; You're A Grand Old Flag; Over There.

Cy Coleman, b. 1929, (U.S.) Sweet Charity; Witchcraft.

Noel Coward, 1899-1973 (Br.) Bitter Sweet; Mad Dogs and Englishmen; Mad About the Boy.

Walter Donaldson, 1893-1947, (U.S.) My Buddy; Carolina in the Morning; You're Driving Me Crazy; Makin' Whoopee.

Neil Diamond, b. 1941, (U.S.) I'm a Believer; Sweet Caroline.

Vernon Duke, 1903-1969, (U.S.) April in Paris.

Bob Dylan, b. 1941, (U.S.) Blowin' in the Wind.

Gus Edwards, 1879-1945, (U.S.) School Days; By the Light of the Silvery Moon; In My Merry Oldsmobile.

Sherman Edwards, 1919-1981, (U.S.) See You in September; Wonderful! Wonderful!

Duke Ellington, 1899-1974, (U.S.) Sophisticated Lady; Satin Doll; It Don't Mean a Thing; Solitude.

Sammy Fain, b. 1902, I'll Be Seeing You; Love Is a Many-Splendored Thing.

Fred Fisher, 1875-1942, (U.S.) Peg O' My Heart; Chicago.

Stephen Collins Foster, 1826-1864, (U.S.) My Old Kentucky Home; Old Folks At Home.

Rudolf Friml, 1879-1972, (naturalized U.S.) The Firefly; Rose Marie; Vagabond King; Bird of Paradise.

John Gay, 1685-1732, (Br.) The Beggar's Opera.

George Gershwin, 1898-1937, (U.S.) Someone to Watch Over Me; I've Got a Crush on You; Embraceable You.

Ferde Grofe, 1892-1972, (U.S.) Grand Canyon Suite.

Marvin Hamlisch, b. 1944, (U.S.) The Way We Were; Nobody Does It Better, A Chorus Line.

W. C. Handy, 1873-1958, (U.S.) St. Louis Blues.

Ray Henderson, 1896-1970, (U.S.) George White's Scandals; That Old Gang of Mine; Five Foot Two, Eyes of Blue.

Victor Herbert, 1859-1924, (Ir.-U.S.) Mlle. Modiste; Babes in Toyland; The Red Mill; Naughty Marietta; Sweethearts.

Jerry Herman, b. 1932, (U.S.) Hello Dolly; Mame.

Brian Holland, b. 1941, **Lamont Dozier,** b. 1941, **Eddie Holland,** b. 1939, (all U.S.) Heat Wave; Stop! In the Name of Love; Baby, I Need Your Loving.

Scott Joplin, 1868-1917, (U.S.) Treemonisha.

John Kander, b. 1927, (U.S.) Cabaret; Chicago; Funny Lady.

Jerome Kern, 1885-1945, (U.S.) Sally; Sunny; Show Boat.

Carole King, b. 1942, (U.S.) Will You Love Me Tomorrow?; Natural Woman; One Fine Day; Up on the Roof.

Burton Lane, b. 1912, (U.S.) Finian's Rainbow.

Franz Lehar, 1870-1948, (Hung.) Merry Widow.

Jerry Leiber, & **Mike Stoller,** both b. 1933, (both U.S.) Hound Dog; Searchin'; Yakety Yak; Love Me Tender.

Mitch Leigh, b. 1928, (U.S.) Man of La Mancha.

John Lennon, 1940-1980, & **Paul McCartney,** b. 1942, (both Br.) I Want to Hold Your Hand; She Loves You; Hard Day's Night; Can't Buy Me Love; And I Love Her.

Frank Loesser, 1910-1969, (U.S.) Guys and Dolls; Where's Charley?; The Most Happy Fella; How to Succeed . . .

Frederick Loewe, 1901-1988, (Aust.-U.S.) The Day Before Spring; Brigadoon; Paint Your Wagon; My Fair Lady; Camelot.

Henry Mancini, b. 1924, (U.S.) Moon River; Days of Wine and Roses; Pink Panther Theme.

Barry Mann, b. 1939, & **Cynthia Weil,** b. 1937, (both U.S.) You've Lost That Loving Feeling, Saturday Night at the Movies.

Jimmy McHugh, 1894-1969 (U.S.) Don't Blame Me; I'm in the Mood for Love; I Feel a Song Coming On.

Joseph Meyer, 1894-1987, (U.S.) If You Knew Susie; California, Here I Come; Crazy Rhythm.

Chauncey Olcott, 1860-1932, (U.S.) Mother Machree.

Cole Porter, 1893-1964, (U.S.) Anything Goes; Kiss Me Kate; Can Can; Silk Stockings.

Richard Rodgers, 1902-1979, (U.S.) Connecticut Yankee; Oklahoma!; Carousel; South Pacific; The King and I; The Sound of Music.

Smokey Robinson, b. 1940, (U.S.) Shop Around; My Guy; My Girl; Get Ready.

Sigmund Romberg, 1887-1951, (Hung.) Maytime; The Student Prince; Desert Song; Blossom Time.

Harold Rome, b. 1908, (U.S.) Pins and Needles; Call Me Mister; Wish You Were Here; Fanny; Destry Rides Again.

Vincent Rose, b. 1880-1944, (U.S.) Avalon; Whispering; Blueberry Hill.

Harry Ruby, 1895-1974, (U.S.) Three Little Words; Who's Sorry Now?

Arthur Schwartz, 1900-1984, (U.S.) The Band Wagon; Dancing in the Dark; By Myself; That's Entertainment.

Neil Sedaka, b. 1939, (U.S.) Breaking Up Is Hard to Do.

Paul Simon, b. 1942, (U.S.) Sounds of Silence; I Am a Rock; Mrs. Robinson; Bridge Over Troubled Waters.

Stephen Sondheim, b. 1930, (U.S.) A Little Night Music; Company; Sweeney Todd; Sunday in the Park with George.

John Philip Sousa. 1854-1932, (U.S.) El Capitan; Stars and Stripes Forever.

Oskar Straus, 1870-1954, (Aus.) Chocolate Soldier.

Johann Strauss, 1825-1899, (Aus.) Gypsy Baron; Die Fledermaus; waltzes: Blue Danube, Artist's Life.

Charles Strouse, b. 1928, (U.S.) Bye Bye, Birdie; Annie.

Jule Styne, b. 1905, (b. Br.-U.S.) Gentlemen Prefer Blondes; Bells Are Ringing; Gypsy; Funny Girl.

Arthur S. Sullivan, 1842-1900, (Br.) H.M.S. Pinafore, Pirates of Penzance; The Mikado.

Deems Taylor, 1885-1966, (U.S.) Peter Ibbetson.

Egbert van Alstyne, 1882-1951, (U.S.) In the Shade of the Old Apple Tree; Memories; Pretty Baby.

Jimmy Van Heusen, 1913-1990, (U.S.) Moonlight Becomes You; Swinging on a Star; All the Way; Love and Marriage.

Albert von Tilzer, 1878-1956, (U.S.) I'll Be With You in Apple Blossom Time; Take Me Out to the Ball Game.

Harry von Tilzer, 1872-1946, (U.S.) Only a Bird in a Gilded Cage; On a Sunday Afternoon.

Fats Waller, 1904-1943, (U.S.) Honeysuckle Rose; Ain't Misbehavin'.

Harry Warren, 1893-1981, (U.S.) You're My Everything; We're in the Money; I Only Have Eyes for You.

Jimmy Webb, b. 1946, (U.S.) Up, Up and Away; By the Time I Get to Phoenix; Didn't We?; Wichita Lineman.

Andrew Lloyd Webber, b. 1948, (Br.) Jesus Christ Superstar, Evita, Cats, The Phantom of the Opera.

Kurt Weill, 1900-1950, (G.-U.S.) Threepenny Opera; Lady in the Dark; Knickerbocker Holiday; One Touch of Venus.

Percy Wenrich, 1887-1952, (U.S.) When You Wore a Tulip; Moonlight Bay; Put On Your Old Gray Bonnet.

Richard A. Whiting, 1891-1938, (U.S.) Till We Meet Again; Sleepytime Gal; Beyond the Blue Horizon; My Ideal.

John Williams, b. 1932, (U.S.) Jaws, E.T., Star Wars series, Raiders of the Lost Ark series.

Meredith Willson, 1902-1984, (U.S.) The Music Man.

Stevie Wonder, b. 1950, (U.S.) You Are the Sunshine of My Life; Signed, Sealed, Delivered, I'm Yours.

Vincent Youmans, 1898-1946, (U.S.) Two Little Girls in Blue; Wildflower; No, No, Nanette; Hit the Deck; Rainbow; Smiles.

Lyricists

Johnny Burke, 1908-1984, (U.S.) What's New?; Misty; Imagination; Polka Dots and Moonbeams.

Sammy Cahn, b. 1913, (U.S.) High Hopes; Love and Marriage; The Second Time Around; It's Magic.

Betty Comden, b. 1919 (U.S.) and **Adolph Green,** b. 1915 (U.S.) The Party's Over; Just in Time; New York, New York.

Hal David, b. 1921 (U.S.) What the World Needs Now Is Love; Close to You.

Buddy De Sylva, 1895-1950, (U.S.) When Day is Done; Look for the Silver Lining; April Showers.

Howard Dietz, 1896-1983, (U.S.) Dancing in the Dark; You and the Night and the Music; That's Entertainment.

Al Dubin, 1891-1945, (U.S.) Tiptoe Through the Tulips; Anniversary Waltz; Lullaby of Broadway.

Fred Ebb, b. 1936 (U.S.) *Cabaret, Zorba, Woman of the Year.*

Dorothy Fields, 1905-1974, (U.S.) On the Sunny Side of the Street; Don't Blame Me; The Way You Look Tonight.

Ira Gershwin, 1896-1983, (U.S.) The Man I Love; Fascinating Rhythm; S'Wonderful; Embraceable You.

William S. Gilbert, 1836-1911, (Br.) *The Mikado; H.M.S. Pinafore, Pirates of Penzance.*

Gerry Goffin, b. 1939, (U.S.) Will You Love Me Tomorrow, Take Good Care of My Baby, Up on the Roof, One Fine Day.

Mack Gordon, 1905-1959, (Pol.-U.S.) You'll Never Know; The More I See You; Chattanooga Choo-Choo; You Make Me Feel So Young.

Oscar Hammerstein II, 1895-1960, (U.S.) Ol' Man River; *Oklahoma; Carousel.*

E. Y. (Yip) Harburg, 1898-1981, (U.S.) Brother, Can You Spare a Dime; April in Paris; Over the Rainbow.

Lorenz Hart, 1895-1943, (U.S.) Isn't it Romantic; Blue Moon, Lover; Manhattan; My Funny Valentine; Mountain Greenery.

DuBose Heyward, 1885-1940, (U.S.) Summertime; A Woman Is A Sometime Thing.

Gus Kahn, 1886-1941, (U.S.) Memories; Ain't We Got Fun.

Alan J. Lerner, 1918-1986, (U.S.) *Brigadoon; My Fair Lady; Camelot; Gigi.; On a Clear Day You Can See Forever.*

Johnny Mercer, 1909-1976, (U.S.) Blues in the Night; Come Rain or Come Shine; Laura; That Old Black Magic.

Bob Merrill, b. 1921, (U.S.) People; Don't Rain on My Parade.

Jack Norworth, 1879-1959, (U.S.) Take Me Out to the Ball Game; Shine On Harvest Moon.

Mitchell Parish, b. 1901, (U.S.) Stairway to the Stars; Stardust.

Andy Razaf, 1895-1973, (U.S.) Honeysuckle Rose, Ain't Misbehavin', S'posin'.

Leo Robin, 1900-1984, (U.S.) Thanks for the Memory; Hooray for Love; Diamonds are a Girl's Best Friend.

Paul Francis Webster, b. 1907, (U.S.) I Got It Bad and That Ain't Good, Secret Love, The Shadow of Your Smile, Love Is a Many-Splendored Thing.

Jack Yellen, b. 1892, (U.S.) Down by the O-Hi-O; Ain't She Sweet; Happy Days Are Here Again.

Noted Jazz Artists

Jazz has been called America's only completely unique contribution to Western culture. The following individuals have made major contributions in this field:

Julian "Cannonball" Adderley, 1928-1975: alto sax.

Louis "Satchmo" Armstrong, 1900-1971: trumpet, singer; originated the "scat" vocal.

Mildred Bailey, 1907-1951: blues singer.

Chet Baker, 1929-1988: trumpet.

Count Basie, 1904-1984: orchestra leader, piano.

Sidney Bechet, 1897-1959: early innovator, soprano sax.

Bix Beiderbecke, 1903-1931: cornet, piano, composer.

Bunny Berrigan, 1909-1942: trumpet, singer.

Barney Bigard, 1906-1980: clarinet.

Art Blakey, b. 1919: drums, leader.

Jimmy Blanton, 1921-1942: bass.

Charles "Buddy" Bolden, 1868-1931: cornet; formed the first jazz band in the 1890s.

Big Bill Broonzy, 1893-1958: blues singer, guitar.

Clifford Brown, 1930-1956: trumpet.

Ray Brown, b. 1926: bass.

Dave Brubeck, b. 1920: piano, combo leader.

Don Byas, 1912-1972: tenor sax.

Harry Carney, 1910-1974: baritone sax.

Benny Carter, b. 1907: alto sax, trumpet, clarinet.

Ron Carter, b. 1937: bass, cello.

Sidney Catlett, 1910-1951: drums.

Charlie Christian, 1919-1942: guitar.

Kenny Clarke, 1914-1985: pioneer of modern drums.

Buck Clayton, b. 1911: trumpet, arranger.

Al Cohn, 1925-1988: tenor sax, composer.

Cozy Cole, 1909-1981: drums.

Ornette Coleman, b. 1930: saxophone; unorthodox style.

John Coltrane, 1926-1967: tenor sax innovator.

Eddie Condon, 1904-1973: guitar, band leader; promoter of Dixieland.

Chick Corea, b. 1941: pianist, composer.

Tadd Dameron, 1917-1965: piano, composer.

Eddie "Lockjaw" Davis, 1921-1986: tenor sax.

Miles Davis, b. 1926: trumpet; pioneer of cool jazz.

Wild Bill Davison, b. 1906: cornet, leader; prominent in early Chicago jazz.

Buddy De Franco, b. 1933: clarinet.

Paul Desmond, 1924-1977: alto sax.

Vic Dickenson, 1906-1984: trombone, composer.

Warren "Baby" Dodds, 1898-1959: Dixieland drummer.

Johnny Dodds, 1892-1940: clarinet.

Eric Dolphy, 1928-1964: alto sax, composer.

Jimmy Dorsey, 1904-1957: clarinet, alto sax; band leader.

Tommy Dorsey, 1905-1956: trombone; band leader.

Roy Eldridge, 1911-1989: trumpet, drums, singer.

Duke Ellington, 1899-1974: piano, band leader, composer.

Bill Evans, 1929-1980: piano.

Gil Evans, 1912-1988: composer, arranger, piano.

Ella Fitzgerald, b. 1918: singer.

"Red" Garland, 1923-1984; piano.

Erroll Garner, 1921-1977: piano, composer, "Misty."

Stan Getz, b. 1927: tenor sax.

Dizzy Gillespie, b. 1917: trumpet, composer; bop developer.

Benny Goodman, 1909-1986: clarinet, band and combo leader.

Dexter Gordon, 1923-1990: tenor sax; bop-derived style.

Stephane Grappelli, b. 1908: violin.

Bobby Hackett, 1915-1976: trumpet, cornet.

Lionel Hampton, b. 1913: vibes, drums, piano, combo leader.

Herbie Hancock, b. 1940: piano, composer.

W. C. Handy, 1873-1958: composer, "St. Louis Blues."

Coleman Hawkins, 1904-1969: tenor sax; 1939 recording of "Body and Soul", a classic.

Roy Haynes, b. 1926: drums.

Fletcher Henderson, 1898-1952: orchestra leader, arranger; pioneered jazz and dance bands of the 30s.

Woody Herman, 1913-87: clarinet, alto sax, band leader.

Jay C. Higginbotham, 1906-1973: trombone.

Earl "Fatha" Hines, 1905-1983: piano, songwriter.

Johnny Hodges, 1906-1971: alto sax.

Billie Holiday, 1915-1959: blues singer, "Strange Fruit."

Sam "Lightnin' " Hopkins, 1912-1982: blues singer, guitar.

Mahalia Jackson, 1911-1972: gospel singer.

Milt Jackson, b. 1923: vibes, piano, guitar.

Illinois Jacquet, b. 1922: tenor sax.

Keith Jarrett, b. 1945: technically phenomenal pianist.

Blind Lemon Jefferson, 1897-1930: blues singer, guitar.

Bunk Johnson, 1879-1949: cornet, trumpet.

James P. Johnson, 1891-1955: piano, composer.

J. J. Johnson, b. 1924: trombone, composer.

Elvin Jones, b. 1927: drums.

Jo Jones, 1911-1985: drums.

Philly Joe Jones, 1923-1985: drums.

Quincy Jones, b. 1933: arranger.

Thad Jones, 1923-1986: trumpet, cornet.

Scott Joplin, 1868-1917: composer; "Maple Leaf Rag."

Stan Kenton, 1912-1979: orchestra leader, composer, piano.

Barney Kessel, b. 1923: guitar.

Lee Konitz, b. 1927: alto sax.

Gene Krupa, 1909-1973: drums, band and combo leader.

Scott LaFaro, 1936-1961: bass.

Huddie Ledbetter (Leadbelly), 1888-1949: blues singer, guitar.

John Lewis, b. 1920: composer, piano, combo leader.

Mel Lewis, b. 1929: drummer, orchestra leader.

Jimmie Lunceford, 1902-1947: band leader, sax.

Herbie Mann, b. 1930: flute.

Wynton Marsalis, b. 1961: trumpet.

Jimmy McPartland, b. 1907: trumpet.

Marian McPartland, b. 1920: piano.

Glenn Miller, 1904-1944: trombone, dance band leader.

Charles Mingus, 1922-1979: bass, composer, combo leader.

Thelonious Monk, 1920-1982: piano, composer, combo leader; a developer of bop.

Wes Montgomery, 1925-1968: guitar.
"Jelly Roll" Morton, 1885-1941: composer, piano, singer.
Bennie Moten, 1894-1935: piano; an early organizer of large jazz orchestras.
Gerry Mulligan, b. 1927: baritone sax, arranger, leader.
Turk Murphy, 1915-1987: trombone, band leader.
Theodore "Fats" Navarro, 1923-1950: trumpet.
Red Nichols, 1905-1965: cornet, combo leader.
Red Norvo, b. 1908: vibes, band leader.
Anita O'Day, b. 1919: singer.
King Oliver, 1885-1938: cornet, band leader; teacher of Louis Armstrong.
Kid Ory, 1886-1973: trombone, "Muskrat Ramble".
Charlie "Bird" Parker, 1920-1955: alto sax, composer; rated by many as the greatest jazz improviser.
Art Pepper, 1925-1982: alto sax.
Oscar Peterson, b. 1925: piano, composer, combo leader.
Oscar Pettiford, 1922-1960: a leading bassist in the bop era.
Bud Powell, 1924-1966: piano; modern jazz pioneer.
Tito Puente, b. 1923: band leader.
Sun Ra, b. 1915?: big band leader, pianist, composer.
Gertrude "Ma" Rainey, 1886-1939: blues singer.
Don Redman, 1900-1964: composer, arranger; pioneer in the evolution of the large orchestra.
Django Reinhardt, 1910-1953: guitar; Belgian gypsy, first European to influence American jazz.
Buddy Rich, 1917-1987: drums, band leader.
Max Roach, b. 1925: drums.
Sonny Rollins, b. 1929: tenor sax.
Frank Rosolino, 1926-1978: trombone.
Jimmy Rushing, 1903-1972: blues singer.
George Russell, b. 1923: composer, piano.
Pee Wee Russell, 1906-1969: clarinet.
Artie Shaw, b. 1910: clarinet, combo leader.
George Shearing, b. 1919: piano, composer, "Lullaby of Birdland."

Horace Silver, b. 1928: piano, combo leader.
Zoot Sims, 1925-1985: tenor, alto sax; clarinet.
Zutty Singleton, 1898-1975: Dixieland drummer.
Bessie Smith, 1894-1937: blues singer.
Clarence "Pinetop" Smith, 1904-1929: piano, singer; pioneer of boogie woogie.
Willie "The Lion" Smith, 1897-1973: stride style pianist.
Muggsy Spanier, 1906-1967: cornet, band leader.
Billy Strayhorn, 1915-67: composer, piano.
Sonny Stitt, 1924-1982: alto, tenor sax.
Art Tatum, 1910-1956: piano; technical virtuoso.
Billy Taylor, b. 1921: piano, composer.
Cecil Taylor, b. 1933: piano, composer.
Jack Teagarden, 1905-1964: trombone, singer.
Dave Tough, 1908-1948: drums.
Lennie Tristano, 1919-1978: piano, composer.
Joe Turner, 1911-1985: blues singer.
McCoy Tyner, b. 1938: piano, composer.
Sarah Vaughan, 1924-1990: singer.
Joe Venuti, 1904-1978: first great jazz violinist.
Thomas "Fats" Waller, 1904-1943: piano, singer, composer. "Ain't Misbehavin' ".
Dinah Washington, 1924-1963: singer.
Chick Webb, 1902-1939: band leader, drums.
Ben Webster, 1909-1973: tenor sax.
Paul Whiteman, 1890-1967: orchestra leader; a major figure in the introduction of jazz to a large audience.
Charles "Cootie" Williams, 1908-1985: trumpet, band leader.
Mary Lou Williams, 1914-1981: piano, composer.
Teddy Wilson, 1912-1986: piano, composer.
Kai Winding, 1922-1983: trombone, composer.
Jimmy Yancey, 1894-1951: piano.
Lester "Pres" Young, 1909-1959: tenor sax, composer; a bop pioneer.

Rock & Roll Notables

For more than a quarter of a century, rock & roll has been an important force in American popular culture. The following individuals or groups have made a significant impact. Next to each is an associated single record or record album.

The Allman Brothers Band: "Ramblin' Man"
The Animals: "House of the Rising Sun"
Paul Anka: "Lonely Boy"
The Association: "Cherish"
Frankie Avalon: "Venus"
The Band: "The Weight"
The Beach Boys: "Surfin' U.S.A."
The Beastie Boys: "(You've Got to) Fight for Your Right to Party"
The Beatles: "Hey Jude"
The Bee Gees: "Stayin' Alive"
Pat Benatar: "Hit Me With Your Best Shot"
Chuck Berry: "Johnny B. Goode"
The Big Bopper: "Chantilly Lace"
Black Sabbath: "Paranoid"
Blind Faith: "Can't Find My Way Home"
Blondie: "Heart of Glass"
Blood, Sweat and Tears: "Spinning Wheel"
Bon Jovi: Slippery When Wet
Gary "U.S." Bonds: "Quarter to Three"
Booker T. and the MGs: "Green Onions"
Earl Bostic: "Flamingo"
David Bowie: "Let's Dance"
James Brown: "Papa's Got a Brand New Bag"
Jackson Browne: "Doctor My Eyes"
Buffalo Springfield: "For What It's Worth"
The Byrds: "Turn! Turn! Turn!"
Canned Heat: "Going Up the Country"
The Cars: "Shake It Up"
Ray Charles: "Georgia on My Mind"
Chubby Checker: "The Twist"
Chicago: "Hard Habit to Break"
Eric Clapton: "Layla"
The Coasters: "Yakety Yak"
Eddie Cochran: "Summertime Blues"
Phil Collins: "Against All Odds"
Sam Cooke: "You Send Me"
Alice Cooper: "School's Out"
Elvis Costello: "Allison"
Cream: "Sunshine of Your Love"
Credence Clearwater Revival: "Proud Mary"
Crosby, Stills, Nash and Young: "Suite: Judy Blue Eyes"
The Crystals: "Da Doo Ron Ron"
Danny and the Juniors: "At the Hop"
Bobby Darin: "Splish Splash"
Spencer Davis Group: "Gimme Some Lovin' "

Bo Diddley: "Who Do You Love?"
Dion and the Belmonts: "A Teenager in Love"
Dire Straits: Brothers in Arms
Fats Domino: "Blueberry Hill"
The Doobie Brothers: "What a Fool Believes"
The Doors: "Light My Fire"
The Drifters: "Save the Last Dance for Me"
Duran Duran: "Hungry Like the Wolf"
Bob Dylan: "Like a Rolling Stone"
The Eagles: "Hotel California"
Earth, Wind and Fire: "Shining Star"
Emerson, Lake and Palmer: "From the Beginning"
The Eurythmics: "Sweet Dreams (Are Made of This)"
Everly Brothers: "Wake Up Little Susie"
Jose Feliciano: "Light My Fire"
The Five Satins: "In the Still of the Night"
Fleetwood Mac: Rumours
Dan Fogelberg: "Missing You"
The Four Seasons: "Sherry"
The Four Tops: "I Can't Help Myself"
Aretha Franklin: "Respect"
Marvin Gaye: "I Heard It through the Grapevine"
Genesis: "Land of Confusion"
The J. Geils Band: Freeze-Frame
Grand Funk Railroad: "We're an American Band"
The Grateful Dead: "Truckin' "
Bill Haley and the Comets: "Rock Around the Clock"
Hall and Oates: "Rich Girl"
Jimi Hendrix: Are You Experienced?
Buddy Holly and the Crickets: "That'll Be the Day"
Whitney Houston: "The Greatest Love"
Janis Ian: "At Seventeen"
The Isley Brothers: "It's Your Thing"
The Jackson 5/The Jacksons: "ABC"
Janet Jackson: "Control"
Michael Jackson: "Beat It"
Jay and the Americans: "This Magic Moment"
The Jefferson Airplane/Jefferson Starship: "White Rabbit"
Jethro Tull: Aqualung
Joan Jett: "I Love Rock n' Roll"
Billy Joel: "Uptown Girl"
Elton John: "Sad Songs"
Janis Joplin: "Me and Bobby McGee"
Chaka Khan: "I Feel for You"
B.B. King: "The Thrill Is Gone"
Carole King: Tapestry

The Kinks: "You Really Got Me"
Kiss: "Rock' n' Roll All Night"
Gladys Knight and the Pips: "Midnight Train to Georgia"
Cyndi Lauper: "Girls Just Want to Have Fun"
Led Zeppelin: "Stairway to Heaven"
Brenda Lee: "I'm Sorry"
Huey Lewis and the News: Sports
Jerry Lee Lewis: "Whole Lotta Shakin' Going On"
Little Anthony and the Imperials: "Tears on My Pillow"
Little Richard: "Tutti Frutti"
Lovin Spoonful: "Do You Believe in Magic?"
Frankie Lymon: "Why Do Fools Fall in Love?"
Lynyrd Skynyrd: "Freebird"
Madonna: "Material Girl"
The Mamas and the Papas: "Monday, Monday"
Bob Marley: "Jamming"
Martha and the Vandellas: "Dancin' in the Streets"
The Marvelettes: "Please Mr. Postman"
Clyde McPhatter: "Money Honey"
John Cougar Mellencamp: "Hurt So Good"
George Michael: "I Want Your Sex"
Steve Miller Band: "Abracadabra"
Joni Mitchell: "Big Yellow Taxi"
The Monkees: "I'm a Believer"
Moody Blues: "Nights in White Satin"
Rick Nelson: "Hello Mary Lou"
Roy Orbison: "Oh Pretty Woman"
Ozzy Osbourne: "You Can't Kill Rock 'n' Roll"
Carl Perkins: "Blue Suede Shoes"
Tom Petty and the Heartbreakers: "Refugee"
Pink Floyd: Dark Side of the Moon
Poco: Deliverin'
The Police: "Every Breath You Take"
Iggy Pop: "Lust for Life"
Elvis Presley: "Love Me Tender"
The Pretenders: Learning to Crawl
Lloyd Price: "Stagger Lee"
Prince: "Purple Rain"
Procul Harum: "A Whiter Shade of Pale"
Gary Puckett and the Union Gap: "Young Girl"
Queen: "Bohemian Rhapsody"
The Rascals: "Good Lovin"
Otis Redding: "The Dock of the Bay"
Lou Reed: "Walk on the Wild Side"
REO Speedwagon: "Keep on Lovin' You"

Righteous Brothers: "You've Lost that Lovin' Feeling"
Johnny Rivers: "Poor Side of Town"
Smokey Robinson and the Miracles: "Ooh Baby Baby"
The Rolling Stones: "Satisfaction"
The Ronettes: "Be My Baby"
Linda Ronstadt: "You're No Good"
Run D.M.C.: "Raisin' Hell"
Sam and Dave: "Soul Man"
Santana: "Black Magic Woman"
Neil Sedaka: "Breaking Up is Hard to Do"
Bob Seger: "Old Time Rock and Roll"
Del Shannon: "Runaway"
The Shirelles: "Soldier Boy"
Simon and Garfunkel: "Bridge Over Troubled Water"
Carly Simon: "You're So Vain"
Sly and the Family Stone: "Everyday People"
Patti Smith: "Because the Night"
Southside Johnny and the Asbury Jukes: This Time
Dusty Springfield: "You Don't Have to Say You Love Me"
Bruce Springsteen: "Born in the U.S.A."
Steely Dan: "Rikki Don't Lose That Number"
Steppenwolf: "Born to Be Wild"
Cat Stevens: "Wild World"
Rod Stewart: "Maggie Mae"
Sting: "If You Love Somebody, Set Them Free"
Donna Summer: "Bad Girls"
The Supremes: "Stop! In the Name of Love"
Talking Heads: "Wild Wild Life"
James Taylor: "You've Got a Friend"
The Temptations: "My Girl"
Three Dog Night: "Joy to the World"
Traffic: "Feelin' Alright"
Big Joe Turner: "Shake, Rattle & Roll"
Tina Turner: "What's Love Got to Do with It?"
U2: "With or Without You"
Van Halen: "Jump"
Dionne Warwick: "I'll Never Fall in Love Again"
Muddy Waters: "Rollin' Stone"
Mary Wells: "My Guy"
The Who: "My Generation"
Jackie Wilson: "That's Why"
Stevie Wonder: "You Are the Sunshine of My Life"
The Yardbirds: "For Your Love"
Yes: "Owner of a Lonely Heart"
Frank Zappa/Mothers of Invention: Sheik Yerbouti

Entertainment Personalities — Where and When Born

Actors, Actresses, Dancers, Musicians, Producers, Radio-TV Performers, Singers

(As of July, 1990)

Name	Birthplace	Born	Name	Birthplace	Born
Abbado, Claudio	Milan, Italy	6/26/33	Ames, Ed	Boston, Mass.	7/9/27
Abbott, George	Forestville, N.Y.	6/25/87	Ames, Leon	Portland, Ind.	1/20/03
Abraham, F. Murray	Pittsburgh, Pa.	10/24/39	Amos, John	Newark, N.J.	12/27/41
Acuff, Roy	Maynardville, Tenn.	9/15/03	Amsterdam, Morey	Chicago, Ill.	12/14/14
Adams, Don	New York, N.Y.	4/19/26	Anderson, Harry	Newport, R.I.	10/14/52
Adams, Edie	Kingston, Pa.	4/16/29	Anderson, Ian	Dunfermline, Scotland	8/10/47
Adams, Joey	New York, N.Y.	1/6/11	Anderson, Judith	Adelaide, Australia	2/10/98
Adams, Mason	New York, N.Y.	2/26/19	Anderson, Loni	St. Paul, Minn.	8/5/46
Adams, Maud	Lulea, Sweden	2/12/45	Anderson, Lynn	Grand Forks, N.D.	9/26/47
Adjani, Isabelle	W. Germany	6/27/55	Anderson, Marian	Philadelphia, Pa.	2/17/02
Adler, Larry	Baltimore, Md.	2/10/14	Anderson, Melissa Sue	Berkeley, Cal.	9/26/62
Agutter, Jenny	London, England	12/20/52	Anderson, Richard	Long Branch, N.J.	8/8/26
Aiello, Danny	New York, N.Y.	6/20/33	Anderson, Richard Dean	Minneapolis, Minn.	1/23/53
Aimee, Anouk	Paris, France	4/27/32	Andersson, Bibi	Stockholm, Sweden	11/11/35
Akins, Claude	Nelson, Ga.	5/25/18	Andress, Ursula	Bern, Switzerland	3/19/36
Albanese, Licia	Bari, Italy	7/22/13	Andrews, Anthony	London, England	1948
Alberghetti, Anna Maria	Pesaro, Italy	5/15/36	Andrews, Dana	Collins, Miss.	1/1/09
Albert, Eddie	Rock Island, Ill.	4/22/08	Andrews, Julie	Walton, England	10/1/35
Albert, Edward	Los Angeles, Cal.	2/20/51	Andrews, Maxene	Minneapolis, Minn.	1/3/18
Albright, Lola	Akron, Oh.	7/20/24	Andrews, Patty	Minneapolis, Minn.	2/16/20
Alda, Alan	New York, N.Y.	1/28/36	Anka, Paul	Ottawa, Ont.	7/30/41
Alexander, Jane	Boston, Mass.	10/28/39	Ann-Margret	Stockholm, Sweden	4/28/41
Allen, Debbie	Houston, Tex.	1/16/51	Anspach, Susan	New York, N.Y.	11/23/39
Allen, Karen	Carrollton, Ill.	10/5/51	Ant, Adam	London, England	11/3/54
Allen, Mel	Birmingham, Ala.	2/14/13	Archer, Anne	Los Angeles, Cal.	8/25/50
Allen, Nancy	New York, N.Y.	6/24/50	Arden, Eve	Mill Valley, Cal.	4/30/12
Allen, Peter	Tenderfield, Australia	2/10/44	Arkin, Alan	New York, N.Y.	3/26/34
Allen, Steve	New York, N.Y.	12/26/21	Arnaz, Desi Jr.	Los Angeles, Cal.	1/19/53
Allen, Woody	Brooklyn, N.Y.	12/1/35	Arnaz, Lucie	Hollywood, Cal.	7/17/51
Alley, Kirstie	Wichita, Kan.	1/12/55	Arness, James	Minneapolis, Minn.	5/26/23
Allman, Gregg	Nashville, Tenn.	12/7/47	Arnold, Eddy	Henderson, Tenn.	5/15/18
Allyson, June	New York, N.Y.	10/7/17	Arquette, Rosanna	New York, N.Y.	8/10/59
Alonso, Maria Conchita	Cuba	1957	Arrau, Claudio	Chillau, Chile	2/6/03
Alpert, Herb	Los Angeles, Cal.	3/31/35	Arroyo, Martina	New York, N.Y.	2/2/37
Altman, Robert	Kansas City, Mo.	2/20/25	Arthur, Beatrice	New York, N.Y.	5/13/26
Ameche, Don	Kenosha, Wis.	5/31/08	Arthur, Jean	New York, N.Y.	10/17/05

Name	Birthplace	Born
Ashcroft, Peggy	Croyden, England	12/22/07
Ashley, Elizabeth	Ocala, Fla.	8/30/41
Asner, Ed.	Kansas City, Mo.	11/15/29
Assante, Armand	New York, N.Y.	10/4/49
Astin, John	Baltimore, Md.	3/30/30
Atherton, William	New Haven, Conn.	7/30/47
Atkins, Chet	Luttrell, Tenn.	6/20/24
Attenborough, Richard	Cambridge, England	8/29/23
Auberjonois, Rene	New York, N.Y.	6/1/40
Aumont, Jean-Pierre	Paris, France	1/5/09
Austin, Patti	New York, N.Y.	1948
Autry, Gene	Tioga, Tex.	9/29/07
Avalon, Frankie	Philadelphia, Pa.	9/18/40
Ax, Emmanuel	Lvov, USSR	6/8/49
Aykroyd, Dan	Ottawa, Ont.	7/1/52
Ayres, Lew	Minneapolis, Minn.	12/28/08
Aznavour, Charles	Paris, France	5/22/24
Bacall, Lauren	New York, N.Y.	9/16/24
Bacon, Kevin	Philadelphia, Pa.	7/8/58
Baez, Joan	Staten Island, N.Y.	1/9/41
Bailey, Pearl	Newport News, Va.	3/29/18
Bain, Conrad	Lethbridge, Alta.	2/4/23
Baio, Scott	Brooklyn, N.Y.	9/22/61
Baker, Anita	Toledo, Oh.	1/26/58
Baker, Carroll	Johnstown, Pa.	5/28/31
Baker, Joe Don	Groesbeck, Tex.	2/12/36
Baldwin, Alec	Massapequa, N.Y.	4/3/58
Ballard, Kaye	Cleveland, Oh.	11/20/26
Balsam, Martin	New York, N.Y.	11/4/19
Bancroft, Anne	New York, N.Y.	9/17/31
Banks, Jonathan	Washington, D.C.	1/31/46
Barber, Red	Columbus, Miss.	2/17/08
Bardot, Brigitte	Paris, France	9/28/34
Barker, Bob	Darrington, Wash.	12/12/23
Barkin, Ellen	New York, N.Y.	4/16/54
Barnes, Priscilla	Ft. Dix, N.J.	12/7/56
Barr, Roseanne	Salt Lake City, Ut.	11/3/52
Barrault, Jean-Louis	Vesinet, France	9/8/10
Barrie, Barbara	Chicago, Ill.	5/23/31
Barrie, Mona	London, England	12/18/09
Barry, Gene	New York, N.Y.	6/14/19
Bartholomew, Freddie	London, England	3/28/24
Barty, Billy	Millsboro, Pa.	10/25/24
Baryshnikov, Mikhail	Riga, Latvia	1/28/48
Basinger, Kim	Athens, Ga.	12/8/53
Bassey, Shirley	Cardiff, Wales.	1/8/37
Bateman, Jason	Rye, N.Y.	1/14/69
Bateman, Justine	Rye, N.Y.	2/19/66
Bates, Alan	Allestree, England	2/17/34
Baxter-Birney, Meredith	Los Angeles, Cal.	6/21/47
Beal, John	Joplin, Mo.	8/13/09
Bean, Orson	Burlington, Vt.	7/22/28
Beasley, Allyce	New York, N.Y.	7/6/54
Beatty, Ned	Louisville, Ky.	7/6/37
Beatty, Warren	Richmond, Va.	3/30/37
Beck, John	Chicago, Ill.	1/28/43
Bedelia, Bonnie	New York, N.Y.	3/25/48
Bee Gees		
Gibb, Barry	Isle of Man, England	9/1/46
Gibb, Robin	" "	12/22/49
Gibb, Maurice	" "	12/22/49
Beery, Noah Jr.	New York, N.Y.	8/10/13
Begley, Ed Jr.	Los Angeles, Cal.	9/16/49
Belafonte, Harry	New York, N.Y.	3/1/27
Belafonte-Harper, Shari	New York, N.Y.	9/22/54
Bel Geddes, Barbara	New York, N.Y.	10/31/22
Bellamy, Ralph	Chicago, Ill.	6/17/04
Belmondo, Jean-Paul	Neuilly-sur-Seine, France	4/9/33
Belushi, Jim	Chicago, Ill.	6/15/54
Benatar, Pat	Brooklyn, N.Y.	1/10/53
Benedict, Dirk	Helena, Mont.	3/1/45
Benjamin, Richard	New York, N.Y.	5/22/38
Bennett, Joan	Palisades, N.J.	2/27/10
Bennett, Tony	New York, N.Y.	8/3/26
Benson, George	Pittsburgh, Pa.	3/22/43
Benson, Robby	Dallas, Tex.	1/21/55
Beradino, John	Los Angeles, Cal.	5/1/17
Berenger, Tom	Chicago, Ill.	5/31/50
Bergen, Candice	Beverly Hills, Cal.	5/9/46
Bergen, Polly	Knoxville, Tenn.	7/14/30
Bergerac, Jacques	Biarritz, France	5/26/27
Bergman, Ingmar	Uppsala, Sweden.	7/14/18
Berle, Milton	New York, N.Y.	7/12/08
Berlinger, Warren	Brooklyn, N.Y.	8/31/37
Berman, Lazar	Leningrad, USSR	2/26/30
Berman, Shelley	Chicago, Ill.	2/3/26
Bernsen, Corbin	No. Hollywood, Cal.	9/7/54

Name	Birthplace	Born
Bernstein, Leonard	Lawrence, Mass.	8/25/18
Berry, Chuck	St. Louis, Mo.	10/18/26
Berry, Ken	Moline, Ill.	11/3/33
Bertinelli, Valerie	Wilmington, Del.	4/23/60
Bikel, Theodore	Vienna, Austria	5/2/24
Birney, David	Washington, D.C.	4/23/39
Bishop, Joey	Bronx, N.Y.	2/3/18
Bisoglio, Val	New York, N.Y.	5/7/26
Bisset, Jacqueline	Weybridge, England	9/13/44
Bixby, Bill	San Francisco, Cal.	1/22/34
Black, Karen	Park Ridge, Ill.	7/1/42
Blackstone Jr., Harry	Three Rivers, Mich.	6/30/34
Blades, Ruben	Panama	1948
Blaine, Vivian	Newark, N.J.	11/21/21
Blair, Linda	St. Louis, Mo.	1/22/59
Blake, Robert	Nutley, N.J.	9/18/33
Bledsoe, Tempestt	Chicago, Ill.	8/1/73
Bloom, Claire	London, England	2/15/31
Blyth, Ann	Mt. Kisco, N.Y.	8/16/28
Bochco, Steven	New York, N.Y.	12/16/43
Bogarde, Dirk	London, England	3/28/20
Bogdanovich, Peter	Kingston, N.Y.	7/30/39
Bonet, Lisa	San Francisco, Cal.	11/16/67
Bonham-Carter, Helena	England	1967
Bon Jovi, Jon	Sayreville, N.J.	3/2/61
Bono, Sonny	Detroit, Mich.	2/16/35
Booke, Sorrell	Buffalo, N.Y.	1/4/30
Boone, Debby	Hackensack, N.J.	9/22/56
Boone, Pat	Jacksonville, Fla.	6/1/34
Booth, Shirley	New York, N.Y.	8/30/07
Borge, Victor	Copenhagen, Denmark	1/3/09
Borgnine, Ernest	Hamden, Conn.	1/24/17
Bosco, Philip	Jersey City, N.J.	9/26/30
Bosley, Tom	Chicago, Ill.	10/1/27
Bosson, Barbara	Charleroi, Pa.	11/1/39
Bostwick, Barry	San Mateo, Cal.	2/24/46
Bottoms, Joseph	Santa Barbara, Cal.	4/22/54
Bottoms, Timothy	Santa Barbara, Cal.	8/30/51
Bowie, David	London, England	1/8/47
Boxleitner, Bruce	Elgin, Ill.	5/12/50
Boy George	London, England	6/14/61
Boyle, Peter	Philadelphia, Pa.	10/18/33
Bracco, Lorraine	New York, N.Y.	1955
Bracken, Eddie	New York, N.Y.	2/7/20
Branagh, Kenneth	Belfast, No. Ireland	1961
Brand, Neville	Kewanee, Ill.	8/13/21
Brando, Marion	Omaha, Neb.	4/3/24
Brazzi, Rossano	Bologna, Italy	9/18/16
Brendel, Alfred	Wiesenberg, Austria	1/5/31
Brennan, Eileen	Los Angeles, Cal.	9/3/35
Brenner, David	Philadelphia, Pa.	2/4/45
Brewer, Teresa	Toledo, Oh.	5/7/31
Brian, David	New York, N.Y.	8/5/14
Bridges, Beau	Hollywood, Cal.	12/9/41
Bridges, Jeff	Los Angeles, Cal.	12/4/49
Bridges, Lloyd	San Leandro, Cal.	1/15/13
Brimley, Wilford	Salt Lake City, Ut.	9/27/34
Broderick, Matthew	New York, N.Y.	3/21/62
Brolin, James	Los Angeles, Cal.	7/18/40
Bronson, Charles	Ehrenfeld, Pa.	11/3/22
Brooks, Albert	Beverly Hills, Cal.	7/22/47
Brooks, Avery	Evansville, Ind.	10/2/-
Brooks, Mel	New York, N.Y.	6/28/26
Brooks, Stephen	Columbus, Oh.	1942
Brosnan, Pierce	Co. Meath, Ireland	5/15/53
Brown, Blair	Washington, D.C.	1948
Brown, Bryan	Australia	1947
Brown, James	Pulaski, Tenn.	6/17/28
Brown, Jim	St. Simons Island, Ga.	2/17/36
Brown, Les	Reinerton, Pa.	3/14/12
Brown, Ray	Pittsburgh, Pa.	10/13/26
Browne, Roscoe Lee	Woodbury, N.J.	5/2/25
Bryant, Anita	Barnsdall, Okla.	3/25/40
Buckley, Betty	Ft. Worth, Tex.	7/3/47
Bujold, Genevieve	Montreal, Que.	7/1/42
Bumbry, Grace	St. Louis, Mo.	1/4/37
Burghoff, Gary	Bristol, Conn.	5/24/40
Burke, Delta	Orlando, Fla.	7/30/56
Burke, Paul	New Orleans, La.	7/21/26
Burnett, Carol	San Antonio, Tex.	4/26/33
Burns, George	New York, N.Y.	1/20/96
Burr, Raymond	New Westminster, B.C.	5/21/17
Burstyn, Ellen	Detroit, Mich.	12/7/32
Burton, LeVar	Landsthul, W. Germany	2/16/57
Busey, Gary	Goose Creek, Tex.	6/29/44
Butkus, Dick	Chicago, Ill.	12/9/42
Button, Dick	Englewood, N.J.	7/18/29
Buttons, Red	New York, N.Y.	2/5/19
Buzzi, Ruth	Westerly, R.I.	7/24/36

Name	Birthplace	Born	Name	Birthplace	Born
Byrne, David	Dumbarton, Scotland	5/14/52	Coburn, James	Laurel, Neb.	8/31/28
Caan, James	New York, N.Y.	3/26/39	Coca, Imogene	Philadelphia, Pa.	11/18/08
Caballe, Montserrat	Barcelona, Spain	4/12/33	Cohn, Mindy	Los Angeles, Cal.	5/20/66
Caesar, Sid	Yonkers, N.Y.	9/8/22	Colbert, Claudette	Paris, France	9/18/05
Cage, Nicolas	Long Beach, Cal.	1965	Cole, Gary	Park Ridge, Ill.	9/20/57
Caine, Michael	London, England	3/14/33	Cole, Natalie	Los Angeles, Cal.	2/6/50
Caldwell, Sarah	Maryville, Mo.	3/6/24	Cole, Olivia	Memphis, Tenn.	11/26/42
Caldwell, Zoe	Melbourne, Australia	9/14/33	Coleman, Dabney	Austin, Tex.	1/3/32
Calhoun, Rory	Los Angeles, Cal.	8/8/23	Coleman, Gary	Zion, Ill.	2/8/68
Callas, Charlie	Brooklyn, N.Y.	12/20/-	Collins, Joan	London, England	5/23/33
Calloway, Cab	Rochester, N.Y.	12/25/07	Collins, Judy	Seattle, Wash.	5/1/39
Cameron, Kirk	Panorama City, Cal.	10/12/70	Collins, Phil.	London, England	1/30/51
Camp, Hamilton	London, England	10/30/34	Comden, Betty	Brooklyn, N.Y.	5/3/19
Campanella, Joseph	New York, N.Y.	11/21/27	Como, Perry	Canonsburg, Pa.	5/18/12
Campbell, Glen	Billstown, Ark.	4/22/36	Conner, Nadine	Compton, Cal.	2/20/13
Candy, John	Toronto, Ont.	10/31/50	Connery, Sean.	Edinburgh, Scotland	8/25/30
Cannell, Stephen J.	Los Angeles, Cal.	2/5/42	Conniff, Ray	Attleboro, Mass.	11/6/16
Cannon, Dyan	Tacoma, Wash.	1/4/37	Connors, Chuck	Brooklyn, N.Y.	4/10/21
Cantrell, Lana	Sydney, Australia	8/7/43	Connors, Mike	Fresno, Cal.	8/15/25
Capra, Frank.	Palermo, Italy	5/18/97	Conrad, Robert	Chicago, Ill.	3/1/35
Cara, Irene	New York, N.Y.	3/18/59	Conrad, William	Louisville, Ky.	9/27/20
Carey, Macdonald.	Sioux City, Ia.	3/15/13	Constantine, Michael	Reading, Pa.	5/22/27
Cariou, Len.	Winnipeg, Canada	9/30/39	Conti, Tom	Paisley, Scotland	11/22/41
Carle, Frankie	Providence, R.I.	3/25/03	Convy, Bert	St. Louis, Mo.	6/23/39
Carlin, George	New York, N.Y.	5/12/38	Conway, Tim.	Willoughby, Oh.	12/15/33
Carlisle, Kitty.	New Orleans, La	9/3/15	Cook, Barbara	Atlanta, Ga.	10/25/27
Carmen, Eric.	Cleveland, Oh.	8/11/49	Cook, Peter	Torquay, England.	11/17/37
Carmichael, Ian	Hull, England	6/18/20	Cooke, Alistair	Manchester, England.	11/20/08
Carnes, Kim	California	1948	Coolidge, Rita	Nashville, Tenn.	5/1/45
Carney, Art.	Mt. Vernon, N.Y.	11/4/18	Cooper, Alice	Detroit, Mich.	2/4/48
Carnovsky, Morris.	St. Louis, Mo.	9/5/97	Cooper, Jackie	Los Angeles, Cal.	9/15/22
Caron, Leslie.	Boulogne, France.	7/1/31	Copperfield, David.	Metuchen, N.J.	1957
Carpenter, John.	Carthage, N.Y.	1/16/48	Coppola, Francis	Detroit, Mich.	4/7/39
Carr, Vikki	El Paso, Tex.	7/19/41	Corby, Ellen	Racine, Wis.	6/3/13
Carradine, David	Hollywood, Cal.	10/8/36	Cord, Alex	New York, N.Y.	8/3/31
Carradine, Keith	San Mateo, Cal.	8/8/50	Corea, Chick.	Chelsea, Mass.	6/12/41
Carreras, Jose.	Barcelona, Spain	12/5/47	Corelli, Franco	Ancona, Italy	4/8/23
Carroll, Diahann	Bronx, N.Y.	7/17/35	Corey, Jeff	New York, N.Y.	8/10/14
Carroll, Pat.	Shreveport, La.	5/5/27	Cosby, Bill	Philadelphia, Pa.	7/12/37
Carson, Johnny	Corning, Ia.	10/23/25	Costas, Bob	New York, N.Y.	3/22/52
Carter, Dixie	McLemoresville, Tenn.	5/25/39	Costello, Elvis	London, England	8/25/54
Carter, Jack	New York, N.Y.	6/24/23	Costner, Kevin	Los Angeles, Cal.	1/18/55
Carter, June	Maces Spring, Va.	6/23/29	Cotten, Joseph	Petersburg, Va.	5/15/05
Carter, Lynda	Phoenix, Ariz.	7/24/51	Cougar, John	Seymour, Ind.	10/7/51
Carter, Nell.	Birmingham, Ala.	9/13/48	Courtenay, Tom	Hull, England	2/25/37
Carvey, Dana	Missoula, Mont.	4/2/55	Cox, Ronny	Cloudcroft, N.M.	8/23/38
Casadesus, Gaby	Marseilles, France	1902	Craddock, Crash	Greensboro, N.C.	6/16/40
Cash, Johnny	Kingsland, Ark.	2/26/32	Crain, Jeanne	Barstow, Cal.	5/25/25
Cash, Rosanne	Memphis, Tenn.	5/24/55	Crawford, Michael	Salisbury, England	1/19/42
Cass, Peggy	Boston, Mass.	5/21/24	Crenna, Richard	Los Angeles, Cal.	11/30/27
Cassidy, David.	New York, N.Y.	4/12/50	Crespin, Regine	Marseilles, France	2/23/26
Cassidy, Shaun	Los Angeles, Cal.	9/27/58	Cronyn, Hume	London, Ont.	7/18/11
Cates, Phoebe.	New York, N.Y.	1964	Crosby, Bob	Spokane, Wash.	8/23/13
Caulfield, Joan.	West Orange, N.J.	6/1/22	Crosby, David	Los Angeles, Cal.	8/14/41
Cavallaro, Carmen	New York, N.Y.	5/6/13	Crosby, Norm	Boston, Mass.	9/15/27
Cavett, Dick	Gibbon, Neb.	11/19/36	Crouse, Lindsay	New York, N.Y.	5/12/48
Chamberlain, Richard.	Beverly Hills, Cal.	3/31/35	Crowell, Rodney.	Houston, Tex.	8/17/50
Champion, Marge	Los Angeles, Cal.	9/2/23	Cruise, Tom	Syracuse, N.Y.	7/3/62
Channing, Carol	Seattle, Wash.	1/31/23	Crystal, Billy	Long Beach, N.Y.	3/14/47
Channing, Stockard	New York, N.Y.	2/13/44	Cugat, Xavier	Barcelona, Spain	1/1/00
Chaplin, Geraldine.	Santa Monica, Cal.	7/31/44	Cullum, John.	Knoxville, Tenn.	3/2/30
Chaplin, Sydney.	Beverly Hills, Cal.	3/31/26	Culp, Robert	Oakland, Cal.	8/16/30
Chapman, Tracy.	Cleveland, OH.	1964	Cummings, Constance	Seattle, Wash.	5/15/10
Charisse, Cyd	Amarillo, Tex.	3/8/21	Cummings, Robert	Joplin, Mo.	6/9/10
Charles, Ray.	Albany, Ga.	9/23/30	Curtin, Jane	Cambridge, Mass.	9/6/47
Charo.	Murcia, Spain	1/15/51	Curtis, Jamie Lee	Los Angeles, Cal.	11/22/58
Chase, Chevy	New York, N.Y.	10/8/43	Curtis, Keene	Salt Lake City, Ut.	2/15/23
Checker, Chubby	Philadelphia, Pa.	10/3/41	Curtis, Ken	Lamar, Col.	7/2/16
Cher	El Centro, Cal.	5/20/46	Curtis, Tony	New York, N.Y.	6/3/25
Chong, Rae Dawn.	California	1961	Cusack, Cyril.	Durban, S. Africa	11/26/10
Chong, Thomas	Edmonton, Alta.	5/24/38	Cusack, Joan	Evanston, Ill.	10/11/62
Christie, Julie.	Assam, India	4/14/40	Cusack, John	Chicago, Ill.	1967
Christopher, William.	Evanston, Ill.	10/20/32	Cushing, Peter.	Surrey, England.	5/26/13
Christy, June.	Springfield, Ill.	11/20/25	Dafoe, Willem	Appleton, Wis.	7/22/55
Clapton, Eric.	Surrey, England.	3/30/45	Dahl, Arlene	Minneapolis, Minn.	8/11/28
Clark, Dane	New York, N.Y.	2/18/13	Dale, Jim	Rothwell, England	8/15/35
Clark, Dick	Mt. Vernon, N.Y.	11/30/29	Dalton, Abby	Las Vegas, Nev.	8/15/32
Clark, Petula	Ewell, Surrey, England.	11/15/32	Dalton, Timothy	Wales	3/21/44
Clark, Roy	Meherrin, Va.	4/15/33	Daltrey, Roger	London, England.	3/1/44
Clark, Susan.	Sarnia, Ont.	3/8/44	Daly, John	Johannesburg, S. Africa	2/20/14
Clary, Robert	Paris, France	3/1/26	Daly, Tyne	Madison, Wis.	2/21/47
Clayburgh, Jill	New York, N.Y.	4/30/44	Damone, Vic	Brooklyn, N.Y.	6/12/28
Cleese, John.	England	10/27/39	D'Angelo, Beverly	Columbus, Oh.	1954
Cleveland, James	Chicago, Ill.	12/5/31	Dangerfield, Rodney	Babylon, N.Y.	11/22/22
Cliburn, Van	Shreveport, La.	7/12/34	Daniels, Charlie	Wilmington, N.C.	10/28/36
Clooney, Rosemary.	Maysville, Ky.	5/23/28	Daniels, Jeff	Georgia	1955
Close, Glenn	Greenwich, Conn.	3/19/47	Daniels, William	Brooklyn, N.Y.	3/31/27
			Danner, Blythe	Philadelphia, Pa.	2/3/44
			Danson, Ted	San Diego, Cal.	12/29/47

Name	Birthplace	Born	Name	Birthplace	Born
Danza, Tony	New York, N.Y.	4/21/50	Dunn, Nora	Chicago, Ill.	4/29/52
Darby, Kim	Hollywood, Cal.	7/8/48	Dunne, Griffin	California	6/8/55
D'Arby, Terence Trent	New York, N.Y.	3/15/62	Dunne, Irene	Louisville, Ky.	12/20/98
Darren, James	Philadelphia, Pa.	6/8/36	Dunnock, Mildred	Baltimore, Md.	1/25/04
Davidson, John	Pittsburgh, Pa.	12/13/41	Durbin, Deanna	Winnipeg, Man.	12/4/21
Davis, Ann B.	Schenectady, N.Y.	5/5/26	Durning, Charles	Highland Falls, N.Y.	2/28/23
Davis, Clifton	Chicago, Ill.	10/4/45	Dussault, Nancy	Pensacola, Fla.	6/30/36
Davis, Geena	Ware, Mass.	1/21/57	Duvall, Robert	San Diego, Cal.	1/5/31
Davis, Judy	Perth, Australia	1956	Duvall, Shelley	Houston, Tex.	1949
Davis, Mac	Lubbock, Tex.	1/21/42	Dylan, Bob	Duluth, Minn.	5/24/41
Davis, Ossie	Cogdell, Ga.	12/18/17	Dysart, Richard	Augusta, Me.	3/30/-
Davis, Skeeter	Dry Ridge, Ky.	12/30/31	Easton, Sheena	Bellshill, Scotland.	4/27/59
Dawber, Pam	Farmington Hills, Mich.	10/18/51	Eastwood, Clint	San Francisco, Cal.	5/31/30
Dawson, Richard	Hampshire, England	11/20/32	Ebert, Roger	Urbana, Ill.	6/18/42
Day, Doris	Cincinnati, Oh.	4/3/24	Ebsen, Buddy	Belleville, Ill.	4/2/08
Day, Laraine	Roosevelt, Ut.	10/13/20	Eckstine, Billy	Pittsburgh, Pa.	7/8/14
Day-Lewis, Daniel	England	1957	Edelman, Herb.	Brooklyn, N.Y.	11/5/33
Dean, Jimmy	Plainview, Tex.	8/10/28	Eden, Barbara	Tucson, Ariz.	8/23/34
De Camp, Rosemary	Prescott, Ariz.	11/14/10	Edwards, Anthony	Santa Barbara, Cal.	1/19/62
DeCarlo, Yvonne	Vancouver, B.C.	9/1/22	Edwards, Blake	Tulsa, Okla.	7/26/22
Dee, Frances	Los Angeles, Cal.	11/26/07	Edwards, Ralph	Merino, Col.	6/13/13
Dee, Ruby	Cleveland, Oh.	10/27/23	Eggar, Samantha	London, England	3/5/39
Dee, Sandra	Bayonne, N.J.	4/23/42	Eichhorn, Lisa	Reading, Pa.	2/4/52
Defore, Don	Cedar Rapids, Ia.	8/25/17	Eikenberry, Jill	New Haven, Conn.	1/21/47
DeHaven, Gloria	Los Angeles, Cal.	7/23/25	Ekberg, Anita	Malmo, Sweden	9/29/31
De Havilland, Olivia	Tokyo, Japan	7/1/16	Ekland, Britt	Stockholm, Sweden	10/6/42
Delany, Dana	New York, N.Y.	3/13/56	Elam, Jack	Miami, Ariz.	11/13/16
Della Chiesa, Vivienne	Chicago, Ill.	10/9/20	Elizondo, Hector	New York, N.Y.	12/22/36
Delon, Alain	Sceaux, France	11/8/35	Elliott, Bob	Boston, Mass.	3/26/23
DeLuise, Dom	Brooklyn, N.Y.	8/1/33	Elliott, Denholm	London, England	5/31/22
De Mille, Agnes	New York, N.Y.	9/18/05	Elliott, Sam	Sacramento, Cal.	8/9/44
De Mornay, Rebecca	Santa Rosa, Cal.	1962	Elvira (Cassandra Peterson)	Manhattan, Kan.	9/17/51
Deneuve, Catherine	Paris, France	10/22/43	Estevan, Gloria	Cuba	1957
De Niro, Robert	New York, N.Y.	8/17/43	Estevez, Emilio	New York, N.Y.	1962
Dennehy, Brian	Bridgeport, Conn.	7/9/40	Estrada, Erik	New York, N.Y.	3/16/49
Dennis, Sandy	Hastings, Neb.	4/27/37	Evans, Dale	Uvalde, Tex.	10/31/12
Denver, Bob	New Rochelle, N.Y.	1/9/35	Evans, Gene	Holbrook, Ariz.	7/11/24
Denver, John	Roswell, N.M.	12/31/43	Evans, Linda	Hartford, Conn.	11/18/42
DePalma, Brian	Newark, N.J.	9/11/40	Evans, Robert	New York, N.Y.	6/29/30
Depp, Johnny	Owensboro, KY.	6/9/63	Everett, Chad	South Bend, Ind.	6/11/36
Derek, Bo	Long Beach, Cal.	11/20/56	Everly, Don	Brownie, Ky.	2/1/37
Derek, John	Hollywood, Cal.	8/12/26	Everly, Phil	Chicago, Ill.	1/19/38
Dern, Bruce	Chicago, Ill.	6/4/36	Evigan, Greg	S. Amboy, N.J.	10/14/53
Devane, William	Albany, N.Y.	9/5/37	Ewell, Tom	Owensboro, Ky.	4/29/09
DeVito, Danny	Neptune, N.J.	11/17/44	Fabares, Shelley	Santa Monica, Cal.	1/19/42
Dewhurst, Colleen	Montreal, Que.	6/3/26	Fabian (Forte)	Philadelphia, Pa.	2/6/43
DeWitt, Joyce	Wheeling, W.Va.	4/23/49	Fabray, Nanette	San Diego, Cal.	10/27/20
Dey, Susan	Pekin, Ill.	12/10/52	Fairbanks, Douglas Jr.	New York, N.Y.	12/9/09
Diamond, Neil	Brooklyn, N.Y.	1/24/41	Fairchild, Morgan	Dallas, Tex.	2/3/50
Dickinson, Angie	Kulm, N.D.	9/30/31	Falana, Lola	Philadelphia, Pa.	9/11/46
Diddley, Bo.	McComb, Miss.	12/20/28	Falk, Peter	New York, N.Y.	9/16/27
Dietrich, Marlene	Berlin, Germany	12/27/01	Farentino, James	Brooklyn, N.Y.	2/24/38
Diller, Phyllis	Lima, Oh.	7/17/17	Fargo, Donna	Mt. Airy, N.C.	11/10/45
Dillman, Bradford	San Francisco, Cal.	4/14/30	Farr, Jamie	Toledo, Oh.	7/1/34
Dillon, Matt	New Rochelle, N.Y.	2/18/64	Farrell, Eileen	Willimantic, Conn.	2/13/20
Dixon, Ivan	New York, N.Y.	4/6/31	Farrell, Mike	St. Paul, Minn.	2/6/39
Dobson, Kevin	New York, N.Y.	3/18/44	Farrow, Mia	Los Angeles, Cal.	2/9/45
Domingo, Placido	Madrid, Spain	1/21/41	Fawcett, Farrah	Corpus Christi, Tex.	2/2/47
Domino, Fats.	New Orleans, La.	2/26/28	Faye, Alice	New York, N.Y.	5/5/12
Donahue, Phil	Cleveland, Oh.	12/21/35	Feld, Fritz.	Berlin, Germany	10/15/00
Donahue, Troy	New York, N.Y.	1/27/36	Feldon, Barbara	Pittsburgh, Pa.	3/12/41
Donovan	Glasgow, Scotland	5/10/43	Feldshuh, Tovah	New York, N.Y.	12/27/52
Dotrice, Roy	Guernsey, England	5/26/23	Feliciano, Jose	Lares, Puerto Rico	9/10/45
Douglas, Kirk	Amsterdam, N.Y.	12/9/18	Fell, Norman	Philadelphia, Pa.	3/24/24
Douglas, Michael	New Brunswick, N.J.	9/25/44	Fellini, Federico	Rimini, Italy	1/20/20
Douglas, Mike	Chicago, Ill.	8/11/25	Fender, Freddy	San Benito, Tex.	6/4/37
Down, Leslie-Ann	London, England	3/17/54	Ferrell, Conchata	Charleston, W. Va.	3/28/43
Downey, Robert Jr.	California	4/4/65	Ferrer, Jose	Santurce, P.R.	1/8/12
Downs, Hugh	Akron, Oh.	2/14/21	Ferrer, Mel	Elberon, N.J.	8/25/17
Doyle, David	Lincoln, Neb.	12/1/29	Ferrigno, Lou	Brooklyn, N.Y.	11/9/52
Dragon, Daryl	Los Angeles, Cal.	8/27/42	Fiedler, John	Platville, Wis.	2/3/25
Drake, Alfred	Bronx, N.Y.	10/7/14	Field, Sally	Pasadena, Cal.	11/6/46
Drake, Larry	Tulsa, Okla.	2/21/-	Fields, Kim	Los Angeles, Cal.	5/12/69
Drew, Ellen	Kansas City, Mo.	11/23/15	Finney, Albert	Salford, England	5/9/36
Dryer, Fred.	Hawthorne, Cal.	7/6/46	Firkusny, Rudolf	Napajedla, Czechoslovakia	2/11/12
Dreyfuss, Richard	Brooklyn, N.Y.	10/29/47	Firth, Peter	Yorkshire, England	10/27/53
Dru, Joanne	Logan, W.Va.	1/31/23	Fischer-Dieskau, Dietrich	Berlin, Germany	5/28/25
Duchin, Peter	New York, N.Y.	7/28/37	Fisher, Carrie	Beverly Hills, Cal.	10/21/56
Duffy, Julia	Minneapolis, Minn.	6/27/51	Fisher, Eddie	Philadelphia, Pa.	8/10/28
Duffy, Patrick	Townsend, Mont.	3/17/49	Fitzgerald, Ella.	Newport News, Va.	4/25/18
Dufour, Val	New Orleans, La.	2/5/27	Fitzgerald, Geraldine	Dublin, Ireland.	11/24/13
Dukakis, Olympia	Massachusetts	1932	Flack, Roberta	Black Mountain, N.C.	2/10/39
Duke, Patty.	New York, N.Y.	12/14/46	Flanagan, Fionnula	Dublin, Ireland.	12/10/41
Dullea, Keir.	Cleveland, Oh.	5/30/36	Flanders, Ed	Minneapolis, Minn.	12/29/34
Dunaway, Faye	Bascom, Fla.	1/14/41	Fleming, Rhonda	Hollywood, Cal.	8/10/23
Duncan, Sandy	Henderson, Tex.	2/20/46	Fletcher, Louise	Birmingham, Ala.	1936
Dunham, Katherine	Joliet, Ill.	6/22/10			

Name	Birthplace	Born
Foch, Nina	Leyden, Netherlands	4/20/24
Fogelberg, Dan	Peoria, Ill.	8/13/51
Fonda, Jane	New York, N.Y.	12/21/37
Fonda, Peter	New York, N.Y.	2/23/40
Fontaine, Joan	Tokyo, Japan	10/22/17
Fonteyn, Margot	Reigate, England	5/18/19
Ford (Tenn.), Ernie	Bristol, Tenn.	2/13/19
Ford, Glenn	Quebec, Canada	5/1/16
Ford, Harrison	Chicago, Ill.	7/13/42
Forrest, Steve	Huntsville, Tex.	9/29/24
Forsythe, John	Penns Grove, N.J.	1/29/18
Foster, Jodie	New York, N.Y.	11/19/62
Fox, James	London, England	5/19/39
Fox, Michael J.	Edmonton, Alta.	6/9/61
Foxworth, Robert	Houston, Tex.	11/1/41
Foxx, Redd	St. Louis, Mo.	12/9/22
Frampton, Peter	Kent, England	4/22/50
Francescatti, Zino	Marseilles, France	8/9/05
Franciosa, Anthony	New York, N.Y.	10/25/28
Francis, Anne	Ossining, N.Y.	9/16/30
Francis, Arlene	Boston, Mass.	10/20/08
Francis, Connie	Newark, N.J.	12/12/38
Francis, Genie	Los Angeles, Cal.	5/26/62
Frankenheimer, John	Malba, N.Y.	2/19/30
Franklin, Aretha	Memphis, Tenn.	3/25/42
Franklin, Bonnie	Santa Monica, Cal.	1/6/44
Franklin, Joe	New York, N.Y.	1929
Frann, Mary	St. Louis, Mo.	2/27/43
Franz, Dennis	Chicago, Ill.	10/28/44
Freeman Jr., Al	San Antonio, Tex.	3/21/34
Frick, Mr. (W. Groebli)	Basel, Switzerland	4/21/15
Friedkin, William	Chicago, Ill.	8/29/39
Frost, David	Tenterden, England	4/7/39
Funicello, Annette	Utica, N.Y.	10/22/42
Funt, Allen	New York, N.Y.	9/16/14
Gabor, Eva	Hungary	1921
Gabor, Zsa Zsa	Hungary	—
Gabriel, John	Niagara Falls, N.Y.	5/25/31
Gabriel, Peter	London, England	5/13/50
Gail, Max	Detroit, Mich.	4/5/43
Gallagher, Megan	Reading, Pa.	2/6/-
Galway, James	Belfast, Ireland	12/8/39
Garagiola, Joe	St. Louis, Mo.	2/12/26
Gardenia, Vincent	Naples, Italy	1/7/22
Garfunkel, Art	New York, N.Y.	10/13/41
Garland, Beverly	Santa Cruz, Cal.	10/17/26
Garner, James	Norman, Okla.	4/7/28
Garr, Teri	Lakewood, Oh.	12/11/49
Garrett, Betty	St. Joseph, Mo.	5/23/19
Garson, Greer	Co. Down, N. Ireland	9/29/08
Gatlin, Larry	Seminole, Tex.	5/2/48
Gayle, Crystal	Paintsville, Ky.	1/9/51
Gaynor, Mitzi	Chicago, Ill.	9/4/30
Gazzara, Ben	New York, N.Y.	8/28/30
Gedda, Nicolai	Stockholm, Sweden	7/11/25
Geldof, Bob	Co. Dublin, Ire.	10/5/51
Gentry, Bobbie	Chickasaw Co., Miss.	7/27/44
Gere, Richard	Philadelphia, Pa.	8/31/49
Getty, Estelle	New York, N.Y.	7/25/24
Ghostley, Alice	Eve, Mo.	8/14/26
Giannini, Giancarlo	Spezia, Italy	8/1/42
Gibb, Cynthia	Bennington, Vt.	12/14/63
Gibbs, Marla	Chicago, Ill.	6/14/31
Gibson, Debbie	Merrick, N.Y.	8/31/70
Gibson, Henry	Germantown, Pa.	9/21/35
Gibson, Mel	Peerskill, N.Y.	1/3/51
Gielgud, John	London, England	4/14/04
Gifford, Frank	Santa Monica, Cal.	8/16/30
Gilbert, Melissa	Los Angeles, Cal.	5/8/64
Gilberto, Astrud	Salvador, Brazil	3/30/40
Gillette, Anita	Baltimore, Md.	8/16/38
Gilley, Mickey	Natchez, Miss.	3/9/36
Ginty, Robert	New York, N.Y.	11/14/48
Gish, Lillian	Springfield, Oh.	10/14/96
Givens, Robin	New York, N.Y.	11/27/64
Glaser, Paul Michael	Cambridge, Mass.	3/25/43
Glass, Ron	Evansville, Ind.	7/10/45
Glenn, Scott	Pittsburgh, Pa.	1/26/42
Gless, Sharon	Los Angeles, Cal.	5/31/43
Glover, Danny	San Francisco, Cal.	1948
Glynn, Carlin	Cleveland, Oh.	2/19/40
Gobel, George	Chicago, Ill.	5/20/19
Godard, Jean Luc	Paris, France	12/3/30
Godunov, Alexander	Sakhalin Is., USSR	11/28/49
Goldberg, Whoopi	New York, N.Y.	1949
Goldblum, Jeff	Pittsburgh, Pa.	10/22/53
Goldsboro, Bobby	Marianna, Fla.	1/18/42
Goldthwait, Bob	Syracuse, N.Y.	1962
Goodman, John	St. Louis, Mo.	6/20/53
Gordon, Gale	New York, N.Y.	2/2/06
Gorman, Cliff	New York, N.Y.	10/13/36
Gorme, Eydie	Bronx, N.Y.	8/16/32
Gorshin, Frank	Pittsburgh, Pa.	4/5/34
Gossett Jr., Louis	Brooklyn, N.Y.	5/27/36
Gould, Elliott	Brooklyn, N.Y.	8/29/38
Gould, Harold	Schenectady, N.Y.	12/10/23
Gould, Morton	Richmond Hill, N.Y.	12/10/13
Goulet, Robert	Lawrence, Mass.	11/26/33
Gowdy, Curt	Green River, Wyo.	7/31/19
Graham, Martha	Pittsburgh, Pa.	5/11/94
Graham, Virginia	Chicago, Ill.	7/4/12
Grammer, Kelsey	Virgin Islands	2/20/-
Granger, Farley	San Jose, Cal.	7/1/25
Granger, Stewart	London, England	5/6/13
Grant, Amy	Augusta, Ga.	1961
Grant, Lee	New York, N.Y.	10/31/29
Graves, Peter	Minneapolis, Minn.	3/18/26
Gray, Coleen	Staplehurst, Neb.	10/23/22
Gray, Erin	Honolulu, Ha.	1/7/52
Gray, Linda	Santa Monica, Cal.	9/12/40
Grayson, Kathryn	Winston-Salem, N.C.	2/9/22
Greco, Buddy	Philadelphia, Pa.	8/14/26
Greco, Jose	Abruzzi, Italy	12/23/18
Green, Adolph	New York, N.Y.	12/2/15
Green, Al	Forest City, Ark.	4/13/46
Greene, Ellen	New York, N.Y.	1950
Greene, Michele	Las Vegas, Nev.	2/3/-
Greene, Shecky	Chicago, Ill.	4/8/26
Gregory, Cynthia	Los Angeles, Cal.	7/8/46
Gregory, Dick	St. Louis, Mo.	10/12/32
Gregory, James	Bronx, N.Y.	12/23/11
Grey, Joel	Cleveland, Oh.	4/11/32
Griffin, Merv	San Mateo, Cal.	7/6/25
Griffith, Andy	Mount Airy, N.C.	6/1/26
Griffith, Melanie	New York, N.Y.	8/9/57
Grimes, Tammy	Lynn, Mass.	1/30/34
Grizzard, George	Roanoke Rapids, N.C.	4/1/28
Grodin, Charles	Pittsburgh, Pa.	4/21/35
Groh, David	New York, N.Y.	5/21/41
Grosbard, Ulu	Antwerp, Belgium	1/19/29
Gross, Michael	Chicago, Ill.	6/21/47
Guardino, Harry	New York, N.Y.	12/23/25
Guillaume, Robert	St. Louis, Mo.	11/30/37
Guinness, Alec	London, England	4/2/14
Guthrie, Arlo	New York, N.Y.	7/10/47
Guttenberg, Steve	New York, N.Y.	8/24/58
Guy, Jasmine	Boston, Mass.	3/10/-
Gwynne, Fred	New York, N.Y.	7/10/26
Hackett, Buddy	Brooklyn, N.Y.	8/31/24
Hackman, Gene	San Bernardino, Cal.	1/30/30
Hagen, Uta	Gottingen, Germany	6/12/19
Haggard, Merle	Bakersfield, Cal.	4/6/37
Haggerty, Dan	Hollywood, Cal.	11/19/41
Hagman, Larry	Weatherford, Tex.	9/21/31
Hague, Albert	Berlin, Germany	10/13/20
Haid, Charles	San Francisco, Cal.	6/2/43
Hale, Barbara	DeKalb, Ill.	4/18/22
Hall, Arsenio	Cleveland, Oh.	2/12/58
Hall, Daryl	Pottstown, Pa.	10/11/49
Hall, Deidre	Milwaukee, Wis.	10/31/48
Hall, Huntz	New York, N.Y.	8/15/19
Hall, Monty	Winnipeg, Man.	8/25/25
Hall, Tom T.	Olive Hill, Ky.	5/25/36
Hamel, Veronica	Philadelphia, Pa.	11/20/43
Hamill, Mark	Oakland, Cal.	9/25/51
Hamilton, George	Memphis, Tenn.	8/12/39
Hamlin, Harry	Pasadena, Cal.	10/30/51
Hampton, Lionel	Birmingham, Ala.	4/12/13
Hancock, Herbie	Chicago, Ill.	4/12/40
Hanks, Tom	Oakland, Cal.	7/9/56
Hannah, Daryl	Chicago, Ill.	1961
Hardison, Kadeem	New York, N.Y.	7/24/-
Harmon, Mark	Burbank, Cal.	9/2/51
Harper, Jessica	Chicago, Ill.	1949
Harper, Tess	Mammoth Springs, Ark.	1952
Harper, Valerie	Suffern, N.Y.	8/22/40
Harrelson, Woody	Midland, Tex.	7/23/-
Harrington, Pat Jr.	New York, N.Y.	8/13/29
Harris, Barbara	Evanston, Ill.	7/25/35
Harris, Ed	Englewood, N.J.	11/28/50
Harris, Emmylou	Birmingham, Ala.	4/2/47
Harris, Julie	Grosse Pte. Park, Mich.	12/2/25
Harris, Phil	Linton, Ind.	6/24/04
Harris, Richard	Co. Limerick, Ireland	10/1/33
Harris, Rosemary	Ashby, England	9/19/30
Harrison, George	Liverpool, England	2/25/43

Name	Birthplace	Born	Name	Birthplace	Born
Harrison, Gregory	Avalon, Cal.	5/31/50	Hurt, William	Washington, D.C.	3/20/50
Harry, Deborah	Miami, Fla.	7/1/45	Hussey, Ruth	Providence, R.I.	10/30/14
Hart, Mary	Sioux Falls, S.D.	1951	Huston, Anjelica	Ireland	1952
Hartley, Mariette	New York, N.Y.	6/21/40	Hutton, Betty	Battle Creek, Mich.	2/26/21
Hartman, David	Pawtucket, R.I.	5/19/35	Hutton, Lauren	Charleston, S.C.	11/17/43
Hartman, Lisa	Houston, Tex.	6/1/56	Hutton, Timothy	Malibu, Cal.	8/16/61
Hartman, Phil	Ontario, Canada	9/24/48	Hyde-White, Wilfrid	Gloucester, England	5/12/03
Hasselhoff, David	Baltimore, Md.	7/17/52	Hyman, Earle	Rocky Mount, N.C.	10/11/26
Hasso, Signe	Stockholm, Sweden	8/15/10			
Hauer, Rutger	Netherlands	1/23/44	Ian, Janis	New York, N.Y.	4/7/51
Haver, June	Rock Island, Ill.	6/10/26	Idol, Billy	London, England	11/30/55
Havoc, June	Seattle, Wash.	11/8/16	Iglesias, Julio	Madrid, Spain	9/23/43
Hawn, Goldie	Washington, D.C.	11/21/45	Ireland, John	Vancouver, B.C.	1/30/14
Hayden, Melissa	Toronto, Ont.	4/25/23	Irons, Jeremy	Cowes, England	9/19/48
Hayes, Helen	Washington, D.C.	10/10/00	Irving, Amy	Palo Alto, Cal.	9/10/53
Hayes, Isaac	Covington, Tenn.	8/20/42	Irving, George S.	Springfield, Mass.	11/1/22
Hays, Robert	Bethesda, Md.	7/24/47	Ives, Burl	Hunt Township, Ill.	6/14/09
Heard, John	Washington, D.C.	5/7/47	Ivey, Judith	El Paso, Tex.	9/4/51
Hearn, George	Memphis, Tenn.	1935			
Heatherton, Joey	Rockville Centre, N.Y.	9/14/44	Jackee	Winston-Salem, N.C.	8/14/-
Heckart, Eileen	Columbus, Oh.	3/29/19	Jackson, Anne	Allegheny, Pa.	9/3/25
Helmond, Katherine	Galveston, Tex.	7/5/34	Jackson, Glenda	Liverpool, England	5/9/36
Hemingway, Margaux	Portland, Ore.	2/19/55	Jackson, Janet	Gary, Ind.	5/16/66
Hemingway, Mariel	Mill Valley, Cal.	11/21/61	Jackson, Jermaine	Gary, Ind.	12/11/54
Hemmings, David	Guildford, England	11/18/41	Jackson, La Toya	Gary, Ind.	1/29/56
Hemsley, Sherman	Philadelphia, Pa.	2/1/38	Jackson, Kate	Birmingham, Ala.	10/29/48
Henderson, Florence	Dale, Ind.	2/14/34	Jackson, Michael	Gary, Ind.	8/29/58
Henderson, Skitch	Halstad, Minn.	1/27/18	Jackson, Victoria	Miami, Fla.	8/2/59
Henner, Marilu	Chicago, Ill.	4/6/52	Jacobi, Derek	London, England	10/22/38
Henning, Doug	Ft. Garry, Man.	5/3/47	Jaeckel, Richard	Long Beach, N.Y.	10/10/26
Henreid, Paul	Trieste, Austria	1/10/08	Jagger, Dean	Lima, Oh.	11/7/03
Hepburn, Audrey	Brussels, Belgium	5/4/29	Jagger, Mick	Dartford, England.	7/26/43
Hepburn, Katharine	Hartford, Conn.	11/8/09	James, Dennis	Jersey City, N.J.	8/24/17
Herman, Pee-wee	Peekskill, N.Y.	1952	James, John	Minneapolis, Minn.	4/18/56
Herrmann, Edward	Washington, D.C.	7/21/43	Janis, Conrad	New York, N.Y.	2/11/28
Hershey, Barbara	Los Angeles, Cal.	2/5/48	Jarreau, Al	Milwaukee, Wis	3/12/40
Hesseman, Howard	Lebanon, Ore.	2/27/40	Jeffreys, Anne	Goldsboro, N.C.	1/26/23
Heston, Charlton	Evanston, Ill.	10/4/23	Jenner, Bruce	Mt. Kisco, N.Y.	10/28/49
Hewitt, Christopher	Sussex, England	4/5/-	Jennings, Waylon	Littlefield, Tex.	6/15/37
Higgins, Joel	Bloomington, Ill.	9/28/43	Jett, Joan	Philadelphia, Pa.	9/22/60
Hildegarde	Adell, Wis.	2/1/06	Jewison, Norman	Toronto, Ont.	7/21/26
Hill, Arthur	Melfort, Sask.	8/1/22	Jillian, Ann	Cambridge, Mass.	1/29/50
Hill, Benny	Southampton, England.	1/21/25	Joel, Billy	Bronx, N.Y.	5/9/49
Hill, George Roy	Minneapolis, Minn.	12/20/22	John, Elton	Middlesex, England.	3/25/47
Hiller, Wendy	Stockport, England.	8/15/12	Johns, Glynis	Durban, S. Africa	10/5/23
Hillerman, John	Denison, Tex.	12/30/32	Johnson, Anne-Marie	Los Angeles, Cal.	7/18/-
Hines, Gregory	New York, N.Y.	2/14/46	Johnson, Arte	Benton Harbor, Mich.	1/20/29
Hines, Jerome	Hollywood, Cal.	11/8/21	Johnson, Ben	Foraker, Okla.	6/13/18
Hingle, Pat	Miami, Fla.	7/19/23	Johnson, Don	Flatt Creek, Mo.	12/15/49
Hirsch, Judd	Bronx, N.Y.	3/15/35	Johnson, Van	Newport, R.I.	8/25/16
Hirt, Al	New Orleans, La.	11/7/22	Jones, Allan	Scranton, Pa.	10/14/07
Ho, Don	Kakaako, Oahu, Ha.	8/13/30	Jones, Charlie	Ft. Smith, Ark.	11/9/30
Hoffman, Dustin	Los Angeles, Cal.	8/8/37	Jones, Dean	Morgan City, Ala.	1/25/35
Hogan, Paul	New South Wales, Australia.	1941	Jones, George	Saratoga, Tex.	9/12/31
			Jones, Grace	Spanishtown, Jamaica.	5/19/52
Holbrook, Hal	Cleveland, Oh.	2/17/25	Jones, Grandpa	Niagara, Ky.	10/20/13
Holder, Geoffrey	Trinidad	8/1/30	Jones, Henry	Philadelphia, Pa.	8/1/12
Holliday, Polly	Jasper, Ala.	7/2/37	Jones, Jack	Hollywood, Cal.	1/14/38
Holliman, Earl	Delhi, La.	9/11/28	Jones, James Earl	Tate Co., Miss.	1/17/31
Holloway, Sterling	Cedartown, Ga.	1/4/05	Jones, Jennifer	Tulsa, Okla.	3/2/19
Holm, Celeste	New York, N.Y.	4/29/19	Jones, Shirley	Smithton, Pa.	3/31/34
Hooks, Jan	Decatur, Ga.	4/23/57	Jones, Tom	Pontypridd, Wales	6/7/40
Hooks, Robert	Washington, D.C.	4/18/37	Jones, Tommy Lee	San Saba, Tex.	9/15/46
Hope, Bob	London, England	5/29/03	Jordan, Richard	New York, N.Y.	7/19/38
Hopkins, Anthony	Wales	12/31/37	Jourdan, Louis	Marseilles, France	6/19/21
Hopkins, Telma	Louisville, Ky.	10/28/48	Julia, Raul	San Juan, P.R.	3/9/40
Hopper, Dennis	Dodge City, Kan.	5/17/36	Jump, Gordon	Dayton, Oh.	4/1/32
Horne, Lena	Brooklyn, N.Y.	6/30/17			
Horne, Marilyn	Bradford, Pa.	1/16/34	Kahn, Madeline	Boston, Mass.	9/29/42
Horsley, Lee	Muleshoe, Tex.	5/15/55	Kanaly, Steve	Burbank, Cal.	3/14/46
Horton, Robert	Los Angeles, Cal.	7/29/24	Kane, Carol	Cleveland, Oh.	6/18/52
Hoskins, Bob	Suffolk, England	10/26/42	Kaplan, Gabe	Brooklyn, N.Y.	3/31/45
Houston, Whitney	E. Orange, N.J.	8/9/63	Karlen, John	New York, N.Y.	5/28/33
Howard, Ken	El Centro, Cal.	3/28/44	Karras, Alex	Gary, Ind.	7/15/35
Howard, Ron	Duncan, Okla.	3/1/54	Kasem, Casey	Detroit, Mich.	1933
Howell, C. Thomas	Los Angeles, Cal.	12/7/66	Katt, William	Los Angeles, Cal.	2/16/51
Howes, Sally Ann	London, England	7/20/30	Kavner, Julie	Los Angeles, Cal.	9/7/51
Hughes, Barnard	Bedford Hills, N.Y.	7/16/15	Kazan, Elia	Istanbul, Turkey.	9/7/09
Hulce, Tom	Whitewater, Wis.	12/6/53	Kazan, Lainie	New York, N.Y.	5/15/42
Humperdinck, Engelbert	Madras, India	5/3/36	Keach, Stacy	Savannah, Ga.	6/2/41
Hunt, Linda	Morristown, N.J.	4/2/45	Keaton, Diane	Santa Ana, Cal.	1/5/46
Hunter, Holly	Conyers, Ga.	1959	Keaton, Michael	Pittsburgh, Pa.	9/9/51
Hunter, Kim	Detroit, Mich.	11/12/22	Keel, Howard	Gillespie, Ill.	4/13/17
Hunter, Ross	Cleveland, Oh.	5/6/21	Keeler, Ruby	Halifax, N.S.	8/25/09
Hunter, Tab	New York, N.Y.	7/11/31	Keeshan, Bob	Lynbrook, N.Y.	6/27/27
Hurt, John	Chesterfield, England	1/22/40	Keitel, Harvey	Brooklyn, N.Y.	1947
Hurt, Mary Beth	Marshalltown, Ia.	9/26/46	Keith, Brian	Bayonne, N.J.	11/14/21
			Keith, David	Knoxville, Tenn.	5/8/54
			Kellerman, Sally	Long Beach, Cal.	6/2/37
			Kelley, DeForest	Atlanta, Ga.	1/20/20
			Kelly, Gene	Pittsburgh, Pa.	8/23/12

Name	Birthplace	Born
Kelly, Jack	Astoria, N.Y.	9/16/27
Kelly, Nancy	Lowell, Mass.	3/25/21
Kennedy, George	New York, N.Y.	2/18/26
Kennedy, Jayne	Washington, D.C.	11/27/51
Kent, Allegra	Los Angeles, Cal.	8/11/37
Kercheval, Ken	Wolcottville, Ind.	7/15/35
Kerns, Joanna	San Francisco, Cal.	2/12/53
Kerr, Deborah	Helensburgh, Scotland.	9/30/21
Kerr, John	New York, N.Y.	11/15/31
Khan, Chaka	Great Lakes. Ill.	3/23/53
Kidder, Margot	Yellowknife, N.W.T.	10/17/48
Kiley, Richard	Chicago, Ill.	3/31/22
King, Alan	Brooklyn, N.Y.	12/26/27
King, B. B.	Itta Bena, Miss.	9/16/25
King, Carole	Brooklyn, N.Y.	2/9/42
King, Larry	New York, N.Y.	11/19/33
King, Perry	Alliance, Oh.	4/30/48
Kingsley, Ben	Yorkshire, England	12/31/43
Kinski, Klaus	Sopot, Poland.	10/8/26
Kinski, Nastassia	Berlin, W. Germany.	1/24/60
Kirby, Durward.	Covington, Ky.	8/24/12
Kirkland, Gelsey	Bethlehem, Pa.	12/29/53
Kirsten, Dorothy	Montclair, N.J.	7/6/19
Kitt, Eartha	North, S.C.	1/26/28
Klein, Robert.	New York, N.Y.	2/8/42
Klemperer, Werner	Cologne, Germany.	3/22/19
Kline, Kevin.	St. Louis, Mo.	10/24/47
Klugman, Jack.	Philadelphia, Pa.	4/27/22
Knight, Gladys	Atlanta, Ga.	5/28/44
Knotts, Don	Morgantown, W. Va.	7/21/24
Knox, Alexander.	Strathroy, Ont.	1/16/07
Kopell, Bernie	New York, N.Y.	6/21/33
Korman, Harvey	Chicago, Ill.	2/15/27
Kotero, Apollonia	Santa Monica, Cal.	8/2/60
Kotto, Yaphet	New York, N.Y.	11/15/44
Kramer, Stanley	New York, N.Y.	9/29/13
Kramer, Stepfanie	Los Angeles, Cal.	8/6/56
Kristofferson, Kris	Brownsville, Tex.	6/22/36
Kubelik, Rafael	Bychori, Czechoslovakia.	6/29/14
Kubrick, Stanley	Bronx, N.Y.	7/26/28
Kulp, Nancy	Harrisburg, Pa.	8/28/21
Kurtz, Swoosie.	Omaha, Neb.	9/6/44
LaBelle, Patti.	Philadelphia, Pa.	10/4/44
Ladd, Cheryl	Huron, S.D.	7/12/51
Ladd, Diane	Meridian, Miss.	11/29/32
Lahti, Christine	Detroit, Mich.	4/5/50
Laine, Cleo.	Middlesex, England.	10/28/27
Laine, Frankie	Chicago, Ill.	3/30/13
Lamarr, Hedy	Vienna, Austria	11/9/13
Lamas, Lorenzo	Santa Monica, Cal.	1/20/58
Lamb, Gil	Minneapolis, Minn.	6/14/06
Lamour, Dorothy	New Orleans, La.	12/10/14
Lancaster, Burt	New York, N.Y.	11/2/13
Landau, Martin.	New York, N.Y.	6/20/34
Landesberg, Steve	New York, N.Y.	11/23/45
Landis, John	Chicago, Ill.	8/3/50
Landon, Michael	Forest Hills, N.Y.	10/21/36
Lane, Abbe.	Brooklyn, N.Y.	12/14/32
Lane, Diane	New York, N.Y.	1/22/63
Lane, Priscilla	Indianola, Ia.	6/12/17
Lang, K.D.	Consort, Alberta	1962
Lang, Stephen	New York, N.Y.	7/11/52
Lange, Hope	Redding Ridge, Conn.	11/28/31
Lange, Jessica	Cloquet, Minn.	4/20/49
Langella, Frank	Bayonne, N.J.	1/1/40
Langford, Frances	Lakeland, Fla.	4/4/13
Lansbury, Angela	London, England	10/16/25
Lansing, Robert	San Diego, Cal.	6/5/28
Laredo, Ruth	Detroit, Mich.	11/20/37
Larroquette, John	New Orleans, La.	11/25/47
Lasser, Louise	New York, N.Y.	4/11/39
Lauper, Cyndi	New York, N.Y.	6/20/53
Laurie, Piper	Detroit, Mich.	1/22/32
Lauter, Ed	Long Beach, N.Y.	10/30/40
Lavin, Linda	Portland, Me.	10/15/37
Lawrence, Carol.	Melrose Park, Ill.	9/5/34
Lawrence, Steve	Brooklyn, N.Y.	7/8/35
Lawrence, Vicki	Inglewood, Cal.	3/26/49
Leach, Robin.	London, England	8/29/41
Leachman, Cloris	Des Moines, Ia.	4/4/26
Lean, David	Croydon, England	3/25/08
Lear, Norman	New Haven, Conn.	7/27/22
Learned, Michael	Washington, D.C.	4/9/39
LeBon, Simon	Bushey, England	10/27/58
Lee, Brenda	Atlanta, Ga.	12/11/44
Lee, Christopher.	London, England	5/27/22
Lee, Michele	Los Angeles, Cal.	6/24/42

Name	Birthplace	Born
Lee, Peggy	Jamestown, N.D.	5/26/20
Lee, Spike	Atlanta, Ga.	3/20/57
Le Gallienne, Eva	London, England	1/11/99
Legrand, Michel	Paris, France	2/24/32
Leibman, Ron	New York, N.Y.	10/11/37
Leifer, Carol	E. Williston, N.Y.	1956
Leigh, Janet	Merced, Cal.	7/6/27
Leinsdorf, Erich	Vienna, Austria	2/4/12
Leisure, David	San Diego, Cal.	11/16/-
Lemmon, Chris	Los Angeles, Cal.	1/22/54
Lemmon, Jack.	Boston, Mass.	2/8/25
Lennon, Julian	London, England	4/8/63
Lennon Sisters		
Dianne	Los Angeles, Cal.	12/1/39
Janet	Culver City, Cal.	11/15/46
Kathy	Santa Monica, Cal.	8/22/42
Peggy	Los Angeles, Cal.	4/8/41
Leno, Jay.	New Rochelle, N.Y.	4/28/50
Lenz, Kay.	Los Angeles, Cal.	3/4/53
Leonard, Sheldon	New York, N.Y.	2/22/07
Leontovich, Eugenie.	Moscow, Russia	3/21/00
Leslie, Joan	Detroit, Mich.	1/26/25
Letterman, David	Indianapolis, Ind.	4/12/47
Levine, James	Cincinnati, Oh.	6/23/43
Levinson, Barry	Baltimore, Md.	1932
Lewis, Emmanuel	New York, N.Y.	3/9/71
Lewis, Dawnn	New York, N.Y.	8/13/-
Lewis, Huey	New York, N.Y.	1952
Lewis, Jerry	Newark, N.J.	3/16/26
Lewis, Jerry Lee	Ferriday, La.	9/29/35
Lewis, Richard.	New York, N.Y.	6/29/47
Lewis, Shari	New York, N.Y.	1/17/34
Light, Judith	Trenton, N.J.	2/9/50
Lightfoot, Gordon	Orillia, Ont.	11/17/38
Linden, Hal	New York, N.Y.	3/20/31
Lindfors, Viveca	Uppsala, Sweden.	12/29/20
Linkletter, Art	Saskatchewan, Canada.	7/17/12
Linn-Baker, Mark	St. Louis, Mo.	6/17/53
Lithgow, John	Rochester, N.Y.	10/19/45
Little, Cleavon	Chickasha, Okla.	6/1/39
Little, Rich	Ottawa, Ont.	11/26/38
Little Richard.	Macon, Ga.	12/5/32
Lloyd, Christopher.	Stamford, Conn.	10/22/38
Lloyd, Emily	England	9/29/70
Locke, Sondra	Shelbyville, Tenn.	5/28/47
Lockhart, June.	New York, N.Y.	6/25/25
Locklear, Heather	Los Angeles, Cal.	9/25/61
Loggia, Robert.	New York, N.Y.	1/3/30
Loggins, Kenny	Everett, Wash.	1/7/48
Lollobrigida, Gina	Subiaco, Italy	7/4/28
Lom, Herbert.	Prague, Czechoslovakia.	1/9/17
London, Julie.	Santa Rosa, Cal.	9/26/26
Long, Shelley	Ft. Wayne, Ind.	8/23/49
Lord, Jack	New York, N.Y.	—
Loren, Sophia	Rome, Italy	9/20/34
Loring, Gloria	New York, N.Y.	12/10/46
Loudon, Dorothy	Boston, Mass.	9/17/33
Louise, Tina	New York, N.Y.	2/11/34
Lovitz, Jon	Tarzana, Cal.	7/21/57
Lowe, Rob	Charlottesville, Va.	3/17/64
Loy, Myrna.	Helena, Mon.	8/2/05
Lucas, George	Modesto, Cal.	5/14/44
Lucci, Susan	Westchester Co., N.Y.	12/23/49
Luckinbill, Laurence	Ft. Smith, Ark.	11/21/34
Ludwig, Christa	Berlin, Germany	3/16/28
Luke, Keye	Canton, China.	1904
Lumet, Sidney	Philadelphia, Pa.	6/25/24
Lupino, Ida	London, England	2/4/18
LuPone, Patti.	Northport, N.Y.	4/21/49
Lynn, Jeffrey	Auburn, Mass.	2/16/09
Lynch, David	Missoula, Mont.	1/1/46
Lynn, Loretta.	Butcher Hollow, Ky.	4/14/-
Maazel, Lorin	Paris, France	3/6/30
MacArthur, James.	Los Angeles, Cal.	12/8/37
MacCorkindale, Simon	Cambridge, England	2/12/53
MacGraw, Ali	Pound Ridge, N.Y.	4/1/39
MacKenzie, Gisele	Winnipeg, Man.	1/10/27
MacLaine, Shirley	Richmond, Va.	4/24/34
MacLeod, Gavin	Mt. Kisco, N.Y.	2/28/30
MacMurray, Fred	Kankakee, Ill.	8/30/08
MacNee, Patrick.	London, England	2/6/22
MacNeil, Cornell.	Minneapolis, Minn.	9/24/22
Macchio, Ralph	Long Island, N.Y.	11/4/62
Macy, Bill	Revere, Mass.	5/18/22
Madden, John	Austin, Minn.	4/10/36
Madonna (Ciccone)	Bay City, Mich.	8/16/58
Majors, Lee	Wyandotte, Mich.	4/23/40
Malbin, Elaine	New York, N.Y.	5/24/32

Name	Birthplace	Born
Malden, Karl	Chicago, Ill.	3/22/13
Malfitano, Catherine	New York, N.Y.	4/18/48
Malkovich, John	Christopher, Ill.	12/9/53
Malle, Louis	Thumeries, France	10/30/32
Malone, Dorothy	Chicago, Ill.	1/30/25
Manchester, Melissa	Bronx, N.Y.	2/15/51
Mancini, Henry	Cleveland, Oh.	4/16/24
Mandel, Howie	Toronto, Ont.	11/29/-
Mandrell, Barbara	Houston, Tex.	12/25/48
Mangione, Chuck	Rochester, N.Y.	11/29/40
Manilow, Barry	New York, N.Y.	6/17/46
Mann, Herbie	New York, N.Y.	4/16/30
Manoff, Dinah	New York, N.Y.	1/25/58
Marceau, Marcel	Strasbourg, France	3/22/23
Marsalis, Wynton	New Orleans, La.	10/18/61
Marchand, Nancy	Buffalo, N.Y.	6/19/28
Margolin, Janet	New York, N.Y.	7/25/43
Marin, Cheech	Los Angeles, Cal.	7/13/46
Markova, Alicia	London, England	12/1/10
Marriner, Neville	Lincoln, England	4/15/24
Marsh, Jean	London, England	7/1/34
Marshall, E. G.	Owatonna, Minn.	6/18/10
Marshall, Penny	New York, N.Y.	10/15/43
Marshall, Peter	Huntington, W.Va.	3/30/27
Martin, Dean	Steubenville, Oh.	6/17/17
Martin, Dick	Detroit, Mich.	1/30/23
Martin, Mary	Weatherford, Tex.	12/1/13
Martin, Pamela Sue	Westport, Conn.	1/5/54
Martin, Steve	Waco, Tex.	1945
Martin, Tony	San Francisco, Cal.	12/25/13
Martins, Peter	Copenhagen, Denmark	10/27/46
Mason, Jackie	Sheboygan, Wis.	6/9/31
Mason, Marsha	St. Louis, Mo.	4/3/42
Mastrantonio, Mary Eliz.	Lombard, Ill.	11/17/58
Mastroianni, Marcello	Rome, Italy	9/28/24
Matheson, Tim	Glendale, Cal.	12/31/47
Mathis, Johnny	San Francisco, Cal.	9/30/35
Matthau, Walter	New York, N.Y.	10/1/20
Mature, Victor	Louisville, Ky.	1/29/16
May, Elaine	Philadelphia, Pa.	4/21/32
Mayfield, Curtis	Chicago, Ill.	6/3/42
Mayo, Virginia	St. Louis, Mo.	11/30/20
Mazurki, Mike	Austria	12/25/09
Mazursky, Paul	Brooklyn, N.Y.	4/25/30
McArdle, Andrea	Philadelphia, Pa.	11/5/63
McBride, Patricia	Teaneck, N.J.	8/23/42
McCallum, David	Glasgow, Scotland	9/19/33
McCambridge, Mercedes	Joliet, Ill.	3/17/18
McCarthy, Andrew	New York, N.Y.	1963
McCarthy, Kevin	Seattle, Wash.	2/15/14
McCartney, Paul	Liverpool, England	6/18/42
McCarver, Tim	Memphis, Tenn.	10/16/41
McClanahan, Rue	Healdton, Okla.	2/21/36
McClure, Doug	Glendale, Cal.	5/11/35
McClurg, Edie	Kansas City, Mo.	7/23/-
McCoo, Marilyn	Jersey City, N.J.	9/30/43
McCrea, Joel	Los Angeles, Cal.	11/5/05
McDowall, Roddy	London, England	9/28/28
McDowell, Malcolm	Leeds, England	6/13/43
McEntire, Reba	McAlester, Okla.	3/28/55
McFarland, Spanky	Dallas, Tex.	10/2/28
McGavin, Darren	Spokane, Wash.	5/7/22
McGillis, Kelly	Newport, Cal.	1957
McGoohan, Patrick	New York, N.Y.	3/19/28
McGovern, Elizabeth	Evanston, Ill.	7/18/61
McGovern, Maureen	Youngstown, Oh.	7/27/49
McGuire, Al	New York, N.Y.	9/7/31
McGuire, Dorothy	Omaha, Neb.	6/14/19
McIntire, John	Spokane, Wash.	6/27/07
McKechnie, Donna	Pontiac, Mich.	11/16/42
McKee, Lonette	Detroit, Mich.	1954
McKellen, Ian	Burnley, England	5/25/39
McKeon, Nancy	Westbury, N.Y.	4/4/66
McLean, Don	New Rochelle, N.Y.	10/2/45
McLerie, Allyn	Grand Mere, Que.	12/1/26
McMahon, Ed	Detroit, Mich.	3/6/23
McNichol, Kristy	Los Angeles, Cal.	9/11/62
McQueen, Butterfly	Tampa, Fla.	1/7/11
McRaney, Gerald	Collins, Miss.	8/19/47
Meadows, Audrey	Wu Chang, China.	2/8/24
Meadows, Jayne	Wu Chang, China.	9/27/20
Meara, Anne	New York, N.Y.	9/20/29
Mehta, Zubin	Bombay, India.	4/29/36
Melanie	New York, N.Y.	2/3/47
Mendes, Sergio	Niteroi, Brazil	2/11/41
Menuhin, Yehudi	New York, N.Y.	4/22/16
Mercer, Marian	Akron, Oh.	11/26/35
Mercouri, Melina	Athens, Greece	10/18/25
Meredith, Burgess	Cleveland, Oh.	11/16/08
Merrick, David	Hong Kong	11/27/12
Merrill, Dina	New York, N.Y.	12/9/25
Merrill, Robert	Brooklyn, N.Y.	6/4/19
Messina, Jim	Maywood, Cal.	12/5/47
Meyers, Ari	San Juan, Puerto Rico	4/6/69
Michael, George	Watford, England	6/26/63
Michaels, Al	New York, N.Y.	11/12/44
Midler, Bette	Paterson, N.J.	12/1/45
Milano, Alyssa	New York, N.Y.	12/19/73
Miles, Sarah	Ingatestone, England.	12/31/41
Miles, Vera	near Boise City, Okla.	8/23/30
Miller, Ann	Houston, Tex.	4/12/19
Miller, Dennis	Pittsburgh, Pa.	11/3/53
Miller, Mitch	Rochester, N.Y.	7/4/11
Miller, Roger	Ft. Worth, Tex.	1/2/36
Mills, Donna	Chicago, Ill.	12/11/43
Mills, John	Suffolk, England	2/22/08
Mills, Juliet	London, England	11/21/41
Milner, Martin	Detroit, Mich.	12/28/27
Milnes, Sherrill	Downers Grove, Ill.	1/10/35
Milsap, Ronnie	Robinsville, N.C.	1/16/44
Milstein, Nathan	Odessa, Russia.	12/31/04
Mimieux, Yvette	Hollywood, Cal.	1/8/39
Minnelli, Liza	Los Angeles, Cal.	3/12/46
Mitchell, Cameron	Dallastown, Pa.	4/11/18
Mitchell, James	Sacramento, Cal.	2/29/20
Mitchell, Joni	McLeod, Alta.	11/7/43
Mitchum, Robert	Bridgeport, Conn.	8/6/17
Moffat, Donald	Plymouth, England	12/26/30
Moffo, Anna	Wayne, Pa.	6/27/27
Molinaro, Al	Kenosha, Wis.	6/24/19
Moll, Richard	Pasadena, Cal.	1/13/43
Montalban, Ricardo	Mexico City, Mexico	11/25/20
Montand, Yves	Monsumagno, Italy	10/13/21
Montgomery, Elizabeth	Hollywood, Cal.	4/15/33
Moody, Ron	London, England	1/8/24
Moore, Clayton	Chicago, Ill.	9/14/14
Moore, Constance	Sioux City, Ia.	1/18/22
Moore, Demi	Roswell, N.M.	11/11/62
Moore, Dudley	London, England	4/19/35
Moore, Garry	Baltimore, Md.	1/31/15
Moore, Mary Tyler	Brooklyn, N.Y.	12/29/37
Moore, Melba	New York, N.Y.	10/29/45
Moore, Roger	London, England	10/14/27
Moore, Terry	Los Angeles, Cal.	1/1/29
Moranis, Rick	Toronto, Ont.	4/18/-
Moreau, Jeanne	Paris, France	1/23/28
Moreno, Rita	Humacao, P.R.	12/11/31
Morgan, Dennis	Prentice, Wis.	12/10/10
Morgan, Harry	Detroit, Mich.	4/10/15
Moriarty, Michael	Detroit, Mich.	4/5/41
Morini, Erika	Vienna, Austria	1/5/10
Morita, Pat	Isleton, Cal.	6/28/32
Morley, Robert	Wiltshire, England	5/26/08
Morris, Greg	Cleveland, Oh.	9/27/34
Morris, Howard	New York, N.Y.	9/4/25
Morse, Robert	Newton, Mass.	5/18/31
Moses, William	Los Angeles, Cal.	11/17/59
Muldaur, Diana	New York, N.Y.	8/19/38
Mulgrew, Kate	Dubuque, Ia.	4/29/55
Mulhare, Edward	Ireland	4/8/23
Mull, Martin	Chicago, Ill.	8/18/43
Mulligan, Richard	New York, N.Y.	11/13/32
Munsel, Patrice	Spokane, Wash.	5/14/25
Murphy, Ben	Jonesboro, Ark.	3/6/42
Murphy, Eddie	Brooklyn, N.Y.	4/3/61
Murphy, George	New Haven, Conn.	7/4/02
Murphy, Michael	Los Angeles, Cal.	5/5/38
Murray, Anne	Springhill, Nova Scotia.	6/20/45
Murray, Arthur	New York, N.Y.	4/4/95
Murray, Bill	Evanston, Ill.	9/21/50
Murray, Don	Hollywood, Cal.	7/31/29
Murray, Kathryn	Jersey City, N.J.	9/15/06
Musante, Tony	Bridgeport, Conn.	6/30/36
Musburger, Brent	Portland, Ore.	5/26/39
Muti, Riccardo	Naples, Italy.	7/28/41
Nabors, Jim	Sylacauga, Ala.	6/12/33
Nash, Graham	Blackpool, England.	2/2/42
Natwick, Mildred	Baltimore, Md.	6/19/08
Naughton, James	Middletown, Conn.	7/6/46
Neal, Patricia	Packard, Ky.	1/20/26
Nealon, Kevin	Bridgeport, Conn.	11/18/53
Neill, Sam	New Zealand	1948
Nelligan, Kate	London, Ontario.	3/16/51
Nelson, Craig T.	Spokane, Wash.	4/4/46
Nelson, Ed	New Orleans, La.	12/21/28

Name	Birthplace	Born
Nelson, Gene	Seattle, Wash.	3/24/20
Nelson, Harriet (Hilliard)	Des Moines, Ia.	7/18/14
Nelson, Judd	Portland, Me.	1959
Nelson, Tracy	Santa Monica, Cal.	10/25/63
Nelson, Willie	Abbott, Tex.	4/30/33
Nero, Peter	New York, N.Y.	5/22/34
New Kids On The Block		
Knight, Jonathan	Worcester, Mass.	11/29/68
Knight, Jordan	Worcester, Mass.	5/17/70
McIntyre, Joe	Needham, Mass.	12/31/72
Wahlberg, Donnie	Boston, Mass.	8/17/69
Wood, Danny	Boston, Mass.	5/14/69
Newhart, Bob	Oak Park, Ill.	9/29/29
Newley, Anthony	Hackney, England	9/24/31
Newman, Laraine	Los Angeles, Cal.	3/2/52
Newman, Paul	Cleveland, Oh.	1/26/25
Newman, Phyllis	Jersey City, N.J.	3/19/35
Newman, Randy	Los Angeles, Cal.	11/28/43
Newton, Wayne	Norfolk, Va.	4/3/42
Newton-John, Olivia	Cambridge, England	9/26/47
Nichols, Mike	Berlin, Germany	11/6/31
Nicholson, Jack	Neptune, N.J.	4/28/37
Nicks, Stevie	Phoenix, Ariz.	5/26/48
Nielsen, Leslie	Regina, Sask.	2/11/26
Nilsson, Birgit	Karup, Sweden	5/17/18
Nimoy, Leonard	Boston, Mass.	3/26/31
Noble, James	Dallas, Tex.	3/5/22
Nolte, Nick	Omaha, Neb.	2/8/40
Norman, Jessye	Augusta, Ga.	9/15/45
Norris, Chuck	Ryan, Okla.	1939
North, Sheree	Los Angeles, Cal.	1/17/33
Novak, Kim	Chicago, Ill.	2/13/33
Novello, Don	Ashtabula, Oh.	1/1/43
Nureyev, Rudolf	Russia	3/17/38
Oates, John	New York, N.Y.	4/7/48
O'Brian, Hugh	Rochester, N.Y.	4/19/30
O'Brien, Margaret	San Diego, Cal.	1/15/37
Ocean, Billy	Trinidad	1/21/52
O'Connell, Helen	Lima, Oh.	5/23/20
O'Connor, Carroll	New York, N.Y.	8/2/24
O'Connor, Donald	Chicago, Ill.	8/28/25
Odetta	Birmingham, Ala.	12/31/30
O'Hara, Maureen	Dublin, Ireland	8/17/20
O'Herlihy, Dan	Wexford, Ireland	5/1/19
Olin, Ken	Chicago, Ill.	7/30/54
Olin, Lena	Sweden	1956
Olmos, Edward James	E. Los Angeles, Cal.	2/24/47
Olsen, Merlin	Logan, Ut.	9/15/40
Olsin, K.T.	Arkansas	1942
O'Neal, Patrick	Ocala, Fla.	9/26/27
O'Neal, Ryan	Los Angeles, Cal.	4/20/41
O'Neal, Tatum	Los Angeles, Cal.	11/5/63
O'Neill, Ed	Youngstown, Oh.	1946
O'Neill, Jennifer	Brazil	2/20/47
Ontkean, Michael	Vancouver, B.C.	1/24/46
Opatoshu, David	New York, N.Y.	1/30/18
Orbach, Jerry	New York, N.Y.	10/20/35
Orlando, Tony	New York, N.Y.	4/3/44
Osbourne, Ozzy	Birmingham, England	12/3/46
O'Shea, Milo	Ireland	1926
Osmond, Donny	Ogden, Ut.	12/9/57
Osmond, Marie	Ogden, Ut.	10/13/59
O'Sullivan, Maureen	Boyle, Ireland	5/17/11
O'Toole, Annette	Houston, Tex.	4/1/52
O'Toole, Peter	Connemara, Ireland	8/2/32
Owens, Buck	Sherman, Tex.	8/12/29
Ozawa, Seiji	Shenyang, China	9/1/35
Paar, Jack	Canton, Oh.	5/1/18
Pacino, Al	New York, N.Y.	4/25/40
Page, Patti	Claremore, Okla.	11/8/27
Paige, Janis	Tacoma, Wash.	9/16/22
Palance, Jack	Lattimer, Pa.	2/18/20
Palin, Michael	England	1943
Palmer, Betsy	East Chicago, Ind.	11/1/29
Papas, Irene	Greece	3/9/26
Papp, Joseph	Brooklyn, N.Y.	6/22/21
Parker, Alan	London, England	2/14/44
Parker, Eleanor	Cedarville, Oh.	6/26/22
Parker, Fess	Ft. Worth, Tex.	8/16/25
Parker, Jameson	Baltimore, Md.	11/18/47
Parker, Jean	Deer Lodge, Mon.	8/11/12
Parks, Bert	Atlanta, Ga.	12/30/14
Parsons, Estelle	Lynn, Mass.	11/20/27
Parton, Dolly	Sevierville, Tenn.	1/19/46
Pasternak, Joseph	Hungary	9/19/01
Patinkin, Mandy	Chicago, Ill.	11/30/52

Name	Birthplace	Born
Pavarotti, Luciano	Modena, Italy	10/12/35
Paycheck, Johnny	Greenfield, Oh.	5/31/41
Pearl, Minnie	Centerville, Tenn.	10/25/12
Peck, Gregory	La Jolla, Cal.	4/5/16
Pendergrass, Teddy	Philadelphia, Pa.	3/26/50
Penn, Arthur	Philadelphia, Pa.	9/27/22
Penn, Sean	Burbank, Cal.	8/17/60
Penny, Joe	London, England	9/14/56
Peppard, George	Detroit, Mich.	10/1/28
Perkins, Elizabeth	Vermont	1961
Perkins, Anthony	New York, N.Y.	4/4/32
Perlman, Itzhak	Tel Aviv, Israel	8/31/45
Perlman, Rhea	Brooklyn, N.Y.	3/31/48
Perlman, Ron	New York, N.Y.	4/13/-
Perrine, Valerie	Galveston, Tex.	9/3/43
Persoff, Nehemiah	Jerusalem, Palestine	8/14/20
Peters, Bernadette	New York, N.Y.	2/28/48
Peters, Brock	New York, N.Y.	7/2/27
Peters, Jean	Canton, Oh.	10/15/26
Peters, Roberta	New York, N.Y.	5/4/30
Petty, Tom	Gainesville, Fla.	10/20/53
Pfeiffer, Michelle	Santa Ana, Cal.	4/29/57
Phillips, MacKenzie	Alexandria, Va.	11/10/59
Phillips, Michelle	Long Beach, Cal.	6/4/44
Phoenix, River	Madras, Ore.	8/23/70
Pickett, Cindy	Norman, Okla.	4/18/47
Picon, Molly	New York, N.Y.	6/1/98
Pinchot, Bronson	New York, N.Y.	5/20/59
Piscopo, Joe	Passaic, N.J.	6/17/51
Pleasence, Donald	Worksop, England	10/5/19
Pleshette, Suzanne	New York, N.Y.	1/31/37
Plowright, Joan	Brigg, England	10/28/29
Plummer, Amanda	New York, N.Y.	3/23/57
Plummer, Christopher	Toronto, Ont.	12/13/29
Poitier, Sidney	Miami, Fla.	2/20/27
Polanski, Roman	Paris, France	8/18/33
Pollack, Sidney	Lafayette, Ind.	7/1/34
Ponti, Carlo	Milan, Italy	12/11/13
Porizkova, Paulina	Czechoslovakia	4/9/65
Post, Markie	Palo Alto, Cal.	11/4/50
Poston, Tom	Columbus, Oh.	10/17/27
Potts, Annie	Nashville, Tenn.	10/28/-
Powell, Jane	Portland, Ore.	4/1/28
Powers, Stefanie	Hollywood, Cal.	11/2/42
Prentiss, Paula	San Antonio, Tex.	3/4/39
Presley, Priscilla	New York, N.Y.	5/24/45
Preston, Billy	Houston, Tex.	9/9/46
Previn, Andre	Berlin, Germany	4/6/29
Price, Leontyne	Laurel, Miss.	2/10/27
Price, Ray	Perryville, Tex.	1/12/26
Price, Vincent	St. Louis, Mo.	5/27/11
Pride, Charlie	Sledge, Miss.	3/18/39
Prince	Minneapolis, Minn.	6/7/58
Principal, Victoria	Japan	—
Prosky, Robert	Philadelphia, Pa.	12/13/30
Prowse, Juliet	Bombay, India	9/25/37
Pryor, Richard	Peoria, Ill.	12/1/40
Pulliam, Keshia Knight	Newark, N.J.	4/9/79
Pyle, Denver	Bethune, Col.	5/11/20
Quaid, Dennis	Houston, Tex.	4/9/54
Quaid, Randy	Houston, Tex.	10/1/50
Quinlan, Kathleen	Pasadena, Cal.	11/19/54
Quinn, Anthony	Chihuahua, Mexico	4/21/15
Quinn, Martha	Albany, N.Y.	5/11/59
Rabb, Ellis	Memphis, Tenn.	6/20/30
Rabbitt, Eddie	Brooklyn, N.Y.	11/27/41
Rachins, Alan	Cambridge, Mass.	10/10/-
Rae, Charlotte	Milwaukee, Wis.	4/22/26
Raffin, Deborah	Los Angeles, Cal.	3/13/53
Rainer, Luise	Vienna, Austria	1/12/09
Raitt, Bonnie	Burbank, Cal.	11/8/49
Raitt, John	Santa Ana, Cal.	1/19/17
Ralston, Esther	Bar Harbor, Me.	9/17/02
Ralston, Vera Hruba	Prague, Czechoslovakia	6/12/19
Rambo, Dack	Delano, Cal.	11/13/41
Rampal, Jean-Pierre	Marseilles, France	1/7/22
Randall, Tony	Tulsa, Okla.	2/26/20
Randolph, John	New York, N.Y.	6/1/15
Rashad, Phylicia	Houston, Tex.	6/17/48
Ratzenberger, John	Bridgeport, Conn.	4/6/47
Rawls, Lou	Chicago, Ill.	12/1/36
Ray, Aldo	Pen Argyl, Pa.	9/25/26
Rayburn, Gene	Christopher, Ill.	12/22/17
Raye, Martha	Butte, Mon.	8/27/16
Raymond, Gene	New York, N.Y.	8/13/08
Reddy, Helen	Melbourne, Australia	10/25/41
Redford, Robert	Santa Monica, Cal.	8/18/37
Redgrave, Lynn	London, England	3/8/43

Name	Birthplace	Born
Redgrave, Vanessa	London, England	1/30/37
Reed, Jerry	Atlanta, Ga.	3/20/37
Reed, Oliver	London, England	2/13/38
Reed, Rex	Ft. Worth, Tex.	10/2/38
Reed, Robert	Highland Park, Ill.	10/19/32
Reese, Della	Detroit, Mich.	7/6/31
Reeve, Christopher	New York, N.Y.	9/25/52
Reid, Kate	London, England	11/4/30
Reid, Tim	Norfolk, Va.	12/19/44
Reilly, Charles Nelson	New York, N.Y.	1/13/31
Reiner, Carl	Bronx, N.Y.	3/20/22
Reiner, Rob	Bronx, N.Y.	3/6/45
Reinhold, Judge	Wilmington, Del.	1956
Reinking, Ann	Seattle, Wash.	11/10/50
Remick, Lee	Quincy, Mass.	12/14/35
Resnik, Regina	New York, N.Y.	8/30/24
Reynolds, Burt	Waycross, Ga.	2/11/36
Reynolds, Debbie	El Paso, Tex.	4/1/32
Rhue, Madlyn	Washington, D.C.	10/3/34
Rich, Charlie	Forest City, Ark.	12/14/32
Richards, Keith	Kent, England	12/18/43
Richardson, Tony	Shipley, England	6/5/28
Richie, Lionel	Tuskegee, Ala.	6/20/50
Rickles, Don	New York, N.Y.	5/8/26
Riegert, Peter	New York, N.Y.	1948
Rigg, Diana	Doncaster, England	7/20/38
Ringwald, Molly	Rosewood, Cal.	2/14/68
Ritter, John	Burbank, Cal.	9/17/48
Rivera, Chita	Washington, D.C.	1/23/33
Rivera, Geraldo	New York, N.Y.	7/4/43
Rivers, Joan	Brooklyn, N.Y.	6/8/33
Robards, Jason Jr.	Chicago, Ill.	7/26/22
Robbins, Jerome	New York, N.Y.	10/11/18
Roberts, Doris	St. Louis, Mo.	11/4/30
Roberts, Eric	Biloxi, Miss.	4/18/56
Roberts, Julia	Smyrna, Ga.	1967
Roberts, Pernell	Waycross, Ga.	5/18/30
Roberts, Tony	New York, N.Y.	10/22/39
Robertson, Cliff	La Jolla, Cal.	9/9/25
Robertson, Dale	Harrah, Okla.	7/14/23
Robinson, Charles	Houston, Tex.	11/9/-
Robinson, Holly	Philadelphia, Pa.	1965
Robinson, Smokey	Detroit, Mich.	2/19/40
Roche, Eugene	Boston, Mass.	9/22/28
Rodgers, Jimmie	Camas, Wash.	1933
Rodrigues, Percy	Montreal, Que.	6/13/24
Rodriquez, Johnny	Sabinal, Tex.	12/10/51
Rogers, Chas. (Buddy)	Olathe, Kan.	8/13/04
Rogers, Fred	Latrobe, Pa.	3/20/28
Rogers, Ginger	Independence, Mo.	7/16/11
Rogers, Kenny	Houston, Tex.	8/21/38
Rogers, Mimi	Coral Gables, Fla.	1/27/-
Rogers, Roy	Cincinnati, Oh.	11/5/12
Rogers, Wayne	Birmingham, Ala.	4/7/33
Roland, Gilbert	Juarez, Mexico	12/11/05
Rolle, Esther	Pompano Beach, Fla.	11/8/33
Rollins, Howard	Baltimore, Md.	10/17/50
Romero, Cesar	New York, N.Y.	2/15/07
Ronstadt, Linda	Tucson, Ariz.	7/15/46
Rooney, Mickey	Brooklyn, N.Y.	9/23/20
Rose Marie	New York, N.Y.	8/15/25
Ross, Diana	Detroit, Mich.	3/26/44
Ross, Katharine	Hollywood, Cal.	1/29/43
Ross, Marion	Albert Lea, Minn.	10/25/28
Rosselini, Isabella	Rome, Italy	6/18/52
Rostropovich, Mstislav	Baku, USSR.	3/12/27
Roth, David Lee	Bloomington, Ind.	10/10/55
Rourke, Mickey	Miami, Fla.	1956
Rowlands, Gena	Cambria, Wis.	6/19/34
Rubinstein, John	Los Angeles, Cal.	12/8/46
Rush, Barbara	Denver, Col.	1/4/30
Russell, Jane	Bemidji, Minn.	6/21/21
Russell, Ken	Southampton, England	7/3/27
Russell, Kurt	Springfield, Mass.	3/17/51
Russell, Mark	Buffalo, N.Y.	8/23/32
Russell, Nipsey	Atlanta, Ga.	10/13/24
Russell, Theresa	San Diego, Cal.	1957
Rutherford, Ann	Toronto, Ont.	11/2/20
Ruttan, Susan	Oregon City, Ore.	9/16/50
Ryan, Meg	Fairfield, Conn.	1962
Ryan, Peggy	Long Beach, Cal.	8/28/24
Ryan, Roz	Detroit, Mich.	7/7/51
Rydell, Bobby	Philadelphia, Pa.	4/26/42
Sahl, Mort	Montreal, Que.	5/11/27
Saint, Eva Marie	Newark, N.J.	7/4/24
St. James, Susan	Los Angeles, Cal.	8/14/46
St. John, Jill	Los Angeles, Cal.	8/19/40
Sainte-Marie, Buffy	Maine	2/20/41
Sajak, Pat	Chicago, Ill.	10/26/47
Saks, Gene	New York, N.Y.	11/8/21
Sales, Soupy	Franklinton, N.C.	1/8/26
Samms, Emma	London, England	8/28/60
Sanderson, William	Memphis, Tenn.	1/10/48
Sandy, Gary	Dayton, Oh.	12/25/45
Sanford, Isabel	New York, N.Y.	8/29/17
Santana, Carlos	Mexico	7/20/47
Sarandon, Chris	Beckley, W.Va.	7/24/42
Sarandon, Susan	New York, N.Y.	10/4/46
Sarnoff, Dorothy	New York, N.Y.	5/25/17
Sarrazin, Michael	Quebec City, Que.	5/22/40
Savage, Fred	Highland Park, Ill.	7/9/66
Savalas, Telly	Garden City, N.Y.	1/21/24
Saxon, John	Brooklyn, N.Y.	8/5/35
Sayles, John	Schenectady, N.Y.	9/28/50
Scaggs, Boz	Dallas, Tex.	6/8/44
Schallert, William	Los Angeles, Cal.	7/6/22
Scheider, Roy	Orange, N.J.	11/10/32
Schell, Maria	Vienna, Austria	1/15/26
Schell, Maximilian	Vienna, Austria	12/8/30
Schell, Ronnie	Richmond, Cal.	12/23/31
Schenkel, Chris	Bippus, Ind.	8/21/23
Schnabel, Stefan	Berlin, Germany	2/2/12
Schneider, Alexander	Vilna, Poland	10/21/08
Schneider, John	Mt. Kisco, N.Y.	4/8/54
Schreiber, Avery	Chicago, Ill.	4/9/35
Schroder, Rick	Staten Island, N.Y.	4/3/70
Schwarzenegger, Arnold	Graz, Austria	7/30/47
Schwarzkopf, Elisabeth	Jarotschin, Poland	12/9/15
Scofield, Paul	Hurst, Pierpont, England	1/21/22
Scolari, Peter	New Rochelle, Ill.	9/12/54
Scorsese, Martin	New York, N.Y.	11/17/42
Scott, George C.	Wise, Va.	10/18/27
Scott, Lizabeth	Scranton, Pa.	9/29/22
Scott, Martha	Jamesport, Mo.	9/22/14
Scotto, Renata	Savona, Italy	2/24/35
Scully, Vin	New York, N.Y.	11/29/27
Sebastian, John	New York N.Y.	3/17/44
Sedaka, Neil	New York, N.Y.	3/13/39
Seeger, Pete	New York, N.Y.	5/3/19
Segal, George	Great Neck, N.Y.	2/13/34
Segal, Vivienne	Philadelphia, Pa.	4/19/97
Seinfeld, Jerry	New York, N.Y.	1954
Sellecca, Connie	New York, N.Y.	5/25/55
Selleck, Tom	Detroit, Mich.	1/29/45
Serkin, Rudolf	Eger, Austria	3/28/03
Severinsen, Doc	Arlington, Ore.	7/7/27
Seymour, Jane	Middlesex, England	2/15/51
Shackelford, Ted	Oklahoma City, Okla.	6/23/46
Shaffer, Paul	Thunder Bay, Ont.	11/28/49
Shandling, Garry	Tucson, Ariz.	11/29/49
Shankar, Ravi	India	4/7/20
Sharif, Omar	Alexandria, Egypt	4/10/32
Shatner, William	Montreal, Que.	3/22/31
Shearer, Moira	Scotland	1/17/26
Sheedy, Ally	New York, N.Y.	6/12/62
Sheen, Charlie	Santa Monica, Cal.	1966
Sheen, Martin	Dayton, Oh.	8/3/40
Shelley, Carole	London, England	8/16/39
Shepard, Sam	Ft. Sheridan, Ill.	11/5/43
Shepherd, Cybill	Memphis, Tenn.	2/18/50
Shields, Brooke	New York, N.Y.	5/31/65
Shire, Talia	New York, N.Y.	4/25/46
Shirley, Ann	New York, N.Y.	4/17/18
Shore, Dinah	Winchester, Tenn.	3/1/17
Short, Bobby	Danville, Ill.	9/15/24
Short, Martin	Hamilton, Ont.	3/26/51
Shull, Richard B.	Evanston, Ill.	2/24/29
Sidney, Sylvia	New York, N.Y.	8/8/10
Siepi, Cesare	Milan, Italy	2/10/23
Sikking, James B.	Los Angeles, Cal.	3/5/34
Sills, Beverly	Brooklyn, N.Y.	5/25/29
Silver, Ron	New York, N.Y.	7/2/46
Simmons, Gene	Haifa, Israel	8/25/49
Simmons, Jean	London, England	1/31/29
Simon, Carly	New York, N.Y.	6/25/45
Simon, Paul	Newark, N.J.	11/5/42
Simone, Nina	Tyron, N.C.	2/21/33
Sinatra, Frank	Hoboken, N.J.	12/12/15
Sinatra, Nancy	Jersey City, N.J.	6/8/40
Sinbad	Benton Harbor, Mich.	11/10/-
Siskel, Gene	Chicago, Ill.	1/26/46
Skelton, Red (Richard)	Vincennes, Ind.	7/18/13
Skerritt, Tom	Detroit, Mich.	8/25/33
Slater, Helen	Massapequa, N.Y.	12/14/63
Slezak, Erika	Hollywood, Cal.	8/5/46

Name	Birthplace	Born	Name	Birthplace	Born
Slick, Grace	Chicago, Ill.	10/30/39	Swayze, Patrick	Houston, Tex.	8/18/54
Smirnoff, Yakov	Odessa, USSR	1/24/51	Swenson, Inga	Omaha, Neb.	12/29/34
Smith, Allison	New York, N.Y.	12/9/69	Swit, Loretta	Passaic, N.J.	11/4/37
Smith, Alexis	Penticton, B.C.	6/8/21	Mr. T (Lawrence Tero)	Chicago, Ill.	5/21/52
Smith, Buffalo Bob	Buffalo, N.Y.	11/27/17	Talbot, Lyle	Pittsburgh, Pa.	2/8/02
Smith, Connie	Elkhart, Ind.	8/14/41	Tallchief, Maria	Fairfax, Okla.	1/24/25
Smith, Jaclyn	Houston, Tex.	10/26/47	Tandy, Jessica	London, England	6/7/09
Smith, Keely	Norfolk, Va.	3/9/35	Tarkenton, Fran	Richmond, Va.	2/3/40
Smith, Maggie	Ilford, England.	12/28/34	Tayback, Vic	New York, N.Y.	1/6/29
Smith, Roger	South Gate, Cal.	12/18/32	Taylor, Elizabeth	London, England	2/27/32
Smits, Jimmy	New York, N.Y.	7/9/58	Taylor, James	Boston, Mass.	3/12/48
Smothers, Dick	New York, N.Y.	11/20/39	Taylor, Rod	Sydney, Australia.	1/11/30
Smothers, Tom	New York, N.Y.	2/2/37	Te Kanawa, Kiri	Gisborne, New Zealand	3/6/44
Snow, Hank	Nova Scotia, Canada	5/9/14	Tebaldi, Renata	Pesaro, Italy.	2/1/22
Snyder, Tom	Milwaukee, Wis.	5/12/36	Temple, Shirley	Santa Monica, Cal.	4/23/28
Solti, Georg	Budapest, Hungary	10/21/12	Tennille, Toni	Montgomery, Ala.	5/8/43
Somers, Suzanne	San Bruno, Cal.	10/16/46	Tharp, Twyla	Portland, Ind.	7/1/41
Somes, Michael	nr. Stroud, England.	9/28/17	Thaxter, Phyllis	Portland, Me.	11/20/19
Sommer, Elke	Berlin, Germany	11/5/41	Thicke, Alan	Kirkland Lake, Ont.	3/1/47
Sorvino, Paul	New York, N.Y.	1939	Thomas, B.J.	Hugo, Okla.	8/7/42
Sothern, Ann	Valley City, N.D.	1/22/09	Thomas, Betty	St. Louis, Mo.	7/27/48
Soul, David	Chicago, Ill.	8/28/43	Thomas, Danny	Deerfield, Mich.	1/6/14
Spacek, Sissy	Quitman, Tex.	12/25/49	Thomas, Heather	Greenwich, Conn.	9/8/57
Spano, Joe	San Francisco, Cal.	7/7/46	Thomas, Marlo	Detroit, Mich.	11/21/43
Spelling, Aaron	Dallas, Tex.	4/22/28	Thomas, Philip Michael	Columbus, Oh.	5/26/49
Spielberg, Steven	Cincinnati, Oh.	12/18/47	Thomas, Richard	New York, N.Y.	6/13/51
Springfield, Dusty	London, England	4/16/39	Thompson, Jack	Sydney, Australia.	8/31/40
Springfield, Rick	Sydney, Australia.	8/23/49	Thompson, Lea	Rochester, Minn.	5/31/61
Springsteen, Bruce	Freehold, N.J.	9/23/49	Thompson, Sada	Des Moines, Ia.	9/27/29
Stack, Robert	Los Angeles, Cal.	1/13/19	Thulin, Ingrid	Sweden	1/27/29
Stafford, Jo	Coalinga, Cal.	11/12/18	Tiegs, Cheryl	Minnesota	9/27/47
Stahl, Richard	Detroit, Mich.	1/4/32	Tierney, Gene	Brooklyn, N.Y.	11/20/20
Stallone, Sylvester	New York, N.Y.	7/6/46	Tiffany	Norwalk, Cal.	10/2/71
Stamos, John	Cypress, Cal.	8/19/63	Tillis, Mel	Tampa, Fla.	8/8/32
Stamp, Terence	Stepney, England.	7/22/39	Tiny Tim	New York, N.Y.	4/12/23
Stander, Lionel	New York, N.Y.	1/11/08	Todd, Richard	Dublin, Ireland.	6/11/19
Stang, Arnold	New York, N.Y.	9/28/25	Tomlin, Lily	Detroit, Mich.	9/1/39
Stanley, Kim	Tularosa, N.M.	2/11/25	Tomlinson, David	Scotland	5/7/17
Stanton, Harry Dean	Kentucky	7/14/26	Toomey, Regis	Pittsburgh, Pa.	8/13/02
Stapleton, Jean	New York, N.Y.	1/19/23	Torme, Mel	Chicago, Ill.	9/13/25
Stapleton, Maureen	Troy, N.Y.	6/21/25	Torn, Rip	Temple, Tex.	2/6/31
Starr, Kay	Dougherty, Okla.	7/21/22	Tracy, Arthur	Russia	6/25/03
Starr, Ringo	Liverpool, England	7/7/40	Travanti, Daniel J.	Kenosha, Wis.	3/7/40
Steber, Eleanor	Wheeling, W. Va.	7/17/14	Travers, Mary	Louisville, Ky.	11/9/36
Steenburgen, Mary	Little Rock, Ark.	1953	Travis, Randy	Marshville, N.C.	1959
Steiger, Rod	W. Hampton, N.Y.	4/14/25	Travolta, John	Englewood, N.J.	2/18/54
Stephens, James	Mt. Kisco, N.Y.	5/18/51	Trebek, Alex	Sudbury, Ont.	7/22/40
Sterling, Jan	New York, N.Y.	4/3/23	Trevor, Claire	New York, N.Y.	3/8/09
Sterling, Robert	New Castle, Pa.	11/13/17	Troyanos, Tatiana	New York, N.Y.	9/12/38
Stern, Isaac	Kreminiecz, Russia	7/21/20	Tucker, Michael	Baltimore, Md.	2/6/44
Sternhagen, Frances	Washington, D.C.	1/13/30	Tucker, Tanya	Seminole, Tex.	10/10/58
Stevens, Andrew	Memphis, Tenn.	6/10/55	Tune, Tommy	Wichita Falls, Tex.	2/28/39
Stevens, Cat	London, England	7/21/48	Turner, Ike	Clarksdale, Miss.	11/5/39
Stevens, Connie	Brooklyn, N.Y.	8/8/38	Turner, Kathleen	Springfield, Mo.	6/19/54
Stevens, Kaye	E. Cleveland, Oh.	7/21/35	Turner, Lana	Wallace, Ida.	2/8/20
Stevens, Rise	New York, N.Y.	6/11/13	Turner, Tina	Nutbush, Tenn.	11/26/39
Stevens, Stella	Yazoo City, Miss.	10/1/36	Tushingham, Rita	Liverpool, England	3/14/40
Stevenson, McLean	Normal, Ill.	11/14/29	Twiggy (Leslie Hornby)	London, England	9/19/49
Stevenson, Parker	Philadelphia, Pa.	6/4/52	Twitty, Conway	Friar's Point, Miss.	9/1/33
Stewart, James	Indiana, Pa.	5/20/08	Tyson, Cicely	New York, N.Y.	12/19/33
Stewart, Rod	London, England	1/10/45	Uecker, Bob	Milwaukee, Wis.	1/26/35
Stickney, Dorothy	Dickinson, N.D.	6/21/00	Uggams, Leslie	New York, N.Y.	5/25/43
Stiers, David Ogden	Peoria, Ill.	10/31/42	Ullman, Tracey	Slough, England	1960
Stiller, Jerry	New York, N.Y.	6/8/29	Ullmann, Liv	Tokyo, Japan	12/16/38
Stills, Stephen	Dallas, Tex.	1/3/45	Underwood, Blair	Tacoma, Wash.	8/25/-
Sting (G. Sumner)	Newcastle, England	10/2/51	Urich, Robert	Toronto, Oh.	12/19/46
Stockwell, Dean	Hollywood, Cal.	3/5/36	Ustinov, Peter	London, England	4/16/21
Stone, Oliver	New York, N.Y.	9/15/46	Vaccaro, Brenda	Brooklyn, N.Y.	11/18/39
Stookey, Paul	Baltimore, Md.	12/30/37	Vale, Jerry	New York, N.Y.	7/8/31
Storch, Larry	New York, N.Y.	1/8/23	Valente, Caterina	Paris, France	1/14/31
Storm, Gale	Bloomington, Tex.	4/5/22	Valentine, Karen	Santa Rosa, Cal.	5/25/47
Straight, Beatrice	Old Westbury, N.Y.	8/2/18	Valli, Frankie	Newark, N.J.	5/3/37
Strasser, Robin	New York, N.Y.	5/7/45	Van Ark, Joan	New York, N.Y.	6/16/43
Stratas, Teresa	Toronto, Ont.	5/26/38	Van Doren, Mamie	Rowena, S.D.	2/6/33
Strauss, Peter	New York, N.Y.	2/20/47	Vandross, Luther	New York, N.Y.	4/20/51
Streep, Meryl	Summit, N.J.	6/22/49	Van Dyke, Dick	West Plains, Mo.	12/13/25
Streisand, Barbra	Brooklyn, N.Y.	4/24/42	Van Dyke, Jerry	Danville, Ill.	7/27/32
Stritch, Elaine	Detroit, Mich.	2/2/26	Van Fleet, Jo	Oakland, Cal.	12/30/22
Struthers, Sally	Portland, Ore.	7/28/48	Van Halen, Eddie	Nijmegan, Netherlands.	1/26/57
Stuarti, Enzo	Rome, Italy	3/3/25	Van Pallandt, Nina	Copenhagen, Denmark	7/15/32
Sullivan, Barry	New York, N.Y.	8/29/12	Van Patten, Dick	New York, N.Y.	12/9/28
Sullivan, Susan	New York, N.Y.	11/18/44	Vaughn, Robert	New York, N.Y.	11/22/32
Sullivan, Tom	Boston, Mass.	3/27/47	Venuta, Benay	San Francisco, Cal.	1/27/11
Sumac, Yma	Ichocan, Peru	9/10/27	Verdon, Gwen	Los Angeles, Cal.	1/13/25
Summer, Donna	Boston, Mass.	12/31/48	Vereen, Ben	Miami, Fla.	10/10/46
Sutherland, Donald	St. John, New Brunswick	7/17/35	Verrett, Shirley	New Orleans, La.	5/31/31
Sutherland, Joan	Sydney, Australia.	11/7/26	Vickers, Jon	Prince Albert, Sask.	10/26/26
			Vigoda, Abe	New York, N.Y.	2/24/21

Name	Birthplace	Born	Name	Birthplace	Born
Villella, Edward	Long Island, N.Y.	10/1/36	Wilder, Gene	Milwaukee, Wis.	6/11/35
Vincent, Jan-Michael	Denver, Col.	7/15/44	Williams, Andy	Wall Lake, Ia.	12/3/30
Vinson, Helen	Beaumont, Tex.	9/17/07	Williams, Billy Dee	New York, N.Y.	4/6/37
Vinton, Bobby	Canonsburg, Pa.	4/16/35	Williams, Cindy	Van Nuys, Cal.	8/22/47
Vitale, Dick	E. Rutherford, N.J.	6/9/40	Williams, Esther	Los Angeles, Cal.	8/8/23
Voight, Jon	Yonkers, N.Y.	12/29/38	Williams, Hal	Columbus, Oh.	12/14/38
Von Stade, Frederica	Somerville, N.J.	6/1/45	Williams Jr., Hank	Shreveport, La.	5/26/49
Von Sydow, Max	Lund, Sweden.	4/10/29	Williams, Joe	Cordele, Ga.	12/12/18
			Williams, JoBeth	Houston, Tex.	1953
Wagner, Lindsay	Los Angeles, Cal.	6/22/49	Williams, Paul	Omaha, Neb.	9/19/40
Wagner, Robert	Detroit, Mich.	2/10/30	Williams, Robin	Chicago, Ill.	7/21/52
Wagoner, Porter	West Plains, Mo.	8/12/27	Williams, Treat.	Rowayton, Conn.	12/1/51
Wahl, Ken	Chicago, Ill.	1956	Williamson, Nicol	Hamilton, Scotland	9/14/38
Wain, Bea	Bronx, N.Y.	4/30/17	Willis, Bruce	W. Germany.	3/19/55
Waite, Ralph	White Plains, N.Y.	6/22/29	Wilson, Demond	Valdosta, Ga.	10/13/46
Walden, Robert	New York, N.Y.	9/25/43	Wilson, Elizabeth	Grand Rapids, Mich.	4/4/25
Walken, Christopher	New York, N.Y.	3/31/43	Wilson, Flip.	Jersey City, N.J.	12/8/33
Walker, Clint	Hartford, Ill.	5/30/27	Wilson, Nancy	Chillicothe, Oh.	2/20/37
Walker, Nancy	Philadelphia, Pa.	5/10/22	Windom, William	New York, N.Y.	9/28/23
Wallach, Eli.	Brooklyn, N.Y.	12/7/15	Winfield, Paul	Los Angeles, Cal.	5/22/41
Walston, Ray	Laurel, Miss.	11/2/24	Winfrey, Oprah	Kosciusko, Miss.	1/29/54
Walter, Jessica	New York, N.Y.	1/31/44	Winger, Debra	Cleveland, Oh.	5/16/55
Wanamaker, Sam	Chicago, Ill.	6/14/19	Winkler, Henry	New York, N.Y.	10/30/45
Ward, Rachel	London, England	1957	Winters, Jonathan	Dayton, Oh.	11/11/25
Ward, Simon	London, England	10/19/41	Winters, Shelley	St. Louis, Mo.	8/18/22
Warden, Jack	Newark, N.J.	9/18/20	Winwood, Steve	Birmingham, England.	5/12/48
Warfield, William.	W. Helena, Ark.	1/22/20	Wiseman, Joseph	Montreal, Que.	5/15/18
Warner, Malcolm-Jamal	Jersey City, N.J.	8/18/70	Withers, Jane	Atlanta, Ga.	4/12/26
Warren, Lesley Ann	New York, N.Y.	8/16/46	Wonder, Stevie	Saginaw, Mich.	5/13/50
Warren, Michael	So. Bend, Ind.	3/5/46	Woodard, Alfre	Tulsa, Okla.	11/2/53
Warrick, Ruth	St. Joseph, Mo.	6/29/16	Woods, James.	Vernal, N.J.	4/18/47
Warwick, Dionne.	E. Orange, N.J.	12/12/41	Woodward, Edward.	Croyden, England	6/1/30
Washington, Denzel.	Mt. Vernon, N.Y.	12/28/54	Woodward, Joanne.	Thomasville, Ga.	2/27/30
Waterston, Sam	Cambridge, Mass.	11/15/40	Worth, Irene	Nebraska	6/23/16
Watkins, Carlene	Hartford, Conn.	6/4/52	Wray, Fay	Alberta, Canada	9/10/07
Watts, Andre.	Nuremberg, Germany	6/20/46	Wright, Martha.	Seattle, Wash.	3/23/26
Wayne, David	Traverse City, Mich.	1/30/14	Wright, Max	Detroit, Mich.	8/2/-
Waxman, Al	Toronto, Ont.	3/2/35	Wright, Steven	New York, N.Y.	12/6/55
Weaver, Dennis	Joplin, Mo.	6/4/24	Wright, Teresa	New York, N.Y.	10/27/18
Weaver, Fritz.	Pittsburgh, Pa.	1/19/26	Wyatt, Jane	Campgaw, N.J.	8/10/11
Weaver, Sigourney	New York, N.Y.	10/8/49	Wyman, Jane	St. Joseph, Mo.	1/4/14
Weir, Peter.	Sydney, Australia.	8/8/44	Wynette, Tammy	Red Bay, Ala.	5/5/42
Weitz, Bruce	Norwalk, Conn.	5/27/43	Yarborough, Glenn	Milwaukee, Wis.	1/12/30
Welch, Raquel	Chicago, Ill.	9/5/40	Yarrow, Peter	New York, N.Y.	5/31/38
Weld, Tuesday.	New York, N.Y.	8/27/43	York, Michael	Fulmer, England	3/27/42
Welk, Lawrence	nr. Strasburg, N.D.	3/11/03	York, Susannah	London, England	1/9/42
Wells, Kitty	Nashville, Tenn.	8/30/19	Yothers, Tina.	Whittier, Cal.	9/5/73
Wendt, George	Chicago, Ill.	10/17/48	Young, Alan	Northumberland, England	11/19/19
Weston, Jack	Cleveland, Oh.	8/21/24	Young, Burt	New York, N.Y.	4/30/40
Whelchel, Lisa	Ft. Worth, Tex.	5/29/63	Young, Loretta	Salt Lake City, Ut.	1/6/13
White, Barry	Galveston, Tex.	9/12/44	Young, Neil.	Toronto, Ont.	11/12/45
White, Betty	Oak Park, Ill.	1/17/22	Young, Robert	Chicago, Ill.	2/22/07
White, Jesse	Buffalo, N.Y.	1/3/19	Youngman, Henny	Liverpool, England	1/12/06
White, Vanna	N. Myrtle Beach, S.C.	2/18/57	Zappa, Frank	Baltimore, Md.	12/21/40
Whiting, Margaret	Detroit, Mich.	7/22/24	Zeffirelli, Franco	Florence, Italy.	2/12/23
Whitmore, James	White Plains, N.Y.	10/1/21	Zimbalist, Efrem Jr.	New York, N.Y.	11/30/23
Widmark, Richard	Sunrise, Minn.	12/26/14	Zimbalist, Stephanie	New York, N.Y.	10/6/56
Wiest, Dianne	Kansas City, Mo.	3/28/48	Zmed, Adrian	Chicago, Ill.	3/14/54
Wilder, Billy	Vienna, Austria	6/22/06	Zukerman, Pinchas	Tel Aviv, Israel	7/16/48

Entertainment Personalities of the Past

(as of mid-1990)

Born	Died	Name	Born	Died	Name	Born	Died	Name
1895	1974	Abbott, Bud	1905	1974	Arquette, Cliff	1878	1954	Barrymore, Lionel
1872	1953	Adams, Maude	1899	1987	Astaire, Fred	1848	1905	Barrymore, Maurice
1855	1926	Adler, Jacob P.	1906	1987	Astor, Mary	1897	1963	Barthelmess, Richard
1903	1984	Adler, Luther	1885	1946	Atwill, Lionel	1890	1962	Barton, James
1898	1933	Adoree, Renee	1845	1930	Auer, Leopold	1914	1984	Basehart, Richard
1902	1986	Aherne, Brian	1905	1967	Auer, Mischa	1904	1984	Basie, Count
1931	1989	Ailey, Alvin	1900	1972	Austin, Gene	1923	1985	Baxter, Anne
1909	1964	Albertson, Frank	1898	1940	Ayres, Agnes	1889	1951	Baxter, Warner
1907	1981	Albertson, Jack				1880	1928	Bayes, Nora
1894	1956	Allen, Fred	1913	1989	Backus, Jim	1904	1965	Beatty, Clyde
1906	1964	Allen, Gracie	1892	1968	Bainter, Fay	1902	1962	Beavers, Louise
1883	1950	Allgood, Sara	1906	1975	Baker, Josephine	1884	1946	Beery, Noah
1915	1967	Andrews, Laverne	1904	1983	Balanchine, George	1889	1949	Beery, Wallace
1876	1958	Anglin, Margaret	1911	1989	Ball, Lucille	1901	1970	Begley, Ed
1887	1933	Arbuckle, Fatty (Roscoe)	1882	1956	Bancroft, George	1854	1931	Belasco, David
1900	1976	Arlen, Richard	1903	1968	Bankhead, Tallulah	1949	1982	Belushi, John
1868	1946	Arliss, George	1890	1952	Banks, Leslie	1906	1968	Benaderet, Bea
1888	1945	Armetta, Henry	1890	1955	Bara, Theda	1906	1964	Bendix, William
1900	1971	Armstrong, Louis	1810	1891	Barnum, Phineas T.	1904	1965	Bennett, Constance
1917	1986	Arnaz, Desi	1879	1959	Barrymore, Ethel	1943	1987	Bennett, Michael
1890	1956	Arnold, Edward	1882	1942	Barrymore, John	1894	1974	Benny, Jack

Born	Died	Name
1924	1970	Benzell, Mimi
1899	1966	Berg, Gertrude
1903	1978	Bergen, Edgar
1915	1982	Bergman, Ingrid
1895	1976	Berkeley, Busby
1923	1986	Bernardi, Herschel
1844	1923	Bernhardt, Sarah
1893	1943	Bernie, Ben
1889	1967	Bickford, Charles
1911	1960	Bjoerling, Jussi
1895	1973	Blackmer, Sidney
1908	1989	Blanc, Mel
1900	1943	Bledsoe, Jules
1928	1972	Blocker, Dan
1909	1979	Blondell, Joan
1888	1959	Blore, Eric
1901	1975	Blue, Ben
1899	1957	Bogart, Humphrey
1880	1965	Boland, Mary
1895	1969	Boles, John
1904	1987	Bolger, Ray
1903	1960	Bond, Ward
1892	1981	Bondi, Beulah
1917	1981	Boone, Richard
1833	1893	Booth, Edwin
1796	1852	Booth, Junius Brutus
1894	1953	Bordoni, Irene
1888	1960	Bori, Lucrezia
1905	1965	Bow, Clara
1874	1946	Bowes, Maj. Edward
1928	1977	Boyd, Stephen
1898	1972	Boyd, William
1899	1978	Boyer, Charles
1893	1939	Brady, Alice
1894	1974	Brennan, Walter
1904	1979	Brent, George
1891	1951	Brice, Fanny
1891	1959	Broderick, Helen
1904	1951	Bromberg, J. Edward
1892	1973	Brown, Joe E.
1926	1966	Bruce, Lenny
1895	1953	Bruce, Nigel
1910	1982	Bruce, Virginia
1920	1985	Brynner, Yul
1903	1979	Buchanan, Edgar
1891	1957	Buchanan, Jack
1885	1957	Buck, Gene
1938	1982	Buono, Victor
1885	1970	Burke, Billie
1911	1967	Burnette, Smiley
1902	1971	Burns, David
1925	1984	Burton, Richard
1897	1946	Busch, Mae
1883	1966	Bushman, Francis X.
1896	1946	Butterworth, Charles
1893	1971	Byington, Spring
1904	1972	Cabot, Bruce
1918	1977	Cabot, Sebastian
1899	1986	Cagney, James
1895	1956	Calhern, Louis
1923	1977	Callas, Maria
1933	1976	Cambridge, Godfrey
1865	1940	Campbell, Mrs. Patrick
1892	1964	Cantor, Eddie
1878	1947	Carey, Harry
1950	1983	Carpenter, Karen
1906	1988	Carradine, John
1880	1961	Carrillo, Leo
1892	1972	Carroll, Leo G.
1905	1965	Carroll, Nancy
1910	1963	Carson, Jack
1862	1937	Carter, Mrs. Leslie
1873	1921	Caruso, Enrico
1876	1973	Casals, Pablo
1929	1989	Cassavetes, John
1893	1969	Castle, Irene
1887	1918	Castle, Vernon
1889	1960	Catlett, Walter
1887	1950	Cavanaugh, Hobart
1873	1938	Chaliapin, Feodor
1919	1980	Champion, Gower
1918	1961	Chandler, Jeff
1883	1930	Chaney, Lon
1905	1973	Chaney Jr., Lon
1942	1981	Chapin, Harry
1889	1977	Chaplin, Charles
1893	1940	Chase, Charlie

Born	Died	Name
1893	1961	Chatterton, Ruth
1888	1972	Chevalier, Maurice
1888	1960	Clark, Bobby
1914	1968	Clark, Fred
1920	1966	Clift, Montgomery
1932	1963	Cline, Patsy
1898	1937	Clive, Colin
1892	1967	Clyde, Andy
1911	1976	Cobb, Lee J.
1877	1961	Coburn, Charles
1878	1942	Cohan, George M.
1902	1986	Cohen, Myron
1919	1965	Cole, Nat (King)
1890	1965	Collins, Ray
1891	1958	Colman, Ronald
1908	1934	Columbo, Russ
1907	1944	Compton, Betty
1887	1940	Connolly, Walter
1917	1982	Conried, Hans
1914	1975	Conte, Richard
1914	1984	Coogan, Jackie
1935	1964	Cooke, Sam
1901	1961	Cooper, Gary
1888	1971	Cooper, Gladys
1896	1973	Cooper, Melville
1914	1968	Corey, Wendell
1893	1974	Cornell, Katherine
1890	1972	Correll, Charles (Andy)
1905	1979	Costello, Dolores
1904	1957	Costello, Helene
1908	1959	Costello, Lou
1877	1950	Costello, Maurice
1899	1973	Coward, Noel
1924	1973	Cox, Wally
1908	1983	Crabbe, Buster
1847	1924	Crabtree, Lotta
1928	1978	Crane, Bob
1911	1986	Crawford, Broderick
1908	1977	Crawford, Joan
1916	1944	Cregar, Laird
1880	1942	Crews, Laura Hope
1880	1974	Crisp, Donald
1942	1973	Croce, Jim
1903	1977	Crosby, Bing
1897	1975	Cross, Milton
1910	1986	Crothers, Scatman
1878	1968	Currie, Finlay
1914	1978	Dailey, Dan
1923	1965	Dandridge, Dorothy
1869	1941	Danforth, William
1894	1963	Daniell, Henry
1901	1971	Daniels, Bebe
1860	1935	Daniels, Frank
1936	1973	Darin, Bobby
1921	1965	Darnell, Linda
1879	1967	Darwell, Jane
1909	1986	Da Silva, Howard
1866	1949	Davenport, Harry
1908	1989	Davis, Bette
1907	1961	Davis, Joan
1925	1990	Davis Jr., Sammy
1931	1955	Dean, James
1905	1968	Dekker, Albert
1908	1983	Del Rio, Dolores
1892	1983	Demarest, William
1881	1959	DeMille, Cecil B.
1891	1967	Denny, Reginald
1901	1974	DeSica, Vittorio
1905	1977	Devine, Andy
1942	1972	De Wilde, Brandon
1907	1974	De Wolfe, Billy
1920	1985	Diamond, Selma
1879	1947	Digges, Dudley
1901	1966	Disney, Walt
1894	1949	Dix, Richard
1905	1958	Donat, Robert
1889	1972	Donlevy, Brian
1901	1981	Douglas, Melvyn
1907	1959	Douglas, Paul
—	1980	Dragonette, Jessica
1889	1956	Draper, Ruth
1881	1965	Dresser, Louise
1869	1934	Dressler, Marie
1820	1897	Drew, Mrs. John
1853	1927	Drew, John (son)
1909	1951	Duchin, Eddy
1890	1974	Dumbrille, Douglass
1889	1965	Dumont, Margaret

Born	Died	Name
1878	1927	Duncan, Isadora
1905	1967	Dunn, James
1935	1973	Dunn, Michael
1893	1980	Durante, Jimmy
1907	1968	Duryea, Dan
1858	1924	Duse, Eleanora
1894	1929	Eagels, Jeanne
1901	1967	Eddy, Nelson
1897	1971	Edwards, Cliff
1879	1945	Edwards, Gus
1899	1974	Ellington, Duke
1941	1974	Elliot, Cass
1891	1967	Elman, Mischa
1881	1951	Errol, Leon
1888	1976	Evans, Edith
1901	1989	Evans, Maurice
1913	1967	Evelyn, Judith
1883	1939	Fairbanks, Douglas
1914	1970	Farmer, Frances
1870	1929	Farnum, Dustin
1876	1953	Farnum, William
1882	1967	Farrar, Geraldine
1904	1971	Farrell, Glenda
1868	1940	Faversham, William
1861	1939	Fawcett, George
1897	1961	Fay, Frank
1895	1962	Fazenda, Louise
1933	1982	Feldman, Marty
1898	1985	Fetchit, Stepin
1894	1979	Fiedler, Arthur
1918	1973	Field, Betty
1898	1979	Fields, Gracie
1879	1946	Fields, W.C.
1931	1978	Fields, Totie
1916	1977	Finch, Peter
1865	1932	Fiske, Minnie Maddern
1888	1961	Fitzgerald, Barry
1895	1962	Flagstad, Kirsten
1900	1971	Flippen, Jay C.
1909	1959	Flynn, Errol
1925	1974	Flynn, Joe
1880	1942	Fokine, Michel
1910	1968	Foley, Red
1905	1982	Fonda, Henry
1920	1978	Fontaine, Frank
1887	1983	Fontanne, Lynn
1895	1973	Ford, John
1901	1976	Ford, Paul
1899	1966	Ford, Wallace
1927	1987	Fosse, Bob
1901	1970	Foster, Preston
1857	1928	Foy, Eddie
1903	1968	Francis, Kay
1887	1966	Frawley, William
1885	1938	Frederick, Pauline
1870	1955	Friganza, Trixie
1890	1958	Frisco, Joe
1901	1960	Gable, Clark
1889	1963	Galli-Curci, Amelita
1905	1990	Garbo, Greta
1877	1967	Garden, Mary
1922	1990	Gardner, Ava
1913	1952	Garfield, John
1922	1969	Garland, Judy
1939	1984	Gaye, Marvin
1906	1984	Gaynor, Janet
1902	1978	Geer, Will
1900	1954	George, Gladys
1892	1962	Gibson, Hoot
1894	1971	Gilbert, Billy
1895	1936	Gilbert, John
1855	1937	Gillette, William
1879	1939	Gilpin, Charles
1897	1987	Gingold, Hermione
1898	1968	Gish, Dorothy
1916	1987	Gleason, Jackie
1886	1959	Gleason, James
1938	1984	Gluck, Alma
1905	1990	Goddard, Paulette
1903	1983	Godfrey, Arthur
1874	1955	Golden, John
1882	1974	Goldwyn, Samuel
1909	1986	Goodman, Benny
1915	1969	Gorcey, Leo
1896	1985	Gordon, Ruth
1899	1982	Gosden, Freeman (Amos)
1869	1944	Gottschalk, Ferdinand

Born	Died	Name
1829	1869	Gottschalk, Louis
1916	1973	Grable, Betty
1925	1981	Grahame, Gloria
1904	1986	Grant, Cary
1915	1987	Greene, Lorne
1879	1954	Greenstreet, Sydney
1874	1948	Griffith, David Wark
1912	1980	Griffith, Hugh
1912	1967	Guthrie, Woody
1875	1959	Gwenn, Edmund
1888	1942	Hackett, Charles
1902	1958	Hackett, Raymond
1892	1950	Hale, Alan
1925	1981	Haley, Bill
1899	1979	Haley, Jack
1902	1985	Hamilton, Margaret
1847	1919	Hammerstein, Oscar
1893	1964	Hardwicke, Cedric
1892	1957	Hardy, Oliver
1911	1937	Harlow, Jean
1844	1911	Harrigan, Edward
1908	1990	Harrison, Rex
1870	1946	Hart, William S.
1928	1973	Harvey, Laurence
1910	1973	Hawkins, Jack
1890	1973	Hayakawa, Sessue
1885	1969	Hayes, Gabby
1902	1971	Hayward, Leland
1917	1975	Hayward, Susan
1918	1987	Hayworth, Rita
1896	1937	Healy, Ted
1910	1971	Heflin, Van
1901	1987	Heifetz, Jascha
1873	1918	Held, Anna
1942	1970	Hendrix, Jimi
1936	1990	Henson, Jim
1910	1969	Henie, Sonja
1879	1942	Herbert, Henry
1887	1951	Herbert, Hugh
1886	1956	Hersholt, Jean
1899	1980	Hitchcock, Alfred
1914	1955	Hodiak, John
1894	1973	Holden, Fay
1918	1981	Holden, William
1922	1965	Holliday, Judy
1936	1959	Holly, Buddy
1888	1951	Holt, Jack
1918	1973	Holt, Tim
1898	1978	Homolka, Oscar
1902	1972	Hopkins, Miriam
1858	1935	Hopper, DeWolf
1874	1959	Hopper, Edna Wallace
1915	1970	Hopper, William
1904	1989	Horowitz, Vladimir
1886	1970	Horton, Edward Everett
1874	1926	Houdini, Harry
1902	1988	Houseman, John
1881	1965	Howard, Eugene
1867	1961	Howard, Joe
1890	1943	Howard, Leslie
1885	1955	Howard, Tom
1916	1988	Howard, Trevor
1885	1949	Howard, Willie
1925	1985	Hudson, Rock
1890	1977	Hull, Henry
1886	1957	Hull, Josephine
1895	1958	Humphrey, Doris
1927	1969	Hunter, Jeffrey
1901	1962	Husing, Ted
1906	1987	Huston, John
1884	1950	Huston, Walter
1892	1950	Ingram, Rex
1895	1969	Ingram, Rex
1895	1980	Iturbi, Jose
1838	1905	Irving, Henry
1871	1944	Irving, Isabel
1872	1914	Irving, Laurence
1875	1942	Jackson, Joe
1911	1972	Jackson, Mahalia
1891	1984	Jaffe, Sam
1916	1983	James, Harry
1889	1956	Janis, Elsie
1888	1950	Jannings, Emil
1930	1980	Janssen, David
1900	1974	Jenkins, Allen
1898	1981	Jessel, George

Born	Died	Name
1892	1962	Johnson, Chic
1886	1950	Jolson, Al
1889	1942	Jones, Buck
1933	1983	Jones, Carolyn
1911	1965	Jones, Spike
1943	1970	Joplin, Janis
1902	1982	Jory, Victor
1905	1981	Joslyn, Allyn
1910	1966	Kane, Helen
1887	1969	Karloff, Boris
1893	1970	Karns, Roscoe
1913	1987	Kaye, Danny
1811	1868	Kean, Charles
1806	1880	Kean, Mrs. Charles
1787	1833	Kean, Edmund
1895	1966	Keaton, Buster
1899	1960	Keith, Ian
1894	1973	Kellaway, Cecil
1898	1979	Kelly, Emmett
1929	1982	Kelly, Grace
1910	1981	Kelly, Patsy
1907	1968	Kelton, Pert
1823	1895	Kemble, Agnes
1775	1854	Kemble, Charles
1809	1893	Kemble, Fannie
1926	1959	Kendall, Kay
1914	1990	Kennedy, Arthur
1890	1948	Kennedy, Edgar
1886	1956	Kibbee, Guy
1888	1964	Kilbride, Percy
1923	1986	Knight, Ted
1901	1980	Kostelanetz, Andre
1919	1962	Kovacs, Ernie
1885	1974	Kruger, Otto
1913	1964	Ladd, Alan
1895	1967	Lahr, Bert
1919	1973	Lake, Veronica
1915	1982	Lamas, Fernando
1902	1986	Lanchester, Elsa
1919	1948	Landis, Carole
1904	1972	Landis, Jessie Royce
1884	1944	Langdon, Harry
1853	1929	Langtry, Lillie
1921	1959	Lanza, Mario
1870	1950	Lauder, Harry
1899	1962	Laughton, Charles
1890	1965	Laurel, Stan
1923	1984	Lawford, Peter
1898	1952	Lawrence, Gertrude
1940	1973	Lee, Bruce
1907	1952	Lee, Canada
1914	1970	Lee, Gypsy Rose
1888	1976	Lehmann, Lotte
1913	1967	Leigh, Vivien
1922	1976	Leighton, Margaret
1940	1980	Lennon, John
1898	1981	Lenya, Lotte
1870	1941	Leonard, Eddie
1900	1987	LeRoy Mervyn
1906	1972	Levant, Oscar
1905	1980	Levene, Sam
1902	1971	Lewis, Joe E.
1892	1971	Lewis, Ted
1919	1987	Liberace
1820	1887	Lind, Jenny
1894	1989	Lillie, Beatrice
1889	1968	Lindsay, Howard
1893	1971	Lloyd, Harold
1870	1922	Lloyd, Marie
1891	1957	Lockhart, Gene
1913	1969	Logan, Ella
1909	1942	Lombard, Carole
1902	1977	Lombardo, Guy
1927	1974	Long, Richard
1895	1975	Lopez, Vincent
1888	1968	Lorne, Marion
1904	1964	Lorre, Peter
1912	1962	Lovejoy, Frank
1890	1971	Lowe, Edmund
1892	1947	Lubitsch, Ernst
1882	1956	Lugosi, Bela
1894	1971	Lukas, Paul
1892	1977	Lunt, Alfred
1853	1932	Lupino, George
1893	1942	Lupino, Stanley
1926	1982	Lynde, Paul
1926	1971	Lynn, Diana

Born	Died	Name
1903	1965	MacDonald, Jeanette
1902	1969	MacLane, Barton
1921	1986	MacRae, Gordon
1909	1973	Macready, George
1908	1973	Magnani, Anna
1896	1967	Mahoney, Will
1890	1975	Main, Marjorie
1933	1967	Mansfield, Jayne
1854	1907	Mansfield, Richard
1905	1980	Mantovani, Annunzio
1897	1975	March, Fredric
1945	1981	Marley, Bob
1890	1965	Marshall, Herbert
1920	1981	Martin, Ross
1885	1969	Martinelli, Giovanni
1924	1987	Marvin, Lee
1888	1964	Marx, Arthur (Harpo)
1890	1977	Marx, Julius (Groucho)
1887	1961	Marx, Leonard (Chico)
1909	1984	Mason, James
1896	1983	Massey, Raymond
1879	1948	May, Edna
1885	1957	Mayer, Louis B.
1895	1973	Maynard, Ken
1884	1945	McCormack, John
1895	1952	McDaniel, Hattie
1913	1975	McGiver, John
1899	1981	McHugh, Frank
1883	1959	McLaglen, Victor
1907	1971	McMahon, Horace
1930	1980	McQueen, Steve
1920	1980	Medford, Kay
1880	1946	Meek, Donald
1861	1931	Melba, Nellie
1890	1973	Melchior, Lauritz
1904	1961	Melton, James
1890	1963	Menjou, Adolphe
1902	1966	Menken, Helen
1908	1984	Merman, Ethel
1905	1986	Milland, Ray
1904	1944	Miller, Glenn
1860	1926	Miller, Henry
1898	1936	Miller, Marilyn
1939	1976	Mineo, Sal
1903	1955	Minnevitch, Borrah
1913	1955	Miranda, Carmen
1892	1962	Mitchell, Thomas
1880	1940	Mix, Tom
1926	1962	Monroe, Marilyn
1911	1973	Monroe, Vaughn
1917	1951	Montez, Maria
1904	1981	Montgomery, Robert
1901	1947	Moore, Grace
1876	1962	Moore, Victor
1906	1974	Moorehead, Agnes
1890	1949	Morgan, Frank
1900	1941	Morgan, Helen
1901	1970	Morris, Chester
1914	1959	Morris, Wayne
1943	1971	Morrison, Jim
1932	1982	Morrow, Vic
1915	1977	Mostel, Zero
1897	1969	Mowbray, Alan
1895	1967	Muni, Paul
1894	1953	Munn, Frank
1915	1970	Munshin, Jules
1924	1971	Murphy, Audie
1885	1965	Murray, Mae
1896	1970	Nagel, Conrad
1900	1973	Naish, J. Carroll
1898	1961	Naldi, Nita
1906	1975	Nelson, Ozzie
1940	1985	Nelson, Rick
1885	1967	Nesbit, Evelyn
1910	1983	Niven, David
1890	1950	Nijinsky, Vaslav
1893	1974	Nilsson, Anna Q.
1902	1985	Nolan, Lloyd
1894	1930	Normand, Mabel
1899	1968	Novarro, Ramon
1893	1951	Novello, Ivor
1903	1978	Oakie, Jack
1860	1926	Oakley, Annie
1928	1982	Oates, Warren
1911	1979	Oberon, Merle
1915	1985	O'Brien, Edmond
1899	1983	O'Brien, Pat

Born	Died	Name	Born	Died	Name	Born	Died	Name
1908	1981	O'Connell, Arthur	1899	1966	Rose, Billy	1892	1960	Thomas, John Charles
1880	1959	O'Connor, Una	1910	1980	Roth, Lillian	1882	1976	Thorndike, Sybil
1908	1968	O'Keefe, Dennis	1922	1987	Rowan, Dan			(Three Stooges)
1880	1938	Oland, Warner	1887	1982	Rubinstein, Artur	1902	1975	Fine, Larry
1860	1932	Olcott, Chauncey	1878	1953	Ruffo, Titta	1906	1952	Howard, Curly
1883	1942	Oliver, Edna May	1886	1970	Ruggles, Charles	1897	1975	Howard, Moe
1907	1989	Olivier, Laurence	1924	1961	Russell, Gail	1896	1960	Tibbett, Lawrence
1892	1963	Olsen, Ole	1861	1922	Russell, Lillian	1909	1958	Todd, Michael
1849	1920	O'Neill, James	1911	1976	Russell, Rosalind	1874	1947	Toler, Sidney
1936	1988	Orbison, Roy	1892	1972	Rutherford, Margaret	1905	1968	Tone, Franchot
1899	1985	Ormandy, Eugene	1903	1973	Ryan, Irene	1867	1957	Toscanini, Arturo
1876	1949	Ouspenskaya, Maria	1909	1973	Ryan, Robert	1898	1968	Tracy, Lee
1887	1972	Owen, Reginald				1900	1967	Tracy, Spencer
			1924	1963	Sabu (Dastagir)	1903	1972	Traubel, Helen
1860	1941	Paderewski, Ignace	1877	1968	St. Denis, Ruth	1894	1975	Treacher, Arthur
1924	1987	Page, Geraldine	1884	1955	Sakall, S.Z.	1853	1917	Tree, Herbert Beerbohm
1889	1954	Pallette, Eugene	1885	1936	Sale (Chic), Charles	1890	1973	Truex, Ernest
1914	1986	Palmer, Lilli	1906	1972	Sanders, George	1932	1984	Truffaut, Francois
1894	1958	Pangborn, Franklin	1934	1973	Sands, Diana	1919	1986	Tucker, Forrest
1914	1975	Parks, Larry	1896	1960	Savo, Jimmy	1915	1975	Tucker, Richard
1881	1940	Pasternack, Josef A.	1895	1964	Schildkraut, Joseph	1884	1966	Tucker, Sophie
1837	1908	Pastor, Tony	1865	1930	Schildkraut, Rudolph	1874	1940	Turpin, Ben
1843	1919	Patti, Adelina	1889	1965	Schipa, Tito	1908	1959	Twelvetrees, Helen
1840	1889	Patti, Carlotta	1882	1951	Schnabel, Artur			
1885	1931	Pavlova, Anna	1938	1982	Schneider, Romy	1894	1970	Ulric, Lenore
1900	1973	Paxinou, Katina	1920	1981	Scott, Hazel	1933	1975	Ure, Mary
1904	1984	Peerce, Jan	1898	1987	Scott, Randolph			
1885	1950	Pemberton, Brock	1914	1965	Scott, Zachary	1895	1926	Valentino, Rudolph
1899	1967	Pendleton, Nat	1843	1896	Scott-Siddons, Mrs.	1901	1986	Vallee, Rudy
1905	1941	Penner, Joe	1938	1979	Seberg, Jean	1911	1975	Vance, Vivian
1892	1937	Perkins, Osgood	1892	1974	Seeley, Blossom	1924	1990	Vaughan, Sarah
1915	1963	Piaf, Edith	1893	1987	Segovia, Andres	1893	1943	Veidt, Conrad
1893	1979	Pickford, Mary	1925	1980	Sellers, Peter	1926	1981	Vera-Ellen
1897	1984	Pidgeon, Walter	1902	1965	Selznick, David O.	1885	1957	Von Stroheim, Erich
1892	1957	Pinza, Ezio	1884	1960	Sennett, Mack	1906	1981	Von Zell, Harry
1898	1963	Pitts, Zasu	1927	1978	Shaw, Robert			
1904	1976	Pons, Lily	1891	1972	Shawn, Ted	1887	1969	Walburn, Raymond
1897	1981	Ponselle, Rosa	1868	1949	Shean, Al	1914	1951	Walker, Robert
1904	1963	Powell, Dick	1902	1983	Shearer, Norma	1898	1983	Wallenstein, Alfred
1912	1982	Powell, Eleanor	1915	1967	Sheridan, Ann	1887	1980	Walsh, Raoul
1892	1984	Powell, William	1875	1953	Shubert, Lee	1876	1962	Walter, Bruno
1913	1958	Power, Tyrone	1755	1831	Siddons, Mrs. Sarah	1876	1958	Warner, H. B.
1905	1986	Preminger, Otto	1921	1985	Signoret, Simone	1924	1963	Washington, Dinah
1935	1977	Presley, Elvis	1912	1985	Silvers, Phil	1900	1977	Waters, Ethel
1918	1987	Preston, Robert	1900	1976	Sim, Alastair	1907	1979	Wayne, John
1911	1978	Prima, Louis	1858	1942	Skinner, Otis	1891	1966	Webb, Clifton
1954	1977	Prinze, Freddie	1863	1948	Smith, C. Aubrey	1920	1982	Webb, Jack
			1907	1986	Smith, Kate	1867	1942	Weber, Joe
1946	1989	Radner, Gilda	1917	1979	Soo, Jack	1905	1973	Webster, Margaret
1895	1980	Raft, George	1854	1932	Sousa, John Philip	1915	1985	Welles, Orson
1890	1967	Rains, Claude	1884	1957	Sparks, Ned	1896	1975	Wellman, William
1889	1970	Rambeau, Marjorie	1876	1948	Speaks, Oley	1922	1984	Werner, Oskar
1892	1967	Rathbone, Basil	1873	1937	Standing, Guy	1892	1980	West, Mae
1897	1960	Ratoff, Gregory	1907	1990	Stanwyck, Barbara	1895	1968	Wheeler, Bert
1891	1943	Ray, Charles	1934	1970	Stevens, Inger	1889	1938	White, Pearl
1941	1967	Redding, Otis	1882	1977	Stokowski, Leopold	1891	1967	Whiteman, Paul
1908	1985	Redgrave, Michael	1873	1959	Stone, Fred	1865	1948	Whitty, May
1921	1986	Reed, Donna	1879	1953	Stone, Lewis	1912	1979	Wilding, Michael
1914	1959	Reeves, George	1904	1980	Stone, Milburn	1895	1968	William, Warren
1923	1964	Reeves, Jim	1898	1959	Sturges, Preston	1877	1922	Williams, Bert
1892	1923	Reid, Wallace	1911	1960	Sullavan, Margaret	1923	1953	Williams, Hank
1873	1943	Reinhardt, Max	1902	1974	Sullivan, Ed	1905	1975	Wills, Bob
1909	1971	Rennie, Michael	1903	1956	Sullivan, Francis L.	1903	1978	Wills, Chill
1902	1983	Richardson, Ralph	1892	1946	Summerville, Slim	1894	1953	Wilson, Dooley
1895	1972	Richman, Harry	1899	1983	Swanson, Gloria	1917	1972	Wilson, Marie
1921	1985	Riddle, Nelson	1904	1969	Swarthout, Gladys	1884	1969	Winninger, Charles
1898	1977	Ritchard, Cyril				1904	1959	Withers, Grant
1907	1974	Ritter, Tex	1893	1957	Talmadge, Norma	1907	1961	Wong, Anna May
1905	1969	Ritter, Thelma	1899	1972	Tamiroff, Akim	1938	1981	Wood, Natalie
1901	1965	Ritz, Al	1878	1947	Tanguay, Eva	1892	1978	Wood, Peggy
1906	1986	Ritz, Harry	1885	1966	Taylor, Deems	1888	1963	Woolley, Monty
1903	1985	Ritz, Jimmy	1899	1958	Taylor, Estelle	1902	1981	Wyler, William
1925	1982	Robbins, Marty	1887	1946	Taylor, Laurette	1886	1966	Wynn, Ed
1898	1976	Robeson, Paul	1911	1969	Taylor, Robert	1916	1986	Wynn, Keenan
1878	1949	Robinson, Bill	1878	1938	Tearle, Conway			
1893	1973	Robinson, Edward G.	1884	1953	Tearle, Godfrey	1890	1960	Young, Clara Kimball
1865	1942	Robson, May	1892	1937	Tell, Alma	1917	1978	Young, Gig
1905	1977	Rochester (E. Anderson)	1864	1942	Tempest, Marie	1887	1953	Young, Roland
1897	1933	Rodgers, Jimmy	1910	1963	Templeton, Alec			
1879	1935	Rogers, Will	1847	1928	Terry, Ellen	1902	1979	Zanuck, Darryl F.
1880	1962	Rooney, Pat	1871	1940	Tetrazzini, Luisa	1869	1932	Ziegfeld, Florenz
			1899	1936	Thalberg, Irving	1873	1976	Zukor, Adolph

Original Names of Selected Entertainers

Edie Adams: Elizabeth Edith Enke
Eddie Albert: Edward Albert Heimberger
Alan Alda: Alphonso D'Abruzzo

Jane Alexander: Jane Quigley
Fred Allen: John Sullivan
Woody Allen: Allen Konigsberg

Julie Andrews: Julia Wells
Eve Arden: Eunice Quedens
Beatrice Arthur: Bernice Frankel
Jean Arthur: Gladys Greene
Fred Astaire: Frederick Austerlitz

Lauren Bacall: Betty Joan Perske
Anne Bancroft: Anna Maria Italiano
Brigitte Bardot: Camille Javal
Gene Barry: Eugene Klass
Orson Bean: Dallas Burrows
Pat Benatar: Patricia Andrejewski
Robbie Benson: Robert Segal
Tony Bennett: Anthony Benedetto
Busby Berkeley: William Berkeley Enos
Jack Benny: Benjamin Kubelsky
Joey Bishop: Joseph Gottlieb
Robert Blake: Michael Gubitosi
Victor Borge: Borge Rosenbaum
David Bowie: David Robert Jones
Boy George: George Alan O'Dowd
Fanny Brice: Fanny Borach
Morgan Brittany: Suzanne Cupito
Charles Bronson: Charles Buchinski
Albert Brooks: Albert Einstein
Mel Brooks: Melvin Kaminsky
George Burns: Nathan Birnbaum
Ellen Burstyn: Edna Gilhooley
Richard Burton: Richard Jenkins
Red Buttons: Aaron Chwatt
Nicolas Cage: Nicholas Coppola
Michael Caine: Maurice Micklewhite
Maria Callas: Maria Kalogeropoulos
Vikki Carr: Florencia Casillas
Diahann Carroll: Carol Diahann Johnson
Cyd Charisse: Tula Finklea
Ray Charles: Ray Charles Robinson
Cher: Cherilyn Sarkisian
Patsy Cline: Virginia Patterson Hensley
Lee J. Cobb: Leo Jacoby
Claudette Colbert: Lily Chauchoin
Michael Connors: Kreker Ohanian
Robert Conrad: Conrad Robert Falk
Alice Cooper: Vincent Furnier
David Copperfield: David Kotkin
Howard Cosell: Howard Cohen
Elvis Costello: Declan Patrick McManus
Lou Costello: Louis Cristillo
Joan Crawford: Lucille Le Sueur
Michael Crawford: Michael Dumbell-Smith
Tom Cruise: Thomas Mopother
Tony Curtis: Bernard Schwartz

Vic Damone: Vito Farinola
Rodney Dangerfield: Jacob Cohen
Bobby Darin: Walden Waldo Cassotto
Doris Day: Doris von Kappelhoff
Yvonne De Carlo: Peggy Middleton
Sandra Dee: Alexandra Zuck
John Denver: Henry John Deutschendorf Jr.
Bo Derek: Cathleen Collins
John Derek: Derek Harris
Angie Dickinson: Angeline Brown
Phyllis Diller: Phyllis Driver
Diana Dors: Diana Fluck
Melvyn Douglas: Melvyn Hesselberg
Bob Dylan: Robert Zimmerman

Sheena Easton: Sheena Shirley Orr
Barbara Eden: Barbara Huffman
Ron Ely: Ronald Pierce
Chad Everett: Raymond Cramton
Tom Ewell: S. Yewell Tompkins

Douglas Fairbanks: Douglas Ullman
Morgan Fairchild: Patsy McClenny
Alice Faye: Ann Leppert
Stepin Fetchit: Lincoln Perry
W.C. Fields: William Claude Dukenfield
Peter Finch: William Mitchell
Barry Fitzgerald: William Joseph Shields
Joan Fontaine: Joan de Havilland
John Ford: Sean O'Fearna
John Forsythe: John Freund
Redd Foxx : John Sanford
Anthony Franciosa: Anthony Papaleo
Arlene Francis: Arlene Kazanjian
Connie Francis: Concetta Franconero

Greta Garbo: Greta Gustafsson
Vincent Gardenia: Vincent Scognamiglio
John Garfield: Julius Garfinkle
Judy Garland: Frances Gumm
James Garner: James Bumgarner
Crystal Gayle: Brenda Gayle Webb
Paulette Goddard: Marion Levy
Eydie Gorme: Edith Gormezano
Stewart Granger: James Stewart
Cary Grant: Archibald Leach
Lee Grant: Lyova Rosenthal
Joel Grey: Joe Katz

Buddy Hackett: Leonard Hacker
Jean Harlow: Harlean Carpentier
Rex Harrison: Reginald Carey
Laurence Harvey: Larushka Skikne
Helen Hayes: Helen Brown
Susan Hayward: Edythe Marriner
Rita Hayworth: Margarita Cansino
Pee-Wee Herman: Paul Rubenfeld
Barbara Hershey: Barbara Herzstine
William Holden: William Beedle
Judy Holliday: Judith Tuvim
Harry Houdini: Ehrich Weiss
Leslie Howard: Leslie Stainer
Moe Howard: Moses Horowitz
Rock Hudson: Roy Scherer Jr. (later Fitzgerald)
Engelbert Humperdinck: Arnold Dorsey
Kim Hunter: Janet Cole
Mary Beth Hurt: Mary Supinger
Betty Hutton: Betty Thornberg

David Janssen: David Meyer
Elton John: Reginald Dwight
Don Johnson: Donald Wayne
Jennifer Jones: Phyllis Isley
Tom Jones: Thomas Woodward
Louis Jourdan: Louis Gendre

Boris Karloff: William Henry Pratt
Danny Kaye: David Kaminsky
Diane Keaton: Diane Hall
Michael Keaton: Michael Douglas
Howard Keel: Harold Leek
Chaka Khan: Yvette Stevens
Carole King: Carole Klein
Ben Kingsley: Krishna Banji
Nastassja Kinski: Nastassja Naksyznyski
Ted Knight: Tadeus Wladyslaw Konopka

Cheryl Ladd: Cheryl Stoppelmoor
Veronica Lake: Constance Ockleman
Dorothy Lamour: Mary Kaumeyer
Michael Landon: Eugene Orowitz
Mario Lanza: Alfredo Cocozza
Stan Laurel: Arthur Jefferson
Steve Lawrence: Sidney Leibowitz
Brenda Lee: Brenda Mae Tarpley
Bruce Lee: Lee Yuen Kam
Gypsy Rose Lee: Rose Louise Hovick
Michelle Lee: Michelle Dusiak
Peggy Lee: Norma Egstrom
Janet Leigh: Jeanette Morrison
Vivien Leigh: Vivien Hartley
Huey Lewis: Hugh Cregg
Jerry Lewis: Joseph Levitch
Hal Linden: Harold Lipshitz
Carole Lombard: Jane Peters
Jack Lord: John Joseph Ryan
Sophia Loren: Sophia Scicoloni
Peter Lorre: Laszio Lowenstein
Myrna Loy: Myrna Williams
Bela Lugosi: Bela Ferenc Blasko

Moms Mabley: Loretta Mary Aitken
Shirley MacLaine: Shirley Beaty
Madonna: Madonna Louise Ciccone
Lee Majors: Harvey Lee Yeary 2d
Karl Malden: Malden Sekulovich
Jayne Mansfield: Vera Jane Palmer
Fredric March: Frederick Bickel
Peter Marshall: Pierre LaCock
Dean Martin: Dino Crocetti
Ethel Merman: Ethel Zimmerman
Ray Milland: Reginald Truscott-Jones
Ann Miller: Lucille Collier
Joni Mitchell: Roberta Joan Anderson
Marilyn Monroe: Norma Jean Mortenson, (later) Baker

(continued)

Yves Montand: Ivo Levi
Ron Moody: Ronald Moodnick
Demi Moore: Demi Guynes
Garry Moore: Thomas Garrison Morfit
Rita Moreno: Rosita Alverio
Harry Morgan: Harry Bratsburg
Paul Muni: Muni Weisenfreund

Mike Nichols: Michael Igor Peschowsky
Sheree North: Dawn Bethel
Hugh O'Brian: Hugh Krampke
Maureen O'Hara: Maureen Fitzsimmons

Patti Page: Clara Ann Fowler
Jack Palance: Walter Palanuik
Lilli Palmer: Lilli Peiser
Bert Parks: Bert Jacobson
Minnie Pearl: Sarah Ophelia Cannon
Bernadette Peters: Bernadette Lazzaro
Edith Piaf: Edith Gassion
Slim Pickens: Louis Lindley
Mary Pickford: Gladys Smith
Stephanie Powers: Stefania Federkiewcz
Paula Prentiss: Paula Ragusa
Robert Preston: Robert Preston Meservey
Prince: Prince Rogers Nelson

Tony Randall: Leonard Rosenberg
Martha Raye: Margaret O'Reed
Donna Reed: Donna Belle Mullenger
Della Reese: Delloreese Patricia Early
Joan Rivers: Joan Sandra Molinsky
Edward G. Robinson: Emmanuel Goldenberg
Ginger Rogers: Virginia McMath
Roy Rogers: Leonard Slye
Mickey Rooney: Joe Yule Jr.
Lillian Russell: Helen Leonard

Susan St. James: Susan Miller
Soupy Sales: Milton Hines
Susan Sarandon: Susan Tomaling
Randolph Scott: George Randolph Crane
Jane Seymour: Joyce Frankenberg
Omar Sharif: Michael Shalhoub
Martin Sheen: Ramon Estevez
Beverly Sills: Belle Silverman
Talia Shire: Talia Coppola
Phil Silvers: Philip Silversmith
Suzanne Somers: Suzanne Mahoney
Ann Sothern: Harriette Lake
Barbara Stanwyck: Ruby Stevens
Jean Stapleton: Jeanne Murray
Ringo Starr: Richard Starkey
Connie Stevens: Concetta Ingolia
Sting: Gordon Sumner
Donna Summers: LaDonna Gaines

Robert Taylor: Spangler Arlington Brugh
Danny Thomas: Amos Jacobs
Sophie Tucker: Sophia Kalish
Tina Turner: Annie Mae Bullock
Conway Twitty: Harold Lloyd Jenkins
Rudolph Valentino: Rudolpho D'Antonguolla
Frankie Valli: Frank Castelluccio

David Wayne: Wayne McMeekan
John Wayne: Marion Morrison
Clifton Webb: Webb Parmalee Hollenbeck
Raquel Welch: Raquel Tejada
Gene Wilder: Jerome Silberman
Shelly Winters: Shirley Schrift
Stevie Wonder: Stevland Morris
Natalie Wood: Natasha Gurdin
Jane Wyman: Sarah Jane Fulks
Gig Young: Byron Barr

Federal Aid to the Arts and Humanities

Source: U.S. National Endowment for the Arts; U.S National Endowment for the Humanities (annual reports)

(millions of dollars)

Type of Fund and Program	1970	1975	1980	1982	1983	1984	1985	1986	1987	1988
National Endowment for the Arts:										
Funds available[1]	15.7	86.9	188.1	133.4	147.5	169.9	171.7	167.1	170.9	171.1
Program appropriation	6.3	67.3	97.0	103.3	101.7	119.0	118.7	115.7	120.8	122.2
Matching funds[2]	2.0	7.5	42.9	14.2	24.9	27.4	29.5	30.0	29.3	32.9
Grants awarded (number)	556	3,071	5,505	5,090	5,174	5,056	4,801	4,484	4,542	4,628
Funds obligated	12.9	81.7	166.4	131.8	127.0	147.4	149.4	146.6	151.4	156.3
Music	2.5	14.9	13.6	14.1	12.9	15.2	15.3	14.6	15.1	15.3
State programs	1.9	14.7	22.1	21.3	21.1	24.6	24.4	23.8	24.6	24.9
Museums	NA	10.8	11.2	11.5	10.0	12.5	11.9	11.5	11.5	12.6
Theater	2.8	6.4	8.4	9.6	9.5	10.7	10.6	10.2	10.8	10.7
Dance	1.7	6.1	8.0	8.5	9.1	9.1	9.0	9.0	9.1	9.2
Media arts	0.2	5.4	8.4	10.1	9.3	9.5	9.4	12.3	12.9	12.4
Challenge[3]	X	X	50.8	14.4	14.0	18.8	20.7	20.7	20.8	24.8
Visual arts	1.0	3.2	7.3	6.5	5.8	6.6	6.2	5.7	6.2	6.0
Other	2.8	20.1	36.6	35.8	35.1	40.6	41.3	38.8	40.4	40.4
National Endowment for the Humanities:										
Funds available[1]	13.0	86.0	186.2	120.9[4]	123.5[5]	127.3	125.6	121.1	128.4	125.2
Program appropriation	6.1	67.3	100.3	90.4	90.4	97.8	95.2	91.9[6]	95.8[6]	96.7
Matching funds[2]	2.0	6.5	38.4	28.8	27.9	29.5	30.4	27.3	28.5	28.5
Grants awarded (number)	542	1,330	2,917	2,143	1,928	2,523	2,241	2,297	2,888	2,113
Funds obligated	10.5	73.1	185.5	115.8	123.3	127.6	125.7	121.1	128.4	125.2
Education programs	4.2	17.1	18.3	13.0	14.7	19.3	17.9	14.8	16.4	16.6
State programs	X	X	26.0	22.8	24.0	26.0	24.4	24.1	25.0	25.3
Research grants	2.0	13.4	32.0	25.7	23.1	24.1	24.4	21.0	21.7	21.9
Fellowship program	1.7	10.9	18.0	16.5	14.1	15.0	15.3	14.4	15.3	15.3
Challenge[3]	X	X	53.5	20.7	21.8	18.3	19.6	16.2	16.5	16.5
General programs	X	X	X	16.2	24.9	24.3	24.1	24.7	25.4	24.9
Preservation[7]	X	X	X	X	X	X	X	4.1	4.1	4.7
National Capital Arts and Cultural Affairs Program	X	X	X	X	X	X	X	1.9	4.0	X
Other	2.6	31.8	37.7	0.9	0.7	0.7	X	X	X	X

NA = Not available. X = Not applicable. (1) Includes other funds, not shown separately. Excludes administrative funds. Gifts are included through 1980; excluded thereafter. (2) Represents Federal funds appropriated only upon receipt or certification by Endowment of matching non-Federal gifts. (3) Program designed to stimulate new sources and higher levels of giving to institutions for the purpose of guaranteeing long-term stability and financial independence. Program requires a match of at least 3 private dollars to each Federal dollar. Funds for challenge grants are not allocated by program area because they are awarded on a grant-by-grant basis. (4) Excludes $5.2 million reappropriated to challenge grants in 1983. (5) Includes reappropriated funds from 1982. (6) Excludes National Capital Arts and Cultural Affairs Program. (7) Program designed to support projects which preserve and guarantee access to print and non-print media in danger of disintegration or deterioration.

CABINETS OF THE U. S.

Secretaries of State

The Department of Foreign Affairs was created by act of Congress July 27, 1789, and the name changed to Department of State on Sept. 15.

President	Secretary	Home	Apptd.
Washington	Thomas Jefferson	Va.	1789
"	Edmund Randolph	"	1794
"	Timothy Pickering	Pa.	1795
Adams, J.	"	"	1797
"	John Marshall	Va.	1800
Jefferson	James Madison	"	1801
Madison	Robert Smith	Md.	1809
"	James Monroe	Va.	1811
Monroe	John Quincy Adams	Mass.	1817
Adams, J.Q.	Henry Clay	Ky.	1825
Jackson	Martin Van Buren	N.Y.	1829
"	Edward Livingston	La.	1831
"	Louis McLane	Del.	1833
"	John Forsyth	Ga.	1834
Van Buren	"	"	1837
Harrison, W.H.	Daniel Webster	Mass.	1841
Tyler	"	"	1841
"	Abel P. Upshur	Va.	1843
"	John C. Calhoun	S.C.	1844
Polk	"	"	1845
"	James Buchanan	Pa.	1845
Taylor	"	"	1849
	John M. Clayton	Del.	1849
Fillmore	"	"	1850
"	Daniel Webster	Mass.	1850
"	Edward Everett	"	1852
Pierce	William L. Marcy	N.Y.	1853
Buchanan	"	"	1857
"	Lewis Cass	Mich.	1857
"	Jeremiah S. Black	Pa.	1860
Lincoln	"	"	1861
"	William H. Seward	N.Y.	1861
Johnson, A.	"	"	1865
Grant	Elihu B. Washburne	Ill.	1869
"	Hamilton Fish	"	1869
Hayes	"	"	1877
"	William M. Evarts	"	1877
Garfield	"	"	1881
"	James G. Blaine	Me.	1881
Arthur	"	"	1881
"	F.T. Frelinghuysen	N.J.	1881
Cleveland	F.T. Frelinghuysen	N.J.	1885
"	Thomas F. Bayard	Del.	1885
Harrison, B.	"	"	1889
"	James G. Blaine	Me.	1889
Harrison, B.	John W. Foster	Ind.	1892
Cleveland	Walter Q. Gresham	Ill.	1893
"	Richard Olney	Mass.	1895
McKinley	"	"	1897
"	John Sherman	Oh.	1897
"	William R. Day	"	1898
"	John Hay	D.C.	1898
Roosevelt, T.	"	"	1901
"	Elihu Root	N.Y.	1905
"	Robert Bacon	"	1909
Taft	"	"	1909
"	Philander C. Knox	Pa.	1909
Wilson	"	"	1913
"	William J. Bryan	Neb.	1913
"	Robert Lansing	N.Y.	1915
"	Bainbridge Colby	"	1920
Harding	Charles E. Hughes	"	1921
Coolidge	"	"	1923
"	Frank B. Kellogg	Minn.	1925
"	"	"	1929
Hoover	"	"	1929
"	Henry L. Stimson	N.Y.	1929
Roosevelt, F.D.	Cordell Hull	Tenn.	1933
"	E.R. Stettinius Jr.	Va.	1944
Truman	"	"	1945
"	James F. Byrnes	S.C.	1945
"	George C. Marshall	Pa.	1947
"	Dean G. Acheson	Conn.	1949
Eisenhower	John Foster Dulles	N.Y.	1953
"	Christian A. Herter	Mass.	1959
Kennedy	Dean Rusk	N.Y.	1961
Johnson, L.B.	"	"	1963
Nixon	William P. Rogers	N.Y.	1969
"	Henry A. Kissinger	D.C.	1973
Ford	"	"	1974
Carter	Cyrus R. Vance	N.Y.	1977
"	Edmund S. Muskie	Me.	1980
Reagan	Alexander M. Haig Jr.	Conn.	1981
"	George P. Shultz	Cal.	1982
Bush	James A. Baker 3d	Tex.	1989

Secretaries of the Treasury

The Treasury Department was organized by act of Congress Sept. 2, 1789.

President	Secretary	Home	Apptd.
Washington	Alexander Hamilton	N.Y.	1789
"	Oliver Wolcott	Conn.	1795
Adams, J.	"	"	1797
"	Samuel Dexter	Mass.	1801
Jefferson	"	"	1801
"	Albert Gallatin	Pa.	1801
Madison	"	"	1809
"	George W. Campbell	Tenn.	1814
"	Alexander J. Dallas	Pa.	1814
"	William H. Crawford	Ga.	1816
Monroe	"	"	1817
Adams, J.Q.	Richard Rush	Pa.	1825
Jackson	Samuel D. Ingham	Pa.	1829
"	Louis McLane	Del.	1831
"	William J. Duane	Pa.	1833
"	Roger B. Taney	Md.	1833
"	Levi Woodbury	N.H.	1834
Van Buren	"	"	1837
Harrison, W.H.	Thomas Ewing	Oh.	1841
Tyler	"	"	1841
"	Walter Forward	Pa.	1841
"	John C. Spencer	N.Y.	1843
Tyler	George M. Bibb	Ky.	1844
Polk	Robert J. Walker	Miss.	1845
Taylor	William M. Meredith	Pa.	1849
Fillmore	Thomas Corwin	Oh.	1850
Pierce	James Guthrie	Ky.	1853
Buchanan	Howell Cobb	Ga.	1857
"	Phillip F. Thomas	Md.	1860
"	John A. Dix	N.Y.	1861
Lincoln	Salmon P. Chase	Oh.	1861
Lincoln	William P. Fessenden	Me.	1864
"	Hugh McCulloch	Ind.	1865
Johnson, A.	"	"	1865
Grant	George S. Boutwell	Mass.	1869
"	William A. Richardson	Mass.	1873
"	Benjamin H. Bristow	Ky.	1874
"	Lot M. Morrill	Me.	1876
Hayes	John Sherman	Oh.	1877
Garfield	William Windom	Minn.	1881
Arthur	Charles J. Folger	N.Y.	1881
"	Walter Q. Gresham	Ind.	1884
"	Hugh McCulloch	Ind.	1884
Cleveland	Daniel Manning	N.Y.	1885
"	Charles S. Fairchild	"	1887
Harrison, B.	William Windom	Minn.	1889
"	Charles Foster	Oh.	1891
Cleveland	John G. Carlisle	Ky.	1893
McKinley	Lyman J. Gage	Ill.	1897
Roosevelt, T.	"	"	1901
"	Leslie M. Shaw	Ia.	1902
"	George B. Cortelyou	N.Y.	1907
Taft	Franklin MacVeagh	Ill.	1909
Wilson	William G. McAdoo	N.Y.	1913
"	Carter Glass	Va.	1918
"	David F. Houston	Mo.	1920
Harding	Andrew W. Mellon	Pa.	1921
Coolidge	"	"	1923
Hoover	"	"	1929
"	Ogden L. Mills	N.Y.	1932
Roosevelt, F.D.	William H. Woodin	"	1933
"	Henry Morgenthau, Jr.	"	1934

President	Secretary	Home	Apptd.	President	Secretary	Home	Apptd.
Truman	Fred M. Vinson	Ky.	1945	Nixon	George P. Shultz	Ill.	1972
"	John W. Snyder	Mo.	1946	"	William E. Simon	N.J.	1974
Eisenhower	George M. Humphrey	Oh.	1953	Ford	"		1974
"	Robert B. Anderson	Conn.	1957	Carter	W. Michael Blumenthal	Mich.	1977
Kennedy	C. Douglas Dillon	N.J.	1961	"	G. William Miller	R.I.	1979
Johnson, L.B.	"		1963	Reagan	Donald T. Regan	N.Y.	1981
"	Henry H. Fowler	Va.	1965	"	James A. Baker 3d	Tex.	1985
"	Joseph W. Barr	Ind.	1968	"	Nicholas F. Brady	N.J.	1988
Nixon	David M. Kennedy	Ill.	1969	Bush	"	"	1989
"	John B. Connally	Tex.	1971				

Secretaries of Defense

The Department of Defense, originally designated the National Military Establishment, was created Sept. 18, 1947. It is headed by the secretary of defense, who is a member of the president's cabinet.

The departments of the army, of the navy, and of the air force function within the Department of Defense, and their respective secretaries are no longer members of the president's cabinet.

President	Secretary	Home	Apptd.	President	Secretary	Home	Apptd.
Truman	James V. Forrestal	N.Y.	1947	Nixon	Melvin R. Laird	Wis.	1969
"	Louis A. Johnson	W.Va.	1949	"	Elliot L. Richardson	Mass.	1973
"	George C. Marshall	Pa.	1950	"	James R. Schlesinger	Va.	1973
"	Robert A. Lovett	N.Y.	1951	Ford	"		1974
Eisenhower	Charles E. Wilson	Mich.	1953	"	Donald H. Rumsfeld	Ill.	1975
"	Neil H. McElroy	Oh.	1957	Carter	Harold Brown	Cal.	1977
"	Thomas S. Gates Jr.	Pa.	1959	Reagan	Caspar W. Weinberger	Cal.	1981
Kennedy	Robert S. McNamara	Mich.	1961	"	Frank C. Carlucci	Pa.	1987
Johnson, L.B.	"		1963	Bush	Richard B. Cheney	Wyo.	1989
"	Clark M. Clifford	Md.	1968				

Secretaries of War

The War (and Navy) Department was created by act of Congress Aug. 7, 1789, and Gen. Henry Knox was commissioned secretary of war under that act Sept. 12, 1789.

President	Secretary	Home	Apptd.	President	Secretary	Home	Apptd.
Washington	Henry Knox	Mass.	1789	Grant	John A. Rawlins	Ill.	1869
"	Timothy Pickering	Pa.	1795	"	William T. Sherman	Oh.	1869
"	James McHenry	Md.	1796	"	William W. Belknap	Ia.	1869
Adams, J.			1797	"	Alphonso Taft	Oh.	1876
"	Samuel Dexter	Mass.	1800	"	James D. Cameron	Pa.	1876
Jefferson	Henry Dearborn	"	1801	Hayes	George W. McCrary	Ia.	1877
Madison	William Eustis	Mass.	1809	"	Alexander Ramsey	Minn.	1879
"	John Armstrong	N.Y.	1813	Garfield	Robert T. Lincoln	Ill.	1881
Madison	James Monroe	Va.	1814	Arthur	"	"	1881
"	William H. Crawford	Ga.	1815	Cleveland	William C. Endicott	Mass.	1885
Monroe	John C. Calhoun	S.C.	1817	Harrison, B.	Redfield Proctor	Vt.	1889
Adams, J.Q.	James Barbour	Va.	1825	"	Stephen B. Elkins	W.Va.	1891
"	Peter B. Porter	N.Y.	1828	Cleveland	Daniel S. Lamont	N.Y.	1893
Jackson	John H. Eaton	Tenn.	1829	McKinley	Russel A. Alger	Mich.	1897
"	Lewis Cass	Mich.	1831	"	Elihu Root	N.Y.	1899
"	Benjamin F. Butler	N.Y.	1837	Roosevelt, T.	"	"	1901
Van Buren	Joel R. Poinsett	S.C.	1837	"	William H. Taft	Oh.	1904
Harrison, W.H.	John Bell	Tenn.	1841	"	Luke E. Wright	Tenn.	1908
Tyler	John Bell	Tenn.	1841	Taft	Jacob M. Dickinson	Tenn.	1909
Tyler	John C. Spencer	N.Y.	1841	"	Henry L. Stimson	N.Y.	1911
"	James M. Porter	Pa.	1843	Wilson	Lindley M. Garrison	N.J.	1913
"	William Wilkins		1844	"	Newton D. Baker	Oh.	1916
Polk	William L. Marcy	N.Y.	1845	Harding	John W. Weeks	Mass.	1921
Taylor	George W. Crawford	Ga.	1849	Coolidge	"		1923
Fillmore	Charles M. Conrad	La.	1850	"	Dwight F. Davis	Mo.	1925
Pierce	Jefferson Davis	Miss.	1853	Hoover	James W. Good	Ill.	1929
Buchanan	John B. Floyd	Va.	1857	Hoover	Patrick J. Hurley	Okla.	1929
"	Joseph Holt	Ky.	1861	Roosevelt, F.D.	George H. Dern	Ut.	1933
Lincoln	Simon Cameron	Pa.	1861	"	Harry H. Woodring	Kan.	1937
"	Edwin M. Stanton	Pa.	1862	Roosevelt, F.D.	Henry L. Stimson	N.Y.	1940
Johnson, A.	"	"	1865	Truman	Robert P. Patterson	N.Y.	1945
"	John M. Schofield	Ill.	1868	"	*Kenneth C. Royall	N.C.	1947

Secretaries of the Navy

The Navy Department was created by act of Congress Apr. 30, 1798.

President	Secretary	Home	Apptd.	President	Secretary	Home	Apptd.
Adams, J.	Benjamin Stoddert	Md.	1798	Van Buren	Mahlon Dickerson	N.J.	1837
Jefferson			1801	"	James K. Paulding	N.Y.	1838
"	Robert Smith	"	1801	Harrison, W.H.	George E. Badger	N.C.	1841
Madison	Paul Hamilton	S.C.	1809	Tyler	"	"	1841
"	William Jones	Pa.	1813	"	Abel P. Upshur	Va.	1841
"	Benjamin Williams Crowninshield	Mass.	1814	"	David Henshaw	Mass.	1843
Monroe			1817	"	Thomas W. Gilmer	Va.	1844
"	Smith Thompson	N.Y.	1818	"	John Y. Mason		1844
"	Samuel L. Southard	N.J.	1823	Polk	George Bancroft	Mass.	1845
Adams, J.Q.	"		1825	"	John Y. Mason	Va.	1846
Jackson	John Branch	N.C.	1829	Taylor	William B. Preston		1849
"	Levi Woodbury	N.H.	1831	Fillmore	William A. Graham	N.C.	1850
"	Mahlon Dickerson	N.J.	1834	"	John P. Kennedy	Md.	1852
				Pierce	James C. Dobbin	N.C.	1853

President	Secretary	Home	Apptd.
Buchanan	Isaac Toucey	Conn.	1857
Lincoln	Gideon Welles	Conn.	1861
Johnson, A.	"		1865
Grant	Adolph E. Borie	Pa.	1869
	George M. Robeson	N.J.	1869
Hayes	Richard W. Thompson	Ind.	1877
	Nathan Goff Jr.	W.Va.	1881
Garfield	William H. Hunt	La.	1881
Arthur	William E. Chandler	N.H.	1882
Cleveland	William C. Whitney	N.Y.	1885
Harrison, B.	Benjamin F. Tracy	N.Y.	1889
Cleveland	Hilary A. Herbert	Ala.	1893
McKinley	John D. Long	Mass.	1897
Roosevelt, T.	"	"	1901
	William H. Moody	"	1902

President	Secretary	Home	Apptd.
Roosevelt, T.	Paul Morton	Ill.	1904
"	Charles J. Bonaparte	Md.	1905
"	Victor H. Metcalf	Cal.	1906
"	Truman H. Newberry	Mich.	1908
Taft	George von L. Meyer	Mass.	1909
Wilson	Josephus Daniels	N.C.	1913
Harding	Edwin Denby	Mich.	1921
Coolidge	"	"	1923
"	Curtis D. Wilbur	Cal.	1924
Hoover	Charles Francis Adams	Mass.	1929
Roosevelt, F.D.	Claude A. Swanson	Va.	1933
"	Charles Edison	N.J.	1940
"	Frank Knox	Ill.	1940
"	*James V. Forrestal	N.Y.	1944
Truman	"	"	1945

*Last members of Cabinet. The War Department became the Department of the Army and it and the Navy Department became branches of the Department of Defense, created Sept. 18, 1947.

Attorneys General

The office of attorney general was organized by act of Congress Sept. 24, 1789. The Department of Justice was created June 22, 1870.

President	Attorney General	Home	Apptd.
Washington	Edmund Randolph	Va.	1789
	William Bradford	Pa.	1794
	Charles Lee	Va.	1795
Adams, J.	"	"	1797
Jefferson	Levi Lincoln	Mass.	1801
	John Breckenridge	Ky.	1805
	Caesar A. Rodney	Del.	1807
Madison	"	"	1809
	William Pinkney	Md.	1811
	Richard Rush	Pa.	1814
Monroe	"	"	1817
	William Wirt	Va.	1817
Adams, J.Q.	"	"	1825
Jackson	John M. Berrien	Ga.	1829
	Roger B. Taney	Md.	1831
	Benjamin F. Butler	N.Y.	1833
Van Buren	"	"	1837
	Felix Grundy	Tenn.	1838
	Henry D. Gilpin	Pa.	1840
Harrison, W.H.	John J. Crittenden	Ky.	1841
Tyler	"	"	1841
	Hugh S. Legare	S.C.	1841
	John Nelson	Md.	1843
Polk	John Y. Mason	Va.	1845
	Nathan Clifford	Me.	1846
	Isaac Toucey	Conn.	1848
Taylor	Reverdy Johnson	Md.	1849
Fillmore	John J. Crittenden	Ky.	1850
Pierce	Caleb Cushing	Mass.	1853
Buchanan	Jeremiah S. Black	Pa.	1857
	Edwin M. Stanton	Pa.	1860
Lincoln	Edward Bates	Mo.	1861
	James Speed	Ky.	1864
Johnson, A.	"	"	1865
	Henry Stanbery	Oh.	1866
	William M. Evarts	N.Y.	1868
Grant	Ebenezer R. Hoar	Mass.	1869
	Amos T. Akerman	Ga.	1870
	George H. Williams	Ore.	1871
	Edwards Pierrepont	N.Y.	1875
	Alphonso Taft	Oh.	1876
Hayes	Charles Devens	Mass.	1877
Garfield	Wayne MacVeagh	Pa.	1881
Arthur	Benjamin H. Brewster	"	1881

President	Attorney General	Home	Apptd.
Cleveland	Augustus Garland	Ark.	1885
Harrison, B.	William H. H. Miller	Ind.	1889
Cleveland	Richard Olney	Mass.	1893
"	Judson Harmon	Oh.	1895
McKinley	Joseph McKenna	Cal.	1897
"	John W. Griggs	N.J.	1898
"	Philander C. Knox	Pa.	1901
Roosevelt, T.	"	"	1901
"	William H. Moody	Mass.	1904
"	Charles J. Bonaparte	Md.	1906
Taft	George W. Wickersham	N.Y.	1909
Wilson	J.C. McReynolds	Tenn.	1913
"	Thomas W. Gregory	Tex.	1914
"	A. Mitchell Palmer	Pa.	1919
Harding	Harry M. Daugherty	Oh.	1921
Coolidge	"	"	1923
"	Harlan F. Stone	N.Y.	1924
"	John G. Sargent	Vt.	1925
Hoover	William D. Mitchell	Minn.	1929
Roosevelt, F.D.	Homer S. Cummings	Conn.	1933
"	Frank Murphy	Mich.	1939
"	Robert H. Jackson	N.Y.	1940
"	Francis Biddle	Pa.	1941
Truman	Thomas C. Clark	Tex.	1945
"	J. Howard McGrath	R.I.	1949
"	J.P. McGranery	Pa.	1952
Eisenhower	Herbert Brownell Jr.	N.Y.	1953
"	William P. Rogers	Md.	1957
Kennedy	Robert F. Kennedy	Mass.	1961
Johnson, L.B.	"	"	1963
"	N. de B. Katzenbach	Ill.	1964
"	Ramsey Clark	Tex.	1967
Nixon	John N. Mitchell	N.Y.	1969
"	Richard G. Kleindienst	Ariz.	1972
"	Elliot L. Richardson	Mass.	1973
"	William B. Saxbe	Oh.	1974
Ford	"	"	1974
"	Edward H. Levi	Ill.	1975
Carter	Griffin B. Bell	Ga.	1977
"	Benjamin R. Civiletti	Md.	1979
Reagan	William French Smith	Cal.	1981
"	Edwin Meese 3d	Cal.	1985
"	Richard Thornburgh	Pa	1988
Bush	"	"	1989

Secretaries of the Interior

The Department of Interior was created by act of Congress Mar. 3, 1849.

President	Secretary	Home	Apptd.
Taylor	Thomas Ewing	Oh.	1849
Fillmore	Thomas M. T. McKennan	Pa.	1850
Fillmore	Alex H. H. Stuart	Va.	1850
Pierce	Robert McClelland	Mich.	1853
Buchanan	Jacob Thompson	Miss.	1857
Lincoln	Caleb B. Smith	Ind.	1861
	John P. Usher	"	1863
Johnson, A.	"	"	1865
	James Harlan	Ia.	1865
	Orville H. Browning	Ill.	1866

President	Secretary	Home	Apptd.
Grant	Jacob D. Cox	Oh.	1869
	Columbus Delano	"	1870
	Zachariah Chandler	Mich.	1875
Hayes	Carl Schurz	Mo.	1877
Garfield	Samuel J. Kirkwood	Ia.	1881
Arthur	Henry M. Teller	Col.	1882
Cleveland	Lucius Q.C. Lamar	Miss.	1885
	William F. Vilas	Wis.	1888
Harrison, B.	John W. Noble	Mo.	1889
Cleveland	Hoke Smith	Ga.	1893

President	Secretary	Home	Apptd.
Cleveland	David R. Francis	Mo.	1896
McKinley	Cornelius N. Bliss	N.Y.	1897
"	Ethan A. Hitchcock	Mo.	1898
Roosevelt, T.	"		1901
"	James R. Garfield	Oh.	1907
Taft	Richard A. Ballinger	Wash.	1909
"	Walter L. Fisher	Ill.	1911
Wilson	Franklin K. Lane	Cal.	1913
"	John B. Payne	Ill.	1920
Harding	Albert B. Fall	N.M.	1921
"	Hubert Work	Col.	1923
Coolidge	"		1923
"	Roy O. West	Ill.	1929
Hoover	Ray Lyman Wilbur	Cal.	1929
Roosevelt, F.D.	Harold L. Ickes	Ill.	1933
Truman	"		1945

President	Secretary	Home	Apptd.
Truman	Julius A. Krug	Wis.	1946
"	Oscar L. Chapman	Col.	1949
Eisenhower	Douglas McKay	Ore.	1953
"	Fred A Seaton	Neb.	1956
Kennedy	Stewart L. Udall	Ariz.	1961
Johnson, L.B.	"		1963
Nixon	Walter J. Hickel	Alas.	1969
"	Rogers C.B. Morton	Md.	1971
Ford	"		1974
"	Stanley K. Hathaway	Wyo.	1975
"	Thomas S. Kleppe	N.D.	1975
Carter	Cecil D. Andrus	Ida.	1977
Reagan	James G. Watt	Col.	1981
"	William P. Clark	Cal.	1983
"	Donald P. Hodel	Ore.	1985
Bush	Manuel Lujan	N.M.	1989

Secretaries of Agriculture

The Department of Agriculture was created by act of Congress May 15, 1862. On Feb. 8, 1889, its commissioner was renamed secretary of agriculture and became a member of the cabinet.

President	Secretary	Home	Apptd.
Cleveland	Norman J. Colman	Mo.	1889
Harrison, B.	Jeremiah M. Rusk	Wis.	1889
Cleveland	J. Sterling Morton	Neb.	1893
McKinley	James Wilson	Ia.	1897
Roosevelt, T.	"	"	1901
Taft	"	"	1909
Wilson	David F. Houston	Mo.	1913
"	Edwin T. Meredith	Ia.	1920
Harding	Henry C. Wallace	Ia.	1921
Coolidge	"		1923
"	Howard M. Gore	W.Va.	1924
"	William M. Jardine	Kan.	1925
Hoover	Arthur M. Hyde	Mo.	1929
Roosevelt, F.D.	Henry A. Wallace	Ia.	1933

President	Secretary	Home	Apptd.
"	Claude R. Wickard	Ind.	1940
Truman	Clinton P. Anderson	N.M.	1945
"	Charles F. Brannan	Col.	1948
Eisenhower	Ezra Taft Benson	Ut.	1953
Kennedy	Orville L. Freeman	Minn.	1961
Johnson, L.B.	"		1963
Nixon	Clifford M. Hardin	Ind.	1969
"	Earl L. Butz	Ind.	1971
Ford	"	"	1974
"	John A. Knebel	Va.	1976
Carter	Bob Bergland	Minn.	1977
Reagan	John R. Block	Ill.	1981
"	Richard E. Lyng	Cal.	1986
Bush	Clayton K. Yeutter	Neb.	1989

Secretaries of Commerce and Labor

The Department of Commerce and Labor, created by Congress Feb. 14, 1903, was divided by Congress Mar. 4, 1913, into separate departments of Commerce and Labor. The secretary of each was made a cabinet member.

Secretaries of Commerce and Labor

President	Secretary	Home	Apptd.
Roosevelt, T.	George B. Cortelyou	N.Y.	1903
"	Victor H. Metcalf	Cal.	1904
"	Oscar S. Straus	N.Y.	1906
Taft	Charles Nagel	Mo.	1909

Secretaries of Labor

President	Secretary	Home	Apptd.
Wilson	William B. Wilson	Pa.	1913
Harding	James J. Davis	Pa.	1921
Coolidge	"	"	1923
Hoover	"	"	1929
"	William N. Doak	Va.	1930
Roosevelt, F.D.	Frances Perkins	N.Y.	1933
Truman	L.B. Schwellenbach	Wash.	1945
"	Maurice J. Tobin	Mass.	1949
Eisenhower	Martin P. Durkin	Ill.	1953
"	James P. Mitchell	N.J.	1953
Kennedy	Arthur J. Goldberg	Ill.	1961
"	W. Willard Wirtz	Ill.	1962
Johnson, L.B.	"		1963
Nixon	George P. Shultz	Ill	1969
"	James D. Hodgson	Cal.	1970
"	Peter J. Brennan	N.Y.	1973
Ford	"		1974
"	John T. Dunlop	Cal.	1975
"	W.J. Usery Jr.	Ga.	1976
Carter	F. Ray Marshall	Tex.	1977
Reagan	Raymond J. Donovan	N.J.	1981
"	William E. Brock	Tenn.	1985
"	Ann D. McLaughlin	D.C.	1987
Bush	Elizabeth Hanford Dole	N.C.	1989

Secretaries of Commerce

President	Secretary	Home	Apptd.
Wilson	William C. Redfield	N.Y.	1913
"	Joshua W. Alexander	Mo.	1919
Harding	Herbert C. Hoover	Cal.	1921
Coolidge	"		1923
"	William F. Whiting	Mass.	1928
Hoover	Robert P. Lamont	Ill.	1929
"	Roy D. Chapin	Mich.	1932
Roosevelt, F.D.	Daniel C. Roper	S.C.	1933
"	Harry L. Hopkins	N.Y.	1939
"	Jesse Jones	Tex.	1940
"	Henry A. Wallace	Ia.	1945
Truman	"	"	1945
"	W. Averell Harriman	N.Y.	1947
"	Charles Sawyer	Oh.	1948
Eisenhower	Sinclair Weeks	Mass.	1953
"	Lewis L. Strauss	N.Y.	1958
"	Frederick H. Mueller	Mich.	1959
Kennedy	Luther H. Hodges	N.C.	1961
Johnson, L.B.	"		1963
"	John T. Connor	N.J.	1965
"	Alex B. Trowbridge	N.J.	1967
"	Cyrus R. Smith	N.Y.	1968
Nixon	Maurice H. Stans	Minn.	1969
"	Peter G. Peterson	Ill.	1972
"	Frederick B. Dent	S.C.	1973
Ford	"	"	1974
"	Rogers C.B. Morton	Md.	1975
"	Elliot L. Richardson	Mass.	1975
Carter	Juanita M. Kreps	N.C.	1977
"	Philip M. Klutznick	Ill.	1979
Reagan	Malcolm Baldrige	Conn.	1981
"	C. William Verity Jr.	Oh.	1987
Bush	Robert A. Mosbacher	Tex.	1989

Secretaries of Housing and Urban Development

The Department of Housing and Urban Development was created by act of Congress Sept. 9, 1965.

President	Secretary	Home	Apptd.	President	Secretary	Home	Apptd.
Johnson, L.B.	Robert C. Weaver	Wash.	1966	Ford	Carla Anderson Hills	Cal.	1975
"	Robert C. Wood	Mass.	1969	Carter	Patricia Roberts Harris	D.C.	1977
Nixon	George W. Romney	Mich.	1969	"	Moon Landrieu	La.	1979
"	James T. Lynn	Oh.	1973	Reagan	Samuel R. Pierce Jr.	N.Y.	1981
Ford	"	"	1974	Bush	Jack F. Kemp	N.Y.	1989

Secretaries of Transportation

The Department of Transportation was created by act of Congress Oct. 15, 1966.

President	Secretary	Home	Apptd.	President	Secretary	Home	Apptd.
Johnson, L.B.	Alan S. Boyd	Fla.	1966	Carter	Neil E. Goldschmidt	Ore.	1979
Nixon	John A. Volpe	Mass.	1969	Reagan	Andrew L. Lewis Jr.	Pa.	1981
"	Claude S. Brinegar	Cal.	1973	"	Elizabeth Hanford Dole	N.C.	1983
Ford	Claude S. Brinegar	Cal.	1974	"	James H. Burnley	N.C.	1987
"	William T. Coleman Jr.	Pa.	1975	Bush	Samuel K. Skinner	Ill.	1989
Carter	Brock Adams	Wash.	1977				

Secretaries of Energy

The Department of Energy was created by federal law Aug. 4, 1977.

President	Secretary	Home	Apptd.	President	Secretary	Home	Apptd.
Carter	James R. Schlesinger	Va.	1977	Reagan	Donald P. Hodel	Ore.	1982
"	Charles Duncan Jr.	Wyo.	1979	"	John S. Herrington	Cal.	1985
Reagan	James B. Edwards	S.C.	1981	Bush	James D. Watkins	Cal.	1989

Secretaries of Health, Education, and Welfare

The Department of Health, Education and Welfare, created by Congress Apr. 11, 1953, was divided by Congress Sept. 27, 1979, into separate departments of Education, and Health and Human Services. The secretary of each is a cabinet member.

President	Secretary	Home	Apptd.	President	Secretary	Home	Apptd.
Eisenhower	Oveta Culp Hobby	Tex.	1953	Nixon	Robert H. Finch	Cal.	1969
"	Marion B. Folsom	N.Y.	1955	"	Elliot L. Richardson	Mass.	1970
"	Arthur S. Flemming	Oh.	1958	"	Caspar W. Weinberger	Cal.	1973
Kennedy	Abraham A. Ribicoff	Conn.	1961	Ford	"	"	1974
"	Anthony J. Celebrezze	Oh.	1962	"	Forrest D. Mathews	Ala.	1975
Johnson, L.B.	"	"	1963	Carter	Joseph A. Califano, Jr.	D.C.	1977
"	John W. Gardner	N.Y.	1965	"	Patricia Roberts Harris	D.C.	1979
Johnson, L.B.	Wilbur J. Cohen	Mich.	1968				

Secretaries of Health and Human Services

President	Secretary	Home	Apptd.	President	Secretary	Home	Apptd.
Carter	Patricia Roberts Harris	D.C.	1979	Reagan	Otis R. Bowen	Ind.	1985
Reagan	Richard S. Schweiker	Pa.	1981	Bush	Louis W. Sullivan	Ga.	1989
"	Margaret M. Heckler	Mass.	1983				

Secretaries of Education

President	Secretary	Home	Apptd.	President	Secretary	Home	Apptd.
Carter	Shirley Hufstedler	Cal.	1979	Reagan	Lauro F. Cavazos	Tex.	1988
Reagan	Terrel Bell	Ut.	1981	Bush	"	"	1989
Reagan	William J. Bennett	N.Y.	1985				

Secretaries of Veterans Affairs

The Department of Veterans Affairs was created Oct. 25, 1988 when Pres. Reagan signed a bill which made the Veterans Administration into a cabinet post as of Mar. 15, 1989.

President	Secretary	Home	Apptd.
Bush	Edward J. Derwinski	Ill.	1989

Librarians of Congress

Librarian	Served	Appointed by President	Librarian	Served	Appointed by President
John J. Beckley	1802-1807	Jefferson	Herbert Putnam	1899-1939	McKinley
Patrick Magruder	1807-1815	Jefferson	Archibald MacLeish	1939-1944	F. Roosevelt
George Watterston	1815-1829	Madison	Luther H. Evans	1945-1953	Truman
John Silva Meehan	1829-1861	Jackson	L. Quincy Mumford	1954-1974	Eisenhower
John G. Stephenson	1861-1864	Lincoln	Daniel J. Boorstin	1975-1987	Ford
Ainsworth Rand Spofford	1864-1897	Lincoln	James H. Billington	1987-	Reagan
John Russell Young	1897-1899	McKinley			

Speakers of the House of Representatives

Party designations: A, American; D, Democratic; DR, Democratic Republican; F, Federalist;
R, Republican; W, Whig. *Served only one day.

Name	Party	State	Tenure	Name	Party	State	Tenure
Frederick Muhlenberg	F	Pa.	1789-1791	*Theodore M. Pomeroy	R	N.Y.	1869-1869
Jonathan Trumbull	F	Conn.	1791-1793	James G. Blaine	R	Me.	1869-1875
Frederick Muhlenberg	F	Pa.	1793-1795	Michael C. Kerr	D	Ind.	1875-1876
Jonathan Dayton	F	N.J.	1795-1799	Samuel J. Randall	D	Pa.	1876-1881
Theodore Sedgwick	F	Mass.	1799-1801	Joseph W. Keifer	R	Oh.	1881-1883
Nathaniel Macon	DR	N.C.	1801-1807	John G. Carlisle	D	Ky.	1883-1889
Joseph B. Varnum	DR	Mass.	1807-1811	Thomas B. Reed	R	Me.	1889-1891
Henry Clay	DR	Ky.	1811-1814	Charles F. Crisp	D	Ga.	1891-1895
Langdon Cheves	DR	S.C.	1814-1815	Thomas B. Reed	R	Me.	1895-1899
Henry Clay	DR	Ky.	1815-1820	David B. Henderson	R	Ia.	1899-1903
John W. Taylor	DR	N.Y.	1820-1821	Joseph G. Cannon	R	Ill.	1903-1911
Philip P. Barbour	DR	Va.	1821-1823	Champ Clark	D	Mo.	1911-1919
Henry Clay	DR	Ky.	1823-1825	Frederick H. Gillett	R	Mass.	1919-1925
John W. Taylor	D	N.Y.	1825-1827	Nicholas Longworth	R	Oh.	1925-1931
Andrew Stevenson	D	Va.	1827-1834	John N. Garner	D	Tex.	1931-1933
John Bell	D	Tenn.	1834-1835	Henry T. Rainey	D	Ill.	1933-1935
James K. Polk	D	Tenn.	1835-1839	Joseph W. Byrns	D	Tenn.	1935-1936
Robert M. T. Hunter	D	Va.	1839-1841	William B. Bankhead	D	Ala.	1936-1940
John White	W	Ky.	1841-1843	Sam Rayburn	D	Tex.	1940-1947
John W. Jones	D	Va.	1843-1845	Joseph W. Martin Jr.	R	Mass.	1947-1949
John W. Davis	D	Ind.	1845-1847	Sam Rayburn	D	Tex.	1949-1953
Robert C. Winthrop	W	Mass.	1847-1849	Joseph W. Martin Jr.	R	Mass.	1953-1955
Howell Cobb	D	Ga.	1849-1851	Sam Rayburn	D	Tex.	1955-1961
Linn Boyd	D	Ky.	1851-1855	John W. McCormack	D	Mass.	1962-1971
Nathaniel P. Banks	A	Mass.	1856-1857	Carl Albert	D	Okla.	1971-1977
James L. Orr	D	S.C.	1857-1859	Thomas P. O'Neill Jr.	D	Mass.	1977-1987
William Pennington	R	N.J.	1860-1861	James Wright	D	Tex.	1987-1989
Galusha A. Grow	R	Pa.	1861-1863	Thomas S. Foley	D	Wash.	1989-
Schuyler Colfax	R	Ind.	1863-1869				

Floor Leaders in the U.S. Senate

Majority Leaders

Name	State	Party	Tenure
Charles Curtis	Kan.	R	1925-1929
James E. Watson	Ind.	R	1929-1933
Joseph T. Robinson	Ark.	D	1933-1937
Alben W. Barkley	Ky.	D	1937-1947
Wallace H. White	Me.	R	1947-1949
Scott W. Lucas	Ill.	D	1949-1951
Ernest W. McFarland	Ariz.	D	1951-1953
Robert A. Taft	Oh.	R	1953
William F. Knowland	Cal.	R	1953-1955
Lyndon B. Johnson	Tex.	D	1955-1961
Mike Mansfield	Mont.	D	1961-1977
Robert C. Byrd	W.Va.	D	1977-1981
Howard H. Baker Jr.	Tenn.	R	1981-1985
Robert J. Dole	Kan.	R	1985-1987
Robert C. Byrd	W.Va.	D	1987-1989
George J. Mitchell	Me.	D	1989-

Minority Leaders

Name	State	Party	Tenure
Oscar W. Underwood	Ala.	D	1920-1923
Joseph T. Robinson	Ark.	D	1923-1933
Charles L. McNary	Ore.	R	1933-1944
Wallace H. White	Me.	R	1944-1947
Alben W. Barkley	Ky.	D	1947-1949
Kenneth S. Wherry	Neb.	R	1949-1951
Henry Styles Bridges	N.H.	R	1952-1953
Lyndon B. Johnson	Tex.	D	1953-1955
William F. Knowland	Cal.	R	1955-1959
Everett M. Dirksen	Ill.	R	1959-1969
Hugh D. Scott	Penn.	R	1969-1977
Howard H. Baker Jr.	Tenn.	R	1977-1981
Robert C. Byrd	W.Va.	D	1981-1987
Robert J. Dole	Kan.	R	1987-

Federal Bureau of Investigation

The Federal Bureau of Investigation was created July 26, 1908 and was referred to as Office of Chief Examiner. It became the Bureau of Investigation (Mar. 26, 1909), United States Bureau of Investigation (July 1, 1932), Division of Investigation (Aug. 10, 1933), and Federal Bureau of Investigation (July 1, 1935).

Director	Assumed office	Director	Assumed office
Stanley W. Finch	July 26, 1908	L. Patrick Gray, act.	May 3, 1972
A(lexander) Bruce Bielaski	Apr. 30, 1912	William D. Ruckelshaus, act.	Apr. 27, 1973
William E. Allen, act.	Feb. 10, 1919	Clarence M. Kelley	July 9, 1973
William J. Flynn	July 1, 1919	William H. Webster	Feb. 23, 1978
William J. Burns	Aug. 22, 1921	John E. Otto, act.	May 27, 1987
J. Edgar Hoover, act.	May 10, 1924	William S. Sessions	Nov. 2, 1987
J. Edgar Hoover	Dec. 10, 1924		

Central Intelligence Agency

On June 13, 1942 President Roosevelt established the Office of Strategic Services (OSS) and named William J. Donovan as its director. The OSS was disbanded Oct. 1, 1945 and its functions absorbed by the State and War departments. President Truman, Jan. 22, 1946, established the Central Intelligence Agency Group (CIG) to operate under the direction of the National Intelligence Authority (NIA). The National Security Act of 1947 replaced the NIA with the National Security Council and the CIG with the Central Intelligence Agency.

Director	Served	Appointed by President	Director	Served	Appointed by President
Adm. Sidney W. Souers	1946	Truman	Richard Helms	1966-1973	Johnson
Gen. Hoyt S. Vandenberg	1946-1947	Truman	James R. Schlesinger	1973	Nixon
Adm. Roscoe H. Hillenkoetter	1947-1950	Truman	William E. Colby	1973-1976	Nixon
Gen. Walter Bedell Smith	1950-1953	Truman	George Bush	1976-1977	Ford
Allen W. Dulles	1953-1961	Eisenhower	Adm. Stansfield Turner	1977-1981	Carter
John A. McCone	1961-1965	Kennedy	William J. Casey	1981-1987	Reagan
Adm. William F. Raborn Jr.	1965-1966	Johnson	William H. Webster	1987-	Reagan

National Political Parties

As of mid-1990

Republican Party

National Headquarters—310 First St., SE, Washington, DC 20003.
Chairman—Lee Atwater.
Co-Chairman—Jeanie Austin.
Vice Chairmen—Bernard M. Shanley, Jack Londen, Martha Moore, Nelda Barton, Ernest Angelo Jr., Kay Riddle, Elsie Vartanian, Duane Acklie.
Secretary—Kit Mehrtens.
Treasurer—William J. McManus.
General Counsel—Jan Baran.

Democratic Party

National Headquarters—430 South Capitol St., SE, Washington, DC 20003.
Chairman—Ronald H. Brown.
Vice Chairpersons—Lynn Cutler, Jack Otero, Carmen Perez, James Ruvolo, Lottie Shackelford.
Secretary—Kathleen M. Vick.
Treasurer—Robert Farmer.

Other Major Political Organizations

American Party of the United States
(P.O. Box 597, Provo, UT 84603)
National Chairman—Arly Pedersen.
Secretary—Doris Feimer.
Treasurer—Florence Bale.

Americans For Democratic Action
(1511 K St., NW, Washington, DC 20005)
President—Charles Rangel
National Director—Amy Isaacs.
Chair, Exec. Comm.—James Bishop.

Communist Party U.S.A.
(235 W. 23d St., New York, NY 10011)
General Secretary—Gus Hall.

Conservative Party of the State of N.Y.
(486 78th St., Ft. Hamilton Sta., NY 11209)
Chairman—Michael R. Long.
Executive Director—Anthony Rudmann.
Secretary—John J. Flynn.

Liberal Party of New York State
(18 W. 56th St., New York, NY 10019)
Chairman—Frank Marin.

Exec. Director—Carl F. Grillo.

Libertarian Party
(1528 Pennsylvania Ave SE, Wash., DC 20003)
Chair—David Walter.
Vice-Chair—Mary Gingell.
Secretary—Joseph Dehn.
National Director—D. Nick Dunbar.

Prohibition National Committee
(P.O. Box 2635, Denver, CO 80201)
National Chairman—Earl F. Dodge.
National Secretary—Margaret L. Storms.

Socialist Labor Party
In Minnesota: Industrial Gov't. Party
(914 Industrial Ave., Palo Alto, CA 94303)
National Secretary—Robert Bills.

Socialist Workers Party
(14 Charles Lane, New York, NY 10014)
National Secretary—Jack Barnes.

America's Third Parties

Since 1860, there have been only 4 presidential elections in which all "third parties" together polled more than 10% of the vote: the Populists (James Baird Weaver) in 1892, the National Progressives (Theodore Roosevelt) in 1912, the La Follette Progressives in 1924, and George Wallace's American Party in 1968. In 1948, the combined "third parties" (Henry Wallace's Progressives, Strom Thurmond's States'

Rights party or Dixiecrats, Prohibition, Socialists, and others) received only 5.75% of the vote. In most elections since 1860, fewer than one vote in 20 has been cast for a third party. The only successful third party in American history was the Republican Party in the election of Abraham Lincoln in 1860.

Notable Third Parties

Party	Presidential nominee	Election	Issues	Strength in
Anti-Masonic	William Wirt	1832	Against secret societies and oaths	Pa., Vt.
Liberty	James G. Birney	1844	Anti-slavery	North
Free Soil	Martin Van Buren	1848	Anti-slavery	New York, Ohio
American (Know Nothing)	Millard Fillmore	1856	Anti-immigrant	Northeast, South
Greenback	Peter Cooper	1876	For "cheap money,"	
Greenback	James B. Weaver	1880	labor rights	National
Prohibition	John P. St. John	1884	Anti-liquor	National
Populist	James B. Weaver	1892	For "cheap money," end of national banks	South, West
Socialist	Eugene V. Debs	1900-20	For public ownership	National
Progressive (Bull Moose)	Theodore Roosevelt	1912	Against high tariffs	Midwest, West
Progressive	Robert M. LaFollette	1924	Farmer & labor rights	Midwest, West
Socialist	Norman Thomas	1928-48	Liberal reforms	National
Union	William Lemke	1936	Anti "New Deal"	National
States' Rights	Strom Thurmond	1948	For states' rights	South
Progressive	Henry Wallace	1948	Anti-cold war	New York, California
American Independent	George Wallace	1968	For states' rights	South
American	John G. Schmitz	1972	For "law and order"	Far West, Oh., La.
None (Independent)	John B. Anderson	1980	A 3d choice	National

UNITED STATES FACTS
Superlative U.S. Statistics
Source: U.S. Geological Survey, U.S. Bureau of the Census

Area for 50 states and D. of C.	Total	3,618,770 sq. mi.
	Land 3,539,289 sq. mi.—Water 79,481 sq. mi.	
Largest state.	Alaska.	591,004 sq. mi.
Smallest state.	Rhode Island.	1,212 sq. mi.
Largest county (excludes Alaska).	San Bernardino County, California.	20,064 sq. mi.
Smallest county.	Kalawo, Hawaii.	14 sq. mi.
Northernmost city.	Barrow, Alaska.	71°17'N.
Northernmost point.	Point Barrow, Alaska.	71°23'N.
Southernmost city.	Hilo, Hawaii.	19°43'N.
Southernmost settlement.	Naalehu, Hawaii.	19°03'N.
Southernmost point.	Ka Lae (South Cape), Island of Hawaii.	18°55'N. (155°41'W.)
Easternmost city.	Eastport, Maine.	66°59'02"W.
Easternmost settlement.	Lubec, Maine.	66°58'49"W.
Easternmost point.	Quoddy Head, Maine.	66°57'W.
Westernmost city.	West Unalaska, Alaska.	166°32'W.
Westernmost settlement.	Adak, Alaska.	176°39'W.
Westernmost point.	Cape Wrangell, Alaska.	172°27'E.
Highest settlement.	Climax, Colorado.	11,560 ft.
Lowest settlement.	Calipatria, California.	−185 ft.
Highest point on Atlantic coast.	Cadillac Mountain, Mount Desert Is., Maine.	1,530 ft.
Oldest national park.	Yellowstone National Park (1872), Wyoming, Montana, Idaho.	3,468 sq. mi.
Largest national park.	Wrangell-St. Elias, Alaska.	13,018 sq. mi.
Largest national monument.	Death Valley, California, Nevada.	3,231 sq. mi.
Highest waterfall.	Yosemite Falls—Total in three sections.	2,425 ft.
	Upper Yosemite Fall.	1,430 ft.
	Cascades in middle section.	675 ft.
	Lower Yosemite Fall.	320 ft.
Longest river.	Mississippi-Missouri.	3,710 mi.
Highest mountain.	Mount McKinley, Alaska.	20,320 ft.
Lowest point.	Death Valley, California.	−282 ft.
Deepest lake.	Crater Lake, Oregon.	1,932 ft.
Rainiest spot.	Mt. Waialeale, Hawaii.	Annual aver. rainfall 460 inches
Largest gorge.	Grand Canyon, Colorado River, Arizona.	277 miles long, 600 ft. to 18 miles wide, 1 mile deep
Deepest gorge.	Hell's Canyon, Snake River, Idaho-Oregon.	7,900 ft.
Strongest surface wind.	Mount Washington, New Hampshire recorded 1934.	231 mph
Biggest dam.	New Cornelia Tailings, Ten Mile Wash, Arizona.	274,026,000 cu. yds. material used
Tallest building.	Sears Tower, Chicago, Illinois.	1,454 ft.
Largest building.	Boeing 747 Manufacturing Plant, Everett, Washington.	205,600,000 cu. ft.; covers 47 acres.
Tallest structure.	TV tower, Blanchard, North Dakota.	2,063 ft.
Longest bridge span.	Verrazano-Narrows, New York.	4,260 ft.
Highest bridge.	Royal Gorge, Colorado.	1,053 ft. above water
Deepest well.	Gas well, Washita County, Oklahoma.	31,441 ft.

The 48 Contiguous States

Area for 48 states.	Total.	3,021,295 sq. mi.
	Land 2,962,031 sq. mi.—Water 59,264 sq. mi.	
Largest state.	Texas.	266,807 sq. mi.
Northernmost city.	International Falls, Minnesota.	48°36'N.
Northernmost settlement.	Angle Inlet, Minnesota.	49°21'N.
Northernmost point.	Northwest Angle, Minnesota.	49°23'N.
Southernmost city.	Key West, Florida.	24°33'N.
Southernmost mainland city.	Florida City, Florida.	25°27'N.
Southernmost point.	Key West, Florida.	24°33'N.
Westernmost town.	La Push, Washington.	124°38'W.
Westernmost point.	Cape Alava, Washington.	124°44'W.
Highest mountain.	Mount Whitney, California.	14,494 ft.

Note to users: The distinction between cities and towns varies from state to state. In this table the U.S. Bureau of the Census usage was followed.

Geodetic Datum of North America

In July 1986, the National Oceanic and Atmospheric Administration's National Geodetic Survey (NGS) completed the readjustment and redefinition of the North American Datum. This new datum is known as the North American Datum of 1983. Rapid advances in economic growth and scientific exploration in the United States after World War II resulted in an increasing need for accurate coordinate information. To facilitate the use of satellite surveying and navigation systems, the new datum was redefined using the Geodetic Reference System 1980 as the reference ellipsoid because this model more closely approximates the true size and shape of the Earth. The readjustment of the datum resulted in position changes of as much as 330 feet in the Continental United States and as much as ¼ mile in Hawaii, the Aleutian Islands, Puerto Rico, and the Virgin Islands.

Statistical Information about the U.S.

In the *Statistical Abstract of the United States* the Bureau of the Census, U.S. Dept. of Commerce, annually publishes a summary of social, political, and economic information. A book of almost 1,000 pages, it presents in 31 sections comprehensive data on population, housing, health, education, employment, income, prices, business, banking, energy, science, defense, trade, government finance, foreign country comparison, and other subjects. Special features include sections on State Rankings and Metropolitan Statistical Areas and a new section on computer technology in the office. The book is prepared under the direction of Glenn W. King, Chief, Statistical Compendia Staff, Bureau of the Census. Supplements to the *Statistical Abstract* are *County and City Data Book, 1988; Historical Statistics of the United States, Colonial Times to 1970;* and *State and Metropolitan Area Data Book, 1986* (1990 forthcoming). Information concerning these and other publications may be obtained from the Supt. of Documents, Government Printing Office, Wash., D.C. 20402, or from the U.S. Bureau of the Census, Data User Services Division, Wash., D.C. 20233.

Highest and Lowest Altitudes in the U.S. and Territories

Source: U.S. Geological Survey (Minus sign means below sea level; elevations are in feet.)

State	Highest Point Name	County	Elev.	Lowest Point Name	County	Elev.
Alabama	Cheaha Mountain	Cleburne	2,405	Gulf of Mexico		Sea level
Alaska	Mount McKinley		20,320	Pacific Ocean		Sea level
Arizona	Humphreys Peak	Coconino	12,633	Colorado R.	Yuma	70
Arkansas	Magazine Mountain	Logan	2,753	Ouachita R.	Ashley-Union	55
California	Mount Whitney	Inyo-Tulare	14,494	Death Valley	Inyo	−282
Colorado	Mount Elbert	Lake	14,433	Arkansas R.	Prowers	3,350
Connecticut	Mount Frissell	Litchfield	2,380	L.I. Sound		Sea level
Delaware	On Ebright Road	New Castle	442	Atlantic Ocean		Sea level
Dist. of Col.	Tenleytown	N. W. part	410	Potomac R.		1
Florida	Sec. 30, T 6N, R 20W.	Walton	345	Atlantic Ocean		Sea level
Georgia	Brasstown Bald	Towns-Union	4,784	Atlantic Ocean		Sea level
Guam	Mount Lamlam	Agat District	1,332	Pacific Ocean		Sea level
Hawaii	Mauna Kea	Hawaii	13,796	Pacific Ocean		Sea level
Idaho	Borah Peak	Custer	12,662	Snake R.	Nez Perce	710
Illinois	Charles Mound	Jo Daviess	1,235	Mississippi R.	Alexander	279
Indiana	Franklin Township	Wayne	1,257	Ohio R.	Posey	320
Iowa	Sec. 29, T 100N, R 41W.	Osceola	1,670	Mississippi R.	Lee	480
Kansas	Mount Sunflower	Wallace	4,039	Verdigris R.	Montgomery	679
Kentucky	Black Mountain	Harlan	4,139	Mississippi R.	Fulton	257
Louisiana	Driskill Mountain	Bienville	535	New Orleans	Orleans	−8
Maine	Mount Katahdin	Piscataquis	5,267	Atlantic Ocean		Sea level
Maryland	Backbone Mountain	Garrett	3,360	Atlantic Ocean		Sea level
Massachusetts	Mount Greylock	Berkshire	3,487	Atlantic Ocean		Sea level
Michigan	Mount Arvon	Baraga	1,979	Lake Erie	Monroe	571
Minnesota	Eagle Mountain	Cook	2,301	Lake Superior		600
Mississippi	Woodall Mountain	Tishomingo	806	Gulf of Mexico		Sea level
Missouri	Taum Sauk Mt.	Iron	1,772	St. Francis R.	Dunklin	230
Montana	Granite Peak	Park	12,799	Kootenai R.	Lincoln	1,800
Nebraska	Johnson Township	Kimball	5,426	Missouri R.	Richardson	840
Nevada	Boundary Peak	Esmeralda	13,140	Mount Manchester	Clark	479
New Hamp.	Mt. Washington	Coos	6,288	Atlantic Ocean	Rockingham	Sea level
New Jersey	High Point	Sussex	1,803	Atlantic Ocean		Sea level
New Mexico	Wheeler Peak	Taos	13,161	Red Bluff Res.	Eddy	2,842
New York	Mount Marcy	Essex	5,344	Atlantic Ocean		Sea level
North Carolina	Mount Mitchell	Yancey	6,684	Atlantic Ocean		Sea level
North Dakota	White Butte	Slope	3,506	Red R.	Pembina	750
Ohio	Campbell Hill	Logan	1,549	Ohio R.	Hamilton	455
Oklahoma	Black Mesa	Cimarron	4,973	Little R.	McCurtain	289
Oregon	Mount Hood	Clackamas-Hood R.	11,239	Pacific Ocean		Sea level
Pennsylvania	Mt. Davis	Somerset	3,213	Delaware R.	Delaware	Sea level
Puerto Rico	Cerro de Punta	Ponce District	4,390	Atlantic Ocean		Sea level
Rhode Island	Jerimoth Hill	Providence	812	Atlantic Ocean		Sea level
Samoa	Lata Mountain	Tau Island	3,160	Pacific Ocean		Sea level
South Carolina	Sassafras Mountain	Pickens	3,560	Atlantic Ocean		Sea level
South Dakota	Harney Peak	Pennington	7,242	Big Stone Lake	Roberts	966
Tennessee	Clingmans Dome	Sevier	6,643	Mississippi R.	Shelby	178
Texas	Guadalupe Peak	Culberson	8,749	Gulf of Mexico		Sea level
Utah	Kings Peak	Duchesne	13,528	Beaverdam Wash.	Washington	2,000
Vermont	Mount Mansfield	Lamoille	4,393	Lake Champlain		95
Virginia	Mount Rogers	Grayson-Smyth	5,729	Atlantic Ocean		Sea level
Virgin Islands	Crown Mountain	St. Thomas Island	1,556	Atlantic Ocean		Sea level
Washington	Mount Rainier	Pierce	14,410	Pacific Ocean		Sea level
West Virginia	Spruce Knob	Pendleton	4,861	Potomac R.	Jefferson	240
Wisconsin	Timms Hill	Price	1,951	Lake Michigan		579
Wyoming	Gannett Peak	Fremont	13,804	B. Fourche R.	Crook	3,099

U.S. Coastline by States

Source: NOAA, U.S. Commerce Department
(statute miles)

State	Coastline[1]	Shoreline[2]	State	Coastline[1]	Shoreline[2]
Atlantic coast	2,069	28,673	Gulf coast	1,631	17,141
Connecticut	0	618	Alabama	53	607
Delaware	28	381	Florida	770	5,095
Florida	580	3,331	Louisiana	397	7,721
Georgia	100	2,344	Mississippi	44	359
Maine	228	3,478	Texas	367	3,359
Maryland	31	3,190			
Massachusetts	192	1,519	Pacific coast	7,623	40,298
New Hampshire	13	131	Alaska	5,580	31,383
New Jersey	130	1,792	California	840	3,427
New York	127	1,850	Hawaii	750	1,052
North Carolina	301	3,375	Oregon	296	1,410
Pennsylvania	0	89	Washington	157	3,026
Rhode Island	40	384			
South Carolina	187	2,876	Arctic coast, Alaska	1,060	2,521
Virginia	112	3,315	United States	12,383	88,633

(1) Figures are lengths of general outline of seacoast. Measurements were made with a unit measure of 30 minutes of latitude on charts as near the scale of 1:1,200,000 as possible. Coastline of sounds and bays is included to a point where they narrow to width of unit measure, and includes the distance across at such point. (2) Figures obtained in 1939-40 with a recording instrument on the largest-scale charts and maps then available. Shoreline of outer coast, offshore islands, sounds, bays, rivers, and creeks is included to the head of tidewater or to a point where tidal waters narrow to a width of 100 feet.

States: Settled, Capitals, Entry into Union, Area, Rank

The original 13 states—The 13 colonies that seceded from Great Britain and fought the War of Independence (American Revolution) became the 13 original states. They were: Delaware, Pennsylvania, New Jersey, Georgia, Connecticut, Massachusetts, Maryland, South Carolina, New Hampshire, Virginia, New York, North Carolina, and Rhode Island. The order for the original 13 states is the order in which they ratified the Constitution.

State	Set-tled*	Capital	Entered Union Date	Order	Long (approx. mean)	Wide (approx. mean)	Land	Inland Water	Total	Rank in area
Ala.	1702	Montgomery	Dec. 14, 1819	22	330	190	50,767	938	51,705	29
Alas.	1784	Juneau	Jan. 3, 1959	49	(a)1,480	810	570,833	20,171	591,004	1
Ariz.	1776	Phoenix	Feb. 14, 1912	48	400	310	113,508	492	114,000	6
Ark.	1686	Little Rock	June 15, 1836	25	260	240	52,078	1,109	53,187	27
Cal.	1769	Sacramento	Sept. 9, 1850	31	770	250	156,299	2,407	158,706	3
Col.	1858	Denver	Aug. 1, 1876	38	380	280	103,595	496	104,091	8
Conn.	1634	Hartford	Jan. 9, 1788	5	110	70	4,872	147	5,018	48
Del.	1638	Dover	Dec. 7, 1787	1	100	30	1,932	112	2,045	49
D.C.		Washington			...	...	63	6	69	51
Fla.	1565	Tallahassee	Mar. 3, 1845	27	500	160	54,153	4,511	58,664	22
Ga.	1733	Atlanta	Jan. 2, 1788	4	300	230	58,056	854	58,910	21
Ha.	1820	Honolulu	Aug. 21, 1959	50	...	...	6,425	46	6,471	47
Ida.	1842	Boise	July 3, 1890	43	570	300	82,412	1,153	83,564	13
Ill.	1720	Springfield	Dec. 3, 1818	21	390	210	55,645	700	56,345	24
Ind.	1733	Indianapolis	Dec. 11, 1816	19	270	140	35,932	253	36,185	38
Ia.	1788	Des Moines	Dec. 28, 1846	29	310	200	55,965	310	56,275	25
Kan.	1727	Topeka	Jan. 29, 1861	34	400	210	81,778	499	82,277	14
Ky.	1774	Frankfort	June 1, 1792	15	380	140	39,669	740	40,410	37
La.	1699	Baton Rouge	Apr. 30, 1812	18	380	130	44,521	3,230	47,752	31
Me.	1624	Augusta	Mar. 15, 1820	23	320	190	30,995	2,270	33,265	39
Md.	1634	Annapolis	Apr. 28, 1788	7	250	90	9,837	623	10,460	42
Mass.	1620	Boston	Feb. 6, 1788	6	190	50	7,824	460	8,284	45
Mich.	1668	Lansing	Jan. 26, 1837	26	490	240	56,954	1,573	58,527	23
Minn.	1805	St. Paul	May 11, 1858	32	400	250	79,548	4,854	84,402	12
Miss.	1699	Jackson	Dec. 10, 1817	20	340	170	47,233	457	47,689	32
Mo.	1735	Jefferson City	Aug. 10, 1821	24	300	240	68,945	752	69,697	19
Mon.	1809	Helena	Nov. 8, 1889	41	630	280	145,388	1,658	147,046	4
Neb.	1823	Lincoln	Mar. 1, 1867	37	430	210	76,644	711	77,355	15
Nev.	1849	Carson City	Oct. 31, 1864	36	490	320	109,894	667	110,561	7
N.H.	1623	Concord	June 21, 1788	9	190	70	8,993	286	9,279	44
N.J.	1660	Trenton	Dec. 18, 1787	3	150	70	7,468	319	7,787	46
N.M.	1610	Santa Fe	Jan. 6, 1912	47	370	343	121,335	258	121,593	5
N.Y.	1614	Albany	July 26, 1788	11	330	283	47,377	1,731	49,108	30
N.C.	1660	Raleigh	Nov. 21, 1789	12	500	150	48,843	3,826	52,669	28
N.D.	1812	Bismarck	Nov. 2, 1889	39	340	211	69,300	1,403	70,702	17
Oh.	1788	Columbus	Mar. 1, 1803	17	220	220	41,004	325	41,330	35
Okla.	1889	Oklahoma City	Nov. 16, 1907	46	400	220	68,655	1,301	69,956	18
Ore.	1811	Salem	Feb. 14, 1859	33	360	261	96,184	889	97,073	10
Pa.	1682	Harrisburg	Dec. 12, 1787	2	283	160	44,888	420	45,308	33
R.I.	1636	Providence	May 29, 1790	13	40	30	1,055	158	1,212	50
S.C.	1670	Columbia	May 23, 1788	8	260	200	30,203	909	31,113	40
S.D.	1859	Pierre	Nov. 2, 1889	40	380	210	75,952	1,164	77,116	16
Tenn.	1769	Nashville	June 1, 1796	16	440	120	41,155	989	42,144	34
Tex.	1682	Austin	Dec. 29, 1845	28	790	660	262,017	4,790	266,807	2
Ut.	1847	Salt Lake City	Jan. 4, 1896	45	350	270	82,073	2,826	84,899	11
Vt.	1724	Montpelier	Mar. 4, 1791	14	160	80	9,273	341	9,614	43
Va.	1607	Richmond	June 25, 1788	10	430	200	39,704	1,063	40,767	36
Wash.	1811	Olympia	Nov. 11, 1889	42	360	240	66,511	1,627	68,139	20
W.Va.	1727	Charleston	June 20, 1863	35	240	130	24,119	112	24,232	41
Wis.	1766	Madison	May 29, 1848	30	310	260	54,426	1,727	56,153	26
Wy.	1834	Cheyenne	July 10, 1890	44	360	280	96,989	820	97,809	9

*First European permanent settlement. (a) Aleutian Islands and Alexander Archipelago are not considered in these lengths.

The Continental Divide

The Continental Divide: watershed, created by mountain ranges or table-lands of the Rocky Mountains, from which the drainage is easterly or westerly; the easterly flowing waters reaching the Atlantic Ocean chiefly through the Gulf of Mexico, and the westerly flowing waters reaching the Pacific Ocean through the Columbia River, or through the Colorado River, which flows into the Gulf of California.

The location and route of the Continental Divide across the United States may briefly be described as follows:

Beginning at point of crossing the United States-Mexican boundary, near long. 108°45'W., the Divide, in a northerly direction, crosses New Mexico along the western edge of the Rio Grande drainage basin, entering Colorado near long. 106°41'W.

Thence by a very irregular route northerly across Colorado along the western summits of the Rio Grande and of the Arkansas, the South Platte, and the North Platte River basins, and across Rocky Mountain National Park, entering Wyoming near long. 106°52'W.

Thence in a northwesterly direction, forming the western rims of the North Platte, Big Horn, and Yellowstone River basins, crossing the southwestern portion of Yellowstone National Park.

Thence in a westerly and then a northerly direction forming the common boundary of Idaho and Montana, to a point on said boundary near long. 114°00'W.

Thence northeasterly and northwesterly through Montana and the Glacier National Park, entering Canada near long. 114°04'W.

Chronological List of Territories

Source: National Archives and Records Service

Name of territory	Date of Organic Act			Organic Act effective			Admission as state			Yrs. terr.
Northwest Territory(a)	July	13,	1787	No fixed date.			Mar.	1,	1803(b)	16
Territory southwest of River Ohio	May	26,	1790	No fixed date.			June	1,	1796(c)	6
Mississippi	Apr.	7,	1798	When president acted.			Dec.	10,	1817	19
Indiana	May	7,	1800	July 4, 1800			Dec.	11,	1816	16
Orleans	Mar.	26,	1804	Oct. 1, 1804			Apr.	30,	1812(d)	7
Michigan	Jan.	11,	1805	June 30, 1805			Jan.	26,	1837	31
Louisiana-Missouri(e)	Mar.	3,	1805	July 4, 1805			Aug.	10,	1821	16
Illinois	Feb.	3,	1809	Mar. 1, 1809			Dec.	3,	1818	9
Alabama	Mar.	3,	1817	When Miss. became a state			Dec.	14,	1819	2
Arkansas	Mar.	2,	1819	July 4, 1819			June	15,	1836	17
Florida	Mar.	30,	1822	No fixed date			Mar.	3,	1845	23
Wisconsin	Apr.	20,	1836	July 3, 1836			May	29,	1848	12
Iowa	June	12,	1838	July 3, 1838			Dec.	28,	1846	7
Oregon	Aug.	14,	1848	Date of act			Feb.	14,	1859	10
Minnesota	Mar.	3,	1849	Date of act			May	11,	1858	9
New Mexico	Sept.	9,	1850	On president's proclamation			Jan.	6,	1912	61
Utah	Sept.	9,	1850	Date of act			Jan.	4,	1896	44
Washington	Mar.	2,	1853	Date of act			Nov.	11,	1889	36
Nebraska	May	30,	1854	Date of act			Mar.	1,	1867	12
Kansas	May	30,	1854	Date of act			Jan.	29,	1861	6
Colorado	Feb.	28,	1861	Date of act			Aug.	1,	1876	15
Nevada	Mar.	2,	1861	Date of act			Oct.	31,	1864	3
Dakota	Mar.	2,	1861	Date of act			Nov.	2,	1889	28
Arizona	Feb.	24,	1863	Date of act			Feb.	14,	1912	49
Idaho	Mar.	3,	1863	Date of act			July	3,	1890	27
Montana	May	26,	1864	Date of act			Nov.	8,	1889	25
Wyoming	July	25,	1868	When officers were qualified			July	10,	1890	22
Alaska(f)	May	17,	1884	No fixed date.			Jan.	3,	1959	75
Oklahoma	May	2,	1890	Date of act			Nov.	16,	1907	17
Hawaii	Apr.	30,	1900	June 14, 1900			Aug.	21,	1959	59

(a) Included Ohio, Indiana, Illinois, Michigan, Wisconsin, eastern Minnesota; (b) as the state of Ohio; (c) as the state of Tennessee; (d) as the state of Louisiana; (e) organic act for Missouri Territory of June 4, 1812, became effective Dec. 7, 1812; (f) Although the May 17, 1884 act actually constituted Alaska as a district, it was often referred to as a territory, and unofficially administered as such. The Territory of Alaska was legally and formally organized by an act of Aug. 24, 1912.

Geographic Centers, U.S. and Each State

Source: U.S. Geological Survey

United States, including Alaska and Hawaii — South Dakota; Butte County, W of Castle Rock, Approx. lat. 44°58'N. long. 103°46'W.

Contiguous U. S. (48 states) — Near Lebanon, Smith Co., Kansas, lat. 39°50'N. long. 98°35'W.

North American continent — The geographic center in Pierce County, North Dakota, 6 miles W of Balta, latitude 48°10', longitude 100°10'W.

State—county, locality

Alabama—Chilton, 12 miles SW of Clanton.
Alaska—lat. 63°50'N. long. 152°W. Approx. 60 mi. NW of Mt. McKinley.
Arizona—Yavapai, 55 miles ESE of Prescott.
Arkansas—Pulaski, 12 miles NW of Little Rock.
California—Madera, 38 miles E of Madera.
Colorado—Park, 30 miles NW of Pikes Peak.
Connecticut—Hartford, at East Berlin.
Delaware—Kent, 11 miles S of Dover.
District of Columbia—Near 4th and L Sts., NW.
Florida—Hernando, 12 miles NNW of Brooksville.
Georgia—Twiggs, 18 miles SE of Macon.
Hawaii—Hawaii, 20°15'N, 156°20'W, off Maui Island.
Idaho—Custer, at Custer, SW of Challis.
Illinois—Logan, 28 miles NE of Springfield.
Indiana—Boone, 14 miles NNW of Indianapolis.
Iowa—Story, 5 miles NE of Ames.
Kansas—Barton, 15 miles NE of Great Bend.
Kentucky—Marion, 3 miles NNW of Lebanon.
Louisiana—Avoyelles, 3 miles SE of Marksville.
Maine—Piscataquis, 18 miles north of Dover.
Maryland—Prince Georges, 4.5 miles NW of Davidsonville.

Massachusetts—Worcester, north part of city.
Michigan—Wexford, 5 miles NNW of Cadillac.
Minnesota—Crow Wing, 10 miles SW of Brainerd.
Mississippi—Leake, 9 miles WNW of Carthage.
Missouri—Miller, 20 miles SW of Jefferson City.
Montana—Fergus, 11 miles west of Lewistown.
Nebraska—Custer, 10 miles NW of Broken Bow.
Nevada—Lander, 26 miles SE of Austin.
New Hampshire—Belknap, 3 miles E of Ashland.
New Jersey—Mercer, 5 miles SE of Trenton.
New Mexico—Torrance, 12 miles SSW of Willard.
New York—Madison, 12 miles S of Oneida and 26 miles SW of Utica.
North Carolina—Chatham, 10 miles NW of Sanford.
North Dakota—Sheridan, 5 miles SW of McClusky.
Ohio—Delaware, 25 miles NNE of Columbus.
Oklahoma—Oklahoma, 8 miles N of Oklahoma City.
Oregon—Crook, 25 miles SSE of Prineville.
Pennsylvania—Centre, 2.5 miles SW of Bellefonte.
Rhode Island—Kent, 1 mile SSW of Crompton.
South Carolina—Richland, 13 miles SE of Columbia.
South Dakota—Hughes, 8 miles NE of Pierre.
Tennessee—Rutherford, 5 mi. NE of Murfreesboro.
Texas—McCulloch, 15 miles NE of Brady.
Utah—Sanpete, 3 miles N of Manti.
Vermont—Washington, 3 miles E of Roxbury.
Virginia—Buckingham, 5 miles SW of Buckingham.
Washington—Chelan, 10 mi. WSW of Wenatchee.
West Virginia—Braxton, 4 miles E of Sutton.
Wisconsin—Wood, 9 miles SE of Marshfield.
Wyoming—Fremont, 58 miles ENE of Lander.

There is no generally accepted definition of geographic center, and no satisfactory method for determining it. The geographic center of an area may be defined as the center of gravity of the surface, or that point on which the surface of the area would balance if it were a plane of uniform thickness.

No marked or monumented point has been established by any government agency as the geographic center of either the 50 states, the contiguous United States, or the North American continent. A monument was erected in Lebanon, Kan., contiguous U.S. center, by a group of citizens. A cairn in Rugby, N.D. marks the center of the North American continent.

International Boundary Lines of the U.S.

The length of the northern boundary of the contiguous U.S. — the U.S.-Canadian border, excluding Alaska — is 3,987 miles according to the U.S. Geological Survey, Dept. of the Interior. The length of the Alaskan-Canadian border is 1,538 miles. The length of the U.S.-Mexican border, from the Gulf of Mexico to the Pacific Ocean, is approximately 1,933 miles (1963 boundary agreement).

Origin of the Names of U.S. States

Source: State officials, the Smithsonian Institution, and the Topographic Division, U.S. Geological Survey.

Alabama—Indian for tribal town, later a tribe (Alabamas or Alibamons) of the Creek confederacy.

Alaska—Russian version of Aleutian (Eskimo) word, alakshak, for "peninsula," "great lands," or "land that is not an island."

Arizona—Spanish version of Pima Indian word for "little spring place," or Aztec arizuma, meaning "silver-bearing."

Arkansas—French variant of Quapaw, a Siouan people meaning "downstream people."

California—Bestowed by the Spanish conquistadors (possibly by Cortez). It was the name of an imaginary island, an earthly paradise, in "Las Serges de Esplandian," a Spanish romance written by Montalvo in 1510. Baja California (Lower California, in Mexico) was first visited by Spanish in 1533. The present U.S. state was called Alta (Upper) California.

Colorado—Spanish, red, first applied to Colorado River.

Connecticut—From Mohican and other Algonquin words meaning "long river place."

Delaware—Named for Lord De La Warr, early governor of Virginia; first applied to river, then to Indian tribe (Lenni-Lenape), and the state.

District of Columbia—For Columbus, 1791.

Florida—Named by Ponce de Leon on Pascua Florida, "Flowery Easter," on Easter Sunday, 1513.

Georgia—For King George II of England by James Oglethorpe, colonial administrator, 1732.

Hawaii—Possibly derived from native word for homeland, Hawaiki or Owhyhee.

Idaho—A coined name with an invented Indian meaning: "gem of the mountains;" originally suggested for the Pike's Peak mining territory (Colorado), then applied to the new mining territory of the Pacific Northwest. Another theory suggests Idaho may be a Kiowa Apache term for the Comanche.

Illinois—French for Illini or land of Illini, Algonquin word meaning men or warriors.

Indiana—Means "land of the Indians."

Iowa—Indian word variously translated as "one who puts to sleep" or "beautiful land."

Kansas—Sioux word for "south wind people."

Kentucky—Indian word variously translated as "dark and bloody ground," "meadow land" and "land of tomorrow."

Louisiana—Part of territory called Louisiana by Sieur de La Salle for French King Louis XIV.

Maine—From Maine, ancient French province. Also: descriptive, referring to the mainland as distinct from the many coastal islands.

Maryland—For Queen Henrietta Maria, wife of Charles I of England.

Massachusetts—From Indian tribe named after "large hill place" identified by Capt. John Smith as being near Milton, Mass.

Michigan—From Chippewa words mici gama meaning "great water," after the lake of the same name.

Minnesota—From Dakota Sioux word meaning "cloudy water" or "sky-tinted water" of the Minnesota River.

Mississippi—Probably Chippewa; mici zibi, "great river" or "gathering-in of all the waters." Also: Algonquin word, "Messipi."

Missouri—Algonquin Indian tribe named after Missouri River, meaning "muddy water."

Montana—Latin or Spanish for "mountainous."

Nebraska—From Omaha or Otos Indian word meaning "broad water" or "flat river," describing the Platte River.

Nevada—Spanish, meaning snow-clad.

New Hampshire—Named 1629 by Capt. John Mason of Plymouth Council for his home county in England.

New Jersey—The Duke of York, 1664, gave a patent to John Berkeley and Sir George Carteret to be called Nova Caesaria, or New Jersey, after England's Isle of Jersey.

New Mexico—Spaniards in Mexico applied term to land north and west of Rio Grande in the 16th century.

New York—For Duke of York and Albany who received patent to New Netherland from his brother Charles II and sent an expedition to capture it, 1664.

North Carolina—In 1619 Charles I gave a large patent to Sir Robert Heath to be called Province of Carolana, from Carolus, Latin name for Charles. A new patent was granted by Charles II to Earl of Clarendon and others. Divided into North and South Carolina, 1710.

North Dakota—Dakota is Sioux for friend or ally.

Ohio—Iroquois word for "fine or good river."

Oklahoma—Choctaw coined word meaning red man, proposed by Rev. Allen Wright, Choctaw-speaking Indian.

Oregon—Origin unknown. One theory holds that the name may have been derived from that of the Wisconsin River shown on a 1715 French map as "Ouaricon-sint."

Pennsylvania—William Penn, the Quaker, who was made full proprietor by King Charles II in 1681, suggested Sylvania, or woodland, for his tract. The king's government owed Penn's father, Admiral William Penn, £16,000, and the land was granted as partial settlement. Charles II added the Penn to Sylvania, against the desires of the modest proprietor, in honor of the admiral.

Puerto Rico—Spanish for Rich Port.

Rhode Island—Exact origin is unknown. One theory notes that Giovanni de Verrazano recorded an island about the size of Rhodes in the Mediterranean in 1524, but others believe the state was named Roode Eylandt by Adriaen Block, Dutch explorer, because of its red clay.

South Carolina—See North Carolina.

South Dakota—See North Dakota.

Tennessee—Tanasi was the name of Cherokee villages on the Little Tennessee River. From 1784 to 1788 this was the State of Franklin, or Frankland.

Texas—Variant of word used by Caddo and other Indians meaning friends or allies, and applied to them by the Spanish in eastern Texas. Also written texias, tejas, teysas.

Utah—From a Navajo word meaning upper, or higher up, as applied to a Shoshone tribe called Ute. Spanish form is Yutta, English Uta or Utah. Proposed name Deseret, "land of honeybees," from Book of Mormon, was rejected by Congress.

Vermont—From French words vert (green) and mont (mountain). The Green Mountains were said to have been named by Samuel de Champlain. When the state was formed, 1777, Dr. Thomas Young suggested combining vert and mont into Vermont.

Virginia—Named by Sir Walter Raleigh, who fitted out the expedition of 1584, in honor of Queen Elizabeth, the Virgin Queen of England.

Washington—Named after George Washington. When the bill creating the Territory of Columbia was introduced in the 32d Congress, the name was changed to Washington because of the existence of the District of Columbia.

West Virginia—So named when western counties of Virginia refused to secede from the United States, 1863.

Wisconsin—An Indian name, spelled Ouisconsin and Mesconsing by early chroniclers. Believed to mean "grassy place" in Chippewa. Congress made it Wisconsin.

Wyoming—The word was taken from Wyoming Valley, Pa., which was the site of an Indian massacre and became widely known by Campbell's poem, "Gertrude of Wyoming." In Algonquin it means "large prairie place."

Territorial Sea of the U.S.

According to a December 27, 1988 proclamation by Pres. Ronald Reagan: "The territorial sea of the United States henceforth extends to 12 nautical miles from the baselines of the United States determined in accordance with international law. In accordance with international law, as reflected in the applicable provisions of the 1982 United Nations Convention on the Law of the Sea, within the territorial sea of the United States, the ships of all countries enjoy the right of innocent passage and the ships and aircraft of all countries enjoy the right of transit passage through international straits."

Accession of Territory by the U.S.

Source: U.S. Bureau of the Census

	Acquisi-tion date	Gross Area (Land and water) Sq. mi.		Acquisi-tion date	Gross Area (Land and water) Sq. mi.		Acquisi-tion date	Gross Area (Land and water Sq. mi.
Total U.S.	(x)	3,623,434	Gadsden Purchase .	1853	29,640	Virgin Islands of		
United States.	(x)	3,618,770	Alaska	1867	591,004	the U.S.	1917	132
Territory in 1790[1] . .	(x)	891,364	Hawaii	1898	6,471	Pacific Islands,		
Louisiana Purchase	1803	831,321	Other areas:			Trust Territory		
Purchase of Florida	1819	69,866	Puerto Rico	[2]1898	3,515	of the[3]	1947	533
Texas	1845	384,958	Guam	[3]1898	209	No. Mariana Islands[5]	1947	184
Oregon	1846	283,439	American Samoa .	[4]1899	77	All other[6].	(x)	14
Mexican Cession .	1848	530,706						

(x) Not applicable. (1) Includes that part of drainage basin of Red River of the North, south of 49th parallel, sometimes considered part of Louisiana Purchase. (2) Ceded by Spain in 1898, ratified in 1899, and became Commonweaith of Puerto Rico by Act of Congress on July 25, 1952. (3) Acquired 1898; ratified 1899. (4) Acquired 1899; ratified 1900. (5) Land area only. (6) Comprises the following islands with gross areas as indicated, in sq. mi.: Midway (2), Wake (3), Palmyra (4), Navassa (2), Baker, Howland, and Jarvis (combined area, 3), Johnston Atoll (combined area, less than .5), and Kingman Reef (less than .5). Excludes Canton and Enderbury Islands (combined area 27 sq. mi.), which are considered to be under the jurisdiction of Kiribati since 1979, and Swan Islands (1 sq. mi.), which were returned to Honduras in 1972.

Public Lands of the U. S.

Source: Bureau of Land Management, U.S. Interior Department

Disposition of Public Lands 1781 to 1988

Disposition by methods not elsewhere classified[1]	Acres	Granted to states for:	Acres
Granted or sold to homesteaders	303,500,000	Support of common schools	77,630,000
Granted to railroad corporations	287,500,000	Reclamation of swampland	64,920,000
Granted to veterans as military bounties. .	94,400,000	Construction of railroads	37,130,000
Confirmed as private land claims[2]	61,000,000	Support of misc. institutions[6]	21,700,000
Sold under timber and stone law[3].	34,000,000	Purposes not elsewhere classified[7] . . .	117,600,000
Granted or sold under timber culture law[4] .	13,900,000	Canals and rivers	6,100,000
Sold under desert land law[5]	10,900,000	Construction of wagon roads	3,400,000
	10,700,000	**Total granted to states . . . . . .**	**328,480,000**

(1) Chiefly public, private, and preemption sales, but includes mineral entries, scrip locations, sales of townsites and townlots. (2) The Government has confirmed title to lands claimed under valid grants made by foreign governments prior to the acquisition of the public domain by the United States. (3) The law provided for the sale of lands valuable for timber or stone and unfit for cultivation. (4) The law provided for the granting of public lands to settlers on condition that they plant and cultivate trees on the lands granted. (5) The law provided for the sale of arid agricultural public lands to settlers who irrigate them and bring them under cultivation. (6) Universities, hospitals, asylums, etc. (7) For construction of various public improvements (individual items not specified in the granting act) reclamation of desert lands, construction of water reservoirs, etc.

Public Lands Administered by Federal Agencies

Agency (Acres, Sept. 30, 1989)	Public domain	Acquired	Total
Forest Service	161,038,854.3	28,341,223.5	189,380,077.8
Bureau of Land Management.	268,093,335.0	2,324,840.0	270,418,175.0
Bureau of Reclamation.	3,533,817.5	1,969,275.9	5,503,093.4
Fish and Wildlife Service	81,321,344	10,097,347	91,318,691
National Park Service	64,325,741.0	8,517,114.8	72,842,855.8
Bureau of Indian Affairs	2,554,358.7	193,079.6	2,747,438.3
Tennessee Valley Authority.	0	1,040,231.3	1,040,231.3
Corps of Engineers	604,971.2	4,869,200.0	5,474,171.2
U.S. Army.	3,187,901.0	6,495,173.0	9,683,074.0
U.S. Navy.	618,005.6	1,743,750.2	2,361,755.8
U.S. Air Force	6,858,510.0	1,255,022.0	8,113,532.0
Department of Energy.	1,465,862.4	700,478.8	2,166,341.2
Total, all agencies (incl. those not shown) . .	**660,976,655.8**	**63,089,515.1**	**724,066,170.9**

National Parks, Other Areas Administered by Nat'l Park Service

Figures given are date area initially protected by Congress or presidential proclamation, date given current designation, and gross area in acres 12/31/88.

National Parks

Acadia, Me. (1916/1929) 41,409. Includes Mount Desert Island, half of Isle au Haut, Schoodic Point on mainland. Highest elevation on Eastern seaboard.

Arches, Ut. (1929/1971) 73,379. Contains giant red sandstone arches and other products of erosion.

Badlands, S.D. (1929/1978) 243,244; eroded prairie, bison, bighorn and antelope. Contains animal fossils of 40 million years ago.

Big Bend, Tex. (1935/1944) 802,541. Rio Grande, Chisos Mts.

Biscayne, Fla. (1968/1980) 173,039. Aquatic park encompasses chain of islands south of Miami.

Bryce Canyon, Ut. (1923/1928) 35,835. Spectacularly colorful natural display of erosion effects.

Canyonlands, Ut. (1964) 337,570. At junction of Colorado and Green rivers, extensive evidence of prehistoric Indians.

Capitol Reef, Ut. (1937/1971) 241,904. A 60-mile uplift of sandstone cliffs dissected by high-walled gorges.

Carlsbad Caverns, N.M. (1923/1930) 46,755. Largest known caverns; not yet fully explored.

Channel Islands, Cal. (1938/1980) 249,354. Seal lion breeding place, nesting sea birds, unique plants.

Crater Lake, Ore. (1902) 183,224. Extraordinary blue lake in crater of extinct volcano encircled by lava walls 500 to 2,000 feet high.

Denali, Alas. (1917/1980) 4,716,726. Name changed from Mt. McKinley NP. Contains highest mountain in U.S.; wildlife.

Everglades, Fla. (1934) 1,508,939. Largest remaining subtropical wilderness in continental U.S.

Gates of the Arctic, Alas. (1978/1980) 7,523,888. Vast wilderness in north central region.

Glacier, Mon. (1910) 1,013,572. Superb Rocky Mt. scenery, numerous glaciers and glacial lakes. Part of Waterton-Glacier Intl. Peace Park established by U.S. and Canada in 1932.

Glacier Bay, Alas. (1925/1980) 3,225,284. Great tidewater glaciers that move down mountain sides and break up into the sea; much wildlife.

Grand Canyon, Ariz. (1908/1919) 1,218,375. Most spectacular part of Colorado River's greatest canyon.

Grand Teton, Wy. (1929) 309,994. Most impressive part of the Teton Mountains, winter feeding ground of largest American elk herd.

Great Basin, Nev. (1922/1986) 77,109. Wide basins and high mountain ranges.

Great Smoky Mountains, N.C.-Tenn. (1926/1934) 520,269. Largest eastern mountain range, magnificent forests.

Guadalupe Mountains, Tex. (1966/1972) 86,416. Extensive Permian limestone fossil reef; tremendous earth fault.

Haleakala, Ha. (1916/1960) 28,655. Dormant volcano on Maui with large colorful craters.

Hawaii Volcanoes, Ha. (1916/1961) 229,177. Contains Kilauea and Mauna Loa, active volcanoes.

Hot Springs, Ark. (1832/1921) 5,839. Government supervised bath houses use waters of 45 of the 47 natural hot springs.

Isle Royale, Mich. (1931) 571,790. Largest island in Lake Superior, noted for its wilderness area and wildlife.

Katmai, Alas. (1918/1980) 3,716,000. Valley of Ten Thousand Smokes, scene of 1912 volcanic eruption.

Kenai Fjords, Alas. (1978/1980) 669,541. Abundant mountain goats, marine mammals, birdlife; the Harding Icefield, one of the major icecaps in U.S.

Kings Canyon, Cal. (1890/1940) 461,901. Mountain wilderness, dominated by Kings River Canyons and High Sierra; contains giant sequoias.

Kobuk Valley, Alas. (1978/1980) 1,750,421. Broad river is core of native culture.

Lake Clark, Alas. (1978/1980) 2,636,839. Across Cook Inlet from Anchorage. A scenic wilderness rich in fish and wildlife.

Lassen Volcanic, Cal. (1907/1916) 106,372. Contains Lassen Peak, recently active volcano, and other volcanic phenomena.

Mammoth Cave, Ky. (1926/1941) 52,419. 144 miles of surveyed underground passages, beautiful natural formations, river 300 feet below surface.

Mesa Verde, Col. (1906) 52,085. Most notable and best preserved prehistoric cliff dwellings in the United States.

Mount Rainier, Wash. (1899) 235,404. Greatest single-peak glacial system in the lower 48 states.

North Cascades, Wash. (1968) 504,781. Spectacular mountainous region with many glaciers, lakes.

Olympic, Wash. (1909/1938) 921,942. Mountain wilderness containing finest remnant of Pacific Northwest rain forest, active glaciers, Pacific shoreline, rare elk.

Petrified Forest, Ariz. (1906/1962) 93,533. Extensive petrified wood and Indian artifacts. Contains part of Painted Desert.

Redwood, Cal. (1968) 110,132. Forty miles of Pacific coastline, groves of ancient redwoods and world's tallest trees.

Rocky Mountain, Col. (1915) 265,200. On the continental divide, includes 107 named peaks over 11,000 feet.

Samoa, American Samoa (1988) 8,000. Features the only paleotropical rain forest.

Sequoia, Cal. (1890) 402,482. Groves of giant sequoias, highest mountain in contiguous United States — Mount Whitney (14,494 feet). World's largest tree.

Shenandoah, Va. (1926/1935) 195,382. Portion of the Blue Ridge Mountains; overlooks Shenandoah Valley; Skyline Drive.

Theodore Roosevelt, N.D. (1947/1978) 70,416. Contains part of T.R.'s ranch and scenic badlands.

Virgin Islands, V.I. (1956) 14,689. Covers 75% of St. John Island, lush growth, lovely beaches, Indian relics, evidence of colonial Danes.

Voyageurs, Minn. (1971/1975) 218,036. Abundant lakes, forests, wildlife, canoeing, boating.

Wind Cave, S.D. (1903) 28,292. Limestone caverns in Black Hills. Extensive wildlife includes a herd of bison.

Wrangell-St. Elias, Alas. (1978/1980) 8,331,604. Largest area in park system, most peaks over 16,000 feet, abundant wildlife; day's drive east of Anchorage.

Yellowstone, Ida., Mon., Wy., (1872) 2,219,791. Oldest national park. World's greatest geyser area has about 3,000 geysers and hot springs; spectacular falls and impressive canyons of the Yellowstone River; grizzly bear, moose, and bison.

Yosemite, Cal. (1890) 761,170. Yosemite Valley, the nation's highest waterfall, 3 groves of sequoias, and mountainous.

Zion, Ut. (1909/1919) 146,598. Unusual shapes and landscapes have resulted from erosion and faulting; Zion Canyon, with sheer walls ranging up to 2,500 feet, is readily accessible.

National Historical Parks

Appomattox Court House, Va. (1930/1954) 1,325. Where Lee surrendered to Grant.

Boston, Mass. (1974) 41. Includes Faneuil Hall, Old North Church, Bunker Hill, Paul Revere House.

Chaco Culture, N.M. (1907/1980) 33,974. Ruins of pueblos built by prehistoric Indians.

Chesapeake and Ohio Canal, Md.-W.Va.-D.C. (1961/1971) 20,781. 184 mile historic canal; D.C. to Cumberland, Md.

Colonial, Va. (1930/1936) 9,327. Includes most of Jamestown Island, site of first successful English colony; Yorktown, site of Cornwallis' surrender to George Washington; and the Colonial Parkway.

Cumberland Gap, Ky.-Tenn.-Va. (1940) 20,274. Mountain pass of the Wilderness Road which carried the first great migration of pioneers into America's interior.

George Rogers Clark, Vincennes, Ind. (1966) 26. Commemorates American defeat of British in west during Revolution.

Harpers Ferry, Md., W. Va. (1944/1963) 2,239. At the confluence of the Shenandoah and Potomac rivers, the site of John Brown's 1859 raid on the Army arsenal.

Independence, Pa. (1948/1956) 45. Contains several properties in Philadelphia associated with the Revolutionary War and the founding of the U.S. Includes Independence Hall.

Jean Laffite (and preserve), La. (1939/1978) 20,020. Includes Chalmette, site of 1814 Battle of New Orleans; French Quarter.

Kalaupapa, Ha. (1980) 10,779. Molokai's former leper colony site and other historic areas.

Kaloko-Honokohau, Ha. (1978) 1,161. Culture center has 234 historic features and grave of first king, Kamehameha.

Klondike Gold Rush, Alas.-Wash. (1976) 13,191. Alaskan Trails in 1898 Gold Rush. Museum in Seattle.

Lowell, Mass. (1978) 137. Seven mills, canal, 19th C. structures, park to show planned city of Industrial Revolution.

Lyndon B. Johnson, Tex. (1969/1980) 1,571. President's birthplace, boyhood home, ranch.

Minute Man, Mass. (1959) 750. Where the colonial Minute Men battled the British, April 19, 1775. Also contains Nathaniel Hawthorne's home.

Morristown, N.J. (1933) 1,671. Sites of important military encampments during the Revolutionary War; Washington's headquarters 1777, 1779-80.

Natchez, Miss. (1988) 80. Mansions, townhouses, and villas concerning history of Natchez, Miss.

Nez Perce, Ida. (1965) 2,109. Illustrates the history and culture of the Nez Perce Indian country. 20 separate sites.

Pu'uhonua o Honaunau, Ha. (1955/1978) 182. Until 1819, a sanctuary for Hawaiians vanquished in battle, and those guilty of crimes or breaking taboos.

San Antonio Missions, Tex. (1978/1983) 493. Four of finest Spanish missions in U.S., 18th C. irrigation system.

San Francisco Maritime (1988) 50. Artifacts, photographs, and historic vessels related to the development of the Pacific Coast.

San Juan Island, Wash. (1966) 1,752. Commemorates peaceful relations of the U.S., Canada and Great Britain since the 1872 boundary disputes.

Saratoga, N.Y. (1938) 3,393. Scene of a major battle which became a turning point in the War of Independence.

Sitka, Alas. (1910/1972) 107. Scene of last major resistance of the Tlingit Indians to the Russians, 1804.

Valley Forge, Pa. (1976) 3,468. Continental Army campsite in 1777-78 winter.

War in the Pacific, Guam (1978) 1,960. Scenic park memorial for WWII combatants in Pacific.

Women's Rights, N.Y. (1980) 6. Seneca Falls site where Susan B. Anthony, Elizabeth Cady Stanton began rights movement in 1848.

Zuni-Cibola, N. Mex. (1988) 800. Historical, archeological, and cultural site associated with the Zuni Tribe over its 1700-year cultural continuum.

National Battlefields

Antietam, Md. (1890/1978) 3,244. Battle ended first Confederate invasion of North, Sept. 17, 1862.

Big Hole, Mon. (1910/1963) 656. Site of major battle with Nez Perce Indians.

Cowpens, S.C. (1929/1972) 842. Revolutionary War battlefield.

Fort Donelson, Tenn. (1928/1985) 536. Site of first major Union victory.

Fort Necessity, Pa. (1931/1961) 903. First battle of French and Indian War.

Monocacy, Md. (1934/1976) 1,647. Civil War battle in defense of Wash., D.C., July 9, 1864.

Moores Creek, N.C. (1926/1980) 87. Pre-Revolutionary War battle.

Petersburg, Va. (1926/1962) 2,735. Scene of 10-month Union campaign 1864-65.

Stones River, Tenn. (1927/1960) 403. Civil War battle leading to Sherman's "March to the Sea."
Tupelo, Miss. (1929/1961) 1. Crucial battle over Sherman's supply line.
Wilson's Creek, Mo. (1960/1970) 1,750. Civil War battle for control of Missouri.

National Battlefield Parks

Kennesaw Mountain, Ga. (1917/1935) 2,885. Two major battles of Atlanta campaign in Civil War.
Manassas, Va. (1940) 5,072. Two battles of Bull Run in Civil War, 1861 and 1862.
Richmond, Va. (1936) 769. Site of battles defending Confederate capital.

National Battlefield Site

Brices Cross Roads, Miss. (1929) 1. Civil War battlefield.

National Military Parks

Chickamauga and Chattanooga, Ga.-Tenn. (1890) 8,106. Four Civil War battlefields.
Fredericksburg and Spotsylvania County, Va. (1927) 5,907. Sites of several major Civil War battles and campaigns.
Gettysburg, Pa. (1895) 3,896. Site of decisive Confederate defeat in North. Gettysburg Address.
Guilford Courthouse, N.C. (1917) 220. Revolutionary War battle site.
Horseshoe Bend, Ala. (1956) 2,040. On Tallapoosa River, where Gen. Andrew Jackson broke the power of the Creek Indian Confederacy.
Kings Mountain, S.C. (1931) 3,945. Revolutionary War battle.
Pea Ridge, Ark. (1956) 4,300. Civil War battle.
Shiloh, Tenn. (1894) 3,838. Major Civil War battle; site includes some well-preserved Indian burial mounds.
Vicksburg, Miss. (1899) 1,620. Union victory gave North control of the Mississippi and split the Confederacy in two.

National Memorials

Arkansas Post, Ark. (1960) 389. First permanent French settlement in the lower Mississippi River valley.
Arlington House, the Robert E. Lee Memorial, Va. (1925/1972) 28. Lee's home overlooking the Potomac.
Chamizal, El Paso, Tex. (1966/1974) 55. Commemorates 1963 settlement of 99-year border dispute with Mexico.
Coronado, Ariz. (1941/1952) 4,750. Commemorates first European exploration of the Southwest.
DeSoto, Fla. (1948) 27. Commemorates 16th-century Spanish explorations.
Federal Hall, N.Y. (1939/1955) 0.45. First seat of U.S. government under the Constitution.
Fort Caroline, Fla. (1950) 138. On St. Johns River, overlooks site of second attempt by French Huguenots to colonize North America.
Fort Clatsop, Ore. (1958) 125. Lewis and Clark encampment 1805-06.
General Grant, N.Y. (1958) 0.76. Tombs of Pres. and wife.
Hamilton Grange, N.Y. (1962) 0.11. Home of Alexander Hamilton.
John F. Kennedy Center for the Performing Arts, D.C. (1958/1964) 18.
Johnstown Flood, Pa. (1964) 164. Commemorates tragic flood of 1889.
Lincoln Boyhood, Ind. (1962) 200. Lincoln grew up here.
Lincoln Memorial, D.C. (1911) 110.
Lyndon B. Johnson Grove on the Potomac, D.C. (1973) 17.
Mount Rushmore, S.D. (1925) 1,278. World famous sculpture of 4 presidents.
Roger Williams, R.I. (1965) 5. Memorial to founder of Rhode Island.
Thaddeus Kosciuszko, Pa. (1972) 0.02. Memorial to Polish hero of American Revolution.
Theodore Roosevelt Island, D.C. (1932) 89.
Thomas Jefferson Memorial, D.C. (1934) 18.
USS Arizona, Ha. (1980) 00. Memorializes American losses at Pearl Harbor.
Washington Monument, D.C. (1848) 106.
Wright Brothers, N.C. (1927/1953) 431. Site of first powered flight.

National Historic Sites

Abraham Lincoln Birthplace, Hodgenville, Ky. (1916/1959) 117.
Adams, Quincy, Mass. (1946/1952) 10. Home of Presidents John Adams, John Quincy Adams, and celebrated descendants.
Allegheny Portage Railroad, Pa. (1964) 1,247. Part of the Pennsylvania Canal system.

Andersonville, Andersonville, Ga. (1970) 476. Noted Civil War prison.
Andrew Johnson, Greeneville, Tenn. (1935/1963) 17. Home of the President.
Bent's Old Fort, Col. (1960) 800. Old West fur-trading post.
Boston African American (1980) Pre-Civil War black history structures.
Carl Sandburg Home, N.C. (1968/1972) 264. Poet's home.
Charles Pinckney, S.C. (1988) 25.
Christiansted, St. Croix; V.I. (1952/1961) 27. Commemorates Danish colony.
Clara Barton, Md. (1974) 9. Home of founder of American Red Cross.
Edgar Allan Poe, Pa. (1978/1980) 1. Poet's home.
Edison, West Orange, N.J. (1955/1962) 21. Home and laboratory.
Eisenhower, Gettysburg, Pa. (1967/1969) 690. Home of 34th president.
Eleanor Roosevelt, Hyde Park, N.Y. (1977) 181. Personal retreat.
Eugene O'Neill, Danville, Cal. (1976) 13. Playwright's home.
Ford's Theatre, Washington, D.C. (1866/1970) 0.29. Includes theater, now restored, where Lincoln was assassinated, house where he died, and Lincoln Museum.
Fort Bowie, Ariz. (1964/1972) 1,000. Focal point of operations against Geronimo and the Apaches.
Fort Davis, Tex. (1961/1963) 460. Frontier outpost battled Comanches and Apaches.
Fort Laramie, Wy. (1938/1960) 833. Military post on Oregon Trail.
Fort Larned, Kan. (1964/1966) 718. Military post on Santa Fe Trail.
Fort Point, San Francisco, Cal. (1970) 29. Largest West Coast fortification.
Fort Raleigh, N.C. (1941) 157. First English settlement.
Fort Scott, Kan. (1965/1978) 17. Commemorates U.S. frontier of 1840-50.
Fort Smith, Ark. (1961) 75. Active post from 1817 to 1890.
Fort Union Trading Post, Mon., N.D. (1966) 442. Principal fur-trading post on upper Missouri, 1829-1867.
Fort Vancouver, Wash. (1948/1961) 209. Hdqts. for Hudson's Bay Company in 1825. Early military and political seat.
Frederick Douglass Home, D.C. (1962/1988) 9. Home of nation's leading black spokesman.
Frederick Law Olmsted, Mass. (1979) 2. Home of famous park planner (1822-1903).
Friendship Hill, Pa. (1978) 675. Home of Albert Gallatin, Jefferson's Sec'y of Treasury. Not open to public.
Golden Spike, Utah (1957) 2,735. Commemorates completion of first transcontinental railroad in 1869.
Grant-Kohrs Ranch, Mon. (1972) 1,498. Ranch house and part of 19th century ranch.
Hampton, Md. (1948) 62. 18th-century Georgian mansion.
Harry S Truman, Mo. (1983). 0.78. Home of Pres. Truman after 1919.
Herbert Hoover, West Branch, Ia. (1965) 187. Birthplace and boyhood home of 31st president.
Home of Franklin D. Roosevelt, Hyde Park, N.Y. (1944) 290. Birthplace, home and "Summer White House".
Hopewell Furnace, Pa. (1938/1985) 848. 19th-century iron making village.
Hubbell Trading Post, Ariz. (1965) 160. Indian trading post.
James A. Garfield, Mentor, Oh. (1980) 8. President's home.
Jefferson National Expansion, Mo. (1935/1954) 191. Commemorates westward expansion.
Jimmy Carter, Ga. (1987) 70. Birthplace and home of 39th president.
John Fitzgerald Kennedy, Brookline, Mass. (1967) 0.09. Birthplace and childhood home of the President.
John Muir, Martinez, Cal. (1964) 339. Home of early conservationist and writer.
Knife River Indian Villages, N.D. (1974) 1,293. Remnants of 5 Hidatsa villages.
Lincoln Home, Springfield, Ill. (1971) 12. Lincoln's residence when he was elected President, 1860.
Longfellow, Cambridge, Mass. (1972) 2. Longfellow's home, 1837-82, and Washington's hq. during Boston Siege, 1775-76.
Maggie L. Walker, Va. (1978) 1. Richmond home of black leader and 1903 founder of bank.
Martin Luther King, Jr., Atlanta, Ga. (1980) 23. Birthplace, grave.
Martin Van Buren, N.Y. (1974) 40. Lindenwald, home of 8th president, near Kinderhook.
Ninety Six, S.C. (1976) 989. Colonial trading village.
Palo Alto Battlefield, Tex. (1978) 50. One of 2 Mexican War battles fought in U.S.
Pennsylvania Avenue, D.C. (1965) NA. Includes area between Capitol and White House, Ford's Theatre.

Puukohola Heiau, Ha. (1972) 80. Ruins of temple built by King Kamehameha.

Sagamore Hill, Oyster Bay, N.Y. (1962) 83. Home of President Theodore Roosevelt from 1885 until his death in 1919.

Saint-Gaudens, Cornish, N.H. (1964/1977) 148. Home, studio and gardens of American sculptor Augustus Saint-Gaudens.

Saint Paul's Church, N.Y. (1943/1978) 6. Eighteenth Century site of John Peter Zenger's "freedom of press" trial.

Salem Maritime, Mass. (1938) 9. Only port never seized from the patriots by the British. Major fishing and whaling port.

San Juan, P.R. (1949) 75. 16th-century Spanish fortifications.

Saugus Iron Works, Mass. (1968) 9. Reconstructed 17th-century colonial ironworks.

Springfield Armory, Mass. (1974) 55. Small arms manufacturing center for nearly 200 years.

Steamtown, Pa. (1986) 42. Railyard, roadhouse and repair shops of former Delaware, Lackawanna and Western Railroad.

Theodore Roosevelt Birthplace, N.Y., N.Y. (1962) 0.11.

Theodore Roosevelt Inaugural, Buffalo, N.Y. (1966) 1. Wilcox House where he took oath of office, 1901.

Thomas Stone, Md. (1978) 328. Home of signer of Declaration, built in 1771. Not open to public.

Tuskegee Institute, Ala. (1974) 74. College founded by Booker T. Washington in 1881 for blacks, includes student-made brick buildings.

Ulysses S. Grant, St. Louis Co., Mo. (1989) 10. Home of Grant during pre-Civil War years.

Vanderbilt Mansion, Hyde Park, N.Y. (1940) 212. Mansion of 19th-century financier.

Whitman Mission, Wash. (1936/1963) 98. Site where Dr. and Mrs. Marcus Whitman ministered to the Indians until slain by them in 1847.

William Howard Taft, Cincinnati, Oh. (1969) 3. Birthplace and early home of the 27th president.

National Monuments

Name	State	Year	Acreage
Agate Fossil Beds	Neb.	1965	3,055
Alibates Flint Quarries	N.M.-Tex.	1965	1,371
Aniakchak	Alas.	1978	137,176
Aztec Ruins	N.M.	1923	319
Bandelier	N.M.	1916	32,737
Black Canyon of the Gunnison	Col.	1933	20,766
Booker T. Washington	Va.	1956	224
Buck Island Reef	V.I.	1961	880
Cabrillo	Cal.	1913	137
Canyon de Chelly	Ariz.	1931	83,840
Cape Krusenstern	Alas.	1978	659,807
Capulin Volcano	N.M.	1916	793
Casa Grande Ruins	Ariz.	1892	473
Castillo de San Marcos	Fla.	1924	20
Castle Clinton	N.Y.	1946	1
Cedar Breaks	Ut.	1933	6,155
Chiricahua	Ariz.	1924	11,985
Colorado	Col.	1911	20,454
Congaree Swamp	S.C.	1976	22,200
Craters of the Moon	Ida.	1924	53,545
Custer Battlefield	Mon.	1879	765
Death Valley	Cal.-Nev.	1933	2,067,628
Devils Postpile	Cal.	1911	798
Devils Tower	Wy.	1906	1,347
Dinosaur	Col.-Ut.	1915	210,844
Effigy Mounds	Ia.	1949	1,481
El Malpais	N.M.	1987	114,942
El Morro	N.M.	1906	1,279
Florissant Fossil Beds**	Col.	1969	5,998
Fort Frederica	Ga.	1936	216
Fort Jefferson	Fla.	1935	64,700
Fort Matanzas	Fla.	1924	228
Fort McHenry National Monument and Historic Shrine	Md.	1925	43
Fort Pulaski	Ga.	1924	5,623
Fort Stanwix	N.Y.	1935	16
Fort Sumter	S.C.	1948	197
Fort Union	N.M.	1954	721
Fossil Butte	Wy.	1972	8,198
G. Washington Birthplace	Va.	1930	538
George Washington Carver	Mo.	1943	210
Gila Cliff Dwellings	N.M.	1907	533
Grand Portage	Minn.	1951	710
Great Sand Dunes	Col.	1932	38,662
Hagerman Fossil Beds	Ida.	1988	4,280
Hohokam Pima*	Ariz.	1972	1,690
Homestead Nat'l. Monument of America	Neb.	1936	195
Hovenweep	Col.-Ut.	1923	785
Jewel Cave	S.D.	1908	1,274
John Day Fossil Beds	Ore.	1974	14,014
Joshua Tree	Cal.	1936	559,955

Name	State	Year	Acreage
Lava Beds	Cal.	1925	46,560
Montezuma Castle	Ariz.	1906	858
Mound City Group	Oh.	1923	270
Muir Woods	Cal.	1908	554
Natural Bridges	Ut.	1908	7,636
Navajo	Ariz.	1909	360
Ocmulgee	Ga.	1934	683
Oregon Caves	Ore.	1909	488
Organ Pipe Cactus	Ariz.	1937	330,689
Pecos	N.M.	1965	365
Pinnacles	Cal.	1908	16,265
Pipe Spring	Ariz.	1923	40
Pipestone	Minn.	1937	282
Poverty Point	La.	1988	911
Rainbow Bridge	Ut.	1910	160
Russell Cave	Ala.	1961	310
Saguaro	Ariz.	1933	83,574
Salinas	N.M.	1909	1,077
Scotts Bluff	Neb.	1919	2,997
Statue of Liberty	N.J.-N.Y.	1924	58
Sunset Crater	Ariz.	1930	3,040
Timpanogos Cave	Ut.	1922	250
Tonto	Ariz.	1907	1,120
Tumacacori	Ariz.	1908	17
Tuzigoot	Ariz.	1939	801
Walnut Canyon	Ariz.	1915	2,249
White Sands	N.M.	1933	143,733
Wupatki	Ariz.	1924	35,253
Yucca House*	Col.	1919	10

National Preserves

Aniakchak	Alas.	1978	465,603
Bering Land Bridge	Alas.	1978	2,784,960
Big Cypress	Fla.	1974	570,000
Big Thicket	Tex.	1974	85,733
City of Rocks	Ida.	1988	14,407
Denali	Alas.	1917	1,311,365
Gates of the Arctic	Alas.	1978	948,629
Glacier Bay	Alas.	1925	57,884
Katmai	Alas.	1918	374,000
Lake Clark	Alas.	1978	1,407,293
Noatak	Alas.	1978	6,574,481
Timucuan Ecological & Historic Preserve	Fla.	1988	35,000
Wrangell-St. Elias	Alas.	1978	4,856,721
Yukon-Charley Rivers	Alas.	1978	2,523,509

National Seashores

Assateague Island	Md.-Va.	1965	39,631
Canaveral	Fla.	1975	57,662
Cape Cod	Mass.	1961	43,557
Cape Hatteras	N.C.	1937	30,319
Cape Lookout**	N.C.	1966	28,243
Cumberland Island	Ga.	1972	36,415
Fire Island	N.Y.	1964	19,579
Gulf Islands	Fla.-Miss.	1971	139,775
Padre Island	Tex.	1962	130,434
Point Reyes	Cal.	1962	71,047

National Parkways

Blue Ridge	Va.-N.C.	1936	85,950
George Washington Memorial	Va.-Md.	1930	7,131
John D. Rockefeller Jr. Mem.	Wy.	1972	23,777
Natchez Trace	Ala.-Miss.-Tenn.	1938	51,756

National Lakeshores

Apostle Islands	Wis.	1970	69,372
Indiana Dunes	Ind.	1966	13,841
Pictured Rocks	Mich.	1966	72,916
Sleeping Bear Dunes	Mich.	1970	71,134

National Rivers

Big South Fork Natl. R. and Recreation	Tenn.-Ky.	1976	122,960
Buffalo	Ark.	1972	94,219
New River Gorge	W.Va.	1978	62,144
Ozark	Mo.	1964	80,788
Mississippi Natl. R. and Recreation	Minn.	1988	50,000

Name	State	Year	Acreage
National Wild and Scenic Rivers			
Alagnak Wild	Alas.	1980	24,038
Bluestone	W.Va.	1988	N.A.
Delaware	N.Y.-N.J.-Pa.	1978	1,973
Lower Saint Croix	Minn.-Wis.	1972	9,475
Missouri Natl. Recreational River.	Neb.	1978	0
Obed Wild	Tenn.	1976	5,075
Rio Grande	Tex.	1978	9,600
Saint Croix	Minn.-Wis.	1968	67,432
Upper Delaware	N.Y.-N.J.	1978	75,000

Name	State	Year	Acreage
Coulee Dam	Wash.	1946	100,390
Curecanti	Col.	1965	42,114
Cuyahoga Valley	Oh.	1974	32,438
Delaware Water Gap	N.J.-Pa.	1965	66,652
Gateway	N.Y.-N.J.	1972	26,311
Gauley R.	W.Va.	1988	N.A.
Glen Canyon	Ariz.-Ut.	1958	1,236,880
Golden Gate	Cal.	1972	73,082
Lake Chelan	Wash.	1968	61,883
Lake Mead	Ariz.-Nev.	1936	1,495,666
Lake Meredith	Tex.	1965	44,978
Ross Lake	Wash.	1968	117,575
Santa Monica Mts.	Cal.	1978	150,050
Whiskeytown	Cal.	1965	42,503

Parks (no other classification)

Name	State	Year	Acreage
Catoctin Mountain	Md.	1954	5,770
Constitution Gardens	D.C.	1978	52
Fort Washington	Md.	1930	341
Greenbelt	Md.	1950	1,176
Perry's Victory	Oh.	1936	25
Piscataway	Md.	1961	4,263
Prince William Forest	Va.	1948	18,572
Rock Creek	D.C.	1890	1,754
Vietnam Veterans	D.C.	1980	2
Wolf Trap Farm Park for the Performing Arts	Va.	1966	130

National Mall .... D.C. 1933 146

National Scenic Trails

Name	State	Year	Acreage
Appalachian	Me. to Ga.	1968	161,546
Natchez Trace	Ga.-Ala.-Tenn.	1983	10,995
Potomac Heritage	Md.-D.C.-Va.-Pa.	1983	***

National Recreation Areas

Name	State	Year	Acreage
Amistad	Tex.	1965	57,292
Bighorn Canyon	Mon.-Wy.	1966	120,296
Chattahoochee R.	Ga.	1978	9,268
Chickasaw	Okla.	1902	9,522

International Historic Sites

Saint Croix Island .... Me. 1949 35

*Not open to the public. **No federal facilities. ***Undetermined.

National Park Service Recreation Visits

Source: National Park Service

The following places had more than 2.5 million recreation visits in 1989:

Park	Recreation Visits	Park	Recreation Visits
Acadia Natl. Park	5,440,952	J.F.K. Center for the Performing Arts	3,450,734
Blue Ridge Natl. Parkway	16,176,170	Lake Mead Natl. Recreation Area	8,495,295
Cape Cod Natl. Seashore	5,020,069	Natchez Trace Parkway	10,837,880
Castle Clinton Natl. Monument	3,285,976	National Capital Parks	8,934,149
Gateway Natl. Recreation Area	6,748,181	Olympic Natl. Park	2,737,611
George Washington Memorial Parkway	3,048,161	Rocky Mountain Natl. Park	2,502,915
Glen Canyon Natl. Recreation Area	3,452,847	San Francisco Maritime Natl. Hist. Park	5,203,302
Golden Gate Natl. Recreation Area	16,656,900	Statue of Liberty Natl. Monument	2,655,797
Grand Canyon Natl. Park	3,966,209	Valley Forge Natl. Hist. Park	4,700,074
Great Smokey Mtns. Natl. Park	8,333,553	Vietnam Veterans Memorial	2,594,694
Gulf Islands Natl. Seashore	4,458,368	Yellowstone Natl. Park	2,644,442
Independence Natl. Hist. Park	5,174,682	Yosemite Natl. Park	3,308,159
Jefferson Natl. Expansion Memorial Hist. Site	2,518,712		

Attendance at all areas administered by the National Park Service in 1989 was 269,399,900 recreation visits.

National Recreation Areas Administered by Forest Service

Name	State	Year	Acreage	Name	State	Year	Acreage
Allegheny	Pa.	1984	23,063	Oregon Dunes	Ore.	1972	31,566
Arapaho	Col.	1978	34,928	Rattlesnake	Mon.	1980	61,000
Flaming Gorge	Ut.-Wyo.	1968	201,114	Sawtooth	Ida.	1972	756,019
Hell's Canyon	Ida.-Ore.	1975	538,115	Spruce Knob-Seneca Rocks	W. Va.	1965	100,000
Mount Baker	Wash.	1984	8,473	Whiskeytown Shasta-Trinity	Cal.	1965	203,587
Mount Rogers	Va.	1966	154,816	White Rocks	Vt.	1984	36,400

Recreational Use of Public Lands Administered by Bureau of Land Management

Source: U.S. Bureau of Land Management

(In thousands. For year ending Sept. 30.)

Year	Number of visits	Total	Type of Recreation Use (visitor hours)							Snow- and ice-based recreational activity, winter sports
			Land-based recreation activities					Water-based recreation activities		
			Motorized travel		Non-motorized travel	Site based				
			Off road vehicle travel	Other motorized travel		Camping	Hunting	Fishing	Boating	
1983	56,270	334,010	24,397	35,534	12,237	84,066	92,974	20,290	16,869	2,917
1984	59,228	271,373	21,348	25,433	9,579	73,032	73,898	14,263	11,184	2,894
1985	51,739	244,612	36,995	24,053	10,047	65,397	51,842	14,254	11,710	5,023
1986	54,253	284,142	49,688	25,866	14,397	95,196	35,570	18,227	15,891	6,025
1987	56,427	514,716[1]	123,325	34,325	19,172	195,315	57,624	22,932	15,140	3,259
1989	60,957	493,214	65,808	74,075	36,676	173,597	46,760	23,392	18,491	3,119

(1) Increase due to an estimated longer length of stay per visit, especially in California.

Federal Indian Reservations and Trust Lands[1]

Source: Bureau of Indian Affairs, U.S. Interior Department (data as of 1988)
The total American Indian population according to the 1980 Census is 1.534 million.

State	No of Reser.	Tribally-owned acreage[2]	Individually-owned acreage[2]	No. of persons[3]	Average (%) unempl. rate[4]	Major tribes and/or nations
Alabama	1	230	0	1,480	30	Poarch Creek
Alaska	1[5]	86,773	884,100	91,106	47	Aleut, Eskimo, Athapascan[6], Haida, Tlingit, Tsimpshian
Arizona.	20	19,766,911	256,927	165,385	48	Navajo, Apache, Papago, Hopi, Yavapai, Pima
California.	83	513,005	67,175	28,815	38	Hoopa, Paiute, Yurok, Karok, Mission Bands
Colorado.	2	785,411	2,964	10,467	17	Ute
Connecticut . . .	1	1,201	0	80	0	Mashantucket Pequot
Florida	4	153,840	0	2,062	28	Seminole, Miccosukee[7]
Idaho	4	464,077	327,301	10,607	45	Shoshone, Bannock, Nez Perce
Iowa	1	4,164	0	737	31	Sac and Fox[8]
Kansas	4	7,620	22,058	2,321	17	Potawatomi, Kickapoo, Iowa
Louisiana.	3	567	0	936	41	Chitimacha, Coushatta, Tunica-Biloxi
Maine.	3	212,699	0	2,859	32	Passamaquoddy, Penobscot, Maliseet
Michigan	8	12,433	9,224	12,723	47	Chippewa, Potawatomi, Ottawa
Minnesota	14	714,271	51,011	19,863	58	Chippewa, Sioux
Mississippi	1	17,715	19	4,832	26	Choctaw
Montana	7	2,327,347	2,881,339	34,001	50	Blackfeet, Crow, Sioux, Assiniboine, Cheyenne
Nebraska	3	21,657	43,186	3,690	46	Omaha, Winnebago, Santee Sioux
Nevada.	22	1,147,163	78,566	9,075	37	Paiute, Shoshone, Washoe
New Mexico . . .	24	7,174,491	675,968	126,346	37	Zuni, Apache, Navajo
New York	8	87,058	0	12,314	51	Seneca, Mohawk, Onondaga, Oneida[9]
North Carolina. .	1	56,461	0	6,110	40	Cherokee
North Dakota . .	3	217,049	634,950	23,629	57	Sioux, Chippewa, Mandan, Arikara, Hidatsa
Oklahoma	1[10]	94,488	1,018,738	231,952	21	Cherokee, Creek, Choctaw, Chickasaw, Osage, Cheyenne, Arapahoe, Kiowa, Comanche
Oregon.	6	643,561	135,052	10,231	37	Warm Springs, Wasco, Paiute, Umatilla, Siletz
Rhode Island. . .	1	1,800	0	2,058	45	Narragansett
South Dakota . .	9	2,660,995	2,421,092	58,201	74	Sioux
Texas.	3	4,574	0	1,320	12	Alabama-Coushatta, Tiwa, Kickapoo
Utah	4	2,298,302	33,343	9,010	23	Ute, Goshute, Southern Paiute
Washington . . .	27	2,102,097	467,785	40,893	53	Yakima, Lummi, Quinault
Wisconsin	11	337,330	80,671	21,037	40	Chippewa, Oneida, Winnebago
Wyoming.	1	1,793,420	93,842	4,935	46	Shoshone, Arapahoe

(1) As of 1988 the federal government recognized and acknowledged that it had a special relationship with, and a trust responsibility for, 307 federally recognized Indian entities in the continental U.S., plus some 200 tribal entities in Alaska. The term "Indian entities" encompasses Indian tribes, bands, villages, groups, pueblos, Eskimos, and Aleuts, eligible for federal services and classified in the following 3 categories: (a) Officially approved Indian organizations pursuant to federal statutory authority (Indian Reorganization Act; Oklahoma Indian Welfare Act and Alaska Native Act.) (b) Officially approved Indian organizations outside of specified federal statutory authority. (c) Traditional Indian organizations recognized without formal federal approval of organizational structure. Some reservation boundaries transcend state boundaries (e.g., Navajo which is in Arizona, New Mexico, and Utah). For statistical convenience under "Number of Reservations," such reservations are counted in the state where population is predominant and/or tribal headquarters is located.

(2) The acreages refer only to Indian lands which are either owned by the tribes or individual Indians, and held in trust by the U.S. government. Many of these parcels are located off reservations. Not all lands within reservation boundaries are necessarily trust lands. Many parcels are privately-owned by tribes, individual Indians, and non-Indians. Also, some internal lands are the property of various governmental agencies.

(3) Number of Indians living on or adjacent to federally recognized reservations comprising the BIA service population.

(4) Unemployment rate of Indian work force consisting of all those 16 years old and over who are able and actively seeking work.

(5) Alaskan Indian Affairs are carried out under the Alaska Native Claims Settlement Act (Dec. 18, 1971). The Act provided for the establishment of regional and village corporations to conduct business for profit and non-profit purposes. There are 13 such regional corporations, each one with organized village corporations. The Annette Island Reservation remains the only federally recognized reservation in Alaska in the sense of specific reservation boundaries, trust lands, etc.

(6) Aleuts and Eskimos are racially and linguistically related. Athapascans are related to the Navaho and Apache Indians.

(7) "Seminole" means "runaways" and these Indians from various tribes were originally refugees from whites in the Carolinas and Georgia. Later joined by runaway slaves, the Seminole were united by their hostility to the United States. Formal peace with the Seminoles in Florida was not achieved until 1934. The Miccosukee are a branch of the Seminole; they retain their Indian religion and have not made formal peace with the United States.

(8) Once two tribes, the Sac and Fox formed a political alliance in 1734.

(9) These 4 tribes along with the Cayuga and Tuscarora made up the Iroquois League, which ruled large portions of New York, New England and Pennsylvania and ranged into the Midwest and South. The Onondaga, who traditionally provide the president of the league, maintain that they are a foreign nation within New York and the United States.

(10) Indian land status in Oklahoma is unique and there are no reservations except for Osage in the sense that the term is used elsewhere in the U.S. Likewise, many of the Oklahoma tribes are unique in their high degree of assimilation to the white culture.

PRESIDENTIAL ELECTIONS

Popular and Electoral Vote, 1984 and 1988

Source: News Election Service

States	1988 Electoral Vote Dukakis	1988 Electoral Vote Bush	1988 Democrat Dukakis	1988 Republican Bush	1984 Electoral Vote Mondale	1984 Electoral Vote Reagan	1984 Democrat Mondale	1984 Republican Reagan
Ala.	0	9	549,506	815,576	0	9	551,899	872,849
Alas. . . .	0	3	72,584	119,251	0	3	62,007	138,377
Ariz. . . .	0	7	454,029	702,541	0	7	333,854	681,416
Ark.. . . .	0	6	349,237	466,578	0	6	338,646	534,774
Cal.. . . .	0	47	4,702,233	5,054,917	0	47	3,815,947	5,305,410
Col.. . . .	0	8	621,453	728,177	0	8	454,975	821,817
Conn. . . .	0	8	676,584	750,241	0	8	569,597	890,877
Del.. . . .	0	3	108,647	139,639	0	3	101,656	152,190
D.C. . . .	3	0	159,407	27,590	3	0	180,408	29,009
Fla.. . . .	0	21	1,655,851	2,616,597	0	21	1,448,344	2,728,775
Ga.	0	12	714,792	1,081,331	0	12	706,628	1,068,722
Ha.	4	0	192,364	158,625	0	4	147,098	184,934
Ida. . . .	0	4	147,272	253,881	0	4	108,510	297,523
Ill.. . . .	0	24	2,215,940	2,310,939	0	24	2,086,499	2,707,103
Ind. . . .	0	12	860,643	1,297,763	0	12	841,481	1,377,230
Ia..	8	0	670,557	545,355	0	8	605,620	703,088
Kan. . . .	0	7	422,636	554,049	0	7	332,471	674,646
Ky.	0	9	580,368	734,281	0	9	536,756	815,345
La.	0	10	717,460	883,702	0	10	651,586	1,037,299
Me.. . . .	0	4	243,569	307,131	0	4	214,515	336,500
Md.. . . .	0	10	826,304	876,167	0	10	787,935	879,918
Mass. . .	13	0	1,401,415	1,194,635	0	13	1,239,606	1,310,936
Mich.. . .	0	20	1,675,783	1,965,486	0	20	1,529,638	2,251,571
Minn.. . .	10	0	1,109,471	962,337	10	0	1,036,364	1,032,603
Miss.. . .	0	7	363,921	557,890	0	7	352,192	582,377
Mo.. . . .	0	11	1,001,619	1,084,953	0	11	848,583	1,274,188
Mon. . . .	0	4	168,936	190,412	0	4	146,742	232,450
Neb. . . .	0	5	259,235	397,956	0	5	187,475	459,135
Nev. . . .	0	4	132,738	206,040	0	4	91,655	188,770
N.H. . . .	0	4	163,696	281,537	0	4	120,377	267,051
N.J.. . . .	0	16	1,317,541	1,740,604	0	16	1,261,323	1,933,630
N.M. . . .	0	5	244,497	270,341	0	5	201,769	307,101
N.Y. . . .	36	0	3,347,882	3,081,871	0	36	3,119,609	3,664,763
N.C. . . .	0	13	890,167	1,237,258	0	13	824,287	1,346,481
N.D. . . .	0	3	127,739	166,559	0	3	104,429	200,336
Oh.. . . .	0	23	1,939,629	2,416,549	0	23	1,825,440	2,678,559
Okla.. . .	0	8	483,423	678,367	0	8	385,080	861,530
Ore.. . .	7	0	616,206	560,126	0	7	536,479	685,700
Pa.. . . .	0	25	2,194,944	2,300,087	0	25	2,228,131	2,584,323
R.I.. . . .	4	0	225,123	177,761	0	4	197,106	212,080
S.C. . . .	0	8	370,554	606,443	0	8	344,459	615,539
S.D. . . .	0	3	145,560	165,415	0	3	116,113	200,267
Tenn.. . .	0	11	679,794	947,233	0	11	711,714	990,212
Tex. . . .	0	29	2,352,748	3,036,829	0	29	1,949,276	3,433,428
Ut.	0	5	207,352	428,442	0	5	155,369	469,105
Vt.	0	3	115,775	124,331	0	3	95,730	135,865
Va.	0	12	859,799	1,309,162	0	12	796,250	1,337,078
Wash.. . .	10	0	933,516	903,835	0	10	798,352	1,051,670
W.Va.. . .	6	0	341,016	310,065	0	6	328,125	405,483
Wis. . . .	11	0	1,126,794	1,047,499	0	11	995,740	1,198,584
Wyo.. . .	0	3	67,113	106,867	0	3	53,370	133,241
Total. . .	**112**	**426**	**41,805,422**	**48,881,221**	**13**	**525**	**37,457,215**	**54,281,858**

Presidential Election Returns by Counties

All results are official. Results for New England states are for selected cities or towns due to unavailability of county results. Totals are always statewide.

Source: News Election Service

Alabama

County	1988 Dukakis (D)	Bush (R)	1984 Mondale (D)	Reagan (R)
Autauga	3,667	7,828	3,366	8,350
Baldwin	9,271	25,933	7,272	24,964
Barbour	3,836	4,958	4,591	5,459
Bibb	2,244	2,885	2,167	3,487
Blount	4,485	8,754	3,738	8,508
Bullock	3,122	1,421	3,537	1,697
Butler	3,465	3,923	3,641	4,941
Calhoun	12,451	19,806	12,752	23,291
Chambers	5,103	7,694	5,302	8,024
Cherokee	3,176	2,868	3,029	3,225
Chilton	3,820	8,761	3,924	8,243
Choctaw	3,491	3,629	3,373	3,960
Clarke	4,217	5,708	4,452	6,282
Clay	1,602	3,496	1,456	3,432
Cleburne	1,383	3,071	1,238	3,259
Coffee	4,319	8,890	4,370	10,558
Colbert	10,397	7,775	11,008	9,530
Conecuh	3,022	3,256	2,737	3,538
Coosa	1,860	2,405	1,781	2,585
Covington	3,845	8,130	3,812	9,944
Crenshaw	1,836	2,617	1,904	3,261
Cullman	8,517	14,351	7,989	14,782
Dale	3,476	9,266	3,215	10,319
Dallas	9,660	7,630	10,955	9,585
DeKalb	7,333	11,478	7,212	12,098
Elmore	4,501	10,852	4,198	11,694
Escambia	4,020	6,807	3,853	8,694
Etowah	17,762	17,828	19,074	19,243
Fayette	3,186	4,338	2,533	4,654
Franklin	4,961	5,146	4,601	5,304
Geneva	2,685	5,703	2,330	6,308
Greene	3,295	1,048	3,675	1,361
Hale	3,187	2,414	3,289	2,691
Henry	2,206	3,613	2,231	3,952
Houston	7,001	19,989	6,488	20,834
Jackson	7,418	6,090	7,425	6,730
Jefferson	107,766	148,879	107,506	158,362
Lamar	2,274	3,214	1,910	3,943
Lauderdale	12,862	12,942	12,907	15,354
Lawrence	4,646	3,616	4,866	4,466
Lee	9,078	17,180	9,077	16,757
Limestone	5,455	9,086	5,410	8,423
Lowndes	3,328	1,405	3,567	1,629
Macon	6,351	1,304	7,857	1,543
Madison	25,800	53,575	26,889	50,428
Marengo	4,402	4,241	4,811	5,261
Marion	4,505	5,955	3,918	6,771
Marshall	7,357	12,148	7,704	12,330
Mobile	45,524	72,203	47,252	81,923
Monroe	3,509	5,379	3,725	5,917
Montgomery	28,709	41,131	31,206	43,328
Morgan	10,594	18,679	11,324	24,103
Perry	3,574	2,107	3,731	2,600
Pickens	3,107	3,851	3,586	4,685
Pike	3,813	5,897	3,541	6,231
Randolph	2,462	4,625	2,439	4,940
Russell	6,589	6,333	7,610	6,654
St. Clair	4,335	10,604	4,000	10,408
Shelby	7,138	27,052	5,884	21,858
Sumter	4,390	2,212	4,478	2,493
Talladega	8,291	12,973	8,490	14,067
Tallapoosa	4,598	8,502	4,458	9,045
Tuscaloosa	18,166	27,396	16,066	28,075
Walker	11,338	11,011	10,591	12,852
Washington	3,402	3,741	3,081	4,434
Wilcox	3,369	1,739	2,663	2,337
Winston	2,954	6,235	2,624	6,845
Totals	549,506	815,576	551,899	872,849

Alabama Vote Since 1940

1940, Roosevelt, Dem., 250,726; Willkie, Rep., 42,174; Babson, Proh., 698; Browder, Com., 509; Thomas, Soc., 100.

1944, Roosevelt, Dem., 198,918; Dewey, Rep., 44,540; Watson, Proh., 1,095; Thomas, Soc., 190.

1948, Thurmond, States' Rights, 171,443; Dewey, Rep., 40,930; Wallace, Prog., 1,522; Watson, Proh., 1,085.

1952, Eisenhower, Rep., 149,231; Stevenson, Dem., 275,075; Hamblen, Proh., 1,814.

1956, Stevenson, Dem., 290,844; Eisenhower, Rep. 195,694; Independent electors, 20,323.

1960, Kennedy, Dem., 324,050; Nixon, Rep., 237,981; Faubus, States' Rights, 4,367; Decker, Proh., 2,106; King, Afro-Americans, 1,485; scattering, 236.

1964, Dem. 209,848 (electors unpledged); Goldwater, Rep., 479,085; scattering, 105.

1968, Nixon, Rep., 146,923; Humphrey, Dem., 196,579; Wallace, 3d party, 691,425; Munn, Proh., 4,022.

1972, Nixon, Rep., 728,701; McGovern, Dem., 219,108 plus 37,815 Natl. Demo. Party of Alabama; Schmitz, Conservative, 11,918; Munn, Proh., 8,551.

1976, Carter, Dem., 659,170; Ford, Rep., 504,070; Maddox, Am. Ind., 9,198; Bubar, Proh., 6,669; Hall, Com., 1,954; MacBride, Libertarian, 1,481.

1980, Reagan, Rep., 654,192; Carter, Dem., 636,730; Anderson, Independent, 16,481; Rarick, Amer. Ind., 15,010; Clark, Libertarian, 13,318; Bubar, Statesman, 1,743; Hall, Com., 1,629; DeBerry, Soc. Work., 1,303; McReynolds, Socialist, 1,006; Commoner, Citizens, 517.

1984, Reagan, Rep., 872,849; Mondale, Dem., 551,899; Bergland, Libertarian, 9,504.

1988, Bush, Rep., 815,576; Dukakis, Dem., 549,506; Paul, Lib., 8,460; Fulani, Ind., 3,311.

Alaska

Election District	1988 Dukakis (D)	Bush (R)	1984 Mondale (D)	Reagan (R)
No. 1	3,167	4,564	2,937	5,256
No. 2	1,879	2,274	1,857	2,645
No. 3	1,884	2,313	1,561	2,540
No. 4	6,057	5,963	5,293	7,322
No. 5	3,696	6,874	2,896	8,188
No. 6	1,543	2,347	1,261	2,883
No. 7	2,088	3,806	1,539	4,363
No. 8	3,815	7,629	2,752	8,603
No. 9	3,980	6,876	3,186	8,361
No. 10	3,786	6,241	3,034	7,634
No. 11	2,590	3,189	2,621	5,176
No. 12	3,733	3,511	4,063	5,348
No. 13	2,643	4,968	2,616	6,106
No. 14	3,387	6,164	2,843	7,465
No. 15	3,726	8,949	2,749	8,993
No. 16	4,174	8,851	2,935	9,942
No. 17	1,302	3,093	1,014	3,793
No. 18	1,674	5,998	967	4,858
No. 19	2,737	4,485	1,905	3,880
No. 20	3,389	5,225	2,914	6,538
No. 21	2,816	3,127	2,433	3,629
No. 22	1,377	1,861	1,319	2,075
No. 23	1,390	1,898	1,546	2,165
No. 24	1,381	1,818	1,473	2,321
No. 25	1,400	1,611	1,825	2,004
No. 26	1,568	2,959	1,216	3,019
No. 27	1,372	2,657	1,252	3,270
Totals	72,584	119,251	62,007	138,377

Alaska Vote Since 1960

1960, Kennedy, Dem., 29,809; Nixon, Rep. 30,953.

1964, Johnson, Dem., 44,329; Goldwater, Rep., 22,930.

1968, Nixon, Rep., 37,600; Humphrey, Dem., 35,411; Wallace, 3d party, 10,024.

1972, Nixon, Rep., 55,349; McGovern, Dem., 32,967; Schmitz, American, 6,903.

1976, Carter, Dem., 44,058; Ford, Rep., 71,555; MacBride, Libertarian, 6,785.

1980, Reagan, Rep., 86,112; Carter, Dem., 41,842; Clark, Libertarian, 18,479; Anderson, Ind., 11,155; Write-in, 857.

1984, Reagan, Rep., 138,377; Mondale, Dem., 62,007; Bergland, Libertarian, 6,378.

1988, Bush, Rep., 119,251; Dukakis, Dem., 72,584; Paul, Lib., 5,484; Fulani, New. Alliance, 1,024.

Arizona

County	1988 Dukakis (D)	Bush (R)	1984 Mondale (D)	Reagan (R)
Apache	8,944	5,347	7,277	5,638
Cochise	11,812	15,815	9,671	16,405
Coconino	14,660	16,649	11,528	17,581
Gila	7,147	7,861	6,509	8,543
Graham	3,407	5,120	3,080	5,247
Greenlee	1,733	1,526	1,963	1,801

La Paz	1,746	2,562	1,502	2,757
Maricopa	230,952	442,337	154,833	411,902
Mohave	10,197	17,651	7,436	17,364
Navajo	9,023	10,393	8,017	11,379
Pima	113,824	117,899	91,585	123,830
Pinal	13,850	14,966	11,923	16,464
Santa Cruz	3,268	3,320	2,463	3,855
Yavapai	14,514	27,842	9,609	24,802
Yuma	8,952	13,253	6,458	13,848
Totals	454,029	702,541	333,854	681,416

Arizona Vote Since 1940

1940, Roosevelt, Dem., 95,267; Willkie, Rep., 54,030; Babson, Proh., 742.

1944, Roosevelt, Dem., 80,926; Dewey, Rep., 56,287; Watson, Proh., 421.

1948, Truman, Dem., 95,251; Dewey, Rep., 77,597; Wallace, Prog., 3,310; Watson, Proh., 786; Teichert, Soc. Labor, 121.

1952, Eisenhower, Rep., 152,042; Stevenson, Dem., 108,528.

1956, Eisenhower, Rep., 176,990; Stevenson, Dem., 112,880; Andrews, Ind. 303.

1960, Kennedy, Dem., 176,781; Nixon, Rep., 221,241; Hass, Soc. Labor, 469.

1964, Johnson, Dem., 237,753; Goldwater, Rep., 242,535; Hass, Soc. Labor, 482.

1968, Nixon, Rep., 266,721; Humphrey, Dem., 170,514; Wallace, 3d party, 46,573; McCarthy, New Party, 2,751; Halstead, Soc. Worker, 85; Cleaver, Peace and Freedom, 217; Blomen, Soc. Labor, 75.

1972, Nixon, Rep., 402,812; McGovern, Dem., 198,540; Schmitz, Amer., 21,208; Soc. Workers, 30,945. (Due to ballot peculiarities in 3 counties (particularly Pima), thousands of voters cast ballots for the Socialist Workers Party and one of the major candidates. Court ordered both votes counted as official.

1976, Carter, Dem., 295,602; Ford, Rep., 418,642; McCarthy, Ind., 19,229; MacBride, Libertarian, 7,647; Camejo, Soc. Workers, 928; Anderson, Amer., 564; Maddox, Am. Ind., 85.

1980, Reagan, Rep., 529,688; Carter, Dem., 246,843; Anderson, Ind., 76,952; Clark, Libertarian, 18,784; De Berry, Soc. Workers, 1,100; Commoner, Citizens, 551; Hall, Com., 25; Griswold, Workers World, 2.

1984, Reagan, Rep., 681,416; Mondale, Dem., 333,854; Bergland, Libertarian, 10,585.

1988, Bush, Rep., 702,541; Dukakis, Dem., 454,029; Paul, Lib., 13,351; Fulani, New Alliance, 1,662.

Arkansas

	1988		1984	
County	Dukakis (D)	Bush (R)	Mondale (D)	Reagan (R)
Arkansas	3,075	4,007	3,153	4,804
Ashley	4,466	4,111	3,373	5,675
Baxter	4,808	8,614	4,528	10,870
Benton	9,399	24,295	7,306	24,296
Boone	3,998	7,567	3,356	7,961
Bradley	2,167	2,089	2,313	2,690
Calhoun	1,024	1,316	1,058	1,474
Carroll	2,632	4,553	2,263	5,041
Chicot	2,426	1,901	3,407	2,502
Clark	4,675	3,389	4,638	4,185
Clay	3,442	2,766	3,279	3,767
Cleburne	3,404	4,932	3,172	5,769
Cleveland	1,404	1,462	1,378	1,773
Columbia	3,706	5,810	3,680	6,526
Conway	4,134	4,066	3,742	5,049
Craighead	9,083	11,887	8,035	14,047
Crawford	3,582	9,092	3,071	9,551
Crittenden	6,702	7,441	6,520	6,663
Cross	2,989	3,186	2,701	3,917
Dallas	1,990	1,947	2,035	2,361
Desha	2,859	2,334	2,918	2,696
Drew	2,578	2,995	2,638	3,407
Faulkner	7,302	10,678	7,169	11,595
Franklin	2,458	3,588	2,399	4,382
Fulton	2,018	1,918	1,864	2,329
Garland	11,406	19,281	11,484	21,213
Grant	2,142	2,717	2,148	3,167
Greene	5,065	5,161	4,730	6,179
Hempstead	3,841	3,938	3,327	4,904
Hot Spring	5,090	4,181	5,836	5,629
Howard	1,818	2,510	1,746	3,079
Independence	4,523	6,637	4,415	7,428
Izard	2,652	2,824	2,345	2,726
Jackson	4,199	3,049	4,038	3,901
Jefferson	16,664	12,520	18,082	14,514
Johnson	2,818	4,046	3,056	4,720

Lafayette	1,915	1,860	1,695	2,290
Lawrence	3,179	3,205	2,594	4,039
Lee	2,878	1,863	2,541	2,101
Lincoln	2,204	1,557	2,406	1,860
Little River	2,740	2,347	2,090	3,155
Logan	1,254	2,203	3,206	5,653
Lonoke	4,786	7,215	4,636	8,425
Madison	2,106	3,067	2,133	3,516
Marion	2,033	2,993	1,945	3,545
Miller	5,437	7,110	4,686	8,302
Mississippi	6,759	7,841	7,548	10,180
Monroe	2,052	1,862	2,413	2,508
Montgomery	1,362	1,752	1,497	2,221
Nevada	1,732	1,714	1,783	2,352
Newton	1,489	2,504	1,414	2,749
Ouachita	5,229	6,297	5,858	6,700
Perry	1,470	1,627	1,404	2,047
Phillips	5,580	3,892	5,946	4,686
Pike	1,681	2,105	1,443	2,665
Poinsett	3,873	3,644	3,906	5,622
Polk	2,390	4,099	2,101	5,181
Pope	4,941	10,084	5,082	10,667
Prairie	1,688	1,947	1,437	2,407
Pulaski	55,857	70,562	54,237	77,651
Randolph	2,781	2,560	2,507	3,188
St. Francis	4,656	4,298	4,866	5,378
Saline	8,436	12,353	5,977	11,709
Scott	1,707	2,507	1,609	3,056
Searcy	1,340	2,743	1,313	2,819
Sebastian	9,684	24,426	8,688	27,595
Sevier	2,037	2,254	1,942	3,302
Sharp	2,955	3,623	2,492	4,392
Stone	1,728	2,186	1,654	2,325
Union	5,931	10,581	6,208	12,333
Van Buren	2,607	3,562	2,529	4,060
Washington	12,557	23,601	11,319	24,993
White	6,957	11,094	6,603	12,566
Woodruff	1,924	1,097	2,055	1,675
Yell	2,763	3,535	2,679	4,051
Totals	349,237	466,578	338,646	534,774

Arkansas Vote Since 1940

1940, Roosevelt, Dem., 158,622; Willkie, Rep., 42,121; Babson, Proh., 793; Thomas, Soc., 305.

1944, Roosevelt, Dem., 148,965; Dewey, Rep., 63,551; Thomas, Soc. 438.

1948, Truman, Dem., 149,659; Dewey, Rep., 50,959; Thurmond, States' Rights, 40,068; Thomas, Soc., 1,037; Wallace, Prog., 751; Watson, Proh., 1.

1952, Eisenhower, Rep., 177,155; Stevenson, Dem., 226,300; Hamblen, Proh., 886; MacArthur, Christian Nationalist, 458; Hass, Soc. Labor, 1.

1956, Stevenson, Dem., 213,277; Eisenhower, Rep., 186,287; Andrews, Ind., 7,008.

1960, Kennedy, Dem., 215,049; Nixon, Rep., 184,508; Nat'l. States' Rights, 28,952.

1964, Johnson, Dem., 314,197; Goldwater, Rep., 243,264; Kasper, Nat'l. States Rights, 2,965.

1968, Nixon, Rep., 189,062; Humphrey, Dem., 184,901; Wallace, 3d party, 235,627.

1972, Nixon, Rep., 445,751; McGovern, Dem., 198,899; Schmitz, Amer. , 3,016.

1976, Carter, Dem., 498,604; Ford, Rep., 267,903; McCarthy, Ind., 639; Anderson, Amer., 389.

1980, Reagan, Rep., 403,164; Carter, Dem., 398,041; Anderson, Ind., 22,468; Clark, Libertarian, 8,970; Commoner, Citizens, 2,345; Bubar, Statesman, 1,350; Hall, Comm., 1,244.

1984, Reagan, Rep., 534,774; Mondale, Dem., 338,646; Bergland, Libertarian, 2,220.

1988, Bush, Rep., 466,578; Dukakis, Dem., 349,237; Duke, Chr. Pop., 5,146; Paul, Lib., 3,297.

California

	1988		1984	
County	Dukakis (D)	Bush (R)	Mondale (D)	Reagan (R)
Alameda	310,263	162,815	279,281	190,029
Alpine	230	306	194	264
Amador	5,197	6,893	4,166	6,970
Butte	30,406	40,143	25,126	44,836
Calaveras	5,674	7,640	3,919	7,339
Colusa	2,022	3,077	1,715	3,362
Contra Costa	169,411	158,652	137,941	167,797
Del Norte	3,587	3,714	2,693	3,989
El Dorado	19,800	30,021	13,969	26,900
Fresno	92,635	94,835	83,416	101,156
Glenn	2,894	4,944	2,480	5,994
Humboldt	29,781	21,460	24,870	27,495
Imperial	10,243	12,889	8,231	13,816
Inyo	2,653	5,042	2,348	5,811

Kern	55,083	90,550	44,523	85,872
Kings	9,142	12,118	7,317	13,357
Lake	9,828	9,366	8,292	10,291
Lassen	3,446	5,157	3,253	5,338
Los Angeles	1,372,352	1,239,716	1,114,578	1,370,813
Madera	10,642	13,255	8,701	13,853
Marin	69,394	46,855	56,796	55,845
Mariposa	2,998	3,768	2,121	3,571
Mendocino	17,152	12,979	14,172	16,107
Merced	20,105	21,717	16,875	25,003
Modoc	1,416	2,518	1,219	2,995
Mono	1,284	2,177	944	2,630
Monterey	48,998	50,022	39,676	54,440
Napa	22,283	23,235	18,234	25,715
Nevada	14,980	21,383	10,941	19,440
Orange	269,013	586,230	200,477	615,099
Placer	27,516	42,096	20,527	36,565
Plumas	4,251	4,603	3,709	5,079
Riverside	133,122	199,979	99,853	178,397
Sacramento	188,557	201,832	153,450	197,957
San Benito	4,559	5,578	3,454	5,530
San Bernardino	151,118	235,167	114,710	217,556
San Diego	333,264	523,143	251,134	487,362
San Francisco	201,887	72,503	190,396	88,683
San Joaquin	61,699	75,309	53,441	81,084
San Luis Obispo	35,667	46,613	26,626	48,331
San Mateo	141,859	109,261	120,853	133,912
Santa Barbara	63,586	77,524	49,505	85,458
Santa Clara	277,810	254,442	224,032	280,425
Santa Cruz	63,133	37,728	47,240	39,862
Shasta	21,171	32,402	19,178	32,854
Sierra	791	860	781	1,078
Siskiyou	8,365	9,056	7,130	10,544
Solano	54,344	50,314	41,435	50,867
Sonoma	91,262	67,725	69,383	74,014
Stanislaus	44,685	51,648	36,599	54,085
Sutter	6,557	14,100	5,526	14,425
Tehama	7,213	9,854	6,511	11,536
Trinity	2,518	3,267	2,204	3,525
Tulare	30,711	46,891	27,707	50,262
Tuolumne	8,717	10,646	7,212	10,376
Ventura	89,065	147,604	64,623	146,647
Yolo	30,429	22,358	25,264	23,604
Yuba	5,444	8,937	4,996	9,265
Totals	**4,702,233**	**5,054,917**	**3,815,947**	**5,305,410**

California Vote Since 1940

1940, Roosevelt, Dem., 1,877,618; Willkie, Rep., 1,351,419; Thomas, Prog., 16,506; Browder, Com., 13,586; Babson, Proh., 9,400.

1944, Roosevelt, Dem., 1,988,564; Dewey, Rep., 1,512,965; Watson, Proh., 14,770; Thomas, Soc., 3,923; Teichert, Soc. Labor, 327.

1948, Truman, Dem., 1,913,134; Dewey, Rep., 1,895,269; Wallace, Prog., 190,381; Watson, Proh., 16,926; Thomas, Soc., 3,459; Thurmond, States' Rights, 1,228; Teichert, Soc. Labor, 195; Dobbs, Soc. Workers, 133.

1952, Eisenhower, Rep., 2,897,310; Stevenson, Dem., 2,197,548; Hallinan, Prog., 24,106; Hamblen, Proh., 15,653; MacArthur, (Tenny Ticket), 3,326; (Kellems Ticket) 178; Hass, Soc. Labor, 273; Hoopes, Soc., 206; scattered, 3,249.

1956, Eisenhower, Rep., 3,027,668; Stevenson, Dem., 2,420,136; Holtwick, Proh., 11,119; Andrews, Constitution, 6,087; Hass, Soc. Labor, 300; Hoopes, Soc., 123; Dobbs, Soc. Workers, 96; Smith, Christian Nat'l., 8.

1960, Kennedy, Dem., 3,224,099; Nixon, Rep., 3,259,722; Decker, Proh., 21,706; Hass, Soc. Labor, 1,051.

1964, Johnson, Dem., 4,171,877; Goldwater, Rep., 2,879,108; Hass, Soc. Labor, 489; DeBerry, Soc. Worker, 378; Munn, Proh., 305; Hensley, Universal, 19.

1968, Nixon, Rep., 3,467,664; Humphrey, Dem., 3,244,318; Wallace, 3d party, 487,270; Peace and Freedom party, 27,707; McCarthy, Alternative, 20,721; Gregory, write-in, 3,230; Mitchell, Com., 260; Munn, Proh., 59; Blomen, Soc. Labor, 341; Soeters, Defense, 17.

1972, Nixon, Rep., 4,602,096; McGovern, Dem., 3,475,847; Schmitz, Amer., 232,554; Spock, Peace and Freedom, 55,167; Hall, Com., 373; Hospers, Libertarian, 980; Munn, Proh., 53; Fisher, Soc. Labor, 197; Jenness, Soc. Workers, 574; Green, Universal, 21.

1976, Carter, Dem., 3,742,284; Ford, Rep., 3,882,244; Mac-Bride, Libertarian, 56,388; Maddox, Am. Ind., 51,098; Wright, People's, 41,731; Camejo, Soc. Workers, 17,259; Hall, Com., 12,766; write-in, McCarthy, 58,412; other write-in, 4,935.

1980, Reagan, Rep. 4,524,858; Carter, Dem., 3,083,661; Anderson, Ind., 739,833; Clark, Libertarian, 148,434; Com-

moner, Ind. 61,063; Smith, Peace & Freedom, 18,116; Rarick, Amer. Ind., 9,856.

1984, Reagan, Rep. 5,305,410; Mondale, Dem., 3,815,947; Bergland, Libertarian, 48,400.

1988, Bush, Rep., 5,054,917; Dukakis, Dem., 4,702,233; Paul, Lib., 70,105; Fulani, Ind., 31,181.

Colorado

	1988		1984	
	Dukakis	Bush	Mondale	Reagan
County	(D)	(R)	(D)	(R)
Adams	49,464	43,163	35,285	55,092
Alamosa	2,146	2,567	1,720	2,953
Arapahoe	61,113	95,926	39,891	107,556
Archuleta	795	1,440	584	1,557
Baca	851	1,670	580	1,903
Bent	1,088	1,032	859	1,314
Boulder	57,265	48,174	42,195	53,535
Chaffee	2,548	3,080	1,779	3,680
Cheyenne	399	760	307	892
Clear Creek	1,698	1,820	1,089	2,151
Conejos	1,976	1,445	1,553	1,669
Costilla	1,120	454	997	621
Crowley	630	862	517	993
Custer	310	753	241	832
Delta	3,521	5,449	2,835	6,678
Denver	127,173	77,753	110,200	105,096
Dolores	230	488	173	667
Douglas	6,931	17,035	3,011	12,249
Eagle	3,314	4,366	2,032	4,500
Elbert	1,566	2,805	802	2,605
El Paso	39,995	96,965	28,185	88,377
Fremont	5,278	7,623	3,895	8,250
Garfield	4,620	6,358	3,076	7,111
Gilpin	804	728	634	896
Grand	1,451	2,306	1,017	2,865
Gunnison	1,897	2,520	1,424	3,100
Hinsdale	111	295	98	310
Huerfano	1,876	1,079	1,602	1,581
Jackson	294	584	191	722
Jefferson	81,824	110,820	53,700	124,496
Kiowa	398	645	265	850
Kit Carson	1,196	2,262	778	2,762
Lake	1,516	969	1,324	1,364
La Plata	5,443	7,714	4,040	8,719
Larimer	35,703	45,967	23,896	49,883
Las Animas	4,075	2,162	3,670	2,992
Lincoln	874	1,356	587	1,661
Logan	3,382	4,485	2,155	5,883
Mesa	14,372	22,150	9,938	23,736
Mineral	174	217	117	333
Moffat	1,634	2,757	1,228	3,630
Montezuma	2,233	4,208	1,665	4,753
Montrose	3,748	6,012	2,864	7,162
Morgan	3,728	4,795	2,331	6,097
Otero	3,910	4,265	3,005	5,373
Ouray	439	814	366	914
Park	1,343	1,909	782	2,041
Philips	923	1,317	651	1,689
Pitkin	3,420	2,801	2,293	3,117
Prowers	2,207	2,978	1,467	3,501
Pueblo	32,788	20,119	27,126	24,634
Rio Blanco	803	1,821	484	2,131
Rio Grande	1,545	2,626	1,104	3,122
Routt	2,922	3,264	2,051	4,239
Saguache	1,033	945	867	1,201
San Juan	192	210	183	320
San Miguel	961	798	654	833
Sedgwick	611	921	429	1,146
Summit	2,595	2,893	1,588	3,253
Teller	1,656	3,760	1,043	3,460
Washington	958	1,707	568	2,080
Weld	20,548	26,497	13,863	31,293
Yuma	1,835	2,513	1,121	3,394
Total	621,453	728,177	454,975	821,817

Colorado Vote Since 1940

1940, Roosevelt, Dem., 265,554; Willkie, Rep., 279,576; Thomas, Soc., 1,899; Babson, Proh., 1,597; Browder, Com., 378.

1944, Roosevelt, Dem., 234,331; Dewey, Rep., 268,731; Thomas, Soc., 1,977.

1948, Truman, Dem., 267,288; Dewey, Rep., 239,714; Wallace, Prog., 6,115; Thomas, Soc., 1,678; Dobbs, Soc. Workers, 228; Teichert, Soc. Labor, 214.

1952, Eisenhower, Rep., 379,782; Stevenson, Dem., 245,504; MacArthur, Constitution, 2,181; Hallinan, Prog., 1,919; Hoopes, Soc., 365; Hass, Soc. Labor, 352.

1956, Eisenhower, Rep., 394,479; Stevenson, Dem., 263,997; Hass, Soc. Lab., 3,308; Andrews, Ind., 759; Hoopes, Soc., 531.

1960, Kennedy, Dem., 330,629; Nixon, Rep., 402,242; Hass, Soc. Labor, 2,803; Dobbs, Soc. Workers, 572.

1964, Johnson, Dem., 476,024; Goldwater, Rep., 296,767; Hass, Soc. Labor, 302; DeBerry, Soc. Worker, 2,537; Munn, Proh., 1,356.

1968, Nixon, Rep., 409,345; Humphrey, Dem., 335,174; Wallace, 3d party, 60,813; Blomen, Soc. Labor, 3,016; Gregory, New-party, 1,393; Munn, Proh., 275; Halstead, Soc. Worker, 235.

1972, Nixon, Rep., 597,189; McGovern, Dem., 329,980; Fisher, Soc. Labor, 4,361; Hospers, Libertarian, 1,111; Hall, Com., 432; Jenness, Soc. Workers, 555; Munn, Proh., 467; Schmitz, Amer., 17,269; Spock, Peoples, 2,403.

1976, Carter, Dem., 460,353; Ford, Rep., 584,367; McCarthy, Ind., 26,107; MacBride, Libertarian, 5,330; Bubar, Proh., 2,882.

1980, Reagan, Rep., 652,264; Carter, Dem., 367,973; Anderson, Ind., 130,633; Clark, Libertarian, 25,744; Commoner, Citizens, 5,614; Bubar, Statesman, 1,180; Pulley, Socialist, 520; Hall, Com., 487.

1984, Reagan, Rep., 821,817; Mondale, Dem., 454,975; Bergland, Libertarian, 11,257.

1988, Bush, Rep., 728,177; Dukakis, Dem., 621,453; Paul, Lib., 15,482; Dodge, Proh., 4,604.

Connecticut

City	1988 Dukakis (D)	Bush (R)	1984 Mondale (D)	Reagan (R)
Bridgeport	23,831	17,084	24,332	24,256
Hartford	27,295	8,100	29,327	11,621
New Britain	15,843	9,569	14,608	13,723
New Haven	31,951	11,616	32,518	16,483
Norwalk	14,518	18,618	12,509	22,447
Stamford	20,773	24,877	19,432	29,167
Waterbury	18,202	20,018	18,217	24,764
West Hartford	19,311	16,482	16,882	20,517
Totals	676,584	750,241	569,597	890,877

Connecticut Vote Since 1940

1940, Roosevelt, Dem., 417,621; Willkie, Rep., 361,021; Browder, Com., 1,091; Aiken, Soc. Labor, 971; Willkie, Union, 798.

1944, Roosevelt, Dem., 435,146; Dewey, Rep., 390,527; Thomas, Soc., 5,097; Teichert, Soc. Labor, 1,220.

1948, Truman, Dem., 423,297; Dewey, Rep., 437,754; Wallace, Prog., 13,713; Thomas, Soc., 6,964; Teichert, Soc. Labor, 1,184; Dobbs, Soc. Workers, 606.

1952, Eisenhower, Rep., 611,012; Stevenson, Dem., 481,649; Hoopes, Soc., 2,244; Hallinan, Peoples, 1,466; Hass, Soc. Labor, 535; write-in, 5.

1956, Eisenhower, Rep., 711,837; Stevenson, Dem., 405,079; scattered, 205.

1960, Kennedy, Dem., 657,055; Nixon, Rep., 565,813.

1964, Johnson, Dem., 826,269; Goldwater, Rep., 390,996; scattered, 1,313.

1968, Nixon, Rep., 556,721; Humphrey, Dem., 621,561; Wallace, 3d party, 76,650; scattered, 1,300.

1972, Nixon, Rep., 810,763; McGovern, Dem., 555,498; Schmitz, Amer., 17,239; scattered, 777.

1976, Carter, Dem., 647,895; Ford, Rep., 719,261; Maddox, George Wallace Party, 7,101; LaRouche, U.S. Labor, 1,789.

1980, Reagan, Rep., 677,210; Carter, Dem., 541,732; Anderson, Ind., 171,807; Clark, Libertarian, 8,570; Commoner, Citizens, 6,130; scattered, 836.

1984, Reagan, Rep., 890,877; Mondale, Dem., 569,597.

1988, Bush, Rep., 750,241; Dukakis, Dem., 676,584; Paul, Lib., 14,071; Fulani; New Alliance, 2,491.

Delaware

County	1988 Dukakis (D)	Bush (R)	1984 Mondale (D)	Reagan (R)
Kent	12,996	19,923	11,789	21,531
New Castle	79,147	92,587	76,238	102,322
Sussex	16,504	27,129	13,629	28,337
Totals	108,647	139,639	101,656	152,190

Delaware Vote Since 1940

1940, Roosevelt, Dem., 74,559; Willkie, Rep., 61,440; Babson, Proh., 220; Thomas, Soc., 115.

1944, Roosevelt, Dem., 68,166; Dewey, Rep., 56,747; Watson, Proh., 294; Thomas, Soc., 154.

1948, Truman, Dem., 67,813; Dewey, Rep., 69,688; Wallace, Prog., 1,050; Watson, Proh., 343; Thomas, Soc., 250; Teichert, Soc. Labor, 29.

1952, Eisenhower, Rep., 90,059; Stevenson, Dem., 83,315; Hass, Soc. Labor, 242; Hamblen, Proh., 234; Hallinan, Prog., 155; Hoopes, Soc., 20.

1956, Eisenhower, Rep., 98,057; Stevenson, Dem., 79,421; Oltwick, Proh., 400; Hass, Soc. Labor, 110.

1960, Kennedy, Dem., 99,590; Nixon, Rep., 96,373; Faubus, States' Rights, 354; Decker, Proh., 284; Hass, Soc. Labor, 82.

1964, Johnson, Dem., 122,704; Goldwater, Rep., 78,078; Hass, Soc. Labor, 113; Munn, Proh., 425.

1968, Nixon, Rep., 96,714; Humphrey, Dem., 89,194; Wallace, 3d party, 28,459.

1972, Nixon, Rep., 140,357; McGovern, Dem., 92,283; Schmitz, Amer., 2,638; Munn, Proh., 238.

1976, Carter, Dem., 122,596; Ford, Rep., 109,831; McCarthy, non-partisan, 2,437; Anderson, Amer., 645; LaRouche, U.S. Labor, 136; Bubar, Proh., 103; Levin, Soc. Labor, 86.

1980, Reagan, Rep., 111,252; Carter, Dem., 105,754; Anderson, Ind., 16,288; Clark, Libertarian, 1,974; Greaves, American, 400.

1984, Reagan, Rep., 152,190; Mondale, Dem., 101,656; Bergland, Libertarian, 268.

1988, Bush, Rep., 139,639; Dukakis, Dem., 108,647; Paul, Lib., 1,162; Fulani, New Alliance, 443.

District of Columbia

County	1988 Dukakis (D)	Bush (R)	1984 Mondale (D)	Reagan (R)
Totals	159,407	27,590	180,408	29,009

District of Columbia Vote Since 1964

1964, Johnson, Dem., 169,796; Goldwater, Rep., 28,801.

1968, Nixon, Rep., 31,012; Humphrey, Dem., 139,566.

1972, Nixon, Rep., 35,226; McGovern, Dem., 127,627; Reed, Soc. Workers, 316; Hall, Com., 252.

1976, Carter, Dem., 137,818; Ford, Rep., 27,873; Camejo, Soc. Workers, 545; MacBride, Libertarian, 274; Hall, Com., 219; LaRouche, U.S. Labor, 157.

1980, Reagan, Rep., 23,313; Carter, Dem., 130,231; Anderson, Ind., 16,131; Commoner, Citizens, 1,826; Clark, Libertarian, 1,104; Hall, Com., 369; De Berry, Soc. Work., 173; Griswold, Workers World, 52; write-ins, 690.

1984, Mondale, Dem., 180,408; Reagan, Rep., 29,009; Bergland, Libertarian, 279.

1988, Bush, Rep., 27,590; Dukakis, Dem., 159,407; Fulani, New Alliance, 2,901; Paul, Lib., 554.

Florida

County	1988 Dukakis (D)	Bush (R)	1984 Mondale (D)	Reagan (R)
Alachua	29,375	30,124	26,551	30,582
Baker	1,353	3,414	1,381	3,485
Bay	11,582	31,712	9,381	29,322
Bradford	2,386	4,218	2,341	4,128
Brevard	42,967	104,721	36,963	102,339
Broward	218,211	220,196	194,542	254,501
Calhoun	1,329	2,420	1,312	2,493
Charlotte	15,967	28,879	11,303	27,464
Citrus	12,177	21,052	10,463	20,754
Clay	7,766	25,882	5,488	21,545
Collier	12,768	38,910	9,065	33,603
Columbia	4,072	7,759	4,261	8,807
Dade	216,847	270,672	223,793	324,216
De Soto	2,181	4,237	2,302	4,822
Dixie	1,366	2,027	1,224	2,204
Duval	74,832	127,875	77,459	128,653
Escambia	29,934	64,774	26,798	66,638
Flagler	4,241	6,494	2,999	4,907
Franklin	1,283	1,911	1,089	2,218
Gadsden	6,368	5,987	7,399	5,805
Gilchrist	1,137	1,854	1,051	2,056
Glades	1,034	1,546	1,070	1,987
Gulf	1,687	3,040	1,783	3,573
Hamilton	1,314	2,062	1,401	1,921
Hardee	1,688	3,636	1,536	3,957
Hendry	2,036	3,962	2,018	4,524
Hernando	15,432	21,179	12,204	21,273
Highlands	8,087	16,713	7,217	16,465
Hillsborough	98,969	150,065	86,189	157,827
Holmes	1,639	4,221	1,231	4,547

Indian River	10,447	24,619	8,731	23,694
Jackson	5,002	8,392	4,956	9,086
Jefferson	2,055	2,326	2,055	2,244
Lafayette	722	1,450	862	1,513
Lake	16,762	37,314	12,215	35,304
Lee	40,709	87,247	30,011	85,006
Leon	33,446	36,032	29,654	36,301
Levy	3,433	5,250	3,103	5,561
Liberty	709	1,419	649	1,409
Madison	1,950	2,556	2,101	2,816
Manatee	26,618	51,160	20,887	55,775
Marion	20,679	41,488	16,221	37,796
Martin	11,486	31,270	8,976	28,897
Monroe	10,151	15,919	7,771	16,316
Nassau	4,138	8,366	3,483	8,033
Okaloosa	9,726	40,295	7,289	36,963
Okeechobee	3,007	4,733	2,226	4,447
Orange	53,991	117,141	48,737	122,007
Osceola	9,811	21,350	6,627	18,344
Palm Beach	144,143	181,408	116,071	186,755
Pasco	50,369	63,788	40,961	66,609
Pinellas	152,374	210,971	128,547	240,535
Polk	38,236	77,065	35,505	84,174
Putnam	8,569	11,621	7,821	11,424
St. Johns	7,999	19,164	6,652	16,493
St. Lucie	17,427	32,241	13,039	28,189
Santa Rosa	5,251	18,948	4,646	21,237
Sarasota	42,095	84,585	30,512	87,713
Seminole	22,627	60,328	17,789	56,229
Sumter	3,900	5,933	3,460	6,252
Suwannee	3,126	5,859	2,788	6,079
Taylor	1,762	4,054	1,728	4,030
Union	691	1,643	761	1,804
Volusia	55,437	74,116	43,811	68,317
Wakulla	1,605	3,157	1,469	3,087
Walton	3,231	7,481	2,500	7,117
Washington	2,139	4,366	1,916	4,603
Totals	1,655,851	2,616,597	1,448,344	2,728,775

Florida Vote Since 1940

1940, Roosevelt, Dem., 359,334; Willkie, Rep., 126,158.

1944, Roosevelt, Dem., 339,377; Dewey, Rep., 143,215.

1948, Truman, Dem., 281,988; Dewey, Rep., 194,280; Thurmond, States' Rights, 89,755; Wallace, Prog., 11,620.

1952, Eisenhower, Rep., 544,036; Stevenson, Dem., 444,950; scattered, 351.

1956, Eisenhower, Rep., 643,849; Stevenson, Dem., 480,371.

1960, Kennedy, Dem., 748,700; Nixon, Rep., 795,476.

1964, Johnson, Dem., 948,540; Goldwater, Rep., 905,941.

1968, Nixon, Rep., 886,804; Humphrey, Dem., 676,794; Wallace, 3d party, 624,207.

1972, Nixon, Rep., 1,857,759; McGovern, Dem., 718,117; scattered, 7,407.

1976, Carter, Dem., 1,636,000; Ford, Rep., 1,469,531; McCarthy, Ind., 23,643; Anderson, Amer., 21,325.

1980, Reagan, Rep., 2,046,951; Carter, Dem., 1,419,475; Anderson, Ind., 189,692; Clark, Libertarian, 30,524; write-ins, 285.

1984, Reagan, Rep., 2,728,775; Mondale, Dem., 1,448,344.

1988, Bush, Rep., 2,616,597; Dukakis, Dem., 1,655,851; Paul, Lib., 19,796, Fulani, New Alliance, 6,655.

Georgia

	1988		1984	
	Dukakis	Bush	Mondale	Reagan
County	(D)	(R)	(D)	(R)
Appling	1,837	3,000	1,958	2,929
Atkinson	887	1,126	901	944
Bacon	780	1,407	1,010	1,778
Baker	707	629	691	675
Baldwin	4,008	5,852	3,853	5,717
Banks	984	1,590	1,063	1,549
Barrow	2,442	4,738	2,367	4,123
Bartow	4,884	8,039	4,780	7,104
Ben Hill	1,867	2,005	1,859	2,313
Berrien	1,381	2,030	1,670	2,395
Bibb	22,084	22,179	26,427	24,170
Bleckley	1,175	1,950	1,465	1,912
Brantley	1,450	1,539	1,517	1,679
Brooks	1,500	2,136	1,661	2,229
Bryan	1,423	2,802	1,398	2,265
Bulloch	3,417	6,354	3,644	6,117
Burke	2,861	2,988	3,127	3,137
Butts	1,730	2,184	1,820	2,141
Calhoun	901	644	1,077	776
Camden	2,090	2,913	2,164	2,841
Candler	877	1,261	1,014	1,497
Carroll	4,706	10,754	5,590	11,436
Catoosa	3,588	9,319	3,089	7,908
Charlton	943	1,327	1,111	1,368
Chatham	25,063	35,623	28,271	38,482
Chattahoochee	362	454	428	459
Chattooga	2,206	3,665	2,576	2,953

Cherokee	4,378	14,593	3,499	11,146
Clarke	11,154	11,150	10,132	11,503
Clay	595	398	750	419
Clayton	14,689	28,225	11,763	31,553
Clinch	594	863	625	862
Cobb	39,297	106,621	28,414	97,429
Coffee	2,777	4,019	2,633	4,200
Colquitt	2,998	5,653	3,208	5,815
Columbia	4,617	16,401	3,727	12,294
Cook	1,226	1,555	1,510	1,860
Coweta	4,212	9,668	3,650	7,981
Crawford	1,340	1,235	1,423	1,298
Crisp	1,690	2,916	2,128	2,895
Dade	1,120	2,539	1,150	2,750
Dawson	761	1,908	643	1,322
Decatur	2,348	3,866	2,656	4,134
DeKalb	92,521	90,179	77,329	104,697
Dodge	2,164	2,677	2,513	2,765
Dooly	1,613	1,386	1,726	1,435
Dougherty	12,579	15,520	12,904	16,920
Douglas	5,086	13,493	4,371	12,428
Early	1,359	1,918	1,494	2,239
Echols	245	422	227	453
Effingham	1,905	3,933	2,055	4,266
Elbert	2,118	2,796	2,670	3,366
Emanuel	2,387	3,530	2,458	3,920
Evans	1,023	1,707	1,193	1,601
Fannin	2,123	4,271	1,965	4,159
Fayette	4,593	16,443	2,861	12,575
Floyd	8,548	14,607	8,873	15,437
Forsyth	2,347	7,947	2,275	6,641
Franklin	1,842	2,615	1,838	2,549
Fulton	120,752	91,785	125,567	95,149
Gilmer	1,363	3,353	1,234	2,972
Glascock	210	580	317	827
Glynn	6,339	11,126	6,574	11,724
Gordon	2,369	6,051	2,607	5,566
Grady	1,883	2,989	2,261	3,866
Greene	1,818	1,432	1,992	1,599
Gwinnett	20,948	66,372	14,139	54,749
Habersham	2,114	4,871	2,125	4,647
Hall	7,782	17,415	7,421	15,076
Hancock	1,947	621	2,109	644
Haralson	2,404	4,529	1,938	3,945
Harris	1,905	3,414	2,096	3,138
Hart	2,476	3,044	2,496	2,842
Heard	874	1,551	810	1,492
Henry	4,348	10,882	4,096	9,142
Houston	8,664	15,748	9,226	14,255
Irwin	918	1,226	905	1,330
Jackson	2,607	4,407	2,717	4,202
Jasper	1,188	1,474	1,122	1,431
Jeff Davis	1,242	2,050	1,380	2,233
Jefferson	2,346	2,788	2,816	2,999
Jenkins	953	1,288	1,108	1,399
Johnson	927	1,567	1,199	1,733
Jones	2,662	3,618	2,781	3,401
Lamar	1,416	2,035	1,605	2,198
Lanier	698	725	741	852
Laurens	4,879	6,929	5,471	7,181
Lee	995	2,875	1,284	2,972
Liberty	2,906	3,100	2,803	3,229
Lincoln	893	1,417	1,115	1,357
Long	681	858	816	1,099
Lowndes	6,427	10,855	6,167	10,437
Lumpkin	1,286	2,688	1,110	1,991
McDuffie	1,704	3,231	2,006	3,284
McIntosh	1,527	1,273	1,796	1,512
Macon	2,268	1,412	2,521	1,515
Madison	1,639	3,724	1,690	3,768
Marion	844	804	951	846
Meriwether	2,934	3,101	2,864	3,195
Miller	515	1,105	526	1,348
Mitchell	2,260	2,590	2,791	2,737
Monroe	1,970	2,570	2,189	2,420
Montgomery	903	1,228	950	1,365
Morgan	1,508	2,108	1,714	2,301
Murray	1,679	3,996	1,649	3,521
Muscogee	18,772	23,058	20,835	23,816
Newton	3,111	5,809	3,389	5,810
Oconee	1,990	4,265	1,467	3,471
Oglethorpe	1,154	1,951	1,238	2,122
Paulding	2,717	7,329	2,621	6,048
Peach	2,972	2,782	3,369	2,652
Pickens	1,430	3,021	1,329	2,801
Pierce	1,558	1,947	1,501	1,978
Pike	1,176	2,074	1,203	1,855
Polk	2,977	5,454	3,262	5,435
Pulaski	1,476	1,400	1,440	1,509
Putnam	1,532	2,111	1,336	1,830
Quitman	436	296	490	361
Rabun	1,301	2,278	1,267	2,191
Randolph	1,369	1,319	1,454	1,578
Richmond	20,489	27,566	21,208	29,869
Rockdale	4,330	12,413	3,291	10,121
Schley	439	635	403	614
Screven	1,461	2,178	1,747	2,583
Seminole	1,171	1,469	1,350	1,636
Spalding	4,318	7,730	4,878	8,571
Stephens	2,185	4,329	2,272	4,057
Stewart	1,136	832	1,308	805

Sumter	3,332	4,289	3,725	4,607
Talbot	1,248	802	1,494	778
Taliaferro	469	306	550	318
Tattnall	1,694	3,172	1,954	3,641
Taylor	1,134	1,145	1,340	1,292
Telfair	1,765	1,805	2,049	1,980
Terrell	1,383	1,517	1,598	1,744
Thomas	3,530	6,572	4,039	6,427
Tift	2,446	4,760	2,736	4,429
Toombs	1,152	4,433	2,385	4,470
Towns	942	1,783	1,007	1,960
Treutlen	726	970	843	1,086
Troup	4,562	9,484	5,272	9,340
Turner	1,122	1,312	1,270	1,329
Twiggs	1,730	1,261	1,755	1,143
Union	1,258	2,396	1,112	1,914
Upson	2,666	4,614	2,943	4,803
Walker	4,753	10,487	5,000	10,734
Walton	3,091	5,974	2,481	4,995
Ware	4,292	4,819	4,435	5,547
Warren	1,091	897	1,258	1,087
Washington	2,615	2,752	3,034	2,887
Wayne	2,417	3,340	2,434	3,698
Webster	427	361	534	402
Wheeler	658	709	774	833
White	1,028	2,648	1,090	2,369
Whitfield	4,618	12,761	5,284	11,957
Wilcox	1,079	1,235	1,212	1,218
Wilkes	1,549	1,810	1,586	1,837
Wilkinson	1,831	1,546	2,102	1,756
Worth	1,311	2,668	1,685	2,910
Totals	714,792	1,081,331	706,628	1,068,722

Georgia Vote Since 1940

1940, Roosevelt, Dem., 265,194; Willkie, Rep., 23,934; Ind. Dem., 22,428; total, 46,362; Babson, Proh., 983.

1944, Roosevelt, Dem., 268,187; Dewey, Rep., 56,506; Watson, Proh., 36.

1948, Truman, Dem., 254,646; Dewey, Rep., 76,691; Thurmond, States' Rights, 85,055; Wallace, Prog., 1,636; Watson, Proh., 732.

1952, Eisenhower, Rep., 198,979; Stevenson, Dem., 456,823; Liberty Party, 1.

1956, Stevenson, Dem., 444,388; Eisenhower, Rep., 222,778; Andrews, Ind., write-in, 1,754.

1960, Kennedy, Dem., 458,638; Nixon, Rep., 274,472; write-in, 239.

1964, Johnson, Dem., 522,557; Goldwater, Rep., 616,600.

1968, Nixon, Rep., 380,111; Humphrey, Dem., 334,440; Wallace, 3d party, 535,550; write-in, 162.

1972, Nixon, Rep., 881,496; McGovern, Dem., 289,529; Schmitz, Amer., 2,288; scattered.

1976, Carter, Dem., 979,409; Ford, Rep., 483,743; write-in, 4,306.

1980, Reagan, Rep., 654,168; Carter, Dem., 890,955; Anderson, Ind., 36,055; Clark, Libertarian, 15,627.

1984, Reagan, Rep., 1,068,722; Mondale, Dem., 706,628.

1988, Bush, Rep., 1,081,331; Dukakis, Dem., 714,792; Paul, Lib., 8,435; Fulani, New Alliance, 5,099.

Hawaii

	1988		1984	
County	Dukakis (D)	Bush (R)	Mondale (D)	Reagan (R)
Hawaii	24,091	17,125	17,866	20,707
Honolulu	138,971	120,258	107,404	140,258
Kauai	11,770	8,298	8,862	9,249
Maui	17,532	12,944	12,966	14,720
Totals	192,364	158,625	147,098	184,934

Hawaii Vote Since 1960

1960, Kennedy, Dem., 92,410; Nixon, Rep., 92,295.

1964, Johnson, Dem., 163,249; Goldwater, Rep., 44,022.

1968, Nixon, Rep., 91,425; Humphrey, Dem., 141,324; Wallace, 3d party, 3,469.

1972, Nixon, Rep., 168,865; McGovern, Dem., 101,409.

1976, Carter, Dem., 147,375; Ford, Rep., 140,003; MacBride, Libertarian, 3,923.

1980, Reagan, Rep., 130,112; Carter, Dem., 135,879; Anderson, Ind., 32,021; Clark, Libertarian, 3,269; Commoner, Citizens, 1,548; Hall, Com., 458.

1984, Reagan, Rep., 184,934; Mondale, Dem., 147,098; Bergland, Libertarian, 2,167.

1988, Bush, Rep., 158,625; Dukakis, Dem., 192,364; Paul, Lib., 1,999; Fulani, New Alliance, 1,003.

Idaho

	1988		1984	
County	Dukakis (D)	Bush (R)	Mondale (D)	Reagan (R)
Ada	30,525	54,951	21,760	60,036
Adams	643	1,107	540	1,381
Bannock	13,074	14,986	9,399	18,742
Bear Lake	867	2,084	481	2,760
Benewah	1,518	1,650	1,447	2,039
Bingham	4,346	10,131	3,064	11,900
Blaine	2,498	3,130	1,971	3,603
Boise	620	1,044	436	1,249
Bonner	5,555	5,721	4,628	6,889
Bonneville	7,032	22,613	4,877	24,392
Boundary	1,336	1,800	1,158	2,159
Butte	521	899	429	1,245
Camas	136	288	123	364
Canyon	10,207	21,426	7,527	24,613
Caribou	867	2,239	535	3,032
Cassias	1,833	5,345	1,036	6,503
Clark	133	281	59	353
Clearwater	1,861	1,659	1,608	2,176
Custer	616	1,253	461	1,653
Elmore	2,078	3,756	1,458	4,595
Franklin	806	2,992	439	3,261
Fremont	1,178	3,401	818	4,006
Gem	2,064	2,926	1,607	3,644
Gooding	1,872	2,908	1,247	3,819
Idaho	2,198	3,541	1,996	4,219
Jefferson	1,198	5,295	743	5,770
Jerome	1,985	3,830	1,284	4,913
Kootenai	11,621	15,093	9,004	17,330
Latah	6,544	6,367	5,571	7,709
Lemhi	1,157	2,378	852	2,810
Lewis	807	786	648	1,000
Lincoln	574	918	386	1,211
Madison	1,009	6,197	483	6,798
Minidoka	2,290	4,623	1,398	5,938
Nez Perce	7,754	7,027	5,981	8,153
Oneida	508	1,269	360	1,528
Owyhee	848	1,707	574	2,141
Payette	1,900	3,786	1,410	4,605
Power	1,095	1,838	678	2,298
Shoshone	3,379	2,134	3,033	3,156
Teton	531	982	370	1,242
Twin Falls	7,078	13,243	4,567	16,974
Valley	1,251	1,897	945	2,299
Washington	1,359	2,380	1,119	3,015
Totals	147,272	253,881	108,510	297,523

Idaho Vote Since 1940

1940, Roosevelt, Dem., 127,842; Willkie, Rep., 106,553; Thomas, Soc., 497; Browder, Com., 276.

1944, Roosevelt, Dem., 107,399; Dewey, Rep., 100,137; Watson, Proh., 503; Thomas, Soc., 282.

1948, Truman, Dem., 107,370; Dewey, Rep., 101,514; Wallace, Prog., 4,972; Watson, Proh., 628; Thomas, Soc., 332.

1952, Eisenhower, Rep., 180,707; Stevenson Dem., 95,081; Hallinan, Prog., 443; write-in, 23.

1956, Eisenhower, Rep., 166,979; Stevenson, Dem., 105,868; Andrews, Ind., 126; write-in, 16.

1960, Kennedy, Dem., 138,853; Nixon, Rep., 161,597.

1964, Johnson, Dem., 148,920; Goldwater, Rep., 143,557.

1968, Nixon, Rep., 165,369; Humphrey, Dem., 89,273; Wallace, 3d party, 36,541.

1972, Nixon, Rep., 199,384; McGovern, Dem., 80,826; Schmitz, Amer., 28,869; Spock, Peoples, 903.

1976, Carter, Dem., 126,549; Ford, Rep., 204,151; Maddox, Amer., 5,935; MacBride, Libertarian, 3,558; LaRouche, U.S. Labor, 739.

1980, Reagan, Rep., 290,699; Carter, Dem., 110,192; Anderson, Ind., 27,058; Clark, Libertarian, 8,425; Rarick, Amer., 1,057.

1984, Reagan, Rep., 297,523; Mondale, Dem., 108,510; Bergland, Libertarian, 2,823.

1988, Bush, Rep., 253,881; Dukakis, Dem., 147,272; Paul, Lib., 5,313; Fulani, Ind., 2,502.

Illinois

	1988		1984	
County	Dukakis (D)	Bush (R)	Mondale (D)	Reagan (R)
Adams	13,768	15,831	10,336	20,225
Alexander	2,693	1,954	2,872	2,574
Bond	3,459	3,608	2,870	4,240
Boone	4,234	6,923	3,717	7,536
Brown	1,267	1,373	959	1,478
Bureau	7,354	8,896	6,925	11,741
Calhoun	1,544	1,238	1,443	1,648

County				
Carroll	2,990	4,464	2,398	5,237
Cass	3,316	2,916	2,937	3,435
Champaign	29,733	33,247	27,266	39,224
Christian	8,295	7,040	7,541	8,534
Clark	3,275	4,508	3,032	5,318
Clay	2,761	3,494	2,524	4,562
Clinton	5,935	7,681	4,628	9,233
Coles	8,327	11,043	7,156	14,044
Cook	1,129,973	878,582	1,112,641	1,055,558
Crawford	3,555	4,951	3,130	6,261
Cumberland	1,904	2,667	1,733	3,002
DeKalb	11,811	17,182	10,942	20,294
DeWitt	2,660	3,942	2,352	4,534
Douglas	3,184	4,378	2,886	5,691
DuPage	94,285	217,907	71,430	227,141
Edgar	3,880	5,538	3,241	6,821
Edwards	1,218	2,212	1,057	2,778
Effingham	4,553	8,431	3,841	9,617
Fayette	4,632	5,452	3,844	6,607
Ford	2,026	4,059	1,763	4,871
Franklin	11,023	7,677	10,667	9,656
Fulton	9,046	6,999	9,131	9,147
Gallatin	2,455	1,580	2,164	1,939
Greene	3,020	3,136	2,563	4,057
Grundy	5,525	8,743	4,671	9,595
Hamilton	2,618	2,622	2,251	3,074
Hancock	4,740	4,568	3,713	6,251
Hardin	1,308	1,504	1,205	1,689
Henderson	2,085	1,726	1,969	2,289
Henry	11,594	11,358	10,679	14,504
Iroquois	4,221	9,596	3,300	11,327
Jackson	11,334	9,687	12,105	13,609
Jasper	2,135	3,024	1,750	3,673
Jefferson	7,729	7,624	7,200	9,642
Jersey	4,376	4,343	3,762	5,146
JoDaviess	4,141	4,923	3,348	5,877
Johnson	1,872	2,797	1,647	3,424
Kane	36,366	66,283	31,875	72,655
Kankakee	15,147	20,316	15,246	23,807
Kendall	4,347	10,653	3,789	10,872
Knox	12,752	10,842	12,027	14,974
Lake	64,327	114,115	53,947	118,401
LaSalle	22,271	22,166	20,532	27,388
Lawrence	3,140	3,655	2,924	4,686
Lee	4,608	8,903	3,919	11,178
Livingston	5,009	10,324	4,567	12,291
Logan	4,727	8,490	4,052	9,932
McDonough	5,247	7,173	4,561	9,383
McHenry	18,919	46,135	14,420	47,282
McLean	18,659	30,572	15,880	32,221
Macon	25,364	23,862	25,463	30,457
Macoupin	12,195	9,362	10,602	12,282
Madison	54,175	44,907	48,352	57,021
Marion	8,592	8,695	7,599	11,300
Marshall	2,742	3,586	2,386	4,060
Mason	3,406	3,424	3,354	4,109
Massac	3,227	3,507	3,194	3,827
Menard	2,103	3,560	1,826	3,925
Mercer	4,204	3,683	3,982	4,907
Monroe	4,529	6,275	3,256	6,936
Montgomery	7,293	6,388	6,360	8,191
Morgan	6,032	8,808	5,361	10,683
Moultrie	3,013	3,167	2,458	3,593
Ogle	5,641	11,644	4,803	13,503
Peoria	35,253	37,605	36,830	45,607
Perry	5,167	4,576	4,584	5,852
Piatt	3,099	4,137	2,840	5,000
Pike	4,614	3,965	3,965	5,295
Pope	996	1,202	940	1,545
Pulaski	1,793	1,666	1,724	1,923
Putnam	1,601	1,516	1,487	1,912
Randolph	7,844	7,396	6,355	9,415
Richland	2,863	4,264	2,182	5,665
Rock Island	40,174	27,412	40,208	35,121
St. Clair	55,465	41,439	52,294	51,046
Saline	6,676	5,798	6,038	7,176
Sangamon	37,729	50,175	34,059	54,086
Schuyler	1,866	2,178	1,533	2,515
Scott	1,243	1,535	943	1,976
Shelby	4,650	5,370	4,317	6,372
Stark	1,274	1,841	1,072	2,228
Stephenson	7,460	11,342	6,723	14,237
Tazewell	24,603	28,861	23,095	33,782
Union	4,197	4,244	3,815	4,721
Vermilion	17,918	16,943	16,530	22,932
Wabash	2,241	3,453	1,795	3,639
Warren	3,617	4,584	3,318	5,846
Washington	2,689	4,127	2,363	5,129
Wayne	3,135	5,481	2,621	6,298
White	4,144	4,354	3,457	5,500
Whiteside	11,328	12,978	11,226	16,743
Will	49,816	73,129	45,193	78,684
Williamson	12,712	12,274	11,614	14,930
Winnebago	45,280	55,699	44,629	64,203
Woodford	4,604	9,474	4,425	10,758
Totals	2,215,940	2,310,939	2,086,499	2,707,103

Illinois Vote Since 1940

1940, Roosevelt, Dem., 2,149,934; Willkie, Rep., 2,047,240; Thomas, Soc., 10,914; Babson, Proh., 9,190.

1944, Roosevelt, Dem., 2,079,479; Dewey, Rep., 1,939,314; Teichert, Soc. Labor, 9,677; Watson, Proh., 7,411; Thomas, Soc., 180.

1948, Truman, Dem., 1,994,715; Dewey, Rep., 1,961,103; Watson, Proh., 11,959; Thomas, Soc., 11,522; Teichert, Soc. Labor, 3,118.

1952, Eisenhower, Rep., 2,457,327; Stevenson, Dem., 2,013,920; Hass, Soc. Labor, 9,363; write-in, 448.

1956, Eisenhower, Rep., 2,623,327; Stevenson, Dem., 1,775,682; Hass, Soc. Labor, 8,342; write-in, 56.

1960, Kennedy, Dem., 2,377,846; Nixon, Rep., 2,368,988; Hass, Soc. Labor, 10,560; write-in, 15.

1964, Johnson, Dem., 2,796,833; Goldwater, Rep., 1,905,946; write-in, 62.

1968, Nixon, Rep., 2,174,774; Humphrey, Dem., 2,039,814; Wallace, 3d party, 390,958; Blomen, Soc. Labor, 13,878; write-in, 325.

1972, Nixon, Rep. 2,788,179; McGovern, Dem., 1,913,472; Fisher, Soc. Labor, 12,344; Schmitz, Amer., 2,471; Hall, Com., 4,541; others, 2,229.

1976, Carter, Dem., 2,271,295; Ford, Rep., 2,364,269; McCarthy, Ind., 55,939; Hall, Com., 9,250; MacBride, Libertarian, 8,057; Camejo, Soc. Workers, 3,615; Levin, Soc. Labor, 2,422; LaRouche, U.S. Labor, 2,018; write-in, 1,968.

1980, Reagan, Rep., 2,358,049; Carter, Dem., 1,981,413; Anderson, Ind., 346,754; Clark, Libertarian, 38,939; Commoner, Citizens, 10,692; Hall, Com., 9,711; Griswold, Workers World, 2,257; DeBerry, Socialist Workers, 1,302; write-ins, 604.

1984, Reagan, Rep., 2,707,103; Mondale, Dem., 2,086,499; Bergland, Libertarian, 10,086.

1988, Bush, Rep., 2,310,939; Dukakis, Dem., 2,215,940; Paul, Lib., 14,944; Fulani, Solid., 10,276.

Indiana

County	1988		1984	
	Dukakis (D)	Bush (R)	Mondale (D)	Reagan (R)
Adams	3,811	8,137	3,923	7,958
Allen	39,238	74,638	38,462	75,505
Bartholomew	8,804	17,364	8,075	18,704
Benton	1,349	2,698	1,357	3,281
Blackford	2,253	3,336	2,395	3,787
Boone	4,168	11,608	3,982	11,790
Brown	2,115	3,348	2,657	3,517
Carroll	2,952	4,981	2,774	5,528
Cass	5,784	10,970	5,521	12,355
Clark	14,528	16,544	14,138	19,419
Clay	3,724	5,852	3,707	6,957
Clinton	4,412	8,570	4,329	8,969
Crawford	2,036	2,532	2,256	2,633
Daviess	3,483	6,768	3,545	7,721
Dearborn	5,066	8,195	4,920	9,149
Decatur	2,979	6,245	2,766	6,551
Dekalb	4,657	9,018	4,617	8,769
Delaware	20,548	27,348	19,791	30,092
Dubois	5,954	9,995	5,423	9,391
Elkhart	14,236	33,793	13,240	34,621
Fayette	4,118	5,949	4,122	7,142
Floyd	11,024	14,291	10,616	15,466
Fountain	3,279	5,113	2,897	5,450
Franklin	2,472	4,777	2,225	5,202
Fulton	2,788	5,234	2,527	6,057
Gibson	7,031	7,610	7,082	8,618
Grant	10,799	18,441	9,986	20,482
Greene	5,979	7,689	5,267	8,438
Hamilton	8,853	36,654	6,364	30,254
Hancock	5,355	13,374	4,550	12,880
Harrison	4,933	6,702	4,634	7,255
Hendricks	7,643	22,090	6,659	21,307
Henry	7,779	11,280	7,064	11,926
Howard	11,518	19,971	10,458	22,386
Huntington	3,873	11,675	4,598	10,805
Jackson	5,550	9,470	5,163	9,879
Jasper	3,237	6,009	2,821	6,537
Jay	3,212	5,363	3,174	5,975
Jefferson	5,221	6,949	4,952	7,482
Jennings	3,667	5,636	3,264	6,356
Johnson	9,001	24,654	7,715	23,482
Knox	7,006	9,813	6,417	10,872
Kosciusko	5,321	17,761	4,877	17,560
LaGrange	2,029	4,495	1,884	4,172
Lake	105,026	79,929	117,984	94,870
LaPorte	17,585	20,537	15,904	22,346
Lawrence	5,787	10,742	5,608	11,440
Madison	24,443	32,596	22,254	36,510
Marion	128,627	184,519	130,185	184,880
Marshall	5,488	10,490	4,931	11,100
Martin	2,132	3,066	1,937	3,363

Miami.	4,613	8,533	4,224	9,551
Monroe.	15,855	20,756	14,719	21,772
Montgomery.	3,623	10,793	3,626	11,119
Morgan.	5,375	14,284	4,627	14,884
Newton.	1,744	3,274	1,596	3,560
Noble.	4,143	7,889	4,237	8,459
Ohio.	1,113	1,412	1,068	1,503
Orange.	2,739	5,245	D2,571	5,909
Owen.	2,484	3,837	2,082	4,204
Parke.	2,563	4,458	2,205	5,052
Perry.	4,804	4,720	4,760	4,785
Pike.	3,037	3,294	3,231	3,689
Porter.	19,390	29,790	17,862	32,505
Posey.	4,468	5,987	4,452	6,472
Pulaski.	2,213	3,677	2,008	4,167
Putnam.	3,850	7,119	3,392	7,820
Randolph.	3,990	6,856	3,805	7,793
Ripley.	3,605	6,414	3,336	7,143
Rush.	2,451	5,112	2,307	5,429
St. Joseph.	48,056	49,481	47,513	54,404
Scott.	3,378	3,455	3,460	4,110
Shelby.	5,382	10,176	5,357	11,056
Spencer.	4,061	4,964	4,005	5,816
Starke.	4,104	4,458	3,674	5,104
Steuben.	3,114	6,855	2,441	6,424
Sullivan.	4,320	4,246	4,006	4,771
Switzerland.	1,479	1,572	1,484	1,857
Tippecanoe.	16,256	27,897	15,789	29,706
Tipton.	2,485	5,148	2,328	5,687
Union.	946	1,814	816	1,970
Vanderburgh.	31,270	38,928	31,049	40,994
Vermillion.	4,044	3,674	3,666	4,428
Vigo.	19,192	21,929	18,429	26,259
Wabash.	4,168	9,153	4,077	9,862
Warren.	1,542	2,243	1,309	2,525
Warrick.	7,999	10,504	6,345	10,202
Washington.	3,370	4,998	3,334	5,874
Wayne.	10,209	16,388	10,173	18,955
Wells.	3,437	7,712	3,274	7,579
White.	3,256	6,220	3,157	7,279
Whitley.	3,642	7,679	3,690	7,763
Totals.	860,643	1,297,763	841,481	1,377,230

Indiana Vote Since 1940

1940, Roosevelt, Dem., 874,063; Willkie, Rep., 899,466; Babson, Proh., 6,437; Thomas, Soc., 2,075; Aiken, Soc. Labor, 706.

1944, Roosevelt, Dem., 781,403; Dewey, Rep., 875,891; Watson, Proh., 12,574; Thomas, Soc., 2,223.

1948, Truman, Dem., 807,833; Dewey, Rep., 821,079; Watson, Proh., 14,711; Wallace, Prog., 9,649; Thomas, Soc., 2,179; Teichert, Soc. Labor, 763.

1952, Eisenhower, Rep., 1,136,259; Stevenson, Dem., 801,530; Hamblen, Proh., 15,335; Hallinan, Prog., 1,222; Hass, Soc. Labor, 979.

1956, Eisenhower, Rep., 1,182,811; Stevenson, Dem., 783,908; Holtwick, Proh., 6,554; Hass, Soc. Labor, 1,334.

1960, Kennedy, Dem., 952,358; Nixon, Rep., 1,175,120; Decker, Proh., 6,746; Hass, Soc. Labor, 1,136.

1964, Johnson, Dem. 1,170,848; Goldwater, Rep., 911,118; Munn, Proh., 8,266; Hass, Soc. Labor, 1,374.

1968, Nixon, Rep., 1,067,885; Humphrey, Dem., 806,659; Wallace, 3d party, 243,108; Munn, Proh., 4,616; Halstead, Soc. Worker, 1,293; Gregory, write-in, 36.

1972, Nixon, Rep., 1,405,154; McGovern, Dem., 708,568; Reed, Soc. Workers, 5,575; Fisher, Soc. Labor, 1,688; Spock, Peace & Freedom, 4,544.

1976, Carter, Dem., 1,014,714; Ford, Rep., 1,185,958; Anderson, Amer., 14,048; Camejo, Soc. Workers, 5,695; LaRouche, U.S. Labor, 1,947.

1980 Reagan, Rep., 1,255,656; Carter, Dem., 844,197; Anderson, Ind., 111,639; Clark, Libertarian, 19,627; Commoner, Citizens, 4,852; Greaves, American, 4,750; Hall, Com., 702; DeBerry, Soc., 610.

1984 Reagan, Rep., 1,377,230; Mondale, Dem., 841,481; Bergland, Libertarian, 6,741.

1988, Bush, Rep., 1,297,763; Dukakis, Dem., 860,643; Fulani, New Alliance, 10,215.

Iowa

	1988		1984	
County	Dukakis (D)	Bush (R)	Mondale (D)	Reagan (R)
Adair	2,261	1,833	1,979	2,615
Adams	1,283	1,080	1,221	1,706
Allamakee	2,768	3,186	2,282	3,997
Appanoose	3,209	2,779	3,289	3,412
Audubon	1,863	1,478	1,854	2,306
Benton	5,873	4,011	4,993	5,566

Black Hawk	31,657	24,112	31,467	32,262
Boone	7,232	4,381	6,485	5,746
Bremer	4,961	5,079	4,084	6,895
Buchanan	4,778	3,495	4,129	4,965
Buena Vista	4,580	4,170	4,109	5,193
Butler	2,593	3,523	2,323	4,570
Calhoun	2,990	2,474	2,541	3,311
Carroll	5,437	3,701	4,960	5,021
Cass	2,934	3,962	2,417	5,053
Cedar	4,032	3,373	3,086	4,617
Cerro Gordo	12,857	9,358	11,570	11,214
Cherokee	3,574	3,218	3,349	4,046
Chickasaw	3,530	2,549	3,186	3,661
Clarke	2,262	1,631	2,030	2,262
Clay	4,173	3,641	3,774	4,450
Clayton	4,320	3,839	3,446	5,029
Clinton	12,549	10,243	11,240	13,914
Crawford	3,868	3,375	3,396	4,552
Dallas	7,501	4,858	6,564	6,080
Davis	2,246	1,563	2,187	1,956
Decatur	2,192	1,406	2,098	2,104
Delaware	3,947	3,425	3,158	4,769
Des Moines	11,593	7,652	11,173	9,559
Dickinson	3,342	3,678	3,025	4,064
Dubuque	23,797	14,530	21,876	19,239
Emmet	2,778	2,173	2,746	2,946
Fayette	5,304	4,921	4,677	6,505
Floyd	4,377	3,266	4,154	4,341
Franklin	2,594	2,320	2,349	3,129
Fremont	1,547	1,946	1,426	2,686
Greene	3,011	2,091	2,831	2,579
Grundy	2,211	3,433	1,915	4,527
Guthrie	2,910	2,005	2,517	2,783
Hamilton	4,156	3,277	3,330	4,279
Hancock	2,831	2,731	2,539	3,362
Hardin	5,088	3,856	4,477	5,195
Harrison	2,883	3,108	2,495	4,352
Henry	3,754	3,951	3,377	4,516
Howard	2,330	1,970	2,135	2,718
Humboldt	2,713	2,594	2,406	3,396
Ida	1,787	1,951	1,559	2,618
Iowa	3,338	3,247	2,815	4,352
Jackson	4,864	3,237	4,400	4,811
Jasper	8,940	6,703	8,023	8,576
Jefferson	3,594	3,614	2,961	4,727
Johnson	28,759	15,453	26,000	18,677
Jones	4,641	3,496	3,825	4,907
Keokuk	2,899	2,278	2,649	2,913
Kossuth	5,088	3,938	4,838	4,872
Lee	10,911	6,228	8,912	8,756
Linn	42,993	33,129	38,528	41,061
Louisa	2,268	2,060	1,927	2,623
Lucas	2,454	1,776	2,422	2,630
Lyon	1,706	3,517	1,401	4,178
Madison	3,421	2,410	3,067	3,168
Mahaska	4,451	4,798	4,107	6,086
Marion	6,922	5,914	6,313	7,259
Marshall	9,760	7,657	8,809	10,839
Mills	2,092	3,212	1,434	3,994
Mitchell	2,870	2,338	2,531	3,144
Monona	2,408	2,068	2,159	2,746
Monroe	2,338	1,313	2,342	1,927
Montgomery	1,898	3,166	1,661	4,224
Muscatine	7,059	6,904	5,986	9,069
O'Brien	2,768	4,241	2,479	5,008
Osceola	1,277	1,951	1,146	2,285
Page	2,185	4,583	1,914	5,876
Palo Alto	3,377	2,041	3,018	2,715
Plymouth	4,220	5,316	3,464	6,482
Pocahontas	2,722	1,871	2,481	2,627
Polk	84,476	57,854	75,413	71,413
Pottawattamie	14,958	17,193	12,329	21,527
Poweshiek	4,876	3,683	4,103	4,715
Ringgold	1,609	1,110	1,593	1,512
Sac	2,613	2,411	2,363	3,298
Scott	34,415	31,025	32,550	38,034
Shelby	2,806	3,019	2,291	4,200
Sioux	2,923	10,270	2,585	11,665
Story	19,051	13,782	18,277	19,804
Tama	4,584	3,362	4,061	4,882
Taylor	1,671	1,647	1,499	2,496
Union	3,236	2,751	2,875	3,583
Van Buren	1,612	1,692	1,606	2,138
Wapello	10,177	5,350	10,545	7,098
Warren	9,627	6,424	8,171	8,277
Washington	3,776	3,741	3,079	4,613
Wayne	1,988	1,467	1,927	2,061
Webster	10,267	6,926	9,930	9,619
Winnebago	2,804	2,863	2,669	3,616
Winneshiek	4,443	4,194	3,724	5,277
Woodbury	20,153	18,790	18,951	23,002
Worth	2,440	1,488	2,263	1,985
Wright	3,353	2,658	2,980	3,675
Totals	670,557	545,355	605,620	703,088

Iowa Vote Since 1940

1940, Roosevelt, Dem., 578,800; Willkie, Rep., 632,370; Babson, Proh., 2,284; Browder, Com., 1,524; Aiken, Soc. Labor, 452.

1944, Roosevelt, Dem., 499,876; Dewey, Rep., 547,267; Watson, Proh., 3,752; Thomas, Soc., 1,511; Teichert, Soc. Labor, 193.

1948, Truman, Dem., 522,380; Dewey, Rep., 494,018; Wallace, Prog., 12,125; Teichert, Soc. Labor, 4,274; Watson, Proh., 3,382; Thomas, Soc., 1,829; Dobbs, Soc. Workers, 26.

1952, Eisenhower, Rep., 808,906; Stevenson, Dem., 451,513; Hallinan, Prog., 5,085; Hamblen, Proh., 2,882; Hoopes, Soc., 219; Hass, Soc. Labor, 139; scattering 29.

1956, Eisenhower, Rep., 729,187; Stevenson, Dem., 501,858; Andrews (A.C.P. of Iowa), 3,202; Hoopes, Soc., 192; Hass, Soc. Labor, 125.

1960, Kennedy, Dem., 550,565; Nixon, Rep., 722,381; Hass, Soc. Labor, 230; write-in, 634.

1964, Johnson, Dem., 733,030; Goldwater, Rep., 449,148; Hass, Soc. Labor, 182; DeBerry, Soc. Worker, 159; Munn, Proh., 1,902.

1968, Nixon, Rep., 619,106; Humphrey, Dem., 476,699; Wallace, 3d party, 66,422; Munn, Proh., 362; Halstead, Soc. Worker, 3,377; Cleaver, Peace and Freedom, 1,332; Blomen, Soc. Labor, 241.

1972, Nixon, Rep., 706,207; McGovern, Dem., 496,206; Schmitz, Amer., 22,056; Jenness, Soc. Workers, 488; Fisher, Soc. Labor, 195; Hall, Com. 272; Green, Universal, 199; scattered, 321.

1976, Carter, Dem., 619,931; Ford, Rep., 632,863; McCarthy, Ind., 20,051; Anderson, Amer., 3,040; MacBride, Libertarian, 1,452.

1980, Reagan, Rep., 676,026; Carter, Dem., 508,672; Anderson, Ind., 115,633; Clark, Libertarian, 13,123; Commoner, Citizens, 2,273; McReynolds, Socialist, 534; Hall Com., 298; DeBerry, Soc. Work., 244; Greaves, American, 189; Bubar, Statesman, 150; scattering, 519.

1984, Reagan, Rep., 703,088; Mondale, Dem., 605,620; Bergland, Libertarian, 1,844.

1988, Bush, Rep., 545,355; Dukakis, Dem., 670,557; LaRouche, Ind., 3,526; Paul, Lib., 2,494.

Kansas

County	1988 Dukakis (D)	1988 Bush (R)	1984 Mondale (D)	1984 Reagan (R)
Allen	2,392	3,429	1,779	4,266
Anderson	1,466	1,781	1,155	2,462
Atchison	3,177	3,243	2,641	4,536
Barber	1,118	1,539	805	2,111
Barton	5,024	7,741	3,111	10,234
Bourbon	2,623	3,660	2,174	4,856
Brown	1,719	3,059	1,303	3,894
Butler	7,690	10,976	6,352	12,920
Chase	538	884	393	1,162
Chautauqua	661	1,247	497	1,688
Cherokee	4,069	4,281	3,663	5,081
Cheyenne	594	1,105	356	1,442
Clark	409	876	324	1,075
Clay	1,112	2,997	919	3,559
Cloud	2,022	3,043	1,878	3,856
Coffey	1,246	2,581	1,037	3,063
Comanche	375	738	285	993
Cowley	6,186	7,778	5,153	9,930
Crawford	7,783	6,940	6,722	9,518
Decatur	793	1,291	467	1,769
Dickinson	2,870	5,121	2,168	6,487
Doniphan	1,312	2,162	952	2,818
Douglas	15,752	16,149	12,877	18,804
Edwards	792	993	606	1,352
Elk	608	1,075	452	1,301
Ellis	5,289	5,194	3,457	7,509
Ellsworth	1,219	1,711	905	2,353
Finney	3,408	5,381	2,398	6,943
Ford	3,817	5,685	2,914	6,738
Franklin	3,592	4,777	2,524	6,283
Geary	2,721	3,782	2,301	4,475
Gove	663	966	426	1,310
Graham	702	1,139	480	1,423
Grant	907	1,654	615	2,043
Gray	696	1,180	514	1,580
Greeley	317	506	227	699
Greenwood	1,421	2,217	1,173	2,900
Hamilton	517	801	408	1,037
Harper	1,235	1,941	893	2,696
Harvey	5,503	6,893	4,599	8,507
Haskell	427	964	281	1,151
Hodgeman	439	732	306	939
Jackson	2,261	2,759	1,667	3,464
Jefferson	2,810	3,605	1,990	4,524
Jewell	684	1,546	583	1,992
Johnson	55,183	95,591	37,782	101,042

County	Dukakis (D)	Bush (R)	Mondale (D)	Reagan (R)
Kearny	524	1,073	321	1,214
Kingman	1,420	2,205	1,047	2,826
Kiowa	485	1,276	361	1,537
Labette	4,433	5,125	3,631	6,542
Lane	450	768	282	1,008
Leavenworth	8,797	9,913	6,583	11,018
Lincoln	796	1,229	551	1,723
Linn	1,497	2,163	1,152	2,794
Logan	503	988	331	1,235
Lyon	5,314	6,820	4,188	9,796
McPherson	4,354	6,563	3,185	8,630
Marion	2,024	3,685	1,633	4,407
Marshall	2,560	3,140	1,813	4,097
Meade	664	1,322	491	1,804
Miami	4,427	4,807	3,076	5,877
Mitchell	1,145	2,257	919	3,036
Montgomery	5,429	9,067	4,933	12,023
Morris	1,165	1,682	820	2,240
Morton	569	1,074	322	1,353
Nemaha	2,261	2,849	1,761	3,653
Neosho	3,402	3,739	2,679	4,968
Ness	687	1,230	539	1,779
Norton	855	1,923	611	2,515
Osage	2,840	3,496	2,072	4,288
Osborne	943	1,541	686	2,171
Ottawa	953	1,836	698	2,343
Pawnee	1,474	1,825	1,092	2,570
Phillips	960	2,316	626	2,810
Pottawatomie	2,544	3,897	1,798	4,596
Pratt	1,651	2,505	1,253	3,240
Rawlins	612	1,318	412	1,625
Reno	11,545	12,753	9,229	16,621
Republic	1,069	2,346	966	2,974
Rice	2,033	2,503	1,559	3,598
Riley	7,283	9,507	5,974	11,306
Rooks	1,012	1,938	699	2,604
Rush	1,020	1,045	718	1,758
Russell	1,448	2,403	1,055	3,673
Saline	7,998	11,371	6,527	15,242
Scott	717	1,590	427	2,017
Sedgwick	65,618	86,124	55,060	95,972
Seward	1,655	4,089	1,198	5,047
Shawnee	33,940	35,489	26,307	43,435
Sheridan	600	901	429	1,274
Sherman	1,082	1,929	714	2,702
Smith	1,004	1,951	684	2,330
Stafford	1,121	1,532	844	2,062
Stanton	310	592	205	783
Stevens	612	1,642	386	1,862
Summer	4,417	5,394	3,713	6,942
Thomas	1,408	2,342	887	3,106
Trego	795	979	598	1,491
Wabaunsee	1,166	1,737	805	2,276
Wallace	257	655	152	838
Washington	1,063	2,269	889	2,979
Wichita	399	721	232	916
Wilson	1,545	2,743	1,343	3,660
Woodson	761	1,062	596	1,408
Wyandotte	38,678	19,097	35,887	27,267
Totals	422,636	554,049	332,471	674,646

Kansas Vote Since 1940

1940, Roosevelt, Dem., 364,725; Willkie, Rep., 489,169; Babson, Proh., 4,056; Thomas, Soc., 2,347.

1944, Roosevelt, Dem., 287,458; Dewey, Rep., 442,096; Watson, Proh., 2,609; Thomas, Soc., 1,613.

1948, Truman, Dem., 351,902; Dewey, Rep., 423,039; Watson, Proh., 6,468; Wallace, Prog., 4,603; Thomas, Soc., 2,807.

1952, Eisenhower, Rep., 616,302; Stevenson, Dem., 273,296; Hamblen, Proh., 6,038; Hoopes, Soc., 530.

1956, Eisenhower, Rep., 566,878; Stevenson, Dem., 296,317; Holtwick, Proh., 3,048.

1960, Kennedy, Dem., 363,213; Nixon, Rep., 561,474; Decker, Proh., 4,138.

1964, Johnson, Dem., 464,028; Goldwater, Rep., 386,579; Munn, Proh., 5,393; Hass, Soc. Labor, 1,901.

1968, Nixon, Rep., 478,674; Humphrey, Dem., 302,996; Wallace, 3d, 88,921; Munn, Proh., 2,192.

1972, Nixon, Rep., 619,812; McGovern, Dem., 270,287; Schmitz, Cons., 21,808; Munn, Proh., 4,188.

1976, Carter, Dem., 430,421; Ford, Rep., 502,752; McCarthy, Ind., 13,185; Anderson, Amer., 4,724; MacBride, Libertarian, 3,242; Maddox, Cons., 2,118; Bubar, Proh., 1,403.

1980, Reagan, Rep., 566,812; Carter, Dem., 326,150; Anderson, Ind., 68,231; Clark, Libertarian, 14,470; Shelton, American, 1,555; Hall, Com., 967; Bubar, Statesman, 821; Rarick, Conservative, 789.

1984, Reagan, Rep., 674,646; Mondale, Dem., 332,471; Bergland, Libertarian, 3,585.

1988, Bush, Rep., 554,049; Dukakis, Dem., 422,636; Paul, Ind., 12,553; Fulani, Ind., 3,806.

Kentucky

County	1988 Dukakis (D)	1988 Bush (R)	1984 Mondale (D)	1984 Reagan (R)
Adair	1,723	4,346	1,812	4,500
Allen	1,573	3,342	1,521	3,427
Anderson	2,176	3,225	1,717	3,425
Ballard	2,162	1,460	2,002	1,663
Barren	4,799	6,653	4,503	7,717
Bath	2,099	1,614	1,781	2,020
Bell	5,182	5,759	5,490	7,249
Boone	5,382	12,667	4,853	12,690
Bourbon	2,793	3,308	2,649	3,936
Boyd	9,552	9,379	9,601	10,925
Boyle	3,575	4,746	3,378	5,675
Bracken	1,176	1,630	1,136	1,812
Breathitt	3,387	2,149	3,435	2,855
Breckinridge	2,765	3,841	2,669	4,432
Bullitt	6,005	8,859	6,005	9,556
Butler	1,245	3,278	1,055	3,121
Caldwell	2,564	2,952	2,427	3,162
Calloway	5,287	6,225	5,028	6,442
Campbell	9,553	19,387	9,068	21,473
Carlisle	1,428	1,104	1,277	1,308
Carroll	1,913	1,702	1,564	1,824
Carter	4,570	4,325	3,985	4,656
Casey	1,216	3,857	1,122	4,356
Christian	5,704	9,250	5,432	10,708
Clark	4,252	5,329	3,595	6,130
Clay	1,709	4,156	1,634	4,772
Clinton	899	3,248	838	3,459
Crittenden	1,443	2,211	1,483	2,167
Cumberland	753	2,231	766	2,729
Daviess	14,815	17,356	13,347	19,495
Edmonson	1,243	2,555	1,200	3,001
Elliott	1,797	550	1,683	601
Estill	1,692	3,077	1,593	3,512
Fayette	32,554	48,065	28,961	51,993
Fleming	2,086	2,409	1,616	2,824
Floyd	12,327	5,296	10,259	5,218
Franklin	9,271	9,805	7,790	11,057
Fulton	1,531	1,474	1,534	1,780
Gallatin	1,060	881	1,042	1,042
Garrard	1,710	2,681	1,566	3,284
Grant	1,896	2,835	1,685	2,840
Graves	7,153	6,274	6,759	7,287
Grayson	2,575	5,186	2,200	5,524
Green	1,595	3,139	1,611	3,210
Greenup	6,956	6,559	6,923	7,451
Hancock	1,478	1,733	1,287	1,967
Hardin	7,262	13,240	6,329	14,293
Harlan	7,341	5,166	7,663	6,959
Harrison	2,748	2,983	2,405	3,467
Hart	2,519	2,927	2,278	3,065
Henderson	7,648	6,911	6,795	7,389
Henry	2,544	2,286	2,279	2,802
Hickman	1,158	1,142	1,049	1,380
Hopkins	7,453	7,979	6,743	9,368
Jackson	678	3,926	542	3,806
Jefferson	127,936	139,711	119,350	161,283
Jessamine	2,955	7,057	2,379	7,081
Johnson	3,538	4,619	3,078	5,225
Kenton	14,838	30,738	14,642	34,304
Knott	5,185	1,691	4,487	1,728
Knox	2,919	4,903	2,932	5,730
Larue	1,822	2,590	1,514	2,873
Laurel	3,620	9,296	3,267	9,621
Lawrence	2,198	2,294	2,223	2,713
Lee	984	1,588	768	1,862
Leslie	1,105	3,280	1,075	3,385
Letcher	4,697	3,601	4,153	3,676
Lewis	1,568	3,108	1,484	3,445
Lincoln	2,677	3,530	2,498	3,996
Livingston	2,052	1,834	2,007	1,866
Logan	3,379	4,295	3,347	4,889
Lyon	1,337	1,077	1,272	969
McCracken	12,208	12,160	12,535	12,903
McCreary	1,644	3,477	1,909	4,028
McLean	2,269	1,829	1,917	1,942
Madison	6,672	9,956	6,509	11,309
Magoffin	2,895	2,138	2,942	2,343
Marion	3,152	2,500	2,835	3,305
Marshall	5,888	5,256	5,725	5,152
Martin	1,581	2,587	1,471	3,248
Mason	2,721	3,158	2,663	2,751
Meade	3,079	3,441	2,503	3,820
Menifee	1,096	670	956	785
Mercer	2,832	3,904	2,516	4,592
Metcalfe	1,705	2,179	1,575	2,349
Monroe	1,025	4,214	1,052	4,670
Montgomery	3,082	3,435	2,490	3,864
Morgan	2,329	1,452	2,481	1,834
Muhlenberg	6,912	5,369	6,157	6,094
Nelson	4,788	5,283	4,199	6,044
Nicholas	1,242	1,271	1,107	1,535
Ohio	3,612	4,910	3,253	5,119
Oldham	4,025	8,716	2,857	8,112
Owen	1,823	1,468	1,575	1,735
Owsley	345	1,266	375	1,466
Pendleton	1,576	2,487	1,529	2,767
Perry	5,557	5,154	5,258	5,218
Pike	16,339	9,976	15,817	11,869
Powell	2,113	2,128	1,575	2,269
Pulaski	4,788	13,482	4,384	14,434
Robertson	515	511	467	567
Rockcastle	1,041	3,880	1,089	4,328
Rowan	2,968	3,093	2,748	3,698
Russell	1,455	4,292	1,448	4,476
Scott	3,380	4,482	2,606	4,461
Shelby	3,834	4,998	3,326	5,390
Simpson	2,138	2,699	2,140	3,073
Spencer	1,121	1,368	910	1,456
Taylor	2,879	5,362	3,286	5,932
Todd	1,632	2,282	1,505	2,364
Trigg	1,991	2,427	1,905	2,512
Trimble	1,342	1,083	1,088	1,389
Union	3,316	2,292	3,090	2,524
Warren	9,684	16,703	7,937	16,167
Washington	1,950	2,445	1,786	2,804
Wayne	2,057	3,672	2,277	4,449
Webster	3,019	2,159	3,042	2,504
Whitley	3,794	7,337	3,575	7,851
Wolfe	1,516	916	1,394	1,257
Woodford	2,653	4,512	2,290	4,746
Totals	580,368	734,281	536,756	815,345

Kentucky Vote Since 1940

1940, Roosevelt, Dem., 557,222; Willkie, Rep., 410,384; Babson, Proh., 1,443; Thomas, Soc., 1,014.

1944, Roosevelt, Dem., 472,589; Dewey, Rep., 392,448; Watson, Proh., 2,023; Thomas, Soc., 535; Teichert, Soc. Labor, 326.

1948, Truman, Dem., 466,756; Dewey, Rep., 341,210; Thurmond, States' Rights, 10,411; Wallace, Prog., 1,567; Thomas, Soc., 1,284; Watson, Proh., 1,245; Teichert, Soc. Labor, 185.

1952, Eisenhower, Rep., 495,029; Stevenson, Dem., 495,729; Hamblen, Proh., 1,161; Hass, Soc. Labor, 893; Hallinan, Proh., 336.

1956, Eisenhower, Rep., 572,192; Stevenson, Dem., 476,453; Byrd, States' Rights, 2,657; Holtwick, Proh., 2,145; Hass, Soc. Labor, 358.

1960, Kennedy, Dem., 521,855; Nixon, Rep., 602,607.

1964, Johnson, Dem., 669,659; Goldwater, Rep., 372,977; John Kasper, Nat'l. States Rights, 3,469.

1968, Nixon, Rep., 462,411; Humphrey, Dem., 397,547; Wallace, 3d p., 193,098; Halstead, Soc. Worker, 2,843.

1972, Nixon, Rep., 676,446; McGovern, Dem., 371,159; Schmitz, Amer., 17,627; Jenness, Soc. Workers, 685; Hall, Com., 464; Spock, Peoples, 1,118.

1976, Carter, Dem., 615,717; Ford, Rep., 531,852; Anderson, Amer., 8,308; McCarthy, Ind., 6,837; Maddox, Amer. Ind., 2,328; MacBride, Libertarian, 814.

1980, Reagan, Rep., 635,274; Carter, Dem., 616,417; Anderson, Ind., 31,127; Clark, Libertarian, 5,531; McCormack, Respect For Life, 4,233; Commoner, Citizens, 1,304; Pulley, Socialist, 393; Hall, Com., 348.

1984, Reagan, Rep., 815,345; Mondale, Dem., 536,756.

1988, Bush, Rep., 734,281; Dukakis, Dem., 580,368; Duke, Pop., 4,494; Paul, Lib., 2,118.

Louisiana

Parish	1988 Dukakis (D)	1988 Bush (R)	1984 Mondale (D)	1984 Reagan (R)
Acadia	11,510	11,319	9,262	14,906
Allen	5,204	3,674	4,842	4,474
Ascension	12,147	10,726	11,048	11,945
Assumption	5,610	4,017	4,660	5,433
Avoyelles	7,353	7,659	6,808	9,402
Beauregard	4,704	6,466	4,199	7,353
Bienville	3,705	3,680	3,530	4,587
Bossier	9,035	20,807	7,006	22,638
Caddo	39,204	54,498	35,727	63,429
Calcasieu	33,932	29,649	33,214	35,566
Caldwell	1,423	2,997	1,348	3,341
Cameron	2,257	1,775	1,608	2,265
Catahoula	1,916	2,862	1,649	3,640
Claiborne	3,158	3,756	2,788	4,349
Concordia	3,461	5,037	3,332	6,177
DeSoto	5,366	5,022	4,642	5,989
E. Baton Rouge	59,270	86,791	56,673	95,704
East Carroll	1,809	1,536	2,089	1,974
East Feliciana	3,659	3,527	4,122	4,166
Evangeline	7,693	7,437	6,981	8,680
Franklin	3,043	5,520	2,937	6,708

Grant	2,628	4,402	2,588	5,334
Iberia	12,166	15,438	10,170	17,727
Iberville	8,678	5,855	8,587	6,455
Jackson	2,842	4,251	2,568	5,034
Jefferson	53,035	110,942	41,183	123,997
Jefferson Davis	6,799	5,851	5,962	8,296
Lafayette	24,133	36,648	19,265	44,344
Lafourche	15,013	16,152	10,186	20,930
LaSalle	1,622	4,559	1,318	5,404
Lincoln	5,427	8,853	5,432	9,087
Livingston	9,659	15,779	8,913	17,465
Madison	2,416	2,334	2,906	2,849
Morehouse	4,496	7,335	4,829	8,585
Natchitoches	6,151	7,224	5,806	8,836
Orleans	116,851	64,763	119,478	86,316
Ouachita	15,429	33,858	15,525	37,270
Plaquemines	3,997	6,084	3,261	7,855
Pointe Coupee	6,308	4,333	6,732	5,477
Rapides	17,928	29,977	16,121	32,879
Red River	2,254	2,266	1,958	3,060
Richland	2,833	5,226	2,918	5,990
Sabine	3,532	4,767	2,980	6,295
St. Bernard	11,406	19,609	8,076	24,428
St. Charles	7,973	9,685	6,784	10,185
St. Helena	3,013	2,006	2,956	2,366
St. James	6,707	3,799	5,989	4,627
St. John The Baptist	8,366	7,464	7,646	9,093
St. Landry	19,091	15,790	17,950	19,055
St. Martin	10,148	7,541	8,589	9,698
St. Mary	10,364	11,540	9,411	15,275
St. Tammany	15,638	38,334	11,719	38,664
Tangipahoa	13,527	16,669	12,799	19,580
Tensas	1,556	1,645	1,628	1,956
Terrebonne	12,686	18,745	9,640	23,696
Union	3,210	5,900	2,916	6,585
Vermilion	12,180	9,224	9,033	12,721
Vernon	4,998	7,453	4,076	9,035
Washington	8,369	9,374	7,680	11,185
Webster	7,434	10,204	6,509	12,055
W. Baton Rouge	4,686	3,972	4,631	4,189
West Carroll	1,607	3,077	1,474	3,874
West Feliciana	2,146	1,854	2,296	2,097
Winn	2,699	4,165	2,633	4,934
Totals	717,460	883,702	651,586	1,037,299

Louisiana Vote Since 1940

1940, Roosevelt, Dem., 319,751; Willkie, Rep., 52,446.

1944, Roosevelt, Dem., 281,564; Dewey, Rep., 67,750.

1948, Thurmond, States' Rights, 204,290; Truman, Dem., 136,344; Dewey, Rep., 72,657; Wallace, Prog., 3,035.

1952, Eisenhower, Rep., 306,925, Stevenson, Dem., 345,027.

1956, Eisenhower, Rep., 329,047; Stevenson, Dem., 243,977; Andrews, States' Rights, 44,520.

1960, Kennedy, Dem., 407,339; Nixon, Rep., 230,890; States' Rights (unpledged) 169,572.

1964, Johnson, Dem., 387,068; Goldwater, Rep., 509,225.

1968, Nixon, Rep., 257,535; Humphrey, Dem., 309,615; Wallace, 3d party, 530,300.

1972, Nixon, Rep., 686,852; McGovern, Dem., 298,142; Schmitz, Amer., 52,099; Jenness, Soc. Workers., 14,398.

1976, Carter, Dem., 661,365; Ford, Rep., 587,446; Maddox, Amer., 10,058; Hall, Com., 7,417; McCarthy, Ind., 6,588; MacBride, Libertarian, 3,325.

1980, Reagan, Rep., 792,853; Carter, Dem., 708,453; Anderson, Ind., 26,345; Rarick, Amer. Ind., 10,333; Clark, Libertarian, 8,240; Commoner, Citizens, 1,584; DeBerry, Soc. Work., 783.

1984, Reagan, Rep., 1,037,299; Mondale, Dem., 651,586; Bergland, Libertarian, 1,876.

1988, Bush, Rep., 883,702; Dukakis, Dem., 717,460; Duke, Pop., 18,612; Paul, Lib., 4,115.

Maine

	1988		1984	
City	Dukakis (D)	Bush (R)	Mondale (D)	Reagan (R)
Auburn	4,629	5,947	4,430	6,994
Augusta	4,576	5,182	4,451	5,995
Bangor	6,534	7,194	6,155	8,389
Bath	1,838	2,543	1,714	2,899
Biddeford	5,017	4,375	5,489	4,147
Brewer	1,784	2,908	1,461	3,093
Gardiner	1,395	1,609	1,216	1,942
Lewiston	9,225	7,265	9,853	9,480
Old Town	2,220	1,640	2,217	2,087
Portland	18,234	11,676	17,543	13,315
Rockland	1,198	1,850	1,051	2,169
Saco	3,169	3,852	3,094	3,761
Sanford	3,456	4,541	3,517	4,578
South Portland	5,820	5,744	5,377	6,653
Waterville	4,031	3,158	4,075	3,873
Westbrook	3,648	4,086	3,345	4,456
Totals	243,569	307,131	214,515	336,500

Maine Vote Since 1940

1940, Roosevelt, Dem., 156,478; Willkie, Rep., 165,951; Browder, Com., 411.

1944, Roosevelt, Dem., 140,631; Dewey, Rep., 155,434; Teichert, Soc. Labor, 335.

1948, Truman, Dem., 111,916; Dewey, Rep., 150,234; Wallace, Prog., 1,884; Thomas, Soc., 547; Teichert, Soc. Labor, 206.

1952, Eisenhower, Rep., 232,353; Stevenson, Dem., 118,806; Hallinan, Prog., 332; Hass, Soc. Labor, 156; Hoopes, Soc., 138; scattered, 1.

1956, Eisenhower, Rep., 249,238; Stevenson, Dem., 102,468.

1960, Kennedy, Dem., 181,159; Nixon, Rep., 240,608.

1964, Johnson, Dem., 262,264; Goldwater, Rep., 118,701.

1968, Nixon, Rep., 169,254; Humphrey, Dem., 217,312; Wallace, 3d party, 6,370.

1972, Nixon, Rep., 256,458; McGovern, Dem., 160,584; scattered, 229.

1976, Carter, Dem., 232,279; Ford, Rep., 236,320; McCarthy, Ind., 10,874; Bubar, Proh., 3,495.

1980, Reagan, Rep., 238,522; Carter, Dem., 220,974; Anderson, Ind., 53,327; Clark, Libertarian, 5,119; Commoner, Citizens, 4,394; Hall, Com., 591; write-ins, 84.

1984, Reagan, Rep., 336,500; Mondale, Dem., 214,515.

1988, Bush, Rep., 307,131; Dukakis, Dem., 243,569; Paul, Lib., 2,700; Fulani, New Alliance, 1,405.

Maryland

	1988		1984	
County	Dukakis (D)	Bush (R)	Mondale (D)	Reagan (R)
Allegany	11,844	17,462	11,143	19,763
Anne Arundel	55,440	98,540	47,565	94,171
Baltimore	121,570	163,881	106,908	171,929
Calvert	6,376	10,956	5,455	8,303
Caroline	2,440	4,661	2,198	4,876
Carroll	12,368	31,224	8,898	27,230
Cecil	7,807	13,224	6,681	13,111
Charles	11,823	20,828	10,264	16,132
Dorchester	3,709	6,343	3,160	6,699
Frederick	17,061	32,575	13,411	29,606
Garrett	2,557	6,665	2,386	7,042
Harford	19,803	38,493	17,133	37,382
Howard	34,007	44,153	25,713	35,841
Kent	2,925	3,761	2,390	3,897
Montgomery	165,187	154,191	146,036	146,924
Prince George's	133,816	86,545	136,063	95,121
Queen Anne's	3,857	7,803	2,938	6,784
St. Mary's	7,434	12,767	6,420	11,201
Somerset	2,911	4,222	2,439	4,508
Talbot	3,948	8,170	3,198	8,028
Washington	14,408	25,912	13,329	27,118
Wicomico	9,413	16,272	8,160	16,124
Worcester	4,787	8,430	3,770	8,208
Totals	826,304	876,167	787,935	879,918

Maryland Vote Since 1940

1940, Roosevelt, Dem., 384,546; Willkie, Rep., 269,534; Thomas, Soc., 4,093; Browder, Com., 1,274; Aiken, Soc. Labor, 657.

1944, Roosevelt, Dem., 315,490; Dewey, Rep., 292,949.

1948, Truman, Dem., 286,521; Dewey, Rep., 294,814; Wallace, Prog., 9,983; Thomas, Soc., 2,941; Thurmond, States' Rights, 2,476; Wright, write-in, 2,294.

1952, Eisenhower, Rep., 499,424; Stevenson, Dem., 395,337; Hallinan, Prog., 7,313.

1956, Eisenhower, Rep., 559,738; Stevenson, Dem., 372,613.

1960, Kennedy, Dem., 565,800; Nixon, Rep., 489,538.

1964, Johnson, Dem., 730,912; Goldwater, Rep., 385,495; write-in, 50.

1968, Nixon, Rep., 517,995; Humphrey, Dem., 538,310; Wallace, 3d party, 178,734.

1972, Nixon, Rep., 829,305; McGovern, Dem., 505,781; Schmitz, Amer., 18,726.

1976, Carter, Dem., 759,612; Ford, Rep., 672,661.

1980, Reagan, Rep., 680,606; Carter, Dem., 726,161; Anderson, Ind., 119,537; Clark, Libertarian, 14,192.

1984, Reagan, Rep., 879,918; Mondale, Dem., 787,935; Bergland, Libertarian, 5,721.

1988, Bush, Rep., 876,167; Dukakis, Dem., 826,304; Paul, Lib., 6,748; Fulani, Alliance, 5,115.

Massachusetts

City	1988 Dukakis (D)	Bush (R)	1984 Mondale (D)	Reagan (R)
Boston	122,349	62,202	131,745	75,311
Brockton	14,776	16,056	14,130	17,161
Cambridge	32,027	8,770	32,582	10,007
Fall River	20,184	8,394	20,722	11,463
Framingham	15,826	12,745	14,368	15,074
Lawrence	9,255	8,265	10,986	9,877
Lowell	16,391	13,998	15,042	16,834
Lynn	18,540	12,182	17,103	14,445
New Bedford	22,609	9,901	22,070	13,147
Newton	29,039	13,892	27,343	16,184
Quincy	20,911	18,403	18,971	20,123
Somerville	21,612	8,931	21,065	11,318
Springfield	30,113	16,244	29,376	21,431
Worcester	34,369	24,355	32,525	27,348
Totals	1,401,415	1,194,635	1,239,606	1,310,936

Massachusetts Vote Since 1940

1940, Roosevelt, Dem., 1,076,522; Willkie, Rep., 939,700; Thomas, Soc., 4,091; Browder, Com., 3,806; Aiken, Soc. Labor, 1,492; Babson, Proh., 1,370.

1944, Roosevelt, Dem., 1,035,296; Dewey, Rep., 921,350; Teichert, Soc. Labor, 2,780; Watson, Proh., 973.

1948, Truman, Dem., 1,151,788; Dewey, Rep., 909,370; Wallace, Prog., 38,157; Teichert, Soc. Labor, 5,535; Watson, Proh., 1,663.

1952, Eisenhower, Rep., 1,292,325; Stevenson, Dem., 1,083,525; Hallinan, Prog., 4,636; Hass, Soc. Labor, 1,957; Hamblen, Proh., 886; scattered, 69; blanks, 41,150.

1956, Eisenhower, Rep., 1,393,197; Stevenson, Dem., 948,190; Hass, Soc. Labor, 5,573; Holtwick, Proh., 1,205; others, 341.

1960, Kennedy, Dem., 1,487,174; Nixon, Rep., 976,750; Hass, Soc. Labor, 3,892; Decker, Proh., 1,633; others, 31; blank and void, 26,024.

1964, Johnson, Dem., 1,786,422; Goldwater, Rep., 549,727; Hass, Soc. Labor, 4,755; Munn, Proh., 3,735; scattered, 159; blank, 48,104.

1968, Nixon, Rep., 766,844; Humphrey, Dem., 1,469,218; Wallace, 3d party, 87,088; Blomen, Soc. Labor, 6,180; Munn, Proh., 2,369; scattered, 53; blanks, 25,394.

1972, Nixon, Rep., 1,112,078; McGovern, Dem., 1,332,540; Jenness, Soc. Workers, 10,600; Fisher, Soc. Labor, 129; Schmitz, Amer., 2,877; Spock, Peoples, 101; Hall, Com., 46; Hospers, Libertarian, 43; scattered, 342.

1976, Carter, Dem., 1,429,475; Ford, Rep., 1,030,276; McCarthy, Ind., 65,637; Camejo, Soc. Workers, 8,138; Anderson, Amer., 7,555; La Rouche, U.S. Labor, 4,922; MacBride, Libertarian, 135.

1980, Reagan, Rep., 1,057,631; Carter, Dem., 1,053,802; Anderson, Ind., 382,539; Clark, Libertarian, 22,038; DeBerry, Soc. Workers, 3,735; Commoner, Citizens, 2,056; McReynolds, Socialist, 62; Bubar, Statesman, 34; Griswold, Workers World, 19; scattered, 2,382.

1984, Reagan, Rep., 1,310,936; Mondale, Dem., 1,239,606.

1988, Bush, Rep., 1,194,635; Dukakis, Dem., 1,401,415; Paul, Lib., 24,251; Fulani, New Alliance, 9,561.

Michigan

County	1988 Dukakis (D)	Bush (R)	1984 Mondale (D)	Reagan (R)
Alcona	1,918	2,966	1,616	3,223
Alger	2,210	1,830	2,018	2,175
Allegan	10,785	22,163	8,389	23,762
Alpena	6,341	6,664	5,136	8,212
Antrim	3,159	5,231	2,507	5,726
Arenac	3,211	3,064	2,436	3,483
Baraga	1,753	1,630	1,818	1,965
Barry	7,983	12,546	5,898	14,245
Bay	28,225	20,710	22,597	26,198
Benzie	2,437	3,240	1,866	3,590
Berrien	21,948	37,799	21,228	43,160
Branch	5,231	9,225	3,860	11,004
Calhoun	22,717	26,771	20,313	34,470
Cass	7,444	10,229	6,634	11,647
Charlevoix	3,875	5,802	3,175	6,355
Cheboygan	3,943	5,395	3,358	6,053
Chippewa	5,222	6,786	4,575	8,135
Clare	4,710	5,661	3,764	6,587
Clinton	9,225	15,497	6,226	17,387
Crawford	1,825	3,097	1,558	3,303
Delta	8,891	7,114	7,934	8,952
Dickinson	6,129	6,158	5,614	6,880
Eaton	15,322	24,193	10,290	27,720
Emmet	4,170	7,105	3,254	7,760
Genesee	104,880	70,922	89,491	92,943
Gladwin	4,164	4,746	3,368	5,401
Gogebic	5,151	3,509	5,554	4,006
Grand Traverse	10,098	17,191	7,271	18,036
Gratiot	5,719	8,447	4,000	10,456
Hillsdale	4,763	10,571	3,616	12,063
Houghton	6,510	7,098	6,434	8,652
Huron	5,714	9,419	3,966	11,073
Ingham	55,984	58,363	46,411	68,753
Ionia	8,160	12,028	5,735	14,162
Iosco	4,929	7,234	3,850	7,907
Iron	3,774	2,866	3,559	3,468
Isabella	7,960	10,362	6,435	12,215
Jackson	21,865	33,885	18,340	40,133
Kalamazoo	39,457	50,205	32,460	58,327
Kalkaska	2,092	3,369	1,595	3,623
Kent	73,467	131,910	66,238	137,417
Keweenaw	631	536	628	599
Lake	1,958	1,713	1,845	2,125
Lapeer	10,736	16,670	7,800	19,222
Leelanau	3,331	5,215	2,498	5,356
Lenawee	13,690	19,115	11,012	22,409
Livingston	13,749	31,331	10,720	31,846
Luce	864	1,528	833	1,715
Mackinac	2,093	3,127	1,949	3,627
Macomb	112,856	175,632	97,816	194,300
Manistee	4,765	5,368	3,917	6,328
Marquette	15,418	11,704	14,074	14,196
Mason	4,531	6,800	3,803	8,202
Mecosta	4,736	8,181	4,048	9,023
Menominee	4,918	5,440	4,425	6,618
Midland	13,452	19,994	10,769	21,521
Missaukee	1,621	3,566	1,256	3,970
Monroe	21,847	26,189	19,617	29,419
Montcalm	7,664	10,963	5,491	13,109
Montmorency	1,563	2,514	1,387	2,913
Muskegon	28,977	33,567	25,247	39,355
Newaygo	5,389	9,896	4,496	10,636
Oakland	174,745	283,359	150,286	306,050
Oceana	3,356	5,693	2,865	6,405
Ogemaw	4,012	4,091	3,132	4,901
Ontonagon	2,517	2,023	2,350	2,464
Osceola	2,860	5,218	2,127	5,923
Oscoda	1,170	1,972	951	2,239
Otsego	2,635	4,620	2,117	4,639
Ottawa	18,769	61,515	15,000	60,142
Presque Isle	3,025	3,614	2,481	4,207
Roscommon	4,394	5,866	3,359	6,419
Saginaw	45,616	42,401	38,420	51,495
St. Clair	20,909	32,336	16,998	36,114
St. Joseph	7,017	13,084	5,795	15,405
Sanilac	5,445	10,653	4,126	12,627
Schoolcraft	2,071	1,802	1,920	2,139
Shiawassee	13,056	15,506	9,514	18,756
Tuscola	9,060	12,093	6,212	14,698
Van Buren	10,668	14,522	8,853	16,426
Washtenaw	61,799	55,029	55,084	58,736
Wayne	450,222	291,996	496,632	367,391
Wexford	4,287	6,043	3,398	7,279
Totals	1,675,783	1,965,486	1,529,638	2,251,571

Michigan Vote Since 1940

1940, Roosevelt, Dem., 1,032,991; Willkie, Rep., 1,039,917; Thomas, Soc., 7,593; Browder, Com., 2,834; Babson, Proh., 1,795; Aiken, Soc. Labor, 795.

1944, Roosevelt, Dem., 1,106,899; Dewey, Rep., 1,084,423; Watson, Proh., 6,503; Thomas, Soc., 4,598; Smith, America First, 1,530; Teichert, Soc. Labor, 1,264.

1948, Truman, Dem., 1,003,448; Dewey, Rep., 1,038,595; Wallace, Prog., 46,515; Watson, Proh., 13,052; Thomas, Soc. 6,063; Teichert, Soc. Labor, 1,263; Dobbs, Soc. Workers, 672.

1952, Eisenhower, Rep., 1,551,529; Stevenson, Dem., 1,230,657; Hamblen, Proh., 10,331; Hallinan, Prog., 3,922; Hass, Soc. Labor, 1,495; Dobbs, Soc. Workers, 655; scattered, 3.

1956, Eisenhower, Rep., 1,713,647; Stevenson, Dem., 1,359,898; Holtwick, Proh., 6,923.

1960, Kennedy, Dem., 1,687,269; Nixon, Rep., 1,620,428; Dobbs, Soc. Workers, 4,347; Decker, Proh., 2,029; Daly, Tax Cut, 1,767; Hass, Soc. Labor, 1,718; Ind. American, 539.

1964, Johnson, Dem., 2,136,615; Goldwater, Rep., 1,060,152; DeBerry, Soc. Workers, 3,817; Hass, Soc. Labor, 1,704; Proh. (no candidate listed), 699, scattering, 145.

1968, Nixon, Rep., 1,370,665; Humphrey, Dem., 1,593,082; Wallace, 3d party, 331,968; Halstead, Soc. Worker, 4,099; Blomen, Soc. Labor, 1,762; Cleaver, New Politics, 4,585; Munn, Proh., 60; scattering, 29.

1972, Nixon, Rep., 1,961,721; McGovern, Dem., 1,459,435; Schmitz, Amer., 63,321; Fisher, Soc. Labor, 2,437; Jenness, Soc. Workers, 1,603; Hall, Com., 1,210.

1976, Carter, Dem., 1,696,714; Ford, Rep., 1,893,742; McCarthy, Ind., 47,905; MacBride, Libertarian, 5,406; Wright, People's, 3,504, Camejo, Soc. Workers, 1,804; LaRouche, U.S. Labor, 1,366; Levin, Soc. Labor, 1,148; scattering, 2,160.

1980, Reagan, Rep., 1,915,225; Carter, Dem., 1,661,532; Anderson, Ind., 275,223; Clark, Libertarian, 41,597; Commoner, Citizens, 11,930; Hall, Com., 3,262; Griswold, Workers World, 30; Greaves, American, 21; Bubar, Statesman, 9.

1984, Reagan, Rep., 2,251,571; Mondale, Dem., 1,529,638; Bergland, Libertarian, 10,055.

1988, Bush, Rep., 1,965,486; Dukakis, Dem., 1,675,783; Paul, Lib., 18,336; Fulani, Ind., 2,513.

Minnesota

County	1988 Dukakis (D)	1988 Bush (R)	1984 Mondale (D)	1984 Reagan (R)
Aitkin	3,863	3,011	3,943	3,422
Anoka	57,953	46,853	50,305	46,578
Becker	5,787	6,738	5,456	7,553
Beltrami	7,566	6,652	7,481	7,414
Benton	5,861	6,060	4,922	6,830
Big Stone	2,026	1,469	1,994	1,821
Blue Earth	12,375	11,959	11,877	14,298
Brown	5,109	6,898	4,469	8,399
Carlton	8,790	4,626	9,189	4,877
Carver	6,439	12,560	6,725	11,963
Cass	5,127	5,895	4,773	6,619
Chippewa	3,238	3,190	3,047	3,964
Chisago	7,875	6,163	6,683	6,279
Clay	11,186	10,380	10,294	11,565
Clearwater	1,769	1,763	1,917	2,066
Cook	1,080	1,078	1,129	1,219
Cottonwood	3,095	3,390	3,073	4,275
Crow Wing	9,674	11,017	8,719	11,362
Dakota	61,942	61,606	49,125	55,119
Dodge	2,925	3,848	2,786	4,428
Douglas	5,803	7,898	5,444	9,005
Faribault	3,879	4,846	3,993	5,690
Fillmore	4,114	5,004	4,351	6,342
Freeborn	8,036	7,226	9,338	8,413
Goodhue	9,438	9,455	8,679	11,171
Grant	1,950	1,693	1,867	2,111
Hennepin	292,909	240,209	272,401	253,921
Houston	3,936	4,777	3,512	5,645
Hubbard	3,306	4,365	2,806	4,621
Isanti	6,075	5,246	5,378	5,660
Itasca	10,517	8,358	11,455	9,306
Jackson	3,275	2,629	3,437	3,131
Kanabec	2,970	2,571	2,660	3,027
Kandiyohi	6,962	8,634	8,402	9,539
Kittson	1,650	1,381	1,610	1,716
Koochiching	3,867	2,842	4,238	3,466
LacQuiParle	2,805	2,116	2,685	2,731
Lake	3,887	1,838	4,468	2,003
Lake O'Woods	798	984	824	1,094
Le Sueur	5,410	5,415	5,070	6,033
Lincoln	1,891	1,479	1,827	1,905
Lyon	5,657	5,969	5,389	7,170
McLeod	5,736	7,967	4,864	8,728
Mahnomen	1,277	1,051	1,241	1,328
Marshall	3,001	2,752	2,705	3,433
Martin	4,922	5,724	4,673	7,308
Meeker	4,544	4,999	4,156	5,511
Mille Lacs	4,327	3,862	4,011	4,307
Morrison	6,469	6,598	6,225	7,556
Mower	11,893	6,969	12,498	8,054
Murray	2,840	2,316	2,741	2,780
Nicollet	6,786	6,878	5,789	7,472
Nobles	4,953	4,348	4,819	4,876
Norman	2,149	1,789	2,202	2,152
Olmsted	19,423	27,683	16,535	28,129
Otter Tail	10,373	14,015	9,714	15,664
Pennington	3,105	2,920	2,913	3,536
Pine	5,540	3,857	5,223	4,493
Pipestone	2,382	2,760	2,391	3,043
Polk	7,523	7,032	7,033	8,617
Pope	3,074	2,627	2,757	3,064
Ramsey	143,767	88,736	141,623	95,667
Red Lake	1,229	918	1,294	1,184
Redwood	3,178	5,076	2,957	6,020
Renville	4,454	4,356	3,972	5,571
Rice	11,570	9,460	10,880	10,456
Rock	2,435	2,737	2,188	2,971
Roseau	2,630	3,500	2,319	3,445
St. Louis	70,344	31,799	77,683	34,162
Scott	11,405	13,050	9,452	12,573
Sherburne	7,959	8,360	6,140	7,738
Sibley	3,154	3,655	2,761	4,638
Stearns	23,798	27,529	20,944	30,216
Steele	5,496	7,981	5,060	8,780
Stevens	2,721	2,679	2,451	3,251
Swift	3,579	2,156	3,531	2,893
Todd	5,023	5,633	4,657	6,585
Traverse	1,399	1,061	1,325	1,399
Wabasha	4,442	4,681	3,872	5,299
Wadena	2,464	3,733	2,454	4,306
Waseca	3,721	4,471	3,527	5,509
Washington	34,952	30,850	28,527	29,046
Watonwan	2,544	2,821	2,425	3,526
Wilkin	1,486	1,933	1,410	2,367
Winona	10,310	11,012	9,577	11,981
Wright	14,177	14,987	12,486	15,399
Yellow Med	3,282	2,925	3,018	3,819
Totals	1,109,471	962,337	1,036,364	1,032,603

Minnesota Vote Since 1940

1940, Roosevelt, Dem., 644,196; Willkie, Rep., 596,274; Thomas, Soc., 5,454; Browder, Com., 2,711; Aiken, Ind., 2,553.

1944, Roosevelt, Dem., 589,864; Dewey, Rep., 527,416; Thomas, Soc., 5,073; Teichert, Ind. Gov't., 3,176.

1948, Truman, Dem., 692,966; Dewey, Rep., 483,617; Wallace, Prog., 27,866; Thomas, Soc., 4,646; Teichert, Soc. Labor, 2,525; Dobbs, Soc. Workers, 606.

1952, Eisenhower, Rep., 763,211; Stevenson, Dem., 608,458; Hallinan, Prog., 2,666; Hass, Soc. Labor, 2,383; Hamblen, Proh., 2,147; Dobbs, Soc. Workers, 618.

1956, Eisenhower, Rep., 719,302; Stevenson, Dem., 617,525; Hass, Soc. Labor (Ind. Gov.), 2,080; Dobbs, Soc. Workers, 1,098.

1960, Kennedy, Dem., 779,933; Nixon, Rep., 757,915; Dobbs, Soc. Workers, 3,077; Industrial Gov., 962.

1964, Johnson, Dem., 991,117; Goldwater, Rep., 559,624; DeBerry, Soc. Workers, 1,177; Hass, Industrial Gov., 2,544.

1968, Nixon, Rep., 658,643; Humphrey, Dem., 857,738; Wallace, 3d party, 68,931; scattered, 2,443; Halstead, Soc. Worker, 808; Blomen, Ind. Gov't., 285; Mitchell, Com., 415; Cleaver, Peace, 935; McCarthy, write-in, 585; scattered, 170.

1972, Nixon, Rep., 898,269; McGovern, Dem., 802,346; Schmitz, Amer., 31,407; Spock, Peoples, 2,805; Fisher, Soc. Labor, 4,261; Jenness, Soc. Workers, 940; Hall, Com., 662; scattered, 962.

1976, Carter, Dem., 1,070,440; Ford, Rep., 819,395; McCarthy, Ind., 35,490; Anderson, Amer., 13,592; Camejo, Soc. Workers, 4,149; MacBride, Libertarian, 3,529; Hall, Com., 1,092.

1980, Reagan, Rep., 873, 268; Carter, Dem., 954,173; Anderson, Ind., 174,997; Clark, Libertarian, 31,593; Commoner, Citizens, 8,406; Hall, Com., 1,117; DeBerry, Soc. Workers, 711; Griswold, Workers World, 698; McReynolds, Socialist, 536; write-ins, 281.

1984, Mondale, Dem., 1,036,364; Reagan, Rep., 1,032,603; Bergland, Libertarian, 2,996.

1988, Bush., 962,337; Dukakis, Dem., 1,109,471; McCarthy, Minn. Prog., 5,403; Paul, Lib., 5,109.

Mississippi

County	1988 Dukakis (D)	1988 Bush (R)	1984 Mondale (D)	1984 Reagan (R)
Adams	7,732	8,116	7,849	9,440
Alcorn	5,335	6,641	4,862	7,203
Amite	2,834	3,333	2,569	3,463
Attala	2,997	4,524	3,327	4,870
Benton	1,718	1,565	1,715	1,737
Bolivar	7,606	6,105	8,769	6,939
Calhoun	2,086	3,375	1,749	3,579
Carroll	1,560	2,628	1,462	2,823
Chickasaw	2,713	3,390	2,329	3,605
Choctaw	1,335	2,297	1,166	2,491
Claiborne	3,085	1,233	3,179	1,294
Clarke	2,576	4,522	2,262	4,551
Clay	3,849	3,645	4,046	4,112
Coahoma	6,139	4,939	6,639	5,759
Copiah	4,175	5,100	4,591	5,806
Covington	2,591	4,005	2,219	4,165
DeSoto	5,449	14,681	4,369	12,576
Forrest	6,953	14,249	6,786	15,719
Franklin	1,563	2,376	1,494	2,564
George	2,435	4,545	1,655	4,346
Greene	1,637	2,837	1,297	2,744
Grenada	3,683	5,352	3,325	5,181
Hancock	3,760	7,763	2,630	7,662
Harrison	14,439	32,892	12,495	33,995
Hinds	41,058	52,749	42,373	56,953

Holmes	5,350	2,737	5,641	3,102
Humphreys	2,644	2,018	2,596	2,309
Issaquena	511	424	501	512
Itawamba	3,143	4,535	2,674	4,587
Jackson	10,328	29,830	8,821	29,585
Jasper	3,184	3,368	3,104	3,727
Jefferson	2,693	702	3,049	856
Jefferson Davis	2,948	2,745	2,644	2,884
Jones	7,383	16,764	7,298	17,586
Kemper	2,069	2,128	2,089	2,354
Lafayette	3,967	5,841	3,646	6,006
Lamar	2,535	9,145	1,964	7,929
Lauderdale	7,967	18,302	7,534	18,807
Lawrence	2,517	3,682	2,274	3,970
Leake	2,787	4,168	2,845	4,663
Lee	6,604	13,767	6,208	13,312
Leflore	5,830	6,409	7,443	7,550
Lincoln	4,534	8,710	4,458	8,898
Lowndes	5,993	11,258	6,078	12,049
Madison	8,242	11,399	8,002	9,298
Marion	4,240	7,019	3,757	7,355
Marshall	6,982	4,668	5,845	4,389
Monroe	4,669	6,447	4,437	7,387
Montgomery	1,893	2,504	1,881	3,093
Neshoba	2,942	6,363	2,630	6,715
Newton	2,332	5,658	2,127	5,911
Noxubee	2,722	1,870	2,928	2,123
Oktibbeha	5,100	7,126	5,097	7,574
Panola	5,222	5,382	5,465	5,850
Pearl River	3,939	10,220	3,085	9,978
Perry	1,326	2,983	1,415	3,098
Pike	6,531	7,637	6,137	8,254
Pontotoc	2,772	4,939	2,494	5,182
Prentiss	3,429	4,348	2,897	4,821
Quitman	2,497	1,832	2,343	2,198
Rankin	6,201	22,937	5,874	22,393
Scott	2,939	5,522	3,274	5,763
Sharkey	1,609	1,277	1,723	1,487
Simpson	3,016	6,151	2,894	5,983
Smith	1,660	4,573	1,573	5,116
Stone	1,452	3,007	1,185	2,980
Sunflower	4,898	4,362	4,913	5,178
Tallahatchie	2,881	2,633	2,725	2,901
Tate	2,872	4,553	2,846	4,677
Tippah	2,958	4,593	2,566	4,706
Tishomingo	3,378	3,646	2,879	3,527
Tunica	1,510	896	1,621	1,109
Union	3,044	5,511	2,766	5,837
Walthall	2,354	3,103	2,219	3,305
Warren	7,437	12,507	8,054	12,959
Washington	10,222	10,229	10,617	12,454
Wayne	2,889	4,496	2,818	5,000
Webster	1,550	3,061	1,397	3,390
Wilkinson	2,678	1,528	2,627	1,722
Winston	3,851	5,317	3,543	5,192
Yalobusha	2,402	2,660	2,337	2,934
Yazoo	4,989	5,538	5,037	6,275
Totals	363,921	557,890	352,192	582,377

Mississippi Vote Since 1940

1940, Roosevelt, Dem., 168,252; Willkie, Ind. Rep., 4,550; Rep., 2,814; total, 7,364; Thomas, Soc., 103.

1944, Roosevelt, Dem., 158,515; Dewey, Rep., 3,742; Reg. Dem., 9,964; Ind. Rep., 7,859.

1948, Thurmond, States' Rights, 167,538; Truman, Dem., 19,384; Dewey, Rep., 5,043; Wallace, Prog., 225.

1952, Eisenhower, Ind. vote pledged to Rep. candidate, 112,966; Stevenson, Dem., 172,566.

1956, Stevenson, Dem., 144,498; Eisenhower, Rep., 56,372; Black and Tan Grand Old Party, 4,313; total, 60,685; Byrd, Ind., 42,966.

1960, Democratic unpledged electors, 116,248; Kennedy, Dem., 108,362; Nixon, Rep., 73,561. Mississippi's victorious slate of 8 unpledged Democratic electors cast their votes for Sen. Harry F. Byrd (D-Va.).

1964, Johnson, Dem., 52,618; Goldwater, Rep., 356,528.

1968, Nixon, Rep., 88,516; Humphrey, Dem., 150,644; Wallace, 3d party, 415,349.

1972, Nixon, Rep., 505,125; McGovern, Dem., 126,782; Schmitz, Amer., 11,598; Jenness, Soc. Workers, 2,458.

1976, Carter, Dem., 381,309; Ford, Rep., 366,846; Anderson, Amer., 6,678; McCarthy, Ind., 4,074; Maddox, Ind., 4,049; Camejo, Soc. Workers, 2,805; MacBride, Libertarian, 2,609.

1980, Reagan, Rep., 441,089; Carter, Dem., 429,281; Anderson, Ind., 12,036; Clark, Libertarian, 5,465; Griswold, Workers World, 2,402; Pulley, Soc. Worker, 2,347.

1984, Reagan, Rep., 582,377; Mondale, Dem., 352,192; Bergland, Libertarian, 2,336.

1988, Bush, Rep., 557,890; Dukakis, Dem., 363,921; Duke, Ind., 4,232; Paul, Lib., 3,329.

Missouri

County	1988 Dukakis (D)	1988 Bush (R)	1984 Mondale (D)	1984 Reagan (R)
Adair	3,571	5,721	3,119	6,430
Andrew	3,108	3,407	2,457	4,252
Atchison	1,468	1,761	1,219	2,277
Audrain	5,226	5,072	4,662	7,261
Barry	4,210	7,231	3,483	7,683
Barton	1,603	3,339	1,348	3,996
Bates	3,332	3,574	2,889	4,223
Benton	2,654	3,467	2,251	3,805
Bollinger	1,883	2,710	1,923	2,778
Boone	24,370	22,948	19,364	26,600
Buchanan	18,601	15,336	15,369	19,735
Butler	5,751	7,968	4,699	8,712
Caldwell	1,726	2,074	1,382	2,678
Callaway	5,209	6,887	4,327	8,262
Camden	3,930	7,773	3,088	8,057
Cape Girardeau	7,904	16,583	7,346	17,404
Carroll	2,330	2,811	1,980	3,495
Carter	1,087	1,429	916	1,402
Cass	10,092	12,799	7,517	14,456
Cedar	1,774	2,966	1,440	3,539
Chariton	2,347	2,193	2,244	2,744
Christian	4,724	7,670	3,223	7,634
Clark	1,925	1,493	1,627	2,068
Clay	29,620	30,293	22,586	36,529
Clinton	3,653	3,282	2,778	4,226
Cole	8,359	18,023	6,702	20,366
Cooper	2,510	3,737	2,219	4,603
Crawford	3,107	3,856	2,610	4,716
Dade	1,315	2,154	1,100	2,600
Dallas	2,293	2,898	1,902	3,577
Daviess	1,743	1,765	1,526	2,414
DeKalb	1,970	1,863	1,464	2,188
Dent	2,421	2,975	2,544	3,490
Douglas	1,735	3,225	1,536	3,662
Dunklin	5,281	5,026	4,967	6,092
Franklin	11,891	16,611	8,319	18,669
Gasconade	1,621	4,216	1,130	4,678
Gentry	1,872	1,554	1,600	2,047
Greene	35,475	52,211	27,965	57,250
Grundy	2,052	2,668	1,861	3,156
Harrison	1,776	2,271	1,649	2,844
Henry	4,135	4,167	3,741	5,419
Hickory	1,677	2,043	1,212	2,190
Holt	1,258	1,583	1,026	2,087
Howard	2,446	1,865	2,014	2,360
Howell	4,324	7,277	3,767	8,204
Iron	2,263	1,877	2,023	2,316
Jackson	147,964	107,810	135,067	132,271
Jasper	11,159	19,934	9,259	23,066
Jefferson	27,738	29,279	20,026	34,525
Johnson	5,373	7,512	4,238	8,413
Knox	1,255	1,212	1,097	1,513
Laclede	3,442	6,070	2,665	6,406
Lafayette	5,654	6,825	4,848	8,581
Lawrence	4,432	6,911	3,720	8,370
Lewis	2,460	1,803	1,977	2,438
Lincoln	4,605	5,305	3,290	6,137
Linn	3,150	3,061	3,112	3,822
Livingston	3,077	3,462	2,699	4,090
McDonald	2,299	3,812	2,109	4,521
Macon	3,215	3,406	3,037	4,542
Madison	2,167	2,528	1,862	2,808
Maries	1,552	1,919	1,388	2,267
Marion	5,617	5,034	4,666	6,831
Mercer	877	875	875	1,229
Miller	2,555	5,662	2,054	6,706
Missouri	2,814	2,218	2,524	2,502
Moniteau	1,936	3,502	1,614	4,197
Monroe	2,461	1,542	1,992	2,163
Montgomery	2,064	2,714	1,668	3,261
Morgan	2,604	3,958	2,169	4,392
New Madrid	3,812	3,387	3,776	4,323
Newton	5,798	10,617	4,623	11,709
Nodaway	4,240	4,103	3,615	5,471
Oregon	2,042	1,717	2,026	1,979
Osage	1,771	3,885	1,343	4,381
Ozark	1,329	2,404	1,110	2,614
Pemiscot	3,288	3,066	3,293	3,733
Perry	2,136	3,836	1,837	4,493
Pettis	5,486	9,648	5,413	10,991
Phelps	5,867	8,329	5,074	9,012
Pike	3,816	3,271	3,313	3,933
Platte	11,225	11,838	7,668	12,859
Polk	3,419	5,030	2,819	5,467
Pulaski	3,446	4,642	2,865	5,330
Putnam	803	1,365	797	1,540
Ralls	2,489	1,494	2,011	2,067
Randolph	5,291	4,384	4,471	5,735
Ray	4,879	3,763	3,979	4,875
Reynolds	1,961	1,162	2,026	1,330
Ripley	1,961	2,647	1,883	2,927
St. Charles	29,286	50,005	17,617	47,784
St. Clair	1,864	2,312	1,655	2,667
St. Francois	8,158	7,923	7,137	9,792
Ste. Genevieve	3,612	2,532	2,723	3,245

	1988		1984	
St. Louis	216,534	262,784	173,144	307,684
Saline	5,039	4,625	4,281	6,042
Schuyler	1,013	1,063	1,141	1,250
Scotland	1,117	1,248	1,075	1,485
Scott	5,914	8,013	5,569	8,727
Shannon	1,796	1,696	1,580	1,779
Shelby	1,818	1,586	1,573	2,243
Stoddard	4,701	5,822	4,294	6,701
Stone	2,889	5,080	2,119	5,706
Sullivan	1,562	1,897	1,784	2,306
Taney	3,888	7,043	2,912	7,082
Texas	3,887	4,584	3,662	5,591
Vernon	3,402	4,149	2,984	5,181
Warren	2,935	4,452	1,964	5,150
Washington	3,744	3,240	2,987	3,755
Wayne	2,456	2,648	2,363	2,867
Webster	3,890	5,123	2,982	5,529
Worth	732	677	734	921
Wright	2,232	4,151	1,973	4,687
Totals	1,001,619	1,084,953	848,583	1,274,188

	1988		1984	
Powell	1,174	1,574	1,066	1,877
Prairie	343	541	289	693
Ravalli	4,763	7,418	3,825	8,161
Richland	1,824	2,628	1,382	3,847
Roosevelt	2,083	1,957	1,962	2,431
Rosebud	1,869	1,822	1,920	2,413
Sanders	1,959	2,152	1,654	2,467
Sheridan	1,354	1,381	1,087	1,774
Silver Bow	11,422	5,043	11,095	6,637
Stillwater	1,407	1,920	1,100	2,118
Sweet Grass	462	1,242	378	1,417
Teton	1,303	1,876	1,102	2,257
Toole	1,070	1,505	789	1,949
Treasure	231	291	209	353
Valley	2,163	2,467	1,849	3,123
Wheatland	443	667	407	753
Wibaux	258	358	216	423
Yellowstone	21,987	28,059	19,437	34,124
Totals	168,936	190,412	146,742	232,450

Missouri Vote Since 1940

1940, Roosevelt, Dem., 958,476; Willkie, Rep., 871,009; Thomas, Soc., 2,226; Babson, Proh., 1,809; Aiken, Soc. Labor, 209.

1944, Roosevelt, Dem., 807,357; Dewey, Rep., 761,175; Thomas, Soc., 1,750; Watson, Proh., 1,175; Teichert, Soc. Labor, 221.

1948, Truman, Dem., 917,315; Dewey, Rep., 655,039; Wallace, Prog., 3,998; Thomas, Soc., 2,222.

1952, Eisenhower, Rep., 959,429; Stevenson, Dem., 929,830; Hallinan, Prog., 987; Hamblen, Proh., 885; MacArthur, Christian Nationalist, 302; America First, 233; Hoopes, Soc., 227; Hass, Soc. Labor, 169.

1956, Stevenson, Dem., 918,273; Eisenhower, Rep., 914,299.

1960, Kennedy, Dem., 972,201; Nixon, Rep., 962,221.

1964, Johnson, Dem., 1,164,344; Goldwater, Rep., 653,535.

1968, Nixon, Rep., 811,932; Humphrey, Dem., 791,444; Wallace, 3d party, 206,126.

1972, Nixon, Rep., 1,154,058; McGovern, Dem., 698,531.

1976, Carter, Dem., 999,163; Ford, Rep., 928,808; McCarthy, Ind., 24,329.

1980, Reagan, Rep., 1,074,181; Carter, Dem., 931,182; Anderson, Ind., 77,920; Clark, Libertarian, 14,422; DeBerry, Soc. Workers, 1,515; Commoner, Citizens, 573; write-ins, 31.

1984, Reagan, Rep., 1,274,188; Mondale, Dem., 848,583.

1988, Bush, Rep., 1,084,953; Dukakis, Dem., 1,001,619; Fulani, New Alliance, 6,656; Paul, write-in, 434.

Montana Vote Since 1940

1940, Roosevelt, Dem., 145,698; Willkie, Rep., 99,579; Thomas, Soc., 1,443; Babson, Proh., 664; Browder, Com., 489.

1944, Roosevelt, Dem., 112,556; Dewey, Rep., 93,163; Thomas, Soc., 1,296; Watson, Proh., 340.

1948, Truman, Dem., 119,071; Dewey, Rep., 96,770; Wallace, Prog., 7,313; Thomas, Soc., 695; Watson, Proh., 429.

1952, Eisenhower, Rep., 157,394; Stevenson, Dem., 106,213; Hallinan, Prog., 723; Hamblen, Proh., 548; Hoopes, Soc., 159.

1956, Eisenhower, Rep., 154,933; Stevenson, Dem., 116,238.

1960, Kennedy, Dem., 134,891; Nixon, Rep., 141,841; Decker, Proh., 456; Dobbs, Soc. Workers, 391.

1964, Johnson, Dem., 164,246; Goldwater, Rep., 113,032; Kasper, Nat'l States Rights, 519; Munn, Proh., 499; DeBerry, Soc. Worker, 332.

1968, Nixon, Rep., 138,835; Humphrey, Dem., 114,117; Wallace, 3d party, 20,015; Halstead, Soc. Worker, 457; Munn, Proh., 510; Caton, New Reform, 470.

1972, Nixon, Rep., 183,976; McGovern, Dem., 120,197; Schmitz, Amer., 13,430.

1976, Carter, Dem., 149,259; Ford, Rep., 173,703; Anderson, Amer., 5,772.

1980, Reagan, Rep., 206,814; Carter, Dem., 118,032; Anderson, Ind., 29,281; Clark, Libertarian, 9,825.

1984, Reagan, Rep., 232,450; Mondale, Dem., 146,742; Bergland, Libertarian, 5,185.

1988, Bush, Rep., 190,412; Dukakis, Dem., 168,936; Paul, Lib., 5,047; Fulani, New Alliance, 1,279.

Montana

County	1988 Dukakis (D)	Bush (R)	1984 Mondale (D)	Reagan (R)
Beaverhead	1,274	2,668	942	3,044
Big Horn	2,233	1,711	2,681	2,390
Blaine	1,460	1,402	1,229	1,736
Broadwater	592	1,054	458	1,345
Carbon	2,039	2,390	1,657	2,877
Carter	242	666	194	823
Cascade	15,718	15,946	14,252	19,846
Chouteau	1,166	1,980	896	2,425
Custer	2,343	3,007	1,982	3,579
Daniels	571	802	473	984
Dawson	2,120	2,658	1,776	3,468
Deer Lodge	3,185	1,168	3,539	1,901
Fallon	612	1,002	569	1,237
Fergus	2,052	3,948	1,804	4,585
Flathead	10,202	14,461	8,310	17,012
Gallatin	9,527	13,214	8,163	15,643
Garfield	196	631	134	770
Glacier	2,151	1,728	2,167	2,228
Golden Valley	203	335	211	384
Granite	511	789	417	880
Hill	4,219	3,467	3,657	4,635
Jefferson	1,746	2,007	1,324	2,226
Judith Basin	590	902	483	1,050
Lake	4,109	4,883	3,473	5,754
Lewis & Clark	11,932	10,946	8,768	13,569
Liberty	418	771	323	895
Lincoln	3,601	3,500	2,959	4,080
Madison	878	2,045	708	2,308
McCone	567	814	459	1,015
Meagher	337	656	283	771
Mineral	789	616	718	943
Missoula	19,178	15,965	16,540	19,777
Musselshell	898	1,280	781	1,541
Park	2,526	3,823	2,387	4,115
Petroleum	91	204	86	258
Phillips	905	1,462	787	1,934
Pondera	1,245	1,795	1,039	2,239
Powder River	395	815	346	1,066

Nebraska

County	1988 Dukakis (D)	Bush (R)	1984 Mondale (D)	Reagan (R)
Adams	4,145	8,063	2,940	9,092
Antelope	933	2,626	697	3,222
Arthur	58	210	33	248
Banner	112	361	58	457
Blaine	72	336	48	363
Boone	976	2,160	699	2,508
Box Butte	2,466	3,253	1,471	4,011
Boyd	480	967	308	1,173
Brown	435	1,305	312	1,513
Buffalo	4,700	9,980	3,083	11,343
Burt	1,458	2,050	1,054	2,645
Butler	1,715	2,083	1,192	2,555
Cass	3,674	4,658	2,495	5,451
Cedar	1,759	2,462	1,201	3,268
Chase	597	1,446	367	1,687
Cherry	642	2,240	463	2,720
Cheyenne	1,333	2,862	857	3,159
Clay	1,097	2,352	811	2,919
Colfax	1,542	2,329	981	2,998
Cuming	1,238	3,201	779	3,931
Custer	1,496	4,202	1,090	4,749
Dakota	2,941	2,744	2,510	3,467
Dawes	1,122	2,618	864	3,325
Dawson	2,184	5,529	1,487	6,878
Deuel	302	769	198	961
Dixon	1,166	1,802	985	2,154
Dodge	6,116	8,412	4,259	10,167
Douglas	76,444	99,806	58,867	112,557
Dundy	333	828	225	992
Fillmore	1,433	1,952	1,009	2,474
Franklin	768	1,294	522	1,597
Frontier	384	1,057	258	1,351
Furnas	791	1,830	579	2,363
Gage	4,008	5,114	2,699	6,102
Garden	366	986	180	1,158

County	Dukakis (D)	Bush (R)	Mondale (D)	Reagan (R)
Garfield	234	803	196	899
Gosper	331	694	201	802
Grant	89	301	51	404
Greeley	670	763	485	948
Hall	6,822	12,020	4,615	13,082
Hamilton	1,289	3,019	840	3,417
Harlan	725	1,403	493	1,692
Hayes	160	512	100	591
Hitchcock	480	1,132	341	1,391
Holt	1,327	4,081	893	4,611
Hooker	91	378	55	433
Howard	1,186	1,526	887	1,899
Jefferson	1,819	2,470	1,366	3,114
Johnson	1,162	1,182	821	1,536
Kearney	1,056	2,120	726	2,505
Keith	1,067	2,879	631	3,423
Keya Paha	145	446	126	505
Kimball	540	1,321	339	1,732
Knox	1,477	2,644	1,149	3,364
Lancaster	44,260	44,605	32,780	48,627
Lincoln	6,070	8,395	4,483	10,692
Logan	93	373	66	445
Loup	97	295	79	323
McPherson	60	229	57	295
Madison	2,779	9,135	1,755	9,786
Merrick	1,192	2,376	818	2,696
Morrill	753	1,554	463	1,888
Nance	794	1,185	524	1,391
Nemaha	1,457	2,293	1,004	2,752
Nuckolls	1,114	1,750	947	2,132
Otoe	2,616	3,724	1,868	4,679
Pawnee	767	975	552	1,306
Perkins	467	1,117	307	1,418
Phelps	1,047	3,316	739	3,739
Pierce	914	2,474	545	3,016
Platte	3,285	9,029	2,057	10,035
Polk	944	1,768	610	2,149
Red Willow	1,505	3,325	1,022	4,101
Richardson	1,926	2,702	1,422	3,634
Rock	198	756	147	873
Saline	3,119	2,352	2,385	2,941
Sarpy	10,936	20,179	6,831	20,155
Saunders	3,524	4,454	2,467	5,217
Scotts Bluff	4,454	8,594	3,060	10,676
Seward	2,682	3,467	1,905	3,969
Sheridan	612	2,251	377	2,661
Sherman	839	914	701	1,144
Sioux	194	568	121	732
Stanton	637	1,709	410	2,080
Thayer	1,322	1,981	946	2,578
Thomas	81	383	73	298
Thurston	1,225	1,105	1,077	1,410
Valley	873	1,603	739	2,052
Washington	2,552	4,567	1,561	5,163
Wayne	1,111	2,473	833	3,075
Webster	891	1,314	645	1,694
Wheeler	141	309	97	365
York	1,748	4,744	1,114	5,012
Totals	**259,235**	**397,956**	**187,475**	**459,135**

Nebraska Vote Since 1940

1940, Roosevelt, Dem., 263,677; Willkie, Rep., 352,201.

1944, Roosevelt, Dem., 233,246; Dewey, Rep., 329,880.

1948, Truman, Dem., 224,165; Dewey, Rep., 264,774.

1952, Eisenhower, Rep., 421,603; Stevenson Dem., 188,057.

1956, Eisenhower, Rep., 378,108; Stevenson, Dem., 199,029.

1960, Kennedy, Dem., 232,542; Nixon, Rep., 380,553.

1964, Johnson, Dem., 307,307; Goldwater, Rep., 276,847.

1968, Nixon, Rep., 321,163; Humphrey, Dem., 170,784; Wallace, 3d party, 44,904.

1972, Nixon, Rep., 406,298; McGovern, Dem., 169,991; scattered 817.

1976, Carter, Dem., 233,287; Ford, Rep., 359,219; McCarthy, Ind., 9,383; Maddox, Amer. Ind., 3,378; MacBride, Libertarian, 1,476.

1980, Reagan, Rep., 419,214; Carter, Dem., 166,424; Anderson, Ind., 44,854; Clark, Libertarian, 9,041.

1984, Reagan, Rep., 459,135; Mondale, Dem., 187,475; Bergland, Libertarian, 2,075.

1988, Bush, Rep., 397,956; Dukakis, Dem., 259,235; Paul, Lib., 2,534; Fulani, New Alliance, 1,740.

Nevada

County	1988 Dukakis (D)	Bush (R)	1984 Mondale (D)	Reagan (R)
Churchill	1,481	4,578	1,304	4,479
Clark	78,359	108,110	53,386	94,133
Douglas	3,107	7,074	1,877	6,385
Elko	2,310	5,722	1,566	5,110
Esmeralda	143	380	158	453
Eureka	151	413	124	439
Humboldt	1,024	2,378	862	2,498
Lander	439	1,214	301	1,222
Lincoln	466	1,035	397	1,175
Lyon	2,301	4,390	1,673	4,370
Mineral	978	1,480	766	1,645
Nye	1,748	3,619	1,269	3,573
Pershing	458	867	333	956
Storey	432	651	252	570
Washoe	32,902	52,654	22,321	50,418
White Pine	1,351	1,774	1,276	1,917
Totals	**132,738**	**206,040**	**91,655**	**188,770**

Nevada Vote Since 1940

1940, Roosevelt, Dem., 31,945; Willkie, Rep., 21,229.

1944, Roosevelt, Dem., 29,623; Dewey, Rep., 24,611.

1948, Truman, Dem., 31,291; Dewey, Rep., 29,357; Wallace, Prog., 1,469.

1952, Eisenhower, Rep., 50,502; Stevenson, Dem., 31,688.

1956, Eisenhower, Rep., 56,049; Stevenson, Dem., 40,640.

1960, Kennedy, Dem., 54,880; Nixon, Rep., 52,387.

1964, Johnson, Dem., 79,339; Goldwater, Rep., 56,094.

1968, Nixon, Rep., 73,188; Humphrey, Dem., 60,598; Wallace, 3d party, 20,432.

1972, Nixon, Rep., 115,750; McGovern, Dem. 66,016.

1976, Carter Dem., 92,479; Ford, Rep., 101,273; MacBride, Libertarian, 1,519; Maddox, Amer. Ind., 1,497; scattered 5,108.

1980, Reagan, Rep., 155,017; Carter, Dem., 66,666; Anderson, Ind., 17,651; Clark, Libertarian, 4,358.

1984, Reagan, Rep., 188,770; Mondale, Dem., 91,655; Bergland, Libertarian, 2,292.

1988, Bush, Rep., 206,040; Dukakis, Dem., 132,738; Paul, Lib., 3,520; Fulani, New Alliance, 835.

New Hampshire

City	1988 Dukakis (D)	Bush (R)	1984 Mondale (D)	Reagan (R)
Berlin City	2,271	2,529	1,863	3,261
Claremont	2,254	2,513	2,006	2,868
Concord	6,698	7,439	5,172	7,190
Dover	4,803	5,357	3,826	5,397
Keene	4,466	4,535	3,238	4,975
Laconia	2,111	3,835	1,552	4,151
Manchester	12,567	23,893	10,283	24,780
Nashua	12,833	19,369	9,305	16,961
Portsmouth	5,377	4,827	4,418	4,967
Rochester	3,591	5,368	2,622	5,457
Totals	**163,696**	**281,537**	**120,377**	**267,051**

New Hampshire Vote Since 1940

1940, Roosevelt, Dem., 125,292; Willkie, Rep., 110,127.

1944, Roosevelt, Dem., 119,663; Dewey, Rep., 109,916; Thomas, Soc., 46.

1948, Truman, Dem., 107,995; Dewey, Rep., 121,299; Wallace, Prog., 1,970; Thomas, Soc., 86; Teichert, Soc. Labor, 83; Thurmond, States' Rights, 7.

1952, Eisenhower, Rep., 166,287; Stevenson, Dem., 106,663.

1956, Eisenhower, Rep., 176,519; Stevenson, Dem., 90,364; Andrews, Const., 111.

1960, Kennedy, Dem., 137,772; Nixon, Rep., 157,989.

1964, Johnson, Dem., 182,065; Goldwater, Rep., 104,029.

1968, Nixon, Rep., 154,903; Humphrey, Dem., 130,589; Wallace, 3d party, 11,173; New Party, 421; Halstead, Soc. Worker, 104.

1972, Nixon, Rep., 213,724; McGovern, Dem., 116,435; Schmitz, Amer., 3,386; Jenness, Soc. Workers, 368; scattered, 142.

1976, Carter, Dem., 147,645; Ford, Rep., 185,935; McCarthy, Ind., 4,095; MacBride, Libertarian, 936; Reagan, write-in, 388; La Rouche, U.S. Labor, 186; Camejo, Soc. Workers, 161; Levin, Soc. Labor, 66; scattered, 215.

1980, Reagan, Rep., 221,705; Carter, Dem., 108,864; Anderson, Ind., 49,693; Clark, Libertarian, 2,067; Commoner, Citizens, 1,325; Hall, Com., 129; Griswold, Workers World, 76; DeBerry, Soc. Workers, 72; scattered, 68.

1984, Reagan, Rep., 267,051; Mondale, Dem., 120,377; Bergland, Libertarian, 735.

1988, Bush, Rep., 281,537; Dukakis, Dem., 163,696; Paul, Lib., 4,502; Fulani, New Alliance, 790.

New Jersey

County	1988 Dukakis (D)	1988 Bush (R)	1984 Mondale (D)	1984 Reagan (R)
Atlantic	34,047	44,748	33,240	49,158
Bergen	160,655	226,885	155,039	268,507
Burlington	61,140	87,416	57,467	89,815
Camden	90,704	100,072	90,233	109,749
Cape May	15,105	28,738	13,378	28,768
Cumberland	21,869	26,024	21,141	29,398
Essex	156,098	111,491	173,295	136,798
Gloucester	35,479	51,708	32,702	54,041
Hudson	95,696	81,807	94,304	112,834
Hunterdon	13,758	31,907	10,972	29,737
Mercer	68,712	65,384	66,398	71,195
Middlesex	117,149	143,361	104,905	160,221
Monmouth	91,844	147,320	79,382	152,595
Morris	58,721	127,420	53,201	137,719
Ocean	64,474	124,587	51,012	124,391
Passaic	66,254	88,070	69,590	101,951
Salem	9,956	15,240	8,935	17,368
Somerset	37,406	67,658	31,924	66,303
Sussex	13,676	36,086	11,502	35,680
Union	93,158	112,967	92,056	135,446
Warren	11,640	21,715	10,647	21,938
Totals	1,317,541	1,740,604	1,261,323	1,933,630

New Jersey Vote Since 1940

1940, Roosevelt, Dem., 1,016,404; Willkie, Rep., 944,876; Browder, Com., 8,814; Thomas, Soc., 2,823; Babson, Proh., 851; Aiken, Soc. Labor, 446.

1944, Roosevelt, Dem., 987,874; Dewey, Rep., 961,335; Teichert, Soc. Labor, 6,939; Watson, Nat'l. Proh., 4,255; Thomas, Soc., 3,385.

1948, Truman, Dem., 895,455; Dewey, Rep., 981,124; Wallace, Prog., 42,683; Watson, Proh., 10,593; Thomas, Soc., 10,521; Dobbs, Soc. Workers, 5,825; Teichert, Soc. Labor, 3,354.

1952, Eisenhower, Rep., 1,373,613; Stevenson, Dem., 1,015,902; Hoopes, Soc., 8,593; Hass, Soc. Labor, 5,815; Hallinan, Prog., 5,589; Krajewski, Poor Man's, 4,203; Dobbs, Soc. Workers, 3,850; Hamblen, Proh., 989.

1956, Eisenhower, Rep., 1,606,942; Stevenson Dem., 850,337; Holtwick, Proh., 9,147; Hass, Soc. Labor, 6,736; Andrews, Conservative, 5,317; Dobbs, Soc. Workers, 4,004; Krajewski, American Third Party, 1,829.

1960, Kennedy, Dem., 1,385,415; Nixon, Rep., 1,363,324; Dobbs, Soc. Workers, 11,402; Lee, Conservative, 8,708; Hass, Soc. Labor, 4,262.

1964, Johnson, Dem., 1,867,671; Goldwater, Rep., 963,843; DeBerry, Soc. Workers, 8,181; Hass, Soc. Labor, 7,075.

1968, Nixon, Rep., 1,325,467; Humphrey, Dem., 1,264,206; Wallace, 3d party, 262,187; Halstead, Soc. Worker, 8,667; Gregory, Peace Freedom, 8,084; Blomen, Soc. Labor, 6,784.

1972, Nixon, Rep., 1,845,502; McGovern, Dem., 1,102,211; Schmitz, Amer., 34,378; Spock, Peoples, 5,355; Fisher, Soc. Labor, 4,544; Jenness, Soc. Workers, 2,233; Mahalchik, Amer. First, 1,743; Hall, Com., 1,263.

1976, Carter, Dem., 1,444,653; Ford, Rep., 1,509,688; McCarthy, Ind., 32,717; MacBride, Libertarian, 9,449; Maddox, Amer., 7,716; Levin, Soc. Labor, 3,686; Hall, Com., 1,662; LaRouche, U.S. Labor, 1,650; Camejo, Soc. Workers, 1,184; Wright, People's, 1,044; Bubar, Proh., 554; Zeidler, Soc., 469.

1980, Reagan, Rep., 1,546,557; Carter, Dem., 1,147,364; Anderson, Ind., 234,632; Clark, Libertarian, 20,652; Commoner, Citizens, 8,203; McCormack, Right to Life, 3,927; Lynen, Middle Class, 3,694; Hall, Com., 2,555; Pulley, Soc. Workers, 2,198; McReynolds, Soc., 1,973; Gahres, Down With Lawyers, 1,718; Griswold, Workers World, 1,288; Wendelken, Ind., 923.

1984, Reagan, Rep., 1,933,630; Mondale, Dem., 1,261,323; Bergland, Libertarian, 6,416.

1988, Bush, Rep., 1,740,604; Dukakis, Dem., 1,317,541; Lewin, Peace & Freedom, 9,953; Paul, Lib., 8,421.

New Mexico

County	1988 Dukakis (D)	1988 Bush (R)	1984 Mondale (D)	1984 Reagan (R)
Bernalillo	78,346	92,830	67,789	104,694
Catron	490	925	418	970
Chaves	6,730	13,367	5,332	15,248
Cibola	3,458	2,640	3,140	3,578
Colfax	2,785	2,256	2,435	2,994
Curry	3,995	8,032	3,108	9,188
De Baca	480	643	386	756
Dona Ana	19,608	21,582	13,678	22,153
Eddy	8,544	9,805	7,364	11,810
Grant	5,443	4,196	5,755	4,979
Guadalupe	1,243	861	946	990
Harding	291	377	224	401
Hidalgo	901	1,100	860	1,282
Lea	5,879	11,309	4,558	14,569
Lincoln	1,690	3,511	1,134	3,992
Los Alamos	3,275	6,622	2,859	6,682
Luna	3,066	3,415	2,557	4,145
McKinley	9,595	5,694	7,915	6,557
Mora	1,601	923	1,235	1,017
Otero	5,284	9,984	4,167	9,751
Quay	1,901	2,454	1,368	2,842
Rio Arriba	7,503	3,024	6,938	4,116
Roosevelt	2,033	3,589	1,696	4,598
Sandoval	9,332	9,411	7,080	9,005
San Juan	11,094	16,202	8,963	18,690
San Miguel	6,131	2,763	5,227	3,485
Santa Fe	23,581	12,891	18,262	15,886
Sierra	1,595	2,507	1,335	2,663
Socorro	2,960	3,114	2,541	3,403
Taos	6,271	2,897	5,144	4,154
Torrance	1,618	2,252	1,274	2,326
Union	638	1,291	488	1,503
Valencia	7,136	7,874	5,393	8,474
Totals	244,497	270,341	201,769	307,101

New Mexico Vote Since 1940

1940, Roosevelt, Dem., 103,699; Willkie, Rep., 79,315.

1944, Roosevelt, Dem., 81,389; Dewey, Rep., 70,688; Watson, Proh., 148.

1948, Truman, Dem., 105,464; Dewey, Rep., 80,303; Wallace, Prog., 1,037; Watson, Proh., 127; Thomas, Soc., 83; Teichert, Soc. Labor, 49.

1952, Eisenhower, Rep., 132,170; Stevenson, Dem., 105,661; Hamblen, Proh., 297; Hallinan, Ind. Prog., 225; MacArthur, Christian National, 220; Hass, Soc. Labor, 35.

1956, Eisenhower, Rep., 146,788; Stevenson, Dem., 106,098; Holtwick, Proh., 607; Andrews, Ind., 364; Hass, Soc. Labor, 69.

1960, Kennedy, Dem., 156,027; Nixon, Rep., 153,733; Decker, Proh., 777; Hass, Soc. Labor, 570.

1964, Johnson, Dem., 194,017; Goldwater, Rep., 131,838; Hass, Soc. Labor, 1,217; Munn, Proh., 543.

1968, Nixon, Rep., 169,692; Humphrey, Dem., 130,081; Wallace, 3d party, 25,737; Chavez, 1,519; Halstead, Soc. Worker, 252.

1972, Nixon, Rep., 235,606; McGovern, Dem., 141,084; Schmitz, Amer., 8,767; Jenness, Soc. Workers, 474.

1976, Carter, Dem., 201,148; Ford, Rep., 211,419; Camejo, Soc. Workers, 2,462; MacBride, Libertarian, 1,110; Zeidler, Soc., 240; Bubar, Proh., 211.

1980, Reagan, Rep., 250,779; Carter, Dem., 167,826; Anderson, Ind., 29,459; Clark, Libertarian, 4,365; Commoner, Citizens, 2,202; Bubar, Statesman, 1,281; Pulley, Soc. Worker, 325.

1984, Reagan, Rep., 307,101; Mondale, Dem., 201,769; Bergland, Libertarian, 4,459.

1988, Bush, Rep., 270,341; Dukakis, Dem., 244,497; Paul, Lib., 3,268; Fulani, New Alliance, 2,237.

New York

County	1988 Dukakis (D)	1988 Bush (R)	1984 Mondale (D)	1984 Reagan (R)
Albany	86,564	59,534	75,447	74,542
Allegany	5,614	11,880	4,720	14,527
Bronx	218,245	76,043	223,112	109,308
Broome	48,130	47,610	37,658	58,109
Cattaraugus	12,447	19,691	10,194	24,162
Cayuga	15,044	16,934	12,207	21,451
Chautauqua	25,814	31,642	22,986	39,597
Chemung	15,966	20,951	14,638	24,909
Chenango	8,021	11,727	6,343	14,254
Clinton	12,670	15,702	10,804	19,549
Columbia	11,585	15,111	8,960	18,814
Cortland	7,673	10,934	6,438	13,691
Delaware	7,463	11,391	5,745	14,002
Dutchess	38,968	62,165	32,867	70,324
Erie	238,779	188,796	237,631	222,882
Essex	6,623	10,350	5,119	12,114
Franklin	7,928	9,135	6,400	10,617
Fulton	9,012	11,757	7,644	14,887
Genesee	9,945	14,182	8,549	16,582
Greene	7,265	11,874	5,858	14,150

	1988		1984	
Hamilton	976	2,320	737	2,637
Herkimer	12,694	15,104	10,346	18,827
Jefferson	14,137	19,304	10,960	23,445
Kings	363,916	178,961	368,518	230,064
Lewis	4,252	5,787	2,757	7,069
Livingston	9,506	14,004	7,399	16,389
Madison	10,665	14,902	8,291	17,568
Monroe	153,650	155,271	132,109	182,696
Montgomery	11,371	11,128	9,044	14,398
Nassau	250,130	337,430	240,697	392,017
New York	385,675	115,927	379,521	144,281
Niagara	43,801	42,537	41,368	51,289
Oneida	47,665	55,039	42,603	65,377
Onondaga	94,751	104,080	81,777	121,857
Ontario	17,341	21,780	12,844	24,507
Orange	38,465	65,446	32,663	69,413
Orleans	5,913	9,028	4,429	10,453
Oswego	18,430	25,362	14,437	31,481
Otsego	11,069	13,021	9,582	16,777
Putnam	12,158	24,086	9,473	25,707
Queens	325,147	217,049	328,379	285,477
Rensselaer	33,066	35,412	26,755	43,892
Richmond	47,812	77,427	44,345	83,187
Rockland	47,634	63,825	44,687	70,020
St. Lawrence	18,921	20,290	15,963	26,062
Saratoga	31,684	43,498	22,166	47,394
Schenectady	36,483	33,364	30,612	42,808
Schoharie	5,389	7,008	3,996	8,692
Schuyler	2,900	4,291	2,422	5,207
Seneca	6,215	7,221	4,825	9,420
Steuben	12,824	25,359	10,471	28,848
Suffolk	199,215	311,242	171,295	335,485
Sullivan	11,635	15,713	10,475	18,037
Tioga	8,102	12,670	5,860	14,856
Tompkins	21,455	14,932	19,357	18,255
Ulster	30,744	41,173	26,445	47,372
Warren	8,580	15,860	5,886	17,616
Washington	8,201	14,103	5,909	16,580
Wayne	12,959	20,613	9,700	24,171
Westchester	169,860	197,956	160,225	229,005
Wyoming	5,228	9,451	4,381	11,199
Yates	3,507	5,488	2,670	6,367
Totals	3,347,882	3,081,871	3,119,609	3,664,763

New York Vote Since 1940

1940, Roosevelt, Dem., 2,834,500; American Lab., 417,418; total, 3,251,918; Willkie, Rep., 3,027,478; Thomas, Soc., 18,950; Babson, Proh., 3,250.

1944, Roosevelt, Dem., 2,478,598; American Lab., 496,405; Liberal, 329,325; total, 3,304,238; Dewey, Rep., 2,987,647; Teichert, Ind. Gov't., 14,352; Thomas, Soc., 10,553.

1948, Truman, Dem., 2,557,642; Liberal, 222,562; total, 2,780,204; Dewey, Rep., 2,841,163; Wallace, Amer. Lab., 509,559; Thomas, Soc., 40,879; Teichert, Ind. Gov't., 2,729; Dobbs, Soc. Workers, 2,675.

1952, Eisenhower, Rep., 3,952,815; Stevenson, Dem., 2,687,890, Liberal, 416,711; total, 3,104,601; Hallinan, American Lab., 64,211; Hoopes, Soc., 2,664; Dobbs, Soc. Workers, 2,212; Hass, Ind. Gov't., 1,560; scattering, 178; blank and void, 87,813.

1956, Eisenhower, Rep., 4,340,340; Stevenson, Dem., 2,458,212; Liberal, 292,557; total, 2,750,769; write-in votes for Andrews, 1,027; Werdel, 492; Hass, 150; Hoopes, 82; others, 476.

1960, Kennedy, Dem., 3,423,909; Liberal, 406,176; total, 3,830,085; Nixon, Rep., 3,446,419; Dobbs, Soc. Workers, 14,319; scattering, 256; blank and void, 88,896.

1964, Johnson, Dem., 4,913,156; Goldwater, Rep., 2,243,559; Hass, Soc. Labor, 6,085; DeBerry, Soc. Workers, 3,215; scattering, 188; blank and void, 151,383.

1968, Nixon, Rep., 3,007,932; Humphrey, Dem., 3,378,470; Wallace, 3d party, 358,864; Blomen, Soc. Labor, 8,432; Halstead, Soc. Worker, 11,851; Gregory, Freedom and Peace, 24,517; blank, void, and scattering, 171,624.

1972, Nixon, Rep., 3,824,642; Conservative, 368,136; McGovern, Dem., 2,767,956; Liberal, 183,128; Reed, Soc. Workers, 7,797; Fisher, Soc. Labor, 4,530; Hall, Com., 5,641; blank, void, or scattered, 161,641.

1976, Carter, Dem., 3,389,558; Ford, Rep., 3,100,791; MacBride, Libertarian, 12,197; Hall, Com., 10,270; Camejo, Soc. Workers, 6,996; LaRouche, U.S. Labor, 5,413; blank, void, or scattered, 143,037.

1980, Reagan, Rep., 2,893,831; Carter, Dem., 2,728,372; Anderson, Lib., 467,801; Clark, Libertarian, 52,648; McCormack, Right to Life, 24,159; Commoner, Citizens, 23,186; Hall, Com., 7,414; DeBerry, Soc. Workers, 2,068; Griswold, Workers World, 1,416; scattering, 1,064.

1984, Reagan, Rep., 3,664,763; Mondale, Dem., 3,119,609; Bergland, Libertarian, 11,949.

1988, Bush, Rep., 3,081,871; Dukakis, Dem., 3,347,882; Marra, Right to Life, 20,497; Fulani, New Alliance, 15,845.

North Carolina

	1988		1984	
	Dukakis	Bush	Mondale	Reagan
County	(D)	(R)	(D)	(R)
Alamance	12,642	24,131	11,230	26,063
Alexander	4,148	7,968	3,581	8,502
Alleghany	2,087	2,174	2,013	2,589
Anson	4,831	2,782	5,015	3,719
Ashe	4,034	6,019	4,009	6,611
Avery	1,367	4,277	1,159	4,702
Beaufort	5,352	8,190	5,987	9,284
Bertie	3,762	2,145	3,953	2,879
Bladen	5,031	3,770	5,064	4,701
Brunswick	7,681	10,007	6,774	9,673
Buncombe	26,964	36,828	23,337	37,698
Burke	10,848	15,933	10,353	18,766
Cabarrus	10,686	22,524	8,477	22,528
Caldwell	7,862	15,176	7,311	17,024
Camden	1,081	1,144	1,075	1,282
Carteret	6,859	11,076	5,882	11,637
Caswell	4,189	3,299	4,157	3,992
Catawba	12,922	28,872	11,700	31,476
Chatham	7,600	6,999	7,458	8,595
Cherokee	2,567	4,557	2,776	4,894
Chowan	1,756	1,884	1,736	2,171
Clay	1,289	2,174	1,340	2,259
Cleveland	10,321	14,039	10,288	17,095
Columbus	9,172	6,659	8,728	9,150
Craven	7,313	12,057	7,186	12,893
Cumberland	23,789	27,057	22,614	31,602
Currituck	1,555	2,443	1,668	2,885
Dare	2,806	5,234	1,839	4,738
Davidson	13,215	28,374	11,469	30,471
Davie	3,166	7,988	2,911	8,201
Duplin	5,945	5,774	6,830	7,708
Durham	35,441	29,928	32,244	29,185
Edgecombe	9,044	6,831	10,545	9,635
Forsyth	39,726	57,688	36,814	59,208
Franklin	5,438	5,499	4,766	5,984
Gaston	14,582	34,775	14,142	39,167
Gates	2,024	1,451	2,225	1,694
Graham	1,313	2,091	1,494	2,514
Granville	5,280	4,880	5,217	6,302
Greene	2,729	2,498	2,772	3,195
Guilford	50,351	66,060	46,027	73,096
Halifax	8,726	7,462	9,276	8,832
Harnett	7,259	9,749	7,106	11,198
Haywood	9,010	8,957	7,956	10,146
Henderson	9,338	19,711	7,222	19,369
Hertford	4,943	2,977	4,498	3,176
Hoke	3,281	2,020	3,214	2,449
Hyde	1,316	940	1,004	1,195
Iredell	10,530	21,536	9,999	23,641
Jackson	4,933	5,166	4,367	5,582
Johnston	8,717	15,563	7,833	16,210
Jones	1,946	1,649	2,025	2,062
Lee	4,231	7,104	3,925	8,198
Lenoir	7,649	10,669	8,556	13,321
Lincoln	6,444	11,651	5,996	12,621
McDowell	4,449	6,526	4,076	7,639
Macon	3,773	6,026	3,570	6,661
Madison	3,033	3,453	2,988	3,666
Martin	3,598	3,149	3,870	4,266
Mecklenburg	71,907	106,236	63,190	106,754
Mitchell	1,377	4,620	1,286	4,737
Montgomery	3,995	4,504	3,831	5,109
Moore	7,642	14,543	7,063	14,681
Nash	8,740	15,906	8,588	17,295
New Hanover	15,401	23,807	12,591	23,771
Northampton	4,599	2,415	5,094	3,198
Onslow	7,162	12,253	5,713	13,928
Orange	22,326	14,503	20,564	15,585
Pamlico	2,188	2,297	2,152	2,554
Pasquotank	3,860	4,006	3,854	4,646
Pender	4,377	4,926	4,354	5,079
Perquimans	1,543	1,781	1,441	1,939
Person	3,777	4,832	3,528	5,854
Pitt	14,777	18,245	13,481	18,983
Polk	2,534	3,874	2,169	4,046
Randolph	8,641	23,881	7,511	25,759
Richmond	7,151	5,073	7,494	6,807
Robeson	16,988	9,908	15,257	12,947
Rockingham	11,551	14,591	10,605	17,895
Rowan	12,127	23,192	10,643	25,207
Rutherford	6,926	10,337	6,862	11,369
Sampson	8,009	8,524	9,115	10,665
Scotland	3,865	3,199	4,028	4,077
Stanly	6,627	11,885	6,138	13,116
Stokes	5,319	8,661	4,950	9,515
Surry	7,245	11,393	7,188	13,340
Swain	1,821	1,795	2,000	2,012
Transylvania	4,280	7,009	3,733	6,956

Tyrrell	785	637	807	774
Union	8,820	17,015	7,048	16,885
Vance	5,631	5,625	5,880	6,836
Wake	61,352	81,613	50,323	81,251
Warren	4,249	2,163	3,946	2,664
Washington	2,806	2,186	3,114	2,731
Watauga	6,048	8,662	5,163	9,370
Wayne	9,135	15,292	10,011	17,961
Wilkes	7,230	15,231	6,852	18,670
Wilson	8,214	10,997	8,343	12,243
Yadkin	3,195	7,918	3,075	8,976
Yancey	3,803	4,160	3,651	4,296
Totals	890,167	1,237,258	824,287	1,346,481

North Carolina Vote Since 1940

1940, Roosevelt, Dem., 609,015; Willkie, Rep., 213,633.

1944, Roosevelt, Dem., 527,399; Dewey, Rep., 263,155.

1948, Truman, Dem., 459,070; Dewey, Rep., 258,572; Thurmond, States' Rights, 69,652; Wallace, Prog., 3,915.

1952, Eisenhower, Rep., 558,107; Stevenson, Dem., 652,803.

1956, Eisenhower, Rep., 575,062; Stevenson, Dem., 590,530.

1960, Kennedy, Dem., 713,136; Nixon, Rep., 655,420.

1964, Johnson, Dem., 800,139; Goldwater Rep., 624,844.

1968, Nixon, Rep., 627,192; Humphrey, Dem., 464,113; Wallace, 3d party, 496,188.

1972, Nixon, Rep., 1,054,889; McGovern, Dem., 438,705; Schmitz, Amer., 25,018.

1976, Dem., 927,365; Ford, Rep., 741,960; Anderson, Amer., 5,607; MacBride, Libertarian, 2,219; LaRouche, U.S. Labor, 755.

1980, Reagan, Rep., 915,018; Carter, Dem., 875,635; Anderson, Ind., 52,800; Clark, Libertarian, 9,677; Commoner, Citizens, 2,287; DeBerry, Soc. Workers, 416.

1984, Reagan, Rep., 1,346,481; Mondale, Dem., 824,287; Bergland, Libertarian, 3,794.

1988, Bush, Rep., 1,237,258; Dukakis, Dem., 890,167; Fulani, New Alliance, 5,682; Paul, write-in, 1,263.

North Dakota

	1988		1984	
County	Dukakis (D)	Bush (R)	Mondale (D)	Reagan (R)
Adams	708	1,018	530	1,343
Barnes	2,858	3,631	2,507	4,348
Benson	1,691	1,316	1,599	1,729
Billings	211	437	133	505
Bottineau	1,684	2,530	1,279	3,356
Bowman	737	1,111	562	1,559
Burke	693	971	543	1,298
Burleigh	10,760	18,000	8,781	19,913
Cass	22,107	26,699	18,054	29,221
Cavalier	1,333	2,096	1,110	2,661
Dickey	1,249	2,064	1,051	2,460
Divide	875	869	626	1,165
Dunn	892	1,263	716	1,583
Eddy	748	891	796	1,049
Emmons	925	1,634	620	1,885
Foster	837	1,218	765	1,422
Golden Valley	388	781	325	964
Grand Forks	12,494	14,801	10,050	15,898
Grant	654	1,351	507	1,607
Griggs	846	1,020	828	1,254
Hettinger	698	1,395	524	1,646
Kidder	678	1,039	506	1,240
La Moure	1,223	1,642	1,086	1,978
Logan	540	1,111	401	1,222
McHenry	1,665	1,888	1,283	2,485
McIntosh	598	1,726	427	2,047
McKenzie	1,273	1,949	974	2,610
McLean	2,428	2,906	2,082	3,673
Mercer	1,843	3,013	1,729	3,705
Morton	4,708	5,588	3,996	7,146
Mountrail	1,977	1,443	1,565	1,959
Nelson	1,151	1,078	1,026	1,445
Oliver	526	696	419	915
Pembina	1,616	2,471	1,367	2,895
Pierce	1,008	1,422	691	1,883
Ramsey	2,665	3,103	2,304	4,150
Ransom	1,459	1,362	1,222	1,706
Renville	837	893	592	1,163
Richland	3,523	4,670	3,047	5,980
Rolette	2,426	1,126	2,179	1,479
Sargent	1,306	1,119	1,295	1,385
Sheridan	428	885	306	1,075
Sioux	701	325	655	442
Slope	202	315	174	419
Stark	3,678	6,137	2,759	7,641
Steele	895	690	781	941
Stutsman	4,214	5,375	3,495	6,591
Towner	970	946	789	1,242
Traill	1,940	2,562	1,580	3,037
Walsh	2,646	3,250	2,264	4,347
Ward	9,906	13,179	7,336	16,077

Wells	1,317	1,901	1,036	2,426
Williams	4,004	5,653	3,177	8,166
Totals	127,739	166,559	104,429	200,336

North Dakota Vote Since 1940

1940, Roosevelt, Dem., 124,036; Willkie, Rep., 154,590; Thomas, Soc., 1,279; Knutson, Com., 545; Babson, Proh., 325.

1944, Roosevelt, Dem., 100,144; Dewey, Rep., 118,535; Thomas, Soc., 943, Watson, Proh., 549.

1948, Truman, Dem., 95,812; Dewey, Rep., 115,139; Wallace, Prog., 8,391; Thomas, Soc., 1,000, Thurmond, States' Rights, 374.

1952, Eisenhower, Rep., 191,712; Stevenson, Dem., 76,694; MacArthur, Christian Nationalist, 1,075; Hallinan, Prog., 344; Hamblen, Proh., 302.

1956, Eisenhower, Rep., 156,766; Stevenson, Dem., 96,742; Andrews, Amer., 483.

1960, Kennedy, Dem., 123,963; Nixon, Rep., 154,310; Dobbs, Soc. Workers, 158.

1964, Johnson, Dem., 149,784; Goldwater, Rep., 108,207; DeBerry, Soc. Worker, 224; Munn, Proh., 174.

1968, Nixon, Rep., 138,669; Humphrey, Dem., 94,769; Wallace, 3d party, 14,244; Halstead, Soc. Worker, 128; Munn, Prohibition, 38; Troxell, Ind., 34.

1972, Nixon, Rep., 174,109; McGovern, Dem., 100,384; Jenness, Soc. Workers, 288; Hall, Com., 87; Schmitz, Amer., 5,646.

1976, Carter, Dem., 136,078; Ford, Rep., 153,470; Anderson, Amer., 3,698; McCarthy, Ind., 2,952; Maddox, Amer. Ind., 269; MacBride, Libertarian, 256; scattering, 371.

1980, Reagan, Rep., 193,695; Carter, Dem., 79,189; Anderson, Ind., 23,640; Clark, Libertarian, 3,743; Commoner, Libertarian, 429; McLain, Nat'l People's League, 296; Greaves, American, 235; Hall, Com., 93; DeBerry, Soc. Workers, 89; McReynolds, Soc., 82; Bubar, Statesman, 54.

1984, Reagan, Rep., 200,336; Mondale, Dem., 104,429; Bergland, Libertarian, 703.

1988, Bush, Rep., 166,559; Dukakis, Dem., 127,739; Paul, Lib., 1,315; LaRouche, Natl. Econ. Recovery, 905.

Ohio

	1988		1984	
County	Dukakis (D)	Bush (R)	Mondale (D)	Reagan (R)
Adams	3,740	5,916	3,534	6,113
Allen	13,727	31,021	12,176	33,506
Ashland	6,072	12,726	4,786	14,339
Ashtabula	20,536	17,654	19,344	21,669
Athens	10,795	9,314	10,201	11,548
Auglaize	4,756	13,562	4,102	14,766
Belmont	19,515	12,214	19,458	15,170
Brown	5,047	7,539	4,067	8,221
Butler	33,770	75,725	27,700	76,216
Carroll	4,667	6,179	3,771	6,703
Champaign	4,272	8,995	3,544	9,935
Clark	23,247	32,729	21,154	35,831
Clermont	15,352	37,417	11,713	35,316
Clinton	3,746	8,856	3,332	9,603
Columbiana	21,561	21,175	20,155	24,552
Coshocton	6,020	8,282	4,392	9,842
Crawford	6,018	12,472	4,932	14,682
Cuyahoga	353,401	242,439	362,626	284,094
Darke	6,851	14,914	5,904	16,379
Defiance	5,448	9,566	5,004	10,951
Delaware	7,590	20,693	5,773	19,050
Erie	15,097	16,670	13,508	19,174
Fairfield	12,504	29,208	9,817	30,843
Fayette	2,623	6,186	2,126	6,838
Franklin	147,585	226,265	131,530	250,360
Fulton	5,076	10,230	4,217	11,412
Gallia	4,834	7,399	4,251	8,194
Geauga	11,874	22,339	9,954	22,369
Greene	18,025	34,432	17,129	34,267
Guernsey	5,926	8,507	4,967	10,252
Hamilton	140,354	227,004	140,350	246,288
Hancock	7,435	19,696	5,758	22,169
Hardin	4,145	7,291	3,813	8,722
Harrison	3,881	3,298	3,370	4,276
Henry	3,764	8,618	2,779	9,317
Highland	4,278	8,776	3,784	9,000
Hocking	3,706	5,426	3,280	6,071
Holmes	2,179	5,064	1,737	5,146
Huron	7,794	12,633	6,609	14,388
Jackson	4,505	6,671	4,369	7,411
Jefferson	22,095	14,141	22,832	17,105
Knox	6,882	12,180	5,730	14,062

County					County			
Lake	39,667	52,963	36,711	54,587	Beaver	777	2,013	536	2,689
Lawrence	11,628	12,937	11,431	14,973	Beckham	3,388	3,463	2,601	5,005
Licking	16,793	34,540	13,995	37,560	Blaine	1,775	2,889	1,484	4,037
Logan	4,484	11,099	3,645	12,230	Bryan	6,849	4,615	5,475	6,246
Lorain	55,600	50,410	52,970	57,379	Caddo	5,387	4,689	4,463	6,811
Lucas	99,755	83,788	97,293	100,285	Canadian	7,453	17,872	5,245	20,929
Madison	3,421	8,303	2,928	8,979	Carter	7,988	8,430	6,161	11,578
Mahoning	75,524	43,722	76,514	53,424	Cherokee	6,483	5,838	5,307	7,614
Marion	9,596	14,864	8,827	17,392	Choctaw	3,362	2,217	2,801	3,155
Medina	19,505	29,962	15,897	30,690	Cimarron	470	1,153	359	1,420
Meigs	3,699	5,486	3,549	6,307	Cleveland	22,067	36,313	16,512	42,806
Mercer	4,978	11,162	4,422	11,542	Coal	1,365	891	1,284	1,259
Miami	11,138	/24,915	9,695	26,300	Comanche	11,441	17,464	8,890	21,382
Monroe	4,269	2,557	3,611	3,302	Cotton	1,482	1,266	1,264	1,796
Montgomery	95,737	131,596	94,016	137,053	Craig	2,940	2,463	2,515	3,629
Morgan	2,085	3,713	1,868	3,994	Creek	9,512	11,308	7,465	15,011
Morrow	3,515	7,130	2,839	8,116	Custer	3,697	6,735	2,700	8,191
Muskingum	11,691	19,736	10,037	21,821	Delaware	4,889	5,248	3,789	6,690
Noble	2,079	3,155	1,777	3,853	Dewey	963	1,543	664	2,098
Ottawa	8,038	9,352	7,053	10,920	Ellis	786	1,422	562	1,881
Paulding	3,114	5,381	2,811	5,545	Garfield	8,067	15,246	5,730	19,642
Perry	5,011	6,602	3,961	7,548	Garvin	5,438	5,109	4,215	7,505
Pickaway	4,905	10,796	4,110	11,942	Grady	6,689	7,994	4,846	11,042
Pike	5,191	5,611	4,895	6,318	Grant	1,249	1,690	825	2,470
Portage	25,607	26,334	21,719	29,536	Greer	1,256	1,225	1,220	1,664
Preble	4,937	10,297	4,198	11,065	Harmon	990	611	765	1,009
Putnam	4,004	11,183	3,194	11,936	Harper	593	1,281	373	1,748
Richland	19,617	30,047	16,141	35,299	Haskell	2,963	1,822	2,535	2,417
Ross	9,271	14,563	8,020	17,015	Hughes	3,259	2,037	2,901	2,663
Sandusky	9,709	14,203	8,564	17,214	Jackson	3,542	4,423	2,996	5,773
Scioto	14,442	16,029	14,120	18,818	Jefferson	1,767	1,063	1,496	1,656
Seneca	9,504	13,704	7,905	16,520	Johnston	2,042	1,518	1,820	2,195
Shelby	5,065	12,198	4,315	13,509	Kay	7,751	12,646	6,044	16,731
Stark	69,639	87,087	65,157	98,434	Kingfisher	1,777	4,011	1,125	5,528
Summit	112,612	101,155	109,569	115,637	Kiowa	2,298	2,030	2,016	2,951
Trumbull	58,674	38,815	56,902	45,623	Latimer	2,365	1,830	1,858	2,210
Tuscarawas	14,185	17,145	13,149	19,366	Le Flore	6,594	6,964	5,990	8,604
Union	3,130	8,846	2,579	9,336	Lincoln	4,225	6,409	3,020	8,088
Van Wert	3,848	9,410	3,338	9,570	Logan	4,603	6,947	3,551	8,356
Vinton	2,385	2,652	1,990	3,041	Love	1,889	1,361	1,359	1,833
Warren	11,145	31,419	9,031	29,848	McClain	3,594	4,771	2,549	6,056
Washington	9,967	14,767	7,920	16,529	McCurtain	4,928	4,920	3,994	6,381
Wayne	13,571	22,320	11,323	24,475	McIntosh	4,041	2,665	3,479	3,646
Williams	4,666	10,782	3,624	10,804	Major	982	2,638	619	3,385
Wood	18,579	26,013	15,907	29,750	Marshall	2,730	1,911	2,039	2,488
Wyandot	2,936	6,178	2,342	7,204	Mayes	6,691	6,115	5,154	8,585
Totals	1,939,629	2,416,549	1,825,440	2,678,559	Murray	2,697	2,056	2,229	3,073
					Muskogee	13,760	11,147	12,343	14,652
					Noble	1,661	3,015	1,238	4,018
					Nowata	2,203	2,000	1,687	3,030
					Okfuskee	2,209	1,851	1,684	2,443
					Oklahoma	75,812	135,376	60,235	159,974
					Okmulgee	8,262	5,674	7,380	8,704
					Osage	7,778	7,162	6,095	10,083
					Ottawa	6,658	5,026	5,781	7,666
					Pawnee	2,781	3,324	2,165	4,699
					Payne	10,568	16,027	7,653	20,811
					Pittsburg	8,623	7,594	6,860	9,778
					Pontotoc	6,484	6,609	5,526	8,301
					Pottawatomie	8,873	12,099	6,966	16,143
					Pushmataha	2,430	1,841	2,079	2,499
					Roger Mills	866	1,132	680	1,550
					Rogers	8,771	12,940	6,013	16,137
					Seminole	4,911	4,078	3,957	6,009
					Sequoyah	4,951	5,710	4,202	7,042
					Stephens	7,833	9,844	6,359	12,871
					Texas	1,717	4,971	1,033	5,968
					Tillman	2,148	1,754	1,674	2,637
					Tulsa	69,044	127,512	58,274	159,549
					Wagoner	7,378	10,219	5,271	12,534
					Washington	6,971	14,613	5,476	19,043
					Washita	2,290	2,402	1,547	3,847
					Woods	1,735	2,835	1,231	3,741
					Woodward	2,408	4,996	1,647	6,376
					Totals	483,423	678,367	385,080	861,530

Ohio Vote Since 1940

1940, Roosevelt, Dem., 1,733,139; Willkie, Rep., 1,586,773.

1944, Roosevelt, Dem., 1,570,763; Dewey, Rep., 1,582,293.

1948, Truman, Dem., 1,452,791; Dewey, Rep., 1,445,684; Wallace, Prog., 37,596.

1952, Eisenhower, Rep., 2,100,391; Stevenson, Dem., 1,600,367.

1956, Eisenhower, Rep., 2,262,610; Stevenson, Dem., 1,439,655.

1960, Kennedy, Dem., 1,944,248; Nixon, Rep., 2,217,611.

1964, Johnson, Dem., 2,498,331; Goldwater, Rep., 1,470,865.

1968, Nixon, Rep., 1,791,014; Humphrey, Dem., 1,700,586; Wallace, 3d party, 467,495; Gregory, 372; Munn, Proh., 19; Blomen, Soc. Labor, 120; Halstead, Soc. Worker, 69; Mitchell, Com., 23.

1972, Nixon, Rep., 2,441,827; McGovern, Dem., 1,558,889; Fisher, Soc. Labor, 7,107; Hall, Com., 6,437; Schmitz, Amer., 80,067; Wallace, Ind., 460.

1976, Carter, Dem., 2,011,621; Ford, Rep., 2,000,505; McCarthy, Ind., 58,258; Maddox, Amer. Ind., 15,529; MacBride, Libertarian, 8,961; Hall, Com., 7,817; Camejo, Soc. Workers, 4,717; LaRouche, U.S. Labor, 4,335; scattered, 130.

1980, Reagan, Rep., 2,206,545; Carter, Dem., 1,752,414; Anderson, Ind., 254,472; Clark, Libertarian, 49,033; Commoner, Citizens, 8,564; Hall, Com., 4,729; Congress, Ind. 4,029; Griswold, Workers World, 3,790; Bubar, Statesman, 27.

1984, Reagan, Rep., 2,678,559; Mondale, Dem., 1,825,440; Bergland, Libertarian, 5,886.

1988, Bush, Rep., 2,416,549; Dukakis, Dem., 1,939,629; Fulani, Ind., 12,017; Paul, Ind., 11,926.

Oklahoma

	1988		1984	
County	Dukakis (D)	Bush (R)	Mondale (D)	Reagan (R)
Adair	2,624	3,558	2,266	4,423
Alfalfa	1,117	1,960	866	2,715
Atoka	2,565	1,971	2,047	2,361

Oklahoma Vote Since 1940

1940, Roosevelt, Dem., 474,313; Willkie, Rep., 348,872; Babson, Proh., 3,027.

1944, Roosevelt, Dem., 401,549; Dewey, Rep., 319,424; Watson, Proh., 1,663.

1948, Truman, Dem., 452,782; Dewey, Rep., 268,817.

1952, Eisenhower, Rep., 518,045; Stevenson, Dem., 430,939.

1956, Eisenhower, Rep., 473,769; Stevenson, Dem., 385,581.

1960, Kennedy, Dem., 370,111; Nixon, Rep., 533,039.

1964, Johnson, Dem., 519,834; Goldwater, Rep. 412,665.

1968, Nixon, Rep., 449,697; Humphrey, Dem., 301,658; Wallace, 3d party, 191,731.

1972, Nixon, Rep. 759,025; McGovern, Dem., 247,147; Schmitz, Amer., 23,728.

1976, Carter, Dem., 532,442; Ford, Rep., 545,708; McCarthy, Ind., 14,101.

1980, Reagan, Rep., 695,570; Carter, Dem., 402,026; Anderson, Ind., 38,284; Clark, Libertarian, 13,828.

1984, Reagan, Rep., 861,530; Mondale, Dem., 385,080; Bergland, Libertarian, 9,066.

1988, Bush, Rep., 678,367; Dukakis, Dem., 483,423; Paul, Lib., 6,261; Fulani, New Alliance, 2,985.

Oregon

County	1988 Dukakis (D)	1988 Bush (R)	1984 Mondale (D)	1984 Reagan (R)
Baker	2,896	3,696	2,591	5,204
Benton	16,930	14,004	16,073	17,836
Clackamas	59,799	61,381	47,254	68,630
Clatsop	8,074	5,956	7,525	7,522
Columbia	8,983	6,424	8,219	7,811
Coos	13,996	10,153	13,582	13,637
Crook	2,719	3,049	2,268	3,773
Curry	4,015	4,761	3,423	5,363
Deschutes	14,264	16,425	11,671	19,323
Douglas	17,255	20,120	14,609	25,243
Gilliam	417	470	359	700
Grant	1,437	2,264	1,344	2,695
Harney	1,379	1,833	1,290	2,197
Hood River	3,275	3,257	3,022	4,531
Jackson	28,028	32,516	22,230	37,895
Jefferson	2,346	2,509	1,920	3,283
Josephine	10,646	15,876	8,539	19,470
Klamath	8,429	13,484	7,575	17,686
Lake	1,237	2,161	1,184	2,466
Lane	69,883	47,563	63,999	61,493
Lincoln	9,598	7,364	8,637	9,110
Linn	17,007	18,312	16,161	23,463
Malheur	2,965	6,285	2,611	8,441
Marion	41,193	45,292	36,440	54,535
Morrow	1,375	1,529	1,254	2,130
Multnomah	161,361	95,561	144,179	119,932
Polk	9,626	10,553	8,709	12,678
Sherman	435	555	398	828
Tillamook	5,529	4,297	4,988	5,267
Umatilla	8,327	10,254	8,246	14,211
Union	4,682	5,061	4,134	6,645
Wallowa	1,425	1,993	1,204	2,619
Wasco	5,141	4,462	5,526	6,905
Washington	59,837	67,018	44,602	75,877
Wheeler	274	367	253	504
Yamhill	11,423	13,321	9,450	15,797
Totals	**616,206**	**560,126**	**536,479**	**685,700**

Oregon Vote Since 1940

1940, Roosevelt, Dem., 258,415; Willkie, Rep., 219,555; Aiken, Soc. Labor, 2,487; Thomas, Soc., 398; Browder, Com., 191; Babson, Proh., 154.

1944, Roosevelt, Dem., 248,635; Dewey, Rep., 225,365; Thomas, Soc., 3,785; Watson, Proh., 2,362.

1948, Truman, Dem., 243,147; Dewey, Rep., 260,904; Wallace, Prog., 14,978; Thomas, Soc., 5,051.

1952, Eisenhower, Rep., 420,815; Stevenson, Dem., 270,579; Hallinan, Ind., 3,665.

1956, Eisenhower, Rep., 406,393; Stevenson, Dem., 329,204.

1960, Kennedy, Dem., 367,402; Nixon, Rep., 408,060.

1964, Johnson, Dem., 501,017; Goldwater, Rep., 282,779; write-in, 2,509.

1968, Nixon, Rep., 408,433; Humphrey, Dem., 358,866; Wallace, 3d party, 49,683; write-in, McCarthy, 1,496; N. Rockefeller, 69; others, 1,075.

1972, Nixon, Rep., 486,686; McGovern, Dem., 392,760, Schmitz, Amer., 46,211; write-in, 2,289.

1976, Carter, Dem., 490,407; Ford, Rep., 492,120; McCarthy, Ind., 40,207; write-in, 7,142.

1980, Reagan, Rep., 571,044; Carter, Dem., 456,890; Anderson, Ind., 112,389; Clark, Libertarian, 25,838; Commoner, Citizens, 13,642; scattered, 1,713.

1984, Reagan, Rep., 658,700; Mondale, Dem., 536,479.

1988, Bush, Rep., 560,126; Dukakis, Dem., 616,206; Paul, Lib., 14,811; Fulani, Ind., 6,487.

Pennsylvania

County	1988 Dukakis (D)	1988 Bush (R)	1984 Mondale (D)	1984 Reagan (R)
Adams	8,299	15,650	7,289	16,786
Allegheny	348,814	231,137	372,576	284,692
Armstrong	13,892	11,509	14,525	13,709
Beaver	50,327	25,764	54,765	32,052
Bedford	5,754	11,123	5,424	13,085
Berks	41,040	70,153	37,849	74,605
Blair	15,588	25,623	15,651	30,104
Bradford	6,635	13,568	5,474	14,808
Bucks	82,472	127,563	74,568	130,119
Butler	22,341	27,777	24,735	31,676
Cambria	38,517	25,626	39,865	32,173
Cameron	901	1,731	990	2,031
Carbon	9,104	10,232	8,836	10,701
Centre	18,357	23,875	16,194	27,802
Chester	44,853	93,522	38,870	92,221
Clarion	5,616	8,026	5,407	9,836
Clearfield	12,235	14,296	11,963	18,653
Clinton	5,759	5,735	4,525	6,678
Columbia	7,767	12,114	8,254	14,402
Crawford	13,021	17,249	12,792	20,181
Cumberland	24,613	47,292	21,374	49,282
Dauphin	35,079	48,917	33,576	54,330
Delaware	96,144	147,656	98,207	161,754
Elk	5,879	6,737	5,486	8,470
Erie	53,913	48,306	52,471	55,860
Fayette	33,096	16,915	35,098	21,314
Forest	865	1,159	839	1,468
Franklin	12,368	27,086	11,480	27,243
Fulton	1,532	3,086	1,309	3,254
Greene	9,126	4,879	9,365	6,376
Huntingdon	4,752	8,800	4,430	10,220
Indiana	16,514	14,983	15,791	18,845
Jefferson	6,235	9,743	5,950	11,334
Juniata	2,834	4,881	2,624	5,059
Lackawanna	45,591	42,083	45,851	48,132
Lancaster	38,982	96,979	31,308	99,090
Lawrence	21,884	15,829	23,981	19,277
Lebanon	11,912	24,415	10,520	27,008
Lehigh	42,801	56,363	41,089	61,799
Luzerne	58,553	59,059	58,482	69,169
Lycoming	13,528	24,792	13,147	28,498
McKean	5,300	9,323	4,818	10,963
Mercer	24,278	21,301	24,659	24,211
Mifflin	4,790	8,170	5,178	9,106
Monroe	9,859	17,185	8,193	16,109
Montgomery	109,834	170,294	99,741	181,426
Montour	2,031	3,617	2,055	4,174
Northampton	39,264	42,748	37,979	44,648
Northumberland	14,255	20,207	13,748	22,109
Perry	3,910	8,545	3,492	9,365
Philadelphia	449,566	219,053	501,369	267,178
Pike	3,097	6,659	2,503	6,343
Potter	2,119	4,432	1,789	5,164
Schuylkill	24,797	32,666	25,758	37,330
Snyder	2,658	9,054	2,383	8,968
Somerset	13,815	16,809	13,900	19,502
Sullivan	1,091	1,808	952	1,926
Susquehanna	4,871	9,077	4,471	10,566
Tioga	4,807	9,471	4,060	10,532
Union	3,163	7,912	2,747	7,792
Venango	8,624	11,468	9,114	13,507
Warren	6,790	8,991	6,244	10,838
Washington	47,527	28,651	50,911	34,782
Wayne	3,775	9,926	3,155	10,061
Westmoreland	76,710	61,472	79,906	71,377
Wyoming	2,797	6,607	2,518	7,230
York	37,691	72,408	33,359	75,020
Totals	**2,194,944**	**2,300,087**	**2,228,131**	**2,584,323**

Pennsylvania Vote Since 1940

1940, Roosevelt, Dem., 2,171,035; Willkie, Rep., 1,889,848; Thomas, Soc., 10,967; Browder, Com., 4,519; Aiken, Ind. Gov., 1,518.

1944, Roosevelt, Dem., 1,940,479; Dewey, Rep., 1,835,054; Thomas, Soc., 11,721; Watson, Proh., 5,750; Teichert, Ind. Gov., 1,789.

1948, Truman, Dem., 1,752,426; Dewey, Rep., 1,902,197; Wallace, Prog., 55,161; Thomas, Soc., 11,325; Watson, Proh., 10,338; Dobbs, Militant Workers, 2,133; Teichert, Ind. Gov., 1,461.

1952, Eisenhower, Rep., 2,415,789; Stevenson, Dem., 2,146,269; Hamblen, Proh., 8,771; Hallinan, Prog., 4,200; Hoopes, Soc., 2,684; Dobbs, Militant Workers, 1,502; Hass, Ind. Gov., 1,347; scattered, 155.

1956, Eisenhower, Rep., 2,585,252; Stevenson, Dem., 1,981,769; Hass, Soc. Labor, 7,447; Dobbs, Militant Workers, 2,035.

1960, Kennedy, Dem., 2,556,282; Nixon, Rep., 2,439,956; Hass, Soc. Labor, 7,185; Dobbs, Soc. Workers, 2,678; scattering, 440.

1964, Johnson, Dem., 3,130,954; Goldwater, Rep., 1,673,657; DeBerry, Soc. Workers, 10,456; Hass, Soc. Labor, 5,092; scattering, 2,531.

1968, Nixon, Rep., 2,090,017; Humphrey, Dem., 2,259,405; Wallace, 3d party, 378,582; Blomen, Soc. Labor, 4,977; Halstead, Soc. Workers, 4,862; Gregory, 7,821; others, 2,264.

1972, Nixon, Rep., 2,714,521; McGovern, Dem., 1,796,951; Schmitz, Amer., 70,593; Jenness, Soc. Workers, 4,639; Hall, Com., 2,686; others, 2,715.

1976, Carter, Dem., 2,328,677; Ford, Rep., 2,205,604; McCarthy, Ind., 50,584; Maddox, Constitution, 25,344;

Camejo, Soc. Workers, 3,009; LaRouche, U.S. Labor, 2,744; Hall, Com., 1,891; others, 2,934.

1980, Reagan, Rep., 2,261,872; Carter, Dem., 1,937,540; Anderson, Ind., 292,921; Clark, Libertarian, 33,263; DeBerry, Soc. Workers, 20,291; Commoner, Consumer, 10,430; Hall, Com., 5,184.

1984, Reagan, Rep., 2,584,323; Mondale, Dem., 2,228,131; Bergland, Libertarian, 6,982.

1988, Bush, Rep., 2,300,087; Dukakis, Dem., 2,194,944; McCarthy, Consumer, 19,158; Paul, Lib., 12,051.

Rhode Island

City	1988 Dukakis (D)	Bush (R)	1984 Mondale (D)	Reagan (R)
Cranston	19,711	17,129	17,742	19,517
East Providence	11,948	8,181	11,064	10,332
Pawtucket	15,985	9,359	14,109	12,460
Providence	34,806	15,310	35,751	19,748
Warwick	21,662	18,052	19,278	22,276
Totals	225,123	177,761	197,106	212,080

Rhode Island Vote Since 1940

1940, Roosevelt, Dem., 182,182; Willkie, Rep., 138,653; Browder, Com., 239; Babson, Proh., 74.

1944, Roosevelt, Dem., 175,356; Dewey, Rep., 123,487; Watson, Proh., 433.

1948, Truman, Dem., 188,736; Dewey, Rep., 135,787; Wallace, Prog., 2,619; Thomas, Soc., 429; Teichert, Soc. Labor, 131.

1952, Eisenhower, Rep., 210,935; Stevenson, Dem., 203,293; Hallinan, Prog., 187; Hass, Soc. Labor, 83.

1956, Eisenhower, Rep., 225,819; Stevenson, Dem., 161,790.

1960, Kennedy, Dem., 258,032; Nixon, Rep., 147,502.

1964, Johnson, Dem., 315,463; Goldwater, Rep., 74,615.

1968, Nixon, Rep., 122,359; Humphrey, Dem., 246,518; Wallace, 3d party, 15,678; Halstead, Soc. Worker, 383.

1972, Nixon, Rep., 220,383; McGovern, Dem., 194,645; Jenness, Soc. Workers, 729.

1976, Carter, Dem., 227,636; Ford, Rep., 181,249; MacBride, Libertarian, 715; Camejo, Soc. Workers, 462; Hall, Com., 334; Levin, Soc. Labor, 188.

1980, Reagan, Rep., 154,793; Carter, Dem., 198,342; Anderson, Ind., 59,819; Clark, Libertarian, 2,458; Hall, Com., 218; McReynolds, Socialist, 170; DeBerry, Soc. Worker, 90; Griswold, Workers World, 77.

1984, Reagan, Rep., 212,080; Mondale, Dem., 197,106; Bergland, Libertarian, 277.

1988, Bush, Rep., 177,761; Dukakis, Dem., 225,123; Paul, Lib., 825; Fulani, New Alliance, 280.

South Carolina

County	1988 Dukakis (D)	Bush (R)	1984 Mondale (D)	Reagan (R)
Abbeville	3,629	3,738	3,051	3,798
Aiken	10,598	27,665	9,872	25,872
Allendale	1,796	1,295	2,170	1,570
Anderson	12,281	25,939	10,324	24,123
Bamberg	2,830	2,403	2,892	2,908
Barnwell	2,564	4,467	2,811	4,346
Beaufort	8,691	16,184	7,347	13,668
Berkeley	9,312	16,779	7,380	16,972
Calhoun	2,175	2,585	2,315	2,742
Charleston	32,977	49,149	29,470	53,779
Cherokee	4,322	7,763	4,101	8,655
Chester	3,737	3,968	3,559	4,441
Chesterfield	4,699	4,999	4,593	5,451
Clarendon	5,030	4,337	5,591	5,102
Colleton	4,508	4,962	4,910	6,200
Darlington	7,625	9,854	7,456	11,100
Dillon	3,251	3,793	3,360	4,646
Dorchester	7,371	14,756	7,037	15,289
Edgefield	3,020	3,814	3,227	3,224
Fairfield	3,827	2,714	4,117	3,147
Florence	12,531	19,490	14,639	22,753
Georgetown	5,402	7,032	6,392	7,370
Greenville	27,188	67,371	24,137	66,766
Greenwood	6,511	9,096	6,339	10,887
Hampton	3,435	2,826	3,736	3,464
Horry	13,316	24,843	8,940	20,396
Jasper	2,894	2,004	3,753	3,102
Kershaw	4,494	8,877	4,323	8,822
Lancaster	6,181	9,152	5,804	10,383
Laurens	5,930	9,731	5,312	9,729
Lee	3,423	2,936	3,912	3,548
Lexington	11,366	41,457	8,828	38,628
McCormick	1,722	1,172	1,526	1,186
Marion	5,008	4,403	5,043	4,698
Marlboro	3,937	2,921	4,294	3,951
Newberry	3,825	6,427	3,790	7,176
Oconee	4,299	10,184	3,333	8,625
Orangeburg	14,655	13,281	15,121	14,286
Pickens	6,103	17,448	4,481	15,155
Richland	36,420	43,841	32,212	46,773
Saluda	3,225	1,962	3,515	
Spartanburg	22,964	40,801	20,130	41,553
Sumter	9,502	13,161	9,566	12,909
Union	4,420	6,019	4,424	6,331
Williamsburg	7,343	5,914	7,586	6,492
York	11,458	21,657	9,273	20,008
Totals	370,554	606,443	344,459	615,539

South Carolina Vote Since 1940

1940, Roosevelt, Dem., 95,470; Willkie, Rep., 1,727.

1944, Roosevelt, Dem., 90,601; Dewey, Rep., 4,547; Southern Democrats, 7,799; Watson, Proh., 365; Rep. Tolbert faction, 63.

1948, Thurmond, States' Rights, 102,607; Truman, Dem., 34,423; Dewey, Rep., 5,386; Wallace, Prog., 154; Thomas, Soc., 1.

1952, Eisenhower ran on two tickets. Under state law vote cast for two Eisenhower slates of electors could not be combined. Eisenhower, Ind., 158,289; Rep., 9,793; total, 168,082; Stevenson, Dem., 173,004; Hamblen, Proh., 1.

1956, Stevenson, Dem., 136,372; Byrd, Ind., 88,509; Eisenhower, Rep., 75,700; Andrews, Ind., 2.

1960, Kennedy, Dem., 198,129; Nixon, Rep., 188,558; write-in, 1.

1964, Johnson, Dem., 215,700; Goldwater, Rep., 309,048; write-ins: Nixon, 1; Wallace, 5; Powell, 1; Thurmond, 1.

1968, Nixon, Rep., 254,062; Humphrey, Dem., 197,486; Wallace, 3d party, 215,430.

1972, Nixon, Rep., 477,044; McGovern, Dem., 184,559; United Citizens, 2,265; Schmitz, Amer., 10,075; write-in, 17.

1976, Carter, Dem., 450,807; Ford, Rep., 346,149; Anderson, Amer., 2,996; Maddox, Amer. Ind., 1,950; write-in, 681.

1980, Reagan, Rep., 439,277; Carter, Dem., 428,220; Anderson, Ind., 13,868; Clark, Libertarian, 4,807; Rarick, Amer. Ind., 2,086.

1984, Reagan, Rep., 615,539; Mondale, Dem., 344,459; Bergland, Libertarian, 4,359.

1988, Bush, Rep., 606,443; Dukakis, Dem., 370,554; Paul, Lib., 4,935; Fulani, United Citizens, 4,077.

South Dakota

County	1988 Dukakis (D)	Bush (R)	1984 Mondale (D)	Reagan (R)
Aurora	987	856	840	1,029
Beadle	4,523	4,611	3,523	5,876
Bennett	579	663	453	856
Bon Homme	1,574	1,826	1,408	2,478
Brookings	4,860	5,394	4,089	6,679
Brown	8,673	8,537	6,852	10,541
Brule	991	971	961	1,578
Buffalo	334	151	236	253
Butte	1,256	2,291	784	2,865
Campbell	334	909	214	1,035
Chas. Mix	2,205	1,966	1,879	2,660
Clark	1,164	1,247	960	1,748
Clay	2,859	2,307	2,711	3,057
Codington	4,570	5,050	3,528	6,108
Corson	722	710	792	955
Custer	1,180	1,806	858	2,183
Davison	3,705	4,024	3,248	4,783
Day	2,137	1,616	1,932	2,150
Deuel	1,246	1,251	941	1,537
Dewey	1,007	765	772	941
Douglas	695	1,438	536	1,713
Edmunds	1,259	1,327	1,007	1,553
Fall River	1,380	2,002	1,135	2,748
Faulk	714	842	579	1,124
Grant	1,988	2,148	1,606	2,738
Gregory	1,138	1,566	780	1,777
Haakon	379	958	237	1,168
Hamlin	1,258	1,380	963	1,782
Hand	1,101	1,461	846	2,030
Hanson	776	786	625	898
Harding	259	633	186	723
Hughes	2,853	4,545	2,072	4,985
Hutchinson	1,594	2,700	1,237	3,372
Hyde	436	546	350	797
Jackson	450	671	365	903
Jerauld	751	777	542	1,012
Jones	261	521	206	689

	Dukakis	Bush	Mondale	Reagan
Kingsbury	1,472	1,592	1,249	2,121
Lake	2,663	2,439	2,367	3,027
Lawrence	3,705	5,570	2,565	5,949
Lincoln	3,190	3,537	2,626	3,988
Lyman	631	843	478	1,120
McCook	1,492	1,501	1,448	1,902
McPherson	571	1,358	418	1,813
Marshall	1,372	1,142	1,111	1,529
Meade	3,212	5,189	2,093	5,908
Mellette	385	460	303	616
Miner	955	795	960	1,004
Minnehaha	29,135	26,765	23,042	29,908
Moody	1,715	1,161	1,586	1,633
Pennington	12,068	19,510	8,224	21,947
Perkins	851	1,326	714	1,686
Potter	701	1,175	482	1,551
Roberts	2,267	2,012	2,063	2,767
Sanborn	770	815	611	1,080
Shannon	1,206	256	1,489	324
Spink	2,071	1,969	1,680	2,627
Stanley	511	698	351	942
Sully	393	571	266	836
Todd	1,117	535	1,022	679
Tripp	1,219	2,113	935	2,483
Turner	1,780	2,436	1,486	3,086
Union	2,612	1,907	2,221	2,431
Walworth	1,094	1,940	779	2,396
Yankton	3,777	4,186	2,932	5,161
Ziebach	427	362	359	429
Totals	145,560	165,415	116,113	200,267

South Dakota Vote Since 1940

1940, Roosevelt, Dem., 131,862; Willkie, Rep., 177,065.

1944, Roosevelt, Dem., 96,711; Dewey, Rep., 135,365.

1948, Truman, Dem., 117,653; Dewey, Rep., 129,651; Wallace, Prog., 2,801.

1952, Eisenhower, Rep., 203,857; Stevenson, Dem., 90,426.

1956, Eisenhower, Rep., 171,569; Stevenson, Dem., 122,288.

1960, Kennedy, Dem., 128,070; Nixon, Rep., 178,417.

1964, Johnson, Dem., 163,010; Goldwater, Rep., 130,108.

1968, Nixon, Rep., 149,841; Humphrey, Dem., 118,023; Wallace, 3d party, 13,400.

1972, Nixon, Rep., 166,476; McGovern, Dem., 139,945; Jenness, Soc. Workers, 994.

1976, Carter, Dem., 147,068; Ford, Rep., 151,505; MacBride, Libertarian, 1,619; Hall, Com., 318; Camejo, Soc. Workers, 168.

1980, Reagan, Rep., 198,343; Carter, Dem., 103,855; Anderson, Ind., 21,431; Clark, Libertarian, 3,824; Pulley, Soc. Workers, 250.

1984, Reagan, Rep., 200,267; Mondale, Dem., 116,113.

1988, Bush, Rep., 165,415; Dukakis, Dem., 145,560; Paul, Lib., 1,060; Fulani, New Alliance, 730.

Tennessee

	1988		1984	
County	Dukakis (D)	Bush (R)	Mondale (D)	Reagan (R)
Anderson	9,589	15,056	10,415	16,783
Bedford	4,046	4,856	4,499	4,699
Benton	2,826	2,167	3,398	2,481
Bledsoe	1,274	1,858	1,316	1,950
Blount	9,602	20,027	9,189	20,525
Bradley	6,122	15,829	6,085	16,322
Campbell	4,188	5,197	4,692	5,685
Cannon	1,726	1,604	1,846	1,669
Carroll	4,151	5,635	4,568	6,017
Carter	4,634	12,036	4,642	13,153
Cheatham	3,067	4,132	3,007	4,109
Chester	1,757	2,781	1,854	2,793
Claiborne	2,977	4,071	2,870	4,474
Clay	1,183	1,291	1,281	1,338
Cocke	2,115	5,430	2,068	6,665
Coffee	5,686	7,837	5,691	7,695
Crockett	1,742	2,214	1,937	2,479
Cumberland	3,964	7,557	3,605	7,083
Davidson	89,270	96,599	89,498	98,115
Decatur	1,880	2,286	2,031	2,390
De Kalb	2,452	2,098	2,645	2,337
Dickson	5,129	5,343	5,809	5,846
Dyer	3,690	6,508	3,991	6,610
Fayette	3,292	3,573	3,634	3,733
Fentress	1,856	3,103	1,755	2,922
Franklin	5,442	5,381	5,846	5,705
Gibson	7,542	8,415	8,334	9,484
Giles	3,918	3,518	3,812	3,875
Grainger	1,423	2,734	1,565	3,212
Greene	5,077	11,947	4,763	13,215
Grundy	2,415	1,429	2,596	1,396
Hamblen	5,061	10,418	4,922	11,144
Hamilton	40,990	68,111	41,449	69,626
Hancock	737	1,303	619	1,491

	Dukakis	Bush	Mondale	Reagan
Hardeman	3,526	3,547	3,797	3,712
Hardin	2,808	4,252	3,051	4,632
Hawkins	5,212	9,356	4,802	9,863
Haywood	2,923	2,687	3,308	2,839
Henderson	2,296	5,418	2,426	5,362
Henry	5,138	4,784	5,407	5,376
Hickman	2,643	2,246	2,941	2,370
Houston	1,467	882	1,716	882
Humphreys	3,037	2,132	3,668	2,249
Jackson	1,962	1,168	2,894	1,544
Jefferson	3,168	6,832	3,185	7,721
Johnson	1,329	3,715	999	3,853
Knox	41,829	73,092	43,448	76,965
Lake	935	806	1,191	878
Lauderdale	3,296	3,308	3,506	3,566
Lawrence	4,903	6,273	5,458	6,034
Lewis	1,419	1,324	1,556	1,733
Lincoln	3,672	4,288	4,103	3,982
Loudon	3,480	7,122	3,227	7,113
McMinn	4,568	8,462	5,141	9,604
McNairy	3,510	4,625	3,825	4,776
Macon	1,538	2,962	1,747	3,330
Madison	11,001	16,952	12,006	17,819
Marion	4,175	4,407	3,942	4,337
Marshall	2,795	2,975	2,935	3,416
Maury	6,280	8,397	6,950	9,008
Meigs	1,048	1,507	1,012	1,575
Monroe	4,000	6,355	4,223	6,665
Montgomery	9,145	12,599	9,939	13,228
Moore	731	786	808	963
Morgan	1,941	2,576	2,121	2,903
Obion	4,785	6,037	4,769	6,384
Overton	2,511	1,873	2,749	2,054
Perry	1,208	854	1,316	948
Pickett	634	1,118	706	1,246
Polk	2,073	2,297	2,112	2,785
Putnam	6,606	9,547	7,443	8,999
Rhea	2,595	5,144	2,804	5,692
Roane	6,535	10,881	6,623	11,882
Robertson	5,884	5,714	5,756	5,445
Rutherford	12,245	20,397	11,618	19,503
Scott	1,611	2,562	1,810	3,107
Sequatchie	1,196	1,659	1,238	1,785
Sevier	3,643	11,920	3,384	12,517
Shelby	149,759	157,457	169,717	165,947
Smith	2,522	2,138	3,258	2,393
Stewart	1,979	1,302	2,174	1,285
Sullivan	17,396	32,996	16,925	36,516
Sumner	11,702	19,523	11,535	18,442
Tipton	3,824	6,052	3,895	5,945
Trousdale	1,193	969	1,142	781
Unicoi	1,794	3,664	1,696	4,249
Union	1,431	2,110	1,495	2,447
Van Buren	796	780	810	718
Warren	4,646	4,529	4,813	4,811
Washington	10,087	19,615	9,452	21,762
Wayne	1,516	3,405	1,534	3,332
Weakley	4,239	5,701	4,752	6,480
White	2,562	2,646	3,033	2,895
Williamson	7,864	20,847	6,929	17,975
Wilson	8,360	13,317	8,433	12,858
Totals	679,794	947,233	711,714	990,212

Tennessee Vote Since 1940

1940, Roosevelt, Dem., 351,601; Willkie, Rep., 169,153; Babson, Proh., 1,606; Thomas, Soc., 463.

1944, Roosevelt, Dem., 308,707; Dewey, Rep., 200,311; Watson, Proh., 882; Thomas, Soc., 892.

1948, Truman, Dem., 270,402; Dewey, Rep., 202,914; Thurmond, States' Rights, 73,815; Wallace, Prog., 1,864; Thomas, Soc., 1,288.

1952, Eisenhower, Rep., 446,147; Stevenson, Dem., 443,710; Hamblen, Proh., 1,432; Hallinan, Prog., 885; MacArthur, Christian Nationalist, 379.

1956, Eisenhower, Rep., 462,288; Stevenson, Dem., 456,507; Andrews, Ind., 19,820; Holtwick, Proh., 789.

1960, Kennedy, Dem., 481,453; Nixon, Rep., 556,577; Faubus, States' Rights, 11,304; Decker, Proh., 2,458.

1964, Johnson, Dem. 635,047; Goldwater, Rep., 508,965; write-in, 34.

1968, Nixon, Rep., 472,592; Humphrey, Dem., 351,233; Wallace, 3d party, 424,792.

1972, Nixon, Rep., 813,147; McGovern, Dem., 357,293; Schmitz, Amer., 30,373; write-in, 369.

1976, Carter, Dem., 825,879; Ford, Rep., 633,969; Anderson, Amer., 5,769; McCarthy, Ind., 5,004; Maddox, Am. Ind., 2,303; MacBride, Libertarian, 1,375; Hall, Com., 547; LaRouche, U.S. Labor, 512; Bubar, Proh., 442; Miller, Ind., 316; write-in, 230.

1980, Reagan, Rep., 787,761; Carter, Dem., 783,051; Anderson, Ind., 35,991; Clark, Libertarian, 7,116; Commoner, Citizens, 1,112; Bubar, Statesman, 521; McReynolds, So-

cialist, 519; Hall, Com., 503; DeBerry, Soc. Worker, 490;
Griswold, Workers World, 400; write-ins, 152.
1984, Reagan, Rep., 990,212; Mondale, Dem., 711,714;
Bergland, Libertarian, 3,072.
1988, Bush, Rep., 947,233; Dukakis, Dem., 679,794; Paul,
Ind., 2,041; Duke, Ind., 1,807.

Texas

County	1988 Dukakis (D)	1988 Bush (R)	1984 Mondale (D)	1984 Reagan (R)
Anderson	6,128	7,858	4,747	8,634
Andrews	1,122	3,052	820	3,918
Angelina	10,849	12,738	9,054	14,685
Aransas	2,305	3,858	1,696	4,352
Archer	1,627	2,010	1,089	2,487
Armstrong	314	720	238	791
Atascosa	4,657	4,777	3,547	5,279
Austin	2,593	4,524	1,941	4,872
Bailey	876	1,459	684	1,888
Bandera	1,251	3,435	771	3,152
Bastrop	8,004	5,991	4,744	6,439
Baylor	1,153	914	1,019	1,314
Bee	4,616	4,620	3,659	5,377
Bell	17,751	29,382	13,322	31,117
Bexar	174,036	193,192	136,947	203,319
Blanco	1,012	1,680	700	1,957
Borden	169	283	140	325
Bosque	2,670	3,458	2,046	3,923
Bowie	12,331	15,454	10,077	18,244
Brazoria	23,436	34,028	18,609	39,166
Brazos	14,885	29,369	12,348	34,733
Brewster	1,569	1,708	1,462	2,066
Briscoe	574	464	471	538
Brooks	2,859	608	2,702	896
Brown	4,763	6,810	4,070	8,468
Burleson	3,085	2,242	2,578	3,076
Burnet	4,343	5,120	2,983	5,895
Caldwell	4,649	3,553	3,401	4,315
Calhoun	3,314	3,183	2,586	4,434
Callahan	2,017	2,887	1,305	3,538
Cameron	30,972	24,263	26,394	29,545
Camp	2,121	1,908	1,917	2,238
Carson	1,034	2,100	826	2,412
Cass	5,941	5,305	5,053	6,677
Castro	1,436	1,604	1,009	2,026
Chambers	3,035	3,694	2,632	4,322
Cherokee	5,604	7,520	4,494	8,187
Childress	1,060	1,201	900	1,574
Clay	2,288	2,043	1,844	2,569
Cochran	681	771	557	1,117
Coke	674	863	532	1,090
Coleman	1,978	2,340	1,420	2,790
Collin	22,934	67,776	13,604	61,095
Collingsworth	809	872	742	1,396
Colorado	2,847	3,723	2,428	4,528
Comal	5,716	13,994	4,179	13,452
Comanche	2,622	2,120	2,248	2,678
Concho	643	617	580	821
Cooke	4,217	7,196	3,278	8,260
Coryell	4,026	7,461	3,113	9,056
Cottle	690	379	623	507
Crane	596	1,219	392	1,473
Crockett	881	932	589	1,094
Crosby	1,435	1,121	1,212	1,376
Culberson	557	417	407	509
Dallam	645	1,205	496	1,594
Dallas	243,198	347,094	203,592	405,444
Dawson	2,155	3,154	1,781	3,685
Deaf Smith	1,930	3,744	1,485	4,762
Delta	1,244	869	973	1,024
Denton	26,204	57,444	16,772	52,865
DeWitt	2,579	3,628	1,882	4,401
Dickens	696	435	692	594
Dimmit	2,735	900	2,546	1,338
Donley	661	1,043	529	1,297
Duval	4,177	907	3,748	1,201
Eastland	3,215	3,929	2,522	4,841
Ector	10,825	23,155	8,913	31,228
Edwards	368	556	159	626
Ellis	11,169	16,422	8,029	16,873
El Paso	62,622	55,573	51,917	66,114
Erath	4,113	5,427	3,234	6,122
Falls	2,877	2,344	2,834	3,133
Fannin	5,163	4,024	4,399	4,692
Fayette	3,390	4,551	2,379	5,711
Fisher	1,516	721	1,384	965
Floyd	1,391	1,741	1,023	2,092
Foard	513	306	448	472
Fort Bend	23,351	39,818	18,729	41,370
Franklin	1,453	1,439	1,104	1,836
Freestone	2,916	3,159	2,489	3,624
Frio	3,016	1,505	2,656	2,003
Gaines	1,310	2,265	797	2,714
Galveston	38,633	34,913	36,092	40,262
Garza	989	1,183	521	1,219
Gillespie	1,588	5,662	1,137	5,496
Glasscock	143	384	128	403
Goliad	1,358	1,427	836	1,540
Gonzales	2,897	2,983	2,196	3,962
Gray	2,460	7,259	2,003	8,955
Grayson	14,347	18,825	11,803	22,554
Gregg	12,486	26,465	10,700	29,697
Grimes	2,735	2,820	2,370	3,365
Guadalupe	7,111	13,265	5,060	14,382
Hale	3,502	6,284	3,202	7,670
Hall	1,029	714	984	1,058
Hamilton	1,355	1,718	1,130	2,116
Hansford	443	1,967	259	2,213
Hardeman	1,143	855	927	1,238
Hardin	8,245	6,897	6,782	8,380
Harris	342,919	464,217	334,135	536,028
Harrison	8,974	11,957	7,773	12,618
Hartley	505	1,229	356	1,419
Haskell	1,715	1,193	1,434	1,701
Hays	11,187	11,716	6,663	12,467
Hemphill	527	1,170	413	1,650
Henderson	9,819	11,005	7,302	12,725
Hidalgo	54,330	29,246	44,147	35,059
Hill	4,381	4,796	3,420	5,344
Hockley	2,850	4,368	2,044	5,462
Hood	4,255	7,400	3,063	6,817
Hopkins	4,984	5,133	3,707	5,772
Houston	3,846	3,882	3,275	4,542
Howard	4,445	6,024	4,115	7,519
Hudspeth	406	405	362	557
Hunt	6,820	12,331	6,971	14,303
Hutchinson	2,950	7,526	2,052	9,078
Irion	326	539	199	619
Jack	1,521	1,542	945	1,825
Jackson	2,141	2,954	1,804	3,661
Jasper	6,613	4,985	5,787	5,965
Jeff Davis	325	524	299	511
Jefferson	55,649	35,754	54,846	45,124
Jim Hogg	1,630	510	1,703	608
Jim Wells	8,495	4,335	7,795	5,896
Johnson	12,507	17,509	9,148	18,254
Jones	2,898	3,000	2,343	4,017
Karnes	2,529	2,383	1,802	3,068
Kaufman	7,358	8,466	5,554	9,343
Kendall	1,446	4,875	938	4,568
Kenedy	119	76	110	96
Kent	398	274	253	332
Kerr	3,587	11,207	3,102	11,829
Kimble	551	1,061	442	1,333
King	64	111	53	141
Kinney	669	771	486	774
Kleberg	5,367	4,443	4,924	5,712
Knox	1,013	765	921	1,027
Lamar	7,553	8,021	5,504	9,273
Lamb	2,230	3,064	1,919	3,892
Lampasas	1,954	3,000	1,356	3,285
LaSalle	1,651	693	1,504	1,007
Lavaca	3,531	4,377	2,464	5,058
Lee	2,527	2,513	1,659	2,957
Leon	2,316	2,778	1,621	3,207
Liberty	8,343	8,524	6,292	10,504
Limestone	3,476	3,257	3,228	4,063
Lipscomb	377	1,111	241	1,451
Live Oak	1,573	2,277	1,260	2,481
Llano	2,629	3,550	1,894	4,042
Loving	23	54	16	57
Lubbock	22,202	50,760	18,793	57,151
Lynn	1,086	1,279	1,009	1,617
McCulloch	1,665	1,618	1,433	2,060
McLennan	27,545	38,606	23,206	42,232
McMullen	94	302	61	337
Madison	1,835	1,896	1,384	2,158
Marion	2,255	1,857	2,111	2,336
Martin	632	1,017	512	1,218
Mason	671	975	570	1,168
Matagorda	5,675	6,787	5,201	8,452
Maverick	4,395	1,592	3,063	1,783
Medina	4,227	5,722	3,053	5,737
Menard	614	552	394	725
Midland	8,487	30,618	7,214	33,706
Milam	4,865	3,512	3,734	4,384
Mills	842	1,043	688	1,262
Mitchell	1,773	1,596	1,332	2,007
Montague	3,689	3,475	2,602	4,406
Montgomery	18,394	40,360	13,293	41,230
Moore	1,537	3,710	1,129	4,649
Morris	3,522	2,104	2,925	2,778
Motley	262	429	282	533
Nacogdoches	6,886	11,767	5,694	13,063
Navarro	6,749	6,445	5,672	7,816
Newton	3,640	1,659	3,296	2,123
Nolan	2,853	2,734	2,524	3,608
Nueces	49,209	46,337	46,721	54,333
Ochiltree	579	2,928	419	3,492
Oldham	303	691	226	762
Orange	17,834	11,959	16,816	15,386
Palo Pinto	3,930	4,649	3,349	5,701
Panola	4,123	4,642	3,179	5,676
Parker	8,517	14,090	6,050	13,647
Parmer	764	2,061	567	2,524
Pecos	1,960	2,483	1,596	3,451
Polk	5,943	5,831	3,826	5,987
Potter	9,563	16,400	8,355	20,396

| County | 1972 D | ... |

Presidio	1,176	586	992	837
Rains	1,448	1,281	1,027	1,560
Randall	8,492	27,986	6,044	30,249
Reagan	418	935	243	1,079
Real	483	795	360	1,004
Red River	3,165	2,475	2,518	2,979
Reeves	2,812	1,724	2,396	2,461
Refugio	1,831	1,883	1,559	2,421
Roberts	135	441	106	539
Robertson	3,630	2,184	3,339	2,663
Rockwall	2,659	7,214	1,639	6,688
Runnels	1,720	2,417	1,179	2,968
Rusk	5,140	9,117	4,599	11,081
Sabine	2,053	1,925	1,940	2,045
San Augustine	2,118	1,946	1,583	1,937
San Jacinto	2,972	2,691	2,466	3,174
San Patricio	9,920	9,159	8,838	11,074
San Saba	1,165	1,099	1,070	1,566
Schleicher	494	653	326	854
Scurry	2,119	3,749	1,564	5,028
Shackelford	681	865	415	1,181
Shelby	4,261	3,999	3,610	4,863
Sherman	340	1,145	246	1,269
Smith	18,719	34,658	15,227	40,740
Somervell	983	1,304	635	1,422
Starr	6,958	1,218	5,047	1,658
Stephens	1,519	2,342	1,046	2,898
Sterling	188	464	129	577
Stonewall	724	421	643	599
Sutton	571	996	465	1,251
Swisher	1,893	1,271	1,642	1,611
Tarrant	151,310	242,660	120,147	248,050
Taylor	13,073	28,563	9,628	34,444
Terrell	390	296	289	407
Terry	1,941	2,645	1,535	3,181
Throckmorton	534	455	388	586
Titus	4,357	4,247	3,631	5,069
Tom Green	12,283	21,463	8,981	23,847
Travis	127,783	105,915	94,124	124,944
Trinity	2,657	2,448	2,115	2,599
Tyler	4,198	3,070	3,119	3,638
Upshur	5,242	5,991	4,614	7,325
Upton	544	1,189	380	1,603
Uvalde	3,684	4,266	2,482	4,790
Val Verde	5,044	5,109	3,857	5,909
Van Zandt	6,153	7,371	4,506	8,474
Victoria	8,923	15,056	7,037	18,787
Walker	5,826	8,473	4,263	8,809
Waller	3,957	3,607	3,828	4,116
Ward	1,858	2,709	1,188	3,474
Washington	2,960	6,041	2,483	6,506
Webb	16,227	7,528	12,308	8,582
Wharton	5,935	6,978	5,072	8,495
Wheeler	1,067	1,703	805	2,251
Wichita	17,956	23,324	16,009	28,932
Wilbarger	2,248	2,669	2,011	3,644
Willacy	3,165	1,750	3,037	2,340
Williamson	19,589	27,322	9,911	25,774
Wilson	3,953	4,436	2,829	4,588
Winkler	947	1,656	752	2,213
Wise	5,288	6,064	3,856	6,958
Wood	4,553	6,216	3,449	7,144
Yoakum	727	1,762	456	2,204
Young	3,007	4,156	2,203	5,282
Zapata	2,171	958	1,577	1,214
Zavala	3,338	628	2,937	924
Totals	2,352,748	3,036,829	1,949,276	3,433,428

Texas Vote Since 1940

1940, Roosevelt, Dem., 840,151; Willkie, Rep., 199,152; Babson, Proh., 925; Thomas, Soc., 728; Browder, Com., 212.

1944, Roosevelt, Dem., 821,605; Dewey, Rep., 191,425; Texas Regulars, 135,439; Watson, Proh., 1,017; Thomas, Soc., 594; America First, 250.

1948, Truman, Dem., 750,700; Dewey, Rep., 282,240; Thurmond, States' Rights, 106,909; Wallace, Prog., 3,764; Watson, Proh., 2,758; Thomas, Soc., 874.

1952, Eisenhower, Rep., 1,102,878; Stevenson, Dem., 969,228; Hamblen, Proh., 1,983; MacArthur, Christian Nationalist, 833; MacArthur, Constitution, 730; Hallinan, Prog., 294.

1956, Eisenhower, Rep., 1,080,619; Stevenson, Dem., 859,958; Andrews, Ind., 14,591.

1960, Kennedy, Dem., 1,167,932; Nixon, Rep., 1,121,699; Sullivan, Constitution, 18,169; Decker, Proh., 3,870; write-in, 15.

1964, Johnson, Dem., 1,663,185; Goldwater, Rep., 958,566; Lightburn, Constitution, 5,060.

1968, Nixon, Rep., 1,227,844; Humphrey, Dem., 1,266,804; Wallace, 3d party, 584,269; write-in, 489.

1972, Nixon, Rep., 2,298,896; McGovern, Dem., 1,154,289; Schmitz, Amer., 6,039; Jenness, Soc. Workers, 8,664; others, 3,393.

1976, Carter, Dem., 2,082,319; Ford, Rep., 1,953,300; McCarthy, Ind., 20,118; Anderson, Amer., 11,442; Camejo, Soc. Workers, 1,723; write-in, 2,982.

1980, Reagan, Rep., 2,510,705; Carter, Dem., 1,881,147; Anderson, Ind., 111,613; Clark, Libertarian, 37,643; write-in, 528.

1984, Reagan, Rep., 3,433,428; Mondale, Dem., 1,949,276.

1988, Bush, Rep., 3,036,829; Dukakis, Dem., 2,352,748; Paul, Lib., 30,355; Fulani, New Alliance, 7,208.

Utah

County	1988 Dukakis (D)	1988 Bush (R)	1984 Mondale (D)	1984 Reagan (R)
Beaver	816	1,286	708	1,516
Box Elder	2,736	12,585	1,983	13,243
Cache	5,871	21,766	4,123	22,127
Carbon	5,521	3,019	4,357	4,393
Daggett	132	272	227	296
Davis	16,868	50,469	11,727	49,863
Duchesne	1,227	3,118	746	4,437
Emery	1,788	2,322	1,326	3,081
Garfield	370	1,470	315	1,609
Grand	1,287	1,895	876	2,463
Iron	1,736	6,038	1,342	6,856
Juab	974	1,505	917	1,902
Kane	398	1,788	294	1,710
Millard	1,124	3,515	1,192	4,345
Morgan	647	1,889	481	1,934
Piute	206	476	151	606
Rich	234	621	131	797
Salt Lake	107,453	163,557	78,488	183,536
San Juan	1,407	2,377	1,145	2,598
Sanpete	1,822	4,579	1,227	5,507
Sevier	1,403	4,747	1,072	5,736
Summit	2,545	3,881	1,539	4,093
Tooele	4,166	5,539	3,584	6,478
Uintah	1,799	5,341	1,186	7,437
Utah	18,533	68,134	14,801	72,284
Wasatch	1,451	2,487	1,015	2,789
Washington	3,054	13,306	1,846	12,049
Wayne	353	784	224	930
Weber	21,431	39,676	18,346	44,590
Totals	207,352	428,442	155,369	469,105

Utah Vote Since 1940

1940, Roosevelt, Dem., 154,277; Willkie, Rep., 93,151; Thomas, Soc., 200; Browder, Com., 191.

1944, Roosevelt, Dem., 150,088; Dewey, Rep., 97,891; Thomas, Soc., 340.

1948, Truman, Dem., 149,151; Dewey, Rep., 124,402; Wallace, Prog., 2,679; Dobbs, Soc. Workers, 73.

1952, Eisenhower, Rep., 194,190; Stevenson, Dem., 135,364.

1956, Eisenhower, Rep., 215,631; Stevenson, Dem., 118,364.

1960, Kennedy, Dem., 169,248; Nixon, Rep., 205,361; Dobbs, Soc. Workers, 100.

1964, Johnson, Dem., 219,628; Goldwater, Rep., 181,785.

1968, Nixon, Rep., 238,728; Humphrey, Dem., 156,665; Wallace, 3d party, 26,906; Halstead, Soc. Worker, 89; Peace and Freedom, 180.

1972, Nixon, Rep., 323,643; McGovern, Dem., 126,284; Schmitz, Amer., 28,549.

1976, Carter, Dem., 182,110; Ford, Rep., 337,908; Anderson, Amer., 13,304; McCarthy, Ind., 3,907; MacBride, Libertarian, 2,438; Maddox, Am. Ind., 1,162; Camejo, Soc. Workers, 268; Hall, Com., 121.

1980, Reagan, Rep., 439,687; Carter, Dem., 124,266; Anderson, Ind., 30,284; Clark, Libertarian, 7,226; Commoner, Citizens, 1,009; Greaves, American, 965; Rarick, Amer. Ind., 522; Hall, Com., 139; DeBerry, Soc. Worker, 124.

1984, Reagan, Rep., 469,105; Mondale, Dem., 155,369; Bergland, Libertarian, 2,447.

1988, Bush, Rep., 428,442; Dukakis, Dem., 207,352; Paul, Lib., 7,473; Dennis, American, 2,158.

Vermont

City	1988 Dukakis (D)	1988 Bush (R)	1984 Mondale (D)	1984 Reagan (R)
Barre City	2,132	2,100	1,903	2,195
Bennington	3,180	2,748	2,879	3,237
Brattleboro	3,136	2,044	2,741	2,645
Burlington	9,748	6,382	10,080	7,857
Montpelier	2,351	2,013	2,120	2,257

Rutland City....	3,590	3,631	3,298	3,970
St. Albans City...	1,441	1,295	1,346	1,748
St. Johnsbury...	1,188	1,974	915	2,152
South Burlington..	3,373	3,136	2,728	3,443
Winooski....	1,426	1,014	1,361	1,264
Totals........	115,775	124,331	95,730	135,865

Vermont Vote Since 1940

1940, Roosevelt, Dem., 64,269; Willkie, Rep., 78,371; Browder, Com., 411.

1944, Roosevelt, Dem., 53,820; Dewey, Rep., 71,527.

1948, Truman, Dem., 45,557; Dewey, Rep., 75,926; Wallace, Prog., 1,279; Thomas, Soc., 585.

1952, Eisenhower, Rep., 109,717; Stevenson, Dem., 43,355; Hallinan, Prog., 282; Hoopes, Soc., 185.

1956, Eisenhower, Rep., 110,390; Stevenson, Dem., 42,549; scattered, 39.

1960, Kennedy, Dem., 69,186; Nixon, Rep., 98,131.

1964, Johnson, Dem., 107.674; Goldwater, Rep., 54,868.

1968, Nixon, Rep., 85,142; Humphrey, Dem., 70,255; Wallace, 3d party, 5,104; Halstead, Soc. Worker, 295; Gregory, New Party, 579.

1972, Nixon, Rep., 117,149; McGovern, Dem., 68,174; Spock, Liberty Union, 1,010; Jenness, Soc. Workers, 296; scattered, 318.

1976, Carter, Dem., 77,798; Carter, Ind. Vermonter, 991; Ford, Rep., 100,387; McCarthy, Ind., 4,001; Camejo, Soc. Workers, 430; LaRouche, U.S. Labor, 196; scattered, 99.

1980, Reagan, Rep., 94,598; Carter, Dem., 81,891; Anderson, Ind., 31,760; Commoner, Citizens, 2,316; Clark, Libertarian, 1,900; McReynolds, Liberty Union, 136; Hall, Com. 118; DeBerry, Soc. Worker, 75; scattering, 413.

1984, Reagan, Rep., 135,865; Mondale, Dem., 95,730; Bergland, Libertarian, 1,002.

1988, Bush, Rep., 124,331; Dukakis, Dem., 115,775; Paul, Lib., 1,000; LaRouche, Ind., 275.

Virginia

	1988		1984	
County	Dukakis (D)	Bush (R)	Mondale (D)	Reagan (R)
Accomack.....	4,443	6,926	4,355	8,047
Albemarle....	10,363	15,117	7,982	14,455
Alleghany....	2,316	2,555	1,932	3,067
Amelia......	1,359	2,187	1,432	2,336
Amherst.....	3,567	6,507	3,409	7,004
Appomattox...	1,740	3,205	1,498	3,386
Arlington....	40,314	34,191	37,031	34,848
Augusta.....	4,170	13,251	3,899	15,308
Bath.......	881	1,273	727	1,434
Bedford.....	5,406	10,702	4,754	10,371
Bland......	937	1,556	867	1,812
Botetourt....	3,763	5,687	3,243	5,959
Brunswick....	3,070	2,742	3,040	2,950
Buchanan....	6,935	3,912	7,828	5,053
Buckingham...	1,941	2,481	1,879	2,627
Campbell....	4,574	12,713	4,380	13,388
Caroline....	3,186	3,065	3,111	2,949
Carroll.....	3,190	6,377	2,914	7,056
Charles City...	1,839	826	1,776	776
Charlotte....	1,923	2,699	1,811	2,999
Chesterfield...	18,723	58,828	13,739	54,896
Clarke......	1,478	2,502	1,215	2,529
Craig......	864	1,112	845	1,173
Culpeper.....	2,555	5,896	2,255	5,596
Cumberland...	1,132	1,978	1,237	2,027
Dickenson....	4,461	3,091	4,848	3,921
Dinwiddie....	3,405	4,165	3,485	4,547
Essex......	1,294	2,038	1,300	2,120
Fairfax.....	125,711	200,631	107,295	183,181
Fauquier....	4,837	11,733	4,056	10,319
Floyd......	1,727	2,921	1,599	3,431
Fluvanna....	1,562	2,447	1,332	2,247
Franklin....	5,734	7,391	4,903	7,684
Frederick....	3,707	9,921	2,671	9,542
Giles......	3,042	3,490	3,047	4,340
Gloucester....	3,372	7,646	2,830	7,109
Goochland....	2,209	3,765	2,178	3,404
Grayson.....	2,441	3,966	2,319	4,508
Greene.....	899	2,234	760	2,216
Greensville...	2,083	1,610	2,352	2,304
Halifax.....	4,282	5,671	4,231	6,726
Hanover.....	5,985	20,570	4,831	18,800
Henrico.....	26,980	62,284	21,336	63,864
Henry......	7,536	10,871	6,976	12,593
Highland....	456	807	398	997
Isle of Wight...	3,747	5,779	3,650	5,664
James City....	4,642	8,945	3,486	7,104
King George....	1,519	2,587	1,450	2,356
King and Queen...	1,309	1,376	1,201	1,449
King William.....	1,561	2,735	1,448	2,803
Lancaster......	1,551	3,380	1,559	3,416
Lee........	4,906	4,080	5,085	5,365
Loudoun.....	10,101	20,448	8,227	17,765
Louisa......	2,789	3,831	2,703	3,789
Lunenburg....	1,870	2,530	1,754	2,713
Madison.....	1,427	2,501	1,302	2,723
Mathews.....	1,235	2,752	1,106	2,868
Mecklenburg...	3,275	5,887	3,438	6,777
Middlesex....	1,361	2,571	1,206	2,612
Montgomery...	8,909	12,326	7,202	12,428
Nelson......	2,272	2,502	2,021	2,777
New Kent....	1,427	2,917	1,204	2,679
Northampton...	2,242	2,562	2,226	2,906
Northumberland...	1,506	2,984	1,407	3,166
Nottoway....	2,217	3,161	2,296	3,418
Orange......	2,592	4,319	2,285	4,483
Page.......	2,499	5,013	2,437	5,021
Patrick.....	2,093	3,990	1,908	4,703
Pittsylvania...	6,612	12,229	7,791	15,743
Powhatan....	1,467	4,040	1,381	3,921
Prince Edward...	2,434	3,147	2,589	3,454
Prince George...	2,469	4,982	2,136	4,999
Prince William...	19,198	39,654	15,631	34,992
Pulaski.....	4,686	6,844	4,364	8,242
Rappahannock...	1,003	1,657	999	1,696
Richmond....	924	1,862	830	1,869
Roanoke.....	12,938	22,011	10,569	23,348
Rockbridge...	2,412	3,541	2,098	4,067
Rockingham...	4,716	13,241	4,220	13,480
Russell.....	6,222	4,374	6,760	5,738
Scott......	3,616	4,986	3,904	5,804
Shenandoah...	3,276	8,612	2,771	9,048
Smyth......	3,989	7,446	4,102	8,593
Southampton...	3,000	3,439	3,300	4,669
Spotsylvania...	5,486	10,978	4,012	8,207
Stafford....	5,380	12,234	4,429	10,283
Surry......	1,602	1,246	1,875	1,462
Sussex......	1,958	1,822	2,408	2,183
Tazewell....	8,096	7,165	8,014	9,645
Warren.....	2,769	4,700	2,551	5,016
Washington...	5,819	10,722	5,573	12,132
Westmoreland...	2,311	2,974	2,363	3,219
Wise.......	7,017	6,189	7,303	7,909
Wythe......	3,201	5,827	2,996	6,773
York.......	4,639	11,103	4,063	10,214
City				
Alexandria....	24,358	20,913	23,552	21,166
Bedford.....	960	1,322	997	1,553
Bristol.....	2,446	4,407	2,429	5,012
Buena Vista...	828	1,121	724	1,335
Charlottesville...	7,671	5,817	7,317	6,947
Chesapeake...	18,828	29,738	16,740	27,542
Clifton Forge...	961	759	896	965
Colonial Heights...	1,581	6,001	1,218	6,387
Covington....	1,567	1,274	1,391	1,722
Danville....	7,353	12,221	5,846	12,141
Emporia.....	977	1,289	807	1,252
Fairfax.....	3,430	5,576	3,263	6,234
Falls Church...	2,484	2,470	2,398	2,684
Franklin....	1,630	1,557	1,537	1,561
Fredericksburg...	2,683	3,401	2,439	3,500
Galax......	907	1,278	814	1,548
Hampton....	19,106	24,034	18,180	25,537
Harrisonburg...	2,799	5,376	2,384	5,221
Hopewell....	2,566	4,672	2,564	5,661
Lexington....	997	994	946	1,197
Lynchburg....	8,279	15,323	8,542	17,447
Manassas....	2,658	5,980	1,824	4,615
Manassas Park...	434	993	375	975
Martinsville...	2,794	3,360	2,942	4,234
Newport News...	21,413	32,570	21,834	33,614
Norfolk.....	37,778	30,538	38,913	36,360
Norton.....	795	608	842	806
Petersburg....	8,177	4,231	9,248	5,753
Poquoson....	877	3,840	647	3,667
Portsmouth...	19,698	16,087	21,623	18,940
Radford.....	1,855	2,481	1,781	2,855
Richmond....	42,155	31,586	49,408	38,754
Roanoke.....	17,185	15,389	17,300	19,008
Salem......	3,760	5,694	3,347	6,419
South Boston...	936	1,694	974	1,899
Staunton....	2,457	5,775	2,012	6,137
Suffolk.....	8,080	9,742	8,842	10,128
Virginia Beach...	33,780	76,481	24,703	72,571
Waynesboro...	2,038	4,672	1,579	4,465
Williamsburg...	1,534	1,648	1,469	1,913
Winchester...	2,300	4,497	2,064	5,055
Total........	859,799	1,309,162	796,250	1,337,078

Virginia Vote Since 1940

1940, Roosevelt, Dem., 235,961; Willkie, Rep., 109,363; Babson, Proh., 882; Thomas, Soc., 282; Browder, Com., 71; Aiken, Soc. Labor, 48.

1944, Roosevelt, Dem., 242,276; Dewey, Rep., 145,243; Watson, Proh., 459; Thomas, Soc., 417; Teichert, Soc. Labor, 90.

1948, Truman, Dem., 200,786; Dewey, Rep., 172,070; Thurmond, States' Rights, 43,393; Wallace, Prog., 2,047; Thomas, Soc., 726; Teichert, Soc. Labor, 234.

1952, Eisenhower, Rep., 349,037; Stevenson, Dem., 268,677; Hass, Soc. Labor, 1,160; Hoopes, Social Dem., 504; Hallinan, Prog., 311.

1956, Eisenhower, Rep., 386,459; Stevenson, Dem., 267,760; Andrews, States' Rights, 42,964; Hoopes, Soc. Dem., 444; Hass, Soc. Labor, 351.

1960, Kennedy, Dem., 362,327; Nixon, Rep., 404,521; Coiner, Conservative, 4,204; Hass, Soc. Labor, 397.

1964, Johnson, Dem., 558,038; Goldwater, Rep., 481,334; Hass, Soc. Labor, 2,895.

1968, Nixon, Rep., 590,319; Humphrey, Dem., 442,387; Wallace, 3d party, *320,272; Blomen, Soc. Labor, 4,671; Munn, Proh., 601; Gregory, Peace and Freedom, 1,680.

*10,561 votes for Wallace were omitted in the count.

1972, Nixon, Rep., 988,493; McGovern, Dem., 438,887; Schmitz, Amer., 19,721; Fisher, Soc. Labor, 9,918.

1976, Carter, Dem., 813,896; Ford, Rep., 836,554; Camejo, Soc. Workers, 17,802; Anderson, Amer., 16,686; LaRouche, U.S. Labor, 7,508; MacBride, Libertarian, 4,648.

1980, Reagan, Rep., 989,609; Carter, Dem., 752,174; Anderson, Ind., 95,418; Commoner, Citizens, 14,024; Clark, Libertarian, 12,821; DeBerry, Soc. Worker, 1,986.

1984, Reagan, Rep., 1,337,078; Mondale, Dem., 796,250.

1988, Bush, Rep., 1,309,162; Dukakis, Dem., 859,799; Fulani, Ind., 14,312; Paul, Lib., 8,336.

2,460; Hass, Soc. Labor, 633; Hoopes, Soc., 254; Dobbs, Soc. Workers, 119.

1956, Eisenhower, Rep., 620,430; Stevenson, Dem., 523,002; Hass, Soc. Labor, 7,457.

1960, Kennedy, Dem., 599,298; Nixon, Rep., 629,273; Hass, Soc. Labor, 10,895; Curtis, Constitution, 1,401; Dobbs, Soc. Workers, 705.

1964, Johnson, Dem., 779,699; Goldwater, Rep., 470,366; Hass, Soc. Labor, 7,772; DeBerry, Freedom Soc., 537.

1968, Nixon, Rep., 588,510; Humphrey, Dem., 616,037; Wallace, 3d party, 96,990; Blomen, Soc. Labor, 488; Cleaver, Peace and Freedom, 1,609; Halstead, Soc. Worker, 270; Mitchell, Free Ballot, 377.

1972, Nixon, Rep., 837,135; McGovern, Dem., 568,334; Schmitz, Amer., 58,906; Spock, Ind., 2,644; Fisher, Soc. Labor, 1,102; Jenness, Soc. Worker, 623; Hall, Com., 566; Hospers, Libertarian, 1,537.

1976, Carter, Dem., 717,323; Ford, Rep., 777,732; McCarthy, Ind., 36,986; Maddox, Amer. Ind., 8,585; Anderson, Amer., 5,046; MacBride, Libertarian, 5,042; Wright, People's, 1,124; Camejo, Soc. Workers, 905; LaRouche, U.S. Labor, 903; Hall, Com., 817; Levin, Soc. Labor, 713; Zeidler, Soc., 358.

1980, Reagan, Rep., 865,244; Carter, Dem., 650,193; Anderson, Ind., 185,073; Clark, Libertarian, 29,213; Commoner, Citizens, 9,403; DeBerry, Soc. Worker, 1,137; McReynolds, Socialist, 956; Hall, Com., 834; Griswold, Workers World, 341.

1984, Reagan, Rep., 1,051,670; Mondale, Dem., 798,352; Bergland, Libertarian, 8,844.

1988, Bush, Rep., 903,835; Dukakis, Dem., 933,516; Paul, Lib., 17,240; LaRouche, Ind., 4,412.

Washington

County	1988 Dukakis (D)	1988 Bush (R)	1984 Mondale (D)	1984 Reagan (R)
Adams	1,612	2,612	1,311	3,449
Asotin	3,422	2,874	3,042	3,876
Benton	14,817	28,686	13,784	32,307
Chelan	8,183	11,601	6,978	13,667
Clallam	11,123	11,200	9,701	13,605
Clark	40,021	37,285	35,248	40,681
Columbia	730	1,172	673	1,404
Cowlitz	16,090	12,009	15,361	14,858
Douglas	3,760	5,378	3,127	6,443
Ferry	972	972	935	1,232
Franklin	4,772	6,488	4,328	7,724
Garfield	593	714	493	913
Grant	7,564	10,859	6,298	12,888
Grays Harbor	14,097	8,860	14,050	11,286
Island	8,510	12,552	6,850	13,548
Jefferson	5,270	4,184	4,602	4,543
King	349,663	290,524	289,620	332,987
Kitsap	33,748	34,743	29,681	36,101
Kittitas	5,318	5,048	4,830	6,580
Klickitat	2,991	2,920	2,712	3,910
Lewis	8,629	14,184	7,634	15,846
Lincoln	1,884	2,689	1,671	3,474
Mason	7,826	7,426	7,007	8,410
Okanogan	5,630	5,856	5,330	7,476
Pacific	5,017	3,073	4,679	3,613
Pend Oreille	1,925	1,802	1,655	2,374
Pierce	96,688	94,167	79,498	112,877
San Juan	3,008	2,660	2,514	2,900
Skagit	15,159	16,550	13,947	18,840
Skamania	1,748	1,356	1,552	1,736
Snohomish	80,694	84,158	66,728	90,362
Spokane	68,520	68,787	59,620	88,043
Stevens	5,068	6,576	4,304	8,211
Thurston	33,860	31,980	26,840	34,442
Wahkiakum	961	629	930	776
Walla Walla	7,448	9,683	6,804	12,361
Whatcom	25,571	23,820	22,670	27,228
Whitman	7,403	7,680	6,621	10,021
Yakima	23,221	30,026	24,724	40,678
Totals	933,516	903,835	798,352	1,051,670

Washington Vote Since 1940

1940, Roosevelt, Dem., 462,145; Willkie, Rep., 322,123; Thomas, Soc., 4,586; Browder, Com., 2,626; Babson, Proh., 1,686; Aiken, Soc. Labor, 667.

1944, Roosevelt, Dem., 486,774; Dewey, Rep., 361,689; Thomas, Soc., 3,824; Watson, Proh., 2,396; Teichert, Soc. Labor, 1,645.

1948, Truman, Dem., 476,165; Dewey, Rep., 386,315; Wallace, Prog., 31,692; Watson, Proh., 6,117; Thomas, Soc., 3,534; Teichert, Soc. Labor, 1,133; Dobbs, Soc. Workers, 103.

1952, Eisenhower, Rep., 599,107; Stevenson, Dem., 492,845; MacArthur, Christian Nationalist, 7,290; Hallinan, Prog.,

West Virginia

County	1988 Dukakis (D)	1988 Bush (R)	1984 Mondale (D)	1984 Reagan (R)
Barbour	3,221	3,023	3,108	3,877
Berkeley	6,313	10,761	6,181	12,887
Boone	6,539	2,786	7,121	4,656
Braxton	3,377	2,024	3,350	2,902
Brooke	6,258	4,006	6,636	4,819
Cabell	15,368	17,197	15,513	21,815
Calhoun	1,644	1,395	1,473	1,765
Clay	2,263	1,536	2,117	1,667
Doddridge	955	1,880	836	2,343
Fayette	11,009	5,143	11,650	7,360
Gilmer	1,661	1,387	1,494	1,953
Grant	893	3,215	828	3,715
Greenbrier	6,091	5,395	5,599	7,337
Hampshire	2,085	3,253	2,102	4,065
Hancock	8,338	5,882	8,708	7,326
Hardy	1,689	2,581	1,641	2,938
Harrison	17,005	13,364	14,969	19,400
Jackson	4,573	5,696	4,147	7,117
Jefferson	4,334	5,349	4,216	5,884
Kanawha	41,144	38,140	37,832	51,499
Lewis	3,272	3,602	2,693	5,297
Lincoln	5,049	3,457	5,467	4,405
Logan	11,317	4,244	10,892	6,425
McDowell	7,204	2,463	8,546	4,284
Marion	14,441	9,229	13,833	13,106
Marshall	7,903	6,793	7,947	8,615
Mason	5,468	5,332	5,701	6,648
Mercer	10,152	10,221	9,164	13,910
Mineral	4,059	6,015	3,832	7,291
Mingo	7,429	2,896	8,434	4,275
Monongalia	14,178	12,091	13,236	14,972
Monroe	2,427	2,719	2,333	3,612
Morgan	1,545	3,002	1,457	3,469
Nicholas	5,173	3,731	4,588	4,656
Ohio	10,121	10,341	10,163	13,447
Pendleton	1,595	1,901	1,464	2,027
Pleasants	1,421	1,761	1,458	2,255
Pocahontas	1,958	1,876	1,903	2,479
Preston	4,357	5,804	4,054	6,955
Putnam	6,640	8,163	5,208	9,238
Raleigh	14,302	10,395	14,442	14,571
Randolph	5,233	4,746	4,839	6,100
Ritchie	1,446	2,874	1,231	3,355
Roane	2,447	2,861	2,468	3,751
Summers	3,072	2,231	2,670	2,975
Taylor	2,852	2,816	2,754	4,007
Tucker	1,869	1,699	1,766	2,240
Tyler	1,501	2,365	1,395	3,170
Upshur	3,065	4,813	2,468	5,951
Wayne	8,621	7,123	8,378	8,811
Webster	2,185	1,016	2,355	1,565
Wetzel	3,928	3,381	3,549	4,626
Wirt	929	1,125	868	1,450
Wood	12,959	19,450	11,357	24,821

Wyoming........	6,138	3,516	5,691	5,379
Totals	341,016	310,065	328,125	405,483

West Virginia Vote Since 1940

1940, Roosevelt, Dem., 495,662; Willkie, Rep., 372,414.

1944, Roosevelt, Dem., 392,777; Dewey, Rep., 322,819.

1948, Truman, Dem., 429,188; Dewey, Rep., 316,251; Wallace, Prog., 3,311.

1952, Eisenhower, Rep., 419,970; Stevenson, Dem., 453,578.

1956, Eisenhower, Rep., 449,297; Stevenson, Dem., 381,534.

1960, Kennedy, Dem., 441,786; Nixon, Rep., 395,995.

1964, Johnson, Dem., 538,087; Goldwater, Rep., 253,953.

1968, Nixon, Rep., 307,555; Humphrey, Dem., 374,091; Wallace, 3d party, 72,560.

1972, Nixon, Rep., 484,964; McGovern, Dem., 277,435.

1976, Carter, Dem., 435,864; Ford, Rep., 314,726.

1980, Reagan, Rep., 334,206; Carter, Dem., 367,462; Anderson, Ind., 31,691; Clark, Libertarian, 4,356.

1984, Reagan, Rep., 405,483; Mondale, Dem., 328,125.

1988, Bush, Rep., 310,065; Dukakis, Dem., 341,016; Fulani, New Alliance, 2,230.

Wisconsin

	1988		1984	
County	Dukakis (D)	Bush (R)	Mondale (D)	Reagan (R)
Adams	3,598	3,258	2,713	3,644
Ashland	4,526	2,926	4,680	3,517
Barron	8,951	8,527	8,060	9,587
Bayfield	4,323	3,095	4,034	3,474
Brown	41,788	43,625	30,208	51,186
Buffalo	3,481	2,783	2,921	3,325
Burnet	3,537	2,884	3,328	3,528
Calumet	6,481	8,107	4,735	8,969
Chippewa	11,447	9,757	10,200	10,983
Clark	6,642	6,296	5,647	8,098
Columbia	9,132	10,475	8,124	11,658
Crawford	3,808	3,236	3,435	4,411
Dane	105,414	69,143	94,638	74,009
Dodge	12,663	17,003	11,052	20,455
Door	5,425	6,907	3,915	8,264
Douglas	13,907	6,440	14,290	7,066
Dunn	9,205	7,273	7,709	8,472
Eau Claire	21,150	17,664	19,344	20,394
Florence	1,018	1,106	870	1,227
Fond duLac	15,887	21,985	13,982	26,067
Forest	2,142	1,845	2,213	2,296
Grant	9,421	10,049	7,890	13,427
Green	5,153	6,636	4,367	7,826
Green Lake	3,033	5,205	2,441	6,198
Iowa	4,268	4,240	3,842	4,982
Iron	2,090	1,599	1,967	1,667
Jackson	3,924	3,555	3,427	4,383
Jefferson	11,816	14,309	10,788	17,779
Juneau	3,734	4,869	3,151	5,627
Kenosha	30,089	21,661	29,233	26,112
Kewaunee	4,786	4,330	3,444	5,705
La Crosse	22,204	21,548	17,787	25,717
La Fayette	3,521	3,665	2,959	4,582
Langlade	4,254	4,884	3,675	5,828
Lincoln	5,819	5,257	5,352	6,681
Manitowoc	19,680	16,020	17,249	19,635
Marathon	24,658	24,482	20,126	27,077
Marinette	8,030	9,637	6,798	11,439
Marquette	2,463	3,059	2,031	3,404
Menominee	1,028	381	852	392
Milwaukee	268,287	168,363	259,134	196,259
Monroe	6,437	7,073	5,564	8,225
Oconto	6,549	7,084	5,288	8,713
Oneida	7,414	8,130	6,416	9,782
Outagamie	27,771	33,113	19,789	36,765
Ozaukee	12,561	22,899	10,763	23,896
Pepin	1,906	1,311	1,629	1,555
Pierce	8,659	6,045	7,285	7,611
Polk	8,981	6,866	8,033	8,101
Portage	16,317	12,057	14,399	13,603
Price	3,987	3,450	3,479	4,286
Racine	39,631	36,342	36,953	42,085
Richland	3,643	4,026	2,844	4,857
Rock	29,576	28,178	26,430	32,483
Rusk	3,888	3,063	3,843	4,061
St. Croix	11,392	9,960	10,126	11,365
Sauk	8,324	10,225	7,157	11,067
Sawyer	3,231	3,260	2,981	3,911
Shawano	6,587	8,352	5,469	10,635
Sheboygan	23,429	23,471	21,111	26,343
Taylor	3,785	4,254	3,271	4,918
Trempealeau	6,212	4,902	5,405	6,007
Vernon	5,754	5,225	5,051	6,468
Vilas	3,781	5,842	2,940	5,963
Walworth	12,203	18,259	9,876	20,590
Washburn	3,393	3,074	3,188	3,847
Washington	15,907	24,328	12,956	25,278

Waukesha	57,598	90,467	47,308	92,415
Waupaca	7,078	11,559	5,894	13,097
Waushara	3,535	4,953	2,782	5,768
Winnebago	28,508	35,085	22,791	39,014
Wood	16,074	16,549	12,118	20,525
Totals	1,126,794	1,047,499	995,740	1,198,584

Wisconsin Vote Since 1940

1940, Roosevelt, Dem., 704,821; Willkie, Rep., 679,260; Thomas, Soc., 15,071; Browder, Com., 2,394; Babson, Proh., 2,148; Aiken, Soc. Labor, 1,882.

1944, Roosevelt, Dem., 650,413; Dewey, Rep., 674,532; Thomas, Soc., 13,205; Teichert, Soc. Labor, 1,002.

1948, Truman, Dem., 647,310; Dewey, Rep., 590,959; Wallace, Prog., 25,282; Thomas, Soc., 12,547; Teichert, Soc. Labor, 399; Dobbs, Soc. Workers, 303.

1952, Eisenhower, Rep., 979,744; Stevenson, Dem., 622,175; Hallinan, Ind., 2,174; Dobbs, Ind., 1,350; Hoopes, Ind., 1,157; Hass, Ind., 770.

1956, Eisenhower, Rep., 954,844; Stevenson, Dem., 586,768; Andrews, Ind., 6,918; Hoopes, Soc., 754; Hass, Soc. Labor, 710; Dobbs, Soc. Workers, 564.

1960, Kennedy, Dem., 830,805; Nixon, Rep., 895,175; Dobbs, Soc. Workers, 1,792; Hass, Soc. Labor, 1,310.

1964, Johnson, Dem., 1,050,424; Goldwater, Rep., 638,495; DeBerry, Soc. Worker, 1,692; Hass, Soc. Labor, 1,204.

1968, Nixon, Rep., 809,997; Humphrey, Dem., 748,804; Wallace, 3d party, 127,835; Blomen, Soc. Labor, 1,338; Halstead, Soc. Worker, 1,222; scattered, 2,342.

1972, Nixon, Rep., 989,430; McGovern, Dem., 810,174; Schmitz, Amer., 47,525; Spock, Ind., 2,701; Fisher, Soc. Labor, 998; Hall, Com., 663; Reed, Ind., 506; scattered, 893.

1976, Carter, Dem., 1,040,232; Ford, Rep., 1,004,987; McCarthy, Ind., 34,943; Maddox, Amer. Ind., 8,552; Zeidler, Soc., 4,298; MacBride, Libertarian, 3,814; Camejo, Soc. Workers, 1,691; Wright, People's, 943; Hall, Com., 749; LaRouche, U.S. Lab., 738; Levin, Soc. Labor, 389; scattered, 2,839.

1980, Reagan, Rep., 1,088,845; Carter, Dem., 981,584; Anderson, Ind., 160,657; Clark, Libertarian, 29,135; Commoner, Citizens, 7,767; Rarick, Constitution, 1,519; McReynolds, Socialist, 808; Hall, Com., 772; Griswold, Workers World, 414; DeBerry, Soc. Workers, 383; scattering, 1,337.

1984, Reagan, Rep., 1,198,584; Mondale, Dem., 995,740; Bergland, Libertarian, 4,883.

1988, Bush, Rep., 1,047,499; Dukakis, Dem., 1,126,794; Paul, Lib., 5,157; Duke, Pop., 3,056.

Wyoming

	1988		1984	
County	Dukakis (D)	Bush (R)	Mondale (D)	Reagan (R)
Albany	5,486	5,653	4,708	7,452
Big Horn	1,469	3,258	1,175	4,019
Campbell	2,288	6,702	1,525	8,387
Carbon	2,555	3,336	2,295	4,557
Converse	1,301	2,885	929	3,542
Crook	553	1,939	450	2,286
Fremont	5,020	7,681	3,969	9,885
Goshen	1,875	3,075	1,364	3,776
Hot Springs	800	1,490	672	1,943
Johnson	707	2,081	558	2,634
Laramie	11,851	15,561	10,110	19,348
Lincoln	1,592	3,237	1,021	3,854
Natrona	9,148	14,005	7,598	18,488
Niobrara	354	825	239	1,098
Park	2,646	6,884	1,965	7,994
Platte	1,482	2,253	1,232	2,813
Sheridan	4,655	5,980	3,648	7,460
Sublette	576	1,636	389	1,976
Sweetwater	6,720	6,780	5,230	8,308
Teton	2,217	3,616	1,565	3,487
Uinta	1,922	3,464	1,276	4,075
Washakie	1,197	2,538	970	3,245
Weston	699	1,988	482	2,614
Totals	67,113	106,867	53,370	133,241

Wyoming Vote Since 1940

1940, Roosevelt, Dem., 59,287; Willkie, Rep., 52,633; Babson, Proh., 172; Thomas, Soc., 148.

1944, Roosevelt, Dem., 49,419; Dewey, Rep., 51,921.

1948, Truman, Dem., 52,354; Dewey, Rep., 47,947; Wallace, Prog., 931; Thomas, Soc., 137; Teichert, Soc. Labor, 56.

1952, Eisenhower, Rep., 81,047; Stevenson, Dem., 47,934; Hamblen, Proh., 194; Hoopes, Soc., 40; Haas, Soc. Labor, 36.

1956, Eisenhower, Rep., 74,573; Stevenson, Dem., 49,554.

1960, Kennedy, Dem., 63,331; Nixon, Rep., 77,451.

1964, Johnson, Dem., 80,718; Goldwater, Rep., 61,998.

1968, Nixon, Rep., 70,927; Humphrey, Dem., 45,173; Wallace, 3d party, 11,105.

1972, Nixon, Rep., 100,464; McGovern, Dem., 44,358; Schmitz, Amer., 748.

1976, Carter, Dem., 62,239; Ford, Rep., 92,717; McCarthy, Ind., 624; Reagan, Ind., 307; Anderson, Amer., 290; Mac-Bride, Libertarian, 89; Brown, Ind., 47; Maddox, Amer. Ind., 30.

1980, Reagan, Rep., 110,700; Carter, Dem., 49,427; Anderson, Ind., 12,072; Clark, Libertarian, 4,514.

1984, Reagan, Rep., 133,241; Mondale, Dem., 53,370; Bergland, Libertarian, 2,357.

1988, Bush, Rep., 106,867; Dukakis, Dem., 67,113; Paul, Lib., 2,026; Fulani, New Alliance, 545.

Official 1988 Presidential General Election Results

Source: Federal Election Commission

Candidate	Party[1]	Official Popular Vote Total	Percent of Total Vote
George Bush	Republican	48,886,097	53.37
Michael S. Dukakis	Democratic	41,809,074	45.65
Delmar Dennis	American	3,475	0.00
Earl Dodge	Prohibition	8,002	0.01
David Duke	Populist	47,047	0.05
Lenora B. Fulani	New Alliance	217,219	0.24
James C. Griffin	American Independent	27,818	0.03
Jack Herer	GrassRoots	1,949	0.00
Larry Holmes	Workers World	7,846	0.01
Willa Kenoyer	Socialist	3,882	0.00
Lyndon H. LaRouche	National Economic	25,542	0.03
Herbert Lewin	Peace & Freedom	10,370	0.01
William A. Marra	Right to Life	20,504	0.02
John G. Martin	Third World Assembly	236	0.00
Eugene J. McCarthy	Consumer	30,905	0.03
Ronald E. Paul	Libertarian	432,116	0.47
James Mac Warren	Socialist Workers	15,604	0.02
Edward Winn	Workers League	18,662	0.02
Louie G. Youngkeit	Independent	372	0.00
Write-In		21,039	0.02
None of Above	(Nevada Option)	6,934	0.01
Total Votes		91,594,693	

Voting Age Population: 182,628,000
(Census Bureau Estimate)

[1] Party designations may vary from one state to another.

Electoral Votes for President

Major Parties' Popular and Electoral Vote for President

(F) Federalist; (D) Democrat; (R) Republican; (DR) Democrat Republican; (NR) National Republican;
(W) Whig; (P) People's; (PR) Progressive; (SR) States' Rights; (LR) Liberal Republican; Asterisk (*)—See notes.

Year	President elected	Popular	Elec.	Losing candidate	Popular	Elec.
1789	George Washington (F)	Unknown	69	No opposition..........	—	—
1792	George Washington (F)	Unknown	132	No opposition..........	—	—
1796	John Adams (F).........	Unknown	71	Thomas Jefferson (DR)	Unknown	68
1800*	Thomas Jefferson (DR)	Unknown	73	Aaron Burr (DR)	Unknown	73
1804	Thomas Jefferson (DR)	Unknown	162	Charles Pinckney (F)	Unknown	14
1808	James Madison (DR)......	Unknown	122	Charles Pinckney (F)	Unknown	47
1812	James Madison (DR)	Unknown	128	DeWitt Clinton (F)	Unknown	89
1816	James Monroe (DR)	Unknown	183	Rufus King (F)	Unknown	34
1820	James Monroe (DR)	Unknown	231	John Quincy Adams (DR)....	Unknown	1
1824*	John Quincy Adams (DR) ...	105,321	84	Andrew Jackson (DR)......	155,872	99
				Henry Clay (DR)........	46,587	37
				William H. Crawford (DR) ...	44,282	41
1828	Andrew Jackson (D)......	647,231	178	John Quincy Adams (NR)....	509,097	83
1832	Andrew Jackson (D)	687,502	219	Henry Clay (NR)	530,189	49
1836	Martin Van Buren (D).....	762,678	170	William H. Harrison (W)	548,007	73
1840	William H. Harrison (W) ...	1,275,017	234	Martin Van Buren (D)	1,128,702	60
1844	James K. Polk (D)	1,337,243	170	Henry Clay (W)........	1,299,068	105
1848	Zachary Taylor (W).......	1,360,101	163	Lewis Cass (D).........	1,220,544	127
1852	Franklin Pierce (D)	1,601,474	254	Winfield Scott (W)	1,386,578	42
1856	James C. Buchanan (D).....	1,927,995	174	John C. Fremont (R)......	1,391,555	114
1860	Abraham Lincoln (R)......	1,866,352	180	Stephen A. Douglas (D)....	1,375,157	12
				John C. Breckinridge (D) ...	845,763	72
				John Bell (Const. Union).....	589,581	39
1864	Abraham Lincoln (R)......	2,216,067	212	George McClellan (D).....	1,808,725	21
1868	Ulysses S. Grant (R)......	3,015,071	214	Horatio Seymour (D).....	2,709,615	80
1872*	Ulysses S. Grant (R)......	3,597,070	286	Horace Greeley (D-LR)	2,834,079	—
1876*	Rutherford B. Hayes (R)....	4,033,950	185	Samuel J. Tilden (D)......	4,284,757	184
1880	James A. Garfield (R)	4,449,053	214	Winfield S. Hancock (D)	4,442,030	155
1884	Grover Cleveland (D)	4,911,017	219	James G. Blaine (R)	4,848,334	182
1888*	Benjamin Harrison (R)	5,444,337	233	Grover Cleveland (D)......	5,540,050	168
1892	Grover Cleveland (D)	5,554,414	277	Benjamin Harrison (R)......	5,190,802	145
				James Weaver (P).......	1,027,329	22
1896	William McKinley (R)......	7,035,638	271	William J. Bryan (D-P).....	6,467,946	176
1900	William McKinley (R)......	7,219,530	292	William J. Bryan (D)......	6,358,071	155
1904	Theodore Roosevelt (R)....	7,628,834	336	Alton B. Parker (D).......	5,084,491	140
1908	William H. Taft (R)	7,679,006	321	William J. Bryan (D)......	6,409,106	162
1912	Woodrow Wilson (D)......	6,286,214	435	Theodore Roosevelt (PR)....	4,216,020	88
				William H. Taft (R)	3,483,922	8
1916	Woodrow Wilson (D)......	9,129,606	277	Charles E. Hughes (R).....	8,538,221	254
1920	Warren G. Harding (R).....	16,152,200	404	James M. Cox (D)	9,147,353	127
1924	Calvin Coolidge (R).......	15,725,016	382	John W. Davis (D)	8,385,586	136
				Robert M. LaFollette (PR)....	4,822,856	13
1928	Herbert Hoover (R)	21,392,190	444	Alfred E. Smith (D).......	15,016,443	87
1932	Franklin D. Roosevelt (D) ...	22,821,857	472	Herbert Hoover (R)	15,761,841	59
				Norman Thomas (Socialist)....	884,781	—
1936	Franklin D. Roosevelt (D) ...	27,751,597	523	Alfred Landon (R).......	16,679,583	8
1940	Franklin D. Roosevelt (D) ...	27,243,466	449	Wendell Willkie (R)......	22,304,755	82
1944	Franklin D. Roosevelt (D) ...	25,602,505	432	Thomas E. Dewey (R).....	22,006,278	99
1948	Harry S Truman (D)	24,105,812	303	Thomas E. Dewey (R).....	21,970,065	189
				J. Strom Thurmond (SR)....	1,169,021	39
				Henry A. Wallace (PR).....	1,157,172	—
1952	Dwight D. Eisenhower (R) ...	33,936,252	442	Adlai E. Stevenson (D).....	27,314,992	89
1956*	Dwight D. Eisenhower (R) ...	35,585,316	457	Adlai E. Stevenson (D).....	26,031,322	73
1960*	John F. Kennedy (D).....	34,227,096	303	Richard M. Nixon (R)......	34,108,546	219
1964	Lyndon B. Johnson (D)....	43,126,506	486	Barry M. Goldwater (R)	27,176,799	52
1968	Richard M. Nixon (R).....	31,785,480	301	Hubert H. Humphrey (D).....	31,275,166	191
				George C. Wallace (3d party) ..	9,906,473	46
1972*	Richard M. Nixon (R).....	47,165,234	520	George S. McGovern (D)	29,170,774	17
1976*	Jimmy Carter (D)........	40,828,929	297	Gerald R. Ford (R)......	39,148,940	240
1980	Ronald Reagan (R)......	43,899,248	489	Jimmy Carter (D).......	35,481,435	49
				John B. Anderson (independent) ..	5,719,437	—
1984	Ronald Reagan (R)......	54,281,858	525	Walter F. Mondale (D)	37,457,215	13
1988*	George Bush (R)........	48,881,221	426	Michael S. Dukakis (D)	41,805,422	111

1800—Elected by House of Representatives because of tied electoral vote. **1824**—Elected by House of Representatives. No candidate polled a majority. In 1824, the Democrat Republicans had become a loose coalition of competing political groups. By 1828, the supporters of Jackson were known as Democrats, and the J.Q. Adams and Henry Clay supporters as National Republicans. **1872**—Greeley died Nov. 29, 1872. His electoral votes were split among 4 individuals. **1876**—Fla., La., Ore., and S. C. election returns were disputed. Congress in joint session (Mar. 2, 1877) declared Hayes and Wheeler elected President and Vice-President. **1888**—Cleveland had more votes than Harrison but the 233 electoral votes cast for Harrison against the 168 for Cleveland elected Harrison president. **1956**—Democrats elected 74 electors but one from Alabama refused to vote for Stevenson. **1960**—Sen. Harry F. Byrd (D-Va.) received 15 electoral votes. **1972**—John Hospers of Cal. and Theodora Nathan of Ore. received one vote from an elector of Virginia. **1976**—Ronald Reagan of Cal. received one vote from an elector of Washington. **1988**—Sen. Lloyd Bentsen (D.-Tex.) received 1 electoral vote.

The Electoral College

The president and the vice president of the United States are the only elective federal officials not elected by direct vote of the people. They are elected by the members of the Electoral College, an institution that has survived since the founding of the nation despite repeated attempts in Congress to alter or abolish it. In the elections of 1824, 1876 and 1888 the presidential candidate receiving the largest popular vote failed to win a majority of the electoral votes.

On presidential election day, the first Tuesday after the first Monday in November of every 4th year, each state chooses as many electors as it has senators and representatives in Congress. In 1964, for the first time, as provided by the 23d Amendment to the Constitution, the District of Columbia voted for 3 electors. Thus, with 100 senators and 435 representatives, there are 538 members of the Electoral College, with a majority of 270 electoral votes needed to elect the president and vice president.

Political parties customarily nominate their lists of electors at their respective state conventions. An elector cannot be a member of Congress or any person holding federal office.

Some states print the names of the candidates for president and vice president at the top of the November ballot while others list only the names of the electors. In either case, the electors of the party receiving the highest vote are elected. The electors meet on the first Monday after the 2d Wednesday in December in their respective state capitals or in some other place prescribed by state legislatures. By long-established custom they vote for their party nominees, although the Constitution does not require them to do so. All of the state's electoral votes are then awarded to the winners. The only Constitutional requirement is that at least one of the persons each elector votes for shall not be an inhabitant of that elector's home state.

Certified and sealed lists of the votes of the electors in each state are mailed to the president of the U.S. Senate. He opens them in the presence of the members of the Senate and House of Representatives in a joint session held on Jan. 6 (the next day if that falls on a Sunday), and the electoral votes of all the states are then counted. If no candidate for president has a majority, the House of Representatives chooses a president from among the 3 highest candidates, with all representatives from each state combining to cast one vote for that state. If no candidate for vice president has a majority, the Senate chooses from the top 2, with the senators voting as individuals.

Voting for President

Source: Federal Election Commission; Commission for Study of American Electorate

Candidates	Voter Participation (% of voting-age population)		Candidates	Voter Participation (% of voting-age population)
1932 Roosevelt-Hoover	52.4		1964 Johnson-Goldwater	61.9
1936 Roosevelt-Landon	56.0		1968 Humphrey-Nixon	60.9
1940 Roosevelt-Willkie	58.9		1972 McGovern-Nixon	55.2(a)
1944 Roosevelt-Dewey	56.0		1976 Carter-Ford	53.5
1948 Truman-Dewey	51.1		1980 Carter-Reagan	54.0
1952 Stevenson-Eisenhower	61.6		1984 Mondale-Reagan	53.1
1956 Stevenson-Eisenhower	59.3		1988 Dukakis-Bush	50.1
1960 Kennedy-Nixon	62.8			

(a) The sharp drop in 1972 reflects the expansion of eligibility with the enfranchisement of 18 to 21 year olds.

Party Nominees for President and Vice President

Asterisk (*) denotes winning ticket

	Democratic		Republican	
Year	President	Vice President	President	Vice President
1844	James K. Polk*	George M. Dallas	Henry Clay (Whig)	Theo. Frelinghuysen
1848	Lewis Cass	William Butler	Zachary Taylor* (Whig)	Millard Fillmore
1852	Franklin Pierce*	William King	Winfield Scott (Whig)	William Graham
1856	James Buchanan*	John Breckinridge	John Freemont	William Dayton
1860	John Breckinridge	Joseph Lane	Abraham Lincoln*	Hannibal Hamlin
1864	George McClellan	G.H. Pendleton	Abraham Lincoln*	Andrew Johnson
1868	Horatio Seymour	Francis Blair	Ulysses S. Grant*	Schuyler Colfax
1872	Horace Greeley	B. Gratz Brown	Ulysses S. Grant*	Henry Wilson
1876	Samuel J. Tilden	Thomas Hendricks	Rutherford B. Hayes*	William Wheeler
1880	Winfield Hancock	William English	James A. Garfield*	Chester A. Arthur
1884	Grover Cleveland*	Thomas Hendricks	James Blaine	John Logan
1888	Grover Cleveland	A.G. Thurman	Benjamin Harrison*	Levi Morton
1892	Grover Cleveland*	Adlai Stevenson	Benjamin Harrison	Whitelaw Reid
1896	William J. Bryan	Adlai Stevenson	William McKinley*	Garret Hobart
1900	William J. Bryan	Adlai Stevenson	William McKinley*	Theodore Roosevelt
1904	Alton Parker	Henry Davis	Theodore Roosevelt*	Charles Fairbanks
1908	William J. Bryan	John Kern	William H. Taft*	James Sherman
1912	Woodrow Wilson*	Thomas Marshall	William H. Taft	James Sherman[1]
1916	Woodrow Wilson*	Thomas Marshall	Charles Hughes	Charles Fairbanks
1920	James M. Cox	Franklin D. Roosevelt	Warren G. Harding*	Calvin Coolidge
1924	John W. Davis	Charles W. Bryan	Calvin Coolidge*	Charles G. Dawes
1928	Alfred E. Smith	Joseph T. Robinson	Herbert Hoover*	Charles Curtis
1932	Franklin D. Roosevelt*	John N. Garner	Herbert Hoover	Charles Curtis
1936	Franklin D. Roosevelt*	John N. Garner	Alfred M. Landon	Frank Knox
1940	Franklin D. Roosevelt*	Henry A. Wallace	Wendell L. Willkie	Charles McNary
1944	Franklin D. Roosevelt*	Harry S. Truman	Thomas E. Dewey	John W. Bricker
1948	Harry S. Truman*	Alben W. Barkley	Thomas E. Dewey	Earl Warren
1952	Adlai E. Stevenson	John J. Sparkman	Dwight D. Eisenhower*	Richard M. Nixon
1956	Adlai E. Stevenson	Estes Kefauver	Dwight D. Eisenhower*	Richard M. Nixon
1960	John F. Kennedy*	Lyndon B. Johnson	Richard M. Nixon	Henry Cabot Lodge
1964	Lyndon B. Johnson*	Hubert H. Humphrey	Barry M. Goldwater	William E. Miller
1968	Hubert H. Humphrey	Edmund S. Muskie	Richard M. Nixon*	Spiro T. Agnew
1972	George S. McGovern	R. Sargent Shriver Jr.	Richard M. Nixon*	Spiro T. Agnew
1976	Jimmy Carter*	Walter F. Mondale	Gerald R. Ford	Robert J. Dole
1980	Jimmy Carter	Walter F. Mondale	Ronald Reagan*	George Bush
1984	Walter F. Mondale	Geraldine Ferraro	Ronald Reagan*	George Bush
1988	Michael S. Dukakis	Lloyd Bentsen	George Bush*	J. Danforth "Dan" Quayle

(1) Died Oct. 30; replaced on ballot by Nicholas Butler.

Presidents of the U.S.

No.	Name	Politics	Born	in	Inaug.	at age	Died	at age
1	George Washington	Fed.	1732, Feb. 22	Va.	1789	57	1799, Dec. 14	67
2	John Adams	Fed.	1735, Oct. 30	Mass.	1797	61	1826, July 4	90
3	Thomas Jefferson	Dem.-Rep.	1743, Apr. 13	Va.	1801	57	1826, July 4	83
4	James Madison	Dem.-Rep.	1751, Mar. 16	Va.	1809	57	1836, June 28	85
5	James Monroe	Dem.-Rep.	1758, Apr. 28	Va.	1817	58	1831, July 4	73
6	John Quincy Adams	Dem.-Rep.	1767, July 11	Mass.	1825	57	1848, Feb. 23	80
7	Andrew Jackson	Dem.	1767, Mar. 15	S.C.	1829	61	1845, June 8	78
8	Martin Van Buren	Dem.	1782, Dec. 5	N.Y.	1837	54	1862, July 24	79
9	William Henry Harrison	Whig	1773, Feb. 9	Va.	1841	68	1841, Apr. 4	68
10	John Tyler	Whig	1790, Mar. 29	Va.	1841	51	1862, Jan. 18	71
11	James Knox Polk	Dem.	1795, Nov. 2	N.C.	1845	49	1849, June 15	53
12	Zachary Taylor	Whig	1784, Nov. 24	Va.	1849	64	1850, July 9	65
13	Millard Fillmore	Whig	1800, Jan. 7	N.Y.	1850	50	1874, Mar. 8	74
14	Franklin Pierce	Dem.	1804, Nov. 23	N.H.	1853	48	1869, Oct. 8	64
15	James Buchanan	Dem.	1791, Apr. 23	Pa.	1857	65	1868, June 1	77
16	Abraham Lincoln	Rep.	1809, Feb. 12	Ky.	1861	52	1865, Apr. 15	56
17	Andrew Johnson	(1)	1808, Dec. 29	N.C.	1865	56	1875, July 31	66
18	Ulysses Simpson Grant	Rep.	1822, Apr. 27	Oh.	1869	46	1885, July 23	63
19	Rutherford Birchard Hayes	Rep.	1822, Oct. 4	Oh.	1877	54	1893, Jan. 17	70
20	James Abram Garfield	Rep.	1831, Nov. 19	Oh.	1881	49	1881, Sept. 19	49
21	Chester Alan Arthur	Rep.	1829, Oct. 5	Vt.	1881	51	1886, Nov. 18	57
22	Grover Cleveland	Dem.	1837, Mar. 18	N.J.	1885	47	1908, June 24	71
23	Benjamin Harrison	Rep.	1833, Aug. 20	Oh.	1889	55	1901, Mar. 13	67
24	Grover Cleveland	Dem.	1837, Mar. 18	N.J.	1893	55	1908, June 24	71
25	William McKinley	Rep.	1843, Jan. 29	Oh.	1897	54	1901, Sept. 14	58
26	Theodore Roosevelt	Rep.	1858, Oct. 27	N.Y.	1901	42	1919, Jan. 6	60
27	William Howard Taft	Rep.	1857, Sept. 15	Oh.	1909	51	1930, Mar. 8	72
28	Woodrow Wilson	Dem.	1856, Dec. 28	Va.	1913	56	1924, Feb. 3	67
29	Warren Gamaliel Harding	Rep.	1865, Nov. 2	Oh.	1921	55	1923, Aug. 2	57
30	Calvin Coolidge	Rep.	1872, July 4	Vt.	1923	51	1933, Jan. 5	60
31	Herbert Clark Hoover	Rep.	1874, Aug. 10	Ia.	1929	54	1964, Oct. 20	90
32	Franklin Delano Roosevelt	Dem.	1882, Jan. 30	N.Y.	1933	51	1945, Apr. 12	63
33	Harry S. Truman	Dem.	1884, May 8	Mo.	1945	60	1972, Dec. 26	88
34	Dwight David Eisenhower	Rep.	1890, Oct. 14	Tex.	1953	62	1969, Mar. 28	78
35	John Fitzgerald Kennedy	Dem.	1917, May 29	Mass.	1961	43	1963, Nov. 22	46
36	Lyndon Baines Johnson	Dem.	1908, Aug. 27	Tex.	1963	55	1973, Jan. 22	64
37	Richard Milhous Nixon (2)	Rep.	1913, Jan. 9	Cal.	1969	56		
38	Gerald Rudolph Ford	Rep.	1913, July 14	Neb.	1974	61		
39	Jimmy (James Earl) Carter	Dem.	1924, Oct. 1	Ga.	1977	52		
40	Ronald Reagan	Rep.	1911, Feb. 6	Ill.	1981	69		
41	George Bush	Rep.	1924, June 12	Mass.	1989	64		

(1) Andrew Johnson — a Democrat, nominated vice president by Republicans and elected with Lincoln on National Union ticket. (2) Resigned Aug. 9, 1974.

Presidents, Vice Presidents, Congresses

	President	Service		Vice President	Congress
1	George Washington	Apr. 30, 1789—Mar. 3, 1797	1	John Adams	1, 2, 3, 4
2	John Adams	Mar. 4, 1797—Mar. 3, 1801	2	Thomas Jefferson	5, 6
3	Thomas Jefferson	Mar. 4, 1801—Mar. 3, 1805	3	Aaron Burr	7, 8
	"	Mar. 4, 1805—Mar. 3, 1809	4	George Clinton	9, 10
4	James Madison	Mar. 4, 1809—Mar. 3, 1813		"(1)	11, 12
	"	Mar. 4, 1813—Mar. 3, 1817	5	Elbridge Gerry (2)	13, 14
5	James Monroe	Mar. 4, 1817—Mar. 3, 1825	6	Daniel D. Tompkins	15, 16, 17, 18
6	John Quincy Adams	Mar. 4, 1825—Mar. 3, 1829	7	John C. Calhoun	19, 20
7	Andrew Jackson	Mar. 4, 1829—Mar. 3, 1833		"(3)	21, 22
	"	Mar. 4, 1833—Mar. 3, 1837	8	Martin Van Buren	23, 24
8	Martin Van Buren	Mar. 4, 1837—Mar. 3, 1841	9	Richard M. Johnson	25, 26
9	William Henry Harrison (4)	Mar. 4, 1841—Apr. 4, 1841	10	John Tyler	27
10	John Tyler	Apr. 6, 1841—Mar. 3, 1845			27, 28
11	James K. Polk	Mar. 4, 1845—Mar. 3, 1849	11	George M. Dallas	29, 30
12	Zachary Taylor (4)	Mar. 5, 1849—July 9, 1850	12	Millard Fillmore	31
13	Millard Fillmore	July 10, 1850—Mar. 3, 1853			31, 32
14	Franklin Pierce	Mar. 4, 1853—Mar. 3, 1857	13	William R. King (5)	33, 34
15	James Buchanan	Mar. 4, 1857—Mar. 3, 1861	14	John C. Breckinridge	35, 36
16	Abraham Lincoln	Mar. 4, 1861—Mar. 3, 1865	15	Hannibal Hamlin	37, 38
	"(4)	Mar. 4, 1865—Apr. 15, 1865	16	Andrew Johnson	39
17	Andrew Johnson	Apr. 15, 1865—Mar. 3, 1869			39, 40
18	Ulysses S. Grant	Mar. 4, 1869—Mar. 3, 1873	17	Schuyler Colfax	41, 42
	"	Mar. 4, 1873—Mar. 3, 1877	18	Henry Wilson (6)	43, 44
19	Rutherford B. Hayes	Mar. 4, 1877—Mar. 3, 1881	19	William A. Wheeler	45, 46
20	James A. Garfield (4)	Mar. 4, 1881—Sept. 19, 1881	20	Chester A. Arthur	47
21	Chester A. Arthur	Sept. 20, 1881—Mar. 3, 1885			47, 48
22	Grover Cleveland (7)	Mar. 4, 1885—Mar. 3, 1889	21	Thomas A. Hendricks (8)	49, 50
23	Benjamin Harrison	Mar. 4, 1889—Mar. 3, 1893	22	Levi P. Morton	51, 52
24	Grover Cleveland (7)	Mar. 4, 1893—Mar. 3, 1897	23	Adlai E. Stevenson	53, 54
25	William McKinley	Mar. 4, 1897—Mar. 3, 1901	24	Garret A. Hobart (9)	55, 56
	"(4)	Mar. 4, 1901—Sept. 14, 1901	25	Theodore Roosevelt	57
26	Theodore Roosevelt	Sept. 14, 1901—Mar. 3, 1905			57, 58
	"	Mar. 4, 1905—Mar. 3, 1909	26	Charles W. Fairbanks	59, 60
27	William H. Taft	Mar. 4, 1909—Mar. 3, 1913	27	James S. Sherman (10)	61, 62
28	Woodrow Wilson	Mar. 4, 1913—Mar. 3, 1921	28	Thomas R. Marshall	63, 64, 65, 66
29	Warren G. Harding (4)	Mar. 4, 1921—Aug. 2, 1923	29	Calvin Coolidge	67

Presidents, Vice Presidents, Congresses

	President	Service		Vice President	Congress
30	Calvin Coolidge	Aug. 3, 1923—Mar. 3, 1925			68
"		Mar. 4, 1925—Mar. 3, 1929	30	Charles G. Dawes	69, 70
31	Herbert C. Hoover	Mar. 4, 1929—Mar. 3, 1933	31	Charles Curtis	71, 72
32	Franklin D. Roosevelt (16)	Mar. 4, 1933—Jan. 20, 1941	32	John N. Garner	73, 74, 75, 76
"		Jan. 20, 1941—Jan. 20, 1945	33	Henry A. Wallace	77, 78
"(4)		Jan. 20, 1945—Apr. 12, 1945	34	Harry S. Truman	79
33	Harry S. Truman	Apr. 12, 1945—Jan. 20, 1949			79, 80
"		Jan. 20, 1949—Jan. 20, 1953	35	Alben W. Barkley	81, 82
34	Dwight D. Eisenhower	Jan. 20, 1953—Jan. 20, 1961	36	Richard M. Nixon	83, 84, 85, 86
35	John F. Kennedy (4)	Jan. 20, 1961—Nov. 22, 1963	37	Lyndon B. Johnson	87, 88
36	Lyndon B. Johnson	Nov. 22, 1963—Jan. 20, 1965			88
"		Jan. 20, 1965—Jan. 20, 1969	38	Hubert H. Humphrey	89, 90
37	Richard M. Nixon	Jan. 20, 1969—Jan. 20, 1973	39	Spiro T. Agnew (11)	91, 92, 93
"(12)		Jan. 20, 1973—Aug. 9, 1974	40	Gerald R. Ford (13)	93
38	Gerald R. Ford (14)	Aug. 9, 1974—Jan. 20, 1977	41	Nelson A. Rockefeller (15)	93, 94
39	Jimmy (James Earl) Carter	Jan. 20, 1977—Jan. 20, 1981	42	Walter F. Mondale	95, 96
40	Ronald Reagan	Jan. 20, 1981—Jan. 20, 1989	43	George Bush	97, 98, 99, 100
41	George Bush	Jan. 20, 1989—	44	Dan Quayle	101

(1) Died Apr. 20, 1812. (2) Died Nov. 23, 1814. (3) Resigned Dec. 28, 1832, to become U.S. Senator. (4) Died in office. (5) Died Apr. 18, 1853. (6) Died Nov. 22, 1875. (7) Terms not consecutive. (8) Died Nov. 25, 1885. (9) Died Nov. 21, 1899. (10) Died Oct. 30, 1912. (11) Resigned Oct. 10, 1973. (12) Resigned Aug. 9, 1974. (13) First non-elected vice president, chosen under 25th Amendment procedure. (14) First non-elected president. (15) 2d non-elected vice president. (16) First president to be inaugurated under 20th Amendment, Jan. 20, 1937.

Vice Presidents of the U.S.

The numerals given vice presidents do not coincide with those given presidents, because some presidents had none and some had more than one.

	Name	Birthplace	Year	Home	Inaug.	Politics	Place of death	Year	Age
1	John Adams	Quincy, Mass.	1735	Mass.	1789	Fed.	Quincy, Mass.	1826	90
2	Thomas Jefferson	Shadwell, Va.	1743	Va.	1797	Dem.-Rep.	Monticello, Va.	1826	83
3	Aaron Burr	Newark, N.J.	1756	N.Y.	1801	Dem.-Rep.	Staten Island, N.Y.	1836	80
4	George Clinton	Ulster Co., N.Y.	1739	N.Y.	1805	Dem.-Rep.	Washington, D.C.	1812	73
5	Elbridge Gerry	Marblehead, Mass.	1744	Mass.	1813	Dem.-Rep.	Washington, D.C.	1814	70
6	Daniel D. Tompkins	Scarsdale, N.Y.	1774	N.Y.	1817	Dem.-Rep.	Staten Island, N.Y.	1825	51
7	John C. Calhoun (1)	Abbeville, S.C.	1782	S.C.	1825	Dem.-Rep.	Washington, D.C.	1850	68
8	Martin Van Buren	Kinderhook, N.Y.	1782	N.Y.	1833	Dem.	Kinderhook, N.Y.	1862	79
9	Richard M. Johnson	Louisville, Ky.	1780	Ky.	1837	Dem.	Frankfort, Ky.	1850	70
10	John Tyler	Greenway, Va.	1790	Va.	1841	Whig	Richmond, Va.	1862	71
11	George M. Dallas	Philadelphia, Pa.	1792	Pa.	1845	Dem.	Philadelphia, Pa.	1864	72
12	Millard Fillmore	Summerhill, N.Y.	1800	N.Y.	1849	Whig	Buffalo, N.Y.	1874	74
13	William R. King	Sampson Co., N.C.	1786	Ala.	1853	Dem.	Dallas Co., Ala.	1853	67
14	John C. Breckinridge	Lexington, Ky.	1821	Ky.	1857	Dem.	Lexington, Ky.	1875	54
15	Hannibal Hamlin	Paris, Me.	1809	Me.	1861	Rep.	Bangor, Me.	1891	81
16	Andrew Johnson	Raleigh, N.C.	1808	Tenn.	1865	(2)	Carter Co., Tenn.	1875	66
17	Schuyler Colfax	New York, N.Y.	1823	Ind.	1869	Rep.	Mankato, Minn.	1885	62
18	Henry Wilson	Farmington, N.H.	1812	Mass.	1873	Rep.	Washington, D.C.	1875	63
19	William A. Wheeler	Malone, N.Y.	1819	N.Y.	1877	Rep.	Malone, N.Y.	1887	68
20	Chester A. Arthur	Fairfield, Vt.	1829	N.Y.	1881	Rep.	New York, N.Y.	1886	57
21	Thomas A. Hendricks	Muskingum Co., Oh.	1819	Ind.	1885	Dem.	Indianapolis, Ind.	1885	66
22	Levi P. Morton	Shoreham, Vt.	1824	N.Y.	1889	Rep.	Rhinebeck, N.Y.	1920	96
23	Adlai E. Stevenson (3)	Christian Co., Ky.	1835	Ill.	1893	Dem.	Chicago, Ill.	1914	78
24	Garret A. Hobart	Long Branch, N.J.	1844	N.J.	1897	Rep.	Paterson, N.J.	1899	55
25	Theodore Roosevelt	New York, N.Y.	1858	N.Y.	1901	Rep.	Oyster Bay, N.Y.	1919	60
26	Charles W. Fairbanks	Unionville Centre, Oh.	1852	Ind.	1905	Rep.	Indianapolis, Ind.	1918	66
27	James S. Sherman	Utica, N.Y.	1855	N.Y.	1909	Rep.	Utica, N.Y.	1912	57
28	Thomas R. Marshall	N. Manchester, Ind.	1854	Ind.	1913	Dem.	Washington, D.C.	1925	71
29	Calvin Coolidge	Plymouth, Vt.	1872	Mass.	1921	Rep.	Northampton, Mass.	1933	60
30	Charles G. Dawes	Marietta, Oh.	1865	Ill.	1925	Rep.	Evanston, Ill.	1951	85
31	Charles Curtis	Topeka, Kan.	1860	Kan.	1929	Rep.	Washington, D.C.	1936	76
32	John Nance Garner	Red River Co., Tex.	1868	Tex.	1933	Dem.	Uvalde, Tex.	1967	98
33	Henry Agard Wallace	Adair County, Ia.	1888	Iowa	1941	Dem.	Danbury, Conn.	1965	77
34	Harry S. Truman	Lamar, Mo.	1884	Mo.	1945	Dem.	Kansas City, Mo.	1972	88
35	Alben W. Barkley	Graves County, Ky.	1877	Ky.	1949	Dem.	Lexington, Va.	1956	78
36	Richard M. Nixon	Yorba Linda, Cal.	1913	Cal.	1953	Rep.			
37	Lyndon B. Johnson	Johnson City, Tex.	1908	Tex.	1961	Dem.	San Antonio, Tex.	1973	64
38	Hubert H. Humphrey	Wallace, S.D.	1911	Minn.	1965	Dem.	Waverly, Minn.	1978	66
39	Spiro T. Agnew (4)	Baltimore, Md.	1918	Md.	1969	Rep.			
40	Gerald R. Ford	Omaha, Neb.	1913	Mich.	1973	Rep.			
41	Nelson A. Rockefeller	Bar Harbor, Me.	1908	N.Y.	1974	Rep.	New York, N.Y.	1979	70
42	Walter F. Mondale	Ceylon, Minn.	1928	Minn.	1977	Dem.			
43	George Bush	Milton, Mass.	1924	Tex.	1981	Rep.			
44	Dan Quayle	Indianapolis, Ind.	1947	Ind.	1989	Rep.			

(1) John C. Calhoun resigned Dec. 28, 1832, having been elected to the Senate to fill a vacancy. (2) Andrew Johnson — a Democrat nominated by Republicans and elected with Lincoln on the National Union Ticket. (3) Adlai E. Stevenson, 23d vice president, was grandfather of Democratic candidate for president, 1952 and 1956. (4) Resigned Oct. 10, 1973.

BIOGRAPHIES OF U.S. PRESIDENTS

George Washington (1789-1797)

George Washington, first president, was born Feb. 22, 1732 (Feb. 11, 1731, old style), the son of Augustine Washington and Mary Ball, at Wakefield on Pope's Creek, Westmoreland Co., Va. His early childhood was spent on the Ferry farm, near Fredericksburg. His father died when George was 11. He studied mathematics and surveying and when 16 went to live with his half brother Lawrence, who built and named Mount Vernon. George surveyed the lands of William Fairfax in the Shenandoah Valley, keeping a diary. He accompanied Lawrence to Barbados, West Indies, contracted small pox, and was deeply scarred. Lawrence died in 1752 and George acquired his property by inheritance. He valued land and when he died owned 70,000 acres in Virginia and 40,000 acres in what is now West Virginia.

Washington's military service began in 1753 when Gov. Dinwiddie of Virginia sent him on missions deep into Ohio country. He clashed with the French and had to surrender Fort Necessity July 3, 1754. He was an aide to Braddock and at his side when the army was ambushed and defeated on a march to Ft. Duquesne, July 9, 1755. He helped take Fort Duquesne from the French in 1758.

After his marriage to Martha Dandridge Custis, a widow, in 1759, Washington managed his family estate at Mount Vernon. Although not at first for independence, he opposed British exactions and took charge of the Virginia troops before war broke out. He was made commander-in-chief by the Continental Congress June 15, 1775.

The successful issue of a war filled with hardships was due to his leadership. He was resourceful, a stern disciplinarian, and the one strong, dependable force for unity. He favored a federal government and became chairman of the Constitutional Convention of 1787. He helped get the Constitution ratified and was unanimously elected president by the electoral college and inaugurated, Apr. 30, 1789, on the balcony of New York's Federal Hall.

He was reelected 1792, but refused to consider a 3d term and retired to Mount Vernon. He suffered acute laryngitis after a ride in snow and rain around his estate, was bled profusely, and died Dec. 14, 1799.

John Adams (1797-1801)

John Adams, 2d president, Federalist, was born in Braintree (Quincy), Mass., Oct. 30, 1735 (Oct. 19, o. s.), the son of John Adams, a farmer, and Susanna Boylston. He was a great-grandson of Henry Adams who came from England in 1636. He was graduated from Harvard, 1755, taught school, studied law. In 1765 he argued against taxation without representation before the royal governor. In 1770 he defended in court the British soldiers who fired on civilians in the "Boston Massacre." He was a delegate to the first Continental Congress, and signed the Declaration of Independence. He was a commissioner to France, 1778, with Benjamin Franklin and Arthur Lee; won recognition of the U.S. by The Hague, 1782; was first American minister to England, 1785-1788, and was elected vice president, 1788 and 1792.

In 1796 Adams was chosen president by the electors. Intense antagonism to America by France caused agitation for war, led by Alexander Hamilton. Adams, breaking with Hamilton, opposed war.

To fight alien influence and muzzle criticism Adams supported the Alien and Sedition laws of 1798, which led to his defeat for reelection. He died July 4, 1826, on the same day as Jefferson (the 50th anniversary of the Declaration of Independence).

Thomas Jefferson (1801-1809)

Thomas Jefferson, 3d president, was born Apr. 13, 1743 (Apr. 2, o. s.), at Shadwell, Va., the son of Peter Jefferson, a civil engineer of Welsh descent who raised tobacco, and Jane Randolph. His father died when he was 14, leaving him 2,750 acres and his slaves. Jefferson attended the College of William and Mary, 1760-1762, read classics in Greek and Latin and played the violin. In 1769 he was elected to the House of Burgesses. In 1770 he began building Monticello, near Charlottesville. He was a member of the Virginia Committee of Correspondence and the Continental Congress. Named a member of the committee to draw up a Declaration of Independence, he wrote the basic draft. He was a member of the Virginia House of Delegates, 1776-79, elected governor to succeed Patrick Henry, 1779, reelected 1780, resigned June 1781, amid charges of ineffectual military preparation. During his term he wrote the statute on religious freedom. In the Continental Congress, 1783, he drew up an ordinance for the Northwest Territory, forbidding slavery after 1800; its terms were put into the Ordinance of 1787. He was sent to Paris with Benjamin Franklin and John Adams to negotiate commercial treaties, 1784; made minister to France, 1785.

Washington appointed him secretary of state, 1789. Jefferson's strong faith in the consent of the governed, as opposed to executive control favored by Hamilton, secretary of the treasury, often led to conflict: Dec. 31, 1793, he resigned. He was the Democrat Republican candidate for president in 1796; beaten by John Adams, he became vice president. In 1800, Jefferson and Aaron Burr received equal electoral college votes for president. The House of Representatives elected Jefferson. Major events of his administration were the Louisiana Purchase, 1803, and the Lewis and Clark Expedition. He established the Univ. of Virginia and designed its buildings. He died July 4, 1826, on the same day as John Adams.

James Madison (1809-1817)

James Madison, 4th president, Democrat Republican, was born Mar. 16, 1751 (Mar. 5, 1750, o. s.) at Port Conway, King George Co., Va., eldest son of James Madison and Eleanor Rose Conway. Madison was graduated from Princeton, 1771; studied theology, 1772; sat in the Virginia Constitutional Convention, 1776. He was a member of the Continental Congress. He was chief recorder at the Constitutional Convention in 1787, and supported ratification in the Federalist Papers, written with Alexander Hamilton and John Jay. He was elected to the House of Representatives in 1789, helped frame the Bill of Rights and fought the Alien and Sedition Acts. He became Jefferson's secretary of state, 1801.

Elected president in 1808, Madison was a "strict constructionist," opposed to the free interpretation of the Constitution by the Federalists. He was reelected in 1812 by the votes of the agrarian South and recently admitted western states. Caught between British and French maritime restrictions, the U.S. drifted into war, declared June 18, 1812. The war ended in a stalemate. He retired in 1817 to his estate at Montpelier. There he edited his famous papers on the Constitutional Convention. He became rector of the Univ. of Virginia, 1826. He died June 28, 1836.

James Monroe (1817-1825)

James Monroe, 5th president, Democrat Republican, was born Apr. 28, 1758, in Westmoreland Co., Va., the son of Spence Monroe and Eliza Jones, who were of Scottish and Welsh descent, respectively. He attended the College of William and Mary, fought in the 3d Virginia Regiment at White Plains, Brandywine, Monmouth, and was wounded at Trenton. He studied law with Thomas Jefferson, 1780, was a member of the Virginia House of Delegates and of Congress, 1783-86. He opposed ratification of the Constitution because it lacked a bill of rights; was U.S. senator, 1790; minister to France, 1794-96; governor of Virginia, 1799-1802, and 1811. Jefferson sent him to France as minister, 1803. He helped Robert Livingston negotiate the Louisiana Purchase, 1803. He ran against Madison for president in 1808. He was elected to the Virginia Assembly, 1810-1811; was secretary of state under Madison, 1811-1817.

In 1816 Monroe was elected president; in 1820 reelected with all but one electoral college vote. Monroe's administration became the "Era of Good Feeling." He obtained Florida from Spain; settled boundaries with Canada, and eliminated border forts. He supported the anti-slavery position that led to the Missouri Compromise. His most significant contribution was the "Monroe Doctrine," which became a cornerstone of U.S. foreign policy. Monroe retired to Oak Hill, Va. Financial problems forced him to sell his property. He moved to New York City to live with a daughter. He died there July 4, 1831.

John Quincy Adams (1825-1829)

John Quincy Adams, 6th president, independent Federalist, was born July 11, 1767, at Braintree (Quincy), Mass., the son of John and Abigail Adams. His father was the 2d president. He was educated in Paris, Leyden, and Harvard, graduating in 1787. He served as American minister in various European capitals, and helped draft the War of 1812 peace treaty. He was U.S. Senator, 1803-08. President Monroe made him secretary of state, 1817, and he negotiated the cession of the Floridas from Spain, supported exclusion of slavery in the Missouri Compromise, and helped formulate the Monroe Doctrine. In 1824 he was elected president by the House after he failed to win an electoral college majority. His expansion of executive powers was strongly opposed and he was beaten in 1828 by Jackson. In 1831 he entered Congress and served 17 years with distinction. He opposed slavery, the annexation of Texas, and the Mexican War. He helped establish the Smithsonian Institution. He had a stroke in the House and died in the Speaker's Room, Feb. 23, 1848.

Andrew Jackson (1829-1837)

Andrew Jackson, 7th president, was a Jeffersonian-Republican, later a Democrat. He was born in the Waxhaws district, New Lancaster Co., S.C., Mar. 15, 1767, the posthumous son of Andrew Jackson and Elizabeth Hutchinson, who were Irish immigrants. At 13, he joined the militia in the Revolution and was captured.

He read law in Salisbury, N.C., moved to Nashville, Tenn., speculated in land, married, and practiced law. In 1796 he helped draft the constitution of Tennessee and for a year occupied its one seat in Congress. He was in the Senate in 1797, and again in 1823. He defeated the Creek Indians at Horseshoe Bend, Ala., 1814. With 6,000 backwoods fighters he defeated Pakenham's 12,000 British troops at the Chalmette, outside New Orleans, Jan. 8, 1815. In 1818 he briefly invaded Spanish Florida to quell Seminoles and outlaws who harassed frontier settlements. In 1824 he ran for president against John Quincy Adams and had the most popular and electoral votes but not a majority; the election was decided by the House, which chose Adams. In 1828 he defeated Adams, carrying the West and South. He was a noisy debater and a duelist and introduced rotation in office called the "spoils system." Suspicious of privilege, he ruined the Bank of the United States by depositing federal funds with state banks. Though "Let the people rule" was his slogan, he at times supported strict constructionist policies against the expansionist West. He killed the congressional caucus for nominating · presidential candidates and substituted the national convention, 1832. When South Carolina refused to collect imports under his protective tariff he ordered army and naval forces to Charleston. Jackson recognized the Republic of Texas, 1836. He died at the Hermitage, June 8, 1845.

Martin Van Buren (1837-1841)

Martin Van Buren, 8th president, Democrat, was born Dec. 5, 1782, at Kinderhook, N.Y., the son of Abraham Van Buren, a Dutch farmer, and Mary Hoes. He was surrogate of Columbia County, N.Y., state senator and attorney general. He was U.S. senator 1821, reelected, 1827, elected governor of New York, 1828. He helped swing eastern support to Jackson in 1828 and was his secretary of state 1829-31. In 1832 he was elected vice president. He was a consummate politician, known as "the little magician," and influenced Jackson's policies. In 1836 he defeated William Henry Harrison for president and took office as the Panic of 1837 initiated a 5-year nationwide depression. He inaugurated the independent treasury system. His refusal to spend land revenues led to his defeat by Harrison in 1840. He lost the Democratic nomination in 1844 to Polk. In 1848 he ran for president on the Free Soil ticket and lost. He died July 24, 1862, at Kinderhook.

William Henry Harrison (1841)

William Henry Harrison, 9th president, Whig, who served only 31 days, was born in Berkeley, Charles City Co., Va., Feb. 9, 1773, the 3d son of Benjamin Harrison, signer of the Declaration of Independence. He attended Hampden Sydney College. He was secretary of the Northwest Territory, 1798; its delegate in Congress, 1799; first governor of Indiana Territory, 1800; and superintendent of Indian affairs. With 900 men he routed Tecumseh's Indians at Tippecanoe, Nov. 7, 1811. A major general, he defeated British and Indians at Battle of the Thames, Oct. 5, 1813. He served in Congress, 1816-19; Senate, 1825-28. In 1840, he was elected president with a "log cabin and hard cider" slogan. He caught pneumonia during the inauguration and died Apr. 4, 1841.

John Tyler (1841-1845)

John Tyler, 10th president, independent Whig, was born Mar. 29, 1790, in Greenway, Charles City Co., Va., son of John Tyler and Mary Armistead. His father was governor of Virginia, 1808-11. Tyler was graduated from William and Mary, 1807; member of the House of Delegates, 1811; in congress, 1816-21; in Virginia legislature, 1823-25; governor of Virginia, 1825-26; U.S. senator, 1827-36. In 1840 he was elected vice president and, on Harrison's death, succeeded him. He favored pre-emption, allowing settlers to get government land; rejected a national bank bill and thus alienated most Whig supporters; refused to honor the spoils system. He signed the resolution annexing Texas, Mar. 1, 1845. He accepted renomination, 1844, but withdrew before election. In 1861, he chaired an unsuccessful Washington conference called to avert civil war. After its failure he supported secession, sat in the provisional Confederate Congress, became a member of the Confederate House, but died in Richmond, Jan. 18, 1862, before it met.

James Knox Polk (1845-1849)

James Knox Polk, 11th president, Democrat, was born in Mecklenburg Co., N.C., Nov. 2, 1795, the son of Samuel Polk, farmer and surveyor of Scotch-Irish descent, and Jane Knox. He graduated from the Univ. of North Carolina, 1818; member of the Tennessee state legislature, 1823-25. He served in Congress 1825-39 and as speaker 1835-39. He was governor of Tennessee 1839-41, but was defeated 1841 and 1843. In 1844, when both Clay and Van Buren announced opposition to annexing Texas, the Democrats made Polk the first dark horse nominee because he demanded control of all Oregon and annexation of Texas. Polk re-established the independent treasury system originated by Van Buren. His expansionist policy was opposed by Clay, Webster, Calhoun; he sent troops under Zachary Taylor to the Mexican border and, when Mexicans attacked, declared war existed. The Mexican war ended with the annexation of California and much of the Southwest as part of America's "manifest destiny." He compromised on the Oregon boundary ("54-40 or fight!") by accepting the 49th parallel and giving Vancouver to the British. Polk died in Nashville, June 15, 1849.

Zachary Taylor (1849-1850)

Zachary Taylor, 12th president, Whig, who served only 16 months, was born Nov. 24, 1784, in Orange Co., Va., the son of Richard Taylor, later collector of the port of Louisville, Ky., and Sarah Strother. Taylor was commissioned first lieutenant, 1808; fought in the War of 1812; the Black Hawk War, 1832; and the second Seminole War, 1837. He was called Old Rough and Ready. He settled on a plantation near Baton Rouge, La. In 1845 Polk sent him with an army to the Rio Grande. When the Mexicans attacked him, Polk declared war. Taylor was successful at Palo Alto and Resaca de la Palma, 1846; occupied Monterrey. Polk made him major general but sent many of his troops to Gen. Winfield Scott. Outnumbered 4-1, he defeated Santa Anna at Buena Vista, 1847. A national hero, he received the Whig nomination in 1848, and was elected president. He resumed the spoils system and though once a slave-holder worked to have California admitted as a free state. He died in office July 9, 1850.

Millard Fillmore (1850-1853)

Millard Fillmore, 13th president, Whig, was born Jan. 7, 1800, in Cayuga Co., N.Y., the son of Nathaniel Fillmore and Phoebe Millard. He taught school and studied law; admitted to the bar, 1823. He was a member of the state assembly, 1829-32; in Congress, 1833-35 and again 1837-43. He opposed the entrance of Texas as slave territory and voted for a protective tariff. In 1844 he was defeated for governor of New York. In 1848 he was elected vice president and succeeded as president July 10, 1850, after Taylor's death. Fillmore favored the Compromise of 1850 and signed the Fugitive Slave Law. His policies pleased neither expansionists nor slave-holders and he was not renominated in 1852. In 1856 he was nominated by the American (Know-Nothing) party and accepted by the Whigs, but defeated by Buchanan. He died in Buffalo, Mar. 8, 1874.

Franklin Pierce (1853-1857)

Franklin Pierce, 14th president, Democrat, was born in Hillsboro, N. H., Nov. 23, 1804, the son of Benjamin Pierce, veteran of the Revolution and governor of New Hampshire, 1827. He graduated from Bowdoin, 1824. A lawyer, he served in the state legislature 1829-33; in Congress, supporting Jackson, 1833-37; U.S. senator, 1837-42. He enlisted in the Mexican War, became brigadier general under Gen. Winfield Scott. In 1852 Pierce was nominated on the 49th ballot over Lewis Cass, Stephen A. Douglas, and James Buchanan, and defeated Gen. Scott, Whig. Though against slavery, Pierce was influenced by pro-slavery Southerners. He ignored the Ostend Manifesto that the U.S. either buy or take Cuba. He approved the Kansas-Nebraska Act, leaving slavery to popular vote ("squatter sovereignty"), 1854. He signed a reciprocity treaty with Canada and approved the Gadsden Purchase from Mexico, 1853. Denied renomination by the Democrats, he spent most of his remaining years in Concord, N.H., where he died Oct. 8, 1869.

James Buchanan (1857-1861)

James Buchanan, 15th president, Federalist, later Democrat, was born of Scottish descent near Mercersburg, Pa., Apr. 23, 1791. He graduated from Dickinson, 1809; was a volunteer in the War of 1812; member, Pennsylvania legislature, 1814-16, Congress, 1820-31; Jackson's minister to Russia, 1831-33; U.S. senator 1834-45. As Polk's secretary of state, 1845-49, he ended the Oregon dispute with Britain, supported the Mexican War and annexation of Texas. As minister to Britain, 1853, he signed the Ostend Manifesto. Nominated by Democrats, he was elected, 1856, over John C. Fremont (Republican) and Millard Fillmore (American Know-Nothing and Whig tickets). On slavery he favored popular sovereignty and choice by state constitutions; he accepted the pro-slavery Dred Scott decision as binding. He denied the right of states to secede. A strict constructionist, he desired to keep peace and found no authority for using force. He died at Wheatland, near Lancaster, Pa., June 1, 1868.

Abraham Lincoln (1861-1865)

Abraham Lincoln, 16th president, Republican, was born Feb. 12, 1809, in a log cabin on a farm then in Hardin Co., Ky., now in Larue. He was the son of Thomas Lincoln, a carpenter, and Nancy Hanks.

The Lincolns moved to Spencer Co., Ind., near Gentryville, when Abe was 7. When his mother died his father married Mrs. Sarah Bush Johnston, 1819; she had a favorable influence on Abe. In 1830 the family moved to Macon Co., Ill. Lincoln lost election to the Illinois General Assembly, 1832, but later won 4 times, beginning in 1834. He enlisted in the militia in the Black Hawk War, 1832. In New Salem he ran a store, surveyed land, and was postmaster.

In 1837 Lincoln was admitted to the bar and became partner in a Springfield, Ill., law office. He was elected to Congress, 1847-49. He opposed the Mexican War. He supported Zachary Taylor, 1848. He opposed the Kansas-Nebraska Act and extension of slavery, 1854. He failed, in his bid for the Senate, 1855. He supported John C. Fremont, 1856.

In 1858 Lincoln had Republican support in the Illinois legislature for the Senate but was defeated by Stephen A. Douglas, Dem., who had sponsored the Kansas-Nebraska Act.

Lincoln was nominated for president by the Republican party on an anti-slavery platform, 1860. He ran against Douglas, a northern Democrat; John C. Breckinridge, southern pro-slavery Democrat; John Bell, Constitutional Union party. When he won the election, South Carolina seceded from the Union Dec. 20, 1860, followed in 1861 by 10 Southern states.

The Civil War erupted when Fort Sumter was attacked Apr. 12, 1861. On Sept. 22, 1862, 5 days after the battle of Antietam, he announced that slaves in territory then in rebellion would be free Jan. 1, 1863, date of the Emancipation Proclamation, His speeches, including his Gettysburg and Inaugural addresses, are remembered for their eloquence.

Lincoln was reelected, 1864, over Gen. George B. McClellan, Democrat. Lee surrendered Apr. 9, 1865. On Apr. 14, Lincoln was shot by actor John Wilkes Booth in Ford's Theatre, Washington. He died the next day.

Andrew Johnson (1865-1869)

Andrew Johnson, 17th president, Democrat, was born in Raleigh, N.C., Dec. 29, 1808, the son of Jacob Johnson, porter at an inn and church sexton, and Mary McDonough. He was apprenticed to a tailor but ran away and eventually settled in Greeneville, Tenn. He became an alderman, 1828; mayor, 1830; state representative and senator, 1835-43; member of Congress, 1843-53; governor of Tennessee, 1853-57; U.S. senator, 1857-62. He supported John C. Breckinridge against Lincoln in 1860. He had held slaves, but opposed secession and tried to prevent his home state, Tennessee, from seceding. In Mar. 1862, Lincoln appointed him military governor of occupied Tennessee. In 1864 he was nominated for vice president with Lincoln on the National Union ticket to win Democratic support. He succeeded Lincoln as president Apr. 15, 1865. In a controversy with Congress over the president's power over the South, he proclaimed, May 26, 1865, an amnesty to all Confederates except certain leaders if they would ratify the 13th Amendment abolishing slavery. States doing so added anti-Negro provisions that enraged Congress, which restored military control over the South. When Johnson removed Edwin M. Stanton, secretary of war, without notifying the Senate, thus repudiating the Tenure of Office Act, the House impeached him for this and other reasons. He was tried by the Senate, and acquitted by only one vote, May 26, 1868. He returned to the Senate in 1875. Johnson died July 31, 1875.

Ulysses Simpson Grant (1869-1877)

Ulysses S. Grant, 18th president, Republican, was born at Point Pleasant, Oh., Apr. 27, 1822, son of Jesse R. Grant, a tanner, and Hannah Simpson. The next year the family moved to Georgetown, Oh. Grant was named Hiram Ulysses, but on entering West Point, 1839, his name was entered as Ulysses Simpson and he adopted it. He was graduated in 1843; served under Gens. Taylor and Scott in the Mexican War; resigned, 1854; worked in St. Louis until 1860, then went to Galena, Ill. With the start of the Civil War, he was named colonel of the 21st Illinois Vols., 1861, then brigadier general; took Forts Henry and Donelson; fought at Shiloh, took Vicksburg. After his victory at Chattanooga, Lincoln placed him in command of the Union Armies. He accepted Lee's surrender at Appomattox, Apr., 1865. President Johnson appointed Grant secretary of war when he suspended Stanton, but Grant was not confirmed. He was nominated for president by the Republicans in 1868 and elected over Horatio Seymour, Democrat. The 15th Amendment, amnesty bill, and civil service reform were events of his administration. The Liberal Republicans and Democrats opposed him with Horace Greeley, 1872, but he

was reelected. An attempt by the Stalwarts (Old Guard) to nominate him in 1880 failed. In 1884 the collapse of Grant & Ward, investment house, left him penniless. He wrote his personal memoirs while ill with cancer and completed them 4 days before his death at Mt. McGregor, N.Y., July 23, 1885. The book realized over $450,000.

Rutherford Birchard Hayes (1877-1881)

Rutherford B. Hayes, 19th president, Republican, was born in Delaware, Oh., Oct. 4, 1822, the posthumous son of Rutherford Hayes, a farmer, and Sophia Birchard. He was raised by his uncle Sardis Birchard. He graduated from Kenyon College, 1842, and Harvard Law School, 1845. He practiced law in Lower Sandusky, Oh., now Fremont; was city solicitor of Cincinnati, 1858-61. In the Civil War, he was major of the 23d Ohio Vols., was wounded several times, and rose to the rank of brevet major general, 1864. He served in Congress 1864-67, supporting Reconstruction and Johnson's impeachment. He was elected governor of Ohio, 1867 and 1869; beaten in the race for Congress, 1872; reelected governor, 1875. In 1876 he was nominated for president and believed he had lost the election to Samuel J. Tilden, Democrat. But a few Southern states submitted 2 different sets of electoral votes and the result was in dispute. An electoral commission, appointed by Congress, 8 Republicans and 7 Democrats, awarded all disputed votes to Hayes allowing him to become president by one electoral vote. Hayes, keeping a promise to southerners, withdrew troops from areas still occupied in the South, ending the era of Reconstruction. He proceeded to reform the civil service, alienating political spoilsmen. He advocated repeal of the Tenure of Office Act. He supported sound money and specie payments. Hayes died in Fremont, Oh., Jan. 17, 1893.

James Abram Garfield (1881-1881)

James A. Garfield, 20th president, Republican, was born Nov. 19, 1831, in Orange, Cuyahoga Co., Oh., the son of Abram Garfield and Eliza Ballou. His father died in 1833. He worked as a canal bargeman, farmer, and carpenter; attended Western Reserve Eclectic, later Hiram College, and was graduated from Williams in 1856. He taught at Hiram, and later became principal. He was in the Ohio senate in 1859. Anti-slavery and anti-secession, he volunteered for the war, became colonel of the 42d Ohio Infantry and brigadier in 1862. He fought at Shiloh, was chief of staff for Rosecrans and was made major general for gallantry at Chickamauga. He entered Congress as a radical Republican in 1863; supported specie payment as against paper money (greenbacks). On the electoral commission in 1877 he voted for Hayes against Tilden on strict party lines. He was senator-elect in 1880 when he became the Republican nominee for president. He was chosen as a compromise over Gen. Grant, James G. Blaine, and John Sherman. This alienated the Grant following but Garfield was elected. On July 2, 1881, Garfield was shot by mentally disturbed office-seeker, Charles J. Guiteau, while entering a railroad station in Washington. He died Sept. 19, 1881, at Elberon, N.J.

Chester Alan Arthur (1881-1885)

Chester A. Arthur, 21st president, Republican, was born at Fairfield, Vt., Oct. 5, 1829, the son of the Rev. William Arthur, from County Antrim, Ireland, and Malvina Stone. He graduated from Union College, 1848, taught school at Pownall, Vt., studied law in New York. In 1853 he argued in a fugitive slave case that slaves transported through N.Y. State were thereby freed. He was made collector of the Port of New York, 1871. President Hayes, reforming the civil service, forced Arthur to resign, 1879. This made the New York machine stalwarts enemies of Hayes. Arthur and the stalwarts tried to nominate Grant for a 3d term in 1880. When Garfield was nominated, Arthur received 2d place in the interests of harmony. When Garfield died, Arthur became president. He supported civil service reform and the tariff of 1883. He was defeated for renomination by James G. Blaine. He died in New York City Nov. 18, 1886.

Grover Cleveland (1885-1889) (1893-1897)

(According to a ruling of the State Dept., Grover Cleveland is both the 22d and the 24th president, because his 2 terms were not consecutive. By individuals, he is only the 22d.)

Grover Cleveland, 22d and 24th president, Democrat, was born in Caldwell, N.J. Mar. 18, 1837, the son of Richard F. Cleveland, a Presbyterian minister, and Ann Neale. He was named Stephen Grover, but dropped the Stephen. He clerked in Clinton and Buffalo, N.Y., taught at the N.Y. City Institution for the Blind; was admitted to the bar in Buffalo, 1859; became assistant district attorney, 1863; sheriff, 1871; mayor, 1881; governor of New York, 1882. He was an independent, honest administrator who hated corruption. He was nominated for president over Tammany Hall opposition, 1884, and defeated Republican James G. Blaine. He enlarged the civil service, vetoed many pension raids on the Treasury. In 1888 he was defeated by Benjamin Harrison, although his popular vote was larger. Reelected over Harrison in 1892, he faced a money crisis brought about by lowering of the gold reserve, circulation of paper and exorbitant silver purchases under the Sherman Act; obtained a repeal of the latter and a reduced tariff. A severe depression and labor troubles racked his administration but he refused to interfere in business matters and rejected Jacob Coxey's demand for unemployment relief. He broke the Pullman strike, 1894. In 1896, the Democrats repudiated his administration and chose silverite William Jennings Bryan as their candidate. Cleveland died in Princeton, N.J., June 24, 1908.

Benjamin Harrison (1889-1893)

Benjamin Harrison, 23d president, Republican, was born at North Bend, Oh., Aug. 20, 1833. His great-grandfather, Benjamin Harrison, was a signer of the Declaration of Independence; his grandfather, William Henry Harrison, was 9th President; his father, John Scott Harrison, was a member of Congress. His mother was Elizabeth F. Irwin. He attended school on his father's farm; graduated from Miami Univ. at Oxford, Oh., 1852; admitted to the bar, 1853, and practiced in Indianapolis. In the Civil War, he rose to the rank of brevet brigadier general, fought at Kennesaw Mountain, Peachtree Creek, Nashville, and in the Atlanta campaign. He failed to be elected governor of Indiana, 1876; but became senator, 1881. In 1888 he defeated Cleveland for president despite having fewer popular votes. He expanded the pension list, signed the McKinley high tariff bill, the Sherman Antitrust Act, and the Sherman Silver Purchase Act. During his administration, 6 states were admitted to the union. He was defeated for reelection, 1892. He represented Venezuela in a boundary arbitration with Great Britain in Paris, 1899. He died in Indianapolis, Mar. 13, 1901.

William McKinley (1897-1901)

William McKinley, 25th president, Republican, was born in Niles, Oh., Jan. 29, 1843, the son of William McKinley, an ironmaker, and Nancy Allison. McKinley attended school in Poland, Oh., and Allegheny College, Meadville, Pa., and enlisted for the Civil War at 18 in the 23d Ohio, in which Rutherford B. Hayes was a major. He rose to captain and in 1865 was made brevet major. He studied law in the Albany, N.Y., law school; opened an office in Canton, Oh., in 1867, and campaigned for Grant and Hayes. He served in the House of Representatives, 1877-83, 1885-91, and led the fight for passage of the McKinley Tarrif, 1890. Defeated for reelection on the issue in 1890, he was governor of Ohio, 1892-96. He had support for president in the convention that nominated Benjamin Harrison in 1892. In 1896 he was elected president on a protective tariff, sound money (gold standard) platform over William Jennings Bryan, Democratic proponent of free silver. McKinley was reluctant to intervene in Cuba but the loss of the battleship Maine at Havana crystallized opinion. He demanded Spain's withdrawal from Cuba; Spain made some concessions but Congress announced state of war as of Apr. 21. He was reelected in the 1900 campaign, defeating Bryan's anti-imperialist arguments with the promise of a "full dinner pail." McKinley was respected for his conciliatory nature, but conservative on business issues. On Sept. 6, 1901, while welcoming citizens at the Pan-American Exposition, Buffalo, N.Y., he was shot by Leon Czolgosz, an anarchist. He died Sept. 14.

Theodore Roosevelt (1901-1909)

Theodore Roosevelt, 26th president, Republican, was born in N.Y. City, Oct. 27, 1858, the son of Theodore Roosevelt, a glass importer, and Martha Bulloch. He was a 5th cousin of Franklin D. Roosevelt and an uncle of Eleanor Roosevelt. Roosevelt graduated from Harvard, 1880; attended Columbia Law School briefly; sat in the N.Y. State Assembly, 1882-84; ranched in North Dakota, 1884-86; failed election as mayor of N.Y. City, 1886; member of U.S. Civil Service Commission, 1889; president, N.Y. Police Board, 1895, supporting the merit system; assistant secretary of the Navy under McKinley, 1897-98. In the war with Spain, he organized the 1st U.S. Volunteer Cavalry (Rough Riders) as lieutenant colonel; led the charge up Kettle Hill at San Juan. Elected New York governor, 1898-1900, he fought the spoils system and achieved taxation of corporation franchises. Nominated for vice president, 1900, he became nation's youngest president when McKinley died. As president he fought corruption of politics by big business; dissolved Northern Securities Co. and others for violating, anti-trust laws; intervened in coal strike on behalf of the public, 1902; obtained Elkins Law forbidding rebates to favored corporations, 1903; Hepburn Law regulating railroad rates, 1906; Pure Food and Drugs Act, 1906, Reclamation Act and employers' liability laws. He organized conservation, mediated the peace between Japan and Russia, 1905; won the Nobel Peace Prize. He was the first to use the Hague Court of International Arbitration. By recognizing the new Republic of Panama he made Panama Canal possible. He was reelected in 1904.

In 1908 he obtained the nomination of William H. Taft, who was elected. Feeling that Taft had abandoned his policies, Roosevelt unsuccessfully sought the nomination in 1912. He bolted the party and ran on the Progressive "Bull Moose" ticket against Taft and Woodrow Wilson, splitting the Republicans and insuring Wilson's election. He was shot during the campaign but recovered. In 1916 he supported Charles E. Hughes, Republican. A strong friend of Britain, he fought American isolation in World War I. He wrote some 40 books on many topics; his *Winning of the West* is best known. He died Jan. 6, 1919, at Sagamore Hill, Oyster Bay, N.Y.

William Howard Taft (1909-1913)

William Howard Taft, 27th president, Republican, was born in Cincinnati, Oh., Sept. 15, 1857, the son of Alphonso Taft and Louisa Maria Torrey. His father was secretary of war and attorney general in Grant's cabinet; minister to Austria and Russia under Arthur. Taft was graduated from Yale, 1878; Cincinnati Law School, 1880; became law reporter for Cincinnati newspapers; was assistant prosecuting attorney, 1881-83; assistant county solicitor, 1885; judge, superior court, 1887; U.S. solicitor-general, 1890; federal circuit judge, 1892. In 1900 he became head of the U.S. Philippines Commission and was first civil governor of the Philippines, 1901-04; secretary of war, 1904; provisional governor of Cuba, 1906. He was groomed for president by Roosevelt and elected over Bryan, 1908. His administration dissolved Standard Oil and tobacco trusts; instituted Dept. of Labor; drafted direct election of senators and income tax amendments. His tariff and conservation policies angered progressives; though renominated he was opposed by Roosevelt; the result was Democrat Woodrow Wilson's election. Taft, with some reservations, supported the League of Nations. He was professor of constitutional law, Yale, 1913-21; chief justice of the U.S. Supreme Court, 1921-30; illness forced him to resign. He died in Washington, Mar. 8, 1930.

Woodrow Wilson (1913-1921)

Woodrow Wilson, 28th president, Democrat, was born at Staunton, Va., Dec. 28, 1856, as Thomas Woodrow Wilson, son of a Presbyterian minister, the Rev. Joseph Ruggles Wilson and Janet (Jessie) Woodrow. In his youth Wilson lived in Augusta, Ga., Columbia, S.C., and Wilmington, N.C. He attended Davidson College, 1873-74; was graduated from Princeton, A.B., 1879; A.M., 1882; read law at the Univ. of Virginia, 1881; practiced law, Atlanta, 1882-83; Ph.D., Johns Hopkins, 1886. He taught at Bryn Mawr, 1885-88; at Wesleyan, 1888-90; was professor of jurisprudence and political economy at Princeton, 1890-1910; president of Princeton, 1902-1910; governor of New Jersey, 1911-13. In 1912 he was nominated for president with the aid of William Jennings Bryan, who sought to block James "Champ" Clark and Tammany Hall. Wilson won the election because the Republican vote for Taft was split by the Progressives under Roosevelt.

Wilson protected American interests in revolutionary Mexico and fought for American rights on the high seas. His sharp warnings to Germany led to the resignation of his secretary of state, Bryan, a pacifist. In 1916 he was reelected by a slim margin with the slogan, "He kept us out of war." Wilson's attempts to mediate in the war failed. After 4 American ships had been sunk by the Germans, he secured a declaration of war against Germany on Apr. 6, 1917.

Wilson proposed peace Jan. 8, 1918, on the basis of his "Fourteen Points," a state paper with worldwide influence. His doctrine of self-determination continues to play a major role in territorial disputes. The Germans accepted his terms and an armistice, Nov. 11.

Wilson went to Paris to help negotiate the peace treaty, the crux of which he considered the League of Nations. The Senate demanded reservations that would not make the U.S. subordinate to the votes of other nations in case of war. Wilson refused to consider any reservations and toured the country to get support. He suffered a stroke, Oct., 1919. An invalid for months, he clung to his executive powers while his wife and doctor sought to shield him from affairs which would tire him.

He was awarded the 1919 Nobel Peace Prize, but the treaty embodying the League of Nations was rejected by the Senate, 1920. He died in Washington, Feb. 3, 1924.

Warren Gamaliel Harding (1921-1923)

Warren Gamaliel Harding, 29th president, Republican, was born near Corsica, now Blooming Grove, Oh., Nov. 2, 1865, the son of Dr. George Tyron Harding, a physician, and Phoebe Elizabeth Dickerson. He attended Ohio Central College. He was state senator, 1900-04; lieutenant governor, 1904-06; defeated for governor, 1910; chosen U.S. senator, 1915. He supported Taft, opposed federal control of food and fuel; voted for anti-strike legislation, woman's suffrage, and the Volstead prohibition enforcement act over President Wilson's veto; and opposed the League of Nations. In 1920 he was nominated for president and defeated James M. Cox in the election. The Republicans capitalized on war weariness and fear that Wilson's League of Nations would curtail U.S. sovereignty. Harding stressed a return to "normalcy"; worked for tariff revision and repeal of excess profits law and high income taxes. Two Harding appointees, Albert B. Fall (interior) and Harry Daugherty (attorney general), became involved in the Teapot Dome scandal that embittered Harding's last days. He called the International Conference on Limitation of Armaments, 1921-22. Returning from a trip to Alaska he became ill and died in San Francisco, Aug. 2, 1923.

Calvin Coolidge (1923-1929)

Calvin Coolidge, 30th president, Republican, was born in Plymouth, Vt., July 4, 1872, the son of John Calvin Coolidge, a storekeeper, and Victoria J. Moor, and named John Calvin Coolidge. Coolidge graduated from Amherst in 1895. He entered Republican state politics and served as mayor of Northampton, Mass., state senator, lieutenant governor, and, in 1919, governor. In Sept., 1919, Coolidge attained national prominence by calling out the state guard in the Boston police strike. He declared: "There is no right to strike against the public safety by anybody, anywhere, anytime." This brought his name before the Republican convention of 1920, where he was nominated for vice president. He succeeded to the presidency on Harding's death. He opposed the League of Nations; approved the World Court; vetoed the soldiers' bonus bill, which was passed over his veto. In 1924 he was elected by a huge majority. He reduced the national debt by $2 billion in 3 years. He twice vetoed the McNary-Haugen farm bill, which would have provided relief to financially hard-pressed farmers. With Republicans eager to renominate him he announced, Aug. 2, 1927: "I do not choose to run for president in 1928." He died in Northampton, Jan. 5, 1933.

Herbert Clark Hoover (1929-1933)

Herbert C. Hoover, 31st president, Republican, was born at West Branch, Ia., Aug. 10, 1874, son of Jesse Clark Hoover, a blacksmith, and Hulda Randall Minthorn. Hoover grew up in Indian Territory (now Oklahoma) and Oregon; won his A.B. in engineering at Stanford, 1891. He worked briefly with U.S. Geological Survey and western mines; then was a mining engineer in Australia, Asia, Europe, Africa, U.S. While chief engineer, imperial mines, China, he directed food relief for victims of Boxer Rebellion, 1900. He directed

American Relief Committee, London, 1914-15; U.S. Comm. for Relief in Belgium, 1915-1919; was U.S. Food Administrator, 1917-1919; American Relief Administrator, 1918-1923, feeding children in defeated nations; Russian Relief, 1918-1923. He was secy. of commerce, 1921-28. He was elected president over Alfred E. Smith, 1928. In 1929 the stock market crashed and the economy collapsed. During the depression, Hoover opposed federal aid to the unemployed. He was defeated in the 1932 election by Franklin D. Roosevelt. President Truman made him coordinator of European Food Program, 1947, chairman of the Commission for Reorganization of the Executive Branch, 1947-49. He founded the Hoover Institution on War, Revolution, and Peace at Stanford Univ. He died in N.Y. City, Oct. 20, 1964.

Franklin Delano Roosevelt (1933-1945)

Franklin D. Roosevelt, 32d president, Democrat, was born near Hyde Park, N.Y., Jan. 30, 1882, the son of James Roosevelt and Sara Delano. He graduated from Harvard, 1904; attended Columbia Law School; was admitted to the bar. He went to the N.Y. Senate, 1910 and 1913. In 1913 President Wilson made him assistant secretary of the navy.

Roosevelt ran for vice president, 1920, with James Cox and was defeated. From 1920 to 1928 he was a N.Y. lawyer and vice president of Fidelity & Deposit Co. In Aug., 1921, polio paralyzed his legs. He learned to walk with leg braces and a cane.

Roosevelt was elected governor of New York, 1928 and 1930. In 1932, W. G. McAdoo, pledged to John N. Garner, threw his votes to Roosevelt, who was nominated. The depression and the promise to repeal prohibition insured his election. He asked emergency powers, proclaimed the New Deal, and put into effect a vast number of administrative changes. Foremost was the use of public funds for relief and public works, resulting in deficit financing. He greatly expanded the controls of the central government over business, and by an excess profits tax and progressive income taxes produced a redistribution of earnings on an unprecedented scale. The Wagner Act gave labor many advantages in organizing and collective bargaining. He was the last president inaugurated on Mar. 4 (1933) and the first inaugurated on Jan. 20 (1937).

Roosevelt was the first president to use radio for "fireside chats." When the Supreme Court nullified some New Deal laws, he sought power to "pack" the court with additional justices, but Congress refused to give him the authority. He was the first president to break the "no 3d term" tradition (1940) and was elected to a 4th term, 1944, despite failing health. He was openly hostile to fascist governments before World War II and launched a lend-lease program on behalf of the Allies. He wrote the principles of fair dealing into the Atlantic Charter, Aug. 14, 1941 (with Winston Churchill), and urged the Four Freedoms (freedom of speech, of worship, from want, from fear) Jan. 6, 1941. When Japan attacked Pearl Harbor, Dec. 7, 1941, the U.S. entered the war. He conferred with allied heads of state at Casablanca, Jan., 1943; Quebec, Aug., 1943; Teheran, Nov.-Dec., 1943; Cairo, Dec., 1943; Yalta, Feb., 1945. He died at Warm Springs, Ga., Apr. 12, 1945.

Harry S. Truman (1945-1953)

Harry S. Truman, 33d president, Democrat, was born at Lamar, Mo., May 8, 1884, the son of John Anderson Truman and Martha Ellen Young. A family disagreement on whether his middle name was Shippe or Solomon, after names of 2 grandfathers, resulted in his using only the middle initial S. He attended public schools in Independence, Mo., worked for the Kansas City Star, 1901, and as railroad timekeeper, and helper in Kansas City banks up to 1905. He ran his family's farm, 1906-17. He was commissioned a first lieutenant and took part in the Vosges, Meuse-Argonne, and St. Mihiel actions in World War I. After the war he ran a haberdashery, became judge of Jackson Co. Court, 1922-24; attended Kansas City School of Law, 1923-25.

Truman was elected U.S. senator in 1934; reelected 1940. In 1944 with Roosevelt's backing he was nominated for vice president and elected. On Roosevelt's death Truman became president. In 1948 he was elected president.

Truman authorized the first uses of the atomic bomb (Hiroshima and Nagasaki, Aug. 6 and 9, 1945), bringing World War II to a rapid end. He was responsible for creating NATO, the Marshall Plan, and what came to be called the Truman Doctrine (to aid nations such as Greece and Turkey, threatened by Russian or other communist takeover). He broke a Russian blockade of West Berlin with a massive airlift, 1948-49. When communist North Korea invaded South Korea, June, 1950, he won UN approval for a "police action" and sent in forces under Gen. Douglas MacArthur. When MacArthur opposed his policy of limited objectives, Truman removed him from command.

Truman was responsible for higher minimum-wage, increased social-security, and aid-for-housing laws. Truman died Dec. 26, 1972, in Kansas City, Mo.

Dwight David Eisenhower (1953-1961)

Dwight D. Eisenhower, 34th president, Republican, was born Oct. 14, 1890, at Denison, Tex., the son of David Jacob Eisenhower and Ida Elizabeth Stover. The next year, the family moved to Abilene, Kan. He graduated from West Point, 1915. He was on the American military mission to the Philippines, 1935-39 and during 4 of those years on the staff of Gen. Douglas MacArthur. He was made commander of Allied forces landing in North Africa, 1942, full general, 1943. He became supreme Allied commander in Europe, 1943, and as such led the Normandy invasion June 6, 1944. He was given the rank of general of the army Dec. 20, 1944, made permanent in 1946. On May 7, 1945, he received the surrender of the Germans at Rheims. He returned to the U.S. to serve as chief of staff, 1945-1948. In 1948, Eisenhower published *Crusade in Europe*, his war memoirs, which quickly became a best seller. From 1948 to 1953, he was president of Columbia Univ., but took leave of absence in 1950, to command NATO forces.

Eisenhower resigned from the army and was nominated for president by the Republicans, 1952. He defeated Adlai E. Stevenson in the election. He again defeated Stevenson, 1956. He called himself a moderate, favored "free market system" vs. government price and wage controls; kept goverment out of labor disputes; reorganized defense establishment; promoted missile programs. He continued foreign aid; sped end of Korean fighting; endorsed Taiwan and SE Asia defense treaties; backed UN in condemning Anglo-French raid on Egypt; advocated "open skies" policy of mutual inspection to USSR. He sent U.S. troops into Little Rock, Ark., Sept., 1957, during the segregation crisis and ordered Marines into Lebanon July-Aug., 1958.

During his retirement at his farm near Gettysburg, Pa., Eisenhower took up the role of elder statesman, counseling his 3 successors in the White House. He died Mar. 28, 1969, in Washington.

John Fitzgerald Kennedy (1961-1963)

John F. Kennedy, 35th president, Democrat, was born May 29, 1917, in Brookline, Mass., the son of Joseph P. Kennedy, financier, who later became ambassador to Great Britain, and Rose Fitzgerald. He entered Harvard, attended the London School of Economics briefly in 1935, received a B.S., from Harvard, 1940. He served in the Navy, 1941-1945, commanded a PT boat in the Solomons and won the Navy and Marine Corps Medal. He wrote *Profiles in Courage*, which won a Pulitzer prize. He served as representative in Congress, 1947-1953; was elected to the Senate in 1952, reelected 1958. He nearly won the vice presidential nomination in 1956.

In 1960, Kennedy won the Democratic nomination for president and defeated Richard M. Nixon, Republican. He was the first Roman Catholic president.

In Apr. 1961, Kennedy's new administration suffered a severe setback when an invasion force of anti-Castro Cubans, trained and directed by the U.S. Central Intelligence Agency, failed to establish a beachhead at the Bay of Pigs in Cuba.

Kennedy's most important act was his successful demand Oct. 22, 1962, that the Soviet Union dismantle its missile bases in Cuba. He established a quarantine of arms shipments to Cuba and continued surveillance by air. He defied Soviet attempts to force the Allies out of Berlin. He made the steel industry rescind a price rise. He backed civil rights, a mental health program, arbitration of railroad disputes, and expanded medical care for the aged. Astronaut flights and satellite orbiting were greatly developed during his administration.

On Nov. 22, 1963, Kennedy was assassinated in Dallas, Tex.

Lyndon Baines Johnson (1963-1969)

Lyndon B. Johnson, 36th president, Democrat, was born near Stonewall, Tex., Aug. 27, 1908, son of Sam Ealy Johnson and Rebekah Baines. He received a B.S. degree at Southwest Texas State Teachers College, 1930, attended Georgetown Univ. Law School, Washington, 1935. He taught public speaking in Houston, 1930-32; served as secretary to Rep. R. M. Kleberg, 1932-35. In 1937 Johnson won a contest to fill the vacancy caused by the death of a representative and in 1938 was elected to the full term, after which he returned for 4 terms. He was elected U.S. senator in 1948 and reelected in 1954. He became Democratic leader, 1953. Johnson was Texas' favorite son for the Democratic presidential nomination in 1956 and had strong support in the 1960 convention, where the nominee, John F. Kennedy, asked him to run for vice president. His campaigning helped overcome religious bias against Kennedy in the South.

Johnson became president on the death of Kennedy. Johnson worked hard for welfare legislation, signed civil rights, anti-proverty, and tax reduction laws, and averted strikes on railroads. He was elected to a full term, 1964. The war in Vietnam overshadowed other developments during his administration.

In face of increasing division in the nation and his own party over his handling of the war, Johnson announced that he would not seek another term, Mar. 31, 1968.

Retiring to his ranch near Johnson City, Tex., Johnson wrote his memoirs and oversaw the construction of the Lyndon Baines Johnson Library. He died Jan. 22, 1973.

Richard Milhous Nixon (1969-1974)

Richard M. Nixon, 37th president, Republican, was the only president to resign without completing an elected term. He was born in Yorba Linda, Cal., Jan. 9, 1913, the son of Francis Anthony Nixon and Hannah Milhous. Nixon graduated from Whittier College, 1934; Duke Univ. Law School, 1937. After practicing law in Whittier and serving briefly in the Office of Price Administration in 1942, he entered the navy, and served in the South Pacific.

Nixon was elected to the House of Representatives in 1946 and 1948. He achieved prominence as the House Un-American Activities Committee member who forced the showdown that resulted in the Alger Hiss perjury conviction. In 1950 Nixon was elected to the Senate.

He was elected vice president in the Eisenhower landslides of 1952 and 1956. With Eisenhower's endorsement, Nixon won the Republican nomination in 1960. He was defeated by Democrat John F. Kennedy, returned to Cal. and was defeated in his race for governor, 1962.

In 1968, he won the presidential nomination and went on to defeat Democrat Hubert H. Humphrey.

Nixon was the first U.S. president to visit China and Russia (1972). He and his foreign affairs advisor, Henry A. Kissinger, achieved a detente with China. Nixon appointed 4 Supreme Court justices, including the chief justice, thus altering the court's balance in favor of a more conservative view.

Reelected 1972, Nixon secured a cease-fire agreement in Vietnam and completed the withdrawal of U.S. troops.

Nixon's 2d term was cut short by a series of scandals beginning with the burglary of Democratic party national headquarters at the Watergate office complex on June 17, 1972. Nixon denied any White House involvement in the Watergate break-in. On July 16, 1973, a White House aide, under questioning by a Senate committee, revealed that most of Nixon's office conversations and phone calls had been recorded. Nixon claimed executive privilege to keep the tapes secret and the courts and Congress sought the tapes for criminal proceedings against former White House aides and for a House inquiry into possible impeachment.

On Oct. 20, 1973, Nixon fired the Watergate special prosecutor and the attorney general resigned in protest. The public outcry which followed caused Nixon to appoint a new special prosecutor and to turn over to the courts a number of subpoenaed tape recordings. Public reaction also brought the initiation of a formal inquiry into impeachment.

On July 24, 1974, the Supreme Court ruled that Nixon's claim of executive privilege must fall before the special prosecutor's subpoenas of tapes relevant to criminal trial proceedings. That same day, the House Judiciary Committee opened debate on impeachment. On July 30, the committee recommended House adoption of 3 articles of impeachment charging Nixon with obstruction of justice, abuse of power, and contempt of Congress.

On Aug. 5, Nixon released transcripts of conversations held 6 days after the Watergate break-in showing that Nixon had known of, approved, and directed Watergate cover-up activities. Nixon resigned from office Aug. 9.

Gerald Rudolph Ford (1974-1977)

Gerald R. Ford, 38th president, Republican, was born July 14, 1913, in Omaha, Neb., son of Leslie King and Dorothy Gardner, and was named Leslie Jr. When he was 2, his parents were divorced and his mother moved with the boy to Grand Rapids, Mich. There she met and married Gerald R. Ford, who formally adopted the boy and gave him his own name.

He graduated from the Univ. of Michigan, 1935 and Yale Law School, 1941.

He began practicing law in Grand Rapids, but in 1942 joined the navy and served in the Pacific, leaving the service in 1946 as a lieutenant commander.

He entered congress in 1949 and spent 25 years in the House, 8 of them as Republican leader.

On Oct. 12, 1973, after Vice President Spiro T. Agnew resigned, Ford was nominated by President Nixon to replace him. It was the first use of the procedures set out in the 25th Amendment.

When Nixon resigned Aug. 9, 1974, Ford became president, the first to serve without being chosen in a national election. On Sept. 8 he pardoned Nixon for any federal crimes he might have committed as president. Ford veoted 48 bills in his first 21 months in office, saying most would prove too costly. He visited China. In 1976, he was defeated in the election by Democrat Jimmy Carter.

Jimmy (James Earl) Carter (1977-1981)

Jimmy (James Earl) Carter, 39th president, Democrat, was the first president from the Deep South since before the Civil War. He was born Oct. 1, 1924, at Plains, Ga., where his parents, James and Lillian Gordy Carter, had a farm and several businesses.

He attended Georgia Tech, and graduated from the U.S. Naval Academy. He entered the Navy's nuclear submarine program as an aide to Adm. Hyman Rickover, and studied nuclear physics at Union College.

His father died in 1953 and Carter left the Navy to take over the family businesses — peanut-raising, warehousing, and cotton-ginning. He was elected to the Georgia state senate, was defeated for governor, 1966, but elected in 1970.

Carter won the Democratic nomination and defeated President Gerald R. Ford in the election of 1976. He played a major role in the peace negotiations between Israel and Egypt. In Nov. 1979, Iranian student militants attacked the U.S. embassy in Teheran and held members of the embassy staff hostage.

Carter was widely criticized for the poor state of the economy and high inflation. He was also viewed as weak in his handling of foreign policy. He reacted to the Soviet invasion of Afghanistan by imposing a grain embargo and boycotting the Moscow Olympic games. His failure to obtain the release of the remaining 52 hostages held in Iran plagued Carter to the end of his term. He was defeated by Ronald Reagan in the 1980 election. Carter finally succeeded in obtaining the release of the hostages on Inauguration Day, as the new president was taking the oath of office.

Ronald Wilson Reagan (1981-1989)

Ronald Wilson Reagan, 40th president, Republican, was born Feb. 6, 1911, in Tampico, Ill., the son of John Edward Reagan and Nellie Wilson. Reagan graduated from Eureka (Ill.) College in 1932. Following his graduation, he worked as a sports announcer in Des Moines, Ia.

Reagan began a successful career as a film actor in 1937, and starred in numerous movies, and later television, until the 1960s. He was a captain in the Army Air Force during World War II.

He served as president of the Screen Actors Guild from 1947 to 1952, and in 1959.

Once a liberal Democrat, Reagan became active in Republican politics during the 1964 presidential campaign of Barry Goldwater. He was elected governor of California in 1966, and reelected in 1970.

In 1980, he gained the Republican nomination and won a landslide victory over Jimmy Carter. He was easily reelected in 1984. Reagan, at 73, was the oldest man ever elected president.

Reagan successfully forged a bipartisan coalition in Congress which led to enactment of an economic program which included the largest budget and tax cuts in U.S. history, and a Social Security reform bill designed to insure the long-term solvency of the system. In 1986, he signed into law a revolutionary tax-reform bill. He was shot in an assassination attempt in 1981, and had major surgery in 1985 and 1987.

In 1983, Reagan sent a task force to lead the invasion of Grenada, and joined 3 European nations in maintaining a peacekeeping force in Beirut, Lebanon. His opposition to international terrorism led to the U.S. bombing of Lybyan military installations in 1986. He strongly supported El Salvador, the Nicaraguan contras, and other anti-communist governments and forces throughout the world. Aid was sent to the rebels fighting Soviet troops in Afghanistan. When the Iran/Iraq war threatened freedom of the seas, U.S. Navy ships were sent to the Persian Gulf.

Reagan held summit meetings with Soviet leader Gorbachev in 1985 in Geneva, 1986 in Iceland, 1987 in Washington, D.C. where an historic treaty eliminating short and medium-range missiles from Europe was signed, and 1988 in Moscow where Reagan criticized the Soviet record on human rights, and met with Soviet dissidents.

Reagan faced a major crisis in 1986-1987, when it was revealed that the U.S. had sold weapons to Iran in exchange for the release of U.S. hostages being held in Lebanon; and that subsequently some of the money was diverted to the Nicaraguan contras. The scandal led to the resignation of leading White House aides; some were indicted and convicted of criminal charges.

As Reagan left office, the nation was experiencing its 6th consecutive year of economic prosperity. Along with the strong economy, the nation enjoyed low unemployment, energy costs, and inflation. Reagan, however, was unable to control the high budget deficits which plagued him throughout his administration.

George Herbert Walker Bush (1989-   )

George Herbert Walker Bush, 41st president, Republican, was born June 12, 1924, in Milton, Mass., the son of Prescott Bush, U.S. senator from Connecticut, and Dorothy Walker. He served as a U.S. Navy pilot in World War II, earning the Distinguished Flying Cross and three Air Medals for service in the Pacific. After graduating from Yale Univ. (1948), he settled in Texas where, in 1953, he helped found an oil company.

After losing a bid for a U.S. Senate seat in Texas, 1964, he was elected to the House of Representatives in 1966 and 1968. He lost a 2d U.S. Senate race in 1970. He served as U.S. ambassador to the United Nations, 1971-73, headed the U.S. Liaison Office in Beijing, 1974-75, and was director of the Central Intelligence Agency, 1976-77.

Following an unsuccessful bid for the 1980 Republican presidential nomination, Bush was chosen by Ronald Reagan as his vice presidential running mate. He served as U.S. vice president, 1981-89.

In 1988, he gained the Republican presidential nomination and defeated Democrat Michael Dukakis in the election. Calling on Americans "to make kinder the face of the nation and gentler the face of the world," Bush took office faced with the ongoing U.S. budget and trade deficits as well as the rescue of insolvent U.S. savings and loan institutions.

Bush has made no major changes from Reagan's policies in his first 2 years in office. He continued to face a severe budget deficit, struggled with military cutbacks in light of reduced "cold war" tensions, and vetoed congressional actions favorable to abortion and a minimum-wage law that didn't reflect his own views.

Bush has supported Soviet reforms and eastern Europe democratization. He was criticized for his failure to support strongly enough the independence efforts of the Baltic republics and for his soft reaction to the quelling of the China democratic movement. He held summit meetings with Soviet leader Gorbachev in 1989 and 1990.

In Dec. 1989, Bush sent military forces to Panama which overthrew the government and captured military strongman Gen. Manuel Noriega.

Wives and Children of the Presidents

Listed in order of presidential administrations.

Name (Born–died, married)	State	Sons/ daughters
Martha Dandridge Custis Washington (1732-1802, 1759)	Va.	None
Abigail Smith Adams (1744-1818, 1764).	Mass.	3/2
Martha Wayles Skelton Jefferson (1748-1782, 1772)	Va.	1/5
Dorothea "Dolley" Payne Todd Madison (1768-1849, 1794)	N.C.	None
Elizabeth Kortright Monroe (1768-1830, 1786)	N.Y.	../2 (A)
Louisa Catherine Johnson Adams (1775-1852, 1797)	Md.(B)	3/1
Rachel Donelson Robards Jackson (1767-1828, 1791)	Va.	None
Hannah Hoes Van Buren (1783-1819, 1807)	N.Y.	4/...
Anna Symmes Harrison (1775-1864, 1795)	N.J.	6/4
Letitia Christian Tyler (1790-1842, 1813)	Va.	3/5
Julia Gardiner Tyler (1820-1889, 1844) .	N.Y.	5/2
Sarah Childress Polk (1803-1891, 1824)	Tenn.	None
Margaret Smith Taylor (1788-1852, 1810)	Md.	1/5
Abigail Powers Fillmore (1798-1853, 1826)	N.Y.	1/1
Caroline Carmichael McIntosh Fillmore (1813-1881, 1858)	N.J.	None
Jane Means Appleton Pierce (1806-1863, 1834)	N.H.	3/...
Mary Todd Lincoln (1818-1882, 1842) . .	Ky.	4/...
Eliza McCardle Johnson (1810-1876, 1827)	Tenn.	3/2
Julia Dent Grant (1826-1902, 1848) . . .	Mo.	3/1
Lucy Ware Webb Hayes (1831-1889, 1852)	Oh.	7/1
Lucretia Rudolph Garfield (1832-1918, 1858)	Oh.	4/1
Ellen Lewis Herndon Arthur (1837-1880, 1859)	Va.	2/1
Frances Folsom Cleveland (1864-1947, 1886)	N.Y.	2/3
Caroline Lavinia Scott Harrison (1832-1892, 1853)	Oh.	1/1
Mary Scott Lord Dimmick Harrison (1858-1948, 1896)	Pa.	../1
Ida Saxton McKinley (1847-1907, 1871) .	Oh.	../2
Alice Hathaway Lee Roosevelt (1861-1884, 1880)	Mass.	../1
Edith Kermit Carow Roosevelt (1861-1948, 1886)	Conn.	4/1
Helen Herron Taft (1861-1943, 1886) . .	Oh.	2/1
Ellen Louise Axson Wilson (1860-1914, 1885)	Ga.	../3
Edith Bolling Galt Wilson (1872-1961, 1915)	Va.	None
Florence Kling De Wolfe Harding (1860-1924, 1891)	Oh.	None
Grace Anna Goodhue Coolidge (1879-1957, 1905)	Vt.	2/...
Lou Henry Hoover (1875-1944, 1899) . .	Ia.	2/...
Anna Eleanor Roosevelt Roosevelt (1884-1962, 1905)	N.Y.	4/1 (A)
Bess Wallace Truman (1885-1982, 1919)	Mo.	../1
Mamie Geneva Doud Eisenhower (1896-1979, 1916)	Ia.	1/ ..(A)
Jacqueline Lee Bouvier Kennedy (b. 1929, 1953)	N.Y.	1/1 (A)
Claudia "Lady Bird" Alta Taylor Johnson (b. 1912, 1934)	Tex.	../2
Thelma Catherine Patricia Ryan Nixon (b. 1912, 1940)	Nev.	../2
Elizabeth Bloomer Warren Ford (b. 1918, 1948)	Ill.	3/1
Rosalynn Smith Carter (b. 1927, 1946) .	Ga.	3/1
Anne Frances "Nancy" Robbins Davis Reagan (b. 1923, 1952)	N.Y.	1/1 (C)
Barbara Pierce Bush (b. 1925, 1945). . .	N.Y.	4/2

James Buchanan, 15th president, was unmarried. (A) plus one infant, deceased. (B) Born London, father a Md. citizen. (C) President Reagan has a son and daughter from a former marriage.

First Lady: Barbara Bush

The first lady was born Barbara Pierce in Rye, N.Y. on June 8, 1925; the daughter of Marvin and Pauline (Robinson) Pierce. She attended Smith College, 1943-44. She married George Bush, Jan. 6, 1945. They have four sons and a daughter (another daughter died in childhood). Mrs. Bush has had a lifelong involvement in a number of causes, especially the promotion of literacy.

Burial Places of the Presidents

Washington . . .	Mt. Vernon, Va.
J. Adams	Quincy, Mass.
Jefferson	Charlottesville, Va.
Madison	Montpelier Station, Va.
Monroe	Richmond, Va.
J.Q. Adams . . .	Quincy, Mass.
Jackson	Nashville, Tenn.
Van Buren	Kinderhook, N.Y.
W.H. Harrison. .	North Bend, Oh.
Tyler	Richmond, Va.
Polk	Nashville, Tenn.
Taylor	Louisville, Ky.
Fillmore	Buffalo, N.Y.
Pierce	Concord, N.H.
Buchanan	Lancaster, Pa.
Lincoln	Springfield, Ill.
A. Johnson . . .	Greeneville, Tenn.
Grant	New York City
Hayes	Fremont, Oh.
Garfield	Cleveland, Oh.
Arthur	Albany, N.Y.
Cleveland	Princeton, N.J.
B. Harrison . . .	Indianapolis, Ind.
McKinley	Canton, Oh.
T. Roosevelt. . .	Oyster Bay, N.Y.
Taft	Arlington Nat'l. Cem'y.
Wilson	Washington Cathedral
Harding	Marion, Oh.
Coolidge	Plymouth, Vt.
Hoover.	West Branch, Ia.
F.D. Roosevelt .	Hyde Park, N.Y.
Truman	Independence, Mo.
Eisenhower . . .	Abilene, Kan.
Kennedy.	Arlington Nat'l. Cem'y.
L.B. Johnson . .	Stonewall, Tex.

UNITED STATES HISTORY

1492
Christopher Columbus and crew sighted land Oct. 12 in the present-day Bahamas.

1497
John Cabot explored northeast coast to Delaware.

1513
Juan Ponce de Leon explored Florida coast.

1524
Giovanni da Verrazano led French expedition along coast from Carolina north to Nova Scotia; entered New York harbor.

1539
Hernando de Soto landed in Florida May 28; crossed Mississippi River, 1541.

1540
Francisco Vazquez de Coronado explored Southwest north of Rio Grande. Hernando de Alarcon reached Colorado River, Don Garcia Lopez de Cardenas reached Grand Canyon. Others explored California coast.

1565
St. Augustine, Fla. founded by Pedro Menendez. Razed by Francis Drake 1586.

1579
Francis Drake claimed California for Britain. Metal plate, found 1936, thought to be left by Drake, termed probable hoax 1979.

1607
Capt. John Smith and 105 cavaliers in 3 ships landed on Virginia coast, started first permanent English settlement in New World at Jamestown, May 13.

1609
Henry Hudson, English explorer of Northwest Passage, employed by Dutch, sailed into New York harbor in Sept., and up Hudson to Albany. The same year, Samuel de Champlain explored Lake Champlain just to the north. Spaniards settled Santa Fe, N.M.

1619
House of Burgesses, first representative assembly in New World, elected July 30 at Jamestown, Va.
First laborers — indentured servants — in English N. American colonies, landed by Dutch at Jamestown in Aug. Chattel slavery legally recognized, 1650.

1620
Plymouth Pilgrims, Puritan separatists from Church of England, some living in Holland, left Plymouth, England Sept. 15 on Mayflower. Original destination Virginia, they reached Cape Cod Nov. 19, explored coast; 103 passengers landed Dec. 21 (Dec. 11 Old Style) at Plymouth. Mayflower Compact was agreement to form a government and abide by its laws. Half of colony died during harsh winter.

1624
Dutch left 8 men from ship New Netherland on Manhattan Island in May. Rest sailed to Albany.

1626
Peter Minuit bought Manhattan for Dutch from Man-a-hat-a Indians May 6 for trinkets valued at $24.

1634
Maryland founded as Catholic colony with religious tolerance.

1636
Harvard College founded Oct. 28, now oldest in U.S., Grammar school, compulsory education established at Boston.
Roger Williams founded Providence, R.I., June, as a democratically ruled colony with separation of church and state. Charter was granted, 1644.

1654
First Jews arrived in New Amsterdam.

1660
British Parliament passed Navigation Act, regulating colonial commerce to suit English needs.

1664
Three hundred British troops Sept. 8 seized New Netherland from Dutch, who yield peacefully. Charles II granted province of New Netherland and city of New Amsterdam to brother, Duke of York; both renamed New York. The Dutch recaptured the colony Aug. 9, 1673, but ceded it to Britain Nov. 10, 1674.

1676
Nathaniel Bacon led planters against autocratic British Gov. Berkeley, burned Jamestown, Va. Bacon died, 23 followers executed.
Bloody Indian war in New England ended Aug. 12. King Philip, Wampanoag chief, and many Narragansett Indians killed.

1682
Robert Cavelier, Sieur de La Salle, claimed lower Mississippi River country for France, called it Louisiana Apr. 9. Had French outposts built in Illinois and Texas, 1684. Killed during mutiny Mar. 19, 1687.

1683
William Penn signed treaty with Delaware Indians and made payment for Pennsylvania lands.

1692
Witchcraft delusion at Salem (now Danvers) Mass. inspired by preaching; 19 persons executed.

1696
Capt. William Kidd, who was born in Scotland and settled in America, was hired by British to fight pirates and take booty, but himself became pirate. Arrested and sent to England, he was hanged 1701.

1699
French settlements made in Mississippi, Louisiana.

1704
Indians attacked Deerfield, Mass. Feb. 28-29, killed 40, carried off 100.
Boston News Letter, first regular newspaper, started by John Campbell, postmaster. (*Publick Occurences* was suppressed after one issue 1690.)

1709
British-Colonial troops captured French fort, Port Royal, Nova Scotia, in Queen Anne's War 1701-13. France yielded Nova Scotia by treaty 1713.

1712
Slaves revolted in New York Apr. 6. Six committed suicide, 21 were executed. Second rising, 1741; 13 slaves hanged, 13 burned, 71 deported.

1716
First theater in colonies opened in Williamsburg, Va.

1728
Pennsylvania Gazette founded by Samuel Keimer in Philadelphia. Benjamin Franklin bought interest 1729.

1732
Benjamin Franklin published first *Poor Richard's Almanac;* published annually to 1757.

1735
Freedom of the press recognized in New York by acquittal of John Peter Zenger, editor of *Weekly Journal,* on charge of libeling British Gov. Cosby by criticizing his conduct in office.

1740-41
Capt. Vitus Bering, Dane employed by Russians, reached Alaska.

1744
King George's War pitted British and colonials vs. French. Colonials captured Louisburg, Cape Breton Is. June 17, 1745. Returned to France 1748 by Treaty of Aix-la-Chapelle.

1752
Benjamin Franklin, flying kite in thunderstorm, proved lightning is electricity June 15; invented lightning rod.

1754
French and Indian War (in Europe called 7 Years War, started 1756) began when French occupied Ft. Duquesne (Pittsburgh). British moved Acadian French from Nova Scotia to Louisiana Oct. 1755. British captured Quebec Sept. 18, 1759 in battles in which French Gen. Montcalm and

British Gen. Wolfe were killed. Peace signed Feb. 10 1763. French lost Canada and American Midwest. British tightened colonial administration in North America.

1764

Sugar Act placed duties on lumber, foodstuffs, molasses and rum in colonies.

1765

Stamp Act required revenue stamps to help defray cost of royal troops. Nine colonies, led by New York and Massachusetts at Stamp Act Congress in New York Oct. 7-25, 1765, adopted Declaration of Rights opposing taxation without representation in Parliament and trial without jury by admiralty courts. Stamp Act repealed Mar. 17, 1766.

1767

Townshend Acts levied taxes on glass, painter's lead, paper, and tea. In 1770 all duties except on tea were repealed.

1770

British troops fired **Mar. 5** into Boston mob, killed 5 including **Crispus Attucks,** a black man, reportedly leader of group; later called **Boston Massacre.**

1773

East India Co. tea ships turned back at Boston, New York, Philadelphia in **May.** Cargo ship burned at Annapolis Oct. 14, cargo thrown overboard at **Boston Tea Party Dec. 16.**

1774

"Intolerable Acts" of Parliament curtailed Massachusetts self-rule; barred use of Boston harbor till tea was paid for.

First Continental Congress held in Philadelphia **Sept. 5-Oct. 26;** protested British measures, called for civil disobedience.

Rhode Island abolished slavery.

1775

Patrick Henry addressed Virginia convention, Mar. 23 said "Give me liberty or give me death."

Paul Revere and **William Dawes** on night of **Apr. 18** rode to alert patriots that British were on way to Concord to destroy arms. At Lexington, Mass. **Apr. 19** Minutemen lost 8 killed. On return from Concord British took 273 casualties.

Col. Ethan Allen (joined by Col. Benedict Arnold) captured Ft. Ticonderoga, N.Y. **May 10;** also Crown Point. Colonials headed for Bunker Hill, fortified **Breed's Hill,** Charlestown, Mass., repulsed British under Gen. William Howe twice before retreating **June 17;** British casualties 1,000; called **Battle of Bunker Hill.** Continental Congress **June 15** named George Washington commander-in-chief.

1776

France and Spain each agreed **May 2** to provide one million livres in arms to Americans.

In Continental Congress **June 7,** Richard Henry Lee (Va.) moved "that these united colonies are and of right ought to be free and independent states." Resolution adopted July 2. **Declaration of Independence** approved **July 4.**

Col. Moultrie's batteries at **Charleston, S.C.** repulsed British sea attack **June 28.**

Washington, with 10,000 men, lost **Battle of Long Island Aug. 27,** evacuated New York.

Nathan Hale executed as spy by British **Sept. 22.**

Brig. Gen. Arnold's Lake Champlain fleet was defeated at Valcour **Oct. 11,** but British returned to Canada. Howe failed to destroy Washington's army at **White Plains Oct. 28.** Hessians captured Ft. Washington, Manhattan, and 3,000 men **Nov. 16;** Ft. Lee, N.J. **Nov. 18.**

Washington in Pennsylvania, recrossed **Delaware River Dec. 25-26,** defeated 1,400 Hessians at Trenton, N.J. **Dec. 26.**

1777

Washington defeated Lord Cornwallis at Princeton **Jan. 3.** Continental Congress adopted Stars and Stripes. *See Flag article.*

Maj. Gen. **John Burgoyne** with 8,000 from Canada captured **Ft. Ticonderoga July 6.** Americans beat back Burgoyne at **Bemis Heights Oct. 7** and cut off British escape route. Burgoyne surrendered 5,000 men at **Saratoga** N.Y. **Oct. 17.**

Marquis de Lafayette, aged 20, made major general. **Articles of Confederation** and Perpetual Union adopted by Continental Congress **Nov. 15**

France recognized independence of 13 colonies **Dec. 17.**

1778

France signed treaty of aid with U.S. **Feb. 6.** Sent fleet; British evacuated Philadelphia in consequence **June 18.**

John Paul Jones on the *Bonhomme Richard* defeated *Serapis* in British North Sea waters **Sept. 23.**

1780

Charleston, S.C. fell to the British **May 12,** but a British force was defeated near **Kings Mountain, N.C. Oct. 7** by militiamen.

Benedict Arnold found to be a traitor **Sept. 23.** Arnold escaped, made brigadier general in British army.

1781

Bank of North America incorporated in Philadelphia **May 26.**

Cornwallis, sapped by patriot victories, retired to **Yorktown, Va.** Adm. De Grasse landed 3,000 French and stopped British fleet in Hampton Roads. Washington and Rochambeau joined forces, arrived near Williamsburg Sept. 26. When siege of Cornwallis began **Oct. 6,** British had 6,000, Americans 8,846, French 7,800. **Cornwallis surrendered Oct. 19.**

1782

New **British cabinet agreed in March to recognize U.S.** independence. Preliminary agreement signed in Paris **Nov. 30.**

1783

Massachusetts Supreme Court outlawed slavery in that state, noting the words in the state Bill of Rights "all men are born free and equal."

Britain, U.S. signed **peace treaty Sept. 3** (Congress ratified it **Jan. 14, 1784**).

Washington ordered army disbanded **Nov. 3,** bade farewell to his officers at Fraunces Tavern, N.Y. City **Dec. 4.**

Noah Webster published *American Spelling Book,* great bestseller.

1784

First successful daily newspaper, **Pennsylvania Packet & General Advertiser,** published **Sept. 21.**

1786

Delegates from 5 states at **Annapolis, Md. Sept. 11-14** asked Congress to call convention in Philadelphia to write practical constitution for the 13 states.

1787

Shays's Rebellion, of debt-ridden farmers in Massachusetts, failed **Jan. 25.**

Northwest Ordinance adopted **July 13** by Continental Congress. Determined government of Northwest Territory north of Ohio River, west of New York; 60,000 inhabitants could get statehood. Guaranteed freedom of religion, support for schools, no slavery.

Constitutional convention opened at Philadelphia **May 25** with George Washington presiding. Constitution adopted by delegates **Sept. 17;** ratification by 9th state, New Hampshire, **June 21, 1788,** meant adoption; declared in effect **Mar. 4, 1789.**

1789

George Washington chosen president by all electors voting (73 eligible, 69 voting, 4 absent); John Adams, vice president, 34 votes. **Feb. 4.** First Congress met at Federal Hall, N.Y. City; regular sessions began **Apr. 6.** Washington inaugurated there **Apr. 30.** Supreme Court created by Federal Judiciary Act **Sept. 24.** Congress submitted Bill of Rights to states **Sept. 25.**

1790

Congress met in Phila. **Dec. 6,** new temporary Capital.

1791

Bill of Rights went into effect **Dec. 15.**

1792

Gen. "Mad" Anthony Wayne made commander in Ohio-Indiana area, trained "American Legion"; established string of forts. Routed Indians at Fallen Timbers on Maumee River Aug. 20, 1794, checked British at Fort Miami, Ohio.

1793

Eli Whitney invented cotton gin, reviving southern slavery.

1794

Whiskey Rebellion, west Pennsylvania farmers protesting liquor tax of 1791, was suppressed by 15,000 militiamen Sept. 1794. Alexander Hamilton used incident to establish authority of the new federal government in enforcing its laws.

1795

U.S. bought peace from Algiers and Tunis by paying $800,000, supplying a frigate and annual tribute of $25,000 Nov. 28.

Gen. Wayne signed peace with Indians at Fort Greenville. Univ. of North Carolina became first operating state university.

1796

Washington's Farewell Address as president delivered Sept. 19. Gave strong warnings against permanent alliances with foreign powers, big public debt, large military establishment and devices of "small, artful, enterprising minority" to control or change government.

1797

U.S. frigate United States launched at Philadelphia July 10; Constellation at Baltimore Sept. 7; Constitution (Old Ironsides) at Boston Sept. 20.

1798

War with France threatened over French raids on U.S. shipping and rejection of U.S. diplomats. Congress voided all treaties with France, ordered Navy to capture French armed ships. Navy (45 ships) and 365 privateers captured 84 French ships. USS Constellation took French warship Insurgente 1799. Napoleon stopped French raids after becoming First Consul.

1801

Tripoli declared war June 10 against U.S., which refused added tribute to commerce-raiding Arab corsairs. Land and naval campaigns forced Tripoli to conclude peace June 4, 1805.

1803

Supreme Court, in Marbury v. Madison case, for the first time overturned a U.S. law Feb. 24.

Napoleon, who had recovered Louisiana from Spain by secret treaty, sold all of Louisiana, stretching to Canadian border, to U.S., for $11,250,000 in bonds, plus $3,750,000 indemnities to American citizens with claims against France. U.S. took title Dec. 20. Purchases doubled U.S. area.

1804

Lewis and Clark expedition ordered by Pres. Jefferson to explore what is now northwest U.S. Started from St. Louis May 14; ended Sept. 23, 1806. Sacagawea, an Indian woman, served as guide.

Vice Pres. Aaron Burr, after long political rivalry, shot Alexander Hamilton in a duel July 11 in Weehawken, N.J.; Hamilton died the next day.

1807

Robert Fulton made first practical steamboat trip; left N.Y. City Aug. 17, reached Albany, 150 mi., in 32 hrs.

1808

Slave importation outlawed. Some 250,000 slaves were illegally imported 1808-1860.

1811

William Henry Harrison, governor of Indiana, defeated Indians under the Prophet, in battle of Tippecanoe Nov. 7.

Cumberland Road begun at Cumberland, Md.; became important route to West.

1812

War of 1812 had 3 main causes: Britain seized U.S. ships trading with France; Britain seized 4,000 naturalized U.S.

sailors by 1810; Britain armed Indians who raided western border. U.S. stopped trade with Europe 1807 and 1809. Trade with Britain only was stopped, 1810.

Unaware that Britain had raised the blockade 2 days before, Congress declared war June 18 by a small majority. The West favored war, New England opposed it. The British were handicapped by war with France.

U.S. naval victories in 1812 included: USS Essex captured Alert Aug. 13; USS Constitution destroyed Guerriere Aug. 19; USS Wasp took Frolic Oct. 18; USS United States defeated Macedonian off Azores Oct. 25; Constitution beat Java Dec. 29. British captured Detroit Aug. 16.

1813

Oliver H. Perry defeated British fleet at Battle of Lake Erie, Sept. 10. U.S. victory at Battle of the Thames, Ont., Oct. 5, broke Indian allies of Britain, and made Detroit frontier safe for U.S. But Americans failed in Canadian invasion attempts. York (Toronto) and Buffalo were burned.

1814

British landed in Maryland in August, defeated U.S. force Aug. 24, burned Capitol and White House. Maryland militia stopped British advance Sept. 12. Bombardment of Ft. McHenry, Baltimore, for 25 hours, Sept. 13-14, by British fleet failed; Francis Scott Key wrote words to Star Spangled Banner.

U.S. won naval Battle of Lake Champlain Sept. 11. Peace treaty signed at Ghent Dec. 24.

1815

Some 5,300 British, unaware of peace treaty, attacked U.S. entrenchments near New Orleans, Jan. 8. British had over 2,000 casualties, Americans lost 71.

U.S. flotilla finally ended piracy by Algiers, Tunis, Tripoli by Aug. 6.

1816

Second Bank of the U.S. chartered.

1817

Rush-Bagot treaty signed Apr. 28-29; limited U.S., British armaments on the Great Lakes.

1819

Spain cedes Florida to U.S. Feb. 22.

American steamship Savannah made first part steam-powered, part sail-powered crossing of Atlantic, Savannah, Ga. to Liverpool, Eng., 29 days.

1820

Henry Clay's Missouri Compromise bill passed by Congress March 3. Slavery was allowed in Missouri, but not elsewhere west of the Mississippi River north of 36° 30' latitude (the southern line of Missouri). Repealed 1854.

1821

Emma Willard founded Troy Female Seminary, first U.S. women's college.

1823

Monroe Doctrine enunciated Dec. 2, opposing European intervention in the Americas.

1824

Pawtucket, R.I. weavers strike in first such action by women.

1825

Erie Canal opened; first boat left Buffalo Oct. 26, reached N.Y. City Nov. 4. Canal cost $7 million but cut travel time one-third, shipping costs nine-tenths; opened Great Lakes area, made N.Y. City chief Atlantic port.

John Stevens, of Hoboken, N.J., built and operated first experimental steam locomotive in U.S.

1828

South Carolina Dec. 19 declared the right of state nullification of federal laws, opposing the "Tariff of Abominations."

Noah Webster published his American Dictionary of the English Language.

Baltimore & Ohio 1st U.S. passenger RR, was begun July 4.

1830

Mormon church organized by Joseph Smith in Fayette, N.Y. Apr. 6.

1831

Nat Turner, black slave in Virginia, led local slave rebellion, killed 57 whites in Aug. Troops called in, Turner captured, tried, and hanged.

1832

Black Hawk War (Ill.-Wis.) Apr.-Sept. pushed Sauk and Fox Indians west across Mississippi.

South Carolina convention passed Ordinance of Nullification in Nov. against permanent tariff, threatening to withdraw from the Union. Congress Feb. 1833 passed a compromise tariff act, whereupon South Carolina repealed its act.

1833

Oberlin College, first in U.S. to adopt coeducation; refused to bar students on account of race, 1835.

1835

Texas proclaimed right to secede from Mexico; Sam Houston put in command of Texas army, Nov. 2-4.

Gold discovered on Cherokee land in Georgia. Indians forced to cede lands Dec. 20 and to cross Mississippi.

1836

Texans besieged in Alamo in San Antonio by Mexicans under Santa Anna Feb. 23-Mar. 6; entire garrison killed. Texas independence declared, Mar. 2. At San Jacinto Apr. 21 Sam Houston and Texans defeated Mexicans.

Marcus Whitman, H.H. Spaulding and wives reached Fort Walla Walla on Columbia River, Oregon. First white women to cross plains.

Seminole Indians in Florida under Osceola began attacks Nov. 1, protesting forced removal. The unpopular 8-year war ended Aug. 14, 1842; Indians were sent to Oklahoma. War cost the U.S. 1,500 soldiers.

1841

First emigrant wagon train for California, 47 persons, left Independence, Mo. May 1, reached Cal. Nov. 4.

Brook Farm commune set up by New England transcendentalist intellectuals. Lasts to 1846.

1842

Webster-Ashburton Treaty signed Aug. 9, fixing the U.S.-Canada border in Maine and Minnesota.

First use of anesthetic (sulphuric ether gas).

Settlement of Oregon begins via Oregon Trail.

1844

First message over first telegraph line sent May 24 by inventor Samuel F.B. Morse from Washington to Baltimore: "What hath God wrought!"

1845

Texas Congress voted for annexation to U.S. July 4. U.S. Congress admits Texas to Union Dec. 29.

1846

Mexican War. Pres. James K. Polk ordered Gen. Zachary Taylor to seize disputed Texan land settled by Mexicans. After border clash, U.S. declared war May 13; Mexico May 23. Northern Whigs opposed war, southerners backed it.

Bear flag of Republic of California raised by American settlers at Sonoma June 14.

About 12,000 U.S. troops took Vera Cruz Mar. 27, 1847, Mexico City Sept. 14, 1847. By treaty, Feb. 1848, Mexico ceded claims to Texas, California, Arizona, New Mexico, Nevada, Utah, part of Colorado. U.S. assumed $3 million American claims and paid Mexico $15 million.

Treaty with Great Britain June 15 set boundary in Oregon territory at 49th parallel (extension of existing line). Expansionists had used slogan "54° 40' or fight."

Mormons, after violent clashes with settlers over polygamy, left Nauvoo, Ill. for West under Brigham Young, settled July 1847 at Salt Lake City, Utah.

Elias Howe invented sewing machine.

1847

First adhesive U.S. postage stamps on sale July 1; Benjamin Franklin 5¢, Washington 10¢.

Ralph Waldo Emerson published first book of poems; Henry Wadsworth Longfellow published Evangeline.

1848

Gold discovered Jan. 24 in California; 80,000 prospectors emigrate in 1849.

Lucretia Mott and Elizabeth Cady Stanton lead Seneca Falls, N.Y. Women's Rights Convention July 19-20.

1850

Sen. Henry Clay's Compromise of 1850 admitted California as 31st state Sept. 9, slavery forbidden; made Utah and New Mexico territories without decision on slavery; made Fugitive Slave Law more harsh; ended District of Columbia slave trade.

1851

Herman Melville's Moby Dick. Nathaniel Hawthorne's House of the Seven Gables published.

1852

Uncle Tom's Cabin, by Harriet Beecher Stowe, published.

1853

Commodore Matthew C. Perry, U.S.N., received by Lord of Toda, Japan July 14; negotiated treaty to open Japan to U.S. ships.

1854

Republican party formed at Ripon, Wis. Feb. 28. Opposed Kansas-Nebraska Act (became law May 30) which left issue of slavery to vote of settlers.

Henry David Thoreau published Walden.

1855

Walt Whitman published Leaves of Grass.

First railroad train crossed Mississippi on the river's first bridge, Rock Island, Ill.-Davenport, Ia. Apr. 21.

1856

Republican party's first nominee for president, John C. Fremont, defeated. Abraham Lincoln made 50 speeches for him.

Lawrence, Kan. sacked May 21 by slavery party; abolitionist John Brown led anti-slavery men against Missourians at Osawatomie, Kan. Aug. 30

1857

Dred Scott decision by U.S. Supreme Court Mar. 6 held, 6-3, that a slave did not become free when taken into a free state, Congress could not bar slavery from a territory, and blacks could not be citizens.

1858

First Atlantic cable completed by Cyrus W. Field Aug. 5; cable failed Sept. 1.

Lincoln-Douglas debates in Illinois Aug. 21-Oct. 15.

1859

First commercially productive oil well, drilled near Titusville, Pa., by Edwin L. Drake Aug. 27.

Abolitionist John Brown with 21 men seized U.S. Armory at Harpers Ferry (then Va.) Oct. 16. U.S. Marines captured raiders, killing several. Brown was hanged for treason by Virginia Dec. 2.

1860

New England shoe-workers, 20,000, strike, win higher wages.

Abraham Lincoln, Republican, elected president in 4-way race.

First Pony Express between Sacramento, Cal. and St. Joseph, Mo. started Apr. 3; service ended Oct. 24, 1861 when first transcontinental telegraph line was completed.

1861

Seven southern states set up Confederate States of America Feb. 8, with Jefferson Davis as president. Civil War began as Confederates fired on Ft. Sumter in Charleston, S.C. Apr. 12; they captured it Apr. 14.

President Lincoln called for 75,000 volunteers Apr. 15. By May, 11 states had seceded. Lincoln blockaded southern ports Apr. 19, cutting off vital exports, aid.

Confederates repelled Union forces at first Battle of Bull Run July 21.

First transcontinental telegraph was put in operation.

1862

Homestead Act was approved May 20; it granted free family farms to settlers.

Land Grant Act approved July 7, providing for public land sale to benefit agricultural education; eventually led to establishment of state university systems.

Union forces were victorious in western campaigns, took New Orleans. Battles in East were inconclusive.

1863

Lincoln issued **Emancipation Proclamation Jan. 1**, freeing "all slaves in areas still in rebellion."

The entire **Mississippi River** was in Union hands by **July 4**. Union forces won a major victory at **Gettysburg, Pa. July 1-July 4.** Lincoln read his **Gettysburg Address Nov. 19.**

Draft riots in N.Y. City killed about 1,000, including blacks who were hanged by mobs **July 13-16.** Rioters protested provision allowing money payment in place of service. Such payments were ended 1864.

1864

Gen. **Sherman** marched through Georgia, taking Atlanta **Sept. 1,** Savannah **Dec. 22.**

Sand Creek massacre of Cheyenne and Arapaho Indians **Nov. 29** in a raid by 900 cavalrymen who killed 150-500 men, women, and children; 9 soldiers died. The tribes were awaiting surrender terms when attacked.

1865

Robert E. Lee surrendered 27,800 Confederate troops to Grant at **Appomattox Court House,** Va. **Apr. 9.** J.E. Johnston surrendered 31,200 to Sherman at Durham Station, N.C. **Apr. 18.** Last rebel troops surrendered **May 26.**

President **Lincoln was shot Apr. 14** by John Wilkes Booth in Ford's Theater, Washington; died the following morning. Booth was reported dead **Apr. 26.** Four co-conspirators were hanged **July 7.**

Thirteenth Amendment, abolishing slavery, took effect **Dec. 18.**

1866

First post of the **Grand Army of the Republic** formed **Apr. 6;** was a major national political force for years. Last encampment, **Aug. 31, 1949,** attended by 6 of the 16 surviving veterans.

Ku Klux Klan formed secretly in South to terrorize blacks who voted. Disbanded **1869-71.** A second Klan was organized **1915.**

Congress took control of southern Reconstruction, backed freedmen's rights.

1867

Alaska sold to U.S. by Russia for $7.2 million **Mar. 30** through efforts of Sec. of State William H. Seward.

Horatio Alger published first book, *Ragged Dick.*

The **Grange** was organized **Dec 4,** to protect farmer interests.

1868

The World Almanac, a publication of the *New York World,* appeared for the first time.

Pres. **Andrew Johnson** tried to remove Edwin M. Stanton, secretary of war; was impeached by House **Feb. 24** for violation of Tenure of Office Act; acquitted by Senate **March-May.** Stanton resigned.

1869

Financial "**Black Friday**" in New York **Sept. 24;** caused by attempt to "corner" gold.

Transcontinental railroad completed; golden spike driven at Promontory, Utah **May 10** marking the junction of Central Pacific and Union Pacific.

Knights of Labor formed in Philadelphia. By **1886,** it had 700,000 members nationally.

Woman suffrage law passed in Territory of Wyoming **Dec. 10.**

1871

Great fire destroyed Chicago **Oct. 8-11;** loss est. at $196 million.

1872

Amnesty Act restored civil rights to citizens of the South **May 22** except for 500 Confederate leaders.

Congress founded first national park — **Yellowstone** in Wyoming.

1873

First U.S. **postal card** issued **May 1.**

Banks failed, panic began in **Sept.** Depression lasted 5 years.

"**Boss**" **William Tweed** of N.Y. City convicted of stealing public funds. He died in jail in **1878.**

Bellevue Hospital in N.Y. City started the first **school of nursing.**

1875

Congress passed **Civil Rights Act Mar. 1** giving equal rights to blacks in public accommodations and jury duty. Act invalidated in **1883** by Supreme Court.

First **Kentucky Derby** held **May 17** at Churchill Downs, Louisville, Ky.

1876

Samuel J. Tilden, Democrat, received majority of popular votes for president over **Rutherford B. Hayes,** Republican, but 22 electoral votes were in dispute; issue left to Congress. Hayes given presidency in **Feb., 1877** after Republicans agree to end Reconstruction of South.

Col. George A. Custer and 264 soldiers of the 7th Cavalry killed **June 25** in "last stand," Battle of the Little Big Horn, Mont., in Sioux Indian War.

Mark Twain published *Tom Sawyer.*

1877

Molly Maguires, Irish terrorist society in Scranton, Pa. mining areas, broken up by hanging of 11 leaders for murders of mine officials and police.

Pres. Hayes sent troops in violent national **railroad strike.**

1878

First commercial **telephone** exchange opened, New Haven, Conn. **Jan. 28.**

1879

F.W. Woolworth opened his first five-and-ten store in Utica, N.Y. **Feb. 22.**

Henry George published *Progress & Poverty,* advocating single tax on land.

1881

Pres. **James A. Garfield shot** in Washington, D.C. **July 2;** died **Sept. 19.**

Booker T. Washington founded Tuskegee Institute for blacks.

Helen Hunt Jackson published *A Century of Dishonor* about mistreatment of Indians.

1883

Pendleton Act, passed **Jan. 16,** reformed federal civil service.

Brooklyn Bridge opened **May 24.**

1886

Haymarket riot and bombing, evening of **May 4,** followed bitter labor battles for 8-hour day in Chicago; 7 police and 4 workers died, 66 wounded. Eight anarchists found guilty. Gov. John P. Altgeld denounced trial as unfair.

Geronimo, Apache Indian, finally surrendered **Sept. 4.**

American Federation of Labor (AFL) formed **Dec. 8** by 25 craft unions.

1888

Great blizzard in eastern U.S. **Mar. 11-14;** 400 deaths.

1889

Johnstown, Pa. flood May 31; 2,200 lives lost.

1890

First execution by **electrocution:** William Kemmler **Aug. 6** at Auburn Prison, Auburn, N.Y., for murder.

Battle of Wounded Knee, S.D. **Dec. 29,** the last major conflict between Indians and U.S. troops. About 200 Indian men, women, and children, and 29 soldiers were killed.

Castle Garden closed as N.Y. immigration depot; **Ellis Island** opened **Dec. 31,** closed 1954.

Sherman Antitrust Act begins federal effort to curb monopolies.

Jacob Riis published *How the Other Half Lives,* about city slums.

1892

Homestead, Pa., strike at Carnegie steel mills; 7 guards and 11 strikers and spectators shot to death **July 6;** setback for unions.

1893

Financial panic began, led to 4-year depression.

1894

Thomas A. Edison's kinetoscope (motion pictures) (invented 1887) given first public showing Apr. 14.

Jacob S. Coxey led 500 unemployed from the Midwest into Washington, D.C. Apr. 29. Coxey was arrested for trespassing on Capitol grounds.

1896

William Jennings Bryan delivered "Cross of Gold" into Washington, D.C. Apr. 29.

Supreme Court, in Plessy v. Ferguson, approved racial segregation under the "separate but equal" doctrine.

1898

U.S. battleship Maine blown up Feb. 15 at Havana. 260 killed.

U.S. blockaded Cuba Apr. 22 in aid of independence forces. U.S. declared war on Spain, Apr. 24, destroyed Spanish fleet in Philippines May 1, took Guam June 20.

Puerto Rico taken by U.S. July 25-Aug. 12. Spain agreed Dec. 10 to cede Philippines, Puerto Rico, and Guam, and approved independence for Cuba.

U.S. annexed independent republic of Hawaii.

1899

Filipino insurgents, unable to get recognition of independence from U.S., started guerrilla war Feb. 4. Crushed with capture May 23, 1901 of leader, Emilio Aguinaldo.

U.S. declared Open Door Policy to make China an open international market and to preserve its integrity as a nation.

John Dewey published School and Society, backing progressive education.

1900

Carry Nation, Kansas anti-saloon agitator, began raiding with hatchet.

U.S. helped suppress "Boxers" in Peking.

1901

Pres. William McKinley was shot Sept. 6 by an anarchist, Leon Czolgosz; died Sept. 14.

1903

Treaty between U.S. and Colombia to have U.S. dig Panama Canal signed Jan. 22, rejected by Colombia. Panama declared independence with U.S. support Nov. 3; recognized by Pres. Theodore Roosevelt Nov. 6. U.S., Panama signed canal treaty Nov. 18.

Wisconsin set first direct primary voting system May 23.

First automobile trip across U.S. from San Francisco to New York May 23-Aug. 1.

First successful flight in heavier-than-air mechanically propelled airplane by Orville Wright Dec. 17 near Kitty Hawk, N.C., 120 ft. in 12 seconds. Fourth flight same day by Wilbur Wright, 852 ft. in 59 seconds. Improved plane patented May 22, 1906.

Jack London published Call of the Wild.

Great Train Robbery, pioneering film, produced.

1904

Ida Tarbell published muckraking History of Standard Oil.

1905

First Rotary Club of businessmen founded in Chicago.

1906

San Francisco earthquake and fire Apr. 18-19 left 503 dead. $350 million damages.

Pure Food and Drug Act and Meat Inspection Act both passed June 30.

1907

Financial panic and depression started Mar. 13.

First round-the-world cruise of U.S. "Great White Fleet"; 16 battleships, 12,000 men.

1909

Adm. Robert E. Peary reached North Pole Apr. 6 on 6th attempt, accompanied by Matthew Henson, a black man, and 4 Eskimos.

National Conference on the Negro convened May 30, leading to founding of the National Association for the Advancement of Colored People.

1910

Boy Scouts of America founded Feb. 8.

1911

Supreme Court dissolved Standard Oil Co.

First transcontinental airplane flight (with numerous stops) by C.P. Rodgers, New York to Pasadena, Sept. 17-Nov. 5; time in air 82 hrs., 4 min.

1912

Amer. Girl Guides founded Mar. 12; name changed in 1913 to Girl Scouts.

U.S. sent marines Aug. 14 to Nicaragua, which was in default of loans to U.S. and Europe.

1913

N.Y. Armory Show brought modern art to U.S. Feb. 17.

U.S. blockaded Mexico in support of revolutionaries.

Charles Beard published his Economic Interpretation of the Constitution.

Federal Reserve System was authorized Dec. 23, in a major reform of U.S. banking and finance.

1914

Ford Motor Co. raised basic wage rates from $2.40 for 9-hr. day to $5 for 8-hr. day Jan. 5.

When U.S. sailors were arrested at Tampico Apr. 9, Atlantic fleet was sent to Veracruz, occupied city.

Pres. Wilson proclaimed U.S. neutrality in the European war Aug. 4.

The Clayton Antitrust Act was passed Oct. 15, strengthening federal anti-monopoly powers.

1915

First telephone talk, New York to San Francisco, Jan. 25 by Alexander Graham Bell and Thomas A. Watson.

British ship Lusitania sunk May 7 by German submarine; 128 American passengers lost (Germany had warned passengers in advance). As a result of U.S. campaign, Germany issued apology and promise of payments Oct. 5. Pres. Wilson asked for a military fund increase Dec. 7.

U.S. troops landed in Haiti July 28. Haiti became a virtual U.S. protectorate under Sept. 16 treaty.

1916

Gen. John J. Pershing entered Mexico to pursue Francisco (Pancho) Villa, who had raided U.S. border areas. Forces withdrawn Feb. 5, 1917.

Rural Credits Act passed July 17, followed by Warehouse Act. Aug. 11; both provided financial aid to farmers.

Bomb exploded during San Francisco Preparedness Day parade July 22, killed 10. Thomas J. Mooney, labor organizer, and Warren K. Billings, shoe worker, were convicted; both pardoned in 1939.

U.S. bought Virgin Islands from Denmark Aug. 4.

Jeannette Rankin, 1st U.S. Congresswoman (R-Montana) elected.

U.S. established military government in the Dominican Republic Nov. 29.

Trade and loans to European Allies soared during the year.

John Dewey published Democracy and Education.

Carl Sandburg published Chicago Poems.

1917

Germany, suffering from British blockade, declared almost unrestricted submarine warfare Jan. 31. U.S. cut diplomatic ties with Germany Feb. 3, and formally declared war Apr. 6.

Conscription law was passed May 18. First U.S. troops arrived in Europe June 26.

The 18th (Prohibition) Amendment to the Constitution was submitted to the states by Congress Dec. 18. On Jan. 16, 1919, the 36th state (Nevada) ratified it. Franklin D. Roosevelt, as 1932 presidential candidate, endorsed repeal; 21st Amendment repealed 18th; ratification completed Dec. 5, 1933.

1918

Over one million American troops were in Europe by July. War ended Nov. 11.

Influenza epidemic killed an estimated 20 million worldwide, 548,000 in U.S.

1919
First transatlantic flight, by U.S. Navy seaplane, left Rockaway, N.Y. May 8, stopped at Newfoundland, Azores, Lisbon May 27.

Boston police strike Sept. 9; National Guard breaks strike.

Sherwood Anderson published *Winesburg, Ohio.*

About 250 alien radicals were deported Dec. 22.

1920
In national Red Scare, some 2,700 Communists, anarchists, and other radicals were arrested Jan.-May.

Senate refused Mar. 19 to ratify the League of Nations Covenant.

Nicola Sacco, 29, shoe factory employee and radical agitator, and Bartolomeo Vanzetti, 32, fish peddler and anarchist, accused of killing 2 men in Mass. payroll holdup Apr. 15. Found guilty 1921. A 6-year worldwide campaign for release on grounds of want of conclusive evidence and prejudice failed. Both were executed Aug. 23, 1927. Vindicated July 19, 1977 by proclamation of Mass. Gov. Dukakis.

First regular licensed radio broadcasting begun Aug. 20.

19th Amendment ratified Aug. 26, giving women right to vote.

League fo Women Voters founded.

Wall St., N.Y. City, bomb explosion killed 30, injured 100, did $2 million damage Sept. 16.

Sinclair Lewis' *Main Street,* F. Scott Fitzgerald's *This Side of Paradise* published.

1921
Congress sharply curbed immigration, set national quota system May 19.

Joint Congressional resolution declaring peace with Germany, Austria, and Hungary signed July 2 by Pres. Harding; treaties were signed in Aug.

Limitation of Armaments Conference met in Washington Nov. 12 to Feb. 6, 1922. Major powers agreed to curtail naval construction, outlaw poison gas, restrict submarine attack on merchantmen, respect integrity of China.

Ku Klux Klan began revival with violence against blacks in North, South, and Midwest.

1922
Violence during coal-mine strike at Herrin, Ill., June 22-23 cost 36 lives, 21 of them non-union miners.

Reader's Digest founded.

1923
First sound-on-film motion picture, "Phonofilm" was shown by Lee de Forest at Rivoli Theater, N.Y. City, beginning in April.

1924
Law approved by Congress June 15 making all Indians citizens.

Nellie Tayloe Ross elected governor of Wyoming Nov. 9 after death of her husband Oct. 2; installed Jan. 5, 1925, first woman governor. Miriam (Ma) Ferguson was elected governor of Texas Nov. 9; installed Jan. 20, 1925.

George Gershwin wrote *Rhapsody in Blue.*

1925
John T. Scopes found guilty of having taught evolution in Dayton, Tenn. high school, fined $100 and costs July 24.

1926
Dr. Robert H. Goddard demonstrated practicality of rockets Mar. 16 at Auburn, Mass. with first liquid fuel rocket; rocket traveled 184 ft. in 2.5 secs.

Air Commerce Act passed, providing federal aid for airlines and airports.

1927
About 1,000 marines landed in China Mar. 5 to protect property in civil war.

Capt. Charles A. Lindbergh left Roosevelt Field, N.Y. May 20 alone in plane Spirit of St. Louis on first New York-Paris nonstop flight. Reached Le Bourget airfield May 21, 3,610 miles in 33 ¹/₂ hours.

The Jazz Singer, with Al Jolson, demonstrated part-talking pictures in N.Y. City Oct. 6.

Show Boat opened in New York Dec. 27.

O. E. Rolvaag published *Giants in the Earth.*

1928
Herbert Hoover elected president against Alfred E. Smith, the Catholic governor of New York.

Amelia Earhart became first woman to fly the Atlantic June 17.

1929
"St. Valentine's Day massacre" in Chicago Feb. 14; gangsters killed 7 rivals.

Farm price stability aided by Agricultural Marketing Act, passed June 15.

Albert B. Fall, former sec. of the interior, was convicted of accepting a bribe of $100,000 in the leasing of the Elk Hills (Teapot Dome) naval oil reserve; sentenced Nov. 1 to $100,000 fine and year in prison.

Stock Market crash Oct. 29 marked end of postwar prosperity as stock prices plummeted. Stock losses for 1929-31 estimated at $50 billion; worst American depression began.

Thomas Wolfe published *Look Homeward, Angel.* William Faulkner published *The Sound and the Fury.*

1930
London Naval Reduction Treaty signed by U.S., Britain, Italy, France, and Japan Apr. 22; in effect Jan. 1, 1931; expired Dec. 31, 1936.

Hawley-Smoot Tariff signed; rate hikes slash world trade.

1931
Empire State Building opened in N.Y. City May 1.

Pearl Buck published *The Good Earth.*

1932
Reconstruction Finance Corp. established Jan. 22 to stimulate banking and business. Unemployment at 12 million.

Charles Lindbergh Jr. kidnaped Mar. 1, found dead May 12.

Bonus March on Washington May 29 by World War I veterans demanding Congress pay their bonus in full.

1933
FDR named Frances Perkins U.S. Secy of Labor; 1st woman in U.S. Cabinet.

All banks in the U.S. were ordered closed by Pres. Roosevelt Mar. 6.

In the "100 days" special session, Mar. 9—June 16, Congress passed New Deal social and economic measures.

Gold standard dropped by U.S.; announced by Pres. Roosevelt Apr. 19, ratified by Congress June 5.

Prohibition ended in the U.S. as 36th state ratified 21st Amendment Dec. 5.

U.S. foreswore armed intervention in Western Hemisphere nations Dec. 26.

1934
U.S. troops pull out of Haiti Aug. 6.

1935
Comedian Will Rogers and aviator Wiley Post killed Aug. 15 in Alaska plane crash.

Social Security Act passed by Congress Aug. 14.

Huey Long, Senator from Louisiana and national political leader, was assassinated Sept. 8.

Porgy and Bess, George Gershwin opera on American theme, opened Oct. 10 in N.Y. City.

Committee for Industrial Organization (CIO) formed to expand industrial unionism Nov. 9.

1936
Boulder Dam completed.

Margaret Mitchell published *Gone With the Wind.*

1937
Amelia Earhart Putnam, aviator, and co-pilot Fred Noonan lost July 2 near Howland Is. in the Pacific.

Pres. Roosevelt asked for 6 additional Supreme Court justices; "packing" plan defeated.

Auto, steel labor unions won first big contracts.

1938
Naval Expansion Act passed May 17.

National minimum wage enacted June 28.

Orson Welles radio dramatization of *War of the Worlds* caused nationwide scare Oct. 30.

1939

Pres. Roosevelt asked defense budget hike Jan. 5, 12.

N.Y. World's Fair opened Apr. 30, closed Oct. 31; reopened May 11, 1940, and finally closed Oct. 21.

Einstein alerts FDR to A-bomb opportunity in Aug. 2 letter.

U.S. declares its neutrality in European war Sept. 5.

Roosevelt proclaimed a limited national emergency Sept. 8, an unlimited emergency May 27, 1941. Both ended by Pres. Truman Apr. 28, 1952.

John Steinbeck published Grapes of Wrath.

1940

U.S. okayed sale of surplus war material to Britain June 3; announced transfer of 50 overaged destroyers Sept. 3.

First peacetime draft approved Sept. 14.

Richard Wright published Native Son.

1941

The Four Freedoms termed essential by Pres. Roosevelt in speech to Congress Jan. 6: freedom of speech and religion, freedom from want and fear.

Lend-Lease Act signed Mar. 11, providing $7 billion in military credits for Britain. Lend-Lease for USSR approved in Nov.

U.S. occupied Iceland July 7.

The Atlantic Charter, 8-point declaration of principles, issued by Roosevelt and Winston Churchill Aug. 14.

Japan attacked Pearl Harbor, Hawaii, 7:55 a.m. Dec. 7, 19 ships sunk or damaged, 2,300 dead. U.S. declared war on Japan Dec. 8, on Germany and Italy Dec. 11 after those countries declared war.

1942

Federal government forcibly moved 110,000 Japanese-Americans (including 75,000 U.S. citizens) from West Coast to detention camps. Exclusion lasted 3 years.

Battle of Midway June 4-7 was Japan's first major defeat.

Marines landed on Guadalcanal Aug. 7; last Japanese not expelled until Feb. 9, 1943.

U.S., Britain invaded North Africa Nov. 8.

First nuclear chain reaction (fission of uranium isotope U-235) produced at Univ. of Chicago, under physicists Arthur Compton, Enrico Fermi, others Dec. 2.

1943

All war contractors barred from racial discrimination May 27.

Pres. Roosevelt signed June 10 the pay-as-you-go income tax bill. Starting July 1 wage and salary earners were subject to a paycheck withholding tax.

Race riot in Detroit June 21; 34 dead, 700 injured. Riot in Harlem section of N.Y. City; 6 killed.

U.S. troops invaded Italy Sept. 9.

Marines advanced in Gilbert Is. in Nov.

1944

U.S., Allied forces invaded Europe at Normandy June 6.

G.I. Bill of Rights signed June 22, providing veterans benefits.

U.S. forces landed on Leyte, Philippines Oct. 20.

1945

Yalta Conference met in the Crimea, USSR, Feb. 3-11. Roosevelt, Churchill, and Stalin agreed Russia would enter war against Japan.

Marines landed on Iwo Jima Feb. 19; U.S. forces invaded Okinawa Apr. 1.

Pres. Roosevelt, 63, died of cerebral hemorrhage in Warm Springs, Ga. Apr. 12; V.P. Harry S. Truman became pres.

Germany surrendered May 7.

First atomic bomb, produced at Los Alamos, N.M., exploded at Alamogordo, N.M. July 16. Bomb dropped on Hiroshima Aug. 6, on Nagasaki Aug. 9. Japan surrendered Aug. 15.

U.S. forces entered Korea south of 38th parallel to displace Japanese Sept. 8.

Gen. Douglas MacArthur took over supervision of Japan Sept. 9.

1946

Strike by 400,000 mine workers began Apr. 1; other industries followed.

Philippines given independence by U.S. July 4.

1947

Truman Doctrine: Pres. Truman asked Congress to aid Greece and Turkey to combat Communist terrorism Mar. 12. Approved May 15.

United Nations Security Council voted unanimously Apr. 2 to place under U.S. trusteeship the Pacific islands formerly mandated to Japan.

Jackie Robinson on Brooklyn Dodgers Apr. 11, broke the color barrier in major league baseball.

Taft-Hartley Labor Act curbing strikes was vetoed by Truman June 20; Congress overrode the veto.

Proposals later known as the Marshall Plan, under which the U.S. would extend aid to European countries, were made by Sec. of State George C. Marshall June 5. Congress authorized some $12 billion in next 4 years.

1948

USSR began a land blockade of Berlin's Allied sectors Apr. 1. This blockade and Western counter-blockade were lifted Sept. 30, 1949, after British and U.S. planes had lifted 2,343,315 tons of food and coal into the city.

Organization of American States founded Apr. 30.

Alger Hiss, former State Dept. official, indicted Dec. 15 for perjury, after denying he had passed secret documents to Whittaker Chambers for transmission to a communist spy ring. His second trial ended in conviction Jan. 21, 1950, and a sentence of 5 years in prison.

Kinsey Report on Sexuality in the Human Male published.

1949

U.S. troops withdrawn from Korea June 29.

North Atlantic Treaty Organization (NATO) established Aug. 24 by U.S., Canada, and 10 West European nations, agreeing that an armed attack against one or more of them would be considered an attack against all.

Mrs. I. Toguri D'Aquino (Tokyo Rose of Japanese wartime broadcasts) was sentenced Oct. 7 to 10 years in prison for treason. Paroled 1956, pardoned 1977.

Eleven leaders of U.S. Communist party convicted Oct. 14, after 9-month trial in N.Y. City, of advocating violent overthrow of U.S. government. Ten defendants sentenced to 5 years in prison each and the 11th to 3 years. Supreme Court upheld the convictions June 4, 1951.

1950

U.S. Jan 14 recalled all consular officials from China after the latter seized the American consulate in Peking.

Masked bandits robbed Brink's Inc., Boston express office, Jan. 17 of $2.8 million, of which $1.2 million was in cash. Case solved 1956, 8 sentenced to life.

Pres. Truman authorized production of H-bomb Jan. 31.

United Nations asked for troops to restore Korea peace June 25.

Truman ordered Air Force and Navy to Korea June 27 after North Korea invaded South. Truman approved ground forces, air strikes against North June 30.

U.S. sent 35 military advisers to South Vietnam June 27, and agreed to provide military and economic aid to antiCommunist government.

Army seized all railroads Aug. 27 on Truman's order to prevent a general strike; roads returned to owners in 1952.

U.S. forces landed at Inchon Sept. 15; UN force took Pyongyang Oct. 20, reached China border Nov. 20, China sent troops across border Nov. 26.

Two members of a Puerto Rican nationalist movement tried to kill Pres. Truman Nov. 1. (see Assassinations)

U.S. Dec. 8 banned shipments to Communist China and to Asiatic ports trading with it.

1951

Sen. Estes Kefauver led Senate investigation into organized crime. Preliminary report Feb. 28 said gambling take was over $20 billion a year.

Julius Rosenberg, his wife, Ethel, and Morton Sobell, all U.S. citizens, were found guilty Mar. 29 of conspiracy to commit wartime espionage. Rosenbergs sentenced to death, Sobell to 30 years. Rosenbergs executed June 19, 1953. Sobell released Jan. 14, 1969.

Gen. Douglas MacArthur was removed from his Korea command Apr. 11 for unauthorized policy statements.

Korea cease-fire talks began in July; lasted 2 years. Fighting ended July 27, 1953.

Tariff concessions by the U.S. to the Soviet Union, Communist China, and all communist-dominated lands were suspended Aug. 1.

The U.S., Australia, and New Zealand signed a mutual security pact Sept. 1.

Transcontinental television inaugurated Sept. 4 with Pres. Truman's address at the Japanese Peace Treaty Conference in San Francisco.

Japanese Peace Treaty signed in San Francisco Sept. 8 by U.S., Japan, and 47 other nations.

J.D. Salinger published Catcher in the Rye.

1952

U.S. seizure of nation's steel mills was ordered by Pres. Truman Apr. 8 to avert a strike. Ruled illegal by Supreme Court June 2.

Peace contract between West Germany, U.S., Great Britain, and France was signed May 26.

The last racial and ethnic barriers to naturalization were removed, June 26-27, with the passage of the Immigration and Naturalization Act of 1952.

First hydrogen device explosion Nov. 1 at Eniwetok Atoll in Pacific.

1953

Pres. Eisenhower announced May 8 that U.S. had given France $60 million for Indochina War. More aid was announced in Sept. In 1954 it was reported that three fourths of the war's costs were met by U.S.

1954

Nautilus, first atomic-powered submarine, was launched at Groton, Conn. Jan. 21.

Five members of Congress were wounded in the House Mar. 1 by 4 Puerto Rican independence supporters who fired at random from a spectators' gallery.

Sen. Joseph McCarthy led televised hearings Apr. 22-June 17 into alleged Communist influence in the Army.

Racial segregation in public schools was unanimously ruled unconstitutional by the Supreme Court May 17, as a violation of the 14th Amendment clause guaranteeing equal protection of the laws.

Southeast Asia Treaty Organization (SEATO) formed by collective defense pact signed in Manila Sept. 8 by the U.S., Britain, France, Australia, New Zealand, Philippines, Pakistan, and Thailand.

Condemnation of Sen. Joseph R. McCarthy (R., Wis.) voted by Senate, 67-22 Dec. 2 for contempt of a Senate elections subcommittee, for abuse of its members, and for insults to the Senate during his Army investigation hearings.

1955

U.S. agreed Feb. 12 to help train South Vietnamese army.

Supreme Court ordered "all deliberate speed" in integration of public schools May 31.

A summit meeting of leaders of U.S., Britain, France, and USSR took place July 18-23 in Geneva, Switzerland.

Rosa Parks refused Dec. 1 to give her seat to a white man on a bus in Montgomery, Ala. Bus segregation ordinance declared unconstitutional by a federal court following boycott and NAACP protest.

Merger of America's 2 largest labor organizations was effected Dec. 5 under the name American Federation of Labor and Congress of Industrial Organizations. The merged AFL-CIO had a membership estimated at 15 million.

1956

Massive resistance to Supreme Court desegregation rulings was called for Mar. 12 by 101 Southern congressmen.

Federal-Aid Highway Act signed June 29, inaugurating interstate highway system.

First transatlantic telephone cable went into operation Sept. 25.

1957

Congress approved first civil rights bill for blacks since Reconstruction Apr. 29, to protect voting rights.

National Guardsmen, called out by Arkansas Gov. Orval Faubus Sept. 4, barred 9 black students from entering previously all-white Central High School in Little Rock. Faubus complied Sept. 21 with a federal court order to remove the National Guardsmen. The blacks entered school Sept. 23 but were ordered to withdraw by local authorities because of fear of mob violence. Pres. Eisenhower sent federal troops Sept. 24 to enforce the court's order.

Jack Kerouac published On the Road.

1958

First U.S. earth satellite to go into orbit, Explorer I, launched by Army Jan. 31 at Cape Canaveral, Fla.; discovered Van Allen radiation belt.

Five thousand U.S. Marines sent to Lebanon to protect elected government from threatened overthrow July-Oct.

First domestic jet airline passenger service in U.S. opened by National Airlines Dec. 10 between N.Y. and Miami.

1959

Alaska admitted as 49th state Jan. 3; Hawaii admitted Aug. 21.

St. Lawrence Seaway opened Apr. 25.

The George Washington, first U.S. ballistic-missile submarine, launched at Groton, Conn. June 9.

N.S. Savannah, world's first atomic-powered merchant ship, launched July 21 at Camden, N.J.

Soviet Premier Khrushchev paid unprecedented visit to U.S. Sept. 15-27, made transcontinental tour.

1960

Sit-ins began Feb. 1 when 4 black college students in Greensboro, N.C. refused to move from a Woolworth lunch counter when denied service. By Sept. 1961 more than 70,000 students, whites and blacks, had participated in sit-ins.

U.S. launched first weather satellite, Tiros I, Apr. 1.

Congress approved a strong voting rights act Apr. 21.

A U-2 reconnaisance plane of the U.S. was shot down in the Soviet Union May 1. The incident led to cancellation of an imminent Paris summit conference.

Mobs attacked U.S. embassy in Panama Sept. 17 in dispute over flying of U.S. and Panamanian flags.

U.S. announced Dec. 15 it backed rightist group in Laos, which took power the next day.

1961

The U.S. severed diplomatic and consular relations with Cuba Jan. 3, after disputes over nationalizations of U.S. firms, U.S. military presence at Guantanamo base, etc.

Invasion of Cuba's "Bay of Pigs" Apr. 17 by Cuban exiles trained, armed, and directed by the U.S., attempting to overthrow the regime of Premier Fidel Castro, was repulsed.

Commander Alan B. Shepard Jr. was rocketed from Cape Canaveral, Fla., 116.5 mi. above the earth in a Mercury capsule May 5 in the first U.S. manned sub-orbital space flight.

1962

Lt. Col. John H. Glenn Jr. became the first American in orbit Feb. 20 when he circled the earth 3 times in the Mercury capsule Friendship 7.

Pres. Kennedy said Feb. 14 U.S. military advisers in Vietnam would fire if fired upon.

Supreme Court Mar. 26 backed one-man one-vote apportionment of seats in state legislatures.

First U.S. communications satellite launched in July.

James Meredith became first black student at Univ. of Mississippi Oct. 1 after 3,000 troops put down riots.

A Soviet offensive missile buildup in Cuba was revealed Oct. 22 by Pres. Kennedy, who ordered a naval and air quarantine on shipment of offensive military equipment to the island. Kennedy and Soviet Premier Khrushchev reached agreement Oct. 28 on a formula to end the crisis.

Kennedy announced Nov. 2 that Soviet missile bases in Cuba were being dismantled.

Rachel Carson's *Silent Spring* launched environmentalist movement.

1963

Supreme Court ruled Mar. 18 that all **criminal defendants** must have counsel and that illegally acquired evidence was not admissible in state as well as federal courts.

Supreme Court ruled, 8-1, **June** 17 that laws requiring **recitation of the Lord's Prayer** or Bible verses in public schools were unconstitutional.

A limited **nuclear test-ban treaty** was agreed upon **July** 25 by the U.S., Soviet Union and Britain, barring all nuclear tests except underground.

Washington demonstration by 200,000 persons **Aug. 28** in support of **black demands** for equal rights. Highlight was speech in which Dr. Martin Luther King said: "I have a dream that this nation will rise up and live out the true meaning of its creed, 'We hold these truths to be self-evident: that all men are created equal.' "

South Vietnam Pres. Ngo Dinh Diem assassinated Nov. 2; U.S. had earlier withdrawn support.

Pres. **John F. Kennedy was shot** and fatally wounded by an assassin Nov. 22 as he rode in a motorcade through downtown Dallas, Tex. Vice Pres. Lyndon B. Johnson was inaugurated president shortly after in Dallas. Lee Harvey Oswald was arrested and charged with the murder. Oswald was shot and fatally wounded Nov. 24 by Jack Ruby, 52, a Dallas nightclub owner, who was convicted of murder Mar. 14, 1964 and sentenced to death. Ruby died of natural causes Jan. 3, 1967 while awaiting retrial.

U.S. troops in Vietnam totalled over 15,000 by year-end; aid to South Vietnam was over $500 million in 1963.

1964

Panama suspended relations with U.S. Jan. 9 after riots. U.S. offered Dec. 18 to negotiate a new canal treaty.

Supreme Court ordered Feb. 17 that **congressional districts** have equal populations.

U.S. reported May 27 it was sending military planes to Laos.

Omnibus **civil rights bill** passed June 29 banning discrimination in voting, jobs, public accommodations, etc.

Three **civil rights workers** were reported missing in Mississippi June 22; found buried Aug. 4. Twenty-one white men were arrested. On Oct. 20, 1967, an all-white federal jury convicted 7 of conspiracy in the slayings.

U.S. Congress Aug. 7 passed **Tonkin Resolution,** authorizing presidential action in Vietnam, after North Vietnam boats reportedly attacked 2 U.S. destroyers Aug. 2.

Congress approved War on Poverty bill Aug. 11.

The **Warren Commission** released Sept. 27 a report concluding that Lee Harvey Oswald was solely responsible for the Kennedy assassination.

1965

Pres. Johnson in Feb. ordered continuous bombing of North Vietnam below 20th parallel.

Some 14,000 U.S. troops sent to **Dominican Republic** during civil war Apr. 28. All troops withdrawn by next year.

New **Voting Rights Act** signed Aug. 6.

Los Angeles riot by blacks living in Watts area resulted in death of 34 persons and property damage est. at $200 million Aug. 11-16.

Water Quality Act passed Sept. 21 to meet pollution, shortage problems.

National origins quota system of **immigration** abolished Oct. 3.

Electric power failure blacked out most of northeastern U.S., parts of 2 Canadian provinces the night of Nov. 9-10.

U.S. forces in **S. Vietnam** reached 184,300 by year-end.

1966

U.S. forces began firing into Cambodia May 1.

Bombing of **Hanoi** area of North Vietnam by U.S. planes began **June 29.** By Dec. 31, 385,300 U.S. troops were stationed in South Vietnam, plus 60,000 offshore and 33,000 in Thailand.

Medicare, government program to pay part of the medical expenses of citizens over 65, began **July 1.**

Edward Brooke (R, Mass.) elected **Nov. 8** as first black U.S. senator in 85 years.

1967

Black representative **Adam Clayton Powell** (D, N.Y.) was denied Mar. 1 his seat in Congress because of charges he misused govt. funds. Reelected in 1968, he was seated, but fined $25,000 and stripped of his 22 years' seniority.

Pres. Johnson and Soviet Premier Aleksei Kosygin met June 23 and 25 at Glassboro State College in N.J.; agreed not to let any crisis push them into war.

Black riots in Newark, N.J. July 12-17 killed 26, injured 1,500; over 1,000 arrested. In Detroit, Mich., July 23-30 at least 40 died; 2,000 injured, 5,000 left homeless by rioting, looting, burning in city's black ghetto. Quelled by 4,700 federal paratroopers and 8,000 National Guardsmen.

Thurgood Marshall sworn in Oct. 2 as first black U.S. Supreme Court Justice. Carl B. Stokes (D, Cleveland) and Richard G. Hatcher (D, Gary, Ind.) were elected first black mayors of major U.S. cities Nov. 7.

By December 475,000 U.S. troops were in South Vietnam, all North Vietnam was subject to bombing. Protests against the war mounted in U.S. during year.

1968

USS **Pueblo** and 83-man crew seized in Sea of Japan Jan. 23 by North Koreans; 82 men released Dec. 22.

"Tet offensive": Communist troops attacked Saigon, 30 province capitals Jan. 30, suffer heavy casualties.

Pres. Johnson curbed bombing of North Vietnam Mar. 31. Peace talks began in Paris May 10. All bombing of North halted Oct. 31.

Martin Luther King Jr., 39, assassinated Apr. 4 in Memphis, Tenn. James Earl Ray, an escaped convict, pleaded guilty to the slaying, was sentenced to 99 years.

Sen. Robert F. Kennedy (D, N.Y.) 42, shot June 5 in Hotel Ambassador, Los Angeles, after celebrating presidential primary victories. Died June 6. Sirhan Bishara Sirhan, Jordanian, convicted of murder.

Rep. Shirley Chisholm (D., N.Y.) became the first black woman elected to Congress.

1969

Expanded four-party **Vietnam peace talks** began Jan. 18. U.S. force peaked at 543,400 in April. Withdrawal started July 8. Pres. Nixon set Vietnamization policy Nov. 3.

U.S. astronaut Neil A. Armstrong, 38, commander of the Apollo 11 mission, became the first man to **set foot on the moon** July 20. Air Force Col. Edwin E. Aldrin Jr. accompanied Armstrong.

Anti-Vietnam War demonstrations reached peak in U.S.; some 250,000 marched in Washington, D.C. Nov. 15.

Massacre of hundreds of civilians at Mylai, South Vietnam in 1968 incident was reported Nov. 16.

1970

United Mine Workers official Joseph A. Yablonski, his wife, and their daughter were found shot Jan. 5 in their Clarksville, Pa. home. UMW chief W. A. (Tony) Boyle was later convicted of the killing.

A federal jury Feb. 18 found the "Chicago 7" innocent of conspiring to incite riots during the 1968 Democratic National Convention. However, 5 were convicted of crossing state lines with intent to incite riots.

Millions of Americans participated in anti-pollution demonstrations Apr. 22 to mark the first Earth Day.

U.S. and South Vietnamese forces crossed **Cambodian** borders Apr. 30 to get at enemy bases. Four students were killed May 4 at Kent St. Univ. in Ohio by National Guardsmen during a protest against the war.

Two women generals, the first in U.S. history, were named by Pres. Nixon May 15.

A postal reform measure was signed Aug. 12, creating an independent U.S. Postal Service, thus relinquishing governmental control of the U.S. mails after almost 2 centuries.

1971

Charles Manson, 36, and 3 of his followers were found guilty Jan. 26 of first-degree murder in the 1969 slaying of actress Sharon Tate and 6 others.

U.S. air and artillery forces aided a 44-day incursion by South Vietnam forces into Laos starting Feb. 8.

A Constitutional Amendment lowering the voting age to 18 in all elections was approved in the Senate by a vote of 94-0 Mar. 10. The proposed 26th Amendment got House approval by a 400-19 vote Mar. 23. Thirty-eighth state ratified June 30.

A court-martial jury Mar. 29, convicted Lt. William L. Calley Jr. of premeditated murder of 22 South Vietnamese at Mylai on Mar. 16, 1968. He was sentenced to life imprisonment Mar. 31. Sentence was reduced to 20 years Aug. 20.

Publication of classified Pentagon papers on the U.S. involvement in Vietnam was begun June 13 by the New York Times. In a 6-3 vote, the U.S. Supreme Court June 30 upheld the right of the Times and the Washington Post to publish the documents under the protection of the First Amendment.

1972

Pres. Nixon arrived in Peking Feb. 21 for an 8-day visit to China, which he called a "journey for peace." The unprecedented visit ended with a joint communique pledging that both powers would work for "a normalization of relations."

By a vote of 84 to 8, the Senate approved Mar. 22 a Constitutional Amendment banning discrimination against women because of their sex and sent the measure to the states for ratification.

North Vietnamese forces launched the biggest attacks in 4 years across the demilitarized zone Mar. 30. The U.S. responded Apr. 15 by resumption of bombing of Hanoi and Haiphong after a 4-year lull.

Nixon announced May 8 the mining of North Vietnam ports. Last U.S. combat troops left Aug. 11.

Alabama Gov. George C. Wallace, campaigning at a Laurel, Md. shopping center May 15, was shot and seriously wounded as he greeted a large crowd. Arthur H. Bremer, 21, was sentenced Aug. 4 to 63 years for shooting Wallace and 3 bystanders.

In the first visit of a U.S. president to Moscow, Nixon arrived May 22 for a week of summit talks with Kremlin leaders which culminated in a landmark strategic arms pact.

Five men were arrested June 17 for breaking into the offices of the Democratic National Committee in the Watergate office complex in Washington, D.C.

The White House announced July 8 that the U.S. would sell to the USSR at least $750 million of American wheat, corn, and other grains over a period of 3 years.

U.S. bombers struck massively in North Vietnam for 5 days starting Dec. 26, in retaliation for alleged violations of agreements reached prior to the 1968 bombing halt. U.S. forces at year-end were down to 140,000.

1973

Five of seven defendants in the Watergate break-in trial pleaded guilty Jan. 11 and 15, and the other 2 were convicted Jan. 30.

The Supreme Court ruled 7-2, Jan. 22, that a state may not prevent a woman from having an abortion during the first 6 months of pregnancy, invalidating abortion laws in Texas and Georgia, and, by implication, overturning restrictive abortion laws in 44 other states.

Four-party Vietnam peace pacts were signed in Paris Jan. 27, and North Vietnam released some 590 U.S. prisoners by Apr. 1. Last U.S. troops left Mar. 29.

The end of the military draft was announced Jan. 27.

China and the U.S. agreed Feb. 22 to set up permanent liaison offices in each other's country.

Top Nixon aides H.R. Haldeman, John D. Ehrlichman, and John W. Dean, and Attorney General Richard Klein-

dienst resigned Apr. 30 amid charges of White House efforts to obstruct justice in the Watergate case.

The Senate Armed Services Committee July 16 began a probe into allegations that the U.S. Air Force had made 3,500 secret B-52 raids into Cambodia in 1969 and 1970.

John Dean, former Nixon counsel, told Senate hearings June 25 that Nixon, his staff and campaign aides, and the Justice Department all had conspired to cover up Watergate facts. Nixon refused July 23 to release tapes of relevant White House conversations. Some tapes were turned over to the court Nov. 26.

The U.S. officially ceased bombing in Cambodia at midnight Aug. 14 in accord with a June Congressional action.

Vice Pres. Spiro T. Agnew Oct. 10 resigned and pleaded "nolo contendere" (no contest) to charges of tax evasion on payments made to him by Maryland contractors when he was governor of that state. Gerald Rudolph Ford Oct. 12 became first appointed vice president under the 25th Amendment; sworn in Dec. 6.

A total ban on oil exports to the U.S. was imposed by Arab oil-producing nations Oct. 19-21 after the outbreak of an Arab-Israeli war. The ban was lifted Mar. 18, 1974.

Atty. Gen. Elliot Richardson resigned, and his deputy William D. Ruckelshaus and Watergate Special Prosecutor Archibald Cox were fired by Pres. Nixon Oct. 20 when Cox threatened to secure a judicial ruling that Nixon was violating a court order to turn tapes over to Watergate case Judge John Sirica.

Leon Jaworski, conservative Texas Democrat, was named Nov. 1 by the Nixon administration to be special prosecutor to succeed Archibald Cox.

Congress overrode Nov. 7 Nixon's veto of the war powers bill which curbed the president's power to commit armed forces to hostilities abroad without Congressional approval.

1974

Impeachment hearings were opened May 9 against Nixon by the House Judiciary Committee.

John D. Ehrlichman and 3 White House "plumbers" were found guilty July 12 of conspiring to violate the civil rights of Dr. Lewis Fielding, formerly psychiatrist to Pentagon Papers leaker Daniel Ellsberg, by breaking into his Beverly Hills, Cal. office.

The U.S. Supreme Court ruled, 8-0, July 24 that Nixon had to turn over 64 tapes of White House conversations sought by Watergate Special Prosecutor Leon Jaworski.

The House Judiciary Committee, in televised hearings July 24-30, recommended 3 articles of impeachment against Nixon. The first, voted 27-11 July 27, charged Nixon with taking part in a criminal conspiracy to obstruct justice in the Watergate cover-up. The second, voted 28-10 July 29, charged he "repeatedly" failed to carry out his constitutional oath in a series of alleged abuses of power. The third, voted 27-17 July 30, accused him of unconstitutional defiance of committee subpoenas. The House of Representatives voted without debate Aug. 20, by 412-3, to accept the committee report, which included the recommended impeachment articles.

Nixon resigned Aug. 9. His support began eroding Aug. 5 when he released 3 tapes, admitting he originated plans to have the FBI stop its probe of the Watergate break-in for political as well as national security reasons. Vice President Gerald R. Ford was sworn in as the 38th U.S. president on Aug. 9.

An unconditional pardon to ex-Pres. Nixon for all federal crimes that he "committed or may have committed" while president was issued by Pres. Gerald Ford Sept. 8.

1975

Found guilty of Watergate cover-up charges Jan. 1 were ex-Atty. Gen. John N. Mitchell, ex-presidential advisers H.R. Haldeman and John D. Ehrlichman.

U.S. civilians were evacuated from Saigon Apr. 29 as communist forces completed takeover of South Vietnam.

U.S. merchant ship Mayaguez and crew of 39 seized by Cambodian forces in Gulf of Siam May 12. In rescue operation, U.S. Marines attacked Tang Is., planes bombed air base; Cambodia surrendered ship and crew.

Congress voted $405 million for South Vietnam refugees May 16; 140,000 were flown to the U.S,

Illegal CIA operations, including records on 300,000 persons and groups, and infiltration of agents into black, antiwar and political movements, were described by a "blue-ribbon" panel headed by Vice Pres. Rockefeller June 10.

FBI agents captured Patricia (Patty) Hearst, kidnaped Feb. 4, 1974, in San Francisco Sept. 18 with others. She was indicted for bank robbery; a San Francisco jury convicted her Mar. 20, 1976.

1976

Payments abroad of $22 million in bribes by Lockheed Aircraft Corp. to sell its planes were revealed Feb. 4 by a Senate subcommittee. Lockheed admitted payments in Japan, Turkey, Italy, and Holland.

The U.S. celebrated its Bicentennial July 4, marking the 200th anniversary of its independence with festivals, parades, and N.Y. City's Operation Sail, a gathering of tall ships from around the world viewed by 6 million persons.

A mystery ailment "legionnaire's disease" killed 29 persons who attended an American Legion convention July 21-24 in Philadelphia. The cause was found to be a bacterium, it was reported June 18, 1977.

The Viking II set down on Mars' Utopia Plains Sept. 3, following the successful landing by Viking I July 20.

1977

Pres. Jimmy Carter Jan. 21 pardoned most Vietnam War draft evaders, who numbered some 10,000.

Convicted murderer Gary Gilmore was executed by a Utah firing squad Jan. 17, in the first exercise of capital punishment anywhere in the U.S. since 1967. Gilmore had opposed all attempts to delay the execution.

Carter signed an act Aug. 4 creating a new Cabinet-level Energy Department.

1978

U.S. Senate voted Apr. 18 to turn over the Panama Canal to Panama on Dec. 31, 1999; Mar. 16 vote had given approval to a treaty guaranteeing the area's neutrality after the year 2000.

The U.S. Supreme Court June 28 voted 5-4 not to allow a firm quota system in affirmative action plans; the Court did uphold programs that were more "flexible" in nature.

The House Select Committee on Assassinations opened hearings Sept. 6 into assassinations of Pres. Kennedy and Martin Luther King Jr.; the committee recessed Dec. 30 after concluding conspiracies likely in both cases, but with no further hard evidence for further prosecutions.

Congress passed the Humphrey-Hawkins "full employment" Bill Oct. 15, which set national goal of reducing unemployment to 4% by 1983, while reducing inflation to 3% in same period; Pres. Carter signed bill, Oct. 27.

1979

A major accident occurred, Mar. 28, at a nuclear reactor on Three Mile Island near Middletown, Pa.

The federal government announced, Nov. 1, a $1.5 billion loan-guarantee plan to aid the nation's 3d largest automaker, Chrysler Corp., which had reported a loss of $460.6 million for the 3d quarter of 1979.

Some 90 people, including 63 Americans, were taken hostage, Nov. 4, at the American embassy in Teheran, Iran, by militant student followers of Ayatollah Khomeini who demanded the return of former Shah Mohammad Reza Pahlavi, who was undergoing medical treatment in New York City.

1980

Pres. Carter announced, Jan. 4, punitive measures against the USSR, inc. an embargo on the sale of grain and high technology, in retaliation for the Soviet invasion of Afghanistan. At Carter's request, the U.S. Olympic Committee voted, Apr. 12, not to attend the Moscow Summer Olympics.

Eight Americans were killed and 5 wounded, Apr. 24, in an ill-fated attempt to rescue the hostages held by Iranian militants at the U.S. Embassy in Teheran.

In Washington, Mt. St. Helens erupted, May 18, in a violent blast estimated to be 500 times as powerful as the Hiroshima atomic bomb. The blast, followed by others on May 25 and June 12, left about 60 dead, and economic losses estimated at nearly $3 billion.

In a sweeping victory, Nov. 4, Ronald Wilson Reagan was elected 40th President of the United States, defeating incumbent Jimmy Carter. The stunning GOP victory extended to the U.S. Congress where Republicans gained control of the Senate and wrested 33 House seats from the Democrats.

Former Beatle John Lennon was shot and killed, Dec. 8, outside his apartment building in New York City.

1981

Minutes after the inauguration of Pres. Ronald Reagan, Jan. 20, the 52 Americans who had been held hostage in Iran for 444 days were flown to freedom following an agreement in which the U.S. agreed to return to Iran $8 billion in frozen assets.

President Reagan was shot in the chest by a would-be assassin, Mar. 30, in Washington, D.C., as he walked to his limousine following an address.

The world's first reusable spacecraft, the Space Shuttle Columbia, was sent into space, Apr. 12, and completed its successful mission 2 days later.

Both houses of Congress passed, July 29, President Reagan's tax-cut legislation. The largest tax cut in the nation's history was expected to reduce taxes by $37.6 bln. in fiscal 1982, and to save taxpayers $750 bln. over the next 5 years.

Federal air traffic controllers, Aug. 3, began an illegal nationwide strike after their union rejected the government's final offer for a new contract. Most of the 13,000 striking controllers defied the back-to-work order, and were dismissed by President Reagan Aug. 5.

In a 99-0 vote, the Senate confirmed, Sept. 21, the appointment of Sandra Day O'Connor as an associate justice of the U.S. Supreme Court. She was the first woman appointed to that body.

President Reagan ordered sanctions against the new Polish military government, Dec. 23, in response to the imposition of martial law in that country.

1982

The 13-year-old lawsuit against AT&T by the Justice Dept. was settled Jan. 8. AT&T agreed to give up the 22 Bell System companies but in return was allowed to expand into previously prohibited areas inc. data processing, telephone and computer equipment sales, and computer communication devices.

On Mar. 2, the Senate voted 57-37 for a bill that virtually eliminated busing for the purposes of racial integration.

On June 12, in N.Y.'s Central Park, hundreds of thousands demonstrated against nuclear arms.

The Equal Rights Amendment was defeated after a 10-year struggle for ratification.

The elections on Nov. 2 resulted in gains for the Democrats—the margin in the new House was 269-166. In the Senate elections, Democrats won 20 out of 33 seats, but were still the minority, 54-46.

The highest unemployment rate since 1940, 10.4%, was reported on Nov. 5. The rate for Nov. reached 10.8%, with over 11 million unemployed.

Lech Walesa, former leader of Solidarity, the Polish labor union, was freed Nov. 13, after 11 months of internment following the imposition of martial law and the outlawing of Solidarity. Pres. Reagan lifted the U.S. embargo on sales of oil and gas equipment to the Soviet Union.

The Space Shuttle Columbia completed its first operational flight Nov. 16.

A retired dentist, Dr. Barney B. Clark, 61, became the first recipient of a permanent artificial heart during a 7½ hour operation in Salt Lake City Dec. 2. The heart was designed by Dr. Robert Jarvik, also on the surgical team.

1983

On Apr. 20, Pres. Reagan signed a compromise, bipartisan bill designed to rescue the Social Security System from bankruptcy.

In an 8-1 decision, the U.S. Supreme Court held, May 24, that the Internal Revenue Service could deny tax exemptions to private schools that practiced racial discrimination.

Sally Ride became the first American woman to travel in space, June 18, when the space shuttle Challenger was launched from Cape Canaveral, Fla.

On Oct. 23, 241 U.S. Marines and sailors, members of the multinational peacekeeping force in Lebanon, were killed when a TNT-laden suicide terrorist blew up Marine headquarters at Beirut Intl. Airport. Almost simultaneously, a second truck bomb blew up a French paratroop barracks two miles away, killing more than 40.

U.S. Marines and Rangers and a small force from 6 Caribbean nations invaded the island of Grenada on Oct. 25, in response to a request from the Organization of Eastern Caribbean States. After a few days, Grenadian militia and Cuban "construction workers" were overcome, hundreds of U.S. citizens evacuated safely, and the Marxist regime deposed. The U.S. Congress applied the War Powers Resolution, requiring U.S. troops to leave Grenada by Dec. 24.

1984

In his State of the Union address, Jan. 25, Pres. Reagan called for budget cuts of $100 billion over 3 years, but opposed increased taxes.

On Feb. 26, as the position of Pres. Amin Gemayel of Lebanon deteriorated and his army crumbled, Pres. Reagan removed U.S. Marines from Beirut and placed them on U.S. ships offshore.

The space shuttle Challenger was launched on its 4th trip into space, Feb. 3. On Feb. 7, Navy Capt. Bruce McCandless, followed by Army Lt. Colonel Robert Stewart, became the first humans to fly free of a spacecraft.

During March, the U.S. Senate rejected 2 Constitutional amendments that would have permitted prayer in the public schools.

The Central Intelligence Agency (CIA) acknowledged in April that it had participated in the mining of Nicaraguan harbors. This touched off a controversy in Congress, and the Senate, Apr. 10, adopted a nonbinding resolution condemning U.S. participation in the mining.

From Apr. 26 to May 1, Pres. Reagan visited China for the first time, holding discussions with Chinese leaders.

On May 7, American veterans of the Vietnam war reached an out-of-court settlement with 7 chemical companies in their class-action suit the herbicide Agent Orange.

A federal judge in Salt Lake City held, May 10, that the U.S. government had been negligent in its above-ground testing of nuclear weapons in Nevada from 1951 to 1962.

On June 6, former vice president Walter Mondale claimed victory in his struggle with Sen. Gary Hart for the Democratic presidental nomination. In a historic move, July 12, Mondale chose a woman, Rep. Geraldine Ferraro (N.Y.) to run with him as candidate for vice president.

Pres. Reagan, Aug. 11, signed a law prohibiting public high schools from barring students who wished to assemble for religious or political activities outside of school hours.

1985

The controversial MX missile survived critical votes in the Senate and House. The Senate, on Mar. 19 and 21, voted to authorize the missiles and then to appropriate $1.5 million for the construction of 21 missiles. The House gave its endorsement Mar. 26 and 28.

E.F. Hutton, one of the nation's largest brokerage companies, pleaded guilty, May 2, to 2,000 federal charges related to the manipulation of its checking accounts. The company agreed to pay $2 million in fines and to pay back up to $8 million to banks it had defrauded.

"Live Aid," a 17-hour rock concert broadcast July 13 on radio and TV from London and Phila. to 152 countries, raised $70 million for the starving peoples of Africa.

On Oct. 7, 5 hijackers seized an Italian cruise ship, the Achille Lauro, in the open sea as it approached Port Said, Egypt. Some 400 persons were aboard, including about 340 crew. The hijackers, members of the Palestine Liberation Front, a faction broken from the PLO, demanded the release of 50 Palestinians held by Israel. On Oct. 9, Egypt said the hijackers had surrendered to a PLO representative and would be given safe conduct from Egypt. Italy then announced that a 69-year-old, wheelchair-bound American had been shot to death and thrown overboard. On Oct. 10, Egyptian Pres. Hosni Mubarek said the hijackers were in the hands of the PLO. However, they did not actually leave Egypt until that evening. The Reagan administration ordered the Egyptian plane intercepted in international air space, and Navy F-14 fighter jets forced the plane to land in Sicily.

In November, for the first time in 6 years, the leaders of the U.S. and the Soviet Union met at a summit conference. In Geneva, Switzerland, Pres. Reagan and Mikhail Gorbachev, the general secretary of the Soviet Communist Party, talked privately for 5 hours, Nov. 19 and 20, which Pres. Reagan called "fresh start."

Congress passed a compromise Gramm-Rudman bill, Dec. 11, that was a last-ditch effort to end the huge federal deficit. Signed by Pres. Reagan Dec. 12, it was expected to require an initial $11.7 billion reduction in the fiscal 1986 budget deficit, then 4 reductions in equal amounts until a balanced budget was achieved in 1991.

The biggest corporate merger yet, outside the oil industry, was announced Dec. 11, when General Electric Corp. agreed to buy RCA Corp. for $6.28 billion.

1986

On Jan. 20, for the 1st time, the U.S. officially observed Martin Luther King Day.

Moments after liftoff, Jan. 28, the space shuttle Challenger exploded, killing 6 astronauts and Christa McAuliffe, a New Hampshire teacher. Subsequent investigations found that NASA had abandoned "good judgment and common sense" regarding safety problems that caused the explosion.

U.S. warplanes struck targets in Tripoli and Benghazi, Libya, Apr. 14—retaliation against the Libyan bombing of a W. Berlin disco that killed 2, injured 200, Apr. 5. On Jan. 7, Pres. Reagan had said that the U.S. had aborted 26 "terrorist missions" in 1985. In an executive order, he banned trade with and travel to Libya, ordering Americans out. A 2nd executive order, Jan. 8, had frozen all Libyan government assets in the U.S. and U.S. bank branches abroad.

U.S. officials said, June 12, that AIDS cases and deaths would increase tenfold in the next 5 years. At that time, the government had recorded 21,517 cases, 11,713 deaths. An anti-viral drug, azidothymidine (AZT) was found to improve the health of some AIDS patient, but was not a cure.

Because of the mounting abuse of illegal drugs in the U.S., specifically cocaine as "crack," Congress passed anti-drug laws and the U.S. joined Bolivia in raids against cocaine processing hideouts.

The Supreme Court, July 7, found a key provision of the Gramm-Rudman "balanced budget" law unconstitutional.

The U.S., via Congress's Sept. override of Pres. Reagan's veto, joined other nations in imposing economic sanctions on So. Africa, pressuring the Botha gvt. to end apartheid.

The U.S. Senate confirmed, Sept. 17, Pres. Reagan's nomination of William Rehnquist as chief justice, Antonin Scalia as associate justice of the Supreme Court.

Congress passed, in late Sept., the comprehensive Tax Reform Law. In effect in 1987, it simplified the system, drastically changing tax brackets, deductions, and more.

The U.S. and USSR reached tentative agreement on a world-wide ban of medium-range missiles, Sept. 18. But hopes of reducing strategic long-range missiles ended in Iceland in Oct., when Gorbachev called for a limit on the development of "Star Wars," and Reagan refused it.

One day before the 1986 Congressional elections, it was reported that the U.S. had sent spare parts and ammunition to Iran. Over the next months it was revealed that additional arms sales had been made to Iran, and profits diverted to a fund for Nicaraguan contras. This brought on the worst crisis in the Reagan administration.

In the Congressional races, Nov. 4, Democrats won a 55-45 Senate majority, after 6 yrs. of a Republican majority, and enlarged their House majority by 5, to 258-177.

The most scandalous year in Wall Street history ended with Ivan Boesky's agreeing, Nov. 14, to plead guilty to an unspecified criminal count, pay a $100 million fine, and return profits; he was barred for life from trading securities.

1987

Pres. Reagan produced the nation's first trillion-dollar budget, Jan. 5.

The stock market continued its phenomenal rise. The Dow closed at 2002.25, Jan. 8, its first finish above 2000. The Dow advanced for 13 consecutive trading days, another record; Jan. 20; the average soared 51.60 points, Jan. 22, a one-day record. At month's end, the cumulative advance was more than 250 points, yet another record.

Condom ads became prominent in the U.S. media in Jan., reflecting concern for "safe sex" to prevent AIDS.

The Tower Commission Report, Feb. 27, found Pres. Reagan confused and uninformed; and further faulted White House Chief of Staff Donald Regan; former Natl. Security Adviser Robert McFarlane; his successor Adm. John Poindexter; and CIA Director William Casey. Casey had resigned, Feb. 2, on doctors' discovery of a brain tumor; McFarlane attempted suicide, Feb. 9; Regan resigned, Feb. 27.

An Iraqi warplane missile killed 37 sailors on the frigate U.S.S. Stark in the Persian Gulf, May 27. Iraq called it an accident. The Stark's officers were found negligent, June 14. The U.S. escorted Kuwaiti oil tankers to the Gulf, reflagging them for the U.S.

Public hearings by the Senate and House committees investigating the Iran-contra affair went on from May-Aug. Former CIA Director Casey died, May 6, 5 months after brain surgery; Lt. Col. Oliver North, a media sensation, said he had believed all his activities authorized by his superiors; Poindexter said his own purpose had been "to provide some future deniability for the president . . ."; Shultz said Casey, McFarlane, and Poindexter had lied to him and deceived Pres. Reagan. Pres. Reagan, Aug. 12, said he had been "stubborn in pursuit of a policy that went astray," but again denied knowing of the funds' diversion to the contras.

Wall Street crashed, Oct. 19, the Dow plummeting a record 508 points—22.6 percent—after a record high of 2722.42, Aug. 25; a 200-point drop by Oct., called a correction by most; and drops of 91.55, Oct. 6; 95.46, Oct. 14; and 108.36, Oct. 16.

The Senate, Oct. 23, rejected Pres. Reagan's nomination of Robert Bork to the Supreme Court. The Judiciary Committee, Oct. 15, had found Bork unfit, due to insensitivity to individual rights and liberties. The 58-42 vote was the biggest margin of rejection for the position in history.

Pres. Reagan and Soviet leader Gorbachev met in Wash., Dec. 8, and signed an unprecedented agreement calling for the dismantling of all 1,752 U.S. and 859 Soviet missiles with a 300-3,400-mile range. The leaders agreed to meet in Moscow in 1988.

1988

Federal grand juries in Miami and Tampa returned indictments, Feb. 4, against Gen. Manuel Noriega, the effective ruler of Panama, charging that he had protected and otherwise assisted the Medellin drug cartel, linked to 80 percent of the cocaine smuggled into the U.S. Attempts by the U.S. to oust Noriega plunged Panama into political and economic turmoil.

Nearly 1.4 million illegal aliens met the May 4 deadline for applying for amnesty under a U.S. Immigration and Naturalization Service policy. It was estimated that more than half the applications were in Calif., and that, nation-wide, about 71 percent of the aliens had entered the U.S. from Mexico.

Congress approved, in June, the greatest expansion ever of Medicare benefits, by protecting the elderly and disabled against "catastrophic" medical costs. Beneficiaries would bear the cost, estimated at more than $32 billion in 5 years.

Much of the U.S. suffered the worst drought in more than 50 years, during the spring, with the northern Great Plains and Southeast especially hard-hit. By June 23, one-half of the nation's agricultural counties had been designated disaster areas.

A missile, fired from the U.S. Navy warship Vincennes, in the Persian Gulf, struck and destroyed a commercial Iranian airliner, July 3, killing all 290 persons on the plane. Navy personnel had mistaken the airliner for an Iranian F-14 jet fighter. Although the Pentagon first said that the plane was outside its designated commercial air corridor, headed directly for the Vincennes, and descending, this was subsequently disproven.

Fire destroyed about 4 million acres of forest land throughout the west, including Alaska, during the late summer. Property damage was also considerable.

Failures at nuclear-power plants posed problems across the U.S., according to congressional testimony, starting Sept. 30. Problems cited including aging equipment, poor management and training, and lax safety standards.

George Bush, vice president under Ronald Reagan, was elected 41st U.S. president, Nov. 8. Bush defeated the Democratic nominee, Gov. Michael Dukakis (Mass.), by 54 to 46 percent of the popular vote, and 426 electoral votes to Dukakis's 112. Sen. Dan Quayle (Ind.) was the successful vice presidential nominee; Sen. Lloyd Bentsen (Tex.) was the Democratic nominee for v.p. Democrats continued to control both houses of Congress.

The securities co. Drexel Burnham Lambert agreed, Dec. 21, to plead guilty to 6 violations of federal law, inc. insider trading, stock manipulation, and falsified records; and to pay penalties of $650 million, by far the largest such settlement.

1989

The Labor Dept. reported, Jan. 6, that unemployment was 5.3%, a 14-year low, at the end of 1988. For the year as a whole, the economy grew at 3.8%, its strongest showing in 4 years.

Ronald Brown was elected chairman of the Democratic Natl. Committee, Feb. 10; he was the first black to lead a major American political party.

The largest oil spill in U.S. history occurred after the Exxon Valdez struck Bligh Reef in Alaska's Prince William Sound, Mar. 24. The off-course tanker was being piloted by the third mate instead of by the captain, Joseph Hazelwood. Exxon Corp. announced, Mar. 25, that it accepted full financial responsibility for the spill, initially estimated at 240,000 barrels, then announced, Mar. 28, that the spill could not be contained; as of Mar. 29, the spill extended 45 miles.

An officially-estimated 300,000 people marched in Washington, D.C., Apr. 9, advocating a woman's right to choose to have an abortion.

Former Natl. Security Council staff member Oliver North became the first person, May 4, convicted in a jury trial in connection with the Iran-contra scandal. The jury acquitted North on 9 charges, found him guilty of 3: aiding and abetting the obstruction of Congress; altering, destroying, removing, or concealing NSC documents; receiving as an illegal gratuity a $13,800 security system for his home. North received, July 6, a 3-year suspended prison sentence, 2 years' probation, a $150,000 fine, and an order to perform 1,200 hours of community service.

House speaker Jim Wright (D. Tex.), who faced 69 ethical charges, announced his resignation as speaker and from the House, May 31. Rep. Tony Coehlho (D. Calif.), also under scrutiny, announced his resignation as majority whip and from the House.

The **U.S. Supreme Court** announced, July 3, its 5-4 decision to put new **restraints** on a **woman's right to have an abortion,** although it did not overturn Roe v. Wade.

Jack Kemp, secy. of **Housing and Urban Development,** acknowledged, **July 11,** that an estimated **$2 billion** had been lost due to **fraud and mismanagement** during the tenure of his predecessor **Samuel Pierce.**

Legislation passed by Congress to **rescue the savings and loan industry** was signed into law, **Aug. 9,** by Pres. George Bush. The bill provided $166 billion over 10 years to close or merge insolvent S&Ls. The total cost was put at $400 billion over 30 years, most of which would be paid by taxpayers.

Army Gen. Colin Powell was nominated by Pres. Bush, Aug. 10, to serve as **chairman of the Joint Chiefs of Staff;** he became the first black to hold the post.

Hurricane Hugo swept through the Caribbean and into S. Carolina, **Sept. 21-22,** causing more than 50 deaths and immense property damage.

Stock prices, advancing fairly steadily since their big plunge in Oct. 1987, **suddenly fell again in Oct. 1989,** the Dow Jones dropping 190.58 points to a close of 2,569.26, the 2d highest one-day decline in points ever.

Minutes before the start of the 3d game of the 1989 World Series between the San Francisco Giants and the Oakland Athletics, **Oct. 17,** an **earthquake struck the San Francisco Bay area,** causing at least 59 deaths and massive property damage.

Figures in American Folklore

Johnny Appleseed: John Chapman, 1774-1845; according to legend, wandered through Ohio, Indiana, and W. Pennsylvania for 40 years, sowing seeds that produced the Midwest orchards.

P(hineas) T. Barnum: 1810-1891; showman known for extravagant ads and exhibits of "freaks," including Tom Thumb and the original Siamese Twins; his circus, "The Greatest Show on Earth," opened in 1871, in 1881 merged with its chief competitor to become Barnum & Bailey.

Judge Roy Bean: c. 1825-1903; frontier trader, cattle rustler, gambler, saloon keeper; in 1882 in Texas he named himself justice of the peace and set up court in his saloon, rendering unorthodox decisions with one law book and a six-shooter, wit, and common sense.

Billy the Kid: William H. Bonney, 1859-1881; range war gunman and cattle rustler accused of 21 murders, the first before he reached his teens.

Nellie Bly: Elizabeth Seaman, 1867-1922; *New York World* reporter who traveled around the world in 72 days, 6 hours, 11 minutes in 1889-90, beating the record of the fictional Phileas Fogg.

Bonnie & Clyde: Clyde Barrow, 1909-1934, and Bonnie Parker, 1910-1934; outlaws accused of 12 murders during a 2-year robbery spree in the Southwest.

Lizzie Borden: 1860-1927; 32-year-old spinster accused of killing her stepmother and father by hacking them with an ax; tried and found not guilty; she was popularly believed guilty.

Daniel Boone: 1734-1820; frontiersman who blazed the Wilderness Road and founded Boonesboro, Kentucky, which he helped defend against the Indians in 1779; many legendary adventures were disproved.

Jim Bowie: 1796-1836; frontiersman, soldier, and popular hero of the Texas Revolution, killed at the Alamo; either he or his brother Rezin invented the Bowie knife.

Diamond Jim Brady: James Buchanan Brady, 1856-1917; financier and bon vivant, noted for ample girth and lavish life-style.

John Brown: 1800-1859; abolitionist who led a raid on the federal arsenal at Harper's Ferry, Virginia, 1859; captured and tried for treason, his dignity and high moral tone in court won Northern sympathy and when convicted and hanged he became a martyr to the antislavery cause.

Buffalo Bill: William Cody, 1846-1917; army scout, buffalo hunter, Indian fighter, and showman who organized Buffalo Bill's Wild West Show, featuring fancy shooting, a buffalo hunt, Annie Oakley, and Chief Sitting Bull.

Paul Bunyan: legendary lumberjack of fantastic size and strength, the hero of many tall tales popular in the Western timber country.

Kit Carson: Christopher Carson, 1809-1868; frontiersman, soldier, and Indian agent who guided John C. Fremont's expeditions into Wyoming and California, 1842-46.

Calamity Jane: Martha Jane Canary, 1852-1903; frontier character who in 1876 appeared in Deadwood, S. Dakota dressed in men's clothes, boasting of her exploits as a pony express rider and Army scout.

Casey Jones: John Luther Jones, 1864-1900; locomotive engineer celebrated in song, who got his nickname from his Cayce, Kentucky workplace; driving the Cannon Ball express from Memphis to Canton, Mississippi, he applied the brakes in time to save the lives of the passengers in a wreck at Vaughn, Mississippi, but he was killed.

Davey Crockett: 1786-1836; a hero of frontier America, he fought in the Creek War under Andrew Jackson, was elected to the Tennessee legislature and the U.S. Congress, joined the Texas independence forces, and was killed at the Alamo.

Wyatt Earp: 1848-1929; law officer and gunfighter who was involved with his brothers and Doc Holliday in the controversial shootout at the OK Corral, 1881, Tombstone, Arizona.

Wild Bill Hickok: James Butler Hickok, 1837-1876; frontier marshal in Hays and Abilene, Kansas, who gained repute as a marksman and became a legend after his murder in Deadwood, S. Dakota by outlaw Jack McCall.

John Henry: legendary black man celebrated for his strength in ballads and tales; in one version of his story, he succeeded in outworking a steam drill but died from the strain.

Hiawatha: c. 1550; chief of the Onandaga Indians, credited with founding the Iroquois Confederacy, and the hero of a well-known poem by Henry Wadsworth Longfellow.

Jesse James: 1847-1882; outlaw who led his gang in daring bank and train robberies in the Midwest from 1866. He was murdered by Robert Ford, one of his gang.

Annie Oakley: Phoebe Anne Oakley Mozee, 1860-1926; rifle and shotgun markswoman who was the star attraction of Buffalo Bill's Wild West Show, 1885-1902.

Pocahontas: c. 1595-1617; daughter of Chief Powhatan, she was said to have saved the life of Capt. John Smith at Jamestown as Powhatan was about to execute him. Later held hostage at Jamestown for the return of her father's English prisoners, she became a Christian and in 1614 married a settler, John Rolfe; in 1616 Rolfe took her to England, where she was received as a princess; she died during the trip home, and was buried at Gravesend, England.

Betsy Ross: 1752-1846; seamstress who made flags during the American Revolution; however, the legend that she designed and made the first American national flag is generally discredited.

Uncle Remus: main character in *Uncle Remus: His Songs and His Sayings,* by Joel Chandler Harris, 1880, based on oral tales of southern blacks. Uncle Remus is depicted as a benign autocratic figure spinning animal fables to a white boy on a plantation.

Squanto: d. 1622; Indian of the Pawtuxet tribe who was kidnapped by Capt. Thomas Hunt in 1615, lived in England, and returned in 1619; he later acted as interpretor in concluding a treaty between the Pilgrim settlers and Massasoit, became friendly with the Plymouth colonists, and helped them, especially with planting and fishing.

Belle Starr: Myra Belle Shirley, 1848-1889; woman who led a band of cattle rustlers and horse thieves that made regular raids on Oklahoma ranches.

Declaration of Independence

The Declaration of Independence was adopted by the Continental Congress in Philadelphia, on July 4, 1776. John Hancock was president of the Congress and Charles Thomson was secretary. A copy of the Declaration, engrossed on parchment, was signed by members of Congress on and after Aug. 2, 1776. On Jan. 18, 1777, Congress ordered that "an authenticated copy, with the names of the members of Congress subscribing the same, be sent to each of the United States, and that they be desired to have the same put upon record." Authenticated copies were printed in broadside form in Baltimore, where the Continental Congress was then in session. The following text is that of the original printed by John Dunlap at Philadelphia for the Continental Congress.

IN CONGRESS, July 4, 1776.

A DECLARATION

By the REPRESENTATIVES of the

UNITED STATES OF AMERICA,

In GENERAL CONGRESS assembled

When in the Course of human Events, it becomes necessary for one People to dissolve the Political Bands which have connected them with another, and to assume among the Powers of the Earth, the separate and equal Station to which the Laws of Nature and of Nature's God entitle them, a decent Respect to the Opinions of Mankind requires that they should declare the causes which impel them to the Separation.

We hold these Truths to be self-evident, that all Men are created equal, that they are endowed by their Creator with certain unalienable Rights, that among these are Life, Liberty, and the Pursuit of Happiness—That to secure these Rights, Governments are instituted among Men, deriving their just Powers from the Consent of the Governed, that whenever any Form of Government becomes destructive of these Ends, it is the Right of the People to alter or to abolish it, and to institute new Government, laying its Foundation on such Principles, and organizing its Powers in such Form, as to them shall seem most likely to effect their Safety and Happiness. Prudence, indeed, will dictate that Governments long established should not be changed for light and transient Causes; and accordingly all Experience hath shewn, that Mankind are more disposed to suffer, while Evils are sufferable, than to right themselves by abolishing the Forms to which they are accustomed. But when a long Train of Abuses and Usurpations, pursuing invariably the same Object, evinces a Design to reduce them under absolute Despotism, it is their Right, it is their Duty, to throw off such Government, and to provide new Guards for their future Security. Such has been the patient Sufferance of these Colonies; and such is now the Necessity which constrains them to alter their former Systems of Government. The History of the present King of Great-Britain is a History of repeated Injuries and Usurpations, all having in direct Object the Establishment of an absolute Tyranny over these States. To prove this, let Facts be submitted to a candid World.

He has refused his Assent to Laws, the most wholesome and necessary for the public Good.

He has forbidden his Governors to pass Laws of immediate and pressing Importance, unless suspended in their Operation till his Assent should be obtained; and when so suspended, he has utterly neglected to attend to them.

He has refused to pass other Laws for the Accommodation of large Districts of People, unless those People would relinquish the Right of Representation in the Legislature, a Right inestimable to them, and formidable to Tyrants only.

He has called together Legislative Bodies at Places unusual, uncomfortable, and distant from the Depository of their Public Records, for the sole Purpose of fatiguing them into Compliance with his Measures.

He has dissolved Representative Houses repeatedly, for opposing with manly Firmness his Invasions on the Rights of the People.

He has refused for a long Time, after such Dissolutions, to cause others to be elected; whereby the Legislative Powers, incapable of Annihilation, have returned to the People at large for their exercise; the State remaining in the mean time exposed to all the Dangers of Invasion from without, and Convulsions within.

He has endeavoured to prevent the Population of these States; for that Purpose obstructing the Laws for Naturalization of Foreigners; refusing to pass others to encourage their Migrations hither, and raising the Conditions of new Appropriations of Lands.

He has obstructed the Administration of Justice, by refusing his Assent to Laws for establishing Judiciary Powers.

He has made Judges dependent on his Will alone, for the Tenure of their Offices, and the Amount and payment of their Salaries.

He has erected a Multitude of new Offices, and sent hither Swarms of Officers to harrass our People, and eat out their Substance.

He has kept among us, in Times of Peace, Standing Armies, without the consent of our Legislatures.

He has affected to render the Military independent of, and superior to the Civil Power.

He has combined with others to subject us to a Jurisdiction foreign to our Constitution, and unacknowledged by our Laws; giving his Assent to their Acts of pretended Legislation:

For quartering large Bodies of Armed Troops among us:

For protecting them, by a mock Trial, from Punishment for any Murders which they should commit on the Inhabitants of these States:

For cutting off our Trade with all Parts of the World:

For imposing Taxes on us without our Consent:

For depriving us, in many Cases, of the Benefits of Trial by Jury:

For transporting us beyond Seas to be tried for pretended Offences:

For abolishing the free System of English Laws in a neighbouring Province, establishing therein an arbitrary Government, and enlarging its Boundaries, so as to render it at once an Example and fit Instrument for introducing the same absolute Rule into these Colonies:

For taking away our Charters, abolishing our most valuable Laws, and altering fundamentally the Forms of our Governments:

For suspending our own Legislatures, and declaring themselves invested with Power to legislate for us in all Cases whatsoever.

He has abdicated Government here, by declaring us out of his Protection and waging War against us.

He has plundered our Seas, ravaged our Coasts, burnt our towns, and destroyed the Lives of our People.

He is, at this Time, transporting large Armies of foreign Mercenaries to complete the works of Death, Desolation, and Tyranny, already begun with circumstances of Cruelty and Perfidy, scarcely paralleled in the most barbarous Ages, and totally unworthy the Head of a civilized Nation.

He has constrained our fellow Citizens taken Captive on the high Seas to bear Arms against their Country, to become the Executioners of their Friends and Brethren, or to fall themselves by their Hands.

He has excited domestic Insurrections amongst us, and has endeavoured to bring on the Inhabitants of our Frontiers, the merciless Indian Savages, whose known Rule of Warfare, is an undistinguished Destruction, of all Ages, Sexes and Conditions.

In every stage of these Oppressions we have Petitioned for Redress in the most humble Terms: Our repeated Petitions have been answered only by repeated Injury. A Prince, whose Character is thus marked by every act which may define a Tyrant, is unfit to be the Ruler of a free People.

Nor have we been wanting in Attentions to our British Brethren. We have warned them from Time to Time of Attempts by their Legislature to extend an unwarrantable Jurisdiction over us. We have reminded them of the Circumstances of our Emigration and Settlement here. We have appealed to their native Justice and Magnanimity, and we have conjured them by the Ties of our common Kindred to disavow these Usurpations, which, would inevitably interrupt our Connections and Correspondence. They too have been deaf to the Voice of Justice and of Consanguinity. We must, therefore, acquiesce in the Necessity, which denounces our Separation, and hold them, as we hold the rest of Mankind, Enemies in War, in Peace, Friends.

We, therefore, the Representatives of the UNITED STATES OF AMERICA, in General Congress, Assembled, appealing to the Supreme Judge of the World for the Rectitude of our Intentions, do, in the Name, and by Authority of the good People of these Colonies, solemnly Publish and Declare, That these United Colonies are, and of Right ought to be, Free and Independent States; that they are absolved from all Allegiance to the British Crown, and that all political Connection between them and the State of Great-Britain, is and ought to be totally dissolved; and that as Free and Independent States, they have full Power to levy War, conclude Peace, contract Alliances, establish Commerce, and to do all other Acts and Things which Independent States may of right do. And for the support of this declaration, with a firm Reliance on the Protection of divine Providence, we mutually pledge to each other our lives, our Fortunes, and our sacred Honor.

JOHN HANCOCK, President

Attest.
CHARLES THOMSON. Secretary.

Signers of the Declaration of Independence

Delegate and state	Vocation	Birthplace	Born	Died
Adams, John (Mass.)	Lawyer	Braintree (Quincy), Mass.	Oct. 30, 1735	July 4, 1826
Adams, Samuel (Mass.)	Political leader	Boston, Mass.	Sept. 27, 1722	Oct. 2, 1803
Bartlett, Josiah (N.H.)	Physician, judge	Amesbury, Mass.	Nov. 21, 1729	May 19, 1795
Braxton, Carter (Va.)	Farmer	Newington Plantation, Va.	Sept. 10, 1736	Oct. 10, 1797
Carroll, Chas. of Carrollton (Md.)	Lawyer	Annapolis, Md.	Sept. 19, 1737	Nov. 14, 1832
Chase, Samuel (Md.)	Judge	Princess Anne, Md.	Apr. 17, 1741	June 19, 1811
Clark, Abraham (N.J.)	Surveyor	Roselle, N.J.	Feb. 15, 1726	Sept. 15, 1794
Clymer, George (Pa.)	Merchant	Philadelphia, Pa.	Mar. 16, 1739	Jan. 23, 1813
Ellery, William (R.I.)	Lawyer	Newport, R.I.	Dec. 22, 1727	Feb. 15, 1820
Floyd, William (N.Y.)	Soldier	Brookhaven, N.Y.	Dec. 17, 1734	Aug. 4, 1821
Franklin, Benjamin (Pa.)	Printer, publisher.	Boston, Mass.	Jan. 17, 1706	Apr. 17, 1790
Gerry, Elbridge (Mass.)	Merchant	Marblehead, Mass.	July 17, 1744	Nov. 23, 1814
Gwinnett, Button (Ga.)	Merchant	Down Hatherly, England.	c. 1735	May 19, 1777
Hall, Lyman (Ga.)	Physician	Wallingford, Conn.	Apr. 12, 1724	Oct. 19, 1790
Hancock, John (Mass.)	Merchant	Braintree (Quincy), Mass.	Jan. 12, 1737	Oct. 8, 1793
Harrison, Benjamin (Va.)	Farmer	Berkeley, Va.	Apr. 5, 1726	Apr. 24, 1791
Hart, John (N.J.)	Farmer	Stonington, Conn.	c. 1711	May 11, 1779
Hewes, Joseph (N.C.)	Merchant	Princeton, N.J.	Jan. 23, 1730	Nov. 10, 1779
Heyward, Thos. Jr. (S.C.)	Lawyer, farmer	St. Luke's Parish, S.C.	July 28, 1746	Mar. 6, 1809
Hooper, William (N.C.)	Lawyer	Boston, Mass.	June 28, 1742	Oct. 14, 1790
Hopkins, Stephen (R.I.)	Judge, educator	Providence, R.I.	Mar. 7, 1707	July 13, 1785
Hopkinson, Francis (N.J.)	Judge, author.	Philadelphia, Pa.	Sept. 21, 1737	May 9, 1791
Huntington, Samuel (Conn.)	Judge	Windham County, Conn.	July 3, 1731	Jan. 5, 1796
Jefferson, Thomas (Va.)	Lawyer	Shadwell, Va.	Apr. 13, 1743	July 4, 1826
Lee, Francis Lightfoot (Va.)	Farmer	Westmoreland County, Va.	Oct. 14, 1734	Jan. 11, 1797
Lee, Richard Henry (Va.)	Farmer	Westmoreland County, Va.	Jan. 20, 1732	June 19, 1794
Lewis, Francis (N.Y.)	Merchant	Llandaff, Wales	Mar., 1713	Dec. 31, 1802
Livingston, Philip (N.Y.)	Merchant	Albany, N.Y.	Jan. 15, 1716	June 12, 1778
Lynch, Thomas Jr. (S.C.)	Farmer	Winyah, S.C.	Aug. 5, 1749	(at sea) 1779
McKean, Thomas (Del.)	Lawyer	New London, Pa.	Mar. 19, 1734	June 24, 1817
Middleton, Arthur (S.C.)	Farmer	Charleston, S.C.	June 26, 1742	Jan. 1, 1787
Morris, Lewis (N.Y.)	Farmer	Morrisania (Bronx County), N.Y.	Apr. 8, 1726	Jan. 22, 1798
Morris, Robert (Pa.)	Merchant	Liverpool, England.	Jan. 20, 1734	May 9, 1806
Morton, John (Pa.)	Judge	Ridley, Pa.	1724	Apr., 1777
Nelson, Thos. Jr. (Va.)	Farmer	Yorktown, Va.	Dec. 26, 1738	Jan. 4, 1789
Paca, William (Md.)	Judge	Abingdon, Md.	Oct. 31, 1740	Oct. 23, 1799
Paine, Robert Treat (Mass.)	Judge	Boston, Mass.	Mar. 11, 1731	May 12, 1814
Penn, John (N.C.)	Lawyer	Near Port Royal, Va.	May 17, 1741	Sept. 14, 1788
Read, George (Del.)	Judge	Near North East, Md.	Sept. 18, 1733	Sept. 21, 1798
Rodney, Caesar (Del.)	Judge	Dover, Del.	Oct. 7, 1728	June 29, 1784
Ross, George (Pa.)	Judge	New Castle, Del.	May 10, 1730	July 14, 1779
Rush, Benjamin (Pa.)	Physician	Byberry, Pa. (Philadelphia).	Dec. 24, 1745	Apr. 19, 1813
Rutledge, Edward (S.C.)	Lawyer	Charleston, S.C.	Nov. 23, 1749	Jan. 23, 1800
Sherman, Roger (Conn.)	Lawyer	Newton, Mass.	Apr. 19, 1721	July 23, 1793
Smith, James (Pa.)	Lawyer	Dublin, Ireland	c. 1719	July 11, 1806
Stockton, Richard (N.J.)	Lawyer	Near Princeton, N.J.	Oct. 1, 1730	Feb. 28, 1781
Stone, Thomas (Md.)	Lawyer	Charles County, Md.	1743	Oct. 5, 1787
Taylor, George (Pa.)	Ironmaster	Ireland.	1716	Feb. 23, 1781
Thornton, Matthew (N.H.)	Physician	Ireland.	1714	June 24, 1803
Walton, George (Ga.)	Judge	Prince Edward County, Va.	1741	Feb. 2, 1804
Whipple, William (N.H.)	Merchant, judge	Kittery, Me.	Jan. 14, 1730	Nov. 28, 1785
Williams, William (Conn.)	Merchant	Lebanon, Conn.	Apr. 23, 1731	Aug. 2, 1811
Wilson, James (Pa.)	Judge	Carskerdo, Scotland	Sept. 14, 1742	Aug. 28, 1798
Witherspoon, John (N.J.)	Clergyman, educator	Gifford, Scotland	Feb. 5, 1723	Nov. 15, 1794
Wolcott, Oliver (Conn.)	Judge	Windsor, Conn.	Dec. 1, 1726	Dec. 1, 1797
Wythe, George (Va.)	Lawyer	Elizabeth City Co. (Hampton), Va.	1726	June 8, 1806

Constitution of the United States
The Original 7 Articles

PREAMBLE

We, the people of the United States, in order to form a more perfect Union, establish justice, insure domestic tranquility, provide for the common defense, promote the general welfare, and secure the blessings of liberty to ourselves and our posterity do ordain and establish this Constitution for the United States of America.

ARTICLE I.

Section 1—Legislative powers; in whom vested:

All legislative powers herein granted shall be vested in a Congress of the United States, which shall consist of a Senate and House of Representatives.

Section 2—House of Representatives, how and by whom chosen. Qualifications of a Representative. Representatives and direct taxes, how apportioned. Enumeration. Vacancies to be filled. Power of choosing officers, and of impeachment.

1. The House of Representatives shall be composed of members chosen every second year by the people of the several States, and the electors in each State shall have the qualifications requisite for electors of the most numerous branch of the State Legislature.

2. No person shall be a Representative who shall not have attained to the age of twenty-five years, and been seven years a citizen of the United States, and who shall not, when elected, be an inhabitant of that State in which he shall be chosen.

3. *(Representatives and direct taxes shall be apportioned among the several States which may be included within this Union, according to their respective numbers, which shall be determined by adding to the whole number of free persons, including those bound to service for a term of years, and excluding Indians not taxed, three-fifths of all other persons.) (The previous sentence was superseded by Amendment XIV, section 2.)* The actual enumeration shall be made within three years after the first meeting of the Congress of the United States, and within every subsequent term of ten years, in such manner as they shall by law direct. The number of Representatives shall not exceed one for every thirty thousand, but each State shall have at least one Representative; and until such enumeration shall be made, the State of New Hampshire shall be entitled to choose three, Massachusetts eight, Rhode Island and Providence Plantations one, Connecticut five, New York six, New Jersey four, Pennsylvania eight, Delaware one, Maryland six, Virginia ten, North Carolina five, South Carolina five, and Georgia three.

4. When vacancies happen in the representation from any State, the Executive Authority thereof shall issue writs of election to fill such vacancies.

5. The House of Representatives shall choose their Speaker and other officers; and shall have the sole power of impeachment.

Section 3—Senators, how and by whom chosen. How classified. Qualifications of a Senator. President of the Senate, his right to vote. President pro tem., and other officers of the Senate, how chosen. Power to try impeachments. When President is tried, Chief Justice to preside. Sentence.

1. The Senate of the United States shall be composed of two Senators from each State, *(chosen by the Legislature thereof), (The preceding five words were superseded by Amendment XVII, section 1.)* for six years; and each Senator shall have one vote.

2. Immediately after they shall be assembled in consequence of the first election, they shall be divided as equally as may be into three classes. The seats of the Senators of the first class shall be vacated at the expiration of the second year, of the second class at the expiration of the fourth year, and of the third class at the expiration of the sixth year, so that one-third may be chosen every second year; *(and if vacancies happen by resignation, or otherwise, during the recess of the Legislature of any State, the Executive thereof may make temporary appointments until the next meeting of the Legislature, which shall then fill such vacancies.) (The words*

in parentheses were superseded by Amendment XVII, section 2.)

3. No person shall be a Senator who shall not have attained to the age of thirty years, and been nine years a citizen of the United States, and who shall not, when elected, be an inhabitant of that State for which he shall be chosen.

4. The Vice President of the United States shall be President of the Senate, but shall have no vote, unless they be equally divided.

5. The Senate shall choose their other officers, and also a President pro tempore, in the absence of the Vice President, or when he shall exercise the office of President of the United States.

6. The Senate shall have the sole power to try all impeachments. When sitting for that purpose, they shall be on oath or affirmation. When the President of the United States is tried, the Chief Justice shall preside: and no person shall be convicted without the concurrence of two-thirds of the members present.

7. Judgment in cases of impeachment shall not extend further than to removal from office, and disqualification to hold and enjoy any office of honor, trust or profit under the United States: but the party convicted shall nevertheless be liable and subject to indictment, trial, judgment and punishment, according to law.

Section 4—Times, etc., of holding elections, how prescribed. One session each year.

1. The times, places and manner of holding elections for Senators and Representatives, shall be prescribed in each State by the Legislature thereof; but the Congress may at any time by law make or alter such regulations, except as to the places of choosing Senators.

2. The Congress shall assemble at least once in every year, and such meeting shall *(be on the first Monday in December,) (The words in parentheses were superseded by Amendment XX, section 2).* unless they shall by law appoint a different day.

Section 5—Membership, quorum, adjournments, rules. Power to punish or expel. Journal. Time of adjournments, how limited, etc.

1. Each House shall be the judge of the elections, returns and qualifications of its own members, and a majority of each shall constitute a quorum to do business; but a smaller number may adjourn from day to day, and may be authorized to compel the attendance of absent members, in such manner, and under such penalties as each House may provide.

2. Each House may determine the rules of its proceedings, punish its members for disorderly behavior, and, with the concurrence of two-thirds, expel a member.

3. Each House shall keep a journal of its proceedings, and from time to time publish the same, excepting such parts as may in their judgment require secrecy; and the yeas and nays of the members of either House on any question shall, at the desire of one-fifth of those present, be entered on the journal.

4. Neither House, during the session of Congress, shall, without the consent of the other, adjourn for more than three days, nor to any other place than that in which the two Houses shall be sitting.

Section 6—Compensation, privileges, disqualifications in certain cases.

1. The Senators and Representatives shall receive a compensation for their services, to be ascertained by law, and paid out of the Treasury of the United States. They shall in all cases, except treason, felony and breach of the peace, be privileged from arrest during their attendance at the session of their respective Houses, and in going to and returning from the same; and for any speech or debate in either House, they shall not be questioned in any other place.

2. No Senator or Representative shall, during the time for which he was elected, be appointed to any civil office under the authority of the United States, which shall have been created, or the emoluments whereof shall have been increased during such time; and no person holding any office under the United States, shall be a member of either House

during his continuance in office.

Section 7—House to originate all revenue bills. Veto. Bill may be passed by two-thirds of each House, notwithstanding, etc. Bill, not returned in ten days, to become a law. Provisions as to orders, concurrent resolutions, etc.

1. All bills for raising revenue shall originate in the House of Representatives; but the Senate may propose or concur with amendments as on other bills.

2. Every bill which shall have passed the House of Representatives and the Senate, shall, before it becomes a law, be presented to the President of the United States; if he approves he shall sign it, but if not he shall return it, with his objections to that House in which it shall have originated, who shall enter the objections at large on their journal, and proceed to reconsider it. If after such reconsideration two-thirds of that House shall agree to pass the bill, it shall be sent, together with the objections, to the other House, by which it shall likewise be reconsidered, and if approved by two-thirds of that House, it shall become a law. But in all such cases the votes of both Houses shall be determined by yeas and nays, and the names of the persons voting for and against the bill shall be entered on the journal of each House respectively. If any bill shall not be returned by the President within ten days (Sundays excepted) after it shall have been presented to him, the same shall be a law, in like manner as if he had signed it, unless the Congress by their adjournment prevent its return, in which case it shall not be a law.

3. Every order, resolution, or vote to which the concurrence of the Senate and House of Representatives may be necessary (except on a question of adjournment) shall be presented to the President of the United States; and before the same shall take effect, shall be approved by him, or being disapproved by him, shall be repassed by two-thirds of the Senate and House of Representatives, according to the rules and limitations prescribed in the case of a bill.

Section 8—Powers of Congress.

The Congress shall have power

1. To lay and collect taxes, duties, imposts and excises, to pay the debts and provide for the common defense and general welfare of the United States; but all duties, imposts and excises shall be uniform throughout the United States;

2. To borrow money on the credit of the United States;

3. To regulate commerce with foreign nations, and among the several States, and with the Indian tribes;

4. To establish a uniform rule of naturalization, and uniform laws on the subject of bankruptcies throughout the United States;

5. To coin money, regulate the value thereof, and of foreign coin, and fix the standard of weights and measures;

6. To provide for the punishment of counterfeiting the securities and current coin of the United States;

7. To establish post-offices and post-roads;

8. To promote the progress of science and useful arts, by securing for limited times to authors and inventors the exclusive right to their respective writings and discoveries;

9. To constitute tribunals inferior to the Supreme Court;

10. To define and punish piracies and felonies committed on the high seas, and offenses against the law of nations;

11. To declare war, grant letters of marque and reprisal, and make rules concerning captures on land and water;

12. To raise and support armies, but no appropriation of money to that use shall be for a longer term than two years;

13. To provide and maintain a navy;

14. To make rules for the government and regulation of the land and naval forces;

15. To provide for calling forth the militia to execute the laws of the Union, suppress insurrections and repel invasions;

16. To provide for organizing, arming, and disciplining the militia, and for governing such part of them as may be employed in the service of the United States, reserving to the States respectively, the appointment of the officers, and the authority of training the militia according to the discipline prescribed by Congress;

17. To exercise exclusive legislation in all cases whatsoever, over such district (not exceeding ten miles square) as may, by cession of particular States, and the acceptance of Congress, become the seat of the Government of the United States, and to exercise like authority over all places purchased by the consent of the Legislature of the State in which the same shall be, for the erection of forts, magazines, arsenals, dockyards, and other needful buildings;—And

18. To make all laws which shall be necessary and proper for carrying into execution the foregoing powers, and all other powers vested by this Constitution in the Government of the United States, or in any department or officer thereof.

Section 9—Provision as to migration or importation of certain persons. Habeas corpus, bills of attainder, etc. Taxes, how apportioned. No export duty. No commercial preference. Money, how drawn from Treasury, etc. No titular nobility. Officers not to receive presents, etc.

1. The migration or importation of such persons as any of the States now existing shall think proper to admit, shall not be prohibited by the Congress prior to the year one thousand eight hundred and eight, but a tax or duty may be imposed on such importation, not exceeding ten dollars for each person.

2. The privilege of the writ of habeas corpus shall not be suspended, unless when in cases of rebellion or invasion the public safety may require it.

3. No bill of attainder or ex post facto law shall be passed.

4. No capitation, or other direct, tax shall be laid, unless in proportion to the census or enumeration herein before directed to be taken. (Modified by Amendment XVI.)

5. No tax or duty shall be laid on articles exported from any State.

6. No preference shall be given by any regulation of commerce or revenue to the ports of one State over those of another: nor shall vessels bound to, or from, one State, be obliged to enter, clear, or pay duties in another.

7. No money shall be drawn from the Treasury, but in consequence of appropriations made by law; and a regular statement and account of the receipts and expenditures of all public money shall be published from time to time.

8. No title of nobility shall be granted by the United States: and no person holding any office of profit or trust under them, shall, without the consent of the Congress, accept of any present, emolument, office, or title, of any kind whatever, from any king, prince, or foreign state.

Section 10—States prohibited from the exercise of certain powers.

1. No State shall enter into any treaty, alliance, or confederation; grant letters of marque and reprisal; coin money; emit bills of credit; make anything but gold and silver coin a tender in payment of debts; pass any bill of attainder, ex post facto law, or law impairing the obligation of contracts, or grant any title of nobility.

2. No State shall, without the consent of the Congress, lay any imposts or duties on imports or exports, except what may be absolutely necessary for executing its inspection laws: and the net produce of all duties and imposts, laid by any State on imports or exports, shall be for the use of the Treasury of the United States; and all such laws shall be subject to the revision and control of the Congress.

3. No State shall, without the consent of Congress, lay any duty of tonnage, keep troops, or ships of war in time of peace, enter into any agreement or compact with another State, or with a foreign power, or engage in war, unless actually invaded, or in such imminent danger as will not admit of delay.

ARTICLE II.

Section 1—President: his term of office. Electors of President; number and how appointed. Electors to vote on same day. Qualification of President. On whom his duties devolve in case of his removal, death, etc. President's compensation. His oath of office.

1. The Executive power shall be vested in a President of the United States of America. He shall hold his office during the term of four years, and together with the Vice President, chosen for the same term, be elected as follows

2. Each State shall appoint, in such manner as the Legis-

lature thereof may direct, a number of electors, equal to the whole number of Senators and Representatives to which the State may be entitled in the Congress: but no Senator or Representative, or person holding an office of trust or profit under the United States, shall be appointed an elector.

(The electors shall meet in their respective States, and vote by ballot for two persons, of whom one at least shall not be an inhabitant of the same State with themselves. And they shall make a list of all the persons voted for, and of the number of votes for each; which list they shall sign and certify, and transmit sealed to the seat of the Government of the United States, directed to the President of the Senate. The President of the Senate shall, in the presence of the Senate and House of Representatives, open all the certificates, and the votes shall then be counted. The person having the greatest number of votes shall be the President, if such number be a majority of the whole number of electors appointed; and if there be more than one who have such majority, and have an equal number of votes, then the House of Representatives shall immediately choose by ballot one of them for President; and if no person have a majority, then from the five highest on the list the said House shall in like manner choose the President. But in choosing the President, the votes shall be taken by States, the representation from each State having one vote; a quorum for this purpose shall consist of a member or members from two-thirds of the States, and a majority of all the States shall be necessary to a choice. In every case, after the choice of the President, the person having the greatest number of votes of the electors shall be the Vice President. But if there should remain two or more who have equal votes, the Senate shall choose from them by ballot the Vice President.)

(This clause was superseded by Amendment XII.)

3. The Congress may determine the time of choosing the electors, and the day on which they shall give their votes; which day shall be the same throughout the United States.

4. No person except a natural born citizen, or a citizen of the United States, at the time of the adoption of this Constitution, shall be eligible to the office of President; neither shall any person be eligible to that office who shall not have attained to the age of thirty-five years, and been fourteen years a resident within the United States.

(For qualification of the Vice President, see Amendment XII.)

5. In case of the removal of the President from office, or of his death, resignation, or inability to discharge the powers and duties of the said office, the same shall devolve on the Vice President, and the Congress may by law provide for the case of removal, death, resignation or inability, both of the President and Vice President, declaring what officer shall then act as President, and such officer shall act accordingly, until the disability be removed, or a President shall be elected.

(This clause has been modified by Amendments XX and XXV.)

6. The President shall, at stated times, receive for his services, a compensation, which shall neither be increased nor diminished during the period for which he shall have been elected, and he shall not receive within that period any other emolument from the United States, or any of them.

7. Before he enter on the execution of his office, he shall take the following oath or affirmation:

"I do solemnly swear (or affirm) that I will faithfully execute the office of President of the United States, and will to the best of my ability, preserve, protect and defend the Constitution of the United States."

Section 2—President to be Commander-in-Chief. He may require opinions of cabinet officers, etc., may pardon. Treaty-making power. Nomination of certain officers. When President may fill vacancies.

1. The President shall be Commander-in-Chief of the Army and Navy of the United States, and of the militia of the several States, when called into the actual service of the United States; he may require the opinion, in writing, of the principal officer in each of the executive departments, upon any subject relating to the duties of their respective offices, and he shall have power to grant reprieves and pardons for offenses against the United States, except in cases of impeachment.

2. He shall have power, by and with the advice and consent of the Senate, to make treaties, provided two-thirds of the Senators present concur; and he shall nominate, and by and with the advice and consent of the Senate, shall appoint ambassadors, other public ministers and consuls, judges of the Supreme Court, and all other officers of the United States, whose appointments are not herein otherwise provided for, and which shall be established by law: but the Congress may by law vest the appointment of such inferior officers, as they think proper, in the President alone, in the courts of law, or in the heads of departments.

3. The President shall have power to fill up all vacancies that may happen during the recess of the Senate, by granting commissions, which shall expire at the end of their next session.

Section 3—President shall communicate to Congress. He may convene and adjourn Congress, in case of disagreement, etc. Shall receive ambassadors, execute laws, and commission officers.

He shall from time to time give to the Congress information of the state of the Union, and recommend to their consideration such measures as he shall judge necessary and expedient; he may, on extraordinary occasions, convene both Houses, or either of them, and in case of disagreement between them, with respect to the time of adjournment, he may adjourn them to such time as he shall think proper; he shall receive ambassadors and other public ministers; he shall take care that the laws be faithfully executed, and shall commission all the officers of the United States.

Section 4—All civil offices forfeited for certain crimes.

The President, Vice President, and all civil officers of the United States, shall be removed from office on impeachment for, and conviction of, treason, bribery, or other high crimes and misdemeanors.

ARTICLE III.

Section 1—Judicial powers, Tenure. Compensation.

The judicial power of the United States, shall be vested in one Supreme Court, and in such inferior courts as the Congress may from time to time ordain and establish. The judges, both of the Supreme and inferior courts, shall hold their offices during good behavior, and shall at stated times, receive for their services, a compensation, which shall not be diminished during their continuance in office.

Section 2—Judicial power; to what cases it extends. Original jurisdiction of Supreme Court; appellate jurisdiction. Trial by jury, etc. Trial, where.

1. The judicial power shall extend to all cases, in law and equity, arising under this Constitution, the laws of the United States, and treaties made, or which shall be made, under their authority; to all cases affecting ambassadors, other public ministers and consuls; to all cases of admiralty and maritime jurisdiction; to controversies to which the United States shall be a party; to controversies between two or more States; between a State and citizens of another State; between citizens of different States, between citizens of the same State claiming lands under grants of different States, and between a State, or the citizens thereof, and foreign states, citizens or subjects.

(This section is modified by Amendment XI.)

2. In all cases affecting ambassadors, other public ministers and consuls, and those in which a State shall be party, the Supreme Court shall have original jurisdiction. In all the other cases before mentioned, the Supreme Court shall have appellate jurisdiction, both as to law and fact, with such exceptions, and under such regulations as the Congress shall make.

3. The trial of all crimes, except in cases of impeachment, shall be by jury; and such trial shall be held in the State where the said crimes shall have been committed; but when not committed within any State, the trial shall be at such place or places as the Congress may by law have directed.

Section 3—Treason Defined, Proof of, Punishment of.

1. Treason against the United States, shall consist only in levying war against them, or in adhering to their enemies,

giving them aid and comfort. No person shall be convicted of treason unless on the testimony of two witnesses to the same overt act, or on confession in open court.

2. The Congress shall have power to declare the punishment of treason, but no attainder of treason shall work corruption of blood, or forfeiture except during the life of the person attainted.

ARTICLE IV.

Section 1—Each State to give credit to the public acts, etc., of every other State.

Full faith and credit shall be given in each State to the public acts, records, and judicial proceedings of every other State. And the Congress may by general laws prescribe the manner in which such acts, records and proceedings shall be proved, and the effect thereof.

Section 2—Privileges of citizens of each State. Fugitives from justice to be delivered up. Persons held to service having escaped, to be delivered up.

1. The citizens of each State shall be entitled to all privileges and immunities of citizens in the several States.

2. A person charged in any State with treason, felony, or other crime, who shall flee from justice, and be found in another State, shall on demand of the Executive authority of the State from which he fled, be delivered up, to be removed to the State having jurisdiction of the crime.

(3. No person held to service or labor in one State, under the laws thereof, escaping into another, shall in consequence of any law or regulation therein, be discharged from such service or labor, but shall be delivered up on claim of the party to whom such service or labor may be due.) (This clause was superseded by Amendment XIII.)

Section 3—Admission of new States. Power of Congress over territory and other property.

1. New States may be admitted by the Congress into this Union; but no new State shall be formed or erected within the jurisdiction of any other State; nor any State be formed by the junction of two or more States, or parts of States, without the consent of the Legislatures of the States concerned as well as of the Congress.

2. The Congress shall have power to dispose of and make all needful rules and regulations respecting the territory or other property belonging to the United States; and nothing in this Constitution shall be so construed as to prejudice any claims of the United States, or of any particular State.

Section 4—Republican form of government guaranteed. Each state to be protected.

The United States shall guarantee to every State in this Union a Republican form of government, and shall protect each of them against invasion; and on application of the Legislature, or of the Executive (when the Legislature cannot be convened) against domestic violence.

ARTICLE V.

Constitution: how amended; proviso.

The Congress, whenever two-thirds of both Houses shall deem it necessary, shall propose amendments to this Constitution, or, on the application of the Legislatures of two-thirds of the several States, shall call a convention for proposing amendments, which, in either case, shall be valid to all intents and purposes, as part of this Constitution, when ratified by the Legislatures of three-fourths of the several States, or by conventions in three-fourths thereof, as the one

or the other mode of ratification may be proposed by the Congress; provided that no amendment which may be made prior to the year one thousand eight hundred and eight shall in any manner affect the first and fourth clauses in the Ninth Section of the First Article; and that no State, without its consent, shall be deprived of its equal suffrage in the Senate.

ARTICLE VI.

Certain debts, etc., declared valid. Supremacy of Constitution, treaties, and laws of the United States. Oath to support Constitution, by whom taken. No religious test.

1. All debts contracted and engagements entered into, before the adoption of this Constitution, shall be as valid against the United States under this Constitution, as under the Confederation.

2. This Constitution, and the laws of the United States which shall be made in pursuance thereof; and all treaties made, or which shall be made, under the authority of the United States, shall be the supreme law of the land; and the judges in every State shall be bound thereby, any thing in the Constitution or laws of any State to the contrary notwithstanding.

3. The Senators and Representatives before mentioned, and the members of the several State Legislatures, and all executive and judicial officers, both of the United States and of the several States, shall be bound by oath or affirmation, to support this Constitution; but no religious test shall ever be required as a qualification to any office or public trust under the United States.

ARTICLE VII.

What ratification shall establish Constitution.

The ratification of the Conventions of nine States, shall be sufficient for the establishment of this Constitution between the States so ratifying the same.

Done in convention by the unanimous consent of the States present the Seventeenth day of September in the year of our Lord one thousand seven hundred and eighty seven, and of the independence of the United States of America the Twelfth. In witness whereof we have hereunto subscribed our names.

George Washington, President and deputy from Virginia.

New Hampshire—John Langdon, Nicholas Gilman.

Massachusetts—Nathaniel Gorham, Rufus King.

Connecticut—Wm. Saml. Johnson, Roger Sherman.

New York—Alexander Hamilton.

New Jersey—Wil: Livingston, David Brearley, Wm. Paterson, Jona: Dayton.

Pennsylvania—B. Franklin, Thomas Mifflin, Robt. Morris, Geo. Clymer, Thos. FitzSimons, Jared Ingersoll, James Wilson, Gouv. Morris.

Delaware—Geo: Read, Gunning Bedford Jun., John Dickinson, Richard Bassett, Jaco: Broom.

Maryland—James McHenry, Daniel of Saint Thomas' Jenifer, Danl. Carroll.

Virginia—John Blair, James Madison Jr.

North Carolina—Wm. Blount, Rich'd. Dobbs Spaight, Hugh Williamson.

South Carolina—J. Rutledge, Charles Cotesworth Pinckney, Charles Pinckney, Pierce Butler.

Georgia—William Few, Abr. Baldwin.

Attest: William Jackson, Secretary.

Ten Original Amendments: The Bill of Rights
In force Dec. 15, 1791

(The First Congress, at its first session in the City of New York, Sept. 25, 1789, submitted to the states 12 amendments to clarify certain individual and state rights not named in the Constitution. They are generally called the Bill of Rights.

(Influential in framing these amendments was the Declaration of Rights of Virginia, written by George Mason (1725-1792) in 1776. Mason, a Virginia delegate to the Constitutional Convention, did not sign the Constitution and opposed its ratification on the ground that it did not sufficiently oppose slavery or safeguard individual rights.

(In the preamble to the resolution offering the proposed amendments, Congress said: "The conventions of a number of the States having at the time of their adopting the Constitution, expressed a desire, in order to prevent misconstruction or abuse of its powers, that further declaratory and restrictive clauses should be added, and as extending the ground of public confidence in the government will best insure the beneficent ends of its institution, be it resolved," etc.

(Ten of these amendments now commonly known as one to 10 inclusive, but originally 3 to 12 inclusive, were ratified by the states as follows: New Jersey, Nov. 20, 1789; Maryland, Dec. 19, 1789; North Carolina, Dec. 22, 1789; South Carolina, Jan. 19, 1790; New Hampshire, Jan 25, 1790; Delaware, Jan 28, 1790; New York, Feb. 27, 1790; Pennsylvania, Mar. 10, 1790; Rhode

Island, June 7, 1790; Vermont, Nov 3, 1791; Virginia, Dec. 15, 1791; Massachusetts, Mar. 2, 1939; Georgia, Mar. 18, 1939; Connecticut, Apr. 19, 1939. These original 10 ratified amendments follow as Amendments I to X inclusive.

(Of the two original proposed amendments which were not ratified by the necessary number of states, the first related to apportionment of Representatives; the second, to compensation of members. See p. 465.)

AMENDMENT I.
Religious establishment prohibited. Freedom of speech, of the press, and right to petition.

Congress shall make no law respecting an establishment of religion, or prohibiting the free exercise thereof; or abridging the freedom of speech, or of the press; or the right of the people peaceably to assemble, and to petition the Government for a redress of grievances.

AMENDMENT II.
Right to keep and bear arms.

A well-regulated militia, being necessary to the security of a free State, the right of the people to keep and bear arms, shall not be infringed.

AMENDMENT III.
Conditions for quarters for soldiers.

No soldier shall, in time of peace be quartered in any house, without the consent of the owner, nor in time of war, but in a manner to be prescribed by law.

AMENDMENT IV.
Right of search and seizure regulated.

The right of the people to be secure in their persons, houses, papers, and effects, against unreasonable searches and seizures, shall not be violated, and no warrants shall issue, but upon probable cause, supported by oath or affirmation, and particularly describing the place to be searched, and the persons or things to be seized.

AMENDMENT V.
Provisions concerning prosecution. Trial and punishment—private property not to be taken for public use without compensation.

No person shall be held to answer for a capital, or otherwise infamous crime, unless on a presentment or indictment of a Grand Jury, except in cases arising in the land or naval forces, or in the militia, when in actual service in time of war or public danger; nor shall any person be subject for the same offense to be twice put in jeopardy of life or limb; nor shall be compelled in any criminal case to be a witness against himself, nor be deprived of life, liberty, or property, without due process of law; nor shall private property be taken for public use without just compensation.

AMENDMENT VI.
Right to speedy trial, witnesses, etc.

In all criminal prosecutions, the accused shall enjoy the right to a speedy and public trial, by an impartial jury of the State and district wherein the crime shall have been committed, which district shall have been previously ascertained by law, and to be informed of the nature and cause of the accusation; to be confronted with the witnesses against him; to have compulsory process for obtaining witnesses in his favor, and to have the assistance of counsel for his defense.

AMENDMENT VII.
Right of trial by jury.

In suits at common law, where the value in controversy shall exceed twenty dollars, the right of trial by jury shall be preserved, and no fact tried by a jury shall be otherwise reexamined in any court of the United States, than according to the rules of the common law.

AMENDMENT VIII.
Excessive bail or fines and cruel punishment prohibited.

Excessive bail shall not be required, nor excessive fines imposed, nor cruel and unusual punishments inflicted.

AMENDMENT IX.
Rule of construction of Constitution.

The enumeration in the Constitution, of certain rights, shall not be construed to deny or disparage others retained by the people.

AMENDMENT X.
Rights of States under Constitution.

The powers not delegated to the United States by the Constitution, nor prohibited by it to the States, are reserved to the States respectively, or to the people.

Amendments Since the Bill of Rights

AMENDMENT XI.
Judicial powers construed.

The judicial power of the United States shall not be construed to extend to any suit in law or equity, commenced or prosecuted against one of the United States by citizens of another State, or by citizens or subjects of any foreign state.

(This amendment was proposed to the Legislatures of the several States by the Third Congress on March 4, 1794, and was declared to have been ratified in a message from the President to Congress, dated Jan. 8, 1798.

(It was on Jan 5, 1798, that Secretary of State Pickering received from 12 of the States authenticated ratifications, and informed President John Adams of that fact.

(As a result of later research in the Department of State, it is now established that Amendment XI became part of the Constitution on Feb. 7, 1795, for on that date it had been ratified by 12 States as follows:

(1. New York, Mar. 27, 1794. 2. Rhode Island, Mar. 31, 1794. 3. Connecticut, May 8, 1794. 4. New Hampshire, June 16, 1794. 5. Massachusetts, June 26, 1794. 6. Vermont, between Oct 9, 1794, and Nov. 9, 1794. 7. Virginia, Nov. 18, 1794. 8. Georgia, Nov. 29, 1794. 9. Kentucky, Dec. 7, 1794. 10. Maryland, Dec. 26, 1794. 11. Delaware, Jan 23, 1795. 12. North Carolina, Feb. 7, 1795.

(On June 1, 1796, more than a year after Amendment XI had become a part of the Constitution (but before anyone was officially aware of this), Tennessee had been admitted as a State; but not until Oct. 16, 1797, was a certified copy of the resolution of Congress proposing the amendment sent to the Governor of Tennessee (John Sevier) by Secretary of State Pickering, whose office was then at Trenton, New Jersey, because of the epidemic of yellow fever at Philadelphia; it seems, however, that the Legislature of Tennessee took no action on Amendment XI, owing doubtless to the fact that public announcement of its adoption was made soon thereafter.

(Besides the necessary 12 States, one other, South Carolina, ratified Amendment XI, but this action was not taken until Dec. 4, 1797; the two remaining States, New Jersey and Pennsylvania, failed to ratify.)

AMENDMENT XII.
Manner of choosing President and Vice-President.

(Proposed by Congress Dec. 9, 1803; ratification completed June 15, 1804.)

The Electors shall meet in their respective States and vote by ballot for President and Vice-President, one of whom, at least, shall not be an inhabitant of the same State with themselves; they shall name in their ballots the person voted for as President, and in distinct ballots the person voted for as Vice-President, and they shall make distinct lists of all persons voted for as President, and of all persons voted for as Vice-President, and of the number of votes for each, which lists they shall sign and certify, and transmit sealed to the seat of the Government of the United States, directed to the President of the Senate; the President of the Senate shall, in the presence of the Senate and House of Representatives, open all the certificates and the votes shall then be counted;—The person having the greatest number of votes for President, shall be the President, if such number be a majority of the whole number of Electors appointed; and if no person have such majority, then from the persons having the highest numbers not exceeding three on the list of those voted for as President, the House of Representatives shall choose immediately, by ballot, the President. But in choosing the President, the votes shall be taken by States, the representation from each State having one vote; a quorum for this purpose shall consist of a member or members from two-thirds of the States, and a majority of all the States shall be necessary to a choice. *(And if the House of Representatives shall not choose a President whenever the right of choice shall devolve upon them, before the fourth day of March next following, then the Vice-President shall act as President, as in the case of the death or other constitutional disability of the President.) (The words in parentheses were superseded by Amendment XX, section 3.)* The person having the greatest number of votes as Vice-President, shall be the Vice-President, if such number be a majority of the whole number of Electors appointed, and if no person have a majority, then from the two highest numbers on the list, the Senate shall choose the Vice-President; a quorum for the purpose shall consist of two-thirds of the whole number of Senators, and a majority of the whole number shall be necessary to a choice. But no person constitutionally ineligible to the office of President shall be eligible to that of Vice-President of the United States.

THE RECONSTRUCTION AMENDMENTS

(Amendments XIII, XIV, and XV are commonly known as the Reconstruction Amendments, inasmuch as they followed the Civil War, and were drafted by Republicans who were bent on imposing their own policy of reconstruction on the South. Post-bellum legislatures there—Mississippi, South Carolina, Georgia, for example—had set up laws which, it was charged, were contrived to perpetuate Negro slavery under other names.)

AMENDMENT XIII.
Slavery abolished.

(Proposed by Congress Jan. 31, 1865; ratification completed Dec. 18, 1865. The amendment, when first proposed by a resolution in Congress, was passed by the Senate, 38 to 6, on Apr. 8, 1864, but was defeated in the House, 95 to 66 on June 15, 1864. On reconsideration by the House, on Jan. 31, 1865, the resolution passed, 119 to 56. It was approved by President Lincoln on Feb. 1, 1865, although the Supreme Court had decided in 1798 that the President has nothing to do with the proposing of amendments to the Constitution, or their adoption.)

1. Neither slavery nor involuntary servitude, except as a punishment for crime whereof the party shall have been duly convicted, shall exist within the United States or any place subject to their jurisdiction.

2. Congress shall have power to enforce this article by appropriate legislation.

AMENDMENT XIV.
Citizenship rights not to be abridged.

(The following amendment was proposed to the Legislatures of the several states by the 39th Congress, June 13, 1866, and was declared to have been ratified in a proclamation by the Secretary of State, July 28, 1868.

(The 14th amendment was adopted only by virtue of ratification subsequent to earlier rejections. Newly constituted legislatures in both North Carolina and South Carolina (respectively July 4 and 9, 1868), ratified the proposed amendment, although earlier legislatures had rejected the proposal. The Secretary of State issued a proclamation, which, though doubtful as to the effect of attempted withdrawals by Ohio and New Jersey, entertained no doubt as to the validity of the ratification by North and South Carolina. The following day (July 21, 1868), Congress passed a resolution which declared the 14th Amendment to be a part of the Constitution and directed the Secretary of State so to promulgate it. The Secretary waited, however, until the newly constituted Legislature of Georgia had ratified the amendment, subsequent to an earlier rejection, before the promulgation of the ratification of the new amendment.)

1. All persons born or naturalized in the United States, and subject to the jurisdiction thereof, are citizens of the United States and of the State wherein they reside. No State shall make or enforce any law which shall abridge the privileges or immunities of citizens of the United States; nor shall

any State deprive any person of life, liberty, or property, without due process of law; nor deny to any person within its jurisdiction the equal protection of the laws.

2. Representatives shall be apportioned among the several States according to their respective numbers, counting the whole number of persons in each State, excluding Indians not taxed. But when the right to vote at any election for the choice of Electors for President and Vice-President of the United States, Representatives in Congress, the executive and judicial officers of a State, or the members of the Legislature thereof, is denied to any of the male inhabitants of such State, being twenty-one years of age, and, citizens of the United States, or in any way abridged, except for participation in rebellion, or other crime, the basis of representation therein shall be reduced in the proportion which the number of such male citizens shall bear to the whole number of male citizens twenty-one years of age in such State.

3. No person shall be a Senator or Representative in Congress, or Elector of President and Vice-President, or hold any office, civil or military, under the United States, or under any State, who, having previously taken an oath, as a member of Congress, or as an officer of the United States, or as a member of any State Legislature, or as an executive or judicial officer of any State, to support the Constitution of the United States, shall have engaged in insurrection or rebellion against the same, or given aid or comfort to the enemies thereof. But Congress may by a vote of two-thirds of each House, remove such disability.

4. The validity of the public debt of the United States, authorized by law, including debts incurred for payment of pensions and bounties for services in suppressing insurrection or rebellion, shall not be questioned. But neither the United States nor any State shall assume or pay any debt or obligation incurred in aid of insurrection or rebellion against the United States, or any claim for the loss or emancipation of any slave; but all such debts, obligations and claims, shall be held illegal and void.

5. The Congress shall have power to enforce, by appropriate legislation, the provisions of this article.

AMENDMENT XV.
Race no bar to voting rights.

(The following amendment was proposed to the legislatures of the several States by the 40th Congress, Feb. 26, 1869, and was declared to have been ratified in a proclamation by the Secretary of State, Mar. 30, 1870.)

1. The right of citizens of the United States to vote shall not be denied or abridged by the United States or by any State on account of race, color, or previous condition of servitude.

2. The Congress shall have power to enforce this article by appropriate legislation.

AMENDMENT XVI.
Income taxes authorized.

(Proposed by Congress July 12, 1909; ratification declared by the Secretary of State Feb. 25, 1913.)

The Congress shall have power to lay and collect taxes on incomes, from whatever source derived, without apportionment among the several States, and without regard to any census or enumeration.

AMENDMENT XVII.
United States Senators to be elected by direct popular vote.

(Proposed by Congress May 13, 1912; ratification declared by the Secretary of State May 31, 1913.)

1. The Senate of the United States shall be composed of two Senators from each State, elected by the people thereof, for six years; and each Senator shall have one vote. The electors in each State shall have the qualifications requisite for electors of the most numerous branch of the State Legislatures.

2. When vacancies happen in the representation of any State in the Senate, the executive authority of such State shall issue writs of election to fill such vacancies: Provided, That the Legislature of any State may empower the Executive thereof to make temporary appointments until the peo-

ple fill the vacancies by election as the Legislature may direct.

3. This amendment shall not be so construed as to affect the election or term of any Senator chosen before it becomes valid as part of the Constitution.

AMENDMENT XVIII.

Liquor prohibition amendment.

(Proposed by Congress Dec. 18, 1917; ratification completed Jan. 16, 1919. Repealed by Amendment XXI, effective Dec. 5, 1933.)

(1. After one year from the ratification of this article the manufacture, sale, or transportation of intoxicating liquors within, the importation thereof into, or the exportation thereof from the United States and all territory subject to the jurisdiction thereof for beverage purposes is hereby prohibited.

(2. The Congress and the several States shall have concurrent power to enforce this article by appropriate legislation.

(3. This article shall be inoperative unless it shall have been ratified as an amendment to the Constitution by the Legislatures of the several States, as provided in the Constitution, within seven years from the date of the submission hereof to the States by the Congress.)

(The total vote in the Senates of the various States was 1,310 for, 237 against—84.6% dry. In the lower houses of the States the vote was 3,782 for, 1,035 against—78.5% dry.

(The amendment ultimately was adopted by all the States except Connecticut and Rhode Island.)

AMENDMENT XIX.

Giving nationwide suffrage to women.

(Proposed by Congress June 4, 1919; ratification certified by Secretary of State Aug. 26, 1920.)

1. The right of citizens of the United States to vote shall not be denied or abridged by the United States or by any State on account of sex.

2. Congress shall have power to enforce this Article by appropriate legislation.

AMENDMENT XX.

Terms of President and Vice President to begin on Jan. 20; those of Senators, Representatives, Jan. 3.

(Proposed by Congress Mar. 2, 1932; ratification completed Jan. 23, 1933.)

1. The terms of the President and Vice President shall end at noon on the 20th day of January, and the terms of Senators and Representatives at noon on the 3rd day of January, of the years in which such terms would have ended if this article had not been ratified; and the terms of their successors shall then begin.

2. The Congress shall assemble at least once in every year, and such meeting shall begin at noon on the 3rd day of January, unless they shall by law appoint a different day.

3. If, at the time fixed for the beginning of the term of the President, the President elect shall have died, the Vice President elect shall become President. If a President shall not have been chosen before the time fixed for the beginning of his term, or if the President elect shall have failed to qualify, then the Vice President elect shall act as President until a President shall have qualified; and the Congress may by law provide for the case wherein neither a President elect nor a Vice President elect shall have qualified, declaring who shall then act as President, or the manner in which one who is to act shall be selected, and such person shall act accordingly until a President or Vice President shall have qualified.

4. The Congress may by law provide for the case of the death of any of the persons from whom the House of Representatives may choose a President whenever the right of choice shall have devolved upon them, and for the case of the death of any of the persons from whom the Senate may choose a Vice President whenever the right of choice shall have devolved upon them.

5. Sections 1 and 2 shall take effect on the 15th day of October following the ratification of this article (Oct., 1933).

6. This article shall be inoperative unless it shall have been ratified as an amendment to the Constitution by the Legislatures of three-fourths of the several States within seven years from the date of its submission.

AMENDMENT XXI.

Repeal of Amendment XVIII.

(Proposed by Congress Feb. 20, 1933; ratification completed Dec. 5, 1933.)

1. The eighteenth article of amendment to the Constitution of the United States is hereby repealed.

2. The transportation or importation into any State, Territory, or Possession of the United States for delivery or use therein of intoxicating liquors, in violation of the laws thereof, is hereby prohibited.

3. This article shall be inoperative unless it shall have been ratified as an amendment to the Constitution by conventions in the several States, as provided in the Constitution, within seven years from the date of the submission hereof to the States by the Congress.

AMENDMENT XXII.

Limiting Presidential terms of office.

(Proposed by Congress Mar. 24, 1947; ratification completed Feb. 27, 1951.)

1. No person shall be elected to the office of the President more than twice, and no person who has held the office of President, or acted as President, for more than two years of a term to which some other person was elected President shall be elected to the office of the President more than once. But this Article shall not apply to any person holding the office of President when this Article was proposed by the Congress, and shall not prevent any person who may be holding the office of President, or acting as President, during the term within which this Article becomes operative from holding the office of President or acting as President during the remainder of such term.

2. This article shall be inoperative unless it shall have been ratified as an amendment to the Constitution by the Legislatures of three-fourths of the several States within seven years from the date of its submission to the States by the Congress.

AMENDMENT XXIII.

Presidential vote for District of Columbia.

(Proposed by Congress June 16, 1960; ratification completed Mar. 29, 1961.)

1. The District constituting the seat of Government of the United States shall appoint in such manner as the Congress may direct:

A number of electors of President and Vice President equal to the whole number of Senators and Representatives in Congress to which the District would be entitled if it were a State, but in no event more than the least populous State; they shall be in addition to those appointed by the States, but they shall be considered, for the purposes of the election of President and Vice President, to be electors appointed by a State; and they shall meet in the District and perform such duties as provided by the twelfth article of amendment.

2. The Congress shall have power to enforce this article by appropriate legislation.

AMENDMENT XXIV.

Barring poll tax in federal elections.

(Proposed by Congress Aug. 27, 1962; ratification completed Jan. 23, 1964.)

1. The right of citizens of the United States to vote in any primary or other election for President or Vice President, for electors for President or Vice President, or for Senator or Representative in Congress, shall not be denied or abridged by the United States or any State by reason of failure to pay any poll tax or other tax.

2. The Congress shall have power to enforce this article by appropriate legislation.

AMENDMENT XXV.

Presidential disability and succession.

(Proposed by Congress July 6, 1965; ratification completed Feb. 10, 1967.)

1. In case of the removal of the President from office or of his death or resignation, the Vice President shall become President.

2. Whenever there is a vacancy in the office of the Vice President, the President shall nominate a Vice President who shall take office upon confirmation by a majority vote of both houses of Congress.

3. Whenever the President transmits to the President pro tempore of the Senate and the Speaker of the House of Representatives his written declaration that he is unable to discharge the powers and duties of his office, and until he transmits to them a written declaration to the contrary, such powers and duties shall be discharged by the Vice President as Acting President.

4. Whenever the Vice President and a majority of either the principal officers of the executive departments or of such other body as Congress may by law provide, transmit to the President pro tempore of the Senate and the Speaker of the House of Representatives their written declaration that the President is unable to discharge the powers and duties of his office, the Vice President shall immediately assume the powers and duties of the office as Acting President.

Thereafter, when the President transmits to the President pro tempore of the Senate and the Speaker of the House of Representatives his written declaration that no inability exists, he shall resume the powers and duties of his office unless the Vice President and a majority of either the principal officers of the executive department or of such other body as Congress may by law provide, transmit within four days to the President pro tempore of the Senate and the Speaker of the House of Representatives their written declaration that the President is unable to discharge the powers and duties of his office. Thereupon Congress shall decide the issue, assembling within forty-eight hours for that purpose if not in session. If the Congress, within twenty-one days after receipt of the latter written declaration, or, if Congress is not in session, within twenty-one days after Congress is required to assemble, determines by two-thirds vote of both houses that the President is unable to discharge the powers and duties of his office, the Vice President shall continue to discharge the same as Acting President; otherwise, the President shall resume the powers and duties of his office.

AMENDMENT XXVI.

Lowering voting age to 18 years.

(Proposed by Congress Mar. 23, 1971; ratification completed July 1, 1971.)

1. The right of citizens of the United States, who are 18 years of age or older, to vote shall not be denied or abridged by the United States or any state on account of age.

2. The Congress shall have the power to enforce this article by appropriate legislation.

PROPOSED AMENDMENT RELATING TO CONGRESSIONAL PAY

(Proposed by the first Congress Sept. 25, 1789 as one of the 12 amendments to the Constitution, the 10 that were accepted became the Bill of Rights; ratified as of May 1989 by 32 states: Maryland, North Carolina, South Carolina, Delaware, Vermont, Virginia 1789-1791; Ohio 1873; Wyoming 1978; Maine 1983; Colorado 1984; South Dakota, New Hampshire, Arizona, Tennessee, Oklahoma 1985; New Mexico, Indiana, Utah 1986; Montana, Connecticut, Wisconsin, Arkansas 1987; Georgia, W. Virginia, Louisiana 1988; Iowa, Idaho, Nevada, Alaska, Oregon, Minnesota, Texas 1989; Kansas, Florida 1990. An additional 4 ratifications are needed to attain the requisite three-quarters of the States.)

No law, varying the compensation for the services of the Senators and Representatives, shall take effect, until an election of Representatives shall have intervened.

Origin of the Constitution

The War of Independence was conducted by delegates from the original 13 states, called the Congress of the United States of America and generally known as the Continental Congress. In 1777 the Congress submitted to the legislatures of the states the Articles of Confederation and Perpetual Union, which were ratified by New Hampshire, Massachusetts, Rhode Island, Connecticut, New York, New Jersey, Pennsylvania, Delaware, Virginia, North Carolina, South Carolina, and Georgia, and finally, in 1781, by Maryland.

The first article of the instrument read: "The stile of this confederacy shall be the United States of America." This did not signify a sovereign nation, because the states delegated only those powers they could not handle individually, such as power to wage war, establish a uniform currency, make treaties with foreign nations and contract debts for general expenses (such as paying the army). Taxes for the payment of such debts were levied by the individual states. The president under the Articles signed himself "President of the United States in Congress assembled," but here the United States were considered in the plural, a cooperating group. Canada was invited to join the union on equal terms but did not act.

When the war was won it became evident that a stronger federal union was needed to protect the mutual interests of the states. The Congress left the initiative to the legislatures. Virginia in Jan. 1786 appointed commissioners to meet with representatives of other states, with the result that delegates from Virginia, Delaware, New York, New Jersey, and Pennsylvania met at Annapolis. Alexander Hamilton prepared for their call by asking delegates from all states to meet in Philadelphia in May 1787 "to render the Constitution of the Federal government adequate to the exigencies of the union." Congress endorsed the plan Feb. 21, 1787. Delegates were appointed by all states except Rhode Island.

The convention met May 14, 1787. George Washington was chosen delegate (presiding officer). The states certified 65 delegates, but 10 did not attend. The work was done by 55, not all of whom were present at all sessions. Of the 55 attending delegates, 16 failed to sign, and 39 actually signed Sept. 17, 1787, some with reservations. Some historians have said 74 delegates (9 more than the 65 actually certified) were named and 19 failed to attend. These 9 additional persons refused the appointment, were never delegates and never counted as absentees. Washington sent the Constitution to Congress with a covering letter and that body, Sept. 28, 1787, ordered it sent to the legislatures, "in order to be submitted to a convention of delegates chosen in each state by the people thereof."

The Constitution was ratified by votes of state conventions as follows: Delaware, Dec. 7, 1787, unanimous; Pennsylvania, Dec. 12, 1787, 43 to 23; New Jersey, Dec. 18, 1787, unanimous; Georgia, Jan 2, 1788, unanimous; Connecticut, Jan. 9, 1788, 128 to 40; Massachusetts, Feb. 6, 1788, 187 to 168; Maryland, Apr. 28, 1788, 63 to 11; South Carolina, May 23, 1788, 149 to 73; New Hampshire, June 21, 1788, 57 to 46; Virginia, June 25, 1788, 89 to 79; New York, July 26, 1788, 30 to 27. Nine states were needed to establish the operation of the Constitution "between the states so ratifying the same" and New Hampshire was the 9th state. The government did not declare the Constitution in effect until the first Wednesday in Mar. 1789 which was Mar. 4. After that North Carolina ratified it Nov. 21, 1789, 194 to 77; and Rhode Island, May 29, 1790, 34 to 32. Vermont in convention ratified it Jan. 10, 1791, and by act of Congress approved Feb. 18, 1791, was admitted into the Union as the 14th state, Mar. 4, 1791.

On Sept. 17, 1987, the nation began a four-year celebration of the 200th anniversary of the signing of the Constitution of the United States.

As of April 1987, 32 states have voted to issue convention calls to hold a second constitutional convention. Convention bills are pending before 11 more state legislatures, while bills to rescind previous calls are under consideration in four states. When the total reaches 34, the Constitution stipulates that a convention must be held. The convention drive began in the mid 1970s to bring about the consideration of an amendment requiring a balanced federal budget.

Selected Landmark Decisions of the U.S. Supreme Court

1803: Marbury v. Madison. The Court ruled that Congress exceeded its power in the Judiciary Act of 1789; thus, the Court established its power to review acts of Congress and declare invalid those it found in conflict with the Constitution.

1819: McCulloch v. Maryland. The Court ruled that Congress had the authority to charter a national bank, under the Constitution's granting of the power to enact all laws "necessary and proper" to exact the responsibilities of government. The Court also held that the national bank was immune to state taxation.

1819: Trustees of Dartmouth College v. Woodward. The Court ruled that a state could not arbitrarily alter the terms of a college's contract. (In later years the Court widened the implications by using the same principle to limit the states' ability to interfere with business contracts.)

1857: Dred Scott v. Sanford. The Court declared unconstitutional the already-repealed Missouri Compromise of 1820 because it deprived a person of his property—a slave—without due process of law. The Court also ruled that slaves were not citizens of any state nor of the U.S. (The latter part of the decision was overturned by ratification of the 14th Amendment in 1868.)

1896: Plessy v. Ferguson. The Court ruled that a state law requiring federal railroad trains to provide separate but equal facilities for black and white passengers neither infringed upon federal authority to regulate interstate commerce nor violated the 13th and 14th Amendments. (The "separate but equal" doctrine remained effective until the 1954 Brown v. Board of Education decision.)

1904: Northern Securities Co. v. U.S. The Court ruled that a holding company formed solely to eliminate competition between two railroad lines was a combination in restraint of trade, thus a violation of the federal antitrust act.

1908: Muller v. Oregon. The Court ruled to uphold a state law limiting the maximum working hours of women. (Instead of presenting legal arguments, Louis D. Brandeis, counsel for the state, brought forth evidence from social workers, physicians, and factory inspectors that the number of hours women worked affected their health and morals.)

1911: Standard Oil. Co. of New Jersey et al. v. U.S. The Court ruled that the Standard Oil Trust must be dissolved because of its unreasonable restraint of trade, not because of its size.

1919: Schenck v. U.S. In its first decision regarding the extent of protection afforded by the First Amendment, the Court sustained the Espionage Act of 1917, maintaining that freedom of speech and press could be constrained if "the words used are in such circumstances and are of such a nature as to create a clear and present danger. . ."

1925: Gitlow v. New York. The Court ruled that the First Amendment prohibition against government abridgement of the freedom of speech applied to the states as well as to the federal government. The decision was the first of a number of rulings holding that the 14th Amendment extended the guarantees of the Bill of Rights to state action.

1935: Schechter Poultry Corp. v. U.S. The Court ruled that Congress exceeded its authority to delegate legislative powers and to regulate interstate commerce when it enacted the National Industrial Recovery Act, which afforded the U.S. president too much discretionary power.

1951: Dennis et al. v. U.S. The Court upheld convictions under the Smith Act of 1940 for speaking about communist theory that advocated the forcible overthrow of the government. (In the 1957 Yates v. U.S. decision, the Court moderated this ruling by allowing such advocacy in the abstract, if not connected to action to achieve the goal.)

1954: Brown v. Board of Education of Topeka. The Court ruled that separate public schools for black and white students were inherently unequal, thus state-sanctioned segregation in public schools violated the equal protection guarantee of the 14th Amendment. And in **Bolling v. Sharpe** the Court ruled that the congressionally-mandated segregated public school system in the District of Columbia violated the Fifth Amendment's due process guarantee of personal liberty. (The Brown ruling also led to the abolition of state-sponsored segregation in other public facilities.)

1957: Roth v. U.S., Alberts v. California. The Court ruled that obscene material was not protected by the First Amendment guarantees of freedom of speech and press, defining obscene as "utterly without redeeming social value" and appealing to "prurient interests" in the view of the average person. (This definition, the first offered by the Court, was modified in several subsequent decisions, and the "average person" standard was replaced by the "local community" standard in the 1973 Miller v. California case.)

1961: Mapp v. Ohio. The Court ruled that evidence obtained in violation of the 4th Amendment guarantee against unreasonable search and seizure must be excluded from use at state as well as federal trials.

1962: Engel v. Vitale. The Court ruled that public school officials could not require pupils to recite a state-composed prayer at the start of each school day, even if the prayer was non-denominational and pupils who so desired could be excused from reciting it, because such official state sanction of religious utterances was an unconstitutional attempt to establish religion.

1962: Baker v. Carr. The Court held that the constitutional challenges to the unequal distribution of voters among legislative districts could be resolved by federal courts, rejecting the doctrine set out in Colegrove v. Green in 1946 that such apportionment challenges were "political questions."

1963: Gideon v. Wainwright. The Court ruled that the due process clause of the 14th Amendment extended to state as well as federal defendants, thus all persons charged with serious crimes must be provided with an attorney, and states were required to appoint counsel for defendants unable to pay their own attorneys' fees.

1964: New York Times Co. v. Sullivan. The Court ruled that the First Amendment guarantee of freedom of the press protected the press from libel suits for defamatory reports on public officials unless the officials proved that the reports were made from actual malice. The Court defined malice as "with knowledge that (the defamatory statement) was false or with reckless disregard of whether it was false or not."

1965: Griswold v. Conn. The Court ruled that a state unconstitutionally interfered with personal privacy in the marriage relationship when it prohibited anyone, including married couples, from using contraceptives.

1966: Miranda v. Arizona. The Court ruled that the guarantee of due process required that before any questioning of suspects in police custody, the suspects must be informed of their right to remain silent, that anything they say may be used against them, and that they have the right to counsel.

1973: Roe v. Wade, Doe v. Bolton. The Court ruled that the right to privacy inherent in the 14th Amendment's due process guarantee of personal liberty protected a woman's decision whether or not to bear a child, and was impermissibly abridged by state laws that made abortion a crime. During the first trimester of pregnancy, the Court maintained, the decision to have an abortion should be left entirely to a woman and her physician.

1974: U.S. v. Nixon. The Court ruled that neither the separation of powers nor the need to preserve the confidentiality of presidential communications could alone justify an absolute executive privilege of immunity from judicial demands for evidence to be used in a criminal trial.

1976: Gregg v. Georgia, Profitt v. Fla, Jurek v. Texas. The Court held that death, as a punishment for persons convicted of first degree murder, was not in and of itself cruel and unusual punishment in violation of the 8th Amendment. The Court also ruled that the Amendment required the sentencing judge and jury to consider the individual character of the offender and the circumstances of the particular crime before deciding whether or not to impose the death sentence. In the associated Woodson v. N.C., Roberts v. LA., the Court ruled that states could not make death the mandatory penalty for first-degree murder, since that would fail to meet the constitutional requirement for the consideration of the individual offender and offense.

1978: Regents of Univ. of Calif. v. Bakke. The Court ruled that a special admissions program for a state medical school under which a set number of places were set aside for minority group members, with white applicants denied the opportunity to compete for those seats, violated Title XIV of the 1964 Civil Rights Act, which forbids the exclusion of anyone, because of race, from participation in a federally-funded program. The Court also ruled that admissions programs that considered race as one of a complex of factors involved in the decision to admit or reject an applicant were not unconstitutional.

1979: United Steelworkers of America v. Weber, Kaiser Aluminum v. Weber, U.S. v. Weber. The Court ruled that Title VII of the 1964 Civil Rights Act, which forbids racial discrimination in employment, did not forbid employers to adopt voluntarily race-conscious affirmative action programs to encourage minority participation in areas in which they traditionally were underrepresented.

1986: Bowers v. Hardwick. The Court refused to extend the right of privacy inherent in the Constitution to homosexual activity, upholding a Georgia law that made sodomy a crime. (Although the Georgia law covered heterosexual sodomy as well as homosexual sodomy, enforcement in Georgia and most other states had been confined to homosexual activity.)

1989: Webster v. Reproductive Health Services. The Court upheld a Missouri abortion law that prohibited public employees from performing abortions unless the mother's life was in danger, barred the use of public buildings for performing abortions, and required physicians, before performing abortions of fetuses more than 20 weeks old, to perform tests to discover whether the fetus could live outside the womb.

Patrick Henry's Speech to the Virginia Convention

The following is an excerpt from Patrick Henry's speech to the Virginia Convention on Mar. 23, 1775:

Gentlemen may cry, peace, peace—but there is no peace. The war is actually begun! The next gale that sweeps from the north will bring to our ears the clash of resounding arms! Our brethren are already in the field! Why stand we here idle? What is it that gentlemen wish? What would they have? Is life so dear, or peace so sweet, as to be purchased at the price of chains and slavery? Forbid it, Almighty God! I know not what course others may take; but as for me, give me liberty, or give me death!

Common Sense

The following is an excerpt from Thomas Paine's *Common Sense.* Paine adopted the doctrine of separation from Britain after the battles of Lexington and Concord, and published his pamphlet in Jan. 1776.

The cause of America is in great measure the cause of all mankind. Many circumstances hath, and will arise, which are not local, but universal, and through which principles of all Lovers of Mankind are affected, and in the Event of which, their Affections are interested. The laying a Country desolate with Fire and Sword, declaring war against natural rights of all Mankind, and extirpating the Defenders thereof from the Face of the Earth, is the Concern of every Man to whom Nature hath given the Power of feeling; . . . It is repugnant to reason, to the universal order of things, to all examples from former ages, to suppose, that this continent can longer remain subject to any external power . . .

The last cord is now broken, the people of England are presenting addresses against us. There are injuries which nature cannot forgive; she would cease to be nature if she did . . .

O ye that love mankind! Ye that dare oppose, not only the tyranny, but the tyrant, stand forth! Every spot of the old world is overrun with oppression. Freedom hath been hunted round the globe. Asia, and Africa, have long expelled her—Europe regards her like a stranger, and England hath given her warning to depart. O! Receive the fugitive, and prepare in time an asylum for mankind.

Law on Succession to the Presidency

If by reason of death, resignation, removal from office, inability, or failure to qualify there is neither a president nor vice president to discharge the powers and duties of the office of president, then the speaker of the House of Representatives shall upon his resignation as speaker and as representative, act as president. The same rule shall apply in the case of the death, resignation, removal from office, or inability of an individual acting as president.

If at the time when a speaker is to begin the discharge of the powers and duties of the office of president there is no speaker, or the speaker fails to qualify as acting president, then the president pro tempore of the Senate, upon his resignation as president pro tempore and as senator, shall act as president.

An individual acting as president shall continue to act until the expiration of the then current presidential term, except that (1) if his discharge of the powers and duties of the office is founded in whole or in part in the failure of both the president-elect and the vice president-elect to qualify, then he shall act only until a president or vice president qualifies, and (2) if his discharge of the powers and duties of the office is founded in whole or in part on the inability of the president or vice president, then he shall act only until the removal of the disability of one of such individuals.

If, by reason of death, resignation, removal from office, or failure to qualify, there is no president pro tempore to act as president, then the officer of the United States who is highest on the following list, and who is not under any disability to discharge the powers and duties of president shall act as president; the secretaries of state, treasury, defense, attorney general; secretaries of interior, agriculture, commerce, labor, health and human services, housing and urban development, transportation, energy, education.

(Legislation approved July 18, 1947; amended Sept. 9, 1965, Oct. 15, 1966, Aug. 4, 1977, and Sept. 27, 1979. (See also Constitutional Amendment XXV.)

Presidential Oath of Office

The Constitution (Article II) directs that the President shall take the following oath or affirmation: "I do solemnly swear (affirm) that I will faithfully execute the office of President of the United States, and will, to the best of my ability, preserve, protect, and defend the Constitution of the United States." (Custom decrees the use of the words "So help me God" at the end of the oath when taken by the President-elect, his/her left hand on the Bible for the duration of the oath, with his/her right hand slightly raised.)

How the Declaration of Independence Was Adopted

On June 7, 1776, Richard Henry Lee, who had issued the first call for a congress of the colonies, introduced in the Continental Congress at Philadelphia a resolution declaring "that these United Colonies are, and of right ought to be, free and independent states, that they are absolved from all allegiance to the British Crown, and that all political connection between them and the state of Great Britain is, and ought to be, totally dissolved."

The resolution, seconded by John Adams on behalf of the Massachusetts delegation, came up again June 10 when a committee of 5, headed by Thomas Jefferson, was appointed to express the purpose of the resolution in a declaration of independence. The others on the committee were John Adams, Benjamin Franklin, Robert R. Livingston, and Roger Sherman.

Drafting the Declaration was assigned to Jefferson, who worked on a portable desk of his own construction in a room at Market and 7th Sts. The committee reported the result June 28, 1776. The members of the Congress suggested a number of changes, which Jefferson called "deplorable." They didn't approve Jefferson's arraignment of the British people and King George III for encouraging and fostering the slave trade, which Jefferson called "an execrable commerce." They made 86 changes, eliminating 480 words and leaving 1,337. In the final form capitalization was erratic. Jefferson had written that men were endowed with "inalienable" rights; in the final copy it came out as "unalienable" and has been thus ever since.

The Lee-Adams resolution of independence was adopted by 12 yeas July 2 — the actual date of the act of independence. The Declaration, which explains the act, was adopted July 4, in the evening.

After the Declaration was adopted, July 4, 1776, it was turned over to John Dunlap, printer, to be printed on broadsides. The original copy was lost and one of his broadsides was attached to a page in the journal of the Congress. It was read aloud July 8 in Philadelphia, Easton, Pa., and Trenton, N.J. On July 9 at 6 p.m. it was read by order of Gen. George Washington to the troops assembled on the Common in New York City (City Hall Park).

The Continental Congress of July 19, 1776, adopted the following resolution:

"Resolved, That the Declaration passed on the 4th, be fairly engrossed on parchment with the title and stile of 'The Unanimous Declaration of the thirteen United States of America' and that the same, when engrossed, be signed by every member of Congress."

Not all delegates who signed the engrossed Declaration were present on July 4. Robert Morris (Pa.), William Williams (Conn.) and Samuel Chase (Md.) signed on Aug. 2, Oliver Wolcott (Conn.), George Wythe (Va.), Richard Henry Lee (Va.) and Elbridge Gerry (Mass.) signed in August and September, Matthew Thornton (N. H.) joined the Congress Nov. 4 and signed later. Thomas McKean (Del.) rejoined Washington's Army before signing and said later that he signed in 1781.

Charles Carroll of Carrollton was appointed a delegate by Maryland on July 4, 1776, presented his credentials July 18, and signed the engrossed Declaration Aug. 2. Born Sept. 19, 1737, he was 95 years old and the last surviving signer when he died Nov. 14, 1832.

Two Pennsylvania delegates who did not support the Declaration on July 4 were replaced.

The 4 New York delegates did not have authority from their state to vote on July 4. On July 9 the New York state convention authorized its delegates to approve the Declaration and the Congress was so notified on July 15, 1776. The 4 signed the Declaration on Aug. 2.

The original engrossed Declaration is preserved in the National Archives Building in Washington.

The Continental Congress: Meetings, Presidents

Meeting places	Dates of meetings	Congress presidents	Date elected
Philadelphia	Sept. 5 to Oct. 26, 1774	Peyton Randolph, Va. (1)	Sept. 5, 1774
"	"	Henry Middleton, S.C.	Oct. 22, 1774
Philadelphia	May 10, 1775 to Dec. 12, 1776	Peyton Randolph, Va.	May 10, 1775
"	"	John Hancock, Mass.	May 24, 1775
Baltimore	Dec. 20, 1776 to Mar. 4, 1777		
Philadelphia	Mar. 5 to Sept. 18, 1777		
Lancaster, Pa.	Sept. 27, 1777 (one day)		
York, Pa.	Sept. 30, 1777 to June 27, 1778	Henry Laurens, S.C.	Nov. 1, 1777(4)
Philadelphia	July 2, 1778 to June 21, 1783	John Jay, N.Y.	Dec. 10, 1778
"	"	Samuel Huntington, Conn.	Sept. 28, 1779
"	"	Thomas McKean, Del.	July 10, 1781
"	"	John Hanson, Md. (2)	Nov. 5, 1781
"	"	Elias Boudinot, N.J.	Nov. 4, 1782
Princeton, N.J.	June 30 to Nov. 4, 1783	Thomas Mifflin, Pa.	Nov. 3, 1783
Annapolis, Md.	Nov. 26, 1783 to June 3, 1784		
Trenton, N.J.	Nov. 1 to Dec. 24, 1784	Richard Henry Lee, Va.	Nov. 30, 1784
New York City	Jan. 11 to Nov. 4, 1785		
"	Nov. 7, 1785 to Nov. 3, 1786	John Hancock, Mass. (3)	Nov. 23, 1785
"		Nathaniel Gorham, Mass.	June 6, 1786
"	Nov. 6, 1786 to Oct. 30, 1787	Arthur St. Clair, Pa.	Feb. 2, 1787
"	Nov. 5, 1787 to Oct. 21, 1788	Cyrus Griffin, Va.	Jan. 22, 1788
"	Nov. 3, 1788 to Mar. 2, 1789		

(1) Resigned Oct. 22, 1774. (2) Titled "President of the United States in Congress Assembled," John Hanson is considered by some to be the first U.S. President as he was the first to serve under the Articles of Confederation. He was, however, little more than presiding officer of the Congress, which retained full executive power. He could be considered the head of government, but not head of state. (3) Resigned May 29, 1786, without serving, because of illness. (4) Articles of Confederation agreed upon, Nov. 15, 1777; last ratification from Maryland, Mar. 1, 1781.

Origin of the United States National Motto

In God We Trust, designated as the U. S. National Motto by Congress in 1956, originated during the Civil War as an inscription for U. S. coins, although it was used by Francis Scott Key in a slightly different form when he wrote The Star Spangled Banner in 1814. On Nov. 13, 1861, when Union morale had been shaken by battlefield defeats, the Rev. M. R. Watkinson, of Ridleyville, Pa., wrote to Secy. of the Treasury Salmon P. Chase. "From my heart I have felt our national shame in disowning God as not the least of our present national disasters," the minister wrote, suggesting "recognition of the Almighty God in some form on our coins." Secy. Chase ordered designs prepared with the inscription *In God We Trust* and backed coinage legislation which authorized use of this slogan. It first appeared on some U. S. coins in 1864, disappeared and reappeared on various coins until 1955, when Congress ordered it placed on all paper money and all coins.

The Great Seal of the U.S.

On July 4, 1776, the Continental Congress appointed a committee consisting of Benjamin Franklin, John Adams and Thomas Jefferson "to bring in a device for a seal of the United States of America." After many delays, a verbal description of a design by William Barton was finally approved by Congress on June 20, 1782. The seal shows an American bald eagle with a ribbon in its mouth bearing the device E pluribus unum (One out of many). In its talons are the arrows of war and an olive branch of peace. On the reverse side it shows an unfinished pyramid with an eye (the eye of Providence) above it.

The American's Creed

William Tyler Page, Clerk of the U.S. House of Representatives, wrote "The American's Creed" in 1917. It was accepted by the House on behalf of the American people on April 3, 1918.

"I believe in the United States of America as a government of the people, by the people, for the people; whose just powers are derived from the consent of the governed; a democracy in a republic; a sovereign Nation of many sovereign States; a perfect union, one and inseparable; established upon those principles of freedom, equality, justice, and humanity for which American patriots sacrificed their lives and fortunes.

"I therefore believe it is my duty to my country to love it, to support its Constitution, to obey its laws, to respect its flag, and to defend it against all enemies."

The Flag of the U.S.—The Stars and Stripes

The 50-star flag of the United States was raised for the first time officially at 12:01 a.m. on July 4, 1960, at Fort McHenry National Monument in Baltimore, Md. The 50th star had been added for Hawaii; a year earlier the 49th, for Alaska. Before that, no star had been added since 1912, when N.M. and Ariz. were admitted to the Union.

The true history of the Stars and Stripes has become so cluttered by a volume of myth and tradition that the facts are difficult, and in some cases impossible, to establish. For example, it is not certain who designed the Stars and Stripes, who made the first such flag, or even whether it ever flew in any sea fight or land battle of the American Revolution.

One thing all agree on is that the Stars and Stripes originated as the result of a resolution offered by the Marine Committee of the Second Continental Congress at Philadelphia and adopted June 14, 1777. It read:

Resolved: that the flag of the United States be thirteen stripes, alternate red and white; that the union be thirteen stars, white in a blue field, representing a new constellation.

Congress gave no hint as to the designer of the flag, no instructions as to the arrangement of the stars, and no information on its appropriate uses. Historians have been unable to find the original flag law.

The resolution establishing the flag was not even published until Sept. 2, 1777. Despite repeated requests, Washington did not get the flags until 1783, after the Revolutionary War was over. And there is no certainty that they were the Stars and Stripes.

Early Flags

Although it was never officially adopted by the Continental Congress, many historians consider the first flag of the U.S. to have been the Grand Union (sometimes called Great Union) flag. This was a modification of the British Meteor flag, which had the red cross of St. George and the white cross of St. Andrew combined in the blue canton. For the Grand Union flag, 6 horizontal stripes were imposed on the red field, dividing it into 13 alternate red and white stripes. On Jan. 1, 1776, when the Continental Army came into formal existence, this flag was unfurled on Prospect Hill, Somerville, Mass. Washington wrote that "we hoisted the Union Flag in compliment to the United Colonies."

One of several flags about which controversy has raged for years is at Easton, Pa. Containing the devices of the national flag in reversed order, this has been in the public library at Easton for over 150 years. Some contend that this flag was actually the first Stars and Stripes, first displayed on July 8, 1776. This flag has 13 red and white stripes in the canton, 13 white stars centered in a blue field.

A flag was hastily improvised from garments by the defenders of Fort Schuyler at Rome, N.Y., Aug. 3-22, 1777. Historians believe it was the Grand Union flag.

The Sons of Liberty had a flag of 9 red and white stripes, to signify 9 colonies, when they met in New York in 1765 to oppose the Stamp Tax. By 1775, the flag had grown to 13 red and white stripes, with a rattlesnake on it.

At Concord, Apr. 19, 1775, the minute men from Bedford, Mass., are said to have carried a flag having a silver arm with sword on a red field.

At Cambridge, Mass., the Sons of Liberty used a plain red flag with a green pine tree on it.

In June 1775, Washington went from Philadelphia to Boston to take command of the army, escorted to New York by the Philadelphia Light Horse Troop. It carried a yellow flag which had an elaborate coat of arms — the shield charged with 13 knots, the motto "For These We Strive" — and a canton of 13 blue and silver stripes.

In Feb., 1776, Col. Christopher Gadsden, member of the Continental Congress, gave the S. Carolina Provincial Congress a flag "such as is to be used by the commander-in-chief of the American Navy." It had a yellow field, with a rattlesnake about to strike and the words "Don't Tread on Me."

At the battle of Bennington, Aug. 16, 1777, patriots used a flag of 7 white and 6 red stripes with a blue canton extending down 9 stripes and showing an arch of 11 white stars over the figure 76 and a star in each of the upper corners. The stars are seven-pointed. This flag is preserved in the Historical Museum at Bennington, Vt.

At the Battle of Cowpens, Jan. 17, 1781, the 3d Maryland Regt. is said to have carried a flag of 13 red and white stripes, with a blue canton containing 12 stars in a circle around one star.

Who Designed the Flag? No one knows for certain. Francis Hopkinson, designer of a naval flag, declared he also had designed the flag and in 1781 asked Congress to reimburse him for his services. Congress did not do so. Dumas Malone of Columbia Univ. wrote: "This talented man ... designed the American flag."

Who Called the Flag Old Glory? — The flag is said to have been named Old Glory by William Driver, a sea captain of Salem, Mass. One legend has it that when he raised the flag on his brig, the Charles Doggett, in 1824, he said: "I name thee Old Glory." But his daughter, who presented the flag to the Smithsonian Institution, said he named it at his 21st birthday celebration Mar. 17, 1824, when his mother presented the homemade flag to him.

The Betsy Ross Legend — The widely publicized legend that Mrs. Betsy Ross made the first Stars and Stripes in June 1776, at the request of a committee composed of George Washington, Robert Morris, and George Ross, an uncle, was first made public in 1870, by a grandson of Mrs. Ross. Historians have been unable to find a historical record of such a meeting or committee.

Adding New Stars

The flag of 1777 was used until 1795. Then, on the admission of Vermont and Kentucky to the Union, Congress passed and Pres. Washington signed an act that after May 1, 1795, the flag should have 15 stripes, alternate red and white, and 15 white stars on a blue field in the union.

When new states were admitted it became evident that the flag would become burdened with stripes. Congress thereupon ordered that after July 4, 1818, the flag should have 13 stripes, symbolizing the 13 original states; that the union have 20 stars, and that whenever a new state was admitted a new star should be added on the July 4 following admission. No law designates the permanent arrangement of the stars. However, since 1912 when a new state has been admitted, the new design has been announced by executive order. No star is specifically identified with any state.

Code of Etiquette for Display and Use of the U.S. Flag

Although the Stars and Stripes originated in 1777, it was not until 146 years later that there was a serious attempt to establish a uniform code of etiquette for the U.S. flag. The War Department issued Feb. 15, 1923, a circular on the rules of flag usage. These were adopted almost in their entirety June 14, 1923, by a conference of 68 patriotic organizations in Washington. Finally, on June 22, 1942, a joint resolution of Congress, amended by Public Law 94-344 July 7, 1976, codified "existing rules and customs pertaining to the display and use of the flag . . ."

When to Display the Flag—The flag should be displayed on all days, especially on legal holidays and other special occasions, on official buildings when in use, in or near polling places on election days, and in or near schools when in session. A citizen may fly the flag at any time he wishes. It is customary to display the flag only from sunrise to sunset on buildings and on stationary flagstaffs in the open. However, it may be displayed at night on special occasions, preferably lighted. In Washington, the flag now flies over the White House both day and night. It flies over the Senate wing of the Capitol when the Senate is in session and over the House wing when that body is in session. It flies day and night over the east and west fronts of the Capitol, without floodlights at night but receiving light from the illuminated Capitol Dome. It flies 24 hours a day at several other places, including the Fort McHenry Nat'l Monument in Baltimore, where it inspired Francis Scott Key to write The Star Spangled Banner.

How to Fly the Flag—The flag should be hoisted briskly and lowered ceremoniously, and should never be allowed to touch the ground or the floor. When hung over a sidewalk from a rope extending from a building to a pole, the union should be away from the building. When hung over the center of a street it should have the union to the north in an east-west street and to the east in a north-south street. No other flag may be flown above or, if on the same level, to the right of the U.S. flag, except that at the United Nations Headquarters the UN flag may be placed above flags of all member nations and other national flags may be flown with equal prominence or honor with the flag of the U.S. At services by Navy chaplains at sea, the church pennant may be flown above the flag.

When two flags are placed against a wall with crossed staffs, the U.S. flag should be at right—its own right, and its staff should be in front of the staff of the other flag; when a number of flags are grouped and displayed from staffs, it should be at the center and highest point of the group.

Church and Platform Use—In an auditorium, the flag may be displayed flat, above and behind the speaker. When displayed from a staff in a church or public auditorium, the flag should hold the position of superior prominence, in advance of the audience, and in the position of honor at the clergyman's or speaker's right as he faces the audience. Any other flag so displayed should be placed on the left of the clergyman or speaker or to the right of the audience.

When the flag is displayed horizontally or vertically against a wall, the stars should be uppermost and at the observer's left.

How to Dispose of Worn Flags—The flag, when it is in such condition that it is no longer a fitting emblem for display, should be destroyed in a dignified way, preferably by burning.

When to Salute the Flag—All persons present should face the flag, stand at attention and salute on the following occasions: (1) When the flag is passing in a parade or in a review, (2) During the ceremony of hoisting or lowering, (3) When the National Anthem is played, and (4) During the Pledge of Allegiance. Those present in uniform should render the military salute. When not in uniform, men should remove the hat with the right hand holding it at the left shoulder, the hand being over the heart. Men without hats should salute in the same manner. Aliens should stand at attention. Women should salute by placing the right hand over the heart.

On Memorial Day, the flag should fly at half-staff until noon, then be raised to the peak.

As provided by Presidential proclamation the flag should fly at half-staff for 30 days from the day of death of a president or former president; for 10 days from the day of death of a vice president, chief justice or retired chief justice of the U.S., or speaker of the House of Representatives; from day of death until burial of an associate justice of the Supreme Court, cabinet member, former vice president, or Senate president pro tempore, majority or minority Senate leader, or majority or minority House leader; for a U.S. senator, representative, territorial delegate, or the resident commissioner of Puerto Rico, on day of death and the following day within the metropolitan area of the District of Columbia and from day of death until burial within the decedent's state, congressional district, territory or commonwealth; and for the death of the governor of a state, territory, or possession of the U.S., from day of death until burial within that state, territory, or possession.

When used to cover a casket, the flag should be placed so that the union is at the head and over the left shoulder. It should not be lowered into the grave nor touch the ground.

Prohibited Uses of the Flag—The flag should not be dipped to any person or thing. (An exception—customarily, ships salute by dipping their colors.) It should never be displayed with the union down save as a distress signal. It should never be carried flat or horizontally, but always aloft and free.

It should not be displayed on a float, motor car or boat except from a staff.

It should never be used as a covering for a ceiling, nor have placed upon it any word, design, or drawing. It should never be used as a receptacle for carrying anything. It should not be used to cover a statue or a monument.

The flag should never be used for advertising purposes, nor be embroidered on such articles as cushions or hankerchiefs, printed or otherwise impressed on boxes or anything that is designed for temporary use and discard; or used as a costume or athletic uniform. Advertising signs should not be fastened to its staff or halyard.

The flag should never be used as drapery of any sort, never festooned, drawn back, nor up, in folds, but always allowed to fall free. Bunting of blue, white and red always arranged with the blue above and the white in the middle, should be used for covering a speaker's desk, draping the front of a platform, and for decoration in general.

An Act of Congress approved Feb. 8, 1917, provided certain penalties for the desecration, mutilation or improper use of the flag within the District of Columbia. A 1968 federal law provided penalties of up to a year's imprisonment or a $1,000 fine or both, for publicly burning or otherwise desecrating any flag of the United States. In addition, many states have laws against flag desecration. In 1989, the Supreme Court ruled that no laws could prohibit political protesters from burning the flag. The decision had the effect of declaring unconstitutional the flag desecration laws of 48 states, as well as a similar Federal statute, in cases of peaceful political expression.

The Supreme Court, June 1990, declared that a new Federal law making it a crime to burn or deface the American flag violates the free-speech guarantee of the First Amendment. The 5-4 decision led to renewed calls in Congress for a constitutional amendment to make it possible to prosecute flag burning.

Pledge of Allegiance to the Flag

I pledge allegiance to the flag of the United States of America and to the republic for which it stands, one nation under God, indivisible, with liberty and justice for all.

This, the current official version of the Pledge of Allegiance, has developed from the original pledge, which was first published in the Sept. 8, 1892, issue of the Youth's Companion, a weekly magazine then published in Boston. The original pledge contained the phrase "my flag," which was changed more than 30 years later to "flag of the United States of America." An act of Congress in 1954 added the words "under God."

The authorship of the pledge had been in dispute for many years. The Youth's Companion stated in 1917 that the original draft was written by James B. Upham, an executive of the magazine who died in 1910. A leaflet circulated by the magazine later named Upham as the originator of the draft "afterwards condensed and perfected by him and his associates of the Companion force."

Francis Bellamy, a former member of the Youth's Companion editorial staff, publicly claimed authorship of the pledge in 1923. The United States Flag Assn., acting on the advice of a committee named to study the controversy, upheld in 1939 the claim of Bellamy, who had died 8 years earlier. The Library of Congress issued in 1957 a report attributing the authorship to Bellamy.

The National Anthem — The Star-Spangled Banner

The Star-Spangled Banner was ordered played by the military and naval services by President Woodrow Wilson in 1916. It was designated the National Anthem by Act of Congress, Mar. 3, 1931. It was written by Francis Scott Key, of Georgetown, D. C., during the bombardment of Fort McHenry, Baltimore, Md., Sept. 13-14, 1814. Key was a lawyer, a graduate of St. John's College, Annapolis, and a volunteer in a light artillery company. When a friend, Dr. Beanes, a physician of Upper Marlborough, Md., was taken aboard Admiral Cockburn's British squadron for interfering with ground troops, Key and J. S. Skinner, carrying a note from President Madison, went to the fleet under a flag of truce on a cartel ship to ask Beanes' release. Admiral Cockburn consented, but as the fleet was about to sail up the Patapsco to bombard Fort McHenry he detained them, first on H. M. S. Surprise, and then on a supply ship.

Key witnessed the bombardment from his own vessel. It began at 7 a.m., Sept. 13, 1814, and lasted, with intermissions, for 25 hours. The British fired over 1,500 shells, each weighing as much as 220 lbs. They were unable to approach closely because the Americans had sunk 22 vessels in the channel. Only four Americans were killed and 24 wounded. A British bomb-ship was disabled.

During the bombardment Key wrote a stanza on the back of an envelope. Next day at Indian Queen Inn, Baltimore, he wrote out the poem and gave it to his brother-in-law, Judge J. H. Nicholson. Nicholson suggested the tune, Anacreon in Heaven, and had the poem printed on broadsides, of which two survive. On Sept. 20 it appeared in the "Baltimore American." Later Key made 3 copies; one is in the Library of Congress and one in the Pennsylvania Historical Society.

The copy that Key wrote in his hotel Sept. 14, 1814, remained in the Nicholson family for 93 years. In 1907 it was sold to Henry Walters of Baltimore. In 1934 it was bought at auction in New York from the Walters estate by the Walters Art Gallery, Baltimore, for $26,400. The Walters Gallery in 1953 sold the manuscript to the Maryland Historical Society for the same price.

The flag that Key saw during the bombardment is preserved in the Smithsonian Institution, Washington. It is 30 by 42 ft., and has 15 alternate red and white stripes and 15 stars, for the original 13 states plus Kentucky and Vermont. It was made by Mary Young Pickersgill. The Baltimore Flag House, a museum, occupies her premises, which were restored in 1953.

The Star-Spangled Banner

I

Oh, say can you see by the dawn's early light
  What so proudly we hailed at the twilight's last gleaming?
Whose broad stripes and bright stars thru the perilous fight,
  O'er the ramparts we watched were so gallantly streaming?
And the rocket's red glare, the bombs bursting in air,
  Gave proof through the night that our flag was still there.
Oh, say does that star-spangled banner yet wave
  O'er the land of the free and the home of the brave?

II

On the shore, dimly seen through the mists of the deep,
  Where the foe's haughty host in dread silence reposes,
What is that which the breeze, o'er the towering steep,
  As it fitfully blows, half conceals, half discloses?
Now it catches the gleam of the morning's first beam,
  In full glory reflected now shines in the stream:
'Tis the star-spangled banner! Oh long may it wave
  O'er the land of the free and the home of the brave!

III

And where is that band who so vauntingly swore
  That the havoc of war and the battle's confusion,
A home and a country should leave us no more!
  Their blood has washed out their foul footsteps' pollution.
No refuge could save the hireling and slave
  From the terror of flight, or the gloom of the grave:
And the star-spangled banner in triumph doth wave
  O'er the land of the free and the home of the brave!

IV

Oh! thus be it ever, when freemen shall stand
  Between their loved home and the war's desolation!
Blest with victory and peace, may the heav'n rescued land
  Praise the Power that hath made and preserved us a nation.
Then conquer we must, when our cause it is just,
  And this be our motto: "In God is our trust."
And the star-spangled banner in triumph shall wave
  O'er the land of the free and the home of the brave!

America
(My Country 'Tis of Thee)

First sung in public on July 4, 1831, at a service in the Park Street Church, Boston, the words were written by Rev. Samuel Francis Smith, a Baptist clergyman, who set them to a melody he found in a German songbook, unaware that it was the tune for the British anthem, "God Save the King/Queen."

My country, 'tis of thee,
Sweet land of liberty, Of thee I sing.
Land where my fathers died!
Land of the Pilgrims' pride!
From ev'ry mountainside,
Let freedom ring!

My native country, thee,
Land of the noble free,
Thy name I love.
I love thy rocks and rills,
Thy woods and templed hills;
My heart with rapture thrills
Like that above.

Let music swell the breeze,
And ring from all the trees
Sweet freedom's song.
Let mortal tongues awake;
Let all that breathe partake;
Let rocks their silence break,
The sound prolong.

Our fathers' God, to Thee,
Author of liberty,
To Thee we sing.
Long may our land be bright
With freedom's holy light;
Protect us by Thy might,
Great God, our King!

America, the Beautiful

Composed by Katherine Lee Bates, a Massachusetts educator and author, in 1893. It was inspired by the view Bates experienced atop Pike's Peak. Its final form was established in 1911 and is set to the music of Samuel A. Ward's "Materna."

O beautiful for spacious skies,
For amber waves of grain,
For purple mountain majesties
Above the fruited plain.
America! America!
God shed His grace on thee,
And crown thy good with brotherhood
From sea to shining sea.
O beautiful for pilgrim feet
Whose stern impassion'd stress
A thorough-fare for freedom beat
Across the wilderness.
America! America!
God mend thine ev'ry flaw,
Confirm thy soul in self control,
Thy liberty in law.

O beautiful for heroes prov'd
In liberating strife,
Who more than self their country lov'd
And mercy more than life.
America! America!
May God thy gold refine
Till all success be nobleness,
And ev'ry gain divine.
O beautiful for patriot dream
That sees beyond the years,
Thine alabaster cities gleam,
Undimmed by human tears.
America! America!
God shed His grace on thee,
And crown thy good with brotherhood
From sea to shining sea.

The Liberty Bell: Its History and Significance

The Liberty Bell, in Independence Hall, Philadelphia, is an object of great reverence to Americans because of its association with the historic events of the War of Independence.

The original Province bell, ordered to commemorate the 50th anniversary of the Commonwealth of Pennsylvania, was cast by Thomas Lister, Whitechapel, London, and reached Philadelphia in Aug. 1752. It bore an inscription from Leviticus XXV, 10: "Proclaim liberty throughout all the land unto all the inhabitants thereof."

The bell was cracked by a stroke of its clapper in Sept. 1752 while it hung on a truss in the State House yard for testing. Pass & Stow, Philadelphia founders, recast the bell, adding 1 1/2 ounces of copper to a pound of the original metal to reduce brittleness. It was found that the bell contained too much copper, injuring its tone, so Pass & Stow recast it again, this time successfully.

In June 1753 the bell was hung in the wooden steeple of the State House, erected on top of the brick tower. In use while the Continental Congress was in session in the State House, it rang out in defiance of British tax and trade restrictions, and proclaimed the Boston Tea Party and the first public reading of the Declaration of Independence.

On Sept. 18, 1777, when the British Army was about to occupy Philadelphia, the bell was moved in a baggage train of the American Army to Allentown, Pa. where it was hidden in the Zion Reformed Church until June 27, 1778. It was moved back to Philadelphia after the British left.

In July 1781 the wooden steeple became insecure and had to be taken down. The bell was lowered into the brick section of the tower. Here it was hanging in July, 1835, when it cracked while tolling for the funeral of John Marshall, chief justice of the United States. Because of its association with the War of Independence it was not recast but remained mute in this location until 1846, the year of the Mexican War, when it was placed on exhibition in the Declaration Chamber of Independence Hall.

In 1876, when many thousands of Americans visited Philadelphia for the Centennial Exposition, it was placed in its old walnut frame in the tower hallway. In 1877 it was hung from the ceiling of the tower by a chain of 13 links. It was returned again to the Declaration Chamber and in 1896 taken back to the tower hall, where it occupied a glass case. In 1915 the case was removed so that the public might touch it. On Jan. 1, 1976, just after midnight to mark the opening of the Bicentennial Year, the bell was moved to a new glass and steel pavilion behind Independence Hall for easier viewing by the larger number of visitors expected during the year.

The measurements of the bell follow: circumference around the lip, 12 ft.; circumference around the crown, 7 ft. 6 in.; lip to the crown, 3 ft.; height over the crown, 2 ft. 3 in.; thickness at lip, 3 in.; thickness at crown, 1 1/4 in.; weight, 2080 lbs.; length of clapper, 3 ft. 2 in.; cost, £60 14s 5d.

Statue of Liberty National Monument

Since 1886, the Statue of Liberty Enlightening the World has stood as a symbol of freedom in New York harbor. It also commemorates French-American friendship for it was given by the people of France, designed by Frederic Auguste Bartholdi (1834-1904). A $2.5 million building housing the American Museum of Immigration was opened by Pres. Nixon Sept. 26, 1972, at the base of the statue. It houses a permanent exhibition of photos, posters, and artifacts tracing the history of American immigration. The Monument is administered by the National Park Service.

Nearby Ellis Island, gateway to America for more than 12 million immigrants between 1892 and 1954, was proclaimed part of the National Monument in 1965 by Pres. Johnson.

Edouard de Laboulaye, French historian and admirer of American political institutions, suggested that the French present a monument to the United States, the latter to provide pedestal and site. Bartholdi visualized a colossal statue at the entrance of New York harbor, welcoming the peoples of the world with the torch of liberty.

On Washington's birthday, Feb. 22, 1877, Congress approved the use of a site on Bedloe's Island suggested by Bartholdi. This island of 12 acres had been owned in the 17th century by a Walloon named Isaac Bedloe. It was called Bedloe's until Aug. 3, 1956, when Pres. Eisenhower approved a resolution of Congress changing the name to Liberty Island.

The statue was finished May 21, 1884, and formally presented to U.S. Minister Morton July 4, 1884, by Ferdinand de Lesseps, head of the Franco-American Union, promoter of the Panama Canal, and builder of the Suez Canal.

On Aug. 5, 1884, the Americans laid the cornerstone for the pedestal. This was to be built on the foundations of Fort Wood, which had been erected by the Government in 1811. The American committee had raised $125,000, but this was found to be inadequate. Joseph Pulitzer, owner of the New York World, appealed on Mar. 16, 1885, for general donations. By Aug. 11, 1885, he had raised $100,000.

The statue arrived dismantled, in 214 packing cases, from Rouen, France, in June, 1885. The last rivet of the statue was driven Oct. 28, 1886, when Pres. Grover Cleveland dedicated the monument.

The statue weighs 450,000 lbs. or 225 tons. The copper sheeting weighs 200,000 lbs. There are 167 steps from the land level to the top of the pedestal, 168 steps inside the statue to the head, and 54 rungs on the ladder leading to the arm that holds the torch.

Two years of restoration work was completed before the statue's centennial celebration on July 4, 1986. Among other repairs, the multi-million dollar project included replacing the 1,600 wrought iron bands that hold its copper skin to its frame, replacing its torch, and installing an elevator.

A four-day extravaganza of concerts, tall ships, ethnic festivals, and fireworks celebrated the 100th anniversary. The festivities included Chief Justice Warren E. Burger's swearing-in of 5,000 new citizens on Liberty Island, while 20,000 others across the country were simultaneously sworn in through a satellite telecast.

The ceremonies were followed by others on Oct. 28, 1986, the statue's 100th birthday.

Emma Lazarus' Famous Poem

A poem by Emma Lazarus is graven on a tablet within the pedestal on which the statue stands.

The New Colossus

Not like the brazen giant of Greek fame,
With conquering limbs astride from land to land;
Here at our sea-washed, sunset gates shall stand

A mighty woman with a torch, whose flame
Is the imprisoned lightning, and her name
Mother of Exiles. From her beacon-hand
Glows world-wide welcome; her mild eyes command
The air-bridged harbor that twin cities frame.
"Keep ancient lands, your storied pomp!" cries she
With silent lips. "Give me your tired, your poor,
Your huddled masses yearning to breathe free,
The wretched refuse of your teeming shore.
Send these, the homeless, tempest-tost to me,
I lift my lamp beside the golden door!"

Dimensions of the Statue	Ft.	In.
Height from base to torch (45.3 meters)	151	1
Foundation of pedestal to torch (91.5 meters). . .	305	1
Heel to top of head	111	1
Length of hand	16	5
Index finger	8	0
Circumference at second joint.	3	6
Size of finger nail . . . . 13x10 in.		
Head from chin to cranium.	17	3
Head thickness from ear to ear	10	0
Distance across the eye	2	6
Length of nose	4	6
Right arm, length	42	0
Right arm, greatest thickness	12	0
Thickness of waist	35	0
Width of mouth	3	0
Tablet, length	23	7
Tablet, width.	13	7
Tablet, thickness	2	0

Lincoln's Address at Gettysburg, 1863

Fourscore and seven years ago our fathers brought forth on this continent a new nation, conceived in liberty and dedicated to the proposition that all men are created equal.

Now we are engaged in a great civil war, testing whether that nation or any nation so conceived and so dedicated can long endure. We are met on a great battle field of that war. We have come to dedicate a portion of that field, as a final resting-place for those who here gave their lives that that nation might live. It is altogether fitting and proper that we should do this.

But, in a larger sense, we can not dedicate — we can not consecrate — we can not hallow — this ground. The brave men, living and dead, who struggled here, have consecrated it, far above our poor power to add or detract. The world will little note, nor long remember, what we say here, but it can never forget what they did here. It is for us the living, rather, to be dedicated here to the unfinished work which they who fought here have thus far so nobly advanced. It is rather for us to be here dedicated to the great task remaining before us — that from these honored dead we take increased devotion to that cause for which they gave the last full measure of devotion — that we here highly resolve that these dead shall not have died in vain — that this nation, under God, shall have a new birth of freedom — and that government of the people, by the people, for the people, shall not perish from the earth.

Confederate States and Secession

The American Civil War, 1861-65, grew out of sectional disputes over the continued existence of slavery in the South and the contention of Southern legislators that the states retained many sovereign rights, including the right to secede from the Union.

The war was not fought by state against state but by one federal regime against another, the Confederate government in Richmond assuming control over the economic, political, and military life of the South, under protest from Georgia and South Carolina.

South Carolina voted an ordinance of secession from the Union, repealing its 1788 ratification of the U.S. Constitution on Dec. 20, 1860, to take effect Dec. 24. Other states seceded in 1861. Their votes in conventions were:

Mississippi, Jan. 9, 84-15; Florida, Jan. 10, 62-7; Alabama, Jan. 11, 61-39; Georgia, Jan. 19, 208-89; Louisiana, Jan. 26, 113-17; Texas, Feb. 1, 166-7, ratified by popular vote Feb. 23 (for 34,794, against 11,325); Virginia, Apr. 17, 88-55, ratified by popular vote May 23 (for 128,884; against

32,134); Arkansas, May 6, 69-1; Tennessee, May 7, ratified by popular vote June 8 (for 104,019, against 47,238); North Carolina, May 21.

Missouri Unionists stopped secession in conventions Feb. 28 and Mar. 9. The legislature condemned secession Mar. 7. Under the protection of Confederate troops, secessionist members of the legislature adopted a resolution of secession at Neosho, Oct. 31. The Confederate Congress seated the secessionists' representatives.

Kentucky did not secede and its government remained Unionist. In a part occupied by Confederate troops, Kentuckians approved secession and the Confederate Congress admitted their representatives.

The Maryland legislature voted against secession Apr. 27, 53-13. Delaware did not secede. Western Virginia held conventions at Wheeling, named a pro-Union governor June 11, 1861; admitted to Union as West Virginia June 20, 1863; its constitution provided for gradual abolition of slavery.

Confederate Government

Forty-two delegates from South Carolina, Georgia, Alabama, Mississippi, Louisiana, and Florida met in convention at Montgomery, Ala., Feb. 4, 1861. They adopted a provisional constitution of the Confederate States of America, and elected Jefferson Davis (Miss.) provisional president, and Alexander H. Stephens (Ga.) provisional vice president.

A permanent constitution was adopted Mar. 11; it abolished the African slave trade. The Congress moved to Richmond, Va. July 20. Davis was elected president in October,

and was inaugurated Feb. 22, 1862.

The Congress adopted a flag, consisting of a red field with a white stripe, and a blue jack with a circle of white stars. Later the more popular flag was the red field with blue diagonal cross bars that held 13 white stars. The stars represented the 11 states actually in the Confederacy plus Kentucky and Missouri.

(See also Civil War, U.S., in Index)

The Mayflower Compact

The threat of James I to "harry them out of the land" sent a little band of religious dissenters from England to Holland in 1608. They were known as "Separatists" because they wished to cut all ties with the Established Church. In 1620, some of them, known now as the Pilgrims, joined with a larger group in England to set sail on the *Mayflower* for the New World. A joint stock company financed their venture.

In November, they sighted Cape Cod and decided to land an exploring party at Plymouth Harbor. However, a rebellious group picked up at Southhampton and London troubled the Pilgrim leaders, and to control their actions forty-one of the Pilgrims drew up the "Mayflower Compact," which was signed before going ashore. The voluntary agreement to govern themselves was America's first written constitution.

In the name of God, Amen. We, whose names are underwritten, the Loyal Subjects of our dread Sovereign Lord, King *James,* by the Grace of God, of *Great Britain, France and Ireland,* King, *Defender of the Faith,* etc.

Having undertaken for the Glory of God, and Advancement of the Christian Faith, and the Honour of our King and Country, a voyage to plant the first colony in the northern Parts of Virginia; do by these Presents, solemnly and mutually in the Presence of God and one of another, convenant and combine ouselves together into a civil Body Politick, for our better Ordering and Preservation, and Furtherance of the Ends aforesaid: And by Virtue hereof to enact, constitute, and frame, such just and equal Laws, Ordinances, Acts, Constitutions and Offices, from time to time, as shall be thought most meet and convenient for the General good of the Colony; unto which we promise all due Submission and Obedience.

In Witness whereof we have hereunto subscribed our names at *Cape Cod* the eleventh of *November,* in the Reign of our Sovereign Lord, King *James* of *England, France* and *Ireland,* the eighteenth, and of *Scotland* the fifty-fourth. *Anno Domini,* 1620.

Forms of Address for Persons of Rank and Public Office

In these examples John Smith is used as a representative American name. The salutation Dear Sir or Dear Madam is always permissible when addressing a person not known to the writer. Female equivalents should be substituted where appropriate.

President of the United States

Address: The President, The White House, Washington, DC 20500. Also, The President and Mrs. ____.

Salutation: Dear Sir or Mr. President or Dear Mr. President. More intimately: My dear Mr. President. Also: Dear Mr. President and Mrs. ____.

The vice president takes the same forms.

Cabinet Officers

Address: Mr. John Smith, Secretary of State, Washington, D.C. or The Hon. John Smith. Similar addresses for other members of the cabinet. Also: Secretary and Mrs. John Smith.

Salutation: Dear Sir, or Dear Mr. Secretary. Also: Dear Mr. and Mrs. Smith.

The Bench

Address: The Hon. John Smith, Chief Justice of the United States. The Hon. John Smith, Associate Justice of the Supreme Court of the United States. The Hon. John Smith, Associate Judge, U.S. District Court.

Salutation: Dear Sir, or Dear Mr. Chief Justice. Dear Mr. Justice. Dear Judge Smith.

Members of Congress

Address: The Hon. John Smith, United States Senate, Washington, DC 20510, or Sen. John Smith, etc. Also The Hon. John Smith, House of Representatives, Washington, DC 20515, or Rep. John Smith, etc.

Salutation: Dear Mr. Senator or Dear Mr. Smith; for Representative, Dear Mr. Smith.

Officers of Armed Forces

Address: Careful attention should be given to the precise rank, thus: General of the Army John Smith, Fleet Admiral John Smith. The rules for Air Force are same as Army.

Salutation: Dear Sir, or Dear General. All general officers, whatever rank, are entitled to be addressed as generals. Likewise a lieutenant colonel is addressed as colonel and first and second lieutenants are addressed as lieutenant.

Warrant officers and flight officers are addressed as Mister. Chaplains are addressed as Chaplain. A Catholic chaplain may be addressed as Father. Cadets of the United States Military Academy and Air Force Academy are addressed as Cadet. Noncommissioned officers are addressed by their titles.

Ambassador, Governor, Mayor

Address: The Hon. John Smith, followed by his or her title. They can be addressed either at their embassy, or at the Department of State, Washington, D.C. An ambassador from a foreign nation may be addressed as His or Her Excellency. An American is not to be so addressed.

Salutation: Dear Mr. or Madam Ambassador. An ambassador from a foreign nation may be called Your Excellency.

Governors and mayors are often addressed as The Hon. Jane Smith, Governor of ____, or The Hon. John Smith, Mayor of ____; also Governor John Smith, State House, Albany, N.Y., or Mayor Jane Smith, City Hall, Erie, Pa.

The Clergy

Address: His Holiness, the Pope, or His Holiness Pope (name), State of Vatican City, Italy.

Salutation: Your Holiness or Most Holy Father.

Also: His Eminence, John, Cardinal Smith; salutation: Your Eminence. An archbishop or a bishop is addressed The Most Reverend, and the salutation is Your Excellency. A monsignor who is a papal chamberlain is The Very Reverend Monsignor and the salutation is Dear Sir or Very Reverend Monsignor; a monsignor who is a domestic prelate is The Right Reverend Monsignor and salutation is Right Reverend Monsignor. A priest is addressed Reverend John Smith. A brother of an order is addressed Brother ——. A sister takes the same form.

A bishop of the Episcopal Church is The Right Reverend John Smith; salutation is Right Reverend Sir, or Dear Bishop Smith. If a clergyman is a doctor of divinity, he is addressed: The Reverend John Smith, D.D., and the salutation is Reverend Sir, or Dear Dr. Smith. When a clergyman does not have the degree the salutation is Dear Mr. Smith.

A bishop of the Methodist Church is addressed Bishop John Smith with titles following.

Royalty and Nobility

An emperor is to be addressed in a letter as Sir, or Your Imperial Majesty.

A king or queen is addressed as His Majesty (Name), King of (Name), or Her Majesty (Name), Queen of (Name), Salutation: Sir, or Madam, or May it please Your Majesty.

Princes and princesses and other persons of royal blood are addressed as His (or Her) Royal Highness, and saluted with May it please Your Royal Highness.

A duke or marquis is My Lord Duke (or Marquis), a duke is His (or Your) Grace.

AFGHANISTAN

ALBANIA

ALGERIA

ANGOLA

ARGENTINA

AUSTRALIA

AUSTRIA

THE BAHAMAS

BAHRAIN

BANGLADESH

BARBADOS

BELGIUM

BELIZE

BENIN

BHUTAN

BOLIVIA

BOTSWANA

BRAZIL

BRUNEI DARUSSALAM

BULGARIA

BURKINA FASO

BURUNDI

CAMBODIA

CAMEROON

CANADA

CAPE VERDE

CENTRAL AFRICAN REPUBLIC

CHAD

CHILE

CHINA

COLOMBIA

COMOROS

CONGO

COSTA RICA

COTE D'IVOIRE

CUBA

CYPRUS

CZECHOSLOVAKIA

DENMARK

DJIBOUTI

DOMINICA

DOMINICAN REPUBLIC

ECUADOR

EGYPT

EL SALVADOR

EQUATORIAL GUINEA

ETHIOPIA

FIJI

FINLAND

FRANCE

GABON

THE GAMBIA

(EAST) GERMANY

(WEST) GERMANY

GHANA

F2

GREECE	GRENADA	GUATEMALA	GUINEA	GUINEA-BISSAU
GUYANA	HAITI	HONDURAS	HUNGARY	ICELAND
INDIA	INDONESIA	IRAN	IRAQ	IRELAND
ISRAEL	ITALY	JAMAICA	JAPAN	JORDAN
KENYA	NORTH KOREA	SOUTH KOREA	KUWAIT	LAOS
LEBANON	LESOTHO	LIBERIA	LIBYA	LIECHTENSTEIN
LUXEMBOURG	MADAGASCAR	MALAWI	MALAYSIA	MALDIVES
MALI	MALTA	MAURITANIA	MAURITIUS	MEXICO
MONACO	MONGOLIA	MOROCCO	MOZAMBIQUE	MYANMAR (BURMA)
NAMIBIA	NEPAL	NETHERLANDS	NEW ZEALAND	NICARAGUA
NIGER	NIGERIA	NORWAY	OMAN	PAKISTAN

PANAMA	PAPUA NEW GUINEA	PARAGUAY	PERU	PHILIPPINES
POLAND	PORTUGAL	QATAR	ROMANIA	RWANDA
ST. KITTS AND NEVIS	SAINT LUCIA	ST. VINCENT AND THE GRENADINES	SAN MARINO	SAO TOME AND PRINCIPE
SAUDI ARABIA	SENEGAL	SEYCHELLES	SIERRA LEONE	SINGAPORE
SOLOMON ISLANDS	SOMALIA	SOUTH AFRICA	SPAIN	SRI LANKA
SUDAN	SURINAME	SWAZILAND	SWEDEN	SWITZERLAND
SYRIA	TAIWAN	TANZANIA	THAILAND	TOGO
TONGA	TRINIDAD AND TOBAGO	TUNISIA	TURKEY	UGANDA
UNION OF SOVIET SOCIALIST REPUBLICS	UNITED ARAB EMIRATES	UNITED KINGDOM	UNITED STATES	URUGUAY
VANUATU	VATICAN CITY	VENEZUELA	VIETNAM	WESTERN SAMOA
YEMEN	YUGOSLAVIA	ZAIRE	ZAMBIA	ZIMBABWE

INTERNATIONAL TIME ZONES

The world is divided into 24 time zones, each 15° longitude wide. The longitudinal meridian passing through Greenwich, England, is the starting point, and is called the *prime meridian*. The 12th zone is divided by the 180th meridian (International Date Line). When the line is crossed going west, the date is advanced one day; when crossed going east, the date becomes a day earlier.

© The World Almanac and Book of Facts, 1991

NORTH AMERICA

ARCTIC OCEAN

Cape Morris Jesup
Nord
Cape Columbia
Alert
Ellesmere
Island
Thule

Greenland (Kalaallit Nunaat) (Denmark)

Ammassalik

Bering Sea
Chukchi Sea
Bering Strait
St. Lawrence I.
Nome
Nunivak
SEWARD PENINSULA
Bethel
Yukon

Alaska
Point Barrow
Barrow
Beaufort Sea
Sachs Harbour
Banks I.
Melville I.
Devon I.
Baffin Bay
Denmark Strait
Cape Farewell
Godthab (Nuuk)

Highest point in North America
Mt. McKinley, 20,320
Fairbanks
Fort McPherson
Inuvik
BROOKS RANGE
Victoria I.
Resolute
Pond Inlet

Anchorage
Seward
Valdez
Mt. Katmai 6,716
Kodiak
Dawson
YUKON PLATEAU
Cambridge Bay
Baffin Island
Panghirtung
Davis Strait

Mt. Logan 19,850
Gulf of Alaska
ALASKA RANGE
Carmacks
Whitehorse
Great Bear Lake
Arctic Circle
Frobisher Bay
60
Cape Farewell

Juneau
Sitka
Alexander Archipelago
Ketchikan
Prince Rupert
Queen Charlotte Islands
Kitimat
Watson Lake
Fort Simpson
Yellowknife
Great Slave Lake
Rankin Inlet
Eskimo Point
Southampton I.
Hudson Strait
UNGAVA PENINSULA
Povungnituk
Hebron
Labrador Sea

Hay River
Fort Nelson
Uranium City
CANADA
Churchill
Hudson Bay
Schefferville
Goose Bay
St. Anthony
LABRADOR

Port Hardy
Vancouver I.
Mt. Waddington 13,175
Prince George
Grande-Prairie
Dawson Creek
Peace River
Fort McMurray
Fort Smith
Lake Athabasca
La Loche
La Ronge
Flin Flon
Thompson
York Factory
Labrador City
CANADIAN SHIELD
Sept-Iles
Chibougamau
Chicoutimi
Gander
Corner Brook
Newfoundland
St. John's

Mt. Robson 12,972
Jasper
Williams Lake
Kamloops
Edmonton
Calgary
Lethbridge
Prince Albert
Saskatoon
Regina
Brandon
Williston
Winnipeg
Lake Winnipeg
Moosonee
James Bay
Val-d'Or
Quebec
Fredericton
NOVA SCOTIA
Sydney
Cape Breton I.

Vancouver
Victoria
Seattle
Spokane
ROCKY MOUNTAINS
GREAT PLAINS
Thunder Bay
Lake Superior
Sudbury
Timmins
Montreal
Ottawa
Halifax
Cape Sable
Bangor
Portland

Mt. Rainier 14,410
Portland
Eugene
Eureka
Missoula
Great Falls
Billings
Bismarck
Fargo
Duluth
Lake Huron
Lake Ontario
Rochester
Boston
Cape Sable

Boise
Butte
Rapid City
Casper
Cheyenne
Sioux Falls
Minneapolis
Green Bay
Lake Michigan
Toronto
Buffalo
Cleveland
New York City
Philadelphia

San Francisco
San Jose
Fresno
Reno
SIERRA NEVADA
GREAT BASIN
Salt Lake City
Great Salt Lake
Denver
Omaha
Des Moines
Milwaukee
Chicago
Detroit
Pittsburgh
Washington, D.C.
Richmond

Santa Barbara
Point Conception
Los Angeles
San Diego
Tijuana
Mexicali
Death Valley
Lowest point in North America
Las Vegas
COLORADO PLATEAU
Mt. Whitney 14,494
Mt. Elbert 14,433
Kansas City
St. Louis
Louisville
Indianapolis
Columbus
Nashville
Mt. Mitchell 6,684
Raleigh
Charlotte
Cape Hatteras

Phoenix
Tucson
Nogales
Hermosillo
Albuquerque
Amarillo
Lubbock
UNITED STATES
Oklahoma City
Little Rock
Memphis
Wichita
Atlanta
APPALACHIAN MTS.
Charleston
Savannah

Ciudad Juarez
Chihuahua
El Paso
Dallas
Austin
Jackson
Birmingham
Mobile
COASTAL PLAIN
Jacksonville

Ciudad Obregon
Cerro Mohinora 13,097
SIERRA MADRE OCCIDENTAL
San Antonio
Nuevo Laredo
Brownsville
Matamoros
Houston
New Orleans
St. Petersburg
Tampa
Miami
Freeport
Nassau
THE BAHAMAS

La Paz
Durango
Monterrey
Gulf of Mexico
Cape Sable
Havana
CUBA
Pico Duarte 10,416
DOMINICAN REPUBLIC

False Cape
Mazatlan
Tampico
Bay of Campeche
Merida
Cancun
Greater Antilles
JAMAICA
HAITI
Port-au-Prince
Santo Domingo

BAJA CALIFORNIA
Aguascalientes
Cape Corrientes
Leon
Guadalajara
MEXICO
Mexico City
Veracruz
Campeche
Villahermosa
YUCATAN PENINSULA
Kingston
Caribbean Sea
Lesser Antilles

Colima
Puebla
Citlaltepetl 18,700
Oaxaca
Tuxtla Gutierrez
BELIZE

Acapulco
SIERRA MADRE DEL SUR
GUATEMALA
Guatemala
Tajumulco 13,845
Belmopan
HONDURAS
Tegucigalpa

EL SALVADOR
San Salvador
NICARAGUA
Managua
Lake Nicaragua
ISTHMUS OF PANAMA

San Jose
COSTA RICA
Panama Canal
Panama
PANAMA

PACIFIC OCEAN
Tropic of Cancer

ATLANTIC OCEAN

Elevation

Meters	Feet
4,000	13,120
2,000	6,560
500	1,640
200	656
0	0
Below Sea Level	Below Sea Level

0   250   500   750   1000 Miles
0   250   500   750   1000   1200 Kilometers

© The World Almanac and Book of Facts, 1991

UNITED STATES,
CANADA, MEXICO

Elevation

Meters		Feet
3,000		9,842
2,000		6,560
1,000		3,280
200		656
0		0
Below Sea Level		Below Sea Level

© The World Almanac and Book of Facts, 1991

0 ___ 250 ___ 500 Miles
0 ___ 250 ___ 500 ___ 750 Kilometers

ATLANTIC

OCEAN

PACIFIC

OCEAN

Tropic of Cancer

Equator

BRAZIL

BRAZILIAN HIGHLANDS

MATO GROSSO PLATEAU

SELVAS

LA MONTAÑA

ANDES

LLANOS

GUIANA HIGHLANDS

Caribbean Sea

THE BAHAMAS

CUBA

MEXICO

GUATEMALA

HONDURAS

NICARAGUA

COSTA RICA

PANAMA

COLOMBIA

ECUADOR

PERU

BOLIVIA

VENEZUELA

GUYANA

SURINAME

French Guiana (Fr.)

HAITI

DOMINICAN REPUBLIC

JAMAICA

EL SALVADOR

BELIZE

Havana

Santa Clara

Camaguey

Holguin

Guantanamo

Santiago de Cuba

Isle of Youth

Cayman Is. (U.K.)

Montego Bay

Kingston

Cap-Haïtien

Port-au-Prince

Santiago

Santo Domingo

San Juan

Puerto Rico (U.S.)

Virgin Islands (U.S., U.K.)

Anguilla (U.K.)

ANTIGUA & BARBUDA

ST. KITTS & NEVIS

Montserrat (U.K.)

Guadeloupe (Fr.)

DOMINICA

Martinique (Fr.)

SAINT LUCIA

ST. VINCENT & THE GRENADINES

BARBADOS

GRENADA

TRINIDAD & TOBAGO

Port-of-Spain

Margarita Island

Bonaire (Neth.)

Curaçao (Neth.)

Aruba (Neth.)

Cumana

Maturin

Barcelona

Caracas

Valencia

Maracay

Barquisimeto

Coro

El Tigre

Ciudad Bolivar

Ciudad Guayana

Maracaibo

San Fernando de Apure

Puerto Ayacucho

Cabimas

Valera

Merida

Pico Bolivar 16,427

San Cristobal

Cucuta

Bucaramanga

Tunja

Bogota

Villavicencio

Medellin

Manizales

Pereira

Armenia

Ibague

Cali

Buenaventura

Palmira

Neiva

Nev. del Huila 16,865

Popayan

Pasto

Quito

Cotopaxi 19,347

Ambato

Riobamba

Chimborazo 20,561

Guayaquil

Machala

Portoviejo

Esmeraldas

Cali

Sincelejo

Monteria

Barranquilla

Santa Marta

Cartagena

Pico Cristobal Colon 18,947

Magdalena

Benjamin Constant

Iquitos

Yurimaguas

Nev. Huascaran 22,205

Cajamarca

Trujillo

Chimbote

Nev. Yerupaja 21,769

Chiclayo

Talara

Sullana

Piura

Tumbes

Aguja Point

Cerro de Pasco

Huanuco

Pucallpa

Cuzco

Ayacucho

Lima

Callao

Ica

Huancayo

Cruzeiro do Sul

Rio Branco

Guajara-Mirim

Trinidad

La Paz

Lake Titicaca

Puerto Maldonado

Cobija

Riberalta

Manaus

Santarem

Macapa

Marajo Island

Belem

Sao Luis

Parnaiba

Imperatriz

Teresina

Fortaleza

Natal

Joao Pessoa

Recife

Maceio

Aracaju

Salvador

Ilheus

Vitoria da Conquista

Feira de Santana

Juazeiro do Norte

Campina Grande

Sao Luis

Brasilia

Cuiaba

Porto Velho

Guajara-Mirim

Georgetown

New Amsterdam

Paramaribo

Cayenne

Kourou

Mt. Roraima 9,094

Boa Vista

Mamore

Madeira

Purus

Jurua

Negro

Amazon

Tapajos

Xingu

Tocantins

Sao Francisco

Paraguay

Orinoco

Angel Falls

Putumayo

Napo

Maranon

Ucayali

Galapagos Islands (Ecuador)

MOSQUITO COAST

ISTHMUS OF PANAMA

Gulf of Panama

Colon

Panama

David

San Jose

Puntarenas

Limon

Volcan Baru 11,401

Volcan Irazu 11,260

Granada

Leon

Managua

Tegucigalpa

La Ceiba

San Pedro Sula

Cerro Las Minas 9,347

Santa Ana

San Salvador

Guatemala

Volcan Tajumulco 13,845

Escuintla

Belize City

Gulf of Honduras

Turks & Caicos Is. (U.K.)

SOUTH AMERICA
CENTRAL AMERICA
& THE CARIBBEAN

Elevation

Meters	Feet
4,000	13,120
2,000	6,560
500	1,640
200	656
0	0
Below Sea Level	Below Sea Level

750 Miles
1,000 Kilometers
0   250   500   750
0   250   500   750

Tropic of Capricorn

BRAZILIAN HIGHLANDS

Governador Valadares
Vitória
Juiz de Fora
Volta Redonda
Niterói
Rio de Janeiro
Pico da Bandeira 9,482
Ribeirão Preto
Campinas
Jundiaí
São Paulo
Santos
São José do Rio Preto
Uberlândia
Uberaba
Belo Horizonte
Campo Grande
Presidente Prudente
Bauru
Londrina
Sorocaba
Curitiba
Joinvile
Florianópolis
Passo Fundo
Caxias do Sul
Porto Alegre
Ponta Grossa

Corumbá
Santa Cruz
Concepción
Paraguay
PARAGUAY
CHACO
GRAN
Asunción
Formosa
Coronel Oviedo
Encarnación
Iguazú Falls
Santa María
Pelotas
Rivera
Paysandú
Salto
Concordia
Melo
Minas
MONTEVIDEO
URUGUAY
Mar del Plata

Pilcomayo
San Salvador de Jujuy
Tarija
Potosí
Sucre
Santa Cruz
ANDES
ALTIPLANO
Nev. Sajama 21,463
Lake Poopó
Tacna
Arica
Iquique
Antofagasta
Calama
ATACAMA DESERT
San Félix Island (Chile)
San Ambrosio Island (Chile)
Copiapó
Cerro Bonete 22,546
Cerro Ojos del Salado 22,572
La Serena
Highest point in South America
Cerro Aconcagua 22,834
Cerro Tupungato 22,310
Coquimbo
Viña del Mar
Valparaíso
Santiago
San Bernardo
Rancagua
Talca
Chillán
Talcahuano
Concepción
Temuco
Valdivia
Osorno
Puerto Montt
Chonos Archipelago
Chiloé Island
Taitao Peninsula
Juan Fernández Islands (Chile)

Salta
Tucumán
San Miguel de Tucumán
Catamarca
La Rioja
Santiago del Estero
Córdoba
San Juan
Mendoza
Río Cuarto
San Rafael
San Luis
CHILE
ARGENTINA
Resistencia
Corrientes
Santo Tomé
Formosa
Curuzú Cuatiá
Santa Fe
Paraná
Rosario
Avellaneda
Buenos Aires
La Plata
Santa Rosa
Río de la Plata
Punta Alta
Bahía Blanca
Neuquén
San Carlos de Bariloche
Esquel
Viedma
San Matías Gulf
Valdés Peninsula — Lowest point in South America
Rawson
Trelew
Gulf of San Jorge
Cape Tres Puntas
Comodoro Rivadavia
PATAGONIA
Bahía Grande
Puerto Deseado
Río Gallegos
Str. of Magellan
Tierra del Fuego
Ushuaia
Cape Horn

Stanley
Falkland Islands (U.K.) (Islas Malvinas)

South Georgia (U.K.)

Tropic of Capricorn

20°   30°   40°
20°
30°
40°
50°
60°
70°
80°
90°
100°
110°
20°   30°   40°   50°   60°   70°   80°

M10

EUROPE

Elevation

Meters		Feet
4,000		13,120
2,000		6,560
500		1,640
200		656
0		0
Below Sea Level		Below Sea Level

Greenland (Den.)

Arctic Circle

ICELAND
Keflavik · Akureyri
Reykjavik ·
▲ Hekla 4,892

Norwegian Sea

North Cape
Hammerfest
Tromso
Ivalo

LAPLAND

Bodo
Kiruna
Rovaniemi

Arctic Circle

NORWAY
Trondheim
Alesund
Ostersund
Lulea
Umea
Oulu

SWEDEN
FINLAND
Kuopio
Vaasa
Tampere

Glittertind 8,113
Bergen
Gavle
Aland (Fin.)
Turku Helsinki

Gulf of Bothnia

Oslo
Skien
Uppsala
Stockholm
Linkoping

Stavanger
Kristiansand

North Sea

ATLANTIC OCEAN

Faeroe Is. (Den.)

Shetland Is. (U.K.)

Orkney Is.
Inverness
Hebrides
Aberdeen
Dundee
Glasgow
Edinburgh
Belfast · Newcastle

Jonkoping
Gotland (Swe.)

Baltic Sea

SOVIET UNION

IRELAND
Dublin
Cork Limerick
UNITED KINGDOM
Liverpool Leeds
Manchester
Sheffield
Birmingham
Cardiff

Alborg
Jutland
Arhus
Copenhagen
DENMARK
Odense
Helsingborg
Malmo
Bornholm (Den.)

Gdansk
Rostock
Szczecin
Bialystok

Land's End
Bristol
London
Plymouth
Portsmouth
English Channel
Channel Is. (U.K.)
Brest

NETHERLANDS
Amsterdam
Hague
Rotterdam
Antwerp
BELGIUM
Brussels
LUX.
Le Havre
Rouen

Hamburg
Bremen
Hannover
(EAST)
Berlin
(WEST)
Magdeburg
Leipzig
Dresden
Essen
Cologne
GERMANY
Bonn
Frankfurt

POLAND
Poznan
Warsaw
Lodz
Lublin
Wroclaw
Katowice
Kracow

Vistula
Oder

Nantes
Orleans
Tours
FRANCE
Limoges
Dijon
Mannheim
Strasbourg
Stuttgart
Nurnberg
Prague
Ostrava
Brno
CZECHO.
Kosice

CARPATHIAN

Miskolc
Debrecen
Iasi

Bordeaux
Lyon
Grenoble
Geneva
Bern
SWITZ.
Munich
Zurich
Salzburg
Linz
Vienna
Bratislava

Cluj-Napoca
MOUNTAINS

Mt. Blanc 14,690
Matterhorn 15,771
AUSTRIA
Graz
HUNGARY
Budapest
Pecs
ROMANIA
Brasov
Timisoara
Bucharest

Toulouse
PYRENEES
Pico de Aneto 11,168
ANDORRA
Turin
Milan
Verona
Venice
Trieste
Ljubljana
Zagreb
Belgrade
YUGOSLAVIA
Constanta

La Coruna
Gijon
Vigo
Bilbao
San Sebastian
Valladolid
Zaragoza
IBERIAN
Madrid
Barcelona

Genoa
Bologna
Florence
SAN MARINO
APENNINES
DINARIC ALPS
Split
Sarajevo
Dubrovnik
BALKAN
Ruse
Varna

Bay of Biscay

Oporto
Coimbra
PORTUGAL
Lisbon
Cape St. Vincent

SPAIN
PENINSULA
Cordoba
Seville
Cadiz
Granada
Malaga
Gibraltar (U.K.)
Strait of Gibraltar

Valencia
Alicante
Palma
Balearic Is. (Sp.)

Corsica (Fr.)
Ajaccio
MONACO
Nice
Marseille

Rome
ITALY
Naples
Vesuvius 4,202
Bari

Sardinia (It.)
Cagliari

Tyrrhenian Sea

Palermo
Messina
Etna 11,053
Catania
Sicily
MALTA

Mediterranean Sea

Adriatic Sea

Tirana
ALBANIA
Vlore
Skopje
Sofia
BULGARIA
Plovdiv
Burgas

Danube

Thessaloniki
Olympus 9,570
Larisa
Volos
GREECE
Corfu
Ionian Sea
Peloponnesus
Patras
Athens

TURKEY

Rhodes
Iraklion
Crete

AFRICA

0	250	500 Miles
0	250 500	750 Kilometers

© The World Almanac and Book of Facts, 1991

SOVIET UNION

Elevation

Meters	Feet
4,000	13,120
2,000	6,560
500	1,640
200	656
0	0
Below Sea Level	Below Sea Level

© The World Almanac and Book of Facts, 1991

① Moldavian S.S.R.
② Georgian S.S.R.
③ Armenian S.S.R.
④ Azerbaijan S.S.R.
⑤ Tajik S.S.R.
⑥ Kirghiz S.S.R.

ARCTIC OCEAN

PACIFIC OCEAN

Russian Soviet Federative Socialist Republic
R.S.F.S.R.

VERKHOYANSK RA.

CENTRAL SIBERIAN PLATEAU

WEST SIBERIAN PLAIN

URAL MOUNTAINS

KAMCHATKA PENINSULA

KOLYMA MOUNTAINS

Moscow
Leningrad
Kiev
Kharkov
Gorky
Kazan
Sverdlovsk
Novosibirsk
Omsk
Chelyabinsk
Vladivostok
Khabarovsk

250 500 750 Miles
250 500 750 1,000 Kilometers

40°

MONGOLIA
MONGOLIAN PLATEAU
GOBI DESERT
ALTAY MOUNTAINS
Hovd
Moron
Darhan
Ulaanbaatar
Bayanhongor
Choybalsan
Hailar
rpan Depression

Amur
Yichuan
Qiqihar
Jixi
Harbin
Changchun
Jilin
Shenyang
Fushun
Chongjin
N. KOREA
Anshan
Hamhung
Pyongyang
Hohhot
Beijing
Luda
Inchon
Seoul
S. KOREA
Taegu
Pusan
Baotou
Datong
Tianjin
Shijiazhuang
Jinan
Qingdao
Yellow Sea
Taiyuan
Handan
Cheju I.
Nagasaki

Hokkaido
Sapporo
Hakodate
Akita
Sendai
Sea of Japan
Niigata
JAPAN
Tokyo
Kanazawa
Yokohama
Fuji-san 12,388
Kyoto
Nagoya
Kobe
Osaka
Hiroshima
Shikoku
Kitakyushu
Fukuoka
Kyushu
Kagoshima
Honshu

Iwo Jima
(Japan)

CHINA
Golmud
Xining
Lanzhou
Chang
Chang
Lhasa
est point
sia
piau
AN
Gauhati
NGLADESH
aka
Imphal
Chittagong
Mandalay
Myitkyina
Kunming
Zigong
Chengdu
Chongqing
Shaoyang
Guiyang
Guilin
Liuzhou
Nanning
Luoyang
Xuzhou
Zhengzhou
Huainan
Hefei
Nanjing
Shanghai
Hangzhou
Wuhan
Jingdezhen
Nanchang
Changsha
Hengyang
Fuzhou
Ganzhou
Xiamen
Yinchuan
Xian
Wenzhou
Taipei
TAIWAN
Kaohsiung

East China Sea

Ryukyu Is.
Naha
Okinawa

PACIFIC
OCEAN
Tropic of Cancer
20°

Huang
Grand Canal
Shandong Pen.
Chang

MYANMAR
Sittwe
Taunggyi
Prome
Bassein
Yangon
Moulmein
Nakhon Sawan
Tavoy
Bangkok
Sattahip
THAILAND
Chiang Mai
LAOS
Louangphrabang
Vientiane
Nakhon Ratchasima
Savannakhet
Phongsali
Haiphong
Hanoi
Vinh
Hue
Da Nang
VIETNAM
Nha Trang
CAMBODIA
Batdambang
Phnom Penh
Kompong Som
Can Tho
Ho Chi Minh City
Haikou
Zhanjiang
Hainan (China)
Macau (Port.)
Hong Kong (U.K.)
Canton (Guangzhou)

Gulf of Tonkin
Hsi
Mekong
Salween
Irrawaddy

Andaman Islands (India)
Gulf of Thailand
Isthmus of Kra
Nicobar Islands (India)
Phuket
Hat Yai
George Town
MALAYSIA
Medan
Kelang
Kuala Lumpur
Sibolga
Singapore
SINGAPORE
Pakanbaru
Padang
Jambi
Sumatra
Palembang
Bengkulu
Tanjungkarang-Telukbetung
Jakarta
Bandung
Banda Aceh

Natuna Is.
Kuching
Sibu
Samarinda
Borneo
Pontianak
Sampit
Banjarmasin

Bandar Seri Begawan
BRUNEI
MALAYSIA
Tarakan
Sandakan

South China Sea

Laoag
Luzon
Baguio
PHILIPPINES
Quezon City
Manila
Naga
Mindoro
Samar
Tacloban
Iloilo
Leyte
Panay
Cebu
Butuan
Negros
Mindanao
Davao
Puerto Princesa
Palawan
Zamboanga

Philippine Sea

10°

Celebes Sea
Manado
Gorontalo
Ternate
Ambon
Moluccas

Celebes
Balikpapan
Parepare
Palopo
Baubau
Ujung Pandang

Banda Sea

Equator

Java Sea
Semarang
Surabaja
Malang
Bali
Mataram
Ende
Kupang
Yogyakarta
Java
I N D O N E S I A

Timor
Dili
Timor Sea

10°

© The World Almanac and Book of Facts, 1991

100°   110°   120°   130°   140°   150°

Map of North Africa and surrounding regions.

60°   50°   40°   30°   20°

A S I A

E U R O P E

Azores
(Portugal)

Madeira Islands
(Portugal)

Canary Islands
(Sp.)
Las Palmás
Santa Cruz
Funchal

Strait of Gibraltar

Ceuta (Sp.)
Tangier
Melilla
Tetouan
Rabat
Kenitra
Casablanca
Safi
Agadir
Jebel Toubkal 13,661
Marrakech
Khouribga
Meknes
Oujda

MOROCCO

El Djazair
(Algiers)
El Asnam
Wahran
Sidi Bel Abbes
Bejaia
Batna
Skikda
Annaba
Tunis
Cape Bon
Tebessa
Qacentina
Biskra
Djebel Chelia 7,637
Touggourt
Ghardaïa
Bechar
I-n-Salah

Tunis
TUNISIA
Sfax
Tripoli
Misratah
Ghadamis

ALGERIA

A T L A S   M O U N T A I N S

Tropic of Cancer

I-n-Aménas
Tamanrasset
Mt. Tahat 9,573
A H A G G A R

Western Sahara
(Occ. by Morocco)

El Aaiún

Atar

MAURITANIA
Nouakchott
Nouadhibou

Ayoun el Atrous

Kaédi
Kayes

Saint-Louis
SENEGAL
Dakar
Thiés
Kaolack
Banjul
GAMBIA
GUINEA-BISSAU
Bissau
Zinguinchor
Labé
GUINEA
Conakry
Freetown
SIERRA LEONE
Monrovia
LIBERIA

Kiffa

S A H A R A

Tombouctou
Gao

MALI
Bamako
Ségou
Mopti

Sikasso
Kankan

Korhogo
Bouake
CÔTE D'IVOIRE
Yamoussoukro
Abidjan

Bobo-Dioulasso
BURKINA FASO
Ouagadougou

Niger

GHANA
Kumasi
Tamale
Accra

TOGO
Lomé
BENIN
Porto Novo
Cotonou

Mediterranean Sea

Gulf of Sidra

Al Bayda
Tobruk

LIBYA
Banghazi

Al Jawf

Waha

Tropic of Cancer

A Î R
Agadez

NIGER
Niamey
Maradi
Zinder

Sokoto
Katsina
Kano
Zaria
NIGERIA
Minna
Ilorin
Oshogbo
Ibadan
Abeokuta
Lagos
Ogbomosho
Enugu
Onitsha
Makurdi
Port

T I B E S T I
Emi Koussi 11,204

CHAD
Faya-Largeau
Abeche
N'Djamena
Lake Chad
Kumo
Maiduguri
Sarh
Moundou

Maroua
Garoua

CENTRAL AFRICAN REPUBLIC
Bouar
Bambari
Bossangoa
Bafoussam

Alexandria
Tanta
al-Jizah
Cairo
Port Said
Suez
Siwah
EGYPT
Al Fayyum
Asyut
Al Kharijah

Luxor
Aswan

SINAI

Nile

L I B Y A N   D E S E R T

Red Sea

N U B I A N   D E S E R T

Port Sudan

Mitsiwa
Asmera
Mekele

Kassala
Atbarah
Marawi

SUDAN
Omdurman
Khartoum
Wad Madani
Al Ubayyid
Al Fashir
Nyala
Waw
Rumbek

Kusti
White Nile
Blue Nile
Malakal

ETHIOPIAN HIGHLANDS
Gonder
Bahir Dar
Ras Dashen 15,158
Guna 13,881
Dire Dawa
Harer
Nazret
Addis Ababa
ETHIOPIA
Jima
Soke 14,131

DJIBOUTI
Gulf of Aden
Cape Guardafui
Djibouti Lowest point in Africa -512
Lake Assal
Berbera
Hargeysa
Keidto

S O M A L I   P E N I N S U L A

AUSTRALIA &
THE PACIFIC

Elevation

Meters	Feet
2,000	6,560
1,000	3,280
200	656
0	0
Below Sea Level	Below Sea Level

PACIFIC OCEAN

Hawaii (U.S.)
Kauai Oahu Maui Hawaii
Honolulu

Marquesas Islands
French Polynesia (Fr.)
Tuamotu Archipelago
Papeete Tahiti
Society Islands
Austral Islands
Tropic of Capricorn

Line Islands
Christmas I.
Palmyra Atoll
Jarvis I. (U.S.)
Cook Islands (N.Z.)
Avarua

KIRIBATI
Howland I. (U.S.) Enderbury
Baker I. (U.S.) Phoenix Islands
Canton I.
Tokelau
W. SAMOA American Samoa (U.S.)
Apia Pago Pago
Niue (N.Z.)
TONGA
Nuku'alofa

Wake I. (U.S.)
Marshall Islands (U.S.)
Bikini Atoll Ratak Chain
Enewetak Atoll Ralik Chain
Kwajalein Atoll Majuro

TUVALU
Funafuti
Tarawa Gilbert Islands
Banaba

NAURU
Yaren

Santa Cruz Is.
SOLOMON ISLANDS
Espiritu Santo
Malakula Vila
VANUATU
Loyalty Is.
New Caledonia (Fr.)
Noumea

Wallis and Futuna (Fr.)
Vanua Levu
Viti Levu Suva
FIJI

Northern Mariana Islands (U.S.)
Saipan

Guam (U.S.)

Caroline Islands
Truk Is.
Yap Is.
Palau (U.S.)
Koror

Federated States of Micronesia (U.S.)
Kolonia

PAPUA NEW GUINEA
Admiralty Is.
Bismarck Arch.
New Ireland
New Britain
Rabaul
Bougainville
Mt. Wilhelm 14,793
Madang Lae
Port Moresby
Solomon Is.
Guadalcanal Honiara

Philippine Sea
Manila Luzon
PHILIPPINES
Mindanao
Celebes Sea
Manado
BRUNEI
MALAYSIA
Borneo Celebes
Banjarmasin
Ujung Pandang
INDONESIA
Ambon
Banda Sea
Seram
Jayapura
Merauke
Timor
Arafura Sea
Melville I.
Darwin
Katherine

Kermadec Is. (N.Z.)

Norfolk I. (Aust.)

Chatham Is. (N.Z.)

Gulf of Carpentaria
Cape York
Weipa
Mount Isa
Weipa
New Guinea

Coral Sea

Great Barrier Reef
Cairns
Townsville
Mackay
Rockhampton
Bundaberg
GREAT DIVIDING RANGE
Longreach
Charleville
Toowoomba Brisbane
Southport
Charters Towers
GREAT ARTESIAN BASIN
Bourke
Tamworth
Newcastle
Orange Sydney
Wagga Wagga Wollongong
Canberra
Mt. Kosciusko
Highest Point in Australia 7,310
Albury
Bendigo Melbourne
Geelong
Bass Strait
Launceston
Tasmania
Hobart

GREAT SANDY DESERT
GIBSON DESERT
Alice Springs
Ayers Rock 2,844
SIMPSON DESERT
GREAT VICTORIA DESERT
Lowest Point in Australia
Lake Eyre
Broken Hill
Murray
Darling

AUSTRALIA
NULLARBOR PLAIN
Great Australian Bight
Port Augusta
Port Lincoln
Adelaide
Ballarat

Woomera
Whyalla
Coober Pedy
Port Hedland
Newman
Dampier
Cape Leveque
Broome

INDIAN OCEAN

North West Cape
Carnarvon
Geraldton
Kalgoorlie
Perth
Bunbury
Albany Esperance
Cape Leeuwin

NEW ZEALAND
North Island
Auckland
Hamilton Tauranga
New Plymouth Gisborne
Napier
Cook Strait
Wellington Nelson
South Island
Christchurch
Mt. Cook 12,349
Dunedin
Invercargill
Stewart I.

Tasman Sea

800 1,200 Miles
400 800 1,200 1,600 Kilometers

© The World Almanac and Book of Facts, 1991

WORLD HISTORY

Prehistory: Our Ancestors Take Over

Homo sapiens. The precise origins of *homo sapiens,* the species to which all humans belong, are subject to broad speculation based on a small number of fossils, genetic and anatomical studies, and the geological record. But most scientists agree that we evolved from ape-like primate ancestors in a process that began millions of years ago.

Current theories say the first hominid (human-like primate) was *Ramapithecus,* who emerged 12 million years ago. Its remains have been found in Asia, Europe, and Africa. Further development was apparently limited to Africa, where 2 lines of hominids appeared some 5 or 6 million years ago. One was *Australopithecus,* a tool-maker and social animal, who lived from perhaps 4 to 3 million years ago, and then apparently became extinct.

The 2nd was a human line, *Homo habilus,* a large-brained specimen that walked upright and had a dextrous hand. *Homo habilus* lived in semi-permanent camps and had a food-gathering and sharing economy.

Homo erectus, our nearest ancestor, appeared in Africa perhaps 1.75 million years ago, and began spreading into Asia and Europe soon after. It had a fairly large brain and a skeletal structure similar to ours. *Homo erectus* learned to control fire, and probably had primitive language skills. The final brain development to *Homo sapiens* and then to our sub-species *Homo sapiens sapiens* occurred between 500,000 and 50,000 years ago, either in one place — probably Africa — or virtually simultaneously and independently in different places in Africa, Europe, and Asia. There is no question that all modern races are members of the same species, *Homo sapiens sapiens.*

The spread of mankind into the remaining habitable continents probably took place during the last ice age up to 100,000 years ago: to the Americas across a land bridge from Asia, and to Australia across the Timor Straits.

Earliest cultures. A variety of cultural modes — in tool-making, diet, shelter, and possibly social arrangements and spiritual expression, arose as early mankind adapted to different geographic and climatic zones.

Three basic tool-making traditions are recognized by archeologists as arising and often coexisting from one million years ago to the near past: the *chopper tradition,* found largely in E. Asia, with crude chopping tools and simple flake tools; the *flake tradition,* found in Africa and W. Eu-rope, with a variety of small cutting and flaking tools, and the *biface tradition,* found in all of Africa, W. and S. Europe, and S. Asia, producing pointed hand axes chipped on both faces. Later biface sites yield more refined axes and a variety of other tools, weapons, and ornaments using bone, antler, and wood as well as stone.

Only sketchy evidence remains for the different stages in man's increasing control over the environment. Traces of 400,000-year-old covered wood shelters have been found at Nice, France. Scraping tools at Neanderthal sites (200,000-30,000 BC in Europe, N. Africa, the Middle East and Central Asia) suggest the treatment of skins for clothing. Sites from all parts of the world show seasonal migration patterns and exploitation of a wide range of plant and animal food sources.

Painting and decoration, for which there is evidence at the Nice site, flourished along with stone and ivory sculpture after 30,000 years ago; 60 caves in France and 30 in Spain show remarkable examples of wall painting. Other examples have been found in Africa. Proto-religious rites are suggested by these works, and by evidence of ritual cannibalism by Peking Man, 500,000 BC, and of ritual burial with medicinal plants and flowers by Neanderthals at Shanidar in Iraq.

The Neolithic Revolution. Sometime after 10,000 BC, among widely separated human communities, a series of dramatic technological and social changes occurred that are summed up as the Neolithic Revolution. The cultivation of previously wild plants encouraged the growth of permanent settlements. Animals were domesticated as a work force and food source. The manufacture of pottery and cloth began. These techniques permitted a huge increase in world population and in human control over the earth.

No region can safely claim priority as the "inventor" of these techniques. Dispersed sites in Cen. and S. America, S.E. Europe, and the Middle East show roughly contemporaneous (10-8,000 BC) evidence of one or another "neolithic" trait. Dates near 6-3,000 BC have been given for E. and S. Asian, W. European, and sub-Saharan African neolithic remains. The variety of crops — field grains, rice, maize, and roots, and the varying mix of other traits suggest that the revolution occurred independently in all these regions.

History Begins: 4000 - 1000 BC

Near Eastern cradle. If history began with writing, the first chapter opened in Mesopotamia, the Tigris-Euphrates river valley. Clay tablets with pictographs were used by the Sumerians to keep records after 4000 BC. A cuneiform (wedge shaped) script evolved by 3000 BC as a full syllabic alphabet. Neighboring peoples adapted the script to their own language.

Sumerian life centered, from 4000 BC, on large cities (Eridu, Ur, Uruk, Nippur, Kish, Lagash) organized around temples and priestly bureaucracies, with the surrounding plains watered by vast irrigation works and worked with traction plows. Sailboats, wheeled vehicles, potters wheels, and kilns were used. Copper was smelted and tempered in Sumeria from c4000 BC and bronze was produced not long after. Ores, as well as precious stones and metals were obtained through long-distance ship and caravan trade. Iron was used from c2000 BC. Improved ironworking, developed partly by the **Hittites,** became widespread by 1200 BC.

Sumerian political primacy passed among cities and their kingly dynasties. Semitic-speaking peoples, with cultures derived from the Sumerian, founded a succession of dynasties that ruled in Mesopotamia and neighboring areas for most of 1800 years; among them the **Akkadians** (first under Sargon c2350 BC), the **Amorites** (whose laws, codified by **Hammurabi,** c1792-1750 BC, have Biblical parallels), and the **Assyrians,** with interludes of rule by the Hittites, Kassites, and Mitanni, all possibly Indo-Europeans. The political and cultural center of gravity shifted northwest with each successive empire.

Mesopotamian learning, maintained by scribes and preserved by successive rulers in vast libraries, was not abstract or theoretical. Algebraic and geometric problems could be solved on a practical basis in construction, commerce, or administration. Systematic lists of astronomical phenomena, plants, animals and stones were kept; medical texts listed ailments and their herbal cures.

The Sumerians worshipped anthropomorphic gods representing natural forces — Anu, god of heaven; Enlil (Ea), god of water. Epic poetry related these and other gods in a hierarchy. Sacrifices were made at ziggurats — huge stepped temples. Gods were thought to control all events, which could be foretold using oracular materials. This religious pattern persisted into the first millenium BC.

The Syria-Palestine area, site of some of the earliest urban remains (Jericho, 7000 BC), and of the recently uncovered **Ebla** civilization (fl. 2500 BC), experienced Egyptian cultural and political influence along with Mesopotamian. The **Phoenician** coast was an active commercial center. A phonetic alphabet was invented here before 1600 BC. It became the ancestor of all European, Middle Eastern, Indian, S.E.

4500

• Thai bronzes

3500
• Bronze Age begins
• Sumerian cities

• 1st pyramids
• Egypt unified

• Indus Valley civilization

2500

2500 BC

Ebla civilization

Egyptian literature begins

Bronze-age Minoan
civilization emerges on Crete

Phonetic alphabet invented before 1600

Peruvian neolithic
ceremonial centers

1750 — Hammurabi

Aryans invade India

Chinese Shang dynasty

Mt. Sinai revelations to Moses

Mexican Olmec
civilization established

1000 BC

Asian, Ethiopian, and Korean alphabets.

Regional commerce and diplomacy were aided by the use of Akkadian as a *lingua franca*, later replaced by Aramaic.

Egypt. Agricultural villages along the Nile were united by 3300 BC into two kingdoms, Upper and Lower Egypt, unified under the Pharaoh Menes c3100 BC; Nubia to the south was added 2600 BC. A national bureaucracy supervised construction of canals and monuments (**pyramids** starting 2700 BC). Brilliant First Dynasty achievements in architecture, sculpture and painting, set the standards and forms for all subsequent Egyptian civilization and are still admired. **Hieroglyphic writing** appeared by 3400 BC, recording a sophisticated literature including romantic and philosophical modes after 2300 BC.

An ordered hierarchy of gods, including totemistic animal elements, was served by a powerful priesthood in Memphis. The pharaoh was identified with the falcon god Horus. Later trends were the belief in an afterlife, and the quasi-monotheistic reforms of **Akhenaton** (c1379-1362 BC).

After a period of conquest by Semitic Hyksos from Asia (c1700-1500 BC), the New Kingdom established an empire in Syria. Egypt became increasingly embroiled in Asiatic wars and diplomacy. Eventually it was conquered by Persia in 525 BC, and it faded away as an independent culture.

India. An urban civilization with a so-far-undeciphered writing system stretched across the Indus Valley and along the Arabian Sea c3000-1500 BC. Major sites are Harappa and **Mohenjo-Daro** in Pakistan, well-planned geometric cities with underground sewers and vast granaries. The entire region (600,000 sq. mi.) may have been ruled as a single state. Bronze was used, and arts and crafts were highly developed. Religious life apparently took the form of fertility cults.

Indus civilization was probably in decline when it was destroyed by **Aryan invaders** from the northwest, speaking an Indo-European language from which all the languages of Pakistan, north India and Bangladesh descend. Led by a warrior aristocracy whose legendary deeds are recorded in the **Rig Veda**, the Aryans spread east and south, bringing their pantheon of sky gods, elaborate priestly (Brahmin) ritual, and the beginnings of the caste system; local customs and beliefs were assimilated by the conquerors.

Europe. On Crete, the bronze-age **Minoan civilization** emerged c2500 BC. A prosperous economy and richly decorative art (e.g. at Knossos palace) was supported by seaborne commerce. Mycenae and other cities in Greece and Asia Minor (e.g. **Troy**) preserved elements of the culture to c1100 BC. Cretan Linear A script, c2000-1700 BC, is undeciphered; Linear B, c1300-1200 BC, records a Greek dialect.

Possible connection between Minoan-Mycenaean monumental stonework, and the great megalithic monuments and tombs of W. Europe, Iberia, and Malta (c4000-1500 BC) is unclear.

China. Proto-Chinese neolithic cultures had long covered northern and southeastern China when the first large political state was organized in the north by the **Shang dynasty** c1500 BC. Shang kings called themselves Sons of Heaven, and presided over a cult of human and animal sacrifice to ancestors and nature gods. The Chou dynasty, starting c1100 BC, expanded the area of the Son of Heaven's dominion, but feudal states exercised most temporal power.

A writing system with 2,000 different characters was already in use under the Shang, with **pictographs** later supplemented by phonetic characters. The system, with modifications, is still in use, despite changes in spoken Chinese.

Technical advances allowed urban specialists to create fine ceramic and jade products, and bronze casting after 1500 BC was the most advanced in the world.

Bronze artifacts have recently been discovered in northern Thailand dating to 3600 BC, hundreds of years before similar Middle Eastern finds.

Americas. Olmecs settled on the Gulf coast of Mexico, 1500 BC, and soon developed the first civilization in the Western Hemisphere. Temple cities and huge stone sculpture date to 1200 BC. A rudimentary calendar and writing system existed. Olmec religion, centering on a jaguar god, and art forms influenced all later Meso-American cultures.

Neolithic ceremonial centers were built on the Peruvian desert coast, c2000 BC.

Classical Era of Old World Civilizations

Greece. After a period of decline during the Dorian Greek invasions (1200-1000 BC), Greece and the Aegean area developed a unique civilization. Drawing upon Mycenaean traditions, Mesopotamian learning (weights and measures, lunisolar calendar, astronomy, musical scales), the Phoenician alphabet (modified for Greek), and Egyptian art, the revived **Greek city-states** saw a rich elaboration of intellectual life. Long-range commerce was aided by metal coinage (introduced by the Lydians in Asia Minor before 700 BC); colonies were founded around the Mediterranean and Black Sea shores (Cumae in Italy 760 BC, Massalia in France c600 BC).

Philosophy, starting with Ionian speculation on the nature of matter and the universe (Thales c634-546), and including mathematical speculation (Pythagoras c580-c500), culminated in Athens in the rationalist idealism of **Plato** (c428-347) and **Socrates** (c470-399); the latter was executed for alleged impiety. **Aristotle** (384-322) united all fields of study in his system. The arts were highly valued. Architecture culminated in the **Parthenon** in Athens (438, sculpture by Phidias); poetry and drama (Aeschylus 525-456) thrived. Male beauty and strength, a chief artistic theme, were enhanced at the gymnasium and the national games at Olympia.

Ruled by local tyrants or oligarchies, the Greeks were never politically united, but managed to resist inclusion in the Persian Empire (Darius defeated at Marathon 490 BC, Xerxes at Salamis, Plataea 479 BC). Local warfare was common; the **Peloponnesian Wars**, 431-404 BC, ended in Sparta's victory over Athens. Greek political power waned, but classical Greek cultural forms spread throughout the ancient world from the Atlantic to India.

Hebrews. Nomadic Hebrew tribes entered Canaan before 1200 BC, settling among other Semitic peoples speaking the same language. They brought from the desert a **monotheistic faith** said to have been revealed to Abraham in Canaan c1800 BC and to Moses at Mt. Sinai c1250 BC, after the Hebrews' escape from bondage in Egypt. David (ruled 1000-961 BC) and Solomon (ruled 961-922 BC) united the Hebrews in a kingdom that briefly dominated the area. Phoenicians to the north established colonies

Paleontology: The History of Life

All dates are approximate, and are subject to change based on new fossil finds or new dating techniques; but the sequence of events is generally accepted. Dates are in years before the present.

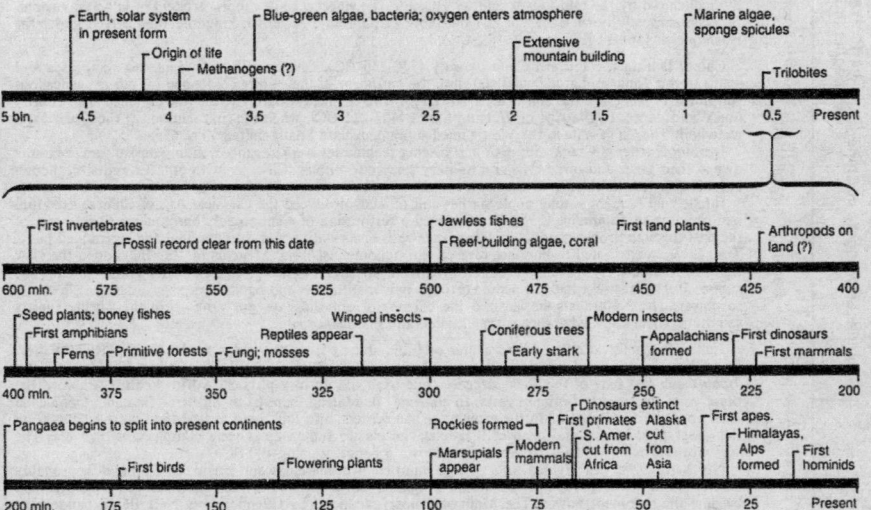

Ancient Near Eastern Civilizations
4000 B.C.-500 B.C.

Timeline (1000 BC – 400 BC):

- 1000 BC
- Chavin dynasty begins in Peru
- Hebrew kingdom divided
- Chou dynasty begins in China
- 800
- Carthage established
- Nubia begins rule of Egypt
- Metal coins in Asia Minor
- Isaiah d.
- Zoroaster b.
- Pythagoras b.
- Indian Buddhism, Jainism begin
- Confucius b.
- 600
- Siddarta b.
- Socrates b.
- Plato b.
- Parthenon
- Peloponnesian Wars
- Aeschylus b.
- 400 BC

around the E. and W. Mediterranean (**Carthage** c814 BC) and sailed into the Atlantic.

A temple in Jerusalem became the national religious center, with sacrifices performed by a hereditary priesthood. Polytheistic influences, especially of the fertility cult of Baal, were opposed by **prophets** (Elijah, Amos, Isaiah).

Divided into **two kingdoms** after Solomon, the Hebrews were unable to resist the revived Assyrian empire, which conquered Israel, the northern kingdom in 722 BC. Judah, the southern kingdom, was conquered in 586 BC by the Babylonians under Nebuchadnezzar II. But with the fixing of most of the Biblical canon by the mid-fourth century BC, and the emergence of rabbis, arbiters of law and custom, Judaism successfully survived the loss of Hebrew autonomy. A Jewish kingdom was revived under the Hasmoneans (168-42 BC).

China. During the **Eastern Chou** dynasty (770-256 BC), Chinese culture spread east to the sea and south to the Yangtze. Large feudal states on the periphery of the empire contended for pre-eminence, but continued to recognize the Son of Heaven (king), while retained a purely ritual role enriched with courtly music and dance. In the Age of Warring States (403-221 BC), when the first sections of the **Great Wall** were built, the Ch'in state in the West gained supremacy, and finally united all of China.

Iron tools entered China c500 BC, and casting techniques were advanced, aiding agriculture. Peasants owned their land, and owed civil and military service to nobles. Cities grew in number and size, though barter remained the chief trade medium.

Intellectual ferment among noble scribes and officials produced the Classical Age of Chinese literature and philosophy. **Confucius** (551-479 BC) urged a restoration of a supposedly harmonious social order of the past through proper conduct in accordance with one's station and through filial and ceremonial piety. The *Analects*, attributed to him, are revered throughout East Asia. **Mencius** (d. 289 BC) added the view that the Mandate of Heaven can be removed from an unjust dynasty. The Legalists sought to curb the supposed natural wickedness of people through new institutions and harsh laws; they aided the Ch'in rise to power. The Naturalists emphasized the balance of opposites — yin, yang — in the world. **Taoists** sought mystical knowledge through meditation and disengagement.

India. The political and cultural center of India shifted from the Indus to the Ganges River Valley. Buddhism, Jainism, and mystical revisions of orthodox Vedism all developed around 500-300 BC. The *Upanishads*, last part of the *Veda*, urged escape from the illusory physical world. Vedism remained the preserve of the priestly Brahmin caste. In contrast, **Buddhism**, founded by Siddarta Gautama (c563-c483 BC), appealed to merchants in the growing urban centers, and took hold at first (and most lastingly) on the geographic fringes of Indian civilization. The classic Indian epics were composed in this era: The *Ramayana* around 300 BC, the *Mahabharata* over a period starting 400 BC.

Northern India was divided into a large number of monarchies and aristocratic republics, probably derived from tribal groupings, when the Magadha kingdom was formed in Bihar c542 BC. It soon became the dominant power. The **Maurya dynasty**, founded by Chandragupta c321 BC, expanded the kingdom, uniting most of N. India in a centralized bureaucratic empire. The third Mauryan king, **Asoka** (ruled c274-236) conquered most of the subcontinent: he converted to Buddhism, and inscribed its tenets on pillars throughout India. He downplayed the caste system and tried to end expensive sacrificial rites.

Before its final decline in India, Buddhism developed the popular worship of heavenly Bodhisatvas (enlightened beings), and produced a refined architecture (stupa—shrine—at Sanchi 100 AD) and sculpture (Gandhara reliefs 1-400 AD).

Persia. Aryan peoples (Persians, Medes) dominated the area of present Iran by the beginning of the first millenium BC. The prophet **Zoroaster** (born c628 BC) introduced a dualistic religion in which the forces of good (Ahura Mazda, Lord of Wisdom) and evil (Ahiram) battle for dominance; individuals are judged by their actions and earn damnation or salvation. Zoroaster's hymns (*Gathas*) are included in the *Avesta*, the Zoroastrian scriptures. A version of this faith became the established religion of the Persian Empire, and probably influenced later monotheistic religions.

Africa. Nubia, periodically occupied by Egypt since the third millenium, ruled Egypt c750-661, and survived as an independent Egyptianized kingdom (Kush; capital Meroe) for 1,000 years.

The Iron Age Nok culture flourished c500 BC-200 AD on the Benue Plateau of Nigeria.

Americas. The Chavin culture controlled north Peru from 900-200 BC. Its ceremonial centers, featuring the jaguar god, survived long after. Chavin architecture, ceramics, and textiles influenced other Peruvian cultures.

Mayan civilization began to develop in Central America in the 5th century BC.

Great Empires Unite the Civilized World: 400 BC - 400 AD

Persia and Alexander. Cyrus, ruler of a small kingdom in Persia from 559 BC, united the Persians and Medes within 10 years, conquered Asia Minor and Babylonia in another 10. His son Cambyses followed by Darius (ruled 522-486) added vast lands to the east and north as far as the Indus Valley and Central Asia, as well as Egypt and Thrace. The whole empire was ruled by an international bureaucracy and army, with Persians holding the chief positions. The resources and styles of all the subject civilizations were exploited to create a rich syncretic art.

The Hellenized kingdom of Macedon, which under Phillip II dominated Greece, passed to his son **Alexander** in 336 BC. Within 13 years, Alexander conquered all the Persian dominions. Imbued by his tutor Aristotle with Greek ideals, Alexander encouraged Greek colonization, and Greek-style cities were founded throughout the empire (e.g. Alexandria, Egypt). After his death in 323 BC, wars of succession divided the empire into three parts — **Macedon**, Egypt (ruled by the **Ptolemies**), and the **Seleucid** Empire.

In the ensuing 300 years (the **Hellenistic Era**), a cosmopolitan Greek-oriented culture permeated the ancient world from W. Europe to the borders of India, absorbing native elites everywhere.

Hellenistic philosophy stressed the private individual's search for happiness. The Cynics followed Diogenes (c372-287), who stressed satisfaction of animal needs and contempt for social convention. Zeno (c335-c263) and the Stoics exalted reason, identified it with virtue, and counseled an ascetic disregard for misfortune. The Epicureans tried to build lives of moderate pleasure without political or emotional

The Rise of the Roman Empire

GERMANIA

SARMATIA

BELGICA

GAUL RAETIA

DACIA

TARRACONENSIS

LUSITANIA ILLYRICUM ARMENIA

Rome ITALY THRACE Constantinople BITHYNIA PONTUS

BAETICA GALATIA

MAURETANIA ACHAEA ASIA CILICIA MESOPOTAMIA

AFRICA Carthage SYRIA

JUDEA

TRIPOLI CYRENAICA ARABIA

EGYPT

- 238 B.C.E.
- 133 B.C.E.
- 44 B.C.E.
- A.D. 14
- A.D. 117

Ancient Asian Empires

Caspian Sea

GOBI DESERT

Sea of Japan

ALTAI MTS.

Great Wall

PAMIR MTS.

TARIM BASIN

East China Sea

Lo-yang

Han Empire 100 B.C.

Chang-an

HIMALAYA MTS.

Tibet

Asoka's Empire 250 B.C.

Pataliputra

Arabian Sea

South China Sea

Bay of Bengal

Khmer Empire

Angkor A.D. 1000

- - - Approximate Borders

*[Left margin timeline markers, top to bottom:]*
400 BC — Alexander becomes king — Aristotle b. — Mahabarata begun — Chinese Age of Warring States — Euclid's geometry — Great Wall of China begun — 200 BC — 1st Roman slave revolt — Hannibal invades Italy — Punic Wars end — Cleopatra defeated — Hellenistic Era — Julius Caesar b. — Julian calendar — Antony, Cleopatra d. — Jesus d. — 1 AD — Mayan civilization begins in Guatemala — Roman Empire — Nero's persecution — 200 AD

involvement. Hellenistic arts imitated life realistically, especially in sculpture and literature (comedies of Menander, 342-292).

The sciences thrived, especially at Alexandria, where the Ptolemies financed a great library and museum. Fields of study included mathematics (**Euclid's** geometry, c300 BC; Menelaus' non-Euclidean geometry, c100 AD); astronomy (heliocentric theory of Aristarchus, 310-230 BC; Julian calendar 45 BC; Ptolemy's *Almagest*, c150 AD); geography (world map of Eratosthenes, 276-194 BC); hydraulics (**Archimedes**, 287-212 BC); medicine (Galen, 130-200 AD), and chemistry. Inventors refined uses for siphons, valves, gears, springs, screws, levers, cams, and pulleys.

A restored Persian empire under the **Parthians** (N. Iranian tribesmen) controlled the eastern Hellenistic world 250 BC-229 AD. The Parthians and the succeeding Sassanian dynasty (229-651) fought with Rome periodically. The **Sassanians** revived Zoroastrianism as a state religion, and patronized a nationalistic artistic and scholarly renaissance.

Rome. The city of Rome was founded, according to legend, by Romulus in 753 BC. Through military expansion and colonization, and by granting citizenship to conquered tribes, the city annexed all of Italy south of the Po in the 100-year period before 268 BC. The Latin and other Italic tribes were annexed first, followed by the Etruscans (a civilized people north of Rome) and the Greek colonies in the south. With a large standing army and reserve forces of several hundred thousand, Rome was able to defeat Carthage in the 3 **Punic Wars,** 264-241, 218-201, 149-146 (despite the invasion of Italy by Hannibal, 218), thus gaining Sicily and territory in Spain and North Africa.

New provinces were added in the East, as Rome exploited local disputes to conquer Greece and Asia Minor in the 2d century BC, and Egypt in the first (after the defeat and suicide of **Antony and Cleopatra,** 30 BC). All the Mediterranean civilized world up to the disputed Parthian border was now Roman, and remained so for 500 years. Less civilized regions were added to the Empire: Gaul (conquered by Julius Caesar, 56-49 BC), Britain (43 AD) and Dacia NE of the Danube (117 AD).

The original aristocratic republican government, with democratic features added in the fifth and fourth centuries BC, deteriorated under the pressures of empire and class conflict (**Gracchus** brothers, social reformers, murdered 133, 121; slave revolts 135, 73). After a series of civil wars (Marius vs. Sulla 88-82, Caesar vs. Pompey 49-45, triumvirate vs. Caesar's assassins 44-43, Antony vs. Octavian 32-30), the empire came under the rule of a deified monarch (first emperor, **Augustus,** 27 BC-14 AD). Provincials (nearly all granted citizenship by Caracalla, 212 AD) came to dominate the army and civil service. Traditional Roman law, systematized and interpreted by independent jurists, and local self-rule in provincial cities were supplanted by a vast tax-collecting bureaucracy in the 3d and 4th centuries. The legal rights of women, children, and slaves were strengthened.

Roman innovations in **civil engineering** included water mills, windmills, and rotary mills, and the use of cement that hardened under water. Monumental architecture (baths, theaters, apartment houses) relied on the arch and the dome. The network of roads (some still standing) stretched 53,000 miles, passing through mountain tunnels as long as 3.5 miles. Aqueducts brought water to cities, underground sewers removed waste.

Roman art and literature were derivative of Greek models. Innovations were made in sculpture (naturalistic busts and equestrian statues), decorative wall painting (as at Pompeii), satire (Juvenal, 60-127), history (Tacitus 56-120), prose romance (Petronius, d. 66 AD). Violence and torture dominated mass public amusements, which were supported by the state.

India. The **Gupta** monarchs reunited N. India c320 AD. Their peaceful and prosperous reign saw a revival of Hindu religious thought and Brahmin power. The old Vedic traditions were combined with devotion to a plethora of indigenous deities (who were seen as manifestations of Vedic gods). **Caste lines** were reinforced, and Buddhism gradually disappeared. The art (often erotic), architecture, and literature of the period, patronized by the Gupta court, are considered to be among India's finest achievements (Kalidasa, poet and dramatist, fl. c400). Mathematical innovations included the use of zero and decimal numbers. Invasions by White Huns from the NW destroyed the empire c550.

Rich cultures also developed in S. India in this era. Emotional Tamil religious poetry aided the Hindu revival. The Pallava kingdom controlled much of S. India c350-880, and helped spread Indian civilization to S.E. Asia.

China. The Ch'in ruler Shih Huang Ti (ruled 221-210 BC), known as the First Emperor, centralized political authority in China, standardized the written language, laws, weights, measures, and coinage, and conducted a census, but tried to destroy most philosophical texts. The **Han dynasty** (206 BC-220 AD) instituted the Mandarin bureaucracy, which lasted for 2,000 years. Local officials were selected by examination in the Confucian classics and trained at the imperial university and at provincial schools. The invention of **paper** facilitated this bureaucratic system. Agriculture was promoted, but the peasants bore most of the tax burden. Irrigation was improved; water clocks and sundials were used; astronomy and mathematics thrived; landscape painting was perfected.

With the expansion south and west (to nearly the present borders of today's China), trade was opened with India, S.E. Asia, and the Middle East, over sea and caravan routes. Indian missionaries brought Mahayana Buddhism to China by the first century AD, and spawned a variety of sects. Taoism was revived, and merged with popular superstitions. Taoist and Buddhist monasteries and convents multiplied in the turbulent centuries after the collapse of the Han dynasty.

The One God Triumphs: 1-750 AD

Christianity. Religions indigenous to particular Middle Eastern nations became international in the first 3 centuries of the Roman Empire. Roman citizens worshiped Isis of Egypt, Mithras of Persia, Demeter of Greece, and the great mother Cybele of Phrygia. Their cults centered on mysteries (secret ceremonies) and the promise of an afterlife, symbolized by the death and rebirth of the god. Judaism, which had begun as the national cult of Judea, also spread by emigration and conversion. It was the only ancient religion west of India to survive.

Christians, who emerged as a distinct sect in the second half of the 1st century AD, revered **Jesus,** a Jewish preacher said to have been killed by the Romans at the request of Jewish authorities in Jerusalem c30 AD. They considered him the Savior (Messiah, or Christ) who rose from the dead and could grant eternal life to the faithful, despite their sinfulness. They believed he was an incarnation of the one god worshipped by the Jews, and that he would return soon to pass final judgment on the world. The missionary activities of such early leaders as **Paul of Tarsus** spread the faith, at first mostly among Jews or among quasi-Jews attracted by the Pauline rejection of such difficult Jewish laws as circumcision. Intermittent persecution, as in Rome under Nero in 64 AD, on grounds of suspected disloyalty, failed to disrupt the Christian communities. Each congregation, generally urban and of plebeian character, was tightly organized under a leader (bishop) elders (presbyters or priests), and assistants (deacons). Stories about Jesus (the Gospels) and the early church (Acts) were written down in the late first and early 2d centuries, and circulated along with letters of Paul. An authoritative canon of these writings was not fixed until the 4th century.

A school for priests was established at Alexandria in the second century. Its teachers (**Origen** c182-251) helped define Christian doctrine and promote the faith in Greek-style philosophical works. Pagan Neoplatonism was given Christian coloration in the works of Church Fathers such as Augustine (354-430). Christian hermits, often drawn from the lower classes, began to associate in monasteries, first in Egypt (St. **Pachomius** c290-345), then in other eastern lands, then in the West (**St. Benedict's rule**, 529). Popular devotion to saints, especially Mary, mother of Jesus, spread.

Under **Constantine** (ruled 306-337), Christianity became in effect the established religion of the Empire. Pagan temples were expropriated, state funds were used to build huge churches and support the hierarchy, and laws were adjusted in accordance with Christian notions. Pagan worship was banned by the end of the fourth century, and severe restrictions were placed on Judaism.

The newly established church was rocked by doctrinal disputes, often exacerbated by regional rivalries both within and outside the Empire. Chief heresies (as defined by church councils backed by imperial authority) were **Arianism**, which denied the divinity of Jesus; **Donatism**, which rejected the convergence of church and state and denied the validity of sacraments performed by sinful clergy; and the **Monophysite** position denying the dual nature of Christ.

Judaism. First century Judaism embraced several sects, including: the **Sadducees**, mostly drawn from the Temple priesthood, who were culturally Hellenized; the **Pharisees**, who upheld the full range of traditional customs and practices as of equal weight to literal scriptural law, and elaborated synagogue worship; and the **Essenes**, an ascetic, millenarian sect. Messianic fervor led to repeated, unsuccessful rebellions against Rome (66-70, 135). As a result, the Temple was destroyed, and the population decimated.

To avoid the dissolution of the faith, a program of codification of law was begun at the academy of Yavneh. The work continued for some 500 years in Palestine and Babylonia, ending in the final redaction of the **Talmud** (c600), a huge collection of legal and moral debates, rulings, liturgy, Biblical exegesis, and legendary materials.

Islam. The earliest Arab civilization emerged by the end of the 2d millenium BC in the watered highlands of Yemen. Seaborne and caravan trade in frankincense and myrrh connected the area with the Nile and Fertile Crescent. The Minaean, Sabean (Sheba), and Himyarite states successively held sway. By Mohammed's time (7th century AD), the region was a province of Sassanian Persia. In the North, the **Nabataean kingdom** at Petra and the kingdom of Palmyra were first Aramaicized and then Romanized, and finally absorbed like neighboring Judea into the Roman Empire. Nomads shared the central region with a few trading towns and oases. Wars between tribes and raids on settled communities were common, and were celebrated in a poetic tradition that by the 6th century helped establish a classic literary Arabic.

In 611 **Mohammed**, a wealthy 40-year-old Arab of Mecca, had a revelation from Allah, the one true god, calling on him to repudiate pagan idolatry. Drawing on elements of Judaism and Christianity, and eventually incorporating some Arab pagan traditions (such as reverence for the black stone at the kaaba shrine in Mecca), Mohammed's teachings, recorded in the **Koran**, forged a new religion, Islam (submission to Allah). Opposed by the leaders of Mecca, Mohammed made a *hejira* (migration) to Medina to the north in 622, the beginning of the Moslem lunar calendar. He and his followers defeated the Meccans in 624 in the first *jihad* (holy war), and by his death (632), nearly all the Arabian peninsula accepted his religious and secular leadership.

Under the first two **caliphs** (successors) Abu Bakr (632-34) and Oman (634-44), Moslem rule was confirmed over Arabia. Raiding parties into Byzantine and Persian border areas developed into campaigns of conquest against the two empires, which had been weakened by wars and by disaffection among subject peoples (including Coptic and Syriac Christians opposed to the Byzantine orthodox church). Syria, Palestine, Egypt, Iraq, and Persia all fell to the inspired Arab armies. The Arabs at first remained a distinct minority, using non-Moslems in the new administrative system, and tolerating Christians, Jews, and Zoroastrians as self-governing "Peoples of the Book," whose taxes supported the empire.

Disputes over the succession, and puritan reaction to the wealth and refinement that empire brought to the ruling strata, led to the growth of schismatic movements. The followers of Mohammed's son-in-law Ali (assassinated 661) and his descendants became the founders of the more mystical **Shi'ite** sect, still the largest non-orthodox Moslem sect. The **Karijites**, puritanical, militant, and egalitarian, persist as a minor sect to the present.

Under the **Ummayad** caliphs (661-750), the boundaries of Islam were extended across N. Africa and into Spain. Arab armies in the West were stopped at Tours in 732 by the Frank Charles Martel. Asia Minor, the Indus Valley, and Transoxiana were conquered in the East. The vast majority of the subject population gradually converted to Islam, encouraged by tax and career privileges. The Arab language supplanted the local tongues in the central and western areas, but Arab soldiers and rulers in the East eventually became assimilated to the indigenous languages.

New Peoples Enter History: 400-900

Barbarian invasions. Germanic tribes infiltrated S and E from their Baltic homeland during the 1st millenium BC, reaching S. Germany by 100 BC and the Black Sea by 214 AD. Organized into large federated tribes under elected kings, most resisted Roman domination and raided the empire in time of civil war (Goths took Dacia 214, raided Thrace 251-269). German troops and commanders came to dominate the Roman armies by the end of the 4th century. **Huns**, invaders from Asia, entered Europe 372, driving more Germans into the western empire. Emperor Valens allowed Visigoths to cross

200 AD

African Axum kingdom expands

Constantinople founded

1st Christian monastery

Augustine b.

350

Ghana begins rule

Japan united

Gupta Empire in India

Huns in Europe

W. Roman Empire ends

Patrick converts Ireland

Justinian code

Benedict founds monastery

500

Clovis unites Franks

Sui dynasty begins

Mohammed's life

Tang dynasty

Talmud completed

650 AD

the Danube 376. Huns under Attila (d. 453) raided Gaul, Italy, Balkans. The western empire, weakened by overtaxation and social stagnation, was overrun in the 5th century. Gaul was effectively lost 406-7, Spain 409, Britain 410, Africa 429-39. Rome was sacked 410 by Visigoths under Alaric, 455 by Vandals. The last western emperor, Romulus Augustulus, was deposed 476 by the Germanic chief Odoacer.

Celts. Celtic cultures, which in pre-Roman times covered most of W. Europe, were confined almost entirely to the British Isles after the Germanic invasions. St. Patrick completed the conversion of Ireland (c457-92). A strong monastic tradition took hold. Irish monastic missionaries in Scotland, England, and the continent (Columba c521-597; Columban c543-615) helped restore Christianity after the Germanic invasions. The monasteries became renowned centers of classic and Christian learning, and presided over the recording of a Christianized Celtic mythology, elaborated by secular writers and bards. An intricate decorative art style developed, especially in book illumination (Lindisfarne Gospels, c700, Book of Kells, 8th century).

Successor states. The Visigoth kingdom in Spain (from 419) and much of France (to 507) saw a continuation of much Roman administration, language, and law (Breviary of Alaric 506), until its destruction by the Moslems, 711. The Vandal kingdom in Africa, from 429, was conquered by the Byzantines, 533. Italy was ruled in succession by an Ostrogothic kingdom under Byzantine suzerainty 489-554, direct Byzantine government, and the German Lombards (568-774). The latter divided the peninsula with the Byzantines and the papacy under the dynamic reformer Pope Gregory the Great (590-604) and his successors.

King Clovis (ruled 481-511) united the Franks on both sides of the Rhine, and after his conversion to orthodox Christianity, defeated the Arian Burgundians (after 500) and Visigoths (507) with the support of the native clergy and the papacy. Under the **Merovingian** kings a feudal system emerged: power was fragmented among hierarchies of military landowners. Social stratification, which in late Roman times had acquired legal, hereditary sanction, was reinforced. The Carolingians (747-987) expanded the kingdom and restored central power. **Charlemagne** (ruled 768-814) conquered nearly all the Germanic lands, including Lombard Italy, and was crowned Emperor by Pope Leo III in Rome in 800. A centuries-long decline in commerce and the arts was reversed under Charlemagne's patronage. He welcomed Jews to his kingdom, which became a center of Jewish learning (Rashi 1040-1105). He sponsored the "Carolingian Renaissance" of learning under the Anglo-Latin scholar Alcuin (c732-804), who reformed church liturgy.

Byzantine Empire. Under Diocletian (ruled 284-305) the empire had been divided into 2 parts to facilitate administration and defense. Constantine founded **Constantinople**, 330, (at old Byzantium) as a fully Christian city. Commerce and taxation financed a sumptuous, orientalized court, a class of hereditary bureaucratic families, and magnificent urban construction (Hagia Sophia, 532-37). The city's fortifications and naval innovations (Greek fire) repelled assaults by Goths, Huns, Slavs, Bulgars, Avars, Arabs, and Scandinavians. Greek replaced Latin as the official language by c700. Byzantine art, a solemn, sacral, and stylized variation of late classical styles (mosaics at S. Vitale, Ravenna, 526-48) was a starting point for medieval art in E. and W. Europe.

Justinian (ruled 527-65) reconquered parts of Spain, N. Africa, and Italy, codified Roman law (codex Justinianus, 529, was medieval Europe's chief legal text), closed the Platonic Academy at Athens and ordered all pagans to convert. Lombards in Italy, Arabs in Africa retook most of his conquests. The Isaurian dynasty from Anatolia (from 717) and the Macedonian dynasty (867-1054) restored military and commercial power. The Iconoclast controversy (726-843) over the permissibility of images, helped alienate the Eastern Church from the papacy.

Arab Empire. Baghdad, founded 762, became the seat of the **Abbasid** Caliphate (founded 750), while Ummayads continued to rule in Spain. A brilliant cosmopolitan civilization emerged, inaugurating an Arab-Moslem golden age. Arab lyric poetry revived; Greek, Syriac, Persian, and Sanskrit books were translated into Arabic, often by Syriac Christians and Jews, whose theology and Talmudic law, respectively, influenced Islam. The arts and music flourished at the court of **Harun al-Rashid** (786-809), celebrated in The Arabian Nights. The sciences, medicine, and mathematics were pursued at Baghdad, Cordova, and Cairo (founded 969). Science and Aristotelian philosophy culminated in the systems of Avicenna (980-1037), Averroes (1126-98), and Maimonides (1135-1204), a Jew; all influenced later Christian scholarship and theology. The Islamic ban on images encouraged a sinuous, geometric decorative tradition, applied to architecture and illumination. A gradual loss of Arab control in Persia (from 874) led to the capture of Baghdad by Persians, 945. By the next century, Spain and N. Africa were ruled by Berbers, while Turks prevailed in Asia Minor and the Levant. The loss of political power by the caliphs allowed for the growth of non-orthodox trends, especially the mystical **Sufi** tradition (theologian Ghazali, 1058-1111).

Africa. Immigrants from Saba in S. Arabia helped set up the **Axum** kingdom in Ethiopia in the 2d century (their language, Ge'ez, is preserved by the Ethiopian Church). In the 4th century, when the kingdom became Christianized, it defeated Kushite Meroe and expanded into Yemen. Axum was the center of a vast ivory trade; it controlled the Red Sea coast until c1100. Arab conquest in Egypt cut Axum's political and economic ties with Byzantium.

The Iron Age entered W. Africa by the end of the 1st millenium BC. **Ghana,** the first known sub-Saharan state, ruled in the upper Senegal-Niger region c400-1240, controlling the trade of gold from mines in the S to trans-Sahara caravan routes to the N. The **Bantu** peoples, probably of W. African origin, began to spread E and S perhaps 2000 years ago, displacing the Pygmies and Bushmen of central and southern Africa over a 1,500-year period.

Japan. The advanced Neolithic Yayoi period, when irrigation, rice farming, and iron and bronze casting techniques were introduced from China or Korea, persisted to c400 AD. The myriad Japanese states were then united by the **Yamato** clan, under an emperor who acted as the chief priest of the animistic **Shinto** cult. Japanese political and military intervention in Korea by the 6th century quickened a Chinese cultural invasion, bringing Buddhism, the Chinese language (which long remained a literary and governmental medium), Chinese ideographs and Buddhist styles in painting, sculpture, literature, and architecture (7th c. Horyu-ji temple at Nara). The Taika Reforms, 646, tried to centralize Japan according to Chinese bureaucratic and Buddhist philosophical values, but failed to curb traditional Japanese decentralization. A nativist reaction against the Buddhist Nara period (710-94) ushered in the

Heian period (794-1185) centered at the new capital, Kyoto. Japanese elegance and simplicity modified Chinese styles in architecture, scroll painting, and literature; the writing system was also simplified. The courtly novel *Tale of Genji* (1010-20) testifies to the enhanced role of women.

Southeast Asia. The historic peoples of southeast Asia began arriving some 2500 years ago from China and Tibet, displacing scattered aborigines. Their agriculture relied on rice and tubers (yams), which they may have introduced to Africa. Indian cultural influences were strongest; literacy and Hindu and Buddhist ideas followed the southern India-China trade route. From the southern tip of Indochina, the kingdom of **Funan** (1st-7th centuries) traded as far west as Persia. It was absorbed by Chenla, itself conquered by the **Khmer Empire** (600-1300). The Khmers, under Hindu god-kings (Suryavarman II, 1113-c1150), built the monumental Angkor Wat temple center for the royal phallic cult. The **Nam-Viet** kingdom in Annam, dominated by China and Chinese culture for 1,000 years, emerged in the 10th century, growing at the expense of the Khmers, who also lost ground in the NW to the new, highly-organized **Thai** kingdom. On Sumatra, the **Srivijaya** Empire at Palembang controlled vital sea lanes (7th to 10th centuries). A Buddhist dynasty, the Sailendras, ruled central **Java** (8th-9th centuries), building at Borobudur one of the largest stupas in the world.

China. The short-lived Sui dynasty (581-618) ushered in a period of commercial, artistic, and scientific achievement in China, continuing under the **T'ang** dynasty (618-906). Such inventions as the magnetic compass, gunpowder, the abacus, and printing were introduced or perfected. Medical innovations included cataract surgery. The state, from the cosmopolitan capital, Ch'ang-an, supervised foreign trade which exchanged Chinese silks, porcelains, and art works for spices, ivory, etc., over Central Asian caravan routes and sea routes reaching Africa. A golden age of poetry bequeathed tens of thousands of works to later generations (Tu Fu 712-70, Li Po 701-62). Landscape painting flourished. Commercial and industrial expansion continued under the **Northern Sung** dynasty (960-1126), facilitated by paper money and credit notes. But commerce never achieved respectability; government monopolies expropriated successful merchants. The population, long stable at 50 million, doubled in 200 years with the introduction of early-ripening rice and the double harvest. In art, native Chinese styles were revived.

Americas. An Indian empire stretched from the Valley of Mexico to Guatemala, 300-600, centering on the huge city **Teotihuacan** (founded 100 BC). To the S, in Guatemala, a high **Mayan** civilization developed, 150-900, around hundreds of rural ceremonial centers. The Mayans improved on Olmec writing and the calendar, and pursued astronomy and mathematics (using the idea of zero). In S. America, a widespread pre-Inca culture grew from **Tiahuanaco** near Lake Titicaca (Gateway of the Sun, c700).

Christian Europe Regroups and Expands: 900-1300

Scandinavians. Pagan Danish and Norse (**Viking**) adventurers, traders, and pirates raided the coasts of the British Isles (Dublin founded c831), France, and even the Mediterranean for over 200 years beginning in the late 8th century. Inland settlement in the W was limited to Great Britain (King Canute, 994-1035) and Normandy, settled under Rollo, 911, as a fief of France. Other Vikings reached Iceland (874), Greenland (c986), and probably N. America (Leif Eriksson c1000). Norse traders (**Varangians**) developed Russian river commerce from the 8th-11th centuries, and helped set up a state at Kiev in the late 9th century. Conversion to Christianity occurred during the 10th century, reaching Sweden 100 years later. Eleventh century Norman bands conquered S. Italy and Sicily. Duke **William of Normandy** conquered England, 1066, bringing continental feudalism and the French language, essential elements in later English civilization.

East Europe. Slavs inhabited areas of E. Central Europe in prehistoric times, and reached most of their present limits by c850. The first Slavic states were in the Balkans (Slav-Turk **Bulgarian Empire**, 680-1018) and Moravia (628). Missions of St. Cyril (whose Greek-based Cyrillic alphabet is still used by S. and E. Slavs) converted Moravia, 863. The Eastern Slavs, part-civilized under the overlordship of the Turkish-Jewish **Khazar** trading empire (7th-10th centuries), gravitated toward Constantinople by the 9th century. The **Kievan state** adopted Eastern Christianity under Prince Vladimir, 989. King Boleslav I (992-1025) began **Poland's** long history of eastern conquest. The Magyars (**Hungarians**) in Europe since 896, accepted Latin Christianity, 1001.

Germany. The German kingdom that emerged after the breakup of Charlemagne's Empire remained a confederation of largely autonomous states. The Saxon Otto I, king from 936, established the **Holy Roman Empire** of Germany and Italy in alliance with Pope John XII, who crowned him emperor, 962; he defeated the Magyars, 955. Imperial power was greatest under the **Hohenstaufens** (1138-1254), despite the growing opposition of the papacy, which ruled central Italy, and the Lombard League cities. Frederick II (1194-1250) improved administration, patronized the arts; after his death German influence was removed from Italy.

Christian Spain. From its northern mountain redoubts, Christian rule slowly migrated south through the 11th century, when Moslem unity collapsed. After the capture of **Toledo** (1085), the kingdoms of Portugal, Castile, and Aragon undertook repeated crusades of reconquest, finally completed in 1492. Elements of Islamic civilization persisted in recaptured areas, influencing all W. Europe.

Crusades. Pope Urban II called, 1095, for a crusade to restore Asia Minor to Byzantium and conquer the Holy Land from the Turks. Some 10 crusades (to 1291) succeeded only in founding 4 temporary Frankish states in the Levant. The 4th crusade sacked Constantinople, 1204. In Rhineland (1096), England (1290), France (1306), Jews were massacred or expelled, and wars were launched against Christian heretics (**Albigensian** crusade in France, 1229). Trade in eastern luxuries expanded, led by the Venetian naval empire.

Economy. The agricultural base of European life benefitted from improvements in **plow design** c1000, and by draining of lowlands and clearing of forests, leading to a rural population increase. Towns grew in N. Italy, Flanders, and N. Germany (Hanseatic League). Improvements in **loom design** permitted factory textile production. Guilds dominated urban trades from the 12th century. Banking (centered in Italy, 12th-15th century) facilitated long-distance trade.

The Church. The split between the Eastern and Western churches was formalized in 1054. W. and

950 —
Otto I emperor
Cairo founded
Leif Eriksson reaches Amer.
Poland begins eastern conquest

Kiev Christian under Vladimir
Tales of Genji in Japan
Choir of St. Denis
1050 —
E. Nr. Church built
Jewish scholar Rashi b.
Christians capture Toledo

Sufi mystic Ghazali b.
Angkor Wat temple built
Univ. Bologna founded
Seljuk Turks take Baghdad
Maimonides b.

German Frederick II born
Zen comes to Japan
Ghengis Khan b.
1150 —
Sultanate of Delhi founded
Crusades

Magna Carta
Aquinas b.
Dominicans, Franciscans founded
Mali replaces Ghana
1250 —

Central Europe was divided into 500 bishoprics under one united hierarchy, but conflicts between secular and church authorities were frequent (German **Investiture Controversy**, 1075-1122). Clerical power was first strengthened through the international monastic reform begun at Cluny, 910. Popular religious enthusiasm often expressed itself in heretical movements (Waldensians from 1173), but was channelled by the **Dominican** (1215) and **Franciscan** (1223) friars into the religious mainstream.

Arts. Romanesque architecture (11th-12th centuries) expanded on late Roman models, using the rounded arch and massed stone to support enlarged basilicas. Painting and sculpture followed Byzantine models. The literature of chivalry was exemplified by the epic (Chanson de Roland, c1100) and by courtly love poems of the troubadours of Provence and minnesingers of Germany. **Gothic architecture** emerged in France (choir of St. Denis, c1040) and spread as French cultural influence predominated in Europe. Rib vaulting and pointed arches were used to combine soaring heights with delicacy, and freed walls for display of stained glass. Exteriors were covered with painted relief sculpture and elaborate architectural detail.

Learning. Law, medicine, and philosophy were advanced at independent universities (Bologna, late 11th century), originally corporations of students and masters. Twelfth century translations of Greek classics, especially Aristotle, encouraged an analytic approach. Scholastic philosophy, from Anselm (1033-1109) to Aquinas (1225-74) attempted to reconcile reason and revelation.

Apogee of Central Asian Power; Islam Grows: 1250-1500

Turks. Turkic peoples, of Central Asian ancestry, were a military threat to the Byzantine and Persian Empires from the 6th century. After several waves of invasions, during which most of the Turks adopted Islam, the **Seljuk Turks** took Baghdad, 1055. They ruled Persia, Iraq, and, after 1071, Asia Minor, where massive numbers of Turks settled. The empire was divided in the 12th century into smaller states ruled by Seljuks, Kurds (**Saladin** c1137-93), and Mamelukes (a military caste of former Turk, Kurd, and Circassian slaves), which governed Egypt and the Middle East until the Ottoman era (c1290-1922).

Osman I (ruled c1290-1326) and succeeding sultans united Anatolian Turkish warriors in a militaristic state that waged holy war against Byzantium and Balkan Christians. Most of the Balkans had been subdued, and Anatolia united, when **Constantinople fell**, 1453. By the mid-16th century, Hungary, the Middle East, and North Africa had been conquered. The Turkish advance was stopped at Vienna, 1529, and at the naval battle of Lepanto, 1571, by Spain, Venice, and the papacy.

The **Ottoman state** was governed in accordance with orthodox Moslem law. Greek, Armenian, and Jewish communities were segregated, and ruled by religious leaders responsible for taxation; they dominated trade. State offices and most army ranks were filled by slaves through a system of child conscription among Christians.

India. Mahmud of Ghazni (971-1030) led repeated Turkish raids into N. India. Turkish power was consolidated in 1206 with the start of the **Sultanate at Delhi.** Centralization of state power under the early Delhi sultans went far beyond traditional Indian practice. Moslem rule of most of the subcontinent lasted until the British conquest some 600 years later.

Mongols. Genghis Khan (c1162-1227) first united the feuding Mongol tribes, and built their armies into an effective offensive force around a core of highly mobile cavalry. He and his immediate successors created the largest land empire in history; by 1279 it stretched from the east coast of Asia to the Danube, from the Siberian steppes to the Arabian Sea. East-West trade and contacts were facilitated (Marco Polo c1254-1324). The western Mongols were Islamized by 1295; successor states soon lost their Mongol character by assimilation. They were briefly reunited under the Turk Tamerlane (1336-1405).

Kublai Khan ruled China from his new capital Peking (founded 1264). Naval campaigns against Japan (1274, 1281) and Java (1293) were defeated, the latter by the Hindu-Buddhist maritime kingdom of Majapahit. The **Yuan** dynasty made use of Mongols and other foreigners (including Europeans) in official posts, and tolerated the return of Nestorian Christianity (suppressed 841-45) and the spread of Islam in the South and West. A native reaction expelled the Mongols, 1367-68.

Russia. The Kievan state in Russia, weakened by the decline of Byzantium and the rise of the Catholic Polish-Lithuanian state, was overrun by the Mongols, 1238-40. Only the northern trading republic of Novgorod remained independent. The grand dukes of Moscow emerged as leaders of a coalition of princes that eventually defeated the Mongols, by 1481. With the fall of Constantinople, the **Tsars** (Caesars) at Moscow (from Ivan III, ruled 1462-1505) set up an independent Russian Orthodox Church. Commerce failed to revive. The isolated Russian state remained agrarian, with the peasant class falling into serfdom.

Persia. A revival of Persian literature, using the Arab alphabet and literary forms, began in the 10th century (epic of Firdausi, 935-1020). An art revival, influenced by Chinese styles, began in the 12th. Persian cultural and political forms, and often the Persian language, were used for centuries by Turkish and Mongol elites from the Balkans to India. Persian mystics from Rumi (1207-73) to Jami (1414-92) promoted Sufism in their poetry.

Africa. Two Berber dynasties, imbued with Islamic militance, emerged from the Sahara to carve out empires from the Sahel to central Spain — the Almoravids, c1050-1140, and the fanatical **Almohads**, c1125-1269. The Ghanaian empire was replaced in the upper Niger by Mali, c1230-c1340, whose Moslem rulers imported Egyptians to help make **Timbuktu** a center of commerce (in gold, leather, slaves) and learning. The Songhay empire (to 1590) replaced Mali. To the S, forest kingdoms produced refined art works (Ife terra cotta, **Benin** bronzes). Other Moslem states in Nigeria (Hausas) and Chad originated in the 11th century, and continued in some form until the 19th century European conquest. Less developed Bantu kingdoms existed across central Africa.

Some 40 Moslem Arab-Persian trading colonies and city-states were established all along the E. African coast from the 10th century (Kilwa, Mogadishu). The interchange with Bantu peoples produced the **Swahili** language and culture. Gold, palm oil, and slaves were brought from the interior, stimulating the growth of the Monamatapa kingdom of the Zambezi (15th century). The Christian Ethiopian empire (from 13th century) continued the traditions of Axum.

Southeast Asia. Islam was introduced into Malaya and the Indonesian islands by Arab, Persian, and

Indian traders. Coastal Moslem cities and states (starting before 1300), enriched by trade, soon dominated the interior. Chief among these was the **Malacca** state, on the Malay peninsula, c1400-1511.

Arts and Statecraft Thrive in Europe: 1350-1600

Italian Renaissance & humanism. Distinctive Italian achievements in the arts in the late Middle Ages (Dante, 1265-1321, Giotto, 1276-1337) led to the vigorous new styles of the Renaissance (14th-16th centuries). Patronized by the rulers of the quarreling petty states of Italy (Medicis in Florence and the papacy, c1400-1737), the plastic arts perfected realistic techniques, including **perspective** (Masaccio, 1401-28, Leonardo 1452-1519). Classical motifs were used in architecture and increased talent and expense were put into secular buildings. The Florentine dialect was refined as a national literary language (Petrarch, 1304-74). Greek refugees from the E strengthened the respect of humanist scholars for the classic sources (Bruni 1370-1444). Soon an international movement aided by the spread of **printing** (Gutenberg c1400-1468), **humanism** was optimistic about the power of human reason (Erasmus of Rotterdam, 1466-1536, Thomas More's *Utopia*, 1516) and valued individual effort in the arts and in politics (Machiavelli, 1469-1527).

France. The French monarchy, strengthened in its repeated struggles with powerful nobles (Burgundy, Flanders, Aquitaine) by alliances with the growing commercial towns, consolidated bureaucratic control under Philip IV (ruled 1285-1314) and extended French influence into Germany and Italy (popes at Avignon, France, 1309-1417). The **Hundred Years War,** 1337-1453, ended English dynastic claims in France (battles of Crécy, 1346, Poitiers, 1356; Joan of Arc executed, 1431). A French Renaissance, dating from royal invasions of Italy, 1494, 1499, was encouraged at the court of Francis I (ruled 1515-47), who centralized taxation and law. French vernacular literature consciously asserted its independence (La Pleiade, 1549).

England. The evolution of England's unique political institutions began with the Magna Carta, 1215, by which King John guaranteed the privileges of nobles and church against the monarchy and assured jury trial. After the Wars of the Roses (1455-85), the **Tudor dynasty** reasserted royal prerogatives (Henry VIII, ruled 1509-47), but the trend toward independent departments and ministerial government also continued. English trade (wool exports from c1300) was protected by the nation's growing maritime power (**Spanish Armada** destroyed, 1588).

English replaced French and Latin in the late 14th century in law and literature (Chaucer, 1340-1400) and English translation of the Bible began (Wycliffe, 1380s). Elizabeth I (ruled 1558-1603) presided over a confident flowering of poetry (Spenser, 1552-99), drama (**Shakespeare,** 1564-1616), and music.

German Empire. From among a welter of minor feudal states, church lands, and independent cities, the **Hapsburgs** assembled a far-flung territorial domain, based in Austria from 1276. The family held the title Holy Roman Emperor from 1452 to the Empire's dissolution in 1806, but failed to centralize its domains, leaving Germany disunited for centuries. Resistance to Turkish expansion brought Hungary under Austrian control from the 16th century. The Netherlands, Luxembourg, and Burgundy were added in 1477, curbing French expansion.

The Flemish painting tradition of naturalism, technical proficiency, and bourgeois subject matter began in the 15th century (Jan Van Eyck, 1366-1440), the earliest northern manifestation of the Renaissance. **Durer** (1471-1528) typified the merging of late Gothic and Italian trends in 16th century German art. Imposing civic architecture flourished in the prosperous commercial cities.

Spain. Despite the unification of Castile and Aragon in 1479, the 2 countries retained separate governments, and the nobility, especially in Aragon and Catalonia, retained many privileges. Spanish lands in Italy (Naples, Sicily) and the Netherlands entangled the country in European wars through the mid-17th century, while explorers, traders, and conquerors built up a Spanish empire in the Americas and the Philippines.

From the late 15th century, a **golden age** of literature and art produced works of social satire (plays of Lope de Vega, 1562-1635; Cervantes, 1547-1616), as well as spiritual intensity (El Greco, 1541-1614; Velazquez, 1599-1660).

Black Death. The bubonic plague reached Europe from the E in 1348, killing as much as half the population by 1350. Labor scarcity forced a rise in wages and brought greater freedom to the peasantry, making possible **peasant uprisings** (Jacquerie in France, 1358, Wat Tyler's rebellion in England, 1381). In the *ciompi* revolt, 1378, Florentine wage earners demanded a say in economic and political power.

Explorations. Organized European maritime exploration began, seeking to evade the Venice-Ottoman monopoly of eastern trade and to promote Christianity. Expeditions from Portugal beginning 1418 explored the west coast of Africa, until **Vasco da Gama** rounded the Cape of Good Hope in 1497 and reached India. A Portuguese trading empire was consolidated by the seizure of Goa, 1510, and Malacca, 1551. Japan was reached in 1542. Spanish voyages (**Columbus,** 1492-1504) uncovered a new world, which Spain hastened to subdue. Navigation schools in Spain and Portugal, the development of large sailing ships (carracks), and the invention of the rifle, c1475, aided European penetration.

Mughals and Safavids. East of the Ottoman empire, two Moslem dynasties ruled unchallenged in the 16th and 17th centuries. The Mughal empire in India, founded by Persianized Turkish invaders from the NW under Babur, dates from their 1526 conquest of Delhi. The dynasty ruled most of India for over 200 years, surviving nominally until 1857. **Akbar** (ruled 1556-1605) consolidated administration at his glorious court, where Urdu (Persian-influenced Hindi) developed. Trade relations with Europe increased. Under Shah Jahan (1629-58), a secularized art fusing Hindu and Moslem elements flourished in miniature painting and architecture (**Taj Mahal**). Sikhism, founded c1519, combined elements of both faiths. Suppression of Hindus and Shi'ite Moslems in S India in the late 17th century weakened the empire.

Fanatical devotion to the Shi'ite sect characterized the Safavids of Persia, 1502-1736, and led to hostilities with the Sunni Ottomans for over a century. The prosperity and strength of the empire is evidenced by the mosques at its capital, **Isfahan.** The dynasty enhanced Iranian national consciousness.

China. The Ming emperors, 1368-1644, the last native dynasty in China, wielded unprecedented personal power, while the Confucian bureaucracy began to suffer from inertia. European trade (Portugese

1500
Brazil discovered
Calvin b.
Vesalius b.
St. Theresa of Avila b.
Watch invented
Luther's 95 Theses
Persian Safavids rule
Cortes conquers Aztecs
Mughal empire starts
So. Ger. peasants rise
Pizarro conquers Incas
Jesuits founded
1550
Council of Trent
Dutch republic founded
Velazquez b.
Japan persecutes Christians
Civil War in France
Descartes b.
1600

monopoly through **Macao** from 1557) was strictly controlled. Jesuit scholars and scientists (Matteo Ricci 1552-1610) introduced some Western science; their writings familiarized the West with China. Chinese technological inventiveness declined from this era, but the arts thrived, especially painting and ceramics.

Japan. After the decline of the first hereditary shogunate (chief generalship) at **Kamakura** (1185-1333), fragmentation of power accelerated, as did the consequent social mobility. Under Kamakura and the Ashikaga shogunate, 1338-1573, the daimyos (lords) and samurai (warriors) grew more powerful and promoted a martial ideology. Japanese pirates and traders plied the China coast. Popular Buddhist movements included the nationalist Nichiren sect (from c1250) and **Zen** (brought from China, 1191), which stressed meditation and a disciplined esthetic (tea ceremony, landscape gardening, judo, Noh drama).

Reformed Europe Expands Overseas: 1500-1700

Reformation begun. Theological debate and protests against real and perceived clerical corruption existed in the medieval Christian world, expressed by such dissenters as Wycliffe (c1320-84) and his followers, the Lollards, in England, and **Huss** (burned as a heretic, 1415) in Bohemia.

Luther (1483-1546) preached that only faith could lead to salvation, without the mediation of clergy or good works. He attacked the authority of the Pope, rejected priestly celibacy, and recommended individual study of the Bible (which he translated, c1525). His 95 Theses (1517) led to his excommunication (1520). **Calvin** (1509-64) said God's elect were predestined for salvation; good conduct and success were signs of election. Calvin in Geneva and Knox (1505-72) in Scotland erected theocratic states.

Henry VIII asserted English national authority and secular power by breaking away from the Catholic church, 1534. Monastic property was confiscated, and some Protestant doctrines given official sanction.

Religious wars. A century and a half of religious wars began with a South German peasant uprising, 1524, repressed with Luther's support. Radical sects—democratic, pacifist, millennarian—arose (Anabaptists ruled Muenster, 1534-35), and were suppressed violently. Civil war in France from 1562 between **Huguenots** (Protestant nobles and merchants) and Catholics ended with the 1598 Edict of Nantes tolerating Protestants (revoked 1685). Hapsburg attempts to restore Catholicism in Germany were resisted in 25 years of fighting; the 1555 Peace of Augsburg guarantee of religious independence to local princes and cities was confirmed only after the **Thirty Years War**, 1618-48, when much of Germany was devastated by local and foreign armies (Sweden, France).

A Catholic Reformation, or **counter-reformation**, met the Protestant challenge, clearly defining an official theology at the Council of Trent, 1545-63. The **Jesuit** order, founded 1534 by Loyola (1491-1556), helped reconvert large areas of Poland, Hungary, and S. Germany and sent missionaries to the New World, India, and China, while the Inquisition helped suppress heresy in Catholic countries. A revival of piety appeared in the devotional literature (Theresa of Avila, 1515-82) and the grandiose Baroque art (Bernini, 1598-1680) of Roman Catholic countries.

Scientific Revolution. The late nominalist thinkers (Ockham, c1300-49) of Paris and Oxford challenged Aristotelian orthodoxy, allowing for a freer scientific approach. But metaphysical values, such as the Neoplatonic faith in an orderly, mathematical cosmos, still motivated and directed subsequent inquiry. **Copernicus** (1473-1543) promoted the heliocentric theory, which was confirmed when Kepler (1571-1630) discovered the mathematical laws describing the orbits of the planets. The Christian-Aristotelian belief that heavens and earth were fundamentally different collapsed when **Galileo** (1564-1642) discovered moving sunspots, irregular moon topography, and moons around Jupiter. He and Newton (1642-1727) developed a mechanics that unified cosmic and earthly phenomena. To meet the needs of the new physics, Newton and Leibnitz (1646-1716) invented calculus, Descartes (1596-1650) invented analytic geometry.

An explosion of observational science included the discovery of blood circulation (Harvey, 1578-1657) and microscopic life (Leeuwenhoek, 1632-1723), and advances in anatomy (Vesalius, 1514-64, dissected corpses) and chemistry (Boyle, 1627-91). Scientific research institutes were founded: Florence, 1657, London (**Royal Society**), 1660, Paris, 1666. Inventions proliferated (Savery's steam engine, 1696).

Arts. Mannerist trends of the high Renaissance (Michelangelo, 1475-1564) exploited virtuosity, grace, novelty, and exotic subjects and poses. The notion of artistic genius was promoted, in contrast to the anonymous medieval artisan. Private connoisseurs entered the art market. These trends were elaborated in the 17th century **Baroque** era, on a grander scale. Dynamic movement in painting and sculpture was emphasized by sharp lighting effects, use of rich materials (colored marble, gilt), realistic details. Curved facades, broken lines, rich, deep-cut detail, and ceiling decoration characterized Baroque architecture, especially in Germany. Monarchs, princes, and prelates, usually Catholic, used Baroque art to enhance and embellish their authority, as in royal portraits by Velazquez (1599-1660) and Van Dyck (1599-1641).

National styles emerged. In France, a taste for rectilinear order and serenity (Poussin, 1594-1665), linked to the new rational philosophy, was expressed in classical forms. The influence of classical values in French literature (tragedies of Racine, 1639-99) gave rise to the "battle of the Ancients and Moderns." New forms included the essay (Montaigne, 1533-92) and novel (Princesse de Cleves, La Fayette, 1678).

Dutch painting of the 17th century was unique in its wide social distribution. The Flemish tradition of undemonstrative realism reached its peak in Rembrandt (1606-69) and Vermeer (1632-75).

Economy. European economic expansion was stimulated by the new trade with the East, New World gold and silver, and a doubling of population (50 mln. in 1450, 100 mln. in 1600). New business and financial techniques were developed and refined, such as joint-stock companies, insurance, and letters of credit and exchange. The Bank of Amsterdam, 1609, and the Bank of England, 1694, broke the old monopoly of private banking families. The rise of a business mentality was typified by the spread of clock towers in cities in the 14th century. By the mid-15th century, portable clocks were available; the first watch was invented in 1502.

By 1650, most governments had adopted the **mercantile system**, in which they sought to amass metallic wealth by protecting their merchants' foreign and colonial trade monopolies. The rise in prices and the new coin-based economy undermined the craft guild and feudal manorial systems. Expanding industries, such as clothweaving and mining, benefitted from technical advances. Coal replaced disappearing wood as the chief fuel; it was used to fuel new 16th century blast furnaces making cast iron.

New World. The Aztecs united much of the Mesoamerican culture area in a militarist empire by 1519, from their capital, Tenochtitlan (pop. 300,000), which was the center of a cult requiring enormous levels of ritual human sacrifice. Most of the civilized areas of S. America were ruled by the centralized Inca Empire (1476-1534), stretching 2,000 miles from Ecuador to N.W. Argentina. Lavish and sophisticated traditions in pottery, weaving, sculpture, and architecture were maintained in both regions.

These empires, beset by revolts, fell in 2 short campaigns to gold-seeking Spanish forces based in the Antilles and Panama. Cortes took Mexico, 1519-21; Pizarro Peru, 1531-35. From these centers, land and sea expeditions claimed most of N. and S. America for Spain. The Indian high cultures did not survive the impact of Christian missionaries and the new upper class of whites and mestizos. In turn, New World silver, and such Indian products as potatoes, tobacco, corn, peanuts, chocolate, and rubber exercised a major economic influence on Europe. While the Spanish administration intermittently concerned itself with the welfare of Indians, the population remained impoverished at most levels, despite the growth of a distinct South American civilization. European diseases reduced the native population.

Brazil, which the Portuguese discovered in 1500 and settled after 1530, and the Caribbean colonies of several European nations developed a plantation economy where sugar cane, tobacco, cotton, coffee, rice, indigo, and lumber were grown commercially by slaves. From the early 16th to the late 19th centuries, some 10 million Africans were transported to slavery in the New World.

Netherlands. The urban, Calvinist northern provinces of the Netherlands rebelled against Hapsburg Spain, 1568, and founded an oligarchic mercantile republic. Their strategic control of the Baltic grain market enabled them to exploit Mediterranean food shortages. Religious refugees — French and Belgian Protestants, Iberian Jews — added to the cosmopolitan commercial talent pool. After Spain absorbed Portugal in 1580, the Dutch seized Portuguese possessions and created a vast, though generally short-lived commercial empire in Brazil, the Antilles, Africa, India, Ceylon, Malacca, Indonesia, and Taiwan, and challenged or supplanted Portuguese traders in China and Japan.

England. Anglicanism became firmly established under Elizabeth I after a brief Catholic interlude under "Bloody Mary," 1553-58. But religious and political conflicts led to a rebellion by Parliament, 1642. Roundheads (Puritans) defeated Cavaliers (Royalists); Charles I was beheaded, 1649. The new Commonwealth was ruled as a military dictatorship by Cromwell, who also brutally crushed an Irish rebellion, 1649-51. Conflicts within the Puritan camp (democratic Levelers defeated 1649) aided the Stuart restoration, 1660, but Parliament was permanently strengthened and the peaceful "Glorious Revolution", 1688, advanced political and religious liberties (writings of Locke, 1632-1704). British privateers (Drake, 1540-96) challenged Spanish control of the New World, and penetrated Asian trade routes (Madras taken, 1639). N. American colonies (Jamestown, 1607, Plymouth, 1620) provided an outlet for religious dissenters.

France. Emerging from the religious civil wars in 1628, France regained military and commercial great power status under the ministries of Richelieu (1624-42), Mazarin (1643-61), and Colbert (1662-83). Under Louis XIV (ruled 1643-1715) royal absolutism triumphed over nobles and local parlements (defeat of Fronde, 1648-53). Permanent colonies were founded in Canada (1608), the Caribbean (1626), and India (1674).

Sweden. Sweden seceded from the Scandinavian Union in 1523. The thinly-populated agrarian state (with copper, iron, and timber exports) was united by the Vasa kings, whose conquests by the mid-17th century made Sweden the dominant Baltic power. The empire collapsed in the Great Northern War (1700-21).

Poland. After the union with Lithuania in 1447, Poland ruled vast territories from the Baltic to the Black Sea, resisting German and Turkish incursions. Catholic nobles failed to gain the loyalty of the Orthodox Christian peasantry in the East; commerce and trades were practiced by German and Jewish immigrants. The bloody 1648-49 cossack uprising began the kingdom's dismemberment.

China. A new dynasty, the Manchus, invaded from the NE and seized power in 1644, and expanded Chinese control to its greatest extent in Central and Southeast Asia. Trade and diplomatic contact with Europe grew, carefully controlled by China. New crops (sweet potato, maize, peanut) allowed an economic and population growth (300 million pop. in 1800). Traditional arts and literature were pursued with increased sophistication (*Dream of the Red Chamber*, novel, mid-18th century).

Japan. Tokugawa Ieyasu, shogun from 1603, finally unified and pacified feudal Japan. Hereditary daimyos and samurai monopolized government office and the professions. An urban merchant class grew, literacy spread, and a cultural renaissance occurred (haiku of Basho, 1644-94). Fear of European domination led to persecution of Christian converts from 1597, and stringent isolation from outside contact from 1640.

Philosophy, Industry, and Revolution: 1700-1800

Science and Reason. Faith in human reason and science as the source of truth and a means to improve the physical and social environment, espoused since the Renaissance (Francis Bacon, 1561-1626), was bolstered by scientific discoveries in spite of theological opposition (Galileo's forced retraction, 1633). Descartes applied the logical method of mathematics to discover "self-evident" scientific and philosophical truths, while Newton emphasized induction from experimental observation.

The challenge of reason to traditional religious and political values and institutions began with Spinoza (1632-77), who interpreted the Bible historically and called for political and intellectual freedom.

French philosophes assumed leadership of the "Enlightenment" in the 18th century. Montesquieu (1689-1755) used British history to support his notions of limited government. Voltaire's (1694-1778) diaries and novels of exotic travel illustrated the intellectual trends toward secular ethics and relativism. Rousseau's (1712-1778) radical concepts of the social contract and of the inherent goodness of the common man gave impetus to anti-monarchical republicanism. The *Encyclopedia*, 1751-72, edited by Diderot and d'Alembert, designed as a monument to reason, was largely devoted to practical technology.

In England, ideals of political and religious liberty were connected with empiricist philosophy and science in the followers of Locke. But the extreme empiricism of Hume (1711-76) and Berkeley

1750

Timeline markers (left margin): Rosseau's Social Contract · Spinning jenny · Brit. rules Bengal · Watt's engine · Encyclopedia · Edinburgh plan · Kant's Critique of Pure Reason · American Revolution! · Austria serfs free · Bastille stormed · China bans opium · Divisions of Poland · Burke d. · Fr. Repub. declared · Adam Smith d. · China pop. at 300 mln.

(1685-1753) posed limits to the identification of reason with absolute truth, as did the evolutionary approach to law and politics of Burke (1729-97) and the utilitarianism of Bentham (1748-1832). Adam Smith (1723-90) and other **physiocrats** called for a rationalization of economic activity by removing artificial barriers to a supposedly natural free exchange of goods.

Despite the political disunity and backwardness of most of Germany, German writers participated in the new philosophical trends popularized by Wolff (1679-1754). **Kant's** (1724-1804) **idealism**, unifying an empirical epistemology with *a priori* moral and logical concepts, directed German thought away from skepticism. Italian contributions included work on electricity by Galvani (1737-98) and Volta (1745-1827), the pioneer **historiography of Vico** (1668-1744), and writings on penal reform by Beccaria (1738-94). The American Franklin (1706-90) was celebrated in Europe for his varied achievements.

The growth of the **press** (*Spectator*, 1711-14) and the wide distribution of realistic but sentimental **novels** attested to the increase of a large bourgeois public.

Arts. Rococo art, characterized by extravagant decorative effects, asymmetries copied from organic models, and artificial pastoral subjects, was favored by the continental aristocracy for most of the century (Watteau, 1684-1721), and had musical analogies in the ornamentalized polyphony of late Baroque. The **Neoclassical** art after 1750, associated with the new scientific archeology, was more streamlined, and infused with the supposed moral and geometric rectitude of the Roman Republic (David, 1748-1825). In England, **town planning** on a grand scale began (Edinburgh, 1767).

Industrial Revolution in England. Agricultural improvements, such as the sowing drill (1701) and livestock breeding, were implemented on the large fields provided by enclosure of common lands by private owners. Profits from agriculture and from colonial and foreign trade (1800 volume, £ 54 million) were channelled through hundreds of banks and the **Stock Exchange** (founded 1773) into new industrial processes.

The Newcomen steam pump (1712) aided coal mining. Coal fueled the new efficient steam engines patented by Watt in 1769, and coke-smelting produced cheap, sturdy iron for machinery by the 1730s. The **flying shuttle** (1733) and **spinning jenny** (1764) were used in the large new cotton textile factories, where women and children were much of the work force. Goods were transported cheaply over **canals** (2,000 miles built 1760-1800).

American Revolution. The British colonies in N. America attracted a mass immigration of religious dissenters and poor people throughout the 17th and 18th centuries, coming from all parts of the British Isles, Germany, the Netherlands, and other countries. The population reached 3 million whites and blacks by the 1770s. The small native population was decimated by European diseases and wars with and between the various colonies. British attempts to control colonial trade, and to tax the colonists to pay for the costs of colonial administration and defense clashed with traditions of local self government, and eventually provoked the colonies to rebellion. (*See American Revolution in Index.*)

Central and East Europe. The monarchs of the three states that dominated eastern Europe — Austria, Prussia, and Russia — accepted the advice and legitimation of philosophes in creating more modern, centralized institutions in their kingdoms, enlarged by the division of Poland (1772-95).

Under **Frederick II** (ruled 1740-86) Prussia, with its efficient modern army, doubled in size. State monopolies and tariff protection fostered industry, and some legal reforms were introduced. Austria's heterogeneous realms were legally unified under **Maria Theresa** (ruled 1740-80) and **Joseph II** (1780-90). Reforms in education, law, and religion were enacted, and the Austrian serfs were freed (1781). With its defeat in the Seven Years' War in 1763, Austria lost Silesia and ceased its active role in Germany, but was compensated by expansion to the E and S (Hungary, Slavonia, 1699, Galicia, 1772).

Russia, whose borders continued to expand in all directions, adopted some Western bureaucratic and economic policies under **Peter I** (ruled 1682-1725) and **Catherine II** (ruled 1762-96). Trade and cultural contacts with the West multiplied from the new Baltic Sea capital, **St. Petersburg** (founded 1703).

French Revolution. The growing French middle class lacked political power, and resented aristocratic tax privileges, especially in light of liberal political ideals popularized by the American Revolution. Peasants lacked adequate land and were burdened with feudal obligations to nobles. Wars with Britain drained the treasury, finally forcing the king to call the **Estates-General** in 1789 (first time since 1614), in an atmosphere of food riots (poor crop in 1788).

Aristocratic resistance to absolutism was soon overshadowed by the reformist Third Estate (middle class), which proclaimed itself the **National Constituent Assembly** June 17 and took the "Tennis Court oath" on June 20 to secure a constitution. The storming of the **Bastille** July 14 by Parisian artisans was followed by looting and seizure of aristocratic property throughout France. Assembly reforms included abolition of class and regional privileges, a Declaration of Rights, suffrage by taxpayers (75% of males), and the **Civil Constitution of the Clergy** providing for election and loyalty oaths for priests. A republic was declared Sept. 22, 1792, in spite of royalist pressure from Austria and Prussia, which had declared war in April (joined by Britain the next year). Louis XVI was beheaded Jan. 21, 1793, Queen Marie Antoinette was beheaded Oct. 16, 1793.

Royalist uprisings in La Vendee in the S and military reverses led to a **reign of terror** in which tens of thousands of opponents of the Revolution and criminals were executed. Radical reforms in the **Convention** period (Sept. 1793-Oct. 1795) included the abolition of colonial slavery, economic measures to aid the poor, support of public education, and a short-lived de-Christianization.

Division among radicals (execution of Hebert, March 1794, Danton, April, and Robespierre, July) aided the ascendance of a moderate **Directory**, which consolidated military victories. **Napoleon Bonaparte** (1769-1821), a popular young general, exploited political divisions and participated in a coup Nov. 9, 1799, making himself first consul (dictator).

India. Sikh and Hindu rebels (Rajputs, Marathas) and Afghans destroyed the power of the Mughals during the 18th century. After France's defeat in the Seven Years War, 1763, Britain was the chief European trade power in India. Its control of inland **Bengal and Bihar** was recognized by the Mughal shah in 1765, who granted the **British East India Co.** (under Clive, 1727-74) the right to collect land revenue there. Despite objections from Parliament (1784 India Act) the company's involvement in local wars and politics led to repeated acquisitions of new territory. The company exported Indian textiles, sugar, and indigo.

1800

World Population Growth 1 AD to 1990

Billions

- 1990 5.3 Billion
- 1975 4 Billion
- 1930 2 Billion
- 1850 1 Billion
- 1650 500 Million
- 1 AD 200 Million

6.0
5.0
4.0
3.0
2.0
1.0
0

1 AD   500   1000   1500   2000

ASIA CIRCA 1900

0   600   1200

Scale of Miles

RUSSIAN EMPIRE

OTTOMAN EMPIRE

Lake Baikal

MANCHURIA

JAPAN

KOREA

MONGOLIA

Peking

Jerusalem

Baghdad

Teheran

PERSIA   AFGHANISTAN

Kabul

SINKIANG

CHINESE EMPIRE

Shanghai

Pacific Ocean

Mecca

KASHMIR

PUNJAB

TIBET

CHINA

Lhasa

Chungking

TAIWAN

ARABIA

BALUCHISTAN

Karachi

Delhi

NEPAL

BHUTAN

Canton

Hong Kong

PHILIPPINE ISLANDS

OMAN

BRITISH INDIA

Calcutta

Mandalay

TONGKING

HAINAN

South China Sea

Bombay

BURMA

Rangoon

LAOS

SIAM

Bangkok

CAMBODIA

Saigon

Arabian Sea

Madras

Bay of Bengal

CEYLON

Singapore

BORNEO

CELEBES

SUMATRA

Indian Ocean

JAVA

Change Gathers Steam: 1800-1840

Timeline (left margin):

- 1800
- Haiti indep.
- Mill b.
- Hugo b. — Dix b.
- Lamarck's Philosophie Zoologique
- Napoleon emperor
- Congress of Vienna
- Byron d. — Grimm's Fairy Tales — Scott's Ivanhoe
- 1815
- Decembrist uprising
- S. Amer. colonies win indep.
- Greek indep. movement
- Brazil indep.
- Blake d. — Volta d. — Beethoven d.
- Belgian indep.
- 1830
- 1st Eng. reform bill
- 1st Brit. Factory Act.
- Brit. Emp. slavery banned
- Opium War
- Telegraph perfected by Morse
- Brook Farm, Mass.
- 1845

French ideals and empire spread. Inspired by the ideals of the French Revolution, and supported by the expanding French armies, new republican regimes arose near France: the **Batavian Republic** in the Netherlands (1795-1806), the **Helvetic Republic** in Switzerland (1798-1803), the **Cisalpine Republic** in N. Italy (1797-1805), the **Ligurian Republic** in Genoa (1797-1805), and the **Parthenopean Republic** in S. Italy (1799). A Roman Republic existed briefly in 1798 after Pope Pius VI was arrested by French troops. In Italy and Germany, new nationalist sentiments were stimulated both in imitation of and reaction to France (anti-French and anti-Jacobin peasant uprisings in Italy, 1796-9).

From 1804, when Napoleon declared himself emperor, to 1812, a succession of military victories (Austerlitz, 1805, Jena, 1806) extended his control over most of Europe, through puppet states (**Confederation of the Rhine** united W. German states for the first time and **Grand Duchy of Warsaw** revived Polish national hopes), expansion of the empire, and alliances.

Among the lasting reforms initiated under Napoleon's absolutist reign were: establishment of the Bank of France, centralization of tax collection, codification of law along Roman models (*Code Napoleon*), and reform and extension of secondary and university education. In an 1801 concordat, the papacy recognized the effective autonomy of the French Catholic Church. Some 400,000 French soldiers were killed in the Napoleonic Wars, along with 600,000 foreign troops.

Last gasp of old regime. France's coastal blockade of Europe (**Continental System**) failed to neutralize Britain. The disastrous 1812 invasion of Russia exposed Napoleon's overextension. After an 1814 exile at Elba, Napoleon's armies were defeated at **Waterloo**, 1815, by British and Prussian troops.

At the **Congress of Vienna**, the monarchs and princes of Europe redrew their boundaries, to the advantage of Prussia (in Saxony and the Ruhr), Austria (in Illyria and Venetia), and Russia (in Poland and Finland). British conquest of Dutch and French colonies (S. Africa, Ceylon, Mauritius) was recognized, and France, under the restored Bourbons, retained its expanded 1792 borders. The settlement brought 50 years of international peace to Europe.

But the Congress was unable to check the advance of liberal ideals and of nationalism among the smaller European nations. The 1825 **Decembrist** uprising by liberal officers in Russia was easily suppressed. But an independence movement in **Greece**, stirred by commercial prosperity and a cultural revival, succeeded in expelling Ottoman rule by 1831, with the aid of Britain, France, and Russia.

A constitutional monarchy was secured in France by an **1830 revolution**; Louis Philippe became king. The revolutionary contagion spread to **Belgium**, which gained its independence from the Dutch monarchy, 1830; to **Poland**, whose rebellion was defeated by Russia, 1830-31; and to Germany.

Romanticism. A new style in intellectual and artistic life began to replace Neo-classicism and Rococo after the mid-18th century. By the early 19th, this style, Romanticism, had prevailed in the European world.

Rousseau had begun the reaction against excessive rationalism and skepticism; in education (*Emile*, 1762) he stressed subjective spontaneity over regularized instruction. In Germany, Lessing (1729-81) and Herder (1744-1803) favorably compared the German folk song to classical forms, and began a cult of Shakespeare, whose passion and "natural" wisdom was a model for the Romantic *Sturm und Drang* (storm and stress) movement. Goethe's *Sorrows of Young Werther* (1774) set the model for the tragic, passionate genius.

A new interest in **Gothic architecture** in England after 1760 (Walpole, 1717-97) spread through Europe, associated with an aesthetic Christian and mystic revival (Blake, 1757-1827). Celtic, Norse, and German mythology and folk tales were revived or imitated (Macpherson's Ossian translation, 1762, Grimm's *Fairy Tales*, 1812-22). The medieval revival (Scott's *Ivanhoe*, 1819) led to a new interest in history, stressing national differences and organic growth (Carlyle, 1795-1881; Michelet, 1798-1874), corresponding to theories of natural evolution (Lamarck's *Philosophie zoologique*, 1809, Lyell's *Geology*, 1830-33).

Revolution and war fed an obsession with freedom and conflict, expressed by poets (**Byron**, 1788-1824, **Hugo**, 1802-85) and philosophers (**Hegel**, 1770-1831).

Wild gardens replaced the formal French variety, and painters favored rural, stormy, and mountainous landscapes (**Turner**, 1775-1851; **Constable**, 1776-1837). Clothing became freer, with wigs, hoops, and ruffles discarded. Originality and genius were expected in the life as well as the work of inspired artists (Murger's *Scenes from Bohemian Life*, 1847-49). Exotic locales and themes (as in "Gothic" horror stories) were used in art and literature (Delacroix, 1798-1863, **Poe**, 1809-49).

Music exhibited the new dramatic style and a breakdown of classical forms (Beethoven, 1770-1827). The use of folk melodies and modes aided the growth of distinct national traditions (Glinka in Russia, 1804-57).

Latin America. Haiti, under the former slave **Toussaint L'Ouverture**, was the first Latin American independent state, 1800. All the mainland Spanish colonies won their independence 1810-24, under such leaders as **Bolivar** (1783-1830). Brazil became an independent empire under the Portuguese prince regent, 1822. A new class of military officers divided power with large landholders and the church.

United States. Heavy immigration and exploitation of ample natural resources fueled rapid economic growth. The spread of the franchise, public education, and antislavery sentiment were signs of a widespread democratic ethic.

China. Failure to keep pace with Western arms technology exposed China to greater European influence, and hampered efforts to bar imports of opium, which had damaged Chinese society and drained wealth overseas. In the **Opium War**, 1839-42, Britain forced China to expand trade opportunities and to cede Hong Kong.

Triumph of Progress: 1840-80

Idea of Progress. As a result of the cumulative scientific, economic, and political changes of the preceding eras, the idea took hold among literate people in the West that continuing growth and improvement was the usual state of human and natural life.

Darwin's statement of the **theory of evolution** and survival of the fittest (*Origin of Species*, 1859), defended by intellectuals and scientists against theological objections, was taken as confirmation that progress was the natural direction of life. The controversy helped define popular ideas of the dedicated scientist and ever-expanding human knowledge of and control over the world (Foucault's demonstration of earth's rotation, 1851, Pasteur's germ theory, 1861).

Liberals following Ricardo (1772-1823) in their faith that unrestrained competition would bring continuous economic expansion sought to adjust political life to the new social realities, and believed that unregulated competition of ideas would yield truth (Mill, 1806-73). In England, successive reform bills (1832, 1867, 1884) gave representation to the new industrial towns, and extended the franchise to the middle and lower classes and to Catholics, Dissenters, and Jews. On both sides of the Atlantic, reformists tried to improve conditions for the mentally ill (Dix, 1802-87), women (Anthony, 1820-1906), and prisoners. Slavery was barred in the British Empire, 1833; the United States, 1865; and Brazil, 1888.

Socialist theories based on ideas of human perfectibility or historical progress were widely disseminated. Utopian socialists like Saint-Simon (1760-1825) envisaged an orderly, just society directed by a technocratic elite. A model factory town, New Lanark, Scotland, was set up by utopian Robert Owen (1771-1858), and utopian communal experiments were tried in the U.S. (Brook Farm, Mass., 1841-7). Bakunin's (1814-76) anarchism represented the opposite utopian extreme of total freedom. Marx (1818-83) posited the inevitable triumph of socialism in the industrial countries through a historical process of class conflict.

Spread of industry. The technical processes and managerial innovations of the English industrial revolution spread to Europe (especially Germany) and the U.S., causing an explosion of industrial production, demand for raw materials, and competition for markets. Inventors, both trained and self-educated, provided the means for larger-scale production (Bessemer steel, 1856, sewing machine, 1846). Many inventions were shown at the 1851 London Great Exhibition at the Crystal Palace, whose theme was universal prosperity.

Local specialization and long-distance trade were aided by a revolution in transportation and communication. Railroads were first introduced in the 1820s in England and the U.S. Over 150,000 miles of track had been laid worldwide by 1880, with another 100,000 miles laid in the next decade. Steamships were improved (*Savannah* crossed Atlantic, 1819). The telegraph, perfected by 1844 (Morse), connected the Old and New Worlds by cable in 1866, and quickened the pace of international commerce and politics. The first commercial telephone exchange went into operation in the U.S. in 1878.

The new class of industrial workers, uprooted from their rural homes, lacked job security, and suffered from dangerous overcrowded conditions at work and at home. Many responded by organizing trade unions (legalized in England, 1824; France, 1884). The U.S. Knights of Labor had 700,000 members by 1886. The First International, 1864-76, tried to unite workers internationally around a Marxist program. The quasi-Socialist Paris Commune uprising, 1871, was violently suppressed. Factory Acts to reduce child labor and regulate conditions were passed (1833-50 in England). Social security measures were introduced by the Bismarck regime in Germany, 1883-89.

Revolutions of 1848. Among the causes of the continent-wide revolutions were an international collapse of credit and resulting unemployment, bad harvests in 1845-7, and a cholera epidemic. The new urban proletariat and expanding bourgeoisie demanded a greater political role. Republics were proclaimed in France, Rome, and Venice. Nationalist feelings reached fever pitch in the Hapsburg empire, as Hungary declared independence under Kossuth, a Slav Congress demanded equality, and Piedmont tried to drive Austria from Lombardy. A national liberal assembly at Frankfurt called for German unification.

But riots fueled bourgeois fears of socialism (Marx and Engels' 1848 *Communist Manifesto*) and peasants remained conservative. The old establishment — The Papacy, the Hapsburgs (using Croats and Romanians against Hungary), the Russian army — was able to rout the revolutionaries by 1849. The French Republic succumbed to a renewed monarchy by 1852 (Emperor Napoleon III).

Great nations unified. Using the "blood and iron" tactics of Bismarck from 1862, Prussia controlled N. Germany by 1867 (war with Denmark, 1864, Austria, 1866). After defeating France in 1870 (loss of Alsace-Lorraine), it won the allegiance of S. German states. A new **German Empire** was proclaimed, 1871. Italy, inspired by Mazzini (1805-72) and Garibaldi (1807-82), was unified by the reformed Piedmont kingdom through uprisings, plebiscites, and war.

The U.S., its area expanded after the 1846-47 Mexican War, defeated a secession attempt by slave states, 1861-65. The Canadian provinces were united in an autonomous **Dominion of Canada**, 1867. Control in India was removed from the East India Co. and centralized under British administration after the 1857-58 Sepoy rebellion, laying the groundwork for the modern Indian State. Queen Victoria was named Empress of India, 1876.

Europe dominates Asia. The Ottoman Empire began to collapse in the face of Balkan nationalisms and European imperial incursions in N. Africa (Suez Canal, 1869). The Turks had lost control of most of both regions by 1882. Russia completed its expansion south by 1884 (despite the temporary setback of the Crimean War with Turkey, Britain, and France, 1853-56) taking Turkestan, all the Caucasus, and Chinese areas in the East and sponsoring Balkan Slavs against the Turks. A succession of reformist and reactionary regimes presided over a slow modernization (serfs freed, 1861). Persian independence suffered as Russia and British India competed for influence.

China was forced to sign a series of unequal treaties with European powers and Japan. Overpopulation and an inefficient dynasty brought misery and caused rebellions (Taiping, Moslems) leaving tens of millions dead. Japan was forced by the U.S. (Commodore Perry's visits, 1853-54) and Europe to end its isolation. The Meiji restoration, 1868, gave power to a Westernizing oligarchy. Intensified empire-building gave Burma to Britain, 1824-86, and Indo-China to France, 1862-95. Christian missionary activity followed imperial and trade expansion in Asia.

Respectability. The fine arts were expected to reflect and encourage the progress of morals and

1845

Communist Manifesto

Sewing machine

Mexican War begins

Freud b.

Perry in Japan

Bessemer steel

Second Empire in France

U.S. Civil War

1860

Sepoy rebellion

Overseas cable

Canada united

Marxist 1st International

1870

Paris commune

Mazzini d.

German empire founded

1st telephone

1880

The Seven Wonders of the World

These ancient works of art and architecture were considered awe-inspiring in splendor and/or size by the Greek and Roman world of the Alexandrian epoch and later. Classical writers disagreed as to which works made up the list of Wonders, but the following were usually included:

The Pyramids of Egypt: The only surviving Wonder, these monumental structures of masonry located on the west bank of the Nile River above Cairo were built from 3000 to 1800 B.C. as royal tombs. Three—Khufu, Khafra, and Menkaura—were often grouped as the first Wonder of the World. The largest, **The Great Pyramid of Khufu,** or Cheops, is a solid mass of limestone blocks covering 13 acres. It is estimated to contain 2.3 million blocks of stone, the stones themselves averaging 2½ tons and some weighing 30 tons. Its construction reputedly took 100,000 laborers 20 years.

The Hanging Gardens of Babylon: These gardens were laid out on a brick terrace about 400 feet square and 75 feet above the ground. To irrigate the trees, shrubs, and flowers, screws were turned to lift water from the Euphrates River. The gardens were probably built by King Nebuchandnezzar II around 600 B.C. **The Walls of Babylon,** long, thick, and made of colorfully glazed brick, were considered by some to be among the Seven Wonders.

The Statue of Zeus (Jupiter) at Olympia: This statue of the king of the gods showed him seated on a throne. His flesh was made of ivory, his robe and ornaments of gold. Reputedly 40 feet high, the statue was made by Phidias and was placed in the great temple of Zeus in the sacred grove of Olympia around 457 B.C.

The Colossus of Rhodes: A bronze statue of the sun god Helios, the Colossus was worked on for 12 years in the early 200's B.C. by the sculptor Chares. It was probably 120 feet high. A symbol of the city of Rhodes at its height, the statue stood on a promontory overlooking the harbor.

The Temple of Artemis (Diana) at Ephesus: This largest and most complex temple of ancient times was built around 550 B.C. and was made of marble except for its tile-covered wooden roof. It was begun in honor of a non-Hellenic goddess who later became identified with the Greek goddess of the same name. Ephesus was one of the greatest of the Ionian cities.

The Mausoleum at Halicarnassus: The source of our word "mausoleum," this marble tomb was built in what is now southeastern Turkey by Artemisia for her husband Mausolus, an official of the Persian Empire who died in 353 B.C. About 135 feet high, it was adorned with the works of 4 sculptors.

The Pharos (Lighthouse) of Alexandria: This sculpture was designed around 270 B.C., during the reign of King Ptolemy II, by the Greek architect Sostratos. Estimates of its height range from 200 to 600 feet.

Africa 1914

British · French · German · Belgian · Italian · Portuguese · Spanish · Independent manners among the different classes. "Victorian" prudery, exaggerated delicacy, and familial piety were heralded by Bowdler's expurgated edition of Shakespeare (1818). Government-supported mass education inculcated a work ethic as a means to escape poverty (Horatio Alger, 1832-99).

The official Beaux Arts school in Paris set an international style of imposing public buildings (Paris Opera, 1861-74, Vienna Opera, 1861-69) and uplifting statues (Bartholdi's *Statue of Liberty*, 1885). Realist painting, influenced by photography (Daguerre, 1837), appealed to a new mass audience with social or historical narrative (Wilkie, 1785-1841, Poynter, 1836-1919) or with serious religious, moral, or social messages (pre-Raphaelites, Millet's Angelus, 1858) often drawn from ordinary life. The Impressionists (Pissarro, 1830-1903, Renoir, 1841-1919) rejected the central role of serious subject matter in favor of a colorful and sensual depiction of a moment, but their sunny, placid depictions of bourgeois scenes kept them within the respectable consensus.

Realistic novelists presented the full panorama of social classes and personalities, but retained sentimentality and moral judgment (Dickens, 1812-70, Eliot, 1819-80, Tolstoy, 1828-1910, Balzac, 1799-1850).

Veneer of Stability: 1880-1900

Imperialism triumphant. The vast **African** interior, visited by European explorers (Barth, 1821-65, Livingstone, 1813-73) was conquered by the European powers in rapid, competitive thrusts from their coastal bases after 1880, mostly for domestic political and international strategic reasons. W. African Moslem kingdoms (Fulani), Arab slave traders (Zanzibar), and Bantu military confederations (Zulu) were alike subdued. Only Christian Ethiopia (defeat of Italy, 1896) and Liberia resisted successfully. France (W. Africa) and Britain ("Cape to Cairo," Boer War, 1899-1902) were the major beneficiaries. The ideology of "the white man's burden" (Kipling, *Barrack Room Ballads*, 1892) or of a "civilizing mission" (France) justified the conquests.

West European foreign capital investments soared to nearly $40 billion by 1914, but most was in E. Europe (France, Germany) the Americas (Britain) and the white colonies. The foundation of the modern interdependent world economy was laid, with cartels dominating raw material trade.

An **industrious world.** Industrial and technological proficiency characterized the 2 new great powers — Germany and the U.S. Coal and iron deposits enabled Germany to reach second or third place status in iron, steel, and shipbuilding by the 1900s. German electrical and chemical industries were world leaders. The U.S. post-civil war boom (interrupted by "panics," 1884, 1893, 1896) was shaped by massive immigration from S. and E. Europe from 1880, government subsidy of railroads, and huge private monopolies (Standard Oil, 1870, U.S. Steel, 1901). The **Spanish-American War**, 1898 (Philippine rebellion, 1899-1901) and the Open Door policy in China (1899) made the U.S. a world power.

England led in **urbanization** (72% by 1890), with **London** the world capital of finance, insurance, and shipping. Electric subways (London, 1890), sewer systems (Paris, 1850s), parks, and bargain department stores helped improve living standards for most of the urban population of the industrial world.

Asians assimilate. Asian reaction to European economic, military, and religious incursions took the form of imitation of Western techniques and adoption of Western ideas of progress and freedom. The Chinese "self-strengthening" movement of the 1860s and 70s included rail, port, and arsenal improvements and metal and textile mills. Reformers like K'ang Yu-wei (1858-1927) won liberalizing reforms in 1898, right after the European and Japanese "scramble for concessions."

A universal education system in Japan and importation of foreign industrial, scientific, and military experts aided Japan's unprecedented rapid modernization after 1868, under the authoritarian Meiji regime. Japan's victory in the **Sino-Japanese War**, 1894-95, put Formosa and Korea in its power.

In India, the British alliance with the remaining princely states masked reform sentiment among the Westernized urban elite; higher education had been conducted largely in English for 50 years. The **Indian National Congress**, founded in 1885, demanded a larger government role for Indians.

"Fin-de-siecle" sophistication. Naturalist writers pushed realism to its extreme limits, adopting a quasi-scientific attitude and writing about formerly taboo subjects like sex, crime, extreme poverty, and corruption (Flaubert, 1821-80, Zola, 1840-1902, Hardy, 1840-1928). Unseen or repressed psychological motivations were explored in the clinical and theoretical works of Freud (1856-1939) and in the fiction of Dostoevsky (1821-81), James (1843-1916), Schnitzler (1862-1931) and others.

A contempt for bourgeois life or a desire to shock a complacent audience was shared by the French symbolist poets (Verlaine, 1844-96, Rimbaud, 1854-91), neo-pagan English writers (Swinburne, 1837-1909), continental dramatists (Ibsen, 1828-1906) and satirists (Wilde, 1854-1900). Nietzsche (1844-1900) was influential in his elitism and pessimism.

Post-impressionist art neglected long-cherished conventions of representation (Cezanne, 1839-1906) and showed a willingness to learn from primitive and non-European art (Gauguin, 1848-1903, Japanese prints).

Racism. Gobineau (1816-82) gave a pseudo-biological foundation to modern racist theories, which spread in the latter 19th century along with **Social Darwinism**, the belief that societies are and should be organized as a struggle for survival of the fittest. The Medieval period was interpreted as an era of natural Germanic rule (Chamberlain, 1855-1927) and notions of superiority were associated with German national aspirations (Treitschke, 1834-96). **Anti-Semitism**, with a new racist rationale, became a significant political force in Germany (Anti-Semitic Petition, 1880), Austria (Lueger, 1844-1910), and France (Dreyfus case, 1894-1906).

Last Respite: 1900-1909

Alliances. While the peace of Europe (and its dependencies) continued to hold (1907 **Hague Conference** extended the rules of war and international arbitration procedures), imperial rivalries, protectionist trade practices (in Germany and France), and the escalating arms race (British *Dreadnought* battleship launched, Germany widens Kiel canal, 1906) exacerbated minor disputes (German-French Moroccan "crises", 1905, 1911).

Security was sought through alliances: **Triple Alliance** (Germany, Austria-Hungary, Italy) renewed

1880

Dostoyevsky d.

Indian Natl. Cong. — Marx d.

1885

Brazil bans slavery

Kipling's *Barrack Room Ballads*

Europe conquers Africa

Rimbaud d.

radio

Sino-Jap. War

Span.-Am. War — 1895

Russ. Soc. Dem. Party

Dreyfus case

Gorky's *Lower Depths*

Boxer rebellion

Wilde d.

Ford Motor Co.

Panama Canal

Australia united

1904

2, 1907; Anglo-Japanese Alliance, 1902; Franco-Russian Alliance, 1899; **Entente Cordiale** (Britain, France) 1904; Anglo-Russian Treaty, 1907; German-Ottoman friendship.

Ottomans decline. The inefficient, corrupt Ottoman government was unable to resist further loss of territory. Nearly all European lands were lost in 1912 to Serbia, Greece, Montenegro, and Bulgaria. Italy took Libya and the Dodecanese islands the same year, and Britain took Kuwait, 1899, and the Sinai, 1906. The **Young Turk** revolution in 1908 forced the sultan to restore a constitution, introduced some social reform, industrialization, and secularization.

British Empire. British trade and cultural influence remained dominant in the empire, but constitutional reforms presaged its eventual dissolution: the colonies of **Australia** were united in 1901 under a self-governing commonwealth. **New Zealand** acquired dominion status in 1907. The old Boer republics joined Cape Colony and Natal in the self-governing **Union of South Africa** in 1910.

The 1909 Indian Councils Act enhanced the role of elected province legislatures in **India.** The Moslem League, founded 1906, sought separate communal representation.

East Asia. Japan exploited its growing industrial power to expand its empire. Victory in the 1904-05 war against Russia (naval battle of Tsushima, 1905) assured Japan's domination of **Korea** (annexed 1910) and Manchuria (took Port Arthur 1905).

In China, central authority began to crumble (empress died, 1908). Reforms (Confucian exam system ended 1905, modernization of the army, building of railroads) were inadequate and secret societies of reformers and nationalists, inspired by the Westernized **Sun Yat-sen** (1866-1925) fomented periodic uprisings in the south.

Siam, whose independence had been guaranteed by Britain and France in 1896, was split into spheres of influence by those countries in 1907.

Russia. The population of the Russian Empire approached 150 million in 1900. Reforms in education, law, and local institutions (*zemstvos*), and an industrial boom starting in the 1880s (oil, railroads) created the beginnings of a modern state, despite the autocratic tsarist regime. Liberals (1903 Union of Liberation), Socialists (Social Democrats founded 1898, Bolsheviks split off 1903), and populists (Social Revolutionaries founded 1901) were periodically repressed, and national minorities persecuted (anti-Jewish pogroms, 1903, 1905-6).

An industrial crisis after 1900 and harvest failures aggravated poverty in the urban proletariat, and the 1904-05 defeat by Japan (which checked Russia's Asian expansion) sparked the revolution of 1905-06. A **Duma** (parliament) was created, and an agricultural reform (under Stolypin, prime minister 1906-11) created a large class of landowning peasants (kulaks).

The world shrinks. Developments in transportation and communication and mass population movements helped create an awareness of an interdependent world. Early **automobiles** (Daimler, Benz, 1885) were experimental, or designed as luxuries. Assembly-line mass production (Ford Motor Co., 1903) made the invention practicable, and by 1910 nearly 500,000 motor vehicles were registered in the U.S. alone. **Heavier-than-air flights** began in 1903 in the U.S. (Wright brothers), preceded by glider, balloon, and model plane advances in several countries. Trade was advanced by improvements in **ship design** (gyrocompass, 1907), speed (Lusitania crossed Atlantic in 5 days, 1907), and reach (Panama Canal begun, 1904).

The first transatlantic **radio** telegraphic transmission occurred in 1901, 6 years after Marconi discovered radio. Radio transmission of human speech had been made in 1900. Telegraphic transmission of photos was achieved in 1904, lending immediacy to news reports. **Phonographs,** popularized by Caruso's recordings (starting 1902) made for quick international spread of musical styles (ragtime). **Motion pictures,** perfected in the 1890s (Dickson, Lumiere brothers), became a popular and artistic medium after 1900; newsreels appeared in 1909.

Emigration from crowded European centers soared in the decade: 9 million migrated to the U.S., and millions more went to Siberia, Canada, Argentina, Australia, South Africa, and Algeria. Some 70 million Europeans emigrated in the century before 1914. Several million Chinese, Indians, and Japanese migrated to Southeast Asia, where their urban skills often enabled them to take a predominant economic role.

Social reform. The social and economic problems of the poor were kept in the public eye by realist fiction writers (Dreiser's *Sister Carrie,* 1900; Gorky's *Lower Depths,* 1902; Sinclair's *Jungle,* 1906), journalists (U.S. muckrakers — Steffens, Tarbell) and artists (Ashcan school). Frequent labor strikes and occasional assassinations by anarchists or radicals (Austrian Empress, 1898; King Umberto I of Italy, 1900; U.S. Pres. McKinley, 1901; Russian Interior Minister Plehve, 1904; Portugal's King Carlos, 1908) added to social tension and fear of revolution.

But democratic reformism prevailed. In Germany, Bernstein's (1850-1932) **revisionist Marxism,** downgrading revolution, was accepted by the powerful Social Democrats and trade unions. The British Fabian Society (the Webbs, Shaw) and the Labour Party (founded 1906) worked for reforms such as social security and union rights (1906), while women's suffragists grew more militant. U.S. **progressives** fought big business (Pure Food and Drug Act, 1906). In France, the 10-hour work day (1904) and separation of church and state (1905) were reform victories, as was universal suffrage in Austria (1907).

Arts. An unprecedented period of experimentation, centered in France, produced several new **painting** styles: fauvism exploited bold color areas (Matisse, *Woman with Hat,* 1905); expressionism reflected powerful inner emotions (the Brücke group, 1905); cubism combined several views of an object on one flat surface (Picasso's *Demoiselles,* 1906-07); futurism tried to depict speed and motion (Italian Futurist Manifesto, 1910). Architects explored new uses of steel structures, with facades either neo-classical (Adler and Sullivan in U.S.); curvilinear Art Nouveau (Gaudi's Casa Mila, 1905-10); or functionally streamlined (Wright's Robie House, 1909).

Music and Dance shared the experimental spirit. Ruth St. Denis (1877-1968) and Isadora Duncan (1878-1927) pioneered modern dance, while Diaghilev in Paris revitalized classic ballet from 1909. Composers explored atonal music (Debussy, 1862-1918) and dissonance (Schönberg, 1874-1951), or revolutionized classical forms (Stravinsky, 1882-1971), often showing jazz or folk music influences.

War and Revolution: 1910-1919

War threatens. Germany under Wilhelm II sought a political and imperial role consonant with its industrial strength, challenging Britain's world supremacy and threatening France, still resenting the loss of Alsace-Lorraine. Austria wanted to curb an expanded Serbia (after 1912) and the threat it posed to its own Slav lands. Russia feared Austrian and German political and economic aims in the Balkans and Turkey. An accelerated arms race resulted: the German standing army rose to over 2 million men by 1914. Russia and France had over a million each, Austria and the British Empire nearly a million each. Dozens of enormous battleships were built by the powers after 1906.

The **assassination of Austrian Archduke Franz Ferdinand** by a Serbian, June 28, 1914, was the pretext for war. The system of alliances made the conflict Europe-wide; Germany's invasion of Belgium to outflank France forced Britain to enter the war. Patriotic fervor was nearly unanimous among all classes in most countries.

World War I. German forces were stopped in France in one month. The rival armies dug **trench networks.** Artillery and improved machine guns prevented either side from any lasting advance despite repeated assaults (600,000 dead at **Verdun**, Feb.-July 1916). Poison gas, used by Germany in 1915, proved ineffective. Over one million U.S. troops tipped the balance after mid-1917, forcing Germany to sue for peace.

In the East, the Russian armies were thrown back (battle of **Tannenberg**, Aug. 20, 1914) and the war grew unpopular. An allied attempt to relieve Russia through Turkey failed (**Gallipoli** 1915). The new Bolshevik regime signed the capitulatory Brest-Litovsk peace in March, 1918. Italy entered the war on the allied side, Apr. 1915, but was pushed back by Oct. 1917. A renewed offensive with Allied aid in Oct.-Nov. 1918 forced Austria to surrender.

The British Navy successfully blockaded Germany, which responded with submarine U-boat attacks; **unrestricted submarine warfare** against neutrals after Jan. 1917 helped bring the U.S. into the war. Other battlefields included Palestine and Mesopotamia, both of which Britain wrested from the Turks in 1917, and the African and Pacific colonies of Germany, most of which fell to Britain, France, Australia, Japan, and South Africa.

From 1916, the civilian population and economy of both sides were mobilized to an unprecedented degree. Over 10 million soldiers died (May 1917 French mutiny crushed).

Settlement. At the **Versailles conference** (Jan.-June 1919) and in subsequent negotiations and local wars (Russian-Polish War 1920), the map of Europe was redrawn with a nod to U.S. Pres. Wilson's principle of self-determination. Austria and Hungary were separated and much of their land was given to Yugoslavia (formerly Serbia), Romania, Italy, and the newly independent Poland and Czechoslovakia. Germany lost territory in the West, North, and East, while Finland and the Baltic states were detached from Russia. Turkey lost nearly all its Arab lands to British-sponsored Arab states or to direct French and British rule.

A huge **reparations** burden and partial demilitarization were imposed on Germany. Wilson obtained approval for a League of Nations, but the U.S. Senate refused to allow the U.S. to join.

Russian revolution. Military defeats and high casualties caused a contagious lack of confidence in Tsar Nicholas, who was forced to abdicate, Mar. 1917. A liberal provisional government failed to end the war, and massive desertions, riots, and fighting between factions followed. A moderate socialist government under Kerensky was overthrown in a violent **coup by the Bolsheviks** in Petrograd under Lenin, who disbanded the elected Constituent Assembly, Nov. 1917.

The Bolsheviks brutally suppressed all opposition and ended the war with Germany, Mar. 1918. **Civil war** broke out in the summer between the Red Army, including the Bolsheviks and their supporters, and monarchists, anarchists, nationalities (Ukrainians, Georgians, Poles) and others. Small U.S., British, French and Japanese units also opposed the Bolsheviks, 1918-19 (Japan in Vladivostok to 1922). The civil war, anarchy, and pogroms devastated the country until the 1920 Red Army victory. The wartime total monopoly of political, economic, and police power by the Communist Party leadership was retained.

Other European revolutions. An unpopular monarchy in **Portugal** was overthrown in 1910. The new republic took severe anti-clerical measures, 1911.

After a century of Home Rule agitation, during which **Ireland** was devastated by famine (one million dead, 1846-47) and emigration, republican militants staged an unsuccessful uprising in Dublin, Easter 1916. The execution of the leaders and mass arrests by the British won popular support for the rebels. The Irish Free State, comprising all but the 6 northern counties, achieved dominion status in 1922.

In the aftermath of the world war, radical revolutions were attempted in Germany (**Spartacist** uprising Jan. 1919), **Hungary** (Kun regime 1919), and elsewhere. All were suppressed or failed for lack of support.

Chinese revolution. The Manchu Dynasty was overthrown and a republic proclaimed, Oct. 1911. First president Sun Yat-sen resigned in favor of strongman Yuan Shih-k'ai. Sun organized the parliamentarian **Kuomintang** party.

Students launched protests May 4, 1919 against League of Nations concessions to China to Japan. Nationalist, liberal, and socialist ideas and political groups spread. The **Communist Party** was founded 1921. A communist regime took power in Mongolia with Soviet support in 1921.

India restive. Indian objections to British rule erupted in nationalist riots as well as in the non-violent tactics of Gandhi (1869-1948). Nearly 400 unarmed demonstrators were shot at **Amritsar**, Apr. 1919. Britain approved limited self-rule that year.

Mexican revolution. Under the long Diaz dictatorship (1876-1911) the economy advanced, but Indian and mestizo lands were confiscated, and concessions to foreigners (mostly U.S.) damaged the middle class. A **revolution in 1910** led to civil wars and U.S. intervention (1914, 1916-17). Land reform and a more democratic constitution (1917) were achieved.

Timeline (1916–1928):

- 1916
- Dada movement
- Bolshevik coup
- World War I
- China May 4 protest
- Amritsar riots
- Russian Civil War
- U.S. prohibition
- Iraq, Transjordan
- U.S. women's vote
- Reza Khan in Persia
- Russia's NEP
- Rathenau killed
- 1922
- Ulysses
- Kafka's *Trial*
- Lenin d.
- Irish Free State
- Eng. Labour govt.
- Fasc. March on Rome
- Portugal coup
- Kellogg-Briand Pact
- *Threepenny Opera*
- 1928

Timeline (left margin):

- 1928
- Stock market crash
- Smoot-Hawley Tariff
- India salt march
- Alfonso leaves Spain
- Japan seizes Manchuria
- Gandhi's fast
- Hitler dictator
- International Style
- 1933
- FDR in office
- Hitler takes Rhineland
- Nuremberg Laws
- Long March in China
- Fr. Popular Front
- Italy takes Ethiopia
- Japan invades China
- Civil War in Spain
- 1938

The Aftermath of War: 1920-29

U.S. Easy credit, technological ingenuity, and war-related industrial decline in Europe caused a long economic boom, in which ownership of the new products — autos, phones, radios — became democratized. Prosperity, an increase in women workers, women's suffrage (1920) and drastic change in fashion (flappers, mannish bob for women, clean-shaven men), created a wide perception of social change, despite prohibition of alcoholic beverages (1919-33). Union membership and strikes increased. Fear of radicals led to Palmer raids (1919-20) and Sacco/Vanzetti case (1921-27).

Europe sorts itself out. Germany's liberal **Weimar constitution** (1919) could not guarantee a stable government in the face of rightist violence (Rathenau assassinated 1922) and Communist refusal to cooperate with Socialists. Reparations and allied occupation of the Rhineland caused staggering inflation which destroyed middle class savings, but economic expansion resumed after mid-decade, aided by U.S. loans. A sophisticated, innovative culture developed in architecture and design (Bauhaus, 1919-28), film (Lang, *M*, 1931), painting (Grosz), music (Weill, *Threepenny Opera*, 1928), theater (Brecht, *A Man's a Man*, 1926), criticism (Benjamin), philosophy (Jung), and fashion. This culture was considered decadent and socially disruptive by rightists.

England elected its first labor governments (Jan. 1924, June 1929). A 10-day general strike in support of coal miners failed, May 1926. In **Italy**, strikes, political chaos and violence by small Fascist bands culminated in the Oct. 1922 Fascist March on Rome, which established Mussolini's dictatorship. Strikes were outlawed (1926), and Italian influence was pressed in the Balkans (Albania a protectorate 1926). A conservative dictatorship was also established in **Portugal** in a 1926 military coup.

Czechoslovakia, the only stable democracy to emerge from the war in Central or East Europe, faced opposition from Germans (in the Sudetenland), Ruthenians, and some Slovaks. As the industrial heartland of the old Hapsburg empire, it remained fairly prosperous. With French backing, it formed the Little Entente with Yugoslavia (1920) and **Romania** (1921) to block Austrian or Hungarian irredentism. **Hungary** remained dominated by the landholding classes and expansionist feeling. Croats and Slovenes in **Yugoslavia** demanded a federal state until King Alexander proclaimed a dictatorship (1929). **Poland** faced nationality problems as well (Germans, Ukrainians, Jews); Pilsudski ruled as dictator from 1926. The **Baltic states** were threatened by traditionally dominant ethnic Germans and by Soviet-supported communists.

An economic collapse and famine in **Russia**, 1921-22, claimed 5 million lives. The New Economic Policy (1921) allowed land ownership by peasants and some private commerce and industry. Stalin was absolute ruler within 4 years of Lenin's 1924 death. He inaugurated a brutal collectivization program 1929-32, and used foreign communist parties for Soviet state advantage.

Internationalism. Revulsion against World War I led to pacifist agitation, the Kellogg-Briand Pact renouncing aggressive war (1928), and **naval disarmament** pacts (Washington, 1922, London, 1930). But the League of Nations was able to arbitrate only minor disputes (Greece-Bulgaria, 1925).

Middle East. Mustafa Kemal (Ataturk) led **Turkish** nationalists in resisting Italian, French, and Greek military advances, 1919-23. The sultanate was abolished 1922, and elaborate reforms passed, including secularization of law and adoption of the Latin alphabet. Ethnic conflict led to persecution of **Armenians** (over 1 million dead in 1915, 1 million expelled), Greeks (forced Greek-Turk population exchange, 1923), and Kurds (1925 uprising).

With evacuation of the Turks from **Arab** lands, the puritanical Wahabi dynasty of eastern Arabia conquered present Saudi Arabia, 1919-25. British, French, and Arab dynastic and nationalist maneuvering resulted in the creation of two more Arab monarchies in 1921: Iraq and Transjordan (both under British control), and two French mandates: Syria and Lebanon. Jewish immigration into British-mandated **Palestine**, inspired by the Zionist movement, was resisted by Arabs, at times violently (1921, 1929 massacres).

Reza Khan ruled **Persia** after his 1921 coup (shah from 1925), centralized control, and created the trappings of a modern state.

China. The Kuomintang under **Chiang Kai-shek** (1887-1975) subdued the warlords by 1928. The Communists were brutally suppressed after their alliance with the Kuomintang was broken in 1927. Relative peace thereafter allowed for industrial and financial improvements, with some Russian, British, and U.S. cooperation.

Arts. Nearly all bounds of subject matter, style, and attitude were broken in the arts of the period. Abstract art first took inspiration from natural forms or narrative themes (Kandinsky from 1911), then worked free of any representational aims (Malevich's suprematism, 1915-19, Mondrian's geometric style from 1917). The **Dada** movement from 1916 mocked artistic pretension with absurd collages and constructions (Arp, Tzara, from 1916). Paradox, illusion, and psychological taboos were exploited by surrealists by the latter 1920s (Dali, Magritte). Architectural schools celebrated industrial values, whether vigorous abstract constructivism (Tatlin, *Monument to 3rd International*, 1919) or the machined, streamlined **Bauhaus** style, which was extended to many design fields (Helvetica type face).

Prose writers explored revolutionary narrative modes related to dreams (Kafka's *Trial*, 1925), internal monologue (Joyce's *Ulysses*, 1922), and word play (Stein's *Making of Americans*, 1925). Poets and novelists wrote of modern alienation (Eliot's *Waste Land*, 1922) and aimlessness (Lost Generation).

Sciences. Scientific specialization prevailed by the 20th century. Advances in knowledge and technological aptitude increased with the geometric increase in the number of practitioners. Physicists challenged common-sense views of causality, observation, and a mechanistic universe, putting science further beyond popular grasp (Einstein's general theory of relativity, 1915; Bohr's quantum mechanics, 1913; Heisenberg's uncertainty principle, 1927).

Rise of the Totalitarians: 1930-39

Depression. A worldwide financial panic and economic depression began with the Oct. 1929 U.S. stock market crash and the May 1931 failure of the Austrian Credit-Anstalt. A credit crunch caused international bankruptcies and **unemployment:** 12 million jobless by 1932 in the U.S., 5.6 million in Germany, 2.7 million in England. Governments responded with **tariff restrictions** (Smoot-Hawley Act 1930; Ottawa Imperial Conference, 1932) which dried up world trade. Government public works programs were vitiated by deflationary budget balancing.

Germany. Years of agitation by violent extremists was brought to a head by the Depression. Nazi leader **Hitler** was named chancellor by Pres. Hindenburg Jan. 1933, and given dictatorial power by the Reichstag in Mar. Opposition parties were disbanded, strikes banned, and all aspects of economic, cultural, and religious life brought under central government and Nazi party control and manipulated by sophisticated propaganda. Severe persecution of Jews began **(Nuremberg Laws** Sept. 1935). Many Jews, political opponents and others were sent to concentration camps (Dachau, 1933) where thousands died or were killed. Public works, renewed conscription (1935), arms production, and a 4-year plan (1936) ended unemployment.

Hitler's expansionism started with reincorporation of the Saar (1935), occupation of the **Rhineland** (Mar. 1936), and annexation of Austria (Mar. 1938). At **Munich,** Sept. 1938, an indecisive Britain and France sanctioned German dismemberment of Czechoslovakia.

Russia. Urbanization and education advanced. Rapid industrialization was achieved through successive **5-year-plans** starting 1928, using severe labor discipline and mass forced labor. Industry was financed by a decline in living standards and exploitation of agriculture, which was almost totally collectivized by the early 1930s (*kolkhoz,* collective farm; *sovkhoz,* state farm, often in newly-worked lands). Successive **purges** increased the role of professionals and management at the expense of workers. Millions perished in a series of man-made disasters: elimination of kulaks (peasant land-owners), 1929-34; severe famine, 1932-33; party purges (Great Purge, 1936-38); suppression of nationalities; and poor conditions in labor camps.

Spain. An industrial revolution during World War I created an urban proletariat, which was attracted to socialism and anarchism; Catalan nationalists challenged central authority. The 5 years after King Alfonso left Spain, Apr. 1931, were dominated by tension between intermittent leftist and anti-clerical governments and clericals, monarchists and other rightists. Anarchist and communist rebellions were crushed, but a July, 1936, extreme right rebellion led by Gen. Francisco Franco and aided by Nazi Germany and Fascist Italy succeeded, after a 3-year **civil war** (over 1 million dead in battles and atrocities). The war polarized international public opinion.

Italy. Despite propaganda for the ideal of the Corporate State, few domestic reforms were attempted. An entente with Hungary and Austria, Mar. 1934, a pact with Germany and Japan, Nov. 1937, and intervention by 50-75,000 troops in Spain, 1936-39, sealed Italy's identification with the fascist bloc (anti-Semitic laws after Mar. 1938). Ethiopia was conquered, 1935-37, and **Albania** annexed, Jan. 1939, in conscious imitation of ancient Rome.

East Europe. Repressive regimes fought for power against an active opposition (liberals, socialists, communists, peasants, Nazis). Minority groups and Jews were restricted within national boundaries that did not coincide with ethnic population patterns. In the destruction of **Czechoslovakia,** Hungary occupied southern Slovakia (Nov. 1938) and Ruthenia (Mar. 1939), and a pro-Nazi regime took power in the rest of Slovakia. Other boundary disputes (e.g. Poland-Lithuania, Yugoslavia-Bulgaria, Romania-Hungary) doomed attempts to build joint fronts against Germany or Russia. Economic depression was severe.

East Asia. After a period of liberalism in **Japan,** nativist militarists dominated the government with peasant support. Manchuria was seized, Sept. 1931-Feb. 1932, and a puppet state set up (Manchukuo). Adjacent Jehol (inner Mongolia) was occupied in 1933. China proper was invaded July 1937; large areas were conquered by Oct. 1938.

In **China** Communist forces left Kuomintang-besieged strongholds in the South in a Long March (1934-35) to the North. The Kuomintang-Communist civil war was suspended Jan. 1937 in the face of threatening Japan.

The democracies. The Roosevelt Administration, in office Mar. 1933, embarked on an extensive program of social reform and economic stimulation, including protection for labor unions (heavy industries organized), social security, public works, wages and hours laws, assistance to farmers. Isolationist sentiment (1937 Neutrality Act) prevented U.S. intervention in Europe, but military expenditures were increased in 1939.

French political instability and polarization prevented resolution of economic and international security questions. The **Popular Front** government under Blum (June 1936-Apr. 1938) passed social reforms (40-hour week) and raised arms spending. National coalition governments ruled Britain from Aug. 1931, brought some economic recovery, but failed to define a consistent foreign policy until Chamberlain's government (from May 1937), which practiced deliberate **appeasement** of Germany and Italy.

India. Twenty years of agitation for autonomy and then for independence (Gandhi's **salt march,** 1930) achieved some constitutional reform (extended provincial powers, 1935) despite Moslem-Hindu strife. Social issues assumed prominence with peasant uprisings (1921), strikes (1928), Gandhi's efforts for untouchables (1932 "fast unto death"), and social and agrarian reform by the provinces after 1937.

Arts. The streamlined, geometric design motifs of Art Deco (from 1925) prevailed through the 1930s. Abstract art flourished (Moore sculptures from 1931) alongside a new realism related to social and political concerns (Socialist Realism the official Soviet style from 1934; Mexican muralists Rivera, 1886-1957, and Orozco, 1883-1949), which was also expressed in fiction and poetry (Steinbeck's *Grapes of Wrath,* 1939; Sandburg's *The People, Yes,* 1936). Modern architecture (*International Style,* 1932) was unchallenged in its use of man-made materials (concrete, glass), lack of decoration, and monumentality (Rockefeller Center, 1929-40). U.S.-made films captured a world-wide audience with their larger-than-life fantasies (*Gone with the Wind,* 1939).

War, Hot and Cold: 1940-49

War in Europe. The Nazi-Soviet non-aggression pact (Aug. '39) freed Germany to attack Poland (Sept.). Britain and France, who had guaranteed Polish independence, declared war on Germany. Russia seized East Poland (Sept.), attacked Finland (Nov.) and took the Baltic states (July '40). Mobile German forces staged "blitzkrieg" attacks Apr.-June, '40, conquering neutral Denmark, Norway, and the low countries and defeating France; 350,000 British and French troops were evacuated at Dunkirk (May). The Battle of Britain, June-Dec. '40, denied Germany air superiority, German-Italian campaigns won the Balkans by Apr. '41. Three million Axis troops invaded Russia June '41, marching through the Ukraine to the Caucasus, and through White Russia and the Baltic republics to Moscow and Leningrad.

Russian winter counterthrusts, '41-'42 and '42-'43 stopped the German advance (Stalingrad Sept. '42-Feb. '43). With British and U.S. Lend-Lease aid and sustaining great casualties, the Russians drove the Axis from all E. Europe and the Balkans in the next 2 years. Invasions of N. Africa (Nov. '42), Italy (Sept. '43), and Normandy (June '44) brought U.S., British, Free French and allied troops to Germany by spring '45. Germany surrendered May 7, 1945.

War in Asia-Pacific. Japan occupied Indochina Sept. '40, dominated Thailand Dec. '41, attacked Hawaii, the Philippines, Hong Kong, Malaya Dec. 7, 1941. Indonesia was attacked Jan. '42, Burma conquered Mar. 42. Battle of Midway (June '42) turned back the Japanese advance. "Island-hopping" battles (Guadalcanal Aug. '42-Jan. '43, Leyte Gulf Oct. '44, Iwo Jima Feb.-Mar. '45, Okinawa Apr. '45) and massive bombing raids on Japan from June '44 wore out Japanese defenses. Two U.S. atom bombs, dropped Aug. 6 and 9, forced Japan to surrender Aug. 14, 1945.

Atrocities. The war brought 20th-century cruelty to its peak. Nazi murder camps (Auschwitz) systematically killed 6 million Jews. Gypsies, political opponents, sick and retarded people, and others deemed undesirable were murdered by the Nazis, as were vast numbers of Slavs, especially leaders.

Civilian deaths. German bombs killed 70,000 English civilians. Some 100,000 Chinese civilians were killed by Japanese forces in the capture of Nanking. Severe retaliation by the Soviet army, E. European partisans, Free French and others took a heavy toll. U.S. and British bombing of Germany killed hundreds of thousands, as did U.S. bombing of Japan (80-200,000 at Hiroshima alone). Some 45 million people lost their lives in the war.

Settlement. The United Nations charter was signed in San Francisco June 26, 1945 by 50 nations. The International Tribunal at Nuremberg convicted 22 German leaders for war crimes Sept. '46, 23 Japanese leaders were convicted Nov. '48. Postwar border changes included large gains in territory for the USSR, losses for Germany, a shift westward in Polish borders, and minor losses for Italy. Communist regimes, supported by Soviet troops, took power in most of E. Europe, including Soviet-occupied Germany (GDR proclaimed Oct. '49). Japan lost all overseas lands.

Recovery. Basic political and social changes were imposed on Japan and W. Germany by the western allies (Japan constitution Nov. '46, W. German basic law May '49). U.S. Marshall Plan aid ($12 billion '47-'51) spurred W. European economic recovery after a period of severe inflation and strikes in Europe and the U.S. The British Labour Party introduced a national health service and nationalized basic industries in 1946.

Cold War. Western fears of further Soviet advances (Cominform formed Oct. '47, Czechoslovakia coup, Feb. '48, Berlin blockade Apr.'48-Sept. '49) led to formation of NATO. Civil War in Greece and Soviet pressure on Turkey led to U.S. aid under the Truman Doctrine (Mar. '47). Other anti-communist security pacts were the Org. of American States (Apr. '48) and Southeast Asia Treaty Org. (Sept. '54). A new wave of Soviet purges and repression intensified in the last years of Stalin's rule, extending to E. Europe (Slansky trial in Czechoslovakia, 1951). Only Yugoslavia resisted Soviet control (expelled by Cominform, June '48; U.S. aid, June '49).

China, Korea. Communist forces emerged from World War II strengthened by the Soviet takeover of industrial Manchuria. In 4 years of fighting, the Kuomintang was driven from the mainland; the People's Republic was proclaimed Oct. 1, 1949. Korea was divided by Russian and U.S. occupation forces. Separate republics were proclaimed in the 2 zones Aug.-Sept. '48.

India. India and Pakistan became independent dominions Aug. 15, 1947. Millions of Hindu and Moslem refugees were created by the partition; riots, 1946-47, took hundreds of thousands of lives; Gandhi himself was assassinated Jan. '48. Burma became completely independent Jan. '48; Ceylon took dominion status in Feb.

Middle East. The UN approved partition of Palestine into Jewish and Arab states. Israel was proclaimed May 14, 1948. Arabs rejected partition, but failed to defeat Israel in war, May '48-July '49. Immigration from Europe and the Middle East swelled Israel's Jewish population. British and French forces left Lebanon and Syria, 1946. Transjordan occupied most of Arab Palestine.

Southeast Asia. Communists and others fought against restoration of French rule in Indochina from 1946; a non-communist government was recognized by France Mar. '49, but fighting continued. Both Indonesia and the Philippines became independent, the former in 1949 after 4 years of war with Netherlands, the latter in 1946. Philippine economic and military ties with the U.S. remained strong; a communist-led peasant rising was checked in '48.

Arts. New York became the center of the world art market; abstract expressionism was the chief mode (Pollock from '43, de Kooning from '47). Literature and philosophy explored existentialism (Camus' *Stranger*, 1942, Sartre's *Being and Nothingness*, 1943). Non-western attempts to revive or create regional styles (Senghor's Negritude, Mishima's novels) only confirmed the emergence of a universal culture. Radio and phonograph records spread American popular music (swing, bebop) around the world.

The American Decade: 1950-59

Polite decolonization. The peaceful decline of European political and military power in Asia and Africa accelerated in the 1950s. Nearly all of N. Africa was freed by 1956, but France fought a bitter war to retain Algeria, with its large European minority, until 1962. **Ghana,** independent 1957, led a parade of new black African nations (over 2 dozen by 1962) which altered the political character of the UN. Ethnic disputes often exploded in the new nations after decolonization (UN troops in Cyprus 1964; **Nigeria** civil war 1967-70). Leaders of the new states, mostly sharing socialist ideologies, tried to create an Afro-Asian bloc (Bandung Conf. 1955), but Western economic influence and U.S. political ties remained strong (Baghdad Pact, 1955).

Trade. World trade volume soared, in an atmosphere of monetary stability assured by international accords (**Bretton Woods** 1944). In Europe, economic integration advanced (**European Economic Community** 1957, European Free Trade Association 1960). Comecon (1949) coordinated the economies of Soviet-bloc countries.

U.S. Economic growth produced an abundance of consumer goods (9.3 million motor vehicles sold, 1955). Suburban housing tracts changed life patterns for middle and working classes (Levittown 1946-51). **Eisenhower's** landslide election victories (1952, 1956) reflected consensus politics. Censure of McCarthy (Dec. '54) curbed the political abuse of anti-communism. A system of alliances and military bases bolstered U.S. influence on all continents. Trade and payments surpluses were balanced by overseas investments and foreign aid ($50 billion, 1950-59).

USSR. In the "thaw" after Stalin's death in 1953, relations with the West improved (evacuation of Vienna, Geneva summit conf., both 1955). Repression of scientific and cultural life eased, and many prisoners were freed or rehabilitated culminating in **de-Stalinization** (1956). Khrushchev's leadership aimed at consumer sector growth, but farm production lagged, despite the virgin lands program (from 1954). The 1956 Hungarian revolution, the 1960 U-2 spy plane episode, and other incidents renewed East-West tension and domestic curbs.

East Europe. Resentment of Russian domination and Stalinist repression combined with nationalist, economic and religious factors to produce periodic violence. East Berlin workers rioted in 1953, Polish workers rioted in Poznan, June 1956, and a broad-based revolution broke out in Hungary, Oct. 1956. All were suppressed by Soviet force or threats (at least 7,000 dead in Hungary). But Poland was allowed to restore private ownership of farms, and a degree of personal and economic freedom returned to Hungary. Yugoslavia experimented with worker self-management and a market economy.

Korea. The 1945 division of Korea left industry in the North, which was organized into a militant regime and armed by Russia. The South was politically disunited. Over 60,000 North Korean troops invaded the South June 25, 1950. The U.S., backed by the UN Security Council, sent troops. UN troops reached the Chinese border in Nov. Some 200,000 Chinese crossed the Yalu River and drove back UN forces. Cease-fire in July 1951 found the opposing forces near the original 38th parallel border. After 2 years of sporadic fighting, an armistice was signed July 27, 1953. U.S. troops remained in the South, and U.S. economic and military aid continued. The war stimulated rapid economic recovery in Japan.

China. Starting in 1952, industry, agriculture, and social institutions were forcibly collectivized. As many as several million people were executed as Kuomintang supporters or as class and political enemies. The Great Leap Forward, 1958-60, unsuccessfully tried to force the pace of development by substituting labor for investment.

Indochina. Ho's forces, aided by Russia and the new Chinese Communist government, fought French and pro-French Vietnamese forces to a standstill, and captured the strategic Dienbienphu camp in May, 1954. The Geneva Agreements divided Vietnam in half pending elections (never held), and recognized Laos and Cambodia as independent. The U.S. aided the anti-Communist Republic of Vietnam in the South.

Middle East. Arab revolutions placed leftist, militantly nationalist regimes in power in Egypt (1952) and Iraq (1958). But Arab unity attempts failed (United Arab Republic joined Egypt, Syria, Yemen 1958-61). Arab refusal to recognize Israel (Arab League economic blockade began Sept. 1951) led to a permanent state of war, with repeated incidents (Gaza, 1955). Israel occupied Sinai, Britain and France took the Suez Canal, Oct. 1956, but were replaced by the UN Emergency Force. The Mossadegh government in Iran nationalized the British-owned oil industry May 1951, but was overthrown in a U.S.-aided coup Aug. 1953.

Latin America. Dictator Juan Peron, in office 1946, enforced land reform, some nationalization, welfare state measures, and curbs on the Roman Catholic Church, but crushed opposition. A Sept. 1955 coup deposed Peron. The 1952 revolution in Bolivia brought land reform, nationalization of tin mines, and improvement in the status of Indians, who nevertheless remained poor. The Batista regime in Cuba was overthrown, Jan. 1959, by Fidel Castro, who imposed a communist dictatorship, aligned Cuba with Russia, improved education and health care. A U.S.-backed anti-Castro invasion (Bay of Pigs, Apr. 1961) was crushed. Self-government advanced in the British Caribbean.

Technology. Large outlays on research and development in the U.S. and USSR focused on military applications (H-bomb in U.S. 1952, USSR 1953, Britain 1957, intercontinental missiles late 1950s). Soviet launching of the Sputnik satellite, Oct. 1957, spurred increases in U.S. science education funds (National Defense Education Act).

Literature and letters. Alienation from social and literary conventions reached an extreme in the theater of the absurd (Beckett's *Waiting for Godot* 1952), the "new novel" (Robbe-Grillet's *Voyeur* 1955), and avant-garde film (Antonioni's *L'Avventura* 1960). U.S. Beatniks (Kerouac's *On the Road* 1957) and others rejected the supposed conformism of Americans (Riesman's *Lonely Crowd* 1950).

Rising Expectations: 1960-69

Economic boom. The longest sustained economic boom on record spanned almost the entire decade in the capitalist world; the closely-watched GNP figure doubled in the U.S. 1960-70, fueled by Vietnam War-related budget deficits. The **General Agreement on Tariffs and Trade,** 1967, stimulated West European prosperity, which spread to peripheral areas (Spain, Italy, E. Germany). Japan became a top economic power ($20 billion exports 1970). Foreign investment aided the industrialization of Brazil. Soviet 1965 economic reform attempts (decentralization, material incentives) were limited; but growth continued.

Reform and radicalization. Pres. John F. Kennedy, inaugurated 1961, emphasized youthful idealism, vigor; he was assassinated Nov. 22, 1963. A series of political and social reform movements took root in the U.S., later spreading to other countries with the help of ubiquitous U.S. film and television programs and heavy overseas travel (2.2 million U.S. passports issued 1970). Blacks agitated peaceably and with partial success against segregation and poverty (1963 March on Washington, 1964 **Civil Rights Act**); but some urban ghettos erupted in extensive riots (Watts, 1965; Detroit, 1967; King assassination, Apr. 4, 1968). New concern for the poor (Harrington's *Other America,* 1963) led to Pres. Johnson's **"Great Society"** programs (Medicare, Water Quality Act, Higher Education Act, all 1965). Concern with the **environment** surged (Carson's *Silent Spring,* 1962). **Feminism** revived as a cultural and political movement (Friedan's *Feminine Mystique,* 1963, National Organization for Women founded 1966) and a movement for homosexual rights emerged (Stonewall riot, in NYC, 1969). Pope John XXIII called Vatican II, 1962-65, which liberalized Roman Catholic liturgy.

Opposition to U.S. involvement in Vietnam, especially among university students (**Moratorium** protest Nov. '69) turned violent (Weatherman Chicago riots Oct. '69). New Left and Marxist theories became popular, and membership in radical groups swelled (Students for a Democratic Society, Black Panthers). Maoist groups, especially in Europe, called for total transformation of society. In France, students sparked a nationwide strike affecting 10 million workers May-June '68, but an electoral reaction barred revolutionary change.

Arts and styles. The boundary between fine and popular arts were blurred by Pop Art (Warhol) and rock musicals (Hair, 1968). Informality and exaggeration prevailed in fashion (beards, miniskirts). A non-political "counterculture" developed, rejecting traditional bourgeois life goals and personal habits, and use of marijuana and hallucinogens spread (Woodstock festival Aug. '69). Indian influence was felt in music (Beatles), religion (Ram Dass), and fashion.

Science. Achievements in space (men on moon July '69) and electronics (lasers, integrated circuits) encouraged a faith in scientific solutions to problems in agriculture ("green revolution"), medicine (heart transplants 1967) and other areas. The harmful effects of science, it was believed, could be controlled (1963 nuclear weapon test ban treaty, 1968 non-proliferation treaty).

China. Mao's revolutionary militance caused disputes with Russia under "revisionist" Khrushchev, starting 1960. The two powers exchanged fire in 1969 border disputes. China used force to capture areas disputed with India 1962. The "Great Proletarian Cultural Revolution" tried to impose a utopian egalitarian program in China and spread revolution abroad; political struggle, often violent, convulsed China 1965-68.

Indochina. Communist-led guerrillas aided by N. Vietnam fought from 1960 against the S. Vietnam government of Ngo Dinh Diem (killed 1963). The U.S. military role increased after the 1964 Tonkin Gulf incident. U.S. forces peaked at 543,400, Apr. '69. Massive numbers of N. Viet troops also fought. Laotian and Cambodian neutrality were threatened by communist insurgencies, with N. Vietnamese aid, and U.S. intrigues.

Third World. A bloc of authoritarian leftist regimes among the newly independent nations emerged in political opposition to the U.S.-led Western alliance, and came to dominate the conference of nonaligned nations (Belgrade 1961, Cairo 1964, Lusaka 1970). Soviet political ties and military bases were established in Cuba, Egypt, Algeria, Guinea, and other countries, whose leaders were regarded as revolutionary heros by opposition groups in pro-Western or colonial countries. Some leaders were ousted in coups by pro-Western groups—Zaire's Lumumba (killed 1961), Ghana's Nkrumah (exiled 1966), and Indonesia's Sukarno (effectively ousted 1965 after a Communist coup failed).

Middle East. Arab-Israeli tension erupted into a brief war June 1967. Israel emerged as a major regional power. Military shipments before and after the war brought much of the Arab world into the Soviet political sphere. Most Arab states broke U.S. diplomatic ties, while Communist countries cut their ties to Israel. Intra-Arab disputes continued: Egypt and Saudi Arabia supported rival factions in a bloody Yemen civil war 1962-70; Lebanese troops fought Palestinian commandos 1969.

East Europe. To stop the large-scale exodus of citizens, E. German authorities built a fortified wall across Berlin Aug. '61. Soviet sway in the Balkans was weakened by Albania's support of China (USSR broke ties Dec. '61) and Romania's assertion of industrial and foreign policy autonomy 1964. Liberalization in Czechoslovakia, spring 1968, was crushed by troops of 5 Warsaw Pact countries. West German treaties with Russia and Poland, 1970, facilitated the transfer of German technology and confirmed post-war boundaries.

Disillusionment: 1970-79

U.S.: Caution and neoconservatism. A relatively sluggish economy, energy and resource shortages (natural gas crunch 1975, gasoline shortage 1979) and environmental problems contributed to a **"limits of growth"** philosophy. Suspicion of science and technology killed or delayed major projects (supersonic transport dropped 1971, DNA recombination curbed 1976, Seabrook A-plant protests 1977-78) and was fed by the Three Mile Island nuclear reactor accident Mar. '79.

Mistrust of big government weakened support for government reform plans among liberals. School busing and racial quotas were opposed (**Bakke decision** June '78); the Equal Rights Amendment for women languished; civil rights for homosexuals were opposed (Dade County referendum June '77).

Completion of communist forces' takeover of S. Vietnam (evacuation of U.S. civilians Apr. '75), revelations of Central Intelligence Agency misdeeds (Rockefeller Commission report June '75), and **Watergate** scandals (Nixon quit Aug. '74) reduced faith in U.S. moral and material capacity to influence world affairs. Revelations of Soviet crimes (Solzhenitsyn's *Gulag Archipelago* from 1974) and Russian intervention in Africa aided a revival of anti-Communist sentiment.

Economy sluggish. The 1960s boom faltered in the 1970s; a severe recession in the U.S. and Europe 1974-75 followed a huge oil price hike Dec. '73. Monetary instability (U.S. cut ties to gold Aug. '71), the decline of the dollar, and **protectionist** moves by industrial countries (1977-78) threatened trade. Business investment and spending for research declined. Severe inflation plagued many countries (25% in Britain 1975; 18% in U.S. 1979).

China picks up pieces. After the 1976 deaths of Mao and Chou, a power struggle for the leadership succession was won by pragmatists. A nationwide purge of orthodox Maoists was carried out and the "Gang of Four" led by Mao's widow Chiang Ching was arrested.

The new leaders freed over 100,000 political prisoners, and reduced public adulation of Mao. Political and trade ties were expanded with Japan, Europe, and U.S. in the late 1970's, as relations worsened with Russia, Cuba, and Vietnam (4-week invasion by China 1979). Ideological guidelines in industry, science, education, and the armed forces, which the ruling faction said had caused chaos and decline, were reversed (bonuses to workers Dec. '77; exams for college entrance Oct. '77). Severe restrictions on cultural expression were eased (Beethoven ban lifted Mar. '77).

Europe. European unity moves (EEC-EFTA trade accord 1972) faltered as economic problems appeared (Britain floated pound 1972; France floated franc 1974). Germany and Switzerland curbed guest workers from S. Europe. Greece and Turkey quarreled over Cyprus (Turks intervened 1974), Aegean oil rights.

All non-Communist Europe was under democratic rule after free elections were held in Spain June '76, 7 months after the death of Franco. The conservative, colonialist regime in **Portugal** was overthrown Apr. '74. In **Greece**, the 7-year-old military dictatorship yielded power in 1974. Northern Europe, though ruled mostly by Socialists (**Swedish Socialists** unseated 1976, after 44 years in power), turned conservative. The **British** Labour government imposed wage curbs 1975, and suspended nationalization schemes. Terrorism in **Germany** (1972 Munich Olympics killings) led to laws curbing some civil liberties. French "new philosophers" rejected leftist ideologies and the shaky Socialist-Communist coalition lost a 1978 election bid.

Religion back in politics. The improvement in Moslem countries' political fortunes by the 1950s (with the exception of Central Asia under Soviet and Chinese rule) and the growth of Arab oil wealth, was followed by a resurgence of traditional piety. **Libyan** dictator Qaddafy mixed strict Islamic laws with socialism in his militant ideology, called for an eventual Moslem return to Spain and Sicily. The illegal Moslem Brotherhood in **Egypt** was accused of violence, while extreme Moslem groups bombed theaters, 1977, to protest secular values.

In **Turkey**, the National Salvation Party was the first Islamic group to share power (1974) since secularization in the 1920s. Religious authorities, such as Ayatollah Ruholla Khomeini, led the **Iranian** revolution and religiously motivated Moslems took part in the insurrection in Saudi Arabia that briefly seized the Grand Mosque in Mecca 1979. Moslem puritan opposition to **Pakistan** Pres. Bhutto helped lead to his overthrow July '77. However, Moslem solidarity could not prevent Pakistan's eastern province (**Bangladesh**) from declaring independence, Dec. '71, after a bloody civil war.

Moslem and Hindu resentment against coerced sterilization in **India** helped defeat the Gandhi government, which was replaced Mar. '77 by a coalition including religious Hindu parties and led by devout Hindu Desai. Moslems in the southern **Philippines**, aided by Libya, conducted a long rebellion against central rule from 1973.

Evangelical Protestant groups grew in numbers and prosperity in the U.S. A revival of interest in Orthodox Christianity occurred among **Russian** intellectuals (Solzhenitsyn). The secularist **Israeli** Labor party, after decades of rule, was ousted in 1977 by conservatives led by Begin, an observant Jew; religious militants founded settlements on the disputed West Bank, part of Biblically-promised Israel. U.S. Reform Judaism revived many previously discarded traditional practices.

The Buddhist Soka Gakkai movement launched the Komeito party in Japan 1964, which became a major opposition party in 1972 and 1976 elections.

Old-fashioned religious wars raged intermittently in **N. Ireland** (Catholic vs. Protestant 1969-   ) and **Lebanon** (Christian vs. Moslem 1975-   ) while religious militancy complicated the Israel-Arab dispute (1973 Israel-Arab war). In spite of a **1979 peace treaty between Egypt and Israel** which looked forward to a resolution of the Palestinian issue, increased religious militancy on the West Bank made a resolution unlikely.

Latin America. Repressive conservative regimes strengthened their hold on most of the continent, with the violent coup against the elected Allende government in **Chile**, Sept. '73, the 1976 military coup in **Argentina**, and coups against reformist regimes in **Bolivia**, 1971 and 1979, and **Peru**, 1976. In Central America, increasing liberal and leftist militancy led to the ouster of the Somoza regime of Nicaragua in 1979 and civil conflict in El Salvador.

Indochina. Communist victory in Vietnam, Cambodia, and Laos by May '75 did not bring peace. Attempts at radical social reorganization left over one million dead in Cambodia 1975-78 and caused hundreds of thousands of ethnic Chinese and others to flee Vietnam ("boat people" 1979). The Vietnamese invasion of Cambodia swelled the refugee population and contributed to widespread starvation in that devastated country.

Russian expansion. Soviet influence, checked in some countries (troops ousted by Egypt 1972) was projected further afield, often with the use of Cuban troops (Angola 1975-89, Ethiopia 1977-88) and aided by a growing navy, merchant fleet, and international banking ability. Detente with the West — 1972 Berlin pact, 1972 strategic arms pact (**SALT**) — gave way to a more antagonistic relationship in the late 1970s, exacerbated by the Soviet invasion of Afghanistan 1979.

Africa. The last remaining European colonies were granted independence (**Spanish Sahara** 1976, **Djibouti** 1977) and, after 10 years of civil war and many negotiation sessions, a black government took over Zimbabwe (**Rhodesia**) 1979; white domination remained in **S. Africa**. Great power involvement in local wars (Russia in **Angola, Ethiopia**; France in **Chad, Zaire, Mauritania**) and the use of tens of thousands of Cuban troops was denounced by some African leaders as neocolonialism. Ethnic or tribal clashes made Africa the chief world locus of sustained warfare in the late 1970s.

Arts. Traditional modes in painting, architecture, and music, pursued in relative obscurity for much of the 20th century, returned to popular and critical attention in the 1970s. The pictorial emphasis in neorealist and photorealist painting, the return of many architects to detail, decoration, and traditional natural materials, and the concern with ordered structure in musical composition were, ironically, novel experiences for artistic consumers after the exhaustion of experimental possibilities. However, these more conservative styles coexisted with modernist works in an atmosphere of variety and tolerance.

*(right-margin timeline, top to bottom)*

1980

Iran-Iraq War begins

Solidarity founded

ERA defeated
Israel invades Lebanon
U.S. Congress O.K.'s tax cut
U.S.-led boycott of Moscow Olympics
U.S. hostages held in Iran

S. Africa gives voice to Coloureds, Asians
U.S. invades Grenada

U.S. mines Nicaragua ports

Gorbachev made USSR Gen-Secy

Reagan landslide re-election

Achille Lauro terrorism
Challenger explodes
150 mln. Africans near famine

U.S. Tax Reform Law

U.S. stock market crash

Nicaragua cease-fire
U.S. bombs Libya
Iran-contra scandal

USSR withdraws from Afghanistan
Iran-Iraq cease-fire

Nicaragua cease-fire

'revolutionary change' S. Africa

Poland free election
Tiananmen Sq. protests crushed

Berlin Wall opens
Eastern Europe Marxist economies fall

1990

Revitalization of Capitalism, Demand for Democracy: 1980-89

USSR, Eastern Europe. A troublesome 1980-85 for the USSR was followed by 5 years of astonishing change: the **surrender of the Communist monopoly, remaking of the Soviet state, and disintegration of the Soviet empire.** After deaths of Brezhnev 1982, Andropov 1984, Chernenko 1985; harsh treatment of dissent; restriction of emigration; invasion of Afghanistan Dec.'79; Gen. Secy. **Mikhail Gorbachev** (1985-) promoted **glasnost, perestroika,** economic and social reform (Jan.'87), supported by Communist Party (July '88); signed **INF treaty** (Dec.'87). Gorbachev pledged to cut the military budget (1988); military withdrawal from Afghanistan was completed Feb.'89; democratization was not hindered in Poland, Hungary; the Soviet people chose part of the new Congress from competing candidates Mar.'89. At decade's end, Gorbachev was widely considered responsible for the **1989 ending of the Cold War.**

Poland. Solidarity, the labor union founded 1980 by Lech Walesa, outlawed 1982, was legalized 1988, after years of unrest. Poland's first free election since the Communist takeover brought Solidarity victory (June '89); Tadeusz Mazowiecki, a Walesa advisor, became Prime Minister in a government with the Communists (Aug.'89).

In the fall of 1989 the failure of Marxist economies in **Hungary, E. Germany, Czechoslovakia, Bulgaria, and Romania** brought the fall of the Communist monopoly, the demand for democracy. The **Berlin Wall** was opened Nov.'89.

U.S. "The Reagan Years" (1981-88) brought the **longest economic boom** in U.S. history via budget and tax cuts, deregulation, "junk bond" financing, leveraged buyouts, mergers and takeovers; a **strong anti-Communist stance,** via increased defense spending, aid to anti-communists in Central America, invasion of Cuba-threatened Grenada, championing of MX missile system and "Star Wars." Four Reagan-Gorbachev summits, 1985-88, climaxed in INF treaty 1987. Financial scandals mounted (E.F. Hutton 1985, Ivan Boesky 1986), the stock market crashed Oct.'87, the trade imbalance grew (esp. with Japan), the budget deficit soared ($3.2 trillion 1988); homelessness, drug abuse (esp. "crack") grew. The Iran-contra affair (North TV testimony July'87) was the low point, but V.P. Bush was elected pres. 1988.

Middle East. This area remained militarily unstable, with sharp divisions on economic, political, racial, and religious lines. In **Iran,** the revolution (1979-80) and violent political upheavals after, brought strong anti-U.S. stance. A dispute with **Iraq** over the Shatt al-Arab waterway became warfare Sept.'80-July'88, with millions killed.

Libya's support for international terrorism caused the U.S. to close the diplomatic mission (May'81), embargo oil (Mar.'82); U.S. accused Muammar al-Qadaffy of aiding terrorists in Dec.'85 Rome, Vienna airport attacks, retaliated by bombing Libya Apr.'86.

Israel affirmed all Jerusalem as its capital (July'80); destroyed an Iraqi atomic reactor 1981; invaded Lebanon 1982, bringing the PLO to agree to withdraw. A **Palestinian uprising,** inc. women, children hurling rocks, bottles at troops, began Dec.'87 in Israeli-occupied Gaza, spread to the West Bank; troops responded with force, killing 300 by 1988's end, with 6,000 more in detention camps.

Israeli withdrawal from **Lebanon** began Feb.'85, ended June'85, as Lebanon continued torn with military and political conflict between rival factions. Premier Karami was assassinated June'87. Artillery duels between Christian East Beirut and Moslem West Beirut, Mar.-Apr.'89, left 200 dead, 700 wounded. At 80s end, violence still dominated.

Central America. In **Nicaragua,** the leftist Sandinista National Liberation Front, in power after the 1979 civil war, faced problems due to Nicaragua's military aid to leftist guerrillas in El Salvador, U.S. backing of anti-government contras. The U.S. CIA admitted directing the mining of Nicaraguan ports 1984; U.S. sent aid, humanitarian 1985, military 1986. Profits from secret arms sales to Iran were found diverted to contras 1987. Cease-fire talks between Sandinista government and contras came in 1988, elections in Feb.'90.

In El Salvador, a military coup (Oct.'79) failed to halt extreme right-wing violence and left-wing activity. Archbishop Oscar Romero was assassinated Mar.'80; Jan.-June some 4,000 civilians reportedly were killed. In 1984, newly-elected Pres. Duarte decreased rights abuses. Leftist guerrillas continued their offensive 1989.

Africa. 1980-85 marked the rapid decline of the economies of virtually all Africa's 61 countries, due to accelerating desertification, the world economic recession, heavy indebtedness to overseas creditors, rapid population growth, political instability. Some 60 million Africans, almost one-fifth of the population, faced prolonged hunger 1981; much of Africa had one of the worst droughts ever 1983, and by year's end **150 million faced near-famine.** "Live Aid" marathon rock concert (July'85), U.S. and Western nations sent aid Sept.'85. Economic hardship fueled political unrest, coups. Wars in Ethiopia, Sudan, military strife in 6 other nations continued through 1989. AIDS took a heavy toll.

South Africa. Anti-apartheid sentiment gathered **force,** demonstrations and violent police response grew. South African white voters approved (Nov.'83) the first constitution to give "Coloureds" Asians a voice, while still excluding blacks—70% of the population. The U.S. imposed economic sanctions Aug.'85, 11 Western nations followed in Sept. P.W. Botha, 80s president, was succeeded by **F.W. deClerk,** Sept.'89, on a platform of "evolutionary" change via negotiation with the black population.

China. From 1980 through mid-1989 the Communist Party, under **Chairman Deng Xiaoping,** pursued **far-reaching changes** in political and economic institutions, expanding commercial and technical ties to the industrialized world, increasing the role of market forces in stimulating urban economic development. But Apr.'89, brought the demand for more changes: students camped out in Tiananmen Sq., Beijing; some 100,000 students and workers marched, at least 20 other cities saw protests. Martial law was imposed; Army troops crushed protests in Tiananmen Sq., June 3-4 with death toll estimates 500-7,000, up to 10,000 injured, up to 10,000 dissidents arrested, 31 tried and executed. The conciliatory Communist Party chief was ousted; the Politburo adopted reforms against official corruption (July).

Japan. Relations with other nations, esp. U.S., 1980-89, were dominated by **trade imbalances favoring Japan.** In 1985 the U.S. trade deficit with Japan was $49.7 billion, one-third of the total U.S. trade deficit. After Japan was found to sell semiconductors, computer memory chips below cost (Apr.'86), the U.S. was assured a "fair share" of the market, but charged Japan with failing to live up to the agreement Mar.'87. The **Omnibus Trade Bill,** Aug.'88, provided for retaliation; Pres. Bush called Japan's practices "unjustifiable," the law gave Japan 18 months to stop or face trade restrictions.

European Community. With the addition of Greece, Portugal, and Spain, the EC became a **common market of over 300 million people,** the West's largest trading entity. **Margaret Thatcher** became the first British prime minister in this century to win 3 consecutive terms 1987. France elected its first socialist president, **Francois Mitterand** 1981, re-elected 1988. Italy elected its first socialist premier, **Bettino Craxi** 1983.

International Terrorism. With the 1979 overthrow of the Shah of Iran, terrorism became a prominent political tactic that increased through the 80s, but with fewer "spectacular" attacks after 1985. Iranian militants held 52 Americans hostage in Iran for 444 days, 1979-81; a TNT-laden suicide terrorist blew up U.S. Marine headquarters in Beirut, killing 241 Americans, while a truck bomb blew up a French paratroop barracks, killing 58, 1984; the *Achille Lauro* was hijacked, an American passenger killed, and the U.S. subsequently intercepted the Egyptian plane flying the terrorists to safety 1985. Incidents rose to 700 in 1985, 1,000+ in 1988. The Pentagon reported 52 terrorist groups Jan.'89.

Assassinations included Egypt's Pres. **Anwar el-Sadat** 1981; India's Prime Minister **Indira Gandhi** 1984; Lebanese Premier **Rashid Karami** 1987; Pakistan's Pres. **Mohammed Zia-ul Haz** 1988.

HISTORICAL FIGURES

Ancient Greeks and Latins

Greeks

Aeschines, orator, 389-314BC.
Aeschylus, dramatist, 525-456BC.
Aesop, fableist, c620-c560BC.
Alcibiades, politician, 450-404BC.
Anacreon, poet, c582-c485BC.
Anaxagoras, philosopher, c500-428BC.
Anaximander, philosopher, 611-546BC.
Antiphon, speechwriter, c480-411BC.
Apollonius, mathematician, c265-170BC.
Archimedes, math. c287-212BC.
Aristophanes, dramatist, c448-380BC.
Aristotle, philosopher, 384-322BC.
Athenaeus, scholar, fl.c200.
Callicrates, architect, fl.5th cent.BC.
Callimachus, poet, c305-240BC.
Cratinus, comic dramatist, 520-421BC.
Democritus, philosopher, c460-370BC.
Demosthenes, orator, 384-322BC.
Diodorus, historian, fl.20BC.
Diogenes, philosopher, c372-c287BC.

Dionysius, historian, d.c7BC.
Empedocles, philosopher, c490-430BC.
Epicharmus, dramatist, c530-440BC.
Epictetus, philosopher, c55-c135.
Epicurus, philosopher, 341-270BC.
Eratosthenes, scientist, c276-194BC.
Euclid, mathematician, fl.c300BC.
Euripides, dramatist, c484-406BC.
Galen, physician, c129-199.
Heraclitus, philosopher, c535-c475BC.
Herodotus, historian, c484-420BC.
Hesiod, poet, 8th cent. BC.
Hippocrates, physician, c460-377BC.
Homer, poet, believed lived c850BC.
Isocrates, orator, 436-338BC.
Menander, dramatist, 342-292BC.
Phidias, sculptor, c500-435BC.
Pindar, poet, c518-c438BC.
Plato, philosopher, c428-c347BC.
Plutarch, biographer, c46-120.

Polybius, historian, c200-c118BC.
Praxiteles, sculptor, 400-330BC.
Pythagoras, phil., math., c580-c500BC.
Sappho, poet, c610-c580BC.
Simonides, poet, 556-c468BC.
Socrates, philosopher, c470-399BC.
Solon, statesman, 640-560BC.
Sophocles, dramatist, C496-406BC.
Strabo, geographer, c63BC-AD24.
Thales, philosopher, c634-c546BC.
Themistocles, politician, c524-c460BC.
Theocritus, poet, c310-250BC.
Theophrastus, phil. c372-c287BC.
Thucydides, historian, fl.5th cent.BC.
Timon, philosopher, c320-c230BC.
Xenophon, historian, c434-c355BC.
Zeno, philosopher, c495-c430BC.

Latins

Ammianus, historian, c330-395.
Apuleius, satirist, c124-c170.
Boethius, scholar, c480-524
Caesar, Julius, general, 100-44BC.
Catilina, politician, c108-62BC.
Cato(Elder), statesman, 234-149BC.
Catullus, poet, c84-54BC.
Cicero, orator, 106-43BC.
Claudian, poet, c370-c404.
Ennius, poet, 239-170BC.
Gellius, author, c130-c165.
Horace, poet, 65-8BC.

Juvenal, satirist, c60-c127.
Livy, historian, 59BC-AD17.
Lucan, poet, 39-65.
Lucilius, poet, c180-c102BC.
Lucretius, poet, c99-c55BC.
Martial, epigrammatist, c38-c103.
Nepos, historian, c100-c25BC.
Ovid,poet, 43BC-AD17.
Persius, satirist, 34-62.
Plautus, dramatist, c254-c184BC.
Pliny, scholar, 23-79.
Pliny(Younger), author, 62-113.

Quintilian, rhetorician, c35-c97.
Sallust, historian, 86-34BC.
Seneca, philosopher, 4BC-AD65.
Silius, poet, c25-101.
Statius, poet, c45-c96.
Suetonius, biographer, c69-c122.
Tacitus, historian, c56-c120.
Terence, dramatist, 185-c159BC.
Tibullus, poet, c55-c19BC.
Virgil, poet, 70-19BC.
Vitruvius, architect, fl.1st cent.BC.

Rulers of England and Great Britain

Name	England	Began	Died	Age	Rgd
Saxons and Danes					
Egbert	King of Wessex, won allegiance of all English	829	839	—	10
Ethelwulf	Son, King of Wessex, Sussex, Kent, Essex	839	858	—	19
Ethelbald	Son of Ethelwulf, displaced father in Wessex	858	860	—	2
Ethelbert	2d son of Ethelwulf, united Kent and Wessex	860	866	—	6
Ethelred I	3d son, King of Wessex, fought Danes	866	871	—	5
Alfred	The Great, 4th son, defeated Danes, fortified London	871	899	52	28
Edward	The Elder, Alfred's son, united English, claimed Scotland	899	924	55	25
Athelstan	The Glorious, Edward's son, King of Mercia, Wessex	924	940	45	16
Edmund I	3d son of Edward, King of Wessex, Mercia	940	946	25	6
Edred	4th son of Edward	946	955	32	9
Edwy	The Fair, eldest son of Edmund, King of Wessex	955	959	18	3
Edgar	The Peaceful, 2d son of Edmund, ruled all English	959	975	32	17
Edward	The Martyr, eldest son of Edgar, murdered by stepmother	975	978	17	4
Ethelred II	The Unready, 2d son of Edgar, married Emma of Normandy	978	1016	48	37
Edmund II	Ironside, son of Ethelred II, King of London	1016	1016	27	0
Canute	The Dane, gave Wessex to Edmund, married Emma	1016	1035	40	19
Harold I	Harefoot, natural son of Canute	1035	1040	—	5
Hardecanute	Son of Canute by Emma, Danish King	1040	1042	24	2
Edward	The Confessor, Son of Ethelred II (Canonized 1161)	1042	1066	62	24
Harold II	Edward's brother-in-law, last Saxon King	1066	1066	44	0
House of Normandy					
William I	The Conqueror, defeated Harold at Hastings	1066	1087	60	21
William II	Rufus, 3d son of William I, killed by arrow	1087	1100	43	13
Henry I	Beauclerc, youngest son of William I	1100	1135	67	35
House of Blois					
Stephen	Son of Adela, daughter of William I, and Count of Blois	1135	1154	50	19
House of Plantagenet					
Henry II	Son of Geoffrey Plantagenet (Angevin) by Matilda, dau. of Henry I	1154	1189	56	35
Richard I	Coeur de Lion, son of Henry II, crusader	1189	1199	42	10
John	Lackland, son of Henry II, signed Magna Carta, 1215	1199	1216	50	17
Henry III	Son of John, acceded at 9, under regency until 1227	1216	1272	65	56
Edward I	Longshanks, son of Henry III	1272	1307	68	35
Edward II	Son of Edward I, deposed by Parliament, 1327	1307	1327	43	20
Edward III	Of Windsor, son of Edward II	1327	1377	65	50
Richard II	Grandson of Edw. III, minor until 1389, deposed 1399	1377	1400	33	22
House of Lancaster					
Henry IV	Son of John of Gaunt, Duke of Lancaster, son of Edw. III	1399	1413	47	13
Henry V	Son of Henry IV, victor of Agincourt	1413	1422	34	9
Henry VI	Son of Henry V, deposed 1461, died in Tower	1422	1471	49	39

Name		Began	Died	Age	Rgd
House of York					
Edward IV	Great-great-grandson of Edward III, son of Duke of York	1461	1483	41	22
Edward V	Son of Edward IV, murdered in Tower of London	1483	1483	13	0
Richard III	Crookback, bro. of Edward IV, fell at Bosworth Field	1483	1485	35	2
House of Tudor					
Henry VII	Son of Edmund Tudor, Earl of Richmond, whose father had married the widow of Henry V; descended from Edward III through his mother, Margaret Beaufort via John of Gaunt. By marriage with dau. of Edward IV he united Lancaster and York	1485	1509	53	24
Henry VIII	Son of Henry VII by Elizabeth, dau. of Edward IV.	1509	1547	56	38
Edward VI	Son of Henry VIII, by Jane Seymour, his 3d queen. Ruled under regents. Was forced to name Lady Jane Grey his successor. Council of State proclaimed her queen July 10, 1553. Mary Tudor won Council, was proclaimed queen July 19, 1553. Mary had Lady Jane Grey beheaded for treason, Feb., 1554	1547	1553	16	6
Mary I	Daughter of Henry VIII, by Catherine of Aragon	1553	1558	43	5
Elizabeth I	Daughter of Henry VIII, by Anne Boleyn	1558	1603	69	44

Great Britain
House of Stuart

Name		Began	Died	Age	Rgd
James I	James VI of Scotland, son of Mary, Queen of Scots. *First to call himself King of Great Britain. This became official with the Act of Union, 1707*	1603	1625	59	22
Charles I	Only surviving son of James I; beheaded Jan. 30, 1649	1625	1649	48	24
Commonwealth, 1649-1660					
Council of State, 1649; Protectorate, 1653					
The Cromwells	Oliver Cromwell, Lord Protector	1653	1658	59	—
	Richard Cromwell, son, Lord Protector, resigned May 25, 1659	1658	1712	86	—
House of Stuart (Restored)					
Charles II	Eldest son of Charles I, died without issue	1660	1685	55	25
James II	2d son of Charles I. Deposed 1688. Interregnum Dec. 11, 1688, to Feb. 13, 1689	1685	1701	68	3
William III	Son of William, Prince of Orange, by Mary, dau. of Charles I	1689	1702	51	13
and Mary II	Eldest daughter of James II and wife of William III		1694	33	6
Anne	2d daughter of James II	1702	1714	49	12
House of Hanover					
George I	Son of Elector of Hanover, by Sophia, grand-dau. of James I	1714	1727	67	13
George II	Only son of George I, married Caroline of Brandenburg	1727	1760	77	33
George III	Grandson of George II, married Charlotte of Mecklenburg	1760	1820	81	59
George IV	Eldest son of George III, Prince Regent, from Feb., 1811	1820	1830	67	10
William IV	3d son of George III, married Adelaide of Saxe-Meiningen	1830	1837	71	7
Victoria	Dau. of Edward, 4th son of George III; married (1840) Prince Albert of Saxe-Coburg and Gotha, who became Prince Consort	1837	1901	81	63
House of Saxe-Coburg and Gotha					
Edward VII	Eldest son of Victoria, married Alexandra, Princess of Denmark	1901	1910	68	9
House of Windsor					
Name Adopted July 17, 1917					
George V	2d son of Edward VII, married Princess Mary of Teck	1910	1936	70	25
Edward VIII	Eldest son of George V; acceded Jan. 20, 1936, abdicated Dec. 11	1936	1972	77	1
George VI	2d son of George V; married Lady Elizabeth Bowes-Lyon	1936	1952	56	15
Elizabeth II	Elder daughter of George VI, acceded Feb. 6, 1952	1952	—	—	—

Rulers of Scotland

Kenneth I MacAlpin was the first Scot to rule both Scots and Picts, 846 AD.

Duncan I was the first general ruler, 1034. Macbeth seized the kingdom 1040, was slain by Duncan's son, Malcolm III MacDuncan (Canmore), 1057.

Malcolm married Margaret, Saxon princess who had fled from the Normans. Queen Margaret introduced English language and English monastic customs. She was canonized, 1250. Her son Edgar, 1097, moved the court to Edinburgh. His brothers Alexander I and David I succeeded. Malcolm IV, the Maiden, 1153, grandson of David I, was followed by his brother, William the Lion, 1165, whose son was Alexander II, 1214. The latter's son, Alexander III, 1249, defeated the Norse and regained the Hebrides. When he died, 1286, his granddaughter, Margaret, child of Eric of Norway and grandniece of Edward I of England, known as the Maid of Norway, was chosen ruler, but died 1290, aged 8.

John Baliol, 1292-1296. (Interregnum, 10 years).

Robert Bruce (The Bruce), 1306-1329, victor at Bannockburn, 1314.

David II, only son of Robert Bruce, ruled 1329-1371.

Robert II, 1371-1390, grandson of Robert Bruce, son of Walter, the Steward of Scotland, was called The Steward, first of the so-called Stuart line.

Robert III, son of Robert II, 1390-1406.

James I, son of Robert III, 1406-1437.

James II, son of James I, 1437-1460.

James III, eldest son of James II, 1460-1488.

James IV, eldest son of James III, 1488-1513.

James V, eldest son of James IV, 1513-1542.

Mary, daughter of James V, born 1542, became queen when one week old; was crowned 1543. Married, 1558, Francis, son of Henry II of France, who became king 1559, died 1560. Mary ruled Scots 1561 until abdication, 1567. She also married (2) Henry Stewart, Lord Darnley, and (3) James, Earl of Bothwell. Imprisoned by Elizabeth I, Mary was beheaded 1587.

James VI, 1566-1625, son of Mary and Lord Darnley, became King of England on death of Elizabeth in 1603. Although the thrones were thus united, the legislative union of Scotland and England was not effected until the Act of Union, May 1, 1707.

Prime Ministers of Great Britain

(W = Whig; T = Tory; Cl = Coalition; P = Peelite; L = Liberal; C = Conservative; La = Labour)

Sir Robert Walpole (W)	1721-1742	Viscount Goderich (T)	1827-1828	Herbert H. Asquith (L)	1908-1915
Earl of Wilmington (W)	1742-1743	Duke of Wellington (T)	1828-1830	Herbert H. Asquith	1915-1916
Henry Pelham (W)	1743-1754	Earl Grey (W)	1830-1834	David Lloyd George (Cl)	1916-1922
Duke of Newcastle (W)	1754-1756	Viscount Melbourne (W)	1834	Andrew Bonar Law (C)	1922-1923
Duke of Devonshire (W)	1756-1757	Sir Robert Peel (T)	1834-1835	Stanley Baldwin (C)	1923-1924
Duke of Newcastle (W)	1757-1762	Viscount Melbourne (W)	1835-1841	James Ramsay MacDonald	
Earl of Bute (T)	1762-1763	Sir Robert Peel (T)	1841-1846	(La)	1924
George Grenville (W)	1763-1765	Lord John Russell (later		Stanley Baldwin (C)	1924-1929
Marquess of Rockingham		Earl) (W)	1846-1852	James Ramsay MacDonald	
(W)	1765-1766	Earl of Derby (T)	1852	(La)	1929-1931
William Pitt the Elder		Earl of Aberdeen (P)	1852-1855	James Ramsay MacDonald	
(Earl of Chatham) (W)	1766-1768	Viscount Palmerston (L)	1855-1858	(Cl)	1931-1935
Duke of Grafton (W)	1768-1770	Earl of Derby (C)	1858-1859	Stanley Baldwin (Cl)	1935-1937
Frederick North (Lord		Viscount Palmerston (L)	1859-1865	Neville Chamberlain (Cl)	1937-1940
North) (T)	1770-1782	Earl Russell (L)	1865-1866	Winston Churchill (Cl)	1940-1945
Marquess of Rockingham		Earl of Derby (C)	1866-1868	Winston Churchill (C)	1945
(W)	1782	Benjamin Disraeli (C)	1868	Clement Attlee (La)	1945-1951
Earl of Shelburne (W)	1782-1783	William E. Gladstone (L)	1868-1874	Sir Winston Churchill	1951-1955
Duke of Portland (Cl)	1783	Benjamin Disraeli (C)	1874-1880	Sir Anthony Eden (C)	1955-1957
William Pitt the Younger		William E. Gladstone (L)	1880-1885	Harold Macmillan (C)	1957-1963
(T)	1783-1801	Marquess of Salisbury (C)	1885-1886	Sir Alec Douglas-Home	
Henry Addington (T)	1801-1804	William E. Gladstone (L)	1886	(C)	1963-1964
William Pitt the Younger		Marquess of Salisbury (C)	1886-1892	Harold Wilson (La)	1964-1970
(T)	1804-1806	William E. Gladstone (L)	1892-1894	Edward Heath (C)	1970-1974
William Wyndham Grenville,		Earl of Rosebery (L)	1894-1895	Harold Wilson (La)	1974-1976
Baron Grenville (W)	1806-1807	Marquess of Salisbury (C)	1895-1902	James Callaghan (La)	1976-1979
Duke of Portland (T)	1807-1809	Arthur J. Balfour (C)	1902-1905	Margaret Thatcher (C)	1979-
Spencer Perceval (T)	1809-1812	Sir Henry			
Earl of Liverpool (T)	1812-1827	Campbell-Bannerman (L)	1905-1908		
George Canning (T)	1827				

Historical Periods of Japan

Yamato	c.300-592	Conquest of Yamato plain c. 300 A.D.	Ashikaga	1338-1573	Ashikaga Takauji becomes shogun, 1338.
Asuka	592-710	Accession of Empress Suiko, 592.	Muromachi	1392-1573	Unification of Southern and Northern Courts, 1392.
Nara	710-794	Completion of Heijo (Nara), 710; capital moves to Naga-oka, 784.	Sengoku	1467-1600	Beginning of the Onin war, 1467
Heian	794-1192	Completion of Heian (Kyoto), 794	Momoyama	1573-1603	Oda Nobunaga enters Kyoto, 1568; Nobunaga deposes last Ashikaga shogun, 1573; Tokugawa Ieyasu victor at Sekigahara, 1600.
Fujiwara	858-1160	Fujiwara-no-Yoshifusa becomes regent, 858.	Edo	1603-1867	Ieyasu becomes shogun, 1603.
Taira	1160-1185	Taira-no-Kiyomori assumes control, 1160; Minamoto-no-Yoritomo victor over Taira, 1185.	Meiji	1868-1912	Enthronement of Emperor Mutsuhito (Meiji), 1867; Meiji Restoration and Charter Oath, 1868.
Kamakura	1192-1333	Yoritomo becomes shogun, 1192.	Taisho	1912-1926	Accession of Emperor Yoshihito, 1912.
Namboku	1334-1392	Restoration of Emperor Godaigo, 1334; Southern Court established by Godaigo at Yoshino, 1336.	Showa	1926-1989	Accession of Emperor Hirohito, 1926.
			Heisei	1989-	Accession of Emperor Akihito, 1989

Rulers of France: Kings, Queens, Presidents

Caesar to Charlemagne

Julius Caesar subdued the Gauls, native tribes of Gaul (France) 57 to 52 BC. The Romans ruled 500 years. The Franks, a Teutonic tribe, reached the Somme from the East ca. 250 AD. By the 5th century the Merovingian Franks ousted the Romans. In 451 AD, with the help of Visigoths, Burgundians and others, they defeated Attila and the Huns at Chalons-sur-Marne.

Childeric I became leader of the Merovingians 458 AD. His son Clovis I (Chlodwig, Ludwig, Louis), crowned 481, founded the dynasty. After defeating the Alemanni (Germans) 496, he was baptized a Christian and made Paris his capital. His line ruled until Childeric III was deposed, 751.

The West Merovingians were called Neustrians, the eastern Austrasians. Pepin of Herstal (687-714) major domus, or head of the palace, of Austrasia, took over Neustria as dux (leader) of the Franks. Pepin's son, Charles, called Martel (the Hammer) defeated the Saracens at Tours-Poitiers, 732; was succeeded by his son, Pepin the Short, 741, who deposed Childeric III and ruled as king until 768.

His son, Charlemagne, or Charles the Great (742-814) became king of the Franks, 768, with his brother Carloman, who died 771. He ruled France, Germany, parts of Italy, Spain, Austria, and enforced Christianity. Crowned Emperor of the Romans by Pope Leo III in St. Peter's, Rome, Dec. 25, 800 AD. Succeeded by son, Louis I the Pious, 814. At death, 840, Louis left empire to sons, Lothair (Roman emperor); Pepin I (king of Aquitaine); Louis II (of Germany); Charles the Bald (France). They quarreled and by the peace of Verdun, 843, divided the empire.

(continued)

AD   Name, year of accession

The Carolingians

843   Charles I (the Bald), Roman Emperor, 875
877   Louis II (the Stammerer), son
879   Louis III (died 882) and Carloman, brothers
885   Charles II (the Fat), Roman Emperor, 881
888   Eudes (Odo) elected by nobles
898   Charles III (the Simple), son of Louis II, defeated by
922   Robert, brother of Eudes, killed in war
923   Rudolph (Raoul) Duke of Burgundy
936   Louis IV, son of Charles III
954   Lothair, son, aged 13, defeated by Capet
986   Louis V (the Sluggard), left no heirs

The Capets

987   Hugh Capet, son of Hugh the Great
996   Robert II (the Wise), his son
1031   Henry I, his son
1060   Philip I (the Fair), son
1108   Louis VI (the Fat), son
1137   Louis VII (the Younger), son
1180   Philip II (Augustus), son, crowned at Reims
1223   Louis VIII (the Lion), son
1226   Louis IX, son, crusader; Louis IX (1214-1270) reigned 44 years, arbitrated disputes with English King Henry III; led crusades, 1248 (captured in Egypt 1250) and 1270, when he died of plague in Tunis. Canonized 1297 as St. Louis.
1270   Philip III (the Hardy), son
1285   Philip IV (the Fair), son, king at 17
1314   Louis X (the Headstrong), son. His posthumous son, John I, lived only 7 days
1316   Philip V (the Tall), brother of Louis X
1322   Charles IV (the Fair), brother of Louis X

House of Valois

1328   Philip VI (of Valois), grandson of Philip III
1350   John II (the Good), his son, retired to England
1364   Charles V (the Wise), son
1380   Charles VI (the Beloved), son
1422   Charles VII (the Victorious), son. In 1429 Joan of Arc (Jeanne d'Arc) promised Charles to oust the English, who occupied northern France. Joan won at Orleans and Patay and had Charles crowned at Reims July 17, 1429. Joan was captured May 24, 1430, and executed May 30, 1431, at Rouen for heresy. Charles ordered her rehabilitation, effected 1455.
1461   Louis XI (the Cruel), son, civil reformer
1483   Charles VIII (the Affable), son
1498   Louis XII, great-grandson of Charles V
1515   Francis I, of Angouleme, nephew, son-in-law. Francis I (1494-1547) reigned 32 years, fought 4 big wars, was patron of the arts, aided Cellini, del Sarto, Leonardo da Vinci, Rabelais, embellished Fontainebleau.
1547   Henry II, son, killed at a joust in a tournament. He was the husband of Catherine de Medicis (1519-1589) and the lover of Diane de Poitiers (1499-1566). Catherine was born in Florence, daughter of Lorenzo de Medicis. By her marriage to Henry II she became the mother of Francis II, Charles IX, Henry III and Queen Margaret (Reine Margot) wife of Henry IV. She persuaded Charles IX to order the massacre of Huguenots on the Feast of St. Bartholomew, Aug. 24, 1572, the day her daughter was married to Henry of Navarre.
1559   Francis II, son. In 1548, Mary, Queen of Scots since infancy, was betrothed when 6 to Francis, aged 4. They were married 1558. Francis died 1560, aged 16; Mary ruled Scotland, abdicated 1567.
1560   Charles IX, brother
1574   Henry III, brother, assassinated

House of Bourbon

1589   Henry IV, of Navarre, assassinated. Henry IV made enemies when he gave tolerance to Protestants by Edict of Nantes, 1598. He was grandson of Queen Margaret of Navarre, literary patron. He married Margaret of Valois, daughter of Henry II and Catherine de Medicis; was divorced; in 1600 married Marie de Medicis, who became Regent of France, 1610-17 for her son, Louis XIII, but was exiled by Richelieu, 1631.

1610   Louis XIII (the Just), son. Louis XIII (1601-1643) married Anne of Austria. His ministers were Cardinals Richelieu and Mazarin.
1643   Louis XIV (The Grand Monarch), son. Louis XIV was king 72 years. He exhausted a prosperous country in wars for thrones and territory. By revoking the Edict of Nantes (1685) he caused the emigration of the Huguenots. He said: "I am the state."
1715   Louis XV, great-grandson. Louis XV married a Polish princess; lost Canada to the English. His favorites, Mme. Pompadour and Mme. Du Barry, influenced policies. Noted for saying "After me, the deluge".
1774   Louis XVI, grandson; married Marie Antoinette, daughter of Empress Maria Therese of Austria. King and queen beheaded by Revolution, 1793. Their son, called Louis XVII, died in prison, never ruled.

First Republic

1792   National Convention of the French Revolution
1795   Directory, under Barras and others
1799   Consulate, Napoleon Bonaparte, first consul. Elected consul for life, 1802.

First Empire

1804   Napoleon I, emperor. Josephine (de Beauharnais) empress, 1804-09; Marie Louise, empress, 1810-1814. Her son, Francois (1811-1832), titular King of Rome, later Duke de Reichstadt and "Napoleon II," never ruled. Napoleon abdicated 1814, died 1821.

Bourbons Restored

1814   Louis XVIII king; brother of Louis XVI.
1824   Charles X, brother; reactionary; deposed by the July Revolution, 1830.

House of Orleans

1830   Louis-Philippe, the "citizen king."

Second Republic

1848   Louis Napoleon Bonaparte, president, nephew of Napoleon I. He became:

Second Empire

1852   Napoleon III, emperor; Eugenie (de Montijo) empress. Lost Franco-Prussian war, deposed 1870. Son, Prince Imperial (1856-79), died in Zulu War. Eugenie died 1920.

Third Republic—Presidents

1871   Thiers, Louis Adolphe (1797-1877)
1873   MacMahon, Marshal Patrice M. de (1808-1893)
1879   Grevy, Paul J. (1807-1891)
1887   Sadi-Carnot, M. (1837-1894), assassinated
1894   Casimir-Perier, Jean P. P. (1847-1907)
1895   Faure, Francois Felix (1841-1899)
1899   Loubet, Emile (1838-1929)
1906   Fallieres, C. Armand (1841-1931)
1913   Poincare, Raymond (1860-1934)
1920   Deschanel, Paul (1856-1922)
1920   Millerand, Alexandre (1859-1943)
1924   Doumergue, Gaston (1863-1937)
1931   Doumer, Paul (1857-1932), assassinated
1932   Lebrun, Albert (1871-1950), resigned 1940
1940   Vichy govt. under German armistice: Henri Philippe Petain (1856-1951) Chief of State, 1940-1944.
     Provisional govt. after liberation: Charles de Gaulle (1890-1970) Oct. 1944-Jan. 21, 1946; Felix Gouin (1884-1977) Jan. 23, 1946; Georges Bidault (1899-1983) June 24, 1946.

Fourth Republic—Presidents

1947   Auriol, Vincent (1884-1966)
1954   Coty, Rene (1882-1962)

Fifth Republic—Presidents

1959   de Gaulle, Charles Andre J. M. (1890-1970)
1969   Pompidou, Georges (1911-1974)
1974   Giscard d'Estaing, Valery (1926-   )
1981   Mitterrand, Francois (1916-   )

Rulers of Middle Europe; Rise and Fall of Dynasties

Carolingian Dynasty

Charles the Great, or Charlemagne, ruled France, Italy, and Middle Europe; established Ostmark (later Austria); crowned Roman emperor by pope in Rome, 800 AD; died 814.

Louis I (Ludwig) the Pious, son; crowned by Charlemagne 814, d. 840.

Louis II, the German, son; succeeded to East Francia (Germany) 843-876.

Charles the Fat, son; inherited East Francia and West Francia (France) 876, reunited empire, crowned emperor by pope, 881, deposed 887.

Arnulf, nephew, 887-899. Partition of empire.

Louis the Child, 899-911, last direct descendant of Charlemagne.

Conrad I, duke of Franconia, first elected German king, 911-918, founded House of Franconia.

Saxon Dynasty; First Reich

Henry I, the Fowler, duke of Saxony, 919-936.

Otto I, the Great, 936-973, son; crowned Holy Roman Emperor by pope, 962.

Otto II, 973-983, son; failed to oust Greeks and Arabs from Sicily.

Otto III, 983-1002, son; crowned emperor at 16.

Henry II, the Saint, duke of Bavaria, 1002-1024, great-grandson of Otto the Great.

House of Franconia

Conrad II, 1024-1039, elected king of Germany.

Henry III, the Black, 1039-1056, son; deposed 3 popes; annexed Burgundy.

Henry IV, 1056-1106, son; regency by his mother, Agnes of Poitou. Banned by Pope Gregory VII, he did penance at Canossa.

Henry V, 1106-1125, son; last of Salic House.

Lothair, duke of Saxony, 1125-1137. Crowned emperor in Rome, 1134.

House of Hohenstaufen

Conrad III, duke of Swabia, 1138-1152. In 2d Crusade.

Frederick I, Barbarossa, 1152-1190; Conrad's nephew.

Henry VI, 1190-1196, took lower Italy from Normans. Son became king of Sicily.

Philip of Swabia, 1197-1208, brother.

Otto IV, of House of Welf, 1198-1215; deposed.

Frederick II, 1215-1250, son of Henry VI; king of Sicily; crowned king of Jerusalem; in 5th Crusade.

Conrad IV, 1250-1254, son; lost lower Italy to Charles of Anjou.

Conradin (1252-1268) son, king of Jerusalem and Sicily, beheaded. Last Hohenstaufen.

Interregnum, 1254-1273, Rise of the Electors.

Transition

Rudolph I of Hapsburg, 1273-1291, defeated King Ottocar II of Bohemia. Bequeathed duchy of Austria to eldest son, Albert.

Adolph of Nassau, 1292-1298, killed in war with Albert of Austria.

Albert I, king of Germany, 1298-1308, son of Rudolph.

Henry VII, of Luxemburg, 1308-1313, crowned emperor in Rome. Seized Bohemia, 1310.

Louis IV of Bavaria (Wittelsbach), 1314-1347. Also elected was Frederick of Austria, 1314-1330 (Hapsburg). Abolition of papal sanction for election of Holy Roman Emperor.

Charles IV, of Luxemburg, 1347-1378, grandson of Henry VII, German emperor and king of Bohemia, Lombardy, Burgundy; took Mark of Brandenburg.

Wenceslaus, 1378-1400, deposed.

Rupert, Duke of Palatine, 1400-1410.

Hungary

Stephen I, house of Arpad, 997-1038. Crowned king 1000; converted Magyars; canonized 1083. After several centuries of feuds Charles Robert of Anjou became Charles I, 1308-1342.

Louis I, the Great, son, 1342-1382; joint ruler of Poland with Casimir III, 1370. Defeated Turks.

Mary, daughter, 1382-1395, ruled with husband. Sigismund of Luxemburg, 1387-1437, also king of Bohemia. As bro. of Wenceslaus he succeeded Rupert as Holy Roman Emperor, 1410.

Albert II, 1438-1439, son-in-law of Sigismund; also Roman emperor. (see under Hapsburg.)

Ulaszlo I of Poland, 1440-1444.

Ladislaus V, posthumous son of Albert II, 1444-1457. John Hunyadi (Hunyadi Janos) governor (1446-1452), fought Turks, Czechs; died 1456.

Matthias I (Corvinus) son of Hunyadi, 1458-1490. Shared rule of Bohemia, captured Vienna, 1485, annexed Austria, Styria, Carinthia.

Ladislas II (king of Bohemia), 1490-1516.

Louis II, son, aged 10, 1516-1526. Wars with Suleiman, Turk. In 1527 Hungary was split between Ferdinand I, Archduke of

Austria, bro.-in-law of Louis II, and John Zapolya of Transylvania. After Turkish invasion, 1547, Hungary was split between Ferdinand, Prince John Sigismund (Transylvania) and the Turks.

House of Hapsburg

Albert V of Austria, Hapsburg, crowned king of Hungary, Jan. 1438, Roman emperor, March, 1438, as Albert II; died 1439.

Frederick III, cousin, 1440-1493. Fought Turks.

Maximilian I, son, 1493-1519. Assumed title of Holy Roman Emperor (German), 1493.

Charles V, grandson, 1519-1556. King of Spain with mother co-regent; crowned Roman emperor at Aix, 1520. Confronted Luther at Worms; attempted church reform and religious conciliation; abdicated 1556.

Ferdinand I, king of Bohemia, 1526, of Hungary, 1527; disputed. German king, 1531. Crowned Roman emperor on abdication of brother Charles V, 1556.

Maximilian II, son, 1564-1576.

Rudolph II, son, 1576-1612.

Matthias, brother, 1612-1619, king of Bohemia and Hungary.

Ferdinand II of Styria, king of Bohemia, 1617, of Hungary, 1618, Roman emperor, 1619. Bohemian Protestants deposed him, elected Frederick V of Palatine, starting Thirty Years War.

Ferdinand III, son, king of Hungary, 1625, Bohemia, 1627, Roman emperor, 1637. Peace of Westphalia, 1648, ended war. Leopold I, 1658-1705; Joseph I, 1705-1711; Charles VI, 1711-1740.

Maria Theresa, daughter, 1740-1780, Archduchess of Austria, queen of Hungary; ousted pretender, Charles VII, crowned 1742; in 1745 obtained election of her husband Francis I as Roman emperor and co-regent (d. 1765). Fought Seven Years' War with Frederick II (the Great) of Prussia. Mother of Marie Antoinette, Queen of France.

Joseph II, son 1765-1790, Roman emperor, reformer; powers restricted by Empress Maria Theresa until her death, 1780. First partition of Poland. Leopold II, 1790-1792.

Francis II, son, 1792-1835. Fought Napoleon. Proclaimed first hereditary emperor of Austria, 1804. Forced to abdicate as Roman emperor, 1806; last use of title. Ferdinand I, son, 1835-1848, abdicated during revolution.

Austro-Hungarian Monarchy

Francis Joseph I, nephew, 1848-1916, emperor of Austria, king of Hungary. Dual monarchy of Austria-Hungary formed, 1867. After assassination of heir, Archduke Francis Ferdinand, June 28, 1914, Austrian diplomacy precipitated World War I.

Charles I, grand-nephew, 1916-1918, last emperor of Austria and king of Hungary. Abdicated Nov. 11-13, 1918, died 1922.

Rulers of Prussia

Nucleus of Prussia was the Mark of Brandenburg. First margrave was Albert the Bear (Albrecht), 1134-1170. First Hohenzollern margrave was Frederick, burgrave of Nuremberg, 1417-1440.

Frederick William, 1640-1688, the Great Elector. Son, Frederick III, 1688-1713, was crowned King Frederick of Prussia, 1701.

Frederick William I, son, 1713-1740.

Frederick II, the Great, son, 1740-1786, annexed Silesia part of Austria.

Frederick William II, nephew, 1786-1797.

Frederick William III, son, 1797-1840. Napoleonic wars.

Frederick William IV, son, 1840-1861. Uprising of 1848 and first parliament and constitution.

Second and Third Reich

William I, 1861-1888, brother. Annexation of Schleswig and Hanover; Franco-Prussian war, 1870-71, proclamation of German Reich, Jan. 18, 1871, at Versailles; William, German emperor (Deutscher Kaiser), Bismarck, chancellor.

Frederick III, son, 1888.

William II, son, 1888-1918. Led Germany in World War I, abdicated as German emperor and king of Prussia, Nov. 9, 1918. Died in exile in Netherlands June 4, 1941. Minor rulers of Bavaria, Saxony, Wurttemberg also abdicated.

Germany proclaimed a republic at Weimar, July 1, 1919. Presidents: Frederick Ebert, 1919-1925, Paul von Hindenburg-Beneckendorff, 1925, reelected 1932, d. Aug. 2, 1934. Adolf Hitler, chancellor, chosen successor as Leader-Chancellor (Fuehrer & Reichskanzler) of Third Reich. Annexed Austria, March, 1938. Precipitated World War II, 1939-1945. Committed suicide April 30, 1945.

Rulers of Poland

House of Piasts

Miesko I, 962?-992; Poland Christianized 966. Expansion under 3 Boleslavs: I, 992-1025, son, crowned king 1024; II,

1058-1079, great-grandson, exiled after killing bishop Stanislav who became chief patron saint of Poland: III, 1106-1138, nephew, divided Poland among 4 sons eldest suzerain.

(continued)

1138-1306, feudal division. 1226 founding in Prussia of military order Teutonic Knights. 1226 invasion by Tartars/Mongols.

Vladislav I, 1306-1333, reunited most Polish territories, crowned king 1320. Casimir III the Great, 1333-1370, son, developed economic, cultural life, foreign policy.

House of Anjou

Louis I, 1370-1382, nephew/identical with Louis I of Hungary. Jadwiga, 1384-1399, daughter, married 1386 Jagiello, Grand Duke of Lituania.

House of Jagelloneans

Vladislav II, 1386-1434, Christianized Lituania, founded personal union between Poland & Lituania. Defeated 1410 Teutonic Knights at Grunwald.

Vladislav III, 1434-1444, son, simultaneously king of Hungary. Fought Turks, killed 1444 in battle of Varna.

Casimir IV, 1446-1492, brother, competed with Hapsburgs, put son Vladislav on throne of Bohemia, later also of Hungary.

Sigismund I, 1506-1548, brother, patronized science & arts, his & son's reign "Golden Age."

Sigismund II, 1548-1572, son, established 1569 real union of Poland and Lituania (lasted until 1795).

Elective kings

Polish nobles proclaimed 1572 Poland a Republic headed by king to be elected by whole nobility.

Stephen Batory, 1576-1586, duke of Transylvania, married Ann, sister of Sigismund II August. Fought Russians.

Sigismund III Vasa, 1587-1632, nephew of Sigismund II. 1592-1598 also king of Sweden. His generals fought Russians, Turks.

Vladislav II Vasa, 1632-1648, son. Fought Russians.

John II Casimir Vasa, 1648-1668, brother. Fought Cossacks, Swedes, Russians, Turks, Tartars (the "Deluge"). Abdicated 1668.

John III Sobieski, 1674-1696. Won Vienna from Turks, 1683.

Stanislav II, 1764-1795, last king. Encouraged reforms; 1791 1st modern Constitution in Europe. 1772, 1793, 1795 Poland partitioned among Russia, Prussia, Austria. Unsuccessful insurrection against foreign invasion 1794 under Kosciuszko, Amer-Polish gen.

1795-1918 Poland under foreign rule

1807-1815 Grand Duchy of Warsaw created by Napoleon I, Frederick August of Saxony grand duke.

1815 Congress of Vienna proclaimed part of Poland "Kingdom" in personal union with Russia.

Polish uprisings: 1830 against Russia, 1846, 1848 against Austria, 1863 against Russia—all repressed.

1918-1939 Second Republic

1918-1922 Head of State Jozef Pilsudski. Presidents: Gabriel Narutowicz 1922, assassinated. Stanislav Wojsiechowski 1922-1926, had to abdicate after Pilsudski's coup d'état. Ignacy Mosciecki, 1926-1939, ruled with Pilsudski as (until 1935) virtual dictator.

1939-1945 Poland under foreign occupation

Nazi aggression Sept. 1939. Polish govt.-in-exile, first in France, then in England. Vladislav Raczkiewicz pres., Gen. Vladislav Sikorski, then Stanislav Mikolajczyk, prime ministers. Polish Committee of Natl. Liberation proclaimed at Lublin July 1944, transformed into govt. Jan. 1, 1945.

Rulers of Denmark, Sweden, Norway

Denmark

Earliest rulers invaded Britain; King Canute, who ruled in London 1016-1035, was most famous. The Valdemars furnished kings until the 15th century. In 1282 the Danes won the first national assembly, Danehof, from King Erik V.

Most redoubtable medieval character was Margaret, daughter of Valdemar IV, born 1353, married at 10 to King Haakon VI of Norway. In 1376 she had her first infant son Olaf made king of Denmark. After his death, 1387, she was regent of Denmark and Norway. In 1388 Sweden accepted her as sovereign. In 1389 she made her grand-nephew, Duke Erik of Pomerania, titular king of Denmark, Sweden, and Norway, with herself as regent. In 1397 she effected the Union of Kalmar of the three kingdoms and had Erik VII crowned. In 1439 the three kingdoms deposed him and elected, 1440, Christopher of Bavaria king (Christopher III). On his death, 1448, the union broke up.

Succeeding rulers were unable to enforce their claims as rulers of Sweden until 1520, when Christian II conquered Sweden. He was thrown out 1522, and in 1523 Gustavus Vasa united Sweden. Denmark continued to dominate Norway until the Napoleonic wars, when Frederick VI, 1808-1839, joined the Napoleonic cause after Britain had destroyed the Danish fleet, 1807. In 1814 he was forced to cede Norway to Sweden and Helgoland to Britain, receiving Lauenburg. Successors Christian VIII, 1839; Frederick VII, 1848; Christian IX, 1863; Frederick VIII, 1906; Christian X, 1912; Frederick IX, 1947; Margrethe II, 1972.

Sweden

Early kings ruled at Uppsala, but did not dominate the country. Sverker, c1130-c1156, united the Swedes and Goths. In 1435 Sweden obtained the Riksdag, or parliament. After the Union of Kalmar, 1397, the Danes either ruled or harried the country until Christian II of Denmark conquered it anew, 1520. This led to a rising under Gustavus Vasa, who ruled Sweden 1523-1560, and established an independent kingdom. Charles IX, 1599-1611, crowned 1604, conquered Moscow. Gustavus II Adolphus, 1611-1632, was called the Lion of the North. Later rulers: Christina, 1632; Charles X, Gustavus 1654; Charles XI, 1660; Charles XII (invader of Russia and Poland, defeated at Poltava, June 28, 1709), 1697; Ulrika Eleanora, sister, elected queen 1718; Frederick I (of Hesse), her husband, 1720; Adolphus Frederick, 1751; Gustavus III, 1771; Gustavus IV Adolphus, 1792; Charles XIII, 1809. (Union with Norway began 1814.) Charles XIV John, 1818. He was Jean Bernadotte, Napoleon's Prince of Ponte Corvo, elected 1810 to succeed Charles XIII. He founded the present dynasty: Oscar I, 1844; Charles XV, 1859; Oscar II, 1872; Gustavus V, 1907; Gustav VI Adolf, 1950; Carl XVI Gustaf, 1973.

Norway

Overcoming many rivals, Harald Haarfager, 872-930, conquered Norway, Orkneys, and Shetlands; Olaf I, great-grandson, 995-1000, brought Christianity into Norway, Iceland, and Greenland. In 1035 Magnus the Good also became king of Denmark. Haakon V, 1299-1319, had married his daughter to Erik of Sweden. Their son, Magnus, became ruler of Norway and Sweden at 6. His son, Haakon VI, married Margaret of Denmark; their son Olaf IV became king of Norway and Denmark, followed by Margaret's regency and the Union of Kalmar, 1397.

In 1450 Norway became subservient to Denmark. Christian IV, 1588-1648, founded Christiania, now Oslo. After Napoleonic wars, when Denmark ceded Norway to Sweden, a strong nationalist movement forced recognition of Norway as an independent kingdom united with Sweden under the Swedish kings, 1814-1905. In 1905 the union was dissolved and Prince Carl of Denmark became Haakon VII. He died Sept. 21, 1957, aged 85; succeeded by son, Olav V, 1957.

Rulers of the Netherlands and Belgium

The Netherlands (Holland)

William Frederick, Prince of Orange, led a revolt against French rule, 1813, and was crowned King of the Netherlands, 1815. Belgium seceded Oct. 4, 1830, after a revolt, and formed a separate government. The change was ratified by the two kingdoms by treaty Apr. 19, 1839.

Succession: William II, son, 1840; William III, son, 1849; Wilhelmina, daughter of William III and his 2d wife Princess Emma of Waldeck, 1890; Wilhelmina abdicated, Sept. 4, 1948, in favor of daughter, Juliana. Juliana abdicated Apr. 30, 1980, in favor of daughter, Beatrix.

Belgium

A national congress elected Prince Leopold of Saxe-Coburg King; he took the throne July 21, 1831, as Leopold I. Succession: Leopold II, son 1865; Albert I, nephew of Leopold II, 1909; Leopold III, son of Albert, 1934; Prince Charles, Regent 1944; Leopold returned 1950, yielded powers to son Baudouin, Prince Royal, Aug. 6, 1950, abdicated July 16, 1951. Baudouin I took throne July 17, 1951.

For political history prior to 1830 see articles on the Netherlands and Belgium.

Roman Rulers

From Romulus to the end of the Empire in the West. Rulers of the Roman Empire in the East sat in Constantinople and for a brief period in Nicaea, until the capture of Constantinople by the Turks in 1453, when Byzantium was succeeded by the Ottoman Empire.

BC	Name	AD	Name	AD	Name
	The Kingdom	98	Trajanus	324	Constantinus I (the Great)
753	Romulus (Quirinus)	117	Hadrianus	337	Constantinus II, Constans I,
716	Numa Pompilius	138	Antoninus Pius		Constantius II
673	Tullus Hostilius	161	Marcus Aurelius and Lucius Verus	340	Constantius II and Constans I
640	Ancus Marcius	169	Marcus Aurelius (alone)	350	Constantius II
616	L. Tarquinius Priscus	180	Commodus	361	Julianus II (the Apostate)
578	Servius Tullius	193	Pertinax; Julianus I	363	Jovianus
534	L. Tarquinius Superbus	193	Septimius Severus		**West (Rome) and East**
	The Republic	211	Caracalla and Geta		**(Constantinople)**
509	Consulate established	212	Caracalla (alone)	364	Valentinianus I (West) and Valens
509	Quaestorship instituted	217	Macrinus		(East)
498	Dictatorship introduced	218	Elagabalus (Heliogabalus)	367	Valentinianus I with
494	Plebeian Tribunate created	222	Alexander Severus		Gratianus (West) and Valens (East)
494	Plebeian Aedileship created	235	Maximinus I (the Thracian)	375	Gratianus with Valentinianus
444	Consular Tribunate organized	238	Gordianus I and Gordianus II;		II (West) and Valens (East)
435	Censorship instituted		Pupienus and Balbinus	378	Gratianus with Valentinianus II
366	Praetorship established	238	Gordianus III		(West) Theodosius I (East)
366	Curule Aedileship created	244	Philippus (the Arabian)	383	Valentinianus II (West) and
362	Military Tribunate elected	249	Decius		Theodosius I (East)
326	Proconsulate introduced	251	Gallus and Volusianus	394	Theodosius I (the Great)
311	Naval Duumvirate elected	253	Aemilianus	395	Honorius (West) and Arcadius
217	Dictatorship of Fabius Maximus	253	Valerianus and Gallienus		(East)
133	Tribunate of Tiberius Gracchus	258	Gallienus (alone)	408	Honorius (West) and Theodosius II
123	Tribunate of Gaius Gracchus	268	Claudius Gothicus		(East)
82	Dictatorship of Sulla	270	Quintillus	423	Valentinianus III (West) and
60	First Triumvirate formed	270	Aurelianus		Theodosius II (East)
	(Caesar, Pompeius, Crassus)	275	Tacitus	450	Valentinianus III (West)
46	Dictatorship of Caesar	276	Florianus		and Marcianus (East)
43	Second Triumvirate formed	276	Probus	455	Maximus (West), Avitus
	(Octavianus, Antonius, Lepidus)	282	Carus		(West); Marcianus (East)
	The Empire	283	Carinus and Numerianus	456	Avitus (West), Marcianus (East)
27	Augustus (Gaius Julius	284	Diocletianus	457	Majorianus (West), Leo I (East)
	Caesar Octavianus)	286	Diocletianus and Maximianus	461	Severus II (West), Leo I (East)
14	Tiberius I	305	Galerius and Constantius I	467	Anthemius (West), Leo I (East)
37	Gaius Caesar (Caligula)	306	Galerius, Maximinus II, Severus I	472	Olybrius (West), Leo I (East)
41	Claudius I	307	Galerius, Maximinus	473	Glycerius (West), Leo I (East)
54	Nero		II, Constantinus I, Licinius,	474	Julius Nepos (West), Leo II (East)
68	Galba		Maxentius	475	Romulus Augustulus (West) and
69	Galba; Otho, Vitellius	311	Maximinus II, Constantinus I,		Zeno (East)
69	Vespasianus		Licinius, Maxentius	476	End of Empire in West; Odovacar,
79	Titus	314	Maximinus II, Constantinus I,		King, drops title of Emperor;
81	Domitianus		Licinius		murdered by King Theodoric of
96	Nerva	314	Constantinus I and Licinius		Ostrogoths 493 AD

Rulers of Modern Italy

After the fall of Napoleon in 1814, the Congress of Vienna, 1815, restored Italy as a political patchwork, comprising the Kingdom of Naples and Sicily, the Papal States, and smaller units. Piedmont and Genoa were awarded to Sardinia, ruled by King Victor Emmanuel I of Savoy.

United Italy emerged under the leadership of Camillo, Count di Cavour (1810-1861), Sardinian prime minister. Agitation was led by Giuseppe Mazzini (1805-1872) and Giuseppe Garibaldi (1807-1882), soldier, Victor Emmanuel I abdicated 1821. After a brief regency for a brother, Charles Albert was King 1831-1849, abdicating when defeated by the Austrians at Novara. Succeeded by Victor Emmanuel II,

1849-1861.

In 1859 France forced Austria to cede Lombardy to Sardinia, which gave rights to Savoy and Nice to France. In 1860 Garibaldi led 1,000 volunteers in a spectacular campaign, took Sicily and expelled the King of Naples. In 1860 the House of Savoy annexed Tuscany, Parma, Modena, Romagna, the Two Sicilies, the Marches, and Umbria. Victor Emmanuel assumed the title of King of Italy at Turin Mar. 17, 1861. In 1866 he allied with Prussia in the Austro-Prussian War, with Prussia's victory received Venetia. On Sept. 20, 1870, his troops under Gen. Raffaele Cadorna entered Rome and took over the Papal States, ending the temporal power of the Roman Catholic Church.

Succession: Umberto I; 1878, assassinated 1900; Victor Emmanuel III, 1900, abdicated 1946, died 1947; Umberto II, 1946, ruled a month. In 1921 Benito Mussolini (1883-1945) formed the Fascist party and became prime minister Oct. 31, 1922. He made the King Emperor of Ethiopia, 1937; entered World War II as ally of Hitler. He was deposed July 25, 1943.

At a plebiscite June 2, 1946, Italy voted for a republic; Premier Alcide de Gasperi became chief of state June 13, 1946. On June 28, 1946, the Constituent Assembly elected Enrico de Nicola, Liberal, provisional president. Successive presidents: Luigi Einaudi, elected May 11, 1948, Giovanni Gronchi, Apr. 29, 1955; Antonio Segni, May 6, 1962; Giuseppe Saragat, Dec. 28, 1964; Giovanni Leone, Dec. 29, 1971; Alessandro Pertini, July 9, 1978; Francesco Cossiga, July 9, 1985.

Rulers of Spain

From 8th to 11th centuries Spain was dominated by the Moors (Arabs and Berbers). The Christian reconquest established small kingdoms (Asturias, Aragon, Castile, Catalonia, Leon, Navarre, and Valencia). In 1474 Isabella, b. 1451, became Queen of Castile & Leon. Her husband, Ferdinand, b. 1452, inherited Aragon 1479, with Catalonia, Valencia, and the Balearic Islands, became Ferdinand V of Castile. By Isabella's request Pope Sixtus IV established the Inquisition, 1478. Last Moorish kingdom, Granada, fell 1492. Columbus opened New World of colonies, 1492. Isabella died 1504, succeeded by her daughter, Juana "the Mad," but Ferdinand ruled until his death 1516.

Charles I, b. 1500, son of Juana and grandson of Ferdinand and Isabella, and of Maximilian I of Hapsburg; succeeded later as Holy Roman Emperor, Charles V, 1520; abdicated 1556. Philip II, son, 1556-1598, inherited only Spanish throne; conquered Portugal, fought Turks, persecuted non-Catholics, sent Armada against England. Was married to Mary I of England, 1554-1558. Succession: Philip III, 1598-1621; Philip IV, 1621-1665; Charles II, 1665-1700, left Spain to Philip of Anjou, grandson of Louis XIV, who as Philip V, 1700-1746, founded Bourbon dynasty. Ferdinand VI, 1746-1759; Charles III, 1759-1788; Charles IV, 1788-1808, abdicated.

Napoleon now dominated politics and made his brother Joseph King of Spain 1808, but the Spanish ousted him in 1813. Ferdinand VII, 1808, 1814-1833, lost American colonies; succeeded by daughter Isabella II, aged 3, with wife Maria Christina of Naples regent until 1843. Isabella deposed by revolution 1868. Elected king by the Cortes, Amadeo of Savoy, 1870; abdicated 1873. First republic, 1873-74. Alphonso XII, son of Isabella, 1875-85. His posthumous son was Alphonso XIII, with his mother, Queen Maria Christina regent; Spanish-American war, Spain lost Cuba, gave up Puerto Rico, Philippines, Sulu Is., Marianas. Alphonso took throne 1902, aged 16, married British Princess Victoria Eugenia of Battenberg. The dictatorship of Primo de Rivera, 1923-30, precipitated the revolution of 1931. Alphonso agreed to leave without formal abdication. The monarchy was abolished and the second republic established, with socialist backing. Presidents were Niceto Alcala Zamora, to 1936, when Manuel Azaña was chosen.

In July, 1936, the army in Morocco revolted against the government and General Francisco Franco led the troops into Spain. The revolution succeeded by Feb., 1939, when Azaña resigned. Franco became chief of state, with provisions that if he was incapacitated the Regency Council by two-thirds vote may propose a king to the Cortes, which must have a two-thirds majority to elect him.

Alphonso XIII died in Rome Feb. 28, 1941, aged 54. His property and citizenship had been restored.

A succession law restoring the monarchy was approved in a 1947 referendum. Prince Juan Carlos, son of the pretender to the throne, was designated by Franco and the Cortes in 1969 as the future king and chief of state. Upon Franco's death, Nov. 20, 1975, Juan Carlos was proclaimed king, Nov. 22, 1975.

Leaders in the South American Wars of Liberation

Simon Bolivar (1783-1830), Jose Francisco de San Martin (1778-1850), and Francisco Antonio Gabriel Miranda (1750-1816), are among the heroes of the early 19th century struggles of South American nations to free themselves from Spain. All three, and their contemporaries, operated in periods of factional strife, during which soldiers and civilians suffered.

Miranda, a Venezuelan, who had served with the French in the American Revolution and commanded parts of the French Revolutionary armies in the Netherlands, attempted to start a revolt in Venezuela in 1806 and failed. In 1810, with British and American backing, he returned and was briefly a dictator, until the British withdrew their support. In 1812 he was overcome by the royalists in Venezuela and taken prisoner, dying in a Spanish prison in 1816.

San Martin was born in Argentina and during 1789-1811 served in campaigns of the Spanish armies in Europe and Africa. He first joined the independence movement in Argentina in 1812 and in 1817 invaded Chile with 4,000 men over the mountain passes. Here he and Gen. Bernardo O'Higgins (1778-1842) defeated the Spaniards at Chacabuco, 1817, and O'Higgins was named Liberator and became first director of Chile, 1817-23. In 1821 San Martin occupied Lima and Callao, Peru, and became protector of Peru.

Bolivar, the greatest leader of South American liberation from Spain, was born in Venezuela, the son of an aristocratic family. He first served under Miranda in 1812 and in 1813 captured Caracas, where he was named Liberator. Forced out next year by civil strife, he led a campaign that captured Bogota in 1814. In 1817 he was again in control of Venezuela and was named dictator. He organized Nueva Granada with the help of General Francisco de Paula Santander (1792-1840). By joining Nueva Granada, Venezuela, and the present terrain of Panama and Ecuador, the republic of Colombia was formed with Bolivar president. After numerous setbacks he decisively defeated the Spaniards in the second battle of Carabobo, Venezuela, June 24, 1821.

In May, 1822, Gen. Antonio Jose de Sucre, Bolivar's lieutenant, took Quito. Bolivar went to Guayaquil to confer with San Martin, who resigned as protector of Peru and withdrew from politics. With a new army of Colombians and Peruvians Bolivar defeated the Spaniards in a battle at Junín in 1824 and cleared Peru.

De Sucre organized Charcas (Upper Peru) as Republica Bolivar (now Bolivia) and acted as president in place of Bolivar, who wrote its constitution. De Sucre defeated the Spanish faction of Peru at Ayacucho, Dec. 19, 1824.

Continued civil strife finally caused the Colombian federation to break apart. Santander turned against Bolivar, but the latter defeated him and banished him. In 1828 Bolivar gave up the presidency he had held precariously for 14 years. He became ill from tuberculosis and died Dec. 17, 1830. He is buried in the national pantheon in Caracas.

Rulers of Russia; Premiers of the USSR

First ruler to consolidate Slavic tribes was Rurik, leader of the Russians who established himself at Novgorod, 862 A.D. He and his immediate successors had Scandinavian affiliations. They moved to Kiev after 972 AD and ruled as Dukes of Kiev. In 988 Vladimir was converted and adopted the Byzantine Greek Orthodox service, later modified by Slav influences. Important as organizer and lawgiver was Yaroslav, 1019-1054, whose daughters married kings of Norway, Hungary, and France. His grandson, Vladimir II (Monomakh), 1113-1125, was progenitor of several rulers, but in 1169 Andrew Bogolubski overthrew Kiev and began the line known as Grand Dukes of Vladimir.

Of the Grand Dukes of Vladimir, Alexander Nevsky, 1246-1263, had a son, Daniel, first to be called Duke of Muscovy (Moscow) who ruled 1294-1303. His successors became Grand Dukes of Muscovy. After Dmitri III Donskoi defeated the Tartars in 1380, they also became Grand Dukes of all Russia. Independence of the Tartars and considerable territorial expansion were achieved under Ivan III, 1462-1505.

Tsars of Muscovy—Ivan III was referred to in church ritual as Tsar. He married Sofia, niece of the last Byzantine emperor. His successor, Basil III, died in 1533 when Basil's son Ivan was only 3. He became Ivan IV, "the Terrible"; crowned 1547 as Tsar of all the Russias, ruled till 1584. Under the weak rule of his son, Feodor I, 1584-1598, Boris Godunov had control. The dynasty died, and after years of tribal strife and intervention by Polish and Swedish armies, the Russians united under 17-year-old Michael Romanov, distantly related to the first wife of Ivan IV. He ruled 1613-1645 and established the Romanov line. Fourth ruler after Michael was Peter I.

Tsars, or Emperors of Russia (Romanovs)—Peter I, 1682-1725, known as Peter the Great, took title of Emperor in 1721. His successors and dates of accession were: Catherine, his widow, 1725, Peter II, his grandson, 1727; Anne, Duchess of Courland, 1730, daughter of Peter the Great's brother, Tsar Ivan V; Ivan VI, 1740, great-grandson of Ivan V, child, kept in prison and murdered 1764; Elizabeth, daughter of Peter I, 1741; Peter III, grandson of Peter I,

1761, deposed 1762 for his consort, Catherine II, former princess of Anhalt Zerbst (Germany) who is known as Catherine the Great; Paul I, her son, 1796, killed 1801; Alexander I, son of Paul, 1801, defeated Napoleon; Nicholas I, his brother, 1825; Alexander II, son of Nicholas, 1855, assassinated 1881 by terrorists; Alexander III, son, 1881.

Nicholas II, son, 1894-1917, last Tsar of Russia, was forced to abdicate by the Revolution that followed losses to Germany in WWI. The Tsar, the Empress, the Tsesarevich (Crown Prince) and the Tsar's 4 daughters were murdered by the Bolsheviks in Ekaterinburg, July 16, 1918.

Provisional Government—Prince Georgi Lvov and Alexander Kerensky, premiers, 1917.

Union of Soviet Socialist Republics

Bolshevik Revolution, Nov. 7, 1917, displaced Kerensky; council of People's Commissars formed, Lenin (Vladimir Ilyich Ulyanov), premier. Lenin died Jan. 21, 1924. Aleksei Rykov (executed 1938) and V. M. Molotov held the office, but actual ruler was Joseph Stalin (Joseph Vissarionovich Djugashvili), general secretary of the Central Committee of the Communist Party. Stalin became president of the Council of Ministers (premier) May 7, 1941, died Mar. 5, 1953. Succeeded by Georgi M. Malenkov, as head of the Council and premier and Nikita S. Khrushchev, first secretary of the Central Committee. Malenkov resigned Feb. 8, 1955, became deputy premier, was dropped July 3, 1957. Marshal Nikolai A. Bulganin became premier Feb. 8, 1955; was demoted and Khrushchev became premier Mar. 27 1958. Khrushchev was ousted Oct. 14-15, 1964, replaced by Leonid I. Brezhnev as first secretary of the party and by Aleksei N. Kosygin as premier. On June 16, 1977, Brezhnev took office as president. Brezhnev died Nov. 10, 1982; 2 days later the Central Committee unanimously elected former KGB head Yuri V. Andropov president. Andropov died Feb. 9, 1984; on Feb. 13, Konstantin U. Chernenko was chosen by Central Committee as its general secretary. Chernenko died Mar. 10, 1985. On Mar. 11, he was succeeded as general secretary by Mikhail Gorbachev, who replaced Andrei Gromyko as president on Oct. 1, 1988.

Governments of China

(Until 221 BC and frequently thereafter, China was not a unified state. Where dynastic dates overlap, the rulers or events referred to appeared in different areas of China.)

Hsia	c1994BC	-	c1523BC	Tang (a golden age of Chinese culture; capital: Sian)	618	-	906
Shang	c1523	-	c1028	Five Dynasties (Yellow River basin)	902	-	960
Western Chou	c1027	-	770	Ten Kingdoms (southern China)	907	-	979
Eastern Chou	770	-	256	Liao (Khitan Mongols; capital: Peking)	947	-	1125
Warring States	403	-	222			
Ch'in (first unified empire)	221	-	206	Sung	960	-	1279
Han	202BC	-	220AD	Northern Sung (reunified central and southern China)	960	-	1126
Western Han (expanded Chinese state beyond the Yellow and Yangtze River valleys)	202BC	-	9AD	Western Hsai (non-Chinese rulers in northwest)	990	-	1227
Hsin (Wang Mang, usurper)	9AD	-	23AD	Chin (Tartars; drove Sung out of central China)	1115	-	1234
Eastern Han (expanded Chinese state into Indo-China and Turkestan)	25	-	220	Yuan (Mongols; Kublai Khan made Peking his capital in 1267)	1271	-	1368
Three Kingdoms (Wei, Shu, Wu)	220	-	265	Ming (China reunified under Chinese rule; capital: Nanking, then Peking in 1420)	1368	-	1644
Chin (western)	265	-	317			
(eastern)	317	-	420	Ch'ing (Manchus, descendents of Tartars)	1644	-	1911
Northern Dynasties (followed several short-lived governments by Turks, Mongols, etc.)	386	-	581	Republic (disunity; provincial rulers, warlords)	1912	-	1949
Southern Dynasties (capital: Nanking)	420	-	589	People's Republic of China	1949	-	—
Sui (reunified China)	581	-	618			

Leaders Since 1949

Mao Zedong	Chairman, Central People's Administrative Council, Communist Party (CPC), 1949-1976
Zhou Enlai	Premier, foreign minister, 1949-1976
Deng Xiaoping	Vice Premier, 1949-1976; 1977-1987
Liu Shaoqi	President, 1959-1969
Hua Guofeng	Premier, 1976-1980; CPC Chairman, 1976-1981
Zhao Ziyong	Premier, 1980-88; CPC Chairman, 1987-89
Hu Yaobang	CPC Chairman, 1981-1987
Li Xiannian	President, 1983-1988
Yong Shang-Kun	President, 1988-
Li Peng	Premier, 1988-

Chronological List of Popes

Source: Annuario Pontificio. Table lists year of accession of each Pope.

The Roman Catholic Church names the Apostle Peter as founder of the Church in Rome. He arrived there c. 42, was martyred there c. 67, and raised to sainthood.

The Pope's temporal title is: Sovereign of the State of Vatican City.

The Pope's spiritual titles are: Bishop of Rome, Vicar of Jesus Christ, Successor of St. Peter, Prince of the Apostles, Supreme Pontiff of the Universal Church, Patriarch of the West, Primate of Italy, Archbishop and Metropolitan of the Roman Province.

Anti-Popes are in *Italics*. Anti-Popes were illegitimate claimants of or pretenders to the papal throne.

Year	Pope	Year	Pope	Year	Pope	Year	Pope
See above.	St. Peter		or Adeodatus	983	John XIV	1316	John XXII
67	St. Linus	619	Boniface V	985	John XV	*1328*	*Nicholas V*
76	St. Anacletus	625	Honorius I	996	Gregory V	1334	Benedict XII
	or Cletus	640	Severinus	*997*	*John XVI*	1342	Clement VI
88	St. Clement I	642	Theodore I	999	Sylvester II	1352	Innocent VI
97	St. Evaristus	649	St. Martin I, Martyr	1003	John XVII	1362	Bl. Urban V
105	St. Alexander I	654	St. Eugene I	1004	John XVIII	1370	Gregory XI
115	St. Sixtus I	657	St. Vitalian	1009	Sergius IV	1378	Urban VI
125	St. Telesphorus	672	Adeodatus II	1012	Benedict VIII	*1378*	*Clement VII*
136	St. Hyginus	676	Donus	*1012*	*Gregory*	1389	Boniface IX
140	St. Pius I	678	St. Agatho	1024	John XIX	*1394*	*Benedict XIII*
155	St. Anicetus	682	St. Leo II	1032	Benedict IX	1404	Innocent VII
166	St. Soter	684	St. Benedict II	1045	Sylvester III	1406	Gregory XII
175	St. Eleutherius	685	John V	1045	Benedict IX	*1409*	*Alexander V*
189	St. Victor I	686	Conon	1045	Gregory VI	*1410*	*John XXIII*
199	St. Zephyrinus	*687*	*Theodore*	1046	Clement II	1417	Martin V
217	St. Callistus I	*687*	*Paschal*	1047	Benedict IX	1431	Eugene IV
217	*St. Hippolytus*	687	St. Sergius I	1048	Damasus II	*1439*	*Felix V*
222	St. Urban I	701	John VI	1049	St. Leo IX	1447	Nicholas V
230	St. Pontian	705	John VII	1055	Victor II	1455	Callistus III
235	St. Anterus	708	Sisinnius	1057	Stephen IX (X)	1458	Pius II
236	St. Fabian	708	Constantine	*1058*	*Benedict X*	1464	Paul II
251	St. Cornelius	715	St. Gregory II	1059	Nicholas II	1471	Sixtus IV
251	*Novatian*	731	St. Gregory III	1061	Alexander II	1484	Innocent VIII
253	St. Lucius I	741	St. Zachary	*1061*	*Honorius II*	1492	Alexander VI
254	St. Stephen I	752	Stephen II (III)	1073	St. Gregory VII	1503	Pius III
257	St. Sixtus II	757	St. Paul I	*1080*	*Clement III*	1503	Julius II
259	St. Dionysius	*767*	*Constantine*	1086	Bl. Victor III	1513	Leo X
269	St. Felix I	*768*	*Philip*	1088	Bl. Urban II	1522	Adrian VI
275	St. Eutychian	768	Stephen III (IV)	1099	Paschal II	1523	Clement VII
283	St. Caius	772	Adrian I	*1100*	*Theodoric*	1534	Paul III
296	St. Marcellinus	795	St. Leo III	*1102*	*Albert*	1550	Julius III
308	St. Marcellus I	816	Stephen IV (V)	*1105*	*Sylvester IV*	1555	Marcellus II
309	St. Eusebius	817	St. Paschal I	1118	Gelasius II	1555	Paul IV
311	St. Melchiades	824	Eugene II	*1118*	*Gregory VIII*	1559	Pius IV
314	St. Sylvester I	827	Valentine	1119	Callistus II	1566	St. Pius V
336	St. Marcus	827	Gregory IV	1124	Honorius II	1572	Gregory XIII
337	St. Julius I	*844*	*John*	*1124*	*Celestine II*	1585	Sixtus V
352	Liberius	844	Sergius II	1130	Innocent II	1590	Urban VII
355	*Felix II*	847	St. Leo IV	*1130*	*Anacletus II*	1590	Gregory XIV
366	St. Damasus I	855	Benedict III	*1138*	*Victor IV*	1591	Innocent IX
366	*Ursinus*	*855*	*Anastasius*	1143	Celestine II	1592	Clement VIII
384	St. Siricius	858	St. Nicholas I	1144	Lucius II	1605	Leo XI
399	St. Anastasius I	867	Adrian II	1145	Bl. Eugene III	1605	Paul V
401	St. Innocent I	872	John VIII	1153	Anastasius IV	1621	Gregory XV
417	St. Zosimus	882	Marinus I	1154	Adrian IV	1623	Urban VIII
418	St. Boniface I	884	St. Adrian III	1159	Alexander III	1644	Innocent X
418	*Eulalius*	885	Stephen V (VI)	*1159*	*Victor IV*	1655	Alexander VII
422	St. Celestine I	891	Formosus	1164	Paschal III	1667	Clement IX
432	St. Sixtus III	896	Boniface VI	*1168*	*Callistus III*	1670	Clement X
440	St. Leo I	896	Stephen VI (VII)	*1179*	*Innocent III*	1676	Bl. Innocent XI
461	St. Hilary	897	Romanus	1181	Lucius III	1689	Alexander VIII
468	St. Simplicius	897	Theodore II	1185	Urban III	1691	Innocent XII
483	St. Felix III (II)	898	John IX	1187	Clement III	1700	Clement XI
492	St. Gelasius I	900	Benedict IV	1187	Gregory VIII	1721	Innocent XIII
496	Anastasius II	903	Leo V	1191	Celestine III	1724	Benedict XIII
498	St. Symmachus	*903*	*Christopher*	1198	Innocent III	1730	Clement XII
498	*Lawrence*	904	Sergius III	1216	Honorius III	1740	Benedict XIV
	(501-505)	911	Anastasius III	1227	Gregory IX	1758	Clement XIII
514	St. Hormisdas	913	Landus	1241	Celestine IV	1769	Clement XIV
523	St. John I, Martyr	914	John X	1243	Innocent IV	1775	Pius VI
526	St. Felix IV (III)	928	Leo VI	1254	Alexander IV	1800	Pius VII
530	Boniface II	928	Stephen VII	1261	Urban IV	1823	Leo XII
530	*Dioscorus*		(VIII)	1265	Clement IV	1829	Pius VIII
533	John II	931	John XI	1271	Bl. Gregory X	1831	Gregory XVI
535	St. Agapitus I	936	Leo VII	1276	Bl. Innocent V	1846	Pius IX
536	St. Silverius, Martyr	939	Stephen VIII	1276	Adrian V	1878	Leo XIII
537	Vigilius		(IX)	1276	John XXI	1903	St. Pius X
556	Pelagius I	942	Marinus II	1277	Nicholas III	1914	Benedict XV
561	John III	946	Agapitus II	1281	Martin IV	1922	Pius XI
575	Benedict I	955	John XII	1285	Honorius IV	1939	Pius XII
579	Pelagius II	963	Leo VIII	1288	Nicholas IV	1958	John XXIII
590	St. Gregory I	964	Benedict V	1294	St. Celestine V	1963	Paul VI
604	Sabinian	965	John XIII	1294	Boniface VIII	1978	John Paul I
607	Boniface III	973	Benedict VI	1303	Bl. Benedict XI	1978	John Paul II
608	St. Boniface IV	*974*	*Boniface VII*	1305	Clement V		
615	St. Deusdedit	974	Benedict VII				

WORLD EXPLORATION AND GEOGRAPHY

Early Explorers of the Western Hemisphere

The first men to discover the New World or Western Hemisphere are believed to have walked across a "land bridge" from Siberia to Alaska, an isthmus since broken by the Bering Strait. From Alaska, these ancestors of the Indians spread through North, Central, and South America. Anthropologists have placed these crossings at between 18,000 and 14,000 B.C.; but evidence found in 1967 near Puebla, Mex., indicates mankind reached there as early as 35,000-40,000 years ago.

At first, these people were hunters using flint weapons and tools. In Mexico, about 7000-6000 B.C., they founded farming cultures, developing corn, squash, etc. Eventually, they created complex civilizations — Olmec, Toltec, Aztec, and Maya and, in South America, Inca. Carbon-14 tests show men lived about 8000 B.C. near what are now Front Royal, Va., Kanawha, W. Va., and Dutchess Quarry, N.Y. The Hopewell Culture, based on farming, flourished about 1000 B.C.; remains of it are seen today in large mounds in Ohio and other states.

Norsemen (Norwegian Vikings sailing out of Iceland and Greenland) are credited by most scholars with being the first Europeans to discover America, with at least 5 voyages around 1000 A.D. to areas they called Helluland, Markland, Vinland—possibly Labrador, Nova Scotia or Newfoundland, and New England.

Christopher Columbus, most famous of the explorers, was born at Genoa, Italy, but made his discoveries sailing for the Spanish rulers Ferdinand and Isabella. Dates of his voyages, places he discovered, and other information follow:

1492—First voyage. Left Palos, Spain, Aug. 3 with 88 men (est.). Discovered San Salvador (Guanahani or Watling Is., Bahamas) Oct. 12. Also Cuba, Hispaniola (Haiti-Dominican Republic); built Fort La Navidad on latter.

1493—Second voyage, first part, Sept. 25, with 17 ships, 1,500 men. Dominica (Lesser Antilles) Nov. 3; Guadeloupe, Montserrat, Antigua, San Martin, Santa Cruz, Puerto Rico, Virgin Islands. Settled Isabela on Hispaniola. **Second part** (Columbus having remained in Western Hemisphere), Jamaica, Isle of Pines, La Mona Is.

1498—Third voyage. Left Spain May 30, 1498, 6 ships. Discovered Trinidad. Saw South American continent Aug. 1, 1498, but called it Isla Sancta (Holy Island). Entered Gulf of Paria and landed, first time on continental soil. At mouth of Orinoco Aug. 14 he decided this was the mainland.

1502—Fourth voyage, 4 caravels, 150 men. St. Lucia, Guanaja off Honduras; Cape Gracias a Dios, Honduras; San Juan River, Costa Rica; Almirante, Portobelo, and Laguna de Chiriqui, Panama.

Year	Explorer	Nationality and employer	Discovery or exploration
1497	John Cabot	Italian-English	Newfoundland or Nova Scotia
1498	John and Sebastian Cabot	Italian-English	Labrador to Hatteras
1499	Alonso de Ojeda	Spanish	South American coast, Venezuela
1500, Feb.	Vicente y Pinzon	Spanish	South American coast, Amazon River
1500, Apr.	Pedro Alvarez Cabral	Portuguese	Brazil (for Portugal)
1500-02	Gaspar Corte-Real	Portuguese	Labrador
1501	Rodrigo de Bastidas	Spanish	Central America
1513	Vasco Nunez de Balboa	Spanish	Pacific Ocean
1513	Juan Ponce de Leon	Spanish	Florida
1515	Juan de Solis	Spanish	Rio de la Plata
1519	Alonso de Pineda	Spanish	Mouth of Mississippi River
1519	Hernando Cortes	Spanish	Mexico
1520	Ferdinand Magellan	Portuguese-Spanish	Straits of Magellan, Tierra del Fuego
1524	Giovanni da Verrazano	Italian-French	Atlantic coast-New York harbor
1532	Francisco Pizarro	Spanish	Peru
1534	Jacques Cartier	French	Canada, Gulf of St. Lawrence
1536	Pedro de Mendoza	Spanish	Buenos Aires
1536	A.N. Cabeza de Vaca	Spanish	Texas coast and interior
1539	Francisco de Ulloa	Spanish	California coast
1539-41	Hernando de Soto	Spanish	Mississippi River near Memphis
1539	Marcos de Niza	Italian-Spanish	Southwest (now U.S.)
1540	Francisco V. de Coronado	Spanish	Southwest (now U.S.)
1540	Hernando Alarcon	Spanish	Colorado River
1540	Garcia de L. Cardenas	Spanish	Grand Canyon of the Colorado
1541	Francisco de Orellana	Spanish	Amazon River
1542	Juan Rodriguez Cabrillo	Portuguese-Spanish	San Diego harbor
1565	Pedro Menendez de Aviles	Spanish	St. Augustine
1576	Martin Frobisher	Engish	Frobisher's Bay, Canada
1577-80	Francis Drake	English	California coast
1582	Antonio de Espejo	Spanish	Southwest (named New Mexico)
1584	Amadas & Barlow (for Raleigh)	English	Virginia
1585-87	Sir Walter Raleigh's men	English	Roanoke Is., N.C.
1595	Sir Walter Raleigh	English	Orinoco River
1603-09	Samuel de Champlain	French	Canadian interior, Lake Champlain
1607	Capt. John Smith	English	Atlantic coast
1609-10	Henry Hudson	English-Dutch	Hudson River, Hudson Bay
1634	Jean Nicolet	French	Lake Michigan; Wisconsin
1673	Jacques Marquette, Louis Jolliet	French	Mississippi S to Arkansas
1682	Sieur de La Salle	French	Mississippi S to Gulf of Mexico
1789	Alexander Mackenzie	Canadian	Canadian Northwest

Arctic Exploration

Early Explorers

1587 — John Davis (England). Davis Strait to Sanderson's Hope, 72° 12' N.

1596 — Willem Barents and Jacob van Heemskerck (Hol-

land). Discovered Bear Island, touched northwest tip of Spitsbergen, 79° 49' N, rounded Novaya Zemlya, wintered at Ice Haven.

1607 — Henry Hudson (England). North along Greenland's east coast to Cape Hold-with-Hope, 73° 30', then north of Spitsbergen to 80° 23'. Returning he discovered Hudson's Touches (Jan Mayen).

1616 — William Baffin and Robert Bylot (England). Baffin Bay to Smith Sound.

1728 — Vitus Bering (Russia). Proved Asia and America were separated by sailing through strait.

1733-40 — Great Northern Expedition (Russia). Surveyed Siberian Arctic coast.

1741 — Vitus Bering (Russia). Sighted Alaska from sea, named Mount St. Elias. His lieutenant, Chirikof, discovered coast.

1771 — Samuel Hearne (Hudson's Bay Co.). Overland from Prince of Wales Fort (Churchill) on Hudson Bay to mouth of Coppermine River.

1778 — James Cook (Britain). Through Bering Strait to Icy Cape, Alaska, and North Cape, Siberia.

1789 — Alexander Mackenzie (North West Co., Britain). Montreal to mouth of Mackenzie River.

1806 — William Scoresby (Britain). N. of Spitsbergen to 81° 30'.

1820-3 — Ferdinand von Wrangel (Russia). Completed a survey of Siberian Arctic coast. His exploration joined that of James Cook at North Cape, confirming separation of the continents.

1845 — Sir John Franklin (Britain) was one of many to seek the Northwest Passage—an ocean route connecting the Atlantic and Pacific via the Arctic. His 2 ships (the Erebus and Terror) were last seen entering Lancaster Sound July 26.

1881 — The steamer *Jeanette* on an expedition led by Lt. Cmdr. George W. DeLong was trapped in ice and crushed, June 1881. DeLong and 11 crewmen died; 12 others survived.

1888 — Fridtjof Nansen (Norway) crossed Greenland's icecap, 1893-96 — Nansen in Fram drifted from New Siberian Is. to Spitsbergen; tried polar dash in 1895, reached Franz Josef Land.

1897 — Salomon A. Andree (Sweden) and 2 others started in balloon from Danes, Is., Spitsbergen, July 11, to drift across pole to America, and disappeared. Over 33 years later, Aug. 6, 1930, their frozen bodies were found on White Is., 82° 57' N 29° 52' E.

1903-06 — Roald Amundsen (Norway) first sailed Northwest Passage.

Discovery of North Pole

Robert E. Peary explored Greenland's coast 1891-92, tried for North Pole 1893. In 1900 he reached northern limit of Greenland and 83° 50' N; in 1902 he reached 84° 06' N; in 1906 he went from Ellesmere Is. to 87° 06' N. He sailed in the *Roosevelt*, July, 1908, to winter off Cape Sheridan, Grant Land. The dash for the North Pole began Mar. 1 from Cape Columbia, Ellesmere Land. Peary reached the pole, 90° N, Apr. 6, 1909.

Peary had several supporting groups carrying supplies until the last group turned back at 87° 47' N. Peary, Matthew Henson, and 4 Eskimos proceeded with dog teams and sleds. They crossed the pole several times, finally built an igloo at 90°, remained 36 hours. Started south Apr. 7 at 4 p.m. for Cape Columbia. The Eskimos were Coqueeh, Ootah, Eginwah, and Seegloo.

1914 — Donald MacMillan (U.S.). Northwest, 200 miles, from Axel Heiberg Island to seek Peary's Crocker Land.

1915-17 — Vihjalmur Stefansson (Canada) discovered Borden, Brock, Meighen, and Lougheed Islands.

1918-20 — Roald Amundsen sailed Northeast Passage.

1925 — Amundsen and Lincoln Ellsworth (U.S.) reached 87° 44' N in attempt to fly to North Pole from Spitsbergen.

1926 — Richard E. Byrd and Floyd Bennett (U.S.) first over North Pole by air, May 9.

1926 — Amundsen, Ellsworth, and Umberto Nobile (Italy) flew from Spitsbergen over North Pole May 12, to Teller, Alaska, in dirigible *Norge*.

1928 — Nobile crossed North Pole in airship May 24, crashed May 25. Amundsen lost while trying to effect rescue by plane.

North Pole Exploration Records

On Aug. 3, 1958, the *Nautilus,* under Comdr. William R. Anderson, became the first ship to cross the North Pole beneath the Arctic ice.

The nuclear-powered U.S. submarine *Seadragon,* Comdr. George P. Steele 2d, made the first east-west underwater transit through the Northwest Passage during August, 1960. It sailed from Portsmouth N.H., headed between Greenland and Labrador through Baffin Bay, then west through Lancaster Sound and McClure Strait to the Beaufort Sea. Traveling submerged for the most part, the submarine made 850 miles from Baffin Bay to the Beaufort Sea in 6 days.

On Aug. 16, 1977, the Soviet nuclear icebreaker *Arktika* reached the North Pole and became the first surface ship to break through the Arctic ice pack to the top of the world.

On April 30, 1978, Naomi Uemura, a Japanese explorer, became the first man to reach the North Pole alone by dog sled. During the 54-day, 600-mile trek over the frozen Arctic, Uemura survived attacks by a marauding polar bear.

In April, 1982, Sir Ranulph Fiennes and Charles Burton, British explorers, reached the North Pole and became the first to circle the earth from pole to pole. They had reached the South Pole 16 months earlier. The 52,000-mile trek took 3 years, involved 23 people, and cost an estimated $18 million. The expedition was also the first to travel down the Scott Glacier and the first to journey up the Yukon and through the Northwest Passage in a single season.

On May 2, 1986, 6 American and Canadian explorers reached the North Pole assisted only by dogs. They became the first to reach the North Pole without mechanical assistance since Robert E. Peary planted a flag there in 1909. The explorers, Americans Will Steger, Paul Schurke, Anne Bancroft, and Geoff Carroll, and Canadians Brent Boddy and Richard Weber completed the 500-mile journey in 56 days.

Antarctic Exploration

Early History

Antarctica has been approached since 1773-75, when Capt. James Cook (Britain) reached 71° 10' S. Many sea and landmarks bear names of early explorers. Bellingshausen (Russia) discovered Peter I and Alexander I Islands, 1819-21. Nathaniel Palmer (U.S.) discovered Palmer Peninsula, 60° W, 1820, without realizing that this was a continent. James Weddell (Britain) found Weddell Sea, 74° 15' S, 1823.

First to announce existence of the continent of Antarctica was Charles Wilkes (U.S.), who followed the coast for 1,500 mi., 1840. Adelie Coast, 140° E, was found by Dumont d'Urville (France), 1840. Ross Ice Shelf was found by James Clark Ross (Britain), 1841-42.

1895 — Leonard Kristensen (Norway) landed a party on the coast of Victoria Land. They were the first ashore on the main continental mass. C.E. Borchgrevink, a member of that party, returned in 1899 with a British expedition, first to winter on Antarctica.

1902-04 — Robert F. Scott (Britain) discovered Edward VII Peninsula. He reached 82° 17' S, 146° 33' E from McMurdo Sound.

1908-09 — Ernest Shackleton (Britain) introduced the use of Manchurian ponies in Antarctic sledging. He reached 88° 23' S, discovering a route on to the plateau by way of the Beardmore Glacier and pioneering the way to the pole.

Discovery of South Pole

1911 — Roald Amundsen (Norway) with 4 men and dog teams reached the pole Dec. 14.

1912 — Capt. Scott reached the pole from Ross Island Jan. 18, with 4 companions. They found Amundsen's tent. None of Scott's party survived. They were found Nov. 12.

1928 — First man to use an airplane over Antarctica was Hubert Wilkins (Britain).

1929 — Richard E. Byrd (U.S.) established Little America on Bay of Whales. On 1,600-mi. airplane flight begun Nov. 28 he crossed South Pole Nov. 29 with 3 others.

1934-35 — Byrd led 2d expedition to Little America, explored 450,000 sq. mi., wintered alone at weather station, 80° 08′ S.

1934-37 — John Rymill led British Graham Land expedition; discovered that Palmer Peninsula is part of Antarctic mainland.

1935 — Lincoln Ellsworth (U.S.) flew south along Palmer Peninsula's east coast, then crossed continent to Little America, making 4 landings on unprepared terrain in bad weather.

1939-41 — U.S. Antarctic Service built West Base on Ross Ice Shelf under Paul Siple, and East Base on Palmer Peninsula under Richard Black. U.S. Navy plane flights discovered about 150,000 sq. miles of new land.

1940 — Byrd charted most of coast between Ross Sea and Palmer Peninsula.

1946-47 — U.S. Navy undertook Operation High-jump under Byrd. Expedition included 13 ships and 4,000 men. Airplanes photomapped coastline and penetrated beyond pole.

1946-48 — Ronne Antarctic Research Expedition, Comdr. Finn Ronne, USNR, determined the Antarctic to be only one continent with no strait between Weddell Sea and Ross Sea; discovered 250,000 sq. miles of land by flights to 79° S Lat., and made 14,000 aerial photographs over 450,000 sq. miles of land. Mrs. Ronne and Mrs. H. Darlington were the first women to winter on Antarctica.

1955-57 — U.S. Navy's Operation Deep Freeze led by Adm. Byrd. Supporting U.S. scientific efforts for the International Geophysical Year, the operation was commanded by Rear Adm. George Dufek. It established 5 coastal stations fronting the Indian, Pacific, and Atlantic oceans and also 3 interior stations; explored more than 1,000,000 sq. miles in Wilkes Land.

1957-58 — During the International Geophysical year, July, 1957, through Dec. 1958, scientists from 12 countries conducted ambitious programs of Antarctic research. A network of some 60 stations on the continent and sub-Arctic islands studied oceanography, glaciology, meteorology, seismology, geomagnetism, the ionosphere, cosmic rays, aurora, and airglow.

Dr. V.E. Fuchs led a 12-man Trans-Antarctic Expedition on the first land crossing of Antarctica. Starting from the Weddell Sea, they reached Scott Station Mar. 2, 1958, after traveling 2,158 miles in 98 days.

1958 — A group of 5 U.S. scientists led by Edward C. Thiel, seismologist, moving by tractor from Ellsworth Station on Weddell Sea, identified a huge mountain range, 5,000 ft. above the ice sheet and 9,000 ft. above sea level. The range, originally seen by a Navy plane, was named the Dufek Massif, for Rear Adm. George Dufek.

1959 — Twelve nations — Argentina, Australia, Belgium, Chile, France, Japan, New Zealand, South Africa, the Soviet Union, the United Kingdom, and the U.S. — signed a treaty suspending any territorial claims for 30 years and reserving the continent for research.

1961-62 — Scientists discovered a trough, the Bentley Trench, running from Ross Ice Shelf, Pacific, into Marie Byrd Land, around the end of the Ellsworth Mtns., toward the Weddell Sea.

1962 — First nuclear power plant began operation at McMurdo Sound.

1963 — On Feb. 22 a U.S. plane made the longest nonstop flight ever made in the S. Pole area, covering 3,600 miles in 10 hours. The flight was from McMurdo Station south past the geographical S. Pole to Shackleton Mtns., southeast to the "Area of Inaccessibility" and back to McMurdo Station.

1964 — A British survey team was landed by helicopter on Cook Island, the first recorded visit since its discovery in 1775.

1964 — New Zealanders completed one of the last and most important surveys when they mapped the mountain area from Cape Adare west some 400 miles to Pennell Glacier.

1989 — Two Americans, Victoria Murden and Shirley Metz, became the first women to reach the South Pole overland when they arrived with 9 others on Jan. 17, 1989. The 51-day trek on skis covered 740 miles.

Volcanoes

Source: Global Volcanism Network, Smithsonian Institution

More than 75 per cent of the world's 850 active volcanoes lie within the "Ring of Fire," a zone running along the west coast of the Americas from Chile to Alaska and down the east coast of Asia from Siberia to New Zealand. Twenty per cent of these volcanoes are located in Indonesia. Other prominent groupings are located in Japan, the Aleutian Islands, and Central America. Almost all active regions are found at the boundaries of the large moving plates which comprise the earth's surface. The "Ring of Fire" marks the boundary between the plates underlying the Pacific Ocean and those underlying the surrounding continents. Other active regions, such as the Mediterranean Sea and Iceland, are located on plate boundaries.

Major Historical Eruptions

Approximately 7,000 years ago, Mazama, a 9,900-feet-high volcano in southern Oregon, erupted violently, ejecting ash and lava. The ash spread over the entire northwestern United States and as far away as Saskatchewan, Canada. During the eruption, the top of the mountain collapsed, leaving a caldera 6 miles across and about a half mile deep, which filled with rain water to form what is now called Crater Lake.

In 79 A.D., Vesuvio, or Vesuvius, a 4,190 feet volcano overlooking Naples Bay became active after several centuries of quiescence. On Aug. 24 of that year, a heated mud and ash flow swept down the mountain engulfing the cities of Pompeii, Herculaneum, and Stabiae with debris over 60 feet deep. About 10 percent of the population of the 3 towns was killed.

The largest eruptions in recent centuries have been in Indonesia. In 1883, an eruption similar to the Mazama eruption occurred on the island of Krakatau. On August 27, the 2,640-feet-high peak of the volcano collapsed to 1,000 feet below sea level, leaving only a small portion of the island standing above the sea. Ash from the eruption colored sunsets around the world for 2 years. A tsunami ("tidal wave") generated by the collapse killed 36,000 people in nearby Java and Sumatra and eventually reached England. A similar, but even more powerful, eruption had taken place 68 years earlier at Tambora volcano on the Indonesian island of Sumbawa.

Notable Active Volcanoes

Name, latest activity	Location	Feet	Name, latest activity	Location	Feet
Africa			**Antarctica**		
Cameroon (1982)	Cameroon	13,354	Erebus (1988)	Ross Island	12,450
Nyirangongo (1977)	Zaire	11,400	Big Ben (1960)	Heard Island	9,007
Nyamuragira (1988)	Zaire	10,028	Deception Island (1970)	South Shetland	
Karthala (1977)	Comoro Is.	8,000		Islands	1,890
Piton de la Fournaise (1990)	Reunion Is.	5,981			
Erta-Ale (1973)	Ethiopia	1,650		*(continued)*	

Name, latest activity	Location	Feet
Asia-Oceania		
Klyuchevskaya (1990)	USSR	15,584
Kerinci (1987)	Sumatra	12,467
Rindjani (1966)	Indonesia	12,224
Semeru (1989)	Java	12,060
Slamet (1988)	Java	11,247
Raung (1989)	Java	10,932
Agung (1964)	Bali	10,308
On-Take (1980)	Japan	10,049
Mayon (1988)	Philippines	9,991
Merapi (1988)	Java	9,551
Bezymianny (1986)	USSR	9,514
Marapi (1988)	Sumatra	9,485
Ruapehu (1990)	New Zealand	9,175
Asama (1988)	Japan	8,300
Niigata Yakeyama (1989)	Japan	8,111
Canlaon (1969)	Philippines	8,070
Yake Dake (1963)	Japan	8,064
Alaid (1972)	Kuril Is.	7,662
Ulawun (1990)	New Britain	7,532
Ngauruhoe (1975)	New Zealand	7,515
Chokai (1974)	Japan	7,300
Galunggung (1982)	Java	7,113
Amburombu (1969)	Indonesia	7,051
Azuma (1978)	Japan	6,700
Tangkuban Prahu (1967)	Java	6,637
Sangeang Api (1988)	Indonesia	6,351
Nasu (1977)	Japan	6,210
Tiatia (1973)	Kuril Islands	6,013
Manam (1990)	Papua New Guinea	6,000
Soputan (1989)	Indonesia	5,994
Siau (1976)	Indonesia	5,853
Kelud (1990)	Java	5,679
Batur (1968)	Bali	5,636
Kirisima (1982)	Japan	5,577
Bagana (1989)	Papua New Guinea	6,558
Keli Mutu (1968)	Indonesia	5,460
Akita Komaga take (1970)	Japan	5,449
Gamkonora (1981)	Indonesia	5,364
Aso (1990)	Japan	5,223
Lewotobi Laki-Laki (1968)	Indonesia	5,217
Lokon-Empung (1988)	Indonesia	5,187
Bulusan (1988)	Philippines	5,115
Sarycheva (1976)	Kuril Islands	4,960
Karkar (1981)	Papua New Guinea	4,920
Karymsky (1985)	USSR	4,869
Lopevi (1982)	New Hebrides	4,755
Ambrym (1979)	New Hebrides	4,376
Awu (1968)	Indonesia	4,350
Sakurajima (1990)	Japan	3,668
Langila (1990)	New Britain	3,586
Dukono (1971)	Indonesia	3,566
Suwanosezima (1989)	Japan	2,640
Oshima (1988)	Japan	2,550
Usu (1976)	Japan	2,400
Pagan (1988)	Mariana Is.	1,870
White Island (1989)	New Zealand	1,075
Taal (1988)	Philippines	984
Central America—Caribbean		
Acatenango (1972)	Guatemala	12,992
Fuego (1990)	Guatemala	12,582
Tacana (1988)	Guatemala	12,400
Santiaguito (Santa Maria) (1990)	Guatemala	12,362
Irazu (1988)	Costa Rica	11,260
Poas (1990)	Costa Rica	8,930

Name, latest activity	Location	Feet
Pacaya (1990)	Guatemala	8,346
Izalco (1966)	El Salvador	7,749
San Miguel (1986)	El Salvador	6,994
Rincon de la Vieja (1987)	Costa Rica	6,234
El Viejo (San Cristobal) (1987)	Nicaragua	5,840
Ometepe (Concepcion) (1986)	Nicaragua	5,106
Arenal (1990)	Costa Rica	5,092
Momotombo (1982)	Nicaragua	4,199
Soufriere (1979)	St. Vincent	4,048
Telica (1987)	Nicaragua	3,409
South America		
Guallatiri (1987)	Chile	19,882
Lascar (1990)	Chile	19,652
Cotopaxi (1975)	Ecuador	19,347
Tupungatito (1986)	Chile	18,504
Ruiz (1989)	Colombia	17,716
Sangay (1988)	Ecuador	17,159
Guagua Pichincha (1988)	Ecuador	15,696
Purace (1977)	Colombia	15,601
Galeras (1990)	Colombia	13,996
Llaima (1990)	Chile	10,239
Villarica (1984)	Chile	9,318
Hudson (1973)	Chile	8,580
Alcedo (1970)	Galapagos Is.	3,599
Mid-Pacific		
Mauna Loa (1987)	Hawaii	13,680
Kilauea (1990)	Hawaii	4,077
Mid-Atlantic Ridge		
Beerenberg (1985)	Jan Mayen Is.	7,470
Hekla (1981)	Iceland	4,892
Leirhnukur (1975)	Iceland	2,145
Krafla (1984)	Iceland	2,145
Surtsey (1967)	Iceland	568
Europe		
Etna (1990)	Italy	11,053
Stromboli (1989)	Italy	3,038
North America		
Colima (1988)	Mexico	14,003
Redoubt (1990)	Alaska	10,197
Iliamna (1978)	Alaska	10,016
Shishaldin (1987)	Aleutian Is.	9,387
Mt. St. Helens (1989)	Washington	8,300+
Pavlof (1988)	Aleutian Is.	8,261
Veniaminof (1987)	Alaska	8,225
El Chichon (1983)	Mexico	7,300
Katmai (1974)	Alaska	6,715
Makushin (1987)	Aleutian Is.	6,680
Pogromni (1964)	Aleutian Is.	6,568
Trident 1963	Alaska	6,010
Great Sitkin (1974)	Aleutian Is.	5,710
Cleveland (1987)	Aleutian Is.	5,675
Gareloi (1982)	Aleutian Is.	5,334
Korovin (1987)	Aleutian Is.	4,852
Akutan (1989)	Aleutian Is.	4,275
Kiska (1969)	Aleutian Is.	4,275
Augustine (1988)	Alaska	3,999
Okmok (1988)	Aleutian Is.	3,519
Seguam (1977)	Alaska	3,458

Notable Volcanic Eruptions

Date	Volcano	Deaths	Date	Volcano	Deaths
			Apr. 8, 1902	Santa Maria, Guatemala	1,000
79 A.D.	Mt. Vesuvius, Italy	16,000	May 8, 1902	Mt. Pelée, Martinique	30,000
1169	Mt. Etna, Sicily	15,000	1911	Mt. Taal, Philippines	1,400
1631	Mt. Vesuvius, Italy	4,000	1919	Mt. Kelud, Java	5,000
1669	Mt. Etna, Sicily	20,000	Jan. 18-21, 1951	Mt. Lamington, New Guinea	3,000
1772	Mt. Papandayan, Java	3,000	Apr. 26, 1966	Mt. Kelud, Java	1,000
1792	Mt. Unzen-Dake, Japan	10,400	May 18, 1980	Mt. St. Helens, U.S.	60
1815	Tamboro, Java	12,000	Nov. 13, 1985	Nevado del Ruiz, Colombia	22,940
Aug. 26-28, 1883	Krakatau, Indonesia	35,000	Aug. 24, 1986	NW Cameroon	1,700+

Mountains

Height of Mount Everest

Mt. Everest was considered to be 29,002 ft. tall when Edmund Hillary and Tenzing Norgay scaled it in 1953. This triangulation figure had been accepted since 1850. In 1954 the Surveyor General of the Republic of India set the height at 29,028 ft., plus or minus 10 ft. because of snow. The National Geographic Society accepts the new figure, but many mountaineering groups still use 29,002 ft.

In 1987, new calculations based on satellite measurements indicate that the Himalayan peak K-2 rose 29,064 feet above sea level and that Mt. Everest is 800 feet higher. The National Geographic Society has not accepted the revised figure.

United States, Canada, Mexico

Name	Place	Feet	Name	Place	Feet	Name	Place	Feet
McKinley	Alas	20,320	Alverstone	Alas-Yukon	14,565	Princeton	Col	14,197
Logan	Yukon	19,850	Browne Tower	Alas	14,530	Crestone Needle	Col	14,197
Citlaltepec (Orizaba)	Mexico	18,700	Whitney	Cal	14,494	Yale	Col	14,196
St. Elias	Alas-Yukon	18,008	Elbert	Col	14,433	Bross	Col	14,172
Popocatepetl	Mexico	17,887	Massive	Col	14,421	Kit Carson	Col	14,165
Foraker	Alas	17,400	Harvard	Col	14,420	Wrangell	Alas	14,163
Iztaccihuatl	Mexico	17,343	Rainier	Wash	14,410	Shasta	Cal	14,162
Lucania	Yukon	17,147	Williamson	Cal	14,375	Sill	Cal	14,162
King	Can	16,971	Blanca Peak	Col	14,345	El Diente	Col	14,159
Steele	Can	16,644	La Plata	Col	14,336	Maroon	Col	14,156
Bona	Alas	16,550	Uncompahgre	Col	14,309	Tabeguache	Col	14,155
Blackburn	Alas	16,390	Crestone	Col	14,294	Oxford	Col	14,153
Kennedy	Alas	16,286	Lincoln	Col	14,286	Sneffels	Col	14,150
Sanford	Alas	16,237	Grays Peak	Col	14,270	Point Success	Wash	14,150
South Buttress	Alas	15,885	Antero	Col	14,269	Democrat	Col	14,148
Wood	Yukon	15,885	Torreys	Col	14,267	Capitol	Col	14,130
Vancouver	Alas-Yukon	15,700	Castle	Col	14,265	Liberty Cap	Wash	14,112
Churchill	Alas	15,638	Quandary	Col	14,265	Pikes Peak	Col	14,110
Fairweather	Alas-Yukon	15,300	Evans	Col	14,264	Snowmass	Col	14,092
Zinantecatl (Toluca)	Mexico	15,016	Longs Peak	Col	14,256	Windom	Col	14,087
Hubbard	Alas-Yukon	15,015	McArthur	Yukon	14,253	Russell	Cal	14,086
Bear	Alas	14,831	Wilson	Col	14,246	Eolus	Col	14,084
Walsh	Yukon	14,780	White	Col	14,246	Columbia	Col	14,073
East Buttress	Alas	14,730	North Palisade	Cal	14,242	Augusta	Alas-Yukon	14,070
Matlalcueyetl	Mexico	14,636	Shavano	Col	14,229	Missouri	Col	14,067
Hunter	Alas	14,573	Belford	Col	14,197	Humboldt	Col	14,064

South America

Peak, country	Feet	Peak, country	Feet	Peak, country	Feet
Aconcagua, Argentina	22,834	Laudo, Argentina	20,997	Polieras, Argentina	20,456
Ojos del Salado, Arg.-Chile	22,572	Ancohuma, Bolivia	20,958	Pular, Chile	20,423
Bonete, Argentina	22,546	Ausangate, Peru	20,945	Chani, Argentina	20,341
Tupungato, Argentina-Chile	22,310	Toro, Argentina-Chile	20,932	Aucanquilcha, Chile	20,295
Pissis, Argentina	22,241	Illampu, Bolivia	20,873	Juncal, Argentina-Chile	20,276
Mercedario, Argentina	22,211	Tres Cruces, Argentina-Chile	20,853	Negro, Argentina	20,184
Huascaran, Peru	22,205	Huandoy, Peru	20,852	Quela, Argentina	20,128
Llullaillaco, Argentina-Chile	22,057	Parinacota, Bolivia-Chile	20,768	Condoriri, Bolivia	20,095
El Libertador, Argentina	22,047	Tortolas, Argentina-Chile	20,745	Palermo, Argentina	20,079
Cachi, Argentina	22,047	Ampato, Peru	20,702	Solimana, Peru	20,068
Yerupaja, Peru	21,709	Condor, Argentina	20,669	San Juan, Argentina-Chile	20,049
Galan, Argentina	21,654	Salcantay, Peru	20,574	Sierra Nevada, Arg.-Chile	20,023
El Muerto, Argentina-Chile	21,457	Chimborazo, Ecuador	20,561	Antofalla, Argentina	20,013
Sajama, Bolivia	21,391	Huancarhuas, Peru	20,531	Marmolejo, Argentina-Chile	20,013
Nacimiento, Argentina	21,302	Famatina, Argentina	20,505	Chachani, Peru	19,931
Illimani, Bolivia	21,201	Pumasillo, Peru	20,492	Licancabur, Argentina-Chile	19,425
Coropuna, Peru	21,083	Solo, Argentina	20,492		

The highest point in the West Indies is in the Dominican Republic, Pico Duarte (10,417 ft.)

Africa, Australia, and Oceania

Peak, country	Feet	Peak, country	Feet	Peak, country	Feet
Kilimanjaro, Tanzania	19,340	Meru, Tanzania	14,979	Toubkal, Morocco	13,661
Kenya, Kenya	17,058	Wilhelm, Papua New Guinea	14,793	Kinabalu, Malaysia	13,455
Margherita Pk., Uganda-Zaire	16,763	Karisimbi, Zaire-Rwanda	14,787	Kerinci, Sumatra	12,467
Jaja, New Guinea	16,500	Elgon, Kenya-Uganda	14,178	Cook, New Zealand	12,349
Trikora, New Guinea	15,585	Batu, Ethiopia	14,131	Teide, Canary Islands	12,198
Mandala, New Guinea	15,420	Guna, Ethiopia	13,881	Semeru, Java	12,060
Ras Dashan, Ethiopia	15,158	Gughe, Ethiopia	13,780	Kosciusko, Australia	7,310

Europe

Peak, country	Feet	Peak, country	Feet	Peak, country	Feet
Alps					
		Liskamm, It., Switz.	14,852	Nadelhorn, Switz.	14,196
Mont Blanc, Fr. It.	15,771	Weisshorn, Switz.	14,780	Grand Combin, Switz.	14,154
Monte Rosa (highest peak of group), Switz.	15,203	Taschhorn, Switz.	14,733	Lenzpitze, Switz.	14,088
		Matterhorn, It., Switz.	14,690	Finsteraarhorn, Switz.	14,022
Dom, Switz.	14,911	Dent Blanche, Switz.	14,293	Castor, Switz.	13,865

Peak, country	Feet
Zinalrothorn, Switz.	13,849
Hohberghorn, Switz.	13,842
Alphubel, Switz.	13,799
Rimpfischhorn, Switz.	13,776
Aletschorn, Switz.	13,763
Strahlhorn, Switz.	13,747
Dent D'Herens, Switz.	13,686
Breithorn, It., Switz.	13,665
Bishorn, Switz.	13,645
Jungfrau, Switz.	13,642
Ecrins, Fr.	13,461
Monch, Switz.	13,448
Pollux, Switz.	13,422
Schreckhorn, Switz.	13,379
Ober Gabelhorn, Switz.	13,330
Gran Paradiso, It.	13,323
Bernina, It., Switz.	13,284
Fiescherhorn, Switz.	13,283

Peak, county	Feet
Grunhorn, Switz.	13,266
Lauteraarhorn, Switz.	13,261
Durrenhorn, Switz.	13,238
Allalinhorn, Switz.	13,213
Weissmies, Switz.	13,199
Lagginhorn, Switz.	13,156
Zupo, Switz.	13,120
Fletschhorn, Switz.	13,110
Adlerhorn, Switz.	13,081
Gletscherhorn, Switz.	13,068
Schalihorn, Switz.	13,040
Scerscen, Switz.	13,028
Eiger, Switz.	13,025
Jagerhorn, Switz.	13,024
Rottalhorn, Switz.	13,022

Peak, country	Feet
Pyrenees	
Aneto, Sp.	11,168
Posets, Sp.	11,073
Perdido, Sp.	11,007
Vignemale, Fr., Sp.	10,820
Long, Sp.	10,479
Estats, Sp.	10,304
Montcalm, Sp.	10,105
Caucasus (Europe-Asia)	
El'brus, USSR	18,510
Shkara, USSR.	17,064
Dykh Tau, USSR	17,054
Kashtan Tau, USSR	16,877
Dzhangi Tau, USSR	16,565
Kazbek, USSR	16,558

Asia

Peak	Country	Feet
Everest	Nepal-Tibet.	29,028
K2 (Godwin Austen)	Kashmir.	28,250
Kanchenjunga	India-Nepal	28,208
Lhotse I (Everest)	Nepal-Tibet.	27,923
Makalu I	Nepal-Tibet.	27,824
Lhotse II (Everest)	Nepal-Tibet.	27,560
Dhaulagiri	Nepal	26,810
Manaslu I	Nepal	26,760
Cho Oyu.	Nepal-Tibet.	26,750
Nanga Parbat.	Kashmir.	26,660
Annapurna I.	Nepal	26,504
Gasherbrum	Kashmir.	26,470
Broad	Kashmir.	26,400
Gosainthan	Tibet.	26,287
Annapurna II	Nepal	26,041
Gyachung Kang	Nepal-Tibet.	25,910
Disteghil Sar	Kashmir.	25,868
Himalchuli.	Nepal.	25,801
Nuptse (Everest)	Nepal-Tibet.	25,726
Masherbrum	Kashmir.	25,660
Nanda Devi	India.	25,645
Rakaposhi.	Kashmir.	25,550
Kamet	India-Tibet.	25,447
Namcha Barwa.	Tibet.	25,445
Gurla Mandhata	Tibet.	25,355
Ulugh Muz Tagh	Sinkiang-Tibet.	25,340
Kungur.	Sinkiang.	25,325
Tirich Mir	Pakistan.	25,230
Makalu II.	Nepal-Tibet.	25,120
Minya Konka	China	24,900
Kula Gangri	Bhutan-Tibet	24,784
Changtzu (Everest)	Nepal-Tibet.	24,780
Muz Tagh Ata.	Sinkiang.	24,757
Skyang Kangri	Kashmir.	24,750
Communism Peak	USSR	24,590
Jongsang Peak.	India-Nepal	24,472
Pobedy Peak	Sinkiang-USSR.	24,406
Sia Kangri	Kashmir.	24,350
Haramosh Peak	Pakistan.	24,270
Istoro Nal	Pakistan.	24,240
Tent Peak	India-Nepal.	24,165
Chomo Lhari	Bhutan-Tibet	24,040
Chamlang.	Nepal	24,012
Kabru	India-Nepal.	24,002
Alung Gangri	Tibet.	24,000
Baltoro Kangri	Kashmir.	23,990
Mussu Shan.	Sinkiang.	23,890
Mana	India.	23,860
Baruntse.	Nepal	23,688
Nepal Peak	India-Nepal.	23,500
Amne Machin.	China	23,490
Gauri Sankar	Nepal-Tibet.	23,440
Badrinath	India.	23,420
Nunkun	Kashmir.	23,410
Lenina Peak.	USSR	23,405
Pyramid	India-Nepal.	23,400
Api	Nepal.	23,399
Pauhunri.	India-Tibet	23,385
Trisul.	India.	23,360
Kangto.	India-Tibet	23,260
Nyenchhen Thanglha	Tibet.	23,255
Trisuli	India.	23,210
Pumori.	Nepal-Tibet.	23,190
Dunagiri	India.	23,184
Lombo Kangra	Tibet.	23,165
Saipal	Nepal.	23,100
Macha Pucchare.	Nepal	22,958
Numbar	Nepal.	22,817
Kanjiroba	Nepal	22,580
Ama Dablam	Nepal.	22,350
Cho Polu	Nepal	22,093
Lingtren	Nepal-Tibet.	21,972
Khumbutse	Nepal-Tibet.	21,785
Hlako Gangri	Tibet.	21,266
Mt. Grosvenor	China	21,190
Thagchhab Gangri	Tibet.	20,970
Damavand	Iran	18,606
Ararat	Turkey	16,804

Antarctica

Peak	Feet
Vinson Massif	16,864
Tyree.	16,290
Shinn.	15,750
Gardner	15,375
Epperly	15,100
Kirkpatrick	14,855
Elizabeth.	14,698
Markham	14,290
Bell	14,117
Mackellar	14,098
Anderson	13,957
Bentley.	13,934
Kaplan	13,878

Peak	Feet
Andrew Jackson	13,750
Sidley	13,720
Ostenso	13,710
Minto.	13,668
Miller.	13,650
Long Gables	13,620
Dickerson	13,517
Giovinetto	13,412
Wade	13,400
Fisher	13,386
Fridtjof Nansen	13,350
Wexler.	13,202
Lister.	13,200

Peak	Feet
Shear	13,100
Odishaw	13,008
Donaldson	12,894
Ray	12,808
Sellery	12,779
Waterman	12,730
Anne	12,703
Press	12,566
Falla.	12,549
Rucker	12,520
Goldthwait	12,510
Morris.	12,500
Erebus	12,450

Peak	Feet
Campbell	12,434
Don Pedro Christophersen	12,355
Lysaght	12,326
Huggins	12,247
Sabine	12,200
Astor	12,175
Mohl	12,172
Frankes	12,064
Jones.	12,040
Gjelsvik	12,008
Coman.	12,000

Ocean Areas and Average Depths

Four major bodies of water are recognized by geographers and mapmakers. They are: the Pacific, Atlantic, Indian, and Arctic oceans. The Atlantic and Pacific oceans are considered divided at the equator into the No. and So. Atlantic; the No. and So. Pacific. The Arctic Ocean is the name for waters north of the continental land masses in the region of the Arctic Circle.

	Sq. miles	Avg. depth in feet		Sq. miles	Avg. depth in feet
Pacific Ocean	64,186,300	12,925	Hudson Bay	281,900	305
Atlantic Ocean.	33,420,000	11,730	East China Sea	256,600	620
Indian Ocean.	28,350,500	12,598	Andaman Sea	218,100	3,667
Arctic Ocean.	5,105,700	3,407	Black Sea	196,100	3,906
South China Sea	1,148,500	4,802	Red Sea	174,900	1,764
Caribbean Sea	971,400	8,448	North Sea	164,900	308
Mediterranean Sea	969,100	4,926	Baltic Sea	147,500	180
Bering Sea.	873,000	4,893	Yellow Sea.	113,500	121
Gulf of Mexico	582,100	5,297	Persian Gulf	88,800	328
Sea of Okhotsk	537,500	3,192	Gulf of California	59,100	2,375
Sea of Japan	391,100	5,468			

How Deep Is the Ocean?

Principal ocean depths. Source: Defense Mapping Agency Hydrographic/Topographic Center

Name of area	Location		Meters	Depth Fathoms	Feet
Pacific Ocean					
Mariana Trench	11°22'N	142°36'E	10,924	5,973	35,840
Tonga Trench	23°16'S	174°44'W	10,800	5,906	35,433
Philippine Trench	10°38'N	126°36'E	10,057	5,499	32,995
Kermadec Trench	31°53'S	177°21'W	10,047	5,494	32,963
Bonin Trench	24°30'N	143°24'E	9,994	5,464	32,788
Kuril Trench	44°15'N	150°34'E	9,750	5,331	31,988
Izu Trench	31°05'N	142°10'E	9,695	5,301	31,808
New Britain Trench	06°19'S	153°45'E	8,940	4,888	29,331
Yap Trench	08°33'N	138°02'E	8,527	4,663	27,976
Japan Trench	36°08'N	142°43'E	8,412	4,600	27,599
Peru-Chile Trench	23°18'S	71°14'W	8,064	4,409	26,457
Palau Trench	07°52'N	134°56'E	8,054	4,404	26,424
Aleutian Trench	50°51'N	177°11'E	7,679	4,199	25,194
New Hebrides Trench	20°36'S	168°37'E	7,570	4,139	24,836
North Ryukyu Trench	24°00'N	126°48'E	7,181	3,927	23,560
Mid. America Trench	14°02'N	93°39'W	6,662	3,643	21,857
Atlantic Ocean					
Puerto Rico Trench	19°55'N	65°27'W	8,605	4,705	28,232
So. Sandwich Trench	55°42'S	25°56'E	8,325	4,552	27,313
Romanche Gap	0°13'S	18°26'W	7,728	4,226	25,354
Cayman Trench	19°12'N	80°00'W	7,535	4,120	24,721
Brazil Basin	09°10'S	23°02'W	6,119	3,346	20,076
Indian Ocean					
Java Trench	10°19'S	109°58'E	7,125	3,896	23,376
Ob' Trench	09°45'S	67°18'E	6,874	3,759	22,553
Diamantina Trench	35°50'S	105°14'E	6,602	3,610	21,660
Verna Trench	09°08'S	67°15'E	6,402	3,501	21,004
Agulhas Basin	45°20'S	26°50'E	6,195	3,387	20,325
Arctic Ocean					
Eurasia Basin	82°23'N	19°31'E	5,450	2,980	17,881
Mediterranean Sea					
Ionian Basin	36°32'N	21°06'E	5,150	2,816	16,896

Note: Deeper depths have been reported in some of the above areas. However, they are not official unless confirmed by research vessels.

Principal World Rivers

Source: U.S. Geological Survey (length in miles)

River	Outflow	Lgth	River	Outflow	Lgth	River	Outflow	Lgth
Albany	James Bay	610	Indus	Arabian Sea	1,800	Red River of N.	Lake Winnipeg	545
Amazon	Atlantic Ocean	4,000	Irrawaddy	Bay of Bengal	1,337	Rhine	North Sea	820
Amu	Aral Sea	1,578	Japura	Amazon River	1,750	Rhone	Gulf of Lions	505
Amur	Tatar Strait	2,744	Jordan	Dead Sea	200	Rio de la Plata	Atlantic Ocean	150
Angara	Yenisey River	1,151	Kootenay	Columbia River	485	Rio Grande	Gulf of Mexico	1,900
Arkansas	Mississippi	1,459	Lena	Laptev Sea	2,734	Rio Roosevelt	Aripuana	400
Back	Arctic Ocean	605	Loire	Bay of Biscay	634	Saguenay	St. Lawrence R.	434
Brahmaputra	Bay of Bengal	1,800	Mackenzie	Arctic Ocean	2,635	St. John	Bay of Fundy	418
Bug, Southern	Dnieper River	532	Madeira	Amazon River	2,013	St. Lawrence	Gulf of St. Law.	800
Bug, Western	Wisla River	481	Magdalena	Caribbean Sea	956	Salween	Andaman Sea	1,500
Canadian	Arkansas River	906	Marne	Seine River	326	Sao Francisco	Atlantic Ocean	1,988
Chang Jiang	E. China Sea	3,964	Mekong	S. China Sea	2,600	Saskatchewan	Lake Winnipeg	1,205
Churchill, Man.	Hudson Bay	1,000	Meuse	North Sea	580	Seine	English Chan.	496
Churchill, Que.	Atlantic Ocean	532	Mississippi	Gulf of Mexico	2,340	Shannon	Atlantic Ocean	230
Colorado	Gulf of Calif.	1,450	Missouri	Mississippi	2,540	Snake	Columbia River	1,038
Columbia	Pacific Ocean	1,243	Murray-Darling	Indian Ocean	2,310	Sungari	Amur River	1,150
Congo	Atlantic Ocean	2,718	Negro	Amazon	1,400	Syr	Aral Sea	1,370
Danube	Black Sea	1,776	Nelson	Hudson Bay	410	Tajo, Tagus	Atlantic Ocean	626
Dnieper	Black Sea	1,420	Niger	Gulf of Guinea	2,590	Tennessee	Ohio River	652
Dniester	Black Sea	877	Nile	Mediterranean	4,160	Thames	North Sea	236
Don	Sea of Azov	1,224	Ob-Irtysh	Gulf of Ob	3,362	Tiber	Tyrrhenian Sea	252
Drava	Danube River	447	Oder	Baltic Sea	567	Tigris	Shatt al-Arab	1,180
Dvina, North	White Sea	824	Ohio	Mississippi	1,310	Tisza	Danube River	600
Dvina, West	Gulf of Riga	634	Orange	Atlantic Ocean	1,300	Tocantins	Para River	1,677
Ebro	Mediterranean	565	Orinoco	Atantic Ocean	1,600	Ural	Caspian Sea	1,575
Elbe	North Sea	724	Ottawa	St. Lawrence R.	790	Uruguay	Rio de la Plata	1,000
Euphrates	Shatt al-Arab	1,700	Paraguay	Parana River	1,584	Volga	Caspian Sea	2,194
Fraser	Str. of Georgia	850	Parana	Rio de la Plata	2,485	Weser	North Sea	454
Gambia	Atlantic Ocean	700	Peace	Slave River	1,210	Wisla	Bay of Danzig.	675
Ganges	Bay of Bengal	1,560	Pilcomayo	Paraguay River	1,000	Yellow (See Huang)		
Garonne	Bay of Biscay	357	Po	Adriatic Sea	405	Yenisey	Kara Sea	2,543
Hsi	S. China Sea	1,200	Purus	Amazon River	2,100	Yukon	Bering Sea	1,979
Huang	Yellow Sea	2,903	Red	Mississippi	1,290	Zambezi	Indian Ocean	1,700

Major Rivers in North America

Source: U.S. Geological Survey

River	Source or Upper Limit of Length	Outflow	Miles
Alabama	Gilmer County, Ga.	Mobile River	729
Albany	Lake St. Joseph, Ontario	James Bay	610
Allegheny	Potter County, Pa.	Ohio River	325
Altamaha-Ocmulgee	Junction of Yellow and South Rivers, Newton County, Ga.	Atlantic Ocean	392
Apalachicola-Chattahoochee	Towns County, Ga.	Gulf of Mexico	524
Arkansas	Lake County, Col.	Mississippi River	1,459
Assiniboine	Eastern Saskatchewan	Red River	450
Attawapiskat	Attawapiskat, Ontario	James Bay	465
Back (N.W.T.)	Contwoyto Lake	Chantrey Inlet	605
Big Black (Miss.)	Webster County, Miss.	Mississippi River	330
Brazos	Junction of Salt and Double Mountain Forks, Stonewall County, Tex.	Gulf of Mexico	923
Canadian	Las Animas County, Col.	Arkansas River	906
Cedar (Iowa)	Dodge County, Minn.	Iowa River	329
Cheyenne	Junction of Antelope Creek and Dry Fork, Converse County, Wyo.	Missouri River	290
Churchill	Methy Lake, Saskatchewan	Hudson Bay	1,000
Cimarron	Colfax County, N.M.	Arkansas River	600
Colorado (Ariz.)	Rocky Mountain National Park, Col. (90 miles in Mexico)	Gulf of Cal.	1,450
Colorado (Texas)	West Texas	Matagorda Bay	862
Columbia	Columbia Lake, British Columbia	Pacific Ocean, bet. Ore. and Wash.	1,243
Columbia, Upper	Columbia Lake, British Columbia	To mouth of Snake River	890
Connecticut	Third Connecticut Lake, N.H.	L.I. Sound, Conn.	407
Coppermine (N.W.T.)	Lac de Gras	Coronation Gulf (Arctic Ocean)	525
Cumberland	Letcher County, Ky.	Ohio River	720
Delaware	Schoharie County, N.Y.	Liston Point, Delaware Bay	390
Fraser	Near Mount Robson (on Continental Divide)	Strait of Georgia	850
Gila	Catron County, N.M.	Colorado River	649
Green (Ut.-Wyo.)	Junction of Wells and Trail Creeks, Sublette County, Wyo.	Colorado River	730
Hamilton (Lab.)	Lake Ashuanipi	Atlantic Ocean	532
Hudson	Henderson Lake, Essex County, N.Y.	Upper N.Y. Bay	306
Illinois	St. Joseph County, Ind.	Mississippi River	420
James (N.D.-S.D.)	Wells County, N.D.	Missouri River	710
James (Va.)	Junction of Jackson and Cowpasture Rivers, Botetourt County, Va.	Hampton Roads	340
Kanawha-New	Junction of North and South Forks of New River, N.C.	Ohio River	352
Kentucky	Junction of North and Middle Forks, Lee County, Ky.	Ohio River	259
Klamath	Lake Ewauna, Klamath Falls, Ore.	Pacific Ocean	250
Koyukuk	Endicott Mountains, Alaska	Yukon River	470
Kuskokwim	Alaska Range	Kuskokwim Bay	724
Liard	Southern Yukon, Alaska	Mackenzie River	693
Little Missouri	Crook County, Wyo.	Missouri River	560
Mackenzie	Great Slave Lake, N.W.T.	Arctic Ocean	2,635
Milk	Junction of North and South Forks, Alberta	Missouri River	625
Minnesota	Big Stone Lake, Minn.	Mississippi River	332
Mississippi	Lake Itasca, Minn.	Mouth of Southwest Pass	2,340
Mississippi, Upper	Lake Itasca, Minn.	To mouth of Missouri River	1,171
Mississippi-Missouri-Red Rock	Source of Red Rock, Beaverhead Co., Mon.	Mouth of Southwest Pass	3,710
Missouri	Junction of Jefferson, Madison, and Gallatin rivers, Madison County, Mon.	Mississippi River	2,315
Missouri-Red Rock	Source of Red Rock, Beaverhead Co., Mon.	Mississippi River	2,540
Mobile-Alabama-Coosa	Gilmer County, Ga.	Mobile Bay	774
Nelson (Manitoba)	Lake Winnipeg	Hudson Bay	410
Neosho	Morris County, Kan.	Arkansas River, Okla.	460
Niobrara	Niobrara County, Wyo.	Missouri River, Neb.	431
North Canadian	Union County, N.M.	Canadian River, Okla.	800
North Platte	Junction of Grizzly and Little Grizzly creeks, Jackson County, Col.	Platte River, Neb.	618
Ohio	Junction of Allegheny and Monongahela rivers, Pittsburgh, Pa.	Mississippi River	981
Ohio-Allegheny	Potter County, Pa.	Mississippi River	1,306
Osage	East-central Kansas	Missouri River	500
Ottawa	Lake Capimitchigama	St. Lawrence River	790
Ouachita	Polk County, Ark.	Red River	605
Peace	Stikine Mountains, B.C.	Slave River	1,210
Pearl	Neshoba County, Miss.	Gulf of Mexico	411
Pecos	Mora County, N.M.	Rio Grande	926
Pee Dee-Yadkin	Watauga County, N.C.	Winyah Bay	435
Pend Oreille-Clark Fork	Near Butte, Mon.	Columbia River	531
Platte	Junction of North and South Platte Rivers, Neb.	Missouri River	310
Porcupine	Ogilvie Mountains, Alaska	Yukon River, Alaska	569
Potomac	Garrett County, Md.	Chesapeake Bay	383
Powder	Junction of South and Middle Forks, Wyo.	Yellowstone River	375
Red (Okla.-Tex.-La.)	Curry County, N.M.	Mississippi River	1,290
Red River of the North	Junction of Otter Tail and Bois de Sioux Rivers, Wilkin County, Minn.	Lake Winnipeg	545
Republican	Junction of North Fork and Arikaree River, Neb.	Kansas River	445
Rio Grande	San Juan County, Col.	Gulf of Mexico	1,900

River	Source or Upper Limit of Length	Outflow	Miles
Roanoke	Junction of North and South Forks, Montgomery County, Va.	Albemarle Sound	380
Rock (Ill.-Wis.)	Dodge County, Wis.	Mississippi River	300
Sabine	Junction of South and Caddo Forks, Hunt County, Tex.	Sabine Lake	380
Sacramento	Siskiyou County, Cal.	Suisun Bay	377
St. Francis	Iron County, Mo.	Mississippi River	425
St. Lawrence	Lake Ontario	Gulf of St. Lawrence (Atlantic Ocean)	800
Salmon (Idaho)	Custer County, Ida.	Snake River	420
San Joaquin	Junction of South and Middle Forks, Madera County, Cal.	Suisun Bay	350
San Juan	Silver Lake, Archuleta County, Col.	Colorado River	360
Santee-Wateree-Catawba	McDowell County, N.C.	Atlantic Ocean	538
Saskatchewan, North	Rocky Mountains	Saskatchewan R.	800
Saskatchewan, South	Rocky Mountains	Saskatchewan R.	865
Savannah	Junction of Seneca and Tugaloo rivers, Anderson County, S.C.	Atlantic Ocean, Ga.-S.C.	314
Severn (Ontario)	Sandy Lake	Hudson Bay	610
Smoky Hill	Cheyenne County, Col.	Kansas River, Kan.	540
Snake	Teton County, Wyo.	Columbia River, Wash.	1,038
South Platte	Junction of South and Middle Forks, Park County, Col.	Platte River	424
Susitna	Alaska Range	Cook Inlet	313
Susquehanna	Otsego Lake, Otsego County, N.Y.	Chesapeake Bay	444
Tallahatchie	Tippah County, Miss.	Yazoo River	301
Tanana	Wrangell Mountains, Alaska	Yukon River	659
Tennessee	Junction of French Broad and Holston Rivers	Ohio River	652
Tennessee-French Broad	Transylvania County, N.C.	Ohio River	883
Tombigbee	Prentiss County, Miss.	Mobile River	525
Trinity	North of Dallas, Tex.	Galveston Bay	360
Wabash	Darke County, Oh.	Ohio River	512
Washita	Hemphill County, Tex.	Red River, Okla.	500
White (Ark.-Mo.)	Madison County, Ark.	Mississippi River	722
Willamette	Douglas County, Ore.	Columbia River	309
Wind-Bighorn	Junction of Wind and Little Wind Rivers, Fremont Co., Wyo. (Source of Wind R. is Togwotee Pass, Teton Co., Wyo.)	Yellowstone River	336
Wisconsin	Lac Vieux Desert, Vilas County, Wis.	Mississippi River	430
Yellowstone	Park County, Wyo.	Missouri River	692
Yukon	Coast Mountains of British Columbia	Bering Sea	1,979

Lakes of the World

Source: U.S. Geological Survey

A lake is a body of water surrounded by land. Although some lakes are called seas, they are lakes by definition. The Caspian Sea is bounded by the Soviet Union and Iran and is fed by eight rivers.

Name	Continent	Area sq. mi.	Length mi.	Depth feet	Elev. feet
Caspian Sea	Asia-Europe	143,244	760	3,363	−92
Superior	North America	31,700	350	1,330	600
Victoria	Africa	26,828	250	270	3,720
Aral Sea	Asia	24,904	280	220	174
Huron	North America	23,000	206	750	579
Michigan	North America	22,300	307	923	579
Tanganyika	Africa	12,700	420	4,823	2,534
Baykal	Asia	12,162	395	5,315	1,493
Great Bear	North America	12,096	192	1,463	512
Nyasa	Africa	11,150	360	2,280	1,550
Great Slave	North America	11,031	298	2,015	513
Erie	North America	9,910	241	210	570
Winnipeg	North America	9,417	266	60	713
Ontario	North America	7,550	193	802	245
Balkhash	Asia	7,115	376	85	1,115
Ladoga	Europe	6,835	124	738	13
Chad	Africa	6,300	175	24	787
Maracaibo	South America	5,217	133	115	Sea level
Onega	Europe	3,710	145	328	108
Eyre	Australia	3,600	90	4	−52
Volta	Africa	3,276	250	.....	.....
Titicaca	South America	3,200	122	922	12,500
Nicaragua	North America	3,100	102	230	102
Athabasca	North America	3,064	208	407	700
Reindeer	North America	2,568	143	720	1,106
Rudolf	Africa	2,473	154	240	1,230
Issyk Kul	Asia	2,355	115	2,303	5,279
Torrens	Australia	2,230	130	.....	92
Vanern	Europe	2,156	91	328	144
Nettilling	North America	2,140	67	.....	95
Winnipegosis	North America	2,075	141	38	830
Albert	Africa	2,075	100	168	2,030
Kariba	Africa	2,050	175	390	1,590
Nipigon	North America	1,872	72	540	1,050
Gairdner	Australia	1,840	90	.....	112
Urmia	Asia	1,815	90	49	4,180
Manitoba	North America	1,799	140	12	813

Large U.S. Lakes

Source: U.S. Geological Survey

Natural U.S. lakes (excluding the Great Lakes) with areas of 100 sq. mi.

Lake	State	Area (sq. mi.)	Lake	State	Area (sq. mi.)
Lake of the Woods	Minn., Ontario, Manitoba	1,697	Naknek	Alas.	242
Great Salt[1]	Ut.	1,361[2]	Winnebago	Wis.	215
Iliamna	Alas.	1,000	Mille Lacs	Minn.	207
Okeechobee	Fla.	700	Flathead	Mon.	197
Pontchartrain[1]	La.	625	Tahoe	Cal., Nev.	193
Becharof	Alas.	458	Leech	Minn.	176
Red Lake (upper and lower)	Minn.	451	Pyramid[1]	Nev.	168[2]
Champlain	N.Y., Vt., Quebec	435	Pend Oreille	Ida.	148
St. Clair	Mich., Ontario	432	Ugashik (upper and lower)	Alas.	147
Salton Sea[1]	Cal.	374[2]	Upper Klamath	Ore.	142
Rainy	Minn., Ontario	360	Utah	Ut.	140
Teshekpuk	Alas.	315	Bear (including Mud Lake)	Ida., Ut.	136

(1) Salty. (2) Variable.

The Great Lakes

Source: National Ocean Service, U.S. Commerce Department

The Great Lakes form the largest body of fresh water in the world and with their connecting waterways are the largest inland water transportation unit. Draining the great North Central basin of the U.S., they enable shipping to reach the Atlantic via their outlet, the St. Lawrence R., and also the Gulf of Mexico via the Illinois Waterway, from Lake Michigan to the Mississippi R. A third outlet connects with the Hudson R. and thence the Atlantic via the N. Y. State Barge Canal System. Traffic on the Illinois Waterway and the N.Y. State Barge Canal System is limited to recreational boating and small shipping vessels.

Only one of the lakes, Lake Michigan, is wholly in the United States; the others are shared with Canada. Ships move from the shores of Lake Superior to Whitefish Bay at the east end of the lake, thence through the Soo (Sault Ste. Marie) locks, through the St. Mary's River and into Lake Huron. To reach Gary, and Port of Indiana and South Chicago, Ill., ships move west from Lake Huron to Lake Michigan through the Straits of Mackinac.

Lake Superior is 600 feet above mean water level at Point-au-Pere, Quebec, on the International Great Lakes Datum (1955). From Duluth, Minn., to the eastern end of Lake Ontario is 1,156 mi.

	Superior	Michigan	Huron	Erie	Ontario
Length in miles	350	307	206	241	193
Breadth in miles	160	118	183	57	53
Deepest soundings in feet	1,330	923	750	210	802
Volume of water in cubic miles	2,900	1,180	850	116	393
Area (sq. miles) water surface—U.S.	20,600	22,300	9,100	4,980	3,560
Canada	11,100	.....	13,900	4,930	3,990
Area (sq. miles) entire drainage basin—U.S.	16,900	45,600	16,200	18,000	15,200
Canada	32,400	.....	35,500	4,720	12,100
Total Area (sq. miles) U.S. and Canada	81,000	67,900	74,700	32,630	34,850
Mean surface above mean water level at Point-au-Pere, Quebec, aver. level in feet (1900-1988)	600.61	578.34	578.34	570.53	244.74
Latitude, North	46° 25'	41° 37'	43° 00'	41° 23'	43° 11'
	49° 00'	46° 06'	46° 17'	42° 52'	44° 15'
Longitude, West	84° 22'	84° 45'	79° 43'	78° 51'	76° 03'
	92° 06'	88° 02'	84° 45'	83° 29'	79° 53'
National boundary line in miles	282.8	None	260.8	251.5	174.6
United States shore line (mainland only) miles	863	1,400	580	431	300

Famous Waterfalls

Source: National Geographic Society, Washington, D.C.

The earth has thousands of waterfalls, some of considerable magnitude. Their importance is determined not only by height but volume of flow, steadiness of flow, crest width, whether the water drops sheerly or over a sloping surface, and in one leap or a succession of leaps. A series of low falls flowing over a considerable distance is known as a cascade.

Sete Quedas or Guaira is the world's greatest waterfall when its mean annual flow (estimated at 470,000 cubic feet per second) is combined with height. A greater volume of water passes over Boyoma Falls (Stanley Falls), though not one of its seven cataracts, spread over nearly 60 miles of the Congo River, exceeds 10 feet.

Estimated mean annual flow, in cubic feet per second, of other major waterfalls are: Niagara, 212,200; Paulo Afonso, 100,000; Urubupunga, 97,000; Iguazu, 61,000; Patos-Maribondo, 53,000; Victoria, 35,400; and Kaieteur, 23,400.

Height = total drop in feet in one or more leaps. † = falls of more than one leap; * = falls that diminish greatly seasonally; ** = falls that reduce to a trickle or are dry for part of each year. If river names not shown, they are same as the falls. R. = river; L. = lake; (C) = cascade type.

Name and location	Ht.	Name and location	Ht.	Name and location	Ht.
Africa		**Zimbabwe-Zambia**		**Asia**	
		*Victoria, Zambezi R.	343		
		South Africa			
Angola		*Augrabies, Orange R.	480		
Duque de Braganca,		Howick, Umgeni R.	364	India—*Cauvery	330
Lucala R.	344	† Tugela	2,014	*Gokak, Ghataprabha R.	170
Ruacana, Cuene R.	406	Highest fall	597	*Jog (Gersoppa), Sharavathi R.	830
Ethiopia		**Tanzania-Zambia**		**Japan**	
Fincha	508	*Kalambo	726	*Kegon, Daiya R.	330
Tesissat, Blue Nile R.	140	**Uganda**		**Laos**	
Lesotho		Kabalega (Murchison) Victoria		Khon Cataracts,	
*Maletsunyane	630	Nile R.	130	Mekong R. (C)	70

Name and location	Ht.
Australasia	
Australia	
New South Wales	
Wentworth.	614
Highest fall.	360
Wollomombi.	1,100
Queensland	
Coomera	210
Tully	885
† Wallaman, Stony Cr. . .	1,137
Highest fall.	937
New Zealand	
Bowen.	540
Helena.	890
Stirling.	505
† Sutherland, Arthur R.	1,904
Highest fall	815
Europe	
Austria—† Gastein	492
Highest fall	280
† *Golling, Schwarzbach R. . . .	250
† Krimml.	1,312
France—*Gavarnie	1,385
Great Britain—Scotland	
Glomach.	370
Wales	
Cain	150
Rhaiadr	240
Iceland—Detti	144
† Gull, Hvita R.	105
Italy—Frua, Toce R. (C).	470
Norway	
Mardalsfossen (Northern)	1,535
† Mardalsfossen (Southern). . . .	2,149
† **Skjeggedal, Nybuai R.	1,378
**Skykje.	984
Vetti, Morka-Koldedola R.	900
Voring, Bjoreio R.	597
Sweden	
† Handol.	427
† Tannforsen, Are R.	120
Switzerland	
† Diesbach	394
Giessbach	984
Handegg, Aare R.	150
Iffigen	120

Name and location	Ht.
Pissevache, Salanfe R.	213
† Reichenbach.	656
Rhine.	79
† Simmen.	459
Staubbach.	984
† Trummelbach.	1,312
North America	
Canada	
Alberta	
Panther, Nigel Cr.	600
British Columbia	
† Della.	1,443
† Takakkaw, Daly Glacier.	1,200
Northwest Territories	
Virginia, S. Nahanni R.	294
Quebec	
Montmorency.	274
Canada—United States	
Niagara: American.	182
Horseshoe.	173
United States	
California	
*Feather, Fall R.	640
Yosemite National Park	
*Bridalveil.	620
*Illilouette	370
*Nevada, Merced R.	594
**Ribbon.	1,612
**Silver Strand, Meadow Br. .	1,170
*Vernal, Merced R.	317
† **Yosemite	2,425
Yosemite (upper).	1,430
Yosemite (lower).	320
Yosemite (middle) (C). . . .	675
Colorado	
† Seven, South Cheyenne Cr. . .	300
Hawaii	
Akaka, Kolekole Str.	442
Idaho	
**Shoshone, Snake R.	212
Twin, Snake R.	120
Kentucky	
Cumberland.	68
Maryland	
*Great, Potomac R. (C)	71
Minnesota	
**Minnehaha.	53

Name and location	Ht.
New Jersey	
Passaic	70
New York	
*Taughannock	215
Oregon	
† Multnomah	620
Highest fall	542
Tennessee	
Fall Creek.	256
Washington	
Mt. Rainier Natl. Park	
Narada, Paradise R.	168
Sluiskin, Paradise R.	300
Palouse	197
**Snoqualmie.	268
Wisconsin	
*Big Manitou, Black R. (C).	165
Wyoming	
Yellowstone Natl. Pk. Tower. . . .	132
*Yellowstone (upper).	109
*Yellowstone (lower).	308
Mexico	
El Salto	218
**Juanacatlan, Santiago R.	72
South America	
Argentina-Brazil	
Iguazu.	230
Brazil	
Glass	1,325
Patos-Maribondo, Grande R.	115
Paulo Afonso, Sao Francisco R. . .	275
Colombia	
Catarata de Candelas,	
Cusiana R.	984
*Tequendama, Bogota R.	427
Ecuador	
*Agoyan, Pastaza R.	200
Guyana	
Kaieteur, Potaro R.	741
Great, Kamarang R.	1,600
† Marina, Ipobe R.	500
Highest fall	300
Venezuela—	
† *Angel.	3,212
Highest fall	2,648
Cuquenan.	2,000

Notable Deserts of the World

Arabian (Eastern), 70,000 sq. mi. in Egypt between the Nile river and Red Sea, extending southward into Sudan.

Atacama, 600 mi. long area rich in nitrate and copper deposits in N. Chile.

Chihuahuan, 140,000 sq. mi. in Tex., N.M., Ariz., and Mexico.

Death Valley, 3,300 sq. mi. in E. Cal. and SW Nev. Contains lowest point below sea level (282 ft.) in Western Hemisphere.

Gibson, 120,000 sq. mi. in the interior of W. Australia.

Gobi, 500,000 sq. mi. in Mongolia and China.

Great Sandy, 150,000 sq. mi. in W. Australia.

Great Victoria, 150,000 sq. mi. in W. and S. Australia.

Kalahari, 225,000 sq. mi. in southern Africa.

Kara-Kum, 120,000 sq. mi. in Turkmen SSR.

Kavir (Dasht-e Kavir), great salt waste in central Iran some 400 mi. long.

Kyzyl Kum, 100,000 sq. mi. in Kazakh and Uzbek SSRs.

Libyan, 450,000 sq. mi. in the Sahara extending from Lybia through SW Egypt into Sudan.

Lut (Dasht-e Lut), 20,000 sq. mi. in E. Iran.

Mojave, 15,000 sq. mi. in S. Cal.

Nafud (An Nafud), 40,000 sq. mi. near Jawf in Saudi Arabia.

Namib, long narrow area extending 800 miles along SW coast of Africa.

Nubian, 100,000 sq. mi. in the Sahara in NE Sudan.

Painted Desert, section of high plateau in N. Ariz. extending 150 mi.

Rub al Khali (Empty Quarter), 250,000 sq. mi. in the south Arabian Peninsula.

Sahara, 3,500,000 sq. mi. in N. Africa extending westward to the Atlantic. Largest desert in the world.

Simpson, 40,000 sq. mi. in central Australia.

Sonoran, 70,000 sq. mi. in SW Ariz. and SE Cal. extending into Mexico.

Syrian, 100,000 sq. mi. arid wasteland extending over much of N. Saudi Arabia, E. Jordan, S. Syria, and W. Iraq.

Taklimakan, 140,000 sq. mi. in Sinkiang Province, China.

Thar (Great Indian), 100,000 sq. mi. arid area extending 400 mi. along India-Pakistan border.

Highest and Lowest Continental Altitudes

Source: National Geographic Society, Washington, D.C.

Continent	Highest point	Feet elevation	Lowest point	Feet below sea level
Asia	Mount Everest, Nepal-Tibet	29,028	Dead Sea, Israel-Jordan	1,312
South America . .	Mount Aconcagua, Argentina	22,834	Valdes Peninsula, Argentina	131
North America . .	Mount McKinley, Alaska	20,320	Death Valley, California	282
Africa	Kilimanjaro, Tanzania	19,340	Lake Assal, Djibouti	512
Europe	Mount El'brus, USSR	18,510	Caspian Sea, USSR	92
Antarctica	Vinson Massif	16,864	Unknown	. . .
Australia	Mount Kosciusko, New South Wales	7,310	Lake Eyre, South Australia	52

Important Islands and Their Areas

Figure in parentheses shows rank among the world's 10 largest islands; some islands have not been surveyed accurately; in such cases estimated areas are shown.

Location-Ownership
Area in square miles

Arctic Ocean
Canadian

Axel Heiberg	16,671
Baffin (5)	195,928
Banks	27,038
Bathurst	6,194
Devon	21,331
Ellesmere (10)	75,767
Melville	16,274
Prince of Wales	12,872
Somerset	9,570
Southampton	15,913
Victoria (9)	83,896

USSR

Franz Josef Land	8,000
Novaya Zemlya (two is.)	35,000
Wrangel	2,800

Norwegian

Svalbard	23,940
Nordaustlandet	5,410
Spitsbergen	15,060

Atlantic Ocean

Anticosti, Canada	3,066
Ascension, UK	34
Azores, Portugal	888
Faial	67
Sao Miguel	291
Bahamas	5,353
Bermuda Is., UK	20
Block, Rhode Island	10
Canary Is., Spain	2,808
Fuerteventura	668
Gran Canaria	592
Tenerife	795
Cape Breton, Canada	3,981
Cape Verde Is.	1,750
Faeroe Is., Denmark	540
Falkland Is., UK	4,700
Fernando de Noronha Archipelago, Brazil	7
Greenland, Denmark (1)	840,000
Iceland	39,769
Long Island, N.Y.	1,396
Bioko Is. Equatorial Guinea	785
Madeira Is., Portugal	307
Marajo, Brazil	15,528
Martha's Vineyard, Mass.	91
Mount Desert, Me.	108
Nantucket, Mass.	46
Newfoundland, Canada	42,030
Prince Edward, Canada	2,184
St. Helena, UK	47
South Georgia, UK	1,450
Tierra del Fuego, Chile and Argentina	18,800
Tristan da Cunha, UK	40

British Isles

Great Britain, mainland (8)	84,200
Channel Islands	75
Guernsey	24
Jersey	45
Sark	2
Hebrides	2,744
Ireland	32,599
Irish Republic	27,136
Northern Ireland	5,463
Man	227
Orkney Is.	390
Scilly Is.	6
Shetland Is.	567
Skye	670
Wight	147

Baltic Sea

Aland Is., Finland	581
Bornholm, Denmark	227
Gotland, Sweden	1,164

Caribbean Sea

Antigua	108
Aruba, Netherlands	75
Barbados	166
Cuba	44,218
Isle of Youth	1,182
Curacao, Netherlands	171
Dominica	290
Guadeloupe, France	687
Hispaniola, Haiti and Dominican Republic	29,530
Jamaica	4,244
Martinique, France	425
Puerto Rico, U.S.	3,515
Tobago	116
Trinidad	1,864
Virgin Is., UK	59
Virgin Is., U.S.	132

Indian Ocean

Andaman Is., India	2,500
Madagascar (4)	226,658
Mauritius	720
Pemba, Tanzania	380
Reunion, France	969
Seychelles	171
Sri Lanka	25,332
Zanzibar, Tanzania	640

Persian Gulf

Bahrain	258

Mediterranean Sea

Balearic Is., Spain	1,936
Corfu, Greece	229
Corsica, France	3,369
Crete, Greece	3,186
Cyprus	3,572
Elba, Italy	86
Euboea, Greece	1,409
Malta	122
Rhodes, Greece	542
Sardinia, Italy	9,262
Sicily, Italy	9,822

Pacific Ocean

Aleutian Is., U.S.	6,821
Adak	289
Amchitka	121
Attu	388
Kanaga	135
Kiska	110
Tanaga	209
Umnak	675
Unalaska	1,064
Unimak	1,600
Canton, Kiribati*	4
Caroline Is., U.S. trust terr.	472
Christmas, Kiribati*	94
Clipperton, France	2
Diomede, Big, USSR	11
Diomede, Little, U.S.	2
Easter, Chile	69
Fiji	7,056
Vanua Levu	2,242
Viti Levu	4,109
Funafuti, Tuvalu*	2
Galapagos Is., Ecuador	3,043
Guadalcanal	2,500
Guam	209
Hainan, China	13,000
Hawaiian Is., U.S.	6,450
Hawaii	4,037
Oahu	593
Hong Kong, UK	29
Japan	145,809
Hokkaido	30,144
Honshu (7)	87,805
Iwo Jima	8
Kyushu	14,114
Okinawa	459
Shikoku	7,049
Kodiak, U.S.	3,670
Marquesas Is., France	492
Marshall Is., U.S. trust terr.	70
Bikini*	2
Nauru	8
New Caledonia, France	6,530
New Guinea (2)	306,000
New Zealand	103,883
Chatham	372
North	44,035
South	58,305
Stewart	674
Northern Mariana Is.	184
Philippines	115,831
Leyte	2,787
Luzon	40,880
Mindanao	36,775
Mindoro	3,790
Negros	4,907
Palawan	4,554
Panay	4,446
Samar	5,050
Quemoy	56
Sakhalin, USSR	29,500
Samoa Is.	1,177
American Samoa	77
Tutuila	52
Samoa (Western)	1,133
Savaii	670
Upolu	429
Santa Catalina, U.S.	72
Tahiti, France	402
Taiwan	13,823
Tasmania, Australia	26,178
Tonga Is.	270
Vancouver, Canada	12,079
Vanuatu	5,700

East Indies

Bali, Indonesia	2,147
Borneo, Indonesia- Malaysia, UK (3)	280,100
Celebes, Indonesia	69,000
Java, Indonesia	48,900
Madura, Indonesia	2,113
Moluccas, Indonesia	28,766
New Britain, Papua New Guinea	14,093
New Ireland, Papua New Guinea	3,707
Sumatra, Indonesia (6)	165,000
Timor	11,570

*Atolls: Bikini (lagoon area, 230 sq. mi., land area 2 sq. mi.), U.S. Trust Territory of the Pacific Islands; Canton (lagoon 20 sq. mi., land 4 sq. mi.), Kiribati; Christmas (lagoon 140 sq. mi., land 94 sq. mi.), Kiribati; Funafuti (lagoon 84 sq. mi., land 2 sq. mi.), Tuvalu. Australia, often called an island, is a continent. Its mainland area is 2,939.975 sq. mi.

Islands in minor waters; Manhattan (22 sq mi.) Staten (59 sq. mi.) and Governors (173 acres), all in New York Harbor, U.S.; Isle Royale (209 sq. mi.), Lake Superior, U.S.; Manitoulin (1,068 sq. mi.), Lake Huron, Canada; Pinang (110 sq. mi.), Strait of Malacca, Malaysia; Singapore (239 sq. mi.), Singapore Strait, Singapore.

DISASTERS
Some Notable Shipwrecks Since 1850
(Figures indicate estimated lives lost; as of mid-1990)

1854, Mar.—City of Glasgow; British steamer missing in North Atlantic; 480.

1854, Sept. 27—Arctic; U.S. (Collins Line) steamer sunk in collision with French steamer Vesta near Cape Race; 285-351.

1856, Jan. 23—Pacific; U.S. (Collins Line) steamer missing in North Atlantic; 186-286.

1858, Sept. 23—Austria; German steamer destroyed by fire in North Atlantic; 471.

1863, Apr. 27—Anglo-Saxon; British steamer wrecked at Cape Race; 238.

1865, Apr. 27—Sultana; a Mississippi River steamer blew up near Memphis, Tenn; 1,450.

1869, Oct. 27—Stonewall; steamer burned on Mississippi River below Cairo, Ill.; 200.

1870, Jan. 25—City of Boston; British (Inman Line) steamer vanished between New York and Liverpool; 177.

1870, Oct 19—Cambria; British steamer wrecked off northern Ireland; 196.

1872, Nov. 7—Mary Celeste; U.S. half-brig sailed from New York for Genoa; found abandoned in Atlantic 4 weeks later in mystery of sea; crew never heard from; loss of life unknown.

1873, Jan. 22—Northfleet; British steamer foundered off Dungeness, England; 300.

1873, Apr. 1—Atlantic; British (White Star) steamer wrecked off Nova Scotia; 585.

1873, Nov. 23—Ville du Havre; French steamer, sunk after collision with British sailing ship Loch Earn; 226.

1875, May 7—Schiller; German steamer wrecked off Scilly Isles; 312.

1875, Nov. 4—Pacific; U.S. steamer sunk after collision off Cape Flattery; 236.

1878, Sept. 3—Princess Alice; British steamer sunk after collision in Thames River; 700.

1878, Dec. 18—Byzantin; French steamer sank after Dardanelles collision; 210.

1881, May 24—Victoria; steamer capsized in Thames River, Canada; 200.

1883, Jan. 19—Cimbria; German steamer sunk in collision with British steamer Sultan in North Sea; 389.

1887, Nov. 15—Wah Yeung; British steamer burned at sea; 400.

1890, Feb. 17—Duburg; British steamer wrecked, China Sea; 400.

1890, Sept. 19—Ertogrul; Turkish frigate foundered off Japan; 540.

1891, Mar. 17—Utopia; British steamer sank in collision with British ironclad Anson off Gibraltar; 562.

1895, Jan. 30—Elbe; German steamer sank in collision with British steamer Craithie in North Sea; 332.

1895, Mar. 11—Reina Regenta; Spanish cruiser foundered near Gibraltar; 400.

1898, Feb. 15—Maine; U.S. battleship blown up in Havana Harbor; 260.

1898, July 4—La Bourgogne; French steamer sunk in collision with British sailing ship Cromartyshire off Nova Scotia; 549.

1898, Nov. 26—Portland; U.S. steamer wrecked off Cape Cod; 157.

1904, June 15—General Slocum; excursion steamer burned in East River, New York City; 1,030.

1904, June 28—Norge; Danish steamer wrecked on Rockall Island, Scotland; 620.

1906, Aug. 4—Sirio; Italian steamer wrecked off Cape Palos, Spain; 350.

1908, Mar. 23—Matsu Maru; Japanese steamer sank in collision near Hakodate, Japan; 300.

1909, Aug. 1—Waratah; British steamer, Sydney to London, vanished; 300.

1910, Feb. 9—General Chanzy; French steamer wrecked off Minorca, Spain; 200.

1911, Sept. 25—Liberté; French battleship exploded at Toulon; 285.

1912, Mar. 5—Principe de Asturias; Spanish steamer wrecked off Spain; 500.

1912, Apr. 14-15—Titanic; British (White Star) steamer hit iceberg in North Atlantic; 1,503.

1912, Sept. 28—Kichemaru; Japanese steamer sank off Japanese coast; 1,000.

1914, May 29—Empress of Ireland; British (Canadian Pacific) steamer sunk in collision with Norwegian collier in St. Lawrence River; 1,014.

1915, May 7—Lusitania; British (Cunard Line) steamer torpedoed and sunk by German submarine off Ireland; 1,198.

1915, July 24—Eastland; excursion steamer capsized in Chicago River; 812.

1916, Feb. 26—Provence; French cruiser sank in Mediterranean; 3,100.

1916, Mar. 3—Principe de Asturias; Spanish steamer wrecked near Santos, Brazil; 558.

1916, Aug. 29—Hsin Yu; Chinese steamer sank off Chinese coast; 1,000.

1917, Dec. 6—Mont Blanc, Imo; French ammunition ship and Belgian steamer collided in Halifax Harbor; 1,600.

1918, Apr. 25—Kiang-Kwan Chinese steamer sank in collision off Hankow; 500.

1918, July 12—Kawachi; Japanese battleship blew up in Tokayama Bay; 500.

1918, Oct. 25—Princess Sophia; Canadian steamer sank off Alaskan coast; 398.

1919, Jan. 17—Chaonia; French steamer lost in Straits of Messina, Italy; 460.

1919, Sept. 9—Valbanera; Spanish steamer lost off Florida coast; 500.

1921, Mar. 18—Hong Kong; steamer wrecked in South China Sea; 1,000.

1922, Aug. 26—Niitaka; Japanese cruiser sank in storm off Kamchatka, USSR; 300.

1927, Oct. 25—Principessa Mafalda; Italian steamer blew up, sank off Porto Seguro, Brazil; 314.

1928, Nov. 12—Vestris; British steamer sank in gale off Virginia; 113.

1934, Sept. 8—Morro Castle; U.S. steamer, Havana to New York, burned off Asbury Park, N.J.; 134.

1939, May 23—Squalus; U.S. submarine sank off Portsmouth, N.H.; 26.

1939, June 1—Thetis; British submarine, sank in Liverpool Bay; 99.

1942, Feb. 18—Truxtun and Pollux; U.S. destroyer and cargo ship ran aground, sank off Newfoundland; 204.

1942, Oct. 2—Curacao; British cruiser sank after collision with liner Queen Mary; 338.

1944, Dec. 17-18—3 U.S. Third Fleet destroyers sank during typhoon in Philippine Sea; 790.

1947, Jan. 19—Himera; Greek steamer hit a mine off Athens; 392.

1947, Apr. 16—Grandcamp; French freighter exploded in Texas City, Tex., Harbor, starting fires; 510.

1948, Nov.—Chinese army evacuation ship exploded and sunk off S. Manchuria; 6,000.

1948, Dec. 3—Kiangya; Chinese refugee ship wrecked in explosion S. of Shanghai; 1,100+.

1949, Sept. 17—Noronic; Canadian Great Lakes Cruiser burned at Toronto dock; 130.

1952, Apr. 26—Hobson and Wasp; U.S. destroyer and aircraft carrier collided in Atlantic; 176.

1953, Jan. 31—Princess Victoria; British ferry sank in storm off northern Irish coast; 134.

1954, Sept. 26—Toya Maru; Japanese ferry sank in Tsugaru Strait, Japan; 1,172.

1956, July 26—Andrea Doria and Stockholm; Italian liner and Swedish liner collided off Nantucket; 51.

1957, July 14—Eshghabad; Soviet ship ran aground in Caspian Sea; 270.

1961, July 8—Save; Portuguese ship ran aground off Mozambique; 259.

1962, Apr. 8—Dara; British liner exploded and sunk in Persian Gulf; 236.

1963, Apr. 10—Thresher; U.S. Navy atomic submarine sank in North Atlantic; 129.

1964, Feb. 10—Voyager, Melbourne; Australian destroyer sank after collision with Australian aircraft carrier Melbourne off New South Wales; 82.

1965, Nov. 13—Yarmouth Castle; Panamanian registered cruise ship burned and sank off Nassau; 90.

1967, July 29—Forrestal; U.S. aircraft carrier caught fire off N. Vietnam; 134.

1968, Jan. 25—Dakar; Israeli submarine vanished in Mediterranean Sea; 69.

1968, Jan. 27—Minerve; French submarine vanished in Mediterranean; 52.

1968, late May—Scorpion; U.S. nuclear submarine sank in Atlantic near Azores; 99 (located Oct. 31).

1969, June 2—Evans; U.S. destroyer cut in half by Australian carrier Melbourne, S. China Sea; 74.

1970, Mar. 4—Eurydice; French submarine sank in Mediterranean near Toulon; 57.

1970, Dec. 15—Namyong-Ho; South Korean ferry sank in Korea Strait; 308.

1974, May 1— Motor launch capsized off Bangladesh; 250.

1974, Sept. 26— Soviet destroyer burned and sank in Black Sea; 200+.

1976, Oct. 20—George Prince and Frosta; ferryboat and Norwegian tanker collided on Mississippi R. at Luling, La.; 77.

1976, Dec. 25—Patria; Egyptian liner caught fire and sank in the Red Sea; c. 100.

1977, Jan. 11—Grand Zenith; Panamanian-registered tanker sank off Cape Cod, Mass.; 38.

1979, Aug. 14—23 yachts competing in Fastnet yacht race sunk or abandoned during storm in S. Irish Sea; 18.

1981, Jan. 27—Tamponas II; Indonesian passenger ship caught fire and sank in Java Sea; 580.

1981, May 26—Nimitz; U.S. Marine combat jet crashed on deck of U.S. aircraft carrier; 14.

1983, Feb. 12—Marine Electric; coal freighter sank during storm off Chincoteague, Va.; 33.

1983, May 25—10th of Ramadan; Nile steamer caught fire and sank in L. Nassar; 357.

1986, Aug. 31—Admiral Nakhimov; Soviet passenger ship and Pyotr Vasev, Soviet freighter, collided in the Black Sea; 398.

1987, Mar. 6—British ferry capsized off Zeebrugge, Belgium; 188.

1987, Dec. 20—Philippine ferry Dona Paz and oil tanker Victor collided in the Tablas Strait; 3,000+.

1988, Aug. 6—Indian ferry capsized on Ganges R.; 400+.

1989, Apr. 7—Soviet submarine caught fire and sank off Norway; 42.

1989, Apr. 19—USS Iowa; U.S. battleship; explosion in gun turret; 47.

1989, Aug. 20—British barge Bowbelle struck British pleasure cruiser Marchioness on Thames R. in central London; 56.

1989, Sept. 10—Romanian pleasure boat and Bulgarian barge collided on Danube R.; 161.

Major Earthquakes

Magnitude of earthquakes (Mag.), distinct from deaths or damage caused, is measured on the Richter scale, on which each higher number represents a tenfold increase in energy measured in ground motion. Adopted in 1935, the scale has been applied in the following table to earthquakes as far back as reliable seismograms are available.

Date	Place	Deaths	Mag.	Date	Place	Deaths	Mag.
526 May 20	Syria, Antioch	250,000	N.A.	1960 May 21-30	Southern Chile	5,000	8.3
856	Greece, Corinth	45,000	"	1962 Sept. 1	Northwestern Iran	12,230	7.1
1057	China, Chihli	25,000	"	1963 July 26	Yugoslavia, Skopje	1,100	6.0
1268	Asia Minor, Cilicia	60,000	"	1964 Mar. 27	Alaska	131	8.4
1290 Sept. 27	China, Chihli	100,000	"	1966 Aug. 19	Eastern Turkey	2,520	6.9
1293 May 20	Japan, Kamakura	30,000	"	1968 Aug. 31	Northeastern Iran	12,000	7.4
1531 Jan. 26	Portugal, Lisbon	30,000	"	1970 Jan. 5	Yunnan Province, China.	10,000	7.7
1556 Jan. 24	China, Shaanxi	830,000	"	1970 Mar. 28	Western Turkey	1,086	7.4
1667 Nov.	Caucasia, Shemaka	80,000	"	1970 May 31	Northern Peru	66,794	7.7
1693 Jan. 11	Italy, Catania	60,000	"	1971 Feb. 9	San Fernando Val-		
1730 Dec. 30	Japan, Hokkaido	137,000	"		ley, Cal.	65	6.6
1737 Oct. 11	India, Calcutta	300,000	"	1972 Apr. 10	Southern Iran	5,057	6.9
1755 June 7	Northern Persia	40,000	"	1972 Dec. 23	Nicaragua	5,000	6.2
1755 Nov. 1	Portugal, Lisbon	60,000	8.75*	1974 Dec. 28	Pakistan (9 towns)	5,200	6.3
1783 Feb. 4	Italy, Calabria	30,000	N.A.	1975 Sept. 6	Turkey (Lice, etc.)	2,312	6.8
1797 Feb. 4	Ecuador, Quito	41,000	"	1976 Feb. 4	Guatemala	22,778	7.5
1811-12	New Madrid, Mo. (series)	—	8.7*	1976 May 6	Northeast Italy	946	6.5
1822 Sept. 5	Asia Minor, Aleppo	22,000	"	1976 June 26	New Guinea, Irian Jaya	443	7.1
1828 Dec. 28	Japan, Echigo	30,000	"	1976 July 28	China, Tangshan	242,000	8.2
1868 Aug. 13-15	Peru and Ecuador	40,000	"	1976 Aug. 17	Philippines, Mindanao	8,000	7.8
1875 May 16	Venezuela, Colombia	16,000	"	1976 Nov. 24	E. Turkey	4,000	7.9
1886 Aug. 31	Charleston, S.C.	60	6.6	1977 Mar. 4	Romania	1,541	7.5
1896 June 15	Japan, sea wave	27,120	N.A.	1977 Aug. 19	Indonesia	200	8.0
1906 Apr. 18-19	San Francisco, Cal.	503	8.3	1977 Nov. 23	Northwestern Argentina	100	8.2
1906 Aug. 16	Chile, Valparaiso	20,000	8.6	1978 June 12	Japan, Sendai	21	7.5
1908 Dec. 28	Italy, Messina	83,000	7.5	1978 Sept. 16	Northeast Iran	25,000	7.7
1915 Jan. 13	Italy, Avezzano	29,980	7.5	1979 Sept. 12	Indonesia	100	8.1
1920 Dec. 16	China, Gansu	100,000	8.6	1979 Dec. 12	Colombia, Ecuador	800	7.9
1923 Sept. 1	Japan, Yokohama	200,000	8.3	1980 Oct. 10	Northwestern Algeria	4,500	7.3
1927 May 22	China, Nan-Shan	200,000	8.3	1980 Nov. 23	Southern Italy	4,800	7.2
1932 Dec. 26	China, Gansu	70,000	7.6	1982 Dec. 13	North Yemen	2,800	6.0
1933 Mar. 2	Japan	2,990	8.9	1983 Mar. 31	Southern Colombia	250	5.5
1933 Mar. 10	Long Beach, Cal.	115	6.2	1983 May 26	N. Honshu, Japan	81	7.7
1934 Jan. 15	India, Bihar-Nepal	10,700	8.4	1983 Oct. 30	Eastern Turkey	1,300	7.1
1935 May 31	India, Quetta	50,000	7.5	1985 Mar. 3	Chile	146	7.8
1939 Jan. 24	Chile, Chillan	28,000	8.3	1985 Sept. 19, 21	Mexico City	4,200+	8.1
1939 Dec. 26	Turkey, Erzincan	30,000	7.9	1987 Mar. 5-6	NE Ecuador	4,000+	7.3
1946 Dec. 21	Japan, Honshu	2,000	8.4	1988 Aug. 20	India/Nepal border.	1,000+	6.5
1948 June 28	Japan, Fukui	5,131	7.3	1988 Nov. 6	China/Burma border	1,000	7.3
1949 Aug. 5	Ecuador, Pelileo	6,000	6.8	1988 Dec. 7	NW Armenia	55,000+	6.8
1950 Aug. 15	India, Assam	1,530	8.7	1989 Oct. 17	San Francisco Bay area.	62	6.9
1953 Mar. 18	NW Turkey	1,200	7.2	1990 May 30	N. Peru	115	6.3
1956 June 10-17	N. Afghanistan	2,000	7.7	1990 May 30	Romania	8	6.5
1957 July 2	Northern Iran	2,500	7.4	1990 June 21	NW Iran	40,000+	7.7
1957 Dec. 13	Western Iran	2,000	7.1				
1960 Feb. 29	Morocco, Agadir	12,000	5.8	(*) estimated from earthquake intensity. (N.A.) not available.			

Some Recent Earthquakes

Source: Global Volcanism Network, Smithsonian Institution

Attached is a list of recent earthquakes. Magnitude of earthquakes is measured on the Richter scale, on which each higher number represents a tenfold increase in energy measured in ground motion. A quake is considered significant if it has a magnitude of 6.5 on the Richter scale or if it causes casualities or considerable damage.

Date	Place	Magnitude	Date	Place	Magnitude
June 20, 1990	NW Iran	7.7	Feb. 20	Japan	6.5
May 30	N. Peru	6.3	Feb. 19	Vanuatu	6.8
May 30	Romania	6.5	Feb. 19	New Zealand	6.3
Mar. 25	Costa Rica	7.1	Feb. 8	Philippines	6.6
Feb. 28	S. California	5.5	Jan. 16	N. California	5.5

Date	Place	Magnitude	Date	Place	Magnitude
Dec. 30, 1989	Bismarck Sea	6.7	Oct. 18	San Francisco Bay area	6.9
Dec. 27	Australia	5.4	Oct. 7	Aleutian Islands	6.7
Dec. 15	Philippines	7.3	Sept. 22	W. China	6.2
Nov. 20	SW China	5.1	Sept. 4	Indonesia	6.1
Nov. 1	Off Japan coast	7.3	Aug. 20	Ethiopia	6.3
Oct. 29	Algeria	6.0	May 23	Macquarie Island	8.3
Oct. 18	NE China	5.3	Apr. 25	Mexico	6.8

Some Notable Tornadoes In U.S. Since 1925

Date		Place	Deaths	Date		Place	Deaths
1925	Mar. 18	Mo., Ill. Ind.	689	1959	Feb. 10	St. Louis, Mo.	21
1927	Apr. 12	Rock Springs, Tex.	74	1960	May 5,6	SE Oklahoma, Arkansas	30
1927	May 9	Arkansas, Poplar Bluff, Mo.	92	1965	Apr. 11	Ind., Ill., Oh., Mich., Wis.	271
1927	May 29	St. Louis, Mo.	90	1966	Mar. 3	Jackson, Miss.	57
1930	May 6	Hill, Navarro, Ellis Co., Tex.	41	1966	Mar. 3	Mississippi, Alabama	61
1932	Mar. 21	Ala. (series of tornadoes)	268	1967	Apr. 21	Ill., Mich.	33
1936	Apr. 5	Miss., Ga.	455	1968	May 15	Midwest	71
1936	Apr. 6	Gainesville, Ga.	203	1969	Jan. 23	Mississippi.	32
1938	Sept. 29	Charleston, S.C.	32	1971	Feb. 21	Mississippi delta	110
1942	Mar. 16	Central to NE Miss.	75	1973	May 26-27	South, Midwest (series)	47
1942	Apr. 27	Rogers & Mayes Co., Okla.	52	1974	Apr. 3-4	Ala., Ga., Tenn., Ky., Oh.	350
1944	June 23	Oh., Pa., W. Va., Md.	150	1977	Apr. 4	Ala., Miss., Ga.	22
1945	Apr. 12	Okla.-Ark.	102	1979	Apr. 10	Tex., Okla.	60
1947	Apr. 9	Tex., Okla. & Kan.	169	1980	June 3	Grand Island, Neb. (series)	4
1948	Mar. 19	Bunker Hill & Gillespie, Ill.	33	1982	Mar. 2-4	South, Midwest (series)	17
1949	Jan. 3	La. & Ark.	58	1982	May 29	So. Ill.	10
1952	Mar. 21	Ark., Mo., Tenn. (series)	208	1983	May 18-22	Tex.	12
1953	May 11	Waco, Tex.	114	1984	Mar. 28	N. Carolina; S. Carolina	67
1953	June 8	Mich., Oh.	142	1984	Apr. 21-22	Mississippi.	15
1953	June 9	Worcester and vicinity, Mass.	90	1984	Apr. 26	Series Okla to Minn.	17
1953	Dec. 5	Vicksburg, Miss.	38	1985	May 31	N.Y., Pa., Oh., Ont. (series)	90
1955	May 25	Kan., Mo., Okla., Tex.	115	1987	May 22	Saragosa, Tex.	29
1957	May 20	Kan., Mo.	48	1990	June 2-3	Midwest, Great Lakes	13
1958	June 4	Northwestern Wisconsin	30				

Hurricanes, Typhoons, Blizzards, Other Storms

Names of hurricanes and typhoons in italics—H.—hurricane; T.—typhoon

Date	Location	Deaths	Date	Location	Deaths
1888 Mar. 11-14	Blizzard, Eastern U.S.	400	1967 July 9	T. *Billie*, SW Japan	347
1900 Aug.-Sept.	H., Galveston, Tex.	6,000	1967 Sept. 5-23	H. *Beulah*, Carib., Mex., Tex.	54
1906 Sept. 11	H., La., Miss.	350	1967 Dec. 12-20	Blizzard, Southwest, U.S.	51
1906 Sept. 18	Typhoon, Hong Kong.	10,000	1968 Nov. 18-28	T. *Nina*, Philippines	63
1926 Sept. 11-22	H., Fla., Ala.	243	1969 Aug. 17-18	H. *Camille*, Miss., La.	256
1926 Oct. 20	H., Cuba.	600	1970 July 30-		
1928 Sept. 6-20	H., So. Fla.	1,836	Aug. 5	H. *Celia*, Cuba, Fla., Tex.	31
1930 Sept. 3	H., Dominican Rep.	2,000	1970 Aug. 20-21	H. *Dorothy*, Martinique	42
1938 Sept. 21	H., Long Island N.Y., New England	600	1970 Sept. 15	T. *Georgia*, Philippines	300
1940 Nov. 11-12	Blizzard, U.S. NE, Midwest	144	1970 Oct. 14	T. *Sening*, Philippines.	583
1942 Oct. 15-16	H., Bengal, India	40,000	1970 Oct. 15	T. *Titang*, Philippines	526
1944 Sept. 9-16	H., N.C. to New Eng.	46	1970 Nov. 13	Cyclone, Bangladesh	300,000
1952 Oct. 22	Typhoon, Philippines	0,300	1971 Aug. 1	T. *Rose*, Hong Kong	130
1954 Aug. 30	H. *Carol*, Northeast U.S.	68	1972 June 19-29	H. *Agnes*, Fla. to N.Y.	118
1954 Oct. 5-18	H. *Hazel*, Eastern, U.S., Haiti	347	1972 Dec. 3	T. *Theresa*, Philippines	169
1955 Aug. 12-13	H. *Connie*, Carolinas, Va., Md.	43	1973 June-Aug.	Monsoon rains in India	1,217
1955 Aug. 7-21	H. *Diane*, Eastern U.S.	400	1974 June 11	Storm Dinah, Luzon Is., Philip.	71
1955 Sept. 19	H. *Hilda*, Mexico	200	1974 July 11	T. *Gilda*, Japan, S. Korea	108
1955 Sept. 22-28	H. *Janet*, Caribbean	500	1974 Sept. 19-20	H. *Fifi*, Honduras	2,000
1956 Feb. 1-29	Blizzard, Western Europe	1,000	1974 Dec. 25	Cyclone leveled Darwin, Aus.	50
1957 June 25-30	H. *Audrey*, Tex. to Ala.	390	1975 Sept. 13-27	H. *Eloise*, Caribbean, NE U.S.	71
1958 Feb. 15-16	Blizzard, NE U.S.	171	1976 May 20	T. *Olga*, floods, Philippines	215
1959 Sept. 17-19	T. *Sarah*, Japan, S. Korea	2,000	1977 July 25, 31	T. *Thelma*, T. *Vera*, Taiwan	39
1959 Sept. 26-27	T. *Vera*, Honshu, Japan	4,466	1978 Oct. 27	T. *Rita*, Philippines	c. 400
1960 Sept. 4-12	H. *Donna*, Caribbean, E. U.S.	148	1979 Aug. 30-		
1961 Sept. 11-14	H. *Carla*, Tex.	46	Sept. 7	H. *David*, Caribbean, East. U.S.	1,100
1961 Oct. 31	H. *Hattie*, Br. Honduras	400	1980 Aug. 4-11	H. *Allen*, Caribbean, Texas	272
1963 May 28-29	Windstorm, Bangladesh	22,000	1981 Nov. 25	T. *Irma*, Luzon Is., Philippines	176
1963 Oct. 4-8	H. *Flora*, Caribbean	6,000	1983 June	Monsoon rains in India	900
1964 Oct. 4-7	H. *Hilda*, La., Miss., Ga.	38	1983 Aug. 18	H. *Alicia*, southern Texas	17
1964 June 30	T. *Winnie*, N. Philippines	107	1984 Sept. 2	T. *Ike*, southern Philippines	1,363
1964 Sept. 5	T. *Ruby*, Hong Kong and China	735	1985 May 25	Cyclone, Bangladesh.	10,000
1965 May 11-12	Windstorm, Bangladesh	17,000	1985 Oct. 26-		
1965 June 1-2	Windstorm, Bangladesh	30,000	Nov. 6	H. *Juan*, SE U.S.	97
1965 Sept. 7-12	H. *Betsy*, Fla., Miss., La.	74	1987 Nov. 25	T. *Nina*, Philippines	650
1965 Dec. 15	Windstorm, Bangladesh	10,000	1989 Sept. 16-22	H. *Hugo*, Caribbean, SE U.S.	504
1966 June 4-10	H. *Alma*, Honduras, SE U.S.	51	1990 May 6-11	Cyclone, SE India.	450
1966 Sept. 24-30	H. *Inez*, Carib., Fla., Mex.	293			

Floods, Tidal Waves

Date		Location	Deaths	Date		Location	Deaths
1228	....	Holland	100,000	1889	May 31	Johnstown, Pa.	2,200
1642	....	China	300,000	1900	Sept. 8	Galveston, Tex.	5,000
1887	....	Huang He River, China	900,000	1903	June 15	Heppner, Ore.	325

(continued)

Date		Location	Deaths	Date		Location	Deaths
1911	....	Chang Jiang River, China	100,000	1970	May 20	Central Romania	160
1913	Mar. 25-27	Ohio, Indiana	732	1970	July 22	Himalayas, India	500
1915	Aug. 17	Galveston, Tex.	275	1971	Feb. 26	Rio de Janeiro, Brazil	130
1928	Mar. 13	Collapse of St. Francis Dam, Saugus, Cal.	450	1972	Feb. 26	Buffalo Creek, W. Va.	118
1928	Sept. 13	Lake Okeechobee, Fla.	2,000	1972	June 9	Rapid City, S.D.	236
1931	Aug.	Huang He River, China	3,700,000	1972	Aug. 7	Luzon Is., Philippines	454
1937	Jan. 22	Ohio, Miss. Valleys	250	1973	Aug. 19-31	Pakistan	1,500
1939	....	Northern China	200,000	1974	Mar. 29	Tubaro, Brazil	1,000
1946	Apr. 1	Hawaii, Alaska	159	1974	Aug. 12	Monty-Long, Bangladesh	2,500
1947	....	Honshu Island, Japan	1,900	1976	June 5	Teton Dam collapse, Ida.	11
1951	Aug.	Manchuria	1,800	1976	July 31	Big Thompson Canyon, Col.	139
1953	Jan. 31	Western Europe	2,000	1976	Nov. 17	East Java, Indonesia	136
1954	Aug. 17	Farahzad, Iran	2,000	1977	July 19-20	Johnstown, Pa.	68
1955	Oct. 7-12	India, Pakistan	1,700	1979	June-Sept.	Northern India	1,200
1959	Nov. 1	Western Mexico	2,000	1979	Jan.-Feb.	Brazil	204
1959	Dec. 2	Frejus, France	412	1979	July 17	Lomblem Is., Indonesia	539
1960	Oct. 10	Bangladesh	6,000	1979	Aug. 11	Morvi, India	5,000-15,000
1960	Oct. 31	Bangladesh	4,000	1980	Feb. 13-22	So. Cal., Ariz.	26
1962	Feb. 17	German North Sea coast	343	1981	Apr.	Northern China	550
1962	Sept. 27	Barcelona, Spain	445	1981	July	Sichuan, Hubei Prov., China	1,300
1963	Oct. 9	Dam collapse, Vaiont, Italy	1,800	1982	Jan. 23	Nr. Lima, Peru	600
1966	Nov. 3-4	Florence, Venice, Italy	113	1982	May 12	Guangdong, China	430
1967	Jan. 18-24	Eastern Brazil	894	1982	June 6	So. Conn.	12
1967	Mar. 19	Rio de Janeiro, Brazil	436	1982	Sept. 17-21	El Salvador, Guatemala	1,300+
1967	Nov. 26	Lisbon, Portugal	464	1982	Dec. 2-9	Ill., Mo., Ark.	22
1968	Aug. 7-14	Gujarat State, India	1,000	1983	Feb.-Mar.	Cal. coast	13
1968	Oct. 7	Northeastern India	780	1983	Apr. 6-12	Ala., La., Miss., Tenn.	15
1969	Jan. 18-26	So. Cal.	100	1984	May 27	Tulsa, Okla.	13
1969	Mar. 17	Mundau Valley, Alagoas, Brazil	218	1984	Aug-Sept.	S. Korea	200+
1969	Aug. 20-22	Western Virginia	189	1987	July 19	Northern Italy, dam burst	361
1969	Sept. 15	South Korea	250	1987	Aug.-Sept.	Northern Bangladesh	1,000+
1969	Oct. 1-8	Tunisia	500	1988	Sept.	Northern India	1,000+
				1990	June 14	Shadyside, Oh.	22

Fires

Date		Location	Deaths	Date		Location	Deaths
1835	Dec. 16	New York City, 500 bldgs. destroyed	—	1961	Jan. 6	Thomas Hotel, San Francisco	20
1845	May	Canton, China, theater	1,670	1961	Dec. 8	Hartford, Conn., hospital	16
1871	Oct. 8	Chicago, $196 million loss	250	1961	Dec. 17	Niteroi, Brazil, circus	323
1871	Oct. 8	Peshtigo, Wis., forest fire	1,182	1963	May 4	Diourbel, Senegal, theater	64
1872	Nov. 9	Boston, 800 bldgs. destroyed	—	1963	Nov. 18	Surfside Hotel, Atlantic City, N.J.	25
1876	Dec. 5	Brooklyn (N.Y.), theater	295	1963	Nov. 23	Fitchville, Oh., rest home	63
1877	June 20	St. John, N. B., Canada	100	1963	Dec. 29	Roosevelt Hotel, Jacksonville, Fla.	22
1881	Dec. 8	Ring Theater, Vienna	850	1964	May 8	Manila, apartment bldg	30
1887	May 25	Opera Comique, Paris	200	1964	Dec. 18	Fountaintown, Ind., nursing home	20
1887	Sept. 4	Exeter, England, theater	200	1965	Mar. 1	LaSalle, Canada, apartment	28
1894	Sept. 1	Minn., forest fire	413	1966	Mar. 11	Numata, Japan, 2 ski resorts	31
1897	May 4	Paris, charity bazaar	150	1966	Aug. 13	Melbourne, Australia, hotel	29
1900	June 30	Hoboken, N. J., docks	326	1966	Sept. 12	Anchorage, Alaska, hotel	14
1902	Sept. 20	Birmingham, Ala., church	115	1966	Oct. 17	N. Y. City bldg. (firemen)	12
1903	Dec. 30	Iroquois Theater, Chicago	602	1966	Dec. 7	Erzurum, Turkey, barracks	68
1908	Jan. 13	Rhoads Theater, Boyertown, Pa.	170	1967	Feb. 7	Montgomery, Ala., restaurant	25
1908	Mar. 4	Collinwood, Oh., school	176	1967	May 22	Brussels, Belgium, store	322
1911	Mar. 25	Triangle factory, N. Y. City	145	1967	July 16	Jay, Fla., state prison	37
1913	Oct. 14	Mid Glamorgan, Wales, colliery	439	1968	Feb. 7	Shrewsbury, England, hospital	22
1918	Apr. 1	Norman Okla., state hospital	38	1968	May 11	Vijayawada, India, wedding hall	58
1918	Oct. 12	Cloquet, Minn., forest fire	400	1968	Nov. 18	Glasgow, Scotland, factory	24
1919	June 20	Mayaguez Theater, San Juan	150	1969	Jan. 26	Victoria Hotel, Dunnville, Ont.	13
1923	May 17	Camden, S. C., school	76	1969	Dec. 2	Notre Dame, Can., nursing home	54
1924	Dec. 24	Hobart, Okla., school	35	1970	Jan. 9	Marietta, Oh., nursing home	27
1929	May 15	Cleveland, Oh., clinic	125	1970	Mar. 20	Seattle, Wash., hotel	19
1930	Apr. 21	Columbus, Oh., penitentiary	320	1970	Nov. 1	Grenoble, France, dance hall	145
1931	July 24	Pittsburgh, Pa., home for aged	48	1970	Dec. 20	Tucson, Arizona, hotel	28
1934	Dec. 11	Hotel Kerns, Lansing, Mich.	34	1971	Mar. 6	Burghoezli, Switzerland, psychiatric clinic	28
1938	May 16	Atlanta, Ga., Terminal Hotel	35	1971	Apr. 20	Hotel, Bangkok, Thailand	24
1940	Apr. 23	Natchez, Miss., dance hall	198	1971	Oct. 19	Honesdale, Pa., nursing home	15
1942	Nov. 28	Cocoanut Grove, Boston	491	1971	Dec. 25	Hotel, Seoul, So. Korea	162
1942		St. John's, Newfoundland, hostel	100	1972	May 13	Osaka, Japan, nightclub	116
1943	Sept. 7	Gulf Hotel, Houston	55	1972	July 5	Sherborne, England, hospital	30
1944	July 6	Ringling Circus, Hartford	168	1973	Feb. 6	Paris, France, school	21
1946	June 5	LaSalle Hotel, Chicago	61	1973	Nov. 6	Fukui, Japan, train	28
1946	Dec. 7	Winecoff Hotel, Atlanta	119	1973	Nov. 29	Kumamoto, Japan, department store	107
1946	Dec. 12	New York, ice plant, tenement	37	1973	Dec. 2	Seoul, Korea, theater	50
1949	Apr. 5	Effingham, Ill., hospital	77	1974	Feb. 1	Sao Paulo, Brazil, bank building	189
1950	Jan. 7	Davenport, Ia., Mercy Hospital	41	1974	June 30	Port Chester, N. Y., discotheque	24
1953	Mar. 12	Largo, Fla., nursing home	35	1974	Nov. 3	Seoul, So. Korea, hotel discotheque	88
1953	Apr. 16	Chicago, metalworking plant	35	1975	Dec. 12	Mina, Saudi Arabia, tent city	138
1957	Feb. 17	Warrenton, Mo., home for aged	72	1976	Oct. 24	Bronx, N.Y., social club	25
1958	Mar. 19	New York City, loft building	24	1977	Feb. 25	Moscow, Rossiya hotel	45
1958	Dec. 1	Chicago, parochial school	95	1977	May 28	Southgate, Ky., nightclub	164
1958	Dec. 16	Bogota, Colombia, store	83	1977	June 9	Abidjan, Ivory Coast, nightclub	41
1959	June 23	Stalheim, Norway, resort hotel	34	1977	June 26	Columbia, Tenn., jail	42
1960	Mar. 12	Pusan, Korea, chemical plant	68	1977	Nov. 14	Manila, hotel	47
1960	July 14	Guatemala City, mental hospital	225	1978	Jan. 28	Kansas City, Coates House Hotel	16
1960	Nov. 13	Amude, Syria, movie theater	152				

Date		Location	Deaths	Date		Location	Deaths
1979	July 14	Saragossa, Spain, hotel	80	1983	Dec. 17	Madrid, Spain, discotheque	83
1979	Dec. 31	Chapais, Quebec, social club	42	1984	May 11	Great Adventure Amusement Park,	
1980	May 20	Kingston, Jamaica, nursing home.	157			N.J.	8
1980	Nov. 21	MGM Grand Hotel, Las Vegas	84	1985	Apr. 27	Tabaco, Philippines, movie theater .	44
1980	Dec. 4	Stouffer Inn, Harrison, N.Y.	26	1985	Apr. 26	Buenos Aires, Argentina hospital	79
1981	Jan. 9	Keansburg, N.J., boarding home	30	1985	May 11	Bradford, England, soccer stadium.	53
1981	Feb. 10	Las Vegas Hilton	8	1986	Dec. 31	Puerto Rico, Dupont Plaza Hotel .	96
1981	Feb. 14	Dublin, Ireland, discotheque	44	1987	May 6-		
1982	Sept. 4	Los Angeles, apartment house	24		June 2	Northern China forest fire	193
1982	Nov. 8	Biloxi, Miss., county jail	29	1987	Nov. 17	London, England subway	30
1983	Feb. 13	Turin, Italy, movie theater	64	1990	Mar. 25	N.Y. City social club	87

Explosions

Date		Location	Deaths	Date		Location	Deaths
1910	Oct. 1	Los Angeles Times Bldg.,	21	1964	July 23	Bone, Algeria, harbor munitions.	100
1913	Mar. 7	Dynamite, Baltimore harbor	55	1965	Mar. 4	Gas pipeline, Natchitoches, La.	17
1915	Sept. 27	Gasoline tank car, Ardmore, Okla.	47	1965	Aug. 9	Missile silo, Searcy, Ark.	53
1917	Apr. 10	Munitions plant, Eddystone, Pa.	133	1965	Oct. 21	Bridge, Tila Bund, Pakistan	80
1917	Dec. 6	Halifax Harbor, Canada.	1,654	1965	Oct. 30	Cartagena, Colombia	48
1918	May 18	Chemical plant, Oakdale, Pa.	193	1965	Nov. 24	Armory, Keokuk, la.	20
1918	July 2	Explosives, Split Rock, N.Y.	50	1966	Oct. 13	Chemical plant, La Salle, Que.	11
1918	Oct. 4	Shell plant, Morgan Station, N.J.	64	1967	Feb. 17	Chemical plant, Hawthorne, N.J.	11
1919	May 22	Food plant, Cedar Rapids, Ia.	44	1967	Dec. 25	Apartment bldg., Moscow	20
1920	Sept. 16	Wall Street, New York, bomb.	30	1968	Apr. 6	Sports store, Richmond, Ind.	43
1924	Jan. 3	Food plant, Pekin, Ill.	42	1970	Apr. 8	Subway construction, Osaka, Japan	73
1928	April 13	Dance hall, West Plains, Mo.	40	1971	June 24	Tunnel, Sylmar, Cal.	17
1937	Mar. 18	New London, Tex., school	413	1971	June 28	School, fireworks, Pueblo, Mex.	13
1940	Sept. 12	Hercules Powder, Kenvil, N.J.	55	1971	Oct. 21	Shopping center, Glasgow, Scot.	20
1942	June 5	Ordnance plant, Elwood, Ill.	49	1973	Feb. 10	Liquified gas tank, Staten Is., N.Y.	40
1944	Apr. 14	Bombay, India, harbor	700	1975	Dec. 27	Chasnala, India, mine	431
1944	July 17	Port Chicago, Cal., pier	322	1976	Apr. 13	Lapua, Finland, munitions works	45
1944	Oct. 21	Liquid gas tank, Cleveland	135	1977	Nov. 11	Freight train, Iri, S. Korea	57
1947	Apr. 16	Texas City, Tex., pier.	561	1977	Dec. 22	Grain elevator, Westwego, La.	35
1948	July 28	Farben works, Ludwigshafen, Ger.	184	1978	Feb. 24	Derailed tank car, Waverly, Tenn.	12
1950	May 19	Munitions barges, S. Amboy, N. J.	30	1978	July 11	Propylene tank truck, Spanish	
1956	Aug. 7	Dynamite trucks, Cali, Colombia .	1,100			coastal campsite.	150
1958	Apr. 18	Sunken munitions ship, Okinawa .	40	1980	Oct. 25	School, Ortuella, Spain	64
1958	May 22	Nike missiles, Leonardo, N.J.	10	1981	Feb. 13	Sewer system, Louisville, Ky.	0
1959	Apr. 10	World War II bomb, Philippines	38	1982	Apr. 7	Tanker truck, tunnel, Oakland, Cal.	7
1959	June 28	Rail tank cars, Meldrin, Ga.	25	1982	Apr. 25	Antiques exhibition, Todi, Italy.	33
1959	Aug. 7	Dynamite truck, Roseburg, Ore.	13	1982	Nov. 2	Salang Tunnel, Afghanistan . 1,000-3,000	
1959	Nov. 2	Jamuri Bazar, India, explosives	46	1984	Feb. 25	Oil pipeline, Cubatao, Brazil.	508
1959	Dec. 13	Dortmund, Ger., 2 apt. bldgs.	26	1984	June 21	Naval supply depot, Severomorsk,	
1960	Mar. 4	Belgian munitions ship, Havana.	100			USSR.	200+
1960	Oct. 25	Gas, Windsor, Ont., store	11	1984	Nov. 19	Gas storage area, NE Mexico City .	334
1962	Jan. 16	Gas pipeline, Edson, Alberta, Canada.	8	1984	Dec. 5	Coal mine, Taipei, Taiwan	94
1962	Oct. 3	Telephone Co. office, N. Y. City	23	1985	June 25	Fireworks factory, Hallett, Okla.	21
1963	Jan. 2	Packing plant, Terre Haute, Ind.	16	1988	July 6	Oil rig, North Sea.	167
1963	Mar. 9	Dynamite plant, S. Africa	45	1989	June 3	Gas pipeline, between Ufa, Asha,	
1963	Aug. 13	Explosives dump, Gauhiti, India .	32			USSR.	650+
1963	Oct. 31	State Fair Coliseum, Indianapolis.	73				

Notable Nuclear Accidents

Oct. 7, 1957 — A fire in the Windscale plutonium production reactor north of Liverpool, England spread radioactive material throughout the countryside. In 1983, the British government said that 39 people probably died of cancer as a result.

1957 — A chemical explosion in Kasli, USSR, in tanks containing nuclear waste, spread radioactive material and forced a major evacuation.

Jan. 3, 1961 — An experimental reactor at a federal installation near Idaho Falls, Id. killed three workers—the only deaths in U.S. reactor operations. The plant had high radiation levels but damage was contained.

Oct. 5, 1966 — A sodium cooling system malfunction caused a partial core meltdown at the Enrico Fermi demonstration breeder reactor near Detroit, Mich. Radiation was contained.

Jan. 21, 1969 — A coolant malfunction from an experimental underground reactor at Lucens Vad, Switzerland resulted in the release of a large amount of radiation into a cavern, which was then sealed.

Nov. 19, 1971 — The water-storage space at the Northern States Power Co.'s reactor in Monticello, Minn. filled to capacity and spilled over, dumping about 50,000 gallons of radioactive waste water into the Mississippi River. Some was taken into the St. Paul water system.

Mar. 22, 1975 — A technician checking for air leaks with a lighted candle caused a $100 million fire at the Brown's Ferry reactor in Decatur, Ala. The fire burned out electrical controls, lowering the cooling water to dangerous levels.

Mar. 28, 1979 — The worst commercial nuclear accident in the U.S. occured as equipment failures and human mistakes led to a loss of coolant, and partial core meltdown at the Three Mile Island reactor in Middletown, Pa.

Aug. 7, 1979 — Highly enriched uranium was released from a top-secret nuclear fuel plant near Erwin, Tenn. About 1,000 people were contaminated with up to 5 times as much radiation as would normally be received in a year.

Feb. 11, 1981 — Eight workers were contaminated when over 100,000 gallons of radioactive coolant leaked into the containment building of the TVA's Sequoyah 1 plant in Tennessee.

Apr. 25, 1981 — Some 100 workers were exposed to radioactive material during repairs of a nuclear plant at Tsuruga, Japan.

Jan. 25, 1982 — A steam-generator pipe broke at the Rochester Gas & Electric Co's Ginna plant near Rochester, N.Y. Small amounts of radioactive steam escaped into the air.

Jan. 6, 1986 — A cylinder of nuclear material burst after being improperly heated at a Kerr-McGee plant at Gore, Okla. One worker died and 100 were hospitalized.

Apr., 1986 — A serious accident at the Chernobyl nuclear plant about 60 miles from Kiev in the Soviet Union spewed clouds of radiation that spread over several European nations.

Some Notable Aircraft Disasters Since 1937

Date		Aircraft	Site of accident	Deaths
1937	May 6	German zeppelin Hindenburg	Burned at mooring, Lakehurst, N.J.	36
1944	Aug. 23	U.S. Air Force B-24	Hit school, Freckelton, England	76[1]
1945	July 28	U.S. Army B-25	Hit Empire State bldg., N.Y.C.	14[1]
1947	May 30	Eastern Air Lines DC-4	Crashed near Port Deposit, Md.	53
1952	Dec. 20	U.S. Air Force C-124	Fell, burned, Moses Lake, Wash.	87
1953	Mar. 3	Canadian Pacific Comet Jet	Karachi, Pakistan	11[2]
1953	June 18	U.S. Air Force C-124	Crashed, burned near Tokyo	129
1955	Nov. 1	United Air Lines DC-6B	Exploded, crashed near Longmont, Col.	44[3]
1956	June 20	Venezuelan Super-Constellation	Crashed in Atlantic off Asbury Park, N.J.	74
1956	June 30	TWA Super-Const., United DC-7	Collided over Grand Canyon, Arizona	128
1960	Dec. 16	United DC-8 jet, TWA Super-Const.	Collided over N.Y. City	134[4]
1962	Mar. 16	Flying Tiger Super-Const.	Vanished in Western Pacific	107
1962	June 3	Air France Boeing 707 jet	Crashed on takeoff from Paris	130
1962	June 22	Air France Boeing 707 jet	Crashed in storm, Guadeloupe, W.I.	113
1963	June 3	Chartered Northw. Airlines DC-7	Crashed in Pacific off British Columbia	101
1963	Nov. 29	Trans-Canada Airlines DC-8F	Crashed after takeoff from Montreal	118
1965	May 20	Pakistani Boeing 720-B	Crashed at Cairo, Egypt, airport	121
1966	Jan. 24	Air India Boeing 707 jetliner	Crashed on Mont Blanc, France-Italy	117
1966	Feb. 4	All-Nippon Boeing 727	Plunged into Tokyo Bay	133
1966	Mar. 5	BOAC Boeing 707 jetliner	Crashed on Mount Fuji, Japan	124
1966	Dec. 24	U.S. military-chartered CL-44	Crashed into village in So. Vietnam	129[1]
1967	Apr. 20	Swiss Britannia turboprop	Crashed at Nicosia, Cyprus	126
1967	July 19	Piedmont Boeing 727, Cessna 310	Collided in air, Hendersonville, N.C.	82
1968	Apr. 20	S. African Airways Boeing 707	Crashed on takeoff, Windhoek, SW Africa	122
1968	May 3	Braniff International Electra	Crashed in storm near Dawson, Tex.	85
1969	Mar. 16	Venezuelan DC-9	Crashed after takeoff from Maracaibo, Venezuela	155[5]
1969	Dec. 8	Olympia Airways DC-6B	Crashed near Athens in storm	93
1970	Feb. 15	Dominican DC-9	Crashed into sea on takeoff from Santo Domingo	102
1970	July 3	British chartered jetliner	Crashed near Barcelona, Spain	112
1970	July 5	Air Canada DC-8	Crashed near Toronto International Airport	108
1970	Aug. 9	Peruvian turbojet	Crashed after takeoff from Cuzco, Peru	101[1]
1970	Nov. 14	Southern Airways DC-9	Crashed in mountains near Huntington, W. Va.	75[6]
1971	July 30	All-Nippon Boeing 727 and Japanese Air Force F-86	Collided over Morioka, Japan	162[7]
1971	Sept. 4	Alaska Airlines Boeing 727	Crashed into mountain near Juneau, Alaska	111
1972	Aug. 14	E. German Ilyushin-62	Crashed on take-off East Berlin	156
1972	Oct. 13	Aeroflot Ilyushin-62	E. German airline crashed near Moscow	176
1972	Dec. 3	Chartered Spanish airliner	Crashed on take-off, Canary Islands	155
1972	Dec. 29	Eastern Airlines Lockheed Tristar	Crashed on approach to Miami Int'l. Airport	101
1973	Jan. 22	Chartered Boeing 707	Burst into flames during landing, Kano Airport, Nigeria	176
1973	Feb. 21	Libyan jetliner	Shot down by Israeli fighter planes over Sinai	108
1973	Apr. 10	British Vanguard turboprop	Crashed during snowstorm at Basel, Switzerland	104
1973	June 3	Soviet Supersonic TU-144	Crashed near Goussainville, France	14[8]
1973	July 11	Brazilian Boeing 707	Crashed on approach to Orly Airport, Paris	122
1973	July 31	Delta Airlines jetliner	Crashed, landing in fog at Logan Airport, Boston	89
1973	Dec. 23	French Caravelle jet	Crashed in Morocco	106
1974	Mar. 3	Turkish DC-10 jet	Crashed at Ermenonville near Paris	346
1974	Apr. 23	Pan American 707 jet	Crashed in Bali, Indonesia	107
1974	Dec. 1	TWA-727	Crashed in storm, Upperville, Va.	92
1974	Dec. 4	Dutch-chartered DC-8	Crashed in storm near Colombo, Sri Lanka	191
1975	Apr. 4	Air Force Galaxy C-5B	Crashed near Saigon, So. Vietnam, after takeoff with load of orphans	172
1975	June 24	Eastern Airlines 727 jet	Crashed in storm, JFK Airport, N.Y. City	113
1975	Aug. 3	Chartered 707	Hit mountainside, Agadir, Morocco	188
1976	Sept. 10	British Airways Trident, Yugoslav DC-9	Collided near Zagreb, Yugoslavia	176
1976	Sept. 19	Turkish 727	Hit mountain, southern Turkey	155
1976	Oct. 13	Bolivian 707 cargo jet	Crashed in Santa Cruz, Bolivia	100[9]
1977	Jan. 13	Aeroflot TU-104	Exploded and crashed at Alma-Ata, Central Asia	90
1977	Mar. 27	KLM 747, Pan American 747	Collided on runway, Tenerife, Canary Islands	582
1977	Nov. 19	TAP Boeing 727	Crashed on Madeira	130
1977	Dec. 4	Malaysian Boeing 737	Hijacked, then exploded in mid-air over Straits of Johore	100
1977	Dec. 13	U.S. DC-3	Crashed after takeoff at Evansville, Ind.	29[10]
1978	Jan. 1	Air India 747	Exploded, crashed into sea off Bombay	213
1978	Sept. 25	Boeing 727, Cessna 172	Collided in air, San Diego, Cal.	150
1978	Nov. 15	Chartered DC-8	Crashed near Colombo, Sri Lanka	183
1979	May 25	American Airlines DC-10	Crashed after takeoff at O'Hare Intl. Airport, Chicago	275[11]
1979	Aug. 17	Two Soviet Aeroflot jetliners	Collided over Ukraine	173
1979	Oct. 31	Western Airlines DC-10	Mexico City Airport	74
1979	Nov. 26	Pakistani Boeing 707	Crashed near Jidda, Saudi Arabia	156
1979	Nov. 28	New Zealand DC-10	Crashed into mountain in Antarctica	257
1980	Mar. 14	Polish Ilyushin 62	Crashed making emergency landing, Warsaw	87[12]
1980	Aug. 19	Saudi Arabian Tristar	Burned after emergency landing, Riyadh	301
1981	Dec. 1	Yugoslavian DC-9	Crashed into mountain in Corsica	174
1982	Jan. 13	Air Florida Boeing 737	Crashed into Potomac River after takeoff	78
1982	July 9	Pan-Am Boeing 727	Crashed after takeoff in Kenner, La.	153[13]
1982	Sept. 11	U.S. Army CH-47 Chinook helicopter	Crashed during air show in Mannheim, W. Germany	46
1983	Sept. 1	S. Korean Boeing 747	Shot down after violating Soviet airspace	269
1983	Nov. 27	Colombian Boeing 747	Crashed near Barajas Airport, Madrid	183
1985	Feb. 19	Spanish Boeing 727	Crashed into Mt. Oiz, Spain	148
1985	June 23	Air-India Boeing 747	Crashed into Atlantic Ocean S. of Ireland	329
1985	Aug. 2	Delta Air Lines jumbo jet	Crashed at Dallas-Ft. Worth Intl. Airport	133
1985	Aug. 12	Japan Air Lines Boeing 747	Crashed into Mt. Ogura, Japan	520[14]
1985	Dec. 12	Arrow Air DC 8	Crashed after takeoff in Gander, Newfoundland	256[15]
1986	Mar. 31	Mexican Boeing 727	Crashed NW of Mexico City	166
1986	Aug. 31	Aeromexico DC-9	Collided with Piper PA-28 over Cerritos, Cal.	82[16]

Date		Aircraft	Site of accident	Deaths
1987	May 9	Ilyushin 62M	Crashed after takeoff in Warsaw, Poland	183
1987	Aug. 16	Northwest Airlines MD-82	Crashed after takeoff in Romulus, Mich.	156
1988	July 3	Iranian A300 Airbus	Shot down by U.S. Navy warship *Vincennes* over Persian Gulf	290
1988	Dec. 21	Pan Am Boeing 747	Exploded and crashed in Lockerbie, Scotland.	270[17]
1989	Feb. 8	Boeing 707	Crashed into mountain in Azores Islands off Portugal	144
1989	June 7	Suriname DC-8	Crashed near Paramaribo Airport, Suriname	168
1989	July 19	United Airlines DC-10	Crashed while landing with a disabled hydrolic system, Sioux City, Ia.	111
1989	Sept. 19	French DC-10	Exploded in air over Niger	171

(1) Including those on the ground and in buildings. (2) First fatal crash of commercial jet plane. (3) Caused by bomb planted by John G. Graham in insurance plot to kill his mother, a passenger. (4) Including all 128 aboard the planes and 6 on ground. (5) Killed 84 on plane and 71 on ground. (6) Including 43 Marshall U. football players and coaches. (7) Airliner-fighter crash, pilot of fighter parachuted to safety, was arrested for negligence. (8) First supersonic plane crash killed 6 crewmen and 8 on the ground; there were no passengers. (9) Crew of 3 killed; 97, mostly children, killed on ground. (10) Including U. of Evansville basketball team. (11) Highest death toll in U.S. aviation history. (12) Including 22 members of U.S. boxing team. (13) including 8 on ground. (14) Worst single-plane disaster. (15) Incl. 248 members of U.S. 101st Airborne Division. (16) Incl. 15 on the ground. (17) Incl. 11 on the ground.

Major U.S. Railroad Wrecks

Date		Location	Deaths	Date		Location	Deaths
1876	Dec. 29	Ashtabula, Oh.	92	1925	June 16	Hackettstown, N. J.	50
1880	Aug. 11	Mays Landing, N. J.	40	1925	Oct. 27	Victoria, Miss.	21
1887	Aug. 10	Chatsworth, Ill.	81	1926	Sept. 5	Waco, Col.	30
1888	Oct. 10	Mud Run, Pa.	55	1928	Aug. 24	I.R.T. subway, Times Sq., N. Y.	18
1896	July 30	Atlantic City, N. J.	60	1938	June 19	Saugus, Mont.	47
1903	July 23	Laurel Run, Pa.	53	1939	Aug. 12	Harney, Nev.	24
1904	Aug. 7	Eden, Col.	96	1940	Apr. 19	Little Falls, N. Y.	31
1904	Sept. 24	New Market Tenn.	56	1940	July 31	Cuyahoga Falls, Oh.	43
1906	Mar. 16	Florence, Col.	35	1943	Aug. 29	Wayland, N. Y.	27
1906	Oct. 28	Atlantic City, N. J.	40	1943	Sept. 6	Frankford Junction, Philadelphia, Pa.	79
1906	Dec. 30	Washington, D. C.	53	1943	Dec. 16	Between Rennert and Buie, N. C.	72
1907	Jan. 2	Volland, Kan.	33	1944	July 6	High Bluff, Tenn.	35
1907	Jan. 19	Fowler, Ind.	29	1944	Aug. 4	Near Stockton, Ga.	47
1907	Feb. 16	New York, N.Y.	22	1944	Sept. 14	Dewey, Ind.	29
1907	Feb. 23	Colton, Cal.	26	1944	Dec. 31	Bagley, Utah	50
1907	July 20	Salem, Mich.	33	1945	Aug. 9	Michigan, N. D.	34
1910	Mar. 1	Wellington, Wash.	96	1946	Apr. 25	Naperville, Ill.	45
1910	Mar. 21	Green Mountain, Ia.	55	1947	Feb. 18	Gallitzin, Pa.	24
1911	Aug. 25	Manchester, N. Y.	29	1950	Feb. 17	Rockville Centre, N. Y.	31
1912	July 4	East Corning, N. Y.	39	1950	Sept. 11	Coshocton, Oh.	33
1912	July 5	Ligonier, Pa.	23	1950	Nov. 22	Richmond Hill, N. Y.	79
1914	Aug. 5	Tipton Ford, Mo.	43	1951	Feb. 6	Woodbridge, N. J.	84
1914	Sept. 15	Lebanon, Mo.	28	1951	Nov. 12	Wyuta, Wyo.	17
1916	Mar. 29	Amherst, Oh.	27	1951	Nov. 25	Woodstock, Ala.	17
1917	Sept. 18	Kellyville, Okla.	23	1953	Mar. 27	Conneaut, Oh.	21
1917	Dec. 20	Shepherdsville, Ky.	46	1956	Jan. 22	Los Angeles, Cal.	30
1918	June 22	Ivanhoe, Ind.	68	1956	Feb. 28	Swampscott, Mass.	13
1918	July 9	Nashville, Tenn.	101	1956	Sept. 5	Springer, N. M.	20
1918	Nov. 1	Brooklyn, N. Y.	97	1957	June 11	Vroman, Col.	12
1919	Jan. 12	South Byron, N. Y.	22	1958	Sept. 15	Elizabethport, N. J.	48
1919	July 1	Dunkirk, N. Y.	12	1960	Mar. 14	Bakersfield, Cal.	14
1919	Dec. 20	Onawa, Maine	23	1962	July 28	Steelton, Pa.	19
1921	Feb. 27	Porter, Ind.	37	1966	Dec. 28	Everett, Mass.	13
1921	Dec. 5	Woodmont, Pa.	27	1971	June 10	Salem, Ill.	11
1922	Aug. 5	Sulphur Spring, Mo.	34	1972	Oct. 30	Chicago, Ill.	45
1922	Dec. 13	Humble, Tex.	22	1977	Feb. 4	Chicago, Ill., elevated train	11
1923	Sept. 12	Lockett, Wy.	31	1987	Jan. 4	Essex, Md.	16

World's worst train wreck occurred Dec. 12, 1917, Modane, France, passenger train derailed, 543 killed.

Principal U.S. Mine Disasters Since 1900

Source: Bureau of Mines, U.S. Interior Department

Note: Prior to 1968, only disasters with losses of 60 or more lives are listed; since 1968, all disasters in which 5 or more people were killed are listed. Only fatalities to mining company employees are included. All bituminous-coal mines unless otherwise noted.

Date		Location	Deaths	Date		Location	Deaths
1900	May 1	Scofield, Ut.	100	1912	Mar. 20	McCurtain, Okla.	73
1902	May 19	Coal Creek, Tenn.	184	1912	Mar. 26	Jed, W. Va.	83
1902	July 10	Johnstown, Pa.	112	1913	Apr. 23	Finleyville, Pa.	96
1903	June 30	Hanna, Wy.	169	1913	Oct. 22	Dawson, N.M.	263
1904	Jan. 25	Cheswick, Pa.	179	1914	Apr. 28	Eccles, W. Va.	181
1905	Feb. 20	Virginia City, Ala.	112	1915	Mar. 2	Layland, W. Va.	112
1907	Jan. 29	Stuart W. Va.	84	1917	Apr. 27	Hastings, Col.	121
1907	Dec. 6	Monongah, W. Va.	361	1917[2]	June 8	Butte, Mon.	163
1907	Dec. 19	Jacobs Creek, Pa.	239	1917	Aug. 4	Clay, Ky.	62
1908	Nov. 28	Marianna, Pa.	154	1919[1]	June 5	Wilkes-Barre, Pa.	92
1909	Jan. 12	Switchback, W. Va.	67	1922	Nov. 6	Spangler, Pa.	77
1909	Nov. 13	Cherry, Ill.	259	1922	Nov. 22	Dolomite, Ala.	90
1910	Jan. 31	Primero, Col.	75	1923	Feb. 8	Dawson, N.M.	120
1910	May 5	Palos, Ala.	90	1923	Aug. 14	Kemmerer, Wy.	99
1910	Nov. 8	Delagua, Col.	79	1924	Mar. 8	Castle Gate, Ut.	171
1911	Apr. 7	Throop, Pa.	72	1924	Apr. 28	Benwood, W. Va.	119
1911	Apr. 8	Littleton, Ala.	128	1926	Jan. 13	Wilburton, Okla.	91
1911	Dec. 9	Briceville, Tenn.	84	1926[2]	Nov. 3	Ishpeming, Mich.	51

(continued)

Date		Location	Deaths	Date		Location	Deaths
1927	Apr. 30	Everettville, W. Va.	97	1968	Nov. 20	Farmington, W. Va.	78
1928	May 19	Mather, Pa.	195	1970	Dec. 30	Hyden, Ky.	38
1929	Dec. 17	McAlester, Okla.	61	1972[2]	May 2	Kellogg, Ida	91
1930	Nov. 5	Millfield, Oh.	79	1976	Mar. 9, 11	Oven Fork, Ky.	26
1940	Jan. 10	Bartley, W. Va.	91	1977	Mar. 1	Tower City, Pa.	9
1940	Mar. 16	St. Clairsville, Oh.	72	1981	Apr. 15	Redstone, Col.	15
1940	July 15	Portage, Pa.	63	1981	Dec. 7	Topmost, Ky.	8
1943	Feb. 27	Washoe, Mon.	74	1981	Dec. 8	nr. Chattanooga, Tenn. . . .	13
1944	July 5	Belmont, Oh.	66	1982	Jan. 20	Floyd County, Ky.	7
1947	Mar. 25	Centralia, Ill.	111	1983	June 21	McClure, Va	7
1951	Dec. 21	West Frankfort, Ill.	119	1984	Dec. 19	Huntington, Ut.	27
1968[3]	Mar. 6	Calumet, La.	21	1989	Sept. 13	Wheatcroft, Ky.	10

(1) Anthracite mine. (2) Metal mine. (3) Nonmetal mine.
World's worst mine disaster killed 1,549 workers in Honkeiko Colliery in Manchuria Apr. 25, 1942.

Record Oil Spills

As a rule, the number of tons can be multiplied by 7 to estimate the number of barrels spilled; the exact number of barrels in a ton varies with the type of oil. Each barrel contains 42 gallons.

Name, place	Date	Cause	Tons
Ixtoc I oil well, southern Gulf of Mexico	June 3, 1979	Blowout	600,000
Nowruz oil field, Persian Gulf	Feb., 1983	Blowout	600,000 (est.)
Atlantic Empress & Aegean Captain, off Trinidad & Tobago	July 19, 1979	Collision	300,000
Castillo de Bellver, off Cape Town, South Africa	Aug. 6, 1983	Fire	250,000
Amoco Cadiz, near Portsall, France	March 16, 1978 . . .	Grounding	223,000
Torrey Canyon, off Land's End, England	March 18, 1967 . . .	Grounding	119,000
Sea Star, Gulf of Oman	Dec. 19, 1972	Collision	115,000
Urquiola, La Coruna, Spain	May 12, 1976	Grounding	100,000
Hawaiian Patriot, northern Pacific	Feb. 25, 1977	Fire	99,000
Othello, Tralhavet Bay, Sweden	March 20, 1970 . . .	Collision	60,000-100,000

Other Notable Oil Spills

Name, place	Date	Cause	Gallons
World Glory, off South Africa	June 13, 1968	Hull failure	13,524,000
Burmah Agate, Galveston Bay, Tex.	Nov. 1, 1979	Collision	10,700,000
Exxon Valdez, Prince William Sound, Alas.	Mar. 24, 1989	Grounding	10,080,000
Keo, off Massachusetts	Nov. 5, 1969	Hull failure	8,820,000
Storage tank, Sewaren, N.J.	Nov. 4, 1969	Tank rupture	8,400,000
Ekofisk oil field, North Sea	Apr. 22, 1977	Well blowout	8,200,000
Argo Merchant, Nantucket, Mass.	Dec. 15, 1976	Grounding	7,700,000
Pipeline, West Delta, La.	Oct. 15, 1967.	Dragging anchor	6,720,000
Tanker off Japan.	Nov. 30, 1971	Ship broke in half	6,258,000
Storage tank, Monongahela River	Jan. 2, 1988	Tank rupture	3,800,000

Historic Assassinations Since 1865

1865—Apr. 14. U. S. Pres. Abraham Lincoln, shot by John Wilkes Booth in Washington, D. C.; died Apr. 15.

1881—Mar. 13. Alexander II, of Russia—July 2. U. S. Pres. James A. Garfield, shot by Charles J. Guiteau, Washington D.C.; died Sept. 19.

1900—July 29. Umberto I, king of Italy.

1901—Sept. 6. U. S. Pres. William McKinley in Buffalo, N. Y., died Sept. 14. Leon Czolgosz executed for the crime Oct. 29.

1913—Feb. 23. Mexican Pres. Francisco I, Madero and Vice Pres. Jose Pino Suarez.—Mar. 18. George, king of Greece.

1914—June 28. Archduke Francis Ferdinand of Austria-Hungary and his wife in Sarajevo, Bosnia (later part of Yugoslavia), by Gavrilo Princip.

1916—Dec. 30. Grigori Rasputin, politically powerful Russian monk.

1918—July 12. Grand Duke Michael of Russia, at Perm.—July 16. Nicholas II, abdicated as czar of Russia; his wife, the Czarina Alexandra, their son, Czarevitch Alexis, and their daughters, Grand Duchesses Olga, Tatiana, Marie, Anastasia, and 4 members of their household were executed by Bolsheviks at Ekaterinburg.

1920—May 20. Mexican Pres. Gen. Venustiano Carranza in Tlaxcalantongo.

1922—Aug. 22. Michael Collins, Irish revolutionary.—Dec. 16. Polish President Gabriel Narutowicz in Warsaw by an anarchist.

1923—July 20. Gen. Francisco "Pancho" Villa, ex-rebel leader, in Parral, Mexico.

1928—July 17. Gen. Alvaro Obregon, president-elect of Mexico, in San Angel, Mexico.

1933—Feb. 15. In Miami, Fla. Joseph Zangara, anarchist, shot at Pres.-elect Franklin D. Roosevelt, but a woman seized his arm, and the bullet fatally wounded Mayor Anton J. Cermak, of Chicago, who died Mar. 6. Zangara was electrocuted on Mar. 20, 1933.

1934—July 25. In Vienna, Austrian Chancellor Engelbert Dollfuss by Nazis.

1935—Sept. 8. U. S. Sen. Huey P. Long, shot in Baton Rouge, La., by Dr. Carl Austin Weiss, who was slain by Long's bodyguards.

1940—Aug. 20. Leon Trotsky (Lev Bronstein), 63, exiled Russian war minister, near Mexico City. Killer identified as Ramon Mercador del Rio, a Spaniard, served 20 years in Mexican prison.

1948—Jan. 30. Mohandas K. Gandhi, 78, shot in New Delhi, India, by Nathuran Vinayak Godse.—Sept. 17. Count Folke Bernadotte, UN mediator for Palestine, ambushed in Jerusalem.

1951—July 20. King Abdullah ibn Hussein of Jordan. Oct. 21. Prime Min. Liaquat Ali Khan of Pakistan shot in Rawalpindi.

1956—Sept. 21. Pres. Anastasio Somoza of Nicaragua, in Leon; died Sept. 29.

1957—July 26. Pres. Carlos Castillo Armas of Guatemala, in Guatemala City by one of his own guards.

1958—July 14. King Faisal of Iraq; his uncle, Crown Prince Abdul Illah, and July 15, Premier Nuri as-Said, by rebels in Baghdad.

1959—Sept. 25. Prime Minister Solomon Bandaranaike of Ceylon, by Buddhist monk in Colombo.

1961—Jan. 17. Ex-Premier Patrice Lumumba of the Congo, in Katanga Province—May 30. Dominican dictator

Rafael Leonidas Trujillo Molina shot to death by assassins near Ciudad Trujillo.

1963—June 12. Medgar W. Evers, NAACP's Mississippi field secretary, in Jackson, Miss.—Nov. 2. Pres. Ngo Dinh Diem of the Republic of Vietnam and his brother, Ngo Dinh Nhu, in a military coup.—Nov. 22. U. S. Pres. John F. Kennedy fatally shot in Dallas, Tex.; accused Lee Harvey Oswald murdered by Jack Ruby while awaiting trial.

1965—Jan. 21. Iranian premier Hassan Ali Mansour fatally wounded by assassin in Teheran; 4 executed.—Feb. 21. Malcolm X, black nationalist, fatally shot in N. Y. City.

1966—Sept. 6. Prime Minister Hendrik F. Verwoerd of South Africa stabbed to death in parliament at Capetown.

1968—Apr. 4. Rev. Dr. Martin Luther King Jr. fatally shot in Memphis, Tenn. by James Earl Ray.—June 5. Sen. Robert F. Kennedy (D-N. Y.) fatally shot in Los Angeles; Sirhan Sirhan, resident alien, convicted of murder.

1971—Nov. 28. Jordan Prime Minister Wasfi Tal, in Cairo, by Palestinian guerrillas.

1973—Mar. 2. U. S. Ambassador Cleo A. Noel Jr., U. S. Charge d'Affaires George C. Moore and Belgian Charge d'Affaires Guy Eid killed by Palestinian guerrillas in Khartoum, Sudan.

1974—Aug. 15. Mrs. Park Chung Hee, wife of president of So. Korea, hit by bullet meant for her husband.—Aug. 19. U. S. Ambassador to Cyprus, Rodger P. Davies, killed by sniper's bullet in Nicosia.

1975—Feb. 11. Pres. Richard Ratsimandrava, of Madagascar, shot in Tananarive.—Mar. 25. King Faisal of Saudi Arabia shot by nephew Prince Musad Abdel Aziz, in royal palace, Riyadh.—Aug. 15. Bangladesh Pres. Sheik Mujibur Rahman killed in coup.

1976—Feb. 13. Nigerian head of state, Gen. Murtala Ramat Mohammed, slain by self-styled "young revolutionaries."

1977—Mar. 16. Kamal Jumblat, Lebanese Druse chieftain, was shot near Beirut.—Mar. 18. Congo Pres. Marien Ngouabi shot in Brazzaville.

1978—July 9. Former Iraqi Premier Abdul Razak Al-Naif shot in London.

1979—Feb. 14. U.S. Ambassador Adolph Dubs shot and killed by Afghan Moslem extremists in Kabul.—Aug. 27. Lord Mountbatten, WW2 hero, and 2 others were killed when a bomb exploded on his fishing boat off the coast of Co. Sligo, Ire. The IRA claimed responsibility. —Oct. 26. So. Korean President Park Chung Hee and 6 bodyguards fatally shot by Kim Jae Kyu, head of Korean CIA, and 5 aides in Seoul.

1980—Apr. 12. Liberian President William R. Tolbert slain in military coup.—Sept. 17. Former Nicaraguan President Anastasio Somoza Debayle and 2 others shot in Paraguay.

1981—Oct. 6. Egyptian President Anwar El-Sadat fatally shot by a band of commandos while reviewing a military parade in Cairo.

1982—Sept. 14. Lebanese President-elect Bishir Gemayel killed by bomb in east Beirut.

1983—Aug. 21. Philippine opposition political leader Benigno Aquino Jr. fatally shot by a gunman at Manila International Airport.—Oct. 9. Four S. Korea cabinet ministers and 15 others killed by bomb blast in Rangoon, Burma.

1984—Oct. 31. Indian Prime Minister Indira Gandhi shot and killed by 2 of her bodyguards, who were members of the minority Sikh sect, in New Delhi.

1986—Feb. 28. Swedish Premier Olof Palme shot and killed by a gunman in Stockholm.

1988—June 1. Lebanese Premier Rashid Karami killed when a bomb exploded aboard a helicopter in which he was traveling. —Apr. 16. PLO military chief Khalil Wazir (Abu Jihad) was gunned down by Israeli commandos in Tunisia.

1989—Aug. 18. Columbian Liberal Party presidential candidate Luis Carlos Galan was killed by Medellin cartel drug traffickers at a campaign rally in Bogota.—Nov. 22. Lebanese president Rene Moawad was killed when a bomb exploded next to his motorcade.

1990—Mar. 22. Columbian Patriotic Union presidential candidate Bernando Jamamillo Ossa was shot by a gunman at an airport in Bogota.

Assassination Attempts

1910—Aug. 6. N. Y. City Mayor William J. Gaynor shot and seriously wounded by discharged city employee.

1912—Oct. 14. Former U. S. President Theodore Roosevelt shot and seriously wounded by demented man in Milwaukee, Wis.

1950—Nov. 1. In an attempt to assassinate President Truman, 2 members of a Puerto Rican nationalist movement—Griselio Torresola and Oscar Collazo—tried to shoot their way into Blair House. Torresola was killed, and a guard, Pvt. Leslie Coffelt was fatally shot. Collazo was convicted Mar. 7. 1951 for the murder of Coffelt.

1970—Nov. 27. Pope Paul VI unharmed by knife-wielding assailant who attempted to attack him in Manila airport.

1972—May 15. Alabama Gov. George Wallace shot in Laurel, Md. by Arthur Bremer; seriously crippled.

1972—Dec. 7. Mrs. Ferdinand E. Marcos, wife of the Philippine president, was stabbed and seriously injured in Pasay City, Philippines.

1975—Sept. 5. Pres. Gerald R. Ford was unharmed when a Secret Service agent grabbed a pistol aimed at him by Lynette (Squeaky) Fromme, a Charles Manson follower, in Sacramento.

1975—Sept. 22. Pres. Gerald R. Ford escaped unharmed when Sara Jane Moore, a political activist, fired a revolver at him.

1980—Apr. 14. Indian Prime Minister Indira Gandhi was unharmed when a man threw a knife at her in New Delhi.

1980—May 29. Civil rights leader Vernon E. Jordan Jr. shot and wounded in Ft. Wayne, Ind.

1981—Jan. 16. Irish political activist Bernadette Devlin McAliskey and her husband were shot and seriously wounded by 3 members of a protestant paramilitary group in Co. Tyrone, Ire.

1981—Mar. 30. Pres. Ronald Reagan, Press Secy. James Brady, Secret Service agent Timothy J. McCarthy, and Washington, D.C. policeman Thomas Delahanty were shot and seriously wounded by John W. Hinckley Jr. in Washington, D.C.

1981—May 13. Pope John Paul II and 2 bystanders were shot and wounded by Mehmet Ali Agca, an escaped Turkish murderer, in St. Peter's Square, Rome.

1982—May 12. Pope John Paul II was unharmed when a man with a knife was overpowered by guards, in Fatima, Portugal.

1982—June 3. Israel's ambassador to Britain Shlomo Argov was shot and seriously wounded by Arab terrorists in London.

1986—Sept. 7. Chile President Gen. Augusto Pinochet Ugarte escaped unharmed when his motorcade was attacked by rebels using rockets, bazookas, grenades, and rifles.

Notable Kidnapings

Edward A. Cudahy Jr., 16, in Omaha, Neb., Dec. 18, 1900. Returned Dec. 20 after $25,000 paid. Pat Crowe confessed.

Robert Franks, 13, in Chicago, May 22, 1924, by 2 youths, Richard Loeb and Nathan Leopold, who killed boy. Demand for $10,000 ignored. Loeb died in prison, Leopold paroled 1958.

Charles A. Lindbergh Jr., 20 mos. old, in Hopewell, N.J., Mar. 1, 1932; found dead May 12. Ransom of $50,000 was paid to man identified as Bruno Richard Hauptmann, 35, paroled German convict who entered U.S. illegally. Haupt-

(continued)

mann was convicted after spectacular trial at Flemington, and electrocuted in Trenton, N.J. prison, Apr. 3, 1936.

William A. Hamm Jr., 39, in St. Paul, **June 15, 1933**. $100,000 paid. Alvin Karpis given life, paroled in 1969.

Charles F. Urschel, in Oklahoma City, **July 22, 1933**. Released July 31 after $200,000 paid. George (Machine Gun) Kelly and 5 others given life.

Brooke L. Hart, 22, in San Jose, Cal. Thomas Thurmond and John Holmes arrested after demanding $40,000 ransom. When Hart's body was found in San Francisco Bay, Nov. 26, 1933, a mob attacked the jail at San Jose and lynched the 2 kidnapers.

George Weyerhaeuser, 9, in Tacoma, Wash., **May 24, 1935**. Returned home June 1 after $200,000 paid. Kidnapers given 20 to 60 years.

Charles Mattson, 10, in Tacoma, Wash., **Dec. 27, 1936**. Found dead Jan. 11, 1937. Kidnaper asked $28,000, failed to contact.

Arthur Fried, in White Plains, N.Y., **Dec. 4, 1937**. Body not found. Two kidnapers executed.

Robert C. Greenlease, 6, taken from Kansas City, Mo. school **Sept. 28, 1953**, and held for $600,000. Body found Oct. 7. Mrs. Bonnie Brown Heady and Carl A. Hall pleaded guilty and were executed.

Peter Weinberger, 32 days old, Westbury, N.Y., **July 4, 1956**, for $2,000 ransom, not paid. Child found dead. Angelo John LaMarca, 31, convicted, executed.

Cynthia Ruotolo, 6 wks old, taken from carriage in front of Hamden, Conn. store **Sept. 1, 1956**. Body found in lake.

Lee Crary, 8 in Everett, Wash., **Sept. 22, 1957**, $10,000 ransom, not paid. He escaped after 3 days, led police to George E. Collins, who was convicted.

Eric Peugeot, 4, taken from playground at St. Cloud golf course, Paris, **Apr. 12, 1960**. Released unharmed 3 days later after payment of undisclosed sum. Two sentenced to prison.

Frank Sinatra Jr., 19, from hotel room in Lake Tahoe, Cal., **Dec. 8, 1963**. Released Dec. 11 after his father paid $240,000 ransom. Three men sentenced to prison; most of ransom recovered.

Barbara Jane Mackle, 20, abducted **Dec. 17, 1968**, from Atlanta, Ga., motel, was found unharmed 3 days later, buried in a coffin-like wooden box 18 inches underground, after her father had paid $500,000 ransom; Gary Steven Krist sentenced to life, Ruth Eisenmann-Schier to 7 years; most of ransom recovered.

Anne Katherine Jenkins, 22, abducted **May 10, 1969**, from her Baltimore apartment, freed 3 days later after her father paid $10,000 ransom.

Mrs. Roy Fuchs, 35, and 3 children held hostage 2 hours, **May 14, 1969**, in Long Island, N. Y., released after her husband, a bank manager, paid kidnapers $129,000 in bank funds; 4 men arrested, ransom recovered.

C. Burke Elbrick, U.S. ambassador to Brazil, kidnaped by revolutionaries in Rio de Janeiro **Sept. 4, 1969**; released 3 days later after Brazil yielded to kidnaper's demands to publish manifesto and release 15 political prisoners.

Patrick Dolan, 18, found shot to death near Sao Paulo, Brazil, **Nov. 5, 1969**, after he was kidnaped and $12,500 paid.

Sean M. Holly, U.S. diplomat, in Guatemala **Mar. 6, 1970**; freed 2 days later upon release of 3 terrorists from prison.

Lt. Col. Donald J. Crowley, U.S. air attache, in Dominican Republic **Mar. 24, 1970**; released after government allowed 20 prisoners to leave the country.

Count Karl von Spreti, W. German ambassador to Guatemala, **Mar. 31, 1970**; slain after Guatemala refused demands for $700,000 and release of 22 prisoners.

Pedro Eugenio Aramburu, former Argentine president, by terrorists **May 29, 1970**; body found July 17.

Ehrenfried von Holleben, W. German ambassador to Brazil, by terrorists **June 11, 1970**; freed after release of 40 prisoners.

Daniel A. Mitrione, U.S. diplomat, **July 31, 1970**, by terrorists in Montevideo, Uruguay; body found Aug. 10 after government rejected demands for release of all political pris-

oners.

James R. Cross, British trade commissioner, **Oct. 5, 1970**, by French Canadian separatists in Quebec; freed Dec. 3 after 3 kidnapers and relatives flown to Cuba by government.

Pierre Laporte, Quebec Labor Minister, by separatists **Oct. 10, 1970**; body found Oct. 18.

Giovanni E. Bucher, Swiss ambassador **Dec. 7, 1970**, by revolutionaries in Rio de Janeiro; freed Jan. 16, 1971, after Brazil released 70 political prisoners.

Geoffrey Jackson, British ambassador, in Montevideo, **Jan. 8, 1971**, by Tupamaro terrorists. Held as ransom for release of imprisoned terrorists; released Sept. 9; prisoners escaped.

Ephraim Elrom, Israel consul general in Istanbul, **May 17, 1971**. Held as ransom for imprisoned terrorists; found dead May 23.

Mrs. Virginia Piper, 49 abducted **July 27, 1972**, from her home in suburban Minneapolis; found unharmed near Duluth 2 days later after her husband paid $1 million ransom to the kidnapers.

Victor E. Samuelson, Exxon executive. **Dec. 6, 1973**, in Campana, Argentina, by Marxist guerrillas, freed Apr. 29, 1974, after payment of record $14.2 million ransom.

J. Paul Getty 3d, 17, grandson of the U.S. oil mogul, released **Dec. 15, 1973**, in southern Italy after $2.8 million ransom paid.

Patricia (Patty) Hearst, 19, taken from her Berkeley, Cal., apartment **Feb. 4, 1974**. Symbionese Liberation Army demanded her father, Randolph A. Hearst, publisher, give millions to poor. She was identified by FBI as taking part in a San Francisco bank holdup, **Apr. 15**. FBI, **Sept. 18, 1975**, captured Patricia and others in San Francisco; they were indicted on various charges. Patricia for bank robbery. Convicted, **Mar. 20, 1976**. She was released from prison under executive clemency, **Feb. 1, 1979**. In 1978, William and Emily Harris were sentenced to 10 years to life for the Hearst kidnaping. Both were paroled in 1983.

J. Reginald Murphy, 40, an editor of *Atlanta* (Ga.) *Constitution*, kidnaped **Feb. 20, 1974**, freed **Feb. 22** after payment of $700,000 ransom by the newspaper. Police arrested William A. H. Williams, a contractor; most of the money was recovered.

J. Guadalupe Zuno Hernandez, 83, father-in-law of Mexican President Luis Echeverria Alvarez, seized by 4 terrorists **Aug. 28, 1974**; government refused to negotiate; he was released **Sept. 8**.

E. B. Reville, Hepzibah, Ga., banker, and wife Jean, kidnaped **Sept. 30, 1974**. Ransom of $30,000 paid. He was found alive; Mrs. Reville was found dead in car trunk Oct. 2.

Jack Teich, Kings Point, N.Y., steel executive, seized **Nov. 12, 1974**; released Nov. 19 after payment of $750,000.

William F. Niehous, a U.S. businessman, was abducted from his suburban Caracas, Venezuela home, **Feb. 27, 1976**. He was rescued by police **June 29, 1979**, ending more than 3 years of captivity.

Hanns-Martin Schleyer, a West German industrialist, was kidnaped in Cologne, **Sept. 5, 1977** by armed terrorists. Schleyer was found dead, **Oct. 19**, in an abandoned car shortly after 3 jailed terrorist leaders of the Baader-Meinhof gang were found dead in their prison cells near Stuttgart, West Germany.

Aldo Moro, former Italian premier, kidnaped in Rome, **Mar. 16, 1978**, by left-wing terrorists. Five of his bodyguards killed during abduction. Moro's bullet-ridden body was found in a parked car, **May 9**, in Rome. Six members of the Red Brigades arrested, charged, June 5, with complicity in the kidnaping.

James L. Dozier, a U.S. Army general, kidnaped from his apartment in Verona, Italy, **Dec. 17, 1981**, by members of the Red Brigades terrorist organization. He was rescued, **Jan. 28, 1982**.

Enrique Camarena Salazar, and **Alfredo Zavala Avelar**, U.S. Drug Enforcement Agency employees were kidnaped in Guadalajara, Mexico, **Feb. 7, 1985**. Their bodies were found Mar. 6.

UNITED STATES POPULATION

The Bicentennial Census

On April 1, 1990, the Bureau of the Census began to take the 21st decennial census of the United States. The Census Bureau took the first census in 1790, when it counted 3.9 million people, and has conducted a census every 10 years over the past 200 years, as mandated by the U.S. Constitution, Article 1, Section 2. The primary purpose of the census was, and is, to provide population counts needed to apportion seats in the U.S. House of Representatives, and to subsequently determine state legislative district boundaries. In addition, the findings of the 1990 census are critical to many other national, state, and local programs, which: determine compliances with the Voting Rights Act and amendments; allocate funds from federal grant programs; identify areas needing bilingual education; assess the need for equal employment opportunity programs; allocate funds and analyze programs for American Indians and Alaska Natives; identify areas needing energy assistance; develop programs to reduce unemployment; identify areas needing programs to stimulate economic growth; establish fair lending practices; assess the need for developing or expanding low-income housing programs; and identify areas requiring child assistance programs. For state and local government programs, the census results will help: develop social services programs, including programs for the elderly and handicapped; assess transportation systems and improve commuting patterns; identify areas for low-cost housing programs; establish occupational and vocational education programs; plan school district boundaries and school construction programs; and assess the need for state housing bonds for below-market interest rates on mortgages.

History of the Census

The first U.S. census was conducted shortly after George Washington became president. It counted the number of free white males age 16 and over, and under 16 (to measure how many men might be available for military service), the number of free white females, all other free persons (including any American Indians who paid taxes), and slaves. It took 18 months to collect the data, often on unofficial sheets of paper supplied by U.S. marshals. In contrast to today's pledge of confidentiality, the 1790 census was displayed "at two of the most public places." The 1790 census resulted in an increase of 41 seats (65 to 106) in the House of Representatives.

As the nation expanded, so did the scope of the census data. The first inquiry on manufactures was made in 1810. Questions on agriculture, mining, and fisheries were added in 1840. In 1850, the census included inquiries on social issues—taxation, churches, pauperism, and crime.

The 1880 census contained so many questions that it took the full 10 years between censuses to publish all the results. Because of this delay, Congress limited the 1900 census to questions on population, manufactures, agriculture, and mortality. (Many of the dropped topics reappeared in later censuses.)

For many years, each census had to be authorized by a specific act of Congress. In 1954, Congress specified the laws under which the Census Bureau operates in Title 13 of the U.S. Code. This title delineates the basic scope of the census, the requirements for the public to provide information as well for the Bureau to keep information confidential, and the penalties for violating any of these obligations. The secretary of commerce (and through him, the Census Bureau) is now directed by law to take censuses of population, housing, agriculture, irrigation, manufactures, mineral in-

dustries, other businesses (wholesale trade, retail trade, services), construction, transportation, and governments at stated intervals, and may take surveys related to any of these subjects.

U.S. marshals supervised their assistants' enumeration of the first nine censuses and reported to the president (1790), the secretary of state (1800-1840), or the secretary of the interior (1850-1870). There was no continuity of personnel from one census to the next. However, in 1902, Congress authorized the president to set up a permanent Census Office in the Interior Dept. In 1903, the agency was transferred to the new Dept. of Commerce and Labor, and when the department split in 1913, the Bureau of the Census was placed in the Commerce Dept.

The Census Bureau began using statistical sampling techniques in the 1940s, computers in the 1950s, and mail enumeration in the 1960s, all in an effort to publish more data sooner and at a lower cost, and with less burden on the public.

1990 Projections

As mandated by Congress, the bureau must report the total population counts (used for congressional apportionment) for each state by race and Hispanic origin, cross tabulated by all ages, to the president by Dec. 31, 1990 (after publication of this edition—for complete census counts, see The World Almanac, 1992). This data is taken from the "short form," sent to all U.S. households, which contains 14 basic population and housing questions. The deadline for all states to receive redistricting counts is April 1, 1991.

Approximately 20 percent of all households received a longer form, which asked the same basic questions plus 45 additional inquiries (no individual had to answer all questions) concerning housing characteristics, citizenship, education, ancestry, residence five years ago, language, military service, disability, labor force participation, transportation, and income. The data from this sample will be statistically inflated to depict the entire population. Information collected on the "long form" should begin to be available to the public in mid-1992. The complete analysis of census data will probably take the entire decade of the 1990s.

Based on the Census Bureau's own estimates, the 1990 census will show that the U.S. population has reached approximately 250 million, a 10.4 percent increase over the 1980 count of 226,545,805. The nation totaled 200 million on Nov. 20, 1967, reached 150 million in 1949, totaled 100 million in 1915, and 50 million in 1880. The bureau's projections indicate that the population could reach 300 million by 2020.

The nation is growing by about 6,300 persons daily, some 4,400 coming from a surplus of births (10,600) over deaths (6,200). The remaining average daily growth of 2,000 comes from immigration. Currently, the U.S. is experiencing a net gain of one person every 14 seconds. This is based on one birth every eight seconds, one death every 14 seconds, one immigrant every 35 seconds, and one person leaving the country every three minutes.

Accounting for one-fifth of the total U.S. population growth during the 1980s were immigrants, particularly Mexicans, Filipinos, Chinese, Koreans, and Vietnamese. The 1990 census will count 21 million Hispanics (8 percent of the total U.S. population), a 44 percent increase since 1980. (An estimated 1 million Hispanics were not counted in 1980, and this undercount is part of the controversy over the 1990 count.) The black population increased by 16 percent and remained at 12

(continued)

percent of the total population between 1980 and 1990. Whites increased by 8 percent during the 1980s, and their percent of the total population decreased from 86 to 84 percent.

During the past 10 years, the number of people aged 40 to 44 grew by 49.8 percent and those 35 to 39 increased by 43.8 percent. The population aged 95 to 99 has increased by 96 percent and those 100 or older (57,000 total) increased by 76.6 percent between 1980 and 1990.

Los Angeles-Long Beach grew by 17 percent since 1980, and replaced New York City, which increased by 4 percent, as the most populated metropolitan area. Among the 25 largest metropolitan areas, Riverside-San Bernardino, Calif. has been the fastest growing, with a 45 percent increase since 1980. Phoenix, Dallas, Tampa-St. Petersburg, Houston, Atlanta, and San Diego increased by more than 25 percent each. Pittsburgh, Detroit, and Cleveland were the only metro areas among the top 25 to lose population during the past decade.

If the projected state counts are accurate, California (5), Texas (4), and Florida (3) are expected to gain the most seats in the House of Representatives after redistricting. It is also projected that Arizona and Georgia will gain two seats each, and North Carolina and Virginia one each. Projected decreases in House seats include New York and Pennsylvania (-3 each), Illinois, Michigan, and Ohio (-2 each), and Idaho, Iowa, Kansas, Massachusetts, West Virginia, and Wisconsin (-1 each).

The Process and the Problems

Planned since 1984, the 1990 census required the hiring of over 500,000 people (about 300,000 working at peak), working at 484 field offices, 13 regional census centers, and 7 processing offices. Over 106 million questionnaire packages were printed, assembled, and mailed. Nearly 7 million maps were generated to help census takers collect questionnaires (from those who did not return theirs by mail). The Census Bureau will use 570 minicomputers in field offices, which were set up and will be dismantled in a one-year period. The bureau estimated that from 1984 to 1993, the total cost of carrying out and providing the results of the 1990 census will be approximately $2.6 billion, with more than $1.3 billion spent in 1990.

In 1980, the return rate for the census questionnaires was approximately 75 percent. When the Census Bureau first mailed 1990 forms in April, it expected to get 70 percent returned, but received only 63 percent. Many reasons were cited for the low rate of return including the public's apathy, distrust of the government, illiteracy, concern about privacy, forgetfulness, as well as problems with the mail. As of mid-July, the bureau reported that 99 percent of the households that did not respond to first mailings had been counted (by enumerators and remailing), but that several areas still lagged far behind. The original deadline for the count's completion was June 7, 1990, but because of the slow return rate it was pushed back to June 30. A 99 percent success rate for the households that did not return the forms in April means less than 1 percent of the total was not counted (as of July 1990). The success rates for previously uncounted residents in New York, Delaware, Maryland, and California were all below 95 percent. New York City, San Jose, San Francisco, and Boston had particularly low return rates, while Detroit, Chicago, and Cleveland returned 100 percent in the follow-up.

In addition to concerns about substantial undercounting of homeless persons, there has been criticism of the Census Bureau regarding the accuracy of the count. Leaders in New York City, Los Angeles, Chicago, Houston, and Miami have urged the bureau to make a statistical adjustment to the 1990 count. In fact, these cities (plus New York State and California) have sued the Commerce Dept. to demand a post-census adjustment, which would require a survey of 150,000 housing units. Those demanding an adjustment claim that the census will undercount due to difficulties in reaching people in urban areas. The Census Bureau estimated that it missed about 2.2 million people in 1980—about 1.6 percent of the population—and some fear that the undercount will be even greater in 1990. In New York City, officials stated that the undercount in 1990 could reach 1 million, resulting in the loss of two congressional seats and more than $1 billion in federal aid in the 1990s. A decision on the statistical adjustment must be made by the secretary of commerce by July 15, 1991. At a congressional hearing (July 1990) to confirm Barbara Everitt Bryant as director of the Census Bureau, Bryant stated that there was a "50-50 chance of having all the work done in time to make an adjustment decision" by that date. The Census Bureau has never made a statistical adjustment of the census like the one being sought.

M.S.H., Editor

Changing Population Patterns

By Barbara Everitt Bryant

Director, U.S. Bureau of the Census

On January 1, 1990, the estimated resident population of the United States was 249.6 million, a 10.2 percent increase over the April 1, 1980 census count of 226.5 million. The growth of 23.1 million was attributable to a natural increase of 16.5 million (36.6 million births less 20.1 million deaths) and a net immigration of 6.6 million.

Changes in age structure during the 1980s reflect past trends in childbearing: the low birth rate in the two decades ending in 1945, the higher birth rate during the "baby boom" (1946-1964), and the lower birth rate subsequently. From 1980 to July 1, 1989, the population 18 to 24 years old declined 12.2 percent while the population 25 to 44 years old increased 28.1 percent. The elderly population (65 years and over) rose 21.3 percent and increased from 11.3 percent to 12.5 percent of the total population. The median age (the age at which half the population is younger and half is older) rose from 30.0 to 32.7. The elderly percentage and the median age in 1989 were the highest in the nation's history.

The South and West accounted for 18.8 million, or 87 percent, of the nation's population growth from 1980 to 1989 and increased their share of the population from 52.3 to 55.3 percent. The share of the population residing in the North (Northeast and Midwest regions) dropped below 50 percent in 1975. During the 1980 to 1989 period, the South and West added 8.9 million population through net migration while the North lost 2.7 million population through net migration. California, Texas, and Florida together accounted for 11.1 million, or 51 percent, of national growth from 1980 to 1989. The highest growth rates were in Nevada (38.8 percent), Alaska (31.1 percent), and Arizona (30.8 percent) while Iowa, West Virginia, and the District of Columbia lost population. In 1989, **11.7 percent of the nation's population resided in California.** This is the highest concentration in any one state since 1860 when 12.3 percent resided in New York. California's population in 1989 (29.1 million) exceeded the combined population of the 21 least populous states.

In 1988, the nation's 37 **metropolitan areas** with at least 1 million population had 120.4 million residents, or 49 percent of the national population. Altogether, 189.4 million persons, or 77 percent, lived in the nation's 283 designated metropolitan areas. From 1980 to 1988, the population in metropolitan areas increased 9.7 percent, about twice the 4.5 percent increase in nonmetropolitan territory. During the 1970s, the growth rate was higher in nonmetropolitan territory than in metropolitan areas. The growth rates in metropolitan areas by size category were similar in the 1980 to 1988 period. In the 1970s, the metropolitan growth rate was lowest in the largest areas (those with 5 million or more population). For nonmetropolitan counties, the growth rate was highest in both periods in counties with 15 percent or more of their resident workers commuting to metropolitan areas. The New York City metropolitan area had 18.1 million residents in 1988, followed by the Los Angeles (13.8 million) and Chicago (8.2 million) metropolitan areas. Among metropolitan areas with at least 1 million population, the highest growth rates in the 1980 to 1988 period were in Phoenix (34.5 percent), Dallas-Ft. Worth (28.5 percent), and Atlanta (28 percent).

In 1988, only 5 million perso s lived on **farms,** down from 15.6 million in 1960 and 32 million in 1920. The 1988 figure represented only 2 percent of the nation's population compared to 8.7 percent in 1960 and 30.2 percent in 1920.

Based on data from the Current Population Survey, there were 92.8 million **households** (occupied housing units) in the United States in March 1989, up 14.9 percent from the March 1980 estimate of 80.8 million.

The more rapid growth rate in households than in population reflects changes in age structure which in turn reflect the changes in childbearing noted earlier. The average number of persons per household dropped from 3.33 in 1964 to 2.76 in 1980 and to a record low of 2.62 in 1989. Most of the decline is attributable to the decline in the average number of children (under 18 years), which dropped from 1.23 in 1964 (at the end of the baby boom) to 0.79 in 1980 and 0.69 in 1989. There were 22.7 million 1-person households in 1989, up from 18.3 million in 1980 and 10.9 million in 1970. Households with 5 or more persons numbered 9.3 million in 1989, down from 10.4 million in 1980 and 13.3 million in 1970. From 1980 to 1989, the number of married-couple families increased from 49.1 million to 52.1 million, and the number of female-householder families (no spouse present) rose from 8.7 million to 10.9 million. (Families have at least two members, including at least one relative of the householder.)

Today's **young adults** are less likely to have married or to be maintaining their own households than in the past. The median age at first marriage for females rose from 20.3 in 1960 to 22.0 in 1980 and 23.8 in 1989. The corresponding figures for males are 22.8, 24.7, and 26.2. In 1989, 52.5 percent of persons 18 to 24 years old lived with one or both parents, up from 48.4 percent in 1980 and 43.0 percent in 1960. Among **children under 18 years,** 73.1 percent lived with both parents in 1989, down from 76.7 percent in 1980 and 87.7 percent in 1960. The decline reflects changing **marital patterns:** the number of divorced persons per 1,000 married persons with spouse present was 138 in 1989, up from 100 in 1980 and 35 in 1960.

The **educational level** of the population continues to rise. Among persons 25 years and over in 1988, 76.2 percent had completed 4 years of high school (or more education), up from 68.6 percent in 1980 and 24.5 percent in 1940; 20.3 percent had completed 4 or more years of college, compared to 17.0 percent in 1980 and 4.6 percent in 1940. In 1988, 24.0 percent of males and 17.0 percent of females had completed 4 or more years of college.

Resident Population by Sex, Race, Residence, and Median Age: 1790 to 1989

Source: U.S. Bureau of the Census (thousands, except as indicated)

Date	Sex		Race				Residence		Median Age (years)		
	Male	Female	White	Black Number	Black Percent	Other	Urban	Rural	All races	White	Black
Conterminous U.S.[1]											
1790 (Aug. 2) . . .	NA	NA	3,172	757	19.3	NA	202	3,728	NA	NA	NA
1810 (Aug. 6). . .	NA	NA	5,862	1,378	19.0	NA	525	6,714	NA	16.0	NA
1820 (Aug. 7). . .	4,897	4,742	7,867	1,772	18.4	NA	693	8,945	16.7	16.5	17.2
1840 (June 1) . .	8,689	8,381	14,196	2,874	16.8	NA	1,845	15,224	17.8	17.9	17.3
1860 (June 1) . .	16,085	15,358	26,923	4,442	14.1	79	6,217	25,227	19.4	19.7	17.7
1870 (June 1) . .	19,494	19,065	33,589	4,880	12.7	89	9,902	28,656	20.2	20.4	18.5
1880 (June 1) . .	25,519	24,637	43,403	6,581	13.1	172	14,130	36,026	20.9	21.4	18.0
1890 (June 1) . .	32,237	30,711	55,101	7,489	11.9	358	22,106	40,841	22.0	22.5	17.8
1900 (June 1) . .	38,816	37,178	66,809	8,834	11.6	351	30,160	45,835	22.9	23.4	19.4
1920 (Jan. 1) . .	53,900	51,810	94,821	10,463	9.9	427	54,158	51,553	25.3	25.6	22.3
1930 (Apr. 1) . . .	62,137	60,638	110,287	11,891	9.7	597	68,955	53,820	26.4	26.9	23.5
1940 (Apr. 1) . . .	66,062	65,608	118,215	12,866	9.8	589	74,424	57,246	29.0	29.5	25.3
United States											
1950 (Apr. 1) . . .	75,187	76,139	135,150	15,045	9.9	1,131	96,847	54,479	30.2	30.7	26.2
1960 (Apr. 1) . . .	88,331	90,992	158,832	18,872	10.5	1,620	125,269	54,054	29.5	30.3	23.5
1970 (Apr. 1)[2] . .	98,926	104,309	178,098	22,581	11.1	2,557	149,325	53,887	28.0	28.9	22.4
1980 (Apr. 1)[3] . .	110,053	116,493	194,713	26,683	11.8	5,150	167,051	59,495	30.0	30.9	24.9
1983 (July 1, est)	113,119	120,365	199,849	28,056	12.0	6,379	NA	NA	30.8	31.7	25.9
1984 (July 1, est)	115,022	121,455	201,290	28,457	12.0	6,730	NA	NA	31.1	32.0	26.3
1985 (July 1, est)	116,160	122,576	202,769	28,870	12.1	7,097	NA	NA	31.4	32.3	26.6
1986 (July 1, est)	117,730	123,737	204,326	29,303	12.2	7,478	NA	NA	31.7	32.7	26.9
1987 (July 1, est)	118,541	124,886	205,833	29,746	12.2	7,846	NA	NA	32.1	33.0	27.2
1988 (July 1, est)	119,724	126,060	207,357	30,201	12.3	8,227	NA	NA	32.4	33.3	27.5
1989 (July 1, est)	120,982	127,258	208,961	30,660	12.4	8,618	NA	NA	32.7	33.8	27.7

(NA) Not available. (1) Excludes Alaska and Hawaii. (2) The revised 1970 resident population count is 203,302,031, which incorporates changes due to errors found after tabulations were completed. The race and sex data shown here reflect the official 1970 census count while the residence data come from the tabulated count. (3) The race data shown for April 1, 1980 have been modified.

U.S. Population by Official

(Members of the Armed Forces overseas or

State	1790	1800	1810	1820	1830	1840	1850	1860	1870	1880
Ala. . .	....	1,250	9,046	127,901	309,527	590,756	771,623	964,201	996,992	1,262,505
Alas. . .										33,426
Ariz. . .									9,658	40,440
Ark. . .	....	....	1,062	14,273	30,388	97,574	209,897	435,450	484,471	802,525
Cal. . .							92,597	379,994	560,247	864,694
Col. . .								34,277	39,864	194,327
Conn. .	237,946	251,002	261,942	275,248	297,675	309,978	370,792	460,147	537,454	622,700
Del. . .	59,096	64,273	72,674	72,749	76,748	78,085	91,532	112,216	125,015	146,608
D.C. . .	....	8,144	15,471	23,336	30,261	33,745	51,687	75,080	131,700	177,624
Fla. . .					34,730	54,477	87,445	140,424	187,748	269,493
Ga. . .	82,548	162,686	252,433	340,989	516,823	691,392	906,185	1,057,286	1,184,109	1,542,180
Ha. . .										
Ida. . .									14,999	32,610
Ill. . . .			12,282	55,211	157,445	476,183	851,470	1,711,951	2,539,891	3,077,871
Ind. . .		5,641	24,520	147,178	343,031	685,866	988,416	1,350,428	1,680,637	1,978,301
Ia. . . .						43,112	192,214	674,913	1,194,020	1,624,615
Kan. . .								107,206	364,399	996,096
Ky. . . .	73,677	220,955	406,511	564,317	687,917	779,828	982,405	1,155,684	1,321,011	1,648,690
La. . .			76,556	153,407	215,739	352,411	517,762	708,002	726,915	939,946
Me. . .	96,540	151,719	228,705	298,335	399,455	501,793	583,169	628,279	626,915	648,936
Md. . .	319,728	341,548	380,546	407,350	447,040	470,019	583,034	687,049	780,894	934,943
Mass. .	378,787	422,845	472,040	523,287	610,408	737,699	994,514	1,231,066	1,457,351	1,783,085
Mich. .			4,762	8,896	31,639	212,267	397,654	749,113	1,184,059	1,636,937
Minn. .							6,077	172,023	439,706	780,773
Miss. .		7,600	31,306	75,448	136,621	375,651	606,526	791,305	827,922	1,131,597
Mo. . .			19,783	66,586	140,455	383,702	682,044	1,182,012	1,721,295	2,168,380
Mon. . .									20,595	39,159
Neb. . .								28,841	122,993	452,402
Nev. . .								6,857	42,491	62,266
N.H. . .	141,885	183,858	214,460	244,161	269,328	284,574	317,976	326,073	318,300	346,991
N.J. . .	184,139	211,149	245,562	277,575	320,823	373,306	489,555	672,035	906,096	1,131,116
N.M. . .							61,547	93,516	91,874	119,565
N.Y. . .	340,120	589,051	959,049	1,372,812	1,918,608	2,428,921	3,097,394	3,880,735	4,382,759	5,082,871
N.C. . .	393,751	478,103	555,500	638,829	737,987	753,419	869,039	992,622	1,071,361	1,399,750
N.D. . .									*2,405	36,909
Oh. . .		45,365	230,760	581,434	937,903	1,519,467	1,980,329	2,339,511	2,665,260	3,198,062
Okla. . .										
Ore. . .							12,093	52,465	90,923	174,768
Pa. . .	434,373	602,365	810,091	1,049,458	1,348,233	1,724,033	2,311,786	2,906,215	3,521,951	4,282,891
R.I. . .	68,825	69,122	76,931	83,059	97,199	108,830	147,545	174,620	217,353	276,531
S.C. . .	249,073	345,591	415,115	502,741	581,185	594,398	668,507	703,708	705,606	995,577
S.D. . .								*4,837	*11,776	98,268
Tenn. .	35,691	105,602	261,727	422,823	681,904	829,210	1,002,717	1,109,801	1,258,520	1,542,359
Tex. . .							212,592	604,215	818,579	1,591,749
Ut. . . .							11,380	40,273	86,786	143,963
Vt. . . .	85,425	154,465	217,895	235,981	280,652	291,948	314,120	315,098	330,551	332,286
Va. . .	691,737	807,557	877,683	938,261	1,044,054	1,025,227	1,119,348	1,219,630	1,225,163	1,512,565
Wash. .							1,201	11,594	23,955	75,116
W. Va. .	55,873	78,592	105,469	136,808	176,924	224,537	302,313	376,688	442,014	618,457
Wis. . .						30,945	305,391	775,881	1,054,670	1,315,497
Wy. . .									9,118	20,789
U.S. . .	3,929,214	5,308,483	7,239,881	9,638,453	12,860,702	17,063,353¹	23,191,876	31,443,321¹	38,558,371	50,189,209

Note: Where possible, population shown is that of 1980 area of state.
*1860 figure is for Dakota Territory; 1870 figures are for parts of Dakota Territory. (1) U.S. total includes persons (5,318 in 1830 and 6,100 in 1840) on public ships in the service of the United States not credited to any region, division, or state.

Density of Population by States

(Per square mile, land area only)

State	1920	1960	1980	1988	State	1920	1960	1980	1988	State	1920	1960	1980	1988
Ala. . .	45.8	64.2	76.6	80.8	La. . .	39.6	72.2	94.5	99.0	Oh. . .	141.4	236.6	263.3	264.7
Alas.*	0.1	0.4	0.7	0.9	Me. . .	25.7	31.3	36.3	38.9	Okla. . .	29.2	33.8	44.1	47.2
Ariz. . .	2.9	11.5	23.9	30.7	Md. . .	145.8	313.5	428.7	469.9	Ore. . .	8.2	18.4	27.4	28.8
Ark. . .	33.4	34.2	43.9	46.0	Mass. .	479.2	657.3	733.3	752.7	Pa. . .	194.5	251.4	264.3	267.4
Cal. . .	22.0	100.4	151.4	181.2	Mich. .	63.8	137.7	162.6	162.2	R.I. . .	566.4	819.3	897.8	940.9
Col. . .	9.1	16.9	27.9	31.9	Minn. .	29.5	43.1	51.2	54.1	S.C. . .	55.2	78.7	103.4	114.9
Conn. .	286.4	520.6	637.8	663.6	Miss. .	38.6	46.0	53.4	55.5	S.D. . .	8.3	9.0	9.1	9.4
Del. . .	113.5	225.2	307.6	341.7	Mo. . .	49.5	62.6	71.3	74.6	Tenn. .	56.1	86.2	111.6	118.9
D.C. . .	7,292.9	12,523.9	10,132.3	9,792.0	Mon. . .	3.8	4.6	5.4	5.5	Tex. . .	17.8	36.4	54.3	64.3
Fla. . .	17.7	91.5	180.0	227.8	Neb. . .	16.9	18.4	20.5	20.9	Ut. . .	5.5	10.8	17.8	20.6
Ga. . .	49.3	67.8	94.1	109.2	Nev. . .	.7	2.6	7.3	9.6	Vt. . .	38.6	42.0	55.2	60.1
Ha.*	39.9	98.5	150.1	170.9	N.H. . .	49.1	67.2	102.4	120.7	Va. . .	57.4	99.6	134.7	151.5
Ida. . .	5.2	8.1	11.5	12.2	N.J. . .	420.0	805.5	986.2	1,033.9	Wash. .	20.3	42.8	62.1	69.9
Ill. . . .	115.7	180.4	205.3	208.7	N.M. . .	2.9	7.8	10.7	12.4	W. Va. .	60.9	77.2	80.8	77.6
Ind. . .	81.3	128.8	152.8	154.6	N.Y. . .	217.9	350.6	370.6	378.0	Wis. . .	47.6	72.6	86.5	89.2
Ia. . . .	43.2	49.2	52.1	50.6	N.C. . .	52.5	93.2	120.4	132.9	Wy. . .	2.0	3.4	4.9	4.9
Kan. . .	21.6	26.6	28.9	30.5	N.D. . .	9.2	9.1	9.4	9.6	U.S. . .	*29.9	50.6	64.0	69.5
Ky. . . .	60.1	76.2	92.3	93.9										

*For purposes of comparison, Alaska and Hawaii included in above tabulation for 1920, even though not states then.

Census from 1790 to 1980

other U.S. nationals overseas are not included.

1890	1900	1910	1920	1930	1940	1950	1960	1970	1980[1]
1,513,401	1,828,697	2,138,093	2,348,174	2,646,248	2,832,961	3,061,743	3,266,740	3,444,354	3,894,025
32,052	63,592	64,356	55,036	59,278	72,524	128,643	226,167	302,583	401,851
88,243	122,931	204,354	334,162	435,573	499,261	749,587	1,302,161	1,775,399	2,716,546
1,128,211	1,311,564	1,574,449	1,752,204	1,854,482	1,949,387	1,909,511	1,786,272	1,923,322	2,286,357
1,213,398	1,485,053	2,377,549	3,426,861	5,677,251	6,907,387	10,586,223	15,717,204	19,971,069	23,667,764
413,249	539,700	799,024	939,629	1,035,791	1,123,296	1,325,089	1,753,947	2,209,596	2,889,735
746,258	908,420	1,114,756	1,380,631	1,606,903	1,709,242	2,007,280	2,535,234	3,032,217	3,107,564
168,493	184,735	202,322	223,003	238,380	266,505	318,085	446,292	548,104	594,338
230,392	278,718	331,069	437,571	486,869	663,091	802,178	763,956	756,668	638,432
391,422	528,542	752,619	968,470	1,468,211	1,897,414	2,771,305	4,951,560	6,791,418	²9,746,961
1,837,353	2,216,331	2,609,121	2,895,832	2,908,506	3,123,723	3,444,578	3,943,116	4,587,930	5,462,982
......	154,001	191,874	255,881	368,300	422,770	499,794	632,772	769,913	964,691
88,548	161,772	325,594	431,866	445,032	524,873	588,637	667,191	713,015	944,127
3,826,352	4,821,550	5,638,591	6,485,280	7,630,654	7,897,241	8,712,176	10,081,158	11,110,285	11,427,409
2,192,404	2,516,462	2,700,876	2,930,390	3,238,503	3,427,796	3,934,224	4,662,498	5,195,392	5,490,214
1,912,297	2,231,853	2,224,771	2,404,021	2,470,939	2,538,268	2,621,073	2,757,537	2,825,368	2,913,808
1,428,108	1,470,495	1,690,949	1,769,257	1,880,999	1,801,028	1,905,299	2,178,611	2,249,071	2,364,236
1,858,635	2,147,174	2,289,905	2,416,630	2,614,589	2,845,627	2,944,806	3,038,156	3,220,711	3,660,324
1,118,588	1,381,625	1,656,388	1,798,509	2,101,593	2,363,880	2,683,516	3,257,022	3,644,637	4,206,116
661,086	694,466	742,371	768,014	797,423	847,226	913,774	969,265	993,722	1,125,043
1,042,390	1,188,044	1,295,346	1,449,661	1,631,526	1,821,244	2,343,001	3,100,689	3,923,897	4,216,933
2,238,947	2,805,346	3,366,416	3,852,356	4,249,614	4,316,721	4,690,514	5,148,578	5,689,170	5,737,093
2,093,890	2,420,982	2,810,173	3,668,412	4,842,325	5,256,106	6,371,766	7,823,194	8,881,826	9,262,044
1,310,283	1,751,394	2,075,708	2,387,125	2,563,953	2,792,300	2,982,483	3,413,864	3,806,103	4,075,970
1,289,600	1,551,270	1,797,114	1,790,618	2,009,821	2,183,796	2,178,914	2,178,141	2,216,994	2,520,770
2,679,185	3,106,665	3,293,335	3,404,055	3,629,367	3,784,664	3,954,653	4,319,813	4,677,623	4,916,766
142,924	243,329	376,053	548,889	537,606	559,456	591,024	674,767	694,409	786,690
1,062,656	1,066,300	1,192,214	1,296,372	1,377,963	1,315,834	1,325,510	1,411,330	1,485,333	1,569,825
47,355	42,335	81,875	77,407	91,058	110,247	160,083	285,278	488,738	800,508
376,530	411,588	430,572	443,083	465,293	491,524	533,242	606,921	737,681	920,610
1,444,933	1,883,669	2,537,167	3,155,900	4,041,334	4,160,165	4,835,329	6,066,782	7,171,112	7,365,011
160,282	195,310	327,301	360,350	423,317	531,818	681,187	951,023	1,017,055	1,303,302
6,003,174	7,268,894	9,113,614	10,385,227	12,588,066	13,479,142	14,830,192	16,782,304	18,241,391	17,558,165
1,617,949	1,893,810	2,206,287	2,559,123	3,170,276	3,571,623	4,061,929	4,556,155	5,084,411	5,880,095
190,983	319,146	577,056	646,872	680,845	641,935	619,636	632,446	617,792	652,717
3,672,329	4,157,545	4,767,121	5,759,394	6,646,697	6,907,612	7,946,627	9,706,397	10,657,423	10,797,603
258,657	790,391	1,657,155	2,028,283	2,396,040	2,336,434	2,233,351	2,328,284	2,559,463	3,025,487
317,704	413,536	672,765	783,389	953,786	1,089,684	1,521,341	1,768,687	2,091,533	2,633,156
5,258,113	6,302,115	7,665,111	8,720,017	9,631,350	9,900,180	10,498,012	11,319,366	11,800,766	11,864,720
345,506	428,556	542,610	604,397	687,497	713,346	791,896	859,488	949,723	947,154
1,151,149	1,340,316	1,515,400	1,683,724	1,738,765	1,899,804	2,117,027	2,382,594	2,590,713	3,120,729
348,600	401,570	583,888	636,547	692,849	642,961	652,740	680,514	666,257	690,768
1,767,518	2,020,616	2,184,789	2,337,885	2,616,556	2,915,841	3,291,718	3,567,089	3,926,018	4,591,023
2,235,527	3,048,710	3,896,542	4,663,228	5,824,715	6,414,824	7,711,194	9,579,677	11,198,655	14,225,513
210,779	276,749	373,351	449,396	507,847	550,310	688,862	890,627	1,059,273	1,461,037
332,422	343,641	355,956	352,428	359,611	359,231	377,747	389,881	444,732	511,456
1,655,980	1,854,184	2,061,612	2,309,187	2,421,851	2,677,773	3,318,680	3,966,949	4,651,448	5,346,797
357,232	518,103	1,141,990	1,356,621	1,563,396	1,736,191	2,378,963	2,853,214	3,413,244	4,132,353
762,794	958,800	1,221,119	1,463,701	1,729,205	1,901,974	2,005,552	1,860,421	1,744,237	1,950,186
1,693,330	2,069,042	2,333,860	2,632,067	2,939,006	3,137,587	3,434,575	3,951,777	4,417,821	4,705,642
62,555	92,531	145,965	194,402	225,565	250,742	290,529	330,066	332,416	469,557
62,979,766	76,212,168	92,228,496	106,021,537	123,202,624	132,164,569	151,323,199	179,323,175	203,302,031	226,542,203

(1) Updated, April 1989. (2) According to 1986 estimates, Florida has passed Illinois in population.

U.S. Center of Population, 1790-1980

Center of Population is that point which may be considered as center of population gravity of the U.S. or that point upon which the U.S. would balance if it were a rigid plane without weight and the population distributed thereon with each individual being assumed to have equal weight and to exert an influence on a central point proportional to his distance from that point.

Year	N. Lat. ° ' "	W.Long. ° ' "	Approximate location
1790	39 16 30	76 11 12	23 miles east of Baltimore, Md.
1800	39 16 6	76 56 30	18 miles west of Baltimore, Md.
1810	39 11 30	77 37 12	40 miles northwest by west of Washington, D.C. (in Va.)[1]
1820	39 5 42	78 33 0	16 miles east of Moorefield, W. Va.[1]
1830	38 57 54	79 16 54	19 miles west-southwest of Moorefield, W. Va.[1]
1840	39 2 0	80 18 0	16 miles south of Clarksburg, W. Va.[1]
1850	38 59 0	81 19 0	23 miles southeast of Parkersburg, W. Va.[1]
1860	39 0 24	82 48 48	20 miles south by east of Chillicothe, Oh.
1870	39 12 0	83 35 42	48 miles east by north of Cincinnati, Oh.
1880	39 4 8	84 39 40	8 miles west by south of Cincinnati, Oh. (in Ky.)
1890	39 11 56	85 32 53	20 miles east of Columbus, Ind.
1900	39 9 36	85 48 54	6 miles southeast of Columbus, Ind.
1910	39 10 12	86 32 20	In the city of Bloomington, Ind.
1920	39 10 21	86 43 15	8 miles south-southeast of Spencer, Owen County, Ind.
1930	39 3 45	87 8 6	3 miles northeast of Linton, Greene County, Ind.
1940	38 56 54	87 22 35	2 miles southeast by east of Carlisle, Haddon township, Sullivan Co., Ind.
1950 (Inc. Alaska & Hawaii)	38 48 15	88 22 8	3 miles northeast of Louisville, Clay County, Ill.
1960	38 35 58	89 12 35	6 1/2 miles northwest of Centralia, Clinton Co., Ill.
1970	38 27 47	89 42 22	5 miles east southeast of Mascoutah, St. Clair County, Ill.
1980	38 8 13	90 34 26	1/4 mile west of De Soto, Jefferson Co., Mo.

(1) West Virginia was set off from Virginia Dec. 31, 1862, and admitted as a state June 20, 1863.

Projections of Total Population by Race: 1990 to 2025

Source: U.S. Bureau of the Census

| Year | Total Population (1,000) | | | | By Race (middle series) | | | | | |
| | Lowest series | Middle series | Highest series | Zero migration | Number (1,000) | | | Percent distribution | | |
					White	Black	Other races	White	Black	Other races
1990 ..	248,656	250,410	251,897	247,943	210,616	31,148	8,645	84.1	12.4	3.5
1992 ..	251,592	254,521	257,235	250,781	213,301	31,988	9,232	83.8	12.6	3.6
1993 ..	252,906	256,466	259,888	252,083	214,542	32,398	9,527	83.7	12.6	3.7
1994 ..	254,121	258,338	262,526	253,308	215,714	32,801	9,823	83.5	12.7	3.8
1995 ..	255,239	260,138	265,151	254,459	216,820	33,199	10,119	83.3	12.8	3.9
2000 ..	259,576	268,266	278,228	259,304	221,514	35,129	11,624	82.6	13.1	4.3
2005 ..	262,363	275,604	291,710	263,189	225,424	37,003	13,177	81.8	13.4	4.8
2010 ..	264,193	282,575	305,882	266,528	228,978	38,833	14,764	81.0	13.7	5.2
2015 ..	265,072	288,997	320,494	269,131	232,081	40,564	16,352	80.3	14.0	5.7
2020 ..	264,536	294,364	335,022	270,493	234,330	42,128	17,906	79.6	14.3	6.1
2025 ..	262,218	298,252	348,985	270,234	235,369	43,473	19,410	78.9	14.6	6.5

For the series shown, the following assumptions were made about fertility (ultimate lifetime births per woman), mortality (ultimate life expectancy in 2080), and immigration (ultimate yearly net immigration). Lowest series: 1.5 births per woman, 77.9 years, and 300,000 net immigration. Middle series: 1.8 births per woman, 81.2 years, and 500,000 net immigration. Highest series: 2.2 births per woman, 88.0 years, and 800,000 net immigration. Zero migration series: 1.8 births per woman and 81.2 years.

U.S. Area and Population: 1790 to 1980

Source: U.S. Bureau of the Census

| Census date | Area (square miles) | | | Population | | Increase over preceding census | |
	Gross	Land	Water	Number	Per sq. mile of land	Number	%
1980 (Apr. 1)	3,618,770	3,539,289	79,481	226,542,203	64.0	23,240,172	11.4
1970 (Apr. 1)	3,618,770	3,536,855	81,915	203,302,031	57.5	23,978,856	13.4
1960 (Apr. 1)	3,618,770	3,540,911	77,859	179,323,175	50.6	27,997,377	18.5
1950 (Apr. 1)	3,618,770	3,552,206	66,564	151,325,798	42.6	19,161,229	14.5
1940 (Apr. 1)	3,618,770	3,554,608	64,162	132,164,569	37.2	8,961,945	7.3
1930 (Apr. 1)	3,618,770	3,551,608	67,162	123,202,624	34.7	17,181,087	16.2
1920 (Jan. 1)	3,618,770	3,546,931	71,839	106,021,537	29.9	13,793,041	15.0
1910 (Apr. 15)	3,618,770	3,547,045	71,725	92,228,496	26.0	16,016,328	21.0
1900 (June 1)	3,618,770	3,547,314	71,456	76,212,168	21.5	13,232,402	21.0
1890 (June 1)	3,612,299	3,540,705	71,594	62,979,766	17.8	12,790,557	25.5
1880 (June 1)	3,612,299	3,540,705	71,594	50,189,209	14.2	11,630,838	30.2
1870 (June 1)	3,612,299	3,540,705	71,594	38,558,371	10.9	7,115,050	22.6
1860 (June 1)	3,021,295	2,969,640	51,655	31,443,321	10.6	8,251,445	35.6
1850 (June 1)	2,991,655	2,940,042	51,613	23,191,876	7.9	6,122,423	35.9
1840 (June 1)	1,792,552	1,749,462	43,090	17,069,453	9.8	4,203,433	32.7
1830 (June 1)	1,792,552	1,749,462	43,090	12,866,020	7.4	3,227,567	33.5
1820 (June 1)	1,792,552	1,749,462	43,090	9,638,453	5.5	2,398,572	33.1
1810 (Aug. 6)	1,722,685	1,681,828	40,857	7,239,881	4.3	1,931,398	36.4
1800 (Aug. 4)	891,364	864,746	26,618	5,308,483	6.1	1,379,269	35.1
1790 (Aug. 2)	891,364	864,746	26,618	3,929,214	4.5		

NOTE: Percent changes are computed on basis of change in population since preceding census date, and period covered therefore is not always exactly 10 years.

Population density figures given for various years represent the area within the boundaries of the United States which was under the jurisdiction on date in question, including in some cases considerable areas not organized or settled and not covered by the census. In 1870, for example, Alaska was not covered by the census.

Revised figure of 39,818,449 for the 1870 population includes adjustments for undernumeration in the Southern states. On the basis of the revised figure, the population increased by 8,375,128, or 26.6 percent between 1860 and 1870, and by 10,370,760, or 26.1 percent between 1870 and 1880.

Congressional Apportionment

	1980	1970		1980	1970		1980	1970		1980	1970		1980	1970
Ala..	7	7	Ida...	2	2	Minn..	8	8	N. D..	1	1	Vt...	1	1
Alas..	1	1	Ill....	22	24	Miss..	5	5	Oh...	21	23	Va...	10	10
Ariz..	5	4	Ind...	10	11	Mo...	9	10	Okla..	6	6	Wash..	8	7
Ark..	4	4	Ia....	6	6	Mon...	2	2	Ore...	5	4	W. Va..	4	4
Cal..	45	43	Kan..	5	5	Neb...	3	3	Pa...	23	25	Wis...	9	9
Col...	6	5	Ky...	7	7	Nev...	2	1	R.I...	2	2	Wy...	1	1
Conn.	6	6	La...	8	8	N. H..	2	2	S. C..	6	6			
Del..	1	1	Me...	2	2	N. J...	14	15	S. D..	1	2	Totals.	435	435
Fla...	19	15	Md...	8	8	N. M..	3	2	Tenn..	9	8			
Ga...	10	10	Mass.	11	12	N. Y...	34	39	Tex...	27	24			
Ha...	2	2	Mich..	18	19	N. C...	11	11	Ut....	3	2			

The primary reason the Constitution provided for a census of the population every 10 years was to give a basis for apportionment of representatives among the states. This apportionment largely determines the number of electoral votes allotted to each state.

The number of representatives of each state in Congress is determined by the state's population, but each state is entitled to one representative regardless of population. A Congressional apportionment has been made after each decennial census except that of 1920.

Under provisions of a law that became effective Nov. 15, 1941, apportionment of representatives is made by the method of equal proportions. In the application of this method, the apportionment is made so that the average population per representative has the least possible variation between one state and any other. The first House of Representatives, in 1789, had 65 members, as provided by the Constitution. As the population grew, the number of representatives was increased, but the total membership has been fixed at 435 since the apportionment based on the 1910 census.

Percent Distribution of the Population by Age

Source: U.S. Bureau of the Census

U.S. Population Abroad, by Selected Country: 1988

Source: U.S. Dept. of State

(In thousands. As of May 1. Data compiled as part of noncombatant personnel evacuation requirements report)

Country	Total[1]	Resident U.S. citizen	U.S. tourists	Country	Total[1]	Resident U.S. citizen	U.S. tourists
Total[2]	4,006.7	2,174.6	1,041.4	Japan	121.0	41.7	9.6
Australia	92.7	68.7	21.0	Mexico	601.8	396.0	203.1
Belgium	19.8	13.9	4.0	Netherlands	48.8	34.5	4.3
Brazil	52.7	40.4	11.2	Panama	40.3	11.3	0.4
Canada	447.3	235.1	209.9	Philippines	273.4	156.3	3.9
Colombia	21.4	19.9	1.2	Portugal	25.0	15.7	6.4
Costa Rica	26.0	17.1	7.4	Saudi Arabia	25.9	21.6	0.3
Dominican Republic	77.5	63.2	13.0	South Africa	26.5	9.4	16.5
France	132.2	43.5	86.2	South Korea	68.4	10.0	26.6
Greece	69.6	54.4	9.8	Spain	110.4	60.1	30.3
Hong Kong	22.2	14.5	6.6	Switzerland	32.3	24.1	7.5
Ireland	34.1	30.0	4.0	United Kingdom	284.8	158.8	80.1
Israel	121.8	60.9	60.0	Venezuela	22.3	20.6	1.3
Italy	174.0	86.4	58.2	West Germany	491.1	134.1	21.2

(1) Includes Dept. of Defense noncombatant employees, other U.S. government employees, and dependents of U.S. military and civilian employees, not shown separately. (2) Includes other countries not shown separately.

Estimated Population of American Colonies: 1630-1780

Source: U.S. Bureau of the Census (thousands)

Colony	1780	1770	1750	1740	1720	1700	1690	1670	1650	1630
Total	2,780.4	2,148.1	1,170.8	905.6	466.2	250.9	210.4	111.9	50.4	4.6
Maine (counties)[1]	49.1	31.3	...	...	...	...	...	...	1.0	0.4
New Hampshire[2]	87.8	62.4	27.5	23.3	9.4	5.0	4.2	1.8	1.3	0.5
Vermont[3]	47.6	10.0	...	...	...	...	...	...	...	...
Plymouth and Massachusetts[1,2,4]	268.6	235.3	188.0	151.6	91.0	55.9	56.9	35.3	15.6	0.9
Rhode Island[2]	52.9	58.2	33.2	25.3	11.7	5.9	4.2	2.2	0.8	...
Connecticut[2]	206.7	183.9	111.3	89.6	58.8	26.0	21.6	12.6	4.1	...
New York[2]	210.5	162.9	76.7	63.7	36.9	19.1	13.9	5.8	4.1	0.4
New Jersey[2]	139.6	117.4	71.4	51.4	29.8	14.0	8.0	1.0	...	...
Pennsylvania[2]	327.3	240.1	119.7	85.6	31.0	18.0	11.4	...	...	...
Delaware[2]	45.4	35.5	28.7	19.9	5.4	2.5	1.5	0.7	0.2	...
Maryland[2]	245.5	202.6	141.1	116.1	66.1	29.6	24.0	13.2	4.5	...
Virginia[2]	538.0	447.0	231.0	180.4	87.8	58.6	53.0	35.3	18.7	2.5
North Carolina[2]	270.1	197.2	73.0	51.8	21.3	10.7	7.6	3.8	...	...
South Carolina[2]	180.0	124.2	64.0	45.0	17.0	5.7	3.9	0.2	...	...
Georgia[2]	56.1	23.4	5.2	2.0	...	...	...	...	...	...
Kentucky[5]	45.0	15.7	...	...	...	...	...	...	...	...
Tennessee[6]	10.0	1.0	...	...	...	...	...	...	...	...

(1) For 1660-1750, Maine counties included with Massachusetts. Maine was a part of Massachusetts until it became a separate state in 1820. (2) One of the original 13 states. (3) Admitted to statehood in 1791. (4) Plymouth became a part of the Province of Massachusetts in 1691. (5) Admitted to statehood in 1792. (6) Admitted to statehood in 1796.

Metropolitan Statistical Areas: 1980–1988

Source: U.S. Bureau of the Census
(MSAs over 297,000 listed by 1988 population)

By current standards, an area qualifies for recognition as a Metropolitan Statistical Area (MSA) in one of two ways: if there is a city of at least 50,000 population; or a Census Bureau-defined urbanized area of at least 50,000 with a total metropolitan population of at least 100,000 (75,000 in New England). In addition to the county containing the main city, an MSA also includes other counties having strong economic and social ties to the central county. If an area has more than one million population and meets certain other specified requirements, it is termed a Consolidated Metropolitan Statistical Area (CMSA). MSAs are defined by the Office of Management and Budget as of June 30, 1988.

MSA	Population 1988 (estimate)	1980	Percent Change 1980 to 1988
New York-Northern New Jersey-Long Island, NY-NJ-CT CMSA	18,120,200	17,539,532	3.3
Los Angeles-Anaheim-Riverside, CA CMSA	13,769,700	11,497,549	19.8
Chicago-Gary-Lake County, IL-IN-WI CMSA	8,180,900	7,937,290	3.1
San Francisco-Oakland-San Jose, CA CMSA	6,041,800	5,367,900	12.6
Philadelphia-Wilmington-Trenton, PA-NJ-DE-MD CMSA	5,963,300	5,680,509	5.0
Detroit-Ann Arbor, MI CMSA	4,620,200	4,752,764	−2.8
Boston-Lawrence-Salem, MA-NH CMSA	4,109,900	3,971,792	3.5
Dallas-Fort Worth, TX CMSA	3,766,100	2,930,568	28.5
Washington, D.C.-MD-VA	3,734,200	3,250,921	14.9
Houston-Galveston-Brazoria, TX CMSA	3,641,500	3,099,942	17.5
Miami-Fort Lauderdale, FL CMSA	8,000,500	2,643,766	13.5
Cleveland-Akron-Lorain, OH CMSA	2,769,000	2,834,062	−2.3
Atlanta, GA.	2,736,600	2,138,136	28.0
St. Louis, MO-IL	2,466,700	2,376,968	3.8
Seattle-Tacoma, WA CMSA	2,420,800	2,093,285	15.6
Minneapolis-St. Paul, MN-WI.	2,387,500	2,137,133	11.7
San Diego, CA.	2,370,400	1,861,846	27.3
Baltimore, MD	2,342,500	2,199,497	6.5
Pittsburgh-Beaver Valley, PA CMSA	2,284,100	2,423,311	−5.7
Phoenix, AZ	2,029,500	1,509,175	34.5
Tampa-St. Petersburg-Clearwater, FL	1,995,100	1,613,600	23.6
Denver-Boulder, CO CMSA	1,858,000	1,618,461	14.8
Cincinnati-Hamilton, OH-KY-IN CMSA	1,728,500	1,660,257	4.1
Kansas City, MO-KS	1,575,400	1,433,464	9.9
Milwaukee-Racine, WI CMSA	1,571,700	1,570,152	0.1
Portland-Vancouver, OR-WA CMSA	1,414,200	1,297,977	9.0
Sacramento, CA.	1,385,200	1,099,814	25.9
Norfolk-Virginia Beach-Newport News, VA	1,380,200	1,160,311	19.0
Columbus, OH.	1,344,300	1,243,827	8.1
San Antonio, TX	1,323,200	1,072,125	23.4
New Orleans, LA	1,306,900	1,256,668	4.0
Indianapolis, IN	1,236,600	1,166,575	6.0
Buffalo-Niagara Falls, NY CMSA	1,175,600	1,242,826	−5.4
Providence-Pawtucket-Fall River, RI-MA CMSA	1,125,400	1,083,139	3.9
Charlotte-Gastonia-Rock Hill, NC-SC.	1,112,000	971,447	14.5
Hartford-New Britain-Middletown, CT CMSA	1,067,800	1,013,508	5.3
Salt Lake City-Ogden, UT	1,085,000	910,222	17.0
Rochester, NY.	980,100	971,230	0.9
Memphis, TN-AK-MS	979,300	913,472	7.2
Nashville, TN.	971,800	850,505	14.3
Orlando, FL	971,200	699,904	38.8
Louisville, KY-IN.	967,000	956,426	1.1
Oklahoma City, OK	963,800	860,969	11.9
Dayton-Springfield, OH.	948,000	942,083	0.6
Greensboro-Winston-Salem-High Point, NC	924,700	851,444	8.6
Birmingham, AL	923,400	883,993	4.5
Jacksonville, FL.	898,100	722,252	24.3
Albany-Schenectady-Troy, NY	850,800	835,880	1.8
Richmond-Petersburg, VA	844,300	761,311	10.9
Honolulu, HI.	838,500	762,565	10.0
West Palm Beach-Boca Raton-Delray Beach, FL.	818,500	576,758	41.9
Austin, TX	748,500	536,688	39.5
Scranton-Wilkes-Barre, PA.	736,600	728,796	1.1
Tulsa, OK	727,600	657,173	10.7
Raleigh-Durham, NC	683,500	560,774	21.9
Allentown-Bethlehem, PA-NJ	677,100	635,481	6.6
Grand Rapids, MI	665,200	601,680	10.6
Syracuse, NY	650,300	642,971	1.1
Tucson, AZ.	636,000	531,443	19.7
Las Vegas, NV.	631,300	463,087	36.3
Omaha, NE-IA.	621,600	585,122	6.2
Greenville-Spartanburg, SC	621,400	570,210	9.0
Toledo, OH	616,500	616,864	−0.1
Fresno, CA.	614,800	514,621	19.5
Knoxville, TN.	599,600	565,970	5.9
Harrisburg-Lebanon-Carlisle, PA	591,100	556,242	6.3
El Paso, TX	585,900	479,899	22.1
Baton Rouge, LA	536,500	494,151	8.6
New Haven-Meriden, CT	523,700	500,462	4.7
Springfield, MA	522,500	515,259	1.4
Bakersfield, CA	520,000	403,089	29.0
Little Rock-North Little Rock, AK	513,100	474,463	8.1
Charleston, SC	510,800	430,346	18.7
Youngstown-Warren, OH.	501,700	531,350	−5.6
Albuquerque, NM	493,100	420,261	17.3
Mobile, AL	485,800	443,536	9.5
Wichita, KS.	483,100	442,401	9.2
Columbia, SC	456,500	409,953	11.3
Stockton, CA.	455,700	347,342	31.2
Johnson City-Kingsport-Bristol, TN-VA	442,300	433,638	2.0
Chattanooga, TN-GA	438,100	426,443	2.7
Flint, MI	430,700	450,449	−4.4
Lansing-East Lansing, MI.	428,400	419,750	2.1
Worcester, MA	415,700	402,918	3.2
Lancaster, PA	414,100	362,346	14.3
York, PA	410,400	381,255	7.6
Saginaw-Bay City-Midland, MI	406,200	421,518	−3.6
Canton, OH	401,400	404,421	−0.8
Augusta, GA-SC.	396,400	345,923	14.6
Jackson, MS.	396,200	362,038	9.4
Lakeland-Winter Haven, FL.	395,800	321,652	23.0
Colorado Springs, CO	393,900	309,424	27.3
Des Moines, IA	391,800	367,561	6.6
Melbourne-Titusville-Palm Bay, FL	388,300	272,959	42.3
McAllen-Edinburg-Mission, TX	387,900	283,323	36.9
Fort Wayne, IN	367,400	354,156	3.7
Davenport-Rock Island-Moline, IA-IL.	364,200	384,749	−5.3
Beaumont-Port Arthur, TX	363,900	373,211	−2.5
Shreveport, LA	359,100	333,158	7.8
Corpus Christi, TX.	358,000	326,228	9.7
Spokane, WA	356,400	341,835	4.3
Madison, WI	352,800	323,545	9.1
Pensacola, FL.	349,900	289,782	20.8
Salinas-Seaside-Monterey, CA	348,800	290,444	20.1
Daytona Beach, FL	348,400	258,762	34.6
Lexington-Fayette, KY	347,900	317,548	9.6
Santa Barbara-Santa Maria-Lompoc, CA.	343,100	298,694	14.9
Modesto, CA.	341,000	265,900	28.3
Peoria, IL.	340,400	365,864	−7.0
Reading, PA	329,100	312,509	5.3
Huntington-Ashland, W.VA-KY-OH.	322,300	336,410	−4.2
Appleton-Oshkosh-Neenah, WI	312,900	291,369	7.4
Utica-Rome, NY	312,600	320,180	−2.4
Atlantic City, NJ.	309,200	276,385	11.9
Fort Myers-Cape Coral, FL	309,100	205,286	50.6
Montgomery, AL.	300,800	272,687	10.3
Visalia-Tulare-Porterville, CA	297,900	245,738	21.2

Population of U.S. Cities

Source: U.S. Bureau of the Census (100 most populated cities ranked by July 1, 1988 estimates)

Rank	City	1988	1980	1970	1960	1950	1900	1850
1	New York, N.Y.	7,352,700	7,071,639	7,895,563	7,781,984	7,891,957	3,437,202	696,115
2	Los Angeles, Cal.	3,352,710	2,966,850	2,811,801	2,479,015	1,970,358	102,479	1,610
3	Chicago, Ill.	2,977,520	3,005,072	3,369,357	3,550,404	3,620,962	1,698,575	29,963
4	Houston, Tex.	1,698,090	1,595,138	1,233,535	938,219	596,163	44,633	2,396
5	Philadelphia, Pa.	1,647,000	1,688,210	1,949,996	2,002,512	2,071,605	1,293,697	121,376
6	San Diego, Cal.	1,070,310	875,538	697,471	573,224	334,387	17,700	...
7	Detroit, Mich.	1,035,920	1,203,339	1,514,063	1,670,144	1,849,568	285,704	21,019
8	Dallas, Tex.	987,360	904,078	844,401	679,684	434,462	42,638	...
9	San Antonio, Tex.	941,150	785,880	654,153	587,718	408,442	53,321	3,488
10	Phoenix, Ariz.	923,750	789,704	584,303	439,170	106,818	5,544	...
11	Baltimore, Md.	751,400	786,775	905,787	939,024	949,708	508,957	169,054
12	San Jose, Cal.	738,420	629,442	459,913	204,196	95,280	21,500	...
13	San Francisco, Cal.	731,600	678,974	715,674	740,316	775,357	342,782	34,776
14	Indianapolis, Ind.	727,130	700,807	736,856	476,258	427,173	169,164	8,091
15	Memphis, Tenn.	645,190	646,356	623,988	497,524	396,000	102,320	8,841
16	Jacksonville, Fla.	635,430	540,920	504,265	201,030	204,517	28,429	1,045
17	Washington, D.C.	617,000	638,333	756,668	763,956	802,178	278,718	40,001
18	Milwaukee, Wis.	599,380	636,212	717,372	741,324	637,392	285,315	20,061
19	Boston, Mass.	577,830	562,994	641,071	697,197	801,444	560,892	136,881
20	Columbus, Oh.	569,570	564,871	540,025	471,316	375,901	125,560	17,882
21	New Orleans, La.	531,700	557,515	593,471	627,525	570,445	287,104	116,375
22	Cleveland, Oh.	521,370	573,822	750,879	876,050	914,808	381,768	17,034
23	El Paso, Tex.	510,970	425,259	322,261	276,687	130,485	15,906	...
24	Seattle, Wash.	502,200	493,846	530,831	557,087	467,591	80,671	...
25	Denver, Col.	492,200	492,365	514,678	493,887	415,786	133,859	...
26	Nashville-Davidson, Tenn.	481,400	455,651	426,029	170,874	174,307	80,865	10,165
27	Austin, Tex.	464,690	345,496	253,539	186,545	132,459	22,258	629
28	Kansas City, Mo.	438,950	448,159	507,330	475,539	456,622	163,752	...
29	Oklahoma City, Okla.	434,380	403,213	368,164	324,253	243,504	10,037	...
30	Fort Worth, Tex.	426,610	385,164	393,455	356,268	278,778	26,688	...
31	Atlanta, Ga.	420,220	425,022	495,039	487,455	331,314	89,872	2,572
32	Portland, Ore.	418,470	366,383	379,967	372,676	373,628	90,426	...
33	Long Beach, Cal.	415,040	361,334	358,879	344,168	250,767	2,252	...
34	St. Louis, Mo.	403,700	453,085	622,236	750,026	856,796	575,238	77,860
35	Tucson, Ariz.	385,720	330,537	262,933	212,892	45,454	7,531	...
36	Albuquerque, N.M.	378,480	331,767	244,501	201,189	96,815	6,238	...
37	Honolulu, Ha.[1]	376,110	762,874	630,528	294,194	248,034	39,306	...
38	Pittsburgh, Pa.	375,230	423,938	520,089	604,332	676,806	321,616	46,601
39	Miami, Fla.	371,100	346,865	334,859	291,688	249,276	1,681	...
40	Cincinnati, Oh.	370,480	385,457	453,514	502,550	503,998	325,902	115,435
41	Tulsa, Okla.	368,330	360,919	330,350	261,685	182,740	1,390	...
42	Charlotte, N.C.	367,860	314,447	241,420	201,564	134,042	18,091	1,065
43	Virginia Beach, Va.	365,300	262,199	172,106	8,091	5,390	...	...
44	Oakland, Cal.	356,860	339,337	361,561	367,548	384,575	66,960	...
45	Omaha, Neb.	353,170	314,255	346,929	301,598	251,117	102,555	...
46	Minneapolis, Minn.	344,670	370,951	434,400	482,872	521,718	202,718	...
47	Toledo, Oh.	340,760	354,635	383,062	318,003	303,616	131,822	3,829
48	Sacramento, Cal.	338,220	275,741	257,105	191,667	137,572	29,282	6,820
49	Newark, N.J.	313,800	329,248	381,930	405,220	438,776	246,070	38,894
50	Buffalo, N.Y.	313,570	357,870	462,768	532,759	580,132	352,387	42,261
51	Fresno, Cal.	307,090	218,202	165,655	133,929	91,669	12,470	...
52	Wichita, Kan.	295,320	279,272	276,554	254,698	168,279	24,671	...
53	Norfolk, Va.	286,500	266,979	307,951	304,869	213,513	46,624	14,326
54	Colorado Springs, Col.	283,110	215,150	135,517	70,194	45,472	21,085	...
55	Louisville, Ky.	281,880	298,451	361,706	390,639	369,129	204,731	43,194
56	Tampa, Fla.	281,790	271,523	277,714	274,970	124,681	15,839	...
57	Mesa, Ariz.	280,360	152,453	63,049	33,772	16,790	722	...
58	Birmingham, Ala.	277,280	284,413	300,910	340,887	326,037	38,415	...
59	Corpus Christi, Tex.	260,930	231,999	204,525	167,690	108,287	4,703	...
60	St. Paul, Minn.	259,110	270,230	309,866	313,411	311,349	163,065	1,112
61	Arlington, Tex.	257,460	160,113	90,229	44,775	7,692	1,079	...
62	Anaheim, Cal.	244,670	219,311	166,408	104,184	14,556	1,456	...
63	Santa Ana, Cal.	239,540	203,713	155,710	100,350	45,533	4,933	...
64	St. Petersburg, Fla.	235,450	238,647	216,159	181,298	96,738	1,575	...
65	Baton Rouge, La.[2]	235,270	346,029	165,921	152,419	125,629	11,269	3,905
66	Rochester, N.Y.	229,780	241,741	295,011	318,611	332,488	162,608	36,403
67	Lexington-Fayette, Ky.	225,700	204,165	108,137	62,810	55,534	26,369	8,159
68	Akron, Oh.	221,510	237,177	275,425	290,351	274,605	42,728	3,266
69	Aurora, Col.	218,720	158,588	74,974	48,548	11,421	202	...
70	Anchorage, Alas.	218,500	174,431	48,081	44,237	11,254	...	...
71	Shreveport, La.	218,010	205,820	182,064	164,372	127,206	16,013	1,728
72	Jersey City, N.J.	217,630	223,532	260,350	276,101	299,017	206,433	6,856
73	Richmond, Va.	213,300	219,214	249,332	219,958	230,310	85,050	27,570
74	Riverside, Cal.	210,630	170,876	140,089	84,332	46,764	7,973	...
75	Las Vegas, Nev.	210,620	164,674	125,787	64,405	24,624	...	...
76	Mobile, Ala.	208,820	200,452	190,026	194,856	129,009	38,469	20,515
77	Jackson, Miss.	201,250	202,895	153,968	144,422	98,271	7,816	1,881
78	Montgomery, Ala.	193,510	177,857	133,386	134,393	106,525	30,346	8,728
79	Des Moines, Ia.	192,910	191,003	201,404	208,982	177,965	62,139	...
80	Stockton, Cal.	190,680	149,779	109,963	86,321	70,853	17,506	...
81	Lubbock, Tex.	188,090	173,979	149,101	126,691	71,747	...	...
82	Lincoln, Neb.	187,890	171,932	149,518	128,521	98,884	40,169	...
83	Huntington Beach, Cal.	186,880	170,505	115,960	11,492	5,237	...	...
84	Raleigh, N.C.	186,720	150,255	122,830	93,931	65,679	13,643	4,518

(continued)

Rank	City	1988	1980	1970	1960	1950	1900	1850
85	Grand Rapids, Mich.	185,370	181,843	197,649	177,313	176,515	87,565	2,686
86	Yonkers, N.Y.	183,000	195,351	204,297	190,634	152,798	47,931	...
87	Greensboro, N.C.	181,970	170,279	144,076	119,574	74,389	10,035	...
88	Garland, Tex.	180,450	138,857	81,437	38,501	10,571	819	...
89	Little Rock, Ark.	180,090	158,461	132,483	107,813	102,213	38,307	2,167
90	Fort Wayne, Ind.	179,810	172,196	178,269	161,776	133,607	45,115	4,282
91	Madison, Wis.	178,180	170,616	171,809	126,706	96,056	19,164	1,525
92	Dayton, Oh.	178,000	203,371	243,023	262,332	243,872	85,333	10,977
93	Columbus, Ga.	177,680	169,441	155,028	116,779	79,611	17,614	9,621
94	Knoxville, Tenn.	172,080	175,030	174,587	111,827	124,769	32,637	2,076
95	Spokane, Wash.	170,900	171,300	170,516	181,608	161,721	36,848	...
96	Fremont, Cal.	166,590	131,945	100,869	43,790	...	...	...
97	Amarillo, Tex.	166,010	149,230	127,010	137,969	74,246	1,442	...
98	Tacoma, Wash.	163,960	158,501	154,407	147,979	143,673	37,714	...
99	Chattanooga, Tenn.	162,670	169,565	119,923	130,009	131,041	30,154	...
100	Hialeah, Fla.	162,080	145,254	102,452	66,972	19,676	...	...

City Population by Race and Hispanic Origin

Source: U.S. Bureau of the Census

This table presents a summary of the final 1980 census population estimates (data are based on sample tabulations) for cities over 250,000, classified by race and Hispanic origin.

	Total	White	Black	Am. Indian Eskimos Aleut.	Asian & Pacific Islander	Race N.E.C.[1]	Hispanic Origin[2]
Albuquerque, NM	331,767	275,758	7,691	7,163	3,755	37,400	112,030
Atlanta, GA	425,022	138,235	283,158	610	2,001	1,018	5,750
Austin, TX	345,544	263,618	42,108	1,516	4,127	34,175	64,945
Baltimore, MD	786,775	346,692	430,934	2,170	4,898	2,081	7,804
Birmingham, AL	284,413	124,767	158,200	220	933	293	2,054
Boston, MA	562,994	396,635	126,438	1,455	16,298	22,168	36,430
Buffalo, NY	357,870	253,507	95,622	2,084	1,335	5,322	8,926
Charlotte, NC	314,447	212,293	97,896	1,162	2,393	703	3,091
Chicago, IL	3,005,078	1,512,411	1,197,174	6,804	73,745	214,944	423,357
Cincinnati, OH	385,457	251,332	130,490	567	2,332	736	3,263
Cleveland, OH	573,822	309,299	251,084	1,282	3,372	8,785	17,896
Columbus, OH	564,866	431,966	124,689	1,024	5,410	1,777	5,300
Dallas, TX	904,074	558,443	265,105	3,878	9,163	67,485	110,511
Denver, CO	492,365	375,628	59,095	4,318	8,934	44,390	92,257
Detroit, MI	1,203,339	420,529	758,468	3,846	7,614	12,882	28,466
El Paso, TX	425,259	306,510	13,641	1,563	3,995	99,550	265,997
Fort Worth, TX	385,166	266,638	87,635	1,841	2,954	26,098	48,568
Honolulu, HI (County)	762,565	262,604	17,203	2,445	463,117	17,196	54,619
Houston, TX	1,595,167	981,563	439,604	3,945	35,448	134,607	280,691
Indianapolis, IN	700,719	540,496	152,590	1,356	4,539	1,738	6,430
Jacksonville, FL	540,920	394,661	137,150	1,950	5,485	1,674	9,879
Kansas City, MO	448,154	313,835	122,336	2,115	3,591	6,277	14,643
Long Beach, CA	361,334	272,272	40,463	3,531	22,025	23,043	50,450
Los Angeles, CA	2,966,850	1,842,050	504,301	19,296	206,536	394,667	815,305
Louisville, KY	298,455	212,052	84,254	408	1,327	414	2,049
Memphis, TN	646,356	334,363	307,573	680	2,864	876	5,730
Miami, FL	346,865	225,200	87,018	334	2,050	32,263	194,185
Milwaukee, WI	636,212	468,064	147,055	5,348	4,451	11,294	26,487
Minneapolis, MN	370,951	325,415	28,469	9,198	5,358	2,511	4,762
Nashville-Davidson, TN	455,663	345,766	105,869	743	2,418	867	3,257
New Orleans, LA	557,515	238,192	308,039	623	7,458	3,203	19,215
New York, NY	7,071,639	4,348,605	1,788,377	13,400	245,759	675,498	1,406,389
Newark, NJ	329,248	107,465	191,968	923	2,421	26,471	61,322
Norfolk, VA	266,979	163,052	93,977	822	7,075	2,053	5,792
Oakland, CA	339,337	131,127	159,351	2,754	28,053	18,052	32,133
Oklahoma City, OK	403,243	323,665	58,550	11,199	4,610	5,219	11,767
Omaha, NE	314,267	268,995	37,889	1,839	2,381	3,163	7,354
Philadelphia, PA	1,688,210	988,337	638,788	2,799	19,950	38,336	64,323
Phoenix, AZ	789,704	673,488	37,747	11,645	8,429	58,395	116,875
Pittsburgh, PA	423,938	318,287	101,549	584	2,818	700	3,370
Portland, OR	366,423	319,220	28,034	3,374	12,980	2,815	7,541
Sacramento, CA	275,741	187,992	36,842	3,506	24,558	22,843	38,905
St. Louis, MO	453,085	242,988	206,170	679	2,214	1,034	5,380
St. Paul, MN	270,230	245,795	13,018	2,558	5,345	3,514	7,553
San Antonio, TX	785,809	621,679	57,566	2,375	5,821	98,368	421,808
San Diego, CA	875,538	674,268	77,508	5,833	61,655	56,274	129,953
San Francisco, CA	678,974	402,131	86,190	3,566	149,269	37,818	84,194
San Jose, CA	629,442	470,458	28,792	5,801	53,205	71,186	140,318
Seattle, WA	493,846	396,275	46,565	6,821	38,936	5,249	12,744
Tampa, FL	271,523	202,507	63,578	607	1,894	2,937	35,781
Toledo, OH	354,635	284,104	61,855	989	2,005	5,682	10,984
Tucson, AZ	330,537	274,750	11,587	4,578	3,427	36,195	82,106
Tulsa, OK	360,919	298,926	42,845	13,816	2,962	2,370	6,291
Virginia Beach, VA	262,199	227,454	26,266	630	6,489	1,360	5,269
Washington, DC	638,333	174,705	448,370	1,014	6,883	7,361	17,777
Wichita, KS	279,272	236,549	30,263	2,942	4,525	4,993	9,455

(1) Not elsewhere classified.
(2) Persons of Hispanic origin may be of any race.

Population by State: 1989

Source: U.S. Bureau of the Census (1989 estimates)
(in thousands)

1989 rank	State	1989 Population	Percent change 1980-89	1989 rank	State	1989 Population	Percent change 1980-89	1989 rank	State	1989 Population	Percent change 1980-89
1	Cal.	29,063	22.8	19	Md.	4,694	11.3	36	Neb.	1,611	2.6
2	N.Y.	17,950	2.2	20	La.	4,382	4.2	37	N.M.	1,528	17.3
3	Tex.	16,991	19.4	21	Minn.	4,353	6.8	38	Me.	1,222	8.7
4	Fla.	12,671	30.0	22	Ala.	4,118	5.8	39	Ha.	1,112	15.3
5	Pa.	12,040	1.5	23	Ky.	3,727	1.8	40	Nev.	1,111	38.8
6	Ill.	11,658	2.0	24	Ariz.	3,556	30.8	41	N.H.	1,107	20.3
7	Oh.	10,907	1.0	25	S.C.	3,512	12.5	42	Id.	1,014	7.4
8	Mich.	9,273	0.1	26	Colo.	3,317	14.8	43	R.I.	998	5.4
9	N.J.	7,736	5.0	27	Conn.	3,239	4.2	44	Mont.	806	2.4
10	N.C.	6,571	11.7	28	Okla.	3,224	6.6	45	S.D.	715	3.5
11	Ga.	6,436	17.8	29	Ia.	2,840	-2.5	46	Del.	673	13.2
12	Va.	6,098	14.0	30	Ore.	2,820	7.1	47	N.D.	660	1.1
13	Mass.	5,913	3.1	31	Miss.	2,621	4.0	48	D. of C.	604	-5.4
14	Ind.	5,593	1.9	32	Kan.	2,513	6.3	49	Vt.	567	10.9
15	Mo.	5,159	4.9	33	Ark.	2,406	5.2	50	Alas.	527	31.1
16	Tenn.	4,940	7.6	34	W.Va.	1,857	-4.8	51	Wyo.	475	1.1
17	Wis.	4,867	3.4	35	Utah	1,707	16.8		U.S. Total	248,239	9.6
18	Wash.	4,761	15.2								

Foreign-Born Population in Twelve Metropolitan Areas of the United States: 1980

Source: U.S. Bureau of the Census

Country of origin	New York City	Chicago	Los Angeles	Philadelphia	Houston	Detroit	Dallas	San Diego	Phoenix	San Antonio	San Francisco	Washington DC
Number of foreign-born persons	1,946,800	744,930	1,664,793	242,658	220,861	282,766	124,697	235,593	82,536	76,944	509,352	249,994
Percent of population foreign-born	21.3	10.5	22.3	5.1	7.6	6.5	4.2	12.7	5.5	7.2	15.7	8.2
Europe	37.7	40.9	13.0	54.8	11.7	47.9	16.4	18.5	30.6	13.8	23.8	26.9
Austria	1.6	1.2	0.4	1.6	0.3	1.2	0.4	0.4	0.9	0.3	0.6	0.8
Czechoslovakia	1.0	1.4	0.3	0.8	0.3	0.9	0.4	0.3	0.7	0.3	0.4	0.6
France	0.8	0.5	0.5	0.9	0.7	0.7	0.9	0.7	1.4	0.8	1.1	1.8
Germany	4.3	6.0	2.1	9.4	2.6	6.3	5.0	3.7	7.2	5.8	4.2	6.2
Greece	2.4	3.2	0.4	2.5	0.7	2.1	0.5	0.5	0.8	0.2	0.8	1.9
Hungary	1.3	0.9	0.7	1.6	0.3	1.6	0.4	0.4	1.2	0.2	0.5	0.7
Ireland	2.7	2.0	0.3	3.8	0.2	1.0	0.4	0.5	0.9	0.5	1.2	0.7
Italy	10.5	6.0	1.3	14.9	0.7	8.0	0.7	2.0	3.4	0.6	3.3	2.4
Netherlands	0.2	0.5	0.5	0.5	0.5	0.6	0.5	0.7	0.9	0.2	0.8	0.6
Poland	4.6	8.4	1.0	4.7	0.5	7.6	0.6	0.7	1.8	0.5	0.6	1.1
Portugal	0.5	0.1	0.2	0.9	0.1	*	*	0.8	0.1	0.1	1.4	0.6
Sweden	0.2	0.9	0.2	0.3	0.1	0.3	0.2	0.5	0.5	0.1	0.6	0.3
United Kingdom	2.5	2.5	2.8	7.8	3.2	8.1	4.6	4.7	6.4	3.0	4.1	5.2
England	1.6	1.6	1.9	4.6	2.2	4.4	3.4	3.2	4.3	2.3	2.8	3.6
Northern Ireland	0.1	0.1	0.1	0.5	*	0.2	0.1	0.1	0.1	0.1	0.1	0.1
Scotland	0.6	0.6	0.5	2.1	0.4	3.0	0.6	1.0	1.4	0.3	0.7	0.7
Wales	*	*	*	0.2	0.1	0.2	0.1	0.1	0.1	*	0.1	0.1
Yugoslavia	1.3	3.0	0.6	1.0	0.2	3.7	0.2	0.5	1.1	0.1	0.5	0.3
U.S.S.R.	4.9	3.3	2.1	8.9	0.7	3.5	0.9	0.9	2.1	0.5	1.9	1.8
Asia	13.1	17.2	20.4	16.7	21.7	18.3	21.2	27.4	12.7	9.7	42.3	32.0
China	3.3	1.2	2.0	1.4	2.1	0.9	1.5	1.0	1.6	0.5	11.0	2.8
India	1.4	2.9	0.6	2.8	3.5	2.2	2.4	0.4	0.8	0.6	1.3	3.6
Japan	0.9	0.8	2.0	0.9	1.1	0.6	1.5	2.8	1.5	1.7	2.7	1.6
Korea	1.2	2.3	3.0	3.4	1.4	1.1	2.0	0.9	1.6	1.1	1.8	5.9
Philippines	1.3	4.3	4.4	2.1	1.9	2.0	1.8	13.0	1.3	1.7	13.2	3.6
Vietnam	0.2	0.6	1.7	1.4	5.3	0.4	3.8	3.3	1.6	1.5	2.2	3.6
North and Central America	27.4	28.7	54.8	9.5	51.0	23.1	48.5	44.9	44.6	69.4	21.9	17.4
Canada	1.2	2.2	3.4	3.2	2.3	19.9	3.8	5.9	10.8	1.6	4.1	3.3
Mexico	0.4	21.6	41.9	0.6	42.4	1.7	40.0	36.9	31.9	64.9	11.0	0.9
West Indies	22.6	3.2	2.7	4.8	3.8	1.2	2.8	0.9	0.8	1.3	1.0	8.4
Cuba	2.8	1.9	2.1	1.2	2.0	0.3	2.0	0.3	0.3	0.7	0.6	2.0
Dominican Republic	6.6	0.1	*	0.3	0.1	0.1	0.1	0.1	0.1	0.1	*	0.5
Jamaica	5.1	0.6	0.2	1.7	0.5	0.4	0.2	0.2	0.1	0.2	0.2	2.8
South America	8.8	2.5	3.5	2.5	3.9	1.0	2.4	1.7	1.9	1.0	2.5	9.6
North Africa	0.6	0.3	0.6	0.5	0.5	0.4	0.6	0.3	0.3	0.3	0.5	1.3
Other Africa	0.7	0.8	0.5	1.1	1.7	0.5	1.5	0.5	0.6	0.3	0.6	3.8
All other countries	0.2	0.2	0.5	0.3	0.3	0.2	0.5	1.0	0.6	0.3	1.6	0.8
Country not reported	6.5	6.2	4.7	5.6	8.5	5.0	7.9	4.8	6.6	4.8	4.9	6.4

Note: * indicates amount less or rounds than 0.1 percent.

Immigration by Country of Last Residence 1820-1989

Source: U.S. Immigration and Naturalization Service

(thousands)

Country	Total 1820-1989	Total 1961-1970	Total 1971-1980	1984	1985	1986	1987	1988[11]	1989[12]	Percent 1820-1989	Percent 1961-1970	Percent 1971-1980
All countries*..	55,458	3,321.7	4,493.3	543.9	570.0	601.7	601.5	643.0	1,090.9	100.0	100.0	100.0
Europe	36,977	1,123.5	800.4	69.9	69.5	69.2	68.0	71.8	94.3	66.7	33.8	17.8
Austria[1]	4,338	20.6	9.5	2.4	1.9	2.0	2.4	2.5	2.8	2.8	.6	0.2
Hungary........		5.4	6.6	0.5	0.6	0.6	—	0.7	0.7		.2	0.1
Belgium.......	210	9.2	5.3	0.8	0.8	0.8	0.9	0.7	0.7	0.4	.3	0.1
Czechoslovakia ..	145	3.3	6.0	0.7	0.7	0.6	0.7	0.7	0.5	0.3	.1	0.1
Denmark.......	370	9.2	4.4	0.5	0.5	0.5	0.5	0.6	0.6	0.7	.3	0.1
Finland	37	4.2	2.9	0.2	0.2	0.3	0.3	0.3	0.3	0.1	.1	0.1
France	783	45.2	25.1	3.3	3.5	3.9	3.8	3.6	4.1	1.4	1.4	0.6
Germany[1]......	7,071	190.8	74.4	9.4	10.2	9.9	9.9	9.7	10.4	12.8	5.7	1.7
Great Britain[2]....	5,100	214.5	137.4	16.5	15.6	16.0	15.9	14.7	17.0	9.2	6.5	3.1
Greece	700	86.0	92.4	3.3	3.5	3.5	4.1	4.7	4.6	1.3	2.6	2.1
Ireland........	4,715	33.0	11.5	1.1	1.3	1.8	3.0	5.1	7.0	8.5	1.0	0.3
Italy.........	5,357	214.1	129.4	6.3	6.4	5.7	4.7	5.3	11.1	9.7	6.4	2.9
Netherlands	373	30.6	10.5	1.3	1.2	1.3	1.3	1.2	1.2	0.7	.9	0.2
Norway[10]	753	15.5	3.9	0.4	0.4	0.4	0.4	0.4	0.6	1.4	.5	0.1
Poland[1]	588	53.5	37.2	7.2	7.4	6.5	5.8	7.3	13.3	1.1	1.6	0.8
Portugal.......	497	76.1	101.7	3.8	3.8	3.8	4.0	3.3	3.9	0.9	2.3	2.3
Spain	282	44.7	39.1	2.2	2.3	2.2	2.1	2.0	2.2	0.5	1.3	0.9
Sweden[10]	1,245	17.1	6.5	1.1	1.2	1.2	1.2	1.2	1.2	2.2	.5	0.1
Switzerland.....	358	18.5	8.2	0.8	1.0	0.9	0.1	0.9	1.1	0.6	.6	0.2
USSR[1,3]	3,429	2.5	39.0	3.3	1.5	1.0	1.1	1.4	4.6	6.2	.1	0.9
Yugoslavia	133	20.4	30.5	1.4	1.5	1.9	1.8	2.0	2.5	0.2	.6	0.7
Other Europe....	290	9.1	18.9	3.4	4.0	4.4	4.0	3.4	4.0	0.5	.2	0.2
Asia	5,697	427.6	1,588.2	247.8	255.2	258.5	248.3	254.7	296.4	10.3	12.9	35.2
China[5]........	874	34.8	124.3	29.1	33.1	16.5	18.6	34.3	39.3	1.6	1.0	2.8
Hong Kong	288	75.0	113.5	12.3	10.8	9.9	8.8	11.8	15.2	0.5	2.3	2.5
India.........	427	27.2	164.1	23.6	24.5	24.8	26.4	25.3	28.6	0.8	.8	3.7
Iran	162	10.3	45.1	11.1	12.3	12.0	10.3	9.8	13.0	0.3	.3	1.0
Israel	132	29.6	37.7	4.1	4.3	5.1	4.8	4.4	5.5	0.2	.9	0.8
Japan	456	40.0	49.8	4.5	4.6	4.4	4.7	5.1	5.4	0.8	1.2	1.1
Jordan	70	11.7	27.5	2.2	2.7	2.8	2.8	3.1	3.8	0.1	.4	0.6
Korea........	611	34.5	267.6	32.5	34.8	35.2	35.4	34.2	33.0	1.1	1.0	6.0
Lebanon	91	15.2	41.3	3.0	2.5	3.0	3.0	3.5	3.8	0.2	.5	0.9
Philippines	955	98.4	355.0	47.0	53.1	61.5	58.3	61.0	66.1	1.7	3.0	7.9
Turkey	409	10.1	13.4	1.7	1.7	2.0	2.1	2.2	2.5	0.7	.3	0.3
Vietnam.......	444	4.3	172.8	25.8	20.4	15.0	13.1	12.8	13.3	0.8	1.1	3.8
Other Asia	779	36.5	176.1	50.9	50.4	66.3	60.0	47.1	66.7	1.4	1.1	3.8
America........	12,017	1,716.4	1,982.5	208.1	225.5	254.1	265.0	294.9	672.6	21.7	51.7	44.3
Argentina	125	49.7	29.9	2.3	1.9	2.3	2.2	2.6	3.8	0.2	1.5	0.7
Brazil	93	29.3	17.8	2.2	2.6	2.7	2.7	3.0	3.7	0.2	.9	0.4
Canada	4,271	413.3	169.9	15.7	16.4	16.1	16.7	15.8	18.3	7.7	12.4	3.8
Colombia......	272	72.0	77.3	10.9	11.8	11.2	11.5	10.2	14.9	0.5	2.2	1.7
Cuba	739	208.5	264.9	5.7	17.1	30.8	27.4	16.6	9.5	1.3	6.3	5.9
Dominican Rep. ..	468	93.3	148.1	23.2	23.9	26.2	24.9	27.2	26.7	0.8	2.8	3.3
Ecuador.......	143	36.8	50.1	4.2	4.6	4.5	4.7	4.7	7.6	0.3	1.1	1.1
El Salvador.....	216	15.0	34.4	8.8	10.1	10.9	10.6	12.0	57.6	0.4	.5	0.8
Guatemala	104	15.9	25.9	4.0	4.4	5.3	5.8	5.8	19.2	0.2	.5	0.6
Haiti	215	34.5	56.3	9.6	9.9	12.4	14.6	34.8	13.3	0.4	1.0	1.3
Honduras	79	15.7	17.4	3.4	3.7	4.6	4.8	4.3	7.6	0.1	.5	0.4
Mexico	3,208	453.9	640.3	57.8	61.3	66.8	72.5	95.2	405.6	5.8	13.7	14.3
Panama.......	90	19.4	23.5	3.2	3.2	3.1	2.8	3.0	3.9	0.2	.6	0.5
Peru.........	106	19.1	29.2	4.3	4.1	4.8	5.8	5.8	10.0	0.2	.6	0.6
West Indies.....	1,168	133.9	271.8	29.9	28.5	29.2	33.7	32.3	38.0	2.1	4.0	6.1
Other America ...	740	106.1	125.7	22.9	22.0	23.2	24.2	21.5	32.7	1.3	3.1	2.8
Africa	301	29.0	80.8	13.6	15.2	15.5	15.7	17.1	22.5	0.5	.9	1.8
Australia and New Zealand.	144	19.6	23.8	2.3	2.5	2.4	2.3	2.5	2.9	0.3	.6	0.5
Other Oceania....	54	5.6	17.6	1.9	2.1	1.9	2.1	1.8	2.0	0.1	.1	0.4
Unknown or Not Reported	267	—	—	—	—	—	—	—	—	0.5	—	—

* Figures may not add to total due to rounding. (1) 1938-1945, Austria included with Germany; 1899-1919, Poland included with Austria-Hungary, Germany, and USSR. (2) Beginning 1952, includes data for United Kingdom not specified, formerly included with "Other Europe". (3) Europe and Asia. (4) Beginning 1957, includes Taiwan. (5) Prior to 1951, included with "Other Asia". (6) Prior to 1951, Philippines included with "All other". (7) Prior to 1953, data for Vietnam not available. (8) Prior to 1951, included with "Other America". (9) Prior to 1951, included with "West Indies". (10) Norway and Sweden were combined from 1820-1868. (11) First full year with Immigration Reform and Control Act of 1986 in effect. (12) Data include 478,814 previously illegal aliens who were granted permanent resident status under section 245A of the Immigration Reform and Control Act of 1986. These aliens are not new residents of the United States.

Poverty by Family Status, Sex, and Race

Source: U.S. Bureau of the Census, Current Population Reports
By thousands

	1988 No.¹	1988 %²	1986 No.¹	1986 %²	1984 No.¹	1984 %²	1978 No.¹	1978 %²
Total poor	31,745	13.0	32,370	13.6	33,700	14.4	24,497	11.4
In families	24,048	11.6	24,754	12.0	26,458	13.1	19,062	10.0
Head.	6,874	10.4	7,023	10.9	7,277	11.6	5,280	9.1
Related children	11,935	19.0	12,257	19.8	12,929	21.0	9,722	15.7
Other relatives	5,238	6.6	5,475	6.9	6,251	8.0	4,509	5.7
Unrelated individuals	7,070	20.6	6,846	21.6	6,609	21.8	5,435	22.1
In families with a female householder, no husband present	11,972	37.2	11,944	38.3	11,831	38.4	9,269	35.6
Head.	3,642	33.4	3,613	34.6	3,498	34.5	2,654	31.4
Related children	6,948	52.7	6,943	54.4	6,772	54.0	5,687	50.6
Other relatives	1,382	17.1	1,388	17.5	1,562	19.1	928	14.6
Unrelated female individuals . . .	4,225	23.1	4,311	25.1	4,035	24.4	3,611	26.0
All other	12,076	6.9	12,811	7.3	14,627	8.5	9,793	5.9
Head.	3,232	5.9	3,410	6.3	3,780	7.2	2,626	5.3
Related children	4,987	10.0	5,313	10.8	6,157	12.5	4,035	7.9
Other relatives	3,857	5.4	4,087	5.8	4,690	6.7	3,131	4.8
Unrelated male individuals	2,844	17.7	2,536	17.5	2,575	18.7	1,824	17.1
Total white poor	20,715	10.1	22,138	11.0	22,955	11.5	16,259	8.7
In families	15,001	8.6	16,393	9.4	17,299	10.1	12,050	7.3
Head.	4,409	7.8	4,811	8.6	4,925	9.1	3,523	6.9
Female.	1,945	26.5	2,041	28.2	1,878	27.1	1,391	23.5
Related children	7,095	14.0	7,714	15.3	8,086	16.1	5,674	11.0
Other relatives	3,497	5.1	3,868	5.7	4,289	6.4	2,852	4.5
Unrelated individuals	5,314	18.1	5,198	19.2	5,181	19.9	4,209	19.8
Total black poor	9,356	31.3	8,983	31.1	9,490	33.8	7,625	30.6
In families	7,650	30.0	7,401	29.7	8,104	33.2	6,493	29.5
Head.	2,089	28.2	1,987	28.0	2,094	30.9	1,622	27.5
Female.	1,579	49.0	1,488	50.1	1,533	51.7	1,208	50.6
Related children	4,148	42.8	4,039	42.7	4,320	46.2	3,781	41.2
Other relatives	1,413	16.8	1,375	16.5	1,691	20.5	1,094	15.7
Unrelated individuals	1,509	36.8	1,431	38.5	1,255	35.8	1,132	38.6

(1) Beginning in 1979, total includes members of unrelated subfamilies not shown separately. For earlier years, unrelated subfamily members are included in the "in family" category. (2) Percent of total population in that general category who fell below poverty level. For example, of all black female heads of households in 1978, 50.6% were poor.

Poverty Level by Family Size 1987, 1988

	1987	1988		1987	1988
1 persons	$ 5,778	$ 6,024	3 persons	$ 9,056	$ 9,435
Under 65 years	5,909	6,155	4 persons	11,611	12,092
65 years and over.	5,447	5,674	5 persons	13,737	14,305
2 persons	7,397	7,704	6 persons	15,509	16,149
Householder under 65 years.	7,641	7,958	7 persons	17,649	18,248
Householder 65 years and			8 persons	19,515	20,279
over	6,872	7,158	9 persons or more	23,105	24,133

Income Distribution by Population Fifths

Families, 1988 Race	Top income of each fifth Lowest	Second	Third	Fourth	Top 5%	Percent distribution of total income Lowest fifth	Second fifth	Third fifth	Fourth fifth	Highest fifth	Top 5%
Total	$15,102	$26,182	$38,500	$55,906	$92,001	4.6	10.7	16.7	24.0	44.0	17.2
White	16,814	28,000	40,000	57,350	93,900	5.1	11.1	16.8	23.7	43.3	17.0
Black and other	(NA)	(NA)	(NA)	(NA)	(NA)	(NA)	(NA)	(NA)	(NA)	(NA)	(NA)
Black.	7,148	14,400	24,425	40,300	65,927	3.3	8.5	15.2	25.1	47.9	17.7
Region											
Northeast.	$17,745	$30,000	$43,002	$62,318	$618,499	4.8	11.1	16.9	24.0	43.3	16.5
Midwest.	16,000	27,340	38,793	54,424	475,199	5.0	11.4	17.3	24.0	42.4	16.5
South	13,044	23,460	35,100	52,400	441,996	4.3	10.2	16.3	24.2	44.9	17.4
West	15,813	26,600	39,280	57,143	636,899	4.8	10.7	16.5	23.5	44.5	18.1

Persons Below Poverty Level, 1960-1988

Year	Number Below Poverty Level (mil.) All races¹	White	Black	Spanish origin²	Percent Below Poverty Level All races¹	White	Black	Spanish origin²	Average income cutoffs for non-farm family of 4³ at poverty level
1960	39.9	28.3	NA	NA	22.2	17.8	NA	NA	$3,022
1965	33.2	22.5	NA	NA	17.3	13.3	NA	NA	3,223
1970	25.4	17.5	7.5	NA	12.6	9.9	33.5	NA	3,968
1975	25.9	17.8	7.5	3.0	12.3	9.7	31.3	26.9	5,500
1980⁴	29.3	19.7	8.6	3.5	13.0	10.2	32.5	25.7	8,414
1986⁴	32.4	22.2	9.0	5.1	13.6	11.0	31.1	27.3	11,203
1987⁴	32.5	21.4	9.7	5.5	13.5	10.5	33.1	28.2	11,611
1988	31.7	20.7	9.4	5.4	13.0	10.1	31.3	26.7	12,092

NA = Not Available. (1) Includes other races not shown separately. (2) Persons of Spanish origin may be of any race. (3) Beginning in 1981, income cutoffs for nonfarm families are applied to both farm and nonfarm families. (4) Data based on revised poverty definition.

Poverty Rate

The poverty rate is the proportion of the population whose income falls below the government's official poverty level, which is adjusted each year to take account of inflation.

The national poverty rate was higher in 1986 than in any year from 1969 through 1980. The rate reached a peak of 15.2 percent in 1983.

Aid to Families with Dependent Children

Source: Family Support Administration. Office of Family Assistance. Social Security Admin.

FY 1989 State	Total Assistance Payments[1]	Average Monthly Caseload	Average Monthly Recipients	Average Monthly Children	Average Payment per Family	Average Payment per Person
Alabama	$61,117,217	44,820	129,037	91,698	$113.64	$39.47
Alaska	54,783,597	7,415	19,423	12,640	615.70	235.05
Arizona	117,043,333	36,044	105,380	73,608	270.60	92.56
Arkansas	55,439,117	23,914	69,633	49,621	193.19	66.35
California	4,436,483,185	604,761	1,762,931	1,186,027	611.33	209.71
Colorado	131,025,819	33,851	97,312	65,562	322.55	112.20
Connecticut	242,437,895	38,311	106,187	71,468	527.35	190.26
Delaware	25,050,732	7,463	19,189	13,137	279.74	108.79
Dist. of Col.	77,531,492	18,108	47,860	38,094	356.80	135.00
Florida	354,574,290	118,582	326,764	234,736	249.18	90.43
Georgia	289,335,398	92,654	265,879	186,915	260.23	90.69
Guam	3,100,547	1,170	4,072	2,916	220.88	63.45
Hawaii	89,114,192	13,873	42,783	28,288	535.30	173.58
Idaho	18,429,755	6,231	16,819	11,438	246.49	91.31
Illinois	786,541,577	206,895	632,181	432,184	316.80	103.68
Indiana	162,240,669	51,611	147,385	100,331	261.96	91.73
Iowa	149,034,319	34,819	97,590	63,039	356.69	127.26
Kansas	104,283,113	25,213	73,869	50,218	344.67	117.64
Kentucky	155,423,930	58,717	155,722	104,508	220.58	83.17
Louisiana	184,829,568	92,194	276,574	194,644	167.07	55.69
Maine	86,062,625	17,948	50,801	31,955	399.59	141.18
Maryland	265,450,435	63,230	176,135	117,494	349.85	125.59
Massachusetts	595,016,889	88,188	241,696	154,158	562.26	205.15
Michigan	1,226,434,609	211,919	639,889	414,187	482.27	159.72
Minnesota	343,392,910	54,639	163,542	105,363	523.73	174.98
Mississippi	84,917,420	59,860	178,834	128,611	118.22	39.57
Missouri	220,042,222	68,067	203,109	134,135	269.39	90.28
Montana	40,565,738	9,329	27,694	17,795	362.36	122.06
Nebraska	56,618,425	14,210	41,026	28,107	332.02	115.00
Nevada	24,222,246	7,293	20,142	14,078	276.79	100.21
New Hampshire	24,303,571	4,901	12,716	8,424	413.25	159.27
New Jersey	440,059,320	102,519	297,796	204,812	357.70	123.14
New Mexico	54,962,877	20,372	58,676	40,541	224.83	78.06
New York	2,153,726,471	337,300	979,135	647,598	532.10	183.30
North Carolina	220,522,505	77,066	200,277	136,163	238.46	91.76
North Dakota	24,025,321	5,489	15,292	10,175	364.74	130.93
Ohio	826,624,751	222,187	629,106	410,938	310.03	109.50
Oklahoma	124,326,583	35,930	103,043	70,742	288.35	100.55
Oregon	137,546,020	32,060	87,288	58,306	357.53	131.31
Pennsylvania	738,456,580	174,577	522,682	348,480	352.50	117.74
Puerto Rico	70,596,887	57,841	185,345	126,470	101.71	31.74
Rhode Island	86,079,829	15,057	41,899	27,535	476.41	171.20
South Carolina	91,286,353	37,466	107,461	76,916	203.04	70.79
South Dakota	21,615,831	6,632	18,928	13,263	271.62	95.17
Tennessee	142,001,084	70,575	195,481	132,975	167.67	60.53
Texas	367,805,132	181,598	539,858	378,245	168.78	56.77
Utah	63,475,434	14,969	43,627	28,369	353.36	121.25
Vermont	41,424,560	7,015	19,723	12,406	492.08	175.02
Virgin Islands	2,908,765	941	3,388	2,544	257.60	71.55
Virginia	168,357,395	53,918	145,622	99,858	260.21	96.34
Washington	420,720,603	78,031	219,273	141,050	449.31	159.89
West Virginia	110,033,577	36,087	109,294	67,173	254.09	83.90
Wisconsin	454,213,644	81,981	244,876	160,787	461.71	154.57
Wyoming	18,797,003	5,123	13,737	9,113	305.79	114.03
U.S. Total	**$17,244,413,360**	**3,770,959**	**10,933,981**	**7,369,835**	**$381.08**	**$131.43**

(1) Total assistance payments include AFDC-Basic, AFDC-Unemployed Parent, grant diversion and home repairs.

Supplemental Security Income (SSI) Program
Recipients and Payments, 1955-1989

Category		1955, Dec.	1965, Dec.	1970, Dec.	1975, Dec.[1]	1980, Dec.	1985, Dec.	1989, Dec.
Aged:	Recipients	2,538,000	2,087,000	2,082,000	2,307,105	1,807,776	1,504,469	1,439,043
	Total amt.	$127,003,000	$131,674,000	$161,642,000	$209,777,000	$221,303,000	$247,133,000	$286,105,000
	Avg. amt.	$50.05	$63.10	$77.65	$90.93	$128.20	$164.26	$198.81
Blind:	Recipients	104,000	85,100	81,000	74,489	78,401	82,220	82,765
	Total amt.	$5,803,000	$6,922,000	$8,446,000	$10,918,000	$16,381,000	$22,555,000	$26,465,000
	Avg. amt.	$55.55	$81.35	$104.35	$146.57	$213.23	$274.32	$319.76
Disabled:	Recipients	241,000	557,000	935,000	1,932,681	2,255,840	2,551,332	3,071,251
	Total amt.	$11,750,000	$37,035,000	$91,325,000	$272,800,000	$444,322,000	$665,774,000	$948,833,000
	Avg. amt.	$48.75	$66.50	$97.65	$141.15	$197.90	$260.95	$308.94

(1) In 1972, Congress replaced the categorical Federal-State programs of Old-Age Assistance, Aid to the Blind, and Aid to the Permanently and Totally Disabled with the Federal Supplemental Security Income (SSI) program effective Jan. 1974. The SSI program is administered by the Social Security Admin.

U.S. Places of 5,000 or More Population—With ZIP and Area Codes

Source: U.S. Bureau of the Census; U.S. Postal Service; N.Y. Telephone Co.

The listings below show the official urban population of the United States. "Urban population" is defined as all persons living in (a) places of 5,000 inhabitants or more, incorporated as cities, villages, boroughs (except Alaska), and towns (except in New England, New York, New Jersey, Pennsylvania and Wisconsin), but excluding those persons living in the rural portions of extended cities; (b) unincorporated places of 5,000 inhabitants or more; and (c) other territory, incorporated or unincorporated, included in urbanized areas.

The non-urban portion of an extended city contains one or more areas, each at least 5 square miles in extent and with a population density of less than 100 persons per square mile. The area or areas constitute at least 25 percent of the legal city's land area of a total of 25 square miles or more.

In New England, New York, New Jersey, Pennsylvania, and Wisconsin, minor civil divisions called "towns" often include rural areas and one or more urban areas. Only the urban areas of these "towns" are included here, except in the case of New England where entire town populations, which may include some rural population, are shown; these towns are indicated by italics. Boroughs in Alaska may contain one or more urban areas which are included here. Population in Hawaii is counted by county subdivisions.

(u) means place is unincorporated.

The ZIP Code of each place appears before the name of that place, if it is obtainable. Telephone Area Code appears in parentheses after the name of the state or, if a state has more than one number, after the name of the place.

CAUTION—Where an asterisk (*) appears before the ZIP Code, ask your local postmaster for the correct ZIP Code for a specific address within the place listed.

ZIP code	Place	1980	1970
	Alabama (205)		
35007	Alabaster.	7,079	2,642
35950	Albertville	12,039	9,963
35010	Alexander City.	13,807	12,358
36420	Andalusia	10,415	10,092
36201	Anniston	29,135	31,533
35016	Arab	6,053	4,399
35611	Athens	14,558	14,360
36502	Atmore.	8,789	8,293
35954	Attalla	7,737	7,510
36830	Auburn	28,471	22,767
36507	Bay Minette	7,455	6,727
35020	Bessemer.	31,729	33,428
*35203	Birmingham	284,413	300,910
35957	Boaz	7,151	5,635
36426	Brewton	6,680	6,747
35020	Brighton	5,308	2,277
35215	Center Point(u)	23,317	15,675
36611	Chickasaw .	7,402	8,447
35044	Childersburg.	5,084	4,831
35045	Clanton.	5,832	5,868
35055	Cullman	13,084	12,601
35601	Decatur.	42,002	38,044
36732	Demopolis	7,678	7,651
36301	Dothan	48,750	36,733
36330	Enterprise	18,033	15,591
36027	Eufaula.	12,097	9,102
35064	Fairfield.	13,242	14,369
36532	Fairhope	7,286	5,720
35555	Fayette.	5,287	4,568
35630	Florence	37,029	34,031
35214	Forestdale(u)	10,814	6,091
35967	Fort Payne	11,485	8,435
36360	Fort Rucker(u).	8,932	14,242
35068	Fultondale .	6,217	5,163
*35901	Gadsden .	47,565	53,928
35071	Gardendale	8,005	6,537
36037	Greenville	7,807	8,033
35976	Guntersville	7,041	6,491
35565	Haleyville	5,306	4,190
35640	Hartselle.	8,858	7,355
35209	Homewood	21,271	21,245
35226	Hoover .	18,996	688
35020	Hueytown	13,452	7,095
*35804	Huntsville	142,513	139,282
35210	Irondale	6,073	5,957
36545	Jackson	5,957	5,957
36265	Jacksonville	9,735	7,715
35501	Jasper	11,894	10,798
36863	Lanett	8,922	6,908
35094	Leeds.	8,638	6,991
35228	Midfield.	6,182	6,621
*36601	Mobile	200,452	190,026
36460	Monroeville	5,674	4,846
*36104	Montgomery .	177,857	133,386
35223	Mountain Brook .	17,400	19,474
35660	Muscle Shoals.	8,911	6,907
35476	Northport.	14,291	9,435
36801	Opelika.	21,896	19,027
36467	Opp.	7,204	6,493
36203	Oxford .	8,939	4,361
36360	Ozark.	13,188	13,555
35124	Pelham.	6,759	931
35125	Pell City	6,616	5,602
36867	Phenix City.	26,928	25,281
36272	Piedmont.	5,544	5,063
35127	Pleasant Grove .	7,102	5,090
36067	Prattville .	18,647	13,116
36610	Prichard .	39,541	41,578
35901	Rainbow City	6,299	3,099
35809	Redstone Arsenal(u)	5,728	....
36274	Roanoke .	5,809	5,251
35653	Russellville.	8,195	7,814
36201	Saks(u).	11,118	....
36571	Saraland .	9,833	7,840
35768	Scottsboro .	14,758	9,324
36701	Selma .	26,684	27,379
36701	Selmont-West Selmont(u)	5,255	2,270
35660	Sheffield .	11,903	13,115
35901	Southside	5,141	983
35150	Sylacauga .	12,708	12,255
35160	Talladega	19,128	17,662
35217	Tarrant City	8,148	6,835
36582	Theodore(u) .	6,392	....
36619	Tillman's Corner(u) .	15,941	....
36081	Troy.	13,124	11,482
35401	Tuscaloosa .	75,143	65,773
35674	Tuscumbia .	9,137	8,828
36083	Tuskegee .	12,716	11,028
35216	Vestavia Hills .	15,733	12,250
36201	West End-Cobb(u)	5,169	5,515
	Alaska (907)		
*99502	Anchorage .	174,431	48,081
99702	Eielson AFB(u) .	5,232	6,149
99701	Fairbanks .	22,645	14,771
99801	Juneau .	19,528	6,050
99611	Kenai Peninsula borough.	25,282	16,586
99901	Ketchikan .	7,198	6,994
99835	Sitka .	7,803	3,370
	Arizona (602)		
85321	Ajo(u).	5,189	5,881
85220	Apache Junction .	9,935	2,443
85323	Avondale .	8,134	6,626
85603	Bisbee .	7,154	8,328
86430	Bullhead City-Riviera(u) .	10,364	....
85222	Casa Grande .	14,971	10,536
85224	Chandler .	29,673	13,763
85228	Coolidge .	6,851	5,314
85707	Davis-Monthan AFB(u) .	6,279	'.....
85205	Dreamland-VeldaRose(u) .	5,969	....
85231	Eloy.	6,240	5,381
86001	Flagstaff .	34,641	26,117
85613	Fort Huachuca(u) .	NA	6,659
85234	Gilbert .	5,717	1,971
*85301	Glendale .	96,988	36,228
85501	Globe.	6,886	7,333
85614	Green Valley(u) .	7,999	....
86025	Holbrook .	5,785	4,759
86401	Kingman .	9,257	7,312
86403	Lake Havasu City .	15,737	4,111
85301	Luke(u).	NA	5,047
*85201	Mesa .	152,404	63,049
85621	Nogales .	15,683	8,946
86040	Page(u).	NA	1,439
85253	Paradise Valley .	10,832	6,637
85345	Peoria .	12,171	4,792
*85026	Phoenix.	789,704	584,303
86301	Prescott .	19,865	13,631
85546	Safford .	7,010	5,493

ZIP code	Place	1980	1970
85631	San Manuel(u)	5,443	
*85251	Scottsdale	88,622	67,823
85635	Sierra Vista	25,968	6,689
85713	South Tucson	6,554	6,220
85351	Sun City(u)	40,505	13,670
*85282	Tempe	106,919	63,550
86045	Tuba City(u)	5,045	
*85726	Tucson	330,537	262,933
85364	West Yuma(u)	NA	5,552
86047	Winslow	7,921	8,066
85364	Yuma	42,481	29,007

Arkansas (501)

ZIP code	Place	1980	1970
71923	Arkadelphia	10,005	9,841
72501	Batesville	8,447	7,209
72015	Benton	17,437	16,499
72712	Bentonville	8,756	5,508
72315	Blytheville	24,314	24,752
71701	Camden	15,356	15,147
72830	Clarksville	5,237	4,616
72032	Conway	20,375	15,510
71635	Crossett	6,706	6,191
71639	Dumas	6,091	4,600
71730	El Dorado	26,685	25,283
72701	Fayetteville	36,604	30,729
71742	Fordyce	5,175	4,837
72335	Forrest City	13,803	12,521
72901	Fort Smith	71,384	62,802
72601	Harrison	9,567	7,239
72342	Helena	9,598	10,415
71801	Hope	10,290	8,830
71901	Hot Springs	35,166	35,631
72076	Jacksonville	27,589	19,832
72401	Jonesboro	31,530	27,050
*72201	Little Rock	159,159	132,483
71753	Magnolia	11,909	11,303
72104	Malvern	10,163	8,739
72360	Marianna	6,220	6,196
71654	McGehee	5,671	4,683
71953	Mena	5,154	4,530
71655	Monticello	8,259	5,085
72110	Morrilton	7,355	6,814
72653	Mountain Home	7,447	3,936
72112	Newport	8,339	7,725
*72114	North Little Rock	64,388	60,040
72370	Osceola	8,881	7,892
72450	Paragould	15,214	10,639
71601	Pine Bluff	56,576	57,389
72455	Pocahontas	5,995	4,544
72756	Rogers	17,429	11,050
72801	Russellville	14,518	11,750
72143	Searcy	13,612	9,040
72116	Sherwood	10,423	2,754
72761	Siloam Springs	7,940	6,009
72764	Springdale	23,458	16,783
72160	Stuttgart	10,941	10,477
75502	Texarkana	21,459	21,682
72472	Trumann	6,395	6,023
72956	Van Buren	12,020	8,373
71671	Warren	7,646	6,433
72390	West Helena	11,367	11,007
72301	West Memphis	28,138	26,070
72396	Wynne	7,927	6,696

California

ZIP code	Place		1980	1970
94501	Alameda	(415)	63,852	70,968
94507	Alamo(u)	(415)	8,505	14,059
94706	Albany	(415)	15,130	15,561
*91802	Alhambra	(818)	64,767	62,125
90249	Alondra Park(u)	(213)	12,096	12,193
92001	Alpine(u)	(619)	5,368	1,570
91001	Altadena(u)	(818)	40,510	42,415
95116	Alum Rock(u)	(408)	17,471	18,355
94590	American Canyon(u)	(707)	5,712	
*92803	Anaheim	(714)	219,494	166,408
96007	Anderson	(916)	7,381	5,492
94509	Antioch	(415)	43,559	28,060
92307	Apple Valley(u)	(619)	14,305	6,702
95003	Aptos(u)	(408)	7,039	8,704
91006	Arcadia	(818)	45,993	45,138
95521	Arcata	(707)	12,849	8,985
95825	Arden-Arcade(u)	(916)	87,570	82,492
93420	Arroyo Grande	(805)	11,290	7,454
90701	Artesia	(213)	14,301	14,757
93203	Arvin	(805)	6,863	5,199
94577	Ashland(u)	(415)	13,893	14,810
93422	Atascadero	(805)	15,930	10,290
94025	Atherton	(415)	7,797	8,085
95301	Atwater	(209)	17,530	11,640
95603	Auburn	(916)	7,540	6,570
92505	August(u)	(714)	6,350	6,293
91746	Avocado Heights(u)	(818)	11,721	9,810
91702	Azusa	(818)	29,380	25,217
*93302	Bakersfield	(805)	105,611	69,515
91706	Baldwin Park	(818)	50,554	47,285

ZIP code	Place		1980	1970
92220	Banning	(714)	14,020	12,034
92311	Barstow	(619)	17,690	17,442
93402	Baywood-Los Osos(u)	(805)	10,933	3,487
95903	Beale AFB East(u)	(916)	6,329	7,029
92223	Beaumont	(714)	6,818	5,484
90201	Bell	(213)	25,450	21,836
90706	Bellflower	(213)	53,441	52,334
90201	Bell Gardens	(213)	34,117	29,308
94002	Belmont	(415)	24,505	23,538
94510	Benicia	(707)	15,376	7,349
95005	Ben Lomond(u)	(408)	7,238	2,793
*94704	Berkeley	(415)	103,328	114,091
*90213	Beverly Hills	(213)	32,646	33,416
92314	Big Bear(u)	(714)	11,151	5,268
92316	Bloomington(u)	(714)	6,674	11,957
92225	Blythe	(619)	6,805	7,047
92002	Bonita(u)	(619)	6,257	
95006	Boulder Creek(u)	(408)	5,662	1,806
92227	Brawley	(619)	14,946	13,746
92621	Brea	(714)	27,913	18,447
95605	Broderick-Bryte(u)	(916)	10,194	12,782
*90620	Buena Park	(714)	64,165	63,646
*91505	Burbank	(818)	84,625	88,871
94010	Burlingame	(415)	26,173	27,320
92231	Calexico	(619)	14,412	10,625
93725	Calwa(u)	(209)	6,640	5,191
93010	Camarillo	(805)	37,732	19,219
93010	Camarillo Heights(u)	(805)	6,341	5,892
95682	Cameron Park(u)	(916)	5,607	
95008	Campbell	(408)	26,843	23,797
91351	Canyon Country(u)	(805)	15,728	
92055	Camp Pendleton South(u)	(714)	7,952	13,692
92624	Capistrano Beach(u)	(714)	6,168	4,149
95010	Capitola	(408)	9,095	5,080
92007	Cardiff-by-the-Sea(u)	(619)	10,054	5,724
92008	Carlsbad	(619)	35,490	14,944
95608	Carmichael(u)	(916)	43,108	37,625
93013	Carpinteria	(805)	10,835	6,982
90744	Carson	(213)	81,221	71,150
92077	Casa De Oro-Mt. Helix(u)	(619)	19,651	
92010	Castle Park-Otay(u)	(619)	21,049	15,445
94546	Castro Valley(u)	(415)	44,011	44,760
95307	Ceres	(209)	13,281	6,029
90701	Cerritos	(213)	52,756	15,856
91724	Charter Oak(u)	(818)	6,840	
94541	Cherryland(u)	(415)	9,425	9,969
92223	Cherry Valley(u)	(714)	5,012	3,165
95926	Chico	(916)	26,716	19,580
95926	Chico North(u)	(916)	11,739	6,656
95926	Chico West(u)	(916)	6,378	4,787
91710	Chino	(714)	40,165	20,411
93610	Chowchilla	(209)	5,122	4,349
*92010	Chula Vista	(619)	83,927	67,901
95610	Citrus(u)	(916)	12,450	
95610	Citrus Heights(u)	(916)	85,911	21,760
91711	Claremont	(714)	31,028	24,776
93612	Clovis	(209)	33,021	13,856
92236	Coachella	(619)	9,129	8,353
93210	Coalinga	(209)	6,593	6,161
92324	Colton	(714)	27,419	20,016
90022	Commerce	(213)	10,509	10,635
*90220	Compton	(213)	81,350	78,547
*94520	Concord	(415)	103,763	85,164
93212	Corcoran	(209)	6,454	5,249
91720	Corona	(714)	37,791	27,519
92118	Coronado	(619)	18,790	20,020
94925	Corte Madera	(415)	8,074	8,464
92626	Costa Mesa	(714)	82,291	72,660
	Country Club(u)	(209)	9,585	
*91722	Covina	(818)	32,746	30,395
92335	Crestline(u)	(714)	6,715	
90201	Cudahy	(213)	18,275	16,998
90230	Culver City	(213)	38,139	34,451
95014	Cupertino	(408)	34,297	17,895
90630	Cypress	(714)	40,738	31,569
*94017	Daly City	(415)	78,519	66,922
94526	Danville	(415)	26,446	
92629	Dana Point(u)	(714)	10,602	4,745
95616	Davis	(916)	36,640	23,488
90250	Del Aire(u)	(213)	8,487	11,930
93215	Delano	(805)	16,491	14,559
92014	Del Mar	(619)	5,017	3,956
92240	Desert Hot Springs	(619)	5,941	2,738
91765	Diamond Bar(u)	(714)	28,045	10,576
93618	Dinuba	(209)	9,907	7,917
95620	Dixon	(916)	7,541	4,432
*90241	Downey	(213)	82,602	88,573
91010	Duarte	(818)	16,766	14,981
94568	Dublin	(415)	13,496	13,641
90220	East Compton(u)	(213)	6,435	5,853
92343	East Hemet(u)	(714)	14,712	8,598
90638	East La Mirada(u)	(213)	9,688	12,339
90022	East Los Angeles(u)	(213)	110,017	104,881
94303	East Palo Alto(u)	(415)	18,191	18,727
93257	East Porterville(u)	(209)	5,218	4,042
92508	Edgemont(u)	(714)	5,215	
93523	Edwards AFB(u)	(805)	8,554	10,331
*92020	El Cajon	(619)	73,892	52,273
92243	El Centro	(619)	23,996	19,272
94530	El Cerrito	(415)	22,731	25,190
95624	Elk Grove(u)	(916)	10,959	3,721

ZIP code	Place		1980	1970
*91734	El Monte	(818)	79,494	69,892
93446	El Paso de Robles	(213)	9,163	7,168
93030	El Rio(u)	(805)	5,674	6,173
90245	El Segundo	(213)	13,752	15,620
94803	El Sobrante(u)	(415)	10,535	----
92630	El Toro(u)	(714)	38,153	8,654
92709	El Toro Station(u)	(714)	7,632	6,970
92024	Encinitas	(619)	10,796	5,375
*92025	Escondido	(619)	62,480	36,792
95501	Eureka	(707)	24,153	24,337
93221	Exeter	(209)	5,619	4,475
94930	Fairfax	(415)	7,391	7,661
94533	Fairfield	(707)	58,099	44,146
95628	Fair Oaks(u)	(916)	20,235	11,256
92028	Fallbrook(u)	(619)	14,041	6,945
93223	Farmersville	(209)	5,544	3,456
93015	Fillmore	(805)	9,602	6,285
90001	Florence-Graham(u)	(213)	48,662	42,900
95828	Florin(u)	(916)	16,523	9,646
95630	Folsom	(916)	11,003	5,810
92335	Fontana	(714)	36,804	20,673
93841	Foothill Farms(u)	(916)	13,700	----
95437	Fort Bragg	(707)	5,019	4,455
95540	Fortuna	(707)	7,591	4,203
94404	Foster City	(415)	23,287	9,522
92708	Fountain Valley	(714)	55,080	31,886
95019	Freedom(u)	(408)	6,416	5,563
*94536	Fremont	(415)	131,945	100,869
*93706	Fresno	(209)	217,491	165,655
*92631	Fullerton	(714)	102,246	85,987
95632	Galt	(209)	5,514	3,200
*90247	Gardena	(213)	45,165	41,021
95205	Garden Acres(u)	(213)	7,361	7,870
*92640	Garden Grove	(714)	123,351	121,155
92392	George AFB(u)	(619)	7,061	7,404
95020	Gilroy	(408)	21,641	12,684
92509	Glen Avon(u)	(714)	8,444	5,759
*91209	Glendale	(818)	139,060	132,664
91740	Glendora	(818)	38,500	32,143
92324	Grand Terrace	(714)	8,498	5,901
95945	Grass Valley	(916)	6,697	5,149
93308	Greenacres(u)	(805)	5,381	2,116
93433	Grover City	(805)	8,827	5,939
91745	Hacienda Heights	(818)	49,422	35,969
94019	Half Moon Bay	(415)	7,282	4,023
93230	Hanford	(209)	20,958	15,179
90716	Hawaiian Gardens	(213)	10,548	9,052
90250	Hawthorne	(213)	56,437	53,304
*94544	Hayward	(415)	93,585	93,058
95448	Healdsburg	(707)	7,217	5,438
92343	Hemet	(714)	22,531	12,252
94547	Hercules	(415)	5,963	252
90254	Hermosa Beach	(213)	18,070	17,412
92345	Hesperia	(619)	13,540	4,592
92346	Highland	(714)	10,908	12,669
94010	Hillsborough	(415)	10,372	8,753
95023	Hollister	(408)	11,488	7,663
91720	Home Gardens(u)	(714)	5,783	5,116
*92647	Huntington Beach	(714)	170,505	115,960
90255	Huntington Park	(213)	45,932	33,744
92032	Imperial Beach	(619)	22,689	20,244
92201	Indio	(619)	21,611	14,459
*90306	Inglewood	(213)	94,162	89,985
*92711	Irvine	(714)	62,134	7,381
94707	Kensington(u)	(415)	5,342	5,823
93930	King City	(408)	5,495	3,717
93631	Kingsburg	(209)	5,115	3,843
91011	La Canada-Flintridge	(818)	20,153	20,714
91214	La Crescenta-Montrose(u)	(818)	16,531	19,620
90045	Ladera Heights(u)	(213)	6,647	6,079
94549	Lafayette	(415)	20,837	20,484
*92651	Laguna Beach	(714)	17,858	14,550
92653	Laguna Hills(u)	(714)	33,600	13,676
92677	Laguna Niguel(u)	(714)	12,237	4,644
90631	La Habra	(213)	45,232	41,350
92352	Lake Arrowhead(u)	(714)	6,272	2,682
92040	Lakeside(u)	(619)	23,921	11,991
92330	Lake Elsinore	(714)	5,982	3,530
*90714	Lakewood	(213)	74,511	83,025
92041	La Mesa	(619)	50,342	39,178
90638	La Mirada	(213)	40,986	30,808
93241	Lamont(u)	(805)	9,616	7,007
93534	Lancaster	(805)	48,027	32,728
92153	La Palma	(213)	15,663	9,687
91747	La Puente	(818)	30,882	31,092
91744	La Riviera(u)	(916)	10,906	----
94939	Larkspur	(415)	11,064	10,487
91750	La Verne	(714)	23,508	12,965
90260	Lawndale	(213)	23,460	24,825
92045	Lemon Grove	(619)	20,780	19,794
93245	Lemoore	(209)	8,832	4,219
93245	Lemoore Station(u)	(209)	5,888	9,210
90304	Lennox(u)	(213)	18,445	16,121
92024	Leucadia(u)	(619)	9,478	----
95207	Lincoln Village(u)	(916)	7,067	6,112
95901	Linda(u)	(916)	10,225	7,112
93247	Lindsay	(209)	6,936	5,206
95062	Live Oak(u) (Santa Cruz)	(916)	11,482	6,443
94550	Livermore	(415)	48,349	37,703
95334	Livingston	(209)	5,326	2,588
*95240	Lodi	(209)	35,221	28,691
92354	Loma Linda	(714)	10,694	7,651
90717	Lomita	(213)	17,191	19,784
93436	Lompoc	(805)	26,267	25,264
*90801	Long Beach	(213)	361,498	358,879
90720	Los Alamitos	(213)	11,529	11,346
94022	Los Altos	(415)	25,769	25,062
94022	Los Altos Hills	(415)	7,421	6,871
*90052	Los Angeles	(213)	2,968,528	2,811,801
93635	Los Banos	(209)	10,341	9,188
95030	Los Gatos	(408)	26,593	22,613
94903	Lucas Valley-Marinwood(u)	(415)	5,409	----
90262	Lynwood	(213)	48,289	43,354
93637	Madera	(209)	21,732	16,044
90266	Manhattan Beach	(213)	31,542	35,352
95336	Manteca	(209)	24,925	13,845
93933	Marina	(408)	20,647	8,343
90292	Marina Del Rey(u)	(213)	8,065	----
94553	Martinez	(415)	22,582	16,506
95901	Marysville	(916)	9,898	9,353
95655	Mather AFB(u)	(916)	5,245	7,027
91016	Mayflower Village(u)	(818)	5,017	----
90270	Maywood	(213)	21,810	16,996
93250	Mc Farland	(805)	5,151	4,177
95521	McKinleyville(u)	(707)	7,772	----
95023	Meiners Oaks-Mira Monte(u)	(805)	9,512	7,025
93640	Mendota	(209)	5,038	2,705
94025	Menlo Park	(415)	26,438	26,826
*95340	Merced	(209)	36,423	22,670
94030	Millbrae	(415)	20,058	20,920
94941	Mill Valley	(415)	12,967	12,942
95035	Milpitas	(408)	37,820	26,561
91752	Mira Loma(u)	(714)	8,707	8,482
92675	Mission Viejo	(714)	48,384	11,933
*95350	Modesto	(209)	106,963	61,712
91016	Monrovia	(818)	30,531	30,562
91763	Montclair	(714)	22,628	22,546
90640	Montebello	(213)	52,929	42,807
93940	Monterey	(408)	27,558	26,302
91754	Monterey Park	(818)	54,338	49,166
94556	Moraga	(415)	15,014	14,205
95037	Morgan Hill	(408)	17,060	5,579
93442	Morro Bay	(805)	9,064	7,109
*94042	Mountain View	(415)	58,655	54,132
92405	Muscoy(u)	(714)	6,188	7,091
94558	Napa	(707)	50,879	36,103
92050	National City	(619)	48,772	43,184
94560	Newark	(415)	32,126	27,153
91321	Newhall(u)	(805)	12,029	9,651
*92660	Newport Beach	(714)	63,475	49,582
93444	Nipomo(u)	(805)	5,247	3,642
91760	Norco	(714)	19,732	14,511
95603	North Auburn(u)	(916)	7,619	----
94025	North Fair Oaks(u)	(415)	10,294	9,740
95660	North Highlands(u)	(916)	37,825	31,854
90650	Norwalk	(213)	84,901	90,164
94947	Novato	(415)	43,916	31,006
95361	Oakdale	(209)	8,474	6,594
*94615	Oakland	(415)	339,337	361,561
92054	Oceanside	(619)	76,698	40,494
93308	Oildale(u)	(805)	23,382	20,879
93023	Ojai	(805)	6,816	5,591
95961	Olivehurst(u)	(916)	8,929	8,100
*91761	Ontario	(714)	88,820	64,118
95060	Opal Cliffs(u)	(408)	5,041	5,425
92667	Orange	(714)	91,450	77,365
95662	Orangevale(u)	(916)	20,585	16,493
94563	Orinda	(415)	16,825	6,790
95965	Oroville	(916)	8,683	7,536
93030	Oxnard	(805)	108,195	71,225
94044	Pacifica	(415)	36,866	36,020
93950	Pacific Grove	(408)	15,755	13,505
93550	Palmdale	(805)	12,277	8,511
92260	Palm Desert	(619)	11,801	6,171
92262	Palm Springs	(619)	32,359	20,936
94302	Palo Alto	(415)	55,225	56,040
90274	Palos Verdes Estates	(213)	14,376	13,631
95969	Paradise	(916)	22,571	14,539
90723	Paramount	(213)	36,407	34,734
95823	Parkway-Sacramento So.(u)	(916)	26,815	28,574
*91109	Pasadena	(818)	118,072	112,951
92370	Perris	(714)	6,740	4,228
94952	Petaluma	(707)	33,834	24,870
90660	Pico Rivera	(213)	53,387	54,170
94611	Piedmont	(415)	10,498	10,917
94564	Pinole	(415)	14,253	13,266
93449	Pismo Beach	(805)	5,364	4,043
94565	Pittsburg	(415)	33,465	21,423
92670	Placentia	(714)	35,041	21,948
95667	Placerville	(916)	6,739	5,416
94523	Pleasant Hill	(415)	25,547	24,610
94566	Pleasanton	(415)	35,160	18,328
*91766	Pomona	(714)	92,742	87,384
93257	Porterville	(209)	19,707	12,602
93041	Port Hueneme	(805)	17,803	14,295
92064	Poway	(619)	32,263	9,422
93534	Quartz Hill(u)	(213)	7,421	4,935
92065	Ramona(u)	(619)	8,173	3,554
95670	Rancho Cordova(u)	(916)	42,881	30,451
91730	Rancho Cucamonga	(714)	55,250	19,484

ZIP code	Place		1980	1970
92270	Rancho Mirage	(619)	6,281	2,767
90274	Rancho Palos Verdes	(213)	35,227	33,285
96080	Red Bluff	(916)	9,490	7,676
96001	Redding	(916)	42,103	16,659
92373	Redlands	(714)	43,619	36,355
*90277	Redondo Beach	(213)	57,102	57,451
*94064	Redwood City	(415)	54,965	55,686
93654	Reedley	(209)	11,071	8,131
92376	Rialto	(714)	37,862	28,370
*94802	Richmond	(415)	74,676	79,043
93555	Ridgecrest	(619)	15,929	7,629
95003	Rio Del Mar(u)	(408)	7,067	----
95673	Rio Linda(u)	(916)	7,359	7,524
95367	Riverbank	(209)	5,695	3,949
*92502	Riverside	(714)	170,591	140,089
95677	Rocklin	(916)	7,344	3,039
94572	Rodeo(u)	(415)	8,286	5,356
94928	Rohnert Park	(707)	22,965	6,133
90274	Rolling Hills Estates	(213)	9,412	6,735
95401	Roseland(u)	(707)	7,915	5,105
91770	Rosemead	(818)	42,604	40,972
95826	Rosemont(u)	(916)	18,888	----
95678	Roseville	(916)	24,347	18,221
90720	Rossmoor(u)	(213)	10,457	12,922
91745	Rowland Heights(u)	(818)	28,252	16,881
92509	Rubidoux(u)	(714)	16,763	13,969
*95813	Sacramento	(916)	275,741	257,105
93901	Salinas	(408)	80,479	58,896
94960	San Anselmo	(415)	12,067	13,031
*92403	San Bernardino	(714)	118,794	105,869
94066	San Bruno	(415)	35,417	36,254
	San Buenaventura (see Ventura)	(805)		
94070	San Carlos	(415)	24,710	26,053
92672	San Clemente	(714)	27,325	17,063
*92109	San Diego	(619)	875,538	697,471
91773	San Dimas	(714)	24,014	15,692
*91340	San Fernando	(818)	17,731	16,571
*94101	San Francisco	(415)	678,974	715,674
91776	San Gabriel	(818)	30,072	29,336
93657	Sanger	(209)	12,558	10,088
92383	San Jacinto	(714)	7,098	4,385
*95101	San Jose	(408)	629,400	459,913
92375	San Juan Capistrano	(714)	18,959	3,781
94577	San Leandro	(415)	63,952	68,698
94580	San Lorenzo(u)	(415)	20,545	24,633
93401	San Luis Obispo	(805)	34,252	28,036
92069	San Marcos	(619)	17,479	3,896
91108	San Marino	(818)	13,307	14,177
*94402	San Mateo	(415)	77,640	78,991
94806	San Pablo	(415)	19,750	21,461
*94901	San Rafael	(415)	44,700	38,977
94583	San Ramon	(415)	22,356	4,084
*92711	Santa Ana	(714)	204,023	155,710
*93102	Santa Barbara	(805)	74,542	70,215
*95050	Santa Clara	(408)	87,700	86,118
95060	Santa Cruz	(408)	41,483	32,076
90670	Santa Fe Springs	(213)	14,559	14,750
93454	Santa Maria	(805)	39,685	32,749
*90406	Santa Monica	(213)	88,314	88,289
93060	Santa Paula	(805)	20,658	18,001
*95402	Santa Rosa	(707)	82,658	50,006
92071	Santee	(619)	47,080	21,107
95070	Saratoga	(408)	29,261	26,810
91350	Seugus-Bouquet Canyon(u)	(805)	16,283	----
94965	Sausalito	(415)	7,090	6,158
95066	Scotts Valley	(408)	6,891	3,621
90740	Seal Beach	(213)	25,975	24,441
93955	Seaside	(408)	36,567	36,883
95472	Sebastopol	(707)	5,500	3,993
93662	Selma	(209)	10,942	7,459
93263	Shafter	(805)	7,010	5,327
91024	Sierra Madre	(818)	10,837	12,140
90806	Signal Hill	(213)	5,734	5,588
*93065	Simi Valley	(805)	77,500	59,832
92075	Solana Beach	(619)	13,047	5,023
93960	Soledad	(408)	5,928	4,222
95476	Sonoma	(707)	6,054	4,259
95073	Soquel(u)	(408)	6,212	5,795
91733	South El Monte	(213)	16,623	13,443
90280	South Gate	(213)	66,784	56,909
92677	South Laguna(u)	(714)	6,013	2,566
95705	South Lake Tahoe	(916)	20,681	12,921
95350	South Modesto(u)	(209)	12,492	7,889
95865	South Oroville(u)	(916)	7,246	4,111
91030	South Pasadena	(818)	22,681	22,979
94080	South San Francisco	(415)	49,393	46,646
91770	South San Gabriel(u)	(213)	5,421	5,051
91744	South San Jose Hills(u)	(213)	16,049	12,386
90605	South Whittier(u)	(213)	43,815	46,641
95991	South Yuba(u)	(916)	7,530	5,352
*92077	Spring Valley(u)	(619)	40,191	29,742
94305	Stanford(u)	(415)	11,045	8,691
90680	Stanton	(714)	21,144	18,185
*95204	Stockton	(209)	148,283	109,963
94585	Suisun City	(707)	11,087	2,917
92381	Sun City(u)	(714)	8,460	5,519
92388	Sunnymead(u)	(714)	11,554	6,708
*94086	Sunnyvale	(408)	106,618	95,976
96130	Susanville	(916)	6,520	6,608
93268	Taft	(805)	5,316	4,285
94806	Tara Hills-Montalvin Manor(u)	(415)	9,471	----
94941	Tamalpais-Homestead Valley(u)	(415)	8,511	----
91780	Temple City	(818)	28,972	31,034
*91360	Thousand Oaks	(805)	77,797	35,873
94920	Tiburon	(415)	6,685	6,209
*90510	Torrance	(213)	131,497	134,968
95396	Tracy	(209)	18,428	14,724
93274	Tulare	(209)	22,530	16,235
95380	Turlock	(209)	26,291	13,992
92680	Tustin	(714)	32,248	22,313
92705	Tustin-Foothills(u)	(714)	26,174	26,699
92277	Twentynine Palms(u)	(619)	7,465	5,667
92278	Twentynine Palms Base	(619)	7,079	5,647
95482	Ukiah	(707)	12,035	10,095
94587	Union City	(415)	39,406	14,724
91786	Upland	(714)	47,647	32,551
95688	Vacaville	(707)	43,367	21,690
91355	Valencia(u)	(805)	12,163	4,243
91744	Valinda(u)	(818)	18,700	18,837
94590	Vallejo	(707)	80,188	71,710
92343	Valle Vista(u)	(714)	5,474	----
93437	Vandenberg AFB(u)	(805)	8,136	13,193
93436	Vandenberg Village(u)	(805)	5,839	----
*93001	Ventura	(805)	73,774	57,964
92392	Victorville	(619)	14,220	10,845
90043	View Park-Windsor Hills(u)	(213)	12,101	12,268
92667	Villa Park	(714)	7,137	2,723
94553	Vine Hill-Pacheco(u)	(415)	6,129	----
93277	Visalia	(209)	49,729	27,130
92083	Vista	(619)	35,834	24,688
*91789	Walnut	(714)	9,978	5,992
*94596	Walnut Creek	(415)	54,033	39,844
94596	Walnut Creek West(u)	(415)	5,893	8,330
90255	Walnut Park(u)	(213)	11,811	8,925
93280	Wasco	(805)	9,613	8,269
95076	Watsonville	(408)	23,662	14,719
90044	West Athens(u)	(213)	8,531	13,311
90502	West Carson(u)	(213)	17,997	15,501
90247	West Compton(u)	(213)	5,907	5,748
*91793	West Covina	(818)	80,292	68,034
90069	West Hollywood	(213)	35,754	34,622
92683	Westminster	(714)	71,133	60,076
95351	West Modesto(u)	(209)	NA	6,135
90047	Westmont(u)	(213)	27,916	29,310
94565	West Pittsburg(u)	(415)	8,773	5,969
91746	West Puente Valley(u)	(818)	20,445	20,733
95691	West Sacramento	(916)	10,875	12,002
*90606	West Whittier-Los Nietos(u)	(213)	20,962	20,845
*90605	Whittier	(213)	68,558	72,863
90222	Willowbrook(u)	(213)	30,845	28,705
93286	Woodlake	(209)	5,375	3,371
95695	Woodland	(916)	30,235	20,677
94062	Woodside	(415)	5,291	4,734
92686	Yorba Linda	(714)	28,254	11,856
96097	Yreka City	(916)	5,916	5,394
95991	Yuba City	(916)	18,736	13,986
92399	Yucaipa(u)	(714)	23,345	19,284
92284	Yucca Valley(u)	(619)	8,294	3,893

Colorado

ZIP code	Place		1980	1970
80840	Air Force Academy	(719)	8,655	----
81101	Alamosa	(719)	6,830	6,985
80401	Applewood(u)	(303)	12,040	8,214
*80001	Arvada	(303)	84,576	49,844
80010	Aurora	(303)	158,588	74,974
*80302	Boulder	(303)	76,685	66,870
80601	Brighton	(303)	12,773	8,309
80020	Broomfield	(303)	20,730	7,261
81212	Canon City	(719)	13,037	9,206
----	Castlewood	(303)	16,413	----
80110	Cherry Hills Village	(303)	5,127	4,605
81220	Cimarron Hills	(303)	6,597	----
81520	Clifton	(303)	5,223	----
*80901	Colorado Springs	(719)	215,105	135,517
80120	Columbine	(303)	23,523	----
80022	Commerce City	(303)	16,234	17,407
81321	Cortez	(303)	7,095	6,032
81625	Craig	(303)	8,133	4,205
*80202	Denver	(303)	492,686	514,678
80022	Derby(u)	(303)	8,578	10,206
81301	Durango	(303)	11,649	10,333
80110	Englewood	(303)	30,021	33,695
80620	Evans	(303)	5,063	2,570
80439	Evergreen	(303)	6,376	2,321
80221	Federal Heights	(303)	7,846	1,502
80913	Fort Carson(u)	(303)	13,219	19,399
*80521	Fort Collins	(303)	64,632	43,337
80701	Fort Morgan	(303)	8,768	7,594
80017	Fountain	(719)	8,324	3,515
80401	Golden	(303)	12,237	9,817
81501	Grand Junction	(303)	27,956	20,170
80631	Greeley	(303)	53,006	38,902
80110	Greenwood Village	(303)	5,729	3,095
80501	Gunbarrel	(303)	5,172	----
81230	Gunnison	(303)	5,785	4,613

ZIP code	Place		1980	1970
.....	Ken Caryl	(303)	10,661	....
80026	Lafayette	(303)	8,985	3,498
81050	La Junta	(719)	8,338	8,205
80215	Lakewood	(303)	113,808	92,743
81052	Lamar	(719)	7,713	7,797
80120	Littleton	(303)	28,631	26,466
80120	Littleton Southeast(u)	(303)	33,029	22,899
80501	Longmont	(303)	42,942	23,209
80027	Louisville	(303)	5,593	2,409
80537	Loveland	(303)	30,215	16,220
81401	Montrose	(303)	8,722	6,496
80233	Northglenn	(303)	29,847	27,785
*81003	Pueblo	(719)	101,686	97,774
80911	Security-Widefield(u)	(719)	18,768	15,297
80110	Sheridan	(719)	5,377	4,787
80221	Sherrelwood(u)	(303)	17,629	18,868
80122	Southglenn	(303)	37,787	....
80477	Steamboat Springs	(303)	5,098	2,340
80751	Sterling	(303)	11,385	10,636
80906	Stratmoor	(719)	5,519	....
80229	Thornton	(303)	40,343	13,326
81082	Trinidad	(719)	9,663	9,901
80229	Welby(u)	(303)	9,668	6,875
80030	Westminster	(303)	50,211	19,512
80221	Westminster East(u)	(303)	6,002	7,576
80033	Wheat Ridge	(303)	30,293	29,778

Connecticut (203)

See Note on Page 563

ZIP code	Place	1980	1970
06401	Ansonia	19,039	21,160
06001	Avon	11,201	8,352
06037	Berlin	15,121	14,149
06801	Bethel	16,004	10,945
06002	Bloomfield	18,608	18,301
06405	Branford	23,363	20,444
*06602	Bridgeport	142,546	156,542
06010	Bristol	57,370	55,487
06804	Brookfield	12,872	9,688
06013	Burlington	5,660	4,070
06234	Brooklyn	5,691	4,965
06019	Canton	7,635	6,868
06410	Cheshire	21,788	19,051
06413	Clinton	11,195	10,267
06415	Colchester	7,761	6,603
06340	Conning Towers-Nautilus Park(u)	9,665	9,791
06238	Coventry	8,895	8,140
06416	Cromwell	10,265	7,400
06810	Danbury	60,470	50,781
06820	Darien	18,892	20,336
06418	Derby	12,346	12,599
06422	Durham	5,143	4,489
06423	East Haddam	5,621	4,676
06424	East Hampton	8,572	7,078
06108	East Hartford	52,563	57,583
06512	East Haven	25,028	25,120
06333	East Lyme	13,870	11,399
06425	Easton	5,962	4,885
06016	East Windsor	8,925	8,513
06029	Ellington	9,711	7,707
06082	Enfield	42,695	46,189
06426	Essex	5,078	4,911
06430	Fairfield	54,849	56,487
06032	Farmington	16,407	14,390
06033	Glastonbury	24,327	20,651
06035	Granby	7,956	6,150
06830	Greenwich	59,578	59,755
06351	Griswold	8,967	7,763
06340	Groton	41,062	38,244
06340	Groton Borough	10,086	8,933
06437	Guilford	17,375	12,033
06438	Haddam	6,383	4,934
06514	Hamden	51,071	49,357
*06101	Hartford	136,392	158,017
06082	Hazardville(u)	5,436	....
06248	Hebron	5,453	3,815
06037	Kensington(u)	7,502	....
06239	Killingly	14,519	13,573
06339	Ledyard	13,735	14,837
06759	Litchfield	7,605	7,399
06443	Madison	14,031	9,768
06040	Manchester	49,761	47,994
06250	Mansfield	20,634	19,994
06450	Meriden	57,118	55,959
06762	Middlebury	5,995	5,542
06457	Middletown	39,040	36,924
06460	Milford	50,898	50,858
06468	Monroe	14,010	12,047
06353	Montville	16,455	15,662
06770	Naugatuck	26,456	23,034
*06050	New Britain	73,840	83,441
06840	New Canaan	17,931	17,451
06810	New Fairfield	11,260	6,991
*06510	New Haven	126,089	137,707
06111	Newington	28,841	26,037
06320	New London	28,842	31,630
06776	New Milford	19,420	14,601
06470	Newtown	19,107	16,942
06471	North Branford	11,554	10,778
06473	North Haven	22,080	22,194
06856	Norwalk	77,767	79,288
06360	Norwich	38,074	41,739
06779	Oakville(u)	8,737	....
06371	Old Lyme	6,159	4,964
06475	Old Saybrook	9,287	8,468
06477	Orange	13,237	13,524
06483	Oxford	6,634	4,480
02891	Pawcatuck(u)	5,216	5,255
06374	Plainfield	12,774	11,957
06062	Plainville	16,401	16,733
06782	Plymouth	10,732	10,321
06480	Portland	8,383	8,812
06712	Prospect	6,807	6,543
06260	Putnam	6,855	6,918
.....	Putnam	8,580	8,598
06875	Redding	7,272	5,590
06877	Ridgefield Center(u)	6,066	5,878
.....	Ridgefield	20,120	18,188
06067	Rocky Hill	14,559	11,103
06483	Seymour	13,434	12,776
06484	Shelton	31,314	27,165
06082	Sherwood Manor(u)	6,303	....
06070	Simsbury	21,161	17,475
06071	Somers	8,473	6,893
06488	Southbury	14,156	7,852
06489	Southington	36,879	30,946
06074	South Windsor	17,198	15,553
06082	Southwood Acres(u)	9,779	....
06075	Stafford	9,268	8,680
*06904	Stamford	102,466	108,798
06378	Stonington	16,220	15,940
06268	Storrs(u)	11,394	10,691
06430	Stratfield-Brooklawn(u)	8,890	....
06497	Stratford	50,541	49,775
06078	Suffield	9,294	8,634
06786	Terryville(u)	5,234	....
06787	Thomaston	6,272	6,233
06277	Thompson	8,141	7,580
06084	Tolland	9,694	7,857
06790	Torrington	30,987	31,952
06611	Trumbull	32,989	31,394
06066	Vernon	27,974	27,237
06492	Wallingford	37,274	35,714
*06701	Waterbury	103,266	108,033
06385	Waterford	17,843	17,227
06795	Watertown	19,489	18,610
06498	Westbrook	5,216	3,820
06107	West Hartford	61,301	68,031
06516	West Haven	53,184	52,851
06880	Weston	8,284	7,417
06880	Westport	25,290	27,318
06109	Wethersfield	26,013	26,662
06226	Willimantic	14,652	14,402
06897	Wilton	15,351	13,572
06094	Winchester	10,841	11,106
06280	Windham	21,062	19,626
06095	Windsor	25,204	22,502
06096	Windsor Locks	12,190	15,080
06098	Winsted	8,092	8,954
06716	Wolcott	13,008	12,495
06525	Woodbridge	7,761	7,673
06798	Woodbury	6,942	5,869
06281	Woodstock	5,117	4,311

Delaware (302)

ZIP code	Place	1980	1970
19713	Brookside(u)	15,255	7,856
19703	Claymont(u)	10,022	6,584
19901	Dover	23,507	17,488
19802	Edgemoor(u)	7,397	....
19805	Elsmere	6,493	8,415
19963	Milford	5,366	5,314
*19711	Newark	25,247	21,298
19973	Seaford	5,256	5,537
19804	Stanton(u)	5,495	....
19803	Talleyville(u)	6,880	....
*19899	Wilmington	70,195	80,386
19720	Wilmington Manor —Chelsea—Leedom	9,233	10,134

District of Columbia (202)

ZIP code	Place	1980	1970
*20013	Washington	638,432	756,668

Florida

ZIP code	Place		1980	1970
*32701	Altamonte Springs	(407)	21,105	4,391
32703	Apopka	(407)	6,019	4,045
33821	Arcadia	(813)	6,002	5,658
32233	Atlantic Beach	(904)	7,847	6,132
33823	Auburndale	(813)	6,501	5,386
.....	Aventura(u)	(305)	10,162	....
33825	Avon Park	(813)	8,026	6,712
32807	Azalea Park(u)	(407)	8,304	7,367
33830	Bartow	(813)	14,780	12,891
.....	Bay Crest(u)	(813)	5,927	....

ZIP code	Place		1980	1970
.....	Bayonet Point(u)	(813)	16,455	....
33504	Bay Pines(u)	(813)	5,757	....
33505	Bayshore Gardens(u).	(813)	14,945	9,255
33589	Beacon Square(u)	(813)	6,513	2,927
32073	Bellair-Meadowbrook			
	Terrace(u).	(904)	12,144	....
33430	Belle Glade	(407)	16,535	15,949
32506	Belleview(u)	(904)	15,439	916
32661	Beverly Hills(u)	(904)	5,024	....
*33467	Boca Raton	(407)	49,447	28,506
33959	Bonita Springs(u)	(813)	5,435	1,932
*33435	Boynton Beach	(407)	35,624	18,115
*34206	Bradenton	(813)	30,228	21,040
33511	Brandon(u).	(813)	41,826	12,749
32525	Brent(u)	(904)	21,872	....
33314	Broadview Park(u)	(305)	6,022	6,049
33313	Broadview-Pompano Park(u)	(305)	5,256	....
*34601	Brooksville	(904)	5,582	4,060
33311	Browardale(u)	(305)	7,571	17,444
33142	Browns Village(u)	(305)	NA	23,442
33142	Brownsville(u)	(305)	18,058	....
33054	Bunche Park(u)	(305)	NA	5,773
32401	Callaway.	(904)	7,154	3,240
32920	Cape Canaveral	(407)	5,733	4,258
33904	Cape Coral	(813)	32,103	11,470
33055	Carol City(u)	(305)	47,349	27,361
32707	Casselberry	(407)	15,037	9,438
33401	Century Village(u).	(305)	10,619	2,679
32324	Chattahoochee	(904)	5,332	7,944
*34615	Clearwater City	(813)	85,170	52,074
32711	Clermont	(904)	5,461	3,661
33440	Clewiston	(813)	5,219	3,896
32922	Cocoa	(407)	16,096	16,110
32931	Cocoa Beach	(407)	10,926	9,952
32922	Cocoa West(u)	(407)	6,432	5,779
33066	Coconut Creek	(305)	6,288	1,359
33060	Collier City(u)	(305)	7135	....
33064	Collier Manor-Cresthaven(u)	(305)	7,045	7,202
33901	Combee Settlement(u) . . .	(813)	5,400	4,963
32809	Conway(u)	(407)	23,940	8,642
33314	Cooper City	(305)	10,140	2,535
33134	Coral Gables	(305)	43,241	42,494
33065	Coral Springs	(305)	37,349	1,489
.....	Coral Terrace(u)	(305)	22,702	....
32536	Crestview	(904)	7,617	7,952
33803	Crystal Lake(u)	(813)	6,827	6,227
33157	Cutler(u)	(305)	15,593	....
33157	Cutler Ridge(u)	(305)	20,886	17,441
33880	Cypress Gardens(u)	(813)	8,043	3,757
.....	Cypress Lake(u)	(813)	8,721	....
33004	Dania.	(305)	11,796	9,013
33314	Davie	(305)	20,515	5,859
*32015	Daytona Beach	(904)	54,176	45,327
33441	Deerfield Beach	(305)	39,193	16,662
32433	DeFuniak Springs	(904)	5,563	4,966
32720	De Land	(904)	15,354	11,641
*33444	Delray Beach	(407)	34,329	19,915
33617	Del Rio(u)	(813)	7,409	....
32725	Deltona(u)	(407)	15,710	4,868
*34698	Dunedin	(813)	30,203	17,639
33610	East Lake-Orient Park (u) . .	(813)	5,612	5,697
33940	East Naples(u)	(813)	12,127	6,152
32032	Edgewater	(904)	6,726	3,348
32542	Eglin AFB(u)	(904)	7,574	7,769
33614	Egypt Lake(u)	(813)	11,932	7,556
34680	Elfers(u)	(813)	11,396	....
*34223	Englewood(u)	(813)	10,242	5,108
32504	Ensley(u)	(904)	14,422	....
32726	Eustis	(904)	9,453	6,722
32804	Fairview Shores(u)	(305)	10,174	....
32034	Fernandina Beach	(904)	7,224	6,955
32730	Fern Park(u)	(407)	8,890	....
32504	Ferry Pass(u)	(904)	16,910	....
33030	Florida City	(305)	6,174	5,133
32751	Forest City(u)	(407)	6,819	....
*33319	Fort Lauderdale	(305)	153,256	139,590
33841	Fort Meade	(813)	5,546	4,374
*33901	Fort Myers	(813)	36,638	27,351
33931	Fort Myers Beach(u)	(813)	5,753	4,305
*34950	Fort Pierce	(407)	33,802	29,721
33452	Fort Pierce NW(u)	(407)	5,929	3,269
32548	Fort Walton Beach	(904)	20,829	19,994
*32601	Gainesville	(904)	81,371	64,510
33801	Gibsonia(u)	(813)	5,011	....
32960	Gifford(u)	(305)	6,240	5,772
.....	Gladeview(u)	(305)	18,919	....
33143	Glenvar Heights(u)	(305)	13,216	....
33055	Golden Glades(u)	(305)	23,154	....
32733	Goldenrod(u)	(407)	13,681	....
32560	Gonzalez(u)	(904)	6,084	....
32503	Goulding(u)	(904)	5,352	....
33170	Goulds(u)	(305)	7,078	6,690
33463	Greenacres City.	(407)	8,780	1,731
32561	Gulf Breeze	(904)	5,478	4,190
33581	Gulf Gate Estates(u)	(813)	9,248	5,874
33707	Gulfport	(813)	11,180	9,976
33844	Haines City	(813)	10,799	8,956
33009	Hallandale	(305)	36,517	23,849
*33010	Hialeah.	(305)	145,254	102,452
33455	Hobe Sound(u)	(407)	6,822	2,029
32805	Holden Heights(u).	(407)	13,840	6,206
34690	Holiday(u)	(813)	18,392	....
32017	Holly Hill	(904)	9,953	8,191
*33022	Hollywood	(305)	117,188	106,873
33030	Homestead	(305)	20,668	13,674
33030	Homestead Base(u)	(305)	7,594	8,257
34667	Hudson(u)	(813)	5,799	2,278
33934	Immokalee(u)	(813)	11,038	3,764
32937	Indian Harbour Beach . . .	(407)	5,967	5,371
33880	Inwood(u)	(813)	6,668	....
33162	Ives Estates(u)	(305)	12,623	....
*32201	Jacksonville	(904)	540,920	504,265
32250	Jacksonville Beach	(904)	15,462	12,779
33568	Jasmine Estates(u)	(813)	11,995	2,967
*34957	Jensen Beach(u)	(407)	6,639	....
33458	Jupiter	(407)	9,868	3,136
.....	Kendale Lakes(u)	(305)	32,769	....
33156	Kendall(u)	(305)	73,758	35,497
.....	Kendall Green(u)	(305)	6,768	....
33149	Key Biscayne(u).	(305)	6,313	....
33037	Key Largo(u)	(305)	7,447	2,866
33040	Key West	(305)	24,292	29,312
32303	Killearn(u)	(904)	8,700	....
.....	Kings Point(u)	(305)	8,724	....
32741	Kissimmee	(407)	15,487	7,119
33618	Lake Carroll(u)	(305)	13,012	5,577
32055	Lake City.	(904)	9,257	10,575
*33802	Lakeland	(813)	47,406	42,803
33801	Lakeland Highlands(u) . . .	(813)	10,426	....
.....	Lake Lorraine(u)	(904)	5,427	....
33054	Lake Lucerne(u)	(305)	9,762	....
33612	Lake Magdalene(u)	(813)	13,331	9,266
33403	Lake Park	(407)	6,909	6,993
.....	Lakeside(u)	(904)	10,534	....
33853	Lake Wales	(813)	8,466	8,240
33460	Lake Worth	(407)	27,048	23,714
33460	Lantana	(407)	8,048	7,126
*34640	Largo	(813)	57,958	24,230
33313	Lauderdale Lakes.	(305)	25,426	10,577
33313	Lauderhill	(305)	37,271	8,465
34272	Laurel(u)	(813)	6,368	....
33717	Lealman(u)	(813)	19,873	....
32748	Leesburg	(904)	13,191	11,869
33936	Lehigh Acres(u)	(813)	9,604	4,394
33033	Leisure City(u)	(305)	17,905	....
33614	Leto(u)	(813)	9,003	8,458
33064	Lighthouse Point	(305)	11,488	9,071
.....	Lindgren Acres(u)	(305)	11,986	....
32060	Live Oak	(904)	6,732	6,830
32810	Lockhart(u)	(407)	10,571	5,809
34228	Longboat Key	(813)	8,221	2,850
*32750	Longwood	(407)	10,029	3,203
33549	Lutz(u)	(813)	5,555	....
32444	Lynn Haven	(904)	6,239	4,044
32751	Maitland	(407)	8,763	7,157
33550	Mango-Seffner(u)	(813)	6,493	....
33050	Marathon(u)	(305)	7,568	4,397
33063	Margate	(305)	35,900	8,867
32446	Marianna	(904)	7,074	7,282
*32901	Melbourne	(407)	46,536	40,236
33314	Melrose Park(u)	(904)	5,725	6,111
33561	Memphis(u)	(813)	5,501	3,207
32952	Merritt Island(u)	(407)	30,708	29,233
*33152	Miami.	(305)	346,681	334,859
33139	Miami Beach	(305)	96,298	87,072
33023	Miami Gardens			
	—Utopia-Carver(u)	(305)	9,025	....
33014	Miami Lakes(u)	(305)	9,809	....
33153	Miami Shores	(305)	9,244	9,425
33166	Miami Springs	(305)	12,350	13,279
32570	Milton	(904)	7,206	5,360
32754	Mims(u)	(407)	7,583	8,309
33023	Miramar	(305)	32,813	23,997
32757	Mount Dora	(904)	5,883	4,646
32506	Myrtle Grove(u)	(904)	14,238	16,186
*33962	Naples	(813)	17,581	12,042
33940	Naples Park(u)	(813)	5,438	1,522
33032	Naranja-Princeton(u)	(305)	10,381	....
32233	Neptune Beach	(904)	5,248	4,281
*34652	New Port Richey	(813)	11,196	6,098
33552	New Port Richey East(u) . .	(813)	6,627	2,758
32069	New Smyrna Beach	(904)	13,557	10,580
32578	Niceville	(904)	8,543	4,155
33169	Norland(u)	(305)	19,471	....
33308	North Andrews Gardens(u) .	(305)	8,967	7,082
33903	North Fort Myers(u).	(813)	22,808	8,798
33068	North Lauderdale	(305)	18,653	1,213
33161	North Miami	(305)	42,566	34,767
33160	North Miami Beach	(305)	36,481	30,544
33940	North Naples(u)	(813)	7,950	3,201
33408	North Palm Beach	(407)	11,344	9,035
33596	North Port	(813)	6,205	2,244
33169	Norwood(u)	(305)	NA	14,973
33308	Oakland Park	(305)	22,944	16,261
33860	Oak Ridge(u)	(813)	15,477	....
32670	Ocala.	(904)	37,170	22,583
32548	Ocean City(u)	(904)	5,582	5,267
32761	Ocoee	(407)	7,803	3,937
33163	Ojus(u)	(305)	17,344	....
33165	Olympia Heights(u)	(305)	33,112	....

ZIP code	Place		1980	1970
33558	Oneco(u)	(813)	6,417	3,246
33054	Opa-Locka	(305)	14,460	11,902
33054	Opa-Locka North(u)	(305)	5,721	.....
32073	Orange Park	(904)	8,766	5,019
*32820	Orlando	(407)	128,394	99,006
32811	Orlovista(u)	(407)	6,474	.....
32074	Ormond Beach	(904)	21,438	14,063
32074	Ormond By-The-Sea(u)	(904)	7,665	6,002
32570	Pace(u)	(904)	5,006	1,776
33476	Pahokee	(407)	6,346	5,663
32077	Palatka	(904)	10,175	9,444
33505	Palma Sola(u)	(813)	5,297	1,745
32905	Palm Bay	(407)	18,560	7,176
33480	Palm Beach	(407)	9,729	9,086
33403	Palm Beach Gardens	(407)	14,407	6,102
34221	Palmetto	(813)	8,637	7,422
33157	Palmetto Estates(u)	(305)	11,116	.....
*34683	Palm Harbor(u)	(813)	5,215	.....
33619	Palm River-Clair Mel(u)	(813)	14,447	8,536
33460	Palm Springs	(407)	8,166	4,340
33012	Palm Springs North(u)	(407)	5,838	.....
32401	Panama City	(904)	33,346	32,096
33866	Pembroke Park	(305)	5,326	2,949
33023	Pembroke Pines	(305)	35,776	15,496
*32502	Pensacola	(904)	57,619	59,507
33157	Perrine(u)	(305)	16,129	10,257
32347	Perry	(904)	8,254	7,701
32809	Pine Castle(u)	(407)	9,992	.....
32808	Pine Hills(u)	(407)	35,771	13,882
*34665	Pinellas Park	(813)	32,811	22,287
33168	Pinewood(u)	(305)	16,216	.....
33566	Plant City	(813)	17,064	15,451
33314	Plantation	(305)	48,653	23,523
*33067	Pompano Beach	(305)	52,618	38,587
33064	Pompano Beach Highlands(u)	(305)	16,154	5,014
33950	Port Charlotte(u)	(813)	25,730	10,769
32019	Port Orange	(904)	18,756	3,781
34952	Port St. Lucie	(407)	14,690	330
*33950	Punta Gorda	(813)	6,797	3,879
32351	Quincy	(904)	8,591	8,334
33156	Richmond Heights(u)	(305)	8,577	6,663
33312	Riverland (u)	(305)	5,919	5,512
33404	Riviera Beach	(407)	26,596	21,401
33314	Rock Island(u)	(813)	5,022	.....
32955	Rockledge	(407)	11,877	10,523
33570	Ruskin(u)	(813)	5,117	2,414
34695	Safety Harbor	(813)	6,461	3,103
32084	St. Augustine	(904)	11,985	12,352
34769	St. Cloud	(407)	7,840	5,041
*33702	St. Petersburg	(813)	238,647	216,159
33706	St. Petersburg Beach	(813)	9,354	8,024
33508	Samoset(u)	(813)	5,747	4,070
33432	Sandalfoot Cove(u)	(305)	5,299	.....
32771	Sanford	(407)	23,176	17,393
*34236	Sarasota	(813)	48,868	40,237
33577	Sarasota Springs(u)	(813)	13,860	4,405
32937	Satellite Beach	(407)	9,163	6,558
	Scott Lake(u)	(305)	14,154	.....
*33870	Sebring	(813)	8,736	7,223
33578	Siesta Key(u)	(813)	7,010	4,460
32809	Sky Lake(u)	(407)	6,692	.....
32703	South Apopka(u)	(407)	5,687	2,293
33505	South Bradenton(u)	(813)	14,297	.....
32021	South Daytona	(904)	9,608	4,979
33579	Southgate(u)	(813)	7,322	6,885
33143	South Miami	(305)	10,895	11,780
33157	South Miami Heights(u)	(305)	23,559	10,395
32937	South Patrick Shores(u)	(407)	9,816	10,313
33595	South Venice(u)	(813)	8,075	4,680
32401	Springfield	(904)	7,220	5,949
34606	Spring Hill(u)	(904)	6,468	.....
32091	Starke	(904)	5,306	4,848
*34994	Stuart	(407)	9,467	4,820
33573	Sun City Center(u)	(813)	5,605	2,143
33160	Sunny Isles(u)	(305)	12,564	.....
33304	Sunrise	(305)	39,681	7,403
33139	Sunset(u)	(305)	13,531	.....
33144	Sweetwater	(305)	8,067	3,357
33614	Sweetwater Creek(u)	(813)	NA	19,453
*32303	Tallahassee	(904)	81,548	72,624
33313	Tamarac	(305)	29,142	5,193
33144	Tamiami(u)	(305)	17,607	.....
*33625	Tampa	(813)	271,577	277,714
	Tanglewood(u)	(813)	8,229	.....
*34689	Tarpon Springs	(813)	13,251	7,118
33617	Temple Terrace	(813)	11,097	7,347
33905	Tice(u)	(813)	6,645	7,254
32780	Titusville	(407)	31,910	30,515
32505	Town 'n' Country(u)	(904)	37,834	.....
33707	Treasure Island	(813)	6,316	6,120
32807	Union Park(u)	(407)	19,175	2,595
33620	University (Hillsborough)(u)	(813)	24,514	10,039
32580	Valparaiso	(904)	6,142	6,504
*34285	Venice	(813)	12,153	6,648
33595	Venice Gardens(u)	(813)	6,568	.....
32960	Vero Beach	(407)	16,176	11,908
32960	Vero Beach South(u)	(407)	12,636	7,330
33901	Villas(u)	(813)	8,724	.....
32507	Warrington(u)	(904)	15,792	15,848
33314	Washington Park(u)	(305)	7,240	.....
32703	Wekiva Springs(u)	(407)	13,386	.....
33505	West Bradenton(u)	(813)	NA	6,162
33155	Westchester(u)	(305)	29,272	.....
32446	West End(u)	(904)	NA	5,289
33138	West Little River(u)	(305)	32,492	.....
32901	West Melbourne	(407)	5,078	3,050
33144	West Miami	(305)	6,076	5,494
*33404	West Palm Beach	(407)	62,530	57,375
32505	West Pensacola(u)	(904)	24,371	20,924
33168	Westview(u)	(305)	9,102	.....
33880	West Winter Haven(u)	(813)	NA	7,716
33165	Westwood Lakes(u)	(305)	11,478	12,811
33305	Wilton Manors	(305)	12,742	10,948
33803	Winston(u)	(813)	9,315	4,505
*32787	Winter Garden	(407)	6,789	5,153
33880	Winter Haven	(813)	21,119	16,136
*32789	Winter Park	(407)	22,314	21,895
32708	Winter Springs	(407)	10,475	1,161
32548	Wright(u)	(904)	13,011	.....
33599	Zephyrhills	(813)	5,742	3,369

Georgia

ZIP code	Place		1980	1970
31620	Adel	(912)	5,592	4,972
*31701	Albany	(912)	74,425	72,623
31709	Americus	(912)	16,120	16,091
*30601	Athens	(404)	42,549	44,342
*30304	Atlanta	(404)	425,022	495,039
*30901	Augusta	(404)	47,532	59,864
31717	Bainbridge	(912)	10,553	10,887
30032	Belvedere Park(u)	(404)	17,766	.....
31723	Blakely	(912)	5,880	5,267
31520	Brunswick	(912)	17,605	19,585
30518	Buford	(404)	6,578	4,640
31728	Cairo	(912)	8,777	8,061
30701	Calhoun	(404)	5,335	4,748
31730	Camilla	(912)	5,414	4,987
30032	Candler-McAfee(u)	(404)	27,306	.....
30117	Carrollton	(404)	14,078	13,520
30120	Cartersville	(404)	9,247	10,138
30125	Cedartown	(404)	8,619	9,253
30341	Chamblee	(404)	7,137	9,127
31014	Cochran	(912)	5,121	5,161
30337	College Park	(404)	24,632	18,203
*31902	Columbus	(404)	169,441	155,028
30027	Conley(u)	(404)	6,033	.....
30207	Conyers	(404)	6,567	4,809
31015	Cordele	(912)	11,184	10,733
30209	Covington	(404)	10,586	10,267
30720	Dalton	(404)	20,581	18,872
31742	Dawson	(912)	5,699	5,383
*30030	Decatur	(404)	18,404	21,943
31520	Dock Junction(u)	(912)	6,189	6,009
30340	Doraville	(404)	7,414	9,157
31533	Douglas	(912)	10,980	10,195
30134	Douglasville	(404)	7,641	5,472
30033	Druid Hills(u)	(404)	12,700	.....
31021	Dublin	(912)	16,083	15,143
30338	Dunwoody(u)	(404)	17,768	.....
31023	Eastman	(912)	5,303	5,416
30344	East Point	(404)	37,486	39,315
30635	Elberton	(404)	5,686	6,438
30060	Fair Oaks(u)	(404)	8,486	.....
30535	Fairview(u)	(404)	6,558	.....
31750	Fitzgerald	(912)	10,187	8,187
30050	Forest Park	(404)	18,782	19,994
31905	Fort Benning South(u)	(404)	15,074	27,495
30905	Fort Gordon(u)	(404)	14,069	15,589
30741	Fort Oglethorpe	(404)	5,443	3,869
31313	Fort Stewart(u)	(912)	15,031	4,467
31030	Fort Valley	(912)	9,000	9,251
30501	Gainesville	(404)	15,280	15,459
31408	Garden City	(912)	6,895	5,790
30316	Gresham Park(u)	(404)	6,232	.....
30223	Griffin	(404)	20,728	22,734
30354	Hapeville	(404)	6,166	9,567
31313	Hinesville	(912)	11,309	4,115
31545	Jesup	(912)	9,418	9,091
30144	Kennesaw	(404)	5,095	3,548
30728	La Fayette	(404)	6,517	6,044
30240	La Grange	(404)	24,204	23,301
30245	Lawrenceville	(404)	8,928	5,207
30057	Lithia Springs(u)	(404)	9,145	.....
30059	Mableton(u)	(404)	25,111	.....
*31201	Macon	(912)	116,860	122,423
30060	Marietta	(404)	30,821	27,216
30907	Martinez(u)	(404)	16,472	.....
31061	Midway-Hardwick(u)	(912)	8,977	14,047
31061	Milledgeville	(912)	12,176	11,601
30655	Monroe	(404)	8,854	8,071
31768	Moultrie	(912)	15,105	14,400
30075	Mountain Park(u)	(404)	9,425	268
30263	Newnan	(404)	11,449	11,205
30319	North Atlanta(u)	(404)	30,521	.....
30033	North Decatur(u)	(404)	11,830	.....
30033	North Druid Hills(u)	(404)	12,438	.....
30032	Panthersville(u)	(404)	11,366	.....
30269	Peachtree City	(404)	6,429	793
31069	Perry	(912)	9,453	7,771
31643	Quitman	(912)	5,188	4,818

ZIP code	Place		1980	1970
*30274	Riverdale	(404)	7,121	2,521
30161	Rome	(404)	28,915	30,759
30075	Roswell	(404)	23,337	5,430
31522	St. Simons(u)	(912)	6,566	5,346
31082	Sandersville	(912)	6,137	5,546
33028	Sandy Springs(u)	(404)	46,877	....
*31401	Savannah	(912)	141,654	118,349
30079	Scottdale(u)	(404)	8,770	....
30080	Smyrna	(404)	20,312	19,157
30278	Snellville	(404)	8,514	1,990
30901	South Augusta(u)	(404)	51,072	....
30458	Statesboro	(912)	14,866	14,616
30401	Swainsboro	(912)	7,602	7,325
31791	Sylvester	(404)	5,860	4,226
30286	Thomaston	(404)	9,682	10,024
31792	Thomasville	(912)	18,463	18,155
30824	Thomson	(404)	7,001	6,503
31794	Tifton	(912)	13,749	12,179
30577	Toccoa	(404)	8,869	6,971
30084	Tucker(u)	(404)	25,399	....
31601	Valdosta	(912)	37,596	32,303
30474	Vidalia	(912)	10,393	9,507
31093	Warner Robins	(912)	39,893	33,491
31501	Waycross	(912)	19,371	18,996
30830	Waynesboro	(404)	5,760	5,530
30901	West Augusta(u)	(404)	24,242	....
31410	Wilmington Island(u)	(912)	7,546	3,284
30680	Winder	(404)	6,705	6,605

Hawaii (808)

See Note on Page 563

ZIP code	Place	1980	1970
96706	Ewa	190,037	132,299
96720	Hilo	37,017	26,412
*96815	Honolulu	365,048	324,871
96732	Kahului	13,026	8,287
96749	Keaau-Mountain View	7,055	3,802
96752	Kekaha-Waimea	5,256	4,159
96753	Kihei	6,035	1,636
.....	Koolauloa	14,195	10,562
.....	Koolaupoko	109,373	92,219
96790	Kula	5,077	2,124
96761	Lahaina	10,284	5,524
96768	Makawao-Paia	10,361	5,788
.....	North Kona	13,748	4,832
96781	Papaikou-Wailea	5,261	5,503
.....	South Kona	5,914	4,400
96786	Wahiawa	41,562	37,329
96791	Waialua	9,849	9,171
96792	Waianae	32,810	24,077
96703	Wailua-Anahola	6,030	3,599
96793	Wailuku	10,674	9,084

Idaho (208)

ZIP code	Place	1980	1970
83221	Blackfoot	10,065	8,716
*83708	Boise City	102,249	74,990
83318	Burley	8,761	8,279
83605	Caldwell	17,699	14,219
83201	Chubbuck	7,052	2,924
83814	Coeur D'Alene	19,913	16,228
83401	Idaho Falls	39,739	35,776
83338	Jerome	6,891	4,183
83501	Lewiston	27,986	26,068
83642	Meridian	6,658	2,616
83843	Moscow	16,513	14,146
83647	Mountain Home	7,540	6,451
83648	Mountain Home AFB(u)	6,403	6,038
83651	Nampa	25,112	20,768
83661	Payette	5,448	4,521
83201	Pocatello	46,340	40,036
83854	Post Falls	5,736	2,371
83440	Rexburg	11,559	8,272
83350	Rupert	5,476	4,563
83301	Twin Falls	26,209	21,914

Illinois

ZIP code	Place		1980	1970
60101	Addison	(708)	29,826	24,482
60102	Algonquin	(708)	5,834	3,515
60658	Alsip	(708)	17,134	11,608
62002	Alton	(618)	34,171	39,700
62906	Anna	(618)	5,408	4,766
*60004	Arlington Heights	(708)	66,116	65,058
*60507	Aurora	(708)	81,293	74,389
60010	Barrington	(708)	9,029	8,581
60103	Bartlett	(708)	13,254	3,501
61607	Bartonville	(309)	6,110	7,221
60510	Batavia	(708)	12,574	9,060
62618	Beardstown	(217)	6,338	6,222
*62220	Belleville	(618)	42,150	41,223
60104	Bellwood	(708)	19,811	22,096
61008	Belvidere	(815)	15,176	14,061
60106	Bensenville	(708)	16,106	12,956
62812	Benton	(618)	7,778	6,833
60162	Berkeley	(708)	5,467	6,152
60402	Berwyn	(708)	46,849	52,502
62010	Bethalto	(618)	8,630	7,074
60108	Bloomingdale	(708)	12,656	2,974
61701	Bloomington	(309)	44,189	39,992
60406	Blue Island	(708)	21,855	22,629
60439	Bolingbrook	(708)	37,261	7,651
60538	Boulder Hill(u)	(708)	9,333	....
60914	Bourbonnais	(815)	13,280	5,909
60915	Bradley	(815)	11,015	9,881
60455	Bridgeview	(708)	14,155	12,506
60153	Broadview	(708)	8,618	9,623
60513	Brookfield	(708)	19,395	20,284
60090	Buffalo Grove	(708)	22,230	12,333
60459	Burbank	(708)	28,462	26,726
62206	Cahokia	(618)	18,904	20,649
62914	Cairo	(618)	5,931	6,277
60409	Calumet City	(708)	39,673	33,107
60643	Calumet Park	(708)	8,788	10,069
61520	Canton	(309)	14,626	14,217
62901	Carbondale	(618)	26,414	22,816
62626	Carlinville	(217)	5,439	5,675
62821	Carmi	(618)	6,107	6,033
60187	Carol Stream	(708)	15,472	4,434
60110	Carpentersville	(708)	23,272	24,059
60013	Cary	(708)	6,640	4,358
62801	Centralia	(618)	15,126	15,966
62206	Centreville	(618)	9,747	11,378
61820	Champaign	(217)	58,267	56,837
61920	Charleston	(217)	19,355	16,421
62629	Chatham	(217)	5,597	2,788
62233	Chester	(618)	8,027	5,310
*60607	Chicago	(312)	3,005,072	3,369,357
60411	Chicago Heights	(708)	37,026	40,900
60415	Chicago Ridge	(708)	13,473	9,187
61523	Chillicothe	(309)	6,176	6,052
60650	Cicero	(708)	61,232	67,058
60514	Clarendon Hills	(708)	6,857	6,750
61727	Clinton	(217)	8,014	7,581
62234	Collinsville	(618)	19,475	18,224
60477	Country Club Hills	(708)	14,676	6,920
60525	Countryside	(708)	6,242	2,864
60435	Crest Hill	(815)	9,252	7,460
60445	Crestwood	(708)	10,712	5,770
60417	Crete	(708)	5,417	4,656
61611	Creve Coeur	(309)	6,851	6,440
60014	Crystal Lake	(815)	18,590	14,541
61832	Danville	(217)	38,985	42,570
60559	Darien	(708)	14,968	7,789
*62521	Decatur	(217)	93,939	90,397
60015	Deerfield	(708)	17,432	18,876
60115	De Kalb	(815)	33,157	32,949
*60016	Des Plaines	(708)	53,568	57,239
61021	Dixon	(815)	15,710	18,147
60419	Dolton	(708)	24,766	25,990
60515	Downers Grove	(708)	42,691	32,544
62832	Du Quoin	(618)	6,594	6,691
62024	East Alton	(618)	7,096	7,309
60411	East Chicago Heights	(708)	5,347	5,000
61244	East Moline	(309)	20,907	20,956
61611	East Peoria	(309)	22,385	18,671
*62201	East St. Louis	(618)	55,200	70,169
62025	Edwardsville	(618)	12,460	11,070
62401	Effingham	(217)	11,270	9,458
62930	Eldorado	(618)	5,198	3,876
60120	Elgin	(708)	63,668	55,691
60007	Elk Grove Village	(708)	28,679	20,346
60126	Elmhurst	(708)	44,251	46,392
60635	Elmwood Park	(708)	24,016	26,160
*60204	Evanston	(708)	73,706	80,113
60642	Evergreen Park	(708)	22,260	25,921
62837	Fairfield	(618)	5,944	5,897
62208	Fairview Heights	(618)	11,244	10,050
62839	Flora	(618)	5,379	5,283
60422	Flossmoor	(708)	8,423	7,846
60130	Forest Park	(708)	15,177	15,472
60020	Fox Lake	(708)	6,831	4,511
60131	Franklin Park	(708)	17,507	20,348
61032	Freeport	(815)	26,406	27,736
60030	Gages Lake-Wildwood(u)	(708)	5,848	5,337
61401	Galesburg	(309)	35,305	36,290
61254	Geneseo	(309)	6,373	5,840
60134	Geneva	(708)	9,881	9,049
62034	Glen Carbon	(618)	5,197	1,897
60022	Glencoe	(708)	9,200	10,542
60137	Glendale Heights	(618)	23,251	11,406
60137	Glen Ellyn	(708)	23,691	21,909
60025	Glenview	(708)	30,842	24,880
60425	Glenwood	(708)	10,538	7,416
62040	Granite City	(618)	36,815	40,685
60030	Grayslake	(708)	5,260	4,907
62246	Greenville	(618)	5,271	4,631
60031	Gurnee	(708)	7,179	2,738
60103	Hanover Park	(708)	28,719	11,735
62946	Harrisburg	(618)	9,322	9,535
60033	Harvard	(815)	5,126	5,177
60426	Harvey	(708)	35,810	34,636
60656	Harwood Heights	(708)	8,228	9,060
60429	Hazel Crest	(708)	13,973	10,329
62948	Herrin	(618)	10,708	9,623
60457	Hickory Hills	(708)	13,778	13,176
62249	Highland	(618)	7,122	5,981

ZIP code	Place		1980	1970
60035	Highland Park	(708)	30,599	32,263
60040	Highwood	(708)	5,455	4,973
60162	Hillside	(708)	8,279	8,888
60521	Hinsdale	(708)	16,726	15,918
60172	Hoffman Estates	(708)	38,258	22,238
60456	Hometown	(708)	5,324	6,729
60430	Homewood	(708)	19,724	18,871
60942	Hoopeston	(217)	6,411	6,461
60143	Itasca	(708)	7,948	4,638
62650	Jacksonville	(217)	20,284	20,553
62052	Jerseyville	(618)	7,506	7,446
*60431	Joliet	(815)	77,956	78,827
60458	Justice	(708)	10,552	9,473
60901	Kankakee	(815)	29,633	30,944
61443	Kewanee	(309)	14,508	15,762
60525	La Grange	(708)	15,693	17,814
60525	La Grange Park	(708)	13,359	15,459
60045	Lake Forest	(708)	15,245	15,642
60102	Lake in the Hills	(708)	5,651	3,240
60047	Lake Zurich	(708)	8,225	4,082
60438	Lansing	(708)	29,039	25,805
61301	La Salle	(815)	10,347	10,736
62439	Lawrenceville	(618)	5,652	5,863
60439	Lemont	(708)	5,640	5,080
60048	Libertyville	(708)	16,520	11,684
62656	Lincoln	(217)	16,327	17,582
60645	Lincolnwood	(708)	11,921	12,929
60046	Lindenhurst	(708)	6,220	3,141
60532	Lisle	(708)	13,638	5,329
62056	Litchfield	(217)	7,204	7,190
60441	Lockport	(815)	9,192	9,861
60148	Lombard	(708)	36,879	34,043
61111	Loves Park	(815)	13,192	12,390
60534	Lyons	(708)	9,925	11,124
61455	Macomb	(309)	19,632	19,643
62060	Madison	(618)	5,301	7,042
62959	Marion	(618)	14,031	11,724
60426	Markham	(708)	15,172	15,987
60443	Matteson	(708)	10,223	4,741
61938	Mattoon	(217)	19,293	19,681
60153	Maywood	(708)	27,998	29,019
60050	McHenry	(815)	10,737	6,772
*60160	Melrose Park	(708)	20,735	22,716
61342	Mendota	(815)	7,134	6,902
62960	Metropolis	(618)	7,171	6,940
60445	Midlothian	(708)	14,274	14,422
61264	Milan	(309)	6,371	4,873
61265	Moline	(309)	46,407	46,237
61462	Monmouth	(309)	10,706	11,022
60450	Morris	(815)	8,833	8,194
61550	Morton	(309)	14,178	10,811
60053	Morton Grove	(708)	23,747	26,369
62863	Mount Carmel	(618)	8,908	8,096
60056	Mount Prospect	(708)	52,634	34,995
62864	Mount Vernon	(618)	16,995	16,270
60060	Mundelein	(708)	17,053	16,128
62966	Murphysboro	(618)	9,866	10,013
60540	Naperville	(708)	42,601	22,794
60451	New Lenox	(815)	5,792	2,855
60648	Niles	(708)	30,363	31,432
61761	Normal	(309)	35,672	26,396
60656	Norridge	(708)	16,483	17,113
60542	North Aurora	(708)	5,205	4,833
60062	Northbrook	(708)	30,735	25,422
60064	North Chicago	(708)	38,774	47,275
60164	Northlake	(708)	12,166	14,191
61111	North Park(u)	(815)	15,806	15,679
60546	North Riverside	(708)	6,764	8,097
60521	Oak Brook	(708)	6,676	4,164
60452	Oak Forest	(708)	25,040	19,271
*60454	Oak Lawn	(708)	60,590	60,305
*60301	Oak Park	(708)	54,887	62,511
62269	O'Fallon	(618)	12,173	7,268
62450	Olney	(618)	9,026	8,974
60462	Orland Park	(708)	23,045	6,391
61350	Ottawa	(815)	18,166	18,716
60067	Palatine	(708)	32,176	26,050
60463	Palos Heights	(708)	11,096	8,544
60465	Palos Hills	(708)	16,654	6,629
62557	Pana	(217)	6,040	6,326
61944	Paris	(217)	9,885	9,971
60466	Park Forest	(708)	26,222	30,638
60466	Park Forest South	(708)	6,245	1,748
60068	Park Ridge	(708)	38,704	42,614
61554	Pekin	(309)	33,967	31,375
*61601	Peoria	(309)	124,160	126,963
61614	Peoria Heights	(309)	7,453	7,943
61354	Peru	(815)	10,886	11,772
61764	Pontiac	(815)	11,227	10,595
61356	Princeton	(815)	7,342	6,959
60070	Prospect Heights	(708)	11,823	13,333
62301	Quincy	(217)	42,352	45,288
61866	Rantoul	(217)	20,161	25,562
60471	Richton Park	(708)	9,403	2,558
60627	Riverdale	(708)	13,233	15,806
60305	River Forest	(708)	12,392	13,402
60171	River Grove	(708)	10,368	11,465
60546	Riverside	(708)	9,236	10,357
60472	Robbins	(708)	8,119	9,641
62454	Robinson	(618)	7,285	7,178
61068	Rochelle	(815)	8,982	8,594
61071	Rock Falls	(815)	10,624	10,287
*61125	Rockford	(815)	139,712	147,370
61201	Rock Island	(309)	46,821	50,166
60008	Rolling Meadows	(708)	20,167	19,178
60441	Romeoville	(815)	15,519	12,888
60172	Roselle	(708)	17,034	6,207
62024	Rosewood Heights(u)	(618)	5,085	3,391
60073	Round Lake Beach	(708)	12,921	5,717
60174	St. Charles	(708)	17,492	12,945
62881	Salem	(618)	7,813	6,187
60548	Sandwich	(815)	5,356	5,056
60411	Sauk Village	(708)	10,906	7,479
60172	Schaumburg	(708)	53,355	18,531
60176	Schiller Park	(708)	11,458	12,712
62225	Scott AFB(u)	(618)	8,648	7,871
62565	Shelbyville	(217)	5,259	4,887
61282	Silvis	(309)	7,130	5,907
60076	Skokie	(708)	60,278	68,322
60177	South Elgin	(708)	5,970	4,289
60473	South Holland	(708)	24,977	23,931
*62703	Springfield	(217)	100,054	91,753
61362	Spring Valley	(815)	5,822	5,605
60475	Steger	(708)	9,269	8,104
61081	Sterling	(815)	16,273	16,113
60402	Stickney	(708)	5,893	6,601
60103	Streamwood	(708)	23,456	18,176
61364	Streator	(815)	14,795	15,600
60501	Summit	(708)	10,110	11,569
62221	Swansea	(618)	5,529	5,432
60178	Sycamore	(815)	9,219	7,843
62568	Taylorville	(217)	11,386	10,644
60477	Tinley Park	(708)	26,178	12,572
61801	Urbana	(217)	35,978	33,976
62471	Vandalia	(618)	5,338	5,160
60061	Vernon Hills	(708)	9,827	1,056
60181	Villa Park	(708)	23,155	25,891
60555	Warrenville	(708)	7,519	3,281
61571	Washington	(309)	10,364	6,790
62204	Washington Park	(618)	8,223	9,524
60970	Watseka	(815)	5,543	5,294
60084	Wauconda	(708)	5,688	5,460
60085	Waukegan	(708)	67,653	65,134
60153	Westchester	(708)	17,730	20,033
60185	West Chicago	(708)	12,550	9,988
60558	Western Springs	(708)	12,876	13,029
62896	West Frankfort	(618)	9,437	8,854
60559	Westmont	(708)	17,353	8,832
61604	West Peoria(u)	(309)	5,219	6,873
60187	Wheaton	(708)	43,043	31,138
60090	Wheeling	(708)	23,266	13,243
60091	Wilmette	(708)	28,221	32,134
60093	Winnetka	(708)	12,772	14,131
60096	Winthrop Harbor	(708)	5,427	4,794
60097	Wonder Lake(u)	(815)	5,917	4,806
60191	Wood Dale	(708)	11,251	8,831
60515	Woodridge	(708)	21,763	11,028
62095	Wood River	(618)	12,446	13,186
60098	Woodstock	(815)	11,725	10,226
60482	Worth	(708)	11,592	11,999
60099	Zion	(708)	17,865	17,268

Indiana

ZIP code	Place		1980	1970
46001	Alexandria	(317)	6,028	5,600
46011	Anderson	(317)	64,695	70,787
46703	Angola	(219)	5,486	5,117
46706	Auburn	(219)	8,122	7,388
47421	Bedford	(812)	14,410	13,087
46107	Beech Grove	(317)	13,196	13,559
47401	Bloomington	(812)	52,667	43,262
46714	Bluffton	(219)	8,705	8,297
47601	Boonville	(812)	6,300	5,736
47834	Brazil	(812)	7,852	8,163
46112	Brownsburg	(317)	6,242	5,751
46032	Carmel	(317)	18,272	6,691
46303	Cedar Lake	(219)	8,754	7,589
47111	Charlestown	(812)	5,596	5,993
46304	Chesterton	(219)	8,531	6,177
47130	Clarksville	(812)	15,164	13,298
47842	Clinton	(317)	5,267	5,340
46725	Columbia City	(219)	5,091	4,911
47201	Columbus	(812)	30,292	26,457
47331	Connersville	(317)	17,023	17,604
47933	Crawfordsville	(317)	13,325	13,842
46307	Crown Point	(219)	16,455	10,931
46733	Decatur	(219)	8,649	8,445
46514	Dunlap(u)	(219)	5,397	....
46311	Dyer	(219)	9,555	4,906
46312	East Chicago	(219)	39,786	46,982
46514	Elkhart	(219)	41,305	43,152
46036	Elwood	(317)	10,867	11,196
*47708	Evansville	(812)	130,496	138,764
*46802	Fort Wayne	(219)	172,391	178,269
46041	Frankfort	(317)	15,168	14,956
46131	Franklin	(317)	11,563	11,477
*46401	Gary	(219)	151,968	175,415
46933	Gas City	(317)	6,370	5,742
46526	Goshen	(219)	19,665	17,871
46135	Greencastle	(317)	8,403	8,852

ZIP code	Place		1980	1970
46140	Greenfield	(317)	11,288	9,986
47240	Greensburg	(812)	9,254	8,620
46142	Greenwood	(317)	19,327	11,869
46319	Griffith	(219)	17,026	18,168
*46320	Hammond	(219)	93,714	107,983
47348	Hartford City	(317)	7,622	8,207
46322	Highland	(219)	25,935	24,947
46342	Hobart	(219)	22,987	21,485
47542	Huntingburg	(812)	5,376	4,794
46750	Huntington	(219)	16,202	16,217
*46206	Indianapolis	(317)	700,807	736,856
47546	Jasper	(812)	9,097	8,641
47130	Jeffersonville	(812)	21,220	20,008
46755	Kendallville	(219)	7,299	6,838
46901	Kokomo	(317)	47,808	44,042
*47901	Lafayette	(317)	43,011	44,955
46405	Lake Station	(219)	15,087	9,858
46350	La Porte	(219)	21,796	22,140
46226	Lawrence	(317)	25,591	16,353
46052	Lebanon	(317)	11,456	9,766
47441	Linton	(812)	6,315	5,450
46947	Logansport	(219)	17,731	19,255
46356	Lowell	(219)	5,827	3,839
47250	Madison	(812)	12,472	13,081
46952	Marion	(317)	35,874	39,607
46151	Martinsville	(317)	11,311	9,723
46410	Merrillville	(219)	27,677	15,918
46360	Michigan City	(219)	36,850	39,369
46544	Mishawaka	(219)	40,224	36,060
47960	Monticello	(219)	5,162	4,869
46158	Mooresville	(317)	5,349	5,800
47620	Mount Vernon	(812)	7,656	6,770
*47302	Muncie	(317)	77,216	69,082
46321	Munster	(219)	20,671	16,514
47150	New Albany	(812)	37,103	38,402
47362	New Castle	(317)	20,056	21,215
46774	New Haven	(219)	6,714	5,346
46060	Noblesville	(317)	12,253	7,548
46962	North Manchester	(219)	5,998	5,791
47265	North Vernon	(812)	5,768	4,582
47130	Oak Park(u)	(812)	5,871	....
46970	Peru	(317)	13,764	14,139
46168	Plainfield	(317)	9,191	8,211
46563	Plymouth	(219)	7,693	7,661
46368	Portage	(219)	27,409	19,127
46371	Portland	(219)	7,074	7,115
47670	Princeton	(812)	8,976	7,431
47374	Richmond	(317)	41,349	43,999
46975	Rochester	(219)	5,050	4,631
46173	Rushville	(317)	6,113	6,686
47167	Salem	(812)	5,290	5,041
46375	Schererville	(219)	13,209	3,663
47170	Scottsburg	(812)	5,068	4,791
47274	Seymour	(812)	15,050	13,352
47176	Shelbyville	(317)	14,989	15,094
*46624	South Bend	(219)	109,727	125,580
46383	South Haven(u)	(219)	6,679	....
46224	Speedway	(317)	12,641	14,523
47586	Tell City	(812)	8,704	7,933
*47808	Terre Haute	(812)	61,125	70,335
46072	Tipton	(317)	5,004	5,313
46383	Valparaiso	(219)	22,247	20,020
47591	Vincennes	(812)	20,857	19,867
46992	Wabash	(219)	12,985	13,379
46580	Warsaw	(219)	10,647	7,506
47501	Washington	(812)	11,325	11,358
47906	West Lafayette	(317)	21,247	19,157
46394	Whiting	(219)	5,630	7,054
47394	Winchester	(317)	5,659	5,493

Iowa

ZIP code	Place		1980	1970
50511	Algona	(515)	6,289	6,032
50009	Altoona	(515)	5,764	2,883
50010	Ames	(515)	45,775	39,505
50021	Ankeny	(515)	15,429	9,151
50022	Atlantic	(712)	7,789	7,306
52722	Bettendorf	(319)	27,381	22,126
50036	Boone	(515)	12,602	12,468
52601	Burlington	(319)	29,529	32,366
51401	Carroll	(712)	9,705	8,716
50613	Cedar Falls	(319)	36,322	29,597
*52401	Cedar Rapids	(319)	110,243	110,642
52544	Centerville	(515)	6,558	6,531
50049	Chariton	(515)	5,116	5,009
50616	Charles City	(515)	8,778	9,268
51012	Cherokee	(712)	7,004	7,272
51632	Clarinda	(712)	5,458	5,420
50428	Clear Lake City	(515)	7,458	6,430
52732	Clinton	(319)	32,828	34,719
50053	Clive	(515)	5,906	3,005
52240	Coralville	(319)	7,687	6,130
51501	Council Bluffs	(712)	56,449	60,348
50801	Creston	(515)	8,429	8,234
*52802	Davenport	(319)	103,264	98,469
52101	Decorah	(319)	7,991	7,237
51442	Denison	(712)	6,675	6,218
*50318	Des Moines	(515)	191,003	201,404
52001	Dubuque	(319)	62,374	62,309

ZIP code	Place		1980	1970
51334	Estherville	(712)	7,518	8,108
52556	Fairfield	(515)	9,428	8,715
50501	Fort Dodge	(515)	29,423	31,263
52627	Fort Madison	(319)	13,520	13,996
51534	Glenwood	(712)	5,280	4,421
50112	Grinnell	(515)	8,868	8,402
51537	Harlan	(712)	5,357	5,049
50644	Independence	(319)	6,392	5,910
50125	Indianola	(515)	10,843	8,852
52240	Iowa City	(319)	50,508	46,850
50126	Iowa Falls	(515)	6,174	6,454
52632	Keokuk	(319)	13,536	14,631
50138	Knoxville	(515)	8,143	7,755
51031	Le Mars	(712)	8,276	8,159
52060	Maquoketa	(319)	6,313	5,677
52302	Marion	(319)	19,474	18,028
50158	Marshalltown	(515)	26,938	26,219
50401	Mason City	(515)	30,144	30,379
52641	Mount Pleasant	(319)	7,322	7,007
52761	Muscatine	(319)	23,467	22,405
50201	Nevada	(515)	5,912	4,952
50208	Newton	(515)	15,292	15,619
50662	Oelwein	(319)	7,564	7,735
52577	Oskaloosa	(515)	10,629	11,224
52501	Ottumwa	(515)	27,381	29,610
50219	Pella	(515)	8,349	6,668
50220	Perry	(515)	7,053	6,906
51566	Red Oak	(712)	6,810	6,210
51201	Sheldon	(712)	5,003	4,535
51601	Shenandoah	(712)	6,274	5,968
*51101	Sioux City	(712)	82,003	85,925
51301	Spencer	(712)	11,726	10,278
50588	Storm Lake	(712)	8,814	8,591
50322	Urbandale	(515)	17,869	14,434
52349	Vinton	(319)	5,040	4,845
52353	Washington	(319)	6,584	6,317
*50701	Waterloo	(319)	75,985	75,533
50677	Waverly	(319)	8,444	7,205
50595	Webster City	(515)	8,572	8,488
50265	West Des Moines	(515)	21,894	16,441
50311	Windsor Heights	(515)	5,632	6,303

Kansas

ZIP code	Place		1980	1970
67410	Abilene	(913)	6,572	6,661
67005	Arkansas City	(316)	13,201	13,216
66002	Atchison	(913)	11,407	12,565
67010	Augusta	(316)	6,968	5,977
67012	Bonner Springs	(913)	6,266	3,884
66720	Chanute	(316)	10,506	10,341
67337	Coffeyville	(316)	15,185	15,116
67701	Colby	(913)	5,544	4,658
66901	Concordia	(913)	6,847	7,221
67037	Derby	(316)	9,786	7,947
67801	Dodge City	(316)	18,001	14,127
67042	El Dorado	(316)	11,551	12,308
66801	Emporia	(316)	25,287	23,327
66442	Fort Riley North(u)	(913)	16,086	12,469
66701	Fort Scott	(316)	8,893	8,967
67846	Garden City	(316)	18,256	14,790
67735	Goodland	(913)	5,708	5,510
67530	Great Bend	(316)	16,608	16,133
67601	Hays	(913)	16,301	15,396
67060	Haysville	(316)	8,006	6,531
67501	Hutchinson	(316)	40,284	36,885
67301	Independence	(316)	10,598	10,347
66749	Iola	(316)	6,938	6,493
66441	Junction City	(913)	19,305	19,018
*66101	Kansas City	(913)	161,148	168,213
66043	Lansing	(913)	5,307	3,797
66044	Lawrence	(913)	52,738	45,698
66048	Leavenworth	(913)	33,656	25,147
66206	Leawood	(913)	13,360	10,645
66215	Lenexa	(913)	18,639	5,549
67901	Liberal	(316)	14,911	13,862
67460	McPherson	(316)	11,753	10,851
66502	Manhattan	(913)	32,644	27,575
66203	Merriam	(913)	10,794	10,955
66222	Mission	(913)	8,643	8,125
67114	Newton	(316)	16,332	15,439
66061	Olathe	(913)	37,258	17,917
66067	Ottawa	(913)	11,016	11,036
66204	Overland Park	(913)	81,784	77,934
67357	Parsons	(316)	12,898	13,015
66762	Pittsburg	(316)	18,770	20,171
66208	Prairie Village	(913)	24,657	28,378
67124	Pratt	(316)	6,885	6,736
66203	Roeland Park	(913)	7,962	9,760
67665	Russell	(913)	5,427	5,371
67401	Salina	(913)	41,843	37,714
*66203	Shawnee	(913)	29,653	20,946
*66603	Topeka	(913)	118,690	125,011
67152	Wellington	(316)	8,212	8,072
*67202	Wichita	(316)	279,838	276,554
67156	Winfield	(316)	10,736	11,405

Kentucky

ZIP code	Place		1980	1970
41101	Ashland	(606)	27,064	29,245
40004	Bardstown	(502)	6,155	5,816

ZIP code	Place		1980	1970
41073	Bellevue	(606)	7,678	8,847
40403	Berea	(606)	8,226	6,956
42101	Bowling Green	(502)	40,450	36,705
40218	Buechel(u)	(502)	6,912	5,359
42718	Campbellsville	(502)	8,715	7,598
42330	Central City	(502)	5,250	5,450
40701	Corbin	(606)	8,075	7,474
*41011	Covington	(606)	49,585	52,535
41031	Cynthiana	(606)	5,881	6,356
40422	Danville	(606)	12,942	11,542
41074	Dayton	(606)	6,979	8,751
41017	Edgewood	(606)	7,243	4,139
42701	Elizabethtown	(502)	15,380	11,748
41018	Elsmere	(606)	7,203	5,161
41018	Erlanger	(606)	14,466	12,676
40118	Fairdale(u)	(502)	7,315	....
40291	Fern Creek(u)	(502)	16,866	....
41139	Flatwoods	(606)	8,354	7,380
41042	Florence	(606)	15,586	11,661
42223	Fort Campbell North(u)	(502)	17,211	13,616
40121	Fort Knox(u)	(502)	31,035	37,608
41017	Fort Mitchell	(606)	7,294	6,982
41075	Fort Thomas	(606)	16,012	16,338
42601	Frankfort	(502)	25,973	21,902
42134	Franklin	(502)	7,738	6,553
40324	Georgetown	(502)	10,972	8,629
42141	Glasgow	(502)	12,958	11,301
40330	Harrodsburg	(606)	7,265	6,741
41701	Hazard	(606)	5,429	5,459
42420	Henderson	(502)	24,834	22,976
40228	Highview(u)	(502)	13,286	....
40229	Hillview	(502)	5,196	....
42240	Hopkinsville	(502)	27,318	21,395
41051	Independence	(606)	7,998	1,715
40299	Jeffersontown	(502)	15,795	9,701
40342	Lawrenceburg	(502)	5,167	3,579
40033	Lebanon	(502)	6,590	5,528
*40511	Lexington-Fayette	(606)	204,165	108,137
*40201	Louisville	(502)	298,694	361,706
42431	Madisonville	(502)	16,979	15,332
42066	Mayfield	(502)	10,705	10,724
41056	Maysville	(606)	7,983	7,411
40965	Middlesborough	(606)	12,251	11,878
42633	Monticello	(606)	5,677	3,618
40351	Morehead	(606)	7,789	7,191
40353	Mount Sterling	(606)	5,820	5,083
42071	Murray	(502)	14,248	13,537
40218	Newburg(u)	(502)	24,612	....
*41071	Newport	(606)	21,587	25,998
40356	Nicholasville	(606)	10,400	5,829
40219	Okolona(u)	(502)	20,039	17,643
42301	Owensboro	(502)	54,450	50,329
42001	Paducah	(502)	29,315	31,627
40361	Paris	(606)	7,935	7,823
40258	Pleasure Ridge Park(u)	(502)	27,332	28,566
42445	Princeton	(502)	7,073	6,292
40160	Radcliff	(502)	14,656	8,426
40475	Richmond	(606)	21,705	16,861
42276	Russellville	(502)	7,520	6,456
40207	St. Matthews	(502)	13,519	13,152
40065	Shelbyville	(502)	5,308	4,182
40216	Shively	(502)	16,645	19,139
42501	Somerset	(606)	10,649	10,436
40272	Valley Station(u)	(502)	24,474	24,471
40383	Versailles	(606)	6,427	5,679
41101	Westwood(u)	(606)	5,973	777
40769	Williamsburg	(606)	5,560	3,687
40391	Winchester	(606)	15,216	13,402

Louisiana

ZIP code	Place		1980	1970
70510	Abbeville	(318)	12,391	10,996
71301	Alexandria	(318)	51,565	41,811
70032	Arabi(u)	(504)	10,248	....
70094	Avondale(u)	(504)	6,699	....
70714	Baker	(504)	12,865	8,281
71220	Bastrop	(318)	15,527	14,713
*70821	Baton Rouge	(504)	220,394	165,921
70360	Bayou Cane(u)	(504)	15,723	9,077
70380	Bayou Vista(u)	(504)	5,605	5,121
70037	Belle Chasse(u)	(504)	5,412	....
70427	Bogalusa	(504)	16,976	18,412
71010	Bossier City	(318)	49,969	43,769
70517	Breaux Bridge	(318)	5,922	4,942
	Broadmoor(u)	(318)	7,051	....
71291	Brownsville-Bawcomville(u)	(318)	7,252	....
71322	Bunkie	(318)	5,364	5,395
70043	Chalmette(u)	(504)	33,847	....
71291	Claiborne(u)	(318)	6,278	....
70433	Covington	(504)	7,892	7,170
70526	Crowley	(318)	16,036	16,104
70345	Cut Off(u)	(504)	5,049	....
70726	Denham Springs	(504)	8,412	6,752
70634	De Ridder	(318)	10,337	8,030
70346	Donaldsonville	(504)	7,901	7,367
70072	Estelle(u)	(504)	12,724	....
70535	Eunice	(318)	12,479	11,390
70538	Franklin	(318)	9,584	9,325
70354	Galliano(u)	(504)	5,159	....
70737	Gonzales	(504)	7,287	4,512
70053	Gretna	(504)	20,615	24,875
70401	Hammond	(504)	15,226	12,487
70123	Harahan	(504)	11,384	13,037
70058	Harvey(u)	(504)	22,709	6,347
70360	Houma	(504)	32,602	30,922
70544	Jeanerette	(318)	6,511	6,322
70121	Jefferson(u)	(504)	15,550	16,489
70546	Jennings	(318)	12,401	11,783
71251	Jonesboro	(318)	5,061	5,072
70548	Kaplan	(318)	5,016	5,540
70062	Kenner	(504)	66,382	29,858
70445	Lacombe(u)	(504)	5,146	....
70501	Lafayette	(318)	80,584	68,908
70601	Lake Charles	(318)	75,051	77,998
71254	Lake Providence	(318)	6,361	6,183
70068	Laplace(u)	(504)	16,112	5,953
70373	Larose(u)	(504)	5,234	4,267
70446	Leesville	(318)	9,054	8,928
70123	Little Farms(u)	(504)	NA	15,713
70448	Mandeville	(504)	6,076	2,571
71052	Mansfield	(318)	6,485	6,432
71351	Marksville	(318)	5,113	4,519
70072	Marrero(u)	(504)	36,548	29,015
*70004	Metairie(u)	(504)	164,160	136,477
71055	Minden	(318)	15,074	13,996
71201	Monroe	(318)	57,597	56,374
70380	Morgan City	(504)	16,114	16,586
70601	Moss Bluff(u)	(318)	7,004	....
71457	Natchitoches	(318)	16,664	15,974
70560	New Iberia	(318)	32,766	30,147
*70113	New Orleans	(504)	557,927	593,471
71463	Oakdale	(318)	7,155	7,301
70570	Opelousas	(318)	18,903	20,387
71360	Pineville	(318)	12,034	8,951
70764	Plaquemine	(504)	7,521	7,739
70454	Ponchatoula	(504)	5,469	4,545
70767	Port Allen	(504)	6,114	5,728
70085	Poydras(u)	(504)	5,722	....
70601	Prien(u)	(318)	6,224	....
70394	Raceland(u)	(504)	6,302	4,880
70578	Rayne	(318)	9,066	9,510
70084	Reserve(u)	(504)	7,288	6,381
70123	River Ridge(u)	(504)	17,146	....
71270	Ruston	(318)	20,585	17,365
70582	St. Martinville	(318)	7,965	7,153
70807	Scotlandville(u)	(504)	15,113	22,599
*71102	Shreveport	(318)	206,989	182,064
70458	Slidell	(504)	26,718	16,101
71459	South Fort Polk(u)	(318)	12,498	15,600
71075	Springhill	(318)	6,516	6,496
70663	Sulphur	(318)	19,709	14,959
71282	Tallulah	(318)	11,341	9,643
71285	Terrytown(u)	(318)	23,548	13,382
70301	Thibodaux	(504)	15,810	15,028
70053	Timberlane(u)	(504)	11,579	....
71373	Vidalia	(318)	5,936	5,538
70586	Ville Platte	(318)	9,201	9,692
70092	Violet(u)	(504)	11,678	....
70094	Waggaman(u)	(504)	9,004	....
70669	Westlake	(318)	5,246	4,082
71291	West Monroe	(318)	14,993	14,868
70094	Westwego	(504)	12,663	11,442
71483	Winnfield	(318)	7,311	7,142
71295	Winnsboro	(318)	5,921	5,349
70791	Zachary	(504)	7,297	4,964

Maine (207)

See Note Page 563

ZIP code	Place	1980	1970
04210	Auburn	23,128	24,151
04330	Augusta	21,819	21,945
04401	Bangor	31,643	33,168
04530	Bath	10,246	9,679
04915	Belfast	6,243	5,957
04005	Biddeford	19,638	19,983
04412	Brewer	9,017	9,300
04011	Brunswick Center(u)	10,990	10,867
04011	Brunswick	17,366	16,195
04093	Buxton	5,775	3,135
04107	Cape Elizabeth	7,838	7,873
04736	Caribou	9,916	10,419
04021	Cumberland	5,284	4,096
04605	Ellsworth	5,179	4,603
04937	Fairfield	6,113	5,684
04105	Falmouth	6,853	6,291
04938	Farmington	6,730	5,657
04032	Freeport	5,863	4,781
04345	Gardiner	6,485	6,685
04038	Gorham	10,101	7,839
04444	Hampden	5,250	4,693
04730	Houlton Center(u)	5,730	6,760
04730	Houlton	6,766	8,111
04239	Jay	5,080	3,954
04043	Kennebunk	6,621	5,646
03904	Kittery Center(u)	5,465	7,363
03904	Kittery	9,314	11,028
04240	Lewiston	40,481	41,779

ZIP code	Place	1980	1970
04750	Limestone	8,719	10,360
04457	Lincoln	5,066	4,759
04250	Lisbon	8,769	6,544
04750	Loring(u)	6,572	7,881
04756	Madawaska	5,282	5,585
04462	Millinocket Center(u)	7,567	7,558
04462	Millinocket	7,567	7,742
04062	North Windham(u)	5,492	....
04963	Oakland	5,162	3,535
04064	Old Orchard Beach Ctr.(u).	6,023	5,273
04064	Old Orchard Beach.	6,291	5,404
04468	Old Town	8,422	8,741
04473	Orono Center(u)	9,891	9,146
04473	Orono	10,578	9,989
*04101	Portland	61,572	65,116
04769	Presque Isle	11,172	11,452
04841	Rockland	7,919	8,505
04276	Rumford Compact(u)	6,256	6,198
04276	Rumford	8,240	9,363
04072	Saco	12,921	11,678
04073	Sanford Center(u).	10,268	10,457
04073	Sanford	18,020	15,812
04074	Scarborough.	11,347	7,845
04976	Skowhegan Center(u)	6,517	6,571
04976	Skowhegan	8,098	7,601
04106	South Portland	22,712	23,267
04084	Standish	5,946	3,122
04086	Topsham.	6,431	5,022
04901	Waterville	17,779	18,192
04090	Wells	8,211	4,448
04092	Westbrook	14,976	14,444
04082	Windham.	11,282	6,593
04901	Winslow Center(u)	5,903	5,389
04901	Winslow	8,057	7,299
04364	Winthrop	5,889	4,335
04096	Yarmouth	6,585	4,854
03909	York	8,465	5,690

Maryland (301)

ZIP code	Place	1980	1970
21001	Aberdeen	11,533	7,403
21005	Aberdeen Proving Ground(u)	5,772	7,403
20783	Adelphi(u)	12,530	....
20331	Andrews AFB(u).	10,064	6,418
*21401	Annapolis	31,740	30,095
21227	Arbutus(u)	20,163	22,745
21012	Arnold(u)	12,285	....
20906	Aspen Hill(u)	47,455	16,887
*21233	Baltimore.	786,741	905,787
21014	Bel Air	7,814	6,307
21050	Bel Air North(u)	5,043	....
21014	Bel Air South(u)	8,461	....
20705	Beltsville(u)	12,760	8,912
*20814	Bethesda(u)	63,022	71,621
20710	Bladensburg	7,691	7,977
*20715	Bowie.	33,695	35,028
21225	Brooklyn Park(u)	11,508	....
20818	Cabin John-Brookmont(u)	5,135	....
20619	California(u)	5,770	....
21613	Cambridge	11,703	11,595
20748	Camp Springs(u)	16,118	22,776
21401	Cape St. Clair(u)	6,022	....
20743	Carmody Hills-Pepper Mill(u)	5,571	6,245
21234	Carney(u)	21,488	....
21228	Catonsville(u)	33,208	54,812
-20785	Cheverly	5,751	6,808
20815	Chevy Chase(u).	12,232	16,424
20783	Chillum(u).	32,775	35,656
20735	Clinton(u).	16,438	....
20904	Cloverly(u).	5,153	....
21030	Cockeysville(u)	17,013	....
20904	Colesville(u)	14,359	9,455
20740	College Park.	23,614	26,156
*21044	Columbia(u).	52,518	8,815
20743	Coral Hills(u).	11,602	9,058
21114	Crofton(u)	12,009	4,478
21502	Cumberland	25,933	29,724
20747	District Heights	6,799	7,846
20785	Dodge Park(u)	5,275	....
21222	Dundalk(u).	71,293	85,377
21601	Easton	7,536	6,809
20737	East Riverdale(u)	14,117	....
21219	Edgemere(u).	9,078	10,352
21040	Edgewood	19,455	8,551
21921	Elkton.	6,468	5,362
21043	Ellicott City(u)	21,784	9,435
21221	Essex(u).	39,614	38,193
20904	Fairland(u).	5,154	....
21047	Fallston(u).	5,572	....
21061	Ferndale(u).	14,314	9,929
20747	Forestville(u).	16,401	16,188
20755	Fort Meade(u).	14,083	16,699
21701	Frederick.	27,557	23,641
	Friendly(u).	8,848	....
21532	Frostburg.	7,715	7,327
*20877	Gaithersburg.	26,424	8,344
20874	Germantown(u).	9,721	....

ZIP code	Place	1980	1970
....	Glassmanor(u)	7,751	....
21061	Glen Burnie(u).	37,263	38,608
20769	Glenn Dale(u)	5,106	....
20771	Goddard(u).	6,147	....
20770	Greenbelt	16,000	18,199
21122	Green Haven(u).	6,577	....
21740	Hagerstown	34,132	35,862
21740	Halfway(u).	8,659	6,106
21204	Hampton(u)	5,220	....
21078	Havre De Grace.	8,763	9,791
20903	Hillandale(u)	9,686	....
20748	Hillcrest Heights.	17,021	24,037
*20780	Hyattsville(u)	12,709	14,998
21085	Joppatowne(u).	11,348	9,092
20785	Kentland(u)	8,596	9,649
20772	Kettering(u)	6,972	....
21122	Lake Shore(u)	10,181	....
20785	Landover(u)	5,374	5,597
20787	Langley Park(u).	14,038	11,564
20706	Lanham-Seabrook(u)	15,814	13,244
21227	Lansdowne-Baltimore Highlands(u)	16,759	17,770
20772	Largo(u)	5,557	....
*20707	Laurel	12,103	10,525
21502	La Vale-Narrows Park(u).	5,523	3,971
20653	Lexington Pk.(u).	10,361	9,136
21090	Linthicum(u)	7,457	9,775
21207	Lochearn(u)	26,908	....
21037	Londontowne(u).	6,052	3,864
21093	Lutherville-Timonium(u).	17,854	24,055
20748	Marlow Heights(u)	5,824	....
20707	Maryland City(u)	6,949	7,102
	Mays Chapel(u).	5,213	....
21220	Middle River(u)	26,756	19,935
	Milford Mill(u)	20,354	....
20879	Montgomery Village(u)	18,725	....
20822	Mount Rainier	7,361	8,180
21402	Naval Academy(u)	5,367	....
20784	New Carrollton	12,632	14,870
20815	North Bethesda(u)	22,671	....
20895	North Kensington(u)	9,039	....
20707	North Laurel(u)	6,093	....
21113	Odenton(u).	13,270	5,969
20832	Olney(u).	13,026	2,138
21206	Overlea(u)	12,965	13,124
21117	Owings Mills(u)	9,526	7,360
20745	Oxon Hill(u)	36,267	11,974
20785	Palmer Park(u)	7,986	6,172
21234	Parkville	35,159	33,589
21122	Pasadena(u)	7,439	....
21128	Perry Hall(u).	13,455	5,446
21208	Pikesville(u).	22,555	25,395
20854	Potomac(u).	40,402	....
21227	Pumphrey(u).	5,666	6,425
20878	Quince Orchard(u)	5,107	....
21133	Randallstown(u).	25,927	33,683
	Redland(u).	10,759	....
21136	Reisterstown(u)	19,385	12,568
21122	Riviera Beach(u)	8,812	7,464
*20850	Rockville.	43,811	42,739
21237	Rosedale(u)	19,956	19,417
21221	Rossville(u).	8,646	....
20601	St. Charles(u).	13,921	....
21801	Salisbury.	16,429	15,252
20743	Seat Pleasant	5,217	7,217
21207	Security(u).	29,453	....
21144	Severn(u).	20,147	....
21146	Severna Park(u)	21,253	16,358
*20907	Silver Spring(u)	72,893	77,411
21061	South Gate(u).	24,185	9,356
20895	South Kensington(u)	9,344	10,289
20707	South Laurel(u).	18,034	13,345
20746	Suitland-Silver Hills(u)	32,164	30,355
20912	Takoma Park	16,231	18,507
....	Tantallon(u)	9,945	....
20748	Temple Hills(u)	6,630	....
21204	Towson(u)	51,083	77,768
20601	Waldorf(u).	9,782	7,368
20743	Walker Mill(u)	10,651	7,103
21157	Westminster.	8,808	7,207
20902	Wheaton Glenmont(u)	48,598	66,280
20903	White Oak(u).	13,700	19,769
21157	White Plains(u).	5,167	....
21207	Woodlawn(u)	5,306	....

Massachusetts

See Note on Page 563

ZIP code	Place		1980	1970
02351	Abington	(617)	13,517	12,334
01720	Acton.	(508)	17,544	14,770
02743	Acushnet.	(508)	8,704	7,767
01220	Adams Center(u)	(413)	6,857	11,256
....	Adams	(413)	10,381	11,772
01001	Agawam	(413)	26,271	21,717
01913	Amesbury Center(u)	(508)	12,236	10,088
....	Amesbury	(508)	13,971	11,388
01002	Amherst Center	(413)	17,773	17,926
....	Amherst	(413)	33,229	26,331
01810	Andover	(508)	26,370	23,695
02174	Arlington	(617)	48,219	53,524
01721	Ashland	(508)	9,165	8,882

ZIP code	Place		1980	1970
01331	Athol Center(u)	(617)	8,708	9,723
.....	Athol	(508)	10,634	11,185
02703	Attleboro	(508)	34,196	32,907
01501	Auburn	(508)	14,845	15,347
02322	Avon	(508)	5,026	5,295
*01432	Ayer	(617)	6,993	8,325
02630	Barnstable	(508)	30,898	19,842
01730	Bedford	(617)	13,067	13,513
01007	Belchertown	(413)	8,339	5,936
02019	Bellingham	(508)	14,300	13,967
02178	Belmont	(617)	26,100	28,285
01915	Beverly	(508)	37,655	38,348
01821	Billerica	(508)	36,727	31,648
01504	Blackstone	(508)	6,570	6,566
*02109	Boston	(617)	562,994	641,071
02532	Bourne	(508)	13,874	12,636
01921	Boxford	(508)	5,374	4,032
02184	Braintree	(617)	36,337	35,050
02631	Brewster	(508)	5,226	1,790
02324	Bridgewater	(508)	17,202	12,911
*02403	Brockton	(508)	95,172	89,040
02146	Brookline	(617)	55,062	58,689
01803	Burlington	(617)	23,486	21,980
*02138	Cambridge	(617)	95,322	100,361
02021	Canton	(617)	18,182	17,100
02330	Carver	(508)	6,988	2,420
01507	Charlton	(508)	6,719	4,654
02633	Chatham	(508)	6,071	4,554
01824	Chelmsford	(508)	31,174	31,432
02150	Chelsea	(617)	25,431	30,625
*01021	Chicopee	(413)	55,112	66,676
01510	Clinton	(508)	12,771	13,383
01778	Cochituate(u)	(617)	6,126	.....
02025	Cohasset	(617)	7,174	6,954
01742	Concord	(508)	16,293	16,148
01226	Dalton	(413)	6,797	7,505
01923	Danvers	(508)	24,100	26,151
02714	Dartmouth	(508)	23,966	18,800
02026	Dedham	(617)	25,298	26,938
02638	Dennis	(508)	12,360	6,454
02715	Dighton	(508)	5,352	4,667
01826	Dracut	(508)	21,249	18,214
01570	Dudley	(508)	8,717	8,087
02332	Duxbury	(617)	11,807	7,636
02333	East Bridgewater	(508)	9,945	8,347
02536	East Falmouth(u)	(617)	5,181	2,971
01027	Easthampton	(413)	15,580	13,012
01028	East Longmeadow	(413)	12,905	13,029
02334	Easton	(508)	16,623	12,157
02149	Everett	(617)	37,195	42,485
02719	Fairhaven	(508)	15,759	16,332
*02722	Fall River	(508)	92,574	96,898
*02540	Falmouth Center(u)	(508)	5,720	5,806
.....	Falmouth	(508)	23,640	15,942
01420	Fitchburg	(508)	39,580	43,343
01433	Fort Devens(u)	(617)	9,546	12,915
02035	Foxborough	(508)	14,148	14,218
01701	Framingham	(508)	65,113	64,048
02038	Franklin Center(u)	(508)	9,296	8,863
.....	Franklin	(508)	18,217	17,830
02702	Freetown	(508)	7,058	4,270
01440	Gardner	(508)	17,900	19,748
01833	Georgetown	(508)	5,687	5,290
01930	Gloucester	(508)	27,768	27,941
01519	Grafton	(508)	11,238	11,659
01033	Granby	(413)	5,380	5,473
01230	Great Barrington	(413)	7,405	7,537
01301	Greenfield Center(u)	(413)	14,198	14,642
.....	Greenfield	(413)	18,436	18,116
01450	Groton	(508)	6,154	5,109
01834	Groveland	(508)	5,040	5,382
02338	Halifax	(617)	5,513	3,537
01936	Hamilton	(508)	6,960	6,373
02339	Hanover	(617)	11,358	10,107
02341	Hanson	(617)	8,508	7,148
01451	Harvard	(508)	12,170	12,494
02645	Harwich	(508)	8,971	5,892
01830	Haverhill	(508)	46,865	46,120
02043	Hingham	(617)	20,339	18,845
02343	Holbrook	(617)	11,140	11,775
01520	Holden	(508)	13,336	12,564
01746	Holliston	(508)	12,622	12,069
01040	Holyoke	(413)	44,678	50,112
01748	Hopkinton	(508)	7,114	5,981
01749	Hudson Center(u)	(508)	14,156	14,283
.....	Hudson	(508)	16,408	16,084
02045	Hull	(617)	9,714	9,961
02601	Hyannis(u)	(617)	9,118	6,847
01938	Ipswich(u)	(508)	NA	5,022
.....	Ipswich	(508)	11,158	10,750
02364	Kingston	(617)	7,362	5,999
02346	Lakeville	(508)	5,931	4,376
01523	Lancaster	(508)	6,334	6,095
*01842	Lawrence	(508)	63,175	66,915
01238	Lee	(413)	6,247	6,426
01524	Leicester	(508)	9,446	9,140
01240	Lenox	(413)	6,523	5,804
01453	Leominster	(508)	34,508	32,939
02173	Lexington	(617)	29,479	31,886
01773	Lincoln	(617)	7,098	7,567
01460	Littleton	(508)	6,970	6,380
01106	Longmeadow	(413)	16,301	15,630
*01853	Lowell	(508)	92,418	94,239
01056	Ludlow	(413)	18,150	17,580
01462	Lunenburg	(508)	8,405	7,419
*01901	Lynn	(617)	78,471	90,294
01940	Lynnfield	(617)	11,267	10,826
02148	Malden	(617)	53,386	56,127
01944	Manchester	(508)	5,424	5,151
02048	Mansfield	(508)	13,453	9,939
01945	Marblehead	(617)	20,126	21,295
01752	Marlborough	(508)	30,508	27,936
02050	Marshfield	(617)	20,916	15,223
02739	Mattapoisett	(508)	5,597	4,500
01754	Maynard	(508)	9,590	9,710
02052	Medfield	(508)	10,220	9,821
02155	Medford	(617)	58,076	64,397
02053	Medway	(508)	8,447	7,938
02176	Melrose	(617)	30,055	33,180
01844	Methuen	(508)	36,701	35,456
02346	Middleborough Center(u)	(508)	7,012	6,259
.....	Middleborough	(508)	16,404	13,607
01757	Milford Center(u)	(508)	NA	13,740
.....	Milford	(508)	23,390	19,352
01527	Millbury	(508)	11,808	11,987
02054	Millis	(508)	6,908	5,686
02186	Milton	(617)	25,860	27,190
01057	Monson	(413)	7,315	7,355
01351	Montague	(413)	8,011	8,451
02554	Nantucket	(508)	5,087	3,774
01760	Natick	(508)	29,461	31,057
02192	Needham	(617)	27,901	29,748
*02741	New Bedford	(508)	98,478	101,777
01950	Newburyport	(508)	15,900	15,807
02158	Newton	(617)	83,622	91,263
02056	Norfolk	(508)	6,363	4,656
01247	North Adams	(413)	18,063	19,195
01002	North Amherst(u)	(413)	5,616	2,854
01060	Northampton	(413)	29,286	29,664
01845	North Andover	(508)	20,129	16,284
*02760	North Attleborough	(508)	21,095	18,665
01532	Northborough	(508)	10,568	9,218
01534	Northbridge	(508)	12,246	11,795
01864	North Reading	(508)	11,455	11,264
02060	North Scituate(u)	(617)	5,221	5,507
02766	Norton	(508)	12,690	9,487
02061	Norwell	(617)	9,182	7,796
02062	Norwood	(617)	29,711	30,815
01364	Orange	(508)	6,844	6,104
02653	Orleans	(508)	5,306	3,055
01253	Otis(u)	(413)	NA	5,596
01540	Oxford Center(u)	(508)	6,369	6,109
.....	Oxford	(508)	11,680	10,345
01069	Palmer	(413)	11,389	11,680
01960	Peabody	(617)	45,976	48,080
02359	Pembroke	(617)	13,487	11,193
01463	Pepperell	(508)	8,061	5,887
01866	Pinehurst(u)	(617)	6,588	.....
01201	Pittsfield	(413)	51,974	57,020
02762	Plainville	(508)	5,857	4,953
*02360	Plymouth Center(u)	(508)	7,232	6,940
.....	Plymouth	(508)	35,913	18,606
02169	Quincy	(617)	84,743	87,966
02368	Randolph	(617)	28,218	27,035
02767	Raynham	(508)	9,085	6,705
01867	Reading	(617)	22,678	22,539
02769	Rehoboth	(508)	7,570	6,512
02151	Revere	(617)	42,423	43,159
02370	Rockland	(617)	15,695	15,674
01966	Rockport	(508)	6,345	5,636
01970	Salem	(508)	38,276	40,556
01950	Salisbury	(508)	5,973	4,179
02563	Sandwich	(508)	8,727	5,239
01906	Saugus	(617)	24,746	25,110
02066	Scituate	(617)	17,317	16,973
02771	Seekonk	(508)	12,269	11,116
02067	Sharon	(617)	13,601	12,367
01464	Shirley	(508)	5,124	4,909
01545	Shrewsbury	(508)	22,674	19,196
02725	Somerset	(508)	18,813	18,088
02143	Somerville	(617)	77,372	88,779
01772	Southborough	(508)	6,193	5,798
01550	Southbridge Center(u)	(508)	12,882	14,261
.....	Southbridge	(508)	16,665	17,057
01075	South Hadley	(413)	16,399	17,033
01077	Southwick	(413)	7,382	6,330
02664	South Yarmouth(u)	(617)	7,525	5,380
01562	Spencer Center	(617)	6,350	5,895
.....	Spencer	(508)	10,774	8,779
*01101	Springfield	(413)	152,319	163,905
01564	Sterling	(508)	5,440	4,247
02180	Stoneham	(617)	21,424	20,725
02072	Stoughton	(617)	26,710	23,459
01775	Stow	(508)	5,144	3,984
01566	Sturbridge	(508)	5,976	4,878
01776	Sudbury	(508)	14,027	13,506
01527	Sutton	(508)	5,855	4,590
01907	Swampscott	(617)	13,837	13,578
02777	Swansea	(508)	15,461	12,640
02780	Taunton	(508)	45,001	43,756

ZIP code	Place		1980	1970
01468	Templeton	(508)	6,070	5,863
01876	Tewksbury	(508)	24,635	22,755
01983	Topsfield	(508)	5,709	5,225
01469	Townsend	(508)	7,201	4,281
01376	Turners Falls(u)	(413)	NA	5,168
01879	Tyngsborough	(508)	5,683	4,204
01569	Uxbridge	(508)	8,374	8,253
01880	Wakefield	(617)	24,895	25,402
02081	Walpole	(508)	18,859	18,149
02154	Waltham	(617)	58,200	61,582
01082	Ware Center(u)	(413)	6,806	6,509
.....	Ware	(413)	8,953	8,187
02571	Wareham	(508)	18,457	11,492
02172	Watertown	(617)	34,384	39,307
01778	Wayland	(508)	12,170	13,461
01570	Webster Center(u)	(508)	11,175	12,432
.....	Webster	(508)	14,480	14,917
02181	Wellesley	(617)	27,209	28,051
01581	Westborough	(508)	13,619	12,594
01583	West Boylston	(508)	6,204	6,369
02379	West Bridgewater	(508)	6,359	6,070
01742	West Concord(u)	(617)	5,331	....
01085	Westfield	(413)	36,465	31,433
01886	Westford	(508)	13,434	10,368
01473	Westminster	(508)	5,139	4,273
02193	Weston	(617)	11,169	10,870
02790	Westport	(508)	13,763	9,791
01089	West Springfield	(413)	27,042	28,461
02090	Westwood	(617)	13,212	12,570
02188	Weymouth	(617)	55,601	54,610
01588	Whitinsville(u)	(508)	5,379	5,210
02382	Whitman	(617)	13,534	13,059
01095	Wilbraham	(413)	12,053	11,984
01267	Williamstown	(413)	8,741	8,454
01887	Wilmington	(508)	17,471	17,102
01475	Winchendon	(508)	7,019	6,635
01890	Winchester	(617)	20,701	22,269
02152	Winthrop	(617)	19,294	20,335
01801	Woburn	(617)	36,626	37,406
*01613	Worcester	(508)	161,799	176,572
02093	Wrentham	(508)	7,580	7,315
02675	Yarmouth	(508)	18,449	12,033

Michigan

ZIP code	Place		1980	1970
49221	Adrian	(517)	21,276	20,382
49224	Albion	(517)	11,059	12,112
48101	Allen Park	(313)	34,196	40,747
48801	Alma	(517)	9,652	9,611
49707	Alpena	(517)	12,214	13,805
*48106	Ann Arbor	(313)	107,969	100,035
48063	Avon(u)	(313)	40,779	....
*49016	Battle Creek	(616)	35,724	38,931
48706	Bay City	(517)	41,593	49,449
48505	Beecher(u)	(313)	17,178	....
48809	Belding	(616)	5,634	5,121
49022	Benton Harbor	(616)	14,707	16,481
49022	Benton Heights(u)	(616)	6,787	....
48072	Berkley	(313)	18,637	21,879
48009	Beverly Hills	(313)	11,598	13,598
49307	Big Rapids	(616)	14,361	11,995
*48012	Birmingham	(313)	21,689	26,170
48013	Bloomfield(u)	(313)	42,876	....
49107	Buchanan	(616)	5,142	4,645
*48502	Burton	(313)	29,976	32,540
49601	Cadillac	(616)	10,199	9,990
48724	Carrollton(u)	(517)	7,482	7,300
48015	Center Line	(313)	9,293	10,379
48813	Charlotte	(517)	8,251	8,244
49721	Cheboygan	(616)	5,106	5,553
48017	Clawson	(313)	15,103	17,617
48043	Clinton(u)	(313)	72,400	1,677
49036	Coldwater	(517)	9,461	9,155
49321	Comstock Park(u)	(616)	5,506	5,766
49508	Cutlerville(u)	(616)	8,256	6,267
48423	Davison	(313)	6,087	5,259
*48120	Dearborn	(313)	90,660	104,199
48127	Dearborn Heights	(313)	67,706	80,069
*48233	Detroit	(313)	1,203,368	1,514,063
49047	Dowagiac	(616)	6,307	6,583
48021	East Detroit	(313)	38,280	45,920
49506	East Grand Rapids	(616)	10,914	12,565
48823	East Lansing	(517)	48,309	47,540
49001	Eastwood(u)	(517)	7,186	9,682
48229	Ecorse	(313)	14,447	17,515
49829	Escanaba	(906)	14,355	15,368
49022	Fair Plain(u)	(616)	8,289	3,680
48024	Farmington	(313)	11,022	10,329
48024	Farmington Hills	(313)	58,056	48,694
48430	Fenton	(313)	8,098	8,284
48220	Ferndale	(313)	26,227	30,850
48134	Flat Rock	(313)	6,853	5,643
*48502	Flint	(313)	159,611	193,317
48433	Flushing	(313)	8,624	7,190
48026	Fraser	(313)	14,560	11,868
48135	Garden City	(313)	35,640	41,864
48439	Grand Blanc	(313)	6,848	5,132
49417	Grand Haven	(616)	11,763	11,844

ZIP code	Place		1980	1970
48837	Grand Ledge	(517)	6,920	6,032
*49501	Grand Rapids	(616)	181,843	197,649
49418	Grandville	(616)	12,412	10,764
48838	Greenville	(616)	8,019	7,493
48138	Grosse Ile(u)	(313)	9,320	8,306
48236	Grosse Pointe	(313)	5,901	6,637
48236	Grosse Pointe Farms	(313)	10,551	11,701
48236	Grosse Pointe Park	(313)	13,562	15,641
48236	Grosse Pointe Woods	(313)	18,886	21,878
48212	Hamtramck	(313)	21,300	26,783
49930	Hancock	(906)	5,122	4,820
48225	Harper Woods	(313)	16,361	20,186
48625	Harrison(u)	(517)	23,649	....
48840	Haslett(u)	(517)	7,025	....
49058	Hastings	(616)	6,418	6,501
48030	Hazel Park	(313)	20,914	23,784
48203	Highland Park	(313)	27,909	35,444
49242	Hillsdale	(517)	7,432	7,728
49423	Holland	(616)	26,281	26,479
48842	Holt(u)	(517)	10,097	6,980
49931	Houghton	(906)	7,512	6,067
48843	Howell	(517)	6,976	5,224
48070	Huntington Woods	(313)	6,937	8,536
48141	Inkster	(313)	35,190	38,595
48846	Ionia	(616)	5,920	6,361
49801	Iron Mountain	(906)	8,341	8,702
49938	Ironwood	(906)	7,741	8,711
49849	Ishpeming	(906)	7,538	8,245
*49201	Jackson	(517)	39,739	45,484
49428	Jenison(u)	(616)	16,330	11,266
*49001	Kalamazoo	(616)	79,722	85,555
49508	Kentwood	(616)	30,438	20,310
49801	Kingsford	(906)	5,290	5,276
49843	K.I. Sawyer(u)	(906)	7,345	8,224
49015	Lakeview(u)	(517)	13,345	11,391
48144	Lambertville(u)	(313)	6,341	5,711
*48924	Lansing	(517)	130,414	131,403
48446	Lapeer	(313)	6,225	6,914
48146	Lincoln Park	(313)	45,105	52,984
*48150	Livonia	(313)	104,814	110,109
49431	Ludington	(616)	8,937	9,021
48071	Madison Heights	(313)	35,375	38,599
49660	Manistee	(616)	7,665	7,723
49855	Marquette	(906)	23,288	21,967
49068	Marshall	(616)	7,201	7,253
48040	Marysville	(313)	7,345	5,610
48854	Mason	(517)	6,019	5,468
48122	Melvindale	(313)	12,322	13,862
49858	Menominee	(906)	10,099	10,748
49254	Michigan Center(u)	(517)	5,244	....
48640	Midland	(517)	37,269	35,176
48042	Milford	(313)	5,041	4,699
48161	Monroe	(313)	23,531	23,894
48043	Mount Clemens	(313)	18,991	20,476
48858	Mount Pleasant	(517)	23,746	20,524
*49440	Muskegon	(616)	40,823	44,631
49444	Muskegon Heights	(616)	14,611	17,304
49866	Negaunee	(906)	5,189	5,248
48047	New Baltimore	(313)	5,439	4,132
49120	Niles	(616)	13,115	12,988
.....	Northview(u)		11,662	....
48167	Northville	(313)	5,698	5,400
49441	Norton Shores	(616)	22,025	22,271
48050	Novi	(313)	22,525	9,668
48237	Oak Park	(313)	31,537	36,762
48864	Okemos(u)	(517)	8,882	7,770
48867	Owosso	(517)	16,455	17,179
49770	Petoskey	(616)	6,097	6,342
48170	Plymouth	(313)	9,986	11,758
*48053	Pontiac	(313)	76,715	85,279
49081	Portage	(616)	38,157	33,590
48060	Port Huron	(313)	33,981	35,794
48239	Redford(u)	(313)	58,441	....
48218	River Rouge	(313)	12,912	15,947
48192	Riverview	(313)	14,569	11,342
48063	Rochester	(313)	7,203	7,054
48174	Romulus	(313)	24,857	22,879
48066	Roseville	(313)	54,311	60,529
*48068	Royal Oak	(313)	70,893	86,238
48601	Saginaw	(517)	77,508	91,849
48083	St. Clair Shores	(313)	76,210	88,093
48879	St. Johns	(517)	7,376	6,672
49085	St. Joseph	(616)	9,622	11,042
48176	Saline	(313)	6,483	4,811
49783	Sault Ste. Marie	(906)	14,448	15,136
*48075	Southfield	(313)	75,568	69,285
48198	Southgate	(313)	32,058	33,909
49090	South Haven	(616)	5,943	6,471
48178	South Lyon	(313)	5,214	2,675
*49015	Springfield	(616)	5,458	3,994
*48078	Sterling Heights	(313)	108,999	61,365
49091	Sturgis	(616)	9,468	9,295
48473	Swartz Creek	(313)	5,013	4,928
48180	Taylor	(313)	77,568	70,020
49286	Tecumseh	(517)	7,320	7,120
49093	Three Rivers	(616)	7,015	7,355
49684	Traverse City	(616)	15,516	18,048
48183	Trenton	(313)	22,762	24,127
48084	Troy	(313)	67,102	39,419
48087	Utica	(313)	5,282	3,504
49504	Walker	(616)	15,088	11,492

ZIP code	Place		1980	1970
*48089	Warren	(313)	161,134	179,260
48095	Waterford(u)	(313)	64,250	----
48184	Wayne	(313)	21,159	21,054
48033	West Bloomfield(u)	(313)	41,962	----
48185	Westland	(313)	84,603	86,749
49007	Westwood(u)	(616)	8,519	9,143
48019	White Lake-Seven Harbors(u)	(313)	7,557	----
48096	Wixom	(313)	6,705	2,010
48183	Woodhaven	(313)	10,902	3,566
48753	Wurtsmith(u)	(517)	5,166	6,832
*48192	Wyandotte	(313)	34,006	41,061
49509	Wyoming	(616)	59,616	56,560
48197	Ypsilanti	(313)	24,031	29,538

Minnesota

ZIP code	Place		1980	1970
56007	Albert Lea	(507)	19,190	19,418
56308	Alexandria	(612)	7,608	6,973
55303	Andover	(612)	9,387	----
55303	Anoka	(612)	15,634	13,298
55124	Apple Valley	(612)	21,818	8,502
55112	Arden Hills	(612)	8,012	5,149
55912	Austin	(507)	23,020	26,210
56601	Bemidji	(218)	10,949	11,490
55433	Blaine	(612)	28,558	20,573
55420	Bloomington	(612)	81,831	81,970
56401	Brainerd	(218)	11,469	11,667
55429	Brooklyn Center	(612)	31,230	35,173
55429	Brooklyn Park	(612)	43,332	26,230
55337	Burnsville	(612)	35,674	19,940
55316	Champlin	(612)	9,006	2,275
55317	Chanhassen	(612)	6,359	4,879
55318	Chaska	(612)	8,346	4,352
55719	Chisholm	(218)	5,930	5,913
55720	Cloquet	(218)	11,142	8,699
55421	Columbia Heights	(612)	20,029	23,997
55433	Coon Rapids	(612)	35,826	30,505
55016	Cottage Grove	(612)	18,994	13,419
56716	Crookston	(218)	8,628	8,312
55428	Crystal	(612)	25,543	30,925
56501	Detroit Lakes	(218)	7,106	5,797
*55806	Duluth	(218)	92,811	100,578
55121	Eagan	(612)	20,532	10,398
55005	East Bethel	(612)	6,626	2,586
56721	East Grand Forks	(218)	8,537	7,607
*55343	Eden Prairie	(612)	16,263	6,938
55435	Edina	(612)	46,073	44,046
55330	Elk River	(612)	6,785	2,252
55734	Eveleth	(218)	5,042	4,721
56031	Fairmont	(507)	11,506	10,751
55113	Falcon Heights	(507)	5,291	5,530
55021	Faribault	(507)	16,241	16,595
56537	Fergus Falls	(218)	12,519	12,443
55432	Fridley	(612)	30,228	29,233
55416	Golden Valley	(612)	22,775	24,246
55744	Grand Rapids	(218)	7,934	7,247
*55303	Ham Lake	(612)	7,832	3,327
55033	Hastings	(612)	12,827	12,195
55811	Hermantown	(218)	6,759	----
55746	Hibbing	(218)	21,193	16,104
55343	Hopkins	(612)	15,336	13,428
55350	Hutchinson	(612)	9,244	8,031
56649	International Falls	(218)	5,611	6,439
55075	Inver Grove Heights	(612)	17,171	12,148
55042	Lake Elmo	(612)	5,296	3,565
55044	Lakeville	(612)	14,790	7,556
55355	Litchfield	(612)	5,904	5,262
55110	Little Canada	(612)	7,102	3,481
56345	Little Falls	(612)	7,250	7,467
56001	Mankato	(507)	28,646	30,895
55369	Maple Grove	(612)	20,525	6,275
55109	Maplewood	(612)	26,990	25,186
56258	Marshall	(507)	11,161	9,886
55118	Mendota Heights	(612)	7,288	6,565
*55401	Minneapolis	(612)	370,951	434,400
55343	Minnetonka	(612)	38,683	35,776
56265	Montevideo	(612)	5,845	5,661
56560	Moorhead	(218)	29,998	29,687
56267	Morris	(612)	5,367	5,366
55364	Mound	(612)	9,280	7,572
55112	Mounds View	(612)	12,593	10,599
55112	New Brighton	(612)	23,269	19,507
54428	New Hope	(612)	23,087	23,180
56073	New Ulm	(507)	13,755	13,051
55057	Northfield	(507)	12,562	10,235
56001	North Mankato	(507)	9,145	7,347
55109	North St. Paul	(612)	11,921	11,950
55119	Oakdale	(612)	12,123	7,795
55323	Orono	(612)	6,845	6,787
55060	Owatonna	(507)	18,632	15,341
55427	Plymouth	(612)	31,615	18,077
55372	Prior Lake	(612)	7,284	1,114
55303	Ramsey	(612)	10,093	----
55066	Red Wing	(612)	13,736	10,441
56283	Redwood Falls	(507)	5,210	4,774
55423	Richfield	(612)	37,851	47,231
55422	Robbinsdale	(612)	14,422	16,845
55901	Rochester	(507)	57,906	53,766

ZIP code	Place		1980	1970
55068	Rosemount	(612)	5,083	1,337
55113	Roseville	(612)	35,820	34,438
55418	St. Anthony	(612)	7,981	9,239
56301	St. Cloud	(612)	42,566	39,691
55426	St. Louis Park	(612)	42,931	48,883
*55101	St. Paul	(612)	270,230	309,866
56082	St. Peter	(507)	9,056	8,339
56379	Sauk Rapids	(612)	5,793	5,051
55379	Shakopee	(612)	9,941	6,876
55126	Shoreview	(612)	17,300	10,978
55075	South St. Paul	(612)	21,235	25,016
55432	Spring Lake Park	(612)	6,477	6,417
55082	Stillwater	(612)	12,290	10,191
56701	Thief River Falls	(218)	9,105	8,618
55110	Vadnais Heights	(612)	5,111	3,411
55792	Virginia	(218)	11,056	12,450
56093	Waseca	(507)	8,219	6,789
55118	West St. Paul	(612)	18,527	18,802
55110	White Bear Lake	(612)	22,538	23,313
56201	Willmar	(612)	15,895	12,869
55987	Winona	(507)	25,075	26,438
55119	Woodbury	(612)	10,297	6,184
56187	Worthington	(507)	10,243	9,916

Mississippi (601)

ZIP code	Place		1980	1970
39730	Aberdeen		7,184	6,507
38821	Amory		7,307	7,236
38606	Batesville		5,162	3,796
39520	Bay St. Louis		7,850	6,752
*39530	Biloxi		49,311	48,486
38829	Booneville		6,199	5,895
39042	Brandon		9,626	2,685
39601	Brookhaven		10,800	10,700
39046	Canton		11,116	10,503
38614	Clarksdale		21,137	21,673
38732	Cleveland		14,524	13,327
39056	Clinton		14,660	7,289
39429	Columbia		7,733	7,587
39701	Columbus		27,503	25,795
38834	Corinth		13,180	11,581
39532	D'Iberville(u)		13,369	7,268
39552	Escatawpa(u)		5,367	1,579
39074	Forest		5,229	4,085
39553	Gautier(u)		8,917	2,087
38701	Greenville		40,613	39,648
38930	Greenwood		20,115	22,400
38901	Grenada		11,508	9,944
39501	Gulfport		39,676	40,791
39401	Hattiesburg		40,829	38,277
38635	Holly Springs		7,285	5,728
38751	Indianola		8,050	8,947
*39205	Jackson		202,895	153,968
39090	Kosciusko		7,415	7,266
39440	Laurel		21,897	24,145
38756	Leland		6,667	6,000
39560	Long Beach		14,199	6,170
39339	Louisville		7,323	6,626
39648	McComb		12,331	11,851
39301	Meridian		46,577	45,083
39563	Moss Point		18,998	19,321
39120	Natchez		22,209	19,704
38652	New Albany		7,072	6,426
39501	North Gulfport(u)		6,660	6,996
39564	Ocean Springs		14,504	9,160
39567	Orange Grove(u)		13,476	----
38655	Oxford		9,882	8,519
39567	Pascagoula		29,318	27,264
39571	Pass Christian		5,014	2,979
39208	Pearl		18,602	9,623
39465	Petal		8,476	6,986
39350	Philadelphia		6,434	6,274
39466	Picayune		10,361	9,760
39157	Ridgeland		5,461	1,650
38668	Senatobia		5,013	4,247
38671	Southaven(u)		16,071	8,931
39759	Starkville		16,139	11,369
38801	Tupelo		23,905	20,471
39180	Vicksburg		25,434	25,478
39367	Waynesboro		5,349	4,368
39773	West Point		8,811	8,714
38967	Winona		6,177	5,521
39194	Yazoo City		12,092	11,688

Missouri

ZIP code	Place		1980	1970
63123	Affton(u)	(314)	23,181	24,264
63010	Arnold	(314)	19,141	17,381
66605	Aurora	(417)	6,437	5,359
63011	Ballwin	(314)	12,750	10,656
63137	Bellefontaine Neighbors	(314)	12,082	14,084
64012	Belton	(816)	12,708	12,270
63134	Berkeley	(314)	15,922	19,743
63031	Black Jack	(314)	5,293	4,145
64015	Blue Springs	(816)	25,936	6,779
65613	Bolivar	(417)	5,919	4,769
65233	Boonville	(816)	6,959	7,514
63114	Breckenridge Hills	(314)	5,666	7,011
63144	Brentwood	(314)	8,209	11,248
63044	Bridgeton	(314)	18,445	19,992

ZIP code	Place		1980	1970
64628	Brookfield	(816)	5,555	5,491
63701	Cape Girardeau	(314)	34,361	31,282
64836	Carthage	(417)	11,104	11,035
63830	Caruthersville	(314)	7,958	7,350
63834	Charleston	(314)	5,230	5,131
64601	Chillicothe	(816)	9,089	9,519
63105	Clayton	(314)	14,306	16,100
64735	Clinton	(816)	8,366	7,504
65201	Columbia	(314)	62,061	58,812
63128	Concord(u)	(314)	20,896	21,217
63126	Crestwood	(314)	12,815	15,123
63141	Creve Coeur	(314)	11,743	8,967
63136	Dellwood	(314)	6,200	7,137
63020	De Soto	(314)	5,993	5,984
63131	Des Peres	(314)	7,953	5,333
63841	Dexter	(314)	7,043	6,024
63011	Ellisville	(314)	6,233	4,681
64024	Excelsior Springs	(816)	10,424	9,411
63640	Farmington	(314)	8,270	6,590
63135	Ferguson	(314)	24,549	28,759
63028	Festus	(314)	7,574	7,530
*63033	Florissant	(314)	55,721	65,908
65473	Fort Leonard Wood(u)	(314)	21,262	33,799
65251	Fulton	(314)	11,046	12,248
64118	Gladstone	(816)	24,990	23,422
63122	Glendale	(314)	6,035	6,981
64030	Grandview	(816)	24,561	17,456
63401	Hannibal	(314)	18,811	18,609
64701	Harrisonville	(816)	6,372	5,052
*63042	Hazelwood	(314)	13,098	14,082
*64051	Independence	(816)	111,797	111,630
63755	Jackson	(314)	7,827	5,896
65101	Jefferson City	(314)	33,619	32,407
63136	Jennings	(314)	16,934	19,379
64801	Joplin	(417)	39,126	39,256
*64108	Kansas City	(816)	448,028	507,330
63857	Kennett	(314)	10,145	10,090
63501	Kirksville	(816)	17,167	15,560
63122	Kirkwood	(314)	27,739	31,679
63124	Ladue	(314)	9,369	10,306
65536	Lebanon	(417)	9,507	8,616
64063	Lee's Summit	(816)	28,741	16,230
63125	Lemay(u)	(314)	35,424	40,529
64067	Lexington	(816)	5,063	5,388
64068	Liberty	(816)	16,251	13,704
63552	Macon	(816)	5,680	5,301
63863	Malden	(314)	6,096	5,374
63011	Manchester	(314)	6,351	5,031
63143	Maplewood	(314)	10,960	12,785
65340	Marshall	(816)	12,781	12,051
63043	Maryland Heights(u)	(314)	5,676	8,805
64468	Maryville	(816)	9,558	9,970
65265	Mexico	(314)	12,276	11,807
65270	Moberly	(816)	13,418	12,988
65708	Monett	(417)	6,148	5,937
63026	Murphy(u)	(314)	8,121	....
64850	Neosho	(417)	9,493	7,517
64772	Nevada	(417)	9,044	9,736
63121	Normandy	(314)	5,174	6,236
63121	Northwoods	(314)	5,831	4,607
63366	O'Fallon	(314)	8,654	7,018
63132	Olivette	(314)	7,952	9,156
63114	Overland	(314)	19,620	24,819
63775	Perryville	(314)	7,343	5,149
63120	Pine Lawn	(314)	6,570	5,745
63901	Poplar Bluff	(314)	17,139	16,653
64133	Raytown	(816)	31,831	33,306
64085	Richmond	(816)	5,499	4,948
63117	Richmond Heights	(314)	11,516	13,802
63124	Rock Hill	(314)	5,702	6,815
65401	Rolla	(314)	13,303	13,571
63074	St. Ann	(314)	15,523	18,215
63301	St. Charles	(314)	37,379	31,834
63114	St. John	(314)	7,854	8,960
*64501	St. Joseph	(816)	76,691	72,748
*63155	St. Louis	(314)	452,801	622,236
63376	St. Peters	(314)	15,700	486
63126	Sappington(u)	(314)	11,388	10,603
65301	Sedalia	(816)	20,927	22,847
63119	Shrewsbury	(314)	5,077	5,896
63801	Sikeston	(314)	17,431	14,699
63138	Spanish Lake(u)	(314)	20,632	15,647
*65801	Springfield	(417)	133,116	120,096
63080	Sullivan	(314)	5,461	5,111
64683	Trenton	(816)	6,811	6,063
63084	Union	(314)	5,506	5,183
63130	University City	(314)	42,690	47,527
64093	Warrensburg	(816)	13,807	13,125
63090	Washington	(314)	9,251	8,499
64870	Webb City	(417)	7,309	6,923
63119	Webster Groves	(314)	23,097	27,457
65775	West Plains	(417)	7,741	6,893

Montana (406)

ZIP code	Place	1980	1970
59711	Anaconda-Deer Lodge County	12,518	9,771
*59101	Billings	66,813	61,581
59101	Billings Heights(u)	8,480	....
59715	Bozeman	21,645	18,670
59701	Butte-Silver Bow	37,205	23,368
59330	Glendive	5,978	6,305
*59401	Great Falls	56,884	60,091
59501	Havre	10,891	10,558
59601	Helena	23,938	22,730
59901	Kalispell	10,689	10,526
59044	Laurel	5,481	4,454
59457	Lewistown	7,104	6,437
59047	Livingston	6,994	6,883
59402	Malmstrom AFB(u)	6,675	8,374
59301	Miles City	9,602	9,023
59801	Missoula	33,351	29,497
59801	Missoula South(u)	5,557	4,886
59801	Orchard Homes(u)	10,837	....
59270	Sidney	5,726	4,543

Nebraska

ZIP code	Place		1980	1970
69301	Alliance	(308)	9,920	6,862
68310	Beatrice	(402)	12,891	12,389
68005	Bellevue	(402)	21,813	21,953
68008	Blair	(402)	6,418	6,106
69337	Chadron	(308)	5,933	5,921
68601	Columbus	(402)	17,328	15,471
68355	Falls City	(402)	5,374	5,444
68025	Fremont	(402)	23,979	22,962
69341	Gering	(308)	7,760	5,639
68801	Grand Island	(308)	33,180	32,358
68901	Hastings	(402)	23,045	23,580
68949	Holdrege	(308)	5,624	5,635
68847	Kearney	(308)	21,158	19,181
68128	La Vista	(402)	9,588	4,858
68850	Lexington	(308)	6,898	5,654
*68501	Lincoln	(402)	171,932	149,518
69001	McCook	(308)	8,404	8,285
68410	Nebraska City	(402)	7,127	7,441
68701	Norfolk	(402)	19,449	16,607
69101	North Platte	(308)	24,509	19,447
68113	Offutt AFB West(u)	(402)	8,787	8,445
69153	Ogallala	(308)	5,638	4,976
*68108	Omaha	(402)	313,939	346,929
68046	Papillion	(402)	6,399	5,606
68048	Plattsmouth	(402)	6,295	6,371
68127	Ralston	(402)	5,143	4,731
69361	Scottsbluff	(308)	14,156	14,507
68434	Seward	(402)	5,713	5,294
69162	Sidney	(308)	6,010	6,403
68776	South Sioux City	(402)	9,339	7,920
68787	Wayne	(402)	5,240	5,379
68467	York	(402)	7,723	6,778

Nevada (702)

ZIP code	Place	1980	1970
89005	Boulder City	9,590	5,223
89701	Carson City	32,022	15,468
89112	East Las Vegas(u)	6,449	6,501
89801	Elko	8,758	7,621
89015	Henderson	24,363	16,395
89450	Incline Village-Crystal Bay(u)	6,225	....
*89114	Las Vegas	164,674	125,787
89110	Nellis AFB(u)	6,205	6,449
89030	North Las Vegas	42,739	46,067
89109	Paradise(u)	84,818	24,477
*89501	Reno	100,756	72,863
89431	Sparks	40,780	24,187
89110	Sunrise Manor(u)	44,155	9,684
89431	Sun Valley(u)	8,822	2,414
89109	Vegas Creek(u)	NA	8,970
89101	Winchester(u)	19,728	13,981

New Hampshire (603)

See note on page 563

ZIP code	Place	1980	1970
03031	Amherst	8,243	4,605
03102	Bedford	9,481	5,859
03570	Berlin	13,084	15,256
03743	Claremont	14,557	14,221
03301	Concord	30,400	30,022
03818	Conway	7,158	4,865
03038	Derry Compact(u)	12,248	6,090
....	Derry	18,875	11,712
03820	Dover	22,377	20,850
03824	Durham Compact(u)	8,448	7,221
....	Durham	10,652	8,869
03833	Exeter Compact(u)	8,947	6,439
....	Exeter	11,024	8,892
03235	Franklin	7,901	7,292
03045	Goffstown	11,315	9,284
03842	Hampton Compact(u)	6,779	5,407
....	Hampton	10,493	8,011
03755	Hanover Compact(u)	6,861	6,147
....	Hanover	9,119	8,494
03106	Hooksett	7,303	5,564
03051	Hudson	14,022	10,638
03431	Keene	21,449	20,467
03246	Laconia	15,575	14,888
03766	Lebanon	11,134	9,725

ZIP code	Place		1980	1970
03561	Littleton		5,558	5,290
03053	Londonderry		13,598	5,346
*03101	Manchester		90,936	87,754
03054	Merrimack		15,406	8,595
03055	Milford		8,685	6,622
*03060	Nashua		67,865	55,820
03773	Newport		6,229	5,899
03076	Pelham		8,090	5,408
03865	Plaistow		5,609	4,712
03801	Portsmouth		26,254	25,717
03077	Raymond		5,453	3,003
03867	Rochester		21,560	17,938
03079	Salem		24,124	20,142
03874	Seabrook		5,917	3,053
03878	Somersworth		10,350	9,026
03087	Windham		5,664	3,008

New Jersey

ZIP code	Place		1980	1970
07747	Aberdeen(u)	(201)	17,235	---
08201	Absecon	(609)	6,859	6,094
07401	Allendale	(201)	5,901	6,240
07712	Asbury Park	(201)	17,015	16,533
*08401	Atlantic City	(609)	40,199	47,859
08106	Audubon	(609)	9,533	10,802
08007	Barrington	(609)	7,416	8,409
07002	Bayonne	(201)	65,047	72,743
08722	Beachwood	(201)	7,687	4,390
07109	Belleville	(201)	35,367	37,629
08031	Bellmawr	(609)	13,721	15,618
07719	Belmar	(201)	6,771	5,782
07621	Bergenfield	(201)	25,568	29,000
07922	Berkeley Hts. Twp.	(201)	12,549	13,078
08009	Berlin	(609)	5,786	4,997
07924	Bernardsville	(201)	6,715	6,652
08012	Blackwood(u)	(609)	5,219	---
07003	Bloomfield	(201)	47,792	52,029
07403	Bloomingdale	(201)	7,867	7,797
07603	Bogota	(201)	8,344	8,960
07005	Boonton	(201)	8,620	9,261
08805	Bound Brook	(201)	9,710	10,450
08723	Brick Twp	(201)	53,629	35,057
08302	Bridgeton	(609)	18,795	20,435
08203	Brigantine	(609)	8,318	6,741
08015	Browns Mills(u)	(609)	10,568	7,144
07828	Budd Lake	(201)	6,523	---
08016	Burlington	(609)	10,246	12,010
07405	Butler	(201)	7,616	7,051
07006	Caldwell	(201)	7,624	8,677
*08101	Camden	(609)	84,910	102,551
08701	Candlewood(u)	(201)	6,750	5,629
07072	Carlstadt	(201)	6,166	6,724
08069	Carney's Point	(609)	7,574	---
07008	Carteret	(201)	20,598	23,137
07009	Cedar Grove Twp	(201)	12,600	15,582
07928	Chatham	(201)	8,537	9,566
*08002	Cherry Hill Twp.	(609)	68,785	64,395
08077	Cinnaminson Twp.	(609)	16,072	16,962
07066	Clark Twp.	(201)	16,699	18,829
08312	Clayton	(609)	6,013	5,193
08021	Clementon	(609)	5,764	4,492
07010	Cliffside Park	(201)	21,464	18,891
07721	Cliffwood-Cliffwood Beach(u)	(201)	NA	1,953
*07015	Clifton	(201)	74,388	82,437
07624	Closter	(201)	8,164	8,604
08108	Collingswood	(609)	15,838	17,422
07016	Cranford Twp.	(201)	24,573	27,391
07626	Cresskill	(201)	7,609	8,298
	Crestwood Village	(201)	7,965	---
08075	Delran Twp.	(609)	14,811	10,065
07834	Denville Twp.	(201)	14,380	14,045
08096	Deptford Twp.	(609)	23,473	24,232
07801	Dover	(201)	14,681	15,039
07628	Dumont	(201)	18,334	20,155
08812	Dunellen	(201)	6,593	7,072
08816	East Brunswick Twp.	(201)	37,711	34,166
07936	East Hanover	(201)	9,319	---
*07019	East Orange	(201)	77,878	75,471
07073	East Rutherford	(201)	7,849	8,536
08520	East Windsor Twp.	(609)	21,041	11,736
07724	Eatontown	(201)	12,703	14,619
08010	Edgewater Park	(609)	9,273	---
08817	Edison Twp.	(201)	70,193	67,120
*07201	Elizabeth	(201)	106,201	112,654
07407	Elmwood Park	(201)	18,377	20,511
07630	Emerson	(201)	7,793	8,428
*07631	Englewood	(201)	23,701	24,985
07632	Englewood Cliffs	(201)	5,698	5,938
08053	Evesham Twp.	(609)	21,659	13,477
08618	Ewing Twp.	(609)	34,842	32,831
07006	Fairfield	(201)	7,987	6,731
07701	Fair Haven	(201)	5,679	6,142
07410	Fair Lawn	(201)	32,229	38,040
07022	Fairview	(201)	10,519	10,698
07023	Fanwood	(201)	7,767	8,920
08518	Florence-Roebling(u)	(609)	7,677	7,551
07932	Florham Park	(201)	9,359	9,373
08640	Fort Dix(u)	(609)	14,297	26,290
07024	Fort Lee	(201)	32,449	30,631
07417	Franklin Lakes	(201)	8,769	7,550
07728	Freehold	(201)	10,020	10,545
07026	Garfield	(201)	26,803	30,797
08753	Gilford Park	(201)	6,528	4,007
08028	Glassboro	(609)	14,574	12,938
08029	Glendora	(609)	5,632	---
07028	Glen Ridge	(201)	7,855	8,518
07452	Glen Rock	(201)	11,497	13,011
08030	Gloucester City	(609)	13,121	14,707
	Gordon's Corner	(201)	6,320	---
07093	Guttenberg	(201)	7,340	5,754
*07602	Hackensack	(201)	36,039	36,008
07840	Hackettstown	(201)	8,850	9,472
08108	Haddon Twp.	(609)	15,875	18,192
08033	Haddonfield	(609)	12,337	13,118
08035	Haddon Heights	(609)	8,361	9,365
07508	Haledon	(201)	6,607	6,767
08650	Hamilton Twp. (Mercer)	(609)	82,801	79,609
08037	Hammonton	(609)	12,298	11,464
07981	Hanover Twp.	(201)	11,846	10,700
07029	Harrison	(201)	12,242	11,811
07604	Hasbrouck Heights	(201)	12,166	13,651
07506	Hawthorne	(201)	18,200	19,173
07730	Hazlet Twp.	(201)	23,013	22,239
08904	Highland Park	(201)	13,396	14,385
07732	Highlands	(201)	5,187	3,916
07642	Hillsdale	(201)	10,495	11,768
07205	Hillside Twp.	(201)	21,440	21,636
07030	Hoboken	(201)	42,460	45,380
08753	Holiday City-Berkeley	(201)	9,019	---
07843	Hopatcong	(201)	15,531	9,052
08560	Hopewell Twp. (Mercer)	(609)	10,893	10,030
07111	Irvington	(201)	61,493	59,743
08527	Jackson Twp.	(201)	25,644	18,276
*07303	Jersey City	(201)	223,532	260,350
07734	Keansburg	(201)	10,613	9,720
07032	Kearny	(201)	35,735	37,585
08824	Kendall Park(u)	(201)	7,419	7,412
07033	Kenilworth	(201)	9,221	9,165
07735	Keyport	(201)	7,413	7,205
07405	Kinnelon	(201)	7,770	7,600
07034	Lake Hiawatha(u)	(201)	NA	11,389
07871	Lake Mohawk(u)	(201)	8,498	6,262
07054	Lake Parsippany(u)	(201)	NA	7,488
08701	Lakewood(u)	(201)	22,863	17,874
08879	Laurence Harbor(u)	(201)	6,737	6,715
07605	Leonia	(201)	8,027	8,847
07035	Lincoln Park	(201)	8,806	9,034
07036	Linden	(201)	37,836	41,409
08021	Lindenwold	(609)	18,196	12,199
07739	Linwood	(609)	6,144	6,159
07424	Little Falls Twp.	(201)	11,496	11,727
07643	Little Ferry	(201)	9,399	9,064
07739	Little Silver	(201)	5,548	6,010
07039	Livingston Twp.	(201)	28,040	30,127
07644	Lodi	(201)	23,956	25,163
07740	Long Branch	(201)	29,819	31,774
07071	Lyndhurst	(201)	20,326	22,729
07940	Madison	(201)	15,357	16,710
08859	Madison Park	(201)	7,447	---
07430	Mahwah Twp.	(201)	12,127	10,800
08736	Manasquan	(201)	5,354	4,971
08835	Manville	(201)	11,278	13,029
08052	Maple Shade Twp.	(609)	20,525	16,464
07040	Maplewood Twp.	(201)	22,950	24,932
08402	Margate City	(609)	9,179	10,576
07746	Marlboro Twp.	(201)	17,560	12,273
08053	Marlton(u)	(609)	9,411	10,180
07747	Matawan	(201)	8,837	9,136
07607	Maywood	(201)	9,895	11,087
08641	McGuire AFB(u)	(609)	7,853	10,933
08619	Mercerville-Hamilton Sq.(u)	(609)	25,446	24,465
08840	Metuchen	(201)	13,762	16,031
08846	Middlesex	(201)	13,480	15,038
07748	Middletown Twp.	(201)	61,615	54,623
07432	Midland park	(201)	7,381	8,159
07041	Milburn Twp.	(201)	19,543	21,089
08850	Milltown	(201)	7,136	6,470
08332	Millville	(609)	24,815	21,366
08094	Monroe Twp. (Gloucester)	(609)	21,639	14,071
*07042	Montclair	(201)	38,321	44,043
07645	Montvale	(201)	7,318	7,327
07045	Montville Twp.	(201)	14,290	11,846
08057	Moorestown-Lenola(u)	(609)	13,695	14,179
07950	Morris Plains	(201)	5,305	5,540
07960	Morristown	(201)	16,614	17,662
07092	Mountainside	(201)	7,118	7,520
08060	Mount Holly Twp.	(609)	10,818	12,713
07753	Neptune Twp.	(201)	28,366	27,863
07753	Neptune City	(201)	5,276	5,502
*07102	Newark	(201)	329,248	381,930
*08901	New Brunswick	(201)	41,442	41,885
08511	New Hanover	(201)	14,248	27,410
07646	New Milford	(201)	16,876	19,149
07974	New Providence	(201)	12,426	13,796
07860	Newton	(609)	7,748	7,297
07032	North Arlington	(201)	16,587	18,096
07047	North Bergen Twp.	(201)	47,019	47,751
08902	North Brunswick Twp.	(201)	22,220	16,691
07006	North Caldwell	(201)	5,832	6,733
08225	Northfield	(609)	7,795	8,646

ZIP code	Place		1980	1970
07508	North Haledon	(201)	8,177	7,614
07060	North Plainfield	(201)	19,108	21,796
07647	Northvale	(201)	5,046	5,177
07110	Nutley	(201)	28,998	31,913
07755	Oakhurst(u)	(201)	NA	5,558
07436	Oakland	(201)	13,443	14,420
08226	Ocean City	(609)	13,949	10,575
07757	Oceanport	(201)	5,888	7,503
08758	Ocean Twp	(609)	23,570	
08857	Old Bridge	(201)	21,815	25,176
08857	Old Bridge Twp	(201)	51,515	48,715
07649	Oradell	(201)	6,658	6,903
*07050	Orange	(201)	31,136	32,566
07650	Palisades Park	(201)	13,732	13,351
08065	Palmyra	(609)	7,085	6,969
07652	Paramus	(201)	26,474	28,381
07656	Park Ridge	(201)	8,515	8,709
07054	Parsippany-Troy Hills	(201)	49,868	
*07055	Passaic	(201)	52,463	55,124
*07510	Paterson	(201)	137,970	144,824
08066	Paulsboro	(609)	6,944	8,084
08110	Pennsauken Twp	(609)	33,775	36,394
08069	Penns Grove	(609)	5,760	5,727
08070	Pennsville Center(u)	(609)	12,467	11,014
07440	Pequannock Twp	(201)	13,776	14,350
08861	Perth Amboy	(201)	38,951	38,798
08865	Phillipsburg	(201)	16,647	17,849
08021	Pine Hill	(609)	8,684	5,132
08854	Piscataway Twp	(201)	42,223	36,418
08071	Pitman	(609)	9,744	10,257
*07061	Plainfield	(201)	45,555	46,862
08232	Pleasantville	(609)	13,435	14,007
08742	Point Pleasant	(201)	17,747	15,968
08742	Point Pleasant Beach	(201)	5,415	4,882
07442	Pompton Lakes	(201)	10,660	11,397
08540	Princeton	(609)	12,035	12,311
08540	Princeton North(u)	(609)	NA	5,488
07508	Prospect Park	(201)	5,142	5,176
*07065	Rahway	(201)	26,723	29,114
08057	Ramblewood(u)	(201)	6,475	5,556
07446	Ramsey	(201)	12,899	12,571
07869	Randolph Twp	(201)	17,828	13,296
08869	Raritan	(201)	6,128	6,691
07701	Red Bank	(201)	12,031	12,847
07657	Ridgefield	(201)	10,294	11,308
07660	Ridgefield Park	(201)	12,738	13,990
*07451	Ridgewood	(201)	25,208	27,547
07456	Ringwood	(201)	12,625	10,393
07661	River Edge	(201)	11,111	12,850
08075	Riverside Twp	(609)	7,941	8,591
07675	River Vale	(201)	9,489	
07726	Robertsville	(201)	8,461	
07662	Rochelle Park Twp	(201)	5,603	6,380
07866	Rockaway	(201)	6,852	6,383
07068	Roseland	(201)	5,330	4,453
07203	Roselle	(201)	20,641	22,585
07204	Roselle Park	(201)	13,377	14,277
07760	Rumson	(201)	7,623	7,421
08078	Runnemede	(609)	9,461	10,475
*07070	Rutherford	(201)	19,068	20,802
07662	Saddle Brook Twp	(201)	14,084	15,910
08079	Salem	(609)	6,959	7,648
08872	Sayreville	(201)	29,969	32,508
07076	Scotch Plains Twp	(201)	20,774	22,279
07094	Secaucus	(201)	13,719	13,228
08753	Silverton	(201)	7,236	
08083	Somerdale	(609)	5,900	6,510
08873	Somerset	(201)	21,731	
08244	Somers Point	(609)	10,330	7,919
08876	Somerville	(201)	11,973	13,652
08879	South Amboy	(201)	8,322	9,338
07079	South Orange Vill. Twp	(201)	15,864	
07080	South Plainfield	(201)	20,521	21,142
08882	South River	(201)	14,361	15,428
07871	Sparta Twp	(201)	13,333	10,819
08884	Spotswood	(201)	7,840	7,891
07081	Springfield Twp	(201)	13,955	15,740
07762	Spring Lake Heights	(201)	5,424	4,602
08084	Stratford	(609)	8,005	9,801
07747	Strathmore(u)	(201)	NA	7,674
07876	Succasunna-Kenvil	(201)	10,931	
07901	Summit	(201)	21,071	23,620
07666	Teaneck Twp	(201)	39,007	42,355
07670	Tenafly	(201)	13,552	14,827
07724	Tinton Falls	(201)	7,740	8,395
*08753	Toms River(u)	(201)	7,465	7,303
07512	Totowa	(201)	11,448	11,580
*08608	Trenton	(609)	92,124	104,786
08520	Twin Rivers	(609)	7,742	
07083	Union Twp	(201)	50,184	53,077
07735	Union Beach	(201)	6,354	6,472
07087	Union City	(201)	55,593	57,305
07458	Upper Saddle River	(201)	7,958	7,949
08406	Ventnor City	(609)	11,704	10,385
07044	Verona	(201)	14,166	15,067
08251	Villas	(609)	5,909	3,155
08360	Vineland	(609)	53,753	47,399
07463	Waldwick	(201)	10,802	12,313
07057	Wallington	(201)	10,741	10,284

ZIP code	Place		1980	1970
07465	Wanaque	(201)	10,025	8,636
07882	Washington	(201)	6,429	5,943
07675	Washington Twp. (Bergen)	(201)	9,550	10,577
07060	Watchung	(201)	5,290	4,750
07470	Wayne Twp	(201)	46,474	49,141
07087	Weehawken Twp	(201)	13,168	13,383
07006	West Caldwell	(201)	11,407	11,913
07701	Westfield	(201)	30,447	33,720
07728	West Freehold	(201)	9,929	
07764	West Long Branch	(201)	7,380	6,845
07480	West Milford Twp	(201)	22,750	17,304
07093	West New York	(201)	39,194	40,627
07052	West Orange	(201)	39,510	43,715
07424	West Paterson	(201)	11,293	11,692
07675	Westwood	(201)	10,714	11,105
07885	Wharton	(201)	5,485	5,535
08610	White Horse	(609)	10,098	
07886	White Meadow Lake(u)	(201)	8,429	8,499
08094	Williamstown	(609)	5,768	4,075
08046	Willingboro Twp	(609)	39,912	43,386
08095	Winslow Twp	(609)	20,034	11,202
07095	Woodbridge Twp	(201)	90,074	98,944
08096	Woodbury	(609)	10,353	12,408
07675	Woodcliff Lake	(201)	5,644	5,506
07075	Wood-Ridge	(201)	7,929	8,311
07481	Wyckoff Twp	(201)	15,500	16,039
08620	Yardville-Groveville	(609)	9,414	
.....	Yorketown	(201)	5,330	

New Mexico (505)

ZIP code	Place	1980	1970
88310	Alamogordo	24,024	23,035
*87101	Albuquerque	332,920	244,501
88210	Artesia	10,385	10,315
87410	Aztec	5,512	3,354
87002	Belen	5,617	4,823
88101	Cannon(u)	NA	5,461
88220	Carlsbad	25,496	21,297
88101	Clovis	31,194	28,495
88030	Deming	9,964	8,343
87532	Espanola	6,803	4,528
87401	Farmington	30,729	21,979
87301	Gallup	18,167	14,596
87020	Grants	11,451	8,768
88240	Hobbs	28,794	26,025
88330	Holloman AFB(u)	7,245	8,001
88001	Las Cruces	45,086	37,857
87701	Las Vegas	14,322	7,528
87544	Los Alamos(u)	11,039	11,310
88260	Lovington	9,727	8,915
87107	North Valley(u)	13,006	10,366
87114	Paradise Hills	5,096	
88130	Portales	9,940	10,554
87740	Raton	8,225	6,962
87124	Rio Rancho Estates	9,985	
88201	Roswell	39,676	33,908
87115	Sandia(u)	5,288	6,867
87501	Santa Fe	49,160	41,167
87420	Shiprock	7,237	
88061	Silver City	9,887	8,557
87801	Socorro	7,576	5,849
87105	South Valley(u)	38,916	29,389
87901	Truth or Consequences	5,219	4,656
88401	Tucumcari	6,765	7,189
87544	White Rock	6,560	3,861
87327	Zuni Pueblo	5,551	3,958

New York

ZIP code	Place		1980	1970
*12207	Albany	(518)	101,727	115,781
11507	Albertson(u)	(516)	5,561	6,825
11701	Amityville	(516)	9,076	9,794
12010	Amsterdam	(518)	21,872	25,524
12603	Arlington(u)	(914)	11,305	11,203
13021	Auburn	(315)	32,548	34,599
*11702	Babylon	(516)	12,388	12,897
11510	Baldwin(u)	(516)	31,630	34,525
13027	Baldwinsville	(315)	6,446	6,298
14020	Batavia	(716)	16,703	17,338
14810	Bath	(607)	6,042	6,053
13088	Bayberry-Lynelle Meadows(u)	(315)	14,813	
11705	Bayport(u)	(516)	9,282	8,232
11706	Bay Shore(u)	(516)	10,784	11,119
11709	Bayville	(516)	7,034	6,147
12508	Beacon	(914)	12,937	13,255
11710	Bellmore(u)	(516)	18,106	18,431
11714	Bethpage(u)	(516)	16,840	18,555
*13902	Binghamton	(607)	55,860	64,123
10913	Blauvelt(u)	(914)	NA	5,426
11716	Bohemia(u)	(516)	9,308	8,926
11717	Brentwood(u)	(516)	44,321	28,327
10510	Briarcliff Manor	(914)	7,115	6,521
14610	Brighton (u)	(716)	35,776	
14420	Brockport	(716)	9,776	7,878
10708	Bronxville	(914)	6,267	6,674
*14240	Buffalo	(716)	357,870	462,768
14424	Canandaigua	(716)	10,419	10,488

ZIP code	Place		1980	1970
13617	Canton	(315)	7,055	6,398
11514	Carle Place(u)	(516)	5,470	6,326
11516	Cedarhurst	(516)	6,162	6,941
11720	Centereach(u)	(516)	30,136	9,427
11934	Center Moriches(u)	(516)	5,703	3,802
11721	Centerport(u)	(516)	6,576	----
11722	Central Islip(u)	(516)	19,734	36,391
14225	Cheektowaga(u)	(716)	92,145	----
12065	Clifton Park	(518)	23,989	14,867
12043	Cobleskill	(518)	5,272	4,368
12047	Cohoes	(518)	18,144	18,653
11724	Cold Spring Harbor(u)	(516)	5,336	5,509
12205	Colonie	(518)	8,869	8,701
11725	Commack(u)	(516)	34,719	24,138
10920	Congers(u).	(914)	7,123	5,928
11726	Copiague(u)	(516)	20,132	19,632
11727	Coram(u)	(516)	24,752	----
14830	Corning	(607)	12,953	15,792
13045	Cortland	(607)	20,138	19,621
10520	Croton-on-Hudson	(914)	6,889	7,523
11729	Deer Park(u)	(516)	30,394	32,274
12054	Delmar(u)	(518)	8,423	----
14043	Depew	(716)	19,819	22,158
13214	DeWitt(u)	(315)	9,024	10,032
11746	Dix Hills(u)	(516)	26,693	10,050
10522	Dobbs Ferry	(914)	10,053	10,353
14048	Dunkirk	(716)	15,310	16,855
14052	East Aurora	(716)	6,803	7,033
10709	Eastchester(u).	(914)	20,305	23,750
11735	East Farmingdale(u)	(516)	5,522	----
12302	East Glenville(u).	(518)	6,537	5,898
11746	East Half Hollow Hills(u)	(516)	NA	9,691
11576	East Hills.	(516)	7,160	8,624
11730	East Islip(u)	(516)	13,852	6,861
11758	East Massapequa(u).	(516)	13,987	15,926
11554	East Meadow(u).	(516)	39,317	46,290
11743	East Neck(u)	(516)	NA	5,221
11731	East Northport(u)	(516)	20,187	12,392
11772	East Patchogue(u)	(516)	18,139	8,082
14445	East Rochester	(716)	7,596	8,347
11518	East Rockaway	(516)	10,917	11,795
13902	East Vestal(u)	(607)	NA	10,472
*14901	Elmira	(607)	35,327	39,945
11003	Elmont(u)	(516)	27,592	29,363
11731	Elwood(u)	(516)	11,847	15,031
13760	Endicott	(607)	14,457	16,556
13760	Endwell(u)	(607)	13,745	15,999
13219	Fairmount(u)	(315)	13,415	15,317
14450	Fairport.	(716)	5,970	6,474
12601	Fairview(u)	(914)	5,852	8,517
11735	Farmingdale	(516)	7,946	9,297
11738	Farmingville(u)	(516)	13,398	----
*11001	Floral Park	(516)	16,805	18,466
11768	Fort Salonga(u)	(516)	9,550	----
11010	Franklin Square(u)	(516)	29,051	32,156
14063	Fredonia	(716)	11,126	10,326
11520	Freeport	(516)	38,272	40,374
13069	Fulton	(315)	13,312	14,003
11530	Garden City	(516)	22,927	25,373
11040	Garden City Park(u)	(516)	7,712	7,488
14624	Gates-North Gates(u)	(716)	15,244	----
14454	Geneseo	(716)	6,746	5,714
14456	Geneva	(315)	15,133	16,793
11542	Glen Cove	(516)	24,618	25,770
12801	Glens Falls.	(518)	15,897	17,222
12801	Glens Falls North(u)	(518)	6,956	NA
12078	Gloversville	(518)	17,836	19,677
*11022	Great Neck	(516)	9,168	10,798
11020	Great Neck Plaza	(516)	5,604	6,043
14616	Greece(u)	(716)	16,177	----
11740	Greenlawn(u)	(516)	13,869	8,493
12083	Greenville(u)	(518)	8,706	----
11746	Half Hollow Hills(u)	(516)	NA	12,081
14075	Hamburg.	(716)	10,582	10,215
11946	Hampton Bays(u)	(516)	7,256	1,862
14221	Harris Hill(u)	(716)	5,087	----
10528	Harrison	(914)	23,046	21,544
10530	Hartsdale(u)	(914)	10,216	12,226
10706	Hastings-on-Hudson	(914)	8,573	9,479
11787	Hauppauge(u)	(516)	20,960	13,957
10927	Haverstraw	(914)	8,300	8,198
10532	Hawthorne(u)	(914)	5,010	----
*11551	Hempstead	(516)	40,404	39,411
13350	Herkimer.	(315)	8,383	8,960
11040	Herricks(u).	(516)	8,123	9,112
11557	Hewlett(u)	(516)	6,986	6,796
*11802	Hicksville(u)	(516)	43,245	49,820
10977	Hillcrest(u)	(914)	5,733	5,357
11741	Holbrook(u)	(516)	24,382	----
11742	Holtsville(u)	(516)	13,515	----
14843	Hornell	(607)	10,234	12,144
14845	Horseheads	(607)	7,348	7,989
12534	Hudson.	(518)	7,986	8,940
12839	Hudson Falls	(518)	7,419	7,917
11743	Huntington	(516)	21,727	12,601
11746	Huntington Station(u)	(516)	28,769	28,817
13357	Ilion	(315)	9,450	9,808
11696	Inwood(u)	(516)	8,228	8,433
14617	Irondequoit(u)	(716)	57,648	----

ZIP code	Place		1980	1970
10533	Irvington	(914)	5,774	5,878
11751	Islip(u)	(516)	13,438	7,692
11752	Islip Terrace(u)	(516)	5,588	----
14850	Ithaca	(607)	28,732	26,226
14701	Jamestown	(716)	35,775	39,795
10535	Jefferson Valley-Yorktown(u)	(914)	13,380	9,008
11753	Jericho(u)	(516)	12,739	14,010
13790	Johnson City.	(607)	17,126	18,025
12095	Johnstown	(518)	9,360	10,045
14217	Kenmore.	(716)	18,474	20,980
11754	Kings Park(u)	(516)	16,131	5,555
11024	Kings Point.	(516)	5,234	5,614
12401	Kingston	(914)	24,481	25,544
14218	Lackawanna.	(716)	22,701	28,657
10512	Lake Carmel(u)	(914)	7,295	4,796
11755	Lake Grove	(516)	9,692	8,133
11779	Lake Ronkonkoma(u)	(516)	38,336	7,284
11552	Lakeview(u)	(516)	5,276	5,471
14086	Lancaster	(716)	13,056	13,365
10538	Larchmont	(914)	6,308	7,603
12110	Latham(u)	(518)	11,182	9,661
11559	Lawrence	(516)	6,175	6,566
11756	Levittown(u)	(516)	57,045	65,440
11757	Lindenhurst	(516)	26,919	28,359
13365	Little Falls	(315)	6,156	7,629
14094	Lockport.	(716)	24,844	25,399
11791	Locust Grove(u)	(516)	9,670	11,626
11561	Long Beach	(516)	34,073	33,127
12211	Loudonville(u)	(518)	11,480	9,299
11563	Lynbrook.	(516)	20,424	23,151
13208	Lyncourt(u)	(315)	5,129	----
10541	Mahopac(u)	(914)	7,681	5,265
12953	Malone	(518)	7,668	8,048
11565	Malverne	(516)	9,262	10,036
10543	Mamaroneck	(914)	17,616	18,909
11030	Manhasset(u)	(516)	8,485	8,541
13104	Manlius.	(315)	5,241	4,295
11050	Manorhaven	(516)	5,384	5,488
11758	Massapequa(u)	(516)	24,454	26,821
11762	Massapequa Park	(516)	19,779	22,112
13662	Massena.	(315)	12,851	14,042
11950	Mastic(u)	(516)	10,413	----
11951	Mastic Beach(u)	(516)	8,318	4,870
13211	Mattydale(u)	(315)	7,511	8,292
12118	Mechanicville	(518)	5,500	6,247
11763	Medford(u)	(516)	20,418	----
14103	Medina	(716)	6,392	6,415
11746	Melville(u)	(516)	8,139	6,641
11566	Merrick(u)	(516)	24,478	25,904
11953	Middle Island(u)	(516)	5,703	----
10940	Middletown	(914)	21,454	22,607
11764	Miller Place(u)	(516)	7,877	----
11501	Mineola.	(516)	20,757	21,845
10950	Monroe.	(914)	5,996	4,439
10952	Monsey(u)	(914)	12,380	8,797
12701	Monticello	(914)	6,306	5,991
10549	Mt. Kisco.	(914)	8,025	8,172
11766	Mount Sinai(u).	(516)	6,591	----
*10551	Mount Vernon	(914)	66,713	72,768
12590	Myers Corner(u)	(914)	5,180	2,826
10954	Nanuet(u)	(914)	12,578	10,447
11767	Nesconset(u)	(516)	10,706	10,048
14513	Newark.	(315)	10,017	11,644
12550	Newburgh	(914)	23,438	26,219
11590	New Cassel(u)	(516)	9,635	8,721
10956	New City(u)	(914)	35,859	27,344
11040	New Hyde Park	(516)	9,801	10,116
*10802	New Rochelle	(914)	70,794	75,385
*12550	New Windsor Center(u)	(914)	7,812	8,803
*10001	New York	(212)	7,071,639	7,895,563
*10451	Bronx	(212)	1,168,972	1,471,701
*11201	Brooklyn	(718)	2,230,936	2,602,102
*10001	Manhattan	(212)	1,428,285	1,539,233
*(Q)	Queens	(718)	1,891,325	1,987,174

(Q) There are 4 P.O.s for Queens: 11101 for L.I. City; 11690 Far Rocka-way; 11351 Flushing; and 11431 Jamaica.

ZIP code	Place		1980	1970
*10314	Staten Island	(718)	352,121	295,443
14301	Niagara(u)	(716)	9,648	----
*14302	Niagara Falls	(716)	71,384	85,615
12309	Niskayuna(u)	(518)	5,223	6,186
11701	North Amityville(u)	(516)	13,140	10,916
11703	North Babylon(u)	(516)	19,019	39,526
11706	North Bay Shore(u)	(516)	35,020	----
11710	North Bellmore(u)	(516)	20,630	22,893
11713	North Bellport(u)	(516)	7,432	5,903
11752	North Great River(u)	(516)	11,416	12,080
11757	North Lindenhurst(u)	(516)	11,511	11,117
11758	North Massapequa(u)	(516)	21,385	23,123
11566	North Merrick(u)	(516)	12,848	13,650
11040	North New Hyde Park(u)	(516)	15,114	18,154
11772	North Patchogue(u)	(516)	7,126	5,232
11768	Northport.	(516)	7,651	7,494
13212	North Syracuse	(315)	7,970	8,687
10591	North Tarrytown(u)	(914)	7,994	8,334
14120	North Tonawanda	(716)	35,760	36,012
11580	North Valley Stream(u)	(516)	14,530	14,881
11793	North Wantagh(u)	(516)	12,677	15,053
13815	Norwich	(607)	8,082	8,843
10960	Nyack	(914)	6,428	6,659
11769	Oakdale(u)	(516)	8,090	7,334

ZIP code	Census Division	1980	1970
11572	Oceanside(u) (516)	33,639	35,372
13669	Ogdensburg (315)	12,375	14,554
11804	Old Bethpage(u) (516)	6,215	7,084
14760	Olean (716)	18,207	19,169
13421	Oneida (315)	10,810	11,658
13820	Oneonta (607)	14,933	16,030
12550	Orange Lake(u) (914)	5,120	4,348
10562	Ossining (914)	20,196	21,659
13126	Oswego (315)	19,793	20,913
11771	Oyster Bay(u) (516)	6,497	6,822
11772	Patchogue (516)	11,291	11,582
10965	Pearl River(u) (914)	15,893	17,146
10566	Peekskill (914)	18,236	19,283
10803	Pelham (914)	6,848	2,076
10803	Pelham Manor (914)	6,130	6,673
14527	Penn Yan (315)	5,242	5,293
13212	Pitcher Hill (315)	6,063	
11714	Plainedge(u) (516)	9,629	10,759
11803	Plainview(u) (516)	28,037	31,695
12901	Plattsburgh (518)	21,057	18,715
12903	Plattsburgh AFB(u) (518)	5,905	7,078
10570	Pleasantville (914)	6,749	7,110
10573	Port Chester (914)	23,565	25,803
11777	Port Jefferson (516)	6,731	5,515
11776	Port Jefferson Station(u) (516)	17,009	7,403
12771	Port Jervis (914)	8,699	8,852
11050	Port Washington(u) (516)	14,521	15,923
13676	Potsdam (315)	10,635	10,303
*12601	Poughkeepsie (914)	29,757	32,029
12603	Red Oaks Mill(u) (914)	5,236	3,919
12144	Rensselaer (518)	9,047	10,136
11961	Ridge(u) (516)	8,977	
11901	Riverhead(u) (516)	6,339	7,585
11901	Riverside-Flanders(u) (516)	5,400	
*14603	Rochester (716)	241,741	295,011
*11570	Rockville Centre (516)	25,412	27,444
11778	Rocky Point(u) (516)	7,012	
12205	Roessleville(u) (518)	11,685	5,476
13440	Rome (315)	43,826	50,148
11575	Roosevelt(u) (516)	14,109	15,008
11577	Roslyn Heights(u) (516)	6,546	7,242
12303	Rotterdam(u) (518)	22,933	25,214
10580	Rye (914)	15,083	15,869
11780	St. James(u) (516)	12,122	10,500
14779	Salamanca (716)	6,890	7,877
12983	Saranac Lake (518)	5,578	6,086
12866	Saratoga Springs (518)	23,906	18,845
11782	Sayville(u) (516)	12,013	11,680
10583	Scarsdale (914)	17,650	19,229
*12301	Schenectady (518)	67,972	77,958
10940	Scotchtown(u) (914)	7,352	2,119
12302	Scotia (518)	7,280	7,370
11579	Sea Cliff (516)	5,364	5,890
11783	Seaford(u) (516)	16,117	17,379
11784	Selden(u) (516)	17,259	11,613
13148	Seneca Falls (315)	7,466	7,794
11733	Setauket-East Setauket(u) (516)	10,176	6,857
11967	Shirley(u) (516)	18,072	6,280
11787	Smithtown(u) (516)	30,906	
13209	Solvay (315)	7,140	8,280
11789	South Beach(u) (516)	8,071	
11735	South Farmingdale(u) (516)	16,439	20,464
14850	South Hill(u) (607)	5,276	
11746	South Huntington(u) (516)	14,854	9,115
14904	Southport(u) (607)	8,329	8,685
11581	South Valley Stream(u) (516)	5,462	6,595
11590	South Westbury(u) (516)	9,732	10,978
10977	Spring Valley (914)	20,537	18,112
11790	Stony Brook(u) (516)	16,155	6,391
10980	Stony Point(u) (914)	8,686	8,270
10901	Suffern(u) (914)	10,794	8,273
11791	Syosset(u) (516)	9,818	10,084
*13201	Syracuse (315)	170,105	197,297
10983	Tappan(u) (914)	8,267	7,424
10591	Tarrytown (914)	10,648	11,115
10594	Thornwood(u) (914)	7,197	6,874
14150	Tonawanda (716)	18,693	21,898
*12180	Troy (518)	56,638	62,918
10707	Tuckahoe (914)	6,076	6,236
11553	Uniondale(u) (516)	20,016	22,077
*13503	Utica (315)	75,632	91,373
10989	Valley Cottage(u) (914)	8,214	6,007
*11580	Valley Stream (516)	35,769	40,413
13850	Vestal (607)	27,238	26,909
10901	Viola(u) (914)	5,340	5,136
12586	Walden (914)	5,659	5,277
11793	Wantagh(u) (516)	19,817	21,783
12590	Wappingers Falls (914)	5,110	5,607
13165	Waterloo (315)	5,303	5,418
13601	Watertown (315)	27,861	30,787
12189	Watervliet (518)	11,354	12,404
14580	Webster (716)	5,499	5,037
14895	Wellsville (716)	5,769	5,815
11758	West Amityville(u) (516)	6,623	6,424
11704	West Babylon(u) (516)	41,699	12,893
11706	West Bay Shore(u) (516)	5,118	
11590	Westbury (516)	13,871	15,362
14905	West Elmira(u) (607)	5,485	5,901
12801	West Glens Falls(u) (518)	5,331	3,363
10993	West Haverstraw (914)	9,181	8,558
11552	West Hempstead(u) (516)	18,536	20,375
11743	West Hills(u) (516)	6,071	
11795	West Islip(u) (516)	29,533	17,374
12203	Westmere(u) (518)	6,881	6,364
10994	West Nyack(u) (914)	8,553	5,510
10996	West Point(u) (914)	8,105	
11796	West Sayville(u) (516)	8,185	7,386
14224	West Seneca(u) (716)	51,210	
13219	Westvale(u) (315)	6,169	7,253
*10602	White Plains (914)	46,999	50,346
14221	Williamsville (716)	6,017	6,878
11596	Williston Park (516)	8,216	9,154
11797	Woodbury(u) (516)	7,043	
11598	Woodmere(u) (516)	17,205	19,831
11798	Wyandach(u) (516)	13,215	15,716
*10701	Yonkers (914)	195,351	204,297
10598	Yorktown Heights(u) (914)	7,696	6,805

North Carolina

ZIP code	Census Division	1980	1970
28001	Albemarle (704)	15,110	11,126
27263	Archdale (919)	5,326	4,874
27203	Asheboro (919)	15,252	10,797
*28801	Asheville (704)	54,022	57,820
28303	Bonnie Doone(u) (919)	5,950	
28607	Boone (704)	10,191	8,754
28712	Brevard (704)	5,323	5,243
27215	Burlington (919)	37,266	35,930
28542	Camp Le Jeune(u) (919)	30,764	34,549
27510	Carrboro (919)	7,517	5,058
27511	Cary (919)	21,612	7,640
27514	Chapel Hill (919)	32,421	26,199
*28202	Charlotte (704)	315,474	241,420
27012	Clemmons(u) (919)	7,401	
28328	Clinton (919)	7,552	7,157
28025	Concord (704)	16,942	18,464
28334	Dunn (919)	8,962	8,302
*27701	Durham (919)	101,149	95,438
28379	East Rockingham(u) (919)	5,190	2,858
27288	Eden (919)	15,672	15,871
27932	Edenton (919)	5,264	4,956
27909	Elizabeth City (919)	13,784	14,381
28728	Enka(u) (704)	5,567	
*28302	Fayetteville (919)	59,507	53,510
28043	Forest City (704)	7,688	7,179
28307	Fort Bragg(u) (919)	37,834	46,995
27529	Garner (919)	9,556	4,923
28052	Gastonia (704)	47,218	47,322
27530	Goldsboro (919)	31,871	26,960
27253	Graham (919)	8,415	8,172
*27420	Greensboro (919)	155,642	144,076
27834	Greenville (919)	35,740	29,063
28532	Havelock (919)	17,718	3,012
27536	Henderson (919)	13,522	13,896
28739	Hendersonville (704)	6,862	6,443
28601	Hickory (704)	20,757	20,569
*27260	High Point (919)	63,479	63,229
28348	Hope Mills (919)	5,412	1,866
28540	Jacksonville (919)	18,237	16,289
28081	Kannapolis(u) (704)	34,564	36,293
27284	Kernersville (919)	5,875	4,815
27021	King(u) (919)	8,757	1,033
	Kings Grant(u) (919)	6,652	
28086	Kings Mountain (704)	9,080	8,465
28501	Kinston (919)	25,234	23,020
28352	Laurinburg (919)	11,480	8,859
28645	Lenoir (704)	13,748	14,705
27292	Lexington (704)	15,711	17,205
28358	Lumberton (919)	18,340	16,961
28212	Mint Hill (704)	9,830	
28110	Monroe (704)	12,639	11,282
28115	Mooresville (704)	8,575	8,808
28655	Morganton (704)	13,763	13,625
27030	Mount Airy (919)	6,862	7,325
28560	New Bern (919)	14,557	14,660
27604	New Hope (Wake)(u) (919)	6,768	
	New Hope (Wayne)(u) (919)	6,685	
	New River Station(u) (919)	5,401	
28658	Newton (704)	7,624	7,857
28012	North Belmont(u) (704)	10,762	10,672
27565	Oxford (919)	7,709	7,178
	Piney Green-White Oak(u) (919)	6,058	
*27611	Raleigh (919)	149,771	122,830
27320	Reidsville (919)	12,492	13,636
27870	Roanoke Rapids (919)	14,702	13,508
28379	Rockingham (704)	8,300	5,852
27801	Rocky Mount (919)	41,526	34,284
27573	Roxboro (919)	7,532	5,370
28601	St. Stephens(u) (704)	10,797	
28144	Salisbury (704)	22,677	22,515
27330	Sanford (919)	14,773	11,716
28150	Shelby (704)	15,310	16,328
27577	Smithfield (919)	7,288	6,677
28387	Southern Pines (919)	8,620	5,937
28390	Spring Lake (919)	6,273	3,968
27045	Stanleyville(u) (704)	5,039	2,362
28677	Statesville (704)	18,622	20,007
28778	Swannanoa(u) (704)	5,586	1,966
27886	Tarboro (919)	8,741	9,425
27360	Thomasville (919)	14,144	15,230

ZIP code	Place		1980	1970
27370	Trinity(u)	(919)	6,726	....
27889	Washington	(919)	8,418	8,961
28786	Waynesville	(704)	6,765	6,488
28025	West Concord(u)	(704)	5,859	5,347
28472	Whiteville	(919)	5,565	4,195
27892	Williamston	(919)	6,159	6,570
28401	Wilmington	(919)	44,000	46,169
27893	Wilson	(919)	34,424	29,347
*27102	Winston-Salem	(919)	131,885	133,683

North Dakota (701)

ZIP code	Place		1980	1970
58501	Bismarck		44,485	34,703
58301	Devils Lake		7,442	7,078
58601	Dickinson		15,924	12,405
58102	Fargo		61,308	53,365
58237	Grafton		5,293	5,946
58201	Grand Forks		43,765	39,008
58201	Grand Forks AFB(u)		9,390	10,474
58401	Jamestown		16,280	15,385
58554	Mandan		15,513	11,093
58701	Minot		32,843	32,290
58701	Minot AFB(u)		9,880	12,077
58072	Valley City		7,774	7,843
58075	Wahpeton		9,064	7,076
58078	West Fargo		10,099	5,161
58801	Williston		13,336	11,280

Ohio

ZIP code	Place		1980	1970
45810	Ada	(419)	5,669	5,309
*44309	Akron	(216)	237,177	275,425
44601	Alliance	(216)	24,315	26,547
44001	Amherst	(216)	10,638	9,902
44805	Ashland	(419)	20,326	19,872
44004	Ashtabula	(216)	23,449	24,313
45701	Athens	(614)	19,743	24,168
44202	Aurora	(216)	8,177	6,549
44515	Austintown(u)	(216)	33,636	29,393
44011	Avon	(216)	7,241	7,214
44012	Avon Lake	(216)	13,222	12,261
44203	Barberton	(216)	29,751	33,052
44140	Bay Village	(216)	17,846	18,163
44122	Beachwood	(216)	9,983	9,631
45385	Beavercreek	(513)	31,589	....
44146	Bedford	(216)	15,056	17,552
44146	Bedford Heights	(216)	13,214	13,063
43906	Bellaire	(614)	8,241	9,655
45305	Bellbrook	(513)	5,174	1,268
43311	Bellefontaine	(513)	11,888	11,255
44811	Bellevue	(419)	8,187	8,604
45714	Belpre	(614)	7,193	7,189
44017	Berea	(216)	19,597	22,465
43209	Bexley	(614)	13,405	14,888
43004	Blacklick Estates(u)	(614)	11,223	8,351
45242	Blue Ash	(513)	9,510	8,324
44512	Boardman(u)	(216)	39,161	30,852
43402	Bowling Green	(419)	25,728	14,656
44141	Brecksville	(216)	10,132	9,137
45231	Brentwood(u)	(513)	5,508	....
45211	Bridgetown(u)	(513)	11,460	13,352
44141	Broadview Heights	(216)	10,920	11,463
44144	Brooklyn	(216)	12,342	13,142
44142	Brook Park	(216)	26,195	30,774
44212	Brunswick	(216)	27,689	15,852
43506	Bryan	(419)	7,879	7,008
44820	Bucyrus	(419)	13,433	13,111
43725	Cambridge	(614)	13,573	13,656
44405	Campbell	(216)	11,619	12,577
44406	Canfield	(216)	5,535	4,997
*44711	Canton	(216)	93,077	110,053
45822	Celina	(419)	9,137	8,072
45459	Centerville	(513)	18,886	10,333
45211	Cheviot	(513)	9,888	11,135
45601	Chillicothe	(614)	23,420	24,842
*45234	Cincinnati	(513)	385,409	453,514
43113	Circleville	(614)	11,700	11,687
*44101	Cleveland	(216)	573,822	750,879
44118	Cleveland Heights	(216)	56,438	60,767
43410	Clyde	(419)	5,489	5,503
*43235	Columbus	(614)	565,032	540,025
44030	Conneaut	(216)	13,835	14,552
44410	Cortland	(216)	5,011	2,525
43812	Coshocton	(614)	13,405	13,747
45238	Covedale(u)	(513)	5,830	6,639
44827	Crestline	(419)	5,406	5,965
*44222	Cuyahoga Falls	(216)	43,710	49,815
*45401	Dayton	(513)	193,536	243,023
45236	Deer Park	(513)	6,745	7,415
43512	Defiance	(419)	16,810	16,281
43015	Delaware	(614)	18,780	15,008
45238	Delhi Hills(u)	(513)	27,647	....
45833	Delphos	(419)	7,314	7,608
44622	Dover	(216)	11,526	11,516
44112	East Cleveland	(216)	36,957	39,600
44094	Eastlake	(216)	22,104	19,690

ZIP code	Place		1980	1970
43920	East Liverpool	(216)	16,687	20,020
44413	East Palestine	(216)	5,306	5,604
45320	Eaton	(513)	6,839	6,020
*44035	Elyria	(216)	57,504	53,427
45322	Englewood	(513)	11,329	7,885
44117	Euclid	(216)	59,999	71,552
45324	Fairborn	(513)	29,702	32,267
45014	Fairfield	(513)	30,777	14,680
44313	Fairlawn	(216)	6,100	6,102
44126	Fairview Park	(216)	19,311	21,699
45840	Findlay	(419)	35,594	35,800
45405	Forest Park	(513)	18,566	15,139
45426	Fort McKinley(u)	(513)	10,161	11,536
44830	Fostoria	(419)	15,743	16,037
45005	Franklin	(513)	10,711	10,075
43420	Fremont	(419)	17,834	18,490
43230	Gahanna	(614)	18,001	12,400
44833	Galion	(419)	12,391	13,123
45631	Gallipolis	(614)	5,576	7,490
44125	Garfield Heights	(216)	33,380	41,417
44041	Geneva	(216)	6,655	6,449
45327	Germantown	(513)	5,015	4,088
44420	Girard	(216)	12,517	14,119
43212	Grandview Heights	(614)	7,420	8,460
45123	Greenfield	(513)	5,150	4,780
45331	Greenville	(513)	12,999	12,380
45239	Groesbeck(u)	(513)	9,594	....
43123	Grove City	(614)	16,793	13,911
*45012	Hamilton	(513)	63,189	67,865
45030	Harrison	(513)	5,855	4,408
43055	Heath	(614)	6,969	6,768
44124	Highland Heights	(216)	5,739	5,926
43026	Hilliard	(614)	8,131	8,369
45133	Hillsboro	(513)	6,356	5,584
44484	Howland(u)	(216)	7,441	....
44425	Hubbard	(216)	9,245	8,583
45424	Huber Heights(u)	(513)	31,731	18,943
43081	Huber Ridge(u)	(614)	5,835	....
44839	Huron	(419)	7,123	6,896
44131	Independence	(216)	8,165	7,034
45638	Ironton	(614)	14,290	15,030
45640	Jackson	(614)	6,675	6,843
44240	Kent	(216)	26,164	28,183
43326	Kenton	(419)	8,605	8,315
45236	Kenwood(u)	(513)	9,928	15,769
45429	Kettering	(513)	61,186	71,864
44094	Kirtland	(216)	5,969	5,530
44107	Lakewood	(216)	61,963	70,173
43130	Lancaster	(614)	34,953	32,911
45036	Lebanon	(513)	9,636	7,934
*45802	Lima	(419)	47,827	53,734
45215	Lincoln Heights	(513)	5,259	6,099
43228	Lincoln Village(u)	(614)	10,548	11,215
43138	Logan	(614)	6,557	6,269
43140	London	(614)	6,958	6,481
*44052	Lorain	(216)	75,416	78,185
44641	Louisville	(216)	7,996	6,298
45140	Loveland	(513)	9,106	7,126
44124	Lyndhurst	(216)	18,092	19,749
44056	Macedonia	(216)	6,571	6,375
45243	Madeira	(513)	9,341	6,713
*44901	Mansfield	(419)	53,927	55,047
44137	Maple Heights	(216)	29,735	34,093
45750	Marietta	(614)	16,467	16,861
43302	Marion	(614)	37,040	38,646
43935	Martins Ferry	(614)	9,331	10,757
43040	Marysville	(513)	7,414	5,744
45040	Mason	(513)	8,692	5,677
44646	Massillon	(216)	30,557	32,539
43537	Maumee	(419)	15,747	15,937
44124	Mayfield Heights	(216)	21,550	22,139
44256	Medina	(216)	15,268	10,913
44060	Mentor	(216)	42,065	36,912
44060	Mentor-on-the-Lake	(216)	7,919	6,517
45342	Miamisburg	(513)	15,304	14,797
44130	Middleburg Heights	(216)	16,218	12,367
45042	Middletown	(513)	43,719	48,767
45042	Middletown South(u)	(513)	5,260	....
45150	Milford	(513)	5,232	4,828
45239	Monfort Heights(u)	(513)	9,745	....
45242	Montgomery	(513)	10,084	5,683
45439	Moraine	(513)	5,325	4,898
45231	Mount Healthy	(513)	7,562	7,446
43050	Mount Vernon	(614)	14,380	13,373
43545	Napoleon	(419)	8,614	7,791
43055	Newark	(614)	41,200	41,836
45344	New Carlisle	(513)	6,496	6,112
43764	New Lexington	(614)	5,179	4,921
44663	New Philadelphia	(216)	16,883	15,184
44446	Niles	(216)	23,088	21,581
45239	Northbrook(u)	(513)	8,357	....
44720	North Canton	(216)	14,228	15,228
45239	North College Hill	(513)	10,990	12,363
44057	North Madison(u)	(216)	8,741	6,982
44070	North Olmsted	(216)	36,486	34,861
45502	Northridge(u) (Clark)	(513)	5,559	12
45414	Northridge(u) (Montgomery)	(513)	9,720	10,084
44039	North Ridgeville	(216)	21,522	13,152
44133	North Royalton	(216)	17,671	12,807
45239	Northview(u)	(513)	9,973	....
43619	Northwood	(419)	5,495	4,222

ZIP code	Place	1980	1970
44203	Norton . . . . (216)	12,242	12,308
44857	Norwalk . . . . (419)	14,358	13,386
45212	Norwood . . . . (513)	26,342	30,420
45873	Oakwood . . . . (419)	9,372	10,095
44074	Oberlin . . . . (216)	8,660	8,761
44138	Olmsted Falls . . . . (216)	5,868	2,504
43615	Oregon . . . . (419)	18,675	16,563
44667	Orrville . . . . (216)	7,511	7,408
45431	Overlook-Page Manor(u). . . (513)	14,825	19,719
45056	Oxford . . . . (513)	17,655	15,868
44077	Painesville . . . . (216)	16,391	16,536
45344	Park Layne(u) . . . . (513)	5,372	.....
44129	Parma . . . . (216)	92,548	100,216
44130	Parma Heights . . . . (216)	23,112	27,192
44124	Pepper Pike . . . . (216)	6,177	5,382
44646	Perry Heights(u). . . . . . . (216)	9,206	.....
43551	Perrysburg . . . . (419)	10,215	7,693
45356	Piqua . . . . (513)	20,480	20,741
45069	Pisgah(u). . . . . (513)	15,660	.....
44319	Portage Lakes(u) . . . . . . (216)	11,310	.....
43452	Port Clinton . . . . (419)	7,223	7,202
45662	Portsmouth . . . . (614)	25,943	27,633
44266	Ravenna . . . . (216)	11,987	11,780
45215	Reading . . . . (513)	12,879	14,617
43068	Reynoldsburg . . . . (614)	20,661	13,921
44143	Richmond Heights . . . . . . (213)	10,095	9,220
44270	Rittman . . . . (216)	6,063	6,308
44116	Rocky River . . . . (216)	21,084	22,958
43460	Rossford . . . . (419)	5,978	5,302
45217	St. Bernard . . . . (513)	5,396	6,131
43950	St. Clairsville . . . . (614)	5,452	4,754
45885	St. Marys . . . . (419)	8,414	7,699
44460	Salem . . . . (216)	12,869	14,186
44870	Sandusky . . . . (419)	31,360	32,674
44870	Sandusky South(u) . . . . . (419)	6,548	8,501
44672	Sebring . . . . (216)	5,078	4,954
44131	Seven Hills . . . . (216)	13,650	12,700
44120	Shaker Heights . . . . (216)	32,487	36,306
45241	Sharonville . . . . (513)	10,108	11,393
44054	Sheffield Lake . . . . (216)	10,484	8,734
44875	Shelby . . . . (419)	9,703	9,847
45365	Sidney . . . . (513)	17,657	16,332
45236	Silverton . . . . (513)	6,172	6,588
44139	Solon . . . . (216)	14,341	11,147
44121	South Euclid . . . . (216)	25,713	29,579
45246	Springdale . . . . (216)	10,111	8,127
*45501	Springfield . . . . (513)	72,563	81,941
43952	Steubenville . . . . (614)	26,400	30,771
44224	Stow . . . . (216)	25,303	20,061
44240	Streetsboro . . . . (216)	9,055	7,966
44136	Strongsville . . . . (216)	28,577	15,182
44471	Struthers . . . . (216)	13,624	15,343
43560	Sylvania . . . . (419)	15,527	12,031
44278	Tallmadge . . . . (216)	15,269	15,274
45243	The Village of Indian Hill . . (513)	5,521	5,651
44883	Tiffin . . . . (419)	19,549	21,596
45371	Tipp City . . . . (513)	5,595	5,090
*43601	Toledo . . . . (419)	354,635	383,062
43964	Toronto . . . . (614)	6,934	7,705
45067	Trenton . . . . (513)	6,401	5,278
45426	Trotwood . . . . (513)	7,802	6,997
45373	Troy . . . . (513)	19,086	17,186
44087	Twinsburg . . . . (216)	7,632	6,432
44683	Uhrichsville . . . . (614)	6,130	5,731
45322	Union . . . . (513)	5,219	3,654
44118	University Heights . . . . . . (216)	15,401	17,055
43221	Upper Arlington . . . . (614)	35,648	38,727
43351	Upper Sandusky . . . . (419)	5,967	5,645
43078	Urbana . . . . (513)	10,762	11,237
45377	Vandalia . . . . (513)	13,161	10,796
45891	Van Wert . . . . (419)	11,035	11,320
44089	Vermilion . . . . (216)	11,012	9,872
44281	Wadsworth . . . . (216)	15,166	13,142
45895	Wapakoneta . . . . (419)	8,402	7,324
*44481	Warren . . . . (216)	56,629	63,494
44122	Warrensville Heights . . . . . (216)	16,565	18,925
43160	Washington C.H. . . . . (614)	12,682	12,495
43567	Wauseon . . . . (419)	6,173	4,932
45692	Wellston . . . . (614)	6,016	5,410
43968	Wellsville . . . . (216)	5,095	5,891
45449	West Carrollton . . . . (513)	13,148	10,748
43081	Westerville . . . . (614)	23,414	12,530
44145	Westlake . . . . (216)	19,483	15,689
43213	Whitehall . . . . (614)	21,299	25,263
45239	White Oak(u) . . . . (513)	9,563	.....
44092	Wickliffe . . . . (216)	16,790	20,632
44890	Willard . . . . (419)	5,674	5,510
44094	Willoughby . . . . (216)	19,329	18,634
44094	Willoughby Hills . . . . (216)	8,612	5,969
44094	Willowick . . . . (216)	17,834	21,237
45177	Wilmington . . . . (216)	10,431	10,051
45459	Woodbourne-Hyde Park(u) . (513)	8,826	.....
44691	Wooster . . . . (216)	19,289	18,703
43085	Worthington . . . . (614)	15,016	15,326
45215	Wyoming . . . . (513)	8,282	9,089
45385	Xenia . . . . (513)	24,653	25,373
*44501	Youngstown . . . . (216)	115,511	140,909
43701	Zanesville . . . . (614)	28,655	33,045

Oklahoma

ZIP code	Place	1980	1970
74820	Ada. . . . . (405)	15,902	14,859
73521	Altus . . . . (405)	23,101	23,302
73717	Alva. . . . . (405)	6,416	7,440
73005	Anadarko . . . . (405)	6,378	6,682
73401	Ardmore . . . . (405)	23,689	20,881
74003	Bartlesville. . . . . (918)	34,568	29,683
73008	Bethany . . . . (405)	22,038	22,694
74008	Bixby . . . . (918)	6,969	3,973
74631	Blackwell. . . . . (405)	8,400	8,645
74012	Broken Arrow . . . . (918)	35,761	11,018
73018	Chickasha . . . . (405)	15,828	14,194
73020	Choctaw . . . . (405)	7,520	4,750
74017	Claremore. . . . . (918)	12,085	9,084
73601	Clinton . . . . (405)	6,796	8,511
74023	Cushing . . . . (918)	7,720	7,529
73115	Del City . . . . (405)	28,523	27,133
73533	Duncan . . . . (405)	22,517	19,718
74701	Durant . . . . (405)	11,972	11,118
73034	Edmond . . . . (405)	34,637	16,633
73644	Elk City. . . . . (405)	9,579	7,323
73036	El Reno . . . . (405)	15,486	14,510
73701	Enid. . . . . (405)	50,363	44,986
73503	Fort Sill(u) . . . . (405)	15,924	21,217
73542	Frederick. . . . . (405)	6,153	6,132
73044	Guthrie . . . . (405)	10,312	9,575
73942	Guymon . . . . (405)	8,492	7,674
74437	Henryetta . . . . (918)	6,432	6,430
74848	Holdenville. . . . . (405)	5,469	5,181
74743	Hugo . . . . (405)	7,172	6,585
74745	Idabel. . . . . (405)	7,622	5,946
74037	Jenks . . . . (918)	5,876	2,685
73501	Lawton. . . . . (405)	80,054	74,470
73055	Marlow . . . . (405)	5,017	3,995
74501	McAlester . . . . (918)	17,255	18,802
74354	Miami . . . . (918)	14,237	13,880
73110	Midwest City. . . . . (405)	49,559	48,212
73060	Moore . . . . (405)	35,063	18,761
74401	Muskogee . . . . (918)	40,011	37,331
73064	Mustang . . . . (405)	7,496	2,637
73069	Norman . . . . (405)	68,020	52,117
*73125	Oklahoma City . . . . (405)	404,014	368,164
74447	Okmulgee . . . . (918)	16,263	15,180
74055	Owasso . . . . (918)	6,149	3,491
73075	Pauls Valley . . . . (405)	5,664	5,769
73077	Perry . . . . (405)	5,796	5,341
74601	Ponca City . . . . (405)	26,238	25,940
74953	Poteau . . . . (918)	7,089	5,500
74361	Pryor Creek . . . . (918)	8,483	7,057
74955	Sallisaw . . . . (918)	6,403	4,888
74063	Sand Springs . . . . (918)	13,121	10,565
74066	Sapulpa . . . . (918)	15,853	15,159
74868	Seminole . . . . (405)	8,590	7,878
74801	Shawnee. . . . . (405)	26,506	25,075
74074	Stillwater. . . . . (405)	38,268	31,126
73086	Sulphur. . . . . (405)	5,516	5,158
74464	Tahlequah. . . . . (918)	9,708	9,254
74873	Tecumseh . . . . (405)	5,123	4,451
73120	The Village. . . . . (405)	11,114	13,695
*74101	Tulsa . . . . (918)	360,919	330,350
74156	Turley(u) . . . . (918)	6,336	.....
74301	Vinita . . . . (918)	6,740	5,847
74467	Wagoner . . . . (918)	6,191	4,959
73132	Warr Acres . . . . (405)	9,940	9,887
73096	Weatherford. . . . . (405)	9,640	7,959
74884	Wewoka . . . . (405)	5,472	5,284
73801	Woodward . . . . (405)	13,781	9,563
73099	Yukon . . . . (405)	17,112	8,411

Oregon (503)

ZIP code	Place	1980	1970
97321	Albany	26,511	18,181
97005	Aloha(u)	28,353	.....
97601	Altamont(u)	19,805	15,746
97520	Ashland	14,943	12,342
97103	Astoria.	9,998	10,244
97814	Baker.	9,471	9,354
97005	Beaverton	31,926	18,577
97701	Bend	17,263	13,710
97013	Canby	7,659	3,813
97225	Cedar Hills(u)	9,619	.....
.....	Centennial(u)	22,118	.....
97502	Central Point.	6,357	4,004
97420	Coos Bay	14,424	13,466
97330	Corvallis	40,960	35,056
97424	Cottage Grove.	7,148	6,004
.....	Cully(u).	10,569	.....
97338	Dallas	8,530	6,361
97266	Errol Heights(u)	10,487	.....
*97401	Eugene.	105,664	79,028
97116	Forest Grove	11,499	8,275
97301	Four Corners(u)	11,331	5,823
97223	Garden Home-Whitford(u). .	6,926	.....
97027	Gladstone	9,500	6,254
97526	Grants Pass	14,997	12,455
97030	Gresham.	33,005	10,030
97303	Hayesville(u).	9,213	5,518
97230	Hazelwood(u)	25,541	.....
97838	Hermiston	9,408	4,893

ZIP code	Place	1980	1970
97123	Hillsboro	27,664	14,675
97303	Keizer(u)	18,592	11,405
97601	Klamath Falls	16,661	15,775
97850	La Grande	11,354	9,645
97034	Lake Oswego	22,527	14,615
97355	Lebanon	10,413	6,636
97367	Lincoln City	5,469	4,198
97128	McMinnville	14,080	10,125
97501	Medford	39,746	28,973
97223	Metzger(u)	5,544	---
97862	Milton-Freewater	5,086	4,105
97222	Milwaukie	17,931	16,444
97361	Monmouth	5,594	5,237
97132	Newberg	10,394	6,507
97365	Newport	7,519	5,188
97459	North Bend	9,779	8,553
	North Springfield(u)	6,140	---
97268	Oak Grove(u)	11,640	---
97914	Ontario	8,814	6,523
97045	Oregon City	14,673	9,176
97220	Parkrose(u)	21,108	---
97801	Pendleton	14,521	13,197
*97208	Portland	368,148	379,967
97236	Powellhurst(u)	20,132	---
97754	Prineville	5,276	4,101
97225	Raleigh Hills(u)	6,517	---
97756	Redmond	6,452	3,721
97404	River Road(u)	10,370	---
97470	Roseburg	16,644	14,461
97051	St. Helens	7,064	6,212
*97301	Salem	89,091	68,725
97401	Santa Clara(u)	14,288	---
97138	Seaside	5,193	4,402
97381	Silverton	5,168	4,301
97477	Springfield	41,621	26,874
97386	Sweet Home	6,921	3,799
97058	The Dalles	10,820	10,423
97223	Tigard	14,799	6,499
97060	Troutdale	5,908	1,661
97062	Tualatin	7,483	750
97068	West Linn	11,358	7,091
97225	West Slope(u)	5,364	---
97501	White City(u).	5,445	---
97233	Wilkes-Rockwood(u)	23,216	---
97071	Woodburn	11,196	7,495

Pennsylvania

ZIP code	Place		1980	1970
19001	Abington Township(u)	(215)	59,084	63,625
15001	Aliquippa	(412)	17,094	22,277
*18101	Allentown	(215)	103,758	109,871
*16603	Altoona	(814)	57,078	63,115
19002	Ambler	(215)	6,628	7,800
15003	Ambridge	(412)	9,575	11,324
18403	Archbald	(717)	6,295	6,118
19003	Ardmore(u)	(215)	NA	5,131
15068	Arnold	(412)	6,853	8,174
19014	Aston Township(u)	(215)	14,530	13,704
15202	Avalon	(412)	6,240	7,010
15005	Baden	(412)	5,318	5,536
15004	Bala-Cynwyd(u).	(215)	NA	6,483
15234	Baldwin	(412)	24,714	26,729
18013	Bangor	(215)	5,006	5,425
15009	Beaver	(412)	5,441	6,100
15010	Beaver Falls	(412)	12,525	14,635
16823	Bellefonte	(814)	6,300	6,828
15202	Bellevue	(412)	10,128	11,586
19020	Bensalem Township(u)	(215)	52,399	33,038
18603	Berwick	(717)	12,189	12,274
15102	Bethel Park	(412)	34,755	34,758
*18016	Bethlehem	(215)	70,419	72,686
18447	Blakely	(717)	7,438	6,391
17815	Bloomsburg	(717)	11,717	11,652
15104	Braddock	(412)	5,634	8,795
16701	Bradford	(814)	11,211	12,672
15227	Brentwood	(412)	11,859	13,732
15017	Bridgeville	(412)	6,154	6,717
19007	Bristol	(215)	10,867	12,085
19007	Bristol Twp(u)	(215)	58,733	67,498
19015	Brookhaven(u)	(215)	7,912	7,370
16001	Butler	(412)	17,026	18,691
15419	California	(412)	5,703	6,635
17011	Camp Hill	(717)	8,422	9,931
15317	Canonsburg	(412)	10,459	11,439
18407	Carbondale	(717)	11,255	12,478
17013	Carlisle	(717)	18,314	18,079
15106	Carnegie	(412)	10,099	10,864
15108	Carnot-Moon(u)	(412)	11,102	13,093
15234	Castle Shannon	(412)	10,164	12,036
18032	Catasauqua	(215)	7,944	5,702
17201	Chambersburg	(717)	16,174	17,315
15022	Charleroi	(412)	5,717	6,723
19012	Cheltenham Twp(u).	(215)	35,509	40,238
*19013	Chester	(215)	45,794	56,331
19013	Chester Twp(u)	(215)	5,687	5,708
15025	Clairton	(412)	12,188	15,051
16214	Clarion	(814)	6,198	6,095
18411	Clarks Summit	(717)	5,272	5,376
16830	Clearfield	(814)	7,580	8,176
19018	Clifton Heights	(215)	7,320	8,348
19320	Coatesville	(215)	10,698	12,331
19023	Collingdale	(215)	9,539	10,605
17512	Columbia	(717)	10,466	11,237
15425	Connellsville	(412)	10,319	11,643
19428	Conshohocken	(215)	8,591	10,195
15108	Coraopolis	(412)	7,308	8,435
16407	Corry	(814)	7,149	7,435
15205	Crafton	(412)	7,623	8,233
17821	Danville	(717)	5,239	6,176
19023	Darby	(215)	11,513	13,729
19036	Darby Twp(u)	(215)	12,264	---
19333	Devon-Berwyn(u)	(215)	5,246	---
18519	Dickson City	(717)	6,699	7,698
15033	Donora	(412)	7,524	8,825
15216	Dormont	(412)	11,275	12,856
19335	Downingtown	(215)	7,650	7,437
18901	Doylestown	(215)	8,717	8,270
15801	Du Bois	(814)	9,290	10,112
18512	Dunmore	(717)	16,781	18,168
15110	Duquesne	(412)	10,094	11,410
18642	Duryea	(717)	5,415	5,264
19401	East Norriton(u)	(215)	12,711	---
18042	Easton	(215)	26,027	29,450
18301	East Stroudsburg	(717)	8,039	7,894
15005	Economy	(412)	9,538	7,176
16412	Edinboro	(814)	6,324	4,871
18704	Edwardsville	(717)	5,729	5,633
17022	Elizabethtown	(717)	8,233	8,072
16117	Ellwood City	(412)	9,998	10,857
18049	Emmaus	(215)	11,001	11,511
17522	Ephrata	(717)	11,095	9,662
*16501	Erie	(814)	119,123	129,265
18643	Exeter	(717)	5,493	4,670
19054	Falls Twp(u)	(215)	36,083	35,630
16121	Farrell	(412)	8,645	11,000
19032	Folcroft	(215)	8,231	9,610
15221	Forest Hills	(412)	8,198	9,561
18704	Forty Fort	(717)	5,590	6,114
15238	Fox Chapel	(412)	5,049	4,684
17931	Frackville	(717)	5,308	5,445
16323	Franklin	(814)	8,146	8,629
15143	Franklin Park	(412)	6,135	5,310
18052	Fullerton(u)	(215)	6,055	7,908
17325	Gettysburg	(717)	7,194	7,275
15045	Glassport	(412)	6,242	7,450
15036	Glenolden	(215)	7,633	8,697
15601	Greensburg	(412)	17,558	17,077
15220	Green Tree	(412)	5,722	6,441
16125	Greenville	(412)	7,730	8,704
16127	Grove City	(412)	8,162	8,312
17331	Hanover	(717)	14,890	15,623
*17105	Harrisburg	(717)	53,264	68,061
19040	Hatboro	(215)	7,579	8,880
19083	Haverford Twp(u)	(215)	52,349	55,132
18201	Hazleton	(717)	27,318	30,426
18055	Hellertown	(215)	6,025	6,615
17033	Hershey(u)	(717)	13,249	7,407
18042	Highland Park (Northampton)(u)	(215)	5,922	5,500
16648	Hollidaysburg	(814)	5,892	6,262
16001	Homeacre-Lyndora(u)	(412)	8,333	8,415
15120	Homestead	(412)	5,092	6,309
18431	Honesdale	(717)	5,128	5,224
19044	Horsham(u)	(215)	9,900	---
17036	Hummelstown	(717)	6,159	4,723
16652	Huntingdon	(814)	7,042	6,987
15701	Indiana	(412)	16,051	16,100
15644	Jeannette	(412)	*13,106	15,209
15344	Jefferson	(412)	8,643	8,512
18229	Jim Thorpe	(717)	5,263	5,456
*15901	Johnstown	(814)	35,496	42,476
15108	Kennedy Twp(u)	(412)	7,159	6,859
18704	Kingston	(717)	15,681	18,325
16201	Kittanning	(412)	5,432	6,231
*17604	Lancaster	(717)	54,725	57,690
19446	Lansdale	(215)	16,526	18,451
19050	Lansdowne	(215)	11,891	14,090
15650	Latrobe	(412)	10,799	11,749
17042	Lebanon	(717)	25,711	28,572
18235	Lehighton	(215)	5,826	6,095
17837	Lewisburg	(717)	5,407	5,718
17044	Lewistown	(717)	9,630	11,098
17543	Lititz	(717)	7,590	7,072
17745	Lock Haven	(717)	9,617	11,427
15068	Lower Burrell	(412)	13,200	13,654
19003	Lower Merion Twp(u)	(215)	59,651	63,392
19006	Lower Moreland Twp(u)	(215)	12,472	11,746
19047	Lower Southampton Twp(u)	(215)	18,305	17,578
19008	Marple Twp(u)	(215)	23,642	25,040
15237	McCandless Twp(u)	(412)	26,250	22,404
15134	McKeesport	(412)	31,012	37,977
15136	McKees Rocks	(412)	8,742	11,901
17948	Mahanoy City	(717)	6,167	7,257
17545	Manheim	(717)	5,015	5,434
16335	Meadville	(814)	15,544	16,573
17055	Mechanicsburg	(717)	9,487	9,385
*19063	Media	(215)	6,119	6,444
17057	Middletown (Dauphin)(u)	(717)	10,122	9,080
18017	Middletown (Northampton)(u)	(215)	5,801	---

ZIP code	Place		1980	1970
.....	Middletown Twp			
	(Delaware)(u)	(215)	12,463	12,878
17551	Millersville	(717)	7,668	6,396
17847	Milton	(717)	6,730	7,723
17954	Minersville	(717)	5,635	6,012
15061	Monaca	(412)	7,661	7,486
15062	Monessen	(412)	11,928	15,216
15063	Monongahela	(412)	5,950	7,113
15146	Monroeville	(412)	30,977	29,011
17754	Montoursville	(717)	5,403	5,985
18507	Moosic	(717)	6,068	4,646
19067	Morrisville	(215)	9,845	11,309
17851	Mount Carmel	(717)	8,190	9,317
17552	Mount Joy	(717)	5,680	5,041
15666	Mount Pleasant	(412)	5,354	5,895
15228	Mount Lebanon(u)	(412)	34,414	39,157
15120	Munhall	(412)	14,535	16,574
15668	Murrysville	(412)	16,036	12,661
18634	Nanticoke	(717)	13,044	14,638
18064	Nazareth	(215)	5,443	5,815
.....	Nether Providence Twp(u) .	(215)	12,730	13,644
15066	New Brighton	(412)	7,364	7,637
*16101	New Castle	(412)	33,621	38,559
17070	New Cumberland	(717)	8,051	9,803
15068	New Kensington	(412)	17,660	20,312
*19401	Norristown	(215)	34,684	38,169
18067	Northampton	(215)	8,240	8,389
15104	North Braddock	(412)	8,711	10,838
15137	North Versailles(u)	(412)	13,294	.....
16421	Northwest Harbor-Creek(u) .	(814)	7,485	.....
19074	Norwood	(215)	6,647	7,229
15139	Oakmont	(412)	7,039	7,550
16301	Oil City	(814)	13,881	15,033
18518	Old Forge	(717)	9,304	9,522
18447	Olyphant	(717)	5,204	5,422
18071	Palmerton	(215)	5,455	5,620
17078	Palmyra	(717)	7,228	7,615
19301	Paoli(u)	(215)	6,698	5,835
17331	Parkville(u)	(717)	5,009	5,120
15235	Penn Hills(u)	(412)	57,632	.....
18944	Perkasie	(215)	5,241	5,451
*19104	Philadelphia	(215)	1,688,210	1,949,996
19460	Phoenixville	(215)	14,165	14,823
*15219	Pittsburgh	(412)	423,959	520,089
*18640	Pittston	(717)	9,930	11,113
18705	Plains(u)	(717)	5,455	6,606
15236	Pleasant Hills	(412)	9,604	10,409
15239	Plum	(412)	25,390	21,932
18651	Plymouth	(717)	7,605	9,536
19462	Plymouth Twp(u)	(215)	17,168	16,876
15133	Port Vue	(412)	5,316	5,862
19464	Pottstown	(215)	22,729	25,355
17901	Pottsville	(717)	18,195	19,715
19076	Prospect Park	(215)	6,593	7,250
15767	Punxsutawney	(814)	7,479	7,792
18951	Quakertown	(215)	8,867	7,276
19087	Radnor Twp(u)	(215)	27,676	27,459
*19603	Reading	(215)	78,686	87,643
17356	Red Lion	(717)	5,824	5,645
18954	Richboro(u)	(215)	5,141	.....
15853	Ridgway	(814)	5,604	6,022
19078	Ridley Park	(215)	7,889	9,025
19033	Ridley Twp(u)	(215)	33,771	39,085
15237	Ross Twp(u)	(412)	35,102	32,892
15857	St. Marys	(814)	6,417	7,470
18840	Sayre	(717)	6,951	7,473
17972	Schuylkill Haven	(717)	5,977	6,125
15683	Scottdale	(412)	5,833	5,818
15106	Scott Twp(u)	(412)	20,413	21,856
*18503	Scranton	(717)	88,117	102,696
17870	Selinsgrove	(717)	5,227	5,116
15116	Shaler Twp(u)	(412)	33,712	33,369
17872	Shamokin	(717)	10,357	11,719
16146	Sharon	(412)	19,057	22,653
19079	Sharon Hill	(215)	6,221	7,464
16150	Sharpsville	(412)	5,375	6,126
17976	Shenandoah	(717)	7,589	8,287
19607	Shillington	(215)	5,601	6,249
17404	Shiloh(u)	(717)	5,315	.....
17257	Shippensburg	(717)	5,261	5,536
15501	Somerset	(814)	6,474	6,269
18964	Souderton	(215)	6,657	6,366
17701	South Williamsport	(717)	6,581	7,153
19064	Springfield(u)	(215)	25,326	.....
19118	Springfield Twp(u)	(215)	20,344	22,394
16801	State College	(814)	36,130	32,833
17113	Steelton	(717)	6,484	8,556
15136	Stowe Twp(u)	(412)	9,202	10,119
18360	Stroudsburg	(717)	5,148	5,451
16323	Sugar Creek	(814)	5,954	5,944
17801	Sunbury	(717)	12,292	13,025
19081	Swarthmore	(215)	5,950	6,156
17111	Swatara Twp(u)	(717)	18,796	17,178
15218	Swissvale	(412)	11,345	13,819
18704	Swoyersville	(717)	5,795	6,786
18252	Tamaqua	(717)	8,843	9,246
15084	Tarentum	(412)	6,419	7,379
18517	Taylor	(717)	7,246	6,977
16354	Titusville	(814)	6,884	7,331
19401	Trooper(u)	(215)	7,370	.....
15145	Turtle Creek	(412)	6,959	8,308
16686	Tyrone	(814)	6,346	7,072
15401	Uniontown	(412)	14,510	16,282
19061	Upper Chichester Twp(u) .	(215)	14,377	11,414
19082	Upper Darby(u)	(215)	84,054	95,910
19034	Upper Dublin Twp(u) . . .	(215)	22,348	19,449
19406	Upper Merion Twp(u) . . .	(215)	26,138	23,699
19090	Upper Moreland Twp(u) . .	(215)	25,874	24,866
19063	Upper Providence Twp(u) .	(215)	9,477	9,234
15241	Upper St. Clair(u)	(412)	19,023	.....
19006	Upper Southampton Twp(u) .	(215)	15,806	13,936
15690	Vandergrift	(412)	6,823	7,889
18974	Warminster(u)	(215)	35,543	.....
16365	Warren	(814)	12,146	12,998
15301	Washington	(412)	18,363	19,827
17268	Waynesboro	(717)	9,726	10,011
.....	Weigelstown(u)	(717)	5,213	.....
19380	West Chester	(215)	17,435	19,301
19930	West Goshen(u)	(215)	7,998	.....
15122	West Mifflin	(412)	26,322	28,070
19401	West Norriton(u)	(215)	14,034	.....
15905	Westmont	(814)	6,113	6,673
18643	West Pittston	(717)	5,980	7,074
15229	West View	(412)	7,648	8,312
18052	Whitehall	(215)	15,143	16,450
19428	Whitemarsh Twp(u)	(215)	15,101	15,886
15131	White Oak	(717)	9,480	9,304
*18701	Wilkes-Barre	(717)	51,551	58,856
15221	Wilkinsburg	(412)	23,669	26,780
15145	Wilkins Twp(u)	(412)	8,472	8,749
17701	Williamsport	(717)	33,401	37,918
15025	Wilson	(412)	7,564	8,406
15963	Windber	(814)	5,585	6,332
19610	Wyomissing	(215)	6,551	7,136
19050	Yeadon	(215)	11,727	12,136
*17405	York	(717)	44,619	50,335

Rhode Island (401)

See Note on Page 563

ZIP code	Place	1980	1970
02806	Barrington	16,174	17,554
02809	Bristol	20,128	17,860
02830	Burrillville	13,164	10,087
02863	Central Falls	16,995	18,716
02816	Coventry	27,065	22,947
02910	Cranston	71,992	74,287
02864	Cumberland	27,069	26,605
02864	Cumberland Hill(u)	5,421	.....
02818	East Greenwich	10,211	9,577
02914	East Providence	50,980	48,207
02814	Glocester	7,550	5,160
02828	Greenville(u)	7,576	.....
02833	Hopkinton	6,406	5,392
02919	Johnston	24,907	22,037
02881	Kingston(u)	5,479	5,601
02865	Lincoln	16,949	16,182
02840	Middletown	17,216	29,290
02882	Narragansett	12,088	7,138
02840	Newport	29,259	34,562
02843	Newport East(u)	11,030	10,285
02852	North Kingstown	21,938	29,793
02908	North Providence	29,188	24,337
02876	North Smithfield	9,972	9,349
*02860	Pawtucket	71,204	76,984
02871	Portsmouth	14,257	12,521
*02904	Providence	156,804	179,116
02857	Scituate	6,405	7,489
02917	Smithfield	16,886	13,468
02879	South Kingstown	20,414	16,913
02878	Tiverton	13,526	12,559
02864	Valley Falls(u)	10,892	.....
*02880	Wakefield-Peacedale(u) . .	6,474	6,331
02885	Warren	10,640	10,523
*02887	Warwick	87,123	83,694
02891	Westerly	18,580	17,248
02891	Westerly Center(u)	14,093	13,654
02893	West Warwick	27,026	24,323
02895	Woonsocket	45,914	46,820

South Carolina (803)

ZIP code	Place	1980	1970
29620	Abbeville	5,863	5,515
29801	Aiken	14,978	13,436
29621	Anderson	27,546	27,556
29407	Avondale-Moorland(u) . . .	5,355	5,236
29812	Barnwell	5,572	4,439
29902	Beaufort	8,634	9,434
29627	Belton	5,312	5,257
29841	Belvedere(u)	5,859	.....
29512	Bennettsville	8,774	7,468
29611	Berea(u)	13,164	7,186
.....	Brookdale(u)	6,123	.....
29020	Camden	7,462	8,532
29209	Capitol View(u)	9,962	.....
29033	Cayce	11,701	9,967
*29401	Charleston	69,779	66,945
29404	Charleston Base(u)	NA	6,238

ZIP code	Place	1980	1970
29408	Charleston Yard(u)	NA	13,565
29520	Cheraw	5,654	5,627
29706	Chester	6,820	7,045
29631	Clemson	8,118	6,690
29325	Clinton	8,596	8,138
*29201	Columbia	101,229	113,542
29526	Conway	10,240	8,151
29532	Darlington	7,989	6,990
29204	Dentsville(u)	13,579	
29536	Dillon	7,042	6,391
29405	Dorchester Terrace-Brentwood(u)	7,862	
29601	Duncan(u)	5,146	1,266
29640	Easley	14,264	11,175
29501	Florence	29,842	25,997
29206	Forest Acres	6,062	6,808
29340	Gaffney	13,453	13,253
29605	Gantt(u)	13,719	11,386
29440	Georgetown	10,144	10,449
29445	Goose Creek	17,811	3,825
*29602	Greenville	58,242	61,436
29203	Greenview(u)	5,515	
29646	Greenwood	21,613	21,069
29651	Greer	10,525	10,642
29410	Hanahan	13,224	9,118
29550	Hartsville	7,631	8,017
29928	Hilton Head Island(u)	11,344	
29621	Homeland Park(u)	6,720	
29412	James Island(u)	24,124	
29456	Ladson(u)	13,246	
29560	Lake City	5,636	6,247
29720	Lancaster	9,703	9,186
29902	Laurel Bay(u)	5,238	
29360	Laurens	10,587	10,298
29571	Marion	7,700	7,435
29662	Mauldin	8,143	3,797
29464	Mount Pleasant	14,464	6,879
29574	Mullins	6,068	6,006
29577	Myrtle Beach	18,758	9,035
29108	Newberry	9,866	9,218
29841	North Augusta	13,593	12,883
29406	North Charleston	62,479	21,211
	North Trenholm(u)	10,962	
29565	Oak Grove(u)	7,092	
29115	Orangeburg	14,933	13,252
29905	Parris Island(u)	7,752	8,868
29483	Pinehurst-Sheppard Park(u)	6,956	1,711
29730	Rock Hill	35,327	33,846
29407	St. Andrews (Charleston)(u)	9,908	9,202
29210	St. Andrews (Richland)(u)	20,245	
29609	Sans Souci(u)	8,393	
29678	Seneca	7,436	6,573
	Seven Oaks(u)	16,604	
29152	Shaw AFB(u)	6,939	5,819
29681	Simpsonville	9,037	3,308
	South Sumter(u)	7,096	
*29301	Spartanburg	43,826	44,546
29483	Summerville	6,492	3,839
29150	Sumter	24,921	24,555
29687	Taylors(u)	15,801	6,831
29379	Union	10,523	10,775
29205	Valencia Heights(u)	5,328	
29607	Wade-Hampton(u)	20,180	17,152
29488	Walterboro	6,036	6,257
29405	Wando Woods(u)	5,266	
29611	Welcome(u)	6,922	
29169	West Columbia	10,409	7,838
29206	Woodfield(u)	9,588	
29388	Woodruff	5,171	4,690
29745	York	6,412	5,081

South Dakota (605)

ZIP code	Place	1980	1970
57401	Aberdeen	25,851	26,476
57006	Brookings	14,951	13,717
57350	Huron	13,000	14,299
57042	Madison	6,210	6,315
57301	Mitchell	13,916	13,425
57501	Pierre	11,973	9,699
57701	Rapid City	46,492	43,836
*57101	Sioux Falls	81,343	72,488
57785	Sturgis	5,184	4,536
57069	Vermillion	9,582	9,128
57201	Watertown	15,649	13,388
57078	Yankton	12,011	11,919

Tennessee

ZIP code	Place		1980	1970
37701	Alcoa	(615)	6,870	7,739
37303	Athens	(615)	12,080	11,790
38134	Bartlett	(901)	17,170	1,150
37660	Bloomingdale(u)	(615)	12,088	8,120
38008	Bolivar	(901)	6,597	6,674
37027	Brentwood	(615)	9,431	4,099
37620	Bristol	(615)	23,986	20,064
38012	Brownsville	(901)	9,307	7,011
*37401	Chattanooga	(615)	169,514	119,923
37040	Clarksville	(615)	54,777	31,719
37311	Cleveland	(615)	26,415	21,446
37716	Clinton	(615)	5,245	4,794
38017	Collierville	(901)	7,839	3,651
37663	Colonial Heights(u)	(615)	6,744	3,027
38401	Columbia	(615)	26,571	21,471
37922	Concord (Knox)(u)	(615)	8,569	....
38501	Cookeville	(615)	20,350	14,403
38019	Covington	(901)	6,065	5,801
38555	Crossville	(615)	6,394	5,381
37321	Dayton	(615)	5,233	4,361
37055	Dickson	(615)	7,040	5,665
38024	Dyersburg	(901)	15,856	14,523
37801	Eagleton Village(u)	(615)	5,331	5,345
37412	East Ridge	(615)	21,236	21,799
37643	Elizabethton	(615)	12,431	12,269
37334	Fayetteville	(615)	7,559	7,691
37064	Franklin	(615)	12,407	9,497
37066	Gallatin	(615)	17,191	13,253
38138	Germantown	(901)	21,482	3,474
37072	Goodlettsville	(615)	8,327	6,168
37075	Greater Hendersonville(u)	(615)	25,029	11,996
37743	Greeneville	(615)	14,097	13,722
37918	Halls(u)	(615)	10,363	....
37748	Harriman	(615)	8,303	8,734
37341	Harrison(u)	(615)	6,206	....
37075	Hendersonville	(615)	26,561	412
38343	Humboldt	(901)	10,209	10,066
38301	Jackson	(901)	49,258	39,996
37760	Jefferson City	(615)	5,612	5,124
37601	Johnson City	(615)	39,753	33,770
*37662	Kingsport	(615)	32,027	31,938
*37901	Knoxville	(615)	175,045	174,587
37766	La Follette	(615)	8,176	6,902
37086	LaVergne	(615)	5,495	5,220
38464	Lawrenceburg	(615)	10,175	5,889
37087	Lebanon	(615)	11,872	12,492
37771	Lenoir City	(615)	5,180	5,324
37091	Lewisburg	(615)	8,760	7,207
38351	Lexington	(901)	5,934	5,024
37665	Lynn Garden(u)	(615)	7,213	....
38201	McKenzie	(901)	5,405	4,873
37110	McMinnville	(615)	10,683	10,662
37355	Manchester	(615)	7,250	6,208
38237	Martin	(901)	8,898	7,781
37701	Maryville	(615)	17,480	13,808
*38101	Memphis	(901)	646,174	623,988
37343	Middle Valley(u)	(615)	11,420	....
38358	Milan	(901)	8,083	7,313
38053	Millington	(901)	20,236	21,177
37814	Morristown	(615)	19,570	20,318
37130	Murfreesboro	(615)	32,845	26,360
*37202	Nashville-Davidson	(615)	455,651	**426,029
37821	Newport	(615)	7,580	7,328
37830	Oak Ridge	(615)	27,662	28,319
38242	Paris	(901)	10,728	9,892
37849	Powell(u)	(615)	7,220	....
38478	Pulaski	(615)	7,184	6,989
37415	Red Bank White Oak	(615)	13,129	12,715
38063	Ripley	(901)	6,366	4,794
37854	Rockwood	(615)	5,687	5,259
38372	Savannah	(901)	6,992	5,576
37160	Shelbyville	(615)	13,530	12,262
37377	Signal Mountain	(615)	5,818	4,839
37167	Smyrna	(615)	8,839	5,698
37379	Soddy-Daisy	(615)	8,388	7,569
37172	Springfield	(615)	10,814	9,720
37363	Summit (Hamilton)(u)	(615)	8,345	....
37388	Tullahoma	(615)	15,800	15,311
38261	Union City	(901)	10,436	11,925
37398	Winchester	(615)	5,821	5,256

**Comprises the Metropolitan Government of Nashville and Davidson County.

Texas

ZIP code	Place		1980	1970
*79604	Abilene	(915)	98,315	89,653
75001	Addison	(214)	5,553	593
78516	Alamo	(512)	5,831	4,291
78209	Alamo Heights	(512)	6,252	6,933
77039	Aldine(u)	(713)	12,623	....
78332	Alice	(512)	20,961	20,121
75002	Allen	(214)	8,314	1,940
79830	Alpine	(915)	5,465	5,971
77511	Alvin	(713)	16,515	10,671
*79105	Amarillo	(806)	149,230	127,010
79714	Andrews	(915)	11,061	8,625
77515	Angleton	(409)	13,929	9,906
78336	Aransas Pass	(512)	7,173	5,813
*76010	Arlington	(817)	160,113	90,229
75751	Athens	(214)	10,197	9,582
75551	Atlanta	(214)	6,272	5,007
*78710	Austin	(512)	345,890	253,539
76020	Azle	(817)	5,822	4,493
75149	Balch Springs	(214)	13,746	10,464
77520	Bay City	(409)	17,837	13,445
77404	Baytown	(713)	56,923	43,980
*77704	Beaumont	(409)	118,102	117,548
76021	Bedford	(817)	20,821	10,049
78102	Beeville	(512)	14,574	13,506
77401	Bellaire	(713)	14,950	19,009

ZIP code	Place		1980	1970
76704	Bellmead	(817)	7,569	7,698
76513	Belton	(817)	10,660	8,696
76126	Benbrook	(817)	13,579	8,169
79720	Big Spring	(915)	24,804	28,735
75418	Bonham	(214)	7,338	7,698
79007	Borger	(806)	15,837	14,195
76230	Bowie	(817)	5,610	5,185
76825	Brady	(915)	5,969	5,557
76024	Breckenridge	(817)	6,921	5,944
77833	Brenham	(409)	10,966	8,922
77611	Bridge City	(409)	7,667	8,164
79316	Brownfield	(806)	10,387	9,647
78520	Brownsville	(512)	84,997	52,522
76801	Brownwood	(915)	19,203	17,368
77801	Bryan	(409)	44,337	33,719
76354	Burkburnett	(817)	10,668	9,230
76028	Burleson	(817)	11,734	7,713
76520	Cameron	(817)	5,721	5,546
79015	Canyon	(806)	10,724	8,333
78834	Carrizo Springs	(512)	6,886	5,374
75006	Carrollton	(214)	40,591	13,855
75633	Carthage	(214)	6,447	5,392
75104	Cedar Hill	(214)	6,849	2,610
75935	Center	(409)	5,827	4,989
....	Champions(u)	(713)	14,692	....
77530	Channelview(u)	(713)	17,471	....
79201	Childress	(817)	5,817	5,408
76031	Cleburne	(817)	19,218	16,015
77327	Cleveland	(713)	5,977	5,627
77015	Clover Leaf(u)	(713)	17,317	....
77531	Clute	(409)	9,577	6,023
76834	Coleman	(915)	5,960	5,608
77840	College Station	(409)	37,272	17,676
76034	Colleyville	(817)	6,700	3,342
79512	Colorado City	(915)	5,405	5,227
75428	Commerce	(214)	8,136	9,534
77301	Conroe	(409)	18,034	11,969
78109	Converse	(512)	5,150	1,383
76522	Copperas Cove	(817)	19,469	10,818
*78408	Corpus Christi	(512)	232,134	204,525
75110	Corsicana	(214)	21,712	19,972
75835	Crockett	(713)	7,405	6,616
76036	Crowley	(817)	5,852	2,662
78839	Crystal City	(512)	8,334	8,104
77954	Cuero	(512)	7,124	6,956
79022	Dalhart	(806)	6,854	5,705
*75260	Dallas	(214)	904,599	844,401
77536	Deer Park	(713)	22,648	12,773
78840	Del Rio	(512)	30,034	21,330
75020	Denison	(214)	23,884	24,923
76201	Denton	(817)	48,063	39,874
75115	De Soto	(214)	15,538	6,617
75941	Diboll	(713)	5,227	3,557
77539	Dickinson	(713)	7,505	10,776
79027	Dimmitt	(806)	5,019	4,327
78537	Donna	(512)	9,952	7,365
79029	Dumas	(806)	12,194	9,771
75116	Duncanville	(214)	27,781	14,105
78852	Eagle Pass	(512)	21,407	15,364
78539	Edinburg	(512)	24,075	17,163
77957	Edna	(512)	5,650	5,332
77437	El Campo	(619)	10,462	9,332
*79910	El Paso	(915)	425,259	322,261
78543	Elsa	(512)	5,061	4,400
75119	Ennis	(214)	12,110	11,046
76039	Euless	(817)	24,002	19,316
76140	Everman	(817)	5,387	4,570
78355	Falfurrias	(512)	6,103	6,355
75234	Farmers Branch	(214)	24,863	27,492
76119	Forest Hill	(817)	11,684	8,236
79906	Fort Bliss(u)	(915)	12,687	13,288
76544	Fort Hood(u)	(817)	31,250	32,597
79735	Fort Stockton	(915)	8,688	8,283
*76101	Fort Worth	(817)	385,164	393,455
78624	Fredericksburg	(512)	6,412	5,326
77541	Freeport	(409)	13,444	11,997
77546	Friendswood	(713)	10,719	5,675
76240	Gainesville	(817)	14,081	13,830
77547	Galena Park	(713)	9,879	10,479
77550	Galveston	(409)	61,902	61,809
*75040	Garland	(214)	138,857	81,437
76528	Gatesville	(817)	6,078	4,683
78626	Georgetown	(512)	9,468	6,395
75644	Gilmer	(214)	5,167	4,196
75647	Gladewater	(214)	6,548	5,574
78629	Gonzales	(512)	7,152	5,854
76046	Graham	(817)	9,055	7,477
75050	Grand Prairie	(214)	71,462	50,904
76051	Grapevine	(817)	11,801	7,049
75401	Greenville	(214)	22,161	22,043
77619	Groves	(409)	17,090	18,067
76117	Haltom City	(817)	29,014	28,127
76541	Harker Heights	(817)	7,345	4,216
78550	Harlingen	(512)	43,543	33,503
77859	Hearne	(713)	5,418	4,982
75652	Henderson	(214)	11,473	10,187
79045	Hereford	(806)	15,853	13,414
76643	Hewitt	(817)	5,247	569
75205	Highland Park	(214)	8,909	10,133
77562	Highlands	(713)	6,467	3,462
76645	Hillsboro	(817)	7,397	7,224
77563	Hitchcock	(713)	6,103	5,565
78861	Hondo	(512)	6,057	5,487
*77013	Houston	(713)	1,595,138	1,233,535
77338	Humble	(713)	6,729	3,272
77340	Huntsville	(409)	23,936	17,610
76053	Hurst	(817)	31,420	27,215
78362	Ingleside	(512)	5,436	3,763
76367	Iowa Park	(817)	6,184	5,796
*75061	Irving	(214)	109,943	97,260
77029	Jacinto City	(713)	8,953	9,563
75766	Jacksonville	(214)	12,264	9,734
75951	Jasper	(409)	6,959	6,251
77450	Katy	(713)	5,660	2,923
79745	Kermit	(915)	8,015	7,884
78028	Kerrville	(512)	15,276	12,672
75662	Kilgore	(214)	11,331	9,495
76541	Killeen	(817)	46,296	35,507
78363	Kingsville	(512)	28,808	28,915
......	Kingwood	(713)	16,261	....
78219	Kirby	(512)	6,435	3,238
78236	Lackland AFB(u)	(512)	14,459	19,141
77566	Lake Jackson	(409)	19,102	13,376
77568	La Marque	(409)	15,372	16,131
79631	Lamesa	(806)	11,790	11,559
76550	Lampasas	(512)	6,165	5,922
75146	Lancaster	(214)	14,807	10,522
77571	La Porte	(713)	14,062	7,149
78040	Laredo	(512)	91,449	69,024
77573	League City	(713)	16,578	10,818
76238	Leon Valley	(512)	9,088	2,487
79336	Levelland	(806)	13,809	11,445
75067	Lewisville	(214)	24,273	9,264
77575	Liberty	(713)	7,945	5,591
79339	Littlefield	(806)	7,409	6,738
78233	Live Oak	(512)	8,183	2,779
78644	Lockhart	(512)	7,953	6,489
75601	Longview	(214)	62,762	45,547
*79408	Lubbock	(806)	173,873	149,101
75901	Lufkin	(409)	28,562	23,049
78648	Luling	(512)	5,039	4,719
78501	McAllen	(512)	67,042	37,636
75069	McKinney	(214)	16,249	15,193
76063	Mansfield	(817)	8,092	3,658
76661	Marlin	(817)	7,099	6,351
75670	Marshall	(214)	24,921	22,937
78368	Mathis	(512)	5,667	5,351
78570	Mercedes	(512)	11,851	9,355
75149	Mesquite	(214)	67,053	55,131
76667	Mexia	(817)	7,094	5,943
79701	Midland	(915)	70,525	59,463
76067	Mineral Wells	(817)	14,468	18,411
78572	Mission	(512)	22,653	13,043
77459	Missouri City	(713)	24,423	4,136
79756	Monahans	(915)	8,397	8,333
75455	Mount Pleasant	(214)	11,003	9,459
75961	Nacogdoches	(409)	27,149	22,544
77868	Navasota	(409)	5,971	5,111
77627	Nederland	(409)	16,855	16,810
78130	New Braunfels	(512)	22,402	17,859
76118	North Richland Hills	(817)	30,592	16,514
*79760	Odessa	(915)	90,027	78,380
77630	Orange	(409)	23,628	24,457
75801	Palestine	(214)	15,948	14,525
79065	Pampa	(806)	21,396	21,726
75460	Paris	(214)	25,498	23,441
*77501	Pasadena	(713)	112,560	89,957
77581	Pearland	(713)	13,248	6,444
78061	Pearsall	(512)	7,383	5,545
79772	Pecos	(915)	12,855	12,682
79070	Perryton	(806)	7,991	7,810
78577	Pharr	(512)	21,381	15,829
79072	Plainview	(806)	22,187	19,096
75075	Plano	(214)	72,331	17,872
78064	Pleasanton	(512)	6,346	5,407
77640	Port Arthur	(409)	61,195	57,371
78374	Portland	(512)	12,023	7,302
77979	Port Lavaca	(512)	10,911	10,491
77651	Port Neches	(409)	13,944	10,894
78580	Raymondville	(512)	9,493	7,987
75080	Richardson	(214)	72,496	48,405
76118	Richland Hills	(817)	7,977	8,865
77469	Richmond	(713)	9,692	5,777
78582	Rio Grande City(u)	(512)	8,930	5,676
77019	River Oaks	(817)	6,890	8,193
76701	Robinson	(817)	6,074	3,807
78380	Robstown	(512)	12,100	11,217
76567	Rockdale	(512)	5,611	4,655
75087	Rockwall	(214)	5,939	3,121
77471	Rosenberg	(713)	17,840	12,098
78664	Round Rock	(512)	12,740	2,811
75088	Rowlett	(214)	7,522	2,243
76179	Saginaw	(817)	5,736	2,382
76901	San Angelo	(915)	73,240	63,884
*78284	San Antonio	(512)	785,940	654,153
78586	San Benito	(512)	17,988	15,176
78384	San Diego	(512)	5,225	4,490
78589	San Juan	(512)	7,608	5,070
78666	San Marcos	(512)	23,420	18,860
77550	Santa Fe	(713)	5,413	....

ZIP code	Place		1980	1970
78154	Schertz	(512)	7,262	4,061
75159	Seagoville	(214)	7,304	4,390
78155	Seguin	(512)	17,854	15,934
79360	Seminole	(915)	6,080	5,007
75090	Sherman	(214)	30,413	29,061
77656	Silsbee	(409)	7,684	7,271
78387	Sinton	(512)	6,044	5,563
79364	Slaton	(806)	6,804	6,583
79549	Snyder	(915)	12,705	11,171
77587	South Houston	(713)	13,293	11,527
76401	Stephenville	(817)	11,881	9,277
77478	Sugar Land	(713)	8,826	3,318
75482	Sulphur Springs	(214)	12,804	10,642
79556	Sweetwater	(915)	12,242	12,020
76574	Taylor	(512)	10,619	9,616
76501	Temple	(817)	42,354	33,431
75160	Terrell	(214)	13,269	14,182
75501	Texarkana	(214)	31,271	30,497
77590	Texas City	(409)	41,201	38,908
75056	The Colony	(214)	11,586	....
77380	The Woodlands	(713)	8,443	....
79088	Tulia	(806)	5,033	5,294
75701	Tyler	(214)	70,508	57,770
78148	Universal City	(512)	10,720	7,613
76308	University Park	(214)	22,254	23,498
78801	Uvalde	(512)	14,178	10,764
76384	Vernon	(817)	12,695	11,454
77901	Victoria	(512)	50,695	41,349
77662	Vidor	(409)	11,834	9,738
*76701	Waco	(817)	101,261	95,326
76148	Watauga	(817)	10,284	3,778
75165	Waxahachie	(214)	14,624	13,452
76086	Weatherford	(817)	12,049	11,750
78596	Weslaco	(512)	19,331	15,313
77005	West University Place	(713)	12,010	13,317
77488	Wharton	(713)	9,033	7,881
76108	White Settlement	(817)	13,508	13,449
*76307	Wichita Falls	(817)	94,201	96,265
78239	Windcrest	(512)	5,332	3,371
76710	Woodway	(817)	7,091	4,819
77995	Yoakum	(512)	6,148	5,755

Utah (801)

ZIP code	Place	1980	1970
84003	American Fork	12,417	7,713
84118	Bennion(u)	9,632	....
84010	Bountiful	32,877	27,751
84302	Brigham City	15,596	14,007
84720	Cedar City	10,972	8,945
84014	Centerville	8,069	3,268
84015	Clearfield	17,982	13,316
84015	Clinton	5,777	1,768
84121	Cottonwood(u)	11,554	8,431
84121	Cottonwood Heights(u)	22,665	....
84020	Draper	5,530	....
84109	East Millcreek(u)	24,150	26,579
84106	Granite Park(u)	5,554	9,573
84117	Holladay(u)	22,189	23,014
84037	Kaysville	9,811	6,192
84118	Kearns(u)	21,353	17,247
84041	Layton	22,862	13,603
84043	Lehi	6,848	4,659
84321	Logan	26,844	22,333
84044	Magna(u)	13,138	5,509
84047	Midvale	10,144	7,840
84532	Moab	5,333	4,793
84117	Mount Olympus(u)	6,068	5,909
84107	Murray	25,750	21,206
84404	North Ogden	9,309	5,257
84054	North Salt Lake	5,548	2,143
*84401	Ogden	64,407	69,478
*84057	Orem	52,399	25,729
84651	Payson	8,246	4,501
84062	Pleasant Grove	10,669	5,327
84501	Price	9,086	6,218
*84601	Provo	74,111	53,131
84701	Richfield	5,482	4,471
84065	Riverton	7,032	2,820
84067	Roy	19,694	14,356
84770	St. George	11,350	7,097
*84101	Salt Lake City	163,034	175,885
*84070	Sandy City	52,210	6,438
84121	South Cottonwood(u)	11,117	....
84065	South Jordan	7,492	2,942
84403	South Ogden	11,366	9,991
84115	South Salt Lake	10,413	7,810
84660	Spanish Fork	9,825	7,284
84663	Springville	12,101	8,790
84015	Sunset	5,733	6,268
84107	Taylorsville(u)	17,448	....
84074	Tooele	14,335	12,539
84047	Union-East Midvale(u)	9,663	....
84010	Val Verda(u)	6,422	....
84078	Vernal	6,600	3,908
84403	Washington Terrace	8,212	7,241
84084	West Jordan	27,325	4,221
*84119	West Valley City	72,299	....
84070	White City(u)	7,180	6,402

Vermont (802)

See Note on Page 563

ZIP code	Place	1980	1970
05641	Barre	9,824	10,209
.....	Barre	7,090	6,509
05201	Bennington	15,815	14,586
.....	Bennington(u)	9,349	7,950
05301	Brattleboro Center(u)	8,596	9,055
.....	Brattleboro	11,886	12,239
05401	Burlington	37,712	38,633
05446	Colchester	12,629	8,776
05451	Essex	14,392	10,951
05452	Essex Junction	7,033	6,511
05753	Middlebury	7,574	6,532
05602	Montpelier	8,241	8,609
05701	Rutland	18,436	19,293
05478	St. Albans	7,308	8,082
05819	St. Johnsbury	7,938	8,409
05401	South Burlington	10,679	10,032
05156	Springfield Center(u)	5,603	5,632
.....	Springfield	10,190	10,063
05404	Winooski	6,318	7,309

Virginia

ZIP code	Place		1980	1970
*22313	Alexandria	(703)	103,217	110,927
22003	Annandale(u)	(703)	49,524	27,405
*22210	Arlington(u)	(703)	152,599	174,284
22041	Bailey's Crossroads(u)	(703)	12,564	7,295
24523	Bedford	(703)	5,991	6,011
22307	Belle Haven(u)	(703)	6,520	....
23234	Bellwood(u)	(804)	6,439	....
23234	Bensley(u)	(804)	5,299	....
24060	Blacksburg	(703)	30,638	9,384
24605	Bluefield	(703)	5,946	5,286
23235	Bon Air(u)	(804)	16,224	10,771
24201	Bristol	(703)	19,042	14,857
24416	Buena Vista	(703)	6,717	6,425
22015	Burke(u)	(703)	33,835	....
24018	Cave Spring(u)	(703)	21,682	....
22020	Centreville(u)	(703)	7,473	....
23227	Chamberlayne(u)	(804)	5,136	....
22021	Chantilly(u)	(703)	12,259	....
*22906	Charlottesville	(804)	45,010	38,880
*23320	Chesapeake	(804)	114,226	89,580
23831	Chester(u)	(804)	11,728	5,556
24073	Christiansburg	(703)	10,345	7,857
24422	Clifton Forge	(703)	5,046	5,501
24078	Collinsville(u)	(703)	7,517	6,015
23834	Colonial Heights	(804)	16,509	15,097
24426	Covington	(703)	9,063	10,060
22701	Culpeper	(703)	6,621	6,056
22191	Dale City(u)	(703)	33,127	13,857
24541	Danville	(804)	45,642	46,391
23228	Dumbarton(u)	(804)	8,149	....
22027	Dunn Loring(u)	(703)	6,077	....
23222	East Highland Park(u)	(804)	11,797	....
22030	Fairfax	(703)	19,390	22,727
*22046	Falls Church	(703)	9,515	10,772
23901	Farmville	(804)	6,067	4,331
22060	Fort Belvoir(u)	(703)	7,726	14,591
22308	Fort Hunt(u)	(703)	14,294	10,415
23801	Fort Lee(u)	(804)	9,784	12,435
22310	Franconia(u)	(703)	8,476	....
23851	Franklin	(804)	7,308	6,880
22401	Fredericksburg	(703)	15,322	14,450
22630	Front Royal	(703)	11,126	8,211
24333	Galax	(703)	6,524	6,278
23060	Glen Allen(u)	(804)	6,202	....
23052	Gloucester Point(u)	(804)	5,841	....
22306	Groveton(u)	(703)	18,860	11,761
*23660	Hampton	(804)	122,617	120,779
22801	Harrisonburg	(703)	19,671	14,605
*22070	Herndon	(703)	11,449	4,301
23075	Highland Springs(u)	(804)	12,146	7,345
24019	Hollins(u)	(703)	12,187	....
23860	Hopewell	(804)	23,397	23,471
22303	Huntington(u)	(703)	5,813	5,559
22306	Hybla Valley(u)	(703)	15,533	....
22043	Idylwood(u)	(703)	11,982	....
22042	Jefferson(u)	(804)	24,342	25,432
22041	Lake Barcroft(u)	(703)	8,725	11,605
22191	Lake Ridge(u)	(703)	11,072	....
23228	Lakeside(u)	(804)	12,289	11,137
23060	Laurel(u)	(804)	10,569	....
22075	Leesburg	(703)	8,357	4,821
24450	Lexington	(703)	7,292	7,597
22312	Lincolnia(u)	(703)	10,350	10,355
22079	Lorton(u)	(703)	5,813	....
*24505	Lynchburg	(804)	66,743	54,083
24572	Madison Heights(u)	(804)	14,146	....
22110	Manassas	(703)	15,438	9,164
22110	Manassas Park	(703)	6,524	6,844
22030	Mantua(u)	(703)	6,523	6,911
24354	Marion	(703)	7,287	8,158
24112	Martinsville	(703)	18,149	19,653
22101	McLean(u)	(703)	35,664	17,698
23111	Mechanicsville(u)	(804)	9,269	5,189
22116	Merrifield(u)	(703)	7,525	....

ZIP code	Place		1980	1970
23231	Montrose(u)	(804)	5,349	....
22121	Mount Vernon(u)	(703)	24,058	....
22122	Newington(u)	(703)	8,313	....
*23607	Newport News	(804)	144,903	138,177
*23501	Norfolk	(804)	266,979	307,951
22151	North Springfield(u)	(703)	9,538	8,631
22124	Oakton(u)	(703)	19,150	....
23803	Petersburg	(804)	41,055	36,103
22043	Pimmit Hills(u)	(703)	6,658	....
23662	Poquoson	(804)	8,726	5,441
*23705	Portsmouth	(804)	104,577	110,963
24301	Pulaski	(703)	10,106	10,279
22134	Quantico Station(u)	(703)	7,121	6,213
22141	Radford	(703)	13,225	11,596
22090	Reston(u)	(703)	36,407	5,723
24641	Richlands	(703)	5,796	4,843
*23232	Richmond	(804)	219,214	249,332
*24001	Roanoke	(703)	100,427	92,115
22310	Rose Hill(u)	(703)	11,926	14,492
24153	Salem	(703)	23,958	21,982
22044	Seven Corners(u)	(703)	6,058	5,590
24592	South Boston	(804)	7,093	6,889
*22150	Springfield	(703)	21,435	11,613
24401	Staunton	(703)	21,857	24,504
22170	Sterling Park(u)	(703)	16,080	8,321
23434	Suffolk	(804)	47,621	9,858
22170	Sugarland Run(u)	(703)	6,258	....
24502	Timberlake(u)	(804)	9,697	....
23229	Tuckahoe(u)	(804)	39,868	....
22101	Tysons Corner(u)	(703)	10,065	....
22180	Vienna	(703)	15,469	17,146
24179	Vinton	(703)	8,027	6,347
*23458	Virginia Beach	(804)	262,199	172,106
22980	Waynesboro	(703)	15,329	16,707
22110	West Gate(u)	(703)	7,119	....
22152	West Springfield(u)	(703)	25,012	14,143
23185	Williamsburg	(804)	9,870	9,069
22601	Winchester	(703)	20,217	14,643
24592	Wolf Trap(u)	(804)	9,875	....
22191	Woodbridge(u)	(703)	24,004	25,412
24382	Wytheville	(703)	7,135	6,069

Washington

ZIP code	Place		1980	1970
98520	Aberdeen	(206)	18,739	18,489
98036	Alderwood Manor(u)	(206)	16,524	....
98221	Anacortes	(206)	9,013	7,701
98002	Auburn	(206)	26,417	21,653
*98009	Bellevue	(206)	73,903	61,196
98225	Bellingham	(206)	45,794	39,375
98390	Bonney Lake	(206)	5,328	2,700
98011	Bothell	(206)	7,943	5,420
	Boulevard Park(u)	(206)	8,382	....
98310	Bremerton	(206)	36,208	35,307
98178	Bryn Mawr-Skyway(u)	(206)	11,754	....
98166	Burien(u)	(206)	23,189	....
98607	Camas	(206)	5,681	5,790
98055	Cascade-Fairwood(u)	(206)	16,939	....
98531	Centralia	(206)	10,809	10,054
98532	Chehalis	(206)	6,100	5,727
99004	Cheney	(509)	7,630	6,358
99403	Clarkston	(509)	6,903	6,312
99324	College Place	(509)	5,771	4,510
98188	Des Moines	(206)	7,378	3,951
99213	Dishman(u)	(509)	10,169	9,079
	Dumas Bay-Twin Lakes(u)	(206)	14,535	....
98004	Eastgate(u)	(206)	8,341	....
	East Renton Highlands(u)	(206)	12,033	....
98801	East Wenatchee Bench(u)	(509)	11,410	2,446
98020	Edmonds	(206)	27,526	23,684
98926	Ellensburg	(509)	11,752	13,568
98022	Enumclaw	(206)	5,427	4,703
98823	Ephrata	(509)	5,359	5,255
99210	Esperance(u)	(509)	11,120	....
*98201	Everett	(206)	54,413	53,622
99011	Fairchild AFB(u)	(509)	5,353	6,754
98201	Fairmont-Intercity(u)	(206)	6,997	....
98055	Fairwood(u)	(206)	5,337	....
98466	Fircrest	(206)	5,477	5,651
98433	Fort Lewis(u)	(206)	23,761	38,054
98930	Grandview	(509)	5,615	3,605
98660	Hazel Dell(u)	(206)	15,386	....
98550	Hoquiam	(206)	9,719	10,466
98011	Inglewood(u)	(206)	12,467	....
98027	Issaquah	(206)	5,536	4,313
98033	Juanita(u)	(206)	17,232	....
98626	Kelso	(206)	11,129	10,296
98028	Kenmore(u)	(206)	7,281	....
99336	Kennewick	(509)	34,397	15,212
98031	Kent	(206)	22,961	17,711
98033	Kingsgate(u)	(206)	12,652	....
98033	Kirkland	(206)	18,785	14,970
98503	Lacey	(206)	13,940	9,696
98155	Lake Forest North(u)	(206)	7,995	....
	Lakeland North(u)	(206)	11,451	....
	Lakeland South(u)	(206)	5,225	....

ZIP code	Place		1980	1970
....	Lake Stickney(u)	(206)	6,135	....
98499	Lakes District(u)	(206)	54,533	48,195
98632	Longview	(206)	31,052	28,373
98036	Lynnwood	(206)	21,937	17,381
	Martha Lake(u)	(206)	7,022	....
98270	Marysville	(206)	5,080	4,343
98438	McChord AFB(u)	(206)	5,746	6,515
98040	Mercer Island	(206)	21,522	19,047
98837	Moses Lake	(509)	10,629	10,310
98043	Mountlake Terrace	(206)	16,534	16,600
98273	Mount Vernon	(206)	13,009	8,804
98006	Newport Hills(u)	(206)	12,245	....
98155	North City-Ridgecrest(u)	(206)	13,551	....
	North Hill(u)	(206)	10,170	....
98270	North Marysville(u)	(206)	15,159	....
98277	Oak Harbor	(206)	12,271	9,167
*98501	Olympia	(206)	27,447	23,296
99214	Opportunity(u)	(509)	21,241	16,604
98662	Orchards(u)	(206)	8,826	....
98444	Parkland(u)	(206)	23,355	21,012
99301	Pasco	(509)	18,428	13,920
98362	Port Angeles	(206)	17,311	16,367
98368	Port Townsend	(206)	6,067	5,241
	Poverty Bay(u)	(206)	8,353	....
99163	Pullman	(509)	23,579	20,509
98371	Puyallup	(206)	18,251	14,742
98052	Redmond	(206)	23,318	11,020
98055	Renton	(206)	31,031	25,878
99352	Richland	(509)	33,578	26,290
98160	Richmond Beach-Innis Arden(u)	(206)	6,700	....
98113	Richmond Highlands(u)	(206)	24,463	....
98188	Riverton(u)	(206)	14,182	....
98033	Rose Hill(u)	(206)	7,616	....
*98109	Seattle	(206)	493,846	530,831
98284	Sedro Woolley	(206)	6,110	4,598
98584	Shelton	(206)	7,629	6,515
98155	Sheridan Beach(u)	(206)	6,873	....
98201	Silver Lake-Fircrest(u)	....	10,299	....
98290	Snohomish	(206)	5,294	5,174
98387	Spanaway(u)	(206)	8,868	5,768
*99210	Spokane	(509)	171,300	170,516
98944	Sunnyside	(509)	9,225	6,751
*98402	Tacoma	(206)	158,501	154,407
98501	Tanglewilde-Thompson Place(u)	....	5,910	3,423
99948	Toppenish	(509)	6,517	5,744
99268	Town and Country(u)	(509)	5,578	6,484
98502	Tumwater	(206)	6,705	5,373
98406	University Place(u)	(206)	20,381	13,230
	Valley Ridge(u)	(206)	17,961	....
*98660	Vancouver	(206)	42,834	41,859
99037	Veradale(u)	(509)	7,256	....
99362	Walla Walla	(509)	25,618	23,619
98801	Wenatchee	(509)	17,257	16,912
98003	West Federal Way(u)	(206)	16,872	....
99301	West Pasco(u)	(509)	6,210	....
98166	White Center-Shorewood(u)	(206)	19,362	....
*99901	Yakima	(509)	49,826	45,588
98188	Zenith-Saltwater(u)	(206)	8,982	....

West Virginia (304)

ZIP code	Place	1980	1970
25801	Beckley	20,492	19,884
24701	Bluefield	16,060	15,921
26330	Bridgeport	6,604	4,777
26201	Buckhannon	6,820	7,261
*25301	Charleston	63,968	71,505
26301	Clarksburg	22,371	24,864
25064	Dunbar	9,285	9,151
26241	Elkins	8,536	8,287
26554	Fairmont	23,863	26,093
26354	Grafton	6,845	6,433
*25701	Huntington	63,684	74,315
26726	Keyser	6,569	6,586
25401	Martinsburg	13,063	14,626
26505	Morgantown	27,605	29,431
26041	Moundsville	12,419	13,560
26155	New Martinsville	7,109	6,528
25143	Nitro	8,074	8,019
25901	Oak Hill	7,120	4,738
26101	Parkersburg	39,946	44,208
25550	Point Pleasant	5,682	6,122
24740	Princeton	7,538	7,253
25177	St. Albans	12,402	14,356
25303	South Charleston	15,968	16,333
26105	Vienna	11,618	11,549
26062	Weirton	25,371	27,131
26452	Weston	6,250	7,323
26003	Wheeling	43,070	48,188
25661	Williamson	5,219	5,831

Wisconsin

ZIP code	Place		1980	1970
54301	Allouez(u)	(414)	14,882	13,753
54409	Antigo	(715)	8,653	9,005
54911	Appleton	(414)	58,913	56,377
54806	Ashland	(715)	9,115	9,615

ZIP code	Place		1980	1970
54304	Ashwaubenon	(414)	14,486	9,323
53913	Baraboo	(608)	8,081	7,931
53916	Beaver Dam	(414)	14,149	14,265
53511	Beloit	(608)	35,207	35,729
53511	Beloit North(u)	(608)	5,457	----
54923	Berlin	(414)	5,478	5,338
53005	Brookfield	(414)	34,035	31,761
53209	Brown Deer	(414)	12,921	12,582
53105	Burlington	(414)	8,395	7,479
53012	Cedarburg	(414)	9,005	7,697
54729	Chippewa Falls	(715)	11,845	12,351
53110	Cudahy	(414)	19,547	22,078
53115	Delavan	(414)	5,684	5,526
54115	De Pere	(414)	14,892	13,309
54701	Eau Claire	(715)	51,509	44,619
53122	Elm Grove	(414)	6,735	7,201
54935	Fond Du Lac	(414)	35,863	35,515
53538	Fort Atkinson	(414)	9,785	9,164
53217	Fox Point	(414)	7,649	7,939
53132	Franklin	(414)	16,871	12,247
53022	Germantown	(414)	10,729	6,974
53209	Glendale	(414)	13,882	13,426
53024	Grafton	(414)	8,381	5,998
54305	Green Bay	(414)	87,809	87,809
53129	Greendale	(414)	16,928	15,089
53220	Greenfield	(414)	31,353	24,424
53130	Hales Corners	(414)	7,110	7,771
53027	Hartford	(414)	7,159	6,499
53029	Hartland	(414)	5,559	2,763
54303	Howard	(414)	8,240	4,911
54016	Hudson	(715)	5,434	5,049
53545	Janesville	(608)	51,071	46,426
53549	Jefferson	(414)	5,647	5,429
54130	Kaukauna	(414)	11,310	11,308
53140	Kenosha	(414)	77,685	78,805
54136	Kimberly	(414)	5,881	6,131
54601	La Crosse	(608)	48,347	50,266
53147	Lake Geneva	(414)	5,612	4,890
54140	Little Chute	(414)	7,907	5,522
53701	Madison	(608)	170,616	171,809
54220	Manitowoc	(414)	32,547	33,430
54143	Marinette	(715)	11,965	12,696
54449	Marshfield	(715)	18,290	15,619
54952	Menasha	(414)	14,728	14,836
53051	Menomonee Falls	(414)	27,845	31,697
54751	Menomonie	(715)	12,769	11,112
53092	Mequon	(414)	16,193	12,150
54452	Merrill	(715)	9,578	9,502
53562	Middleton	(608)	11,851	8,246
53203	Milwaukee	(414)	636,297	717,372
53716	Monona	(608)	8,809	10,420
53566	Monroe	(608)	10,027	8,654
53150	Muskego	(414)	15,277	11,573
54956	Neenah	(414)	23,272	22,902
53151	New Berlin	(414)	30,529	26,910
54961	New London	(414)	6,210	5,801
53154	Oak Creek	(414)	16,932	13,928
53066	Oconomowoc	(414)	9,909	8,741
54650	Onalaska	(608)	9,249	4,909
54901	Oshkosh	(414)	49,678	53,082
53818	Platteville	(608)	9,580	9,599
54457	Plover	(715)	5,310	----
53073	Plymouth	(414)	6,027	5,810
53901	Portage	(608)	7,896	7,821
53074	Port Washington	(414)	8,612	8,752
53821	Prairie du Chien	(608)	5,859	5,540
53401	Racine	(414)	85,725	95,162
53959	Reedsburg	(608)	5,038	4,585
54501	Rhinelander	(715)	7,873	8,218
54868	Rice Lake	(715)	7,691	7,278
54971	Ripon	(414)	7,111	7,053
54022	River Falls	(715)	9,019	7,238
53207	St. Francis	(414)	10,095	10,489
54166	Shawano	(715)	7,013	6,488
53081	Sheboygan	(414)	48,085	48,484
53085	Sheboygan Falls	(414)	5,253	4,771
53211	Shorewood	(414)	14,327	15,576
53172	South Milwaukee	(414)	21,069	23,297
54656	Sparta	(608)	6,934	6,258
54481	Stevens Point	(715)	22,970	23,479
53589	Stoughton	(608)	7,589	6,096
54235	Sturgeon Bay	(414)	8,847	6,776
53590	Sun Prairie	(608)	12,931	9,935
54880	Superior	(715)	29,571	32,237
54660	Tomah	(608)	7,204	5,647
54241	Two Rivers	(414)	13,354	13,732
53094	Watertown	(414)	18,113	15,683
53186	Waukesha	(414)	50,365	39,695
53963	Waupun	(414)	8,132	7,946
54401	Wausau	(715)	32,426	32,806
54401	Wausau West Rib Mt.(u)	(715)	6,005	----
53213	Wauwatosa	(414)	51,308	58,676
53214	West Allis	(414)	63,982	71,649
53095	West Bend	(414)	21,484	16,555
54476	Weston(u)	(715)	8,775	3,375
53217	Whitefish Bay	(414)	14,930	17,402
53190	Whitewater	(414)	11,520	12,038
54494	Wisconsin Rapids	(715)	17,995	18,587

Wyoming (307)

82601	Casper	51,016	39,361
82001	Cheyenne	47,283	41,254
82414	Cody	6,599	5,161
82633	Douglas	6,030	2,677
82930	Evanston	6,265	4,462
82716	Gillette	12,134	7,194
82335	Green River	12,807	4,196
82520	Lander	9,126	7,125
82070	Laramie	24,410	23,143
82435	Powell	5,310	4,807
82301	Rawlins	11,547	7,855
82501	Riverton	9,562	7,995
82901	Rock Springs	19,458	11,657
82801	Sheridan	15,146	10,856
82240	Torrington	5,441	4,237
82201	Wheatland	5,816	2,498
82401	Worland	6,391	5,055

Census and Areas of Counties and States

Source: U.S. Bureau of the Census
With names of county seats or court houses

Population figures listed below are final counts in the 1980 census, conducted on Apr. 1, 1990, and updated in April 1990, for all counties and states. Figures are subject to change pending the outcome of various lawsuits dealing with the census counts.

Alabama

(67 counties, 50,767 sq. mi. land; pop., 3,894,025)

County	Pop.	County seat or court house	Land area sq. mi.
Autauga	32,259	Prattville	597
Baldwin	78,440	Bay Minette	1,589
Barbour	24,756	Clayton	884
Bibb	15,723	Centreville	625
Blount	36,459	Oneonta	643
Bullock	10,596	Union Springs	625
Butler	21,680	Greenville	779
Calhoun	116,936	Anniston	611
Chambers	39,191	Lafayette	596
Cherokee	18,760	Centre	553
Chilton	30,612	Clanton	695
Choctaw	16,839	Butler	909
Clarke	27,702	Grove Hill	1,230
Clay	13,703	Ashland	605
Cleburne	12,595	Heflin	561
Coffee	38,533	Elba	680
Colbert	54,519	Tuscumbia	589
Conecuh	15,884	Evergreen	854
Coosa	11,377	Rockford	657
Covington	36,850	Andalusia	1,038
Crenshaw	14,110	Luverne	611
Cullman	61,642	Cullman	738
Dale	47,821	Ozark	561
Dallas	53,981	Selma	975
De Kalb	53,658	Fort Payne	778
Elmore	43,390	Wetumpka	622
Escambia	38,392	Brewton	951
Etowah	103,057	Gadsden	542
Fayette	18,809	Fayette	630
Franklin	28,350	Russellville	643
Geneva	24,253	Geneva	578
Greene	11,021	Eutaw	631
Hale	15,604	Greensboro	661
Henry	15,302	Abbeville	557
Houston	74,632	Dothan	577
Jackson	51,407	Scottsboro	1,070
Jefferson	671,371	Birmingham	1,119
Lamar	16,453	Vernon	605
Lauderdale	80,504	Florence	661
Lawrence	30,170	Moulton	693
Lee	76,283	Opelika	609
Limestone	46,005	Athens	559
Lowndes	13,253	Hayneville	714
Macon	26,829	Tuskegee	614
Madison	196,966	Huntsville	806
Marengo	25,047	Linden	982
Marion	30,041	Hamilton	743
Marshall	65,622	Guntersville	567
Mobile	364,379	Mobile	1,238
Monroe	22,651	Monroeville	1,019
Montgomery	197,038	Montgomery	793
Morgan	90,231	Decatur	575
Perry	15,012	Marion	718
Pickens	21,481	Carrollton	890
Pike	28,050	Troy	672
Randolph	20,075	Wedowee	584

County	Pop.	County Seat or court house	Land area sq. mi.
Russell	47,356	Phenix City	634
St. Clair	41,205	Ashville & Pell City	646
Shelby	66,298	Columbiana	800
Sumter	16,908	Livingston	907
Talladega	73,826	Talladega	753
Tallapoosa	38,766	Dadeville	701
Tuscaloosa	137,473	Tuscaloosa	1,336
Walker	68,660	Jasper	804
Washington	16,821	Chatom	1,081
Wilcox	14,755	Camden	883
Winston	21,953	Double Springs	613

Alaska
(23 divisions, 570,833 sq. mi. land; pop., 401,851)

Census area	Pop.	Land area sq. mi.
Aleutian Islands	7,768	10,890
Anchorage Borough	173,017	1,732

Census division	Pop.	Land area sq. mi.
Bethel	10,999	36,104
Bristol Bay Borough	1,094	531
Dillingham	4,616	46,042
Fairbanks North Star Borough	53,983	7,404
Haines Borough	1,680	2,374
Juneau Borough	19,528	2,626
Kenai Peninsula Borough	25,282	16,056
Ketchikan Gateway Borough	11,316	1,242
Kobuk	4,831	31,593
Kodiak Island Borough	9,939	4,796
Matanuska-Susitna Borough	17,766	24,502
Nome	6,537	23,871
North Slope Borough	4,199	90,955
Prince of Wales-Outer Ketchikan	3,822	7,660
Sitka Borough	7,803	2,938
Skagway-Yakutat-Angoon	3,478	13,239
Southeast Fairbanks	5,770	24,169
Valdez-Cordova	8,348	39,229
Wade Hampton	4,665	17,816
Wrangell-Petersburg	6,167	5,965
Yukon-Koyukuk	7,873	159,099

Arizona
(15 counties, 113,508 sq. mi. land; pop. 2,716,546)

County	Pop.	County seat or court house	Land area sq. mi.
Apache	52,083	Saint Johns	11,211
Cochise	86,717	Bisbee	6,218
Coconino	74,947	Flagstaff	18,608
Gila	37,080	Globe	4,752
Graham	22,862	Safford	4,630
Greenlee	11,406	Clifton	1,837
La Paz	12,487	Parker	4,430
Maricopa	1,509,175	Phoenix	9,127
Mohave	55,693	Kingman	13,285
Navajo	67,709	Holbrook	9,965
Pima	531,263	Tucson	9,187
Pinal	90,918	Florence	5,343
Santa Cruz	20,459	Nogales	1,238
Yavapai	68,145	Prescott	8,123
Yuma	88,762	Yuma	5,564

Arkansas
(75 counties, 52,078 sq. mi. land; pop. 2,286,357)

County	Pop.	County Seat or court house	Land area sq. mi.
Arkansas	24,175	DeWitt & Stuttgart	1,006
Ashley	26,538	Hamburg	934
Baxter	27,409	Mountain Home	546
Benton	78,115	Bentonville	843
Boone	26,067	Harrison	584
Bradley	13,803	Warren	654
Calhoun	6,079	Hampton	628
Carroll	16,203	Berryville and Eureka Sp.	634
Chicot	17,793	Lake Village	649
Clark	23,326	Arkadelphia	867
Clay	20,616	Corning; Piggott	641
Cleburne	16,909	Heber Springs	551
Cleveland	7,868	Rison	599
Columbia	26,644	Magnolia	767
Conway	19,505	Morrilton	558
Craighead	63,218	Jonesboro and Lake City	713
Crawford	36,892	Van Buren	594
Crittenden	49,097	Marion	624
Cross	20,434	Wynne	622
Dallas	10,515	Fordyce	668
Desha	19,760	Arkansas City	746
Drew	17,910	Monticello	831
Faulkner	46,192	Conway	645
Franklin	14,705	Charleston and Ozark	609
Fulton	9,975	Salem	616
Garland	69,916	Hot Spgs. Nat'l Pk.	657
Grant	13,008	Sheridan	633
Greene	30,744	Paragould	579
Hempstead	23,635	Hope	725
Hot Spring	26,819	Malvern	615
Howard	13,459	Nashville	574
Independence	30,147	Batesville	763
Izard	10,768	Melbourne	581
Jackson	21,646	Newport	633
Jefferson	90,718	Pine Bluff	882
Johnson	17,423	Clarksville	676
Lafayette	10,213	Lewisville	518
Lawrence	18,447	Walnut Ridge	589
Lee	15,539	Marianna	602
Lincoln	13,369	Star City	562
Little River	13,952	Ashdown	516
Logan	20,144	Booneville & Paris	717
Lonoke	34,518	Lonoke	783
Madison	11,373	Huntsville	837
Marion	11,334	Yellville	587
Miller	37,766	Texarkana	619
Mississippi	59,517	Blytheville and Osceola	896
Monroe	14,052	Clarendon	609
Montgomery	7,771	Mount Ida	774
Nevada	11,097	Prescott	620
Newton	7,756	Jasper	823
Ouachita	30,541	Camden	737
Perry	7,266	Perryville	550
Phillips	34,772	Helena	685
Pike	10,373	Murfreesboro	598
Poinsett	27,032	Harrisburg	762
Polk	17,007	Mena	860
Pope	38,964	Russellville	820
Prairie	10,140	Des Arc and De Valls Bluff	656
Pulaski	340,597	Little Rock	767
Randolph	16,834	Pocahontas	656
St. Francis	30,858	Forrest City	638
Saline	53,156	Benton	725
Scott	9,685	Waldron	896
Searcy	8,847	Marshall	668
Sebastian	94,930	Fort Smith; Greenwood	535
Sevier	14,060	De Queen	560
Sharp	14,607	Ash Flat	606
Stone	9,022	Mountain View	606
Union	49,988	El Dorado	1,053
Van Buren	13,357	Clinton	709
Washington	99,735	Fayetteville	951
White	50,835	Searcy	1,040
Woodruff	11,222	Augusta	592
Yell	17,026	Danville and Dardanelle	930

California
(58 counties, 156,299 sq. mi. land; pop. 23,667,764)

County	Pop.	County seat or court house	Land area sq. mi.
Alameda	1,105,379	Oakland	736
Alpine	1,097	Markleeville	738
Amador	19,314	Jackson	589
Butte	143,851	Oroville	1,646
Calaveras	20,710	San Andreas	1,021
Colusa	12,791	Colusa	1,152
Contra Costa	656,331	Martinez	730
Del Norte	18,217	Crescent City	1,007
El Dorado	85,812	Placerville	1,715
Fresno	515,013	Fresno	5,978
Glenn	21,350	Willows	1,319
Humboldt	108,525	Eureka	3,579
Imperial	92,110	El Centro	4,173
Inyo	17,895	Independence	10,223
Kern	403,089	Bakersfield	8,130
Kings	73,738	Hanford	1,392
Lake	36,366	Lakeport	1,262
Lassen	21,661	Susanville	4,553
Los Angeles	7,477,238	Los Angeles	4,070
Madera	63,116	Madera	2,145
Marin	222,592	San Rafael	523
Mariposa	11,108	Mariposa	1,455
Mendocino	66,738	Ukiah	3,512
Merced	134,558	Merced	1,944
Modoc	8,610	Alturas	4,064
Mono	8,577	Bridgeport	3,018
Monterey	290,444	Salinas	3,303
Napa	99,199	Napa	744
Nevada	51,645	Nevada City	960
Orange	1,932,921	Santa Ana	798
Placer	117,247	Auburn	1,416
Plumas	17,340	Quincy	2,573
Riverside	663,199	Riverside	7,214
Sacramento	783,381	Sacramento	971
San Benito	25,005	Hollister	1,388
San Bernardino	893,157	San Bernardino	20,064
San Diego	1,861,846	San Diego	4,212
San Francisco	678,974	San Francisco	46
San Joaquin	347,342	Stockton	1,415
San Luis Obispo	155,345	San Luis Obispo	3,308
San Mateo	588,164	Redwood City	447
Santa Barbara	298,660	Santa Barbara	2,748
Santa Clara	1,295,071	San Jose	1,293
Santa Cruz	188,141	Santa Cruz	446
Shasta	115,613	Redding	3,786
Sierra	3,073	Downieville	959
Siskiyou	39,732	Yreka	6,281
Solano	235,203	Fairfield	834
Sonoma	299,827	Santa Rosa	1,604
Stanislaus	265,902	Modesto	1,506
Sutter	52,246	Yuba City	602
Tehama	38,888	Red Bluff	2,953
Trinity	11,858	Weaverville	3,190

County	Pop.	County seat or court house	Land area sq. mi.
Tulare	245,751	Visalia	4,808
Tuolumne	33,920	Sonora	2,234
Ventura	529,899	Ventura	1,862
Yolo	113,374	Woodland	1,014
Yuba	49,733	Marysville	640

Colorado
(63 counties, 103,595 sq. mi. land; pop. 2,889,735)

County	Pop.	County seat or court house	Land area sq. mi.
Adams	245,944	Brighton	1,235
Alamosa	11,799	Alamosa	719
Arapahoe	293,300	Littleton	800
Archuleta	3,664	Pagosa Springs	1,353
Baca	5,419	Springfield	2,554
Bent	5,945	Las Animas	1,517
Boulder	189,625	Boulder	742
Chaffee	13,227	Salida	1,008
Cheyenne	2,153	Cheyenne Wells	1,783
Clear Creek	7,308	Georgetown	396
Conejos	7,794	Conejos	1,284
Costilla	3,071	San Luis	1,227
Crowley	2,988	Ordway	790
Custer	1,528	Westcliffe	740
Delta	21,225	Delta	1,141
Denver	492,686	Denver	111
Dolores	1,658	Dove Creek	1,064
Douglas	25,153	Castle Rock	841
Eagle	13,171	Eagle	1,690
Elbert	6,850	Kiowa	1,851
El Paso	309,424	Colorado Springs	2,129
Fremont	28,676	Canon City	1,538
Garfield	22,514	Glenwood Springs	2,952
Gilpin	2,441	Central City	149
Grand	7,475	Hot Sulphur Springs	1,854
Gunnison	10,689	Gunnison	3,238
Hinsdale	408	Lake City	1,115
Huerfano	6,440	Walsenburg	1,584
Jackson	1,863	Walden	1,614
Jefferson	371,741	Golden	768
Kiowa	1,936	Eads	1,758
Kit Carson	7,599	Burlington	2,160
Lake	8,830	Leadville	379
La Plata	27,195	Durango	1,692
Larimer	149,184	Fort Collins	2,604
Las Animas	14,897	Trinidad	4,771
Lincoln	4,663	Hugo	2,586
Logan	19,800	Sterling	1,818
Mesa	81,530	Grand Junction	3,309
Mineral	604	Creede	877
Moffat	13,133	Craig	4,732
Montezuma	16,510	Cortez	2,038
Montrose	24,352	Montrose	2,240
Morgan	22,513	Fort Morgan	1,276
Otero	22,567	LaJunta	1,247
Ouray	1,925	Ouray	542
Park	5,333	Fairplay	2,192
Phillips	4,542	Holyoke	688
Pitkin	10,338	Aspen	968
Prowers	13,070	Lamar	1,629
Pueblo	125,972	Pueblo	2,377
Rio Blanco	6,255	Meeker	3,222
Rio Grande	10,511	Del Norte	913
Routt	13,404	Steamboat Springs	2,367
Saguache	3,935	Saguache	3,167
San Juan	833	Silverton	388
San Miguel	3,192	Telluride	1,287
Sedgwick	3,266	Julesburg	540
Summit	8,848	Breckenridge	607
Teller	8,034	Cripple Creek	559
Washington	5,304	Akron	2,520
Weld	123,438	Greeley	3,990
Yuma	9,682	Wray	2,365

Connecticut
(8 counties, 4,872 sq. mi. land; pop. 3,107,564)

County	Pop.	County seat or court house	Land area sq. mi.
Fairfield	807,143	Bridgeport	632
Hartford	807,766	Hartford	739
Litchfield	156,769	Litchfield	921
Middlesex	129,017	Middletown	373
New Haven	761,325	New Haven	610
New London	238,409	Norwich	669
Tolland	114,823	Rockville	412
Windham	92,312	Putnam	515

Delaware
(3 counties, 1,932 sq. mi. land; pop. 594,338)

County	Pop.	County seat or court house	Land area sq. mi.
Kent	98,219	Dover	595
New Castle	399,002	Wilmington	396
Sussex	98,004	Georgetown	942

District of Columbia
(63 sq. mi. land; pop. 638,432)

Florida
(67 counties, 54,153 sq. mi. land; pop. 9,746,961)

County	Pop.	County seat or court house	Land area sq. mi.
Alachua	151,369	Gainesville	901
Baker	15,289	Macclenny	585
Bay	97,740	Panama City	758
Bradford	20,023	Starke	293
Brevard	272,959	Titusville	995
Broward	1,018,257	Fort Lauderdale	1,211
Calhoun	9,294	Blountstown	568
Charlotte	59,115	Punta Gorda	690
Citrus	54,703	Inverness	629
Clay	67,052	Green Cove Spgs.	592
Collier	85,791	Naples	1,994
Columbia	35,399	Lake City	796
Dade	1,625,509	Miami	1,955
De Soto	19,039	Arcadia	636
Dixie	7,751	Cross City	701
Duval	570,981	Jacksonville	776
Escambia	233,794	Pensacola	660
Flagler	10,913	Bunnell	491
Franklin	7,661	Apalachicola	545
Gadsden	41,674	Quincy	518
Gilchrist	5,767	Trenton	354
Glades	5,992	Moore Haven	763
Gulf	10,658	Port St. Joe	559
Hamilton	8,761	Jasper	517
Hardee	20,357	Wauchula	637
Hendry	18,599	La Belle	1,163
Hernando	44,469	Brooksville	477
Highlands	47,526	Sebring	1,029
Hillsborough	646,939	Tampa	1,053
Holmes	14,723	Bonifay	488
Indian River	59,896	Vero Beach	497
Jackson	39,154	Marianna	942
Jefferson	10,703	Monticello	609
Lafayette	4,035	Mayo	545
Lake	104,870	Tavares	954
Lee	205,266	Fort Myers	803
Leon	148,655	Tallahassee	676
Levy	19,870	Bronson	1,100
Liberty	4,260	Bristol	837
Madison	14,894	Madison	710
Manatee	148,445	Bradenton	747
Marion	122,488	Ocala	1,610
Martin	64,014	Stuart	555
Monroe	63,098	Key West	1,034
Nassau	32,894	Fernandina Beach	649
Okaloosa	109,920	Crestview	936
Okeechobee	20,264	Okeechobee	770
Orange	470,865	Orlando	910
Osceola	49,287	Kissimmee	1,350
Palm Beach	576,758	West Palm Beach	1,993
Pasco	193,661	Dade City	738
Pinellas	728,409	Clearwater	280
Polk	321,652	Bartow	1,823
Putnam	50,549	Palatka	733
St. Johns	51,303	Saint Augustine	617
St. Lucie	87,182	Fort Pierce	581
Santa Rosa	55,988	Milton	1,024
Sarasota	202,251	Sarasota	573
Seminole	179,752	Sanford	298
Sumter	24,272	Bushnell	561
Suwannee	22,287	Live Oak	690
Taylor	16,532	Perry	1,058
Union	10,166	Lake Butler	246
Volusia	258,762	De Land	1,113
Wakulla	10,887	Crawfordville	601
Walton	21,300	De Funiak Springs	1,066
Washington	14,509	Chipley	590

Georgia
(159 counties, 58,056 sq. mi. land; pop. 5,462,982)

County	Pop.	County seat or court house	Land area sq. mi.
Appling	15,565	Baxley	510
Atkinson	6,141	Pearson	344
Bacon	9,379	Alma	286
Baker	3,808	Newton	347
Baldwin	34,686	Milledgeville	257
Banks	8,702	Homer	234
Barrow	21,293	Winder	163
Bartow	40,760	Cartersville	456
Ben Hill	16,000	Fitzgerald	254
Berrien	13,525	Nashville	456
Bibb	151,085	Macon	253
Bleckley	10,767	Cochran	219
Brantley	8,701	Nahunta	445
Brooks	15,255	Quitman	491
Bryan	10,175	Pembroke	441
Bulloch	35,785	Statesboro	678
Burke	19,349	Waynesboro	833
Butts	13,665	Jackson	187
Calhoun	5,717	Morgan	284
Camden	13,371	Woodbine	649
Candler	7,518	Metter	248
Carroll	56,346	Carrollton	501
Catoosa	36,991	Ringgold	162
Charlton	7,343	Folkston	780
Chatham	202,226	Savannah	443
Chattahoochee	21,732	Cusseta	250
Chattooga	21,856	Summerville	313
Cherokee	51,699	Canton	424
Clarke	74,498	Athens	122
Clay	3,553	Fort Gaines	196
Clayton	150,357	Jonesboro	148
Clinch	6,660	Homerville	821
Cobb	297,694	Marietta	343
Coffee	26,894	Douglas	602
Colquitt	35,376	Moultrie	557

County	Pop.	County seat or court house	Land area sq. mi.
Columbia	40,118	Appling	290
Cook	13,490	Adel	233
Coweta	39,268	Newnan	444
Crawford	7,684	Knoxville	328
Crisp	19,489	Cordele	275
Dade	12,318	Trenton	176
Dawson	4,774	Dawsonville	212
Decatur	25,495	Bainbridge	586
De Kalb	483,024	Decatur	270
Dodge	16,955	Eastman	504
Dooly	10,826	Vienna	397
Dougherty	100,710	Albany	330
Douglas	54,573	Douglasville	203
Early	13,158	Blakely	516
Echols	2,297	Statenville	421
Effingham	18,327	Springfield	482
Elbert	18,758	Elberton	367
Emanuel	20,795	Swainsboro	688
Evans	8,428	Claxton	186
Fannin	14,748	Blue Ridge	384
Fayette	29,043	Fayetteville	199
Floyd	79,800	Rome	519
Forsyth	27,958	Cumming	226
Franklin	15,185	Carnesville	264
Fulton	589,904	Atlanta	534
Gilmer	11,110	Ellijay	427
Glascock	2,382	Gibson	144
Glynn	54,981	Brunswick	412
Gordon	30,070	Calhoun	355
Grady	19,845	Cairo	459
Greene	11,391	Greensboro	389
Gwinnett	166,808	Lawrenceville	435
Habersham	25,020	Clarkesville	278
Hall	75,649	Gainesville	379
Hancock	9,466	Sparta	470
Haralson	18,422	Buchanan	283
Harris	15,464	Hamilton	464
Hart	18,585	Hartwell	230
Heard	6,520	Franklin	292
Henry	36,309	McDonough	321
Houston	77,605	Perry	380
Irwin	8,988	Ocilla	362
Jackson	25,343	Jefferson	342
Jasper	7,553	Monticello	371
Jeff Davis	11,473	Hazlehurst	335
Jefferson	18,403	Louisville	529
Jenkins	8,841	Millen	353
Johnson	8,660	Wrightsville	306
Jones	16,579	Gray	394
Lamar	12,215	Barnesville	186
Lanier	5,654	Lakeland	194
Laurens	36,990	Dublin	816
Lee	11,684	Leesburg	358
Liberty	37,583	Hinesville	517
Lincoln	6,949	Lincolnton	196
Long	4,524	Ludowici	402
Lowndes	67,972	Valdosta	507
Lumpkin	10,762	Dahlonega	287
McDuffie	18,546	Thomson	256
McIntosh	8,046	Darien	425
Macon	14,003	Oglethorpe	404
Madison	17,747	Danielsville	285
Marion	5,297	Buena Vista	366
Meriwether	21,229	Greenville	506
Miller	7,038	Colquitt	284
Mitchell	21,114	Camilla	512
Monroe	14,610	Forsyth	397
Montgomery	7,011	Mount Vernon	244
Morgan	11,572	Madison	349
Murray	19,685	Chatsworth	345
Muscogee	170,108	Columbus	218
Newton	34,666	Covington	277
Oconee	12,427	Watkinsville	186
Og"lethorpe	8,929	Lexington	442
Paulding	26,042	Dallas	312
Peach	19,151	Fort Valley	152
Pickens	11,652	Jasper	232
Pierce	11,897	Blackshear	344
Pike	8,937	Zebulon	219
Polk	32,382	Cedartown	311
Pulaski	8,950	Hawkinsville	249
Putnam	10,295	Eatonton	344
Quitman	2,357	Georgetown	146
Rabun	10,466	Clayton	370
Randolph	9,599	Cuthbert	431
Richmond	181,629	Augusta	326
Rockdale	36,570	Conyers	132
Schley	3,433	Ellaville	169
Screven	14,043	Sylvania	655
Seminole	9,057	Donalsonville	225
Spalding	47,899	Griffin	199
Stephens	21,761	Toccoa	177
Stewart	5,896	Lumpkin	452
Sumter	29,360	Americus	489
Talbot	6,536	Talbotton	395
Taliaferro	2,032	Crawfordville	196
Tattnall	18,134	Reidsville	484
Taylor	7,902	Butler	382
Telfair	11,445	McRae	444
Terrell	12,017	Dawson	337
Thomas	38,098	Thomasville	551
Tift	32,862	Tifton	268
Toombs	22,592	Lyons	371
Towns	5,638	Hiawassee	165
Treutlen	6,087	Soperton	202
Troup	50,003	La Grange	414
Turner	9,510	Ashburn	289
Twiggs	9,354	Jeffersonville	362
Union	9,390	Blairsville	320
Upson	25,998	Thomaston	326
Walker	56,470	La Fayette	446
Walton	31,211	Monroe	330
Ware	37,180	Waycross	907
Warren	6,583	Warrenton	286
Washington	18,842	Sandersville	684
Wayne	20,750	Jesup	647
Webster	2,341	Preston	210
Wheeler	5,155	Alamo	299
White	10,120	Cleveland	242
Whitfield	65,775	Dalton	291
Wilcox	7,682	Abbeville	382
Wilkes	10,951	Washington	470
Wilkinson	10,368	Irwinton	451
Worth	18,064	Sylvester	575

Hawaii

(4 counties, 6,645 sq. mi. land; pop. 964,691)

County	Pop.	County seat or court house	Land area sq. mi.
Hawaii	92,053	Hilo	4,034
Honolulu	762,874	Honolulu	596
Kauai	39,082	Lihue	620
Maui*	70,991	Wailuku	1,175

*Includes population of Kalawao County (146).

Idaho

(44 counties, 82,412 sq. mi. land; pop. 944,127)

County	Pop.	County seat or court house	Land area sq. mi.
Ada	173,125	Boise	1,052
Adams	3,347	Council	1,362
Bannock	65,421	Pocatello	1,112
Bear Lake	6,931	Paris	990
Benewah	8,292	Saint Maries	784
Bingham	36,489	Blackfoot	2,096
Blaine	9,841	Hailey	2,634
Boise	2,999	Idaho City	1,901
Bonner	24,163	Sandpoint	1,726
Bonneville	65,980	Idaho Falls	1,840
Boundary	7,289	Bonners Ferry	1,268
Butte	3,342	Arco	2,236
Camas	818	Fairfield	1,071
Canyon	83,756	Caldwell	584
Caribou	8,695	Soda Springs	1,763
Cassia	19,427	Burley	2,560
Clark	798	Dubois	1,763
Clearwater	10,390	Orofino	2,236
Custer	3,385	Challis	4,927
Elmore	21,565	Mountain Home	3,071
Franklin	8,895	Preston	664
Fremont	10,813	Saint Anthony	1,852
Gem	11,972	Emmett	558
Gooding	11,874	Gooding	728
Idaho	14,769	Grangeville	8,497
Jefferson	15,304	Rigby	1,093
Jerome	14,840	Jerome	601
Kootenai	59,770	Coeur d'Alene	1,240
Latah	28,749	Moscow	1,077
Lemhi	7,460	Salmon	4,564
Lewis	4,118	Nezperce	478
Lincoln	3,436	Shoshone	1,205
Madison	19,480	Rexburg	468
Minidoka	19,718	Rupert	757
Nez Perce	33,220	Lewiston	845
Oneida	3,258	Malad City	1,200
Owyhee	8,272	Murphy	7,643
Payette	15,825	Payette	405
Power	6,844	American Falls	1,403
Shoshone	19,226	Wallace	2,641
Teton	2,897	Driggs	448
Twin Falls	52,927	Twin Falls	1,944
Valley	5,604	Cascade	3,670
Washington	8,803	Weiser	1,454

Illinois

(102 counties, 55,645 sq. mi. land; pop. 11,427,409)

County	Pop.	County seat or court house	Land area sq. mi.
Adams	71,622	Quincy	852
Alexander	12,264	Cairo	236
Bond	16,224	Greenville	377
Boone	28,630	Belvidere	282
Brown	5,411	Mount Sterling	306
Bureau	39,114	Princeton	869
Calhoun	5,967	Hardin	250
Carroll	18,779	Mount Carroll	444
Cass	15,084	Virginia	374
Champaign	168,392	Urbana	998
Christian	36,446	Taylorville	710
Clark	16,913	Marshall	506
Clay	15,283	Louisville	469
Clinton	32,617	Carlyle	472
Coles	52,992	Charleston	509

Illinois

County	Pop.	County seat or court house	Land area sq. mi.
Cook	5,253,628	Chicago	958
Crawford	20,818	Robinson	446
Cumberland	11,062	Toledo	346
De Kalb	74,628	Sycamore	634
De Witt	18,108	Clinton	397
Douglas	19,774	Tuscola	417
Du Page	658,858	Wheaton	337
Edgar	21,725	Paris	623
Edwards	7,961	Albion	223
Effingham	30,944	Effingham	478
Fayette	22,167	Vandalia	709
Ford	15,265	Paxton	486
Franklin	43,201	Benton	414
Fulton	43,687	Lewiston	871
Gallatin	7,590	Shawneetown	325
Greene	16,661	Carrollton	543
Grundy	30,582	Morris	423
Hamilton	9,172	McLeansboro	436
Hancock	23,877	Carthage	796
Hardin	5,383	Elizabethtown	181
Henderson	9,114	Oquawka	373
Henry	57,968	Cambridge	824
Iroquois	32,976	Watseka	1,118
Jackson	61,649	Murphysboro	590
Jasper	11,318	Newton	496
Jefferson	36,558	Mount Vernon	570
Jersey	20,538	Jerseyville	373
Jo Daviess	23,520	Galena	603
Johnson	9,624	Vienna	346
Kane	278,405	Geneva	524
Kankakee	102,926	Kankakee	679
Kendall	37,202	Yorkville	322
Knox	61,607	Galesburg	720
Lake	440,388	Waukegan	454
La Salle	109,139	Ottawa	1,139
Lawrence	17,807	Lawrenceville	374
Lee	36,328	Dixon	725
Livingston	41,381	Pontiac	1,046
Logan	31,802	Lincoln	619
McDonough	37,236	Macomb	590
McHenry	147,724	Woodstock	606
McLean	119,149	Bloomington	1,185
Macon	131,375	Decatur	581
Macoupin	49,384	Carlinville	865
Madison	247,661	Edwardsville	728
Marion	43,523	Salem	573
Marshall	14,479	Lacon	388
Mason	19,492	Havana	536
Massac	14,990	Metropolis	241
Menard	11,700	Petersburg	315
Mercer	19,286	Aledo	559
Monroe	20,117	Waterloo	388
Montgomery	31,686	Hillsboro	705
Morgan	37,502	Jacksonville	568
Moultrie	14,546	Sullivan	325
Ogle	46,338	Oregon	759
Peoria	200,466	Peoria	621
Perry	21,714	Pinckneyville	443
Piatt	16,581	Monticello	439
Pike	18,896	Pittsfield	830
Pope	4,404	Golconda	374
Pulaski	8,840	Mound City	203
Putnam	6,085	Hennepin	160
Randolph	35,566	Chester	583
Richland	17,587	Olney	360
Rock Island	166,759	Rock Island	423
St. Clair	265,469	Belleville	672
Saline	27,360	Harrisburg	385
Sangamon	176,070	Springfield	866
Schuyler	8,365	Rushville	436
Scott	6,142	Winchester	251
Shelby	23,923	Shelbyville	747
Stark	7,389	Toulon	288
Stephenson	49,536	Freeport	564
Tazewell	132,078	Pekin	650
Union	16,851	Jonesboro	414
Vermilion	95,222	Danville	900
Wabash	13,713	Mt. Carmel	224
Warren	21,943	Monmouth	543
Washington	15,472	Nashville	563
Wayne	18,059	Fairfield	715
White	17,864	Carmi	497
Whiteside	65,970	Morrison	682
Will	324,460	Joliet	844
Williamson	56,538	Marion	427
Winnebago	250,884	Rockford	516
Woodford	33,320	Eureka	527

Indiana
(92 counties, 35,932 sq. mi. land; pop. 5,490,214)

County	Pop.	County seat	Land area sq. mi.
Adams	29,619	Decatur	340
Allen	294,335	Fort Wayne	659
Bartholomew	65,088	Columbus	409
Benton	10,218	Fowler	407
Blackford	15,570	Hartford City	166
Boone	36,446	Lebanon	423
Brown	12,377	Nashville	312
Carroll	19,722	Delphi	372
Cass	40,936	Logansport	414
Clark	88,838	Jeffersonville	376
Clay	24,862	Brazil	360
Clinton	31,545	Frankfort	405
Crawford	9,820	English	307
Daviess	27,836	Washington	432
Dearborn	34,291	Lawrenceburg	307
Decatur	23,841	Greensburg	373
DeKalb	33,606	Auburn	364
Delaware	128,587	Muncie	392
Dubois	34,238	Jasper	429
Elkhart	137,330	Goshen	466
Fayette	28,272	Connersville	215
Floyd	61,205	New Albany	150
Fountain	19,033	Covington	398
Franklin	19,612	Brookville	385
Fulton	19,335	Rochester	369
Gibson	33,156	Princeton	490
Grant	80,934	Marion	415
Greene	30,416	Bloomfield	546
Hamilton	82,381	Noblesville	398
Hancock	43,939	Greenfield	307
Harrison	27,276	Corydon	486
Hendricks	69,804	Danville	409
Henry	53,336	New Castle	394
Howard	86,896	Kokomo	293
Huntington	35,596	Huntington	366
Jackson	36,523	Brownstown	513
Jasper	26,138	Rensselaer	561
Jay	23,239	Portland	384
Jefferson	30,419	Madison	363
Jennings	22,854	Vernon	378
Johnson	77,240	Franklin	321
Knox	41,838	Vincennes	520
Kosciusko	59,555	Warsaw	540
Lagrange	25,550	Lagrange	380
Lake	522,917	Crown Point	501
La Porte	108,632	La Porte	600
Lawrence	42,472	Bedford	452
Madison	139,336	Anderson	453
Marion	765,233	Indianapolis	396
Marshall	39,155	Plymouth	444
Martin	11,001	Shoals	339
Miami	39,820	Peru	369
Monroe	98,787	Bloomington	385
Montgomery	35,501	Crawfordsville	505
Morgan	51,999	Martinsville	409
Newton	14,844	Kentland	401
Noble	35,443	Albion	413
Ohio	5,114	Rising Sun	87
Orange	18,677	Paoli	408
Owen	15,840	Spencer	386
Parke	16,372	Rockville	444
Perry	19,346	Cannelton	382
Pike	13,465	Petersburg	341
Porter	119,816	Valparaiso	418
Posey	26,414	Mount Vernon	409
Pulaski	13,258	Winamac	435
Putnam	29,163	Greencastle	482
Randolph	29,997	Winchester	454
Ripley	24,398	Versailles	447
Rush	19,604	Rushville	408
St. Joseph	241,617	South Bend	459
Scott	20,422	Scottsburg	191
Shelby	39,887	Shelbyville	413
Spencer	19,361	Rockport	400
Starke	21,997	Knox	309
Steuben	24,694	Angola	308
Sullivan	21,107	Sullivan	452
Switzerland	7,153	Vevay	223
Tippecanoe	121,702	Lafayette	502
Tipton	16,819	Tipton	260
Union	6,860	Liberty	162
Vanderburgh	167,515	Evansville	236
Vermillion	18,229	Newport	260
Vigo	112,385	Terre Haute	405
Wabash	36,640	Wabash	398
Warren	8,976	Williamsport	366
Warrick	41,474	Boonville	391
Washington	21,932	Salem	516
Wayne	76,058	Richmond	404
Wells	25,401	Bluffton	370
White	23,867	Monticello	506
Whitley	26,215	Columbia City	336

Iowa
(99 counties; 55,965 sq. mi. land; pop. 2,913,808)

County	Pop.	County seat	Land area sq. mi.
Adair	9,509	Greenfield	570
Adams	5,731	Corning	425
Allamakee	15,108	Waukon	633
Appanoose	15,511	Centerville	498
Audubon	8,559	Audubon	444
Benton	23,649	Vinton	718
Black Hawk	137,961	Waterloo	573
Boone	26,184	Boone	573
Bremer	24,820	Waverly	439
Buchanan	20,844	Independence	572
Buena Vista	20,774	Storm Lake	575
Butler	17,668	Allison	582
Calhoun	13,542	Rockwell City	571

County	Pop.	County seat or court house	Land area sq. mi.
Carroll	22,951	Carroll	570
Cass	16,932	Atlantic	565
Cedar	18,635	Tipton	582
Cerro Gordo	48,458	Mason City	569
Cherokee	16,238	Cherokee	577
Chickasaw	15,437	New Hampton	505
Clarke	8,612	Osceola	431
Clay	19,576	Spencer	569
Clayton	21,098	Elkader	779
Clinton	57,122	Clinton	695
Crawford	18,935	Denison	714
Dallas	29,513	Adel	591
Davis	9,104	Bloomfield	504
Decatur	9,794	Leon	535
Delaware	18,933	Manchester	578
Des Moines	46,203	Burlington	414
Dickinson	15,629	Spirit Lake	381
Dubuque	93,745	Dubuque	607
Emmet	13,336	Estherville	394
Fayette	25,488	West Union	731
Floyd	19,597	Charles City	501
Franklin	13,036	Hampton	583
Fremont	9,401	Sidney	515
Greene	12,119	Jefferson	571
Grundy	14,366	Grundy Center	501
Guthrie	11,983	Guthrie Center	590
Hamilton	17,862	Webster City	576
Hancock	13,833	Garner	571
Hardin	21,776	Eldora	569
Harrison	16,348	Logan	697
Henry	18,890	Mount Pleasant	436
Howard	11,114	Cresco	473
Humboldt	12,246	Dakota City	436
Ida	8,908	Ida Grove	432
Iowa	15,429	Marengo	587
Jackson	22,503	Maquoketa	638
Jasper	36,425	Newton	731
Jefferson	16,316	Fairfield	440
Johnson	81,717	Iowa City	614
Jones	20,401	Anamosa	576
Keokuk	12,921	Sigourney	580
Kossuth	21,891	Algona	974
Lee	43,106	Fort Madison and Keokuk	522
Linn	169,775	Cedar Rapids	724
Louisa	12,055	Wapello	402
Lucas	10,313	Chariton	432
Lyon	12,896	Rock Rapids	588
Madison	12,597	Winterset	563
Mahaska	22,507	Oskaloosa	571
Marion	29,669	Knoxville	560
Marshall	41,652	Marshalltown	573
Mills	13,406	Glenwood	439
Mitchell	12,329	Osage	470
Monona	11,692	Onawa	697
Monroe	9,209	Albia	434
Montgomery	13,413	Red Oak	424
Muscatine	40,436	Muscatine	442
O'Brien	16,972	Primghar	574
Osceola	8,371	Sibley	399
Page	19,063	Clarinda	535
Palo Alto	12,721	Emmetsburg	562
Plymouth	24,743	Le Mars	864
Pocahontas	11,369	Pocahontas	577
Polk	303,170	Des Moines	582
Pottawattamie	86,500	Council Bluffs	953
Poweshiek	19,306	Montezuma	585
Ringgold	6,112	Mount Ayr	535
Sac	14,118	Sac City	576
Scott	160,022	Davenport	459
Shelby	15,043	Harlan	591
Sioux	30,813	Orange City	769
Story	72,326	Nevada	574
Tama	19,533	Toledo	721
Taylor	8,353	Bedford	537
Union	13,858	Creston	426
Van Buren	8,626	Keosauqua	484
Wapello	40,241	Ottumwa	434
Warren	34,878	Indianola	573
Washington	20,141	Washington	570
Wayne	8,199	Corydon	526
Webster	45,953	Fort Dodge	718
Winnebago	13,010	Forest City	401
Winneshiek	21,876	Decorah	690
Woodbury	100,884	Sioux City	873
Worth	9,075	Northwood	401
Wright	16,319	Clarion	579

Kansas

(105 counties, 81,778 sq. mi. land; pop. 2,364,236)

County	Pop.	County seat or court house	Land area sq. mi.
Allen	15,654	Iola	505
Anderson	8,749	Garnett	584
Atchison	18,397	Atchison	431
Barber	6,548	Medicine Lodge	1,136
Barton	31,343	Great Bend	895
Bourbon	15,969	Fort Scott	638
Brown	11,955	Hiawatha	572
Butler	44,782	El Dorado	1,443
Chase	3,309	Cottonwood Falls	777
Chautauqua	5,016	Sedan	644
Cherokee	22,304	Columbus	590
Cheyenne	3,678	Saint Francis	1,021
Clark	2,599	Ashland	975
Clay	9,802	Clay Center	632
Cloud	12,494	Concordia	718
Coffey	9,370	Burlington	615
Comanche	2,554	Coldwater	789
Cowley	36,624	Winfield	1,128
Crawford	37,916	Girard	595
Decatur	4,509	Oberlin	894
Dickinson	20,175	Abilene	852
Doniphan	9,268	Troy	388
Douglas	67,640	Lawrence	461
Edwards	4,271	Kinsley	620
Elk	3,918	Howard	650
Ellis	26,098	Hays	900
Ellsworth	6,640	Ellsworth	717
Finney	23,825	Garden City	1,302
Ford	24,315	Dodge City	1,099
Franklin	21,813	Ottawa	577
Geary	29,852	Junction City	377
Gove	3,726	Gove	1,072
Graham	3,995	Hill City	898
Grant	6,977	Ulysses	575
Gray	5,138	Cimarron	868
Greeley	1,845	Tribune	778
Greenwood	8,764	Eureka	1,135
Hamilton	2,514	Syracuse	998
Harper	7,778	Anthony	802
Harvey	30,531	Newton	540
Haskell	3,814	Sublette	578
Hodgeman	2,269	Jetmore	860
Jackson	11,644	Holton	658
Jefferson	15,207	Oskaloosa	535
Jewell	5,241	Mankato	910
Johnson	270,269	Olathe	478
Kearny	3,435	Lakin	868
Kingman	8,960	Kingman	865
Kiowa	4,046	Greensburg	723
Labette	25,682	Oswego	653
Lane	2,472	Dighton	717
Leavenworth	54,809	Leavenworth	463
Lincoln	4,145	Lincoln	720
Linn	8,234	Mound City	601
Logan	3,478	Oakley	1,073
Lyon	35,108	Emporia	844
McPherson	26,855	McPherson	900
Marion	13,522	Marion	944
Marshall	12,720	Marysville	878
Meade	4,788	Meade	979
Miami	21,618	Paola	590
Mitchell	8,117	Beloit	717
Montgomery	42,281	Independence	646
Morris	6,419	Council Grove	693
Morton	3,454	Elkhart	731
Nemaha	11,211	Seneca	719
Neosho	18,967	Erie	576
Ness	4,498	Ness City	1,074
Norton	6,689	Norton	873
Osage	15,319	Lyndon	695
Osborne	5,959	Osborne	882
Ottawa	5,971	Minneapolis	721
Pawnee	8,065	Larned	755
Phillips	7,406	Phillipsburg	887
Pottawatomie	14,782	Westmoreland	828
Pratt	10,275	Pratt	735
Rawlins	4,105	Atwood	1,069
Reno	64,983	Hutchinson	1,259
Republic	7,569	Belleville	719
Rice	11,900	Lyons	728
Riley	63,505	Manhattan	593
Rooks	7,006	Stockton	888
Rush	4,516	LaCrosse	718
Russell	8,868	Russell	869
Saline	48,905	Salina	721
Scott	5,782	Scott City	718
Sedgwick	367,088	Wichita	1,007
Seward	17,071	Liberal	640
Shawnee	154,916	Topeka	549
Sheridan	3,544	Hoxie	895
Sherman	7,759	Goodland	1,057
Smith	5,947	Smith Center	897
Stafford	5,539	Saint John	788
Stanton	2,339	Johnson	681
Stevens	4,736	Hugoton	727
Sumner	24,928	Wellington	1,183
Thomas	8,451	Colby	1,075
Trego	4,165	Wakeeney	890
Wabaunsee	6,867	Alma	797
Wallace	2,045	Sharon Springs	914
Washington	8,543	Washington	898
Wichita	3,041	Leoti	719
Wilson	12,128	Fredonia	575
Woodson	4,600	Yates Center	498
Wyandotte	172,335	Kansas City	149

Kentucky

(120 counties, 39,669 sq. mi. land; pop. 3,660,324)

County	Pop.	County seat or court house	Land area sq. mi.
Adair	15,233	Columbia	407

County	Pop.	County seat or court house	Land area sq. mi.
Allen	14,128	Scottsville	338
Anderson	12,567	Lawrenceburg	204
Ballard	8,798	Wickliffe	254
Barren	34,009	Glasgow	482
Bath	10,025	Owingsville	277
Bell	34,330	Pineville	361
Boone	45,842	Burlington	246
Bourbon	19,405	Paris	292
Boyd	55,513	Catlettsburg	160
Boyle	25,066	Danville	182
Bracken	7,738	Brooksville	203
Breathitt	17,004	Jackson	495
Breckinridge	16,861	Hardinsburg	565
Bullitt	43,346	Shepherdsville	300
Butler	11,064	Morgantown	431
Caldwell	13,473	Princeton	347
Calloway	30,031	Murray	386
Campbell	83,317	Alexandria	152
Carlisle	5,487	Bardwell	191
Carroll	9,270	Carrollton	130
Carter	25,060	Grayson	407
Casey	14,818	Liberty	445
Christian	66,878	Hopkinsville	722
Clark	28,322	Winchester	255
Clay	22,752	Manchester	471
Clinton	9,321	Albany	196
Crittenden	9,207	Marion	360
Cumberland	7,289	Burkesville	304
Daviess	85,949	Owensboro	463
Edmonson	9,962	Brownsville	302
Elliott	6,908	Sandy Hook	234
Estill	14,495	Irvine	256
Fayette	204,165	Lexington	285
Fleming	12,323	Flemingsburg	351
Floyd	48,764	Prestonsburg	393
Franklin	41,830	Frankfort	212
Fulton	8,971	Hickman	211
Gallatin	4,842	Warsaw	99
Garrard	10,853	Lancaster	232
Grant	13,308	Williamstown	259
Graves	34,049	Mayfield	557
Grayson	20,854	Leitchfield	493
Green	11,043	Greensburg	289
Greenup	39,132	Greenup	347
Hancock	7,742	Hawesville	189
Hardin	88,911	Elizabethtown	629
Harlan	41,889	Harlan	468
Harrison	15,166	Cynthiana	310
Hart	15,402	Munfordville	412
Henderson	40,849	Henderson	438
Henry	12,740	New Castle	291
Hickman	6,065	Clinton	245
Hopkins	46,174	Madisonville	552
Jackson	11,996	McKee	346
Jefferson	684,638	Louisville	386
Jessamine	26,065	Nicholasville	174
Johnson	24,432	Paintsville	264
Kenton	137,058	Independence	163
Knott	17,940	Hindman	352
Knox	30,239	Barbourville	388
Larue	11,983	Hodgenville	263
Laurel	38,982	London	434
Lawrence	14,121	Louisa	420
Lee	7,754	Beattyville	211
Leslie	14,882	Hyden	402
Letcher	30,687	Whitesburg	339
Lewis	14,545	Vanceburg	484
Lincoln	19,053	Stanford	337
Livingston	9,219	Smithland	312
Logan	24,138	Russellville	556
Lyon	6,490	Eddyville	209
McCracken	61,310	Paducah	251
McCreary	15,634	Whitley City	427
McLean	10,090	Calhoun	256
Madison	53,352	Richmond	443
Magoffin	13,515	Salyersville	310
Marion	17,910	Lebanon	347
Marshall	25,637	Benton	304
Martin	13,925	Inez	230
Mason	17,760	Maysville	241
Meade	22,854	Brandenburg	306
Menifee	5,117	Frenchburg	203
Mercer	19,011	Harrodsburg	250
Metcalfe	9,484	Edmonton	291
Monroe	12,353	Tompkinsville	331
Montgomery	20,046	Mount Sterling	199
Morgan	12,103	West Liberty	382
Muhlenberg	32,238	Greenville	478
Nelson	27,584	Bardstown	424
Nicholas	7,157	Carlisle	197
Ohio	21,765	Hartford	596
Oldham	28,094	La Grange	190
Owen	8,924	Owenton	354
Owsley	5,709	Booneville	198
Pendleton	10,989	Falmouth	281
Perry	33,763	Hazard	341
Pike	81,123	Pikeville	785
Powell	11,101	Stanton	180
Pulaski	45,803	Somerset	660
Robertson	2,270	Mount Olivet	100
Rockcastle	13,973	Mount Vernon	318
Rowan	19,049	Morehead	282
Russell	13,708	Jamestown	250
Scott	21,813	Georgetown	286
Shelby	23,328	Shelbyville	385
Simpson	14,673	Franklin	236
Spencer	5,929	Taylorsville	192
Taylor	21,178	Campbellsville	270
Todd	11,874	Elkton	377
Trigg	9,384	Cadiz	421
Trimble	6,253	Bedford	148
Union	17,821	Morganfield	341
Warren	71,828	Bowling Green	548
Washington	10,764	Springfield	301
Wayne	17,022	Monticello	446
Webster	14,832	Dixon	336
Whitley	33,396	Williamsburg	443
Wolfe	6,698	Campton	223
Woodford	17,778	Versailles	192

Louisiana

(64 parishes, 44,521 sq. mi. land; pop. 4,206,116)

County	Pop.	County seat or court house	Land area sq. mi.
Acadia	56,427	Crowley	657
Allen	21,408	Oberlin	765
Ascension	50,068	Donaldsville	296
Assumption	22,084	Napoleonville	342
Avoyelles	41,393	Marksville	846
Beauregard	29,692	De Ridder	1,163
Bienville	16,387	Arcadia	816
Bossier	80,721	Benton	845
Caddo	252,437	Shreveport	894
Calcasieu	167,048	Lake Charles	1,082
Caldwell	10,761	Columbia	541
Cameron	9,336	Cameron	1,417
Catahoula	12,287	Harrisonburg	732
Claiborne	17,095	Homer	765
Concordia	22,981	Vidalia	717
De Soto	25,664	Mansfield	880
East Baton Rouge	366,164	Baton Rouge	458
East Carroll	11,772	Lake Providence	426
East Feliciana	19,015	Clinton	455
Evangeline	33,343	Ville Platte	667
Franklin	24,141	Winnsboro	635
Grant	16,703	Colfax	653
Iberia	63,752	New Iberia	589
Iberville	32,159	Plaquemine	638
Jackson	17,321	Jonesboro	579
Jefferson	454,592	Gretna	348
Jefferson Davis	32,168	Jennings	655
Lafayette	150,017	Lafayette	270
Lafourche	82,483	Thibodaux	1,141
La Salle	17,004	Jena	638
Lincoln	39,763	Ruston	472
Livingston	58,655	Livingston	661
Madison	15,682	Tallulah	631
Morehouse	34,803	Bastrop	807
Natchitoches	39,863	Natchitoches	1,264
Orleans	557,927	New Orleans	199
Ouachita	139,241	Monroe	627
Plaquemines	26,049	Pointe a la Hache	1,035
Pointe Coupee	24,045	New Roads	566
Rapides	135,282	Alexandria	1,341
Red River	10,433	Coushatta	394
Richland	22,187	Rayville	583
Sabine	25,280	Many	855
St. Bernard	64,097	Chalmette	486
St. Charles	37,259	Hahnville	286
St. Helena	9,827	Greensburg	409
St. James	21,495	Convent	248
St. John The Baptist	31,924	Edgard	213
St. Landry	84,128	Opelousas	936
St. Martin	40,214	Saint Martinville	749
St. Mary	64,395	Franklin	613
St. Tammany	110,554	Covington	873
Tangipahoa	80,698	Amite	783
Tensas	8,525	Saint Joseph	623
Terrebonne	94,393	Houma	1,367
Union	21,167	Farmerville	884
Vermilion	48,458	Abbeville	1,205
Vernon	53,475	Leesville	1,332
Washington	44,207	Franklinton	676
Webster	43,631	Minden	602
West Baton Rouge	19,086	Port Allen	194
West Carroll	12,922	Oak Grove	360
West Feliciana	12,186	Saint Francisville	406
Winn	17,253	Winnfield	953

Maine

(16 counties, 30,995 sq. mi. land; pop. 1,125,043)

County	Pop.	County seat or court house	Land area sq. mi.
Androscoggin	99,509	Auburn	477
Aroostook	91,344	Houlton	6,721
Cumberland	215,789	Portland	876
Franklin	27,447	Farmington	1,699
Hancock	41,781	Ellsworth	1,537
Kennebec	109,889	Augusta	876
Knox	32,941	Rockland	370
Lincoln	25,691	Wiscasset	458
Oxford	49,043	South Paris	2,053

County	Pop.	County seat or court house	Land area sq. mi.
Penobscot	137,015	Bangor	3,430
Piscataquis	17,634	Dover-Foxcroft	3,986
Sagadahoc	28,795	Bath	257
Somerset	45,049	Skowhegan	3,930
Waldo	28,414	Belfast	730
Washington	34,963	Machias	2,586
York	139,739	Alfred	1,008

Maryland
(23 cos., 1 ind. city, 9,837 sq. mi. land; pop. 4,216,933)

County	Pop.	County seat or court house	Land area sq. mi.
Allegany	80,548	Cumberland	421
Anne Arundel	370,775	Annapolis	418
Baltimore	655,615	Towson	598
Calvert	34,638	Prince Frederick	213
Caroline	23,143	Denton	321
Carroll	96,356	Westminster	452
Cecil	60,430	Elkton	360
Charles	72,751	La Plata	452
Dorchester	30,623	Cambridge	593
Frederick	114,263	Frederick	663
Garrett	26,490	Oakland	657
Harford	145,930	Bel Air	448
Howard	118,572	Ellicott City	251
Kent	16,695	Chestertown	278
Montgomery	579,053	Rockville	495
Prince Georges	665,071	Upper Marlboro	487
Queen Annes	25,508	Centreville	372
St. Mary's	59,895	Leonardtown	373
Somerset	19,188	Princess Anne	338
Talbot	25,604	Easton	259
Washington	113,086	Hagerstown	455
Wicomico	64,540	Salisbury	379
Worcester	30,889	Snow Hill	475
Independent City			
Baltimore	786,775		80

Massachusetts
(14 counties; 7,824 sq. mi. land; pop. 5,737,093)

County	Pop.	County seat or court house	Land area sq. mi.
Barnstable	147,925	Barnstable	400
Berkshire	145,110	Pittsfield	929
Bristol	474,641	Taunton	557
Dukes	8,942	Edgartown	102
Essex	633,688	Salem	495
Franklin	64,317	Greenfield	702
Hampden	443,018	Springfield	618
Hampshire	138,813	Northampton	528
Middlesex	1,367,034	Cambridge	822
Nantucket	5,087	Nantucket	47
Norfolk	606,587	Dedham	400
Plymouth	405,437	Plymouth	655
Suffolk	650,142	Boston	57
Worcester	646,352	Worcester	1,513

Michigan
(63 counties; 56,954 sq. mi. land; pop. 9,262,044)

County	Pop.	County seat or court house	Land area sq. mi.
Alcona	9,740	Harrisville	679
Alger	9,225	Munising	912
Allegan	81,555	Allegan	832
Alpena	32,315	Alpena	567
Antrim	16,194	Bellaire	480
Arenac	14,706	Standish	367
Baraga	8,484	L'Anse	901
Barry	45,781	Hastings	560
Bay	119,881	Bay City	447
Benzie	11,205	Beulah	322
Berrien	171,276	Saint Joseph	576
Branch	40,188	Coldwater	508
Calhoun	141,579	Marshall	712
Cass	49,499	Cassopolis	495
Charlevoix	19,907	Charlevoix	421
Cheboygan	20,649	Cheboygan	720
Chippewa	29,029	Sault Sainte Marie	1,590
Clare	23,822	Harrison	570
Clinton	55,893	Saint Johns	573
Crawford	9,465	Grayling	559
Delta	38,947	Escanaba	1,173
Dickinson	25,341	Iron Mountain	770
Eaton	88,337	Charlotte	579
Emmet	22,992	Petoskey	468
Genesee	450,449	Flint	642
Gladwin	19,957	Gladwin	505
Gogebic	19,686	Bessemer	1,105
Grand Traverse	54,899	Traverse City	466
Gratiot	40,448	Ithaca	570
Hillsdale	42,071	Hillsdale	603
Houghton	37,872	Houghton	1,014
Huron	36,459	Bad Axe	830
Ingham	272,437	Mason	560
Ionia	51,815	Ionia	577
Iosco	28,349	Tawas City	546
Iron	13,635	Crystal Falls	1,163
Isabella	54,110	Mount Pleasant	577
Jackson	151,495	Jackson	705
Kalamazoo	212,378	Kalamazoo	562
Kalkaska	10,952	Kalkaska	563
Kent	444,506	Grand Rapids	862
Keweenaw	1,963	Eagle River	543
Lake	7,711	Baldwin	568
Lapeer	70,038	Lapeer	658
Leelanau	14,007	Leland	341
Lenawee	89,948	Adrian	753
Livingston	100,289	Howell	574
Luce	6,659	Newberry	904
Mackinac	10,178	Saint Ignace	1,025
Macomb	694,600	Mount Clemens	482
Manistee	23,019	Manistee	543
Marquette	74,101	Marquette	1,821
Mason	26,365	Ludington	494
Mecosta	36,961	Big Rapids	560
Menominee	26,201	Menominee	1,045
Midland	73,578	Midland	525
Missaukee	10,009	Lake City	565
Monroe	134,659	Monroe	557
Montcalm	47,555	Stanton	713
Montmorency	7,492	Atlanta	550
Muskegon	157,589	Muskegon	507
Newaygo	34,917	White Cloud	847
Oakland	1,011,793	Pontiac	875
Oceana	22,002	Hart	541
Ogemaw	16,436	West Branch	570
Ontonagon	9,861	Ontonagon	1,311
Osceola	18,928	Reed City	569
Oscoda	6,858	Mio	568
Otsego	14,993	Gaylord	516
Ottawa	157,174	Grand Haven	567
Presque Isle	14,267	Rogers City	656
Roscommon	16,374	Roscommon	528
Saginaw	228,059	Saginaw	815
St. Clair	138,802	Port Huron	734
St. Joseph	56,083	Centreville	503
Sanilac	40,789	Sandusky	964
Schoolcraft	8,575	Manistique	1,173
Shiawassee	71,140	Corunna	540
Tuscola	56,961	Caro	812
Van Buren	66,814	Paw Paw	611
Washtenaw	264,740	Ann Arbor	710
Wayne	2,337,843	Detroit	615
Wexford	25,102	Cadillac	566

Minnesota
(87 counties; 79,548 sq. mi. land; pop. 4,075,970)

County	Pop.	County seat or court house	Land area sq. mi.
Aitkin	13,404	Aitkin	1,834
Anoka	195,998	Anoka	430
Becker	29,336	Detroit Lakes	1,312
Beltrami	30,982	Bemidji	2,507
Benton	25,187	Foley	408
Big Stone	7,716	Ortonville	497
Blue Earth	52,314	Mankato	749
Brown	28,645	New Ulm	610
Carlton	29,936	Carlton	864
Carver	37,046	Chaska	351
Cass	21,050	Walker	2,033
Chippewa	14,941	Montevideo	584
Chisago	25,717	Center City	417
Clay	49,327	Moorhead	1,049
Clearwater	8,761	Bagley	999
Cook	4,092	Grand Marais	1,412
Cottonwood	14,854	Windom	640
Crow Wing	41,722	Brainerd	1,008
Dakota	194,111	Hastings	574
Dodge	14,773	Mantorville	439
Douglas	27,839	Alexandria	643
Faribault	19,714	Blue Earth	714
Fillmore	21,930	Preston	862
Freeborn	36,329	Albert Lea	705
Goodhue	38,749	Red Wing	763
Grant	7,171	Elbow Lake	547
Hennepin	941,411	Minneapolis	541
Houston	19,617	Caledonia	564
Hubbard	14,098	Park Rapids	936
Isanti	23,600	Cambridge	440
Itasca	43,006	Grand Rapids	2,661
Jackson	13,690	Jackson	699
Kanabec	12,161	Mora	527
Kandiyohi	36,763	Willmar	784
Kittson	6,672	Hallock	1,104
Koochiching	17,571	International Falls	3,108
Lac qui Parle	10,592	Madison	772
Lake	13,043	Two Harbors	2,053
Lake of the Woods	3,764	Baudette	1,296
Le Sueur	23,434	Le Center	446
Lincoln	8,207	Ivanhoe	538
Lyon	25,207	Marshall	714
McLeod	29,657	Glencoe	489
Mahnomen	5,535	Mahnomen	559
Marshall	13,027	Warren	1,760
Martin	24,687	Fairmont	708
Meeker	20,594	Litchfield	624
Mille Lacs	18,430	Milaca	578
Morrison	29,311	Little Falls	1,124
Mower	40,390	Austin	711
Murray	11,507	Slayton	702
Nicollet	26,929	Saint Peter	440
Nobles	21,840	Worthington	714
Norman	9,379	Ada	877
Olmsted	91,971	Rochester	655
Otter Tail	51,937	Fergus Falls	1,973

County	Pop.	County seat or court house	Land area sq. mi.
Pennington	15,258	Thief River Falls	618
Pine	19,871	Pine City	1,421
Pipestone	11,690	Pipestone	466
Polk	34,844	Crookston	1,982
Pope	11,657	Glenwood	668
Ramsey	459,784	Saint Paul	154
Red Lake	5,471	Red Lake Falls	433
Redwood	19,341	Redwood Falls	882
Renville	20,401	Olivia	984
Rice	46,087	Faribault	501
Rock	10,703	Luverne	483
Roseau	12,574	Roseau	1,677
St. Louis	222,229	Duluth	6,125
Scott	43,784	Shakopee	357
Sherburne	29,908	Elk River	435
Sibley	15,448	Gaylord	593
Stearns	108,161	Saint Cloud	1,338
Steele	30,328	Owatonna	431
Stevens	11,322	Morris	560
Swift	12,920	Benson	743
Todd	24,991	Long Prairie	941
Traverse	5,542	Wheaton	575
Wabasha	19,335	Wabasha	537
Wadena	14,192	Wadena	538
Waseca	18,448	Waseca	422
Washington	113,571	Stillwater	390
Watonwan	12,361	Saint James	435
Wilkin	8,382	Breckenridge	751
Winona	46,256	Winona	630
Wright	58,962	Buffalo	672
Yellow Medicine	13,653	Granite Falls	758

Mississippi
(82 counties, 47,233 sq. mi. land; pop. 2,520,770)

County	Pop.	County seat or court house	Land area sq. mi.
Adams	38,071	Natchez	456
Alcorn	33,036	Corinth	401
Amite	13,369	Liberty	732
Attala	19,865	Kosciusko	737
Benton	8,153	Ashland	407
Bolivar	45,965	Cleveland & Rosedale	892
Calhoun	15,664	Pittsboro	573
Carroll	9,776	Carrollton & Vaiden	634
Chickasaw	17,851	Houston & Okolona	503
Choctaw	8,996	Ackerman	420
Claiborne	12,279	Port Gibson	494
Clarke	16,945	Quitman	692
Clay	21,082	West Point	415
Coahoma	36,918	Clarksdale	559
Copiah	26,503	Hazlehurst	779
Covington	15,927	Collins	416
De Soto	53,930	Hernando	483
Forrest	66,018	Hattiesburg	469
Franklin	8,208	Meadville	566
George	15,297	Lucedale	483
Greene	9,827	Leakesville	718
Grenada	21,115	Grenada	421
Hancock	24,496	Bay Saint Louis	478
Harrison	157,665	Gulfport	581
Hinds	250,998	Jackson & Raymond	875
Holmes	22,970	Lexington	759
Humphreys	13,931	Belzoni	430
Issaquena	2,513	Mayersville	406
Itawamba	20,518	Fulton	540
Jackson	118,015	Pascagoula	731
Jasper	17,265	Bat Springs & Paulding	678
Jefferson	9,181	Fayette	523
Jefferson Davis	13,846	Prentiss	409
Jones	61,912	Ellisville & Laurel	696
Kemper	10,148	De Kalb	766
Lafayette	31,030	Oxford	669
Lamar	23,821	Purvis	499
Lauderdale	77,285	Meridian	705
Lawrence	12,518	Monticello	435
Leake	18,790	Carthage	584
Lee	57,061	Tupelo	451
Leflore	41,525	Greenwood	605
Lincoln	30,174	Brookhaven	587
Lowndes	57,304	Columbus	517
Madison	41,613	Canton	718
Marion	25,708	Columbia	548
Marshall	29,296	Holly Springs	709
Monroe	36,404	Aberdeen	772
Montgomery	13,366	Winona	408
Neshoba	23,789	Philadelphia	572
Newton	19,967	Decatur	580
Noxubee	13,212	Macon	698
Oktibbeha	36,018	Starkville	459
Panola	28,164	Batesville & Sardis	694
Pearl River	33,795	Poplarville	818
Perry	9,864	New Augusta	651
Pike	36,173	Magnolia	410
Pontotoc	20,918	Pontotoc	499
Prentiss	24,025	Booneville	418
Quitman	12,636	Marks	405
Rankin	69,427	Brandon	782
Scott	24,556	Forest	610
Sharkey	7,964	Rolling Fork	435
Simpson	23,441	Mendenhall	591
Smith	15,077	Raleigh	635
Stone	9,716	Wiggins	446
Sunflower	34,844	Indianola	706
Tallahatchie	17,157	Charleston & Sumner	651
Tate	20,119	Senatobia	406
Tippah	18,739	Ripley	458
Tishomingo	18,434	Iuka	434
Tunica	9,652	Tunica	460
Union	21,741	New Albany	416
Walthall	13,761	Tylertown	404
Warren	51,627	Vicksburg	596
Washington	72,344	Greenville	733
Wayne	19,135	Waynesboro	813
Webster	10,300	Walthall	424
Wilkinson	10,021	Woodville	678
Winston	19,474	Louisville	610
Yalobusha	13,183	Coffeeville & Water Valley	478
Yazoo	27,349	Yazoo City	933

Missouri
(114 cos., 1 ind. city, 68,945 sq. mi. land; pop. 4,916,766)

County	Pop.	County seat or court house	Land area sq. mi.
Adair	24,870	Kirksville	567
Andrew	13,980	Savannah	435
Atchison	8,605	Rockport	542
Audrain	26,458	Mexico	697
Barry	24,408	Cassville	773
Barton	11,292	Lamar	596
Bates	15,873	Butler	849
Benton	12,183	Warsaw	729
Bollinger	10,301	Marble Hill	621
Boone	100,376	Columbia	687
Buchanan	87,888	Saint Joseph	409
Butler	37,693	Poplar Bluff	698
Caldwell	8,660	Kingston	430
Callaway	32,252	Fulton	842
Camden	19,963	Camdenton	641
Cape Girardeau	58,837	Jackson	577
Carroll	12,131	Carrollton	695
Carter	5,532	Van Buren	509
Cass	51,029	Harrisonville	701
Cedar	11,894	Stockton	470
Chariton	10,489	Keytesville	758
Christian	22,402	Ozark	564
Clark	8,493	Kahoka	507
Clay	136,488	Liberty	403
Clinton	15,916	Plattsburg	423
Cole	56,663	Jefferson City	392
Cooper	14,643	Boonville	567
Crawford	18,300	Steelville	744
Dade	7,383	Greenfield	491
Dallas	12,096	Buffalo	543
Daviess	8,905	Gallatin	568
De Kalb	8,222	Maysville	425
Dent	14,517	Salem	755
Douglas	11,594	Ava	814
Dunklin	36,320	Kennett	547
Franklin	71,129	Union	922
Gasconade	13,181	Hermann	521
Gentry	7,887	Albany	493
Greene	185,302	Springfield	677
Grundy	11,959	Trenton	437
Harrison	9,890	Bethany	725
Henry	19,672	Clinton	729
Hickory	6,367	Hermitage	379
Holt	6,882	Oregon	457
Howard	10,008	Fayette	465
Howell	28,807	West Plains	928
Iron	11,084	Ironton	552
Jackson	629,180	Independence	611
Jasper	86,958	Carthage	641
Jefferson	146,814	Hillsboro	661
Johnson	39,059	Warrensburg	834
Knox	5,508	Edina	507
Laclede	24,323	Lebanon	768
Lafayette	29,931	Lexington	632
Lawrence	28,973	Mount Vernon	613
Lewis	10,901	Monticello	509
Lincoln	22,193	Troy	627
Linn	15,495	Linneus	620
Livingston	15,739	Chillicothe	537
McDonald	14,917	Pineville	540
Macon	16,313	Macon	797
Madison	10,725	Fredericktown	497
Maries	7,551	Vienna	528
Marion	28,638	Palmyra	438
Mercer	4,685	Princeton	454
Miller	18,539	Tuscumbia	593
Mississippi	15,726	Charleston	410
Moniteau	12,068	California	417
Monroe	9,716	Paris	670
Montgomery	11,537	Montgomery City	540
Morgan	13,807	Versailles	594
New Madrid	22,945	New Madrid	658
Newton	40,555	Neosho	627
Nodaway	21,996	Maryville	875
Oregon	10,238	Alton	792
Osage	12,014	Linn	606
Ozark	7,961	Gainesville	731
Pemiscot	24,987	Caruthersville	517
Perry	16,784	Perryville	473

County	Pop.	County seat or court house	Land area sq. mi.
Pettis	36,378	Sedalia	686
Phelps	33,633	Rolla	674
Pike	17,568	Bowling Green	673
Platte	46,341	Platte City	421
Polk	18,822	Bolivar	636
Pulaski	42,011	Waynesville	550
Putnam	6,092	Unionville	520
Rails	8,984	New London	482
Randolph	25,460	Huntsville	477
Ray	21,378	Richmond	568
Reynolds	7,230	Centerville	809
Ripley	12,458	Doniphan	631
St. Charles	143,455	St. Charles	558
St. Clair	8,622	Osceola	699
St. Francois	42,600	Farmington	451
St. Louis	974,180	Clayton	506
Ste. Genevieve	15,180	Ste. Genevieve	504
Saline	24,913	Marshall	755
Schuyler	4,979	Lancaster	309
Scotland	5,415	Memphis	438
Scott	39,647	Benton	423
Shannon	7,885	Eminence	1,004
Shelby	7,826	Shelbyville	501
Stoddard	29,009	Bloomfield	815
Stone	15,587	Galena	451
Sullivan	7,434	Milan	651
Taney	20,467	Forsyth	608
Texas	21,070	Houston	1,180
Vernon	19,806	Nevada	837
Warren	14,900	Warrenton	429
Washington	17,983	Potosi	762
Wayne	11,277	Greenville	762
Webster	20,414	Marshfield	594
Worth	3,008	Grant City	266
Wright	16,188	Hartville	682
Independent City			
St. Louis	452,801	.....	61

Montana

(56 counties, 145,388 sq. mi. land; pop., 786,690)

County	Pop.	County seat	Land area sq. mi.
Beaverhead	8,186	Dillon	5,529
Big Horn	11,096	Hardin	4,983
Blaine	5,999	Chinook	4,257
Broadwater	3,267	Townsend	1,189
Carbon	8,099	Red Lodge	2,056
Carter	1,799	Ekalaka	3,342
Cascade	80,696	Great Falls	2,699
Chouteau	6,092	Fort Benton	3,987
Custer	13,109	Miles City	3,776
Daniels	2,835	Scobey	1,427
Dawson	11,805	Glendive	2,374
Deer Lodge	12,518	Anaconda	740
Fallon	3,763	Baker	1,623
Fergus	13,076	Lewistown	4,340
Flathead	51,966	Kalispell	5,112
Gallatin	42,865	Bozeman	2,510
Garfield	1,656	Jordan	4,491
Glacier	10,628	Cut Bank	2,994
Golden Valley	1,026	Ryegate	1,172
Granite	2,700	Philipsburg	1,729
Hill	17,985	Havre	2,897
Jefferson	7,029	Boulder	1,657
Judith Basin	2,646	Stanford	1,871
Lake	19,056	Polson	1,445
Lewis & Clark	43,039	Helena	3,461
Liberty	2,329	Chester	1,426
Lincoln	17,752	Libby	3,616
McCone	2,702	Circle	2,626
Madison	5,448	Virginia City	3,590
Meagher	2,154	White Sulphur Springs	2,392
Mineral	3,675	Superior	1,216
Missoula	76,016	Missoula	2,582
Musselshell	4,428	Roundup	1,871
Park	12,869	Livingston	1,665
Petroleum	655	Winnett	1,652
Phillips	5,367	Malta	5,130
Pondera	6,731	Conrad	1,632
Powder River	2,520	Broadus	3,288
Powell	6,958	Deer Lodge	2,329
Prairie	1,836	Terry	1,732
Ravalli	22,493	Hamilton	2,384
Richland	12,243	Sidney	2,081
Roosevelt	10,467	Wolf Point	2,357
Rosebud	9,899	Forsyth	5,019
Sanders	8,675	Thompson Falls	2,749
Sheridan	5,414	Plentywood	1,681
Silver Bow	38,092	Butte	718
Stillwater	5,598	Columbus	1,793
Sweet Grass	3,216	Big Timber	1,903
Teton	6,491	Choteau	2,275
Toole	5,559	Shelby	1,931
Treasure	981	Hysham	975
Valley	10,250	Glasgow	4,935
Wheatland	2,359	Harlowton	1,419
Wibaux	1,476	Wibaux	688
Yellowstone	108,035	Billings	2,624

Nebraska

(93 counties, 76,644 sq. mi. land; pop., 1,569,825)

County	Pop.	County seat	Land area sq. mi.
Adams	30,656	Hastings	564
Antelope	8,675	Neligh	859
Arthur	513	Arthur	711
Banner	918	Harrisburg	747
Blaine	867	Brewster	714
Boone	7,391	Albion	687
Box Butte	13,696	Alliance	1,077
Boyd	3,331	Butte	532
Brown	4,377	Ainsworth	1,214
Buffalo	34,797	Kearney	945
Burt	8,813	Tekamah	486
Butler	9,330	David City	584
Cass	20,297	Plattsmouth	557
Cedar	10,852	Hartington	740
Chase	4,758	Imperial	894
Cherry	6,758	Valentine	5,961
Cheyenne	10,057	Sidney	1,196
Clay	8,106	Clay Center	574
Colfax	9,890	Schuyler	410
Cuming	11,664	West Point	575
Custer	13,877	Broken Bow	2,571
Dakota	16,573	Dakota City	258
Dawes	9,609	Chadron	1,397
Dawson	22,162	Lexington	982
Deuel	2,462	Chappell	437
Dixon	7,137	Ponca	474
Dodge	35,847	Fremont	534
Douglas	397,884	Omaha	333
Dundy	2,861	Benkelman	920
Fillmore	7,920	Geneva	576
Franklin	4,377	Franklin	576
Frontier	3,647	Stockville	976
Furnas	6,486	Beaver City	721
Gage	24,456	Beatrice	858
Garden	2,802	Oshkosh	1,680
Garfield	2,363	Burwell	570
Gosper	2,140	Elwood	461
Grant	877	Hyannis	775
Greeley	3,462	Greeley	570
Hall	47,690	Grand Island	537
Hamilton	9,301	Aurora	543
Harlan	4,292	Alma	555
Hayes	1,356	Hayes Center	713
Hitchcock	4,079	Trenton	709
Holt	13,552	O'Neill	2,406
Hooker	990	Mullen	721
Howard	6,773	Saint Paul	564
Jefferson	9,817	Fairbury	575
Johnson	5,285	Tecumseh	377
Kearney	7,053	Minden	519
Keith	9,364	Ogallala	1,039
Keya Paha	1,301	Springview	769
Kimball	4,882	Kimball	952
Knox	11,457	Center	1,105
Lancaster	192,884	Lincoln	839
Lincoln	36,455	North Platte	2,525
Logan	983	Stapleton	571
Loup	859	Taylor	574
McPherson	593	Tryon	859
Madison	31,382	Madison	575
Merrick	8,945	Central City	478
Morrill	6,085	Bridgeport	1,405
Nance	4,740	Fullerton	439
Nemaha	8,367	Auburn	409
Nuckolls	6,726	Nelson	576
Otoe	15,183	Nebraska City	615
Pawnee	3,937	Pawnee City	433
Perkins	3,637	Grant	885
Phelps	9,769	Holdrege	540
Pierce	8,481	Pierce	575
Platte	28,852	Columbus	669
Polk	6,320	Osceola	437
Red Willow	12,615	McCook	718
Richardson	11,315	Falls City	553
Rock	2,383	Bassett	1,003
Saline	13,131	Wilber	575
Sarpy	86,015	Papillion	238
Saunders	18,716	Wahoo	753
Scotts Bluff	38,344	Gering	725
Seward	15,789	Seward	575
Sheridan	7,544	Rushville	2,453
Sherman	4,226	Loup City	564
Sioux	1,845	Harrison	2,070
Stanton	6,549	Stanton	431
Thayer	7,582	Hebron	575
Thomas	973	Thedford	713
Thurston	7,186	Pender	391
Valley	5,633	Ord	567
Washington	15,508	Blair	386
Wayne	9,858	Wayne	443
Webster	4,858	Red Cloud	575
Wheeler	1,060	Bartlett	575
York	14,798	York	576

Nevada

(16 cos., 1 ind. city, 109,894 sq. mi. land; pop., 800,508)

County	Pop.	County seat	Land area sq. mi.
Churchill	13,917	Fallon	4,990
Clark	461,816	Las Vegas	7,881

County	Pop.	County seat or court house	Land area sq. mi.
Douglas	19,421	Minden	708
Elko	17,269	Elko	17,135
Esmeralda	777	Goldfield	3,587
Eureka	1,198	Eureka	4,175
Humboldt	9,449	Winnemucca	9,698
Lander	4,082	Battle Mountain	5,515
Lincoln	3,732	Pioche	10,635
Lyon	13,594	Yerington	2,007
Mineral	6,217	Hawthorne	3,744
Nye	9,048	Tonopah	18,155
Pershing	3,408	Lovelock	6,036
Storey	1,459	Virginia City	264
Washoe	193,623	Reno	6,317
White Pine	8,167	Ely	8.902
Independent City			
Carson City	32,022	Carson City	146

New Hampshire
(10 counties, 8,993 sq. mi. land; pop., 920,610)

County	Pop.	County seat or court house	Land area sq. mi.
Belknap	42,884	Laconia	404
Carroll	27,931	Ossipee	933
Cheshire	62,116	Keene	711
Coos	35,147	Lancaster	1,804
Grafton	65,806	Woodsville	1,719
Hillsborough	276,608	Nashua	876
Merrimack	98,302	Concord	936
Rockingham	190,345	Exeter	699
Strafford	85,408	Dover	370
Sullivan	36,063	Newport	540

New Jersey
(21 counties, 7,468 sq. mi. land; pop., 7,365,011)

County	Pop.	County seat or court house	Land area sq. mi.
Atlantic	194,119	Mays Landing	568
Bergen	845,385	Hackensack	237
Burlington	362,542	Mount Holly	808
Camden	471,650	Camden	223
Cape May	82,266	Cape May Court House	263
Cumberland	132,866	Bridgeton	498
Essex	851,304	Newark	127
Gloucester	199,917	Woodbury	327
Hudson	556,972	Jersey City	46
Hunterdon	87,361	Flemington	426
Mercer	307,863	Trenton	227
Middlesex	595,893	New Brunswick	316
Monmouth	503,173	Freehold	472
Morris	407,630	Morristown	470
Ocean	346,038	Toms River	641
Passaic	447,585	Paterson	187
Salem	64,676	Salem	338
Somerset	203,129	Somerville	305
Sussex	116,119	Newton	526
Union	504,094	Elizabeth	103
Warren	84,429	Belvidere	359

New Mexico
(33 counties, 121,335 sq. mi. land; pop., 1,303,302)

County	Pop.	County seat or court house	Land area sq. mi.
Bernalillo	420,261	Albuquerque	1,169
Catron	2,720	Reserve	6,929
Chaves	51,103	Roswell	6,066
Cibola	30,347	Grants	4,468
Colfax	13,706	Raton	3,762
Curry	42,019	Clovis	1,408
De Baca	2,454	Fort Sumner	2,323
Dona Ana	96,340	Las Cruces	3,819
Eddy	47,855	Carlsbad	4,184
Grant	26,204	Silver City	3,969
Guadalupe	4,496	Santa Rosa	3,032
Harding	1,090	Mosquero	2,122
Hidalgo	6,049	Lordsburg	3,445
Lea	55,634	Lovington	4,389
Lincoln	10,997	Carrizozo	4,832
Los Alamos	17,599	Los Alamos	109
Luna	15,585	Deming	2,965
McKinley	56,536	Gallup	5,442
Mora	4,205	Mora	1,930
Otero	44,665	Alamogordo	6,626
Quay	10,577	Tucumcari	2,874
Rio Arriba	29,282	Tierra Amarilla	5,856
Roosevelt	15,695	Portales	2,453
Sandoval	34,400	Bernalillo	3,707
San Juan	80,833	Aztec	5,521
San Miguel	22,751	Las Vegas	4,709
Santa Fe	75,519	Santa Fe	1,905
Sierra	8,454	Truth or Consequences	4,178
Socorro	12,969	Socorro	6,625
Taos	18,862	Taos	2,204
Torrance	7,491	Estancia	3,335
Union	4,725	Clayton	3,830
Valencia	60,853	Los Lunas	5,616

New York
(62 counties, 47,377 sq. mi. land; pop., 17,558,165)

County	Pop.	County seat or court house	Land area sq. mi.
Albany	285,909	Albany	524
Allegany	51,742	Belmont	1,032
Bronx	1,168,972	Bronx	42
Broome	213,648	Binghamton	712
Cattaraugus	85,697	Little Valley	1,306
Cayuga	79,894	Auburn	695
Chautauqua	146,925	Mayville	1,064
Chemung	97,656	Elmira	411
Chenango	49,344	Norwich	897
Clinton	80,750	Plattsburgh	1,043
Columbia	59,487	Hudson	638
Cortland	48,820	Cortland	500
Delaware	46,824	Delhi	1,440
Dutchess	245,055	Poughkeepsie	804
Erie	1,015,472	Buffalo	1,046
Essex	36,176	Elizabethtown	1,806
Franklin	44,929	Malone	1,642
Fulton	55,153	Johnstown	497
Genesee	59,400	Batavia	495
Greene	40,861	Catskill	648
Hamilton	5,034	Lake Pleasant	1,721
Herkimer	66,714	Herkimer	1,416
Jefferson	88,151	Watertown	1,273
Kings	2,231,028	Brooklyn	70
Lewis	25,035	Lowville	1,283
Livingston	57,006	Geneseo	633
Madison	65,150	Wampsville	656
Monroe	702,238	Rochester	663
Montgomery	53,439	Fonda	404
Nassau	1,321,582	Mineola	287
New York	1,428,285	New York	22
Niagara	227,354	Lockport	526
Oneida	253,466	Utica	1,219
Onondaga	463,920	Syracuse	784
Ontario	88,909	Canandaigua	644
Orange	259,603	Goshen	826
Orleans	38,496	Albion	391
Oswego	113,901	Oswego	954
Otsego	59,075	Cooperstown	1,004
Putnam	77,193	Carmel	231
Queens	1,891,325	Jamaica	109
Rensselaer	151,966	Troy	655
Richmond	352,029	Saint George	59
Rockland	259,530	New City	175
St. Lawrence	114,347	Canton	2,728
Saratoga	153,759	Ballston Spa	810
Schenectady	149,946	Schenectady	206
Schoharie	29,710	Schoharie	624
Schuyler	17,686	Watkins Glen	329
Seneca	33,733	Ovid & Waterloo	327
Steuben	99,217	Bath	1,396
Suffolk	1,284,231	Riverhead	911
Sullivan	65,155	Monticello	976
Tioga	49,812	Owego	519
Tompkins	87,085	Ithaca	477
Ulster	158,158	Kingston	1,131
Warren	54,854	Queensbury	882
Washington	54,795	Hudson Falls	836
Wayne	84,581	Lyons	605
Westchester	866,599	White Plains	438
Wyoming	39,895	Warsaw	595
Yates	21,459	Penn Yan	339

North Carolina
(100 counties, 48,843 sq. mi. land; pop., 5,880,095)

County	Pop.	County seat or court house	Land area sq. mi.
Alamance	99,136	Graham	433
Alexander	24,999	Taylorsville	259
Alleghany	9,587	Sparta	235
Anson	25,562	Wadesboro	533
Ashe	22,325	Jefferson	426
Avery	14,409	Newland	247
Beaufort	40,266	Washington	826
Bertie	21,024	Windsor	701
Bladen	30,448	Elizabethtown	879
Brunswick	35,767	Southport	860
Buncombe	160,934	Asheville	659
Burke	72,504	Morganton	504
Cabarrus	85,895	Concord	364
Caldwell	67,746	Lenoir	471
Camden	5,829	Camden	240
Carteret	41,092	Beaufort	526
Caswell	20,705	Yanceyville	428
Catawba	105,208	Newton	396
Chatham	33,415	Pittsboro	708
Cherokee	18,933	Murphy	452
Chowan	12,558	Edenton	182
Clay	6,619	Hayesville	214
Cleveland	83,435	Shelby	468
Columbus	51,037	Whiteville	938
Craven	71,043	New Bern	701
Cumberland	247,160	Fayetteville	657
Currituck	11,089	Currituck	256
Dare	13,377	Manteo	391
Davidson	113,162	Lexington	548
Davie	24,599	Mocksville	267
Duplin	40,952	Kenansville	819
Durham	152,235	Durham	298
Edgecombe	55,988	Tarboro	506
Forsyth	243,704	Winston-Salem	412
Franklin	30,055	Louisburg	494
Gaston	162,568	Gastonia	357
Gates	8,875	Gatesville	338
Graham	7,217	Robbinsville	289
Granville	33,995	Oxford	534
Greene	16,117	Snow Hill	266

County	Pop.	County seat or court house	Land area sq. mi.
Guilford	317,154	Greensboro	651
Halifax	55,076	Halifax	724
Harnett	59,570	Lillington	601
Haywood	46,495	Waynesville	555
Henderson	58,580	Hendersonville	374
Hertford	23,368	Winton	356
Hoke	20,383	Raeford	391
Hyde	5,873	Swanquarter	624
Iredell	82,538	Statesville	574
Jackson	25,811	Sylva	491
Johnston	70,599	Smithfield	795
Jones	9,705	Trenton	470
Lee	36,718	Sanford	259
Lenoir	59,819	Kinston	402
Lincoln	42,372	Lincolnton	298
McDowell	35,135	Marion	437
Macon	20,178	Franklin	517
Madison	16,827	Marshall	451
Martin	25,948	Williamston	461
Mecklenburg	404,270	Charlotte	528
Mitchell	14,428	Bakersville	222
Montgomery	22,469	Troy	490
Moore	50,505	Carthage	701
Nash	67,153	Nashville	540
New Hanover	103,471	Wilmington	185
Northampton	22,195	Jackson	538
Onslow	112,784	Jacksonville	763
Orange	77,055	Hillsboro	400
Pamlico	10,398	Bayboro	341
Pasquotank	28,462	Elizabeth City	228
Pender	22,262	Burgaw	875
Perquimans	9,486	Hertford	246
Person	29,164	Roxboro	398
Pitt	83,651	Greenville	657
Polk	12,984	Columbus	238
Randolph	91,300	Asheboro	789
Richmond	45,161	Rockingham	477
Robeson	101,577	Lumberton	949
Rockingham	83,426	Wentworth	569
Rowan	99,186	Salisbury	519
Rutherford	53,787	Rutherfordton	568
Sampson	49,687	Clinton	947
Scotland	32,273	Laurinburg	319
Stanly	48,517	Albemarle	396
Stokes	33,086	Danbury	452
Surry	59,449	Dobson	539
Swain	10,283	Bryson City	526
Transylvania	23,417	Brevard	378
Tyrrell	3,975	Columbia	407
Union	70,436	Monroe	639
Vance	36,748	Henderson	249
Wake	301,429	Raleigh	854
Warren	16,232	Warrenton	427
Washington	14,801	Plymouth	332
Watauga	31,678	Boone	314
Wayne	97,054	Goldsboro	554
Wilkes	58,657	Wilkesboro	752
Wilson	63,132	Wilson	374
Yadkin	28,439	Yadkinville	336
Yancey	14,934	Burnsville	314

North Dakota

(53 counties, 69,300 sq. mi. land; pop., 652,717)

County	Pop.	County seat	Land area sq. mi.
Adams	3,584	Hettinger	988
Barnes	13,960	Valley City	1,498
Benson	7,944	Minnewaukan	1,412
Billings	1,138	Medora	1,152
Bottineau	9,338	Bottineau	1,668
Bowman	4,229	Bowman	1,162
Burke	3,822	Bowbells	1,118
Burleigh	54,811	Bismarck	1,616
Cass	88,247	Fargo	1,767
Cavalier	7,636	Langdon	1,507
Dickey	7,207	Ellendale	1,139
Divide	3,494	Crosby	1,288
Dunn	4,627	Manning	1,993
Eddy	3,554	New Rockford	634
Emmons	5,877	Linton	1,499
Foster	4,611	Carrington	640
Golden Valley	2,391	Beach	1,003
Grand Forks	66,100	Grand Forks	1,440
Grant	4,274	Carson	1,660
Griggs	3,714	Cooperstown	708
Hettinger	4,275	Mott	1,133
Kidder	3,833	Steele	1,362
La Moure	6,473	La Moure	1,150
Logan	3,493	Napoleon	1,000
McHenry	7,858	Towner	1,887
McIntosh	4,800	Ashley	984
McKenzie	7,132	Watford City	2,754
McLean	12,288	Washburn	2,065
Mercer	9,378	Stanton	1,044
Morton	25,177	Mandan	1,921
Mountrail	7,679	Stanley	1,837
Nelson	5,233	Lakota	991
Oliver	2,495	Center	723
Pembina	10,399	Cavalier	1,120

County	Pop.	County seat	Land area sq. mi.
Pierce	6,166	Rugby	1,037
Ramsey	13,048	Devils Lake	1,241
Ransom	6,698	Lisbon	862
Renville	3,608	Mohall	874
Richland	19,207	Wahpeton	1,436
Rolette	12,177	Rolla	914
Sargent	5,512	Forman	857
Sheridan	2,819	McClusky	989
Sioux	3,620	Fort Yates	1,099
Slope	1,157	Amidon	1,219
Stark	23,697	Dickinson	1,338
Steele	3,106	Finley	713
Stutsman	24,154	Jamestown	2,263
Towner	4,052	Cando	1,035
Traill	9,624	Hillsboro	861
Walsh	15,371	Grafton	1,290
Ward	58,392	Minot	2,041
Wells	6,979	Fessenden	1,288
Williams	22,237	Williston	2,074

Ohio

(88 counties, 41,004 sq. mi. land; pop., 10,797,603)

County	Pop.	County seat	Land area sq. mi.
Adams	24,328	West Union	586
Allen	112,241	Lima	405
Ashland	46,178	Ashland	424
Ashtabula	104,215	Jefferson	703
Athens	56,399	Athens	508
Auglaize	42,554	Wapakoneta	398
Belmont	82,569	Saint Clairsville	537
Brown	31,920	Georgetown	493
Butler	258,787	Hamilton	470
Carroll	25,598	Carrollton	393
Champaign	33,649	Urbana	429
Clark	150,236	Springfield	398
Clermont	128,483	Batavia	456
Clinton	34,603	Wilmington	410
Columbiana	113,572	Lisbon	534
Coshocton	36,024	Coshocton	566
Crawford	50,075	Bucyrus	403
Cuyahoga	1,498,295	Cleveland	459
Darke	55,096	Greenville	600
Defiance	39,987	Defiance	414
Delaware	53,840	Delaware	443
Erie	79,655	Sandusky	264
Fairfield	93,678	Lancaster	506
Fayette	27,467	Washington C. H.	405
Franklin	869,126	Columbus	543
Fulton	37,751	Wauseon	407
Gallia	30,098	Gallipolis	471
Geauga	74,474	Chardon	408
Greene	129,769	Xenia	416
Guernsey	42,024	Cambridge	522
Hamilton	873,203	Cincinnati	412
Hancock	64,581	Findlay	532
Hardin	32,719	Kenton	471
Harrison	18,152	Cadiz	400
Henry	28,383	Napoleon	415
Highland	33,477	Hillsboro	553
Hocking	24,304	Logan	423
Holmes	29,416	Millersburg	424
Huron	54,608	Norwalk	494
Jackson	30,592	Jackson	420
Jefferson	91,564	Steubenville	410
Knox	46,309	Mount Vernon	529
Lake	212,801	Painesville	231
Lawrence	63,849	Ironton	457
Licking	120,981	Newark	686
Logan	39,155	Bellefontaine	458
Lorain	274,909	Elyria	495
Lucas	471,741	Toledo	341
Madison	33,004	London	467
Mahoning	289,487	Youngstown	417
Marion	67,974	Marion	403
Medina	113,150	Medina	422
Meigs	23,641	Pomeroy	432
Mercer	38,334	Celina	457
Miami	90,381	Troy	410
Monroe	17,382	Woodsfield	457
Montgomery	571,697	Dayton	458
Morgan	14,241	McConnelsville	420
Morrow	26,480	Mount Gilead	406
Muskingum	83,340	Zanesville	654
Noble	11,310	Caldwell	399
Ottawa	40,076	Port Clinton	253
Paulding	21,302	Paulding	419
Perry	31,032	New Lexington	412
Pickaway	43,662	Circleville	503
Pike	22,802	Waverly	443
Portage	135,856	Ravenna	493
Preble	38,223	Eaton	426
Putnam	32,991	Ottawa	484
Richland	131,205	Mansfield	497
Ross	65,004	Chillicothe	692
Sandusky	63,267	Fremont	410
Scioto	84,545	Portsmouth	613
Seneca	61,901	Tiffin	553
Shelby	43,089	Sidney	409
Stark	378,823	Canton	574
Summit	524,472	Akron	412
Trumbull	241,863	Warren	612
Tuscarawas	84,614	New Philadelphia	570

County	Pop.	County seat or court house	Land area sq. mi.
Union	29,536	Marysville	437
Van Wert	30,458	Van Wert	410
Vinton	11,584	McArthur	414
Warren	99,276	Lebanon	403
Washington	64,266	Marietta	640
Wayne	97,408	Wooster	557
Williams	36,369	Bryan	422
Wood	107,372	Bowling Green	619
Wyandot	22,651	Upper Sandusky	406

Oklahoma
(77 counties, 68,655 sq. mi. land; pop., 3,025,487)

County	Pop.	County seat or court house	Land area sq. mi.
Adair	18,575	Stilwell	577
Alfalfa	7,077	Cherokee	864
Atoka	12,748	Atoka	980
Beaver	6,806	Beaver	1,808
Beckham	19,243	Sayre	904
Blaine	13,443	Watonga	920
Bryan	30,535	Durant	902
Caddo	30,905	Anadarko	1,286
Canadian	56,452	El Reno	901
Carter	43,610	Ardmore	828
Cherokee	30,684	Tahlequah	748
Choctaw	17,203	Hugo	762
Cimarron	3,648	Boise City	1,842
Cleveland	133,173	Norman	529
Coal	6,041	Coalgate	520
Comanche	112,456	Lawton	1,076
Cotton	7,338	Walters	656
Craig	15,014	Vinita	763
Creek	59,210	Sapulpa	930
Custer	25,995	Arapaho	981
Delaware	23,946	Jay	720
Dewey	5,922	Taloga	1,007
Ellis	5,596	Arnett	1,232
Garfield	62,820	Enid	1,060
Garvin	27,856	Pauls Valley	813
Grady	39,490	Chickasha	1,106
Grant	6,518	Medford	1,004
Greer	6,877	Mangum	638
Harmon	4,519	Hollis	537
Harper	4,715	Buffalo	1,039
Haskell	11,010	Stigler	570
Hughes	14,338	Holdenville	806
Jackson	30,356	Altus	817
Jefferson	8,294	Waurika	769
Johnston	10,356	Tishomingo	639
Kay	49,852	Newkirk	921
Kingfisher	14,187	Kingfisher	906
Kiowa	12,711	Hobart	1,019
Latimer	9,840	Wilburton	728
Le Flore	40,698	Poteau	1,585
Lincoln	26,601	Chandler	964
Logan	26,881	Guthrie	748
Love	7,469	Marietta	519
McClain	20,291	Purcell	582
McCurtain	36,151	Idabel	1,826
McIntosh	15,495	Eufaula	599
Major	8,772	Fairview	958
Marshall	10,550	Madill	372
Mayes	32,261	Pryor	644
Murray	12,147	Sulphur	420
Muskogee	67,033	Muskogee	815
Noble	11,573	Perry	736
Nowata	11,486	Nowata	540
Okfuskee	11,125	Okemah	628
Oklahoma	568,933	Oklahoma City	708
Okmulgee	39,169	Okmulgee	698
Osage	39,327	Pawhuska	2,265
Ottawa	32,870	Miami	465
Pawnee	15,310	Pawnee	551
Payne	62,435	Stillwater	691
Pittsburg	40,524	McAlester	1,251
Pontotoc	32,598	Ada	717
Pottawatomie	55,239	Shawnee	783
Pushmataha	11,773	Antlers	1,417
Roger Mills	4,799	Cheyenne	1,146
Rogers	46,436	Claremore	683
Seminole	27,465	Wewoka	639
Sequoyah	30,749	Sallisaw	678
Stephens	43,419	Duncan	884
Texas	17,727	Guymon	2,040
Tillman	12,398	Frederick	904
Tulsa	470,593	Tulsa	572
Wagoner	41,801	Wagoner	559
Washington	48,113	Bartlesville	423
Washita	13,798	Cordell	1,006
Woods	10,923	Alva	1,291
Woodward	21,172	Woodward	1,242

Oregon
(36 counties, 96,184 sq. mi. land; pop., 2,633,156)

County	Pop.	County seat or court house	Land area sq. mi.
Baker	16,134	Baker	3,072
Benton	68,211	Corvallis	679
Clackamas	241,911	Oregon City	1,870
Clatsop	32,489	Astoria	805
Columbia	35,646	Saint Helens	651
Coos	64,047	Coquille	1,606
Crook	13,091	Prineville	2,984
Curry	16,992	Gold Beach	1,629
Deschutes	62,142	Bend	3,025
Douglas	93,748	Roseburg	5,044
Gilliam	2,057	Condon	1,213
Grant	8,210	Canyon City	4,525
Harney	8,314	Burns	10,174
Hood River	15,835	Hood River	521
Jackson	132,456	Medford	2,787
Jefferson	11,599	Madras	1,789
Josephine	58,820	Grants Pass	1,640
Klamath	59,117	Klamath Falls	5,954
Lake	7,532	Lakeview	8,251
Lane	275,226	Eugene	4,562
Lincoln	35,264	Newport	980
Linn	89,495	Albany	2,296
Malheur	26,896	Vale	9,861
Marion	204,692	Salem	1,184
Morrow	7,519	Heppner	2,044
Multnomah	562,647	Portland	431
Polk	45,203	Dallas	741
Sherman	2,172	Moro	827
Tillamook	21,164	Tillamook	1,101
Umatilla	58,861	Pendleton	3,218
Union	23,921	La Grande	2,035
Wallowa	7,273	Enterprise	3,150
Wasco	21,732	The Dalles	2,384
Washington	245,860	Hillsboro	725
Wheeler	1,513	Fossil	1,713
Yamhill	55,332	McMinnville	715

Pennsylvania
(67 counties, 44,888 sq. mi. land; pop., 11,864,720)

County	Pop.	County seat or court house	Land area sq. mi.
Adams	68,292	Gettysburg	521
Allegheny	1,450,195	Pittsburgh	727
Armstrong	77,768	Kittanning	646
Beaver	204,441	Beaver	436
Bedford	46,784	Bedford	1,017
Berks	312,509	Reading	861
Blair	136,621	Hollidaysburg	527
Bradford	62,919	Towanda	1,152
Bucks	479,180	Doylestown	610
Butler	147,912	Butler	789
Cambria	183,263	Ebensburg	691
Cameron	6,674	Emporium	398
Carbon	53,285	Jim Thorpe	384
Centre	112,760	Bellefonte	1,106
Chester	316,660	West Chester	758
Clarion	43,362	Clarion	607
Clearfield	83,578	Clearfield	1,149
Clinton	38,971	Lock Haven	891
Columbia	61,967	Bloomsburg	486
Crawford	88,869	Meadville	1,011
Cumberland	179,625	Carlisle	547
Dauphin	232,317	Harrisburg	528
Delaware	555,029	Media	184
Elk	38,338	Ridgeway	830
Erie	279,780	Erie	804
Fayette	160,395	Uniontown	794
Forest	5,072	Tionesta	428
Franklin	113,629	Chambersburg	774
Fulton	12,842	McConnellsburg	438
Greene	40,355	Waynesburg	577
Huntingdon	42,253	Huntingdon	877
Indiana	92,281	Indiana	829
Jefferson	48,303	Brookville	657
Juniata	19,188	Mifflintown	392
Lackawanna	227,908	Scranton	461
Lancaster	362,346	Lancaster	952
Lawrence	107,150	New Castle	363
Lebanon	109,829	Lebanon	363
Lehigh	273,582	Allentown	348
Luzerne	343,079	Wilkes-Barre	891
Lycoming	118,416	Williamsport	1,237
McKean	50,635	Smethport	979
Mercer	128,299	Mercer	672
Mifflin	46,908	Lewistown	413
Monroe	69,409	Stroudsburg	609
Montgomery	643,371	Norristown	486
Montour	16,675	Danville	131
Northampton	225,418	Easton	376
Northumberland	100,381	Sunbury	461
Perry	35,718	New Bloomfield	557
Philadelphia	1,688,210	Philadelphia	136
Pike	18,271	Milford	550
Potter	17,726	Coudersport	1,081
Schuylkill	160,630	Pottsville	782
Snyder	33,584	Middleburg	329
Somerset	81,243	Somerset	1,073
Sullivan	6,349	Laporte	451
Susquehanna	37,876	Montrose	826
Tioga	40,973	Wellsboro	1,131
Union	32,870	Lewisburg	317
Venango	64,444	Franklin	679
Warren	47,449	Warren	885
Washington	217,074	Washington	958
Wayne	35,237	Honesdale	731
Westmoreland	392,184	Greensburg	1,033
Wyoming	26,433	Tunkhannock	399
York	312,963	York	906

County	Pop.	County seat or court house	Land area sq. mi.

Rhode Island
(5 counties, 1,055 sq. mi. land; pop., 947,154)

County	Pop.	County seat or court house	Land area sq. mi.
Bristol	46,942	Bristol	26
Kent	154,163	East Greenwich	172
Newport	81,383	Newport	107
Providence	571,349	Providence	416
Washington	93,317	West Kingston	333

South Carolina
(46 counties, 30,203 sq. mi. land; pop., 3,120,729)

County	Pop.	County seat or court house	Land area sq. mi.
Abbeville	22,627	Abbeville	508
Aiken	105,630	Aiken	1,092
Allendale	10,700	Allendale	413
Anderson	133,235	Anderson	718
Bamberg	18,118	Bamberg	395
Barnwell	19,868	Barnwell	558
Beaufort	65,364	Beaufort	579
Berkeley	94,745	Moncks Corner	1,108
Calhoun	12,206	Saint Matthews	380
Charleston	276,556	Charleston	938
Cherokee	40,983	Gaffney	396
Chester	30,148	Chester	580
Chesterfield	38,161	Chesterfield	802
Clarendon	27,464	Manning	602
Colleton	31,676	Walterboro	1,052
Darlington	62,717	Darlington	563
Dillon	31,083	Dillon	406
Dorchester	59,045	Saint George	575
Edgefield	17,528	Edgefield	490
Fairfield	20,700	Winnsboro	685
Florence	110,163	Florence	804
Georgetown	42,461	Georgetown	822
Greenville	287,895	Greenville	795
Greenwood	55,859	Greenwood	451
Hampton	18,159	Hampton	561
Horry	101,419	Conway	1,143
Jasper	14,504	Ridgeland	655
Kershaw	39,015	Camden	723
Lancaster	53,361	Lancaster	552
Laurens	52,214	Laurens	712
Lee	18,929	Bishopville	411
Lexington	140,353	Lexington	707
McCormick	7,797	McCormick	350
Marion	34,179	Marion	493
Marlboro	31,634	Bennettsville	483
Newberry	31,111	Newberry	634
Oconee	48,611	Walhalla	629
Orangeburg	82,276	Orangeburg	1,111
Pickens	79,292	Pickens	499
Richland	269,600	Columbia	762
Saluda	16,136	Saluda	456
Spartanburg	203,023	Spartanburg	814
Sumter	88,243	Sumter	665
Union	30,764	Union	515
Williamsburg	38,226	Kingstree	934
York	106,720	York	685

South Dakota
(67 counties, 75,952 sq. mi. land; pop., 690,768)

County	Pop.	County seat or court house	Land area sq. mi.
Aurora	3,628	Plankinton	707
Beadle	19,195	Huron	1,259
Bennett	3,236	Martin	1,182
Bon Homme	8,059	Tyndall	552
Brookings	24,332	Brookings	795
Brown	36,962	Aberdeen	1,722
Brule	5,245	Chamberlain	815
Buffalo	1,795	Gannvalley	475
Butte	8,372	Belle Fourche	2,251
Campbell	2,243	Mound City	732
Charles Mix	9,680	Lake Andes	1,090
Clark	4,894	Clark	953
Clay	13,135	Vermillion	409
Codington	20,885	Watertown	694
Corson	5,196	McIntosh	2,467
Custer	6,000	Custer	1,559
Davison	17,820	Mitchell	436
Day	8,133	Webster	1,022
Deuel	5,289	Clear Lake	631
Dewey	5,366	Timber Lake	2,310
Douglas	4,181	Armour	434
Edmunds	5,159	Ipswich	1,149
Fall River	8,439	Hot Springs	4,742
Faulk	3,327	Faulkton	1,004
Grant	9,013	Milbank	681
Gregory	6,015	Burke	1,013
Haakon	2,794	Philip	1,822
Hamlin	5,261	Hayti	512
Hand	4,948	Miller	1,437
Hanson	3,415	Alexandria	433
Harding	1,700	Buffalo	2,678
Hughes	14,220	Pierre	757
Hutchinson	9,350	Olivet	816
Hyde	2,069	Highmore	860
Jackson	3,437	Kadoka	1,872
Jerauld	2,929	Wessington Spgs.	530
Jones	1,453	Murdo	971
Kingsbury	6,679	De Smet	824
Lake	10,724	Madison	560
Lawrence	18,339	Deadwood	800
Lincoln	13,942	Canton	578
Lyman	3,864	Kennebec	1,679
McCook	6,444	Salem	576
McPherson	4,027	Leola	1,148
Marshall	5,404	Britton	848
Meade	20,717	Sturgis	3,481
Mellette	2,249	White River	1,311
Miner	3,739	Howard	570
Minnehaha	109,435	Sioux Falls	810
Moody	6,692	Flandreau	520
Pennington	70,133	Rapid City	2,783
Perkins	4,700	Bison	2,884
Potter	3,674	Gettysburg	869
Roberts	10,911	Sisseton	1,102
Sanborn	3,213	Woonsocket	569
Shannon	11,323	(Attached to Fall River)	2,094
Spink	9,201	Redfield	1,505
Stanley	2,533	Fort Pierre	1,431
Sully	1,990	Onida	972
Todd	7,328	(Attached to Tripp)	1,388
Tripp	7,268	Winner	1,618
Turner	9,255	Parker	617
Union	10,938	Elk Point	453
Walworth	7,011	Selby	707
Washabaugh	—	(Attached to Jackson)	—
Yankton	18,952	Yankton	518
Ziebach	2,308	Dupree	1,969

Tennessee
(95 counties, 41,155 sq. mi. land; pop., 4,591,023)

County	Pop.	County seat or court house	Land area sq. mi.
Anderson	67,346	Clinton	339
Bedford	27,916	Shelbyville	475
Benton	14,901	Camden	392
Bledsoe	9,478	Pikeville	407
Blount	77,770	Maryville	558
Bradley	67,547	Cleveland	327
Campbell	34,841	Jacksboro	479
Cannon	10,234	Woodbury	266
Carroll	28,285	Huntingdon	600
Carter	50,205	Elizabethton	341
Cheatham	21,616	Ashland City	304
Chester	12,727	Henderson	289
Claiborne	24,595	Tazewell	432
Clay	7,676	Celina	227
Cocke	28,792	Newport	432
Coffee	38,311	Manchester	428
Crockett	14,941	Alamo	266
Cumberland	28,676	Crossville	682
Davidson	477,811	Nashville	501
Decatur	10,857	Decaturville	330
De Kalb	13,589	Smithville	291
Dickson	30,037	Charlotte	491
Dyer	34,663	Dyersburg	520
Fayette	25,305	Somerville	705
Fentress	14,826	Jamestown	498
Franklin	31,983	Winchester	543
Gibson	49,467	Trenton	602
Giles	24,625	Pulaski	610
Grainger	16,751	Rutledge	273
Greene	54,406	Greeneville	619
Grundy	13,787	Altamont	361
Hamblen	49,300	Morristown	156
Hamilton	287,643	Chattanooga	539
Hancock	6,887	Sneedville	223
Hardeman	23,873	Bolivar	670
Hardin	22,280	Savannah	578
Hawkins	43,751	Rogersville	486
Haywood	20,318	Brownsville	534
Henderson	21,390	Lexington	520
Henry	28,656	Paris	560
Hickman	15,151	Centerville	610
Houston	6,871	Erin	200
Humphreys	15,957	Waverly	528
Jackson	9,398	Gainesboro	308
Jefferson	31,284	Dandridge	265
Johnson	13,745	Mountain City	297
Knox	319,694	Knoxville	506
Lake	7,455	Tiptonville	169
Lauderdale	24,555	Ripley	474
Lawrence	34,110	Lawrenceburg	617
Lewis	9,700	Hohenwald	282
Lincoln	26,483	Fayetteville	571
Loudon	28,553	Loudon	235
McMinn	41,878	Athens	429
McNairy	22,525	Selmer	562
Macon	15,700	Lafayette	307
Madison	74,546	Jackson	558
Marion	24,416	Jasper	512
Marshall	19,698	Lewisburg	376
Maury	51,095	Columbia	616
Meigs	7,431	Decatur	189
Monroe	28,700	Madisonville	648
Montgomery	83,342	Clarksville	539
Moore	4,510	Lynchburg	129
Morgan	16,604	Wartburg	523
Obion	32,781	Union City	550
Overton	17,575	Livingston	433
Perry	6,111	Linden	412
Pickett	4,358	Byrdstown	159

County	Pop.	County seat or court house	Land area sq. mi.
Polk	13,602	Benton	438
Putnam	47,601	Cookeville	399
Rhea	24,235	Dayton	309
Roane	48,425	Kingston	357
Robertson	37,021	Springfield	476
Rutherford	84,058	Murfreesboro	606
Scott	19,259	Huntsville	528
Sequatchie	8,605	Dunlap	266
Sevier	41,418	Sevierville	590
Shelby	777,113	Memphis	772
Smith	14,935	Carthage	313
Stewart	8,665	Dover	454
Sullivan	143,968	Blountville	415
Sumner	85,790	Gallatin	529
Tipton	32,747	Covington	454
Trousdale	6,137	Hartsville	114
Unicoi	16,362	Erwin	186
Union	11,707	Maynardville	218
Van Buren	4,728	Spencer	273
Warren	32,653	McMinnville	431
Washington	88,755	Jonesboro	326
Wayne	13,946	Waynesboro	734
Weakley	32,896	Dresden	581
White	19,567	Sparta	373
Williamson	58,108	Franklin	584
Wilson	56,064	Lebanon	570

Texas

(254 counties, 262,017 sq. mi. land; pop., 14,225,513)

County	Pop.	County seat or court house	Land area sq. mi.
Anderson	38,381	Palestine	1,077
Andrews	13,323	Andrews	1,501
Angelina	64,172	Lufkin	807
Aransas	14,260	Rockport	280
Archer	7,266	Archer City	907
Armstrong	1,994	Claude	909
Atascosa	25,055	Jourdanton	1,218
Austin	17,726	Bellville	656
Bailey	8,168	Muleshoe	826
Bandera	7,084	Bandera	793
Bastrop	24,726	Bastrop	895
Baylor	4,919	Seymour	862
Bee	26,030	Beeville	880
Bell	157,820	Belton	1,055
Bexar	988,971	San Antonio	1,248
Blanco	4,681	Johnson City	714
Borden	859	Gail	900
Bosque	13,401	Meridian	989
Bowie	75,301	Boston	891
Brazoria	169,587	Angleton	1,407
Brazos	93,588	Bryan	589
Brewster	7,573	Alpine	6,169
Briscoe	2,579	Silverton	887
Brooks	8,428	Falfurrias	942
Brown	33,057	Brownwood	936
Burleson	12,313	Caldwell	669
Burnet	17,803	Burnet	994
Caldwell	23,637	Lockhart	546
Calhoun	19,574	Port Lavaca	540
Callahan	10,992	Baird	899
Cameron	209,680	Brownsville	906
Camp	9,275	Pittsburg	203
Carson	6,672	Panhandle	924
Cass	29,430	Linden	937
Castro	10,556	Dimmitt	899
Chambers	18,538	Anahuac	616
Cherokee	38,127	Rusk	1,052
Childress	6,950	Childress	707
Clay	9,582	Henrietta	1,086
Cochran	4,825	Morton	775
Coke	3,196	Robert Lee	908
Coleman	10,439	Coleman	1,277
Collin	144,490	McKinney	851
Collingsworth	4,648	Wellington	909
Colorado	18,823	Columbus	965
Comal	36,446	New Braunfels	555
Comanche	12,617	Comanche	930
Concho	2,915	Paint Rock	992
Cooke	27,656	Gainesville	893
Coryell	56,767	Gatesville	1,057
Cottle	2,947	Paducah	895
Crane	4,600	Crane	782
Crockett	4,608	Ozona	2,806
Crosby	8,859	Crosbyton	899
Culberson	3,315	Van Horn	3,815
Dallam	6,531	Dalhart	1,505
Dallas	1,556,419	Dallas	880
Dawson	16,184	Lamesa	903
Deaf Smith	21,165	Hereford	1,497
Delta	4,839	Cooper	278
Denton	143,126	Denton	911
Dewitt	18,903	Cuero	910
Dickens	3,539	Dickens	907
Dimmit	11,367	Carrizo Springs	1,307
Donley	4,075	Clarendon	929
Duval	12,517	San Diego	1,795
Eastland	19,480	Eastland	924
Ector	115,374	Odessa	903
Edwards	2,033	Rocksprings	2,121
Ellis	59,743	Waxahachie	939
El Paso	479,899	El Paso	1,014
Erath	22,560	Stephenville	1,080
Falls	17,946	Marlin	770
Fannin	24,285	Bonham	895
Fayette	18,832	La Grange	950
Fisher	5,891	Roby	897
Floyd	9,834	Floydada	992
Foard	2,158	Crowell	703
Fort Bend	130,962	Richmond	876
Franklin	6,893	Mount Vernon	294
Freestone	14,830	Fairfield	888
Frio	13,785	Pearsall	1,133
Gaines	13,150	Seminole	1,504
Galveston	195,738	Galveston	399
Garza	5,336	Post	895
Gillespie	13,532	Fredericksburg	1,061
Glasscock	1,304	Garden City	900
Goliad	5,193	Goliad	859
Gonzales	16,949	Gonzales	1,068
Gray	26,386	Pampa	921
Grayson	89,796	Sherman	934
Gregg	99,495	Longview	273
Grimes	13,580	Anderson	799
Guadalupe	46,708	Seguin	713
Hale	37,592	Plainview	1,005
Hall	5,594	Memphis	877
Hamilton	8,297	Hamilton	836
Hansford	6,209	Spearman	921
Hardeman	6,368	Quanah	688
Hardin	40,721	Kountze	898
Harris	2,409,544	Houston	1,734
Harrison	52,265	Marshall	908
Hartley	3,987	Channing	1,462
Haskell	7,725	Haskell	901
Hays	40,594	San Marcos	678
Hemphill	5,304	Canadian	903
Henderson	42,606	Athens	888
Hidalgo	283,323	Edinburg	1,569
Hill	25,024	Hillsboro	968
Hockley	23,230	Levelland	908
Hood	17,714	Granbury	425
Hopkins	25,247	Sulphur Springs	789
Houston	22,299	Crockett	1,234
Howard	33,142	Big Spring	901
Hudspeth	2,728	Sierra Blanca	4,567
Hunt	55,248	Greenville	840
Hutchinson	26,304	Stinnett	872
Irion	1,386	Mertzon	1,052
Jack	7,408	Jacksboro	920
Jackson	13,352	Edna	844
Jasper	30,781	Jasper	921
Jeff Davis	1,647	Fort Davis	2,257
Jefferson	248,652	Beaumont	937
Jim Hogg	5,168	Hebbronville	1,136
Jim Wells	36,498	Alice	867
Johnson	67,649	Cleburne	730
Jones	17,268	Anson	931
Karnes	13,593	Karnes City	753
Kaufman	39,038	Kaufman	788
Kendall	10,635	Boerne	663
Kenedy	543	Sarita	1,389
Kent	1,145	Jayton	878
Kerr	28,780	Kerrville	1,107
Kimble	4,063	Junction	1,250
King	425	Guthrie	914
Kinney	2,279	Brackettville	1,359
Kleberg	33,358	Kingsville	853
Knox	5,329	Benjamin	845
Lamar	42,156	Paris	919
Lamb	18,669	Littlefield	1,013
Lampasas	12,005	Lampasas	714
La Salle	5,514	Cotulla	1,517
Lavaca	19,004	Hallettsville	971
Lee	10,952	Giddings	631
Leon	9,594	Centerville	1,079
Liberty	47,088	Liberty	1,174
Limestone	20,224	Groesbeck	930
Lipscomb	3,766	Lipscomb	933
Live Oak	9,606	George West	1,057
Llano	10,144	Llano	939
Loving	91	Mentone	670
Lubbock	211,651	Lubbock	900
Lynn	8,605	Tahoka	888
McCulloch	8,735	Brady	1,071
McLennan	170,755	Waco	1,031
McMullen	789	Tilden	1,163
Madison	10,649	Madisonville	472
Marion	10,360	Jefferson	385
Martin	4,684	Stanton	914
Mason	3,683	Mason	934
Matagorda	37,828	Bay City	1,127
Maverick	31,398	Eagle Pass	1,287
Medina	23,164	Hondo	1,331
Menard	2,346	Menard	902
Midland	82,636	Midland	902
Milam	22,732	Cameron	1,019
Mills	4,477	Goldthwaite	748
Mitchell	9,088	Colorado City	912
Montague	17,410	Montague	928
Montgomery	127,222	Conroe	1,047

County	Pop.	County seat or court house	Land area sq. mi.
Moore.	16,575	Dumas.	905
Morris.	14,629	Daingerfield.	256
Motley.	1,950	Matador.	959
Nacogdoches.	46,786	Nacogdoches.	939
Navarro.	35,323	Corsicana.	1,068
Newton.	13,254	Newton.	935
Nolan.	17,359	Sweetwater.	915
Nueces.	268,215	Corpus Christi.	847
Ochiltree.	9,588	Perryton.	919
Oldham.	2,283	Vega.	1,485
Orange.	83,838	Orange.	362
Palo Pinto.	24,062	Palo Pinto.	949
Panola.	20,724	Carthage.	812
Parker.	44,609	Weatherford.	902
Parmer.	11,038	Farwell.	885
Pecos.	14,618	Fort Stockton.	4,777
Polk.	24,407	Livingston.	1,061
Potter.	98,637	Amarillo.	902
Presidio.	5,188	Marfa.	3,857
Rains.	4,839	Emory.	243
Randall.	75,062	Canyon.	917
Reagan.	4,135	Big Lake.	1,173
Real.	2,469	Leakey.	697
Red River.	16,101	Clarksville.	1,054
Reeves.	15,801	Pecos.	2,626
Refugio.	9,289	Refugio.	771
Roberts.	1,187	Miami.	915
Robertson.	14,653	Franklin.	864
Rockwall.	14,528	Rockwall.	128
Runnels.	11,872	Ballinger.	1,056
Rusk.	41,382	Henderson.	932
Sabine.	8,702	Hemphill.	486
San Augustine.	8,785	San Augustine.	524
San Jacinto.	11,434	Coldspring.	572
San Patricio.	58,013	Sinton.	693
San Saba.	5,841	San Saba.	1,136
Schleicher.	2,820	Eldorado.	1,309
Scurry.	18,192	Snyder.	900
Shackelford.	3,915	Albany.	915
Shelby.	23,084	Center.	791
Sherman.	3,174	Stratford.	923
Smith.	128,366	Tyler.	932
Somervell.	4,154	Glen Rose.	188
Starr.	27,266	Rio Grande City.	1,226
Stephens.	9,926	Breckenridge.	894
Sterling.	1,206	Sterling City.	923
Stonewall.	2,406	Aspermont.	925
Sutton.	5,130	Sonora.	1,455
Swisher.	9,723	Tulia.	902
Tarrant.	860,880	Fort Worth.	868
Taylor.	110,932	Abilene.	917
Terrell.	1,595	Sanderson.	2,357
Terry.	14,581	Brownfield.	887
Throckmorton.	2,053	Throckmorton.	912
Titus.	21,442	Mount Pleasant.	412
Tom Green.	84,784	San Angelo.	1,515
Travis.	419,335	Austin.	989
Trinity.	9,450	Groveton.	692
Tyler.	16,223	Woodville.	922
Upshur.	28,595	Gilmer.	587
Upton.	4,619	Rankin.	1,243
Uvalde.	22,441	Uvalde.	1,564
Val Verde.	35,910	Del Rio.	3,150
Van Zandt.	31,426	Canton.	855
Victoria.	68,807	Victoria.	887
Walker.	41,789	Huntsville.	786
Waller.	19,798	Hempstead.	514
Ward.	13,976	Monahans.	836
Washington.	21,998	Brenham.	610
Webb.	99,258	Laredo.	3,362
Wharton.	40,242	Wharton.	1,086
Wheeler.	7,137	Wheeler.	904
Wichita.	121,082	Wichita Falls.	606
Wilbarger.	15,931	Vernon.	947
Willacy.	17,495	Raymondville.	589
Williamson.	76,521	Georgetown.	1,137
Wilson.	16,756	Floresville.	807
Winkler.	9,944	Kermit.	840
Wise.	26,525	Decatur.	902
Wood.	24,697	Quitman.	689
Yoakum.	8,299	Plains.	800
Young.	19,001	Graham.	919
Zapata.	6,628	Zapata.	999
Zavala.	11,666	Crystal City.	1,298

Utah

(29 counties, 82,073 sq. mi. land; pop. 1,461,037)

Beaver.	4,378	Beaver.	2,586
Box Elder.	33,222	Brigham City.	5,614
Cache.	57,176	Logan.	1,171
Carbon.	22,179	Price.	1,479
Daggett.	769	Manila.	699
Davis.	146,540	Farmington.	299
Duchesne.	12,565	Duchesne.	3,233
Emery.	11,451	Castle Dale.	4,449
Garfield.	3,673	Panguitch.	5,148
Grand.	8,241	Moab.	3,689
Iron.	17,349	Parowan.	3,301

Juab.	5,530	Nephi.	3,396
Kane.	4,024	Kanab.	3,898
Millard.	8,970	Fillmore.	6,818
Morgan.	4,917	Morgan.	603
Piute.	1,329	Junction.	759
Rich.	2,100	Randolph.	1,034
Salt Lake.	619,066	Salt Lake City.	756
San Juan.	12,253	Monticello.	7,725
Sanpete.	14,620	Manti.	1,587
Sevier.	14,727	Richfield.	1,910
Summit.	10,198	Coalville.	1,865
Tooele.	26,033	Tooele.	6,919
Uintah.	20,506	Vernal.	4,479
Utah.	218,106	Provo.	2,018
Wasatch.	8,523	Heber City.	1,191
Washington.	26,065	Saint George.	2,422
Wayne.	1,911	Loa.	2,461
Weber.	144,616	Ogden.	566

Vermont

(14 counties, 9,273 sq. mi. land; pop. 511,456)

Addison.	29,406	Middlebury.	773
Bennington.	33,345	Bennington.	677
Caledonia.	25,808	Saint Johnsbury.	651
Chittenden.	115,534	Burlington.	540
Essex.	6,313	Guildhall.	666
Franklin.	34,788	Saint Albans.	649
Grand Isle.	4,613	North Hero.	89
Lamoille.	16,767	Hyde Park.	461
Orange.	22,739	Chelsea.	690
Orleans.	23,440	Newport.	697
Rutland.	58,347	Rutland.	932
Washington.	52,393	Montpelier.	690
Windham.	36,933	Newfane.	787
Windsor.	51,030	Woodstock.	972

Virginia

(95 cos., 41 ind. cities, 39,704 sq. mi. land; pop. 5,346,797)

Accomack.	31,268	Accomac.	476
Albemarle.	50,689	Charlottesville.	725
Alleghany.	14,333	Covington.	446
Amelia.	8,405	Amelia, C.H..	357
Amherst.	29,122	Amherst.	479
Appomattox.	11,971	Appomattox.	336
Arlington.	152,599	Arlington.	26
Augusta.	53,732	Staunton.	989
Bath.	5,860	Warm Springs.	538
Bedford.	34,927	Bedford.	747
Bland.	6,349	Bland.	359
Botetourt.	23,270	Fincastle.	545
Brunswick.	15,632	Lawrenceville.	563
Buchanan.	37,989	Grundy.	504
Buckingham.	11,751	Buckingham.	583
Campbell.	45,424	Rustburg.	505
Caroline.	17,904	Bowling Green.	535
Carroll.	27,270	Hillsville.	478
Charles City.	6,692	Charles City.	181
Charlotte.	12,266	Charlotte Courthouse.	477
Chesterfield.	141,372	Chesterfield.	434
Clarke.	9,965	Berryville.	178
Craig.	3,948	New Castle.	330
Culpeper.	22,620	Culpeper.	382
Cumberland.	7,881	Cumberland.	300
Dickenson.	19,806	Clintwood.	331
Dinwiddie.	22,602	Dinwiddie.	507
Essex.	8,864	Tappahannock.	263
Fairfax.	596,901	Fairfax.	394
Fauquier.	35,889	Warrenton.	651
Floyd.	11,563	Floyd.	381
Fluvanna.	10,244	Palmyra.	290
Franklin.	35,740	Rocky Mount.	683
Frederick.	34,150	Winchester.	415
Giles.	17,810	Pearisburg.	362
Gloucester.	20,107	Gloucester.	225
Goochland.	11,761	Goochland.	281
Grayson.	16,579	Independence.	446
Greene.	7,625	Standardsville.	157
Greensville.	10,903	Emporia.	300
Halifax.	30,418	Halifax.	816
Hanover.	50,398	Hanover.	467
Henrico.	180,735	Richmond.	238
Henry.	57,654	Martinsville.	382
Highland.	2,937	Monterey.	416
Isle of Wight.	21,603	Isle of Wight.	319
James City.	22,763	Williamsburg.	153
King and Queen.	5,968	King and Queen.	317
King George.	10,543	King George.	180
King William.	9,327	King William.	278
Lancaster.	10,129	Lancaster.	133
Lee.	25,956	Jonesville.	437
Loudoun.	57,427	Leesburg.	521
Louisa.	17,825	Louisa.	497
Lunenburg.	12,124	Lunenburg.	432
Madison.	10,232	Madison.	322
Mathews.	7,995	Mathews.	87
Mecklenburg.	29,444	Boydton.	616
Middlesex.	7,719	Saluda.	134
Montgomery.	63,516	Christiansburg.	390
Nelson.	12,204	Lovingston.	474
New Kent.	8,781	New Kent.	213

County	Pop.	County seat or court house	Land area sq. mi.
Northampton	14,625	Eastville	226
Northumberland	9,828	Heathsville	185
Nottoway	14,666	Nottoway	316
Orange	17,827	Orange	342
Page	19,401	Luray	313
Patrick	17,585	Stuart	481
Pittsylvania	66,147	Chatham	995
Powhatan	13,062	Powhatan	261
Prince Edward	16,456	Farmville	354
Prince George	25,733	Prince George	266
Prince William	144,703	Manassas	339
Pulaski	35,229	Pulaski	318
Rappahannock	6,093	Washington	267
Richmond	6,952	Warsaw	193
Roanoke	72,945	Salem	251
Rockbridge	17,911	Lexington	603
Rockingham	57,038	Harrisonburg	865
Russell	31,761	Lebanon	479
Scott	25,068	Gate City	535
Shenandoah	27,559	Woodstock	512
Smyth	33,345	Marion	452
Southampton	18,731	Courtland	603
Spotsylvania	34,435	Spotsylvania	404
Stafford	40,470	Stafford	271
Surry	6,046	Surry	281
Sussex	10,874	Sussex	491
Tazewell	50,511	Tazewell	520
Warren	21,200	Front Royal	217
Washington	46,487	Abingdon	562
Westmoreland	14,041	Montross	227
Wise	43,863	Wise	405
Wythe	25,522	Wytheville	465
York	35,463	Yorktown	113

Independent cities

City	Pop.	Land area sq. mi.
Alexandria	103,217	15
Bedford	5,991	7
Bristol	19,042	12
Buena Vista	6,717	3
Charlottesville	45,010	10
Chesapeake	114,226	340
Clifton Forge	5,046	3
Colonial Heights	16,509	8
Covington	9,063	4
Danville	45,642	17
Emporia	4,840	2
Fairfax	19,390	6
Falls Church	9,515	2
Franklin	7,308	4
Fredericksburg	15,322	6
Galax	6,524	6
Hampton	122,617	51
Harrisonburg	19,671	6
Hopewell	23,397	10
Lexington	7,292	2
Lynchburg	66,743	50
Manassas	15,438	8
Manassas Park	6,524	2
Martinsville	18,149	11
Newport News	144,903	65
Norfolk	266,979	53
Norton	4,757	7
Petersburg	41,055	23
Poquoson	8,726	17
Portsmouth	104,577	30
Radford	13,225	7
Richmond	219,214	60
Roanoke	100,427	43
Salem	23,958	14
South Boston	7,093	6
Staunton	21,857	9
Suffolk	47,621	409
Virginia Beach	262,199	256
Waynesboro	15,329	8
Williamsburg	9,870	5
Winchester	20,217	9

Washington

(39 counties, 66,511 sq. mi. land; pop., 4,132,353)

County	Pop.	County seat or court house	Land area sq. mi.
Adams	13,267	Ritzville	1,921
Asotin	16,823	Asotin	635
Benton	109,444	Prosser	1,715
Chelan	45,061	Wenatchee	2,916
Clallam	51,648	Port Angeles	1,753
Clark	192,227	Vancouver	627
Columbia	4,057	Dayton	865
Cowlitz	79,548	Kelso	1,140
Douglas	22,144	Waterville	1,817
Ferry	5,811	Republic	2,200
Franklin	35,025	Pasco	1,243
Garfield	2,468	Pomeroy	706
Grant	48,522	Ephrata	2,660
Grays Harbor	66,314	Montesano	1,918
Island	44,048	Coupeville	212
Jefferson	15,965	Port Townsend	1,805
King	1,269,898	Seattle	2,128
Kitsap	146,609	Port Orchard	393
Kittitas	24,877	Ellensburg	2,308
Klickitat	15,822	Goldendale	1,880
Lewis	55,279	Chehalis	2,409
Lincoln	9,604	Davenport	2,310
Mason	31,184	Shelton	961
Okanogan	30,663	Okanogan	5,281
Pacific	17,237	South Bend	908
Pend Oreille	8,580	Newport	1,400
Pierce	485,667	Tacoma	1,675
San Juan	7,838	Friday Harbor	179
Skagit	64,138	Mount Vernon	1,735
Skamania	7,919	Stevenson	1,672
Snohomish	337,016	Everett	2,098
Spokane	341,835	Spokane	1,762
Stevens	28,979	Colville	2,470
Thurston	124,264	Olympia	727
Wahkiakum	3,832	Cathlamet	261
Walla Walla	47,435	Walla Walla	1,261
Whatcom	106,701	Bellingham	2,125
Whitman	40,103	Colfax	2,151
Yakima	172,508	Yakima	4,287

West Virginia

(55 counties, 24,119 sq. mi. land; pop., 1,950,186)

County	Pop.	County seat or court house	Land area sq. mi.
Barbour	16,639	Philippi	343
Berkeley	46,775	Martinsburg	321
Boone	30,447	Madison	503
Braxton	13,894	Sutton	513
Brooke	31,117	Wellsburg	90
Cabell	106,835	Huntington	282
Calhoun	8,250	Grantsville	280
Clay	11,265	Clay	346
Doddridge	7,433	West Union	321
Fayette	57,863	Fayetteville	667
Gilmer	8,334	Glenville	340
Grant	10,210	Petersburg	480
Greenbrier	37,665	Lewisburg	1,025
Hampshire	14,867	Romney	644
Hancock	41,053	New Cumberland	84
Hardy	10,030	Moorefield	585
Harrison	77,710	Clarksburg	417
Jackson	25,794	Ripley	464
Jefferson	30,302	Charles Town	209
Kanawha	231,414	Charleston	901
Lewis	18,813	Weston	389
Lincoln	23,675	Hamlin	439
Logan	50,679	Logan	456
McDowell	49,899	Welch	535
Marion	65,789	Fairmont	312
Marshall	41,608	Moundsville	305
Mason	27,045	Point Pleasant	433
Mercer	73,870	Princeton	420
Mineral	27,234	Keyser	329
Mingo	37,336	Williamson	424
Monongalia	75,024	Morgantown	363
Monroe	12,873	Union	473
Morgan	10,711	Berkeley Springs	230
Nicholas	28,126	Summersville	650
Ohio	61,389	Wheeling	106
Pendleton	7,910	Franklin	698
Pleasants	8,236	St. Marys	131
Pocahontas	9,919	Marlinton	942
Preston	30,460	Kingwood	651
Putnam	38,181	Winfield	346
Raleigh	86,821	Beckley	608
Randolph	28,734	Elkins	1,040
Ritchie	11,442	Harrisville	454
Roane	15,952	Spencer	484
Summers	15,875	Hinton	353
Taylor	16,584	Grafton	174
Tucker	8,675	Parsons	421
Tyler	11,320	Middlebourne	258
Upshur	23,427	Buckhannon	355
Wayne	46,021	Wayne	508
Webster	12,245	Webster Springs	556
Wetzel	21,874	New Martinsville	359
Wirt	4,922	Elizabeth	235
Wood	93,627	Parkersburg	367
Wyoming	35,993	Pineville	502

Wisconsin

(72 counties, 54,426 sq. mi. land; pop., 4,705,642)

County	Pop.	County seat or court house	Land area sq. mi.
Adams	13,457	Friendship	648
Ashland	16,783	Ashland	1,048
Barron	38,730	Barron	865
Bayfield	13,822	Washburn	1,462
Brown	175,280	Green Bay	524
Buffalo	14,309	Alma	699
Burnett	12,340	Grantsburg	818
Calumet	30,867	Chilton	326
Chippewa	51,702	Chippewa Falls	1,017
Clark	32,910	Neillsville	1,218
Columbia	43,222	Portage	771
Crawford	16,556	Prairie du Chien	566
Dane	323,545	Madison	1,205
Dodge	74,747	Juneau	887
Door	25,029	Sturgeon Bay	492
Douglas	44,421	Superior	1,305
Dunn	34,314	Menomonie	853
Eau Claire	78,805	Eau Claire	638
Florence	4,172	Florence	486

County	Pop.	County seat or court house	Land area sq. mi.
Fond Du Lac	88,952	Fond du Lac	725
Forest	9,044	Crandon	1,011
Grant	51,736	Lancaster	1,144
Green	30,012	Monroe	583
Green Lake	18,370	Green Lake	357
Iowa	19,802	Dodgeville	760
Iron	6,730	Hurley	751
Jackson	16,831	Black River Falls	998
Jefferson	66,152	Jefferson	562
Juneau	21,037	Mauston	774
Kenosha	123,137	Kenosha	273
Kewaunee	19,539	Kewaunee	343
La Crosse	91,056	La Crosse	457
Lafayette	17,412	Darlington	634
Langlade	19,978	Antigo	873
Lincoln	26,311	Merrill	886
Manitowoc	82,918	Manitowoc	594
Marathon	111,270	Wausau	1,559
Marinette	39,314	Marinette	1,395
Marquette	11,672	Montello	455
Menominee	3,373	Keshena	359
Milwaukee	964,988	Milwaukee	241
Monroe	35,074	Sparta	904
Oconto	28,947	Oconto	1,002
Oneida	31,216	Rhinelander	1,130
Outagamie	128,730	Appleton	642
Ozaukee	66,981	Port Washington	235
Pepin	7,477	Durand	231
Pierce	31,149	Ellsworth	577
Polk	32,351	Balsam Lake	919
Portage	57,420	Stevens Point	810
Price	15,788	Phillips	1,256
Racine	173,132	Racine	335
Richland	17,476	Richland Center	585
Rock	139,420	Janesville	723
Rusk	15,589	Ladysmith	913
St. Croix	43,872	Hudson	723
Sauk	43,469	Baraboo	838

	Pop.		Land area sq. mi.
Sawyer	12,843	Hayward	1,255
Shawano	35,928	Shawano	897
Sheboygan	100,935	Sheboygan	515
Taylor	18,817	Medford	975
Trempealeau	26,158	Whitehall	736
Vernon	25,642	Viroqua	808
Vilas	16,535	Eagle River	867
Walworth	71,507	Elkhorn	556
Washburn	13,174	Shell Lake	815
Washington	84,848	West Bend	430
Waukesha	280,203	Waukesha	554
Waupaca	42,831	Waupaca	754
Waushara	18,526	Wautoma	628
Winnebago	131,772	Oshkosh	449
Wood	72,799	Wisconsin Rapids	801

Wyoming

(23 counties, 96,989 sq. mi. land; pop., 469,557)

County	Pop.		Land area sq. mi.
Albany	29,062	Laramie	4,268
Big Horn	11,896	Basin	3,139
Campbell	24,367	Gillette	4,796
Carbon	21,896	Rawlins	7,877
Converse	14,069	Douglas	4,271
Crook	5,308	Sundance	2,855
Fremont	40,251	Lander	9,181
Goshen	12,040	Torrington	2,186
Hot Springs	5,710	Thermopolis	2,005
Johnson	6,700	Buffalo	4,166
Laramie	68,649	Cheyenne	2,684
Lincoln	12,177	Kemmerer	4,070
Natrona	71,856	Casper	5,347
Niobrara	2,924	Lusk	2,684
Park	21,639	Cody	6,936
Platte	11,975	Wheatland	2,023
Sheridan	25,048	Sheridan	2,532
Sublette	4,548	Pinedale	4,872
Sweetwater	41,723	Green River	10,352
Teton	9,355	Jackson	4,011
Uinta	13,021	Evanston	2,085
Washakie	9,496	Worland	2,243
Weston	7,106	Newcastle	2,402

Population of Outlying Areas

Source: U.S. Bureau of the Census
Population figures are final counts from the census conducted on Apr. 1, 1980.

Puerto Rico

ZIP code	Municipios	Pop.	Land area sq. mile	ZIP code	Municipios	Pop.	Land area sq. mile	ZIP code	Municipios	Pop.	Land area sq. mile
00601	Adjuntas	18,786	67	00650	Florida	7,232	10	00720	Orocovis	19,332	64
00602	Aguada	31,567	31	00653	Guanica	18,799	37	00723	Patillas	17,774	47
00603	Aguadilla	54,606	37	00654	Guayama	40,183	65	00724	Penuelas	19,116	45
00607	Aguas Buenas	22,429	30	00656	Guayanilla	21,050	42	00731	Ponce	189,046	117
00609	Aibonito	22,167	31	00657	Guaynabo	80,742	27	00742	Quebradillas	19,728	23
00610	Anasco	23,274	40	00658	Gurabo	23,574	28	00743	Rincon	11,788	14
00612	Arecibo	86,766	127	00659	Hatillo	28,958	42	00745	Rio Grande	34,283	62
00615	Arroyo	17,014	15	00660	Hormigueros	14,030	11	00747	Sabana Grande	20,207	36
00617	Barceloneta	18,942	24	00661	Humacao	46,134	45	00751	Salinas	26,438	71
00618	Barranquitas	21,639	34	00662	Isabela	37,435	56	00753	San German	32,922	54
00619	Bayamon	196,206	45	00664	Jayuya	14,722	44	*00936	San Juan	434,849	47
00623	Cabo Rojo	34,045	72	00665	Juana Diaz	43,505	61	00754	San Lorenzo	32,428	53
00625	Caguas	117,959	59	00666	Juncos	25,397	27	00755	San Sebastian	35,690	71
00627	Camuy	24,884	47	00667	Lajas	21,236	60	00757	Santa Isabel	19,854	35
00629	Canovanas	31,880	33	00669	Lares	26,743	62	00758	Toa Alta	31,910	28
00630	Carolina	165,954	48	00670	Las Marias	8,747	46	00759	Toa Baja	78,246	24
00632	Catano	26,243	6	00671	Las Piedras	22,412	34	00760	Trujillo Alto	51,389	21
00633	Cayey	41,099	52	00672	Loiza	20,867	21	00761	Utuado	34,505	115
00635	Ceiba	14,944	27	00673	Luquillo	14,895	26	00762	Vega Alta	28,696	28
00638	Ciales	16,211	67	00701	Manati	36,562	46	00763	Vega Baja	47,115	48
00639	Cidra	28,365	36	00706	Maricao	6,737	37	00765	Vieques	7,662	53
00640	Coamo	30,822	78	00707	Maunabo	11,813	21	00766	Villalba	20,734	37
00642	Comerio	18,212	29	00708	Mayaguez	96,193	77	00767	Yabucoa	31,425	55
00643	Corozal	28,221	43	00716	Moca	29,165	50	00768	Yauco	37,742	69
00645	Culebra	1,265	13	00717	Morovis	21,142	39		Total	3,196,520	3,459
00646	Dorado	25,511	24	00718	Naguabo	20,617	52				
00648	Fajardo	32,087	31	00719	Naranjito	23,633	28				

ZIP code	Area	Pop.	Land area sq. mile	ZIP code	Area	Pop.	Land area sq. mile	ZIP code	Area	Pop.	Land area sq. mile
	American Samoa				Mongmong-Toto-Maite	5,245	2	00820	Christiansted	2,904	
96799	American Samoa	32,297	77		Piti	2,866	7	00840	Frederiksted	1,046	
				96915	Santa Rita	9,183	17		Total	96,569	132
	Guam				Sinajana	2,485	1				
96910	Agana	896	1		Talofofo	2,006	17		**Trust Territory of Pacific Islands**		
	Agana Hts.	3,284	1	96911	Tamuning	13,580	6				
96915	Agat	3,999	10		Umatac	732	6		Kosrae	NA	42
	Asan	2,034	6		Yigo	10,359	35		Marshall Islands	NA	70
96913	Barrigada	7,756	9	96914	Yona	4,228	20		Palau	NA	192
	Chalan-Pago-Ordot	3,120	5		Total	105,979	209		Ponape	NA	176
96912	Dededo	23,644	30						Truk	NA	49
96916	Inarajan	2,059	19		**Virgin Islands**				Yap	NA	46
	Mangilao	6,840	10		St. Croix	49,725	80		Total	NA	533
96916	Merizo	1,663	6		St. John	2,472	20				
					St. Thomas	44,372	32		**No. Mariana Islands**	16,758	184
				00801	Charlotte Amalie	11,671					

RELIGIOUS INFORMATION

Census of Religious Groups in the U.S.

Source: *1990 Yearbook of American and Canadian Churches*

The 1990 Yearbook of American and Canadian Churches reported a total of 145,383,738 members of religious groups in the U.S.—58.7 percent of the population; membership rose 1.1 percent from the previous year.

Comparisons of membership statistics from group to group are not necessarily meaningful. Membership definitions vary —e.g., Roman Catholics count members from infancy, but some Protestant groups count only "adult" members, usually 13 years or older; some groups compile data carefully, but others estimate; not all groups report annually.

The number of churches appear in parentheses. Asterisk (*) indicates church declines to publish membership figures; (**) indicates figures date from 1980 or earlier.

Group	Members
Adventist churches:	
Advent Christian Ch. (251)	19,900
Primitive Advent Christian Ch. (10)	546
Seventh-day Adventists (4,145)	687,200
American Rescue Workers (20)	2,700
Anglican Orthodox Church (40)	6,000
Baha'i Faith (1,700)	110,000
Baptist churches:	
Amer. Baptist Assn. (1,705)	250,000
Amer. Baptist Chs. in U.S.A. (5,839)	1,549,563
Baptist General Conference (789)	135,125
Baptist Missionary Assn. of America (1,347)	227,897
Conservative Baptist Assn. of America (1,121)	204,496
Duck River (and Kindred) Assn. of Baptists (85)	**8,632
Free Will Baptists (2,496)	204,382
Gen. Assn. of Regular Baptist Chs. (1,585)	260,000
Natl. Baptist Convention of America (11,398)	**2,668,799
Natl. Baptist Convention, U.S.A. (26,000)	**5,500,000
Natl. Primitive Baptist Convention (616)	**250,000
No. Amer. Baptist Conference (259)	42,629
Seventh Day Baptist General Conference (81)	5,149
Southern Baptist Convention (37,517)	14,812,844
Brethren (German Baptists):	
Brethren Ch. (Ashland, Ohio) (124)	14,753
Fellowship of Grace Brethren (312)	41,767
Brethren, River:	
Brethren in Christ Ch. (193)	17,081
Buddhist Churches of America (100)	100,000
Christadelphians (850)	**15,800
The Christian and Missionary Alliance (1,793)	259,612
Christian Catholic Church (6)	2,500
Christian Church (Disciples of Christ) (4,159)	1,073,119
Christian Churches and Churches of Christ (5,579)	1,070,616
Christian Methodist Episcopal Church (2,340)	718,922
Christian Nation Church U.S.A. (5)	200
Christian Union (114)	6,000
Churches of Christ (13,375)	1,626,000
Churches of Christ in Christian Union (260)	10,418
Churches of God:	
Chs. of God, General Conference (343)	33,778
Ch. of God (Anderson, Ind.) (2,336)	198,842
Ch. of God (Seventh Day), Denver, Col. (135)	6,498
Church of Christ, Scientist (3,000)	*
Church of God by Faith (106)	**4,500
Church of the Nazarene (5,129)	552,264
Conservative Congregational Christian Conference (176)	29,015
Eastern Orthodox churches:	
Albanian Orth. Diocese of America (2)	586
American Carpatho-Russian Orth. Greek Catholic Ch. (74)	**100,000
Antiochian Orth. Christian Archdiocese of No. Amer. (150)	300,000
Diocese of the Armenian Ch. of America (66)	**450,000
Bulgarian Eastern Orth. Ch. (13)	**86,000
Coptic Orthodox Ch. (40)	160,000
Greek Orth. Archdiocese of N. and S. America (535)	**1,950,000
Orthodox Ch. in America (440)	**1,000,000
Patriarchal Parishes of the Russian Orth. Ch. in the U.S.A. (38)	9,780
Romanian Orth. Episcopate of America (34)	60,000
Serbian Eastern Orth. Ch. (68)	67,000
Syrian Orth. Ch. of Antioch (Archdiocese of the U.S.A. and Canada) (28)	30,000
Ukrainian Orth. Ch. of America (Ecumenical Patriarchate) (27)	5,000
Ukrainian Orthodox Church in the U.S.A. (107)	**87,745
The Episcopal Church in the U.S.A. (7,360)	2,455,422

Group	Members
American Ethical Union (Ethical Culture Movement) (21)	3,212
Evangelical Church of North America (155)	17,417
Evangelical Congregational Church (156)	33,318
The Evangelical Covenant Church of America (584)	87,750
Evangelical Free Church of America (880)	95,722
Evangelical associations:	
Apostolic Christian Chs. of America (80)	11,300
Apostolic Christian Ch. (Nazarean) (48)	2,799
Christian Congregation (1,456)	107,902
Friends:	
Evangelical Friends Alliance (217)	24,095
Friends General Conference (505)	31,690
Friends United Meeting (545)	55,501
Grace Gospel Fellowship (52)	4,500
Independent Fundamental Churches of America (1,019)	120,446
Jehovah's Witnesses (8,851)	804,639
Jewish organizations:	
Union of Amer. Hebrew Congregations (Reform) (839)	1,300,000
Union of Orthodox Jewish Congregations of America (1,000)	1,000,000
United Synagogue of America (Conservative) (850)	2,000,000
Latter-day Saints:	
Ch. of Jesus Christ (Bickertonites) (70)	2,986
Ch. of Jesus Christ of Latter-day Saints (Mormon) (8,682)	4,000,000
Reorganized Ch. of Jesus Christ of Latter Day Saints (1,137)	190,950
Lutheran churches:	
Ch. of the Lutheran Brethren of America (128)	13,695
Ch. of the Lutheran Confession (67)	8,655
Evangelical Luthern Church in America (11,120)	5,251,534
Evangelical Lutheran Synod (123)	21,378
Assn. of Free Lutheran Congregations (193)	26,870
Latvian Evangelical Lutheran Church of America (56)	13,211
Lutheran Ch.-Missouri Synod (5,939)	2,604,278
Protestant Conference (Lutheran) (7)	1,035
Wisconsin Evangelical Lutheran Synod (1,191)	418,691
Mennonite churches:	
Beachy Amish Mennonite Chs. (100)	6,800
Evangelical Mennonite Ch. (26)	3,888
General Conference of Mennonite Brethren Chs. (128)	17,065
The General Conference Mennonite Ch. (224)	34,693
Hutterian Brethren (77)	3,988
Mennonite Ch. (1,023)	92,682
Old Order Amish Ch. (756)	64,040
Old Order (Wisler) Mennonite Ch. (36)	9,731
Methodist churches:	
African Methodist Episcopal Ch. (6,200)	2,210,000
African Methodist Episcopal Zion Ch. (6,060)	1,220,260
Evangelical Methodist Ch. (130)	8,282
Free Methodist Ch. of North America (1,071)	73,647
Fundamental Methodist Ch. (13)	733
Primitive Methodist Ch., U.S.A. (85)	8,244
Reformed Methodist Union Episcopal Ch. (18)	3,800
Southern Methodist Ch. (150)	7,283
United Methodist Ch. (37,641)	9,055,575
Moravian churches:	
Moravian Ch. (Unitas Fratrum), Northern Province (100)	31,468
Moravian Ch. in America (Unitas Fratrum), Southern Province (54)	21,467
Unity of the Brethren (26)	2,873
Moslems	**6,000,000+

Group	Members	Group	Members
New Apostolic Church of North America (491) .	36,972	Orthodox Presbyterian Ch. (188)	19,094
North American Old Roman Catholic Church		Presbyterian Ch. in America (1,067)	208,394
(133).	62,611	Presbyterian Ch. (U.S.A.) (11,505)	2,929,608
Old Catholic churches:		Reformed Presbyterian Ch. in No. Amer. (68) . .	5,174
Christ Catholic Ch. (6)	2,500	Reformed churches:	
Pentecostal churches:		Christian Reformed Ch. in N. America (699) . . .	222,408
Apostolic Faith (Portland, Ore.) (45)	4,100	Hungarian Reformed Ch. in America (31)	12,500
Assemblies of God (11,123)	2,147,041	Protestant Reformed Chs. in America (21). . . .	4,544
Bible Church of Christ (6)	6,405	Reformed Ch. in America (925)	333,798
Bible Way Church of Our Lord Jesus Christ		Reformed Ch. in the U.S. (34)	3,778
World Wide (350).	**30,000	The Roman Catholic Church (23,091)	54,918,949
Church of God (Cleveland, Tenn.) (5,763)	582,203	The Salvation Army (1,097).	433,448
Church of God of Prophecy (2,111).	73,977	The Schwenkfelder Church (5).	2,516
Congregational Holiness Ch. (174)	8,347	Social Brethren (40)	**1,784
Gen. Council, Christian Ch. of No. Amer. (104) . .	13,500	Natl. Spiritualist Assn. of Churches (142).	5,558
Intl. Ch. of the Foursquare Gospel (1,363)	198,715	Gen. Convention, The Swedenborgian	
Open Bible Standard Chs. (325)	46,000	Church (50)	2,423
Pentecostal Assemblies of the World (550) . . .	**4,500	Unitarian Universalist Assn. (956)	178,623
Pentecostal Church of God (1,157)	86,000	United Brethren:	
Pentecostal Free-Will Baptist Ch. (130)	10,700	Ch. of the United Brethren in Christ (256)	26,869
United Pentecostal Ch. Intl. (3,592)	500,000	United Christian Ch. (12)	420
Polish Natl. Catholic Church of America (162). .	**282,411	United Church of Christ (6,362)	1,644,787
Presbyterian churches:		Universal Fellowship of Metropolitan	
Associate Reformed Presbyterian Ch. (Gen.		Community Chs. (230).	34,000
Synod) (181)	36,949	Vedanta Society (13)	2,500
Cumberland Presbyterian Ch. (752)	91,491	Volunteers of America (607)	**36,634
Evangelical Presbyterian Ch. (155)	50,300	The Wesleyan Church (3,217).	185,861

Religious Population of the U.S.

Source: *1990 Yearbook of American and Canadian Churches*

(Membership in thousands, except as indicated)

Religious Body	Membership						
	1960	1965	1970	1975	1980	1988	1989
Total	114,449	124,682	131,045	131,013	134,817	143,830	145,384
Members as percent of popu-							
lation	64	64	63	61	59	58.6	58.7
Buddhists	20	92	100	60	60	100	100
Eastern Churches	2,699	3,172	3,850	3,696	3,823	3,973	4,077
Jews	5,367	5,600	5,870	6,115	5,920	5,944	5,935
Old Catholic, Polish National							
Catholic, Armenian Churches	590	484	848	846	924	829	827
Roman Catholics	42,105	46,246	48,125	48,882	50,450	53,497	54,919
Protestants	63,669	69,088	71,173	71,043	73,479	79,296	79,329
Miscellaneous	—	—	449	372	161	192	197

Estimated Religious Population of the World, mid-1989

Source: The 1989 Encyclopedia Britannica Book of the year (in thousands)

	Africa	Asia	Europe	Latin America	Northern America	Oceania	U.S.S.R.	World	%
Christians	293,547	236,700	410,310	410,240	234,600	21,700	104,800	1,711,897	32.9
Roman Catholics	110,264	111,028	260,450	381,800	95,200	7,660	5,300	971,702	18.7
Protestants	77,327	73,563	73,330	15,500	94,600	7,600	9,300	351,220	6.7
Orthodox	26,262	3,300	35,860	1,660	5,900	540	90,100	163,622	3.1
Anglicans	24,108	645	32,690	1,230	7,200	5,336	—	71,209	1.4
Other Christians	55,586	48,164	7,980	10,050	31,700	564	99	154,143	3.0
Muslims	263,132	608,500	12,360	1,200	5,220	99	34,100	924,611	17.8
Nonreligious	1,700	690,000	52,158	16,000	21,700	3,100	84,855	869,513	16.7
Hindus	1,450	685,000	594	750	1,100	310	1	689,205	13.2
Buddhists	14	310,000	222	495	400	17	290	311,438	6.0
Atheists	250	150,000	18,460	2,900	1,200	530	58,500	231,840	4.5
Chinese folk reli-									
gionists	10	170,000	50	60	101	15	—	170,236	3.3
New Religionists	15	125,000	35	460	1,300	9	—	126,819	2.4
Tribal Religionists	66,240	23,500	—	950	50	70	—	90,810	1.7
Sikhs	23	17,350	217	7	230	8	—	17,735	0.3
Jews	300	4,310	1,447	1,010	7,100	90	3,100	17,357	0.3
Shamanists	—	10,500	—	—	—	—	200	10,702	0.2
Confucians	—	5,800	1	—	18	—	—	5,821	0.1
Baha'is	1,310	2,510	85	750	340	71	6	5,072	0.1
Jains	45	3,520	10	3	2	1	—	3,581	0.1
Shintoists	—	3,200	—	1	3	—	—	3,205	0.1
Other religionists	279	5,719	736	4,237	405	87	7	11,570	0.2
Total Population	628,317	3,051,609	496,686	439,064	273,770	26,109	285,861	5,201,416	100.0

Headquarters, Leaders of U.S. Religious Groups

Year organized in parentheses. See Associations and Societies section for religious organizations.

Adventist churches:

Advent Christian Church (1854) — Pres., Rev. Donald E. Wrigley; sec., Rev. Marshall Tidwell, 1002 Grove Ave. SW, Lenoir, NC 28645.

Primitive Advent Christian Church — Pres., Donald Young; sec.-treas., Hugh W. Good, 395 Frame Rd., Elkview, WV 25071.

Seventh-day Adventists (1863) — Pres., Neal C. Wilson; sec., G. Ralph Thompson, 6840 Eastern Ave. NW, Wash., DC 20012.

Baptist churches:

American Baptist Assn. (1905) — Pres., Ken Ashlock; sec.-treas., D.S. Madden, P.O. Box 1050, Texarkana, AR 75504.

American Baptist Churches in the U.S.A. (1907) — Pres., Harold Davis; gen. sec., Daniel E. Weiss, P.O. Box 851, Valley Forge, PA 19482.

Baptist General Conference (1879) — Pres., Dr. Robert S. Ricker, 2002 S. Arlington Heights Rd., Arlington Heights, IL 60005.

Baptist Missionary Assn. of America (formerly **North American Baptist Assn.**) (1950) — Pres., Rev. Gary D. Divine, rec. sec., Rev. Ralph Cottrell, P.O. Box 1203, Van, TX 75790.

Conservative Baptist Assn. of America (1947) — Gen. Dir., Dr. Tim Blanchard, Box 66, Wheaton, IL 60189.

Free Will Baptists (1727) — Mod., Rev. Ralph Hampton; exec. sec., Dr. Melvin Worthington, P.O. Box 1088, Nashville, TN 37202.

General Assn. of General Baptists (1823) — Mod., Rev. Dean Trivitt; clerk, Rev. Edwin Runyon, 801 Kendall, Poplar Bluff, MO 63901.

General Assn. of Regular Baptist Churches (1932) — Chpsn., Dr. David Nettleton; sec., Dr. John White, 1300 N. Meacham Rd., Schaumburg, IL 60173.

Natl. Baptist Convention, U.S.A. (1880) — Pres., Dr. T.J. Jemison; gen. sec., W. Franklyn Richardson, 52 S. 6th Ave., Mt. Vernon, NY 10550.

North American Baptist Conference (1865) — Mod., Rev. Harvey Mehlhaff; exec. dir., Dr. John Binder, 1 S. 210 Summit Ave., Oakbrook Terrace, IL 60181.

Southern Baptist Convention (1845) — Pres., C. Jerry Vines; rec. sec., Martin B. Bradley, 127 9th Ave. N., Nashville, TN 37234.

Brethren in Christ Church (1798) — Mod., Bishop John A. Byers; gen. sec., Dr. R. Donald Shafer, P.O. Box 245, Upland, CA 91785.

Brethren (German Baptists):

Brethren Church (Ashland, Oh.) (1882) — Mod., Dr. Dale Stoffer, sec., Norma Waters, RR 1, Box 421, McGaheysville, VA 22840.

Buddhist Churches of America (1899) — Bishop, Rt. Rev. Seigen H. Yamaoka; exec. asst., Rev. Seikan Fukuma, 1710 Octavia St., San Francisco, CA 94109.

The Christian and Missionary Alliance (1887) — Pres., David L. Rambo; sec., Elwood N. Nielsen, 350 N. Highland Ave., Nyack, NY 10960.

Christian Church (Disciples of Christ) (1809) — Gen. minister and pres., John O. Humbert; v.p. for communication, Carolyn W. Day, 222 S. Downey Ave., Box 1986, Indianapolis, IN 46206.

Christian Methodist Episcopal Church (1870) — Exec. sec., Dr. W. Clyde Williams, 2805 Shoreland Dr., Atlanta, GA 30331. sec., Rev. Edgar L. Wade, P.O. Box 3403, Memphis, TN 38101.

Churches of Christ in Christian Union (1909) — Gen. supt., Rev. Robert Kline; gen. sec., Rev. Robert Barth, P.O. Box 188, Alma, GA 31510.

Grace Brethren Church, Fellowship of (1882) — Mod., Dr. John Davies; sec., Rev. Kenneth Koontz, 855 Turnbull St., Delona, FL 32725.

Churches of God:

Churches of God, General Conference (1825) — Pres., Pastor Larry G. White; journalizing sec., Rev. Harry G. Cadamore, 157 N. Second St., W. Newton, PA 15089.

Church of God (Anderson, Ind.) (1880) — Chpsn., Samuel G. Hines; exec. sec., Edward L. Foggs, Box 2420, Anderson, IN 46018.

Church of Christ, Scientist (1879) — Pres., Pearline B. Thompson; clk., Mrs. Virginia S. Harris, The First Church of Christ, Scientist, 175 Huntington Ave., Boston, MA 02115.

Church of the Nazarene (1908) — Gen. sec., B. Edgar Johnson, 6401 The Paseo, Kansas City, MO 64131.

National Association of Congregational Christian Churches (1955) — Mod., Rev. Cliff Schutger; exec. sec., J. Fred Rennebohm, Box 1620, Oak Creek, WI 53154.

Eastern Orthodox churches:

Antiochian Orthodox Christian Archdiocese of North America (formerly **Syrian Antiochian Orthodox Archdiocese**) (1894) — Primate, Metropolitan Archbishop Philip (Saliba); aux., Archbishop Michael (Shaheen), Bishop Antoun (Khouri), 358 Mountain Rd., Englewood, NJ 07631.

Diocese of the Armenian Church of America (1889) — Primate, Eastern Diocese, Archbishop Torkom Manoogian; sec., Edward Onanian, 13010 Hathaway Dr., Wheaton, MD 20906; Western Diocese, Primate, His Eminence Archbishop Vatche Hovsepian, 1201 N. Vine St., Hollywood, CA 90038.

Coptic Orthodox Ch. — Archpriest Fr. Gabriel Abdelsayed, 427 West Side Ave., Jersey City, NJ 07304.

Greek Orthodox Archdiocese of North and South America (1864) — Pres., Archbishop Iakovos; sec., Peter Kourides, 8-10 E. 79th St., N.Y., NY 10021.

Orthodox Church in America (formerly **Russian Orthodox Greek Catholic Church of North America**) (1792) — Primate, Metropolitan Theodosius; chancellor, V. Rev. Robert S. Kondratick, P.O. Box 675, Syosset, NY 11791.

Romanian Orthodox Episcopate of America (1929) — Archbishop Victorin (Urache); sec., Rev. Fr. Felix Dubneae, 3355 Ridgewood Rd., Akron, OH 44313.

Serbian Orthodox Church for the U.S.A. and Canada — Bishops, Rt. Rev. Bishop Firmilian, Rt. Rev. Bishop Chrysostom; Bishop Christopher; St. Sava Monastery, Box 519, Libertyville, IL 60048.

Syrian Orthodox Church of Antioch, Archdiocese of the U.S.A. and Canada (1957) — Primate, Archbishop Mar-Athanasius Y. Samuel; gen. sec., Very Rev. Chorepiscopus John Meno, 45 Fairmount Ave., Hackensack, NJ 07601.

Ukrainian Orthodox Church in America (Ecumenical Patriarchate) (1928) — Primate, Rev. Bishop Vsevolod; sec., Rt. Rev. Ivan Tkaczuk, 90-34 139th St., Jamaica, NY 11435.

Ukrainian Orthodox Church of the U.S.A. (1919) — Metropolitan, Most Rev. Mstyslav S. Skrypnyk, Box 495, South Bound Brook, NJ 08880.

The Episcopal Church (1789) — Presiding bishop and primate, Most Rev. Edmond L. Browning; sec., Rt. Rev. Herbert A. Donovan Jr., Box 6120, Little Rock, AR 72216.

The Evangelical Covenant Church (1885) — Pres., Dr. Paul E. Larsen; sec., Rev. Timothy C. Ek, 5101 N. Francisco Ave., Chicago, IL 60625.

Friends:

Evangelical Friends Alliance (1965) — Mid-America YM, Ed Key, 2018 Maple, Wichita, KS 67213.

Friends General Conference (1900) — Gen. sec., Meredith Walton, 1520B Race St., Phila., PA 19102.

Friends United Meeting (formerly **Five Years Meeting of Friends**) (1902) — Presiding clerk, Paul Enyart, 101 Quaker Hill Dr., Richmond, IN 47374.

Independent Fundamental Churches of America (1930) — Natl. Exec. Dir., Dr. Richard Gregory, 2684 Meadow Ridge Dr., Bryon Ctr., MI 49315.

Jehovah's Witnesses (1879) — Pres., Frederick W. Franz, 25 Columbia Heights, Brooklyn, NY 11201.

Jewish congregations:

Union of American Hebrew Congregations (Reform) — Pres., Rabbi Alexander M. Schindler, 838 5th Ave., N.Y., NY 10021.

Union of Orthodox Jewish Congregations of America — Pres., Sidney Kwestel, 45 W. 36th St., N.Y., NY 10018.

United Synagogue of America (Conservative) — Pres., Franklin D. Kreutzer, 155 5th Ave., N.Y., NY 10010.

Latter-day Saints:

The Church of Jesus Christ of Latter-day Saints (Mormon) (1830) — Pres., Ezra Taft Benson, 50 E. North Temple St., Salt Lake City, UT 84150.

Reorganized Church of Jesus Christ of Latter Day Saints (1830) — Pres., Wallace B. Smith; sec., W. Grant McMurray, The Auditorium, P.O. Box 1059, Independence, MO 64051.

Lutheran churches:

Church of the Lutheran Brethren of America (1900) — Pres., Rev. Robert M. Overgard Sr.; sec., Rev. Richard Vettrus, 707 Crestview Dr., W. Union, IA 52175.

Church of the Lutheran Confession (1961) — Pres., Rev. Daniel Fleischer; sec., Rev. Paul F. Nolting, 620 E. 50th St., Loveland, CO 80537.

Evangelical Lutheran Church in America (1987) — Bishop, Rev. Dr. Herbert W. Chilstrom; sec., Rev. Dr. Lowell G. Almen, 8765 W. Higgins Rd., Chicago, IL 60631.

Evangelical Lutheran Synod (1853) — Pres., Rev. George Orvick; sec., Rev. Alf Merseth, 106 13th St. S., Northwood, IA 50459.

Assn. of Free Lutheran Congregations (1962) — Pres. Rev. Richard Snipstead; sec., Rev. Ronald Knutson, 402 W. 11th St., Canton, SD 57013.

Lutheran Church — Missouri Synod (1847) — Pres., Dr. Ralph A. Bohlmann; sec., Dr. Walter L. Rosin, 1333 S. Kirkwood, St. Louis, MO 63122.

Wisconsin Evangelical Lutheran Synod (1850) — Pres., Rev. Carl H. Mischke; sec., Prof. David Worgull, 1270 N. Dobson, Chandler, AZ 85224.

Mennonite churches:

The General Conference of Mennonite Brethren Churches (1860) — Chpsn., Herb Brandt; sec., Roland Reimer, 8000 W. 21st St., Wichita, KS 67212.

Mennonite Church (1690) — Mod., George R. Brunk, II, 421 S. Second St. Ste. 600, Elkhart, IN 46516.

Methodist churches:

African Methodist Episcopal Zion Church (1796) — Sr. Bishop, William Milton Smith; sec., Bd. of Bishops, Bishop John Henry Miller, Sr., 8605 Caswell Court, Raleigh, NC 27612.

Free Methodist Church of North America (1860) — Bishops R.F. Andrews, D. Bastian, G.E. Bates, D.M. Foster, N. Nzeyimana, C.E. Van Valin; gen. conf. sec., Melvin J. Spencer, 901 College Ave., Winona Lake, IN 46590.

The United Methodist Church (1968) — Sec., Gen. Conference, Faith Richardson, 168 Mt. Vernon St., Newtonville, MA 02160.

Universal Fellowship of Metropolitan Community Churches — Mod., Rev. Elder Troy D. Perry; clerk, Rev. Elder Nancy L. Wilson, 5300 Santa Monica Blvd., Los Angeles, CA 90029.

Moravian Church (Unitas Fratrum) (1740) **Northern Province** — Pres., Dr. Gordon L. Sommers, 1021 Center St., P.O. Box 1245, Bethlehem, PA 18016. **Southern Province** — Pres., Rev. Graham H. Rights, 459 S. Church St., Winston-Salem, NC 27108.

Pentecostal churches:

Assemblies of God (1914) — Gen. supt., G. Raymond Carlson; gen. sec., Joseph R. Flower, 1445 Boonville Ave., Springfield, MO 65802.

Bible Way Church of Our Lord Jesus Christ World Wide (1927) — Presiding bishop, Smallwood E. Williams; gen. sec., Bishop Edward William, 5118 Clarendon Rd., Brooklyn, NY 11226.

Gen. Council, Christian Church of No. America (1948) — Gen. overseer; Rev. Guy BonGiovanni; gen. sec.-treas., Rev. Richard A. Tedesco, Rt. 18 & Rutledge Rd., Box 141-A, RD #1, Transfer, PA 16154.

The Church of God (1903) — Gen. overseer, Bishop Voy M. Bullen; gen. sec.-treas., Marie Powell, Box 13036, 1207 Willow Brook, Huntsville, AL 35802.

Church of God (Cleveland, Tenn.) (1886) — Gen. overseer, Raymond Crowley; gen. sec.-treas., John Nichols, P.O. Box 2430, Cleveland, TN 37320.

International Church of the Foursquare Gospel (1927) — Pres., Dr. John R. Holland; sec., Rev. John W. Bowers, 1100 Glendale Blvd., Los Angeles, CA 90026.

National Gay Pentecostal Alliance (1980) — Pres., Rev. Wm. H. Carey, P.O. Box 1391, Schenectady, NY 12301.

Open Bible Standard Churches (1919) — Gen. supt., Ray E. Smith; sec.-treas., Patrick L. Bowlin, 2020 Bell Ave., Des Moines, IA 50315.

Pentecostal Church of God (1919) — Gen. supt., Dr. James D. Gee; gen. sec.-treas., Dr. Ronald R. Minor, 4901 Pennsylvania, P.O. Box 850, Joplin, MO 64802.

Pentecostal Free Will Baptist Church (1959) — Gen. supt., Rev. Don Sauls; gen. sec., Rev. J.T. Hammond, Box 1568, Dunn, NC 28334.

United Pentecostal Church International (1945) — Gen. supt., Rev. Nathaniel A. Urshan; gen. sec.-treas., Rev. C. M. Becton, 8855 Dunn Rd., Hazelwood, MO 63042.

Presbyterian churches:

Cumberland Presbyterian Church (1810) — Mod., Beverly St. John; stated clerk, Robert Prosser, 1978 Union Ave., Memphis, TN 38104.

Evangelical Presbyterian Church (1981) — Mod., Richard Heidtman; stated clerk, Rev. L. Edward Davis, 26049 Five Mile Rd., Detroit, MI 48239.

The Orthodox Presbyterian Church (1936) — Mod., Mark T. Bube; stated clerk, John P. Galbraith, 2345 Willow Brook Dr., Huntingdon Valley, PA 19006.

Presbyterian Church in America (1973) — Mod., Dr. D. James Kennedy; stated clerk, Dr. Paul R. Gilchrist, 1852 Century Pl., Atlanta, GA 30345.

Presbyterian Church (U.S.A.) (1983) — Mod., C. Kenneth Hall; stated clerk, Rev. James E. Andrews, 100 Witherspoon St., Louisville, KY 40202.

Reformed Presbyterian Church of No. America (1871) — Mod., Dr. John H. White; clerk, Rev. Paul M. Martin, 1117 E. Devonshire, Phoenix, AZ 85014.

Reformed churches:

Christian Reformed Church in North America (1857) — Stated clerk, Rev. Leonard J. Hofman, 2850 Kalamazoo Ave., SE, Grand Rapids, MI 49560.

Reformed Church in America (1628) — Pres., Wilbur T. Washington; gen. sec., Edwin G. Mulder, 475 Riverside Dr., N.Y., NY 10115.

Reformed Episcopal Church (1873) — Pres., and Presid. Bishop, Rev. William H. S. Jerden Jr; sec., Rev. Roger F. Spence, 6300 Greenwood Pkwy., 203, Sagamore Hills, OH 44067.

Roman Catholic Church — National Conference of Catholic Bishops. Pres., Archbishop John L. May; sec., Archbishop Eugene Marino, 1312 Massachusetts Ave. NW, Wash., DC 20005.

The Salvation Army (1880) — Natl. Cmdr. Commissioner Andrew S. Miller; natl. chief sec., Col. Harold E. Shoults, 799 Bloomfield Ave., Verona, NJ 07044.

Sikh (1972) — Chief adm., Siri Singh Sahib, Harbhajan Singh Khalsa Yogiji; sec. gen., Mukhia Sardarni Sahiba, Sardarni Premka Kaur Khalsa, 1649 S. Robertson Blvd., Los Angeles, CA 90035.

Unitarian Universalist Assn. (1961) — Pres., Rev. William Schulz; sec., Barry Johnson-Fay, 25 Beacon St., Boston, MA 02108.

United Brethren in Christ (1789) — Chpsn., Bishop C. Ray Miller; 302 Lake St., Huntington, IN 46750.

United Church of Christ (1957) — Pres., Rev. Avery D. Post; sec., Rev. Carol Joyce Brun, 105 Madison Ave., N.Y., NY 10016.

Volunteers of America (1896) — Pres., Raymond C. Tremont; 3813 N. Causeway Blvd., Metairie, LA 70002.

The Wesleyan Church (1968) — Gen. supt., Rev. J. Stevan Manley; gen. sec., Rev. Robert W. Wilson, 10880 State Rt. 170, Negley, OH.

Religious Preference of Teens

Source: The Gallup Organization, Jan. 1990

	Protestant	Catholic		Protestant	Catholic		Protestant	Catholic
National	53%	32%	Whites	49	33	South	72	18
Sex			Non-Whites	64	28	West	36	33
Male	48	33	**Family**			**Urbanization**		
Female	55	31	White-collar	48	35	Central cities	49	36
Age			Blue-collar	56	30	Suburbs	49	32
Ages 13 to 15	54	30	**Region**			Non-metropolitan areas	60	27
Ages 16 to 17	54	30	East	40	42			
Race			Midwest	49	40			

Church Attendance By Teens & Adults

Source: The Gallup Organization, Jan. 1990

Worship Service Attendance In Past Seven Days

	Adults	Teens		Adults	Teens		Adults	Teens
1989	43%	57%	1985	42%	52%	1982	41%	50%
1988	42	51	1984	40	52	1981	41	54
1987	40	52	1983	40	53	1980	41	50
1986	40	54						

Jewish Holy Days, Festivals, and Fasts

	1990 (5750-51)	1991 (5751-52)	1992 (5752-53)	1993 (5753-54)	1994
Tu B'Shvat	Feb. 10 Sat.	Jan. 30 Wed.	Jan. 20 Mon.	Feb. 6 Sat.	Jan. 27 Thu.
Ta'anis Esther (Fast of Esther)	Mar. 8 Thu.*	Feb. 27 Wed.	Mar. 18 Wed.	Mar. 4 Thu.*	Feb. 24 Thu.
Purim	Mar. 11 Sun.	Feb. 28 Thu.	Mar. 19 Thu.	Mar. 7 Sun.	Feb. 25 Fri.
Passover	Apr. 10 Tue.	Mar. 30 Sat.	Apr. 18 Sat.	Apr. 6 Tue.	Mar. 27 Sun.
	Apr. 17 Tue.	Apr. 6 Sat	Apr. 25 Sat.	Apr. 13 Tue.	Apr. 3 Sun.
Lag B'Omer	May 13 Sun.	May 2 Thu.	May 21 Thu.	May 9 Sun.	Apr. 29 Fri.
Shavuot	May 30 Wed.	May 19 Sun.	June 7 Sun.	May 26 Wed.	May 16 Mon.
	May 31 Thu.	May 20 Mon.	June 8 Mon.	May 27 Thu.	May 17 Tue.
Fast of the 17th Day of Tammuz	July 10 Tue.	June 30 Sun.*	July 19 Sun.*	July 6 Tue.	June 26 Sun.
Fast of the 9th Day of Ac	July 31 Tue.	July 21 Sun.*	Aug. 9 Sun.*	July 27 Tue.	July 17 Sun.
Rosh Hashanah	Sept. 20 Thu.	Sept. 9 Mon.	Sept. 28 Mon.	Sept. 16 Thu.	Sept. 6 Tue.
	Sept. 21 Fri	Sept. 10 Tue.	Sept. 29 Tue.	Sept. 17 Fri.	Sept. 7 Wed.
Fast of Gedalya	Sept. 23 Sun.*	Sept. 11 Wed.	Sept. 30 Wed.	Sept. 19 Sun.*	Sept. 8 Thu.
Yom Kippur	Sept. 29 Sat.	Sept. 18 Wed.	Oct. 7 Wed.	Sept. 25 Sat.	Sept. 15 Thu.
Sukkot	Oct. 4 Thu.	Sept. 23 Mo.n	Oct. 12 Mon.	Sept. 30 Thu.	Sept. 20 Tue.
	Oct. 10 Wed.	Sept. 29 Sun.	Oct. 18 Sun.	Oct. 6 Wed.	Sept. 26 Mon.
Shmini Atzeret	Oct. 11 Thu.	Sept. 30 Mon.	Oct. 19 Mon.	Oct. 7 Thu.	Sept. 27 Tue.
	Oct. 12 Fri.	Oct. 1 Tue.	Oct. 20 Tue.	Oct. 8 Fri.	Sept. 28 Wed.
Chanukah	Dec. 12 Wed.	Dec. 2 Mon.	Dec. 20 Sun.	Dec. 9 Thu.	Nov. 28 Mon.
	Dec. 19 Wed.	Dec. 9 Mon.	Dec. 27 Sun.	Dec. 16 Thu.	Dec. 5 Mon.
Fast of the 10th of Tevet	Dec. 27 Thu.	Dec. 17 Tue.	Jan. 3, Sun. 1993	Dec. 24 Fri.	Dec. 13 Tue.

The months of the Jewish year are: 1) Tishri; 2) Cheshvan (also Marcheshvan); 3) Kislev; 4) Tebet (also Tebeth); 5) Shebat (also Shebhat); 6) Adar; 6a) Adar Sheni (II) added in leap years; 7) Nisan; 8) Iyar; 9) Sivan; 10) Tammuz; 11) Av (also Abh); 12) Elul. All Jewish holy days, etc., begin at sunset on the day previous. *Date changed to avoid Sabbath.

Greek Orthodox Movable Ecclesiastical Dates

	1991	1992	1993	1994
Triódion begins	January 27	February 16	February 7	February 20
Sat. of Souls	February 9	February 29	February 20	March 5
Meat Fare	February 10	March 1	February 21	March 6
2nd Sat. of Souls	February 16	March 7	February 27	March 12
Lent Begins	February 18	March 9	March 1	March 14
St. Theodore 3rd Sat. of Souls	February 23	March 14	March 6	March 19
Sunday of Orthodoxy	February 24	March 15	March 7	March 20
Sat. of Lazarus	March 30	April 18	April 10	April 23
Palm Sunday	March 31	April 19	April 11	April 24
Holy (Good) Friday	April 5	April 24	April 16	April 29
Western Easter	March 31	April 19	April 11	April 3
Orthodox Easter	April 7	April 26	April 18	May 1
Ascension	May 16	June 4	May 27	June 9
Sat. of Souls	May 25	June 13	June 5	June 18
Pentecost	May 26	June 14	June 6	June 19
All Saints	June 2	June 21	June 13	June 26

Islamic (Moslem) Calendar 1990-1991 (1411-1412)

The Islamic Calendar is a lunar reckoning from the year of the *hegira*, 622 A.D., when Muhammed moved from Mecca to Medina. It runs in cycles of 30 years, of which the 2d, 5th, 7th, 10th, 13th, 16th, 18th, 21st, 24th, 26th, and 29th are leap years; 1411 is the 1st year, 1412 the 2d year of the cycle. Common years have 354 days, leap years 355, the extra day being added to the last month, Zu'lhijjah. Except for this case, the 12 months beginning with Muharram have alternately 30 and 29 days.

Year	Name of month	Month begins	Year	Name of month	Month begins
1411	Muharram (New Year)	July 24, 1990	1411	Shawwai	Apr. 16, 1991
1411	Safar	Aug. 23, 1990	1411	Zu'lkadah	May 15, 1991
1411	Rabia I	Sept. 21, 1990	1411	Zu'lhijjah	June 14, 1991
1411	Rabia II	Oct. 21, 1990	1412	Muharram (New Year)	July 13, 1991
1411	Jumada I	Nov. 19, 1990	1412	Safar	Aug. 12, 1991
1411	Jumada II	Dec. 19, 1990	1412	Rabia I	Sept. 10, 1991
1411	Rajab	Jan. 17, 1991	1412	Rabia II	Oct. 10, 1991
1411	Shaban	Feb. 16, 1991	1412	Jamada I	Nov. 8, 1991
1411	Ramadan	Mar. 17, 1991			

Episcopal Church Calendar and Liturgical Colors

White—from Christmas Day through the First Sunday after Epiphany; Maundy Thursday (as an alternative to crimson at the Eucharist); from the Vigil of Easter to the Day of Pentecost (Whitsunday); Trinity Sunday; Feasts of the Lord (except Holy Cross Day); the Confession of St. Peter; the Conversion of St. Paul; St. Joseph; St. Mary Magdalene; St. Mary the Virgin; St. Michael and All Angels; All Saint's Day; St. John the Evangelist; memorials of other saints who were not martyred; Independence Day and Thanksgiving Day; weddings and funerals. Red.—the Day of Pentecost; Holy Cross Day; feasts of apostles and evangelists (except those listed above); feasts and memorials of martyrs (including Holy Innocents' Day). Violet—Advent and Lent. Crimson (dark red)—Holy Week. Green—the seasons after Epiphany and after Pentecost. Black—optional alternative for funerals. Alternative colors used in some churches: Blue—Advent; Lenten White—Ash Wednesday to Palm Sunday. *(continued)*

In the Episcopal Church the days of fasting are Ash Wednesday and Good Friday. Other days of special devotion (abstinence) are the 40 days of Lent and all Fridays of the year, except those in Christmas and Easter seasons and any Feasts of the Lord which occur on a Friday or during Lent. Ember Days (optional) are days of prayer for the Church's ministry. They fall on the Wednesday, Friday, and Saturday after the first Sunday in Lent, the Day of Pentecost, Holy Cross Day, and the Third Sunday of Advent. Rogation Days (also optional) are the three days before Ascension Day, and are days of prayer for God's blessing on the crops, on commerce and industry, and for the conservation of the earth's resources.

Days, etc.	1987	1988	1989	1990	1991	1992
Golden Number	12	13	14	15	16	17
Sunday Letter	D	CB	A	G	F	ED
Sundays after Epiphany	8	6	5	8	5	8
Ash Wednesday	Mar. 4	Feb. 17	Feb. 8	Feb. 28	Feb. 13	Mar. 4
First Sunday in Lent	Mar. 8	Feb. 21	Feb. 12	Mar. 4	Feb. 17	Mar. 8
Passion/Palm Sunday	Apr. 12	Mar. 27	Mar. 19	Apr. 8	Mar. 24	Apr. 12
Good Friday	Apr. 17	Apr. 1	Mar. 24	Apr. 13	Mar. 29	Apr. 17
Easter Day	Apr. 19	Apr. 3	Mar. 26	Apr. 15	Mar. 31	Apr. 19
Ascension Day	May 28	May 12	May 4	May 24	May 9	May 28
The Day of Pentecost	June 7	May 22	May 14	June 3	May 19	June 7
Trinity Sunday	June 14	May 29	May 21	June 10	May 26	June 14
Numbered Proper of 2 Pentecost	#7	#5	#3	#6	#4	#7
First Sunday of Advent	Nov. 29	Nov. 27	Dec. 3	Dec. 2	Dec. 1	Nov. 29

Ash Wednesday and Easter Sunday

Year	Ash Wed.	Easter Sunday	Year	Ash Wed.	Easter Sunday	Year	Ash Wed.	Easter Sunday	Year	Ash Wed.	Easter Sunday
1901	Feb. 20	Apr. 7	1951	Feb. 7	Mar. 25	2001	Feb. 28	Apr. 15	2051	Feb. 15	Apr. 2
1902	Feb. 12	Mar. 30	1952	Feb. 27	Apr. 13	2002	Feb. 13	Mar. 31	2052	Mar. 6	Apr. 21
1903	Feb. 25	Apr. 12	1953	Feb. 18	Apr. 5	2003	Mar. 5	Apr. 20	2053	Feb. 19	Apr. 6
1904	Feb. 17	Apr. 3	1954	Mar. 3	Apr. 18	2004	Feb. 25	Apr. 11	2054	Feb. 11	Mar. 29
1905	Mar. 8	Apr. 23	1955	Feb. 23	Apr. 10	2005	Feb. 9	Mar. 27	2055	Mar. 3	Apr. 18
1906	Feb. 28	Apr. 15	1956	Feb. 15	Apr. 1	2006	Mar. 1	Apr. 16	2056	Feb. 16	Apr. 2
1907	Feb. 13	Mar. 31	1957	Mar. 6	Apr. 21	2007	Feb. 21	Apr. 8	2057	Mar. 7	Apr. 22
1908	Mar. 4	Apr. 19	1958	Feb. 19	Apr. 6	2008	Feb. 6	Mar. 23	2058	Feb. 27	Apr. 14
1909	Feb. 24	Apr. 11	1959	Feb. 11	Mar. 29	2009	Feb. 25	Apr. 12	2059	Feb. 12	Mar. 30
1910	Feb. 9	Mar. 27	1960	Mar. 2	Apr. 17	2010	Feb. 17	Apr. 4	2060	Mar. 3	Apr. 18
1911	Mar. 1	Apr. 16	1961	Feb. 15	Apr. 2	2011	Mar. 9	Apr. 24	2061	Feb. 23	Apr. 10
1912	Feb. 21	Apr. 7	1962	Mar. 7	Apr. 22	2012	Feb. 22	Apr. 8	2062	Feb. 8	Mar. 26
1913	Feb. 5	Mar. 23	1963	Feb. 27	Apr. 14	2013	Feb. 13	Mar. 31	2063	Feb. 28	Apr. 15
1914	Feb. 25	Apr. 12	1964	Feb. 12	Mar. 29	2014	Mar. 5	Apr. 20	2064	Feb. 20	Apr. 6
1915	Feb. 17	Apr. 4	1965	Mar. 3	Apr. 18	2015	Feb. 18	Apr. 5	2065	Feb. 11	Mar. 29
1916	Mar. 8	Apr. 23	1966	Feb. 23	Apr. 10	2016	Feb. 10	Mar. 27	2066	Feb. 24	Apr. 11
1917	Feb. 21	Apr. 8	1967	Feb. 8	Mar. 26	2017	Mar. 1	Apr. 16	2067	Feb. 16	Apr. 3
1918	Feb. 13	Mar. 31	1968	Feb. 28	Apr. 14	2018	Feb. 14	Apr. 1	2068	Mar. 7	Apr. 22
1919	Mar. 5	Apr. 20	1969	Feb. 19	Apr. 6	2019	Mar. 6	Apr. 21	2069	Feb. 27	Apr. 14
1920	Feb. 18	Apr. 4	1970	Feb. 11	Mar. 29	2020	Feb. 26	Apr. 12	2070	Feb. 12	Mar. 30
1921	Feb. 9	Mar. 27	1971	Feb. 24	Apr. 11	2021	Feb. 17	Apr. 4	2071	Mar. 4	Apr. 19
1922	Mar. 1	Apr. 16	1972	Feb. 16	Apr. 2	2022	Mar. 2	Apr. 17	2072	Feb. 24	Apr. 10
1923	Feb. 14	Apr. 1	1973	Mar. 7	Apr. 22	2023	Feb. 22	Apr. 9	2073	Feb. 8	Mar. 26
1924	Mar. 5	Apr. 20	1974	Feb. 27	Apr. 14	2024	Feb. 14	Mar. 31	2074	Feb. 28	Apr. 15
1925	Feb. 25	Apr. 12	1975	Feb. 12	Mar. 30	2025	Mar. 5	Apr. 20	2075	Feb. 20	Apr. 7
1926	Feb. 17	Apr. 4	1976	Mar. 3	Apr. 18	2026	Feb. 18	Apr. 5	2076	Mar. 4	Apr. 19
1927	Mar. 2	Apr. 17	1977	Feb. 23	Apr. 10	2027	Feb. 10	Mar. 28	2077	Feb. 24	Apr. 11
1928	Feb. 22	Apr. 8	1978	Feb. 8	Mar. 26	2028	Mar. 1	Apr. 16	2078	Feb. 16	Apr. 3
1929	Feb. 13	Mar. 31	1979	Feb. 28	Apr. 15	2029	Feb. 14	Apr. 1	2079	Mar. 8	Apr. 23
1930	Mar. 5	Apr. 20	1980	Feb. 20	Apr. 6	2030	Mar. 6	Apr. 21	2080	Feb. 21	Apr. 7
1931	Feb. 18	Apr. 5	1981	Mar. 4	Apr. 19	2031	Feb. 26	Apr. 13	2081	Feb. 12	Mar. 30
1932	Feb. 10	Mar. 27	1982	Feb. 24	Apr. 11	2032	Feb. 11	Mar. 28	2082	Mar. 4	Apr. 19
1933	Mar. 1	Apr. 16	1983	Feb. 16	Apr. 3	2033	Mar. 2	Apr. 17	2083	Feb. 17	Apr. 4
1934	Feb. 14	Apr. 1	1984	Mar. 7	Apr. 22	2034	Feb. 22	Apr. 9	2084	Feb. 9	Mar. 26
1935	Mar. 6	Apr. 21	1985	Feb. 20	Apr. 7	2035	Feb. 7	Mar. 25	2085	Feb. 28	Apr. 15
1936	Feb. 26	Apr. 12	1986	Feb. 12	Mar. 30	2036	Feb. 27	Apr. 13	2086	Feb. 13	Mar. 31
1937	Feb. 10	Mar. 28	1987	Mar. 4	Apr. 19	2037	Feb. 18	Apr. 5	2087	Mar. 5	Apr. 20
1938	Mar. 2	Apr. 17	1988	Feb. 17	Apr. 3	2038	Mar. 10	Apr. 25	2088	Feb. 25	Apr. 11
1939	Feb. 22	Apr. 9	1989	Feb. 8	Mar. 26	2039	Feb. 23	Apr. 10	2089	Feb. 16	Apr. 3
1940	Feb. 7	Mar. 24	1990	Feb. 28	Apr. 15	2040	Feb. 15	Apr. 1	2090	Mar. 1	Apr. 16
1941	Feb. 26	Apr. 13	1991	Feb. 13	Mar. 31	2041	Mar. 6	Apr. 21	2091	Feb. 21	Apr. 8
1942	Feb. 18	Apr. 5	1992	Mar. 4	Apr. 19	2042	Feb. 19	Apr. 6	2092	Feb. 13	Mar. 30
1943	Mar. 10	Apr. 25	1993	Feb. 24	Apr. 11	2043	Feb. 11	Mar. 29	2093	Feb. 25	Apr. 12
1944	Feb. 23	Apr. 9	1994	Feb. 16	Apr. 3	2044	Mar. 2	Apr. 17	2094	Feb. 17	Apr. 4
1945	Feb. 14	Apr. 1	1995	Mar. 1	Apr. 16	2045	Feb. 22	Apr. 9	2095	Mar. 9	Apr. 24
1946	Mar. 6	Apr. 21	1996	Feb. 21	Apr. 7	2046	Feb. 7	Mar. 25	2096	Feb. 29	Apr. 15
1947	Feb. 19	Apr. 6	1997	Feb. 12	Mar. 30	2047	Feb. 27	Apr. 14	2097	Feb. 13	Mar. 31
1948	Feb. 11	Mar. 28	1998	Feb. 25	Apr. 12	2048	Feb. 19	Apr. 5	2098	Mar. 5	Apr. 20
1949	Mar. 2	Apr. 17	1999	Feb. 17	Apr. 4	2049	Mar. 3	Apr. 18	2099	Feb. 25	Apr. 12
1950	Feb. 22	Apr. 9	2000	Mar. 8	Apr. 23	2050	Feb. 23	Apr. 10	2100	Feb. 10	Mar. 28

The Ten Commandments

According to Judeo-Christian tradition, as related in the Bible, the Ten Commandments were revealed by God to Moses, and form the basic moral component of God's covenant with Israel. The Ten Commandments appear in two different places in the Old Testament—Exodus 20:1-17 and Deuterotomy 5:6-21—the phrasing similar but not identical. Most Protestant, Anglican, and Orthodox Christians enumerate the commandments differently from Roman Catholics and Lutherans. Jewish tradition considers the introduction, "I am the Lord·.." to be the first commandment and makes the prohibition against "other gods" and idolatry the second.

Abridged Text of the Ten Commandments in Exodus 20:1-17

I. I am the Lord your God, who brought you out of the land of Egypt, out of the house of bondage. You shall have no other gods before me.
II. You shall not make for yourself a graven image. You shall not bow down to them or serve them.
III. You shall not take the name of the Lord your God in vain.
IV. Remember the sabbath day, to keep it holy.
V. Honor your father and your mother.
VI. You shall not kill.
VII. You shall not commit adultery.
VIII. You shall not steal.
IX. You shall not bear false witness against your neighbor.
X. You shall not covet.

Books of the Bible

Old Testament—Standard Protestant English Versions

Genesis	II Chronicles	Daniel
Exodus	Ezra	Hosea
Leviticus	Nehemiah	Joel
Numbers	Esther	Amos
Deuteronomy	Job	Obadiah
Joshua	Psalms	Jonah
Judges	Proverbs	Micah
Ruth	Ecclesiastes	Nahum
I Samuel	Song of Solomon	Habakkuk
II Samuel	Isaiah	Zephaniah
I Kings	Jeremiah	Haggai
II Kings	Lamentations	Zechariah
I Chronicles	Ezekiel	Malachi

New Testament—Standard Protestant English Versions

Matthew	Ephesians	Hebrews
Mark	Phillippians	James
Luke	Colossians	I Peter
John	I Thessalonians	II Peter
Acts	II Thessalonians	I John
Romans	I Timothy	II John
I Corinthians	II Timothy	III John
II Corinthians	Titus	Jude
Galatians	Philemon	Revelation

Catholic Versions

All the Catholic books of the Bible (Old Testament and New Testament) have the same names as Protestant Versions. A Catholic Version (and Pre-Reformation Bibles) simply has the books **Tobit, Judith, Wisdom, Sirach (Ecclesiasticus), Baruch, I Maccabees,** and **II Maccabees** as part of the Old Testament. The Old Testament books that a Catholic Bible includes and a Protestant Bible does not are called "Deuterocanonical Books."

Roman Catholic Hierarchy
Source: U.S. Catholic Conference; Mid-year, 1990
Supreme Pontiff

At the head of the Roman Catholic Church is the Supreme Pontiff, Pope John Paul II, Karol Wojtyla, born at Wadowice (Krakow), Poland, May 18, 1920; ordained priest Nov. 1, 1946; promoted to Archbishop of Krakow Jan. 13, 1964; proclaimed Cardinal June 26, 1967; elected pope as successor of Pope John Paul I Oct. 16, 1978; solemn commencement as pope Oct. 22, 1978.

College of Cardinals

Members of the Sacred College of Cardinals are chosen by the Pope to be his chief assistants and advisors in the administration of the church. Among their duties is the election of the Pope when the Holy See becomes vacant. The title of cardinal is a high honor, but it does not represent any increase in the powers of holy orders.

In its present form, the College of Cardinals dates from the 12th century. The first cardinals, from about the 6th century, were deacons and priests of the leading churches of Rome, and bishops of neighboring diocese. The title of cardinal was limited to members of the college in 1567. The number of cardinals was set at 70 in 1586 by Pope Sixtus V. From 1959 Pope John XXIII began to increase the number. However, the number of cardinals eligible to participate in papal elections was limited to 120. There were lay cardinals until 1918, when the Code of Canon Law specified that all cardinals must be priests. Pope John XXIII in 1962 established that all cardinals must be bishops. The first age limits were set in 1971 by Pope Paul VI, who decreed that at age 80 cardinals must retire from curial departments and offices and from participation in papal elections. They continue as members of the college, with all rights and privileges.

U.S. Cardinals

Name	Office	Born	Named Cardinal
Aponte Martinez, Luis	Archbishop of San Juan	1922	1973
Baum, William	Prefect of Congregation for Seminaries and Institutes of Study	1926	1976
Bernardin, Joseph	Archbishop of Chicago	1928	1983
Carberry, John*	Archbishop emeritus of St. Louis	1904	1969
Hickey, James	Archbishop of Washington	1920	1988
Krol, John	Archbishop emeritus of Philadelphia	1910	1967
Law, Bernard F.	Archbishop of Boston	1931	1985
O'Connor, John J	Archbishop of New York	1920	1985
Szoka, Edmund	Archbishop of Detroit	1927	1988

*Asterisk indicates cardinals ineligible to take part in papal elections.

Major Christian Denominations:

Italics indicate that area which, generally speaking, most

Denomination	Origins	Organization	Authority	Special rites
Baptists	In radical Reformation objections to infant baptism, demands for church-state separation; John Smyth, English Separatist in 1609; Roger Williams, 1638, Providence, R.I.	Congregational, *i.e.*, each local church is autonomous.	Scripture; some Baptists, particularly in the South, interpret the Bible literally.	Baptism, after about age 12, by total immersion; Lord's Supper.
Church of Christ (Disciples)	Among evangelical Presbyterians in Ky. (1804) and Penn. (1809), in distress over Protestant factionalism and decline of fervor. Organized 1832.	Congregational.	*"Where the Scriptures speak, we speak; where the Scriptures are silent, we are silent."*	Adult baptism, Lord's Supper (weekly).
Episcopalians	Henry VIII separated English Catholic Church from Rome, 1534, for political reasons. Protestant Episcopal Church in U.S. founded 1789.	*Bishops, in apostolic succession, are elected by diocesan representatives; part of Anglican Communion, symbolically headed by Archbishop of Canterbury.*	Scripture as interpreted by tradition, esp. *39 Articles* (1563); not dogmatic. Tri-annual convention of bishops, priests, and laymen.	Infant baptism, Holy Communion, others. Sacrament is symbolic, but has real spiritual effect.
Lutherans	Martin Luther in Wittenberg, Germany, 1517, objected to Catholic doctrine of salvation by merit and sale of indulgences; break complete by 1519.	Varies from congregational to episcopal; in U.S. a combination of regional synods and congregational polities is most common.	*Scripture, and tradition as spelled out in Augsburg Confession (1530) and other creeds. These confessions of faith are binding although interpretations vary.*	Infant baptism, Lord's Supper. Christ's true body and blood present "in, with, and under the bread and wine."
Methodists	Rev. John Wesley began movement, 1738, within Church of England. First U.S. denomination Baltimore, 1784.	Conference and superintendent system. *In United Methodist Church, general superintendents are bishops—not a priestly order, only an office—who are elected for life.*	Scripture as interpreted by tradition, reason, and experience.	Baptism of infants or adults, Lord's Supper commanded. Other rites, inc. marriage, ordination, solemnize personal commitments.
Mormons	In visions of the Angel Moroni by Joseph Smith, 1827, in New York, in which he received a new revelation on golden tablets: *The Book of Mormon*.	Theocratic; all male adults are in priesthood which culminates in Council of 12 Apostles and 1st Presidency (1st President, 2 counselors).	*The Bible, Book of Mormon and other revelations to Smith, and certain pronouncements of the 1st Presidency.*	Adult baptism, laying on of hands (which confers the gift of the Holy Spirit), Lord's Supper. Temple rites: baptism for the dead, marriage for eternity, others.
Orthodox	Original Christian proselytizing in 1st century; broke with Rome, 1054, after centuries of doctrinal disputes and diverging traditions.	Synods of bishops in autonomous, usually national, churches elect a patriarch, archbishop or metropolitan. These men, as a group, are the heads of the church.	Scripture, tradition, and the first 7 church councils up to Nicaea II in 787. Bishops in council have authority in doctrine and policy.	Seven sacraments: infant baptism and anointing, Eucharist (both bread and wine), ordination, penance, anointing of the sick, marriage.
Pentecostal	In Topeka, Kansas (1901), and Los Angeles (1906) in reaction to loss of evangelical fervor among Methodists and other denominations.	Originally a movement, not a formal organization. Pentecostalism now has a variety of organized forms and continues also as a movement.	Scripture, individual charismatic leaders, the teachings of the Holy Spirit.	*Spirit baptism, esp. as shown in "speaking in tongues"; healing and sometimes exorcism; adult baptism, Lord's Supper.*
Presbyterians	In Calvinist Reformation in 1500s; differed with Lutherans over sacraments, church government. John Knox founded Scotch Presbyterian church about 1560.	*Highly structured representational system of ministers and laypersons (presbyters) in local, regional and national bodies. (synods).*	Scripture.	Infant baptism, Lord's Supper; bread and wine symbolize Christ's spiritual presence.
Roman Catholics	Traditionally, by Jesus who named St. Peter the 1st Vicar; historically, in early Christian proselytizing and the conversion of imperial Rome in the 4th century.	Hierarchy with supreme power vested in Pope elected by cardinals. Councils of Bishops advise on matters of doctrine and policy.	*The Pope, when speaking for the whole church in matters of faith and morals, and tradition, which is partly recorded in scripture and expressed in church councils.*	Seven sacraments: baptism, contrition and penance, confirmation, Eucharist, marriage, ordination, and anointing of the sick (unction).
United Church of Christ	*By ecumenical union, 1957, of Congregationalists and Evangelical & Reformed, representing both Calvinist and Lutheran traditions.*	Congregational; a General Synod, representative of all congregations, sets general policy.	Scripture.	Infant baptism, Lord's Supper.

How Do They Differ?

distinguishes that denomination from any other.

Practice	Ethics	Doctrine	Other	Denomination
Worship style varies from staid to evangelistic. Extensive missionary activity.	Usually opposed to alcohol and tobacco; sometimes tends toward a perfectionist ethical standard.	*No creed; true church is of believers only, who are all equal.*	Since no authority can stand between the believer and God, the Baptists are strong supporters of church-state separation.	Baptists
Tries to avoid any rite or doctrine not explicitly part of the 1st century church. Some congregations may reject instrumental music.	Some tendency toward perfectionism; increasing interest in social action programs.	Simple New Testament faith; avoids any elaboration not firmly based on Scripture.	Highly tolerant in doctrinal and religious matters; strongly supportive of scholarly education.	Church of Christ (Disciples)
Formal, based on *Book of Common Prayer* (1549); services range from austerely simple to highly elaborate.	Tolerant; sometimes permissive; some social action programs.	*Apostles' Creed* is basic; otherwise, considerable variation ranges from rationalist and liberal to acceptance of most Roman Catholic dogma.	Strongly ecumenical, holding talks with all other branches of Christendom.	Episcopalians
Relatively simple formal liturgy with emphasis on the sermon.	Generally, conservative in personal and social ethics; doctrine of "2 kingdoms" (worldly and holy) supports conservatism in secular affairs.	Salvation by faith alone through grace. Lutheranism has made major contributions to Protestant theology.	Though still somewhat divided along ethnic lines (German, Swede, etc.), main divisions are between funamentalists and liberals.	Lutherans
Worship style varies widely by denomination, local church, geography.	Originally pietist and perfectionist; always strong social activist elements	No distinctive theological development; 25 Articles abriged from Church of England's 39 not binding.	In 1968, United Methodist Church joined pioneer English- and German-speaking groups. UMs leaders in ecumenical movement.	Methodists
Staid service with hymns, sermon. Secret temple ceremonies may be more elaborate. Strong missionary activity.	Temperance; strict tithing. Combine a strong work ethic with communal self-reliance.	God is a material being; he created the universe out of pre-existing matter; all persons can be saved and many will become divine. Most other beliefs are traditionally Christian.	Mormons regard mainline churches as apostate, corrupt. Reorganized Church (founded 1860) rejects most Mormon doctrine and practice except Book of Mormon.	Mormons
Elaborate liturgy, usually in the vernacular, though extremely traditional. The liturgy is the essence of Orthodoxy. Veneration of icons.	Tolerant; very little social action; divorce, remarriage permitted in some cases. Priests need not be celibate; bishops are.	Emphasis on Christ's resurrection, rather than crucifixion; the Holy Spirit proceeds from God the Father only.	Orthodox Church in America, orginally under Patriarch of Moscow, was granted autonomy in 1970. Greek Orthodox do not recognize this autonomy.	Orthodox
Loosely structured service with rousing hymns and sermons, culminating in spirit baptism.	Usually, emphasis on perfectionism with varying degrees of tolerance.	Simple traditional beliefs, usually Protestant, with emphasis on the immediate presence of God in the Holy Spirit	Once confined to lower-class "holy rollers," Pentecostalism now appears in mainline churches and has established middle-class congregations.	Pentecostal
A simple, sober service in which the sermon is central.	Traditionally, a tendency toward strictness with firm church- and self-discipline; otherwise tolerant.	Emphasizes the sovereignty and justice of God; no longer doctrinaire.	While traces of belief in predestination (that God has foreordained salvation for the "elect") remain, this idea is no longer a central element in Presbyterianism.	Presbyterians
Relatively elaborate ritual; wide variety of public and private rites, e.g., rosary recitation, processions, novenas.	Theoretically very strict; tolerant in practice on most issues. Divorce and remarriage not accepted. Celibate clergy, except in Eastern rite.	Highly elaborated. Salvation by merit gained through faith. Unusual development of doctrines surrounding Mary. Dogmatic.	Roman Catholicism went through a period of relatively rapid change as a result of Vatican Councils I and II.	Roman Catholics
Usually simple services with emphasis on the sermon.	Tolerant; some social action emphasis.	Standard Protestant; *Statement of Faith* (1959) is not binding.	The 2 main churches in the 1957 union represented earlier unions with small groups of almost every Protestant denomination.	United Church of Christ

The Major World Religions

Buddhism

Founded: About 525 BC, reportedly near Benares, India.
Founder: Gautama Siddhartha (ca. 563-480), the Buddha, who achieved enlightenment through intense meditation.
Sacred Texts: The *Tripitaka*, a collection of the Buddha's teachings, rules of monastic life, and philosophical commentaries on the teachings; also a vast body of Buddhist teachings and commentaries, many of which are called *sutras*.
Organization: The basic institution is the *sangha* or monastic order through which the traditions are passed to each generation. Monastic life tends to be democratic and anti-authoritarian. Large lay organizations have developed in some sects.
Practice: Varies widely according to the sect and ranges from austere meditation to magical chanting and elaborate temple rites. Many practices, such as exorcism of devils, reflect pre-Buddhist beliefs.
Divisions: A wide variety of sects grouped into 3 primary branches: Therevada (sole survivor of the ancient Hinayana schools) which emphasizes the importance of pure thought and deed; Mahayana, which includes Zen and Soka-gakkai, ranges from philosophical schools to belief in the saving grace of higher beings or ritual practices, and to practical meditative disciplines; and Tantrism, an unusual combination of belief in ritual magic and sophisticated philosophy.
Location: Throughout Asia, from Ceylon to Japan. Zen and Soka-gakkai have several thousand adherents in the U.S.
Beliefs: Life is misery and decay, and there is no ultimate reality in it or behind it. The cycle of endless birth and rebirth continues because of desire and attachment to the unreal "self". Right meditation and deeds will end the cycle and achieve Nirvana, the Void, nothingness.

Hinduism

Founded: Ca. 1500 BC by Aryan invaders of India where their Vedic religion intermixed with the practices and beliefs of the natives.
Sacred texts: The *Veda*, including the *Upanishads*, a collection of rituals and mythological and philosophical commentaries; a vast number of epic stories about gods, heroes and saints, including the *Bhagavadgita*, a part of the *Mahabharata*, and the *Ramayana;* and a great variety of other literature.
Organization: None, strictly speaking. Generally, rituals should be performed or assisted by Brahmins, the priestly caste, but in practice simpler rituals can be performed by anyone. Brahmins are the final judges of ritual purity, the vital element in Hindu life. Temples and religious organizations are usually presided over by Brahmins.
Practice: A variety of private rituals, primarily passage rites (eg. initiation, marriage, death, etc.) and daily devotions, and a similar variety of public rites in temples. Of the latter, the *puja*, a ceremonial dinner for a god, is the most common.
Divisions: There is no concept of orthodoxy in Hinduism, which presents a bewildering variety of sects, most of them devoted to the worship of one of the many gods. The 3 major living traditions are those devoted to the gods Vishnu and Shiva and to the goddess Shakti; each of them divided into further sub-sects. Numerous folk beliefs and practices, often in amalgamation with the above groups, exist side-by-side with sophisticated philosophical schools and exotic cults.
Location: Confined to India, except for the missionary work of Vedanta, the Krishna Consciousness society, and individual *gurus* (teachers) in the West.
Beliefs: There is only one divine principle; the many gods are only aspects of that unity. Life in all its forms is an aspect of the divine, but it appears as a separation from the divine, a meaningless cycle of birth and rebirth (*samsara*) determined by the purity or impurity of past deeds (*karma*). To improve one's *karma* or escape *samsara* by pure acts, thought, and/or devotion is the aim of every Hindu.

Islam

Founded: 622 AD in Medina, Arabian peninsula.
Founder: Mohammed (ca. 570-632), the Prophet.
Sacred texts: *Koran*, the words of God. *Hadith*, collections of the sayings of the Prophet.
Organization: Theoretically the state and religious community are one, administered by a caliph. In practice, Islam is a loose collection of congregations united by a very conservative tradition. Islam is basically egalitarian and non-authoritarian.
Practice: Every Moslem has 5 duties: to make the profession of faith ("There is no god but Allah ..."), pray 5 times a day, give a regular portion of his goods to charity, fast during the day in the month of Ramadan, and make at least one pilgrimage to Mecca if possible.
Divisions: The 2 major sects of Islam are the Sunni (orthodox) and the Shi'ah. The Shi'ah believe in 12 *imams*, perfect teachers, who still guide the faithful from Paradise. Shi'ah practice tends toward the ecstatic, while the Sunni is staid and simple. The Shi'ah sect affirms man's free will; the Sunni is deterministic. The mystic tradition in Islam is Sufism. A Sufi adept believes he has acquired a special inner knowledge direct from Allah.
Location: From the west coast of Africa to the Philipines across a broad band that includes Tanzania, southern USSR and western China, India, Malaysia and Indonesia. Islam claims over 2 million adherents in the U.S.
Beliefs: Strictly monotheistic. God is creator of the universe, omnipotent, just, and merciful. Man is God's highest creation, but limited and commits sins. He is misled by Satan, an evil spirit. God revealed the *Koran* to Mohammed to guide men to the truth. Those who repent and sincerely submit to God return to a state of sinlessness. In the end, the sinless go to Paradise, a place of physical and spiritual pleasure, and the wicked burn in Hell.

Judaism

Founded: About 1300 BCE.
Founder: Abrahm is regarded as the founding patriarch, but the Torah of Moses is the basic source of the teachings.
Sacred Texts: The five books of Moses constitute the written Torah. Special sanctity is also assigned other writings of the Hebrew Bible—the teachings of oral Torah are recorded in the Talmud, the Midrash, and various commentaries.
Organization: Originally theocratic, Judaism has evolved a congregational polity. The basic institution is the local synagogue, operated by the congregation and led by a rabbi of their choice. Chief Rabbis in France and Great Britain have authority only over those who accept it; in Israel, the 2 Chief Rabbis have civil authority in family law.
Practice: Among traditional practitioners, almost all areas of life are governed by strict religious discipline. Sabbath and holidays are marked by special observances, and attendance at public worship is regarded as especially important then. The chief annual observances are Passover, celebrating the liberation of the Israelites from Egypt and marked by the ritual Seder meal in the home, and the 10 days from Rosh Hashana (New Year) to Yom Kippur (Day of Atonement), a period of fasting and penitence.
Divisions: Judaism is an unbroken spectrum from ultra conservative to ultra liberal, largely reflecting different points of view regarding the binding character of the prohibitions and duties—particularly the dietary and Sabbath observations—prescribed in the daily life of the Jew.
Location: Almost worldwide, with concentrations in Israel and the U.S.
Beliefs: Strictly monotheistic. God is the creator and absolute ruler of the universe. Men are free to choose to rebel against God's rule. God established a particular relationship with the Hebrew people: by obeying a divine law God gave them they would be a special witness to God's mercy and justice. The emphasis in Judaism is on ethical behavior (and, among the traditional, careful ritual obedience) as the true worship of God.

STATES AND OTHER AREAS OF THE U.S.

Sources: Population: Commerce Dept., Bureau of the Census (July, 1989 provisional estimates, inc. armed forces personnel in each state but excluding such personnel stationed overseas); area: Bureau of the Census, Geography Division; forested land: Agriculture Dept., Forest Service; lumber production: Bureau of the Census, Industry Division; mineral production: Interior Dept., Bureau of Mines (preliminary); commercial fishing: Commerce Dept., Natl. Marine Fisheries Service; value of construction: McGraw-Hill Information Systems Co., F.W. Dodge Division; per capita income (estimate): Commerce Dept., Bureau of Economic Analysis; unemployment: Labor Dept., Bureau of Labor Statistics; finance: Federal Deposit Insurance Corp., U.S. League of Savings Institutions; federal employees: Labor Dept., Office of Personnel Management; energy: Energy Dept., Energy Information Administration; education: Education Dept., National Education Assn. Other information from sources in individual states, usually Commerce Dept.

Alabama

Heart of Dixie, Camellia State

People. Population (1989): 4,118,000; **rank:** 22. **Pop. density:** 79.6 per sq. mi. **Urban** (1985): 60%. **Racial distrib.** (1985): 73.8% White; 26.2% Black; Hispanic 18,300. **Net change** (1985-89): +96,000; 2.4%.

Geography. Total area: 51,705 sq. mi.; **rank:** 29. **Land area:** 50,708 sq. mi. **Acres forested land:** 21,361,100. **Location:** in the east south central U.S., extending N-S from Tenn. to the Gulf of Mexico; east of the Mississippi River. **Climate:** long, hot summers; mild winters; generally abundant rainfall. **Topography:** coastal plains inc. Prairie Black Belt give way to hills, broken terrain; highest elevation, 2,407 ft. **Capital:** Montgomery.

Economy. Principal industries: pulp and paper, chemicals, electronics, apparel, textiles, primary metals, lumber and wood, food processing, fabricated metals, automotive tires. **Principal manufactured goods** (1988-1989): electronics, cast iron and plastic pipe, fabricated steel prods., ships, paper products, chemicals, steel, mobile homes, fabrics, poultry processing. **Agriculture: Chief crops** (1988-89): peanuts, cotton, soybeans, hay, corn, wheat, potatoes, pecans, sweet potatoes, cottonseed, catfish. **Livestock** (1989): 1.8 mln. cattle; 345,000 hogs/pigs; 16.3 mln. poultry. **Timber/lumber** (1988): pine, hardwoods; 2.1 bln. bd. ft. **Nonfuel Minerals** (1989): $483 mln., mostly cement, clays, lime, sand & gravel, stone. **Commercial fishing** (1989): $38.3 mln. **Chief ports:** Mobile. **Value of construction** (1989): $2.9 bln. **Employment distribution** (1989): 24% mfg.; 21.9% trade; 18.4% serv. **Per capita income** (1989): $13,679. **Unemployment** (1989): 7.0%. **Tourism** (1988): tourists spent $2.3 bln. **Sales Tax** (1989): 4%.

Finance. FDIC-insured commercial banks & trust companies (1987): 228. **Deposits:** $23.4 bln. **Savings institutions** (1990): 36. **Assets:** $9.3 bln.

Federal government. No. federal civilian employees (Mar. 1989): 47,133. **Avg. salary:** $29,396. **Notable federal facilities:** George C. Marshall NASA Space Center, Huntsville; Gunter & Maxwell AFB, Montgomery; Ft. Rucker, Ozark; Ft. McClellan, Anniston; Natl. Fertilizer Development Center, Muscle Shoals; Navy Station & U.S. Corps of Engineers, Mobile; Redstone Arsenal, Huntsville.

Energy. Electricity production (1989, mwh, by source): Hydroelectric: 5.4 mln. Mineral: 49.2 mln. Nuclear: 13.0 mln.

Education. Student-teacher ratio (1988): 18.7. **Avg. salary, public school teachers** (1990): $25,500.

State data. Motto: We dare defend our rights. **Flower:** Camellia. **Bird:** Yellowhammer. **Tree:** Southern Pine. **Song:** Alabama. **Entered union** Dec. 14, 1819; **rank,** 22d. **State fair** at: Birmingham; early Oct.

History. First Europeans were Spanish explorers in the early 1500s. The French made the first permanent settlement, on Mobile Bay, 1701-02; later, English settled in the northern areas. France ceded the entire region to England at the end of the French and Indian War, 1763, but Spanish Florida claimed the Mobile Bay area until U.S. troops took it, 1813. Gen. Andrew Jackson broke the power of the Creek Indians, 1814, and they were removed to Oklahoma. The Confederate States were organized Feb. 4, 1861, at Montgomery, the first capital.

Tourist attractions. Jefferson Davis' "first White House" of the Confederacy; Ivy Green, Helen Keller's birthplace, Tuscumbia; statue of Vulcan, Birmingham; George Washington Carver Museum, Tuskegee Univ.; W.C. Handy Home & Museum, Florence; Alabama Space and Rocket Center, Huntsville; Alabama Shakespeare Festival, Montgomery; Moundville State Monument, Moundville; Pike Pioneer Museum, Troy, USS Alabama Memorial Park, Mobile; 28 hunting areas, 24 public lakes, 82 campgrounds, 21 state parks.

At Russell Cave National Monument, near Bridgeport: a detailed record of occupancy by humans from about 10,000 BC to 1650 AD.

Famous Alabamians include Hank Aaron, Tallulah Bankhead, Hugo L. Black, Paul "Bear" Bryant, George Washington Carver, Nat King Cole, William C. Handy, Helen Keller, Harper Lee, Joe Louis, Willie Mays, John Hunt Morgan, Jesse Owens, George Wallace, Booker T. Washington, Hank Williams.

Alabama Business Council (State Chamber of Commerce). 468 S. Perry St., P.O. Box 76, Montgomery, AL 36195; 1-800-248-5033.

Toll-free travel information. 1-800-392-8096; 1-800-ALABAMA out of state.

Alaska

Unofficial nickname: "The Last Frontier"

People. Population (1989): 527,000; **rank:** 49. **Pop. density:** 0.89 per sq. mi. **Urban** (1980): 64.3%. **Net change** (1985-89): +5,000; 1.0%.

Geography. Total area: 591,000 sq. mi.; **rank:** 1. **Land area:** 570,833 sq. mi. **Acres forested land:** 119,145,000. **Location:** NW corner of North America, bordered on east by Canada. **Climate:** SE, SW, and central regions, moist and mild; far north extremely dry. Extended summer days, winter nights, throughout. **Topography:** includes Pacific and Arctic mountain systems, central plateau, and Arctic slope. Mt. McKinley, 20,320 ft., is the highest point in North America. **Capital:** Juneau.

Economy. Principal industries: oil, gas, tourism, commercial fishing. **Principal manufactured goods:** fish products, lumber and pulp, furs. **Agriculture** (1988): Chief crops: barley, hay, greenhouse nursery prods., potatoes, lettuce, milk. **Livestock** (1988): 9,500 cattle; 2,400 sheep; 6,000 poultry; 23,000 reindeer. **Timber/lumber:** spruce, yellow cedar, hemlock. **Nonfuel minerals** (1989): $252 mln.; gold, sand & gravel, crushed and broken stone. **Commercial fishing** (1989): $1.2 bln. **Chief ports:** Anchorage, Dutch Harbor, Kodiak, Seward, Skagway, Juneau, Sitka, Valdez, Wrangell. **International airports at:** Anchorage, Fairbanks, Ketchikan, Juneau. **Value of construction** (1989): $609 mln. **Employment distribution** (1989): 30.8% gvt.; 20.3% serv.; 19.9% trade. **Per capita income** (1989): $21,173. **Unemployment** (1989): 6.7%. **Tourism** (1987-88): $500 mln.

Finance. Commercial bank deposits, per capita (1985): $7,475. **Savings institutions** (1990): 3. **Assets:** $287 mln.

Federal government. No. federal civilian employees (Mar. 1989): 11,528. **Avg. salary:** $33,501.

Energy. Electricity production (1988, mwh, by source): Hydroelectric: 935,000. Mineral: 3.3 mln.

Education. Student-teacher ratio (1988): 17.0. **Avg. salary, public school teachers** (1990.): $43,153.

State data. Motto: North to the future. **Flower:** Forget-Me-Not. **Bird:** Willow Ptarmigan. **Tree:** Sitka Spruce. **Song:** Alaska's Flag. **Entered union:** Jan. 3, 1959; rank, 49th. **State fair at:** Palmer; late Aug.—early Sept.

History. Vitus Bering, a Danish explorer working for Russia, was the first European to land in Alaska, 1741. Alexander Baranov, first governor of Russian America, set up headquarters at Archangel, near present Sitka, in 1799. Secretary of State William H. Seward in 1867 bought Alaska from Russia for $7.2 million, a bargain some called "Seward's Folly." In 1896 gold was discovered and the famed Gold Rush was on.

Tourist attractions: Portage Glacier, Mendenhall Glacier, Glacier Bay National Park, Katmai National Park & Preserve, Denali National Park, one of North America's great wildlife sanctuaries, surrounding Mt. McKinley, No. America's highest peak. Pribilof Islands fur seal rookeries, restored St. Michael's Russian Orthodox Cathedral, Sitka.

Famous Alaskans include Tom Bodett, Susan Butcher, Ernest Gruening, Sydney Laurence, Libby Riddles, Jefferson "Soapy" Smith.

Tourist information. Alaska Division of Tourism, P.O. Box E, Juneau, AK 99811-0800.

Arizona

Grand Canyon State

People. Population (1989): 3,556,000; **rank:** 24. **Pop. density:** 31.2 per sq. mi. **Urban** (1980): 83.8% **Racial distrib.** (1985): 91.6% White; 2.0% Black; 6.6% Other (includes American Indians); Hispanic 533,200. **Net change** (1985-89): +395,000; 12.5%.

Geography. Total area: 114,000 sq. mi.; **rank:** 6. **Land area:** 113,508 sq. mi. **Acres forested land:** 18,493,900. **Location:** in the southwestern U.S. **Climate:** clear and dry in the southern regions and northern plateau; high central areas have heavy winter snows. **Topography:** Colorado plateau in the N, containing the Grand Canyon; Mexican Highlands running diagonally NW to SE; Sonoran Desert in the SW. **Capital:** Phoenix.

Economy. Principal industries: manufacturing, tourism, mining, agriculture. **Principal manufactured goods:** electronics, printing and publishing, foods, primary and fabricated metals, aircraft and missiles, apparel. **Agriculture:** Chief crops: cotton, sorghum, barley, corn, wheat, sugar beets, citrus fruits. **Livestock** (1989): 830,000 cattle; 100,000 hogs/pigs; 262,000 sheep; 320,000 poultry. **Timber/lumber** (1988): pine, fir, spruce; 435 mln. bd. ft. **Nonfuel Minerals** (1989): $3.2 bln.; copper, molybdenum, gold, silver. **International airports at:** Phoenix, Tucson, Yuma. **Value of construction** (1989): $5.0 bln. **Employment distribution** (1989): 26.7% services; 25.2% trade; 16.9% gvt.; 12.9% mfg. **Per capita income** (1989): $15,881. **Unemployment** (1989): 5.2%. **Tourism** (1989): tourists spent $5.6 bln. **Sales tax:** 5.0% (Maricopa, Pinal Countries, 5.5%).

Finance. FDIC-insured commercial bank & trust companies (1987): 54. **Deposits:** $23.8 bln. **Savings institutions** (1990): 12. **Assets:** $20.4 bln.

Federal government. No. federal civilian employees (Mar. 1989): 28,149. **Avg. salary:** $27,195. **Notable federal facilities:** Williams, Luke, Davis-Monthan AF bases; Ft. Huachuca Army Base; Yuma Proving Grounds.

Energy. Electricity production (1989, mwh, by source): Hydroelectric: 7.8 mln.; Mineral: 30.8; Nuclear: 22.9.

Education. Student-teacher ratio (1988): 18.1. **Avg. salary, public school teachers** (1990): $29,600.

State data. Motto: Ditat Deus (God enriches). **Flower:** Blossom of the Saguaro cactus. **Bird:** Cactus wren. **Tree:** Paloverde. **Song:** Arizona. **Entered union** Feb. 14, 1912; rank, 48th. **State fair** at: Phoenix; late Oct.–early Nov.

History. Marcos de Niza, a Franciscan, and Estevan, a black slave, explored the area, 1539. Eusebio Francisco Kino, Jesuit missionary, taught Indians Christianity and farming, 1690-1711, left a chain of missions. Spain ceded Arizona to Mexico, 1821. The U. S. took over at the end of the Mexican War, 1848. The area below the Gila River was obtained from Mexico in the Gadsden Purchase, 1854. Long Apache wars did not end until 1886, with Geronimo's surrender.

Tourist attractions. The Grand Canyon of the Colorado, an immense, vari-colored fissure 217 mi. long, 4 to 13 mi. wide at the brim, 4,000 to 5,500 ft. deep; the Painted Desert, extending for 30 mi. along U.S. 66; the Petrified Forest; Canyon Diablo, 225 ft. deep and 500 ft. wide; Meteor Crater, 4,150 ft. across, 570 ft. deep, made by a prehistoric meteor. Also, London Bridge at Lake Havasu City.

Famous Arizonans include Cochise, Geronimo, Barry Goldwater, Zane Grey, Carl Hayden, George W. P. Hunt, Helen Jacobs, Percival Lowell, Sandra Day O'Connor, William H. Pickering, John J. Rhodes, Morris Udall, Stewart Udall, Frank Lloyd Wright.

Tourist information. Phoenix & Valley of the Sun Visitor and Convention Bureau, 1-602-254-6500.

Arkansas

Land of Opportunity

People. Population (1989): 2,406,000; **rank:** 33. **Pop. density:** 46.2 per sq. mi. **Urban** (1980): 51.5%. **Racial distrib.** (1985): 83.4% White; 16.6% Black; Hispanic 13,500. **Net change** (1985-89): +46,000; 1.9%.

Geography. Total area: 53,187 sq. mi.; **rank:** 27. **Land area:** 52,078 sq. mi. **Acres forested land:** 18,281,500. **Location:** in the west south-central U.S. **Climate:** long, hot summers; mild winters; generally abundant rainfall. **Topography:** eastern delta and prairie, southern lowland forests, and the northwestern highlands, which include the Ozark Plateaus. **Capital:** Little Rock.

Economy. Principal industries: manufacturing, agriculture, tourism, forestry. **Principal manufactured goods:** food prods., chemicals, lumber, paper, electric motors, furniture, home appliances, auto components, airplane parts, apparel, machinery, petroleum prods. **Agriculture:** Chief crops: soybeans, rice, cotton, tomatoes, watermelons, winegrapes, blueberries, apples, commercial vegetables. **Livestock** (1988): 1.75 mln. cattle; 540,000 hogs/pigs; $1.65 bln. poultry. **Timber/lumber** (1988): oak, hickory, gum, cypress, pine; 1.5 bln. bd. ft. **Nonfuel Minerals** (1989): $342 mln.; abrasives, bauxite, bromine. **Commercial fishing** (1986): $7.3 mln. **Chief ports:** Little Rock, Pine Bluff, Osceola, Helena, Fort Smith, Van Buren, Camden, Dardanelle, North Little Rock, West Memphis, Crosset. **Value of construction** (1989): $1.8 bln. **Employment distribution** (1989): 21.8% mfg.; 19.4% trade; 16.5% serv.; 4.1% agric. **Per capita income** (1989): $12,984. **Unemployment** (1989): 7.2% **Tourism** (1988): travelers spent $2.1 bln.

Finance. FDIC-insured commercial banks & trust companies (1987): 256. **Deposits:** $15.9 bln. **Savings institutions** (1990): 34. **Assets:** $5.3 bln.

Federal government. No. federal civilian employees (Mar. 1989): 12,414. **Avg. salary:** $26,306. **Notable federal facilities:** Nat'l. Center for Toxicological Research, Jefferson; Pine Bluff Arsenal, Little Rock AFB.

Energy. Electricity production (1987, mwh, by source): Hydroelectric: 2.8 mln.; Mineral: 22.1 mln.; Nuclear: 8.9 mln.

Education. Student-teacher ratio (1988): 15.7. **Avg. salary, public school teachers** (1990): $22,000.

State data. Motto: Regnat Populus (The people rule). **Flower:** Apple Blossom. **Bird:** Mockingbird. **Tree:** Pine. **Song:** Arkansas. **Entered union:** June 15, 1836; rank, 25th. **State fair at:** Little Rock; late Sept.- early Oct.

History. First European explorers were de Soto, 1541, Jolliet, 1673; La Salle, 1682. First settlement was by the French under Henri de Tonty, 1686, at Arkansas Post. In 1762 the area was ceded by France to Spain, then back again in 1800, and was part of the Louisiana Purchase by the U.S. in 1803. Arkansas seceded from the Union in 1861, only after the Civil War began, and more than 10,000 Arkansans fought on the Union side.

Tourist attractions. 5 natl. parks & 45 state parks, inc. Hot Springs National Park, water ranging from 95° to 147°F. Eureka Springs, resort since 1880s; Blanchard Caverns, near Mountain View, are among the nation's largest; Crater of Diamonds, near Murfreesboro, only U.S. diamond mine; Buffalo Natl. River; Mid-America Museum, Ozark Folk Center.

Famous Arkansans include Dee Brown, Glen Campbell, Johnny Cash, Hattie Caraway, "Dizzy" Dean, Orval Faubus, James W. Fulbright, Douglas MacArthur, John L. McClellan, James S. McDonnel, Dick Powell, Winthrop Rockefeller, Mary Steenburgen, Edward Durell Stone, Archibald Yell.

Chamber of Commerce. One Spring Bldg., Little Rock, AR 72201.

Toll-free travel information. 1-800-828-8974.

California
Golden State

People. Population (1989): 29,063,000; **rank:** 1. **Pop. density:** 185.9 per sq. mi. **Urban** (1985): 91.3%. **Racial distrib.** (1985): 85.6% White; 7.8% Black; 6.6% Other (includes American Indians, Asian Americans, and Pacific Islanders); Hispanic 5.9%. **Net change** (1985-89): +2,709; 10.3%.

Geography. Total area 158,706 sq. mi.; **rank:** 3. **Land area:** 156,299 sq. mi. **Acres forested land:** 40,152,100. **Location:** on western coast of the U.S. **Climate:** moderate temperatures and rainfall along the coast; extremes in the interior. **Topography:** long mountainous coastline; central valley; Sierra Nevada on the east; desert basins of the southern interior; rugged mountains of the north. **Capital:** Sacramento.

Economy. Principal industries: agriculture, manufacturing, services, trade. **Principal manufactured goods:** foods, primary and fabricated metals, machinery, electric and electronic equipment, transportation equipment. **Agriculture: Chief crops:** grapes, cotton, flowers, oranges, nursery products, hay, tomatoes, lettuce, strawberries, almonds, broccoli, walnuts, sugar beets, peaches, potatoes. **Livestock** (1990): 4.9 mln. cattle & calves; 140,000 hogs/pigs; 955,000 sheep; 281.5 mln. poultry. **Timber/lumber** (1988): fir, pine, redwood, oak; 4.9 bln. bd. ft. **Nonfuel Minerals:** (1989): $2.84 bln.; mostly asbestos, boron minerals, cement, diatomite, calcined gypsum, construction sand & gravel. **Commercial fishing** (1989): $123.3 mln. **Chief ports:** Long Beach, San Diego, Oakland, San Francisco, Sacramento, Stockton. **International airports at:** Los Angeles, San Francisco, San Jose. **Value of construction** (1989): $41.5 bln. **Employment distribution** (1989): 26.3% serv.; 23.7% trade; 17.2% mfg.; 15.9% gvt. **Per capita income** (1989): $19,740. **Unemployment** (1989): 5.1% **Tourism** (1989): $39.9 bln. **Sales tax:** 6-7%.

Finance. FDIC-insured commercial banks & trust companies (1987): 484. **Deposits:** $241 bln. **Savings institutions** (1990): 182. **Assets:** $370.5 bln.

Federal government. No. federal civilian employees (Mar. 1989): 212,217. **Avg. salary:** $29,008. **Notable federal facilities:** Vandenberg, Beale, Travis, McClellan AF bases, San Francisco Mint.

Energy. Electricity production (1989, mwh, by source): Hydroelectric: 23.5 mln.; Mineral: 61.5 mln.; Nuclear: 30.9 mln.

Education. Student-teacher ratio (1988): 22.7. **Avg. salary, public school teachers** (1988): $38,996.

State Data. Motto: Eureka (I have found it). **Flower:** Golden poppy. **Bird:** California valley quail. **Tree:** California redwood. **Song:** I Love You, California. **Entered Union** Sept. 9, 1850; **rank,** 31st. **State fair at:** Sacramento; late Aug.—early Sept.

History. First European explorers were Cabrillo, 1542, and Drake, 1579. First settlement was the Spanish Alta California mission at San Diego, 1769, first in a string founded by Franciscan Father Junipero Serra. U. S. traders and settlers arrived in the 19th century and staged the abortive Bear Flag Revolt, 1846; the Mexican War began later in 1846 and U.S. forces occupied California; Mexico ceded the province to the U.S., 1848, the same year the Gold Rush began.

Tourist attractions. Scenic regions are Yosemite Valley; Lassen and Sequoia-Kings Canyon national parks; Lake Tahoe; the Mojave and Colorado deserts; San Francisco Bay; and Monterey Peninsula. Oldest living things on earth are believed to be a stand of Bristlecone pines in the Inyo National Forest, est. to be 4,600 years old. The world's tallest tree, the Howard Libbey redwood, 362 ft. with a girth of 44 ft., stands on Redwood Creek, Humboldt County.

Also, RMS Queen Mary, Spruce Goose, both Long Beach; Palomar Observatory; Disneyland; J. Paul Getty Museum, Malibu; Tournament of Roses and Rose Bowl.

Famous Californians include Luther Burbank, John C. Fremont, Bret Harte, Wm. R. Hearst, Jack London, Aimee Semple McPherson, John Muir, Richard M. Nixon, William Saroyan, Junipero Serra, Leland Stanford, John Steinbeck, Earl Warren.

Chamber of Commerce: 1027 10th, Sacramento, CA 95814.

Toll-free travel information. 1-800-862-2543, x T100.

Colorado
Centennial State

People. Population (1989): 3,317,000; **rank:** 26. **Pop. density:** 31.9 per sq. mi. **Urban** (1980): 80.6%. **Racial distrib.** (1985): 96.3% White; 3.7% Black; Hispanic 383,500. **Net change** (1985-89): +65,000; 2.6%.

Geography. Total area: 104,091 sq. mi.; **rank:** 8. **Land area:** 103,595 sq. mi. **Acres forested land:** 22,271,000. **Location:** in west central U.S. **Climate:** low relative humidity, abundant sunshine, wide daily, seasonal temperatures ranges; alpine conditions in the high mountains. **Topography:** eastern dry high plains; hilly to mountainous central plateau; western Rocky Mountains of high ranges alternating with broad valleys and deep, narrow canyons. **Capital:** Denver.

Economy. Principal industries: manufacturing, government, tourism, agriculture, aerospace, electronics equipment. **Principal manufactured goods:** computer equipment, instruments, foods, machinery, aerospace products. **Agriculture: Chief crops:** corn, wheat, hay, sugar beets, barley, potatoes, apples, peaches, pears, dry edible beans, sorghum, onions, oats. **Livestock** (1989): 2.8 mln. cattle; 220,000 hogs/pigs; 825,000 sheep; 4.0 mln. poultry. **Timber/lumber** (1988): oak, ponderosa pine, Douglas fir; 147 mln. bd. ft. **Nonfuel Minerals** (1989): $443 mln.; gold, construction sand & gravel, crushed stone. **International airports at:** Denver. **Value of construction** (1989): $2.8 bln. **Employment distribution** (1987 est.): 26.7% serv.; 20.8% trade; 17.0% gvt.; 10.0% mfg. **Per capita income** (1989): $17,494. **Unemployment** (1989): 5.8%. **Tourism** (1989): $5.6 bln. **Sales Tax:** 3%.

Finance. FDIC-insured commercial banks & trust companies (1987): 471. **Deposits:** $21.6 bln. **Savings institutions** (1990): 35. **Assets:** $13.3 bln.

Federal government. No. federal civilian employees (Mar. 1989): 36,286. **Avg. salary:** $29,939. **Notable federal facilities:** U.S. Air Force Academy; U.S. Mint; Ft. Carson, Lowry AFB; Solar Energy Research Institute; U.S. Rail Transport. Test Center; N. Amer. Aerospace Defense Command; Consolidated Space Operations Center; U.S. Documents Center, Fitzsimons Army Medical Center, Federal Center.

Energy. Electricity production (1989, mwh, by source): Hydroelectric: 1.7 mln.; Mineral: 28.5 mln. Nuclear: 0.6 mln.

Education. Student-teacher ratio (1988): 17.8. **Avg. salary, public school teachers** (1990): $30,700.

State data. Motto: Nil Sine Numine (Nothing without Providence). **Flower:** Rocky Mountain columbine. **Bird:** Lark bunting. **Tree:** Colorado blue spruce. **Song:** Where the Columbines Grow. Entered union Aug. 1, 1876; rank 38th. **State fair** at: Pueblo; last week in Aug.

History. Early civilization centered around Mesa Verde 2,000 years ago. The U.S. acquired eastern Colorado in the Louisiana Purchase, 1803; Lt. Zebulon M. Pike explored the area, 1806, discovering the peak that bears his name. After the Mexican War, 1846-48, U.S. immigrants settled in the east, former Mexicans in the south.

Tourist attractions. 310 or more sunshine days per year; more than 1,000 peaks of 2 or more miles; Rocky Mountain National Park; Garden of the Gods; Great Sand Dunes, Dinosaur, Black Canyon of the Gunnison, and Colorado national monuments; Pikes Peak and Mt. Evans highways; Mesa Verde National Park (Ancient Anasazi Indian cliff dwellings); 35 major ski areas; the Grand Mesa tableland comprises Grand Mesa Forest, 659,584 acres, with 200 lakes stocked with trout. Mining towns of Central City, Silverton, Cripple Creek; Burlington's Old Town; Bent's Fort, outside La Junta; Georgetown Loop Historic Mining Railroad Park, Cumbres & Toltec Scenic Railroad.

Famous Coloradans include Frederick Bonfils, Molly Brown, William N. Byers, M. Scott Carpenter, Jack Dempsey, Mamie Eisenhower, Douglas Fairbanks, Scott Hamilton, "Baby Doe" Tabor, Lowell Thomas, Byron R. White, Paul Whiteman.

Toll-free travel information. 1-800-433-2656.

Connecticut

Constitution State, Nutmeg State

People. Population (1989): 3,239,000; **rank:** 27. **Pop. density:** 645.5 per sq. mi. **Urban** (1980): 78.8% **Racial distrib.** (1985): 92.3% White; 7.7% Black; Hispanic 139,200. **Net change** (1985-89): +62,000; 2.0%.

Geography. Total area: 5,018 sq. mi.; **rank:** 48. **Land area:** 4,872 sq. mi. **Acres forested land:** 1,860,800. **Location:** New England state in the northeastern corner of the U.S. **Climate:** moderate; winters avg. slightly below freezing, warm, humid summers. **Topography:** western upland, the Berkshires, in the NW, highest elevations; narrow central lowland N-S; hilly eastern upland drained by rivers. **Capital:** Hartford.

Economy. Principal industries: manufacturing, retail trade, government, services, finances, insurance, real estate. **Principal manufactured goods:** aircraft engines and parts, submarines, helicopters, instruments, machinery & computer equipment, electronics & electrical equipment. **Agriculture: Chief crops:** nursery stock, vegetables, sweet corn, tobacco, apples. **Livestock** (1989): 73,000 cattle; 6,800 hogs/pigs; 8,400 sheep; 5.6 mln. poultry. **Timber/lumber:** oak, birch, beech, maple. **Nonfuel Minerals** (1989): $115 mln; crushed stone; construction sand & gravel. **Commercial fishing** (1989): $18.3 mln. **Chief ports:** New Haven, Bridgeport, New London. **International airports at:** Windsor Locks. **Value of construction** (1989): $3.6 bln. **Employment distribution** (1989): 21.4% mfg.; 25.3% serv. **Per capita income** (1989): $24,604. **Unemployment** (1989): 3.7%. **Tourism** (1989): out-of-state visitors spent $3.2 bln. **Sales tax:** 8.0%.

Finance. FDIC-insured commercial banks & trust companies (1987): 59. **Deposits:** $26.7 bln. **Savings institutions** (1990): 26. **Assets:** $92.5 bln.

Federal Government. No. federal civilian employees (Mar. 1989): 9,403. **Avg. salary:** $30,696. **Notable federal facilities:** U.S. Coast Guard Academy; U.S. Navy Submarine Base.

Energy. Electricity production (1989, mwh, by source): Hydroelectric: 324,000; Mineral: 13.6 mln.; Nuclear: 22.3 mln.

Education. Student-teacher ratio (1988): 13.1. **Avg. salary, public school teachers** (1990): $40,496.

State data. Motto: Qui Transtulit Sustinet (He who transplanted still sustains). **Flower:** Mountain laurel. **Bird:** American robin. **Tree:** White oak. **Song:** Yankee Doodle Dandy. **Fifth** of the 13 original states to ratify the Constitution, Jan. 9, 1788.

History. Adriaen Block, Dutch explorer, was the first European visitor, 1614. By 1634, settlers from Plymouth Bay started colonies along the Connecticut River and in 1637 defeated the Pequot Indians. In the Revolution, Connecticut men fought in most major campaigns and turned back British raids on Danbury and other towns, while Connecticut privateers captured British merchant ships.

Tourist attractions. Mark Twain House, Hartford; Yale University's Art Gallery, Peabody Museum, all in New Haven; Mystic Seaport; Mystic Marine Life Aquarium; P.T. Barnum Museum, Bridgeport; Gillette Castle, Hadlyme; U.S.S. Nautilus Memorial, Groton (1st nuclear-powered submarine).

Famous "Nutmeggers" include Ethan Allen, Phineas T. Barnum, Samuel Colt, Jonathan Edwards, Nathan Hale, Katharine Hepburn, Isaac Hull, J. Pierpont Morgan, Israel Putnam, Harriet Beecher Stowe, Mark Twain, Noah Webster, Eli Whitney.

Tourist information. State Dept. of Economic Development, 865 Brook St., Rocky Hill, CT 06067.

Toll-free travel information. 1-800-CT-BOUND (282-6863).

Delaware

First State, Diamond State

People. Population (1989): 673,000; **rank:** 46. **Pop. density:** 329.1 per sq. mi. **Urban** (1980): 70.6%. **Racial distrib.** (1985): 82.9% White; 17.1% Black; Hispanic 10,000. **Net change** (1985-89): +47,000; 7.5%.

Geography. Total area: 2,045 sq. mi.; **rank:** 49. **Land area:** 1,932 sq. mi. **Acres forested land:** 391,800. **Location:** occupies the Delmarva Peninsula on the Atlantic coastal plain. **Climate:** moderate. **Topography:** Piedmont plateau to the N, sloping to a near sea-level plain. **Capital:** Dover.

Economy. Principal industries: chemistry, agriculture, finance, poultry, shellfish, tourism, auto assembly, food processing, transportation equipment. **Principal manufactured goods:** nylon, apparel, luggage, foods, autos, processed meats and vegetables, railroad and aircraft equipment. **Agriculture: Chief crops:** soybeans, potatoes, corn, mushrooms, lima beans, green peas, barley, cucumbers, snap beans, watermelons, apples. **Livestock** (1988): 29,000 cattle; 217.5 mln. broilers. **Nonfuel Minerals** (1989): $6 mln; construction sand & gravel, magnesium compounds, greensand marl. **Commercial fishing** (1989): $3.5 mln. **Chief ports:** Wilmington. **International airports at:** Philadelphia/Wilmington. **Value of construction** (1989): $877.3 mln. **Employment distribution** (1988): 78.9% non-manufacturing; 21.1% mfg. **Per capita income** (1989): $19,116. **Unemployment** (1989): 3.5%. **Tourism** (1985): out-of-state visitors spent $666 mln.

Finance. FDIC-insured commercial banks & trust companies (1987): 42. **Deposits:** $16.4 bln. **Savings institutions** (1990): 4. **Assets:** $5.1 bln.

Federal government. No. federal civilian employees (Mar. 1989): 2,960. **Avg. salary:** $27,377. **Notable federal facilities:** Dover Air Force Base, Federal Wildlife Refuge, Bombay Hook.

Energy. Electricity production (1988, mwh, by source): Mineral: 9.0 mln.

Education. Student-teacher ratio (1988): 16.4. **Avg. salary, public school teachers** (1990): $33,480.

State data. Motto: Liberty and independence. **Flower:** Peach blossom. **Bird:** Blue hen chicken. **Tree:** American holly. **Song:** Our Delaware. **First** of original 13 states to ratify the Constitution, Dec. 7, 1787. **State fair** at: Harrington; end of July.

History. The Dutch first settled in Delaware near present Lewes, 1631, but were wiped out by Indians. Swedes settled at present Wilmington, 1638; Dutch settled anew, 1651, near New Castle and seized the Swedish settlement, 1655, only to lose all Delaware and New Netherland to the British, 1664.

Tourist attractions. Ft. Christina Monument, the site of founding of New Sweden; John Dickinson "Penman of the

Revolution" home, Dover; Henry Francis du Pont Winterthur Museum; Hagley Museum, Wilmington; Rehoboth Beach, "nation's summer capitol," Rehoboth; Dover Downs Intl. Speedway, Dover; Old Swedes (Trinity Parish) Church, erected 1698, is the oldest Protestant church in the U.S. still in use.

Famous Delawareans include Thomas F. Bayard, Henry Seidel Canby, E. I. du Pont, John P. Marquand, Howard Pyle, Caesar Rodney.

Chamber of Commerce. One Commerce Center, Wilmington, DE 19801.

Toll-free travel information. 1-800-441-8846.

Florida
Sunshine State

People. Population (1989): 12,671,000; **rank: 4. Pop. density:** 216.0 per sq. mi. **Urban** (1980): 84.3%. **Racial distrib.** (1985): 86.1% White; 13.9% Black; Hispanic 1.1 mln. **Net change** (1985-89): +1.3 mln.; 11.5%.

Geography. Total area: 58,664 sq. mi.; **rank: 22. Land area:** 54,153 sq. mi. **Acres forested land:** 17,039,700. **Location:** peninsula jutting southward 500 mi. bet. the Atlantic and the Gulf of Mexico. **Climate:** subtropical N of Bradenton-Lake Okeechobee-Vero Beach line; tropical S of line. **Topography:** land is flat or rolling; highest point is 345 ft. in the NW. **Capital:** Tallahassee.

Economy. Principal industries: services, trade, gvt., manufacturing, tourism. **Principal manufactured goods:** electric & electronic equip., transp. equipment; food; printing & publishing; machinery. **Agriculture: Chief crops:** citrus fruits, vegetables, potatoes, melons, strawberries, sugar cane. **Livestock** (1987): 1.97 mln. cattle; 150,000 hogs/pigs; 7,360 sheep; 13.5 mln. poultry. **Timber/lumber** (1988): pine, cypress, cedar; 602 mln. bd. ft. **Nonfuel Minerals** (1989): $1.6 bln.; mostly cement, phosphate rock, crushed stone. **Commercial fishing** (1989): $185.9 mln. **Chief ports:** Pensacola, Tampa, Miami, Port Everglades, Jacksonville, St. Petersburg, Canaveral. **International airports at:** Miami, Tampa, Jacksonville, Orlando, Ft. Lauderdale, W. Palm Beach. **Value of construction** (1989): $20.5 bln. **Per capita income** (1989): $17,694. **Unemployment** (1989): 5.6% **Tourism** (1989): out-of-state visitors spent $24.3 bln. **Sales tax:** 6%.

Finance. FDIC-insured commercial banks & trust companies (1987): 417. **Deposits:** $87.2 bln. **Savings institutions** (1990): 141. **Assets:** $79.4 bln.

Federal government. No. federal civilian employees (Mar. 1989): 61,458. **Avg. salary:** $28,999. **Notable federal facilities:** John F. Kennedy Space Center, NASA-Kennedy Space Center's Spaceport USA; Eglin Air Force Base.

Energy. Electricity production (1989, mwh, by source): Hydroelectric: 209,000; Mineral: 97.7 mln.; Nuclear: 26.2 mln.

Education. Student-teacher ratio (1988): 17.1. **Avg. salary, public school teachers** (1990): $28,525.

State data. Motto: In God we trust. **Flower:** Orange blossom. **Bird:** Mockingbird. **Tree:** Sabal palmetto palm. **Song:** Old Folks at Home. **Entered union** Mar. 3, 1845; rank, 27th. **State fair at:** Tampa; early to mid-Feb.

History. First European to see Florida was Ponce de Leon, 1513. France established a colony, Fort Caroline, on the St. Johns River, 1564; Spain settled St. Augustine, 1565, and Spanish troops massacred most of the French. Britain's Francis Drake burned St. Augustine, 1586. Britain held the area briefly, 1763-83, returning it to Spain. After Andrew Jackson led a U.S. invasion, 1818, Spain ceded Florida to the U.S., 1819. The Seminole War, 1835-42, resulted in removal of most Indians to Oklahoma. Florida seceded from the Union, 1861, was readmitted, 1868.

Tourist attractions. Miami, with a variety of luxury hotels at Miami Beach; St. Augustine, oldest city in U.S.; Walt Disney World's Magic Kingdom and EPCOT; Spaceport U.S.A.

Everglades National Park preserves the beauty of the vast Everglades swamp. Castillo de San Marcos, St. Au-

gustine, is a national monument. Also, the Ringling Museum of Art, and the Ringling Museum of the Circus, both in Sarasota; Sea World, Orlando; Busch Gardens, Tampa; Universal Studios.

Famous Floridians include Henry M. Flagler, James Weldon Johnson, MacKinlay Kantor, Henry B. Plant, Marjorie Kinnan Rawlings, Joseph W. Stilwell, Charles P. Summerall.

Tourist information. Florida Division of Tourism, 126 Van Buren St., Tallahassee, FL 32399-2000, 1-904-487-1462.

Georgia
Empire State of the South, Peach State

People. Population (1989): 6,436,000; **rank: 11. Pop. density:** 109.3 per sq. mi. **Urban** (1980): 62.4%. **Racial distrib.** (1985): 73.0% White; 27.0% Black; Hispanic 47,700. **Net** (1985-89): +460,000; 7.7%.

Geography. Total area: 58,910 sq. mi.; **rank: 21. Land area:** 58,056 sq. mi. **Acres forested land:** 25,256,000. **Location:** South Atlantic state. **Climate:** maritime tropical air masses dominate in summer; continental polar air masses in winter; east central area drier. **Topography:** most southerly of the Blue Ridge Mtns. cover NE and N central; central Piedmont extends to the fall line of rivers; coastal plain levels to the coast flatlands. **Capital:** Atlanta.

Economy. Principal industries: manufacturing, forestry, agriculture, chemicals. **Principal manufactured goods** (1989): textiles, apparel, food, electric, electronic machinery, transportation equipment, lumber, paper. **Agriculture: Chief crops:** (1989): peanuts, soybeans, corn, tobacco, cotton, corn. **Livestock** (1989): 7.9 mln. poultry; 1.5 mln. cattle; 500,000 hogs/pigs; 8,726 sheep; **Timber/lumber** (1988): pine, hardwood; 2.6 bln. bd. ft. **Nonfuel Minerals** (1989): $1.2 bln.; clays, crushed stone. **Commercial fishing** (1989): $19.8 mln. **Chief ports:** Savannah, Brunswick. **International airports at:** Atlanta. **Value of construction** (1989): $7.8 bln. **Employment distribution:** 26% trade; 21% serv.; 19% mfg.; 17% gvt. **Per capita income** (1989): $16,188. **Unemployment** (1989): 5.5%. **Tourism** (1989): tourists spent $9.1 bln. **Sales tax:** 4%.

Finance. FDIC-insured commercial banks & trust companies (1987): 369. **Deposits:** $39.0 bln. **Savings institutions** (1990): 69. **Assets:** $18.9 bln.

Federal government. No. federal civilian employees (Mar. 1989): 67,518. **Avg. salary:** $27,824. **Notable federal facilities:** Dobbins AFB, Fts. Benning, Gordon, McPherson; Fed. Law Enforcement Training Ctr., Glynco, Warner Robins AFB; Centers for Disease Control, Atlanta.

Energy. Electricity production (1987, mwh, by source): Hydroelectric: 2.0 mln.; Mineral: 64.9 mln.; Nuclear: 15.2 mln.

Education. Student-teacher ratio (1988): 18.5. **Avg. salary, public school teachers** (1990): $27,892.

State data. Motto: Wisdom, justice and moderation. **Flower:** Cherokee rose. **Bird:** Brown thrasher. **Tree:** Live oak. **Song:** Georgia On My Mind. **Fourth** of the 13 original states to ratify the Constitution, Jan. 2, 1788.

History. Gen. James Oglethorpe established the first settlements, 1733, for poor and religiously-persecuted Englishmen. Oglethorpe defeated a Spanish army from Florida at Bloody Marsh, 1742. In the Revolution, Georgians seized the Savannah armory, 1775, and sent the munitions to the Continental Army; they fought seesaw campaigns with Cornwallis' British troops, twice liberating Augusta and forcing final evacuation by the British from Savannah, 1782.

Tourist attractions. Atlanta area: State Capitol, Stone Mt. Park, Six Flags over Georgia, Kennesaw Mt. Natl. Battlefield Park, Martin Luther King Center, Underground Atlanta, Jimmy Carter Lib. & Museum. NW: Chickamauga Battlefield Park, Chattahoochee Natl. Forest. NE: alpine village of Helen; Dahlonega, site of America's first gold rush; Brasstown Bald Mt., Lake Lanier. SW: Roosevelt's Little White House, Callaway Gardens, Andersonville Natl. Historic Site. SE: Okefenokee Swamp. Coastal: Jekyll Island, St. Simons Island, Cumberland Island Natl. Seashore, historic riverfront district in Savannah, Ft. Pulaski.

Famous Georgians include Hank Aaron, Griffin Bell, James Bowie, Erskine Caldwell, Jimmy Carter, Ray Charles, Lucius D. Clay, Ty Cobb, John C. Fremont, Joel Chandler Harris, Gladys Knight, Juliette Gordon Low, Martin Luther King Jr., Sidney Lanier, Margaret Mitchell, Flannery O'Connor, Jackie Robinson, Joseph Wheeler.

Chamber of Commerce. 235 International Blvd., Atlanta, GA 30303.

Toll-free travel information. 1-800-VISIT GA.

Hawaii
The Aloha State

People. Population (1989): 1,112,000; **rank:** 39. **Pop. density:** 171.8 per sq. mi. **Urban** (1980): 86.5%. **Racial distrib.** (1985): 24.5% Caucasian; 23.2% Japanese; 11.3% Filipino; 20% Hawaiian and part-Hawaiian. **Net change** (1985-89): +63,000; 6.0%.

Geography. Total area: 6,471 sq. mi.; **rank:** 47. **Land area:** 6,425 sq. mi. **Acres forested land:** 1,986,000. **Location:** Hawaiian Islands lie in the North Pacific, 2,397 mi. SW from San Francisco. **Climate:** subtropical, with wide variations in rainfall; Waialeale, on Kauai, wettest spot in U.S. (annual rainfall 444 in.) **Topography:** islands are tops of a chain of submerged volcanic mountains; active volcanoes: Mauna Loa, Kilauea. **Capital:** Honolulu.

Economy. Principal industries: tourism, defense and other government, sugar refining, pineapple and diversified agriculture, aquaculture, fishing, motion pictures. **Principal manufactured goods:** sugar, canned pineapple, clothing, foods, printing and publishing. **Agriculture: Chief crops:** sugar, pineapples, macadamia nuts, fruits, coffee, vegetables, melons, and floriculture. **Livestock** (1988): 208,000 cattle and calves; 43,000 hogs/pigs; 1.22 mln. chickens. **Nonfuel Minerals** (1989): $93 mln.; mostly crushed stone & cement. **Commercial fishing** (1989): $47.1 mln. **Chief ports:** Honolulu, Nawiliwili, Barbers Point, Kahului, Hilo. **International airports at:** Honolulu. **Value of construction** (1989): $2.0 bln. **Employment distribution** (1989): 24% trade; 24.5% serv.; 19.3% gvt. **Per capita income** (1989): $18,306. **Unemployment** (1989): 2.6%. **Tourism** (1988): visitors spent $9.2 bln. **General excise tax:** 4%.

Finance. FDIC-insured **commercial banks & trust companies:** (1987): 22. **Deposits:** $9.8 bln. **Savings institutions** (1990): 6. **Assets:** $7.2 bln.

Federal government. No. federal civilian employees (Mar. 1989): 23,117. **Avg. salary:** $29,824. **Notable federal facilities:** Pearl Harbor Naval Shipyard; Hickam AFB; Schofield Barracks.

Energy. Electricity production (1989, mwh, by source): Hydroelectric: 14,000; Mineral: 7.6 mln.

Education. Student-teacher ratio (1988): 21.1. **Avg. Salary, public school teachers** (1990): $32,047.

State data. Motto: The life of the land is perpetuated in righteousness. **Flower:** Yellow Hibiscus. **Bird:** Hawaiian goose. **Tree:** Candlenut. **Song:** Hawaii Ponoi. **Entered union** Aug. 21, 1959; rank, 50th. **State fair** at: Honolulu; late May–mid-June.

History. Polynesians from islands 2,000 mi. to the south settled the Hawaiian Islands, probably between 300 A.D. and 600 A.D. First European visitor was British Capt. James Cook, 1778. Missionaries arrived, 1820, taught religion, reading and writing. King Kamehameha III and his chiefs created the first Constitution and a Legislature which set up a public school system. Sugar production began in 1835 and it became the dominant industry. In 1893, Queen Liliuokalani was deposed, followed, 1894, by a republic headed by Sanford B. Dole. Annexation by the U.S. came in 1898.

Tourist attractions. Hawaii Volcanoes, Haleakala National Parks; Polynesian Cultural Center, Waikiki Beach, Nuuanu Pali, Bishop Museum, Waimea Canyon, Wailua River State Park, Honolulu Academy of Arts.

Famous Islanders include Bernice Pauahi Bishop, John A. Burns, Father Damien de Veuster, Daniel K. Inouye, Duke Kahanamoku, King Kamehameha the Great, Queen Kaahumanu, Queen Liliuokalani, Ellison Onizuka.

Chamber of Commerce. Dillingham Bldg., 735 Bishop St., Honolulu, HI 96813.

Idaho
Gem State

People. Population (1989): 1,014,000; **rank:** 42. **Pop. density:** 12.1 per sq. mi. **Urban** (1980): 54.0%. **Racial distrib.** (1980): 95.5% White; 0.3% Black; Hispanic 41,800. **Net change** (1985-89): +9,000; 0.9%.

Geography. Total area: 83,564 sq. mi.; **rank:** 13. **Land area:** 82,412 sq. mi. **Acres forested land:** 21,726,600. **Location:** Pacific Northwest-Mountain state bordering on British Columbia. **Climate:** tempered by Pacific westerly winds; drier, colder, continental clime in SE; altitude an important factor. **Topography:** Snake R. plains in the S; central region of mountains, canyons, gorges (Hells Canyon, 7,900 ft., deepest in N.A.); subalpine northern region. **Capital:** Boise.

Economy. Principal industries: agriculture, manufacturing, tourism, lumber, mining, electronics. **Principal manufactured goods:** processed foods, lumber and wood products, chemical products, primary metals, fabricated metal products, machinery, electronic components. **Agriculture:** Chief crops: potatoes, peas, sugar beets, alfalfa seed, wheat, hops, barley, plums and prunes, mint, onions, corn, cherries, apples, hay. **Livestock:** 1.62 mln. cattle; 80,000 hogs/pigs; 324,000 sheep; 1.28 mln. poultry. **Timber/lumber** (1988): yellow, white pine; Douglas fir; white spruce; 2.1 bln. bd. ft. **Nonfuel Minerals** (1989): $323 mln.; phosphate rock, silver, gold, sand & gravel. **Chief ports:** Lewiston. **Value of construction** (1989) $740 mln. **Employment distribution:** 21% trade; 15% serv., 14% mfg.; 10% agric. **Per capita income** (1989): $13,762. **Unemployment** (1989): 5.1%. **Tourism** (1989): travellers spent $1.4 bln. **Sales tax:** 5%.

Finance. FDIC-insured **commercial banks & trust companies** (1987): 24. **Deposits:** $5.9 bln. **Savings institutions** (1990): 5. **Assets:** $904 mln.

Federal government. No. federal civilian employees (Mar. 1989): 7,079. **Avg. salary:** $29,027. **Notable federal facilities:** Ida. Nat'l. Engineering Lab, Idaho Falls; Mt. Home Air Force Base, Mt. Home.

Energy. Electricity production (1989, mwh, by source): Hydroelectric: 6.8 mln.

Education: Student-teacher ratio (1988): 20.6. **Avg. salary, public school teachers** (1990): $23,494.

State data. Motto: Esto Perpetua (It is perpetual). **Flower:** Syringa. **Bird:** Mountain bluebird. **Tree:** White pine. **Song:** Here We Have Idaho. **Entered union** July 3, 1890; rank, 43d. **State fair** at: Boise, late Aug.; and Blackfoot, early Sept.

History. Exploration of the Idaho area began with Lewis and Clark, 1805-06. Next came fur traders, setting up posts, 1809-34, and missionaries, establishing missions, 1830s-1850s. Mormons made their first permanent settlement at Franklin, 1860. Idaho's Gold Rush began that same year, and brought thousands of permanent settlers. Strangest of the Indian Wars was the 1,300-mi. trek in 1877 of Chief Joseph and the Nez Perce tribe, pursued by troops that caught them a few miles short of the Canadian border. In 1890, Idaho adopted a progressive Constitution and became a state.

Tourist attractions. Hells Canyon, deepest gorge in N.A.; Craters of the Moon; Sun Valley, year-round resort in the Sawtooth Mtns.; Crystal Falls Cave; Shoshone Falls; Lava Hot Springs; Lake Pend Oreille; Lake Coeur d'Alene; Sawtooth Natl. Recreation Area; River of No Return Wilderness Area.

Famous Idahoans include William E. Borah, Frank Church, Fred T. Dubois, Chief Joseph, Sacagawea.

Tourist information. Department of Commerce, 700 W. State St., Boise, ID 83720.

Toll-free travel information. 1-800-635-7820.

Illinois
The Prairie State

People. Population (1989): 11,658,000; **rank: 6. Pop. density:** 206.9 per sq. mi. **Urban** (1980): 83.3%. **Racial distrib.** (1985): 84.6% White; 15.4% Black; Hispanic 754,900. **Net change** (1985-89): +119,000; 1.6%.

Geography. Total area: 56,345 sq. mi.; **rank: 24. Land area:** 55,645 sq. mi. **Acres forested land:** 3,810,400. **Location:** east-north central state; western, southern, and eastern boundaries formed by Mississippi, Ohio, and Wabash Rivers, respectively. **Climate:** temperate; typically cold, snowy winters, hot summers. **Topography:** prairie and fertile plains throughout; open hills in the southern region. **Capital:** Springfield.

Economy. Principal industries: manufacturing, wholesale and retail trade, finance, insurance, foods, agriculture. **Principal manufactured goods:** machinery, electric and electronic equipment, primary and fabricated metals, chemical products, printing and publishing. **Agriculture: Chief crops:** corn, soybeans, wheat, oats, hay. **Livestock** (1989): 1.9 mln. cattle; 5.6 mln. hogs/pigs; 140,000 sheep; 3.76 mln. poultry. **Timber/lumber** (1988): oak, hickory, maple, cottonwood; 120 mln. bd. ft. **Nonfuel Minerals** (1989): $644 mln.; mostly crushed stone, cement, construction & industrial sand & gravel. **Commercial fishing** (1989): $304,000. **Chief ports:** Chicago. **International airports at:** Chicago. **Value of construction** (1989): $11.8 bln. **Employment distribution** (1989): 24.7% serv.; 24.6% trade; 19.0% mfg. **Per capita income** (1989): $18,858. **Unemployment** (1989) 6.0%. **Tourism** (1989): out-of-state visitors spent $12.0 bln. **Sales tax:** 6.25%.

Finance. FDIC-insured **commercial banks & trust companies** (1987): 1,219. **Deposits:** $134.7 bln. **Savings institutions** (1990): 240. **Assets:** $64.1 bln.

Federal government. No. federal civilian employees (Mar. 1989): 53,587. **Avg. salary:** $29,426. **Notable federal facilities:** Fermi Nat'l. Accelerator Lab; Argonne Nat'l. Lab; Ft. Sheridan; Rock Island; Great Lakes, Naval Training Station, Scott AFB.

Energy. Electricity production (1989, mwh, by source): Hydroelectric: 48,000; Mineral: 54.1 mln.; Nuclear: 69.2 mln.

Education. Student-teacher ratio (1988): 17.1. **Avg. salary, public school teachers** (1990): $33,014.

State data. Motto: State sovereignty—national union. **Flower:** Native violet. **Bird:** Cardinal. **Tree:** White oak. **Song:** Illinois. **Entered union** Dec. 3, 1818; **rank,** 21st. **State fair** at: Springfield; early Aug.; DuQuoin, late Aug.

History. Fur traders were the first Europeans in Illinois, followed shortly, 1673, by Jolliet and Marquette, and, 1680, La Salle, who built a fort near present Peoria. First settlements were French, at Fort St. Louis on the Illinois River, 1692, and Kaskaskia, 1700. France ceded the area to Britain, 1763; Amer. Gen. George Rogers Clark, 1778, took Kaskaskia from the British without a shot. Defeat of Indian tribes in Black Hawk War, 1832, and railroads in 1850s, inspired change.

Tourist attractions: Chicago museums, parks; Lincoln shrines at Springfield, New Salem, Sangamon; Cahokia Mounds, E. St. Louis; Starved Rock State Park; Crab Orchard Wildlife Refuge; Mormon settlement at Nauvoo; Fts. Kaskaskia, Chartres, Massac (parks); Shawnee Natl. Forest, Southern Illinois; Illinois State Museum, Springfield; Dickson Mounds Museum, btwn. Havana & Lewistown.

Famous Illinoisans include Jane Addams, Saul Bellow, Jack Benny, Ray Bradbury, Gwendolyn Brooks, William Jennings Bryan, St. Francis Xavier Cabrini, Clarence Darrow, John Deere, Stephen A. Douglas, James T. Farrell, George W. Ferris, Marshall Field, Betty Friedan, Benny Goodman, Ulysses S. Grant, Ernest Hemingway, Wild Bill Hickock, Abraham Lincoln, Vachel Lindsay, Edgar Lee Masters, Oscar Mayer, Cyrus McCormick, Ronald Reagan, Carl Sandburg, Adlai Stevenson, Frank Lloyd Wright, Philip Wrigley.

Tourist information. Illinois Dept. of Commerce and Community Affairs, 620 E. Adams St., Springfield, IL 62701.
Toll-free literature on Illinois events. 1-800-223-0121.

Indiana
Hoosier State

People. Population (1989): 5,593,000; **rank: 14. Pop. density:** 154.6 per sq. mi. **Urban** (1980): 64.2%. **Racial distrib.** (1985): 92.0 White; 8.0% Black; Hispanic 182,600. **Net change** (1985-89): +92,000; 1.7%.

Geography. Total area: 36,185 sq. mi.; **rank: 38. Land area:** 35,932 sq. mi. **Acres forested land:** 3,942,900. **Location:** east north-central state; Lake Michigan on northern border. **Climate:** 4 distinct seasons with a temperate climate. **Topography:** hilly southern region; fertile rolling plains of central region; flat, heavily glaciated north; dunes along Lake Michigan shore. **Capital:** Indianapolis.

Economy. Principal industries: manufacturing, wholesale and retail trade, agriculture, government, services. **Principal manufactured goods:** primary and fabricated metals, transportation equipment, electrical and electronic equipment, non-electrical machinery, plastics, chemical products, foods. **Agriculture: Chief crops** (1987): corn, sorghum, oats, wheat, rye, soybeans, hay. **Livestock** (1987): 1.2 mln. cattle; 4.4 mln. hogs/pigs; 82,757 sheep; 28 mln. chickens. **Timber/lumber** (1988): oak, tulip, beech, sycamore; 365 mln. bd. ft. **Nonfuel Minerals** (1989): $437 mln.; mostly crushed stone, abrasives, cement, construction sand & gravel. **Commercial fishing** (1989): $1.9 mln. **Chief ports:** Burns Harbor, Portage; Southwind Maritime, Mt. Vernon; Clark Maritime, Jeffersonville. **International airports at:** Indianapolis. **Value of construction** (1989): $5.5 bln. **Employment distribution** (1986): 27.1% mfg.; 23.6% trade; 19.2% serv. **Per capita income** (1989): $16,005. **Unemployment** (1989): 4.7%. **Tourism** (1985): tourists spent $3 bln. **Sales tax:** 5%, with exemptions.

Finance. FDIC-insured **commercial banks & trust companies** (1987): 355. **Deposits:** $40.7 bln. **Savings institutions** (1990): 101. **Assets:** $13.5 bln.

Federal government. No. federal civilian employees (Mar. 1989): 25,461. **Avg. salary:** $27,469. **Notable federal facilities:** Naval Avionics Ctr.; Ft. Benjamin Harrison; Grissom AFB; Navy Weapons Support Ctr., Crane.

Energy. Electricity production (1989 mwh, by source): Hydroelectric: 441,000; Mineral: 83.5 mln.

Education. Student-teacher ratio (1988): 17.8. **Avg. salary, public school teachers** (1990): $30,493.

State data. Motto: Crossroads of America. **Flower:** Peony. **Bird:** Cardinal. **Tree:** Tulip poplar. **Song:** On the Banks of the Wabash, Far Away. **Entered union** Dec. 11, 1816; **rank,** 19th. **State fair** at: Indianapolis; mid-Aug.

History. Pre-historic Indian Mound Builders of 1,000 years ago were the earliest known inhabitants. A French trading post was built, 1731-32, at Vincennes and La Salle visited the present South Bend area, 1679 and 1681. France ceded the area to Britain, 1763. During the Revolution, American Gen. George Rogers Clark captured Vincennes, 1778, and defeated British forces 1779; at war's end Britain ceded the area to the U.S. Miami Indians defeated U.S. troops twice, 1790, but were beaten, 1794, at Fallen Timbers by Gen. Anthony Wayne. At Tippecanoe, 1811, Gen. William H. Harrison defeated Tecumseh's Indian confederation.

Tourist attractions. Lincoln Boyhood, George Rogers Clark memorials; Wyandotte Cave; Vincennes, Tippecanoe sites; Indiana Dunes; Hoosier Nat'l. Forest; Benjamin Harrison Home.

Famous "Hoosiers" include Larry Bird, Ambrose Burnside, Hoagy Carmichael, Jim Davis, James Dean, Eugene V. Debs, Theodore Dreiser, Paul Dresser, Gil Hodges, David Letterman, Jane Pauley, Cole Porter, Gene Stratton Porter, Ernie Pyle, James Whitcomb Riley, Oscar Robertson, Red Skelton, Booth Tarkington, Lew Wallace, Wendell L. Willkie, Wilbur Wright.

Chamber of Commerce. One North Capital, Suite 200, Indianapolis, IN 46204.

Toll-free travel information. 1-800-289-6646.

Iowa

Hawkeye State

People. Population (1989): 2,840,000; **rank:** 29. **Pop. density:** 50.5 per sq. mi. **Urban** (1980): 58.6%. **Racial distrib.** (1985): 98.4% White; 1.6% Black; 0.5% Hispanic 25,800. **Net change** (1985-89): —30,000; —1.1%.

Geography. Total area: 56,275 sq. mi.; **rank:** 25. **Land area:** 55,965 sq. mi. **Acres forested land:** 1,561,300. **Location:** Midwest state bordered by Mississippi R. on the E and Missouri R. on the W. **Climate:** humid, continental. **Topography:** Watershed from NW to SE; soil especially rich and land level in the N central counties. **Capital:** Des Moines.

Economy. Principal industries: insurance, manufacturing, agriculture. **Principal manufactured goods:** tires, farm machinery, electronic products, appliances, office furniture, chemicals, fertilizers, auto accessories. **Agriculture: Chief crops:** silage and grain corn, soybeans, oats, hay. **Livestock** (1989): 4.8 mln. cattle; 13.5 mln. hogs/pigs; 400,000 sheep; 7.6 mln. turkeys. **Timber/lumber** (1988): red cedar; 52 mln. bd. ft. **Nonfuel Minerals** (1989): $292 mln.; mostly crushed stone, portland cement, construction sand & gravel. **Value of construction** (1989): 1.8 bln. **Employment distribution** (1989): 25.7% trade; 22.8% serv; 19.7% mfg.; 18.0% gvt. **Per capita income** (1989): $15,524. **Unemployment** (1989): 4.3%. **Tourism** (1988): tourists spent $2.1 bln. **Sales tax:** 4%.

Finance. FDIC-insured commercial banks & trust companies (1987): 614. **Deposits:** $26.0 bln. **Savings institutions** (1990): 45. **Assets:** $9.0 bln.

Federal government. No. federal civilian employees (Mar. 1989): 7,708. **Avg. salary:** $27,642.

Energy. Electricity production (1989, mwh, by source): Hydroelectric: 698,000; Mineral: 23.1 mln.; Nuclear: 3.2 mln.

Education. Student-teacher ratio (1988): 15.8. **Avg. salary, public school teachers** (1990): $26,747.

State data. Motto: Our liberties we prize and our rights we will maintain. **Flower:** Wild rose. **Bird:** Eastern goldfinch. **Tree:** Oak. **Rock:** Geode. **Entered union** Dec. 28, 1846; rank, 29th. **State fair** at: Des Moines; mid-Aug.

History. A thousand years ago several groups of prehistoric Indian Mound Builders dwelt on Iowa's fertile plains. Marquette and Jolliet gave France its claim to the area, 1673. It became U.S. territory through the 1803 Louisiana Purchase. Indian tribes were moved into the area from states further east, but by mid-19th century were forced to move on to Kansas. Before and during the Civil War, Iowans strongly supported Abraham Lincoln and became traditional Republicans.

Tourist attractions. Herbert Hoover birthplace and library, West Branch; Effigy Mounds Nat'l. Monument, Marquette, a pre-historic Indian burial site; Amana colonies; Davenport Municipal Art Gallery's collection of Grant Wood's paintings and memorabilia; Living History Farms, Des Moines; Adventureland, Altoona; Boone & Scenic Valley Railroad, Boone; Greyhound Parks in Dubuque, Council Bluffs & Waterloo; Prairie Meadows horse racing, Altoona.

Famous Iowans include James A. Van Allen, Marquis Childs, Buffalo Bill Cody, Mamie Dowd Eisenhower, George Gallup, Susan Glaspell, James Norman Hall, Harry Hansen, Herbert Hoover, Glenn Miller, Billy Sunday, Carl Van Vechten, Henry Wallace, John Wayne, Meredith Willson, Grant Wood.

Tourist information. Bureau of Tourism & Visitors, Iowa Dept. of Economic Development, 200 E. Grand Ave. Des Moines, IA 50309.

Toll-free travel information. 1-800-345-IOWA.

Kansas

Sunflower State

People. Population (1989): 2,513,000; **rank:** 32. **Pop. density:** 30.5 per sq. mi. **Urban** (1980): 66.7%. **Racial distrib.** (1985): 94.4% White; 5.6% Black; Hispanic 69,900. **Net change** (1985-89): +64,000; 2.6%.

Geography. Total area: 82,277 sq. mi.; **rank:** 14. **Land area:** 81,778 sq. mi. **Acres forested land:** 1,344,400. **Location:** West North Central state, with Missouri R. on E. **Climate:** temperate but continental, with great extremes bet. summer and winter. **Topography:** hilly Osage Plains in the E; central region level prairie and hills; high plains in the W. **Capital:** Topeka.

Economy. Principal industries: agriculture, machinery, mining, aerospace. **Principal manufactured goods:** processed foods, aircraft, petroleum products, farm machinery. **Agriculture: Chief crops:** wheat, sorghum, corn, hay. **Livestock** (1989): 5.86 mln. cattle; 1.45 mln. hogs/pigs; 277,000 sheep; 2.1 mln. poultry. **Timber/lumber:** oak, walnut. **Nonfuel Minerals** (1989): $292 mln.; cement, salt, crushed stone. **Chief ports:** Kansas City. **International airports at:** Wichita. **Value of construction** (1989): $2.1 bln. **Employment distribution** (1989): 25.0% trade; 20.5% serv.; 19.9% gvt.; 17.1% mfg. **Per capita income** (1989): $16,182. **Unemployment** (1989): 4.0%. **Tourism** (1985): out-of-state visitors spent $1.9 bln. **Sales tax:** 6.25% maximum.

Finance. FDIC-insured commercial banks & trust companies (1987): 613. **Deposits:** $21.5 bln. **Savings institutions** (1990): 53. **Assets:** $22.0 bln.

Federal government. No. federal civilian employees (Mar. 1989): 15,828. **Avg. salary:** $27,086. **Notable federal facilities:** McConnell AFB; Fts. Riley, Leavenworth.

Energy. Electricity production (1989, mwh, by source): Hydroelectric: 12,000; Mineral: 24.7 mln; Nuclear: 6.7 mln.

Education. Student-teacher ratio (1988): 15.2. **Avg. salary, public school teachers** (1990): $28,671.

State data. Motto: Ad Astra per Aspera (To the stars through difficulties). **Flower:** Native sunflower. **Bird:** Western meadowlark. **Tree:** Cottonwood. **Song:** Home on the Range. **Entered union** Jan. 29, 1861; rank, 34th. **State fair** at: Hutchinson; 2d week of Sept.

History. Coronado marched through the Kansas area, 1541; French explorers came next. The U.S. took over in the Louisiana Purchase, 1803. In the pre-war North-South struggle over slavery, so much violence swept the area it was called Bleeding Kansas. Railroad construction after the war made Abilene and Dodge City terminals of large cattle drives from Texas.

Tourist attractions. Eisenhower Center and "Place of Meditation," Abilene; Agricultural Hall of Fame and National Ctr., Bonner Springs, displays farm equipment; Dodge City-Boot Hill & Frontier Town; Cowtown-historic frontier town, Wichita; Ft. Scott & Ft. Larned-restored 1800s cavalry forts. Kansas Cosmosphere and Space Discovery Center, Hutchinson.

Famous Kansans include Thomas Hart Benton, John Brown, Walter P. Chrysler, John Steuart Curry, Amelia Earhart, Dwight D. Eisenhower, Ron Evans, Wild Bill Hickok, Cyrus Holliday, William Inge, Walter Johnson, Alf Landon, Carry Nation, Gordon Parks, Jim Ryun, William Allen White.

Tourist information. Kansas Dept. of Commerce, Travel and Tourism Div., 400 SW 8th St., 5th Fl., Topeka, KS 66603; 1-913-296-2009.

Toll-free travel information. 1-800-2KANSAS in state.

Kentucky

Bluegrass State

People. Population (1989): 3,727,000 **rank:** 23. **Pop. density:** 92.2 per sq. mi. **Urban** (1980): 50.9% **Racial Distrib.** (1985): 92.9% White; 7.1% Black; Hispanic 14,300. **Net change** (1985-89): +2,000; 0.1%.

Geography. Total area: 40,410 sq. mi.; **rank:** 37. **Land area:** 39,669 sq. mi. **Acres forested land:** 12,160,800. **Location:** east south central state, bordered on N by Illinois, Indiana, Ohio; on E by West Virginia and Virginia; in S by Tennessee; on W by Missouri. **Climate:** moderate, with plentiful rainfall. **Topography:** mountainous in E; rounded hills of the Knobs in the N; Bluegrass, heart of state; wooded rocky hillsides of the Pennyroyal; Western Coal Field; the fertile Purchase the SW. **Capital:** Frankfort.

Economy. Principal industries: manufacturing, coal mining, construction, agriculture. **Principal manufactured goods:** nonelectrical machinery, food products, electrical & electronic products, apparel, primary metals, chemicals and allied prods. **Agriculture: Chief crops** (1986): tobacco, soybeans, corn. **Livestock** (1987): 2.5 mln. cattle; 880,000 hogs/pigs; 32,000 sheep; 1.8 mln. chickens; 1985 receipts for horse & mule sales, $450 mln. **Timber/lumber** (1988): hardwoods, pines; 423 mln. bd. ft. **Nonfuel Minerals** (1989): $331 mln.; mostly crushed stone. **Chief ports:** Paducah, Louisville, Covington, Owensboro, Ashland, Henderson County, Lyon County, Hickman-Fulton County. **International airports at:** Covington. **Value of construction** (1989): $3.3 bln. **Employment distribution:** 23.8% trade; 20.4% mfg.; 19.7% serv.; 18.4% gvt. **Per capita income** (1989): $13,777. **Unemployment** (1989): 6.2%. **Tourism** (1989): tourists spent $4.3 bln. **Sales tax:** 5%.

Finance. FDIC-insured commercial banks & trust companies (1987): 331. **Deposits:** $26.5 bln. **Savings institutions** (1990): 62. **Assets:** $7.8 bln.

Federal government. No. federal civilian employees (Mar. 1989): 27,747. **Avg. salary:** $24,809. **Notable federal facilities:** U.S. Gold Bullion Depository, Fort Knox; Federal Correctional Institution, Lexington.

Energy. Electricity production (1988, mwh, by source): Hydroelectric: 2.4 mln.; Mineral: 74.0 mln.

Education. Student-teacher ratio (1988): 17.8. **Avg. salary, public school teachers** (1990): $26,275.

State data. Motto: United we stand, divided we fall. **Flower:** Goldenrod. **Bird:** Cardinal. **Tree:** Kentucky coffee tree. **Song:** My Old Kentucky Home. **Entered union** June 1, 1792; rank, 15th. **State fair at:** Louisville.

History. Kentucky was the first area west of the Alleghenies settled by American pioneers; first permanent settlement, Harrodsburg, 1774. Daniel Boone blazed the Wilderness Trail through the Cumberland Gap and founded Fort Boonesborough, 1775. Indian attacks, spurred by the British, were unceasing until, during the Revolution, Gen. George Rogers Clark captured British forts in Indiana and Illinois, 1778. In 1792, after Virginia dropped its claims to the region, Kentucky became the 15th state.

Tourist attractions. Kentucky Derby and accompanying festivities, Louisville; Land Between the Lakes Nat'l. Recreation Area encompassing Kentucky Lake and Lake Barkley; Mammoth Cave National Park with 300 mi. of explored passageways, 200-ft. high rooms, blind fish, and Echo River, 360 ft. below ground; Shaker Village of Pleasant Hill, Harrodsburg; Lincoln birthplace, Hodgenville; My Old Kentucky Home, Bardstown; Cumberland Gap Natl. Historical Park, Middlesboro; Kentucky Horse Park, Lexington.

Famous Kentuckians include Muhammad Ali, John James Audubon, Alben Barkley, Daniel Boone, Louis D. Brandeis, John C. Breckinridge, Kit Carson, Albert B. "Happy" Chandler, Cassius Marcellus Clay, Henry Clay, Jefferson Davis, "Casey" Jones, Abraham Lincoln, Mary Todd Lincoln, Thomas Hunt Morgan, Carry Nation, Col. Harland Sanders, Diane Sawyer, Jesse Stuart, Adlai Stevenson, Zachary Taylor, Robert Penn Warren, Whitney Young, Jr.

Chamber of Commerce. 452 Versailles Rd., P.O. Box 817, Frankfort, KY 40602.

Toll-free travel information. 1-800-225-TRIP in U.S., Ontario & Quebec, Canada.

Louisiana

Pelican State

People. Population (1989): 4,382,000; **rank:** 20. **Pop. density:** 91.8 per sq. mi. **Urban** (1980): 68.7%. **Racial distrib.** (1985): 70.0% White; 30.0% Black; Hispanic 98,400. **Net change** (1985-89): −103,000; −2.3%.

Geography. Total area: 47,752 sq. mi.; **rank:** 31. **Land area:** 44,521 sq. mi. **Acres forested land:** 14,558,100. **Location:** south central Gulf Coast state. **Climate:** subtropical, affected by continental weather patterns. **Topography:** lowlands of marshes and Mississippi R. flood plain; Red R. Valley lowlands; upland hills in the Florida Parishes; average elevation, 100 ft. **Capital:** Baton Rouge.

Economy. Principal industries: wholesale and retail trade, government, manufacturing, construction, transportation, mining. **Principal manufactured goods:** chemical products, foods, transportation equipment, electronic equipment, apparel, petroleum products. **Agriculture: Chief crops:** soybean, sugarcane, rice, corn, cotton, sweet potatoes, melons, pecans. **Livestock** (1989): 573,000 cattle; 154,000 hogs/pigs; 21,000 sheep; 600,000 poultry. **Timber/lumber** (1988): pines, hardwoods, oak; 816 mln. bd. ft. **Nonfuel Minerals** (1989): $392 mln., mostly salt, sand & gravel, sulfur. **Commercial fishing** (1989): $264.2 mln. **Chief ports:** New Orleans, Baton Rouge, Lake Charles, S. Louisiana Port Commission at La Place. **International airports at:** New Orleans. **Value of construction** (1989): $3.2 bln. **Employment distribution** (1985): 23.8% trade; 21.5% gvt.; 21.3% serv.; 10.9% mfg. **Per capita income** (1989): $13,041. **Unemployment** (1989): 7.9%. **Tourism** (1989): out-of-state visitors spent $4.4 bln. **Sales tax:** .04%.

Finance. FDIC-insured commercial banks & trust companies (1987): 298. **Deposits:** $31.7 bln. **Savings institutions** (1990): 86. **Assets:** $13.3 bln.

Federal government. No. federal civilian employees (Mar. 1989): 21,212. **Avg. salary:** $27,115. **Notable federal facilities:** Barksdale, England, Ft. Polk military bases; Strategic Petroleum Reserve, New Orleans; Michoud Assembly Plant, New Orleans; U.S. Public Service Hospital, Carville.

Energy. Electricity production (1989, mwh, by source): Hydroelectric: 2.1 mln.; Mineral: 43.0 mln; Nuclear: 13.8 mln.

Education. Student-teacher ratio (1988): 18.2. **Avg. salary, public school teachers** (1990): $22,993.

State data. Motto: Union, justice and confidence. **Flower:** Magnolia. **Bird:** Eastern brown pelican. **Tree:** Cypress. **Song:** Give Me Louisiana. **Entered union** Apr. 30, 1812; rank, 18th. **State fair at:** Shreveport; Oct.

History. The area was first visited, 1530, by Cabeza de Vaca and Panfilo de Narvaez. The region was claimed for France by LaSalle, 1682. First permanent settlement was by French at Biloxi, now in Mississippi, 1699. France ceded the region to Spain, 1762, took it back, 1800, and sold it to the U.S., 1803, in the Louisiana Purchase. During the Revolution, Spanish Louisiana aided the Americans. Admitted to statehood, 1812, Louisiana was the scene of the Battle of New Orleans, 1815.

Louisiana Creoles are descendants of early French and/or Spanish settlers. About 4,000 Acadians, French settlers in Nova Scotia, Canada, were forcibly transported by the British to Louisiana in 1755 (an event commemorated in Longfellow's *Evangeline*) and settled near Bayou Teche; their descendants became known as Cajuns. Another group, the Islenos, were descendants of Canary Islanders brought to Louisiana by a Spanish governor in 1770. Traces of Spanish and French survive in local dialects.

Tourist attractions. Mardi Gras, French Quarter, Superdome, Dixieland jazz, all New Orleans; Battle of New Orleans site; Longfellow-Evangeline Memorial Park; Kent House Museum, Alexandria; Hodges Gardens, Natchilotches.

Famous Louisianans include Louis Armstrong, Pierre Beauregard, Judah P. Benjamin, Braxton Bragg, Grace

King, Huey Long, Leonidas K. Polk, Henry Miller Shreve, Edward D. White Jr.

Tourist Information. State Dept. of Culture, Recreation & Tourism, P.O. Box 94291, Baton Rouge, LA 70804-9291.

Toll-free travel information. 1-800-33-GUMBO.

Maine

Pine Tree State

People. Population (1989): 1,222,000; **rank: 38. Pop. density:** 36.7 per sq. mi. **Urban** (1980): 47.5% **Racial distrib.** (1980): 98.3% White; 0.3% Black; Hispanic: 4,400. **Net change** (1985-89): +58,000; 5.0%.

Geography. Total area: 33,265 sq. mi.; **rank: 39. Land area:** 33,215 sq. mi. **Acres forested land:** 17,718,300. **Location:** New England state at northeastern tip of U.S. **Climate:** Southern interior and coastal, influenced by air masses from the S and W; northern clime harsher, avg. +100 in. snow in winter. **Topography:** Appalachian Mtns. extend through state; western borders have rugged terrain; long sand beaches on southern coast; northern coast mainly rocky promontories, peninsulas, fjords. **Capital:** Augusta.

Economy. Principal industries: manufacturing, services, trade, government, finance, insurance, real estate, construction. **Principal manufactured goods:** paper and wood products, leather goods. **Agriculture: Chief crops:** potatoes, apples, hay, blueberries. **Livestock** (1986): 135,000 cattle; 79,000 hogs/pigs; 17,000 sheep; 4.9 mln. poultry. **Timber/lumber** (1988): pine, spruce, fir; 769 mln. bd ft. **Nonfuel Minerals** (1989): $66 mln.; construction sand & gravel, cement, crushed stone, dimension stone. **Commercial fishing** (1989): $132.5 mln. **Chief ports:** Searsport, Portland, Eastport. **International airports at:** Portland, Bangor. **Value of construction** (1989): $961.3 mln. **Employment distribution** (1987): 24.3% trade; 21.4% serv.; 20.1% mfg.; 18.9% gvt. **Per capita income** (1989): $16,310. **Unemployment** (1989): 4.1%. **Tourism** (1989): $2 bln. **Sales tax:** 5%.

Finance. FDIC-insured commercial banks & trust companies (1987): 22. **Deposits:** $5.2 bln. **Savings institutions** (1990): 14. **Assets:** $7.4 bln.

Federal government. No. federal civilian employees (Mar. 1989): 12,858. **Avg. salary:** $26,545. **Notable federal facilities:** Kittery Naval Shipyard; Brunswick Naval Air Station; Loring Air Force Base.

Energy. Electricity production (1989, mwh, by source): Hydroelectric: 1.6 mln.; Mineral: 2.9 mln.; Nuclear: 5.0 mln.

Education. Student-teacher ratio (1988): 14.6. **Avg. salary, public school teachers** (1990): $26,881.

State data. Motto: Dirigo (I direct). **Flower:** White pine cone and tassel. **Bird:** Chickadee. **Tree:** Eastern white pine. **Song:** State of Maine Song. **Entered union:** Mar. 15, 1820; rank, 23d.

History. Maine's rocky coast was explored by the Cabots, 1498-99. French settlers arrived, 1604, at the St. Croix River; English, 1607, on the Kennebec. In 1691, Maine was made part of Massachusetts. In the Revolution, a Maine regiment fought at Bunker Hill; a British fleet destroyed Falmouth (now Portland), 1775, but the British ship Margaretta was captured near Machiasport. In 1820, Maine broke off from Massachusetts, became a separate state.

Tourist attractions. Acadia Nat'l. Park, Bar Harbor, on Mt. Desert Is.; Funtown, Saco; Bath Iron Works and Marine Museum; Boothbay (Harbor) Railway Museum; Portland Art Museum; Sugarloaf/USA Ski Area; Ogunquit, Portland, York.

Famous "Down Easters" include James G. Blaine, Cyrus H.K. Curtis, Hannibal Hamlin, Longfellow, Sir Hiram and Hudson Maxim, Edna St. Vincent Millay, Kate Douglas Wiggin, Ben Ames Williams.

Chamber of Commerce and Industry. 126 Sewall St., Augusta, ME 04330.

Toll-free travel information. 1-800-533-9595, winter only, out of state only; 1-207-289-2423 year round.

Maryland

Old Line State, Free State

People. Population (1989): 4,694,000; **rank: 19 Pop. density:** 448.8 per sq. mi. **Urban** (1980): 80.3% **Racial distrib.** (1985): 75.8% White; 24.2% Black; Hispanic 71,400. **Net change** (1985-89): +301,000; 6.8%.

Geography. Total area: 10,460 sq. mi.; **rank: 42. Land area:** 9,837 sq. mi. **Acres forested land:** 2,653,200. **Location:** Middle Atlantic state stretching from the Ocean to the Allegheny Mtns. **Climate:** continental in the west; humid subtropical in the east. **Topography:** Eastern Shore of coastal plain and Maryland Main of coastal plain, piedmont plateau, and the Blue Ridge, separated by the Chesapeake Bay. **Capital:** Annapolis.

Economy. Principal industries: manufacturing, tourism. **Principal manufactured goods:** electric and electronic equipment; food and kindred products; chemicals and allied products. **Agriculture: Chief crops** (1989): corn, soybeans, greenhouse & nursery prods. **Livestock** (1989): 328,000 cattle; 180,000 hogs/pigs; 32,000 sheep; 257.8 mln. poultry. **Timber/lumber:** hardwoods. **Nonfuel Minerals** (1989): $367 mln.; crushed stone, sand & gravel, Portland cement. **Commercial fishing** (1989): $52.1 mln. **Chief ports:** Baltimore. **International airports at:** Baltimore. **Value of construction** (1989): $7.3 bln. **Employment distribution** (1988): 27.4% serv.; 25.9% trade; 18.3% gvt. **Per capita income** (1989): $21,020. **Unemployment** (1989): 3.7%. **Tourism** (1988): tourists spent $5.9 bln. **Sales tax:** 5%.

Finance. FDIC-insured commercial banks & trust companies (1987): 93. **Deposits:** $30.0 bln. **Savings institutions** (1990): 102. **Assets:** $23.5 bln.

Federal government. No. federal civilian employees (Mar. 1989): 104,172. **Avg. salary:** $33,389. **Notable federal facilities:** U.S. Naval Academy, Annapolis; Natl. Agric. Research Cen.; Ft. George G. Meade, Aberdeen Proving Ground; Goddard Space Flight Center.

Energy. Electricity production (1989, mwh, by source): Hydroelectric: 1.3 mln.; Mineral: 27.3 mln.; Nuclear: 11.7 mln.

Education. Student-teacher ratio (1988): 16.8. **Avg. salary, public school teachers** (1990): $36,092.

State data. Motto: Fatti Maschii, Parole Femine (Manly deeds, womanly words). **Flower:** Black-eyed susan. **Bird:** Baltimore oriole. **Tree:** White oak. **Song:** Maryland, My Maryland. **Seventh** of the original 13 states to ratify Constitution, Apr. 28, 1788. **State fair at:** Timonium; late Aug.-early Sept.

History. Capt. John Smith first explored Maryland, 1608. William Claiborne set up a trading post on Kent Is. in Chesapeake Bay, 1631. Britain granted land to Cecilius Calvert, Lord Baltimore, 1632; his brother led 200 settlers to St. Marys River, 1634. The bravery of Maryland troops in the Revolution, as at the Battle of Long Island, won the state its nickname, The Old Line State. In the War of 1812, when a British fleet tried to take Fort McHenry, Marylander Francis Scott Key, 1814, wrote *The Star-Spangled Banner.*

Tourist Attractions. Racing events include the Preakness, at Pimlico track, Baltimore; the International at Laurel Race Course; the Maryland Million at Pimlico. Also Annapolis yacht races; Ocean City summer resort; restored Ft. McHenry, Baltimore, near which Francis Scott Key wrote *The Star-Spangled Banner;* Antietam Battlefield, 1862, near Hagerstown; South Mountain Battlefield, 1862; Edgar Allan Poe house, Baltimore; The State House, Annapolis, 1772, the oldest still in use in the U.S.; Montgomery & Prince George's County gateway to Washington, D.C.

Famous Marylanders include Benjamin Banneker, Francis Scott Key, H.L. Mencken, William Pinkney, Upton Sinclair, Roger B. Taney, Charles Willson Peale.

Chamber of Commerce. 60 West St., Suite 405, Annapolis, MD 21401.

Toll-free travel information. 1-800-543-1036.

Massachusetts

Bay State, Old Colony

People. Population (1989): 5,913,000; **rank:** 13. **Pop. density:** 713.8 per sq. mi. **Urban** (1980): 83.8% **Racial distrib.** (1985): 96.5% White; 3.5% Black; Hispanic 154,100. **Net change** (1985-89): +89,000; 1.5%.

Geography. Total area: 8,284 sq. mi.; **rank:** 45. **Land area:** 7,824 sq. mi. **Acres forested land:** 2,952,300. **Location:** New England state along Atlantic seaboard. **Climate:** temperate, with colder and drier clime in western region. **Topography:** jagged indented coast from Rhode Island around Cape Cod; flat land yields to stony upland pastures near central region and gentle hilly country in west; except in west, land is rocky, sandy, and not fertile. **Capital:** Boston.

Economy. Principal industries: services, trade, manufacturing. **Principal manufactured goods** (1989): electric and electronic equipment, machinery, printing and publishing, instruments, fabricated metal products. **Agriculture: Chief crops:** cranberries, greenhouse, nursery, vegetables. **Livestock** (1983): 120,000 cattle; 50,000 hogs/pigs; 8,000 sheep; 125,000 horses, ponies; 3.6 mln. poultry. **Timber/lumber** (1988): white pine, oak, other hard woods; 85 mln. bd. ft. **Nonfuel Minerals** (1989): $144 mln.; mostly construction sand & gravel, crushed stone. **Commercial fishing** (1989): $272.9 mln. **Chief ports:** Boston, Fall River, New Bedford, Salem, Gloucester. **International airport at:** Boston. **Value of construction** (1989): $6.4 bln. **Employment distribution** (1989): 29.7% serv.; 23.9% trade; 18.1% mfg. **Per capita income** (1989): $22,196. **Unemployment** (1989): 4.0%. **Tourism** (1987): out-of-state visitors spent $12.9 bln. **Sales tax:** 5%.

Finance. FDIC-insured commercial banks & trust companies (1987): 107. **Deposits:** $66.9 bln. **Savings institutions** (1990): 29. **Assets:** $98.2 bln.

Federal government. No. federal civilian employees (Mar. 1989): 30,755. **Avg. salary:** $29,425. **Notable federal facilities:** Ft. Devens; Thomas P. O'Neill Jr. Federal Bldg., J.W. McCormack Bldg., John Fitzgerald Kennedy Federal Bldg., Boston; Q.M. Laboratory, Natick.

Energy. Electricity production (1989, mwh, by source): Hydroelectric: 150,000; Mineral: 33.3 mln.; Nuclear: 1.1 mln.

Education. Student-teacher ratio (1988): 13.7. **Avg. salary, public school teachers** (1990): $34,225.

State data. Motto: Ense Petit Placidam Sub Libertate Quietem (By the sword we seek peace, but peace only under liberty). **Flower:** Mayflower. **Bird:** Chickadee. **Tree:** American elm. **Song:** All Hail to Massachusetts. **Sixth** of the original 13 states to ratify Constitution, Feb. 6, 1788.

History. Pilgrims settled in Plymouth, 1620; the following year they gave thanks for their survival with the first Thanksgiving Day. Indian opposition reached a high point in King Philip's War, 1675-76, won by the colonists. Demonstrations against British restrictions set off the "Boston Massacre," 1770, and Boston "tea party," 1773. First bloodshed of the Revolution was at Lexington, 1775.

Tourist attractions. Cape Cod—Plymouth Rock, Plymouth Plantation, Mayflower II, Provincetown artists colony; Boston—Freedom Trail, Museum of Fine Arts, Children's Museum, Museum of Science, New England Aquarium, JFK Library, Boston Ballet, Boston Pops, Boston Symphony Orchestra; Berkshires—Tanglewood, Jacob's Pillow Dance Festival, Hancock Shaker Village, Berkshire Scenic Railroad; Old Sturbridge Village; Walden Pond; Naismith Memorial Basketball Hall of Fame, Springfield.

Famous "Bay Staters" include John Adams, John Quincy Adams, Samuel Adams, Louisa May Alcott, Horatio Alger, Susan B. Anthony, Crispus Attucks, Clara Barton, Alexander Graham Bell, Emily Dickinson, Ralph Waldo Emerson, John Hancock, Nathaniel Hawthorne, Oliver W. Holmes, Winslow Homer, Elias Howe, John Fitzgerald Kennedy, Samuel F.B. Morse, Edgar Allan Poe,

Paul Revere, Henry David Thoreau, James McNeil Whistler, John Greenleaf Whittier.

Tourist information. Massachusetts Office of Travel & Tourism, 100 Cambridge St., 13th Floor, Boston, MA 02202.

Toll-free travel information. 1-800-624-MASS.

Michigan

Great Lakes State, Wolverine State

People. Population (1989): 9,273,000; **rank:** 8. **Pop. density:** 158.4 per sq. mi. **Urban** (1980): 70.7%. **Racial distrib.** (1985): 86.5% White; 13.5% Black; Hispanic 155,200. **Net change** (1985-89) +185,000; 2.0%.

Geography. Total area: 58,527 sq. mi.; **rank:** 23. **Land area:** 56,954 sq. mi. **Acres forested land:** 19,270,400. **Location:** east north central state bordering on 4 of the 5 Great Lakes, divided into an Upper and Lower Peninsula by the Straits of Mackinac, which link lakes Michigan and Huron. **Climate:** well-defined seasons tempered by the Great Lakes. **Topography:** low rolling hills give way to northern tableland of hilly belts in Lower Peninsula; Upper Peninsula is level in the east, with swampy areas; western region is higher and more rugged. **Capital:** Lansing.

Economy. Principal industries: manufacturing, services, tourism, agriculture, mining. **Principal manufactured goods:** transportation equipment, machinery, fabricated metals, primary metals, food prods., rubber & plastics. **Agriculture: Chief crops:** corn, winter wheat, soybeans, dry beans, oats, hay, sugar beets, honey, asparagus, sweet corn, apples, cherries, grapes, peaches, blueberries, flowers. **Livestock** (1986): 1.4 mln. cattle; 1.2 mln. hogs/pigs; 108,000 sheep; 8.9 mln. poultry. **Timber/lumber** (1988): maple, oak, aspen; 298 mln. bd. ft. **Nonfuel Minerals** (1989): $1.59 bln.; iron ore, Portland cement, crushed stone, sand & gravel. **Commercial fishing** (1989): $9.9 mln. **Chief ports:** Detroit, Saginaw River, Escanaba, Muskegon, Saulte Ste. Marie, Port Huron. **International airports at:** Detroit, Sault St. Marie. **Value of construction** (1989): $8.1 bln. **Employment distribution** (1989): 22% mfg.; 20% serv.; **Per capita income** (1989): $17,745. **Unemployment** (1989): 7.1%. **Tourism** (1989): travellers spent $16.5 bln. **Sales tax:** 4%.

Finance. FDIC-insured commercial banks & trust companies (1987): 345. **Deposits:** $64.7 bln. **Savings institutions** (1990): 44. **Assets:** $35.1 bln.

Federal government. No. federal civilian employees (Mar. 1989): 27,118. **Avg. salary:** $29,016. **Notable federal facilities:** Isle Royal, Sleeping Bear Dunes national parks.

Energy. Electricity production (1989, mwh, by source): Hydroelectric: 483,000 mln; Mineral: 70.6 mln.; Nuclear: 17.8 mln.

Education. Student-teacher ratio (1988): 19.8. **Avg. salary, public school teachers** (1990): $36,010.

State data. Motto: Si Quaeris Peninsulam Amoenam Circumspice (If you seek a pleasant peninsula, look about you). **Flower:** Apple blossom. **Bird:** Robin. **Tree:** White pine. **Song:** Michigan, My Michigan. **Entered union** Jan. 26, 1837; **rank,** 26th. **State fair at:** Detroit, late Aug.-early Sept.; Upper Peninsula (Escanaba) mid-Aug; Michigan Festival, mid.-Aug.

History. French fur traders and missionaries visited the region, 1616, set up a mission at Sault Ste. Marie, 1641, and a settlement there, 1668. The whole region went to Britain, 1763. Anthony Wayne defeated their Indian allies at Fallen Timbers, Ohio, 1794. The British returned, 1812, seized Ft. Mackinac and Detroit. Oliver H. Perry's Lake Erie victory and William H. Harrison's troops, who carried the war to the Thames River in Canada, 1813, freed Michigan once more.

Tourist attractions. Henry Ford Museum, Greenfield Village, reconstruction of a typical 19th cent. American village, both in Dearborn; Michigan Space Ctr., Jackson; Tahquamenon *(Hiawatha)* Falls; DeZwaan windmill and Tulip Festival, Holland; "Soo Locks," St. Marys Falls Ship Canal, Sault Ste. Marie.

Famous Michiganians include Ralph Bunche, Thomas A. Edison, Gerald R. Ford, Paul de Kruif, Edna Ferber, Henry Ford, Aretha Franklin, Edgar Guest, Lee Iacocca, Robert Ingersoll, Magic Johnson, Will Kellogg, Ring Lardner, Elmore Leonard, Charles Lindbergh, Joe Louis, Madonna, Pontiac, Diana Ross, Tom Selleck, Lily Tomlin, Stewart Edward White, Malcolm X.

Chamber of Commerce: 200 N. Washington Sq., Suite 400, Lansing, MI 48933.

Toll-free travel information. 1-800-543-2937.

Minnesota

North Star State, Gopher State

People. Population (1989): 4,353,000; **rank:** 21. **Pop. density:** 51.6 per sq. mi. **Urban** (1980): 66.9%. **Racial distrib.** (1985): 98.5% White; 1.5% Black; Hispanic 33,500. **Net change** (1985-89): +162,000; 3.9%.

Geography. Total area: 84,402 sq. mi.; **rank:** 12. **Land area:** 79,548 sq. mi. **Acres forested land:** 16,709,200. **Location:** north central state bounded on the E by Wisconsin and Lake Superior, on the N by Canada, on the W by the Dakotas, and on the S by Iowa. **Climate:** northern part of state lies in the moist Great Lakes storm belt; the western border lies at the edge of the semi-arid Great Plains. **Topography:** central hill and lake region covering approx. half the state; to the NE, rocky ridges and deep lakes; to the NW, flat plain; to the S, rolling plains and deep river valleys. **Capital:** St. Paul.

Economy. Principal industries: agri business, forest products, mining, manufacturing, tourism. **Principal manufactured goods:** food processing, non-electrical machinery, chemicals, paper, electric and electronic equipment, printing and publishing, instruments, fabricated metal products. **Agriculture: Chief crops:** corn, soybeans, wheat, sugar beets, sunflowers, barley. **Livestock** (1989): 2.9 mln. cattle; 4.7 mln. hogs/pigs; 263,000 sheep; 11.7 mln. poultry. **Timber/lumber** (1988): needleleaves and hardwoods; 158 mln. bd. ft. **Nonfuel Minerals** (1989): 1.3 bln.; mostly iron ore. **Commercial fishing** (1989): $73,000. **Chief ports:** Duluth, St. Paul, Minneapolis. **International airports at:** Minneapolis-St. Paul. **Value of construction** (1989): $5.0 bln. **Employment distribution** (1989): 25.1% trade; 24.3% serv.; 19.5% mfg.; 15.9% gvt. **Per capita income** (1989): $17,746. **Unemployment** (1989): 4.3%. **Tourism** (1987): out-of-state visitors spent $3.6 bln. **Sales tax:** 6%.

Finance. FDIC-insured commercial banks & trust companies (1987): 733. **Deposits:** $41.2 bln. **Savings institutions** (1990): 32. **Assets:** $13.5 bln.

Federal government. No. federal civilian employees (Mar. 1989): 14,379. **Avg. salary:** $29,502.

Energy. Electricity production (1989, mwh, by source): Hydroelectric: 532,000; Mineral: 25.4 mln.; Nuclear: 12.3 mln.

Education. Student-teacher ratio (1988): 17.0. **Avg. salary, public school teachers** (1990): $32,190.

State data. Motto: L'Etoile du Nord (The star of the north). **Flower:** Pink and white lady's-slipper. **Bird:** Common loon. **Tree:** Red pine. **Song:** Haill Minnesota. **Entered union** May 11, 1858; rank, 32d. **State fair at:** Saint Paul; late Aug. to early Sept.

History. Fur traders and missionaries from French Canada opened the region in the 17th century. Britain took the area east of the Mississippi, 1763. The U.S. took over that portion after the Revolution and in 1803 bought the western area as part of the Louisiana Purchase. The U.S. built present Ft. Snelling, 1820, bought lands from the Indians, 1837. Sioux Indians staged a bloody uprising, 1862, and were driven from the state.

Tourist attractions. Minnehaha Falls, Minneapolis, inspiration for Longfellow's *Hiawatha;* over 10,000 lakes; 64 state parks; 20 historical sites; Minneapolis Aquatennial; Ordway Theater, St. Paul; Guthrie Theater, Minneapolis; professional baseball, football, hockey. Voyageurs Nat'l. Park, a water wilderness along the Canadian border; Mayo Clinic, Rochester; St. Paul Winter Carnival.

Famous Minnesotans include F. Scott Fitzgerald, Cass Gilbert, Hubert Humphrey, Sister Elizabeth Kenny, Sinclair Lewis, Paul Manship, E. G. Marshall, William and Charles Mayo, Walter F. Mondale, Charles Schulz, Harold Stassen, Thorstein Veblen.

Tourist information. Minnesota Office of Tourism, 375 Jackson St., 250 Skyway Level, St. Paul, MN 55101.

Toll-free travel information. 1-800-328-1461.

Mississippi

Magnolia State

People. Population (1989): 2,621,000; **rank:** 31. **Pop. density:** 55.0 per sq. mi. **Urban** (1980): 47.3%. **Racial distrib.** (1985): 63.7% White; 36.3% Black; Hispanic 11,700. **Net change** (1985-89): +8,000; 0.3%.

Geography. Total area: 47,689 sq. mi.; **rank:** 32. **Land area:** 47,233 sq. mi. **Acres forested land:** 16,715,600. **Location:** south central state bordered on the W by the Mississippi R. and on the S by the Gulf of Mexico. **Climate:** semi-tropical, with abundant rainfall, long growing season, and extreme temperatures unusual. **Topography:** low, fertile delta bet. the Yazoo and Mississippi rivers; loess bluffs stretching around delta border; sandy Gulf coastal terraces followed by piney woods and prairie; rugged, high sandy hills in extreme NE followed by black prairie belt. Pontotoc Ridge, and flatwoods into the north central highlands. **Capital:** Jackson.

Economy. Principal industries: manufacturing, food processing, seafood, government, wholesale and retail trade, agriculture. **Principal manufactured goods:** apparel, furniture, lumber and wood products, foods and kindred products, electrical machinery and equipment, transportation equip. **Agriculture: Chief crops:** cotton, soybeans, catfish, rice. **Livestock** (1989): 1.4 mln. cattle; 180,000 hogs/pigs; 387 mln. broilers. **Timber/lumber** (1988): pine, oak, hardwoods; 2.2 bln. bd. ft. **Nonfuel Minerals** (1989): $108 mln., mostly construction sand & gravel. **Commercial fishing** (1989): $44.0 mln. **Chief ports:** Pascagoula, Vicksburg, Gulfport, Natchez, Greenville. **Value of construction** (1989): $1.6 bln. **Employment distribution** (1989): 26.4% mfg.; 21.7% gvt.; 21.4% trade; 16.6% serv. **Per capita income** (1989): $11,835. **Unemployment** (1989): 7.8%. **Tourism** (1989): out-of-state visitors spent $1.5 bln. **Sales tax:** 6%.

Finance. FDIC-insured commercial banks & trust companies (1987): 138. **Deposits:** $15.1 bln. **Savings institutions** (1990): 40. **Assets:** $4.8 bln.

Federal government. No. federal civilian employees (Mar. 1989): 17,749. **Avg. salary:** $27,963. **Notable federal facilities:** Columbus, Keesler AF bases; Meridian Naval Air Station, John F. Stennis Space Center.

Energy. Electricity production (1988, mwh, by source): Mineral 15.5 mln; Nuclear 9.6 mln.

Education. Student-teacher ratio (1988): 18.4. **Avg. salary, public school teachers** (1990): $24,363.

State data. Motto: Virtute et Armis (By valor and arms). **Flower:** Magnolia. **Bird:** Mockingbird. **Tree:** Magnolia. **Song:** Go, Mississippi! **Entered union** Dec. 10, 1817; rank, 20th. **State fair at:** Jackson; Fall.

History. De Soto explored the area, 1540, discovered the Mississippi River, 1541. La Salle traced the river from Illinois to its mouth and claimed the entire valley for France, 1682. First settlement was the French Ft. Maurepas, near Ocean Springs, 1699. The area was ceded to Britain, 1763; American settlers followed. During the Revolution, Spain seized part of the area and refused to leave even after the U.S. acquired title at the end of the Revolution, finally moving out, 1798. Mississippi seceded 1861. Union forces captured Corinth and Vicksburg and destroyed Jackson and much of Meridian.

Tourist attractions. Vicksburg National Military Park and Cemetery, other Civil War sites; Natchez Trace; Indian mounds; Antebellum Home; pilgrimages at Natchez, Columbus, Vicksburg; Mardi Gras and blessing of the shrimp fleet, June, both in Biloxi.

Famous Mississippians include Dana Andrews, Jimmy Buffet, Hodding Carter III, William Faulkner, Shelby Foote, Fannie Lou Hamer, Jim Henson, L.Q.C. Lamar, Elvis Presley, Leontyne Price, Charlie Pride, Eudora Welty, Tennessee Williams.

Chamber of Commerce. P.O. Box 1849, Jackson, MS 39205.

Toll-free travel information. 1-800-962-2346; 1-800-647-2290 out of state.

Missouri

Show Me State

People. Population (1989): 5,159,000; **rank:** 15. **Pop. density:** 74.0 per sq. mi. **Urban** (1980): 68.1%. **Racial distrib.** (1985): 89.1% White; 10.9% Black; Hispanic 48,300. **Net change** (1985-89): +123,000; 2.4%.

Geography. Total area: 69,697 sq. mi.; **rank:** 19. **Land area:** 68,945 sq. mi. **Acres forested land:** 12,876,000. **Location:** West North central state near the geographic center of the conterminous U.S.; bordered on the E by the Mississippi R., on the NW by the Missouri R. **Climate:** continental, susceptible to cold Canadian air, moist, warm Gulf air, and drier SW air. **Topography:** Rolling hills, open, fertile plains, and well-watered prairie N of the Missouri R.; south of the river land is rough and hilly with deep, narrow valleys; alluvial plain in the SE; low elevation in the west. **Capital:** Jefferson City.

Economy. Principal industries: agriculture, manufacturing, aerospace, tourism. **Principal manufactured goods:** transportation equipment, food and related products, electrical and electronic equipment, chemicals. **Agriculture: Chief crops:** soybeans, corn, wheat, cotton. **Livestock** (1988): 4.5 mln. cattle; 2.9 mln. hogs/pigs; 125,000 sheep; 7.9 mln. chickens, 16.5 mln. turkeys. **Timber/lumber** (1988): oak, hickory; 371 mln. bd. ft. **Nonfuel Minerals** (1989): $1.1 bln., mostly lead, crushed stone, Portland cement. **Chief ports:** St. Louis, Kansas City. **International airports at:** St. Louis, Kansas City. **Value of construction** (1989): $4.2 bln. **Employment distribution** (1987): 24% trade; 23% serv.; 19% mfg.; 16% gvt. **Per capita income** (1989): $16,431. **Unemployment** (1989): 5.5%. **Tourism** (1987): total travelers spent $5 bln. **Sales tax:** 4.225%.

Finance. FDIC-insured commercial banks & trust companies (1987): 610. **Deposits:** $43.9 bln. **Savings institutions** (1990): 80. **Assets:** $23.0 bln.

Federal government. No. federal civilian employees (Mar. 1989): 45,268. **Avg. salary:** $27,861. **Notable federal facilities:** Federal Reserve banks, St. Louis, Kansas City; Ft. Leonard Wood, Rolla; Jefferson Barracks, St. Louis; Whiteman AFB, Knob Noster.

Energy. Electricity production (1988 mwh, by source): Hydroelectric: 1.5 mln.; Mineral: 49.3 mln; Nuclear: 8.9 mln.

Education. Student-teacher ratio (1988): 15.9. **Avg. salary, public school teachers** (1990): $27,229.

State data. Motto: Salus Populi Suprema Lex Esto (The welfare of the people shall be the supreme law). **Flower:** Hawthorn. **Bird:** Bluebird. **Tree:** Dogwood. **Song:** Missouri Waltz. **Entered union** Aug. 10, 1821; rank, 24th. **State fair** at: Sedalia; late week in Aug.

History. DeSoto visited the area, 1541. French hunters and lead miners made the first settlement, c. 1735, at Ste. Genevieve. The U.S. acquired Missouri as part of the Louisiana Purchase, 1803. The fur trade and the Santa Fe Trail provided prosperity; St. Louis became the "jump-off" point for pioneers on their way West. Pro- and anti-slavery forces battled each other there during the Civil War.

Tourist attractions. Mark Twain Area, Hannibal; Pony Express Museum, St. Joseph; Harry S. Truman Library, Independence; Gateway Arch, St. Louis; Silver Dollar City, Branson Worlds of Fun, Kansas City; Lake of the Ozarks, Churchill Memorial, Fulton.

Famous Missourians include Josephine Baker, Thomas Hart Benton, George Caleb Bingham, Gen. Omar Bradley, George Washington Carver, Walter Cronkite, Dale Carnegie, Walt Disney, T.S. Eliot, Betty Grable, Jesse James, J. C. Penney, John J. Pershing, Joseph Pulitzer, Ginger Rogers, Bess Truman, Harry S. Truman, Mark Twain, Tennessee Williams.

Chamber of Commerce: 400 E. High St., P.O. Box 149, Jefferson City, MO 65101.

Toll-free travel information. 1-800-877-1234.

Montana

Treasure State

People. Population (1989): 806,000; **rank:** 44. **Pop. density:** 5.48 per sq. mi. **Urban** (1980): 52.9%. **Racial distrib.** (1980): 94.0% White; 0.2% Black; Hispanic 10,800. **Net change** (1985-89): −20,000; −2.4%.

Geography. Total area: 147,046 sq. mi.; **rank:** 4. **Land area:** 145,388 sq. mi. **Acres forested land:** 22,559,300. **Location:** Mountain state bounded on the E by the Dakotas, on the S by Wyoming, on the S/SW by Idaho, and on the N by Canada. **Climate:** colder, continental climate with low humidity. **Topography:** Rocky Mtns. in western third of the state; eastern two-thirds gently rolling northern Great Plains. **Capital:** Helena.

Economy. Principal industries: agriculture, timber, mining, tourism, oil & gas. **Principal manufactured goods:** food prods., wood & paper prods., primary metals, printing & publishing, petroleum & coal prods. **Agriculture: Chief crops:** wheat, barley, sugar beets, hay, oats. **Livestock** (1989): 2.35 mln. cattle; 245,000 hogs/pigs; 568,000 sheep; 910,000 poultry. **Timber/lumber** (1988): Douglas fir, pines, larch; 1.7 bln. bd. ft. **Nonfuel Minerals** (1989): $637 mln. mostly metallics. **International airports at:** Great Falls, Billings, Kalispell, Missoula. **Value of construction** (1989): $482.9 mln. **Employment distribution** (1988): 26.0% serv.; 21.9% trade; 18.5% govt.; 7.7% agric; 5.9% mfg. **Per capita income** (1989): $13,852. **Unemployment** (1989): 5.9%. **Tourism** (1988-89): non-resident visitors spent $658 mln.

Finance. FDIC-insured commercial banks & trust companies (1987): 169. **Deposits:** $6.1 bln. **Savings institutions** (1990): 10. **Assets:** $1.2 bln.

Federal government. No. federal civilian employees (Mar. 1989): 8,292. **Avg. salary:** $28,606. **Notable federal facilities:** Malmstrom AFB; Ft. Peck, Hungry Horse, Libby, Yellowtail dams, numerous missile silos.

Energy. Electricity production (1988, mwh, by source): Hydroelectric: 8.3 mln; Mineral: 16.5 mln.

Education. Student-teacher ratio (1988): 15.8. **Avg. salary, public school teachers** (1990): $25,081.

State data. Motto: Oro y Plata (Gold and silver). **Flower:** Bitterroot. **Bird:** Western meadowlark. **Tree:** Ponderosa pine. **Song:** Montana. **Entered union** Nov. 8, 1889; rank, 41st. **State fair** at: Great Falls; late July to early Aug.

History. French explorers visited the region, 1742. The U.S. acquired the area partly through the Louisiana Purchase, 1803, and partly through the explorations of Lewis and Clark, 1805-06. Fur traders and missionaries established posts in the early 19th century. Indian uprisings reached their peak with the Battle of the Little Big Horn, 1876. Mining activity and the coming of the Northern Pacific Railway, 1883, brought population growth.

Tourist attractions. Glacier Natl. Park, on the Continental Divide, is a scenic and recreational wonderland, with 60 glaciers, 200 lakes, and many trout streams. Yellowstone Natl. Park has 3 or 5 entrances in Montana, with 2,221,000 acres of scenic beauty, inc. geysers, mountains, canyons, streams, lakes, forests, waterfalls.

Also, Museum of the Plains Indian, Blackfeet Reservation near Browning; Custer Battlefield National Cemetery; Flathead Lake, in the NW, Lewis and Clark Caverns State Park, near Whitehall; 7 Indian reservations, covering over 5 million acres; state capitol and historical society, Helena.

Famous Montanans include Gary Cooper, Marcus Daly, Chet Huntley, Will James, Myrna Loy, Mike Mansfield, Brent Musberger, Jeannette Rankin, Charles M. Russell, Lester Thurow.

Chamber of Commerce. 2030 11th Ave., P.O. Box 1730, Helena, MT 59624.

Toll-free travel information. 1-800-541-1447.

Nebraska

Cornhusker State

People. Population (1989): 1,611,000; **rank:** 36. **Pop. density:** 20.8 per sq. mi. **Urban** (1980): 62.9%. **Racial distrib.** (1985): 96.7% White; 3.3% Black; Hispanic 29,900. **Net change** (1985-89): +6,000; 0.4%.

Geography. Total area: 77,355 sq. mi.; **rank:** 15. **Land area:** 76,644 sq. mi. **Acres forested land:** 1,029,100. **Location:** West North Central state with the Missouri R. for a NE/E border. **Climate:** continental semi-arid. **Topography:** till plains of the central lowland in the eastern third rising to the Great Plains and hill country of the north central and NW. **Capital:** Lincoln.

Economy. Principal industries: agriculture, food processing, manufacturing. **Principal manufactured goods:** foods, machinery, electric and electronic equipment, primary and fabricated metal products, transportation equipment, instruments & related prod. **Agriculture:** Chief **crops:** corn, sorghum, soybeans, hay, wheat, beans, oats, potatoes, sugar beets. **Livestock** (1989): 5.5 mln. cattle; 4.0 mln. hogs/pigs; 180,000 sheep; 4.5 mln. poultry. **Nonfuel Minerals** (1989): $85 mln.; mostly Portland cement, crushed stone, construction sand & gravel. **Chief ports:** Omaha, Sioux City, Brownville, Blair, Plattsmouth, Nebraska City. **Value of construction** (1989): $1.1 bln. **Employment distribution** (1989): 25.8% trade; 23.0% serv.; 20.1% gvt.; 13.8% mfg.; 8.8% agric. **Per capita income** (1989): $15,360. **Unemployment** (1989): 3.1%. **Tourism** (1989): traveler expenditures $3.6 bln. **Sales tax:** 4%, + some local sales taxes of .5-1.5%.

Finance. FDIC-insured commercial banks & trust companies (1987): 437. **Deposits:** $14.5 bln. **Savings institutions** (1990): 23. **Assets:** $11.0 bln.

Federal government. No. federal civilian employees (Mar. 1989): 9,039. **Avg. salary:** $28,148. **Notable federal facilities:** Strategic Air Command Base, Omaha.

Energy. Electricity production (1988, mwh, by source): Hydroelectric: 1.4 mln.; Mineral: 12.5 mln.; Nuclear: 6.8 mln.

Education. Student-teacher ratio (1968): 15.0. **Avg. salary, public school teachers** (1990): $24,751.

State data. Motto: Equality before the law. **Flower:** Goldenrod. **Bird:** Western meadowlark. **Tree:** Cottonwood. **Song:** Beautiful Nebraska. **Entered union** Mar. 1, 1867; rank, 37th. **State fair** at: Lincoln; Aug. 31-Sept. 9, 1990.

History. Spanish and French explorers and fur traders visited the area prior to the Louisiana Purchase, 1803. Lewis and Clark passed through, 1804-06. First permanent settlement was Bellevue, near Omaha, 1823. Many Civil War veterans settled under free land terms of the 1862 Homestead Act; struggles followed between homesteaders and ranchers.

Tourist attractions. Architecturally unique, 400' tall state capitol, Lincoln; Stuhr Museum of the Prairie Pioneer, Grand Island; Museum of the Fur Trade, Chadron; State Museum (Elephant Hall), Lincoln; Joslyn Art Museum, Omaha; Strategic Air Command Museum, Bellevue; Boys Town, founded by Fr. Flanagan, west of Omaha; Arbor Lodge State Park, Nebraska City; Buffalo Bill Ranch State Historical Park, North Platte; Pioneer Village, Minden; Oregon Trail landmarks, Scotts Bluff National Monument, Chimney Rock Historic Site, Ft. Robinson; Hastings Museum, McDonald Planetarium, Hastings.

Famous Nebraskans include Fred Astaire, William E. and William Jennings Bryan, Johnny Carson, Willa Cather, William F. "Buffalo Bill" Cody, Loren Eiseley, Rev. Edward J. Flanagan, Henry Fonda, Gerald R. Ford, Rollin Kirby, Harold Lloyd, Wright Morris, J. Sterling Morton, John

Neidhardt, George Norris, Gen. John J. Pershing, Chief Red Cloud, Mari Sandoz, Malcolm X, Roscoe Pound.

Chamber of Commerce. 1320 Lincoln Mall, Box 95128, Lincoln, NE 68501.

Toll-free travel information. 1-800-742-7595; 1-800-228-4307 out of state.

Nevada

Sagebrush State, Battle Born State, Silver State

People. Population (1989): 1,111,000; **rank:** 40. **Pop. density:** 10.0 per sq. mi. **Urban** (1980): 85.3%. **Racial distrib.** (1985): 93.4% White; 6.6% Black; Hispanic 69,700. **Net change** (1985-89): +171,000; 18.3%.

Geography. Total area: 110,561 sq. mi.; **rank:** 7. **Land area:** 109,894 sq. mi. **Acres forested land:** 7,683,300. **Location:** Mountain state bordered on N by Oregon and Idaho, on E by Utah and Arizona, on SE by Arizona, and on SW/W by California. **Climate:** semi-arid and arid. **Topography:** rugged N-S mountain ranges; highest elevation, Boundary Peak, 13,140 ft.; southern area is within the Mojave Desert; lowest elevation, Colorado R. Canyon, 470 ft. **Capital:** Carson City.

Economy. Principal industries: gaming, tourism, mining, manufacturing, government, agriculture, warehousing, trucking. **Principal manufactured goods:** gaming devices, chemicals, aerospace prods.; lawn & garden irrigation equip.; seismic & machinery-monitoring devices. **Agriculture:** Chief **crops:** alfalfa seed, potatoes, hay, barley, wheat. **Livestock** (1988): 500,000 cattle; 16,000 hogs/ pigs; 96,000 sheep; 18,000 poultry. **Timber/lumber:** piñon, juniper, other pines. **Nonfuel Minerals** (1989): $2.0 bln.; mostly gold, silver, barite, construction sand & gravel. **International airports** at Las Vegas, Reno. **Value of construction** (1989): $3.3 bln. **Employment distribution** (1989): 43% serv.; 21% trade; 12% gvt. **Per capita income** (1989): $18,827. **Unemployment** (1989): 5.0%. **Tourism** (1987): out-of-state travelers spent $8.2 bln. **Sales tax:** 5.75-6%.

Finance. FDIC-insured commercial banks & trust companies (1987): 18. **Deposits:** $6.1 bln. **Savings institutions** (1990): 6. **Assets:** $5.0 bln.

Federal government. No. federal civilian employees (Mar. 1989): 6,718. **Avg. salary:** $29,851. **Notable federal facilities:** Nevada Test Site; Hawthorne Army Ammunition Plant, Nellis Air Force Base & Gunnery Range; Fallon Naval Air Station; Palomino Valley Wild Horse & Burro Placement Center.

Energy. Electricity production (1988, mwh, by source): Hydroelectric: 2.1 mln.; Mineral: 18.2 mln.

Education. Student-teacher ratio (1988): 20.3. **Avg. salary, public school teachers** (1990): $30,587.

State data. Motto: All for our country. **Flower:** Sagebrush. **Bird:** Mountain bluebird. **Trees:** Single-leaf pinon and bristlecone pine. **Song:** Home Means Nevada. **Entered union** Oct. 31, 1864; rank, 36th. **State fair** at Reno; early Sept.

History. Nevada was first explored by Spaniards in 1776. Hudson's Bay Co. trappers explored the north and central region, 1825; trader Jedediah Smith crossed the state, 1826 and 1827. The area was acquired by the U.S., in 1848, at the end of the Mexican War. First settlement, Mormon Station, now Genoa, was est. 1849. In the early 20th century, Nevada adopted progressive measures such as the initiative, referendum, recall, and woman suffrage.

Tourist attractions. Legalized casino gambling provided the impetus for the development of resort facilities at Lake Tahoe, Reno, Las Vegas, and elsewhere. Ghost towns, rodeos, mountain climbing, skiing, golfing, trout fishing, water sports and hunting important. Notable are Hoover Dam, Lake Mead Natl. Recreation Area, Lake Tahoe, Great Basin Natl. Park, Valley of Fire State Park & Virginia City. Annual events inc. Helldorado Days & Rodeo, Las Vegas; Reno Rodeo; Basque Festival, Elko; Nevada Day, Carson City; Cowboy Poetry Gathering, Elko.

Famous Nevadans include Walter Van Tilburg Clark, Sarah Winnemucca Hopkins, Paul Laxalt, John William Mackay, Pat McCarran, Dat So La Lee, Key Pittman, William Morris Stewart.

Tourist Information. Commission on Tourism, Capitol Complex, Carson City, NV 89710.

Toll-free travel information. 1-800-638-2328.

New Hampshire
Granite State

People. Population (1989): 1,107,000; **rank: 41. Pop. density:** 119.3 per sq. mi. **Urban** (1980): 52.2%. **Racial distrib.** (1980): 98.8% White; 0.4% Black; Hispanic 5,700. **Net change** (1985-89): +109,000; 10.9%.

Geography. Total area: 9,279 sq. mi.; **rank: 44. Land area:** 8,993 sq. mi. **Acres forested land:** 5,013,500. **Location:** New England state bounded on S by Massachusetts, on W by Vermont, on N/NW by Canada, on E by Maine and the Atlantic O. **Climate:** highly varied, due to its nearness to high mountains and ocean. **Topography:** low, rolling coast followed by countless hills and mountains rising out of a central plateau. **Capital:** Concord.

Economy. Principal industries: tourism, manufacturing, agriculture, trade, mining. **Principal manufactured goods:** machinery, electrical & electronic products, plastics, fabricated metal products, leather goods. **Agriculture: Chief crops:** dairy products, nursery and greenhouse products, hay, vegetables, fruit, maple syrup & sugar prods. **Livestock** (1988): 55,000 cattle; 9,000 hogs/pigs; 12,000 sheep; 365,000 poultry. **Timber/lumber** (1988): white pine, hemlock, oak, birch; 158 mln. bd. ft. **Nonfuel Minerals** (1989): $49 mln.; mostly construction sand & gravel, crushed & dimension stone. **Commercial fishing** (1989): $10.3 mln. **Chief ports:** Portsmouth, Hampton, Rye. **Value of construction** (1989): $1.3 bln. **Employment distribution** (1988): 22.5% mfg.; 25.7% trade; 22.4% serv; 12.9% gvt. **Per capita income** (1989): $20,251. **Unemployment** (1989): 3.5%. **Tourism** (1989): out-of-state visitors spent $2.2 bln.

Finance. FDIC-insured commercial banks & trust companies (1987): 60. **Deposits:** $6.9 bln. **Savings institutions** (1990): 11. **Assets:** $1.9 bln.

Federal government. No. federal civilian employees (Mar. 1989): 3,644. **Avg. salary:** $30,434.

Energy. Electricity production (1988, mwh, by source): Hydroelectric: 968,000; Mineral: 6.0 mln.

Education. Student-teacher ratio (1988): 16.2. **Avg. salary, public school teachers** (1990): $28,939.

State data. Motto: Live free or die. **Flower:** Purple lilac. **Bird:** Purple finch. **Tree:** White birch. **Song:** Old New Hampshire. **Ninth** of the original 13 states to ratify the Constitution, June 21, 1788.

History. First explorers to visit the New Hampshire area were England's Martin Pring, 1603, and Champlain, 1605. First settlement was Odiorne's Point (now port of Rye), 1623. Indian raids were halted, 1759, by Robert Rogers' Rangers. Before the Revolution, New Hampshire men seized a British fort at Portsmouth, 1774, and drove the royal governor out, 1775. Three regiments served in the Continental Army and scores of privateers raided British shipping.

Tourist attractions. Mt. Washington, highest peak in Northeast, hub of network of trails; Lake Winnipesaukee; White Mt. Natl. Forest; Crawford, Franconia, Pinkham notches in White Mt. region—Franconia famous for the Old Man of the Mountains, described by Hawthorne as the Great Stone Face; the Flume, a spectacular gorge; the aerial tramway on Cannon Mt; Strawbery Banke, Portsmouth; Shaker Village, Canterbury.

Famous New Hampshirites include Salmon P. Chase, Ralph Adams Cram, Mary Baker Eddy, Daniel Chester French, Robert Frost, Horace Greeley, Sarah Buell Hale, Franklin Pierce, Augustus Saint-Gaudens, Daniel Webster.

Tourist Information. Department of Resources and Economic Development, Office of Vacation Travel, P.O. Box 856, Concord, NH 03301.

Toll-free travel information. 1-800-258-3608 in northeast; to obtain guidebook, 1-800-441-5370.

New Jersey
Garden State

People. Population (1989): 7,736,000; **rank: 9. Pop. density:** 993.5 per sq. mi. **Urban** (1980): 89.0%. **Racial distrib.** (1985): 86.4% White; 13.6% Black; Hispanic 573,200. **Net change** (1985-89): +168,000; 2.2%.

Geography. Total area: 7,787 sq. mi.; **rank: 46. Land area:** 7,468 sq. mi. **Acres forested land:** 1,928,400. **Location:** Middle Atlantic state bounded on the N and E by New York and the Atlantic O., on the S and W by Delaware and Pennsylvania. **Climate:** moderate, with marked difference bet. NW and SE extremities. **Topography:** Appalachian Valley in the NW also has highest elevation, High Pt., 1,801 ft.; Appalachian Highlands, flat-topped NE-SW mountain ranges; Piedmont Plateau, low plains broken by high ridges (Palisades) rising 400-500 ft.; Coastal Plain, covering three-fifths of state in SE, gradually rises from sea level to gentle slopes. **Capital:** Trenton.

Economy. Principal industries: services, trade, manufacturing. **Principal manufactured goods:** chemicals, electronic and electrical equipment, non-electrical machinery, fabricated metals. **Agriculture: Chief crops:** hay, corn, soybeans, tomatoes, blueberries, peaches, cranberries. **Livestock** (1987): 77,500 cattle; 32,000 hogs/pigs; 12,600 sheep; 2.1 mln. poultry. **Timber/lumber** (1988): pine, cedar, mixed hardwoods; 7 mln. bd. ft. **Nonfuel Minerals** (1989): $230 mln.; mostly crushed stone, construction sand & gravel. **Commercial fishing** (1989): $78.8 mln. **Chief ports:** Newark, Elizabeth, Hoboken, Camden. **International airports at:** Newark. **Value of construction** (1989): $7.3 bln. **Employment distribution** (1989): 25.7% serv.; 24.0% trade; 17.6% mfg.; 15.1% gvt. **Per capita income** (1989): $23,764. **Unemployment** (1989): 4.1%. **Tourism** (1988): tourists spent $13.6 bln. **Sales tax:** 6%.

Finance. FDIC-insured commercial banks & trust companies (1987): 125. **Deposits:** $59.6. **Savings institutions** (1990): 130. **Assets:** $52.0 bln.

Federal government. No. federal civilian employees (Mar. 1989): 37,644. **Avg. salary:** $29,946. **Notable federal facilities:** McGuire AFB Fort Dix; Fort Monmouth; Picatinny Arsenal; Lakewood Naval Air Station, Lakehurst Naval Air Engineering Center.

Energy. Electricity production (1988, mwh, by source): Mineral: 16.7 mln.; Nuclear: 23.9 mln.

Education. Student-teacher ratio (1988): 13.6. **Avg. salary, public school teachers** (1990): $36,030.

State Data. Motto: Liberty and prosperity. **Flower:** Purple violet. **Bird:** Eastern goldfinch. **Tree:** Red oak. **Third** of the original 13 states to ratify the Constitution, Dec. 18, 1787. **State fair:** usually Aug.

History. The Lenni Lenape (Delaware) Indians had mostly peaceful relations with European colonists who arrived after the explorers Verrazano, 1524, and Hudson, 1609. The Dutch were first; when the British took New Netherland, 1664, the area between the Delaware and Hudson Rivers was given to Lord John Berkeley and Sir George Carteret. New Jersey was the scene of nearly 100 battles, large and small, during the Revolution, including Trenton, 1776, Princeton, 1777, Monmouth, 1778.

Tourist attractions. 127 miles of beaches; Miss America Pageant and hotel-casinos, Atlantic City; Grover Cleveland birthplace, Caldwell. Cape May Historic District; Edison Labs, W. Orange; Great Adventure amusement park; Liberty State Park; Meadowlands Sports Complex; Pine Barrens wilderness area; Princeton University; numerous Revolutionary War historical sites.

Famous New Jerseyans include Count Basie, Aaron Burr, Grover Cleveland, James Fenimore Cooper, Stephen Crane, Thomas Edison, Albert Einstein, Alexander Hamilton, Joyce Kilmer, Gen. George McClellan,

Thomas Paine, Molly Pitcher, Paul Robeson, Walter Schirra, Frank Sinatra, Bruce Springsteen, Walt Whitman, Woodrow Wilson.

Chamber of Commerce. 51 Commerce St., Newark, NJ 07102.

Toll-free travel information. 1-800-JERSEY-7.

New Mexico
Land of Enchantment

People. Population (1989): 1,528,000; **rank:** 37. **Pop. density:** 12.6 per sq. mi. **Urban** (1980): 72.1%. **Racial distrib.** (1985): 89.0% White; 2.0% Black; 9.0% Other (includes American Indians); Hispanic 550,600. **Net change** (1985-89): +78,000; 5.4%.

Geography. Total area: 121,593 sq. mi.; **rank:** 5. **Land area:** 121,335 sq. mi. **Acres forested land:** 18,059,800. **Location:** southwestern state bounded by Colorado on the N, Oklahoma, Texas, and Mexico on the E and S, and Arizona on the W. **Climate:** dry, with temperatures rising or falling 5°F with every 1,000 ft. elevation. **Topography:** eastern third, Great Plains; central third Rocky Mtns. (85% of the state is over 4,000 ft. elevation); western third high plateau. **Capital:** Santa Fe.

Economy. Principal industries: extractive industries, tourism, agriculture. **Principal manufactured goods:** foods, electrical machinery, apparel, lumber, printing, transportation equipment. **Agriculture: Chief crops:** wheat, hay, sorghum, grain, onions, cotton, corn. **Livestock:** 1.72 mln. cattle; 72,000 hogs/pigs; 578,000 sheep; 1.21 mln. poultry. **Timber/lumber** (1988): Ponderosa pine, Douglas fir; 176 mln. bd. ft. **Nonfuel Minerals** (1989): $1.2 bln.; copper, potash, construction sand & gravel. **International airports at:** Albuquerque. **Value of construction** (1989): $1.3 bln. **Employment distribution:** 22.3% serv.; 18.0% agric.; 10% mfg.; 26.2% gvt. **Per capita income** (1989): $13,191. **Unemployment** (1989): 6.7%. **Tourism** (1989): out-of-state visitors spent $2.2 bln. **Sales tax:** 4¾%.

Finance. FDIC-insured commercial banks & trust companies (1987): 94. **Deposits:** $8.5 bln. **Savings institutions** (1990): 24. **Assets:** $4.9 bln.

Federal government. No. federal civilian employees (Mar. 1989): 23,369. **Avg. salary:** $28,182. **Notable federal facilities:** Kirtland, Cannon, Holloman AF bases; Los Alamos Scientific Laboratory; White Sands Missile Range.

Energy. Electricity production (1988, mwh, by source): Hydroelectric: 100,000; Mineral: 26.3 mln.

Education. Student-teacher ratio (1988): 18.5. **Avg. salary, public school teachers** (1990): $25,120.

State data. Motto: Crescit Eundo (It grows as it goes). **Flower:** Yucca. **Bird:** Roadrunner. **Tree:** Pinon. **Song:** O, Fair New Mexico, Asi Es Nuevo Mexico. **Entered union** Jan. 6, 1912; **rank,** 47th. **State fair** at: Albuquerque; mid-Sept.

History. Franciscan Marcos de Niza and a black slave Estevan explored the area, 1539, seeking gold. First settlements were at San Juan Pueblo, 1598, and Santa Fe, 1610. Settlers alternately traded and fought with the Apaches, Comanches, and Navajos. Trade on the Santa Fe Trail to Missouri started 1821. The Mexican War was declared May, 1846, Gen. Stephen Kearny took Santa Fe, August. In the 1870s, cattlemen staged the famed Lincoln County War in which Billy (the Kid) Bonney played a leading role. Pancho Villa raided Columbus, 1916.

Tourist Attractions. Carlsbad Caverns, a national park, has caverns on 3 levels and the largest natural cave "room" in the world, 1,500 by 300 ft., 300 ft. high; White Sands Natl. Monument, the largest gypsum deposit in the world.

Pueblo ruins from 100 AD, Chaco Canyon; Acoma, the "sky city," built atop a 357-ft. mesa; 19 Pueblo, 4 Navajo, and 2 Apache reservations. Also, ghost towns, dude ranches, skiing, hunting, and fishing.

Famous New Mexicans include Billy (the Kid) Bonney, Kit Carson, Peter Hurd, Archbishop Jean Baptiste Lamy,

Nancy Lopez, Bill Mauldin, Georgia O'Keeffe, Kim Stanley, Al Unser, Bobby Unser, Lew Wallace.

Tourist information. New Mexico Travel Division, Joseph M. Montoya Bldg., 1100 St. Francis Dr., Santa Fe, N.M. 87503.

Toll-free travel information. 1-800-545-2040.

New York
Empire State

People. Population (1989): 17,950,000; **rank:** 2. **Pop. density:** 365.5 per sq. mi. **Urban** (1980): 84.6%. **Racial distrib.** (1985): 84.6% White; 15.4% Black; Hispanic: 1.9 mln. **Net change** (1985-89): +182,000; 1.0%.

Geography. Total area: 49,108 sq. mi.; **rank:** 30. **Land area:** 47,377 sq. mi. **Acres forested land:** 17,218,400. **Location:** Middle Atlantic state, bordered by the New England states, Atlantic Ocean, New Jersey and Pennsylvania, Lakes Ontario and Erie, and Canada. **Climate:** variable; the SE region moderated by the ocean. **Topography:** highest and most rugged mountains in the NE Adirondack upland; St. Lawrence-Champlain lowlands extend from Lake Ontario NE along the Canadian border; Hudson-Mohawk lowland follows the flows of the rivers N and W, 10-30 mi. wide; Atlantic coastal plain in the SE; Appalachian Highlands, covering half the state westward from the Hudson Valley, include the Catskill Mtns., Finger Lakes; plateau of Erie-Ontario lowlands. **Capital:** Albany.

Economy. Principal industries: manufacturing, finance, communications, tourism, transportation, services. **Principal manufactured goods:** books and periodicals, clothing and apparel, pharmaceuticals, machinery, instruments, toys and sporting goods, electronic equipment, automotive and aircraft components. **Agriculture: Chief crops:** apples, cabbage, cauliflower, celery, cherries, grapes, corn, peas, snap beans, sweet corn. **Products:** milk, cheese, maple syrup, wine. **Livestock** (1988): 1.7 mln. cattle; 151,000 hogs/pigs; 63,000 sheep; 10.9 mln. poultry. **Timber/lumber** (1988): saw log production; 304 mln. bd. ft. **Nonfuel Minerals** (1989): $746 mln.; mostly crushed stone, cement, construction sand & gravel, zinc. **Commercial fishing** (1989): $51.1 mln. **Chief ports:** New York, Buffalo, Albany. **International airports at:** New York, Buffalo, Syracuse, Massena, Ogdensburg, Watertown, Niagara Falls, Newburgh, Sullivan county. **Value of construction** (1989): $16.4 bln. **Employment distribution** (1989): 18% mfg.; 32% serv.; 26% trade. **Per capita income** (1989): $20,540. **Unemployment** (1989): 5.1%. **Tourism** (1988): tourists spent $20.0 bln. **Sales tax:** 4-8¼%.

Finance. FDIC-insured commercial banks & trust companies (1987): 200. **Deposits:** $468.8 bln. **Savings institutions** (1990): 86. **Assets:** $56.7 bln.

Federal government. No. federal civilian employees (Mar. 1989): 68,719. **Avg. salary:** $28,365. **Notable federal facilities:** West Point Military Academy; Merchant Marine Academy; Ft. Drum; Griffiss, Plattsburgh AF bases; Watervliet Arsenal.

Energy. Electricity production (1988, mwh, by source): Hydroelectric: 24.0 mln.; Mineral: 76.6 mln.; Nuclear: 24.2 mln.

Education. Student-teacher ratio (1988): 14.9. **Avg. salary, public school teachers** (1990): $38,800.

State data. Motto: Excelsior (Ever upward). **Flower:** Rose. **Bird:** Bluebird. **Tree:** Sugar maple. **Song:** I Love New York. **Eleventh** of the original 13 states to ratify the Constitution, July 26, 1788. **State fair** at: Syracuse, late Aug.-early Sept.

History. In 1609 Henry Hudson discovered the river that bears his name and Champlain explored the lake, far upstate, which was named for him. Dutch built posts near Albany 1614 and 1624; in 1626 they settled Manhattan. A British fleet seized New Netherland, 1664. Ninety-two of the 300 or more engagements of the Revolution were fought in New York, including the Battle of Bemis Heights-Saratoga, a turning point of the war.

Tourist attractions. New York City; Adirondack and Catskill mtns.; Finger Lakes, Great Lakes; Long Island beaches; Thousand Islands; Niagara Falls; Saratoga Springs racing and spas; Philipsburg Manor, Sunnyside, the restored home of Washington Irving, The Dutch Church of Sleepy Hollow, all in North Tarrytown; Corning Glass Center and Steuben factory, Corning; Fenimore House, National Baseball Hall of Fame and Museum, both in Cooperstown; Ft. Ticonderoga overlooking lakes George and Champlain; Albany's Empire State Plaza, Lake Placid Olympic Village.

The Franklin D. Roosevelt National Historic Site, Hyde Park, includes the graves of Pres. and Mrs. Roosevelt, the family home since 1867, the Roosevelt Library. Sagamore Hill, Oyster Bay, the Theodore Roosevelt estate, includes his home.

Famous New Yorkers include Susan B. Anthony, Peter Cooper, George Eastman, Millard Fillmore, Julia Ward Howe, Charles Evans Hughes, Henry and William James, Herman Melville, Franklin Delano Roosevelt, Theodore Roosevelt, Alfred E. Smith, Elizabeth Cady Stanton, Martin Van Buren, Walt Whitman.

Tourist information: N.Y. State Dept. of Economic Development, 1 Commerce Plaza, Albany, NY 12245.

Toll-free travel information. 1-800-CALLNYS, from the 48 contiguous states; 1-518-474-4116 from other areas and Canada.

North Carolina

Tar Heel State, Old North State

People. Population (1989): 6,571,000; **rank: 10. Pop. density:** 124.8 per sq. mi. **Urban** (1980): 42.9%. **Racial distrib.** (1985): 77.5% White; 22.5% Black; Hispanic: 38,900. **Net change** (1985-89): +312,000; 5.0%.

Geography. Total area: 52,669 sq. mi.; **rank: 28. Land area:** 48,843 sq. mi. **Acres forested land:** 20,043,300. **Location:** South Atlantic state bounded by Virginia, South Carolina, Georgia, Tennessee, and the Atlantic O. **Climate:** sub-tropical in SE, medium-continental in mountain region; tempered by the Gulf Stream and the mountains in W. **Topography:** coastal plain and tidewater, two-fifths of state, extending to the fall line of the rivers; piedmont plateau, another two-fifths, 200 mi. wide of gentle to rugged hills; southern Appalachian Mtns. contains the Blue Ridge and Great Smoky mtns. **Capital:** Raleigh.

Economy. Principal industries: manufacturing, agriculture, tobacco, tourism. **Principal manufactured goods:** textiles, tobacco products, electrical/electronic equip., chemicals, furniture, food products, non-electrical machinery. **Agriculture: Chief crops:** tobacco, soybeans, corn, peanuts, small sweet potatoes, feed grains, vegetables, fruits. **Livestock** (1987): 950,000 cattle; 2.6 mln. hogs/pigs; 20.9 mln. chickens. **Timber/lumber** (1988): yellow pine, oak, hickory, poplar, maple. 1.7 bln. bd. ft. **Nonfuel Minerals** (1989): Total $584 mln., mostly clay, sand & gravel, crushed stone. **Commercial fishing** (1989): $70.6 mln. **Chief ports:** Morehead City, Wilmington. **Value of construction** (1989): $7.2 bln. **Employment distribution** (1989): 29.2% mfg.; 22.9% trade; 17.6% serv.; 15.3% gvt. **Per capita income** (1989): $15,221. **Unemployment** (1989): 3.5%. **Tourism** (1989): out-of-state visitors spent $6.2 bln. **Sales tax:** 5.0%.

Finance. FDIC-insured commercial banks & trust companies (1987): 65. **Deposits:** $41.0 bln. **Savings institutions** (1990): 129. **Assets:** $21.2 bln.

Federal government. No. federal civilian employees (Mar. 1989): 28,990. **Avg. salary:** $26,802. **Notable federal facilities:** Ft. Bragg; Camp LeJeune Marine Base; U.S. EPA Research and Development Labs, Cherry Point Marine Corps Air Station; Natl. Humanities Center; Natl. Inst. of Environmental Health Science; Natl. Center for Health Statistics Lab, Research Triangle Park.

Energy. Electricity production (1988, mwh, by source): Hydroelectric: 2.9 mln.; Mineral: 46.4 mln.; Nuclear: 29.2 mln.

Education. Student-teacher ratio (1988): 17.5. **Avg. salary, public school teachers** (1990): $27,814.

State data. Motto: Esse Quam Videri (To be rather than to seem). **Flower:** Dogwood. **Bird:** Cardinal. **Tree:**

Pine. **Song:** The Old North State. **Twelfth** of the original 13 states to ratify the Constitution, Nov. 21, 1789. **State fair** at: Raleigh; mid-Oct.

History. The first English colony in America was the first of 2 established by Sir Walter Raleigh on Roanoke Is., 1585 and 1587. The first group returned to England; the second, the "Lost Colony," disappeared without trace. Permanent settlers came from Virginia, c. 1660. Roused by British repressions, the colonists drove out the royal governor, 1775; the province's congress was the first to vote for independence; ten regiments were furnished to the Continental Army. Cornwallis' forces were defeated at Kings Mountain, 1780, and forced out after Guilford Courthouse, 1781.

Tourist attractions. Cape Hatteras and Cape Lookout national seashores; Great Smoky Mtns. (half in Tennessee); Guilford Courthouse and Moore's Creek parks, 66 Revolutionary battle sites; Bennett Place, NW of Durham, where Gen. Joseph Johnston surrendered the last Confederate army to Gen. Wm. Sherman; Ft. Raleigh, Roanoke Is., where Virginia Dare, first child of English parents in the New World, was born Aug. 18, 1587; Wright Brothers National Memorial, Kitty Hawk; N.C. Zoo, Asheboro; N. Carolina Symphony, Raleigh.

Famous North Carolinians include Richard J. Gatling, Billy Graham, Andrew Jackson, Andrew Johnson, Wm. Rufus King, Dolley Madison, Edward R. Murrow, James K. Polk, Enos Slaughter, Moses Waddel, Thomas Wolfe.

Tourist information. Division of Travel & Tourism Development, P.O. Box 25249, Raleigh, NC 27611.

Toll-free travel information. 1-800-VISITNC.

North Dakota

Peace Garden State

People. Population (1989): 660,000; **rank: 47. Pop. density:** 9.3 per sq. mi. **Urban** (1980): 48.8%. **Racial distrib.** (1980): 95.8% White; 0.39% Black; Hispanic (1980): 3,700. **Net change** (1985-89): -25,000; -3.6%.

Geography. Total area: 70,702 sq. mi.; **rank: 17. Land area:** 69,300 sq. mi. **Acres forested land:** 421,800. **Location:** West North Central state, situated exactly in the middle of North America, bounded on the N by Canada, on the E by Minnesota, on the S by South Dakota, on the W by Montana. **Climate:** continental, with a wide range of temperature and moderate rainfall. **Topography:** Central Lowland in the E comprises the flat Red River Valley and the Rolling Drift Prairie; Missouri Plateau of the Great Plains on the W. **Capital:** Bismarck.

Economy. Principal industries: agriculture, mining, tourism, manufacturing. **Principal manufactured goods:** farm equipment, processed foods. **Agriculture: Chief crops:** spring wheat, durum, barley, rye, flaxseed, oats, potatoes, dried edible beans, honey, soybeans, sugarbeets, sunflowers, hay. **Livestock** (1987): 2.0 mln. cattle; 285,000 hogs/pigs; 180,000 sheep; 1.4 mln. poultry. **Nonfuel Minerals** (1989): $14 mln. mostly lime, construction sand & gravel, crushed stone. **International airports at:** Fargo, Grand Forks, Bismarck, Minot. **Value of construction** (1989): $458.3 mln. **Employment distribution:** 21.9% trade; 20.4% gvt.; 18.6% serv.; 17.2% agric. **Per capita income** (1989): $13,261. **Unemployment** (1989): 4.2%. **Tourism** (1988): $565 mln. **Sales tax:** 6.5%-7.5%.

Finance. FDIC-insured commercial banks & trust companies (1987): 176. **Deposits:** $6.1 bln. **Savings institutions** (1990): 6. **Assets:** $4.2 bln.

Federal government. No. federal civilian employees (Mar. 1989): 5,552. **Avg. salary:** $26,291. **Notable federal facilities:** Strategic Air Command bases at Minot, Grand Forks; Northern Prairie Wildlife Research Center; Garrison Dam; Theodore Roosevelt Natl. Park; Grand Forks Energy Research Center; Ft. Union Natl. Historic Site.

Energy. Electricity production (1988, mwh, by source): Hydroelectric: 1.9 mln.; Mineral: 25.5 mln.

Education. Student-teacher ratio (1988): 15.4. **Avg. salary, public school teachers** (1990): $23,016.

State data. Motto: Liberty and union, now and forever, one and inseparable. **Flower:** Wild prairie rose. **Bird:** Western Meadowlark. **Tree:** American elm. **Song:** North Dakota Hymn. **Entered union** Nov. 2, 1889; rank, 39th. **State fair** at: Minot; 3d week in July.

History. Pierre La Verendrye was the first French fur trader in the area, 1738, followed later by the English. The U.S. acquired half the territory in the Louisiana Purchase, 1803. Lewis and Clark built Ft. Mandan, spent the winter of 1804-05 there. In 1818, American ownership of the other half was confirmed by agreement with Britain. First permanent settlement was at Pembina, 1812. Missouri River steamboats reached the area, 1832; the first railroad, 1873, bringing many homesteaders. The state was first to hold a presidential primary, 1912.

Tourist attractions. North Dakota Heritage Center, state capitol grounds; Bonanzaville, Fargo, restored pioneer town; Ft. Union Trading Post Natl. Historic Site, built 1829; Lake Sakakawea, 180 miles of fishing, boating, 1,600 miles of shoreline. Interntl. Peace Garden, 2,200-acre tract extending across the border into Manitoba; 65,000-acre Theodore Roosevelt National Park, Badlands, contains the president's Elkhorn Ranch; Ft. Abraham Lincoln State Park and Museum, S of Mandan.

Famous North Dakotans include Maxwell Anderson, Angie Dickinson, John Bernard Flannagan; Louis L'Amour, Peggy Lee, Eric Sevareid, Vilhjalmur Stefansson, Lawrence Welk.

Chamber of Commerce. P.O. Box 2467, Fargo, ND 58108.

Toll-free travel information. 1-800-437-2077.

Ohio
Buckeye State

People. Population (1989): 10,907,000; rank: 7. **Pop. density:** 263.9 per sq. mi. **Urban** (1980): 73.3%. **Racial distrib.** (1985): 89.4% White; 10.6% Black; Hispanic (1980): 107,700. **Net change** (1985-89): +132,000; 1.2%.

Geography. Total area: 41,330 sq. mi.; rank: 35. **Land area:** 41,004 sq. mi. **Acres forested land:** 6,146,600. **Location:** East North Central state bounded on the N by Michigan and Lake Erie; on the E and S by Pennsylvania, West Virginia; and Kentucky; on the W by Indiana. **Climate:** temperate but variable; weather subject to much precipitation. **Topography:** generally rolling plain; Allegheny plateau in E; Lake [Erie] plains extend southward; central plains in the W. **Capital:** Columbus.

Economy. Principal industries: manufacturing, trade, services. **Principal manufactured goods:** transportation equipment, machinery, primary and fabricated metal products. **Agriculture: Chief crops:** corn, hay, winter wheat, oats, soybeans. **Livestock** (1985): 1.8 mln. cattle; 2.0 mln. hogs/pigs; 275,000 sheep; 22.0 mln. poultry. **Timber/lumber** (1988): oak, ash, maple, walnut, beech; 303 mln. bd. ft. **Nonfuel Minerals** (1989): $787 mln.; mostly crushed stone, construction sand & gravel, lime, Portland cement. **Commercial fishing** (1989): $1.3 mln. **Chief ports:** Toledo, Conneaut, Cleveland, Ashtabula. **International airports at:** Cleveland, Cincinnati, Columbus, Dayton. **Value of construction** (1989): $10.3 bln. **Employment distribution** (1985): 25.6% mfg.; 24.2% trade; 21.8% serv.; 15.2% gvt. **Per capita income** (1989): $16,499. **Unemployment** (1989): 5.5%. **Tourism** (1982): travelers spent nearly $5.4 bln.

Finance. FDIC-insured commercial banks & trust companies (1987): 308. **Deposits:** $70.4 bln. **Savings institutions** (1990): 217. **Assets:** $50.5.

Federal government. No. federal civilian employees (Mar. 1989): 54,732. **Avg. salary:** $30,506. **Notable federal facilities:** Wright Patterson AF base; Defense Construction Supply Center; Lewis Research Ctr.; Portsmouth Gaseous Diffusion Plant; Mound Laboratory.

Energy. Electricity production (1988, mwh, by source): Hydroelectric: 176,000; Mineral: 115.0 mln.; Nuclear: 8.5.

Education. Student-teacher ratio (1988): 17.6. **Avg. salary, public school teachers** (1990): $31,170.

State data. Motto: With God, all things are possible. **Flower:** Scarlet carnation. **Bird:** Cardinal. **Tree:** Buckeye. **Song:** Beautiful Ohio. **Entered union** Mar. 1, 1803; rank, 17th. **State fair** at: Columbus; mid-Aug.

History. LaSalle visited the Ohio area, 1669. American fur-traders arrived, beginning 1685; the French and Indians sought to drive them out. During the Revolution, Virginians defeated the Indians, 1774, but hostilities were renewed, 1777. The region became U.S. territory after the Revolution. First organized settlement was at Marietta, 1788. Indian warfare ended with Anthony Wayne's victory at Fallen Timbers, 1794. In the War of 1812, Oliver H. Perry's victory on Lake Erie and William H. Harrison's invasion of Canada, 1813, ended British incursions.

Tourist attractions. Mound City Group National Monuments, a group of 24 prehistoric Indian burial mounds; Neil Armstrong Air and Space Museum, Wapakoneta; Air Force Museum, Dayton; Pro Football Hall of Fame, Canton; King's Island amusement park, King's Island; Cedar Point amusement park, Sandusky. birthplaces, homes, and memorials to Ohio's 8 U.S. presidents: Wm. Henry Harrison, Grant, Garfield, Hayes, McKinley, Harding, Taft, Benjamin Harrison; Lake Erie Islands, Sandusky; Amish Region, Tuscarawas/Holmes counties; German Village, Columbus; Sea World, Aurora; Jack Nicklaus Sports Center, Mason; Bob Evans Farm, Rio Grande.

Famous Ohioans include Sherwood Anderson, Neil Armstrong, George Bellows, Ambrose Bierce, Clarence Darrow, Paul Laurence Dunbar, Thomas Edison, Clark Gable, John Glenn, Bob Hope, Jack Nicklaus, Jesse Owens, Eddie Rickenbacker, John D. Rockefeller Sr. and Jr., Pete Rose, Gen. Wm. Sherman, Harriet Beecher Stowe, Charles Taft, Robert A. Taft, William H. Taft, James Thurber, Orville Wright.

Chamber of Commerce. 35 E. Gay St., Columbus, OH 43215.

Toll-free travel information. 1-800-BUCKEYE.

Oklahoma
Sooner State

People. Population (1989): 3,224,000; rank: 28. **Pop. density:** 46.1 per sq. mi. **Urban** (1980): 67.3%. **Racial distrib.** (1985): 85.6% White; 6.9% Black; 6.3% Amer. Ind; Hispanic 69,800. **Net change** (1985-89): −90,000; −2.7%.

Geography. Total area: 69,919 sq. mi.; rank: 18. **Land area:** 68,782 sq. mi. **Acres forested land:** 8,513,300. **Location:** West South Central state bounded on the N by Colorado and Kansas; on the E by Missouri and Arkansas; on the S and W by Texas and New Mexico. **Climate:** temperate; southern humid belt merging with colder northern continental; humid eastern and dry western zones. **Topography:** high plains predominate the W, hills and small mountains in the E; the east central region is dominated by the Arkansas R. Basin, and the Red R. Plains, in the S. **Capital:** Oklahoma City.

Economy. Principal industries: manufacturing, mineral and energy exploration and production, agriculture, printing & publishing. **Principal manufactured goods:** non-electrical machinery, fabricated metal products, petroleum. **Agriculture: Chief crops:** wheat, hay, peanuts, grain sorghum, soybeans, corn, pecans, oats, barley, rye. **Livestock** (1989): 5.2 mln. cattle; 240,000 hogs/pigs; 136,000 sheep; 4.65 mln. poultry. **Timber/lumber** (1988): pine, oaks, hickory; 283 mln. bd. ft. **Nonfuel Minerals** (1989): $221 mln.; mostly crushed stone, Portland cement, sand & gravel. **Chief ports:** Catoosa, Muskogee. **International airports at:** Oklahoma City, Tulsa. **Value of construction** (1989): $1.9 bln. **Employment distribution** (1988): 20.2% trade; 19.4% gvt.; 23.2% serv.; 10.7% mfg. **Per capita income** (1989): $14,151. **Unemployment** (1989): 5.6%. **Tourism** (1987): tourists spent $2.9 bln.

Finance. FDIC-insured commercial banks & trust companies (1987): 520. **Deposits:** $25.4 bln. **Savings institutions** (1990): 39. **Assets:** $10.2 bln.

Federal government. No. federal civilian employees (Mar. 1989): 37,465. **Avg. salary:** $27,234. **Notable federal facilities:** Federal Aviation Agency and Tinker AFB, both Oklahoma City; Ft. Sill, Lawton; Altus AFB, Altus; Vance AFB, Enid.

Energy. Electricity production (1988, mwh, by source): Hydroelectric: 2.1 mln.; Mineral: 42.0 mln.

Education. Student-teacher ratio (1988): 16.5. **Avg. salary, public school teachers** (1990): $23,070.

State data. Motto: Labor Omnia Vincit (Labor conquers all things). **Flower:** Mistletoe. **Bird:** Scissortailed flycatcher. **Tree:** Redbud. **Song:** Oklahoma! **Entered union** Nov. 16, 1907; rank, 46th. **State fair at:** Oklahoma City; last week of Sept.

History. Part of the Louisiana Purchase, 1803, Oklahoma was known as Indian Territory (but was not given territorial government) after it became the home of the "Five Civilized Tribes"—Cherokee, Choctaw, Chickasaw, Creek, and Seminole—1828-1846. The land was also used by Comanche, Osage, and other Plains Indians. As white settlers pressed west, land was opened for homesteading by runs and lottery, the first run taking place Apr. 22, 1889. The most famous run was to the Cherokee Outlet, 1893.

Tourist attractions. Will Rogers Memorial, Claremore; National Cowboy Hall of Fame, Oklahoma City; restored Ft. Gibson Stockade, near Muskogee, the Army's largest outpost in Indian lands; Indian pow-wows; rodeos; fishing; hunting; Ouachita National Forest; Enterprise Square, museum devoted to American economic system.

Famous Oklahomans include Carl Albert, L. Gordon Cooper, Woody Guthrie, Gen. Patrick J. Hurley, Karl Jansky, Mickey Mantle, Carry Nation, Wiley Post, Oral Roberts, Will Rogers, Maria Tallchief, Jim Thorpe.

Chamber of Commerce. 4020 N. Lincoln Blvd., Oklahoma City, OK 73105.

Tourism Dept. P.O. Box 60000, Oklahoma City, OK 73146.

Toll-free travel information. 1-800-652-6552.

Oregon

Beaver State

People. Population (1989): 2,820,000; **rank:** 30. **Pop. density:** 29.1 per sq. mi. **Urban** (1980): 67.9%. **Racial distrib.** (1985): 98.5% White; 1.5% Black; Hispanic; 76,000. **Net change** (1985-89): +132,000; 4.9%.

Geography. Total area: 97,073 sq. mi.; **rank:** 10. **Land area:** 96,184 sq. mi. **Acres forested land:** 29,810,000. **Location:** Pacific state, bounded on N by Washington; on E by Idaho; on S by Nevada and California; on W by the Pacific. **Climate:** coastal mild and humid climate; continental dryness and extreme temperatures in the interior. **Topography:** Coast Range of rugged mountains; fertile Willamette R. Valley to E and S; Cascade Mtn. Range of volcanic peaks E of the valley; plateau E of Cascades, remaining two-thirds of state. **Capital:** Salem.

Economy. Principal industries: forestry, agriculture, tourism, high technology, manufacturing. **Principal manufactured goods:** lumber & wood products, foods, machinery, fabricated metals, paper, printing & publishing, primary metals. **Agriculture: Chief crops:** hay, grass seed, farm forest prods., wheat, potatoes, onions, pears. **Livestock** (1988): 1.4 mln. cattle; 100,000 hogs/pigs; 475,000 sheep; 21.9 mln. poultry. **Timber/lumber** (1988): Douglas fir, hemlock, ponderosa pine; 8.4 bln. bd. ft. **Nonfuel Minerals** (1989): $199 mln.; mostly crushed stone, construction sand & gravel. **Commercial fishing** (1989): $76.9 mln. **Chief ports:** Portland, Astoria, Newport, Coos Bay. **International airports at:** Portland. **Value of construction** (1989): $2.4 bln. **Employment distribution** (1985): 25.2% trade; 20.8% serv.; 19.4% mfg.; 19.2% gvt. **Per capita income** (1989): $15,785. **Un-**

employment (1989): 5.7%. **Tourism** (1988): travel expenditures, $2 bln.

Finance. FDIC-insured commercial banks & trust companies (1987): 59. **Deposits:** $14.5 bln. **Savings institutions** (1990): 12. **Assets:** $11.1 bln

Federal government. No. federal civilian employees (Mar. 1989): 19,081. **Avg. salary:** $29,551. **Notable federal facilities:** Bonneville Power Administration.

Energy. Electricity production (1988, mwh, by source): Hydroelectric: 34.7 mln.; Nuclear: 6.3 mln.

Education. Student-teacher ratio (1988): 18.4. **Avg. salary, public school teachers** (1990): $30,563.

State data. Motto: She flies with her own wings. **Flower:** Oregon grape. **Bird:** Western meadowlark. **Tree:** Douglas fir. **Song:** Oregon, My Oregon. **Entered union** Feb. 14, 1859; rank, 33d. **State fair** at: Salem; late Aug. to early Sept.

History. American Capt. Robert Gray discovered and sailed into the Columbia River, 1792; Lewis and Clark, traveling overland, wintered at its mouth 1805-06; fur traders followed. Settlers arrived in the Willamette Valley, 1834. In 1843 the first large wave of settlers arrived via the Oregon Trail. Early in the 20th century, the "Oregon System," reforms which included the initiative, referendum, recall, direct primary, and woman suffrage, was adopted.

Tourist attractions. John Day Fossil Beds National Monument; Columbia River Gorge; Mt. Hood & Timberline Lodge; Crater Lake National Park; Oregon Dunes National Recreation Area; Ft. Clatsop National Memorial; Oregon Caves National Monument; Shakespearean Festival, Ashland; High Desert Museum, Bend. Also, skiing, fishing; Annual Albany Timber Carnival, Pendelton Round-Up, Portland Rose Festival.

Famous Oregonians include Ernest Bloch, Ernest Haycox, Chief Joseph, Edwin Markham, Tom McCall, Dr. John McLoughlin, Joaquin Miller, Linus Pauling, John Reed, Alberto Salazar, Mary Decker Slaney, William Simon U'Ren.

Tourist Information: Economic Development Department, 775 Summer St. NE, Salem, OR 97310.

Toll-free travel information. 1-800-543-8838; 1-800-547-7842 out of state.

Pennsylvania

Keystone State

People. Population (1989): 12,040,000; **rank:** 5. **Pop. density:** 265.7 per sq. mi. **Urban** (1980): 69.3%. **Racial distrib.** (1985): 90.7% White; 9.3% Black; Hispanic; 158,500. **Net change** (1985-89): +174,000; 1.5%.

Geography. Total area: 45,308 sq. mi.; **rank:** 33. **Land area:** 44,888 sq. mi. **Acres forested land:** 16,825,900. **Location:** Middle Atlantic state, bordered on the E by the Delaware R., on the S by the Mason-Dixon Line; on the W by West Virginia and Ohio; on the N/NE by Lake Erie and New York. **Climate:** continental with wide fluctuations in seasonal temperatures. **Topography:** Allegheny Mtns. run SW to NE, with Piedmont and Coast Plain in the SE triangle; Allegheny Front a diagonal spine across the state's center; N and W rugged plateau falls to Lake Erie Lowland. **Capital:** Harrisburg.

Economy. Principal industries: steel, travel, health, apparel, machinery, food & agriculture. **Principal manufactured goods:** primary metals, foods, fabricated metal products, non-electrical machinery, electrical machinery. **Agriculture: Chief crops:** corn, hay, mushrooms, apples, potatoes, winter wheat, oats, vegetables, tobacco, grapes. **Livestock** (1985): 1.96 mln. cattle; 800,000 hogs/pigs; 88,000 sheep; 22.5 mln. poultry. **Timber/lumber** (1988): pine, oak, maple; 611 mln. bd. ft. **Nonfuel Minerals** (1989): $1.0 bln.; mostly crushed stone, cement, lime, construction sand & gravel. **Commercial fishing** (1989): $264,000. **Chief ports:** Philadelphia, Pittsburgh, Erie. **International airports at:** Philadelphia, Pittsburgh, Erie, Harrisburg. **Value of construction** (1989): $10.5 bln. **Employment distribution** (1986): 24.4% serv.;

23.9% trade; 23.3% mfg.; 14.9% gvt. **Per capita income** (1989): $17,422 **Unemployment** (1989): 4.5%. **Tourism** (1985): out-of-state visitors spent $8.9 bln.

Finance. FDIC-insured commercial banks & trust companies (1987): 299. **Deposits:** $109.1 bln. **Savings institutions** (1990): 161. **Assets:** $42.6 bln.

Federal government. No. federal civilian employees (Mar. 1989): 87,890. **Avg. salary:** $26,878. **Notable federal facilities:** Army War College, Carlisle; Ships Control Ctr., Mechanicsburg; New Cumberland Army Depot; Philadelphia Navy Yard, Philadelphia.

Energy. Electricity production (1988, mwh, by source): Hydroelectric: 705,000 Mineral: 114.4 mln. Nuclear: 37.9 mln.

Education. Student-teacher ratio (1988): 15.9. **Avg. salary, public school teachers** (1990): $32,809.

State data. Motto: Virtue, liberty and independence. **Flower:** Mountain laurel. **Bird:** Ruffed grouse. **Tree:** Hemlock. **Second** of the original 13 states to ratify the Constitution, Dec. 12, 1787. **State fair** at: Harrisburg; 2d week in Jan.

History. First settlers were Swedish, 1643, on Tinicum Is. In 1655 the Dutch seized the settlement but lost it to the British, 1664. The region was given by Charles II to William Penn, 1681, Philadelphia (brotherly love) was the capital of the colonies during most of the Revolution, and of the U.S., 1790-1800. Philadelphia was taken by the British, 1777; Washington's troops encamped at Valley Forge in the bitter winter of 1777-78. The Declaration of Independence, 1776, and the Constitution, 1787, were signed in Philadelphia.

Tourist attractions. Independence Hall & Natl. Historic Park, Franklin Institute Science Museum, Philadelphia Museum of Art, all in Philadelphia; Valley Forge Natl. Historic Park, Gettysburg Natl. Military Park; Pennsylvania Dutch Country; Hershey; Dusquesne Incline, Carnegie Institute, Heinz Hall, all in Pittsburgh; year 'round outdoor sports in Pocono Mtns., Pine Creek River Gorge, Alleghenies, Laurel Highlands & Presque Isle State Park.

Famous Pennsylvanians include Marian Anderson, Maxwell Anderson, James Buchanan, Andrew Carnegie, Stephen Foster, Benjamin Franklin, George C. Marshall, Andrew W. Mellon, Robert E. Peary, Mary Roberts Rinehart, Betsy Ross.

Chamber of Commerce. 222 N. 3d St., Harrisburg, PA 17101.

Toll-free travel information. 1-800-VISITPA.

Rhode Island

Little Rhody, Ocean State

People. Population (1989): 998,000; **rank:** 43. **Pop. density:** 823.4 per sq. mi. **Urban** (1980): 87.0% **Racial distrib.** (1985): 96.5% White; 3.5% Black; Hispanic: 19,700. **Net change** (1985-89): +32,000; 3.3%.

Geography. Total area: 1,212 sq. mi.; **rank:** 50. **Land area:** 1,055 sq. mi. **Acres forested land:** 404,200. **Location:** New England state. **Climate:** invigorating and changeable. **Topography:** eastern lowlands of Narragansett Basin; western uplands of flat and rolling hills. **Capital:** Providence.

Economy. Principal industries: manufacturing, services. **Principal manufactured goods:** costume jewelry, machinery, textiles, electronics, silverware. **Agriculture: Chief crops:** nursery prods., turf, potatoes, apples. **Livestock:** 7,000 cattle; 6,400 hogs/pigs; 6,500 sheep; 430,000 poultry. **Timber/lumber:** oak, chestnut. **Nonfuel Minerals** (1989): $11 mln.; construction sand & gravel, crushed stone. **Commercial fishing** (1989): $75.0 mln. **Chief ports:** Providence, Quonset Point, Newport, Tiverton. **Value of construction** (1989): $1.3 bln. **Employment distribution** (1989): 25.0% mfg.; 25.4% serv.; 22.8% trade. **Per capita income** (1989): $18,061. **Unemployment** (1989): 4.1%. **Tourism** (1987): visitors spent $1.1 bln. **Sales tax:** 6%.

Finance. FDIC-insured commercial banks & trust companies (1987): 15. **Deposits:** $9.0 bln. **Savings institutions** (1990): 4. **Assets:** $3.4 bln.

Federal government. No. federal civilian employees (Mar. 1989): 5,917. **Avg. salary:** $29,779. **Notable federal facilities:** Naval War College; Naval Underwater Systems Center.

Energy. Electricity production (1988, mwh, by source): Mineral: 764,000.

Education. Student-teacher ratio (1988): 14.5. **Avg. salary, public school teachers** (1990): $36,057.

State data. Motto: Hope. **Flower:** Violet. **Bird:** Rhode Island red. **Tree:** Red maple. **Song:** Rhode Island. **Thirteenth** of original 13 states to ratify the Constitution, May 29, 1790. **State fair** at: E. Greenwich; mid-Aug.

History. Rhode Island is distinguished for its battle for freedom of conscience and action, begun by Roger Williams, founder of Providence, who was exiled from Massachusetts Bay Colony in 1636, and Anne Hutchinson, exiled in 1638. Rhode Island gave protection to Quakers in 1657 and to Jews from Holland in 1658.

The colonists broke the power of the Narragansett Indians in the Great Swamp Fight, 1675, the decisive battle in King Philip's War. British trade restrictions angered the colonists and they burned the British revenue cutter Gaspee, 1772. The colony declared its independence May 4, 1776. Gen. John Sullivan and Lafayette won a partial victory, 1778, but failed to oust the British.

Tourist attractions. Newport mansions; summer resorts and water sports; various yachting races inc. Newport to Bermuda. Touro Synagogue, Newport, 1763; first Baptist Church in America, Providence, 1638; Gilbert Stuart birthplace, Saunderstown; Narragansett Indian Fall Festival.

Famous Rhode Islanders include Ambrose Burnside, George M. Cohan, Nelson Eddy, Jabez Gorham, Nathanael Greene, Christopher and Oliver La Farge, Matthew C. and Oliver Perry, Gilbert Stuart.

Chamber of Commerce. 30 Exchange Terr., Providence, RI 02908.

Toll-free travel information. 1-800-556-2484.

South Carolina

Palmetto State

People. Population (1989): 3,512,000. **rank:** 25. **Pop. density:** 112.9 per sq. mi. **Urban** (1980): 54.1%. **Racial distrib.** (1985): 69.5% White; 30.5% Black; Hispanic: 20,100. **Net change** (1985-89): +177,000; 5.3%.

Geography. Total area: 31,113 sq. mi.; **rank:** 40. **Land area:** 30,203 sq. mi. **Acres forested land:** 12,249,400. **Location:** south Atlantic coast state, bordered by North Carolina on the N; Georgia on the SW and W; the Atlantic O. on the E, SE and S. **Climate:** humid sub-tropical. **Topo- graphy:** Blue Ridge province in NW has highest peaks; piedmont lies between the mountains and the fall line; coastal plain covers two-thirds of the state. **Capital:** Columbia.

Economy. Principal industries: tourism, agriculture, manufacturing. **Principal manufactured goods:** textiles, chemicals and allied products, machinery & fabricated metal products, apparel and related products. **Agriculture: Chief crops:** tobacco, soybeans, corn, cotton, peaches, hay. **Livestock** (1989): 620,000 cattle; 400,000 hogs/pigs; 8.1 mln. poultry. **Timber/lumber** (1988): pine, oak; 1.5 bln. **Nonfuel Minerals** (1989): $399 mln.; mostly crushed stone, Portland cement, clay. **Commercial fishing** (1989): $24.9 mln. **Chief ports:** Charleston, Georgetown, Port Royal. **International airports at:** Charleston. **Value of construction** (1989): $3.4 bln. **Employment distribution** (1987): 26.8% mfg.; 18.3% gvt.; 17.3% serv. **Per capita income** (1989): $13,616. **Unemployment** (1989): 4.7%. **Tourism** (1987): $4.3 bln. **Sales tax:** 5%.

Finance. FDIC-insured commercial banks & trust companies (1987): 73. **Deposits:** $13.2 bln. **Savings institutions** (1990): 48. **Assets:** $11.7 bln.

Federal government: No. federal civilian employees (Mar. 1989): 25,872. **Avg. Salary:** $26,696. **Notable federal facilities:** Polaris Submarine Base; Barnwell Nuclear Power Plant; Ft. Jackson; Parris Island; Savannah River Plant.

Energy. Electricity production (1988, mwh, by source): Hydroelectric: 631,000; Mineral: 23.8 mln.; Nuclear: 40.8 mln.

Education. Student-teacher ratio (1988): 17.2. **Avg. salary, public school teachers** (1990): $27,076.

State data. Motto: Dum Spiro Spero (While I breathe, I hope). **Flower:** Yellow jessamine. **Bird:** Carolina wren. **Tree:** Palmetto. **Song:** Carolina. **Eighth** of the original 13 states to ratify the Constitution, May 23, 1788. **State fair** at: Columbia; mid-Oct.

History. The first English colonists settled, 1670, on the Ashley River, moved to the site of Charleston, 1680. The colonists seized the government, 1775, and the royal governor fled. The British took Charleston, 1780, but were defeated at Kings Mountain that year, and at Cowpens and Eutaw Springs, 1781. In the 1830s, South Carolinians, angered by federal protective tariffs, adopted the Nullification Doctrine, holding a state can void an act of Congress. The state was the first to secede and, in 1861, Confederate troops fired on and forced the surrender of U. S. troops at Ft. Sumter, in Charleston Harbor, launching the Civil War.

Tourist attractions. Restored historic Charleston harbor area and Charleston gardens: Middleton Place, Magnolia, Cypress; other gardens at Brookgreen, Edisto, Glencairn; state parks; coastal islands; shore resorts such as Myrtle Beach and Hilton Head Island; fishing and quail hunting; Ft. Sumter National Monument, in Charleston Harbor; Charleston Museum, est. 1773, is the oldest museum in the U.S.; South Carolina State Museum, one of largest museums in South, Columbia.

Famous South Carolinians include Charles Bolden, James F. Byrnes, John C. Calhoun, DuBose Heyward, Ernest F. Hollings, Andrew Jackson, Jesse Jackson, James Longstreet, Francis Marion, Ronald McNair, Charles Pinckney, John Rutledge, Thomas Sumter, Strom Thurmond.

Chamber of Commerce. 1301 Gervais St., Suite 520, No. Carolina National Bank Tower, Columbia, SC 29201.

South Dakota

Coyote State, Sunshine State

People. Population (1989): 715,000; **rank:** 45. **Pop. density:** 9.3 per sq. mi. **Urban** (1980): 46.4%. **Racial distrib.** (1980): 92.6% White; 0.31% Black; 7.1% Other (includes American Indians); Hispanic: 3,700. **Net change** (1985-89): +7,000; 1.0%.

Geography. Total area: 77,116 sq. mi.; **rank:** 16. **Land area:** 75,952 sq. mi. **Acres forested land:** 1,702,000. **Location:** West North Central state bounded on the N by North Dakota; on the E by Minnesota and Iowa; on the S by Nebraska; on the W by Wyoming and Montana. **Climate:** characterized by extremes of temperature, persistent winds, low precipitation and humidity. **Topography:** Prairie Plains in the E; rolling hills of the Great Plains in the W; the Black Hills, rising 3,500 ft. in the SW corner. **Capital:** Pierre.

Economy. Principal industries: agriculture, services, manufacturing. **Principal manufactured goods** (1986): food & kindred prods., machinery, electric & electronic equipment. **Agriculture:** Chief crops (1989): corn, oats, wheat, sunflowers, soybeans, sorghum. **Livestock** (1989): 3.4 mln. cattle; 1.7 mln. hogs/ pigs; 590,000 sheep. **Timber/lumber** (1989): ponderosa pine; 192 mln. bd. ft. **Nonfuel Minerals** (1989): $296 mln.; mostly gold, Portland cement. **Value of construction** (1989): $498.3 mln. **Employment distribution** (1989): 24.4% serv.; 11.5% mfg. **Per capita income** (1989): $13,244. **Unemployment** (1989): 4.2%. **Tourism** (1989): travellers spent $755 mln. **Sales tax:** 4%.

Finance. FDIC-insured commercial banks & trust companies (1987): 135. **Deposits:** $8.1 bln. **Savings institutions** (1990): 12. **Assets:** $1.5 bln.

Federal government. No. federal civilian employees (Mar. 1989): 6,871. **Avg. salary:** $26,280. **Notable federal facilities:** Bureau of Indian Affairs, Ellsworth AFB, Corp of Engineers, Nat'l Park Service.

Energy. Electricity production (1988, mwh, by source): Hydroelectric: 5.3 mln.; Mineral: 2.6 mln.

Education. Student-teacher ratio (1988): 15.4. **Avg. salary, public school teachers** (1990): $21,300.

State data. Motto: Under God, the people rule. **Flower:** Pasque flower. **Bird:** Ringnecked pheasant. **Tree:** Black Hills spruce. **Song:** Hail, South Dakota. **Entered union** Nov. 2, 1889; rank, 40th. **State fair** at: Huron; late Aug.-early Sept.

History. Les Verendryes explored the region, 1742-43. Lewis and Clark passed through the area, 1804 and 1806. First white American settlement was at Fort Pierre, 1817. Gold was discovered, 1874, on the Sioux Reservation; miners rushed in. The U.S. first tried to stop them, then relaxed its opposition. The Sioux relinquished the land, 1877, and the "great Dakota Boom" began, 1879. A new Indian uprising came in 1890, climaxed by the massacre of Indian families at Wounded Knee.

Tourist attractions. Black Hills; Mt. Rushmore, with colossal likeness of the faces of U.S. Presidents Washington, Jefferson, Lincoln & T. Roosevelt carved by sculptor Gutzon Borglum; Needles Highway; Harney Peak, at 7,242 ft. the tallest peak between the Rockies and the Alps; Deadwood, an 1876 Gold Rush town; Custer State Park's buffalo and burro herds; Jewel Cave, the 4th largest cave in the world; Badlands Natl. Park's "moonscape"; "Great Lakes of So. Dakota"; Ft. Sisseton, restored 1864 army frontier post; Great Plains Zoo & Museum; Corn Palace in Mitchell; Wind Cave; Mammoth Site, ongoing excavation of prehistoric mammoths; Crazy Horse, mountain carving in progress.

Famous South Dakotans include Sparky Anderson, Catherine Bach, Tom Brokaw, "Calamity Jane", Mary Hart, Crazy Horse, Myron Floren, Alvin H. Hansen, Cheryl Ladd, Dr. Ernest O. Lawrence, George McGovern, Billy Mills, Allen Neuharth, Pat O'Brien, Sitting Bull.

Tourist information. South Dakota Tourism, 711 Wells Ave., Pierre, SD 57501-3335.

Toll-free travel information. 1-800-952-2217; 1-800-843-1930 out of state.

Tennessee

Volunteer State

People. Population (1989): 4,940,000; **rank:** 16. **Pop. density:** 117.2 per sq. mi. **Urban** (1980): 60.4%. **Racial distrib.** (1985): 83.8% White; 16.2% Black; Hispanic: 18,200. **Net change** (1985-89): +173,000; 3.6%.

Geography. Total area: 42,144 sq. mi.; **rank:** 34. **Land area:** 41,155 sq. mi. **Acres forested land:** 13,160,500. **Location:** East South Central state bounded on the N by Kentucky and Virginia; on the E by North Carolina; on the S by Georgia, Alabama, and Mississippi; on the W by Arkansas and Missouri. **Climate:** humid continental to the N; humid sub-tropical to the S. **Topography:** rugged country in the E; the Great Smoky Mtns. of the Unakas; low ridges of the Appalachian Valley; the flat Cumberland Plateau; slightly rolling terrain and knobs of the Interior Low Plateau, the largest region; Eastern Gulf Coastal Plain to the W, is laced with meandering streams; Mississippi Alluvial Plain, a narrow strip of swamp and flood plain in the extreme W. **Capital:** Nashville.

Economy. Principal industries: trade, services, construction; transp., commun., public utilities; finance, ins., real estate. **Principal manufactured goods:** chemicals & allied prods.; food & kindred prods.; nonelectrical machinery; electric/electronic equip.; apparel; fabr. metal prods.; transp. equip.; rubber/misc. plastic prods.; paper & allied prods., printing and publishing. **Agriculture:** Chief crops (1987): greenhouse nursery, soybeans, lint, cotton, tobacco. **Livestock** (1988): 2.3 mln. cattle; 1.1 mln. hogs/

pigs; 10,000 sheep; 2.1 mln. poultry. **Timber/lumber** (1988): red oak, white oak, yellow poplar, hickory; 684 mln. bd. ft. **Nonfuel Minerals** (1989): $650 mln.; mostly clay, sand and gravel, crushed stone. **Chief ports:** Memphis, Nashville, Chattanooga, Knoxville. **International airports at:** Memphis, Nashville. **Value of construction** (1989): $4.8 bln. **Employment distribution** (1989): 24.3% mfg.; 23.6% trade; 21.6% serv.; 15.5% gvt. **Per capita income** (1989): $14,765. **Unemployment** (1989): 5.1%. **Tourism** (1989): out-of-state visitors spent $3.3 bln. **Sales tax:** 5½%.

Finance. FDIC-insured commercial banks & trust companies (1987): 283. **Deposit:** $32.3 bln. **Savings institutions** (1990): 56. **Assets:** $11.6 bln.

Federal government. No. federal civilian employees (Mar. 1989): 41,116. **Avg. salary:** $29,158. **Notable federal facilities:** Tennessee Valley Authority; Oak Ridge Nat'l. Laboratories.

Energy. Electricity production (1988, mwh, by source): Hydroelectric: 4.6 mln.; Mineral: 51.3 mln.

Education. Student-teacher ratio (1988): 19.3. **Avg. salary, public school teachers** (1990): $27,052.

State data. Motto: Agriculture and commerce. **Flower:** Iris. **Bird:** Mockingbird. **Tree:** Tulip poplar. **Song:** The Tennessee Waltz. **Entered union** June 1, 1796; rank, 16th. **State fair at:** Nashville; mid-Sept.

History. Spanish explorers first visited the area, 1541. English traders crossed the Great Smokies from the east while France's Marquette and Joliet sailed down the Mississippi on the west, 1673. First permanent settlement was by Virginians on the Watauga River, 1769. During the Revolution, the colonists helped win the Battle of Kings Mountain, N.C., 1780, and joined other eastern campaigns. The state seceded from the Union 1861, and saw many engagements of the Civil War, but 30,000 soldiers fought for the Union.

Tourist attractions. Natural wonders include Reelfoot Lake, the reservoir basin of the Mississippi R. formed by the 1811 earthquake; Lookout Mountain, Chattanooga; Fall Creek Falls, 256 ft. high; Great Smoky Mountains National Park; Lost Sea, Sweetwater; Cherokee Natl. Forest.

Also, the Hermitage, 13 mi. E of Nashville, home of Andrew Jackson; the homes of presidents Polk and Andrew Johnson; American Museum of Science, Oak Ridge; the Parthenon, Nashville, a replica of the Parthenon of Athens; the Grand Old Opry, Nashville, Opryland, USA, theme park, Nashville; Graceland, home of Elvis Presley, Memphis; Alex Haley Home & Museum, Henning; Casey Jones Home & Museum, Jackson.

Famous Tennesseans include Davy Crockett, David Farragut, William C. Handy, Sam Houston, Cordell Hull, Grace Moore, Dinah Shore, Alvin York.

Tourist information. Dept. of Tourist Development, 5th Floor, Rachel Jackson Bldg., Nashville, TN 37219.

Texas

Lone Star State

People. Population (1989): 16,991,000; **rank: 3. Pop. density:** 63.7 per sq. mi. **Urban** (1980): 79.6%. **Racial distrib.** (1985): 88.2% White; 11.8% Black; Hispanic 3.7 mln. **Net change** (1985-89): +612,000; 3.7%.

Geography. Total area: 266,807 sq. mi.; **rank: 2. Land area:** 262,017 sq. mi.; **Acres forested land:** 23,279,300. **Location:** Southwestern state, bounded on the SE by the Gulf of Mexico; on the SW by Mexico, separated by the Rio Grande; surrounding states are Louisiana, Arkansas, Oklahoma, New Mexico. **Climate:** extremely varied; driest region is the Trans-Pecos; wettest is the NE. **Topography:** Gulf Coast Plain in the S and SE; North Central Plains slope upward with some hills; the Great Plains extend over the Panhandle, are broken by low mountains; the Trans-Pecos is the southern extension of the Rockies. **Capital:** Austin.

Economy. Principal industries: trade, services, manufacturing. **Principal manufactured goods:** machinery, transportation equipment, foods, refined petroleum, ap-

parel. **Agriculture: Chief crops:** cotton, grain sorghum, grains, vegetables, citrus and other fruits, pecans, peanuts. **Livestock** (1985): 14.1 mln. cattle; 415,000 hogs/pigs; 1.81 mln. sheep; 17.4 mln. poultry. **Timber/ lumber** (1988): pine, cypress; 1.3 bln. bd. ft. **Nonfuel Minerals** (1989): $1.5 bln.; mostly cement, stone, sand & gravel. **Commercial fishing** (1989): $170.1 mln. **Chief ports:** Houston, Galveston, Brownsville, Beaumont, Port Arthur, Corpus Christi. **Major international airports at:** Houston, Dallas/Ft. Worth, San Antonio. **Value of construction** (1989) $12.8 bln. **Employment distribution** (1989): 24.8% trade; 23.7% serv.; 18.0% gvt.; 14.2% mfg. **Per capita income** (1989): $15,483. **Unemployment** (1989): 6.7%. **Tourism** (1987): out-of-state visitors spent $17.6 bln. **Sales tax:** 6%, + optional 1% local, 1% transit.

Finance. FDIC-insured commercial banks & trust companies (1987): 1,972. **Deposits:** $165.0 bln. **Savings institutions** (1990): 196. **Assets:** $90.6 bln.

Federal government. No. federal civilian employees (Mar. 1989): $121,266. **Avg. salary:** $27,108. **Notable federal facilities:** Fort Hood (Killeen); Kelly AFB, and Ft. Sam Houston, both San Antonio.

Energy. Electricity production (1988, mwh, by source): Hydroelectric: 1.2 mln.; Mineral: 215.2 mln. Nuclear: 3.7 mln.

Education. Expenditures per pupil, public schools (1987): $3,409 **Avg. salary, public school teachers** (1990): $27,502.

State data. Motto: Friendship. **Flower:** Bluebonnet. **Bird:** Mockingbird. **Tree:** Pecan. **Song:** Texas, Our Texas. **Entered union** Dec. 29, 1845; rank, 28th. **State fair at:** Dallas; mid-Oct.

History. Pineda sailed along the Texas coast, 1519; Cabeza de Vaca and Coronado visited the interior, 1541. Spaniards made the first settlement at Ysleta, near El Paso, 1682. Americans moved into the land early in the 19th century. Mexico, of which Texas was a part, won independence from Spain, 1821; Santa Anna became dictator, 1835. Texans rebelled; Santa Anna wiped out defenders of the Alamo, 1836. Sam Houston's Texans defeated Santa Anna at San Jacinto and independence was proclaimed the same year. In 1845, Texas was admitted to the Union.

Tourist attractions. Padre Island National Seashore; Big Bend, Guadalupe Mtns. national parks; The Alamo; Ft. Davis; Six Flags Amusement Park. Named for Pres. Lyndon B. Johnson are a state park, a natl. historic site marking his birthplace, boyhood home, and ranch, all near Johnson City, and a library in Austin.

Famous Texans include Stephen F. Austin, James Bowie, Carol Burnett, J. Frank Dobie, Dwight D. Eisenhower, Sam Houston, Howard Hughes, Lyndon B. Johnson, Mary Martin, Chester Nimitz, Katharine Ann Porter, Sam Rayburn.

Chamber of Commerce. 300 W. 15th, #875, Austin, TX 78701.

Utah

Beehive State

People. Population (1989): 1,707,000; **rank: 35. Pop. density:** 20.1 per sq. mi. **Urban** (1980): 84.4%. **Racial distrib.** (1985): 97.1% White; Hispanic 70,600. **Net change** (1985-89): +63,000; 3.8%.

Geography. Total area: 84,899 sq. mi.; **rank: 11. Land area:** 82,073 sq. mi. **Acres forested land:** 15,557,400. **Location:** Middle Rocky Mountain state; its southeastern corner touches Colorado, New Mexico, and Arizona, and is the only spot in the U.S. where 4 states join. **Climate:** arid; ranging from warm desert in SW to alpine in NE. **Topography:** high Colorado plateau is cut by brilliantly-colored canyons of the SE; broad, flat, desert-like Great Basin of the W; the Great Salt Lake and Bonneville Salt Flats to the NW; Middle Rockies in the NE run E-W; valleys and plateaus of the Wasatch Front. **Capital:** Salt Lake City.

Economy. Principal industries: services, trade, manufacturing, government, construction. **Principal manufactured goods:** guided missiles and parts, electronic components, food products, fabricated metals, steel, electrical equipment. **Agriculture: Chief crops:** hay, wheat, apples, barley, alfalfa seed, corn, potatoes, cherries, onions. **Livestock:** 855,000 cattle; 34,000 hogs/pigs; 600,000 sheep; 3.8 mln. poultry. **Timber/lumber:** aspen, spruce, pine. **Nonfuel Minerals** (1989): $1.2 mln.; copper, gold, magnesium. **International airports at:** Salt Lake City. **Value of construction** (1989): $1.4 bln. **Employment distribution:** (1989) 24.2% serv.; 29.0% trade; 21.2% govt; 14.9% mfg. **Per capita income** (1989): $13,027. **Unemployment** (1989): 4.6%. **Tourism** (1986): travellers spent $2.0 bln. **Sales tax:** 6.25%.

Finance. FDIC-insured commercial banks & trust companies (1987): 61. **Deposits:** $9.1 bln. **Savings institutions** (1990): 13. **Assets:** $6.9 bln.

Federal government. No. federal civilian employees (Mar. 1989): 33,138. **Avg. salary:** $26,355. **Notable federal facilities:** Hill AFB; Tooele Army Depot, IRS Western Service Center.

Energy. Electricity production (1988, mwh, by source): Hydroelectric: 593,000 mln.; Mineral: 28.9 mln.

Education. Student-teacher ratio (1988): 24.5. **Avg. salary, public school teachers** (1990): $23,652.

State data. Motto: Industry. **Flower:** Sego lily. **Bird:** Seagull. **Tree:** Blue spruce. **Song:** Utah, We Love Thee. **Entered union** Jan. 4, 1896; rank, 45th. **State fair at:** Salt Lake City; Sept.

History. Spanish Franciscans visited the area, 1776, the first white men to do so. American fur traders followed. Permanent settlement began with the arrival of the Mormons, 1847. They made the arid land bloom and created a prosperous economy, organized the State of Deseret, 1849, and asked admission to the Union. This was not achieved until 1896, after a long period of controversy over the Mormon Church's doctrine of polygamy, which it discontinued in 1890.

Tourist attractions. Temple Square, Mormon Church hdqtrs., Salt Lake City; Great Salt Lake; fishing streams, lakes and reservoirs, numerous winter sports; campgrounds. Natural wonders may be seen at Zion, Canyonlands, Bryce Canyon, Arches, and Capitol Reef national parks; Dinosaur, Rainbow Bridge, Timpanogos Cave, and Natural Bridges national monuments. Also Lake Powell and Flaming Gorge reservoirs.

Famous Utahans include Maude Adams, Ezra Taft Benson, John Moses Browning, Mariner Eccles, Philo Farnsworth, James Fletcher, David M. Kennedy, J. Willard Marriott, Osmond Family, Merlin Olsen, Ivy Baker Priest, George Romney, Brigham Young, Loretta Young.

Tourist information. Utah Travel Council, Council Hall, Salt Lake City, UT 84114.

Vermont
Green Mountain State

People. Population (1989): 567,000; **rank:** 48. **Pop. density:** 59.0 per sq. mi. **Urban** (1980): 33.8%. **Racial distrib.** (1980): 96.0% White; 0.22% Black; Hispanic 3,700. **Net change** (1985-89): +32,000; 6.0%.

Geography. Total area: 9,614 sq. mi.; **rank:** 43. **Land area:** 9,273 sq. mi. **Acres forested land:** 4,511,700. **Location:** northern New England state. **Climate:** temperate, with considerable temperature extremes; heavy snowfall in mountains. **Topography:** Green Mtns. N-S backbone 20-36 mi. wide; avg. altitude 1,000 ft. **Capital:** Montpelier.

Economy. Principal industries: manufacturing, tourism, agriculture, trade; finance, insurance, real estate, government. **Principal manufactured goods:** machine tools, furniture, scales, books, computer components, fishing rods. **Agriculture: Chief crops:** dairy products, apples, maple syrup, silage corn, hay. **Livestock** (1989): 320,000 cattle; 5,100 hogs/ pigs; 20,456 sheep; 406,000 poultry. **Timber/lumber** (1988): pine, spruce, fir, hemlock; 138 mln. bd. ft. **Nonfuel Minerals** (1989): $520 mln.; mostly dimension stone, crashed stone, construction sand & gravel. **International airports at:** Burlington. **Value of construction** (1989): $627.6 mln. **Employment distribution** (1990): 26% serv.; 23% trade; 19% mfg. **Per capita**

income (1989): $16,399. **Unemployment** (1989): 3.7%. **Tourism** (1988): visitors spent $1.25 bln. **Sales tax.** 4%.

Finance. FDIC-insured commercial banks & trust companies (1987): 25. **Deposits:** $4.2 bln. **Savings institutions** (1990): 4. **Assets** $ 565 mln.

Federal government. No. federal civilian employees (Mar. 1989): 2,527. **Avg. salary:** $27,421.

Energy. Electricity production (1987, mwh, by source): Hydroelectric: 809,000; Mineral: 26,000; Nuclear: 4.1 mln.

Education. Student-teacher ratio (1988): 13.6. **Avg. salary, public school teachers** (1990): $28,798.

State data. Motto: Freedom and unity. **Flower:** Red clover. **Bird:** Hermit thrush. **Tree:** Sugar maple. **Song:** Hail, Vermont. **Entered union** Mar. 4, 1791; rank, 14th. **State fair at:** Rutland; early Sept.

History. Champlain explored the lake that bears his name, 1609. First American settlement was Ft. Dummer, 1724, near Brattleboro. Ethan Allen and the Green Mountain Boys captured Ft. Ticonderoga, 1775; John Stark defeated part of Burgoyne's forces near Bennington, 1777. In the War of 1812, Thomas MacDonough defeated a British fleet on Champlain off Plattsburgh, 1814.

Tourist attractions. Year-round outdoor sports, esp. hiking, camping and skiing; there are over 56 ski areas in the state. Popular are the Shelburne Museum; Rock of Ages Tourist Center, Graniteville; Vermont Marble Exhibit, Proctor; Bennington Battle Museum; Pres. Coolidge homestead, Plymouth; Maple Grove Maple Museum, St. Johnsbury.

Famous Vermonters include Ethan Allen, Chester A. Arthur, Calvin Coolidge, Adm. George Dewey, John Dewey, Stephen A. Douglas, Dorothy Canfield Fisher, James Fisk.

Tourist information. Vermont Travel Division, 134 State St., Montpelier, VT 05602.

Virginia
Old Dominion

People. Population (1989): 6,098,000; **rank:** 12. **Pop. density:** 149.6 per sq. mi. **Urban** (1980): 66.0%. **Racial distrib.** (1985): 81.0% White; 19.0% Black; Hispanic 87,000. **Net change** (1985-89): +394,000; 6.9%.

Geography. Total area: 40,767 sq. mi.; **rank:** 36. **Land area:** 39,704 sq. mi. **Acres forested land:** 16,417,400. **Location:** South Atlantic state bounded by the Atlantic O. on the E and surrounded by North Carolina, Tennessee, Kentucky, West Virginia, and Maryland. **Climate:** mild and equable. **Topography:** mountain and valley region in the W, including the Blue Ridge Mtns.; rolling piedmont plateau; tidewater, or coastal plain, including the eastern shore. **Capital:** Richmond.

Economy. Principal industries: services, trade, government, manufacturing, tourism, agriculture. **Principal manufactured goods:** textiles, transportation equipment, electric & electronic equipment, food processing, chemicals. **Agriculture: Chief crops** (1988): tobacco, soybeans, peanuts, winterwheat, corn, far grain, tomatoes. **Livestock** (1989): 1.67 mln. cattle; 450,000 hogs/pigs; 158,000 sheep; 5.82 mln. poultry. **Timber/lumber** (1988): pine and hardwoods; 1.1 bln. bd. ft. **Nonfuel Minerals** (1989): $59 mln.; mostly crushed stone. **Commercial fishing** (1989): $100.0 mln. **Chief ports:** Hampton Roads, Richmond, Alexandria. **International airports at:** Norfolk, Dulles, Richmond, Newport News. **Value of construction** (1989): $9.0 bln. **Employment distribution** (1988): 24% serv.; 23% trade; 20% govt.; 15.4% mfg. **Per capita income** (1989): $16,399. **Unemployment** (1989): 3.9%. **Tourism** (1988): out-of-state visitors spent $4.4 bln. **Sales tax:** 4.5%.

Finance. FDIC-insured commercial banks & trust companies (1987): 171. **Deposits:** $41.2 bln. **Savings institutions** (1990): 63. **Assets:** $29.9 bln.

Federal government. No. federal civilian employees (Mar. 1989): 135,379. **Avg. salary:** $31,488. **Notable federal facilities:** Pentagon; Naval Sta., Norfolk; Naval Air

Sta., Norfolk, Virginia Beach; Naval Shipyard, Portsmouth; Marine Corps Base, Quantico; Langley AFB; NASA at Langley.

Energy. Electricity production (1988, mwh, by source): Mineral: 24.4 mln.; Nuclear: 21.0 mln.

Education. Student-teacher ratio (1988): 16.1. **Avg. salary, public school teachers** (1990): $30,926.

State data. Motto: Sic Semper Tyrannis (Thus always to tyrants). **Flower:** Dogwood. **Bird:** Cardinal. **Tree:** Dogwood. **Song:** Carry Me Back to Old Virginia. **Tenth** of the original 13 states to ratify the Constitution, June 25, 1788. **State fair** at: Richmond; late Sept.-early Oct.

History. English settlers founded Jamestown, 1607. Virginians took over much of the government from royal Gov. Dunmore in 1775, forcing him to flee. Virginians under George Rogers Clark freed the Ohio-Indiana-Illinois area of British forces. Benedict Arnold burned Richmond and Petersburg for the British, 1781. That same year, Britain's Cornwallis was trapped at Yorktown and surrendered.

Tourist attractions. Colonial Williamsburg; Busch Gardens; Wolf Trap Farm, near Falls Church; Arlington National Cemetery; Mt. Vernon, home of George Washington; Jamestown Festival Park; Yorktown; Jefferson's Monticello, Charlottesville; Robert E. Lee's birthplace, Stratford Hall, and grave, at Lexington; Appomattox; Shenandoah National Park; Blue Ridge Parkway; Virginia Beach.

Famous Virginians include Richard E. Byrd, James B. Cabell, William Henry Harrison, Patrick Henry, Thomas Jefferson, Joseph E. Johnston, Robert E. Lee, Meriwether Lewis and William Clark, James Madison, George Mason, James Monroe, John Marshall, Edgar Allan Poe, Walter Reed, Zachary Taylor, John Tyler, Maggie Walker, Booker T. Washington, George Washington, Woodrow Wilson.

Chamber of Commerce: 9th South Fifth St., Richmond, VA 23219.

Toll-free travel information. 1-800-VISITVA.

Washington
Evergreen State

People. Population (1989): 4,761,000; rank: 18. **Pop. density:** 69.9 per sq. mi. **Urban** (1980): 73.5%. **Racial distrib.** (1985): 97.2% White; 2.8% Black; Hispanic 142,000. **Net change** (1985-89) +354,000; 8.0%.

Geography. Total area: 68,139 sq. mi.; rank: 20. **Land area:** 66,511 sq. mi. **Acres forested land:** 23,181,000. **Location:** northwestern coastal state bordered by Canada on the N; Idaho on the E; Oregon on the S; and the Pacific O. on the W. **Climate:** mild, dominated by the Pacific O.; flat terrain of Puget Sound Lowland; Cascade Mtns. region's high peaks to the E; Columbia Basin in central portion; highlands to the NE; mountains to the SE. **Capital:** Olympia.

Economy. Principal industries: aerospace, forest products, food products, primary metals, agriculture. **Principal manufactured goods:** aircraft, pulp and paper, lumber and plywood, aluminum, processed fruits and vegetables. **Agriculture:** Chief crops: hops, spearmint oil, raspberries, apples, asparagus, pears, cherries, peppermint oil, potatoes. **Livestock** (1986): 1.3 mln. cattle; 50,000 hogs/pigs; 59,000 sheep; 5.7 mln. poultry. **Timber/lumber** (1988): Douglas fir, hemlock, cedar, pine; 4.5 bln. bd. ft. **Nonfuel Minerals** (1989): $451 mln.; mostly construction sand & gravel, crushed stone, Portland cement. **Commercial fishing** (1989): $134.6 mln. **Chief ports:** Seattle, Tacoma, Vancouver, Kelso-Longview. **International airports at:** Seattle/Tacoma, Spokane, Boeing Field. **Value of construction** (1989): $5.2 bln. **Employment distribution** (1989): 24.4% trade; 20.7% serv.; 18.3% gvt.; 17.3% mfg. **Per capita income** (1989): $17,640. **Unemployment** (1989): 6.2%. **Tourism** (1988): $4.6 bln. **Sales tax:** 6.5%.

Finance. FDIC-insured commercial banks & trust companies (1987): 94. **Deposits:** $26.9 bln. **Savings institutions** (1990): 32. **Assets:** $17.5 bln.

Federal government. No. federal civilian employees (Mar. 1989): 48,161. **Avg. salary:** $29,562. **Notable federal facilities:** Bonneville Power Admin.; Ft. Lewis; McChord AFB; Hanford Nuclear Reservation; Bremerton Naval Shipyards.

Energy. Electricity production (1988, mwh, by source): Hydroelectric: 68.4 mln.; Mineral: 8.8 mln.; Nuclear: 6.0 mln.

Education. Student-teacher ratio (1988): 20.4. **Avg. salary, public school teachers** (1990): $30,475.

State data. Motto. Alki (By and by). **Flower:** Western rhododendron. **Bird:** Willow goldfinch. **Tree:** Western hemlock. **Song:** Washington, My Home. **Entered union** Nov. 11, 1889; rank, 42d. **State fairs at:** S.E. Washington, W. Washington, N. Cent. Washington District, Cent. Washington.

History. Spain's Bruno Hezeta sailed the coast, 1775. American Capt. Robert Gray sailed up the Columbia River, 1792. Canadian fur traders set up Spokane House, 1810; Americans under John Jacob Astor established a post at Fort Okanogan, 1811. Missionary Marcus Whitman settled near Walla Walla, 1836. Final agreement on the border of Washington and Canada was made with Britain, 1846, and gold was discovered in the state's northeast, 1855, bringing new settlers.

Tourist attractions. Mt. Rainier, Olympic and North Cascades National Parks; Mt. St. Helens; Pacific beaches; Puget Sound; wineries; Indian cultures; year-round outdoor recreation: Seattle Waterfront, Seattle Center, Space Needle, San Juan Islands, Grand Coulee Dam, Spokane's Riverfront Park.

Famous Washingtonians include Bing Crosby, William O. Douglas, Henry M. Jackson, Gary Larson, Mary McCarthy, Edward R. Murrow, Theodore Roethke, Marcus Whitman, Minoru Yamasaki.

Local Chambers of Commerce. P.O. Box 658, Olympia, WA 98507.

Toll-free travel information. 1-800-544-1800.

West Virginia
Mountain State

People. Population (1989): 1,857,000. rank: 34. **Pop. density:** 76.6 per sq. mi. **Urban** (1980): 36.2. **Racial distrib.** (1985): 96.7% White; 3.3% Black; Hispanic (1980): 7,900. **Net change** (1985-89): −80,000; −4.1%.

Geography. Total area: 24,232 sq. mi.; rank: 41. **Land area:** 24,119 sq. mi. **Acres forested land:** 11,668,600. **Location:** South Atlantic state bounded on the N by Ohio, Pennsylvania, Maryland; on the S and W by Virginia, Kentucky, Ohio; on the E by Maryland and Virginia. **Climate:** humid continental climate except for marine modification in the lower panhandle. **Topography:** ranging from hilly to mountainous; Allegheny Plateau in the W, covers two-thirds of the state; mountains here are the highest in the state, over 4,000 ft. **Capital:** Charleston.

Economy. Principal industries: manufacturing, services, mining, tourism. **Principal manufactured goods:** machinery, plastic and hardwood prods., fabricated metals, basic organic and inorganic chemicals, aluminum, steel. **Agriculture:** Chief crops: apples, peaches, hay, tobacco, corn, wheat, oats. **Chief products:** dairy prods., eggs. **Livestock** (1989): 500,000 cattle; 37,000 hogs/pigs; 82,000 sheep; 810,000 chickens. **Timber/ lumber** (1988): oak, yellow poplar, hickory, walnut, cherry; 402 mln. bd. ft. **Nonfuel Minerals** (1989): $110 mln.; mostly crushed stone. **Chief port:** Huntington. **Value of construction** (1989): $844.2 mln. **Employment distribution** (1989): 23% trade; 21% gvt.; 22% serv.; 14% mfg. **Per capita income** (1989): $12,529. **Unemployment** (1989): 8.6%. **Tourism** (1989): travel-related expenditures were $2.3 bln. **Sales tax:** 6%.

Finance. FDIC-insured commercial banks & trust companies (1987): 213. **Deposits:** $12.8 bln. **Savings institutions** (1990): 16. **Assets:** $2.2 bln.

Federal government. No. federal civilian employees (Mar. 1989): 10,126. **Avg. salary:** $27,506. **Notable federal facilities:** National Radio Astronomy Observatory, Green Bank; Bureau of Public Debt. Bldg., Parkersburg; Natl. Park, Harper's Ferry; Correctional Institution for Women, Alderson.

Energy. Electricity production (1988, mwh, by source): Hydroelec c: 298,000; Mineral: 61.0 mln.

Education. Student-teacher ratio (1988): 15.1. **Avg. salary, public school teachers** (1990): $22,842.

State Data. Motto: Montani Semper Liberi (Mountaineers are always free) **Flower:** Big rhododendron. **Bird:** Cardinal. **Tree:** Sugar maple. **Songs:** The West Virginia Hills; This Is My West Virginia; West Virginia, My Home, Sweet Home. **Entered union** June 20, 1863; rank, 35th. **State fair at:** Lewisburg (Fairlea), late Aug.

History. Early explorers included George Washington, 1753, and Daniel Boone. The area became part of Virginia and often objected to rule by the eastern part of the state. When Virginia seceded, 1861, the Wheeling Conventions repudiated the act and created a new state, Kanawha, subsequently changed to West Virginia. It was admitted to the Union as such, 1863.

Tourist attractions. Harpers Ferry National Historic Park has been restored to its condition in 1859, when John Brown seized the U.S. Armory.

Also Science and Cultural Center, Charleston; White Sulphur and Berkeley Springs mineral water spas; Monongahela Natl. Forest; state parks and forests; trout fishing; turkey, deer, and bear hunting; white water rafting, paddleboat tours, skiing; glass tours at Fenton Glass in Williamstown, Viking Glass in New Martinsville, Blenko Glass in Milton; Sternwheel Regatta, Charleston; Mountain State Forest Festival; Mountain State Arts & Crafts Fair, Ripley.

Famous West Virginians include Newton D. Baker, Pearl Buck, John W. Davis, Thomas "Stonewall" Jackson, Don Knotts, Dwight Whitney Morrow, Nick Nolte, Michael Owens, Cyrus Vance, Col. Charles "Chuck" Yeager.

Tourist information. Dept. of Commerce, State Capitol, Charleston WV 25305.

Toll-free travel information. 1-800-CALLW.VA.

Wisconsin

Badger State

People. Population (1989): 4,867,000; **rank:** 17. **Pop. density:** 86.7 per sq. mi. **Urban** (1980): 64.2%. **Racial distrib.** (1985): 95.7% White; 4.3% Black; Hispanic 66,300. **Net change** (1985-89): +114,000; 2.4%.

Geography. Total area: 56,153 sq. mi.; **rank:** 26. **Land area:** 54,426 sq. mi. **Acres forested land:** 14,907,700. **Location:** North central state, bounded on the N by Lake Superior and Upper Michigan; on the E by Lake Michigan; on the S by Illinois; on the W by the St. Croix and Mississippi rivers. **Climate:** long, cold winters and short, warm summers tempered by the Great Lakes. **Topography:** narrow Lake Superior Lowland plain met by Northern Highland which slopes gently to the sandy crescent Central Plain; Western Upland in the SW; 3 broad parallel limestone ridges running N-S are separated by wide and shallow lowlands in the SE. **Capital:** Madison.

Economy. Principal industries: manufacturing, trade, services, government, transportation, communications, agriculture, tourism. **Principal manufactured goods:** machinery, foods, fabricated metals, transportation equipment, paper and wood products. **Agriculture: Chief crops:** corn, beans, beets, peas, hay, oats, cabbage, cranberries. **Chief products:** milk, butter, cheese. **Livestock** (1989): 4.1 mln. cattle, 1.3 mln. hogs/pigs; 84,000 sheep; 4.1 mln. poultry. **Timber/lumber** (1988): maple, birch, oak, evergreens; 429 mln. bd. ft. **Nonfuel Minerals** (1989): $202 mln.; mostly crushed stone, construction & industrial sand & gravel, lime. **Commercial fishing**

(1989): $5.6 mln. **Chief ports:** Superior, Ashland, Milwaukee, Green Bay, Kewaunee, Pt. Washington, Manitowoc, Sheboygan, Marinette, Kenosha. **International airports at:** Milwaukee. **Value of construction** (1989): $4.4 bln. **Employment distribution** (1989): 23.6% trade; 25.2% mfg.; 22.4% serv.; 15.0% gvt. **Per capita income** (1989): $16,759. **Unemployment** (1989): 4.4%. **Tourism** (1987): out-of-state visitors spent $5.0 bln. **Sales tax:** 5%.

Finance. FDIC-insured commercial banks & trust companies (1987): 566. **Deposits:** $34.1 bln. **Savings institutions** (1990): 70. **Assets:** $17.1 bln.

Federal government. No. federal civilian employees (Mar. 1989): 12,119. **Avg. salary:** $27,266. **Notable federal facilities:** Ft. McCoy.

Energy. Electricity production (1988, mwh, by source): Hydroelectric: 1.2 mln.; Mineral: 32.1 mln.; Nuclear: 11.5 mln.

Education. Student-teacher ratio (1988): 16.0. **Avg. salary, public school teachers** (1990): $32,320.

State data. Motto: Forward. **Flower:** Wood violet. **Bird:** Robin. **Tree:** Sugar maple. **Song:** On, Wisconsin! **Entered union** May 29, 1848; rank, 30th. **State fair at:** West Allis; mid-Aug.

History. Jean Nicolet was the first European to see the Wisconsin area, arriving in Green Bay, 1634; French missionaries and fur traders followed. The British took over, 1763. The U.S. won the land after the Revolution but the British were not ousted until after the War of 1812. Lead miners came next, then farmers. Railroads were started in 1851, serving growing wheat harvests and iron mines.

Tourist attractions. Old Wade House and Carriage Museum, Greenbush; Villa Louis, Prairie du Chien; Circus World Museum, Baraboo; Wisconsin Dells; Old World Wisconsin, Eagle; Door County peninsula; Chequamegon and Nicolet national forests; Lake Winnebago; numerous lakes for water sports, ice boating and fishing; skiing and hunting.

Famous Wisconsinites include Edna Ferber, King Camp Gillette, Harry Houdini, Robert LaFollette, Alfred Lunt, Georgia O'Keeffe, Spencer Tracy, Thorstein Veblen, Orson Welles, Thornton Wilder, Frank Lloyd Wright.

Tourist information. Wisconsin Dept. of Development, Division of Tourism, 123 W. Washington Ave., Madison, WI 53702.

Toll-free travel information. 1-800-372-2737.

Wyoming

Equality State

People. Population (1989): 475,000; **rank:** 50. **Pop. density:** 4.9 per sq. mi. **Urban** (1980): 62.7%. **Racial distrib.** (1980): 95.0% White; 0.71% Black; Hispanic (1980): 26,500. **Net change** (1985-89): −35,000; −6.8%.

Geography. Total area: 97,809 sq. mi.; **rank:** 9. **Land area:** 96,989 sq. mi. **Acres forested land:** 10,028,300. **Location:** Mountain state lying in the high western plateaus of the Great Plains. **Climate:** semi-desert conditions throughout; true desert in the Big Horn and Great Divide basins. **Topography:** the eastern Great Plains rise to the foothills of the Rocky Mtns.; the Continental Divide crosses the state from the NW to the SE. **Capital:** Cheyenne.

Economy. Principal industries: mineral extraction, tourism and recreation, agriculture. **Principal manufactured goods:** refined petroleum products, foods, wood products, stone, clay and glass products. **Agriculture: Chief crops:** wheat, beans, barley, oats, sugar beets, hay. **Livestock** (1989): 1.38 mln. cattle; 16,000 hogs/pigs; 837,000 sheep. **Timber/lumber** (1988): aspen, yellow pine; 301 mln. bd. ft. **Nonfuel Minerals** (1989): $799 mln.; mostly Portland cement, crushed stone. **International airports at:** Casper. **Value of construction** (1989): $407.6 mln. **Employment distribution** (1988): 21.4% serv.; 19.7% trade; 13% mining. **Per capita income** (1989): $14,135. **Unemployment** (1989): 6.3%. **Tourism** (1989): out-of-state visitors spent $1.5 bln. **State sales tax.** 3%.

Finance. FDIC-insured commercial banks & trust companies: 106. **Deposits:** $3.9 bln. **Savings institutions** (1990): 10. **Assets:** $1.2 bln.

Federal government. No. federal civilian employees (Mar. 1989): 4,886. **Avg. salary:** $28,110. **Notable federal facilities:** Warren AFB.

Energy. Electricity production (1986, mwh, by source): Hydroelectric: 789,000; Mineral: 38.4 mln.

Education. Student-teacher ratio (1988): 14.6. **Avg. salary, public school teachers** (1990): $28,184.

State data. Motto: Equal Rights. **Flower:** Indian paintbrush. **Bird:** Meadowlark. **Tree:** Cottonwood. **Song:** Wyoming. **Entered union** July 10, 1890; rank, 44th. **State fair** at: Douglas; late Aug.

History. Francés Francois and Louis Verendrye were the first Europeans, 1743. John Colter, American, was first to traverse Yellowstone Park, 1807-08. Trappers and fur traders followed in the 1820s. Forts Laramie and Bridger became important stops on the pioneer trail to the West Coast. Indian wars followed massacres of army detachments in 1854 and 1866. Population grew after the Union Pacific crossed the state, 1869. Women won the vote, for the first time in the U.S., from the Territorial Legislature, 1869.

Tourist attractions. Yellowstone National Park, 3,472 sq. mi. in the NW corner of Wyoming and the adjoining edges of Montana and Idaho, the oldest U.S. national park, est. 1872, has some 10,000 geysers, hot springs, mud volcanoes, fossil forests, a volcanic glass (obsidian) mountain, the 1,000-ft.-deep canyon and 308-ft.-high waterfall of the Yellowstone River, and a wide variety of animals living free in their natural habitat.

Also, Grand Teton National Park, with mountains 13,000 ft. high; National Elk Refuge, covering 25,000 acres; Devils Tower, a columnar rock of igneous origin 1,280 ft. high; Fort Laramie and surrounding areas of pioneer trails; Buffalo Bill Museum, Cody; Cheyenne Frontier Days Celebration, last full week in July, the state's largest rodeo, and world's largest purse.

Famous Wyomingites include James Bridger, Buffalo Bill Cody, Nellie Tayloe Ross.

Tourist information. Travel Commission, Etchepare Circle, Cheyenne, WY 82002.

Toll-free travel information. 1-800-CALLWYO.

District of Columbia

Area: 69 sq. mi. **Population:** (1989): 604,000. **Motto:** Justitia omnibus, Justice for all. **Flower:** American beauty rose. **Tree:** Scarlet oak. **Bird:** Wood thrush. The city of Washington is coextensive with the District of Columbia.

The District of Columbia is the seat of the federal government of the United States. It lies on the west central edge of Maryland on the Potomac River, opposite Virginia. Its area was originally 100 sq. mi. taken from the sovereignty of Maryland and Virginia. Virginia's portion south of the Potomac was given back to that state in 1846.

The 23d Amendment, ratified in 1961, granted residents the right to vote for president and vice president for the first time and gave them 3 members in the Electoral College. The first such votes were cast in Nov. 1964.

Congress, which has legislative authority over the District under the Constitution, established in 1878 a government of 3 commissioners appointed by the president. The Reorganization Plan of 1967 substituted a single commissioner (also called mayor), assistant, and 9-member City Council. Funds were still appropriated by Congress; residents had no vote in local government, except to elect school board members.

In Sept. 1970, Congress approved legislation giving the District one delegate to the House of Representatives. The delegate could vote in committee but not on the House floor. The first was elected 1971.

In May 1974 voters approved a charter giving them the right to elect their own mayor and a 13-member city council; the first took office Jan. 2, 1975. The district won the right to levy its own taxes but Congress retained power to veto council actions, and approve the city's annual budget.

Proposals for a "federal town" for the deliberations of the Continental Congress were made in 1783, 4 years before the adoption of the Constitution that gave the Confederation a national government. Rivalry between northern and southern delegates over the site appeared in the First Congress, 1789. John Adams, presiding officer of the Senate, cast the deciding vote of that body for Germantown, Pa. In 1790 Congress compromised by making Philadelphia the temporary capital for 10 years. The Virginia members of the House wanted a capital on the eastern bank of the Potomac; they were defeated by the Northerners, while the Southerners defeated the Northern attempt to have the nation assume the war debts of the 13 original states, the Assumption Bill fathered by Alexander Hamilton. Hamilton and Jefferson arranged a compromise: the Virginia men voted for the Assumption Bill, and the Northerners conceded the capital to the Potomac. President Washington chose the site in Oct. 1790 and persuaded landowners to sell their holdings to the government at £25, then about $66, an acre. The capital was named Washington.

Washington appointed Pierre Charles L'Enfant, a French engineer who had come over with Lafayette, to plan the capital on an area not over 10 mi. square. The L'Enfant plan, for streets 100 to 110 feet wide and one avenue 400 feet wide and a mile long, seemed grandiose and foolhardy. But Washington endorsed it. When L'Enfant ordered a wealthy landowner to remove his new manor house because it obstructed a vista, and demolished it when the owner refused, Washington stepped in and dismissed the architect. The official map and design of the city was completed by Benjamin Banneker, a distinguished black architect and astronomer, and Andrew Ellicott.

On Sept. 18, 1793, Pres. Washington laid the cornerstone of the north wing of the Capitol. On June 3, 1800, Pres. John Adams moved to Washington and on June 10, Philadelphia ceased to be the temporary capital. The City of Washington was incorporated in 1802; the District of Columbia was created as a municipal corporation in 1871, embracing Washington, Georgetown, and Washington County.

Outlying U.S. Areas

Commonwealth of Puerto Rico

(Estado Libre Asociado de Puerto Rico)

People. Population (1986): 3,286,000. **Pop. density:** 956.6 per sq. mi. **Urban** (1980): 66.8%. **Racial distribution** (1980): 99.9% Hispanic. **Net migration** (1985): −27,691.

Geography. Total area: 3,435 sq. mi. **Land area:** 3,421 sq. mi. **Location:** island lying between the Atlantic to the N and the Caribbean to the S; it is easternmost of the West Indies group called the Greater Antilles, of which Cuba, Hispaniola, and Jamaica are the larger islands. **Climate:** mild, with a mean temperature of 77°. **Topography:** mountainous throughout three-fourths of its rectangular area, surrounded by a broken coastal plain; highest peak is Cerro de Punta, 4,389 ft. **Capital:** San Juan.

Economy. Principal industries: manufacturing. **Principal manufactured goods:** pharmaceuticals; chemicals; machinery and metals, electric machinery and equipment, petroleum refining, food products, apparel. **Agriculture. Chief crops:** coffee; plantains; bananas; yams; taniers; pineapples; pidgeon peas; peppers; pumpkins; coriander; lettuce; tobacco. **Livestock** (1985): 579,810 cattle; 210,013 pigs; 7.4 mln. poultry. **Nonfuel Minerals** (1987): $111.6 mln., mostly cement. **Commercial fishing** (1984): $7.9 mln. **Chief ports/river shipping:** San Juan, Ponce, Mayaguez, Guayanillá, Guánica, Yabucoa, Aguirre. **Major airports at:** San Juan, Ponce, Mayaguez, Aguadilla. **Value of construction** (1987): $2.5 bln. **Employment distribution:** 24% gvt.; 18% manuf.; 19% trade; 20% serv. **Per capita income** (1985): $4,301. **Unemployment**

(1988): 15%. **Tourism** (1987): Out-of-area visitors spent $1 bln.

Finance. No. FDIC-insured commercial banks & trust companies (1987): 14. **Deposits:** $9.7 bln. **No. savings institutions** (1987): 10. **Assets:** $6.2 bln.

Federal government. No. federal civilian employees (1985): 9,989. **Notable federal facilities:** U.S. Naval Station at Roosevelt Roads; U.S. Army Salinas Training Area and Ft. Allen; Sabana SECA Communications Center (U.S. Navy); Ft. Buchanan.

Energy Production (1985): Steam and gas: 11,938 mln. kwh; Other: 209 mln. kwh.

Education. No. schools (1985): 1,782 public, 818 private elem. and second.; 69 higher ed. **Avg. salary, public school teachers** (1985): $12,000.

Misc. Data. Motto. Joannes Est Nomen Eius (John is his name). **Flower:** Maga. **Bird:** Reinita. **Tree:** Ceiba. **National anthem:** La Borinqueña.

History: Puerto Rico (or Borinquen, after the original Arawak Indian name Boriquen), was discovered by Columbus, Nov. 19, 1493. Ponce de Leon conquered it for Spain, 1509, and established the first settlement at Caparra, across the bay from San Juan.

Sugar cane was introduced, 1515, and slaves were imported 3 years later. Gold mining petered out, 1570. Spaniards fought off a series of British and Dutch attacks; slavery was abolished, 1873. Under the treaty of Paris, Puerto Rico was ceded to the U.S. after the Spanish-American War, 1898. In 1952 the people voted in favor of Commonwealth status.

The Commonwealth of Puerto Rico is a self-governing part of the U.S. with a primary Hispanic culture. Puerto Ricans are U.S. citizens and about 2.0 million now live on the mainland, although since 1974 there has also been a reverse migration flow.

The current commonwealth political status of Puerto Rico gives the island's citizens virtually the same control over their internal affairs as the fifty states of the U.S. However, they do not vote in national elections, although they do vote in national primary elections.

Puerto Rico is represented in Congress solely by a resident commissioner who has a voice but no vote, except in committees.

No federal income tax is collected from residents on income earned from local sources in Puerto Rico.

Puerto Rico's famous "Operation Bootstrap," begun in the late 1940s, succeeded in changing the island from "The Poorhouse of the Caribbean" to an area with the highest per capita income in Latin America. This pioneering program encouraged manufacturing and the development of the tourist trade by selective tax exemption, low-interest loans, and other incentives. Despite the marked success of Puerto Rico's development efforts over an extended period of time, per capita income in Puerto Rico is low in comparison to that of the U.S. In calendar year 1985, the transfer payments from the U.S. government to individuals and governments in Puerto Rico totalled $3.2 bln., or 22% of the Gross Domestic Product of $14.8 bln.

General tourist attractions: Ponce Museum of Art; forts El Morro and San Cristobal; Old Walled City of San Juan; Arecibo Observatory; Cordillera Central and state parks; El Yunque Rain Forest; San Juan Cathedral; Porta Coeli Chapel and Museum of Religious Art, Interamerican Univ., San Germán; Condado Convention Center; Casa Blanca, Ponce de León family home, Puerto Rican Family Museum of 16th and 17 centuries and the Fine Arts Center in San Juan.

Cultural facilities, festivals, etc.: Festival Casals classical music concerts, mid-June; Puerto Rico Symphony Orchestra at Music Conservatory; Botanical Garden and Museum of Anthropology, Art, and History at the University of Puerto Rico; Institute of Puerto Rican Culture, at the Dominican Convent, and many popular festivals throughout the island.

Famous Puerto Ricans include: José Celso Barbosa, Julia de Burgos, Pablo Casals, Orlando Cepeda, Roberto Clemente, José de Diego, José Feliciano, Luis A. Ferré, José Ferrer, Doña Felisa Rincón de Gautier, Commodore Diégo E. Hernández, Rafael Hernández (El Jibarito), Raúl Juliá, Luis Muñoz Marín, René Marqués, Luis Palés Matos, Concha Meléndez, Rita Moreno, Adm. Horacio Rivero, Rafael Hernández Colón, Marta Casals Istomier, Miguel Hernándo Agosto.

Chamber of Commerce: 100 Tetuán P.O.Box. S-3789, San Juan, PR 00904; Ponce & South: El Señorial Bldg., Ponce, PR 00731.

Guam

Where America's Day Begins

People. Population (1987): 127,675. **Pop. density:** 589 per sq. mi. **Urban** (1980): 39.5%. **Major ethnic groups** (1987): Chamorro 48.8%, Filipino 25.2%, stateside immigrants 20%, remainder Micronesians. Native Guamanians, ethnically called Chamorros, are basically of Indonesian stock, with a mixture of Spanish and Filipino. In addition to the offical language, they speak the native Chamorro.

Geography. Total area: 209 sq. mi. land, 30 mi. long and 4 to 8.5 mi. wide. **Location:** largest and southernmost of the Mariana Islands in the West Pacific, 3,700 mi. W of Hawaii. **Climate:** tropical, with temperatures from 70° to 90°F; avg. annual rainfall, about 70 in. **Topography:** coral-line limestone plateau in the N; southern chain of low volcanic mountains sloping gently to the W, more steeply to coastal cliffs on the E; general elevation, 500 ft.; highest pt., Mt. Lamlam, 1,334 ft. **Capital:** Agana.

Economy. Principal industries: construction, light manufacturing, tourism, banking, defense. **Principal manufactured goods:** textiles, foods. **Agriculture: Chief crops:** cabbages, eggplants, cucumber, long beans, tomatoes, bananas, coconuts, watermelon, yams, canteloupe, papayas, maize, sweet potatoes. **Livestock** (1984): 2,000 cattle; 14,000 hogs/pigs. **Chief ports:** Apra Harbor. **International airports at:** Tamuning. **Value of construction** (1980): $80.60 mln. **Employment distribution** (1987): 61.3% private sector; 38.7% gvt. **Per capita income** (1986): $7,116. **Unemployment** (1987): 3%. **Tourism** (1980): visitors' receipts $117.9 mln.

Finance. Notable industries: insurance, real estate, finance. **No. banks:** 13; **No. savings and loan assns.:** 2.

Federal government. No. federal employees (1980): 6,600. **Notable federal facilities:** Anderson AFB; naval, air and port bases.

Education. No. public schools: 37 elementary; 19 secondary; 2 higher education.

Misc. Data. Flower: Puti Tai Nobio (Bougainvillea). **Bird:** Toto (Fruit dove). **Tree:** Ifit (Intsiabijuga). **Song:** Stand Ye Guamians.

History. Magellan arrived in the Marianas Mar. 6, 1521. They were colonized in 1668 by Spanish missionaries who named them the Mariana Islands in honor of Maria Anna, queen of Spain. When Spain ceded Guam to the U.S., it sold the other Marianas to Germany. Japan obtained a League of Nations mandate over the German islands in 1919; in Dec. 1941 it seized Guam; the island was retaken by the U.S. in July 1944.

Guam is a self-governing organized unincorporated U.S. territory. Under the jurisdiction of the Interior Department, it is administered under the Organic Act of 1950, which provides for a governor and a 21-member unicameral legislature, elected biennially by the residents who are American citizens but do not vote for president.

Beginning in Nov., 1970, Guamanians elected their own governor, previously appointed by the U.S. president. He took office in Jan. 1971. In 1972 a U.S. law gave Guam one delegate to the U.S. House of Representatives; the delegate may vote in committee but not on the House floor.

General tourist attractions. annual mid-Aug. Merizo Water Festival; Tarzan Falls; beaches; water sports, duty-free port shopping.

Virgin Islands

St. John, St. Croix, St. Thomas

People. Population (1988): 106,000 (52,400, St. Croix; 50,860, St. Thomas; 2,740, St. John). **Pop. density:** 814.47 per sq. mi. **Urban** (1980): 39%. **Racial distribution:** 15% White; 85% Black. **Major ethnic groups:** West Indian, French, Hispanic.

Geography. Total area: 133 sq. mi.; **Land area:** 136 sq. mi. **Location:** 3 larger and 50 smaller islands and cays in the S and W of the V.I. group (British V.I. colony to the N and E) which is situated 70 mi. E of Puerto Rico, located W of the Anegada Passage, a major channel connecting the Atlantic O. and the Caribbean Sea. **Climate:** subtropical; the sun tempered by gentle trade winds; humidity is low; average temperature, 78° F. **Topography:** St. Thomas is mainly a ridge of hills running E and W, and has little tillable land; St. Croix rises abruptly in the N but slopes to the S to flatlands and lagoons; St. John has steep, lofty hills and valleys with little level tillable land. **Capital:** Charlotte Amalie, St. Thomas.

Economy. Principal industries: tourism, rum, alumina prod., petroleum refining, watch industry, textiles, electronics. **Principal manufactured goods:** rum, textiles, pharmaceuticals, perfumes. **Gross Domestic Product** (1987): $1.246 bln. **Agriculture: Chief crops:** truck garden produce. **Minerals:** sand, gravel. **Chief ports:** Cruz Bay, St. John; Frederiksted and Christiansted, St. Croix; Charlotte Amalie, St. Thomas. **International airports on:** St. Thomas, St. Croix. **Value of construction** (1987): $167.0 mln. **Per capita income** (1987): $7,465. **Unemployment** (1989): 4.4%. **Tourism** (1988): $662.8. **No. banks** (1990): 8.

Education (1987): **No. public schools:** 34 elem. and second.; 1 college. **Avg. starting salary, public school teachers:** $18,001.

Misc. data. Flower: Yellow elder or yellow trumpet, local designation Ginger Thomas. **Bird:** Yellow breast. **Song:** Virgin Islands March.

History. The islands were discovered by Columbus in 1493. Spanish forces, 1555, defeated the Caribes and claimed the territory; by 1596 the native population was annihilated. First permanent settlement in the U.S. territory, 1672, by the Danes; U.S. purchased the islands, 1917, for defense purposes.

The Virgin Islands has a republican form of government, headed by a governor and lieut. governor elected, since 1970, by popular vote for 4-year terms. There is a 15-member unicameral legislature, elected by popular vote. Residents of the V.I. have been U.S. citizens since 1927. Since 1973 they have elected a delegate to the U.S. House of Representatives, who may vote in committee but not in the House.

General tourist attractions. Magens Bay, St. Thomas; duty-free shopping; Virgin Islands National Park, 14,488 acres on St. John of lush growth, beaches, Indian relics, and evidence of colonial Danes.

Tourist information. Dept. of Economic Development & Agriculture, St. Thomas, P.O. Box 6400, St. Thomas, VI 00801; St. Croix, P.O. Box 4535, Christiansted, St. Croix 00820.

American Samoa

Capital: Pago Pago, Island of Tutuila. **Area:** 77 sq. mi. **Population:** (1988) 38,000. **Motto:** Samoa Muamua le Atua (In Samoa, God Is First). **Song:** Amerika Samoa. **Flower:** Paogo (Ula-fala). **Plant:** Ava.

Blessed with spectacular scenery and delightful South Seas climate, American Samoa is the most southerly of all lands under U. S. sovereignty. It is an unincorporated territory consisting of 6 small islands of the Samoan group: Tutuila, Aunu'u, Manu'a Group (Ta'u, Olosega and Ofu), and Rose. Also administered as part of American Samoa is Swain's Island, 210 mi. to the NW, acquired by the U.S. in 1925. The islands are 2,300 mi. SW of Honolulu.

American Samoa became U. S. territory in Feb., 1900 by a treaty with the United Kingdom and Germany in 1899. The islands were ceded by local chiefs in April, 1900 and July, 1904, and became U.S territories. The U.S. acquired commercial rights pursuant to the convention 1899, a tripartite agreement among Great Britain, Germany, and the U.S.

Samoa (Western), comprising the larger islands of the Samoan group, was a New Zealand mandate and UN Trusteeship until it became an independent nation Jan. 1, 1962 *(see Index.)*

Tutuila and Annu'u have an area of 53 sq. mi. Ta'u has an area of 17 sq. mi., and the islets of Ofu and Olosega, 5 sq. mi. with a population of a few thousand. Swain's Island has nearly 2 sq. mi. and a population of about 100.

About 70% of the land is bush. Chief products and exports are fish products, copra, and handicrafts. Taro, bread-fruit, yams, coconuts, pineapples, oranges, and bananas are also produced.

From 1900-1951, American Samoa was under the jurisdiction of the U.S. Navy. Since 1951, it has been under the Interior Dept. On Jan. 3, 1978, the first popularly elected Samoan governor and lieutenant governor were inaugurated. Previously, the governor was appointed by the Secretary of the Interior. American Samoa has a bicameral legislature and elects its own member of Congress, who can introduce legislation and vote in committee, but not in the House.

The American Samoans are of Polynesian origin. They are nationals of the U.S.; 20,000 live in Hawaii, 65,000 in California and Washington.

Minor Caribbean Islands

Quita Sueño Bank, Roncador and Serrana, lie in the Caribbean between Nicaragua and Jamaica. They are uninhabited. U.S. claim to the islands was relinquished in a treaty with Colombia, which entered into force on Sept. 17, 1981.

Navassa lies between Jamaica and Haiti, covers about 2 sq. mi., is reserved by the U.S. for a lighthouse and is uninhabited. It is administered by the U.S. Coast Guard.

Wake, Midway, Other Islands

Wake Island, and its sister islands, **Wilkes** and **Peale,** lie in the Pacific Ocean on the direct route from Hawaii to Hong Kong, about 2,300 mi. W of Hawaii and 1,290 mi. E of Guam. The group is 4.5 mi. long, 1.5 mi. wide, and totals less than 3 sq. mi.

The U.S. flag was hoisted over Wake Island, July 4, 1898, formal possession taken Jan. 17, 1899; Wake has been administered by the U.S. Air Force since 1972. The population consists of a number of USAF personnel.

The **Midway Islands,** acquired in 1867, consist of 2, **Sand** and **Eastern,** in the North Pacific 1,150 mi. NW of Hawaii, with area of about 3 sq. mi., administered by the U.S. Navy. There is no indigenous population; it is currently populated with several U.S. military personnel.

Johnston Atoll, SW of Hawaii, area 1 sq. mi. is operated by The Defense Nuclear Agency, and **Kingman Reef,** S of Hawaii, is under Navy control.

Howland, Jarvis, and **Baker Islands,** 1,500-1,650 miles southwest of the Hawaiian group, uninhabited since World War II, are under the Interior Dept.

Palmyra is an atoll about 1,000 miles south of Hawaii, 4 sq. mi. Privately owned, it is under the Interior Dept.

Islands Under Trusteeship

The Trust Territory of the Pacific Islands was established in 1947, as the only strategic trusteeship of the 11 trusteeships established by the U.N. The territory has a heterogeneous population of about 140,000 people scattered among more than 2,100 islands and atolls in 3 major archipelagos: the Carolines, the Marshalls, and the Marianas. The entire geographic area is sometimes referred to as "Micronesia," meaning "little islands." The area of the Trust Territory covered some 3 million sq.

miles of the Pacific Ocean, slightly larger than the continental U.S. However, its islands constituted a land area of only 715.8 sq. miles—half the size of Rhode Island. It formerly contained 4 political jurisdictions: The Commonwealth of the Northern Mariana Islands (CNMI), the Federated States of Micronesia (FSM), the Republic of the Marshall Islands (RMI), and the Republic of Palau (RP). As of Oct. 21, 1986, the RMI entered into free association with the U.S., as did the FSM effective Nov. 3, 1986. The CNMI became a commonwealth of the U.S., also effective Nov. 3. Only the RP remains under trusteeship.

Commonwealth of the Northern Mariana Islands

Located in the perpetually warm climes between Guam and the Tropic of Cancer, the 16 islands of the Northern Marianas form a 300-mile-long archipelago, comprising a total land area of 183.5 sq. miles. The native population, estimated at 21,777, is concentrated on the 3 largest of the 6 inhabited islands: **Saipan**, the seat of government and commerce (19,156), **Rota** (1,507), and **Tinian** (975).

The people of the Northern Marianas are predominantly of Chamorro cultural extraction, although numbers of Carolinians and immigrants from other areas of E. Asia and Micronesia have also settled in the islands. Pursuant to the Covenant of 1975, which established the Northern Marianas as a commonwealth in political union with the U.S., most natives and many domiciliaries of these islands achieved U.S. citizenship on Nov. 13, 1986, when the U.S. terminated its administration of the U.N. trusteeship as it affected the Northern Marianas. From July 18, 1947, the U.S. had administered the Northern Marianas under a trusteeship agreement with the U.N. Security Council. English is among the several languages commonly spoken.

The Northern Mariana Islands has been self-governing since 1978, when both a constitution drafted and adopted by the people became effective, and a bicameral legislature with offices of governor and lieutenant governor was inaugurated. Commercial activity has increased steadily in the last few years, with 3,537 business licenses issued in the CNM, mostly in tourism, construction, and light industry. In 1989, more than 300,000 tourists visited, an increase of 7.5% over previous years. An agreement with the U.S. for 1986-1992 entitles the Northern Marianna Islands to $228 million for capital development, government operations and special programs.

Federated States of Micronesia

The Federated States of Micronesia extends across the 1,800-mile-long Caroline Island archipelago. The 4 states of the FSM are Pohnpei, Kosrae, Truk, and Yap. Each state consists of several islands, except for Kosrae, a single island. The capital of the FSM is Pohnpei. Populations are: Pohnpei 52,000; Truk, 31,000; Kosrae, 16,500; Yap, 12,000. Pohnpei is 2,900 miles SW of Honolulu and 1,000 miles SE of Guam. The islands vary geologically from high, mountainous islands to low, coral atolls. The FSM lies between the equator and 9 degrees N and 138 degrees and 168 degrees E. Average year-round temperature is 80 degrees. Pohnpei gets the highest annual rainfall, averaging up to 250 inches.

The cultures of the FSM are very diverse. Several languages, each with dialects, are spoken throughout: Yapese, Ulithian, Woleaian, Ponapean, Nukuoran, Kapingamarangi, Trukese, and Kosraean. Each state has a constitution and government, headed by a governor. The status of free association recognizes that the FSM is a sovereign-self-governing state, with the U.S. responsible for defense and also extending agreed-upon amounts of economic and service assistance. Each of the state's constitutions recognizes a role for traditional leaders and customs.

Republic of the Marshall Islands

The Republic of the Marshall Islands consists of 2 island/atoll chains, the Ratak (sunrise) Chain, and the Ralik (sunset) Chain, totalling 31 atolls. Each atoll is a cluster of several small islands circling a lagoon. Total land area is 70 sq. miles. The capital is **Majuro**, 2,000 miles SW of Honolulu and 1,300 SE of Guam. Population is 43,000, 20,000 in Majuro. Average year-round temperature is 81 degrees.

Marshallese culture revolves around the complex clan system. Land is owned by each clan and passed down over the generations. In the late 1970's, the U.S. embarked upon an ambitious Capital Improvement Program, with a goal of building a major infrastructure (airport, dock, roads, water-power-sewer system) in Majuro. Funding was completed in 1985.

The Marshall Islands' Constitution includes both American and British concepts. The executive branch is the Nitijela (parliament) and is consulted by a Council of Iroij (local chiefs). The Nitijela elects the President from among its own members. The status of free association recognizes that the Marshall Islands is a sovereign, self-governing state, with the U.S. responsible for defense, and for extending agreed-upon amounts of economic and service assistance. A subsidiary agreement allows the U.S. continued use of Kwajalein Missile Range for 30 years. Another subsidiary agreement provides for settlement of all claims arising out of the nuclear testing programs conducted by the U.S. at Bikini and Enewetak Atolls from 1946 to 1958.

Republic of Palau

Palau consists of more than 200 islands in the Caroline chain, of which 8 are permanently inhabited. The capital of Palau, Koror, lies 3,997 miles SW of Honolulu and 813 miles S of Guam. Population of Palau is approximately 14,000, 8,100 in Koror. Average year-round temperature is 80 degrees, average annual rainfall 150 inches.

Until 1979, a High Commissioner appointed by the U.S. president, himself appointed a district administrator for Palau to oversee programs and administration there. In support of the evolving political status, the U.S. recognized the Constitution of Palau and the establishment of the Government of Palau. The Constitution became effective in 1980. The President and Vice President are elected by popular vote. A Council of Chiefs advises the President on matters concerning traditional law and custom. Palau has a bicameral national legislature composed of a House of Delegates and a Senate.

Washington, Capital of the U.S.

Arlington National Cemetery

Arlington National Cemetery, on the former Custis estate in Virginia, is the site of the **Tomb of the Unknown Soldier** and the final resting place of John Fitzgerald Kennedy, president of the United States, who was buried there Nov. 25, 1963. A torch burns day and night over his grave. The remains of his brother Sen. Robert F. Kennedy (N.Y.) were interred on June 8, 1968, in an area adjacent. Many other famous Americans are also buried at Arlington, as well as 175,000 American soldiers from every major war.

U.S. Marine Corps War Memorial (Iwo Jima)

North of the National Cemetery, approximately 350 yards, stands the bronze statue of the raising of the United States flag on Mt. Suribachi during WWII, executed by Felix de Weldon from the photograph by Joe Rosenthal, and presented to the nation by members and friends of the U.S. Marine Corps.

Vietnam War Memorial

Dedicated on November 13, 1982, it is a symbol of the U.S.' honor and recognition of the men and women who served in the armed forces in the Vietnam War. It is in-

(continued)

scribed with the names of the more than 58,000 who gave their lives or remain missing.

The Capitol

The United States Capitol was originally designed by Dr. William Thornton, an amateur architect, who submitted a plan in the spring of 1793 that won him $500 and a city lot.

The south, or House wing, was completed in 1807 under the direction of Benjamin H. Latrobe.

The present Senate and House wings and the iron dome were designed and constructed by Thomas U. Walter, the 4th architect of the Capitol, between 1851-1863.

The present cast iron dome at its greatest exterior measures 135 ft. 5 in., and it is topped by the bronze Statue of Freedom that stands 19$\frac{1}{2}$ ft. and weighs 14,985 pounds. On its base are the words "E Pluribus Unum" (Out of Many One).

The Capitol is normally open from 9 a.m. to 4:30 p.m. Tours through the Capitol, including the House and Senate galleries, are conducted from 9 a.m. to 4 p.m. without charge.

Folger Shakespeare Library

The Folger Shakespeare Library on Capitol Hill, Washington, D. C., is a research institution devoted to the advancement of learning in the background of Anglo-American civilization in the 16th and 17th centuries, and in most aspects of the continental Renaissance. It has the largest collection of Shakespeareana in the world, with 79 copies of the First Folio.

Library of Congress

Established by and for Congress in 1800, the Library of Congress has extended its services over the years to other government agencies and other libraries, to scholars, and to the general public, and it now serves as the national library. It contains over 80 million items in 470 languages.

The library's exhibit halls are open to the public. Guided tours are given every hour from 9 a.m. through 4 p.m. Monday through Friday.

Thomas Jefferson Memorial

Dedicated in 1943, The Thomas Jefferson Memorial stands on the south shore of the Tidal Basin in West Potomac park. It is a circular stone structure, with Vermont marble on the exterior and Georgia white marble inside and combines architectural elements of the dome of the Pantheon in Rome and the rotunda designed by Jefferson for the University of Virginia.

The memorial is open daily from 8 a.m. to midnight. An elevator and curb ramps for the handicapped are in service.

Lincoln Memorial

The Lincoln Memorial in West Potomac Park, on the axis of the Capitol and the Washington Monument, consists of a large marble hall enclosing a heroic statue of Abraham Lincoln in meditation sitting on a large armchair. It was dedicated on Memorial Day, May 30, 1922. The Memorial was designed by Henry Bacon. The statue was made by Daniel Chester French and sculpted by the Piccirilli family. Murals and ornamentation on the bronze ceiling beams are by Jules Guerin.

The memorial is open daily from 8 a.m. to midnight. An elevator for the handicapped is in service.

John F. Kennedy Center

John F. Kennedy Center for the Performing Arts, designated by Congress as the National Cultural Center and the official memorial in Washington to President Kennedy, opened September 8, 1971. Tours are available daily between 10:00 a.m. and 1:00 p.m.

Mount Vernon

Mount Vernon on the south bank of the Potomac R., 16 miles below Washington, D. C., is part of a large tract of land in northern Virginia.

The present house is an enlargement of one apparently built on the site of an earlier one by Augustine Washington, who lived there 1735-1738. His son Lawrence came there in 1743, when he renamed the plantation Mount Vernon in honor of Admiral Vernon under whom he had served in the West Indies. Lawrence Washington died in 1752 and was succeeded as proprietor of Mount Vernon by his half-brother, George Washington.

National Archives

The Declaration of Independence, the Constitution of the United States, and the Bill of Rights are on permanent display in the National Archives Exhibition Hall. They are sealed in glass-and-bronze cases. The National Archives also holds the permanently valuable federal records of the United States government.

National Gallery of Art

The National Gallery of Art, situated in an area bounded by Constitution Avenue and the Mall, between Third and Seventh Streets, was established by Joint Resolution of Congress Mar. 24, 1937, and opened Mar. 17, 1941.

Normally open daily from 10 a.m. to 5 p.m.; noon to 9 p.m. Sunday. Summer, 10 a.m. to 9 p.m., noon to 9 p.m. on Sunday.

The Pentagon

The Pentagon, headquarters of the Department of Defense, is one of the world's largest office buildings. Situated in Arlington, Va., it houses more than 23,000 employees in offices that occupy 3,707,745 square feet.

Tours are available Monday through Friday (excluding federal holidays), from 9 a.m. to 3:30 p.m.

Smithsonian Institution

The Smithsonian Institution, established in 1846, the world's largest museum complex, is comprised of 14 museums and the National Zoo. It holds some 100 million artifacts and specimens in its trust "for the increase and diffusion of knowledge among men." Nine museums are located on the National Mall between the Washington Monument and the Capitol; 4 other museums and the zoo are elsewhere in Washington, and the Cooper-Hewitt Museum in New York City. The National Air and Space Museum, National Museum of Natural History, and the National Portrait Gallery are some of the more popular museums. They are open daily, except Dec. 25, from 10 a.m. to 5:30 p.m. unless otherwise noted.

Washington Monument

The Washington Monument, dedicated in 1885, is a tapering shaft or obelisk of white marble, 555 ft., 5-$\frac{1}{8}$ inches in height and 55 ft., 1-$\frac{1}{2}$ inches square at base. Eight small windows, 2 on each side, are located at the 500-ft. level, where points of interest are indicated.

Open daily except Dec. 25, 9 a.m. to 5 p.m., 8 a.m. to 12 p.m. in summer.

The White House

The White House, the president's residence, stands on 18 acres on the south side of Pennsylvania Avenue, between the Treasury and the Executive Office Building.

The walls are of sandstone, quarried at Aquia Creek, Va. The exterior walls were painted, causing the building to be termed the "White House." On Aug. 24, 1814, during Madison's administration, the house was burned by the British. James Hoban rebuilt it by Oct. 1817.

The White House is normally open from 10 a.m. to 12 noon, Tuesday through Saturday. Only the public rooms on the ground floor and state floor may be visited.

CITIES OF THE U.S. [1]

Sources: Bureau of the Census: population (1988 estimates); population growth (1970-1980); population over 65 and under 35 (1980). Geography Division, Bureau of the Census: population density (1980); area (1980). Bureau of Labor Statistics: employment (Jan. 1990). Bureau of Economic Analysis: per capita personal income (MSA, 1988).

Akron, Ohio

Population: 221,510; **Pop. density:** 4,312 per sq. mi.; **Pop. growth:** −13.9%; **Pop. over 65:** 13.5%; **Pop. under 35:** 57.1%. **Area:** 55 sq. mi. **Employment:** 101,401 employed, 8.6% unemployed; **Per capita income:** $15,946; % change 1983-88: 34.4.

History: settled 1825; inc. as city 1865; located on Ohio-Erie Canal and is a port of entry; since 1870 the rubber capital of the U.S.

Transportation: 1 airport; major trucking industry; Conrail; metro transit system. **Communications:** 4 TV, 7 radio stations; CATV. **Medical facilities:** 11 hospitals; specialized children's treatment center. **Educational facilities:** 13 univ. and colleges; 68 public schools. **Further information:** Akron Regional Development Board or Akron-Summit Convention and Visitors Bureau, Cascade Plaza, Akron, OH 44308.

Albuquerque, New Mexico

Population: 378,480; **Pop. density:** 3,492 per sq. mi.; **Pop. growth:** 35.7%; **Pop. over 65:** 8.4%; **Pop. under 35:** 61.6%. **Area:** 95 sq. mi. **Employment:** 204,485 employed, 4.0% unemployed; **Per capita income:** $15,019; % change 1983-88: 31.4.

History: founded 1706 by the Spanish; inc. 1890.

Transportation: 1 international airport; 2 railroads; 2 bus lines. **Communications:** 5 TV, 31 radio stations; CATV. **Medical facilities:** 10 major hospitals. **Educational facilities:** 1 university. **Further information:** Convention & Visitors Bureau, 625 Silver S.W., Albuquerque, NM 87125.

Amarillo, Texas

Population: 166,010; **Pop. density:** 1,863 per sq. mi.; **Pop. growth:** 17.5%; **Pop. over 65:** 10.1%; **Pop. under 35:** 60.1%. **Area:** 80 sq. mi. **Employment:** 76,698 employed, 6.5% (Mar.) unemployed; **Per capita income:** $14,634; % change 1983-88: 17.9.

History: founded 1887 as a junction of two railroads; inc. 1899; became industrial city after discovery of oil (1921) and helium gas.

Transportation: 1 airport; 2 railroads; 3 bus lines; city transit system. **Communications:** 5 TV, 17 radio stations; CATV. **Medical facilities:** 5 hospitals; Amarillo Medical Ctr. **Educational facilities:** 47 public schools; 1 college. **Further information:** Chamber of Commerce, P.O. Box 9480, Amarillo, TX 79105.

Anaheim, California

Population: 244,670; **Pop. density:** 5,349 per sq. mi.; **Pop. growth:** 31.6%; **Pop. over 65:** 7.7%; **Pop. under 35:** 60.7%. **Area:** 41 sq. mi. **Employment:** 156,827 employed. 3.3% unemployed; **Per capita income:** $22,753; % change 1983-88: 42.4.

History: founded 1858; inc. 1876; now known as home of Disneyland (since 1955).

Transportation: 3 municipal airports; 4 railroads; Greyhound buses. **Communications:** 12 TV, 4 radio stations; CATV. **Medical facilities:** 6 general hospitals. **Educational facilities:** 3 colleges, 5 junior colleges; 62 elementary, 8 junior high, 8 high schools. **Further information:** Chamber of Commerce, 100 South Anaheim Blvd., Suite 300, Anaheim, CA 92805.

Anchorage, Alaska

Population: 218,500 **Pop. density:** 100 per sq. mi.; **Pop. growth:** 259.5%; **Pop. over 65:** 2.0%; **Pop. under 35:** 70.2%. **Area:** 1,732 sq. mi.. **Employment:** 109,506 employed, 5.9% unemployed; **Per capita income:** $21,840; % change 1983-88: 8.9.

History: founded 1914 as a construction camp for railroad; HQ of Alaska Defense Command, WWII; severely damaged in earthquake 1964.

Transportation: 1 international airport, 3 other airports. **Communications:** 6 TV, 16 radio stations. **Medical facilities:** 3 hospitals. **Educational facilities:** 2 univ., 1 comm. college. **Further information:** Chamber of Commerce, 437 E St., Anchorage, AK 99501.

Arlington, Texas

Population: 257,460; **Pop. density:** 2,024 per sq. mi.; **Pop. growth:** 77.5%; **Pop. over 65:** 4.5%; **Pop. under 35:** 67.3%. **Area:** 79 sq. mi.; **Employment:** 123,977 employed, 3.8% unemployed; **Per capita income:** $16,551; % change 1983-88: 26.9.

History: settled in 1840s between Dallas & Ft. Worth; inc. 1884.

Transportation: Dallas/Ft. Worth airport is 20 minutes away; 11 railway lines; intercity transport system in planning stage. **Communications:** 13 TV, 53 radio stations; CATV. **Medical facilities:** 4 hospitals. **Educational facilities:** 51 public schools; 1 univ. **Further information:** Chamber of Commerce, 316 W. Main St., Arlington, TX 76010.

Atlanta, Georgia

Population: 420,220; **Pop. density:** 3,244 per sq. mi.; **Pop. growth:** −14.1%; **Pop. over 65:** 11.5%; **Pop. under 35:** 60.7%. **Area:** 131 sq. mi.. **Employment:** 212,861 employed, 6.8% unemployed; **Per capita income:** $18,400; % change 1983-88: 42.3.

History: founded as "Terminus" 1837; renamed Atlanta 1845 after Atlantis; inc. 1847; played major role in Civil War and burned during Gen. Sherman's "March to the Sea."

Transportation: 1 international airport; 7 railroad lines, 2 systems; 2 bus terminals; rapid rail. **Communications:** 9 TV, 41 radio stations; 21 cable TV companies. **Medical facilities:** 60 hospitals; VA hospital; Natl. Centers for Disease Control; Natl. Cancer Center. **Educational facilities:** 37 colleges, universities, seminaries, junior colleges. **Further information:** Chamber of Commerce, 235 International Blvd., Atlanta, GA 30303.

Aurora, Colorado

Population: 218,720; **Pop. density:** 2,652 per sq. mi.; **Pop. growth:** 111.5%; **Pop. over 65:** 4.3%; **Pop. under 35:** 67.3%. **Area:** 60 sq. mi. **Employment:** 106,728 employed, 4.5% unemployed; **Per capita income:** $18,155; % change 1983-88: 22.4.

History: residential suburb 5 mi. east of Denver; fast-growing trade center for large livestock and farm area.

Transportation: 1 international airport; 4 railroads; 2 bus lines; city bus system. **Further information:** ECO Aurora, Inc., 1470 S. Havana, Ste. 708, Aurora, CO 80012.

Austin, Texas

Population: 464,690; **Pop. density:** 2,978 per sq. mi.; **Pop. growth:** 36.3%; **Pop. over 65:** 7.5%; **Pop. under 35:** 69%. **Area:** 116 sq. mi.. **Employment:** 262,866 employed, 4.3% unemployed; **Per capita income:** $15,342; % change 1983-88: 22.7.

History: first permanent settlement 1835; capital of Rep. of Texas 1838; named after Stephen Austin; inc. 1840.

Transportation: 1 international airport; 4 railroads. **Communications:** 5 TV, 18 radio stations. **Medical facilities:** 15 hospitals. **Educational facilities:** 7 universities

(1) Based on 1988 estimates, the 100 most populated cities (inc.=incorporated; est.=established; NA=not available).

649

and colleges. **Further information:** Chamber of Commerce, P.O. Box 1967, Austin, TX 78767.

Baltimore, Maryland

Population: 751,400; **Pop. density:** 9,835 per sq. mi.; **Pop. growth:** −13.1%; **Pop. over 65:** 12.8%; **Pop. under 35%:** 56.9%. **Area:** 80 sq. mi.. **Employment:** 316,832 employed, 6.7% unemployed; **Per capita income:** $19,010; % change 1983-88: 41.8.

History: founded by Maryland legislature 1729; inc. 1797; bombing of its Ft. McHenry 1814 inspired Francis Scott Key to write "Star-Spangled Banner;" rebuilt after fire 1904.

Transportation: 1 major airport; 3 railroads, bus system; subway system, 2 underwater tunnels. **Communications:** 6 TV, 33 radio stations. **Medical facilities:** 29 hospitals; 2 major medical centers. **Educational facilities:** 189 public schools; over 30 universities and colleges. **Further information:** Greater Baltimore Committee, Suite 900, Two Hopkins Plaza, Baltimore, MD 21202.

Baton Rouge, Louisiana

Population: 235,270; **Pop. density:** 5,673 per sq. mi.; **Pop. growth:** 32.2%; **Pop. over 65:** 8.7%; **Pop. under 35:** 64.0%. **Area:** 61 sq. mi.. **Employment:** 111,429 employed, 5.4% unemployed; **Per capita income:** $13,784; % change 1983-88: 20.6.

History: claimed by Spain at time of La. Purchase 1803; est. independence by rebellion 1810; inc. as town 1817; held by Union during most of Civil War.

Transportation: 1 airport, 7 airlines; 1 bus line; 3 railroad trunk lines. **Communications:** 5 TV, 19 radio stations; CATV. **Medical facilities:** 7 hospitals. **Educational facilities:** 96 public, 46 private schools; 2 univ. **Further information:** Chamber of Commerce, P.O. Box 3217, Baton Rouge, LA 70821.

Birmingham, Alabama

Population: 277,280; **Pop. density:** 2,872 per sq. mi.; **Pop. growth:** −5.5%; **Pop. over 65%:** 13.9%; **Pop. under 35:** 57.5%. **Area:** 99 sq. mi.. **Employment:** 119,986 employed, 6.9% unemployed; **Per capita income:** $14,798; % change 1983-88: 37.0.

History: settled due to discovery of elements needed for steel production; inc. 1871; named after Great Britain's steel making center.

Transportation: 1 airport; 4 major rail freight lines, Amtrak; 1 bus line; 75 truck line terminals; 4 interstate highways. **Communications:** 5 TV, 22 radio stations; 1 educational TV, 1 educational radio station. **Medical facilities:** Univ. of Alabama in Birmingham Medical Center; VA hospital with organ transplant program; 15 other hospitals. **Educational facilities:** 1 university, 12 colleges, 2 junior colleges. **Further information:** Chamber of Commerce, 2027 First Ave. N., Birmingham, AL 35202.

Boston, Massachusetts

Population: 577,830; **Pop. density:** 11,979 per sq. mi.; **Pop. growth:** −12.2%; **Pop. over 65:** 12.7%; **Pop. under 35:** 60.4%. **Area:** 46 sq. mi.. **Employment:** 284,704 employed, 4.4% unemployed; **Per capita income:** $22,248; % change 1983-88: 52.3.

History: settled 1630 by John Winthrop; capital of Mass. Bay Colony; figured strongly in Am. Revolution, earning distinction as the "Cradle of Liberty;" inc. 1822.

Transportation: 1 major airport; 2 railroads; city rail and subway system; 2 underwater tunnels. **Communications:** 8 TV, 17 radio stations; CATV. **Medical facilities:** 16 hospitals; 8 major medical research centers. **Educational facilities:** 11 universities and colleges. **Further information:** Chamber of Commerce, Federal Reserve Bank, 600 Atlantic Ave., 13th Fl., Boston, MA 02106.

Buffalo, New York

Population: 313,570; **Pop. density:** 8,520 per sq. mi.; **Pop. growth:** −22.7%; **Pop. over 65:** 15.0%; **Pop. under 35:** 55.3%. **Area:** 42 sq. mi.. **Employment:** 135,115 employed, 7.6% unemployed; **Per capita income:** $16,342; % change 1983-88: 37.1.

History: founded 1790 by the Dutch; raided twice by British during War of 1812; as western terminus for Erie Canal became a center for trade and manufacturing; inc. 1832.

Transportation: 1 international airport; 6 major railroads; metro rail system; water service to Great Lakes-St. Lawrence seaways system, and Atlantic seaboard. **Communications:** 5 TV, 23 radio stations, 2 cable systems. **Medical facilities:** 21 hospitals. **Educational facilities:** 2 universities, 9 colleges; 78 public schools. **Further information:** Greater Buffalo Chamber of Commerce, 107 Delaware Ave., Buffalo, NY 14202.

Charlotte, North Carolina

Population: 367,860; **Pop. density:** 2,278 per sq. mi.; **Pop. growth:** 30.2%; **Pop. over 65:** 8.6%; **Pop. under 35:** 60.4%. **Area:** 138 sq. mi. **Employment:** 211,622 employed, 3.4% unemployed; **Per capita income:** $16,348; % change 1983-88: 45.2.

History: settled by Scotch-Irish immigrants 1740s; inc. 1767 and named after Queen Charlotte, George III's wife; scene of first major U.S. gold discovery 1799.

Transportation: 1 airport; 2 major railway lines; 2 bus lines; 200 trucking firms. **Communications:** 6 TV, 20 radio stations. **Medical facilities:** 12 hospitals, 1 medical center. **Educational facilities:** 2 universities, 5 colleges. **Further information:** Chamber of Commerce, P.O. Box 32785, Charlotte, NC 28232.

Chattanooga, Tennessee

Population: 162,670; **Pop. density:** 1,370 per sq. mi.; **Pop. growth:** 41.4%; **Pop. over 65:** 12.7%; **Pop. under 35:** 57.3%. **Area:** 124 sq. mi. **Employment:** 77,435 employed, 4.5% unemployed; **Per capita income:** $14,304; % change 1983-88: 40.9.

History: first permanent white settlement 1835; chartered 1839, as city 1851.

Transportation: 1 airport, 7 airlines; 1 bus line and local service; 2 railroads. **Communications:** 6 TV stations; CATV; 23 radio stations. **Medical facilities:** 17 hospitals. **Educational facilities:** 53 public schools; 2 universities; 3 junior colleges, 4 colleges. **Further information:** Partners for Economic Progress, Civic Forum, 1001 Market St., Chattanooga, TN 37402.

Chicago, Illinois

Population: 2,977,520; **Pop. density:** 13,180 per sq. mi.; **Pop. growth:** −10.8%; **Pop. over 65:** 11.4%; **Pop. under 35:** 58.5%. **Area:** 228 sq. mi. **Employment:** 1,332,912 employed, 7.7% unemployed; **Per capita income:** $19,060; % change 1983-88: 35.9.

History: site acquired from Indians 1795; area began settlement with opening of Erie Canal 1825; chartered as city 1837; boomed with arrival of railroads from east and canal to Mississippi R.; much of city destroyed by fire 1871; major grain & livestock market.

Transportation: 3 airports; major railroad system; major trucking industry. **Communications:** 9 TV, 31 radio stations. **Medical facilities:** over 123 hospitals. **Educational facilities:** 95 institutions of higher learning. **Further information:** Association of Commerce and Industry, 200 N. LaSalle St., Chicago, IL 60601.

Cincinnati, Ohio

Population: 370,480; **Pop. density:** 4,941 per sq. mi.; **Pop. growth:** −15.0%; **Pop. over 65:** 14.5%; **Pop. under 35:** 58.5%. **Area:** 78 sq. mi.. **Employment:** 190,038 employed, 6.3% unemployed; **Per capita income:** $16,633; % change 1983-88: 36.4.

History: founded 1788 and named after the Society of Cincinnati, an organization of Revolutionary War officers; chartered as village 1802; inc. as city 1819.

Transportation: 1 international airport; 3 railroads; 1 bus system. **Communications:** 6 TV, 3 CATV systems; 27 radio stations. **Medical facilities:** 32 hospitals; Children's Hospital Medical Center; VA hospital. **Educational facilities:** 4 universities; 5 colleges, 8 technical & 2-year colleges. **Further information:** Chamber of Commerce, 300 Carew Tower, 441 Vine St., Cincinnati, OH 45202.

Cleveland, Ohio

Population: 521,370; **Pop. density:** 7,264 per sq. mi.; **Pop. growth:** −23.6%; **Pop. over 65:** 13.0%; **Pop. under 35:** 56.7%. **Area:** 79 sq. mi.. **Employment:** 221,074 employed, 9.1% unemployed; **Per capita income:** $18,168; % change 1983-88: 35.3.

History: surveyed in 1796; inc. as village 1814, as city 1836; annexed Ohio City 1854.

Transportation: 1 intl. airport; rail service; major port; rapid transit system. **Communications:** 7 TV, 20 radio stations. **Medical facilities:** numerous hospitals; major medical research center. **Educational facilities:** 124 public schools; 8 universities and colleges. **Further information:** Convention & Visitor's Bureau, 3100 Terminal Tower, Cleveland, OH 44115.

Colorado Springs, Colorado

Population: 283,110; **Pop. density:** 2,088 per sq. mi.; **Pop. growth:** 58.8%; **Pop. over 65:** 8.3%; **Pop. under 35:** 62.3%. **Area:** 103 sq. mi.. **Employment:** 133,948 employed, 6.4% unemployed; **Per capita income:** $15,464; % change 1983-88: 29.2.

History: founded 1859 at the foot of Pikes Peak; inc. 1886.

Transportation: 1 municipal airport; 2 railroads; Greyhound-Trailways bus line. **Communications:** 5 TV, 22 radio stations. **Medical facilities:** 9 hospitals. **Educational facilities:** 3 universities, 7 colleges. **Further information:** Chamber of Commerce, P.O. Drawer B, Colorado Springs, CO 80901.

Columbus, Georgia

Population: 178,680; **Pop. density:** 779 per sq. mi.; **Pop. growth:** 9.3%; **Pop. over 65:** 8.9%; **Pop. under 35:** 61.5%. **Area:** 218 sq. mi. **Employment:** 69,816 employed, 5.6% unemployed; **Per capita income:** $12,726; % change 1983-88: 37.9.

History: settled and inc. 1828; a port city on Chattahouchee R.

Transportation: 1 airport; metro bus system; 2 bus lines; 2 railroads. **Communications:** 5 TV, 11 radio stations. **Medical facilities:** 5 hospitals. **Educational facilities:** 53 public schools; 1 college. **Further information:** Chamber of Commerce, P.O. Box 1200, Columbus, GA 31902.

Columbus, Ohio

Population: 569,570; **Pop. density:** 3,121 per sq. mi.; **Pop. growth:** 4.6%; **Pop. over 65:** 8.9%; **Pop. under 35:** 64.4%. **Area:** 181 sq. mi.. **Employment:** 314,959 employed, 5.9% unemployed; **Per capita income:** $16,251; % change 1983-88: 37.7.

History: first settlement 1797; laid out as new capital 1812 with current name; became city 1834.

Transportation: 2 airports; 3 railroads; 4 intercity bus lines. **Communications:** 5 TV, 19 radio stations. **Medical facilities:** 22 hospitals. **Educational facilities:** 12 universities and colleges. **Further information:** Chamber of Commerce, P.O. Box 1527, Columbus, OH 43216.

Corpus Christi, Texas

Population: 260,930; **Pop. density:** 2,230 per sq. mi.; **Pop. growth:** 13.4%; **Pop. over 65:** 8.2%; **Pop. under 35:** 63.2%. **Area:** 104 sq. mi.. **Employment:** 109,635 employed, 6.2% unemployed; **Per capita income:** $12,408; % change 1983-88: 16.5.

History: settled 1839 and inc. 1852.

Transportation: 1 international airport; 2 bus lines, metro bus system; 3 freight railroads. **Communications:** 6 TV, 17 radio stations. **Medical facilities:** 14 hospitals including a children's center. **Educational facilities:** 54 public schools; 1 univ., 1 college. **Further information:** Chamber of Commerce, PO Box 640, Corpus Christi, TX 78403.

Dallas, Texas

Population: 987,360; **Pop. density:** 2,715 per sq. mi.; **Pop. growth:** 7%; **Pop. over 65:** 9.5%; **Pop. under 35:** 61.1%. **Area:** 333 sq. mi. **Employment:** 602,974 employed, 5.2% unemployed; **Per capita income:** $18,580; % change 1983-88: 24.9.

History: first settled 1841; platted 1846; inc. 1871; developed as the financial and commercial center of Southwest; known for its oil industry and cotton market.

Transportation: 1 international airport; Amtrak; major transit system. **Communications:** 10 TV, 49 radio stations. **Medical facilities:** 70 hospitals; major medical center. **Educational facilities:** 7 univ., 2 colleges. **Further information:** Chamber of Commerce, 1507 Pacific Ave., Dallas, TX 75201.

Dayton, Ohio

Population: 178,000; **Pop. density:** 4,236 per sq. mi.; **Pop. growth:** −16.3%; **Pop. over 65:** 11.8%; **Pop. under 35:** 59.8%. **Area:** 48 sq. mi. **Employment:** 81,808 employed, 9.9% unemployed; **Per capita income:** $16,107; % change 1983-88: 36.9.

History: settled 1796; inc. 1805; disastrous flood 1913; site where Wright Bros. invented first airplane to sustain flight 1903.

Transportation: 1 international airport, 12 airlines, 2 railroads; 4 bus lines; countywide Dayton Regional Transit Authority. **Communications:** 5 TV, 8 radio stations. **Medical facilities:** 15 hospitals including VA facility. **Educational facilities:** 26 institutions of higher learning. **Further information:** Dayton Area Chamber of Commerce, Fifth and Main, Chamber Plaza, Dayton, OH 45402.

Denver, Colorado

Population: 492,200; **Pop. density:** 4,435 per sq. mi.; **Pop. growth:** −4.3%; **Pop. over 65:** 12.6%; **Pop. under 35:** 58.9%. **Area:** 111 sq. mi. **Employment:** 245,794 employed, 5.9% unemployed; **Per capita income:** $18,155; % change 1983-88: 22.4.

History: settled 1858 by gold prospectors and miners; inc. 1861; growth spurred by gold and silver boom; the financial and industrial center of Rocky Mt. region.

Transportation: 1 international airport; 5 major rail freight lines, Amtrak, 2 bus lines. **Communications:** 7 TV, 35 radio stations. **Medical facilities:** 34 hospitals. **Educational facilities:** 2 universities; 3 colleges. **Further information:** Chamber of Commerce, 1301 Welton St., Denver, CO 80204.

Des Moines, Iowa

Population: 192,910 **Pop. density:** 2,890 per sq. mi.; **Pop. growth:** −5.2%; **Pop. over 65:** 12.5%; **Pop. under 35:** 58.4%. **Area:** 66 sq. mi. **Employment:** 117,793 employed, 4.4% unemployed; **Per capita income:** $17,156; % change 1983-88: 31.2.

History: Fort Des Moines built 1843; settled and inc. 1851; chartered as city 1857.

Transportation: 1 international airport; 3 bus lines; 4 railroads; metro bus system. **Communications:** 5 TV, 18 radio stations; CATV. **Medical facilities:** 8 hospitals. **Educational facilities:** 1 univ., 2 colleges. **Further information:** Chamber of Commerce, 8th & High Sts., Des Moines, IA 50309.

Detroit, Michigan

Population: 1,035,920; **Pop. density:** 8,848 per sq. mi.; **Pop. growth:** −20.5%; **Pop. over 65:** 11.7%; **Pop. under 35:** 59.5%. **Area:** 136 sq. mi. **Employment:** 399,742 employed, 12.0% unemployed; **Per capita income:** $18,554; % change 1983-88: 43.5.

History: founded by French 1701; controlled by British 1760; acquired by U.S. 1796; destroyed by fire 1805; capital of state 1837-47; inc. as city 1824; auto manufacturing began 1899.

Transportation: 1 international airport; 10 railroads; major international port; public transit system. **Communications:** 9 TV, 37 radio stations. **Medical facilities:** 28 hospitals, major medical center. **Educational facilities:** 13 universities and colleges. **Further information:** Chamber of Commerce, 150 Michigan Avenue, Detroit, MI 48226.

El Paso, Texas

Population: 510,970; **Pop. density:** 1,779 per sq. mi.. **Pop. growth:** 32.0%; **Pop. over 65:** 6.9%; **Pop. under 35:** 65%. **Area:** 239 sq. mi. **Employment:** 207,907 employed, 9.5% unemployed; **Per capita income:** $10,008; % change 1983-88: 23.7.

History: first settled 1827; inc. 1873; arrival of railroad 1881 boosted city's population and industries.

Transportation: International airport; 5 major rail lines; 8 bus lines; 9 major highways; gateway to Mexico. **Communications:** 6 TV, 23 radio stations. **Medical facilities:** 16 hospitals; cancer treatment center. **Educational facilities:** 2 colleges and universities. **Further information:** Convention and Visitors Bureau, 5 Civic Center Plaza, El Paso, TX 79901.

Fort Wayne, Indiana

Population: 179,810; **Pop. density:** 3,274 per sq. mi.; **Pop. growth:** −3.4%; **Pop. over 65:** 11.9%; **Pop. under 35:** 60.5%. **Area:** 52 sq. mi. **Employment:** 92,911 employed, 7.4% unemployed; **Per capita income:** $16,336; % change 1983-88: 44.1.

History: French fort 1680; U.S. fort 1794; settled by 1832; inc. 1840 prior to Wabash-Erie canal completion 1843.

Transportation: 1 airport, 9 airlines; 3 railroads; 5 bus lines. **Communications:** 5 TV stations; 13 radio stations. **Medical facilities:** 3 major hospitals; VA hospital. **Educational facilities:** 82 public schools; 5 colleges. **Further information:** Chamber of Commerce, 826 Ewing Street, Fort Wayne, IN 46802.

Fort Worth, Texas

Population: 426,610; **Pop. density:** 1,604 per sq. mi.; **Pop. growth:** −2.1%; **Pop. over 65:** 11.8%; **Pop. under 35:** 58.5%. **Area:** 240 sq. mi. **Employment:** 256,009 employed, 5.8% unemployed; **Per capita income:** $16,551; % change 1983-88: 26.9.

History: est. as military post 1849; inc. 1873; oil discovered 1917; Fort Worth is a sister city to Dallas.

Transportation: 1 intl. airport; 8 major railroads, Amtrak; local bus service; 2 transcontinental, 2 intrastate bus lines. **Communications:** 9 TV, 37 radio stations. **Medical facilities:** 35 hospitals; 2 children's hospitals; 4 government hospitals. **Educational facilities:** 8 colleges & universities. **Further information:** Chamber of Commerce, 700 Throckmorton, Fort Worth, TX 76102.

Fremont, California

Population: 166,590; **Pop. density:** 1,683 per sq. mi.; **Pop. growth:** 30.8%; **Pop. over 65:** 5.2%; **Pop. under 18:** 30.1%. **Area:** 78.4 sq. mi. **Employment:** NA **Per capita income:** NA

History: area first settled by Spanish 1769; during 1800s a collection of towns formed the area; inc. 1956.

Transportation: intracity bus line; Bay Area Rapid Transit System (southern terminal). **Communications:** NA **Medical facilities:** 1 hospital. **Educational facilities:** 43 public schools; 1 jr. college. **Further information:** Chamber of Commerce, One Fremont Pl., 39650 Liberty St., Ste. 130, Fremont, CA 94538.

Fresno, California

Population: 307,090; **Pop. density:** 3,356 per sq. mi.; **Pop. growth:** 31.7%; **Pop. over 65:** 10.9%; **Pop. under 35:** 62.5%. **Area:** 65 sq. mi. **Employment:** 116,853 employed, 9.4% unemployed; **Per capita income:** $15,012; % change 1983-88: 32.4.

History: founded 1872; inc. as city 1885.

Transportation: 2 municipal airports; Amtrak; 1 bus line; intracity bus system. **Communications:** 11 TV stations, 5 CATV services; 58 radio stations. **Medical facilities:** 6 general hospitals including a VA facility. **Educational facilities:** 8 colleges and univ.; 85 public schools. **Further information:** Chamber of Commerce, P.O. Box 1469, Fresno, CA 93721.

Garland, Texas

Population: 180,450; **Pop. density:** 2,493 per sq. mi.; **Pop. growth:** 70.5%; **Pop. over 65:** 4.1%; **Pop. under 35:** 33.7%. **Area:** 56 sq. mi. **Employment:** 94,283 employed, 4.5% unemployed; **Per capita income:** $18,580; % change 1983-88: 24.9.

History: city in Dallas co., 14 mi. NE of Dallas.

Transportation: 45 miles from Dallas/Ft. Worth airport; 2 railroads. **Communications:** 3 TV stations (from Dallas). **Medical facilities:** total of 306 hospital beds. **Educational facilities:** 53 public schools; 1 univ.; 2 community colleges. **Further information:** Chamber of Commerce, P.O. Box 460939, Garland, TX 75046.

Grand Rapids, Michigan

Population: 185,370; **Pop. density:** 4,190 per sq. mi.; **Pop. growth:** −8.0%; **Pop. over 65:** 13.4%; **Pop. under 35:** 60.5%. **Area:** 43.4 sq. mi. **Employment:** 98,396 employed, 8.2% unemployed; **Per capita income:** $16,713; % change 1983-88: 42.3.

History: originally site of Ottawa Indian village; trading post 1826; became lumbering center and chartered as town 1850.

Transportation: 1 international airport; 4 railroads; 5 bus lines; transit bus system. **Communications:** 6 TV, 25 radio stations. **Medical facilities:** 10 hospitals. **Educational facilities:** 64 public schools; 8 colleges. **Further information:** Chamber of Commerce, 17 Fountain St., NW, Grand Rapids, MI 49503.

Greensboro, North Carolina

Population: 181,970; **Pop. density:** 2,581 per sq. mi.; **Pop. growth:** 8.0%; **Pop. over 65:** 9.8%; **Pop. under 35:** 57%. **Area:** 60 sq. mi.; **Employment:** 87,309 employed, 4.2% unemployed; **Per capita income:** $16,614; % change 1983-88: 43.7.

History: settled 1749; site of Revolutionary War conflict 1781 between Nathanael Greene and Cornwallis; inc. 1807.

Transportation: 1 regional airport; 2 railroads; Trailways/Greyhound bus service. **Communications:** all cable TV stations; 11 radio stations. **Medical facilities:** 4 hospitals. **Educational facilities:** 38 public schools; 2 univ., 1 college. **Further information:** Chamber of Commerce, P.O. Box 3246, Greensboro, NC 27402.

Hialeah, Florida

Population: 162,080; **Pop. density:** 7,487 per sq. mi.; **Pop. growth:** 41.8%; **Pop. over 65:** 11.4%; **Pop. under 18:** 24.2%. **Area:** 19.4 sq. mi.; **Employment:** NA **Per capita income:** $16,874; % change 1983-88: 38.3.

History: inc. 1925; built over drained swamplands NW of Miami.

Transportation: Miami Int'l. airport is 5 miles away; Amtrak; 2 rail freight lines. **Communications:** NA. **Medical facilities:** 3 hospitals. **Educational facilities:** 2 universities. **Further information:** Hialeah Dept. of Eco. Development, Office of the Mayor, 501 Palm Ave., Hialeah, FL 33010.

Honolulu, Hawaii

Population: 376,110; **Pop. density:** 1,280 per sq. mi.; **Pop. growth:** 20.9%; **Pop. over 65:** 7.4%; **Pop. under 35:** 62.4%. **Area:** 596 sq. mi.. **Employment:** 375,385 employed, 2.7% unemployed (MSA); **Per capita income:** $17,540; % change 1983-88: 33.8.

History: harbor first discovered 1794; city began 1816; became capital 1816.

Transportation: 1 major airport; large, active port for passengers and cargo. **Communications:** 10 TV, 28 radio stations. **Medical facilities:** 33 hospitals. **Educational facilities:** 163 public schools (state); 102 private schools (state); 4 univ., 1 college. **Further information:** Visitors Bureau, 2270 Kalakaua Avenue, Honolulu, HI 96815.

Houston, Texas

Population: 1,698,090; **Pop. density:** 2,869 per sq. mi.; **Pop. growth:** 29.3%; **Pop. over 65:** 6.9%; **Pop. under 35:** 64.4%. **Area:** 556 sq. mi.. **Employment:** 938,333 employed, 5.1% unemployed; **Per capita income:** $16,192; % change 1983-88: 15.7.

History: founded 1836; inc. 1837; capital of Rep. of Texas 1837-39, 1842-45; developed rapidly after completion of canal to Gulf of Mexico 1914; important oil center.

Transportation: 2 commercial airports; 5 railroads; major bus transit system; major international port. **Communications:** 9 TV, 45 radio stations. **Medical facilities:** 59 hospitals; major medical center. **Educational facilities:** 27 universities and colleges. **Further information:** Chamber of Commerce, 1100 Milam, Houston, TX 77002.

Huntington Beach, California

Population: 186,880; **Pop. density:** 6,315 per sq. mi.; **Pop. growth:** 47%. **Area:** 27 sq. mi.. **Employment:** 124,148 employed, 2.9% unemployed; **Per capita income:** $22,753; % change 1983-88: 42.4.

History: settled in early 1880s; inc. 1909; oil discovered 1920, led to city's development.

Transportation: 1 airport; 1 railroad; 2 bus lines. **Communications:** 1 TV station; CATV. **Medical facilities:** 2 hospitals. **Educational facilities:** 45 public schools; 1 junior college. **Further information:** Chamber of Commerce, Seacliff Village, 2213 Main #32, Huntington Beach, CA 92648.

Indianapolis, Indiana

Population: 727,130; **Pop. density:** 1,991 per sq. mi.; **Pop. growth:** −4.9%; **Pop. over 65:** 10.3%; **Pop. under 35:** 59.4%. **Area:** 352 sq. mi.. **Employment:** 385,237 employed, 4.6% unemployed; **Per capita income:** $16,987; % change 1983-88: 40.4.

History: settled in 1820, made into capital 1825.

Transportation: 1 international airport; 5 railroads; 3 interstate bus lines. **Communications:** 7 TV, 25 radio stations. **Medical facilities:** 17 hospitals; 1 major medical and research center. **Educational facilities:** 6 universities and colleges; major public library system. **Further information:** Chamber of Commerce, 320 N. Meridian Street, Indianapolis, IN 46204.

Jackson, Mississippi

Population: 201,250; **Pop. density:** 1,914 per sq. mi.; **Pop. growth:** 31.8%; **Pop. over 65:** 9.9%; **Pop. under 35:** 59.3%. **Area:** 106.2 sq. mi.. **Employment:** 102,130 employed, 5.3% unemployed; **Per capita income:** $14,311; % change 1983-88: 32.2.

History: originally known as Le Fleur's Bluff, selected as capital 1821 and named for Andrew Jackson; inc. 1833; scene of secession convention 1861; captured by Sherman 1863.

Transportation: 5 airlines; 2 bus lines; Ill. Central railroad. **Communications:** 5 TV, 25 radio stations. **Medical facilities:** 12 hospitals including a VA facility. **Educational facilities:** 1 univ., 5 colleges. **Further information:**

Chamber of Commerce, P.O. Box 22548, Jackson, MS 39225.

Jacksonville, Florida

Population: 635,430; **Pop. density:** 712 per sq. mi.; **Pop. growth:** 7.3%; **Pop. over 65:** 9.6%; **Pop. under 35:** 60.0%. **Area:** 760 sq. mi.. **Employment:** 301,986 employed, 6.2% unemployed; **Per capita income:** $15,452; % change 1983-88: 34.6.

History: settled 1816 as Cowford; renamed after Andrew Jackson 1822; inc. 1832; rechartered 1851; scene of conflicts in Seminole and Civil Wars.

Transportation: 1 international airport; 3 railroads; 2 interstate bus lines. **Communications:** 6 TV, 21 radio stations. **Medical facilities:** 14 hospitals. **Educational facilities:** 5 universities and colleges. **Further information:** Chamber of Commerce, 3 Independent Drive, P.O. Box 329, Jacksonville, FL 32201.

Jersey City, New Jersey

Population: 217,630; **Pop. density:** 16,934 per sq. mi.; **Pop. growth:** −14.1%; **Pop. over 65:** 11.8%; **Pop. under 35:** 57.6%. **Area:** 13.2 sq. mi. **Employment:** 92,146 employed, 8.8% unemployed; **Per capita income:** $16,915; % change 1983-88: 44.5

History: bought from Indians 1830; chartered as town by British 1668; scene of Revolutionary War conflict 1779; chartered under present name 1838; important station on Underground Railroad.

Transportation: bus and subway system. **Medical facilities:** 10 hospitals. **Educational facilities:** 3 colleges. **Further information:** Chamber of Commerce & industry of Hudson County, 911 Bergen Ave., Jersey City, NJ 07303.

Kansas City, Kansas

Population: 162,070; **Pop. density:** 1,500 per sq. mi.; **Pop. growth:** −4.2%; **Pop. over 65:** 11.7%; **Pop. under 35:** 57.1%. **Area:** 107 sq. mi. **Employment:** 76,739 employed, 8.4% unemployed; **Per capita income:** $16,309.

Transportation: 1 airport, 11 airlines; 9 railroads; bus system. **Communications:** 4 TV stations; 32 radio stations. **Medical facilities:** 3 hospitals, medical center. **Educational facilities:** 50 public schools; 1 junior college, Univ. of Kansas Medical Ctr. **Further information:** Chamber of Commerce, P.O. Box 1310, Kansas City, KS 66117.

Kansas City, Missouri

Population: 438,950; **Pop. density:** 1,418 per sq. mi.; **Pop. growth:** −11.7%; **Pop. over 65:** 12.3%; **Pop. under 35:** 57.1%. **Area:** 316 sq. mi. **Employment:** 230,452 employed, 7.3% unemployed; **Per capita income:** $17,078; % change 1983-88: 32.1.

History: settled by 1838 at confluence of the Missouri and Kansas Rivers; inc. 1851.

Transportation: 1 international airport; a major rail center; 191 trunk lines; several barge companies. **Communications:** 7 TV, 29 radio stations. **Medical facilities:** 14 hospitals; VA facility. **Educational facilities:** 9 colleges & universities. **Further information:** Chamber of Commerce, 600 Boatmen's Center, 920 Main St., Kansas City, MO 64105.

Knoxville, Tennessee

Population: 172,080; **Pop. density:** 2,273 per sq. mi.; **Pop. growth:** .25%; **Pop. over 65:** 13.8%; **Pop. under 35:** 57.8%. **Area:** 77 sq. mi.. **Employment:** 81,649 employed, 4.5% unemployed; **Per capita income:** $14,218; % change 1983-88: 42.6.

History: founded 1785; city officially founded 1791; territorial capital 1792; named after Washington's Sec. of War.

Transportation: 1 airport, 2 bus lines, 61 motor freight carriers; 2 railroads. **Communications:** 5 TV, 17 radio stations; CATV. **Medical facilities:** 8 hospitals. **Educa-**

tional facilities: 85 public schools; 1 univ., 1 college. **Further information:** Chamber of Commerce, P.O. Box 2688, Knoxville, TN 37901.

Las Vegas, Nevada

Population: 210,620; **Pop. density:** 2,994 per sq. mi.; **Pop. growth:** 30.9%; **Pop. over 65:** 8.3%; **Pop. under 35:** 58.4%. **Area:** 55 sq. mi. **Employment:** 125,540 employed, 4.7% unemployed; **Per capita income:** $16,979; % change 1983-88: 36.1.

History: occupied by Mormons 1855-57; bought by railroad 1903; city of Las Vegas inc. 1911; gambling legalized 1931.

Transportation: 1 international airport; 2 railroads; bus system. **Communcations:** 7 TV and 28 radio stations. **Medical facilities:** 8 hospitals. **Educational facilities:** 130 public schools; 1 college; 1 univ. **Further information:** Chamber of Commerce, 2301 E. Sahara Ave., Las Vegas, NV, 89104.

Lexington–Fayette, Kentucky

Population: 225,700; **Pop. density:** 719 per sq. mi.; **Pop. growth:** 88.8%; **Pop. over 65:** 8.6%; **Pop. under 35:** 63.3%. **Area:** 284 sq. mi.. **Employment:** 128,163 employed, 3.0% unemployed; **Per capita income:** $15,725; % change 1983-88: 32.1.

History: site was founded and named 1775 by hunters who heard of the Revolutionary War battle at Lexington, Mass.; settled 1779; inc. 1832.

Transportation: 8 airlines, 2 railroads; city buses. **Communications:** 5 TV stations, CATV; 9 radio stations. **Medical facilities:** 5 general, 5 specialized hospitals. **Educational facilities:** 2 univ., 2 colleges. **Further information:** Chamber of Commerce, 330 East Main, Lexington, KY 40507.

Lincoln, Nebraska

Population: 187,890; **Pop. density:** 2,866 per sq. mi.; **Pop. growth:** 15.0%; **Pop. over 65:** 10.3%; **Pop. under 35:** 63.9%. **Area:** 60 sq. mi.. **Employment:** 112,958 employed, 2.2% unemployed; **Per capita income:** $15,078; % change 1983-88: 28.4.

History: originally called Lancaster, chosen state capital 1867 and renamed after Abraham Lincoln; inc. 1869.

Transportation: 1 airport; Greyhound, Amtrak, 2 railroads. **Communications:** 1 TV, 13 radio stations. **Medical facilities:** 4 hospitals including a VA facility. **Educational facilities:** 2 univ., 1 college, 46 public, 15 private schools. **Further information:** Chamber of Commerce, 1221 N St., Lincoln, NE 68508.

Little Rock, Arkansas

Population: 180,450; **Pop. density:** 1,996 per sq. mi.; **Pop. growth:** 19.6%; **Pop. over 65:** 11.0%; **Pop. under 35:** 60.8%. **Area:** 79 sq. mi. **Employment:** 91,460 employed, 4.7% unemployed; **Per capita income:** $14,688; % change 1983-88: 31.3.

History: founded 1821; inc. as city 1835.

Transportation: 1 airport, 7 airlines; 3 railroads; 1 bus line. **Communications:** 7 TV stations; 34 radio stations. **Medical facilities:** 16 hospitals; veterans' medical center. **Educational facilities:** 49 public schools; 8 colleges and universities; Univ. of Arkansas. **Further information:** Chamber of Commerce, One Spring St., Little Rock, AR 72201.

Long Beach, California

Population: 415,040; **Pop. density:** 7,256 per sq. mi.; **Pop. growth:** 0.7%; **Pop. over 65:** 14.0%; **Pop. under 35:** 56.6%. **Area:** 50 sq. mi.. **Employment:** 193,030 employed, 5.7% unemployed; **Per capita income:** $18,790; % change 1983-88: 34.7.

History: settled as early as 1769 by Spanish; by 1884 present site developed due to its harbor; inc. 1888; oil discovered 1921.

Transportation: 1 airport; 3 railroads; major international port; 6 bus lines, "lite" rail service. **Communications:** CATV; 4 radio stations. **Medical facilities:** 10 hospitals. **Educational facilities:** 78 public schools; 1 university, 1 college. **Further information:** Chamber of Commerce, One World Trade Center, Long Beach, CA 90831.

Los Angeles, California

Population: 3,352,700; **Pop. density:** 6,380 per sq. mi.; **Pop. growth:** +5.5%; **Pop. over 65:** 10.6%; **Pop. under 35:** 58.1%. **Area:** 465 sq. mi.. **Employment:** 1,653,691 employed, 6.6% unemployed; **Per capita income:** $18,790; % change 1983-88: 34.7.

History: founded by Spanish 1781; captured by U.S. 1846; inc. 1850; Hollywood a district of L.A.

Transportation: 1 intl. airport; 4 railroads; major freeway system; intracity transit system. **Communications:** 19 TV, 71 radio stations. **Medical facilities:** 822 hospitals and clinics. **Educational facilities:** 11 universities and colleges; 1,642 public schools; 800 private schools. **Further information:** Chamber of Commerce, 404 S. Bixel St., P.O. Box 3696, Los Angeles, CA 90051.

Louisville, Kentucky

Population: 281,800; **Pop. density:** 4,974 per sq. mi.; **Pop. growth:** −17.5%; **Pop. over 65:** 15.3%; **Pop. under 35:** 54.1%. **Area:** 60 sq. mi. **Employment:** 133,153 employed, 5.6% unemployed. **Per capita income:** $15,682; % change 1983-88: 35.7.

History: settled 1778; named for Louis XVI of France; inc. 1828; base for Union forces in Civil War.

Transportation: 2 municipal airports; 1 terminal, 6 trunk-line railroads; 3 bus lines; 5 barge lines. **Communications:** 4 TV, 20 radio stations, 2 educational, CATV. **Medical facilities:** 21 hospitals. **Educational facilities:** 10 colleges & universities, 9 business colleges & technical schools. **Further information:** Chamber of Commerce, One Riverfront Plaza, Louisville, KY 40202.

Lubbock, Texas

Population: 188,090; **Pop. density:** 1,933 per sq. mi.; **Pop. growth:** 16.7%; **Pop. over 65:** 7.8%; **Pop. under 35:** 66.9%. **Area:** 90 sq. mi. **Employment:** 91,592 employed, 4.3% unemployed; **Per capita income:** $13,432; % change 1983-88: 21.0.

History: settled 1879; inc. in 1909 through merger of two towns.

Transportation: 1 international airport; 2 railroads, bus line. **Communications:** 5 TV, 18 radio stations. **Medical facilities:** 7 hospitals. **Educational facilities:** 51 public schools; 2 univ., 1 college. **Further information:** Chamber of Commerce, P.O. Box 561, Lubbock, TX 79408.

Madison, Wisconsin

Population: 178,180; **Pop. density:** 3,165 per sq. mi.; **Pop. growth:** −.7%; **Pop. over 65:** 8.7%; **Pop. under 35:** 65.1%. **Area:** 60 sq. mi. **Employment:** 108,268 employed, 2.8% unemployed; **Per capita income:** $17,909; % change 1983-88: 36.2.

History: first white settlement 1832; named after James Madison who died in 1836; chartered 1856.

Transportation: 1 airport, 8 airlines; 2 railroads; intracity bus system. **Communications:** 6 TV, 18 radio stations. **Medical facilities:** 6 hospitals. **Educational facilities:** 39 public schools; 3 colleges and universities; Univ. of Wisconsin. **Further information:** Chamber of Commerce, P.O. Box 71, Madison, WI 53701.

Memphis, Tennessee

Population: 645,190; **Pop. density:** 2,448 per sq. mi.; **Pop. growth:** 3.6%; **Pop. over 65:** 10.4%; **Pop. under 35:** 60.5%. **Area:** 264 sq. mi.. **Employment:** 308,476 employed, 4.5% unemployed; **Per capita income:** $15,456; % change 1983-88: 40.9.

History: French, Spanish and U.S. forts by 1797; settled by 1819; inc. as town 1826, as city 1840; surrendered charter to state 1879 after yellow fever epidemics; rechartered as city 1893.

Transportation: 1 international airport; 6 railroads; bus system. **Communications:** 6 TV, 29 radio stations. **Medical facilities:** 21 hospitals. **Educational facilities:** 12 universities and colleges; 205 public, 76 private schools. **Further information:** Memphis Area Chamber of Commerce, 22 N. Front St., Box 224, Memphis TN 38101.

Mesa, Arizona

Population: 280,360; **Pop. density:** 2,242 per sq. mi.; **Pop. growth:** 141.8%; **Pop. over 65:** 11.2%; **Pop. under 35:** 62.4%. **Area:** 68 sq. mi. **Employment:** 100,091 employed, 3.5% unemployed; **Per capita income:** $16,815; % change 1983-88: 34.8.

History: founded by Mormons 1878; inc. 1883; 15 mi. from Phoenix; population boomed fivefold from 1960-80.

Transportation: 1 intl. airports; 2 railroads; trolley and bus lines. **Medical facilities:** 4 major hospitals. **Educational facilities:** 49 public schools; 1 college, 1 univ. **Further information:** Convention and Visitor's Bureau, 120 N. Center, Mesa, AZ 85201.

Miami, Florida

Population: 371,100; **Pop. density:** 11,256 per sq. mi.; **Pop. growth:** 3.6%; **Pop. over 65:** 17.0%; **Pop. under 35:** 46.5%. **Area:** 34 sq. mi.. **Employment:** 187,563 employed; 7.9% unemployed; **Per capita income:** $16,874; % change 1983-88: 38.3.

History: site of fort 1836; settlement began 1870; inc. 1896 and modern city developed into resort and recreation center; land speculation 1920s added to city's growth, as did Cuban immigration in 1970s and 1980s.

Transportation: 1 international airport; 2 passenger railroads, 1 all-freight; 2 bus lines; 65 truck lines. **Communications:** 6 commercial, 5 educational TV stations; 31 radio stations. **Medical facilities:** 41 hospitals, VA Hospital. **Educational facilities:** 6 colleges & universities. **Further information:** Metro-Dade Department of Tourism, 234 W. Flagler St., Miami, FL 33130.

Milwaukee, Wisconsin

Population: 599,380; **Pop. density:** 6,627 per sq. mi.; **Pop. growth:** −11.3%; **Pop. over 65:** 12.5%; **Pop. under 35:** 59.8%. **Area:** 96 sq. mi.. **Employment:** 297,374 employed, 5.6% unemployed; **Per capita income:** $17,880; % change 1983-88: 34.9.

History: Indian trading post by 1674; settlement began 1835; inc. as city 1848; beer industry is famous.

Transportation: 1 international airport; 2 railroads; major port; 4 bus lines. **Communications:** 12 TV, 33 radio stations. **Medical facilities:** 25 hospitals; major medical center. **Educational facilities:** 12 universities and colleges. **Further information:** Association of Commerce, 756 N. Milwaukee Street, Milwaukee, WI 53202.

Minneapolis, Minnesota

Population: 344,670; **Pop. density:** 6,744 per sq. mi.; **Pop. growth:** −14.6%; **Pop. over 65:** 15.4%; **Pop. under 35:** 59.4%. **Area:** 55 sq. mi.. **Employment:** 198,052 employed; 3.3% unemployed; **Per capita income:** $19,371; % change 1983-88: 37.7.

History: site visited by Hennepin 1680; included in area of military reservations 1819; inc. 1867.

Transportation: 1 international airport; 6 railroads; mass transit systems; 5 major barge lines. **Communications:** 6 TV, 39 radio stations. **Medical facilities:** 36 hospitals, including leading heart hospital at Univ. of Minnesota. **Educational facilities:** 48 public school districts; 13 colleges and universities. **Further information:** Greater Minneapolis Chamber of Commerce, 81 S. 9th St., Ste. 200, Minneapolis, MN 55402.

Mobile, Alabama

Population: 208,820; **Pop. density:** 1,630 per sq. mi.; **Pop. growth:** 5.5%; **Pop. over 65:** 11.1%; **Pop. under 35:** 59.3%. **Area:** 123 sq. mi.. **Employment:** 86,113 employed, 7.0% unemployed; **Per capita income:** $12,233; % change 1983-88: 28.5.

History: settled by French 1711; later occupied by U.S. 1813; inc. as town 1814, as city 1819; only seaport of Alabama.

Transportation: 4 rail freight lines, Amtrak, 4 major airlines, 65 truck lines; leading river system. **Communications:** 7 TV, 19 radio stations; CATV. **Medical facilities:** 7 hospitals. **Educational facilities:** 1 univ., 2 colleges. **Further information:** Chamber of Commerce, P.O. Box 2187, Mobile, AL 36652.

Montgomery, Alabama

Population: 193,510; **Pop. density:** 1,389 per sq. mi.; **Pop. growth:** 33.3%; **Pop. over 65:** 10.1%; **Pop. under 35:** 60.7%. **Area:** 128 sq. mi.. **Employment:** 84,456 employed, 6.3% unemployed; **Per capita income:** $14,053; % change 1983-88: 37.4.

History: inc. as town 1819, as city 1837; first capital of Confederacy 1861.

Transportation: 12 airlines; 2 railroads; 1 bus line; Alabama River is navigable to Gulf of Mexico. **Communications:** 5 TV, 6 radio stations; CATV. **Medical facilities:** 16 hospitals; VA and 32 clinics. **Educational facilities:** 48 public, 28 private schools, 5 universities. **Further information:** Chamber of Commerce, P.O. Box 79, Montgomery, AL 36101.

Nashville-Davidson, Tennessee

Population: 481,400; **Pop. density:** 949 per sq. mi.; **Pop. growth:** 7.0%; **Pop. over 65:** 11.0%; **Pop. under 35:** 58.7%. **Area:** 480 sq. mi.. **Employment:** 260,459 employed, 3.4% unemployed; **Per capita income:** $16,258; % change 1983-88: 43.6.

History: settled 1779; first chartered 1806; important Union base during Civil War.

Transportation: 1 airport, 2 railroads; 3 bus lines; transit system. **Communications:** 7 TV, 30 radio stations. **Medical facilities:** 14 hospitals; VA Hospital, speech-hearing center. **Educational facilities:** 16 colleges & universities. **Further information:** Chamber of Commerce, 161 4th Ave., Nashville, TN 37219.

Newark, New Jersey

Population: 313,800; **Pop. density:** 13,718 per sq. mi.; **Pop. growth:** −13.8%; **Pop. over 65:** 8.8%; **Pop. under 35:** 61.6%. **Area:** 24 sq. mi.. **Employment:** 115,665 employed, 10.0% unemployed; **Per capita income:** $22,963; % change 1983-88: 47.3.

History: settled by Puritans 1666; used as supply base by Washington 1776; inc. as town 1833, as city 1836.

Transportation: 1 international airport; 2 railroads; bus system; 2 subways. **Communications:** 3 TV, 5 radio stations. **Medical facilities:** 6 hospitals. **Educational facilities:** 5 universities and colleges; 71 public schools. **Further information:** Metro Newark Chamber of Commerce, 40 Clinton St., Newark, NJ 07102.

New Orleans, Louisiana

Population: 531,700; **Pop. density:** 2,802 per sq. mi.; **Pop. growth:** −6%; **Pop. over 65:** 11.7%; **Pop. under 35:** 60.1%. **Area:** 199 sq. mi.. **Employment:** 207,030 employed, 6.5% unemployed; **Per capita income:** $14,034; % change 1983-88: 18.5.

History: founded by French 1718, became major seaport on Mississippi R.; acquired by U.S. as part of La. Purchase 1803; inc. as city 1805; 29-day Battle of New Orleans fought during War of 1812.

Transportation: 2 airports; major railroad center; major international port. **Communications:** 7 TV, 18 radio stations. **Medical facilities:** numerous hospitals; major medical research center. **Educational facilities:** 13 universities and colleges. **Further information:** Chamber of Commerce, 301 Camp Street, New Orleans, LA 70130.

New York City, New York

Population: 7,352,700; **Pop. density:** 23,494 per sq. mi.; **Pop. growth:** −10.4%; **Pop. over 65:** 13.5%; **Pop. under 35:** 53.7%. **Area:** 301 sq. mi.. **Employment:** 3,174,000 employed, 7.0% unemployed; **Per capita income:** $20,396; % change 1983-88: 40.6.

History: trading post established by H. Hudson 1609; British took control from Dutch 1664 and named New York; briefly capital of U.S.; Washington inaugurated as president 1789; comprised of 5 boroughs: The Bronx, Brooklyn, Manhattan, Queens, Staten Island.

Transportation: 2 airports; 2 rail terminals; major subway network; ferry system; 4 underwater tunnels. **Communications:** 13 TV stations, 117 radio stations. **Medical facilities:** 100 hospitals; 5 medical research centers. **Educational facilities:** 94 universities and colleges; 976 public schools, 914 private schools. **Further information:** Convention and Visitors Bureau, 2 Columbus Circle, New York, NY 10019.

Norfolk, Virginia

Population: 286,500; **Pop. density:** 5,037 per sq. mi.; **Pop. growth:** −13.3%; **Pop. over 65:** 9.2%; **Pop. under 35:** 68.6%. **Area:** 53 sq. mi.. **Employment:** 90,369 employed, 5.4% unemployed; **Per capita income:** $15,051; % change 1983-88: 30.8.

History: founded 1682; burned by patriots to prevent capture by British during Revolutionary War; rebuilt and inc. as town 1805, as city 1845; location of world's largest naval base.

Transportation: 1 international airport; 4 major railroad systems in area. **Communications:** 7 TV, 38 radio stations. **Medical facilities:** 11 hospitals. **Educational facilities:** 53 public schools; 2 universities, 1 college. **Further information:** Hampton Roads Chamber of Commerce, 480 Bank St., Norfolk, VA 23510.

Oakland, California

Population: 356,860; **Pop. density:** 6,284 per sq. mi.; **Pop. growth:** −6.2%; **Pop. over 65:** 13.2%; **Pop. under 35:** 57%. **Area:** 54 sq. mi.. **Employment:** 181,820 employed, 5.5% unemployed; **Per capita income:** $21,096; % change 1983-88: 36.4.

History: area settled by Spanish 1820; inc. as city under present name 1854.

Transportation: 1 international airport; western terminus for 3 railroads; underground, underwater 75-mile subway. **Communications:** 1 TV, 3 radio stations. **Medical facilities:** 7 hospitals, including Children's Hospital Medical Center, VA hospital. **Educational facilities:** 94 public schools; 8 "eastbay" colleges and universities. **Further information:** Chamber of Commerce, 475 14th St., Oakland, CA 94612-1903.

Oklahoma City, Oklahoma

Population: 434,380; **Pop. density:** 667 per sq. mi.; **Pop. growth:** 9.5%; **Pop. over 65:** 11.3%; **Pop. under 35:** 58.2%. **Area:** 604 sq. mi.. **Employment:** 214,405 employed, 7.2% unemployed; **Per capita income:** $14,612; % change 1983-88: 15.7.

History: settled during landrush in Midwest 1889; inc. 1890; oil discovered 1928.

Transportation: 1 international airport; 3 railroads; public transit system; 5 major bus lines. **Communications:** 8 TV, 24 radio stations; cable TV. **Medical facilities:** 12 hospitals, VA hospital. **Educational facilities:** 87 public schools; 17 colleges and universities. **Further information:** Chamber of Commerce, One Santa Fe Plaza, Oklahoma City, OK 73102.

Omaha, Nebraska

Population: 353,170; **Pop. density:** 3,453 per sq. mi.; **Pop. growth:** −9.5%; **Pop. over 65:** 12.2%; **Pop. under 35:** 41.9%. **Area:** 91 sq. mi. **Employment:** 179,257 employed, 3.5% unemployed; **Per capita income:** $15,873; % change 1983-88: 28.9.

History: founded 1854; inc. 1857; large livestock market; home for U.S. Strategic Air Command.

Transportation: 8 major airlines; 4 major railroads; intercity bus line. **Communications:** 8 TV, 22 radio stations. **Medical facilities:** 17 hospitals; institute for cancer research. **Educational facilities:** 229 public, 138 private schools; 3 universities, 6 colleges. **Further information:** Chamber of Commerce, 1301 Harney St., Omaha, NE 68102.

Philadelphia, Pennsylvania

Population: 1,647,000; **Pop. density:** 12,413 per sq. mi.; **Pop. growth:** −13.4%; **Pop. over 65:** 14.1%; **Pop. under 35:** 54.4%. **Area:** 136 sq. mi.. **Employment:** 681,906 employed, 5.8% unemployed; **Per capita income:** $18,504; % change 1983-88: 39.3.

History: first settled by Swedes 1636; by English 1681; named Philadelphia 1682; chartered 1701; Continental Congress met 1774, 1775; Dec. of Independence signed 1776; national capital 1790-1800; cap. of Penn. 1683-1799.

Transportation: 1 major airport; 3 railroads; major freshwater port; subway, el, rail commuter, bus, and streetcar system. **Communications:** 6 TV stations; 53 radio stations. **Medical facilities:** 124 hospitals. **Educational facilities:** 88 degree-granting institutions. **Further information:** Office of City Representative, 1660 Municipal Services Bldg., Philadelphia, PA 19107.

Phoenix, Arizona

Population: 923,750; **Pop. density:** 2,438 per sq. mi.; **Pop. growth:** 35.1%; **Pop. over 65:** 9.3%; **Pop. under 35:** 60.4%. **Area:** 324 sq. mi. **Employment:** 557,227 employed, 3.8% unemployed; **Per capita income:** $16,815; % change 1983-88: 34.8.

History: settled in 1870; inc. as city 1881.

Transportation: 1 intl. airport; 2 railroads; 2 transcontinental bus lines; public transit system. **Communications:** 8 TV, 35 radio stations; CATV. **Medical facilities:** 42 hospitals, 1 medical research center. **Educational facilities:** 411 public schools; 11 institutions of higher learning. **Further information:** Chamber of Commerce, 34 W. Monroe, Suite 900, Phoenix, AZ 85003.

Pittsburgh, Pennsylvania

Population: 375,230; **Pop. density:** 7,707 per sq. mi.; **Pop. growth:** −18%; **Pop. over 65:** 16.0%; **Pop. under 35:** 52.9%. **Area:** 55 sq. mi.. **Employment:** 163,170 employed, 5.1% unemployed; **Per capita income:** $16,484; % change 1983-88: 32.4.

History: settled around Ft. Pitt 1758; inc. as city 1816; has one of largest inland ports; by Civil War, already a center for iron production.

Transportation: 1 international airport; 20 railroads; 2 bus lines; trolley/subway system. **Communications:** 6 TV, 25 radio stations. **Medical facilities:** 32 hospitals; VA installation. **Educational facilities:** 86 public schools; 3 universities, 6 colleges. **Further information:** Chamber of Commerce, 3 Gateway Ctr., Pittsburgh, PA 15222.

Portland, Oregon

Population: 418,470; **Pop. density:** 3,557 per sq. mi.; **Pop. growth:** −3.6%; **Pop. over 65:** 10.9%; **Pop. under 35:** 58.9%. **Area:** 103 sq. mi.. **Employment:** 198,573 employed, 5.1% unemployed; **Per capita income:** $16,837; % change 1983-88: 32.0.

History: settled by pioneers 1845, developed as trading center, aided by California Gold Rush 1849; chartered as city 1851.

Transportation: 1 international airport; 3 major rail freight lines, Amtrak; 2 intercity bus lines; 27-mi. frontage freshwater port; mass transit bus and rail system. **Communications:** 5 TV, 23 radio stations. **Medical facilities:** 32 hospitals; VA hospital. **Educational facilities:** 11 colleges and universities, 3 community colleges. **Further Information:** Chamber of Commerce, 221 N.W. 2nd Ave., Portland, OR 97209.

Raleigh, North Carolina

Population: 186,720; **Pop. density:** 2,793 per sq. mi.; **Pop. growth:** 22.3%; **Pop. over 65:** 8.3%; **Pop. under 35:** 62.8%. **Area:** 54 sq. mi. **Employment:** 115,428 employed, 3.2% unemployed; **Per capita income:** $17,671; % change 1983-88: 45.9.

History: named after Sir Walter Raleigh, site chosen for capital 1788; laid out 1792; inc. 1795; occupied by Gen. Sherman 1865.

Transportation: 1 airport, 7 airlines; 3 railroads; 1 bus line. **Communications:** 6 TV stations; 20 radio stations. **Medical facilities:** 11 hospitals. **Educational facilities:** 4 colleges and universities, 4 junior colleges; 82 public schools. **Further information:** Chamber of Commerce, 800 S. Salisbury St., P.O. Box 2978, Raleigh, NC 27602.

Richmond, Virginia

Population: 213,300; **Pop. density:** 3,650 per sq. mi.; **Pop. growth:** −12.1%; **Pop. over 65:** 14.1%; **Pop. under 35:** 56.9%. **Area:** 60 sq. mi. **Employment:** 105,363 employed, 4.8% unemployed; **Per capita income:** $18,617; % change 1983-88: 40.1.

History: first settled 1607; attacked by British under Benedict Arnold 1781; inc. as city 1782; capital of Confederate States of America, 1861.

Transportation: 1 international airport; 4 railroads, 3 intracity bus lines; deepwater terminal accessible to ocean-going ships. **Communications:** 6 TV, 26 radio stations; CATV. **Medical facilities:** Medical Coll. of Virginia renowned for heart and kidney transplants; 19 other hospitals including VA facility. **Educational facilities:** 173 public, 45 private schools; 9 colleges and universities. **Further information:** Chamber of Commerce, P.O. Box 12324, Richmond, VA 23241.

Riverside, California

Population: 210,630; **Pop. density:** 2,406 per sq. mi.; **Pop. growth:** 22.0%; **Pop. over 65:** 8.8%; **Pop. under 35:** 62.8%. **Area:** 71 sq. mi. **Employment:** 123,514 employed, 5.9% unemployed; **Per capita income:** $15,655; % change 1983-88: 31.8.

History: founded 1870; inc. 1886; known for its citrus industry.

Communications: 11 TV, 13 radio stations. **Educational facilities:** 1 univ., 1 college. **Further information:** Chamber of Commerce, 4261 Main St., Riverside, CA 92501.

Rochester, New York

Population: 229,780; **Pop. density:** 7,068 per sq. mi.; **Pop. growth:** −18.1%; **Pop. over 65:** 14.0%; **Pop. under 35:** 60.0%. **Area:** 34 sq. mi. **Employment:** 110,656 employed, 5.6% unemployed; **Per capita income:** $18,299; % change 1983-88: 34.2.

History: first permanent white settlement 1812; inc. as village 1817, as city 1834; developed as Erie Canal town.

Transportation: 1 airport; Amtrak; 3 bus lines; intracity transit service; Port of Rochester. **Communications:** 5 TV, 18 radio stations. **Medical facilities:** 8 general hospitals. **Educational facilities:** 10 colleges, 3 community colleges. **Further information:** Chamber of Commerce, 55 St. Paul St., Rochester, NY 14604.

Sacramento, California

Population: 338,220; **Pop. density:** 2,872 per sq. mi.; **Pop. growth:** 10.7%; **Pop. over 65:** 9.6%; **Pop. under**

35: 59%. **Area:** 96 sq. mi. **Employment:** 162,963 employed, 5.3% unemployed; **Per capita income:** $17,050; % change 1983-88: 37.2.

History: settled 1839; important trading center during California Gold Rush 1840s.

Transportation: metropolitan airport; 2 mainline transcontinental rail carriers; bus and light rail system. **Communications:** 7 TV, 25 radio stations. **Medical facilities:** 8 hospitals. **Educational facilities:** 2 universities, 4 community colleges. **Further information:** Chamber of Commerce, 917 7th St., P.O. Box 1017, Sacramento, CA 95805.

St. Louis, Missouri

Population: 403,700; **Pop. density:** 7,427 per sq. mi.; **Pop. growth:** −27.2%; **Pop. over 65:** 17.6%; **Pop. under 35:** 54%. **Area:** 61 sq. mi. **Employment:** 166,624 employed, 8.9% unemployed; **Per capita income:** $17,806; % change 1983-88: 35.4.

History: founded 1764 as a fur trading post by French; acquired by U.S. 1803; chartered as city 1822; gateway to Missouri R.

Transportation: 1 international airport; major rail center, 17 trunk line railroads; major inland port; 14 bus lines; 14 barge lines. **Communications:** 6 TV, 35 radio stations. **Medical facilities:** 65 hospitals. **Educational facilities:** 5 universities, 26 colleges and seminaries. **Further information:** Regional Commerce and Growth Assoc., Ten Broadway, St. Louis, MO 63102.

St. Paul, Minnesota

Population: 259,110; **Pop. density:** 5,196 per sq. mi.; **Pop. growth:** −12.8%; **Pop. over 65:** 15.0%; **Pop. under 35:** 41.5%. **Area:** 52 sq. mi. **Employment:** 138,470 employed, 3.9% unemployed; **Per capita income:** $19,371; % change 1983-88: 37.7.

History: founded in early 1840s as "Pig's Eye Landing;" became capital of the Minnesota territory 1849 and chartered as St. Paul.

Transportation: 1 international airport; 6 major rail lines; 3 interstate bus lines; public transit system. **Communications:** 6 TV, 35 radio stations; CATV. **Medical facilities:** 7 hospitals. **Educational facilities:** 2 univ., 5 colleges. **Further information:** Chamber of Commerce, 600 N. Central Tower, 445 Minnesota St., St. Paul, MN 55101.

St. Petersburg, Florida

Population: 235,450; **Pop. density:** 4,186 per sq. mi.; **Pop. growth:** 10.4%; **Pop. over 65:** 25.8%; **Pop. under 35:** 43.7%. **Area:** 57 sq. mi. **Employment:** 127,530 employed, 5.7% unemployed; **Per capita income:** $16,409; % change 1983-88: 36.7.

History: settled in 1888; inc. 1892.

Transportation: 1 international airport; bus system; 1 full-service port. **Communications:** 9 TV, 49 radio stations. **Medical facilities:** 9 hospitals. **Educational facilities:** 128 public schools; 6 colleges. **Further information:** Chamber of Commerce, P.O. Box 1371, St. Petersburg, FL 33731.

San Antonio, Texas

Population: 941,150; **Pop. density:** 2,988 per sq. mi.; **Pop. growth:** 20%; **Pop. over 65:** 9.5%; **Pop. under 35:** 62.1%. **Area:** 263 sq. mi. **Employment:** 411,731 employed, 6.6% unemployed; **Per capita income:** $13,436; % change 1983-88: 24.1.

History: first Spanish garrison 1718; Battle at the Alamo fought here 1835; city subsequently captured by Texans; inc. 1837.

Transportation: 1 intl. airport; 4 railroads; 6 bus lines; public transit system. **Communications:** 7 TV, 31 radio stations. **Medical facilities:** 26 hospitals; major medical center. **Educational facilities:** 14 universities and colleges. **Further information:** Chamber of Commerce, 602 E. Commerce, P.O. Box 1628, San Antonio, TX 78296.

San Diego, California

Population: 1,070,310; **Pop. density:** 2,736 per sq. mi.; **Pop. growth:** 25.5%; **Pop. over 65:** 9.7%; **Pop. under 35:** 62.1%. **Area:** 320 sq. mi.. **Employment:** 532,319 employed, 3.8% unemployed; **Per capita income:** $17,576; % change 1983-88: 35.1.

History: claimed by the Spanish 1542, first mission est. 1769; scene of conflict during Mexican-American War 1846; inc. 1850.

Transportation: 1 major airport; 1 railroad; major freeway system; bus system. **Communications:** 7 TV, 27 radio stations. **Medical facilities:** 20 hospitals. **Educational facilities:** 5 universities, 3 colleges. **Further information:** Chamber of Commerce, 110 West "C," Suite 1600, San Diego, CA 92101.

San Francisco, California

Population: 731,600, **Pop. density:** 14,760 per sq. mi.; **Pop. growth:** --5.1%; **Pop. over 65:** 15.4%; **Pop. under 35:** 51.7%. **Area:** 46 sq. mi.. **Employment:** 378,093 employed, 4.0% unemployed; **Per capita income:** $26,309; % change 1983-88: 38.9.

History: sited by Spanish 1542, settled by 1776; claimed by U.S. 1846; became a major city during California Gold Rush 1849; inc. as city 1850; earthquake devasted city 1906.

Transportation: 1 major airport; intracity railway system; 2 railway transit systems; bus and railroad service; ferry system; 1 underwater tunnel. **Communications:** 14 TV and cable stations; 69 radio stations. **Medical facilities:** 23 hospitals; 1 major medical center. **Educational facilities:** 4 universities and colleges. **Further information:** Chamber of Commerce, 465 California Street, San Francisco, CA 94104.

San Jose, California

Population: 738,420; **Pop. density:** 3,984 per sq. mi.; **Pop. growth:** 36.9%; **Pop. over 65:** 6.2%; **Pop. under 35:** 64.7%. **Area:** 158 sq. mi.. **Employment:** 366,657 employed, 4.3% unemployed; **Per capita income:** $23,181; % change 1983-88: 39.4.

History: founded by the Spanish 1777 between San Francisco and Monterey; briefly capital of Calif. 1849-51; inc. 1850.

Transportation: 1 international airport; 2 railroads; bus system. **Communications:** 4 TV, 14 radio stations. **Medical facilities:** 6 hospitals. **Educational facilities:** 3 universities and colleges. **Further information:** Chamber of Commerce, 180 S. Market St., San Jose, CA 95113.

Santa Ana, California

Population: 239,540; **Pop. density:** 7,544 per sq. mi.; **Pop. growth:** 30.8%; **Pop. over 65:** 7.4%; **Pop. under 35:** 66.9%. **Area:** 27 sq. mi.. **Employment:** 131,972 employed, 3.8% unemployed (county); **Per capita income:** $22,753; % change 1983-88: 42.4.

History: founded 1869; inc. as city 1886.

Transportation: 1 airport; 5 major freeways including main Los Angeles-San Diego artery; Amtrak. **Communications:** CATV system. **Medical facilities:** 4 hospitals. **Educational facilities:** 1 university, 1 community college. **Further information:** Chamber of Commerce, 600 W. Santa Ana Blvd., P.O. Box 205, Santa Ana, CA 92702.

Seattle, Washington

Population: 502,200; **Pop. density:** 5,879 per sq. mi.; **Pop. growth:** −7.0%; **Pop. over 65:** 15.4%; **Pop. under 35:** 54.9%. **Area:** 84 sq. mi.. **Employment:** 336,284 employed, 4.5% unemployed; **Per capita income:** $19,703; % change 1983-88: 34.0.

History: settled 1851; inc. 1869; suffered severe fire 1889; played prominent role during Alaska Gold Rush 1897; growth followed opening of Panama Canal 1914; center of aircraft industry WWII.

Transportation: 1 international airport; 2 railroads; ferries serve Puget Sound, Alaska, Canada. **Communications:** 7 TV, 42 radio stations. **Medical facilities:** 27 hospitals. **Educational facilities:** 4 colleges; 11 community colleges. **Further information:** Greater Seattle Chamber of Commerce, 600 University St., Ste. 1200, Seattle, WA 98101-3186.

Shreveport, Louisiana

Population: 218,010; **Pop. density:** 2,572 per sq. mi.; **Pop. growth:** 13%; **Pop. over 65:** 11.7%; **Pop. under 35:** 59.4%. **Area:** 80 sq. mi.. **Employment:** 88,149 employed, 10.2% unemployed; **Per capita income:** $13,156; % change 1983-88: 17.2.

History: founded 1833 near site of a 160-mile log jam cleared by Capt. Henry Shreve; inc. 1839; oil discovered 1906.

Transportation: 1 airport; 2 bus lines. **Communications:** 5 TV, 16 radio stations; CATV. **Medical facilities:** 11 hospitals. **Educational facilities:** 3 univ., 3 colleges. **Further information:** Chamber of Commerce, P.O. Box 20074, Shreveport, LA 71120.

Spokane, Washington

Population: 170,900; **Pop. density:** 3,313 per sq. mi.; **Pop. growth:** .5; **Pop. over 65:** 15.3%; **Pop. under 35:** 59.2%. **Area:** 52 sq. mi. **Employment:** 81,115 employed, 7.7% unemployed; **Per capita income:** $14,373; % change 1983-88: 28.3.

History: settled 1872; inc. as village of Spokane Falls 1881 but destroyed in fire 1889; reinc. as city of Spokane 1891.

Transportation: 1 international airport; 2 railroads; bus system. **Communications:** 5 TV and 25 radio stations. **Medical facilities:** 6 major hospitals. **Educational facilities:** 8 colleges and universities; 14 public school districts, 11 high schools. **Further information:** Chamber of Commerce, W. 1020 Riverside Ave., P.O. Box 2147, Spokane, WA 99210.

Stockton, California

Population: 190,680; **Pop. density:** 3,744 per sq. mi.; **Pop. growth:** 36.2%; **Pop. over 65:** 11.0%; **Pop. under 35:** 58.0%. **Area:** 40 sq. mi. **Employment:** 75,276 employed, 10.8% unemployed; **Per capita income:** $11,288; % change 1983-88: 25.7.

History: site purchased 1842; settled 1847; inc. 1850; chief distributing point for agricultural products of San Joaquin Valley.

Transportation: 1 airport, 7 railroads; 2 bus lines, city bus system. **Communications:** 5 TV stations. **Medical facilities:** 4 hospitals; regional burn center. **Educational facilities:** 45 public schools; 4 colleges and universities. **Further information:** Chamber of Commerce, 445 W. Weber Ave., Suite 220, Stockton, CA 95203.

Tacoma, Washington

Population: 163,960; **Pop. density:** 3,316 per sq. mi.; **Pop. growth:** 2.7%; **Pop. over 65:** 14%; **Pop. under 35:** 42%. **Area:** 47.8 sq. mi. **Employment:** 82,038 employed, 6.4% unemployed; **Per capita income:** $14,661; % change 1983-88: 27.1.

History: discovered 1792 by the British; first permanent settlement 1864; terminus for the Northern Pacific Railroad; inc. 1884.

Transportation: 1 airport; 1 railroad; transit system; Port of Tacoma. **Communications:** NA **Medical facilities:** 6 hospitals, VA facility. **Educational facilities:** 2 univ., 2 colleges. **Further information:** Chamber of Commerce, P.O. Box 1933, Tacoma, WA 98401-1933.

Tampa, Florida

Population: 281,790; **Pop. density:** 3,232 per sq. mi.; **Pop. growth:** −2.2%; **Pop. over 65:** 14.8%; **Pop. under 35:** 54%. **Area:** 84 sq. mi.. **Employment:** 173,685 employed, 5.5% unemployed; **Per capita income:** $16,409; % change 1983-88: 36.7

History: U.S. army fort on site 1824; inc. 1855.

Transportation: 1 international airport; Port of Tampa, 140 steamship lines; 2 bus lines. **Communications:** 7 TV, 27 radio stations. **Medical facilities:** 19 hospitals. **Educational facilities:** 131 public schools; 4 colleges and universities. **Further information:** Chamber of Commerce, 801 E. Kennedy Blvd., P.O. Box 420, Tampa, FL 33601.

Toledo, Ohio

Population: 340,760; **Pop. density:** 4,221 per sq. mi.; **Pop. growth:** −7.4%; **Pop. over 65:** 12.5%; **Pop. under 35:** 58.5%. **Area:** 84 sq. mi.. **Employment:** 155,203 employed, 12.3% unemployed; **Per capita income:** $16,083; % change 1983-88: 34.5.

History: site of Ft. Industry, 1794; settled 1817; figured in "Toledo War" 1835-36 between Ohio and Michigan over their borders; inc. 1837.

Transportation: 10 major airlines; 9 railroads; 100 motor freight lines; 2 interstate bus lines. **Communications:** 5 TV, 17 radio stations; 4 cablevision co. **Medical facilities:** 9 major hospital complexes. **Educational facilities:** 7 colleges and universities. **Further information:** Office of Tourism and Conventions, 218 Huron, Toledo, OH 43604.

Tucson, Arizona

Population: 385,720; **Pop. density:** 3,338 per sq. mi.; **Pop. growth:** 25.7%; **Pop. over 65:** 11.7%; **Pop. under 35:** 60.7%. **Area:** 99 sq. mi.. **Employment:** 191,242 employed, 3.7% unemployed; **Per capita income:** $14,362; % change 1983-88: 32.5.

History: settled 1775 by Spanish as a presidio; acquired by U.S. in Gadsen Purchase 1853; inc. 1877.

Transportation: 1 international airport; 3 railroads; bus system. **Communications:** 6 TV, 27 radio stations; CATV. **Medical facilities:** 15 hospitals. **Educational facilities:** 2 univ., 1 college; 165 public schools. **Further information:** Chamber of Commerce, P.O. Box 991, Tucson, AZ 85702.

Tulsa, Oklahoma

Population: 368,330; **Pop. density:** 1,940 per sq. mi.; **Pop. growth:** 9.3%; **Pop. over 65:** 10.8%; **Pop. under 35:** 58.1%. **Area:** 185.6 sq. mi.. **Employment:** 182,916 employed, 5.5% unemployed; **Per capita income:** $15,075; % change 1983-88: 18.6.

History: settled in 1830s by Creek Indians; modern town founded 1882 and inc. 1898; oil discovered early 20th century.

Transportation: 1 international airport; 5 rail lines; 2 bus lines; transit bus system. **Communications:** 7 TV, 23 radio stations. **Medical facilities:** 6 hospitals. **Educational facilities:** 57 public and 23 private schools; 6 colleges and universities. **Further information:** Chamber of Commerce, 616 S. Boston Ave., Tulsa, OK 74119.

Virginia Beach, Virginia

Population: 365,300; **Pop. density:** 1,028 per sq. mi.; **Pop. growth:** 52.3%; **Pop. over 65:** 4.5%; **Pop. under 35:** 66.0%. **Area:** 255 sq. mi.. **Employment:** 159,315 employed, 4.7% unemployed; **Per capita income:** $15,051; % change 1983-88: 30.8.

History: area founded by Capt. John Smith 1607; formed by merger with Princess Anne co. 1963.

Transportation: 1 airport; 2 railroads; 2 bus lines; public transit system. **Communications:** 6 TV, 40 radio stations. **Medical facilities:** 2 hospitals. **Educational facilities:** 62 public schools; 1 university, 2 colleges. **Further information:** Chamber of Commerce, 4512 Virginia Beach Blvd., Virginia Beach, VA 23462.

Washington, District of Columbia

Population: 617,000; **Pop. density:** 10,121 per sq. mi.; **Pop. growth:** −15.7%; **Pop. over 65:** 11.6%; **Pop. under 35:** 56.9%. **Area:** 63 sq. mi.. **Employment:** 292,068 employed, 4.9% unemployed; **Per capita income:** $23,175; % change 1983-88: 43.9.

History: capital of the U.S.; 10-mile-square diamond at Potomac R. chosen by George Washington 1790 on land ceded from Va. and Md.; Congress first met 1800; inc. 1802; sacked by British, War of 1812.

Transportation: 2 airports; rail transit system; extensive local bus service; 1 bus, 2 rail lines. **Communications:** 5 TV, 61 radio stations. **Medical facilities:** 43 hospitals; major medical research center. **Educational facilities:** 6 universities and colleges. **Further information:** Convention and Visitors Association, 1411 K St. NW, Suite 500, Washington, DC 20005.

Wichita, Kansas

Population: 295,320; **Pop. density:** 2,765 per sq. mi.; **Pop. growth:** 1.0%; **Pop. over 65:** 10.6%; **Pop. under 35:** 59.9%. **Area:** 101 sq. mi.. **Employment:** 157,302 employed, 4.6% unemployed; **Per capita income:** $16,467; % change 1983-88: 25.6.

History: founded 1864; inc. 1871.

Transportation: 1 airport; 3 major rail freight lines; 2 bus lines. **Communications:** 5 TV, 23 radio stations. **Medical facilities:** 7 hospitals. **Educational facilities:** 95 public schools; 2 univ., 2 colleges. **Further information:** Chamber of Commerce, 350 W. Douglas, Wichita, KS 67202.

Yonkers, New York

Population: 183,000; **Pop. density:** 10,852 per sq. mi.; **Pop. growth:** −4%. **Pop. over 65:** 14.8%. **Area:** 18 sq. mi.. **Employment:** 100,311 employed, 4.2% unemployed; **Per capita income:** $20,396; % change 1983-88: 40.6.

History: founded 1641 by the Dutch; inc. as town 1855; chartered as city 1872; borders NYC to the North.

Transportation: intracity bus system; rail service. **Communications:** see New York City. **Medical facilities:** 3 hospitals. **Educational facilities:** 30 public schools; 3 colleges. **Further information:** Chamber of Commerce, 480 N. Broadway, Yonkers, NY 10701.

Percentage of the U.S. Population Living in Metropolitan Areas: 1987

Source: U.S. Bureau of the Census

New Jersey	100.0	Hawaii	76.7	Kansas	52.8
California	95.7	Arizona	76.2	New Mexico	48.4
Maryland	92.9	Virginia	71.7	Nebraska	47.2
Connecticut	92.6	Louisiana	69.0	Kentucky	45.8
Rhode Island	92.6	Oregon	67.6	Iowa	43.1
Florida	90.8	Indiana	68.0	Alaska	42.4
Massachusetts	90.7	Alabama	67.2	Arkansas	39.5
New York	90.5	Tennessee	67.0	North Dakota	38.0
Pennsylvania	84.7	Wisconsin	66.5	West Virginia	36.3
Nevada	82.6	Minnesota	66.1	Maine	36.1
Illinois	82.5	Delaware	66.0	Mississippi	30.3
Colorado	81.7	Missouri	66.0	Wyoming	29.0
Washington	81.2	Georgia	64.6	South Dakota	28.7
Texas	81.0	South Carolina	60.4	Montana	24.2
Michigan	80.2	Oklahoma	58.8	Vermont	23.1
Ohio	78.9	New Hampshire	56.3	Idaho	19.6
Utah	77.2	North Carolina	55.3		

Notable Tall Buildings in North American Cities

Height from sidewalk to roof, including penthouse and tower if enclosed as integral part of structure; actual number of stories beginning at street level. Asterisks (*) denote buildings still under construction Jan. 1991. Year is date of completion

City	Hgt. ft.	Stories
Akron, Oh.		
First National Tower	330	28
National City Center	301	23
Albany, N.Y.		
Erastus Corning II Tower	589	44
State Office Building	388	34
Agency (4 bldgs.), So. Mall	310	23
Atlanta, Ga.		
*C & S Plaza, 600 Peachtree St.	1,024	55
*One Peachtree Center	843	61
IBM Tower, 1179 W. Peachtree (1988)	828	52
191 Peachtree (1990)	770	54
Westin Peachtree Plaza	723	71
Georgia Pacific Tower	697	51
Southern Bell Telephone	677	47
Promenade II (1989)	617	40
Concourse Tower #6	567	32
First Atlanta Bank, 2 Peachtree	556	44
Marriott Marquis	554	52
Concourse Tower, (1988)	570	32
Equitable Building, 100 Peachtree	453	34
101 Marietta Tower, 101 Marietta St.	446	36
*Ravinia #3	444	34
Bell South Enterprises (1990)	428	28
Atlanta Plaza I	425	32
Park Place, 2660 Peachtree	420	40
Club Towers Apts. (1989)	410	38
First American Bank	409	32
Peachtree Summit	406	31
North Avenue Tower, 310 North Ave.	403	26
Tower Place, 3361 Piedmont Road	401	29
First Union Bank, 999 Peachtree	396	30
Richard B. Russell, Federal Bldg.	383	26
Atlanta Hilton Hotel	383	32
Peachtree Center, Harris Bldg.	382	31
AT&T Long Line Bldg.	380	
Marquis One	378	30
Marquis Two, 275 Peachtree	378	30
Trust Company Bank	377	28
Coastal States Insurance	377	27
Peachtree Center Cain Building	376	30
Peachtree Center Building	374	31
One Georgia Center	371	29
The Campanile, 1145 Peachtree	367	25
Riverwood Tower (1989)	362	26
Austin, Tex.		
One American Center, 600 Congress	395	32
One Congress Plaza, 111 Congress	391	30
First RepublicBank Tower, 515 Congress	328	26
Baltimore, Md.		
U.S. Fidelity & Guaranty Co.	529	40
Maryland National Bank Bldg.	509	34
6 St. Paul Place	493	37
World Trade Center Bldg.	395	32
Tremont Plaza Hotel	395	37
250 W. Pratt St.	360	26
Harbor Court	356	28
Blaustein Bldg.	342	30
Union Trust Tower	335	24
Central Savings Bank Bldg.	330	30
Charles Center South	330	26
Baton Rouge, La.		
State Capitol	460	34
American Bank Bldg.	315	24
Birmingham, Ala.		
South Trust Tower	454	34
First Natl. Southern Natural Bldg.	390	30
South Central Bell Hdqts. Bldg.	390	30
City Federal Bldg.	325	27
Boston, Mass.		
John Hancock Tower	790	60
Prudential Center	750	52
Boston Co. Bldg., Court St.	605	41
Federal Reserve Bldg.	604	32
International Place, 100 Oliver St.	600	46

City	Hgt. ft.	Stories
First National Bank of Boston	591	37
One Financial Center	590	46
Shawmut Bank Bldg.	520	38
Exchange Place, 53 State St.	510	39
Sixty State St.	509	38
One Post Office Sq.	507	40
One Beacon St.	507	40
New England Merch. Bank Bldg.	500	40
U.S. Custom House	496	32
John Hancock Bldg.	495	26
State St. Bank Bldg.	477	34
125 High St. (1990)	455	30
One Hundred Summer St.	450	33
McCormack Bldg.	401	22
Keystone Custodian Funds	400	32
Saltonstall Office Bldg.	396	22
Devonshire, 250 Wash. St.	396	40
Harbor Towers (2 bldgs.)	396	40
Westin Hotel, Copley Place	395	36
Federal Center (1988)	393	28
75 State St. (1988)	390	31
John F. Kennedy Bldg.	387	24
Marriott Hotel, Copley Place	383	39
101 Federal St. (1988)	382	31
Longfellow Towers (2 bldgs.)	380	38
Buffalo, N.Y.		
Marine Midland Center	529	40
City Hall	378	32
Rand Bldg., not incl. 40-ft. beacon	351	29
Main Place Tower	350	26
Calgary, Alta.		
Petro-Canada Tower #2	689	52
Benkers Hall (1989)	645	50
Calgary Tower	626	
Canterra Tower (1988)	580	46
First Canadian Centre	547	44
Scotia Centre	504	38
Nova Bldg., 801 7th Ave. SW	500	37
Petro-Canada Tower #1	469	33
Two Bow Valley Square	468	39
Fifth & Fifth Bldg.	460	35
Home Oil Tower	463	34
Shell Tower	460	34
Dome Oil Tower	449	33
Four Bow Valley Square	441	37
Esso Plaza (twin towers)	435	34
Oxford Square	421	33
Family Life Bldg.	410	33
Pan Canadian Bldg., 150 9th Ave. SW	410	28
Norcen Tower	408	33
Alberta Stock Exchange Bldg.	407	33
Amoco Centre (1988)	396	30
Western Centre	385	40
Calgary Place	385	30
Three Bow Valley Square	382	33
Charlotte, N.C.		
One First Union Center	580	42
NCNB Plaza	503	40
Interstate Tower	462	32
Two First Union Center	433	32
Wachovia Center	420	32
Charlotte Plaza	388	27
First Citizens Plaza	320	23
Chicago, Ill.		
Sears Tower (world's tallest)	1,454	110
Amoco	1,136	80
John Hancock Center	1,127	100
311 S. Wacker	970	65
Two Prudential Plaza	901	64
AT&T Corporate Center (1989)	891	60
900 N. Michigan	871	66
Water Tower Place	859	74
First Natl. Bank	852	60
Three First National Plaza	775	57
Olympia Centre	727	63
Leo Burnett Bldg. (1989)	700	46
600 N. Lakeshore Dr.	697	75
IBM Plaza	695	52

City	Hgt. ft.	Stories
One Magnificent Mile	673	58
Daley Center	662	31
1,000 Lake Shore Plaza	648	55
Lake Point Tower	645	70
Board of Trade, incl. 81 ft. statue	605	44
Prudential Bldg., 130 E. Randolph	601	41
Antenna tower, 311 ft., makes total	912	...
CNA Plaza	600	44
Huron Apts.	599	56
Marina City Apts., 2 buildings	588	61
Mid Continental Plaza, 55 E. Monroe	580	50
Associates Center	575	41
Pittsfield, 55 E. Washington St.	572	38
Onterie Center (1985)	570	58
Civic Opera Bldg.	555	45
Newberry Plaza, State & Oak	553	56
One South Wacker Dr.	550	40
Harbor Point	550	54
Madison Plaza	551	45
190 S. LaSalle	550	40
LaSalle Natl. Bank, 135 S. LaSalle St.	535	44
One LaSalle Street	530	49
111 E. Chestnut St.	529	56
Chicago Mercantile Exchange (2 Bldgs)	525	40
River Plaza, Rush & Hubbard	524	56
35 E. Wacker Drive	523	40
United Ins. Bldg., 1 E. Wacker Dr.	522	41
Lincoln Tower, 75 E. Wacker Dr.	519	42
Quaker Tower	518	35
Carbide & Carbon, 230 N. Mich.	503	37
Walton Colonnade	500	44
Xerox Center	500	40
One Financial Place	498	40
LaSalle-Wacker, 221 N. LaSalle St.	491	41
Amer. Nat'l. Bank, 33 N. LaSalle St.	479	40
Bankers, 105 W. Adams St.	476	41
Brunswick Bldg.	475	37
310 Center	475	37
American Furniture Mart	474	24
333 Wacker Dr.	472	36
Sheraton Hotel, 505 N. Mich. Ave.	471	42
Playboy Bldg., 919 N. Mich. Ave.	468	37

Cincinnati, Oh.

City	Hgt. ft.	Stories
Carew Tower	568	49
Central Trust Tower	504	33
Dubois Tower, 5th & Walnut	423	32
Netherland Plaza	372	31
Central Trust Center	355	27
Atrium Two	350	30
Star Bank Center	351	26
Clarion North Tower	350	33
Cinn. Commerce Center	346	29

Cleveland, Oh.

City	Hgt. ft.	Stories
*Ameritrust Center/Hyatt Hotel	920	61
*Society Center	888	57
Tower City	708	52
BP America	658	46
Plaza Tower at Erieview	529	40
One Cleveland Center	450	31
*Bank One Tower	446	38
Justice Center, 1250 Ontario	420	26
Federal Bldg.	419	32
National City Center	410	35
Ameritrust	383	29
Cleveland St. J. F. Rhodes Tower	373	20
Eaton Center	360	28
Ohio-Bell	360	22

Columbus, Oh.

City	Hgt. ft.	Stories
James A. Rhodes (State Office Tower)	629	41
LeVeque Tower, 50 W. Broad	555	47
Ohio Bureau of Worker's Compensation & Ind. Comm. (1990)	530	33
Huntington Center, 41 S. High St.	512	37
Verne-Riffe State Office Tower	503	33
One Nationwide Plaza	482	40
One Riverside Plaza	456	31
Borden Bldg., 180 E. Broad	438	34
Three Nationwide Plaza (1989)	408	27
One Columbus	366	26
Columbus Center, 100 E. Broad	357	24
Capitol Square	348	26
Ohio Bell Bldg., 150 E. Gay St.	346	26

Dallas, Tex.

City	Hgt. ft.	Stories
First RepublicBank Plaza, 901 Main St.	939	73
Momentum Place	787	61

City	Hgt. ft.	Stories
Texas Commerce Tower	738	55
Allied Bank Tower	721	60
Renaissance Tower	710	56
Trammell Crow Tower	686	50
Arco Tower, 1601 Bryan St.	660	49
First City Center	655	49
Thanksgiving Tower, 1600 Pacific Ave.	645	50
First National Bank	625	52
Republic Bank Tower	598	50
SW Bell Admin. Tower	580	37
One Lincoln Plaza	579	45
Olympia York, 1999 Bryan St.	562	37
Reunion Tower	560	50
Southland Life Tower	550	42
Maxus Energy, 717 N. Harwood St.	550	34
2001 Bryan St.	512	40
San Jacinto Tower	456	33
Republic Bank Bldg., not incl. 150-ft. ornamental tower	452	36
Stouffer Hotel	451	29
Skyway Tower	448	31
One Main Place	445	34
1600 Pacific Bldg.	434	31
Mercantile Natl. Bank Bldg., not incl. 115-ft. weather beacon	430	31
Magnolia Bldg.	430	31
Mart Hotel	400	29
Complex Union Tower	400	33
One Dallas Centre	386	30
Southwestern Bell Toll Bldg.	372	22

Dayton, Oh.

City	Hgt. ft.	Stories
Kettering Tower, 2d & Main	405	30
Mead World Hqtrs, 10 W. 2d St.	365	28
Centre City Office Bldg, 40 S. Main St.	297	20

Denver, Col.

City	Hgt. ft.	Stories
Republic Plaza	714	56
Mountain Bell Center	709	54
United Bank of Denver	698	52
1999 Broadway	544	43
Arco Tower	527	41
Anaconda Tower	507	40
Amoco Bldg., 17th Ave. & Broadway	448	36
17th Street Plaza	438	35
Stellar Plaza	437	31
First Interstate Tower North	434	32
One Denver Place	428	34
Brooks Towers, 1020 15th St.	420	42
Tabor Center, #1	408	32
Manville Plaza	404	29
Colorado Nat'l. Bank, 17th & Curtis	389	26
First Interstate Tower South	385	28
Security Life Bldg.	384	33
Mellon Financial Center	374	31
Dominion Plaza	368	30
Lincoln Center	366	30
Denver Natl. Bank Plaza	363	29
Bank Western	357	27
Colorado State Bank	352	26

Des Moines, Ia.

City	Hgt. ft.	Stories
Principal Financial Group Bldg.	630	44
Ruan Center	457	36
Financial Center, 7th & Walnut	345	25
Marriott Hotel, 700 Grand Ave.	340	33
Plaza, 3d & Walnut	340	25

Detroit, Mich.

City	Hgt. ft.	Stories
Westin Hotel	720	71
Penobscot Bldg.	557	47
Guardian	485	40
Renaissance Center (4 bldgs.)	479	39
Book Tower	472	35
150 W. Jefferson Bldg.	470	29
Prudential 3000 Town Center	448	32
Cadillac Tower	437	40
David Stott	436	38
ANR Bldg.	430	32
Fisher	420	28
J. L. Hudson Bldg.	397	28
McNamara Federal Office Bldg.	393	27
2000 Prudential Town Ctr.	392	28
American Center	374	27
Top of Troy Bldg.	374	27
Comerica Bldg., 211 N. Fort	370	28
Edison Plaza	365	25
David Broderick Tower	358	34
1st National Bldg.	350	25
Buhl, 535 Griswold	350	26

City	Hgt. ft.	Stories
Edmonton, Alta.		
Manulife Place, 10170-101 St.	479	39
Royal Trust Tower.	476	30
AGT Tower, 10020-100 St.	441	34
CCB Tower, 10124-103 Ave.	410	34
Principal Plaza, 10303 Jasper Ave.	370	30
Scotia Place, 10060 Jasper Ave.	366	30
CN Tower, 1004-104 Ave.	365	26
Phipps McKinnon	359	21
Fort Wayne, Ind.		
One Summit Square, (1981)	442	26
Ft. Wayne Natl. Bank (1970)	339	26
Fort Worth, Tex.		
City Center Tower II.	546	38
1st United Tower	536	40
Continental Plaza	525	40
1st City Bank Tower.	475	33
Texas American Bank.	454	37
Texas Bldg.	380	30
Hamilton, Ont.		
Century Twenty One	418	43
Stelco Tower.	339	25
Harrisburg, Pa.		
State Office Tower #2.	334	21
333 Market St. (incl. tower).	327	19
Hartford, Conn.		
City Place	535	38
Travelers Ins. Co. Bldg.	527	34
Goodwin Square.	522	30
Hartford Plaza	420	22
Hartford Natl. Bank & Trust	360	26
One Commercial Plaza.	349	27
Bushnell Tower	349	27
One Financial Plaza, 755 Main.	335	26
Honolulu, Hi.		
Ala Moana Hotel.	396	38
Pacific Tower.	350	30
Franklin Towers	350	41
Honolulu Tower	350	40
Discovery Bay	350	42
Hyatt Regency Waikiki	350	39
Maile Court Hotel	350	43
Regency Tower, 2525 Date St.	350	42
Pearlridge Square.	350	43
Yacht Harbor Towers	350	40
Canterbury Place	350	40
Royal Iolani.	350	38
Island Colony	350	44
Century Center	350	41
Pacific Beach Hotel	350	43
Hawaiian Monarch Hotel	350	43
Waikiki Hobron.	350	43
Honolulu Tower 2	350	40
Tapa Tower, 2005 Kalia Rd.	350	36
Executive Center, 1088 Bishop St.	350	41
1001 Bishop	350	28
Houston, Tex.		
Texas Commerce Tower	1,002	75
Allied Bank Plaza, 1000 Louisiana.	992	71
Transco Tower.	901	64
RepublicBank Center	780	56
Heritage Plaza, 1111 Bagby	762	53
InterFirst Plaza.	744	55
1600 Smith St.	729	55
Gulf Tower, 1301 McKinney	725	52
One Shell Plaza		
(not incl. 285 ft. TV tower)	714	50
Four Allen Center	692	50
Capital Natl. Bank Plaza	685	50
One Houston Center	678	47
First City Tower	662	47
1100 Milam Bldg.	651	47
San Felipe Plaza.	620	45
Exxon Bldg.	606	44
The America Tower	577	42
Marathon Oil Tower	572	41
Two Houston Center	570	40
Dresser Tower	550	40
1415 Louisiana Tower.	550	44
Pennzoil, 700 Milam (2 bldgs.)	523	36
Two Allen Center	521	36

City	Hgt. ft.	Stories
Entex Bldg.	518	35
Huntington	506	34
Tenneco Bldg.	502	33
Conoco Tower	465	32
One Allen Center	452	34
Summit Tower West	441	31
Coastal Tower	441	31
Four Leafs Towers (2 bldgs.).	439	40
Phoenix Tower.	434	34
Gulf Bldg.	428	37
The Spires	426	41
Central Tower (4 Oaks Place)	420	30
First City Natl. Bank.	410	32
Houston Lighting & Power	410	27
Niels Esperson Bldg.	409	31
Hyatt Regency Houston	401	34
Indianapolis, Ind.		
Bank One Tower (1989)	728	51
AUL Tower.	533	38
Market Tower (1988)	515	32
Indiana Natl. Bank Tower.	504	35
Riley Towers (2 bldgs.)	427	30
300 N. Meridian Bldg. (1988).	408	28
First Indiana Plaza.	396	31
City-County Bldg.	375	28
Indiana Bell Telephone	321	20
Jacksonville, Fla.		
Barnett Tower	631	43
Independent Life & Acccident Ins. Co.	535	37
Southern Bell (1983)	447	32
Gulf Life Tower	435	27
American Heritage Ins. Bldg.	357	23
Blue Cross-Blue Shield (1973)	350	22
Kansas City, Mo.		
One Kansas City Place	626	42
AT&T Town Pavilion.	590	38
Hyatt Regency.	504	40
Kansas City Power and Light Bldg.	476	32
City Hall	443	29
Federal Office Bldg.	413	35
Commerce Tower	402	32
City Center Sq.	402	30
Southwest Bell Telephone Bldg.	394	27
Pershing Road Associates	352	28
Las Vegas, Nev.		
Fitzgerald Casino-Hotel.	400	34
Landmark Hotel	356	31
Las Vegas Hilton	345	30
Lexington, Ky.		
Lexington Financial Center	410	30
Kincaid Tower	333	22
Little Rock, Ark.		
TCBY Towers	546	40
First Commercial Bank	454	30
Worthen Bank & Trust	375	24
First South Bldg.	365	25
Tower Bldg.	350	18
Union National Bank.	331	21
Los Angeles, Cal.		
First Interstate World Center (1989).	1,017	73
First Interstate Bank.	858	62
*Cal. Plaza 11A.	750	57
Wells Fargo Tower	750	54
Security Pacific Plaza	735	55
So. Cal. Gas Center (1990)	733	55
*777 Tower.	725	52
Mitsui Fudoson (1990)	716	52
Atlantic Richfield Tower.	699	52
Bank of America Tower.	699	52
444 S. Flower St.	625	48
AT&T Bldg..	620	42
One California Plaza	578	42
Century Plaza Towers (2 bldgs.)	571	44
IBM Tower	560	45
Citicorp Plaza	534	42
1999 Ave. of the Stars (1989)	533	39
Manulife Tower (1990)	517	37
Union Bank Square	516	41
MCA-Getty	506	40
WTC Bldg.	496	36
Fox Plaza.	492	34
ARCO Center	462	33
City Hall	454	28

City	Hgt. ft.	Stories
Equitable Life Bldg.	454	34
Transamerica Center	452	32
Mutual Benefit Life Ins. Bldg.	435	31
Warner Center Plaza III	415	25
Broadway Plaza	414	33
1900 Ave. of Stars	398	27
1 Wilshire Bldg.	395	28
The Evian	390	31
400 S. Hope St.	375	26
Westin Bonaventure Hotel	367	35
Beaudry Center	365	29
Cal. Fed. Savings & Loan Bldg.	363	28
Century City North	363	26
Home Savings Tower	356	25

Louisville, Ky.

City	Hgt. ft.	Stories
First Natl. Bank	512	40
Citizen's Plaza	420	30
Humana Bldg.	350	27
Meindinger Tower	338	26
Brown & Williamson Tower	338	26

Memphis, Tenn.

City	Hgt. ft.	Stories
100 N. Main Bldg.	430	37
Commerce Square	396	31
Sterick Bldg.	365	31
Clark, 5100 Poplar	365	32
Morgan Keegan Tower, 50 Front St.	341	23
First Natl. Bank Bldg.	332	25

Miami, Fla.

City	Hgt. ft.	Stories
Southeast Financial Center (1983)	764	55
Centrust Tower (1987)	562	35
Metro-Dade Administration Bldg.	510	30
Florida National Tower (1986)	484	35
One Biscayne Corp.	456	40
Amerifirst Bldg. (1973)	375	32
Hotel Inter-Continental Miami	366	35
Venitia, 1635 Bayshore Dr.	365	42
Dade County Court House	357	28

Milwaukee, Wis.

City	Hgt. ft.	Stories
First Wis. Center & Office Tower	625	42
Milwaukee Center	422	28
Faison Bldg. (1989)	417	34
411 Bldg.	385	30
Northwestern Mutual Insurance (1989)	359	19
City Hall	350	9
Allen-Bradley Co.	333	17

Minneapolis, Minn.

City	Hgt. ft.	Stories
IDS Center	775	57
Norwest	772	57
Multifoods Tower	668	52
Piper Jaffray Tower	579	42
Pillsbury Center, 200 S. 6th St.	561	42
Opus, 150 S. 5th.	503	36
Plaza VII, 45 S. 7th	475	36
Lincoln Centre, 333 S. 7th	454	32
Foshay Tower, not including 163-ft. antenna tower.	447	32
Marriott Hotel	440	32
Northwestern Bell	416	26
Hennepin County Government Center	403	24
First Natl. Bank Bldg.	366	28
100 South Fifth.	356	25
Municipal Building	355	14
100 Washington Square	340	22

Montreal, Que.

City	Hgt. ft.	Stories
Place Victoria	624	47
Place Ville Marie	616	42
Canadian Imperial Bank of Commerce	604	43
Le Complexe Desjardins		
La Tour du Sud	498	40
La Tour du L'Est.	428	32
La Tour du Nord	355	27
La Tour Laurier	425	36
C.I.L. House	429	32
Chateau Champlain Hotel	420	38
Port Royal Apts.	400	33
Royal Bank Tower	397	22
Sun Life Bldg.	390	26
Banque Canadienne National	390	32

Nashville, Tenn.

City	Hgt. ft.	Stories
Third National Financial Center	490	30
American General Center	452	31

City	Hgt. ft.	Stories
Landmark Center	409	30
James K. Polk State Office Bldg.	392	32
Stouffer Hotel (1987)	385	35
First American N.A. Bank.	354	28
One Nashville Plaza.	346	23

Newark, N.J.

City	Hgt. ft.	Stories
Natl. Newark & Essex Bldg.	465	36
Raymond-Commerce	448	37
Park Plaza Bldg.	400	26
Prudential Plaza	370	24
Public Service Elec. & Gas.	360	26
Prudential Ins. Co., 753 Broad St.	360	26
AT&T Bldg.	359	31
Gateway 1	355	28

New Orleans, La.

City	Hgt. ft.	Stories
One Shell Square	697	51
Place St. Charles	645	53
Plaza Tower	531	45
Energy Centre	530	39
LL&E Tower, 901 Poydras	481	36
Sheraton Hotel	478	47
Marriott Hotel	450	42
Texaco Bldg.	442	33
Canal Place One	439	32
1010 Common.	438	31
Int'l. Trade Mart Bldg.	407	33
225 Baronne St.	362	28
One Poydras Plaza	360	28
Hyatt-Regency Hotel, Poydras Plaza	360	25
Hibernia Bank Bldg.	355	23

New York, N.Y.

City	Hgt. ft.	Stories
World Trade Center (2 towers) (1973)	1,368/ 1,362	110/110
Empire State, 34th St. & 5th Ave.	1,250	102
TV tower, 164 ft., makes total (1931).	1,414	...
Chrysler, Lexington & 43d (1930)	1,046	77
Amer. International, 70 Pine (1932)	950	67
40 Wall Tower (1929)	927	71
Citicorp Center (1977)	914	46
G.E. Bldg., Rockefeller Center (1933).	850	70
Chase Manhattan Plaza (1960)	813	60
Pan Am Bldg., 200 Park Ave. (1963)	808	59
Cityspire (1989)	802	72
Woolworth, 233 Broadway (1913).	792	60
1 Worldwide Plaza	778	47
1 Penn Plaza (1972)	764	57
Carnegie Tower	756	59
Exxon, 1251 Ave. of Americas (1971).	750	54
Equitable Center Tower West (1985)	750	58
60 Wall St. (1989).	745	50
1 Liberty Plaza (1972)	743	50
Citibank (1907)	741	57
World Financial Center, Tower C (1988)	739	54
One Astor Plaza (1969).	730	54
Solow Bldg. (1979)	725	50
Marine Midland	724	52
Metropolitan Tower (1988)	716	66
Union Carbide Bldg. (1960).	707	52
General Motors Bldg. (1968).	705	50
Metropolitan Life, (1909)	700	50
500 5th Ave. (1928).	697	58
Chem. Bank, N.Y. Trust Bldg. (1963)	687	50
55 Water St.	687	53
1585 Broadway	685	42
Chanin, Lexington & 42d (1929)	680	56
15 Columbus Circle (1970).	679	44
McGraw Hill, 1221 Ave. of Am. (1972)	674	51
Citicorp (Queens) (1990)	673	50
Lincoln, 60 E. 42d Street (1939).	673	53
1633 Broadway	670	48
Trump Tower, 725 5th Ave. (1983)	664	68
599 Lexington Ave. (1988).	653	47
Museum Tower Apts. (1985).	650	58
712 5th Ave. (1990).	650	56
American Brands, 245 Park Ave.	648	47
A. T. & T. Tower, (1983)	648	37
World Financial Center Tower B (1986).	645	50
General Electric, 570 Lexington (1931)	640	50
Irving Trust, 1 Wall St. (1932)	640	50
345 Park Ave.	634	44
Grace Plaza, 1114 Ave. of Am.	630	50
1 New York Plaza (1969).	630	50
Home Insurance Co. Bldg.	630	44
N.Y. Telephone, 1095 Ave. of Am.	630	40
Central Park Place (1988)	628	56
888 7th Ave.	628	42

City	Hgt. ft.	Stories
1 Hammarskjold Plaza	628	50
Waldorf-Astoria, 301 Park Ave. (1931)	625	47
Burlington House, (1970)	625	50
Olympic Tower, 645 5th Ave. (1976)	620	51
10 E. 40th St.	620	48
101 Park Ave.	618	50
750 7th Ave.	615	35
New York Life, 51 Madison Ave. (1928)	615	40
Rihga Royal Hotel	610	54
17 State St.	610	41
Penney Bldg., 1301 Ave. of Am.	609	46
IBM, 590 Madison Ave. (1983)	603	41
780 3rd Ave.	600	50
560 Lexington Ave.	600	22
Celanese Bldg. (1973)	592	45
U.S. Court House, 505 Pearl St. (1976)	590	37
*Kalikow Hotel	588	58
Federal Bldg., Foley Square	587	41
Time & Life, 1271 Ave. of Am. (1959)	587	47
Cooper Bregstein Bldg., 1250 Bway.	580	40
Stevens Tower, 1185 Ave. of Am.	580	42
Municipal, Bldg. (1919)	580	34
520 Madison Ave. (1983)	577	42
1 Madison Square Plaza (1968)	576	42
World Financial Center Tower A (1986)	575	42
One Financial Sq. (1987)	575	37
Park Ave. Plaza (1987)	575	44
Westvaco Bldg. 299 Park Ave.	574	42
Marriott Marquis Hotel (1985)	574	42
Socony Mobil Bldg., East 42d St.	572	45
Sperry Rand Bldg., 1290 Ave. of Am.	570	43
600 3d Ave.	570	42
Helmsley Bldg., 230 Park (1929)	565	35
1 Bankers Trust Plaza	565	40
Hemsley Palace Hotel (1980)	563	51
30 Broad St.	562	48
Park Ave Tower (1986)	561	36
Sherry-Netherland, 5th Ave. & 59th St.	560	40
Continental Can, 633 3d Ave. (1983)	557	39
Sperry & Hutchinson, 330 Madison	555	39
Continental Corp., 180 Maiden Lane	555	41
Galleria, 117 E. 57th St. (1975)	552	57
Interchem Bldg., 1133 Ave. of Am.	552	45
151 E. 44th St.	550	44
N.Y. Telephone, 323 Bway. (1979)	550	45
919 3d Ave.	550	47
Burroughs Bldg., 605 3d Ave.	550	44
Bankers Trust, 33 E. 48 St. (1963)	547	41
Transportation Bldg., 225 Bway.	546	45
Equitable, 120 Broadway (1915)	545	42
1 Brooklyn Bridge Plaza (1976)	540	42
Paine Webber Bldg. (1961)	540	42
Ritz Tower, Park Ave. & 57th St.	540	41
Bankers Trust, 6 Wall St.	540	39
1166 Ave. of Americas	540	44
1700 Broadway	533	41
Downtown Athletic Club, 19 West St.	530	45
Nelson Towers, 7th Ave. & 34th St.	525	45
767 3d Ave.	525	39
Hotel Pierre, 5th Ave. & 61st St. (1928)	525	44
House of Seagram, (1958)	525	38
7 World Trade Center (1985)	525	44
Random House, 825 3d Ave.	522	40
3 Park Ave.	522	42
North American Plywood, 800 3d Ave.	520	41
Du Mont Bldg., 515 Madison Ave.	520	42
26 Broadway	520	31
Newsweek Bldg., 444 Madison Ave.	518	43
Sterling Drug Bldg., 90 Park Ave.	515	41
First National City Bank	515	41
Bank of New York, 48 Wall St.	513	32
Navarre, 512 7th Ave.	513	43
Manhattan Savings Bank, Bklyn.	512	42
ITT—American, 437 Madison Ave.	512	40
International, Rockefeller Ctr.	512	41
1407 Broadway Realty Corp.	512	44
United Nations, 405 E. 42 St. (1953)	505	39

Oakland, Cal.

City	Hgt. ft.	Stories
Ordway Bldg., 2150 Valdez St.	404	28
Kaiser Bldg.	390	28
Lake Merritt Plaza	371	27
American President Lines (1990)	360	29
Raymond Kaiser Engineer Bldg.	336	25
Clorox Bldg.	330	24

Oklahoma City, Okla.

City	Hgt. ft.	Stories
Liberty Tower (1971)	500	36
First National Center (1974)	493	33
City Place (1935)	440	32
First Oklahoma Tower (1982)	425	31
Kerr-McGee Center	393	30
Mid America Tower (1981)	362	19
Citizens Plaza (1984)	321	22

Omaha, Neb.

City	Hgt. ft.	Stories
Woodmen Tower	469	30
Northwestern Bell Telephone Hdqrs.	334	16
Masonic Manor	320	22
First Natl. Center	320	22

Orlando, Fla.

City	Hgt. ft.	Stories
Sun Bank Center Tower (1988)	441	31
First F.A. Bldg. (1988)	409	28

Ottawa, Ont.

City	Hgt. ft.	Stories
Place de Ville, Tower C	368	29
R.H. Coats Bldg.	326	27

Philadelphia, Pa.

City	Hgt. ft.	Stories
One Liberty Place (1987)	945	61
Two Liberty Place (1989)	809	58
Mellon Bank Center (1969)	792	53
Bell Atlantic Tower	725	53
Blue Cross Tower	700	50
1919 Market St.	700	50
Commerce Sq., #1	559	41
City Hall Tower, incl. 37-ft. statue of Wm. Penn.	548	7
1818 Market St.	500	40
Provident Mutual Life	491	40
Fidelity Mutual Life Ins. Bldg. (1972)	492	38
Phila. Saving Fund Society (1932)	492	39
Central Penn Natl. Bank	490	36
Centre Square (2 towers) (1973)	490/416	38/32
Industrial Valley Bank	482	32
Philadelphia National Bank	475	25
Two Mellon Plaza	450	30
2000 Market St.	435	29
Two Logan Square	435	34
Fidelity Bank Bldg.	405	30
2 Girard Plaza	404	30
One Logan Square	400	32
Lewis Tower, 15th & Locust	400	33
1500 Locust St.	390	44
Philadelphia Electric Co.	384	27
INA Annex	383	27
Academy House, 1420 Locust St.	377	37
Penn Mutual Life	375	20
The Drake, 15th & Spruce	375	33
Medical Tower, 255 So. 17th.	364	33
State Bldg., 1400 Spring Garden	351	18
United Engineers, 17th & Ludlow	344	20
Packard, 15th & Chestnut	340	25
Inquirer Building	340	18

Phoenix, Ariz.

City	Hgt. ft.	Stories
Valley National Bank (1972)	483	40
Arizona Bank Downtown(1976)	407	31
Phoenix Plaza (1989)	397	25
First Interstate Bank Plaza (1971)	372	27
Phoenix Center (1979)	361	28
Citibank Plaza (1964)	356	27
One Renaissance Sq. (1987)	347	26
Two Renaissance Sq. (1989)	347	26
Merabank Tower	341	26

Pittsburgh, Pa.

City	Hgt. ft.	Stories
USX Towers	841	64
One Mellon Bank Center	725	54
One PPG Place	635	40
Fifth Avenue Place (1987)	616	32
One Oxford Centre	615	46
Gulf, 7th Ave. and Grant St.	582	44
University of Pittsburgh	535	42
Mellon Bank Bldg.	520	41
1 Oliver Plaza	511	40
Grant, Grant St. at 3rd Ave.	485	40
Koppers, 7th Ave. and Grant	475	34
Equibank Bldg.	445	34
CNG Tower (1987)	430	32
Pittsburgh National Bldg.	424	30
Alcoa Bldg., 425 Sixth Ave.	410	30
Liberty Tower	358	29
Westinghouse Bldg.	355	23
Oliver, 535 Smithfield St.	347	24
Gateway Bldg. No. 3	344	24
Centre City Tower	341	26

City	Hgt. ft.	Stories
Federal Bldg., 1000 Liberty Ave..	340	23
Bell Telephone, 416 7th Ave..	339	21
Hilton Hotel.	333	22
Frick, 437 Grant St..	330	20

Portland, Ore.

City	Hgt. ft.	Stories
First Interstate Tower	546	41
U.S. Bancorp Tower.	536	39
Koin Tower Plaza	509	35
Standard Insurance Center.	367	27
Pacwest Center	356	31

Providence, R.I.

City	Hgt. ft.	Stories
Fleet National Bank	420	26
Rhode Island Hospital Trust Tower	410	30
40 Westminster Bldg.	301	24

Raleigh, N.C.

City	Hgt. ft.	Stories
2 Hanover Sq..	431	29
*First Citizens	406	30
*First Union	400	30

Richmond, Va.

City	Hgt. ft.	Stories
James Monroe Bldg.	450	29
City Hall (incl. penthouse)	425	17
Crestar Bank Hdqt. Bldg..	400	24
Federal Reserve Bank	393	26
Sovran Center	333	25

Rochester, N.Y.

City	Hgt. ft.	Stories
Xerox Tower	443	30
Lincoln First Tower	390	26
Eastman Kodak Bldg..	360	19

St. Louis, Mo.

City	Hgt. ft.	Stories
Gateway Arch	630	. . .
Metropolitan Square Tower	591	42
S.W. Bell Telephone Bldg.	587	44
Mercantile Center Tower	550	37
Centerre Plaza.	433	31
Laclede Gas. Bldg., 8th & Olive	400	31
S.W. Bell Telephone Bldg.	398	31
Civil Courts.	387	13
Queeny Tower	321	24
Counsel Tower.	320	30

St. Paul, Minn.

City	Hgt. ft.	Stories
First Natl. Bank Bldg., incl.		
100-ft. sign.	517	32
Minn. World Trade Center	471	36
Galtier Plaza's Jackson Tower.	440	46
Osborn Bldg., 320 Wabasha	368	20
Kellogg Square Apts.	366	32
Northwestern Bell Telephone (2 bldgs.). .	340	16
Pointe of St. Paul	340	34
American National Bank Bldg.	335	25
North Central Tower, 445 Minn.	328	27
Amhoist/Park Tower	324	26

Salt Lake City, Ut.

City	Hgt. ft.	Stories
L.D.S. Church Office Bldg.	420	30
Beneficial Life Tower	351	21
Amer. Towers (2 bldgs.)	324	27

San Antonio, Tex.

City	Hgt. ft.	Stories
Tower of the Americas	622	. . .
Marriott Rivercenter (1988).	546	38
NBC Plaza (1988)	444	32
Tower Life	404	30
NCNB Plaza	387	28
Nix Professional Bldg..	375	23

San Diego, Cal.

City	Hgt. ft.	Stories
Symphony Tower (1989)	499	34
First Interstate Bank (1985)	398	23
Union Bank (1969).	388	27
First National Bank (1982)	379	27
The Meridan	375	27
Imperial Bank	355	24
Executive Complex (1963)	350	25
Wells Fargo Bldg. (1982)	348	20
Great American Bldg. (1974).	339	24

San Francisco, Cal.

City	Hgt. ft.	Stories
Transamerica Pyramid	853	48
Bank of America.	778	52
101 California St.	600	48
5 Fremont Center	600	43
Embarcadero Center, No. 4	570	45
Security Pacific Bank	569	45
One Market Plaza, Spear St..	565	43
Wells Fargo Bldg..	561	43
Standard Oil, 575 Market St..	551	39
One Sansome-Citicorp	550	39
Shaklee Bldg., 444 Market	537	38
Aetna Life	529	38
First & Market Bldg..	529	38
Metropolitan Life.	524	38
Crocker National Bank	500	38
Hilton Hotel.	493	46
Pacific Gas & Electric.	492	34
Union Bank.	487	37
Pacific Insurance	476	34
Bechtel Bldg., Fremont St.	475	33
333 Market Bldg.	474	33
Hartford Bldg..	465	33
Mutual Benefit Life.	438	32
Russ Bldg.	435	31
Pacific Telephone Bldg..	435	26
Pacific Gateway	416	30
Embarcadero Center, No. 3	412	31
Embarcadero Center, No. 2	412	31
595 Market Bldg.	410	31
101 Montgomery St.	405	28
Cal. State Automobile Assn.	399	29
Alcoa Bldg..	398	27
St. Francis Hotel.	395	32
Shell Bldg.	386	29
Del Monte	378	28
Pacific 3-Apparel Mart	376	30
Meridien Hotel	374	34

Seattle, Wash.

City	Hgt. ft.	Stories
Columbia Seafirst Center.	954	76
Two Union Square.	740	56
Washington Mutual Tower	730	55
*AT&T Gateway Tower.	722	62
1001 4th Pl.	609	50
Space Needle	605	. . .
Pacific First Center	580	44
First Interstate Center.	574	48
Seafirst 5th Ave. Plaza	543	42
Bank of Cal., 900 4th Ave.	536	42
Rainier Bank Tower, 4th & Univ..	514	42
Smith Tower	500	42
Key Tower	493	40
Federal Office Bldg..	487	37
Pacific Northwest Bell.	466	33
One Union Square.	456	38
1111 3d Ave. Bldg..	454	35
Washington Plaza Second Tower	448	44
Westin Bldg., 2001 6th Ave.	409	34
Westin Hotel	397	40
Financial Center	389	30
Daon Bldg., 840 Olive Way.	381	19
Sheraton Seattle Hotel	371	34
Sixth & Pike Bldg.	365	29
Fourth & Blanchard Bldg..	360	24
Crown Plaza Hotel	352	33

Tampa, Fla.

City	Hgt. ft.	Stories
Barnett Plaza	577	42
Tampa City Center	537	39
First Financial Tower	458	36
NCNB Plaza (1988)	454	33

Toledo, Oh.

City	Hgt. ft.	Stories
Owens-Illinois Corp. Headquarters	411	32
Owens-Corning Fiberglas Tower	400	30
Ohio Citizens Bank Bldg.	368	27
Toledo Govt. Center.	327	26

Toronto, Ont.

City	Hgt. ft.	Stories
CN Tower, World's tallest		
self-supporting structure	1,821	. . .
First Canadian Place	952	72
*Bay/Adelaide Project	902	57
Scotia Plaza	886	68
Canada Trust Tower (1990)	846	52
BCE Place (2 towers) (1990).	790/705	53/43
Commerce Court West	784	57
Toronto-Dominion Tower (TD Centre). . .	758	56
Royal Trust Tower (TD Centre)	600	46
Royal Bank Plaza—South Tower	589	41
Manulife Centre	545	53
IBM Tower TD Centre.	520	36
Two Bloor West	486	34
Exchange Tower.	480	36
Commerce Court North.	476	34

City	Hgt. ft.	Stories	City	Hgt. ft.	Stories
Simpson Tower	473	33	4th Natl. Bank of Tulsa	412	33
*Eaton Centre	471	31	320 South Boston Bldg.	400	24
Cadillac-Fairview Bldg., 10 Queen St.	465	36	Cities Service Bldg.	388	28
Palace Place (1990)	455	46	Univ. Club Tower	377	32
Palace Pier	452	46	City of Faith Hospital	348	30
Continental Bank Bldg.	450	35	Philtower	343	24
Sheraton Centre	443	43			
Hudson's Bay Centre	442	35	**Vancouver, B.C.**		
Old Toronto Exchange Bldg. (1990)	436	31	Royal Centre Tower (1973)	460	36
Leaside Towers (2 bldgs.)	423	44	Canada Trust Tower, 1055 Melville	454	35
*Metro Hall	420	27	Scotiabank Tower	451	36
Commercial Union Tower (TD Centre)	420	32	Bentall IV (1981)	450	35
Maple Leaf Mills Tower	419	30	Vancouver Center (1977)	450	36
Plaza 2 Hotel	415	41	Park Place (1984)	450	35
Sun Life Bldg., 150 King St.	410	28	T-D Bank Tower (1978)	440	30
Royal York Hotel	399	27	200 Granville Square (1973)	438	28
			Harbour Centre (1977)	428	21
Tulsa, Okla.			Bentall III (1974)	399	31
Bank of Oklahoma Tower	667	52			
City of Faith Clinic Tower	648	60	**Winston-Salem, N.C.**		
Mid-Continent Tower	530	36	Wachovia Bldg.	410	30
1st National Tower	516	41	Reynolds Bldg.	315	21

Other Notable Tall Buildings in U.S.

Cape Canaveral, Fla., Vehicle Assembly Bldg., 40 (552); Allentown, Pa., Power & Light Bldg., 23 (320); Amarillo, Tex., American Natl. Bank, 33 (374); Atlantic City, N.J., Taj Mahal, 51 (429); Bethlehem, Pa., Martin Tower, 21 (332); Charleston, W. Va., Kanawha Valley Bldg., 20 (384); Frankfort, Ky., Capital Plaza Office Tower, 28 (338); Galveston, Tex., American National Ins., 20 (358); Knoxville, Tenn., United American Bank, 30 (400); Lincoln, Neb., State Capitol (432); Mobile, Ala., First Natl. Bank, 33 (420); Niagara Falls, Ont., Skylon, (520); Shreveport La., Commercial National Tower, 24 (365); Springfield, Mass., Valley Bank Tower, 29 (370); Tallahassee, Fla., State Capitol Tower, 22 (345).

Notable Bridges in North America

Source: State Highway Engineers: Canadian Civil Engineering — ASCE

Asterisk (*) designates railroad bridge. Span of a bridge is distance (in feet) between its supports.

Year	Bridge	Location	Longest span	Year	Bridge	Location	Longest span
	Suspension			1958	Mississippi R.	New Orleans, La.	1,575
1964	Verrazano-Narrows	New York, N.Y.	4,260	1936	Transbay	San Fran. Bay	1,400
1937	Golden Gate	San Fran. Bay, Cal.	4,200	1968	W. 17th St.	Huntington, W. Va.	1,312
1957	Mackinac	Sts. of Mackinac	3,800	1968	Mississippi R.	Baton Rouge, La.	1,235
1931	Geo. Washington	Hudson River, N.Y.-N.J.	3,500	1955	Tappan Zee	Hudson River	1,212
1950	Tacoma Narrows	Washington	2,800	1930	Longview, Wash.	Columbia River	1,200
1936	*Transbay	San Fran. Bay, Cal.	2,310	1909	Queensboro	East R., N.Y.C.	1,182
1939	Bronx-Whitestone	East R., N.Y.C.	2,300	1927	Carquinez Strait	California	1,100
1970	Pierre Laporte	Quebec	2,190	1958	Parallel Span	"	1,100
1951	Del. Memorial	Wilmington, Del.	2,150	1930	Jacques Cartier	Montreal, P.Q.	1,097
1968	Del. Mem. (new)	Wilmington, Del.	2,150	1968	Isaiah D. Hart	Jacksonville, Fla.	1,088
1957	Walt Whitman	Phila., Pa.	2,000	1957	*Richmond	San Fran. Bay, Cal.	1,070
1929	Ambassador	Detroit-Canada	1,850	1929	Grace Memorial	Charleston, S.C.	1,050
1961	Throgs Neck	Long Is. Sound	1,800	1963	Newburgh-Beacon	Hudson, R., N.Y.	1,000
1926	Benjamin Franklin	Philadelphia	1,750	1982	Yeager	Charleston, W. Va.	947
1924	Bear Mt., N.Y.	Hudson River	1,632	1975	Caruthersville, Mo.	Mississippi R.	920
1952	*Wm. Preston Lane Mem.	Sandy Point, Md.	1,600	1977	Saint Marys	Saint Marys, W. Va.	900
				1969	Silver Memorial	Pt. Pleasant, W. Va.	900
1903	Williamsburg	East R., N.Y.C.	1,600	1987	Carl Perkins	Ohio River/So. Portsmouth, Ky.	900
1969	Newport	Narragansett Bay, R.I.	1,600				
1883	Brooklyn	East R., N.Y.C.	1,595	1940	Natchez	Mississippi R.	875
1939	Lion's Gate	Burrard Inlet, B.C.	1,550	1938	Blue Water	Pt. Huron, Mich.	871
1930	Mid-Hudson, N.Y.	Poughkeepsie	1,500	1972	Vicksburg	Mississippi River.	870
1964	Vincent Thomas	Los Angeles Harbor	1,500	1972	N. Fork American R.	Auburn, Cal.	862
1909	Manhattan	East R., N.Y.C.	1,470	1940	*Baton Rouge	Mississippi R.	848
1936	Triboro	East R., N.Y.C.	1,380	1899	*Cornwall	St. Lawrence R.	843
1931	St. Johns	Portland, Ore.	1,207	1940	Greenville	Mississippi R.	840
1929	Mount Hope	Rhode Island	1,200	1961	Helena, Ark.	Mississippi R.	840
1960	Ogdensburg, N.Y.	St. Lawrence R.	1,150	1963	Brent Spence	Covington, Ky.	831
1939	Deer Isle	Maine.	1,080	1963	Cincinnati, Oh.	Ohio River	830
1931	Maysville (Ky.)	Ohio River	1,060	1963	Mississippi, R.	Donaldsonville, La.	825
1867	Cincinnati	Ohio River	1,057	1930	*Vicksburg	Mississippi R.	825
1971	Dent	Clearwater Co., Ida.	1,050	1929	Louisville	Ohio River	820
1900	Miampimi	Mexico	1,030	1961	Campbellton-Cross Point	New Brunswick-Quebec	815
1849	Wheeling, W. Va.	Ohio River	1,010	1950	Maurice J. Tobin	Boston, Mass.	800
	Cantilever			1935	Rip Van Winkle	Catskill, N.Y.	800
				1938	Cairo	Ohio River, Ill.-Ky.	800
1917	Quebec	Quebec	1,800	1932	Washington Mem.	Seattle, Wash.	800
1981	Ravenswood	W. Va.	1,723	1936	McCullough	Coos Bay, Ore.	793
1974	Commodore Barry	Chester, Pa.	1,622				

(continued)

Year	Bridge	Location	Longest span
1935	[4]Huey P Long	New Orleans	790
1916	*Memphis (Harahan)	Mississippi R.	790
1892	*Memphis	Mississippi R.	790
1949	Memphis-Arkansas	Mississippi R.	790
1904	*Mingo Jct., W. Va.	Ohio River	769
1910	*Beaver, Pa.	Ohio River	767
1965	[5]S.N. Pearman	Charleston, S.C.	760
1940	Owensboro.	Ohio River	750
1928	Outerbridge, N.Y.-N.J.	Arthur Kill	750
1910	*P&LE	Beaver, Pa.	750

Simple Truss

Year	Bridge	Location	Longest span
1976	Chester	Chester, W. Va.	745
1917	*Metropolis.	Ohio River	720
1929	Irvin S. Cobb	Ohio River-Ill.-Ky.	716
1922	*Tanana River	Nenana, Alaska	700
1933	*Henderson	Ohio River-Ind.-Ky.	665
1967	I-77, Ohio River	Williamstown, W. Va.	650
1917	[4]MacArthur, Ill.-Mo.	St. Louis	647
1919	Louisville	Ohio River	644
1933	Atchafalaya	Morgan City, La.	608
1924	*Castleton	Hudson River	598
1937	Delaware R.	Easton, Pa.	550
1889	*Cincinnati	Ohio River	542
1951	Allegheny River	Allegheny Co., Pa.	533
1914	Pittsburgh	Allegheny R.	531
1930	*Martinez.	California.	528
1951	Rankin	Pittsburgh, Pa.	525
1913	Old Brownsville	Brownsville, Pa.	520
1906	Donora-Webster.	Donora-Webster, Pa.	515
1909	Hulton.	Pittsburgh, Pa.	505
1967	Tanana River	Alaska	500

Steel Truss

Year	Bridge	Location	Longest span
1973	Atchafalaya R.	Krotz Springs, La.	780
1972	Atchafalaya R.	Simmesport, La.	720
1975	I-24	Tenn R., Ky.	720
1938	US-62, Ky.	Green River	700
1952	US-62, Ky.	Cumberland River.	700
1940	Jamestown.	Jamestown, R.I.	640
1940	Greenville	Mississippi R., Ark.	640
1949	Memphis	Mississippi R., Ark.	621
1978	Atchafalaya R.	Morgan City, La.	607
1938	US-22.	Delaware River, N.J.	540
1955	Interstate (I-5)	Columbia River, Ore.-Wash.	531
1910	[4]McKinley, St. Louis	Mississippi River.	517
1972	Mississippi River.	Muscatine, Ia.	512
1896	Newport	Ohio River, Ky.	511
1970	Lake Koocanusa.	Lincoln Co., Mon.	500
1931	US-60.	Cumberland R., Ky.	500
1958	Lake Oahe	Mobridge, S.D.	500
1958	Lake Oahe	Gettysburg, S.D.	500

Continuous Truss

Year	Bridge	Location	Longest span
1966	Columbia R. (Astoria)	Ore.-Wash.	1,232
1977	Francis Scott Key	Baltimore, Md.	1,200
1943	Dubuque, Ia.	Mississippi R.	845
1956	[6]Earl C. Clements	Ohio R., Ill-Ky.	825
1953	John E. Mathews	Jacksonville, Fla.	810
1940	Gov. Nice Mem.	Potomac River, Md.	800
1957	Kingston-Rhinecliff	Hudson R., N.Y.	800
1986	Rochester-Monaca	Rochester-Monaca, Pa.	780
1918	*Sciotoville	Ohio River	775
1981	Sewickley	Sewickley, Pa.	750
1984	13th St. Bridge, Ohio R.	Ashland, Ky.	740
1959	Monaca-E. Rochester.	Monaca-East Rochester, Pa.	730
1976	Betsy Ross.	Philadelphia, Pa.	729
1929	Madison-Milton	Ohio River	727
1970	Vanport.	Vanport, Pa.	715
1966	[6]Matthew E. Welsh	Mauckport	707
1962	Champlain	Montreal, P.Q.	707
1973	Girard Point	Philadelphia, Pa.	700
1954	Pa. Tpk., Delaware R.	Philadelphia, Pa.	682
1949	George Platt	Philadelphia, Pa.	680
1938	Port Arthur-Orange	Texas.	680
1929	*Cincinnati	Ohio River	675
1928	Cape Girardeau, Mo.	Mississippi R.	672
1946	Chester, Ill.	Mississippi R.	670
1970	Gulfgate	Port Arthur, Tex.	664
1930	Quincy, Ill.	Mississippi R.	628
1961	Shippingport	Shippingport, Pa.	620
1972	US 181, over harbor	Corpus Christi, Tex.	620
1934	Bourne	Cape Cod Canal	616
1935	Sagamore	Cape Cod Canal	616
1965	Clarion R. (I-80)	Clarion Co., Pa.	612
1975	Donora-Monesson.	Donora-Monesson, Pa.	608
1957	Blatnik	Duluth, Minn.	600
1965	Rio Grande Gorge.	Taos, N.M.	600
1941	Columbia River	Kettle Falls, Wash.	600
1954	Columbia River	Umatilla, Ore.	600
1954	Columbia River	The Dalles, Ore.	576
1962	W. Br. Feather River	Oroville, Cal.	576
1967	Glenwood	Pittsburgh, Pa.	567
1936	Meredosia	Illinois River	567
1936	Mark Twain Mem.	Hannibal, Mo.	562
1957	Mackinac	Mackinac Straits, Mich.	560
1937	Homestead.	Pittsburgh	553
1961	Ship Canal	Seattle, Wash.	552
1932	Pulaski Skyway	Passaic R., N.J.	550
1973	I-95, Thames River	New London, Conn.	540
1966	Emlenton	Emlenton, Pa.	540

Continuous Box and Plate Girder

Year	Bridge	Location	Longest span
1988	Piney Creek-US19	Beckley, W. Va.	1,760
1973	Danville-US119	Danville, W. Va.	1,545
1983	Mississippi R.	Luling, La.	1,222
1974	Dunbar-S. Charleston.	South Charleston, W. Va.	842
1988	Beaver Creek-I-64.	Beckley, W. Va.	764
1967	San Mateo-Hayward No. 2.	San Fran. Bay, Cal.	750
1977	Intracoastal Canal.	Gibbstown, La.	750
1976	Intracoastal Canal.	Forked Is., La.	750
1963	Gunnison River	Gunnison, Col.	720
1969	[7]San Diego-Coronado.	San Diego Bay, Cal.	660
1973	Ship Channel (I-610)	Houston, Tex.	630
1981	Douglas.	Juneau, Alaska	620
1976	Wax L. Outlet	Calumet, La.	618
1975	S. Charleston-I-64	South Charleston, W. Va.	612
1981	Glenn Jackson (I-205)	Columbia R., Ore.-Wash.	600
1967	Poplar St.	St. Louis, Mo.	600
1982	Illinois R.	Pekin, Ill.	550
1982	I-440	Arkansas R.	540
1977	US-64, Tennessee R.	Savannah, Tenn.	525
1988	Mon City	Monongahela, Pa.	520
1965	McDonald-Cartier	Ottawa, Ont.	520
1972	Sitka Harbor	Sitka, Alaska	450
1986	Veterans	Pittsburgh, Pa.	440
1986	SR 76, Cumberland R.	Dover, Tenn.	440
1985	SR 20, Tennessee R.	Perryville, Tenn.	440
1970	Willamette R., I-205	West Linn, Ore.	430
1974	I-430	Arkansas R.	430
1985	I-435	Missouri R., Ks.-Mo.	425
1984	US-36	Missouri R., Ks.-Mo.	425
1972	I-635, Kansas City.	Missouri R., Kan.-Mo.	425
1985	FAU 3456, Tennessee R.	Chattanooga, Tenn.	420
1967	I-24, Tennessee R.	Marion Co., Tenn.	420
1978	Snake River	Clarkston, Wash.	420
1976	35th St. Bridge, Kanawha	Charleston, W. Va.	415
1986	SR 1, Tennessee R.	New Johnsonville, Tenn.	411
1979	Arkansas R.	Clarksville, Ark.	410
1975	Yukon River	Alaska	410
1973	Intracoastal Waterway	Corpus Christi, Tex.	400
1972	I-75, Tennessee River.	Loudon Co., Tenn.	400
1941	Susquehanna	Susquehanna R., Md.	400
1987	Clairton-Glassport.	Clairton-Glassport, Pa	400

Continuous Plate

Year	Bridge	Location	Longest span
1982	Houston Ship Chan	Texas.	750
1971	W. Atchafalaya	Henderson, La.	573
1981	Illinois 23	Illinois R., Ill.	510
1968	Trinity R.	Dallas, Tex.	480
1978	San Joaquin R.	Antioch, Cal.	460
1977	Thomas Johnson Mem.	Solomons, Md.	451
1975	I-129	Missouri R., Ia.	450
1967	Mississippi River.	LaCrescent, Minn.	450
1966	I-480	Missouri R., Ia.-Neb.	425
1970	I-435	Missouri R., Mo.	425
1972	I-80	Missouri R., Ia.-Neb.	425
1971	St. Croix River	Hudson, Wisc.	390
1968	Lafayette St.	St. Paul, Minn.	362
1967	San Mateo Creek	Hillsborough, Cal.	360
1961	Whiskey Creek	Shasta Co., Cal.	350
1964	Lexington Ave.	St. Paul, Minn.	340

I-Beam Girder

Year	Bridge	Location	Longest span
1980	Shreveport Int.	Louisiana.	438
1941	US-31E.	Rolling Fork R., Ky.	340
1948	US-27.	Licking River, Ky.	316
1947	US-31E.	Green River, Ky.	316

Year	Bridge	Location	Longest span
1941	US-62	Rolling Fork, Ky.	240
1942	Licking River	Owingsville, Ky.	240
1954	Fuller Warren	Jacksonville, Fla.	224

Steel Arch

Year	Bridge	Location	Longest span
1977	New River Gorge	Fayetteville, W. Va.	1,700
1931	Bayonne, N.J.	Kill Van Kull	1,652
1973	Fremont	Portland, Ore.	1,255
1964	Port Mann	British Columbia.	1,200
1916	*Hell Gate	East R., N.Y.C.	1,038
1959	Glen Canyon	Colorado River	1,028
1967	Trois-Rivieres	St. Lawrence R., P.Q.	1,100
1962	Lewiston-Queenston	Niagara River, Ont.	1,000
1976	Perrine	Twin Falls, Ida.	993
1941	Rainbow	Niagara Falls	984
1986	Moundsville Bridge, Ohio R.	Moundsville, W. Va.	912
1984	I-255	Mississippi R., Mo.	909
1972	¹⁰I-40, Mississippi R.	Memphis, Tenn.	900
1970	Lake Quinsigamond	Worcester, Mass.	849
1966	Charles Braga	Somerset, Mass.	840
1936	Henry Hudson	Harlem River, N.Y.C.	840
1967	Lincoln Trail	Ohio R., Ind.-Ky.	825
1978	I-57, Cairo, Ill.	Mississippi R.	821
1961	Sherman Minton	Louisville, Ky.	800
1936	French King	Conn. R. (Rt. 2, Mass.)	782
1978	I-470 Bridge, Ohio R.	Wheeling, W. Va.	780
1930	West End	Pittsburgh	780
1976	I-471, Ohio R.	Newport, Ky.	760

Concrete Arch

Year	Bridge	Location	Longest span
1971	Selah Creek (twin)	Selah, Wash.	549
1968	Cowlitz River	Mossyrock, Wash.	520
1931	Westinghouse	Pittsburgh	460
1923	Cappelen	Minneapolis	400
1973	Elwha River	Port Angeles, Wash.	380

Twin Concrete Trestle

Year	Bridge	Location	Longest span
1979	I-55/I-10	Manchae, La.	181,157
1969	L. Pontchartrain Cswy.	Mandeville, La.	126,720
1972	Atchafalaya Flwy.	Baton Rouge, La.	93,984
1963	⁹L. Pontchartrain	Slidell, La.	28,547

Concrete Slab Dam

Year	Bridge	Location	Longest span
1927	Conowingo Dam	Maryland	4,611
1952	SR-4, Roanoke R.	Mecklenburg Co., Va.	2,785
1936	Hoover Dam	Boulder City, Nev.	1,324

Drawbridges

Vertical Lift

Year	Bridge	Location	Longest span
1937	Marine Parkway	Jamaica Bay, N.Y.C.	590
1959	*Arthur Kill	N.Y.-N.J.	558
1935	*Cape Cod Canal	Massachusetts	544
1960	*Delair, N.J.	Delaware River	542
1931	Burlington, N.J.	Delaware R.	534
1968	Second Narrows	Vancouver, B.C.	493
1912	*A-S-B Fratt	Kansas City	428

Year	Bridge	Location	Longest span
1945	*Harry S. Truman	Kansas City	427
1955	Roosevelt Island	East River, N.Y.C.	418
1980	US-17, James R.	Isle of Wight, Co., Va.	415
1932	*M-K-T R.R.	Missouri R.	414
1969	Wilm'gtn Mem.	Wilmington, N.C.	408
1930	Aerial	Duluth, Minn.	386
1941	Main St.	Jacksonville, Fla.	386
1962	Burlington	Ontario.	370
1941	Acosta	St. Johns R., Fla.	365
1922	*Cincinnati	Ohio River	365
1967	SR-156, James R.	Prince George Co., Va.	364
1964	Red R.	Alexandria, La.	360
1957	Industrial Canal	New Orleans, La.	360
1950	Red R.	Moncla, La.	360
1936	Tribo	Harlem River, N.Y.C.	344
1961	⁴Corpus Christi Harbor	Corpus Christi, Tex.	344
1939	U.S. 1&9, Passaic R.	Newark, N.J.	333
1929	Carlton	Bath-Woolwich, Me.	328
1930	*Martinez	California.	328
1960	St. Andrews Bay	Panama City, Fla.	327
1929	*Penn-Lehigh	Newark Bay	322
1920	*Chattanooga	Tennessee R.	310

Bascule

Year	Bridge	Location	Longest span
1969	E. Pearl River	Slidell, La.	482
1955	Chehalis R.	Aberdeen, Wash.	340
1917	SR-8, Tennessee River	Chattanooga, Tenn.	306
1940	Lorain, Ohio	Black River	300
1968	Elizabeth River	Chesapeake, Va.	280
1913	Broadway	Portland, Ore.	278
1982	Columbus Drive	Chicago R.	269
1954	Fuller Warren	St. Johns R., Fla.	267
1958	Morrison	Portland, Ore.	262
1926	Burnside	Portland, Ore.	252
1977	Curtis Creek	Baltimore, Md.	251

Swing Bridges

Year	Bridge	Location	Longest span
1926	⁴Fort Madison	Mississippi R.	525
1930	Rigolets Pass	New Orleans, La.	400
1950	Douglass Memorial	Wash. D.C.	386
1916	Keokuk Municipal	Mississippi R., Ia.	377
1945	Lord Delaware	Mattaponi River, Va.	252
1957	Eltham	Pamunkey River, Va.	237

Swing Span

Year	Bridge	Location	Longest span
1908	*Willamette R.	Portland, Ore.	521
1903	*East Omaha	Missouri R.	519
1952	US-17	York River, Va.	500
1897	*Duluth, Minn.	St. Louis Bay	486
1899	*C.M.&N.R.R.	Chicago	474
1913	Rt. 82, Conn-R.	E. Haddam, Ct.	465
1914	*Coos Bay	Oregon.	458

Floating Pontoon

Year	Bridge	Location	Longest span
1963	Evergreen Pt.	Seattle, Wash.	7,518
1940	Lacey V. Murrow	Seattle	6,561
1961	Hood Canal	Pt. Gamble, Wash.	6,471
1989	3rd Lake Washington Bridge	Seattle, Wash.	6,130

(1) The Transbay Bridge has 2 spans of 2,310 ft. each. (2) A second bridge in parallel was completed in 1973. (3) The Richmond Bridge has twin spans 1,070 ft. each. (4) Railroad and vehicular bridge. (5) Two spans each 760 ft. (6) Two spans each 707 ft. (7) Two spans each 660 ft. (8) Two spans each 825 ft. (9) Total length of bridge. (10) Two spans each 900 ft.

Notable International Bridges

Angostura, suspension type, span 2,336 feet, 1967 at Ciudad Bolivar, Venezuela. Total length, 5,507.

Bendorf Bridge on the Rhine River, 5 mi. n. of Coblenz, completed 1965, is a 3-span cement girder bridge, 3,378 ft. overall length, 101 ft. wide, with the main span 682 ft.

Bosporus Bridge linking Europe and Asia opened at Istanbul in 1973, at 3,524 ft. is the fifth longest suspension bridge in the world.

Gladesville Bridge at Sydney, Australia, has the longest concrete arch in the world (1,000 ft. span).

Humber Bridge, with a suspension span of 4,626 ft., the longest in the world, crosses the Humber estuary 5 miles west of the city of Kingston upon Hull, England. Unique in a large suspension bridge are the towers of reinforced concrete instead of steel.

Second Narrow's Bridge, Canada's longest railway lift span connecting Vancouver and North Vancouver over Burrard Inlet.

Oland Island Bridge in Sweden was completed in 1972. It is 19,882 feet long, Europe's longest.

Oosterscheldebrug, opened Dec. 15, 1965, is a 3.125-mile causeway for automobiles over a sea arm in Zeeland, the Netherlands. It completes a direct connection between Flushing and Rotterdam.

Rio-Niteroi, Guanabara Bay, Brazil, completed in 1972, is world's longest continuous box and plate girder bridge, 8 miles, 3,363 feet long, with a center span of 984 feet and a span on each side of 656 feet.

Tagus River Bridge near Lisbon, Portugal, has a 3,323-ft. main span. Opened Aug. 6, 1966, it was named Salazar Bridge for the former premier.

Zoo Bridge across the Rhine at Cologne, with steel box girders, has a main span of 850 ft.

Oldest Bridge in Continuous Use

Completed in 1841, the 178 ft. long, wood truss (with orthotropic steel deck) covered bridge spans the Housatonic River on Rt. 128 in West Cornwall, Connecticut.

Underwater Vehicular Tunnels in North America

(3,000 feet in length or more)

Name	Location	Waterway	Lgth. Ft.
Bart Trans-Bay Tubes (Rapid Transit)	San Francisco, Cal.	S.F. Bay	3.6 miles
Brooklyn-Battery	New York, N.Y.	East River	9,117
Holland Tunnel	New York, N.Y.	Hudson River	8,557
Lincoln Tunnel	New York, N.Y.	Hudson River	8,216
Thimble Shoal Channel	Newport News, Va.	Chesapeake Bay	8,187
Chesapeake Channel	Northampton Co., Va.	Chesapeake Bay	7,941
Baltimore Harbor Tunnel	Baltimore, Md.	Patapsco River	7,650
Hampton Roads	Newport News, Va.	Hampton Roads	7,479
Fort McHenry Tunnel (2)	Baltimore, Md.	Baltimore Harbor	7,200
Queens Midtown	New York, N.Y.	East River	6,414
Sumner Tunnel	Boston, Mass.	Boston Harbor	5,650
Louis-Hippolyte Lafontaine Tunnel	Montreal, Que.	St. Lawrence River	5,280
Detroit-Windsor	Detroit, Mich.	Detroit River	5,135
Callahan Tunnel	Boston, Mass.	Boston Harbor	5,046
Midtown Tunnel	Norfolk, Va.	Elizabeth River	4,194
Baytown Tunnel	Baytown, Tex.	Houston Ship Channel	4,111
Posey Tube	Oakland, Cal.	Oakland Estuary	3,500
Downtown Tunnel	Norfolk, Va.	Elizabeth River	3,350
Webster St.	Alameda, Cal.	Oakland Estuary	3,350
Bankhead Tunnel	Mobile, Ala.	Mobile River	3,109
I-10 Twin Tunnel	Mobile, Ala.	Mobile River	3,000

Land Vehicular Tunnels in U.S.

(over 2,000 feet in length.)

Name	Location	Lgth. Ft.	Name	Location	Lgth. Ft.
			Fort Pitt	Pittsburgh, Pa.	3,560
E. Johnson Memorial	I-70, Col.	8,959	Mall Tunnel	Dist. of Columbia	3,400
Eisenhower Memorial	I-70, Col.	8,941	Caldecott	Oakland, Cal.	3,371
Allegheny (twin)	Penna. Turnpike	6,072	Cody No. 1	U.S. 14, 16, 20, Wyo.	3,202
Liberty Tubes	Pittsburgh, Pa.	5,920	Kalihi	Honolulu, Ha.	2,780
Zion Natl. Park	Rte. 9, Utah.	5,766	Memorial	W. Va. Tpke. (I-77)	2,669
East River Mt. (twin)	Interstate 77, W. Va.-Va.	5,412	Ft. Cronkhite	Sausalito, Cal.	2,690
Tuscarora (twin)	Penna. Turnpike	5,400	Cross-Town	178 St. N.Y.C.	2,414
Kittatinny (twin)	Penna. Turnpike	4,660	F.D. Roosevelt Dr.	81-89 Sts. N.Y.C.	2,400
Blue Mountain (twin)	Penna. Turnpike	4,435	Dewey Sq.	Boston, Mass.	2,400
Lehigh	Penna. Turnpike	4,379	Battery Park	N.Y.C.	2,300
Wawona	Yosemite Natl. Park	4,233	Battery St.	Seattle, Wash.	2,140
Big Walker Mt.	Route I-77, Va.	4,229	Big Oak Flat	Yosemite Natl. Park	2,083
Squirrel Hill	Pittsburgh, Pa.	4,225			

World's Longest Railway Tunnels

Source: Railway Directory & Year Book. Tunnels over 5 miles in length.

Tunnel	Date	Miles	Operating railway	Country
Seikan	1985	33.5	Japanese National	Japan
Dai-shimizu	1979	14	Japanese National	Japan
Simplon No. 1 and 2	1906, 1922	12	Swiss Fed. & Italian St.	Switz.-Italy
Kanmon	1975	12	Japanese National	Japan
Apennine	1934	11	Italian State	Italy
Rokko	1972	10	Japanese National	Japan
Mt. MacDonald	1989	9.1	Canadian Pacific	Canada
Gotthard	1882	9	Swiss Federal	Switzerland
Lotschberg	1913	9	Bern-Lotschberg-Simplon	Switzerland
Hokuriku	1962	9	Japanese National	Japan
Mont Cenis (Frejus)	1871	8	Italian State	France-Italy
Shin-Shimizu	1961	8	Japanese National	Japan
Aki	1975	8	Japanese National	Japan
Cascade	1929	8	Burlington Northern	U.S.
Flathead	1970	8	Burlington Northern	U.S.
Keijo	1970	7	Japanese National	Japan
Lierasen	1973	7	Norwegian State	Norway
Santa Lucia	1977	6	Italian State	Italy
Arlberg	1884	6	Austrian Federal	Austria
Moffat	1928	6	Denver & Rio Grande Western	U.S.
Shimizu	1931	6	Japanese National	Japan

ASSOCIATIONS AND SOCIETIES

Source: World Almanac questionnaire

Arranged according to key words in titles. Founding year of organization in parentheses; last figure after ZIP code indicates membership.

AFS Intercultural Programs (1917), 313 E. 43rd Street, N.Y., NY 10017; approx. 7,000.

Aaron Burr Assn. (1946), 2064 Faculty Dr., Winston-Salem, NC 27106; 400.

Abortion Federation, Natl. (1977), 1436 U St. NW, Suite 103, Washington, DC 20009; 300 organizations.

Accountants, Amer. Institute of Certified Public (1887), 1211 Ave. of the Americas, N.Y., NY 10036; 294,000.

Accountants, Natl. Assn. of (1919), 10 Paragon Dr., Box 433, Montvale, NJ 07645-1760; 85,000.

Accountants, Natl. Society of Public (1945), 1010 N. Fairfax St., Alexandria, VA 22314.

Accountants for Cooperatives, Natl. Soc. of (1936), 6320 Augusta Dr., Ste. 802-C Springfield, VA 22150; 2,000.

Acoustical Society of America (1929), 500 Sunnyside Blvd., Woodbury, NY 11797; 6,500.

Actors' Equity Assn. (1913), 165 W. 46 St., N.Y., NY 10036.

Actors' Fund of America (1882), 1501 Broadway, N.Y., NY 10036; 3,500.

Actuaries, American Academy of (1965), 1720 I St. NW, Wash., DC 20006; 9,500.

Actuaries, Society of (1949), 475 N. Martingale Rd., Suite 800, Schaumburg, IL 60173-2226; 12,200.

Adirondack Mountain Club (1922), RR 3, Box 3055, Lake George, NY 12845; 17,858.

Advertisers, Assn. of Natl. (1910), 155 E. 44th St., N.Y., NY 10017.

Advertising Agencies, Amer. Assn. of (1917), 666 Third Ave., N.Y., NY 10017; 765 agencies.

Aeronautic Assn., Natl. (1905), 1815 N. Fort Myer Dr., Ste. 700, Arlington, VA 22209; 7,392.

Aeronautics and Astronautics, Amer. Institute of (1963), 1633 Broadway, N.Y., NY 10019; 38,000.

Aerospace Industries Assn. of America (1919), 1250 Eye St. NW, Wash., DC 20005; 53 cos.

Aerospace Medical Assn. (1929), 320 S. Henry St., Alexandria, VA 22314-3524; 4,350.

Afro-American Life and History, Assn. for the Study of (1915), 1401 14th St. NW, Wash., DC 20005; 1,800.

Aging Assn., Amer. (1970), 600 South 42nd St., Omaha, NE 68198-4635; 400.

Agricultural Chemicals Assn., Natl. (1933), 1155 15th St. NW, Wash., DC 20005; 125 cos.

Agricultural Economics Assn., Amer. (1910), 80 Heady Hall, Iowa State Univ., Ames, IA 50011; 4,500.

Agricultural History Society (1919), Room 928, 1301 New York Ave. NW, Wash., DC 20005-4788; 1,400.

Agronomy, Amer. Society of (1907), 677 S. Segoe Rd., Madison, WI 53711; 12,443.

Aircraft Assn., Experimental (1953), EAA Aviation Center, Oshkosh, WI 54903-3086; 125,000.

Aircraft Owners and Pilots Assn. (1939), 421 Aviation Way, Frederick, MD 2I701; 300,000.

Air Force Assn. (1946), 1501 Lee Hwy., Arlington, VA 22209; 200,000.

Air Force Sergeants Assn. (1961), P.O. Box 31050, Temple Hills, MD 20748.

Air Line Employees Assn. (1951), 5600 S. Central Ave., Chicago, IL 60638.

Air Line Pilots Assn. (1931), 1625 Massachusetts Ave. NW, Wash., DC 20036; 41,000.

Air Pollution Control Assn. (1907), P.O. Box 2861, Pittsburgh, PA 15230; 8,500.

Air Transport Assn. of America (1936), 1709 New York Ave. NW, Wash., DC 20006; 27 airlines.

Air & Waste Management Assn. (1907), P.O. Box 2861, Pittsburgh, PA 15230; 11,000.

Al-Anon Family Groups (1950), P.O. Box 862, Midtown Sta., N.Y., NY 10018; 24,918.

Alcohol Problems, Amer. Council on (1964), 3426 Bridgeland Dr., Bridgeton, MO 63044.

Alcoholics Anonymous (1935), 468 Park Ave. So., N.Y., NY 10016; 1 mln.+.

Alcoholism and Drug Dependence, Natl. Council on (1944), 12 W. 21st St., N.Y., NY 10010; 200 affiliates.

All-Terrain Vehicle Owners Assn., Natl. (1972), P.O. Box 1272, Bensalem, PA 19020; 2,514.

Allergy and Immunology, Amer. Academy of (1943), 611 E. Wells St., Milwaukee, WI 53202; 4,000.

Alpine Club, Amer. (1902), 113 E. 90th St., N.Y., NY 10028.

Altrusa Intl. (1917), 332 S. Michigan Ave., Chicago, IL 60604.

Alzheimer's Disease and Related Disorders Assn. (1980), 70 E. Lake St., Chicago, IL 60601-5997; 170 chapters.

Amer. Indian Affairs, Assn. on (1923), 95 Madison Ave., N.Y., NY, 10016; 40,000.

American Legion, The (1919), 700 N. Pennsylvania St., Indianapolis, IN 46204; 3.0 mln. **American Legion Auxiliary** (1920), 777 N. Meridian St., Indianapolis, IN 46204; 950,000.

Amer. States, Organization of (1890), 17th & Constitution Ave. NW, Wash., DC 20006; 32 countries.

Amer. Veterans of World War II, Korea & Vietnam (AMVETS), (1944), 4647 Forbes Blvd., Lanham, MD 20706; 200,000. **AMVETS Auxiliary** (1946), 4647 Forbes Blvd., Lanham, MD 20706; 20,000.

Amideast (Amer. Mideast Educational & Training Services) (1951), 1100 17th St. NW, Suite 300, Wash., DC 20036; 225 institutions.

Amnesty Intl. USA (1961), 322 Eighth Ave., N.Y., NY 10001; 700,000+.

Amputation Foundation, Natl. (1923), 157-12 89th St., Whitestone, NY 11357; 2,200.

Anderson, Inc., Historical (1973), P.O. Box 268, Anderson, TX 77830; 250.

Andersonville, Natl. Soc. of (1975), P.O. Box 65, Andersonville, GA 31711; 140.

Animal Protection Institute of America (1968), 2831 Fruitridge Rd., P.O. Box 95822, Sacramento, CA 95822; 135,000.

Animal Welfare Institute (1951), 1686 34th St. NW, Wash., DC 20007; 8,000.

Animals, Amer. Society for Prevention of Cruelty to (ASPCA) (1866), 441 E. 92d St., N.Y., NY 10128; 300,000.

Animals, The Fund for (1967), 200 W. 57th St., N.Y., NY 10019; 200,000.

Antelopes, Grand United Order of (1925), 162 Fourth Ave., E. Orange, NJ 01017; 499.

Anthropological Assn., Amer. (1902), 1703 New Hampshire Ave. NW, Wash., DC 20009; 10,000.

Antiquarian Society, Amer. (1812), 185 Salisbury St., Worcester, MA 01609-1634; 522.

Anti-Vivisection Society, Amer. (1883), Suite 204, Noble Plaza, 801 Old York Rd., Jenkintown, PA 19046; 10,000+.

Appalachian Mountain Club (1876), 5 Joy St., Boston, MA 02108; 37,500.

Appalachian Trail Conference (1925), Washington & Jackson Sts., Harpers Ferry, WV 25425; 23,000.

Appraisers, Amer. Society of (1936), 535 Herndon Pkwy., #150, Herndon, VA 22070; 5,600.

Arab Americans, Natl. Assn. of (1972), 2033 M St. NW, Wash., DC 20036.

Arbitration Assn., Amer. (1926), 140 W. 51st St., N.Y., NY 10020-1203; 6,523.

Arboriculture, Intl. Society of (1924), 5 Lincoln Sq., Urbana, IL 61801; 4,500.

Archaeological Institute of America (1879), 675 Commonwealth Ave., Boston, MA 02215; 8,200.

Archaeology, Institute of Nautical (1976), P.O. Drawer HG, College Station, TX 77841; 800.

Archery Assn., Natl. (1879), 1750 E. Boulder St., Colorado Springs, CO 80909; 3,500.

Architects, Amer. Institute of (1857), 1735 New York Ave. NW, Wash., DC 20006; 51,000.

Architectural Historians, Society of (1940), 1232 Pine Street, Phila., PA 19107-5944; 3,600.

Armed Forces Communications and Electronics Assn. (1946), 4400 Fair Lakes Ct., Fairfax, VA 22033; 37,000.

Army, Assn. of the United States (1950), 2425 Wilson Blvd., Arlington, VA 22201; 160,000.

Arts, Amer. Council for the (1960), 1285 Avenue of the Americas, N.Y., NY 10019; 3,000.

Arts, Amer. Federation of (1909), 41 E. 65th St., N.Y., NY 10021; 1,100.

Arts and Letters, Amer. Academy and Institute of (1898), 633 W. 155th St., N.Y., NY 10032; 250.

Arts and Letters, Natl. Society of (1944), 2800 Quebec St. NW, Washington, DC 20008; 1,700.

Arts & Sciences, Amer. Academy of (1780), Norton's Woods, 136 Irving St., Cambridge, MA 02138; 3,370.

Assistance League, Natl. (1949), 5627 Fernwood Ave., Los Angeles, CA 90038; 17,000.

Association Executives, American Society of (1920), 1575 Eye St. NW, Wash., DC 20005; 18,000.

Association Publications, Society of Natl. (1963), 3299 K St. NW, Suite 700, Wash., DC 20007; 210 publications.

Astrologers, Amer. Federation of (1938), P.O. Box 22040, Tempe, AZ 85285; 4,500.

Astronautical Society, Amer. (1954), 6352 Rolling Mill Pl., Suite 102, Springfield, VA 22152; 1,500.

Astronomical Society, Amer. (1899), 2000 Florida Ave., NW, Suite 300, Wash., DC 20009; 5,000.

Ataxia Foundation, Natl. (1957), 600 Twelve Oaks Cntr., 15500 Wayzata Blvd., Wayzata MN 55391; 1,400.

Atheist Assn. (1925), Box 2832, San Diego, CA 92112.

Atheists, Amer. (1963), P.O. Box 2117, Austin, TX 78768.

Athetic Assn., Natl. Jr. College (1949), 1825 Austin Bluffs Pkwy., Colorado Springs, CO 80918; 556.

Athletic Assn., Natl. Scholastic (1985), 6991 Simson St., Oakland, CA 94605-2226.

Athletic Associations, Natl. Federation of State H. S. (1920), 11724 Plaza Circle, Box 20626, Kansas City, MO 64195.

Athletic Union of the U.S., Amateur (1888), 3400 W. 86th St., Indianapolis, IN 46268.

Athletics Congress/USA, The (1979), One Hoosier Dome, Indianapolis, IN 46225; 125,000.

Auctioneers Assn., Natl. (1949), 8880 Ballentine, Overland Park, KS 66214; 5,000.

Audubon Society, Natl. (1905), 950 Third Ave., N.Y., NY 10022; 578,000.

Authors League of America (1912), 234 W. 44th St., N.Y., NY 10036; 15,000.

Autism, Natl. Society for Children and Adults with, (1965), 1234 Massachusetts Ave. NW, Wash., DC 20005; 6,000.

Autograph Collectors Club, Universal (1965), P.O. Box 6181, Wash., DC 20044-6181; 2,447.

Automobile Assn., Amer. (1902), 8111 Gatehouse Rd., Falls Church, VA 22047; 28 million+.

Automobile Club, Natl. (1924), One Market Plaza, San Francisco, CA 94105; 316,000.

Automobile Club of America, Antique (1935), 501 W. Governor Rd., Hershey, PA 17033; 53,000.

Automobile Dealers Assn., Natl. (1917), 8400 Westpark Dr., McLean, VA 22102; 20,000.

Automobile License Plate Collectors' Assn. (1954), P.O. Box 712, Weston, W. VA 26452; 2,384.

Automotive Hall of Fame (1939), 3225 Cook Rd., Midland, MI 48640; 2,500.

Avon Collectors, Inc., Natl. Assn. of (1971), P.O. Box 68, W. Newton, IN 46183; 100 clubs.

Badminton Assn., U.S. (1936), 501 W. Sixth Street, Papillion, NE 68046; 2,000.

Bald-Headed Men of America (1973), 3819 Bridges St., Morehead City, N.C. 28557; approx. 20,000.

Ball Players of Amer., Assn. of Professional (1924), 12062 Valley View St., #211, Garden Grove, CA 92645; 58,000.

Band & Choral Directors Hall of Fame, Natl. (1985), 519 N. Halifax Ave., Daytona Beach, FL 32118.

Bankers Assn., Amer. (1875), 1120 Connecticut Ave. NW, Wash., DC 20036.

Bankers Assn. of America, Independent (1930), One Thomas Circle NW, Suite 950, Wash. DC 20005; 6,400 banks.

Bar Assn., Federal (1920), 1815 H St. NW, Wash., DC 20006; 15,000.

Barbershop Quartet Singing in Amer., Soc. for Preservation & Encouragement of (1938), 6315 Third Ave., Kenosha, WI 53140-5199; 38,000.

Baseball Congress, Amer. Amateur (1935), 118-19 Redfield Plaza, Marshall, MI 49068; 14,200 teams.

Baseball Congress, Natl. (1931), P.O. Box 1420, Wichita, KS 67201.

Baseball Research, Society for Amer. (1971), P.O. Box 470, Garrett Pk., MD 20896; 5,800.

Basketball Assn., Natl. (1946), 645 Fifth Ave., N.Y., NY 10022.

Battleship Assn., Amer. (1964), P.O. Box 11247, San Diego, CA 92111; 2,100.

Beer Can Collectors of America (1970), 747 Merus Ct., Fenton, MO 63026-2092; 4,000.

Beta Gamma Sigma (1913), 605 Old Ballas Rd., Suite 200, St. Louis, MO 63141; 285,000.

Beta Sigma Phi (1931), P.O. Box 8500, Kansas City, MO 64114; 250,000.

Bible Society, Amer. (1816), 1865 Broadway, N.Y., NY 10023; 500,000.

Biblical Literature, Society of (1880), 819 Houston Mill Rd. NE, Atlanta, GA 30329.

Bibliographical Society of America (1904), P.O. Box 397, Grand Central Sta., N.Y., NY 10163; 1,300.

Big Brothers/Big Sisters of America (1903), 230 No. 13th St., Philadelphia, PA 19107; 80,000.

Biochemistry and Molecular Biology, Amer. Society for (1906), 9650 Rockville Pike, Bethesda, MD 20814.

Blind, Amer. Council of the (1961) 1010 Vermont Ave. NW, Suite 1100, Wash., DC 20005; 20,000.

Blind, Amer. Foundation for the (1921), 15 W. 16th St., N.Y., NY 10011; 250.

Blind, Natl. Federation of the (1940), 655 15th St. NW, Suite 300, Washington, DC 20005.

Blindness, Natl. Society to Prevent (1908), 500 E. Remington Rd., Schaumburg, IL 60173; 26 affiliates.

Blindness, Research to Prevent (1960), 598 Madison Ave., N.Y., NY 10023; 1,400.

Blue Angels Assn. (1982), 4600 Twin Oaks Dr., Apt. 702, Warrington, FL 32506; 250.

Blue Cross and Blue Shield Assn. (1946), 676 St. Clair, Chicago, IL 60611; 74 plans.

Blueberry Council, No. Amer. (1965), P.O. Box 166, Marmora, NJ 08223; 37 members, 19 assoc., 13 contributing.

Bluebird Society, No. Amer. (1978), 2 Countryside Ct., Silver Spring, MD 20906; 5,000.

B'nai B'rith Intl. (1843), 1640 Rhode Island Ave. NW, Wash., DC 20036; 500,000.

Boat Assn., Amer. Power (1903), 17640 E. Nine Mile Rd., E. Detroit, MI 48021; 5,000.

Boat Club, Chris Craft Antique (1973), 217 S. Adams St., Tallahassee, FL 32301; 1,600.

Boat Owners Assn. of the U.S. (1966), 880 S. Pickett St., Alexandria, VA 22304; 350,000.

Bodybuilders Assn., Amer. (1981), 6991 Simson St., Oakland, CA 94605-2226; 854.

Bookplate Collectors and Designers, Amer. Soc. of (1922), 605 N. Stoneman Ave. #F, Alhambra, CA 91801; 250.

Booksellers Assn., Amer. (1900), 122 E. 42d St., N.Y., NY 10168; 5,557.

Botanical Gardens & Arboreta, Amer. Assn. of (1940), 786 Church Rd, Wayne, PA 19087; 1,800.

Bottle Clubs, Federation of Historical (1969), 5001 Queen Ave. N., Minneapolis, MN 55430; 90 clubs.

Bowling Congress, Amer. (1895), 5301 S. 76th St., Greendale, WI 53129; 3.1 mln.

Boys' Brigades of America, United (1893), 2803 Glendale Ave., Baltimore, MD 21234; 150.

Boys' Clubs of America (1906), 771 First Ave., N.Y., NY 10017; 1.2 mln.

Boy Scouts of America (1910), 1325 Walnut Hill Lane, Irving, TX 75015-2079; 5.3 mln.

Bread for the World (1974), 802 Rhode Island Ave. NE, Washington, DC 20018; 40,000.

Bridge, Tunnel and Turnpike Assn., Intl. (1932), 2120 L St. NW, Suite 305, Wash., DC 20037; 275 organizations.

Brith Sholom, Natl. (1905), 3939 Conshohocken Ave., Philadelphia, PA 19131; 5,000.

Broadcasters, Natl. Assn. of (1922), 1771 N St. NW, Wash., DC 20036; 6,170 radio & TV stations.

Burroughs Bibliophiles, The (1960), 454 Elaine Dr., Pittsburgh, PA 15236; 256.

Bus Assn., Amer. (1928), 1015 15th St. NW, Suite 250, Wash., DC 20005; 3,000.

Business Bureaus, Council of Better (1970), 4200 Wilson Blvd., Arlington, VA 22203; 180 bureaus.

Business Clubs, Natl. Assn. of Amer. (1922), 3315 No. Main St., High Point, NC 27262; 7,000.

Business Communication, Assn. for (1935), 608 S. Wright St., Urbana, IL 61801; 1,650.

Business Communicators, Intl. Assn. of (1970), One Hallidie Pl., Suite 600, San Francisco, CA 94920; 11,000.

Business Education Assn., Natl. (1946), 1906 Association Dr., Reston, VA 22091; 18,000.

Business Real Estate & Law Assn., Amer. (1923), Dept. of Legal Studies, Univ. of Georgia, Athens, GA 30602; 1,200.

Business-Professional Advertising Assn. (1922), 100 Metroplex Dr., Edison, NJ 08817; 4,500.

Button Society, Natl. (1938), 2733 Juno Pl., Akron, OH 44313; 2,400+.

Byron Society, The (1971 England, 1973 in U.S.), 259 New Jersey Ave., Collingswood, NJ 08108; 300.

CARE (Cooperative For American Relief Everywhere) (1945), 660 First Ave., N.Y., NY 10016.

CB Radio Patrol of Amer., Federation of Police (1977), 1100 NE 125th St., N. Miami, FL 33161; 35,000.

CLU & CHFC, Amer. Soc. of (1928), 270 Bryn Mawr Ave., Bryn Mawr, PA 19010; 32,000.

CORE (Congress of Racial Equality) (1942), 1457 Flatbush Ave., Brooklyn, NY 11210.

CPCU, The Society of (1944), 720 Providence Rd., Malvern, PA 19355; 18,000.

Campers & Hikers Assn., Natl. (1954), 4804 Transit Rd., Bld. 2, Depew, NY 14043; 24,000 families.

Camp Fire Boys & Girls (1910), 4601 Madison Ave., Kansas City, MO 64112; 600,000.

Campers & Hikers Assn., inc. (1954), 7172 Transit Rd., Buffalo, NY 14221; 30,000.

Camping Assn., Amer. (1910), 5000 SR 67 N., Martinsville, IN 46151; 5,200.

Cancer Society, Amer. (1913), 90 Park Ave., N.Y., NY 10017; 257.

Canoe Assn., U.S. (1968), 606 Ross St., Middletown, OH 45044; 1,300.

Carillonneurs in North America, Guild of (1936), 3718 Settle Rd., Cincinnati, OH 45227; 483.

Carnegie Hero Fund Commission (1904), 2307 Oliver Bldg., Pittsburgh, PA 15222.

Cartoonists Society, Natl. (1946), 157 W. 57th St., Suite 904, N.Y., NY 10019; 500.

Cat Fanciers' Assn. (1906), 1309 Allaire Ave., Ocean, NJ 07712; 600 member clubs.

Catholic Bishops, Natl. Conference of/U.S. Cath. Conference (1966), 1312 Massachusetts Ave. NW, Wash., DC 20005.

Catholic Charities, USA (1910), 1319 F St. NW, Wash., DC 20004; 3,350.

Catholic Church Extension Society of the U.S.A. (1905), 35 E. Wacker Dr., Chicago, IL 60601.

Catholic Daughters of the Americas (1903), 10 W. 71st St., N.Y., NY 10023; 150,000.

Catholic Educational Assn., Natl. (1904), 1077-30th St. NW, Suite 100, Wash., DC 20007; 18,353.

Catholic Historical Soc., Amer. (1884), 263 S. Fourth St., Philadelphia, PA 19106; 815.

Catholic Library Assn. (1921), 461 W. Lancaster Ave., Haverford, PA 19041; 1,518.

Catholic Press Assn. of U.S. and Canada (1911), 119 N. Park Ave., Rockville Centre, NY 11570.

Catholic Rural Life Conference, Natl. (1923), 4625 NW Beaver Ave., Des Moines, IA 50310; 2,000.

Catholic War Veterans of the U.S.A. (1935), 419 North Lee Street, Alexandria, VA 22314; 25,000.

Celiac Sprue Assn./USA (1986), 2313 Rocklyn Dr., Suite 1, Des Moines, IA 50322; 1,800.

Cemetery Assn., Amer. (1887), 5201 Leesburg Pike, Falls Church, VA 22041; 2,300.

Ceramic Society, Amer. (1898), 757 Brooksedge Plaza Dr., Westerville, OH 43081; 13,500.

Cerebral Palsy Assns., United (1949), 7 Penn Plaza, N.Y., NY 10001; 180 affiliates.

Chamber of Commerce of the U.S.A. (1912), 1615 H St. NW, Wash., DC 20062; 200,000.

Chamber Music Players, Amateur (1948), 545 Eighth Ave., N.Y., NY 10018; 4,000.

Chaplain's Intl. Assn. (1962), U.S. Box 4266, Norton Air Force Base, San Bernardino, CA 92409; 790.

Chaplains Assn. of the U.S.A., The Military (1925), P.O. Box 645, Riverdale, MD 20737-0645; 1,500.

Checker Federation, Amer., (1948), 3475 Belmont Ave., Baton Rouge, LA 70808; 1,000.

Chemical Manufacturers Assn. (1872), 2501 M St. NW, Wash., DC 20037; 171 companies.

Chemical Society, Amer. (1876), 1155 16th St. NW, Wash., DC 20036; 135,000.

Chemistry, Amer. Assn. for Clinical (1948), 2029 K St. NW, 7th fl. Wash., DC 20006; 9,600.

Chemists, Amer. Institute of (1923), 7315 Wisconsin Ave., Bethesda, Md. 20814; 6,500

Chemists, Amer. Society of Brewing (1934), 3340 Pilot Knob Rd., St. Paul MN 55121; 857.

Chemists, Amer. Assn. of Cereal (1915), 3340 Pilot Knob Rd., St. Paul, MN 55121; 3,523.

Chess Federation, U.S. (1939), 186 Rte. 9W, New Windsor, NY 12550; 60,000.

Chess League of Amer., Correspondence (1897), P.O. Box 416, Warrenville, IL 60555; 1,000.

Child Welfare League of America (1920), 440 First St. NW, Wash., DC 20001; 600 agencies.

Childbirth Without Pain Education Assn. (1959), 20134 Snowden, Detroit, MI 48235; 3,000.

Childhood Education Intl., Assn. for (1892), 11141 Georgia Ave., Suite 200, Wheaton, MD 20902; 14,000.

Children of the Amer. Revolution, Natl. Society of the (1895), 1776 D St. NW, Wash., DC 20006; 10,000.

Children's Aid Society (1853), 105 E. 22d St., N.Y., NY 10010; 1,207.

Children's Book Council (1945), 568 Broadway, Suite 404, N.Y., NY 10012; 65 publishing houses.

Chiropractic Assn., Amer. (1930), 1916 Wilson Blvd., Arlington, VA 22201; 20,000.

Chiropractors Assn., Intl. (1926), 1901 L St. NW, Wash., DC 20036; 7,000.

Christian Endeavor, Intl. Society of (1881), 1221 E. Broad St., Columbus, OH 43216.

Christian Laity Counseling Board (1970), 5901 Plainfield Dr., Charlotte, NC 28215; 38 mln.

Christians and Jews, Natl. Conference of (1927), 71 Fifth Ave., Suite 1100 N.Y., NY 10003.

Church Business Administration, Natl. Assn. of (1956), 7001 Grapevine Hwy., Suite 324, Ft. Worth, TX 76180; 1,500.

Church Federation, Ecumenical (1982), 13014-270, N. Dalemabry, Tampa, FL 33618-2808.

Churches, U.S. Conference for the World Council of (1948), 475 Riverside Dr., N.Y., NY 10115; 27 churches.

Church Women United (1941), The Interchurch Center, 475 Riverside Dr., Rm. 812, N.Y., NY 10115.

Cincinnati, Society of the (1783), 2118 Massachusetts Ave. NW, Wash., DC 20008; 3,200.

Circulation Managers Assn., Intl. (1889), 11600 Sunrise Valley Dr., Reston, VA 22091; 1,536.

Circus Fans Assn. of America (1926), P.O. Box 3187, Flint, MI 48502; 2,400.

Cities, Natl. League of (1924), 1301 Pennsylvania Ave. NW, Wash., DC 20004; 15,000 cities.

Citizens Band Radio Patrol (1977), 1100 NE 125th St., N. Miami, FL 33161; 35,000.

City Management Assn., Intl. (1914), 1120 G St. NW, Wash., DC 20005; 7,240.

Civic League, Natl. (1894), 1601 Grant St., Suite 250, Denver, CO 80203; 1,500.

Civil Air Patrol, (1941), Bldg. 714, Maxwell AFB, AL 36112-5572; 73,000.

Civil Engineers, Amer. Society of (1852), 345 E. 47th St., N.Y., NY 10017; 104,000.

Civil Liberties Union, Amer. (1920), 132 W. 43rd St., N.Y. NY 10036; 250,000.

Civil War Round Table of New York (1951), P.O. Box 3485, N.Y., NY 10185; 150+.

Civic League, Natl. (1894), 55 West 44th St., N.Y., NY 10036; 3,000.

Civitan Internatl. (1920), 1401 52nd St. S., Birmingham, AL 35213-1903; 35,000.

Classical League, Amer. (1919), Hall, Miami Univ., Oxford, OH 45056; 3,604.

Clinical Pastoral Education, Assn. for (1967), 1549 Clairmont Rd., Decatur, GA 30033; 4,366.

Clinical Pathologists, Amer. Society of (1922), 2100 W. Harrison St., Chicago, IL 60612; 47,300.

Coal Association, Natl. (1917), 1130 17th St. NW, Wash., DC 20036; 175 corporate members.

College Athletic Assn., Natl. Junior (1949), 1825 Austin Bluffs Pkwy., Colorado Springs, CO 80918; 565 schools.

College Athletic Conference, Eastern (1938), 1311 Craigville Beach Rd., P.O. Box 3, Centerville, MA 02632.

College Board, The (1900), 45 Columbus Ave., N.Y., NY 10023; 2,600 institutions.

College Music Society (1958), P.O. Box 18000, Boulder, CO 80308; 6,000.

College Physical Education Assn. for Men, Natl. (1897), 108 Cooke Hall, Univ. of Minnesota, Minneapolis, MN 55455.

College Placement Council (1956), 62 Highland Ave., Bethlehem, PA 18017; 3,010.

Colleges, Amer. Assn. of Community and Jr. (1921), One Dupont Circle NW, Suite 410, Wash., DC 20036.

Colleges, Assn. of Amer. (1915), 1818 R St. NW, Wash., DC 20009; 620 institutions.

Colleges and Universities, Assn. of Intl. (1973), I301 S. Ireland Rd., Independence, MO 64055; 11,825.

Collegiate Athletic Assn., Natl. (1906), 6201 College Blvd., Overland Park, KS 66211-2422.

Collegiate Body-Building Assn., Natl. (1983), 6991 Simson St., Oakland, CA 94605; 683.

Collegiate Schools of Business, Amer. Assembly of (1916), 605 Old Ballas Rd., St. Louis, MO 63141-7077; 800+ schools.

Colonial Dames of Amer. (1899), 421 E. 61 St., N.Y., NY 10021; 2,049.

Colonial Dames XVII Century, Natl. Society (1915), 1300 New Hampshire Ave. NW, Wash., DC 20036; 13,000.

Colonial Wars, General Society of (1892), 840 Woodbine Ave., Glendale, OH 45246; 4,400.

Commercial Collectors Assn., Amer. (1969), 4040 W. 70th St., Minneapolis, MN 55435; 3,159.

Commercial Law League of America (1895), 175 W. Jackson, #1541, Chicago, IL 60604; 5,300.

Commercial Travelers of America, Order of United (1888), 632 N. Park St., Columbus, OH 43215; 186,000.

Common Cause (1970), 2030 M St. NW, Wash., DC 20036; 270,000.

Communication, Intl. Training in (1938), 2519 Woodland Dr., Anaheim, CA 92801; 20,000.

Communication, Soc. for Technical (1953), 815 15th St. NW, Wash., DC 20005; 15,000.

Communication Administration, Assn. for (1971), 5105 Backlick Rd., Annadale, VA 22003; 700.

Communities, Federation of Egalitarian (1976), E. Wind, Rt. 3WA, Box 6B2, Tecumseh, MO 65760; 200.

Community Cultural Center Assoc., Amer. (1978), 19 Foothills Dr., Pompton Plains, NJ 07444.

Composers/USA, Natl. Assn. of (1932), P.O. Box 49652, Barrington Sta., Los Angeles, CA 90049; 600.

Composers, Authors & Publishers, Amer. Society of (ASCAP) (1914), One Lincoln Plaza, N.Y., NY 10023; 24,000.

Computing Machinery, Assn. for (1947), 11 W. 42nd St., N.Y., NY 10036; 55,000.

Concrete Institute, Amer. (1904), 22400 W. Seven Mile Rd., Detroit, MI 48219-1849; 16,770.

Conscientious Objection, Central Committee for (1948), 2208 South St., Phila., PA 19146.

Conservation Engineers, Assn. of (1961), Missouri Dept. of Conservation, P.O. Box 180, Jefferson City, MO 65076.

Constantian Society, The (1970), 123 Orr Rd., Pittsburgh, PA 15241; 420.

Construction Industry Manufacturers Assn. (1911), 111 E. Wisconsin Ave., Milwaukee, WI 53202; 150 companies.

Construction Specifications Institute (1948), 601 Madison St., Alexandria, VA 22314-1791; 19,200.

Consumer Credit Assn., intl. (1912), 243 N. Lindbergh, St. Louis, MO 63141; 20,000.

Consumer Federation of America (1968), 1314 14th St. NW, Wash., DC 20005; 200+.

Consumer Interests, Amer. Council on (1953), 240 Stanley Hall, Univ. of Missouri, Columbia, MO 65211; 1,680.

Consumer Protection Institute (1970), 5901 Plainfield Dr., Charlotte, NC 28215.

Consumers League, Natl. (1899), 815 15th St. NW, Suite 516, Wash., DC 20005.

Consumers Union of the U.S. (1936), 256 Washington St., Mount Vernon, NY 10553; 291,000.

Contraception, Assn. for Voluntary Surgical (1943), 122 E. 42nd St., New York, NY 10168; 5,000.

Contract Bridge League, Amer. (1937), 2200 Democrat Rd., Memphis, TN 38132; 190,000.

Contract Management Assn., Natl. (1959), 6728 Old McLean Village Dr., McLean, VA 22101; 20,176.

Contractors, Natl. Assn. of Education and Training (1989), 50 E St. SE, Wash., DC 20003; 18.

Contractors of Amer., General (1918), 1957 E St. NW, Wash., DC 20036; 30,000.

Cooperative Business Assn., Natl. (1916), 1401 New York Ave. NW, #1100, Wash., DC 20005; 180 organizations, 50 indvls.

Cooperative League of the U.S.A. (1916), 1401 New York Ave. NW, Suite 1100, Wash., DC 20005; 285 co-ops.

Correctional Assn., Amer. (1870), 8025 Laurel Lakes Court, Laurel, MD 20707; 24,000.

Correctional Officers, Intl. Assn. of (1977), P.O. Box 7051, Marquette, MI 49855; 10,000.

Cosmetology Assn., Natl. (1921), 3510 Olive St., St. Louis, MO 63103; 47,000.

Cosmopolitan Intl. (1919), 7341 W. 80th, Overland Park, KS 66204; 3,200.

Cotton Council of America, Natl. (1938), 1918 North Parkway, Memphis, TN 38112; 297 delegates.

Counseling and Development, Amer. Assn. for (1952), 5999 Stevenson Ave., Alexandria, VA 22304; 55,000.

Counselors and Family Therapists, Natl. Academy of (1970), 55 Morris Ave., Springfield, NJ 07081-1422; 500.

Country Music Assn. (1958), P.O. Box 22299, Nashville, TN 37202; 8,000+.

Creative Children and Adults, Natl. Assn. for (1974), 8080 Springvalley Dr., Cincinnati, OH 45236; 1,500.

Credit Assn., International (1912), 243 N. Lindberg, St. Louis, MO 63141; 13,500.

Credit Management, Nat. Assn. of (1896), 8815 Centre Park Dr., Columbia, MD 21045.

Credit Union Natl. Assn. (1934), 5710 Mineral Point Rd., Madison, WI 53705; 52 state credit union leagues.

Crime and Delinquency, Natl. Council on (1907), 685 Market St., Suite 620, San Francisco, CA 94105; 200.

Criminal Investigators Assn., intl. (1970), P.O. Box 15350, Chevy Chase, MD 20815; 1,000.

Criminology, Amer. Society of (1941), 1314 Kinnear Rd., Suite 212, Columbus, OH 43212; 2,200.

Crop Science Society of America (1955), 677 S. Segoe Rd., Madison, WI 53711; 5,464.

Cross-Examination Debate Assn. (1971), California State Univ.-Northridge, Northridge, CA 91330.

Cryptogram Assn., Amer. (1929) 4 Hawthorne Dr., Cherry Hill, NJ 08003; 1,100.

Cyprus, Sovereign Order of (1192, 1964 in U.S.), 853 Seventh Ave., N.Y., NY 10019; 474.

Dairy Council, Natl. (1915), 6300 N. River Rd., Rosemont, IL 60018.

Dairy and Food Industries Supply Assn. (1912), 6245 Executive Blvd., Rockville, MD 20852; 632.

Dairy Goat Assn., American (1904), 209 W. Main St., Spindale, NC 28160; 12,000.

Dairylea Cooperative (1907), 831 James St., Syracuse, NY13203; 3,000.

Danish Brotherhood in America (1882), 3717 Harney St., Omaha, NE 68131; 9,534.

Daughters of the American Revolution, Natl. Society, (1890), 1776 D St. NW, Wash., DC 20006-5392; 202,197.

Daughters of the Confederacy, United (1894), 328 N. Blvd., Richmond, VA 23220-4057; 26,000.

Daughters of 1812, Natl. Society, U.S. (1892), 1461 Rhode Island Ave. NW, Wash., DC 20005; 4,700.

Daughters of the Republic of Texas (1891), 5758 Balcones Dr., Ste. 201, Austin, TX 78731; 6,008.

Daughters of Union Veterans of the Civil War (1885), 503 S. Walnut St., Springfield, IL 62704; 4,000.

Deaf, Alexander Graham Bell Assn. for the (1890), 3417 Volta Pl. NW, Wash., DC 20007; 5,000.

Deaf, Natl. Assn. of the (1880), 814 Thayer Ave., Silver Spring, MD 20910; 20,000.

Death and Dying, Natl. Council on (1990), 250 W. 50th St., N.Y., NY 10019; 120,000.

Defense Preparedness Assn., Amer. (1919), 2101 Wilson Blvd., Ste. 400, Arlington, VA 22209; 40,000.

Delta Kappa Gamma Society Intl. (1929), P.O. Box 1589, Austin, TX 78767; 164,000.

Deltiologists of America (1960), P.O. Box 8, Norwood, PA 19074; 1,600.

Democratic Natl. Committee, (1792), 430 S. Capitol St. SE, Wash., DC 20003; 380.

DeMolay, Intl. Council, Order of (1919), 10200 N. Executive Hills Blvd., Kansas City, MO 64153; 2 mln.

Dental Assn., Amer. (1859), 211 E. Chicago Ave., Chicago, IL 60611; 140,000.

Descendants of the Colonial Clergy, Society of the (1933), 30 Leewood Rd., Wellesley, MA 02181; 1,400.

Descendants of the Signers of the Declaration of Independence (1907), 1300 Locust St., Phila., PA 19107; 937.

Descendants of Washington's Army at Valley Forge, Society of (1976), P.O. Box 915, Valley Forge, PA 19482-0915.

Diabetes Assn., Amer. (1940), 1660 Duke St., Alexandria, VA 22314; 259,000.

Dialect Society, Amer. (1889), c/o Allan Metcalf, English Dept., MacMurray College, Jacksonville, IL 62650; 600.

Direct Marketing Assn. (1917), 6 E. 43d St., N.Y., NY 10017.

Directors Guild of America (1936), 7950 Sunset Blvd., Los Angeles, CA 90046; 7,800.

Disabled Amer. Veterans (1920), 3725 Alexandria Pike, Cold Spring, KY 41076; 1.09 mln.

Disc Sports, U.S. (1982), 1090 S. Avenue, #3, Rochester, NY 14620; 14,750.

Dogs on Stamps Study Unit, Amer. Topical Assn. (1979), 3208 Hana Rd., Edison, NJ 08817; 250.

Dowsers, Amer. Society of (1961), Brainerd St., Danville, VT 05828; 3,500.

Dozenal Society of America (1945), Math Dept., Nassau Community College, Garden City, NY 11530; 130.

Dracula Society, Count (1962), 334 W. 54th St., Los Angeles, CA 90037; 500.

Drug, Chemical and Allied Trades Assn. (1890), 2 Roosevelt Ave., Syosset, NY 11791; 2,000.

Ducks Unlimited (1937), One Waterfowl Way at Gilmer Rd., Long Grove, IL 60014; 640,000.

Dutch Settlers Soc. of Albany (1924), 6 DeLucia Terr., Albany, NY 12211; 271.

Eagles, Fraternal Order of (1898), 12660 West Capitol Dr., Brookfield, WI 53055; 1.1 mln.

Earth, Friends of the (1969), 530 7th St. SE, Washington, DC 20003; 20,000.

Easter Seal Society, Natl. (1919), 70 E. Lake St., Chicago, IL 60601.

Eastern Star, General Grand Chapter, Order of the (1876), 1618 New Hampshire Ave. NW, Wash., DC 20009; 1.5 mln.

Economic Assn., Amer. (1885), 1313 21st Ave. So., #809, Nashville, TN 37212; 20,000.

Economic Development, Committee for (1942), 1700 K St., NW, Suite 700, Washington, DC 20006; 365.

Edison Electric Institute (1933), 701 Pennsylvania Ave. NW, Wash., DC 20004-2696; 180 corporations.

Education, Amer. Assn. for Adult and Continuing (1982), 1201 16th St. NW, Suite 230, Wash., DC 20036; 3,500.

Education, Amer. Council on (1918), One Dupont Circle NW, #800, Wash., DC 20036; 1,600 schools.

Associations and Societies

Education, Amer. Soc. for Engineering (1893), 11 Dupont Circle NW, Suite 200, Washington, DC 20036; 10,000+.

Education, Council for Advancement & Support of (1974), 11 Dupont Circle NW, Wash., DC 20036; 2,500 schools.

Education, Council for Basic (1956), 725 15th St. NW, Wash., DC 20005; 10,000.

Education, Institute of Intl. (1919), 809 United Nations Plaza, N.Y., NY 10017.

Education, Natl. Committee for Citizens in (1973), 10840 Little Patuxent Pwky., Suite 301, Columbia, MD 21044.

Education, Natl. Society for the Study of (1901), 5835 Kimbark Ave., Chicago, IL 60637; 2,400.

Education Assn., Natl. (1857), 1201 16th St. NW, Wash., DC 20036; 1.9 mln.

Education Society, Comparative and Intl. (1956), Univ. of S. California, Univ. Park, Los Angeles, CA 90089; 2,500.

Education of Young Children, Natl. Assn. for the (1926), 1834 Connecticut Ave. NW, Wash., DC 20009; 70,000.

Educational Exchange, Council on Intl. (1947), 205 E. 42d St., N.Y., NY 10017; 180 organizations.

Educational Research Assn., Amer. (1916), 1230 17th St. NW, Wash., DC 20036; 14,000+.

8th Air Force Historical Society (1975), P.O. Box 727, Oldsmar, FL 34677; 15,000.

82nd Airborne Division Assn., Inc. (1944), P.O. Box 1442, Bloomington, IN 47402; 20,200.

88th Infantry Division Assn., Inc. (1948), P.O. Box 925, Havertown, PA 19083; 5,152.

Electrical and Electronics Engineers, Institute of (1884), 345 E. 47th St., N.Y., NY 10017; 300,000.

Electrical Manufacturers Assn., Natl. (1926), 2101 L St. NW, Wash., DC 20037; 560 companies.

Electrochemical Society (1902), 10 S. Main St., Pennington, NJ 08534-2896; 6,000.

Electronic Industries Assn. (1924), 2001 Pennsylvania Ave., Wash., DC 20006-1813; 1,058 companies.

Electronics Sales & Service Dealers Assn., Natl. (1973), 2708 W. Berry, Ft. Worth, TX 76109; 1,400.

Electronics Technicians, Intl. Society of Certified (1970), 2708 W. Berry, Ft. Worth, TX 76109; 1,400.

Electroplaters' and Surface Finishers' Society, Amer. (1909), 12644 Research Pkwy, Orlando, FL 32826; 8,600.

Elks of the U.S.A., Benevolent and Protective Order of (1868), 2750 Lakeview Ave., Chicago, IL 60614; 1.5 mln.

Energy Research Institute, Clean (1974), 1251 Memorial Dr., 219 MacArthur Engineering Bldg., Coral Gables, FL, 33146.

Energy, Intl. Assn. for Hydrogen (1975), P.O. Box 242866, Miami, FL 33124-8266; 2,500.

Engine and Boat Manufacturers, Natl. Assn. of (1904), 401 N. Michigan Ave., Chicago, IL 60611.

Engineering, Natl. Academy of (1964), 2101 Constitution Ave. NW, Wash., DC 20418; 1,535.

Engineering, Soc. for the Advancement of Material & Process (1944), P.O. Box 2459, Covina, CA 91722; 10,000.

Engineering Societies, Amer. Assn. of (1979), 345 E. 47th St., N.Y., NY 10017; 38 societies.

Engineering Society of N. America, Illuminating (1906), 345 E. 47th St., N.Y., NY 10017; 9,641.

Engineering Trustees, United (1904), 345 E. 47th St., N.Y., NY 10017.

Engineers, Amer. Inst. of Chemical (1908), 345 E. 47th St., N.Y., N.Y. 10003; 52,000.

Engineers, Amer. Institute of Mining, Metallurgical and Petroleum (1871), 345 E. 47th St., N.Y., NY 10017.

Engineers, Amer. Soc. of Agricultural (1907), 2950 Niles Rd., St. Joseph, MI 49085-9659; 10,000.

Engineers, Amer. Soc. of Civil (1852), 345 E. 47th St., N.Y., NY 10017; 111,112.

Engineers, Amer. Soc. of Naval (1888), 1452 Duke St., Alexandria, VA 22314; 8,500.

Engineers, Amer. Soc. of Plumbing (1964), 3617 Thousand Oaks Blvd., #210, Westlake Vlge, CA 91362-3625; 4,500.

Engineers, Amer. Soc. of Safety (1911), 1800 E. Oakton St., Des Plains, IL 60018; 21,000.

Engineers, Assn. of Conservation (1961), Missouri Conservation Dept., P.O. Box 180, Jefferson City, MO 65102; 200.

Engineers, Assn. of Energy (1977), 4025 Pleasantdale Rd., Suite 420, Atlanta, GA 30340; 6,200.

Engineers, Inst. of Industrial (1948), 25 Technology Park, Atlanta, GA 30092; 43,000.

Engineers, Inst. of Transportation (1930), Suite 410, 525 School St. NW, Wash., DC 20024, 7,700.

Engineers, Natl. Society of Professional (1934), 1420 King St., Alexandria, VA 22314; 75,000.

Engineers, Soc. of Fire Protection (1950), 60 Batterymarch St., Boston, MA 02110; 3,550.

Engineers, Soc. of Logistics (1966), 125 W. Park Loop, Suite 201, Huntsville, AL 35806; 10,000.

Engineers, Soc. of Manufacturing (1932), One SME Drive, P.O. Box 930, Dearborn, MI 48121; 80,000.

Engineers, Society of Mining (1871), 8307 Shaffer Pkwy., Littleton, CO 80127; 23,058.

Engineers, Society of Plastics (1942), 14 Fairfield Dr., Brookfield Ctr., CT 06805; 25,000.

Engineers, Society of Tribologists & Lubrication (1944), 838 Busse Hwy., Park Ridge, IL 60068; 4,100.

English Assn., College (1939), English Dept., Nazareth College, 4245 East Ave., Rochester, NY 14610; 1,450.

English-Speaking Union of the U.S. (1920), 16 E. 69th St., N.Y., NY 10021; 27,000.

Entomological Society of America (1889), 9301 Annapolis Rd., Lanham, MD 20706.

Environmental Health Assn., Natl. (1937), 720 S. Colorado Blvd., Suite 970, Denver, CO 80222; 5,000.

Epigraphic Society, Inc., The (1974), 6625 Bamburgh Dr., San Diego, CA 92117; 1,100.

Esperanto League for North America (1932), P.O. Box 1129, El Cerrito, CA 94530; 937.

Evangelism Crusades, Intl. (1959), 14617 Victory Blvd., Van Nuys, CA 91411.

Exchange Club, Natl. (1911), 3050 Central Ave., Toledo, OH 43606-1757; 41,949.

Executive Management Services Corp. (1973), P.O. Box 58, Atlantic Beach, NY 11509.

Experiment in Intl. Living/School for Intl. Training (1932), P.O. Box 676, Kipling Rd., Brattleboro, VT 05302; 65,000.

Fairs & Expositions, Intl. Assn. of (1919), P.O. Box 985, Springfield, MO 65801; 1,500.

Family Life, Natl. Alliance for, Inc. (1973), Ste. 4, 225 Jericho Tpk., Floral Park, NY 11001; 499.

Family Relations, Natl. Council on (1938), 3989 Central Ave. NE, Suite 550, Minneapolis, MN 55421; 4,000.

Family Service Assn. of America (1911), 11700 W. Lake Park Dr., Park Pl, Milwaukee, WI 53224; 286 agencies.

Farm Bureau Federation, Amer. (1919), 225 Touhy Ave., Park Ridge, IL 60068; 3.8 mln. families.

Farmers of America, Future (1928), 5632 Mt. Vernon Memorial Hwy., Alexandria, VA 22309-0160; 397,107.

Farmers Union, Natl. (1902), Denver, CO 80251; 250,000.

Farmers' Educational and Co-Operative Union of America (1902), 10065 E. Harvard Ave., Denver, CO 80231; 250,000.

Fast Draw Assn., World (1975), 1026 Llagas Rd., Morgan Hill, CA 95037; 320.

Fat Acceptance, Natl. Assn. to Advance (NAAFA) (1969), P.O. Box 188620, Sacramento, CA 95818; 2,500.

Federal Employees Veterans Assn. (1954), Leslie Harris, 1024 E. Cliveden St., Phila., PA 19119; 4,562.

Feminists for Life of America (1972), 811 E. 47th St., Kansas City, MO 64110; 2,000.

Fencers League of America, Amateur (1893), 601 Curtis St., Albany, CA 94706; 8,000.

Film Library Assn., Educational (1943), 45 John St., Suite 301, N.Y., NY 10038; 1,600.

Financial Analysts Federation (1945), #5 Boar's Head Lane, Charlottesville, VA 22901; 17,000.

Financial Executives Institute (1931), 10 Madison Ave., P.O. Box 1938, Morristown, NJ 07960, 13,200.

Financiers, Intl. Soc. of (1979), P.O. Box 18508, Asheville, NC 28814; 400.

Fire Chiefs, Intl. Assn. of (1873), 1329 18th St. NW, Wash., DC 20036; 9,500.

Fire Marshals Assn. of No. America (1906), NFPA, Batterymarch Pk., Quincy, MA 02269-9101.

Fire Protection Assn., Natl. (1896), Batterymarch Park, Quincy MA 02269; 38,000.

Fish Assn., Intl. Game (1939), 3000 E. Las Olas Blvd., Ft. Lauderdale, FL 33316; 25,000.

Fisheries Institute, Natl. (1945), 2000 M St., Washington, DC 20036; 1,250.

Fishes, Soc. for the Protection of Old (1967), School of Fisheries, WH-10 Univ. of Washington, Seattle, WA 98195; 250.

Fishing Institute, Sport (1949), 1010 Massachusetts Ave. NW, Suite 100, Wash., DC 20001; 230.

Fishing Tackle Manufacturers Assn., Amer. (1950), 1250 Grove Ave., Barrington, IL 60010.

Flag Research Center, The (1962), 3 Edgehill Rd., Winchester, MA 01890; 1,200.

Flight Attendants, Assn. of (1973), 1625 Massachusetts Ave. NW, Wash., DC 20036; 28,000.

Florida Tobacco & Candy Assn. (1976), 217 S. Adams St., Tallahassee, FL 32302; 35.

Fly Fishers, Fed. of (1965), Box 1088, 200 Yellowstone Ave., W. Yellowstone, MT 59758; 12,000.

Flying Disc Fed., World (1985), Gnejsvägen 24, 85240; Sundsvall, Sweden; 34,592.

Food Brokers Assn., Natl. (1904), 1010 Massachusetts Ave. NW, Wash., DC 20001; 1,800 companies.

Food Institute, Amer. Frozen (1942), 1764 Old Meadow Ln., Suite 350, McLean, VA 22102; 500 firms.

Footwear Industries Assn., Amer. (1871), 3700 Market St., Philadelphia, PA 19104; 180.

Foreign Relations, Council on (1921), 58 E. 68th St., N.Y., NY 10021; 2,510.

Foreign Student Affairs, Natl. Assn. for (1948), 1860 19th St. NW, Wash., DC 20009; 5,500.

Foreign Study, Amer. Institute for (1964), 102 Greenwich Ave., Greenwich, CT 06830; 300,000.

Foreign Trade Council, Inc., Natl. (1914), 1625 K St. NW, Washington, DC 20002; 500 companies.

Forensic Sciences, Amer. Academy of (1948), 218 E. Cache La Poudre, Colorado Springs, CO 80903; 3,500.

Forest Council (1932), 1250 Connecticut Ave. NW, Suite 320, Washington, DC 20036.

Forest History Society (1946), 701 Vickers Ave., Durham, NC 27701.

Forest Products Assn., Natl. (1902), 1250 Connecticut Ave. NW, Wash., DC 20036; 700 companies.

Forest Products Research Society (1947), 2801 Marshall Ct., Madison, WI 53705; 3,600.

Foresters, Society of Amer. (1900), 5400 Grosvenor La., Bethesda, MD 20814; 19,500.

Forestry Assn., Amer. (1875), 1516 P St. NW, Wash., DC 20005; 40,000.

Fortean Organization, Intl. (1965), P.O. Box 367, Arlington, VA 22205; 700+.

Founders and Patriots of Amer., The Order of the (1896), 3813 Acapulco Ct., Irving, TX 75062; 1,250.

Foundrymen's Society, Amer. (1896), Golf & Wolf Rds., Des Plaines, IL 60016; 13,255.

4-H Clubs (1901-1905), Extension Service, U.S. Dept of Agriculture, Wash., DC 20250; 5.8 mln.

Franklin D. Roosevelt Philatelic Society (1963), 154 Laguna Ct., St. Augustine Shores, FL 32086; 696.

Freedom, Young Americans for (1960), Box 1002, Woodland Rd. Sterling, VA 22170; 80,000.

Freedom of Information Center (1958), School of Journalism, Univ. of Missouri, Columbia, MO 65211.

Freedoms Foundation at Valley Forge (1949), Valley Forge, PA 19481; 5,000.

Friedreich's Ataxia Group in America (1969), P.O. Box 11116, Oakland, CA 94611; 2,100+.

French Institute (1911), 22 E. 60th St., N.Y., NY 10022.

Friendship and Good Will, Intl. Soc. of (1978), 211 W. 4th Ave., P.O. Box 2637, Gastonia, NC 28053-2637.

Frisbee Assn., Intl. (1967), 900 E. El Monte, San Gabriel, CA 91776; 110,000.

Funeral and Memorial Societies, Continental Assn. of (1963), 2001 S. St. NW, Suite 530, Washington, DC 20009.

GASP (Group Against Smokers' Pollution) (1971), P.O. Box 632, College Park, MD 20740; 10,000.

Gamblers Anonymous (1957), 3255 Wilshire Blvd., #610, Los Angeles, CA 90010; 1,200 groups.

Garden Club of Amer. (1913), 598 Madison Ave., N.Y., NY 10022; 15,000.

Garden Clubs, Natl. Council of State (1929), 4401 Magnolia Ave., St. Louis, MO 63110; 308,623.

Garden Clubs of America, Men's (1932), 5560 Merle Hay Rd., Johnston, IA 50131; 9,500.

Gas Appliance Manufacturers Assn. (1935), 1901 N. Ft. Myer Dr., Arlington, VA 22209; 240 companies.

Gas Assn., Amer. (1918), 1515 Wilson Blvd., Arlington, VA 22209; 300 companies; 3,000 individuals.

Gay and Lesbian Task Force, Natl. (1973), 1517 U St. NW, Washington, DC 20009; 17,000.

Genealogical Society, Natl. (1903), 4527 17th St. N., Arlington, VA 22207; 9,500.

Genetic Assn., Amer. (1903), P.O. Box 39, Buckeystown, MD 21717; 3,000.

Geographers, Assn. of Amer. (1904), 1710 16th St. NW, Wash., DC 20009-3198; 6,300.

Geographic Education, Natl. Council for (1915), 16A Leonard Hall, IUPA, Indiana, PA 15705; 3,500.

Geographic Society, Natl. (1888), 1145 17 St. NW, Wash., DC 20036; 10 mln.

Geographical Society, Amer. (1851), 156 Fifth Ave., Suite 600, N.Y., NY 10010-7002; 1,400.

Geolinguistics, Amer. Society of (1965), University of Rhode Island, Kingston, RI 02892; 70.

Geological Institute, Amer. (1948), 4220 King St., Alexandria, VA 22302; 21 societies.

Geological Society of America (1888), 3300 Penrose Pl., P.O. Box 9140, Boulder, CO 80301; 16,300.

Geologists, Assn. of Engineering (1960), 323 Boston Post Rd. Suite 2D, Sudbury, MA 01776; 2,800.

Geologists, Amer. Assn. of Petroleum (1917), 1444 S. Boulder, Tulsa, OK 74119; 32,000.

Geophysicists, Society of Exploration (1930), 8801 S. Yale Ave., Tulsa OK 74137; 14,854.

Geriatrics Society, Amer. (1942), 770 Lexington Ave., Suite 400, N.Y., NY 10021; 6,000.

Gideons Intl. (1899), 2900 Lebanon Rd., Nashville, TN 37214; 104,000.

Gifted & Talented Club, Natl. (1987), 4049 Ross Park Dr., San Jose, CA 95118; 200.

Gifted Children, Amer. Assn. for (1946), 15 Gramercy Park, N.Y., NY 10003.

Gifted Children, Natl. Assn. for (1954), 4175 Lovell Rd., Suite 140, Circle Pines, MN 55014; 6,500.

Girls Clubs of America (1945), 30 E. 33d St., N.Y., NY 10016; 250,000+.

Girl Scouts of the U.S.A. (1912), 830 Third Ave., N.Y., NY 10022; 2.9 mln.

Gladiolus Council, No. Amer. (1945), 9338 Manzanita Dr., Sun City, AZ 85373; 1,275.

Gold Star Mothers, Amer. (1929), 2128 Leroy Pl. NW, Wash., DC 20008; 4,000.

Golf Association, U.S. (1894), Liberty Corner Rd., Far Hills, NJ 07931; 6,187 clubs.

Goose Island Bird & Girl Watching Society (1960), 301 Arthur Ave., Park Ridge, IL 60068; 831.

Gospel Music Assn. (1964), 38 Music Square W., Nashville, TN 37203; 3,000.

Governing Boards, Assn. of (1922), 1 Dupont Circle, Ste. 400, Washington, DC 20036; 1,107.

Government Finance Officers Assn. (1906), 180 N. Michigan Ave., Suite 800, Chicago, IL 60601; 12,000.

Gov't. Funding of Soc. Serv., Greater Wash. Organizations for (1981), 6612 Virginia View Ct. NW, Wash., DC 20816.

Graduate Schools in the U.S., Council of (1961), One Dupont Circle NW, Wash., DC 20036; 365 institutions.

Grandmother Clubs of America, Natl. Federation of (1934), 203 N. Wabash Ave., Chicago, IL 60601; 10,000.

Grange, Natl. (1867), 1616 H St. NW, Wash., DC 20006; 330,000.

Graphic Artists, Society of Amer. (1915), 32 Union Sq., East, N.Y., NY 10003; 203.

Graphic Arts, Amer. Institute of (1914), 1059 Third Ave., N.Y., NY 10021; 6,000.

Gray Panthers (1970), 1424 16th St. NW, Suite L-1, Wash., DC 20036; 70,000.

Greek-Amer. War Veterans in America, Natl. Legion of (1938), 739 W. 186th St., N.Y., NY 10033; 11.

Green Mountain Club, The (1910), 43 State St., Box 889, Montpelier, VT 05601; 5,550.

Grocers, Natl. Assn. of (1893), 1825 Samuel Morse Dr., Reston, VA 22090.

Grocery Manufacturers of America (1908), 1010 Wisconsin Ave., Suite 800, Wash., DC 20007; 137 companies.

Guide Dog Foundation for the Blind (1946), 341 E. Jericho Tpke., Smithtown, NY 11787-2976.

Gyro Intl. (1912), 1096 Mentor Ave., Painesville, OH 44077; 5,044.

HIAS (Hebrew Immigrant Aid Society) (1880), 200 Park Ave. S, N.Y., NY 10003; 6,000.

Hadassah, the Women's Zionist Organization of America (1912), 50 W. 58th St., N.Y., NY 10019; 385,000.

Hairdressers and Cosmetologists Assn., Natl. (1921), 3510 Olive St., St. Louis, MO 63103; 50,406.

Handball Assn., U.S. (1951), 930 N. Benton Ave., Tucson, AZ 85711; 10,000.

Handgun, Intl. Metallic Silhouette Assn. (1976), P.O. Box 368, Burlington, IA 52601; 1,300.

Handicapped, Federation of the (1935), 211 W. 14th St., N.Y., NY 10011; 650.

Handicapped, Natl. Assn. of the Physically (1958), Bethesda Scarlet Oaks, #117, 440 Lafayette Ave., Cincinnati, OH 45220-1000; 700.

Health Council, Natl. (1920), 350 Fifth Ave., Suite 1118, N.Y., NY 10017; 90 natl. organizations.

Health, Physical Education, Recreation and Dance, Amer. Alliance for (1885), 1900 Association Dr., Reston, VA 22091.

Hearing Aid Society, Natl. (1951), 20361 Middlebelt Rd., Livonia, MI 48152; 4,000.

Hearing and Speech Action, Natl. Assn. for (1910), 10801 Rockville Pike, Rockville, MD 20852; 3,500.

Heart Assn., Amer. (1924), 7320 Greenville Ave., Dallas TX 75231; 144,000.

Hearts, Mended (1951), 7320 Greenville Ave., Dallas TX 75231; 18,000.

Heating, Refrigerating & Air Conditioning Engineers, Amer. Soc. of (1894), 1791 Tullie Circle NE, Atlanta, GA 30329.

Helicopter Assn. Intl. (1948), 1619 Duke St., Alexandria, VA 22314; 1,500.

Helicopter Society Intl., Amer. (1943), 217 N. Washington St., Alexandria VA 22314; 8,000.

Hemispheric Affairs, Council on (1975), 1612 20th St. NW, Wash., DC 20009; 2,400.

High School Assns., Natl. Federation of State (1920), P.O. Box 20626, 11724 Plaza Circle, Kansas City, MO 64195; 51.

High Twelve Internatl. (1921), 11155-B2 South Towne Square, St. Louis, MO 63123; 26,000.

Hiking Society, Amer. (1977), 1015 31st St. NW, Wash., DC 20007-4490; 4,500.

Historians, Organization of Amer. (1907), 112 N. Bryan St., Bloomington, IN 47408; 12,000.

Historical Assn., Amer. (1884), 400 A St. SE, Wash., DC 20003; 14,000.

Historic Preservation, Natl. Trust for (1966), 1785 Massachusetts Ave. NW, Wash., DC 20036; 240,000.

Hockey Assn. of the U.S., Amateur (1937), 2997 Broadmoor Valley Rd., Colorado Springs, CO 80906; 300,000.

Holy Cross of Jerusalem, Order of (1965), 853 Seventh Ave., N.Y., NY 10019; 2,225.

Home Builders, Natl. Assn. of (1942), 15th & M Sts. NW, Wash., DC 20005; 157,479.

Home Economics Assn., Amer. (1909), 1555 King St., Alexandria, VA 22314; 23,038.

Homemakers of America, Future (1945), 1910 Association Dr., Reston, VA 22091; 281,000+.

Homemakers Council, Natl. Extension (1936), 4089 Snake Island Rd., Sturgeon Bay, WI 54235; 355,000.

Hospital Marketing and Public Relations of the Amer. Hospital, Amer. Soc. for (1964), 840 N. Lake Shore Dr., 9E, Chicago, IL 60611; 3,100.

Horatio Alger Soc. (1965), 4907 Allison Dr., Lansing, MI 48910; 300.

Horse Council, American (1969), 1700 K St. NW, #300, Washington, DC 20006; 2,100.

Horse Protection Assn., Amer. (1966), 1000 29th St. NW, Suite T-100, Wash., DC 20007; 8,000.

Horse Show Assn. of America Ltd., Natl. (1883), 680 5th Ave., #1602, N.Y., NY 10019.

Horse Shows Assn., Amer. (1917), 220 E. 42 St., N.Y., NY 10017-5806; 54,000+.

Hospital Association, Amer. (1899), 840 N. Lake Shore Dr., Chicago, IL 60611; 40,000.

Hospital Marketing and Public Relations, Amer. Society for (1964), 840 N. Lake Shore Dr., Chicago, IL 60611; 3,167.

Hotel & Motel Assn., Amer. (1910), 888 Seventh Ave., N.Y., NY 10106; 10,000.

Human Resource Management, Society for (1947), 606 N. Washington St., Alexandria, VA 22314; 44,200.

Human Rights and Social Justice, Americans for (1977), P.O. Box 6258, Ft. Worth, TX 76115.

Humane Society of the U.S. (1954), 2100 L St. NW, Wash., DC 20037; 1 mln.+.

Humanics, American (1949), 4601 Madison Ave., Kansas City, MO 64112; 2,000.

Hydrogen Energy, Intl. Assn. for (1975), P.O. Box 248266, Coral Gables, FL 33124; 2,000.

Idaho, U.S.S. (BB-42) Assn. (1957), P.O. Box 11247, San Diego, CA 92111; 1,100.

Identification, Intl. Assn. for (1916), P.O. Box 2423, Alameda, CA 94501; 2,850.

Illustrators, Society of (1901), 128 E. 63 St., N.Y., NY 10021; 975.

Industrial Democracy, League for (1905), 181 Hudson St., N.Y., NY 10013; 1,500.

Industrial Designers Society of America (1965), 1142-E Walker Rd., Great Falls, VA 22066; 2,030.

Industrial Engineers, Amer. Institute of (1948), 25 Technology Park, Norcross, GA 30092; 35,000.

Industrial Health Foundation (1935), 34 Penn Circle West, Pittsburgh, PA 15206; 170 companies.

Industrial Security, Amer. Soc. for (1955), 1655 N. Ft. Myer Dr., Suite 1200, Arlington, VA 22209; 25,000.

Information, Freedom of, Center (1958), P.O. Box 858, Columbia, MO 65205.

Information and Image Management, Assn. for (1945), 1100 Wayne Ave., Ste. 1100, Silver Springs, MD 20910; 7,808.

Information Industry Assn. (1968), 555 New Jersey Ave. NW, Suite 800, Wash., DC 20001; 600 companies.

Insurance Assn., Amer. (1964), 1130 Connecticut Ave. NW, Suite 1000, Wash., DC 20036; 220 companies.

Insurance Society, Inc., Intl. (1965), Rm. 328, Farrah Hall, Tuscaloosa, AL 35487; 900.

Intelligence Officers, Assn. of Former (1975), 6723 Whittier Ave., Suite 303A, McLean, VA 22101; 3,500.

Intercollegiate Athletics, Natl. Assn. of (1936), 1221 Baltimore Ave., Kansas City, MO 64105; 490 schools.

Interior Designers, Amer. Society of (1975), 1430 Broadway, N.Y., NY 10018; 28,000.

International Interculture Programs, AFS (1947), 313 E. 43rd St., N.Y., NY 10017; 100,000.

Intertel, Inc. (1966), P.O. Box 150580, Lakewood, CO 80215; 2,200.

Inventors, Amer. Assn. of (1891), 2020 Pennsylvania Ave. NW, Wash., DC 20006; 5,727.

Investment Clubs, Natl. Assn. of (1951), 1515 E. Eleven Mile Rd., Royal Oak, MI 48067; 65,000.

Investment Management and Research, Assn. for (1990), 5 Boar's Head Ln., Charlottesville, VA 22901; 21,000.

Investors Corp., Natl. Assn. of (1951), 1515 E. Eleven Mile Rd., Royal Oak, MI 48067; 115,000.

Irish-American Cultural Inst. (1962), 2115 Summit Ave., St. Paul, MN 55105.

Iron Castings Society (1897), 455 State St., Des Plaines, IL 60016; 200 firms.

Iron and Steel Engineers, Assn. of (1907), Three Gateway Center, Suite 2350, Pittsburgh, PA 15222; 11,856.

Iron and Steel Institute, Amer. (1908), 1133 15th St. NW, Wash., DC 20005-2701; 1,200.

Italian Historical Society of America (1949), 111 Columbia Heights, Bklyn., NY 11201.

Italy-America Chamber of Commerce (1887), 350 Fifth Ave., N.Y., NY 10118; 850.

Izaak Walton League of America, The (1922), 1401 Wilson Blvd., Level B, Arlington, VA 22209; 50,000.

(Jesse) James Farm, Friends of, (1979), Rt. 2, Box 236, Kearney, MO 64060; 300.

Jamestowne Society (1936), P.O. Box 14523, Richmond, VA 23221; 2,721.

Jane Austen Society of N. Amer. (1979), 4169 Lions Ave., N. Vancouver, B.C., Canada, V7R 3S2; 2,400.

Japanese Amer. Citizens League (1929), 1765 Sutter St., San Francisco, CA 94115; 27,000.

Jaycees, U.S. (1920), 4 W. 21st St., Tulsa, OK 74114; 240,000.

Jewish Appeal, United (1939), 99 Park Avenue, N.Y., NY 10016.

Jewish Book Council (1943), 15 E. 26th St., N.Y., NY 10010.

Jewish Committee, Amer. (1906), 165 E. 56th St., N.Y., NY 10022; 50,000.

Jewish Congress, Amer. (1918), 15 E. 84th St., N.Y., NY 10028; 50,000.

Jewish Federations, Council of (1932), 730 Broadway, N.Y., NY 10003; 200 agencies.

Jewish Historical Society, Amer. (1892), 2 Thornton Rd., Waltham, MA 02154; 3,400.

Jewish War Veterans of the U.S.A. (1896), 1811 R St. NW, Wash., DC 20009; 100,000.

Jewish Welfare Bd. Natl. (1917), 15 E. 26th St., N.Y., NY 10010.

Jewish Women, Natl. Council of (1893), 53 W. 23rd St., N.Y., NY 10010; 100,000.

Job's Daughters, Internatl. Order of (1920), 233 W. 6th St., Papillion, NE 68046; 32,000.

Jockey Club (1894), 380 Madison Ave., N.Y., NY 10017; 90.

John Birch Society (1958), 395 Concord Ave., Belmont, MA 02178; 25,000.

John Pelham Historical Assn. (1982), 7 Carmel Terr., Hampton, VA 23666; 125.

Joseph Diseases Foundation, Intl. (1977), P.O. Box 2550, Livermore, CA 94550; 4,500.

Journalists, Society of Professional (Sigma Delta Chi) (1909), 53 W. Jackson Blvd., Suite 731, Chicago, IL 60604.

Journalists and Authors, Amer. Society of (1948), 1501 Broadway, Suite 1907, N.Y., NY 10036; 750+.

Judaism, Amer. Council for (1943), 298 Fifth Ave., N.Y., NY 10001; 20,000.

Judicature Society, Amer. (1913), 25 E. Washington, Chicago, IL 60602; 20,000.

Juggler's Assn., Intl. (1947), P.O. Box 3707, Akron, OH 44314-3707; 3,000.

Junior Achievement (1919), 550 Summer St., Stamford, CT 06901; 300,000.

Junior Auxiliaries, Natl. Assn. of (1941), 845 S. Main, Greenville, MS 38701; 8,950.

Junior Colleges, Amer. Assn. of Community and (1920), One Dupont Circle NW, Wash., DC 20036; 900.

Junior Leagues, Assn. of (1921), 660 First Ave., N.Y., NY 10016; 189,000.

Kennel Club, Amer. (1884), 51 Madison Ave., N.Y., NY 10010; 130 clubs.

Kidney Fund, Amer. (1971), 6110 Executive Blvd., #1010, Rockville, MD 20852.

Kiwanis Intl. (1915), 3636 Woodview Trace, Indianapolis, IN 46268-3196; 320,000.

Klinefelter's Syndrome Assn. of Canada (1988), P.O. Box 5000, Penetanguishene, Ontario, Canada L0K 1P0.

Knights of Columbus (1882), One Columbus Plaza, New Haven, CT 06507; 1.4 mln.

Knights of Pythias (1864), 2785 E. Desert Inn Rd., #150, Las Vegas, NV 89121; 96,000.

Knights Templar U.S.A., Grand Encampment (1816), 14 E. Jackson Blvd., Suite 1700, Chicago, IL 60604-2293; 295,000.

La Leche League Intl. (1956), 9616 Minneapolis Ave., P.O. Box 1209, Franklin Park, IL 60131; 50,000.

Lambs, The (1874), 3 W. 51st St., N.Y., NY 10019; 185.

Landscape Architects, Amer. Society of (1899), 1733 Connecticut Ave., NW, Wash., DC 20009; 7,000.

Law, Amer. Society of International (1906), 2223 Massachusetts Ave. NW, Washington, DC 20008; 4,300.

Law Enforcement Officers Assn., Amer. (1966), 1000 Connecticut Ave. NW, Suite 9, Wash., DC 20036; 50,000.

Law Libraries, Amer. Assn. of (1906), 53 W. Jackson Blvd., Chicago, IL 60604; 4,700.

Law and Social Policy, Center for (1969), 1751 N St. NW, Wash., DC 20036.

Learned Societies, Amer. Council of (1919), 228 E. 45th St., N.Y., NY 10017; 45 societies.

Lefthanders, League of (1975), P.O. Box 89, New Milford, NJ 07646; 1,200.

Lefthanders Intl. (1975), P.O. Box 8249, Topeka, KS 66608; 30,000.

Legal Administrators, Assn. of (1971), 175 E. Hawthorn Pkwy. #325, Vernon Hills, IL 60061-1428; 6,700.

Legion of Valor of the U.S.A. (1890), 92 Oak Leaf Lane, Chapel Hill, NC 27516; 750.

Leif Ericson Society (1962), Box 301, Chicago, IL 60690-0301; 1,200.

Leprosy Missions, Amer. (1906), One Broadway, Elmwood Park, NJ 07407.

Leukemia Society of America (1949), 733 Third Ave., N.Y., NY 10017; 57 chapters.

Lewis and Clark Trail Heritage Foundation, Inc. (1969), P.O. Box 3434, Great Falls, MT 59403; 1,450.

Lewis Carroll Society of N. America (1974), 617 Rockford Rd., Silver Spring, MD 20902; 325.

Liberty Lobby (1955), 300 Independence Ave. SE, Wash., DC 20003; 25,000.

Libraries Assn., Special (1909), 1700 18th St., NW, Wash., DC 20009; 12,500.

Library Administration & Management Assn. (1957), 50 E. Huron St., Chicago, IL 60611; 5,074.

Library Assn., Amer. (1876), 50 E. Huron St., Chicago, IL 60611; 50,000.

Library Assn., Medical (1898), 6 N. Michigan Ave., Suite 300, Chicago, IL 60602; 5,000+.

Life, Americans United for (1971), 343 S. Dearborn, Chicago, IL 60604.

Life Insurance, Amer. Council of (1975), 1001 Pennsylvania Ave., NW, Wash., DC 20004; 612 firms.

Life Office Management Assn. (1924), 5770 Powers Ferry Rd., Atlanta, GA 30327; 870 companies.

Life Underwriters, Amer. Soc. of Certified (1929), 270 Bryn Mawr Ave., Byrn Mawr, PA 19010; 28,000.

Life Underwriters, Natl. Assn. of (1890), 1922 F St. NW, Wash., DC 20006; 135,000.

Lighter-Than-Air Society (1952), 1800 Triplett Blvd., Akron, OH 44306; 1,200.

Lions Clubs, Intl. Assn. of (1917), 300 22d St., Oak Brook, IL 60521-8842; 1,363,000.

Litchfield Institute, The (1984), 151 N. Main St., Bristol, CT 06010-0483; 43.

Literacy Intl., Laubach (1955), 1320 Jamesville Ave., Box 131, Syracuse, NY 13210.

Literacy Volunteers of America (1962), 5795 Widewaters Parkway, Syracuse, NY 13214; 80,000.

Little League Baseball (1939), P.O. Box 3485, Williamsport, PA 17701; 16,450 leagues.

Little People of America (1957), P.O. Box 9897, Washington, DC 20016; 5,000.

London Club (1975), Rt. One, Big Springs, KS 66050; 200.

Longwave Club of America (1974), 45 Wildflower Rd., Levittown, PA 19057; 536.

Lung Assn., Amer. (1904), 1740 Broadway, N.Y., NY 10019.

Lutheran Education Assn. (1942), 7400 Augusta St., River Forest, IL 60305; 3,750.

Magazine Publishers Assn. (1919), 575 Lexington Ave., N.Y., NY 10022; 215 publishers.

Magicians, Intl. Brotherhood of (1926), 103 N. Main St., Bluffton, OH 45817; 13,000.

Magicians Assn. Worldwide, Amateur (1988), P.O. Box 8073, East Lynne, MA 01904-0073; 16,000.

Magicians, Society of Amer. (1902), 1333 Cory St., Yellow Springs, OH 45387; 5,500.

Management Assn., Amer. (1923), 135 W. 50th St., N.Y., NY 10020; 75,000.

Management Consultants, Institute of (1968), 230 Park Ave., Suite 544, N.Y., NY 10169; 2,200.

Management Consulting Firms, Assn. of (1929), 230 Park Ave., N.Y., NY 10169; 53 firms.

Manufacturers, Natl. Assn. of (1897), 1776 F St. NW, Wash., DC 20006; 13,000 companies.

Manufacturer's Agents Natl. Assn. (1947), 23016 Mill Creek Rd., P.O. Box 3467, Laguna Hills, CA 92654; 10,000.

March of Dimes Birth Defects Foundation (1938), 1275 Mamaroneck Ave., White Plains, NY 10605.

Marijuana Laws, Natl. Organization for the Reform of (NORML) (1970), 1636 R St. NW, #3, Wash., DC 20009; 10,000.

Marine Corps League (1923), P.O. Box 3070, Merrifield, VA 22116-3070; 34,000.

Marine Manufacturers Assn., Natl. (1904), 401 N. Michigan Ave., Chicago, IL 60611; 1,650 companies.

Marine Technology Society (1963), 1825 K St. NW, Suite 218, Wash., DC 20006; 2,500.

Marketing Assn., Amer. (1934), 250 S. Wacker Dr., Chicago, IL 60606; 49,122.

Masonic Relief Assn. of U.S. and Canada (1885), 32613 Seidel Dr., Burlington, WS 53105; 14,700.

Masonic Service Assn. of the U.S. (1919), 8120 Fenton St., Silver Spring, MD 20910; 43 Grand Lodges.

Masons, Ancient and Accepted Scottish Rite, Southern Jurisdiction, Supreme Council (1801), 1733 16th St. NW, Wash., DC 20009; 575,746.

Masons, Supreme Council 33°, Ancient and Accepted Scottish Rite, Northern Masonic Jurisdiction (1813), 33 Marrett Rd., Lexington, MA 02173; 424,602.

Masons, Royal Arch, General Grand Chapter (1797), 1084 New Circle Rd. NE, Lexington, KY 40805; 290,500.

Mathematical Assn. of America (1915), 1529 Eighteenth Street, NW, Wash., DC 20036; 26,000.

Mathematical Society, Amer. (1888), 201 Charles St., Providence, RI 02904; 27,000.

Mathematical Statistics, Institute of (1935), 3401 Investment Blvd., #7, Hayward, CA 94545; 3,704.

Mathematics, Society for Industrial and Applied (1952), 3600 University City Science Ctr., Phila., PA 19104-2688; 7,645.

Mayflower Descendants, General Society of (1897), 4 Winslow St., P.O. Box 3297, Plymouth, MA 02361; 25,000.

Mayors, U.S. Conference of (1932), 1620 Eye St. NW, Wash., DC 20006; 946 cities.

Mechanical Engineers, Amer. Society of (1880), 345 E. 47th St., N.Y., NY 10017; 120,000.

Mechanics, Amer. Academy of (1969), Dept. of Civil Engineering, Northwestern Univ., Evanston, IL 60201; 1,200.

Medical Assn., Amer. (1847), 535 N. Dearborn St., Chicago, IL 60610; 290,000.

Medical Assn., Natl. (1895), 1012 Tenth St. NW, Wash., DC 20001; 16,000.

Medical Record Assn., Amer. (1928), 875 N. Michigan Ave., Chicago, IL 60611; 28,000.

Medical Technologists, Amer. College of (1942), 5608 Lane, Raytown, MO 64133; 368.

Medieval Academy of America (1926), 1430 Massachusetts Ave., Cambridge, MA 02138; 3,700.

Mensa, Amer. (1960), 2626 E. 14th St., Brooklyn, NY 11235; 55,000.

Mental Health Assn., Natl. (1909), 1021 Prince St., Alexandria, VA 22314; 1 mln.

Mental Health Program Directors, Natl. Assn. of State (1963), 1101 King St., Suite 160, Alexandria, VA 22314; 55.

Mentally Ill, Natl. Alliance for the (1979), 2101 Wilson Blvd., Suite 302, Arlington, VA 22201; 80,000.

Merchant Marine Library Assn., Amer. (1921), One World Trade Center, Suite 1365, N.Y., NY 10048.

Merchant Marine Veterans, Amer. (1983), 905 Cape Coral Pkwy., Cape Coral, FL 33904; 1,734.

Merchant Marine Veterans of WWII, U.S. (1944), P.O. Box 629, San Pedro, CA 90731; 7,126.

Merchants Assn., Natl. Retail (1911), 100 W. 31st St., N.Y., NY 10001; 45,000.

Metal Finishers, Natl. Assn. of (1950), 111 E. Wacker Dr., Suite 600, Chicago, IL 60601; 900.

Metallurgy Institute, Amer. Powder (1959), 105 College Rd. East, Princeton, NJ 08540; 2,750.

Metal Powder Industries Federation, (1943), 105 College Rd. East, Princeton, NJ 08540; 260 cos.

Metals, Amer. Society for (ASM Internatl.) (1913), Metals Park, OH 44073; 53,000.

Meteorological Society, Amer. (1919), 45 Beacon St., Boston, MA 02108; 10,200.

Metric Assn., U.S. (1916), 10245 Andasol Ave., Northridge, CA 91325; 2,000.

Microbiology, Amer. Society for (1899), 1325 Massachusetts Ave. NW, Wash. DC 20005; 37,000.

Mideast Educational and Training Services, America-, (1951), 1100 17th Street, NW, Wash., DC 20036.

Military Order of the Loyal Legion of the U.S.A. (1865), 1805 Pine St., Phila., PA 19103; 792.

Military Order of the Purple Heart of the USA (1932), 5413-B Backlick Rd., Springfield, VA 22151; 21,000.

Military Order of the World Wars (1919), 435 N. Lee St., Alexandria, VA 22314; 15,000.

Mining and Metallurgical Society of America (1908), 275 Madison Ave., N.Y., NY 10016; 295.

Mining, Metallurgy and Exploration, Inc., Society for (1871), 8307 Shaffer Pkwy., Littleton, CO 80127; 20,279.

Ministerial Assn., Amer. (1929), 2210 Wilshire Blvd., Suite 582, Santa Monica, CA 90403; 2,500+.

Missouri Alliance for Historic Preservation (1970), P.O. Box 895, Jefferson City, MO 65102; 250.

Model Railroad Assn., Natl. (1935), 4121 Cromwell Rd., Chattanooga, TN 37421; 24,008.

Modern Language Assn. of America (1883), 10 Astor Pl., N.Y., NY 10003; 31,291.

Modern Language Teachers Assns., Natl. Federation of (1916), Gannon Univ., Erie, PA 16541; 7,200.

Moose, Loyal Order of (1888), Mooseheart, IL 60539; 1.8 mln.

Mothers, American (1935), 301 Park Ave., N.Y., NY 10022; 4,000.

Mothers-in-Law Club Intl. (1970), 420 Adelberg Ln., Cedarhurst, NY 11516; 5,000.

Mothers of Twins Clubs, Natl. Organization of (1960), 12404 Princess Jeanne NE, Albuquerque, NM 87112-4640; 12,000.

Motion Picture Arts & Sciences, Academy of (1927), 8949 Wilshire Blvd., Beverly Hills, CA 90211; 5,300.

Motion Pictures, Natl. Board of Review of (1909), P.O. Box 589, Lenox Hill Sta., N.Y., NY 10021.

Motion Picture & Television Engineers, Society of (1916), 595 West Hartsdale Ave., White Plains, NY 10607; 9,500.

Motor Vehicle Administrators, Amer. Assn. of (1933), 4200 Wilson Blvd.; Suite 600, Arlington, VA 22203; 1,000.

Motor Vehicle Manufacturers Assn. (1900), 7430 2nd Ave., Suite 300, Detroit, MI 48202; 17 companies.

Motorcyclist Assn., American (1924), 33 Collegeview Rd., Westerville, OH 43081; 160,000.

Multiple Sclerosis Society, Natl. (1946), 205 E. 42d St., N.Y., NY 10017; 360,000.

Murray Hill Assn., The (1940), 237 Madison Ave., The Morgan Hotel, N.Y., NY 10016; 100.

Muscular Dystrophy Assn. (1950), 810 Seventh Ave., N.Y., NY 10019.

Museums, Amer. Assn. of (1906), 1055 Thomas Jefferson St. NW, Wash., DC 20007; 8,780.

Music Center, Amer. (1939), 30 W. 26th St., N.Y., NY 10010; 1,800.

Music Council, Natl. (1940), 40 W. 37th St., N.Y., NY 10018; 50 organizations.

Music Educators Natl. Conference (1907), 1902 Association Dr., Reston, VA 22090; 54,069.

Music Scholarship Assn., Amer. (1956), 1826 Carew Tower, Cincinnati, OH 45202; 1,400.

Music Teachers Natl. Assn. (1876), 617 Vine St., Suite 1432, Cincinnati, OH 45202-2439; 22,000+.

Musicological Society, Amer. (1934), 201 S. 34th St., Phila., PA 19104-6313, 3,500.

Music Publishers' Assn., Natl. (1917), 205 E. 42nd St., N.Y., NY 10017; 300.

Muzzle Loading Rifle Assn., Natl. (1933), P.O. Box 67, Friendship, IN 47021; 25,300.

NAACP (Natl. Assn. for the Advancement of Colored People) (1909), 4805 Mt. Hope Drive, Baltimore, MD 21215.

NOT-SAFE (1981), Box 5743-WA, Montecito, CA 93150; 1,491.

Na'amat USA (1925), 200 Madison Ave., N.Y., NY 10016; 50,000.

Narcolepsy and Cataplexy Foundation of Amer. (1975), 1410 York Ave., Suite 2D, N.Y. NY 10021; 3,991.

Narcolepsy Assoc., Amer. (1975), P.O. Box 1187, San Carlos, CA 94070; 4,000.

Narcotics Anonymous (1953), P.O. Box 9999, Van Nuys, CA 91409; 1 million.

National Guard Assn. of the U.S. (1878), One Massachusetts Ave. NW, Wash., DC 20001; 54,000.

Nature Conservancy (1951), 1815 N. Lynn St., Arlington, VA 22209; 436,407.

Naturist Society, The (1980), P.O. Box 132, Oshkosh, WI 54902; 15,000.

Naturopathy Institute, The (1984), P.O. Box 56, Malverne, NY 11565.

Navajo Code Talkers Assn. (1971), Box 1182, Window Rock, AZ 86515; 295.

Naval Institute, U.S. (1873), Preble Hall, U.S. Naval Academy, Annapolis, MD 21402; 105,000.

Naval Reserve Assn. (1954), 1619 King St., Alexandria, VA 22314; 24,500.

Navigation, Institute of (1945), 1026 16th St. NW, Suite 104, Wash., DC 20036; 3,200.

Navy Club of the U.S.A. Auxiliary (1941), 418 W. Pontiac St., Ft. Wayne, IN 46807; 1,000.

Navy League of the U.S. (1902); 2300 Wilson Blvd., Arlington, VA 22201; 71,000.

Needlework Guild of America (1885), 1007-B St. Road, Southhampton, PA 18966.

Negro College Fund, United (1944), 500 E. 62d St., N.Y., NY 10021; 42 institutions.

Neurofibromatosis Foundation, Natl. (1978), 141 Fifth Ave., Suite 7-S, N.Y., NY 10010; 25,000.

New Age Walker's (1982), 3301 Bellaire Dr., Altadena, CA 91001; 4,500.

Newspaper Editors, Amer. Society of (1922), P.O. Box 17004, Wash., DC 20041; 1,000.

Newspaper Marketing Assn., Intl. (1930), 11600 Sunrise Valley Dr., Reston, VA 22091; 1,300+.

Newspaper Publishers Assn., Amer. (1887), 11600 Sunrise Valley Dr., Reston, VA 22091; 1,416 newspapers.

Ninety-Nines (Intl. Organization of Women Pilots) (1929), P.O. Box 59965; Will Rogers Airport, Oklahoma City, OK 73159; .6,600.

Nobel Anniversary Committee, Amer. (1942), 1 Morningside Dr. N., Westport, CT 06880; 1,000.

Non-Commissioned Officers Assn. (1960), 10635 IH 35 No., San Antonio, TX 78233; 151,416.

Northern Cross Society (1983), Route One, Lecompton, KS 66050; 100.

Notaries, Amer. Society of (1965), 918 16th St. NW, Wash., DC 20006; 27,169.

Nuclear Society, Amer. (1954), 555 N. Kensington Ave., La Grange Park, IL 60525; 15,000.

Numismatic Assn., Amer. (1891), 818 N. Cascade Ave., Colorado Springs, CO 80903-3279; 30,528.

Numismatic Society, Amer. (1858), Broadway at 155th St., N.Y., NY 10032; 2,400.

Nurses' Assn., Amer. (1896), 2420 Pershing Rd., Kansas City, MO 64108.

Nursing, Natl. League for (1952), 350 Hudson St., N.Y., NY 10014; 18,000.

Nutrition, Amer. Institute of (1928), 9650 Rockville Pike, Bethesda, MD 20814; 2,750.

ORT Federation, Amer. (Org. for Rehabilitation through Training) (1922), 817 Broadway, N.Y., NY 10003; 17,000.

Odd Fellows, Sovereign Grand Lodge Independent Order of (1819), 422 N. Trade St., Winston Salem, NC 27101.

Old Crows, Assn. of (1964), 1000 N. Payne St., Alexandria, VA 22314-1696; 25,000.

Olympic Committee, U.S. (1921), 1750 E. Boulder St., Colorado Springs, CO 80909; 70 organizations.

Opthalmology, Amer. Academy of (1979), 655 Beach St., San Francisco, CA 94109; 16,250.

Optical Society of America (1916), 2010 Massachusetts Ave. NW, Wash., DC 20036; 11,208.

Optimist Intl. (1919), 4494 Lindell Blvd., St. Louis, MO 63108; 170,000.

Optometric Assn., Amer. (1898), 243 N. Lindbergh Blvd., St. Louis, MO 63141; 27,800.

Oral and Maxillofacial Surgeons, Amer. Assn. of (1918), 9700 W. Bryn Mawr Ave., Rosemont, IL 60018; 5,302.

Organists, Amer. Guild of (1896), 475 Riverside Dr., Suite 1260, N.Y., NY 10115; 24,300.

Oriental Society, Amer. (1842), 329 Sterling Memorial Library, Yale Sta., New Haven, CT 06520; 1,440.

Ornithologists' Union, Amer. (1883), c/o National Museum of Natural History, Smithsonian, Wash., DC 20560; 5,000.

Osteopathic Assn., Amer. (1887), 212 E. Ohio St., Chicago, IL 60611; 23,292.

Ostomy Assn., United (1962), 36 Executive Park, Suite 120, Irving, CA 92714, 45,000.

Outlaw and Lawman History, Natl. Organization for (1974), 615-C N. 8th St., Killeen, TX 76541; 500.

Overeaters Anonymous (1960), 4025 Spencer St., #203, Torrance, CA 90503; 120,000.

PTA (Natl. Congress of Parents and Teachers), Natl. (1897), 700 N. Rush St., Chicago, IL 60611; 6.6 mln.

Paleontological Research Institution (1932), 1259 Trumansburg Rd., Ithaca, NY 14850; 700+.

Paper Industry, Technical Assn. of the Pulp and (1916), P.O. Box 105113, Atlanta, GA 30348; 28,000.

Paper Institute, Amer. (1964), 260 Madison Ave., N.Y., NY 10016; 166 companies.

Parasitologists, Amer. Society of (1924), 1041 New Hampshire St., Box 368, Lawrence, KS 66044; 1,491.

Parents Without Partners (1957), 8807 Colesville Rd., Silver Spring, MD 20910; 250,000.

Parkinson's Disease Foundation (1957), 650 W. 168th St., N.Y., NY 10032; 580,000.

Parliamentarians, Amer. Institute of (1958), 124 W. Washington Blvd. Suite 144, Ft. Wayne, IN 46802; 1,350.

Parliamentarians, Natl. Assn. of (1930), 6601 Winchester, Kansas City, MO 64133-4600; 4,500.

Parliamentary Law, Intl. Organization of Professionals in (1976), 3611 Victoria Ave., Los Angeles, CA 90016; 200.

Pasta Assn., Natl. (1904), 1901 N. Ft. Myer Dr., Suite 1000, Arlington, VA 22209; 100 member companies.

Pathologists, Amer. Assn. of (1976), 9650 Rockville Pike, Bethesda, MD 20814; 2,350.

Patriotism, Natl. Committee for Responsible (1967), P.O. Box 665, Grand Central Sta., N.Y., NY 10163; 160.

Pearl Harbor History Associates (1985), P.O. Box 205, Sperryville, VA 22740-0205; 375.

Pearl Harbor Survivors Assn. (1958), 3215 Albert St., Orlando, FL 32806.

PEN Amer. Center (1922), 568 Broadway, N.Y., NY 10012; 2,500.

PEN Women, Natl. League of Amer. (1897), 1300 17th St. NW, Wash., DC 20036-1973; 5,000.

Pen Friends, Intl. (1967), P.O. Box 290065, Homecrest Station, Brooklyn, NY 11229-0001; 250,000.

Pennsylvania Society of New York (1899), 80 N. Main St., Sellersville, PA 18960; 1,800.

Pension Actuaries, Amer. Society of (1966), 2029 K St. NW, Wash., DC 20006; 3,000.

Pension Plan, Committee for a Natl. (1979), P.O. Box 27851, Las Vegas, NV 89126; 2,000.

P.E.O. (Philanthropic Educational Organization) Sisterhood (1869), 3700 Grand Ave., Des Moines, IA 50312; 240,000.

Personnel Administration, Amer. Society for (1948), 606 N. Washington St., Alexandria, VA 22314; 40,000.

Petroleum Equipment Inst. (1951), 3739 E. 31st St., Tulsa, OK 74135; 1,200 member companies.

Petroleum Institute, Amer. (1919), 1220 L St. NW, Wash., DC 20005; 200+ corporations.

Petroleum Landmen, Amer. Assn. of (1955), 777 Main St., Suite 1470, Fort Worth, TX 76102; 11,200.

Pharmaceutical Assn., Amer. (1852), 2215 Constitution Ave. NW, Wash., DC 20037; 38,200.

Phi Delta Kappa (1906), 8th & Union, Box 789, Bloomington, IN 47401-0789; 132,000.

Philatelic Pages & Panels, Amer. Soc. for (1984), 1138 Princeton Dr., Richardson, TX 75081-3615; 679.

Philatelic Society, Amer. (1886), 100 Oakwood Ave., State College, PA 16803; 57,400.

Philological Assn., Amer. (1869), Dept. of Classics, Fordham Univ., Bronx, NY 10458; 2,500.

Philosophical Assn., Amer. (1900), Univ. of Delaware, Newark, DE 19716; 7,600.

Philosophical Enquiry, Intl. Society for (1974), c/o Betty Hansen, 227 Wash. Blvd., Hudson, NY 12534; 474.

Philosophical Society, Amer. (1743), 104 S. 5th St., Phila., PA 19106; 650.

Photogrammetry and Remote Sensing, Amer. Society of (1934), 210 Little Falls St., Falls Church, VA 22046; 8,753.

Photographers of America, Professional (1880), 1090 Executive Way, Des Plaines, IL 60018; 15,000.

Photographic Society of Amer. (1934), 3000 United Founders Blvd. #103, Oklahoma City, OK 73112.

Physical Therapy Assn., Amer. (1921), 1111 N. Fairfax St., Alexandria, VA 22314; 48,000.

Physicians, Amer. Academy of Family (1947), 8880 Ward Pkwy., Kansas City, MO 64114; 68,000.

Physics, Amer. Inst. of (1931), 335 E. 45th St., N.Y., NY 10017-3483.

Physiological Society, Amer. (1887), 9650 Rockville Pike, Bethesda, MD 20814; 6,700.

Phytopathological Soc., The Amer. (1908), 3340 Pilot Knob Rd., St. Paul, MN 55121; 4,300+.

Pilgrim Society (1820), 75 Court St., Plymouth, MA 02360-3891; 900.

Pilgrims of the U.S. (1903), 80 Broadway, N.Y., NY 10005.

Pilot Club Intl. (1921), P.O. Box 4844, 244 College St., Macon, GA 31213-0599; 20,000.

Planetary Society (1980), 65 N. Catalina Ave., Pasadena, CA 91106; 120,000.

Planned Parenthood Federation of America (1916), 810 Seventh Ave., N.Y., NY 10019; 187 affiliates.

Planning Assn., Amer. (1909), 1776 Massachusetts Ave. NW, Wash., DC 20036; 26,000.

Plastic Modelers Society, Intl. (1965), P.O. Box 2890, Sacramento, CA 95812; 3,568.

Plastics Industry, Society of (1937), 1275 K St. NW, Suite 400, Washington, DC 20005; 2,099.

Platform Assn., Intl. (1831), Box 250, Winnetka, IL 60093; 5,000.

Poetry Day Committee, Natl. (1947), 1110 N. Venetian Dr., Miami, FL 33139-1019; 17,500.

Poetry Society of America (1910), 15 Gramercy Park, N.Y., NY 10003; 1,700.

Poets, Academy of Amer. (1934), 177 E. 87th St., N.Y., NY 10121; 2,000.

Polar Society, Amer. (1934), c/o Byrd Polar Research Ctr., 125 S. Oval Mall, Columbus, OH 43210; 2,000.

Police, Internatl. Assn. of Chiefs of (1893), 1110 N. Glebe Rd., Suite 200, Arlington, VA 22201; 13,500.

Police Officers Assn., Natl. Police Reserve Officers Assn., Natl. (1955/1967), 1316 Gardiner Lane, Louisville, KY 40213; 6,000.

Polish Army Veterans Assn. of America (1921), 19 Irving Pl., N.Y., NY 10003; 9,762.

Polish Cultural Society of America (1940), P.O. Box 31, Wall Street, N.Y., NY 10005; 103,111.

Polish Genealogical Society of CT (1984), 8 Lyle Rd., New Britain, CT 06053.

Polish Legion of American Veterans (1921), 3024 N. Laramie Ave., Chicago, IL 60641; 15,000.

Political Items Collectors, Amer. (1945), P.O. Box 340339, San Antonio, TX 78234; 2,800.

Political Science, Academy of (1880), 475 Riverside Dr., Suite 1274, N.Y., NY 10115-0012; 9,000.

Political Science Assn., Amer. (1903), 1527 New Hampshire Ave. NW, Wash., DC 20036; 13,000.

Political & Social Science, Amer. Academy of (1891), 3937 Chestnut St., Phila., PA 19104; 15,000.

Pollution Control, Internatl. Assn. for (1970), 444 N. Capital St. NW, Wash. DC 20001; 500.

Polo Assn., U.S. (1890), 4059 Iron Works Pike, Lexington, KY, 40511; 3,200.

Population Assn. of America (1931), 1429 Duke St., Alexandria, VA 22314-3402; 2,700.

Portuguese Continental Union of the U.S.A. (1925), 899 Boylston St., Boston, MA 02115; 7,457.

Postmasters of the U.S., Natl. Assn. of (1898), 4212 King St., Arlington, VA 22302; 3,000.

Postmasters of the U.S., Natl. League of (1904), 1023 N. Royal St., Alexandria, VA 22003; 22,000.

Poultry Science Assn. (1908), 309 W. Clark St., Champaign, IL 61820; 3,500.

Power Boat Assn., Amer. (1903), 17640 E. Nine Mile Rd., P.O. Box 377, E. Detroit, MI 48021; 9,000.

Precancel Collectors, Natl. Assn. of (1950), 5121 Park Blvd., Wildwood, NJ 08260; 6,500+.

Press, Associated (1848), 50 Rockefeller Plaza, N.Y., NY 10020; 1,365 newspapers & 3,600 broadcast stations.

Press Club, Natl. (1908), 529 14th St. NW, Wash., DC 20045; 4,500.

Press Intl., United (1907), 1400 I St. NW, Wash. DC 20005.

Press and Radio Club (1948), P.O. Box 70023, Montgomery, AL 36107; 736.

Press Women, Natl. Federation of (1937), 1105 Main St., Box 99, Blue Springs, MO 64015; 5,000.

Printing Industries of America (1887), 1730 N. Lynn St., Arlington, VA 22209; 13,000+ companies.

Prisoners of War, Amer. Ex- (1949), 3201 E. Pioneer Pkwy. #40, Arlington, TX 76010-5396; 33,000.

Procrastinators Club of America (1956), Box 712, Bryn Athyn, PA 19009; 6,500.

Propeller Club of the U.S. (1927), 3927 Old Lee Highway, Ste. 101A, Fairfax, VA 22030; 13,000.

Psychiatric Assn., Amer. (1844), 1400 K St. NW, Wash., DC 20005; 35,000.

Psychical Research, Amer. Society for (1885), 5 W. 73d St., N.Y., NY 10023; 1,800.

Psychoanalytic Assn., Amer. (1911), 309 E. 49th St., N.Y., NY 10017; 3,020.

Psychological Assn., Amer. (1892), 1200 17th St. NW, Wash., DC 20036; 60,000.

Psychological Assn. for Psychoanalysis, Natl. (1948), 150 W. 13th St., N.Y., NY 10011; 228.

Psychological Minorities, Society for the Aid of (1953), 42-25 Hampton St., Elmhurst, NY 11373; 553.

Psychotherapy Assn., Amer. Group (1942), 25 E. 21st St., N.Y., NY 10010; 3,400.

Psoriasis Foundation, Natl (1968), 6443 SW Beaverton Hwy., #210, Portland, OR 97221; 14,000.

Public Administration, Amer. Soc. for (1939), 1120 G St. NW, Wash, DC 20005; 14,800.

Public Health Assn., Amer. (1972), 1015 15th St. NW, Wash., DC 20005; 30,000.

Public Relations Soc. of Amer. (1947), 33 Irving Pl. N.Y., NY 10003.

Publicly Traded Cos., Assn. of (1973), 1707 L St. NW, Suite 950, Wash., DC 20036; 791.

Publishers, Assn. of Amer. (1970), One Park Ave., N.Y., NY 10016; 330 publishing houses.

Puppeteers of Amer. (1937), 5 Cricklewood Path, Pasadena, CA 91107; 2,401.

Quality Control, Amer. Society for (1946), 310 W. Wisconsin Ave., Milwaukee, WI 53203; 60,000.

Quota Internatl. (1919), 1828 L St. NW, Wash., DC 20036.

Rabbinical Alliance of America (1942), 3 W. 16th St. N.Y., NY 10011; 500.

Rabbinical Assembly (1900), 3080 Broadway, N.Y., NY 10027; 1,265.

Rabbis, Central Conference of Amer. (1889), 192 Lexington Ave., N.Y., NY 10016; 1,550.

Radio, Natl. Assn. of Business and Educational (1965), 1501 Duke St., Suite 200, Alexandria, VA 22314; 4,873.

Radio Union, Intl. Amateur (1925), P.O. Box AAA, Newington, CT 06111; 126 societies.

Radio and TV Society, Intl. (1939), 420 Lexington Ave., N.Y., NY 10170; 1,900.

Radio Relay League, Amer. (1914), 225 Main St., Newington, CT 06111; 160,000.

Railroad Club of Chicago, The (1934), 506 5th St., Wilmette, IL 60091; 100.

Railroad Passengers, Natl. Assn. of (1967), 236 Massachusetts Ave. NE, Suite 603, Wash., DC 20002; 12,659.

Railroads, Assn. of Amer. (1934), 50 F St. NW, Wash., DC 20001; 113.

Railway Historical Society, Natl. (1935), P.O. Box 58153, Phila., PA 58153; 17,704.

Railway Progress Institute (1908), 700 N. Fairfax St., Suite 601, Alexandria, VA 22314-2098; 130 companies.

Rainbow Walkers (1982), 4370 Fairlawn Dr., Lake Canada, CA 91011; 1,444.

Range Management, Society for (1946), 2760 W. 5th Ave., Denver, CO 80204; 5,500.

Rape, Feminist Alliance Against (1974), P.O. Box 21033, Wash., DC 20009.

Reading Assn., Intl. (1956), P.O. Box 8139, 800 Barksdale Rd., Newark, DE 19714-8139; 90,000.

Real Estate Institute, Intl. (1975), 8383 E. Evans Rd., Scottsdale, AZ 85260; 3,000.

Rebekah Assemblies, Intl. Assn. of (1922), 422 N. Trade St., Suite "R" Winston-Salem, NC 27101; 214,451.

Reconciliation, Fellowship of (1915), 523 N. Broadway, Nyack, NY 10960; 35,000.

Records Managers & Administrators, Assn. of (1975), 4200 Somerset Dr., Suite 215, Prairie Village, KS 66208; 10,000.

Recreation and Park Assn., Natl. (1965), 3101 Park Ctr. Dr., 12th Fl., Alexandria, VA 22302; 20,727.

Red Cross, American (1881), 17th & D Sts. NW, Wash., DC 20006; 1.2 mln. volunteers.

Red Men, Improved Order of (1813), 4007 W. Waco Dr., Waco, TX, 76710; 33,000.

Redwoods League, Save-the- (1918), 114 Sansome St., Rm. 605, San Francisco, CA 94104; 45,000.

Reed Organ Society, Inc. (1981), The Musical Museum, Deansboro, NY 13328; 800.

Regional Plan Assn. (1929), 1040 Ave. of the Americas, N.Y., NY 10018; 1,200.

Rehabilitation Assn., Natl. (1925), 633 S. Washington St., Alexandria, VA 22314; 16,000.

Religion, Amer. Academy of (1909), 501 Hall of Languages, Syracuse Univ., Syracuse, NY 13244-1170; 5,600.

Religion, Freedom from, Foundation (1978), P.O. Box 750, Madison, WI 53701; 3,000.

Remodeling Industry, Natl. Assn. of the (1956), 1901 N. Moore St., Suite 808, Arlington, VA 22209.

Renaissance Society of America (1954), 1161 Amsterdam Ave., N.Y., NY 10027; 3,000.

Republican National Committee (1856), 310 1st Street SE, Washington, DC 20003-1801.

Reserve Officers Assn. of the U.S. (1922), One Constitution Ave., NE, Wash., DC 20002; 123,000.

Restaurant Assn., Natl. (1919), 1200 17th St. NW, Wash., DC 20036; 15,000.

Retarded Citizens of the U.S., Assn. for (1950), 2501 Ave. J, Arlington, TX 76006; 160,000.

Retired Credit Union People, Natl. Assn. for (1978), 5910 Mineral Pt. Rd., Madison, WI 53705; 71,036.

Retired Federal Employees, Natl. Assn. of (1921), 1533 New Hampshire Ave. NW, Wash., DC 20036; 490,000.

Retired Officers Assn. (1929), 201 N. Washington St., Alexandria, VA 22314-2529; 365,000.

Retired Persons, Amer. Assn. of (1958), 1909 K St. NW, Wash., DC 20049; 18 mln.

Retired Teachers Assn., Natl. (1947), 1909 K St. NW, Wash., DC 20049; 540,000.

Revolver Assn., U.S. (1900), 96 W. Union St., Ashland, MA 01721; 1,400.

Reye's Syndrome Foundation, Natl. (1974), 426 N. Lewis, Bryan, OH 43506; 143.

Richard III Society (1969), P.O. Box 13787, New Orleans, LA 70185; 700.

Rifle Assn., Natl. (1871), 1600 Rhode Island Ave. NW, Wash., DC 20036; 2.8 mln.

Road & Transportation Builders' Assn., Amer. (1902), 501 School St. SW, Wash., DC 20024-2713; 3,600.

Rodeo Cowboys Assn., Professional (1936), 101 Pro Rodeo Dr., Colorado Springs, CO 80919; 10,091.

Roller Skating, U.S. Amateur Confederation of (1937), 1500 S. 70th St., Lincoln, NE 68506; 23,000.

Roller Skating Rink Operators Assn. (1937), 7700 A St., Lincoln, NE 68510; 1,150 rinks.

Rose Society, Amer. (1899) 8877 Jefferson Paige Rd., Shreveport, LA 71119; 20,000.

Rotary Intl. (1905), 1560 Sherman Ave., Evanston, IL 60201; 1.1 mln.

Running and Fitness Assn., Amer. (1968), 9310 Old Georgetown Rd., Bethesda, MD 20814; 18,500.

Ruritan Natl. (1928), Ruritan Natl. Rd., Dublin, VA 24084; 37,000.

SANE/FREEZE (1988), 1819 H St. NW, Suite 1000, Wash., DC 20006-3603; 170,000.

Safety and Fairness Everywhere, Natl. Assn. Taunting (1980), P.O. Box 5743WA, Montecito, CA 93150; 12,000.

Safety Council, Natl. (1913), 444 N. Michigan Ave., Chicago, IL 60611; 12,500.

Sailors, Tin Can (1976), Battleship Cove, Fall River, MA 02721; 12,050. .

St. Andrew the Apostle, The Soc. of (1983), Route 3, Sylvester, WV 25193; 450.

St. Dennis of Zante, Sovereign Greek Order of (1096; 1953 in U.S.), 739 W. 186th St., N.Y., NY 10333; 91.

St. George the Martyr, Knightly Assn. of (1980), State Route #3, Sylvester, WV 25193; 10,000.

St. Luke, Physician of Amer., Order of (1952), 2210 Wilshire Blvd., Santa Monica, CA 90403; 300+.

St. Paul, Natl. Guild of (1937), 601 Hill 'n Dale, Lexington, KY 40503; 13,652.

Salespersons, Natl. Assn. of Professional (1970), P.O. Box 76461, Atlanta, GA 30358; 35,000.

Salt Institute (1914), 700 N. Fairfax St., Ste. 600, Alexandria, VA, 22314-2040; 23 companies.

Sane Nuclear Policy, Committee for a (1957), 711 G St. SE, Wash., DC 20003; 130,000.

Savings Institutions, Natl. Council of (1983), 1101 15th St. NW, Wash., DC 20005; 550 members.

Savings & Loan League, Natl. (1943), 1101 15th St. NW, Wash., DC 20005; 300 associations.

School Administrators, Amer. Assn. of (1865), 1801 N. Moore St., Arlington, VA 22209; 19,000.

School Boards Assn., Natl. (1940), 1680 Duke St., Alexandria, VA 22314.

School Counselor Assn., Amer. (1953), 5999 Stevenson Ave., Alexandria, VA 22304; 12,500.

Schools of Art, Natl. Assn. of (also: School of Art and Design, School of Dance, Music, and Theater) (1944), 11250 Roger Bacon Dr., Reston, VA 22090; 161.

Schools & Colleges, Amer. Council on (1927), 13014 Dale Mabry Hwy., Ste. 270-B, Tampa, FL 33180-2808; 137.

Science, Amer. Assn. for the Advancement of (1848), 1333 H St. NW, Wash., DC 20005; 132,000.

Science Fiction Society, World (1939), P.O. Box 1270, Kendall Sq. Sta., Cambridge, MA 02142; 5,000.

Science Service (1921), 1719 N St. NW, Wash., DC 20036.

Science Teachers Assn., Natl. (1965), 1742 Connecticut Ave. NW, Wash., DC 20009; 50,000.

Science Writers, Natl. Assn. of (1934), P.O. Box 294, Greenlawn, NY 11740; 1,500.

Sciences, Natl. Academy of (1863), 2101 Constitution Ave. NW, Wash., DC 20418; 1,816.

Scientists, Federation of American (1945), 307 Massachusetts Ave. NE, Wash., DC 20002; 5,000.

Screen Actors Guild (1933), 7065 Hollywood Blvd. Hollywood, CA 90028; 73,000.

Screen Printing Assn. Intl. (1948), 10015 Main St., Fairfax, VA 22031; 3,000 corporations.

Sculpture Soc., Natl. (1893), 15 E. 26th St., N.Y., NY 10010; 4,500.

Seamen's Service, United (1942), One World Trade Ctr., Suite 1365, N.Y., NY 10048.

2d Air Division Assn. (1947), 1 Jeffrey's Neck Rd., Ipswich, MA 01938; 7,852.

Secondary School Principals, Natl. Assn. of (1916), 1904 Association Dr., Reston, VA 22091; 42,000.

Secretaries, Natl. Assn. of Legal (1950), 2250 E 73, Ste. 550, Tulsa, OK 74136-6805; 16,000.

Securities Industry Assn. (1972), 120 Broadway, N.Y., NY 10271; 600 firms.

Separation of Church & State, Americans United for (1947), 8120 Fenton St., Silver Spring, MD 20910; 50,000.

Sertoma Internatl. (1912), 1912 E. Meyer Blvd., Kansas City, MO 64132; 35,000.

Sex Information & Education Council of the U.S. (SIECUS) (1964), New York University, 32 Washington Place, Rm. 52, N.Y., NY 10003; 2,600.

Shakespeare Assn. of America (1972), Box 6328, Vanderbilt Sta. B, Nashville, TN 37235; 812.

Sheet Metal & Air Conditioning Contractor's Natl. Assn., Inc. (1943), 8224 Old Courthouse Rd., Vienna, VA 22182; 2,290.

Shipbuilders Council of America (1921), 1110 Vermont Ave. NW, Wash., DC 20005; 54 organizations.

Ships in Bottles Assn. of Amer. (1983), P.O. Box 550, Coronado, CA 92118; 300.

Shore & Beach Preservation Assn., Amer. (1926), 3000 Citrus Circle, Suite 230, Walnut Creek, CA 94598; 1,000.

Shrine, Ancient Arabic Order of the Nobles of the Mystic (1872), 2900 Rocky Pt. Dr., Tampa, FL 33607; 799,000.

Shut-Ins, Natl. Society for (1970), 237 Franklin St., Reading, PA 19602; 85.

Sierra Club (1892), 730 Polk St., San Francisco, CA 94109; 440,000.

Silurians, Soc. of the (1924), 164 Lexington Ave., N.Y., NY 10016; 500.

Skating Union of the U.S., Amateur (1928), 1033 Shady Lane, Glen Ellyn, IL 60137; 2,400.

Skeet Shooting Assn., Natl. (1946), P.O. Box 680007, San Antonio, TX 78268; 15,800.

Ski Assn., U.S. (1904), P.O. Box 100, Park City, UT 84060; 30,000.

Small Business, Amer. Federation of (1938), 407 S. Dearborn St., Chicago, IL 60605; 25,000.

Small Business United, Natl. (1986), 1155 15th St. NW, Suite 710, Wash., DC 20005; 50,000.

Smoking & Health, Natl. Clearinghouse for (1965), Center for Disease Control, 1600 Clifton Road NE, Atlanta, GA 30333.

Soccer Federation, U.S. (1913), Viscount Hotel, 40 JFK Intl. Airport, Jamaica, NY 11430; 700,000.

Social Biology, Society for the Study of (1926), Medical Dept., Brookhaven Natl. Laboratory, Upton, NY 11973; 415.

Social Sciences, Natl. Institute of (1865), 444 Madison Ave., Ste. 2901, N.Y., NY 10022; 350.

Social Work Education, Council on (1952), 1600 Duke Street, Alexandria, VA 22314; 3,000.

Social Workers, Natl. Assn. of (1955), 7981 Eastern Ave., Silver Spring, MD 20910; 127,000.

Socialists of America, Democratic (1981), 15 Dutch St., Suite 500, N.Y., NY 10038; 5,000.

Sociological Assn., Amer. (1905), 1722 N St. NW, Wash., DC 20036; 12,666.

Softball Association, Amateur (1933), 2801 N.E. 50th St., Oklahoma City, OK 73111; 226,000 teams.

Softball League, Cinderella (1958), P.O. Box 1411, Corning, NY 14830.

Soft Drink Assn., Natl. (1921), 1101 16th St. NW, Wash., DC 20036; 1,000.

Soil Conservation Society of America (1945), 7515 N.E. Ankeny Rd., Ankeny, IA 50021; 12,000.

Soil Science Society of America (1936), 677 S. Segoe Rd., Madison, WI 53711; 6,114.

Sojourners, Natl. (1919), 8301 E. Boulevard Dr., Alexandria, VA 22308; 9,500.

Soldier's, Sailor's and Airmen's Club (1919), 283 Lexington Ave., N.Y., NY 10016.

Songwriters Guild of America, The (1931), 276 Fifth Ave., N.Y., NY 10001; 5,000.

Sons of the Amer. Legion (1932), Box 1055, Indianapolis, IN 46206; 109,643.

Sons of the American Revolution, Natl. Society of (1889), 1000 S. 4th, Louisville, KY 40203; 26,000.

Sons of Confederate Veterans (1896), Southern Station, Box 5164, Hattiesburg, MS 39406-5164; 9,000.

Sons of the Desert (1965), P.O. Box 8341, Universal City, CA 91608; 10,000.

Sons of Italy in America, The Order (1905), 219 E. St., NE, Wash. DC 20002; 450,000.

Sons of Norway (1895), 1455 W. Lake St., Minneapolis, MN 55408; 85,000.

Sons of Poland, Assn. of the (1903), 591 Summit Ave., Rm. 702, Jersey City, NJ 07306; 10,000.

Sons of the Republic of Texas, The (1893), 5942 Abrams Rd., #222, Dallas, TX 75231; 2,200.

Sons of the Revolution in the State of New York/ Fraunces Tavern Museum (1876), 54 Pearl St., N.Y., NY 10004; 1,350.

Sons of St. Patrick, Society of the Friendly (1784), 80 Wall St., N.Y., NY 10005; 1,400.

Sons of Sherman's March to the Sea (1966), 1725 Farmers Ave., Tempe, AZ 85281; 660.

Sons of Union Veterans of the Civil War (1881), 411 Bartlett St., Lansing, MI 48915; 3,570.

Soroptimist Intl. of the Americas (1921), 1616 Walnut St., Phila., PA 19103; 50,000.

Southern Christian Leadership Conference (1957), 334 Auburn Ave. NE, Atlanta, GA 30303; 1 mln.

Space Education Assoc., U.S. (1973), 746 Turnpike Rd., Elizabethtown, PA 17022-1161; 1,000.

Speech Communication Assn. (1914), 5105 Backlick Rd., Annandale, VA 22003; 6,700.

Speech-Language-Hearing Assn., Amer. (1925), 10801 Rockville Pike, Rockville, MD 20852; 55,000.

Speleological Society, Natl. (1941), 2813 Cave Ave., Huntsville, AL 35810; 6,500.

Spiritual Awareness, Assn. for (1985), P.O. Box 224, Clarence, MO 63437; 2,050.

Sports Car Club of America (1944), P.O. Box 3278, Englewood, CO 80155-3278; 51,081.

Sports Club, Indoor (1930), 1145 Highland St., Napoleon, OH 43545.

Sportscasters Assn., Amer. (1979), 5 Beekman St., N.Y., NY 10038; 500.

Standards Institute, Amer. Natl. (1918), 1430 Broadway, N.Y., NY 10018; 1,000.

State Communities Aid Assn. (1872), 151 Chestnut St., Albany, NY 12210; 95.

State Governments, Council of (1933), P.O. Box 11910, Iron Works Pike, Lexington, KY 40578; 50 states.

State & Local History, Amer. Assn. for (1940), 172 Second Ave. N., Nashville, TN 37201; 6,000.

Statistical Assn., Amer. (1839), 1429 Duke St., Alexandria, VA 22314-3402; 15,000.

Steamship Historical Society of America (1935), H.C. Hall Bldg., 345 Blackstone Blvd., Providence, RI 02906; 3,364.

Steel Construction, Amer. Institute of (1921), 400 N. Michigan Ave., Chicago, IL 60611-4185; 2,600+.

Stock Car Auto Racing, Natl. Assn. for (NASCAR) (1948), 1801 Speedway Blvd., Daytona Beach, FL 32015; 17,000.

Stock Exchange, Amer. (1911), 86 Trinity Pl., N.Y., NY 10006; 871.

Stock Exchange, N.Y. (1792), 11 Wall St., N.Y., NY 10005.

Stock Exchange, Phila. (1790), 1900 Market St., Phila., PA 19103; 505.

Structural Stability Research Council (1944), Fritz Engineering Laboratory No. 13, Lehigh Univ., Bethlehem, PA 18015.

Student Assn., U.S. (1947), 1012 14th St. NW, Suite 403, Wash., DC 20005.

Student Councils, Natl. Assn. of (1931), 1904 Association Dr., Reston, VA 22091; 200,000.

Stuttering Project, Natl. (1977), 4601 Irving St., San Francisco, CA 94122-1020; 4,000.

Sudden Infant Death Syndrome Foundation, Natl. (1962), 8200 Professional Pl., Landover, MA 20785-2264.

Sugar Brokers Assn., Natl. (1903), 1 World Trade Center, N.Y., NY 10047; 100.

Sunbathing Assn., Amer. (1931), 1703 N. Main St., Kissimmee, FL 34744; 34,000.

Sunday League (1933), 279 Highland Ave., Newark, NJ 07104; 25,000.

Surgeons, Amer. College of (1913), 55 E. Erie St., Chicago IL 60611-2797; 50,904.

Surgeons, Intl. College of (1935), 1516 N. Lake Shore Dr., Chicago IL 60610; 6,800.

Surgeons of the U.S., Assn. of Military (1891), 9320 Old Georgetown Rd., Bethesda, MD 20895; 16,600.

Surveying & Mapping, Amer. Congress on (1941), 210 Little Falls, Falls Church, VA 22046; 10,800.

Symphony Orchestra League, Amer. (1942), 777 14th St. NW, Wash., DC 20005; 870 orchestras.

Systems Management, Assn. for (1947), 24587 Bagley Rd., Cleveland, OH 44138; 8,000.

Table Tennis Assn., U.S. (1933), Olympic Complex, 1750 E. Boulder St., Colorado Springs, CO 80909; 6,500.

Tailhook Assn., The (1957), 4849 Ronson Ct., #109, San Diego, CA 92111; 15,000.

Tall Buildings and Urban Habitat, Council on (1969), Lehigh Univ., Bethlehem, PA 18015; 2,500.

Tax Accountants, Natl. Assn. of Enrolled Federal (1960), 6108 N. Harding Ave., Chicago, IL 60659-3108; 450.

Tax Administrators, Federation of (1937), 444 N. Capitol St. NW, Wash., DC 20001.

Tax Assn., Natl.–Tax Institute of America (1907), 5310 E. Main St., Suite 104, Columbus, OH 43213; 1,800.

Tax Foundation, Inc. (1937), 1 Thomas Circle NW, Suite 500, Wash., DC 20005; 568 corporations.

Tax Free America (1986), 11015 Cumpston St., N. Hollywood, CA 91601; 400,000.

Taxpayers Union, Natl. (1969), 325 Pennsylvania Ave. SE, Washington, DC 20003; 200,000.

Tea Assn. of the U.S.A. (1899), 230 Park Ave., N.Y., NY 10169; 179.

Teachers Assn., Amer. String (1946), UGA Sta. Box 2066, Athens, GA 30612-0066; 6,800.

Teachers of English, Natl. Council of (1911), 1111 Kenyon Rd., Urbana, IL 61801; 68,000.

Teachers of English to Speakers of Other Languages (1966), 1600 Cameron St., Suite 300, Alexandria, VA 22314; 14,500.

Teachers of French, Amer. Assn. of (1927), 57 E. Armory Ave., Champaign, IL 61820; 11,000.

Teachers of German, American Assn. of (1926), 112 Haddontowne Court #104, Cherry Hill, NJ 08034; 6,500.

Teachers of Mathematics, Natl. Council of (1920), 1906 Association Dr., Reston, VA 22091; 56,000.

Teachers of Singing, Natl. Assn. of (1944), 2800 Univ. Blvd. N, J.U. Sta., Jacksonville, FL 32211; 4,600.

Teachers of Spanish & Portuguese, Amer. Assn. of (1917), P.O. Box 6349, 218 Lee Hall, MSU., Mississippi State, MS 39762-6349; 13,000.

Telephone Pioneers of Amer. (1911), 22 Cortland, St., 25th fl., N.Y., NY 10007; 780,000.

Television Arts & Sciences, Natl. Academy of (1956), 111 W. 57th St., Suite 1020, N.Y., NY 10019; 11,000.

Television Bureau of Advertising (1954), 485 Lexington Ave., N.Y., NY 10017.

Television & Radio Artists, Amer. Federation of (1937), 1350 Ave. of the Americas, N.Y., NY 10019; 66,000.

Telluride Assn. (1911), 217 West Ave., Ithaca, NY 14850.

Tennis Assn., U.S. (1881), 1212 Ave. of Americas, N.Y., NY 10036.

Terraplane Club, Hudson-Essex (1959), 100 E. Cross St., Ypsilanti, MI 48198; 2,850.

Tesla Memorial Soc., Inc. (1979), 453 Martin Rd., Lackawanna, NY 14216; 1,200+.

Testing & Materials, Amer. Society for (1898), 1916 Race St., Phila., PA 19103; 32,000.

Texas State Genealogical Society (1960), 2507 Tannehill, Houston, TX 77008-3052; 1,000.

Textile Assn., Northern (1854), 230 Congress St., Boston, MA 02110; 150.

Textile Manufacturers Institute, Amer. (1949), 1801 K St. NW, Suite 900, Wash., DC 20006.

Theatre Organ Society, Amer. (1955), P.O. Box 3043, Olivenhain, CA 92024; 6,000.

Theodore Roosevelt Assn. (1920), P.O. Box 720, Oyster Bay, NY 11771; 1,500.

Theological Schools in the U.S. and Canada, Assn. of (1918), 42 E. National Rd., Vandalia, OH 45377; 204.

Theosophical Society in America, The (1875), 1926 N. Main St., Wheaton, IL 60187; 5,486.

Thoreau Society (1941), 156 Belknap St., Concord, MA 01742; 1,400.

Thoroughbred Racing Assns. (1942), 3000 Marcus Ave., Lake Success, NY 11042; 50 racing associations.

Titanic Historical Society (1963), P.O. Box 51053, Indian Orchard, MA 01151-0053; 4,127.

Toastmasters Intl. (1924), 23182 Arroyo Vista, Rancho Santa Margarita, CA 92688; 155,000.

Topical Assn., Amer. (1949), P.O. Box 630, Johnstown, PA 15907; 7,000.

Torch Clubs, Internatl. Assn. of (1924), 435 N. Michigan Ave., #1717, Chicago, IL 60611; 3,250.

Toy Manufacturers of America (1916), 200 Fifth Ave., N.Y., NY 10010; 240.

Traffic and Transportation, Amer. Society of (1946), 1816 Norris Pl. #4, Louisville, KY 40205; 2,400.

Trail Association, North Country (1980), 2780 Mundy Ave., White Cloud, MI 49349; 200.

Transit Assn., Amer. Public (1975), 1201 New York Ave. NW, Wash., DC 20005; 940.

Translators Assn., Amer. (1959), 109 Croton Ave., Ossining, NY 10562; 3,400.

Transportation and Logistics, Inc., Amer. Society of (1946), 1816 Norris Pl., #4, Louisville, KY 40205; 1,800.

Trapshooting Assn., Amateur (1923), 601 W. National Rd. Vandalia, OH 45377; 100,000+.

Travel Agents, Amer. Society of (1931), 1101 King St., Alexandria, VA 22314; 19,135.

Travel Industry Assn. of America (1941), 1133 21st St. NW, Wash., DC 20036; 1,700.

Travelers Protective Assn. of America (1890), 3755 Lindell Blvd., St. Louis, MO 63108; 184,556.

Triple Nine Society (1979), 2119 College St., Cedar Falls, IA 50613; 700.

Trucking Assn., Amer. (1933), 2200 Mill Rd., Alexandria, VA 22314.

True Sisters, United Order (1846), 212 Fifth Ave., N.Y., NY 10010; 8,500.

Tuberous Sclerosis Assn. of Amer. (1970), P.O. Box 44, Rockland, MA 02370; 2,500.

UFOs, Natl. Investigation Committee on (1957), 14617 Victory Blvd., Suite 4, Van Nuys, CA 91411.

UNICEF, U.S. Committee for (1947), 333 E. 38th St., N.Y., NY 10016.

USO (United Service Organizations) (1941), 601 Indiana Ave., NW, Wash., DC 20004.

Underwriters, Amer. Soc. of Chartered Life (1927), 270 Bryn Mawr Ave., Bryn Mawr, PA 19010; 30,000.

Underwriters, Soc. of Chartered Property and Casualty (1944), Kahler Hall, 720 Providence Rd., Malvern, PA 19355.

Uniformed Services Society of Military Widows, Natl. Assn. for (1968), 5535 Hempstead Way, Springfield, VA 22151; 55,000.

United Nations Assn. of the U.S.A. (1923, as League of Nations Assn.) 485 Fifth Ave., N.Y., NY 10017; 21,000.

U.S., Amer. Assn. for Study of the, in World Affairs (1948), 3813 Annandale Rd., Annandale, VA 22003; 1,500.

United Way of America (1918), 801 N. Fairfax St., Alexandria, VA 22309; 1,200.

Universities, Assn. of Amer. (1900), One Dupont Circle, Suite 730, Wash., DC 20036; 58 institutions.

Universities & Colleges, Assn. of Governing Bds. of (1921), One Dupont Circle NW, Suite 400, Wash., DC 20036.

University Extension Assn., Natl. (1915), One Dupont Circle, Suite 400, NW, Wash., DC 20036; 1,100.

University Foundation, Intl. (1973), 1301 S. Noland Rd., Independence, MO 64055; 11,750.

University Professors, Amer. Assn. of (1915), 1012 14th St. NW, Suite 500, Wash., DC 20005; 41,000.

University Women, Amer. Assn. of (1881), 2401 Virginia Ave. NW, Wash., DC 20037; 140,000.

Urban Coalition, Natl. (1967), 1120 G St. NW, Suite 900, Wash., DC 20005; 42 affiliates.

Urban League, Natl. (1910), 500 E. 62d St., N.Y., NY 10020; 50,000.

Utility Commissioners, Natl. Assn. of Regulatory (1889), 1102 Interstate Commerce Commission Bldg., 12th & Constitution NW, Wash., DC 20044-0684; 96 agencies.

Vampire Research Center (1972), P.O. Box 252, Elmhurst, NY 11373; 450.

Variety Clubs Intl. (1928), 1560 Bdway., N.Y., NY 10036.

VASA Order of America (1896), 65 Bryant Rd., Cranston, R.I. 02910; 32,000.

Ventriloquists, No. American Assn. of (1944), 800 W. Littleton Blvd., Box 420, Littleton, CO 80120; 1,750.

Veterans Assn., Blinded (1945), 477 H St. NW, Wash., DC 20001; 7,007.

Veterans Assn., China-Burma-India (1947), 750 N. Lincoln Memorial Dr., Milwaukee, WI 53201; 3,221+.

Veterans Committee, Amer. (1944), 1735 De Sales St. NW, Suite 402, Wash., DC 20817; 25,000.

Veterans of Foreign Wars of the U.S. (1899) **& Ladies Auxiliary** (1914), 406 W. 34th St., Kansas City, MO 64111.

Veterans of the Vietnam War (1980), 2090 Bald Mountain Rd., Wilkes-Barre, PA 18702-9699; 32,000.

Veterans of World War I (1958), 941 N. Capitol St. NE, Room 1201-C, Wash., DC 20002-4234; 98,000.

Veterans of WWII, Submarine (1955), 6523 San Joaquin St., Sacramento, CA 95820; 8,100.

Veterinary Medical Assn., Amer. (1863), 930 N. Meacham Rd., Schaumburg, IL 60196; 49,000.

Victorian Society in America (1966), 219 S. Sixth St., Phila., PA 19106; 4,000.

Volleyball Assn., U.S. (1928), 1750 E. Boulder St., Colorado Springs, CO 80909; 45,000.

Walking Association (1976), 655 E. Rancho Catalina Pl., Tucson, AZ 98704.

Walking Society, American (1980), Viana House, Box 1315, Beverly Hills, CA 90213; 2.8 mln.

War Mothers, Amer. (1917), 2615 Woodley Pl. NW, Wash., DC 20008; 3,000.

Warrant and Warrant Officers' Assn., Chief, U.S. Coast Guard (1929), c/o Fort McNair Yacht Basin, 200 V Street, SW, Wash., DC 20024; 3,346.

Washington, DC Area Trucking Assn. (1933), 2200 Mill Rd., Alexandria, VA 22314; 130 companies.

Watch & Clock Collectors, Natl. Assn. of (1940), 514 Poplar St., Columbia, PA 17512; 33,000.

Watercolor Soc., American (1866), 47 Fifth Ave., N.Y., NY 10003; 491.

Water Pollution Control Admin., Assn. of State and Interstate (1961), 444 N. Capital St. NW, Suite 330, Wash., DC 20001.

Water Pollution Control Federation (1928), 601 Wythe St., Alexandria, VA 22314-1994; 32,000.

Water Resources Assn., Amer. (1964), 5410 Grosvenor Ln., Suite 220, Bethesda, MD 20814-2192; 4,000.

Water Ski Assn., Amer. (1939), 799 Overlook Dr. SE, Winter Haven, FL 33884; 20,000.

Water Well Assn., Natl. (1948), 6375 Riverside Drive, Dublin, OH 43017; 19,650.

Water Works Assn., Amer. (1881), 6666 W. Quincy Ave., Denver, CO 80235; 36,500.

Watts Family Assn. (1969), 12401 Burton St., N. Hollywood, CA 91605; 12 branches.

Weather Modification Assn. (1950), P.O. Box 8116, Fresno, CA 93747; 200.

Welding Society, Amer. (1919), 550 NW LeJeune Rd., Miami, FL 33126; 35,600.

Wheelchair Athletic Assn., Natl. (1956), 3617 Betty Dr., Suite 5, Colorado Springs, CO 80917; 2,000.

Widows, Society of Military (1968), 5535 Hemstead Way, Springfield, VA 22151; 2,000.

Wilderness Society (1935), 900 17th St. NW, Wash., DC 20006; 350,000.

Wild Horse Organized Assistance (WHOA!) (1971), 140 Greenstone Dr., Reno, NV 89512; 10,000.

Wildlife, Defenders of (1947), 1244 19th St. NW, Wash., DC 20036; 80,000.

Wildlife Federation, Natl. (1936), 1400 16th St. NW, Wash., DC 20036; 5.1 mln.

Wildlife Foundation, No. Amer. (1929), 102 Wilmot Rd., #410, Deerfield, IL 60015; 6,000.

Wildlife Fund, World (1961), 1255 23rd St. NW, Wash., DC 20037; 230,000.

Wildlife Management Institute (1911), 1101-14th St., Suite 725, NW, Wash., DC 20005.

William Penn Assn. (1886), 709 Brighton Rd., Pittsburgh, PA 15233; 90,000.

Wireless Pioneers, Society of (1968), 146 Coleen St., Livermore, CA 94550; 5,233.

Wizard of Oz Club, Intl. (1957), Box 95, Kinderhook, IL 62345; 2,500.

Women, Natl. Assn. of Bank (1920), 500 No. Michigan Ave., Suite 1400, Chicago, IL 60611; 30,000.

Women, Natl. Council of (1888), 777 United Nations Plaza, N.Y., NY 10017; approx. 800.

Women, Natl. Organization for (NOW) (1966), 1401 New York Ave. NW, Wash., DC 20005; 150,000.

Women Artists, Natl. Assn. of (1889), 41 Union Sq., N.Y., NY 10003; 700.

Women Engineers, Society of (1950), 345 E. 47th St., N.Y., NY 10017; 15,000.

Women in Communications (1909), 2101 Wilson Blvd., Arlington, VA 22201; 11,500.

Women in Radio and TV, Inc. (1951), 1321 Connecticut Ave. NW, Washington, DC 20036; 3,000.

Women Geographers, Society of (1925), 1619 New Hampshire Ave. NW, Wash., DC 20009; 500.

Women Marines Assn. (1960), P.O. Box 387, Quantico, VA 22134; 3,009.

Women Strike for Peace (1961), 145 S. 13th St., Rm. 706, Phila., PA 19107; 8,000.

Women of the U.S., Natl. Council of (1888), 777 U.N. Plaza, N.Y., NY 10017; 28 organizations.

Women Voters of the U.S., League of (1920), 1730 M St. NW, Wash., DC 20036; 120,000.

Women World War Veterans (1919), 237 Madison Ave., N.Y., NY 10016; 35,000.

Women's Army Corps Veterans Assn. (1947), Hwy. 21, Anniston, AL 36206; 3,500.

Women's Association, American Business (1949), 9100 Ward Parkway, P.O. Box 8728, Kansas City, MO 64114; 100,000.

Women's Christian Temperance Union, Natl. (1874), 1730 Chicago Ave., Evanston, IL 60201; 50,000.

Women's Clubs, General Federation of (1890), 1734 N St. NW., Wash. DC, 20036.

Women's Clubs, National Federation of Business & Professional (1919), 2012 Massachusetts Ave. NW, Wash., DC 20036; 110,000.

Women's Educational & Industrial Union (1877), 356 Boylston St., Boston, MA 02116; 1,131.

Women's Intl. League for Peace & Freedom (1915), 1213 Race St., Phila., PA 19107; 50,000.

Women's Legal Defense Fund (1971), 2000 P St. NW, Suite 400, Washington, DC 20036; 1,900.

Women's Overseas Service League (1921), P.O. Box 39058, Friendship Station, Washington, DC 20016; 1,450.

Woodmen of America, Modern (1883), Mississippi River at 17th St., Rock Island, IL 61201; 600,000.

Woodmen of the World Life Insurance Soc. (1890), 1700 Farnam St., Omaha, NE 68102; 900,000.

Workmen's Circle (1900), 45 E. 33d St., N.Y., NY 10016; 45,000.

World Federalist Assn. (1976), 418 7th St. SE, Washington, DC 20003; 9,000.

World Future Society (1966), 4916 St. Elmo Ave., Bethesda, MD 20814; 30,000.

World Health, Amer. Assn. for (1953), 2001 S St., NW, Suite 530, Washington, DC 20009; 1,100.

World Peace, Intl Assn. of Educators for (1969), P.O. Box 3282, Mastin Lake Sta., Huntsville, AL 35810-0282; 20,000.

World's Fair Collectors Soc. (1968), P.O. Box 20806, Sarasota, FL 34238; 350.

Writers Guild of America, West (1933), 8955 Beverly Blvd., W. Hollywood, CA 90048; 19,500.

Yeoman F. Natl. (1936), 223 El Camino Real, Vallejo, CA 94590; 800.

Young Men's Christian Assns. of the U.S.A., (1851), 101 N. Wacker Dr., Chicago, IL 60606; 13 mln.

YM-YMHAs of Greater New York, Associated (1957), 130 E. 59th St., N.Y., NY 10020; 55,100.

Young Women's Christian Assn. of the U.S.A. (1906), 726 Broadway, N.Y., NY 10003; 1.6 mln.

Youth Hostels, American (1934), P.O. Box 37613, Wash., DC 20013; 100,000.

Zero Population Growth (1968), 1400 16th St. NW, Suite 320, Wash., DC 20036; 25,000.

Ziegfeld Club (1936), 593 Park Ave., N.Y., NY 10021; 303.

Zionist Organization of America (1897), 4 E. 34th St., N.Y., NY 10016; 140,000.

Zoological Parks & Aquariums, Amer. Assn. of (1924), Oglebay Park, Wheeling, WV 26003; 5,800.

Zoologists, Amer. Society of (1890), 104 Sirius Circle, Thousand Oaks, CA 91360; 4,000.

National Nonprofit Associations

Source: *Encyclopedia of Associations*

Type	1980	1985	1989	Type	1980	1985	1989
Trade, business, commercial	3,118	3,719	3,806	Fraternal, foreign interest	435	492	570
Agriculture	677	882	914	Religious	797	953	1,169
Legal, governmental, public				Veteran, hereditary, patriotic	208	281	404
administration, military	529	658	775	Hobby	910	1,311	1,471
Scientific, engineering, tech.	1,039	1,270	1,363	Athletic sports	504	737	839
Educational	2,376	2,822	1,268	Labor unions	235	252	254
Cultural			1,872	Chambers of Commerce	105	142	168
Social welfare	994	1,450	1,686	Letter societies	318	331	337
Health, medical	1,413	1,886	2,162	Fan clubs	NA	NA	561
Public affairs	1,068	1,935	2,292	**Total**	**14,726**	**19,121**	**21,911**

NATIONS OF THE WORLD

As of mid-1990

The nations of the world are listed in alphabetical order. Initials in the following articles include UN (United Nations), OAS (Org. of American States), NATO (North Atlantic Treaty Org.), EC (European Communities or Common Market), OAU (Org. of African Unity), ILO (Intl. Labor Org.), FAO (Food & Agricultural Org.), WHO (World Health Org.), IMF (Intl. Monetary Fund), GATT (General Agreements on Tarriffs & Trade). **Sources:** U.S. Dept. of State; U.S. Census Bureau; The World Factbook; International Monetary Fund; UN Statistical Yearbook; UN Demographic Yearbook; International Iron and Steel Institute; The Statesman's Year-Book; Encyclopaedia Britannica. All embassy addresses are Wash., DC; area codes (202), unless otherwise noted. Literacy rates are usually based on the ability to read and write on a lower elementary school level. The concept of literacy is changing in the industrialized countries, where literacy is defined as the ability to read instructions necessary for a job or a license. By these standards, illiteracy may be more common than present rates suggest. Per person figures in communications and health sections are post-1985.

See special color section for maps and flags.

Afghanistan

Republic of Afghanistan

De Afghanistan Jamhuriat

People: Population (1989 est.): 15,592,000. **Pop. density:** 65 per sq. mi. **Ethnic groups:** Pushtun 50%; Tajik 25%; Uzbek 9%; Hazara 9%. **Languages:** Pushtu, Dari Persian (spoken by Tajiks, Hazaras), Uzbek (Turkic). **Religions:** Sunni Moslem 74%, Shi'a Mosle:n 11%.

Geography: Area: 251,773 sq. mi., about the size of Texas. **Location:** Between Soviet Central Asia and the Indian subcontinent. **Neighbors:** Pakistan on E, S, Iran on W, USSR on N; the NE tip touches China. **Topography:** The country is landlocked and mountainous, much of it over 4,000 ft. above sea level. The Hindu Kush Mts. tower 16,000 ft. above Kabul and reach a height of 25,000 ft. to the E. Trade with Pakistan flows through the 35-mile long Khyber Pass. The climate is dry, with extreme temperatures, and large desert regions, though mountain rivers produce intermittent fertile valleys. **Capital:** Kabul. **Cities** (1987 est.): Kabul 1.2 mln.

Government: Type: Communist. **Head of state, and President of the Revolutionary Council:** Pres. Mohammad Najibullah; in office: Nov. 30, 1987. **Head of Government:** Prime Min. Sultan Ali Keshtmand; in office: Feb. 21, 1989. **Head of Communist Party:** Secy. Gen. Mohammad Najibullah; in office: May 4, 1986. **Local divisions:** 29 provinces, each under a governor. **Defense:** 7.7% of GNP (1984).

Economy: Industries: Textiles, furniture, cement. **Chief crops:** Nuts, wheat, fruits. **Minerals:** Copper, coal, zinc, iron. **Other resources:** Wool, hides, karacul pelts. **Arable land:** 13%. **Livestock** (1988): cattle: 7.7 mln.; sheep: 19 mln. **Electricity prod.** (1988): 1.7 bln. kwh. **Labor force:** agriculture supports about 80% of the population.

Finance: Currency: Afghani (Mar. 1990: 50.60 = $1 US). **Gross national product** (1988): $3.1 bln. **Per capita GNP:** $220. **Imports** (1988): $900 mln.; partners: USSR 30%, Jap. 10%. **Exports** (1988): $433 mln.; partners: USSR 86%. **International reserves less gold** (Feb. 1990): $254 mln. **Gold:** 965,000 oz t. **Consumer prices** (change in 1988): 20%.

Transport: Motor vehicles: in use (1982): 30,000 passenger cars, 35,000 comm. vehicles. **Civil aviation** (1987): 174 mln. passenger-km.

Communications: Television sets: 1 per 709 persons; **Radios:** 1 per 93 persons. **Telephones in use:** 1 per 443 persons. **Daily newspaper circ.** (1988): 10 per 1,000 pop.

Health: Life expectancy at birth (1989): 43 male; 42 female. **Births** (per 1,000 pop. 1989): 44. **Deaths** (per 1,000 pop. 1989): 21. **Natural increase:** 2.4%. **Hospital beds:** 1 per 2,054 persons. **Physicians:** 1 per 4,797 persons. **Infant mortality** (per 1,000 live births 1989): 173.

Education (1987): **Literacy:** 12%. Over 88% of adults have no formal schooling.

Major international Organizations: UN (World Bank, IMF) **Embassy:** 2341 Wyoming Ave. NW, 20008; 234-3770.

Afghanistan, occupying a favored invasion route since antiquity, has been variously known as Ariana or Bactria (in ancient times) and Khorasan (in the Middle Ages). Foreign empires alternated rule with local emirs and kings until the 18th century, when a unified kingdom was established. In 1973, a military coup ushered in a republic.

Pro-Soviet leftists took power in a bloody 1978 coup, and concluded an economic and military treaty with the USSR.

Late in Dec. 1979, the USSR began a massive military airlift into Kabul. The three-month old regime of Hafizullah Amin ended with a Soviet backed coup, Dec. 27th. He was replaced by Babrak Karmal, a more pro-Soviet leader. Soviet troops fanned out over Afghanistan fighting rebels. Fighting continued for 9 years as the Soviets found themselves engaged in a long, protracted guerrilla war.

An UN-mediated agreement was signed Apr. 14, 1988 providing for the withdrawal of Soviet troops from Afghanistan, creation of a neutral Afghan state, and repatriation of millions of Afghan refugees. The U.S. and USSR pledged to serve as guarantors of the agreement. Afghan rebels rejected the pact and vowed to continue fighting while the "Soviets and their puppets" remained in Afghanistan.

The Soviets disclosed that during the war some 15,000 soldiers were killed. They completed their troop withdrawal Feb. 15, 1989 as Afghan rebels and the government began a civil war; the rebels elected a government-in-axile Feb. 23.

There was a failed coup attempt, led by Afghan military forces, Mar. 6-8, 1990.

Albania

Peoples Socialist Republic of Albania

Republika Popullore Socialiste e Shqipërisë

People: Population (1990 est.): 3,268,000. **Pop. density:** 288 per sq. mi. **Urban** (1989): 35%. **Ethnic groups:** Albanians (Gegs in N, Tosks in S) 96%, Greeks 2.5%. **Languages:** Albanian (Tosk is official dialect), Greek. **Religions:** officially atheist; (historically) mostly Moslems. All public worship and religious institutions were outlawed in 1967. In 1990, the right to practice religion was restored.

Geography: Area: 11,100 sq. mi., slightly larger than Maryland. **Location:** On SE coast of Adriatic Sea. **Neighbors:** Greece on S, Yugoslavia on N, E. **Topography:** Apart from a narrow coastal plain, Albania consists of hills and mountains covered with scrub forest, cut by small E-W rivers. **Capital:** Tirana. **Cities** (1987 est.): Tirana 272,000; Durres 127,000; Vlore 90,000.

Government: Type: Communist. **Head of state:** Pres. Ramiz Alia, b. Oct. 18, 1925; in office: Nov. 22, 1982. **Head of government:** Premier Adil Carcani; in office: Jan. 18, 1982. **Head of Communist Party:** Ramiz Alia; in office: Apr. 13, 1985. **Local divisions:** 26 districts. **Defense:** 5.3% of GNP (1986).

Economy: Industries: Cement, textiles. **Chief crops:** Corn, wheat, cotton, potatoes, tobacco, fruits. **Minerals:** Chromium, coal, oil. **Other resources:** Forests. **Arable land:** 21%. **Livestock** (1987): 610,000 cattle; 1.4 mln. sheep. **Electricity prod.** (1988): 5.2 bln. kwh. **Labor force:** 50% agric; 50% ind. & comm.

Finance: Currency: Lek (Nov. 1989: 6.20 = $1 US). **Gross national product** (1986 est.) $2.8 bln. **Per capita GNP** (1986): $930. **Imports** (1986): $335 mln.; partners: Czech., Yugoslavia, Rom. **Exports** (1985): $345 mln.; partners: Czech., Yugoslavia, N. Korea, Italy.

Chief ports: Durres, Vlone, Shengjih.

Communications: Television sets: 1 per 10 persons. **Radios:** 1 per 6 persons. **Daily newspaper circ.** 48 per 1,000 pop.

Health: Life expectancy at birth (1987): 72.0 yrs. **Births** (per 1,000 pop. 1989): 25. **Deaths** (per 1,000 pop. 1989): 6. **Natural increase:** 1.9%. **Hospital beds:** 1 per 182 persons.

684

Physicians: 1 per 489 persons. **Infant mortality** (per 1,000 live births 1989): 59.

Major International Organizations: UN (FAO, WHO).

Education (1989): Literacy: 75%. Free and compulsory ages 7-15.

Ancient Illyria was conquered by Romans, Slavs, and Turks (15th century); the latter Islamized the population. Independent Albania was proclaimed in 1912, republic was formed in 1920. Self-styled King Zog I ruled 1925-39, until Italy invaded.

Communist partisans took over in 1944, allied Albania with USSR, then broke with USSR in 1960 over de-Stalinization. Strong political alliance with China followed, leading to several billion dollars in aid, which was curtailed after 1974. China cut off aid in 1978 when Albania attacked its policies after the death of Chinese ruler Mao Tse-tung.

Large-scale purges of officials occurred during the 1970s. Enver Hoxha, the nation's ruler for 4 decades, died Apr. 11, 1985.

There was some liberization in 1990, including measures providing for freedom to travel abroad and restoration of the right to practice religion.

Algeria

Democratic and Popular Republic of Algeria

al-Jumhuriya al-Jazāiriya ad-Dimuqratiya ash-Shabiya

People: Population (1990 est.): 25,714,000. **Age distrib. (%):** 0–14: 43.9; 15–59: 50.3; 60+: 5.8. **Pop. density:** 27 per sq. mi. **Urban** (1987): 49%. **Ethnic groups:** Arabs 75%, Berbers 25%. **Languages:** Arabic (official), Berber (indigenous language), French. **Religions:** Sunni Moslem (state religion).

Geography: Area: 918,497 sq. mi., more than 3 times the size of Texas. **Location:** In NW Africa, from Mediterranean Sea into Sahara Desert. **Neighbors:** Morocco on W, Mauritania, Mali, Niger on S, Libya, Tunisia on E. **Topography:** The Tell, located on the coast, comprises fertile plains 50-100 miles wide, with a moderate climate and adequate rain. Two major chains of the Atlas Mts., running roughly E-W, and reaching 7,000 ft., enclose a dry plateau region. Below lies the Sahara, mostly desert with major mineral resources. **Capital:** Algiers (El Djazair). **Cities** (1987 est.): El Djazair 1,483,000; Wahran 590,000; Qacentina 483,000.

Government: Type: Republic. **Head of state:** Pres. Chadli Benjedid; b. Apr. 14, 1929; in office: Feb. 9, 1979. **Head of government:** Premier Kasdi Merbah; in office: Nov. 5, 1988. **Local divisions:** 48 wilayaat (provinces). **Defense:** 3.0% of GNP (1987).

Economy: Industries: Oil, light industry, food processing. **Chief crops:** Grains, wine-grapes, potatoes, dates, olives, oranges. **Minerals:** Mercury, iron, zinc, lead. **Crude oil reserves** (1987): 4.8 bln. bbls. **Other resources:** Cork trees. **Arable land:** 17%; **Livestock** (1988): cattle: 1.7 mln.; sheep: 14 mln. **Electricity prod.** (1988): 13.6 bln. kwh. **Crude steel prod.** (1988): 1.4 mln. metric tons **Labor force:** 30% agric.; 30% ind. and commerce; 27% government, & services.

Finance: Currency: Dinar (Mar. 1990: 7.96 = $1 US). **Gross national product** (1987): $63.5 bln. **Per capita income** (1987): $2,760. **Imports** (1988): $7.7 bln.; partners: EEC 64%. **Exports** (1988): $8.6 bln.; partners: EEC 74%. **National budget** (1987): $21.3 bln. **International reserves less gold** (Mar. 1990): $837 mln. **Gold:** 5.58 mln. oz t. **Consumer prices** (change in 1988): 5.9%

Transport: Motor vehicles: in use (1986): 712,000 passenger cars, 471,000 comm. vehicles. **Chief ports:** El Djazair.

Communications: Television sets: 1 per 15 persons. **Radios:** 1 per 4 persons. **Telephones in use:** 1 per 26 persons. **Daily newspaper circ.** (1987): 47 per 1,000 pop.

Health: Life expectancy at birth (1989): 63 male; 67 female. **Births** (per 1,000 pop. 1987): 34.6. **Deaths** (per 1,000 pop. 1987): 7.0. **Natural increase** (1987): 2.7%. **Hospital beds:** 1 per 367 persons. **Physicians:** 1 per 1,302 persons. **Infant mortality** (per 1,000 live births 1986): 82.4

Education (1989): **Literacy:** 52%. **School:** Free and compulsory to age 16; Attendance: 94% primary, 47% secondary.

Major International Organizations: UN (FAO, IMF, WHO), OAU, Arab League, OPEC.

Embassy: 2118 Kalorama Rd. NW, 20008; 328-5300.

Earliest known inhabitants were ancestors of Berbers, followed by Phoenicians, Romans, Vandals, and, finally, Arabs. Turkey ruled 1518 to 1830, when France took control.

Large-scale European immigration and French cultural inroads did not prevent an Arab nationalist movement from launching guerilla war. Peace, and French withdrawal, was negotiated with French Pres. Charles de Gaulle. One million Europeans left.

Ahmed Ben Bella was the victor of infighting, and ruled 1962-65, when an army coup installed Col. Houari Boumedienne as leader.

In 1967, Algeria declared war with Israel, broke with U.S., and moved toward eventual military and political ties with the USSR. Some 500 died in riots protesting economic hardship in 1988. In 1989, voters approved a new constitution which cleared the way for a multiparty system and guaranteed "fundamental rights and freedoms" of Algerians.

Andorra

Principality of Andorra

Principat d'Andorra

People: Population (1990 est.): 51,000. **Age distrib. (%):** 0–14: 19.0; 14–59: 68.5; 60+: 12.5. **Pop. density:** 302 per sq. mi. **Ethnic groups:** Catalan 61%, Spanish 30%, Andorran 6%, French 3%. **Languages:** Catalan (official), Spanish, French. **Religion:** Roman Catholic.

Geography: Area: 185 sq. mi., half the size of New York City. **Location:** In Pyrenees Mtns. **Neighbors:** Spain on S, France on N. **Topography:** High mountains and narrow valleys over the country. **Capital:** Andorra la Vella.

Government: Type: Co-principality. **Head of state:** Co-princes are the president of France and the Roman Catholic bishop of Urgel in Spain. **Local divisions:** 7 parishes.

Economy: Industries: Tourism, tobacco products. **Labor force:** 20% agric.; 80% ind. and commerce; services; government.

Finance: Currency: French franc, Spanish peseta.

Communications: Television sets: 1 per 12 persons . **Radios:** 1 per 6 persons. **Telephones in use:** 1 per 2 persons.

Health: Births (per 1,000 pop. 1989): 10. **Deaths** (per 1,000 pop. 1989): 4. **Natural increase:** 0.7%.

Education (1989): **Literacy:** 99%. School compulsory to age 16.

The present political status, with joint sovereignty by France and the bishop of Urgel, dates from 1278.

Tourism, especially skiing, is the economic mainstay. A free port, allowing for an active trading center, draws some 10 million tourists annually. The ensuing economic prosperity accompanied by Andorra's virtual law-free status, has given rise to calls for reform.

Angola

People's Republic of Angola

República Popular de Angola

People: Population (1990 est.): 8,802,000. **Pop. density:** 18 per sq. mi. **Ethnic groups:** Ovimbundu 36%, Kimbundu 25%; Bakongo 13%. **Languages:** Portuguese (official), various Bantu languages. **Religions:** Roman Catholic 38%, Protestant 15%, indigenous beliefs 47%.

Geography: Area: 481,353 sq. mi., larger than Texas and California combined. **Location:** In SW Africa on Atlantic coast. **Neighbors:** Namibia (SW Africa) on S, Zambia on E, Zaire on N; Cabinda, an enclave separated from rest of country by short Atlantic coast of Zaire, borders Congo Republic. **Topography:** Most of Angola consists of a plateau elevated 3,000 to 5,000 feet above sea level, rising from a narrow coastal strip. There is also a temperate highland area in the west-central region, a desert in the S, and a tropical rain forest covering Cabinda. **Capital:** Luanda (1988 est.): 1.1 mln.

Government: Type: Marxist people's republic, one-party rule. **Head of state:** Pres. Jose Eduardo dos Santos b. Aug. 28, 1942; in office: Sept. 20, 1979. **Local divisions:** 18 provinces. **Defense:** 14.3% of GNP (1984).

Economy: Industries: Food processing, textiles, mining, tires, petroleum. Chief crops: Coffee, bananas. Minerals: Iron, diamonds (over 2 mln. carats a year), copper, phosphates, oil. Crude oil reserves (1987): 1.9 bln. bbls. Arable land: 3%. Fish catch (1987): 81,000 metric tons. Electricity prod. (1988): 737 mln.kwh. Labor force: 85% agric., 15% industry.

Finance: Currency: Kwanza (Nov. 1989: 29.38 = $1 US). Gross domestic product (1987): $4.7 bln. Imports (1986): $1.1 bln.; partners: Portugal 9%, Fra. 12%; U.S. 9.2%. Exports (1986): $1.4 bln.; partners: U.S. 38%.

Transport: Motor vehicles: in use (1984): 56,000 passenger cars, 29,000 comm. vehicles. Chief ports: Cabinda, Lobito, Luanda.

Communications: Television sets: 1 per 228 persons. Radios: 1 per 22 persons. Telephones in use: 1 per 122 persons. Daily newspaper circ. (1984): 13 per 1,000 pop.

Health: Life expectancy at birth (1989): 42.0 male; 45.0 female. Births (per 1,000 pop. 1989): 47. Deaths (per 1,000 pop. 1989): 21. Natural increase: 2.6%. Hospital beds: 1 per 672 persons. Physicians: 1 per 13,489 persons. Infant mortality (per 1,000 live births 1989): 161.

Education (1989): Literacy: 30%.

Major International Organizations: UN (ILO, WHO), OAU.

From the early centuries AD to 1500, Bantu tribes penetrated most of the region. Portuguese came in 1583, allied with the Bakongo kingdom in the north, and developed the slave trade. Large-scale colonization did not begin until the 20th century, when 400,000 Portuguese immigrated.

A guerrilla war begun in 1961 lasted until 1974, when Portugal offered independence. Violence between the National Front, based in Zaire, the Soviet-backed Popular Movement, and the National Union, aided by the U.S. and S. Africa, killed thousands of blacks, drove most whites to emigrate, and completed economic ruin. Cuban troops and Soviet aid helped the Popular Movement win most of the country after independence Nov. 11, 1975, igniting a Civil War.

S. African troops crossed the southern Angolan border June 7, 1981, killing more than 300 civilians and occupying several towns. The S. Africans withdrew in Sept.

Jonas Savimbi, leader of the National Union for Total Independence of Angola (UNITA), a rebel group fighting to overthrow the government, visited the U.S. in 1986 and was favorably received by the Reagan administration.

An agreement was signed Dec. 1988 between Angola, Cuba, and S. Africa on a timetable for withdrawal of Cuban troops (1991), and for the independence of Namibia. The 14-year war ended June 22, 1989, as the government and the rebels agreed to a cease fire.

Antigua and Barbuda

People: Population (1990 est.) 64,000. Urban: (1985) 34%. Ethnic groups: Mostly African. Language: English (official). Religion: Predominantly Church of England.

Geography: Area: 171 sq. mi. Location: Eastern Caribbean. Neighbors: approx. 30 mi. north of Guadeloupe. Capital: St. John's, (1988 est.) 27,000.

Government: Type: Constitutional monarchy with British-style parliament. Head of State: Queen Elizabeth II; represented by Sir Wilfred E. Jacobs. Head of Government: Prime Min. Vere Cornwall Bird; b. Dec. 7, 1910; in office Nov. 1, 1981.

Economy: Industries: manufacturing, tourists (195,000 in 1984). Arable Land: 18%.

Finance: Currency: East Caribbean dollar (Apr. 1990): 2.70 = $1 U.S. Gross national product (1988): $215 mln.

Health: infant mortality (per 1,000 live births 1989): 11.

Education (1990): Literacy: 90%.

Major International Organizations: UN, Commonwealth of Nations.

Embassy: 2400 International Dr., NW 20008; 362-5122.

Antigua was discovered by Columbus in 1493. The British colonized it in 1632.

The British associated state of Antigua achieved independence as Antigua and Barbuda on Nov. 1, 1981. The government maintains close relations with the U.S., United Kingdom, and Venezuela.

Argentina
Argentine Republic
República Argentina

People: Population (1990 est.): 32,291,000. Age distrib. (%): 0–14: 31.1; 15–59: 56.6; 60+: 12.3. Pop. density: 30 per sq. mi. Urban (1987): 85%. Ethnic groups: Europeans 85% (Spanish, Italian), Indians, Mestizos, Arabs. Languages: Spanish (official), English, Italian, German, French. Religions: Roman Catholic 92%.

Geography: Area: 1,065,189 sq. mi., 4 times the size of Texas, second largest in S. America. Location: Occupies most of southern S. America. Neighbors: Chile on W, Bolivia, Paraguay on N, Brazil, Uruguay on NE. Topography: The mountains in W: the Andean, Central, Misiones, and Southern. Aconcagua is the highest peak in the Western hemisphere, alt. 22,834 ft. E of the Andes are heavily wooded plains, called the Gran Chaco in the N, and the fertile, treeless Pampas in the central region. Patagonia, in the S, is bleak and arid. Rio de la Plata, 170 by 140 mi., is mostly fresh water, from 2,485-mi. Parana and 1,000-mi. Uruguay rivers. Capital: Buenos Aires. (The Senate has approved the moving of the capital to the Patagonia Region). Cities (1982 est.): Buenos Aires 2,908,000; Cordoba 969,000; Rosario 750,455; Mendoza 597,000; San Miguel de Tucuman 497,000.

Government: Type: Republic. Head of state: Pres. Carlos Saúl Menem; b. July 2, 1930; in office: July 8, 1989. Local divisions: 22 provinces, 1 natl. terr. and 1 federal dist., under military governors. Defense: 1.4% of GNP (1987).

Economy: Industries: Meat processing, flour milling, chemicals, textiles, machinery, autos. Chief crops: Grains, corn, grapes, linseed, sugar, tobacco, rice, soybeans, citrus fruits. Minerals: Oil, lead, zinc, iron, copper, uranium. Crude oil reserves (1987): 2.1 bln. bbls. Arable land: 13%. Livestock (1988): cattle: 50 mln.; sheep: 29 mln. Fish catch (1987): 420,000 metric tons. Electricity prod. (1988): 48.0 bln. kwh. Crude steel prod. (1988): 3.6 mln. metric tons. Labor force: 12% agric.; 31% ind. and comm.; 57% services.

Finance: Currency: Austral (June 1990: 5,330 = $1 US). Gross national product (1987): $74.3 bln. Per capita GNP (1987): $2,360. Imports (1988): $5.3 bln.; partners: U.S. 18%, W. Ger. 9%, Braz. 16%, Jap. 7%. Exports (1988): $9.1 bln.; partners: USSR 13%, Neth. 9%, U.S. 12%. Tourists (1987): receipts: $614 mln. National budget (1987): $9.5 bln. expenditures. International reserves less gold (Jan. 1990): $1.4 bln. Gold: 4.37 mln. oz t. Consumer prices (change in 1989): 3,079%.

Transport: Railway traffic (1986): 10.7 bln. passenger-km. Motor vehicles: in use (1986): 3.8 mln. passenger cars, 1.4 mln. comm. vehicles. Civil aviation: (1988) 7.7 mln. passenger-km. Chief ports: Buenos Aires, Bahia Blanca, La Plata.

Communications: Television sets: 1 per 4 persons. Radios: 1 per 1 person. Telephones in use: 1 per 9 persons. Daily newspaper circ. (1986): 88 per 1,000 pop.

Health: Life expectancy at birth (1989): 67 male; 74 female. Births (per 1,000 pop. 1989): 20. Deaths (per 1,000 pop. 1989): 9. Natural increase: 1.2%. Hospital beds: 1 per 186 persons. Physicians: 1 per 370 persons. Infant mortality (per 1,000 live births 1989): 32.

Education (1989): Literacy: 94%. School attendence: 21.5% through secondary school.

Major International Organizations: UN (WHO, IMF, FAO), OAS.

Embassy: 1600 New Hampshire Ave. NW 20009; 939-6400.

Nomadic Indians roamed the Pampas when Spaniards arrived, 1515-1516, led by Juan Diaz de Solis. Nearly all the Indians were killed by the late 19th century. The colonists won independence, 1810-1819, and a long period of disorders ended in a strong centralized government.

Large-scale Italian, German, and Spanish immigration in the decades after 1880 spurred modernization, making Argentina the most prosperous, educated, and industrialized of the major Latin American nations. Social reforms were enacted in the 1920s, but military coups prevailed 1930-46, until the election of Gen. Juan Peron as president.

Peron, with his wife Eva Duarte effected labor reforms, but also suppressed speech and press freedoms, closed religious schools, and ran the country into debt. A 1955 coup exiled Peron, who was followed by a series of military and civilian regimes. Peron returned in 1973, and was once more elected president. He died 10 months later, succeeded by his wife, Isabel, who had been elected vice president, and who became the first woman head of state in the Western hemisphere.

A military junta ousted Mrs. Peron in 1976 amid charges of corruption. Under a continuing state of siege, the army battled guerrillas and leftists, killed 5,000 people, and jailed and tortured others. On Dec. 9, 1985, after a trial of 5 months and nearly 1,000 witnesses, 5 former junta members, including ex-presidents Jorge Videla and Gen. Roberto Eduardo Viola, were found guilty of murder and human rights abuses.

A severe worsening in economic conditions placed extreme pressure on the military government.

Argentine troops seized control of the British-held Falkland Islands on Apr. 2, 1982. Both countries had claimed sovereignty over the islands, located 250 miles off the Argentine coast, since 1833. The British dispatched a task force and declared a total air and sea blockade around the Falklands. Fighting began May 1; several hundred lost their lives as the result of the destruction of a British destroyer and the sinking of an Argentine cruiser.

British troops landed in force on East Falkland Island May 21. By June 2, the British had surrounded Stanley, the capital city and Argentine stronghold. The Argentine troops surrendered, June 14; Argentine President Leopoldo Galtieri resigned June 17.

Democratic rule returned to Argentina in 1983 as Raul Alfonsin's Radical Civic Union gained an absolute majority in the presidential electoral college and Congress. In 1989 the nation was plagued by severe financial problems as inflation reached crisis levels; over 6,000%. The hyperinflation sparked a week of looting and rioting in several cities; the government declared a 30-day state of siege May 29.

The International Monetary Fund approved a renewal of a $1.44 bln. loan package to Argentina, May 1990.

Australia
Commonwealth of Australia

People: Population (1990 est.): 16,646,000. **Age distrib.** (%): 0–14: 22.1; 15–59; 62.5; ; 59 +: 15.4. **dop. density:** 5.4 per sq. mi. **Urban** (1984): 85%. **Ethnic groups:** European 95%, Asian 4%, aborigines (including mixed) 1.5%. **Languages:** English, aboriginal languages. **Religions:** Anglican 26%, other Protestant 25%, Roman Catholic 25%.

Geography: Area: 2,966,200 sq. mi., almost as large as the continental U.S. **Location:** SE of Asia, Indian O. is W and S, Pacific O. (Coral, Tasman seas) is E; they meet N of Australia in Timor and Arafura seas; Tasmania lies 150 mi. S of Victoria state, across Bass Strait. **Neighbors:** Nearest are Indonesia, Papua New Guinea on N, Solomons, Fiji, and New Zealand on E. **Topography:** An island continent. The Great Dividing Range along the E coast has Mt. Kosciusko, 7,310 ft. The W plateau rises to 2,000 ft., with arid areas in the Great Sandy and Great Victoria deserts. The NW part of Western Australia and Northern Terr. are arid and hot. The NE has heavy rainfall and Cape York Peninsula has jungles. The Murray R. rises in New South Wales and flows 1,600 mi. to the Indian O. **Capital:** Canberra. **Cities** (1987 est.): Sydney 3,500,000; Melbourne 3,000,000; Brisbane 1,200,000; Adelaide 993,000; Perth 1,100,000.

Government: Type: Democratic, federal state system. **Head of state:** Queen Elizabeth II, represented by Gov.-Gen. William Hayden; in office: Feb. 16, 1989. **Head of government:** Prime Min. Robert James Lee Hawke; b. Dec. 9, 1929; in office: Mar. 11, 1983. **Local divisions:** 6 states, 2 territories. **Defense:** 2.7% of GNP (1988).

Economy: Industries: iron, steel, textiles, electrical equip., chemicals, autos, aircraft, ships, machinery. **Chief crops:** Wheat (a leading export), barley, oats, corn, hay, sugar, wine, fruit, vegetables. **Minerals:** Coal, copper, iron, lead, tin, uranium, zinc. **Crude oil reserves** (1987): 1.6 bln. bbls. **Other resources:** Wool (30% of world output). **Arable land:** 9%. **Livestock** (1989): cattle: 22 mln.; sheep: 162 mln.; pigs: 2.5 mln. **Fish catch** (1987): 156,000 metric tons. **Electricity prod.** (1988): 135 bln. kwh. **Crude steel prod.** (1988): 6.1 mln. metric tons. **Labor force:** 6% agric.; 33% finance & services; 36% trade & manuf.

Finance: Currency: Dollar (June 1990: 1.30 = $1.00 US). **Gross national product** (1988): $220 bln. **Per capita income**

(1988): $14,458. **Imports** (1989): $44.6 bln; partners: U.S. 21%, Jap. 20%, UK 7%. **Exports** (1989): $33.0 bln.; partners: Jap. 27%, U.S. 11%, NZ 5%. **Tourists** (1988): $2.1 bln. receipts. **National budget** (1989): $65 bln. expenditures. **International reserves less gold** (Mar. 1990): $12.8 bln. **Gold:** 7.93 mln. oz t. **Consumer prices** (change in 1989): 7.6%.

Transport: Motor vehicles: in use (1986): 8.7 mln. passenger cars, 1.2 mln. comm. vehicles. **Civil aviation** (1988): 26.2 mln. passenger-km.; 441 airports with scheduled flights. **Chief ports:** Sydney, Melbourne, Newcastle, Port Kembla, Fremantle, Geelong.

Communications: Television sets: 1 per 2 persons. **Radios:** 1 per 2 persons. **Telephones in use:** 1 per 2 persons. **Daily newspaper circ.** (1985): 308 per 1,000 pop.

Health: Life expectancy at birth (1989): 73 male; 80 female. **Births** (per 1,000 pop. 1989): 15. **Deaths** (per 1,000 pop. 1989): 8. **Natural increase:** 8%. **Hospital beds:** 1 per 186 persons. **Physicians:** 1 per 438 persons. **Infant mortality** (per 1,000 live births 1989): 8.1.

Education (1989): **Literacy:** 99%. **School:** compulsory to age 15; attendance 94%.

Major International Organizations: UN and all its specialized agencies, OECD, Commonwealth of Nations.

Embassy: 1601 Massachusetts Ave NW 20036; 797-3000.

Capt. James Cook explored the E coast in 1770, when the continent was inhabited by a variety of different tribes. The first settlers, beginning in 1788, were mostly convicts, soldiers, and government officials. By 1830, Britain had claimed the entire continent, and the immigration of free settlers began to accelerate. The commonwealth was proclaimed Jan. 1, 1901. Northern Terr. was granted limited self-rule July 1, 1978. Their capitals and 1988 population estimates:

	Area (sq. mi.)	Population
New South Wales, Sydney	309,500	5,699,300
Victoria, Melbourne	87,900	4,260,300
Queensland, Brisbane	666,990	2,742,900
Western Aust., Perth	975,100	1,543,900
South Aust., Adelaide	379,900	1,408,000
Tasmania, Hobart	26,200	448,400
Aust. Capital Terr., Canberra	900	273,300
Northern Terr., Darwin	519,800	155,800

Australia's racially discriminatory immigration policies were abolished in 1973, after 3 million Europeans (half British) had entered since 1945. The 50,000 aborigines and 150,000 part-aborigines are mostly detribalized, but there are several preserves in the Northern Territory. They remain economically disadvantaged.

On Jan. 26, 1988, some 15,000 aborigines demonstrated in Sydney to protest discrimination while the rest of the nation celebrated the 200th anniversary of the landing of the first European settlers.

Australia's agricultural success makes it among the top exporters of beef, lamb, wool, and wheat. Major mineral deposits have been developed as well, largely for exports. Industrialization has been completed.

Australia harbors many plant and animal species not found elsewhere, including the kangaroo, koalas, platypus, dingo (wild dog), Tasmanian devil (racoon-like marsupial), wombat (bear-like marsupial), and barking and frilled lizards.

Australian External Territories

Norfolk Is., area 13½ sq. mi., pop. (1985) 1,800, was taken over, 1914. The soil is very fertile, suitable for citrus fruits, bananas, and coffee. Many of the inhabitants are descendants of the Bounty mutineers, moved to Norfolk 1856 from Pitcairn Is. Australia offered the island limited home rule, 1978.

Coral Sea Is. Territory, 1 sq. mi., is administered from Norfolk Is.

Territory of Ashmore and Cartier Is., area 2 sq. mi., in the Indian O. came under Australian authority 1934 and are administered as part of Northern Territory. **Heard** and **McDonald Is.** are administered by the Dept. of Science.

Cocos (Keeling) Is., 27 small coral islands in the Indian O. 1,750 mi. NW of Australia. Pop. (1981) 569, area: 5½ sq. mi. The residents voted to become part of Australia, Apr. 1984.

Christmas Is., 52 sq. mi., pop. 3,000 (1983), 230 mi. S of Java, was transferred by Britain in 1958. It has phosphate deposits.

Australian Antarctic Territory was claimed by Australia in 1933, including 2,360,000 sq. mi. of territory S of 60th parallel S Lat. and between 160th-45th meridians E Long. It does not include Adelie Coast.

Austria

Republic of Austria

Republik Österreich

People: Population (1990 est.): 7,595,000. **Age distrib.** (%): 0–14: 17.7; 15–59: 62.1; 60+: 20.2. **Pop. density:** 233 per sq. mi. **Urban** (1986): 55.0%. **Ethnic groups:** German 98%, Slovene, Croatian. **Languages:** German 98%. **Religions:** Roman Catholic 85%.

Geography: Area: 32,374 sq. mi., slightly smaller than Maine. **Location:** In S Central Europe. **Neighbors:** Switzerland, Liechtenstein on W, W. Germany, Czechoslovakia on N, Hungary on E, Yugoslavia, Italy on S. **Topography:** Austria is primarily mountainous, with the Alps and foothills covering the western and southern provinces. The eastern provinces and Vienna are located in the Danube River Basin. **Capital:** Vienna. **Cities** (1987 cen.): Vienna 1,500,000.

Government: Type: Federal republic. **Head of state:** Pres. Kurt Waldheim; b. Dec. 21, 1918; in office: June 8, 1986. **Head of government:** Chancellor Franz Vranitzky; b. Oct. 4, 1937; in office: June 16, 1986. **Local divisions:** 9 lander (states), each with a legislature. **Defense:** 1.2% of GNP (1987).

Economy: Industries: Steel, machinery, autos, electrical and optical equip., glassware, sport goods, paper, textiles, chemicals, cement. **Chief crops:** Grains, potatoes, beets. **Minerals:** Iron ore, oil, magnesite. **Crude oil reserves** (1985): 116 mln. bbls. **Other resources:** Forests, hydro power. **Arable land:** 18.3%. **Livestock:** (1986): Cattle: 2.6 mln.; pigs: 3.8 mln. **Electricity prod.** (1988): 47.8 bln. kwh. **Crude steel prod.** (1988): 4.5 mln. metric tons. **Labor force:** 8% agric.; 35% ind. & comm.; 56% service.

Finance: Currency: Schilling (June 1990: 11.79 = $1 US). **Gross national product** (1987): $118.1 bln. **Per capita income** (1986): $12,521. **Imports** (1989): $38.9 bln.; partners: W. Ger. 44%, It. 9%, Switz. 5%. **Exports** (1989): $31.9 bln.; partners: W. Ger. 33%, It. 9%, Switz. 7%. **Tourists** (1987): receipts: $7.6 bln. **National budget** (1987): $37.5 bln. expenditures. **International reserves less gold** (Mar. 1990): $8.0 bln. **Gold:** 20.3 mln. oz t. **Consumer prices** (change in 1989): 2.6%.

Transport: Railway traffic (1987): 7.3 bln. passenger-km. **Motor vehicles:** in use (1987): 2.6 mln. passenger cars, 212,000 comm. **Civil aviation** (1987): 1.0 bln. passenger-km; 6 airports with scheduled flights.

Communications: Television sets: 1 per 2.8 persons. **Radios:** 1 per 1.6 persons. **Telephones in use:** 1 per 1.9 persons. **Daily newspaper circ.** (1986): 312 per 1,000 pop.

Health: Life expectancy at birth (1989): 71 male; 79 female. **Births** (per 1,000 pop. 1989): 12. **Deaths** (per 1,000 pop. 1989): 12. **Natural increase:** –.0%. **Hospital beds:** 1 per 92 persons. **Physicians:** 1 per 370 persons. **Infant mortality** (per 1,000 live births 1989): 8.

Education (1989): Literacy: 99%. School years compulsory 9; attendance 95%.

Major International Organizations: UN and all of its specialized agencies, EFTA, OECD.

Embassy: 2343 Massachusetts Ave. NW 20008; 483-4474.

Rome conquered Austrian lands from Celtic tribes around 15 BC. In 788 the territory was incorporated into Charlemagne's empire. By 1300, the House of Hapsburg had gained control; they added vast territories in all parts of Europe to their realm in the next few hundred years.

Austrian dominance of Germany was undermined in the 18th century and ended by Prussia by 1866. But the Congress of Vienna, 1815, confirmed Austrian control of a large empire in southeast Europe consisting of Germans, Hungarians, Slavs, Italians, and others.

The dual Austro-Hungarian monarchy was established in 1867, giving autonomy to Hungary and almost 50 years of peace.

World War I, started after the June 28, 1914 assassination of Archduke Franz Ferdinand, the Hapsburg heir, by a Serbian nationalist, destroyed the empire. By 1918 Austria was reduced to a small republic, with the borders it has today.

Nazi Germany invaded Austria Mar. 13, 1938. The republic was reestablished in 1945, under Allied occupation. Full independence and neutrality were restored in 1955.

Austria produces most of its food, as well as an array of industrial products. A large part of Austria's economy is controlled by state enterprises. Socialists have shared or alternated power with the conservative People's Party.

Economic agreements with the Common Market give Austria access to a free-trade area encompassing most of West Europe.

An international panel of historians issued a report in 1988 which concluded that Pres. Kurt Waldheim knew of war crimes in Greece and Yugoslavia while serving in the German army during WW 2, did nothing to stop them, and later covered up his war record. The panel found no evidence that Waldheim committed war crimes.

The Bahamas

The Commonwealth of the Bahamas

People: Population (1990 est.). 251,000. **Age distrib.** (%): 0–14: 38.0; 15–59: 56.3; 60+: 5.7. **Pop. density:** 45 per sq. mi. **Urban** (1987): 75%. **Ethnic groups:** black 85%, white (British, Canadian, U.S.) 15%. **Languages:** English. **Religions:** Baptist 29%, Anglican 23%, Roman Catholic 22%.

Geography: Area: 5,380 sq. mi., about the size of Connecticut. **Location:** In Atlantic O., E of Florida. **Neighbors:** Nearest are U.S. on W, Cuba on S. **Topography:** Nearly 700 islands (30 inhabited) and over 2,000 islets in the western Atlantic extend 760 mi. NW to SE. **Capital:** Nassau. **Cities:** (1985 est.) New Providence 135,437; Freeport 16,000.

Government: Type: Independent commonwealth. **Head of state:** Queen Elizabeth II, represented by Gov.-Gen. Henry Taylor, in office: June 25, 1988. **Head of government:** Prime Min. Lynden Oscar Pindling; b. Mar. 22, 1930; in office: Jan. 16, 1967. **Local divisions:** 21 districts.

Economy: Industries: Tourism (50% of GNP), rum, banking, pharmaceuticals. **Chief crops:** Fruits, vegetables. **Minerals:** Salt. **Other resources:** Lobsters. **Arable land:** 2%. **Electricity prod.** (1988): 828 mln. kwh. **Labor force:** 5% agric.; 25% tourism, 30% government.

Finance: Currency: Dollar (Jan. 1990: 1 = $1 US). **Gross national product** (1986): $1.7 bln. **Per capita income** (1986): $7,598. **Imports** (1987): $1.7 bln.; partners: U.S. 74%, EC 30%. **Exports** (1987): $733 mln. (not incl. oil); partners: U.S. 41%, U.K. 7%. **Tourists** (1988): $1.1 bln. **National budget** (1987): $404 mln. expenditures. **International reserves less gold** (Mar. 1990): $163 mln. **Consumer prices** (change in 1989): 5.4%.

Transport: Motor vehicles: in use (1984): 88,000 passenger cars, 5,600 comm. vehicles. **Chief ports:** Nassau, Freeport.

Communications: Radios: 1 per 2 persons. **Television sets:** 1 per 4.6 persons. **Telephones in use:** 1 per 2 persons. **Daily newspaper circ.** (1988): 143 per 1,000 pop.

Health: Life expectancy at birth (1989): 67 male; 74 female. **Births** (per 1,000 pop. 1989): 23. **Deaths** (per 1,000 pop. 1989): 6. **Natural increase:** 1.7%. **Infant mortality** (per 1,000 live births 1989): 17.

Education (1989): Literacy: 95%; School compulsory through age 14.

Major International Organizations: UN (World Bank, IMF, WHO), OAS.

Embassy: 600 New Hampshire Ave. NW 20037; 338-3940.

Christopher Columbus first set foot in the New World on San Salvador (Watling I.) in 1492, when Arawak Indians inhabited the islands. British settlement began in 1647; the islands became a British colony in 1783. Internal self-government was granted in 1964; full independence within the Commonwealth was attained July 10, 1973.

International banking and investment management has become a major industry alongside tourism, despite controversy over financial irregularities.

Bahrain

State of Bahrain

Dawlat al-Bahrayn

People: Population (1990 est.): 512,000. **Age distrib. (%):** 0-14: 33.4; 15-59: 62.8; 60+ 3.8. **Pop. density:** 1,872 per sq. mi. **Urban** (1986): 82%. **Ethnic groups:** Bahraini 63%, Asian 13%, other Arab 10%, Iranian 6%. **Languages:** Arabic (official), Farsi, Urdu. **Religions:** Sunni Moslem 30%, Shi'ah Moslem 70%.

Geography: Area: 258 sq. mi., smaller than New York City. **Location:** In Persian Gulf. **Neighbors:** Nearest are Saudi Arabia on W. Qatar on E. **Topography:** Bahrain Island, and several adjacent, smaller islands, are flat, hot and humid, with little rain. **Capital:** Manama. **Cities** (1987 est.): Manama 146,000.

Government: Type: Traditional monarchy. **Head of state:** Amir Isa bin Sulman al-Khalifa; b. July 3, 1933; in office: Nov. 2, 1961. **Head of government:** Prime Min. Kahlifa ibn Sulman al-Khalifa; b. 1935; in office: Jan. 19, 1970. **Local divisions:** 11 municipalities. **Defense:** 4.0% of GNP (1985).

Economy: Industries: Oil products, aluminum smelting. **Chief crops:** Fruits, vegetables. **Minerals:** Oil, gas. **Crude oil reserves** (1985): 173 mln. bbls. **Arable land:** 5%. **Electricity prod.** (1988): 5.4 bln. kwh. **Labor force:** 5% agric.; 85% ind. and commerce; 5% services; 3% gov.

Finance: Currency: Dinar (Mar. 1990): 1.00 = $2.66 US). **Gross national product** (1987): $4.6 bln. **Per capita GNP** (1987): $9,994. **Imports** (1988): $2.6 bln.; partners: Sau. Ar. 60%, UK 6%, U.S. 9%. **Exports** (1988): $2.3 bln.; partners: UAE 18%, Jap. 12%, Sing. 10%, U.S. 6%. **National Budget** (1987): $2.6 bln. expenditures. **International reserves less gold** (Mar. 1990): $855 mln. **Gold:** 150,000 oz t. **Consumer prices** (change in 1989): 0.3%.

Transport: Motor vehicles: in use (1986): 81,000 passenger cars, 24,000 comm. vehicles. **Chief ports:** Sitra.

Communications: Television sets: 1 per 2.3 persons. **Radios:** 1 per 1.7 persons. **Telephones in use:** 1 per 3.4 persons.

Health: Life Expectancy at Birth (1989): 70 male; 75 female. **Births** (per 1,000 pop. 1989): 25. **Deaths** (per 1,000 pop. 1989): 4. **Natural Increase:** 2.1. Medical services are free. **Infant Mortality** (per 1,000 live births 1989): 22.

Education (1989): **Literacy:** 40%.

Major International Organizations: UN (GATT, IMF, WHO), Arab League.

Embassy: 3502 International Dr. NW 20008; 342-0741.

Long ruled by the Khalifa family, Bahrain was a British protectorate from 1861 to 1971, when it regained independence.

Pearls, shrimp, fruits, and vegetables were the mainstays of the economy until oil was discovered in 1932. By the 1970s, oil reserves were depleted; international banking thrived.

Bahrain took part in the 1973-74 Arab oil embargo against the U.S. and other nations. The government bought controlling interest in the oil industry in 1975.

Saudi Arabia has built a 15-mile causeway linking Bahrain with the Arab mainland.

Bangladesh

People's Republic of Bangladesh

Gama Prajätantri Bangladesh

People: Population (1990 est.): 117,976,000. **Age distrib. (%):** 0-14: 44.3; 15-59: 50.4; 60+: 5.3. **Pop. density:** 2,028 per sq. mi. **Urban** (1988): 22%. **Ethnic groups:** Bengali 98%, Bihari, tribesmen. **Languages:** Bengali (official), English. **Religions:** Moslem 83%, Hindu 16%.

Geography: Area: 55,598 sq. mi. slightly smaller than Wisconsin. **Location:** In S Asia, on N bend of Bay of Bengal. **Neighbors:** India nearly surrounds country on W, N, E; Burma on SE. **Topography:** The country is mostly a low plain cut by the Ganges and Brahmaputra rivers and their delta. The land is alluvial and marshy along the coast, with hills only in the extreme SE and NE. A tropical monsoon climate prevails, among the rainiest in the world. **Capital:** Dhaka. **Cities** (1987 est.): Dhaka (met.) 3.4 mln.; Chittagong (met.) 1.4 mln.; Khulna (met.) 646,000.

Government: Type: Islamic republic. **Head of state:** Pres. Hossain Mohammad Ershad, b. Feb. 1, 1930, in office: Dec. 11, 1983. **Head of Government:** Prime Min. Kazi Zafar Ahmed, in office: Aug. 12, 1989. **Local divisions:** 21 districts. **Defense:** 1.8% of GNP (1987).

Economy: Industries: Cement, jute, textiles, fertilizers, petroleum products. **Chief crops:** Jute (most of world output), rice, tea. **Minerals:** Natural gas, offshore oil, coal. **Arable land:** 67%. **Livestock** (1987): cattle: 23 mln.; goats: 10.7 mln. **Fish catch** (1987): 837,000 metric tons. **Electricity prod.** (1988): 4.8 bln. kwh. **Labor force:** 74% agric; 11% ind.; 15% services.

Finance: Currency: Taka (Mar. 1990: 33.80 = $1 US). **Gross national product** (1988): $18.1 bln. **Per capita income** (1986) $113. **Imports** (1989): $3.6 bln.; partners: Jap. 13%, U.S. 13%. **Exports** (1989): $1.3 bln.; partners: U.S. 31%, lt. 9%; Pak 5%. **Tourists** (1987): $13.0 mln. receipts. **National budget** (1988): $3.3 bln. expenditures. **International reserves less gold** (Mar. 1990): $426 mln. **Gold:** 77,000 oz t. **Consumer prices** (change in 1989): 10.0%.

Transport: Railway traffic (1987): 6.0 bln. passenger-km. **Motor vehicles:** in use (1987): 41,000 passenger cars, 25,000 comm. vehicles. **Chief ports:** Chittagong, Chalna.

Communications: Radios: 1 per 24 persons. **Television sets:** 1 per 244 persons. **Telephones in use:** 1 per 568 persons. **Daily newspaper circ.** (1986) 6 per 1,000 pop.

Health: Life expectancy at birth (1989): 54 male; 53 female. **Births** (per 1,000 pop. 1989): 43. **Deaths** (per 1,000 pop. 1989): 15. **Natural increase:** 2.8%. **Hospital beds:** 1 per 3,187 persons. **Physicians:** 1 per 6,219 persons. **Infant mortality** (per 1,000 live births 1989): 138.

Education (1989): **Literacy:** 29%. **Attendance:** 24% primary school; 4% secondary school.

Major International Organizations: UN (GATT, IMF, WHO). **Embassy:** 2201 Wisconsin Ave. NW 20007; 342-8372.

Moslem invaders conquered the formerly Hindu area in the 12th century. British rule lasted from the 18th century to 1947, when East Bengal became part of Pakistan.

Charging West Pakistani domination, the Awami League, based in the East, won National Assembly control in 1971. Assembly sessions were postponed; riots broke out. Pakistani troops attacked Mar. 25; Bangladesh independence was proclaimed the next day. In the ensuing civil war, one million died and 10 million fled to India.

War between India and Pakistan broke out Dec. 3, 1971. Pakistan surrendered in the East Dec. 15. Sheik Mujibur Rahman became prime minister. The country moved into the Indian and Soviet orbits, in response to U.S. support of Pakistan, and much of the economy was nationalized.

In 1974, the government took emergency powers to curb widespread violence; Mujibur was assassinated and a series of coups followed.

Chronic destitution among the densely crowded population has been worsened by the decline of jute as a major world commodity.

On May 30, 1981, Pres. Ziaur Rahman was shot and killed in an unsuccessful coup attempt by army rivals. Vice President Abdus Sattar assumed the presidency but was ousted in a coup led by army chief of staff Gen. H.M. Ershad, Mar. 1982. Ershad declared Bangladesh an Islamic Republic in 1988. Bangladesh remains one of the world's poorest countries.

In 1988 and 1989, natural disasters and, monsoon rains brought devastation to Bangladesh: over 4,000 died, 30 million were made homeless.

Barbados

People: Population (1990 est.): 260,000 **Age distrib. (%):** 0-14: 25.1%; 15-59: 60.3; 60+: 14.6. **Pop. density:** 1,542 per sq. mi. **Urban** (1985): 42%. **Ethnic groups:** African 80%, mixed 16%, Caucasian 4%. **Languages:** English. **Religions:** Anglican 70%, Methodist 9%, Roman Catholic 4%.

Geography: Area: 166 sq. mi. **Location:** In Atlantic, farthest E of W. Indies. **Neighbors:** Nearest are Trinidad, Grenada on SW. **Topography:** The island lies alone in the Atlantic almost completely surrounded by coral reefs. Highest point is Mt. Hillaby, 1,115 ft. **Capital:** Bridgetown. **Cities** (1986): Bridgetown 7,400.

Government: Type: Independent sovereign state within the Commonwealth. **Head of state:** Queen Elizabeth II, represented by Gov.-Gen. Hugh Springer. **Head of government:** Prime Min.

Erskine Sandiford; b. Mar. 24, 1937; in office: June 1, 1987. **Local divisions:** 11 parishes and Bridgetown.

Economy: Industries: Rum, molasses, tourism. **Chief crops:** Sugar, corn. **Minerals:** Lime. **Other resources:** Fish. **Arable land:** 76%. **Electricity prod.** (1987): 425 mln. kwh. **Labor force:** 8% agric.; 22% ind. and comm.; 37% services and government.

Finance: Currency: Dollar (June 1990: 2.01 = $1 US). **Gross national product** (1987): $1.4 bln. **Per capita GNP** (1987): $5,330. **Imports** (1988): $582 mln.; partners: U.S. 32%, CARACOM 12%. **Exports** (1988): $173 mln.; partners: U.S. 26%, CARACOM 30%. **Tourists** (1986): $326 mln. receipts. **National budget** (1987): $470 mln. expenditures. **International reserves less gold** (Mar. 1990): $147 mln. **Consumer prices** (change in 1989): 6.2%.

Transport: Motor vehicles: in use (1987): 34,000 passenger cars; 7,000 comm. vehicles. **Chief ports:** Bridgetown.

Communications: Television sets: 1 per 3.9 persons. **Radios:** 1 per 1.1 persons. **Telephones in use:** 1 per 2.8 persons. **Daily newspaper circ.** (1987): 156 per 1,000 pop.

Health: Life expectancy at birth (1989): male: 73 female: 77. **Births** (per 1,000 pop. 1989): 16. **Deaths** (per 1,000 pop. 1989): 8. **Natural increase:** 1.0%. **Hospital beds** (1986): 2,054. **Physicians** (1986): 243. **Infant mortality** (per 1,000 live births 1989): 17.

Education (1989): **Literacy:** 99%. **Years compulsory:** 9. **Major International Organizations:** UN (FAO, GATT, ILO, IMF, WHO), OAS.

Embassy: 2144 Wyoming Ave. NW 20008; 387-7374.

Barbados was probably named by Portuguese sailors in reference to bearded fig trees. An English ship visited in 1605, and British settlers arrived on the uninhabited island in 1627. Slaves worked the sugar plantations, but were freed in 1834.

Self-rule came gradually, with full independence proclaimed Nov. 30, 1966. British traditions have remained.

Belgium

Kingdom of Belgium

Koninkrijk België (Dutch)
Royaume de Belgique (French)

People: Population (1990 est.): 9,895,000. **Age distrib.** (%): 0–14: 19.3; 15–59: 61.5; 60+: 19.2 **Pop. density:** 840 per sq. mi. **Urban** (1980): 73%. **Ethnic groups:** Fleming 55%, Walloon 33%. **Languages:** Flemish (Dutch) 57%, French 33%, legally bilingual 10%, German 1%. **Religions:** Roman Catholic 75%.

Geography: Area: 11,799 sq. mi., slightly larger than Maryland. **Location:** In NW Europe, on N. Sea. **Neighbors:** France on W, S, Luxembourg on SE, W. Germany on E, Netherlands on N. **Topography:** Mostly flat, the country is trisected by the Scheldt and Meuse, major commercial rivers. The land becomes hilly and forested in the SE (Ardennes) region. **Capital:** Brussels. **Cities** (1988 est.): Brussels (met.) 970,000; Antwerp (met.) 479,000; Ghent 233,000; Charleroi 209,000; Liege 200,000.

Government: Type: Parliamentary democracy under a constitutional monarch. **Head of state:** King Baudouin; b. Sept. 7, 1930; in office: July 17, 1951. **Head of government:** Premier Wilfried Martens; b. Apr. 19, 1936; in office: Dec. 17, 1981. **Local divisions:** 9 provinces; 3 regions; 3 cultural communities. **Defense:** 3.1% of GNP (1988).

Economy: Industries: Steel, glassware, diamond cutting, textiles, chemicals. **Chief crops:** Wheat, potatoes, sugar beets. **Minerals:** Coal. **Other resources:** Forests. **Arable land** (incl. Lux.): 26.5%. **Livestock** (1987): cattle: 3.0 mln; pigs: 5.7 mln. **Fish catch** (1988): 23.3 metric tons. **Electricity prod.** (1989): 60 bln. kwh. **Crude steel prod.** (1988): 11.2 mln. metric tons. **Labor force:** 2% agric.; 26% ind. & comm.; 37% services & transportation; 23% public service.

Finance: Currency: Franc (June 1990: 34.81 = $1 US). **Gross national product** (1988): $153 bln. **Per capita income** (1987): $10,340. *Note:* the following trade and tourist data includes Luxembourg. **Imports** (1988): $95 bln.; partners: W. Ger. 23%, Neth. 17%, France 15%, UK 8%, U.S. 5%. **Exports** (1988): $104 bln.; partners: W. Ger. 19%, France 18%, Neth.

15%, UK 6%. **Tourists** (1987): receipts: $2.9 bln. **National budget** (1989): $51 bln. expenditures. **International reserves less gold** (Mar. 1990): $10.3 bln. **Gold:** 30.2 mln. oz t. **Consumer prices** (change in 1989): 3.1%.

Transport: Railway traffic (1988): 6.3 bln. passenger-km. **Motor vehicles:** in use (1987): 3.4 mln. passenger cars, 296,000 comm. vehicles. **Civil aviation** (1987): 5.9 bln. passenger-km; 4 airports with scheduled flights. **Chief ports:** Antwerp, Zeebrugge, Ghent.

Communications: Television sets: 1 per 3.2 persons. **Radios:** 1 per 2.2 persons; **Telephones in use:** 1 per 2.1 persons. **Daily newspaper circ.** (1988): 195 per 1,000 pop.

Health: Life expectancy at birth (1989): 69.8 male; 76.6 female. **Births** (per 1,000 pop. 1989): 12. **Deaths** (per 1,000 pop. 1989): 11. **Natural increase** 0.1%. **Hospital beds** (1984): 1 per 109 persons. **Physicians:** 1 per 331 persons. **Infant mortality** (per 1,000 live births 1989): 9.4

Education (1989): Literacy: 98%. School compulsory to age 18.

Major International Organizations: UN and all of its specialized agencies, NATO, EC, OECD.

Embassy: 3330 Garfield St. NW 20008; 333-6900

Belgium derives its name from the Belgae, the first recorded inhabitants, probably Celts. The land was conquered by Julius Caesar, and was ruled for 1800 years by conquerors, including Rome, the Franks, Burgundy, Spain, Austria, and France. After 1815, Belgium was made a part of the Netherlands, but it became an independent constitutional monarchy in 1830.

Belgian neutrality was violated by Germany in both world wars. King Leopold III surrendered to Germany, May 28, 1940. After the war, he was forced by political pressure to abdicate in favor of his son, King Baudouin.

The Flemings of northern Belgium speak Dutch while French is the language of the Walloons in the south. The language difference has been a perennial source of controversy and led to antagonism between the 2 groups. Parliament has passed measures aimed at transferring power from the central government to 3 regions—Wallonia, Flanders, and Brussels.

Belgium lives by its foreign trade; about 50% of its entire production is sold abroad.

Belize

People: Population (1990 est.): 180,400. **Age distrib.** (%): 0–14: 44.5; 15–59: 47.8; 60+: 7.6. **Pop. density:** 20 per sq. mi. **Ethnic groups:** African, Mestizo, Amerindian, Creole. **Languages:** English (official), Spanish, native Creole dialects. **Religions:** Roman Catholic 60%, Protestant 40%.

Geography: Area: 8,867 sq. mi. **Location:** eastern coast of Central America. **Neighbors:** Mexico on N., Guatemala on W. and S. **Capital:** Belmopan. **Cities:** (1987 est.): Belize City 48,000.

Government: Type: Parliamentary. **Head of State:** Gov. Gen. Minita Gordon. **Head of government:** Prime Min. George Cadle Price; in office: Nov. 7, 1989. **Local divisions:** 6 districts.

Economy: Sugar is the main export.

Finance: Currency: Belize dollar (Mar. 1990) 2 = $1 U.S. **Gross national product** (1987): 219 mln. **Per capita GNP** (1987): $1,250. **Imports** (1988) $176 mln.; partners: U.S. 55%, UK 8%. **Exports:** (1988): 120 mln.; partners: U.S. 46%, UK 31%. **National Budget** (1988): $89 mln. expenditures.

Health: life expectancy (1989) male: 67; female: 72. **Births** (per 1,000 pop. 1989): 36. **Deaths** (per 1,000 pop. 1989): 6. **Hospital beds:** 1 per 300 persons. **Physicians:** 1 per 2,061 persons. **Infant mortality** (per 1,000 live births, 1989): 36.

Education: (1989) **Literacy:** 93%.; **Years compulsory:** 9; attendance 55%.

Major International Organizations: UN (IMF, World Bank), Commonwealth of Nations.

Embassy: 3400 International Dr., NW 20005; 363-4505.

Belize (formerly called British Honduras), Great Britain's last colony on the American mainland, achieved independence on Sept. 21, 1981. Guatemala claims territorial sovereignty over the country and has refused to recognize Belize's independence. British troops in Belize guarantee security.

Benin

People's Republic of Benin

République Populaire du Benin

People: Population (1990 est.): 4,840,000. **Age distrib. (%):** 0–14: 46.5; 15–59: 49.0; 60+: 4.5. **Pop. density:** 104 per sq. mi. **Urban** (1985): 20%. **Ethnic groups:** Fon, Adja, Bariba, Yoruba. **Languages:** French (official), local dialects. **Religions:** Mainly animist with Christian, Moslem minorities.

Geography: Area: 43,483 sq. mi., slightly smaller than Pennsylvania. **Location:** In W Africa on Gulf of Guinea. **Neighbors:** Togo on W, Burkina Faso, Niger on N, Nigeria on E. **Topography:** most of Benin is flat and covered with dense vegetation. The coast is hot, humid, and rainy. **Capital:** Porto–Novo. **Cities** (1984 est.): Cotonou 330,000.

Government: Type: In transition. **Head of state:** Pres. Gen. Mathieu Kerekou; b. Sept. 2, 1933; in office: Oct. 27, 1972. **Head of Government:** Prime Min. Nicephore Soglo; in office Mar. 12, 1990. **Local divisions:** 6 provinces. **Defense:** 2.1% of GNP (1987).

Economy: Chief crops: Palm products, peanuts, cotton, coffee, tobacco. **Minerals:** Oil. **Arable land:** 12%. **Livestock** (1987): sheep: 1.1 mln.; goats: 1.1 mln. **Fish catch** (1988): 41,000 metric tons. **Electricity prod.** (1988): 24 mln. kwh. **Labor force:** 60% agric; 38% serv. & comm.

Finance: Currency: CFA franc (Mar. 1990: 284 = $1 US). **Gross national product** (1987): $1.4 bln. **Per capita income** (1987): $374. **Imports** (1986): $314 mln.; partners: Fr. 27%, UK 13%, W. Ger. 6%, Neth. 6%. **Exports** (1986): $100 mln.; partners: Neth. 28%, Jap. 27%, Fr. 24%. **National Budget** (1987): $159 bln. expenditures. **International reserves less gold** (Feb. 1990): $3.4 mln.

Transport: Railway traffic (1985): 137 mln. passenger-km; 176 mln. net ton-km. **Chief ports:** Cotonou.

Communications: Radios: 1 per 14 persons. **Televisions:** 1 per 272 persons. **Daily newspaper circ.** (1988): 3 per 1,000 pop.

Health: Life expectancy at birth (1989): 48 male; 51 female. **Births** (per 1,000 pop. 1989): 54. **Deaths** (per 1,000 pop. 1989): 17. **Natural increase:** 3.7%. **Hospital beds:** 1 per 749 persons. **Physicians:** 1 per 16,025 persons. **Infant mortality** (per 1,000 live births 1989): 124.

Education (1987): **Literacy:** 28%. Years compulsory 6; attendance 43%.

Major International Organizations: UN (GATT, IMF, WHO), OAU.

Embassy: 2737 Cathedral Ave. NW 20008; 232-6656.

The Kingdom of Abomey, rising to power in wars with neighboring kingdoms in the 17th century, came under French domination in the late 19th century, and was incorporated into French West Africa by 1904.

Under the name Dahomey, the country became independent Aug. 1, 1960. The name was changed to Benin in 1975. In the fifth coup since independence Col. Ahmed Kerekou took power in 1972; two years later he declared a socialist state with a "Marxist-Leninist" philosophy. In Dec. 1989, Kerekou announced that Marxism-Leninism would no longer be the state ideology. The economy relies on the development of agriculturally-based industries.

Bhutan

Kingdom of Bhutan

Druk-Yul

People: Population (1990 est.): 1,566,000. **Age distrib. (%):** 0–14: 39.8; 15–59: 53.8; over 60: 6.4 **Pop. density:** 84 per sq. mi. **Ethnic groups:** Ngalops and Sharchops 70%. Nepalese 25%, Lepcha (indigenous), Indians. **Languages:** Dzongkha (official), Nepali, English. **Religions:** Buddhist (state religion) 75%, Hindu 25%.

Geography: Area: 18,147 sq. mi., the size of Vermont and New Hampshire combined. **Location:** In eastern Himalayan Mts. **Neighbors:** India on W (Sikkim) and S, China on N. **Topography:** Bhutan is comprised of very high mountains in the N, fertile valleys in the center, and thick forests in the Duar Plain in the S.

Capital: Thimphu (Paro Dzong is administrative capital). **City** (1987 est.): Thimphu 20,000.

Government: Type: Monarchy. **Head of state:** King Jigme Singye Wangchuk; b. Nov. 11, 1955; in office: July 21, 1972. **Local divisions:** 18 districts.

Economy: Industries: Handicrafts. **Chief crops:** Rice, corn, wheat. **Other resources:** Timber. **Arable land:** 2%. **Labor force:** 95% agric.

Finance: Currency: Ngultrum (Jan. 1990: 17 = 1 US) (Indian Rupee also used). **Gross national product** (1987): $252 mln. **Per capita GNP** (1987): $150. **Tourism** (1987): 2.4 mln. **Imports** (1988): $105.1 mln.; partners India 75%. **Exports** (1988): $60.8 mln.; partners India 99%.

Communications: Radios: 1 per 64 persons. **Telephones in use:** 1 per 675 persons.

Health: Life expectancy at birth (1987): 48.1 male; 46.8 female. **Births** (per 1,000 pop. 1989): 38. **Deaths** (per 1,000 pop. 1989): 17. **Natural increase:** 2.0%. **Hospital beds:** 1 per 1,457 persons. **Physicians:** 1 per 9,736 persons. **Infant mortality** (per 1,000 live births 1989): 139.

Education (1989): **Literacy:** 15%. School attendance: 21%.

Major International Organizations: UN (IMF, World Bank).

The region came under Tibetan rule in the 16th century. British influence grew in the 19th century. A monarchy, set up in 1907, became a British protectorate by a 1910 treaty. The country became independent in 1949, with India guiding foreign relations and supplying aid.

Links to India have been strengthened by airline service and a road network. Most of the population engages in subsistence agriculture.

Bolivia

Republic of Bolivia

República de Bolivia

People: Population (1990 est.): 6,730,000. **Age distrib. (%):** 0–14: 43; 15–59: 51.8; 60+: 5.2. **Pop. density:** 16 per sq. mi. **Urban** (1988): 49%. **Ethnic groups:** Quechua 30%, Aymara 25%, mixed 30%, European 14%. **Languages:** Spanish, Quechua, Aymara (all official). **Religions:** Roman Catholic 95%.

Geography: Area: 424,165 sq. mi., the size of Texas and California combined. **Location:** In central Andes Mtns. **Neighbors:** Peru, Chile on W, Argentina, Paraguay on S, Brazil on E and N. **Topography:** The great central plateau, at an altitude of 12,000 ft., over 500 mi. long, lies between two great cordilleras having 3 of the highest peaks in S. America. Lake Titicaca, on Peruvian border, is highest lake in world on which steamboats ply (12,506 ft.). The E central region has semitropical forests; the llanos, or Amazon-Chaco lowlands are in E. **Capitals:** Sucre, (legal), La Paz (de facto). **Cities** (1986 est.): La Paz 955,000; Santa Cruz 419,000; Cochabamba 304,000.

Government: Type: Republic. **Head of state:** Pres. Jaime Paz Zamora, in office: Aug. 6, 1989. **Local divisions:** 9 departments. **Defence:** 3% of GNP (1987).

Economy: Industry: Textiles, food processing, mining, clothing. **Chief crops:** Potatoes, sugar, coffee, corn, coca (sold for cocaine processing). **Minerals:** Antimony, tin, tungsten, silver, zinc, oil, gas, iron. **Crude oil reserves** (1985): 157 mln. bbls. **Other resources:** rubber, cinchona bark. **Arable land:** 3%. **Livestock** (1987): cattle: 5.3 mln.; sheep: 9.5 mln.; pigs: 1.6 mln. **Electricity prod.** (1988): 1.6 bln. kwh. **Labor force:** 50% agric., 10% ind. & comm, 26% serv. & govt.

Finance: Currency: Peso (Mar. 1990: 3,090 = $1 US). **Gross national product** (1987): $4.6 bln. **Per capita GNP** (1987): $570. **Imports** (1988): $604 mln.; partners: U.S. 8%, Jap. 4%, Arg. 6%, Braz. 10%. **Exports** (1988): $601 mln.; partners: Arg. 45%, U.S. 17%. **National budget** (1988): $2.8 bln. expenditures. **International reserves less gold** (Mar. 1990): $109.6 mln. **Gold:** 894,000 oz t. **Consumer prices** (change in 1989): 15%.

Transport: Railway traffic (1987): 790 mln. passenger-km. **Motor vehicles:** in use (1987): 78,000 passenger cars, 142,000 comm. vehicles. **Civil aviation** (1988): 1.1 bln. passenger-km.; 19 airports with scheduled flights.

Communications: Television sets: 1 per 16 persons. **Radios:** 1 per 1.8 persons. **Telephones in use:** 1 per 37 persons. **Daily newspaper circ.** (1984): 40 per 1,000 pop.

Health: Life expectancy at birth (1989): 52 male; 56 female. **Births** (per 1,000 pop. 1989): 36. **Deaths** (per 1,000 pop. 1989): 13. **Natural increase:** 2.3%. **Hospital beds:** 1 per 472 persons. **Physicians:** 1 per 1,595 persons. **Infant mortality** (per 1,000 live births 1989): 123.

Education (1989): **Literacy:** 63%. **Years compulsory:** ages 7-14; attendance 82%.

Major International Organizations: UN (IMF, FAO, WHO), OAS.

Embassy: 3014 Massachusetts Ave. NW 20008; 483-4410.

The Incas conquered the region from earlier Indian inhabitants in the 13th century. Spanish rule began in the 1530s, and lasted until Aug. 6, 1825. The country is named after Simon Bolivar, independence fighter.

In a series of wars, Bolivia lost its Pacific coast to Chile, the oilbearing Chaco to Paraguay, and rubber-growing areas to Brazil, 1879-1935.

Economic unrest, especially among the militant mine workers, has contributed to continuing political instability. A reformist government under Victor Paz Estenssoro, 1951-64, nationalized tin mines and attempted to improve conditions for the Indian majority, but was overthrown by a military junta. A series of coups and countercoups continued through 1981, until the military junta elected Gen. Villa as president.

In July 1982, the military junta assumed power amid a growing economic crisis and foreign debt difficulties. The junta resigned in October and allowed the Congress, elected democratically in 1980, to take power.

U.S. pressure on the government to reduce the country's output of coca, the raw material for cocaine, has led to clashes between police and coca growers and increased anti-U.S. feeling among Bolivians.

Botswana
Republic of Botswana

People: Population (1990 est.): 1,218,000. **Age distrib.** (%): 0-14: 48.1; 15-59: 46.1; 60+: 5.8. **Pop. density:** 5 per sq. mi. **Urban** (1986): 21%. **Ethnic groups:** Batswana, 95%. **Languages:** English (official), Setswana (national). **Religions:** indigenous beliefs (majority), Christian 15%.

Geography: Area: 231,804 sq. mi., slightly smaller than Texas. **Location:** In southern Africa. **Neighbors:** Namibia (S.W. Africa) on N and W, S. Africa on S, Zimbabwe on NE; Botswana claims border with Zambia on N. **Topography:** The Kalahari Desert, supporting nomadic Bushmen and wildlife, spreads over SW; there are swamplands and farming areas in N, and rolling plains in E where livestock are grazed. **Capital:** Gaborone. **Cities** (1986): Gaborone 96,000.

Government: Type: Republic, parliamentary democracy. **Head of state:** Pres. Quett Masire; b. 1925; in office: July 13, 1980. **Local divisions:** 10 district councils and 4 town councils. **Defense:** 4.1% of national budget (1988).

Economy: Industries: Livestock processing, mining. **Chief crops:** Corn, sorghum, peanuts. **Minerals:** Copper, coal, nickel, diamonds. **Other resources:** Big game. **Arable land:** 2%. **Electricity prod.** (1988): 631 mln. kwh. **Labor force:** 70% agric.

Finance: Currency: Pula (Mar. 1990: 1.00 = $.52 US). **Gross national product** (1987): $1.5 bln. **Imports** (1988): $1.1 bln.; partners: S. Africa 88%. **Exports** (1988): $1.0 bln.; partners: Europe 67%, U.S. 17%, S. Africa 7%. **National budget** (1990): $1.0 bln. **International reserves less gold** (Mar. 1990): $2.8 bln. **Consumer prices** (change in 1989): 11.6%

Transport: Railway traffic (1987): 257 mln. passenger km. **Motor vehicles:** in use (1987): 17,000 passenger cars, 26,000 comm. vehicles.

Communications: Radios: 1 per 8 persons. **Daily newspaper circ.** (1989): 22 per 1,000 pop.

Health: Life expectancy at birth (1989): male: 56; female: 62. **Births** (1,000 pop. 1989): 38. **Deaths** (per 1,000 pop. 1989): 11. **Natural increase:** 2.8%. **Hospital beds** (1985): 2,367. **Physicians** (1985): 155. **Infant mortality** (per 1,000 live births 1989): 63.

Education (1989): **Literacy:** 35% (in English).

Major International Organizations: UN (GATT, IMF, WHO), OAU, Commonwealth of Nations.

Embassy: 4301 Connecticut Ave. NW 20008; 244-4990.

First inhabited by bushmen, then by Bantus, the region became the British protectorate of Bechuanaland in 1886, halting encroachment by Boers and Germans from the south and southwest. The country became fully independent Sept. 30, 1966, changing its name to Botswana.

Cattle-raising and mining (diamonds, copper, nickel) have contributed to the country's economic growth. The economy is closely tied to S. Africa.

Brazil
Federative Republic of Brazil
República Federativa do Brasil

People: Population (1990 est.): 153,771,000. **Age distrib.** (%): 0-14: 36.4; 15-59: 57.0; 60+: 6.6. **Pop. density:** 47 per sq. mi. **Urban** (1989): 76%. **Ethnic groups:** Portuguese, Africans, and mulattoes make up the vast majority; Italians, Germans, Japanese, Indians, Jews, Arabs. **Languages:** Portuguese (official), English. **Religions:** Roman Catholic 89%.

Geography: Area: 3,286,470 sq. mi., larger than contiguous 48 U.S. states; largest country in S. America. **Location:** Occupies eastern half of S. America. **Neighbors:** French Guiana, Suriname, Guyana, Venezuela on N, Colombia, Peru, Bolivia, Paraguay, Argentina on W, Uruguay on S. **Topography:** Brazil's Atlantic coastline stretches 4,603 miles. In N is the heavily-wooded Amazon basin covering half the country. Its network of rivers navigable for 15,814 mi. The Amazon itself flows 2,093 miles in Brazil, all navigable. The NE region is semiarid scrubland, heavily settled and poor. The S central region, favored by climate and resources, has almost half of the population, produces 75% of farm goods and 80% of industrial output. The narrow coastal belt includes most of the major cities. Almost the entire country has a tropical or semitropical climate. **Capital:** Brasilia. **Cities** (1985 est.): Sao Paulo 10.1 mln.; Rio de Janeiro 5.6 mln.; Belo Horizonte 2.1 mln.; Fortaleza 1.9 mln.; Salvador 1.8 mln.; Porto Alegre 2.6 mln.

Government: Type: Federal republic. **Head of state:** Pres. Fernando Collor de Mello; b. Aug. 12, 1949; in office: Mar. 15, 1990. **Local divisions:** 23 states, with individual constitutions and elected governments; 3 territories, federal district. **Defense:** 0.8% of GNP (1987).

Economy: Industries: Steel, autos, textiles, ships, appliances, petrochemicals, machinery. **Chief crops:** Coffee (largest grower), cotton, soybeans, sugar, cocoa, rice, corn, fruits. **Minerals:** Chromium, iron, manganese, columbium, titanium, diamonds, gold, nickel, gem stones, coal, tin, tungsten, bauxite, oil. **Crude oil reserves** (1987): 2.3 bln. bbls. **Arable land:** 8%. **Livestock** (1987): cattle: 131 mln.; pigs: 32 mln.; sheep: 19 mln. **Fish catch** (1987): 793,000 metric tons. **Electricity prod.** (1987): 202 bln. kwh. **Crude steel prod.** (1988): 24.6 mln. metric tons. **Labor force:** 40% services, 35% agric.; 25% ind.

Finance: Currency: New Cruzado (June 1990: 54 = $1 US). **Gross national product** (1987): $313 bln. **Per capita GNP** (1987): $2,020. **Imports** (1989): $20 bln.; partners: U.S. 28%, EC 23%. **Exports** (1989): $34 bln.; partners: U.S. 26%, EC 27%. **Tourists** (1986): receipts: $1.5 bln. **National budget** (1986): $40.1 bln expenditures. **International reserves less gold** (Jan. 1989): $5.9 bln. **Gold:** 2.9 mln. oz t. **Consumer prices** (change in 1989): 1,287%.

Transport: Railway traffic (1986): 15.7 bln. passenger-km. **Motor vehicles:** in use (1986): 10 mln. passenger cars, 1.1 mln. **Civil aviation** (1987): 23.5 bln. passenger-km.; 126 airports with scheduled flights. **Chief ports:** Santos, Rio de Janeiro, Vitoria, Salvador, Rio Grande, Recife.

Communications: Television sets: 1 per 4 persons. **Radios:** 1 per 2.5 persons. **Telephones in use:** 1 per 11 persons. **Daily newspaper circ.** (1986): 62 per 1,000 pop.

Health: Life expectancy at birth (1989): 64 male; 69 female. **Births** (per 1,000 pop. 1989): 27. **Deaths** (per 1,000 pop. 1989): 7. **Natural increase:** 2.0%. **Hospital beds:** 1 per 282 persons. **Physicians:** 1 per 684 persons. **Infant mortality** (per 1,000 live births 1989): 67.

Education (1989): **Literacy:** 76%.

Major International Organizations: UN and most of its specialized agencies, OAS.

Embassy: 3006 Massachusetts Ave. NW 20008; 745-2700.

Pedro Alvares Cabral, a Portuguese navigator, is generally credited as the first European to reach Brazil, in 1500. The country was thinly settled by various Indian tribes. Only a few have survived to the present, mostly in the Amazon basin.

In the next centuries, Portuguese colonists gradually pushed inland, bringing along large numbers of African slaves. Slavery was not abolished until 1888.

The King of Portugal, fleeing before Napoleon's army, moved the seat of government to Brazil in 1808. Brazil thereupon became a kingdom under Dom Joao VI. After his return to Portugal, his son Pedro proclaimed the independence of Brazil, Sept. 7, 1822, and was acclaimed emperor. The second emperor, Dom Pedro II, was deposed in 1889, and a republic proclaimed, called the United States of Brazil. In 1967 the country was renamed the Federative Republic of Brazil.

A military junta took control in 1930; dictatorial power was assumed by Getulio Vargas, who alternated with military coups until finally forced out by the military in 1954. A democratic regime prevailed 1956-64, during which time the capital was moved from Rio de Janeiro to Brasilia in the interior.

The next 5 presidents were all military leaders. Censorship was imposed, and much of the opposition was suppressed amid charges of torture. In 1974 elections, the official opposition party made gains in the chamber of deputies; some relaxation of censorship occurred.

Since 1930, successive governments have pursued industrial and agricultural growth and the development of interior areas. Exploiting vast mineral resources, fertile soil in several regions, and a huge labor force, Brazil became the leading industrial power of Latin America by the 1970s, while agricultural output soared. Democratic elections were held in 1985 as the nation returned to civilian rule.

However, income maldistribution, inflation and government land policies have all led to severe economic recession. Foreign debt is among the largest in the world.

Brazil unveiled a comprehensive environmental program for the Amazon region in 1989, amid an international outcry by environmentalists and others concerned about the ongoing destruction of the Amazon ecosystem. The Amazon rain forest was considered a global resource because of its impact on world weather patterns.

Brunei Darussalam
State of Brunei Darussalam
Negara Brunei Darussalam

People: Population (1990 est.): 372,000. **Pop. Density:** 119 per sq. mi. **Ethnic groups:** Malay 65%, Chinese 20%. **Language:** Malay (official), English, Chinese. **Religion:** Moslem 60%, Buddhist 14%, Christian 10%.

Geography: Area: 2,226 sq. mi.; smaller than Delaware. **Location:** on the north coast of the island of Borneo; it is surrounded on its landward side by the Malaysian state of Sarawak. **Capital:** Bandar Seri Begawan. **Cities** (1982 est.): Bandar Seri Begawan 51,000.

Government: Type: Independent sultanate. **Head of Government:** Sultan Sir Muda Hassanal Bolkiah Mu'izzadin Waddaulah; in office: Jan. 1, 1984.

Economy: Industries: petroleum (about 90% of revenue is derived from oil exports). **Chief crops:** rice, bananas, cassava.

Finance: Currency: Brunei dollar (Dec. 1989: 1.96 = $1). **Gross domestic product** (1987): $3.1 bln. **Per capita income** (1987): $20,000.

Communications: Television sets: 1 per 4.7 persons. **Radios:** 1 per 3 persons. **Telephones:** 1 per 6 persons.

Education (1987): **Literacy:** 95% among young.

Health: Life expectancy at birth: (1989): 74 male; 77 female. **Infant Mortality** (per 1,000 live births 1989): 10.

Major International Organizations: UN and some of its specialized agencies.

The Sultanate of Brunei was a powerful state in the early 16th century with authority over all of the island of Borneo as well as parts of the Sulu Islands and the Philippines. In 1888, a treaty was signed which placed the state under the protection of Great Britain.

Brunei became a fully sovereign and independent state on Jan. 1, 1984.

The Sultan of Brunei donated $10 million to the Nicaraguan *contras* in 1987; the subsequent misplacement of the funds generated much media attention in the U.S.

Bulgaria
People's Republic of Bulgaria
Narodna Republika Bulgaria

People: Population (1990 est.): 8,978,000. **Age distrib. (%):** 0–14: 21.2; 15–59: 60.5; 60+: 18.3. **Pop. density:** 203 per sq. mi. **Urban** (1988): 65%. **Ethnic groups:** Bulgarian 85%, Turk 8.5%. **Languages:** Bulgarian, Turkish, Greek. **Religions:** Government promotes atheism; background of people is 85% Orthodox.

Geography: Area: 44,365 sq. mi., about the size of Ohio. **Location:** in eastern Balkan Peninsula on Black Sea. **Neighbors:** Romania on N, Yugoslavia on W, Greece, Turkey on S. **Topography:** The Stara Planina (Balkan) Mts. stretch E-W across the center of the country, with the Danubian plain on N, the Rhodope Mts. on SW, and Thracian Plain on SE. **Capital:** Sofia. **Cities** (1987 est.): Sofia 1,119,000; Plovdiv 346,000; Varna 303,000.

Government: Type: in transition. **Head of state:** Pres. Zhelyu Zhelev; in office: Aug. 1, 1990. **Head of government:** Premier Andrei Lukanov; in office: Feb. 3, 1990. **Head of Communist Party:** First Sec. Alexander Lilov; in office: Feb. 2, 1990. **Local divisions:** 9 administrative regions. **Defense:** 10.3% of GNP (1987).

Economy: Industries: Chemicals, machinery, metals, textiles, fur, leather goods, vehicles, wine, processed food. **Chief crops:** Grains, fruit, corn, potatoes, tobacco. **Minerals:** Lead, manganese, lignite, coal. **Arable land:** 38%. **Livestock** (1988): cattle: 1.8 mln.; pigs: 4.0 mln.; sheep: 8.8 mln. **Fish catch** (1988): 110,000 metric tons. **Electricity prod.** (1988): 43 bln. kwh. **Crude steel prod.** (1988): 3.0 mln. metric tons. **Labor force:** 20% agric.; 33% ind.

Finance: Currency: Lev (Dec. 1989: 1.00 = $.82 US). **Gross National Product** (1988): $67 bln. **Per capita GNP** (1988): $7,510. **Imports** (1987): $16.9 bln.; partners: USSR 56%, E. Ger. 6%, W. Ger. 5%. **Exports** (1987): $16.8 bln.; partners: USSR 61%, E. Ger. 6%. **Tourists** (1986): revenues $345 mln. **National budget** (1987): $23.7 bln. expenditures.

Transport: Railway traffic (1987): 8.0 bln. passenger-km. **Motor vehicles:** in use (1987) 1.1 mln. passenger cars, 587,000 commercial. **Civil aviation** (1987): 3.7 bln. passenger km. 13 airports. **Chief ports:** Burgas, Varna.

Communications: Television sets: 1 per 5.3 persons. **Radios:** 1 per 4.5 persons. **Telephones in use:** 1 per 4.3 persons. **Daily newspaper circ.** (1988): 316 per 1,000 pop.

Health: Life expectancy at birth (1989): 68 male; 74 female. **Births** (per 1,000 pop. 1989): 13. **Deaths** (per 1,000 pop. 1989): 12. **Hospital beds:** 84,300. **Physicians:** 25,000. **Infant mortality** (per 1,000 live births 1989): 18.

Education (1990): **Literacy:** 98%. **Years compulsory:** 8.

Major International Organizations: UN, Warsaw Pact.

Embassy: 1621-22d St. NW 20008; 387-7969.

Bulgaria was settled by Slavs in the 6th century. Turkic Bulgars arrived in the 7th century, merged with the Slavs, became Christians by the 9th century, and set up powerful empires in the 10th and 12th centuries. The Ottomans prevailed in 1396 and remained for 500 years.

A revolt in 1876 led to an independent kingdom in 1908. Bulgaria expanded after the first Balkan War but lost its Aegean coastline in World War I, when it sided with Germany. Bulgaria joined the Axis in World War II, but withdrew in 1944. Communists took power with Soviet aid; the monarchy was abolished Sept. 8, 1946.

On Nov. 10, 1989, Todor Zhivkov, who had held power for 35 years, resigned. Zhivkov was imprisoned, Jan. 1990, pending the outcome of charges of corruption and abuse of power. In Jan. 1990, parliament voted to revoke the constitutionally guaranteed dominant role of the Communist Party.

Burkina Faso

People: Population (1990 est.): 8,941,000. **Pop. density:** 72 per sq. mi. **Urban** (1986): 8%. **Ethnic groups:** Voltaic groups (Mossi, Bobo), **bande. Languages:** French (official), Sudanic tribal languages. **Religions:** animist 65%, Moslems 25%, Christian 10%.

Geography: Area: 105,869 sq. mi., the size of Colorado. **Location:** in W. Africa, S of the Sahara. **Neighbors:** Mali on NW,

Niger on NE, Benin, Togo, Ghana, Côte d' Ivoire on S. **Topography:** Landlocked Burkina Faso is in the savannah region of W. Africa. The N is arid, hot, and thinly populated. **Capital:** Ouagadougou. **Cities** (1986): Ouagadougou 366,000; Bobo-Dioulasso 202,000.

Government: Type: Military. **Head of state:** Pres. Blaise Compaore; in office: Oct. 15, 1987. **Local divisions:** 30 provinces. **Defense:** 3.1% of GNP (1987).

Economy: Chief crops: Millet, sorghum, rice, peanuts, grain. **Minerals:** Manganese, gold, limestone. **Arable land:** 10%. **Electricity prod.** (1987): 144 mln. kwh. **Labor force:** 83% agric.; 12% industry.

Finance: Currency: CFA franc (Mar. 1989: 284 = $1 US). **Gross national product** (1987): $1.4 bln. **Per capita GNP** (1987): $170. **Imports** (1988): $489 mln.; partners: EC, Côte d' Ivoire. **Exports** (1988): $142 mln.; partners: Côte d' Ivoire, EC, China. **International reserves less gold** (Jan. 1990): $265 mln. **Gold:** 11,000 oz t. **Consumer prices** (change in 1989): -.5%.

Transport: Motor vehicles: in use (1983): 21,000 passenger cars, 6,600 comm. vehicles.

Communications: Television sets: 1 per 205 persons. **Radios:** 1 per 26 persons. **Telephones in use:** 1 per 482 persons. **Daily newspaper circ.** (1987): 1 per 1,000 pop.

Health: Life expectancy at birth (1989): 45 male; 49 female. **Births** (per 1,000 pop. 1989): 47. **Deaths** (per 1,000 pop. 1989): 18. **Natural increase:** 2.9%. **Hospital beds:** 1 per 1,359 persons. **Physicians:** 1 per 29,914 persons. **Infant mortality** (per 1,000 live births 1989): 138.

Education (1989): **Literacy:** 8%. Only 8% attend school.

Major International Organizations: UN and many of its specialized agencies, OAU.

Embassy: 2340 Massachusetts Ave. NW 20008; 332-5577.

The Mossi tribe entered the area in the 11th to 13th centuries. Their kingdoms ruled until defeated by the Mali and Songhai empires.

French control came by 1896, but Upper Volta (name changed to Burkina Faso on Aug. 4, 1984), was not finally established as a separate territory until 1947. Full independence came Aug. 5, 1960, and a pro-French government was elected. A 1982 coup established the current regime.

Several hundred thousand farm workers migrate each year to Cote D'Ivoire and Ghana. Burkina Faso is heavily dependent on foreign aid.

Burma

(*See Myanmar*)

Burundi

Republic of Burundi

Republika y'Uburundi

People: Population (1990 est.): 5,647,000. **Age distrib. (%):** 0–14: 44.3; 15–59: 49.6; 60+: 6.1. **Pop. density:** 486 per sq. mi. **Urban** (1986): 8%. **Ethnic groups:** Hutu 85%, Tutsi 14%, Twa (pygmy) 1%. **Languages:** French, Rundi (both official). **Religions:** Christian 67%, traditional African 32%.

Geography: Area: 10,759 sq. mi., the size of Maryland. **Location:** In central Africa. **Neighbors:** Rwanda on N, Zaire on W, Tanzania on E. **Topography:** Much of the country is grassy highland, with mountains reaching 8,900 ft. The southernmost source of the White Nile is located in Burundi. Lake Tanganyika is the second deepest lake in the world. **Capital:** Bujumbura. **Cities** (1986 est.): Bujumbura 272,000.

Government: Type: Republic. **Head of state:** Pres. Maj. Pierre Buyoya; in office: Sept. 9, 1987. **Head of government:** Prime Min: Adrien Sibomana, in office: Oct. 19, 1988. **Local divisions:** 15 provinces. **Defense** (1988): 3.1% of GNP.

Economy: Chief crops: Coffee (87% of exports), cotton, tea. **Minerals:** Nickel. **Arable land:** 43%. **Electricity prod.** (1987): 54 mln. kwh. **Labor force:** 93% agric.

Finance: Currency: Franc (Apr. 1990: 179 = $1 US). **Gross national product** (1987): $1.2 bln. **Per capita income** (1986) $239. **Imports** (1986): $202 mln.; partners: Belg.-Lux. 17%; W. Ger. 18%. **Exports** (1986): $128 mln; partners: W. Ger. 31%, Belg. 20%. **Tourism** (1987): $35 mln. receipts. **National budget** (1986): $203 mln. expenditures. **International reserves less**

gold (Mar. 1990): $93.5 mln. **Gold:** 17,000 oz t. **Consumer prices** (change in 1989): 12.0%.

Transport: Motor vehicles: in use (1987): 9,000 passenger cars, 8,000 comm. vehicles.

Communications: Radios: 1 per 21 persons. **Telephones in use:** 1 per 622 persons.

Health: Life expectancy at birth (1989): 50 male; 53 female. **Births** (per 1,000 pop. 1989): 48. **Deaths** (per 1,000 pop. 1989): 15. **Natural increase:** 3.3%. **Hospital beds:** 1 per 857 persons. **Physicians:** 1 per 26,494 persons. **Infant mortality** (per 1,000 live births 1989): 114.

Education (1988): **Literacy:** 30%.

Major International Organizations: UN (GATT, IMF, WHO), OAU.

Embassy: 2233 Wisconsin Ave. NW 20007; 342-2574.

The pygmy Twa were the first inhabitants, followed by Bantu Hutus, who were conquered in the 16th century by the tall Tutsi (Watusi), probably from Ethiopia. Under German control in 1899, the area fell to Belgium in 1916, which exercised successively a League of Nations mandate and UN trusteeship over Ruanda-Urundi (now 2 countries).

Independence came in 1962, and the monarchy was overthrown in 1966. An unsuccessful Hutu rebellion in 1972-73 left 10,000 Tutsi and 150,000 Hutu dead. Over 100,000 Hutu fled to Tanzania and Zaire. Burundi is pledged to ethnic reconciliation, but remains one of the poorest and most densely populated countries in Africa.

Cambodia

Republic of Cambodia

People: Population (1990 est.): 6,993,000. **Pop. density:** 98 per sq. mi. **Urban** (1985): 10%. **Ethnic groups:** Khmers 90%, Vietnamese 4%, Chinese 5%. **Languages:** Khmer (official), French. **Religions:** Theravada Buddhism 95%.

Geography: Area: 69,898 sq. mi., the size of Missouri. **Location:** In Indochina Peninsula. **Neighbors:** Thailand on W, N, Laos on NE, Vietnam on E. **Topography:** The central area, formed by the Mekong R. basin and Tonle Sap lake, is level. Hills and mountains arise in SE, a long escarpment separates the country from Thailand on NW. 75% of the area is forested. **Capital:** Phnom Penh. **Cities** (1987 est.): Phnom Penh 300,000.

Government: Type: No single authority controls the whole country. **Head of State:** Pres., People's Revolutionary Party Heng Samrin; in office: Jan. 7, 1979. **Head of Government:** Premier Hun Sen; in office: Jan. 14, 1985. **Local divisions:** 20 provinces.

Economy: Industries: Rice milling, wood & rubber. **Chief crops:** Rice, corn. **Minerals:** Iron, copper, manganese. **Other resources:** Forests, rubber, kapok. **Arable land:** 16%. **Livestock** (1987): cattle: 1.5 mln. pigs: 1.3 mln. **Fish catch** (1986): 70,000 metric tons. **Electricity prod.** (1988): 142.00 mln. kwh. **Labor force:** 74% agri.

Finance: Currency: Riel (Jan. 1990: 150 = $1 US). **Gross National Product** (1987): $10.4 bln. **Per capita GNP** (1987): $960. **Imports** (1983): $30 mln. **Exports** (1983): $10 mln.

Transport: Railway traffic (1986): 54 mln. passenger-miles. **Motor vehicles:** in use (1986): 86,000 passenger cars, 32,000 trucks. **Chief ports:** Kompong Som.

Communications: Television sets: 1 per 2,216 persons. **Radios:** 1 per 11 persons. **Telephones in use:** 1 per 179 persons.

Health: Life expectancy at birth (1989): 47 male; 50 female. **Births** (per 1,000 pop. 1989): 39. **Deaths** (per 1,000 pop. 1989): 17. **Natural increase:** 2. **Infant Mortality** (per 1,000 live births 1989): 131.

Education (1989): **Literacy:** 48%.

Major International Organizations: UN.

Early kingdoms dating from that of Funan in the 1st century AD culminated in the great Khmer empire which flourished from the 9th century to the 13th, encompassing present-day Thailand, Cambodia, Laos, and southern Vietnam. The peripheral areas were lost to invading Siamese and Vietnamese, and France established a protectorate in 1863. Independence came in 1953.

Prince Norodom Sihanouk, king 1941-1955 and head of state from 1960, tried to maintain neutrality. Relations with the U.S. were broken in 1965, after South Vietnam planes attacked Vietcong forces within Cambodia. Relations were restored in

1969, after Sihanouk charged Viet communists with arming Cambodian insurgents.

In 1970, pro-U.S. premier Lon Nol seized power, demanding removal of 40,000 North Viet troops; the monarchy was abolished. Sihanouk formed a government-in-exile in Peking, and open war began between the government and Khmer Rouge. The U.S. provided heavy military and economic aid.

Khmer Rouge forces captured Phnom Penh April 17, 1975. The new government evacuated all cities and towns, and shuffled the rural population, sending virtually the entire population to clear jungle, forest, and scrub, which covered half the country. Over one million people were killed in executions and enforced hardships.

Severe border fighting broke out with Vietnam in 1978; developed into a full-fledged Vietnamese invasion. The Vietnamese-backed Kampuchean National United Front for National Salvation, a Cambodian rebel movement, announced, Jan. 8, 1979, the formation of a government one day after the Vietnamese capture of Phnom Pehn. Thousands of refugees flowed into Thailand and widespread starvation was reported.

On Jan. 10, 1983, Vietnam launched an offensive against rebel forces in the west. They overran a refugee camp, Jan. 31, driving 30,000 residents into Thailand. In March, Vietnam launched a major offensive against camps on the Cambodian-Thailand border, engaged Khmer Rouge guerrillas, and crossed the border instigating clashes with Thai troops. Vietnam announced that it would withdraw all its troops by Sept. 1989.

Efforts to create a new government have been hampered by the fear both in Cambodia and internationally that the Khmer Rouge would return to power.

Cameroon
Republic of Cameroon

People: Population (1990 est.): 11,109,000. **Age distrib.** (%): 0–14: 44.6; 15–59: 49.8; 60+: 5.6. **Pop. density:** 58 per sq. mi. **Urban** (1988): 40%. **Ethnic groups:** Some 200 tribes; largest are Bamileke 30%, Fulani 7%. **Languages:** English, French (both official), 24 African groups. **Religions:** Animist 51%, Moslem 16%, Christian 33%.

Geography: Area: 185,568 sq. mi., somewhat larger than California. **Location:** Between W and central Africa. **Neighbors:** Nigeria on NW, Chad, Central African Republic on E, Congo, Gabon, Equatorial Guinea on S. **Topography:** A low coastal plain with rain forests is in S; plateaus in center lead to forested mountains in W, including Mt. Cameroon, 13,000 ft.; grasslands in N lead to marshes around Lake Chad. **Capital:** Yaounde. **Cities** (1988 est.): Douala 852,000; Yaounde 700,000.

Government: Type: Republic, one party presidential regime. **Head of state:** Pres. Paul Biya; b. Feb. 13, 1933; in office: Nov. 6, 1982. **Local divisions:** 10 provinces. **Defense:** 6.5% of budget (1987).

Economy: Industries: Aluminum processing, oil prod., palm products. **Chief crops:** Cocoa, coffee, cotton. **Crude oil reserves** (1985): 531 mln. bbls. **Other resources:** Timber. **Arable land:** 14%. **Livestock** (1986): cattle: 4.3 mln.; sheep: 2.5 mln.; pigs: 1.1 mln. **Fish catch** (1988): 83,000 metric tons. **Electricity prod.** (1988): 2.5 bln. kwh. **Labor force:** 74% agric., 11% ind. and commerce.

Finance: Currency: CFA franc (Mar. 1990: 284 = $1 US). **Gross national product** (1987): $12.3 bln. **Per capita income** (1986): $1,171. **Imports** (1988): 1.2 bln.; partners: Fr. 42%, W. Ger. 10%. **Exports** (1988): $928 mln.; partners: Fr. 21%, U.S. 16%, Neth. 28%. **National budget** (1988): $2.2 bln. **International reserves less gold** (Jan. 1990): $55 mln. **Gold:** 30,000 oz t. **Consumer prices** (change in 1988): 8.6%.

Transport: Railway traffic (1986): 432 mln. passenger-km. **Motor vehicles:** in use (1986): 86,000 passenger cars, 32,000 comm. vehicles. **Chief ports:** Douala.

Communications: Radios: 1 per 11 persons. **Telephones in use:** 1 per 179 persons. **Daily newspaper circ.** (1988): 6 per 1,000 pop.

Health: Life expectancy at birth (1989): 48 male; 52 female. **Births** (per 1,000 pop. 1989): 42. **Deaths** (per 1,000 pop. 1989): 16. **Natural increase:** 2.6%. **Hospital beds** (1981): 24,541. **Physicians** (1982): 604. **Infant mortality** (per 1,000 live births 1989): 123.

Education (1988): **Literacy:** 65%. About 70% attend school.

Major International Organizations: UN, OAU, EC (Associate).

Embassy: 2349 Massachusetts Ave. NW 20008; 265-8790.

Portuguese sailors were the first Europeans to reach Cameroon, in the 15th century. The European and American slave trade was very active in the area. German control lasted from 1884 to 1916, when France and Britain divided the territory, later receiving League of Nations mandates and UN trusteeships. French Cameroon became independent Jan. 1, 1960; one part of British Cameroon joined Nigeria in 1961, the other part joined Cameroon. Stability has allowed for development of roads, railways, agriculture, and petroleum production. Some 3,000 died in 1986 as a result of clouds of toxic gas of volcanic origin emanating from Lake Nyos.

Canada

People: Population (1990 est.): 26,527,000. **Age distrib.** (%): 0–14: 21.4; 15–59: 63.6; 60+: 15.0. **Pop. density:** 6 per sq. mi. **Urban** (1985): 75.9%. **Ethnic groups:** British Isles origin 40%; French 27%, other European 20%. **Language:** English, French (both official). **Religion:** Roman Catholic 46%, Protestant 41%.

Geography: Area: 3,558,096 sq. mi., the 2d largest country in land size, Canada stretches 3,223 miles from east to west and extends southward from the North Pole to the U.S. border. Its seacoast includes 36,356 miles of mainland and 115,133 miles of islands, including the Arctic islands almost from Greenland to near the Alaskan border. Climate, while generally temperate, varies from freezing winter cold to blistering summer heat. **Capitol:** Ottawa. **Cities** (met. 1986 est.): Montreal 2,921,000; Toronto 3,427,000; Vancouver 1,380,000; Ottawa-Hull 819,000; Winnipeg 625,000; Edmonton 785,000, Calgary 671,000, Quebec 603,000.

Government: Type: Confederation with parliamentary democracy. **Head of state:** Queen Elizabeth II, represented by Gov.-Gen. Ray Hnatyshyn; in office: Jan. 29, 1990. **Head of government:** Prime Min. Brian Mulroney; born: Mar. 20, 1939; in office: Sept. 4, 1984. **Local divisions:** 10 provinces, 2 territories. **Defense:** 2% of GNP (1988).

Economy: Minerals: Nickel, zinc, copper, gold, lead, molybdenum, potash, silver. **Crude oil reserves** (1987): 4.8 bln. bbls. **Arable land:** 5%. **Livestock** (1988): cattle: 12.0 mln.; pigs: 10.8 mln.; sheep: 722,000. **Fish catch** (1988): 1.5 mln. metric tons. **Electricity prod.** (1988): 468 bln. kwh. **Crude steel prod.** (1988): 15.1 mln. metric tons. **Labor force:** 4% agric.; 52% ind. & comm., 28% services.

Finance: Currency: Dollar (Aug. 1990: 1.15 = $1 US). **Gross national product** (1988): $486 bln. **Per capita income** (1984 est.) $13,000. **Imports** (1989): $121 bln.; partners: U.S. 69%, EC 8%, Jap. 5%. **Exports** (1989): $121 bln.; partners: U.S. 78%, EC 9%, Jap. 5%. **Tourists** (1988): receipts: $4.6 bln. **National budget** (1987-88): Can $122 bln. expenditures. **International reserves less gold** (Mar. 1990): $13.7 bln. **Gold:** 16.0 mln. oz t. **Consumer prices** (change in 1989): 5.0%.

Transport: Railway traffic (1988): 1.9 bln. passenger-km. **Motor vehicles:** in use (1986): 11.1 mln. passenger cars, 3 mln. comm. **Civil aviation** (1988): 52.6 bln. passenger-km: 61 airports with scheduled flights.

Communications: Television sets: 1 per 1.7 persons. **Radios:** 1 per 1.2 persons. **Telephones in use:** 1 per 1.3 persons. **Daily newspaper circ.** (1988): 211 per 1,000 pop.

Health: Life expectancy at birth (1989): 73 male; 80 female. **Births** (per 1,000 pop. 1989): 14. **Deaths** (per 1,000 pop. 1989): 7. **Natural increase:** .7%. **Hospital beds:** 1 per 148 persons. **Physicians:** 1 per 467 persons. **Infant mortality** (per 1,000 live births 1989): 7.3.

Education (1989): **Literacy:** 99%.

Major International Organizations: UN and all of its specialized agencies, NATO, OECD, Commonwealth of Nations.

Embassy: 501 Pennsylvania Ave. NW 20001; 682-1740.

French explorer Jacques Cartier, who discovered the Gulf of St. Lawrence in 1534, is generally regarded as the founder of Canada. But English seaman John Cabot sighted Newfoundland 37 years earlier, in 1497, and Vikings are believed to have reached the Atlantic coast centuries before either explorer.

Canadian settlement was pioneered by the French who established Quebec City (1608) and Montreal (1642) and declared New France a colony in 1663.

Britain, as part of its American expansion, acquired Acadia (later Nova Scotia) in 1717 and, through military victory over French forces in Canada (an extension of a European conflict between the 2 powers), captured Quebec (1759) and obtained control of the rest of New France in 1763. The French, through the Quebec Act of 1774, retained the rights to their own language, religion, and civil law.

The British presence in Canada increased during the American Revolution when many colonials, proudly calling themselves United Empire Loyalists, moved north to Canada.

Fur traders and explorers led Canadians westward across the continent. Sir Alexander Mackenzie reached the Pacific in 1793 and scrawled on a rock by the ocean, "from Canada by land."

In Upper and Lower Canada (later called Ontario and Quebec) and in the Maritimes, legislative assemblies appeared in the 18th century and reformers called for responsible government. But the War of 1812 intervened. The war, a conflict between Great Britain and the United States fought mainly in Upper Canada, ended in a stalemate in 1814.

In 1837 political agitation for more democratic government culminated in rebellions in Upper and Lower Canada. Britain sent Lord Durham to investigate and, in a famous report (1839), he recommended union of the 2 parts into one colony called Canada. The union lasted until Confederation, July 1, 1867, when proclamation of the British North America (BNA) Act launched the Dominion of Canada, consisting of Ontario, Quebec, and the former colonies of Nova Scotia and New Brunswick.

Since 1840 the Canadian colonies had held the right to internal self-government. The BNA act, which became the country's written constitution, established a federal system of government on the model of a British parliament and cabinet structure under the crown. Canada was proclaimed a self-governing Dominion within the British Empire in 1931.

In 1982 Canada severed its last formal legislative link with Britain by obtaining the right to amend its constitution (the British North America Act of 1867).

The Meech Lake Agreement was signed June 3, 1987. The historic accord, subject to ratification by Parliament and the provincial legislatures, assured constitutional protection for Quebec's efforts to preserve its French language and culture. Critics of the accord charged that it did not make any provision for other minority groups, and that it gave Quebec too much power, which might enable it to pass laws that conflicted with the nation's 1982 Charter of Rights and Freedoms. In 1988, Quebec had overridden a Canadian Supreme Court decision striking down a provincial language law that had restricted the use of any language other than French on public signs. The accord died June 22, 1990, as Newfoundland and Manitoba failed to approve it. The defeat set the stage for a possible reconsideration of Quebec separatism.

Canadian Provinces

	Sq. mi.	Population, 1989 est.
Alberta	248,800	2,423,200
British Columbia	358,971	3,044,200
Manitoba	211,723	1,083,300
New Brunswick	27,834	717,600
Newfoundland	143,510	529,200
Nova Scotia	20,402	885,700
Ontario	344,090	9,546,200
Prince Edward Island	2,165	130,000
Quebec	523,859	6,679,000
Saskatchewan	220,348	1,007,100
Territories		
Northwest Territories	1,271,442	53,100
Yukon	184,931	25,700

Prime Ministers of Canada

Canada is a constitutional monarchy with a parliamentary system of government. It is also a federal state. Canada's offical head of state is the King or Queen of England, represented by a resident Governor-General. However, in practice the nation is governed by the Prime Minister, leader of the party that commands the support of a majority of the House of Commons, dominant chamber of Canada's bicameral Parliament.

Name	Party	Term	Name	Party	Term
Sir John A. MacDonald	Conservative	1867-1873 1878-1891			1935-1948
Alexander Mackenzie	Liberal	1873-1878	R. B. Bennett	Conservative	1930-1935
Sir John J. C. Abbott	Conservative	1891-1892	Louis St. Laurent	Liberal	1948-1957
Sir John S. D. Thompson	Conservative	1892-1894	John G. Diefenbaker	Prog. Cons.	1957-1963
Sir Mackenzie Bowell	Conservative	1894-1896	Lester B. Pearson	Liberal	1963-1968
Sir Charles Tupper	Conservative	1896	Pierre Elliott Trudeau	Liberal	1968-1979
Sir Wilfrid Laurier	Liberal	1896-1911	Joe Clark	Prog. Cons.	1979-1980
Sir Robert L. Borden	Cons. Union.	1911-1920	Pierre Elliott Trudeau	Liberal	1980-1984
Arthur Meighen	Cons. Union.	1920-1921	John Turner	Liberal	1984
W.L. Mackenzie King	Liberal	1921-1926[1] 1926-1930	Brian Mulroney	Prog. Cons.	1984-

(1) King's term was interrupted from June 26-Sept. 25, 1926, when Arthur Meighen again served as prime minister.

Cape Verde
Republic of Cape Verde
República de Cabo Verde

People: Population (1990 est.): 375,000. **Age distrib.** (%): 0-14: 45.6; 15-59: 47.7; 60+: 6.7. **Pop. density:** 337 per sq. mi. **Urban** (1980): 26.2%. **Ethnic groups:** Creole (mulatto) 71%, African 28%, European 1%. **Languages:** Portuguese (official), Crioulo. **Religions:** 80% Roman Catholic.

Geography: Area: 1,557 sq. mi., a bit larger than Rhode Island. **Location:** In Atlantic O., off western tip of Africa. **Neighbors:** Nearest are Mauritania, Senegal. **Topography:** Cape Verde Islands are 15 in number, volcanic in origin (active crater on Fogo). The landscape is eroded and stark, with vegetation mostly in interior valleys. **Capital:** Praia. **Cities** (1986 est.): Mindelo 40,000; Praia 50,000.

Government: Type: Republic. **Head of state:** Pres. Aristides Pereira; b. Nov. 17, 1923; in office: July 5, 1975. **Head of government:** Prime Min. Pedro Pires, b. Apr. 29, 1934; in office: July 5, 1975. **Local divisions:** 14 administrative districts.

Economy: Chief crops: Bananas, coffee, beans, corn, beans. **Minerals:** Salt. **Other resources:** Fish. **Arable land:** 10%. **Electricity prod.** (1989): 18 mln. kwh.

Finance: Currency: Escudo (Dec. 1989: 82.21 = $1 US). **Gross national product** (1987): $136 mln. **Per capita GNP** (1987): $500. **Imports** (1986): $108 mln.; partners: Port. 33%, Neth. 12%. **Exports** (1986): $4.5 mln.; partners: Port. 32%, Ang. 21%.

Transport: Motor vehicles: in use (1981): 4,000 passenger cars, 1,343 comm. vehicles. **Chief ports:** Mindelo, Praia.

Communications: Radios: 1 per 6.8 persons. **Telephones in use:** 1 per 76 persons.

Health: Life expectancy at birth (1989): 59 male; 63 female. **Births** (per 1,000 pop. 1989): 48. **Deaths** (per 1,000 pop. 1989): 11. **Natural increase:** 3.8%. **Hospital beds** (1980): 632. **Physicians** (1980): 51. **Infant mortality** (per 1,000 live births 1989): 66.

Education (1989): **Literacy:** 37%.

Major International Organizations: UN (GATT, IMF, WHO), OAU.

Embassy: 3415 Massachusetts Ave. NW 20007; 965-6820.

The uninhabited Cape Verdes were discovered by the Portuguese in 1456 or 1460. The first Portuguese colonists landed in 1462; African slaves were brought soon after, and most Cape Verdeans descend from both groups. Cape Verde independence came July 5, 1975. The islands have suffered from repeated extreme droughts and famines. Emphasis is placed on the development of agriculture and on fishing.

Central African Republic
République Centrafricaine

People: Population (1990 est.): 2,879,000. **Pop. density:** 12 per sq. mi. **Urban** (1988): 37%. **Ethnic groups:** Banda 27%, Baya 34%, Mandja 21%, Sara 10%. **Languages:** French (official), local dialects. **Religions:** Protestant 25%, Roman Catholic 25%, traditional 24%.

Geography: Area: 240,534 sq. mi., slightly smaller than Texas. **Location:** In central Africa. **Neighbors:** Chad on N, Cameroon on W, Congo, Zaire on S, Sudan on E. **Topography:** Mostly rolling plateau, average altitude 2,000 ft., with rivers draining S to the Congo and N to Lake Chad. Open, well-watered savanna covers most of the area, with an arid area in NE, and tropical rainforest in SW. **Capital:** Bangui. **Cities** (1988 est.): Bangui (met.) 596,000.

Government: Type: Republic. (under military rule). **Head of state:** Gen. Andre Kolingba; in office: Sept. 1, 1981. **Local divisions:** 16 prefectures. **Defense:** 2% of GNP (1984).

Economy: Industries: Textiles, light manuf., mining. **Chief crops:** Cotton, coffee, peanuts, tobacco. **Minerals:** Diamonds (chief export), uranium. **Other resources:** Timber. **Arable land:** 3%. **Electricity prod.** (1987): 91 mln. kwh. **Labor force:** 72% agric.

Finance: Currency: CFA franc (Mar. 1990: 284 = $1 US). **Gross national product** (1988): $1.1 bln. **Per capita income** (1988): $376. **Imports** (1988): $285 mln.; partners: Fr. 52%. **Exports** (1988): $138 mln.; partners: Fr. 17%, Bel.-Lux. 42%. **National budget** (1988): $204 mln. **International reserves less gold** (Jan. 1990): $97 mln. **Gold:** 11,000 oz t.

Transport: Motor vehicles: in use (1986): 1,000 passenger cars, 20,000 comm. vehicles.

Communications: Radios: 1 per 22 persons. **Telephones:** 1 per 380 persons.

Health: Life expectancy at birth (1989): 45 male; 48 female. **Births** (per 1,000 pop. 1989): 44. **Deaths** 1 per 1,000 pop. 1989): 19. **Natural increase:** 2.5%. **Hospital beds** (1984): 3,774. **Physicians** (1984): 112. **Infant mortality** (per 1,000 live births 1989): 143.

Education (1989): **Literacy:** 40%. **Attendance:** primary school 79%; secondary school 18%.

Major International Organizations: UN (GATT, IMF, WHO), OAU.

Embassy: 1618 22d St. NW 20008; 483-7800.

Various Bantu tribes migrated through the region for centuries before French control was asserted in the late 19th century, when the region was named Ubangi-Shari. Complete independence was attained Aug. 13, 1960.

All political parties were dissolved in 1960, and the country became a center for Chinese political influence in Africa. Relations with China were severed after 1965. Elizabeth Domitien, premier 1975-76, was the first woman to hold that post in an African country. Pres. Jean-Bedel Bokassa, who seized power in a 1965 military coup, proclaimed himself constitutional emperor of the renamed Central African Empire Dec. 1976.

Bokassa's rule was characterized by ruthless and cruel authority, and human rights violations. Bokassa was ousted in a bloodless coup aided by the French government, Sept. 20, 1979, and replaced by his cousin David Dacko, former president from 1960 to 1965. In 1981, the political situation deteriorated amid strikes and economic crisis. Gen. Kolingba replaced Dacko as head of state in a bloodless coup.

Chad
Republic of Chad
République du Tchad

People: Population (1990 est.): 5,064,000. **Age distrib. (%):** 0–14: 42.5; 15–59: 51.7; 60+: 5.8. **Pop. density:** 11 per sq. mi. **Urban** (1986): 23%. **Ethnic groups:** 200 distinct groups. **Languages:** French, Arabic, (both official), some 100 other languages. **Religions:** Moslem 44%, animist 23%, Christian 33%.

Geography: Area: 495,755 sq. mi., four-fifths the size of Alaska. **Location:** In central N. Africa. **Neighbors:** Libya on N, Niger, Nigeria, Cameroon on W, Central African Republic on S, Sudan on E. **Topography:** Southern wooded savanna, steppe, and desert, part of the Sahara, in the N. Southern rivers flow N to Lake Chad, surrounded by marshland. **Capital:** N'Djamena. **Cities** (1986 est.): N'Djamena 511,000.

Government: Type: Republic. **Head of state:** Pres. Hissen Habre; b. 1942; in office: June 19, 1982. **Local divisions:** 14 prefectures. **Defense:** 1.9% of GNP (1985).

Economy: Chief crops: Cotton. **Minerals:** Uranium, salt. **Arable land:** 2%. **Fish catch** (1987): 110,000 metric tons. **Electricity prod.** (1988): 69 mln. kwh. **Labor force:** 85% agric.

Finance: Currency: CFA franc (Mar. 1990: 284 = $1 US). **Gross national product** (1987): $805 mln. **Per capita income** (1986): $158. **Imports** (1988): $419 mln.; partners: Fr. 47%. **Exports** (1988): $141 mln.; partners Fra, EDEAC countries. **International reserves less gold** (Jan. 1990): $92 mln. **Gold:** 11,000 oz t.

Transport: Motor vehicles: in use (1985): 2,500 passenger cars, 4,000 comm. vehicles.

Communications: Radios: 1 per 4.3 persons. **Telephones in use:** 1 per 1,114 persons.

Health: Life expectancy at birth (1989): 38 male; 40 female. **Births** (per 1,000 pop. 1989): 42. **Deaths** (per 1,000 pop. 1989): 22. **Natural increase:** 2.0%. **Hospital beds** (1980): 3,500. **Physicians** (1980): 94. **Infant mortality** (per 1,000 live births 1989): 139.

Education (1989): **Literacy:** 17%.

Major International Organizations: UN, (GATT, IMF, WHO), OAU, EEC.

Embassy: 2002 R St. NW 20009; 462-4009.

Chad was the site of paleolithic and neolithic cultures before the Sahara Desert formed. A succession of kingdoms and Arab slave traders dominated Chad until France took control around 1900. Independence came Aug. 11, 1960.

Northern Moslem rebels, have fought animist and Christian southern government and French troops from 1966, despite numerous cease-fires and peace pacts.

Libyan troops entered the country at the request of the Chad government, December 1980. On Jan. 6, 1981 Libya and Chad announced their intention to unite. France together with several African nations condemned the agreement as a menace to African security. The Libyan troops were withdrawn from Chad in November 1981.

Rebel forces, led by Hissen Habre, captured the capital and forced Pres. Oueddei to flee the country in June 1982.

In 1983, France sent some 3,000 troops to Chad to assist Habre in opposing Libyan-backed rebels. France and Libya agreed to a simultaneous withdrawal of troops from Chad in September 1984 but Libyan forces remained in the north until Mar. 1987 when Chad forces drove them from their last major stronghold. Libyan troops abandoned almost $1 billion of military equipment during their retreat.

Chile
Republic of Chile
República de Chile

People: Population (1990 est.): 13,000,000. **Age distrib. (%):** 0–14: 31.1; 15–59: 60.6; 60+: 8.3. **Pop. density:** 44 per sq. mi. **Urban** (1988): 83%. **Ethnic groups:** Mestizo 66%, Spanish 25%, Indian 5%. **Languages:** Spanish. **Religions:** Roman Catholic 89%, Protestant 11%.

Geography: Area: 292,257 sq. mi., larger than Texas. **Location:** Occupies western coast of southern S. America. **Neigh-**

bors: Peru on N, Bolivia on NE, Argentina on E. **Topography:** Andes Mtns. are on E border including some of the world's highest peaks; on W is 2,650-mile Pacific Coast. Width varies between 100 and 250 miles. In N is Atacama Desert, in center are agricultural regions, in S are forests and grazing lands. **Capital:** Santiago. **Cities** (1987 metro est.) Santiago 4,858,000.

Government: Type: Republic. **Head of state:** Pres. Patricio Aylwin; b. 1918; in office: Mar. 11, 1990. **Local divisions:** 12 regions and Santiago region. **Defense:** 3.6% of GNP (1988).

Economy: Industries: Steel, fish processing, wood products. **Chief crops:** Grain, onions, beans, potatoes, peas, fruits, grapes. **Minerals:** Copper (27% world resources and 40% of export revenues), molybdenum, nitrates, iodine (half world output), iron, coal, oil, gas, gold, cobalt, zinc, manganese, borate, mica, mercury, salt, sulphur, marble, onyx. **Crude oil reserves** (1985): 224 mln. bbls. **Other resources:** Water, forests. **Arable land:** 7%. **Livestock** (1988): cattle: 3.3 mln.; sheep: 6.5 mln.; pigs: 1.1 mln. **Fish catch** (1988): 4.7 mln. metric tons. **Electricity prod.** (1988): 15.5 bln. kwh. **Labor force:** 21% agric., forestry, fishing; 32% ind & comm., 28% serv.

Finance: Currency: Peso (June 1990: 294 = $1 US). **Gross national product** (1988): $19.4 bln. **Per capita GNP** (1988): $1,520. **Imports** (1989): $6.4 bln.; partners: U.S. 19%, Braz. 9%. **Exports** (1988): $8.1 bln.; partners: W. Ger. 10%, Jap. 11%, U.S. 22%. **Tourists** (1986): $172 mln. receipts. **National budget** (1988): $5.7 bln. expenditures. **International reserves less gold** (Mar. 1990): $3.3 bln. **Gold:** 1.53 mln. oz. t. **Consumer prices** (change in 1989): 17.0%

Transport: Railway traffic (1987): 1.2 bln. passenger-km. **Motor vehicles:** in use (1987): 660,000 passenger cars, 278,000 comm. vehicles. **Civil aviation** (1988): 2.4 bln. passenger-km.; 18 airports with scheduled flights. **Chief ports:** Valparaiso, Arica, Antofagasta.

Communications: Television sets: 1 per 5.5 persons. **Radios:** 1 per 3.3 persons. **Telephones in use:** 795,000.

Health: Life expectancy at birth (1989): 68 male; 75 female. **Births** (per 1,000 pop. 1989): 21. **Deaths** (per 1,000 pop. 1989): 6. **Natural increase:** 1.5%. **Hospital beds:** 1 per 372 persons. **Physicians:** 1 per 983 persons. **Infant mortality** (per 1,000 live births 1989): 18.

Education (1988): **Literacy:** 92%. Compulsory ages 6-14.

Major International Organizations: UN and all of its specialized agencies, OAS.

Embassy: 1732 Massachusetts Ave. NW 20036; 785-1746.

Northern Chile was under Inca rule before the Spanish conquest, 1536-40. The southern Araucanian Indians resisted until the late 19th century. Independence was gained 1810-18, under Jose de San Martin and Bernardo O'Higgins; the latter, as supreme director 1817-23, sought social and economic reforms until deposed. Chile defeated Peru and Bolivia in 1836-39 and 1879-84, gaining mineral-rich northern land.

Eduardo Frei Montalva came into office in 1964, instituting social programs and gradual nationalization of foreign-owned mining companies. In 1970, Salvador Allende Gossens, a Marxist, became president with a third of the national vote.

The Allende government furthered nationalizations, and improved conditions for the poor. But illegal and violent actions by extremist supporters of the government, the regime's failure to attain majority support, and poorly planned socialist economic programs led to political and financial chaos.

A military junta seized power Sept. 11, 1973, and said Allende killed himself. The junta named a mostly military cabinet, and announced plans to "exterminate Marxism."

Repression continued during the 1980s with little sign of any political liberalization. In a plebiscite held Oct. 5, 1988, voters rejected junta-candidate Gen. Pinochet who, if victorious, would have governed Chile until 1997. Pinochet accepted the rejection and called for presidential elections. In Dec. 1989 voters removed Pinochet from office and elected Patricio Aylwin as president.

Tierra del Fuego is the largest (18,800 sq. mi.) island in the archipelago of the same name at the southern tip of South America, an area of majestic mountains, tortuous channels, and high winds. It was discovered 1520 by Magellan and named the Land of Fire because of its many Indian bonfires. Part of the island is in Chile, part in Argentina. Punta Arenas, on a mainland peninsula, is a center of sheep-raising and the world's southernmost city (pop. 67,600); Puerto Williams, pop. 949, is the southernmost settlement.

China

People's Republic of China

Zhonghua Renmin Gonghe Guo

People: Population (1990 est.): 1,130,065,000. **Pop. density:** 288 per sq. mi. **Urban** (1987): 46%. **Ethnic groups:** Han Chinese 94%, Mongol, Korean, Manchu, others. **Languages:** Mandarin Chinese (official), Yue, Wu Minbei, Minnan, Xiang, Gan. **Religions:** officially atheist; Confucianism, Buddhism, Taoism are traditional.

Geography: Area: 3,705,390 sq. mi., slightly larger than the conterminous U.S. **Location:** Occupies most of the habitable mainland of E. Asia. **Neighbors:** Mongolia on N, USSR on NE and NW, Afghanistan, Pakistan on W, India, Nepal, Bhutan, Myanmar, Laos, Vietnam on S, N. Korea on NE. **Topography:** Two-thirds of the vast territory is mountainous or desert, and only one-tenth is cultivated. Rolling topography rises to high elevations in the N in the Daxinganlingshanmai separating Manchuria and Mongolia; the Tienshan in Xinjiang; the Himalayan and Kunlunshanmai in the SW and in Tibet. Length is 1,860 mi. from N to S, width E to W is more than 2,000 mi. The eastern half of China is one of the best-watered lands in the world. Three great river systems, the Changjiang, the Huanghe, and the Xijiang provide water for vast farmlands. **Capital:** Beijing. **Cities** (1987 est.): Shanghai 7 mln.; Beijing 5.9 mln.; Tianjin 5.4 mln.; Canton 3.3 mln.; Shenyang 4.2 mln.; Wuhan 3.4 mln.; Chengdu 2.6 mln.

Government: Type: Communist Party led state. **Head of state:** Pres. Yang Shangkun; in office: Apr. 8, 1989. **Head of government:** Premier Li Peng; in office: Apr. 9, 1989. **Gen. Secy. of Communist Party:** Jiang Zemin; b. 1926; in office June 24, 1989. **Local divisions:** 22 provinces, 5 autonomous regions, and 3 cities. **Defense:** 4.4% of GNP (1987).

Economy: Industries: Iron and steel, textiles, agriculture implements, trucks. **Chief crops:** Grain, rice, cotton, tea. **Minerals:** tungsten, antimony, coal, iron, lead, manganese, molybdenum, tin. **Crude oil reserves** (1987): 18.5 bln. bbls. **Other resources:** Silk. **Arable land:** 11%. **Livestock** (1987): cattle: 71.3 mln.; pigs: 328 mln.; sheep: 178 mln. **Fish catch** (1988): 9.3 mln. metric tons. **Electricity prod.** (1987): 898 bln. kwh. **Crude steel prod.** (1988): 59.0 mln. metric tons. **Labor force:** 68% agric.; 18% ind. & comm.

Finance: Currency: Yuan (Mar. 1990): 4.72 = $1 US). **Gross national product** (1988): $350 bln. **Per capita income** (1986): $258. **Imports** (1989): $58.2 bln.; partners: Jap. 23%, U.S. 11%, Hong Kong 20%. **Exports** (1989): $51.6 bln.; partners: Hong Kong 35%, Jap. 16%, U.S. 9%. **Tourism** (1988): $2.2 bln. receipts. **National budget** (1987): $66.1 bln. expenditures. **International reserves less gold** (Feb. 1990): $19.9 bln. **Gold:** 12.7 mln. oz t. **Consumer prices** (change in 1989): 16.3%.

Transport: Railway traffic (1988): 326 passenger-km. **Motor vehicles:** in use (1987): 1.1 mln. passenger cars, 2.8 mln. comm. vehicles. **Civil aviation** (1988): 21.4 bln. passenger km, 80 airports with scheduled flights. **Chief ports:** Shanghai, Tianjin, Luda.

Communications: Television sets: 1 per 12 persons. **Radios:** 1 per 8.9 persons. **Telephones:** 1 per 134 persons. **Daily newspaper circ.** (1986): 50 per 1,000 pop.

Health: Life expectancy at birth (1989): 68 male; 70 female. **Births** (per 1,000 pop. 1989): 23. **Deaths** (per 1,000 pop. 1989): 7. **Natural increase:** 1.6%. **Infant Mortality** (per 1,000 live births 1989): 33. **Hospital beds:** 1 per 432 persons. **Physicians:** 1 per 668 persons.

Education (1987): **Literacy:** 70%. Years compulsory 9; first grade enrollment 93%.

Major International Organizations: UN (IMF, FAO, WHO). **Embassy:** 2300 Conn. Ave. NW 20008; 328-2500.

History. Remains of various man-like creatures who lived as early as several hundred thousand years ago have been found in many parts of China. Neolithic agricultural settlements dotted the Huanghe basin from about 5,000 BC. Their language, religion, and art were the sources of later Chinese civilization.

Bronze metallurgy reached a peak and Chinese pictographic writing, similar to today's, was in use in the more developed culture of the Shang Dynasty (c. 1500 BC-c. 1000 BC) which ruled much of North China.

A succession of dynasties and interdynastic warring kingdoms ruled China for the next 3,000 years. They expanded Chinese political and cultural domination to the south and west, and developed a brilliant technologically and culturally advanced society. Rule by foreigners (Mongols in the Yuan Dynasty, 1271-1368, and Manchus in the Ch'ing Dynasty, 1644-1911) did not alter the underlying culture.

A period of relative stagnation left China vulnerable to internal and external pressures in the 19th century. Rebellions left tens of millions dead, and Russia, Japan, Britain, and other powers exercised political and economic control in large parts of the country. China became a republic Jan. 1, 1912, following the Wuchang Uprising inspired by Dr. Sun Yat-sen.

For a period of 50 years, 1894-1945, China was involved in conflicts with Japan. In 1895, China ceded Korea, Taiwan, and other areas. On Sept. 18, 1931, Japan seized the Northeastern Provinces (Manchuria) and set up a puppet state called Manchukuo. The border province of Jehol was cut off as a buffer state in 1933. Japan invaded China proper July 7, 1937. After its defeat in World War II, Japan gave up all seized land.

Following World War II, internal disturbances arose involving the Kuomintang, communists, and other factions. China came under domination of communist armies, 1949-1950. The Kuomintang government moved to Taiwan, 90 mi. off the mainland, Dec. 8, 1949.

The People's Republic of China was proclaimed in Peking Sept. 21, 1949, by the Chinese People's Political Consultative Conference under Mao Zedong.

China and the USSR signed a 30-year treaty of "friendship, alliance and mutual assistance," Feb. 15, 1950.

The U.S. refused recognition of the new regime. On Nov. 26, 1950, the People's Republic sent armies into Korea against U.S. troops and forced a stalemate.

By the 1960s, relations with the USSR deteriorated, with disagreements on borders, ideology and leadership of world communism. The USSR cancelled aid accords, and China, with Albania, launched anti-Soviet propaganda drives. High level talks have been held with the USSR to seek improved trade and cultural contracts; little progress was reported.

On Oct. 25, 1971, the UN General Assembly ousted the Taiwan government from the UN and seated the People's Republic in its place. The U.S. had supported the mainland's admission but opposed Taiwan's expulsion.

U.S. Pres. Nixon visited China Feb. 21-28, 1972, on invitation from Premier Zhou Enlai, ending years of antipathy between the 2 nations. China and the U.S. opened liaison offices in each other's capitals, May-June 1973. The U.S., Dec. 15, 1978, formally recognized the People's Republic of China as the sole legal government of China; diplomatic relations between the 2 nations were established, Jan. 1, 1979.

In a continuing "reassessment" of the policies of Mao Zedong, Mao's widow, Jiang Quing, and other Gang of Four members were convicted of "committing crimes during the 'Cultural Revolution,'" Jan. 25, 1981.

Internal developments. After an initial period of consolidation, 1949-52, industry, agriculture, and social and economic institutions were forcibly molded according to Maoist ideals. However, frequent drastic changes in policy and violent factionalism interfered with economic development.

In 1957, Mao Tse-tung admitted an estimated 800,000 people had been executed 1949-54; opponents claimed much higher figures.

The Great Leap Forward, 1958-60, tried to force the pace of economic development through intensive labor on huge new rural communes, and through emphasis on ideological purity and enthusiasm. The program caused resistance and was largely abandoned. Serious food shortages developed, and the government was forced to buy grain from the West.

The Great Proletarian Cultural Revolution, 1965, was an attempt to oppose pragmatism and bureaucratic power and instruct a new generation in revolutionary principles. Massive purges took place. A program of forcibly relocating millions of urban teenagers into the countryside was launched.

By 1968 the movement had run its course; many purged officials returned to office in subsequent years, and reforms in education and industry that had placed ideology above expertise were gradually weakened.

In the mid-1970s, factional and ideological fighting increased, and emerged into the open after the 1976 deaths of Mao and

Premier Zhou Enlai. Mao's widow and 3 other leading leftists were purged and placed under arrest, after reportedly trying to seize power. Their opponents said the "gang of four" had used severe repression and mass torture, had sparked local fighting and had disrupted production. The new ruling group modified Maoist policies in education, culture, and industry, and sought better ties with non-communist countries.

Relations with Vietnam deteriorated in 1978 as China charged persecution of ethnic Chinese. In retaliation for Vietnam's invasion of Cambodia, China attacked 4 Vietnamese border provinces Feb. 17, 1979; heavy border fighting ensued.

Sweeping reforms of the central bureaucracy were announced March 1982. By the mid 1980's, China had enacted far-reaching economic reforms highlighted by the departure from rigid central planning and the stressing of market-oriented socialism.

Some 100,000 students and workers staged a march in Beijing to demand democratic reforms, May 4, 1989. The demonstrations continued during a visit to Beijing by Soviet leader Mikhail Gorbachev May 15-18. It was the first Sino-Soviet summit since 1959. A million people gathered in Beijing to demand democratic reforms and the removal of Deng and other leaders. There were protests in at least 20 other Chinese cities. Martial law was imposed, May 20, but was mostly ignored by the protesters.

Chinese army troops entered Beijing, June 3-4, and crushed the pro-democracy protests. Tanks and armored personnel carriers attacked Tiananmen Square, outside the Great Hall of the People, which was the main scene of the demonstrations and hunger strikes. It was estimated that 5,000 died, 10,000 were injured, and hundreds of students and workers arrested.

China's population, the world's largest, is still increasing, but with more couples following the government's one-child policy some experts predict that the nation's population will actually decline after peaking in the early 21st century.

Manchuria. Home of the Manchus, rulers of China 1644-1911, Manchuria has accommodated millions of Chinese settlers in the 20th century. Under Japanese rule 1931-45, the area became industrialized. China no longer uses the name Manchuria for the region, which is divided into the 3 NE provinces of Heilongjiang, Jilin, and Liaoning.

Guandong is the southernmost part of Manchuria. Russia in 1898 forced China to lease it Guandong, and built Port Arthur (Lushun) and the port of Dairen (Luda). Japan seized Port Arthur in 1905. It was turned over to the USSR by the 1945 Yalta agreement, but finally returned to China in 1950.

Inner Mongolia was organized by the People's Republic in 1947. Its boundaries have undergone frequent changes, reaching its greatest extent (and restored in 1979) in 1956, with an area of 454,000 sq. mi., allegedly in order to dilute the minority Mongol population. Chinese settlers outnumber the Mongols more than 10 to 1. Pop. (1988 est.): 20.0 mln. Capital: Hohhot.

Xinjiang Uygur Autonomous Region, in Central Asia, is 633,802 sq. mi., pop. (1983 est.): 13.6 mln. (75% Uygurs, a Turkic Moslem group, with a heavy Chinese increase in recent years). Capital: Urumqi. It is China's richest region in strategic minerals. Some Uygurs have fled to the USSR, claiming national oppression.

Tibet, 470,000 sq. mi., is a thinly populated region of high plateaus and massive mountains, the Himalayas on the S, the Kun-luns on the N. High passes connect with India and Nepal; roads lead into China proper. Capital: Lhasa. Average altitude is 15,000 ft. Jiachan, 15,870 ft., is believed to be the highest inhabited town on earth. Agriculture is primitive. Pop. (1988 est.): 2 mln. (of whom 500,000 are Chinese). Another 4 million Tibetans form the majority of the population of vast adjacent areas that have long been incorporated into China.

China ruled all of Tibet from the 18th century, but independence came in 1911. China reasserted control in 1951, and a communist government was installed in 1953, revising the theocratic Lamaist Buddhist rule. Serfdom was abolished, but all land remained collectivized.

A Tibetan uprising within China in 1956 spread to Tibet in 1959. The rebellion was crushed with Chinese troops, and Buddhism was almost totally suppressed. The Dalai Lama and 100,000 Tibetans fled to India.

Colombia

Republic of Colombia
República de Colombia

People: Population (1990 est.): 32,598,000. **Age distrib. (%):** 0–14: 36.4; 15–59: 57.5; 60+: 6.1. **Pop. density:** 72 per sq. mi. **Urban** (1983): 65.4%. **Ethnic groups:** Mestizo 58%, Caucasian 20%, Mulatto 14%. **Languages:** Spanish. **Religions:** Roman Catholic 95%.
Geography: Area: 439,735 sq. mi., about the size of Texas, and New Mexico combined. **Location:** At the NW corner of .S. America. **Neighbors:** Panama on NW, Ecuador, Peru on S, Brazil, Venezuela on E. **Topography:** Three ranges of Andes, the Western, Central, and Eastern Cordilleras, run through the country from N to S. The eastern range consists mostly of high table lands, densely populated. The Magdalena R. rises in Andes, flows N to Carribean, through a rich alluvial plain. Sparsely-settled plains in E are drained by Orinoco and Amazon systems. **Capital:** Bogota. **Cities** (1985 cen.): Bogota 3,967,000; Medellin 1,664,000; Cali 1,450,000; Barranquilla 924,000.
Government: Type: Republic. **Head of state:** Pres. Cesar Gaviria Trujillo; b. 1947; in office: Aug. 7, 1990. **Local divisions:** 23 departments, 8 national territories, and special district of Bogota. **Defense:** 2.1% of GNP (1985).
Economy: Industries: Textiles, processed goods, hides, steel, cement, chemicals. **Chief crops:** Coffee (50% of exports), rice, corn, cotton, sugar, bananas. **Minerals:** Oil, gas, emeralds (90% world output), gold, copper, lead, coal, iron, nickel, salt. **Crude oil reserves** (1987): 1.6 bln. bbls. **Other resources:** Rubber, balsam, dye-woods, copaiba, hydro power. **Arable land:** 5%. **Livestock** (1987): cattle: 23.5 mln.; pigs: 2.4 mln.; sheep: 2.6 mln. **Fish catch** (1987): 80,000 metric tons. **Electricity prod.** (1988): 34.7 bln. kwh. **Crude steel prod.** (1986): 500,000 metric tons. **Labor force:** 26% agric.; 21% ind.; 53% services.
Finance: Currency: Peso (June 1990: 480 = $1 US). **Gross national product** (1988): $39 bln. **Per capita GNP** (1987): $1,140. **Imports** (1988): $5.0 bln.; partners: U.S. 34%, EEC 14%, Jap. 11%. **Exports** (1988): $5.0 bln.; partners: U.S. 20%, EEC 38%. **Tourists** (1987): $213 mln. receipts. **National budget** (1987): $4.5 bln. expenditures. **International reserves less gold** (Mar. 1990): $3.6 bln. **Gold** 643,000 oz t. **Consumer prices** (change in 1989): 25.8.
Transport: Railway traffic (1988): 147 mln. passenger-km. **Motor vehicles:** in use (1986): 840,000 passenger cars, 391,000. **Civil aviation** (1987): 3.9 bln. passenger-km. **Chief ports:** Buena Ventura, Santa Marta, Barranquilla, Cartagena.
Communications: Television sets: 1 per 5.6 persons. **Radios:** 1 per 7.3 persons. **Telephones:** 1 per 12 persons. **Daily newspaper circ.** (1987): 61 per 1,000 pop.
Health: Life expectancy at birth (1989): 64 male; 68 female. **Births** (per 1,000 pop. 1989): 27. **Deaths** (per 1,000 pop. 1989): 7. **Natural increase:** 2.3%. **Hospital beds** (1982): 26,880. **Physicians** (1983): 21,778. **Infant mortality** (per 1,000 live births 1989): 54%.
Education (1990): **Literacy:** 80%. Only 28% finish primary school.
Major International Organizations: UN (World Bank, GATT), OAS.
Embassy: 2118 Leroy Pl. NW, 20008; 387-8338.

Spain subdued the local Indian kingdoms (Funza, Tunja) by the 1530s, and ruled Colombia and neighboring areas as New Granada for 300 years. Independence was won by 1819. Venezuela and Ecuador broke away in 1829-30, and Panama withdrew in 1903.
One of the Latin American democracies, Colombia is plagued by rural and urban violence, though scaled down from "La Violencia" of 1948-58, which claimed 200,000 lives. Attempts at land and social reform, and progress in industrialization have not succeeded in reducing massive social problems aggravated by a very high birth rate. In 1989, the government's increased activity against local drug traffickers sparked a series of retaliation killings. On Aug. 18, Luis Carlos Galán, the ruling party's presidential hopeful in the 1990 election, was assassinated. In 1990, 2 other presidential candidates were slain as the drug traffickers carried on a campaign of intimidation to stop the presidential election. Cesar Gaviria Trujillo, a strong advocate of maintaining the government's war against the nation's drug cartels, was elected president in May.

Comoros

Federal Islamic Republic of the Comoros
Jumhurīyat al-Qumur al-Itthādīyah al-Islāmīyah

People: Population (1990 est.): 459,000. **Pop. density:** 547 per sq. mi. **Ethnic groups:** Arabs, Africans, East Indians. **Languages:** Shaafi Islam, (a Swahili dialect), French (official), Malagasy. **Religions:** Islam (official), Roman Catholic.
Geography: Area: 838 sq. mi., half the size of Delaware. **Location:** 3 islands (Grande Comore, Anjouan, and Moheli) in the Mozambique Channel between NW Madagascar and SE Africa. **Neighbors:** Nearest are Mozambique on W, Madagascar on E. **Topography:** The islands are of volcanic origin, with an active volcano on Grand Comoro. **Capital:** Moroni. **Cities** (1988 est.): Moroni (met.) 28,000.
Government: Type: Republic. **Head of state:** Pres. Said Mohammed Djohar; in office: Nov. 26, 1989. **Local divisions:** each of the 3 main islands is a prefecture.
Economy: Industries: Perfume. **Chief crops:** Vanilla, copra, perfume plants, fruits. **Arable land:** 35%. **Electricity prod.** (1986): 5 mln. kwh. **Labor force:** 80% agric.
Finance: Currency: CFA franc (Mar. 1990: 264 = $1 US). **Gross national product** (1987): $160 mln. **Per capita income** (1986): $340. **Imports** (1986): $38 mln.; partners: Fr. 56%. **Exports** (1986): $20 mln.; partners: Fr. 35%, U.S. 18%.
Transport: Chief ports: Dzaoudzi.
Communications: Radios: 1 per 4.2 persons. **Telephones in use:** 1 per 740 persons.
Health: Life expectancy at birth (1989): 54 male; 58 female. **Births** (per 1,000 pop. 1989): 47. **Deaths** (per 1,000 pop. 1989): 13. **Natural increase:** 3.5%. **Infant mortality** (per 1,000 live births 1989): 91.
Education: (1989): **Literacy:** 15%; less than 20% attend secondary school.
Major International Organizations: UN (IMF, World Bank); OAU.
Embassy: 336 E. 45th St., New York, NY 10017; (212) 972-8010.

The islands were controlled by Moslem sultans until the French acquired them 1841-1909. A 1974 referendum favored independence, with only the Christian island of Mayotte preferring association with France. The French National Assembly decided to allow each of the islands to decide its own fate. The Comoro Chamber of Deputies declared independence July 6, 1975. In a referendum in 1976, Mayotte voted to remain French. A leftist regime that seized power in 1975 was deposed in a pro-French 1978 coup.
In Nov. 1989, Pres. Ahmed Abdallah was assassinated.

Congo

People's Republic of the Congo
République Populaire du Congo

People: Population (1990 est.): 2,305,000. **Pop. density:** 15 per sq. mi. **Urban** (1986): 51%. **Ethnic groups:** Bakongo 45%, Bateke 20%, others. **Languages:** French (official), Bantu dialects. **Religions:** Christians 47% (two-thirds Roman Catholic), animists 47%, Moslem 2%.
Geography: Area: 132,046 sq. mi., slightly smaller than Montana. **Location:** In western central Africa. **Neighbors:** Gabon, Cameroon on W, Central African Republic on N, Zaire on E, Angola (Cabinda) on SW. **Topography:** Much of the Congo is covered by thick forests. A coastal plain leads to the fertile Niari Valley. The center is a plateau; the Congo R. basin consists of flood plains in the lower and savanna in the upper portion. **Capital:** Brazzaville. **Cities** (1984 est.): Brazzaville (met.) 595,000; Pointe-Noire 297,000; Loubomo 35,000.
Government: Type: People's republic. **Head of state:** Pres. Denis Sassou-Nguesso; b. 1943; in office: Feb. 8, 1979. **Head of government:** Prime Min. Alphonse Poaty-Souchlaty; in office: Aug. 7, 1989. **Local divisions:** 9 regions and capital district. **Defense:** 4.6% of GNP (1987).

Economy: Chief crops: Palm oil and kernels, cocoa, coffee, tobacco. **Minerals:** Gold, lead, copper, zinc. **Crude oil reserves** (1988): 750 mln. bbls. **Arable land:** 2%. **Fish catch** (1987): 31,000 metric tons. **Electricity prod.** (1988): 301 mln. kwh. **Labor force:** 90% agric.

Finance: Currency: CFA franc (Mar. 1990: 284 = $1 US). **Gross national product** (1987): $1.7 bln. **Per capita income** (1988): $1,100. **Imports** (1988): $564 mln.; partners: Fr. 52%. **Exports** (1988): $673 mln.; partners: U.S. 45%, Fr. 15%. **Tourist receipts** (1987): $6 mln. **International reserves less gold** (Jan. 1990): $4.4 mln. **Gold:** 11,000 oz t. **Consumer prices** (change in 1989): 3.7%.

Transport: Railway traffic (1986): 456 mln. passenger-km. **Motor vehicles:** in use (1982): 41,000 passenger cars, 79,000 comm. vehicles. **Chief ports:** Pointe-Noire, Brazzaville.

Communications: Television sets: 1 per 375 persons. **Radios:** 1 per 9.4 persons. **Telephones:** in use: 1 per 111 persons.

Health: Life expectancy at birth (1989): 54 male; 58 female. **Births** (per 1,000 pop. 1989): 46. **Deaths** (per 1,000 pop. 1989): 13. **Natural increase:** 3.4%. **Hospital beds:** 1 per 572 persons. **Physicians:** 1 per 4,334 persons. **Infant mortality** (per 1,000 live births 1989): 110.

Education (1989): **Literacy:** 80%. Years compulsory 10; attendance 80%.

Major International Organizations: UN (GATT, IMF, WHO), OAU.

Embassy: 4891 Colorado Ave. NW 20011; 726-5500.

The Loango Kingdom flourished in the 15th century, as did the Anzico Kingdom of the Batekes; by the late 17th century they had become weakened. France established control by 1885. Independence came Aug. 15, 1960.

After a 1963 coup sparked by trade unions, the country adopted a Marxist-Leninist stance, with the USSR and China vying for influence. Tribal divisions remain strong. France remains a dominant trade partner and source of technical assistance, and French-owned private enterprise retained a major economic role. However, the government of Pres. Sassou-Nguesso favored a strengthening of relations with the USSR, a socialist constitution was adopted, 1979.

Costa Rica
Republic of Costa Rica
República de Costa Rica

People: Population (1990 est.): 3,032,000. **Age distrib.** (%): 0–14: 35; 15–49: 51.8; 50+: 13.2. **Pop. density:** 149 per sq. mi. **Urban** (1989): 50%. **Ethnic groups:** Spanish (with Mestizo minority). **Language:** Spanish (official). **Religions:** Roman Catholic 88%.

Geography: Area: 19,575 sq. mi., smaller than W. Virginia. **Location:** In central America. **Neighbors:** Nicaragua on N, Panama on S. **Topography:** Lowlands by the Caribbean are tropical. The interior plateau, with an altitude of about 4,000 ft., is temperate. **Capital:** San Jose. **Cities** (1988 met. est.): San Jose 890,000.

Government: Type: Democratic republic. **Head of state:** Pres. Rafael Angel Calderon; b. 1949; in office May 8, 1990. **Local divisions:** 7 provinces.

Economy: Industries: Furniture, pharmaceuticals, aluminum, textiles, fertilizers, roofing, cement. **Chief crops:** Coffee (chief export), bananas, sugar, cocoa, cotton, hemp. **Minerals:** Gold, salt, sulphur, iron. **Other resources:** Fish, forests. **Arable land:** 12%. **Livestock** (1987): cattle: 2.4. mln. **Fish catch** (1988): 20,000 metric tons. **Electricity prod.** (1988): 2.9 bln. kwh. **Labor force:** 27% agric.; 35% ind. & comm.; 33% service and government.

Finance: Currency: Colone (Mar. 1990: 86 = $1 US). **Gross national product** (1988): $4.2 bln. **Per capita income** (1987): $1,584. **Imports** (1988): $1.4 bln.; partners: U.S. 38%, CACM 10%, Jap. 10%. **Exports** (1988): $1.3 bln.; partners: U.S. 41%, CACM 18%. **Tourists** (1986): receipts: $164 mln. **National budget** (1987): $791 mln. expenditures. **International reserves less gold** (Mar. 1990): $697 mln. **Gold:** 9,000 oz t. **Consumer prices** (change in 1989): 16.5%.

Transport: Motor vehicles: in use (1988): 134,000 passenger cars, 89,000 comm. vehicles. **Civil aviation** (1988): 787 mln. passenger-km; 8 airports with scheduled flights. **Chief ports:** Limon, Puntarenas, Golfito.

Communications: Television sets: 1 per 6.1 persons. **Radios:** 1 per 11 persons. **Telephones:** 1 per 6.9 persons. **Daily newspaper circ.** (1988): 110 per 1,000 pop.

Health: Life expectancy at birth (1989): 74 male; 78 female. **Births** (per 1,000 pop. 1989): 29. **Deaths** (per 1,000 pop. 1989): 4. **Natural increase:** 2.5%. **Hospital beds:** 1 per 368 persons. **Physicians:** 1 per 1,011 persons. **Infant mortality** (per 1,000 live births 1989): 17.

Education (1989): **Literacy:** 93%. Years compulsory 6; attendance 99%.

Major International Organizations: UN (FAO, ILO, IMF, WHO), OAS.

Embassy: 1825 Connecticut Ave. NW, 20009; 234-2945.

Guaymi Indians inhabited the area when Spaniards arrived, 1502. Independence came in 1821. Costa Rica seceded from the Central American Federation in 1838. Since the civil war of 1948-49, there has been little violent social conflict, and free political institutions have been preserved.

Costa Rica, though still a largely agricultural country, has achieved a relatively high standard of living and social services, and land ownership is widespread.

Côte d'Ivoire
Ivory Coast
République de la Côte d'Ivoire

People: Population (1990 est.): 12,070,000. **Age distrib.** (%): 0–14: 45.1; 15–59: 50.2; 60+: 4.7. **Pop. density:** 94 per sq. mi. **Urban** (1986): 47%. **Ethnic groups:** Baule 23%, Bete 18%, Senufo 15%, Malinke 11%, over 60 tribes. **Languages:** French (official), tribal languages. **Religions:** Moslem 20%, Christian 20%, indigenous 60%.

Geography: Area: 124,503 sq. mi., slightly larger than New Mexico. **Location:** On S. coast of W. Africa. **Neighbors:** Liberia, Guinea on W, Mali, Burkina Faso on N, Ghana on E. **Topography:** Forests cover the W half of the country, and range from a coastal strip to halfway to the N on the E. A sparse inland plain leads to low mountains in NW. **Capital:** Abidjan. **Cities** (1985 est.): Abidjan 1,850,000 (met.).

Government: Type: Republic. **Head of state:** Pres. Felix Houphouet-Boigny; b. Oct. 18, 1905; in office: Aug. 7, 1960. **Local divisions:** 49 departments.

Economy: Chief crops: Coffee, cocoa. **Minerals:** Diamonds, manganese. **Other resources:** Timber, rubber, petroleum. **Arable land:** 9%. **Livestock** (1987): goats: 1.4 mln.; sheep: 1.5 mln.; cattle: 965,000. **Fish catch** (1987): 102,000 metric tons. **Electricity prod.** (1988): 2.4 bln. kwh. **Labor force:** 85% agric., forestry.

Finance: Currency: CFA franc (Mar. 1990: 284 = $1 US). **Gross national product** (1987): $10.3 bln. **Per capita income** (1986): $921. **Imports** (1987): $4.6 bln.; partners: Fr. 31%, Jap. 5%, U.S. 5%. **Exports** (1987): $6.2 bln.; partners: Fr. 14%, Neth. 19%, U.S. 11%, It. 8%. **Tourists** (1987): $53 mln receipts; **International reserves less gold** (Jan. 1990): $15.0 mln. **Gold:** 45,000 oz t. **Consumer prices** (changed in 1988): 4.4%.

Transport: Railway traffic (1987): 857 mln. passenger-km. **Motor vehicles:** in use (1984): 182,000 passenger cars, 52,000 comm. vehicles. **Chief ports:** Abidjan, Sassandra.

Communications: Television sets: 1 per 19 persons. **Radios:** 1 per 7.9 persons. **Telephones:** 1 per 97 persons. **Daily newspaper circ.** (1988): 12 per 1,000 pop.

Health: Life expectancy at birth (1989): 52 male; 55 female. **Births** (per 1,000 pop. 1989): 46. **Deaths** (per 1,000 pop. 1989): 13. **Natural increase:** 3.3%. **Hospital beds** (1982): 10,062. **Physicians** (1982): 502. **Infant mortality** (per 1,000 live births 1989): 102.

Education (1988): **Literacy:** 35%. **Years compulsory:** none; attendance 75%.

Major International Organizations: UN and all of its specialized agencies, OAU.

Embassy: 2424 Massachusetts Ave. NW 20008; 797-0300.

A French protectorate from 1842, Côte D'Ivoire became independent in 1960. It is the most prosperous of tropical African nations, due to diversification of agriculture for export, close ties to France, and encouragement of foreign investment. About 20% of the population are workers from neighboring countries. Côte

D'Ivoire, which officially changed its name from Ivory Coast in Oct. 1985, is a leader of the pro-Western bloc in Africa.

Students and workers staged protests, Feb. 1990, demanding the ouster of Pres. Houphouet-Boigny and multiparty democracy.

Cuba

Republic of Cuba

República de Cuba

People: Population (1990 est.): 10,582,000. **Age distrib.** (%): 0–under 15: 24.8; 15–59: 63.6; 60+: 11.6. **Pop. density:** 239 per sq. mi. **Urban** (1989): 72%. **Ethnic groups:** Spanish, African. **Languages:** Spanish. **Religions:** Roman Catholic 42%, none 49%.

Geography: Area: 44,218 sq. mi., nearly as large as Pennsylvania. **Location:** Westernmost of West Indies. **Neighbors:** Bahamas, U.S., on N, Mexico on W, Jamaica on S, Haiti on E. **Topography:** The coastline is about 2,500 miles. The N coast is steep and rocky, the S coast low and marshy. Low hills and fertile valleys cover more than half the country. Sierra Maestra, in the E is the highest of 3 mountain ranges. **Capital:** Havana. **Cities** (1988 est.): Havana 2,059,000; Santiago de Cuba 389,000; Camaguey 274,000.

Government: Type: Communist state. **Head of state:** Pres. Fidel Castro Ruz; b. Aug. 13, 1926; in office: Dec. 3, 1976 (formerly Prime Min. since Feb. 16, 1959). **Local divisions:** 14 provinces, 169 municipal assemblies. **Defense:** 5.4% of GNP (1985).

Economy: Industries: Textiles, wood products, cement, chemicals, cigars. **Chief crops:** Sugar (75% of exports), tobacco, coffee, pineapples, bananas, citrus fruit, coconuts. **Minerals:** Cobalt, nickel, iron, copper, manganese, salt. **Other resources:** Forests. **Arable land:** 29%. **Livestock** (1986); cattle: 6.5 mln.; pigs: 2.4 mln. **Fish catch** (1986): 244,000 metric tons. **Electricity prod.** (1987): 14.0 bln. kwh. **Crude steel prod.** (1985): 412,000 metric tons. **Labor force:** 13% agric.; 40% ind. & comm.; 30% services & govt.

Finance: Currency: Peso (Dec. 1989: .76 = $1 US). **Gross national product** (1984): $26.9 bln. **Per capita income** (1983): $1,590. **Imports** (1985): $8.6 bln.; partners: USSR 72%. **Exports** (1985): $6.5 bln.; partners: USSR 72%. **Tourists** (1986): Revenues: 130 mln.

Transport: Railway traffic (1988): 2.6 bln. passenger-km. **Motor vehicles:** in use (1985): 200,000 passenger cars, 164,000 comm. vehicles. **Civil aviation** (1988): 2.7 bln. passenger-km.; 12 airports with scheduled flights. **Chief ports:** Havana, Matanzas, Cienfuegos, Santiago de Cuba.

Communications: Television sets: 2.0 mln. in use (1987). **Radios:** 3.2 mln. in use (1986). **Telephones in use** (1986): 543,000. **Daily newspaper circ.** (1986): 126 per 1,000 pop.

Health: Life expectancy at birth: (1989): 72 male; 74 female. **Births** (per 1,000 pop. 1989): 17.2. **Deaths** (per 1,000 pop. 1989): 6. **Natural increase:** 1.0%. **Hospital beds** (1986): 56,000. **Physicians** (1986): 25,418. **Infant mortality** (per 1,000 live births 1989): 16.

Education (1989): **Literacy:** 98%. 92% of those between ages 6–14 attend school.

Major International Organizations: UN (GATT, WHO).

Some 50,000 Indians lived in Cuba when it was discovered by Columbus in 1492. Its name derives from the Indian Cubanacan. Except for British occupation of Havana, 1762-63, Cuba remained Spanish until 1898. A slave-based sugar plantation economy developed from the 18th century, aided by early mechanization of milling. Sugar remains the chief product and chief export despite government attempts to diversify.

A ten-year uprising ended in 1878 with guarantees of rights by Spain, which Spain failed to carry out. A full-scale movement under Jose Marti began Feb. 24, 1895.

The U.S. declared war on Spain in April, 1898, after the sinking of the U.S.S. Maine in Havana harbor, and defeated it in the Spanish-American War. Spain gave up all claims to Cuba. U.S. troops withdrew in 1902, but under 1903 and 1934 agreements, the U.S. leases a site at Guantanamo Bay in the SE as a naval base. U.S. and other foreign investments acquired a dominant role in the economy. In 1952, former president Fulgencio Batista seized control and established a dictatorship, which grew increasingly harsh and corrupt. Fidel Castro assembled a rebel

band in 1956; guerrilla fighting intensified in 1958. Batista fled Jan. 1, 1959, and in the resulting political vacuum Castro took power, becoming premier Feb. 16.

The government began a program of sweeping economic and social changes, without restoring promised liberties. Opponents were imprisoned and some were executed. Some 700,000 Cubans emigrated in the years after the Castro takeover, mostly to the U.S.

Cattle and tobacco lands were nationalized, while a system of cooperatives was instituted. By 1960 all banks and industrial companies had been nationalized, including over $1 billion worth of U.S.-owned properties, mostly without compensation.

Poor sugar crops resulted in collectivization of farms, stringent labor controls, and rationing, despite continued aid from the USSR and other communist countries.

The U.S. imposed an export embargo in 1962, severely damaging the economy. In 1961, some 1,400 Cubans, trained and backed by the U.S. Central Intelligence Agency, unsuccessfully tried to invade and overthrow the regime.

In the fall of 1962, the U.S. learned that the USSR had brought nuclear missiles to Cuba. After an Oct. 22 warning from Pres. Kennedy, the missiles were removed.

In 1977, Cuba and the U.S. signed agreements to exchange diplomats, without restoring full ties, and to regulate offshore fishing. In 1978, and again in 1980, the U.S. agreed to accept political prisoners released by Cuba some of whom, it was later discovered, were criminals and mental patients. A 1987 agreement provided for 20,000 Cubans to immigrate to the U.S. each year; Cuba agreed to take back some 2,500 jailed in the U.S. since the 1980 Mariel boat lift.

In 1975-78, Cuba sent troops to aid one faction in the Angola Civil War. Cuba's involvement in Central America, Africa, and the Caribbean, has contributed to poor relations with the U.S. In Dec. 1988, Cuba agreed to a peace accord in which Cuban troops would withdraw from Angola by July 1991.

In 1983, 24 Cubans died and over 700 were captured, later repatriated, as a result of the U.S.-led invasion of Grenada.

Cuba has resisted the social and economic reforms that have taken place in the USSR and other eastern bloc countries

Cyprus

Republic of Cyprus

Kypriaki Dimokratia (Greek)
Kibris Cumhuriyeti (Turkish)

People: Population (1990 est.): 708,000. **Age distrib.** (%): 0–14: 25.4; 15–59: 60.4; 60+: 14.2. **Pop. density:** 194 per sq. mi. **Urban** (1982): 53%. **Ethnic groups:** Greeks 78%, Turks 18.7%, Armenians, Maronites. **Languages:** Greek, Turkish (both official), English. **Religions:** Orthodox 77%, Moslems 18%.

Geography: Area: 3,572 sq. mi., smaller than Connecticut. **Location:** In eastern Mediterranean Sea, off Turkish coast. **Neighbors:** Nearest are Turkey on N, Syria, Lebanon on E. **Topography:** Two mountain ranges run E-W, separated by a wide, fertile plain. **Capital:** Nicosia. **Cities** (1984 est.): Nicosia 124,300.

Government: Type: Republic. **Head of state:** Pres. George Vassiliou; b. May 21, 1931; in office: Feb. 28, 1988. **Local divisions:** 6 districts. **Defense:** 11% of govt. budget (1984).

Economy: Industries: Light manuf. **Chief crops:** Grains, grapes, carobs, citrus fruits, potatoes, olives. **Minerals:** Copper, pyrites, asbetos. **Arable land:** 40%. **Electricity prod.** (1988): 1.6 mln. kwh. **Labor force:** 21% agric.; 20% ind., 18% comm., 19% serv.

Finance: Currency: Pound (Mar. 1990: 1.00 = $2.08 US). **GNP** (1987): $3.5 bln. **Per capita GNP** (1987): $5,210. **Imports** (1988): $1.8 bln.; partners: UK 13%, Itl. 12%. **Exports** (1988): $767 mln.; partners: UK 21%, Libya 9%. **Tourists** (1988): receipts: $782 mln. **National budget** (1987): $911 mln. expenditures. **International reserves less gold** (Mar. 1990): $1.0 bln. **Gold:** 459,000 oz. t. **Consumer prices** (change in 1989): 3.8%.

Transport: Motor vehicles: in use (1987): 142,000 passenger cars, 54,000 comm. vehicles. **Civil aviation** (1987): 2.1 bln. passenger-km; one airport. **Chief ports:** Famagusta, Limassol.

Communications: Television sets: 1 per 3.4 persons. **Radios:** 1 per 2.7 persons. **Telephones:** 1 per 2.0 persons. **Daily newspaper circ.** (1987): 157 per 1,000 pop.

Health: Life expectancy at birth (1989): 74 male; 80 female. **Births** (per 1,000 pop. 1989): 19. **Deaths** (per 1,000 pop. 1989):

7. **Natural increase:** 1.1%. **Hospital beds:** 1 per 160 persons. **Physicians :** 1 per 570 persons. **Infant mortality** (per 1,000 live births 1989): 8.

Education (1989): **Literacy:** 99%. **Years compulsory:** 9; attendance 99%.

Major International Organizations: UN (GATT, IMF, WHO), Commonwealth of Nations, EC (Assoc.).

Embassy: 2211 R St. NW, 20008; 462-5772.

Agitation for enosis (union) with Greece increased after World War II, with the Turkish minority opposed, and broke into violence in 1955-56. In 1959, Britain, Greece, Turkey, and Cypriot leaders approved a plan for an independent republic, with constitutional guarantees for the Turkish minority and permanent division of offices on an ethnic basis. Greek and Turkish Communal Chambers dealt with religion, education, and other matters.

Archbishop Makarios, formerly the leader of the enosis movement, was elected president, and full independence became final Aug. 16, 1960. Makarios was re-elected in 1968 and 1973.

Further communal strife led the United Nations to send a peace-keeping force in 1964; its mandate has been repeatedly renewed.

The Cypriot National Guard, led by officers from the army of Greece, seized the government July 15, 1974, and named Nikos Sampson, an advocate of union with Greece, president. Makarios fled the country. On July 20, Turkey invaded the island; Greece mobilized its forces but did not intervene. A cease-fire was arranged July 22. On the 23d, Sampson turned over the presidency to Glafkos Clerides (on the same day, Greece's military junta resigned). A peace conference collapsed Aug. 14; fighting resumed. By Aug. 16 Turkish forces had occupied the NE 40% of the island, despite the presence of UN peace forces. Makarios resumed the presidency in Dec., until his death, 1977.

Turkish Cypriots voted overwhelmingly, June 8, 1975, to form a separate Turkish Cypriot federated state. A president and assembly were elected in 1976. Some 200,000 Greeks have been expelled from the Turkish-controlled area, replaced by thousands of Turks, some from the mainland.

Turkish Republic of Northern Cyprus

A declaration of independence was announced by Turkish-Cypriot leader Rauf Denktash, Nov. 15, 1983. The new state is not internationally recognized although it does have trade relations with some countries. TRNC contains 1,295 sq mi., pop. (1989 est.): 169,000, 99% Turkish.

Czechoslovakia

Czech and Slovak Federative Republic

People: Population (1990 est.): 15,695,000. **Age distrib.** (%): 0–14: 24.2; 15–59: 59.3; 60+: 16.5. **Pop. density:** 317 per sq. mi. **Urban** (1985): 73%. **Ethnic groups:** Czechs 64%, Slovaks 31%, Hungarian, German, Ukrainian, Polish. **Languages:** Czech, Slovak (both official). **Religions:** Roman Catholic 77%.

Geography: Area: 49,365 sq. mi., the size of New York. **Location:** In E central Europe. **Neighbors:** Poland, E. Germany on N, W. Germany on W. Austria, Hungary on S, USSR on E. **Topography:** Bohemia, in W, is a plateau surrounded by mountains; Moravia is hilly, Slovakia, in E, has mountains (Carpathians) in N, fertile Danube plain in S. Vltava (Moldau) and Labe (Elbe) rivers flow N from Bohemia to G. **Capital:** Prague. **Cities** (1990 est.): Prague 1.2 mln.; Brno 385,000; Bratislava 413,000; Ostrava 327,000.

Government: Type: Socialist (in transition). **Head of state:** Pres. Vaclav Havel; b. Oct. 5, 1936; in office: Dec. 29, 1989; **Head of government:** Prime Min. Marian Calfa; in office: Dec. 10, 1989. **Local divisions:** Czech and Slovak republics each have an assembly. **Defense:** 5.8% of GNP (1985).

Economy: Industries: Machinery, oil products, iron and steel, glass, chemicals, motor vehicles, cement. **Chief crops:** Wheat, sugar beets, potatoes, rye, corn, barley. **Minerals:** coke, coal, iron. **Arable land:** 40%. **Livestock:** (1987): cattle: 5 mln.; pigs: 6.6 mln.; sheep: 1 mln. **Electricity prod.** (1988): 84.0 bln. kwh. **Crude steel prod.** (1988): 15.4 mln. metric tons. **Labor force:** 12% agric.; 37% ind.; 22% service, govt.

Finance: Currency: Koruna (Jan. 1990: 15 = $1 US). **Gross national product** (1988): $158 bln. **Per capita GNP** (1988): $10,130. **Imports** (1985): $18.1 bln.; partners: USSR 31%, E.

Ger. 10%, Pol. 6%, W. Ger. 9%. **Exports** (1985): $18.0 bln.; partners: USSR 35%, E. Ger. 7%, Pol. 7%.

Transport: Railway traffic (1987): 20.0 bln. passenger-km. **Motor vehicles:** in use (1985): 2.6 mln. passenger cars, 425,000 comm. **Civil aviation** (1987): 2.4 bln. passenger-km.; 14 airports.

Communications: Television sets: 1 per 3.7 persons. **Radios:** 1 per 3.6 persons. **Telephones:** 1 per 4.1 persons. **Daily newspaper circ.** (1986): 280 per 1,000 pop.

Health: Life expectancy at birth (1989): 68 male; 75 female. **Births** (per 1,000 pop. 1989): 14. **Deaths** (per 1,000 pop. 1989): 12. **Natural increase:** .2%. **Hospital beds:** 1 per 99 persons; **Physicians:** 1 per 312 persons. **Infant mortality** (per 1,000 live births 1989): 13.

Education (1989): **Literacy:** 99%.

Major International Organizations: UN (GATT, WHO), Warsaw Pact.

Embassy: 3900 Linnean Ave. NW 20008; 263-6315.

Bohemia, Moravia and Slovakia were part of the Great Moravian Empire in the 9th century. Later, Slovakia was overrun by Magyars, while Bohemia and Moravia became part of the Holy Roman Empire. Under the kings of Bohemia, Prague in the 14th century was the cultural center of Central Europe. Bohemia and Hungary became part of Austria-Hungary.

In 1914-1918 Thomas G. Masaryk and Eduard Benes formed a provisional government with the support of Slovak leaders including Milan Stefanik. They proclaimed the Republic of Czechoslovakia Oct. 28, 1918.

By 1938 Nazi Germany had worked up disaffection among German-speaking citizens in Sudetenland and demanded its cession. Prime Min. Neville Chamberlain of Britain, with the acquiescence of France, signed with Hitler at Munich, Sept. 30, 1938, an agreement to the cession, with a guarantee of peace by Hitler and Mussolini. Germany occupied Sudetenland Oct. 1-2.

Hitler on Mar. 15, 1939, dissolved Czechoslovakia, made protectorates of Bohemia and Moravia, and supported the autonomy of Slovakia, which was proclaimed independent Mar. 14, 1939.

Soviet troops with some Czechoslovak contingents entered eastern Czechoslovakia in 1944 and reached Prague in May 1945; Benes returned as president. In May 1946 elections, the Communist Party won 38% of the votes, and Benes accepted Klement Gottwald, a communist, as prime minister.

In February, 1948, the communists seized power in advance of scheduled elections. In May 1948 a new constitution was approved. Benes refused to sign it. On May 30 the voters were offered a one-slate ballot and the communists won full control. Benes resigned June 7 and Gottwald became president. A harsh Stalinist period followed, with complete and violent suppression of all opposition.

In Jan. 1968 a liberalization movement spread explosively through Czechoslovakia. Antonin Novotny, long the Stalinist boss of the nation, was deposed as party leader and succeeded by Alexander Dubcek, a Slovak, who declared he intended to make communism democratic. On Mar. 22 Novotny resigned as president and was succeeded by Gen. Ludvik Svoboda. On Apr. 6, Premier Joseph Lenart resigned and was succeeded by Oldrich Cernik, whose new cabinet was pledged to carry out democratization and economic reforms.

In July 1968 the USSR and 4 Warsaw Pact nations demanded an end to liberalization. On Aug. 20, the Russian, Polish, East German, Hungarian, and Bulgarian armies invaded Czechoslovakia.

Despite demonstrations and riots by students and workers, press censorship was imposed, liberal leaders were ousted from office and promises of loyalty to Soviet policies were made by some old-line Communist Party leaders.

On Apr. 17, 1969, Dubcek resigned as leader of the Communist Party and was succeeded by Gustav Husak. In Jan. 1970, Premier Cernik was ousted. Censorship was tightened and the Communist Party expelled a third of its members. In 1973, amnesty was offered to some of the 40,000 who fled the country after the 1968 invasion, but repressive policies remained in force.

More than 700 leading Czechoslovak intellectuals and former party leaders signed a human rights manifesto in 1977, called Charter 77, prompting a renewed crackdown by the regime.

Czechoslovakia has long been an industrial and technological leader of the eastern European countries, though this has declined in recent years because of the government's rejection of economic reforms.

The police crushed the largest anti-government protests since 1968, when tens of thousands of demonstrators took to the streets of Prague, Nov. 17, 1989. As protesters demanded free elections, the Communist Party leadership resigned Nov. 24; millions went on strike Nov. 27.

On Dec. 10, 1989 the first Cabinet in 41 years without a communist majority took power; Vaclav Havel, playwright and human rights campaigner, was chosen president, Dec. 29.

Denmark

Kingdom of Denmark

Kongeriget Danmark

People: Population (1990 est.): 5,134,000. **Age distrib. (%):** 0–14: 17.6; 15–59: 62.0; 60+: 20.4. **Pop. density:** 305 per sq. mi. **Urban** (1986): 84%. **Ethnic groups:** Almost all Scandinavian. **Languages:** Danish. **Religions:** Evangelical Lutheran 90%.

Geography: Area: 16,633 sq. mi., the size of Massachusetts and New Hampshire combined. **Location:** In northern Europe, separating the North and Baltic seas. **Neighbors:** W. Germany on S., Norway on NW, Sweden on NE. **Topography:** Denmark consists of the Jutland Peninsula and about 500 islands, 100 inhabited. The land is flat or gently rolling, and is almost all in productive use. **Capital:** Copenhagen. **Cities** (1988, met.): Copenhagen 619,000.

Government: Type: Constitutional monarchy. **Head of state:** Queen Margrethe II; b. Apr. 16, 1940; in office: Jan. 14, 1972. **Head of government:** Prime Min. Poul Schluter; b. 1929; in office: Sept. 10, 1982. **Local divisions:** 14 counties and one city (Copenhagen). **Defense:** 2.3% of GNP (1988).

Economy: Industries: Machinery, textiles, furniture, electronics. **Chief crops:** Dairy products. **Crude oil reserves** (1985): 533 mln. bbls. **Arable land:** 62%. **Livestock** (1987): cattle: 2.3 mln.; pigs: 9.2 mln. **Fish catch** (1987): 1.5 mln. metric tons. **Electricity prod.** (1987): 27.5 bln. kwh. **Crude steel prod.** (1985): 560,000 metric tons. **Labor force:** 6% agric.; 31% serv.; 27% govt.

Finance: Currency: Krone (June 1990: 6.44 = $1 US). **Gross national product** (1987): $101.3 bln. **Per capita income** (1988): $19,750. **Imports** (1989): $26.6 bln.; partners: W. Ger. 24%, Swed. 12%, UK 9%, Neth. 5%. **Exports** (1989): $28.1 bln.; partners: W. Ger. 15%, EC 42%, U.S. 8%. **Tourists** (1988): $2.4 bln. receipts. **International reserves less gold** (Mar. 1990): $8.3 bln. **Gold:** 2.0 mln. oz t. **Consumer prices** (change in 1989): 4.8%.

Transport: Railway traffic (1987): 4.7 bln. passenger-km. **Motor vehicles:** in use (1987): 1.5 mln. passenger cars, 282,000 comm. vehicles. **Civil aviation** (1988): 3.5 bln. passenger-km; 12 airports with scheduled flights. **Chief ports:** Copenhagen, Alborg, Arhus, Odense.

Communications: Television sets: 1 per 2.7 persons. **Radios:** 1 per 2.4 persons. **Telephones:** 1 per 1.2 persons. **Daily newspaper circ.** (1986): 367 per 1,000 pop.

Health: Life expectancy at birth (1989): 72 male; 79 female. **Births** (per 1,000 pop. 1989): 11. **Deaths** (per 1,000 pop. 1989): 11. **Hospital beds:** 1 per 159 persons. **Physicians:** 1 per 390 persons. **Infant mortality** (per 1,000 live births 1989): 7.8.

Education (1986): **Literacy:** 99%. Years compulsory 9; attendance 100%.

Major International Organizations: UN and all of its specialized agencies, OECD, EC.

Embassy: 3200 Whitehaven St. NW 20008; 234-4300.

The origin of Copenhagen dates back to ancient times, when the fishing and trading place named Havn (port) grew up on a cluster of islets, but Bishop Absalon (1128-1201) is regarded as the actual founder of the city.

Danes formed a large component of the Viking raiders in the early Middle Ages. The Danish kingdom was a major north European power until the 17th century, when it lost its land in southern Sweden. Norway was separated in 1815, and Schleswig-Holstein in 1864. Northern Schleswig was returned in 1920.

The **Faeroe Islands** in the N. Atlantic, about 300 mi. NE of the Shetlands, and 850 mi. from Denmark proper, 18 inhabited, have an area of 540 sq. mi. and pop. (1987) of 46,000. They are self-governing in most matters.

Greenland

(Kalaallit Nunaat)

Greenland, a huge island between the N. Atlantic and the Polar Sea, is separated from the North American continent by Davis Strait and Baffin Bay. Its total area is 840,000 sq. mi., 84% of which is ice-capped. Most of the island is a lofty plateau 9,000 to 10,000 ft. in altitude. The average thickness of the cap is 1,000 ft. The population (1989 est.) is 55,415. Under the 1953 Danish constitution the colony became an integral part of the realm with representatives in the Folketing. The Danish parliament, 1978, approved home rule for Greenland, effective May 1, 1979. Accepting home rule the islanders elected a socialist-dominated legislature, Apr. 4th. With home rule, Greenlandic place names came into official use. The technically-correct name for Greenland is now Kalaallit Nunaat; its capital is Nuuk, rather than Gothab. Fish is the principal export.

Djibouti

Republic of Djibouti

Jumhouriyya Djibouti

People: Population (1990 est.): 337,000. **Pop. density:** 38 per sq. mi. **Ethnic groups:** Issa (Somali) 60%; Afar 35%; European 5%. **Languages:** French, Arabic (both official); Somali, Saho-Afar, Arabic. **Religions:** Sunni Moslem 94%.

Geography: Area: 8,494 sq. mi., about the size of New Hampshire. **Location:** On E coast of Africa, separated from Arabian Peninsula by the strategically vital strait of Bab el-Mandeb. **Neighbors:** Ethiopia on N (Eritrea) and W, Somalia on S. **Topography:** The territory, divided into a low coastal plain, mountains behind, and an interior plateau, is arid, sandy, and desolate. The climate is generally hot and dry. **Capital:** Djibouti. **Cities** (1982): Djibouti (met.) 200,000.

Government: Type: Republic. **Head of state:** Pres. Hassan Gouled Aptidon b. 1916; in office: June 24, 1977; **Head of government:** Prem. Barkat Gourad Hamadou; in office: Sept. 30, 1978. **Local divisions:** 5 cercles (districts).

Economy: Minerals: Salt. **Electricity prod.** (1986): 140 mln. kwh.

Finance: Currency Franc (Mar. 1990: 177=$1 US). **Gross national product** (1986): $344 mln. **Per capita income** (1982): $400. **Imports** (1986): $197 mln.; partners: Fr. 47%, Jap. 8%, UK 8%. **Exports** (1986): $96 mln.; partners: Fr. 87%.

Transport: Motor vehicles: in use (1985): 12,000 passenger cars, 950 commercial vehicles. **Chief ports:** Djibouti.

Communications: Television sets: 1 per 35 persons. **Radios:** 1 per 16 persons. **Telephones:** 1 per 55 persons.

Health: Life expectancy at birth (1989): 45 male; 49 female. **Births** (per 1,000 pop. 1989): 43. **Deaths** (per 1,000 pop. 1989): 17. **Natural increase:** 2.6%. **Infant mortality** (per 1,000 live births 1989): 121.

Education (1988): **Literacy:** 20%.

Major International Organizations: UN, OAU, Arab League.

Embassy: 866 United Nations Plaza, New York, NY 10017; (212) 753-3163.

France gained control of the territory in stages between 1862 and 1900.

Ethiopia and Somalia have renounced their claims to the area, but each has accused the other of trying to gain control. There were clashes between Afars (ethnically related to Ethiopians) and Issas (related to Somalis) in 1976. Immigrants from both countries continued to enter the country up to independence, which came June 27, 1977.

Unemployment is high and there are few natural resources. French aid is the mainstay of the economy and some 5,000 French troops are present.

Dominica

Commonwealth of Dominica

People: Population (1990 est.): 85,000. **Pop. density:** 262 per sq. mi. **Ethnic groups:** nearly all African or mulatto, Caribs.

Languages: English (official), French patois. **Religions:** mainly Roman Catholic.

Geography: Area: 290 sq. mi., about one-fourth the size of Rhode Island. **Location:** In Eastern Caribbean, most northerly Windward Is. **Neighbors:** Guadeloupe to N, Martinique to S. **Topography:** Mountainous, a central ridge running from N to S, terminating in cliffs; volcanic in origin, with numerous thermal springs; rich deep topsoil on leeward side, red tropical clay on windward coast. **Capital** (1983 est.) Roseau 18,000.

Government: Type: Parliamentary democracy; republic within Commonwealth. **Head of state:** Pres. Clarence Augustus Seignoret; in office: 1984. **Head of government:** Prime Min. Mary Eugenia Charles; b. 1919; in office: July 21, 1980. **Local divisions:** 10 parishes.

Economy: Industries: Agriculture, tourism. **Chief crops:** Bananas, citrus fruits, coconuts. **Minerals:** Pumice. **Other resources:** Forests. **Arable land:** 23%. **Electricity prod.** (1987): 16 mln. kwh. **Labor force:** 40% agric.; 32% ind & comm.; 28% services.

Finance: Currency: East Caribbean dollar (May 1990: 2.70 = $1 US). **Gross domestic product** (1987): $115 mln. **Imports** (1986): $63 mln.; partners: UK 17%, U.S. 27%. **Exports** (1986): $35 mln.; partners: UK 50%. **Tourists** (1987): $11 mln. receipts. **Consumer prices** (change in 1988): 1.7%.

Transport: Chief ports: Roseau.

Communications: Telephones: 1 per 11 persons.

Health: Life expectancy at birth (1989): 73 male; 78 female. **Births** (per 1,000 pop. 1989): 26. **Deaths** (per 1,000 pop. 1989): 5. **Natural increase:** 2.1%. **Hospital beds** (1988): 245. **Physicians** (1988): 31. **Infant mortality** (per 1,000 live births 1989): 14.

Education: Literacy: 80%.

Major International Organizations: UN, OAS.

A British colony since 1805, Dominica was granted self government in 1967. Independence was achieved Nov. 3, 1978.

Hurricane David struck, Aug. 30, 1979, devastating the island and destroying the banana plantations, Dominica's economic mainstay. Coups were attempted in 1980 and 1981.

Dominica took a leading role in the instigation of the 1983 invasion of Grenada.

Dominican Republic

República Dominicana

People: Population (1990 est.): 7,253,000. **Age distrib. (%):** 0–14: 40.7; 15–59: 54.6; 60+: 4.7. **Pop. density:** 388 per sq. mi. **Urban** (1986): 55%. **Ethnic groups:** Caucasian 16%, mixed 73%, black 11%. **Languages:** Spanish. **Religions:** Roman Catholic 92%.

Geography: Area: 18,816 sq. mi., the size of Vermont and New Hampshire combined. **Location:** In West Indies, sharing I. of Hispaniola with Haiti. **Neighbors:** Haiti on W. **Topography:** The Cordillera Central range crosses the center of the country, rising to over 10,000 ft., highest in the Caribbean. The Cibao valley to the N is major agricultural area. **Capital:** Santo Domingo. **Cities** (1987 est.): Santo Domingo 1,700,000; Santiago de Los Caballeros 422,000.

Government: Type: Representative democracy. **Head of state:** Pres. Joaquin Balaguer; in office: Aug. 16, 1986. **Local divisions:** 29 provinces and Santo Domingo. **Defense:** 1.4% of GDP. (1987).

Economy: Industries: Sugar refining, cement, pharmaceuticals. **Chief crops:** sugar, cocoa, coffee, tobacco, rice. **Minerals:** Nickel, gold, silver. **Other resources:** Timber. **Arable land:** 23%. **Livestock.** (1987): cattle: 2.0 mln.; pigs: 2.6 mln. **Electricity prod.** (1988): 3.8 bln. kwh. **Labor force:** 49% agric.; 18% ind.; 34% serv. & govt.

Finance: Currency: Peso (Mar. 1990: 6.34 = $1 US). **Gross national product** (1987): $5.5 bln. **Per capita GNP** (1987): $800. **Imports** (1989): $2.2 mln.; partners: U.S. 35%, Venez. 26%, Mex. 11%. **Exports** (1989): $928 mln.; partners: U.S. 69%, Neth. 4%. **Tourists** (1987): $500 mln. receipts. **National budget** (1987): $898 mln. expenditures. **International reserves less gold** (Mar. 1990): $170 mln. **Gold:** 18,000 oz t. **Consumer prices** (change in 1987): 15.9%.

Transport: Motor vehicles: in use (1985): 99,000 passenger cars, 59,000 comm. vehicles. **Chief ports:** Santo Domingo, San Pedro de Macoris, Puerto Plata.

Communications: Television sets: 1 per 12 persons. **Radios:** 1 per 6 persons. **Telephones:** 1 per 22 persons. **Daily newspaper circ.** (1987): 44 per 1,000 pop.

Health: Life expectancy at birth (1985): 60.7 male; 64.6 female. **Births** (per 1,000 pop. 1989): 30. **Deaths** (per 1,000 pop. 1989): 8. **Natural increase:** 2.2%. **Hospital beds:** 1 per 985 persons. **Physicians:** 1 per 2,100 persons. **Infant mortality** (per 1,000 live births 1989): 66.

Education (1987): Literacy: 68%. Years compulsory 6; attendance 60%.

Major International Organizations: UN (World Bank, IMF, GATT), OAS.

Embassy: 1712 22d St. NW 20008; 332-6280.

Carib and Arawak Indians inhabited the island of Hispaniola when Columbus landed in 1492. The city of Santo Domingo, founded 1496, is the oldest settlement by Europeans in the hemisphere and has the supposed ashes of Columbus in an elaborate tomb in its ancient cathedral.

The western third of the island was ceded to France in 1697. Santo Domingo itself was ceded to France in 1795. Haitian leader Toussaint L'Ouverture seized it, 1801. Spain returned intermittently 1803-21, as several native republics came and went. Haiti ruled again, 1822-44, and Spanish occupation occurred 1861-63.

The country was occupied by U.S. Marines from 1916 to 1924, when a constitutionally elected government was installed.

In 1930, Gen. Rafael Leonidas Trujillo Molina was elected president. Trujillo ruled brutally until his assassination in 1961. Pres. Joaquin Balaguer, appointed by Trujillo in 1960, resigned under pressure in 1962. Juan Bosch, elected president in the first free elections in 38 years, was overthrown in 1963.

On April 24, 1965, a revolt was launched by followers of Bosch and others, including a few communists. Four days later U.S. Marines intervened against the pro-Bosch forces. Token units were later sent by 5 So. American countries as a peacekeeping force.

A provisional government supervised a June 1966 election, in which Balaguer defeated Bosch by a 3-2 margin; there were some charges of election fraud. The Inter-American Peace Force completed its departure Sept. 20, 1966.

Continued depressed world prices have affected the main export commodity, sugar.

Ecuador

Republic of Ecuador

República del Ecuador

People: Population (1990 est.): 10,506,000. **Age distrib. (%):** 0–14: 41.3; 15–64: 55.0; 65+: 3.7. **Pop. density:** 95 per sq. mi. **Urban** (1988): 54% **Ethnic groups:** Indians 25%, Mestizo 55%, Spanish 10%, African 10%. **Languages:** Spanish (official), Quechuan, Jivaroan. **Religions:** Roman Catholic 95%.

Geography: Area: 109,483 sq. mi., the size of Colorado. **Location:** In NW S. America, on Pacific coast, astride Equator. **Neighbors:** Colombia to N, Peru to E and S. **Topography:** Two ranges of Andes run N and S, splitting the country into 3 zones: hot, humid lowlands on the coast; temperate highlands between the ranges, and rainy, tropical lowlands to the E. **Capital:** Quito. **Cities** (1989 est.): Guayaquil 1,600,000; Quito 1,200,000.

Government: Type: Republic. **Head of state:** Pres. Rodrigo Borja Cevallos; in office: Aug. 10, 1988. **Local divisions:** 20 provinces. **Defense:** 1.6% of GNP (1984).

Economy: Industries: Food processing, wood prods., textiles. **Chief crops:** Bananas (largest exporter), coffee, rice, sugar, corn. **Minerals:** Oil, copper, iron, lead, silver, sulphur. **Crude oil reserves** (1987): 1.2 bln. bbls. **Other resources:** Rubber, bark. **Arable land:** 6%. **Livestock** (1988): cattle: 3.8 mln.; pigs: 4.1 mln.; sheep: 2.1 mln. **Fish catch** (1987): 679,000 metric tons. **Electricity prod.** (1988): 5.7 bln. kwh. **Labor force:** 34% agric., 12% ind., 35% services.

Finance: Currency: Sucre (June 1990: 805 = $1 US). **Gross national product** (1988): $9.4 bln. **Per capita GNP** (1988): $1,040. **Imports** (1989): $1.8 bln.; partners: U.S. 26%, EC 16%, Jap. 13%. **Exports** (1989): $2.0 bln.; partners: U.S. 54%. **Tourism** (1986): $135 mln. receipts. **National budget** (1987): $2.6 bln. expenditures. **International reserves less gold** (Mar. 1990): $363 mln. **Gold:** 414,000 oz t. **Consumer prices** (change in 1988): 58.2%.

Transport: Railway traffic (1987) 20 mln. passenger-km.
Motor vehicles: in use (1986): 256,000 passenger cars, 36,000
comm. vehicles. Civil aviation (1984): 893 mln. passenger-km;
42.6 mln. net ton-km. Chief ports: Guayaquil, Manta, Esmeraldas, Puerto Bolivar.
Communications: Television sets: 1 per 17 persons. Radios: 1 per 3.4 persons. Telephones: 1 per 28 persons. Daily
newspaper circ. (1985): 57 per 1,000 pop.
Health: Life expectancy at birth (1989): 64 male, 68 female.
Births (per 1,000 pop. 1989): 31. Deaths (per 1,000 pop. 1989):
7. Natural increase: 2.4%. Hospital beds (1984): 15,455. Physicians (1984): 11,000. Infant mortality (per 1,000 live births
1989): 63.
Education (1986): Literacy: 90%. Attendance through 6th
grade—76% urban, 33% rural.
Major International Organizations: UN (IMF, WHO), OAS,
OPEC.
Embassy: 2535 15th St. NW 20009; 234-7200.

Spain conquered the region, which was the northern Inca empire, in 1633. Liberation forces defeated the Spanish May 24,
1822, near Quito. Ecuador became part of the Great Colombia
Republic but seceded, May 13, 1830.
Ecuador had been ruled by civilian and military dictatorships
since 1968. A peaceful transfer of power from the military junta
to the democratic civilian government took place, 1979.
Since 1972, the economy has revolved around its petroleum
exports, which have declined since 1982 causing severe economic problems. Ecuador suspended interest payments for 1987
on its estimated $8.2 billion foreign debt following a Mar. 5-6
earthquake which left 20,000 homeless, and destroyed a stretch
of the country's main oil pipeline.
Ecuador and Peru have long disputed their Amazon Valley
boundary.
The Galapagos Islands, 600 mi. to the W, are the home of
huge tortoises and other unusual animals.

Egypt
Arab Republic of Egypt
Jumhūrīyah Misr al-Arabiya

People: Population (1990 est.): 54,139,000. Age distrib (%)
0-14: 41.8; 15-59: 52.7; 60+: 5.5. Pop. density: 141 per sq. mi.
Urban (1986): 44%. Ethnic groups: Eastern Hamitic stock
90%, Bedouin, Nubian. Languages: Arabic (official), English.
Religions: 94% Sunni Moslem.
Geography: Area: 386,650 sq. mi, about the size of Texas,
Oklahoma, and Arkansas combined. Location: NE corner of
Africa. Neighbors: Libya on W, Sudan on S, Israel on E. Topography: Almost entirely desolate and barren, with hills and mountains in E and along Nile. The Nile Valley, where most of the
people live, stretches 550 miles. Capital: Cairo. Cities (1986
est.): Cairo 6,305,000; Alexandria 2,800,000; al-Jizah 1,600,000.
Government: Type: Republic. Head of state: Pres. Hosni
Mubarak; b. 1929; in office: Oct. 14, 1981. Head of Government: Atef Sedki in office: Nov. 10, 1986. Local divisions: 26
governorates. Defense: 9.2% of GNP (1987).
Economy: Industries: Textiles, chemicals, petrochemicals,
food processing, cement. Chief crops: Cotton (one of largest
producers), rice, beans, fruits, grains, vegetables, sugar, corn.
Minerals: Oil, phosphates, gypsum, iron, manganese, limestone.
Crude oil reserves (1987): 4 bln. bbls. Arable land: 4%. Livestock (1988): cattle: 1.9 mln.; sheep: 1.1 mln. Fish catch
(1987): 250,000 metric tons. Electricity prod. (1988): 42 bln.
kwh. Labor force: 44% agric.; 22% services; 14% industry.
Finance: Currency: Pound (June 1990: 2.66 = $1 US).
Gross national product (1987): $25.6 bln. Per capita GNP
(1987): $490. Imports (1989): $7.3 bln.; partners: U.S. 19%, W.
Ger. 10%, It. 8%, France 8%. Exports (1989): $2.6 bln.; part-
ners: It. 22%, Rom. 12%. Tourists (1987): $1.5 bln. receipts.
National budget (1987): $12.2 bln. expenditures. International
reserves less gold (Jan. 1990): $1.5 bln. Gold: 2.43 mln. oz t.
Consumer prices (change in 1989): 21.3%.
Transport: Railway traffic (1986): 28.3 bln. passenger-km.
Motor vehicles: in use (1987): 783,000 passenger cars,
371,000 comm. vehicles. Civil aviation (1987): 4.4 bln. passen-
ger-km.; 10 airports. Chief ports: Alexandria, Port Said, Suez.

Communications: Television sets: 1 per 13 persons. Ra-
dios: 1 per 3.9 persons. Telephones: 1 per 34 persons. Daily
newspaper circ. (1986): 88 per 1,000 pop.
Health: Life expectancy at birth (1989): 59 male; 60 female.
Births (per 1,000 pop. 1989): 35. Deaths (per 1,000 pop. 1989):
10. Natural increase: 2.5%. Hospital beds: 1 per 505 persons.
Physicians: 1 per 616 persons. Infant mortality (per 1,000 live
births 1989): 93.
Education (1988): Literacy: 44%. Compulsory ages 6-12.
Major International Organizations: UN (IMF, World Bank,
GATT), OAU.
Embassy: 2310 Decatur Pl. NW 20008; 232-5400.

Archeological records of ancient Egyptian civilization date
back to 4000 BC. A unified kingdom arose around 3200 BC, and
extended its way south into Nubia and north as far as Syria. A
high culture of rulers and priests was built on an economic base
of serfdom, fertile soil, and annual flooding of the Nile banks.
Imperial decline facilitated conquest by Asian invaders (Hyksos, Assyrians). The last native dynasty fell in 341 BC to the
Persians, who were in turn replaced by Greeks (Alexander and
the Ptolemies), Romans, Byzantines, and Arabs, who introduced
Islam and the Arabic language. The ancient Egyptian language is
preserved only in the liturgy of the Coptic Christians.
Egypt was ruled as part of larger Islamic empires for several
centuries. The Mamluks, a military caste of Caucasian origin,
ruled Egypt from 1250 until defeat by the Ottoman Turks in
1517. Under Turkish sultans the khedive as hereditary viceroy
had wide authority. Britain intervened in 1882 and took control of
administration, though nominal allegiance to the Ottoman Empire
continued until 1914.
The country was a British protectorate from 1914 to 1922. A
1936 treaty strengthened Egyptian autonomy, but Britain retained bases in Egypt and a condominium over the Sudan. Britain fought German and Italian armies from Egypt, 1940-42, but
Egypt did not declare war against Germany until 1945. In 1951
Egypt abrogated the 1936 treaty. The Sudan became independent in 1956.
The uprising of July 23, 1952, led by the Society of Free Officers, named Maj. Gen. Mohammed Naguib commander in chief
and forced King Farouk to abdicate. When the republic was proclaimed June 18, 1953, Naguib became its first president and
premier. Lt. Col. Gamal Abdel Nasser removed Naguib and became premier in 1954. In 1956, he was voted president. Nasser
died in 1970 and was replaced by Vice Pres. Anwar Sadat.
The Aswan High Dam, completed 1971, provides irrigation for
more than a million acres of land. Artesian wells, drilled in the
Western Desert, reclaimed 43,000 acres, 1960-66.
When the state of Israel was proclaimed in 1948, Egypt joined
other Arab nations invading Israel and was defeated.
After terrorist raids across its border, Israel invaded Egypt's
Sinai Peninsula, Oct. 29, 1956. Egypt rejected a cease-fire demand by Britain and France; on Oct. 31 the 2 nations dropped
bombs and on Nov. 5-6 landed forces. Egypt and Israel accepted a UN cease-fire; fighting ended Nov. 7.
A UN Emergency Force guarded the 117-mile long border
between Egypt and Israel until May 19, 1967, when it was withdrawn at Nasser's demand. Egyptian troops entered the Gaza
Strip and the heights of Sharm el Sheikh and 3 days later closed
the Strait of Tiran to all Israeli shipping. Full-scale war broke out
June 5 and before it ended under a UN cease-fire June 10, Israel had captured Gaza and the Sinai Peninsula, controlled the
east bank of the Suez Canal and reopened the gulf.
Sporadic fighting with Israel broke out late in 1968 and continued almost daily, 1969-70. Military and economic aid was received from the USSR. Israel and Egypt agreed, Aug. 7, 1970, to
a cease-fire and peace negotiations proposed by the U.S. Negotiations failed to achieve results, but the cease-fire continued.
In a surprise attack Oct. 6, 1973, Egyptian forces crossed the
Suez Canal into the Sinai. (At the same time, Syrian forces attacked Israelis on the Golan Heights.) Egypt was supplied by a
USSR military airlift; the U.S. responded with an airlift to Israel.
Israel counter-attacked, crossed the canal, surrounded Suez
City. A UN cease-fire took effect Oct. 24.
A disengagement agreement was signed Jan. 18, 1974. Under
it, Israeli forces withdrew from the canal's W bank; limited numbers of Egyptian forces occupied a strip along the E bank. A
second accord was signed in 1975, with Israel yielding Sinai oil
fields. Pres. Sadat's surprise visit to Jerusalem, Nov. 1977,
opened the prospect of peace with Israel, but worsened relations with Libya. On Mar. 26, 1979, Egypt and Israel signed a
formal peace treaty, ending 30 years of war, and establishing

diplomatic relations. Israel returned control of the Sinai to Egypt in April 1982.

Tension between Moslem fundamentalists and Christians in 1981 caused street riots and culminated in a nationwide security crackdown in Sept. Pres Sadat was assassinated on Oct. 6.

Relations with the U.S. were strained in 1985 because of the U.S. interception of an Egyptian airliner carrying the hijackers of the *Achille Lauro*.

The **Suez Canal**, 103 mi. long, links the Mediterranean and Red seas. It was built by a French corporation 1859-69, but Britain obtained controlling interest in 1875. The last British troops were removed June 13, 1956. On July 26, Egypt nationalized the canal.

Egypt had barred Israeli ships and cargoes destined for Israel since 1948, and closed the canal to all shipping after the 1967 Arab-Israeli War. The canal was reopened in 1975.

El Salvador

Republic of El Salvador

República de El Salvador

People: Population (1990 est.): 5,221,000. **Age distrib.** (%): 0–14: 45.3; 15–59: 51; 60+: 4.7. **Pop. density:** 671 per sq. mi. **Urban** (1987): 47%. **Ethnic groups:** Mestizo 89%, Indian 10%. **Languages:** Spanish, Nahuatl (among some Indians). **Religions:** Roman Catholic 93%.

Geography: Area: 8,260 sq. mi., the size of Massachusetts. **Location:** In Central America. **Neighbors:** Guatemala on W, Honduras on N. **Topography:** A hot Pacific coastal plain in the south rises to a cooler plateau and valley region, densely populated. The N is mountainous, including many volcanoes. **Capital:** San Salvador. **Cities** (1985 est.): San Salvador 1.4 mln.

Government: Type: Republic. **Head of state:** Pres., Alfredo Cristiani; b. Nov, 22, 1947; in office: June 1, 1989. **Local divisions:** 14 departments. **Defense:** 3.9% of GNP (1987).

Economy: Industries: Food and beverages, textiles, petroleum products. **Chief crops:** Coffee (21% of GNP), cotton, corn, sugar. **Other resources:** Rubber, forests. **Arable land:** 27%. **Livestock** (1988): cattle: 1.1 mln.; pigs: 440,000. **Electricity prod.** (1988): 1.7 bln. kwh. **Labor force:** 40% agric.; 16% ind.; 27% services.

Finance: Currency: Colon (Mar. 1990: 5.00 = $1 US). **Gross national product** (1988): $4.1 bln. **Per capita income** (1986): $700. **Imports** (1987): $1.9 bln.; partners: U.S. 39%, CACM 22%. **Exports** (1987): $1.1 bln.; partners: U.S. 49%, CACM 23%. **National budget** (1987): $642 mln. expenditures. **International reserves less gold** (Mar. 1990): $237 mln. **Gold:** 469,000 oz t. **Consumer prices** (change in 1989): 17.6%.

Transport: Railway traffic (1986): 4.9 mln. passenger-km. **Motor vehicles:** in use (1987): 138,000 passenger cars, 23,000 comm. vehicles. **Chief ports:** La Union, Acajutla.

Communications: Television sets: 1 per 12 persons. **Radios:** 1 per 2.6 persons. **Telephones:** 1 per 36 persons. **Daily newspaper circ.** (1988): 65 per 1,000 pop.

Health: Life expectancy at birth (1985): 62.6 male; 66.3 female. **Births** (per 1,000 pop. 1989): 33. **Deaths** (per 1,000 pop. 1989): 8. **Natural increase:** 2.5%. **Hospital beds:** 1 per 1,129 persons. **Physicians:** 1 per 2,891 persons. **Infant mortality** (per 1,000 live births 1989): 62.

Education (1987): **Literacy:** 62% (urban areas); 40% (rural areas). Years compulsory 6; attendance 82%.

Major International Organizations: UN (IMF, WHO, ILO), OAS, CACM.

Embassy: 2308 California St. NW 20008; 265-3480.

El Salvador became independent of Spain in 1821, and of the Central American Federation in 1839.

A fight with Honduras in 1969 over the presence of 300,000 Salvadorean workers left 2,000 dead. Clashes were renewed 1970 and 1974.

A military coup overthrew the Romero government, 1979, but the ruling military-civilian junta failed to quell the civil war which has resulted in some 50,000 deaths. Some 10,000 leftists insurgents, armed by Cuba and Nicaragua, control about 25% of the country, mostly in the east. Extreme right-wing death squads organized to eliminate suspected leftists were blamed for over 1,000 deaths in 1983. The Reagan administration has staunchly supported the government with military aid.

Voters turned out in large numbers in the May 1984 presidential election. Christian Democrat Jose Napoleon Duarte, a moderate, was victorious with 54% of the vote. Duarte was diagnosed as having terminal cancer in 1988.

Leftist guerrillas continued their offensive in 1990 as the civil war entered its 10th year. Nine soldiers, including 3 officers, were indicted Jan. 1990 in the Nov. 1989 slaying of 6 Jesuit priests at a university in San Salvador.

Equatorial Guinea

Republic of Equatorial Guinea

República de Guinea Ecuatorial

People: Population (1990 est.): 360,000. **Age distrib.** (%): 0–14: 38.1; 15–59: 55.2; 60+: 6.7. **Pop. density:** 35 per sq. mi. **Ethnic groups:** Fangs 80%, Bubi 15%. **Languages:** Spanish (official), Fang, English. **Religions:** Mostly Roman Catholic.

Geography: Area: 10,832 sq. mi., the size of Maryland. **Location:** Bioko Is. off W. Africa coast in Gulf of Guinea, and Rio Muni, mainland enclave. **Neighbors:** Gabon on S, Cameroon on E, N. **Topography:** Bioko Is. consists of 2 volcanic mountains and a connecting valley. Rio Muni, with over 90% of the area, has a coastal plain and low hills beyond. **Capital:** Malabo. **Cities** (1989 est.): Malabo 38,000.

Government: Type: Unitary Republic. **Head of state:** Pres., Supreme Military Council Teodoro Obiang Nguema Mbasogo; b. June 5, 1942; in office: Oct. 10, 1979. **Head of government:** Prime Min. Cristino Seriche Bioko. **Local divisions:** 7 provinces.

Economy: Chief crops: Cocoa, coffee, bananas, sweet potatoes. **Other resources:** Timber. **Arable land:** 8%. **Electricity prod.** (1989): 17 mln. kwh. **Labor force:** agric. 50%; public sector 40%.

Finance: Currency: Bipkwele (Mar. 1990: 284 = $1 US). **Gross national product** (1987): $130 mln. **Per capita income** (1987): $300. **Imports** (1987): $50 mln.; partners: Spain 54%, China 17%. **Exports** (1987): $39 mln.; partners: Sp. 40%, Neth. 28%, W. Ger. 23%.

Transport: Chief ports: Malabo, Bata.

Communications: Radios: 1 per 3.5 persons.

Health: Life expectancy at birth (1989): 44.0 male; 48.0 female. **Births** (per 1,000 pop. 1989): 38. **Deaths** (per 1,000 pop. 1989): 19. **Natural increase:** 1.9% **Hospital beds** (1982): 3,200. **Infant mortality** (per 1,000 live births 1989): 125.

Education (1989): **Literacy:** 55%. About 65% attend primary school.

Major International Organizations: UN (IMF, World Bank), OAU.

Embassy: 801 2d Ave., New York, NY 10017; (212) 599-1523.

Fernando Po (now Bioko) Island was discovered by Portugal in the late 15th century and ceded to Spain in 1778. Independence came Oct. 12, 1968. Riots occurred in 1969 over disputes between the island and the more backward Rio Muni province on the mainland. Masie Nguema Biyogo, himself from the mainland, became president for life in 1972.

Masie's 11-year reign was one of the most brutal in Africa, resulting in a bankrupted nation. Most of the nation's 7,000 Europeans emigrated. In 1976, 45,000 Nigerian workers were evacuated amid charges of a reign of terror. Masie was ousted in a military coup, Aug., 1979.

The nation is heavily dependent on external aid.

Ethiopia

People's Democratic Republic of Ethiopia

Ye Etiyop'iya Hezbawi Dimokrasiyawi Republek

People: Population (1990 est.): 51,375,000. **Age distrib.** (%): 0–14: 46.5; 15–59: 47.3; 60+: 6.2. **Pop. density:** 101 per sq. mi. **Urban** (1989): 11%. **Ethnic groups:** Oromo 40%, Amhara 25%, Tigre 12%, Sidama 9%. **Languages:** Amharic (official), Tigre (Semitic languages); Galla (Hamitic), Arabic, others. **Religions:** Orthodox Christian 40%, Moslem 40%.

Geography: Area: 471,776 sq. mi., four-fifths the size of Alaska. **Location:** In E. Africa. **Neighbors:** Sudan on W, Kenya on S, Somalia, Djibouti on E. **Topography:** A high central plateau, between 6,000 and 10,000 ft. high, rises to higher mountains near the Great Rift Valley, cutting in from the SW. The Blue Nile and other rivers cross the plateau, which descends to plains on both W and SE. **Capital:** Addis Ababa. **Cities** (1984 est.): Addis Ababa 1,412,000.

Government: Type: Communist state. **Head of state:** Pres. Mengistu Haile Mariam; b. 1937; in office: Feb. 11, 1977. **Head of Government:** Prime Min. Hailuyemeneu; in office: Nov. 8, 1989. **Local divisions:** 24 administrative zones, 5 autonomous regions. **Defense:** 8% of GNP (1987).

Economy: Industries: Food processing, cement, textiles. **Chief crops:** Coffee (61% export earnings), grains. **Minerals:** Platinum, gold, copper, potash. **Arable Land:** 13%. **Livestock** (1988): cattle: 23.4 mln.; sheep: 17.5 mln. **Electricity prod.** (1987): 765 mln. kwh. **Labor force:** 90% agric.

Finance: Currency: Birr (Mar. 1990: 2.07 = $1 US). **Gross national product** (1987): $5.7 bln. **Per capita income** (1986): $121. **Imports** (1989): $1.2 bln.; partners: USSR 22%, U.S. 15%, Italy 10%, Jap. 6%, W.Ger. 10%. **Exports** (1988): $429 mln.; partners: U.S. 20%, W. Ger. 18%, Italy 7%. **National budget** (1987): $2.0 bln. expenditures. **International reserves less gold** (Mar. 1990): $33 mln. **Gold:** 162,000 oz t. **Consumer prices** (change in 1988): 7.1%.

Transport: Railway traffic (1986): 350 mln. passenger-km. **Motor vehicles:** in use (1988): 41,300 passenger cars, 19,000 comm. vehicles. **Civil aviation** (1987): 553 mln. passenger-km; 37 airports with scheduled flights. **Chief ports:** Masewa, Aseb.

Communications: Television sets: 1 per 679 persons. **Radios:** 1 per 5.5 persons. **Telephones:** 1 per 341 persons. **Daily newspaper circ.** (1986): 1 per 1,000 pop.

Health: Life expectancy at birth (1989): 50 male; 53 female. **Births** (per 1,000 pop. 1989): 45. **Deaths** (per 1,000 pop. 1989): 15. **Natural increase:** 3.1%. **Hospital beds:** 1 per 3,873 persons. **Physicians:** 1 per 36,660 persons. **Infant mortality** (per 1,000 live births 1989): 113.

Education (1985): Literacy: 18%.

Major International Organizations: UN (IMF, WHO), OAU. **Embassy:** 2134 Kalorama Rd. NW 20008; 234-2281.

Ethiopian culture was influenced by Egypt and Greece. The ancient monarchy was invaded by Italy in 1880, but maintained its independence until another Italian invasion in 1936. British forces freed the country in 1941.

The last emperor, Haile Selassie I, established a parliament and judiciary system in 1931, but barred all political parties.

A series of droughts since 1972 have killed hundreds of thousands. An army mutiny, strikes, and student demonstrations led to the dethronement of Selassie in 1974. The ruling junta pledged to form a one-party socialist state, and instituted a successful land reform; opposition was violently suppressed. The influence of the Coptic Church, embraced in 330 AD, was curbed, and the monarchy was abolished in 1975.

The regime, torn by bloody coups, faced uprisings by tribal and political groups in part aided by Sudan and Somalia. Ties with the U.S., once a major arms and aid source, deteriorated, while cooperation accords were signed with the USSR in 1977. In 1978, Soviet advisors and Cuban troops helped defeat Somalia forces. Ethiopia and Somalia signed a peace agreement in 1988.

A world-wide relief effort began in 1984, as an extended drought caused millions to face starvation and death. In 1988, victories by Eritean guerrillas forced the government to curtail the work of foreign aid workers in drought-stricken regions. Foreign relief officials expressed the fear that suspension of their operations would lead to the starvation death of hundreds of thousands.

Fiji
Republic of Fiji

People: Population (1990 est.): 772,000. **Age distrib.** (%): 0–14: 38.2; 15–59: 56.9; 60+: 4.9. **Pop. density:** 107 per sq. mi. **Urban** (1986): 39%. **Ethnic groups:** Indian 48%, Fijian (Melanesian-Polynesian) 46%, Europeans 2%. **Languages:** English (official), Fijian, Hindustani. **Religions:** Christian 52%, Hindu 38%, Moslem 8%.

Geography: Area: 7,056 sq. mi., the size of Massachusetts. **Location:** In western S. Pacific O. **Neighbors:** Nearest are Solomons on NW, Tonga on E. **Topography:** 322 islands (106 in-

habited), many mountainous, with tropical forests and large fertile areas, Viti Levu, the largest island, has over half the total land area. **Capital:** Suva. **Cities** (1986 est.): Suva 69,000.

Government: Type: Republic. **Head of state:** Pres. Penaia Ganilau; in office: Dec. 5, 1987. **Head of government:** Prime Min. Kamisese Mara; b. May 13, 1920; in office: Oct. 10, 1970. **Local divisions:** 4 divisions, 1 dependency.

Economy: Industries: Sugar refining, light industry, tourism. **Chief crops:** Sugar, bananas, ginger. **Minerals:** Gold. **Other resources:** Timber. **Arable land:** 8%. **Electricity prod.** (1988): 325 mln. kwh. **Labor force:** 44% agric.

Finance: Currency: Dollar (Mar. 1990: 1.54 = $1.00 US). **Gross national product** (1987): $1.1 bln. **Per capita GNP** (1987): $1,680. **Imports** (1988): $462 mln.; partners: Austral. 29%, Jap. 12%, N.Z. 19%. **Exports** (1988): $307 mln.; partners: UK 32%, Aust. 25%. **Tourists** (1988): $180 mln. receipts. **National budget** (1987): $340 mln. expenditures. **International reserves less gold** (Mar. 1989): $216 mln. **Gold:** 10,000 oz t. **Consumer prices** (change in 1989): 6.2%.

Transport: Motor vehicles: in use (1987): 34,000 passenger cars, 24,000 comm. vehicles. **Civil aviation** (1988): 540 mln. passenger-km; 18 airports with scheduled flights. **Chief ports:** Suva, Lautoka.

Communications: Radios: 1 per 1.7 persons. **Telephones:** 1 per 12 persons. **Daily newspaper circ.** (1985): 76 per 1,000 pop.

Health: Life expectancy at birth (1987): 68.0 male; 72.4 female. **Births** (per 1,000 pop. 1989): 28. **Deaths** (per 1,000 pop. 1989): 5. **Natural increase:** 2.3%. **Hospital beds:** 1 per 417 persons. **Physicians:** 1 per 2,649 persons. **Infant mortality** (per 1,000 live births 1989): 19.

Education (1985): Literacy: 80%. 95% attend school.

Major International Organizations: UN (IMF, WHO), Commonwealth of Nations.

Embassy: 2233 Wisconsin Ave. NW 20007; 337-8320.

A British colony since 1874, Fiji became an independent parliamentary democracy Oct. 10, 1970.

Cultural differences between the majority Indian community, descendants of contract laborers brought to the islands in the 19th century, and the less modernized native Fijians, who by law own 83% of the land in communal villages, have led to political polarization.

The discovery of copper on Viti Levu along with increased sugar production bode well for the economy.

In 1987, a military coup ousted the government; order was restored May 21 when a compromise was reached granting Lt. Col. Sitiveni Rabuka, the coup's leader, increased power. Rabuka staged a second coup Sept. 25 and in Oct. declared Fiji a republic. A civilian government was restored to power in Dec.

Finland
Republic of Finland
Suomen Tasavalta

People: Population (1990 est.): 4,977,000. **Age distrib.** (%): 0–14: 19.3; 15–59: 62.9; 60+: 17.8. **Pop. density:** 38 per sq. mi. **Urban** (1989): 61%. **Ethnic groups:** Finns 94%, Swedes, Lapps. **Languages:** Finnish, Swedish (both official). **Religions:** Lutheran 97%.

Geography: Area: 130,119 sq. mi., slightly smaller than Montana. **Location:** In northern Europe. **Neighbors:** Norway on N, Sweden on W, USSR on E. **Topography:** South and central Finland are mostly flat areas with low hills and many lakes. The N has mountainous areas, 3,000-4,000 ft. **Capital:** Helsinki. **Cities** (1988 est.): Helsinki 487,000; Tampere 170,000; Turku 160,000.

Government: Type: Republic. **Head of state:** Pres. Mauno Koivisto; b. Nov. 25, 1923; in office: Jan. 27, 1982. **Head of government:** Prime Min. Harri Holkeri; b. Jan. 6, 1937; in office: Apr. 30, 1987. **Local divisions:** 12 laanit (provinces). **Defense:** 1.6% of GNP (1987).

Economy: Industries: Machinery, metal, shipbuilding, textiles, clothing. **Chief crops:** Grains, potatoes, dairy prods. **Minerals:** Copper, iron, zinc. **Other resources:** Forests (40% of exports). **Arable land:** 8%. **Livestock** (1988): cattle: 1.5 mln. pigs: 1.3 mln. **Fish catch** (1987): 160,000 metric tons. **Electricity prod.** (1988): 47.8 bln. kwh. **Crude steel prod.** (1988): 2.7 min. metric tons. **Labor force:** 11% agric.; 46% ind. & comm.; 28% services.

Finance: Currency: Markkaa (June 1990: 3.97 = $1 US). **Gross national product** (1987): $96.9 bln. **Per capita income** (1986): $11,900. **Imports** (1989): $24.4 bln.; partners: USSR 14%, Swed. 12%, W. Ger. 18%, UK 7%. **Exports** (1989): $23.2 bln.; partners: USSR 15%, Swed. 13%, UK 11%, W. Ger. 11%. **Tourists** (1988): $1.0 bln. receipts. **National budget** (1988): $28.1 bln. expenditures. **International reserves less gold** (Mar. 1990): $7.8 bln. **Gold** 1.9 mln. oz t. **Consumer prices** (change in 1989): 6.6%.

Transport: Railway traffic (1988): 3.1 bln. passenger-km. **Motor vehicles:** in use (1989): 1.7 mln. passenger cars, 238,000 comm. vehicles; **Civil aviation** (1988): 4.0 bln. passenger-km; 21 airports. **Chief ports:** Helsinki, Turku.

Communications: Television sets: 1 per 2.7 persons. **Radios:** 1 per person. **Telephones:** 1 per 2.1 persons. **Daily newspaper circ.** (1986): 543 per 1,000 pop.

Health: Life expectancy at birth (1989): 71 male; 79 female. **Births** (per 1,000 pop. 1989): 12. **Deaths** (per 1,000 pop. 1989): 10. **Natural increase:** .02%. **Hospital beds:** 1 per 81 persons. **Physicians:** 1 per 453 persons. **Infant mortality** (per 1,000 live births 1989): 6.

Education (1988): **Literacy:** 99%. Years compulsory 9; attendance 99%.

Major International Organizations: UN (IMF, GATT), EFTA, OECD.

Embassy: 3216 New Mexico Ave. NW 20016; 363-2430.

The early Finns probably migrated from the Ural area at about the beginning of the Christian era. Swedish settlers brought the country into Sweden, 1154 to 1809, when Finland became an autonomous grand duchy of the Russian Empire. Russian exactions created a strong national spirit; on Dec. 6, 1917, Finland declared its independence and in 1919 became a republic. On Nov. 30, 1939, the Soviet Union invaded, and the Finns were forced to cede 16,173 sq. mi., including the Karelian Isthmus, Viipuri, and an area on Lake Ladoga. After World War II, in which Finland tried to recover its lost territory, further cessions were exacted. In 1948, Finland signed a treaty of mutual assistance with the USSR. In 1956 Russia returned Porkkala, which had been ceded as a military base.

Finland is an integral member of the Nordic group of five countries and maintains good relations with the Soviet Union.

Aland, constituting an autonomous department, is a group of small islands, 572 sq. mi., in the Gulf of Bothnia, 25 mi. from Sweden, 15 mi. from Finland. Mariehamn is the principal port.

France
French Republic
République Française

People: Population (1990 est.): 56,184,000. **Age distrib. (%):** 0–14: 20.5; 15–60: 60.8; 60+: 18.7. **Pop. density:** 252 per sq. mi. **Urban** (1985): 77.2%. **Ethnic groups:** A mixture of various European and Mediterranean groups. **Languages:** French; minorities speak Breton, Alsatian German, Flemish, Italian, Basque, Catalan. **Religions:** Mostly Roman Catholic.

Geography: Area: 220,668 sq. mi., four-fifths the size of Texas. **Location:** In western Europe, between Atlantic O. and Mediterranean Sea. **Neighbors:** Spain on S, Italy, Switzerland, W. Germany on E, Luxembourg, Belgium on N. **Topography:** A wide plain covers more than half of the country, in N and W, drained to W by Seine, Loire, Garonne rivers. The Massif Central is a mountainous plateau in center. In E are Alps (Mt. Blanc is tallest in W. Europe, 15,771 ft.), the lower Jura range, and the forested Vosges. The Rhone flows from Lake Geneva to Mediterranean. Pyrenees are in SW, on border with Spain. **Capital:** Paris. **Cities** (1982 cen.): Paris 2,188,918; Marseille 878,689; Lyon 418,476; Toulouse 354,289; Nice 338,486; Nantes 247,227; Strasbourg 252,264; Bordeaux 211,197.

Government: Type: Republic. **Head of state:** Pres. François Mitterrand; b. Oct. 26, 1916; in office: May 21, 1981. **Head of government:** Prime Min. Michel Rocard; b. Aug. 23, 1930; in office: May 10, 1988. **Local divisions:** 22 administrative regions containing 95 departments. **Defense:** 4% of GNP (1987).

Economy: Industries: Steel, chemicals, autos, textiles, wine, perfume, aircraft, electronic equipment. **Chief crops:** Grains, corn, rice, fruits, vegetables. France is largest food producer, exporter, in W. Eur. **Minerals:** Bauxite, iron, coal. **Crude oil reserves** (1985): 221 mln. bbls. **Other resources:** Forests. Arable land: 32%. **Livestock** (1988): cattle: 21.1 mln.; pigs: 12.5 mln.; sheep: 10.3 mln. **Fish catch** (1988): 843,000 metric tons. **Electricity prod.** (1988): 384 bln. kwh. **Crude steel prod.** (1988): 18.9 mln. metric tons. **Labor force:** 9% agric.; 45% ind. & comm.; 46% services.

Finance: Currency: Franc (June 1990: 5.57 = $1 US). **Gross national product** (1988): $943 mln. **Per capita income** (1986): $13,046. **Imports** (1989): $193 bln.; partners: EC 51%. **Exports** (1989): $179 bln.; partners: EC 50%, U.S. 9%.**Tourists** (1987) receipts: $12.0 bln. **National budget** (1988): $208 bln. expenditures. **International reserves less gold** (Feb. 1990): $24.8 bln. **Gold:** 81.85 mln. oz t. **Consumer prices** (change in 1989): 3.5%.

Transport: Railway traffic (1988): 63.2 bln. passenger-km. **Motor vehicles:** in use (1987): 21.9 mln. passenger cars, 3.9 mln. **Civil aviation** (1988): 40.0 bln. passenger-km; 69 airports with scheduled flights. **Chief ports:** Marseille, LeHavre, Nantes, Bordeaux, Rouen.

Communications: Television sets: 1 per 2.5 persons. **Radios:** 1 per 1.1 persons. **Telephones:** 1 per 1.7 persons. **Daily newspaper circ.** (1986): 205 per 1,000 pop.

Health: Life expectancy at birth (1989): 72 male; 80 female. **Births** (per 1,000 pop. 1989): 14. **Deaths** (per 1,000 pop. 1989): 10. **Natural increase:** .3%. **Hospital beds:** 1 per 80 persons. **Physicians:** 1 per 399 persons. **Infant mortality** (per 1,000 live births 1989): 8.2.

Education (1989): **Literacy:** 99%. Years compulsory 10.

Major International Organizations: UN and most of its specialized agencies, OECD, EC, NATO.

Embassy: 4101 Reservoir Rd. NW 20007; 944-6000.

Celtic Gaul was conquered by Julius Caesar 58-51 BC; Romans ruled for 500 years. Under Charlemagne, Frankish rule extended over much of Europe. After his death France emerged as one of the successor kingdoms.

The monarchy was overthrown by the French Revolution (1789-93) and succeeded by the First Republic; followed by the First Empire under Napoleon (1804-15), a monarchy (1814-48), the Second Republic (1848-52), the Second Empire (1852-70), the Third Republic (1871-1946), the Fourth Republic (1946-58), and the Fifth Republic (1958 to present).

France suffered severe losses in manpower and wealth in the first World War, 1914-18, when it was invaded by Germany. By the Treaty of Versailles, France exacted return of Alsace and Lorraine, French provinces seized by Germany in 1871. Germany invaded France again in May, 1940, and signed an armistice with a government based in Vichy. After France was liberated by the Allies Sept. 1944, Gen. Charles de Gaulle became head of the provisional government, serving until 1946.

De Gaulle again became premier in 1958, during a crisis over Algeria, and obtained voter approval for a new constitution, ushering in the Fifth Republic. Using strong executive powers, he promoted French economic and technological advances in the context of the European Economic Community, and guarded French foreign policy independence.

France had withdrawn from Indochina in 1954, and from Morocco and Tunisia in 1956. Most of its remaining African territories were freed 1958-62, but France retained strong economic and political ties.

In 1966, France withdrew all its troops from the integrated military command of NATO, though 60,000 remained stationed in Germany. France continued to attend political meetings of NATO.

In May 1968 rebellious students in Paris and other centers rioted, battled police, and were joined by workers who launched nationwide strikes. The government awarded pay increases to the strikers May 26. In elections to the Assembly in June, de Gaulle's backers won a landslide victory. Nevertheless, he resigned from office in April, 1969, after losing a nationwide referendum on constitutional reform. De Gaulle's policies were largely continued after his death in 1970.

On May 10, 1981, France elected François Mitterrand, a Socialist candidate, president in a stunning victory over Valéry Giscard d'Estaing. In September, the government nationalized 5 major industries and most private banks. In 1986, France began a privatization program in which some 80 state-owned companies would be sold. Mitterrand was elected to a 2d 7-year term in 1988.

Agents of France's external security service were responsible for the July 10, 1985 sinking of the *Rainbow Warrior*, flagship of the Greenpeace environmental movement, in the port of Auckland, New Zealand.

The island of **Corsica**, in the Mediterranean W of Italy and N of Sardinia, is an official region of France comprising 2 departments. Area: 3,369 sq. mi.; pop. (1986 est.): 248,000. The capital is Ajaccio, birthplace of Napoleon.

Overseas Departments

French Guiana is on the NE coast of South America with Suriname on the W and Brazil on the E and S. Its area is 43,740 sq. mi.; pop. (1989): 94,000. Guiana sends one senator and one deputy to the French Parliament. Guiana is administered by a prefect and has a Council General of 16 elected members; capital is Cayenne.

The famous penal colony, Devil's Island, was phased out between 1938 and 1951.

Immense forests of rich timber cover 90% of the land. Placer gold mining is the most important industry. Exports are shrimp, timber, and machinery.

Guadeloupe, in the West Indies' Leeward Islands, consists of 2 large islands, Basse-Terre and Grande-Terre, separated by the Salt River, plus Marie Galante and the Saintes group to the S and, to the N, Desirade, St. Barthelemy, and over half of St. Martin (the Netherlands portion is St. Maarten). A French possession since 1635, the department is represented in the French Parliament by 2 senators and 3 deputies; administration consists of a prefect (governor) and an elected general and regional councils.

Area of the islands is 660 sq. mi.; pop. (1989 est.) 340,000, mainly descendants of slaves; capital is Basse-Terre on Basse-Terre Is. The land is fertile; sugar, rum, and bananas are exported; tourism is an important industry.

Martinique, the northernmost of the Windward Islands, in the West Indies, has been a possession since 1635, and a department since March, 1946. It is represented in the French Parliament by 2 senators and 3 deputies. The island was the birthplace of Napoleon's Empress Josephine.

It has an area of 425 sq. mi.; pop. (1988 est.) 336,000, mostly descendants of slaves. The capital is Fort-de-France (pop. 1988: 117,000). It is a popular tourist stop. The chief exports are rum, bananas, and petroleum products.

Mayotte, formerly part of Comoros, voted in 1976 to become an overseas department of France. An island NW of Madagascar, area is 144 sq. mi., pop. (1988 est.) 77,000.

Reunion is a volcanic island in the Indian O. about 420 mi. E of Madagascar, and has belonged to France since 1665. Area, 969 sq. mi.; pop. (1988 est.) 575,000, 30% of French extraction. Capital: Saint-Denis. The chief export is sugar. It elects 3 deputies, 2 senators to the French Parliament.

St. Pierre and Miquelon, formerly an Overseas Territory, made the transition to department status in 1976. It consists of 2 groups of rocky islands near the SW coast of Newfoundland, inhabited by fishermen. The exports are chiefly fish products. The St. Pierre group has an area of 10 sq. mi.; Miquelon, 83 sq. mi. Total pop. (1987 est.), 6,300. The capital is St. Pierre. A deputy and a senator are elected to the French Parliament.

Overseas Territories

French Polynesia Overseas Territory, comprises 130 islands widely scattered among 5 archipelagos in the South Pacific; administered by a governor. Territorial Assembly and a Council with headquarters at Papeete, Tahiti, one of the **Society Islands** (which include the **Windward** and **Leeward** islands). A deputy and a senator are elected to the French Parliament.

Other groups are the **Marquesas Islands**, the **Tuamotu Archipelago**, including the **Gambier Islands**, and the **Austral Islands**.

Total area of the islands administered from Tahiti is 1,544 sq. mi.; pop. (1987 est.), 185,000, more than half on Tahiti. Tahiti is picturesque and mountainous with a productive coastline bearing coconut, banana and orange trees, sugar cane and vanilla.

Tahiti was visited by Capt. James Cook in 1769 and by Capt. Bligh in the Bounty, 1788-89. Its beauty impressed Herman Melville, Paul Gauguin, and Charles Darwin.

French Southern and Antarctic Lands Overseas Territory, comprises **Adelie Land**, on Antarctica, and 4 island groups in the Indian O. Adelie, discovered 1840, has a research station, a coastline of 185 mi. and tapers 1,240 mi. inland to the South Pole. The U.S. does not recognize national claims in Antarctica. There are 2 huge glaciers, Ninnis, 22 mi. wide, 99 mi. long, and Mentz, 11 mi. wide, 140 mi. long. The Indian O. groups are:

Kerguelen Archipelago, discovered 1772, one large and 300 small islands. The chief is 87 mi. long, 74 mi. wide, and has Mt.

Ross, 6,429 ft. tall. Principal research station is Port-aux-Francais. Seals often weigh 2 tons; there are blue whales, coal, peat, semi-precious stones. **Crozet Archipelago**, discovered 1772, covers 195 sq. mi. Eastern Island rises to 6,560 ft. **Saint Paul**, in southern Indian O., has warm springs with earth at places heating to 120° to 390° F. **Amsterdam** is nearby; both produce cod and rock lobster.

New Caledonia and its dependencies, an overseas territory, are a group of islands in the Pacific O. about 1,115 mi. E of Australia and approx. the same distance NW of New Zealand. Dependencies are the **Loyalty Islands**, the **Isle of Pines, Huon Islands** and the **Chesterfield Islands.**

New Caledonia, the largest, has 6,530 sq. mi. Total area of the territory is 8,548 sq. mi.; population (1988 est.) 156,000. The group was acquired by France in 1853.

The territory is administered by a governor and government council. There is a popularly elected Territorial Assembly. A deputy and a senator are elected to the French Parliament. Capital: Noumea.

Mining is the chief industry. New Caledonia is one of the world's largest nickel producers. Other minerals found are chrome, iron, cobalt, manganese, silver, gold, lead, and copper. Agricultural products include coffee, copra, cotton, manioc (cassava), corn, tobacco, bananas and pineapples.

In 1987, New Caledonian voters chose by referendum to remain within the French Republic. There were clashes between French and Melanesians (Kanaks) in 1988.

Wallis and Futuna Islands, 2 archipelagos raised to status of overseas territory July 29, 1961, are in the SW Pacific S of the Equator between Fiji and Samoa. The islands have a total area of 106 sq. mi. and population (1987 est.) of 14,800. **Alofi**, attached to Futuna, is uninhabited. Capital: Mata-Utu. Chief products are copra, yams, taro roots, bananas. A senator and a deputy are elected to the French Parliament.

Gabon
Gabonese Republic
République Gabonaise

People: Population (1990 est.): 1,069,000. **Pop. density:** 11 per sq. mi. **Urban** (1985): 40%. **Ethnic groups:** Fangs 25%, Bapounon 10%, others. **Languages:** French (official), Bantu dialects. **Religions:** Tribal beliefs, Christian minority.

Geography: Area: 103,346 sq. mi., the size of Colorado. **Location:** On Atlantic coast of central Africa. **Neighbors:** Equatorial Guinea, Cameroon on N, Congo on E, S. **Topography:** Heavily forested, the country consists of coastal lowlands plateaus in N, E, and S, mountains in N, SE, and center. The Ogooue R. system covers most of Gabon. **Capital:** Libreville. **Cities** (1987 est.): Libreville 352,000.

Government: Type: Republic. **Head of state:** Pres. Omar Bongo; b. Dec. 30, 1935; in office: Dec. 2, 1967. **Head of government:** Prime Min. Leon Mebiame, b. Sept. 1, 1934; in office: Apr. 16, 1975. **Local divisions:** 9 provinces. **Defense:** 4.8% of GNP (1987).

Economy: Industries: Oil products. **Chief crops:** Cocoa, coffee, rice, peanuts, palm products, cassava, bananas. **Minerals:** Manganese, uranium, oil, iron, gas. **Crude oil reserves** (1985): 623 mln. bbls. **Other resources:** Timber. **Arable land:** 2%. **Electricity prod.** (1986): 981 mln. kwh. **Labor force:** 65% agric.; 30% ind. & comm.

Finance: Currency: CFA franc (Mar. 1990: 284 = $1 US). **Gross national product** (1987) $2.8 bln. **Per capita GNP** (1987): $2,890. **Imports** (1988): $930 mln.; partners: Fr. 51%, U.S. 14%. **Exports** (1987): $1.7 bln.; partners: Fr. 26%, U.S. 25%. **Tourists receipts** (1987): $5 mln. **National budget** (1987): $1.2 bln. **International reserves less gold** (Jan. 1990): $1.7 mln. **Gold:** 13,000 oz t. **Consumer prices** (change in 1987): −.09%.

Transport: Motor vehicles: in use (1985): 16,000 passenger cars, 10,000 comm. vehicles. **Civil aviation** (1986): 417 mln. passengers -km. **Chief ports** Port-Gentil, Owendo, Mayumba.

Communications: Television sets: 1 per 33 persons. **Radios:** 1 per 12 persons. **Telephones:** 1 per 81 persons.

Health: Life expectancy at birth (1985): 48.0 male; 51.4 female. **Births** (per 1,000 pop. 1989): 28. **Deaths** (per 1,000 pop. 1989): 15. **Natural increase:** 1.4%. **Hospital beds** (1985):

4,617. **Physicians** (1985): 265. **Infant mortality** (per 1,000 live births 1989): 108.

Education (1988): **Literacy:** 70%. Compulsory to age 16; attendance: 100% primary, 14% secondary.

Major International Organizations: UN (World Bank), OAU, OPEC.

Embassy: 2034 20th St NW 20009; 797-1000.

France established control over the region in the second half of the 19th century. Gabon became independent Aug. 17, 1960. It is one of the most prosperous black African countries, thanks to abundant natural resources, foreign private investment, and government development programs.

The Gambia
Republic of The Gambia

People: Population (1990 est.): 820,000. **Age distrib. (%):** 0–14: 45.9; 15–59: 54.4; 60+: 3.8. **Pop. density:** 192 per sq. mi. **Urban** (1985): 21%. **Ethnic groups:** Mandinka 42%, Fula 16%, Wolof 16%, others. **Languages:** English (official), Mandinka, Wolof. **Religions:** Moslem 90%.

Geography: Area: 4,361 sq. mi., smaller than Connecticut. **Location:** On Atlantic coast near western tip of Africa. **Neighbors:** Surrounded on 3 sides by Senegal. **Topography:** A narrow strip of land on each side of the lower Gambia. **Capital:** Banjul. **Cities** (1986 est.): Banjul 40,000.

Government: Type: Republic. **Head of state:** Pres. Dawda Kairaba Jawara; b. May 16, 1924; in office: Apr. 24, 1970 (prime min. from June 12, 1962). **Local divisions:** 5 divisions and Banjul.

Economy: Industries: Tourism. **Chief crops:** Peanuts (main export), rice. **Arable land:** 16%. **Fish catch** (1988): 14,000 metric tons. **Electricity prod.** (1988): 63 mln. kwh. **Labor force:** 75% agric.; 18% ind. & comm.

Finance: Currency: Dalasi (Mar. 1990: 8.33 = $1.00 US). **Gross national product** (1988): $145 mln. **Per capita income** (1985): $255. **Imports** (1987): $127 mln.; partners: EEC 53%. **Exports** (1987): $40 mln.; partners: EEC 45%. **Tourists** (1987): 36,000. **National budget** (1985): $57 mln. expenditures. **International reserves less gold** (Mar. 1988): $15.5 mln. **Consumer prices** (change in 1989): 8.3%.

Transport: Motor vehicles: in use (1986): 5,200 passenger cars, 720 comm. vehicles. **Chief ports:** Banjul.

Communications: Radios: 1 per 6.1 persons. **Telephones:** 1 per 216 persons.

Health: Life expectancy at birth (1989): 39 male; 44 female. **Births** (per 1,000 pop. 1989): 48. **Deaths** (per 1,000 pop. 1989): 23. **Natural increase:** 2.5%. **Hospital beds** (1980): 635. **Physicians** (1980): 65. **Infant mortality** (per 100,000 live births 1989): 172.

Education (1989): **Literacy:** 12%.

Major International Organizations: UN (GATT, IMF, WHO), OAU.

Embassy: 19 E. 42 St., New York, NY 10017.

The tribes of Gambia were at one time associated with the West African empires of Ghana, Mali, and Songhay. The area became Britain's first African possession in 1588.

Independence came Feb. 18, 1965; republic status within the Commonwealth was achieved in 1970. Gambia is one of the only functioning democracies in Africa. The country suffered from severe famine in 1977-78.

Gambia has a treaty with Senegal to form a confederation of the 2 countries under the name of Senegambia. However, each country will retain its sovereignty.

Germany

Now comprises 2 nations: **Federal Republic of Germany (West Germany), German Democratic Republic (East Germany).**

Germany, prior to World War II, was a central European nation composed of numerous states which had a common language and traditions and which had been united in one country since 1871; since World War II it has been split in 2 parts.

History and government. Germanic tribes were defeated by Julius Caesar, 55 and 53 BC, but Roman expansion N of the Rhine was stopped in 9 AD. Charlemagne, ruler of the Franks,

consolidated Saxon, Bavarian, Rhenish, Frankish, and other lands; after him the eastern part became the German Empire. The Thirty Years' War, 1618-1648, split Germany into small principalities and kingdoms. After Napoleon, Austria contended with Prussia for dominance, but lost the Seven Weeks' War to Prussia, 1866. Otto von Bismarck, Prussian chancellor, formed the North German Confederation, 1867.

In 1870 Bismarck maneuvered Napoleon III into declaring war. After the quick defeat of France, Bismarck formed the **German Empire** and on Jan. 18, 1871, in Versailles, proclaimed King Wilhelm I of Prussia German emperor (Deutscher kaiser).

The German Empire reached its peak before World War I in 1914, with 208,780 sq. mi., plus a colonial empire. After that war Germany ceded Alsace-Lorraine to France; West Prussia and Posen (Poznan) province to Poland; part of Schleswig to Denmark; lost all of its colonies and the ports of Memel and Danzig.

Republic of Germany, 1919-1933, adopted the Weimar constitution; met reparation payments and elected Friedrich Ebert and Gen. Paul von Hindenburg presidents.

Third Reich, 1933-1945, Adolf Hitler led the National Socialist German Workers' (Nazi) party after World War I. In 1923 he attempted to unseat the Bavarian government and was imprisoned. Pres. von Hindenburg named Hitler chancellor Jan. 30, 1933; on Aug. 3, 1934, the day after Hindenburg's death, the cabinet joined the offices of president and chancellor and made Hitler fuehrer (leader). Hitler abolished freedom of speech and assembly, and began a long series of persecutions climaxed by the murder of millions of Jews and opponents.

Hitler repudiated the Versailles treaty and reparations agreements. He remilitarized the Rhineland 1936 and annexed Austria (Anschluss, 1938). At Munich he made an agreement with Neville Chamberlain, British prime minister, which permitted Hitler to annex part of Czechoslovakia. He signed a non-aggression treaty with the USSR, 1939. He declared war on Poland Sept. 1, 1939, precipitating World War II.

With total defeat near, Hitler committed suicide in Berlin Apr. 1945. The victorious Allies voided all acts and annexations of Hitler's Reich.

Postwar changes. The zones of occupation administered by the Allied Powers and later relinquished gave the USSR Saxony, Saxony-Anhalt, Thuringia, and Mecklenburg, and the former Prussian provinces of Saxony and Brandenburg.

The territory E of the Oder-Neisse line within 1937 boundaries comprising the provinces of Silesia, Pomerania, and the southern part of East Prussia, totaling about 41,220 sq. mi., was taken by Poland. Northern East Prussia was taken by the USSR.

The Western Allies ended the state of war with Germany in 1951. The USSR did so in 1955.

There was also created the area of Greater Berlin, within but not part of the Soviet zone, administered by the 4 occupying powers under the Allied Command. In 1948 the USSR withdrew, established its single command in East Berlin, and cut off supplies. The Allies utilized a gigantic airlift to bring food to West Berlin, 1948-1949. In Aug. 1961 the East Germans built a wall dividing Berlin, after over 3 million E. Germans had emigrated.

On Nov. 9, 1989 the E. German government announced the decision to open the border with the West signaling the end of the infamous Berlin Wall.

A New Era: A communism was being rejected in E. Germany, talks began concerning German reunification. At a meeting in Ottawa, Feb. 1990, the foreign ministers of the World War II "Big Four" Allied nations—U.S., USSR, UK, and France—as well as the foreign ministers of E. Germany and W. Germany reached agreement on a format for high-level talks on German reunification.

In May, NATO ministers adopted a package of proposals on reunification including the inclusion of the united Germany as a full member of NATO, and the barring of the new Germany from having its own nuclear, chemical, or biological weapons. In July, the USSR agreed to conditions that would allow Germany to become a member of NATO.

The 2 nations agreed to monetary unification under the W. German mark beginning in July. The merger of the 2 Germanys was to take place on Oct. 3, 1990, and the first all-German elections since 1933 were scheduled for Dec. 2. (*See Chronology and Index for details.*)

East Germany

People: Population (1990 est.): 16,578,000. **Age distrib. (%):** 0–14: 19.2; 15–59: 61.5; 60+: 19.3. **Pop. density:** 400 per sq. mi. **Urban** (1988): 76.6%. **Ethnic groups:** German 99%. **Languages:** German. **Religions:** Protestant 47%, Roman Catholic 7%; none 45%.

Geography: Area: 41,768 sq. mi., the size of Virginia. **Location:** In E. Central Europe. **Neighbors:** W. Germany on W, Czechoslovakia on S, Poland on E. **Topography:** E. Germany lies mostly on the North German plains, with lakes in N, Harz Mtns., Elbe Valley, and sandy soil of Bradenburg in center, and highlands in S. **Capital:** East Berlin. **Cities** (1988 est.): East Berlin 1,260,000; Leipzig 549,000; Dresden 521,000.

Government: Type: In transition. **Head of state:** Pres. Manfred Gerlach; in office: Dec. 6, 1989. **Head of government:** Prime Min. Lothar de Maiziere; b. Mar. 2, 1940; in office: Mar. 18, 1990. **Local divisions:** 14 districts. **Defense:** 7.3% of GNP (1987).

Economy: Industries: Steel, chemicals, electrical prods., textiles, machinery. **Chief crops:** Grains, potatoes, sugarbeets. **Minerals:** Potash, lignite, uranium, coal. **Arable land:** 47%. **Livestock** (1987): cattle: 5.8 mln.; pigs: 12.9 mln.; sheep: 2.5 mln. **Fish catch** (1988): 193,000 metric tons. **Electricity prod.** (1988): 118 bln. kwh. **Crude steel prod.** (1988): 8.2 mln metric tons. **Labor force:** 10% agric.; 42.5% ind. & construction.

Finance: Currency: Mark (July 1990: 1.67 = $1 US). **Gross national product** (1988): $207.2 bln. **Per capita income** (1987): $10,000. **Imports:** (1987): $31 bln.; partners: USSR, E. Europe. **Exports** (1987): $30 bln.; partners: USSR, E. Europe. **Tourists** (1986): 1 mln. **National budget** (1986): $123 bln.

Transport: Railway traffic (1987): 22.4 bln. passenger-km. **Motor vehicles:** in use (1987): 3.6 mln. passenger cars, 435,000 comm. vehicles. **Civil aviation** (1987): 2.8 bln. passenger-km; 4 airports with scheduled flights. **Chief ports:** Rostack, Wismar, Stralsund.

Communications: Television sets: 1 per 2.7 persons. **Radios:** 1 per 2.5 persons. **Telephones:** 1 per 4.3 persons. **Daily newspaper circ.** (1986): 559 per 1,000 pop.

Health: Life expectancy at birth (1989): 70 male; 76 female. **Births** (per 1,000 pop. 1989): 13. **Deaths** (per 1,000 pop. 1989): 13. **Natural increase:** 0.0%. **Hospital beds:** 1 per 99 persons. **Physicians:** 1 per 411 persons. **Infant mortality** (per 1,000 live births 1989): 10.

Education (1989): **Literacy:** 99%. **Years compulsory:** 10.

Major International Organizations: UN (IMF, GATT), Warsaw Pact.

Embassy: 1717 Massachusetts Ave. NW 20036; 232-3134.

The German Democratic Republic was proclaimed in the Soviet sector of Berlin Oct. 7, 1949. It was proclaimed fully sovereign in 1954, but Soviet troops remain on grounds of security and the 4-power Potsdam agreement.

Coincident with the entrance of W. Germany into the European Defense community in 1952, the East German government decreed a prohibited zone 3 miles deep along its 600-mile border with W. Germany and cut Berlin's telephone system in two. Berlin was further divided by erection of a fortified wall in 1961, but the exodus of refugees to the West continued, though on a smaller scale.

E. Germany suffered severe economic problems until the mid-1960s. A "new economic system" was introduced, easing the former central planning controls and allowing factories to make profits provided they were reinvested in operations or redistributed to workers as bonuses. By the early 1970s, the economy was highly industrialized. In May 1972 the few remaining private firms were ordered sold to the government. The nation was credited with the highest standard of living among Warsaw Pact countries. But growth slowed in the late 1970s, due to shortages of natural resources and labor, and a huge debt to lenders in the West. Comparison with the lifestyle in the West caused many of the young to leave the country; some 40,000 in 1988.

The government firmly resisted following the USSR's policy of *glasnost*, but by Oct. 1989, was faced with nationwide demonstrations demanding reform. Pres. Erich Honecker, in office since 1976, was forced to resign, Oct. 18. On Nov. 4, the border with Czechoslovakia was opened and permission granted for refugees to travel on to the West, On Nov. 9, the decision was made to open the border with the West, signaling the end of the "Berlin Wall," which separated the 2 Germanys and was the supreme emblem of the cold war. On the first weekend after the wall was opened, 3 million E. Germans crossed to visit the West.

On Aug. 23, 1990, the E. German Parliament agreed to formal unification with W. Germany to take place on Oct. 3. The first

all-German elections since 1933 were scheduled for Dec. 2. (*See Chronology and Index for details.*)

West Germany
Federal Republic of Germany
Bundesrepublik Deutschland

People: Population (1990 est.): 60,977,000. **Age distrib.** (%): 0–14: 14.7; 15–59: 64.7; 60+: 20.6. **Pop. density:** 626 per sq. mi. **Urban** (1985): 86% **Ethnic groups:** German 93%. **Languages:** German. **Religions:** Protestant 44%, Roman Catholic 47%.

Geography: Area: 95,826 sq. mi. (incl. W. Berlin), the size of Wyoming. **Location:** In central Europe. **Neighbors:** Denmark on N, Netherlands, Belgium, Luxembourg, France on W, Switzerland, Austria on S, Czechoslovakia, E. Germany on E. **Topography:** West Germany is flat in N, hilly in center and W, and mountainous in Bavaria. Chief rivers are Elbe, Weser, Ems, Rhine, and Main, all flowing toward North Sea, and Danube, flowing toward Black Sea. **Capital:** Bonn. **Cities** (1989 est.): Berlin 1.8 mln.; Hamburg 1.6 mln.; Munich 1.3 mln.; Cologne 919,000; Essen 622,000; Frankfurt 598,000; Dortmund 575,000; Dusseldorf 593,000; Stuttgart 561,000.

Government: Type: Federal republic. **Head of state:** Pres. Richard von Weizsacker; b. Apr. 15, 1920; in office: May 23, 1984. **Head of government:** Chan. Helmut Kohl; b. Apr. 3, 1930; in office: Oct. 1, 1982. **Local divisions:** West Berlin and 10 laender (states) with substantial powers. **Defense:** 3.2% of GNP (1989).

Economy: Industries: Steel, ships, vechicles, machinery, coal, chemicals. **Chief crops:** Grains, potatoes, sugar beets. **Minerals:** Coal, potash, lignite, iron. **Crude oil reserves** (1985): 289 mln. bbls. **Arable land:** 30%. **Livestock** (1987): cattle: 14.8 mln.; pigs: 24.3 mln.; sheep: 1.2 mln. **Fish catch** (1987): 159,000 metric tons. **Electricity prod.** (1988): 439 bln. kwh. **Crude steel prod.** (1988): 41.0 mln. metric tons. **Labor force:** 5% agric.; 40% ind. & comm.; 54% services.

Finance: Currency: Mark (July 1990: 1.67 = $1 US). **Gross national product** (1988): $1,208 bln. **Per capita income** (1988): $19,750. **Imports** (1988): $250 bln.; partners: EC 52%; other European 16%. **Exports** (1988): $323 bln.; partners: EC 55%; other European 19%. **Tourists** (1988): receipts $15 bln. **National budget** (1989): $153 bln. **International reserves less gold** (Mar. 1990): $61 bln. **Gold:** 95.18 mln. oz t. **Consumer prices** (change in 1989): 2.8%.

Transport: Railway traffic (1988): 44 bln. passenger-km. **Motor vehicles:** in use (1988): 28.8 mln. passenger cars, 1.3 mln. comm. **Civil aviation** (1988): 34.0 bln. passenger-km; 27 airports with scheduled flights. **Chief ports:** Hamburg, Bremen, Lubeck.

Communications: Television sets: 1 per 2.6 persons. **Radios:** 1 per 2.3 persons. **Telephones:** 1 per 1.5 persons. **Daily newspaper circ.** (1987): 417 per 1,000 pop.

Health: Life expectancy at birth (1989): 71.5 male; 78.1 female. **Births** (per 1,000 pop. 1989): 11. **Deaths** (per 1,000 pop. 1989): 12. **Natural increase:** −.1%. **Hospital beds:** 1 per 91 persons. **Physicians:** 1 per 357 persons. **Infant mortality** (per 1,000 live births 1988): 8.3.

Education (1989): **Literacy:** 99%. **Years compulsory:** 10; attendance 100%.

Major International Organizations: UN and all of its specialized agencies, EC, OECD, NATO.

Embassy: 4645 Reservoir Rd. NW 20007; 298-4000.

The Federal Republic of Germany was proclaimed May 23, 1949, in Bonn, after a constitution had been drawn up by a consultative assembly formed by representatives of the 11 laender (states) in the French, British, and American zones. Later reorganized into 9 units, the laender numbered 10 with the addition of the Saar, 1957. Berlin also was granted land (state) status, but the 1945 occupation agreements placed restrictions on it.

The occupying powers, the U.S., Britain, and France, restored the civil status, Sept. 21, 1949. The U. S. resumed diplomatic relations July 2, 1951. The powers lifted controls and the republic became fully independent May 5, 1955.

Dr. Konrad Adenauer, Christian Democrat, was made chancellor Sept. 15, 1949, re-elected 1953, 1957, 1961. Willy Brandt, heading a coalition of Social Democrats and Free Democrats, became chancellor Oct. 21, 1969.

In 1970 Brandt signed friendship treaties with the USSR and Poland. In 1971, the U.S., Britain, France, and the USSR signed an agreement on Western access to West Berlin. In 1972 the Bundestag approved the USSR and Polish treaties and East and West Germany signed their first formal treaty, implementing the agreement easing access to West Berlin. In 1973 a West Germany-Czechoslovakia pact normalized relations and nullified the 1938 "Munich Agreement."

In May 1974 Brandt resigned, saying he took full responsibility for "negligence" for allowing an East German spy to become a member of his staff.

West Germany has experienced economic growth since the 1950s. The country leads Europe in provisions for worker participation in the management of industry.

The NATO decision to deploy medium-range nuclear missiles in Western Europe sparked a demonstration by some 400,000 protesters in 1983. In 1989, Chancellor Kohl's call for early negotiations with the Soviets on reducing short-range missiles caused a rift with the NATO allies, especially the U.S. and Great Britain.

In 1989, the changes in the E. German government and the opening of the Berlin Wall sparked talk of reunification of the 2 Germanys. In 1990, under the leadership of Chancellor Kohl, W. Germany moved rapidly to reunite with E. Germany.

On Aug. 23, 1990, the E. German Parliament agreed to formal unification with W. Germany to take place on Oct. 3, 1990. The first all-German elections since 1933 were scheduled for Dec. 2. (*See Chronology and Index for details.*)

Helgoland, an island of 130 acres in the North Sea, was taken from Denmark by a British Naval Force in 1807 and later ceded to Germany to become a part of Schleswig-Holstein province in return for rights in East Africa. The heavily fortified island was surrendered to UK, May 22, 1945, demilitarized in 1947, and returned to W. Germany, Mar 1, 1952. It is a free port.

Ghana
Republic of Ghana

People: Population (1990 est.): 15,310,000. **Age distrib. (%):** 0–14: 46.6; 15-59: 48.9; 60+: 4.5. **Pop. density:** 160 per sq. mi. **Urban** (1984): 31%. **Ethnic groups:** Akan 44%, Moshi-Dagomba 16%, Ewe 13%, Ga 8%, others. **Languages:** English (official), 50 tribal languages. **Religions:** Christian 52%, traditional beliefs 30%, Moslem 13%.

Geography: Area: 92,098 sq. mi., slightly smaller than Oregon. **Location:** On southern coast of W. Africa. **Neighbors:** Ivory Coast on W, Burkina Faso on N, Togo on E. **Topography:** Most of Ghana consists of low fertile plains and scrubland, cut by rivers and by the artificial Lake Volta. **Capital:** Accra. **Cities** (1988 est.): Accra 949,000.

Government: Type: Military. **Head of government:** Pres. Jerry Rawlings; b. 1947; in office: Dec. 31, 1981. **Local divisions:** 9 regions.

Economy: Industries: Aluminum, light industry. **Chief crops:** Cocoa (70% of exports), coffee. **Minerals:** Gold, manganese, industrial diamonds, bauxite. **Crude oil reserves:** (1980): 7 mln. bbls. **Other resources:** Timber, rubber. **Arable land:** 12%. **Livestock** (1987): Cattle: 1.4 mln.; sheep: 1.9 mln. **Fish catch** (1987): 324,000 metric tons. **Electricity prod.** (1988): 4.1 bln. kwh. **Labor force:** 55% agric.; 19% ind.

Finance: Currency: Cedi (Mar. 1990: 313 = $1.00 US). **Gross national product** (1987): $5.3 bln. **Per capita GNP** (1987): $390. **Imports** (1987): $988 mln.; partners: UK 18%, W. Ger. 12%, Nigeria 12%. **Exports** (1987): $977 mln.; partners: UK 16%, U.S. 16%, Neth. 9%, W. Ger. 9%. **International reserves less gold** (Mar. 1990): 347 mln. **Gold:** 217,000 oz t. **Consumer prices** (change in 1988): 31.4%.

Transport: Railway traffic (1988): 389 mln. passenger-km. **Motor vehicles:** in use (1986): 26,000 passenger cars, 28,000 comm. vehicles. **Civil aviation** (1986): 298 mln. passenger-km; 4 airports with scheduled flights. **Chief ports:** Tema, Takoradi.

Communications: Television sets: 1 per 77 persons. **Radios:** 1 per 4.7 persons. **Telephones:** 1 per 179 persons.

Health: Life expectancy at birth (1989): 57 male; 62 female. **Births** (per 1,000 pop. 1989): 46. **Deaths** (per 1,000 pop. 1989): 13. **Natural increase:** 3.3%. **Physicians:** 1 per 6,640 persons. **Infant mortality** (per 1,000 live births 1989): 68.

Education (1983): **Literacy:** 30%.

Major International Organizations: UN and all of its specialized agencies, OAU.

Embassy: 2460 16th St. NW 20009; 462-0761.

Named for an African empire along the Niger River, 400-1240 AD, Ghana was ruled by Britain for 113 years as the Gold Coast. The UN in 1956 approved merger with the British Togoland trust territory. Independence came March 6, 1957. Republic status within the Commonwealth was attained in 1960.

Pres. Kwame Nkrumah built hospitals and schools, promoted development projects like the Volta R. hydroelectric and aluminum plants, but ran the country into debt, jailed opponents, and was accused of corruption. A 1964 referendum gave Nkrumah dictatorial powers and set up a one-party socialist state.

Nkrumah was overthrown in 1966 by a police-army coup, which expelled Chinese and East German teachers and technicians. Elections were held in 1969, but 4 further coups occurred in 1972, 1978, 1979, and 1981. The 1979 and 1981 coups were led by Flight Lieut. Jerry Rawlings.

Greece
Hellenic Republic
Elliniki Dimokratia

People: Population (1990 est.): 10,066,000. **Age distrib. (%):** 0–14: 20.5; 15-59: 61.1; 60+: 20.4. **Pop. density:** 196 per sq. mi. **Urban** (1985): 58.0%. **Ethnic groups:** Greeks 98.5%. **Languages:** Greek, others. **Religions:** Greek Orthodox 97%.

Geography: Area: 51,146 sq. mi., the size of Alabama. **Location:** Occupies southern end of Balkan Peninsula in SE Europe. **Neighbors:** Albania, Yugoslavia, Bulgaria on N, Turkey on E. **Topography:** About 75% of Greece is non-arable, with mountains in all areas. Pindus Mts. run through the country N to S. The heavily indented coastline is 9,385 mi. long. Of over 2,000 islands, only 169 are inhabited, among them Crete, Rhodes, Milos, Kerkira (Corfu), Chios, Lesbos, Samos, Euboea, Delos, Mykonos. **Capital:** Athens. **Cities** (1981 est.): Athens (met.) 3,016,457; Thessaloniki (met.) 800,000; Patras 120,000.

Government: Type: Presidential parliamentary republic. **Head of state:** Pres. Constantine Karamanlis; in office: May, 1990. **Head of government:** Prime Min. Constantine Mitsotakis; b. Oct. 18, 1918, in office: Apr. 11, 1990. **Local divisions:** 51 prefectures. **Defense:** 6.2% of GNP (1987).

Economy: Industries: Textiles, chemicals, metals, wine, food processng, cement. **Chief crops:** Grains, corn, rice, cotton, tobacco, olives, citrus fruits, raisins, figs. **Minerals:** Bauxite, lignite, oil, manganese. **Crude oil reserves** (1985): 35 mln. bbls. **Arable land:** 23%. **Livestock** (1987): sheep: 11.0 mln.; goats: 5.6 mln. **Fish catch** (1988): 135,000 metric tons. **Electricity prod.** (1988): 33.1 bln. kwh. **Crude steel prod.** (1988): 970,000 metric tons. **Labor force:** 28% agric.; 29% ind., 42% service.

Finance: Currency: Drachma (June 1990: 161.00 = $1 US). **Gross national product** (1987): $43.5 bln. **Per capita GNP** (1987): $4,350. **Imports** (1988): $12.3 bln.; partners: W. Ger. 22%, It. 12%, Fr. 7%. **Exports** (1988): $5.4 bln.; partners: W. Ger. 25%, It. 18%, U.S. 8%. **Tourists** (1987): $2.1 bln. receipts. **National budget** (1987): $20.2 bln. expenditures. **International reserves less gold** (Mar. 1990): $2.4 bln. **Gold:** 3.3 mln. oz t. **Consumer prices** (change in 1989): 13.7%.

Transport: Railway traffic (1987): 1.9 bln. passenger-km. **Motor vehicles:** in use (1988): 1.4 mln. passenger cars, 680,000 comm. vehicles. **Civil aviation** (1987): 7.1 bln. passenger-km; 29 airports with scheduled flights. **Chief ports:** Piraeus, Thessaloniki, Patrai.

Communications: Television sets: 1 per 5.7 persons. **Radios:** 1 per 2.4 persons. **Telephones:** 1 per 2.4 persons. **Daily newspaper circ.** (1986): 88 per 1,000 pop.

Health: Life expectancy at birth (1989): 75 male; 80 female. **Births** (per 1,000 pop. 1989): 12. **Deaths** (per 1,000 pop. 1989): 9. **Natural increase:** .2%. **Hospital beds:** 1 per 193 persons. **Physicians:** 1 per 341 persons. **Infant mortality** (per 1,000 live birth 1989): 11.

Education (1989): **Literacy:** men 96%, women 89%. **Years compulsory:** 9.

Major International Organizations: UN (GATT, IMF, WHO, ILO), EC, NATO, OECD.

Embassy: 2221 Massachusetts Ave. NW 20008; 667-3168.

The achievements of ancient Greece in art, architecture, science, mathematics, philosophy, drama, literature, and democracy became legacies for succeeding ages. Greece reached the height of its glory and power, particularly in the Athenian city-state, in the 5th century BC.

Greece fell under Roman rule in the 2d and 1st centuries BC. In the 4th century AD it became part of the Byzantine Empire and, after the fall of Constantinople to the Turks in 1453, part of the Ottoman Empire.

Greece won its war of independence from Turkey 1821-1829, and became a kingdom. A republic was established 1924; the monarchy was restored, 1935, and George II, King of the Hellenes, resumed the throne. In Oct., 1940, Greece rejected an ultimatum from Italy. Nazi support resulted in its defeat and occupation by Germans, Italians, and Bulgarians. By the end of 1944 the invaders withdrew. Communist resistance forces were defeated by Royalist and British troops. A plebiscite recalled King George II. He died Apr. 1, 1947, was succeeded by his brother, Paul I.

Communists waged guerrilla war 1947-49 against the government but were defeated with the aid of the U.S.

A period of reconstruction and rapid development followed, mainly with conservative governments under Premier Constantine Karamanlis. The Center Union led by George Papandreou won elections in 1963 and 1964. King Constantine, who acceded in 1964, forced Papandreou to resign. A period of political maneuvers ended in the military takeover of April 21, 1967, by Col. George Papadopoulos. King Constantine tried to reverse the consolidation of the harsh dictatorship Dec. 13, 1967, but failed and fled to Italy. Papadopoulos was ousted Nov. 25, 1973.

Greek army officers serving in the National Guard of Cyprus staged a coup on the island July 15, 1974. Turkey invaded Cyprus a week later, precipitating the collapse of the Greek junta, which was implicated in the Cyprus coup.

The military turned the government over to Karamanlis, who named a civilian cabinet, freed political prisoners, and sought to solve the Cyprus crisis. In Nov. 1974 elections his party won a large parliamentary majority, reduced by socialist gains in 1977. A Dec. 1974 referendum resulted in the proclamation of a republic.

Greece was reintegrated into the military wing of NATO in October 1980, and it became the 10th full member of the European Community on Jan. 1, 1981.

The 1981 victory of the Panhellenic Socialist Movement (Pasok) of Andreas Papandreou has brought about substantial changes in the internal and external policies that Greece has pursued for the past 5 decades. Greece has been victimized in the 1980s by incidents of international terrorism.

A scandal centered on George Kostokas, a banker and publisher, led to the arrest or investigation of about a dozen leading Socialists, implicated Papandreou, and led to the defeat of the Socialists at the polls in 1989.

Grenada
State of Grenada

People: Population (1990 est.): 84,000. **Pop. density:** 654 per sq. mi. **Ethnic groups:** Mostly African descent. **Languages:** English (official), French-African patois. **Religions:** Roman Catholic 64%, Anglican 22%.

Geography: Area: 133 sq. mi., twice the size of Washington, D.C. **Location:** 90 mi. N. of Venezuela. **Topography:** Main island is mountainous; country includes Carriacon and Petit Martinique islands. **Capital:** St. George's. **Cities** (1980 est.): St. George's 7,500.

Government: Type: Independent state. **Head of state:** Queen Elizabeth II, represented by Gov.-Gen. Paul Scoon, b. July 4, 1935; in office: Sept. 30, 1978. **Head of government:** Prime Minister: Nicholas Braithwaite; in office: Mar. 16, 1990. **Local divisions:** 6 parishes and one dependency.

Economy: Industries: Rum. **Chief crops:** Nutmegs, bananas, cocoa, mace. **Arable land:** 41%. **Electricity prod.** (1988): 24.00 mln. kwh. **Labor force:** 33% agric.; 31% services.

Finance: Currency: East Caribbean dollar (Apr. 1990: 2.70 = $1 US). **Gross national product** (1987): $118 mln. **Per capita GNP** (1987): $1,400. **Imports** (1987): $89 mln.; partners: UK 19%, Trin./Tob. 25%. U.S. 17%. **Exports** (1987): $32 mln.; partners: UK 35%, CARICOM countries 38%. **Tourists** (1988):

$28 mln. receipts. **National budget** (1987): $83.8 mln. expenditures. **International reserves less gold** (Jan. 1990): $17 mln.

Transport: Motor vehicles: in use (1981): 4,700 passenger cars, 1,000 comm. vehicles. **Chief ports:** Saint George's.

Communications: Radios: 1 per 2.4 persons. **Telephones:** 1 per 18 persons.

Health: Life expectancy at birth (1989): 69 male; 74 female. **Births** (per 1,000 pop. 1989): 37. **Deaths** (per 1,000 pop. 1989): 7. **Natural increase:** 2.9%. **Infant mortality** (per 1,000 live births 1989): 30.

Education (1989): **Literacy:** 95%; **Years compulsory:** 6. **Major International Organizations:** UN (IMF, WHO), OAS. **Embassy:** 1701 New Hampshire Ave. NW 20009; 265-2561.

Columbus sighted the island 1498. First European settlers were French, 1650. The island was held alternately by France and England until final British occupation, 1784. Grenada became fully independent Feb. 7, 1974 during a general strike. It is the smallest independent nation in the Western Hemisphere. The U.S. has criticized the government for following Soviet and Cuban policies.

On Oct. 14, 1983, a military coup ousted Prime Minister Maurice Bishop, who was put under house arrest, later freed by supporters, rearrested, and, finally, on Oct. 19, executed. U.S. forces, with a token force from 6 area nations, invaded Grenada, Oct. 25. Resistance from the Grenadian army and Cuban advisors was quickly overcome as most of the population welcomed the invading forces as liberators. U.S. troops left Grenada in June 1985.

Guatemala
Republic of Guatemala
República de Guatemala

People: Population (1990 est.): 9,340,000. **Age distrib. (%):** 0–14: 45.9; 15–59: 49.4; 60+: 4.7. **Pop. density:** 233 per sq. mi. **Urban** (1986): 33%. **Ethnic groups:** Maya 55%, Mestizos 44%. **Languages:** Spanish, Indian dialects. **Religions:** Mostly Roman Catholics.

Geography: Area: 42,042 sq. mi., the size of Tennessee. **Location:** in Central America. **Neighbors:** Mexico N, W; El Salvador on S, Honduras, Belize on E. **Topography:** The central highland and mountain areas are bordered by the narrow Pacific coast and the lowlands and fertile river valleys on the Caribbean. There are numerous volcanoes in S, more than half a dozen over 11,000 ft. **Capital:** Guatemala City. **Cities** (1988 est.): Guatemala City 1,800,000.

Government: Type: Republic. **Head of state:** Pres. Marco Vinicio Cerezo Arevalo; b. Dec. 26, 1942; in office: Jan. 14, 1986. **Local divisions:** Guatemala City and 22 departments. **Defense:** 2.2% of GNP (1986).

Economy: Industries: Prepared foods, tires, textiles. **Chief crops:** Coffee (one third of exports), sugar, bananas, cotton, corn. **Minerals:** Oil, nickel. **Crude oil reserves** (1985): 500 mln. bbls. **Other resources:** Rare woods, fish, chicle. **Arable land:** 16%. **Electricity prod.** (1987): 2.8 bln. kwh. **Labor force:** 57% agric.; 21% ind. & comm., 12% services.

Finance: Currency: Quetzal (Apr. 1990: 3.85 = $1 US). **Gross national product** (1987): $9.6 bln. **Per capita GNP** (1987): $810. **Imports** (1988): $1.5 bln.; partners: U.S. 40%, CACM 8%. **Exports** (1988): $1.0 bln.; partners: U.S. 50%, CACM 20%. **Tourism** (1987): $124 mln. **National budget** (1987): $1.0 bln. expenditures. **International reserves less gold** (Mar. 1990): $256 mln. **Gold:** 523,000 oz t. **Consumer prices** (change in 1988): 10.8%.

Transport: Motor vehicles: in use (1983): 188,000 passenger cars, 58,000 comm. vehicles. **Civil aviation** (1987) 164 mln. passenger-km; 3 airports with scheduled flights. **Chief ports:** Puerto Barrios, San Jose.

Communications: Television sets: 1 per 18 persons. **Radios:** 1 per 21 persons. **Telephones:** 1 per 63 persons. **Daily newspaper circ.** (1983): 30 per 1,000 pop.

Health: Life expectancy at birth (1989): 59 male; 63 female. **Births** (per 1,000 pop. 1989): 36. **Deaths** (per 1,000 pop. 1989): 9. **Natural increase:** 2.7% **Health: Physicians** (1984) 3,500. **Infant mortality** (per 1,000 live births 1989): 66.

Education (1989): **Literacy:** 48%. **Years compulsory:** 6; **Attendance:** 35%.

Major International Organizations: UN (IMF, World Bank), OAS.
Embassy: 2220 R St. NW 20008; 745-4952.

The old Mayan Indian empire flourished in what is today Guatemala for over 1,000 years before the Spanish.

Guatemala was a Spanish colony 1524-1821; briefly a part of Mexico and then of the U.S. of Central America, the republic was established in 1839.

Since 1945 when a liberal government was elected to replace the long-term dictatorship of Jorge Ubico, the country has seen a swing toward socialism, an armed revolt, renewed attempts at social reform, a military coup, and, in 1986, civilian rule. The Guerrilla Army of the Poor, an insurgent group founded 1975, led a military offensive by attacking army posts and succeeded in incorporating segments of the large Indian population in its struggle against the government.

Dissident army officers seized power, Mar. 23, 1982, denouncing the Mar. 7 Presidential election as fraudulent and pledging to restore "authentic democracy" to the nation. Political violence has caused some 200,000 Guatemalans to seek refuge in Mexico. A second military coup occurred Oct. 8, 1983. The nation returned to civilian rule in 1986. A military coup was thwarted May, 1989.

Guinea
Republic of Guinea
République de Guinée

People: Population (1990 est.): 7,269,000. **Pop. density:** 64 per sq. mi. **Urban** (1986): 26%. **Ethnic groups:** Foulah 40%, Malinké 25%, Soussous 10%, 15 other tribes. **Languages:** French (official), tribal languages. **Religions:** Moslem 85%, Christian 10%.

Geography: Area: 94,964 sq. mi., slightly smaller than Oregon. **Location:** On Atlantic coast of W. Africa. **Neighbors:** Guinea-Bissau, Senegal, Mali on N, Côte d'Ivoire on E, Liberia on S. **Topography:** A narrow coastal belt leads to the mountainous middle region, the source of the Gambia, Senegal, and Niger rivers. Upper Guinea, farther inland, is a cooler upland. The SE is forested. **Capital:** Conakry. **Cities** (1989 est.): Conakry 705,000; Labe 273,000; N'Zerekore 250,000; Kankan 278,000.

Government: Type: Republic under Military Committee For National Redressment. **Head of state:** Pres. Brig. Gen. Lansana Conte; b. 1944; in office: Apr. 5, 1984. **Local divisions:** 29 administrative regions. **Defense:** 3.2% of GNP (1985).

Economy: Chief crops: Bananas, pineapples, rice, corn, palm nuts, coffee, honey. **Minerals:** Bauxite, iron, diamonds. **Arable land:** 6%. **Electricity prod.** (1988) 243 mln. kwh. **Labor force:** 82% agric.; 9% ind. & comm.

Finance: Currency: Franc (Jan. 1990: 615 = $1 US). **Gross national product** (1988): $2.4 bln. **Per capita income** (1984): $305. **Imports** (1988): $509 mln.; partners: Fr. 31%, U.S. 6% It. 6%. **Exports** (1988): $553 mln.; partners: U.S. 18%, Fr. 13%, W. Ger. 12%, USSR 12%. **National budget** (1988): $417 mln.

Transport: Motor vehicles: in use (1982): 10,000 passenger cars, 10,000 comm. vehicles. **Chief ports:** Conakry.

Communications: Radios: 1 per 31 persons.

Health: Life expectancy at birth (1989): 40 male; 44 female. **Births** (per 1,000 pop. 1989): 48. **Deaths** (per 1,000 pop. 1989): 22. **Natural increase:** 2.5%. **Physicians:** 1 per 9,732 persons. **Infant mortality** (per 1,000 live births 1987): 176.

Education (1989): **Literacy:** 35% (in French). Years compulsory: 8; attendance: 36% primary, 15% secondary.

Major International Organizations: UN and most specialized agencies, OAU.

Embassy: 2112 Leroy Pl. NW 20008; 483-9420.

Part of the ancient West African empires, Guinea fell under French control 1849-98. Under Sekou Toure, it opted for full independence in 1958, and France withdrew all aid.

Toure turned to communist nations for support, and set up a militant one-party state. Western firms, as well as the Soviet government, have invested in Guinea's vast bauxite mines.

Thousands of opponents were jailed in the 1970s, in the aftermath of an unsuccessful Portuguese invasion. Many were tortured and killed.

The military took control of the government in a bloodless coup after the March 1984 death of Toure.

Guinea-Bissau
Republic of Guinea-Bissau
República da Guiné-Bissau

People: Population (1990 est.): 998,000. **Pop. density:** 66 per sq. mi. **Ethnic groups:** Balanta 27%, Fula 23%, Manjaca 11%, Mandinka 12%. **Languages:** Portuguese (official), Criolo, tribal languages. **Religion:** Traditional 65%, Moslem 30%, Christian 4%.

Geography: Area: 13,948 sq. mi. about the size of Connecticut and New Hampshire combined. **Location:** On Atlantic coast of W. Africa. **Neighbors:** Senegal on N, Guinea on E, S. **Topography:** A swampy coastal plain covers most of the country; to the east is a low savanna region. **Capital:** Bissau. **Cities** (1979): Bissau 109,500.

Government: Type: Republic. **Head of government:** Gen. Joao Bernardo Vieira; b. 1939; in office: Nov. 14,1980. **Local divisions:** 8 regions. **Defense:** 8.4% of GNP (1984).

Economy: Chief crops: Peanuts, cotton, rice. **Minerals:** Bauxite. **Arable land:** 10%. **Electricity prod.** (1986): 28 mln. kwh. **Labor force:** 90% agric.

Finance: Currency: Peso (Jan. 1990: 650 = $1 US). **Gross national product** (1987): $152 mln. **Per capita GNP** (1987): $170. **Imports** (1986): $63 mln.; partners: Port. 20%, It. 15%, Fr. 6%. **Exports** (1987): $16 mln.; partners: Port. 65%. **National Budget** (1987): $40 mln. expenditures.

Communications: Radios: 1 per 30 persons. **Daily newspaper circ.** (1988): 7 per 1,000 pop.

Health: Life expectancy at birth (1989): 44 male; 47 female. **Births** (per 1,000 pop. 1989): 43. **Deaths** (per 1,000 pop. 1989): 19. **Natural increase:** 2.4%. **Infant mortality** (per 1,000 live births 1989): 137.

Education (1989): Literacy 19%. **Years compulsory:** 4.
Major International Organizations: UN, OAU.

Embassy: 211 E 43d St., New York, NY 10017; (212) 611-3977.

Portuguese mariners explored the area in the mid-15th century; the slave trade flourished in the 17th and 18th centuries, and colonization began in the 19th.

Beginning in the 1960s, an independence movement waged a guerrilla war and formed a government in the interior that achieved international support. Full independence came Sept. 10, 1974, after the Portuguese regime was overthrown.

The November 1980 coup gave Joao Bernardo Vieira absolute power.

Guyana
Co-operative Republic of Guyana

People: Population (1990 est.): 765,000. **Age distrib. (%):** 0–14: 37.5; 5–59: 56.5; 60+: 6.0. **Pop. density:** 9.2 per sq. mi. **Urban** (1987): 32%. **Ethnic groups:** East Indians 51%, African 30%; mixed 14%. **Languages:** English (official), Amerindian dialects. **Religions:** Christian 46%, Hindu 37%; Moslem 9%.

Geography: Area: 83,000 sq. mi., the size of Idaho. **Location:** On N coast of S. America. **Neighbors:** Venezuela on W, Brazil on S, Suriname on E. **Topography:** Dense tropical forests cover much of the land, although a flat coastal area up to 40 mi. wide, where 90% of the population lives, provides rich alluvial soil for agriculture. A grassy savanna divides the 2 zones. **Capital:** Georgetown. **Cities** (1985 est.): Georgetown 170,000.

Government: Type: Republic within the Commonwealth of Nations. **Head of state:** President Hugh Desmond Hoyte; b. Mar. 9, 1929; in office: Aug. 6, 1985. **Head of Government:** Prime Min. Hamilton Green; in office: Aug. 6, 1985. **Local divisions:** 10 regions. **Defense:** 8.9% of GDP (1989).

Economy: Industries: Cigarettes, rum, clothing, furniture, drugs. **Chief crops:** Sugar, rice, citrus and other fruits. **Minerals:** Bauxite, diamonds. **Other resources:** Timber, shrimp. **Arable land:** 2%. **Electricity prod.** (1988): 530 bln. kwh. **Labor force:** 33% agric.; 45% ind. & comm.; 22% services.

Finance: Currency: Dollar (Mar. 1990: 33.00 = $1 US). **Gross national product** (1987): $344 mln. **Per capita income** (1987): $317. **Imports** (1986): $242 mln.; partners: U.S. 21%, CARICOM 33%. **Exports** (1986): $242 mln.; partners: UK 28%, U.S. 18%, CARICOM 17%. **National budget** (1987): $229.1

mln. **International reserves less gold** (Feb. 1990): $3.5 mln. **Consumer prices** (change in 1988): 39.9%.
Transport: Motor vehicles: in use (1985): 25,000 passenger cars, 7,000 comm. vehicles. **Chief ports:** Georgetown.
Communications: Radios: 1 per 2.5 persons. **Telephones:** 1 per 25 persons. **Daily newspaper circ.** (1988): 77 per 1,000 pop.
Health: Life expectancy at birth (1988): 64 male; 69 female. **Births** (per 1,000 pop. 1989): 25. **Deaths** (per 1,000 pop. 1989): 6. **Natural increase:** 1.8% **Hospital beds:** 1 per 206 persons. **Physicians:** 1 per 5,307 persons. **Infant mortality** (per 1,000 live births 1989): 49.
Education (1989): **Literacy:** 91%. **Years compulsory:** ages 5-14.
Major International Organizations: UN (GATT, ILO, IMF, World Bank), CARICOM, Commonwealth of Nations.
Embassy: 2490 Tracy Pl. NW 20008; 276-6900.

Guyana became a Dutch possession in the 17th century, but sovereignty passed to Britain in 1815. Indentured servants from India soon outnumbered African slaves. Ethnic tension has affected political life.
Guyana became independent May 26, 1966. A Venezuelan claim to the western half of Guyana was suspended in 1970 but renewed in 1982. The Suriname border is also disputed. The government has nationalized most of the economy which has remained severely depressed.
The Port Kaituma ambush of U.S. Rep. Leo J. Ryan and others investigating mistreatment of American followers of the Rev. Jim Jones' People's Temple cult, triggered a mass suicide-execution of 911 cultists in the Guyana jungle, Nov. 18, 1978.

Haiti

Republic of Haiti

Républiqe d'Haiti

People: Population (1990 est.): 6,409,000. **Age distrib.** (%): 4-14: 39.2; 15-59: 52.5; 60+: 8.3. **Pop. density:** 580 per sq. mi. **Urban** (1986): 29%. **Ethnic groups:** African descent 95%. **Languages:** French, Creole (both official). **Religions:** Roman Catholics 80%, Protestants 10%; Voodoo widely practiced.
Geography: Area: 10,714 sq. mi., the size of Maryland. **Location:** In West Indies, occupies western third of I. of Hispaniola. **Neighbors:** Dominican Republic on E, Cuba on W. **Topography:** About two-thirds of Haiti is mountainous. Much of the rest is semiarid. Coastal areas are warm and moist. **Capital:** Port-au-Prince. **Cities** (1987 est.): Port-au-Prince 472,000.
Government: Type: Republic. **Head of state:** Ertha Pascal-Trouillot; b. Aug. 13, 1943; in office: Mar. 13, 1990. **Local divisions:** 9 departments. **Defense:** 1.8% of GNP (1987).
Economy: Industries: Sugar refining; textiles. **Chief crops:** Coffee, sugar, bananas, cocoa, tobacco, rice. **Minerals:** Bauxite. **Other resources:** Timber. **Arable land:** 20%. **Livestock** (1987): cattle: 1.3 mln.; goats: 1.1 mln. **Electricity prod.** (1988): 447 mln. kwh. **Labor force:** 66% agric.; 9% ind. & comm.; 25% services.
Finance: Currency: Gourde (Apr. 1990: 5.00 = $1 US). **Gross national product** (1987): $2.2 bln. **Per capita GNP** (1987): $360. **Imports** (1988): $344 mln.; partners: U.S. 45%. **Exports** (1988): $183 mln.; partners: U.S. 52%. **Tourists** (1987): receipts $93 mln. **National budget** (1987): $258 mln. expenditures. **International reserves less gold** (Mar. 1990): $9.1 mln. **Gold:** 18,000 oz t. **Consumer prices** (change in 1988): 4.1%.
Transport: Motor vehicles: in use (1985): 34,000 passenger cars, 11,000 comm. vehicles. **Chief ports:** Port-au-Prince, Les Cayes.
Communications: Television sets: 1 per 218 persons. **Radios:** 1 per 41 persons. **Telephones in use:** 1 per 65 persons. **Daily newspaper circ.** (1988): 8 per 1,000 pop.
Health: Life expectancy at birth (1989): 55 male; 56 female. **Births** (per 1,000 pop. 1989): 31. **Deaths** (per 1,000 pop. 1989): 12. **Natural increase:** 1.9%. **Hospital beds:** 1 per 1,060 persons. **Physicians:** 1 per 6,539 persons. **Infant mortality rate** (per 1,000 live births, 1989): 92.
Education (1987): **Literacy:** 23%. **Years compulsory:** 6; attendance 20%.
Major International Organizations: UN and some of its specialized agencies, OAS.

Embassy: 2311 Massachusetts Ave. NW 20008; 332-4090.

Haiti, visited by Columbus, 1492, and a French colony from 1677, attained its independence, 1804, following the rebellion led by former slave Toussaint L'Ouverture. Following a period of political violence, the U.S. occupied the country 1915-34.
Dr. Francois Duvalier was voted president in 1957; in 1964 he was named president for life. Upon his death in 1971, he was succeeded by his son, Jean-Claude. Drought in 1975-77 brought famine, and Hurricane Allen in 1980 destroyed most of the rice, bean, and coffee crops.
Haiti is the poorest nation in the Western hemisphere; unemployment was estimated at 50% in 1987.
Following several weeks of unrest, President Jean Claude Duvalier fled Haiti aboard a U.S. Air Force jet Feb. 7, 1986, ending the 28-year dictatorship by the Duvalier family. A military-civilian council headed by Gen. Henri Namphy assumed control. In 1987, voters approved a new constitution.
The Jan. 17, 1988 elections led to Leslie Manigat being named president; opposition leaders charged widespread fraud. Gen. Namphy seized control, June 20, and named himself president of a military government. Namphy was ousted by a military coup in Sept. By mid-1990, there had been 5 governments since Duvalier fled.

Honduras

Republic of Honduras

República de Honduras

People: Population (1990 est.): 5,261,000. **Age distrib.** (%): 0-14: 46.9; 15-59: 48.6; 60+: 4.5. **Pop. density:** 117 per sq. mi. **Urban** (1988): 40.0%. **Ethnic groups:** Mestizo 90%, Indian 7%. **Languages:** Spanish, Indian dialects. **Religions:** Roman Catholic 95%.
Geography: Area: 43,277 sq. mi., slightly larger than Tennessee. **Location:** In Central America. **Neighbors:** Guatemala on W, El Salvador, Nicaragua on S. **Topography:** The Caribbean coast is 500 mi. long. Pacific coast, on Gulf of Fonseca, is 40 mi. long. Honduras is mountainous, with wide fertile valleys and rich forests. **Capital:** Tegucigalpa. **Cities** (1989 est.) Tegucigalpa 550,000; San Pedro Sula 399,000.
Government: Type: Democratic constitutional republic. **Head of State:** Pres. Rafael Leonardo Callejas; in office: Jan. 27, 1990. **Local divisions:** 18 departments. **Defense:** 3.8% of GNP (1987).
Economy: Industries: Textiles, wood prods, cigars. **Chief crops:** Bananas (chief export), coffee, corn, beans. **Minerals:** Gold, silver, copper, lead, zinc, iron, antimony, coal. **Other resources:** Timber. **Arable land:** 16%. **Livestock** (1987): cattle: 2.8 mln. **Electricity prod.** (1988): 1.9 bln. kwh. **Labor force:** 62% agric.; 20% services; 9% manuf.
Finance: Currency: Lempira (Apr. 1990): 2.00 = $1 US). **Gross national product** (1988): $4.4 bln. **Per capita income** (1988): $1,000. **Imports** (1987): $1.7 bln.; partners: U.S. 39%, Jap. 8%. **Exports** (1987): $1.5 bln.; partners: U.S. 54%, Europe 34%. **Tourists** (1987): $26 mln. receipts. **International reserves less gold** (Mar. 1990): $20.5 mln. **Gold:** 16,000 oz t. **Consumer prices** (change in 1989): 9.9%.
Transport: Motor vehicles: in use (1987) 77,000 passenger cars, 18,000 comm. vehicles. **Civil aviation** (1985): 390 mln. passenger-km; 9 airports with scheduled flights. **Chief ports:** Puerto Cortes, La Ceiba.
Communications: Television sets: 1 per 31 persons. **Radios:** 1 per 2.4 persons. **Telephones:** 1 per 79 persons. **Daily newspaper circ.** (1987): 51 per 1,000 pop.
Health: Life expectancy at birth (1989): 63 male; 67 female. **Births** (per 1,000 pop. 1989): 38. **Deaths** (per 1,000 pop. 1989): 7. **Natural increase:** 3.0%. **Hospital beds:** 1 per 820 persons. **Physicians:** 1 per 2,100 persons. **Infant mortality** (per 1,000 live births 1989): 60.
Education (1989): **Literacy:** 56%. **Years compulsory:** 6; attendance 70%.
Major International Organizations: UN, (IMF, WHO, ILO), OAS.
Embassy: 4301 Connecticut Ave. NW 20008; 966-7700.

Mayan civilization flourished in Honduras in the 1st millenium AD. Columbus arrived in 1502. Honduras became independent after freeing itself from Spain, 1821 and from the Fed. of Central America, 1838.

Gen. Oswaldo Lopez Arellano, president for most of the period 1963-75 by virtue of one election and 2 coups, was ousted by the army in 1975 over charges of pervasive bribery by United Brands Co. of the U.S.

The government has resumed land distribution, raised minimum wages, and started a literacy campaign. An elected civilian government took power in 1982, the country's first in 10 years.

The U.S. has provided military aid and advisors to help withstand pressures from Nicaragua and help block arms shipments from Nicaragua to rebel forces in El Salvador. Some 3,200 U.S. troops were sent to Honduras after the Honduran border was violated by Nicaraguan forces, Mar. 1988.

Hungary
Republic of Hungary

People: Population (1990 est.): 10,546,000. **Age distrib. (%):** 0–14: 20.8; 15–59: 60.5; 60+: 18.7. **Pop. density:** 293 per sq. mi. **Urban** (1989): 60%. **Ethnic groups:** Magyar 92%, German 2.5%, Gypsy 3%. **Languages:** Hungarian (Magyar). **Religions:** Roman Catholic 67%, Protestant 25%.

Geography: Area: 35,919 sq. mi., slightly smaller than Indiana. **Location:** In East Central Europe. **Neighbors:** Czechoslovakia on N, Austria on W, Yugoslavia on S, Romania, USSR on E. **Topography:** The Danube R. forms the Czech border in the NW, then swings S to bisect the country. The eastern half of Hungary is mainly a great fertile plain, the Alfold; the W and N are hilly. **Capital:** Budapest. **Cities** (1989 est.): Budapest 2,115,000; Miskolc 208,000; Debrecen 220,000.

Government: Type: Republic (in transition). **Head of state:** Pres. Arpad Goncz; in office: May 2, 1990. **Head of government:** Prime Min. Jozsef Antall; in office: May 3, 1990. **Local divisions:** 20 regions. **Defense:** 5.2% of GNP (1987).

Economy: Industries: Iron and steel, machinery, pharmaceuticals, vehicles, communications equip., milling, distilling. **Chief crops:** Grains, vegetables, fruits, grapes. **Minerals:** Bauxite, coal, natural gas. **Arable land:** 57%. **Livestock** (1987): cattle: 1.7 mln.; pigs: 8.2 mln.; sheep: 2.4 mln. **Electricity prod.** (1987): 29.7 bln. kwh. **Crude steel prod.** (1988): 3.5 mln. metric tons. **Labor force:** 19% agric.; 48% ind. & comm.; 27% services.

Finance: Currency: Forint (Mar. 1990: 59 = $1 US). **Gross national product** (1988): $91.6 bln. **Per capita GNP** (1988): $8,650. **Imports** (1988): $9.3 bln.; partners: USSR 25%, W. Ger. 14%, E. Ger. 7%, Czech. 5%. **Exports** (1988): $9.9 bln.; partners: USSR 27%, E. Ger. 6%, W. Ger. 9%, Czech. 6%. **National budget** (1987): $14.9 bln. **Tourists** (1988): $913 mln. receipts. **Consumer prices** (change in 1988): 15.6%.

Transport: Railway traffic (1988): 11.2 bln. passenger-km. **Motor vehicles:** in use (1988): 1.7 mln. passenger cars, 218,000 comm. vehicles. **Civil aviation** (1988): 1.2 bln. passenger-km; 4 airports.

Communications: Television sets: 1 per 2.5 persons. **Radios:** 1 per 1.7 persons. **Telephones:** 1 per 6.6 persons. **Daily newspaper circ.** (1986): 236 per 1,000 pop.

Health: Life expectancy at birth (1989): 65.3 male; 73.2 female. **Births** (per 1,000 pop. 1989): 12. **Deaths** (per 1,000 pop. 1989): 14. **Natural increase:** –2%. **Hospital beds:** 1 per 101 persons. **Physicians:** 1 per 343 persons. **Infant mortality** (per 1,000 live births 1989): 20.2.

Education (1989): **Literacy:** 98%. **Years compulsory:** to age 16; attendance 96%.

Major International Organizations: UN (IMF, World Bank, GATT), Warsaw Pact.

Embassy: 3910 Shoemaker St. NW 20008; 362-6737.

Earliest settlers, chiefly Slav and Germanic, were overrun by Magyars from the east. Stephen I (997-1038) was made king by Pope Sylvester II in 1000 AD. The country suffered repeated Turkish invasions in the 15th-17th centuries. After the defeats of the Turks, 1686-1697, Austria dominated, but Hungary obtained concessions until it regained internal independence in 1867, with the emperor of Austria as king of Hungary in a dual monarchy with a single diplomatic service. Defeated with the Central Powers in 1918, Hungary lost Transylvania to Romania, Croatia and Bacska to Yugoslavia, Slovakia and Carpatho-Ruthenia to Czechoslovakia, all of which had large Hungarian minorities. A republic under Michael Karolyi and a bolshevist revolt under

Bela Kun were followed by a vote for a monarchy in 1920 with Admiral Nicholas Horthy as regent.

Hungary joined Germany in World War II, and was allowed to annex most of its lost territories. Russian troops captured the country, 1944-1945. By terms of an armistice with the Allied powers Hungary agreed to give up territory acquired by the 1938 dismemberment of Czechoslovakia and to return to its borders of 1937.

A republic was declared Feb. 1, 1946; Zoltan Tildy was elected president. In 1947 the communists forced Tildy out. Premier Imre Nagy, in office since mid-1953, was ousted for his moderate policy of favoring agriculture and consumer production, April 18, 1955.

In 1956, popular demands for the ousting of Erno Gero, Communist Party secretary, and for formation of a government by Nagy, resulted in the latter's appointment Oct. 23; demonstrations against communist rule developed into open revolt. Gero called in Soviet forces. On Nov. 4 Soviet forces launched a massive attack against Budapest with 200,000 troops, 2,500 tanks and armored cars.

About 200,000 persons fled the country. In the spring of 1963 the regime freed many anti-communists and captives from the revolution in a sweeping amnesty. Nagy was executed by the Russians. In 1989, Nagy was exhumed from an unmarked grave and reburied. In Mar. 1987, some 2,000 marched in Budapest calling for democracy.

Soviet troops are stationed in Hungary. Hungarian troops participated in the 1968 Warsaw Pact invasion of Czechoslovakia. Major economic reforms were launched early in 1968, switching from a central planning system to one in which market forces and profit control much of production.

Hungary has embraced *glasnost;* the media comments freely on most topics. In 1989 parliament passed legislation legalizing freedom of assembly and association and it was apparent that Hungary was shifting away from communism toward democracy. In Oct., the communist party was formally dissolved.

Iceland
Republic of Iceland
Lýoveldio Island

People: Population (1990 est.): 251,000. **Age distrib. (%):** 0–14: 25.5; 15–59: 60.1; 60+: 14.4. **Pop. density:** 6 per sq. mi. **Urban** (1989): 90% **Ethnic groups:** Homogeneous, descendants of Norwegians, Celts. **Language:** Icelandic (Islenska). **Religion:** Evangelical Lutheran 95%.

Geography: Area: 39,769 sq. mi., the size of Virginia. **Location:** At N end of Atlantic O. **Neighbors:** Nearest is Greenland. **Topography:** Iceland is of recent volcanic origin. Three-quarters of the surface is wasteland: glaciers, lakes, a lava desert. There are geysers and hot springs, and the climate is moderated by the Gulf Stream. **Capital:** Reykjavik. **Cities** (1988 est.): Reykjavik 93,000.

Government: Type: Constitutional republic. **Head of state:** Pres. Vigdis Finnbogadottir; b. Apr. 15, 1930; in office: Aug. 1, 1980. **Head of government:** Prime Min. Steingrimur Hermannsson; in office: Sept. 28, 1988. **Local divisions:** 23 counties.

Economy: Industries: Fish products (some 80% of exports), aluminum. **Chief crops:** Potatoes, turnips, hay. **Arable land:** 0.5%. **Livestock** (1988): sheep: 586,000. **Fish catch** (1988): 1,700,000 metric tons. **Electricity prod.** (1988): 4.9 bln. kwh. **Labor force:** 11% agric.; 55% comm. & services, 14% fisheries.

Finance: Currency: Kronur (Mar. 1990: 61.06 = $1 US). **Gross national product** (1987): $5.3 bln. **Per capita GNP** (1987): $21,660. **Imports** (1989): $1.4 bln.; partners: W. Ger. 15%, UK 9%, Den. 10%. **Exports** (1989): $1.4 bln.; partners: U.S. 88%, UK 19%. **Tourists** (1988): receipts $108 mln. **National budget** (1987): $1.2 bln. expenditures. **International reserves less gold** (Mar. 1990): $337 mln. **Gold:** 49,000 oz t. **Consumer prices** (change in 1989): 20.8%.

Transport: Motor vehicles: in use (1988): 121,000 passenger cars, 12,000 comm. vehicles. **Civil aviation** (1988): 2.3 bln. passenger-km; 31 airports with scheduled flights. **Chief ports:** Reykjavik.

Communications: Television sets: 1 per 3.3 persons. **Radios:** 1 per 1.6 persons. **Telephones:** 1 per 2.2 persons. **Daily newspaper circ.** (1986): 415 per 1,000 pop.

Health: Life expectancy at birth (1989): 75 male; 81 female. **Births** (per 1,000 pop. 1989): 15. **Deaths** (per 1,000 pop. 1989): 7. **Natural increase:** 0.8%. **Hospital beds:** 1 per 86 persons. **Physicians:** 1 per 385 persons. **Infant mortality** per (1,000 live births 1989): 6.

Education (1989): **Literacy:** 99%. **Years compulsory:** 8; **Attendance:** 99%.

Major International Organizations: UN (GATT), NATO, OECD.

Embassy: 2022 Connecticut Ave. NW 20008; 265-6653.

Iceland was an independent republic from 930 to 1262, when it joined with Norway. Its language has maintained its purity for 1,000 years. Danish rule lasted from 1380-1918; the last ties with the Danish crown were severed in 1941. The Althing, or assembly, is the world's oldest surviving parliament.

India

Republic of India

Bharat

People: Population (1990 est.): 850,067,000. **Age distrib.** (%): 0–14: 36.8; 15–59: 56.4; 60+: 5.8. **Pop. density:** 658 per sq. mi. **Urban** (1989): 28%. **Ethnic groups:** Indo-Aryan groups 72%, Dravidians 25%, Mongoloids 3%. **Languages:** 16 languages, including Hindi (official) and English (associate official). **Religions:** Hindu 83%, Moslem 11%, Christian 3%, Sikh 2%.

Geography: Area: 1,266,595 sq. mi., one third the size of the U.S. **Location:** Occupies most of the Indian subcontinent in S. Asia. **Neighbors:** Pakistan on W, China, Nepal, Bhutan on N, Myanmar, Bangladesh on E. **Topography:** The Himalaya Mts., highest in world, stretch across India's northern borders. Below, the Ganges Plain is wide, fertile, and among the most densely populated regions of the world. The area below includes the Deccan Peninsula. Close to one quarter the area is forested. The climate varies from tropical heat in S to near-Arctic cold in N. Rajasthan Desert is in NW; NE Assam Hills get 400 in. of rain a year. **Capital:** New Delhi. **Cities** (1988 est.): Calcutta 9.9 mln.; Bombay (met.) 8.7 mln.; New Delhi 7.2 mln.; Madras 4.9 mln.; Bangalore 3.9 mln.; Hyderabad 2.8 mln.; Ahmedabad 2.3 mln.

Government: Type: Federal republic. **Head of state:** Pres. Ramaswamy Venkataraman; b. Dec. 4, 1910; in office: July 25, 1987. **Head of government:** Prime Min. Vishwanath Pratap Singh; in office: Dec. 2, 1989. **Local divisions:** 24 states, 7 union territories. **Defense:** 3.8% of GNP (1987).

Economy: Type: Federal republic. **Industries:** Textiles, steel, processed foods, cement, machinery, chemicals, fertilizers, consumer appliances, autos. **Chief crops:** Rice, grains, coffee, sugar cane, spices, tea, cashews, cotton, copra, coir, juta, linseed. **Minerals:** Chromium, coal, iron, manganese, mica salt, bauxite, gypsum, oil. **Crude oil reserves** (1987): 4.3 bln. bbls. **Other resources:** Rubber, timber. **Arable land:** 57%. **Livestock** (1987): cattle: 199 mln.; pigs: 9 mln.; sheep: 55 mln. **Fish catch** (1988): 14.2 mln. metric tons. **Electricity prod.** (1987): 198 bln. kwh. **Crude steel prod.** (1988): 14.2 mln. metric tons. **Labor force:** 70% agric.; 19% ind. & comm.

Finance: Currency: Rupee (June 1990: 17.51 = $1 US). **Gross national product** (1988): $246 bln. **Per capita GNP** (1988): $300. **Imports** (1988): $19.1 bln.; partners: Jap. 12%, U.S. 12%, W. Ger. 10%, UK 8%. **Exports** (1988): $13.3 bln.; partners: U.S. 18%, USSR 15%, UK 6%, Jap. 9%. **Tourists** (1987): receipts: $1.4 bln. **National budget** (1988): $56 bln. expenditures. **International reserves less gold** (Mar. 1990): $4.1 bln. **Gold:** 10.6 mln. oz. t. **Consumer prices** (change in 1988): 9.0%.

Transport: Railway traffic (1988): 269 bln. passenger-km. **Motor vehicles:** in use (1987): 1.6 mln. passenger cars, 1.2 mln. comm. vehicles. **Civil aviation:** (1987): 17.1 bln. passenger-km; 95 airports with scheduled flights. **Chief ports:** Calcutta, Bombay, Madras, Cochin, Vishakhapatnam.

Communications: Television sets: 1 per 62 persons. **Radios:** 1 per 15 persons. **Telephones:** 1 per 180 persons. **Daily newspaper circ.** (1986): 16 per. 1,000 pop.

Health: Life expectancy at birth (1989): 57 male; 58 female. **Births** (per 1,000 pop. 1989): 31. **Deaths** (per 1,000 pop. 1989): 11. **Natural increase:** 2.0%. **Hospital beds:** 1 per 1,130 persons. **Physicians:** 1 per 2,471 persons. **Infant mortality** (per 1,000 live births 1989): 91.

Education (1989): **Literacy:** 36%. **Years Compulsory:** to age 14.

Major International Organizations: UN (IMF, World Bank). **Embassy:** 2107 Massachusetts Ave. NW 20008; 939-7000.

India has one of the oldest civilizations in the world. Excavations trace the Indus Valley civilization back for at least 5,000 years. Paintings in the mountain caves of Ajanta, richly carved temples, the Taj Mahal in Agra, and the Kutab Minar in Delhi are among relics of the past.

Aryan tribes, speaking Sanskrit, invaded from the NW around 1500 BC, and merged with the earlier inhabitants to create classical Indian civilization.

Asoka ruled most of the Indian subcontinent in the 3d century BC, and established Buddhism. But Hinduism revived and eventually predominated. During the Gupta kingdom, 4th-6th century AD, science, literature, and the arts enjoyed a "golden age."

Arab invaders established a Moslem foothold in the W in the 8th century, and Turkish Moslems gained control of North India by 1200. The Mogul emperors ruled 1526-1857.

Vasco de Gama established Portuguese trading posts 1498-1503. The Dutch followed. The British East India Co. sent Capt. William Hawkins, 1609, to get concessions from the Mogul emperor for spices and textiles. Operating as the East India Co. the British gained control of most of India. The British parliament assumed political direction; under Lord Bentinck, 1828-35, rule by rajahs was curbed. After the Sepoy troops mutinied, 1857-58, the British supported the native rulers.

Indonesia

Republic of Indonesia

Republik Indonesia

People: Population (1990 est.): 191,266,000. **Age distrib.** (%): 0–14: 39.2; 15–59: 56.5; 60+: 5.3. **Pop. density:** 255 per sq. mi. **Urban** (1985): 25%. **Ethnic groups:** Malay, Chinese, Irianese. **Languages:** Bahasa Indonesian (Malay) (official), Javanese, other Austronesian languages. **Religions:** Moslem 88%.

Geography: Area: 735,268 sq. mi. **Location:** Archipelago SE of Asia along the Equator. **Neighbors:** Malaysia on N, Papua New Guinea on E. **Topography:** Indonesia comprises 13,500 islands, including Java (one of the most densely populated areas in the world with 1,500 persons to the sq. mi.), Sumatra, Kalimantan (most of Borneo), Sulawesi (Celebes), and West Irian (Irian Jaya, the W. half of New Guinea). Also: Bangka, Billiton, Madura, Bali, Timor. The mountains and plateaus on the major islands have a cooler climate than the tropical lowlands. **Capital:** Jakarta. **Cities** (1988 est.): Jakarta 8,800,000; Surabaja 2,500,000; Bandung 1,400,000; Medan 1,700,000.

Government: Type: Independent republic. **Head of state:** Pres. Suharto; b. June 8, 1921; in office: Mar. 6, 1967. **Local divisions:** 27 provinces, 246 districts & 55 municipalities. **Defense:** 2.5% of GNP (1985).

Economy: Industries: Food processing, textiles, light industry. **Chief crops:** Rice, coffee, sugar. **Minerals:** Nickel, tin, oil, bauxite, copper, natural gas. **Crude oil reserves** (1987): 8.4 bln. bbls. **Other resources:** Rubber. **Arable land:** 8%. **Livestock** (1987): cattle: 6.4 mln.; sheep: 5.1 mln. **Fish catch** (1987): 1.9 mln. metric tons. **Electricity prod.** (1987): 34.8 bln. kwh. **Labor force:** 56% agric.; 23% ind. & comm.; 16% services.

Finance: Currency: Rupiah (June 1990: 1,823 = $1 US). **Gross national product** (1988): $75 bln. **Per capita income** (1988): $435. **Imports** (1988): $13.2 bln.; partners: Jap. 26%, U.S. 12%, Sing. 6%. **Exports** (1988): $19.2 bln.; partners: Jap. 41%, U.S. 16%, Sing. 10%. **Tourists** (1987): $803 mln. receipts. **National budget** (1990): $21.1 bln. **International reserves less gold** (Feb. 1990): $4.9 bln. **Gold:** 3.10 mln. oz t. **Consumer prices** (change in 1988): 8.0%.

Transport: Railway traffic (1988): 7.3 bln. passenger-km. **Motor vehicles:** in use (1988): 1.1 mln. passenger cars, 1.2 mln. comm. **Civil aviation** (1988): 13.8 bln. passenger-km; 134 airports. **Chief ports:** Jakarta, Surabaja, Medan, Palembang, Semarang.

Communications: Television sets: 1 per 24 persons. **Radios:** 1 per 8 persons. **Telephones:** 1 per 193 persons.

Health: Life expectancy at birth (1989): male: 57; female 61 years. **Births** (per 1,000 pop. 1989): 28. **Deaths** (per 1,000 pop. 1989): 9. **Natural increase:** 1.9%. **Hospital beds:** 1 per 1,495 persons. **Physicians:** 1 per 8,000 persons. **Infant mortality** (per 1,000 live births 1989): 58.0.

Education (1988): **Literacy:** 85%. 84% attend primary school.

Major International Organizations: UN and all of its specialized agencies, ASEAN, OPEC.

Embassy: 2020 Massachusetts Ave. NW 20036; 775-5200.

Hindu and Buddhist civilization from India reached the peoples of Indonesia nearly 2,000 years ago, taking root especially in Java. Islam spread along the maritime trade routes in the 15th century, and became predominant by the 16th century. The Dutch replaced the Portuguese as the most important European trade power in the area in the 17th century. They secured territorial control over Java by 1750. The outer islands were not finally subdued until the early 20th century, when the full area of present-day Indonesia was united under one rule for the first time.

Following Japanese occupation, 1942-45, nationalists led by Sukarno and Hatta proclaimed a republic. The Netherlands ceded sovereignty Dec. 27, 1949, after 4 years of fighting. West Irian, on New Guinea, remained under Dutch control.

After the Dutch in 1957 rejected proposals for new negotiations over West Irian, Indonesia stepped up the seizure of Dutch property. A U.S. mediator's plan was adopted in 1962. In 1963 the UN turned the area over to Indonesia, which promised a plebiscite. In 1969, voting by tribal chiefs favored staying with Indonesia, despite an uprising and widespread opposition.

Sukarno suspended Parliament in 1960, and was named president for life in 1963. Russian-armed Indonesian troops staged raids in 1964 and 1965 into Malaysia, whose formation Sukarno had opposed.

Indonesia's popular, pro-Peking Communist Party tried to seize control in 1965; the army smashed the coup, later intimated that Sukarno had played a role in it. In parts of Java, communists seized several districts before being defeated; over 300,000 communists were executed.

Gen. Suharto, head of the army, was named president in 1968, reelected 1973, 1978, and 1988. A coalition of his supporters won a strong majority in House elections in 1971. Moslem opposition parties made gains in 1977 elections but lost ground in the 1982 elections. The military retains a predominant political role.

In 1966 Indonesia and Malaysia signed an agreement ending hostility. After ties with Peking were cut in 1967, there were riots against the economically important ethnic Chinese minority. Riots against Chinese and Japanese also occurred in 1974.

Oil export earnings, and political stability have made Indonesia's economy stable.

Iran

Islamic Republic of Iran

Jomhori-e-Islami-e-Irân

People: Population (1990 est.): 55,647,000. **Age distrib.** (%): 0-14: 44.4; 15-59: 50.3; 60+: 5.2. **Pop. density:** 80 per sq. mi. **Urban** (1987): 55%. **Ethnic groups:** Persian 63%, Turkomans & Baluchis 19%, Kurds 3%, Arabs 4%. **Languages:** Persian, Turk, Kurdish, Arabic, English, French. **Religions:** Shi'a Moslem 93%.

Geography: Area: 636,293 sq. mi. slightly larger than Alaska. **Location:** In the Middle East and S. Asia. **Neighbors:** Turkey, Iraq on W, USSR of N (Armenia, Azerbaijan, Turkmenistan), Afghanistan, Pakistan on E. **Topography:** Interior highlands and plains are surrounded by high mountains, up to 18,000 ft. Large salt deserts cover much of the area, but there are many oases and forest areas. Most of the population inhabits the N and NW. **Capital:** Teheran. **Cities** (1986 cen.): Teheran 6,022,000; Esfahan 1,001,000; Mashhad 1,466,000; Tabriz 994,000; Shiraz 848,000.

Government: Type: Islamic republic. **Religious head:** Ayatollah Sayyed Ali Khamenei; b. 1939; in office: June 4, 1989. **Head of state:** Pres. Hashemi Rafsanjani; in office: Aug 3, 1989. **Local divisions:** 24 provinces. **Defense:** 7.9% of GNP (1986).

Economy: Industries: Cement, sugar refining, carpets. **Chief crops:** Grains, rice, fruits, sugar beets, cotton, grapes. **Minerals:** Chromium, oil, gas. **Crude oil reserves** (1987): 36.5 bln. bbls. **Other resources:** Gums, wool, silk, caviar. **Arable land:** 9%. **Livestock** (1987): cattle: 8.3 mln.; sheep: 34.5 mln. **Electricity prod.** (1988): 43.3 bln. kwh. **Crude steel prod.** (1988) 1.2 mln.

metric tons. **Labor force:** 33% agric.; 21% ind. & comm; 27% services.

Finance: Currency: Rial (Mar. 1990: 71.45 = $1 US). **Gross national product** (1988): $93 bln. **Per capita income** (1986): $1,667. **Imports** (1988): $9.5 bln.; partners: W. Ger. 20%, Jap. 13%, UK 6%. **Exports** (1987): $8.3 bln.; partners: Jap. 16%, It. 10%. **National budget** (1988): $55 bln. expenditures.

Transport: Motor vehicles: in use (1983): 2.1 mln. passenger cars, 313,000 comm. vehicles. **Civil Aviation** (1986): 5.4 bln. passenger km.; 17 airports. **Chief ports:** Bandar Abbas.

Communications: Television sets: 1 per 23 persons. **Radios:** 1 per 4.7 persons. **Telephones:** 1 per 25 persons. **Daily newspaper circ.** (1988): 13 per 1,000 pop.

Health: Life expectancy at birth (1989): 57 male; 57 female. **Births** (per 1,000 pop. 1989): 44. **Deaths** (per 1,000 pop. 1989): 10. **Natural increase:** 3.4%. **Hospital beds:** 1 per 704 persons. **Physicians:** 1 per 2,992 persons. **Infant mortality** (per 1,000 live births 1989): 113.

Education (1986): **Literacy:** 48%.

Major International Organizations: UN (IMF, WHO), OPEC.

Iran was once called Persia. The Iranians, who supplanted an earlier agricultural civilization, came from the E during the 2d millenium BC; they were an Indo-European group related to the Aryans of India.

In 549 BC Cyrus the Great united the Medes and Persians in the Persian Empire, conquered Babylonia in 538 BC, restored Jerusalem to the Jews. Alexander the Great conquered Persia in 333 BC, but Persians regained their independence in the next century under the Parthians, themselves succeeded by Sassanian Persians in 226 AD. Arabs brought Islam to Persia in the 7th century, replacing the indigenous Zoroastrian faith. After Persian political and cultural autonomy was reasserted in the 9th century, the arts and sciences flourished for several centuries.

Turks and Mongols ruled Persia in turn from the 11th century to 1502, when a native dynasty reasserted full independence. The British and Russian empires vied for influence in the 19th century, and Afghanistan was severed from Iran by Britain in 1857.

The previous dynasty was founded by Reza Khan, a military leader, in 1925. He abdicated as shah in 1941, and was succeeded by his son, Mohammad Reza Pahlavi.

Parliament, under Premier Mohammed Mossadegh, nationalized the oil industry in 1951, leading to a British blockade. Mossadegh was overthrown in 1953; the shah assumed control. Under his rule, Iran underwent economic and social change but political opposition was not tolerated.

Conservative Moslem protests led to 1978 violence. Martial law in 12 cities was declared Sept. 8. A military government was appointed Nov. 6 to deal with striking oil workers. Prime Min. Shahpur Bakhtiar was designated by the shah to head a regency council in his absence. The shah left Iran Jan. 16, 1979.

Exiled religious leader Ayatollah Ruhollah Khomeini named a provisional government council in preparation for his return to Iran, Jan. 31. Clashes between Khomeini's supporters and government troops culminated in a rout of Iran's elite Imperial Guard Feb. 11, leading to the fall of Bakhtiar's government.

The Iranian revolution was marked by revolts among the ethnic minorities and by a continuing struggle between the clerical forces and westernized intellectuals and liberals. The Islamic Constitution established final authority to be vested in a Faghi, the Ayatollah Khomeini.

Iranian militants seized the U.S. embassy, Nov. 4, 1979, and took hostages including 62 Americans. The militants vowed to stay in the embassy until the deposed shah was returned to Iran. Despite international condemnations and U.S. efforts, including an abortive Apr., 1980, rescue attempt, the crisis continued. The U.S. broke diplomatic relations with Iran, Apr. 7th. The shah died in Egypt, July 27th. The hostage drama finally ended Jan. 21, 1981 when an accord, involving the release of frozen Iranian assets, was reached.

The ruling Islamic Party, increasingly dissatisfied with President Abolhassan Bani-Sadr, declared him unfit for office. In the weeks following Bani-Sadr's dismissal, June 22, 1981, a new wave of executions began. The political upheavals have brought Iran to almost total isolation from other countries.

A dispute over the Shatt al-Arab waterway that divides the two countries brought Iran and Iraq, Sept. 22, 1980, into open warfare. Iraqi planes attacked Iranian air fields including Teheran airport. Iranian planes bombed Iraqi bases. Iraqi troops occupied Iranian territory including the port city of Khorramshahr in October. Iranian troops recaptured the city and drove Iraqi troops back across the border, May 1982. Iraq, and later Iran, attacked several oil tankers in the Persian Gulf during 1984. Saudi Arabian war planes shot down 2 Iranian jets, June 5, which they felt were threatening Saudi shipping. In Aug. 1988, Iran agreed to accept a UN resolution calling for a cease fire.

In Nov. 1986, senior U.S. officials secretly visited Iran and exchanged arms for Iran's help in obtaining the release of U.S. hostages held by terrorists in Lebanon. The exchange sparked a major scandal in the Reagan administration.

A U.S. Navy warship shot down an Iranian commercial airliner, July 3, 1988, after mistaking it for an F-14 fighter jet; all 290 aboard the plane died.

In 1989, Ayatollah Khomeini offered a $1 million reward for the killing of Salman Rushdie, author of *The Satanic Verses*, a novel perceived as blasphemous to Islam. Khomeini died following a long illness, June 4, 1989.

A major earthquake struck northern Iran June 21, 1990, killing over 35,000, injuring 100,000, and leaving 400,000 homeless. A U.S. offer of assistance was accepted by the Iranian government.

Iraq

Republic of Iraq

al Jumhouriya al 'Iraqia

People: Population (1990 est.): 18,782,000. **Age distrib. (%):** 0–14: 45.3; 15–59: 49.6; 60+: 5.1. **Pop. density:** 104 per sq. mi. **Urban** (1988): 72%. **Ethnic groups:** Arabs, 75% Kurds, 15% Turks. **Languages:** Arabic (official), Kurdish, others. **Religions:** Moslem 95% (Shiites 60%, Sunnis 35%), Christian 5%.
Geography: Area: 167,924 sq. mi., larger than California. **Location:** In the Middle East, occupying most of historic Mesopotamia. **Neighbors:** Jordan, Syria on W, Turkey on N, Iran on E, Kuwait, Saudi Arabia on S. **Topography:** Mostly an alluvial plain, including the Tigris and Euphrates rivers, descending from mountains in N to desert in SW. Persian Gulf region is marshland. **Capital:** Baghdad. **Cities** (1985 est.): Baghdad (met.) 3,400,000.
Government: Type: Republic. **Head of state:** Pres. Saddam Hussein At-Takriti, b. 1935 in office: July 16, 1979. **Local divisions:** 18 provinces. **Defense:** 32% of GNP (1986).
Economy: Industries: Textiles, petrochemicals, oil refining, cement. **Chief crops:** Grains, rice, dates, cotton. **Minerals:** Oil, gas. **Crude oil reserves** (1987): 40 bln. bbls. **Other resources:** Wool, hides. **Arable land:** 13%. **Livestock** (1988): cattle: 1.5 mln.; sheep 8.7 mln; goats: 1.4 mln. **Electricity prod.** (1988): 22.5 bln. kwh. **Labor force:** 33% agric.; 39% services; 28% ind.
Finance: Currency: Dinar (Mar. 1990: 1.00 = $3.21 US). **Gross national product** (1988): $34 bln. **Per capita GNP** (1988): $1,950. **Imports** (1988): $10.6 bln.; partners: Tur. 16%, U.S. 11%. **Exports** (1987): $9.0 bln.; partners: It. 13%, Tur. 8%, Braz. 17%, Jap. 6%.
Transport: Railway traffic (1986): 1.0 bln. passenger-km. **Motor vehicles:** in use (1986): 491,000 passenger cars, 246,700 comm. vehicles. **Civil aviation** (1985): 1.2 bln. passenger-km; 3 airports. **Chief ports:** Basra.
Communications: Television sets: 1 per 18 persons. **Radios:** 1 per 5 persons. **Telephones:** 1 per 17 persons. **Daily newspaper circ.** (1987): 21 per 1,000 pop.
Health: Life expectancy at birth (1989): 65 male; 67 female. **Births** (per 1,000 pop. 1989): 45. **Deaths** (per 1,000 pop. 1989): 8. **Natural increase:** 3.8%. **Hospital beds:** 1 per 552 persons. **Physicians:** 1 per 3,324 persons. **Infant mortality** (per 1,000 live births 1989): 69.
Major International Organizations: UN (IMF, ILO), Arab League, OPEC.
Education (1987): **Literacy:** 70%. Compulsory age 6 to grade 6.
Embassy: 1801 P St. NW 20036; 483-7500.

The Tigris-Euphrates valley, formerly called Mesopotamia, was the site of one of the earliest civilizations in the world. The Sumerian city-states of 3,000 BC originated the culture later developed by the Semitic Akkadians, Babylonians, and Assyrians.
Mesopotamia ceased to be a separate entity after the conquests of the Persians, Greeks, and Arabs. The latter founded Baghdad, from where the caliph ruled a vast empire in the 8th and 9th centuries. Mongol and Turkish conquests led to a decline in population, the economy, cultural life, and the irrigation system.

Britain secured a League of Nations mandate over Iraq after World War I. Independence under a king came in 1932. A leftist, pan-Arab revolution established a republic in 1958, which oriented foreign policy toward the USSR. Most industry has been nationalized, and large land holdings broken up.

A local faction of the international Baath Arab Socialist party has ruled by decree since 1968. Russia and Iraq signed an aid pact in 1972, and arms were sent along with several thousand advisers. The 1978 execution of 21 communists and a shift of trade to the West signalled a more neutral policy, straining relations with the USSR. In the 1973 Arab-Israeli war Iraq sent forces to aid Syria. Within a month of assuming power, Saddam Hussein instituted a bloody purge in the wake of a reported coup attempt against the new regime.

Years of battling with the Kurdish minority resulted in total defeat for the Kurds in 1975, when Iran withdrew support. Kurdish rebels continued their war, 1979; fighting led to Iraqi bombing of Kurdish villages in Iran, causing relations with Iran to deteriorate.

After skirmishing intermittently for 10 months over the sovereignty of the disputed Shatt al-Arab waterway that divides the two countries, Iraq and Iran, Sept. 22, 1980, entered into open warfare when Iraqi fighter-bombers attacked 10 Iranian airfields, including Teheran airport, and Iranian planes retaliated with strikes on 2 Iraqi bases. In the following days, there was heavy ground fighting around Abadan and the adjacent port of Khorramshahr as Iraq pressed its attack on Iran's oil-rich province of Khuzistan. In May 1982, Iraqi troops were driven back across the border.

Israeli airplanes destroyed a nuclear reactor near Baghdad on June 7, 1981, claiming that it could be used to produce nuclear weapons.

Iraq and Iran expanded their war to the Persian Gulf in Apr. 1984. There were several attacks on oil tankers. An Iraqi warplane launched a missile attack on the U.S.S. *Stark*, a U.S. Navy frigate on patrol in the Persian Gulf, May 17, 1987; 37 U.S. sailors died. Iraq apologized for the attack, claiming it was inadvertent. The fierce war ended Aug. 1988, when Iraq accepted a UN resolution for a ceasefire.

Iraq attacked and overran Kuwait Aug. 1, 1990, sparking an international crisis. (*See Chronology and Index for details.*)

Ireland

People: Population (1990 est.): 3,557,000. **Age distrib. (%):** 0–14: 30.5; 15–59: 54.5; 60+:15.0. **Pop. density:** 137 per sq. mi. **Urban** (1985): 57%. **Ethnic groups:** Celtic, English minority. **Languages:** English predominates, Irish (Gaelic) spoken by minority. **Religions:** Roman Catholic 95%, Anglican 3%.
Geography: Area: 27,137 sq. mi. slightly larger than W. Va. **Location:** In the Atlantic O. just W of Great Britain. **Neighbors:** United Kingdom (Northern Ireland). **Topography:** Ireland consists of a central plateau surrounded by isolated groups of hills and mountains. The coastline is heavily indented by the Atlantic O. **Capital:** Dublin. **Cities** (1988 est.): Dublin 502,000; Cork (met.) 133,000.
Government: Type: Parliamentary republic. **Head of State:** Pres. Patrick J. Hillery; b. May 2, 1923; in office: Dec. 3, 1976. **Head of government:** Prime Min. Charles Haughey; in office: Mar. 10, 1987. **Local divisions:** 26 counties. **Defense:** 1.3% of GNP (1988).
Economy: Industries: Food processing, metals, textiles, chemicals, brewing, electrical and non-electrical machinery, tourism. **Chief crops:** Potatoes, grain, sugar beets, fruits, vegetables. **Minerals:** Zinc, lead, silver, gas. **Arable land:** 14%. **Livestock** (1988): cattle: 6.7 mln.; pigs: 994,000; sheep: 2.7 mln. **Fish catch** (1988): 247,000 metric tons. **Electricity prod.** (1986): 12.6 bln. kwh. **Crude steel prod.** (1985): 203,000 metric tons. **Labor force:** 13% agric.; 21% ind. 47% services.
Finance: Currency: Pound (June 1990: 0.60 = $1 US). **Gross national product** (1988): $28.6 bln. **Per capita income** (1988): $6,200. **Imports** (1989): $17.4 bln.; partners: UK 42%, U.S. 17%, W. Ger. 8%, Fr. 5%. **Exports** (1989): $20.6 bln.; partners: UK 33%, Fr. 9%, W. Ger. 9%. **Tourists** (1987); receipts: $811 mln. **National budget** (1986): $8.6 bln. expenditures. **International reserves less gold** (Mar. 1990): $3.8 bln. **Gold:** 352,000 oz. t. **Consumer prices** (change in 1989): 4.1%.
Transport: Railway traffic (1987): 1.2 bln. passenger-km. **Motor vehicles:** in use (1986): 711,000 passenger cars,

106,000 comm. vehicles. **Civil aviation:** (1987): 2.7 bln. passenger-km; 6 airports. **Chief ports:** Dublin, Cork.

Communications: Television sets: 1 per 3.8 persons. **Radios:** 1 per 1.7 persons. **Telephones:** 1 per 3.8 persons. **Daily newspaper circ.** (1986): 200 per 1,000 pop.

Health: Life expectancy at birth (1989): 72 male; 78 female. **Births** (per 1,000 pop. 1989): 16. **Deaths** (per 1,000 pop. 1989): 9. **Natural increase:** 8%. **Hospital beds:** 1 per 128 persons. **Physicians:** 1 per 681 persons. **Infant mortality** (per 1,000 live births 1989): 6.

Education (1988): **Literacy:** 99%. **Years compulsory:** 9; attendance 91%.

Major International Organizations: UN (GATT, IMF, World Bank), EC, OECD.

Embassy: 2234 Massachusetts Ave. NW 20008; 462-3939.

Celtic tribes invaded the islands about the 4th century BC; their Gaelic culture and literature flourished and spread to Scotland and elsewhere in the 5th century AD, the same century in which St. Patrick converted the Irish to Christianity. Invasions by Norsemen began in the 8th century, ended with defeat of the Danes by the Irish King Brian Boru in 1014. English invasions started in the 12th century; for over 700 years the Anglo-Irish struggle continued with bitter rebellions and savage repressions.

The Easter Monday Rebellion (1916) failed but was followed by guerrilla warfare and harsh reprisals by British troops, the "Black and Tans." The Dail Eireann, or Irish parliament, reaffirmed independence in Jan. 1919. The British offered dominion status to Ulster (6 counties) and southern Ireland (26 counties) Dec. 1921. The constitution of the Irish Free State, a British dominion, was adopted Dec. 11, 1922. Northern Ireland remained part of the United Kingdom.

A new constitution adopted by plebiscite came into operation Dec. 29, 1937. It declared the name of the state Eire in the Irish language (Ireland in the English) and declared it a sovereign democratic state.

On Dec. 21, 1948, an Irish law declared the country a republic rather than a dominion and withdrew it from the Commonwealth. The British Parliament recognized both actions, 1949, but reasserted its claim to incorporate the 6 northeastern counties in the United Kingdom. This claim has not been recognized by Ireland. *(See United Kingdom — Northern Ireland.)*

Irish governments have favored peaceful unification of all Ireland. Ireland cooperated with England against terrorist groups.

Ireland has suffered economic hardship in the 1980's; unemployment reached 17% in 1989.

Israel
State of Israel
Medinat Israel

People: Population (1990 est.): 4,371,000. **Age distrib.** (%): 0–14: 32.4; 15–59: 55.3; 60+: 13.3. **Pop. density:** 570 per sq. mi. **Urban** (1986): 89%. **Ethnic groups:** Jewish 83%, Arab 16%. **Languages:** Hebrew and Arabic (official), Yiddish, various European and West Asian languages. **Religions:** Jewish 83%, Moslem 13%.

Geography: Area: 7,847 sq. mi. about the size of New Jersey. **Location:** On eastern end of Mediterranean Sea. **Neighbors:** Lebanon on N, Syria, Jordan on E, Egypt on W. **Topography:** The Mediterranean coastal plain is fertile and well-watered. In the center is the Judean Plateau. A triangular-shaped semi-desert region, the Negev, extends from south of Beersheba to an apex at the head of the Gulf of Aqaba. The eastern border drops sharply into the Jordan Rift Valley, including Lake Tiberias (Sea of Galilee) and the Dead Sea, which is 1,312 ft. below sea level, lowest point on the earth's surface. **Capital:** Jerusalem. Most countries maintain their embassy in Tel Aviv. **Cities** (1986 est.): Jerusalem 457,000; Tel Aviv-Yafo 322,000; Haifa 224,000.

Government: Type: Parliamentary democracy. **Head of state:** Pres. Chaim Herzog; b. Sept. 17, 1918; in office: May 5, 1983. **Head of government:** Prime Min. Yitzhak Shamir; b. 1915; in office: June 11, 1990. **Local divisions:** 6 administrative districts. **Defense:** 16.6% of GNP (1987).

Economy: Industries: Diamond cutting, textiles, electronics, machinery, food processing. **Chief crops:** Citrus fruit, vegetables. **Minerals:** Potash, copper, phosphates, manganese, sulphur. **Crude oil reserves** (1987): 700,000 mln. bbls. **Arable land:** 17%. **Livestock** (1987): cattle: 319,000; sheep: 281,000.

Fish catch (1987): 22,000 metric tons. **Electricity prod.** (1988): 17.3 bln. kwh. **Labor force:** 6% agric.; 23% ind., 30% public services.

Finance: Currency: Shekel (May 1990: 2.01 = $1 US). **GNP** (1988): $36 bln. **Per capita income** (1988): $5,995. **Imports** (1989): $10.6 bln.; partners: U.S. 16%, W. Ger. 13%, UK 9%. **Exports** (1989): $9.6 bln.; partners: U.S. 34%, W. Ger. 5%, UK 7%. **Tourists** (1987): receipts $1.3 bln. **National budget** (1987): $23 bln. expenditures. **International reserves less gold** (Jan. 1990): $5.2 bln. **Gold:** 1.01 mln. oz t. **Consumer prices** (change in 1989): 20.2%.

Transport: Railway traffic (1987): 173 mln. passenger-km. **Motor vehicles:** in use (1987): 696,000 passenger cars, 140,000 comm. vehicles. **Civil aviation** (1987): 7.2 mln. passenger-km; 5 airports with scheduled flights. **Chief ports:** Haifa, Ashdod, Eilat.

Communications: Television sets: 1 per 6.9 persons. **Radios:** 1 per 2.2 persons. **Telephones:** 1 per 2.2 persons. **Daily newspaper circ.** (1988): 357 per 1,000 pop.

Health: Life expectancy at birth (1989) Jewish pop. only: 75 male; 79 female. **Births** (per 1,000 pop. 1989): 22. **Deaths** (per 1,000 pop. 1989): 7%. **Natural increase:** 1.5%. **Hospital beds:** 1 per 159 persons. **Physicians:** 1 per 345 persons. **Infant mortality** (per 1,000 live births 1989): 9.

Education (1989): **Literacy:** 88% (Jewish), 70% (Arab). **Major International Organizations:** UN (GATT).

Embassy: 3541 International Dr. NW 20008; 364-5500.

Occupying the SW corner of the ancient Fertile Crescent, Israel contains some of the oldest known evidence of agriculture and of primitive town life. A more advanced civilization emerged in the 3d millenium BC. The Hebrews probably arrived early in the 2d millenium BC. Under King David and his successors (c.1000 BC-597 BC), Judaism was developed and secured. After conquest by Babylonians, Persians, and Greeks, an independent Jewish kingdom was revived, 168 BC, but Rome took effective control in the next century, suppressed Jewish revolts in 70 AD and 135 AD, and renamed Judea Palestine, after the earlier coastal inhabitants, the Philistines.

Arab invaders conquered Palestine in 636. The Arabic language and Islam prevailed within a few centuries, but a Jewish minority remained. The land was ruled from the 11th century as a part of non-Arab empires by Seljuks, Mamluks, and Ottomans (with a crusader interval, 1098-1291).

After 4 centuries of Ottoman rule, during which the population declined to a low of 350,000 (1785), the land was taken in 1917 by Britain, which in the Balfour Declaration that year pledged to support a Jewish national homeland there, as foreseen by the Zionists. In 1920 a British Palestine Mandate was recognized; in 1922 the land east of the Jordan was detached.

Jewish immigration, begun in the late 19th century, swelled in the 1930s with refugees from the Nazis; heavy Arab immigration from Syria and Lebanon also occurred. Arab opposition to Jewish immigration turned violent in 1920, 1921, 1929, and 1936. The UN General Assembly voted in 1947 to partition Palestine into an Arab and a Jewish state. Britain withdrew in May 1948.

Israel was declared an independent state May 14, 1948; the Arabs rejected partition. Egypt, Jordan, Syria, Lebanon, Iraq, and Saudi Arabia invaded, but failed to destroy the Jewish state, which gained territory. Separate armistices with the Arab nations were signed in 1949; Jordan occupied the West Bank, Egypt occupied Gaza, but neither granted Palestinian autonomy.

After persistent terrorist raids, Israel invaded Egypt's Sinai, Oct. 29, 1956, aided briefly by British and French forces. A UN cease-fire was arranged Nov. 6.

An uneasy truce between Israel and the Arab countries, supervised by a UN Emergency Force, prevailed until May 19, 1967, when the UN force withdrew at the demand of Egypt's Pres. Nasser. Egyptian forces reoccupied the Gaza Strip and closed the Gulf of Aqaba to Israeli shipping. In a 6-day war that started June 5, the Israelis took the Gaza Strip, occupied the Sinai Peninsula to the Suez Canal, and captured Old Jerusalem, Syria's Golan Heights, and Jordan's West Bank. The fighting was halted June 10 by UN-arranged cease-fire agreements.

Egypt and Syria attacked Israel, Oct. 6, 1973 (Yom Kippur, most solemn day on the Jewish calendar). Israel counter-attacked, driving the Syrians back, and crossed the Suez Canal.

A cease fire took effect Oct. 24; a UN peace-keeping force went to the area. A disengagement agreement was signed Jan. 18, 1974. Israel withdrew from the canal's W bank. A second withdrawal was completed in 1976; Israel returned the Sinai to Egypt in 1982.

In the wake of the war, Golda Meir, long Israel's premier, resigned; severe inflation gripped the nation. Palestinian guerrillas staged massacres, killing scores of civilians 1974-75. Israel aided Christian forces in the 1975-76 Lebanese civil war.

Israeli forces raided Entebbe, Uganda, July 3, 1976, and rescued 103 hostages seized by Arab and German terrorists.

In 1977, the conservative opposition, led by Menachem Begin, was voted into office for the first time. Egypt's Pres. Sadat visited Jerusalem Nov. 1977 and on Mar. 26, 1979. Egypt and Israel signed a formal peace treaty, ending 30 years of war, and establishing diplomatic relations.

Israel invaded S. Lebanon, March 1978, following a Lebanon-based terrorist attack in Israel. Israel withdrew in favor of a 6,000-man UN force, but continued to aid Christian militiamen. Violence on the Israeli-occupied West Bank rose in 1982 when Israel announced plans to build new Jewish settlements. Israel affirmed the entire city of Jerusalem as its capital, July, 1980, encompassing the annexed Arab East Jerusalem.

Israel shot down, Apr. 28, 1981, two Syrian helicopters Israel claimed were attacking Lebanese Christian militia forces in the Beirut-Zahle area of Lebanon. Syria responded by installing Soviet-built surface-to-air missiles in Lebanon. Both the U.S. and Israel were unable to persuade Syria to withdraw the missiles, and Israel threatened to destroy them.

On June 7, 1981, Israeli jets destroyed an Iraqi atomic reactor near Baghdad that, Israel claimed, would have enabled Iraq to manufacture nuclear weapons.

Israeli jets bombed Palestine Liberation Organization (PLO) strongholds in Lebanon April, May 1982. In reaction to the wounding of the Israeli ambassador to Great Britain, Israeli forces in a coordinated land, sea, and air attack invaded Lebanon, June 6, to destroy PLO strongholds in that country. Israeli and Syrian forces engaged in the Bekka Valley, June 9, but quickly agreed to a truce. Israeli forces encircled Beirut June 14. Following massive Israeli bombing of West Beirut, the PLO agreed to evacuate the city.

Israeli troops entered West Beirut after newly-elected Lebanese president Bashir Gemayel was assassinated on Sept. 14. Israel received widespread condemnation when Lebanese Christian forces, Sept. 16, entered 2 West Beirut refugee camps and slaughtered hundreds of Palestinian refugees. Israeli troops withdrew from Lebanon in June 1986.

In 1989, violence continued over the Israeli military occupation of the West Bank and Gaza Strip; protesters and Israeli troops clashed frequently.

The Knesset approved a new right-wing coalition government led by Prime Minister Yitzhak Shamir, June 11, 1990, following a 3-month political crisis that began with the fall of the previous "National Unity" government of Shamir and the Labor Party of Shimon Peres.

Italy
Italian Republic
Repubblica Italiana

People: Population (1990 est.): 57,657,000. **Age distrib. (%):** 0–14: 19.9; 15–59: 61.3; 60+: 18.8. **Pop. density:** 493 per sq. mi. **Urban** (1988): 67%. **Ethnic groups:** Italians, small minorities of Germans, Slovenes, Albanians. **Languages:** Italian. **Religions:** Predominantly Roman Catholic.

Geography: Area: 116,303 sq. mi., about the size of Florida and Georgia combined. **Location:** In S Europe, jutting into Mediterranean S. **Neighbors:** France on W, Switzerland, Austria on N, Yugoslavia on E. **Topography:** Occupies a long boot-shaped peninsula, extending SE from the Alps into the Mediterranean, with the islands of Sicily and Sardinia offshore. The alluvial Po Valley drains most of N. The rest of the country is rugged and mountainous, except for intermittent coastal plains, like the Campania, S of Rome. Apennine Mts. run down through center of peninsula. **Capital:** Rome. **Cities** (1988 est.): Rome 2.8 mln.; Milan 1.4 mln.; Naples 1.2 mln.; Turin 1.0 mln.

Government: Type: Republic. **Head of state:** Pres. Francesco Cossiga; b. July 26, 1929; in office: July 9, 1985; **Head of government:** Prime Min. Giulio Andreotti; in office: July 23, 1989. **Local divisions:** 20 regions with some autonomy, 94 provinces. **Defense:** 2.1% of GNP (1988).

Economy: Industries: Steel, machinery, autos, textiles, shoes, machine tools, chemicals. **Chief crops:** Grapes, olives,

citrus fruits, vegetables, wheat, rice. **Minerals:** Mercury, potash, sulphur. **Crude oil reserves** (1987): 951 mln. bbls. **Arable land:** 32%. **Livestock** (1987): cattle: 8.9 mln.; pigs: 9.1 mln.; sheep: 9.6 mln. **Fish catch** (1988): 554,000 metric tons. **Electricity prod.** (1988): 197 bln. kwh. **Crude steel prod.** (1988): 23.6 mln. metric tons. **Labor force:** 5% agric.; 32% ind. and comm.; 58% services and govt.

Finance: Currency: Lira (June 1990: 1,214 = $1 US). **Gross national product** (1988): $825 bln. **Per capita income** (1988): $14,383. **Imports** (1989): $153 bln.; partners: W. Ger. 20%, Fr. 15%, U.S. 7%. **Exports** (1989): $140 bln.; partners: W. Ger. 16%, Fr. 15%, U.S. 10%, UK 6%. **Tourists** (1987): receipts $12.1 bln. **National budget** (1987): $311 bln. expenditures. **International reserves less gold** (Apr. 1990): $51 bln. **Gold:** 66.67 mln. oz t. **Consumer prices** (change in 1989): 6.2%.

Transport: Railway traffic (1987): 41 bln. passenger-km. **Motor vehicles:** in use (1986): 23.3 mln. passenger cars, 1.9 mln. comm. vehicles. **Civil aviation** (1988): 15.6 bln. passenger-km; 36 airports. **Chief ports:** Genoa, Venice, Trieste, Taranto, Naples, La Spezia.

Communications: Television sets: 1 per 3.9 persons. **Radios:** 1 per 3.9 persons. **Telephones:** 1 per 2.0 persons. **Daily newspaper circ.** (1987): 121 per 1,000 pop.

Health: Life expectancy at birth (1989): 73 male; 80 female. **Births** (per 1,000 pop. 1989): 11. **Deaths** (per 1,000 pop. 1989): 10. **Natural increase:** .1%. **Hospital beds:** 1 per 127 persons. **Physicians:** 1 per 233 persons. **Infant mortality** (per 1,000 live births 1989): 8.

Education (1989): **Literacy:** 97%. **Years compulsory:** 8.

Major International Organizations: UN and all of its specialized agencies, NATO, OECD, EC.

Embassy: 1601 Fuller St. NW 20009; 328-5500.

Rome emerged as the major power in Italy after 500 BC, dominating the more civilized Etruscans to the N and Greeks to the S. Under the Empire, which lasted until the 5th century AD, Rome ruled most of Western Europe, the Balkans, the Near East, and North Africa. In 1988, archeologists unearthed evidence showing Rome as a dynamic society in the 6th and 7th centuries B.C.

After the Germanic invasions, lasting several centuries, a high civilization arose in the city-states of the N, culminating in the Renaissance. But German, French, Spanish, and Austrian intervention prevented the unification of the country. In 1859 Lombardy came under the crown of King Victor Emmanuel II of Sardinia. By plebiscite in 1860, Parma, Modena, Romagna, and Tuscany joined, followed by Sicily and Naples, and by the Marches and Umbria. The first Italian parliament declared Victor Emmanuel king of Italy Mar. 17, 1861. Mantua and Venetia were added in 1866 as an outcome of the Austro-Prussian war. The Papal States were taken by Italian troops Sept. 20, 1870, on the withdrawal of the French garrison. The states were annexed to the kingdom by plebiscite. Italy recognized the State of Vatican City as independent Feb. 11, 1929.

Fascism appeared in Italy Mar. 23, 1919, led by Benito Mussolini, who took over the government at the invitation of the king Oct. 28, 1922. Mussolini acquired dictatorial powers. He made war on Ethiopia and proclaimed Victor Emmanuel III emperor, defied the sanctions of the League of Nations, joined the Berlin-Tokyo axis, sent troops to fight for Franco against the Republic of Spain and joined Germany in World War II.

After Fascism was overthrown in 1943, Italy declared war on Germany and Japan and contributed to the Allied victory. It surrendered conquered lands and lost its colonies. Mussolini was killed by partisans Apr. 28, 1945.

Victor Emmanuel III abdicated May 9, 1946; his son Humbert II was king until June 10, when Italy became a republic after a referendum, June 2-3.

Reorganization of the Fascist party is forbidden. The cabinet normally represents a coalition of the Christian Democrats, largest of Italy's many parties, and one or 2 other parties.

The Vatican agreed in 1976 to revise its 1929 concordat with the state, depriving Roman Catholicism of its status as state religion. In 1974 Italians voted by a 3-to-2 margin to retain a 3-year-old law permitting divorce, which was opposed by the church.

Italy has enjoyed an extraordinary growth in industry and living standards since World War II, in part due to membership in the Common Market. Italy joined the European Monetary System, 1980. A wave of left-wing political violence began in the late 1970s with kidnappings and assassinations and continued through the 1980s. Christian Dem. leader and former Prime Min. Moro was murdered May 1978 by Red Brigade terrorists.

The Cabinet of Prime Min. Arnaldo Forlani resigned, May 26, 1981, in the wake of revelations that numerous high-ranking officials were members of an illegally secret Masonic lodge. The June 1983 elections saw Bettino Craxi chosen the nation's first Socialist premier. Craxi's government faced a severe crisis as the result of a chain of events sparked by the Oct. 17, 1985 hijacking of the Italian cruise ship *Achille Lauro* and the subsequent U.S. downing on Italian soil of an Egyptian aircraft carrying the 4 hijackers and Abul Abbas, a PLO leader suspected of planning the hijacking. Craxi's release of Abbas and refusal to turn the 4 hijackers over to the U.S. caused an internal crisis that almost saw his government fall. Craxi ended the longest tenure of an Italian leader since World War II by resigning Mar. 1987.

Sicily, 9,926 sq. mi., pop. (1987) 5,112,000, is an island 180 by 120 mi., seat of a region that embraces the island of **Pantelleria,** 32 sq. mi., and the **Lipari** group, 44 sq. mi., 63 14,000, including 2 active volcanoes: **Vulcano,** 1,637 ft. and **Stromboli,** 3,038 ft. From prehistoric times Sicily has been settled by various peoples; a Greek state had its capital at Syracuse. Rome took Sicily from Carthage 215 BC. **Mt. Etna,** 11,053 ft. active volcano, is tallest peak.

Sardinia, 9,301 sq. mi., pop. (1986) 1,638,000, lies in the Mediterranean, 115 mi. W of Italy and 7-½ mi. S of Corsica. It is 160 mi. long, 68 mi. wide, and mountainous, with mining of coal, zinc, lead, copper. In 1720 Sardinia was added to the possessions of the Dukes of Savoy in Piedmont and Savoy to form the Kingdom of Sardinia. Giuseppe Garibaldi is buried on the nearby isle of Caprera. **Elba,** 86 sq. mi., lies 6 mi. W of Tuscany. Napoleon I lived in exile on Elba 1814-1815.

Trieste. An agreement, signed Oct. 5, 1954, by Italy and Yugoslavia, confirmed, Nov. 10, 1975, gave Italy provisional administration over the northern section and the seaport of Trieste, and Yugoslavia the part of Istrian peninsula it has occupied.

Jamaica

People: Population (1990 est.): 2,513,000. **Age distrib. (%):** 0–14: 36.7; 15–59: 52.8; 60+: 8.5. **Pop. density:** 556 per sq. mi. **Urban** (1989): 48%. **Ethnic groups:** African 76%, mixed 15%, Chinese, Caucasians, East Indians. **Languages:** English, Jamaican Creole. **Religions:** Protestant 70%.

Geography: Area: 4,232 sq. mi., slightly smaller than Connecticut. **Location:** In West Indies. **Neighbors:** Nearest are Cuba on N, Haiti on E. **Topography:** The country is four-fifths covered by mountains. **Capital:** Kingston. **Cities** (1984 est.): St. Andrew 393,000, Kingston 100,000.

Government: Type: Constitutional monarchy. **Head of state:** Queen Elizabeth II, represented by Gov.-Gen. Florizel A. Glasspole; b. Sept. 25, 1909; in office: Mar. 2, 1973. **Head of government:** Prime Min. Michael N. Manley; in office: Feb. 9, 1989. **Local divisions:** 14 parishes; Kingston and St. Andrew corporate area. **Defense:** 1.0% of GDP (1989).

Economy: Industries: Rum, molasses, cement, paper, tourism. **Chief crops:** Sugar cane, coffee, bananas, coconuts, citrus fruits. **Minerals:** Bauxite, limestone, gypsum. **Arable land:** 19%. **Livestock** (1987): cattle: 290,000; goats: 420,000. **Electricity prod.** (1988): 2.4 bln. kwh. **Labor force:** 31% agric.; 27% services; 41% ind.

Finance: Currency: Dollar (Apr. 1990: 6.95 = $1 US). **Gross national product** (1987): $2.9 bln. **Per capita GNP** (1987): $1,160. **Imports** (1989): $1.8 bln.; partners: U.S. 44%, UK 17%. **Exports** (1989): $967 mln.; partners: U.S. 33%, UK 17%, Can. 16%. **Tourists** (1987): receipts: $525 mln. **National budget** (1989): $1.0 bln. **International reserves less gold** (Feb. 1990): $107 mln. **Consumer prices** (change in 1989): 14.3%.

Transport: Railway traffic (1986): 40 mln. passenger-km. **Motor vehicles:** in use (1988): 52,000 passenger cars, 23,000 comm. vehicles. **Civil aviation** (1988): 1.9 bln. passenger km.; 6 airports with scheduled flights. **Chief ports:** Kingston, Montego Bay.

Communications: Television sets: 1 per 6.1 persons. **Radios:** 1 per 2.1 persons. **Telephones:** 1 per 14 persons. **Daily newspaper circ.** (1987): 36 per 1,000 pop.

Health: Life expectancy at birth (1989): 75 male; 78 female. **Births** (per 1,000 pop. 1989): 27. **Deaths** (per 1,000 pop. 1989). **Natural increase:** 2.2%. **Hospital beds:** 1 per 414 persons. **Physicians:** 1 per 6,421 persons. **Infant mortality** (per 1,000 live births 1989): 17.

Education (1990): **Literacy:** 82%. Compulsory to age 14.

Major International Organizations: UN (World Bank, GATT), OAS.

Embassy: 1850 K St. NW 20006; 452-0660.

Jamaica was visited by Columbus, 1494, and ruled by Spain (under whom Arawak Indians died out) until seized by Britain, 1655. Jamaica won independence Aug. 6, 1962.

In 1974 Jamaica sought an increase in taxes paid by U.S. and Canadian companies which mine bauxite on the island. The socialist government acquired 50% ownership of the companies' Jamaican interests in 1976, and was reelected that year. Rudimentary welfare state measures were passed, but unemployment increased. Relations with the U.S. improved greatly in the 1980s following the election of Edward Seaga.

Jamaica took part in the October 1983 invasion of Grenada.

Hurricane Gilbert struck Jamaica Sept. 12, 1988, killing some 45 and causing extensive damage including half the nation's houses.

Japan
Nippon

People: Population (1990 est.): 123,778,000. **Age distrib. (%):** 0–14: 19.0; 15–59: 64.1; 60+: 16.9. **Pop. density:** 844 per sq. mi. **Urban** (1985): 76.7%. **Language:** Japanese. **Ethnic groups:** Japanese 99.4%, Korean 0.5%. **Religions:** Buddhism, Shintoism shared by large majority.

Geography: Area: 145,856 sq. mi., slightly smaller than California. **Location:** Archipelago off E. coast of Asia. **Neighbors:** USSR on N, S. Korea on W. **Topography:** Japan consists of 4 main islands: Honshu ("mainland"), 87,805 sq. mi.; Hokkaido, 30,144 sq. mi.; Kyushu, 14,114 sq. mi.; and Shikoku, 7,049 sq. mi. The coast, deeply indented, measures 16,654 mi. The northern islands are a continuation of the Sakhalin Mts. The Kunlun range of China continues into southern islands, the ranges meeting in the Japanese Alps. In a vast transverse fissure crossing Honshu E-W rises a group of volcanoes, mostly extinct or inactive, including 12,388 ft. Fuji-San (Fujiyama) near Tokyo. **Capital:** Tokyo. **Cities** (1987 est.): Tokyo 8.3 mln.; Osaka 2.6 mln.; Yokohama 3.1 mln.; Nagoya 2.1 mln.; Kyoto 1.4 mln.; Kobe 1.4 mln.; Sapporo 1.6 mln.; Kitakyushu 1 mln.; Kawasaki 1.1 mln; Fukuoka 1.2 mln.

Government: Type: Parliamentary democracy. **Head of state:** Emp. Akihito; b. Dec. 23, 1933; in office: Jan. 7, 1989. **Head of government:** Prime Min. Toshiki Kaifu; b. Jan. 2, 1931; in office: Aug. 9, 1989. **Local divisions:** 47 prefectures. **Defense:** Less than 1% of GNP (1987).

Economy: Industries: Electrical & electronic equip., autos, machinery, chemicals. **Chief crops:** Rice, grains, vegetables, fruits. **Minerals:** negligible. **Crude oil reserves** (1985): 26 mln. bbls. **Arable land:** 13%. **Livestock** (1986): cattle: 4.6 mln.; pigs: 11.7 mln. **Fish catch** (1987): 12.4 mln. metric tons. **Electricity prod.** (1988): 696 bln. kwh. **Crude steel prod.** (1987): 98.5 mln. metric tons. **Labor force:** 8% agric.; 34% manuf. & mining; 53% services & trade.

Finance: Currency: Yen (June 1990: 151 = $1 US). **Gross national product** (1989): $1.8 trl. **Per capita GNP** (1989): $15,030. **Imports** (1989): $209 bln.; partners: U.S. 20%, Middle East 26%, SE Asia 22%, EC 6%. **Exports** (1989): $273 bln.; partners: U.S. 37%, EC 12%, SE Asia 23%. **Tourists** (1988): $2.8 bln. receipts. **National budget** (1989): $470 bln. expenditures. **International reserves less gold** (Mar. 1990): $73 bln. **Gold:** 24.23 mln. oz. t. **Consumer prices** (change in 1989): 2.3%.

Transport: Railway traffic (1987): 341 bln. passenger-km. **Motor vehicles:** in use (1988): 29.4 mln. passenger cars, 19.1 mln. **Civil aviation** (1988): 83.7 bln. passenger-km; 65 airports with scheduled flights. **Chief ports:** Yokohama, Tokyo, Kobe, Osaka, Nagoya, Chiba, Kawasaki, Hakodate.

Communications: Television sets: 1 per 4.1 persons. **Radios:** 1 per 1.3 persons. **Telephones:** 1 per 1.8 persons. **Daily newspaper circ.** (1988): 569 per 1,000 pop.

Health: Life expectancy at birth (1989): 76 male; 82 female. **Births** (per 1,000 pop. 1989): 11. **Deaths** (per 1,000 pop. 1989): 7. **Natural increase:** 0.5%. **Hospital beds:** 1 per 77 persons. **Physicians:** 1 per 668 persons. **Infant mortality** (per 1,000 live births 1989): 5.

Education (1989): **Literacy:** 99%. Most attend school for 12 years.

Major International Organizations: UN (IMF, GATT, ILO), OECD.

Embassy: 2520 Massachusetts Ave. NW 20008; 939-6700.

According to Japanese legend, the empire was founded by Emperor Jimmu, 660 BC, but earliest records of a unified Japan date from 1,000 years later. Chinese influence was strong in the formation of Japanese civilization. Buddhism was introduced before the 6th century.

A feudal system, with locally powerful noble families and their samurai warrior retainers, dominated from 1192. Central power was held by successive families of shoguns (military dictators), 1192-1867, until recovered by the Emperor Meiji, 1868. The Portuguese and Dutch had minor trade with Japan in the 16th and 17th centuries; U.S. Commodore Matthew C. Perry opened it to U.S. trade in a treaty ratified 1854. Japan fought China, 1894-95, gaining Taiwan. After war with Russia, 1904-05, Russia ceded S half of Sakhalin and gave concessions in China. Japan annexed Korea 1910. In World War I Japan ousted Germany from Shantung, took over German Pacific islands. Japan took Manchuria 1931, started war with China 1932. Japan launched war against the U.S. by attack on Pearl Harbor Dec. 7, 1941. Japan surrendered Aug. 14, 1945.

In a new constitution adopted May 3, 1947, Japan renounced the right to wage war; the emperor gave up claims to divinity; the Diet became the sole law-making authority.

The U.S. and 48 other non-communist nations signed a peace treaty and the U.S. a bilateral defense agreement with Japan, in San Francisco Sept. 8, 1951, restoring Japan's sovereignty as of April 28, 1952. Japan signed separate treaties with China, 1952; India, 1952; a declaration with USSR ending a technical state of war, 1956. In Dec. 1965 Japan and South Korea agreed to resume diplomatic relations.

On June 26, 1968, the U.S. returned to Japanese control the Bonin Is., the Volcano Is. (including Iwo Jima) and Marcus Is. On May 15, 1972, Okinawa, the other Ryukyu Is. and the Daito Is. were returned to Japan by the U.S.; it was agreed the U.S. would continue to maintain military bases on Okinawa. Japan and the USSR have failed to resolve disputed claims of sovereignty over 4 of the Kurile Is. and over offshore fishing rights.

In 1972, Japan and China resumed diplomatic relations.

Industrialization was begun in the late 19th century. After World War II, Japan emerged as one of the most powerful economies in the world, and as a leader in technology.

The U.S. and EC member nations have criticized Japan for its restrictive policy on imports which has given Japan a substantial trade surplus.

In Apr. 1987, the U.S. imposed 100% tariffs on Japanese electronics imports in retaliation for what the U.S. considered various unfair trade practices.

The Recruit scandal, the nation's worst political scandal since World War II, which involved illegal political donations and stock trading, led to the resignation of Premier Noboru Takeshita in May 1989.

Premier Toshiki Kaifu visited the U.S. Mar. 2-3, 1990, and met with Pres. Bush in an effort to ease the increasing economic tension between the 2 countries over the long-standing trade imbalance.

Jordan

Hashemite Kingdom of Jordan

al Mamlaka al Urduniya al Hashemiyah

Population (1990 est.): 3,065,000. **Age distrib.** (%): 0-14: 48.1; 15-59: 46.9; 60+: 4.0. **Pop. density:** 80 per sq. mi. **Urban** (1986): 70%. **Ethnic groups:** Arab 98%. **Languages:** Arabic (official), English. **Religions:** Sunni Moslem 92%, Christian 8%.

Geography: Area: 37,737 sq. mi., slightly larger than Indiana. **Location:** In W Asia. **Neighbors:** Israel on W, Saudi Arabia on S, Iraq on E, Syria on N. **Topography:** About 88% of Jordan is arid. Fertile areas are in W. Only port is on short Aqaba Gulf coast. Country shares Dead Sea (1,296 ft. below sea level) with Israel. **Capital:** Amman. **Cities** (1988 est.): Amman 900,000; az-Zarqa 306,000; Irbid 161,000.

Government: Type: Constitutional monarchy. **Head of state:** King Hussein I; b. Nov. 14, 1935; in office: Aug. 11, 1952. **Head of government:** Prime Min. Field Marshal Sharif Zeid bin Shaker; in office: Apr. 27, 1989. **Local divisions:** 8 governorates. **Defense:** 13% of GNP (1987).

Economy: Industries: Textiles, cement, food processing. **Chief crops:** Grains, olives, vegetables, fruits. **Minerals:** Phosphate, potash. **Arable land:** 5%. **Electricity prod.** (1988): 3.3 bln. kwh. **Labor force:** 20% agric. 20% manuf. & mining.

Finance: Currency: Dinar (Mar. 1990: 0.66 = $1 US). **Gross national product** (1987): $4.3 bln. **Imports** (1988): $2.7 bln.; partners: Saudi Ar. 6%, U.S. 11%, Jap. 8%. **Exports** (1988): $1.0 bln.; partners: Saudi Ar. 12%, Ind. 13%, Iraq. 18%. **Tourists** (1986): receipts: $534 mln. **National budget** (1989): $2.3 bln. expenditures. **International reserves less gold** (Mar. 1990): $407 mln. **Gold:** 749,000 oz t. **Consumer prices** (change in 1988): 3.2%.

Transport: Motor vehicles: in use (1986): 158,000 passenger cars, 158,000 comm. vehicles. **Civil aviation** (1988): 3.9 bln. passenger-km; 3 airports with scheduled flights. **Chief ports:** Aqaba.

Communications: Television sets: 1 per 12 persons. **Radios:** 1 per 2.7 persons. **Telephones:** 1 per 10 persons. **Daily newspaper circ.** (1987): 68 per 1,000 pop.

Health: Life expectancy at birth (1989): 67 male; 71 female. **Births** (per 1,000 pop. 1989): 42.7. **Deaths** (per 1,000 pop. 1989): 6. **Natural increase:** 3.6%. **Hospital beds:** 1 per 523 persons. **Physicians:** 1 per 881 persons. **Infant mortality** (per 1,000 live births 1989): 55.

Education (1989): **Literacy:** 71%.

Major International Organizations: UN (WHO, IMF), Arab League.

Embassy: 3504 International Dr. NW 20008; 966-2664.

From ancient times to 1922 the lands to the E of the Jordan were culturally and politically united with the lands to the W. Arabs conquered the area in the 7th century; the Ottomans took control in the 16th. Britain's 1920 Palestine Mandate covered both sides of the Jordan. In 1921, Abdullah, son of the ruler of Hejaz in Arabia, was installed by Britain as emir of an autonomous Transjordan, covering two-thirds of Palestine. An independent kingdom was proclaimed, 1946.

During the 1948 Arab-Israeli war the West Bank and old city of Jerusalem were added to the kingdom, which changed its name to Jordan. All these territories were lost to Israel in the 1967 war, which swelled the number of Arab refugees on the East Bank. A 1974 Arab summit conference designated the Palestine Liberation Organization as the sole representative of Arabs on the West Bank. Jordan accepted the move, and was granted an annual subsidy by Arab oil states.

In 1988 Jordan cut legal and administrative ties with the Israeli-occupied West Bank. In Apr. 1989, riots broke out over price increases imposed under an agreement with the International Monetary Fund.

Kenya

Republic of Kenya

Jamhuri ya Kenya

People: Population (1990 est.): 25,393,000. **Age distrib.** (%): 0-14: 51.2; 15-59: 45.4; 60+: 3.4. **Pop. density:** 105 per sq. mi. **Urban** (1986): 20%. **Ethnic groups:** Kikuyu 21%, Luo 13%, Luhya 14%, Kalenjin 11%, Kamba 11%, others, including Asians, Arabs, Europeans. **Languages:** Swahili (official), English. **Religions:** Protestant 38%, Roman Catholic 26%, Moslem 6%, others.

Geography: Area: 224,960 sq. mi., slightly smaller than Texas. **Location:** On Indian O. coast of E. Africa. **Neighbors:** Uganda on W, Tanzania on S, Somalia on E, Ethopia, Sudan on N. **Topography:** The northern three-fifths of Kenya is arid. To the S, a low coastal area and a plateau varying from 3,000 to 10,000 ft. The Great Rift Valley enters the country N-S, flanked by high mountains. **Capital:** Nairobi. **Cities** (1987 est.): Nairobi 959,000; Mombasa 401,000.

Government: Type: Republic. **Head of state:** Pres. Daniel arap Moi, b. Sept., 1924; in office: Aug. 22, 1978. **Local divisions:** Nairobi and 7 provinces. **Defense:** 2.4% of GDP (1987).

Economy: Industries: Tourism, light industry, petroleum prods. **Chief crops:** Coffee, corn, tea, cereals, cotton, sisal. **Minerals:** Gold, limestone, diatomite, salt, barytes, magnesite, felspar, sapphires, fluospar, garnets. **Other resources:** Timber, hides. **Arable land:** 4%. **Livestock** (1986): cattle: 12.5 mln. **Fish catch** (1987): 131,000 metric tons. **Electricity prod.**

(1987): 2.4 bln. kwh. **Labor force:** 21% agric.; 21% ind. and commerce; 13% services; 40% public sector.

Finance: Currency: Shilling (Mar. 1990: 22.12 = $1 US). **Gross national product** (1987): $8.1 bln. **Per capita income** (1986): $322. **Imports** (1988): $1.9 bln.; partners: UK 14%, W. Ger. 11%, Jap. 11%, Fra. 11%. **Exports** (1988): $1.0 bln.; partners: W. Ger. 11%, UK 18%, Ugan. 9%. **Tourists** (1987): receipts: $355 mln. **National budget** (1987): $2.6 bln expenditures. **International reserves less gold** (Mar. 1990): $197 mln. **Gold:** 80,000 oz t. **Consumer prices** (change in 1988): 8.3%.

Transport: Motor vehicles: in use (1987): 133,000 passenger cars, 110,000 comm. vehicles. **Civil Aviation** (1988): 753 mln. passenger-km; 16 airports with scheduled flights. **Chief ports:** Mombasa.

Communications: Television sets: 1 per 118 persons. **Radios:** 1 per 12 persons. **Telephones:** 1 per 70 persons. **Daily newspaper circ.** (1986): 16 per 1,000 pop.

Health: Life expectancy at birth (1989): 59 male; 63 female. **Births** (per 1,000 pop. 1989): 51. **Deaths** (per 1,000 pop. 1989): 9. **Natural increase:** 4.2%. **Hospital beds:** 1 per 657 persons. **Physicians:** 1 per 7,122 persons. **Infant mortality** (per 1,000 live births 1989): 70.

Education (1989): **Literacy:** 50%. 86% attend primary school.

Major International Organizations: UN and all of its specialized agencies, OAU, Commonwealth of Nations.

Embassy: 2249 R St. NW 20008; 387-6101.

Arab colonies exported spices and slaves from the Kenya coast as early as the 8th century. Britain obtained control in the 19th century. Kenya won independence Dec. 12, 1963, 4 years after the end of the violent Mau Mau uprising.

Kenya has shown steady growth in industry and agriculture under a modified private enterprise system, and has had a relatively free political life. But stability was shaken in 1974-5, with opposition charges of corruption and oppression.

In 1968 ties with Somalia were restored after 4 years of skirmishes. Tanzania closed its Kenya border in 1977 in a dispute over the collapse of the East African Community.

Kenya has close ties to the West.

Kiribati
Republic of Kiribati

People: Population (1990 est.): 65,000. **Pop. density:** 244 per sq. mi. **Ethnic groups:** nearly all Micronesian, some Polynesians. **Languages:** Gilbertese and English (official). **Religions:** evenly divided between Protestant and Roman Catholic.

Geography: Area: 266 sq. mi., slightly smaller than New York City. **Location:** 33 Micronesian islands (the Gilbert, Line, and Phoenix groups) in the mid-Pacific scattered in a 2-mln. sq. mi. chain around the point where the International Date Line cuts the Equator. **Neighbors:** Nearest are Nauru to SW, Tuvalu and Tokelau Is. to S. **Topography:** except Banaba (Ocean) I., all are low-lying, with soil of coral sand and rock fragments, subject to erratic rainfall. **Capital:** Tarawa 22,000.

Government: Type: Republic. **Head of state and of government:** Pres. Ieremia Tabai, b. Dec. 16, 1950; in office: July 12, 1979.

Economy: Industries: Copra. **Chief crops:** Coconuts, breadfruit, pandanus, bananas, paw paw. **Other resources:** Fish. **Electricity prod.** (1988): 8 mln. kwh.

Finance: Currency: Australian dollar. **Gross national product** (1987): $24 mln.

Transport: Chief port: Tarawa.

Communications: Radios: 1 per 6.8 persons. **Telephones:** 1 per 48 persons.

Health: Hospital beds: 1 per 231 persons. **Physicians:** 1 per 4,094 persons.

Education: Literacy (1985): 90%.

A British protectorate since 1892, the Gilbert and Ellice Islands colony was completed with the inclusion of the Phoenix Islands, 1937. Self-rule was granted 1971; the Ellice Islands separated from the colony 1975 and became independent Tuvalu, 1978. Kiribati (pronounced *Kiribass*) independence was attained July 12, 1979. Under a Treaty of Friendship the U.S. relinquished its claims to several of the Line and Phoenix islands, including Christmas, Canton, and Enderbury.

Tarawa Atoll was the scene of some of the bloodiest fighting in the Pacific during WW II.

North Korea
Democratic People's Republic of Korea
Chosun Minchu-chui Inmin Konghwa-guk

People: Population (1990 est.): 23,059,000. **Pop. density:** 471 per sq. mi. **Urban** (1985): 62%. **Ethnic groups:** Korean. **Languages:** Korean. **Religions:** activities almost nonexistent; traditionally Buddhism, Confucianism, Chondokyo.

Geography: Area: 46,540 sq. mi., slightly smaller than Mississippi. **Location:** In northern E. Asia. **Neighbors:** China, USSR on N, S. Korea on S. **Topography:** Mountains and hills cover nearly all the country, with narrow valleys and small plains in between. The N and the E coast are the most rugged areas. **Capital:** Pyongyang. **Cities** (1981 est.): Pyongyang 1,283,000.

Government: Type: Communist state. **Head of state:** Pres. Kim Il-Sung; b. Apr. 15, 1912; in office: Dec. 28, 1972. **Head of government:** Premier Yong Hyong Muk; in office: Dec. 12, 1988. **Head of Communist Party:** Gen. Sec. Kim Il-Sung; in office: 1945. **Local divisions:** 9 provinces, 3 special cities. **Defense** (1988): 24% of GNP.

Economy: Industries: Textiles, petrochemicals, food processing. **Chief crops:** Corn, potatoes, fruits, vegetables, rice. **Minerals:** Coal, lead tungsten, graphite, magnesite, iron, copper, gold, phosphate, salt, fluorspar. **Arable land:** 19%. **Livestock** (1987): cattle: 1.1 mln; pigs: 3.0 mln. **Fish catch** (1987): 1.8 mln. metric tons. **Crude steel prod.** (1987) 6.1 mln. metric tons. **Electricity prod.** (1988): 41 bln. kwh. **Labor force:** 48% agric.

Finance: Currency: Won (Mar. 1990): 0.97 = $1 US). **Gross national product** (1988): $20 bln. **Imports** (1988): $3.1 bln.; partners: China 17%, USSR 36%, Jap. 19%. **Exports** (1988): $2.4 bln.; partners: USSR 43% China 13%, Jap. 15%.

Communications: Television sets: 1 mln. in use (1984). **Radios:** 4.1 mln. in use (1984).

Transport: Chief ports: Chonglin, Hamhung, Nampo.

Health: Life expectancy at birth (1989): 67 male; 73 female. **Births** (per 1,000 pop. 1989): 29. **Deaths** (per 1,000 pop. 1989): 5. **Natural increase:** 2.4%. **Hospital beds:** 1 per 74 persons. **Physicians:** 1 per 370 persons. **Infant mortality** (per 1,000 live births, 1989): 32.

Education (1989): **Literacy:** 99%. **Years compulsory:** 11.

The Democratic People's Republic of Korea was founded May 1, 1948, in the zone occupied by Russian troops after World War II. Its armies tried to conquer the south, 1950. After 3 years of fighting with Chinese and U.S. intervention, a cease-fire was proclaimed.

Industry, begun by the Japanese during their 1910-45 occupation, and nationalized in the 1940s, had grown substantially, using N. Korea's abundant mineral and hydroelectric resources.

Two N. Korean Army officers were sentenced to death by Burmese authorities after they confessed to the October 9, 1983 bombing which killed 17, including 4 S. Korean cabinet ministers, in Rangoon.

South Korea
Republic of Korea
Taehan Min'guk

People: Population (1990 est.): 43,919,000. **Age distrib.** (%): 0–14: 30.6; 15–59: 52.7; 60+: 6.7. **Pop. density:** 1,189 per sq. mi. **Urban** (1988): 68%. **Ethnic groups:** Korean. **Languages:** Korean. **Religions:** Buddhism, Confucianism, Christian.

Geography: Area: 38,025 sq. mi., slightly larger than Indiana. **Location:** In Northern E. Asia. **Neighbors:** N. Korea on N. **Topography:** The country is mountainous, with a rugged east coast. The western and southern coasts are deeply indented, with many islands and harbors. **Capital:** Seoul. **Cities** (1989 cen.): Seoul 10.2 mln.; Pusan 3,700,000; Taegu 2,200,000; Inchon 1,600,000; Kwangju 1,100,000; Taejon 1,000,000.

Government: Type: Republic, with power centralized in a strong executive. **Head of state:** Pres. Roh Tae Woo; b. 1932; in office: Feb. 25, 1988. **Head of government:** Prime Min. Kang Young Hoon; in office: Dec. 5, 1988. **Local divisions:** 9 provinces and Seoul, Pusan, Inchon, and Taegu. **Defense:** 5.8% of GNP (1987).

Economy: Industries: Electronics, ships, textiles, clothing, motor vehicles. **Chief crops:** Rice, barley, vegetables, wheat. **Minerals:** Tungsten, coal, graphite. **Arable land:** 22%. **Livestock** (1987): cattle: 2.8 mln.; pigs: 3.3 mln. **Fish catch:** (1988): 3.2 mln. metric tons. **Electricity prod.** (1988): 85.0 bln. kwh. **Crude steel prod.** (1987): 16.7 mln. metric tons. **Labor force:** 21% agric.; 27% manuf. & mining; 52% services.

Finance: Currency: Won (Mar. 1990: 702 = $1 US). **Gross national product** (1988): $171 bln. **Per capita income** (1986): $2,180. **Imports** (1989): $63 bln.; partners: Jap. 33%, U.S. 21%. **Exports** (1989): $62 bln.; partners: U.S. 40%, Jap. 15%. **Tourists** (1988): receipts: $1.3 bln. **National budget** (1988): $22.0 bln. expenditures. **International reserves less gold** (Mar. 1990): $13 bln. **Gold:** 320,000 oz t. **Consumer prices** (change in 1989): 5.7%.

Transport: Railway traffic (1987): 24 bln. passenger-km. **Motor vehicles:** in use (1988): 975,000 passenger cars, 748,000 comm. vehicles. **Civil aviation** (1987): 14.4 bln. passenger-km; 6 airlines with scheduled flights. **Chief ports:** Pusan, Inchon.

Communications: Television sets: 1 per 4.9 persons. **Radios:** 1 per 1.0 persons. **Telephones:** 1 per 4.1 persons. **Daily newspaper circ.** (1986): 24 per 1,000 pop.

Health: Life expectancy at birth (1989): 66 male; 73 female. **Births** (per 1,000 pop. 1989): 20. **Deaths** (per 1,000 pop. 1989): 6. **Natural increase:** 1.4%. **Hospital beds:** 1 per 487 persons. **Physicians:** 1 per 1,216 persons. **Infant mortality** (per 1,000 live births 1989): 25.0.

Education (1989): **Literacy:** 92%. **Attendance:** High school 90%, college 14%.

Embassy: 2320 Massachusetts Ave. NW 20008; 939-5600.

Korea, once called the Hermit Kingdom, has a recorded history since the 1st century BC. It was united in a kingdom under the Silla Dynasty, 668 AD. It was at times associated with the Chinese empire; the treaty that concluded the Sino-Japanese war of 1894-95 recognized Korea's complete independence. In 1910 Japan forcibly annexed Korea as Chosun.

At the Potsdam conference, July, 1945, the 38th parallel was designated as the line dividing the Soviet and the American occupation. Russian troops entered Korea Aug. 10, 1945, U.S. troops entered Sept. 8, 1945. The Soviet military organized socialists and communists and blocked efforts to let the Koreans unite their country. *(See Index for Korean War.)*

The South Koreans formed the Republic of Korea in May 1948 with Seoul as the capital. Dr. Syngman Rhee was chosen president but a movement spearheaded by college students forced his resignation Apr. 26, 1960.

In an army coup May 16, 1961, Gen. Park Chung Hee became chairman of the ruling junta. He was elected president, 1963; a 1972 referendum allowed him to be reelected for 6 year terms unlimited times. Park was assassinated by the chief of the Korean CIA, Oct. 26, 1979. The calm of the new government was halted by the rise of Gen. Chun Doo Hwan, head of the military intelligence, who reinstated martial law, and reverted South Korea to the police state it was under Park.

North Korean raids across the border tapered off in 1971, but incidents occurred in 1973 and 1974. In July 1972 South and North Korea agreed on a common goal of reunifying the 2 nations by peaceful means. But there had been no sign of a thaw in relations between the two regimes until 1985 when they agreed to discuss economic issues. In 1988, radical students demanding reunification clashed with police.

A Korean Air Lines passenger airliner was shot down by a Soviet jet fighter, Sept. 1, 1983, after it strayed into Soviet airspace; all 269 people aboard died.

On June 10, 1987, middle class office workers, shopkeepers, and business executives joined students in antigovernment protests in Seoul. They were protesting President Chun's decision to choose his successor and not allow the next president to be chosen by direct vote of the people. Following weeks of rioting and violence, Chun, July 1, agreed to permit election of the next president by direct popular vote and other constitutional reforms. In Dec., Roh Tae Woo was elected president. In 1990, the nation's 3 largest political parties merged; some 100,000 students demonstrated, charging that the merger was undemocratic.

Kuwait

State of Kuwait

Dowlat al-Kuwait

People: Population (1990 est.): 2,080,000. **Age distrib.** (%): 0–14: 40.2; 15–59: 57.6; 60+: 2.3. **Pop. density:** 285 per sq. mi. **Urban** (1986): 90%. **Ethnic groups:** Kuwaiti 39%, other Arab 39%, Iranians, Indians, Pakistanis. **Languages:** Arabic, others. **Religions:** Moslem 85%.

Geography: Area: 6,880 sq. mi., slightly smaller than New Jersey. **Location:** In Middle East, at N end of Persian Gulf. **Neighbors:** Iraq on N, Saudi Arabia on S. **Topography:** The country is flat, very dry, and extremely hot. **Capital:** Kuwait. **Cities** (1985 est.): Hawalli 145,000; as-Salimiyah 153,000.

Government: Type: Constitutional monarchy. **Head of state:** Emir Shaikh Jabir al-Ahmad al-Jabir as-Sabah; b. 1928; in office: Jan. 1, 1978. **Head of government:** Prime Min. Shaikh Saad Abdulla as-Salim as-Sabah; in office: Feb. 8, 1978. **Local divisions:** 4 governorates. **Defense:** 5.2% of GNP (1987).

Economy: Industries: Oil products. **Minerals:** Oil, gas. **Crude oil reserves** (1987): 94 bln. bbls. **Cultivated land:** 1%. **Electricity prod.** (1988): 19.5 bln. kwh. **Labor force:** social services 45%; construction 20%.

Finance: Currency: Dinar (May 1990: 1.00 = $3.40 US). **Gross national product** (1988): $19.1 bln. **Per capita GNP** (1988): $10,410. **Imports** (1988): $6.1 bln.; partners: Jap. 21%, U.S. 9%. **Exports** (1988): $7.6 bln.; partners: Jap. 16%, It. 10%. **Tourists** (1988): $100 mln. receipts. **National budget** (1988): $10.5 bln. expenditures. **International reserves less gold** (Mar. 1990): $3.1 bln. **Gold:** 2.53 mln. oz t. **Consumer prices** (change in 1989): 3.3%.

Transport: Motor vehicles: in use (1988): 424,000 passenger cars, 114,000 comm. vehicles. **Civil aviation** (1988): 3.3 bln. passenger-km. 1 airport with scheduled flight. **Chief ports:** Mina al-Ahmadi.

Communications: Television sets: 1 per 2.4 persons. **Radios:** 1 per 1.8 persons. **Telephones:** 1 per 5.9 persons. **Daily newspaper circ.** (1986): 253 per 1,000 pop.

Health: Life expectancy at birth (1989): 72 male; 76 female. **Births** (per 1,000 pop. 1989): 30. **Deaths** (per 1,000 pop. 1989): 2.9. **Natural increase:** 2.7%. **Hospital beds:** 1 per 340 persons. **Physician:** 1 per 669 persons. **Infant mortality** (per 1,000 live births 1989): 14.

Education (1989): **Literacy:** 71%. **Years compulsory:** 8.

Major International Organizations: UN (World Bank, IMF, GATT), Arab League, OPEC.

Embassy: 2940 Tilden St. NW 20008; 966-0702.

Kuwait is ruled by the Al-Sabah dynasty, founded 1759. Britain ran foreign relations and defense from 1899 until independence in 1961. The majority of the population is non-Kuwaiti, with many Palestinians, and cannot vote.

Oil, first exported in 1946, is the fiscal mainstay, providing most of Kuwait's income. Oil pays for free medical care, education, and social security. There are no taxes, except customs duties.

Kuwaiti oil tankers have come under frequent attack by Iran because of Kuwait's support of Iraq in the Iran-Iraq War. In July 1987, U.S. Navy warships began escorting Kuwaiti tankers in the Persian Gulf.

In 1988, a Kuwaiti Airways jet was hijacked by pro-Iranian Shiite Moslem terrorists who demanded the release of 17 Shiite terrorists. The ordeal lasted 16 days as Kuwait refused to release the terrorists.

Kuwait was attacked and overrun by Iraqian forces Aug. 1, 1990. *(See Chronology and Index for details.)*

Laos

Lao People's Democratic Republic

Sathalanalat Paxathipatai Paxaxōn Lao

People: Population (1990 est.): 4,024,000. **Pop. density:** 42 per sq. mi. **Urban** (1987): 15%. **Ethnic groups:** Lao 48%, Mon-Khmer tribes 25%, Thai 14%, Meo and Yao 13%, others. **Languages:** Lao (official), French. **Religions:** Buddhists 50%, tribal 50%.

Geography: Area: 91,428 sq. mi., slightly larger than Utah. **Location:** In Indochina Peninsula in SE Asia. **Neighbors:** Burma, China on N, Vietnam on E, Cambodia on S, Thailand on W. **Topography:** Landlocked, dominated by jungle. High mountains along the eastern border are the source of the E-W rivers slicing across the country to the Mekong R., which defines most of the western border. **Capital:** Vientiane. **Cities** (1984 est.): Vientiane 120,000.

Government: Type: Communist. **Head of state:** Pres. Phoumi Vongvichit in office: Oct. 31, 1986. **Head of government:** Prime Min. Kaysone Phomvihan; b. Dec. 13, 1920; in office: Dec. 2, 1975. **Local divisions:** 17 provinces. **Armed forces: Defense:** 10.5% of GNP (1984).

Economy: Industries: Wood products. **Chief crops:** Rice, corn, tobacco, cotton, opium, citrus fruits, coffee. **Minerals:** Tin. **Other resources:** Forests. **Arable land:** 4%. **Livestock** (1988): pigs: 1.5 mln. **Fish catch** (1988): 20,000 metric tons. **Electricity prod.** (1988): 900 mln. kwh. **Labor force:** 85% agric.; 6% ind.

Finance: Currency: New kip (Mar. 1990): 583 = $1 US). **Gross national product** (1987): $500 mln. **Per capita income** (1985 est.): $500. **Imports** (1988): $240 mln.; partners: Thai. 45%, Jap. 20%. **Exports** (1988): $52 mln.; partners: Chi. 40%.

Transport: Motor vehicles: in use (1987): 15,800 passenger cars, 3,000 comm. vehicles. **Civil Aviation** (1985): 9 mln. passenger km; 7 airports with scheduled flights.

Communications: Radios: 1 per 10 persons.

Health: Life expectancy at birth (1989): 48 male; 51 female. **Births** (per 1,000 pop. 1989): 38. **Deaths** (per 1,000 pop. 1989): 16. **Natural increase:** 2.2%. **Hospital beds:** 1 per 369 persons. **Physicians:** 1 per 6,495 persons. **Infant mortality** (per 1,000 live births, 1989): 128.

Education: (1986): **Literacy:** 41%.

Major International Organizations: UN (FAO, IMF, WHO). **Embassy:** 2222 S St. NW 20008; 332-6416.

Laos became a French protectorate in 1893, but regained independence as a constitutional monarchy July 19, 1949.

Conflicts among neutralist, communist and conservative factions created a chaotic political situation. Armed conflict increased after 1960.

The 3 factions formed a coalition government in June 1962, with neutralist Prince Souvanna Phouma as premier. A 14-nation conference in Geneva signed agreements, 1962, guaranteeing neutrality and independence. By 1964 the Pathet Lao had withdrawn from the coalition, and, with aid from N. Vietnamese troops, renewed sporadic attacks. U.S. planes bombed the Ho Chi Minh trail, supply line from N. Vietnam to communist forces in Laos and S. Vietnam. An estimated 2.75 million tons of bombs were dropped on Laos during the fighting.

In 1970 the U.S. stepped up air support and military aid. After Pathet Lao military gains, Souvanna Phouma in May 1975 ordered government troops to cease fighting; the Pathet Lao took control. A Lao People's Democratic Republic was proclaimed Dec. 3, 1975; it is strongly influenced by Vietnam.

Lebanon

Republic of Lebanon

al-Jumhouriya al-Lubnaniya

People: Population (1990 est.): 3,340,000. **Age distrib.** (%): 0–14: 37.0; 15–59: 55.1; 60+: 7.9. **Pop. density:** 710 per sq. mi. **Urban** (1986): 81%. **Ethnic groups:** Lebanese 82%, Armenians 5%, Palestinian 9%. **Languages:** Arabic (official), French, Armenian. **Religions:** Moslem 57%; Christian 42%.

Geography: Area: 4,015 sq. mi., smaller than Connecticut. **Location:** On Eastern end of Mediterranean Sea. **Neighbors:** Syria on E. Israel on S. **Topography:** There is a narrow coastal strip, and 2 mountain ranges running N-S enclosing the fertile Beqaa Valley. The Litani R. runs S through the valley, turning W to empty into the Mediterranean. **Capital:** Beirut. **Cities** (1985 est.): Beirut 1,500,000; Tripoli 500,000.

Government: Type: Republic. **Head of state:** vacant. **Head of government:** Prime Min. Michel Aoun in office: Sept. 23, 1988. **Local divisions:** 5 governorates. **Defense:** 18% of govt. budget (1984).

Economy: Industries: Trade, food products, textiles, cement, oil products. **Chief crops:** Fruits, olives, tobacco, grapes, vegetables, grains. **Minerals:** Iron. **Arable land:** 21%. **Livestock** (1987): goats: 465,000; sheep: 140,000. **Electricity prod.**

(1988): 4.8 bln. kwh. **Labor force:** 11% agric.; 79% ind., comm., services.

Finance: Currency: Pound (June 1990: 667 = $1 US). **Gross national product** (1986): $1.8 bln. **Per capita GNP** (1986): $690. **Imports** (1988): $2.4 bln.; partners: It. 15%, Fr. 10%, U.S. 9%, Saudi Ar. 6%. **Exports** (1988): $709 mln.; partners: Saudi Ar. 33%, Syria 8%, Jor. 6%, Kuw. 8%. **National budget** (1988): $202 mln. **International reserves less gold** (Mar. 1990): $828 mln. **Gold:** 9.22 mln. oz t.

Transport: Railway traffic (1982): 5.3 mln. passenger-km. **Motor vehicles:** in use (1982): 460,000 passenger cars, 21,000 comm. vehicles. **Civil aviation** (1988): 891 mln. passenger-km. **Chief ports:** Beirut, Tripoli, Sidon.

Communications: Television sets: 1 per 3.4 persons. **Radios:** 1 per 1.3 persons. **Telephones:** 1 per 18.4 persons. **Daily newspaper circ.** (1986): 211 per 1,000 pop.

Health: Life expectancy at birth (1989): 65 male; 70 female. **Births** (per 1,000 pop. 1989): 28. **Deaths** (per 1,000 pop. 1989): 7. **Natural increase:** 2.1%. **Hospital beds:** 1 per 263 persons. **Physicians:** 1 per 771 persons. **Infant mortality** (per 1,000 live births 1989): 48.

Education: (1989): **Literacy:** 75%. **Years compulsory:** 5; attendance 93%.

Major International Organizations: UN (IMF, ILO, WHO). **Embassy:** 2560 28th St. NW 20008; 939-6300.

Formed from 5 former Turkish Empire districts, Lebanon became an independent state Sept. 1, 1920, administered under French mandate 1920-41. French troops withdrew in 1946.

Under the 1943 National Covenant, all public positions were divided among the various religious communities, with Christians in the majority. By the 1970s, Moslems became the majority, and demanded a larger political and economic role.

U.S. Marines intervened, May-Oct. 1958, during a Syrian-aided revolt. Lebanon's efforts to restrain Palestinian commandos caused armed clashes in 1969. Continued raids against Israeli civilians, 1970-75, brought Israeli attacks against guerrilla camps and villages. Israeli troops occupied S. Lebanon, March 1978, and again in Apr. 1980.

An estimated 60,000 were killed and billions of dollars in damage inflicted in a 1975-76 civil war. Palestinian units and leftist Moslems fought against the Maronite militia, the Phalange, and other Christians. Several Arab countries provided political and arms support to the various factions, while Israel aided Christian forces. Up to 15,000 Syrian troops intervened in 1976, and fought Palestinian groups. Arab League troops from several nations tried to impose a cease-fire.

Clashes between Syrian troops and Christian forces erupted, Apr. 1, 1981, near Zahle, Lebanon, bringing to an end the cease-fire that had been in place. By Apr. 22, fighting had broken out not only between Syrians and Christians, but also between two Moslem factions. Israeli commandos attacked Palestinian positions at Tyre and Tulin. In July, Israeli air raids on Beirut killed or wounded some 800 persons. A cease-fire between Israel and the Palestinians was concluded July 24, but hostilities continued.

Israeli forces invaded Lebanon June 6, 1982, in a coordinated land, sea, and air attack aimed at crushing strongholds of the Palestine Liberation Organization (PLO). Israeli and Syrian forces engaged in the Bekka Valley. By June 14, Israeli troops had encircled Beirut. On Aug. 21, the PLO evacuated west Beirut following massive Israeli bombings of the city. The withdrawal was supervised by U.S., French, and Italian troops. Israeli troops withdrew from Lebanon in June 1985.

Israeli troops entered west Beirut following the Sept. 14 assassination of newly-elected Lebanese Pres. Bashir Gemayel. On Sept. 16, Lebanese Christian troops entered 2 refugee camps and massacred hundreds of Palestinian refugees.

In 1983, terrorist bombings became a way of life in Beirut as some 50 people were killed in an explosion at the U.S. Embassy, Apr. 18; 241 U.S. servicemen and 58 French soldiers died in separate Moslem suicide attacks, Oct. 23.

PLO leader Yasir Arafat and PLO dissidents backed by Syria fought a 6-week battle in Tripoli until negotiations allowed Arafat and some 4,000 followers to evacuate the city.

On Apr. 26, 1984, pro-Syrian Rashid Karami was appointed premier. The appointment failed to end virtual civil war in Beirut between Christian forces, and Druse and Shiite Moslem militias. There was heavy fighting between Shiite militiamen and Palestinian guerrillas in May 1985. In June, Beirut Airport was the scene of a hostage crisis where Shiite terrorists held U.S. citizens for 17 days. Fierce artillery duels between Christian east Beirut and

Moslem west Beirut, Mar.-Apr., 1989, left some 200 dead and 700 wounded.

Kidnapping of foreign nationals by Islamic militants has become common in the 1980s. U.S., British, French, and Soviet citizens have been victims.

Premier Karami was assassinated June 1, 1987, when a bomb exploded aboard a helicopter in which he was traveling.

Lesotho
Kingdom of Lesotho

People: Population (1990 est.): 1,757,000. **Age distrib.** (%): 0–14: 42.3; 15–59: 52.2; 60+: 5.7. **Pop. density:** 143 per sq. mi. **Ethnic groups:** Sotho 99%. **Languages:** English, Sesotho (official). **Religions:** Roman Catholic 38%, Protestant 42%.

Geography: Area: 11,716 sq. mi., slightly larger than Maryland. **Location:** In Southern Africa. **Neighbors:** Completely surrounded by Republic of South Africa. **Topography:** Landlocked and mountainous, with altitudes ranging from 5,000 to 11,000 ft. **Capital:** Maseru. **Cities** (1987 est.): Maseru 109,000.

Government: Type: Military. **Head of state:** King Moshoeshoe II, b. May 2, 1938; in office: Mar. 12, 1960. **Head of government:** Gen. Justin Lekhanya; b. Apr. 7, 1938; in office: Jan. 20, 1986. **Local divisions:** 10 districts. **Defense:** 6.5% of GNP (1984).

Economy: Industries: Diamond polishing, food processing. **Chief crops:** Corn, grains, peas, beans. **Other resources:** Wool, mohair. **Arable land:** 10%. **Electricity prod.** (1988): 1 mln. kwh. **Labor force:** 31% agric.; 8% ind. and comm., 45% services.

Finance: Currency: Maloti (Mar. 1990: 1.00 = $.37 US). **Gross national product** (1988): $408 mln. **Per capita GNP** (1987): $360. **Imports** (1985): $326 mln.; partners: Mostly So. Afr. **Exports** (1985): $21 mln.; partners: Mostly So. Afr. **National budget** (1988): $219 mln.

Transport: Motor vehicles: in use (1982): 5,000 passenger cars, 11,000 comm. vehicles.

Communications: Radios: 1 per 36 persons. **Daily newspaper circ.** (1985): 28 per 1,000 pop.

Health: Life expectancy at birth (1989): 59 male; 62 female. **Births** (per 1,000 pop. 1989): 37. **Deaths** (per 1,000 pop. 1989): 10. **Natural increase:** 2.7%. **Hospital beds** (1982): 2,300. **Physicians** (1982): 114. **Infant mortality** (per 1,000 live births 1989): 81.

Education (1987): **Literacy:** 59%.

Major International Organizations: UN (IMF, UNESCO, WHO), OAU.

Embassy: 2511 Massachusetts Ave. NW 20008; 797-5534.

Lesotho (once called Basutoland) became a British protectorate in 1868 when Chief Moshesh sought protection against the Boers. Independence came Oct. 4, 1966. Elections were suspended in 1970. Over 50% of Lesotho's GNP is provided by citizens working in S. Africa. Livestock raising is the chief industry; diamonds are the chief export.

S. Africa imposed a blockade, Jan. 1, 1986, because of Lesotho's giving sanctuary to rebel groups fighting to overthrow the S. African Government. The blockade sparked a Jan. 20 military coup, and was lifted, Jan. 25, when the new leaders agreed to expel the rebels.

In 1990, King Moshoeshoe was sent into exile by the military government.

Liberia
Republic of Liberia

People: Population (1990 est.): 2,644,000. **Age distrib.** (%): 0–14: 46.8; 15–59: 48.3; 60+: 4.9. **Pop. density:** 66 per sq. mi. **Urban** (1985): 39.5%. **Ethnic groups:** Americo-Liberians 5%, indigenous tribes 95% **Languages:** English (official), tribal dialects. **Religions:** Moslem 20%, Christian 10%, traditional beliefs 70%.

Geography: Area: 38,250 sq. mi., slightly smaller than Pennsylvania. **Location:** On SW coast of W. Africa. **Neighbors:** Sierra Leone on W, Guinea on N, Côte d'Ivoire on E. **Topography:** Marshy Atlantic coastline rises to low mountains and plateaus in the forested interior; 6 major rivers flow in parallel courses to the ocean. **Capital:** Monrovia. **Cities** (1987 est.): Monrovia 400,000.

Government: Type: Civilian republic. **Head of state:** Pres. Samuel K. Doe; in office: Apr. 12, 1980. **Local divisions:** 13 counties. **Defense:** 3.8% of GDP (1987).

Economy: Industries: Food processing, mining. **Chief crops:** Rice, cassava, coffee, cocoa, sugar. **Minerals:** Iron, diamonds, gold. **Other resources:** Rubber, timber. **Arable land:** 1%. **Fish catch** (1988): 18,000 metric tons. **Electricity prod.** (1988): 728 mln. kwh. **Labor force:** 82% agric.

Finance: Currency: Dollar (May 1990: 1.00 = $1 US). **Gross national product** (1987): $973 mln. **Per capita GNP** (1987): $410. **Imports** (1988): $308 mln.; partners: U.S. 27%, W. Ger. 10%, Jap. 6%, Neth. 7%. **Exports** (1987): $382 mln.; partners: W. Ger. 31%, U.S. 17%, It. 14%, Fr. 9%. **National budget** (1988): $240 mln. **International reserves less gold** (Feb. 1990): $7,000. **Consumer prices** (change in 1988): 12.2%.

Transport: Motor vehicles: in use (1984): 12,000 passenger cars, 8,000 comm. vehicles. **Chief ports:** Monrovia, Buchanan, Greenville.

Communications: Television sets: 1 per 55 persons. **Radios:** 1 per 4.4 persons. **Telephones:** 1 per 278 persons. **Daily newspaper circ.** (1987): 9 per 1,000 pop.

Health: Life expectancy at birth (1989): 53 male; 56 female. **Births** (per 1,000 pop. 1989): 45. **Deaths** (per 1,000 pop. 1989): 13. **Natural increase:** 3%. **Hospital beds** (1981): 3,000. **Physicians** (1981): 236. **Infant mortality** (per 1,000 live births 1989): 119.

Education (1989): **Literacy:** 25%; 35% attend primary school.

Major International Organizations: UN and most specialized agencies, OAU.

Embassy: 5201 16th St. NW 20011; 723-0437.

Liberia was founded in 1822 by U.S. black freedmen who settled at Monrovia with the aid of colonization societies. It became a republic July 26, 1847, with a constitution modeled on that of the U.S. Descendants of freedmen dominated politics.

Charging rampant corruption, an Army Redemption Council of enlisted men staged a bloody predawn coup, April 12, 1980, in which Pres. Tolbert was killed and replaced as head of state by Sgt. Samuel Doe. Doe was chosen president in a disputed election, and survived a subsequent coup, in 1985.

Rebel forces seeking to depose Pres. Doe made major territorial gains and advanced on the capital, June 1990. (*See Chronology*).

Libya
Socialist People's Libyan Arab Jamahiriya
al-Jamahiriyah al-Arabiya al-Libya al-Shabiya al-Ishtirakiya

People: Population (1990 est.): 4,280,000. **Age distrib.** (%): 0–14: 45.0; 15–59: 51.2; 60+: 3.8. **Pop. density:** 6 per sq. mi. **Urban** (1985): 64%. **Ethnic groups:** Arab-Berber 97%. **Languages:** Arabic. **Religions:** Sunni Moslem 97%.

Geography: Area: 679,359 sq. mi., larger than Alaska. **Location:** On Mediterranean coast of N. Africa. **Neighbors:** Tunisia, Algeria on W, Niger, Chad on S, Sudan, Egypt on E. **Topography:** Desert and semidesert regions cover 92% of the land, with low mountains in N, higher mountains in S, and a narrow coastal zone. **Capital:** Tripoli. **Cities** (1988 est.): Tripoli 591,000.

Government: Type: Islamic Arabic Socialist "Mass-State." **Head of state:** Col. Muammar al-Qaddafi; b. Sept. 1942; in office: Sept. 1969. **Head of government:** Premier Umar Mustafa al-Muntasir; in office: Mar. 1, 1987. **Local divisions:** 46 municipalities. **Defense:** 11.1% of GNP (1987).

Economy: Industries: Carpets, textiles, petroleum. **Chief crops:** Dates, olives, citrus and other fruits, grapes, wheat. **Minerals:** Gypsum, oil, gas. **Crude oil reserves** (1987): 22 bln. bbls. **Arable land:** 2%. **Livestock** (1987): sheep: 5.7 mln.; goats: 1.0 mln. **Electricity prod.** (1988): 13.3 bln. kwh. **Labor force:** 18% agric.; 31% ind.; 27% services; 24% govt.

Finance: Currency: Dinar (Feb. 1990: 1.00 = $2.60 US). **Gross national product** (1988): $20 bln. **Per capita income** (1986): $5,500. **Imports** (1987): $4.8 bln.; partners: It. 30%, W. Ger. 11%, Fr. 6%, Jap. 8%. **Exports** (1987): $5.7 bln.; partners:

t. 24%, W. Ger. 10%, Sp. 7%. **International reserves less gold** (Mar. 1990): $4.4 bln. **Gold:** 3.6 mln. oz t.

Transport: Motor vehicles: in use (1986): 428,000 passenger cars, 334,000 comm. vehicles. **Chief ports:** Tripoli, Benghazi.

Communications: Television sets: 1 per 13 persons. **Radios:** 1 per 3.9 persons. **Daily newspaper circ.** (1988): 10 per 1,000 pop.

Health: Life expectancy at birth (1989): 64 male; 69 female. **Births** (per 1,000 pop. 1989): 38. **Deaths** (per 1,000 pop. 1989): 7. **Natural increase:** 3.1%. **Hospital beds** (1982): 16,051. **Physicians** (1982): 5,200. **Infant mortality** (per 1,000 live births 1989): 70.

Education (1989): Literacy: 60%. **Years compulsory:** 7; **Attendance:** 90%.

Major International Organizations: UN, Arab League, OAU, OPEC.

First settled by Berbers, Libya was ruled by Carthage, Rome, and Vandals, the Ottomans, Italy from 1912, and Britain and France after WW II. It became an independent constitutional monarchy Jan. 2, 1952. In 1969 a junta lead by Col. Muammar al-Qaddafi seized power.

In the mid-1970s, Libya helped arm violent revolutionary groups in Egypt and Sudan, and had aided terrorists of various nationalities.

Libya and Egypt fought several air and land battles along their border in July, 1977. Chad charged Libya with military occupation of its uranium-rich northern region in 1977. Libya's 1979 offensive into the Aouzou Strip was repulsed by Chadian forces. Libyan forces withdrew from Chad, Nov. 1981 but returned. Libyan troops were driven from their last major stronghold by Chad forces in 1987, leaving over $1 billion in military equipment behind.

Widespread nationalization, arrests, imposition of currency regulations, wholesale conscription of civil servants into the army, and the fall in crude oil prices have hurt the economy.

On May 6, 1981, the U.S., citing "a wide range of Libyan provocations and misconduct," closed the Libyan mission in Wash. In August, 2 Libyan jets were shot down by U.S. Navy planes taking part in naval exercises in the Gulf of Sidra which Libya claims as its territory.

The U.S. has accused Libya of masterminding numerous international terrorist actions, including the Dec. 1985 attacks on the Rome and Vienna airports.

On Jan. 7, 1986, the U.S. imposed economic sanctions against Libya, ordered all Americans to leave that country and froze all Libyan assets in the U.S. The U.S. commenced flight operations over the Gulf of Sidra, Jan. 27, and a U.S. Navy task force began conducting exercises in the Gulf, Mar. 23. When Libya fired antiaircraft missiles at American warplanes, the U.S. responded by sinking 2 Libyan ships and bombing a missile installation in Libya. The U.S. withdrew from the Gulf, Mar. 27.

The U.S. accused Libyan leader Qaddafi of having ordered the April 5 bombing of a West Berlin discotheque which killed 2, including a U.S. serviceman. After failing to get their European allies to join them in imposing economic sanctions against Libya, the U.S. sent warplanes to attack terrorist-related targets in Tripoli and Benghazi, Libya, Apr. 14.

At the economic summit of the 7 major industrial democracies in Tokyo, May 4–6, a joint statement was issued which condemned terrorism and singled out Libya as a target for action.

Liechtenstein
Principality of Liechtenstein
Fürstentum Liechtenstein

People: Population: (1990 est.): 30,000. **Age distrib.** (%): 0–14: 20.1; 15–59: 66.3; 60+: 11.6. **Pop. density:** 483 per sq. mi. **Ethnic groups:** Alemannic 95%, Italian 5%. **Languages:** German (official), Alemannic dialect. **Religions:** Roman Catholic 87%, Protestant 8%.

Geography: Area: 62 sq. mi., the size of Washington, D.C. **Location:** In the Alps. **Neighbors:** Switzerland on W, Austria on E. **Topography:** The Rhine Valley occupies one-third of the country, the Alps cover the rest. **Capital:** Vaduz. **Cities** (1989 cen.): Vaduz 4,920, Schaan 4,883.

Government: Type: Hereditary constitutional monarchy. **Head of state:** Prince Franz Josef II; b. Aug. 16, 1906; in office: Mar. 30, 1938. **Head of government:** Hans Brunhart; b. Mar. 28, 1945; in office: Apr. 26, 1978. **Local divisions:** 2 districts, 11 communities.

Economy: Industries: Machines, instruments, chemicals, furniture, ceramics. **Arable land:** 25%. **Labor force:** 54% industry, trade and building; 41% services; 4% agric., fishing, forestry.

Finance: Currency: Swiss Franc. **Gross National Product** (1986): $450 mln. **Tourists** (1988): 71,000.

Communications: Radios: 1 per 2.9 persons. **Telephones:** 1 per 1.0 persons. **Daily newspaper circ.** (1987): 546 per 1,000 pop.

Health: Births (per 1,000 pop. 1989): 13. **Deaths** (per 1,000 pop. 1989): 7. **Natural increase:** .6%. **Infant mortality** (per 1,000 live births 1989): 5.

Education (1989): Literacy: 100%. **Years compulsory** 9; attendance 100%.

Liechtenstein became sovereign in 1866. Austria administered Liechtenstein's ports up to 1920; Switzerland has administered its postal services since 1921. Liechtenstein is united with Switzerland by a customs and monetary union. Taxes are low; many international corporations have headquarters there. Foreign workers comprise a third of the population.

The 1986 general elections were the first in which women were allowed to vote.

Luxembourg
Grand Duchy of Luxembourg
Grand-Duché de Luxembourg

People: Population: (1990 est.): 369,000. **Age distrib.** (%): 0–14: 17.3; 15–59: 64.5; 60+: 18.2. **Pop. density:** 369 per sq. mi. **Urban** (1985): 81%. **Ethnic groups:** Mixture of French and Germans predominate. **Languages:** French, German, Luxembourgian. **Religions:** Roman Catholic 97%.

Geography: Area: 998 sq. mi., smaller than Rhode Island. **Location:** In W. Europe. **Neighbors:** Belgium on W, France on S, W. Germany on E. **Topography:** Heavy forests (Ardennes) cover N, S is a low, open plateau. **Capital:** Luxembourg. **Cities** (1987 est.): Luxembourg 86,000.

Government: Type: Constitutional monarchy. **Head of state:** Grand Duke Jean; b. Jan. 5, 1921; in office: Nov. 12, 1964. **Head of government:** Prime Min. Jacques Santer; in office: July 21, 1984. **Local divisions:** 3 districts. **Defense:** 0.8% of GNP (1988).

Economy: Industries: Steel, chemicals, beer, tires, tobacco, metal products, cement. **Chief crops:** Corn, wine. **Minerals:** Iron. **Arable land:** 25%. **Electricity prod.** (1988): 1.0 bln. kwh. **Crude steel prod.** (1984): 3.9 min. metric tons. **Labor force:** 1% agric.; 42% ind. & comm.; 45% services.

Finance: Currency: Franc (Mar. 1990: 35.06 = $1 US). **Gross national product** (1988): $4.9 bln. **Per capita GNP** (1988): $13,380. **Note:** trade and tourist data included in Belgian statistics. **Consumer prices** (change in 1989): 3.4%.

Transport: Railway traffic (1988): 276 mln. passenger-km. **Motor vehicles:** in use (1988): 168,000 passenger cars, 13,000 comm. vehicles.

Communications: Television sets: 1 per 4.0 persons. **Radios:** 1 per 1.6 persons. **Telephones:** 1 per 2.3 persons. **Daily newspaper circ.** (1986): 365 per 1,000 pop.

Health: Life expectancy at birth (1989): 71 male; 78 female. **Births** (per 1,000 pop. 1989): 12. **Deaths** (per 1,000 pop. 1989): 11. **Hospital beds:** 1 per 80 persons. **Physicians:** 1 per 557 persons. **Infant mortality** (per 1,000 live births 1989): 8.

Education (1989): Literacy: 100%. **Years compulsory** 9; attendance 100%.

Major International Organizations: UN, OECD, EC, NATO. **Embassy:** 2200 Massachusetts Ave. NW 20008; 265-4171.

Luxembourg, founded about 963, was ruled by Burgundy, Spain, Austria, and France from 1448 to 1815. It left the Germanic Confederation in 1866. Overrun by Germany in 2 world wars, Luxembourg ended its neutrality in 1948, when a customs union with Belgium and Netherlands was adopted.

Madagascar

Democratic Republic of Madagascar
Repoblika Demokratika Malagasy

People: Population (1990 est.): 11,802,000. **Pop. density:** 49 per sq. mi. **Urban** (1985): 21.8%. **Ethnic groups:** 18 Malayan-Indonesian tribes (Merina 26%), with Arab and African presence. **Languages:** Malagasy (official), French. **Religions:** animists 52%, Christian 41%, Moslem 7%.

Geography: Area: 226,657 sq. mi., slightly smaller than Texas. **Location:** In the Indian O., off the SE coast of Africa. **Neighbors:** Comoro Is., Mozambique (across Mozambique Channel). **Topography:** Humid coastal strip in the E, fertile valleys in the mountainous center plateau region, and a wider coastal strip on the W. **Capital:** Antananarivo. **Cities** (1985 est.): Antananarivo 650,000.

Government: Type: Republic, strong presidential authority. **Head of state:** Pres. Didier Ratsiraka; b. Nov. 4, 1936; in office: June 15, 1975. **Head of government:** Prime Min. Victor Ramahatra; in office: Feb. 12, 1988. **Local divisions:** 6 provinces. **Defense:** 2.4% of GNP (1987).

Economy: Industries: Food processing, textiles. **Chief crops:** Coffee (over 50% of exports), cloves, vanilla, rice, sugar, sisal, tobacco, peanuts. **Minerals:** Chromium, graphite, coal, bauxite. **Arable land:** 5%. **Livestock** (1988): cattle: 10.4 mln.; pigs: 1.3 mln. **Fish catch** (1988): 63,000 metric tons. **Electricity prod.** (1988): 430 mln. kwh. **Labor force:** 90% agric.

Finance: Currency: Franc (Mar. 1990: 1,538 = $1 US). **Gross national product** (1987): $2.1 bln. **Per capita income** (1986): $255. **Imports** (1986): $438 mln.; partners: Fr. 32%, U.S. 15%. **Exports** (1986): $326 mln.; partners: Fr. 34%, U.S. 14%. **Tourists** (1987): $10 mln. receipts. **National budget** (1987): $480 mln. **International reserves less gold** (Jan. 1990): $208 mln. **Consumer prices** (change in 1987): 15.0%.

Transport: Railway traffic (1987): 208 mln. passenger-km. **Motor vehicles:** in use (1986): 21,000 passenger cars, 14,000 comm. vehicles. **Civil aviation:** (1987): 422 mln. passenger-km; 51 airports with scheduled flights. **Chief ports:** Tamatave, Diego-Suarez, Majunga, Tulear.

Communications: Television sets: 100,000 in use (1987). **Radios:** 2 mln. in use (1986). **Telephones in use** (1987): 43,000.

Health: Life expectancy at birth (1989): 50 male; 53 female. **Births** (per 1,000 pop. 1989): 47. **Deaths** (per 1,000 pop. 1989): 15. **Natural increase:** 3.2%. **Hospital beds** (1982): 20,800. **Physicians** (1982): 940. **Infant mortality** (per 1,000 live births 1989): 99.

Education (1987): Literacy: 53%. Years compulsory: 5; attendance 83%.

Major International Organizations: UN (GATT, WHO, IMF), OAU.

Embassy: 2374 Massachusetts Ave. NW 20008; 265-5525.

Madagascar was settled 2,000 years ago by Malayan-Indonesian people, whose descendants still predominate. A unified kingdom ruled the 18th and 19th centuries. The island became a French protectorate, 1885, and a colony 1896. Independence came June 26, 1960.

Discontent with inflation and French domination led to a coup in 1972. The new regime nationalized French-owned financial interests, closed French bases and a U.S. space tracking station, and obtained Chinese aid. The government conducted a program of arrests, expulsion of foreigners, and repression of strikes, 1979.

In 1990, Madagascar ended a ban on multiparty politics that had been in place since 1975.

Malawi

Republic of Malawi

People: Population (1990 est.): 9,080,000. **Age distrib.** (%): 0–14: 47.8; 15–59: 48.0; 60+: 4.2. **Pop. density:** 176 per sq. mi. **Urban** (1987): 12%. **Ethnic groups:** Chewa, 90%, Nyanja, Lomwe, other Bantu tribes. **Languages:** English, Chichewa (both official). **Religions:** Christian 75%, Moslem 20%.

Geography: Area: 45,747 sq. mi., the size of Pennsylvania. **Location:** In SE Africa. **Neighbors:** Zambia on W, Mozambique

on SE, Tanzania on N. **Topography:** Malawi stretches 560 m. N-S along Lake Malawi (Lake Nyasa), most of which belongs t. Malawi. High plateaus and mountains line the Rift Valley th. length of the nation. **Capital:** Lilongwe. **Cities** (1987 est.): Blantyre 402,000; Lilongwe 220,000.

Government: Type: One-party state. **Head of state:** Pres. Hastings Kamuzu Banda, b. May 14, 1906; in office: July 1966. **Local divisions:** 24 administrative districts. **Defense** 1.4% of GNP (1987).

Economy: Industries: Textiles, sugar, cement. **Chief crops** Tea, tobacco, sugar, coffee. **Other resources:** Rubber. **Arable land:** 25%. **Fish catch** (1988): 88 metric tons. **Electricity prod.** (1988): 535 mln. kwh. **Labor force:** 43% agric.; 23% ind. and comm.; 17% services.

Finance: Currency: Kwacha (Mar. 1990: 2.63 = $1 US). **Gross national product** (1987): $1.2 bln. **Imports** (1988): $40 mln.; partners: So. Afr. 29%, UK 24%, Jap. 6%. **Exports** (1988): $292 mln.; partners: UK 27%, S. Afr. 8%., W. Ger. 10%. **National budget** (1988): $390 mln. **International reserves less gold** (Mar. 1990): $179 mln. **Gold:** 13,000 oz t. **Consumer prices** (change in 1988): 25.0%.

Transport: Railway traffic (1987): 102 mln. passenger-km. **Motor vehicles:** in use (1987): 15,000 passenger cars, 15,000 comm. vehicles. **Civil aviation** (1988) 86 mln. passenger-km; airports with scheduled flights.

Communications: Radios: 1 per 4.3 persons. **Telephones:** per 172 persons. **Daily newspaper circ.** (1985): 5 per 1,000 pop.

Health: Life expectancy at birth (1989): 46 male; 50 female. **Births** (per 1,000 pop. 1989): 51. **Deaths** (per 1,000 pop. 1989): 18. **Natural increase:** 3.3%. **Hospital beds:** 1 per 600 persons. **Physicians:** 1 per 27,094 persons. **Infant mortality** (per 1,000 live births 1989): 132.

Education (1989): Literacy: 25%. About 45% attend school.

Major International Organizations: UN (World Bank, IMF), OAU, Commonwealth of Nations.

Embassy: 2408 Massachusetts Ave. NW 20008; 797-1007.

Bantus came in the 16th century, Arab slavers in the 19th. The area became the British protectorate Nyasaland, in 1891. It became independent July 6, 1964, and a republic in 1966. It has a pro-West foreign policy and cooperates economically with S. Africa.

Malaysia

People: Population (1990 est.): 17,053,000. **Age distrib.** (%): 0–14: 37.8; 15–59: 56.5; 60+: 5.7. **Pop. density:** 132 per sq. mi. **Urban** (1985): 38%. **Ethnic groups:** Malays 59%, Chinese 32%, Indian 9%. **Languages:** Malay (official), English, Chinese, Indian languages. **Religions:** Moslem, Hindu, Buddhist, Confucian, Taoist, local religions.

Geography: Area: 127,316 sq. mi., slightly larger than New Mexico. **Location:** On the SE tip of Asia, plus the N. coast of the island of Borneo. **Neighbors:** Thailand on N, Indonesia on S. **Topography:** Most of W. Malaysia is covered by tropical jungle including the central mountain range that runs N-S through the peninsula. The western coast is marshy, the eastern, sandy. E. Malaysia has a wide, swampy coastal plain, with interior jungles and mountains. **Capital:** Kuala Lumpur. **Cities** (1986 est.): Kuala Lumpur 1 mln.

Government: Type: Federal parliamentary democracy with a constitutional monarch. **Head of state:** Paramount Ruler Sultan Azlan Shah; in office: Apr. 26, 1989. **Head of government:** Prime Min. Datuk Seri Mahathir bin Mohamad; b. Dec. 20, 1925, in office: July 16, 1981. **Local divisions:** 13 states and capital. **Defense:** 4.2% of GNP (1987).

Economy: Industries: Rubber goods, steel, electronics. **Chief crops:** Palm oil, copra, rice, pepper. **Minerals:** Tin (35% world output), iron. **Crude oil reserves** (1987): 3.2 bln. bbls. **Other resources:** Rubber (35% world output). **Arable land:** 13%. **Livestock** (1987): pigs: 2.2 mln. **Fish catch** (1986): 571,000 metric tons. **Electricity prod.** (1988): 15.8 bln. kwh. **Labor force:** 21% agric.; 22% manuf.; 11% tourism & trade.

Finance: Currency: Ringgit (Mar. 1990: 2.72 = $1 US). **Gross national product** (1988): $34.3 bln. **Imports** (1987): $12.1 bln.; partners: Jap. 21%, U.S. 18%, Sing. 14%. **Exports** (1987): $18.0 bln.; partners: Jap. 20%, U.S. 17% Sing. 19%., Neth. 6%. **Tourists** (1987): $717 mln. receipts. **National budget** (1988): $10.8 bln. **International reserves less gold** (Mar.

1990): $7.7 bln. Gold: 2.37 mln. oz t. Consumer prices (change in 1989): 3.0%.

Transport: Railway traffic (incl. Singapore) (1986): 1.3 bln. passenger-km. Motor vehicles: in use (1987): 1.5 mln. passenger cars, 338,000 comm. vehicles. Civil aviation: (1988): 8.5 bln. passenger-km; 38 airports with scheduled flights. Chief ports: George Town, Kelang, Melaka, Kuching.

Communications: Television sets: 1 per 10 persons. Radios: 1 per 2.4 persons. Telephones: 1 per 11 persons. Daily newspaper circ. (1985): 133 per 1,000 pop.

Health: Life expectancy at birth (1989): 65 male; 70 female. Births (per 1,000 pop. 1989): 26. Deaths (per 1,000 pop. 1989): 6. Natural increase: 2.0%. Hospital beds: 1 per 489 persons. Physicians: 1 per 2,853 persons. Infant mortality (per 1,000 live births 1989): 31.

Education (1989): Literacy: 80%; 96% attend primary school, 48% attend secondary.

Major International Organizations: UN (World Bank, IMF, GATT), ASEAN.

Embassy: 2401 Massachusetts Ave. NW 20008; 328-2700.

European traders appeared in the 16th century; Britain established control in 1867. Malaysia was created Sept. 16, 1963. It included Malaya (which had become independent in 1957 after the suppression of Communist rebels), plus the formerly-British Singapore, Sabah (N Borneo), and Sarawak (NW Borneo). Singapore was separated in 1965, in order to end tensions between Chinese, the majority in Singapore, and Malays in control of the Malaysian government.

A monarch is elected by a council of hereditary rulers of the Malayan states every 5 years.

Abundant natural resources have assured prosperity, and foreign investment has aided industrialization.

Maldives
Republic of Maldives
Divehi Jumhuriya

People: Population (1990 est.): 219,000. Age distrib. (%): 0–14: 44.4; 15–59: 51.7; 60+: 3.9. Pop. density: 1,756 per sq. mi. Urban (1985): 26%. Ethnic groups: Sinhalese, Dravidian, Arab mixture. Languages: Divehi (Sinhalese dialect). Religions: Sunni Moslem.

Geography: Area: 115 sq. mi., twice the size of Washington, D.C. Location: In the Indian O. SW of India. Neighbors: Nearest is India on N. Topography: 19 atolls with 1,087 islands, about 200 inhabited. None of the islands are over 5 sq. mi. in area, and all are nearly flat. Capital: Male. Cities (1985 est.): Male 46,334.

Local divisions: 19 districts.

Economy: Industries: Fish processing, tourism. Chief crops: Coconuts, fruit, millet. Other resources: Shells. Arable land: 10%. Fish catch (1987): 56,000 metric tons. Electricity prod. (1987): 4.0 mln. kwh. Labor force: 80% fishing, agriculture, & manufacturing.

Finance: Currency: Rufiyaa (Mar. 1990: 9.19 = $1 US). Gross national product (1987): $69 mln. Per capita income (1985): $470. Imports (1987): $74 min.; partners: Sing., Jap., Sri Lan. Exports (1987): $35 mln.; partners: Jap., Europe. Tourists (1987): $39 mln. receipts.

Transport: Chief ports: Male Atoll.

Communications: Radios: 1 per 9.2 persons. Telephones: 1 per 75 persons.

Health: Life expectancy at birth (1989): 60 male; 63 female. Births (per 1,000 pop. 1989): 47. Deaths (per 1,000 pop. 1989): 10. Natural increase: 3.7%. Infant morality (per 1,000 live births 1989): 80.

Education (1989): Literacy: 36%. Only 6% of those aged 11-15 attend school.

Major International Organizations: UN.

The islands had been a British protectorate since 1887. The country became independent July 26, 1965. Long a sultanate, the Maldives became a republic in 1968. Natural resources and tourism are being developed; however, it remains one of the world's poorest countries.

Mali
Republic of Mali
République du Mali

People: Population (1990 est.): 9,182,000. Age distrib. (%): 0–14: 46.0; 15–59: 49.4; 60+: 4.6. Pop. density: 17 per sq. mi. Urban (1985): 20.8%. Ethnic groups: Mande (Bambara, Malinke, Sarakole) 50%, Peul 17%, Voltaic 12%, Songhai 6%, Tuareg and Moor, 5%. Languages: French (official), Bambara. Religions: Moslem 90%.

Geography: Area: 478,764 sq. mi., about the size of Texas and California combined. Location: In the interior of W. Africa. Neighbors: Mauritania, Senegal on W, Guinea, Côte d'Ivoire, Burkina Faso on S, Niger on E, Algeria on N. Topography: A landlocked grassy plain in the upper basins of the Senegal and Niger rivers, extending N into the Sahara. Capital: Bamako. Cities (1989 est.): Bamako (met.) 800,000.

Government: Type: Republic. Head of state: Pres. Moussa Traore; b. Sept. 25, 1936; in office: Dec. 6, 1968. Local divisions: 7 regions and a capital district. Defense: 3% of GDP (1987).

Economy: Chief crops: Millet, rice, peanuts, cotton. Other resources: Bauxite, iron, gold. Arable land: 2%. Livestock (1987): sheep: 5.7 mln.; cattle: 4.4 mln. Fish catch (1987): 55,000 metric tons. Electricity prod. (1987): 204 mln. kwh. Labor force: 72% agric.; 12% ind. & comm.; 16% services.

Finance: Currency: Franc (Mar. 1990: 284 = $1 US). Gross national product (1987): $1.6 bln. Per capita income (1987): $200. Imports (1987): $493 mln.; partners: Fr. 22%, Ivory Coast 25%. Exports (1987): $260 mln.; partners: Belg.-Lux. 25%, Fr. 15%. Tourists (1987): $16 mln. receipts. National budget (1987): $240 mln. expenditures. International reserves less gold (Feb. 1990): $115 mln. Gold: 19,000 oz t.

Transport: Railway traffic (1987): 772 mln. passenger-km. Motor vehicles: in use (1987): 29,000 passenger cars, 7,500 comm. vehicles.

Communications: Radios: 1 per 59 persons. Telephones: 1 per 580 persons.

Health: Life expectancy at birth (1989): 44 male; 47 female. Births (per 1,000 pop. 1989): 49. Deaths (per 1,000 pop. 1989): 20. Natural increase: 2.9%. Hospital beds (1983): 4,215. Physicians (1983): 283. Infant mortality (per 1,000 live births 1989): 173.

Education (1989): Literacy: 10%. Attendance: 21% attend primary school.

Major International Organizations: UN and all of its specialized agencies, OAU, EC.

Embassy: 2130 R St. NW 20008; 332-2250.

Until the 15th century the area was part of the great Mali Empire. Timbuktu was a center of Islamic study. French rule was secured, 1898. The Sudanese Rep. and Senegal became independent as the Mali Federation June 20, 1960, but Senegal withdrew, and the Sudanese Rep. was renamed Mali.

Mali signed economic agreements with France and, in 1963, with Senegal. In 1968, a coup ended the socialist regime. Famine struck in 1973-74, killing as many as 100,000 people. Drought conditions returned in the 1980s.

Malta
Repubblika Ta' Malta

People: Population (1990 est.): 373,000. Age distrib. (%): 0–14: 23.9; 15–59: 61.6; 60+: 14.5. Pop. density: 2,934 per sq. mi. Ethnic groups: Italian, Arab, French. Languages: Maltese, English both official. Religions: Mainly Roman Catholic.

Geography: Area: 122 sq. mi., twice the size of Washington, D.C. Location: In center of Mediterranean Sea. Neighbors: Nearest is Italy on N. Topography: Island of Malta is 95 sq. mi.; other islands in the group: Gozo, 26 sq. mi., Comino, 1 sq. mi. The coastline is heavily indented. Low hills cover the interior. Capital: Valletta. Cities (1988 est.): Birkirkara 20,000, Qormi 18,000.

Government: Type: Republic. Head of state: Pres. Paul Xuerub; in office: Feb. 15, 1987. Head of government: Prime Min. Eddie Fenech Adami; b. Feb. 7, 1934; in office: May 12, 1987. Local Divisions: 13 electoral districts.

Economy: Industries: Textiles, tourism. **Chief crops:** Potatoes, onions, beans. **Arable land:** 41%. **Electricity prod.** (1988): $1 bln. kwh. **Labor force:** 49% agric.; 24% manuf.; 30% services; 22% gov.

Finance: Currency: Pound (Mar. 1990: 1.00 = $3.01 US). **Gross national product** (1988): $1.6 bln. **Per capita income** (1986): $4,750. **Imports** (1988): $1.3 bln.; partners: UK 18%, It. 23%, W. Ger. 14%, U.S. 7%. **Exports** (1988): $714 mln.; partners: W. Ger. 31%, UK 20%, Libya 8%. **Tourists** (1987): receipts: $363 mln. **National budget** (1987): $762 mln. expenditures. **International reserves less gold** (Mar. 1990): 1.2 bln. **Gold:** 226,000 oz t. **Consumer prices** (change in 1989): 0.9% .

Transport: Motor vehicles: in use (1988): 85,000 passenger cars, 18,000 comm. vehicles. **Civil aviation** (1987): 636 mln. passenger-km; 1 airport. **Chief ports:** Valletta.

Communications: Television sets: 137,000 licensed (1988). **Radios:** 92,000 in use (1986). **Telephones in use** (1988): 163,000.

Health: Life expectancy at birth (1987): 72.5 male; 77.0 female. **Births** (per 1,000 pop. 1989): 14. **Deaths** (per 1,000 pop. 1989): 8. **Natural increase:** .6%. **Hospital beds:** 1 per 108 persons. **Physicians:** 1 per 489 persons. **Infant mortality** (per 1,000 live births 1989): 10.1.

Education (1988): Literacy: 90%. **Compulsory:** until age 16. **Major International Organizations:** UN (GATT, WHO, IMF), Commonwealth of Nations.

Embassy: 2017 Connecticut Ave. NW 20008; 462-3611.

Malta was ruled by Phoenicians, Romans, Arabs, Normans, the Knights of Malta, France, and Britain (since 1814). It became independent Sept. 21, 1964. Malta became a republic in 1974. The withdrawal of the last of its sailors, Apr. 1, 1979, ended 179 years of British military presence on the island.

With Malta's approval, Egyptian commandos stormed a hijacked EgyptAir passenger plane at Valletta airport Nov. 23, 1985; 57 died in the battle.

Malta is democratic but nonaligned.

Mauritania
Islamic Republic of Mauritania
République Islamique de Mauritanie

People: Population (1990 est.): 2,038,000. **Age distrib. (%):** 0–14: 46.4; 15–59: 49.0; 60+: 4.6. **Pop. density:** 4.5 per sq. mi. **Urban** (1983): 6%. **Ethnic groups:** Arab-Berber 80%, Negroes 20%. **Languages:** French (official), Hassanya Arabic (national), Toucouleur, Fula, Sarakole, Wolof. **Religion:** Nearly 100% Moslem.

Geography: Area: 397,954 sq. mi., the size of Texas and California combined. **Location:** In W. Africa. **Neighbors:** Morocco on N, Algeria, Mali on E, Senegal on S. **Topography:** The fertile Senegal R. valley in the S gives way to a wide central region of sandy plains and scrub trees. The N is arid and extends into the Sahara. **Capital:** Nouakchott. **Cities** (1987 est.): Nouakchott 400,000; Nouadhibou 70,000; Kaedi 22,000.

Government: Type: Military republic. **Head of Government:** President & Premier Maaouya Ould Sidi Ahmed Taya; in office: Apr. 25, 1981. **Local divisions:** 12 regions, one capital district. **Defense:** 20% of GNP (1986).

Economy: Chief crops: Dates, grain. **Industries:** iron mining. **Minerals:** Iron, ore, gypsum. **Livestock** (1988): sheep: 4.1 min.; goats: 3.9 min.; cattle: 1.2 mln. **Fish catch** (1987): 99,000 metric tons. **Electricity prod.** (1987): 120 mln. kwh. **Labor force:** 47% agric., 14% ind. & comm., 29% services.

Finance: Currency: Ouguiya (Mar. 1990: 83 = $1 US). **Gross national product** (1988): $843 mln. **Per capita income** (1986): $450. **Imports** (1987): $235 mln.; partners: Fr. 29%, Sp. 9%. **Exports** (1987): $428 mln.; partners: Fr. 21%, It. 26%, Jap. 20%. **International reserves less gold** (Feb. 1989): $43 mln.

Transport: Motor vehicles: in use (1985): 15,000 passenger cars, 2,000 comm. vehicles. **Chief ports:** Nouakchott, Nouadhibou.

Communications: Radios: 1 per 8.1 persons.

Health: Life expectancy at birth (1989): 43 male; 48 female. **Births** (per 1,000 pop. 1989): 49. **Deaths** (per 1,000 pop. 1989): 19. **Natural increase:** 3.0%. **Hospital beds** (1984): 1,325. **Physicians** (1984): 170. **Infant mortality** (per 1,000 live births 1989): 97.

Education (1987): **Literacy:** 17%. **Attendance:** 41% in primary school, 10% in secondary school.

Major International Organizations: UN (GATT, IMF, WHO) OAU, Arab League.

Embassy: 2129 Leroy Pl. NW 20008; 232-5700.

Mauritania became independent Nov. 28, 1960. It annexed the south of former Spanish Sahara in 1976. Saharan guerrillas stepped up attacks in 1977; 8,000 Moroccan troops and French bomber raids aided the government. Mauritania signed a peace treaty with the Polisario Front, 1980, resumed diplomatic relations with Algeria while breaking a defense treaty with Morocco, and renounced sovereignty over its share of former Spanish Sahara. Morocco annexed the territory.

Famine struck repeatedly during the 1980s.

Mauritius

People: Population (1990 est.): 1,141,900. **Age distrib. (%):** 0–14: 36.3; 15–59: 57.2; 60+: 6.4. **Pop. density:** 1,325 per sq. mi. **Urban** (1987): 41%. **Ethnic groups:** Indo-Mauritian 68%, Creole 27%, others. **Languages:** English (official), French, Creole. **Religions:** Hindu 51%, Christian 30%, Moslem 16%.

Geography: Area: 790 sq. mi., about the size of Rhode Island. **Location:** In the Indian O., 500 mi. E of Madagascar. **Neighbors:** Nearest is Madagascar on W. **Topography:** A volcanic island nearly surrounded by coral reefs. A central plateau is encircled by mountain peaks. **Capital:** Port Louis. **Cities** (1986 est.): Port Louis 155,000.

Government: Type: Parliamentary democracy. **Head of state:** Queen Elizabeth II, represented by Gov.-Gen. Sir Veerasamy Ringadoo; in office: Jan. 17, 1986. **Head of government:** Prime Min. Aneerood Jugnauth; in office: June 12, 1982. **Local divisions:** 8 administrative divisions.

Economy: Industries: Tourism. **Chief crops:** Sugar cane, tea. **Arable land:** 58%. **Electricity prod.** (1988): 423 mln. kwh. **Labor force:** 20% agric. & fishing; 38% manuf.; 19% govt. services.

Finance: Currency: Rupee (Mar. 1990: 15.02 = $1 US). **Gross national product** (1987): $1.4 bln. **Per capita income** (1987): $1,400. **Imports** (1988): $1.2 bln.; partners: UK 9%, Fr. 12%, So. Afr. 9%. **Exports** (1988): $997 mln.; partners: UK 50%, Fr. 22%, U.S. 8%. **Tourists** (1987): $138 min. receipts. **National budget** (1985): $310 mln. **International reserves less gold** (Feb. 1990): $561 mln. **Gold:** 61,000 oz t. **Consumer prices** (change in 1989): 12.7%.

Transport: Motor vehicles: in use (1987): 24,000 passenger cars, 6,000 comm. vehicles. **Chief ports:** Port Louis.

Communications: Television sets: 1 per 8.2 persons. **Radios:** 1 per 4.2 persons. **Telephones:** 1 per 15 persons. **Daily newspaper circ.** (1987): 75 per 1,000 pop.

Health: Life expectancy at birth (1988): 64.4 male; 71.2 female. **Births** (per 1,000 pop. 1989): 21. **Deaths** (per 1,000 pop. 1989): 6. **Natural increase:** 1.5%. **Hospital beds:** 1 per 364 persons. **Physicians:** 1 per 784 persons. **Infant mortality** (per 1,000 live births 1989): 22.

Education (1989): **Literacy:** 94%. **Attendance:** almost all children attend school.

Major International Organizations: UN and all of its specialized agencies, OAU, Commonwealth of Nations.

Embassy: 4301 Connecticut Ave. NW 20008; 244-1491.

Mauritius was uninhabited when settled in 1638 by the Dutch, who introduced sugar cane. France took over in 1721, bringing African slaves. Britain ruled from 1810 to Mar. 12, 1968, bringing Indian workers for the sugar plantations.

The economy suffered in the 1980s because of low world sugar prices.

Mexico
United Mexican States
Estados Unidos Mexicanos

People: Population (1990 est.): 88,335,000. **Age distrib. (%):** 0–14: 37.5; 15–59: 57.0; 60+: 5.5. **Pop. density:** 115 per sq. mi. **Urban** (1988): 70%. **Ethnic groups:** Mestizo 60%, American Indian 29%, Caucasian 9%. **Languages:** Spanish. **Religions:** Roman Catholic 97%.

Geography: Area: 761,604 sq. mi., three times the size of Texas. **Location:** In southern N. America. **Neighbors:** U.S. on N, Guatemala, Belize on S. **Topography:** The Sierra Madre Occidental Mts. run NW-SE near the west coast; the Sierra Madre Oriental Mts., run near the Gulf of Mexico. They join S of Mexico City. Between the 2 ranges lies the dry central plateau, 5,000 to 8,000 ft. alt., rising toward the S, with temperate vegetation. Coastal lowlands are tropical. About 45% of land is arid. **Capital:** Mexico City. **Cities** (1986 est.): Mexico City (metro) 18 mln.; Guadalajara (metro) 3 mln.; Monterrey (metro) 2.7 mln.

Government: Type: Federal republic. **Head of state:** Pres. Carlos Salinas de Gortari; b. Apr. 3, 1948; in office: Dec. 1, 1988. **Local divisions:** Federal district and 31 states. **Defense:** 0.6% of GNP (1988).

Economy: Industries: Steel, chemicals, electric goods, textiles, rubber, petroleum, tourism. **Chief crops:** Cotton, coffee, wheat, rice, sugar cane, vegetables, corn. **Minerals:** Silver, lead, zinc, gold, oil, natural gas. **Crude oil reserves** (1987): 54 bln. bbls. **Arable land:** 13%. **Livestock** (1987): cattle: 31.1 mln.; pigs: 19 mln.; sheep: 5.8 mln. **Fish catch** (1987): 1.4 mln. metric tons. **Electricity prod.** (1988): 91.2 bln. kwh. **Crude steel prod.** (1988): 7.7 mln. metric tons. **Labor force:** 26% agric.; 13% manuf; 31% services; 14% comm.

Finance: Currency: Peso (June 1990: 2,849 = $1 US). **Gross national product** (1987): $126 bln. **Per capita income** (1984): $2,082. **Imports** (1988): $19.5 bln.; partners: U.S. 64%, EC 11%. **Exports** (1988): $20.7 bln.; partners: U.S. 64%, EC 10%. **Tourists** (1987): receipts: $2.2 bln. **National budget** (1985): $86.5 bln. expenditures. **International reserves less gold** (Jan. 1990): $6.3 bln. **Gold:** 1.0 mln. oz t. **Consumer prices** (change in 1989): 20.0%.

Transport: Railway traffic (1989): 3.6 bln. passenger-km. **Motor vehicles:** in use (1985): 5.0 mln. passenger cars, 2.1 mln. comm. **Civil aviation** (1988): 14.8 bln. passenger-km; 78 airports. **Chief ports:** Veracruz, Tampico, Mazatlan, Coatzacoalcos.

Communications: Television sets: 1 in 8.7 persons. **Radios:** 1 in 5.1 persons. **Telephones:** 1 in 8.8 persons. **Daily newspaper circ.** (1986): 142 per 1,000 pop.

Health: Life expectancy at birth (1989): 67 male; 73 female. **Births** (per 1,000 pop. 1989): 30. **Deaths** (per 1,000 pop. 1989): 6. **Natural increase:** 2.5%. **Hospital beds** (1984): 72,000. **Physicians** (1980): 53,053. **Infant mortality** (per 1,000 live births 1989): 42.

Education (1989): **Literacy:** 88%. **Years compulsory:** 10. **Major International Organizations:** UN (IMF, GATT), OAS. **Embassy:** 2829 16th St. NW 20009; 234-6000.

Mexico was the site of advanced Indian civilizations. The Mayas, an agricultural people, moved up from Yucatan, built immense stone pyramids, invented a calendar. The Toltecs were overcome by the Aztecs, who founded Tenochtitlan 1325 AD, now Mexico City. Hernando Cortes, Spanish conquistador, destroyed the Aztec empire, 1519-1521.

After 3 centuries of Spanish rule the people rose, under Fr. Miguel Hidalgo y Costilla, 1810, Fr. Morelos y Payon, 1812, and Gen. Agustin Iturbide, who made independence effective Sept. 27, 1821, but made himself emperor as Agustin I. A republic was declared in 1823.

Mexican territory extended into the present American Southwest and California until Texas revolted and established a republic in 1836; the Mexican legislature refused recognition but was unable to enforce its authority there. After numerous clashes, the U.S.-Mexican War, 1846-48, resulted in the loss by Mexico of the lands north of the Rio Grande.

French arms supported an Austrian archduke on the throne of Mexico as Maximilian I, 1864-67, but pressure from the U.S. forced France to withdraw. A dictatorial rule by Porfirio Diaz, president 1877-80, 1884-1911, led to fighting by rival forces until the new constitution of Feb. 5, 1917 provided social reform. Since then Mexico has developed large-scale programs of social security, labor protection, and school improvement. A constitutional provision requires management to share profits with labor.

The Institutional Revolutionary Party has been dominant in politics since 1929. Radical opposition, including some guerrilla activity, has been contained by strong measures.

The presidency of Luis Echeverria, 1970-76, was marked by a more leftist foreign policy and domestic rhetoric. Some land redistribution begun in 1976 was reversed under the succeeding administration.

Some gains in agriculture, industry, and social services have been achieved. The land is rich, but the rugged topography and

lack of sufficient rainfall are major obstacles. Crops and farm prices are controlled, as are export and import. Economic prospects brightened with the discovery of vast oil reserves, perhaps the world's greatest. But much of the work force is jobless or underemployed.

Inflation and the drop in world oil prices caused economic problems in the 1980s. The peso was devalued and private banks were nationalized to restore financial stability.

Many thousands died when a disastrous earthquake struck Mexico City, Sept. 19, 1985.

The U.S. has been critical of Mexico for its failure to combat the production of illegal drugs.

Monaco
Principality of Monaco

People: Population (1989 est.): 29,000. **Age distrib.** (%): 0–14: 12.7; 15–59: 56.3 60+: 30.7. **Pop. density:** 28,072 per sq. mi. **Ethnic groups:** French 47%, Italian 16%, Monegasque 16%. **Languages:** French (official). **Religions:** Predominantely Roman Catholic.

Geography: Area: 0.6 sq. mi. **Location:** On the NW Mediterranean coast. **Neighbors:** France to W, N, E. **Topography:** Monaco-Ville sits atop a high promontory, the rest of the principality rises from the port up the hillside. **Capital:** Monaco-Ville (1985 est.): 1,700.

Government: Type: Constitutional monarchy. **Head of state:** Prince Rainier III; b. May 31, 1923; in office: May 9, 1949. **Head of government:** Min. of State Jean Ausseil; in office: Sept. 1985.

Economy: Industries: Tourism, gambling, chemicals, precision instruments, plastics.

Finance: Currency: French franc or Monégasque franc.

Transport: Chief ports: La Condamine.

Communications: Television sets: 17,000 in use (1984). **Telephones in use** (1984): 18,000.

Health: Births (per 1,000 pop. 1989): 7. **Deaths** (per 1,000 pop. 1989): 7. **Infant mortality** (per 1,000 live births 1989): 9.

Education (1989): **Literacy:** 99%. **Years compulsory:** 10; attendance 99%.

An independent principality for over 300 years, Monaco has belonged to the House of Grimaldi since 1297 except during the French Revolution. It was placed under the protectorate of Sardinia in 1815, and under that of France, 1861. The Prince of Monaco was an absolute ruler until a 1911 constitution.

Monaco's fame as a tourist resort is widespread. It is noted for its mild climate and magnificent scenery. The area has been extended by land reclamation.

Mongolia
Mongolian People's Republic
Bügd Nayramdakh Mongol Ard Uls

People: Population (1990 est.): 2,185,000. **Pop. density:** 3 per sq. mi. **Urban** (1988): 52%. **Ethnic groups:** Mongol 90%. **Languages:** Khalkha Mongolian (official, written in Cyrillic letters since 1941), Russian, Chinese. **Religions:** curbed by govt., traditionally Lama Buddhism.

Geography: Area: 604,247 sq. mi., more than twice the size of Texas. **Location:** In E Central Asia. **Neighbors:** USSR on N, China on S. **Topography:** Mostly a high plateau with mountains, salt lakes, and vast grasslands. Arid lands in the S are part of the Gobi Desert. **Capital:** Ulaanbaatar. **Cities** (1985 est.): Ulaanbaatar 488,000, Darhan 69,000.

Government: Type: Socialist (in transition). **Head of state:** Pres. Punsalmaagiyn Ochirbat; b. 1942; in office: Mar. 21, 1990. **Head of government:** Premier Sharavyn Gunjaador; in office: Mar. 21, 1990. **Local divisions:** 18 provinces, 3 municipalities. **Defense:** 11.5% of GNP (1984).

Economy: Industries: Food processing, textiles, chemicals, cement. **Chief crops:** Grain. **Minerals:** Coal, tungsten, copper, molybdenum, gold, tin. **Arable land:** 1%. **Livestock** (1988): sheep: 13.5 mln.; cattle 2.4 mln. **Electricity prod.** (1988): 2.8 bln. kwh. **Labor force:** 52% agric.; 10% manuf.

Finance: Currency: Tugrik (Jan. 1990: 3.35 = $1 US). **Gross national product** (1986): $3.6 bln. **Per capita GNP** (1986):

$1,820. **Imports** (1987): $1.2 bln.; **partners:** USSR 91%. **Exports** (1987): $768 mln.; **partners:** USSR 80%.

Transport: Railway traffic (1987): 487 mln. passenger-km.
Communications: Television sets: 1 per 18 persons. **Radios:** 1 per 9.4 persons. **Telephones:** 1 per 36 persons. **Daily newspaper circ.** (1988): 91 per 1,000 pop.

Health: Life expectancy at birth (1989): 63 male; 67 female. **Births** (per 1,000 pop. 1989): 35. **Deaths** (per 1,000 pop. 1989): 8. **Natural increase:** 2.8%. **Hospital beds:** 1 per 88 persons. **Physicians:** 1 per 403 persons. **Infant mortality** (per 1,000 live births 1989): 49.

Major International Organizations: UN (ILO, WHO).

Education (1985): **Literacy:** 89%. **Years compulsory:** 7 in major population centers.

One of the world's oldest countries, Mongolia reached the zenith of its power in the 13th century when Genghis Khan and his successors conquered all of China and extended their influence as far W as Hungary and Poland. In later centuries, the empire dissolved and Mongolia came under the suzerainty of China.

With the advent of the 1911 Chinese revolution, Mongolia, with Russian backing, declared its independence. A Mongolian Communist regime was established July 11, 1921.

Mongolia has been changed from a nomadic culture to one of settled agriculture and growing industries with aid from the USSR and East European nations.

In 1990, the Mongolian Communist Party surrendered its monopoly on power. Free elections were held July 1990; the communists were victorious.

Morocco

Kingdom of Morocco

al-Mamlaka al-Maghrebia

People: Population (1990 est.): 26,249,000. **Age distrib. (%):** 0–14: 46.4; 15–59: 49.2; 60+: 4.2. **Pop. density:** 147 per sq. mi. **Urban** (1988): 44%. **Ethnic groups:** Arab-Berber 99%. **Languages:** Arabic (official), with Berber, French, Spanish minorities. **Religions:** Sunni Moslems 99%.

Geography: Area: 172,413 sq. mi., larger than California. **Location:** on NW coast of Africa. **Neighbors:** W. Sahara on S, Algeria on E. **Topography:** Consists of 5 natural regions: mountain ranges (Riff in the N, Middle Atlas, Upper Atlas, and Anti-Atlas); rich plains in the W; alluvial plains in SW; well-cultivated plateaus in the center; a pre-Sahara arid zone extending from SE. **Capital:** Rabat. **Cities** (1984): Casablanca 2,600,000; Rabat 556,000, Fes 852,000.

Government: Type: Constitutional monarchy. **Head of state:** King Hassan II; b. July 9, 1929; in office: Mar. 3, 1961. **Head of government:** Prime Min. Azzedine Laraki, in office: Sept. 30, 1986. **Local divisions:** 2 prefectures, 36 provinces. **Defense:** 5.0% of GNP (1988).

Economy: Industries: Carpets, clothing, leather goods, mining, tourism. **Chief crops:** Grain, fruits, dates, grapes. **Minerals:** Copper, cobalt, manganese, phosphates, lead, oil. **Crude oil reserves** (1980): 100 mln. bbls. **Arable land:** 18%. **Livestock** (1986): cattle: 3.3 mln.; sheep; 12 mln.; goats: 4.5 mln. **Fish catch** (1986): 591,000 metric tons. **Electricity prod.** (1988): 7.7 bln. kwh. **Labor force:** 39% agric., 20% services; 17% ind.

Finance: Currency: Dirham (Mar. 1990: 8.05 = $1 US). **Gross national product** (1988): $18.7 bln. **Per capita income** (1984): $630. **Imports** (1988): $4.4 bln.; **partners:** Fr. 25%, Sp. 7%, Saudi Ar. 15%. **Exports** (1988): $3.5 bln.; **partners:** Fr. 22%, W. Ger. 7%, Sp. 7%, It. 5%. **Tourists** (1987): $1 bln. receipts. **National budget** (1987): $5.0 bln. expenditures. **International reserves less gold** (Mar. 1990): $687 mln. **Gold:** 704,000 oz t. **Consumer prices** (change in 1988): 2.4%.

Transport: Railway traffic (1987): 2.0 bln. passenger-km. **Motor vehicles:** in use (1987): 554,000 passenger cars, 255,000 comm. vehicles. **Civil aviation** (1987): 2.2 bln. passenger-km; 15 airports. **Chief ports:** Tangier, Casablanca, Kenitra.

Communications: Television sets: 1 per 19.2 persons. **Radios:** 1 per 5.4 persons. **Telephones in use:** 1 per 68 persons. **Daily newspaper circ.** (1988): 12 per 1,000 pop.

Health: Life expectancy at birth (1989): 62 male; 65 female. **Births** (per 1,000 pop. 1989): 35. **Deaths** (per 1,000 pop. 1989): 9. **Natural increase:** 2.6%. **Hospital beds:** 1 per 918 persons. **Physicians:** 1 per 4,725 persons. **Infant mortality** (per 1,000 live births 1989): 79.

Education (1985): **Literacy:** 35%.

Major International Organizations: UN (ILO, IMF, WHO), OAU, Arab League.

Embassy: 1601 21st St. NW 20009; 462-7979.

Berbers were the original inhabitants, followed by Carthaginians and Romans. Arabs conquered in 683. In the 11th and 12th centuries, a Berber empire ruled all NW Africa and most of Spain from Morocco.

Part of Morocco came under Spanish rule in the 19th century; France controlled the rest in the early 20th. Tribal uprisings lasted from 1911 to 1933. The country became independent Mar. 2, 1956. Tangier, an internationalized seaport, was turned over to Morocco, 1956. Ifni, a Spanish enclave, was ceded in 1969.

Morocco annexed over 70,000 sq. mi. of phosphate-rich land Apr. 14, 1976, two-thirds of former Spanish Sahara, with the remainder annexed by Mauritania. Spain had withdrawn in February. Polisario, a guerrilla movement, proclaimed the region independent Feb. 27, and launched attacks with Algerian support. Morocco accepted U.S. military and economic aid. When Mauritania signed a treaty with the Polisario Front, and gave up its portion of the former Spanish Sahara, Morocco occupied the area, 1980. Morocco accused Algeria of instigating Polisario attacks.

After years of bitter fighting, Morocco controls the main urban areas, but the Polisario Front's guerrillas move freely in the vast, sparsely populated deserts.

Mozambique

People's Republic of Mozambique

República Popular de Moçambique

People: Population (1990 est.): 14,718,000. **Age distrib. (%):** 0–14: 45.3; 15–59: 50.6; 60+: 4.1. **Pop. density:** 49 per sq. mi. **Ethnic groups:** Bantu tribes. **Languages:** Portuguese (official), Bantu languages predominate. **Religions:** Traditional beliefs 60%, Christian 30%, Moslem 10%.

Geography: Area: 303,769 sq. mi., about the size of Texas. **Location:** On SE coast of Africa. **Neighbors:** Tanzania on N, Malawi, Zambia, Zimbabwe on W, South Africa, Swaziland on S. **Topography:** Coastal lowlands comprise nearly half the country with plateaus rising in steps to the mountains along the western border. **Capital:** Maputo. **Cities:** (1989 est.): Maputo 1.0 mln., Beira 291,604

Government: Type: Socialist one-party state. **Head of state:** Pres. Joaquim Chissano; b. Oct. 22, 1939; in office: Oct. 19, 1986. **Head of Government:** Mario de Graca Machungo; in office: July 17, 1986. **Local divisions:** 10 provinces. **Defense:** 8.4% of GNP (1988).

Economy: Industries: Cement, alcohol, textiles. **Chief crops:** Cashews, cotton, sugar, copra, tea. **Minerals:** Coal, copper, bauxite. **Arable land:** 4%. **Livestock** (1987): cattle: 1.3 mln. **Fish catch** (1985): 37,000 metric tons. **Electricity prod.** (1988): 1.7 bln. kwh. **Labor force:** 85% agric., 9% ind. & comm., 2% services.

Finance: Currency: Metical (Jan. 1990: 808 = $1 US). **Gross national product** (1987): $4.7 bln. **Per capita income** (1987): $319. **Imports** (1987): $627 mln.; **partners:** So. Afr. 11%, U.S. 13%, USSR 12%, It. 14%. **Exports** (1987): $97 mln.; **partners:** U.S. 16%, Jap. 15%. **National budget** (1987): $427 mln.

Transport: Railway traffic (1987): 104 mln. passenger-km. **Motor vehicles:** in use (1981): 49,000 passenger cars, 24,700 comm. vehicles. **Chief ports:** Maputo, Beira, Nacala, Quelimane.

Communications: Television sets: 1 per 425 persons. **Radios:** 1 per 31 persons. **Telephones:** 1 per 235 persons. **Daily newspaper circ.** (1988): 5 per 1,000 pop.

Health: Life expectancy at birth (1989): 45 male; 48 female. **Births** (per 1,000 pop. 1989): 47. **Deaths** (per 1,000 pop. 1989): 18. **Natural increase:** 2.8%. **Hospital beds:** 1 per 1,244 persons. **Physicians:** 1 per 44,392 persons. **Infant mortality** (per 1,000 live births 1989): 200.

Education (1989): **Literacy:** 14%.

Major International Organization: UN (IMF, World Bank), OAU.

The first Portuguese post on the Mozambique coast was established in 1505, on the trade route to the East. Mozambique became independent June 25, 1975, after a ten-year war against Portuguese colonial domination. The 1974 revolution in Portugal paved the way for the orderly transfer of power to Frelimo (Front for the Liberation of Mozambique). Frelimo took over local administration Sept. 20, 1974, over the opposition, in part violent, of some blacks and whites. The new government, led by Maoist Pres. Samora Machel, promised a gradual transition to a communist system. Private schools were closed, rural collective farms organized, and private homes nationalized. Economic problems included the emigration of most of the country's 160,000 whites, a politically untenable economic dependence on white-ruled South Africa, and a large external debt.

In the 1980s, severe drought and civil war caused famine and heavy loss of life.

Myanmar (Formerly Burma)

Union of Myanmar

Pyeidaungzu Myanma Naingngandaw

People: Population (1990 est.): 41,279,000. **Age distrib. (%):** 0–14: 41.2; 15–59: 52.8; 60+: 6.0. **Pop. density:** 152 per sq. mi. **Urban** (1986): 24%. **Ethnic groups:** Burmans (related to Tibetans) 68%; Karen 4%, Shan 7%, Rakhine 3%. **Languages:** Burmese (official). **Religions:** Buddhist 85%; animist, Christian.

Geography: Area: 261,789 sq. mi., nearly as large as Texas. **Location:** Between S. and S.E. Asia, on Bay of Bengal. **Neighbors:** Bangladesh, India on W, China, Laos, Thailand on E. **Topography:** Mountains surround Myanmar on W, N, and E, and dense forests cover much of the nation. N-S rivers provide habitable valleys and communications, especially the Irrawaddy, navigable for 900 miles. The country has a tropical monsoon climate. **Capital:** Yangon. **Cities** (1983 est.): Yangon 2,458,712; Mandalay 458,000; Karbe ('73 cen.): 253,600; Moulmein 188,000.

Government: Type: Military. **Head of state and head of government:** Gen. Saw Maung; in office: Sept. 21, 1988. **Local divisions:** 7 states and 7 divisions. **Defense:** 3.0% of GNP (1987).

Economy: Chief crops: Rice, sugarcane, peanuts, beans. **Minerals:** Oil, lead, silver, tin, tungsten, precious stones. **Crude oil reserves** (1985): 733 mln. bbls. **Other resources:** Rubber, teakwood. **Arable land:** 15%. **Livestock.** (1988): cattle 9.9 mln.; pigs: 3.1 mln. **Fish catch** (1987): 643,000 metric tons. **Electricity prod.** (1988): 2.9 bln. kwh. **Labor force:** 66% agric; 12% ind.

Finance: Currency: Kyat (Mar. 1990: 6.64 = $1 US). **Gross national product** (1988): $9.3 bln. **Per capita income** (1989): $210. **Imports** (1988): $244 mln.; partners: Jap. 50%, EEC 20%. **Exports** (1988): $138 mln.; partners: SE Asian countries 30%; EEC 12%. **Tourism** (1987): $14 mln. receipts. **National budget** (1988): $2.2 bln. **International reserves less gold** (Mar. 1990): $560 mln. **Gold:** 251,000 oz t. **Consumer prices** (change in 1989): 16%.

Transport: Railway traffic (1987): 3.1 bln. passenger-km. **Motor vehicles:** in use (1985): 35,000 passenger cars, 50,000 comm. vehicles. **Civil aviation** (1988): 214 mln. passenger-km.; 21 airports with scheduled flights. **Chief ports:** Yangon, Sittwe, Bassein, Moulmein, Tavoy.

Communications: Television sets: 1 per 592 persons. **Radios:** 1 per 13 persons. **Telephones:** 1 per 624 persons. **Daily newspaper circ.** (1987): 14 per 1,000 pop.

Health: Life expectancy at birth (1989): 53 male; 56 female. **Births** (per 1,000 pop. 1989): 33. **Deaths** (per 1,000 pop. 1989): 13. **Natural increase:** 2.0%. **Hospital beds:** 1 per 1,498 persons. **Physicians:** 1 per 3,485 persons. **Infant mortality** (per 1,000 live births 1989): 99.

Education (1989): **Literacy:** 66%. **Years compulsory:** 4; **Attendance:** 84%.

Major International Organizations: UN (World Bank, IMF, GATT).

Embassy: 2300 S St. NW 20008; 332-9044.

The Burmese arrived from Tibet before the 9th century, displacing earlier cultures, and a Buddhist monarchy was established by the 11th. Burma was conquered by the Mongol dynasty of China in 1272, then ruled by Shans as a Chinese tributary, until the 16th century.

Britain subjugated Burma in 3 wars, 1824-84, and ruled the country as part of India until 1937, when it became self-governing. Independence outside the Commonwealth was achieved Jan. 4, 1948.

Gen. Ne Win dominated politics from 1962 to 1988, when he abdicated power, following waves of anti-government demonstrations. He led a Revolutionary Council set up in 1962, which drove Indians from the civil service and Chinese from commerce. Socialization of the economy was advanced, isolation from foreign countries enforced.

In 1987 Burma, once the richest nation in SE Asia, was granted least developed country status by the UN. Following Ne Win's resignation, Sein Lwin and later Maung Maung, a civilian, took power but rioting and street violence continued. In Sept., Gen. Saw Maung, a close associate of Ne Win, seized power.

In 1989 the country's name was changed to Myanmar.

The first free, multiparty elections in 30 years took place May 27, 1990, with the main opposition party winning a decisive victory.

Namibia

Republic of Namibia

People: Population (1990 est.): 1,372,000. **Pop density:** 4 per sq. mi. **Ethnic groups:** black 86%, white 8%. **Languages:** Afrikaans, English, several indigenous languages. **Religion:** mostly indigenous.

Geography: Area: 317,818 sq. mi., slightly more than half the size of Alaska. **Location:** In S. Africa on the coast of the Atlantic Ocean. Angola on the N., Botswana on the E., and South Africa on the S. **Capital:** Windhoek. **Cities** (1990 est.): Windhoek, 114,000.

Government: Head of state: Pres. Sam Nujoma; in office: Feb. 16, 1990. **Local divisions:** 26 districts.

Economy: Mining accounts for over 40% of GNP. **Electricity prod.** (1988): 432,000 kwh.

Finance: Currency: South African Rand. **Gross National Product** (1988): $1.6 bln. **Per capital GNP** (1988): $1,300. **Imports** (1987): $842 mln. **Exports** (1987): $889,000 mln.

Communications: Television sets: 1 per 42 persons. **Radios:** 1 per 5.8 persons. **Telephones:** 1 per 17 persons.

Health: Life Expectancy at Birth (1989): 57 male; 62 female. **Births** (per 1,000 pop. 1989): 45. **Deaths** (per 1,000 pop 1989): 10. **Natural increase:** 3.5. **Hospital beds:** 1 per 166 persons. **Physicians:** 1 per 4,450 persons. **Infant Mortality** (per 1,000 live births 1989): 72.

Education (1989): **Literacy:** 16% nonwhite.

Namibia was declared a protectorate by Germany in 1890 and officially called South-West Africa. South Africa seized the territory from Germany in 1915 during World War 1; the League of Nations gave South Africa a mandate over the territory in 1920. In 1966, the Marxist South-West Africa People's Organization (SWAPO) launched a guerrilla war for independence.

In 1968 the UN General Assembly gave the area the name Namibia. In Jan. 1970 the UN Security Council condemned S. Africa for "illegal" control of the area. In an advisory opinion, June 1971, the International Court of Justice declared S. Africa was occupying the area illegally.

In a 1977 referendum, white voters backed a plan for a multiracial interim government to lead to independence. SWAPO rejected the plan. Both S. Africa and Namibian rebels agreed to a UN plan for independence by the end of 1978. S. Africa rejected the plan, Sept. 20, 1978, and held elections, without UN supervision, for Namibia's constituent assembly, Dec., that were ignored by the major black opposition parties.

In 1982, So. African and SWAPO agreed in principle on a cease-fire and the holding of UN-supervised elections. So. Africa, however, insisted on the withdrawal of Cuban forces from Angola as a precondition to Namibian independence. On Jan. 18, 1983, South Africa dissolved the Namibian National Assembly and resumed direct control of the territory.

In 1988, A U.S. mediated plan was agreed upon by So. Africa, Angola, and Cuba, which called for withdrawal of Cuban troops from Angola and black majority rule in Namibia.

Namibia became an independent nation March 21, 1990.

Walvis Bay, the only deepwater port in the country, was turned over to South African administration in 1922. S. Africa said in 1978 it would discuss sovereignty only after Namibian independence.

Nauru

Republic of Nauru

Naoero

People: Population (1990): 8,100. **Pop density:** 987 per sq. mi. **Ethnic groups:** Nauruans 57%, Pacific Islanders 26%, Chinese 8%, European 8%. **Languages:** Nauruan (official), English. **Religions:** Predominately Christian.

Geography: Area: 8 sq. mi. **Location:** In Western Pacific O. just S of Equator. **Neighbors:** Nearest are Solomon Is. **Topography:** Mostly a plateau bearing high grade phosphate deposits, surrounded by a coral cliff and a sandy shore in concentric rings. **Capital:** Yaren.

Government: Type: Republic. **Head of state:** Pres. Kenos Aroi; in office: Aug. 17, 1989. **Local divisions:** 14 districts.

Economy: Phosphate mining. **Electricity prod.** (1988): 48 mln. kwh.

Finance: Currency: Australian dollar. **Gross national product** (1986): $160 mln. **Imports** (1984): $14 mln. **Exports** (1984): $93 mln.

Communications: Radios: 4,000 in use (1985). **Telephones in use** (1980): 1,500.

Health: Births (per 1,000 pop. 1989): 21. **Deaths** (per 1,000 pop. 1989): 5. **Natural increase:** 1.6%. **Infant mortality** (per 1,000 live births 1989): 41.

Education (1988): Literacy 99%; compulsory ages 6-16.

The island was discovered in 1798 by the British but was formally annexed to the German Empire in 1886. After World War I, Nauru became a League of Nations mandate administered by Australia. During World War II the Japanese occupied the island and shipped 1,200 Nauruans to the fortress island of Truk as slave laborers.

In 1947 Nauru was made a UN trust territory, administered by Australia. Nauru became an independent republic Jan. 31, 1968.

Phosphate exports provide one of the world's highest per capita revenues for the Nauru people.

Nepal

Kingdom of Nepal

Sri Nepala Sarkar

People: Population (1990 est.): 19,158,000. **Age distrib. (%):** 0–14: 42.2; 15–59: 52.9; 60+: 4.9. **Pop. density:** 334 per sq. mi. **Urban** (1987): 8%. **Ethnic groups:** The many tribes are descendants of Indian, Tibetan, and Central Asian migrants. **Languages:** Nepali (official) (an Indic language), 12 others. **Religions:** Hindu (official) 90%, Buddhist 7%.

Geography: Area: 56,136 sq. mi., the size of North Carolina. **Location:** Astride the Himalaya Mts. **Neighbors:** China on N, India on S. **Topography:** The Himalayas stretch across the N, the hill country with its fertile valleys extends across the center, while the southern border region is part of the flat, subtropical Ganges Plain. **Capital:** Kathmandu. **Cities** (1987 est.): Kathmandu 422,000, Pokhara, Biratnagar, Birganj.

Government: Type: Constitutional monarchy. **Head of state:** King Birendra Bir Bikram Shah Dev; b. Dec. 28, 1945; in office: Jan. 31, 1972. **Head of government:** Prime Min. Krishma Prasad Bhattarai; in office: Apr. 19, 1990. **Local divisions:** 14 zones; 75 districts. **Defense:** 1.2% of GNP (1987).

Economy: Industries: Sugar, jute mills, tourism. **Chief crops:** Jute, rice, grain. **Minerals:** Quartz. **Other resources:** Forests. **Arable land:** 17%. **Livestock** (1986): cattle: 7 mln. **Electricity prod.** (1988): 530 mln. kwh. **Labor force:** 91% agric.

Finance: Currency: Rupee (Mar. 1990: 28.90 = $1 US). **Gross national product** (1988): $3.1 bln. **Per capita income** (1986): $160. **Imports** (1988): $681 mln.; partners: India 47%, Jap. 25%. **Exports** (1988): $190 mln.; partners: India 68%. **Tourists** (1988): receipts: $28 mln. **National budget** (1987): $618 mln. **International reserves less gold** (Mar. 1990): $255 mln. **Gold:** 152,000 oz t. **Consumer prices** (change in 1989): 9.0%.

Transport: Civil aviation (1986): 300 mln. passenger-km.

Communications: Radios: 1 per 8.5 persons. **Telephones:** 1 per 686 persons. **Daily newspaper circ.** (1985): 5 per 1,000 pop.

Health: Life expectancy at birth (1989): 50 male; 49 female. **Births** (per 1,000 pop. 1989): 40. **Deaths** (per 1,000 pop. 1989): 15. **Natural increase:** 2.4%. **Hospital beds:** 1 per 4,572 persons. **Physicians:** 1 per 20,356 persons. **Infant mortality** (per 1,000 live births 1989): 101.

Education (1989): **Literacy:** 29%. **Years compulsory:** 3; **Attendance:** 79% primary, 22% secondary.

Major International Organizations: UN (IMF).

Embassy: 2131 Leroy Pl. NW 20008; 667-4550.

Nepal was originally a group of petty principalities, the inhabitants of one of which, the Gurkhas, became dominant about 1769. In 1951 King Tribhubana Bir Bikram, member of the Shah family, ended the system of rule by hereditary premiers of the Ranas family, who had kept the kings virtual prisoners, and established a cabinet system of government.

Virtually closed to the outside world for centuries, Nepal is now linked to India and Pakistan by roads and air service and to Tibet by road. Polygamy, child marriage, and the caste system were officially abolished in 1963.

In response to numerous pro-democracy protests, the government, which had banned all political parties since 1960, announced the legalization of political parties in 1990. Multi-party elections were scheduled for 1991.

Netherlands

Kingdom of the Netherlands

Konindrijk der Nederlanden

People: Population (1990 est.) 14,864,000. **Age distrib. (%):** 0–14: 18.8; 15–60: 64.2; 60+: 17.0. **Pop. density:** 931 per sq. mi. **Urban** (1988): 88.3%. **Ethnic groups:** Dutch 97%. **Languages:** Dutch. **Religions:** Roman Catholic 40%, Dutch Reformed 19.3%.

Geography: Area: 15,770 sq. mi., the size of Mass., Conn., and R.I. combined. **Location:** In NW Europe on North Sea. **Topography:** The land is flat, an average alt. of 37 ft. above sea level, with much land below sea level reclaimed and protected by 1,500 miles of dikes. Since 1927 the government has been draining the IJsselmeer, formerly the Zuider Zee. By 1972, 410,000 of a planned 550,000 acres had been drained and reclaimed. **Capital:** Amsterdam. **Cities** (1988): Amsterdam 691,000; Rotterdam 574,100; Hague 443,500.

Government: Type: Parliamentary democracy under a constitutional monarch. **Head of state:** Queen Beatrix; b. Jan. 31, 1938; in office: Apr. 30, 1980. **Head of government:** Prime Min. Ruud Lubbers; in office: Nov. 4, 1982. **Seat of govt.:** The Hague. **Local divisions:** 12 provinces. **Defense:** 3.2% of GNP (1987).

Economy: Industries: Metals, machinery, chemicals, oil refinery, diamond cutting, electronics, tourism. **Chief crops:** Grains, potatoes, sugar beets, vegetables, fruits, flowers. **Minerals:** Natural gas, oil. **Crude oil reserves** (1987): 195 mln. bbls. **Arable land:** 26%. **Livestock** (1988): cattle: 4.7 mln.; pigs: 13.4 mln. **Fish catch** (1987): 435,000 metric tons. **Electricity prod.** (1988): 63.0 bln. kwh. **Crude steel prod.** (1988): 5.5 mln. metric tons. **Labor force:** 1% agric.; 47% ind. and commerce, 44% services, 15% govt.

Finance: Currency: Guilder (June 1990: 1.86 = $1 US). **Gross national product** (1988): $223 bln. **Per capita income** (1987): $13,065. **Imports** (1989): $104.2 bln.; partners: W. Ger. 22%, Belg. 11%, U.S. 9%, U.K. 9%. **Exports** (1989): $107.8 bln.; partners: W. Ger. 30%, Belg. 14%, Fr. 10%, UK 9%. **Tourists** (1987): receipts: $2.6 bln. **National budget** (1988): $91 bln. expenditures. **International reserves less gold** (Mar. 1990): $16.8 bln. **Gold:** 43.94 mln. oz t. **Consumer prices** (change in 1989): 1.1%.

Transport: Railway traffic (1988): 9.3 bln. passenger-km. **Motor vehicles:** in use (1987): 5.1 mln. passenger cars, 401,000 comm. vehicles. **Civil aviation** (1987): 27.7 bln. passenger-km; 4 airports. **Chief ports:** Rotterdam, Amsterdam, IJmuiden.

Communications: Television sets: 1 per 3.2 persons. **Radios:** 1 per 1.2 persons. **Telephones:** 1 per 1.6 persons. **Daily newspaper circ.** (1987): 312 per 1,000 pop.

Health: Life expectancy at birth (1989): 74 male; 81 female. **Births** (per 1,000 pop. 1989): 13 **Deaths** (per 1,000 pop. 1989): 9. **Natural increase:** .4%. **Hospital beds** (1988): 67,445. **Physicians** (1988): 34,573. **Infant mortality** (per 1,000 live births 1989): 7

Education (1989): **Literacy:** 99%. **Years compulsory:** 10; attendance: 100%.

Major International Organizations: UN and all of its specialized agencies, NATO, EC, OECD.

Embassy: 4200 Linnean Ave. NW 20008; 244-5300.

Julius Caesar conquered the region in 55 BC, when it was inhabited by Celtic and Germanic tribes.

After the empire of Charlemagne fell apart, the Netherlands (Holland, Belgium, Flanders) split among counts, dukes and bishops, passed to Burgundy and thence to Charles V of Spain. His son, Philip II, tried to check the Dutch drive toward political freedom and Protestantism (1568-1573). William the Silent, prince of Orange, led a confederation of the northern provinces, called Estates, in the Union of Utrecht, 1579. The Estates retained individual sovereignty, but were represented jointly in the States-General, a body that had control of foreign affairs and defense. In 1581 they repudiated allegiance to Spain. The rise of the Dutch republic to naval, economic, and artistic eminence came in the 17th century.

The United Dutch Republic ended 1795 when the French formed the Batavian Republic. Napoleon made his brother Louis king of Holland, 1806; Louis abdicated 1810 when Napoleon annexed Holland. In 1813 the French were expelled. In 1815 the Congress of Vienna formed a kingdom of the Netherlands, including Belgium, under William I. In 1830, the Belgians seceded and formed a separate kingdom.

The constitution, promulgated 1814, and subsequently revised, assures a hereditary constitutional monarchy.

The Netherlands maintained its neutrality in World War I, but was invaded and brutally occupied by Germany from 1940 to 1945.

In 1949, after several years of fighting, the Netherlands granted independence to Indonesia, where it had ruled since the 17th century. In 1963, West New Guinea was turned over to Indonesia, after five years of controversy and seizure of Dutch property in Indonesia.

The independence of former Dutch colonies has instigated mass emigrations to the Netherlands, adding to problems of unemployment.

Though the Netherlands has been heavily industrialized, its productive small farms export large quantities of pork and dairy foods.

The Netherlands has agreed to allow NATO to deploy cruise missles on their soil.

Rotterdam, located along the principal mouth of the Rhine, handles the most cargo of any ocean port in the world. Canals, of which there are 3,478 miles, are important in transportation.

Netherlands Antilles

The **Netherlands Antilles,** constitutionally on a level of equality with the Netherlands homeland within the kingdom, consist of 2 groups of islands in the West Indies. **Curacao, Aruba,** and **Bonaire** are near the South American coast; **St. Eustatius, Saba,** and the southern part of **St. Maarten** are SE of Puerto Rico. Northern two-thirds of St. Maarten belong to French Guadeloupe; the French call the island St. Martin. Total area of the 2 groups is 385 sq. mi., including: Aruba 75, Bonaire 111, Curacao 171, St. Eustatius 11, Saba 5, St. Maarten (Dutch part) 13.

Aruba was separated from The Netherlands Antilles on Jan. 1, 1986; it is an autonomous member of The Netherlands, the same status as the Netherland Antilles.

Total pop. (est. 1989) was 187,000. Willemstad, on Curacao, is the capital. Chief products are corn, pulse, salt and phosphate; principal industry is the refining of crude oil from Venezuela. Tourism is an important industry, as are electronics and shipbuilding.

New Zealand

People: Population: (1990 est.): 3,397,000. **Age distrib. (%):** 0-14: 23.7, 15-59: 61.4; 60+: 14.9 **Pop. density:** 32 per sq. mi. **Urban** (1988): 84.0%. **Ethnic groups:** European (mostly British) 87%, Polynesian (mostly Maori) 9%. **Languages:** English (official), Maori. **Religions:** Anglican 29%, Presbyterian 18%, Roman Catholic 15%, others.

Geography: Area: 103,736 sq. mi., the size of Colorado. **Location:** In SW Pacific O. **Neighbors:** Nearest are Australia on W, Fiji, Tonga on N. **Topography:** Each of the 2 main islands (North and South Is.) is mainly hilly and mountainous. The east coasts consist of fertile plains, especially the broad Canterbury Plains on South Is. A volcanic plateau is in center of North Is. South Is. has glaciers and 15 peaks over 10,000 ft. **Capital:** Wellington. **Cities** (1988 est.): Auckland 149,000; Christchurch 168,000; Wellington 137,000; Manukau 181,000.

Government: Type: Parliamentary. **Head of state:** Queen Elizabeth II, represented by Gov.-Gen. Paul Reeves. **Head of government:** Prime Min. Geoffrey Palmer; in office: Aug. 8, 1989. **Local divisions:** 93 counties, 12 towns & districts. **Defense:** 2.2% of GNP (1987).

Economy: Industries: Food processing, textiles, machinery, fish, forest prods. **Chief crops:** Grain. **Minerals:** Oil, gas, iron, coal **Crude oil reserves** (1987): 182 mln. bbls. **Other resources:** Wool, timber. **Arable land:** 2%. **Livestock** (1987): cattle: 8.2 mln.; sheep: 64 mln. **Fish catch** (1987): 430,000 metric tons. **Electricity prod.** (1988): 27.0 bln. kwh. **Labor force:** 11% agric. & mining; 41% ind. and commerce, 47% services and gov.

Finance: Currency: Dollar (June 1990: 1.70 = $1 US). **Gross national product** (1988): $37 bln. **Per capita income** (1988): $11,040. **Imports** (1989): $8.8 bln.; partners: Austral. 18%, U.S. 16%, Jap. 20%. **Exports** (1989): $8.8 bln.; partners: UK 9%, U.S. 15%, Jap. 15%, Austral. 16%. **Tourists** (1987): receipts $286 mln. **National budget** (1988): $15.6 bln. **International reserves less gold** (Feb. 1990): $2.8 bln. **Gold:** 1,000 oz t. **Consumer prices** (change in 1989): 5.7%.

Transport: Railway traffic (1987): 458 mln. passenger-km. **Motor vehicles:** in use (1988): 1.3 mln. passenger cars; 334,000 comm. vehicles. **Civil aviation:** (1988): 10.7 bln. passenger-km, 36 airports. **Chief ports:** Auckland, Wellington, Lyttleton, Tauranga.

Communications: Television sets: 1 per 3.5 persons. **Radios:** 1 per 1.1 persons. **Telephones:** 1 per 1.4 persons. **Daily newspaper circ.** (1987): 323 per 1,000 pop.

Health: Life expectancy at birth (1989): 72 male; 78 female. **Births** (per 1,000 pop. 1989): 16. **Deaths** (per 1,000 pop. 1989): 8. **Natural increase:** .8%. **Hospital beds:** 1 per 111 persons. **Physicians:** 1 per 522 persons. **Infant mortality** (per 1,000 live births 1989): 10.

Education (1989): **Literacy:** 99%. Compulsory ages 6-15; attendance: 100%.

Major International Organizations: UN (GATT, World Bank, IMF), Commonwealth of Nations, OECD.

Embassy: 37 Observatory Cir. NW 20008; 328-4800.

The Maoris, a Polynesian group from the eastern Pacific, reached New Zealand before and during the 14th century. The first European to sight New Zealand was Dutch navigator Abel Janszoon Tasman, but Maoris refused to allow him to land. British Capt. James Cook explored the coasts, 1769-1770.

British sovereignty was proclaimed in 1840, with organized settlement beginning in the same year. Representative institutions were granted in 1853. Maori Wars ended in 1870 with British victory. The colony became a dominion in 1907, and is an independent member of the Commonwealth.

New Zealand fought on the side of the Allies in both world wars, and signed the ANZUS Treaty of Mutual Security with the U.S. and Australia in 1951. New Zealand's refusal to allow U.S. ships with nuclear weapons to use their port facilities caused an end to the alliance in 1986.

In July 1985, the Rainbow Warrior, flagship of the Greenpeace organization, was bombed and sunk in Auckland harbour by French secret service agents.

A labor tradition in politics dates back to the 19th century. Private ownership is basic to the economy, but state ownership or regulation affects many industries. Transportation, broadcasting, mining, and forestry are largely state-owned.

The native Maoris number about 250,000. Four of 92 members of the House of Representatives are elected directly by the Maori people.

New Zealand comprises **North Island**, 44,035 sq. mi.; **South Island**, 58,304 sq. mi.; **Stewart Island**, 674 sq. mi.; **Chatham Islands**, 372 sq. mi.

In 1965, the **Cook Islands** (pop. 1986 est., 17,185; area 93 sq. mi.) became self-governing although New Zealand retains responsibility for defense and foreign affairs. **Niue** attained the same status in 1974; it lies 400 mi. to W (pop. 1981 est., 3,400; area 100 sq. mi.). **Tokelau Is.,** (pop. 1981 est., 1,600; area 4 sq. mi.) are 300 mi. N of Samoa.

Ross Dependency, administered by New Zealand since 1923, comprises 160,000 sq. mi. of Antarctic territory.

Nicaragua
Republic of Nicaragua
República de Nicaragua

People: Population (1990 est.): 3,606,000. **Age distrib. (%):** 0–14: 46.6; 15–59: 49.3; 60+: 4.1. **Pop. density:** 73 per sq. mi. **Urban** (1988): 60%. **Ethnic groups:** Mestizo 69%, Caucasian 17%, black 9%, Indian 5%. **Languages:** Spanish, (official), English (on Caribbean coast). **Religion:** Roman Catholic 88%.

Geography: Area: 50,193 sq. mi., about the size of Iowa. **Location:** In Central America. **Neighbors:** Honduras on N, Costa Rica on S. **Topography:** Both Atlantic and Pacific coasts are over 200 mi. long. The Cordillera Mtns., with many volcanic peaks, runs NW-SE through the middle of the country. Between this and a volcanic range to the E lie Lakes Managua and Nicaragua. **Capital:** Managua. **Cities** (1986): Managua 1 mln.

Government: Type: Republic. **Head of Government:** Violeta Barrios de Chamorro; b. 1929; in office Apr. 25, 1990. **Local divisions:** 16 departments. **Defense:** 16.8% of GNP (1985).

Economy: Industries: Oil refining, food processing, chemicals, textiles. **Chief crops:** Bananas, cotton, fruit, yucca, coffee, sugar, corn, beans, cocoa, rice, sesame, tobacco, wheat. **Minerals:** Gold, silver, copper, tungsten. **Other resources:** Forests, shrimp. **Arable land:** 10%. **Livestock** (1986): cattle: 2.1 mln.; pigs: 750,000. **Fish catch:** (1987): 4,983 metric tons. **Electricity prod.** (1988): 1.2 bln. kwh. **Labor force:** 44% agric.; 13% ind.; 43% services.

Finance: Currency: Cordoba (May 1990: 100,000 = $1 US). **Gross national product** (1988): $2.1 bln. **Per capita GNP** (1988): $610. **Imports** (1987): $923 mln.; partners Comecon, CACM, EC. **Exports** (1987): $300 mln.; partners EC, Japan, Comecon. **National budget** (1987): $1.4 bln. expenditures. **Consumer prices** (change in 1989): 10,000%.

Transport: Railway traffic (1986): 25.5 mln. passengermiles. **Motor vehicles** in use (1986): 46,000 passenger cars, 30,000 comm. vehicles. **Chief ports:** Corinto, Puerto Somoza, San Juan del Sur.

Communications: Television sets: 1 per 17 persons. **Radios:** 1 per 4.1 persons. **Telephones:** 1 per 77 persons. **Daily newspaper circ.** (1987): 62 per 1,000 pop.

Health: Life expectancy at birth (1989): 61 male; 63 female. **Births** (per 1,000 pop. 1989): 39. **Deaths** (per 1,000 pop. 1989): 8. **Natural increase:** 3.1%. **Hospital beds:** 1 per 761 persons. **Physicians:** 1 per 1,678 persons. **Infant mortality** (per 1,000 live births 1989): 65.

Education (1986): **Literacy:** 66%. **Years compulsory:** 11 years or 16 years old.

Major International Organizations: UN and all of its specialized agencies, OAS.

Embassy: 1627 New Hampshire Ave. NW 20009; 939-6570.

Nicaragua, inhabited by various Indian tribes, was conquered by Spain in 1552. After gaining independence from Spain, 1821, Nicaragua was united for a short period with Mexico, then with the United Provinces of Central America, finally becoming an independent republic, 1838.

U.S. Marines occupied the country at times in the early 20th century, the last time from 1926 to 1933.

Gen. Anastasio Somoza-Debayle was elected president 1967. He resigned 1972, but was elected president again in 1974. Martial law was imposed in Dec. 1974, after officials were kidnapped by the Marxist Sandinista guerrillas. Violent opposition spread to nearly all classes, 1978; a nationwide strike called against the government Aug. 25 touched off a state of civil war at Matagalpa.

Months of simmering civil war erupted when Sandinist guerrillas invaded Nicaragua May 29, 1979, touching off a 7-week-offensive that culminated in the resignation and exile of Somoza, July 17.

Relations with the U.S. were strained due to Nicaragua's military aid to leftist guerrillas in El Salvador and the U.S. backing

anti-Sandinista contra guerrilla groups. Nicaragua accused the U.S. CIA of directing the mining of its ports, Apr. 6, 1984. It asked the International Court of Justice in The Hague to order the U.S. to halt the mining and cease aiding attacks on its territory. The Court ruled, May 10, that the U.S. should immediately halt any actions to blockade or mine Nicaragua's ports.

In 1983, the contras launched their first major offensive; the Sandinistas imposed rule by decree. In 1985, the U.S. House rejected Pres. Reagan's request for military aid to the contras; but in June voted to provide $27 mln. in humanitarian aid. In June 1986, the House approved $100 mln. in contra aid.

The diversion of funds to the contras from the proceeds of a secret arms sale to Iran caused a major scandal in the U.S. The plan, masterminded by the administration's national security advisor and his deputy, took place at a time when military aid to the contras was forbidden by law.

Cease-fire talks between the Sandinista government and the contras were held in 1988 but were ended by Ortega, Nov. 1989.

In a stunning upset, Violeta Barrios de Chamorro defeat Ortega in national elections, Feb. 25, 1990.

Niger
Republic of Niger
République du Niger

People: Population (1990 est.): 7,691,000. **Age distrib. (%):** 0–14: 46.7; 15–59: 48.5; 60+: 4.8. **Pop. density:** 15 per sq. mi. **Urban** (1988): 21%. **Ethnic groups:** Hausa 56%, Djerma 22%, Fulani 8%, Tuareg 8%. **Languages:** French (official), Hausa, Djerma. **Religions:** Sunni Moslem 80%.

Geography: Area: 489,189 sq. mi., almost 3 times the size of California. **Location:** In the interior of N. Africa. **Neighbors:** Libya, Algeria on N, Mali, Burkina Faso on W, Benin, Nigeria on S, Chad on E. **Topography:** Mostly arid desert and mountains. A narrow savanna in the S and the Niger R. basin in the SW contain most of the population. **Capital:** Niamey. **Cities** (1987 est.): Niamey 350,000.

Government: Type: Republic; military in power. **Head of state and government:** Pres. Ali Seibou; in office: Dec. 20, 1989. **Local divisions:** 7 departments. **Defense:** 0.8% of GNP (1985).

Economy: Chief crops: Peanuts, cotton. **Minerals:** Uranium, coal, iron. **Arable land:** 3%. **Livestock** (1986): cattle: 3.5 mln.; sheep 505,000. **Electricity prod.** (1988): 227 mln. kwh. **Labor force:** 90% agric.

Finance: Currency: CFA franc (Mar. 1990: 284 = $1 US). **Gross national product** (1987): $2.2 bln. **Per capita GNP** (1987): $310. **Imports** (1988): $441 mln.; partners: Fr. 36%, Nig. 13%. **Exports** (1988): $371 mln.; partners: Fr. 36%, Nig. 17%. **National budget** (1988): $452 mln. expenditures. **International reserves less gold** (Jan. 1990): $212 mln. **Gold:** 11,000 oz t. **Consumer prices** (change in 1988): −1.4%.

Transport: Motor vehicles in use (1988): 27,000 passenger cars, 25,000 comm. vehicles.

Communications: Television sets: 1 per 277 persons. **Radios:** 1 per 19 persons. **Telephones:** 1 per 563 persons. **Daily newspaper cir.** (1988): 1 per 1,000 pop.

Health: Life expectancy at birth (1989): 48 male; 50 female. **Births** (per 1,000 pop. 1989): 49. **Deaths** (per 1,000 pop. 1989): 17. **Natural increase:** 3.2%. **Infant mortality** (per 1,000 live births 1989): 137.

Education (1989): **Literacy:** 13%. **Years compulsory:** 6; attendance: 15%.

Major International Organizations: UN (GATT, IMF, WHO, FAO), OAU.

Embassy: 2204 R St. NW 20008; 483-4224.

Niger was part of ancient and medieval African empires. European explorers reached the area in the late 18th century. The French colony of Niger was established 1900-22, after the defeat of Tuareg fighters, who had invaded the area from the N a century before. The country became independent Aug. 3, 1960. The next year it signed a bilateral agreement with France retaining close economic and cultural ties, which have continued. Hamani Diori, Niger's first president, was ousted in a 1974 coup. Drought and famine struck in 1973-74, and again in 1975.

Nigeria
Federal Republic of Nigeria

People: Population (1990 est.): 118,865,000. **Pop. density:** 322 per sq. mi. **Urban** (1985): 23%. **Ethnic groups:** Hausa 21%, Yoruba 20%, Ibo 17%, Fulani 9%, others. **Languages:** English (official), Hausa, Yoruba, Ibo. **Religions:** Moslem 50% (in N), Christian 40% (in S), others.

Geography: Area: 356,667 sq. mi., more than twice the size of California. **Location:** On the S coast of W. Africa. **Neighbors:** Benin on W, Niger on N, Chad, Cameroon on E. **Topography:** 4 E-W regions divide Nigeria: a coastal mangrove swamp 10-60 mi. wide, a tropical rain forest 50-100 mi. wide, a plateau of savanna and open woodland, and semidesert in the N. **Capital:** Lagos. **Cities:** (1988): Lagos 1,243,000; Ibadan 1,172,000.

Government: Type: Military. **Head of state:** Gen. Ibrahim Babangida; b. Aug. 17, 1941; in office: Aug. 30, 1985. **Local divisions:** 21 states plus federal capital territory. **Defense:** 1.0% of GNP (1987).

Economy: Industries: Crude oil (95% of export), food processing, assembly of vehicles, textiles. **Chief crops:** Cocoa (main export crop), tobacco, palm products, peanuts, cotton, soybeans. **Minerals:** Oil, gas, coal, iron, limestone, columbium, tin. **Crude oil reserves** (1987): 16.8 bln. bbls. **Other resources:** Timber, rubber, hides. **Arable land:** 31%. **Livestock** (1987): cattle: 12.1 mln.; goats: 26.3 mln.; sheep: 13.1 mln. **Fish catch** (1987): 268,000 metric tons. **Electricity prod.** (1988): 11.2 bln. kwh. **Labor force:** 54% agric., 19% ind., comm. and serv.

Finance: Currency: Naira (Feb. 1990: 7.92 = $1.00 US). **Gross national product** (1987): $78.0 bln. **Per capita income** (1984): $790. **Imports** (1987): $7.8 bln.; partners: U.S., EC. **Exports** (1987): $7.3 bln.; partners: U.S., EC. **Tourist receipts** (1986): $125 mln. **National budget** (1987): $4.8 bln. expenditures. **International reserves less gold** (Jan. 1990): $1.4 bln. **Gold:** 687,000 oz t. **Consumer prices** (change in 1989): 40.9%.

Transport: Motor vehicles: in use (1981): 262,000 passenger cars, 90,000 comm. vehicles. **Civil aviation** (1987): 1.6 bln. passenger-km; 14 airports. **Chief ports:** Port Harcourt, Lagos, Warri, Calabar.

Communications: Television sets: 1 per 20 persons. **Radios:** 1 per 12 persons. **Telephones:** 1 per 397 persons. **Daily newspaper circ.** (1987): 12 per 1,000 pop.

Health: Life expectancy at birth (1989): 47 male; 49 female. **Births** (per 1,000 pop. 1989): 46. **Deaths** (per 1,000 pop. 1989): 17. **Natural increase:** 2.9%. **Hospital beds:** 1 per 1,142 persons. **Physicians:** 1 per 6,900 persons. **Infant mortality** (per 1,000 live births 1989): 121.

Education (1989): **Literacy:** 42%. **Primary school attendance:** 42%.

Major International Organizations: UN (GATT, IMO, WHO), OPEC, OAU, Commonwealth of Nations.

Embassy: 2201 M St. NW 20037; 822-1500.

Early cultures in Nigeria date back to at least 700 BC. From the 12th to the 14th centuries, more advanced cultures developed in the Yoruba area, at Ife, and in the north, where Moslem influence prevailed.

Portuguese and British slavers appeared from the 15th-16th centuries. Britain seized Lagos, 1861, during an anti-slave trade campaign, and gradually extended control inland until 1900. Nigeria became independent Oct. 1, 1960, and a republic Oct. 1, 1963.

On May 30, 1967, the Eastern Region seceded, proclaiming itself the Republic of Biafra, plunging the country into civil war. Casualties in the war, at over 1 million, including many "Biafrans" (mostly Ibos) who died of starvation despite international efforts to provide relief. The secessionists, after steadily losing ground, capitulated Jan. 12, 1970. Within a few years, the Ibos were reintegrated into national life, but mistrust among the regions persists.

Oil revenues have made possible a massive economic development program, largely using private enterprise, but agriculture has lagged. Oil revenues continued to decline in 1987.

After 13 years of military rule, the nation experienced a peaceful return to civilian government, Oct., 1979.

Military rule returned to Nigeria, Dec. 31, 1983 as a coup ousted the democratically-elected government. The government has promised a return to civilian rule by 1992.

Norway
Kingdom of Norway
Kongeriket Norge

People: Population (1990 est.): 4,214,000. **Age distrib. (%):** 0-14: 19.4; 15-59: 59.3; 60+: 21.3. **Pop. density:** 33 per sq. mi. **Urban** (1985): 80%. **Ethnic groups:** Germanic (Nordic, Alpine, Baltic), minority Lapps. **Languages:** Norwegian (official), Lappish. **Religions:** Evangelical Lutheran 94%.

Geography: Area: 125,181 sq. mi., slightly larger than New Mexico. **Location:** Occupies the W part of Scandinavian peninsula in NW Europe (extends farther north than any European land). **Neighbors:** Sweden, Finland, USSR on E. **Topography:** A highly indented coast is lined with tens of thousands of islands. Mountains and plateaus cover most of the country, which is only 25% forested. **Capital:** Oslo. **Cities** (1988): Oslo 449,000; Bergen 207,000.

Government: Type: Hereditary constitutional monarchy. **Head of state:** King Olav V, b. July 2, 1903; in office: Sept. 21, 1957. **Head of government:** Prime Min. Jan Peder Syse; b. Nov. 25, 1930; in office: Oct. 16, 1989. **Local divisions:** Oslo, Svalbard and 18 fylker (counties). **Defense:** 3.2% of GNP (1989).

Economy: Industries: Paper, shipbuilding, engineering, metals, chemicals, food processing oil, gas. **Chief crops:** Grains, potatoes, fruits. **Minerals:** Oil, copper, pyrites, nickel, iron, zinc, lead. **Crude oil reserves** (1987): 11.1 bln. bbls. **Other resources:** Timber. **Arable land:** 3%. **Livestock** (1987): sheep: 2.3 mln.; cattle: 967,000; pigs: 837,000. **Fish catch** (1988): 1.8 mln. metric tons. **Electricity prod.** (1988): 118 bln. kwh. **Crude steel prod.** (1988): 900,000 metric tons. **Labor force:** 7% agric.; 47% ind., banking, comm.; 18% services, 26% govt.

Finance: Currency: Kroner (June 1990: 6.36 = $1 US). **Gross national product** (1988): $89 bln. **Per capita income** (1984): $13,790. **Imports** (1989): $23.1 mln.; partners: Swed. 17%, W. Ger. 16%, UK 10%, U.S. 9%. **Exports** (1989): $26.9 bln.; partners: UK 27%, W. Ger. 17%, Swed. 9%. **Tourists** (1988): receipts: $1.4 bln. **National budget** (1988): $40.6 bln. expenditures. **International reserves less gold** (Mar. 1990): $13.7 bln. **Gold:** 1.18 mln. oz t. **Consumer prices** (change in 1989): 4.6%.

Transport: Railway traffic (1987): 2.2 bln. passenger-km. **Motor vehicles:** in use (1987): 1.5 mln. passenger cars, 264,000 comm. vehicles. **Civil aviation** (1987): 8.8 bln. passenger-km; 49 airports. **Chief ports:** Bergen, Stavanger, Oslo, Tonsberg.

Communications: Television sets: 1 per 2.9 persons. **Radios:** 1 per 1.3 persons. **Telephones:** 1 per 1.6 persons. **Daily newspaper circ.** (1986): 482 per 1,000 pop.

Health: Life expectancy at birth (1989): 72.7 male; 79.7 female. **Births** (per 1,000 pop. 1989): 13. **Deaths** (per 1,000 pop. 1989): 11. **Natural increase:** .2%. **Hospital beds:** 1 per 171 persons. **Physicians:** 1 per 441 persons. **Infant mortality** (per 1,000 live births 1989): 7.1.

Education (1989): **Literacy:** 100%. **Years Compulsory:** 9.

Major International Organizations: UN and all of its specialized agencies, NATO, OECD.

Embassy: 2720 34th St. NW 20008; 333-6000.

The first supreme ruler of Norway was Harald the Fairhaired who came to power in 872 AD. Between 800 and 1000, Norway's Vikings raided and occupied widely dispersed parts of Europe.

The country was united with Denmark 1381-1814, and with Sweden, 1814-1905. In 1905, the country became independent with Prince Charles of Denmark as king.

Norway remained neutral during World War I. Germany attacked Norway Apr. 9, 1940, and held it until liberation May 8, 1945. The country abandoned its neutrality after the war, and joined the NATO alliance. Norway rejected membership in the Common Market in a 1972 referendum.

Abundant hydroelectric resources provided the base for Norway's industrialization, producing one of the highest living standards in the world.

Norway's merchant marine is one of the world's largest.

Norway and the Soviet Union have disputed their territorial waters boundary in the Barents Sea, north of the 2 countries' common border.

Petroleum output from oil and mineral deposits under the continental shelf has raised state revenues.

Svalbard is a group of mountainous islands in the Arctic O., c. 23,957 sq. mi., pop. varying seasonally from 1,500 to 3,600. The largest, Spitsbergen (formerly called West Spitsbergen), 15,060 sq. mi., seat of governor, is about 370 mi. N of Norway. By a treaty signed in Paris, 1920, major European powers recognized the sovereignty of Norway, which incorporated it in 1925. Both Norway and the USSR mine rich coal deposits. Mt. Newton (Spitsbergen) is 5,633 ft. tall.

Oman

Sultanate of Oman

Saltanat 'Uman

People: Population (1990 est.): 1,305,000. **Pop. density:** 16 per sq. mi. **Urban** (1986): 9%. **Ethnic groups:** Arab 88%, Baluchi 4%, Persian 3%, Indian 2%, African 2%. **Languages:** Arabic (official), English, Urdu, others. **Religions:** Ibadhi Moslem 75%, Sunni Moslem.

Geography: Area: 82,030 sq. mi., about the size of New Mexico. **Location:** On SE coast of Arabian peninsula. **Neighbors:** United Arab Emirates, Saudi Arabia, South Yemen on W. **Topography:** Oman has a narrow coastal plain up to 10 mi. wide, a range of barren mountains reaching 9,900 ft., and a wide, stony, mostly waterless plateau, avg. alt. 1,000 ft. Also the tip of the Ruus-al-Jebal peninsula controls access to the Persian Gulf. **Capital:** Muscat. **Cities** (1982 est.): Muscat 85,000.

Government: Type: Absolute monarchy. **Head of state:** Sultan Qabus bin Said; b. Nov. 18, 1942; in office: July 23, 1970. **Local divisions:** 1 province, numerous districts. **Defense:** 24% of GNP (1989).

Economy: Chief crops: Dates, fruits vegetables, wheat, bananas. **Minerals:** Oil (95% of exports). **Crude oil reserves** (1987): 4.5 bln. bbls. **Fish catch** (1986): 96,000 metric tons. **Electricity prod.** (1988): 3.5 bln. kwh. **Labor force:** 60% agric. & fishing.

Finance: Currency: Rial Omani (Mar. 1990: .38 = $1 US). **Gross national product** (1987): $7.5 bln. **Imports** (1988): $2.2 bln.; partners: Jap. 21%, UAE 17%, UK 14%. **Exports** (1988): $2.6 bln.; partners: Jap. 58%, Europe 30%. **National budget** (1987): $4.2 bln. revenues; $5.4 bln. expenditures. **International reserves less gold** (Mar. 1990): $1.0 bln. **Gold:** 289,000 oz t.

Transport: Chief ports: Matrah, Muscat.

Communications: Television sets: 1 per 1.4 persons. **Radios:** 1 per 1.6 persons. **Telephones:** 1 per 17 persons.

Health: Life expectancy at birth (1989): 55 male; 58 female. **Hospital beds:** 1 per 331 persons. **Physicians:** 1 per 1,071 persons. **Infant Mortality** (per 1,000 live births 1989): 107.

Education (1989): **Literacy:** 20%. **Attendance:** 80% primary, 30% secondary.

Major International Organizations: UN (World Bank, IMF), Arab League.

Embassy: 2342 Massachusetts Ave. NW 20008; 387-1980.

A long history of rule by other lands, including Portugal in the 16th century, ended with the ouster of the Persians in 1744. By the early 19th century, Muscat and Oman was one of the most important countries in the region, controlling much of the Persian and Pakistan coasts, and ruling far-away Zanzibar, which was separated in 1861 under British mediation.

British influence was confirmed in a 1951 treaty, and Britain helped suppress an uprising by traditionally rebellious interior tribes against control by Muscat in the 1950s. Enclaves on the Pakistan coast were sold to that country in 1958.

On July 23, 1970, Sultan Said bin Taimur was overthrown by his son. The new sultan changed the nation's name to Sultanate of Oman. He launched a domestic development program, and battled leftist rebels in the southern Dhofar area to their defeat, Dec. 1975.

Oil has been the major source of income.

Pakistan

Islamic Republic of Pakistan

People: Population (1990 est.): 113,163,000. **Pop. density:** 335 per sq. mi. **Urban** (1988): 32%. **Ethnic groups:** Punjabi 66%, Sindhi 13%, Pushtun (Iranian) 8.5%, Urdu 7.6%, Baluchi 2.5%, others. **Languages:** Urdu, English are both official. **Religions:** Moslem 97%.

Geography: Area: 310,403 sq. mi., about the size of Texas. **Location:** In W part of South Asia. **Neighbors:** Iran on W, Afghanistan, China on N, India on E. **Topography:** The Indus R. rises in the Hindu Kush and Himalaya mtns. in the N (highest is K2, or Godwin Austen, 28,250 ft., 2d highest in world), then flows over 1,000 mi. through fertile valley and empties into Arabian Sea. Thar Desert, Eastern Plains flank Indus Valley. **Capital:** Islamabad. **Cities** (1981 cen.): Karachi 5.1 mln.; Lahore 2.9 mln.; Faisalabad 1 mln.; Hyderabad 795,000; Rawalpindi 928,000.

Government: Type: Parliamentary democracy in a federal setting. **Head of government:** Pres. Ishaq Khan; in office: Dec. 12, 1988. **Head of state:** Prime Min. Benazir Bhutto; in office: Dec. 2, 1988. **Local divisions:** Federal capital, 4 provinces, tribal areas. **Defense:** 6.4% of GNP (1987).

Economy: Industries: Textiles, food processing, chemicals, tobacco, **Chief crops:** Rice, wheat. **Minerals:** Natural gas, iron ore. **Crude oil reserves** (1987): 116 mln. bbls. **Other resources:** Wool. **Arable land:** 26%. **Livestock** (1986): cattle: 16.7 mln.; sheep: 26.6 mln.; goats: 31.9 mln. **Fish catch** (1985): 399,000 metric tons. **Electricity prod.** (1988): 29 bln. kwh. **Labor force:** 53% agric.; 13% ind; 33% services.

Finance: Currency: Rupee (June 1990: 21.70 = $1 US). **Gross national product** (1984): $360. **Imports** (1988): $6.5 bln.; partners: Sau. Ar. 5%, Jap. 16%, U.S. 11%, Kuwait 7%. **Exports** (1988): $4.5 bln.; partners: Jap. 10%, U.S. 10%. **Tourist** (1987): $171 mln. receipts. **National budget** (1987): $9.1 bln. expenditures. **International reserves less gold** (Mar. 1990): $549 mln. **Gold:** 1.94 mln. oz t. **Consumer prices** (change in 1989): 7.8%.

Transport: Railway traffic (1987): 16.9 bln. passenger-km. **Motor vehicles:** in use (1987): 540,000 passenger cars, 158,000 comm. vehicles. **Civil aviation** (1988): 7.7 bln. passenger-km; 32 airports with scheduled flights. **Chief ports:** Karachi.

Communications: Television sets: 1 per 73 persons. **Radios:** 1 per 11 persons. **Telephones:** 1 per 159 persons. **Daily newspaper circ.** (1988): 12 per 1,000 pop.

Health: Life expectancy at birth (1989): 54 male; 55 female. **Births** (per 1,000 pop. 1989): 43 **Deaths** (per 1,000 pop. 1989): 14. **Natural increase:** 2.9%. **Hospital beds:** 1 per 1,783 persons. **Physicians:** 1 per 2,176 persons. **Infant mortality** (per 1,000 live births 1989): 120.

Education (1989): **Literacy:** 26%.

Major International Organizations: UN (GATT, ILO, IMF, WHO).

Embassy: 2315 Massachusetts Ave. NW 20008; 939-6200.

Present-day Pakistan shares the 5,000-year history of the India-Pakistan sub-continent. At present day Harappa and Mohenjo Daro, the Indus Valley Civilization, with large cities and elaborate irrigation systems, flourished c. 4,000-2,500 BC.

Aryan invaders from the NW conquered the region around 1,500 BC, forging a Hindu civilization that dominated Pakistan as well as India for 2,000 years.

Beginning with the Persians in the 6th century BC, and continuing with Alexander the Great and with the Sassanians, successive nations to the west ruled or influenced Pakistan, eventually separating the area from the Indian cultural sphere.

The first Arab invasion, 712 AD, introduced Islam. Under the Mogul empire (1526-1857), Moslems ruled most of India, yielding to British encroachment and resurgent Hindus.

After World War I the Moslems of British India began agitation for minority rights in elections. Mohammad Ali Jinnah (1876-1948) was the principal architect of Pakistan. A leader of the Moslem League from 1916, he worked for dominion status for India; from 1940 he advocated a separate Moslem state.

When the British withdrew Aug. 14, 1947, the Islamic majority areas of India acquired self-government as Pakistan, with dominion status in the Commonwealth. Pakistan was divided into 2 sections, West Pakistan and East Pakistan. The 2 areas were nearly 1,000 mi. apart on opposite sides of India.

Pakistan became a republic in 1956. Pakistan had a National Assembly (legislature) with equal membership from East and West Pakistan, and 2 Provincial Assemblies. In Oct. 1958, Gen. Mohammad Ayub Khan took power in a coup. He was elected president in 1960, reelected in 1965.

As a member of the Central Treaty Organization, Pakistan had been aligned with the West. Following clashes between India and China in 1962, Pakistan made commercial and aid agreements with China.

Ayub resigned Mar. 25, 1969, after several months of violent rioting and unrest, most of it in East Pakistan, which demanded autonomy. The government was turned over to Gen. Agha Mohammad Yahya Khan and martial law was declared.

The Awami League, which sought regional autonomy for East Pakistan, won a majority in Dec. 1970 elections to a National Assembly which was to write a new constitution. In March, 1971 Yahya postponed the Assembly. Rioting and strikes broke out in the East.

On Mar. 25, 1971, government troops launched attacks in the East. The Easterners, aided by India, proclaimed the independent nation of Bangladesh. In months of widespread fighting, countless thousands were killed. Some 10 million Easterners fled into India.

Full scale war between India and Pakistan had spread to both the East and West fronts by Dec. 3. Pakistan troops in the East surrendered Dec. 16; Pakistan agreed to a cease-fire in the West Dec. 17. On July 3, 1972, Pakistan and India signed a pact agreeing to withdraw troops from their borders and seek peaceful solutions to all problems.

Zulfikar Ali Bhutto, leader of the Pakistan People's Party, which had won the most West Pakistan votes in the Dec. 1970 elections, became president Dec. 20.

Bhutto was overthrown in a military coup July, 1977. Convicted of complicity in a 1974 political murder, Bhutto was executed Apr.4, 1979. Benazir Bhutto, his daughter, returned to Pakistan from exile in Europe in 1986. Her efforts to relaunch the Pakistan People's Party sparked violence and antigovernment riots.

Pres. Mohammad Zia ul-Haq was killed when his plane exploded in Aug. 1988. Following Nov. elections, Benazir Bhutto was named Prime Minister, the first woman leader of a Moslem nation.

There are several million Afghan refugees now in Pakistan.

Panama
Republic of Panama
República de Panamá

People: Population (1990 est.): 2,423,000. **Age distrib.** (%): 0–14: 37.0; 15–59: 56.3; 60+: 6.7. **Pop. density:** 81 per sq. mi. **Urban** (1987): 53%. **Ethnic groups:** Mestizo 70%, West Indian 14%, Caucasian 10%, Indian 6%. **Languages:** Spanish (official), English. **Religions:** Roman Catholic 93%, Protestant 6%.

Geography: Area: 29,208 sq. mi., slightly larger than West Virginia. **Location:** In Central America. **Neighbors:** Costa Rica on W., Colombia on E. **Topography:** 2 mountain ranges run the length of the isthmus. Tropical rain forests cover the Caribbean coast and eastern Panama. **Capital:** Panama. **Cities** (1989 est.): Panama City 1.2 mln.

Government: Type: Constitutional democracy, centralized republic. **Head of state and head of government:** Pres. Guillermo Endara; in office: Dec. 20, 1989. **Local divisions:** 9 provinces, 1 territory. **Defense:** 3% of GNP (1987).

Economy: Industries: Oil refining, international banking. **Chief crops:** Bananas, pineapples, cocoa, corn, coconuts, sugar. **Minerals:** Copper. **Other resources:** Forests (mahogany), shrimp. **Arable land:** 8%. **Livestock** (1986): cattle: 1.4 mln.; pigs: 215,000. **Fish catch** (1985): 245,000 metric tons. **Electricity prod.** (1988): 3.3 bln. kwh. **Labor force:** 26% agric., 28%, govt. & community services.

Finance: Currency: Balboa (Apr. 1990: 1.00 = $1 US). **Gross national product** (1988): $4.2 bln. **Per capita income** (1984): $1,970. **Imports** (1988): $709 mln.; partners: U.S. 34%, Mexico 15%. **Exports** (1988): $280 mln.; partners: U.S. 66%, EC 16%. **Tourists** (1988): $168 mln. receipts. **National budget** (1988): $800 mln. **International reserves less gold** (Jan. 1990): $115 mln. **Consumer prices** (change in 1988): 0.3%.

Transport: Motor vehicles: in use (1986): 134,000 passenger cars, 46,000 comm. vehicles. **Civil aviation** (1986): 505 mln. passenger-km; 6 airports with scheduled flights. **Chief ports:** Balboa, Cristobal.

Communications: Television sets: 1 per 4.9 persons. **Radios:** 1 per 2.5 persons. **Telephones:** 1 per 9.3 persons. **Daily newspaper circ.** (1988): 43 per 1,000 pop.

Health: Life expectancy at birth (1989): 71 male; 75 female. **Births** (per 1,000 pop. 1989): 27. **Deaths** (per 1,000 pop. 1989): 5. **Natural increase:** 2.1%. **Hospital beds:** 1 per 292 persons.

Physicians: 1 per 839 persons. **Infant mortality** (per 1,000 live births 1989): 23.

Education (1989): **Literacy:** 87%. **Primary school attendance:** almost 100%.

Major International Organizations: UN (IMF, IMO, World Bank), OAS.

Embassy: 2862 McGill Terrace NW 20008; 483-1407.

The coast of Panama was sighted by Rodrigo de Bastidas, sailing with Columbus for Spain in 1501, and was visited by Columbus in 1502. Vasco Nunez de Balboa crossed the isthmus and "discovered" the Pacific O. Sept. 13, 1513. Spanish colonies were ravaged by Francis Drake, 1572-95, and Henry Morgan, 1668-71. Morgan destroyed the old city of Panama which had been founded in 1519. Freed from Spain, Panama joined Colombia in 1821.

Panama declared its independence from Colombia Nov. 3, 1903, with U.S. recognition. U.S. naval forces deterred action by Colombia. On Nov. 18, 1903, Panama granted use, occupation and control of the Canal Zone to the U.S. by treaty, ratified Feb. 26, 1904.

New treaties were proposed in 1967 and 1974. In 1978, a new treaty provided for a gradual takeover by Panama of the canal, and withdrawal of U.S. troops, to be completed by 1999. U.S. payments were substantially increased in the interim. The permanent neutrality of the canal was also guaranteed.

Due to easy Panama ship regulations and strictures in the U.S., merchant tonnage registered in Panama since World War II ranks high in size.

President Delvalle was ousted by the National Assembly, Feb. 26, 1988, after he tried to fire the head of the Panama Defense Forces, Gen. Manuel Antonio Noriega. Noriega had been indicted by 2 U.S. federal grand juries on drug charges. A general strike followed. Despite U.S.-imposed economic sanctions Noriega remained in power. Voters went to the polls to elect a new president May 7, 1989. Noriega claimed victory but foreign observers said that the opposition had won overwhelmingly and that Noriega was trying to steal the election. The government voided the election May 10, charging foreign interference. There was an attempted coup against Noriega Oct. 3.

U.S. troops invaded Panama Dec. 20 following a series of incidents, including the killing of a U.S. Marine by Panamanian soldiers. The operation, called Operation Just Cause, had as its chief objective the capture of Noriega, who was wanted in the U.S. on drug trafficking charges.

Noriega took refuge in the Vatican diplomatic mission, but surrendered after 10 days to U.S. officials Jan. 3, 1990.

Papua New Guinea

People: Population (1989 est.): 3,613,000. **Age distrib.** (%): 0–14: 41.6; 15–59: 52.8; 60+: 5.6. **Pop. density:** 20 per sq. mi. **Urban** (1985): 14.0%. **Ethnic groups:** Papuans (in S and interior), Melanesian (N,E), pygmies, minorities of Chinese, Australians, Polynesians. **Languages:** English (official), Melanesian Pidgin, Police Motu, numerous local languages. **Religions:** Protestant 63%, Roman Catholic 31%, local religions.

Geography: Area: 178,260 sq. mi., slightly larger than California. **Location:** Occupies eastern half of island of New Guinea. **Neighbors:** Indonesia (West Irian) on W, Australia on S. **Topography:** Thickly forested mtns. cover much of the center of the country, with lowlands along the coasts. Included are some of the nearby islands of Bismarck and Solomon groups, including Admiralty Is., New Ireland, New Britain, and Bougainville. **Capital:** Port Moresby. **Cities** (1987): Port Moresby 152,000; Lae 79,000.

Government: Type: Parliamentary democracy. **Head of state:** Queen Elizabeth II, represented by Gov. Gen. Sir Kingsford Dibela; in office: Mar. 1, 1983. **Head of government:** Prime Min. Rabbie Namaliu; in office: July 4, 1988. **Local divisions:** National capital and 19 provinces with elected legislatures. **Defense:** approx. 1.5% of GDP (1985).

Economy: Chief crops: Coffee, coconuts, cocoa. **Minerals:** Gold, copper, silver. **Arable land:** 1%. **Livestock** (1986): pigs: 1.4 mln. **Electricity prod.** (1988): 1.3 bln. kwh. **Labor force:** 82% agric., 3% ind. and commerce, 8% services.

Finance: Currency: Kina (Mar. 1990: 1.00 = $1.02 US). **Gross national product** (1987): $2.5 bln. **Per capita GNP** (1987): $730. **Imports** (1989): $1.5 bln.; partners: Austral. 40%, Jap. 17%; U.S. 9%. **Exports** (1989): $1.2 bln.; partners: Jap.

26%, W. Ger. 36%, Austral. 8%. **National budget** (1989): $1.4 bln. **International reserves less gold** (Mar. 1990): $314 mln. **Gold:** 63,000 oz t. **Consumer prices** (change in 1989): 4.4%.
Transport: Motor vehicles: in use (1986): 19,000 passenger cars, 30,000 comm. vehicles. **Chief ports:** Port Moresby, Lae.
Communications: Television sets: 1 per 14 persons. **Radios:** 1 per 15 persons. **Telephones:** 1 per 48 persons. **Daily newspaper circ.** (1988): 8 per 1,000 pop.
Health: Life expectancy at birth (1987): 53.0 male; 54.6 female. **Births** (per 1,000 pop. 1989): 35. **Deaths** (per 1,000 pop. 1989): 12. **Natural increase:** 2.3%. **Hospital beds** (1984): 14,661. **Physicians** (1984): 280. **Infant mortality** (per 1,000 live births 1989): 72.0.
Education (1989): **Literacy:** 32%. **Attendance:** 65% primary school; 13% secondary school.
Major International Organizations: UN (GATT), Commonwealth of Nations.
Embassy: 1330 Connecticut Ave., NW 20036.

Human remains have been found in the interior of New Guinea dating back at least 10,000 years and possibly much earlier. Successive waves of peoples probably entered the country from Asia through Indonesia. Europeans visited in the 15th century, but land claims did not begin until the 19th century, when the Dutch took control of the western half of the island.

The southern half of eastern New Guinea was first claimed by Britain in 1884, and transferred to Australia in 1905. The northern half was claimed by Germany in 1884, but captured in World War I by Australia, which was granted a League of Nations mandate and then a UN trusteeship over the area. The 2 territories were administered jointly after 1949, given self-government Dec. 1, 1973, and became independent Sept. 16, 1975.

The indigenous population consists of a huge number of tribes, many living in almost complete isolation with mutually unintelligible languages.

Paraguay
Republic of Paraguay
República del Paraguay

People: Population (1990 est.): 4,660,000. **Age distrib.** (%): 0–14: 41.0; 15–59: 52.0; 60+: 7.0. **Pop. density:** 28 per sq. mi. **Urban** (1987): 43%. **Ethnic groups:** Mestizo 95%, small Caucasian, Indian, black minorities. **Languages:** Spanish (official), Guaraní (used by 90%). **Religions:** Roman Catholic (official) 97%.
Geography: Area: 157,047 sq. mi., the size of California. **Location:** One of the 2 landlocked countries of S. America. **Neighbors:** Bolivia on N, Argentina on S, Brazil on E. **Topography:** Paraguay R. bisects the country. To E are fertile plains, wooded slopes, grasslands. To W is the Chaco plain, with marshes and scrub trees. Extreme W is arid. **Capital:** Asunción. **Cities** (1985 cen.): Asunción 477,000.
Government: Type: Republic. **Head of state:** Pres. Gen. Andres Rodriguez; in office: Feb. 3, 1989. **Local divisions:** 19 departments. **Defense:** 1.0% of GNP (1987).
Economy: Industries: Food processing, wood products, textiles, cement. **Chief crops:** Corn, cotton, beans, sugarcane. **Minerals:** Iron, manganese, limestone. **Other resources:** Forests. **Arable land:** 20%. **Livestock** (1986): cattle: 7.1 mln.; pigs: 1.4 mln. **Electricity prod.** (1988): 1.1 bln. kwh. **Labor force:** 44% agric., 34% ind. and commerce, 18% services.
Finance: Currency: Guaraní (Mar. 1990 1,213 = $1 US). **Gross national product** (1987): $7.4 bln. **Per capita GNP** (1987): $1,000. **Imports** (1988): $494 mln.; partners: Braz. 32%, Arg. 12%, U.S. 8%. **Exports** (1988): $509 mln.; partners: Arg. 6%, Neth. 18%, Braz. 22%. **Tourists** (1987): $121 mln. receipts. **National budget** (1987): $1 bln. expenditures. **International reserves less gold** (Mar. 1990): $434 mln. **Gold:** 35,000 oz t. **Consumer prices** (change in 1988): 24.5%.
Transport: Motor vehicles: in use (1985): 84,000 passenger cars, 41,000 comm. vehicles. **Civil aviation** (1988): 872 mln. passenger-km; 1 airport with scheduled flight. **Chief ports:** Asuncion.
Communications: Television sets: 1 per 12 persons. **Radios:** 1 per 5.4 persons. **Telephones:** 1 per 42 persons. **Daily newspaper circ.** (1987): 32 per 100,000 pop.
Health: Life expectancy at birth (1989): 67 male; 72 female. **Births** (per 1,000 pop. 1989): 36. **Deaths** (per 1,000 pop. 1989):

6. **Natural increase:** 3.0%. **Hospital beds:** 1 per 1,489 persons. **Physicians:** 1 per 1,458 persons. **Infant mortality** (per 1,000 live births 1989):49.
Education (1989): **Literacy:** 81%. **Years compulsory:** 7; **Attendance:** 83%.
Major International Organizations: UN (IMF, WHO, ILO), OAS.
Embassy: 2400 Massachusetts Ave. NW 20008; 483-6960.

The Guarani Indians were settled farmers speaking a common language before the arrival of Europeans.

Visited by Sebastian Cabot in 1527 and settled as a Spanish possession in 1535, Paraguay gained its independence from Spain in 1811. It lost much of its territory to Brazil, Uruguay, and Argentina in the War of the Triple Alliance, 1865-1870. Large areas were won from Bolivia in the Chaco War, 1932-35.

Gen. Alfredo Stroessner, who ruled since 1954, was ousted in a military coup led by Gen. Andres Rodriguez on Feb. 3, 1989. Rodriguez was elected president May 1.

Peru
Republic of Peru
República del Peru

People: Population (1990 est.): 21,904,000. **Age distrib.** (%): 0–14: 40.5; 15–59: 46.0; 60+: 5.5. **Pop. density:** 43 per sq. mi. **Urban** (1987): 70%. **Ethnic groups:** Indians 45%, Mestizos 37%, Caucasians 15%, blacks, Asians. **Languages:** Spanish, Quechua both official; Aymara; 30% speak no Spanish. **Religions:** Roman Catholic 90%.
Geography: Area: 496,222 sq. mi., 3 times larger than California. **Location:** On the Pacific coast of S. America. **Neighbors:** Ecuador, Colombia on N, Brazil, Bolivia on E, Chile on S. **Topography:** An arid coastal strip, 10 to 100 mi. wide, supports much of the population thanks to widespread irrigation. The Andes cover 27% of land area. The uplands are well-watered, as are the eastern slopes reaching the Amazon basin, which covers half the country with its forests and jungles. **Capital:** Lima. **Cities** (1988 est.): Lima 5,493,000; Arequipa 591,000; Callao 560,000.
Government: Type: Constitutional republic. **Head of state:** Pres. Alberto Fujimori; b. 1938; in office: June 10, 1990. **Head of government:** Prime Min. Guillermo Larco Cox; in office: Sept. 30, 1989. **Local divisions:** 24 departments, 1 province. **Defense:** 4.9% of GNP (1987).
Economy: Industries: Fish meal, mineral processing, light industry, textiles. **Chief crops:** Cotton, sugar, coffee, corn. **Minerals:** Copper, lead, molybdenum, silver, zinc, iron, oil. **Crude oil reserves** (1987): 535 mln. bbls. **Other resources:** Wool, sardines. **Arable land:** 3%. **Livestock** (1986): cattle: 3.8 mln.; pigs: 2.1 mln.; sheep: 13.5 mln. **Fish catch** (1987): 4.5 mln. metric tons. **Electricity prod.** (1988): 14.8 bln. kwh. **Labor force:** 38% agric.; 17% ind. and mining; 45% govt. and other services.
Finance: Currency: Intl (June 1990: 7,289 = $1 US). **Gross national product** (1988): $19.6 bln. **Per capita income** (1984): $940. **Imports** (1988): $3.0 bln.; partners: U.S. 25%, EC 19%. **Exports** (1988): $2.6 bln.; partners: U.S. 36%, EC 23%, Jap. 10%. **Tourists** (1987): $393 mln. receipts. **National budget** (1987): $3.9 bln. **International reserves less gold** (Mar. 1990): $553 mln. **Gold:** 1.7 mln. oz t. **Consumer prices** (change in 1989): 3,398%.
Transport: Railway traffic (1987): 517 mln. passenger-km. **Motor vehicles:** in use (1987): 377,000 passenger cars, 226,000 comm. vehicles. **Civil aviation** (1987): 2.5 bln. passenger-km; 24 airports. **Chief ports:** Callao, Chimbate, Mollendo.
Communications: Television sets: 1 per 13 persons. **Radios:** 1 per 4.9 persons. **Telephones:** 1 per 32 persons. **Daily newspaper circ.** (1985): 57 per 1,000 pop.
Health: Life expectancy at birth (1989): 61 male; 66 female. **Births** (per 1,000 pop. 1989): 29. **Deaths** (per 1,000 pop. 1989): 8. **Natural increase:** 2.1%. **Hospital beds:** 1 per 625 persons. **Physicians:** 1 per 1,026 persons. **Infant mortality** (per 1,000 live births 1989): 69.
Education (1989): **Literacy:** 79%. **Years compulsory:** 10.
Major International Organizations: UN and all of its specialized agencies, OAS.
Embassy: 1700 Massachusetts Ave. NW 20036; 833-9860.

The powerful Inca empire had its seat at Cuzco in the Andes covering most of Peru, Bolivia, and Ecuador, as well as parts of Colombia, Chile, and Argentina. Building on the achievements of 800 years of Andean civilization, the Incas had a high level of skill in architecture, engineering, textiles, and social organization.

A civil war had weakened the empire when Francisco Pizarro, Spanish conquistador, began raiding Peru for its wealth, 1532. In 1533 he had the seized ruling Inca, Atahualpa, fill a room with gold as a ransom, then executed him and enslaved the natives.

Lima was the seat of Spanish viceroys until the Argentine liberator, Jose de San Martin, captured it in 1821; Spain was defeated by Simon Bolivar and Antonio J. de Sucre; recognized Peruvian independence, 1824. Chile defeated Peru and Bolivia, 1879-84, and took Tarapaca, Tacna, and Arica; returned Tacna, 1929.

On Oct. 3, 1968, a military coup ousted Pres. Fernando Belaunde Terry. In 1968-74, the military government put through sweeping agrarian changes, and nationalized oil, mining, fish-meal, and banking industries.

Food shortages, escalating foreign debt, and strikes led to another coup, Aug. 29, 1976, and to a slowdown of socialist programs.

After 12 years of military rule, Peru returned to democratic leadership under former Pres. Fernando Belaunde Terry, July 1980.

There were strikes by police, oil workers, and other labor unions in 1987 and 1988. Terrorist activity, mostly by Maoist groups, continued; the government said that guerrilla insurgency caused nearly 13,000 deaths in the 1980s.

Philippines
Republic of the Philippines

People: Population (1990 est.): 66,647,000. **Age distrib. (%): 0–14:** 39.0; **15–59:** 56.2; **60+:** 4.8. **Pop. density:** 535 per sq. mi. **Urban** (1987): 41%. **Ethnic groups:** Malays the large majority, Chinese, Americans, Spanish are minorities. **Languages:** Pilipino (based on Tagalog), English both official; numerous others spoken. **Religions:** Roman Catholics 83%, Protestants 9%, Moslems 5%.

Geography: Area: 115,831 sq. mi., slightly larger than Nevada. **Location:** An archipelago off the SE coast of Asia. **Neighbors:** Nearest are Malaysia, Indonesia on S, Taiwan on N. **Topography:** The country consists of some 7,100 islands stretching 1,100 mi. N-S. About 95% of area and population are on 11 largest islands, which are mountainous, except for the heavily indented coastlines and for the central plain on Luzon. **Capital:** Quezon City (Manila is de facto capital). **Cities** (1985 est.): Manila 1.7 mln.; Quezon City 1.3 mln.; Cebu 552,000.

Government: Type: Republic. **Head of state:** Pres. Corazon C. Aquino; b. 1932; in office: Feb. 25, 1986. **Local divisions:** 12 regions, 73 provinces, 61 cities. **Defense:** 1.3% of GNP (1987).

Economy: Industries: Food processing, textiles, clothing, drugs, wood prods., appliances. **Chief crops:** Sugar, rice, corn, pineapple, coconut. **Minerals:** Cobalt, copper, gold, nickel, silver, iron, petroleum. **Crude oil reserves** (1987): 19 mln. bbls. **Other resources:** Forests (42% of area). **Arable land:** 26%. **Livestock** (1987): cattle: 1.7 mln.; pigs: 7.0 mln. **Fish catch** (1984): 1.8 mln. metric tons. **Electricity prod.** (1988): 25.0 bln. kwh. **Labor force:** 47% agric., 20% ind. and comm., 13% services.

Finance: Currency: Peso (May 1990: 22.89 = $1 US). **Gross national product** (1988): $38.2 bln. **Per capita income** (1988): $667. **Imports** (1988): $8.1 bln.; partners: U.S. 25%, Jap. 16%. **Exports** (1988): $7.0 bln.; partners: U.S. 35%, Jap. 17%. **Tourists** (1987): $458 mln. receipts. **National budget** (1989): $10.7 bln. expenditures. **International reserves less gold** (Mar. 1990): $789 mln. **Gold:** 2.5 mln. oz t. **Consumer prices** (change in 1989): 10.6%.

Transport: Railway traffic (1987): 142 mln. passenger-km. **Motor vehicles:** in use (1986): 773,000 passenger cars, 110,000 comm. vehicles. **Civil aviation** (1988): 8.6 bln. passenger-km; 18 airports with scheduled flights. **Chief ports:** Cebu, Manila, Iloilo, Davao.

Communications: Television sets: 1 per 8.8 persons. **Radios:** 1 per 7.5 persons. **Telephones:** 1 per 6.5 persons. **Daily newspaper circ.** (1985): 44 per 1,000 pop.

Health: Life expectancy at birth (1989): 63 male; 69 female. **Births** (per 1,000 pop. 1989): 34. **Deaths** (per 1,000 pop. 1989): 7. **Natural increase:** 2.8%. **Hospital beds:** 1 per 628 persons. **Physicians:** 1 per 1,090 persons. **Infant mortality** (per 1,000 live births 1986): 52.9.

Education (1989): Literacy: 88%. **Attendance:** 97% in elementary, 55% secondary.

Major International Organizations: UN (World Bank, IMF, GATT), ASEAN.

Embassy: 1617 Massachusetts Ave. NW 20036; 483-1414

The Malay peoples of the Philippine archipelago, whose ancestors probably migrated from Southeast Asia, were mostly hunters, fishers, and unsettled cultivators when first visited by Europeans.

The archipelago was visited by Magellan, 1521. The Spanish founded Manila, 1571. The islands, named for King Philip II of Spain, were ceded by Spain to the U.S. for $20 million, 1898, following the Spanish-American War. U.S. troops suppressed a guerrilla uprising in a brutal 6-year war, 1899-1905.

Japan attacked the Philippines Dec. 8, 1941 (Far Eastern time). Japan occupied the islands during WW II.

On July 4, 1946, independence was proclaimed in accordance with an act passed by the U.S. Congress in 1934. A republic was established.

A rebellion by Communist-led Huk guerrillas was put down by 1954. But urban and rural political violence periodically reappears.

The Philippines and the U.S. have treaties for U.S. military and naval bases and a mutual defense treaty. Riots by radical youth groups and terrorism by leftist guerrillas and outlaws, increased from 1970. On Sept. 21, 1972, President Marcos declared martial law. Ruling by decree, he ordered some land reform and stabilized prices. But opposition was suppressed, and a high population growth rate aggravated poverty and unemployment. Political corruption was believed to be widespread. On Jan. 17, 1973, Marcos proclaimed a new constitution with himself as president. His wife received wide powers in 1978 to supervise planning and development.

Government troops battled Moslem (Moro) secessionists, 1973-76, in southern Mindanao. Fighting resumed, 1977, after a Libyan-mediated agreement on autonomy was rejected by the region's mainly Christian voters.

Martial law was lifted Jan. 17, 1981. Marcos turned over legislative power to the National Assembly, released political prisoners, and said he would no longer rule by decree. He was reelected to a new 6-year term as president.

The assassination of prominent opposition leader Benigno S. Aquino Jr, Aug. 21, 1983, sparked demonstrations calling for the resignation of Marcos. An independent commission appointed by Marcos concluded that a military conspiracy was responsible for Aquino's death. The May 1984 elections saw Marcos retain his majority in the National Assembly although opponents made a strong showing in key areas like Manila.

A bitter presidential election campaign ended Feb. 7, 1986 as elections were held amid allegations of widespread fraud. On Feb. 16, Marcos was declared the victor over Corazon Aquino, widow of slain opposition leader Benigno Aquino. Aquino declared herself president and announced a nonviolent "active resistance" to overthrow the Marcos government; the 2 held separate inaugurals on Feb. 25.

On Feb. 22, 2 leading military allies of Marcos quit their posts to protest the rigged elections. Marcos, Feb. 24, declared a state of emergency as his military and religious support continued to erode. That same day U.S. President Ronald Reagan urged Marcos to resign. Marcos ended his 20-year tenure as president Feb. 26 as he fled the country. Aquino was recognized immediately as president by the U.S. and other nations.

In 1987, Aquino announced the start of land reforms. Candidates endorsed by Aquino won large majorities in legislative elections held in May, attesting to her popularity. She is plagued, however, by a weak economy, widespread poverty, communist insurgents, and lukewarm support from the military.

Rebel troops seized military bases, TV stations, and bombed the presidential palace, Dec. 1, 1989. Government forces defeated the attempted coup with the aid of air cover provided by U.S. F-4s.

The archipelago has a coastline of 10,850 mi. Manila Bay, with an area of 770 sq. mi., and a circumference of 120 mi., is the finest harbor in the Far East.

All natural resources of the Philippines belong to the state; their exploitation is limited to citizens of the Philippines or corporations of which 60% of the capital is owned by citizens.

Poland

Republic of Poland

People: Population (1990 est.): 38,363,000. **Age distrib. (%):** 0–14: 25.7; 15–59: 60.2; 60+: 14.1. **Pop. density:** 317 per sq. mi. **Urban** (1989): 60%. **Ethnic groups:** Polish 98%, Germans, Ukrainians, Byelorussians. **Language:** Polish. **Religion:** Roman Catholic 94%.

Geography: Area: 120,727 sq. mi. **Location:** On the Baltic Sea in E Central Europe. **Neighbors:** E. Germany on W, Czechoslovakia on S, USSR (Lithuania, Byelorussia, Ukraine) on E. **Topography:** Mostly lowlands forming part of the Northern European Plain. The Carpathian Mts. along the southern border rise to 8,200 ft. **Capital:** Warsaw. **Cities** (1987 est.): Warsaw 1.6 mln., Lodz 848,000, Kracow 740,000, Wroclaw 631,000, Poznan 570,000.

Government: Type: Socialist (in transition). **Head of state:** Pres. Wojciech Jaruzelski; in office: July 19, 1989. **Head of government: Prime Min.:** Tadeusz Mazowiecki; b. Apr. 17, 1927; in office: Aug. 24, 1989. **Local divisions:** 49 provinces. **Defense:** 6% of GNP (1987).

Economy: Industries: Shipbuilding, chemicals, metals, autos, food processing. **Chief crops:** Grains, potatoes, sugar beets, tobacco, flax. **Minerals:** Coal, copper, zinc, silver, zinc, sulphur, natural gas. **Arable land:** 49%. **Livestock** (1987): cattle: 10.9 mln.; pigs: 18.9 mln.; sheep: 5 mln. **Fish catch** (1985): 650,000 metric tons. **Electricity prod.** (1987): 146 bln. kwh. **Crude steel prod.** (1988): 17.1 mln. metric tons. **Labor force:** 30% agric.; 44% ind. & comm.; 11% services.

Finance: Currency: Zloty (Mar. 1990: 9,500 = $1 US). **Gross national product** (1988): $276 bln. **Per capita income** (1986): $2,000. **Imports** (1989): $10.4 bln.; partners: USSR 38%, E. Ger. 7% W. Ger. 10% Czech. 5%. **Exports** (1989): $13.1 bln.; partners: USSR 30%, E. Ger. 6%, Czech. 6%, W. Ger. 10%. **National budget** (1988): $24 bln. expenditures. **Tourists** (1986): $136 mln. receipts. **International Reserves Less Gold** (Mar. 1990): $2.3 bln. **Gold:** 472,000. **Consumer prices** (change in 1989): 244%.

Transport: Railway traffic (1987): 48 bln. passenger-km. **Motor vehicles:** in use (1987): 4.2 mln. passenger cars, 953,000 comm. vehicles. **Civil aviation** (1987): 3.3 bln. passenger-km; 12 airports. **Chief ports:** Gdansk, Gdynia, Szczecin.

Communications: Television sets: 1 per 3.8 persons. **Radios:** 1 per 3.5 persons. **Telephones:** 1 per 3.8 persons. **Daily newspaper circ.** (1986): 217 per 1,000 pop.

Health: Life expectancy at birth (1989): 66 male; 74 female. **Births** (per 1,000 pop. 1989): 16. **Deaths** (per 1,000 pop. 1989): 10. **Natural increase:** .6%. **Hospital beds:** 1 per 187 persons. **Physicians:** 1 per 487 persons. **Infant mortality** (per 1,000 live births 1989): 21.

Education (1989): **Literacy:** 98%. **Years compulsory:** 8; attendance 97%.

Major International Organizations: UN (GATT, WHO), Warsaw Pact.

Embassy: 2640 16th St. NW 20009; 234-3800.

Slavic tribes in the area were converted to Latin Christianity in the 10th century. Poland was a great power from the 14th to the 17th centuries. In 3 partitions (1772, 1793, 1795) it was apportioned among Prussia, Russia, and Austria. Overrun by the Austro-German armies in World War I, its independence, self-declared on Nov.11, 1918, was recognized by the Treaty of Versailles, June 28, 1919. Large territories to the east were taken in a war with Russia, 1921.

Nazi Germany and the USSR invaded Poland Sept. 1-27, 1939, and divided the country. During the war, some 6 million Polish citizens were killed by the Nazis, half of them Jews. With Germany's defeat, a Polish government-in-exile in London was recognized by the U.S., but the USSR pressed the claims of a rival group. The election of 1947 was completely dominated by the Communists.

In compensation for 69,860 sq. mi. ceded to the USSR, 1945, Poland received approx. 40,000 sq. mi. of German territory E of the Oder-Neisse line comprising Silesia, Pomerania, West Prussia, and part of East Prussia.

In 12 years of rule by Stalinists, large estates were abolished, industries nationalized, schools secularized, and Roman Catholic prelates jailed. Farm production fell off. Harsh working conditions caused a riot in Poznan June 28-29, 1956.

A new Politburo, committed to development of a more independent Polish Communism, was named Oct. 1956, with Wla-

dyslaw Gomulka as first secretary of the Communist Party. Collectivization of farms was ended and many collectives were abolished.

In Dec. 1970 workers in port cities rioted because of price rises and new incentive wage rules. On Dec. 20 Gomulka resigned as party leader; he was succeeded by Edward Gierek; the incentive rules were dropped, price rises were revoked.

Poland was the first communist state to get most-favored nation trade terms from the U.S.

A law promulgated Feb. 13, 1953, required government consent to high Roman Catholic church appointments. In 1956 Gomulka agreed to permit religious liberty and religious publications, provided the church kept out of politics. In 1961 religious studies in public schools were halted. Government relations with the Church improved in the 1970s. The number of priests and churches was greater in 1971 than in 1939.

After 2 months of labor turmoil had crippled the country, the Polish government, Aug. 30, 1980, met the demands of striking workers at the Lenin Shipyard, Gdansk. Among the 21 concessions granted were the right to form independent trade unions and the right to strike — unprecedented political developments in the Soviet bloc. By 1981, 9.5 mln. workers had joined the independent trade union (Solidarity). Farmers won official recognition for their independent trade union in May. Solidarity leaders proposed, Dec. 12, a nationwide referendum on establishing a non-Communist government if the government failed to agree to a series of demands which included access to the mass media and free and democratic elections to local councils in the provinces.

Spurred by the fear of Soviet intervention, the government, Dec. 13, imposed martial law. Public gatherings, demonstrations, and strikes were banned and an internal and external blackout was imposed. Solidarity leaders called for a nationwide strike, but there were only scattered work stoppages. Lech Walesa and other Solidarity leaders were arrested. The U.S. imposed economic sanctions which were lifted when martial law was suspended December 1982.

On Apr. 5, 1989, an accord was reached between the government and opposition factions on a broad range of political and economic reforms incl. free elections. In the first free elections in over 40 years, candidates endorsed by Solidarity swept the parliamentary elections, June 4. On Aug. 19, Tadeusz Mazowiecki became the first non-Communist to head an Eastern bloc nation, when he became prime minister. President Bush visited Poland in July. He praised the reforms and pledged modest U.S. economic aid.

The radical economic program designed to transform the economy into a free-market system drew protests from unions, farmers, and miners. Steep price increases took effect Jan 1, 1990; wages were frozen.

Portugal

Republic of Portugal

República Portuguesa

People: Population (1990 est.): 10,528,000. **Age distrib. (%):** 0–14: 22.7; 15–59: 59.9; 60+: 17.4. **Pop. density:** 281 per sq. mi. **Urban** (1983): 30%. **Ethnic groups:** Homogeneous Mediterranean stock with small African minority. **Languages:** Portuguese. **Religions:** Roman Catholics 97%.

Geography: Area: 36,390 sq. mi., incl. the Azores and Madeira Islands, slightly smaller than Indiana. **Location:** At SW extreme of Europe. **Neighbors:** Spain on N, E. **Topography:** Portugal N of Tajus R, which bisects the country NE-SW, is mountainous, cool and rainy. To the S there are drier, rolling plains, and a warm climate. **Capital:** Lisbon. **Cities** (1987 est.): Lisbon 2 mln. (met.), Oporto, 1.5 mln. (met).

Government: Type: Parliamentary democracy. **Head of state:** Pres. Mario Soares; b. Dec. 7, 1924; in office: Mar. 9, 1986. **Head of government:** Prime Min. Anibal Cavaco Silva; in office: Nov. 6, 1985. **Local divisions:** 18 districts, 2 autonomous regions, one dependency. **Defense:** 3.2% of GNP (1987).

Economy: Industries: Textiles, footwear, cork, chemicals, fish canning, wine, paper. **Chief crops:** Grains, potatoes, rice, grapes, olives, fruits. **Minerals:** Tungsten, uranium, copper, iron. **Other resources:** Forests (world leader in cork production). **Arable land:** 32%. **Livestock** (1987): sheep: 2.4 mln.; pigs: 1.2 mln; cattle: 1 mln. **Fish catch** (1987): 395,000 metric tons. **Elec-**

tricity prod. (1988): 15.5 bln. kwh. **Crude steel prod.** (1985): 420,000 metric tons. **Labor force:** 21% agric.; 34% ind. and comm.; 44% services and govt.

Finance: Currency: Escudo (June 1990: 145.40 = $1 US). **Gross national product** (1987): $33.5 bln. **Per capita income** (1986): $2,970. **Imports** (1989): $18.7 bln.; partners: W. Ger. 12%, UK 8%, Fr. 11%. **Exports** (1989): $12.5 bln.; partners: UK 15%, W. Ger. 13%, Fr. 13%. **Tourists** (1986): $1.5 bln. receipts. **National budget** (1987): $11.3 bln. expenditures. **International reserves less gold** (Mar. 1990): $11.1 bln. **Gold:** 15.7 mln. oz t. **Consumer prices** (change in 1989): 12.6%.

Transport: Railway traffic (1987): 5.8 bln. passenger-km. **Motor vehicles:** in use (1987): 2.5 mln. passenger cars, 189,000 comm. vehicles. **Civil aviation** (1987): 4.8 bln. passenger-km; 20 airports. **Chief ports:** Lisbon, Setubal, Leixoes.

Communications: Television sets: 1 per 6.4 persons. **Radios:** 1 per 4.7 persons. **Telephones:** 1 per 4.9 persons. **Daily newspaper circ.** (1986): 84 per 1,000 pop.

Health: Life expectancy at birth (1989): 71 male; 78 female. **Births** (per 1,000 pop. 1989): 15. **Deaths** (per 1,000 pop. 1989): 9. **Natural increase:** .5%. **Hospital beds:** 1 per 209 persons. **Physicians:** 1 per 388 persons. **Infant mortality** (per 1,000 live births 1989): 15.

Education (1989): **Literacy:** 83%, **Years compulsory:** 6; attendance 60%.

Major International Organizations: UN (GATT, IMF, WHO), NATO, EC, OECD.

Embassy: 2125 Kalorama Rd. NW 20008; 328-8610.

Portugal, an independent state since the 12th century, was a kingdom until a revolution in 1910 drove out King Manoel II and a republic was proclaimed.

From 1932 a strong, repressive government was headed by Premier Antonio de Oliveira Salazar. Illness forced his retirement in Sept. 1968; he was succeeded by Marcello Caetano.

On Apr. 25, 1974, the government was seized by a military junta led by Gen. Antonio de Spinola, who was named president.

The new government reached agreements providing independence for Guinea-Bissau, Mozambique, Cape Verde Islands, Angola, and Sao Tome and Principe. Spinola resigned Sept. 30, 1974, in face of increasing pressure from leftist officers. Despite a 64% victory for democratic parties in April 1975, the Soviet-supported Communist party increased its influence. Banks, insurance companies, and other industries were nationalized.

Parliament approved, June 1, 1989, a package of reforms that did away with the socialist economy and created a "democratic" economy and the denationalization of industries.

Azores Islands, in the Atlantic, 740 mi. W. of Portugal, have an area of 888 sq. mi. and a pop. (1987) of 252,000. A 1951 agreement gave the U.S. rights to use defense facilities in the Azores. The **Madeira Islands,** 350 mi. off the NW coast of Africa, have an area of 307 sq. mi. and a pop. (1987) of 269,000. Both groups were offered partial autonomy in 1976.

Macau, area of 6 sq. mi., is an enclave, a peninsula and 2 small islands, at the mouth of the Canton R. in China. Portugal granted broad autonomy in 1976. In 1987, Portugal and China agreed that Macau would revert to China in 1999. Macao, like Hong Kong, was guaranteed 50 years of noninterference in its way of life and capitalist system. Pop. (1989 est.): 484,000.

Qatar
State of Qatar
Dawlet al-Qatar

People: Population (1990 est.): 498,000. **Pop. density:** 80 per sq. mi. **Ethnic groups:** Arab 40%, Pakistani 18%, Indian 10%, Iranian 14%, others. **Languages:** Arabic (official), English. **Religions:** Moslem 95%.

Geography: Area: 4,247 sq. mi., smaller than Connecticut and Rhode Island combined. **Location:** Occupies peninsula on W coast of Persian Gulf. **Neighbors:** Saudi Arabia on W, United Arab Emirates on S. **Topography:** Mostly a flat desert, with some limestone ridges, vegetation of any kind is scarce. **Capital:** Doha. **Cities** (1987 est.): Doha 250,000.

Government: Type: Traditional emirate. **Head of state and head of government:** Emir & Prime Min. Khalifah ibn Hamad ath-Thani; b. 1932; in office: Feb. 22, 1972 (amir), 1970 (prime min.) **Defense** 47% of GNP (1985).

Economy: Crude oil reserves (1987): 3.3 mln. bbls. **Arable land:** 2.9%. **Electricity prod.** (1987): 4.4 bln. kwh. **Labor force:** 10% agric., 70% ind., services and commerce.

Finance: Currency: Riyal (Mar. 1990: 3.64 = $1.00 US). **Gross national product** (1987): $5.4 bln. **Per capita income** (1985): $27,000. **Imports** (1987): $1.1 bln.; partners: Jap. 20%, UK 16%, U.S. 11%. **Exports** (1987): $2.6 bln.; partners: Jap. 38%, Sing. 13%. **National budget** (1988): $3.4 bln. expenditures.

Transport: Chief ports: Doha, Musayid.

Communications: Television sets: 1 per 2.5 persons. **Radios:** 1 per 2.5 persons. **Telephones:** 1 per 3.4 persons.

Health: Life expectancy at birth (1989): 68 male; 72 female. **Hospital beds:** 1 per 403 persons. **Physicians:** 1 per 679 persons. **Infant mortality** (per 1,000 live births 1989): 29.

Education (1987): **Literacy:** 60%. **Compulsory:** ages 6-16; attendance: 98%.

Major International Organizations: UN (FAO, GATT, IMF, World Bank), Arab League, OPEC.

Embassy: 600 New Hampshire Ave. NW 20037; 338-0111.

Qatar was under Bahrain's control until the Ottoman Turks took power, 1872 to 1915. In a treaty signed 1916, Qatar gave Great Britain responsibility for its defense and foreign relations. After Britain announced it would remove its military forces from the Persian Gulf area by the end of 1971, Qatar sought a federation with other British protected states in the area; this failed and Qatar declared itself independent, Sept. 1 1971.

Oil revenues give Qatar a per capita income among the highest in the world, but lack of skilled labor hampers development plans.

Romania

People: Population (1990 est.): 23,269,000. **Age distrib.** (%): 0–14: 24.7; 15–59: 60.9; 60+: 14.4. **Pop. density:** 252 per sq. mi. **Urban** (1987): 51%. **Ethnic groups:** Romanians 89%, Hungarians 7.9%, Germans 1.6%. **Languages:** Romanian (official), Hungarian, German. **Religions:** Orthodox 80%, Roman Catholic 6%.

Geography: Area: 91,699 sq. mi., slightly smaller than New York and Pennsylvania combined. **Location:** In SE Europe on the Black Sea. **Neighbors:** USSR on E (Moldavia) and N (Ukraine), Hungary, Yugoslavia on W, Bulgaria on S. **Topography:** The Carpathian Mts. encase the north-central Transylvanian plateau. There are wide plains S and E of the mountains, through which flow the lower reaches of the rivers of the Danube system. **Capital:** Bucharest. **Cities** (1986 est.): Bucharest 1,900,000, Brasov 346,000, Timisoara 319,000, Constanta 323,000.

Government: Type: In transition. **Head of state:** Pres. Ion Iliescu; in office; Dec. 25, 1989. **Head of government:** Prime Min. Petre Roman; in office; Dec. 26, 1989. **Local divisions:** Bucharest and 40 counties. **Defense:** 4.3% of GNP (1985).

Economy: Industries: Steel, metals, machinery, oil products, chemicals, textiles, shoes, tourism. **Chief crops:** Grains, sunflower, vegetables, potatoes. **Minerals:** Oil, gas, coal. **Other resources:** Timber. **Arable land:** 45%. **Livestock** (1988): cattle: 7.2 mln.; pigs: 14.7 mln.; sheep: 18.7 mln. **Fish catch** (1988): 264,000 metric tons. **Electricity prod.** (1988): 75.3 bln. kwh. **Crude steel prod.** (1988): 15.0 mln. metric tons. **Labor force:** 28% agric.; 34% ind. & comm.

Finance: Currency: Lei (Mar. 1990: 21.28 = $1 US). **Gross national product** (1988): $151 bln. **Per Capita GNP** (1988): $6,400. **Imports** (1986): $10.6 bln.; partners: USSR 22%, Egypt 10%, Iran 8%. **Exports** (1986): $12.6 bln.; partners: USSR 21%, W. Ger. 7%. **Tourists** (1986): $178 mln. receipts. **National budget** (1982): $142 mln. expenditures.

Transport: Railway traffic (1987): 33 bln. passenger-km. **Motor vehicles:** in use (1986): 105,000 passenger cars; 100,000 comm. vehicles. **Civil aviation** (1988): 3.9 bln. passenger-km; 15 airports. **Chief ports:** Constanta, Galati, Braila.

Communications: Television sets: 1 per 6.0 persons. **Radios:** 1 per 7.3 persons. **Telephones:** 1 per 11 persons. **Daily newspaper circ.** (1987): 159 per 1,000 pop.

Health: Life expectancy at birth (1989): 67 male; 73 female. **Births** (per 1,000 pop. 1989): 16. **Deaths** (per 1,000 pop. 1989): 11. **Natural increase:** 0.5%. **Hospital beds:** 1 per 107 persons. **Physicians:** 1 per 559 persons. **Infant mortality** (per 1,000 live births 1989): 25.

Education (1988): **Literacy:** 98%. **Years compulsory:** 10; attendance 98%.

Major International Organizations: UN (World Bank, IMF, GATT), Warsaw Pact.
Embassy: 1607 23d St. NW 20008; 232-4748.

Romania's earliest known people merged with invading Proto-Thracians, preceding by centuries the Dacians. The Dacian kingdom was occupied by Rome, 106 AD-271 AD; people and language were Romanized. The principalities of Wallachia and Moldavia, dominated by Turkey, were united in 1859, became Romania in 1861. In 1877 Romania proclaimed independence from Turkey, became an independent state by the Treaty of Berlin, 1878, a kingdom, 1881, under Carol I. In 1886 Romania became a constitutional monarchy with a bicameral legislature.

Romania helped Russia in its war with Turkey, 1877-78. After World War I it acquired Bessarabia, Bukovina, Transylvania, and Banat. In 1940 it ceded Bessarabia and Northern Bukovina to the USSR, part of southern Dobrudja to Bulgaria, and Transylvania to Hungary.

In 1941, Romanian premier Marshal Ion Antonescu led his country in support of Germany against the USSR. In 1944 Antonescu was overthrown by King Michael and Romania joined the Allies.

With occupation by Soviet troops the communist-headed National Democratic Front displaced the National Peasant party. A People's Republic was proclaimed, Dec. 30, 1947; Michael was forced to abdicate. Land owners were dispossessed; most banks, factories and transportation units were nationalized.

On Aug. 22, 1965, a new constitution proclaimed Romania a Socialist, rather than a People's Republic. Since 1959, USSR troops have not been permitted to enter Romania.

Internal policies were oppressive. Ethnic Hungarians protested cultural and job discrimination, which has led to strained relations with Hungary.

Romania became industrialized, but lagged in consumer goods and in personal freedoms. All industry was state owned, and state farms and cooperatives owned almost all the arable land.

On Dec. 16, 1989, security forces opened fire on demonstrators in Timisoara; hundreds were buried in mass graves. President Nicolae Ceausescu declared a state of emergency as protests spread to other cities. By Dec. 21, the protests had spread to Bucharest where security forces fired on protestors. Army units joined the rebellion. Dec. 22, and a group known as the "Council of National Salvation" announced that it had overthrown the government. Fierce fighting took place between the army, which backed the new government, and forces loyal to Ceausescu.

Ceausescu was captured, Dec. 23 and, following a trial in which he and his wife were found guilty of genocide, was executed Dec. 25. The U.S. and USSR quickly recognized the new provisional government.

Following months of unrest, Bucharest was beset by violence, as anti-government protestors and pro-government coal miners clashed, June 13-15, 1990.

Rwanda

Republic of Rwanda
Republika y'u Rwanda

People: Population (1990 est.): 7,603,000. **Age distrib.** (%): 0–14: 48.7; 15–59: 47.1; 60+: 4.2. **Pop. density:** 715 per sq. mi. **Urban** (1985): 5.1%. **Ethnic groups:** Hutu 85%, Tutsi 14%, Twa (pygmies) 1%. **Languages:** French, Kinyarwanda (both official), Swahili. **Religions:** Christian 74%, traditional 25%, Moslem 1%.

Geography: Area: 10,169 sq. mi., the size of Maryland. **Location:** In E central Africa. **Neighbors:** Uganda on N, Zaire on W, Burundi on S, Tanzania on E. **Topography:** Grassy uplands and hills cover most of the country, with a chain of volcanoes in the NW. The source of the Nile R. has been located in the headwaters of the Kagera (Akagera) R., SW of Kigali. **Capital:** Kigali. **Cities** (1989 est.): Kigali 300,000.

Government: Type: Republic. **Head of state:** Pres. Juvenal Habyarimana; b. Mar. 8, 1937; in office: July 5, 1973. **Local divisions:** 10 prefectures, 143 communes. **Defense:** 2.0% of GNP (1987).

Economy: Chief crops: Coffee, tea. **Minerals:** Tin, gold, wolframite. **Arable land:** 29%. **Electricity prod.** (1988): 110 mln. kwh. **Labor force:** 91% agric.

Finance: Currency: Franc (Apr. 1990: 79 = $1 US). **Gross national product** (1987): $2.3 bln. **Per capita income** (1986): $323. **Imports** (1987): $354 mln.; partners: Ken. 21%, Belg. 16%, Jap. 12%, W. Ger. 9%. **Exports** (1987): $113 mln.; partners: Belg.-Lux. 17%, Ugan. 12%. **National budget** (1987): $247 mln. revenues; $280 mln. expenditures. **International reserves less gold** (Mar. 1990): $73 mln. **Consumer prices** (change in 1988): 3.0%.

Transport: Motor vehicles: in use (1987): 7,000 passenger cars, 10,000 comm. vehicles.

Communications: Radios: 1 per 16 persons. **Telephones:** 1 per 652 persons.

Health: Life expectancy at birth (1989): 49 male; 53 female. **Births** (per 1,000 pop. 1989): 53. **Deaths** (per 1,000 pop. 1989): 16. **Natural increase:** 3.8%. **Hospital beds** (1984): 9,000. **Physicians** (1984): 177. **Infant mortality** (per 1,000 live births 1989): 117.

Education (1989): **Literacy:** 50%. **Years compulsory:** 8; **attendance:** 70%.

Major International Organizations: UN (GATT, IMF, WHO), OAU.

Embassy: 1714 New Hampshire Ave. NW 20009; 232-2882.

For centuries, the Tutsi (an extremely tall people) dominated the Hutus (90% of the population). A civil war broke out in 1959 and Tutsi power was ended. A referendum in 1961 abolished the monarchic system.

Rwanda, which had been part of the Belgian UN trusteeship of Rwanda-Urundi, became independent July 1, 1962. The government was overthrown in a 1973 military coup. Rwanda is one of the most densely populated countries in Africa. All available arable land is being used, and is being subject to erosion. The government has carried out economic and social improvement programs, using foreign aid and volunteer labor on public works projects.

St. Kitts and Nevis

Federation of St. Kitts & Nevis

People: Population (1990 est.): 40,000. **Ethnic groups:** black African 95%. **Language:** English. **Religion:** Protestant 76%.

Geography: Area: 101 sq. mi. in the northern part of the Leeward group of the Lesser Antilles in the eastern Caribbean Sea. **Capitol:** Basseterre. (1989): 15,000.

Government: Head of State: Queen Elizabeth represented by Sir Clement Arrindell. **Head of Government:** Prime Minister Kennedy A. Simmonds; b. Apr. 12, 1936; in office: Sept. 19, 1983.

Economy: Sugar is the principal industry.

Finance: Currency: E. Caribbean Dollar (Mar. 1990): 2.70 = $1 U.S. **Gross national product** (1986): $66 mln. **Tourists** (1986): $34 mln. receipts.

Communications: Telephones: 1 per 11 persons.

Health: Infant mortality (per 1,000 live births, 1989): 41.

Education: Literacy (1987): 90%.

St. Kitts (known by the natives as Liamuiga) and Nevis were discovered and named by Columbus in 1493. They were settled by Britain in 1623, but ownership was disputed with France until 1713. They were part of the Leeward Islands Federation, 1871-1956, and the Federation of the W. Indies, 1958-62. The colony achieved self-government as an Associated State of the UK in 1967, and became fully independent Sept. 19, 1983. Nevis, the smaller of the islands, has the right of secession.

Saint Lucia

People: Population (1990 est.): 153,000. **Age distrib.** (%): 0–20: 44.5; 21–64: 47.5; 65+: 8.0. **Pop. density:** 537 per sq. mi. **Ethnic groups:** Predominantly African descent. **Languages:** English (official), French patois. **Religions:** Roman Catholic 90%.

Geography: Area: 238 sq. mi., about one-fifth the size of Rhode Island. **Location:** In Eastern Caribbean, 2d largest of the Windward Is. **Neighbors:** Martinique to N, St. Vincent to SW. **Topography:** Mountainous, volcanic in origin; Soufriere, a volcanic crater, in the S. Wooded mountains run N-S to Mt. Gimie,

3,145 ft., with streams through fertile valleys. **Capital:** Castries. **City:** Castries (1986 est.): 52,000.

Government: Type: Parliamentary democracy. **Head of state:** Queen Elizabeth II, represented by Gov.-Gen. S.A. James; **Head of government:** Prime Min. John Compton; in office: May 3, 1982. **Local divisions:** 11 quarters

Economy: Industries: Agriculture, tourism, manufacturing. **Chief crops:** Bananas, coconuts, cocoa, citrus fruits. **Other resources:** Forests. **Arable land:** 8%. **Electricity prod.** (1988): 80 mln. kwh. **Labor force:** 36% agric., 20% ind. & commerce, 18% services.

Finance: Currency: East Caribbean dollar (Mar. 1990: 2.70 = $1 US). **Gross national product** (1987): $166 mln. **Per capita GNP** (1987): $1,370. **Imports** (1986): $155 mln.; partners: U.S. 36%, UK 12%, Trin./Tob. 11%. **Exports** (1986): $83 mln.; partners: U.S. 28%, UK 25%. **Tourists** (1987): receipts: $78 mln.

Transport: Motor vehicles: in use (1984): 7,000 passenger cars, 2,000 comm. vehicles. **Chief ports:** Castries, Vieux Fort.

Communications: Television sets: 1 per 28 persons. **Radios:** 1 per 1.5 persons. **Telephones:** 1 per 10 persons.

Health: Life expectancy at birth (1989): 68 male; 73 female. **Births** (per 1,000 pop. 1989): 34. **Deaths** (per 1,000 pop. 1989): 5. **Natural increase:** 2.8%. **Hospital beds:** 1 per 284 persons. **Physicians:** 1 per 2,636 persons. **Infant mortality** (per 1,000 live births 1989): 18.

Education: Literacy (1989) 78%; **Years compulsory:** ages 5-15; **Attendance:** 80%.

Major International Organizations: UN (IMF, ILO), CARICOM, OAS.

St. Lucia was ceded to Britain by France at the Treaty of Paris, 1814. Self government was granted with the West Indies Act, 1967. Independence was attained Feb. 22, 1979.

Saint Vincent and the Grenadines

People: Population (1990 est.): 106,000. **Pop. density:** 746 per sq. mi. **Ethnic groups:** Mainly of African descent. **Languages:** English. **Religions:** Methodists, Anglicans, Roman Catholics.

Geography: Area: 150 sq. mi., about twice the size of Washington, D.C. **Location:** In the eastern Caribbean, St. Vincent (133 sq. mi.) and the northern islets of the Grenadines form a part of the Windward chain. **Neighbors:** St. Lucia to N, Barbados to E, Grenada to S. **Topography:** St. Vincent is volcanic, with a ridge of thickly-wooded mountains running its length; Soufriere, rising in the N, erupted in Apr. 1979. **Capital:** Kingstown. **Cities** (1985 est.): Kingstown 18,378.

Government: Head of state: Queen Elizabeth II, represented by Gov.-Gen. David Jack; in office: Sept. 20 1989. **Head of government:** James Mitchell; in office: July 30, 1984.

Economy: Industries: Agriculture, tourism. **Chief crops:** Bananas (62% of exports), arrowroot, coconuts. **Arable land:** 50%. **Electricity prod.** (1988): 63 mln. kwh. **Labor force:** 30% agric.

Finance: Currency: East Caribbean dollar (Mar. 1990: 2.70 = $1 US). **Gross national product** (1987): $188 mln. **Per capita GNP** (1987): $1,070. **Tourists** (1987): $35 mln. receipts. **National budget** (1984): $34 mln. expenditures.

Transport: Motor vehicles: in use (1987): 5,000 passenger cars, 2,500 comm. vehicles. **Chief port:** Kingstown.

Communications: Telephones: 1 per 13 persons.

Health: Life expectancy at birth (1989): 69 male; 74 female. **Births** (per 1,000 pop. 1989): 27. **Deaths** (per 1,000 pop. 1989): 6. **Natural increase:** 2.2%. **Infant mortality** (per 1,000 live births 1989): 26.

Education (1989): **Literacy:** 85%.

Columbus landed on St. Vincent on Jan. 22, 1498 (St. Vincent's Day). Britain and France both laid claim to the island in the 17th and 18th centuries; the Treaty of Versailles, 1783, finally ceded it to Britain. Associated State status was granted 1969; independence was attained Oct. 27, 1979.

The entire economic life of St. Vincent is dependent upon agriculture and tourism.

San Marino
Most Serene Republic of San Marino
Serenissima Repubblica di San Marino

People: Population (1990 est.): 23,000. **Age distrib. (%):** 0–14: 19.0; 15–59: 63.7; 60+: 17.3. **Pop. density:** 958 per sq. mi. **Urban** (1988): 90.5%. **Ethnic groups:** Sanmarinese 88%, Italian 11%. **Languages:** Italian. **Religion:** mostly Roman Catholic.

Geography: Area: 24 sq. mi. **Location:** In N central Italy near Adriatic coast. **Neighbors:** Completely surrounded by Italy. **Topography:** The country lies on the slopes of Mt. Titano. **Capital:** San Marino. **City** (1987 est.): San Marino 4,179.

Government: Type: Independent republic. **Head of state:** Two co-regents appt. every 6 months. **Local divisions:** 11 districts, 9 sectors.

Economy: Industries: Postage stamps, tourism, woolen goods, paper, cement, ceramics. **Arable land:** 17%.

Finance: Currency: Italian lira. **Gross national product** (1987): $188 mln. **Tourists** (1988): 2.9 mln.

Communications: Television sets: 1 per 3.4 persons. **Radios:** 1 per 1.8 persons. **Telephones:** 1 per 1.6 persons.

Births (per 1,000 pop. 1989): 8. **Deaths** (per 1,000 pop. 1989): 7. **Natural increase:** 0.1%. **Infant mortality** (per 1,000 live births 1989): 9.6.

Education (1987): **Literacy:** 97%. **Years compulsory:** 8. **Attendance:** 93%.

San Marino claims to be the oldest state in Europe and to have been founded in the 4th century. A communist-led coalition ruled 1947-57; a similar coalition ruled 1978-86. It has had a treaty of friendship with Italy since 1862.

Sao Tome and Principe
Democratic Republic of Sao Tome and Principe
República Democrática de Sao Tome e Principe

People: Population (1990 est.): 125,000. **Pop. density:** 306 per sq. mi. **Ethnic groups:** Portuguese-African mixture, African minority (Angola, Mozambique immigrants). **Languages:** Portuguese. **Religions:** Christian 80%.

Geography: Area: 372 sq. mi., slightly larger than New York City. **Location:** In the Gulf of Guinea about 125 miles off W Central Africa. **Neighbors:** Gabon, Equatorial Guinea on E. **Topography:** Sao Tome and Principe islands, part of an extinct volcano chain, are both covered by lush forests and croplands. **Capital:** Sao Tome. **Cities** (1988 est.): Sao Tome 40,000.

Government: Type: Republic. **Head of state:** Pres. Manuel Pinto da Costa, b. 1910; in office: July 12, 1975. **Head of government:** Prime Min. Celestino Rocha da Costa; in office: Jan. 8, 1988. **Local divisions:** 7 counties.

Economy: Chief crops: Cocoa (82% of exports), coconut products. **Arable land:** 38%. **Electricity prod.** (1987): 15 mln. kwh.

Finance: Currency: Dobra (Jan. 1990: 106 = $1 US). **Gross national product** (1987): $32 mln. **Per capita income** (1986): $384. **Imports** (1986): $25.6 mln.; partners: Port. 61%, Angola 13%. **Exports** (1986): $9.3 mln.; partners: Neth. 52%, Port. 33%, W. Ger. 8%.

Transport: Chief ports: Sao Tome, Santo Antonio.

Communications: Radios: 1 per 3.9 persons.

Health: Births (per 1,000 pop. 1989): 38. **Deaths** (per 1,000 pop. 1989): 7. **Natural increase:** 3.0%. **Physicians:** 1 per 2,819 persons. **Infant mortality** (per 1,000 live births 1989): 51.

Education (1988): **Literacy:** 50%.

Major International Organizations: UN, OAU.

Embassy: 801 2d Ave., New York, NY 10017; 212-697-4211.

The islands were uninhabited when discovered in 1471 by the Portuguese, who brought the first settlers — convicts and exiled Jews. Sugar planting was replaced by the slave trade as the chief economic activity until coffee and cocoa were introduced in the 19th century.

Portugal agreed, 1974, to turn the colony over to the Gabon-based Movement for the Liberation of Sao Tome and Principe, which proclaimed as first president its East German-trained leader Manuel Pinto da Costa. Independence came July 12, 1975. Democratic reforms were instituted in 1987.

Agriculture and fishing are the mainstays of the economy.

Saudi Arabia
Kingdom of Saudi Arabia
al-Mamlaka al-'Arabiya as-Sa'udiya

People: Population (1990 est.): 16,758,000. **Pop. density:** 15 per sq. mi. **Urban** (1986): 73%. **Ethnic groups:** Arab tribes, immigrants from other Arab and Moslem countries. **Language:** Arabic. **Religion:** Moslem 99%.

Geography: Area: 839,996 sq. mi., one-third the size of the U.S. **Location:** Occupies most of Arabian Peninsula in Middle East. **Neighbors:** Kuwait, Iraq, Jordan on N, Yemen, South Yemen, Oman on S, United Arab Emirates, Qatar on E. **Topography:** The highlands on W, up to 9,000 ft., slope as an arid, barren desert to the Persian Gulf. **Capital:** Riyadh. **Cities** (1986 est.): Riyadh 1,380,000; Jidda 1,210,000; Mecca 463,000.

Government: Type: Monarchy with council of ministers. **Head of state and head of government:** King Fahd; b. 1922; in office: June 13, 1982. **Local divisions:** 14 provinces. **Defense:** 12.8% of GNP (1987).

Economy: Industries: Oil products. **Chief crops:** Dates, wheat, barley, fruit. **Minerals:** Oil, gas, gold, copper, iron. **Crude oil reserves** (1987): 169 bln. bbls. **Arable land:** 2%. **Livestock** (1987): sheep: 3.8 mln.; goats: 2.3 mln. **Electricity prod.** (1988): 53 bln. kwh. **Labor force:** 14% agric.; 11% ind; 53% serv., comm., & govt.; 20% construction.

Finance: Currency: Riyal (May 1990: 3.74 = $1 US). **Gross national product** (1988): $70 bln. **Imports** (1987): $24.3 bln.; partners: US 18%, Jap. 18%, W. Ger. 7%. **Exports** (1987): $26.9 bln.; partners: U.S. 19%, Jap., 22%. **National budget** (1988): $38 bln. expenditures. **International reserves less gold** (Mar. 1990): $11.4 bln. **Gold:** 4.59 mln. oz t. **Consumer prices** (change in 1989): 1.1%.

Transport: Railway traffic (1988): 92 mln. passenger-km. **Motor vehicles:** in use (1987): 2.2 mln. passenger cars, 1.9 mln. comm. vehicles. **Civil aviation** (1988): 14.9 bln.; passenger-km.; 23 airports. **Chief ports:** Jidda, Ad-Dammam, Ras Tannurah.

Communications: Television sets: 1 per 3.5 persons. **Radios:** 1 per 3.3 persons. **Telephones:** 1 per 13 persons. **Daily newspaper circ.** (1986): 41 per 1,000 pop.

Health: Life expectancy at birth (1989): 64 male; 67 female. **Births** (per 1,000 pop. 1989): 38. **Deaths** (per 1,000 pop. 1989): 7. **Natural increase:** 3.1%. **Hospital beds:** 1 per 406 persons. **Physicians:** 1 per 973 persons. **Infant mortality** (per 1,000 live births 1989): 74.

Education (1986): **Literacy:** 50% (men).

Major International Organizations: UN (IMF, WHO, FAO), Arab League, OPEC.

Embassy: 601 New Hampshire Ave. NW 20037; 342-3800.

Arabia was united for the first time by Mohammed, in the early 7th century. His successors conquered the entire Near East and North Africa, bringing Islam and the Arabic language. But Arabia itself soon returned to its former status.

Nejd, long an independent state and center of the Wahhabi sect, fell under Turkish rule in the 18th century, but in 1913 Ibn Saud, founder of the Saudi dynasty, overthrew the Turks and captured the Turkish province of Hasa; took the Hejaz in 1925 and by 1926, most of Asir. The discovery of oil in the 1930s transformed the new country.

Crown Prince Khalid was proclaimed king on Mar. 25, 1975, after the assassination of King Faisal. Fahd became king on June 13, 1982 following Khalid's death. There is no constitution and no parliament. The king exercises authority together with a Council of Ministers. The Islamic religious code is the law of the land. Alcohol and public entertainments are restricted, and women have an inferior legal status.

Saudi units fought against Israel in the 1948 and 1973 Arab-Israeli wars. Many billions of dollars of advanced arms have been purchased from Britain, France, and the U.S., including jet fighters, missiles, and, in 1981, 5 airborne warning and control system (AWACS) aircraft from the U.S., despite strong opposition from Israel. Beginning with the 1967 Arab-Israeli war, Saudi Arabia provided large annual financial gifts to Egypt; aid was later

extended to Syria, Jordan, and Palestinian guerrilla groups, as well as to other Moslem countries. The country has aided anti-radical forces in Yemen and Oman.

Faisal played a leading role in the 1973-74 Arab oil embargo against the U.S. and other nations in an attempt to force them to adopt an anti-Israel policy. Saudi Arabia joined most other Arab states, 1979, in condemning Egypt's peace treaty with Israel.

Between 1973 and 1976, Saudi Arabia acquired full ownership of Aramco (Arabian American Oil Co.). In the 1980s, Saudi Arabia's moderate position on crude oil prices often prevailed at OPEC meetings.

The Hejaz contains the holy cities of Islam — Medina where the Mosque of the Prophet enshrines the tomb of Mohammed, who died in the city June 7, 632, and Mecca, his birthplace. More than 600,000 Moslems from 60 nations pilgrimage to Mecca annually. The regime faced its first serious opposition when Moslem fundamentalists seized the Grand Mosque in Mecca, Nov. 20, 1979.

Two Saudi oil tankers were attacked May 1984, as Iran and Iraq began air attacks against shipping in the Persian Gulf. On May 29, the U.S., citing grave concern over the growing escalation of the Iran-Iraq war in the Persian Gulf, authorized the sale of 400 Stinger antiaircraft missiles. In 1986, U.S. President Reagan vetoed a congressional resolution that would have blocked sale of advanced U.S. missiles to the Saudis.

In 1987, Iranians making a pilgrimage to Mecca clashed with anti-Iranian pilgrims and Saudi police; over 400 were killed. Saudi Arabia broke diplomatic relations with Iran in 1988. Some 1,426 Moslem pilgrims died July 2, 1990 when a stampede occurred in a pedestrian tunnel leading to Mecca.

There were some 25,000 U.S. troops on Saudi soil by Aug. 1990, following Iraq's attack on Kuwait. (*See Chronology and Index for details.*)

Senegal
Republic of Senegal
République du Sénégal

People: Population (1990 est.): 7,740,000. **Age distrib.** (%): 0–14: 46.5; 15–59: 48.9; 60+: 4.6. **Pop. density:** 101 per sq. mi. **Urban** (1986): 30%. **Ethnic groups:** Wolof 36%, Serer 17%, Peulh 17%, Diola 9%, Toucouleur 9%, Mandingo 6%. **Languages:** French (official), tribal languages. **Religions:** Moslems 92%, Christians 2%.

Geography: Area: 75,750 sq. mi., the size of South Dakota. **Location:** At western extreme of Africa. **Neighbors:** Mauritania on N, Mali on E, Guinea, Guinea-Bissau on S, Gambia surrounded on three sides. **Topography:** Low rolling plains cover most of Senegal, rising somewhat in the SE. Swamp and jungles are in SW. **Capital:** Dakar. **Cities** (1986): Dakar 1.3 mln. Thies 156,000; Kaolack 132,000.

Government: Type: Republic. **Head of state:** Pres. Abdou Diouf; b. Sept. 7, 1935; in office: Jan. 1, 1981. **Local divisions:** 10 regions. **Defense:** 2.2% of GNP (1987).

Economy: Industries: Food processing, fishing. **Chief crops:** Peanuts are chief export; millet, rice. **Minerals:** Phosphates. **Arable land:** 27%. **Livestock** (1986): cattle: 2.2 mln.; sheep: 2.2 mln.; goats: 1 mln. **Fish catch** (1986): 255,000 metric tons. **Electricity prod.** (1988): 758 mln. kwh. **Labor force:** 77% agric.

Finance: Currency: CFA franc (Mar. 1990: 284 = $1 US). **Gross national product** (1987): $2.0 bln. **Per capita income** (1984): $380. **Imports** (1986): $705 mln.; partners Fr. 37%, U.S. 6%. **Exports** (1986): $483 mln.; partners Fr. 25%, UK 6%. **Tourists** (1987): $123 mln. receipts. **International reserves less gold** (Jan. 1990): $19.0 mln. **Gold:** 29,000 oz t. **Consumer prices** (change in 1989): 0.4%.

Transport: Railway traffic (1984): 133 mln. passenger-km. **Motor vehicles:** in use (1985): 76,000 passenger cars, 36,000 comm. vehicles. **Chief ports:** Dakar, Saint-Louis.

Communications: Television sets: 1 per 31 persons. **Radios:** 1 per 8.7 persons. **Telephones:** 1 per 192 persons. **Daily newspaper circ.** (1984): 4 per 1,000 pop.

Health: Life expectancy at birth (1989): 51 male, 54 female. **Births** (per 1,000 pop. 1989): 46. **Deaths** (per 1,000 pop. 1989): 15. **Natural increase:** 3.1%. **Hospital beds** (1982): 6,200. **Physicians** (1982): 470. **Infant mortality** (per 1,000 live births 1989): 96.

Education (1988): **Literacy:** 10%. **Attendance:** 48% primary, 11% secondary.

Major International Organizations: UN and all of its specialized agencies, OAU.

Embassy: 2112 Wyoming Ave. NW 20008; 234-0540.

Portuguese settlers arrived in the 15th century, but French control grew from the 17th century. The last independent Moslem state was subdued in 1893. Dakar became the capital of French West Africa.

Independence as part, along with the Sudanese Rep., of the Mali Federation, came June 20, 1960. Senegal withdrew Aug. 20 that year. French political and economic influence is strong.

A long drought brought famine, 1972-73, and again in 1978. Senegal is recognized as the most democratic of the French-speaking West African nations.

Senegal, Dec. 17, 1981, signed an agreement with The Gambia for confederation of the 2 countries under the name of Senegambia. The confederation began Feb. 1, 1982. The 2 nations retained their individual sovereignty but adopted joint defense and monetary policies.

In 1989, a border incident sparked ethnic violence against Senegalese in Mauritania and, in retaliation, against Mauritanians in Senegal.

Seychelles
Republic of Seychelles

People: Population (1990 est.): 71,000. **Age distrib. (%):** 0–14: 36.3; 15–64: 57.3; 65+: 6.4. **Pop. density:** 409 per sq. mi. **Urban** (1986): 50% **Ethnic groups:** Creoles (mixture of Asians, Africans, and French) predominate. **Languages:** English, French Creole, (all official). **Religions:** Roman Catholic 90%.

Geography: Area: 171 sq. mi. **Location:** In the Indian O. 700 miles NE of Madagascar. **Neighbors:** Nearest are Madagascar on SW, Somalia on NW. **Topography:** A group of 86 islands, about half of them composed of coral, the other half granite, the latter predominantly mountainous. **Capital:** Victoria. **Cities** (1986): Victoria 23,000.

Government: Type: Single party republic. **Head of state:** Pres. France-Albert Rene, b. Nov. 16, 1935; in office: June 5, 1977. **Defense:** 5.6% of GNP (1984).

Economy: Industries: Food processing. **Chief crops:** Coconut products, cinnamon, vanilla, patchouli. **Electricity prod.** (1988): 67 mln. kwh. **Labor force:** 12% agric.; 19.4% tourism, comm.; 32% serv.; 40% govt.

Finance: Currency: Rupee (Mar. 1990: 5.59 = $1 US). **Gross national product** (1987): $175 mln. **Per capita income** (1987): $2,600. **Imports** (1988): $138 mln.; partners: UK 20%, So. Afr. 13%. **Exports** (1988): $13.6 mln.; partners: Pak. 38%; Jap. 26%. **National Budget** (1989): $168 mln. **Tourists** (1988): $80 mln. receipts. **International reserves less gold** (Mar. 1990): $6.9 mln. **Consumer prices** (change in 1989): 1.5%.

Transport: Motor vehicles: in use (1985): 3,500 passenger cars, 1,000 comm. vehicles. **Port:** Victoria.

Communications: Radios: 1 per 3 persons. **Telephones:** 1 per 5 persons. **Daily newspaper circ.** (1987): 60 per 1,000 pop.

Health: Life expectancy at birth (1989): 65 male; 71 female. **Births** (per 1,000 pop. 1989): 28.2 **Deaths** (per 1,000 pop. 1989): 7. **Natural increase:** 2.2%. **Hospital beds:** 1 per 189 persons. **Physicians:** 1 per 980 persons. **Infant mortality** (per 1,000 live births 1989): 18.4.

Education (1989): **Literacy:** 80%. **Years compulsory** 9; attendance 98%.

Major International Organizations: UN, OAU, Commonwealth of Nations.

The islands were occupied by France in 1768, and seized by Britain in 1794. Ruled as part of Mauritius from 1814, the Seychelles became a separate colony in 1903. The ruling party had opposed independence as impractical, but pressure from the OAU and the UN became irresistible, and independence was declared June 29, 1976. The first president was ousted in a coup a year later by a socialist leader.

A new constitution, announced Mar. 1979, turned the country into a one-party state.

Sierra Leone
Republic of Sierra Leone

People: Population (1990 est.): 4,168,000. **Age distrib. (%):** 0–14: 41.4; 15–59: 53.5; 60+: 5.1. **Pop. density:** 154 per sq. mi. **Ethnic groups:** Temne 30%, Mende 29%, others. **Languages:** English (official), tribal languages. **Religions:** animist 30%, Moslem 30%, Christian 10%.

Geography: Area: 27,925 sq. mi., slightly smaller than South Carolina. **Location:** On W coast of W. Africa. **Neighbors:** Guinea on N, E, Liberia on S. **Topography:** The heavily-indented, 210-mi. coastline has mangrove swamps. Behind are wooded hills, rising to a plateau and mountains in the E. **Capital:** Freetown. **Cities** (1985 est.): Freetown 469,000; Bo, Kenema, Makeni.

Government: Type: Republic. **Head of state and head of government:** Pres. Gen. Joseph Saidu Momoh; b. Jan. 26, 1937; in office: Nov. 28, 1985. **Local divisions:** 12 districts and one region including Freetown.

Economy: Industries: Mining, tourism. **Chief crops:** Cocoa, coffee, palm kernels, rice, ginger. **Minerals:** Diamonds, bauxite. **Arable land:** 25%. **Fish catch** (1986): 52,000 metric tons. **Electricity prod.** (1988): 116 mln. kwh. **Labor force:** 75% agric.; 15% ind. & serv.

Finance: Currency: Leone (Mar. 1990: 1.00 = $.08 US). **Gross national product** (1987): $965 mln. **Per capita income** (1984): $320. **Imports** (1988): $156 mln.; partners: UK 22%, Fr. 11%. **Exports** (1988): $106 mln.; partners: Neth. 31%; UK 15%, U.S. 9%. **National budget** (1987): $181 mln. expenditures. **International reserves less gold** (Mar. 1990): $4 mln. **Consumer prices** (change in 1988): 34.3%.

Transport: Motor Vehicles: in use (1985): 23,000 passenger cars, 36,000 comm. vehicles. **Chief ports:** Freetown, Bonthe.

Communications: Television sets: 1 per 114 persons. **Radios:** 1 per 4.2 persons. **Telephones:** 1 per 251 persons. **Daily newspaper circ.** (1987): 3 per 1,000 pop.

Health: Life expectancy at birth (1989): 41 male; 47 female. **Births** (per 1,000 pop. 1989): 46. **Deaths** (per 1,000 pop. 1989): 21. **Natural increase:** 2.5%. **Hospital beds** (1984): 4,754. **Physicians** (1984): 197. **Infant mortality** (per 1,000 live births 1989): 157.

Education (1989): **Literacy:** 15%.

Major International Organizations: UN (GATT, IMF, WHO), Commonwealth of Nations, OAU.

Embassy: 1701 19th St. NW 20009; 939-9261.

Freetown was founded in 1787 by the British government as a haven for freed slaves. Their descendants, known as Creoles, number more than 60,000.

Successive steps toward independence followed the 1951 constitution. Full independence arrived Apr. 27, 1961. Sierra Leone became a republic Apr. 19, 1971. A one-party state approved by referendum 1978, brought political stability, but the economy has been plagued by inflation, corruption, and dependence upon the International Monetary Fund and creditors.

Singapore
Republic of Singapore

People: Population (1990 est.): 2,703,000. **Age distrib. (%):** 0–14: 23.4; 15–59: 68.4; 60+: 8.2. **Pop. density:** 11,910 per sq. mi. **Ethnic groups:** Chinese 77%, Malays 15%, Indians 6%. **Languages:** Chinese, Malay, Tamil, English all official. **Religions:** Buddhism 29%, Taoism 13%, Moslem 16%, Christian 19%.

Geography: Area: 224 sq. mi., smaller than New York City. **Location:** Off tip of Malayan Peninsula in S.E. Asia. **Neighbors:** Nearest are Malaysia on N, Indonesia on S. **Topography:** Singapore is a flat, formerly swampy island. The nation includes 40 nearby islets. **Capital:** Singapore.

Government: Type: Republic within the Commonwealth. **Head of state:** Pres. Wee Kim Wee; in office: Sept. 3, 1985. **Head of government:** Prime Min. Lee Kuan Yew; b. Sept. 16, 1923; in office: June 5, 1959. **Defense:** 6% of GNP (1987).

Economy: Industries: Shipbuilding, oil refining, electronics, banking, textiles, food, rubber, lumber processing, tourism. **Arable land:** 11%. **Livestock** (1986): pigs: 700,000. **Fish catch** (1987): 15,000 metric tons. **Electricity prod.** (1988): 11.5 bln.

kwh. **Crude steel prod.** (1985): 350,000 metric tons. **Labor force:** 1% agric.; 58% ind. & comm.; 35% services.

Finance: Currency: Dollar (May 1990: 1.88 = $1 US). **Gross national product** (1988): $23.7 bln. **Per capita income** (1985): $6,200. **Imports** (1989): $49.6 bln.; partners: Jap. 18%, Malay. 13%, U.S. 13%, Sau. Ar. 9%. **Exports** (1989): $44.6 bln., partners: U.S. 20%, Malay. 16%, Jap. 11%, HK 6%. **Tourists** (1987): $2.2 bln. receipts. **National budget** (1989): $6.2 bln. expenditures. **Consumer prices** (change in 1989): 2.4%.

Transport: Motor vehicles: in use (1988): 251,000 passenger cars, 114,000 comm. vehicles. **Civil aviation:** (1987) 24.9 bln. passenger-km; 1 airport.

Communications: Television sets: 1 per 4.9 persons. **Radios:** 1 per 3.5 persons. **Telephones:** 1 per 2.1 persons. **Daily newspaper circ.** (1986): 270 per 1,000 pop.

Health: Life expectancy at birth (1989): 71 male; 77 female. **Births** (per 1,000 pop. 1989): 16. **Deaths** (per 1,000 pop. 1989): 5. **Natural increase:** 1.1%. **Hospital beds:** 1 per 267 persons. **Physicians:** 1 per 888 persons. **Infant mortality** (per 1,000 live births 1989): 9.

Education (1987): **Literacy:** 85%. **Years compulsory:** none; attendance 85%.

Major International Organizations: UN (GATT, IMF, WHO), ASEAN.

Embassy: 1824 R St. NW 20009; 667-7555.

Founded in 1819 by Sir Thomas Stamford Raffles, Singapore was a British colony until 1959 when it became autonomous within the Commonwealth. On Sept. 16, 1963, it joined with Malaya, Sarawak and Sabah to form the Federation of Malaysia.

Tensions between Malayans, dominant in the federation, and ethnic Chinese, dominant in Singapore, led to an agreement under which Singapore became a separate nation, Aug. 9, 1965.

Singapore is one of the world's largest ports. Standards in health, education, and housing are high. International banking has grown.

Solomon Islands

People: Population (1989 est.): 314,000. **Age distrib.** (%): 0–14: 49; 15–59: 45.5; 60+: 5.5. **Pop. density:** 29 per sq. mi. **Urban** (1986): 15%. **Ethnic groups:** Melanesian 93%, Polynesian 4%. **Languages:** English (official), Pidgin, local languages. **Religions:** Anglican 34%, Roman Catholic 19%, Evangelical 24%, traditional religions.

Geography: Area: 10,640 sq. mi., slightly larger than Maryland. **Location:** Melanesian archipelago in the western Pacific O. **Neighbors:** Nearest is Papua New Guinea on W. **Topography:** 10 large volcanic and rugged islands and 4 groups of smaller ones. **Capital:** Honiara. **Cities:** (1988): Honiara 30,000.

Government: Type: Parliamentary democracy within the Commonwealth of Nations. **Head of state:** Queen Elizabeth II, represented by Gov.-Gen. George Lepping. **Head of government:** Prime Min. Solomon Mamaloni; in office: Mar. 28, 1989. **Local divisions:** 7 provinces and Honiara.

Economy: Industries: Fish canning. **Chief crops:** Coconuts, rice, bananas, yams. **Other resources:** Forests, marine shell. **Arable land:** 2%. **Fish catch** (1984): 35,000 metric tons. **Electricity prod.** (1988): 30.0 mln. kwh. **Labor force:** 32% agric., 32% services, 18% ind. & comm.

Finance: Currency: Dollar (Mar. 1990: 2.50 = $1 US). **Gross national product** (1987): $141 mln. **Per capita GNP** (1987): $420. **Imports** (1989): $117 mln.; partners: Austral. 31%, Jap. 14%, Sing. 18%. **Exports** (1989): $77 mln.; partners: Jap. 37%, UK 11%.

Communications: Radios: 1 per 4.6 persons. **Telephones:** 1 per 58 persons.

Health: Life expectancy at birth (1989): 66 male; 71 female. **Births:** (per 1,000 pop. 1989): 41. **Deaths** (per 1,000 pop. 1989): 5. **Natural increase:** 3.6%. **Infant mortality** (per 1,000 live births 1989): 41.

Education (1989): **Literacy:** 60%. **Primary school** 78%. **Secondary school:** 21%.

Major International Organizations: UN, Commonwealth of Nations.

The Solomon Islands were sighted in 1568 by an expedition from Peru. Britain established a protectorate in the 1890s over most of the group, inhabited by Melanesians. The islands saw major World War II battles. Self-government came Jan. 2, 1976, and independence was formally attained July 7, 1978.

Somalia
Somali Democratic Republic
Jamhuriyadda Dimugradiga Somaliya

People: Population (1990 est.): 8,415,000. **Pop. density:** 34 per sq. mi. **Ethnic groups:** mainly Hamitic, others. **Languages:** Somali, Arabic (both official). **Religions:** Sunni Moslems 99%.

Geography: Area: 246,300 sq. mi., slightly smaller than Texas. **Location:** Occupies the eastern horn of Africa. **Neighbors:** Djibouti, Ethiopia, Kenya on W. **Topography:** The coastline extends for 1,700 mi. Hills cover the N; the center and S are flat. **Capital:** Mogadishu. **Cities** (1986 est.): Mogadishu 700,000.

Government: Type: Independent republic. **Head of state:** Pres. Mohammed Siad Barrah; b. 1919; in office: Oct. 21, 1969. **Head of government:** Prime Min. Gen. Muhammad Ali Samatar; in office: Feb. 1, 1987. **Local divisions:** 16 regions. **Defense:** 6.5% of GNP (1984).

Economy: Chief crops: Incense, sugar, bananas, sorghum, corn, gum. **Minerals:** Iron, tin, gypsum, bauxite, uranium. **Arable land:** 2%. **Livestock** (1986): cattle: 4 mln.; goats: 18 mln.; sheep: 6 mln. **Fish catch** (1987): 17,000 metric tons. **Electricity prod.** (1988): 86 mln. kwh. **Labor force:** 82% agric.

Finance: Currency: Shilling (Mar. 1990: 1,106 = $1 US). **Gross national product** (1987): $1.5 bln. **Per capita GNP** (1987): $290. **Imports** (1987): $418 mln.; partners: It. 35%, UK 8%, U.S. 9%. **Exports** (1987): $95 mln.; partners: Saudi Ar. 66%, It. 12%. **International reserves less gold** (Nov. 1989): $10.3 mln. **Gold:** 19,000 oz t. **Consumer prices** (change in 1989): 101%.

Transport: Motor vehicles: in use (1986): 17,000 passenger cars, 9,500 comm. vehicles. **Chief ports:** Mogadishu, Berbera.

Communications: Radios: 1 per 20 persons.

Health: Life expectancy at birth (1989): 53 male; 53 female. **Births** (per 1,000 pop. 1989): 47. **Deaths** (per 1,000 pop. 1989): 15. **Natural increase:** 3.2%. **Hospital beds:** 1 per 1,053 persons. **Physicians:** 1 per 13,315 persons. **Infant mortality** (per 1,000 live births 1989): 128.

Education (1986): **Literacy:** 40%. 50% attend primary school, 7% attend secondary school.

Major International Organizations: UN, OAU, Arab League.

Embassy: 600 New Hampshire Ave. NW 20037; 342-1575.

Arab trading posts developed into sultanates. The Italian Protectorate of Somalia, acquired from 1885 to 1927, extended along the Indian O. from the Gulf of Aden to the Juba R. The UN in 1949 approved eventual creation of Somalia as a sovereign state and in 1950 Italy took over the trusteeship held by Great Britain since World War II.

British Somaliland was formed in the 19th century in the NW. Britain gave it independence June 26, 1960; on July 1 it joined with the former Italian part to create the independent Somali Republic.

On Oct. 21, 1969, a Supreme Revolutionary Council seized power in a bloodless coup, named a Council of Secretaries of State, and abolished the Assembly. In May, 1970, several foreign companies were nationalized.

A severe drought in 1975 killed tens of thousands, and spurred efforts to resettle nomads on collective farms.

Somalia has laid claim to Ogaden, the huge eastern region of Ethiopia, peopled mostly by Somalis. Ethiopia battled Somali rebels in 1977. Some 11,000 Cuban troops with Soviet arms defeated Somali army troops and ethnic Somali rebels in Ethiopia, 1978. As many as 1.5 mln. refugees entered Somalia. Guerrilla fighting in Ogaden continued until 1988 when a peace agreement was reached with Ethiopia.

South Africa
Republic of South Africa
Republiek van Suid-Afrika

People: Population (1990 est.): 39,550,000. **Age distrib.** (%): 0–14: 41.0; 15–59: 52.8; 60+: 6.2. **Pop. density:** 75 per sq. mi. **Urban** (1985): 55%. **Ethnic groups:** black 73%, white 18%, coloured 3%, Asian 3%. **Religions:** Mainly Christian, Hindu, Moslem minorities. **Languages:** Afrikaans, English (both official), Bantu languages predominate.

Geography: Area: 472,359 sq. mi., about twice the size of Texas. **Location:** At the southern extreme of Africa. **Neighbors:** Namibia (SW Africa), Botswana, Zimbabwe on N, Mozambique, Swaziland on E; surrounds Lesotho. **Topography:** The large interior plateau reaches close to the country's 2,700-mi. coastline. There are few major rivers or lakes; rainfall is sparse in W, more plentiful in E. **Capitals:** Cape Town (legislative). Pretoria (administrative), and Bloemfontein (judicial). **Cities** (1985 met.): Durban 982,000; Cape Town 1,900,000; Johannesburg 1,600,000; Pretoria 822,000.

Government: Type: Tricameral parliament with one chamber each for whites, coloureds, and Asians. **Head of State:** State Pres. Frederik W. De Klerk; b. Mar. 18, 1936; in office: Sept. 20, 1989. **Local divisions:** 4 provinces, 10 "homelands" for black Africans. **Defense:** 3.7 of GNP (1986).

Economy: Industries: Steel, tires, motors, textiles, plastics. **Chief crops:** Corn, wool, dairy products, grain, tobacco, sugar, fruit, peanuts, grapes. **Minerals:** Gold (largest producer), chromium, antimony, coal, iron, manganese, nickel, phosphates, tin, uranium, gem diamonds, platinum, copper, vanadium. **Other resources:** Wool. **Arable land:** 12%. **Livestock** (1987): cattle: 12.7 mln.; sheep: 30.3 mln. **Fish catch** (1987): 902,000 metric tons. **Electricity prod.** (1988): 155 bln. kwh. **Crude steel prod.** (1988): 8.7 mln. metric tons. **Labor force:** 30% agric.; 29% ind. and commerce; 34% serv.; 7% mining.

Finance: Currency: Rand (June 1990: 2.64 = $1 US). **Gross national product** (1987): $81 bln. **Per capita GNP** (1987): $1,890. **Imports** (1989): $18.4 bln.; partners: W. Ger. 19%, U.S. 16%, UK. 12%. **Exports** (1988): $21.5 bln.; partners: U.S. 43%, Jap. 9%. **Tourism** (1987): $587 mln. receipts. **National budget** (1989): $23.3 bln. **International reserves less gold** (Mar. 1990): $1.0 bln. **Gold:** 3.5 mln. oz t. **Consumer prices** (change in 1989): 14.7%.

Transport: Railway traffic (1987): 15.1 bln. passenger-km. **Motor vehicles:** in use (1987): 3.1 mln. passenger cars, 1.2 mln. comm. vehicles. **Civil aviation:** (1986): 4.5 bln. passenger-km: 39 airports. **Chief ports:** Durban, Cape Town, East London, Port Elizabeth.

Communications: Television sets: 1 per 13 persons. **Radios:** 1 per 3.6 persons. **Telephones:** 1 per 8.5 persons. **Daily newspaper circ.** (1988): 41 per 1,000 pop.

Health: Life expectancy at birth (1982): Whites: 70 years; Asians: 65 years; Africans: 59 years. **Births** (per 1,000 pop. 1989): 35. **Deaths** (per 1,000 pop. 1989): 8. **Natural increase:** 2.7%. **Physicians:** 1 per 1,510 persons. **Infant mortality** (per 1,000 live births 1982): Africans 94, Asians 25.3, whites 14.9.

Education (1989): **Literacy:** 99% (whites), 69% (Asians), 62% (coloureds), 50% (Africans).

Major International Organizations: UN (GATT).

Embassy: 3051 Massachusetts Ave. NW 20008; 232-4400.

Bushmen and Hottentots were the original inhabitants. Bantus, including Zulu, Xhosa, Swazi, and Sotho, had occupied the area from Transvaal to south of Transkei before the 17th century.

The Cape of Good Hope area was settled by Dutch, beginning in the 17th century. Britain seized the Cape in 1806. Many Dutch trekked north and founded 2 republics, the Transvaal and the Orange Free State. Diamonds were discovered, 1867, and gold, 1886. The Dutch (Boers) resented encroachments by the British and others; the Anglo-Boer War followed, 1899-1902. Britain won and, effective May 31, 1910, created the Union of South Africa, incorporating the British colonies of the Cape and Natal, the Transvaal and the Orange Free State. After a referendum, the Union became the Republic of South Africa, May 31, 1961, and withdrew from the Commonwealth.

With the election victory of Daniel Malan's National party in 1948, the policy of separate development of the races, or apartheid, already existing unofficially, became official. This called for separate development, separate residential areas, and ultimate political independence for the whites, Bantus, Asians, and Coloreds. In 1959 the government passed acts providing the eventual creation of several Bantu nations or Bantustans on 13% of the country's land area, though most black leaders have opposed the plan.

Under apartheid, blacks are severely restricted to certain occupations, and are paid far lower wages than are whites for similar work. Only whites may vote or run for public office, and militant white opposition has been curbed. There is an advisory Indian Council, partly elected, partly appointed. In 1969, a Colored People's Representative Council was created. Some liberalization measures were allowed in the 1980s.

At least 600 persons, mostly Bantus, were killed in 1976 riots protesting apartheid. Black protests continued through 1985 as violence broke out in several black townships. Police reaction to the protests caused several hundred deaths. A new constitution was approved by referendum, Nov. 1983, which extended the parliamentary franchise to the Coloured and Asian minorities. Laws banning interracial sex and marriage were repealed in 1985.

In 1963, the Transkei, an area in the SE, became the first of these partially self-governing territories or "Homelands." Transkei became independent on Oct. 26, 1976, Bophuthatswana on Dec. 6, 1977, and Venda on Sept. 13, 1979; none received international recognition.

In 1981, So. Africa launched military operations in Angola and Mozambique to combat terrorists groups; So. African troops attacked the South West African People's Organization (SWAPO) guerrillas in Angola, March, 1982. South Africa and Mozambique signed a non-agression pact in 1984.

A car bomb exploded outside air force headquarters in Pretoria, May 20, 1983, killing or injuring hundreds of people. The African National Congress (ANC), a black nationalist group, claimed responsibility. In the U.S., there were numerous antiapartheid protests in the 1980's.

In 1986, Nobel Peace Prize winner Bishop Desmond Tutu called for Western nations to apply sanctions against S. Africa to force an end to apartheid. President Botha announced in Apr. the end to the nation's system of racial pass laws and offered blacks an advisory role in government.

On May 19, S. Africa attacked 3 neighboring countries—Zimbabwe, Botswana, Zambia—to strike at guerrilla strongholds of the African National Congress.

A nationwide state of emergency was declared June 12, giving almost unlimited power to the security forces. On Apr. 22, 1987, a 6-week-old walkout by railway workers erupted into violence after the dismissal of 16,000 strikers. As confrontation between blacks and government increased, there was widespread support in Western nations for a complete trade embargo on S. Africa.

Some 2 million South African black workers staged a massive strike, June 6-8, 1988, to protest the government's new labor laws and the banning of political activity by trade unions and antiapartheid groups. P.W. Botha, head of the government since 1978, resigned Aug. 14, 1989 and was replaced by Frederik W. De Klerk.

In 1990, the government lifted its ban on the African National Congress, the primary black group fighting to end white minority rule. On Feb. 11, black nationalist leader Nelson Mandela was freed after more than 27 years in prison. Mandela went on a 6-week, 14-nation tour, June-July, highlighted by an 11-day, 8-city tour of the U.S.

Bophuthatswana: Population (1989 est.): 1,914,000. **Area:** 16,988 sq. mi., 6 discontinuous geographic units. **Capital:** Mmabatho. **Head of state:** Pres. Kgosi Lucas Manyane Mangope, b. Dec. 27, 1923; in office: Dec. 6, 1977.

Ciskei: Population (1989 est.): 824,000. **Area:** 2,996 sq. mi. **Capitol:** Bisho. **Head of State:** Military council.

Transkei: Population (1989 est.): 3,224,000. **Area:** 16,855 sq. mi., 3 discontinuous geographic units. **Capital:** Umtata. **Head of government:** Gen. Bantu Holomisa; in office: Dec. 30, 1987.

Venda: Population (1989 est.): 506,000. **Area:** 2,771 sq. mi., 2 discontinuous geographic units. **Capital:** Thohoyandou. **Head of state:** Frank Ravele; in office: Apr. 18, 1988.

Spain

España

People: Population (1990 est.): 39,623,000 **Age distrib.** (%): 0-14: 24.6; 15-59: 59.5; 60+: 15.9. **Pop. density:** 204 per sq. mi. **Urban** (1987): 75%. **Ethnic groups:** Spanish (Castilian, Valencian, Andalusian, Asturian) 72.8%, Catalan 16.4%, Galician 8.2%, Basque 2.3%. **Languages:** Spanish (official), Catalan, Galician, Basque. **Religions:** Roman Catholic 90%.

Geography: Area: 194,896 sq. mi., the size of Arizona and Utah combined. **Location:** In SW Europe. **Neighbors:** Portugal on W, France on N. **Topography:** The interior is a high, arid plateau broken by mountain ranges and river valleys. The NW is heavily watered, the south has lowlands and a Mediterranean climate. **Capital:** Madrid. **Cities** (1987 est.): Madrid 3,500,000; Barcelona 2,000,000; Valencia 700,000; Seville 580,000.

Government: Type: Constitutional monarchy. **Head of state:** King Juan Carlos I de Borbon y Borbon, b. Jan. 5, 1938; in office: Nov. 22, 1975. **Head of government:** Prime Min. Felipe Gonzalez Marquez; in office: Dec. 2, 1982. **Local divisions:** 50 provinces, 2 territories, 3 islands. **Defense:** 2.4% of GNP (1987).

Economy: Industries: Machinery, steel, textiles, shoes, autos, processed foods. **Chief crops:** Grains, olives, grapes, citrus fruits, vegetables, olives. **Minerals:** Lignite, uranium, lead, iron, copper, zinc, coal. **Crude oil reserves** (1987): 34 mln. bbls. **Other resources:** Forests (cork). **Arable land:** 31%. **Livestock** (1987): cattle: 4.9 mln.; pigs: 16.9 mln.; sheep: 17.3 mln. **Fish catch** (1987): 1.0 mln. tons. **Electricity prod.** (1988): 149 bln. kwh. **Crude steel prod.** (1988): 11.8 min. metric tons. **Labor force:** 16% agric.; 24% ind. and comm.; 52% serv.

Finance: Currency: Peseta (May 1990: 101.55 = $1 US). **Gross national product** (1987): $288 bln. **Per capita income** (1984): $4,490. **Imports** (1989): $71.4 bln.; partners: U.S. 11%, EC 33%. **Exports** (1989): $44.4 bln.; partners: EC 49%, U.S. 10%. **Tourists** (1987): $14.7 bln. receipts. **National budget** (1987): $66.7 bln. expenditures. **International reserves less gold** (Mar. 1990): $41.0 bln. **Gold:** 15.7 min. oz t. **Consumer prices** (change in 1989): 6.8%.

Transport: Railway traffic (1988): 15 bln. passenger-km. **Motor vehicles:** in use (1987): 9.7 mln. passenger cars, 1.7 mln. comm. **Civil aviation:** (1987): 22.2 bln. passenger-km; 30 airports with scheduled flights. **Chief ports:** Barcelona, Bilbao, Valencia, Cartagena, Gijon.

Communications: Television sets: 1 per 2.6 persons. **Radios:** 1 per 3.4 persons. **Telephones:** 1 per 2.5 persons. **Daily newspaper circ.** (1987): 76 per 1,000 pop.

Health: Life expectancy at birth (1989): 74 male; 80 female. **Births** (per 1,000 pop. 1989): 13. **Deaths** (per 1,000 pop. 1989): 8. **Natural increase:** .2%. **Hospital beds:** 1 per 213 persons. **Physicians:** 1 per 287 persons. **Infant mortality** (per 1,000 live births 1989): 11.

Education (1989): Literacy: 97%. **School compulsory:** to age 14.

Major international Organizations: UN and all of its specialized agencies, NATO, OECD, EC.

Embassy: 2700 15th St. NW 20009; 265-0190.

Spain was settled by Iberians, Basques, and Celts, partly overrun by Carthaginians, conquered by Rome c.200 BC. The Visigoths, in power by the 5th century AD, adopted Christianity but by 711 AD lost to the Islamic invasion from Africa. Christian reconquest from the N led to a Spanish nationalism. In 1469 the kingdoms of Aragon and Castile were united by the marriage of Ferdinand II and Isabella I, and the last Moorish power was broken by the fall of the kingdom of Granada, 1492. Spain became a bulwark of Roman Catholicism.

Spain obtained a colonial empire with the discovery of America by Columbus, 1492, the conquest of Mexico by Cortes, and Peru by Pizarro. It also controlled the Netherlands and parts of Italy and Germany. Spain lost its American colonies in the early 19th century. It lost Cuba, the Philippines, and Puerto Rico during the Spanish-American War, 1898.

Primo de Rivera became dictator in 1923. King Alfonso XIII revoked the dictatorship, 1930, but was forced to leave the country 1931. A republic was proclaimed which disestablished the church, curtailed its privileges, and secularized education. A conservative reaction occurred 1933 but was followed by a Popular Front (1936-1939) composed of socialists, communists, republicans, and anarchists.

Army officers under Francisco Franco revolted against the government, 1936. In a destructive 3-year war, in which some one million died, Franco received massive help and troops from Italy and Germany, while the USSR, France, and Mexico supported the republic. War ended Mar. 28, 1939. Franco was named caudillo, leader of the nation. Spain was neutral in World War II but its relations with fascist countries caused its exclusion from the UN until 1955.

In July 1969, Franco and the Cortes designated Prince Juan Carlos as the future king and chief of state. After Franco's death, Nov. 20, 1975, Juan Carlos was sworn in as king. He presided over the formal dissolution of the institutions of the Franco regime. In free elections June 1977, moderates and democratic socialists emerged as the largest parties.

Catalonia and the Basque country were granted autonomy, Jan. 1980, following overwhelming approval in home-rule referendums. Basque extremists, however, have continued their campaign for independence.

The **Balearic Islands** in the western Mediterranean, 1,935 sq. mi., are a province of Spain; they include **Majorca** (Mallorca), with the capital, Palma; **Minorca, Cabrera, Ibiza** and **Formentera.** The **Canary Islands,** 2,807 sq. mi., in the Atlantic W of Morocco, form 2 provinces, including the islands of **Tenerife, Palma, Gomera, Hierro, Grand Canary, Fuerteventura,** and **Lanzarote** with Las Palmas and Santa Cruz thriving ports. **Ceuta** and **Melilla,** small enclaves on Morocco's Mediterranean coast, are part of Metropolitan Spain.

Spain has sought the return of Gibraltar, in British hands since 1704.

Sri Lanka

Democratic Socialist Republic of Sri Lanka

Sri Lanka Prajathanthrika Samajavadi Janarajaya

People: Population (1990 est.): 17,135,000. **Age distrib.** (%): 0–14: 35.3; 15–59: 58.1; 60+: 6.6. **Pop. density:** 692 per sq. mi. **Urban** (1985): 21.5%. **Ethnic groups:** Sinhalese 74%, Tamils 17%, Moors 7%. **Languages:** Sinhala and Tamil, (both official); English. **Religions:** Buddhist 69%, Hindu 15%, Christian 8%, Moslem 7%.

Geography: Area: 25,332 sq. mi. about the size of W. Va. **Location:** In Indian O. off SE coast of India. **Neighbors:** India on NW. **Topography:** The coastal area and the northern half are flat; the S-central area is hilly and mountainous. **Capital:** Colombo. **Cities** (1989): Colombo 1.2 mln.; Jaffna, 270,000; Galle, 168,000; Kandy, 147,000.

Government: Type: Republic. **Head of state:** Pres. Ranasinghe Premadasa; b. June 24, 1924; in office: Jan. 2, 1989. **Head of government:** Prime Minister Dingiri Banda Wijetunge, b. 1923, in office: Mar. 3, 1989. **Local divisions:** 8 provinces, 24 districts. **Defense:** 4% of GNP (1988).

Economy: Industries: Plywood, paper, milling, chemicals, textiles. **Chief crops:** Tea, coconuts, rice. **Minerals:** Graphite, limestone, gems, phosphate. **Other resources:** Forests, rubber. **Arable land:** 16%. **Livestock** (1987): cattle: 1.8 mln. **Fish catch** (1986): 183,000 metric tons. **Electricity prod.** (1988): 4.2 bln. kwh. **Labor force:** 46% agric.; 27% ind. and comm.; 26% serv.

Finance: Currency: Rupee (Mar. 1990: 40 = $1 US). **Gross national product** (1988): $7.2 bln. **Per capita GNP** (1988): $400. **Imports** (1988): $2.2 bln.; partners: Jap. 15%, Saudi Ar. 12%, UK 7%. **Exports** (1988): $1.7 bln.; partners: U.S. 22%, UK 7%. **Tourists** (1988): $82 mln. receipts. **National budget** (1988): $2.7 bln. expenditures. **International reserves less gold** (Mar. 1990): $317 mln. **Gold:** 63,000 oz t. **Consumer prices** (change in 1989): 11.6%.

Transport: Railway traffic (1987): 1.9 bln. passenger-km. **Motor vehicles:** in use (1987): 147,000 passenger cars, 243,000 comm. vehicles. **Civil aviation** (1988): 2.4 bln. passenger-km; 1 airport. **Chief ports:** Colombo, Trincomalee, Galle.

Communications: Television sets: 1 per 33 persons. **Radios:** 1 per 5.1 persons. **Telephones:** 1 per 130 persons.

Health: Life expectancy at birth (1989): 67 male; 72 female. **Births** (per 1,000 pop. 1989): 21. **Deaths** (per 1,000 pop. 1989): 6. **Natural increase:** 1.5%. **Hospital beds:** 1 per 357 persons. **Physicians:** 1 per 6,989 persons. **Infant mortality** (per 1,000 live births 1989): 31.

Education (1988): Literacy: 87%. **Years compulsory:** To age 12; attendance 98%.

Major International Organizations: UN (World Bank, IMF), Commonwealth of Nations.

Embassy: 2148 Wyoming Ave. NW 20008; 483-4025.

The island was known to the ancient world as Taprobane (Greek for copper-colored) and later as Serendip (from Arabic). Colonists from northern India subdued the indigenous Veddahs about 543 BC; their descendants, the Buddhist Sinhalese, still form most of the population. Hindu descendants of Tamil immigrants from southern India account for one-fifth of the population. Parts were occupied by the Portuguese in 1505 and by the Dutch in 1658. The British seized the island in 1796. As Ceylon it became an independent member of the Commonwealth in 1948. On May 22, 1972, Ceylon became the Republic of Sri Lanka.

Prime Min. W. R. D. Bandaranaike was assassinated Sept. 25, 1959. In new elections, the Freedom Party was victorious under Mrs. Sirimavo Bandaranaike, widow of the former prime minister. After May 1970 elections, Mrs. Bandaranaike became prime minister again. In 1971 the nation suffered economic problems and terrorist activities by ultra-leftists, thousands of whom were executed. Massive land reform and nationalization of foreign-owned plantations was undertaken in the mid-1970s. Mrs. Bandaranaike was ousted in 1977 elections by the United Nationals. A presidential form of government was installed in 1978 to restore stability.

Tension between the Sinhalese and Tamil separatists erupted into violence repeatedly in the 1980s. In 1987, hundreds died in an attack by Tamil rebels Apr. 17. Sri Lanka forces retaliated in June with attacks on the rebel-held Jaffna peninsula. Over 11,000 have died in the civil war since 1983.

Sudan

Republic of the Sudan

Jamhuryat as-Sudan

People: Population (1990 est.): 25,164,000. **Pop. density:** 25 per sq. mi. **Urban** (1983): 35%. **Ethnic groups:** black 52%, Arab 39%, Beja 6%. **Languages:** Arabic (official), various tribal languages. **Religions:** Sunni Moslem 70%, animist 18%, Christians 5%.

Geography: Area: 966,757 sq. mi., the largest country in Africa, over one-fourth the size of the U.S. **Location:** At the E end of Sahara desert zone. **Neighbors:** Egypt on N, Libya, Chad, Central African Republic on W, Zaire, Uganda, Kenya on S, Ethiopia on E. **Topography:** The N consists of the Libyan Desert in the W, and the mountainous Nubia desert in E, with narrow Nile valley between. The center contains large, fertile, rainy areas with fields, pasture, and forest. The S has rich soil, heavy rain. **Capital:** Khartoum. **Cities** (1983 est.): Khartoum 476,000; Omdurman 526,000; North Khartoum 341,000; Port Sudan 206,000.

Government: Type: Military. **Head of government:** Prime Min. Gen. Omar Al-Bashir; in office: June 30, 1989. **Local divisions:** 9 regions. **Defense:** 2.1% of GNP (1985).

Economy: Industries: Textiles, food processing. **Chief crops:** Gum arabic (principal world source), durra (sorghum), cotton (main export), sesame, peanuts, rice, coffee, sugar cane, wheat, dates. **Minerals:** Chrome, copper, **Other resources:** Mahogany. **Arable land:** 5%. **Livestock** (1986): cattle: 22 mln.; sheep: 12 mln.; goats: 15 mln. **Electricity prod.** (1988): 1.2 bln. kwh. **Labor force:** 78% agric.; 9% ind., comm.

Finance: Currency: Pound (Mar. 1990: 1.00 = $.22 US). **Gross national product** (1988): $8.5 bln. **Per capita GNP** (1987): $330. **Imports** (1988): $1.0 bln.; partners: UK 13%, W. Ger. 8%, Saudi Ar. 11%. **Exports** (1988): $504 mln.; partners: China 6%, It. 9%, Saudi Ar. 21%. **National budget** (1988): $1.5 bln. expenditures. **International reserves less gold** (Mar. 1990): $39.7 mln.

Transport: Railway traffic (1988): 357 mln. passenger km. **Motor vehicles:** in use (1985): 99,000 passenger cars, 17,000 comm. vehicles. **Civil aviation:** (1988): 671 mln. passenger-km; 10 airports with scheduled flights. **Chief ports:** Port Sudan.

Communications: Television sets: 1 per 23 persons. **Radios:** 1 per 4.6 persons. **Telephones:** 1 per 338 persons. **Daily newspaper circ.** (1987): 6 per 1,000 pop.

Health: Life expectancy at birth (1989): 51 male; 55 female. **Births** (per 1,000 pop. 1989): 44. **Deaths** (per 1,000 pop. 1989): 14. **Natural increase:** 3.0%. **Hospital beds** (1985): 17,328. **Physicians** (1983): 2,169. **Infant mortality** (per 1,000 live births 1989): 98.

Education (1986): Literacy: 30%. **Years compulsory:** 9; attendance 50%.

Major International Organizations: UN (IMF, WHO, FAO), Arab League, OAU.

Embassy: 2210 Massachusetts Ave. NW 20008; 338-8565.

Northern Sudan, ancient Nubia, was settled by Egyptians in antiquity, and was converted to Coptic Christianity in the 6th century. Arab conquests brought Islam in the 15th century.

In the 1820s Egypt took over the Sudan, defeating the last of earlier empires, including the Fung. In the 1880s a revolution was led by Mohammed Ahmed who called himself the Mahdi (leader of the faithful) and his followers, the dervishes.

In 1898 an Anglo-Egyptian force crushed the Mahdi's successors. In 1951 the Egyptian Parliament abrogated its 1899 and 1936 treaties with Great Britain, and amended its constitution, to provide for a separate Sudanese constitution.

Sudan voted for complete independence as a parliamentary government effective Jan. 1, 1956. Gen. Ibrahim Abboud took power 1958, but resigned under pressure, 1964.

In 1969, in a second military coup, a Revolutionary Council took power, but a civilian premier and cabinet were appointed; the government announced it would create a socialist state. The northern 12 provinces are predominantly Arab-Moslem and have been dominant in the central government. The 3 southern provinces are black and predominantly pagan. A 1972 peace agreement gave the South regional autonomy. The 2 halves of the nation began a civil war in 1988.

Economic problems plagued the nation in the 1980s, aggravated by a huge influx of refugees from neighboring countries. After 16 years in power, Pres. Nimeiry was overthrown in a bloodless military coup, Apr. 6, 1985. The Sudan held its first democratic parliamentary elections in 18 years in 1986. The elected government was overthrown in a bloodless coup June 30, 1989. Some 2 million were made homeless by torrential rains, Aug. 1988.

Suriname

Republic of Suriname

People: Population (1990 est.): 408,000. **Pop. density:** 6 per sq. mi. **Ethnic groups** Hindustanis 37%, Creole 31%, Javanese 15%. **Languages:** Dutch (official), Sranan (Creole), English, others. **Religions:** Moslem 23%, Hindu 27%, Christian 25%.

Geography: Area: 63,037 sq. mi., slightly larger than Georgia. **Location:** On N shore of S. America. **Neighbors:** Guyana on W, Brazil on S, French Guiana on E. **Topography:** A flat Atlantic coast, where dikes permit agriculture. Inland is a forest belt; to the S, largely unexplored hills cover 75% of the country. **Capital:** Paramaribo. **Cities** (1984): Paramaribo 180,000.

Government: Type: Republic. **Head of State:** Pres. Ramsewak Shankar; in office: Jan. 25, 1988. **Prime Min.** Henck Arron; in office: Jan. 29, 1988. **Local divisions:** 9 districts.

Economy: Industries: Aluminum. **Chief crops:** Rice, sugar, fruits. **Minerals:** Bauxite. **Other resources:** Forests, shrimp. **Arable land:** 1%. **Electricity prod.** (1988): 1.9 bln. kwh. **Labor force:** 29% agric.; 15% ind. and commerce; 42% govt.

Finance: Currency: Guilder (Mar. 1990: 1.78 = $1 US). **Gross national product** (1987): $1.1 bln. **Per capita income** (1985): $2,920. **Imports** (1986): $487 mln.; partners: U.S. 30%, Neth. 9%, Trin./Tob. 21%, Jap. 7%. **Exports** (1986): $482 mln.; partners: U.S. 13%, Neth. 26%. **Tourists** (1987): receipts: $4 mln. **National budget** (1988): $650 mln. expenditures. **International reserves less gold** (Mar. 1990): $9.7 mln. **Gold:** 54,000 oz t.

Transport: Motor vehicles: in use (1987): 33,000 passenger cars, 12,000 comm. vehicles. **Chief ports:** Paramaribo, Nieuw-Nickerie.

Communications: Television sets: 1 per 10 persons. **Radios:** 1 per 1.6 persons. **Telephones:** 1 per 10 persons. **Daily newspaper circ.** (1987): 80 per 1,000 pop.

Health: Life expectancy at birth (1989): 66 male; 71 female. **Births** (per 1,000 pop. 1989): 27. **Deaths** (per 1,000 pop. 1989): 5. **Natural increase:** 2.1%. **Infant mortality** (per 1,000 live births 1989): 40.

Education (1989): Literacy: 65%; compulsory ages 6–12.

Major International Organizations: UN (WHO, ILO, FAO, World Bank, IMF), OAS.

Embassy: 2600 Virginia Ave. NW 20037; 338-6980.

The Netherlands acquired Suriname in 1667 from Britain, in exchange for New Netherlands (New York). The 1954 Dutch constitution raised the colony to a level of equality with the Netherlands and the Netherlands Antilles. In the 1970s the Dutch government pressured for Suriname independence, which came Nov. 25, 1975, despite objections from East Indians. Some 40% of the population (mostly East Indians) emigrated to the Netherlands in the months before independence.

The National Military Council took over control of the government, Feb. 1982. The government came under democratic leadership in 1988.

Swaziland

Kingdom of Swaziland

People: Population (1990 est.): 779,000. **Age distrib.** (%): 0–14: 47.3; 15–59: 47.4; 60+: 5.3. **Pop. density:** 112 per sq. mi. **Urban** (1985): 26%. **Ethnic groups:** Swazi 90%, Zulu 2.3%, European 2.1%, other African, non-African groups. **Languages:** Swazi, English, (both official). **Religions:** Christians 57%, indigenous beliefs 43%.

Geography: Area: 6,704 sq. mi., slightly smaller than New Jersey. **Location:** In southern Africa, near Indian O. coast. **Neighbors:** South Africa on N, W, S, Mozambique on E. **Topography:** The country descends from W-E in broad belts, becoming more arid in the lowveld region, then rising to a plateau in the E. **Capital:** Mbabane. **Cities** (1986 est.): Mbabane 52,000.

Government: Type: Monarchy. **Head of state:** King Mswati 3d; as of: Apr. 25, 1986. **Head of government:** Prime Min. Obed Dlamini; in office: July 12, 1989. **Local divisions:** 4 districts, 2 municipalities, 40 regions.

Economy: Industries: Wood pulp. **Chief crops:** Sugar, corn, cotton, rice, pineapples, sugar, citrus fruits. **Minerals:** Asbestos, iron, coal. **Other resources:** Forests. **Arable land:** 8%. **Electricity prod.** (1988): 130 mln. kwh. **Labor force:** 53% agric.; 9% ind. and commerce; 9% serv.

Finance: Currency: Lilangeni (Mar. 1990: 1.00 = $.39 US). **Gross national product** (1987): $539 mln. **Per capita GNP** (1987): $750. **Imports** (1987): $416 mln.; partners: So. Afr., 96%. **Exports** (1987): $311 mln.; partners: UK 33%, So. Afr. 20%. **National budget** (1986): $120 mln. **International reserves less gold** (Feb. 1990): $176 mln. **Consumer prices** (change in 1989): 11.7%.

Transport: Motor vehicles: in use (1986): 20,000 passenger cars, 20,000 comm. vehicles.

Communications: Radios: 1 per 6.3 persons. **Telephones:** 1 per 34 persons. **Daily newspaper circ.** (1985): 35 per 1,000 pop.

Health: Life expectancy at birth (1989): 47 male; 54 female. **Births** (per 1,000 pop. 1989): 46. **Deaths** (per 1,000 pop. 1989): 15. **Natural increase:** 3.1%. **Hospital beds** (1984): 1,608. **Physicians** (1984): 80. **Infant mortality rate** (per 1,000 live births 1989): 127.

Education (1985): **Literacy:** 65%. Almost all attend primary school.

Major International Organizations: UN (IMF, WHO, FAO), OAU, Commonwealth of Nations.

Embassy: 4301 Connecticut Ave. NW 20008; 362-6683.

The royal house of Swaziland traces back 400 years, and is one of Africa's last ruling dynasties. The Swazis, a Bantu people, were driven to Swaziland from lands to the N by the Zulus in 1820. Their autonomy was later guaranteed by Britain and Transvaal, with Britain assuming control after 1903. Independence came Sept. 6, 1968. In 1973 the king repealed the constitution and assumed full powers.

Under the constitution political parties are forbidden; parliament's role in government is limited to debate and advice.

Sweden

Kingdom of Sweden

Konungariket Sverige

People: Population (1990 est.): 8,407,000. **Age distrib.** (%): 0–14: 17.9; 15–59: 59.0; 60+: 23.1. **Pop. density:** 48 per sq. mi. **Urban** (1985): 85%. **Ethnic groups:** Swedish 91%, Finnish 3%, Lapps, European immigrants. **Languages:** Swedish, Finnish. **Religions:** Lutheran (official) 95%.

Geography: Area: 173,731 sq. mi., larger than California. **Location:** On Scandinavian Peninsula in N. Europe. **Neighbors:** Norway on W, Denmark on S (across Kattegat), Finland on E. **Topography:** Mountains along NW border cover 25% of Sweden, flat or rolling terrain covers the central and southern areas, which includes several large lakes. **Capital:** Stockholm. **Cities** (1988): Stockholm 663,000; Goteborg 429,000; Malmo 230,000.

Government: Type: Constitutional monarchy. **Head of state:** King Carl XVI Gustaf; b. Apr. 30, 1946; in office: Sept. 19, 1973. **Head of government:** Prime Min. Ingvar Carlsson; b. Nov. 9,

1934; in office: Mar. 1, 1986. **Local divisions:** 24 lan (counties), 278 municipalities. **Defense:** 2.9% of GNP (1987).

Economy: Industries: Steel, machinery, instruments, autos, shipbuilding, shipping, paper. **Chief crops:** Grains, potatoes, sugar beets. **Minerals:** Zinc, iron, lead, copper, gold, silver. **Other resources:** Forests (half the country); yield one fourth exports. **Arable land:** 7%. **Livestock** (1987): cattle: 1.7 mln.; pigs: 2.2 mln. **Fish catch** (1987): 197,000 metric tons. **Electricity prod.** (1988): 182 bln. kwh. **Crude steel prod.** (1988): 4.6 mln. metric tons. **Labor force:** 5% agric.; 24% manuf. & mining; 37% social services.

Finance: Currency: Krona (May 1990: 6.00 = $1 US). **Gross national product** (1989): $179 bln. **Per capita income** (1989): $11,783 **Imports** (1989): $47.8 bln.; partners: W. Ger. 21%, UK 9%, U.S. 7%. **Exports** (1989): $51.5 bln.; partners: UK 10%, W. Ger. 12%, Nor. 10%. **Tourists** (1987): $2.0 bln. receipts. **National budget** (1989): $60.5 bln. expenditures. **International reserves less gold** (Mar. 1990): $9.8 bln. **Gold:** 6.06 mln. oz t. **Consumer prices** (change in 1989): 6.4%.

Transport: Railway traffic (1987): 5.9 bln. passenger-km. **Motor vehicles:** in use (1988): 3.3 mln. passenger cars, 259,000 comm. vehicles. **Civil aviation** (1987): 5.7 bln. passenger-km; 43 airports. **Chief ports:** Goteborg, Stockholm, Malmo.

Communications: Television sets: 1 per 2.4 persons. **Radios:** 1 per 1.2 persons. **Telephones:** 1 per 1.1 persons. **Daily newspaper circ.** (1986): 586 per 1,000 pop.

Health: Life expectancy at birth (1989): 74 male; 81 female. **Births** (per 1,000 pop. 1989): 12. **Deaths** (per 1,000 pop. 1989): 12. **Natural increase:** .0%. **Hospital beds:** 1 per 148 persons. **Physicians:** 1 per 373 persons. **Infant mortality** (per 1,000 live births (1989): 6.

Education (1989): **Literacy:** 99%. **Years compulsory:** 12; attendance 100%.

Major International Organizations: UN and all of its specialized agencies, EFTA, OECD.

Embassy: 600 New Hampshire Ave. NW 20037; 944-5600.

The Swedes have lived in present-day Sweden for at least 5,000 years, longer than nearly any other European people. Gothic tribes from Sweden played a major role in the disintegration of the Roman Empire. Other Swedes helped create the first Russian state in the 9th century.

The Swedes were Christianized from the 11th century, and a strong centralized monarchy developed. A parliament, the Riksdag, was first called in 1435, the earliest parliament on the European continent, with all classes of society represented.

Swedish independence from rule by Danish kings (dating from 1397) was secured by Gustavus I in a revolt, 1521-23; he built up the government and military and established the Lutheran Church. In the 17th century Sweden was a major European power, gaining most of the Baltic seacoast, but its international position subsequently declined.

The Napoleonic wars, in which Sweden acquired Norway (it became independent 1905), were the last in which Sweden participated. Armed neutrality was maintained in both world wars.

Over 4 decades of Social Democratic rule was ended in 1976 parliamentary elections but the party was returned to power in the 1982 elections. Although 90% of the economy is in private hands, the government holds a large interest in water power production and the railroads are operated by a public agency.

Consumer cooperatives are in extensive operation and also are important in agriculture and housing.

A labor crisis of strikes locking out more than 800,000 workers, May 1980, brought the country to an industrial standstill.

A Soviet submarine went aground inside Swedish territorial waters near the Karlskrona Naval Base, Oct. 27, 1981. Sweden claimed the submarine was armed with nuclear weapons and the incident a "flagrant violation" of Swedish neutrality. The submarine was towed back to international waters Nov. 6.

Premier Olof Palme was shot and killed on a Stockholm street Feb. 28, 1986. A man with a history of substance abuse and psychiatric treatment was convicted of the crime July, 1989. The conviction was overturned Oct. 12.

Switzerland

Swiss Confederation

People: Population (1990 est.): 6,628,000. **Age distrib.** (%): 0–14: 17.8; 15–59: 63.2; 60+: 19.0. **Pop. density:** 406 per sq. mi. **Urban** (1987): 60.4%. **Ethnic groups:** Mixed European stock. **Languages:** German 65%, French 18%, Italian 12%, Romansh 1%. (all official). **Religions:** Roman Catholic 49%, Protestant 48%.

Geography: Area: 15,941 sq. mi., as large as Mass., Conn., and R.I., combined. **Location:** In the Alps Mts. in Central Europe. **Neighbors:** France on W, Italy on S, Austria on E, W. Germany on N. **Topography:** The Alps cover 60% of the land area, the Jura, near France, 10%. Running between, from NE to SW, are midlands, 30%. **Capital:** Bern. **Cities** (1989): Zurich 346,000; Basel 171,200; Geneva 161,000.

Government: Type: Federal republic. **Head of government:** Pres. Otto Stich; in office: Jan. 1, 1988. **Local divisions:** 20 full cantons, 6 half cantons. **Defense:** 2.2% of GNP (1987).

Economy: Industries: Machinery, machine tools, steel, instruments, watches, textiles, foodstuffs (cheese, chocolate), chemicals, drugs, banking, tourism. **Chief crops:** Grains, potatoes, sugar beets, vegetables, tobacco. **Minerals:** Salt. **Other resources:** Hydro power potential. **Arable land:** 10%. **Livestock** (1987): cattle: 1.8 mln.; pigs: 1.9 mln. **Electricity prod.** (1988): 58.4 bln. kwh. **Crude steel prod.** (1988): 825,000 metric tons. **Labor force:** 39% ind. and commerce, 7% agric., 50% serv.

Finance: Currency: Franc (May 1990: 1.41 = $1 US). **Gross national product** (1988): $111 bln. **Per capita income** (1987): $26,309. **Imports** (1989): $58.1 bln.; partners: W. Ger. 30%, Fr. 11%, It. 10%, U.K. 5%. **Exports** (1989): $51.5 bln.; partners: W. Ger. 18%, Fr. 9%, It. 8%, U.S. 8%. **Tourists** (1988); receipts: $5.6 bln. **National budget** (1988): $17.4 bln. **International reserves less gold** (Mar. 1990): $22.5 bln. **Gold:** 83.28 mln. oz t. **Consumer prices** (change in 1989): 3.2%.

Transport: Railway traffic (1988): 10.8 bln. passenger-km. **Motor vehicles:** in use (1987): 2.7 mln. passenger cars, 218,000 comm. vehicles. **Civil aviation:** (1988): 14.3 bln. passenger-km; 5 airports with scheduled flights.

Communications: Television sets: 1 per 2.9 persons. **Radios:** 1 per 2.6 persons. **Telephones:** 1 per 1.2 persons. **Daily newspaper circ.** (1986): 491 per 1,000 pop.

Health: Life expectancy at birth (1989): 74 male; 82 female. **Births** (per 1,000 pop. 1989): 12 **Deaths** (per 1,000 pop. 1989): 10 **Natural increase:** .2%. **Physicians:** 1 per 620 persons. **Infant mortality** (per 1,000 live births 1989): 6.9.

Education (1989): Literacy: 99%. **Years compulsory:** 9; attendance 100%.

Major International Organizations: Many UN specialized agencies (though not a member).

Embassy: 2900 Cathedral Ave. NW 20008; 745-7900.

Switzerland, the Roman province of Helvetia, is a federation of 23 cantons (20 full cantons and 6 half cantons), 3 of which in 1291 created a defensive league and later were joined by other districts. Voters in the French-speaking part of Canton Bern voted for self-government, 1978; Canton Jura was created Jan. 1, 1979.

In 1648 the Swiss Confederation obtained its independence from the Holy Roman Empire. The cantons were joined under a federal constitution in 1848, with large powers of local control retained by each canton.

Switzerland has maintained an armed neutrality since 1815, and has not been involved in a foreign war since 1515. Switzerland is a member of several UN agencies and of the European Free Trade Assoc. and has ties with the EC. It is also the seat of many UN and other international agencies.

Switzerland is a leading world banking center; stability of the currency brings funds from many quarters.

Syria
Syrian Arab Republic
al-jamhouriya al Arabia as-Souriya

People: Population (1990 est.): 12,471,000. **Age distrib.** (%): 0–14: 49.3; 15–59: 44.2; 60+: 6.5. **Pop. density:** 170 per sq. mi. **Urban** (1988): 50%. **Ethnic groups:** Arab 90%, Kurd, Armenian, others. **Languages:** Arabic (official), Kurdish, Armenian, French, English. **Religions:** Sunni Moslem 74%, other Moslem 16%, Christian 10%.

Geography: Area: 71,498 sq. mi., the size of North Dakota. **Location:** At eastern end of Mediterranean Sea. **Neighbors:** Lebanon, Israel on W, Jordan on S, Iraq on E, Turkey on N. **Topography:** Syria has a short Mediterranean coastline, then

stretches E and S with fertile lowlands and plains, alternating with mountains and large desert areas. **Capital:** Damascus. **Cities** (1989 est.): Damascus 1,361,000; Aleppo 1,308,000; Homs 464,000.

Government: Type: Republic (under military regime). **Head of state:** Pres. Hafez al-Assad; b. Mar. 1930; in office: Feb. 22, 1971. **Head of government:** Prime Min. Mahmoud Zuabi; in office: Nov. 1, 1987. **Local divisions:** Damascus and 13 provinces. **Defense:** 11.9% of GNP (1987).

Economy: Industries: Oil products, textiles, cement, tobacco, glassware, sugar, brassware. **Chief crops:** Cotton, grain, olives, fruits, vegetables. **Minerals:** Oil, phosphate, gypsum. **Crude oil reserves** (1987): 1.4 bln. bbls. **Other resources:** Wool. **Arable land:** 28%. **Livestock** (1986): sheep: 13 mln., goats: 1 mln. **Electricity prod.** (1988): 9.1 bln. kwh. **Labor force:** 32% agric.; 29% ind. & comm.; 39% services.

Finance: Currency: Pound (Mar. 1990: 11.22 = $1 US). **Gross national product** (1986): $17.0 bln. **Imports** (1988): $2.2 bln.; partners: Iran, It., W. Ger., Fr. **Exports** (1988): $1.3 bln.; partners: It. 20%, Rom. 28%. **Tourists** (1987): receipts: $477 mln. **National budget** (1988): $4.6 bln. expenditures. **Consumer prices** (change in 1987): 59.5%.

Transport: Railway traffic (1987): 900 mln. passenger-km. **Motor vehicles:** in use (1987): 112,000 passenger cars, 127,000 comm. vehicles **Civil aviation** (1987): 847 mln. passenger-km; 5 airports with scheduled flights. **Chief ports:** Latakia, Tartus.

Communications: Television sets: 1 per 26.5 persons. **Radios:** 1 per 5.3 persons. **Telephones:** 1 per 17 persons. **Daily newspaper circ.** (1986): 19 per 1,000 pop.

Health: Life expectancy at birth (1989): 67 male; 69 female. **Births** (per 1,000 pop. 1989): 44. **Deaths** (per 1,000 1989): 6. **Natural increase:** 3.8%. **Hospital beds:** 1 per 870 persons. **Physicians:** 1 per 1,347 persons. **Infant mortality** (per 1,000 live births 1989): 40.

Education (1986): Literacy: 78% males. **Years compulsory:** 6; attendance: 94%.

Major International Organizations: UN (IMF, WHO, FAO), Arab League.

Embassy: 2215 Wyoming Ave. NW 20008; 232-6313.

Syria contains some of the most ancient remains of civilization. It was the center of the Seleucid empire, but later became absorbed in the Roman and Arab empires. Ottoman rule prevailed for 4 centuries, until the end of World War I.

The state of Syria was formed from former Turkish districts, made a separate entity by the Treaty of Sevres 1920 and divided into the states of Syria and Greater Lebanon. Both were administered under a French League of Nations mandate 1920-1941.

Syria was proclaimed a republic by the occupying French Sept. 16, 1941, and exercised full independence effective Jan. 1, 1944. Syria joined in the Arab invasion of Israel in 1948.

Syria joined with Egypt in Feb. 1958 in the United Arab Republic but seceded Sept. 30, 1961. The Socialist Baath party and military leaders seized power in Mar. 1963. The Baath, a pan-Arab organization, became the only legal party. The government has been dominated by members of the minority Alawite sect.

In the Arab-Israeli war of June 1967, Israel seized and occupied the Golan Heights area inside Syria, from which Israeli settlements had for years been shelled by Syria.

On Oct. 6, 1973, Syria joined Egypt in an attack on Israel. Arab oil states agreed in 1974 to give Syria $1 billion a year to aid anti-Israel moves. Some 30,000 Syrian troops entered Lebanon in 1976 to mediate in a civil war, and fought Palestinian guerrillas and, later, fought Christian militiamen. Syrian troops again battled Christian forces in Lebanon, Apr. 1981, ending a ceasefire that had been in place.

Following the June 6, 1982 Israeli invasion of Lebanon, Israeli planes destroyed 17 Syrian antiaircraft missile batteries in the Bekka Valley, June 9. Some 25 Syrian planes were downed during the engagement. Syrian and Israeli troops exchanged fire in central Lebanon. Israel and Syria agreed to a cease fire June 11. In 1983, Syria backed the PLO rebels who ousted Yasir Arafat's forces from Tripoli.

Syria's alleged role in promoting acts of international terrorism led to the breaking of diplomatic relations with Great Britain and the implementation of limited sanctions by the European Communities in 1986.

Taiwan

Republic of China

Chung-hua Min-kuo

People: Population (1990 est.): 20,454,000. **Age distrib.** (%): 0-14: 29.6; 15-59: 53.2; 60+: 8.1. **Pop. density:** 1,460 per sq. mi. **Urban** (1987): 72%. **Ethnic groups:** Taiwanese 85%, Chinese 14%. **Languages:** Mandarin Chinese (official), Taiwan, Hakka dialects. **Religions:** Buddhism, Taoism, Confucianism prevail.

Geography: Area: 13,885 sq. mi., about the size of Connecticut & New Hampshire combined. **Location:** Off SE coast of China, between E. and S. China Seas. **Neighbors:** Nearest is China. **Topography:** A mountain range forms the backbone of the island; the eastern half is very steep and craggy, the western slope is flat, fertile, and well-cultivated. **Capital:** Taipei. **Cities** (1989): Taipei (met.) 2,637,000; Kaohsiung 1,342,000; Taichung 715,000; Tainan 656,000.

Government: Type: One-party system. **Head of state and Nationalist Party chmn.:** Pres. Lee Teng-hui; b. Jan. 15, 1923; in office: Jan. 13, 1988. **Head of government:** Prime Min. Hau Pei-tsum; in office: May 2, 1990. **Local divisions:** 16 counties, 5 cities, Taipei & Kao-Hsiung. **Defense:** 4.6% of GNP (1987).

Economy: Industries: Textiles, clothing, electronics, processed foods, chemicals, plastics. **Chief crops:** Rice, bananas, pineapples, sugarcane, sweet potatoes, peanuts. **Minerals:** Coal, limestone, marble. **Crude oil reserves** (1987): 10 mln. bbls. **Arable land:** 25%. **Livestock** (1986): pigs: 6.6 mln. **Fish catch** (1988): 1.2 mln. metric tons. **Electricity prod.** (1988): 71.6 bln. kwh. **Crude steel prod.** (1988): 8.3 mln. metric tons. **Labor force:** 17% agric.; 41% ind. & comm.; 42% services.

Finance: Currency: New Taiwan dollar (June 1990: 27.02 = $1 US). **Gross national product** (1988): $119.1 bln. **Per capita GNP** (1988): $6,200. **Imports** (1989): $52.5 bln.; partners: U.S. 27%, Jap. 30%. **Exports** (1989): $66.1 bln.; partners: U.S. 39%, Jap. 13%, Hong Kong 8%. **Tourists** (1987): $1.6 bln. receipts. **National budget** (1988): $15.6 bln.

Transport: Motor vehicles: in use (1988): 1.5 mln. passenger cars, 524,000 commercial vehicles. **Civil Aviation** (1988): 17.6 bln. passenger-km; 9 airports. **Chief ports:** Kaohsiung, Keelung, Hualien, Taichung.

Communications: Television sets: 1 per 3.2 persons. **Radios:** 1 per 1.5 persons. **Telephones:** 1 per 3.0 persons. **Daily newspaper circ.** (1987): 179 per 1,000 pop.

Health: Life expectancy at birth (1986): 70.0 male; 75.9 female. **Births** (per 1,000 pop. 1989): 16. **Deaths** (per 1,000 pop. 1989): 5. **Natural increase:** 1.1%. **Physicians:** 1 per 1,010 persons. **Hospital beds:** 1 per 227 persons. **Infant mortality** (per 1,000 live births 1987): 6.3.

Education (1986): **Literacy:** 90%. Years compulsory 9; attendance 99%.

Large-scale Chinese immigration began in the 17th century. The island came under mainland control after an interval of Dutch rule, 1620-62. Taiwan (also called Formosa) was ruled by Japan 1895-1945. Two million Kuomintang supporters fled to Taiwan in 1949. Both the Taipei and Peking governments consider Taiwan an integral part of China. Taiwan has rejected Pekings efforts at reunification, but unofficial dealings with the mainland are growing more flexible.

The U.S. upon its recognition of the People's Republic of China, Dec. 15, 1978, severed diplomatic ties with Taiwan. It maintains the unofficial American Institute in Taiwan, while Taiwan has established the Coordination Council for North American Affairs in Washington, D.C.

Land reform, government planning, U.S. aid and investment, and free universal education have brought huge advances in industry, agriculture, and mass living standards. In 1987, martial law was lifted after 38 years.

The Penghu (Pescadores), 50 sq. mi., pop. 120,000, lie between Taiwan and the mainland. **Quemoy** and **Matsu,** pop. (1980) 61,000 lie just off the mainland.

Tanzania

United Republic of Tanzania

Jamhuri ya Mwungano wa Tanzania

People: Population (1990 est.) 26,070,000. **Pop. density:** 67 per sq. mi. **Urban** (1988): 18%. **Ethnic groups:** African. **Languages:** Swahili, English are official. **Religions:** Moslems 33%, Christians 33%, traditional beliefs 33%.

Geography: Area: 364,886 sq. mi., more than twice the size of California. **Location:** On coast of E. Africa. **Neighbors:** Kenya, Uganda on N, Rwanda, Burundi, Zaire on W, Zambia, Malawi, Mozambique on S. **Topography:** Hot, arid central plateau, surrounded by the lake region in the W, temperate highlands in N and S, the coastal plains. Mt. Kilimanjaro, 19,340 ft., is highest in Africa. **Capital:** Dar-es-Salaam. **Cities** (1986): Dar-es-Salaam 1.4 mln.

Government: Type: Republic. **Head of state:** Pres. Ali Hassan Mwinyi; b. May 8, 1925; in office: Nov. 5, 1985. **Head of government:** Prime Min. Joseph Warioba. **Local divisions:** 25 regions (20 on mainland). **Defense:** 3.4% of GNP (1985).

Economy: Industries: Food processing, clothing. **Chief crops:** Sisal, cotton, coffee, tea, tobacco. **Minerals:** Diamonds, gold, nickel. **Other resources:** Hides. **Arable land:** 6%. **Livestock** (1986): cattle: 14 mln.; goats: 6.4 mln.; sheep: 4.1 mln. **Fish catch** (1986): 309,000 metric tons. **Electricity prod.** (1988): 870 mln. kwh. **Labor force:** 90% agric., 10% ind., comm. & govt.

Finance: Currency: Shilling (Mar. 1990: 193 = $1 US). **Gross national product** (1987): $4.9 bln. **Per capita GNP** (1987): $258. **Imports** (1988): $800 mln.; partners: UK 14%, Jap. 12%, W. Ger. 10%. **Exports** (1988): $276 mln.; partners: W. Ger. 15%, UK 13%. **Tourists** (1986): $11 mln. receipts. **National budget** (1985): $1.0 mln. expenditures. **International reserves less gold** (Jan. 1990): $54.2 mln. **Consumer prices** (change in 1989): 24.5%.

Transport: Motor vehicles: in use (1986): 49,000 passenger cars; 33,000 comm. vehicles. **Civil aviation** (1988): $249 mln. passenger-km; 19 airports. **Chief ports:** Dar-es-Salaam, Mtwara, Tanga.

Communications: Radios: 1 per 12 persons. **Telephones:** 1 per 186 persons. **Daily newspaper circ.** (1988): 8 per 1,000 pop.

Health: Life expectancy at birth (1989): 49 male; 54 female. **Births** (per 1,000 pop. 1989): 50. **Deaths** (per 1,000 pop. 1989): 16. **Natural increase:** 3.4%. **Hospital beds** (1984): 22,800. **Physicians** (1984): 1,065. **Infant mortality** (per 1,000 live births 1989): 110.

Education (1987): **Literacy:** 85%. **Attendance:** 87% attend primary school.

Major International Organizations: UN and all of its specialized agencies, OAU, Commonwealth of Nations.

Embassy: 2139 R. St. NW 20008; 939-6125.

The Republic of Tanganyika in E. Africa and the island Republic of Zanzibar, off the coast of Tanganyika, joined into a single nation, the United Republic of Tanzania, Apr. 26, 1964. Zanzibar retains internal self-government.

Tanganyika. Arab colonization and slaving began in the 8th century AD; Portuguese sailors explored the coast by about 1500. Other Europeans followed.

In 1885 Germany established German East Africa of which Tanganyika formed the bulk. It became a League of Nations mandate and, after 1946, a UN trust territory, both under Britain. It became independent Dec. 9, 1961, and a republic within the Commonwealth a year later.

In 1967 the government set on a socialist course; it nationalized all banks and many industries. The government also ordered that Swahili, not English, be used in all official business. Nine million people have been moved into cooperative villages.

Tanzanian forces drove Idi Amin from Uganda, Mar., 1979.

Zanzibar, the Isle of Cloves, lies 23 mi. off the coast of Tanganyika; its area is 640 sq. mi. The island of **Pemba,** 25 mi. to the NE, area 380 sq. mi., is included in the administration. The total population (1985 est.) is 571,000.

Chief industry is the production of cloves and clove oil of which Zanzibar and Pemba produce the bulk of the world's supply.

Zanzibar was for centuries the center for Arab slave-traders. Portugal ruled for 2 centuries until ousted by Arabs around 1700.

Zanzibar became a British Protectorate in 1890; independence came Dec. 10, 1963. Revolutionary forces overthrew the Sultan Jan. 12, 1964. The new government ousted Western diplomats and newsmen, slaughtered thousands of Arabs, and nationalized farms. Union with Tanganyika followed, 1964. The ruling parties of Tanganyika and Zanzibar were united in 1977, as political tension eased.

Thailand
Kingdom of Thailand
Muang Thai or Prathet Thai

People: Population (1990 est.): 54,890,000. **Age distrib.** (%): 0–14: 36.2; 15–59: 58.1; 60+: 5.7. **Pop. density:** 277 per sq. mi. **Urban** (1985): 20%. **Ethnic groups:** Thais 75%, Chinese 14%, others 11%. **Languages:** Thai, regional dialects. **Religions:** Buddhist 95%, Moslem 4%.

Geography: Area: 198,456 sq. mi., about the size of Texas. **Location:** On Indochinese and Malayan Peninsulas in S.E. Asia. **Neighbors:** Myanmar on W. Laos on N, Cambodia on E, Malaysia on S. **Topography:** A plateau dominates the NE third of Thailand, dropping to the fertile alluvial valley of the Chao Phraya R. in the center. Forested mountains are in N, with narrow fertile valleys. The southern peninsula region is covered by rain forests. **Capital:** Bangkok. **Cities** (1980 est.): Bangkok (met.): 4.7 mln.

Government: Type: Constitutional monarchy. **Head of state:** King Bhumibol Adulyadej; b. Dec. 5, 1927; in office: June 9, 1946. **Head of government:** Prime Min. Chatichai Choonhavan; in office: Aug. 2, 1988. **Local divisions:** 73 provinces. **Defense:** 3.7% of GNP (1987).

Economy: Industries: Textiles, mining, wood products. **Chief crops:** Rice (a major export), corn tapioca, sugarcane. **Minerals:** Antimony, tin (among largest producers), tungsten, iron, gas. **Other resources:** Forests (teak is exported), rubber. **Arable land:** 34%. **Livestock** (1987): cattle: 4.9 mln.; pigs: 4.2 mln. **Fish catch** (1988): 2.1 mln. metric tons. **Electricity prod.** (1988): 27.0 bln. kwh. **Labor force:** 59% agric.; 26% ind. & comm.; 10% serv.; 8% govt.

Finance: Currency: Baht (Mar. 1990: 25.98 = $1 US). **Gross national product** (1988): $52.2 bln. **Per capita income** (1988): $771. **Imports** (1986): $19.7 bln.; partners: Jap. 24%, U.S. 13%. **Exports** (1986): $11.6 bln.; partners: Jap. 14%, U.S. 17%, Sing. 14%. **Tourists** (1987): $1.9 mln. receipts. **National budget** (1988): $9.4 bln. **International reserves less gold** (Mar. 1990): $11.0 bln. **Gold:** 2.47 mln. oz t. **Consumer prices** (change in 1989): 5.4%.

Transport: Railway traffic (1987): 9.5 bln. passenger-km. **Motor vehicles:** in use (1986): 545,000 passenger cars, 856,000 comm. vehicles. **Civil aviation** (1987): 13.4 bln. passenger-km; 23 airports with scheduled flights. **Chief ports:** Bangkok, Sattahip.

Communication: Television sets: 1 per 11 persons. **Radios:** 1 per 5.7 persons. **Telephones:** 1 per 53 persons. **Daily newspaper circ.** (1985): 50 per 1,000 pop.

Health: Life expectancy at birth (1989): 62 male; 68 female. **Births** (per 1,000 pop. 1989): 20 **Deaths** (per 1,000 pop. 1989): 7. **Natural increase:** 1.3%. **Hospital beds:** 1 per 627 persons. **Physicians:** 1 per 5,564 persons. **Infant mortality** (per 1,000 live births 1989): 50.

Education (1988): **Literacy:** 89%. **Years compulsory:** 6; attendance 96%.

Major International Organizations: UN (GATT, World Bank). **Embassy:** 2300 Kalorama Rd. NW 20008; 483-7200.

Thais began migrating from southern China in the 11th century. Thailand is the only country in SE Asia never taken over by a European power, thanks to King Mongkut and his son King Chulalongkorn who ruled from 1851 to 1910, modernized the country, and signed trade treaties with both Britain and France. A bloodless revolution in 1932 limited the monarchy.

Japan occupied the country in 1941. After the war, Thailand followed a pro-West foreign policy.

The military took over the government in a bloody 1976 coup. Kriangsak Chomanan, prime minister resigned, Feb. 1980, under opposition over soaring inflation, oil price increases, labor unrest and growing crime.

Vietnamese troops have crossed the border and been repulsed by Thai forces in the 1980s.

Togo
Republic of Togo
République Togolaise

People: Population (1990 est.): 3,566,000. **Age distrib.** (%): 0–14: 49.8; 15–59: 44.6; 60+: 5.6. **Pop. density:** 158 per sq. mi. **Urban** (1987): 23%. **Ethnic groups:** Ewe 35%, Mina 6%, Kabye 22%. **Languages:** French (official), others. **Religions:** Traditional 58%, Christian 22%, Moslem 20%.

Geography: Area: 21,622 sq. mi., slightly smaller than West Virginia. **Location:** On S coast of W. Africa. **Neighbors:** Ghana on W, Burkina Faso on N, Benin on E. **Topography:** A range of hills running SW-NE splits Togo into 2 savanna plains regions. **Capital:** Lomé. **Cities** (1985 est.): Lomé 300,000.

Government: Type: Republic; one-party presidential regime. **Head of state:** Pres. Gnassingbe Eyadema; b. Dec. 26, 1937; in office: Apr. 14, 1967. **Local divisions:** 21 prefectures.

Economy: Industries: Textiles, shoes. **Chief crops:** Coffee, cocoa, yams, manioc, millet, rice. **Minerals:** Phosphates. **Arable land:** 26%. **Electricity prod.** (1988): 155 mln. kwh. **Labor force:** 67% agric.; 15% industry.

Finance: Currency: CFA franc (Mar. 1990: 284 = $1 US). **Gross national product** (1987): $1.3 bln. **Per capita income** (1985): $240. **Imports** (1986): $300 mln.; partners: Fr., U.K., W. Ger. **Exports** (1986): $235 mln.; partners: Neth., Fr., W. Ger. **Tourists** (1987): $21 mln. receipts. **International reserves less gold** (Jan. 1990): $285 mln. **Gold:** 13,000 oz t. **Consumer prices** (change in 1989): .08%.

Transport: Railway traffic (1987): 105 mln. passenger-km. **Motor vehicles:** in use (1988): 47,000 passenger cars, 22,000 comm. vehicles. **Chief ports:** Lomé.

Communications: Television sets: 1 per 152 persons. **Radios:** 1 per 5.0 persons. **Telephones:** 1 per 255 persons. **Daily newspaper circ.** (1988): 3 per 1,000 pop.

Health: Life expectancy at birth (1989): 53 male; 57 female. **Births** (per 1,000 pop. 1989): 47. **Deaths** (per 1,000 pop. 1989): 13. **Natural increase:** 3.3%. **Hospital beds:** 1 per 752 persons. **Physicians:** 1 per 12,992 persons. **Infant mortality** (per 1,000 live births 1989): 113.

Education (1985): **Literacy:** 45% (males).

Major International Organizations: UN (GATT, IMF), OAU. **Embassy:** 2208 Massachusetts Ave. NW 20008; 234-4212.

The Ewe arrived in southern Togo several centuries ago. The country later became a major source of slaves. Germany took control in 1884. France and Britain administered Togoland as UN trusteeships. The French sector became the republic of Togo Apr. 27, 1960.

The population is divided between Bantus in the S and Hamitic tribes in the N. Togo has actively promoted regional integration, as a means of stimulating the economy.

Tonga
Kingdom of Tonga
Pule 'anga Tonga

People: Population (1989 est.): 108,000. **Age distrib.** (%): 0–14: 44.4; 15–59: 50.5; 60+: 5.1. **Pop. density:** 400 per sq. mi. **Ethnic groups:** Tongans 98%, other Polynesian, European. **Languages:** Tongan, English. **Religions:** Free Wesleyan 47%, Roman Catholics 14%, Free Church of Tonga 14%, Mormons 9%, Church of Tonga 9%.

Geography: Area: 270 sq. mi., smaller than New York City. **Location:** In western S. Pacific O. **Neighbors:** Nearest is Fiji, on W, New Zealand, on S. **Topography:** Tonga comprises 169 volcanic and coral islands, 45 inhabited. **Capital:** Nuku'alofa. **Cities** (1986): Nuku'alofa (met.) 29,000.

Government: Type: Constitutional monarchy. **Head of state:** King Taufa'ahau Tupou IV; b. July 4, 1918; in office: Dec. 16, 1965. **Head of government:** Prime Min. Fatafehi Tu'ipelehake; b. Jan. 7, 1922; in office: Dec. 16, 1965. **Local divisions:** 3 main island groups.

Economy: Industries: Tourism. **Chief crops:** Coconut products, bananas are exported. **Other resources:** Fish. **Arable land:** 25%. **Electricity prod.** (1988): 8 mln. kwh. **Labor force:** 45% agric, 27% services.

Finance: Currency: Pa'anga (Jan. 1990: 1.32 = $1 US). **Gross national product** (1987): $65 mln. **Imports** (1985): $41 mln.; partners: N Z 45%, Fiji 7%. **Exports** (1985): $7 mln.; partners: Aust. 29%, N Z 56%.

Transport: Motor vehicles: in use (1983): 443 passenger cars, 1,300 comm. vehicles. **Chief ports:** Nuku'alofa.

Communications: Radios: 1 per 1.2 persons. **Telephones:** 1 per 24 persons.

Health: Life expectancy at birth (1989): 69 male; 74 female. **Births** (per 1,000 pop. 1989): 27. **Deaths** (per 1,000 pop. 1989): 5. **Natural increase:** 2.2%. **Infant mortality** (per 1,000 live births 1989): 25.

Education (1988): **Literacy:** 93%. **Years compulsory:** 8. **Attendance:** 77%.

The islands were first visited by the Dutch in the early 17th century. A series of civil wars ended in 1845 with establishment of the Tupou dynasty. In 1900 Tonga became a British protectorate. On June 4, 1970, Tonga became independent and a member of the Commonwealth.

Trinidad and Tobago
Republic of Trinidad and Tobago

People: Population (1990 est.): 1,270,000. **Age distrib. (%):** 0–14: 32.9; 15–59: 58.7; 60+: 8.4. **Pop. density:** 636 per sq. mi. **Ethnic groups:** Africans 43%, East Indians 40%, mixed 14%. **Languages:** English (official). **Religions:** Roman Catholic 32%, Protestant 29%, Hindu 25%, Moslem 6%.

Geography: Area: 1,980 sq. mi., the size of Delaware. **Location:** Off southeast coast of Venezuela. **Neighbors:** Nearest is Venezuela on SW. **Topography:** Three low mountain ranges cross Trinidad E–W, with a well-watered plain between N and Central Ranges. Parts of E and W coasts are swamps. Tobago, 116 sq. mi., lies 20 mi. NE. **Capital:** Port-of-Spain. **Cities** (1989 met. est.): Port-of-Spain 300,000; San Fernando 50,000.

Government: Type: Parliamentary democracy. **Head of state:** Pres. Noor Hassanali; in office: Mar. 19, 1987. **Head of government:** Prime Min. Arthur Robinson; in office: Dec. 18, 1986. **Local divisions:** 8 counties, 3 municipalities.

Economy: Industries: Oil products, rum, cement, tourism. **Chief crops:** Sugar, cocoa, coffee, citrus fruits, bananas. **Minerals:** Asphalt, oil, **Crude oil reserves** (1987): 567 mln. bbls. **Arable land:** 14%. **Electricity prod.** (1988): 3.3 bln. kwh. **Labor force:** 18% construction-utilities, 14% manuf., mining, commerce, 47% services.

Finance: Currency: Dollar (Mar. 1990: 4.25 = $1 US). **Gross national product** (1987): $4.5 bln. **Per capita income** (1987): $3,731. **Imports** (1988): $1.1 bln.; partners: U.S. 41%, UK 11%. **Exports** (1988): $1.4 bln.; partners: U.S. 56%. **Tourists** (1988): $89 mln. receipts. **National budget** (1988): $2.1 bln. expenditures. **International reserves less gold** (Mar. 1990): $274 mln. **Gold:** 54,000 oz t. **Consumer prices** (change in 1989): 11.5%.

Transport: Motor vehicles: in use (1985): 241,000 passenger cars, 82,000 comm. vehicles. **Civil aviation:** (1986): 2.1 bln. passenger-km; 2 airports. **Chief ports:** Port-of-Spain.

Communications: Television sets: 1 per 3.6 persons. **Radios:** 1 per 3.1 persons. **Telephones:** 1 per 6.2 persons. **Daily newspaper circ.** (1988): 146 per 1,000 pop.

Health: Life expectancy at birth (1989): 68 male; 72 female. **Births** (per 1,000 pop. 1989): 27. **Deaths** (per 1,000 pop. 1989): 6. **Natural increase:** 2.1%. **Hospital beds:** 1 per 290 persons. **Physicians:** 1 per 1,055 persons. **Infant mortality** (per 1,000 pop. 1989): 15.

Education (1988): **Literacy:** 97%. **Years compulsory:** 8. **Major International Organizations:** UN (GATT, IMF, WHO), Commonwealth of Nations, OAS.

Embassy: 1708 Massachusetts Ave. NW 20036; 467-6490.

Columbus sighted Trinidad in 1498. A British possession since 1802, Trinidad and Tobago won independence Aug. 31, 1962. It became a republic in 1976. The People's National Movement party has held control of the government since 1956.

The nation is one of the most prosperous in the Caribbean. Oil production has increased with offshore finds. Middle Eastern oil is refined and exported, mostly to the U.S.

In July 1990, some 120 Moslem extremists captured the parliament building and TV station and took about 50 hostages including Prime Minister Arthur Robinson, who was beaten, shot in the legs, and tied to explosives. After a 6-day siege, the rebels surrendered. (*See Chronology*).

Tunisia
Republic of Tunisia
al Jumhuriyah at-Tunisiyah

People: Population (1990 est.): 8,094,000. **Age distrib. (%)** 0–14: 39.0; 15–59: 54.2; 60+: 6.8. **Pop. density:** 125 per sq. mi. **Ethnic groups:** Arab 98%. **Languages:** Arabic (official), French. **Religions:** Moslem 99%.

Geography: Area: 63,170 sq. mi., about the size of Missouri. **Location:** On N coast of Africa. **Neighbors:** Algeria on W, Libya on E. **Topography:** The N is wooded and fertile. The central coastal plains are given to grazing and orchards. The S is arid, approaching Sahara Desert. **Capital:** Tunis. **Cities** (1984 est.) Tunis 1,000,000, Sfax 475,000.

Government: Type: Republic. **Head of state:** Pres. Gen. Zine al-Abidine Ben Ami; b. Sept 3, 1936; in office: Nov. 7, 1987. **Head of government:** Prime Min. Hamed Karoui; in office: Sept. 27, 1989. **Local divisions:** 23 governorates. **Defense:** 3.1% of GNP (1987).

Economy: Industries: Food processing, textiles, oil products, construction materials, tourism. **Chief crops:** Grains, dates, olives, citrus fruits, figs, vegetables, grapes. **Minerals:** Phosphates, iron, oil, lead, zinc. **Crude oil reserves** (1987): 1.7 bln. bbls. **Arable land:** 20%. **Livestock** (1986): sheep: 5.4 mln.; goats: 1 mln. **Fish catch** (1988): 99,000 metric tons. **Electricity prod.** (1988): 4.2 bln. kwh. **Crude steel prod.** (1986): 188,000 metric tons. **Labor force:** 35% agric.; 22% industry; 11% serv.

Finance: Currency: Dinar (Mar. 1990: .99 = $1 US). **Gross national product** (1987): $9.6 bln. **Per capita income** (1986) $1,163. **Imports** (1989): $4.3 bln.; partners: Fr. 26%, It. 12%. **Exports** (1989): $2.9 bln.; partners: It. 17%, Fr. 26%, W. Ger. 10%, U.S. 19%. **Tourists** (1987): $672 mln. receipts. **National budget** (1987): $3.4 bln. expenditures. **International reserves less gold** (Mar. 1990): $916 mln. **Gold:** 187,000 oz t. **Consumer prices** (change in 1989): 7.4%.

Transport: Railway traffic (1988): 630 mln. passenger-km. **Motor vehicles:** in use (1987): 271,000 passenger cars, 182,000 comm. vehicles; **Civil aviation:** (1987): 2.3 bln. passenger-km; 6 airports. **Chief ports:** Tunis, Sfax, Bizerte.

Communications: Television sets: 1 per 15 persons. **Radios:** 1 per 4.7 persons. **Telephones:** 1 per 24 persons. **Daily newspaper circ.** (1987): 30 per 1,000 pop.

Health: Life expectancy at birth (1989): 68 male; 71 female. **Births** (per 1,000 pop. 1989): 29. **Deaths** (per 1,000 pop. 1989): 6. **Natural increase:** 2.3%. **Hospital beds:** 1 per 482 persons. **Physicians:** 1 per 2,198 persons. **Infant mortality** (per 1,000 pop. live births 1989): 44.

Education (1985): **Literacy:** 46%. **Years compulsory:** 8; attendance 85%.

Major International Organizations: UN, Arab League, OAU. **Embassy:** 1515 Massachusetts Ave. NW 20005; 862-1850.

Site of ancient Carthage, and a former Barbary state under the suzerainty of Turkey, Tunisia became a protectorate of France under a treaty signed May 12, 1881. The nation became independent Mar. 20, 1956, and ended the monarchy the following year. Habib Bourguiba has headed the country since independence.

Although Tunisia is a member of the Arab League, Bourguiba in the 1960s urged negotiations to end Arab-Israeli disputes and was denounced by other members.

Tunisia survived a Libyan-engineered raid against the southern mining center of Gafsa, Jan. 1980.

Turkey
Republic of Turkey
Turkiye Cumhuriyeti

People: Population (1990 est.): 56,549,000. **Age distrib. (%):** 0–14: 38.5; 15–59: 54.9; 60+: 6.6. **Pop. density:** 183 per sq. mi. **Urban** (1987): 55%. **Ethnic groups:** Turks 85%, Kurds 12%. **Languages:** Turkish (official), Kurdish, Arabic. **Religions:** Moslem 98%, Christian, Jewish.

Geography: Area: 301,381 sq. mi., twice the size of California. **Location:** Occupies Asia Minor, between Mediterranean and Black Seas. **Neighbors:** Bulgaria, Greece on W, USSR (Georgia, Armenia) on N, Iran on E, Iraq, Syria on S. **Topography:** Central Turkey has wide plateaus, with hot, dry summers and cold winters. High mountains ring the interior on all but N, with more than 20 peaks over 10,000 ft. Rolling plains are in W; mild, fertile coastal plains are in S, W. **Capital:** Ankara. **Cities** (1988 est.): Istanbul 5,800,000; Ankara 1,700,000; Izmir 2,300,000; Adana 1,700,000.

Government: Type: Republic. **Head of state:** Pres. Turgut Ozal; b. 1927; in office: Nov. 9, 1989. **Head of government:** Prime Min. Yildirim Akbulut; in office: Nov. 9, 1989. **Local divisions:** 67 provinces. **Defense:** 4.5% of GNP (1987).

Economy: Industries: Iron, steel, machinery, metal prods., cars, processed foods. **Chief crops:** Tobacco, cereals, cotton, barley, corn, fruits, potatoes, sugar beets. **Minerals:** Chromium, mercury, borate, copper, coal. **Crude oil reserves** (1987): 139 mln. bbls. **Other resources:** Wool, silk, forests. **Arable land:** 30%. **Livestock** (1987): cattle: 12.0 mln.; sheep: 40.4 mln. **Fish catch** (1987): 562,000 metric tons. **Electricity prod.** (1988): 46.9 bln. kwh. **Crude steel prod.** (1988): 8.0 mln. metric tons. **Labor force:** 56% agric.; 14% ind. and comm.; 30% serv.

Finance: Currency: Lira (Mar. 1990: 2,486 = $1 US). **Gross national product** (1987): $62 bln. **Per capita income** (1986): $1,160 **Imports** (1988): $14.3 bln.; partners: W. Ger. 16%, U.S. 10%. **Exports** (1988): $11.6 bln.; partners: W. Ger. 19%. **Tourists** (1987): $1 bln. receipts. **National budget** (1986): $10.7 bln. expenditures. **International reserves less gold** (Feb. 1990): $5.0 bln. **Gold:** 3.8 mln. oz t. **Consumer prices** (change in 1989): 69.6%.

Transport: Railway traffic (1987): 6.1 bln. passenger-km. **Motor vehicles:** in use (1987): 1.1 mln. passenger cars, 553,000 comm. vehicles. **Civil aviation** (1986): 2.6 bln. passenger-km; 14 airports with scheduled flights. **Chief ports:** Istanbul, Izmir, Mersin, Samsun.

Communications: Television sets: 1 per 6.8 persons. **Radios:** 1 per 7.8 persons. **Telephones:** 1 per 14 persons.

Health: Life expectancy at birth (1989): 63 male; 66 female. **Births** (per 1,000 pop. 1989): 30. **Deaths** (per 1,000 pop. 1989): 8. **Natural increase:** 2.2%. **Hospital beds:** 1 per 476 persons. **Physicians:** 1 per 1,360 persons. **Infant mortality** (per 1,000 live births 1989): 80.

Education (1988): **Literacy:** 70%. **Years compulsory:** 8; attendance 95%.

Major International Organizations: UN (GATT, WHO, IMF), NATO, OECD.

Embassy: 1606 23d St. NW 20008; 387-3200.

Ancient inhabitants of Turkey were among the worlds first agriculturalists. Such civilizations as the Hittite, Phrygian, and Lydian flourished in Asiatic Turkey (Asia Minor), as did much of Greek civilization. After the fall of Rome in the 5th century, Constantinople was the capital of the Byzantine Empire for 1,000 years. It fell in 1453 to Ottoman Turks, who ruled a vast empire for over 400 years.

Just before World War I, Turkey, or the Ottoman Empire, ruled what is now Syria, Lebanon, Iraq, Jordan, Israel, Saudi Arabia, Yemen, and islands in the Aegean Sea.

Turkey joined Germany and Austria in World War I and its defeat resulted in loss of much territory and fall of the sultanate. A republic was declared Oct. 29, 1923. The Caliphate (spiritual leadership of Islam) was renounced 1924.

Long embroiled with Greece over Cyprus, off Turkey's south coast, Turkey invaded the island July 20, 1974, after Greek officers seized the Cypriot government as a step toward unification with Greece. Turkey sought a new government for Cyprus, with Greek Cypriot and Turkish Cypriot zones. In reaction to Turkey's moves, the U.S. cut off military aid in 1975. Turkey, in turn, suspended the use of most U.S. bases. Aid was restored in 1978. There was a military takeover, Sept. 12, 1980.

Religious and ethnic tensions and active left and right extremists have caused endemic violence. Martial law, imposed in 1978, was lifted in 1984. The military formally transferred power to an elected parliament in 1983.

Tuvalu

People: Population (1990 est.): 9,000. **Pop. density:** 900 per sq. mi. **Ethnic group:** Polynesian. **Languages:** Tuvaluan, English. **Religions:** mainly Protestant.

Geography: Area: 10 sq. mi., less than one-half the size of Manhattan. **Location:** 9 islands forming a NW-SE chain 360 mi. long in the SW Pacific O. **Neighbors:** Nearest are Samoa on SE, Fiji on S. **Topography:** The islands are all low-lying atolls, nowhere rising more than 15 ft. above sea level, composed of coral reefs. **Capital:** Funafuti (pop. 1985): 2,800.

Government: Head of state: Queen Elizabeth II, represented by Gov.-Gen. Tupua Leupena; in office: Mar. 1, 1986. **Head of government:** Prime Min. Bikenibeu Paeniu; in office: Oct. 16, 1989. **Local divisions:** 8 island councils on the permanently inhabited islands.

Economy: Industries: Copra. **Chief crops:** Coconuts. **Labor force:** Approx. 1,500 Tuvaluans work overseas in the Gilberts' phosphate industry, or as overseas seamen.

Finance: Currency: Australian dollar.

Transport: Chief port: Funafuti.

Health: (including former Gilbert Is.) **Life expectancy at birth** (1989): 60 male; 63 female. **Births** (per 1,000 pop. 1989): 27. **Deaths** (per 1,000 pop. 1989): 10. **Natural increase:** 1.7%. **Infant mortality** (per 1,000 live births 1989) : 30.

Education (1985): **Literacy:** 96%.

The Ellice Islands separated from the British Gilbert and Ellice Islands colony, 1975, and became independent Tuvalu Oct. 1, 1978.

Britain and New Zealand provide extensive economic aid.

Uganda
Republic of Uganda

People: Population (1990 est.): 17,593,000. **Age distrib.** (%): 0–14: 48.5; 15–59: 47.3; 60+: 4.2. **Pop. density:** 180 per sq. mi. **Urban** (1984): 14%. **Ethnic groups:** Bantu, Nilotic, Nilo-Hamitic, Sudanic tribes. **Languages:** English (official), Luganda, Swahili. **Religions:** Christian 63%, Moslem 6%, traditional beliefs.

Geography: Area: 93,354 sq. mi., slightly smaller than Oregon. **Location:** In E. Central Africa. **Neighbors:** Sudan on N, Zaire on W, Rwanda, Tanzania on S, Kenya on E. **Topography:** Most of Uganda is a high plateau 3,000-6,000 ft. high, with high Ruwenzori range in W (Mt. Margherita 16,750 ft.), volcanoes in SW, NE is arid, W and SW rainy. Lakes Victoria, Edward, Albert form much of borders. **Capital:** Kampala. **Cities** (1988): Kampala 331,000.

Government: Type: Military. **Head of state:** Pres. Yoweri Kaguta Museveni; b. 1944; in office: Jan. 29, 1986. **Head of government:** Prime Min. Samson Kisekka; in office: Jan. 3, 1986. **Local divisions:** 10 provinces, 34 districts. **Defense:** 1% of GNP (1984).

Economy: Chief Crops: Coffee, cotton, tea, corn, bananas, sugar. **Minerals:** Copper, cobalt. **Arable land:** 23%. **Livestock** (1987): cattle: 5.2 mln.; goats: 3.3 mln.; sheep: 1.3 mln. **Fish catch** (1986): 212,000 metric tons. **Electricity prod.** (1988): 312 mln. kwh. **Labor force:** 90% agric.

Finance: Currency: Shilling (Mar. 1990: 379 = $1 US). **Gross national product** (1987): $3.6 bln. **Per capita GNP** (1987): $220. **Imports** (1988): $499 mln.; partners: Kenya 24%, U.K. 17%. **Exports** (1988): $272 mln.; partners: U.S. 27%, U.K. 18%. **National budget** (1988): $790 mln. expenditures. **International reserves less gold** (Jan. 1990): $30.9 mln. **Consumer prices** (change in 1989): 66%.

Transport: Motor vehicles: in use (1988): 32,000 passenger cars, 6,000 comm. vehicles.

Communications: Television sets: 1 per 178 persons. **Radios:** 1 per 46 persons. **Telephones:** 1 per 255 persons. **Daily newspaper circ.** (1984): 2 per 1,000 pop.

Health: Life expectancy at birth (1989): 49 male; 51 female. **Births** (per 1,000 pop. 1989): 49. **Deaths** (per 1,000 pop. 1989): 15. **Natural increase:** 3.4%. **Hospital beds** (1983): 19,650. **Physicians** (1983): 655. **Infant mortality** (per 1,000 live births 1989): 99.

Education (1989): **Literacy:** 52%. About 50% attend primary school.

Major International Organizations: UN (GATT, WHO, IMF), OAU, Commonwealth of Nations.
Embassy: 5909 16th St. NW 20011; 726-7100.

Britain obtained a protectorate over Uganda in 1894. The country became independent Oct. 9, 1962, and a republic within the Commonwealth a year later. In 1967, the traditional kingdoms, including the powerful Buganda state, were abolished and the central government strengthened.

Gen. Idi Amin seized power from Prime Min. Milton Obote in 1971. As many as 300,000 of his opponents were reported killed in subsequent years. Amin was named president for life in 1976. In 1972 Amin expelled nearly all of Uganda's 45,000 Asians. In 1973 the U.S. withdrew all diplomatic personnel.

Amid worsening economic and domestic crises, Uganda's troops exchanged invasion attacks with long-standing foe Tanzania, 1978 to 1979. Tanzanian forces, coupled with Ugandan exiles and rebels, ended the dictatorial rule of Amin, Apr. 11, 1979.

Union of Soviet Socialist Republics
Soyuz Sovetskykh Sotsialisticheskikh Respublic

People: Population (1990 est.): 290,939,000. **Age distrib.** (%): 0–19: 25.5; 20-59: 61.0; 60+: 13.5. **Pop. density:** 33 per sq. mi. **Urban** (1988): 66%. **Ethnic groups:** Russians 52% Ukrainians 16%, Uzbeks 5%, Byelorussians 4%, many others. **Languages:** Slavic (Russian, Ukrainian, Byelorussian, Polish), Altaic (Turkish, etc.), other Indo-European, Uralian, Caucasian. **Religions:** Russian Orthodox 18%, Moslem 9%, non-religious or atheist 70%.

Geography: Area: 8,649,496 sq. mi., the largest country in the world, nearly 2½ times the size of the U.S. **Location:** Stretches from E. Europe across N Asia to the Pacific O. **Neighbors:** Finland, Poland, Czechoslovakia, Hungary, Norway, Romania on W, Turkey, Iran, Afghanistan, China, Mongolia, N. Korea on S. **Topography:** Covering one-sixth of the earth's land area, the USSR contains every type of climate except the distinctly tropical, and has a varied topography.

The European portion is a low plain, grassy in S, wooded in N with Ural Mtns. on the E. Caucasus Mts. on the S. Urals stretch N-S for 2,500 mi. The Asiatic portion is also a vast plain, with mountains on the S and in the E; tundra covers extreme N, with forest belt below; plains, marshes are in W, desert in SW. **Capital:** Moscow. **Cities** (1989 est.): Moscow 8.5 mln.; Leningrad 4.8 mln.; Kiev 2.4 mln.; Tashkent 2.1 mln.; Kharkov 1.5 mln.; Baku 1.7 mln.; Gorky 1.4 mln.; Novosibirsk 1.4 mln.; Minsk 1.5 mln.; Kuibyshev 1.2 mln.; Sverdlovsk 1.3 mln.

Government: Type: Federal union. **Head of state:** Exec. Pres. Mikhail S. Gorbachev; b. Mar. 2, 1931; in office: Mar. 15, 1990. **Head of government:** Premier Nikolai I. Ryzhkov; b. 1929; in office: Sept. 27, 1985. **Local divisions:** 15 union republics, within which are 20 autonomous republics, 6 krays (territories), 123 oblasts (regions), 8 autonomous oblasts. **Defense:** 15-17% of GNP (1988).

Economy: Industries: Steel, machinery, machine tools, vehicles, chemicals, cement, textiles, appliances, paper. **Chief crops:** Grain, cotton, sugar beets, potatoes, vegetables, sunflowers. **Minerals:** Manganese, mercury, potash, bauxite, cobalt, chromium, copper, coal, gold, lead, molybdenum, nickel, phosphates, silver, tin, tungsten, zinc, oil (59%), potassium salts. **Crude oil reserves** (1987): 60 bln. bbls. **Other resources:** Forests (25% of world reserves). **Arable land:** 11%. **Livestock** (1989): cattle: 118 mln.; sheep: 142 mln.; pigs: 77 mln.; goats 142 mln. **Fish catch** (1989): 10.9 mln. metric tons. **Electricity prod.** (1988): 1,730 bln. kwh. **Crude steel prod.** (1988): 164 mln. metric tons. **Labor force:** 22% agric.; 29% industry, 26% services.

Finance: Currency: Ruble (Jan. 1990: 1.00 = $1.61 US). **Gross national product** (1988): $2.5 trl. **Per capita income** (1987): $3,000. **Imports** (1988): $107.3 bln.; partners: E. Ger. 10%, Pol. 7%, Czech. 8%, Bulg. 8%. **Exports** (1988): $110.7 bln.; partners: E. Ger. 10%, Pol. 8%, Bulg. 8%, Czech. 8%. **National budget** (1989): $310 bln. expenditures. **Tourists** (1987): receipts: $198 mln.

Transport: Railway traffic (1987): 402 bln. passenger-km. **Motor vehicles:** in use (1980): 9.2 mln. passenger cars, 7.9 mln. comm. vehicles; manuf. (1982): 1.3 mln. passenger cars; 874,000 comm. vehicles. **Civil aviation** (1988): 213 bln. passenger-km; 52 airports with scheduled flights. **Chief ports:** Leningrad, Odessa, Murmansk, Kaliningrad, Archangelsk, Riga, Vladivostok.

Communications: Television sets: 1 per 3.2 persons. **Radios:** 1 per 1.5 persons. **Telephones:** 1 per 6.7 persons. **Daily newspaper circ.** (1986): 345 per 1,000 pop.

Health: Life expectancy at birth (1989): 64 male; 74 female. **Births** (per 1,000 pop. 1989): 18. **Deaths** (per 1,000 pop. 1989): 11. **Natural increase:** .8%. **Hospital beds:** 1 per 72 persons. **Physicians:** 1 per 259 persons. **Infant mortality** (per 1,000 live births 1989): 25.2.

Education (1989): **Literacy:** 99%. Most receive 11 years of schooling.

Major International Organizations: UN (ILO, UNESCO, WHO), Warsaw Pact.
Embassy: 1125 16th St. NW 20036; 628-7551.

The USSR is nominally a federation consisting of 15 union republics, the largest being the Russian Soviet Federated Socialist Republic. Many of the republics experienced unrest in 1989 and 1990, with several demanding freedom from Moscow. Pres. Gorbachev warned that the unrest posed an "enormous danger" to the USSR. By Sept. 1990, 13 of the 15 Soviet republics had made some move toward greater autonomy.

Beginning in 1939 the USSR by means of military action and negotiation overran contiguous territory and independent republics, including all or part of Lithuania, Latvia, Estonia, Poland, Czechoslovakia, Romania, Germany, Finland, Tannu Tuva, and Japan. Census figures released in 1989 showed a 9.3 percent increase in the Soviet population in the past decade, with the largest increases in the central Asian republics. The figures also showed an increase in persons leaving rural areas to live in cities. The union republics are:

Republic	Area sq. mi.	Pop. (1988 est.)
Russian SFSR	6,592,800	146,000,000
Ukrainian SSR	233,100	51,377,000
Uzbek SSR	172,700	19,569,000
Kazakh SSR	1,049,200	16,470,000
Byelorussian SSR	80,200	10,141,000
Azerbaijan SSR	33,400	6,921,000
Georgian SSR	26,911	5,297,000
Tadzhik SSR	54,019	4,969,000
Moldavian SSR	13,012	4,224,000
Kirghiz SSR	76,642	4,238,000
Lithuanian SSR	26,173	3,682,000
Armenian SSR	11,306	3,459,000
Turkmen SSR	188,417	3,455,000
Latvian SSR	24,695	2,673,000
Estonian SSR	17,413	1,571,000

The **Russian Soviet Federated Socialist Republic** contains over 50% of the population of the USSR and includes 76% of its territory. It extends from the old Estonian, Latvian, and Finnish borders and the Byelorussian and Ukrainian lines on the W, to the shores of the Pacific, and from the Arctic on the N to the Black and Caspian seas and the borders of Kazakh SSR, Mongolia, and Manchuria on the S. Siberia encompasses a large part of the RSFSR area. Capital: Moscow.

Boris N. Yeltsin, a critic of the slow pace of national renewal, was elected President of the SFSR in May, 1990. He called for economic and political sovereignty for the republic.

Parts of eastern and western Siberia have been transformed by steel mills, huge dams, oil and gas industries, electric railroads, and highways.

The **Ukraine**, the most densely populated of the republics, borders on the Black Sea, with Poland, Czechoslovakia, Hungary, and Romania on the W and SW. Capital: Kiev.

The Ukraine contains the arable black soil belt, the chief wheat-producing section of the Soviet Union. Sugar beets, potatoes, and livestock are important.

The Donets Basin has large deposits of coal, iron and other metals. There are chemical and machine industries and salt mines.

There is a strong independence movement in the western part of the republic.

Byelorussia (White Russia). Capital: Minsk. Chief industries include machinery, tools, appliances, tractors, clocks, cameras, steel, cement, textiles, paper, leather, glass. Main crops are grain, flax, potatoes, sugar beets.

Azerbaijan boasts near Baku, the capital, important oil fields. Its natural wealth includes deposits of iron ore, cobalt, etc. A high-yield winter wheat is grown, as are fruits. It produces iron, steel, cement, fertilizers, synthetic rubber, electrical and chemical equipment. It borders on Iran and Turkey. In 1988, clashes were reported between Moslem Azerbaijanis and the minority Christian ethnic Armenians. Soviet troops were sent to quell the ethnic civil war between the 2 factions, Jan. 1990.

Georgia, in the western part of Transcaucasia, contains the largest manganese mines in the world. There are rich timber resources and coal mines. Basic industries are food, textiles, iron, steel. Grain, tea, tobacco, fruits, grapes are grown. Capital: Tbilisi (Tiflis). Despite massive party and government purges since 1972, illegal private enterprise and Georgian nationalist feelings persist; attempts to repress them have led to violence; in Apr. 1989, soviet troops attacked nationalist demonstrators, killing some 20 persons.

Armenia is mountainous, sub-tropical, extensively irrigated. Copper, zinc, aluminum, molybdenum, and marble are mined. Instrument making is important. Armenia has sought a reunification with the Nagorno-Karabakh autonomous region of neighboring Azerbaijan. On Dec. 7, 1988, an earthquake struck in the north killing over 55,000 and leaving 500,000 homeless. An international relief effort was mounted. Soviet troops were sent to quell the ethnic civil war with Azerbaijan, Jan. 1990. Capital: Erevan.

Uzbekistan, most important economically of the Central Asia republics, produces 67% of USSR cotton, 50% of rice, 33% of silk, 34% of astrakhan, 85% of hemp. Industries include iron, steel, cars, tractors, TV and radio sets, textiles, food. Mineral wealth includes coal, sulphur, copper, and oil. Capital: Tashkent.

Turkmenistan in Central Asia, produces cotton, maize, carpets, chemicals. Minerals: oil, coal, sulphur, barite, lime, salt, gypsum. The Kara Kum desert occupies 80% of the area. Capital: Ashkhabad.

Tadzhikistan borders on China and Afghanistan. Over half the population are Tadzhiks, mostly Moslems, speaking an Iranian dialect. Chief occupations are farming and cattle breeding. Cotton, grain, rice, and a variety of fruits are grown. Heavy industry, based on rich mineral deposits, coal and hydroelectric power, has replaced handicrafts. Tadzhikistan declared sovereignty in 1990. Capital: Dushanbe.

Kazakhstan extends from the lower reaches of the Volga in Europe to the Altai Mtns. on the Chinese border. It has vast deposits of coal, oil, iron, tin, copper, lead, zinc, etc. Fish for its canning industry are caught in Lake Balkhash and the Caspian and Aral seas. The capital is Alma-Ata. About 50% of the population is Russian or Ukrainian, working in the virgin-grain lands opened up after 1954, and in the growing industries. Capital: Alma-Ata.

Kirghizia is the eastern part of Soviet Central Asia, on the frontier of Xinjiang, China. The people breed cattle and horses and grow tobacco, cotton, rice, sugar beets. Industries include machine and instrument making, chemicals. Capital: Frunze.

Moldavia, in the SW part of the USSR, is a fertile black earth plain bordering Romania and includes Bessarabia. It is an agricultural region that grows grains, fruits, vegetables, and tobacco. Textiles, wine, food and electrical equipment industries have been developed. Capital: Kishinev. The region was taken from Romania in 1940; the people speak Romanian.

Lithuania, on the Baltic, was an independent nation, 1918-40, when it was annexed by the USSR along with Latvia and Estonia. Produces cattle, hogs, electric motors, and appliances. The capital is Vilnius (Vilna). The supreme Soviet agreed to allow Lithuania to develop a market-oriented economy. Lithuania formally declared its independence from the Soviet Union Mar. 11, 1990. Soviet forces began large-scale maneuvers Mar. 18; border controls were tightened Mar. 21. Pres. Gorbachev warned Lithuania to annul its declaration of independence or face "grave consequences." The Soviets cut off oil and gas supplies Apr. 19. Lithuania agreed to suspend independence May 17, and the oil and gas supplies were renewed.

Latvia, on the Baltic, is the main producer electric railway passenger cars and long distance telephone exchanges in the USSR. From 1917, Latvia was occupied by the Soviets, and Germans. The Aug. 1939 Soviet-German agreement assigned it to the Soviet sphere of influence. It was officially accepted as part of the USSR on Aug. 5, 1940. It attempted to establish independence, 1990. Capital: Riga.

Estonia, also on the Baltic, has textiles, shipbuilding, timber, roadmaking and mining equipment industries and a shale oil refining industry. Capital: Tallinn. The 3 Baltic states were provinces of imperial Russia before World War I, were independent

nations between World Wars I and II, but were conquered by the USSR in 1940. The supreme soviety agreed to allow Estonia to develop a market-oriented economy. Estonia declared itself an "occupied territory," and proclaimed itself a free nation Mar. 1990.

Economy. Almost all legal economic enterprises are state-owned. A huge illegal black market plays an important role in distribution.

The USSR is rich in natural resources; distant Siberian reserves are being exploited. Its heavy industry is 2d only to the U.S. It leads the world in oil and steel production. Consumer industries have lagged comparatively. Agricultural output has expanded, but in poor crop years the USSR has been forced to make huge grain purchases from the West. Shortages and rationing of basic food products periodically occur.

Industrial growth has dropped, due to short falls in oil, coal, and steel industries.

History. Slavic tribes began migrating into Russia from the W in the 5th century AD. The first Russian state, founded by Scandinavian chieftains, was established in the 9th century, centering in Novgorod and Kiev.

In the 13th century the Mongols overran the country. It recovered under the grand dukes and princes of Muscovy, or Moscow, and by 1480 freed itself from the Mongols. Ivan the Terrible was the first to be formally proclaimed Tsar (1547). Peter the Great (1682-1725), extended the domain and in 1721, founded the Russian Empire.

Western ideas and the beginnings of modernization spread through the huge Russian empire in the 19th and early 20th centuries. But political evolution failed to keep pace.

Military reverses in the 1905 war with Japan and in World War I led to the breakdown of the Tsarist regime. The 1917 Revolution began in March with a series of sporadic strikes for higher wages by factory workers. A provisional democratic government under Prince Georgi Lvov was established but was quickly followed in May by the second provisional government, led by Alexander Kerensky. The Kerensky government and the freely-elected Constituent Assembly were overthrown in a communist coup led by Vladimir Ilyich Lenin Nov. 7.

Lenin's death Jan. 21, 1924, resulted in an internal power struggle from which Joseph Stalin eventually emerged the absolute ruler of Russia. Stalin secured his position at first by exiling opponents, but from the 1930s to 1953, he resorted to a series of "purge" trials, mass executions, and mass exiles to work camps. These measures resulted in millions of deaths, according to most estimates.

Germany and the USSR signed a non-aggression pact Aug. 1939; Germany launched a massive invasion of the Soviet Union, June 1941. Notable heroic episode was the "900 days" siege of Leningrad, lasting to Jan. 1944, and causing a million deaths; the city was never taken. Russian winter counterthrusts, 1941 to '42 and 1942 to '43, stopped the German advance. Turning point was the failure of German troops to take and hold Stalingrad, Sept. 1942 to Feb. 1943. With British and U.S. Lend-Lease aid and sustaining great casualties, the Russians drove the German forces from eastern Europe and the Balkans in the next 2 years.

After Stalin died, Mar. 5, 1953, Nikita Khrushchev was elected first secretary of the Central Committee. In 1956 he condemned Stalin. "De-Stalinization" of the country on all levels was effected after Stalin's body was removed from the Lenin-Stalin tomb in Moscow.

Under Khrushchev the open antagonism of Poles and Hungarians toward domination by Moscow was brutally suppressed in 1956. He advocated peaceful co-existence with the capitalist countries, but continued arming the USSR with nuclear weapons. He aided the Cuban revolution under Fidel Castro but withdrew Soviet missiles from Cuba during confrontation by U.S. Pres. Kennedy, Sept.-Oct. 1962.

Khrushchev was suddenly deposed, Oct. 1964, and replaced as party first secretary by Leonid I. Brezhnev.

In Aug. 1968 Russian, Polish, East German, Hungarian, and Bulgarian military forces invaded Czechoslovakia to put a curb on liberalization policies of the Czech government.

The USSR in 1971 continued heavy arms shipments to Egypt. In July 1972 Egypt ordered most of the 20,000 Soviet military personnel in that country to leave. When Egypt and Syria attacked Israel in Oct. 1973, the USSR launched huge arms airlifts to the 2 Arab nations. In 1974, the Soviet replenished the arms used or lost by the Syrians in the 1973 war, and continued some shipments to Egypt.

Massive Soviet military aid to North Vietnam in the late 1960s and early 1970s helped assure communist victories throughout Indo-China. Soviet arms aid and advisers were sent to several African countries in the 1970s, including Algeria, Angola, Somalia, and Ethiopia.

More than 130,000 Jews and over 40,000 ethnic Germans were allowed to emigrate from the USSR in the 1970s, following pressure from the West. Many leading figures in the arts also left the country.

In 1979, Soviet forces entered Afghanistan to support that government against rebels. In 1988, the Soviets announced withdrawal of their troops, which will end a futile 8-year war.

There were serious food shortages reported in the early 1980s and a new agricultural program, covering 1982-90, was announced amid Soviet fears of becoming dependent on foreign, especially U.S., grain imports.

Mikhail Gorbachev was chosen Gen. Secy. of the Communist Party, Mar. 1985. He was the youngest member of the Politburo and signaled a change in Soviet leadership from those whose attitudes were shaped by Stalinism and World War II.

He held 4 summit meetings with U.S. Pres. Reagan. In 1987, in Washington, an INF treaty was signed.

The Soviets received worldwide criticism for their secrecy regarding the Apr. 25, 1986 accident at the Chernobyl nuclear plant.

In 1987, Gorbachev initiated a program of reforms, including expanded freedoms and the democratization of the political process, through openness (*glasnost*) and restructuring (*perestroika*). The reforms were opposed by some Eastern bloc countries and many old-line communists in the USSR. In 1989, the first Soviet Parliament was held since 1918.

Gorbachev faced ethnic and nationalist unrest in the republics in 1989 and 1990.

Government. The communist party leadership dominated all areas of National life since 1917.

In Mar. 1990, the National Parliament repealed the party's political monopoly, revamped and strengthened the presidency, and elected Gorbachev to a 5-year term as a new-style executive president.

United Arab Emirates
Ittihād al-Imarat al-Arabiyah

People: Population (1990 est.): 2,250,000. **Pop. density:** 45 per sq. mi. **Ethnic groups:** Arab, Iranian, Pakistani, Indian. **Languages:** Arabic (official), Farsi, English, Hindi, Urdu. **Religions:** Moslem 94%, Christian, Hindu.

Geography: Area: 32,000 sq. mi., the size of Maine. **Location:** On the S shore of the Persian Gulf. **Neighbors:** Qatar on N, Saudi Ar. on W, S, Oman on E. **Topography:** A barren, flat coastal plain gives way to uninhabited sand dunes on the S. Hajar Mtns. are on E. **Capital:** Abu Dhabi. **Cities** (1984 est.): Abu Dhabi 537,000; Dubai 278,000.

Government: Type: Federation of emirates. **Head of state:** Pres. Zaid ibn Sultan an-Nahayan b. 1923; in office: Dec. 2, 1971. **Head of government:** Prime Min. Rashid ibn Said al-Maktum; in office: June 25, 1979. **Local divisions:** 7 autonomous emirates: Abu Dhabi, Ajman, Dubai, Fujaira, Ras al-Khaimah, Sharjah, Umm al-Qaiwain. **Defense:** 5.7% of GNP (1985).

Economy: Chief crops: Vegetables, dates, limes. **Minerals:** Oil. **Crude oil reserves** (1987): 33 bln. bbls. **Arable land:** 1%. **Electricity prod.** (1988): 14.5 bln. kwh. **Labor force:** 5% agric.; 85% ind. and commerce; 5% serv.; 5% gvt.

Finance: Currency: Dirham (Apr. 1990: 3.67 = $1 US). **Gross national product** (1987): $22 bln. **Per capita GNP** (1987) $11,900. **Imports** (1988): $8.5 bln.; partners: Jap. 18%, UK 11%, W. Ger. 6%. **Exports** (1987): $15.0 bln.; partners: Jap. 36%, U.S. 7%, Fr. 10%. **International reserves less gold** (Feb. 1990): $4.7 bln. **Gold:** 817,000 oz t.

Transport: Motor Vehicles (1985): 62,000 passenger cars; 17,000 commercial vehicles. **Chief ports:** Dubai, Abu Dhabi.

Communications: Television sets: 1 per 12 persons. **Radios:** 1 per 4.7 persons. **Telephones:** 1 per 4.3 persons.

Health: Life Expectancy at Birth (1990): 68 male, 72 female. **Hospital beds:** 1 per 267 persons. **Physicians:** 1 per 659 persons. **Infant mortality** (per 1,000 live births 1989): 29%.

Education (1989): **Literacy:** 68%. **Years Compulsory:** ages 6-12.

Major International Organizations: UN (World Bank, IMF, ILO), Arab League, OPEC. **Embassy:** 600 New Hampshire Ave. NW 20037; 338-6500.

The 7 "Trucial Sheikdoms" gave Britain control of defense and foreign relations in the 19th century. They merged to become an independent state Dec. 2, 1971.

The Abu Dhabi Petroleum Co. was fully nationalized in 1975. Oil revenues have given the UAE one of the highest per capita GNPs in the world. International banking has grown in recent years.

United Kingdom of Great Britain and Northern Ireland

People: Population (1990 est.): 57,121,000. **Age distrib.** (%): 0-14: 18.9; 15-59: 60.5; 60+: 19.6. **Pop. density:** 601 per sq. mi. **Urban** (1985): 92.5%. **Ethnic groups:** English 81.5%, Scottish 9.6%, Irish 2.4%, Welsh 1.9%, Ulster 1.8%; West Indian, Indian, Pakistani over 2%; others. **Languages:** English, Welsh spoken in western Wales; Gaelic. **Religions:** Church of England, Roman Catholic.

Geography: Area: 94,226 sq. mi., slightly smaller than Oregon. **Location:** Off the NW coast of Europe, across English Channel, Strait of Dover, and North Sea. **Neighbors:** Ireland to W, France to SE. **Topography:** England is mostly rolling land, rising to Uplands of southern Scotland; Lowlands are in center of Scotland, granite Highlands are in N. Coast is heavily indented, especially on W. British Isles have milder climate than N Europe, due to the Gulf Stream, and ample rainfall. Severn, 220 mi., and Thames, 215 mi., are longest rivers. **Capital:** London. **Cities** (1987 est.): London 6,700,000; Birmingham 1,008,000; Glasgow 715,000; Leeds 710,000; Sheffield 532,000; Liverpool 476,000; Manchester 451,000; Edinburgh 440,000; Bradford 463,000; Bristol 384,000.

Government: Type: Constitutional monarchy. **Head of state:** Queen Elizabeth II; b. Apr. 21, 1926; in office: Feb. 6, 1952. **Head of government:** Prime Min. Margaret Thatcher; b. Oct. 13, 1925; in office: May 4, 1979. **Local divisions:** England and Wales: 47 non-metro counties, 6 metro counties, Greater London; Scotland: 9 regions, 3 island areas; N. Ireland: 26 districts. **Defense:** 4.7% of GDP (1987).

Economy: Industries: Steel, metals, vehicles, shipbuilding, banking, textiles, chemicals, electronics, aircraft, machinery, distilling. **Chief crops:** Grains, sugar beets, fruits, vegetables. **Minerals:** Coal, tin, oil, gas, limestone, iron, salt, clay, chalk, gypsum, lead, silica. **Crude oil reserves** (1987): 5.8 bln. bbls. **Arable land:** 30%. **Livestock** (1987): cattle: 12.6 mln.; pigs: 7.9 mln.; sheep: 38.7 mln. **Fish catch** (1987): 716,000 metric tons. **Electricity prod.** (1988): 344 bln. kwh. **Crude steel prod.** (1988): 19.0 mln. metric tons. **Labor force:** 1.7% agric.; 24% manuf. & eng.; 52% services.

Finance: Currency: Pound (June 1990: .56 = $1 US). **Gross national product** (1988): $758 bln. **Per capita GNP** (1988): $13,329. **Imports** (1989): $197 bln.; partners: W. Ger. 17%, U.S. 12%, Fr. 7%, Neth. 8%. **Exports** (1989): $152 bln.; partners: U.S. 13%, W. Ger. 10%, Fr. 8%, Neth. 8%. **Tourists** (1987): receipts $10.2 bln.; **National budget** (1988): $320 bln. expenditures. **International reserves less gold** (Mar. 1990): $34 bln. **Gold:** 19.0 mln. oz t. **Consumer prices** (change in 1989): 7.8%.

Transport: Railway traffic (1987): 32.1 bln. passenger-km. **Motor vehicles:** in use (1989): 18.4 mln. passenger cars, 2.7 mln. comm. vehicles. **Civil aviation** (1987): 59.1 bln. passenger-km: 47 airports with scheduled flights. **Chief ports:** London, Liverpool, Glasgow, Southampton, Cardiff, Belfast.

Communications: Television sets: 1 per 3 persons. **Radios:** 1 per 1 person. **Telephones:** 1 per 1.9 persons. **Daily newspaper circ.** (1989): 443 per 1,000 pop.

Health: Life expectancy at birth: (1989): 72 male; 78 female. **Births:** (per 1,000 pop. 1989): 13.2. **Deaths:** (per 1,000 pop. 1989): 12 **Natural increase:** 0.2%. **Hospital beds:** 1 per 138 persons. **Physicians:** 1 per 611 persons. **Infant mortality:** (per 1,000 live births 1989): 13.3.

Education (1989): **Literacy:** 99%. **Years compulsory:** 12; attendance 99%.

Major International Organizations: UN all of and its specialized agencies, NATO, EC, OECD.

Embassy: 3100 Massachusetts Ave. NW 20008; 462-1340.

The United Kingdom of Great Britain and Northern Ireland comprises England, Wales, Scotland, and Northern Ireland.

Queen and Royal Family. The ruling sovereign is Elizabeth II of the House of Windsor, born Apr. 21, 1926, elder daughter of King George VI. She succeeded to the throne Feb. 6, 1952, and was crowned June 2, 1953. She was married Nov. 20, 1947, to Lt. Philip Mountbatten, born June 10, 1921, former Prince of Greece. He was created Duke of Edinburgh, Earl of Merioneth, and Baron Greenwich, and given the style H.R.H., Nov. 19, 1947; he was given the title Prince of the United Kingdom and Northern Ireland Feb. 22, 1957. Prince Charles Philip Arthur George, born Nov. 14, 1948, is the Prince of Wales and heir apparent. His son, William Philip Arthur Louis, born June 21, 1982, is second in line to the throne.

Parliament is the legislative governing body for the United Kingdom, with certain powers over dependent units. It consists of 2 houses: The **House of Lords** includes 763 hereditary and 314 life peers and peeresses, certain judges, 2 archbishops and 24 bishops of the Church of England. Total membership is over 1,000. The **House of Commons** has 650 members, who are elected by direct ballot and divided as follows: England 516; Wales 36; Scotland 71; Northern Ireland 12.

Resources and Industries. Great Britain's major occupations are manufacturing and trade. Metals and metal-using industries contribute more than 50% of the exports. Of about 60 million acres of land in England, Wales and Scotland, 46 million are farmed, of which 17 million are arable, the rest pastures.

Large oil and gas fields have been found in the North Sea. Commercial oil production began in 1975. There are large deposits of coal.

The railroads, nationalized since 1948, have been reduced in total length, with a basic network, Dec. 1978, of 11,123 mi. The merchant marine totaled 126,000 gross registered tons in 1982.

A year-long coal strike costing some $3 bln. ended March 1985. The issue of the closing of uneconomic mines was unresolved.

Britain imports all of its cotton, rubber, sulphur, 80% of its wool, half of its food and iron ore, also certain amounts of paper, tobacco, chemicals. Manufactured goods made from these basic materials have been exported since the industrial age began. Main exports are machinery, chemicals, woolen and synthetic textiles, clothing, autos and trucks, iron and steel, locomotives, ships, jet aircraft, farm machinery, drugs, radio, TV, radar and navigation equipment, scientific instruments, arms, whisky.

Religion and Education. The Church of England is Protestant Episcopal. The queen is its temporal head, with rights of appointments to archbishoprics, bishoprics, and other offices. There are 2 provinces, Canterbury and York, each headed by an archbishop. The most famous church is Westminster Abbey (1050-1760), site of coronations, tombs of Elizabeth I, Mary of Scots, kings, poets, and of the Unknown Warrior.

The most celebrated British universities are Oxford and Cambridge, each dating to the 13th century. There are about 40 other universities.

History. Britain was part of the continent of Europe until about 6,000 BC, but migration of peoples across the English Channel continued long afterward. Celts arrived 2,500 to 3,000 years ago. Their language survives in Welsh, and Gaelic enclaves.

England was added to the Roman Empire in 43 AD. On the withdrawal of Roman legions in 410, waves of Jutes, Angles, and Saxons arrived from German lands. They contended with Danish raiders for control from the 8th through 11th centuries.

The last successful invasion was by French speaking Normans in 1066, who united the country with their dominions in France.

Opposition by nobles to royal authority forced King John to sign the Magna Carta in 1215, a guarantee of rights and the rule of law. In the ensuing decades, the foundations of the parliamentary system were laid.

English dynastic claims to large parts of France led to the Hundred Years War, 1338-1453, and the defeat of England. A long civil war, the War of the Roses, lasted 1455-85, and ended with the establishment of the powerful Tudor monarchy. A distinct English civilization flourished. The economy prospered over long periods of domestic peace unmatched in continental Europe. Religious independence was secured when the Church of England was separated from the authority of the Pope in 1534.

Under Queen Elizabeth I, England became a major naval power, leading to the founding of colonies in the new world and the expansion of trade with Europe and the Orient. Scotland was united with England when James VI of Scotland was crowned James I of England in 1603.

A struggle between Parliament and the Stuart kings led to a bloody civil war, 1642-49, and the establishment of a republic under the Puritan Oliver Cromwell. The monarchy was restored in 1660, but the "Glorious Revolution" of 1688 confirmed the sovereignty of Parliament: a Bill of Rights was granted 1689.

In the 18th century, parliamentary rule was strengthened. Technological and entrepreneurial innovations led to the Industrial Revolution. The 13 North American colonies were lost, but replaced by growing empires in Canada and India. Britain's role in the defeat of Napoleon, 1815, strengthened its position as the leading world power.

The extension of the franchise in 1832 and 1867, the formation of trade unions, and the development of universal public education were among the drastic social changes which accompanied the spread of industrialization and urbanization in the 19th century. Large parts of Africa and Asia were added to the empire during the reign of Queen Victoria, 1837-1901.

Though victorious in World War I, Britain suffered huge casualties and economic dislocation. Ireland became independent in 1921, and independence movements became active in India and other colonies.

The country suffered major bombing damage in World War II, but held out against Germany singlehandedly for a year after the fall of France in 1940.

Industrial growth continued in the postwar period, but Britain lost its leadership position to other powers. Labor governments passed socialist programs nationalizing some basic industries and expanding social security. The Thatcher government has however, tried to increase the role of private enterprise. In 1987, Margaret Thatcher became the first British leader in 160 years to be elected to a 3d consecutive term as prime minister.

Britain broke diplomatic relations with Libya, Apr. 22, 1984, 5 days after a policewoman was killed and 10 Libyan exile demonstrators wounded by machine-gun fire from within the Libyan embassy in London. The embassy occupants, including the killer, left Britain, Apr. 27.

Wales

The Principality of Wales in western Britain has an area of 8,019 sq. mi. and a population (1987 est.) of 2,836,000. Cardiff is the capital, pop. (1981 est.) 273,856.

England and Wales are administered as a unit. Less than 20% of the population of Wales speak both English and Welsh; about 32,000 speak Welsh solely. A 1979 referendum rejected, 4-1, the creation of an elected Welsh Assembly.

Early Anglo-Saxon invaders drove Celtic peoples into the mountains of Wales, terming them Waelise (Welsh, or foreign). There they developed a distinct nationality. Members of the ruling house of Gwynedd in the 13th century fought England but were crushed, 1283. Edward of Caernarvon, son of Edward I of England, was created Prince of Wales, 1301.

Scotland

Scotland, a kingdom now united with England and Wales in Great Britain, occupies the northern 37% of the main British island, and the Hebrides, Orkney, Shetland and smaller islands. Length, 275 mi., breadth approx. 150 mi., area, 30,405 sq. mi., population (1987 est.) 5,121,000.

The Lowlands, a belt of land approximately 60 mi. wide from the Firth of Clyde to the Firth of Forth, divide the farming region of the Southern Uplands from the granite Highlands of the North, contain 75% of the population and most of the industry. The Highlands, famous for hunting and fishing, have been opened to industry by many hydroelectric power stations.

Edinburgh, pop. (1986 est.) 439,000, is the capital. Glasgow, pop. (1986 est.) 733,000, is Britain's greatest industrial center. It is a shipbuilding complex on the Clyde and an ocean port. Aberdeen, pop. (1986 est.) 215,000, NE of Edinburgh, is a major port, center of granite industry, fish processing, and North Sea oil exploitation. Dundee, pop. (1986 est.) 177,000, NE of Edinburgh, is an industrial and fish processing center. About 90,000 persons speak Gaelic as well as English.

History. Scotland was called Caledonia by the Romans who battled early Celtic tribes and occupied southern areas from the 1st to the 4th centuries. Missionaries from Britain introduced Christianity in the 4th century; St. Columba, an Irish monk, converted most of Scotland in the 6th century.

The Kingdom of Scotland was founded in 1018. William Wallace and Robert Bruce both defeated English armies 1297 and 1314, respectively.

In 1603 James VI of Scotland, son of Mary, Queen of Scots, succeeded to the throne of England as James I, and effected the Union of the Crowns. In 1707 Scotland received representation in the British Parliament, resulting from the union of former separate Parliaments. Its executive in the British cabinet is the Secretary of State for Scotland. The growing Scottish National Party urges independence. A 1979 referendum on the creation of an elected Scotland Assembly was defeated.

There are 8 universities. Memorials of Robert Burns, Sir Walter Scott, John Knox, Mary, Queen of Scots draw many tourists, as do the beauties of the Trossachs, Loch Katrine, Loch Lomond and abbey ruins.

Industries. Engineering products are the most important industry, with growing emphasis on office machinery, autos, electronics and other consumer goods. Oil has been discovered offshore in the North Sea, stimulating on-shore support industries.

Scotland produces fine woolens, worsteds, tweeds, silks, fine linens and jute. It is known for its special breeds of cattle and sheep. Fisheries have large hauls of herring, cod, whiting. Whisky is the biggest export.

The **Hebrides** are a group of c. 500 islands, 100 inhabited, off the W coast. The Inner Hebrides include **Skye, Mull,** and **Iona,** the last famous for the arrival of St. Columba, 563 AD. The Outer Hebrides include **Lewis** and **Harris.** Industries include sheep raising and weaving. The **Orkney Islands,** c. 90, are to the NE. The capital is Kirkwall, on Pomona Is. Fish curing, sheep raising and weaving are occupations. NE of the Orkneys are the 200 **Shetland Islands,** 24 inhabited, home of Shetland pony. The Orkneys and Shetlands have become centers for the North Sea oil industry.

Northern Ireland

Six of the 9 counties of Ulster, the NE corner of Ireland, constitute Northern Ireland, with the parliamentary boroughs of Belfast and Londonderry. Area 5,463 sq. mi., 1987 est. pop. 1,575,000, capital and chief industrial center, Belfast, (1987 cen.) 303,000.

Industries. Shipbuilding, including large tankers, has long been an important industry, centered in Belfast, the largest port. Linen manufacture is also important, along with apparel, rope, and twine. Growing diversification has added engineering products, synthetic fibers, and electronics. They are large numbers of cattle, hogs, and sheep, potatoes, poultry, and dairy foods are also produced.

Government. An act of the British Parliament, 1920, divided Northern from Southern Ireland, each with a parliament and government. When Ireland became a dominion, 1921, and later a republic, Northern Ireland chose to remain a part of the United Kingdom. It elects 12 members to the British House of Commons.

During 1968-69, large demonstrations were conducted by Roman Catholics who charged they were discriminated against in voting rights, housing, and employment. The Catholics, a minority comprising about a third of the population, demanded abolition of property qualifications for voting in local elections. Violence and terrorism intensified, involving branches of the Irish Republican Army (outlawed in the Irish Republic), Protestant groups, police, and British troops.

A succession of Northern Ireland prime ministers pressed reform programs but failed to satisfy extremists on both sides. Over 2,000 were killed in over 15 years of bombings and shootings through 1988, many in England itself. Britain suspended the Northern Ireland parliament Mar. 30, 1972, and imposed direct British rule. A coalition government was formed in 1973 when moderates won election to a new one-house Assembly. But a Protestant general strike overthrew the government in 1974 and direct rule was resumed.

The turmoil and agony of Northern Ireland was dramatized in 1981 by the deaths of 10 imprisoned Irish nationalist hunger strikers in Maze Prison near Belfast. The inmates had starved themselves to death in an attempt to achieve status as political prisoners, but the British government refused to yield to their demands. In 1985, the Hillsborough agreement gave the Rep. of Ireland a voice in the governing of Northern Ireland; the accord was strongly opposed by Ulster loyalists.

Education and Religion. Northern Ireland is 2/3 Protestant, 1/3 Roman Catholic. Education is compulsory through age 15.

Channel Islands

The Channel Islands, area 75 sq. mi., est. pop. 1986 145,000, off the NW coast of France, the only parts of the one-time Dukedom of Normandy belonging to England, are **Jersey, Guernsey** and the dependencies of Guernsey — **Alderney, Brechou, Great Sark, Little Sark, Herm, Jethou and Lihou.** Jersey and Guernsey have separate legal existences and lieutenant governors named by the Crown. The islands were the only British soil occupied by German troops in World War II.

Isle of Man

The Isle of Man, area 227 sq. mi., 1986 est. pop. 64,000, is in the Irish Sea, 20 mi. from Scotland, 30 mi. from Cumberland. It is rich in lead and iron. The island has its own laws and a lieutenant governor appointed by the Crown. The Tynwald (legislature) consists of the Legislative Council, partly elected, and House of Keys, elected. Capital: Douglas. Farming, tourism (328,000 visitors in 1988), fishing (kippers, scallops) are chief occupations. Man is famous for the Manx tailless cat.

Gibraltar

Gibraltar, a dependency on the southern coast of Spain, guards the entrance to the Mediterranean. The Rock has been in British possession since 1704. The Rock is 2.75 mi. long, 3/4 of a mi. wide and 1,396 ft. in height; a narrow isthmus connects it with the mainland. Est. pop. 1987, 29,048.

In 1966 Spain called on Britain to give "substantial sovereignty" of Gibraltar to Spain and imposed a partial blockade. In 1967, residents voted for remaining under Britain. A new constitution, May 30, 1996, gave an elected House of Assembly more control in domestic affairs. A UN General Assembly resolution requested Britain to end Gibraltar's colonial status by Oct. 1, 1996. No settlement has been reached.

British West Indies

Swinging in a vast arc from the coast of Venezuela NE, then N and NW toward Puerto Rico are the Leeward Islands, forming a coral and volcanic barrier sheltering the Caribbean from the open Atlantic. Many of the islands are self-governing British possessions. Universal suffrage was instituted 1951-54; ministerial systems were set up 1956-1960.

The **Leeward Islands,** still associated with the UK are **Montserrat** (1980 pop. 11,600, area 32 sq. mi., capital Plymouth), the small **British Virgin Islands** (pop. 1987: 12,000), and **Anguilla** (pop. 1985: 7,000), the most northerly of the Leeward Islands.

The three **Cayman Islands,** a dependency, lie S of Cuba, NW of Jamaica. Pop. 23,000 (1987), most of it on Grand Cayman. It is a free port; in the 1970s Grand Cayman became a tax-free refuge for foreign funds and branches of many Western banks were opened there. Total area 102 sq. mi., capital Georgetown.

The **Turks and Caicos Islands,** at the SE end of the Bahama Islands, are a separate possession. There are about 30 islands, only 6 inhabited, 1987 pop. est. 9,000, area 193 sq. mi., capital Grand Turk. Salt, crayfish and conch shells are the main exports.

Bermuda

Bermuda is a British dependency governed by a royal governor and an assembly, dating from 1620, the oldest legislative body among British dependencies. Capital is Hamilton.

It is a group of 360 small islands of coral formation, 20 inhabited, comprising 20.6 sq. mi. in the western Atlantic, 580 mi. E of North Carolina. Pop., 1989 est., was 58,800 (about 61% of African descent). Density is high.

The U.S. has air and naval bases under long-term lease, and a NASA tracking facility.

Bermuda boasts many resort hotels. Receipts from tourists totalled $436 mln. in 1988. The government raises most revenue from import duties. Exports: petroleum products, medicine.

South Atlantic

Falkland Islands and Dependencies, a British dependency, lies 300 mi. E of the Strait of Magellan at the southern end of South America.

The Falklands or Islas Malvinas include about 200 islands, area 4,700 sq. mi., pop. (1980 est.) 1,800. Sheep-grazing is the main industry; wool is the principal export. There are indications of large oil and gas deposits. The islands are also claimed by Argentina though 97% of inhabitants are of British origin. Argentina invaded the islands Apr. 2, 1982. The British responded by sending a task force to the area, landing their main force on the Falklands, May 21, and forcing an Argentine surrender at Port Stanley, June 14. **South Georgia**, area 1,450 sq. mi., and the uninhabited **South Sandwich Is.** are dependencies of the Falklands.

British Antarctic Territory, south of 60° S lat., was made a separate colony in 1962 and comprises mainly the **South Shetland Islands**, the **South Orkneys** and **Graham's Land**. A chain of meteorological stations is maintained.

St. Helena, an island 1,200 mi. off the W coast of Africa and 1,800 E of South America, has 47 sq. mi. and est. pop., 1981 of 5,300. Flax, lace and rope making are the chief industries. After Napoleon Bonaparte was defeated at Waterloo the Allies exiled him to St. Helena, where he lived from Oct. 16, 1815, to his death, May 5, 1821. Capital is Jamestown.

Tristan da Cunha is the principal of a group of islands of volcanic origin, total area 40 sq. mi., half way between the Cape of Good Hope and South America. A volcanic peak 6,760 ft. high erupted in 1961. The 262 inhabitants were removed to England, but most returned in 1963. The islands are dependencies of St. Helena.

Ascension is an island of volcanic origin, 34 sq. mi. in area, 700 mi. NW of St. Helena, through which it is administered. It is a communications relay center for Britain, and has a U.S. satellite tracking center. Est. pop., 1976, was 1,179, half of them communications workers. The island is noted for sea turtles.

Hong Kong

A Crown Colony at the mouth of the Canton R. in China, 90 mi. S of Canton. Its nucleus is Hong Kong Is., 35½ sq. mi., acquired from China 1841, on which is located Victoria, the capital. Opposite is Kowloon Peninsula, 3 sq. mi. and Stonecutters Is., ¼ sq. mi., added, 1860. An additional 355 sq. mi. known as the New Territories, a mainland area and islands, were leased from China, 1898, for 99 years. Britain and China, Dec. 19, 1985, signed an agreement under which Hong Kong would be allowed to keep its capitalist system for 50 years after 1997, the year that the 99-year lease will expire. Total area of the colony is 409 sq. mi., with a population, 1989 est., of 5.7 million including fewer than 20,000 British. From 1949 to 1962 Hong Kong absorbed more than a million refugees from China.

Hong Kong harbor was long an important British naval station and one of the world's great trans-shipment ports.

Principal industries are textiles and apparel; also tourism, $4.2 bln. expenditures (1988), shipbuilding, iron and steel, fishing, cement, and small manufactures.

Spinning mills, among the best in the world, and low wages compete with textiles elsewhere and have resulted in the protective measures in some countries. Hong Kong also has a booming electronics industry.

British Indian Ocean Territory

Formed Nov. 1965, embracing islands formerly dependencies of Mauritius or Seychelles: the Chagos Archipelago (including Diego Garcia), Aldabra, Farquhar and Des Roches. The latter 3 were transferred to Seychelles, which became independent in 1976. Area 22 sq mi. No civilian population remains.

Pacific Ocean

Pitcairn Island is in the Pacific, halfway between South America and Australia. The island was discovered in 1767 by Carteret but was not inhabited until 23 years later when the mutineers of the Bounty landed there. The area is 18 sq. mi. and pop. 1983, was 61. It is a British colony and is administered by a British Representative in New Zealand and a local Council. The uninhabited islands of **Henderson**, **Ducie** and **Oeno** are in the Pitcairn group.

United States of America

People: Population (1990 est.): 250,372,000. **Age distrib.(%):** 0–14: 21.5; 15–59: 61.8; 60+: 16.7. **Pop. density:** 68 per sq. mi. **Urban** (1987): 76%.

Geography: 3,618,770 sq. mi. (incl. 50 states and D. of C.) about four-tenths the size of USSR; world's 4th largest country. Vast central plain, mountains in west, hills and low mountains in east. **Government:** Federal republic, strong democratic tradition. **Head of state:** George Bush; b. June 12, 1924; in office:

Jan. 20, 1989. **Administrative divisions:** 50 states and Dist. of Columbia. **Defense:** 5.7% of GNP (1988).

Economy: Minerals: Coal, copper, lead, molybdenum, phosphates, uranium, bauxite, gold, iron, mercury, nickel, potash, silver, tungsten, zinc. **Crude oil reserves** (1987): 27 bln. bbls. **Arable land:** 21%. **Livestock** (1988): cattle: 98 mln.; pigs: 56 mln.; sheep: 10.7 mln. **Fish catch** (1987): 3.1 mln. metric tons. **Electricity prod.** (1988): 2,900 bln. kwh. **Crude steel prod.** (1988): 90.7 mln. metric tons.

Finance: Gross national product (1988): 4.8 trl. **Per capita income** (1988): $16,444. **Imports** (1989): $492 bln.; partners: Can. 17%, Jap. 20%, Mex. 6%. **Exports** (1989): $363 bln.; partners: Can. 22%, Jap. 10%, Mex. 6%, UK 5%. **Tourists** (1987): receipts $14.7 bln. **International reserves less gold** (Mar. 1990): $65.2 bln. **Gold:** 261.0 mln. oz t. **Consumer prices** (change in 1989): 4.8%.

Transport: Railway traffic (1987): 19.2 bln. passenger-km. **Motor vehicles:** in use (1987): 139 mln. passenger cars, 40 mln. comm. vehicles. **Civil aviation** (1988): 629 bln. passenger-km; 834 airports with scheduled flights.

Communications: Television sets: 1 per 1.3 persons. **Radios:** 1 per 0.5 persons. **Telephones:** 1 per 1.9 persons. **Daily newspaper circ.** (1989): 255 per 1,000 pop.

Health: Life expectancy at birth (1989): 72 male; 79 female. **Births** (per 1,000 pop. 1989): 15. **Deaths** (per 1,000 pop. 1989): 9. **Natural increase:** .6%. **Hospital beds:** 1 per 188 persons. **Physicians:** 1 per 410 persons. **Infant mortality** (per 1,000 live births 1989): 10.0.

Major International Organizations: UN (GATT, IMF, WHO, FAO), OAS, NATO, OECD.

Education (1987): **Literacy:** 99%.

Uruguay
Oriental Republic of Uruguay
República Oriental del Uruguay

People: Population (1990 est.): 3,002,000. **Age distrib. (%):** 0–14: 26.9; 15–59: 57.7; 60+: 15.4. **Pop. density:** 43 per sq. mi. **Urban** (1985): 86.0%. **Ethnic groups:** Caucasians (Iberians, Italians) 89%, mestizos 10%, mulatto and black. **Languages:** Spanish. **Religions:** 66% Roman Catholic.

Geography: Area: 68,037 sq. mi., the size of Washington State. **Location:** In southern S. America, on the Atlantic O. **Neighbors:** Argentina on W, Brazil on N. **Topography:** Uruguay is composed of rolling, grassy plains and hills, well-watered by rivers flowing W to Uruguay R. **Capital:** Montevideo. **Cities** (1986 est.): Montevideo 1,246,000.

Government: Type: Republic. **Head of state:** Pres. Luis Alberto Lacalle; in office: Nov. 26, 1989. **Local divisions:** 19 departments. **Defense:** 2.5% of GNP (1987).

Economy: Industries: Meat-packing, metals, textiles, wine, cement, oil products. **Chief crops:** Corn, wheat, citrus fruits, rice, oats, linseed. **Arable land:** 8%. **Livestock** (1987): cattle: 9.9 mln.; sheep: 20.6 mln. **Fish catch** (1987): 134,000 metric tons. **Electricity prod.** (1988): 4.2 bln. kwh. **Labor force** 11% agric.; 19% manuf.; 21% serv.; 25% govt.

Finance: Currency: New Peso (May 1990: 969 = $1 US). **Gross national product** (1988): $7.5 bln. **Per capita income** (1986): $1,701. **Imports** (1988): $1.1 bln.; partners: EC 23%, Braz. 24%, Arg. 14%, U.S. 8%. **Exports** (1988): $1.4 bln.; partners: Braz. 17%, U.S. 14%, Arg. 14%, EC 30%. **Tourists** (1986): $259 mln. receipts. **National budget** (1987): $1.3 bln. expeditures. **International reserves less gold** (Jan. 1990): $464 mln. **Gold:** 2.60 mln. oz t. **Consumer prices** (change in 1989): 80.8%.

Transport: Railway traffic (1987): 140 mln. passenger-km. **Motor vehicles:** in use (1981): 281,000 passenger cars, 43,000 comm. vehicles. **Civil aviation** (1985): 240 mln. passenger-km; 7 airports. **Chief ports:** Montevideo.

Communications: Television sets: 1 per 5.9 persons. **Radios:** 1 per 1.7 persons. **Telephones:** 1 per 6.8 persons. **Daily newspaper circ.** (1985): 185 per 1,000 pop.

Health: Life expectancy at birth (1989): 68 male; 75 female. **Births** (per 1,000 pop. 1989): 17. **Deaths** (per 1,000 pop. 1989): 10. **Natural increase:** .7%. **Hospital beds:** 1 per 127 persons. **Physicians:** 1 per 447 persons. **Infant mortality** (per 1,000 live births 1989): 34.

Education (1984): **Literacy:** 96%.

Major International Organizations: UN (GATT, IMF, WHO), OAS.

Embassy: 1919 F St. NW 20006; 331-1313.

Spanish settlers did not begin replacing the indigenous Charrua Indians until 1624. Portuguese from Brazil arrived later, but Uruguay was attached to the Spanish Viceroyalty of Rio de la Plata in the 18th century. Rebels fought against Spain beginning in 1810. An independent republic was declared Aug. 25, 1825.

Liberal governments adopted socialist measures as far back as 1911. The state owns the power, telephone, railroad, cement, oil-refining and other industries.

Uruguay's standard of living was one of the highest in South America, and political and labor conditions among the freest. Economic stagnation, inflation, plus floods and drought in 1967 and a general strike in 1968 brought government attempts to strengthen the economy through devaluation of the peso and wage and price controls. But inflation continued in the 80's and the country asked international creditors to restructure $2.7 bln. in debt in 1983.

Tupamaros, leftist guerrillas drawn from the upper classes, increased terrorist actions in 1970. Violence continued and in Feb. 1973 Pres. Juan Maria Bordaberry agreed to military control of his administration. In June he abolished Congress and set up a Council of State in its place. By 1974 the military had apparently defeated the Tupamaros, using severe repressive measures. Bordaberry was removed by the military in a 1976 coup. Civilian government was restored to the country in 1985.

Vanuatu
Republic of Vanuatu
Ripablik Blong Vanuatu

People: Population (1989 est.): 150,000. **Population density:** 26 per sq. mi. **Ethnic groups:** Mainly Melanesian, some European, Polynesian, Micronesian. **Languages:** Bislama (national), French and English both official. **Religions:** Presbyterian 40%, Anglican 14%, Roman Catholic 16%, animist 15%.

Geography: Area: 5,700 sq. mi. **Location:** SW Pacific, 1,200 mi NE of Brisbane, Australia. **Topography:** dense forest with narrow coastal strips of cultivated land. **Capital:** Vila. **Cities:** Vila (1987): 15,000.

Government: Type: Republic. **Head of state:** Pres. Fred Timakata; in office: Jan. 12, 1989. **Head of gov't:** Prime Min. Rev. Walter Lini; in office: July 30, 1980.

Economy: Industries: Fish-freezing, meat canneries, tourism. **Chief crops:** Copra (38% of export), cocoa, coffee. **Minerals:** Manganese. **Other resources:** Forests, cattle. **Fish catch** (1987): 2.9 metric tons.

Finance: Currency: Australian dollar and Vanuatu franc (Mar. 1990: 120 vatu = $1 US). **Imports** (1987): $68 mln.; partners: Aus. 36%, Fr. 8%, Japan 13%. **Exports** (1987): $17 mln.; partners: Neth. 48%, Jap. 17%, Fr. 12%, Belg.-Lux. 14%.

Health: Life expectancy at birth (1989): 67 male, 71 female. **Infant mortality** (per 1,000 live births 1989): 37.

Education: Education not compulsory, but 85-90% of children of primary school age attend primary schools.

The Anglo-French condominium of the New Hebrides, administered jointly by France and Great Britain since 1906, became the independent Republic of Vanuatu on July 30, 1980.

Vatican City
The Holy See

People: Population (1989 est.): 750. **Ethnic groups:** Italians, Swiss. **Languages:** Italian, Latin.

Geography: Area: 108.7 acres. **Location:** In Rome, Italy. **Neighbors:** Completely surrounded by Italy.

Currency: Lira.

Apostolic Nunciature in U.S.: 3339 Massachusetts Ave. NW 20008; 333-7121.

The popes for many centuries, with brief interruptions, held temporal sovereignty over mid-Italy (the so-called Papal States), comprising an area of some 16,000 sq. mi., with a population in the 19th century of more than 3 million. This territory was incorporated in the new Kingdom of Italy, the sovereignty of the pope being confined to the palaces of the Vatican and the Lateran in Rome and the villa of Castel Gandolfo, by an Italian law, May 13, 1871. This law also guaranteed to the pope and his successors a yearly indemnity of over $620,000. The allowance, however, remained unclaimed.

A Treaty of Conciliation, a concordat and a financial convention were signed Feb. 11, 1929, by Cardinal Gasparri and Premier Mussolini. The documents established the independent state of Vatican City, and gave the Catholic religion special status in Italy. The treaty (Lateran Agreement) was made part of the Constitution of Italy (Article 7) in 1947. Italy and the Vatican reached preliminary agreement in 1976 on revisions of the concordat, that would eliminate Roman Catholicism as the state religion and end required religious education in Italian schools.

Vatican City includes St. Peter's, the Vatican Palace and Museum covering over 13 acres, the Vatican gardens, and neighboring buildings between Viale Vaticano and the Church. Thirteen buildings in Rome, outside the boundaries, enjoy extraterritorial rights; these buildings house congregations or officers necessary for the administration of the Holy See.

The legal system is based on the code of canon law, the apostolic constitutions and the laws especially promulgated for the Vatican City by the pope. The Secretariat of State represents the Holy See in its diplomatic relations. By the Treaty of Conciliation the pope is pledged to a perpetual neutrality unless his mediation is specifically requested. This, however, does not prevent the defense of the Church whenever it is persecuted.

The present sovereign of the State of Vatican City is the Supreme Pontiff John Paul II, Karol Wojtyla, born in Wadowice, Poland, May 18, 1920, elected Oct. 16, 1978 (the first non-Italian to be elected Pope in 456 years).

The U.S. restored formal relations in 1984 after the U.S. Congress repealed an 1867 ban on diplomatic relations with the Vatican.

Venezuela
Republic of Venezuela
Republica de Venezuela

People: Population (1990 est.): 19,753,000. **Age distrib. (%):** 0–14: 38.8; 15–59: 55.7; 60+: 5.5. **Pop. density:** 54 per sq. mi. **Urban** (1989): 83%. **Ethnic groups:** Mestizo 69%, white (Spanish, Portuguese, Italian) 20%, black 9%, Indian 2%. **Languages:** Spanish (official), Indian languages 2%. **Religions:** Roman Catholic 96%.

Geography: Area: 352,143 sq. mi., more than twice the size of California. **Location:** On the Caribbean coast of S. America. **Neighbors:** Colombia on W, Brazil on S, Guyana on E. **Topography:** Flat coastal plain and Orinoco Delta are bordered by Andes Mtns. and hills. Plains, called llanos, extend between mountains and Orinoco. Guyana Highlands and plains are S of Orinoco, which stretches 1,600 mi. and drains 80% of Venezuela. **Capital:** Caracas. **Cities** (1989 est.): Caracas 1,275,000; Maracaibo 1,179,000; Barquisimeto 702,000; Valencia 922,000.

Government: Type: Federal republic. **Head of state:** Pres. Carlos Andres Perez; b. Oct. 27, 1922; in office: Feb. 2, 1989. **Local divisions:** 20 states, 2 federal territories, federal district, federal dependency. **Defense:** 1.4% of GNP (1985).

Economy: Industries: Steel, oil products, textiles, containers, paper, shoes. **Chief crops:** Coffee, rice, fruits, sugar. **Minerals:** Oil (5th largest producer), iron (extensive reserves and production), gold. **Crude oil reserves** (1987): 55 bln. bbls. **Arable land:** 4%. **Livestock** (1986): cattle: 12.3 mln.; pigs: 2.8 mln. **Fish catch** (1988): 290,000 metric tons. **Electricity prod.** (1988): 51.9 bln. kwh. **Crude steel prod.** (1988): 3.6 mln. metric tons. **Labor force:** 15% agric.; 28% ind.; 56% services.

Finance: Currency: Bolivar (Apr. 1990: 43.56 = $1 US). **Gross national product** (1988): $47.3 bln. **Per capita income** (1985): $2,629. **Imports** (1989): $8.7 bln.; partners: U.S. 48%, W. Ger. 6%, Jap. 8%. **Exports** (1988): $10.1 bln.; partners: U.S. 25%, Neth Ant. 21%, Can. 9%. **Tourists** (1987): $409 mln. receipts. **National budget** (1987): $16.6 bln. expenditures. **International reserves less gold** (Mar. 1990): $4.0 bln. **Gold:** 11.46 mln. oz t. **Consumer prices** (change in 1989): 84.5%.

Transport: Railway traffic (1987): 22 mln. passenger-km. **Motor vehicles:** in use (1986): 2.3 mln. passenger cars, 1.2 mln. mm. vehicles. **Civil aviation** (1987): 3.5 mln. passenger-km; 29 airports with scheduled flights. **Chief ports:** Maracaibo, La Guaira, Puerto Cabello.

Communications: Television sets: 1 per 6.6 persons. **Radios:** 1 per 11 persons. **Telephones:** 1 per 2.3 persons. **Daily newspaper circ.** (1982): 120 per 1,000 pop.

Health: Life expectancy at birth (1989): 67 male; 73 female. **Births** (per 1,000 pop. 1989): 30. **Deaths** (per 1,000 pop. 1989): 6. **Natural increase:** 2.5%. **Hospital beds:** 1 per 384 persons. **Physicians:** 1 per 643 persons. **Infant mortality** (per 1,000 live births 1989): 38.

Education (1989): **Literacy:** 88%. **Years compulsory:** 8; attendance 82%.

Major International Organizations: UN (IMF, WHO, FAO), OAS, OPEC.

Embassy: 2445 Massachusetts Ave. NW 20008; 797-3800.

Columbus first set foot on the South American continent on the peninsula of Paria, Aug. 1498. Alonso de Ojeda, 1499, found Lake Maracaibo, called the land Venezuela, or Little Venice, because natives had houses on stilts. Venezuela was under Spanish domination until 1821. The republic was formed after secession from the Colombian Federation in 1830.

Military strongmen ruled Venezuela for most of the 20th century. They promoted the oil industry; some social reforms were implemented. Since 1959, the country has enjoyed progressive, democratically-elected governments.

Venezuela helped found the Organization of Petroleum Exporting States (OPEC). The government, Jan. 1, 1976, nationalized the oil industry with compensation. Development has begun of the Orinoco tar belt, believed to contain the world's largest oil reserves. Oil accounts for much of total export earnings and the economy suffered a severe cash crisis in the 1980s as the result of falling oil revenues.

The government has attempted to reduce dependence on oil.

Vietnam

Socialist Republic of Vietnam

Cong Hoa Xa Hoi Chu Nghia Viet Nam

People: Population (1990 est.): 68,488,000. **Age distrib.** (%): 0-14: 40.8; 15-59: 53.6; 60+: 5.6 **Pop. density:** 519 per sq. mi. **Urban** (1988): 19%. **Ethnic groups:** Vietnamese 84%, Chinese 2%, remainder Muong, Thai, Meo, Khmer, Man, Cham. **Languages:** Vietnamese (official), French, English. **Religions:** Buddhists, Confucians, and Taoists most numerous, Roman Catholics, animists, Muslims, Protestants.

Geography: Area: 128,401 sq. mi., the size of New Mexico. **Location:** On the E coast of the Indochinese Peninsula in SE Asia. **Neighbors:** China on N, Laos, Cambodia on W. **Topography:** Vietnam is long and narrow, with a 1,400-mi. coast. About 24% of country is readily arable, including the densely settled Red R. valley in the N, narrow coastal plains in center, and the wide, often marshy Mekong R. Delta in the S. The rest consists of semi-arid plateaus and barren mountains, with some stretches of tropical rain forest. **Capital:** Hanoi. **Cities** (1989): Ho Chi Minh City 3.9 mln.; Hanoi 3.1 mln.

Government: Type: Communist. **Head of state:** Pres. Vo Chi Cong; in office: June 18, 1987. **Head of government:** Prime Min. Do Muoi; in office: June 22, 1988. **Head of Communist Party:** Nguyen Van Linh; in office: Dec. 18, 1986. **Local divisions:** 39 provinces. **Defense:** 19.4% of GNP (1986).

Economy: Industries: Food processing, textiles, cement, chemical fertilizers, steel. **Chief crops:** Rice, rubber, fruits and vegetables, corn, manioc, sugarcane. **Minerals:** Phosphates, coal, iron, manganese, bauxite, apatite, chromate. **Other resources:** Forests. **Arable land:** 23%. **Livestock** (1987): cattle: 2.7 mln.; pigs: 11.7 mln. **Fish catch** (1988): 871,000 metric tons. **Electricity prod.** (1988): 5.5 bln. kwh. **Labor force:** 70% agric.; 8% ind. and commerce.

Finance: Currency: Dong (Jan. 1990: 4,500 = $1 US). **Gross national product** (1987): $12.6 bln. **Per capita income** (1987): $180. **Imports** (1987): $3.1 bln.; partners: USSR 67%, Jap. 8%. **Exports** (1987): $1.4 bln.; partners: Hong Kong 12%; USSR 53%, Jap. 17%. **National budget** (1987): $4.3 bln. expenditures.

Transport: Motor vehicles: in use (1976): 100,000 passenger cars, 200,000 comm. vehicles. **Civil Aviation** (1987): 10.3 bln. passenger km; 3 airports with scheduled flights. **Chief ports:** Ho Chi Minh City, Haiphong, Da Nang.

Communications: Television sets: 1 per 30 persons. **Radios:** 1 per 10 persons. **Telephones:** 1 per 544 persons. **Daily newspaper circ.** (1987): 38 per 1,000 pop.

Health: Life expectancy at birth (1989): 62 male; 66 female. **Births** (per 1,000 pop. 1989): 33. **Deaths** (per 1,000 pop. 1989): 8. **Natural increase:** 2.5%. **Hospital beds:** 1 per 292 persons. **Physicians:** 1 per 3,140 persons. **Infant mortality** (per 1,000 live births 1989): 51.

Education (1989): **Literacy:** 78%.

Major International Organizations: UN (IMF, WHO).

Vietnam's recorded history began in Tonkin before the Christian era. Settled by Viets from central China, Vietnam was held by China, 111 BC-939 AD, and was a vassal state during subsequent periods. Vietnam defeated the armies of Kublai Khan, 1288. Conquest by France began in 1858 and ended in 1884 with the protectorates of Tonkin and Annam in the N. and the colony of Cochin-China in the S.

In 1940 Vietnam was occupied by Japan; nationalist aims gathered force. A number of groups formed the Vietminh (Independence) League, headed by Ho Chi Minh, communist guerrilla leader. In Aug. 1945 the Vietminh forced out Bao Dai, former emperor of Annam, head of a Japan-sponsored regime. France, seeking to reestablish colonial control, battled communist and nationalist forces, 1946-1954, and was finally defeated at Dienbienphu, May 8, 1954. Meanwhile, on July 1, 1949, Bao Dai had formed a State of Vietnam, with himself as chief of state, with French approval. China backed Ho Chi Minh.

A cease-fire accord signed in Geneva July 21, 1954, divided Vietnam along the Ben Hai R. It provided for a buffer zone, withdrawal of French troops from the North and elections to determine the country's future. Under the agreement the communists gained control of territory north of the 17th parallel, 22 provinces with area of 62,000 sq. mi. and 13 million pop., with its capital at Hanoi and Ho Chi Minh as president. South Vietnam came to comprise the 39 southern provinces with approx. area of 65,000 sq. mi. and pop. of 12 million. Some 900,000 North Vietnamese fled to South Vietnam. Neither South Vietnam nor the U.S. signed the agreement.

On Oct. 26, 1955, Ngo Dinh Diem, premier of the interim government of South Vietnam, proclaimed the Republic of Vietnam and became its first president.

The Democratic Republic of Vietnam, established in the North, adopted a constitution Dec. 31, 1959, based on communist principles and calling for reunification of all Vietnam. North Vietnam sought to take over South Vietnam beginning in 1954. Fighting persisted from 1956, with the communist Vietcong, aided by North Vietnam, pressing war in the South. Northern aid to Vietcong guerrillas was intensified in 1959, and large-scale troop infiltration began in 1964, with Soviet and Chinese arms assistance. Large Northern forces were stationed in border areas of Laos and Cambodia.

A serious political conflict arose in the South in 1963 when Buddhists denounced authoritarianism and brutality. This paved the way for a military coup Nov. 1-2, 1963, which overthrew Diem. Several military coups followed.

In 1964, the U.S. began air strikes against North Vietnam. Beginning in 1965, the raids were stepped up and U.S. troops became combatants. U.S. troop strength in Vietnam, which reached a high of 543,400 in Apr. 1969, was ordered reduced by President Nixon in a series of withdrawals, beginning in June 1969. U.S. bombings were resumed in 1972-73.

A ceasefire agreement was signed in Paris Jan. 27, 1973 by the U.S., North and South Vietnam, and the Vietcong. It was never implemented. U.S. aid was curbed in 1974 by the U.S. Congress. Heavy fighting continued for two years throughout Indochina.

North Vietnamese forces launched attacks against remaining government outposts in the Central Highlands in the first months of 1975. Government retreats turned into a rout, and the Saigon regime surrendered April 30. A Provisional Revolutionary Government assumed control, and first steps were taken to transform society along communist lines. All businesses and farms were collectivized.

The U.S. accepted over 165,000 Vietnamese refugees, while scores of thousands more sought refuge in other countries.

The war's toll included — Combat deaths: U.S. 47,752; South Vietnam over 200,000; other allied forces 5,225. Civilian casualties were over a million. Displaced war refugees in South Vietnam totaled over 6.5 million.

The first National Assembly of both parts of the country met and the country was officially reunited July 2, 1976. The Northern capital, flag, anthem, emblem, and currency were applied to the new state. Nearly all major government posts went to officials of the former Northern government.

Heavy fighting with Cambodia took place, 1977-80, amid mutual charges of aggression and atrocities against civilians. Increasing numbers of Vietnamese civilians, ethnic Chinese, escaped the country, via the sea, or the overland route across Cambodia. Vietnam launched an offensive against Cambodian refugee strongholds along the Thai-Cambodian border in 1985; they also engaged Thai troops. Vietnam declared that it had removed all its troops from Cambodia, Sept. 1989.

Relations with China soured as 140,000 ethnic Chinese left Vietnam charging discrimination; China cut off economic aid. Reacting to Vietnam's invasion of Cambodia, China attacked 4 Vietnamese border provinces, Feb., 1979, instigating heavy fighting.

Vietnam announced a package of reforms aimed at reducing central control of the economy in 1987, as many of the old revolutionary followers of Ho Chi Minh were removed from office. By 1990, the economy was in a dire state with inflation estimated at 1,000% a year.

Progress has been made with the U.S. over the repatriating of "Amerasians," the children fathered by U.S. servicemen.

Western Samoa

Independent State of Western Samoa

Malotuto'atasi o Samoa i Sisifo

People: Population (1989 est.): 169,000. **Age distrib. (%):** 0-14: 50.4; 15-59: 45.4; 60+: 4.3. **Pop. density:** 149 per sq. mi. **Urban** (1981): 21.2%. **Ethnic groups:** Samoan (Polynesian) 88%, Euronesian (mixed) 10%, European, other Pacific Islanders. **Languages:** Samoan, English both official. **Religions:** Protestant 70%, Roman Catholic 20%.

Geography: Area: 1,133 sq. mi., the size of Rhode Island. **Location:** In the S. Pacific O. **Neighbors:** Nearest are Fiji on W, Tonga on S. **Topography:** Main islands, Savai'i (670 sq. mi.) and Upolu (429 sq. mi.), both ruggedly mountainous, and small islands Manono and Apolima. **Capital:** Apia. **Cities** (1983 est.): Apia 35,000.

Government: Type: Parliamentary democracy. **Head of state:** King Malietoa Tanumafili II; b. Jan. 4, 1913; in office: Jan. 1, 1962. **Head of government:** Prime Min. Tofilau Eti Alesana; in office: Apr. 11, 1988. **Local divisions:** 11 districts.

Economy: Chief crops: Cocoa, copra, bananas. **Other resources:** Hardwoods, fish. **Arable land:** 43%. **Electricity prod.** (1988): 30 mln. kwh. **Labor force:** 67% agric.

Finance: Currency: Tala (Mar. 1990: 1.00 = $.44 US). **Gross national product** (1987): $110 mln. **Imports** (1989): $67 mln.; partners: NZ 28% Austral. 10%, Jap. 13%, U.S. 30%. **Exports** (1989): $13 mln.; partners: W. Ger. 31%, NZ 26%, U.S. 12%. **International reserves less gold** (Mar. 1990): $63.3 mln. **Consumer prices** (change in 1989): 5.4%.

Transport: Motor vehicles: in use (1985): 1,700 passenger cars, 2,400 comm. vehicles. **Chief ports:** Apia, Asau.

Communications: Radios: 1 per 2.3 persons. **Telephones:** 1 per 23 persons.

Health: Life expectancy at birth (1989): 64 male; 69 female. **Births** (per 1,000 pop. 1989): 34. **Deaths** (per 1,000 pop. 1989): 7. **Natural increase:** 2.8%. **Hospital beds:** 1 per 236 persons. **Physicians:** 1 per 3,685 persons. **Infant mortality** (per 1,000 live births 1989): 48.

Education (1989): **Literacy:** 90%. 95% attend elementary school.

Major international Organizations: UN (IMF, World Bank), Commonwealth of Nations.

Western Samoa was a German colony, 1899 to 1914, when New Zealand landed troops and took over. It became a New Zealand mandate under the League of Nations and, in 1945, a New Zealand UN Trusteeship.

An elected local government took office in Oct. 1959 and the country became fully independent Jan. 1, 1962.

Yemen

Republic of Yemen

People: Population (1990 est.): 11,000,000. **Pop. density:** 53 per sq. mi. **Ethnic groups:** Arabs, Indians, some Negroids. **Languages:** Arabic. **Religions:** Mostly Sunni Moslem.

Geography: Area: 207,000 sq. mi., slightly smaller than France. **Location:** On the southern coast of the Arabian Peninsula. **Neighbors:** Saudi Arabia on NE, Oman on the E. **Topography:** A sandy coastal strip leads to well-watered fertile mountains in interior. **Capital:** Sana. **Cities** (1986 est.): Sana 427,000; Aden 250,000.

Government: Type: Republic; military in power. **Head of state:** Pres. Ali Abdullah Saleh, b. 1942; in office: July 17, 1978. **Head of government:** Prime Min. Haydar Abu Bakr-al attas; in office: May 22, 1990. **Local divisions:** 17 provinces. **Defense:** 10% of GNP (1985).

Economy: Industries: Food processing, mining, petroleum refining. **Chief crops:** Wheat, sorghum, fruits, coffee, cotton. **Minerals:** Salt. **Crude oil reserves** (1984): 600 mln. bbls. **Arable land:** 14%. **Livestock** (1986): goats: 3.5 mln.; sheep: 2.8 mln. **Fish catch** (1988): 70,000 metric tons. **Electricity prod.** (1988): 1 bln. kwh. **Labor force:** 64% agric.; 22% ind. and commerce; 14% serv.

Finance: (N. Yemen only) Currency: Rial (Apr. 1990: 12.01 = $1 US). **Gross national product** (1987): $4.5 bln. **Imports** (1987): $7.1 bln.; partners: Saudi Ar. 20%, Fr. 8%, Jap. 16%. **Exports** (1987): $3.8 mln.; partners: S. Yemen 23%, Saudi Ar. 8%, Pak. 19%. **National budget** (1986): $1.6 bln. **International reserves less gold** (Mar. 1990): $243 mln.

Transport: Motor vehicles in use (1987): 150,000 passenger cars, 220,000 commercial vehicles. **Chief ports:** Al-Hudaydah, Al-Mukha, Aden.

Communications: (N. Yemen only) Television sets: 1 per 56 persons. **Radios:** 1 per 57 persons. **Telephones:** 1 per 104 persons.

Health: (N. Yemen only) Life expectancy at birth (1989): 47 male; 49 female. **Births** (per 1,000 pop. 1989): 52. **Deaths** (per 1,000 pop. 1989): 18. **Natural increase:** 3.5%. **Hospital beds** (1986): 5,900. **Infant mortality** (per 1,000 live births 1989): 132.

Education (1989): **Literacy:** 25%. **Primary school attendance:** 59%.

Major International Organizations: UN (IMF, WHO), Arab League.

Embassy: 600 New Hampshire Ave. NW 20037; 965-4760.

Yemen's territory once was part of the ancient kindgom of Sheba, or Saba, a prosperous link in trade between Africa and India. A Biblical reference speaks of its gold, spices and precious stones as gifts borne by the Queen of Sheba to King Solomon.

Yemen became independent in 1918, after years of Ottoman Turkish rule, but remained politically and economically backward. Imam Ahmed ruled 1948-1962. Army officers headed by Brig. Gen. Abdullah al-Salal declared the country to be the Yemen Arab Republic.

The Imam Ahmed's heir, the Imam Mohamad al-Badr, fled to the mountains where tribesmen joined royalist forces; internal warfare between them and the republican forces continued. Egypt sent troops and Saudi Arabia military aid to the royalists. About 150,000 people died in the fighting.

There was a bloodless coup Nov. 5, 1967.

In April 1970 hostilities ended with an agreement between Yemen and Saudi Arabia and appointment of several royalists to the Yemen government.

On June 13, 1974, an army group, led by Col. Ibrahim al-Hamidi, seized the government. He was assassinated in 1977.

Meanwhile, South Yemen won independence from Britain in 1967, formed out of the British colony of Aden and the British protectorate of South Arabia. It became the Arab world's only Marxist state, taking the name People's Democratic Republic of Yemen in 1970 and signing a 20-year friendship treaty with the USSR in 1979 that allowed for the stationing of Soviet troops in the south.

More than 300,000 Yemenis fled from the south to the north after independence, contributing to 2 decades of hostility between the 2 states that flared into warfare twice in the 1970's.

An Arab League-sponsored agreement between North and South Yemen on unification of the 2 countries was signed Mar. 29, 1979. An agreement providing for widespread political and economic cooperation was signed in 1988.

The 2 countries were formally united on May 22, 1990.

Yugoslavia
Socialist Federal Republic of Yugoslavia
Socijalistička Federativna Republika Jugoslavija

People: Population (1990 est.): 23,864,000. **Age distrib. (%):** 0–14: 23.5; 15-59: 63.7; 60+: 12.8. **Pop. density:** 240 per sq. mi. **Urban** (1985): 46.5%. **Ethnic groups:** Serbs 36%, Croats 20%, Bosnian Moslems 9%, Slovenes 8%, Macedonians 6%, Albanians 8%. **Languages:** Serbo-Croatian, Macedonian, Slovenian (all official), Albanian. **Religions:** Eastern Orthodox 41%, Roman Catholic 12%, Moslem 3%.

Geography: Area: 98,766 sq. mi., the size of Wyoming. **Location:** On the Adriatic coast of the Balkan Peninsula in SE Europe. **Neighbors:** Italy on W, Austria, Hungary on N, Romania, Bulgaria on E, Greece, Albania on S. **Topography:** The Dinaric Alps run parallel to the Adriatic coast, which is lined by offshore islands. Plains stretch across N and E river basins. S and NW are mountainous. **Capital:** Belgrade. **Cities** (1988 est.): Belgrade 1,300,000; Zagreb 700,000; Skopje 440,000; Sarajevo 400,000; Ljubljana 300,000.

Government: Type: Communist state; Federal republic in form. **Head of state:** Pres. Janez Drnovsek; in office: May 15, 1989. **Head of government:** Prime Min. Ante Markovic; in office: Mar. 16 1989. **Head of Communist Party:** Milan Pancevski; b. May 16, 1935; in office: May 17, 1989. **Local divisions:** 6 republics, 2 autonomous provinces. **Defense:** 2.2% of GNP (1987).

Economy: Industries: Steel, wood products, cement, textiles, tourism. **Chief crops:** Corn, grains, tobacco, sugar beets. **Minerals:** Antimony, bauxite, lead, mercury, coal, iron, copper, chrome, zinc, salt. **Crude oil reserves** (1987): 263 mln. bbls. **Arable land:** 28%. **Livestock** (1986): cattle: 5 mln.; pigs: 7.8 mln.; sheep: 7.6 mln. **Fish catch:** (1988): 81,000 metric tons. **Electricity prod.** (1988): 83.5 bln. kwh. **Crude steel prod.** (1988): 4.4 mln. metric tons. **Labor force:** 22% agric.; 70% ind.

Finance: Currency: New Dinar (Mar. 1990: 11.87 = $1 US). **Gross national product** (1988): $154.1 bln. **Per capita GNP** (1988): $6,540. **Imports** (1989): $14.8 bln.; partners: W. Ger. 19%, USSR 15%, It. 8%, U.S. 6%. **Exports** (1989): $13.4 bln.; partners: USSR 17%, W. Ger. 12%, It. 13%. **Tourists** (1986): $1 bln. receipts. **National budget** (1989): $4.5 bln. expenditures. **International reserves less gold** (Mar. 1990): $5.8 bln. **Gold:** 1.90 mln. oz t. **Consumer prices** (change in 1989): 1,239%.

Transport: Railway traffic (1988): 11.5 bln. passenger-km. **Motor vehicles:** in use (1987): 2.9 mln. passenger cars, 283,000 comm. vehicles. **Civil aviation** (1988): 8.8 bln. passenger-km; 17 airports. **Chief ports:** Rijeka, Split, Koper, Bar, Ploce.

Communications: Television sets: 1 per 5.7 persons. **Radios:** 1 per 6 persons. **Telephones:** 1 per 4.9 persons. **Daily newspaper circ.** (1988): 107 per 1,000 pop.

Health: Life expectancy at birth (1989): 69 male; 75 female. **Births** (per 1,000 pop. 1989): 15. **Deaths** (per 1,000 pop. 1989): 9. **Natural increase:** .6%. **Hospital beds:** 1 per 163 persons. **Physicians:** 1 per 712 persons. **Infant mortality** (per 1,000 live births 1989): 25.

Education (1989): Literacy: 90%. Almost all attend primary school.

Major International Organizations: UN (IMF, World Bank, GATT).

Embassy: 2410 California St. NW 20008; 462-6566.

Serbia, which had since 1389 been a vassal principality of Turkey, was established as an independent kingdom by the Treaty of Berlin, 1878. Montenegro, independent since 1389, also obtained international recognition in 1878. After the Balkan wars Serbia's boundaries were enlarged by the annexation of Old Serbia and Macedonia, 1913.

When the Austro-Hungarian empire collapsed after World War I, the Kingdom of the Serbs, Croats, and Slovenes was formed from the former provinces of Croatia, Dalmatia, Bosnia, Herzegovina, Slovenia, Voyvodina and the independent state of Montenegro. The name was later changed to Yugoslavia.

Nazi Germany invaded in 1941. Many Yugoslav partisan troops continued to operate. Among these were the Chetniks led by Draja Mikhailovich, who fought other partisans led by Josip Broz, known as Marshal Tito. Tito, backed by the USSR and Britain from 1943, was in control by the time the Germans had been driven from Yugoslavia in 1945. Mikhailovich was executed July 17, 1946, by the Tito regime.

A constituent assembly proclaimed Yugoslavia a republic Nov. 29, 1945. It became a federated republic Jan. 31, 1946, and Marshal Tito, a communist, became head of the government.

The Stalin policy of dictating to all communist nations was rejected by Tito. He accepted economic aid and military equipment from the U.S. and received aid in foreign trade also from France and Great Britain. Tito also supported the liberal government of Czechoslovakia in 1968 before the Soviet invasion.

A separatist movement among Croatians, 2d to the Serbs in numbers, brought arrests and a change of leaders in the Croatian Republic in Jan. 1972. Violence by extreme Croatian nationalists and fears of Soviet political intervention led to restrictions on political and intellectual dissent. Serbians, Montenegrins, and Macedonians use Cyrillic, Croatians and Slovenians use Latin letters.

Beginning in 1965, reforms designed to decentralize the administration of economic development and to force industries to produce more efficiently in competition with foreign producers were introduced. Yugoslavia has developed considerable trade with the West.

Pres. Tito died May 4, 1980; with his death, the post as head of the Collective Presidency and also that as head of the League of Communists became a rotating system of succession among the members representing each republic and autonomous province.

On Jan. 22, 1990, a Communist Party conference renounced its constitutionally guaranteed leading role in society and called on parliament to enact "Political Pluralism, including a multiparty system."

Zaire
Republic of Zaire
République du Zaïre

People: Population (1990 est.): 35,330,000. **Pop. density:** 37 per sq. mi. **Urban** (1988): 44.2%. **Ethnic groups:** Bantu tribes 80%, over 200 other tribes. **Languages:** French (official), Bantu dialects. **Religions:** Christian 70%, Moslem 10%.

Geography: Area: 905,563 sq. mi., one-fourth the size of the U.S. **Location:** In central Africa. **Neighbors:** Congo on W, Central African Republic, Sudan on N, Uganda, Rwanda, Burundi, Tanzania on E, Zambia, Angola on S. **Topography:** Zaire includes the bulk of the Zaire (Congo) R. Basin. The vast central region is a low-lying plateau covered by rain forest. Mountainous terraces in the W, savannas in the S and SE, grasslands toward the N, and the high Ruwenzori Mtns. on the E surround the central region. A short strip of territory borders the Atlantic O. The Zaire R. is 2,718 mi. long. **Capital:** Kinshasa. **Cities** (1985 est.): Kinshasa 3,000,000; Kananga 601,239.

Government: Type: Republic with strong presidential authority (in transition). **Head of state:** Pres. Mobutu Sese Seko; b. Oct. 14, 1930; in office: Nov. 25, 1965. **Head of Government:** Prime Min. Lunda Bululu; in office: Apr. 25, 1990. **Local divisions:** 8 regions, Kinshasa. **Defense:** 3.0% of GNP (1987).

Economy: Chief crops: Coffee, rice, sugar cane, bananas, plantains, manioc, mangoes, tea, cocoa, palm oil. **Minerals:** Cobalt (60% of world reserves), copper, cadmium, gold, silver, tin, germanium, zinc, iron, manganese, uranium, radium. **Crude oil reserves** (1987): 111 mln. bbls. **Other resources:** Forests, rubber, ivory. **Arable land:** 3%. **Livestock** (1986): cattle: 1.3 mln.; goats: 2.9 mln. **Fish catch** (1987): 177,000 metric tons. **Electricity prod.** (1988): 5.5 bln. kwh. **Labor force:** 75% agric..

Finance: Currency: Zaire (Mar. 1990: 508 = $1 US). **Gross national product** (1987): $5.0 bln. **Imports** (1988): $756 mln.; partners: Chi. 38%, Belg. 16%, W. Ger. 7%, Fra. 7%. **Exports** (1988): $1.1 bln.; partners: Belg.-Lux. 36%, U.S. 19%. **International reserves less gold** (Mar. 1990): $198 mln. **Gold:** 208,000 oz t. **Consumer prices** (change in 1989): 104%.

Transport: Railway traffic (1988): 359 mln. passenger-km. **Motor vehicles:** in use (1985): 24,000 passenger cars, 60,000 comm. vehicles. **Civil aviation** (1988): 506 mln. passenger-km; 22 airports with scheduled flights. **Chief ports:** Matadi, Boma.

Communications: Television sets: 1 per 2,035 persons. **Radios:** 1 per 9.7 persons. **Telephones:** 1 per 800 persons. **Daily newspaper circ.** (1988): 1 per 1,000 pop.

Health: Life expectancy at birth (1989): 51 male; 54 female. **Births** (per 1,000 pop. 1989): 45. **Deaths** (per 1,000 pop. 1989): 14. **Natural increase:** 3.1%. **Hospital beds:** 1 per 476 persons. **Physicians:** 1 per 23,193 persons. **Infant mortality** (per 1,000 live births 1989): 107.

Education (1988): **Literacy:** 55%.

Major International Organizations: UN and all of its specialized agencies, OAU.

Embassy: 1800 New Hampshire Ave. NW 20008; 234-7690.

The earliest inhabitants of Zaire may have been the pygmies, followed by Bantus from the E and Nilotic tribes from the N. The large Bantu Bakongo kingdom ruled much of Zaire and Angola when Portuguese explorers visited in the 15th century.

Leopold II, king of the Belgians, formed an international group to exploit the Congo in 1876. In 1877 Henry M. Stanley explored the Congo and in 1878 the king's group sent him back to organize the region and win over the native chiefs. The Conference of Berlin, 1884-85, organized the Congo Free State with Leopold as king and chief owner. Exploitation of native laborers on the rubber plantations caused international criticism and led to granting of a colonial charter, 1908.

Belgian and Congolese leaders agreed Jan. 27, 1960, that the Congo would become independent June 30. In the first general elections, May 31, the National Congolese movement of Patrice Lumumba won 35 of 137 seats in the National Assembly. He was appointed premier June 21, and formed a coalition cabinet.

Widespread violence caused Europeans and others to flee. The UN Security Council Aug. 9, 1960, called on Belgium to withdraw its troops and sent a UN contingent. President Kasavubu removed Lumumba as premier. Lumumba fought for control backed by Ghana, Guinea and India; he was murdered in 1961.

The last UN troops left the Congo June 30, 1964, and Moise Tshombe became president.

On Sept. 7, 1964, leftist rebels set up a "People's Republic" in Stanleyville. Tshombe hired foreign mercenaries and sought to rebuild the Congolese Army. In Nov. and Dec. 1964 rebels slew scores of white hostages and thousands of Congolese; Belgian paratroops, dropped from U.S. transport planes, rescued hundreds. By July 1965 the rebels had lost their effectiveness.

In 1965 Gen. Joseph D. Mobutu was named president. He later changed his name to Mobutu Sese Seko. The country changed its name to Republic of Zaire on Oct. 27, 1971; in 1972 Zairians with Christian names were ordered to change them to African names.

In 1969-74, political stability under Mobutu was reflected in improved economic conditions.

Serious economic difficulties, amid charges of corruption by government officials, have plagued Zaire in the 1980s. In 1990, Pres. Mobutu announced an end to a 20-year ban on multiparty politics.

Zambia
Republic of Zambia

People: Population (1990 est.): 8,119,000. **Age distrib.** (%): 0–14: 48.2; 15–59: 47.8; 60+: 4.0. **Pop. density:** 26 per sq. mi. **Urban** (1985): 49%. **Ethnic groups:** Mostly Bantu tribes. **Languages:** English (official), Bantu dialects. **Religions:** Predominantly animist, Roman Catholic 21%, Protestant, Hindu, Moslem minorities.

Geography: Area: 290,586 sq. mi., larger than Texas. **Location:** In southern central Africa. **Neighbors:** Zaire on N, Tanzania, Malawi, Mozambique on E, Zimbabwe, Namibia on S, Angola on W. **Topography:** Zambia is mostly high plateau country covered with thick forests, and drained by several important rivers, including the Zambezi. **Capital:** Lusaka. **Cities** (1988): Lusaka 870,000; Kitwe 472,000; Ndola 442,000.

Government: Type: Republic. **Head of state:** Pres. Kenneth David Kaunda; b. Apr. 28, 1924; in office: Oct. 24, 1964. **Head of government:** Prime Min. Malimba Masheke; in office: Mar. 15, 1989. **Local divisions:** 9 provinces. **Defense:** 6.8% of GDP (1985).

Economy: Chief crops: Corn, tobacco, peanuts, cotton, sugar. **Minerals:** Cobalt, copper, zinc, gold, lead, vanadium, manganese, coal. **Other resources:** Rubber, ivory. **Arable land:** 7%. **Livestock** (1987): cattle: 2.8 mln. **Fish catch** (1987): 68,000 metric tons. **Electricity prod.** (1988): 8.2 bln. kwh. **Labor force:** 60% agric.; 40% ind. and commerce.

Finance: Currency: Kwacha (Mar. 1990: 1.00 = $.03 US). **Gross national product** (1987): $2.1 bln. **Per capita income** (1986): $304. **Imports** (1988): $835 mln.; partners: UK 26%, Saudi Ar. 18%, W. Ger. 18%, U.S. 9%. **Exports** (1988): $1.1 bln.; partners: Jap. 19%, Fr. 15%, UK 13%, U.S. 10%, W. Ger. 9%. **National budget** (1987): $787 mln. expenditures. **International reserves less gold** (Jan. 1990): $135 mln. **Gold:** 12,000 oz t. **Consumer prices** (change in 1989): 154%.

Transport: Motor vehicles: in use (1982): 105,000 passenger cars, 97,000 comm. vehicles. **Civil aviation** (1987): 609 mln. passenger-km; 9 airports with scheduled flights.

Communications: Television sets: 1 per 94 persons. **Radios:** 1 per 7.3 persons. **Telephones:** 1 per 94 persons. **Daily newspaper circ.** (1987): 15 per 1,000 pop.

Health: Life expectancy at birth (1989): 54 male; 57 female. **Births** (per 1,000 pop. 1989): 50. **Deaths** (per 1,000 pop. 1989): 12. **Natural increase:** 3.7%. **Hospital beds:** 1 per 297 persons. **Physicians:** 1 per 10,008 persons. **Infant mortality** (per 1,000 live births 1989): 87.

Education (1988): **Literacy:** 54%. **Attendance:** less than 50% in grades 1–7.

Major International Organizations: UN (GATT, IMF, WHO), OAU, Commonwealth of Nations.

Embassy: 2419 Massachusetts Ave. NW 20008; 265-9717.

As Northern Rhodesia, the country was under the administration of the South Africa Company, 1889 until 1924, when the office of governor was established, and, subsequently, a legislature. The country became an independent republic within the Commonwealth Oct. 24, 1964.

After the white government of Rhodesia declared its independence from Britain Nov. 11, 1965, relations between Zambia and Rhodesia became strained.

As part of a program of government participation in major industries, a government corporation in 1970 took over 51% of the ownership of 2 foreign-owned copper mining companies. Privately-held land and other enterprises were nationalized in 1975, as were all newspapers. In the 1980s, decline in copper prices has hurt the economy and severe drought has caused famine.

Food riots erupted in June 1990, as the nation suffered its worst violence since independence.

Zimbabwe

People: Population (1990 est.): 10,205,000. **Age distrib.** (%): 0–14: 44.9; 15–59: 51.1; 60+: 4.0. **Pop. density:** 66 per sq. mi. **Urban** (1985): 25%. **Ethnic groups:** Shona 80%, Ndebele 19%. **Languages:** English (official), Shona, Sindebele. **Religions:** Predominantly traditional tribal beliefs, Christian minority.

Geography: Area: 150,803 sq. mi., slightly larger than Montana. **Location:** In southern Africa. **Neighbors:** Zambia on N, Botswana on W, S. Africa on S, Mozambique on E. **Topography:** Rhodesia is high plateau country, rising to mountains on eastern border, sloping down on the other borders. **Capital:** Harare. **Cities** (1988 est.): Harare 730,000; Bulawayo (met.) 415,000.

Government: Type: Parliamentary democracy. **Head of state:** Pres. Robert Mugabe; b. Apr. 14, 1928; in office: Jan. 1, 1988. **Local divisions:** 8 provinces. **Defense:** 6.2% of GNP (1985).

Economy: Industries: Clothing, chemicals, light industries. **Chief crops:** Tobacco, sugar, cotton, corn, wheat. **Minerals:** Chromium, gold, nickel, asbestos, copper, iron, coal. **Arable land:** 7%. **Livestock** (1985): cattle: 5.3 mln.; goats: 1.8 mln. **Electricity prod.** (1987): 7.6 bln. kwh. **Labor force:** 74% agric.; 16% serv.

Finance: Currency: Dollar (Mar. 1990: 1.00 = $.41 US). **Gross national product** (1988): $5.5 bln. **Per capita income** (1986): $275. **Imports** (1987): $1.2 bln. partners: UK 10%, So. Afr. 27%, U.S. 7%, W. Ger. 7%. **Exports** (1987): $1.4 bln.; partners: UK 7%, So. Afr. 22%, W. Ger. 8%. **National budget** (1988): $2.8 bln. expenditures. **Total reserves less gold** (Mar. 1990): $117.7 mln. **Consumer prices** (change in 1989): 12.9%.

Transport: Motor vehicles: in use (1985): 253,000 passenger cars, 28,000 comm. vehicles. **Civil aviation** (1987): 648 mln. passenger-km. 8 airports with scheduled flights.

Communications: Television sets: 1 per 71 persons. **Radios:** 1 per 23 persons. **Telephones:** 1 per 33 persons. **Daily newspaper circ.** (1985): 23 per 1,000 pop.

Health: Life expectancy at birth (1989): 59 male; 63 female. **Births** (per 1,000 pop. 1989): 42. **Deaths** (per 1,000 pop. 1989):

9. Natural increase: 3.3%. Physicians: 1 per 6,687 persons.
Infant mortality (per 1,000 live births 1989): 67.

Education (1988): Literacy: 50%. Attendance: 90% primary, 15% secondary for Africans; higher for whites, Asians.

Major international Organizations: UN (IMF, World Bank), OAU, Commonwealth of Nations.

Embassy: 2852 McGill Terrace NW 20008; 332-7100.

Britain took over the area as Southern Rhodesia in 1923 from the British South Africa Co. (which, under Cecil Rhodes, had conquered the area by 1897) and granted internal self-government. Under a 1961 constitution, voting was restricted to maintain whites in power. On Nov. 11, 1965, Prime Min. Ian D. Smith announced his country's unilateral declaration of independence. Britain termed the act illegal, and demanded Rhodesia broaden voting rights to provide for eventual rule by the majority Africans.

Urged by Britain, the UN imposed sanctions, including embargoes on oil and gasoline shipments to Rhodesia. Some oil and gasoline reached Rhodesia, however, from South Africa and Mozam-

bique, before the latter became independent in 1975. In May 1968, the UN Security Council ordered a trade embargo.

A new constitution came into effect, Mar. 2, 1970, providing for a republic with a president and prime minister. The election law effectively prevented full black representation through income tax requirements.

Intermittent negotiations between the government and various black nationalist groups failed to prevent increasing skirmishes. By mid-1978, over 6,000 soldiers and civilians had been killed. An "internal settlement" signed Mar. 1978 in which Smith and 3 popular black leaders share control until transfer of power to the black majority was rejected by guerrilla leaders.

In the country's first universal-franchise election, Apr. 21, 1979, Bishop Abel Muzorewa's United African National Council gained a bare majority control of the black-dominated parliament. Britain, 1979, began efforts to normalize its relationship with Zimbabwe. A British cease-fire was accepted by all parties, Dec. 5th. Independence was finally achieved Apr. 18, 1980.

Population of World's Largest Cities
Source: U.S. Bureau of the Census

The table below represents one attempt at comparing the world's largest cities. The cities are defined as population clusters of continuous built-up areas with a population density of a least 5,000 persons per square mile. The boundary of the city was determined by examining detailed maps of each city in conjunction with the most recent official population statistics. Exclaves of areas exceeding the minimum population density were added to the city if the intervening gap was less than one mile. To the extent practical, nonresidential areas such as parks, airports, industrial complexes and water were excluded from the area reported for each city, thus making the population density reflective of the concentrations in the residential portions of the city. By using a consistent definition for the city, it is possible to make comparisons of the cities on the basis of total population, area, and population density.

Political and administrative boundaries were disregarded in determining the population of the city. Berlin includes both East and West Berlin, as well as population from East Germany. Detroit includes Windsor, Canada.

The population of each city was projected based on the proportion each city was of its country total at the time of the last 2 censuses and projected country populations. Figures in the table below may differ from city population figures elsewhere in the World Almanac because of different methods of determining population.

City, Country	1990 (thousands)	2000 (thousands projected)	Area (sq. mi.)	Density 1989 (pop per sq. mi.)	City, Country	1990 (thousands)	2000 (thousands projected)	Area (sq. mi.)	Density 1989 (pop per sq. mi.)
Tokyo-Yokahama, Japan	26,952	29,971	1,089	24,463	Dhaka, Bangladesh	4,224	6,492	32	125,511
Mexico City, Mexico	20,207	27,872	522	37,314	Barcelona, Spain	4,163	4,834	87	47,138
Sao Paolo, Brazil	18,052	25,354	451	38,528	Manchester, U.K.	4,050	3,827	357	11,397
Seoul, South Korea	16,268	21,976	342	45,953	Philadelphia, U.S.	4,007	3,979	471	8,515
New York, U.S.	14,622	14,648	1,274	11,473	San Francisco, U.S.	3,958	4,214	428	9,167
Osaka-Kobe-Kyoto, Japan	13,826	14,287	495	27,833	Belo Horizonte, Brazil	3,941	5,239	97	39,304
Bombay, India	11,777	15,357	95	120,299	Ho Chi Minh City, Vietnam	3,683	5,125	79	44,922
Calcutta, India	11,663	14,088	209	54,607		3,645	4,481	31	114,914
Buenos Aires, Argentina	11,518	12,911	535	21,233	Ahmadabad, India	3,595	4,837	32	108,618
Rio de Janeiro, Brazil	11,428	14,169	260	42,894	Kinshasa, Zaire	3,575	5,646	57	59,704
Moscow, USSR	10,367	11,121	379	27,117	Hyderabad, India	3,563	4,765	88	39,180
Los Angeles, U.S.	10,060	10,714	1,110	8,985	Sydney, Australia	3,515	3,708	338	10,328
Manila, Philippines	9,880	12,846	188	50,978	Athens, Greece	3,468	3,866	116	29,511
Cairo, Egypt	9,851	12,512	104	92,168	Miami, U.S.	3,421	3,894	448	7,498
Jakarta, Indonesia	9,588	12,804	76	122,033	Guangzhou, China	3,330	3,652	79	41,942
London, U.K.	9,170	8,574	874	10,551	Guadalajara, Mexico	3,262	4,451	78	40,364
Teheran, Iran	9,354	14,251	112	79,594	Surabaya, Indonesia	3,205	3,632	43	73,368
Paris, France	8,709	8,803	432	20,123	Caracas, Venezuela	3,188	3,435	54	58,296
Delhi, India	8,475	11,849	138	59,102	Wuhan, China	3,169	3,495	65	48,376
Karachi, Pakistan	7,711	11,299	190	39,038	Toronto, Canada	3,108	3,296	154	20,001
Lagos, Nigeria	7,602	12,528	56	129,705	Greater Berlin, Germany	3,022	3,006	274	11,036
Essen, W. Germany	7,474	7,239	704	10,653	Rome, Italy	3,021	3,129	69	43,556
Shanghai, China	6,873	7,540	78	87,659	Detroit, U.S.	2,995	2,735	468	6,457
Lima, Peru	6,578	9,241	120	54,789	Porto Alegre, Brazil	3,015	4,109	231	12,608
Chicago, U.S.	6,526	6,568	762	8,560	Naples, Italy	2,960	3,134	62	47,424
Taipei, Taiwan	6,513	8,516	138	45,710	Melbourne, Australia	2,907	2,968	327	8,856
Istanbul, Turkey	6,461	8,875	165	37,760	Alexandria, Egypt	2,899	3,304	35	81,420
Bangkok, Thailand	5,791	7,587	102	55,126	Montreal, Canada	2,896	3,071	164	17,572
Beijing, China	5,736	5,993	151	37,816	Casablanca, Morocco	2,891	3,795	35	80,202
Madras, India	5,743	7,384	115	48,541	Monterrey, Mexico	2,837	3,974	77	35,448
Bogota, Colombia	5,710	7,935	79	69,638	Yangon, Myanmar	2,813	3,332	47	58,724
Hong Kong	5,656	5,956	23	247,004	Ankara, Turkey	2,782	3,777	55	48,852
Santiago, Chile	5,275	6,294	128	40,269	Kiev, USSR	2,751	3,237	62	43,548
Pusan, S. Korea	4,838	6,700	54	86,284	Dallas, U.S.	2,743	3,257	419	6,418
Tianjin, China	4,804	5,298	49	97,291	Singapore, Singapore	2,695	2,913	78	34,185
Milan, Italy	4,738	4,839	344	13,741	Harbin, China	2,618	2,887	30	86,591
Nagoya, Japan	4,736	5,303	307	15,236	Washington, U.S.	2,547	2,707	357	7,082
Leningrad, USSR	4,667	4,738	139	33,474	Taegu, South Korea	2,529	4,051	NA	NA
Bangalore, India	4,612	6,764	50	88,191	Boston, U.S.	2,475	2,485	303	8,162
Madrid, Spain	4,451	5,104	66	66,527	Poona, India	2,447	3,647	NA	NA
Shenyang, China	4,248	4,684	39	108,080	Lisbon, Portugal	2,396	2,717	NA	NA
Lahore, Pakistan	4,236	5,864	57	71,949					(continued)

City, Country	1990 (thousands)	2000 (thousands projected)	Area (sq. mi.)	Density 1989 (pop per sq. mi.)	City, Country	1990 (thousands)	2000 (thousands projected)	Area (sq. mi.)	Density 1989 (pop per sq. mi.)
Tashkent, USSR	2,365	2,947	NA	NA	Salvador, Brazil	2,209	3,286	NA	NA
Chengdu, China	2,349	2,591	25	93,242	Birmingham, U.K.	2,170	2,078	223	9,768
Chongqing, China	2,339	2,961	NA	NA	Bucharest, Romania	2,150	2,271	52	41,132
Vienna, Austria	2,313	2,647	NA	NA	Havana, Cuba	2,109	2,333	NA	NA
Budapest, Hungary	2,301	2,335	138	16,666	Kanpur, India	2,076	2,673	NA	NA
Houston, U.S.	2,298	2,651	310	7,284	NA-not available				

Population Projections, by Region and for Selected Countries: 1995 to 2025

Source: Population Division of the United Nations

(in millions)

Region and Country	1995	2000	2025	Region and Country	1995	2000	2025
World, total	5,679.3	6,127.1	8,177.1	East Asia[2]	1,390.4	1,470.0	1,696.1
More developed[1]	1,242.8	1,275.7	1,396.7	China: mainland	1,184.2	1,255.7	1,460.1
Less developed[1]	4,436.4	4,851.5	6,780.4	Hong Kong	6.6	6.9	7.9
Africa	753.2	877.4	1,642.9	Japan	125.1	127.7	127.6
Eastern Africa[2]	224.7	266.2	531.4	Korea, North	24.9	27.3	37.6
Burundi	6.1	7.0	11.0	Korea, South	46.8	49.5	58.6
Ethiopia	50.1	58.4	112.0	South Asia	1,909.4	2,073.7	2,770.6
Kenya	31.4	38.5	82.9	Eastern So. Asia[2]	480.8	519.7	684.7
Madagascar	13.4	15.6	29.7	Cambodia	9.2	9.9	12.5
Malawi	9.8	11.7	23.2	Indonesia	191.9	204.5	255.3
Mozambique	18.8	21.8	39.7	Laos	5.6	6.2	9.2
Rwanda	8.8	10.6	22.2	Malaysia[5]	19.1	20.6	26.9
Somalia	6.2	7.1	13.2	Myanmar[5]	49.8	55.2	82.2
Uganda	22.5	26.8	52.3	Philippines	68.3	74.8	102.3
Tanzania	32.5	39.1	83.8	Singapore	2.9	3.0	3.2
Zambia	9.4	11.2	23.8	Thailand	61.1	66.1	86.3
Zimbabwe	12.6	15.1	32.7	Vietnam	71.7	78.1	105.1
Middle Africa[2]	83.0	96.1	183.5	Middle So. Asia[2]	1,279.9	1,385.7	1,815.9
Angola	11.5	13.2	24.5	Afghanistan	21.7	24.2	35.9
Cameroon	12.6	14.4	25.2	Bangladesh	130.3	145.8	219.4
Cen. African Rep.	3.3	3.7	6.7	India	899.1	961.5	1,188.5
Chad	6.4	7.3	13.1	Iran	58.7	65.5	96.2
Zaire	44.8	52.4	104.4	Nepal	20.7	23.0	33.9
Northern Africa[2]	164.3	185.7	295.0	Pakistan	128.0	142.6	212.8
Algeria	30.5	35.2	57.3	Sri Lanka	19.5	20.8	26.2
Egypt	58.9	65.2	97.4	Western So. Asia[2]	148.7	168.3	270.0
Libya	5.2	6.1	11.1	Iraq	21.6	24.9	42.7
Morocco	31.9	36.3	59.9	Israel	5.0	5.4	7.0
Sudan	28.7	32.9	55.4	Jordan	5.2	6.4	13.4
Tunisia	8.9	9.7	13.6	Lebanon	3.3	3.6	5.2
Southern Africa[2]	48.1	54.5	90.7	Saudi Arabia	16.1	18.9	33.5
South Africa	41.6	46.9	76.3	Syria	15.3	18.1	32.3
Western Africa[2]	233.1	275.0	542.4	Turkey	62.4	68.5	99.3
Benin	5.4	6.4	12.2	Yemen Arab Rep.	8.6	9.9	16.5
Burkina Faso[3]	9.1	10.5	19.5	Europe (excl. Soviet Union)	506.5	513.1	526.9
Côte d'Ivoire[4]	13.4	15.6	28.1	Eastern Europe[2]	118.2	121.0	131.2
Ghana	18.7	21.9	37.7	Bulgaria	9.6	9.7	10.2
Guinea	7.0	7.9	13.9	Czechoslovakia	16.3	16.8	18.8
Mali	10.7	12.4	21.4	Germany E.	16.5	16.6	16.1
Niger	8.3	9.8	18.9	Hungary	10.8	10.9	10.9
Nigeria	135.5	161.9	338.1	Poland	40.2	41.4	45.9
Senegal	8.7	10.0	18.9	Romania	24.8	25.6	29.2
Togo	3.9	4.6	9.0	Northern Europe[2]	83.0	83.4	83.6
Latin America	501.3	550.0	786.6	Denmark	5.1	5.1	4.8
Caribbean[2]	37.7	40.8	57.7	Finland	5.0	5.0	4.8
Cuba	11.2	11.7	13.6	Ireland	4.0	4.2	5.2
Dominican Rep.	7.7	8.4	12.2	Norway	4.2	4.2	4.3
Haiti	8.6	9.9	18.3	Sweden	8.2	8.1	7.5
Middle America[2]	134.4	149.6	222.6	United Kingdom	56.0	56.2	56.4
El Salvador	7.5	8.7	15.0	Southern Europe[2]	150.0	153.1	162.8
Guatemala	11.1	12.7	21.7	Albania	3.8	4.1	5.8
Honduras	6.0	7.0	13.3	Greece	10.5	10.7	11.8
Mexico	99.2	109.2	154.1	Italy	57.9	58.2	56.9
Nicaragua	4.5	5.3	9.2	Portugal	10.7	11.0	11.9
Temperate South America[2]	52.3	55.5	70.1	Spain	42.0	43.4	49.2
Argentina	35.1	37.2	47.4	Yugoslavia	24.6	25.2	26.6
Chile	14.0	14.9	18.8	Western Europe[2]	155.3	155.6	149.3
Uruguay	3.2	3.4	3.9	Austria	7.5	7.5	7.3
Tropical South America[2]	276.9	304.1	436.3	Belgium	9.9	9.9	9.8
Bolivia	8.4	9.7	18.3	France	56.3	57.1	58.5
Brazil	165.1	179.5	245.8	Germany, W.	60.3	59.8	53.8
Colombia	34.9	38.0	51.7	Netherlands	14.9	15.0	14.6
Ecuador	12.7	14.6	25.7	Switzerland	6.0	5.9	4.9
Paraguay	4.8	5.4	8.6	Soviet Union	303.1	314.8	367.1
Peru	25.1	28.0	41.0	Oceania[2]	28.5	30.4	39.5
Venezuela	24.2	27.2	42.8	Australia	17.7	18.7	23.5
Northern America[2]	286.8	297.7	347.3	New Zealand	3.6	3.7	4.2
Canada	28.3	29.4	34.4	Papua New Guinea	4.8	5.3	8.2
United States	258.3	268.1	312.7				

(1) Regions. (2) Includes countries not shown separately. (3) Formerly Upper Volta. (4) Ivory Coast. (5) Formerly Burma.

Area and Population of the World

Source: U.S. Bureau of the Census; prior to 1950, Rand McNally & Co.

Continent	Area (1,000 sq. mi.)	% of Earth	Population (est., thousands)							% World Total, 1990
			1650	1750	1850	1900	1950	1980	1990	
North America	9,400	16.2	5,000	5,000	39,000	106,000	166,000	252,000	277,000	5.1
South America	6,900	11.9	8,000	7,000	20,000	38,000	—	—	—	—
Latin America, Caribbean	—	—	—	—	—	—	166,000	364,000	450,000	8.4
Europe	3,800	6.6	100,000	140,000	265,000	400,000	392,000	484,000	499,000	9.3
Asia	17,400	30.1	335,000	476,000	754,000	932,000	1,368,000	2,494,000	2,994,000	56.1
Africa	11,700	20.2	100,000	95,000	95,000	118,000	281,000	594,000	795,000	14.9
USSR	—	—	—	—	—	—	180,000	266,000	291,000	5.4
Oceania, incl. Australia	3,300	5.7	2,000	2,000	2,000	6,000	12,000	23,000	26,000	0.4
Antarctica	5,400	9.3	Uninhabited							
World	57,900	—	550,000	725,000	1,175,000	1,600,000	2,565,000	4,477,000	5,333,000	—

The World's Refugees in 1989

The following information is from the *World Refugee Survey 1989*, a publication of the U.S. Committee for Refugees, a nonprofit corp. The refugees in this table include only those who are in need of protection and/or assistance, and do not include refugees who have resettled.

Country of Asylum	From	Number
Total Africa		**4,524,800**
Algeria	Mostly Western Sahara . .	170,000[1]
Angola	Namibia, Zaire, S. Africa . . .	26,500
Benin	Chad	900
Botswana	S. Africa, Angola	800
Burkina Faso	Chad	300
Burundi	Rwanda, Zaire.	90,200[1]
Cameroon	Chad	4,200
Central African Rep.	Chad	2,800
Congo	Chad, Zaire	2,100
Côte d'Ivoire	Liberia	55,800
Djibouti	Ethiopia, Somalia	46,500
Egypt	Palestinians	7,500
Ethiopia	Sudan, Somalia	740,000[1]
Gabon	various	100
Ghana	various	100
Guinea	Liberia	13,000
Kenya	Ethiopia, Rwanda, Uganda. .	15,500[1]
Lesotho	South Africa	4,000[1]
Liberia	various	200
Malawi	Mozambique.	812,000
Morocco	various	800
Mozambique.	S. Africa	400
Namibia	Angola	25,000[1]
Nigeria	Chad, others.	5,100
Rwanda	Burundi	20,500[1]
Senegal	Guinea Bissau, Mauritania .	48,000
Sierra Leone.	various	100
Somalia	Ethiopia	350,000[1]
S. Africa	Mozambique.	201,000[1]
Sudan	Ethiopia, Chad, Zaire . . .	694,300[1]
Swaziland	South Africa, Mozambique. .	71,700[1]
Tanzania	Burundi, Mozambique. . .	266,200
Togo	Ghana	500
Tunisia	various	200
Uganda	Rwanda, Zaire, Sudan . . .	170,500[1]
Zaire	Angola, Rwanda, Burundi .	338,800
Zambia	Angola, Mozambique, Zaire .	131,700
Zimbabwe	Mozambique.	185,500[1]
Total East Asia/Pacific		**574,100**
Hong Kong.	Vietnam	55,400
Indonesia.	Vietnam	8,000
Japan.	Vietnam	2,000
Korea.	Vietnam	200
Macau	Vietnam	400
Malaysia	Vietnam	19,900
Papua New Guinea	Indonesia	8,100
Philippines	Vietnam, Cambodia, Laos . .	26,300
Singapore	Vietnam	300
Taiwan.	Vietnam	200
Thailand	Burma, Laos, Cambodia . . .	436,600
Vietnam	Cambodia	16,700

(1) Significant variance among sources in number reported.

Country of Asylum	From	Number
Total Europe & No. America		**700,600+**
Austria	various	22,800
Canada	various	21,700+
Cyprus	various	1,000
Denmark.	various	4,600
France	various	60,000
Germany.	various	121,000
Hungary.	various	27,000
Netherlands	various	14,000
Norway.	various	4,400
Sweden	various	32,000
Switzerland	various	24,400+
Turkey	Iran, Iraq	233,000[1]
United Kingdom . . .	various	10,000
United States	Nicaragua, El Salvador, Gua- temala.	101,700+
Yugoslavia	various	8,000
Other European. . .	various	7,000
Total Latin America/Caribbean		**152,800**
Argentina	Chile, SE Asia	2,100[1]
Belize.	El Salvador, Guatemala . .	5,100
Bolivia	Guatemala, El Salvador . .	200
Brazil	Europe, other	200
Chile	Europe	100
Colombia	Chile	700
Costa Rica.	El Salvador, Nicaragua. .	33,400[1]
Cuba	Haiti	3,000
Dominican Rep. . . .	Haiti	1,600[1]
Ecuador	Chile, various	700
El Salvador	Nicaragua	500
French Guiana. . . .	Suriname	10,000
Guatemala.	El Salvador, Nicaragua. .	4,400[1]
Honduras	El Salvador, Nicaragua. .	34,900[1]
Mexico	El Salvador, Guatemala . .	46,300[1]
Nicaragua	El Salvador, Guatemala . .	7,000
Panama	El Salvador, others . . .	1,200
Peru	various	700
Uruguay	various	100
Venezuela	Caribbean	200
Total Middle East/South Asia		**9,141,600**
India	Bangladesh, Tibet, Sri Lanka	260,800[1]
Iran	Afghanistan, Iraq	2,825,000[1]
Iraq	Iran	60,000[1]
Nepal	Tibet	12,000
Pakistan	Afghanistan	3,588,000[1]
Yemen, North	S. Yemen, Ethiopia . . .	56,700[1]
Palestinians		
Gaza Strip		469,400
Jordan		899,800
Lebanon		298,700
Syria		272,800
West Bank		398,400
Total Refugees		**15,093,900**

Principal Sources of Refugees

Afghanistan	5,934,500[1]	Somalia	388,600[1]	Nicaragua	89,700[1]
Palestinians	2,340,500	Iran	270,100[1]	Laos	69,044
Mozambique	1,354,000[1]	Rwanda	233,000[1]	Liberia	68,000
Ethiopia	1,035,900	Burundi	186,600[1]	El Salvador	61,100[1]
Iraq	508,200	Western Sahara	165,000[1]	Guatemala	58,700[1]
Angola	438,000	Vietnam	124,779	Yemen (Aden)	55,000[1]
Sudan	435,100	Tibet	112,000	Zaire	50,400
Cambodia	334,166	Sri Lanka	103,000	Bangladesh	50,000[1]

(1) Significant variance among sources in number reported.

U.S. Immigration Law

Source: Immigration and Naturalization Service, U.S. Justice Department

The Immigration and Nationality Act, as amended, provides for the numerical limitation of most immigration. Not subject to any numerical limitations are immigrants classified as immediate relatives who are spouses or children of U.S. citizens, or parents of citizens who are 21 years of age or older; returning residents; certain former U.S. citizens; ministers of religion; and certain long-term U.S. government employees.

The Refugee Act of 1980 (P.L. 96-212) became effective on April 1, 1980. Congress stated that the objectives of the Refugee Act are to provide a permanent and systematic procedure for the admission of refugees who are of special humanitarian concern to the U.S. and to provide uniform provisions for the effective settlement and absorption of those refugees. The number of refugees who may be admitted is determined by the President, after consultation with the Committees on the Judiciary of the Senate and of the House of Representatives.

Numerical Limitation of Immigrants

Immigration to the U.S. is numerically limited to 270,000 per year. Within this quota there is an annual limitation of 20,000 for each country. The colonies and dependencies of foreign states are limited to 5,000 per year, chargeable to the country limitation of the mother country.

Visa Categories

Of those immigrants subject to numerical limitations, applicants for immigration are classified as either preference or nonpreference. The preference visa categories are based on certain relationships to persons in the U.S., i.e., unmarried sons and daughters over 21 of U.S. citizens, spouses and unmarried sons and daughters of resident aliens, married sons and daughters of U.S. citizens, brothers and sisters of U.S. citizens 21 or over (first, 2d, 4th, and 5th preference, respectively); members of the professions or persons of exceptional ability in the sciences and arts whose services are sought by U.S. employers (3d preference); and skilled and unskilled workers in short supply (6th preference). Spouses and children of preference applicants are entitled to the same preference if accompanying or following to join such persons.

Preference status is based upon approved petitions, filed with the Immigration and Naturalization Service, by the appropriate relative or employer (or in the 3d preference by the alien himself).

Other immigrants not within one of the above-mentioned preference groups may qualify as nonpreference applicants and receive only those visa numbers not needed by preference applicants. The nonpreference category has not been available since 1978 due to 6 preferences using the allocation.

Labor Certification

The Act of October 3, 1965, established controls to protect the U.S. labor market from an influx of skilled and unskilled foreign labor. Prior to the issuance of a visa, the potential 3d, 6th, and nonpreference immigrant must obtain the Secretary of Labor's certification, establishing that there are not sufficient workers in the U.S. at the alien's destination who are able, willing, and qualified to perform the job; and that the employment of the alien will not adversely affect the wages and working conditions of workers in the U.S. similarly employed; or that there is satisfactory evidence that the provisions of that section do not apply to the alien's case.

The Immigration Reform and Control Act of 1986

The Immigration Reform and Control Act, PL 99-603, was signed into law on November 6, 1986. The legislation contains 3 major segments—legalization, employer sanctions, and temporary agricultural worker provisions. The legalization segment of the law provides a method for legalizing the status of many of the aliens who have been in the U.S. unlawfully since before January 1, 1982. Legalization is a 2-tiered program which provides for temporary resident status for qualified applicants. After 18 months residence in the U.S., temporary residents are eligible to apply to adjust to permanent resident status. Aliens who were employed in seasonal agricultural work for a minimum of 90 days between May 1985 and May 1986 are also eligible to apply for temporary residence. The agricultural workers will adjust to permanent resident status beginning in December, 1989.

The employer sanctions section of the legislation, for the first time, imposes civil and criminal penalties on employers who knowingly hire, recruit, or refer aliens who are not authorized to work in the U.S. The civil fines range from $250 to $10,000 per alien. Criminal penalties are possible for habitual violators. Employer sanction provisions were to begin in May 1987 but were delayed by Congress until Sept. 1 when a 12-month education period began.

The temporary agricultural worker provisions of the act expand the existing temporary worker (H2) program. The law divides H2 workers into two categories: temporary workers for agricultural labor or services, and all other temporary H2 workers. The changes made by the law affect only the agricultural area and are effective as of June 1, 1987. A grower wishing to hire H2 workers must file a petition with the Department of Labor. The Department will grant the petition provided there are insufficient workers who are able, willing, qualified, and available where and when needed to perform the labor, and there will be no adverse effect on the wages and working conditions of workers similarly employed in the U.S.

In addition to these major provisions, there are many other provisions of the act, including anti-discrimination provisions as well as increasing the numerical limitation for colonies of foreign states from 600 to 5,000 immigrant visas a year. Qualified aliens who are in the category Cuban/Haitian Entrant (Status Pending) are eligible to adjust to permanent resident status. The act also provided an additional 5,000 nonpreference visa numbers in fiscal years 1987 and 1988 to natives of countries which were adversely effected by the changes in the preference system created by the 1965 Immigration and Nationality Act amendments. Section 2 of the Immigration Amendments of 1988, extended this category through fiscal years 1989 and 1990, with 15,000 visa numbers provided for each of those years.

As of May 16, 1990, about 1,762,100 aliens have sought legal status under the pre-1982 provisions of the new immigration law and 1,276,700 have applied for legal status under the agricultural worker provision.

During fiscal 1989, 478,814 temporary resident aliens who qualified under the pre-1982 provisions became lawful permanent residents of the U.S.

Naturalization: How to Become an American Citizen
Source: The Federal Statutes

A person who desires to be naturalized as a citizen of the United States may obtain the necessary application form as well as detailed information from the nearest office of the Immigration and Naturalization Service or from the clerk of a court handling naturalization cases.

An applicant must be at least 18 years old. He must have been a lawful resident of the United States continuously for 5 years. For husbands and wives of U.S. citizens the period is 3 years in most instances. Special provisions apply to certain veterans of the Armed Forces.

An applicant must have been physically present in this country for at least half of the required 5 years' residence.

Every applicant for naturalization must:

(1) demonstrate an understanding of the English language, including an ability to read, write, and speak words in ordinary usage in the English language (persons physically unable to do so, and persons who, on the date of their examinations, are over 50 years of age and have been lawful permanent residents of the United States for 20 years or more are exempt).

(2) have been a person of good moral character, attached to the principles of the Constitution, and well disposed to the good order and happiness of the United States for five years just before filing the petition or for whatever other pe-riod of residence is required in his case and continue to be such a person until admitted to citizenship; and

(3) demonstrate a knowledge and understanding of the fundamentals of the history, and the principles and form of government, of the U.S.

When the applicant files his petition he pays the court clerk $50. At the preliminary hearing he may be represented by a lawyer or social service agency. There is a 30-day wait. If action is favorable, there is a final hearing before a judge, who administers the following oath of allegiance:

I hereby declare, on oath, that I absolutely and entirely renounce and abjure all allegiance and fidelity to any foreign prince, potentate, state or sovereignty, to whom or which I have heretofore been a subject or citizen; that I will support and defend the Constitution and laws of the United States of America against all enemies, foreign and domestic; that I will bear true faith and allegiance to the same; that I will bear arms on behalf of the United States when required by the law; that I will perform noncombatant service in the armed forces of the United States when required by the law; that I will perform work of national importance under civilian direction when required by the law; and that I take this obligation freely without any mental reservation or purpose of evasion; so help me God.

Customs Exemptions and Advice to Travelers
Source: U.S. Customs Service

U.S. residents returning after a stay abroad of at least 48 hours are usually granted customs exemptions of $400 each. The duty-free articles must accompany the traveler at the time of his return, be for personal or household use, have been acquired as an incident of his trip, and be properly declared to Customs. Not more than one liter of alcoholic beverages may be included in the $400 exemption.

If a U.S. resident arrives directly or indirectly from American Samoa, Guam, or the U.S. Virgin Islands, the purchase may be valued up to $800 fair retail value, but not more than $400 of the exemption may be applied to the value of articles acquired elsewhere than in such insular possessions, and 5 liters of alcoholic beverages may be included in the exemption, but not more than 1 liter of such beverages may have been acquired elsewhere than in the designated islands.

The exemption for alcoholic beverages is accorded only when the returning resident has attained 21 years of age at the time of his arrival. One hundred cigars and 200 cigarettes may be included in either exemption. Cuban cigars may be included if obtained in Cuba and all articles acquired there do not exceed $100 in retail value.

The $400 or $800 exemption may be granted only if the exemption, or any part of it, has not been used within the preceding 30-day period and the stay abroad was for at least 48 hours. The 48-hour absence requirement does not apply if you return from Mexico or the U.S. Virgin Islands.

Gifts costing no more than $50 fair retail value or $100 from American Samoa, Guam, or the Virgin Islands, may be mailed duty-free.

Most items—including alcoholic beverages, cigars, cigarettes and perfume—made in designated Caribbean and Central American countries may enter the U.S. duty-free under the Caribbean Basin Economic Recovery Act. Countries currently designated for such duty-free treatment are: Aruba, Antigua and Barbuda, Bahamas, Barbados, Belize, British Virgin Islands, Costa Rica, Dominica, Dominican Republic, El Salvador, Grenada, Guatemala, Guyana, Haiti, Honduras, Jamaica, Montserrat, Netherlands Antilles, Saint Christopher-Nevis, Saint Lucia, Saint Vincent and the Grenadines, and Trinidad and Tobago. Exceptions are: most textiles (incl. clothing), footwear, handbags, luggage, flat goods, work gloves and leather wearing apparel, and certain watches and watch parts. Alcoholic beverages and perfumes, remain subject to IRS tax.

Health Expenditures—Selected Countries: 1980 and 1987
Source: Organization for Economic Cooperation and Development

Country	Total Health Expenditures			Public Health	
	Percent of G.D.P.		Per capita, 1987	Expenditures, 1987—	
	1980	1987	Exchange rates	Percent of gross domestic product	Percent of total health expenditures[1]
United States	9.2	11.2	$2,051	4.6	41.4
Austria	7.9	8.4	1,305	5.7	67.6
Belgium	6.6	7.2	1,048	5.6	76.9
Canada	7.4	8.6	1,376	6.4	74.8
Denmark	6.8	6.0	1,181	5.1	85.5
France	7.6	8.6	1,366	6.8	78.3
Greece	4.3	5.3	203	4.0	75.3
Ireland	8.5	7.4	617	6.5	87.0
Italy	6.8	6.9	907	5.4	78.0
Japan	6.4	6.8	1,347	5.0	73.2
Netherlands	8.2	8.5	1,233	6.6	77.8
New Zealand	7.2	6.9	731	5.7	82.5
Norway	6.6	7.5	1,473	7.3	97.6
Spain	5.9	6.0	447	4.3	71.5
Sweden	9.5	9.0	1,690	8.1	90.6
Switzerland	7.3	7.7	¹1,991	5.3	68.0
Turkey	4.1	3.5	45	1.4	41.3
United Kingdom	5.8	6.1	723	5.3	86.6
West Germany	7.9	8.2	1,502	6.3	77.0

(1) Preliminary estimates. G.D.P. = gross domestic product.

Foreign Trade of Selected Countries—Source of Imports and Destination of Exports: 1988

Source: Organization for Economic Cooperation and Development

(In billions of dollars, except percent. All exports are f.o.b. (free on board) and all imports are c.i.f. (cost insurance freight) except for U.S., Australian and Canadian imports, which are f.o.b.)

Country	Total[1]	O.E.C.D.[2] Total	E.E.C.[3]	Soviet Union and Eastern Europe	China, Vietnam, North Korea	O.P.E.C.[4]	Other developing countries[5]	Africa	America[6]	Middle East[7]	Far East[8]
Imports											
United States	441.3	275.0	85.0	2.2	8.5	23.1	132.6	10.9	51.3	11.5	80.9
Australia	33.3	25.6	7.8	.2	.7	.9	5.9	.2	.5	.8	5.2
Austria	36.6	31.1	24.9	2.3	.2	.6	2.4	.6	.5	.3	-1.2
Belgium[9]	92.1	80.1	67.3	1.9	.2	2.3	7.5	3.8	1.6	2.0	2.3
Canada	106.8	93.9	13.0	.4	.8	1.0	9.8	.8	3.5	.3	6.1
Denmark	26.5	22.8	13.6	.7	.3	.5	2.2	.2	.9	.4	1.0
France	176.8	143.3	106.7	4.7	1.5	6.1	18.4	9.0	4.2	3.4	7.0
Italy	139.0	107.0	80.0	5.6	1.4	8.1	16.6	9.9	3.8	4.0	4.5
Japan	187.5	93.0	24.2	3.5	10.4	26.9	53.8	4.2	8.2	19.2	48.0
Netherlands	99.3	82.9	71.2	2.1	5.1	4.8	4.4	2.7	2.8	3.5	4.7
Spain	60.3	46.8	34.3	1.5	.4	4.0	7.5	3.8	3.2	1.9	2.4
Sweden	45.5	40.0	25.5	1.7	.3	.5	3.1	.2	.9	.4	1.8
Switzerland	56.3	50.5	40.1	.7	.2	.6	4.3	1.1	1.3	.5	1.9
United Kingdom	189.3	160.3	99.4	2.8	.8	3.0	21.1	4.2	3.5	3.1	12.5
West Germany	250.5	202.6	129.8	9.1	2.5	6.2	30.0	8.1	7.6	2.8	13.9
Percent distribution:											
United States	100.0	62.3	19.3	.5	1.9	5.2	30.0	2.5	11.6	2.6	18.3
Australia	100.0	76.6	23.5	.5	2.1	2.8	17.7	.5	1.4	2.3	15.7
Austria	100.0	85.0	68.1	6.3	.5	1.6	6.6	1.7	1.3	.7	3.4
Belgium[9]	100.0	87.0	73.1	2.0	.3	2.5	8.1	4.1	1.7	2.2	2.5
Canada	100.0	87.9	12.2	.4	.7	1.0	9.2	.7	3.3	.3	5.7
Denmark	100.0	86.0	51.4	2.6	1.2	1.7	8.4	.7	3.3	1.6	3.8
France	100.0	81.0	60.4	2.7	.8	3.5	10.4	5.1	2.4	1.9	3.9
Italy	100.0	77.0	57.5	4.0	1.0	5.8	11.9	7.1	2.8	2.9	3.2
Japan	100.0	49.6	12.9	1.8	5.5	14.3	28.7	2.2	4.4	10.3	25.6
Netherlands	100.0	83.4	71.6	2.1	5.2	4.9	4.4	2.7	2.8	3.5	4.7
Spain	100.0	77.5	56.9	2.6	.6	6.7	12.4	6.3	5.3	3.1	3.9
Sweden	100.0	87.9	56.0	3.7	.6	1.0	6.8	.4	2.1	.8	4.0
Switzerland	100.0	89.7	71.3	1.2	.4	1.1	7.6	1.9	2.3	1.0	3.3
United Kingdom	100.0	84.7	52.5	1.5	.4	1.6	11.2	2.2	1.8	1.6	6.6
West Germany	100.0	80.9	51.8	3.6	1.0	2.5	12.0	3.2	3.0	1.1	5.5
Exports											
United States	320.4	202.1	75.9	3.6	5.1	14.0	95.4	7.4	43.9	10.9	46.1
Australia	32.7	19.8	4.8	.9	.9	1.4	9.1	.5	.3	1.1	7.5
Austria	31.0	25.2	19.8	2.8	.2	.9	1.9	.6	.2	.7	.6
Belgium[9]	92.0	80.7	68.3	1.1	.4	1.5	7.6	2.2	.7	2.5	3.4
Canada	111.9	100.5	9.0	1.1	2.1	1.4	6.8	1.0	2.4	.6	6.2
Denmark	27.9	20.7	13.8	.5	.1	.6	2.7	.7	.7	.6	.8
France	161.7	129.7	99.7	3.3	1.0	5.9	21.7	11.7	5.1	3.7	5.4
Italy	129.1	103.7	73.9	3.6	1.3	6.0	13.8	6.2	2.7	4.4	4.1
Japan	265.0	160.5	47.2	3.9	9.9	11.4	79.2	5.8	8.7	8.0	67.1
Netherlands	103.1	90.9	77.0	1.5	.3	2.5	7.1	2.8	1.2	1.8	3.4
Spain	40.2	32.6	26.4	.5	.2	1.8	4.6	2.2	1.6	1.3	.9
Sweden	49.7	43.3	26.0	1.0	.3	1.2	3.9	.9	.9	.9	2.0
Switzerland	50.6	39.8	28.3	1.7	.4	2.0	6.7	1.2	1.5	2.2	3.3
United Kingdom	144.9	114.0	73.0	2.1	.7	7.7	19.0	6.0	2.6	7.9	9.1
West Germany	323.3	271.1	176.0	11.2	2.8	8.8	28.9	9.0	5.6	7.3	11.8
Percent distribution:											
United States	100.0	63.1	23.7	1.1	1.6	4.4	29.8	2.3	13.7	3.4	14.4
Australia	100.0	60.7	14.6	2.8	2.8	4.3	28.0	1.4	1.0	3.3	23.1
Austria	100.0	81.3	63.8	9.1	.6	3.0	6.0	2.0	.7	2.4	1.9
Belgium[9]	100.0	87.8	74.3	1.2	.4	1.6	8.3	2.4	.8	2.7	3.7
Canada	100.0	89.8	8.0	1.0	1.9	1.2	6.1	.9	2.1	.6	5.6
Denmark	100.0	74.3	49.4	1.9	.5	2.1	9.7	2.4	2.6	2.1	2.9
France	100.0	80.2	61.6	2.1	.6	3.7	13.4	7.3	3.1	2.3	3.3
Italy	100.0	80.3	57.2	2.8	1.0	4.7	10.7	4.8	2.1	3.4	3.2
Japan	100.0	60.6	17.8	1.5	3.7	4.3	29.9	2.2	3.3	3.0	25.3
Netherlands	100.0	88.2	74.7	1.4	.3	2.4	6.9	2.7	1.1	1.8	3.3
Spain	100.0	80.9	65.6	1.3	.6	4.5	11.4	5.4	3.9	3.1	2.2
Sweden	100.0	87.1	52.3	2.1	.5	2.4	7.9	1.9	1.8	1.8	4.1
Switzerland	100.0	78.6	56.0	3.3	.8	3.9	13.3	2.4	3.0	4.4	6.6
United Kingdom	100.0	78.6	50.4	1.5	.5	5.3	13.1	4.1	1.8	5.5	6.3
West Germany	100.0	83.8	54.4	3.5	.9	2.7	8.9	2.8	1.7	2.3	3.6

(1) Includes other areas not shown separately. (2) Organization for Economic Cooperation and Development. (3) European Economic Community comprises Belgium-Luxembourg, Denmark, France, Greece, Ireland, Italy, Netherlands, Portugal, Spain, United Kingdom, and West Germany. (4) Organization of Petroleum Exporting Countries. (5) Comprises trade with all countries other than China, North Korea, Vietnam, South Africa, Soviet Union, Eastern Europe, and members of O.P.E.C. and O.E.C.D. (6) All countries comprising the continent except Canada and the United States. (7) Comprises Syria, Lebanon, Israel, Gaza Strip, Jordan, Iraq, Saudi Arabia, Yemen, Kuwait, Bahrain, United Arab Emirates, Qatar, Oman, and Iran. (8) All countries comprising the continent of Asia except Japan, China, North Korea, Vietnam, and those countries listed under Middle East. (9) Includes Luxembourg.

Foreign Exchange Rates: 1970 to 1989

Source: Board of Governors of the Federal Reserve System

(National currency units per dollar, except as noted. Except as indicated, data are annual averages of certified noon buying rates for cable transfers)

Year	Australia[1] (dollar)	Austria (schilling)	Belgium (franc)	Canada (dollar)	China: Taiwan (dollar)	Denmark (krone)	France (franc)	Greece (drachma)	Hong Kong (dollar)
1970	111.36	25.880	49.680	-1.0103	40.050	7.4890	5.5200	30.00	6.0600
1975	130.77	17.443	36.799	1.0175	38.000	5.7481	4.2876	32.29	4.9390
1977	110.82	16.545	35.848	1.0633	38.000	6.0049	4.9160	36.84	4.6620
1978	114.41	14.525	31.493	1.1405	37.054	5.5162	4.5090	36.75	4.6850
1979	111.77	13.387	29.342	1.1603	36.048	5.2622	4.2566	37.04	5.0030
1980	114.00	12.945	29.237	1.1693	36.015	5.6345	4.2250	42.62	4.9760
1981	114.95	15.948	37.194	1.1990	36.849	7.1350	5.4396	55.41	5.5678
1982	101.65	17.060	45.780	1.2344	39.124	8.3443	6.5793	66.87	6.0697
1983	90.14	17.968	51.121	1.2325	40.065	9.1483	7.6203	87.90	7.2569
1984	87.94	20.005	57.749	1.2953	39.633	10.3540	8.7355	112.73	7.8188
1985	70.03	20.676	59.336	1.3658	39.889	10.5980	8.9799	138.40	7.7911
1986	67.09	15.260	44.662	1.3896	37.837	8.0954	6.9256	139.93	7.8037
1987	70.14	12.649	37.357	1.3259	31.756	6.8477	6.0121	135.47	7.7985
1988	78.41	12.357	36.783	1.2306	28.636	6.7411	5.9594	142.00	7.8071
1989, June	81.11	13.320	39.651	1.1928	26.959	7.3727	6.4235	160.13	7.7929

Year	India (rupee)	Ireland[1] (pound)	Italy (lira)	Japan (yen)	Malaysia (ringgit)	Netherlands (guilder)	New Zealand[1] (dollar)	Norway (krone)	Portugal (escudo)
1970	7.576	239.59	623.00	357.60	3.0900	3.5970	111.48	7.1400	28.75
1975	8.409	222.16	653.09	296.78	2.4030	2.5293	121.16	5.2282	25.51
1977	8.769	174.49	882.76	268.62	2.4625	2.4547	96.89	5.3239	38.34
1978	8.198	191.84	849.12	210.38	2.3168	2.1642	103.64	5.2466	44.03
1979	8.156	204.65	831.10	219.02	2.1721	2.0072	102.23	5.0650	48.95
1980	7.887	205.77	856.20	226.63	2.1767	1.9875	97.34	4.9381	50.08
1981	8.681	161.32	1,138.60	220.63	2.3048	2.4998	86.85	5.7430	61.74
1982	9.485	142.05	1,345.00	249.06	2.3395	2.6719	75.10	6.4567	80.10
1983	10.104	124.81	1,519.30	237.55	2.3204	2.8543	66.79	7.3012	111.61
1984	11.348	108.64	1,756.10	237.45	2.3448	3.2083	57.84	8.1596	147.70
1985	12.332	106.62	1,908.90	238.47	2.4806	3.3184	49.75	8.5933	172.07
1986	12.597	134.14	1,491.16	168.35	2.5830	2.4484	52.46	7.3984	149.80
1987	12.943	148.79	1,297.03	144.60	2.5185	2.0263	59.33	6.7408	141.20
1988	13.899	152.49	1,302.39	128.17	2.6189	1.9778	65.56	6.5242	144.26
1989, June	15.690	141.14	1,383.80	133.48	2.7222	2.1361	60.76	6.8784	156.37

Year	Singapore (dollar)	South Africa[1] (rand)	South Korea (won)	Spain (peseta)	Sweden (krona)	Switzerland (franc)	Thailand (baht)	United Kingdom[1] (pound)	West Germany (deutsche mark)
1970	3.0800	139.24	310.57	69.72	5.1700	4.3160	21.000	239.59	3.6480
1975	2.3713	136.47	484.00	57.43	4.1530	2.5839	20.379	222.16	2.4613
1977	2.4394	114.99	484.00	75.99	4.4801	2.4064	20.400	174.49	2.3236
1978	2.2740	115.01	484.00	76.72	4.5206	1.7906	20.336	191.84	2.0096
1979	2.1746	118.72	484.00	67.16	4.2892	1.6643	20.419	212.24	1.8342
1980	2.1412	128.54	607.43	71.76	4.2309	1.6772	20.476	232.43	1.8175
1981	2.1053	114.77	681.03	92.40	5.0659	1.9674	21.731	202.43	2.2631
1982	2.1406	92.30	731.93	110.09	6.2838	2.0327	23.014	174.80	2.4280
1983	2.1136	89.85	776.04	143.50	7.6717	2.1006	22.991	151.59	2.5539
1984	2.1325	69.53	807.91	160.78	8.2706	2.3500	23.582	133.66	2.8454
1985	2.2008	45.57	861.89	169.98	8.6031	2.4551	27.193	129.74	2.9419
1986	2.1782	43.95	884.61	140.04	7.1272	1.7979	26.314	146.77	2.1704
1987	2.1059	49.08	825.93	123.54	6.3468	1.4918	25.774	163.98	1.7981
1988	2.0132	44.15	734.51	116.52	6.1369	1.4642	25.312	178.13	1.7569
1989, June	1.9461	39.03	675.23	118.64	6.4429	1.6410	25.581	168.46	1.8936

(1) Value is U.S. cents per unit of foreign currency.

Exchange Rates—Indexes of Value of Foreign Currency Relative to U.S. Dollar: 1970 to 1988

Source: U.S. Bureau of Labor Statistics

(1977 = 100)

Year	United States	Canada	Japan	Belgium	Denmark	France	Italy	Sweden	United Kingdom	West Germany
1970	100.0	101.8	74.8	72.2	80.0	88.9	140.8	86.1	137.3	63.7
1975	100.0	104.4	90.3	97.6	104.7	114.8	135.3	107.9	127.3	94.5
1977	100.0	100.0	100.0	100.0	100.0	100.0	100.0	100.0	100.0	100.0
1978	100.0	93.2	128.5	114.0	109.0	109.2	104.0	98.2	109.9	115.8
1979	100.0	90.7	112.7	122.2	114.1	115.5	106.2	104.2	121.6	126.7
1980	100.0	90.9	118.7	112.7	106.7	116.5	103.2	105.6	133.3	127.9
1981	100.0	88.6	121.4	96.8	84.1	90.4	77.5	88.2	116.0	103.0
1982	100.0	86.1	107.5	78.3	71.9	74.7	65.2	71.1	100.2	95.6
1983	100.0	86.2	112.7	70.1	65.6	64.5	58.1	58.2	86.9	90.9
1984	100.0	82.0	112.8	62.0	58.0	56.3	50.3	54.0	76.6	81.6
1985	100.0	77.8	112.3	60.4	56.6	54.7	46.2	51.9	74.4	78.9
1986	100.0	76.5	159.1	80.2	74.2	71.0	59.2	62.7	84.1	107.0
1987	100.0	80.1	185.2	95.9	87.7	81.8	68.1	70.4	94.0	129.1
1988	100.0	86.3	208.9	97.4	89.1	82.5	67.8	72.8	102.1	132.1

Public Expenditure for Education and Illiteracy, by Selected Country

Source: United Nations Educational, Scientific, and Cultural Organization

(Expenditure: Includes both capital and current expenditures on public education and subsidized private education. Illiteracy: Defined as inability both to read and write in any, or a specified, language.)

Country	Year	Public Expenditure for Education Percent of total public expenditure	Percent of gross national product	Percent of adult population illiterate,[1] 1985	Country	Year	Public Expenditure for Education Percent of total public expenditure	Percent of gross national product	Percent of adult population illiterate,[1] 1985
United States...	1985	NA	6.7[2]	NA	Morocco	1987	25.5	8.3	66.9
Afghanistan	1987	4.0	NA	76.3	Nepal........	1985	10.8	2.8	74.4
Algeria	1987	27.8	9.8	50.4	Netherlands	1985	16.5	16.4	NA
Argentina......	1987	8.9[3]	1.9[3]	4.5	Nigeria	1986	12.0[10]	1.4[10]	57.6
Australia	1986	12.6	5.8	NA	Pakistan	1987	NA	2.1	70.4
Bangladesh	1986	10.5[3]	2.2[3]	66.9	Peru........	1987	NA	3.3	15.2
Brazil.......	1986	17.7	4.5[3]	22.3	Philippines	1987	NA	2.0	14.3
Burma (Myanmar).	1977	12.2	1.6	NA	Poland	1987	12.5	4.4	NA
Canada.......	1987	15.4	7.2	NA	Portugal	1987	NA	4.5[3]	16.0[4]
Chile.......	1987	NA	3.6	5.6[4]	Romania	1985	NA	2.1	NA
China	1985	NA	2.7	30.7	Saudi Arabia....	1987	13.6	NA	NA
Colombia......	1987	22.4[3]	2.7[3]	11.9	South Korea	1987	26.6	4.2	NA
Czechoslovakia ..	1987	8.0	NA	NA	Soviet Union	1987	NA	7.3[6]	NA
East Germany ...	1987	5.4[5]	5.1[5,6]	NA	Spain	1987	NA	3.2	5.6
Egypt.......	1987	NA	5.5	55.5	Sri Lanka.....	1987	NA	3.8	12.9
Ethiopia......	1986	9.9	4.2	44.8[4,7]	Sudan........	1985	15.0[5]	4.3[5]	NA
France	1986	NA	5.7[8]	NA	Syria	1987	14.0	4.7	40.0
Ghana	1987	NA	3.4[3]	46.8	Tanzania	1987	9.7	4.1	NA
Hungary	1987	6.3	5.6	NA	Thailand	1987	17.9	3.6	9.0
India........	1986	NA	3.4	56.5	Turkey	1987	NA	1.7[11]	25.8[4]
Indonesia	1981	9.3	2.0	25.9	Uganda	1987	22.5[3]	3.9[3]	42.7
Iran	1987	18.1	NA	49.2	United Kingdom ..	1986	NA	5.0	NA
Iraq	1987	6.4	NA	10.7[4,9]	Venezuela	1985	21.3	5.4	11.4
Italy	1986	8.6[3]	4.0[3]	3.0[4]	West Germany...	1986	9.2	4.4	NA
Japan........	1986	17.7	5.0	NA	Yugoslavia.....	1986	NA	3.8	8.8
Kenya.......	1987	22.7	7.0	40.8	Zaire	1980	32.3[5]	3.4[5]	38.8
Malaysia	1987	NA	7.0	26.6	Zimbabwe	1986	16.2	8.5	26.0
Mexico	1987	NA	3.4	9.7[4]					

NA = Not available. (1) Population, 15 years old and over. Estimated by source, except as noted. (2) Data refer to total public and private expenditure on education. (3) Ministry of Education expenditures only. (4) Estimates made by country itself. (5) Current expenditures only. (6) Percent of net material product. (7) Population, 10 years old and over. (8) Metropolitan France only. (9) Population, 15-45 years old. (10) Federal government expenditures only. (11) Expenditure on third level education is not included.

United Nations

The 45th regular session of the United Nations General Assembly opened in September, 1990.

UN headquarters are in New York, N.Y., between First Ave. and Roosevelt Drive and E. 42d St. and E. 48th St. The General Assembly Bldg., Secretariat, Conference and Library bldgs. are interconnected.

A European office at Geneva includes Secretariat and agency staff members. Other offices of UN bodies and related organizations with a staff of some 23,000 from some 150 countries are scattered throughout the world.

The UN has a post office originating its own stamps.

Proposals to establish an organization of nations for maintenance of world peace led to the United Nations Con-

ference on International Organization at San Francisco, Apr. 25-June 26, 1945, where the charter of the United Nations was drawn up. It was signed June 26 by 50 nations, and by Poland, one of the original 51, on Oct. 15, 1945. The charter came into effect Oct. 24, 1945, upon ratification by the permanent members of the Security Council and a majority of other signatories.

Purposes: To maintain international peace and security; to develop friendly relations among nations; to achieve international cooperation in solving economic, social, cultural, and humanitarian problems and in promoting respect for human rights and fundamental freedoms; to be a center for harmonizing the actions of nations in attaining these common ends.

Roster of the United Nations

(As of mid–1990)

The 159 members of the United Nations, with the years in which they became members.

Member	Year	Member	Year	Member	Year	Member	Year
Afghanistan	1946	Burkina Faso.....	1960	Djibouti	1977	Guinea-Bissau	1974
Albania.........	1955	Burundi........	1962	Dominica........	1978	Guyana........	1966
Algeria.........	1962	Byelorussia.......	1945	Dominican Rep....	1945	Haiti	1945
Angola.........	1976	Cambodia.......	1955	Ecuador........	1945	Honduras.......	1945
Antigua and Barbuda .	1981	Cameroon	1960	Egypt[2]........	1945	Hungary	1955
Argentina........	1945	Canada........	1945	El Salvador......	1945	Iceland........	1946
Australia........	1945	Cape Verde.....	1975	Equatorial Guinea...	1968	India.........	1945
Austria.........	1955	Central Afr. Rep....	1960	Ethiopia........	1945	Indonesia[a].....	1950
Bahamas........	1973	Chad	1960	Fiji	1970	Iran..........	1945
Bahrain.........	1971	Chile	1945	Finland........	1955	Iraq..........	1945
Bangladesh.......	1974	China[2]........	1945	France	1945	Ireland........	1955
Barbados........	1966	Colombia.......	1945	Gabon	1960	Israel.........	1949
Belgium.........	1945	Comoros	1975	Gambia	1965	Italy.........	1955
Belize..........	1981	Congo.........	1960	Germany, East...	1973	Jamaica.......	1962
Benin..........	1960	Costa Rica.....	1945	Germany, West...	1973	Japan........	1956
Bhutan.........	1971	Côte d'Ivoire.....	1960	Ghana	1957	Jordan	1955
Bolivia.........	1945	Cuba.........	1945	Greece	1945	Kenya........	1963
Botswana........	1966	Cyprus........	1960	Grenada	1974	Kuwait	1963
Brazil..........	1945	Czechoslovakia....	1945	Guatemala	1945	Laos.........	1955
Brunei..........	1984	Denmark........	1945	Guinea	1958	Lebanon	1945
Bulgaria.........	1955						

Member	Year	Member	Year	Member	Year	Member	Year
Lesotho	1966	New Zealand	1945	Saint Vincent and		Thailand	1946
Liberia	1945	Nicaragua	1945	the Grenadines	1980	Togo	1960
Libya	1955	Niger	1960	Samoa (Western)	1976	Trinidad & Tobago	1962
Luxembourg	1945	Nigeria	1960	Sao Tome e Principe	1975	Tunisia	1956
Madagascar (Malagasy)	1960	Norway	1945	Saudi Arabia	1945	Turkey	1945
Malawi	1964	Oman	1971	Senegal	1960	Uganda	1962
Malaysia[1]	1957	Pakistan	1947	Seychelles	1976	Ukraine	1945
Maldives	1965	Panama	1945	Sierra Leone	1961	USSR	1945
Mali	1960	Papua New Guinea	1975	Singapore[1]	1965	United Arab Emirates	1971
Malta	1964	Paraguay	1945	Solomon Islands	1978	United Kingdom	1945
Mauritania	1961	Peru	1945	Somalia	1960	United States	1945
Mauritius	1968	Philippines	1945	South Africa[5]	1945	Uruguay	1945
Mexico	1945	Poland	1945	Spain	1955	Vanuatu	1981
Mongolia	1961	Portugal	1955	Sri Lanka	1955	Venezuela	1945
Morocco	1956	Qatar	1971	Sudan	1956	Vietnam	1977
Mozambique	1975	Romania	1955	Suriname	1975	Yemen	1947
Myanmar (Burma)	1948	Rwanda	1962	Swaziland	1968	Yugoslavia	1945
Namibia	1990	Saint Christopher		Sweden	1946	Zaire	1960
Nepal	1955	& Nevis	1983	Syria[2]	1945	Zambia	1964
Netherlands	1945	Saint Lucia	1979	Tanzania[3]	1961	Zimbabwe	1980

(1) Malaya joined the UN in 1957. In 1963, its name was changed to Malaysia following the accession of Singapore, Sabah, and Sarawak. Singapore became an independent UN member in 1965. (2) Egypt and Syria were original members of the UN. In 1958, the United Arab Republic was established by a union of Egypt and Syria and continued as a single member of the UN. In 1961, Syria resumed its separate membership. (3) Tanganyika was a member of the United Nations from 1961 and Zanzibar was a member from 1963. Following the ratification in 1964 of Articles of Union between Tanganyika and Zanzibar, the United Republic of Tanganyika and Zanzibar continued as a single member of the United Nations, later changing its name to United Republic of Tanzania. (4) The General Assembly voted in 1971 to expel the Chinese government on Taiwan and admit the Peking government in its place. (5) The General Assembly rejected the credentials of the South African delegates in 1974, and suspended the country from the Assembly. (6) Indonesia withdrew from the UN in 1965 and rejoined in 1966.

Organization of the United Nations

The text of the UN Charter, and further information, may be obtained from the Office of Public Information, United Nations, New York, NY 10017.

General Assembly. The General Assembly is composed of representatives of all the member nations. Each nation is entitled to one vote.

The General Assembly meets in regular annual sessions and in special session when necessary. Special sessions are convoked by the Secretary General at the request of the Security Council or of a majority of the members of the UN.

On important questions a two-thirds majority of members present and voting is required; on other questions a simple majority is sufficient.

The General Assembly must approve the budget and apportion expenses among members. A member in arrears will have no vote if the amount of arrears equals or exceeds the amount of the contributions due for the preceeding two full years.

Security Council. The Security Council consists of 15 members, 5 with permanent seats. The remaining 10 are elected for 2-year terms by the General Assembly; they are not eligible for immediate reelection.

Permanent members of the Council: China, France, USSR, United Kingdom, United States.

Non-permanent members are Canada, Colombia, Ethiopia, Finland, and Malaysia (until Dec. 31, 1990); Cote D'Ivoire, Cuba, Romania, Yemen, Zaire (until Dec. 31, 1991).

The Security Council has the primary responsiblity within the UN for maintaining international peace and security. The Council may investigate any dispute that threatens international peace and security.

Any member of the UN at UN headquarters may participate in its discussions and a nation not a member of UN may appear if it is a party to a dispute.

Decisions on procedural questions are made by an affirmative vote of 9 members. On all other matters the affirmative vote of 9 members must include the concurring votes of all permanent members; it is this clause which gives rise to the so-called "veto." A party to a dispute must refrain from voting.

The Security Council directs the various truce supervisory forces deployed throughout the world.

Economic and Social Council. The Economic and Social Council consists of 54 members elected by the General Assembly for 3-year terms of office. The council is responsible under the General Assembly for carrying out the functions of the United Nations with regard to international economic, social, cultural, educational, health and related matters. The council meets usually twice a year.

Trusteeship Council. The administration of trust territories is under UN supervision. The only remaining trust territory is Palau, administered by the U.S.

Secretariat. The Secretary General is the chief administrative officer of the UN. He may bring to the attention of the Security Council any matter that threatens international peace. He reports to the General Assembly.

Budget: The General Assembly approved a total budget for 90-91 of $1.56 billion.

International Court of Justice (World Court). The International Court of Justice is the principal judicial organ of the United Nations. All members are *ipso facto* parties to the statute of the Court, as are three nonmembers — Liechtenstein, San Marino, and Switzerland. Other states may become parties to the Court's statute.

The jurisdiction of the Court comprises cases which the parties submit to it and matters especially provided for in the charter or in treaties. The Court gives advisory opinions and renders judgments. Its decisions are only binding between the parties concerned and in respect to a particular dispute. If any party to a case fails to heed a judgment, the other party may have recourse to the Security Council.

The 15 judges are elected for 9-year terms by the General Assembly and the Security Council. Retiring judges are eligible for re-election. The Court remains permanently in session, except during vacations. All questions are decided by majority. The Court sits in The Hague, Netherlands.

Judges: 9-year term of office ending 1997: Mohamed Shahabuddeen, Guyana. Roberto Ago, Italy. Stephen Schwebel, U.S. Nikolai K. Tarasov, USSR. Mohammed Bedjaoui, Algeria. **9-year term in office ending 1994:** Ni Zhengyo, China. Jens Evensen, Norway. Manfred Lachs, Poland. Taslim Olawala Elias, Nigeria, Shigeru Oda, Japan. **9-year term in office ending 1991:** Nagendra Singh, India. Jose Maria Ruda, Argentina. Robert Y. Jennings, United Kingdom. Guy Ladreit de Lacharriere, France. Keba Mbaye, Senegal.

United Nations Secretaries General

Year	Secretary, Nation	Year	Secretary, Nation	Year	Secretary, Nation
1946	Trygve Lie, Norway	1961	U Thant, Burma	1982	Javier Perez de Cuellar, Peru
1953	Dag Hammarskjold, Sweden	1972	Kurt Waldheim, Austria		

U.S. Representatives to the United Nations

The U.S. Representative to the United Nations is the Chief of the U.S. Mission to the United Nations in New York and holds the rank and status of Ambassador Extraordinary and Plenipotentiary.

Year	Representative	Year	Representative	Year	Representative
1946	Edward R. Stettinius Jr.	1968	George W. Ball	1976	William W. Scranton
1946	Herschel V. Johnson (act.)	1968	James Russell Wiggins	1977	Andrew Young
1947	Warren R. Austin	1969	Charles W. Yost	1979	Donald McHenry
1953	Henry Cabot Lodge Jr.	1971	George Bush	1981	Jeane J. Kirkpatrick
1960	James J. Wadsworth	1973	John A. Scali	1985	Vernon A. Walters
1961	Adlai E. Stevenson	1975	Daniel P. Moynihan	1989	Thomas R. Pickering
1965	Arthur J. Goldberg				

Visitors to the United Nations

United Nations headquarters is open to the public every day of the year except Christmas and New Year's Day. The public entrance is at 46th Street and First Avenue and opens at 9 a.m.

Guided tours begin from the main lobby of the General Assembly building and are given approximately every half hour from 9:15 a.m. to 4:45 p.m. daily. The tours last about one hour. Tours in languages other than English may be arranged.

Groups of 15 or more persons should make arrangements as far in advance as possible by writing to the Group Program Unit, Visitors' Service, Room GA-56, United Nations, New York, NY 10017, or telephone (212) 963-7713. Children under 5 are not permitted on tours.

Specialized and Related Agencies

These agencies are autonomous, with their own memberships and organs which have a functional relationship or working agreement with the UN (headquarters.)

Food & Agriculture Org. (FAO) aims to increase production from farms, forests, and fisheries; improve distribution, marketing, and nutrition; better conditions for rural people. (Viale delle Terme di Caracalla, 00100 Rome, Italy.)

General Agreement on Tariffs and Trade (GATT) is the only treaty setting rules for world trade. Provides a forum for settling trade disputes and negotiating trade liberalization. (Centre William Rappard, 154 rue de Lausanne, 1211 Geneva 21, Switzerland.)

International Atomic Energy Agency (IAEA) aims to promote the safe, peaceful uses of atomic energy. (Vienna International Centre, PO Box 100, A-1400, Vienna, Austria.)

International Bank for Reconstruction and Development (IBRD) (World Bank) provides loans and technical assistance for economic development projects in developing member countries; encourages cofinancing for projects from other public and private sources. **International Development Association (IDA)**, an affiliate of the Bank, provides funds for development projects on concessionary terms to the poorer developing member countries. (both 1818 H St., NW, Washington, DC 20433.) **International Finance Corporation (IFC)** an affiliate of the Bank, promotes the growth of the private sector in developing member countries; encourages the development of local capital markets; stimulates the international flow of private capital. (1818 H St., NW, Washington, DC 20433.)

International Civil Aviation Org. (ICAO) promotes international civil aviation standards and regulations. (1000 Sherbrooke St. W., Montreal, Quebec, Canada H3A 2R2.)

International Fund for Agricultural Development (IFAD) aims to mobilize funds for agricultural and rural projects in developing countries. (107 Via del Serafico, Rome, Italy.)

International Labor Org. (ILO) aims to promote employment; improve labor conditions and living standards. (4 route de Morillons, CH-1211, Geneva 22, Switzerland.)

International Maritime Org. (IMO) aims to promote cooperation on technical matters affecting international shipping. (4 Albert Embankment, London, SE1 7SR, England.)

International Monetary Fund (IMF) aims to promote international monetary co-operation and currency stabilization; expansion of international trade. (700 19th St., NW, Washington, DC, 20431.)

International Telecommunication Union (ITU) sets up international regulations of radio, telegraph, telephone and space radio-communications. Allocates radio frequencies. (Place des Nations, 1211 Geneva 20, Switzerland.)

United Nations Educational, Scientific, & Cultural Org. (UNESCO) aims to promote collaboration among nations through education, science, and culture. The U.S. withdrew from this organization in 1985 because of UNESCO's anti-Western bias. (9 Place de Fontenoy, 75700 Paris, France.)

United Nations Children's Fund (UNICEF) provides aid and development assistance to children and mothers in developing countries. (1 UN Plaza, New York, NY 10017.)

Universal Postal Union (UPU) aims to perfect postal services and promote international collaboration. (Weltpoststrasse 4, 3000 Berne, 15 Switzerland.)

World Health Org. (WHO) aims to aid the attainment of the highest possible level of health. (1211 Geneva 27, Switzerland.)

World Intellectual Property Organization (WIPO) seeks to protect, through international cooperation, literary, industrial, scientific, and artistic works. (34, Chemin des Colom Bettes, 1211 Geneva, Switzerland.)

World Meteorological Org. (WMO) aims to co-ordinate and improve world meteorological work. (Case Postale 5, CH-1211, Geneva 20, Switzerland.)

Major International Organizations

As of mid-1990

Association of Southeast Asian Nations (ASEAN), was formed in 1967 to promote economic, social, and cultural cooperation and development among the non-communist states of the region. Members in 1990 are Brunei Darussalam, Indonesia, Malaysia, Philippines, Singapore, Thailand. Annual ministerial meetings set policy; a central Secretariat in Jakarta and specialized intergovernmental committees work in trade, transportation, communications, agriculture, science, finance, and culture.

Caribbean Community (Caricom) was established July 4, 1973. Its function is to further co-operation in economics, health, education, culture, science and technology, and tax

(continued)

administration, as well as the co-ordination of foreign policy. Members in 1990 are Antigua, Bahamas, Barbados, Belize, Dominica, Grenada, Guyana, Jamaica, Montserrat, St. Kitts, St. Lucia, St. Vincent, Trinidad & Tobago. Observers are Dominican Republic, Haiti, and Suriname.

Commonwealth of Nations originally called the British Commonwealth of Nations, is an association of nations and dependencies loosely joined by a common interest based on having been parts of the old British Empire. The British monarch is the symbolic head of the Commonwealth.

There are 50 self-governing independent nations in the Commonwealth, plus various colonies and protectorates. As of May 1990, the members were the United Kingdom of Great Britain and Northern Ireland and 16 other nations recognizing the British monarch, represented by a governor-general, as their head of state: Antigua and Barbuda, Australia, Bahamas, Barbados, Belize, Canada, Grenada, Jamaica, Mauritius, New Zealand, Papua New Guinea, St. Kitts-Nevis, St. Lucia, St. Vincent and the Grenadines, Solomon Islands, and Tuvalu (a special member); and 32 countries with their own heads of state: Bangladesh, Botswana, Brunei, Cyprus, Dominica, The Gambia, Ghana, Guyana, India, Kenya, Kiribati, Lesotho, Malawi, Malaysia, The Maldives, Malta, Namibia, Nauru (a special member), Nigeria, Pakistan, Samoa, Seychelles, Sierra Leone, Singapore, Sri Lanka, Swaziland, Tanzania, Tonga, Trinidad and Tobago, Uganda, Vanuatu, Zambia, and Zimbabwe. In addition various Caribbean dependencies take part in certain Commonwealth activities.

The Commonwealth facilitates consultation among member states through meetings of prime ministers and finance ministers, and through a permanent Secretariat. Members consult on economic, scientific, educational, financial, legal, and military matters, and try to coordinate policies.

European Communities (EC, the Common Market) is the collective designation of three organizations with common membership: the European Economic Community (Common Market), the European Coal and Steel Community, and the European Atomic Energy Community (Euratom). The 12 full members are: Belgium, Denmark, France, West Germany, Greece, Ireland, Italy, Luxembourg, Netherlands, Portugal, Spain, United Kingdom. Some 60 nations in Africa, the Caribbean, and the Pacific are affiliated under the Lomé Convention.

A merger of the 3 communities executives went into effect July 1, 1967, though the component organizations date back to 1951 and 1958. A Council of Ministers, a Commission, a European Parliament, and a Court of Justice comprise the permanent structure. The communities aim to integrate their economies, coordinate social developments, and bring about political union of the democratic states of Europe.

The members have agreed that a single European market which will remove all barriers to free trade and free movement of capital and people will take effect at the end of 1992.

European Free Trade Association (EFTA), consisting of Austria, Iceland, Norway, Portugal, Sweden, Switzerland and associated member Finland, was created Jan. 4, 1960, to gradually reduce customs duties and quantitative restrictions between members on industrial products. By Dec. 31, 1966, all tariffs and quotas had been eliminated. The association entered into free trade agreements with the EC, Jan. 1, 1973. Trade barriers were removed July 1, 1976.

League of Arab States (The Arab League) was created Mar. 22, 1945, by Egypt, Iraq, Jordan, Lebanon, Saudi Arabia, Syria, and Yemen. Joining later were Algeria, Bahrain, Djibouti, Kuwait, Libya, Mauritania, Morocco, Oman, Qatar, The Palestine Liberation Org., Somalia, Sudan, Tunisia, United Arab Emirates. The League fosters cultural, economic, and communication ties and mediates disputes among the Arab states; it represents Arab states in certain international negotiations, and coordinates a military, economic, and diplomatic offensive against Israel. As a result of Egypt signing a peace treaty with Israel, the League, Mar. 1979, suspended Egypt's membership and transferred the League's headquarters from Cairo to Tunis. Egypt was readmitted to the organization in 1989.

North Atlantic Treaty Org. (NATO) was created by treaty (signed Apr. 4, 1949; in effect Aug. 24, 1949). Members in 1990 include Belgium, Canada, Denmark, France, Iceland, Italy, Luxembourg, Netherlands, Norway, Portugal, United Kingdom, and the U.S. Greece, Turkey, West Germany, and Spain have joined since. The members agreed to settle disputes by peaceful means; to develop their individual and collective capacity to resist armed attack; to regard an attack on one as an attack on all, and to take necessary action to repel an attack under Article 51 of the United Nations Charter.

The NATO structure consists of a Council and a Military Committee of 3 commands (Allied Command Europe, Allied Command Atlantic, Allied Command Channel) and the Canada-U.S. Regional Planning Group.

Following announcement in 1966 of nearly total French withdrawal from the military affairs of NATO, organization hq. moved, 1967, from Paris to Brussels.

At their summit conference in July 1990, members called for a reshaping of the alliance to assure the Soviet Union of their peaceful intentions.

The reunified Germany became a member late in 1990. (*See Chronology and Index for details.*)

Organization of African Unity (OAU), formed May 25, 1963, by 32 African countries (50 in 1989) to coordinate cultural, political, scientific and economic policies; to end colonialism in Africa; and to promote a common defense of members' independence. It holds annual conferences of heads of state. Hq. is in Addis Ababa, Ethiopia.

Organization of American States (OAS) was formed in Bogota, Colombia, in 1948. Hq. is in Washington, D.C. It has a Permanent Council, Inter-American Economic and Social Council, and Inter-American Council for Education, Science and Culture, a Juridical Committee and a Commission on Human Rights. The Permanent Council can call meetings of foreign ministers to deal with urgent security matters. A General Assembly meets annually. A secretary general and assistant are elected for 5-year terms. There are 32 members, each with one vote in the various organizations: Antigua, Argentina, Bahamas, Barbados, Bolivia, Brazil, Chile, Colombia, Costa Rica, Cuba, Dominica, Dominican Republic, Ecuador, El Salvador, Grenada, Guatemala, Haiti, Honduras, Jamaica, Mexico, Nicaragua, Panama, Paraguay, Peru, St. Kitts-Nevis, St. Lucia, St. Vincent, Suriname, Trinidad & Tobago, U.S., Uruguay, Venezuela. In 1962, the OAS excluded Cuba from OAS activities but not from membership.

Organization for Economic Cooperation and Development (OECD) was established Sept. 30, 1961 to promote economic and social welfare in member countries, and to stimulate and harmonize efforts on behalf of developing nations. Nearly all the industrialized "free market" countries belong, with Yugoslavia as an associate member. OECD collects and disseminates economic and environmental information. Members in 1990 are: Australia, Austria, Belgium, Canada, Denmark, Finland, France, West Germany, Greece, Iceland, Ireland, Italy, Japan, Luxembourg, Netherlands, New Zealand, Norway, Portugal, Spain, Sweden, Switzerland, Turkey, United Kingdom, United States, Yugoslavia (special member). Hq. is in Paris.

Organization of Petroleum Exporting Countries (OPEC) was created Nov. 14, 1960 at Venezuelan initiative. The group attempts to set world oil prices by controlling oil production. It is also involved in advancing members' interests in trade and development dealings with industrialized oil-consuming nations. Members in 1990 are Algeria, Ecuador, Gabon, Indonesia, Iran, Iraq, Kuwait, Libya, Nigeria, Qatar, Saudi Arabia, United Arab Emirates, Venezuela.

Warsaw Pact was created May 14, 1955, as a mutual defense alliance. Members in 1990 are Bulgaria, Czechoslovakia, Hungary, Poland, Romania, and the USSR. Hq. is in Moscow. It provides for a unified military command; if one member is attacked, the others will aid it with all necessary steps including armed force.

The alliance is not expected to survive the reforms among the member nations that occurred in 1989-90.

Ambassadors and Envoys

As of mid-1990

The address of U.S. embassies abroad is the appropriate foreign capital. The U.S. does not have diplomatic relations with the following countries: Albania,[1] Angola,[2] Cambodia,[3] Taiwan,[4] Cuba,[5] Iran,[6] Libya,[6] Vietnam,[1] N. Korea. There are informal relations with Bhutan and Vanuatu.

Countries	Envoys from United States	Envoys to United States
Afghanistan	Vacancy	Vacancy
Algeria	Christopher W.S. Ross, Amb.	Adberrahmane Bensid, Amb.
Antigua & Barbuda	R. James McHugh, Chargé	Edmund H. Lake, Amb.
Argentina	Terence A. Todman, Amb.	Guido DiTella, Amb.
Australia	Melvin F. Sembler, Amb.	Michael J. Cook, Amb.
Austria	Michael J. Habib, Chargé	Friedrich Hoess, Amb.
Bahamas	Chic Hecht, Amb.	Margaret E. McDonald, Amb.
Bahrain	Charles W. Hostler, Amb.	Ghazi M. Algosaibi, Amb.
Bangladesh	Willard De Pree, Amb.	A.H.S. Ataul Karim, Amb.
Barbados	John Clark, Chargé	William Douglas, Amb.
Belgium	Maynard W. Glitman, Amb.	Herman Dehennin, Amb.
Belize	Robert G. Rich, Jr., Amb.	Edward A. Laing, Amb.
Benin	Harriet W. Isom, Amb.	Theophile Nata, Amb.
Bolivia	Robert S. Gelbard, Amb.	Jose Crespo-Velasco, Amb.
Botswana	Johnnie Carson, Chargé	Botsweletse K. Sebele, Amb.
Brazil	Richard H. Melton, Amb.	Marcilio M. Moreira, Amb.
Brunei	Christopher H. Phillips, Amb.	D.P.H. Mohammad Suni, Amb.
Bulgaria	Sol Polansky, Amb.	Velichko F. Velichkov Amb.
Burkina Faso	David H. Shinn, Amb.	Paul-Désiré Kabore, Amb.
Burundi	Cynthia S. Perry, Amb.	Julien Kavakure, Amb.
Cameroon	Frances D. Cook, Amb.	Paul Pondi, Amb.
Canada	Edward N. Ney, Amb.	Derek H. Burney, Amb.
Cape Verde	Francis T. McNamara, Amb.	Jose Luis Fernandes Lopes, Amb.
Central African Rep.	Daniel H. Simpson, Amb.	Jean-Pierre Sohahong-Kombet, Amb.
Chad	Vacancy	Mahamat Ali Adoum, Amb.
Chile	Charles A. Gillespie Jr., Amb.	Octavio Errazuriz, Amb.
China	James R. Lilley, Amb.	Zhu Qizhen, Amb.
Colombia	Thomas E. McNamara, Amb.	Victor Mosquera, Amb.
Comoros	Howard K. Walker, Amb.	Amini Ali Moumin, Amb.
Congo	Leonard G. Shurtleff, Amb.	Benjamin Bounkoulou, Amb.
Costa Rica	Deane R. Hinton, Amb.	Danilo Jimenez, Amb.
Côte d'Ivoire	Kenneth L. Brown, Amb.	Charles Gomis, Amb.
Cyprus	John U. Nix, Chargé	Michael E. Sherifis, Amb.
Czechoslovakia	Shirley Temple Black, Amb.	Miroslav Houstecky, Amb.
Denmark	Keith L. Brown, Amb.	Peter P. Dyvig, Amb.
Djibouti	Robert S. Barrett, Amb.	Roble Olhale, Amb.
Dominica	John Clark, Chargé	Vacancy
Dominican Republic	Paul D. Taylor, Amb.	Carlos A. Morales, Amb.
Ecuador	Adolph H. Eisner, Chargé	Jaime Moncayo, Amb.
Egypt	Frank G. Wisner, Amb.	El Sayed A. R. El Reedy, Amb.
El Salvador	William G. Walker, Amb.	Miguel A. Salaverria, Amb.
Equatorial Guinea	Chester E. Norris Jr., Amb.	Damaso Obiang Ndong, Amb.
Estonia[7]		Ernst Jaakson, Consul General
Ethiopia	Robert G. Houdek, Chargé	Girma Amare, Chargé
Fiji	Evelyn I.H. Teegen, Amb.	Abdul H. Yusuf, Chargé
Finland	John G. Weinmann, Amb.	Jukka Valtasaari, Amb.
France	Walter J.P. Curley, Amb.	Jacques Andreani, Amb.
Gabon	Keith L. Wauchope, Amb.	Jean Robert Odzaga, Amb.
Gambia, The	Vacancy	Ousman A. Sallah, Amb.
Germany, East	Richard C. Barkley, Amb.	Gerhard Herder, Amb.
Germany, West	Vernon A. Walters, Amb.	Juergen Ruhfus, Amb.
Ghana	Raymond C. Ewing, Amb.	Eric K. Otoo, Amb.
Greece	Michael G. Sotirhos, Amb.	Christos Zacharakis, Amb.
Grenada	Ford Cooper, Chargé	Albert O. Xavier, Amb.
Guatemala	Thomas F. Stroock, Amb.	Ricardo Aguirre-Murga, Chargé
Guinea	Samuel E. Lupo, Amb.	Kekoura Camara, Amb.
Guinea-Bissau	William L. Jacobsen Jr., Amb.	Alfredo Lopes Cabral, Amb.
Guyana	Theresa A. Tull, Amb.	Cedric H. Grant, Amb.
Haiti	Alvin P. Adams Jr., Amb.	Fritz Fougy, Amb.
Honduras	Cresencio S. Arcos, Amb.	Jorge Hernandez-Alcerro, Amb.
Hungary	Mark H. Palmer, Amb.	Peter Varkonyi, Amb.
Iceland	Charles E. Cobb Jr., Amb.	Ingvi S. Ingvarsson, Amb.
India	William Clark Jr., Amb.	Karen Singh, Amb.
Indonesia	John C. Monjo, Amb.	Abdul Rachman Ramly, Amb.
Iraq	April C. Glaspie, Amb.	Mohamed Sadiq Al-Mashat, Amb.
Ireland	Richard A. Moore, Amb.	Padraic N. McKernan, Amb.
Israel	William A. Brown, Amb.	Moshe Arad, Amb.
Italy	Peter F. Secchia, Amb.	Rinaldo Petrignani, Amb.
Jamaica	Glen A. Holden, Amb.	Keith Johnson, Amb.
Japan	Michael H. Armacost, Amb.	Ryohei Murata, Amb.
Jordan	Roscoe S. Suddarth, Amb.	Hussein A. Hammami, Amb.
Kenya	Smith Hempstone Jr., Amb.	Dennis D. Afande, Amb.
Kiribati	Evelyn I.H. Teegen, Amb.	Vacancy
Korea, South	Donald P. Gregg, Amb.	Tong-Jin Park, Amb.
Kuwait	W. Nathaniel Howell, Amb.	Shaikh S. N. Al-Sabah, Amb.
Laos	Charles B. Salmon Jr., Amb.	Done Somvorachit, Chargé
Latvia[7]		Anatol Dinbergs, Chargé
Lebanon	John T. McCarthy, Amb.	Bassam Namani, Chargé
Lesotho	Vacancy	W. T. van Tonder, Amb.
Liberia	James K. Bishop, Amb.	Eugenia A. Wordsworth-Stevenson, Amb.

Lithuania[7]		Stasys Lozoraitis Jr., Chargé
Luxembourg	Jean B.S. Gerard	Andre Philippe, Amb.
Madagascar	Howard K. Walker, Amb.	Pierrot J. Rajaonarivelo, Amb.
Malawi	George A. Trail 3d, Amb.	Robert Mbaya, Amb.
Malaysia	Paul M. Cleveland, Amb.	Albert S. Talalla, Amb.
Mali	Robert M. Pringle, Amb.	Mohamed A. Toure, Amb.
Malta	Sally J. Novetzke, Amb.	Salv Stellini, Amb.
Mauritania	William H. Twaddell, Amb.	Abdellah Ould Daddah, Amb.
Mauritius	Penne Percy Korth, Amb.	Chitmansing Jesseramsing, Amb.
Mexico	John Negroponte, Amb.	Gustavo Petricioli, Amb.
Mongolia	Richard L. Williams, Amb.	Gendengiin Nyamdoo, Amb
Morocco	E. Michael Ussery, Amb.	Ali Bengelloun, Amb.
Mozambique	Melissa F. Wells, Amb.	Valeriano Ferrao, Amb.
Myanmar	Burton Levin, Amb.	U. Myo Aung, Amb.
Namibia	Vacancy	Vacancy
Nauru	Melvin F. Sembler, Amb.	Vacancy
Nepal	Julia Chang Bloch, Amb.	Mohan Man Sainju, Amb.
Netherlands	C. Howard Wilkins Jr., Amb.	Johan H. Meesman, Amb.
New Zealand	Della M. Newman, Amb.	Harold H. Francis, Amb.
Nicaragua	John P. Leonard, Chargé	Leonor de Huper, Chargé
Niger	Carl C. Cundiff, Amb.	Moumouni A. Djermakoye, Amb.
Nigeria	Lannon Walker, Amb.	Hamzat Ahmadu, Amb.
Norway	Loret Miller Ruppe, Amb.	Kjeld Vibe, Amb.
Oman	Richard W. Boehm, Amb.	Awadh Bader Al-Shanfari, Amb.
Pakistan	Robert B. Oakley, Amb.	Zulfiqar Ali Khan, Amb.
Panama	Deane R. Hinton, Amb.	Carlos F. Rodriguez, Amb.
Papua New Guinea	Dean L. Welty, Chargé	Margaret Taylor, Amb.
Paraguay	Timothy L. Towell, Amb.	Marcos Martinez Mendieta, Amb.
Peru	Anthony C.E. Quainton, Amb.	Cesar G. Atala, Amb.
Philippines	Nicholas Platt, Amb.	Emmanuel Pelaez, Amb.
Poland	John R. Davis Jr., Amb.	Kazimierz Dziewanowski, Amb.
Portugal	Edward M. Rowell, Amb.	Joao Eduardo M. Periera Bastos, Amb.
Qatar	Mark G. Hambley, Amb.	Hamad A. Al-Kawari, Amb.
Romania	Alan Green Jr., Amb.	Mihai Croitoru, Chargé
Rwanda	Leonard H.O. Spearman Sr., Amb.	Aloys Uwimana, Amb.
St. Kitts & Nevis	John Clark, Chargé	Erstein Edwards, Chargé
St. Lucia	John Clark, Chargé	Joseph E. Edmunds, Amb.
St. Vincent and The Grenadines	John Clark, Chargé	Vacancy
Sao Tome and Principe	Keith L. Wauchope, Amb.	Joaquim R. Branco, Amb.
Saudi Arabia	Charles W. Freeman Jr., Amb.	Bandar Bin Sultan, Amb.
Senegal	George E. Moose, Amb.	Ibra Deguene Ka, Amb.
Seychelles	James Moran, Amb.	Marc Marengo, Chargé
Sierra Leone	Johnny Young, Amb.	George Carew, Amb.
Singapore	Robert D. Orr, Amb.	Tommy T. B. Koh, Amb.
Solomon Islands	Vacancy	Vacancy
Somalia	T. Frank Crigler, Amb.	Abdikarim Ali Omar, Amb.
South Africa	William L. Swing, Amb.	Piet G.J. Koornhof, Amb.
Spain	Joseph Zappala, Amb.	Julian Santamaria, Amb.
Sri Lanka	Marion V. Creekmore Jr., Amb.	W. Susanta de Alwis, Amb.
Sudan	James R. Cheek, Amb.	Abdalla Ahmed Abdalla, Amb.
Suriname	Richard Howland, Amb.	Willem A. Udenhout, Amb.
Swaziland	Mary A. Ryan, Amb.	Absalom V. Mamba, Amb.
Sweden	Charles E. Redman, Amb.	Anders I. Thunborg, Amb.
Switzerland	Joseph B. Gildenhorn, Amb.	Edouard Brunner, Amb.
Syria	Edward P. Djerejian, Amb.	Bushra Kanafani, Amb.
Tanzania	Edward DeJarnette Jr., Amb.	Ali Karume, Chargé
Thailand	Daniel A. O' Donohue, Amb.	Vitthya Vejjajiva, Amb.
Togo	Rush W. Taylor Jr., Amb.	Ellom-Kodjo Schuppius, Amb.
Tonga	Evelyn I.H. Teegen, Amb.	Siosaia Ma'Ulupekotova, Amb.
Trinidad and Tobago	Charles A. Gargano, Amb.	Angus A. Khan, Amb.
Tunisia	Robert H. Pelletreau, Jr., Amb.	Abdelaziz Hamzaoui, Amb.
Turkey	Morton I. Abramowitz, Amb.	Nuzhet Kandemir, Amb.
Tuvalu	Evelyn I.H. Teegen, Amb.	Vacancy
Uganda	John A. Burroughs Jr., Amb.	Stephen K. Katenta-Apuli, Amb.
USSR	John F. Matlock, Jr., Amb.	Yuri Dubinin, Amb.
United Arab Emirates	Edward S. Walker, Amb.	Abdulla Al-Nahayyan, Amb.
United Kingdom	Henry E. Catto, Amb.	Antony Acland, Amb.
Uruguay	Malcolm R. Wilkey, Amb.	Juan Podesta Pinon, Chargé
Vatican	Thomas P. Melady, Amb.	Pio Laghi, Pro-Nuncio
Venezuela	Kenneth N. Skoug Jr., Chargé	Simon A. Consalvi, Amb.
Western Samoa	Della Newman, Amb.	Tuaopepe F. Wendt, Amb.
Yemen	Charles F. Dunbar, Amb.	Mohsin A. Alaini, Amb.
Yugoslavia	Warren Zimmerman, Amb.	Dzevad Mujezinovic, Amb.
Zaire	William C. Harrop, Amb.	Mushobekwa Kalimba wa Katana, Amb.
Zambia	Jeffrey Davidow, Amb.	Paul J.F. Lusaka, Amb.
Zimbabwe	Vacancy	Stanislaus G. Chigwedere, Amb.

Special Missions

U.S. Mission to North Atlantic Treaty Organization, Brussels—William H. Taft 4th
U.S. Mission to the European Communities, Brussels—Thomas M.T. Niles, Amb.
U.S. Mission to the United Nations, New York—Thomas P. Pickering, Amb.
U.S. Mission to the European Office of the UN, Geneva—Morris B. Abram, Amb.
U.S. Mission to the Organization for Economic Cooperation and Development, Paris—Dennis Lamb, Amb.
U.S. Mission to the Organization of American States, Washington—Luigi R. Einaudi, Amb.

(1) Relations severed in 1939. (2) Post closed in 1975. (3) U.S. embassy closed in 1975. (4) U.S. severed relations in 1978; unofficial relations are maintained. (5) Relations severed in 1961; limited ties restored in 1977. (6) U.S. severed relations on Apr. 7, 1980. (7) U.S. does not officially recognize 1940 annexation by USSR. (8) Embassy closed, May 2, 1980. U.S. closed the Libyan mission, May 6, 1981.

U.S. Aid to Foreign Nations

Source: Bureau of Economic Analysis, U.S. Commerce Department

Figures are in millions of dollars. (*Less than $500,000.) Data include military supplies and services furnished under the Foreign Assistance Act and direct Defense Department appropriations, and include credits extended to private entities.

Net grants and credits take into account all known returns to the U.S., including reverse grants, returns of grants, and payments of principal. A minus sign (−) indicates that the total of these returns is greater than the total of grants or credits. Nations with net grant or credit under $2 mln. not incl.

Other assistance represents the transfer of U.S. farm products in exchange for foreign currencies, less the government's disbursements of the currencies as grants, credits, or for purchases.

Amounts do not include investments in the following: Asian Development Bank, $160 mln.; Inter-American Development Bank, $97 mln.; International Development Assn., $852 mln.; International Bank for Reconstruction and Development, $23 mln.; African Development Bank, $7 mln.; African Development Fund, $34 mln.

Calendar Year 1989	Total	Net grants	Net credits	Net other
Total	8,733	10,962	−2,220	−8
Western Europe	−565	82	−647	(*)
Austria	−11	(*)	−11	—
Belgium	−9		−9	—
Finland	7	(*)	7	(*)
France	−14	(*)	−14	—
Ireland	−7		−7	—
Italy	−28	(*)	−29	—
Portugal	71	75	−5	—
Spain	−474	5	−480	1
United Kingdom	−109		−109	—
Yugoslavia	11	(*)	11	(*)
Other & unspecified	−1	(*)	−2	—
Eastern Europe	414	11	420	−17
Poland	519	11	525	−17
Romania	−59		−59	—
USSR	−46		−46	—
Near East & South Asia	4,371	5,787	−1,421	4
Afghanistan	63	66	−3	(*)
Bangladesh	138	54	84	—
Cyprus	19	19	(*)	(*)
Egypt	2,085	2,020	65	−1
Greece	306	(*)	306	−1
India	44	134	−91	−1
Iraq	−16		−16	—
Israel	1,902	2,897	−996	—
Jordan	150	88	62	(*)
Lebanon	−3	17	−20	—
Oman	8	5	3	—
Pakistan	−398	231	−631	2
Sri Lanka	40	20	17	3
Turkey	−91	127	−219	(*)
Yemen	42	26	16	—
UNRWA	39	39	—	—
Other & unspecified	28	28		—
East Asia & Pacific	375	582	−207	(*)
Australia	−18		−18	—
Burma (Myanmar)	1	2	−1	—
Cambodia	5	5	(*)	—
China	35	(*)	35	—
Hong Kong	−8	(*)	−8	—
Indonesia	35	56	−21	—
Korea, South	−132	1	−130	—
Malaysia	−36	1	−37	—
New Zealand	−4		−4	—
Philippines	305	269	36	(*)
Taiwan	−7	(*)	−7	1
Thailand	12	62	−49	—
Fed. States of Micronesia	87	87	—	—
Marshall Islands	69	69	—	—
Other & unspecified	32	33	−1	—
Africa	835	921	−85	−1
Algeria	−77	(*)	−77	—
Angola	−13	(*)	−14	—
Benin	6	6	(*)	—
Botswana	15	16	−1	—
Burkina Faso	13	13	—	(*)
Burundi	3	3	—	(*)
Cameroon	18	23	−5	—
Cape Verde	3	3	—	—
Cen. African Rep.	5	5	—	—
Chad	15	15		—

	Total	Net grants	Net credits	Net other
Djibouti	5	5	—	—
Ethiopia	18	24	−7	(*)
Gabon	8	1	7	—
Gambia	11	11	—	—
Ghana	26	24	2	(*)
Guinea	4	5	−1	(*)
Guinea-Bissau	3	3	—	—
Kenya	53	65	−13	(*)
Lesotho	18	18	—	—
Liberia	13	19	−6	—
Madagascar	6	5	1	—
Malawi	36	36	(*)	—
Mali	23	23	(*)	(*)
Mauritania	11	11	(*)	—
Mauritius	3	(*)	2	—
Morocco	−17	63	−78	−3
Mozambique	32	33	—	(*)
Niger	34	33	1	—
Nigeria	36	7	29	—
Rwanda	9	9	(*)	(*)
Senegal	44	39	6	(*)
Seychelles	4	4	—	—
Sierra Leone	10	6	3	—
Somalia	32	31	1	—
South Africa	18	18	—	—
Sudan	108	79	29	(*)
Swaziland	11	11	(*)	—
Tanzania	11	6	5	—
Togo	−15	15	(*)	—
Tunisia	52	54	−4	2
Uganda	20	15	5	—
Zaire	57	34	23	1
Zambia	21	7	13	—
Zimbabwe	12	17	−5	—
Other & unspecified	108	104	−1	—
Western Hemisphere	1,036	1,312	−280	4
Argentina	−6	(*)	−6	—
Bahamas	−2	(*)	−2	—
Belize	14	12	2	—
Bolivia	113	55	57	—
Brazil	−202	4	−206	—
Canada	−30		−30	—
Chile	−46	1	−47	(*)
Colombia	−36	19	−55	—
Costa Rica	143	129	14	1
Dominican Republic	51	33	18	—
Ecuador	22	25	−2	—
El Salvador	404	377	27	—
Guatemala	161	130	26	4
Guyana	8	(*)	7	—
Haiti	65	72	−7	(*)
Honduras	133	101	32	—
Jamaica	118	71	47	−1
Mexico	−121	21	−142	—
Panama	8	8	—	—
Paraguay	1	2	−1	(*)
Peru	31	28	−7	—
St. Kitts-Nevis	8	(*)	8	—
Trinidad-Tobago	16	(*)	16	—
Uruguay	−6	1	−7	—
Venezuela	−21	(*)	−21	—
Other & unspecified	210	214	2	—
Intl. orgs. & unspecified	2,268	2,268	—	—

NATIONAL DEFENSE

Data as of July, 1990

Chairman, Joint Chiefs of Staff
Gen. Colin L. Powell

The Joint Chiefs of Staff consists of the Chairman and Vice Chairman of the Joint Chiefs of Staff; the Chief of Staff, U.S. Army; the Chief of Naval Operations; the Chief of Staff, U.S. Air Force; and the Commandant of the Marine Corps.

Army

Chief of Staff—Carl E. Vuono

Generals	Date of Rank
Burba, Edwin H. Jr.	Sept. 27, 1989
Foss, John W.	Aug. 2, 1989
Galvin, John R.	Feb. 25, 1985
Lindsay, James J.	Oct. 10, 1986
Menetrey, Louis C.	June 24, 1987
Powell, Colin L.	Apr. 4, 1989
RisCassi, Robert W.	Jan. 17, 1989
Saint, Crosbie E.	June 24, 1988
Schwarzkopf, H. Norman	Nov. 23, 1989
Sullivan, Gordon R.	June 4, 1990
Thurman, Maxwell R.	June 23, 1983
Tuttle, William G.T. Jr.	Oct. 1, 1989

Air Force

Chief of Staff—John M. Loh (act.)

Generals	Date of Rank
Chain, John T., Jr.	July 1, 1985
Johnson, Hansford T.	Oct. 1, 1989
Kutyna, Donald J.	Apr. 1, 1990
Loh, John M.	June 1, 1990
McCarthy, James P.	Oct. 1, 1989
McDonald, Charles C.	Nov. 1, 1989
McPeak, Merrill, A.	Aug. 1, 1988
Oaks, Robert C.	—
Russ, Robert D.	May 22, 1985
Shaud, John A.	July 1, 1988
Yates, Ronald W.	Apr. 1, 1990

Navy

Chief of Naval Operations
Admiral Frank B. Kelso II (submariner)

Admirals	Date of Rank
Carter, Powell F., Jr. (submariner). . .	Oct. 1, 1987
DeMars, Bruce (submariner).	Nov. 1, 1988
Edney, Leon A. (aviator).	Oct. 1, 1988
Hardisty, Huntington (aviator)	Mar. 11, 1987
Hogg, James R. (surface warfare) . . .	Dec. 1, 1988
Howe, Johnathan T. (surface warfare).	June 1, 1989
Jeremiah, David E. (surface warfare) .	Oct. 1, 1987
Trost, Carlisle A.H. (submariner) . . .	Oct. 4, 1985

Marine Corps

Corps Commandant, with rank of General
Alfred M. Gray. . . . . July 1, 1987

ACMC/Chief of Staff, with rank of Gen.
John R. Dailey . . . . Aug. 1, 1990

Coast Guard

Commandant, with rank of Admiral
J. William Kime. . . . . May 31, 1990

Vice Commandant, with rank of Vice Admiral
Martin H. Daniell Jr. . . . . May 31, 1990

Unified Defense Commands Commanders-in-Chief

U.S. European Command, Brussels — Gen. John R. Galvin (USA) (concurrently NATO Supreme Allied Commander).

U.S. Southern Command, Quarry Heights, Panama Canal Zone — Gen. Maxwell R. Thurman (USA).

U.S. Atlantic Command, Norfolk, Virginia — Adm. Lee Baggett, Jr., (USN) (concurrently NATO Supreme Allied Commander, Atlantic).

U.S. Pacific Command, Hawaii — Adm. Huntington Hardisty (USN)

U.S. Space Command, Gen. John L. Piotrowski (USAF)

*Strategic Air Command, Omaha — Gen. John T. Chain (USAF)

*US Forces Command — Gen. Edwin H. Burba (USA)

*U.S. Transportation Command, Gen. Hansford T. Johnson (USAF)

U.S. Special Operations Command, MacDill AFB, Fla. — Gen. James J. Lindsay (USA)

U.S. Central Command, Gen. H. Norman Schwarzkopf (USA)

*A Specified Command.

North Atlantic Treaty Organization International Commands

Supreme Allied Commander, Europe (SACEUR) — Gen. John R. Galvin (USA)

Deputy Supreme Allied Commander Europe (DSACEUR) — Gen. Sir Brian Kenny, UK, Army (UKA)

Deputy Supreme Allied Commander Europe (DSACEUR) — Gen. Eberhard Eimler (GEAF)

Commander-in-Chief Allied Forces Northern Europe — Gen. Sir Patrick Palmer, UK, Army, KBE, MC (UKA)

Commander-in-Chief Allied Forces Central Europe — Gen. Hans-Henning von Sandrart (GEA)

Commander-in-Chief Allied Forces Southern Europe — Adm. J. T. Howe

Commander-in-Chief United Kingdom Air Forces — Air Chief Marshal Sir Patrick Hine (UKAF)

Chairman, NATO Military Committee — Adm. James R. Hogg (USN)

Principal U.S. Military Training Centers

Army

Name, P.O. address	Zip	Nearest city	Name, P.O. address	Zip	Nearest city
Aberdeen Proving Ground, MD . .	21005	Aberdeen	Fort Knox, KY	40121	Louisville
Carlisle Barracks, PA	17013	Carlisle	Fort Leavenworth, KS	66027	Leavenworth
Fort Belvoir, VA.	22060	Alexandria	Fort Lee, VA.	23801	Petersburg
Fort Benning, GA	31905	Columbus	Fort McClellan, AL	36205	Anniston
Fort Bliss, TX	79916	El Paso	Fort Monmouth, NJ.	07703	Red Bank
Fort Bragg, NC	28307	Fayetteville	Fort Rucker, AL.	36362	Dothan
Fort Devens, MA	01433	Ayer	Fort Sill, OK.	73503	Lawton
Fort Dix, NJ	08640	Trenton	Fort Leonard Wood, MO.	65473	Rolla
Fort Eustis, VA	23604	Newport News	Joint Readiness, Ft. Chaffee, AR .	72905	Fort Smith
Fort Gordon, GA	30905	Augusta	National Training Center.	92311	Barstow, CA
Fort Benjamin Harrison, IN . . .	46216	Indianapolis	Redstone Arsenal, AL	35809	Huntsville
Fort Sam Houston, TX.	78234	San Antonio	The Judge Advocate		Charlottes-
Fort Huachuca, AZ.	85613	Sierra Vista	General School, VA	22901	ville
Fort Jackson, SC	29207	Columbia	U.S. Military Acad., NY.	10996	West Point

Navy

Name, P.O. address	Zip	Nearest city	Name, P.O. address	Zip	Nearest city
Great Lakes, IL	60088	North Chicago	Orlando, FL	32813	Orlando
San Diego, CA	92133	San Diego			

Marine Corps

Name, P.O. address	Zip	Nearest city	Name, P.O. address	Zip	Nearest city
MCB Camp Lejeune, NC	28542	Jacksonville		Seattle	Iwakuni
MCB Camp Pendleton, CA	92055	Oceanside		98764	
MCB Camp Butler, Okinawa	FPO		MCAS Kaneohe Bay,		
	Seattle	Futenma,	Oahu, HI	San	
	98773	Okinawa		Fran-	
MCAGCC Twentynine Palms, CA	92278	Palm Springs		cisco	Kailua
MCCDC Quantico, VA	22134	Quantico		96863	
MCRD Parris Island, SC	29905	Beaufort	MCAS Futenma,		
MCRD San Diego, CA	92140	San Diego	Okinawa FPO Seattle	98772	Futenma
MCAS Cherry Point, NC	28533	Havelock	MCAS Beaufort, SC	29904	Beaufort
MCAS El Toro (Santa Ana), CA .	92709	Santa Ana	MCAS Yuma, AZ	85369	Yuma
MCAS Tustin, CA.	92780	Santa Ana	MCMWTC Bridgeport, CA.	93517	Bridgeport
MCAS New River, NC	28545	Jacksonville	MCLB Albany, GA	31704	Albany
MCAS Iwakuni, Japan	FPO		MCLB Barstow, CA	92311	Barstow

MCB = Marine Corps Base. MCCDC = Marine Corps Combat Development Command. MCAS = Marine Corps Air Station. MCRD = Marine Corps Recruit Depot. MCAGCC = Marine Corps Air-Ground Combat Center. MCMWTC = Marine Corps Mountain Warfare Training Center. MCLB = Marine Corps Logistics Base.

Air Force*

Name	Zip	Nearest city	Name	Zip	Nearest city
Chanute AFB, IL	61868	Rantoul	Mather AFB, CA	95655	Sacramento
Columbus AFB, MS	39701	Columbus	Maxwell AFB, AL**	36112	Montgomery
Goodfellow AFB, TX	76903	San Angelo	Randolph AFB, TX	78150	San Antonio
Gunter AFS, AL**	36114	Montgomery	Reese AFB, TX	79489	Lubbock
Keesler AFB, MS	39534	Biloxi	Sheppard AFB, TX	76311	Wichita Falls
Lackland AFB, TX	78236	San Antonio	Vance AFB, OK.	73702	Enid
Laughlin AFB, TX	78843	Del Rio	Williams AFB, AZ	85224	Phoenix
Lowry AFB, CO	80230	Denver	Wright Patterson AFB, OH	45433	Dayton

*Air Training Command Bases. **Air University Bases.

Personal Salutes and Honors

The United States national salute, 21 guns, is also the salute to a national flag. The independence of the United States is commemorated by the salute to the union — one gun for each state — fired at noon on July 4 at all military posts provided with suitable artillery.

A-21-gun salute on arrival and departure, with 4 ruffles and flourishes, is rendered to the President of the United States, to an ex-President and to a President-elect. The national anthem or *Hail to the Chief,* as appropriate, is played for the President, and the national anthem for the others. A 21-gun salute on arrival and departure with 4 ruffles and flourishes, also is rendered to the sovereign or chief of state of a foreign country or a member of a reigning royal family; the national anthem of his or her country is played. The music is considered an inseparable part of the salute and will immediately follow the ruffles and flourishes without pause.

Rank	Salute—guns Arrive	Salute—guns Leave	Ruffles, flourishes	Music
Vice President of United States	19		4	Hail Columbia
Speaker of the House	19		4	March
American or foreign ambassador.	19		4	Nat. anthem of official
Premier or prime minister	19		4	Nat. anthem of official
Secretary of Defense, Army, Navy or Air Force	19	19	4	Honors March
Other Cabinet members, Senate President pro tempore, Governor, or Chief Justice of U.S.	19		4	Honors March
Chairman, Joint Chiefs of Staff.	19	19	4	
Army Chief of Staff, Chief of Naval Operations, Air Force Chief of Staff, Marine Commandant	19	19	4	General's or Admiral's March
General of the Army, General of the Air Force, Fleet Admiral. . . .	19	19	4	
Generals, Admirals	17	17	4	
Assistant secretaries of Defense, Army, Navy or Air Force	17	17	4	Honors March
Chairman of a committee of Congress	17	17	4	Honors March

Other salutes (on arrival only) include 15 guns for U.S. envoys or ministers and foreign envoys or ministers accredited to the U.S.; 15 guns for a lieutenant general or vice admiral; 13 guns for a major general or rear admiral (upper half); 13 guns for U.S. ministers resident and ministers resident accredited to the U.S.; 11 guns for a brigadier general or rear admiral (lower half); 11 guns for U.S. charges d'affaires and like officials accredited to U.S.; and 11 guns for consuls general accredited to U.S.

Military Units, U.S. Army and Air Force

Army units. Squad. In infantry usually ten men under a staff sergeant. Platoon. In infantry 4 squads under a lieutenant. Company. Headquarters section and 4 platoons under a captain. (Company in the artillery is a battery; in the cavalry, a troop.) Battalion. Hdqts. and 4 or more companies under a lieutenant colonel. (Battalion size unit in the cavalry is a squadron.) Brigade. Hdqts. and 3 or more battalions under a colonel. Division. Hdqts. and 3 brigades with artillery, combat support, and combat service support units under a major general. Army Corps. Two or more divisions with corps troops under a lieutenant general. Field Army. Hdqts. and two or more corps with field Army troops under a general.

Air Force Units. Flight. Numerically designated flights are the lowest level unit in the Air Force. They are used primarily where there is a need for small mission elements to be incorporated into an organized unit. Squadron. A squadron is the basic unit in the Air Force. It is used to designate the mission units in operational commands. Group. The group is a flexible unit composed of two or more squadrons whose functions may be either tactical, support or administrative in nature. Wing. An operational wing normally has two or more assigned mission squadrons in an area such as combat, flying training or airlift. Air Division. The organization of the air division may be similar to that of the numbered air force, though on a much smaller scale. Functions are usually limited to operations and logistics. Numbered Air Forces. Normally an operationally oriented agency, the numbered air force is designed for the control of two or more air divisions or units of comparable strength. It is a flexible organization and may be of any size. Its wings may be assigned to air divisions or directly under the numbered air force. Major Command. A major subdivision of the Air Force that is assigned a major segment of the USAF mission.

U.S. Army Insignia and Chevrons

Source: Department of the Army

Grade	Insignia

General of the Armies

General John J. Pershing, the only person to have held this rank, was authorized to prescribe his own insignia, but never wore in excess of four stars. The rank originally was established by Congress for George Washington in 1799, and he was promoted to the rank by joint resolution of Congress, approved by Pres. Ford Oct. 19, 1976.

General of Army... Five silver stars fastened together in a circle and the coat of arms of the United States in gold color metal with shield and crest enameled.

General . . . . Four silver stars
Lieutenant General . . . . . Three silver stars
Major General . . . . Two silver stars
Brigadier General . . . . . One silver star
Colonel . . . . Silver eagle
Lieutenant Colonel . . . . Silver oak leaf
Major . . . . Gold oak leaf
Captain . . . . Two silver bars
First Lieutenant . . . . . . One silver bar
Second Lieutenant . . . . . One gold bar

Warrant officers

Grade Four—Silver bar with 4 enamel black squares.
Grade Three—Silver bar with 3 enamel black squares.
Grade Two—Silver bar with 2 enamel black squares.
Grade One—Silver bar with 1 enamel black squares.

Non-commissioned Officers

Sergeant Major of the Army (E-9). Same as Command Sergeant Major (below) but with 2 stars. Also wears distinctive red and white shield on lapel.

Command Sergeant Major (E-9). Three chevrons above three arcs with a 5-pointed star with a wreath around the star between the chevrons and arcs.

Sergeant Major (E-9). Three chevrons above three arcs with a five-pointed star between the chevrons and arcs.

First Sergeant (E-8). Three chevrons above three arcs with a lozenge between the chevrons and arcs.

Master Sergeant (E-8). Three chevrons above three arcs.

Platoon Sergeant or Sergeant First Class (E-7). Three chevrons above two arcs.

Staff Sergeant (E-6). Three chevrons above one arc.

Sergeant (E-5). Three chevrons.

Corporal (E-4). Two chevrons.

Specialists

Specialist (E-4). Eagle device only.

Other enlisted

Private First Class (E-3). One chevron above one arc.

Private (E-2). One chevron.

Private (E-1). None.

U.S. Army

Source: Department of the Army

Army Military Personnel on Active Duty[1]

June 30[2]	Total strength	Commissioned officers Total	Male	Female[3]	Warrant officers Male[4]	Female	Enlisted personnel Total	Male	Female
1940	267,767	17,563	16,624	939	763	———	249,441	249,441	
1942	3,074,184	203,137	190,662	12,475	3,285	———	2,867,762	2,867,762	
1943	6,993,102	557,657	521,435	36,222	21,919	0	6,413,526	6,358,200	55,325
1944	7,992,868	740,077	692,351	47,726	36,893	10	7,215,888	7,144,601	71,287
1945	8,266,373	835,403	772,511	62,892	56,216	44	7,374,710	7,283,930	90,780
1946	1,889,690	257,300	240,643	16,657	9,826	18	1,622,546	1,605,847	16,699
1950	591,487	67,784	63,375	4,409	4,760	22	518,921	512,370	6,551
1955	1,107,606	111,347	106,173	5,174	10,552	48	985,659	977,943	7,716
1960	871,348	91,056	86,832	4,224	10,141	39	770,112	761,833	8,279
1965	967,049	101,812	98,029	3,783	10,285	23	854,929	846,409	8,520
1969	1,509,637	148,836	143,699	5,137	23,734	20	1,327,047	1,316,326	10,721
1970	1,319,735	143,704	138,469	5,235	23,005	13	1,153,013	1,141,537	11,476
1975	781,316	89,756	85,184	4,572	13,214	22	678,324	640,621	37,703
1980 (Sept 30)	772,661	85,339	77,843	7,496	13,265	113	673,944	612,593	61,351
1984 (Sept. 30)	775,594	92,484	82,497	9,987	15,156	243	667,711	601,095	66,616
1985 (Sept. 30)	776,244	94,103	83,563	10,540	15,296	288	666,557	598,639	67,918
1987 (Mar. 30)	770,075	93,973	82,886	11,087	14,923	332	660,847	589,789	71,058
1988 (Mar. 30)	764,247	93,173	81,904	11,269	14,664	363	656,047	584,305	71,742
1989 (Mar. 30)	760,237	91,550	80,113	11,437	14,517	417	653,753	581,106	72,647
1990 (Mar. 30)	746,220	91,330	79,520	11,810	15,177	470	639,713	567,015	72,698

(1) Represents strength of the active Army, including Philippine Scouts, retired Regular Army personnel on extended active duty, and National Guard and Reserve personnel on extended active duty; excludes U.S. Military Academy cadets, contract surgeons, and National Guard and Reserve personnel not on extended active duty.

(2) Data for 1940 to 1947 include personnel in the Army Air Forces and its predecessors (Air Service and Air Corps).

(3) Includes: women doctors, dentists, and Medical Service Corps officers for 1946 and subsequent years, women in the Army Nurse Corps for all years, and the Women's Army Corps and Women's Medical Specialists Corps (dieticians, physical therapists, and occupational specialists) for 1943 and subsequent years.

(4) Act of Congress approved April 27, 1926, directed the appointment as warrant officers of field clerks still in active service. Includes flight officers as follows: 1943, 5,700; 1944, 13,615; 1945, 31,117; 1946, 2,580.

The Federal Service Academies

U.S. Military Academy, West Point, N.Y. Founded 1802. Awards B.S. degree and Army commission for a 5-year service obligation. For admissions information, write Admissions Office, USMA, West Point, NY 10996.

U.S. Naval Academy, Annapolis, Md. Founded 1845. Awards B.S. degree and Navy or Marine Corps commission for a 5-year service obligation. For admissions information, write Dean of Admissions, Naval Academy, Annapolis, MD 21402.

U.S. Air Force Academy, Colorado Springs, Col. Founded 1954. Awards B.S. degree and Air Force commission for a 5-year service obligation. For admissions information, write Registrar, U.S. Air Force Academy, CO 80840.

U.S. Coast Guard Academy, New London, Conn. Founded 1876. Awards B.S. degree and Coast Guard commission for a 5-year service obligation. For admissions information, write Director of Admissions, Coast Guard Academy, New London, CT 06320.

U.S. Merchant Marine Academy, Kings Point, N.Y. Founded 1943. Awards B.S. degree, a license as a deck, engineer, or dual officer, and a U.S. Naval Reserve commission. Service obligations vary according to options taken by the graduate. For admissions information, write Admission Office, U.S. Merchant Marine Academy, Kings Point, NY 11024.

U.S. Navy Insignia

Source: Department of the Navy

Navy

Stripes and corps device are of gold embroidery.

Stripes

Fleet Admiral . . . . . 1 two inch with 4 one-half inch.
Admiral . . . . 1 two inch with 3 one-half inch.
Vice Admiral. . . . . . 1 two inch with 2 one-half inch.
Rear Admiral (upper
    half) . . . . 1 two inch with 1 one-half inch.
Rear Admiral (lower
    half) . . . . 1 two inch.
Captain. . . . . 4 one-half inch.
Commander . . . . . . 3 one-half inch.
Lieut. Commander . . 2 one-half inch, with 1 one-quarter
                      inch between.
Lieutenant . . . . . . 2 one-half inch.
Lieutenant (j.g.) . . . . 1 one-half inch with one-quarter
                      inch above.
Ensign . . . . 1 one-half inch.
Warrant Officers—One 1/2″ broken with 1/2″ intervals of
blue as follows:

Warrant Officer W-4—1 break

Warrant Officer W-3—2 breaks, 2″ apart
Warrant Officer W-2—3 breaks, 2″ apart
The breaks are symmetrically centered on outer face of the
sleeve.
Enlisted personnel (non-Commissioned petty officers)...A
rating badge worn on the upper left arm, consisting of a
spread eagle, appropriate number of chevrons, and centered specialty mark.

Marine Corps

Marine Corps and Army officer insignia are similar. Marine Corps and Army enlisted insignia, although basically
similar, differ in color, design, and fewer Marine Corps subdivisions. The Marine Corps' distinctive cap and collar orna-
ment is a combination of the American eagle, globe, and anchor.

Coast Guard

Coast Guard insignia follow Navy custom, with certain
minor changes such as the officer cap insignia. The Coast
Guard shield is worn on both sleeves of officers and on the
right sleeve of all enlisted personnel.

U.S. Navy Personnel on Active Duty

June 30	Officers	Nurses	Enlisted	Off. Cand.	Total
1940.	13,162	442	144,824	2,569	160,997
1945.	320,293	11,086	2,988,207	61,231	3,380,817
1950.	42,687	1,964	331,860	5,037	381,538
1960.	67,456	2,103	544,040	4,385	617,984
1970.	78,488	2,273	605,899	6,000	692,660
1980.	63,100[1]	—	464,100[2]	—	527,200
1985 (Jan.)	70,291[1]	—	500,810[2]	—	571,101
1988 (Jan.)	72,038[1]	—	510,208[2]	—	582,246
1989 (Sept.)	74,416	—	533,939	—	608,355

(1) Nurses are included. (2) Officer candidates are included.

Marine Corps Personnel On Active Duty

Year	Officers	Enlisted	Total	Year	Officers	Enlisted	Total	Year	Officers	Enlisted	Total
1955 . .	18,417	186,753	205,170	1970 . .	24,941	234,796	259,737	1987 . .	20,047	179,478	199,525
1960 . .	16,203	154,418	170,621	1980 . .	18,198	170,271	188,469	1988 . .	20,079	177,271	197,350
1965 . .	17,258	172,955	190,213	1985 . .	20,175	177,850	198,025	1989 . .	20,099	176,857	196,956

Veteran Population

Source: Dept. of Veterans Affairs

	March 1990
Veterans in civil life, end of month — Total[a,b]	27,001,000
War Veterans — Total	20,754,000
Vietnam Era — Total	8,301,000
And service in Korean Conflict	592,000
No service in Korean Conflict.	7,709,000
Korean Conflict — Total	4,854,000
And service in WW II.	880,000
No service in WW II	3,973,000
World War II	8,982,000
World War I	90,000
Prior periods of war	(c)
Peacetime Veterans — Total	6,247,000
Post-Vietnam Era	2,976,000
Peacetime service between Korean Conflict and Vietnam Era only	2,943,000
Peacetime Service — other	328,000

NOTE: Detail may not add to total shown due to rounding. (a) The category "War veterans" equals the sum of Vietnam
era (no service in Korean conflict), Korean conflict (no service in World War II), World War II and World War I. The data
refer only to veterans living in the U.S. and Puerto Rico since data on veterans living elsewhere are not available. (b) The
March 1990 figures reflect updated estimates of mortality for the 1980–90 period. These new estimates of mortality are used
to improve the accuracy of the veteran population data. As a result, the 1990 figures are not totally comparable with data
from earlier years. (c) The number of living Spanish-American War veterans in March 1990 was 1. The number of Mexican
Border period veterans reported on the compensation and pension rolls for March 1990 was 61.

Compensation and Pension Case Payments

Fiscal year	Living veteran cases no.	Deceased veteran cases no.	Total cases no.	Total dis- bursement dollars	Fiscal year	Living veteran cases no.	Deceased veteran cases no.	Total cases no.	Total dis- bursement dollars
1900. . .	752,510	241,019	993,529	138,462,130	1950. . .	2,368,238	658,123	3,026,361	2,009,462,298
1910. . .	602,622	318,461	921,083	159,974,056	1960. . .	3,008,935	950,802	3,959,737	3,314,761,383
1920. . .	419,627	349,916	769,543	316,418,029	1970. . .	3,127,338	1,487,176	4,614,514	5,113,649,490
1930. . .	542,610	298,223	840,833	418,432,808	1980. . .	3,195,395	1,450,785	4,646,180	11,045,412,000
1940. . .	610,122	239,176	849,298	429,138,465	1989 . .	2,775,616	878,074	3,653,690	14,938,608,939

USAF and Air Reserve Forces Personnel by Categories

Category	FY '86[2]	FY '87[2]	FY '88[2]	FY '89	FY '90[1]	FY '91[1]
Air Force Military						
Officers	109,400	109,400	105,538	105,538	102,300	98,800
Airmen	494,700	493,000	465,648	465,645	464,400	426,800
Cadets	4,500	4,400	4,400	4,400	4,400	4,400
Total, Air Force Military	608,200	606,800	575,603	575,600	571,000	530,000
Career Reenlistments	38,900	43,000	40,400	37,100	39,000	40,100
Rate	88%	88%	89%	69%	89%	90%
First-Term Reenlistments	23,500	22,100	23,000	25,300	22,500	19,500
Rate	58%	58%	65%	65%	60%	60%
Civilian Personnel						
Direct Hire (including Technicians)	249,604	250,266	252,188	250,416	249,044	255,187
Indirect Hire—Foreign Nationals	13,644	13,496	13,237	13,340	13,399	12,500
Total, Civilian Personnel	263,248	263,762	265,425	263,756	262,443	267,687
Total, Military and Civilian[1]	871,448	870,562	841,028	839,356	833,543	797,687
Technicians (included above as Direct Hire Civilians)						
AFRES Technicians	8,866	9,178	9,994	10,004	10,124	9,923
ANG Technicians	22,497	23,221	23,530	23,613	23,948	23,949
Air Reserve Forces						
Air National Guard, Selected Reserve	112,592	113,767	115,900	115,200	116,300	116,300
Air Force Reserve, Paid	78,519	79,562	82,400	83,600	84,800	85,200
Air Force Reserve, Nonpaid	47,153	49,941	49,920	31,225	43,900	51,700
Total, Ready Reserve	238,264	243,270	248,220	230,055	245,000	253,200
Standby	25,823	28,325	26,200	26,200	26,200	17,000
Total, Air Reserve Forces[3]	264,087	271,595	274,420	256,255	271,200	270,200

Note: Totals may not add due to rounding. (1) President's budget request. (2) FY '84-87 are actual figures; FY '88-89 are estimates; excludes nonchargeable personnel. (3) Excludes Retired Air Force Reserve.

U.S. Air Force Personnel Strength: 1907–1990

Year[2]	Strength	Year	Strength	Year	Strength	Year	Strength
1907	3	1941	152,125	1950	411,277	1987	606,900
1918	195,023	1942	764,415	1960	814,213	1988	575,603
1920	9,050	1943	2,197,114	1970	791,078	1989	570,965
1930	13,531	1944	2,372,292	1980	557,969	1990	571,100[1]
1940	51,165	1945	2,282,259	1986	608,200		

(1) Programmed. (2) Prior to 1947, data are for U.S. Army Air Corps and Air Service of the Signal Corps.

Coast Guard Personnel on Active Duty: 1970-1990

Source: U.S. Dept. of Transportation. *Annual Report of the Secretary of Transportation.*

Year	Total	Officers	Cadets	Enlisted	Year	Total	Officers	Cadets	Enlisted
1970	37,689	5,512	653	31,524	1984	38,705	6,790	759	31,156
1975	36,788	5,630	1,177	29,981	1985	38,595	6,775	733	31,087
1979	38,559	6,340	806	31,413	1986	37,284	6,577	754	29,953
1980	39,381	6,463	877	32,041	1987	38,576	6,644	859	31,073
1981	39,760	6,519	981	32,260	1988	37,723	6,530	887	30,306
1982	38,248	6,431	902	30,915	1990	37,308	6,475	820	29,860
1983	39,708	6,535	811	32,362					

Women in the Armed Forces

Women in the Army, Navy, Air Force, Marines, and Coast Guard are all fully integrated with male personnel. Expansion of military women's programs began in the Department of Defense in fiscal year 1973.

As of mid-1990, women made up 10.8 percent of the armed forces. Almost 25% of all medical and dental specialists are women; only 0.8 percent serve in the infantry, gun crews, or seamanship.

Although women are prohibited by law and directives based on law from serving in combat positions, policy changes in the Department of Defense have made possible the assignment of women to almost all other career fields. Career progression for women is now comparable to that for male personnel. Women are routinely assigned to overseas locations formerly closed to female personnel. Women are in command of activities and units that have missions other than administration of women.

Admission of women to the service academies began in the fall of 1976.

Army — Information: Chief, Office of Public Affairs, Dept. of Army, Wash., DC 20310; (as of Mar. 1990): 84,978 women, 72,698 enlisted women, 11,810 women commissioned officers, 470 women warrant officers.

Army Nurse Corps — Brig. Gen. Clara Adams-Ender, Chief Army Nurse Corps, Office of the Surgeon General, Dept. of Army, 5111 Leesburg Pike, Falls Church, VA 22041.

Navy — Information: Chief of Information, Dept. of Navy, Wash., DC 20350-1200; 7,646 women officers; 51,633 enlisted women; 433 cadets and midshipwomen, as of 9/30/89.

Navy Nurse Corps — Rear Adm. Mary F. Hall, Dir., Navy Nurse Corps, Dept. of Navy, Wash., DC 20372-2000; 2,205 women officers; 779 men. (As of 3/31/89).

Air Force — Information: Office of Public Affairs, Dept. of the Air Force, Wash., DC 20330; 13,403 women officers; 63,175 enlisted women.

Air Force Nurse Corps — Brig. Gen. Barbara A. Goodwin, Chief, Air Force Nurse Corps, Office of the Surgeon Gen., USAF, Bolling AFB, Wash., DC 20332.

Marine Corps — Information: Commandant of the Marine Corps (Code PA), Headquarters, Marine Corps, Wash., DC 20380-0001; 685 women officers; 8,875 enlisted women.

Coast Guard — Information: Commandant (G-CP), U.S. Coast Guard, 2100 Second St., SW, Wash., DC 20593-0001; 219 women commissioned officers; 8 woman warrant officer; 1,337 enlisted women.

U.S. Military Personnel Strengths—Worldwide

(As of Dec. 31, 1989)

Source: U.S. Department of Defense

U.S. Territories & Special Locations					
Continental U.S.	1,262,869	Netherlands	2,859	Bahrain	179
Alaska	23,039	Norway	226	British Indian Ocean Terr.	994
Hawaii	45,589	Portugal	2,022	Egypt	1,140
Guam	7,998	Spain	8,574	Saudi Arabia	432
Johnston Atoll	144	Turkey	4,805	Afloat	10,085
Puerto Rico	2,984	United Kingdom	27,200	Total[1]	13,806
Transients	65,813	Afloat	18,384	Other Western Hemisphere	
Afloat	191,917	Total[1]	336,136	Bermuda	1,556
Total[1]	1,600,482	European NATO	317,614	Canada	541
Western & Southern Europe		East Asia & Pacific		Cuba (Guantanamo)	2,455
		Australia	708	Honduras	1,060
Belgium	2,278	Japan	49,422	Panama	18,856
W. Germany	246,687	Philippines	14,829	Afloat	6,962
Greece	3,298	Rep. of Korea	44,089	Total[1]	32,079
Greenland	191	Thailand	163	Total Worldwide	2,112,128
Iceland	3,209	Afloat	19,787	Ashore	1,864,993
Italy	16,108	Total[1]	129,235	Afloat	247,135
		Africa, Near East & South Asia			

(1) Area totals include countries with less than 100 assigned U.S. military members.

Major U.S. Military Forces: 1980-1988

Source: The Congress of the United States, Congressional Budget Office, *An Analysis of the President's Budgetary Proposals for Fiscal Year 1989.* Data from Dept. of Defense.

	1980	1981	1982	1983	1984	1985	1986	1987	1988
Strategic forces:									
Land-based ICBMs	1,054	1,053	1,053	1,042	1,037	1,028	1,013	1,005	1,000
Sea-launched BMs	576	600	592	568	640	648	640	640	674
Strategic bombers	413	410	410	356	328	328	347	389	423
Strategic interceptors	292	279	261	261	266	264	264	252	252
General purpose forces (active):									
Army Divisions	16	16	16	16	16	17	18	18	18
Marine Corps Divisions	3	3	3	3	3	3	3	3	3
Air Force Tactical Aircraft	3,813	3,991	4,133	4,303	4,352	4,406	4,461	4,396	4,470
Navy/Marine Corps Tactical Aircraft	2,013	2,029	1,968	1,929	1,905	1,970	1,974	1,982	1,962
Naval forces:									
Aircraft carriers	13	12	13	13	13	13	13	14	14
Battleships	-	-	-	1	2	3	3	3	3
Nuclear attack submarines	74	82	91	93	94	96	97	98	96
Other warships	180	188	197	191	197	204	204	206	195
Amphibious assaults[1]	63	59	59	61	59	60	60	61	62
Airlift and sealift forces:									
C-5 aircraft (PAA)	70	70	70	70	70	70	75	84	102
Other Air Force aircraft (PAA)	820	808	795	782	769	787	789	789	781
Navy and Marine Corps Tactical Support Aircraft (PAA)	88	88	88	88	88	88	88	87	87
Ships (NDRF)	164	173	183	192	202	214	220	221	209

(-) Represents zero.   (1) Excludes reserve forces' amphibious ships.

The Medal of Honor

The Medal of Honor is the highest military award for bravery that can be given to any individual in the United States. The first Army Medals were awarded on March 25, 1863, and the first Navy Medals went to sailors and Marines on April 3, 1863.

The Medal of Honor, established by Joint Resolution of Congress, 12 July 1862 (amended by Act of 9 July 1918 and Act of 25 July 1963) is awarded in the name of Congress to a person who, while a member of the Armed Forces, distinguishes himself conspicuously by gallantry and intrepidity at the risk of his life above and beyond the call of duty while engaged in an action against any enemy of the United States; while engaged in military operations involving conflict with an opposing foreign force; or while serving with friendly foreign forces engaged in an armed conflict against an opposing armed force in which the United States is not a belligerent party. The deed performed must have been one of personal bravery or self-sacrifice so conspicuous as to clearly distinguish the individual above his comrades and must have involved risk of life. Incontestable proof of the performance of service is exacted and each recommendation for award of this decoration is considered on the standard of extraordinary merit.

Prior to World War I, the 2,625 Army Medal of Honor awards up to that time were reviewed to determine which past awards met new stringent criteria. The Army removed 911 names from the list, most of them former members of a volunteer infantry group during the Civil War who had been induced to extend their enlistments when they were promised the Medal.

Since that review Medals of Honor have been awarded in the following numbers:

World War I 123   Korean War 131
World War II 433   Vietnam 239

Armed Services Senior Enlisted Adviser

The U.S. Army, Navy and Air Force in 1966-67 each created a new position of senior enlisted adviser whose primary job is to represent the point of view of his services' enlisted men and women on matters of welfare, morale, and any problems concerning enlisted personnel. The senior adviser will have direct access to the military chief of his branch of service and policy-making bodies.

The senior enlisted adviser for each Dept. is:

Army—Sgt. Major of the Army Julius W. Gates.

Navy—Master Chief Petty Officer of the Navy Duane R. Bushey.

Air Force—Chief Master Sgt. of the AF James C. Binnicker.

Marines—Sgt. Major of the Marine Corps David W. Sommers.

Intercontinental Ballistic Missiles (ICBMs), Submarines, and Bombers—U.S. and Soviet Union Balance: 1980 to 1988

Source: The Congress of the United States, Library of Congress, Congressional Research Service, *U.S./Soviet Military Balance, Statistical Trends, 1980-1988,* June 1989

Weapons System	1980	1981	1982	1983	1984	1985	1986	1987	1988	Net Change 1980-1988	1987-1988
ICBMs:											
United States[1]	1,052	1,052	1,049	1,040	1,030	1,017	999	996	1,000	−52	4
Minuteman II	450	450	450	450	450	450	450	450	450	—	—
Minuteman III	550	550	550	550	550	550	534	514	500	−50	−14
Peacekeeper (MX) . . .	—	—	—	—	—	—	10	32	50	50	18
Soviet Union	1,398	1,398	1,398	1,398	1,398	1,398	1,418	1,389	1,348	−50	−41
SS-11	640	580	550	520	520	448	440	420	400	−240	−20
SS-13	60	60	60	60	60	60	60	60	60	—	—
SS-17	150	150	150	150	150	150	150	145	125	−25	−20
SS-18	308	308	308	308	308	308	308	308	296	−12	−12
SS-19	240	300	330	360	360	360	360	350	330	90	−20
SS-24	—	—	—	—	—	—	—	6	12	12	6
SS-25	—	—	—	—	—	72	100	100	125	125	25
Warheads:											
United States	2,152	2,152	2,149	2,140	2,130	2,117	2,157	2,312	2,450	298	138
Soviet Union	5,002	5,302	5,862	6,420	6,420	6,420	6,440	6,400	6,265	1,263	−135
Submarine systems:											
SLBMs[2]:											
United States	576	512	520	568	592	600	640	640	608	32	−32
Trident I	80	112	200	264	288	312	384	384	384	304	—
Poseidon	416	384	320	304	304	288	256	256	224	−192	−32
Polaris A-3	80	16	—	—	—	—	—	—	—	−80	—
Soviet Union	985	985	969	961	946	931	967	969	966	−19	−3
SS-N-5	57	57	57	45	42	39	39	27	24	−33	−3
SS-N-6	464	416	384	368	336	304	272	256	240	−224	−16
SS-N-8	292	292	292	292	292	292	292	286	286	−6	—
SS-N-17	12	12	12	12	12	12	12	12	12	—	—
SS-N-18	160	208	224	224	224	224	224	224	224	64	—
SS-N-20	—	—	—	20	40	60	80	100	100	100	—
SS-N-23	—	—	—	—	—	—	48	64	80	80	16
Warheads:											
United States	4,880	4,752	4,800	5,152	5,344	5,376	5,632	5,632	5,312	432	−320
Soviet Union	1,625	1,817	1,865	1,957	2,122	2,307	2,695	2,941	3,082	1,457	141
Bombers:											
United States	376	376	355	297	297	297	312	363	372	−4	9
B-1B	—	—	—	—	—	—	26	81	90	90	9
B-52D	75	75	58	—	—	—	—	—	—	−75	—
B-52G	151	151	151	151	151	151	150	150	150	−1	—
B-52H	90	90	90	90	90	90	84	84	84	−6	—
FB-111	60	60	56	56	56	56	52	48	48	−12	—
Soviet Union	220	235	245	260	300	325	325	326	350	130	24
M-4 Bison	45	45	45	45	45	30	15	1	—	−45	−1
Tu-95 BEAR	100	100	100	100	100	100	100	100	100	—	—
Tu-95 BEAR-H	—	—	—	—	25	50	50	60	75	75	15
Tu-22M Backfire	75	90	100	115	130	145	160	165	175	100	10

— = zero. (1) Includes weapons not shown separately. (2) Submarine-launched ballistic missile.

Nuclear Weapon Tests

Source: Natural Resources Defense Council

(Known nuclear tests, 1945-1988)

	United States	Soviet Union	Britain	France	China		United States	Soviet Union	Britain	France	China
1945-49	8	1	0	0	0	1970-79[3]	190	196	5	59	16
1950-59[1]	188	71	21	0	0	1980-88[4]	152	186	12	88	8
1960-69[2]	383	170	4	31	10	**Total**	921	624	42	178	34

(1) Stockholm International Peace Research Institute and the Swedish National Defense Research Institute report 18 additional Soviet tests conducted between 1949 and 1958. (2) Since 1962, British underground nuclear tests have been conducted jointly with the United States in Nevada. (3) French Ministry of Defense reports 16 additional Soviet tests conducted between 1963 and 1977. India reported one test in 1974. (4) A French Ministry of Defense document revealed 5 additional French tests between 1975 and 1984.

General and Commander in Chief

	Date of Rank
George Washington	15 June 1775

General of the Armies

John J. Pershing	3 Sept. 1919

General of the Army

	Date of Rank
George C. Marshall	16 Dec. 1944
Douglas MacArthur	18 Dec. 1944
Dwight D. Eisenhower	20 Dec. 1944
Henry H. Arnold	21 Dec. 1944
Omar N. Bradley	20 Sept. 1950

Fleet Admiral

	Date of Rank
William D. Leahy	15 Dec. 1944
Ernest J. King	17 Dec. 1944
Chester W. Nimitz	19 Dec. 1944
William F. Halsey	11 Dec. 1945

Nuclear Arms Treaties and Negotiations: An Historical Overview

Aug. 4, 1963—Nuclear Test Ban Treaty, signed in Moscow by the U.S., USSR, and Great Britain, prohibited testing of nuclear weapons in space, above ground, and under water.

Jan. 1967—Outer Space Treaty banned the introduction of nuclear weapons into space.

1968—Non-proliferation of Nuclear Weapons Treaty, with U.S., USSR, and Great Britain as major signers, limited the spread of military nuclear technology by agreement not to assist nonnuclear nations in getting or making nuclear weapons.

May 26, 1972—SALT I (Strategic Arms Limitations Talks) agreement, in negotiation since Nov. 17, 1969, signed in Moscow by U.S. and USSR. In the area of defensive nuclear weapons, the treaty limited antiballistic missiles to 2 sites of 100 antiballistic missile launchers in each country (amended in 1974 to one site in each country). The treaty also imposed a 5-year freeze on testing and deployment of intercontinental ballistic missiles and submarine-launched ballistic missiles. An interim short-term agreement putting a ceiling on numbers of offensive nuclear weapons was also signed. SALT I was in effect until Oct. 3, 1977.

July 3, 1974—Protocol on antiballistic missile systems and a treaty and protocol on limiting underground testing of nuclear weapons was signed by U.S. and USSR in Moscow.

Nov. 24, 1974—Vladivostok Agreement announced establishing the framework for a more comprehensive agreement on offensive nuclear arms, setting the guidelines of a second SALT treaty.

Sept. 1977—U.S. and USSR agreed to continue to abide by SALT I, despite its expiration date.

June 18, 1979—SALT II, signed in Vienna by the U.S. and USSR, constrained offensive nuclear weapons, limiting each side to 2,400 missile launchers and heavy bombers with

that ceiling to apply until Jan. 1, 1985. The treaty also set a combined total of 1,320 ICBMs and SLBMs with multiple warheads on each side. Although approved by the U.S. Senate Foreign Relations Committee, the treaty never reached the Senate floor because Pres. Jimmy Carter withdrew his support for the treaty following the December 1979 invasion of Afghanistan by Soviet troops.

Nov. 18, 1981—U.S. Pres. Ronald Reagan proposed his controversial "zero option" to cancel deployment of new U.S. intermediate-range missiles in Western Europe in return for Soviet dismantling of comparable forces (600 SS-20, SS-4, and SS-5 missiles already stationed in the European part of its territory).

Nov. 30, 1981—Geneva talks on limiting intermediate nuclear forces based in and around Europe began.

May 9, 1982—U.S. Pres. Ronald Reagan proposed 2-step plan for strategic arms reductions and announced that he had proposed to the USSR that START (Strategic Arms Reduction Talks) begin in June.

May 18, 1982—Soviet Pres. Leonid Brezhnev rejected Reagan's plan as one-sided, but responded positively to the call for arms reduction talks.

June 29, 1982—START (Strategic Arms Reduction Talks) began in Geneva.

1985-1987—Disarmament talks between the U.S. and the USSR began in Geneva, Switzerland on March 12, 1985.

Dec. 8, 1987—I.N.F. (Intermediate-Range Nuclear Forces) Treaty signed in Washington, D.C. by USSR leader Mikhail Gorbachev and U.S. Pres. Ronald Reagan eliminating all medium- and shorter-range nuclear missiles; ratified with conditions by U.S Senate on May 27, 1988.

(For details and 1989-1990 developments see Index and Chronology.)

Estimates of Total Dollar Costs of American Wars

(In millions of dollars, except percent)

Source: *The Military Budget and National Economic Priorities*, revised and updated by James L. Clayton, Univ. of Utah.

Item	World War II	Vietnam Conflict	Korean Conflict	World War I	Civil War: Union	Civil War: Confederacy	Spanish American War	American Revolution	War of 1812	Mexican War
Original increment, direct costs:[1]										
Current dollars	360,000	140,600	50,000	32,700	2,300	1,000	270	100-140	89	82
Constant (1967) dollars.	816,300	148,800	69,300	100,000	8,500	3,700	1,100	400-680	170	300
Percent 1 year's GNP. .	188	14	15	43	74	123	2	104	14	4
Service-connected veterans' benefits[2]	87,629	26,175	17,024	19,273	3,290	—	2,111	28	20	26
Interest, pmts. on war loans[3]	(⁵)	(⁵)	(⁵)	11,000	1,200	(⁵)	60	20	14	10
Current cost to 1986[4] . . .	447,629	166,775	67,024	62,973	6,790	(⁵)	2,441	170	120	120

(1) Figures are rounded and taken from Claudia D. Goldin, *Encyclopedia of American Economic History.* (2) Total cost to Oct. 1, 1986. For World War I and later wars, benefits are actual service-connected figures from 1986 *Annual Report* of Veterans Administration. For earlier wars, service-connected veterans' benefits are estimated at 40 percent of total, the approximate ratio of service-connected to total benefits since World War I. (3) Total cost to 1986. Interest payments are a very rough approximation based on the percentage of the original costs of each war financed by money creation and debt, the difference between the level of public debt at the beginning of the war and at its end, and the approximate time required to pay off the war debts. (4) Figures are rounded estimates. (5) Unknown.

Armed Forces Personnel—Number and Rate, 1987

Source: U.S. Arms Control and Disarmament Agency, *World Military Expenditures and Arms Transfers 1987*

(Number 1,000), Rate per 1,000 population)

Armed forces refer to active-duty military personnel, including paramilitary forces where those forces resemble regular units in their organization, equipment, training or mission. Reserve forces are not included.

	Number	Rate		Number	Rate		Number	Rate
United States	2,279	9.3	Greece	203	20.3	Nigeria	138	1.3
Argentina	118	3.8	India	1,502	1.9	Pakistan	573	5.5
Brazil	541	3.7	Indonesia	281	1.6	Poland	441	11.7
Bulgaria	191	21.3	Iran	350	7.0	Romania	248	10.8
Chile	127	10.2	Iraq	900	53.0	Soviet Union	4,400	15.5
China	3,530	3.3	Israel	180	42.6	Sudan	59	2.5
Cuba	297	28.9	Italy	531	9.3	Syria	400	35.9
Czechoslovakia	215	13.8	Japan	244	2.0	Taiwan	365	18.5
Egypt	450	8.7	Korea, Dem. People's Rep. of			Thailand	275	5.1
El Salvador	49	9.3		838	39.1	Turkey	879	16.6
France	559	10.1	Korea, Rep. of	604	14.3	United Kingdom	328	5.8
German Dem. Rep. . .	241	14.5	Nicaragua	80	24.1	Vietnam	1,300	20.4
Germany, Fed. Rep. . .	495	8.1						

Casualties in Principal Wars of the U.S.

Data on Revolutionary War casualties is from *The Toll of Independence*, Howard H. Peckham, ed., U. of Chicago Press, 1974.

Data prior to World War I are based on incomplete records in many cases. Casualty data are confined to dead and wounded personnel and therefore exclude personnel captured or missing in action who were subsequently returned to military control. Dash (—) indicates information is not available.

Wars	Branch of service	Number serving	Casualties Battle deaths	Casualties Other deaths	Casualties Wounds not mortal[8]	Casualties Total
Revolutionary War	**Total**	—	**6,824**	**18,500**	**8,445**	**33,769**
1775-1783	Army	184,000	5,992	—	7,988	13,980
	Navy &	to	—	—	—	—
	Marines	250,000	832	—	457	1,289
War of 1812	**Total**	**286,730[9]**	**2,260**	**—**	**4,505**	**6,765**
1812-1815	Army	—	1,950	—	4,000	5,950
	Navy	—	265	—	439	704
	Marines	—	45	—	66	111
Mexican War	**Total**	**78,718[9]**	**1,733**	**11,550**	**4,152**	**17,435**
1846-1848	Army	—	1,721	11,500	4,102	17,373
	Navy	—	1	—	3	4
	Marines	—	11	—	47	58
Civil War	**Total**	**2,213,363[9]**	**140,414**	**224,097**	**281,881**	**646,392**
(Union forces only)	Army	2,128,948	138,154	221,374	280,040	639,568
1861-1865	Navy	—	2,112	2,411	1,710	6,233
	Marines	84,415	148	312	131	591
Confederate forces	**Total**	—	**74,524**	**59,297**	**—**	**133,821**
(estimate)[1]	Army	600,000	—	—	—	—
1863-1866	Navy	to	—	—	—	—
	Marines	1,500,000	—	—	—	—
Spanish-American	**Total**	**306,760**	**385**	**2,061**	**1,662**	**4,108**
War	Army[4]	280,564	369	2,061	1,594	4,024
1898	Navy	22,875	10	0	47	57
	Marines	3,321	6	0	21	27
World War I	**Total**	**4,743,826**	**53,513**	**63,195**	**204,002**	**320,710**
April 6, 1917-	Army[5]	4,057,101	50,510	55,868	193,663	300,041
Nov. 11, 1918	Navy	599,051	431	6,856	819	8,106
	Marines	78,839	2,461	390	9,520	12,371
	Coast Guard	8,835	111	81	—	192
World War II	**Total**	**16,353,659**	**292,131**	**115,185**	**670,846**	**1,078,162**
Dec. 7, 1941-	Army[6]	11,260,000	234,874	83,400	565,861	884,135
Dec. 31, 1946[2]	Navy[7]	4,183,466	36,950	25,664	37,778	100,392
	Marines	669,100	19,733	4,778	67,207	91,718
	Coast Guard	241,093	574	1,343	—	1,917
Korean War	**Total**	**5,764,143**	**33,629**	**20,617**	**103,284**	**157,530**
June 25, 1950-	Army	2,834,000	27,704	9,429	77,596	114,729
July 27, 1953[3]	Navy	1,177,000	458	4,043	1,576	6,077
	Marines	424,000	4,267	1,261	23,744	29,272
	Air Force	1,285,000	1,200	5,884	368	7,452
	Coast Guard	44,143	—	—	—	—
Vietnam (preliminary)[10]	**Total**	**8,744,000**	**47,356**	**10,795**	**153,303**	**211,324**
Aug. 4, 1964-	Army	4,368,000	30,904	7,274	96,802	134,972
Jan. 27, 1973	Navy	1,842,000	1,626	923	4,178	6,697
	Marines	794,000	13,082	1,754	51,392	66,213
	Air Force	1,740,000	1,739	842	931	3,435
	Coast Guard	—	5	2	—	7

(1) Authoritative statistics for the Confederate Forces are not available. An estimated 26,000-31,000 Confederate personnel died in Union prisons.

(2) Data are for the period Dec. 1, 1941 through Dec. 31, 1946 when hostilities were officially terminated by Presidential Proclamation, but few battle deaths or wounds not mortal were incurred after the Japanese acceptance of Allied peace terms on Aug. 14, 1945. Numbers serving from Dec. 1, 1941-Aug. 31, 1945 were: Total—14,903,213; Army—10,420,000; Navy—3,883,520; and Marine Corps—599,693.

(3) Tentative final data based upon information available as of Sept. 30, 1954, at which time 24 persons were still carried as missing in action.

(4) Number serving covers the period April 21-Aug. 13, 1898, while dead and wounded data are for the period May 1-Aug. 31, 1898. Active hostilities ceased on Aug. 13, 1898, but ratifications of the treaty of peace were not exchanged between the United States and Spain until April 11, 1899.

(5) Includes Air Service Battle deaths and wounds not mortal include casualties suffered by American forces in Northern Russia to Aug. 25, 1919 and in Siberia to April 1, 1920. Other deaths covered the period April 1, 1917-Dec. 31, 1918.

(6) Includes Army Air Forces.

(7) Battle deaths and wounds not mortal include casualties incurred in Oct. 1941 due to hostile action.

(8) Marine Corps data for World War II, the Spanish-American War and prior wars represent the number of individuals wounded, whereas all other data in this column represent the total number (incidence) of wounds.

(9) As reported by the Commissioner of Pensions in his Annual Report for Fiscal Year 1903.

(10) Number serving covers the period Aug. 4 1964-Jan. 27, 1973 (date of ceasefire). Number of casualties incurred in connection with the conflict in Vietnam from Jan. 1, 1961-Sept. 30, 1977. Includes casualties incurred in Mayaguez Incident. Wounds not mortal exclude 150,375 persons not requiring hospital care.

POSTAL INFORMATION

U.S. Postal Service

The Postal Reorganization Act, creating a government-owned postal service under the executive branch and replacing the old Post Office Department, was signed into law by President Nixon on Aug. 12, 1970. The service officially came into being on July 1, 1971.

The new U.S. Postal Service is governed by an 11-person Board of Governors. Nine members are appointed to 9-year terms by the president with Senate approval. These 9, in turn, choose a postmaster general, who is no longer a member of the president's cabinet. The board and the new postmaster general choose the 11th member, who serves as deputy postmaster general. An independent Postal Rate Commission of 5 members, appointed by the president, recommends postal rates to the governors for their approval.

As of July 28, 1990, there were 34,255 post offices throughout the U.S. and possessions.

U.S. Domestic Rates

In effect from April 3, 1988. Note: On March 6, 1990, a **general domestic rate increase** was proposed by the Postal Service to the Postal Rate Commission. As of mid-September, 1990, a recommendation was pending. **At least some rate increases were most likely to occur in Feb. 1991.**

Domestic includes the U.S., territories and possessions, APO and FPO.

First Class

Letters written, and matter sealed against inspection, 25¢ for 1st oz. or fraction, 20¢ for each additional oz. or fraction. U.S. Postal cards; single 15¢; double 30¢; private postcards, same.

First class includes written matter, namely letters, postal cards, postcards (private mailing cards) and all other matter wholly or partly in writing, whether sealed or unsealed, except manuscripts for books, periodical articles and music, manuscript copy accompanying proofsheets or corrected proofsheets of the same and the writing authorized by law on matter of other classes. Also matter sealed or closed against inspection, bills and statements of accounts.

Express Mail

Express Mail Service is available for any mailable article up to 70 pounds, and guarantees delivery between major U.S. cities or your money back. Articles received by the acceptance time authorized by the postmaster at a postal facility offering Express Mail will be delivered by 3 p.m. the next day to some locations or will be delivered by noon the next day to other destinations. Or, if you prefer, your shipment can be picked up as early as 10 a.m. the next business day. Second day service is available to locations not on the Next Day Delivery Network. Rates include insurance, Shipment Receipt, and Record of Delivery at the destination post office.

Consult Postmaster for other Express Mail Services and rates. (The Postal Service will refund, upon application to originating office, the postage for any Express Mail shipments not meeting the service standard except for those delayed by strike or work stoppage, delay or cancellation of flights, or governmental action beyond the control of the Postal Service.)

Third Class

Third class (limit up to but not including 16 ounces): Mailable matter not in 1st and 2d classes.

Single mailing: Publications, small parcels, printed matter, booklets and catalogs, 25¢ the first ounce, 45¢ for over 1 to 2 ozs., 65¢ for over 2 to 3 ozs., 85¢ for over 3 to 4 ozs., $1.00 for over 4 to 6 ozs., $1.10 for over 6 to 8 ozs., $1.20 for over 8 to 10 ozs., $1.30 for over 10 to 12 ozs., $1.40 for over 12 to 14 ozs., $1.50 for over 14 but less than 16 ozs.

Bulk mailing: At least 200 pieces or 50 pounds of such items as solicitations, newsletters, advertising materials, books and cassettes, each item of which individually weighs less than one pound. Minimum rate per piece: Basic presort, $0.167; Basic presort ZIP+4, $0.162; 5-Digit presort, $0.132; 5-Digit presort ZIP+4, $0.127; ZIP+4 Barcoded, $0.122; Carrier route presort, $0.101. For pieces weighing more than 3.3667 ounces, the following rates apply: Basic presort, 48¢ per pound + 6.6¢ per piece; 5-Digit presort, 48¢ per pound + 3.1¢ per piece; Carrier route presort, 48¢ per pound.

Separate rates for some nonprofit organizations. Bulk mailing fee, $60 per calendar year. Apply to postmaster for permit. One-time fee for permit imprint, $60.

Parcel Post—Fourth Class

Fourth class or parcel post (16 ounces and over): merchandise, printed matter, etc., may be sealed, subject to inspection.

Priority Mail

First class mail of more than 11 ounces can be sent "Priority Mail" service. The most expeditious handling and transportation available will be used for fastest delivery.

On parcels weighing less than 15 lbs. and measuring more than 84 inches, but not more than 108 inches in length and girth combined, the minimum postal charge shall be the zone charge applicable to a 15-pound parcel.

Forwarding Addresses

The mailer, in order to obtain a forwarding address, must endorse the envelope or cover "Address Correction Requested." The destination post office then will determine whether a forwarding address has been left on file and provide it for a fee of 30¢.

Priority Mail

Packages weighing up to 70 pounds and not exceeding 108 inches in length and girth combined, including written and other material of the first class, whether sealed or unsealed, fractions of a pound being charged as a full pound.

Rates according to zone apply between the U.S. and Puerto Rico and Virgin Islands.

Parcels weighing less than 15 pounds, measuring over 84 inches but not exceeding 108 inches in length and girth combined are chargeable with a minimum rate equal to that for a 15 pound parcel for the zone to which addressed.

Zones	To 2	3	4	5	Zones	To 2	3	4	5
1, 2, 3, ...	$2.40	$2.74	$3.18	$3.61	6	$2.40	$3.74	$4.53	$5.27
4	2.40	3.16	3.75	4.32	7	2.40	3.96	4.92	5.81
5	2.40	3.45	4.13	4.86	8	2.40	4.32	5.33	6.37

*Consult postmaster for parcels over 5 lbs.

Special Handling

Third and fourth class parcels will be handled and delivered as expeditiously as practicable (but not special delivery) upon payment, in addition to the regular postage: up to 10 lbs., $1.55; over 10 lbs., $2.25. Such parcels must be endorsed, Special Handling.

Special Delivery

First class mail up to 2 lbs. $5.35, over 2 lbs. and up to 10 lbs., $5.75; over 10 lbs. $7.25. All other classes up to 2 lbs. $5.65, over 2 and up to 10 lbs., $6.50, over 10 lbs. $8.10.

Bound Printed Matter Rates
(Single Piece Zone Rate)

Weight lbs.	Local	1&2	3	4	5	6	7	8
1.5	$0.67	$0.92	$0.96	$1.04	$1.16	$1.28	$1.43	$1.56
2	0.69	0.96	1.02	1.12	1.28	1.44	1.64	1.81
2.5	0.71	0.99	1.07	1.20	1.39	1.60	1.85	2.06
3	0.73	1.03	1.12	1.27	1.51	1.76	2.06	2.31
3.5	0.75	1.07	1.17	1.35	1.63	1.91	2.26	2.56
4	0.77	1.10	1.22	1.43	1.74	2.07	2.47	2.81
4.5	0.79	1.14	1.27	1.50	1.86	2.23	2.68	3.06
5	0.81	1.18	1.33	1.58	1.98	2.39	2.89	3.31
6	0.85	1.25	1.43	1.73	2.21	2.70	3.30	3.80
7	0.89	1.32	1.53	1.89	2.44	3.02	3.72	4.30
8	0.93	1.39	1.63	2.04	2.67	3.33	4.13	4.80
9	0.97	1.47	1.74	2.20	2.91	3.65	4.55	5.30
10	1.01	1.54	1.84	2.35	3.14	3.96	4.96	5.80

(Bound printed matter must weigh at least 1 pound and not more than 10 pounds. Bound printed matter includes catalogs, directories and books not eligible for special fourth-class rates.)

Domestic Mail Special Services

Registry — Only matter prepaid with postage at First-class postage rates may be registered. Stamps or meter stamps must be attached. The face of the article must be at least 5" long, 3½" high. The mailer is required to declare the value of mail presented for registration.

Registered Mail

	Insured	Uninsured
0.00 to $100	$4.50	$4.40
100.01 to $500	4.85	4.70
500.01 to $1,000 . . .	5.25	5.05
1,000.01 to $2,000 . . .	5.65	5.35
2,000.01 to $3,000 . . .	6.05	5.70
3,000.01 to $4,000 . . .	6.45	6.00
4,000.01 to $5,000 . . .	6.85	6.35
5,000.01 to $6,000 . . .	7.25	6.65
6,000.01 to $7,000 . . .	7.65	7.00
7,000.01 to $8,000 . . .	8.10	7.30
8,000.01 to $9,000 . . .	8.55	7.65
9,000.01 to $10,000 . . .	9.00	7.95

Consult postmaster for registry rates above $10,000.

C.O.D.: Unregistered — is applicable to first-, third-, fourth-class, and express mail matter. Such mail must be based on bona fide orders or be in conformity with agreements between senders and addressees. **Registered** — for details consult postmaster.

Insurance — is applicable to third and fourth class matter. Matter for sale addressed to prospective purchasers who have not ordered it or authorized its sending will not be insured.

Insured Mail

$0.01 to $50.	$0.70
50.01 to 100.	1.50
100.01 to 150.	1.90
150.01 to 200.	2.20
200.01 to 300.	3.15
300.01 to 400.	4.30
400.01 to 500.	5.00

Liability for insured mail is limited to $500.

Certified mail — service is available for any matter having no intrinsic value on which 1st class or air mail postage is paid. Receipt is furnished at time of mailing and evidence of delivery obtained. The fee is 85¢ in addition to postage. Return receipt, restricted delivery, and special delivery are available upon payment of additional fees. No indemnity.

Special Fourth Class Rate
(limit 70 lbs.)

First pound or fraction, 90¢ (65¢ if 500 pieces or more of special rate matter are presorted to 5 digit ZIP code or 83¢ if 500 pieces or more are presorted to Bulk Mail Cntrs.); each additional pound or fraction through 7 pounds, 35¢; each additional pound, 20¢. Only the following specific articles: Books of at least 8 printed pages consisting wholly of reading matter or scholarly bibliography, or reading matter with incidental blank spaces for notations and containing no advertising matter other than incidental announcements of books; 16-millimeter or narrower width films in final form and catalogs of such films of 24 pages or more (at least 22 of which are printed) except films and film catalogs sent to or from commercial theaters; printed music in bound or sheet form; printed objective test materials; sound recordings, playscripts and manuscripts for books, periodicals, and music; printed educational reference charts; loose-leaf pages and binders thereof consisting of medical information for distribution to doctors, hospitals, medical schools, and medical students; computer-readable media containing prerecorded information and guides for use with such media. Package must be marked "Special 4th Class Rate" stating item contained.

Library Rate (limit 70 lbs.)

First pound 64¢, each additional pound through 7

Parcel Post Rate Schedule
(Inter BMC/ASF Zip Codes Only, Machinable Parcels, No Discount, No Surcharge)

Weight up to but not exceeding—(pounds)	1 and 2	3	4	Zones 5	6	7	8
2.	$1.69	$1.81	$1.97	$2.24	$2.35	$2.35	$2.35
3.	1.78	1.95	2.20	2.59	2.98	3.42	4.25
4.	1.86	2.10	2.42	2.94	3.46	4.05	5.25
5.	1.95	2.24	2.65	3.29	3.94	4.67	6.25
6.	2.04	2.39	2.87	3.64	4.43	5.30	7.34
7.	2.12	2.53	3.10	4.00	4.91	5.92	8.30
8.	2.21	2.68	3.32	4.35	5.39	6.55	9.26
9.	2.30	2.82	3.55	4.70	5.87	7.17	10.22
10.	2.38	2.97	3.78	5.05	6.35	7.79	11.18
11.	2.47	3.11	4.00	5.40	6.83	8.42	12.14
12.	2.56	3.25	4.22	5.75	7.30	9.03	13.09
13.	2.64	3.40	4.44	6.10	7.78	9.65	14.03
14.	2.69	3.48	4.56	6.27	8.02	9.96	14.50
15.	2.75	3.55	4.67	6.44	8.24	10.24	14.94
16.	2.79	3.63	4.78	6.60	8.45	10.52	15.35
17.	2.84	3.70	4.88	6.75	8.66	10.77	15.74
18.	2.89	3.76	4.98	6.90	8.85	11.02	16.11
19.	2.93	3.83	5.07	7.03	9.03	11.25	16.45
20.	2.98	3.89	5.16	7.16	9.20	11.47	16.79
21.	3.02	3.95	5.25	7.29	9.37	11.68	17.10
22.	3.06	4.01	5.33	7.41	9.53	11.88	17.41
23.	3.10	4.07	5.41	7.53	9.68	12.08	17.70
24.	3.14	4.12	5.49	7.64	9.83	12.26	17.97
25.	3.18	4.18	5.56	7.75	9.97	12.44	18.24

pounds, 23¢; each additional pound, 12¢. Books when loaned or exchanged between and sent to or from schools, colleges, public libraries, and certain non-profit organizations; books, printed music, bound academic theses, periodicals, sound recordings, other library materials, museum materials (specimens, collections), scientific or mathematical kits, instruments or other devices; also catalogs, guides or scripts for some of these materials. Must be marked "Library Rate".

Also qualifying for library rate are: Books mailed from publishers or distributors to schools, libraries, colleges or universities or to bookstores owned, operated and controlled by schools, colleges or universities.

Postal Union Mail Special Services

Registration — available to practically all countries. Fee $4.40. The maximum indemnity payable — generally only in case of complete loss (of both contents and wrapper) — is $24.60. To Canada only the fee is $4.50 providing indemnity for loss up to $100, $4.85 for loss up to $500, and $5.25 for loss up to $1,000.

Return receipt — showing to whom and date delivr'd. 90¢.

Special delivery — Available to most countries. Consult post office. Fees for International Special Delivery same for air or surface: for letters, letter packages and post cards not over 2 pounds, $5.35. If over 2 pounds, $5.75, for printed matter, matter for the blind, or small packets, $5.65 if not over 2 pounds; if over 2 pounds, $6.50.

Marking — an article intended for special delivery service must have affixed to the cover near the name of the country

of destination "EXPRES" (special delivery) label, obtainable at the post office, or it may be marked on the cover boldly in red "EXPRES" (special delivery).

Special handling — entitles AO surface packages to priority handling between mailing point and U.S. point of dispatch. Fees: $1.55 for packages to 10 pounds, and $2.25 for packages over 10 pounds.

Airmail — there is daily air service to practically all countries.

Prepayment of replies from other countries — a mailer who wishes to prepay a reply by letter from another country may do so by sending his correspondent one or more international reply coupons, which may be purchased at United States post offices. One coupon should be accepted in any country in exchange for stamps to prepay a surface letter of the first unit of weight to the U.S.

Additional international special services: Insurance Available to many countries for loss of or damage to items paid at parcel post rate. Consult postmaster for indemnity limits for individual countries.

Limit of Indemnity Not Over	Fees Canada	All other Countries
$50	$0.70	$1.50
100	1.50	1.90
150	1.90	3.15
200	2.20	3.15
300	3.15	4.30
400	4.30	5.00
500	5.00	5.70

Restricted Delivery: Available to many countries for registered mail, limits who may receive an item. Fee: $2.00.

Post Office-Authorized 2-Letter State Abbreviations

The abbreviations below are approved by the U.S. Postal Service for use in addresses only. They do not replace the traditional abbreviations in other contexts. The official list follows, including the District of Columbia, Guam, Puerto Rico, the Canal Zone, and the Virgin Islands (all capital letters are used):

Alabama	AL	Idaho	ID	Nebraska	NE	South Carolina	S
Alaska	AK	Illinois	IL	Nevada	NV	South Dakota	SI
American Samoa	AS	Indiana	IN	New Hampshire	NH	Tennessee	TN
Arizona	AZ	Iowa	IA	New Jersey	NJ	Texas	T
Arkansas	AR	Kansas	KS	New Mexico	NM	Trust Territories	T
California	CA	Kentucky	KY	New York	NY	Utah	U
Canal Zone	CZ	Louisiana	LA	North Carolina	NC	Vermont	V
Colorado	CO	Maine	ME	North Dakota	ND	Virginia	V
Connecticut	CT	Maryland	MD	Northern Mariana Is.	CM	Virgin Islands	V
Delaware	DE	Massachusetts	MA	Ohio	OH	Washington	W
Dist. of Col.	DC	Michigan	MI	Oklahoma	OK	West Virginia	W
Florida	FL	Minnesota	MN	Oregon	OR	Wisconsin	W
Georgia	GA	Missouri	MO	Pennsylvania	PA	Wyoming	W
Guam	GU	Mississippi	MS	Puerto Rico	PR		
Hawaii	HI	Montana	MT	Rhode Island	RI		

Also approved for use in addressing mail are the following abbreviations:

Alley	Aly	Court	Ct	Grove	Grv	Rural	
Arcade	Arc	Courts	Cts	Heights	Hts	Square	S
Avenue	Ave	Crescent	Cres	Highway	Hwy	Street	S
Boulevard	Blvd	Drive	Dr	Lane	Ln	Terrace	Te
Branch	Br	Expressway	Expy	Manor	Mnr	Trail	T
Bypass	Byp	Extended	Ext	Place	Pl	Turnpike	Tpk
Causeway	Cswy	Extension	Ext	Plaza	Plz	Viaduct	V
Center	Ctr	Freeway	Fwy	Point	Pt	Vista	V
Circle	Cir	Gardens	Gdns	Road	Rd		

Size Standards for Domestic Mail

Minimum Size

Pieces which do not meet the following requirements are prohibited from the mails:

   a. All pieces must be at least .007 of an inch thick, and

   b. All pieces (except keys and identification devices) which are ¼ inch or less thick must be:
      (1) Rectangular in shape,
      (2) At least 3½ inches high, and
      (3) At least 5 inches long.

Note: Pieces greater than ¼ inch thick can be mailed even if they measure less than 3½ by 5 inches.

Nonstandard Mail

All First-Class Mail, except presort and carrier route First-Class mail, weighing one ounce or less and all single-piece rate Third-Class mail weighing one ounce or less is nonstandard (and subject to a 10¢ surcharge in addition to the applicable postage and fees) if:

   1. Any of the following dimensions are exceeded:
      Length—11½ inches,
      Height—6⅛ inches,
      Thickness—¼ inch, or

   2. The length divided by the height is not between 1. and 2.5, inclusive. The nonstandard surcharge for presort and carrier route First-Class mail is 5¢.

Air Mail, Parcel Post International Rates

Aerogrammes — 39¢ each to all countries.
Air mail postcards (single) - 36¢ to all countries except Canada (21¢) and Mexico (15¢)

Country	First pound	Air parcel post rates — Each add'l. pound or fraction up to first 5 lbs.	Each add'l pound or fraction	Country	First pound	Air parcel post rates — Each add'l. pound or fraction up to first 5 lbs.	Each add'l pound or fraction
Afghanistan	$10.30	$5.80	$5.00	Guatemala	$5.50	$2.80	$2.00
Albania	8.70	4.80	4.00	Guinea	7.15	4.00	3.00
Algeria	10.30	5.80	5.00	Guinea-Bissau	7.15	4.00	3.00
Andorra	7.15	4.00	6.00	Guyana	7.15	4.00	3.00
Angola	11.95	6.80	6.00	Haiti	5.50	2.80	2.00
Anguilla	5.50	2.80	2.00	Honduras	7.15	4.00	3.00
Antigua & Barbados	5.50	2.80	2.00	Hong Kong	8.70	4.80	4.00
Argentina	10.30	5.80	5.00	Hungary	8.70	4.80	4.00
Aruba	5.50	2.80	2.00	Iceland	8.70	4.80	4.00
Ascension	No Air Service			India	10.30	5.80	5.00
Australia	10.30	5.80	5.00	Indonesia	11.95	6.80	6.00
Austria	7.15	4.00	3.00	Iran	10.30	5.80	5.00
Azores	8.70	4.80	4.00	Iraq	10.30	5.80	5.00
Bahamas	5.50	2.80	2.00	Ireland (Eire)	8.70	4.80	4.00
Bahrain	10.30	5.80	5.00	Israel	8.70	4.80	4.00
Bangladesh	11.95	6.80	3.00	Italy	8.70	4.80	4.00
Barbados	7.15	4.00	3.00	Ivory Coast	10.30	5.80	5.00
Belgium	10.30	5.80	5.00	Jamaica	5.50	2.80	2.00
Belize	5.50	2.80	2.00	Japan	11.95	6.80	6.00
Benin	8.70	4.80	4.00	Jordan	8.70	4.80	4.00
Bermuda	5.50	2.80	2.00	Kampuchea	No Parcel Post Service		
Bhutan	11.95	6.80	6.00	Kenya	10.30	5.80	5.00
Bolivia	7.15	4.00	3.00	Kiribati	7.15	4.00	3.00
Botswana	11.95	6.80	6.00	Korea, Democratic People's Rep. (North)	No Parcel Post Service		
Brazil	11.95	6.80	6.00				
British Virgin Islands	5.50	2.80	2.00	Korea, Rep. of (South)	8.70	4.80	4.00
Brunei	10.30	5.80	5.00	Kuwait	8.70	4.80	4.00
Bulgaria	10.30	5.80	5.00	Lao	11.95	6.80	6.00
Burkina Faso	10.30	5.80	5.00	Latvia	11.95	6.80	6.00
Burma	10.30	5.80	5.00	Lebanon	8.70	4.80	4.00
Burundi	11.95	6.80	6.00	Leeward Islands	5.50	2.80	2.00
Cameroon	10.30	5.80	5.00	Lesotho	11.95	6.80	6.00
Canada[1]	Separate rate schedule			Liberia	8.70	4.80	4.00
Cape Verde	10.30	5.80	5.00	Libya	10.30	5.80	5.00
Cayman Islands	5.50	2.80	2.00	Liechtenstein	7.15	4.00	3.00
Central African Rep.	11.95	6.80	6.00	Lithuania	11.95	6.80	6.00
Chad	10.30	5.80	5.00	Luxembourg	7.15	4.00	3.00
Chile	10.30	5.80	5.00	Macao	8.70	4.80	4.00
China (People's Republic of)	10.30	5.80	5.00	Madagascar	11.95	6.80	6.00
				Madeira Islands	7.15	4.00	3.00
Colombia	7.15	4.00	3.00	Malawi	10.30	5.80	5.00
Comoros	11.95	6.80	6.00	Malaysia	10.30	5.80	5.00
Congo	10.30	5.80	5.00	Maldives	10.30	5.80	5.00
Corsica	11.95	6.80	6.00	Mali	8.70	4.80	4.00
Costa Rica	5.50	2.80	2.00	Malta	8.70	4.80	4.00
Cuba	No Parcel Post Service			Martinique	5.50	2.80	2.00
Cyprus	8.70	4.80	4.00	Mauritania	10.30	5.80	5.00
Czechoslovakia	8.70	4.80	4.00	Mauritius	11.95	6.80	6.00
Denmark	8.70	4.80	4.00	Mexico	5.50	2.80	2.00
Djibouti	10.30	5.80	5.00	Mongolia	No Parcel Post Service		
Dominica	5.50	2.80	2.00	Morocco	8.70	4.80	4.00
Dominican Republic	5.50	2.80	2.00	Mozambique	11.95	6.80	6.00
East Timor	No Parcel Post Service			Namibia	10.30	5.80	5.00
Ecuador	8.70	4.80	4.00	Nauru	8.70	4.80	4.00
Egypt	10.30	5.80	5.00	Nepal	10.30	5.80	5.00
El Salvador	7.15	4.00	3.00	Netherlands	8.70	4.80	4.00
Equatorial Guinea	10.30	5.80	5.00	Netherlands Antilles	5.50	2.80	2.00
Estonia	11.95	6.80	6.00	New Caledonia	10.30	5.80	5.00
Ethiopia	10.30	5.80	5.00	New Zealand	10.30	5.80	5.00
Faeroe Islands	8.70	4.80	4.00	Nicaragua	7.15	4.00	3.00
Falkland Islands	10.30	5.80	5.00	Namilia	10.30	5.80	5.00
Fiji	7.15	4.00	3.00	Niger	10.30	5.80	5.00
Finland	10.30	5.80		Nigeria	8.70	4.80	4.00
France (Including Monaco)	11.95	6.80	6.00	Norway	10.30	5.80	5.00
				Oman	10.30	5.80	5.00
French Guiana	8.70	4.80	4.00	Pakistan	10.30	5.80	5.00
French Polynesia	10.30	5.80	5.00	Panama	5.50	2.80	2.00
Gabon	10.30	5.80	5.00	Papua New Guinea	10.30	5.80	5.00
Gambia	7.15	4.00	3.00	Paraguay	10.30	5.80	5.00
Germany	8.70	4.80	4.00	Peru	7.15	4.00	3.00
Ghana	10.30	5.80	5.00	Philippines	10.30	5.80	5.00
Gibraltar	8.70	4.80	4.00	Pitcairn Islands	7.15	4.00	3.00
Great Britain	8.70	4.80	4.00	Poland	7.15	4.00	3.00
Greece	8.70	4.80	4.00	Portugal	8.70	4.80	4.00
Greenland	10.30	5.80	5.00	Qatar	8.70	4.80	4.00
Grenada	5.50	2.80	2.00	Reunion	11.95	6.80	6.00
Guadeloupe	5.50	2.80	2.00	Romania	8.70	4.80	4.00
				Rwanda	10.30	5.80	5.00

Country	First pound	Air parcel post rates—Each add'l pound or fraction up to first 5 lbs.	Each add'l pound or fraction	Country	First pound	Air parcel post rates—Each add'l pound or fraction up to first 5 lbs.	Each add'l pound or fraction
St. Helena	$8.70	$4.80	$4.00	Tanzania	$11.95	$6.80	$6.00
St. Lucia	5.50	2.80	2.00	Thailand	10.30	5.80	5.00
St. Pierre & Miquelon	5.50	2.80	2.00	Togo	10.30	5.80	5.00
St. Thomas & Principe	10.30	5.80	5.00	Tonga	7.15	4.00	3.00
St. Vincent & The Grenadines	5.50	2.80	2.00	Trinidad & Tobago	7.15	4.00	3.00
San Marino	8.70	4.80	4.00	Tristan da Cunha	11.95	6.80	6.00
Santa Cruz Islands	8.70	4.80	4.00	Tunisia	8.70	4.80	4.00
Saudi Arabia	10.30	4.80	5.00	Turkey	8.70	4.80	4.00
Senegal	10.30	5.80	5.00	Turks & Caicos Islands	5.50	2.80	2.00
Seychelles	10.30	5.80	5.00	Tuvalu (Ellice Islands)	7.15	4.00	3.00
Sierra Leone	10.30	5.80	5.00	Uganda	10.30	5.80	5.00
Singapore	10.30	5.80	5.00	USSR[2]	11.95	6.80	6.00
Solomon Islands	8.70	4.80	4.00	United Arab Emirates	10.30	5.80	5.00
Somalia	10.30	5.80	5.00	Uruguay	7.15	4.00	3.00
South Africa	10.30	5.80	5.00	Vanuatu	7.15	4.00	3.00
Spain	8.70	4.80	4.00	Vatican City State	8.70	4.80	4.00
Sri Lanka	10.30	5.80	5.00	Venezuela	7.15	4.00	3.00
Sudan	10.30	5.80	5.00	Vietnam[1]	No Parcel Post Service		
Suriname	7.15	4.00	3.00	Wallis & Futura Islands	10.30	5.80	5.00
Swaziland	10.30	5.80	5.00	Western Samoa	7.15	4.00	3.00
Sweden	10.30	5.80	5.00	Yemen	10.30	5.80	5.00
Switzerland	7.15	4.00	3.00	Yugoslavia	8.70	4.80	4.00
Syria	8.70	4.80	4.00	Zaire	11.95	6.80	6.00
Taiwan	8.70	4.80	4.00	Zambia	11.95	6.80	6.00
				Zimbabwe	11.95	6.80	6.00

Weight limits: minimum 1 lb., maximum 66 lbs.; up to 2 lbs., $4.32; each add'l pound or fraction, $1.24.

(1) Restrictions apply; consult post office. (2) To facilitate distribution and delivery, include "Union of Soviet Socialist Republics" or "USSR" as part of the address.

Miscellaneous International Rates

Letters and Letter Pkgs (Surface)

Weight steps Over Lbs.	Over Ozs.	Through Lbs.	Through Ozs.	Canada	Mexico	All other countries
0	0	0	1	$.30	$.25	$.40
0	1	0	2	.52	.45	.63
0	2	0	3	.74	.65	.86
0	3	0	4	.96	.85	1.09
0	4	0	5	1.18	1.05	1.32
0	5	0	6	1.40	1.25	1.55
0	6	0	7	1.62	1.45	1.78
0	7	0	8	1.84	1.65	2.01
0	8	0	9	2.06	1.85	3.80
0	9	0	10	2.28	2.05	3.80
0	10	0	11	2.50	2.25	3.80
0	11	0	12	2.72	2.45	3.80
0	12	1	0	3.08	3.25	3.80
1	0	1	8	3.70	4.05	5.20
1	8	2	0	4.32	4.85	6.60
2	0	2	8	4.94	5.65	7.60
2	8	3	0	5.56	6.45	8.60
3	0	3	8	6.18	7.25	9.60
3	8	4	0	6.80	8.05	10.60

Maximum limit: 66 pounds to Canada, 4 pounds to Mexico and all other countries.

Letters and Letter Pkgs (Air)

Canada and Mexico: Refer to rates listed under Letter and Letter Pkgs. (Surface). Mail paid at this rate receives First-Class service in the United States and air service in Canada and Mexico.

All Other Countries: 45 cents per half ounce up to and including 2 ounces; 42 cents each additional half ounce up to and including 32 ounces; 42 cents per additional ounce over 32 ounces.

Parcel Post (Surface)

Canada: $3.95 for over 1 lb. and up to 2 lbs.; $1.20 each add'l lb.

Mexico, Central America, The Caribbean Islands, Bahamas, Bermuda, St. Pierre and Miquelon: $4.40 for the first 2 pounds and $1.40 each additional pound or fraction.

All Other Countries: $4.60 for the first 2 pounds and $1.50 for each additional pound or fraction.

For Parcel Post air rates, see tables, pages 796-797.

Postcards

Surface rates to Canada, 21¢, and Mexico, 15¢; to all other countries, 28¢. By air, Canada, 21¢, and Mexico, 15¢; to all other countries, 36¢. Maximum size permitted, 6 x 4¼ in.; minimum, 5½ x 3½.

Gross Postal Revenues at Large Cities

Fiscal year	Boston	Chicago	L.A.	New York	Phila.	St. Louis	Wash., D.C.
1975	$136,453,079	$365,378,795	$193,229,077	$453,905,277	$134,571,376	$85,591,774	$115,489,343
1980	224,428,760	528,233,991	271,136,828	666,377,778	221,161,624	127,427,555	187,334,312
1981	256,524,082	551,988,015	301,159,594	741,286,845	235,116,018	142,548,957	201,191,995
1982	292,971,572	597,246,568	338,798,409	848,507,590	265,242,959	160,596,946	215,772,861
1983	294,932,399	589,476,264	330,734,928	856,569,717	273,210,529	165,000,437	212,117,368
1984	314,230,399	598,141,605	338,760,060	907,426,500	295,917,848	177,041,331	225,378,646
1985	339,550,469	563,693,370	358,859,412	938,829,064	300,811,081	194,786,119	236,131,464
1986	378,861,842	579,432,633	381,254,469	960,987,314	330,671,509	211,134,497	253,607,563
1987	405,124,317	612,014,066	389,819,485	962,000,684	367,123,549	221,972,462	290,840,099
1988	428,049,178	618,237,375	415,847,750	999,747,864	384,189,378	245,040,401	341,131,117
1989	421,170,296	610,124,516	439,708,491	1,052,810,676	374,566,877	264,109,672	307,918,572

Other cities for fiscal year 1989: Dallas, $431,138,189; Atlanta, $404,563,044; Houston, $346,017,468; Minneapolis, $289,155,599; San Francisco, $270,079,172; Baltimore, $253,333,221; Hartford, CT, $235,122,191; Columbus, OH, $264,224,150.

SOCIAL SECURITY

Social Security Programs

Source: Social Security Administration, U.S. Department of Health and Human Services

Old-Age, Survivors, and Disability Insurance; Medicare; Supplemental Security Income

Social Security Benefits

Social Security benefits are based on a worker's primary insurance amount (PIA), which is related by law to the average indexed monthly earnings (AIME) on which social security contributions have been paid. The full PIA is payable to a retired worker who becomes entitled to benefits at age 65 and to an entitled disabled worker at any age. Spouses and children of retired or disabled workers and survivors of deceased workers receive set proportions of the PIA subject to a family maximum amount. The PIA is calculated by applying varying percentages to succeeding parts of the AIME. The formula is adjusted annually to reflect changes in average annual wages.

Automatic increases in Social Security benefits are initiated for December of a year whenever the Consumer Price Index (CPI) of the Bureau of Labor Statistics for the third calendar quarter of a year increases relative to the CPI for the base quarter, which is either the third calendar quarter of the preceding year or the quarter in which an increase legislated by Congress becomes effective. The size of the benefit increase is determined by the actual percentage rise of the CPI between the quarters measured.

Average monthly benefits payable to all retired workers was $567.00 in December 1989. The average amount for disabled workers in that month was $556.00.

Minimum and maximum monthly retired-worker benefits payable to individuals who retired at age 65[1]

Year of attainment of age 65[2]	Minimum benefit Payable at the time of retirement	Minimum benefit Payable effective December 1989	Maximum benefit Payable at the time of retirement Men[3]	Maximum benefit Payable at the time of retirement Women	Maximum benefit Payable effective December 1989 Men[3]	Maximum benefit Payable effective December 1989 Women
1965 . . .	$44.00	$331.90	$131.70	$135.90	$619.90	$639.70
1970 . . .	64.00	331.90	189.80	196.40	687.00	711.30
1980 . . .	133.90	331.90	572.00	. . .	990.90	. . .
1985 . . .	(4)	(4)	717.20	. . .	849.70	. . .
1989 . . .	(4)	(4)	899.60	. . .	941.80	. . .

(1) Assumes retirement at beginning of year. (2) The final benefit amount payable after SMI premium or any other deductions is rounded to next lower $1 (if not already a multiple of $1). (3) Benefit for both men and women are shown in men's columns except where women's benefit appears between. (4) Minimum eliminated for workers who reach age 62 after 1981.

Amount of Work Required

To qualify for benefits, the worker must have worked in covered employment long enough to become insured. Just how long depends on when the worker reaches age 62 or, if earlier, when he or she dies or becomes disabled.

A person is fully insured if he or she has one quarter of coverage for every year after 1950 (or year age 21 is reached, if later) up to but not including the year in which the worker reaches age 62, dies, or becomes disabled. In 1990, a person earns one quarter of coverage for each $520 of annual earnings in covered employment, up to a maximum of 4 quarters per year.

The law permits special monthly payments under the Social Security program to certain very old persons who are not eligible for regular social security benefits since they had little or no opportunity to earn social security work credits during their working lifetime.

To get disability benefits, in addition to being fully insured, the worker must also have credit for 20 quarters of coverage out of the 40 calendar quarters before he or she becomes disabled. A disabled blind worker need meet only the fully insured requirement. Persons disabled before age 31 can qualify with a briefer period of coverage. Certain survivor benefits are payable if the deceased worker had 6 quarters of coverage in the 13 quarters preceding death.

Work credit for fully insured status for benefits Born after 1929; die, become disabled, or reach age 62 in

	Years needed
1981	7½
1982	7¾
1983	8
1984	8¼
1985	8½
1986	8¾
1987	9
1988	9¼
1989	9½
1990	9¾

Contribution and benefit base

Calendar year	Base
1981	$29,700
1982	32,400
1983	35,700
1984	37,800
1985	39,600
1986	42,000
1987	43,800
1988	45,000
1989	48,000
1990	51,300

Tax-rate schedule
[Percent of covered earnings]

Year	Total Employees and employers, each	OASDI	HI
1979-80	6.13	5.08	1.05
1981	6.65	5.35	1.30
1982-83	6.70	5.40	1.30
1984	7.00	5.70	1.30
1985	7.05	5.70	1.35
1986-87	7.15	5.70	1.45
1988-89	7.51	6.06	1.45
1990 and after	7.65	6.20	1.45

	Self-employed		
1979-80	8.10	7.05	1.05
1981	9.30	8.00	1.30
1982-83	9.35	8.05	1.30
1984	14.00	11.40	2.60
1985	14.10	11.40	2.70
1986-87	14.30	11.40	2.90
1988-89	15.02	12.12	2.90
1990 and after	15.30	12.40	2.90

What Aged Workers Get

When a person has enough work in covered employment and reaches retirement age (currently 65 for full benefit, 62 for reduced benefit), he or she may retire and get monthly old-age benefits. The age at which unreduced benefits are payable will be increased gradually from 65 to 67 over a 21-year period beginning with workers age 62 in the year 2000; (reduced benefits will still be available as early as age 62 but with a larger reduction at age 62.) If a person aged 65 or older continues to work and has earnings of more than $9,360 in 1990, $1 in benefits will be withheld for every $3 above $9,360. The annual exempt amount for people under age 65 is $6,840 in 1990 and $1 in benefits is withheld for every $2 in earnings above the exempt amount for them. The annual exempt amount is raised automatically as the general earnings level rises. The eligible worker who is 70 receives the full benefit regardless of earnings.

For workers who reach age 65 from 1982 through 1989, the worker's benefit is raised by 3% for each year for which the worker between 65 and 70 (72 before 1984) did not receive benefits because of earnings from work or because the worker had not applied for benefits. The delayed retirement credit is 1 percent a year for workers reaching age 65 before 1982. The delayed retirement credit will gradually rise to 8% per year from 1990 through 2008. The rate for 1990 is 3½%.

Effective December 1989, the special benefit for persons aged 72 or over who do not meet the regular coverage requirements is $159.00 a month. Like the monthly benefits, these payments are subject to cost-of-living increases. The special payment is not made to persons on the public assistance or supplemental security income rolls.

Workers retiring before age 65 have their benefits permanently reduced by 5/9 of 1% for each month they receive benefits before age 65. Thus, workers entitled to benefits in the month they reach age 62 receive 80% of the PIA, while a worker retiring at age 65 receives a benefit equal to 100% of the PIA. The nearer to age 65 the worker is when he or she begins collecting a benefit, the larger the benefit will be.

Benefits for Worker's Spouse

The spouse of a worker who is getting Social Security retirement or disability payments may become entitled to a spouse's insurance benefit when he or she reaches 65 of one-half of the worker's PIA. Reduced spouse's benefits are available at age 62 (25/36 of 1% reduction for each month of entitlement before age 65). Benefits are also payable to the aged-divorced spouse of an insured worker if he or she was married to the worker for at least 10 years.

Benefits for Children of
Retired or Disabled Workers

If a retired or disabled worker has a child under 18 the child will get a benefit that is half of the worker's unreduced benefit, and so will the worker's spouse, even if he or she is under 62 if he or she is caring for an entitled child of the worker who is under 16 or who became disabled before age 22. Total benefits paid on a worker's earnings record are subject to a maximum and if the total that would be paid to a family exceeds that maximum, the individual dependents' benefits are adjusted downward. (Total benefits paid to the family of a worker who retired in January 1989 at age 65 and who always had the maximum amount of earnings creditable under Social Security can be no higher than $1,575.60.)

When entitled children reach 18, their benefits will generally stop, except that a child disabled before 22 may get a benefit as long as his or her disability meets the definition in the law. Additionally, benefits will be paid to a child until age 19 if the child is in full-time attendance at an elementary or secondary school.

Benefits may also be paid to a grandchild or step-grandchild of a worker or of his or her spouse, in special circumstances.

OASDI	May 1990	May 1989	May 1988
Monthly beneficiaries, total (in thousands)	39,440	38,835	38,419
Aged 65 and over, total	28,979	28,393	27,875
Retired workers	21,960	21,455	21,009
Survivors and dependents . . .	7,010	6,926	6,849
Special age-72 beneficiaries . .	9	12	16
Under age 65, total	10,462	10,442	10,544
Retired workers	2,545	2,560	2,575
Disabled workers	2,934	2,850	2,804
Survivors and dependents . . .	4,982	5,032	5,165
Total monthly benefits (in millions).	$20,244	$18,870	$17,787

What Disabled Workers Get

If a worker becomes so severely disabled that he or she is unable to work, he or she may be eligible to receive a monthly disability benefit. Benefits continue until it is determined that the individual is no longer disabled. Each beneficiary's eligibility is reviewed periodically. When a disabled worker beneficiary reaches 65, the disability benefit becomes a retired-worker benefit.

Benefits generally like those provided for dependents of retired-worker beneficiaries may be paid to dependents of

disabled beneficiaries. However, the maximum family benefit in disability cases is generally lower than in retirement cases.

Survivor Benefits

If an insured worker should die, one or more types of benefits may be payable to survivors, again subject to a maximum family benefit as described above.

1. If claiming benefits at 65, the surviving spouse will receive a benefit that is 100% of the deceased worker's PIA. The surviving spouse may choose to get the benefit as early as age 60, but the benefit is then reduced by 19/40 of 1% for each month it is paid before age 65. However, for those aged 62 and over whose spouses claimed their benefits before 65, the benefit is the reduced amount the worker would be getting if alive but not less than 82 1/2% of the worker's PIA.

Disabled widows and widowers may under certain circumstances qualify for benefits after attaining age 50 at the rate of 71.5% of the deceased worker's PIA. The widow or widower must have become totally disabled before or within 7 years after the spouse's death, the last month in which he or she received mother's or father's insurance benefits, or the last month he or she previously received surviving spouse's benefits.

2. A benefit for each child until the child reaches 18. The monthly benefit of each child of a worker who has died is three-quarters of the amount the worker would have received if he or she had lived and drawn full retirement benefits. A child with a disability that began before age 22 may receive benefits. Also, a child may receive benefits until age 19 if he or she is in full-time attendance at an elementary or secondary school.

3. A mother's or father's benefit for the widow(er), if children of the worker under 16 are in his or her care. The benefit is 75% of the PIA and he or she draws it until the youngest child reaches 16, at which time payments stop even if the child's benefit continues. They may start again when he or she is 60 (50 if disabled) unless he or she is married. If he or she marries and the marriage is ended, he or she regains benefit rights (A marriage after age 60, 50 if disabled, is deemed not to have occurred for benefit purposes.). If he or she has a disabled child beneficiary aged 16 or over in care, benefits also continue. This benefit may also be paid to the divorced spouse, if the marriage lasted for at least 10 years.

4. Dependent parents may be eligible for benefits, if they have been receiving at least half their support from the worker before his or her death, have reached age 62, and (except in certain circumstances) have not remarried since the worker's death. Each parent gets 75% of the worker's PIA; if only one parent survives the benefit is 82 1/2%.

5. A lump sum cash payment of $255. Payment is made only when there is a spouse who was living with the worker or a spouse or child eligible for immediate monthly survivor benefits.

Self-Employed

A self-employed person who has net earnings of $400 or more in a year must report such earnings for social security tax and credit purposes. The person reports net returns from the business. Income from real estate, savings, dividends, loans, pensions or insurance policies may not be included unless they are part of the business.

A self-employed person gets a quarter of coverage for each $520 (for 1990), up to a maximum of 4 quarters of coverage.

The nonfarm self-employed have the option of reporting their earnings as 2/3 of their gross income from self-employment but not more than $1,600 a year and not less than their actual net earnings. This option can be used only if actual net earnings from self-employment income is less than $1,600 and may be used only 5 times. Also, the self-employed person must have actual net earnings of $400 or more in 2 of the 3 taxable years immediately preceding the year in which he or she uses the option.

When a person has both taxable wages and earnings from self-employment, the wages are credited for Social Security purposes first; only as much of the self-employment income as will bring total earnings up to the current taxable maximum is subject to the self-employment tax.

Farm Owners and Workers

Self-employed farmers whose gross annual earnings from farming are $2,400 or less may report 2/3 of their gross earnings instead of net earnings for social security purposes. Farmers whose gross income is over $2,400 and whose net earnings are less than $1,600 can report $1,600. Cash or crop shares received from a tenant or share farmer count if the owner participated materially in production or management. The self-employed farmer pays contributions at the same rate as other self-employed persons.

Agricultural employees. A worker's earnings from farm work count toward benefits (1) if the employer pays him $150 or more in cash during the year; or (2) if the employer spends $2,500 or more in the year for agricultural labor. Under these rules a person gets credit for one calendar quarter for each $520 in cash pay in 1990 up to four quarters.

Foreign farm workers admitted to the United States on a temporary basis are not covered.

Household Workers

Anyone working as maid, cook, laundress, nursemaid, baby-sitter, chauffeur, gardener and at other household tasks in the house of another is covered by Social Security if he or she is paid $50 or more in cash in a calendar quarter by any one employer. Room and board do not count, but carfare counts if paid in cash. The job does not have to be regular or fulltime. The employee should get a Social Security card at the social security office and show it to the employer.

The employer deducts the amount of the employee's social security tax from the worker's pay, adds an identical amount as the employer's social security tax and sends the total amount to the federal government, with the employee's social security number.

Medicare

Under Medicare, protection against the costs of hospital care is provided for Social Security and Railroad Retirement beneficiaries aged 65 and over and, for persons entitled for 24 months to receive a social security disability benefit, certain persons (and their dependents) with end-stage renal disease, and, on a voluntary basis with payment of a special premium, persons aged 65 and over not otherwise eligible for hospital benefits; all those eligible for hospital benefits may enroll for medical benefits and pay a monthly premium and so may persons aged 65 and over who are not eligible for hospital benefits.

Persons eligible for both hospital and medical insurance may choose to have their covered services provided through a Health Maintenance Organization.

Hospital insurance.—In 1988, nearly $52.7 billion was withdrawn from the hospital insurance trust fund for hospital and related benefits.

The hospital insurance program pays the cost of covered services for hospital and posthospital care as follows:

* Medicare will cover all *medically necessary* inpatient hospital care 365 days a year. The Medicare hospital patient must pay a deductible sum each year (about $560 in 1987).
* Up to 150 days' care in a skilled-nursing facility (skilled-nursing home) in each year. Hospital insurance pays for all covered services except for coinsurance for the first 8 days of SNF care each year (about $20.50 per day in 1989).
* Visits by nurses or other health workers (not doctors) from a home health agency.
* Hospice care for terminally ill individuals.

Medical insurance. Aged persons can receive benefits under this supplementary program only if they sign up for them and agree to a monthly premium ($24.80 in 1988). The Federal Government pays the rest of the cost.

In 1988, about $35 billion was paid out for medical insurance benefits. As of September 1987, about 33 million persons were enrolled — 3 million of them disabled persons under age 65.

The medical insurance program pays 80% of the reasonable charges (after the first $75 in each calendar year) for the following services:

* Physicians' and surgeons' services, whether in the doctor's office, a clinic, or hospital or at home (but physician's charges for X-ray or clinical laboratory services for hospital bed-patients are paid in full and without meeting the deductible).
* Other medical and health services, such as diagnostic tests, surgical dressings and splints, and rental or purchase of medical equipment. Services of a physical therapist in independent practice, furnished in his office or the patient's home. A hospital or extended-care facility may provide covered outpatient physical therapy services under the medical insurance program to its patients who have exhausted their hospital insurance coverage.
* Physical therapy services furnished under the supervision of a practicing hospital, clinic, skilled nursing facility, or agency.
* Certain services by podiatrists.
* All outpatient services of a participating hospital (including diagnostic tests).
* Outpatient speech pathology services, under the same requirements as physical therapy.
* Services of licensed chiropractors who meet uniform standards, but only for treatment by means of manual manipulation of the spine and treatment of subluxation of the spine demonstrated by X-ray.
* Supplies related to colostomies are considered prosthetic devices and payable under the program.
* Home health services even without a hospital stay are paid up to 100% *when medically necessary*.

To get medical insurance protection, persons approaching age 65 may enroll in the 7-month period that includes 3 months before the 65th birthday, the month of the birthday, and 3 months after the birthday, but if they wish coverage to begin in the month they reach 65 they must enroll in the 3 months before their birthday. Persons not enrolling within their first enrollment period may enroll later, during the first 3 months of each year but their premium is 10% higher for each 12-month period elapsed since they first could have enrolled.

The monthly premium is deducted from the cash benefit for persons receiving Social Security, Railroad Retirement, or Civil Service retirement benefits. Income from the medical premiums and the federal matching payments are put in a Supplementary Medical Insurance Trust Fund, from which benefits and administrative expenses are paid.

Medicare card. Persons qualifying for hospital insurance under Social Security receive a health insurance card similar to cards now used by Blue Cross and other health agencies. The card indicates whether the individual has taken out medical insurance protection. It is to be shown to the hospital, skilled-nursing facility, home health agency, doctor, or whoever provides the covered services.

Payments are made only in the 50 states, Puerto Rico, the Virgin Islands, Guam, and American Samoa, except that hospital services may be provided in border areas immediately outside the U.S. if comparable services are not accessible in the U.S. for a beneficiary who becomes ill or is injured in the U.S.

Social Security Financing

Social Security is paid for by a tax on earnings (for 1990, up to $51,300; the taxable earnings base is now subject to automatic adjustment to reflect increases in average wages). The employed worker and his or her employer share the tax equally.

Employers remit amounts withheld from employee wages for Social Security and income taxes to the Internal Revenue Service; employer Social Security taxes are also payable at the same time. (Self-employed workers pay their Social Security taxes along with their regular income tax forms.) The Social Security taxes (along with revenues arising from partial taxation of the Social Security benefits of certain high-income people) are transferred to the Social Security Trust Funds (Federal Old-Age and Survivors Insurance Trust Fund, the Federal Disability Insurance Trust Fund, and the Federal Hospital Insurance Trust Fund); they can be used only to pay benefits, the cost of rehabilitation services, and administrative expenses. Money not immediately needed for these purposes is by law invested in obligations of the Federal Government, which must pay interest on the money borrowed and must repay the principal when the obligations are redeemed or mature.

Supplemental Security Income

On Jan. 1, 1974, the Supplemental Security Income (SSI) program established by the 1972 Social Security Act amendments replaced the former federal grants to states for aid to the needy aged, blind, and disabled in the 50 states and the District of Columbia. The program provides both for federal payments based on uniform national standards and eligibility requirements and for state supplementary payments varying from state to state. The Social Security Administration administers the federal payments financed from general funds of the Treasury—and the state supplements as well, if the state elects to have its supplementary program federally administered. The states may supplement the federal payment for all recipients and must supplement it for persons otherwise adversely affected by the transition from the former public assistance programs. In May 1990, the number of persons receiving federal payments and federally administered state payments was 4,677,635 and the amount of these payments was $1.36 billion.

The maximum monthly federal SSI payment for an individual with no other countable income, living in his own household, was $386.00 in 1990. For a couple it was $579.00.

Examples of monthly cash benefit awards for selected beneficiary families with first entitlement in 1990, effective January 1990

Beneficiary Family	Low Earnings ($9,719 in 1990) (45% of average)	Career Earnings Level Average Earnings ($21,597 in 1990)[1]	Maximum Earnings ($51,300 in 1990)
Primary Insurance amount (worker retiring at 65)	$437.60	$720.70	$975.00
Maximum family benefit (worker retiring at 65)	656.80	1,311.60	1,750.70
Disability maximum family benefit (worker disabled at 55)	634.10	1,105.50	1,737.30
Disabled worker: (worker disabled at 55)			
Worker alone	455.20	737.00	1,158.20
Worker, spouse, and 1 child	634.00	1,105.00	1,737.00
Retired worker claiming benefits at age 62:			
Worker alone[2]	351.00	578.00	774.00
Worker with spouse claiming benefits at—			
Age 65 or over	570.00	939.00	1,258.00
Age 62[2]	526.00	866.00	1,161.00
Widow or widower claiming benefits at—			
Age 65 or over[3]	437.00	720.00	975.00
Age 60	312.00	515.00	697.00
Disabled widow or widower claiming benefits at age 50-59[4]	312.00	515.00	697.00
1 surviving child	328.00	540.00	731.00
Widow or widower age 65 or over and 1 child[5]	656.00	1,260.00	1,705.00
Widowed mother or father and 1 child[5]	656.00	1,080.00	1,462.00
Widowed mother or father and 2 children[5]	656.00	1,311.00	1,705.00

(1) Estimate. (2) Assumes maximum reduction. (3) A widow(er)'s benefit amount is limited to the amount the spouse would have been receiving if still living but not less than 82.5 percent of the PIA. (4) Effective January 1984, disabled widow(er)s claiming benefit at ages 50-59 will receive benefit equal to 71.5 percent of the PIA (based on 1983 Social Security Amendment provision). (5) Based on worker dying at age 65.

Social Security Trust Funds

Old-Age and Survivors Insurance Trust Fund, 1940-1989

[in millions]

Fiscal year[1]	Income					Disbursements					
	Total	Net contri- butions[2]	Income from taxation of benefits	Payments from the general fund of the Treasury[3]	Net interest[4]	Total	Benefit pay- ments[5]	Adminis- trative expenses	Transfers to Rail- road Retire- ment program	Interfund borrow- ing trans- fers[6]	Net increase in fund	Fund at end of period
1940	$592	$550	—	—	$42	$28	$16	$12	—	—	$564	$1,745
1950	2,367	2,106	—	$4	257	784	727	57	—	—	1,583	12,893
1960	10,360	9,843	—	—	517	11,073	10,270	202	$600	—	−713	20,829
1970	31,746	29,955	—	442	1,350	27,321	26,268	474	579	—	4,425	32,616
1980	100,051	97,608	—	557	1,886	103,228	100,626	1,160	1,442	—	−3,177	24,566
1985	179,881	175,305	$3,151	105	1,321	165,310	165,310	1,589	2,310	$−4,364	6,308	33,877
1988	235,720	226,409	3,335	55	5,922	197,021	192,502	1,729	2,790	—	38,700	96,964
1989	260,457	247,116	3,638	43	9,660	209,102	204,600	1,657	2,845	—	51,355	148,319

(1) Under the Congressional Budget Act of 1974 (Public Law 93-344), fiscal years 1977 and later consist of the 12 months ending on September 30 of each year. The act further provides that the calendar quarter July-September 1976 is a period of transition from fiscal year 1976, which ended on June 30, 1976, to fiscal year 1977, which began on October 1, 1976.

(2) Beginning in 1983, includes government contributions on deemed wage credits for military service in 1957 and later.

(3) Includes payments (1) in 1947-52 and in 1967 and later, for costs of noncontributory wage credits for military service performed before 1957; (2) in 1972-83, for costs of deemed wage credits for military service performed after 1956; and (3) in 1969 and later, for costs of benefits to certain uninsured persons who attained age 72 before 1968.

(4) Net interest includes net profits or losses on marketable investments. Beginning in 1967, administrative expenses are charged currently to the trust fund on an estimated basis, with a final adjustment, including interest, made in the following fiscal year. The amounts of these interest adjustments are included in net interest. For years prior to 1967, a description of the method of accounting for administrative expenses is contained in the 1970 Annual Report of the Board of Trustees of the Fedeal Old-Age and Survivors Insurance and Disability Insurance Trust Funds. Beginning in 1983, these figures reflect payments from a borrowing trust fund to a lending trust fund for interest on amounts owed under the interfund borrowing provisions. Also, beginning in 1983, interest paid from the trust fund to the general fund on advance tax transfers is reflected. The amounts shown for 1985 and 1986 include interest adjustments of $76.5 million and $11.5 million, respectively, on unnegotiated checks issued before April 1985.

(5) Beginning in 1967, includes payments for vocational rehabilitation services furnished to disabled persons receiving benefits because of their disabilities. Beginning in 1983, amounts are reduced by amount of reimbursement for unnegotiated benefit checks. The amount shown for 1983 is reduced by $288 million for all unnegotiated checks issued before 1983; reductions in subsequent years are relatively small.

(6) Positive figure represents amounts lent to the OASI Trust Fund from the DI and HI Trust Funds. Negative figures represent amounts repaid from the OASI Trust Fund to the DI and HI Trust Funds.

Disability Insurance Trust Fund, 1960-1989

[in millions]

Fiscal year[1]	Income					Disbursements					Net increase in fund	Fund at end of period
	Total	Net contri-butions[2]	Income from taxation of benefits	Payments from the general fund of the Treasury[3]	Net interest[4]	Total	Benefit pay-ments[5]	Adminis-trative expenses	Transfers to Rail-road Retire-ment program	Interfund borrow-ing trans-fers[6]		
1960	$1,034	$987	—		$47	$533	$528	$32	—$27		$501	$2,167
1970	4,380	4,141	—	$16	223	2,954	2,795	149	10		1,426	5,104
1980	17,376	16,805	—	118	453	15,320	14,998	334	—12		2,056	7,680
1985	17,984	16,876	$217	—	891	19,294	18,648	603	43	$2,540	1,230	5,873
1987	20,047	19,324	—16[7]	—	738	21,222	20,427	738	57	—	—1,175	7,173
1988	22,369	21,736	56	—	577	22,269	21,405	803	61	—	100	7,273
1989	24,479	23,694	135	—	650	23,389	22,550	751	88	—	1,090	8,363

(1) Under the Congressional Budget Act of 1974 (Public Law 93-344), fiscal years 1977 and later consist of the 12 months ending on September 30 of each year. The act further provides that the calendar quarter July-September 1976 is a period of transition from fiscal year 1976, which ended on June 30, 1976, to fiscal year 1977, which began on October 1, 1976.
(2) Beginning in 1983, includes government contributions on deemed wage credits for military service in 1957 and later.
(3) Includes payments (1) in 1967 and later, for costs of noncontributory wage credits for military service performed before 1957; and (2) in 1972-83, for costs of deemed wage credits for military service performed after 1956.
(4) Net interest includes net profits or losses on marketable investments. Beginning in 1967, administrative expenses are charged currently to the trust fund on an estimated basis, with a final adjustment, including interest, made in the following fiscal year. The amounts of these interest adjustments are included in net interest. For years prior to 1967, a description of the method of accounting for administrative expenses is contained in the 1970 Annual Report of the Board of Trustees of the Federal Old-Age and Survivors Insurance and Disability Insurance Trust Funds. Beginning in 1983, these figures reflect payments from a borrowing trust fund to a lending trust fund for interest on amounts owed under the interfund borrowing provisions. Also, beginning in 1983, interest paid from the trust fund to the general fund on advance tax transfers is reflected. The amount shown for 1985 includes an interest adjustment of $14.8 million on unnegotiated checks issued before April 1985.
(5) Beginning in 1967, includes payments for vocational rehabilitation services furnished to disabled persons receiving benefits because of their disabilities. Beginning in 1983, amounts are reduced by amount of reimbursement for unnegotiated benefit checks. The amount shown for 1983 is reduced by $48 million for all unnegotiated checks issued before 1983; reductions in subsequent years are relatively small.
(6) Negative figure represents amounts lent by the DI Trust Fund to the OASI Trust Fund. Positive figures represent repayment of these amounts.
(7) Reflects $195 million in transfers from the DI Trust Fund to the general fund of the Treasury to correct estimated amounts transferred for calendar years 1984 and 1985.

Supplementary Medical Insurance Trust Fund, 1970-1989

[In millions]

Fiscal year[1]	Income				Disbursements			Balance in fund at end of year[4]
	Premium from participants	Government contribu-tions[2]	Interest and other income[3]	Total income	Benefit payments	Adminis-trative expenses	Total disburse-ments	
1970	$ 936	$ 928	$ 12	$1,876	$ 1,979	$ 217	$ 2,196	$ 57
1975	1,887	2,330	105	4,322	3,765	405	4,170	1,424
1980	2,928	6,932	415	10,275	10,144	593	10,737	4,532
1985	5,524	17,898	1,155	24,577	21,808	922	22,730	10,646
1988	8,756	25,418	828	35,002	33,682	1,265	34,947	6,447
1989	11,548[5]	30,712	1,022[5]	43,282[5]	36,867	1,450[5]	38,317[5]	11,412[5]

(1) For 1967 through 1976, fiscal years cover the interval from July 1 through June 30; fiscal year 1977-86 cover the interval from October 1 through September 30. (2) The payments shown as being from the general fund of the Treasury include certain interest-adjustment items. (3) Other income includes recoveries of amounts reimbursed from the trust fund which are not obligations of the trust fund and other miscellaneous income. (4) The financial status of the program depends on both the total net assets and the liabilities of the program. (5) Includes the impact of the Medicare Catastrophic Coverage Act of 1988 (Public Law 100-360).

Hospital Insurance Trust Fund, 1970-1989

[In millions]

Fiscal Year[1]	Income						Disbursements			Trust Fund	
	Payroll taxes	Transfers from railroad retirement account	Reimburse-ment for uninsured persons	Premiums from voluntary enrollees	Payments for military wage credits	Interest on invest-ments and other income[2]	Total income	Benefits payments[3]	Adminis-trative expense[4]	Total disburse-ments	Net increase fund	Fund at end of year
1970	$4,785	$64	617	—	$11	$137	$5,614	$4,804	$149	$4,953	$661	$2,677
1975	11,291	132	481	6	48	609	12,568	10,353	259	10,612	1,956	9,870
1980	23,244	244	697	17	141	1,072	25,415	23,790	497	24,288	1,127	14,490
1985	46,490	371	766	38	86	3,182	50,933	47,841	813	48,654	4,103[5]	21,277[5]
1987	57,820	368	447	40	94	3,982	62,751	49,967	836	50,803	11,949	50,956
1988	61,901	364	475	42	80	5,148	68,010	52,022	707	52,730	15,281	65,877
1989	67,527	379	515	42	86	6,567	75,116	57,433	805	58,238	16,878	82,755

(1) Fiscal years 1976 and earlier consist of the 12 months ending on June 30 of each year; fiscal years 1977 and later consist of the 12 months ending on September 30 of each year. (2) Other income includes recoveries of amounts reimbursed from the trust fund which are not obligations of the trust fund and a small amount of miscellaneous income. (3) Includes costs of Peer Review Organizations (beginning with the implementation of the Prospective Payment System on October 1, 1983). (4) Includes costs of experiments and demonstration projects. (5) In fiscal year 1983, $12,437 million was loaned to the Old-Age and Survivors Insurance Trust Fund under the interfund borrowing provisions of the Social Security Act. Repayments of $1,824 million and $10,613 million were made in fiscal years 1985 and 1986, respectively.
NOTE: Totals do not necessarily equal the sum of rounded components.

LANGUAGE

Sources for this section: *The World Almanac Guide to Good Word Usage; The Columbia Encyclopedia; Webster's Third New International Dictionary; The Oxford English Dictionary, 2nd ed.; The Associated Press Stylebook and Libel Manual; The Encyclopedia Americana.*

Neologisms

("New" words; from the Second Edition of the *Oxford English Dictionary*, Oxford Univ. Press, 1989.)

antiquark: the antiparticle of a quark.

arcade game: a (mechanical or electronic) game of a type orig. popularized in amusement arcades.

assertiveness training: a technique by which diffident persons are trained to behave (more) assuredly.

astroturfed: carpeted with astroturf.

birth parent: a natural (as opposed to an adoptive) parent.

build-down: a systematic reduction of nuclear armaments, by destroying two or more for each new one deployed.

bulimarexic: suffering from or characteristic of bulimia nervosa; one who suffers from bulimia nervosa.

camp-on: a facility of some telephone systems by which the caller of an engaged number can arrange for the system to ring it automatically as soon as it becomes free (in some cases ringing the caller also if he has replaced his receiver).

car-phone: a radio-telephone designed for use in a motor vehicle.

designer drug: a drug synthesized to mimic a legally restricted or prohibited drug without itself being subject to restriction.

fast tracker: a high-flyer; an ambitious or thrusting person.

foodie: also foody. One who is particular about food, a gourmet.

gender gap: the difference in (esp. political) attitudes between men and women.

hate mail: letters (often anonymous) in which the senders express their hostility towards the recipient.

Jazzercise: a proprietary name for a program of physical exercises arranged to be carried out in a class to the accompaniment of jazz music; also, exercise of this kind.

microwavable: of food and food containers: suitable for cooking or heating in a microwave oven.

NIMBY, nimby: "not in my backyard," a slogan expressing objection to the siting of something considered unpleasant, such as nuclear waste, in one's own locality.

passive smoking: the inhalation of smoke involuntarily from the tobacco being smoked by others, considered as a health risk.

rainbow coalition: a political grouping of minority peoples and other disadvantaged elements, esp. for the purpose of electing a candidate.

right to die: the alleged right of a brain-damaged or otherwise incurably ill person to the termination of life-sustaining treatment.

skanking: a style of West Indian dancing to reggae music, in which the body bends forward at the waist, and the knees are raised and the hands claw the air in time to the beat; dancing in this style.

street credibility: popularity with, or accessibility to, ordinary people, esp. those involved in urban street culture; the appearance or fact of being "street-wise"; hence (apparent) familiarity with contemporary trends, fashions, social issues.

yuppiedom: the condition or fact of being a yuppie; the domain of yuppies; yuppies as a class.

Eponyms (words named for people)

Bloody Mary—a vodka and tomato juice drink; after the nickname of Mary I, Queen of England, 1553-58, notorious for her persecution of Protestants.

Bloomers—full, loose trousers gathered at the knee; after Mrs. Amelia Bloomer, an American social reformer who advocated such clothing, 1851.

Bobbies—in Great Britain, police officers; after Sir Robert Peel, the statesman who organized the London police force, 1850.

Bowdlerize—to delete written matter considered indelicate; after Thomas Bowdler, British editor of an expurgated Shakespeare, 1825.

Boycott—to combine against in a policy of nonintercourse for economic or political reasons; after Charles C. Boycott, an English land agent in County Mayo, Ireland, ostracized in 1880 for refusing to reduce rents.

Braille—a system of writing for the blind; after Louis Braille, the French teacher of the blind who invented it, 1852.

Caesarean section—surgical removal of a child from the uterus through an abdominal incision; after Julius Caesar, born c. 102 B.C., in this manner, according to legend.

Casanova—a man who is a promiscuous and unscrupulous lover; after Giovanni Casanova, an Italian adventurer, 1725-98.

Chauvinist—excessively patriotic; after Nicolas Chauvin, a legendary French soldier devoted to Napoleon.

Derby—a stiff felt hat with a dome-shaped crown and rather narrow rolled brim; after Edward Stanley, 12th Earl of Derby, who in 1780 founded the Derby horse race at Epsom Downs, England, to which these hats are worn.

Gerrymander—to divide an election district in an unnatural way, to favor one political party; after Elbridge Gerry, and the salamander, for the salamander-like shape of a Mass. election district created, 1812, during Gerry's governorship.

Guillotine—a machine for beheading; after Joseph Guillotine, a French physician who proposed its use in 1789 as more humane than hanging.

Leotard—a close-fitting garment for the torso, worn by dancers, acrobats, and the like; after Julius Leotard, a 19th-century French aerial gymnast.

Silhouette—an outline image; from Etienne de Silhouette, the French finance minister, 1757, who advocated economies that included buying such paper portraits instead of painted miniatures.

Foreign Words and Phrases

(L=Latin; F=French; Y=Yiddish; R=Russian; G=Greek; I=Italian; S=Spanish)

ad hoc (L; ad HOK): for the particular end or purpose at hand

ad infinitum (L; ad in-FI-NITE-UM): endless

ad nauseum (L; ad NAWZ-ee-um): to a sickening degree

apropos (L; ap-ruh-POH): to the point; appropriate

bête noire (F; BET NWAHR): a thing or person viewed with particular dislike

bon appetit (F; BOH nap-uh-teet): good appetite

bona fide (L; BOH nuh-feyed): genuine

carte blanche (F; kahrt BLANNSH): full discretionary power

cause celebre (F; kawz suh-LEB-ruh): a notorious incident

C'est la vie (F; se lah VEE): That's life

chutzpah (Y; KHOOT-spuh): amazing nerve bordering on arrogance

coup de grace (F; kooh duh GRAHS): the final blow

coup d'etat (F; kooh duh tah): forceful overthrow of a government

creme de la creme (F; KREM duh luh KREM): the best of the best

cum laude/magna cum laude/summa cum laude (L; KUHM loud-ay; MAHN-ya . . .; SOO-ma . . .): with praise or honor; with great praise or honor; with the highest praise or honor

de facto (L; di FAK-toh): in fact; generally agreed to without a formal decision

deja vu (F; DAY-zhah VOOH): the sensation that something happening has happened before

de jure (L; dee JOOR-ee, day YOOR-ay): determined by law, as opposed to de facto

de rigueur (F; duh ree-GUR): necessary according to convention

detente (F; day-TAHNT): an easing or relaxation of strained relations

éminence grise (F; ay-meh-NAHNN-suh GREEZ): one who wields power behind the scenes

enfant terrible (F; ahnn-FAHNN te-REE-bluh): one whose unconventional behavior causes embarrassment

en masse (F; ahn MAHS): in a large body

ergo (L; ER-goh): therefore

esprit de corps (F; es-PREE duh KAWR): group spirit; feeling of camaraderie

Eureka (G; YOOR-EE-kuh): I have found it

ex post facto (L; eks pohst FAK-toh): an explanation or regulation concocted after the event

fait accompli (F; fayt uh-kom-PLEE): an accomplished fact

faux pas (F; fowe PAH): a social blunder

glasnost (R; glahs-nust): openness, candor

hoi polloi (G; hoy puh-LOY): the masses

in loco parentis (L; in LO H-Koh puh-REN-tis): in place of a parent

in memoriam (L; in muh-MAWR-ee-uhm): in memory of

in situ (L; in SEYE-tyooh): in the original arrangement

in toto (L; in TOH-toh): totally

je ne sais quoi (F; zhuh nuh say KWAH): I don't know what; the little something that eludes description

joie de vivre (F; zhwah duh VEEV-ruh): joy of living, love of life

mea culpa (L; MAY-uh CUL-puh): my fault

meshugga (Y; meh-SHOOG-uh): crazy

modus operandi (L; MOH-duhs op-uh-RAN-dee): method of operation

noblesse oblige (F; noh-BLES uh-BLEEZH): the obligation of nobility to help the less fortunate

non compos mentis (L; non KOM-puhs MEN-tis): out of control of the mind; insane

nouveau riche (L; nooh-voh REESH): pejorative for recent rich who spend money conspicuously

perestroika (R; PAIR-es TROY-kuh): restructuring

persona non grata (L; per-SOH-nah non GRAH-tah): unacceptable person

post-mortem (L; pohst-MORE-tuhm): after death; autopsy; analysis after event

prima donna (I; pree-muh DAH-nuh): temperamental person

pro tempore (L; proh TEM-puh-ree): for the time being

que sera sera (S; keh sair-ah sair-AH): what will be, will be

quid pro quo (L; kwid proh KWOH): something given or received for something else

raison d'etre (F; RAY-zohnn DET-ruh): reason for being

shlemiel (Y; shleh-MEEL): an unlucky bungling person

savoir-faire (F; sav-wahr-FAIR): dexterity in social and practical affairs

semper fidelis (L; SEM-puhr fee-DAY-lis): always faithful

status quo (L; STAY-tus QWOH): existing order of things

tour de force (L; TOOR duh FAWRS): feat accomplished through great skill

terra firma (L; TER-uh FUR-muh): solid ground

verbatim (L; ver-BAY-tuhm): word for word

vis-a-vis (F; vee-ZUH-VEE): compared with

Esperanto

In 1887, Dr. L. L. Zamenhof, a linguist and physician, published a slim textbook on his "Internacia Lingvo" (International Language) under the pseudonym "Doktoro Esperanto." The term "Esperanto" became attached to the language itself as it gained adherents rapidly until the outbreak of World War I. Hardly recovered from the effects of the war, Esperanto was savaged by Nazism, Stalinism, Fascism, the Japanese militarists of the 1930's, and chauvinistic groups in many other countries. Not until the late 1950's did the number of speakers begin to show the steady increase which continues as Esperanto begins its second century.

Controlled experiments show that because of its logical structure, phonemic spelling, and regular grammar Esperanto can be learned to a given criterion of performance in from one-twentieth to one-fifth the time needed for the learning of a typical national language.

Inteligenta persono lernas la lingvon Esperanto rapide kaj facile. Esperanto estas la moderna, kultura lingvo por la tuta mondo.

Commonly Confused English Words

adverse: unfavorable
averse: opposed

affect: to influence
effect: to cause

aggravate: to make worse
annoy: to irritate

allusion: an indirect reference
illusion: an unreal impression

anxious: apprehensive
eager: avid

censor: to subject to examination by an official empowered to demand alteration or withdrawal
censure: a judgment involving condemnation

complement: to make complete; something that completes
compliment: to praise; praise

capital: the seat of government
capitol: the building in which a legislative body meets

emigrate: to leave for another place of residence

immigrate: to come to another place of residence

elicit: to draw or bring out
illicit: illegal

denote: to mean
connote: to suggest beyond the explicit meaning

farther: more distant in space
further: an extension of time or degree

historic: an important occurrence
historical: any occurrence in the past

imply: to relay information but not explicitly
infer: to understand information that is not relayed explicitly

imminent: ready to take place
eminent: standing out

incredible: unbelievable
incredulous: skeptical

include: used when the items following are part of a whole

comprise: used when the items following are all of a whole

ingenious: clever
ingenuous: innocent

insidious: intended to trick
invidious: detrimental to reputation

literally: actually
figuratively: metaphorically

oral: spoken, as opposed to written
verbal: referring to skill with language, as opposed to other skills

prevaricate: to lie
procrastinate: to put off

pestilence: a contagious or infectious epidemic disease
petulance: rudeness

prostrate: stretched out flat, face down
prostate: of or relating to the prostate gland

qualitative: relating to quality
quantitative: relating to number

National Spelling Bee Champions

The Scripps Howard National Spelling Bee, conducted by Scripps Howard Newspapers and other leading newspapers since 1939, was instituted by the Louisville (Ky.) Courier-Journal in 1925. Children under 16 years of age and not beyond the eighth grade are eligible to compete for cash prizes at the finals, which are held annually in Washington, D.C. The 1990 winners are: first prize, **Amy Marie Dimak,** Seattle, Wash. (*The Seattle Times*); second prize, **Eric Enders,** El Paso, Tex. (*El Paso Herald-Post*); third prize, **Tessa Alfonsaamary Sandaram,** Newtown Sq., Pa. (*Delaware Cty. Daily & Sunday Times,* Primos, Pa.).

Winning Words

These were the last words given in each of the years 1965-1990 at the Scripps Howard National Spelling Bee. They were all correctly spelled, thereby determining the national champion.

1965 — eczema	1972 — macerate	1979 — maculature	1986 — odontalgia
1966 — ratoon	1973 — vouchsafe	1980 — elucubrate	1987 — staphylococci
1967 — chihuahua	1974 — hydrophyte	1981 — sarcophagus	1988 — elegiacal
1968 — abalone	1975 — incisor	1982 — psoriasis	1989 — spoliator
1969 — interlocutory	1976 — narcolepsy	1983 — purim	1990 — fibranne
1970 — croissant	1977 — cambist	1984 — luge	
1971 — shalloon	1978 — deification	1985 — milieu	

Commonly Misspelled English Words

accidentally	convenience	government	miniature
accommodate	deceive	grammar	mysterious
acquainted	describe	humorous	necessary
all right	description	hurrying	opportunity
already	desirable	incidentally	optimistic
amateur	despair	independent	performance
appearance	desperate	inoculate	permanent
appropriate	eliminate	irresistible	rhythm
bureau	embarrass	laboratory	ridiculous
character	fascinating	lightning	similar
commitment	finally	maintenance	sincerely
conscious	foreign	marriage	transferred
conscientious	forty		

Some Common Abbreviations

Usage of periods after abbreviations varies, but recently the tendency has been toward omission. Definitions preceding those in parentheses are in Latin.

A.A. = Alcoholics Anonymous
A.A.A. = American Automobile Association
AC = alternating current
A.D. = anno Domini (in the year of the Lord)
A.M. = ante meridiem (before noon)
A.F.L. = American Federation of Labor
A.M.A. = American Medical Association
anon. = anonymous
ASAP = as soon as possible
ASCAP = American Society of Composers, Authors, and Publishers
B.A. = Bachelor of Arts
bbl. = barrel(s)
B.C. = before Christ
B.C.E. = before the Christian era
B.S. = Bachelor of Science
B.T.U. = British thermal unit
bu. = bushel
C. = centigrade, Celsius
c. = copyright
c. (or ca.) = circa (about)
C.I.A. = Central Intelligence Agency
C.E.O. = chief executive officer
C.I.O. = Congress of Industrial Organizations
cm = centimeter
C.O.D. = cash (or collect) on delivery
C.P. = Communist Party
C.P.A. = Certified Public Accountant
C.P.R. = cardio-pulmonary resuscitation
D.A. = District Attorney
D.A.R. = Daughters of the American Revolution
DC = direct current
D.D. = Doctor of Divinity
D.D.S. = Doctor of Dental Surgery

DNA = deoxyribonucleic acid
DOA = dead on arrival
ed. = edited, edition, editor
e.g. = exempli gratia (for example)
esp. = especially
et. al. = et alii (and others)
etc. = et cetera (and so forth)
F. = Fahrenheit
F.B.I. = Federal Bureau of Investigation
f.o.b. = freight on board
FYI = for your information
g.n.p. = gross national product
G.O.P. = Grand Old party (Republican)
Hon. = the Honorable
H.R.H. = His (Her) Royal Highness
i.e. = id est (that is)
I.Q. = Intelligence Quotient
I.R.A. = Irish Republican Army
I.R.S. = Internal Revenue Service
J.D. = Juris Doctor (Doctor of Laws)
J.P. = Justice of the Peace
K = 1,000
k. = karat
kg. = kilogram
km. = kilometer
l = liter
lb. = libra (pound)
M.A. = Master of Arts
M.D. = Medicineae Doctor (Doctor of Medicine)
mfg. = manufacturing
ml = milliliter
mm = millimeter
M.S. = Master of Science

mph = miles per hour
MS = manuscript
MSG = monosodium glutamate
Msgr. = Monsignor
NCO = Noncommissioned Officer
No. = numero (number)
op. = opus (work)
oz. = ounce
p. = page
P.M. = post meridiem (afternoon)
POW = prisoner of war
P.S. = post scriptum (postscript)
pt. = pint(s), part, point
qt. = quart(s)
REM = rapid eye movement
R.F.D. = rural free delivery
R.I.P. = Requiescat in pace (May he rest in peace)
R.N. = Registered Nurse
ROTC = Reserve Officers' Training Corps
rpm = revolutions per minute
RR = railroad
R.S.V.P. = Répondez, s'il, vous plait (Please answer)
S.A.S.E. = self-addressed stamped envelope
S.P.C.A. = Society for the Prevention of Cruelty to Animals
St. = saint, street
T. = ton
T.N.T. = trinitrotoluene
UFO = unidentified flying object
UHF = ultra-high frequency
U.S.S. = United States Ship
v. (or vs.) = versus (against)
VHF = very high frequency
w = watt

Latin and Greek Prefixes and Suffixes

Latin prefix/English meaning
a, abs/from
alti, alto/high
ambi/both
ante/before
aqui/water
arbori/tree
audio/hearing
avi/bird
brevi/short
centi/hundred
cerebro/brain
circum/around
ferri, ferro/iron
fissi/split
igni/fire
inter/between
juxta/close
lacto/milk
luni/moon
magni/great
mal/bad
multi/many
naso/nose
nati/birth
oculo/eye
oleo/oil
omni/all
ovi, ovo/egg
plano/flat
post/after

pre/before
pro/for
pulmo/lung
re/again
recti/straight
retro/backward
somni/sleep
stelli/star
sub/under
super/above
terri/land
trans/through
ultra/beyond
uni/one
Latin suffix/English meaning
cide, cidal/kill
fid/split
fuge, fugal/flee from
grade/walking
pennale/wing
vorous/eating
Greek prefix/English meaning
a/not
anti/against
astro/star
auto/self
biblio/book
bio/life
cardio/heart

chloro/green
chrono/time
cosmo/universe
ex/outside
geo/earth
geronto/old age
gluc/sweet
grapho/writing
helio/sun
hemi/half
hetero/different
homeo/similar
homo/same
hydro/water
hyper/above
kinesi/movement
litho/stone
logo/word
macro/large
mega/great
meso/middle
meta/beyond
micro/small
mono/one
necro/dead body
neo/new
ornitho/bird
osteo/bone
pan/all
para/close
phono/sound

photo/light
poly/many
proto/first
pseudo/false
psycho/mind, spirit
pyro/fire
rhino/nose
theo/god
thermo/heat
toxico/poison
zoo/living
Greek suffix/English meaning
algia/pain
archy/government
gamy/marriage
gnomy/knowledge
iasis/disease
itis/inflammation
lepsy/seizure
logy/science of
machy/battle
meter/measure
oid/like
oma/tumor
phobe/fear
scope/observation
sect/cutting
soma/body
sophy/wisdom

A Collection of Animal Collectives

The English language boasts an abundance of names to describe groups of things, particularly pairs or aggregations of animals. Some of these words have fallen into comparative disuse, but many of them are still in service, helping to enrich the vocabularies of those who like their language to be precise, who tire of hearing a group referred to as "a bunch of," or who enjoy the sound of words that aren't overworked.

band of gorillas	**crash** of rhinoceri	**knot** of toads	**shoal** of fish, pilchards
bed of clams, oysters	**cry** of hounds	**leap** of leopards	**skein** of geese
bevy of quail, swans	**down** of hares	**leash** of greyhounds, foxes	**skulk** of foxes
brace of ducks	**drift** of swine	**litter** of pigs	**sleuth** of bears
brood of chicks	**drove** of cattle, sheep	**mob** of kangaroos	**sounder** of boars, swine
cast of hawks	**exaltation** of larks	**murder** of crows	**span** of mules
cete of badgers	**flight** of birds	**muster** of peacocks	**spring** of teals
charm of goldfinches	**flock** of sheep, geese	**mute** of hounds	**swarm** of bees
chattering of choughs	**gaggle** of geese	**nest** of vipers	**team** of ducks, horses
cloud of gnats	**gam** of whales	**nest, nide** of pheasants	**tribe** or **trip** of goats
clowder of cats	**gang** of elks	**pack** of hounds, wolves	**troop** of kangaroos,
clutch of chicks	**grist** of bees	**pair** of horses	monkeys
clutter of cats	**herd** of elephants	**pod** of whales, seals	**volery** of birds
colony of ants	**horde** of gnats	**pride** of lions	**watch** of nightingales
congregation of plovers	**husk** of hares	**school** of fish	**wing** of plovers
covey of quail, partridge	**kindle** or **kendle** of kittens	**sedge** or **siege** of cranes	**yoke** of oxen

Young of Animals Have Special Names

The young of many animals, birds and fish have come to be called by special names. A young eel, for example, is an elver. Many young animals, of course, are often referred to simply as infants, babies, younglets, or younglings.

bunny: rabbit.
calf: cattle, elephant, antelope, rhino, hippo, whale, etc.
cheeper: grouse, partridge, quail.
chick, chicken: fowl.
cockerel: rooster.
codling, sprag: codfish.
colt: horse (male).
cub: lion, bear, shark, fox, etc.
cygnet: swan.
duckling: duck.
eaglet: eagle.
elver: eel.
eyas: hawk, others.
fawn: deer.

filly: horse (female).
fingerling: fish generally.
flapper: wild fowl.
fledgling: birds generally.
foal: horse, zebra, others.
fry: fish generally.
gosling: goose.
heifer: cow.
joey: kangaroo, others.
kid: goat.
kit: fox, beaver, rabbit, cat.
kitten, kitty, catling: cats, other fur-bearers.
lamb, lambkin, cosset, hog: sheep.
leveret: hare.

nestling: birds generally.
owlet: owl.
parr, smolt, grilse: salmon.
piglet, shoat, farrow, suckling: pig.
polliwog, tadpole: frog.
poult: turkey.
pullet: hen.
pup: dog, seal, sea lion, fox.
puss, pussy: cat.
spike, blinker, tinker: mackerel.
squab: pigeon.
squeaker: pigeon, others.
whelp: dog, tiger, beasts of prey.
yearling: cattle, sheep, horse, etc.

The Principal Languages of the World

Source: Sidney S. Culbert, Guthrie Hall NI-25 — University of Washington, Seattle, Wash. 98195

Total number of speakers (native plus non-native) of languages spoken by at least one million persons (midyear 1989)

Language	Millions	Language	Millions	Language	Millions
Achinese (N Sumatra, Indonesia) . .	3	Cantonese (or Yue) (China;		Fon (SC Benin; S Togo)	1
Afrikaans (So. Africa).	10	Hong-kong)	63	French	121
Akan (or Twi-Fante) Ghana	7	Catalan (NE Spain; S France;		Fula (or Peulh) (Cameroon; Nigeria)	13
Albanian (Albania; Yugoslavia) . . .	5	Andorra)	9	Fulakunda (Senegambia; Guinea	
Amharic (Ethiopia)	17	Cebuano (Bohol Sea area,		Bissau).	2
Arabic	197	Philippines)	12	Futa Jalon (NW Guinea; Sierra	
Armenian[1] (USSR).	5	Chagga (Kilimanjaro area, Tanzania)	1	Leone)	3
Assamese[1] (Assam, India;		Chiga (Ankole, Uganda)	1	Galician (Galicia, NW Spain)	3
Bangladesh)	22	Chinese[3]		Galla (see Oromo)	
Aymara (Bolivia; Peru)	2	Chuvash (Chuvash ASSR, USSR) . .	2	Ganda (or Luganda) (S Uganda) . .	3
Azerbaijani (Iran; Azer. SSR, USSR)	14	Czech (Czechoslovakia)	12	Georgian (Georgian SSR, USSR). .	4
Balinese (Indonesia)	3	Danish (Denmark).	5	German	118
Baluchi (Baluchistan, Pakistan) . . .	4	Dimli (EC Turkey)	1	Gilaki (Gilan, NW Iran)	2
Bashkir (Bashkir ASSR, USSR) . . .	1	Dogri (Jammu-Kashmir, C and E		Gogo (Riff Valley; Tanzania)	1
Batak Toda (including Anakola		India).	1	Gondi (Central India)	2
Indonesia (see also Karo-Dairi) . .	4	Dong (Guizhou, Hunan, Guangxi,		Greek (Greece)	12
Baule (Côte d' Ivoire)	2	China)	2	Guarani (Paraguay)	4
Beja (Kassala, Sudan; Ethiopia) . . .	1	Dutch-Flemish (Netherlands;		Gujarati[1] (W and C India; S Pakistan)	38
Bemba (Zambia)	2	Belgium).	21	Gusii (Kisii District, Nyanza, Kenya).	2
Bengali[1]	184	Dyerma (SW Niger).	2	Hadiyya (Arusi, Ethiopia).	2
Berber[2]		Edo (Bendel, S Nigeria)	1	Hakka (or Kejia) (SE China)	32
Beti (Cameroon; Gabon; Eq. Guinea)	2	Efik (incl. Ibibio) (SE Nigeria; W.		Hani (S China).	1
Bhili (India).	3	Cam.)	6	Hausa (N Nigeria; Niger; Cameroon)	34
Bikol (SE Luzon, Philippines).	4	English	443	Haya (Kagera, NW Tanzania) . . .	1
Brahui (Pakistan; Afghan.; Iran) . . .	1	Esperanto	2	Hebrew (Israel)	3
Bugis (Indonesia, Malaysia)	4	Estonian (Estonian SSR, USSR) . . .	1	Hindi[1,4]	352
Bulgarian (Bulgaria).	9	Ewe (SE Ghana; S Togo)	3	Ho (Bihar and Orissa States, India).	1
Burmese (Burma)	30	Fang-Bulu (Dialects of Beti, q. v.)		Hungarian (or Magyar) (Hungary). .	14
Buyi (S Guizhou, S China)	2	Farsi (Iranian form of Persian, q. v.)		Iban (Kalimantan, Indonesia;	
Byelorussian (Byelorussian SSR,		Finnish (Finland; Sweden)	6	Malaysia)	1
USSR).	10	Flemish (see Dutch-Flemish)		Ibibio (see Efik)	

Language	Millions	Language	Millions	Language	Millions
Igbo (or Ibo) (lower Niger R., Nigeria)	16	Meithei (NE India; Bangladesh) . . .	1	Sinhalese (Sri Lanka).	13
Ijaw (Niger River delta, Nigeria) . . .	2	Mende (Central, S and E Sierra		Slovak (Czechoslovakia).	5
Ilocano (NW Luzon, Philippines) . . .	7	Leone).	2	Slovene (Slovenia, NW Yugoslavia)	2
Indonesian (see Malay-Indonesian)		Meru (Eastern Province, C Tanzania)	1	Soga (Busoga, Uganda).	1
Italian (Italy).	63	Miao (or Hmong) (S China; SE Asia)	5	Somali (Somalia; Eth.; Ken.; Djibouti)	7
Japanese . . . . :	125	Mien (China; Viet.; Laos; Thailand) .	2	Songye (Kasai Or., NW Shala, Zaire)	1
Javanese (Java, Indonesia)	58	Min (SE China; Taiwan; Malaysia). .	48	Soninke (Mali; countries to W S E) .	1
Kabyle (W Kabylia, N Algeria). . . .	3	Minangkabau (W Sumatra,		Sotho, Northern (So. Africa).	3
Kamba (E Kenya).	3	Indonesia).	6	Sotho, Southern (So. Africa;
Kannada[1] (S India).	41	Moldavian (included with Romanian)		Lesotho).	4
Kanuri (Nigeria; Niger; Chad; Cam.)	4	Mongolian (Mongolia; NE China) . .	5	Spanish	341
Karen (see Pho and Sgaw)		Mordvin (in and near Mord. SSR.		Sundanese (Sunda Strait, Indonesia)	24
Karo-Dairi (N Sumatra, Indonesia) .	2	USSR).	1	Swahili (Kenya; Tanz.; Zaire;
Kashmiri[1] (N India; NE Pakistan). . .	3	Moré (central part of Burkina Faso).	4	Uganda).	43
Kazakh (Kazakh SSR, USSR). . . .	8	Nepali (Nepal; NE India; Bhutan) . .	13	Swati (Swaziland; So. Africa)	1
Kenuzi-Dongola (S Egypt; Sudan). .	1	Ngulu (Zambezia, Mozambique;		Swedish (Sweden; Finland)	9
Khalka (see Mongolian)		Malawi).	2	Sylhetti (Bangladesh).	5
Khmer (Kampuchea; Vietnam;		Nkole (Western Prov., Uganda) . . .	1	Tagalog (Philippines)	36
Thailand)	7	Norwegian (Norway)	5	Tajiki (Tajik Uzbek Kirghiz SSRs,
Khmer, Northern (Thailand)	1	Nung (NE of Hanoi, Vietnam; China)	1	USSR).	4
Kikuyu (or Gekoyo) (W and C		Nupe (Kwara, Niger States, Nigeria)	1	Tamazight (N Morocco; W Algeria) .	3
Kenya).	5	Nyamwezi-Sukuma (NW Tanzania) .	4	Tamil[1] (Tamil Nadu, India; Sri Lanka)	65
Kirghiz (Kirghiz SSR, USSR).	2	Nyanja (Malawi; Zambia; N		Tatar (Tatar SSR, USSR)	7
Kituba (Bas-Zaire, Bandundu, Zaire)	4	Zimbabwe)	4	Tausug (Philippines; Malaysia) . . .	1
Kongo (W Zaire; S Congo; NW		Oriya[1] (Central and E India).	30	Telugu[1] (Andhra Pradesh, SE India)	68
Angola)	3	Oromo (W Ethiopia; N Kenya)	10	Temne (central Sierra Leone)	1
Konkani (Maharashtra and SW India)	4	Pampangan (NW of Manila,		Thai[5] (Thailand)	48
Korean (So., No. Korea; China;		Philippines)	2	Tho (N Vietnam; S China)	1
Japan).	71	Panay-Hiligaynon (Philippines) . . .	6	Thonga (Mozambique; So. Africa). .	3
Kurdish (south-west of Caspian Sea)	9	Pangasinan (Lingayen G.,		Tibetan (SW China; N India; Nepal) .	5
Kurukh (or Oraon) (C and E India) .	2	Philippines)	2	Tigrinya (S Eritrea, Tigre, Ethiopia) .	4
Lao[5] (Laos)	2	Pashtu (Pakistan; Afghanistan; Iran)	21	Tiv (SE Nigeria; Cameroon)	2
Lampung (Sumatra, indonesia) . . .	1	Pedi (see Sotho, Northern)		Tong (see Dong)
Latvian (Latvian SSR, USSR)	1	Persian (Iran; Afghanistan)	32	Tonga (SW Zambia; NW Zimbabwe)	2
Lingala (including Bangala) (Zaire) .	6	Polish (Poland)	43	Tswana (Botswana; So. Africa) . . .	3
Lithuanian (Lithuanian SSR, USSR).	3	Portuguese	173	Tudza (N Vietnam; S China)	1
Luba-Lulua (or Chiluba) (Kasai,		Provençal (S France).	4	Tulu (S India)	2
Zaire)	6	Punjabi[1] (Punjab, Pakistan; NW		Tumbuka (N Malawi; NE Zambia) . .	2
Luba-Shaba (Shaba, Zaire)	1	India).	84	Turkish (Turkey).	55
Lubu (E Sumatra, Indonesia)	1	Pushto (see Pashtu) (many spellings)		Turkmen (S USSR; NE Iran;
Luhya (W Kenya)	3	Quechua (Peru; Bol. Ec.; Arg.) . . .	8	Afghanistan)	3
Luo (Kenya; Nyanza, Tanzania) . . .	3	Rejang (SW Sumatra, Indonesia) . .	1	Twi-Fante (see Akan)
Luri (SW Iran; Iraq)	3	Riff (N Morocco; Algerian coast) . . .	1	Uighur (Xinjiang, NW China; SC
Lwena (E Angola; W Zambia)	1	Romanian (Romania; Moldavia,		USSR).	7
Macedonian (Macedonia,		USSR).	25	Ukrainian (Ukraine, USSR; Poland).	45
Yugoslavia)	2	Romany (Vlach only) (Europe;		Urdu[1,4] (Pakistan; India).	92
Madurese (Madura, Indonesia) . . .	10	Amer.)	1	Uzbek (Uzbek SSR, USSR)	13
Magindanaon (Moro Gulf, S		Ruanda (Rwanda; S Uganda; E		Vietnamese (Vietnam)	57
Philippines)	1	Zaire)	8	Wolaytta (SW Ethiopia).	2
Makassar (S Sulawesi, Indonesia) .	2	Rundi (Burundi)	6	Wolof (Senegal).	6
Makua (S Tanzania; N Mozambique)	3	Russian	293	Wu (Shanghai and nearby prov.,
Malagasy (Madagascar)	11	Samar-Leyte (Central E Philippines)	3	China)	62
Malay-Indonesian	142	Sango (Central African Republic) . .	3	Xhosa (SW Cape Province, So.
Malay, Pattani (SE pennisular		Santali (E India; Nepal).	5	Africa)	7
Thailand)	1	Sasak (Lombok, Atas Strait,		Yao (see Mien)
Malayalam[1] (Kerala, India).	34	Indonesia)	1	Yao (Malawi; Tanzania; Mozambique)
Malinke-Bambara-Dyula (W Africa).	9	Serbo-Croatian (Yugoslavia)	20	Yi (S and SW China)	6
Mandarin.	864	Sgaw (SW W N of Rangoon, SW		Yiddish[6]
Marathi[1] (Maharashtra, India)	64	Burma)	1	Yoruba (SW Nigeria; Zou, Benin) . .	18
Mazandarani (S Mazandaran, N Iran)	2	Shan (Shan, E Burma)	3	Zande (NE Zaire; SW Sudan)	1
Mbundu (or Umbundu) (Benguela,		Shilha (W Algeria; S Morocco)	3	Zhuang (S China).	14
Angola)	3	Shona (Zimbabwe)	7	Zulu (N Natal, So. Africa; Lesotho) .	7
Mbundu (or Kimbundu) (Luanda,		Sidamo (Sidamo, S Ethiopia)	1	
Angola)	3	Sindhi[1] (SE Pakistan; W India). . . .	16	

(1) One of the fifteen languages of the Constitution of India. (2) See Kabyle, Riff, Shilha, and Tamazight. (3) See Mandarin, Cantonese, Wu, Min, and Hakka. The "common speech" (Putonghua) or the "national language" (Guoyu) is a standardized form of Mandarin as spoken in the area of Beijing. (4) Hindi and Urdu are essentially the same language, Hindustani. As the official language of Pakistan it is written in a modified Arabic script and called Urdu. As the official language of India it is written in the Devanagari script and called Hindi. (5) The distinctions between some Thai dialects and Lao is political rather than linguistic. (6) Yiddish is usually considered a variant of German, though it has its own standard grammar, dictionaries, a highly developed literature, and is written in Hebrew characters.

Computer Language

Source: The Computer Glossary by Alan Freedman. The Computer Language Co. Inc., 1991

access: (used as a verb) to store data on and retrieve data from a disk or other device connected to the computer.

acoustic coupler: a device that connects a terminal or computer to the handset of a telephone. It may also include the modem.

address: a number of a particular memory or disk location. Like a post office box.

analog: a representation of an object that resembles the original. For example, the telephone system converts sound waves into analogous electrical waves.

artificial intelligence: a broad range of computer applications that resemble human intelligence and behavior, such as expert systems and robots.

ASCII: acronym for American Standard Code for Information Interchange. A widely-used code for storing data.

assembly language: a machine oriented language using mnemonics to represent each machine-language instruction. Each CPU has its own assembly language.

authorization code: an identification number or password used to gain access to a computer system.

backup file: a copy of a current file used if the current file is destroyed.

(continued)

BASIC: Beginner's All-purpose Symbolic Instruction Code; a computer language used by many small and personal computer systems.

baud rate: the switching speed of a line. One baud equals one bit per second or more.

binary: refers to the base-2 number system in which the only allowable digits are 0 and 1.

bit: short for binary digit, the smallest unit of information stored in a computer. It always has the binary value of "O" or "1."

bubble memory: a memory that circulates tiny bubble-like magnetic bits in a solid state structure. Not widely used.

buffer: a temporary place to put information for processing.

bug: a mistake that occurs in a program within a computer or in the unit's electrical system. When a mistake is found and corrected, it's called debugging.

byte: an 8-bit sequence of binary digits. Each byte corresponds to 1 character of data, representing a single letter, number, or symbol. Bytes are the most common unit for measuring computer and disk storage capacity.

c: a high-level programming language often used to write commercial products due to its transportability to many different computer systems.

CAD/CAM: abbreviation for computer-aided design/computer-aided manufacturing.

cathode ray tube terminal: a device used as a computer terminal which contains a television-like screen for displaying data. Most CRT terminals also have a typewriter-like keyboard.

CD-ROM: Information is retrieved by a laser beam that scans tracks of microscopic holes in a rotating compact disk. They can store 550 million characters, but cannot store new information.

COBOL: Common Business Oriented Language; one of the most widely used business programming languages.

chip: a common term for an integrated circuit, a collection of interconnected microminiature electronic components.

command: an action statement or order to the computer.

compiler: a program that translates a high-level language, such as BASIC, into machine language.

connect time: the time a user at a terminal (a work station away from the main computer) is logged-on to a computer system.

CPU: the Central Processing Unit within the computer that executes the instructions the user gives the system.

cursor: the symbol on the computer monitor that marks the place where the operator is working.

database: a large amount of data stored in a well organized format. A database management system is a program that allows access to the information.

dedicated: designed for a single use.

density: the number of bits that can be stored in a linear inch.

desktop publishing: using a personal computer to produce high-quality printed output camera ready for the printer.

diagnostics: software programs that test the operational capability of hardware components.

directory: an index to the location of files on a disk.

disk: a revolving plate on which information and programs are stored. See also **Floppy disk.**

disk drive: a peripheral machine that stores information on disks.

documentation: user or operator instructions that come with some hardware and software that tells how to use the material.

DOS: a single-user operating system commonly used on PCs.

download: to transmit data from a central to a remote computer or from a file server to a personal computer.

dump: a printout of the contents of memory or a file.

error message: a statement by the computer indicating that the user has done something incorrectly.

fax: facsimile, the communication of a printed page between remote locations.

field: the physical unit of data in a record.

file: any collection of data treated as a single unit.

file server: a computer that stores data and programs that are shared by many users in a network.

floppy disk: a small inexpensive disk used to record and

store information. It must be used in conjunction with a disk drive.

font: a set of characters of a particular design and size.

foreground/background: an operating system prioritizing method in multitasking computer systems. Programs running in the foreground have highest priority.

format: the arrangement by which information is stored.

function: in programming, a routine, or set of instructions, that performs a particular task.

gigabyte: one billion bytes.

hacker: a very technical person in the computer field; the term is sometimes used in a derogatory manner to refer to people who gain unauthorized access into computer systems and data banks.

hardware: the physical apparatus that makes up a computer, silicon chips, transformers, boards and wires. Also used to describe various pieces of equipment including the CPU, printer, modem, CRT (cathode ray tube).

hexadecimal: refers to the base-16 number system, which is used as a shorthand for referencing machine codes.

intelligent terminal: a terminal with built-in processing capability. It has memory, but no disk or tape storage.

interface: the hardware or software necessary to connect one device or system to another.

K: abbreviation for Kilo-byte used to denote 1,024 units of stored matter.

language: any set of compiled, unified, or related commands or instructions that are acceptable to a computer.

laptop computer: a portable computer that usually weighs less than 12 pounds and has a self-contained power supply.

light pen: an input device that uses a light-sensitive stylus connected by a wire to a video terminal.

load: the actual operation of putting information and data into the computer or memory.

loop: in programming, the repetition of some function within the program.

machine readable: any paper form or storage medium that can be automatically read by the computer.

master file: a collection of records pertaining to one of the main subjects of an information system.

megabyte: one million bytes.

memory: the computer's internal work space.

menu: programs, functions or other choices displayed on the monitor for user selection.

microcomputer: a computer that uses a microprocessor for its CPU. All personal computers are microcomputers.

microprocessor: a complete CPU on a single chip.

minicomputer: an intermediate computer system sized between the very small microcomputer and the large computer.

modem: stands for Modulator-Demodulator. A device that adapts a terminal or computer to an analog telephone line.

mouse: a puck-like object that is used as a pointing and drawing device.

multitasking: the ability to run more than one program at the same time.

network: in communications, the path between terminals and computers. In database management, a database design.

noise: random disturbances that degrade or disrupt data communications.

operating system: a master control program that runs the computer and acts as a scheduler and traffic cop.

OS/2: a single-user, multitasking operating system that was designed to be the successor to DOS.

password: a word or code used to identify an authorized user.

peripheral: any hardware device connected to a computer, such as printers or joy sticks.

pixel: picture element, the smallest display element on a video display screen.

program: coded instructions telling a computer how to perform a specific function.

RAM: stands for Random Access Memory. Same as **memory.**

random access: the ability to retrieve records in a file without reading any previous records.

record: a group of related fields that are used to store data about a subject. A collection of records is a *file*, and a collection of files is a *database*.

ROM: stands for Read Only Memory. A permanent memory.

semiconductor: a solid state substance that can be electrically altered, such as a transistor.

software: the programs, or sets of instructions, that tell the computer what to do.

spreadsheet: a software program that simulates a paper spreadsheet, or worksheet, in which columns of numbers are totaled.

superconductor: a material that has almost no resistance to the flow of electricity.

telecommuting: working at home and communicating via computer with the office.

user friendly: hardware or software that is easy to use.

virus: a program that infects a computer system. It is secretly attached to a program and does its dirty work after the program has been run once.

voice recognition: the understanding of spoken words by a machine.

window: a separate viewing area on a display screen.

word processor: a text–editing program or system that allows electronic writing and correcting of articles, etc.

Economic and Financial Glossary

Acquisition: The purchase of one company by another.

Balanced Budget: The federal government budget is balanced when receipts are equal to current expenditure.

Balance of payments: The difference between all payments made to and from foreign countries over a set period of time. A *favorable* balance exists when more payments are coming in than going out; an *unfavorable* balance, when the reverse is true. Payments include gold, the cost of merchandise and services, interest and dividend payments, money spent by travelers, and repayment of principal on loans.

Balance of trade (trade gap): The difference between exports and imports, both in actual funds and credit. A nation's balance of trade is *favorable* when exports exceed imports and *unfavorable* when the reverse is true.

Bear Market: A market in which prices are falling.

Bearer Bond: A bond issued in bearer form rather than being registered in the owner's name. Ownership is determined by possession.

Bond: A written promise or IOU by the issuer to repay a fixed amount of borrowed money on a specified date and to pay a set annual rate of interest in the meantime, usually at semi-annual intervals. Bonds are generally considered safe because the borrower (whether a company or the government) usually must make interest payments before the money is spent on anything else.

Bull Market: A market in which prices are on the rise.

Commercial Paper: An extremely short-term corporate IOU, generally due in 270 days or less. Available in face amounts of $100,000, $250,000, $500,000, $1,000,000 and combinations thereof.

Convertible Bond: A corporate bond (see below) which may be converted into a stated number of shares of common stock. Its price tends to fluctuate along with fluctuations in the price of the stock and with changes in interest rates.

Corporate Bond: Evidence of debt by a corporation. The bond normally has a stated life and pays a fixed rate of interest. Considered safer than the common or preferred stock of the same company.

Cost of living: The cost of maintaining a standard of living measured in terms of purchased goods and services. A rise in the cost of living mirrors the rate of inflation.

Cost-of-living benefits: Benefits that go to those persons whose money receipts increase automatically as prices rise.

Credit crunch (liquidity crisis): The period when cash for lending to business and consumers is in short supply.

Debenture: An unsecured long-term debt obligation backed only by the general credit of the issuing corporation.

Deficit spending: The practice whereby a government goes into debt to finance some of its expenditures.

Depression: A long period of economic decline when prices are low, unemployment is high, and there are many business failures.

Devaluation: The official lowering of a nation's currency, decreasing its value in relation to foreign currencies.

Discount Rate: The rate of interest set by the Federal Reserve that member banks are charged when borrowing money through the Federal Reserve System.

Disposable income: Income after taxes which is available to persons for spending and saving.

Dividend: Payment by a corporation to its shareholders, usually in the form of cash, stock shares, or other property.

Dow-Jones Industrial Average: A measure of stock market prices, based on 30 leading companies on the New York Stock Exchange.

Econometrics: The application of mathematical and statistical methods to the study of economic and financial data.

Economic Growth: The steady process of increasing productive capacity of the economy, and hence of increasing national income.

Federal Deposit Insurance Corporation (FDIC): A government-sponsored corporation that insures accounts in national banks and other qualified institutions.

Federal Reserve System: The entire banking system of the U.S., incorporating 12 Federal Reserve banks (one in each of 12 Federal Reserve districts), and 24 Federal Reserve branch banks, all national banks and state-chartered commercial banks and trust companies that have been admitted to its membership. The system greatly influences the nation's monetary and credit policies.

Full employment: The economy is said to be at full employment when only fractional unemployment exists. That is, everyone who wishes to work at the going wage-rate for his type of labor is employed. Since it takes time to switch from one job to another, there will be at any given time a small amount of unemployment.

Golden Parachute: Provisions in the employment contracts of executives guaranteeing substantial severance benefits if they lose their position in a corporate takeover.

Government Bond: An IOU of the U.S. Treasury, considered the safest security in the investment world. They are divided into two categories, those that are not marketable and those that are. *Savings Bonds* cannot be bought and sold once the original purchase is made. These include the familiar Series EE bonds. You buy them at 50 percent of their face value and when they mature, 12 years later, they will pay you back 100 percent of face value if you cash them in. Another type, Series H, are not discounted, but issued in amounts of $500, $1,000, $5,000, and $10,000 and pay their interest in semiannual checks. Marketable bonds fall into 12 categories. *Treasury Bills* are short-term U.S. obligations, maturing in 3, 6, or 12 months. They are sold at a discount of the face value, and the minimum denomination is $10,000. *Treasury Notes* mature in up to 10 years. Denominations range from $500, $1,000 to $5,000, $10,000 and up. *Treasury Bonds* mature in 10 to 30 years. The minimum investment is $1,000.

Greenmail: A company buys back its own shares from a suitor for more than the going market price to avoid a hostile takeover.

Gross National Product (GNP): The market value of all goods and services that have been bought for final use during a year. The GNP is generally considered to be the most comprehensive measure of a nation's economic activity. The *Real* GNP is the GNP adjusted for inflation.

Individual Retirement Account (IRA): A self-funded retirement plan that allows employed individuals to contribute a maximum yearly sum toward their retirement. Interest earned in the account is tax deferred.

Inflation: An increase in the average level of prices; double-digit inflation occurs when the percent increase rises above 9.9.

Insider Information: Important facts about the condition or plans of a corporation that have not been released to the general public.

Junk Bonds: Debt securities that sell at relatively low prices, because of the low credit rating of their issuers. They pay significantly higher yields than top-grade bonds to reflect their added risk. In the 1980s, they have been used to finance hostile takeovers.

(continued)

Key leading indicators: A series of eleven indicators from different segments of the economy used by the Commerce Department to foretell what will happen in the economy in the near future.

Leveraged Buy-Out: An acquisition of a public company by a small group, often including the company's management, which takes the company private. Much of the purchase price is borrowed with the debt repaid from company profits or by selling company assets.

Liquid Assets: Assets that include cash or those items that are easily converted into cash.

Margin Account: A brokerage account that allows a person to trade securities on credit.

Money supply: The currency held by the public plus checking accounts in commercial banks and savings institutions.

Mortgage-Backed Securities: Created when a bank, builder or government agency gathers together a group of mortgages and then sells bonds to other institutions and the public. The investors receive their proportionate share of the interest payments on the loans as well as the principal payments. Usually, these mortgages are guaranteed by the government, making them a fairly safe investment despite the fact that their market value does fluctuate.

Municipal Bond: Issued by governmental units such as states, cities, local taxing authorities and other agencies. Interest is exempt from U.S. — and sometimes state and local — income tax. *Municipal Bond Unit Investment Trusts* allow you to invest with as little as $1,000 in a portfolio of many different municipal bonds chosen by professionals. The income is exempt from federal income taxes.

Mutual Fund: A portfolio, or selection, of professionally bought and managed stocks in which you pool your money along with thousands of other people. A share price is based on net asset value, or the value of all the investments owned by the funds, less any debt, and divided by the total number of shares. The major advantage is less risk — it is spread out over many stocks and, if one or two do badly, the remainder may shield you from the losses. *Bond Funds* are mutual funds that deal in the bond market exclusively. *Money Market Mutual Funds* buy in the so-called "Money Market" — institutions that need to borrow large sums of money for short terms. Usually the individual investor cannot afford the denominations required in the "Money Market" (i.e. treasury bills, commercial paper, certificates of deposit), but through a money market mutual fund he can take advantage of these instruments when interest rates are high. These funds offer special checking account advantages. The minimum investment is generally $1,000.

National debt: The debt of the national government as distinguished from the debts of the political subdivisions of the nation and private business and individuals.

National debt ceiling: Limit set by Congress beyond which the national debt cannot rise. This limit is periodically raised by congressional vote.

Option: A contractual agreement between a buyer and a seller to buy or sell shares of a security. A *Call* option contract gives the right to purchase shares of a specific stock at a stated price within a given period of time. A *Put* option contract gives the buyer the right to sell shares of a specific stock at a stated price within a given period of time.

Per capita income: The nation's total income divided by the number of people in the nation.

Prime interest rate: The rate charged by banks on short-term loans to large commercial customers with the highest credit rating.

Producer price index: A statistical measure of the change in the price of wholesale goods. It is reported for 3 different stages of the production chain: crude, intermediate, and finished goods.

Program Trading: A term used for trading techniques involving large numbers and large blocks of stocks, usually used in conjunction with computer programs. Techniques include *Index Arbitrage* in which traders profit from price differences between stocks and futures contracts on stock indexes, and *Portfolio Insurance* which is the use of stock-index futures to protect stock investors from large losses when the market drops.

Public debt: The total of the nation's debts owed by state, local, and national government. This is considered a good measure of how much of the nation's spending is financed by borrowing rather than taxation.

Recession: A mild decrease in economic activity marked by a decline in real GNP, employment, and trade, usually lasting 6 months to a year, and marked by widespread decline in many sectors of the economy.

Savings Association Insurance Fund (SAIF): Created in 1989 to insure accounts in savings and loan associations up to $100,000.

Seasonal adjustment: Statistical changes made to compensate for regular fluctuations in data that are so great they tend to distort the statistics and make comparisons meaningless. For instance, seasonal adjustments are made in midwinter for a slowdown in housing construction and for the rise in farm income in the fall after the summer crops are harvested.

Stagnation: A period of economic slowdown in which there is little growth in GNP, capital investment, and real income.

Stock: *Common Stocks* are shares of ownership in a corporation; they are the most direct way to participate in the fortunes of a company. There can be wide swings in the prices of this kind of stock. *Preferred Stock* is a type of stock on which a fixed dividend must be paid before holders of common stock are issued their share of the issuing corporation's earnings. Prices are higher and yields lower than comparable bonds. However, they are attractive to corporate investors because 85 percent of preferred dividends are tax exempt to corporations. *Convertible Preferred Stock* can be converted into the common stock of the company that issued the preferred. This stock has the advantage of producing a higher yield than common stock and it also has appreciation potential. *Over-the-Counter Stock* is not traded on the major or regional exchanges, but rather through dealers from whom you buy directly. These stocks tend to belong to smaller companies. Prices of OTC stocks are based on the dealer's supply and demand. *Blue Chip* stocks are so called because they have been leading stocks for a long time. *Growth* stocks are stocks whose earnings have grown over several years.

Stock-index Futures: A futures contract is an agreement to buy or sell a specific amount of a commodity or financial instrument at a particular price at a set date. Futures on a stock index (such as the Standard & Poor's 500) are bets on the future price of that group of stocks.

Supply-side economics: The school of economic thinking which stresses the importance of the costs of production as a means of revitalizing the economy. Advocates policies that raise capital and labor output by increasing the incentives to produce.

Takeover: The passing of control of one company by another company or group by sale or merger. A friendly takeover occurs when the acquired company's management is agreeable to the merger; when management is opposed to the merger it is an unfriendly takeover. Takeover *arbitrage* is the purchase and/or selling of the securities of companies involved in takeover situations in order to realize a profit.

Tender Offer: A public offer to buy a company's stock; usually priced at a premium above the market.

Unit Investment Trust: A portfolio of many different corporate bonds, preferred stocks, government-backed securities or utility common stocks in which you can invest with as little as $1,000. Professional managers choose the securities, arrange for safe-keeping and collect the income. You receive your pro rata share of income every month.

Zero Coupon Bond: A corporate or government bond that is issued at a deep discount from the maturity value and pays no interest during the life of the bond. It is redeemable at face value.

CONSUMER INFORMATION

Consumer Information Catalog

Source: Consumer Information Center, U.S. General Services Administration

The *Consumer Information Catalog* is a free listing of about 200 of the best federal consumer publications. They range from booklets on financial planning to planning a diet, from learning about federal benefits to getting an education, from fixing a car to dealing effectively with consumer problems. It also lists many resources that will help you get a passport or a birth certificate, find government documents or national parks, learn your rights and stand up for them. Many of these booklets are free.

The *Consumer Information Catalog* is published quarterly by the Consumer Information Center of the U.S. General Services Administration, so you will be able to send for the most current booklets. For your free copy of the *Consumer Information Catalog*, send your name and address to: Consumer Information Catalog, Pueblo, CO 81009. Educators, libraries, and other non-profit groups who are able to distribute 25 or more copies of the *Consumer Information Catalog* on a quarterly basis should write to the same address for an application to be placed on the mailing list. Costs prevent the Consumer Information Center from maintaining a mailing list for individuals.

The booklets listed below are available *free* from the *Consumer Information Catalog* as of Fall, 1989. Quantities of some may be limited. There is a $1 fee for handling. To order, please send your name and address, the item numbers of the booklets you want, and the $1 fee to: S. James, Consumer Information Center, Pueblo, CO 81009.

Free Publications

Children

Handbook on Child Support Enforcement. The basic steps to follow if you need child support enforcement services; tips on solving enforcement problems. 40 pp. (1989) **505W.**

Growing Up Drug Free. Shows what children should understand about drugs, including alcohol and tobacco, identifies classes and types of drugs, and resource contacts. 55 pp. (1989) **576W.**

Education

Schools Without Drugs. Guide for parents, schools, students, and communities on how to fight drug use by children. Describes extent of the problem, effects of various drugs, and signs of use. Includes legal considerations and an extensive list of resources. 94 pp. (1989) **511W.**

Federal Student Aid Fact Sheet. Describes Federal grants, loans, and work/study programs for college, vocational and technical school students after high school. 13 pp. (1990) **578W.**

AIDS and the Education of Our Children. Facts about AIDS, its transmission, and how teens are at risk. Methods of protection, guidelines for selecting educational materials, and sources for more information. 34 pp. (1988) **509W.**

Choosing a School for Your Child. How to find the right public or private school. Includes a checklist to help you evaluate schools and suggestions on how to transfer from one public school district to another. 36 pp. (1989) **508W.**

Federal Benefits

Medicare and Prepayment Plans. You don't have to give up Medicare benefits to join a Health Maintenance Organization or Competitive Medical Plan. Here's how these plans work and how you are covered. 8 pp. (1987) **515W.**

Request for Earnings and Benefit Estimate Statement. A form to complete and return to Social Security to get your earnings history and an estimate of future benefits. 3 pp. (1989) **517W.**

Hospice Benefits Under Medicare. Describes the scope of medical and support services available to Medicare beneficiaries with a terminal illness. 5 pp. (1989) **513W.**

Food & Nutrition

The Grazing of America: A Guide to Healthy Snacking. "Grazing" is becoming the American way of eating. Learn how to choose the best snacks for your age and lifestyle. 6 pp. (1989) **583W.**

A Simple Guide to Complex Carbohydrates. What they are and why they are vital to a healthy diet. Dispels the popular myth that starch equals calories and lists healthy sources of starch and fiber. 5 pp. (1989) **595W.**

Sweetness Minus Calories Equals Controversy. Discusses research findings on the three artificial sweeteners—saccharin, cyclamate, and aspartame (Nutra-Sweet). 4 pp. (1985) **579W.**

Talking about Turkey. A complete guide with recipes and charts on thawing, cooking, and stuffing. 20 pp. (1984) **528W.**

A Word About Low Sodium Diets. Tips on how to reduce your sodium intake. Gives recipes with salt substitutes. 5 pp. (1986) **527W.**

Diet, Nutrition, and Cancer Prevention: The Good News. This booklet will help you select, prepare and serve healthier food. Includes lists of high-fiber and low-fat foods. 15 pp. (1986) **522W.**

Planning a Diet for a Healthy Heart. How dietary fat and cholesterol increase the risk of heart disease; what to eat to reduce that risk. 6 pp. (1989) **525W.**

Health

Quackery. Discusses how bogus remedies for cancer, arthritis, and the "battle of the bulge" can hurt you much more than help. 4 pp. (1985) **530W.**

Take ACTION against Drug Abuse. Here are examples of volunteer anti-drug programs and how they got started. Offers suggestions on how to set goals, apply for ACTION grants, raise funds, recruit volunteers, publicize, manage the project, and more. 48 pp. (1989) **580W.**

Comparing Contraceptives. Discusses effectiveness and possible side effects of various contraceptives with comparisons and statistics on use. 8 pp. (1986) **533W.**

A Doctor's Advice on Self-Care. Many over-the-counter drugs are now available that can cure, prevent, and diagnose illnesses. The U.S. Commissioner of Food and Drugs tells how to use them safely and effectively. 7 pp. (1989) **534W.**

Breast Exams: What You Should Know. Eighty percent of breast lumps are not cancer: how to check for lumps, how doctors examine them, what types of treatment are available. 17 pp. (1986) **540W.**

Smart Advice for Women 40 and Over: Have a Mammogram. A mammogram is an X-ray of the breast designed to find cancer in its earliest stages. Learn how often, and why, you should have one. 4 pp. (1990) **591W.**

Food and Drug Interactions. Learn how some commonly used drugs affect nutritional needs. 6 pp. (1988) **549W.**

Some Things You Should Know About Prescription Drugs. Even prescription drugs can be dangerous. Here are tips for safe use. 4 pp. (1984) **537W.**

Infertility and How It's Treated. Causes and treatment of infertility. 2 pp. (1983) **548W.**

Clearing the Air: A Guide to Quitting Smoking. No-nonsense tips on kicking the habit. 45 pp. (1988) **543W.**

Facing Surgery: Get a Second Opinion. Answers questions of the prospective patient. Includes toll-free number for locating specialists. 5 pp. (1989) **545W.**

Mental Health

A Consumer's Guide to Mental Health Services. Answers commonly asked questions about mental health and the different methods of treating mental illness. Lists resources for further help and information. 28 pp. (1987) **552W.**

Plain Talk About Depression. Nine million Americans suffer from depressive illness during any six month period. Learn about the symptoms and causes; how it's diagnosed and treated; and how to help. 4 pp. (1989) **575W.**

Plain Talk About Mutual Help Groups. Gain strength through sharing with others who have similiar problems: An overview of the many support groups available. 6 pp. (1989) **553W.**

What to Do When a Friend Is Depressed: A Guide for Students. Increases teen sensitivity to this often misunderstood condition. Identifies common myths, warning signals, and suggests ways to help. 8 pp. (1989) **557W.**

When Someone Close Has AIDS. Sensitive, practical advice about living with, and caring for, someone who has AIDS. Discusses realities and stresses that caregivers and patients deal with. 15 pp. (1989) **577W.**

Plain Talk about Stress. What stress is and how to deal with it. 2 pp. (1987) **554W.**

Plain Talk About Wife Abuse. The causes, emotional and physical consequences, and where an abused wife can get help. 3 pp. (1983) **555W.**

Schizophrenia: Questions and Answers. Describes this chronic, debilitating illness affecting millions of Americans: its nature, causes, treatments, how others can help, and the outlook for recovery. 25 pp. (1986) **556W.**

Money Management

Investment Swindles: How They Work and How to Avoid Them. How to protect yourself against illegal telemarketing and direct mail offers. 20 pp. (1987) **561W.**

Investors' Bill of Rights. Tips to help you make an informed decision on investment risks and costs. 7 pp. (1987) **562W.**

How to Get the Most for Your Money

Source: *Consumer's Resource Handbook.*

Before Making a Purchase:

(1) Analyze what you need and what features are important to you.
(2) Compare brands. Use word-of-mouth recommendations and formal product comparison reports. Check with your local library for magazines and other publicatons containing consumer information.
(3) Compare stores. Look for a store with a good reputation and take advantage of sales.
(4) Check for any additional charges, such as delivery and service costs.
(5) Compare warranties.
(6) Read terms of contracts carefully.
(7) Check the return or exchange policy.

After Your Purchase:

(1) Follow proper use and care instructions for products.
(2) Read and understand the warranty provisions. Keep in mind that you may have additional warranty rights in your state. Check with your state or local consumer office to find out.
(3) If trouble develops, report the problem as soon as possible. Do not try to fix the product yourself as this may void the warranty.
(4) Keep a record of efforts to have your problem remedied. This record should include names of people you speak to, times, dates, and other relevant information.
(5) Send for the *Consumer's Resource Handbook* (see Source, above) to find out where and how to get your problem resolved.
(6) Clearly state your problem and the solution you want.
(7) Include all relevant details, along with copies of documents (proof of purchase).
(8) Briefly describe what you have done to resolve the problem.
(9) Allow each person you contact a reasonable period of time to resolve your problem before contacting another source for assistance.

Handling Your Own Complaint:

(1) Identify your problem and what you believe would be a fair settlement. Do you want your money back? Would you like the product repaired? Will an exchange do?
(2) Gather documentation regarding your complaint. Sales receipts, work orders, warranties, cancelled checks, or contracts will back up your complaint and help the company solve your problem.
(3) Go back to where you made the purchase. Contact the person who sold you the item or performed the service.

Calmly and accurately explain the problem and what action you would like taken. If that person is not helpful, ask for the supervisor or manager and repeat your complaint. A large percentage of consumer problems are resolved at this level. Chances are yours will be too.
(4) Don't give up if you are not satisfied with the response. If the company operates nationally or the product is a national brand, write a letter to the person responsible for consumer complaints at the company's headquarters. A listing of many of these companies can be found in the World Almanac's Business Directory on pages 781–787. If the company doesn't have a consumer office, direct your letter to the president of the company.

How to Write a Complaint Letter:

(1) If you have already contacted the person who sold you the product or service or the company is out of town, you will need to write a letter to pursue your complaint.
(2) If you need the president's name and the address of the company, first check in your phone directory to see if the company has a local office. If it does, call and ask for the name and address of the company's president. If there is no local listing, check *Standard & Poor's Register of Corporations, Directors and Executives.* It lists over 37,000 American business firms and can be found in most libraries.
(3) If you don't have the name of the manufacturer of the product, check your local library for the *Thomas Register.* It lists the manufacturers of thousands of products.

Basic Tips on Letter Writing:

(1) Include your name, address, and home and work phone numbers.
(2) Type your letter if possible. If it is handwritten, make sure it is neat and easy to read.
(3) Make your letter brief and to the point. Include all important facts about your purchase, including the date and place where you made the purchase, and any information you can give about the product or service such as serial or model numbers or specific type of service.
(4) State exactly what you want done about the problem and how long you are willing to wait to get it resolved. Be reasonable.
(5) Include all documents regarding your problems. Be sure to send COPIES, not originals.
(6) Avoid writing an angry, sarcastic, or threatening letter. The person reading your letter probably was not responsible for your problem, but may be very helpful in resolving it.
(7) Keep a copy of the letter for your records.

Business Directory

Listed below are major U.S. corporations, and major foreign corporations, whose operations—products and services—directly concern the American consumer. At the end of each listing is a representative sample of some of the company's products.

Company...Address...Phone Number...Chief executive officer...Business.

AMR Corp....PO Box 619616, Dallas/Ft. Worth Airport, TX 75261...(817) 355-1234...R.L. Crandell...Air transportation (American Airlines).

Abbott Laboratories...One Abbott Park Rd., Abbot Park, IL 60064-3500 (708) 937-6100...D.L. Burnham...health care prods.

Aetna Life & Casualty Co....151 Farmington Ave., Hartford, CT 06156...(203) 273-0123...James T. Lynn...insurance, financial services.

H.F. Ahmanson & Co....660 S. Figueroa St., Los Angeles, CA 90017...(213) 955-4200...R.H. Deihi...operates largest S&L assn. in U.S. (Home Savings of America).

Alberto-Culver Co....2525 Armitage Ave., Melrose Park, IL 60160...(312) 450-3000...Leonard H. Lavin...hair care preparations, feminine hygiene products, household and grocery items.

Albertson's Inc....250 Parkcenter Blvd., Boise, ID 83726...(208) 385-6200...W.E. McCain...supermarkets

Alcan Aluminium Ltd....1188 Sherbrooke St. W., Montreal, Que., Canada H3A 3G2...(514) 848-8050...D.M. Culver...aluminum producer.

Alexander & Alexander Services Inc....1211 Ave. of the Amer., New York, NY 10036...(212) 840-8500...T.H. Irvin...insurance & financial services.

Allied-Signal Inc....Box 2245R, Morristown, NJ 07960...(201) 455-2000...Edward L. Hennessy Jr....aerospace, engineered materials, automotive prods.

Alltel Corp....100 Executive Pkwy., Hudson, OH 44236...(216) 650-7000...J.T. Ford...telephone service in Midwest, South, and Eastern U.S.

Aluminum Co. of America...1501 Alcoa Bldg., Pittsburgh, PA 15219...(412) 553-4545...P.H. O'Neill...mining, refining, & processing of aluminum.

Amerada Hess Corp....1185 Ave. of the Americas, N.Y., NY 10036...(212) 997-8500...L. Hess...integrated petroleum co.

American Brands, Inc....1700 E. Putnam Ave., Old Greenwich, CT 06870 (203) 698-5000...W.J. Alley...tobacco (Pall Mall, Carlton), Half and Half, Paleden pipe tobacco), whiskey (Jim Beam), snack foods, life insurance, office prods., food, financial services, toiletries.

American Cyanamid Co....One Cyanamid Plaza, Wayne, NJ 07470...(201) 831-2000...G.J. Sella Jr....medical, agricultural, chemical, and consumer prods.

American Express Co....American Express Tower, N.Y., NY 10285 (212) 640-2000...J.D. Robinson 3d...travelers checks, credit card services, insurance, investment services (Shearson Lehman Hutton).

American Greetings Corp....10500 American Rd., Cleveland, OH 44144...(216) 252-7300...M. Weiss...greeting cards, stationery, gift items.

American Home Products Corp....685 3d Ave., N.Y., NY 10017...(212) 986-1000...J.R. Stafford...prescription drugs, household prods. (Woolite, Easy-Off oven cleaner; Black Flag, Wizard air fresheners), food (Chef Boy-ar-dee), drugs (Anacin, Advil, Dristan).

American Stores Co....5201 W. Amelia Earhart Dr., Salt Lake City, UT...(801) 539-0112...J.L. Scott...retail food markets, dept. & drug stores.

American Telephone & Telegraph Co....550 Madison Ave. N.Y., NY 10022...(212) 605-5500...R.E. Allen...communications.

Amoco Corp....200 E. Randolph Dr., Chicago, IL 60601...(312) 856-6111...R.M. Morrow...oil and gas exploration, production, and marketing.

Anheuser-Busch, Inc....One Busch Place, St. Louis, MO 63118...(314) 577-2000...H.A. McInnes...brewing (Budweiser, Michelob, Bud Light, Natural Light, King Cobra, Busch), theme parks.

Armstrong World Industries...P.O. Box 3001, 313 W. Liberty St., Lancaster, PA 17604...(717) 397-0611...W.W. Adams...interior furnishings.

Arvin Industries, Inc....One Noblitt Plaza, Box 3000, Columbus, IN 47201...(812) 379-3000...J.K. Baker...auto exhaust systems, electric heaters, stereos.

Ashland Oil, Inc....P.O. Box 391, Ashland, KY 41114...(606) 329-3333...J.R. Hall...petroleum refiner, chemicals.

Atlantic Richfield Co....515 S. Flower St., Los Angeles, CA 90071...(213) 486-3511...L.M. Cook...petroleum, chemicals, other natural resources.

Avery Denison Corp....150 N. Orange Grove Blvd., Pasadena, CA 91103...(818) 304-2000...Charles D. Miller...self-adhesive labels (merged with Denison Manuf. Co. in 1990).

Avon Products, Inc....9 West 57th St., N.Y., NY 10019...(212) 546-6015...J. E. Preston...cosmetics, fragrances, toiletries, health care.

Bally Manufacturing Corp....8700 W. Bryn Mawr Ave., Chicago, IL 60631...(312) 399-1300...R.E. Mullane...lottery and gaming equip., hotel-casino operator, health & fitness centers.

Bausch & Lomb...One Lincoln First Square, Rochester, NY 14601...(716) 338-6000...D.E. Gill...manuf. of vision care products, accessories.

Baxter International Inc....One Baxter Pky., Deerfield, IL. 60015...(708) 948-2000...Vernon R. Loucks Jr....medical care prods & services.

Bell Atlantic Corp....1600 Market St., Philadelphia, PA 19103...(215) 963-6000...R.W. Smit c15 telephone service in mid-Atlantic region.

BellSouth Corp....1155 Peachtree St. NE, Atlanta, GA 30367...(404) 249-2000...J.L. Clendenin...telephone service in the South.

Bethlehem Steel Corp....8th & Eaton Ave., Bethlehem, PA 18016...(215) 694-2424...W.F. Williams...steel & steel prods.

Bic Corporation...Wiley Street, Milford, CT 06401...(203) 783-2000...Bruno Bich...writing instruments, disposable lighters, and shavers.

Black & Decker Mfg. Co....701 E. Joppa Rd., Towson, MD 21204...(301) 583-3900...N.D. Archibald...manuf. power tools, household prods., small appliances.

H & R Block, Inc....4410 Main St., Kansas City, MO 64111...(816) 753-6900...Henry W. Bloch...tax preparation.

Boeing Company...7755 E. Marginal Way So., Seattle, WA 98108...(206) 655-6123...F.A. Shrontz...aircraft manuf.

Boise Cascade Corp....One Jefferson Square, Boise, ID 83728...(208) 384-6161...J.B. Fery...timber, paper, wood prod.

Borden, Inc....277 Park Ave., N.Y., NY 10172...(212) 573-4000...R.J. Ventres...food, cheese and cheese products, snacks (Cracker Jack), beverages.

Bristol-Myers Squibb Co....345 Park Ave., N.Y., NY 10154...(212) 546-4000...Richard L. Gelb...toiletries (Ban anti-perspirant), hair items (Clairol), drugs (Bufferin, Comtrex, Excedrin), household prods.(Drano), infant formula (Enfamil).

Brown-Forman Inc....P.O. Box 1080 Louisville, KY 40210...(502) 585-1100...W.L.L. Brown Jr....distilled spirits (Jack Daniel's Early Times), wines (Bolla, Fontana Candita), champagne (Korbel), liquor (Southern Comfort), Lenox china and crystal.

Brown Group, Inc....8400 Maryland Ave., St. Louis, MO 63166...(314) 854-4000...B.A. Brightwater Jr....manuf. and wholesaler of women's and children's shoes (Buster Brown, Regal Shoes); specialty retailing.

Brunswick Corp....One Brunswick Plaza, Skokie, IL 60077...(708) 470-4700...J.F. Reichert...marine, recreation prods, bowling centers & equip., fishing equip.

Burlington Coat Factory Warehouse Corp....1830 Route 130 North, Burlington, NJ 08016...(609) 387-7800...M.G. Milstein...discount apparel stores.

Burlington Northern Inc....3800 Continental Plaza, 777 Moun St., Ft. Worth, TX 76102...(817) 878-2000...G. Grinstein...rail transportation.

CBS Inc....51 W. 52d St., N.Y., NY 10019...(212) 975-4321...L.A. Tisch...broadcasting, video cassettes, recorded music, leisure prods.

CPC International, Inc....International Plaza, Englewood Cliffs, NJ 07632...(201) 894-4000...J.R. Eiszner...branded food items (Hellman's, Best Foods, Mazola oil, Skippy peanut butter, Knorr Soups, Mueller's pasta prods., Thomas English muffins), corn wet milling prods.

Caesar's World, Inc....1801 Century Park East, Los Angeles, CA 90067...(213) 552-2711...H. Gluck...hotels & casinos, resort hotels.

Campbell Soup Co....Campbell Pl., Camden, NJ 08103...(609) 342-4800...D.W. Johnson...canned soups, spaghetti (Franco-American), vegetable juice (V-8), pork and beans, pet foods, restaurants, confections, Le Menu frozen dinners, Prego spaghetti sauce, Mrs. Paul's frozen fish, Pepperidge Farm breads.

Capital Cities/ABC Inc....77 W. 66th Street, New York, NY 10023...(212) 456-7777...T.S. Murphy...operates television and radio stations, newspapers, cable TV (ESPN); newspapers, specialized business and consumer periodicals.

Carter Hawley Hale Stores, Inc....444 S. Flower St., Los Angeles, CA 90071...(213) 620-0150...P.M. Hawley...dept. stores, specialty stores.

Carter-Wallace, Inc....767 5th Ave., New York, NY 10153...(212) 339-5000...H.H. Hoyt Jr....personal care items, anti-perspirant (Arrid), shave lathers (Rise), condoms (Trojan), laxative (Carter's Pills), pet products.

Castle & Cooke, Inc....10900 Wilshire Blvd., Los Angeles, CA 90024...(213) 842-1500...D.H. Murdock...food processing, Dole.

Caterpillar Inc....100 N.E. Adams St., Peoria, IL 61629...(309) 675-1000...G.A. Schaefer...heavy duty earth-moving equip.

Champion International Corp....1 Champion Plaza, Stamford, CT 06921...(203) 358-7000...A.C. Sigler...forest prods.

Chase Manhattan Corp....1 Chase Manhattan Plaza, New York, NY 10081...(212) 552-2222...W.C. Butcher...Bank holding co.

Chevron Corp....225 Bush St., San Francisco, CA 94104...(415) 894-7700...K.T. Derr...integrated oil co.

Chrysler Corp....12000 Chrysler Dr., Highland Pk., MI 48288...(313) 956-5252...Lee Iacocca...cars, trucks.

Circle K Corp....1601 N 7th St., Phoenix, AZ 85006...(602) 253-9600...R.A. Dearth...convenience store chain.

Circuit City Stores, Inc....2040 Thalbro St., Richmond, VA 23230...(804) 257-4292...R.L. Sharp...retailer of electronic equip., consumer appliances.

Circus Circus Enterprises, Inc....2880 Las Vegas Blvd. S., Las Vegas, NV 89109...(702) 734-0410...W.G. Bennett...casino operator.

Citicorp...399 Park Ave., N.Y., NY 10043...(212) 559-1000...J.S. Reed...largest U.S. commercial bank.

Clayton Homes...P.O. Box 15169, Knoxville, TN 37901...(615) 970-7200...J.L. Clayton...produces & sells manufactured homes.

Clorox Co....1221 Broadway, Oakland, CA 94612...(415) 271-7000...C.R. Weaver...retail consumer prods (Formula 409, Twice As Fresh, Lucite paints, Kingsford charcoal briquets, Hidden Valley Ranch salad dressing, Deer Park bottled water, Soft Scrub cleanser).

Coachman Industries Inc....601 E. Beardsley Ave., Elkhart, IN 46515...(219) 262-0123...T.H. Corson...manuf. recreational vehicles.

Coca-Cola Co....One Coca-Cola Plaza N.W., Atlanta, GA 30313...(404) 676-2121...R.C. Goizueta...soft drink (Coca Cola, Sprite, Ramblin root beer), syrups, citrus and fruit juices (Minute Maid, Hi-C).

Colgate-Palmolive Co....300 Park Ave., N.Y., NY 10022...(212) 310-2000...R Mark...soaps (Palmolive, Irish Spring), detergents (Fab, Ajax, Fresh Start), tooth paste (Colgate, Ultra Brite), household prods. (Handy Wipes, Curad bandages).

Commodore International Ltd....1200 Wilson Dr., West Chester, PA 19380...(215) 431-9100...I. Gould...microcomputer systems, semiconductors component, consumer electronics, office equipment.

Compaq Computer Corp....20555 SH 249, Houston, TX 77070...(713) 370-0670...J.R. Canion...portable, desktop computers.

Control Data Corp....8100 34th Ave. South, Minneapolis, MN 55420...(612) 853-8100...L. Perlman...computer systems & services.

Adolph Coors Co....Golden, CO 80401...(303) 279-6565...W. K. Coors...brewery.

Corning Inc....Houghton Park, Corning, NY 14831...(607) 974-9000...J.R. Houghton...glass mfg.

Crane Co....737 3d Ave., N.Y., NY 10017...(212)

415-7300...R.S. Evans...fluid & pollution controls, aircraft and aerospace, building prods.

A.T. Cross Co....One Albion Rd., Lincoln, RI 02865...(401) 333-1200...B.R. Boss...writing instruments.

Crystal Brands, Inc....Crystal Brands Rd., Southport, CT 06490...(203) 254-6200...R.F. Kral...apparel, accessories.

Culbro Corp....387 Park Avenue South, New York, NY 10016...(212) 561-8700...E. M. Cullman...cigars (Corina, Robert Burns, White Owl, Tiparillo's), snack foods.

Dana Corp....4500 Dorr St., Toledo, OH 43697...(419) 535-4500...S.J. Morcott...truck and auto parts supplies.

Data General Corp....4400 Computer Dr., Westboro, MA 01580...(508) 366-8911...R.L. Skates...computer & communications sytems manuf.

Dayton Hudson Corp....777 Nicollet Mall, Minneapolis, MN 55402...(612) 370-6948...K.A. Macke...department, specialty, stores, Mervyn's, Target.

Deere & Company...John Deere Rd., Moline, IL 61265...(309) 765-8000...H.W. Becherer...farm, industrial, and outdoor power equip.

Delta Air Lines, Inc....Hartsfield Atlanta Intl. Airport, Atlanta, GA 30320...(404) 765-2600...R.W. Allen...air transportation.

Diebold, Inc....P.O. Box 8230, Canton, OH 44711...(216) 489-4000...R.W. Mahoney...equip. for financial insts.

Digital Equipment Corp....146 Main St., Maynard, MA 01754...(508) 493-5111...Kenneth H. Olsen...computer manuf.

Walt Disney Co....500 S. Buena Vista St., Burbank, CA 91521...(818) 560-1000...M.D. Eisner...motion pictures, CATV, amusement parks, Disneyland, Walt Disney World, Epcot Center.

R.R. Donnelly & Sons Co....2223 S. Martin Luther King Drive, Chicago, IL 60616...(312) 326-8000...J.R. Walter...largest commercial printer.

Dow Chemical Co....2030 Dow Center, Midland, MI 48674...(517) 636-1000...F.P. Popoff...chemicals, plastics, metals, consumer prods.

Dow Jones & Co....World Financial Center, New York, NY 10281...(212) 416-2000...W. H. Phillips...financial news service, publishing (Wall Street Journal, Barron's, Ottaway Newspapers).

Dresser Industries, Inc....1600 Pacific Bldg., Dallas, TX 75201...(214) 740-6000...J.J. Murphy...supplier of technology and services to energy related industries.

Dun & Bradstreet Corp....299 Park Ave., New York, NY 10171...(212) 593-6800...C.W. Moritz...business information and computer services, publishing, broadcasting.

E.I. du Pont de Nemours & Co....1007 Market St., Wilmington, DE 19898...(302) 774-1000...E.S. Woolard Jr....chemicals, petroleum, consumer prods., coal.

Eastman Kodak Co....343 State St., Rochester, NY 14650...(716) 724-4000...C.C. Chandler...photographic prods, chemicals, health care (Sterling Drug).

Eaton Corp....Eaton Center, Cleveland, OH 44114...(216) 523-5000...J.R. Stover...manuf. of electronic, electrical prods., vehicle components.

Emerson Electric Co....8000 W. Florissant Ave., St. Louis, MO 63136...(314) 553-2000...C.F. Knight...electrical/electronics products & systems

Ethyl Corp....330 S. 4th St., Richmond, VA 23217...(804) 788-5000...Floyd D. Gottwald Jr....petroleum and industrial chemicals.

Exxon Corp....1251 Ave. of the Americas, N.Y., NY 10020...(212) 333-6900...L.G. Rawl...world's largest oil co.

Family Dollar Stores, Inc....10401 Old Monroe Rd., Charlotte, NC 28212...(704)847-6961...L. Levine...discount variety stores.

Fabri-Centers of America, Inc...5555 Darrow Rd., Hudson, OH. 44236...(216) 656-2600...A. Ross Kamm...Specialty fabric stores.

Fedders Corp....158 Highway 206, P.O. Box 265, Princeton, NJ 07977...(201) 234-2100...S. Giordano...manuf. of room air conditioners.

Federal Express Corp....2005 Corporate Ave., Memphis, TN 38132...(901) 369-3600...F.W. Smith...small package delivery service.

Fieldcrest Cannon, Inc....326 East Stadium Dr., Eden, NC 27288...(919) 627-3000...J.B. Ely 2d...household textile prods., rugs (Karastan, Laurelcrest).

Fleetwood Enterprises, Inc. . . .3125 Myers St., Riverside, CA 92523 . . .(714) 351-3500 . . .John C. Crean . . .manufactured homes, recreational vehicles.

Fluor Corp. . . .3333 Michelson Dr., Irvine, CA 92730 . . .(714) 975-2000 . . .D.S. Tappan Jr. . . .engineering and construction, natural resources.

Ford Motor Co. . . .The American Rd., Dearborn, MI 48121 . . .(313) 322-3000 . . .H.A. Poling . . .motor vehicles, Ford Tractor, Lincoln-Mercury.

Fruit of The Loom, Inc. . . .6300 Sears Tower, Chicago, IL 60606 . . .(312) 876-1724 . . .W. Farley . . .Manuf. of men's and boy's underwear.

GTE Corp. . . .One Stamford Forum, Stamford, CT 06904 . . .(203) 965-2000 . . .J.L. Johnson . . .communications prods. (U.S. Sprint), electronics.

Gannett Co., Inc. . . .P.O. Box 7858, Washington, DC 20044 . . .(703) 284-6000 . . .J.J. Curley . . .newspaper publishing (USA Today), TV stations, outdoor advertising.

The GAP, Inc . . .1 Harrison, San Francisco, CA 94066 . . .(415) 952-4400 . . .D.G. Fisher . . .casual and activewear retailer.

Gencorp . . .175 Ghent Rd., Fairlawn, OH 44313 . . .(216) 869-4200 . . .A.W. Reynolds . . .aerospace, auto prods., polymer prods.

Genentech, Inc. . . .460 Point San Bruno Blvd., S. San Francisco, CA 94080 . . .(415) 266-1000 . . .R.A. Swanson . . .world's largest biotechnology corp.

General Cinema Corp. . . .27 Boylston St., Chestnut Hill, MA 02167 . . .(617) 232-8200 . . .R. A. Smith . . .movie exhibitor, soft drinks (Sunkist), speciality retailing.

General Dynamics Corp. . . .Pierre Laclede Ctr., St. Louis, MO 63105 . . .(314) 889-8200 . . .S.C. Pace . . .military and commercial aircraft, tactical missiles.

General Electric Co. . . .3135 Easton Ave., Fairfield, CT 06431 . . .(203) 373-2211 . . .J. F. Welch Jr. . . .electrical, electronic equip, finance (Kidder, Peabody & Co.), radio, television (NBC), polymer plastic prods.

General Instrument Corp. . . .767 5th Ave., New York, NY 10153 . . .(212) 207-6230 . . .F. G. Hickey . . .race track betting systems, CATV, semiconductors, electronic equip.

General Mills, Inc. . . .9200 Wayzata Blvd., Minneapolis, MN 55440 . . .(612) 540-2311 . . .H.B. Atwater Jr. . . .foods, toys, restaurants, fashion and specialty retailing, Total, Bisquick, Wheaties, Cheerios, Hamburger Helper, Gorton's, Betty Crocker, Red Lobster Inns.

General Motors Corp. . . .3044 W. Grand Rapids, Detroit, MI 48202 . . .(313) 556-5000 . . .R. C. Stempel . . .world's largest auto manuf.

Genesco Inc. . . .Genesco Park, Nashville, TN 37202 . . .(615) 367-7000 . . .W.S. Wire 2d . . .footwear and men's clothing, Hardy, Laredo, Jarman, Flagg Bros., Johnston & Murphy.

Genuine Parts Co. . . .2999 Circle 75 Pkwy, Atlanta, GA 30339 . . .(404) 953-1700 . . .L. L. Prince . . .distributes auto replacement parts (NAPA).

Georgia-Pacific Corp. . . .133 Peachtree St., NE, Atlanta, GA 30303 . . .(404) 521-4000 . . .T.M. Hahn Jr. . . .building prods., pulp, paper, chemicals.

Gerber Products Co. . . .445 State St., Fremont, MI 49412 . . .(616) 928-2718 . . .A.A. Piergallini . . .baby foods, clothing, nursery accessories.

Giant Food Inc. . . .P.O. Box 1804, Washington, DC 20013 . . .(301) 341-4100 . . .I. Cohen . . .supermarkets.

Gillette Co. . . .Prudential Tower Bldg., Boston, MA 02199 . . .(617) 421-7000 . . .Colman M. Mockler Jr. . . .razors, pens (Paper Mate; Flair), toiletries (Right Guard deodorants, Foamy shaving cream, Earth Born shampoo), hair products (Toni, Adorn, White Rain).

Golden Nugget, Inc. . . .3400 Las Vegas Blvd., Las Vegas, NV 89101 . . .(702) 385-7111 . . .Steve Wynn . . .operates casino-hotels.

B.F. Goodrich Company . . .3925 Embassy Pkwy, Akron, OH 44313 . . .(216) 374-3985 . . .John D. Ong . . .chemical, aerospace prods.

Goodyear Tire & Rubber Co. . . .1144 E. Market St., Akron, OH 44316 . . .(216) 796-2121 . . .T.H. Barrett . . .tires, rubber prods.

W.R. Grace & Co. . . .Grace Plaza, 1114 Ave. of the Americas, N.Y., NY 10036 . . .(212) 819-5500 . . .J. Peter Grace . . .chemicals, natural resources, consumer prods. and services, restaurants, Channel Home Centers.

Great Atlantic & Pacific Tea Co. . . .2 Paragon Dr., Montvale, NJ 07645 . . .(201) 573-9700 . . .James Wood . . .supermarket chain.

Greyhound Dial Corp. . . .Greyhound Tower, Phoenix, AZ 85077 . . .(602) 248-4000 . . .John W. Teets . . .bus manuf., household prods. (Dial soap, Purex, Armour Star, Lunch Bucket meals), financial services, food services.

Grumman Corp. . . .1111 Stewart Ave., Bethpage, NY 11714 . . .(516) 575-0574 . . .J. O'Brien . . .aerospace, truck bodies, electronics.

Hannaford Bros. Co. . . .145 Pleasant Hill Rd., Scarborough, ME 04074 . . .(207) 883-2911 . . .J.L. Moody Jr. . . .operates supermarkets, drug stores.

Harcourt Brace Jovanovich, Inc. . . .Orlando, FL 32887 . . .(407) 345-2000 . . .P. Jovanovich . . .textbook publisher, insurance.

Harley-Davidson, Inc. , . . .3700 W. Junear Ave., Milwaukee, WI 53201 . . .(414) 342-4680 . . .R.F. Terrlink . . .manuf. of motorcycles, parts & accessories.

Hartmarx . . .101 N. Wacker Dr., Chicago, IL 60606 . . .(312) 372-6300 . . .H.A. Weinberg . . .apparel manufacturer and retailer (Hickey-Freeman).

Hasbro Inc. . . .1027 Newport Ave., P.O. Box 1059, Pawtucket, R.I. 02862 . . .(401) 727-5000 . . .A.G. Hassenfeld . . .toy manuf. & marketer (Milton Bradley, Playskool, G.I. Joe, Cabbage Patch Kids, Scrabble).

H.J. Heinz Co. . . .P.O. Box 57, Pittsburgh, PA 15230 . . .(412) 456-5700 . . .Anthony J.F. O'Reilly . . .foods (Star-Kist, Ore-Ida, '57 Varieties), 9-Lives cat food, Weight Watchers.

Helene Curtis Industries, Inc. . . .325 N. Wells St., Chicago, IL 60610 . . .(312) 661-0222 . . .R.J. Gidwitz . . .hair care prods. (Finesse, Sauve, Salon Selectives).

Hershey Foods Corp. . . .100 Mansion Rd., Hershey, PA 17033 . . .(717) 534-4000 . . .R.A. Zimmerman . . .chocolate & confectionery prods., (Reese's peanut butter cups, Life Savers, Kit Kat, Peter Paul Mounds, Almond Joy), pasta (San Giorgio, Ronzoni).

Hewlett-Packard Co. . . .3000 Hanover Street, Palo Alto, CA 94304 . . .(415) 857-1501 . . .John A. Young . . .electronic instruments.

Hillenbrand Industries, Inc. . . .Highway 46, Batesville, IN 47006 . . .(812) 934-7000 . . .W.A. Hillenbrand . . .manuf. burial caskets, electronically operated hospital beds.

Home Depot, Inc. . . .2727 Paces Ferry Rd., Atlanta, GA 30339 . . .(404) 433-8211 . . .Bernard Marcus . . .retailer of building materials & home improvement prods.

Honda Motor Co., LTD. . . .1270 Ave. of the Americas, N.Y., NY 10020 . . .(212) 765-3804 . . .N. Kawamoto . . .manuf. autos, motorcycles.

Honeywell, Inc. . . .Honeywell Plaza, Minneapolis, MN 55408 . . .(612) 870-5200 . . .J.J. Renier . . .industrial systems & controls, aerospace guidance systems, information systems.

Geo. A. Hormel & Co. . . .501 16th Ave. N.E., Austin, MN 55912 . . .(507) 437-5611 . . .R.L. Knowlton . . .meat packaging, pork and beef prods (Spam, Light & Lean, Dinty Moore, Mary Kitchen).

Houghton Mifflin Co. . . .One Beacon St., Boston, MA 02108 . . .(617) 725-5000 . . .H.T. Miller . . .book publishing.

Household International Inc. . . .2700 Sanders Rd., Prospect Heights, IL 60070 . . .(708) 564-3663 . . .D.C. Clark . . .financial and insurance services.

Huffy Corp. . . .7701 Byers Rd., Miamisburg, OH 45342 . . .(513) 866-6251 . . .H.A. Shaw 3d . . .bicycle manuf.

Humana, Inc. . . .500 W. Main St., Louisville, KY 40201 . . .(502) 580-1000 . . .D. A. Jones . . .operates hospitals, provides health care plans.

ITT Corp. . . .320 Park Ave., N.Y., NY 10022 . . .(212) 752-6000 . . .R.V. Araskog . . .manuf., installs communcation and electronic equip., auto equip., insurance, financial services, hotels, educational services.

Imperial Oil Ltd. . . .111 St. Clair Ave. W., Toronto, Ont., Canada M5W 1K3 . . .(416) 968-4111 . . .A.R. Haynes . . .Canada's largest oil co.

International Business Machines Corp. . . .Armonk, NY 10504 . . .(914) 765-1900 . . .J.F. Akers . . .information-handling systems, equip., and services.

International Paper Co. . . .2 Manhattanville Rd., Purchase , NY 10577 . . .(914) 397-1500 . . .J.A. Georges . . .paper, wood prods.

Johnson & Johnson . . .One Johnson & Johnson Plaza, New Brunswick, NJ 08933 . . .(201) 524-0400 . . .R.S. Larsen . . .surgical dressings, pharmaceuticals (Tylenol, Medipren), health and baby prods.

Jostens, Inc. . . .5501 Norman Center Dr., Minneapolis, MN 55437 . . .(612) 830-3300 . . .H. W. Lurton . . .school rings, yearbooks.

K mart Corp. . . .3100 W. Big Beaver Rd., Troy, MI 48084 . . .(313) 643-1000 . . .J. E. Antonini . . .largest U.S. chain of discount stores, book stores (Walden Book), cafeterias, drug stores (Pay Less Drug Stores), home improvement retail stores.

Kellogg Co. . . .One Kellogg Sq., Battle Creek, MI 49016 . . .(616) 961-2000 . . .William E. LaMothe . . .ready to eat cereals & other food prods., Mrs. Smith's Pie Co., Salada Foods, Eggo.

Kimberly-Clark Corp. . . .P.O. Box 619100, DFW Airport Station, Dallas, TX 75261 . . .(214) 830-1200 . . .Darwin E. Smith . . .paper and lumber prods., consumer prods. (Kleenex, Huggies).

King World Productions, Inc. . . .830 Morris Turnpike, Short Hills, NJ 07078 . . .(201) 376-1313 . . .M. King . . .syndicator of first-run TV programs.

Knight-Ridder, Inc. . . .One Herold Plaza, Miami, FL 33132 . . .(305) 376-3800 . . .A.J.K. Batten . . .newspaper publishing, TV broadcasting, book publishing, information services.

Kroger Co. . . .1014 Vine St., Cincinnati, OH 45201 . . .(513) 762-4000 . . .Lyle Everingham . . .grocery chain, drugstores (SupeRx).

L.A. Gear, Inc. . . .4221 Redwood Ave., Los Angeles, CA 91204 . . .(213) 822-1995 . . .R.Y. Greenberg . . .athletic & leisure footwear, casual apparel.

La-Z-Boy Chair Co. . . .1284 N. Telegraph Rd., Monroe, MI 48161 . . .(313) 242-1444 . . .C. T. Knabusch . . .reclining chair mfg.

Land's End, Inc. . . .One Land's End Lane, Dodgeville, WI 53595 . . .(608) 935-9341 . . .R.C. Anderson . . .direct-mail catalog co.

Eli Lilly & Company . . .Lilly Corp. Center, Indianapolis, IN 46285 . . .(317) 276-6070 . . .Richard D. Wood . . .mfg. human health and agricultural products.

The Limited, Inc. . . .Two Limited Pkwy., Columbus, OH 43216 . . .(614) 479-7000 . . .L.H. Wexner . . .women's apparel stores (Lane Bryant, Lerner, Victoria's Secret), Abercrombie & Fitch.

Litton Industries, Inc. . . .360 N. Crescent Dr., Beverly Hills, CA 90210 . . .(213) 859-5000 . . .O.L. Hoch . . .industrial systems & services, advanced electronic systems, electronic & electrical prods., marine engineering.

Lockheed Corp. . . .4500 Park Granada Blvd., Calabasas, CA 91399 . . .(818) 712-2380 . . .D.M. Tellep . . .commercial and military aircraft, missiles.

Loews Corp. . . .667 Madison Ave., N.Y., NY 10021 . . .(212) 545-2000 . . .Laurence A. Tisch . . .tobacco prods. (Kent, Newport, True), watches, hotels, real estate, insurance.

Long's Drug Stores Corp. . . .141 North Civic Dr., Walnut Creek, CA 94596 . . .(415) 937-1170 . . .R.M. Long . . .drug store chain.

Lowe's Cos., Inc. . . .Hway. 268 East, N. Wilkesboro, NC 28659 . . .(919) 651-4000 . . .L.G. Herring . . .retailer of building materials & related prods.

Luby's Cafeterias, Inc. . . .211 Northeast Loop 410, San Antonio, TX 78265 . . .(512) 654-9000 . . .R. Erben . . .operates cafeterias in SW U.S.

MCA Inc. . . .100 Universal City Plaza, Universal City, CA 91608 . . .(818) 777-1000 . . .Lew R. Wasserman . . .motion pictures, television, music publishing, mail order, novelty, and gift merchandise.

Manor Care, Inc. . . .10750 Columbia Pike, Silver Spring, MD 20901 . . .(301) 681-9400 . . .S. Bainum Jr . . .operates nursing centers.

Marriott Corp. . . .Marriott Dr., Wash., DC 20058 . . .(301) 380-9000 . . .J. Willard Marriott Jr.

Martin Marietta Corp. . . .6801 Rockledge Dr., Bethesda, MD 20817 . . .(301) 897-6000 . . .N.R. Augustine . . .electronics, aerospace.

Mattel, Inc. . . .5150 Rosecrans Ave., Hawthorne, CA 90250 . . .(213) 978-5150 . . .J.W. Amerman . . .toy & hobby prods (Barbie doll, Masters of the Universe, Hot Wheels, Li'l Miss Makeup).

May Department Stores Co. . . .611 Olive Street, St. Louis, MO 63101 . . .(314) 342-6300 . . .D.C. Farrell . . .department stores (Hecht's, Famous Barr, G. Fox, Lord & Taylor, Foley's), discount chain (Caldor).

Maytag Corp. . . .403 W. 4th St. North, Newton, IA 50208 . . .(515) 792-8000 . . .Daniel J. Krumm . . .manuf. home laundry equip, appliances (Magic Chef, Admiral, Norge).

McCormick & Co., Inc. . . .11350 McCormick Rd., Hunt Valley, MD 21031 . . .(301) 771-7301 . . .C.P. McCormick Jr. . . .world's leading manuf. of seasoning & flavoring prods.

McDonald's Corp. . . .McDonald's Plaza, Oak Brook, IL 60521 . . .(708) 575-3000 . . .M.R. Quinlan . . .fast service restaurants.

McDonnell Douglas Corp. . . .P.O. Box 516, St. Louis, MO 63166 . . .(314) 232-0232 . . .J. F. McDonnell . . .commercial & military aircraft, space systems & missiles.

McGraw-Hill, Inc. . . .1221 Ave. of the Americas, New York, NY 10020 . . .(212) 512-2000 . . .J.L. Dionne . . .book, magazine publishing (Business Week), information & financial services (Standard and Poor's), TV stations.

Mead Corporation . . .Courthouse Plaza Northeast, Dayton, OH 45463 . . .(513) 495-6323 . . .B.R. Roberts . . .printing and writing paper, paperboard, packaging, shipping containers, pulp and lumber.

Media General, Inc. . . .333 E. Grace St., Richmond, VA 23219 . . .(804) 649-6000 . . .D.T. Bryan . . .broadcasting, newspaper publishing.

Medtronic, Inc. . . .7000 Central Ave. N.E., Minneapolis, MN 55432 . . .(612) 574-4000 . . .W.R. Wallin . . .manuf. prosthetic and theraputic devices.

Melville Corp. . . .1 Theall Rd., Rye, NY 10580 . . .(914) 925-4000 . . .S.P. Goldstein . . .shoe stores (Thom McAn), apparel (Marshalls, Chess King), drug stores.

Merck & Co., Inc. . . .P.O. Box 2000, Rahway, NJ 07065 . . .(201) 594-4000 . . .P. Roy Vagelos . . .human & animal health care prods.

Meredith Corp. . . .1716 Locust St., Des Moines, IA 50336 . . .(515) 284-3000 . . .J.D. Rehm . . .magazine publishing (Better Homes and Gardens, Ladies Home Journal), book publishing, broadcasting, commercial printing.

Merrill Lynch & Co., Inc. . . .World Financial Center, N.Y., NY 10281 . . .(212) 449-1000 . . .W.A Schreyer . . . securities broker, financial services, real estate.

Minnesota Mining & Manuf. Co. . . .3M Center, St. Paul, MN 55144 . . .(612) 733-1110 . . .A.F. Jacobson . . .abrasives, adhesives, building services & chemicals, electrical, health care, photographic, printing, recording materials, consumer prods. (Scotch Tape, Post-It).

Mobil Corp. . . .150 E. 42d St., N.Y., NY 10017 . . .(212) 883-4242 . . .A.E. Murray . . .international oil co., chemicals.

Monsanto Company . . .800 N. Lindbergh Blvd., St. Louis, MO 63167 . . .(314) 694-1000 . . .R. J. Mahoney . . .chemicals, electronics, agricultural prods., pharmaceuticals, consumer prods. (NutraSweet).

Motorola, Inc. . . .1303 E. Algonquin Rd., Schaumburg, IL 60196 . . .(312) 397-5000 . . .G.M.C. Fisher . . .electronic equipment and components.

NCR Corp. . . .1700 S. Patterson Blvd., Dayton, OH 45479 . . .(513) 445-5000 . . .Charles E. Exley Jr. . . .business information processing systems.

National Medical Enterprises, Inc. . . .11620 Wilshire Blvd, Los Angeles, CA 90025 . . .(213) 479-5526 . . .R.K. Eamer . . .operates hospitals.

National Semiconductor Corp. . . .2900 Semiconductor Dr., Santa Clara, CA 95052 . . .(408) 721-5000 . . .Charles E. Sporck . . .manuf. of semiconductors.

Navistar Intl. Corp. . . .455 N. Cityfront Plaza Dr., Chicago, IL 60611 . . .(312) 836-2000 . . .J.C. Cotting . . .manuf. heavy duty trucks, parts.

New York Times Co. . . .229 W. 43rd St., N.Y., NY 10036 . . .(212) 556-1234 . . .A. O. Sulzberger . . .newspapers, radio, CATV stations, magazines (Family Circle, Golf Digest).

Norfolk Southern Corp. . . .Three Commercial Place, Norfolk, VA 23510 . . .(804) 629-2680 . . .A.B. McKinnon . . .operates Norfolk & Southern railways, freight carrier (North American Van Lines).

Northrop Corp. . . .1840 Century Park E., Los Angeles, CA 90067 . . .(213) 553-6262 . . .K. Kresa . . .aircraft, electronics, communications.

Noxell Corp. . . .11050 York Rd., Hunt Valley, MD 21030 . . .(301) 785-7300 . . .G. L. Bunting Jr . . .toiletry, household, consumer prods. (Noxzema, Lestoil, Clarion, Cover Girl).

Nynex Corp. . . .335 Madison Ave., N.Y., NY 10017 . . .(212) 370-7400 . . .W.C. Ferguson . . .telephone co. in northeast U.S.

Occidental Petroleum Corp. ...10889 Wilshire Blvd., Los Angeles, CA 90024...(213) 879-1700...Dr. Armand Hammer...oil, gas, chemicals, coal, agriculture.

Ogden Corp. ...2 Pennsylvania Plaza, New York NY 10121...(212) 868-6100...R. Ablon...transportation, foods, metals, financial services.

Olin Corp. ...120 Long Ridge Rd., Stamford, CT 06904...(203) 356-2000...J.W. Johnstone Jr....chemicals, water treatment prods., aerospace.

Olsten Corp. ...One Merrick Ave., Westbury, NY 11590...(516) 832-8200...F. N. Liguori...provides temporary workers.

Outboard Marine Corp. ...100 Sea Horse Dr., Waukegan, IL 60085...(312) 689-6200...J.C. Chapman...outboard motors (Evinrude, Johnson), boats (Four Winns, Stratos, Hydra-Sports).

Owens-Corning Fiberglas Corp. ...Fiberglas Tower, Toledo, OH 43659. (419) 248-8000...W.W. Boeschenstein...glass fiber and related prods.

Oxford Industries, Inc. ...222 Piedmont Ave., N.E., Atlanta, GA 30308...(404) 659-2424...J.H. Lanier...men's and women's apparel products.

Pacific Telesis Group ...130 Kearny St., San Francisco, CA 94108...(415) 882-8000...S. L. Ginn...telephone service.

Pan Am Corp. ...Pan Am Bldg., 200 Park Ave., N.Y., NY 10166...(212) 880-1234...T. G. Plaskett...air transportation.

Paramount Communications Inc., ...15 Columbus Circle, N.Y., NY 10023...(212) 373-8000...M.S. Davis...entertainment (Paramount Pictures, Madison Square Garden), publishing (Simon & Schuster, Prentice Hall).

J.C. Penney Co. ...14841 N. Dallas Pkwy., Dallas, TX 75240...(214) 591-2010...W. R. Howell, chmn....dept. stores, catalog sales, drug stores, insurance.

Pennzoil Co. ...P.O. Box 2967, Houston, TX 77252...(713) 546-4000...J.L. Pate...Integrated oil and gas co.

Pep Boys—Manny, Moe & Jack ...3111 W. Allegheny Ave., Philadelphia, Pa. 19132...(215) 229-9300...M. G. Leibovitz...automotive parts and accessories, retail stores, household items, hardware, bicycles.

PepsiCo, Inc. ...PepsiCo., Inc., Purchase, NY 10577...(914) 253-2000...D.W. Calloway...soft drinks, (Pepsi-Cola, Slice), snack foods (Ruffles, Lays, Doritos) restaurants (Pizza Hut, Kentucky Fried Chicken, Taco Bell).

Perry Drug Stores, Inc. ...5400 Perry Dr., Pontiac, MI 48056...(313) 334-1300...J.A. Robinson...drug stores, health care.

Petrie Stores Corp. ...70 Enterprise Ave., Seacaucus, NJ 07094...(201) 866-3600...M.J. Petrie...operates chain of women's specialty stores.

Pfizer Inc. ...235 E. 42d St., N.Y., NY 10017...(212) 573-2323...E.T. Pratt Jr....pharmaceutical, hospital, agricultural, chemical prods., consumer prods (Plax oral rinse).

Philip Morris Cos., Inc. ...120 Park Ave., N.Y., NY 10017...(212) 880-5000...H. Maxwell...cigarettes (Marlboro, Virginia Slims), beer (Miller High Life, Lite, Lowenbrau brands), packaged foods (Jell-o, Ronzoni pasta, Entenman baked goods, Maxwell House coffee, Kool Aid, Tang, Cheez Whiz & Velveeta cheese prods.).

Phillips-Van Heusen Corp. ...1290 Ave. of the Americas, New York, NY 10104...(212) 541-5200...L. S. Phillips...manuf. apparel for men & women; operates retail stores.

Pitney Bowes, Inc., ...Stamford, CT 06926...(203) 356-5000...G. B. Harvey...postage meters, mail handling equip., office equipment.

Playboy Enterprises, Inc. ...680 N. Lake Shore Dr., Chicago, IL 60611...(312) 751-8000...C. Hefner...magazine publishing, CATV, merchandising.

Polaroid Corp. ...549 Technology Sq., Cambridge, MA 02139...(617) 577-2000...I.M. Booth...photographic equip., supplies and optical goods.

Premark Intl., Inc ...1717 Deerfield Rd. Deerfield, IL 60015...(312) 405-6000...W.L. Batts...consumer prods. (Tupperware, Hobart, West Bend).

Primerica, Corp. ...65 E. 55 St., N.Y., NY 10022...(212) 891-8900...S. I. Weill...insurance financial services (Smith Barney).

Procter & Gamble Co. ...One Procter & Gamble Plaza, Cincinnati, OH 45202...(513) 983-1100...E. L. Artzt...soap & detergent (Ivory, Cheer, Tide, Spic and Span), shortenings (Crisco), toiletries (Crest toothpaste, Prell, and Head and Shoulders shampoos), pharmaceuticals (Pepto-Bismol), Pam-pers disposable diapers, Folgers coffee, Hawaiian Punch, Charmin toilet tissues, Bounty towels, Vicks cough medicines.

Quaker Oats Co. ...321 N. Clark St., Chicago, IL 60610...(312) 222-7111...William D. Smithburg...foods, cereal (Quaker Oat Bran, Life, Cap'n Crunch, Puffed Wheat, Puffed Rice), foods (Aunt Jemima, Celeste pizza, Van Camp's pork and beans, Gatorade), pet foods (Ken-L-Ration, Gaines, Puss 'Boots), Magic Pan restaurants.

Quaker State Corp. ...255 Elm St., Oil City, PA 16301...(814) 676-7676...J.W. Corn refining, marketing petroleum prods., filters, mining & marketing coal.

Ralston Purina Co. ...Checkerboard Sq., St. Louis, MO 63164...(314) 982-1000...W. P. Stiritz...pet and livestock food, consumer prods. (Chex cereal, Beech-Nut baby food, Wonder bread, Hostess baked goods, Eveready batteries).

Raytheon Company ...141 Spring St., Lexington, MA 02173...(617) 862-6600...Thomas L. Phillips...electronics, aviation, appliances...Amana Refrigeration, Beech Aircraft.

Reebok Intl. Ltd. ...100 Technology Ctr. Dr., Stoughton, MA 02072...(617) 821-2800...P.B. Fireman...athletic & casual footwear, sportswear.

Promus Cos. Inc. ...1023 Cherrry Rd., Memphis, TN 38117...(901) 762-8600...M.D. Rose...casinos (Harrah), lodging (Hampton Inn, Embassy Suites).

Reynolds Metals Co. ...6601 W. Broad St., Richmond, VA 23261...(804) 281-2000...W.O. Bourke...aluminum prods.

Rite Aid Corp. ...Shiremanstown, PA 17011...(717) 761-2633...A. Grass...discount drug stores, beauty aid stores, auto parts stores.

Rockwell Intl. Corp. ...2230 E. Imperial Hwy., El Segundo, CA...(213) 647-5000...D. R. Beall...aerospace, electronic, automotive prods.

Rorer Group Inc. ...500 Virginia Dr., Ft. Washington, PA 19034...(215) 628-6000...R.E. Cawthorn...pharmaceuticals (Maalox, Ascriptin).

Rubbermaid Inc. ...1147 Akron Rd., Wooster, OH 44691...(216) 264-6464...S. C. Gault...rubber and plastic consumer prods.

Russell Corp. ...P.O. Box 272, Alexander City, AL 35010...(205) 329-4000...D.L. Carlisle Jr....leisure apparel, athletic uniforms.

Ryder System, Inc. ...3600 NW 82d Ave., Miami, FL 33166...(305) 593-3726...M. A. Burns...truck leasing service.

Santa Fe Pacific Corp., ...224 S. Michigan Ave., Chicago, IL 60604...(312) 786-6422...Robert D. Krebs...railroad, real estate, construction, natural resources.

Sara Lee Corp. ...3 First National Plaza, Chicago, IL 60602...(312) 726-2600...J.H. Bryan Jr....baked goods, fresh and processed meats, fresh and frozen fruits and vegetables and other packaged foods, beverages, tobacco products, hosiery, intimate apparel and knitwear, Electrolux, Fuller Brush, Hanes, Gant, Kiwi, Shasta, Hillshire Farm, L' eggs, Isotoner.

Schering-Plough Corp. ...One Giraldal Farms, Madison, NJ 07940...(201) 822-7000...R. P. Luciano...pharmaceuticals, consumer prods.

Schlumberger Ltd. ...277 Park Ave., New York, NY 10172...(212) 350-9400...E. Baird...oilfield services, electronics, measurement and control devices.

Scott Paper Co. ...Scott Plaza, Phila., PA 19113...(215) 522-5000...P. E. Lippincott...sanitary paper prods.

Seagram Co. ...1430 Peel St., Montreal, Que., Canada H3A 1S9...(514) 849-5271...E.M. Bronfman...distilled spirits & wine (Crown Royal, Chivas Regal, Calvert, Wolfschmidt Vodka, Paul Masson, Christian Brothers, Martell, Myer's Jamaica Rum); juice (Tropicana).

Sears, Roebuck & Co. ...Sears Tower, Chicago, IL 60684...(312) 875-2500...E.A. Brennan...merchandising, insurance (Allstate), financial services (Dean Witter), real estate (Coldwell Banker).

Service Merchandise, Inc. ...P.O. Box 24600, Nashville, TN 37202...(615) 251-6666...R. Zimmerman...operates catalog showrooms.

Shaw Industries, Inc. ...616 E. Walnut Ave., Dalton, GA 30722...(404) 278-3812...R.E. Shaw...manuf. tufted carpeting (Magee, Philadelphia).

Sherwin-Williams Co. ...101 Prospect Ave. N.W., Cleveland, OH 44115...(216) 566-2000...John G. Breen...world's largest paint producer (Dutch Boy, Kem-Tone).

Skyline Corp. ...2520 By-Pass Rd., Elkhart, IN 46515...(219)

294-6521...Arthur J. Decio...mfg. housing and recreational vehicles.

Smucker (J.M.) Co....Strawberry Lane, Orville, OH 44667...(216) 682-0015...P. H. Smucker...preserves, jams, jellies, toppings.

Snap-on Tools Corp....2801 80th St., Kenosha, WI 53141...(414) 656-5200...M. F. Gregory...manuf. mechanic's tools, equip.

Sony Corp....9 W. 57th St., New York, NY 10019...(212) 317-5800...N. Ohga...manuf. televisions, radios, tape recorders, audio equip., video tape recorders, entertainment (Columbia Pictures).

Southwest Airlines Co....P.O. Box 37611, Love Field, Dallas, TX 75235...(214) 902-1100...H.D. Kelleher...air transportation.

Southwestern Bell Corp....One Bell Center, St. Louis, MO 63101...(314) 235-9800...E.E. Whitacre Jr....telephone communications.

Standard Brands Paint Co....4300 W 190th St., Torrance, CA 90509...(213) 214-2411...S.D. Buchalter...retailer of home decorating prods.

Stanley Works...1000 Stanley Drive, P.O. Box 7000, New Britain CT 06050...(203) 225-5111...R.H. Ayers...hand tools, hardware, door opening equipment.

Stride Rite Corp....5 Cambridge Center, Cambridge, MA 02142...(617) 491-8800...A. Hiatt...manuf. & retailer children's footwear.

Sun Company, Inc....100 Matsonford Rd., Radnor, PA 19087...(215) 293-6000...R. McClements Jr....energy resources co.

Syms Corp....Syms Way, Secaucus, NJ 07094...(201) 902-9600...S. Syms...operates off-price apparel stores.

Thomas), technical prods.

Tambrands Inc....One Marcus Ave., Lake Success, NY 11042...(516) 358-8300...M.F.C. Emmett...menstrual tampons (Tampax, Maxithins).

Tandem Computers...19333 Vallco Pkwy., Cupertino, CA 95014...(408) 725-6000...T.G. Treybig...supplier of computer systems and networks.

Tandy Corp....1800 One Tandy Center, Fort Worth, TX 76102...(817) 390-3700...J.V. Roach...consumer electronics retailing & mfg, Radio Shack.

Teledyne, Inc....1901 Ave. of the Stars, Los Angeles, CA 90067...(213) 277-3311...G. A. Roberts...electronics, aerospace prods., industrial prods., insurance, finance.

Tenneco, Inc....P.O. Box 2511, Houston, TX 77252...(713) 757-2131...J. L. Ketelsen...oil, natural gas pipelines, shipbuilding, farm equip.

Texaco Inc....2000 Westchester Ave., White Plains, NY 10650...(914) 253-4000...J.W. Kinnear...petroleum and petroleum prods.

Texas Instruments Inc....7610 Stemmons Freeway, Dallas, TX 75247...(214) 647-6700...R.D. Rogers...electrical & electronics prods.

Textron Inc....40 Westminster St., Providence, RI 02903...(401) 421-2800...B.F. Dolan...aerospace, consumer, industrial, metal prods, consumer finance, insurance, management services.

Tiffany & Co....727 5th Ave, New York, NY 10022...(212) 755-8000...W.R. Chaney...designs, manuf., and distributes jewelry & gift items.

Time Warner Inc....Rockefeller Center, New York, NY 10020...(212) 522-1212...J.R. Munro...magazine publisher (Time, Sports Illustrated, Fortune, Money, People), CATV (HBO, Cinemax), publishing (Little, Brown, Warner Books).

Tonka Corp....6000 Clearwater Dr., Minnetonka, MN 55343...(612) 936-3300...S.G. Shank...toy manuf. (Monopoly, Play-Doh, Pound Puppies, Trivial Pursuit, Risk, Clue).

Tootsie Roll Industries, Inc.,...7401 S. Cicero Ave., Chicago, IL 60629...(312) 838-3400...M.J. Gordon...candy (Tootsie Roll, Mason Dots, Mason Crows, Bonomo Turkish Taffy, Charms).

The Toro Company...8111 Lyndale Ave. South, Bloomington, MN 55420...(612) 887-8526...K. B. Melrose...lawn and turf maintenance, (Lawn Boy); snow removal equipment.

Toys "R" Us...461 From Rd., Paramus, NJ 07652...(201) 262-7800...Charles Lazarus...toy retailer, clothing stores (Kids "R" Us).

Transamerica Corp....600 Montgomery St., San Francisco, CA 94111...(415) 983-4000...J.R. Harvey...insurance, financial, business services (Occidental Life Ins.).

Travelers Corp....One Tower Sq., Hartford, CT 06183...(203) 277-0111...E. H. Budd...insurance.

Tribune Co....435 N. Michigan Ave., Chicago, IL 60611...(312) 222-9100...S.R. Cook...newpaper publishing, broadcasting, entertainment (Chicago Cubs baseball team).

Trinity Industries, Inc....2525 Stemmons Freeway, P.O. Box 10587, Dallas, TX 75207...(214) 631-4420...W.R. Wallace...manufactures variety of metal products.

TRW Inc....1900 Richmond Rd., Cleveland, OH 44124...(216) 291-7000...J.T. Gorman...car and truck operations, electronics, and space systems. (201) 712-0500...F. L. Salizzoni...food service, restaurants (Denny's), nursing homes.

USAIR Group, Inc....1911 Jefferson Hwy., Arlington, VA 22002...(703) 418-7000...E.I. Colodny...air carrier of passengers, property, and mail.

UST Inc....100 W. Putnam Ave., Greenwich, CT 06830...(203) 661-1100...L.F. Bantle...smokeless tobacco (Copenhagen, Skoal, Happy Days), pipes, pipe tobacco.

USX Corp....600 Grant St., Pittsburgh, PA 15230...C.A. Corry...steel manuf., oil & gas.

Unilever, N.V....Burgemeester's Jacobplein 1, Rotterdam, The Netherlands...F. A. Maljers, Chmn....soap, detergent, margarine, frozen food, toothpaste, tea, dried soups, ice cream, cosmetics, fragrances, (Lever Brothers, Lipton, Pond's Vaseline Intensive Care, Obsession, Q-Tips, Cutex).

Union Carbide Corp....39 Old Ridgebury Rd., Danbury, CT 06817...(203) 794-2000...R.D. Kennedy...chemicals, industrial gases.

Union Pacific Corp....Martin Tower, Bethlehem, PA 18018...(215) 861-3200...D. Lewis...railroad, natural resources.

Unisys Corp....P.O. Box 500, Blue Bell, PA 19424...(215) 542-6050...W. Michael Blumenthal...business equip., data processing prods.

U.S. Home Corp....1800 W. Loop South, Houston, TX 77252...(713) 877-2311...R. J. Strudler...leading single-family homebuilder in U.S.

United States Shoe Corp....One Eastwood Dr., Cincinnati, OH 45227...(513) 527-7000...B.B. Hudson...apparel, retailer (Casual Corner), shoes (Red Cross, Joyce), eye-care stores (LensCrafters).

United Technologies Corp....United Technologies Bldg., Hartford, CT 06101...(203) 728-7000...R.F. Daniell...aerospace, industrial prods. & services, Carrier Corp., Otis Elevator; Pratt & Whitney, Sikorsky Aircraft.

Univar Corp....1600 Norton Building, Seattle, WA 98104...(206) 447-5911...J.W. Bernard...industrial and agricultural chemicals, laboratory and graphic arts products distributor, home furnishing supplies and fabrics distributors.

Universal Foods Corp....433 East Michigan St., Milwaukee, WI 53202...(414) 271-6755...G.A. Osborn...yeast products, cheese products, dehydrated seasonings, food colors and flavors, imported gourmet foods.

Upjohn Co....7000 Portage Rd., Kalamazoo, MI 49001...(616) 323-4000...T. Cooper...pharmaceuticals (Motrin, Nuprin, Xanax, Halcion, Cleocin), chemicals, agricultural and health care prods.

VF Corp....1047 No. Park Rd., Wyomissing, PA 19610...(215) 378-1151...L.R. Pugh...apparel, Vanity Fair, Lee jeans, Bassett-Walker, Jantzen.

Vulcan Materials Co....One Metroplex Dr., Birmingham, AL 35209...(205) 877-3000...H.A. Sklenar...construction materials, chemicals, metals.

Wal-Mart Stores Inc....702 W. 8th St., Bentonville, AK 72716...(501) 273-4000...D.D. Glass...discount dept. stores.

Walgreen Co....200 Wilmot Rd., Deerfield, IL 60015...(708) 940-2500...Charles R. Walgreen 3d...retail drug chain, restaurants.

Wang Laboratories, Inc....One Industrial Ave., Lowell, MA 01851...(508) 459-5000...H.H.S. Chou...word processors.

Warner-Lambert Co....201 Tabor Rd., Morris Plains, NJ 07950...(201) 540-2000...J.D. Williams...health care prods. (Benadryl), consumer prods. (Efferdent dental cleanser, Hall cough tablets, Schick razors, Clorets breath mints, Rolaids antacid, Listerine mouth wash).

Washington Post Co....1150 15th St., N.W., Washington, DC 20071...(202) 334-6000...Katharine Graham...newspapers, magazines (Newsweek), TV stations.

Weis Markets, Inc....1000 South Second Street, Sunbury, PA 17801...(717) 286-4571...S. Weis...operates supermarkets, distributes frozen foods and grocery items.

Wells Fargo & Co....420 Montgomery St., San Francisco, CA 94163...(415) 477-1000...C.E. Reichardt...banking.

Wendy's Intl., Inc....4288 W. Dublin-Granville Rd., Dublin, OH 43017...(614) 764-3100...J.W. Near...quick service restaurants.

Westinghouse Electric Corp....Westinghouse Bldg., Gateway Center, Pittsburgh, PA 15222...(412) 244-2000...P.E. Lego...manuf. electrical, mechanical equip., radio and television stations.

Westvaco Corp....299 Park Avenue, New York, NY 10171...(212) 688-5000...J.A. Luke..manufactures paper for graphic reproduction, communications, and packaging (largest producer of envelopes in the world).

Weyerhaeuser Co....Tacoma, WA 98477...(206) 924-2345...George H. Weyerhaeuser...manuf., distribution of forest prods.

Whirlpool Corp....2000 M-63 N., Benton Harbor, MI 49022...(616) 926-5000...D.R. Whitwam...major home appliances.

Whitman Corp. ...One Illinois Ctr., 111 E. Wacker Dr., Chicago, IL 60601...(312) 565-3000...J.W. Cozad... diversified prods. and services, consumer products, food, auto prods (Midas).

Willamette Industries, Inc....3800 1st Interstate Tower, Portland, OR 97201...(503) 227-5581...William Swindells...building materials and paper prods.

Winn-Dixie Stores, Inc....5050 Edgewood Ct., Jacksonville, FL 32205...(904) 783-5000...A.D. Davis, chmn....retail grocery chain.

Winnebago Industries, Inc....P.O. Box 152, Forest City, IA 50436...(515) 582-3535...J.K. Hanson, chmn....manuf. of motor homes, recreation vehicles.

Wolverine World Wide, inc....9341 Courtland Dr., Rockford, MI 49351...(616) 866-5500...T.D. Gleason...manuf. footwear (Hush Puppies).

Woolworth Corp....233 Broadway, N.Y., NY 10279...(212) 553-2000...H.E. Sells...variety stores, shoe stores (Kinney), men's clothing (Richman Brothers), children's apparel (Little Folk shop), athletic footwear (Foot Locker).

Wm. Wrigley Jr. Co....410 N. Michigan Ave., Chicago, IL 60611...(312) 644-2121...William Wrigley...chewing gum.

Xerox Corp....P.O. Box 1600, Stamford, CT 06904...(203) 968-3000...D. T. Kearns...equip. for reproduction, reduction, and transmission of printed information.

Zenith Electronics Corp....1000 Milwaukee Ave., Glenview, IL 60025...(708) 391-7000...Jerry K. Pearlman...consumer electronic prods.

Who Owns What: Familiar Consumer Products

The following is a list of familiar consumer products and their parent companies. The address of the parent company can be found on pages 815-821.

Admiral appliances: Maytag
Ajax cleanser: Colgate-Palmolive
Allstate Insurance Co.: Sears, Roebuck
Almond Joy candy: Hershey
Anacin: American Home Products
Arrid anti-perspirant: Carter-Wallace

Ban anti-perspirant: Bristol-Myers
Beech Aircraft: Raytheon
Beech Nut babyfood: Ralston Purina
Betty Crocker products: General Mills
Budweiser beer: Anheuser-Busch
Bufferin: Bristol-Myers
Business Week magazine: McGraw-Hill
Buster Brown shoes: Brown Group

Cap'n Crunch cereal: Quaker Oats
Carrier air conditioners: United Technologies
Celeste Pizza: Quaker Oats
Charmin toilet tissues: Procter & Gamble
Chef Boy-ar-dee products: American Home Products
Cheer detergent: Procter & Gamble
Cheerios cereal: General Mills
Clairol hair products: Bristol-Myers
Clorets mints: Warner-Lambert
Columbia Pictures: Sony
Copenhagen snuff: UST
Cracker Jack: Borden
Crest toothpaste: Procter & Gamble
Crisco shortening: Procter & Gamble

Dean Witter financial services: Sears, Roebuck
Deer Park bottled water: Clorox
Doritos chips: PepsiCo
Drano: Bristol-Meyers
Dristan: American Home Products
Duncan Hines cookies: Procter & Gamble
Easy-Off oven cleaner: American Home Products
Efferdent dental cleanser: Warner-Lambert
ESPN: Capital Cities/ABC
Eveready batteries: Ralston Purina
Excedrin: Bristol-Myers

Fab detergent: Colgate-Palmolive
Family Circle magazine: New York Times
Flagg Bros. shoe stores: Genesco
Foamy shaving cream: Gillette
Folger coffee: Procter & Gamble
Formula 409 spray cleaner: Clorox
Franco-American foods: Campbell Soup
Frito-Lay snacks: PepsiCo
Fuller Brush prods.: Sara Lee
Gatorade: Quaker Oats
Gleem toothpaste: Procter & Gamble
Hampton inns—Promus
Handy Wipes: Colgate-Palmolive
Hanes hosiery: Sara Lee
Hawaiian Punch: Procter & Gamble
Head and Shoulders shampoo: Procter & Gamble

Hellman's mayonnaise: CPC International
Hi-C fruit drinks: Coca Cola
Hillshire Farm meats: Sara Lee
Home Box Office: Time
Hostess baked goods: Ralston Purina
Hush Puppies shoes: Wolverine World Wide
Ivory soap products: Procter & Gamble
Jack Daniel bourbon: Brown-Forman
Jell-o: Philip Morris
Jim Beam whiskey: American Brands
Ken-L-Ration pet foods: Quaker Oats
Kent cigarettes: Loews
Kinney shoe stores: Woolworth
Knorr soups: CPC International
Kool Aid: Philip Morris
La Menu frozen dinners: Campbell Soup
Ladies Home Journal magazine: Meredith
Lee jeans: VF Corp.
Lenox china: Brown-Forman
Lens Crafters: U.S. Shoe
Lerner stores: The Limited
Lestoil: Procter & Gamble
Life Savers: Hershey
Lipton tea: Unilever
Listerine mouth wash: Warner-Lambert
Log Cabin syrup: Philip Morris
Lord & Taylor dept. stores: May Dept. Stores
Lucite paints: Clorox
Lunch Bucket meals: Greyhound Dial

Maalox: Rorer Group
Marlboro cigarettes: Philip Morris
Mazola oil: CPC International
Maxwell House coffee: Philip Morris
Michelob beer: Anheuser-Busch
Midas automotive centers: Whitman
Miller beer: Philip Morris
Milton Bradley games: Hasbro
Minute Rice: Philip Morris
Mrs. Paul's frozen fish: Campbell Soup
Mueller's pasta prods.: CPC International
NBC Broadcasting: General Electric
Newsweek magazine: Washington Post
9-Lives cat food: H.J. Heinz
North American Van Lines: Norfolk Southern

Obsession fragrance: Unilever
Ore-Ida frozen foods: H.J. Heinz
Pampers: Procter & Gamble
Paper Mate pens: Gillette
People magazine: Time
Pepto-Bismol: Procter & Gamble
Pepperidge Farm products: Campbell Soup
Pizza Hut restaurants: PepsiCo
Plax oral rinse: Pfizer
Playskool toys: Hasbro
Prego spaghetti sauce: Campbell Soup

(continued)

Prell shampoo: Procter & Gamble
Prentice-Hall publishing: Paramount
Post-It stickers: Minn. Min. & Manuf.
Purex detergent: Greyhound Dial
Q-Tips: Unilever
Radio Shack retail outlets: Tandy
Ramblin root beer: Coca Cola
Red Lobster Inns: General Mills
Reese's peanut butter cups: Hershey
Right Guard deodorant: Gillette
Rise shave lathers: Carter-Wallace
Rolaids antacid: Warner-Lambert
Ronzoni pasta: Hershey
Ruffles chips: PepsiCo
San Giorgio pasta: Hershey
Scotch tape: Minn. Min. & Manuf.
Scrabble: Hasbro
Skippy peanut butter: CPC International
Simon & Schuster publishing: Paramount
Southern Comfort liquor: Brown-Forman
Sports Illustrated magazine: Time
Sprite soda: Coca-Cola
Sugartwin: Alberto Culver

Sunkist soft drink: General Cinema
Taco Bell restaurants: PepsiCo
Thom McAn shoe stores: Melville
Thomas English muffins: CPC International
Tide detergent: Procter & Gamble
Trojan condoms: Carter-Wallace
Tropicana juices: Seagram
Tupperware: Premark
Tylenol: Johnson & Johnson
Ultra Brite toothpaste: Colgate-Palmolive
V-8 vegetable juice: Campbell Soup
Vanity Fair apparel: VF Corp.
Velveeta cheese prods.: Philip Morris
Vicks cough medicines: Procter & Gamble
Virginia Slims cigarettes: Philip Morris
Walden Book stores: K mart
Wall Street Journal: Dow Jones
Weight Watchers: H.J. Heinz
Wheaties cereal: General Mills
White Owl cigars: Culbro
Wizard air freshener: American Home Products
Wyler's drink mixes: Borden

Credit Card Rates

(As of Aug. 1, 1990)
(Prepared by Christian T. Jones, San Diego, CA)

Nearly all states have special laws dealing with rates charged for credit cards issued by state banks and other financial institutions. Although some state laws apply only to banks, under Federal parity law, the same charges can be made by other financial institutions. A national bank can charge the highest rates allowed for revolving credit extended by any other creditor in the state where the bank is located for similar types of credit, and such rates may also be charged to residents of any other state. Rates are yearly.

Ala.	No limit.	La.	18%; 4% cash advance and $12 annual fees.
Alas.	17% plus fee.		
Ariz.	No limit.	Me.	18%; $12 annual fee.
Ark.	5% over FRB discount rate (max. 17%).	Md.	24%; 2% fee.
		Mass.	23% to $6,000; no limit over $6,000; $20 annual fee.
Cal.	No limit.		
Colo.	21%.	Mich.	18%; no limit on annual fee.
Conn.	15%; $10 annual fee.	Minn.	18%; $50 annual fee.
D.C.	24%.	Miss.	21%; or 18% plus $12 annual fee.
Del.	No limit.		
Fla.	18%.	Mo.	22-10% @ $1,000.
Ga.	No limit on rate or fee.	Mont.	No limit.
Ha.	24%.	Neb.	18% plus fees.
Ida.	No limit.	Nev.	No limit.
Ill.	No limit; plus fees.	N.H.	No limit.
Ind.	36-21-15%, @ $810, $2,700; or 21%.	N.J.	30%; $15 annual fee or $50 over $5,000.
Ia.	No limit.	N.M.	No limit.
Kan.	18-14.45% @ $1,000.	N.Y.	25% plus annual fee to 6/30/93.
Ky.	21%; $20 annual fee.	N.C.	18%; $20 annual fee.
		N.D.	No limit.
Oh.	25% to 1/1/92.		
Okla.	30-21-15% @ $780, $2,600; or 21%.		
Ore.	No limit.		
Pa.	12% loans; 15% purchases; $15 annual fee.		
P.R.	17% loans; 26% purchases.		
R.I.	18%.		
S.C.	No limit.		
S.D.	No limit.		
Tenn.	24%.		
Tex.	18%.		
Utah	No limit.		
Vt.	18%; no limit on annual fee.		
Va.	No limit.		
Wash.	12% or 4% over U.S. T-bill rate.		
W.Va.	18%.		
Wis.	No limit.		
Wyo.	36-21% @ $1,000; no limit over $25,000.		

Fair Credit: What You Should Know

Source: Federal Trade Commission

Billing. The Fair Credit Billing Act permits you to dispute the accuracy of charges listed on your credit card statement and provides other important rights (such as limits on liability for unauthorized charges). To file a notice of a "billing error," send a letter to the card issuer at the address specified for "billing inquiries" within 60 days of the date that the card issuer mailed the first statement that shows the alleged error. Be sure to include your name, address, account number, the amount of the charge you dispute, and why you think an error was made. Do not send the letter in the same envelope as your payment and keep a copy.

Equal Credit. The Equal Credit Opportunity Act (ECOA) prohibits discrimination on the grounds of sex, marital status, age (provided the applicant has the capacity under state law to enter a contract), race, color, religion, or national origin. The ECOA also protects applicants whose income derives in whole or in part from any public assistance program, or those who have in good faith exercised any right under the Federal Consumer Credit Protection Act, which includes the FCBA and ECOA, among other provisions.

The creditor may inquire about your marital status, for example, if it needs to do so to determine its rights and not to discriminate in a determination of creditworthiness. An-

other example involves considering the age of the applicant if the inquiry is for the purpose of determining the amount and probable continuation of income levels or other elements of creditworthiness. However, a creditor may not consider race, national origin, or religion in deciding whether to extend credit.

The ECOA also requires the creditor to respond to applications within 30 days of receiving a completed application and to provide rejected applicants with a statement of specific reasons why credit was denied or a notice disclosing the consumer's rights to have the reasons if he or she requests them in writing.

Mail-Order Merchandise. By law, you have the right to have merchandise ordered through the mail shipped within 30 days, unless another shipping date has been specified in the advertisement for the merchandise. Promises such as "one week" or "4 to 6 weeks" must be met. However, if the seller is unable to ship your order when promised (or within the 30-day limit), the seller must provide you with a notice informing you that you have the right to cancel your order and get a prompt refund. If you experience a problem with late or non-delivery of merchandise ordered through the mail, contact the Federal Trade Commission.

Interest Laws and Consumer Finance Loan Rates

Source: Revised by Christian T. Jones. Editor, Consumer Finance Law Bulletin, San Diego, Ca.

All states have laws regulating interest rates. These laws fix a legal or conventional rate which applies when there is no contract for interest. They also fix a general maximum contract rate, but there are so many exceptions that the general contract maximum actually applies only to exceptional cases. Also, federal law has preempted state limits on first home mortgages, subject to each state's right to reinstate its own law, and given depository institutions parity with other state lenders.

Legal rate of interest. The legal or conventional rate of interest applies to money obligations when no interest rate is contracted for and also to judgments. The rate is usually somewhat below the general interest rate.

General maximum contract rates. General interest laws in most states set the maximum rate between 8% and 16% per year. The general maximum is fixed by the state constitution at 5% over the Federal Reserve Discount rate in Arkansas. Loans to corporations are frequently exempted or subject to a higher maximum. In recent years, it has also been common to provide special rates for home mortgage loans and variable usury rates that are indexed to market rates.

Specific enabling acts. In many states special statutes permit industrial loan companies, second mortgage lenders, and banks to charge 1.5% a month or more. Laws regulating revolving loans, charge accounts and credit cards generally limit charges between 1.5% and 2% per month plus annual fees for credit cards. Rates for installment sales contracts in most states are somewhat higher. Credit unions may generally charge 1% to 1.5% a month. Pawnbrokers' rates vary widely. Savings and loan associations, and loans insured by federal agencies, are also specially regulated. A number of states allow regulated lenders to charge any rate agreed to with the customer either for all credit or over a certain dollar amount.

Consumer finance loan statutes. Most consumer finance loan statutes are based on early models drafted by the Russell Sage Foundation (1916-42) to provide small loans to wage earners under license and other protective regulations. Since 1969 the model has frequently been the Uniform Consumer Credit Code which applies to credit sales and loans for consumer purposes. In general, licensed lenders may charge 3% a month and reduced rates for additional amounts. An add-on of 17% ($17 per $100) per year yields about 2.5% per month if paid in equal monthly installments. Discount rates produce higher yields than add-on rates of the same amount. In the table below, unless otherwise stated, monthly and annual rates are based on reducing principal balances, annual add-on rates are based on the original principal for the full term, and two or more rates apply to different portions of balance or original principal.

States with consumer finance loan laws and the rates of charge as of August 1, 1990

Maximum monthly rates computed on unpaid balances, unless otherwise stated.

Ala.. . . Annual add-on: 15% to $750, 10% to $2,000 (min. 1.5% on unpaid balances). Higher rates for loans up to $749. Over $2,000, any agreed rate. Fee: 4% (max. $25); 5% real estate.

Alas.. . 3% to $850, 2% to $10,000. Over $10,000, any agreed rate.

Ariz.. . To $1,000: 3%. Over $1,000: 3% to $500, 2% to $10,000. Over $10,000, any agreed rate.

Cal.. . 2.5% to $225, 2% to $900, 1.5% to $1,650, 1% to $2,500 (1.6% min.). Over $2,500, any agreed rate. 5% fee (max. $50) to $2,500

Colo.. . 36% per year to $630, 21% to $2,100, 15% to $25,000 (21% min.).

Conn. . Annual Add-on: 17% to $600, 11% to $5,000; 11% over $1,800 to $5,000 for certain secured loans. Any agreed rate for second mortgages.

Del.. . . Any agreed rate.

D.C. . . 24% per year.

Fla.. . . 30% per year to $1,000, 24% to $2,000, 18% to $25,000.

Ga.. . . 10% per year discount to 18 months, add-on to 36¹/₂ months; 8% fee to $600, 4% on excess plus $2 per month. Over $3,000, any agreed rate.

Ha.. . . 3.5% to $100, 2.5% to $300; 2% on entire balance over $300 or discount rates.

Ida.. . . Any agreed rate.

Ill.. . . . Any agreed rate.

Ind.. . . 36% per year to $810, 21% to $2,700, 15% to $25,000 (21% min.).

Ia.. . . 3% to $1,000, 2% to $2,800, 1.5% to $25,000; or equivalent flat rate. Over $25,000: 21% per year.

Kan.. . 36% per year to $690, 21% to $2,300, 14.45% to $25,000 (18% min.). Fee: 2% (max. $100); 3% real estate.

Ky.. . . 3% to $1,000, 2% to $3,000. Over $3,000, 2%.

La.. . . 36% per year to $1,400, 27% to $4,000, 24% to $7,000, 21% over $7,000, plus $25 fee.

Me.. . . 30% per year to $700, 21% to $2,000, 15% to $25,000 (18% min.).

Md.. . . 2.75% to $1,000, 2% to $2,000. Over $2,000, 2%.

Mass.. . 23% per year plus $20 fee to $6,000; any agreed rate over $6,000.

Mich.. . 31% per year to $500, 13% to $3,000 (18% min.); 18% for second mortgages, plus 2% fee (max. $200).

Minn.. . 33% per year to $750, 19% over $750 (21.75% min.).

Miss.. . 36% per year to $1,000, 33% to $1,800, 24% to $5,000, 14% over $5,000. Over $25,000, 18%. 2% fee (max. $50).

Mo.. . . 2.218% to $1,200, 1.67% over $1,200, plus 5% fee (max. $15); 1.67% plus 2% for second mortgages.

Mont.. . Any agreed rate.

Neb.. . 24% per year to $1,000. 21% over, plus fee of 7% to $2,000 and 5% over (max. $500).

Nev.. . . Any agreed rate.

N.H. . . 2% to $600, 1.5% to $1,500; Any agreed rate over $1,500 or for real estate mortgages.

N.J.. . . 30% per year to $5,000 or for second mortgages.

N.M. . . Any agreed rate.

N.Y. . . 25% per year to 6/30/93.

N.C. . . 3% to $1,000, 1.5% to $7,500; 1.5% on entire amount to $10,000. 1.5% or variable plus 2% fee for second mortgages.

N.D.. . 2.5% to $250, 2% to $500, 1.75% to $750, 1.5% to $1,000; any agreed rate over $1,000.

Ohio . . 28% per year to $1,000, 22% to $5,000; 25% on entire amount over $5,000; plus fee.

Okla.. . 30% per annum to $780, 21% to $2,600, 15% to $45,000. (21% min.). Special rates to $500.

Ore. . . Any agreed rate.

Pa.. . . 9.5% per year discount to 48 months, 6% for remaining time plus 2% fee (max. $100); or 2% on unpaid balances; 1.85% for second mortgages over $5,000, plus 2% fee.

P.R. . . 24% per year.

R.I. . . 3% to $300, 2.5% for loans between $300 and $800; 2% for larger loans to $5,000. 1.75% over $5,000.

S.C. . . Any agreed and posted rate.

S.D. . . Any agreed rate.

Tenn.. . Over $100, 24% per year or discount rates plus fees.

Texas . Annual add-on: 18% to $1,080, 8% to $9,000 or formula rate (18% to 24% per year on unpaid balances.)

Utah . . Any agreed rate.

Vt. . . . 2% to $1,000, 1% to $3,000 (min. 1.5%); 1.5% for second mortgages.

Va.. . . 2³⁄₄% to $800, 2% to $2,000, 1.5% to $3,500; or annual add-on of 19% to $800, 15% to $2,000, 12% to $2,800; 2% fee. Any agreed rate over $3,500 for second mortgages, plus 2% fee.

Wash. . 2.5% to $500, 1.5% to $1,000, 1% to $2,500. Over $2,500, 25% per year or discount rates.

W.Va. . 36% per year to $500, 24% to $1,500, 18% to $2,000. Over $2,000, 27% per year to $2,000, 25% to $10,000, 18% on remainder, 2% fee.

Wis. . . Any agreed rate.

Wyo.. . 36% per year to $1,000, 21% to $25,000. No limit over $25,000.

U.S. Passport, Visa, and Health Requirements

Source: Passport Services, U.S. State Department as of June, 1990

Passports are issued by the U.S. Department of State to citizens and nationals of the United States for the purpose of documenting them for foreign travel and identifying them as Americans.

How to Obtain a Passport

Applicants who have never been issued a passport in their own name must execute an application in person before (1) a passport agent; (2) a clerk of any federal court or state court of record or a judge or clerk of any probate court accepting applications; (3) a postal employee designated by the postmaster at a post office which has been selected to accept passport applications; or (4) a U.S. diplomatic or consular officer abroad. A DSP-11 is the correct form to use for applicants who must apply in person. All persons are required to obtain individual passports in their own name. An applicant who is 13 years of age or older is required to appear in person before the clerk or agent executing the application. A parent or legal guardian may execute the application for children under 13.

A passport previously issued to the applicant, or one in which he was included, will be accepted as proof of U.S. citizenship. If the applicant has no prior passport and was born in the U.S. a certified copy of their birth certificate shall be presented to the agent accepting the passport application. To be acceptable, the certificate must show the given name and surname, the date and place of birth, and that the birth record was filed shortly after birth. A delayed birth certificate (a record filed more than one year after the date of birth) is acceptable provided that it shows acceptable secondary evidence was used for creating this record.

If such primary evidence is not obtainable, a notice from state registrar shall be submitted stating that no birth record exists. The notice shall be accompanied by the best obtainable secondary evidence such as a baptismal certificate, or a hospital birth record.

A naturalized citizen with no previous passport should present a Certificate of Naturalization. A person born abroad claiming U.S. citizenship through either a native-born or naturalized citizen parent must submit a Certificate of Citizenship issued by the Immigration and Naturalization Service; or a Consular Report of Birth or Certification of Birth issued by the Dept. of State. If one of the above documents has not been obtained, evidence of citizenship of the parent(s) through whom citizenship is claimed and evidence which would establish the parent/child relationship must be submitted. Additionally, if citizenship is derived through birth to citizen parent(s), the following documents will be required: parents' marriage certificate plus an affidavit from parent(s) showing periods and places of residence or physical presence in the U.S. and abroad, specifying periods spent abroad in the employment of the U.S. government, including the armed forces, or with certain international organizations. If citizenship is derived through naturalization of parents, evidence of admission to the U.S. for permanent residence also will be required.

Persons who possess a passport in their own name issued within the last 12 years and after their 16th birthday may be eligible to apply for a new passport by mail. A form DSP-82, Application for Passport by Mail must be filled out and mailed to the nearest passport agency, together with their previous passport, 2 recent identical photographs and $35.00.

Contract Employees — Persons traveling because of a contract with the U.S. Government must submit with their application: letters from their employer stating position, destination and purpose of travel, armed forces contract number, and expiration date of contract when pertinent.

Photographs, Fees and Identity

Photographs — Submit 2 identical photographs which are sufficiently recent (normally not more than 6 months old) to be a good likeness of and satisfactorily identify the applicant. Photographs should be 2×2 inches in size. The image size measured from the bottom of the chin to the top of the head (including hair) should be not less than one inch nor more than 1 3/8 inches. Photographs should be portrait-type prints. They must be clear, front view, full face, with a plain, white or off-white background. Photographs which depict the applicant as relaxed and smiling are encouraged.

Fees — The passport fee is $20.00 for passports issued to persons under 18 years of age. These passports are valid for 5 years from the date of issue. The passport fee is $35.00 for passports issued to persons 18 and older. These passports are valid for 10 years from the date of issuance. An additional fee of $7.00 is charged for the execution of the application. There is no acceptance fee when using DSP-82, "Application For Passport By Mail." Applicants eligible to use this form pay only the $35.00 passport fee.

Identity—Applicants must also establish their identity to the satisfaction of the person accepting the application. To establish identity, applicants may use a previous U.S. passport, a Certificate of Naturalization, a Certificate of Citizenship, a valid driver's license, or a government identification card. Applicants may not use a Social Security card, learner's or temporary driver's license, credit card, or expired identity card. Applicants unable to establish their identity must take the identification cards they have in their own name (i.e. Social Security card) and in addition, they must be accompanied by a person who has known them for at least 2 years and who is a U.S. citizen or legal U.S. permanent resident alien. That person must sign an affidavit before the individual who executes the passport application. The witness will be required to establish his or her own identity.

The loss or theft of a valid passport is a serious matter and should be reported immediately to Passport Services, 1425 K Street, N.W., Dept. of State, Wash., D.C. 20524, tel: (202) 647-0508 or to the nearest passport agency if you are in the U.S. or the nearest U.S. embassy or consulate when abroad.

Foreign Regulations

A visa, usually rubber stamped in a passport by a representative of the country to be visited, indicates that the bearer of the passport is permitted to enter that country for a certain purpose and length of time. In most instances, you must obtain necessary visas before you leave the U.S. Apply directly to the embassy or nearest consulate of each country you plan to visit, or consult a travel agent.

The State Dept. publication, "Foreign Visa Requirements," contains entry requirements and application instructions for most foreign countries and is available for 50¢ from the Consumer Information Center, Dept. 438T, Pueblo, CO 81009.

The process may take several weeks, so it is important to apply well in advance and verify requirements with the embassy or nearest consulate of each country before applying.

Aliens — An alien leaving the U.S. must request a passport from the embassy of the country of their nationality, must have a permit from his local Collector of Internal Revenue, and if they wish to return, should request a re-entry permit from the Immigration and Naturalization Service if it is required.

How to Obtain Birth, Marriage, Death Records

The United States government has published a series of inexpensive booklets entitled: Where to Write for Birth & Death Records; Where to Write for Marriage Records; Where to Write for Divorce Records; Where to Write for Birth and Death Records of U. S. Citizens Who were Born or Died Outside of the U. S.; Birth Certifications for Alien Children Adopted by U. S. Citizens; You May Save Time Proving Your Age and Other Birth Facts. They tell where to write to get a certified copy of an original vital record. Supt. of Documents, Government Printing Office, Washington, DC 20402.

Tourism, 1989

Source: U.S. Travel and Tourism Admin.

International tourism reached record levels in 1989, when 38.3 million people visited the U.S. About 70 percent of those visits were for leisure and vacation. The foreign visitors spent $43 billion, while Americans traveling to other nations spent $42.6. The difference was in the U.S.'s favor for the first time, and was expected to increase in 1990. According to the Commerce Dept., tourism became the nation's largest export industry in 1989. The states which showed the largest increase in foreign visitors in 1989 were: New Mexico and South Dakota (+266%); Utah (+254%); Arizona (+205%); Tennessee (+190%); and Alabama and Iowa (+175%).

Share of International Travelers' Spending in the U.S.

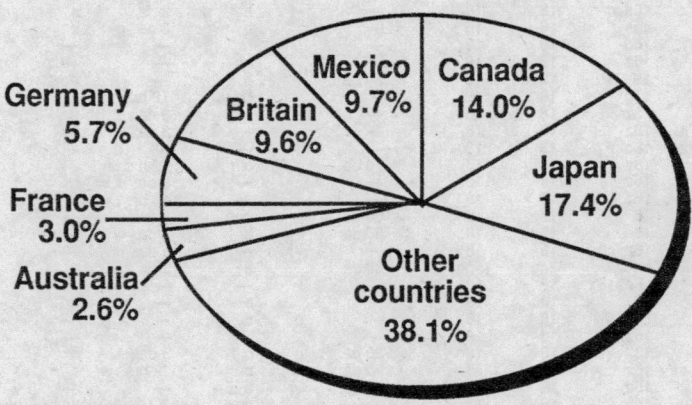

Top U.S. Places Visited by Overseas Travelers
(in millions)

Marriage Laws

Source: Gary N. Skoloff, Skoloff & Wolfe, Livingston, N.J.; as of June 1, 1990

State	Age with parental consent Male	Female	Age without consent Male	Female	Physical exam & blood test for male and female Maximum period between exam and license	Scope of medical exam	Waiting period Before license	After license
Alabama*	14a	14a	18	18	—	b	—	s
Alaska	16z	16z	18	18	—	b	3 da., w	—
Arizona	16z	16z	18	18	—	b	—	—
Arkansas	17c	16c	18	18	—	v	—	—
California	aa	aa	18	18	30 da., w	bb	—	h
Colorado*	16z	16z	18	18	—	—	—	s
Connecticut	16z	16z	18	18	—	bb	4 da., w	ttt
Delaware	18c	16c	18	18	—	b	—	e, s
Florida	16a, c	16a, c	18	18	—	b	3 da.	s
Georgia*	aa	aa	16	16	—	b	3 da., g	s*
Hawaii	16d	16d	18	18	—	b	—	—
Idaho*	16z	16z	18	18	—	bb	—	—
Illinois	16	16	18	18	30 da.	b, n	—	ee
Indiana*	17c	17c	18	18	—	bb	72 hrs.	t
Iowa*	18z	18z	18	18	—	b	3 da., v	tt
Kansas*	18z	18z	18	18	—	b	3 da., w	—
Kentucky	18c, z	18c, z	18	18	—	b	—	—
Louisiana	18z	18z	18	18	10 da.	b	72 hrs., w	—
Maine	16z	16z	18	18	—	b	3 da., v, w	h
Maryland	16c, f	16c, f	18	18	—	b	48 hrs., w	ff
Massachusetts	16d	16	18	18	60 da.	bb	3 da., v	—
Michigan	16c, d	16c	18	18	30 da.	b	3 da., w	—
Minnesota	16z	16z	18	18	—	b	5 da., w	—
Mississippi	aa	aa	17gg	15gg	30 da.	b	3 da., w	—
Missouri	15d, 18z	15d, 18z	18	18	—	b	—	—
Montana* w	16	16	18	18	—	b	—	ff
Nebraska w	17	17	18	18	—	bb	—	—
Nevada	16z	16z	18	18	—	—	—	—
New Hampshire	14j	13j	18	18	30 da.	b, l	3 da., v	h
New Jersey	16z, c	16z, c	18	18	30 da.	b	72 hrs., w	s
New Mexico	16d	16d	18	18	30 da.	b	—	—
New York	14j	14j	18	18	—	nn	—	24 hrs., w, t
North Carolina	16c, g	16c, g	18	18	—	m	v	—
North Dakota	16	16	18	18	—	—	—	t
Ohio*	18c, z	16c, z	18	18	30 da.	b	5 da.	t, w
Oklahoma*	16c	16c	18	18	30 da., w	b	—	s
Oregon	17	17	18	18	—	—	3 da., w	—
Pennsylvania*	16d	16d	18	18	30 da.	b	3 da., w	t
Puerto Rico	18c, d, z	16c, d, z	21	21	—	b	—	—
Rhode Island*	18d	16d	18	18	—	bb	—	—
South Carolina*	16c	14c	18	18	—	—	1 da.	—
South Dakota	16c	16c	18	18	—	—	—	tt
Tennessee	16d	16d	18	18	—	—	3 da., cc	s
Texas*	14j, k	14j, k	18	18	—	—	—	s
Utah	14	14	18x	18x	30 da.	b	—	s
Vermont	16z	16z	18	18	30 da.	b	3 da., w	—
Virginia	16a, c	16a, c	18	18	—	b	—	t
Washington	17d	17d	18	18	—	bbb	3 da.	t
West Virginia	18c	18c	18	18	—	b	3 da., w	—
Wisconsin	16	16	18	18	—	b	5 da., w	s
Wyoming	16d	16d	18	18	—	bb	—	—
Dist. of Columbia*	16a	16a	18	18	30 da., w	b	3 da., w	—

*Indicates 1987 common-law marriage recognized; in many states, such marriages are only recognized if entered into many years before. (a) Parental consent not required if minor was previously married. (aa) No age limits. (b) Veneral diseases. (bb) Veneral diseases and Rubella (for female). In Colorado, Rubella for female under 45 and Rh type. (bbb) No medical exam required; however, applicants must file affidavit showing non-affliction of contagious venereal disease. (c) Younger parties may obtain license in case of pregnancy or birth of child. (cc) Unless parties are over 18 years of age. (d) Younger parties may obtain license in special circumstances. (e) Residents before expiration of 24-hour waiting period; non-residents formerly residents, before expiration of 96-hour waiting period; others 96 hours. (ee) License effective 1 day after issuance, unless court orders otherwise, valid for 60 days only. (f) If parties are under 16 years of age, proof of age and the consent of parents in person is required. If a parent is ill, an affidavit by the incapacitated parent and a physician's affidavit to that effect required. (ff) License valid for 180 days only. (g) Unless parties are 18 years of age or more, or female is pregnant, or applicants are the parents of a living child born out of wedlock. (gg) Notice to parents necessary if parties are under 21. (h) License valid for 90 days only. (j) Parental consent and/or permission of judge required. (k) Below age of consent parties need parental consent and permission of judge. (l) With each certificate issued to couples, a list of family planning agencies and services available to them is provided. (m) Mental incompetence, infectious tuberculosis, venereal diseases and Rubella (certain counties only). (n) Venereal diseases; test for sickle cell anemia given at request of examining physician. (nn) Tests for sickle cell anemia may be required for certain applicants. Marriage prohibited unless it is established that procreation is not possible. (p) If one or both parties are below the age for marriage without parental consent (3 day waiting period). (s) License valid for 30 days only. (t) License valid for 60 days only. (tt) License valid for 20 days only. (ttt) License valid for 65 days. (v) Parties must file notice of intention to marry with local clerk. (w) Waiting period may be avoided. (x) Authorizes counties to provide for premarital counseling as a requisite to issuance of license to persons under 19 and persons previously divorced. (y) Marriages by proxy are valid. (yy) Proxy marriages are valid under certain conditions. (z) Younger parties may marry with parental consent and/or permission of judge. In Connecticut, judicial approval. (zz) With consent of court.

Divorce Laws

Adapted from a revision by Gary N. Skoloff of the N.J. Bar, as of June 1, 1990. Important: almost all states also have other laws, as well as qualifications of the laws shown below and proposed divorce-reform laws pending. It would be wise to consult a lawyer in conjunction with the use of this chart.

Some grounds for absolute divorce

	Residence	Adultery	Cruelty	Desertion	Alcoholism	Impotency	Non-support	Insanity	Pregnancy at marriage	Bigamy	Separation	Felony conviction or imprisonment	Drug addiction	Fraud force, duress
PR	1 yr.	Yes	Yes	1 yr.	Yes	Yes	No	Yes	No	A	2 yrs.	Yes*	Yes	No
AL	6 mos.*	Yes	Phys. only	1 yr.	Yes	Yes*	2 yrs.	5 yrs.	Yes	A	2 yrs.*	2 yrs*	Yes	A
AK	*	Yes	Yes	1 yr.	1 yr.	Yes	No	18 mos.	No	A	No	Yes	Yes	A
AZ	90 da.	No	No	No	No	No	No	No	No	A	No	No	No	No
AR	60 da.	Yes	Yes	1 yr.	1 yr.	Yes	Yes	3 yrs.	No	No	3 yrs.	Yes	No	A
CA	6 mos.	No	No	No	No	A	No	Yes, A	No	A	No	No	No	A
CO	90 da.	No	No	No	No	No	No	No	No	A	No	No	No	A
CT	1 yr.*	Yes	Yes	1 yr.	Yes	A	No	5 yrs.	Yes*	A	18 mos.*	life*	No	Yes
DE	6 mos.	Yes	Yes	Yes	Yes	A	No	A	No	Yes	6 mos.	Yes	No	No
FL	6 mos.	No	No	No	No	No	No	3 yrs.	No	No	No	No	No	No
GA	6 mos.	Yes	Yes	1 yr.	Yes	Yes	No	2 yrs.	Yes	A	No	Yes*	Yes	Yes
HI	6 mos.*	No	No	No	No	No	No	A	No	A	2 yrs.*	No	No	A
ID	6 wks.	Yes	Yes	Yes	Yes	A	Yes	3 yrs.	Yes	A	5 yrs.	Yes	No	A
IL	90 da.	Yes	Yes	1 yr.	2 yrs.	Yes	No	No	No	Yes	2 yrs.*	Yes	2 yrs.	No
IN	6 mos.*	No	No	No	No	Yes	No	2 yrs.	No	A	No	Yes	No	No
IA	1 yr.*	No	No	No	No	A	No	A	No	A	No	No	No	No
KS	60 da.	No	No	No	No	No	Yes	2 yrs.	A	A	No	No	No	A
KY	180 da.	No	No	No	No	A	No	No	No	No	No	No	No	A
LA	1 yr.*	Yes	Yes	Yes	Yes	No	No	No	No	A	6 mos.	Yes*	No	A
ME	6 mos.*	Yes	Yes	3 yrs.	Yes	Yes	Yes	No	No	No	No	No	Yes	No
MD	1 yr.	Yes	No	1 yr.*	No	No	No	3 yrs.	No	A	1 yr.*	1 yr.*	No	No
MA	1 yr.*	Yes	Yes	1 yr.	Yes	Yes	Yes	No	No	A	No	5 yrs.	Yes	No
MI	180 da.	No	No	No	No	No	No	No	No	A	No	No	No	A
MN	180 da.	No	No	No	No	No	No	No	No	No	No	No	No	A
MS	6 mos.	Yes	Yes	1 yr.	Yes	Yes	No	3 yrs.	Yes	A	No	Yes*	Yes	A
MO	90 da.	No	No	No	No	No	No	No	No	No	No	No	No	A
MT	90 da.	No	No	No	No	A	No	No	No	No	180 da.*	No	No	A
NE	1 yr.*	No	No	No	No	A	No	No	No	A	No	No	No	A
NV	6 wks.	No	No	No	No	A	No	2 yrs.	No	A	1 yr.	No	No	A
NH	1 yr.*	Yes	Yes	2 yrs.	2 yrs.	Yes	2 yrs.	No	No	No	No	1 yr.*	No	No
NJ	1 yr.*	Yes	Yes	1 yr.	1 yr.	A	No	2 yrs.	No	A	18 mos.	18 mos.	1 yr.	No
NM	6 mos.	Yes	Yes	Yes*	No	No	No	No	No	No	No	No	No	No
NY	1 yr.*	Yes	Yes	1 yr.	No	A	No	No	No	A	1 yr.	3 yrs.	No	No
NC	6 mos.	No	No	No	No	A	No	3 yrs.	No	A	1 yr.	No	No	No
ND	6 mos.	Yes	Yes	1 yr.	1 yr.	A	1 yr.	5 yrs.*	No	A	No	Yes	1 yr.	A
OH	6 mos.	Yes	Yes	1 yr.	Yes	Yes	Yes	No	No	Yes, A	1 yr.	Yes	No	Yes
OK	6 mos.	Yes	Yes	1 yr.	Yes	Yes	Yes	5 yrs.	Yes	No	No	Yes	No	Yes
OR	6 mos.*	No	No	No	No	A	No	No	No	No	No	No	No	A
PA	6 mos.	Yes	Yes	1 yr.	No	No	No	18 mos.*	No	Yes	2 yrs.*	Yes	No	No
RI	1yr.	Yes	Yes	5 yrs.*	Yes	Yes	1 yr.	No	Yes	Yes	3 yrs.	No	Yes	No
SC	1 yr.*	Yes	Phys. only	1 yr.	Yes	No	No	No	No	A	1 yr.	No	Yes	No
SD	none*	Yes	Yes	1 yr.	1 yr.	A	1 yr.	5 yrs.	No	A	No	Yes	No	A*
TN	6 mos.	Yes	Yes	2 yrs.	Yes	Yes	Yes	No	Yes	Yes	2 yrs.	Yes	Yes	A
TX	6 mos.*	Yes	Yes	1 yr.	*	A	No	3 yrs.	No	A	3 yrs.	1 yr.	No	No
UT	3 mos.	Yes	Yes	1 yr.	Yes	Yes	Yes	Yes	No	A	3 yrs.*	Yes	No	A
VT	6 mos.*	Yes	Yes	7 yrs.*	No	No	Yes	5 yrs.	No	No	6 mos.	3 yrs.	No	A
VA	6 mos.*	Yes	Yes*	1 yr.	No	A	No	No	A	A	1 yr.*	1 yr.*	No	No
WA	bona fide res.	No	No	No	No	No	No	No	No	No	No	No	No	No
WV	1 yr.	Yes	Yes	6 mos.	Yes	A	A	3 yrs.	A	A	1 yr.	Yes	Yes	No
WI	6 mos.	No	No	No	No	A	No	No	No	A	1 yr.	No	No	A
WY	60 da.*	No	No	No	No	No	No	2 yrs.	No	A	No	No	No	A
DC	6 mos.	No	No	No	No	No	No	A*	No	A	6 mos.-1 yr.	No	No	A

(*) indicates qualification-check local statutes; (A) indicates grounds for annulment.

Wedding Anniversaries

The traditional names for wedding anniversaries go back many years in social usage. As such names as wooden, crystal, silver, and golden were applied it was considered proper to present the married pair with gifts made of these products or of something related. The list of traditional gifts, with a few allowable revisions in parentheses, is presented below, followed by modern gifts in bold face.

1st-Paper, **clocks**
2d-Cotton, **china**
3d-Leather, **crystal & glass**
4th-Linen (silk), **electrical appliances**
5th-Wood, **silverware**
6th-Iron, **wood**
7th-Wool (copper), **desk sets**
8th-Bronze, **linens & lace**
9th-Pottery (china), **leather**

10th-Tin (aluminum), **diamond jewelry**
11th-Steel, **fashion jewelry, accessories**
12th-Silk, **pearls or colored gems**
13th-Lace, **textiles & furs**
14th-Ivory, **gold jewelry**
15th-Crystal, **watches**
20th-China, **platinum**

25th-Silver, **sterling silver jubliee**
30th-Pearl, **diamond**
35th-Coral (jade), **jade**
40th-Ruby, **ruby**
45th-Sapphire, **sapphire**
50th-Gold, **gold**
55th-Emerald, **emerald**
60th-Diamond, **diamond**

Copyright Law of The United States

Source: Copyright Office, Library of Congress

What Copyright Is

Copyright is a form of protection provided by the laws of the United States (title 17, U.S. Code) to the authors of "original works of authorship" including literary, dramatic, musical, artistic, and certain other intellectual works. This protection is available to both published and unpublished works. Section 106 of the Copyright Act generally gives the owner of copyright the exclusive right to do and to authorize others to do the following:

• To *reproduce* the copyrighted work in copies or phonorecords;

• To prepare *derivative works* based upon the copyrighted work;

• To *distribute copies or phonorecords* of the copyrighted work to the public by sale or other transfer of ownership, or by rental, lease, or lending;

• To *perform the copyrighted work publicly*, in the case of literary, musical, dramatic, and choreographic works, pantomimes, and motion pictures and other audiovisual works; and

• To *display the copyrighted work publicly*, in the case of literary, musical, dramatic, and choreographic works, pantomimes, and pictorial, graphic, or sculptural works, including the individual images of a motion picture or other audiovisual work.

It is illegal for anyone to violate any of the rights provided by the Act to the owner of copyright. These rights, however, are not unlimited in scope. Sections 107 through 118 of the Copyright Act establish limitations on these rights. In some cases, these limitations are specified exemptions from copyright liability. One major limitation is the doctrine of "fair use," which is given a statutory basis by section 107 of the Act. In other instances, the limitation takes the form of a "compulsory license" under which certain limited uses of copyrighted works are permitted upon payment of specified royalties and compliance with statutory conditions.

Copyright protection subsists from the time the work is created in fixed form; that is, it is an incident of the process of authorship. The copyright in the work of authorship *immediately* becomes the property of the author who created it. Only the author or those deriving their rights from the author can rightfully claim copyright.

In the case of works made for hire, the employer and not the employee is presumptively considered the author. Section 101 of the copyright statute defines a "work made for hire" as:

(1) a work prepared by an employee within the scope of his or her employment; or-

(2) a work specially ordered or commissioned for use as a contribution to a collective work, as a part of a motion picture or other audiovisual work, as a translation, as a supplementary work, as a compilation, as an instructional text, as a test, as answer material for a test, or as an atlas, if the parties expressly agree in a written instrument signed by them that the work shall be considered a work made for hire.

The authors of a joint work are co-owners of the copyright in the work, unless there is an agreement to the contrary.

Copyright in each separate contribution to a periodical or other collective work is distinct from copyright in the collective work as a whole and vests initially with the author of the contribution.

Works published on or after January 1, 1978, are subject to protection under the copyright statute if, on the date of first publication, one or more of the authors is a national or domiciliary of the U.S., or is a national, domiciliary, or soverign authority of a foreign nation that is a party to a copyright treaty to which the U.S. is also a party, or is a stateless person, regardless of domicile, or if the work is first published either in the U.S. or in a foreign nation that on the date of first publication is a party to the Universal Copyright Convention or the Berne Union.

What Works Are Protected

Copyright protects "original works of authorship" that are fixed in a tangible form of expression. The fixation need not be directly perceptible, so long as it may be communicated with the aid of a machine or device. Copyrightable works include the following categories:

(1) literary works;

(2) musical works, including any accompanying words;

(3) dramatic works, including any accompanying music;

(4) pantomimes and choreographic works;

(5) pictorial, graphic, and sculptural works;

(6) motion pictures and other audiovisual works; and

(7) sound recordings.

These categories should be viewed quite broadly: for example, computer programs and most "compilations" are registrable as "literary works"; maps and architectural plans are registrable as "pictorial, graphic, and sculptural works."

What Is Not Protected By Copyright

Several categories of material are generally not eligible for statutory copyright protection. These include among others:

• Works that have *not* been fixed in a tangible form of expression. For example: choreographic works that have not been notated or recorded, or improvisational speeches or performances that have not been written or recorded.

• Titles, names, short phrases, and slogans; familiar symbols or designs; mere variations of typographic ornamentation, lettering, or coloring; mere listings of ingredients or contents.

• Ideas, procedures, methods, systems, processes, concepts, principles, discoveries, or devices, as distinguished from a description, explanation, or illustration.

• Works consisting *entirely* of information that is common property and containing no original authorship. For example: standard calendars, height and weight charts, tape measures and rulers, and lists or tables taken from public documents or other common sources.

Notice of Copyright

For works first published on and after March 1, 1989, use of the copyright notice is optional, though highly recommended. Before March 1, 1989, the use of the notice was mandatory on all published works, and any work first published before that date *must* bear a notice or risk loss of copyright protection.

Use of the notice is recommended because it informs the public that the work is protected by copyright, identifies the copyright owner, and shows the year of first publication. Furthermore, in the event that a work is infringed, if the work carries a proper notice, the court will not allow a defendant to claim "innocent infringement"—that is, that he or she did not realize that the work is protected. (A successful innocent infringement claim may result in a reduction in damages that the copyright owner would otherwise receive.)

The use of the copyright notice is the responsibility of the copyright owner and does not require advance permission from, or registration with, the Copyright Office.

For visually perceptible copies, the form of the notice consists of the following: © (the letter C in a circle), the word "Copyright," or "Copr.," and the year of first publication, and the name of the owner of copyright in the work. Example: © 1989 Judy Smith. The notice must be affixed in such manner and location as to give reasonable notice of the claim of copyright.

The notice of copyright prescribed for all published phonorecords of sound recordings consists of the symbol ℗ (the letter P in a circle), the year of first publication of the sound recording, and the name of the owner of copyright in the sound recording. Example ℗ 1990 XYZ Records, Inc. The notice on phonorecords may appear on the surface of the phonorecord or on the phonorecord label or container, provided the manner of placement and location give reasonable notice of the claim.

How Long Copyright Protection Endures

Works Originally Copyrighted on or After January 1, 1978

A work that is created (fixed in tangible form for the first time) on or after January 1, 1978, is automatically protected from the moment of its creation, and is ordinarily given a term enduring for the author's life, plus an additional 50 years after the author's death. In the case of "a joint work prepared by two or more authors who did not work for hire," the term lasts for 50 years after the last surviving author's death. For works made for hire, and for anonymous and pseudonymous works (unless the author's identity is revealed in Copyright Office records), the duration of copyright will be 75 years from publication or 100 years from creation, whichever is shorter.

Works that were created but not published or registered for copyright before January 1, 1978, have been automatically brought under the statute and are now given Federal copyright protection. The duration of copyright in these works will generally be computed in the same way as for works created on or after January 1, 1978: the life-plus-50 or 75/100-year terms will apply to them as well. The law provides that in no case will the term of copyright for works in this category expire before December 31, 2002, and for works published on or before December 31, 2002, the term of copyright will not expire before December 31, 2027.

Works Copyrighted Before January 1, 1978

Under the law in effect before 1978, copyright was secured either on the date a work was published or on the date of registration if the work was registered in unpublished form. In either case, the copyright endured for a first term of 28 years from the date it was secured. During the last (28th) year of the first term, the copyright was eligible for renewal. The current copyright law has extended the renewal term from 28 to 47 years for copyrights that were subsisting on January 1, 1978, making these works eligible for a total term of protection of 75 years. However, the copyright *must* be renewed to receive the 47-year period of added protection. This is accomplished by filing a properly completed Form RE accompanied by a $6 filing fee in the Copyright Office before the end of the 28th calendar year of the original term.

International Copyright Protection

There is no such thing as an "international copyright" that will automatically protect an author's writings throughout the entire world. Protection against unauthorized use in a particular country depends, basically, on the national laws of that country. However, most countries do offer protection to foreign works under certain conditions, and these conditions have been greatly simplified by international copyright treaties and conventions. The U.S. belongs to both global, multilateral copyright treaties—the Universal Copyright Convention (UCC) and the Berne Convention for the Protection of Literary and Artistic Works.

A U.S. author may obtain copyright protection in all countries that are members of the Berne Union and the Universal Copyright Convention. A work first published in the U.S. or another Berne Union country (or first published in a non-Berne Union country, followed by publication within 30 days in a Berne Union country) is eligible for protection in all Berne member countries. There are no special requirements. In UCC member countries, where no formalities are required, the works of U.S. authors are also automatically protected. Member countries whose laws impose formalities protect U.S. works if all published copies bear a Convention notice, which consists of the symbol ©, together with the name of the copyright owner and the year of publication. Example: © JOHN DOE 1990.

For a list of countries that maintain copyright relations with the U.S., write or call the Copyright Office and ask for Circular 38a.

Copyright Registration

Copyright registration is a legal formality intended to make a public record of the basic facts of a particular copyright and is not a condition of copyright protection. Even though registration is not generally a requirement for protection, the copyright law provides several inducements or advantages to encourage copyright owners to register. Among these advantages are the following:

• Registration establishes a public record of the copyright claim;

• Before an infringement suit may be filed in court, registration is necessary for works of U.S. origin and for foreign works not originating in a Berne Union country. (For more information on when a work is of U.S. origin, contact the Copyright Office);

• If made before or within 5 years of first publication, registration will establish prima facie evidence in court of the validity of the copyright and of the facts stated in the certificate; and

• If registration is made within 3 months after first publication of the work or prior to an infringement of the work, statutory damages and attorney's fees will be available to the copyright owner in court actions. Otherwise, only an award of actual damages and profits is available to the copyright owner.

Registration may be made at any time within the life of the copyright. When a work has been registered in unpublished form, it is not necessary to make another registration when the work becomes published (although the copyright owner may register the published edition, if desired).

The process of registration is quite simple. An appropriate form is requested from the Copyright Office and completed. It is returned to the Copyright Office along with a $10 ($20, effective 1/3/91) nonrefundable filing fee and the appropriate deposit(s) of the work for which registration is sought. In a common example—a published book—the deposit is two copies of the best edition of the book. A certificate of registration is sent once the paperwork is completed, a process that usually takes several months due to the large volume of registrations the Office must handle.

Although a copyright registration is not required, the Copyright Act establishes a mandatory deposit requirement for works published in the U.S. In general, the owner of copyright, or the owner of the exclusive right of publication in the work, has a legal obligation to deposit in the Copyright Office, within three months of publication in the U.S., two copies (or, in the case of sound recordings, two phonorecords) for the use of the Library of Congress. Failure to make the deposit can result in fines and other penalties, but does not affect copyright protection. Certain categories of works are *exempt entirely* from the mandatory deposit requirements, and the obligation is reduced for certain other categories.

Information on registration and application forms may be obtained free of charge by writing the Copyright Office, Information Section, LM-455, Library of Congress, Washington, DC 20559. Registration application forms and circulars may be ordered on a 24-hour basis by calling (202) 707-9100. Request Circular 1 for additional general information on copyright, including a list of which application forms to use when registering specific types of works.

Birthstones

Source: Jewelry Industry Council

Month	Ancient	Modern
January	Garnet	Garnet
February	Amethyst	Amethyst
March	Jasper	Bloodstone or Aquamarine
April	Sapphire	Diamond
May	Agate	Emerald
June	Emerald	Pearl, Moonstone, or Alexandrite
July	Onyx	Ruby
August	Carnelian	Sardonyx or Peridot
September	Chrysolite	Sapphire
October	Aquamarine	Opal or Tourmaline
November	Topaz	Topaz
December	Ruby	Turquoise or Zircon

Home Buyer's Glossary

Amortization: The gradual repayment of a mortgage over time, usually according to a predetermined schedule.

Appraisal: An opinion or estimate of the value of property, usually made by lenders before they will determine how much of a mortgage they will extend.

Assumable mortgage: The purchaser takes ownership of real estate encumbered by an existing mortgage and assumes responsibility as the guarantor for the unpaid balance of the mortgage.

Balloon payment: The final payment on a loan, usually substantially larger than previous payments, which repays the loan in full.

Binder: A preliminary and temporary agreement between the seller and the buyer, generally agreeing to the price of a house before a formal contract.

Broker: Usually, a licensed agent of, and paid by, the seller to serve as an intermediary in real estate transactions.

Closing: The day of judgment, when after writing numerous checks to cover various fees, the title passes to the buyer.

Commission: The fee paid by a seller to a broker for the sale of the house. Fee is negotiable.

Condominium: A form of ownership, not a kind of development, in which the owner gets title to a housing unit and an interest in the common areas.

Cooperative: A type of ownership in which buyers get shares in the cooperative corporation that owns the building. Those shares give the buyer a proprietary lease on an apartment in that building.

Deed: A written document that conveys title in the property.

Equity: The value of property minus the mortgage and other liens against it.

Escrow: Money paid monthly to the lender, along with the mortgage payment, for use in paying taxes and sometimes insurance. The lender keeps the funds separately and pays bills when due.

Foreclosure: Forced sale of property to meet debt obligations; usually to a lending or taxing institution.

Freddie Mac: The Federal Home Loan Mortgage Corp., a major secondary mortgage market agency that buys mortgages from lenders, allowing them to make new loans with the proceeds.

FHA: The Federal Housing Administration, a division of the Department of Housing and Urban Development that insures, but does not make, mortgages.

Fannie Mae: Federal National Mortgage Association, the largest secondary mortgage agency.

Ginnie Mae: Government National Mortgage Association, a government-owned secondary market agency that buys FHA-insured loans from lenders.

Indexing: Adjusting the interest rate on a loan in accordance with the movements of an index or economic indicator, i.e., the U.S. Treasury bill rate or the consumer price index.

Interest: Money paid for the use of money. There are two kinds of interest. Simple interest is interest that is earned and paid. Compound interest is the accumulated interest that is added to the principal amount.

Lien: A right to property obtained as collateral to a loan or debt. A mortgage is a lien.

Mortgage: A written pledge of property as collateral for a loan.

The most common type of mortgage is the *fixed rate mortgage*, in which the monthly payments remain the same over the life of the loan; and the *adjustable rate mortgage* (ARM) where the interest rate is tied to a financial index (the one-year Treasury bill rate and the savings and loan cost-of-funds index are most common). With an ARM, the monthly payments usually vary over the life of the loan. In some cases, the total number of monthly payments can be increased or decreased with the amount remaining the same. In 1989, nearly half of new mortgages were ARMs.

Another type of mortgage is the *graduated payment mortgage*, which has a fixed interest rate but lower initial payments, usually for the first 5 years of the loan. This type of mortgage is advantageous to the first-time homeowner. There is also the *shared-appreciation mortgage*, in which a borrower agrees to share the appreciation of the property with the lender in return for a lower interest rate. *Reverse mortgages* allow elderly homeowners to convert some of their accumulated housing equity into cash.

Origination Fee: A fee paid by a borrower for the cost of evaluating and documenting a loan.

Points: Additional payments made by a borrower to a lender; a point equals 1 percent of the loan.

Prepayment penalty: An extra fee charged for paying off a mortgage before it is due.

Principal: The total amount of a mortgage debt. The amount upon which the interest is computed.

Title: Evidence of a person's ownership of a piece of property.

Median Price of Existing Single-Family Homes

Source: National Association of Realtors

The median sale price for existing single-family homes rose 5.2 percent in the first quarter of 1990 from the same period in 1989.

City[1]	Median price first quarter 1989	1990	Pct. chng.	City[1]	Median price First quarter 1989	1990	Pct. chng.
Akron, Oh.	$56,000	$65,800	+17.5	Los Angeles, Cal.	$201,000	211,500	+6.0
Albuquerque, N.M.	82,000	82,800	+1.0	Louisville, Ky.	56,700	59,300	+3.0
Anaheim/Santa Ana, Cal.	237,900	243,600	+3.9	Madison, Wis.	74,700	78,700	+5.4
Atlanta, Ga.	80,300	85,300	+6.2	Memphis, Tenn.	77,000	77,900	+1.2
Baltimore, Md.	92,200	104,200	+13.0	Miami/Hialeah, Fla.	82,600	90,200	+8.7
Baton Rouge, La.	61,100	64,000	+4.7	Milwaukee, Wis.	74,500	81,800	+7.6
Birmingham, Ala.	77,300	77,500	+0.3	Minneapolis/St. Paul, Minn.	85,900	87,800	+2.2
Boston, Mass.	178,500	182,300	+3.4	Mobile, Ala.	50,900	56,700	+6.5
Buffalo, N.Y.	68,700	77,300	+12.5	Nashville/Davidson, Tenn.	79,600	80,800	+1.5
Charleston, S.C.	72,400	74,400	+2.8	New Haven, Conn.	166,700	148,300	−11.0
Charlotte, N.C.	85,200	89,600	+5.2	New Orleans, La.	71,200	67,700	−1.0
Chattanooga, Tenn.	65,600	66,800	+1.8	New York, N.Y.	181,700	173,700	−4.9
Chicago, Ill.	99,300	112,300	+12.8	Oklahoma City, Okla.	52,300	50,600	−3.3
Cincinnati, Oh.	73,200	78,000	+7.1	Omaha, Neb.	60,900	64,800	+9.3
Cleveland, Oh.	69,400	77,100	+11.1	Orlando, Fla.	79,100	79,900	+1.0
Columbia, S.C.	71,900	74,900	+4.2	Philadelphia, Pa.	100,400	98,400	+2.1
Columbus, Oh.	73,900	79,200	+7.2	Phoenix, Ariz.	78,500	82,300	+4.8
Corpus Christi, Tex.	63,200	62,500	−1.1	Pittsburgh, Pa.	62,400	68,600	+9.9
Dallas, Tex.	88,400	94,000	+4.7	Portland, Ore.	67,100	75,600	+12.7
Daytona Beach, Fla.	59,500	62,400	+4.9	Providence, R.I.	128,800	127,000	−1.4
Denver, Col.	80,800	84,500	+4.6	Raleigh/Durham, N.C.	102,000	108,500	+6.4
Des Moines, Ia.	57,300	62,300	+11.2	Sacramento, Cal.	100,300	127,700	+27.3
Detroit, Mich.	71,900	75,500	+6.5	St. Louis, Mo.	81,400	82,600	+8.1
El Paso, Tex.	57,200	62,100	+8.6	San Antonio, Tex.	60,800	62,900	+2.1
Grand Rapids, Mich.	59,600	67,500	+14.0	San Diego, Cal.	163,900	182,300	+6.4
Hartford, Conn.	165,500	157,100	−5.1	San Francisco, Cal.	243,900	262,200	+7.5
Honolulu, Hi.	236,000	290,400	+18.5	Seattle, Wash.	99,700	136,100	+36.5
Houston, Tex.	62,900	70,700	+12.4	Spokane, Wash.	50,200	52,000	+3.6
Indianapolis, Ind.	68,000	73,200	+7.6	Syracuse, N.Y.	76,900	78,100	+1.6
Jacksonville, Fla.	65,900	67,300	+2.1	Tampa, Fla.	71,700	74,300	+8.3
Kansas City, Mo.	73,800	73,900	+0.1	Toledo, Oh.	57,700	61,300	+6.2
Knoxville, Tenn.	69,800	73,600	+5.4	Tulsa, Okla.	60,500	62,000	+2.5
Las Vegas, Nev.	80,500	88,600	+10.1	Washington, D.C.	143,700	144,700	+0.7
Little Rock, Ark.	63,400	NA	NA	U.S. average	$91,200	$95,900	+5.2

(1) All areas are metropolitan statistical areas as defined by the U.S. Office of Management and Budget. They include the named central city and surrounding suburban areas.

Housing Affordability

Source: National Association of Realtors

	Median-priced existing home	Average mortgage rate	Monthly principal and interest payment	Payment as percentage of median income		Median-priced existing home	Average mortgage rate	Monthly principal and interest payment	Payment as percentage of median income
1981	$66,400	15.12%	$677	36.3%	1986	$80,300	10.25%	$563	23.0%
1982	67,800	15.38	702	35.9	1987	85,600	9.28	565	21.8
1983	70,300	12.85	616	30.1	1988	90,600	9.31	599	22.5
1984	72,400	12.49	618	28.2	1989	93,200	10.59	687	25.2
1985	75,500	11.74	609	26.2	1990	97,500	10.16	694	24.3

Note: The average mortgage rate is based on the effective rate of loans closed on existing homes monitored by the Federal Home Loan Bank Board.
The 1988 and 1989 numbers are for June.

Income Needed to Get a Mortgage

Source: National Association of Realtors

The following shows the minimum annual gross income needed for various size home loans at different rates. The figures are based on a 30-year loan and assume that the borrower's monthly payments can't exceed 28% of gross income, the ceiling most lenders use. The figures do not include property taxes and insurance as part of the monthly payment.

Interest rate (Percent)	$50,000	$75,000	$100,000 income needed	$150,000	$200,000
8	$15,724	$23,586	$31,447	$47,171	$62,895
8½	16,477	24,715	32,954	49,430	65,907
9	17,242	25,863	34,484	51,726	68,968
9½	18,018	27,028	36,037	54,055	72,074
10	18,085	28,208	37,611	56,415	75,221
10½	19,602	29,403	39,203	58,805	78,406
11	20,407	30,611	40,814	61,221	81,628
11½	21,221	31,831	42,441	63,662	84,883
12	22,042	33,063	44,084	66,125	88,167
12½	22,870	34,305	45,740	68,610	91,479
13	23,704	35,556	47,409	71,113	94,817

Tips on Cutting Energy Costs in Your Home

Source: Con Edison Conservation Services, New York City

Heating

In many homes, in areas where temperatures drop during the winter, more energy is used for heating than anything else. Installing the right amount of insulation, storm windows and doors, caulking and weatherstripping pays off. Also consider the following advice:

- Make sure the thermostat and heating system are in good working order. An annual checkup is recommended.
- If your heating system has air filters, make sure they are clean.
- Set the thermostat no higher than 68 degrees. When no one is home, or when everyone is sleeping, the setting should be turned down to 60 degrees or lower. An automatic setback thermostat can raise and lower your home's temperature at times you specify.
- Close off and do not heat unused areas.
- Cover all air conditioner units.
- If you do not have conventional storm windows or doors, use kits to make plastic storm windows.
- Special glass fireplace doors help keep a room's heat from being drawn up the chimney when the fire is burning low. Close the damper when a fireplace is not in use.
- Use the sun's heat by opening blinds and draperies on sunny days.
- Keep radiators and warm air outlets clean. Do not block them with furniture or draperies.

Water Heater

In many homes, the water heater ranks second only to the heating system in total energy consumption.

- Put an insulation blanket on your water heater; when you go on vacation turn it to a minimum setting.
- If you have a dishwasher, set the water heater thermostat no higher than 140 degrees. If not, or if you have a separate water heater for baths, a setting as low as 110 degrees may be sufficient.
- Run the dishwasher and clothes washer only when you have a full load. Use warm or cold water cycles for laundry when you can.
- Take showers instead of tub baths. About half as much hot water is used for a shower.
- Install a water-saver shower head.
- Install aerators or restrictors on all your sink faucets.
- Do not leave the hot water running when rinsing dishes or shaving. Plug and partially fill the basin, or fill a pan with water.
- Use the right size water heater for your needs. An oversized unit wastes energy heating unneeded water. An undersized unit will not deliver all the hot water you want when you need it.
- When shopping for a water heater, look for the yellow-and-black federal EnergyGuide label to learn the estimated yearly energy cost of a unit.

Air Conditioning

- Clean or replace the filter in an air conditioner at the beginning of the cooling season. Then check it once a month and clean or change the filter if necessary. A dirty filter blocks the flow of air.
- Adjust the temperature control setting to provide a room temperature no lower than 78 degrees. Use a good wall thermometer to tell which setting will provide the desired temperature.

- Close draperies and shades to block out the sun's heat.
- When shopping for a new room air conditioner, look for the yellow-and-black federal EnergyGuide label to learn the Energy Efficiency Rating (EER) and the estimated yearly operating cost. The higher the EER, the less electricity will be used for a cooling job.
- Read the manufacturer's instructions; follow closely.
- If you have a central air conditioning system, run your hands along the ducts while it is operating to check for air leaks. Repair leaks with duct tape. Make sure the duct system is properly insulated.
- On many days, a window fan can cool an apartment as effectively as an air conditioner, and it is less costly.

Refrigerators and Freezers

The refrigerator operates 24 hours a day, every day, so it is one of the biggest users of energy in the home all year.

- Keep the condenser coils clean. The coils are on the back or at the bottom of the refrigerator. Carefully wipe, vacuum or brush the coils to remove dust and dirt at least once a year.
- Examine door gaskets and hinges regularly for air leaks. The doors should fit tightly. To check, place a piece of paper between the door and the cabinet. Close the door with normal force, then try to pull the paper straight out. There should be a slight resistance. Test all around the door, including the hinge side. If there are any places where the paper slides out easily, you need to adjust the hinges or replace the gasket, or both.
- Pause before opening your refrigerator door. Think of everything you will need before you open the door so you do not have to go back several times. When you open the door, close it quickly to keep the cool air in.
- Adjust the temperature-setting dial of the refrigerator as the manufacturer recommends. Use a thermometer to check the temperature (38 to 40 degrees is usually recommended for the refrigerator; zero degrees for the freezer). Settings that are too cold waste electricity.
- If you have a manual-defrost refrigerator, do not allow the ice to build up more than $1/4$ inch thick.
- Keep your refrigerator well-stocked but allow room for air to circulate around the food.
- The freezer, on the other hand, should be packed full. If necessary, fill empty spaces with bags of ice cubes or fill milk cartons with water and freeze.
- When you are going to be away from home for a week or more, turn off and unplug the refrigerator, empty and clean it, and prop the door open.
- If you are buying a new refrigerator, look for one with a humid-dry ("power-saver") switch. This switch is used to turn off "anti-sweat" heaters in the doors to save electricity when the heaters are not needed.
- When shopping for a new refrigerator or freezer, eliminate those too large for your needs; look for the federal EnergyGuide label to help you select an efficient unit.

Cooking

- Cook as many dishes in the oven at one time as you can instead of cooking each separately. If recipes call for slightly different temperatures, say 325, 350, and 375 degrees, pick the middle temperature of 350 to cook all 3 dishes and remove each dish as it's done.

Tips for Fuel-Efficient Driving
Source: U.S. Environmental Protection Agency

When Buying a New Vehicle

- **Buy the type of vehicle that best suits your needs.** Check the federal *Gas Mileage Guide,* available free at all auto dealerships, to compare the fuel economy of similar models. In general, *larger displacement engines and higher horsepower ratings will result in lower fuel economy.* The additional power and torque may be useful for mountain driving or trailer towing situations, but your fuel economy will suffer during almost all types of driving. *Avoid unnecessary optional equipment* (especially heavy options such as four-wheel drive and options such as air conditioning that tax the engine). Extra equipment adds weight and decreases the fuel economy of the vehicle. Beware of "sport" packages, which often include fuel-guzzling features such as energy robbing tires that are not reflected by *Guide* mileage values.

Conserving Fuel with your Current Vehicle:

- **Drive your vehicle wisely.** *Avoid idles* of more than one minute (turn off your engine in traffic jams, limit vehicle warm-ups in winter, park and go in instead of using drive-up lanes at restaurants and banks). *Go easy on the brakes and gas pedal* (anticipate stops and avoid "jack-rabbit" starts). Pay attention to speed. *You can improve your fuel economy about 15 percent by driving 55 mph rather than*

65 mph. Put your vehicle's transmission into overdrive or a "fuel economy" position when cruising on the highway. If you have manual transmission, follow recommended shift guidelines or heed your shift indicator light. *Do not carry unneeded items* that add weight. Reduce drag by placing items inside the vehicle or trunk rather than on roof racks. *Use air conditioning only when necessary.*

- **Maintain your vehicle regularly.** *Periodic tune-ups improve vehicle fuel economy and performance.* Dragging brakes, low transmission fluid levels, out of tune engines, and old plugged fuel or air filters all hurt fuel economy. *Inflate tires* to maximum recommended pressure and perform periodic *wheel alignments. Use energy conserving oils* which increase fuel economy by reducing internal engine friction (the best are labeled "Energy Conserving II").

- **Keep track of your vehicle's fuel economy.** A marked increase in the amount of fuel you use could indicate the need for a tune-up, or serve as an early signal for necessary repairs.

- **Use your vehicle effectively.** *Use your vehicle only when necessary.* Combine errands into one trip. If you have access to more than one vehicle, drive the one that's most fuel efficient whenever possible. Consider carpooling, bicycling, walking, or public transportation.

Fuel Economy in 1991 Cars: Comparative Miles per Gallon
Source: U.S. Environmental Protection Agency

Fuel economy estimates for 1991 model-year vehicles rank the 1,875-pound subcompact Geo Metro XFI as the most fuel efficient car at 53 miles per gallon (mpg) for city driving and 58 mpg on the highway. The car is made by Suzuki and sold by General Motors. The Lamborghini DB132/Diablo receives the lowest fuel economy rating of 9 mpg city/14 mpg highway, and purchasers will pay a $3,200 gas guzzler tax. MPG ratings appear on window stickers of all new cars prior to sale. By choosing models that obtain fuel economies of just one mile per gallon more than the average for each vehicle class, the Environmental Protection Agency says, consumers could save more than $400 in fuel costs over the life of the vehicle.

Model	Highest Mileage by Class Engine Description Size/No. Cylinders	Trans.	City/Hwy.	Avg. Annual Fuel Cost	Model	Lowest Mileage by Class Engine Description Size/No. Cylinders	Trans.	City/Hwy.	Avg. Annual Fuel Cost
Two Seaters					**Two Seaters**				
Honda					Lamborghini:				
Civic CRX	1.5-liter				DB132/	5.7-liter			
HF	/4	M5	49/52	$375	Diablo	/12	M5	9/14	$1,977
Minicompact					**Minicompact**				
Nissan	1.6-liter				Porsche	5.0-liter			
NX Coupe	/4	M5	28/38	585	928 S4	/8	M5	13/19	1,451
Subcompact					**Subcompact**				
Geo Metro	1.0-liter				Rolls Royce:				
XFI	/3	M5	53/58	341	Corniche	6.8-liter			
					III	/8	A3	10/13	1,977
					Bentley	6.8-liter			
Compact					Continental	/8	A3	10/13	1,977
Volkswagen	1.6-liter				**Compact**				
	/4	M5	37/43	450	BMW M5	3.5-liter			
Jetta (Diesel)						/6	M5	11/20	1,553
Mid-size					**Mid-size**				
Chrysler					Rolls Royce:				
Acclaim	2.5-liter				Silver	6.8-liter			
	/4	M5	24/34	669	Spirit	/8	A3	10/13	1,977
Spirit	2.5-liter				Bentley	6.8-liter			
	/4	M5	24/34	669	TurboR	/8	A3	10/13	1,977
Large					Bentley	6.8-liter			
Saab 9000	2.3-liter				8/	/8	A3	10/13	1,977
	/4	M5	20/26	853	Mulsanne S				
					Large				
					Cadillac				
Small Station Wag.					Brougham	5.0-liter			
Honda	1.5-liter					/8	L4	16/25	986
Civic	/4	M5	31/35	568	**Small Station Wag.**				
Wagon					Toyota				
Mid-Size Station Wag.					Camry	2.5-liter			
Volvo					Wag.	/6	L4	18/24	892
240	2.3-liter				**Mid-Size Station Wag.**				
Wagon	/4	M5	22/28	782	Mercedes				
740	2.3-liter				300TE-	3.0-liter			
Wagon	/4	M5	22/28	782	4MATIC	/6	A4	16/20	1,279
Large Station Wag.					**Large Station Wag.**				
Ford					General Motors				
Grand	5.0-liter				Caprice	5.0-liter			
Marquis	/8	L4	17/24	938	Wagon	/8	L4	26/25	986
LTD					Custom	5.0-liter			
Crown	5.0-liter				Cruiser	/8	L4	16/25	986
Vic	/8	L4	17/24	938	Road-	5.0-liter			
					master	/8	L4	16/25	986

*Transmission Types: M5 = Manual 5-speed; A3 = Automatic 3-speed; L4 = Automatic w lockup feature.

VITAL STATISTICS

Source: National Center for Health Statistics, U.S. Department of Health and Human Services

Births

According to provisional statistics for the first quarter of 1990, there were 986,000 live births, 5 percent more than the estimated number reported for the same 3-month period in 1989 (937,000). The birth rate (16.0) was 4 percent above the rate for the first quarter of 1989 (15.4); the fertility rate (68.2) was 5 percent higher than the rate for the comparable period in 1989 (65.2).

During the 12 months ending with March 1990, there were an estimated 4,070,000 live births, 4 percent more than the number reported for the comparable period ending a year earlier (3,912,000). The birth rate was 16.3, 3 percent above the rate for the 12 months ending with March 1989 (15.9).

Marriages

The total number of marriages for the first quarter of 1990 was 422,000. The marriage rate was 6.8 per 1,000 population, 3 percent above the rate for the first quarter of 1989 (6.6). Marriage rates for the first quarter of the year typically are lower than rates for the rest of the year.

During the 12 months ending with March 1990, an estimated 2,423,000 couples married, an increase of 48,000 over the number who married during the previous 12-month period. The marriage rate for the 12 months ending with March 1990 was 9.7 per 1,000 population, compared with 9.6 for the previous 12-month period.

Divorces

A total of 299,000 couples divorced during the first quarter of 1990. The divorce rate was 4.9 per 1,000 population, 4 percent above the rate for the first quarter of 1989 (4.7).

During the 12 months ending with March 1990, an estimated 1,177,000 couples divorced. The divorce rate was 4.7

per 1,000 population, a decline from 4.8 during the comparable period a year earlier.

Deaths

According to provisional statistics, there were 586,000 deaths during the first quarter of 1990, 2 percent more than for the first quarter of 1989 (574,000). The death rate was 9.5 per 1,000 population, 1 percent higher than the Jan.-March 1989 rate. Among the 586,000 deaths for the first quarter of 1990, were 9,900 deaths at ages under 1 year, yielding an infant mortality rate of 9.8 per 1,000 live births, 5 percent lower than the rate of 10.3 for the first quarter of 1989.

The death rate for the 12 months ending with March 1990 (8.7 deaths per 1,000 population) was the same as the rate for the comparable 12-month period a year earlier. The infant mortality rate for this 12-month-period was 9.6 per 1,000 live births, 2 percent lower than the rate of 9.8 for the 12 months ending with March 1989.

Provisional Statistics
12 months ending with March

	Number		Rate*	
	1990	1989	1990	1989
Live births	4,070,000	3,923,000	16.3	15.9
Deaths	2,167,000	2,152,000	8.7	8.7
Natural increase.	1,903,000	1,771,000	7.6	7.2
Marriages	2,423,000	2,375,000	9.7	9.6
Divorces	1,177,000	1,192,000	4.7	4.8
Infant deaths. . .	38,900	38,400	9.6	9.8
Population base (in millions)			249.0	246.3

*Per 1,000 population
Note: Rates are based on the 1980 Census of Population.

Annual Report for the Year 1989 (Provisional Statistics)

Highlights

The provisional number of live births in 1989 was higher than the number reported in 1988, and was the largest number reported since 1964. The birth rate and the fertility rate also increased in 1989 and were the highest since 1982.

In 1989 the provisional number of marriages was 2,404,000, an increase of 1 percent over 2,389,000 in 1989. The marriage rate remained the same as in 1988 (9.7). The number of divorces decreased by 20,000 from 1988 to 1989 (1,183,000 to 1,163,000) and the divorce rate dropped 2 percent, from 4.8 to 4.7.

Births

During 1989 an estimated 4,021,000 babies were born in the United States, 3 percent more than in 1988 (3,913,000). This was the largest number reported since 1964. The birth rate was 16.2 per 1,000 total population, 2 percent above the rate for 1988 (15.9). The fertility rate was 68.8 live births per 1,000 women aged 15-44 years, 2 percent higher than 1988 (67.3) rate.

The birth and fertility rates, which increased dramatically in the 1940's and 1950's, followed by rapid declines in the 1960's and early 1970's, have been fairly steady since 1975. The current birth and fertility rates are the highest since 1982. The 3-percent number of births increase in the general fertility rate between 1988 and 1989 is the result of a 2-per-

cent increase in the fertility rate and of less than a 1-percent increase in the number of women in the childbearing ages. Within the childbearing ages, the number of women 15-29 years declined, while the number of women 30-44 years increased, which suggests an increase in some age-specific birth rates.

Deaths

The provisional count of deaths in the United States during 1989 totaled 2,155,000, about 16,000 fewer than in 1988. The provisional death rate of 8.7 deaths per 1,000 population was 1 percent lower than the provisional rate for 1988 (8.8).

The infant mortality rate for 1989 was 9.7 per 1,000 live births, compared with the rate of 9.9 for 1988. It was the lowest rate ever recorded in the U.S.

Marriages and Divorces

The number of marriages in 1989 was 2,404,000, 1 percent more than in 1988. The national marriage rate remained relatively stable compared with 1988, increasing 1 percent. The marriage rate per 1,000 population for 1989 was identical to the 1988 rate.

According to provisional data, 1,163,000 couples were divorced during 1989, 20,000 fewer than in 1988. The divorce rate for 1989, 4.7 per 1,000 population, was a 2-percent drop from the rate for 1988.

Births and Deaths in the U.S.

Refers only to events occurring within the U.S., including Alaska and Hawaii beginning in 1960. Excludes fetal deaths. Rates per 1,000 population enumerated as of April 1 for 1960, and 1970; estimated as of July 1 for all other years. Beginning 1970 excludes births and deaths occurring to nonresidents of the U.S.

Year	Births Total number	Rate	Deaths Total number	Rate
1955.	4,097,000	25.0	1,528,717	9.3
1960.	4,257,850	23.7	1,711,962	9.5
1965.	3,760,358	19.4	1,828,136	9.4
1970.	3,731,386	18.4	1,921,031	9.5
1975.	3,144,198	14.6	1,892,879	8.8
1980.	3,612,258	15.9	1,986,000	8.7
1985.	3,749,000	15.7	2,084,000	8.7
1989.	4,021,000	16.2	2,155,000	8.7

Births and Deaths by States and Regions

Source: National Center for Health Statistics.

	Births 1988 Number	Births 1988 Rate	Births 1989 Number	Births 1989 Rate	Deaths 1988 Number	Deaths 1988 Rate	Deaths 1989 Number	Deaths 1989 Rate
New England	195,022	15.0	202,027	15.5	121,658	9.4	117,320	9.0
Maine	15,961	13.2	16,842	13.8	11,331	9.4	11,029	9.0
New Hampshire	17,186	15.8	17,946	16.2	8,658	8.0	8,391	7.6
Vermont	8,538	15.3	7,920	14.0	5,267	9.5	4,501	7.9
Massachusetts	91,988	15.6	96,457	16.3	57,715	9.8	55,472	9.4
Rhode Island	14,481	14.6	15,302	15.3	9,930	10.0	9,757	9.8
Connecticut	46,868	14.5	47,560	14.7	28,757	8.9	28,170	8.7
Middle Atlantic	558,553	14.8	577,960	15.3	373,228	9.9	363,176	9.6
New York	277,291	15.5	291,145	16.2	174,299	9.7	169,634	9.5
New Jersey	114,118	14.8	116,554	15.1	71,773	9.3	69,393	9.0
Pennsylvania	167,144	13.9	170,261	14.1	127,156	10.6	124,149	10.3
East North Central	637,327	15.1	646,830	15.3	374,467	8.9	368,631	8.7
Ohio	165,258	15.2	162,793	14.9	100,625	9.3	98,224	9.0
Indiana	81,421	14.7	82,764	14.8	50,396	9.1	49,421	8.8
Illinois	180,526	15.5	186,500	16.0	101,165	8.7	100,686	8.6
Michigan	140,229	15.2	142,673	15.4	78,882	8.5	77,660	8.4
Wisconsin	69,893	14.4	72,100	14.8	43,399	8.9	42,640	8.8
West North Central	265,917	15.0	265,762	14.9	167,896	9.5	164,478	9.2
Minnesota	66,579	15.5	66,593	15.3	35,246	8.2	34,484	7.9
Iowa	38,506	13.6	37,241	13.1	27,753	9.8	25,201	8.9
Missouri	75,844	14.8	80,126	15.5	54,495	10.6	55,648	10.8
North Dakota	11,433	17.1	10,862	16.5	6,055	9.1	5,865	8.9
South Dakota	11,297	15.8	10,991	15.4	6,564	9.2	6,535	9.1
Nebraska	24,363	15.2	24,317	15.1	15,123	9.4	15,226	9.5
Kansas	37,895	15.2	35,632	14.2	22,660	9.1	21,519	8.6
South Atlantic	655,130	15.4	678,872	15.7	390,957	9.2	395,197	9.2
Delaware	10,915	16.5	11,492	17.1	5,866	8.9	5,968	8.9
Maryland	68,412	14.8	67,550	14.4	37,789	8.2	38,078	8.1
District of Columbia	19,290	31.3	22,549	37.3	8,972	14.5	9,862	16.3
Virginia	90,498	15.0	93,453	15.3	46,984	7.8	46,342	7.6
West Virginia	22,585	12.0	23,079	12.4	19,649	10.5	19,472	10.5
North Carolina	98,183	15.1	102,817	15.6	58,164	9.0	57,859	8.8
South Carolina	53,285	15.4	55,214	15.7	28,348	8.2	28,958	8.2
Georgia	107,108	16.9	109,905	17.1	52,815	8.3	53,761	8.4
Florida	184,854	15.0	192,813	15.2	132,370	10.7	133,897	10.6
East South Central	230,975	15.1	229,994	14.9	149,298	9.7	143,249	9.3
Kentucky	51,109	13.7	52,591	14.1	35,557	9.5	34,005	9.1
Tennessee	79,140	16.2	76,780	15.5	50,720	10.4	47,454	9.6
Alabama	59,611	14.5	58,360	14.2	39,016	9.5	37,420	9.1
Mississippi	41,115	15.7	42,263	16.1	24,005	9.2	24,370	9.3
West South Central	463,380	17.2	451,625	16.7	217,605	8.1	215,141	8.0
Arkansas	34,554	14.4	34,997	14.5	25,278	10.6	24,519	10.2
Louisiana	75,170	17.1	68,813	15.7	38,640	8.8	36,221	8.3
Oklahoma	46,874	14.5	46,455	14.4	29,174	9.0	28,779	8.9
Texas	306,782	18.2	301,360	17.7	124,514	7.4	125,622	7.4
Mountain	235,526	17.7	235,645	17.4	96,664	7.3	96,645	7.2
Montana	11,356	14.1	11,394	14.1	6,736	8.4	6,682	8.3
Idaho	15,564	15.5	15,459	15.2	7,391	7.4	7,150	7.1
Wyoming	6,697	14.0	6,491	13.7	3,042	6.4	3,065	6.5
Colorado	53,014	16.1	52,863	15.9	21,712	6.6	21,764	6.6
New Mexico	27,438	18.2	27,324	17.9	10,476	7.0	10,525	6.9
Arizona	65,608	18.8	67,609	19.0	28,446	8.2	28,882	8.1
Utah	37,260	22.0	36,208	21.2	9,695	5.7	9,483	5.6
Nevada	18,589	17.6	18,297	16.5	9,166	8.7	9,094	8.2
Pacific	653,886	17.5	705,189	18.4	227,784	7.4	290,059	7.6
Washington	68,242	14.7	73,261	15.4	36,372	7.8	36,341	7.6
Oregon	41,305	14.9	43,835	15.5	24,868	9.0	27,469	9.7
California	514,247	18.2	557,003	19.2	208,161	7.4	217,489	7.5
Alaska	11,037	21.1	11,545	21.9	2,059	3.9	2,052	3.9
Hawaii	19,055	17.4	19,545	17.6	6,324	5.8	6,708	6.0

Infant Mortality Rates by Race and Sex

Source: National Center for Health Statistics

	All races Both sexes	All races Male	All races Female	White Both sexes	White Male	White Female	Black Both sexes	Black Male	Black Female
1960	26.0	29.3	22.6	22.9	26.0	19.6	44.3	49.1	39.4
1970	20.0	22.4	17.5	17.8	20.0	15.4	32.6	36.2	29.0
1980	12.6	13.9	11.2	11.0	12.3	9.6	21.4	23.3	19.4
1981	11.9	13.1	10.7	10.5	11.7	9.2	20.0	21.7	18.3
1982	11.5	12.8	10.2	10.1	11.2	8.9	19.6	21.5	17.7
1983	11.2	12.3	10.0	9.7	10.8	8.6	19.2	21.1	17.2
1984	10.8	11.9	9.6	9.4	10.5	8.3	18.4	19.8	16.9
1985	10.6	11.9	9.3	9.3	10.6	8.0	18.2	19.9	16.5
1986	10.4	11.5	9.1	8.9	10.0	7.8	18.0	20.0	16.0
1987	10.1	1.2	8.9	8.6	9.6	7.6	17.9	19.6	16.0

Estimated Death Rates for Selected Causes, 1988-89

Source: Natl. Center for Health Statistics. U.S. Depart. of Health and Human Services

Cause of death	Rate* 1988	Rate*ᴾ 1989	Cause of death	Rate* 1988	Rate*ᴾ 1989
All causes	884.2	862.0	Influenza and pneumonia.	31.3	29.8
Viral hepatitis	0.5	0.6	Influenza	0.8	0.5
Tuberculosis, all forms	0.8	0.7	Pneumonia	30.5	29.3
Septicemia.	8.5	7.4	Chronic obstructive pulmonary diseases	33.3	33.6
Syphilis.	0.0	0.0	Chronic and unspecified bronchitis .	1.4	1.5
All other infectious and parasitic dis-			Emphysema	6.4	6.2
eases	8.9	11.1	Asthma	1.9	1.9
Malignant neoplasms, including			Ulcer of stomach and duodenum	2.6	2.4
neoplasms of lymphatic and			Hernia and intestinal obstruction	2.1	2.2
hematopoietic tissues	198.3	199.2	Cirrhosis and chronic liver disease . . .	10.6	10.4
Diabetes mellitus	16.2	18.5	Cholelithiasis, cholecystitis, and cholan-		
Meningitis	0.5	0.4	gitis	1.3	1.2
Major cardiovascular diseases	394.5	372.2	Nephritis, nephrosis and nephrotic syn..	9.2	8.7
Diseases of heart	311.9	293.6	Infections of kidney	0.6	0.5
Rheumatic fever and			Hyperplasia of prostate.	0.2	0.2
rheumatic heart disease	2.7	2.4	Congenital anomalies.	5.2	5.1
Hypertensive heart disease . . .	8.3	8.2	Certain causes of mortality in early in-		
Ischemic heart disease	208.0	198.6	fancy	1.7	1.8
Acute myocardial infarction. . . .	101.6	98.4	Symptoms, signs, ill-defined conditions .	17.7	16.2
All other forms of heart disease .	87.5	78.8	All other diseases	67.2	68.2
Hypertension.	3.0	3.2	Accidents	38.9	37.2
Cerebrovascular diseases	60.8	58.3	Motor vehicle accidents.	19.7	18.9
Artherosclerosis	9.6	7.6	Suicide	11.9	12.3
Other diseases of arteries,			Homicide	8.8	8.8
arterioles, and capillaries	9.2	9.5	All other external causes.	0.9	1.0
Acute bronchitis and bronchiolitis	0.3	0.2			

*Per 100,000 population; based on a 10-percent sample of deaths. from Jan. through Nov. p = provisional.

Principal Types of Accidental Deaths

Source: National Safety Council

Year	Motor vehicle	Falls	Drowning	Fires, Burns	Injestion of Food, Object	Firearms	Poison (solid, liquid)	Poison by Gas
1970 . .	54,633	16,926	7,860	6,718	2,753	2,406	3,679	1,620
1975 . .	45,853	14,896	8,000	6,071	3,106	2,380	4,694	1,577
1980 . .	53,172	13,294	7,257	5,822	3,249	1,955	3,089	1,242
1982 . .	45,779	12,077	6,351	5,210	3,254	1,756	3,474	1,259
1983 . .	44,452	12,024	6,353	5,028	3,387	1,695	3,382	1,251
1985 . .	45,901	12,001	5,316	4,938	3,551	1,649	4,091	1,079
1986 . .	47,865	11,444	5,700	4,835	3,692	1,452	4,731	1,009
1987 . .	48,290	11,733	5,100	4,710	3,688	1,440	4,415	900
1988 . .	48,900	12,200	4,600	4,700	4,000	1,500	5,100	900
1989 . .	46,900	12,400	4,600	4,400	3,900	1,600	5,600	900
			Death rates per 100,000 population					
1970 . .	26.8	8.3	3.9	3.3	1.4	1.2	1.8	0.8
1975 . .	21.3	6.9	3.7	2.8	1.4	1.1	2.2	0.7
1980 . .	23.4	5.9	3.2	2.6	1.4	0.9	1.4	0.5
1982 . .	19.7	5.2	2.7	2.2	1.4	0.8	1.4	0.5
1983 . .	19.0	5.1	2.7	2.1	1.4	0.7	1.4	0.5
1985 . .	19.2	5.0	2.2	2.1	1.5	0.7	1.7	0.5
1986 . .	19.9	4.7	2.4	2.0	1.5	0.6	2.0	0.4
1987 . .	19.8	4.8	2.1	1.9	1.5	0.6	1.8	0.4
1988 . .	19.9	5.0	1.9	1.9	1.6	0.6	2.1	0.4
1989 . .	18.9	5.0	1.9	1.8	1.6	0.6	2.3	0.4

U.S. Civil Aviation Accidents

Source: National Safety Council

1989	Accidents Total	Accidents Fatal	Deaths[1]	Accident Rates Per 100,000 Aircraft-Hours Total	Accident Rates Per 100,000 Aircraft-Hours Fatal	Accident Rates Per million Aircraft-Miles Total	Accident Rates Per million Aircraft-Miles Fatal
Large airlines	24	8	131	0.230	0.077	0.0055	0.0018
Commuter airlines. . .	18	5	31	0.882	0.245	0.047	0.013
On-demand air taxis .	110	23	80	3.83	0.80	—	—
General aviation	2,167	420	763	7.25	1.40	—	—

(1) Includes passengers. crew members and others.

Transportation Accident Passenger Death Rates, 1988

Source: National Safety Council

Kind of transportation	Passenger miles (billions)	Passenger deaths	Rate per 100 min. pass. miles	1986-1988 aver. death rate
Passenger automobiles and taxis[1]	2,143.9	25,614	1.19	1.23
Buses	127.9	44	0.03	0.03
Intercity buses	23.1	6	0.03	0.03
Railroad passenger trains	12.8	2	0.02	0.06
Scheduled airlines	334.2	273	0.01	0.03

(1) Drivers of passenger automobiles are considered passengers.

Ownership of Life Insurance in the U.S. and Assets of U.S. Life Insurance Companies

Source: American Council of Life Insurance

Legal Reserve Life Insurance Companies (millions of dollars)

	Purchases of life insurance				Insurance in force					
Year	Ordi-nary	Group	Indus-trial	Total	Ordi-nary	Group	Indus-trial	Credit	Total	Assets
1940	6,689	691	3,350	10,730	79,346	14,938	20,866	380	115,530	30,802
1950	17,326	6,068	5,402	28,796	149,116	47,793	33,415	3,844	234,168	64,020
1960	52,883	14,645	6,880	74,408	341,881	175,903	39,563	29,101	586,448	119,576
1965	83,485	51,385*	7,296	142,166*	499,638	308,078	39,818	53,020	900,554	158,884
1970	122,820	63,690*	6,612	193,122*	734,730	551,357	38,644	77,392	1,402,123	207,254
1975	188,003	95,190*	6,729	289,922*	1,083,421	904,695	39,423	112,032	2,139,571	289,304
1980	385,575	183,418	3,609	572,602	1,760,474	1,579,355	35,994	165,215	3,541,038	479,210
1981	481,895	346,702*	2,517	831,114*	1,978,080	1,888,612	34,547	162,356	4,063,595	525,803
1982	585,444	250,532	1,898	837,874	2,216,388	2,066,361	32,766	161,144	4,476,659	588,163
1983	753,444	271,609	1,388	1,026,441	2,544,275	2,219,573	31,354	170,659	4,965,861	654,948
1984	820,315	293,521	943	1,114,779	2,887,574	2,392,558	30,104	189,951	5,499,987	722,979
1985	910,944	319,503	722	1,231,169	3,247,289	2,561,595	28,250	215,973	6,053,107	825,901
1986	933,592	374,741*	418	1,308,751*	3,658,203	2,801,049	27,168	233,859	6,720,279	937,551
1987	986,660	365,529	324	1,352,513	4,139,071	3,043,782	26,668	242,977	7,452,498	1,044,459
1988	995,686	410,848	320	1,406,854	4,511,608	3,232,080	25,456	251,015	8,020,159	1,166,870
1989	1,020,719	420,707	252	1,441,678	4,939,964	3,469,498	24,446	260,107	8,694,015	1,299,756

*Includes Servicemen's Group Life Insurance $27.8 billion in 1965, $17.1 billion in 1970, $1.7 billion in 1975, $45.6 billion in 1981, and $51.0 in 1986, as well as $84.4 billion of Federal Employees' Group Life Insurance in 1981 and $10.8 billion in 1986.

Accidental Deaths and Injuries by Severity of Injury

Source: National Safety Council

In 1989 accidental deaths were estimated to number 94,500, a decrease of 2,000 or 2 percent from the 1988 total. This was the eighth consecutive year that accidental deaths were estimated at less than 100,000. The death rate per 100,000 population was 39.8, down 3 percent from 1988. The rates for work and motor vehicle deaths in 1989 were the lowest on record.

1989 Severity of injury	Total*	Motor vehicle	Work	Home	Public
Deaths*	94,500	46,900	10,400	22,500	19,000
Disabling injuries*	9,000,000	1,700,000	1,700,000	3,400,000	2,400,000
Permanent impairments.	340,000	140,000	60,000	90,000	60,000
Temporary total disabilities . . .	8,600,000	1,600,000	1,600,000	3,300,000	2,300,000

Certain Costs of Accidental Deaths or Injuries, 1989 (billions)					
Total*	$148.5	$72.2	$48.5	$18.2	$12.5
Wage loss	37.7	19.5	8.3	6.1	5.5
Medical expense	23.7	5.2	8.1	6.6	5.0
Insurance administration	28.4	20.7	6.1	0.9	0.7

*Duplication between motor vehicle, work, and home are eliminated in the total column.

Home Accident Deaths

Source: National Safety Council

Year	Total home	Falls	Fires, burns[2]	Suffo., ingesting object	Suffo., mech-anical	Poison (solid, liquid)	Poison by gas	Fire-arms	Other
1950	29,000	14,800	5,000	(1)	1,600	1,300	1,250	950	4,100
1955	28,500	14,100	5,400	(1)	1,250	1,150	900	1,100	4,600
1960	28,000	12,300	6,350	1,850	1,500	1,350	900	1,200	2,550
1965	26,500	11,700	6,100	1,300*	1,200	1,700	1,100	1,300	4,100
1970	27,000	9,700	5,600	1,800	1,100	3,000	1,100	1,400	3,300
1975	25,000	8,000	5,000	1,800	800	3,700	1,000	1,300	3,400
1980	22,800	7,100	4,800	2,000	500	2,500	700	1,100	4,100[3]
1985	21,600	6,500	4,000	2,400	600	3,200	700	900	3,300
1987	21,400	6,300	3,900	2,500	600	3,500	600	800	3,200
1988	22,500	6,400	3,800	2,800	500	4,200	600	900	3,300
1989	22,500	6,600	3,300	2,700	700	4,700	600	900	3,000

*Data for this year and subsequent years not comparable with previous years due to classification changes. (1) Included in Other. (2) Includes deaths resulting from conflagration, regardless of nature of injury. (3) Includes about 1,000 excessive deaths due to summer heat wave.

Pedalcycle Accidents

Source: National Safety Council

	Pedalcycles (millions)		Death Rate[1]	Percent of Deaths by Age		
Year		Deaths		0-14	15-24	25 & over
1940	7.8	750	9.59	48	39	13
1950	13.8	440	3.18	82	9	9
1960	28.2	460	1.63	78	9	13
1970	56.5	780	1.38	66	15	19
1980	82.3	1,200	1.46	35	36	29
1985	92.7	1,100	1.19	49	24	27
1987	100.2	1,000[2]	1.00	41[2]	27[2]	32[2]
1988	100.7	900	0.89	35	24	41
1989	100.6	1,000	0.99	32	22	46

(1) Deaths per 100,000 pedalcycles. (2) Data for 1987 and later are not comparable to prior years due to changes in estimating procedures.

The 15 Leading Causes of Death, 1989

Source: National Center for Health Statistics

Rank		Number	Death rate	Rank		Number	Death rate
1	All causes	1,957,000	862.0	8	Motor vehicle accidents . .	43,050	18.9
2	Major cardiovascular diseases	844,830	372.2	9	Diabetes mellitus.	41,970	18.5
3	Malignant neoplasms, inc. of lymphatic & hematopoletic tissues.	452,230	199.2	10	All other accidents & adverse affects	41,370	18.2
4	Cerebrovascular diseases	132,370	58.3	11	Symptoms, signs, ill-defined conditions	36,710	16.2
5	Accidents & adverse affects.	84,420	37.2	12	Suicide	27,800	12.3
6	Chronic obstructive pulmonary diseases, allied conditions	76,150	33.6	13	Chronic liver disease and cirrhosis.	23,640	10.4
				14	Homicide & legal intervention	19,930	8.8
7	Pneumonia	66,530	29.3	15	Nephritis & nephrotic syndrome, & nephrosis	19,890	8.7

Note: Data are provisional, estimated from a 10-percent sample of deaths, from Jan. through Nov. Rates per 100,000 population.

Accidental Death Rate Declines 21% in 1980s

The death rate from accidents has dropped 21 percent in the last decade, according to the National Safety Council in Aug. 1990. Increased safety consciousness was cited in the 20 percent decrease in the rate of motor vehicle deaths, which have consistently made up almost half the total accidental deaths, as well as the 29 percent drop in the death rate from public accidents, including plane crashes, falls, and drownings, and the 16 percent drop in the death rate from home accidents, such as fires, falls, and poisonings.

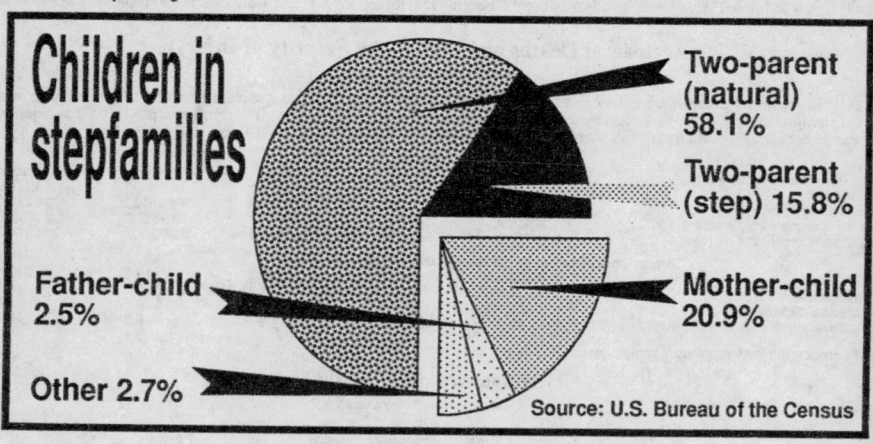

Children in stepfamilies

Two-parent (natural) 58.1%

Two-parent (step) 15.8%

Father-child 2.5%

Mother-child 20.9%

Other 2.7%

Source: U.S. Bureau of the Census

Living Arrangements of the Elderly, 1989

Source: Bureau of the Census

(Noninstitutional population. Numbers in thousands)

Living arrangement and age	1989 Total	Men	Women	Percent distribution Total	Men	Women
65 years and over	29,022	12,078	16,944	100.0	100.0	100.0
Living—						
Alone	8,851	1,916	6,935	30.5	15.9	40.9
With spouse.	15,773	8,977	6,796	54.3	74.3	40.1
With other relatives	3,797	927	2,870	13.1	7.7	16.9
With nonrelatives only	601	258	343	2.1	2.1	2.0
65 to 74 years	17,747	7,880	9,867	100.0	100.0	100.0
Living—						
Alone	4,355	1,045	3,310	24.5	13.3	33.5
With spouse.	11,252	6,176	5,075	63.4	78.4	51.4
With other relatives	1,832	502	1,331	10.3	6.4	13.5
With nonrelatives only	308	157	151	1.7	2.0	1.5
75 to 84 years	9,175	3,506	5,669	100.0	100.0	100.0
Living—						
Alone	3,509	645	2,864	38.2	18.4	50.5
With spouse.	4,060	2,468	1,593	44.3	70.4	28.1
With other relatives	1,386	305	1,080	15.1	8.7	19.1
With nonrelatives only	220	88	132	2.4	2.5	2.3
85 years and over	2,101	693	1,408	100.0	100.0	100.0
Living—						
Alone	987	226	760	47.0	32.6	54.0
With spouse.	462	334	128	22.0	48.2	9.1
With other relatives	579	121	459	27.6	17.5	32.6
With nonrelatives only	73	12	61	3.5	1.7	4.3

Marriages and Divorces by States and Regions
Source: National Center for Health Statistics

	Marriages 1988 Number	Rate	Marriages 1989 Number	Rate	Divorces 1988 Number	Rate	Divorces 1989 Number	Rate
New England	116,059	9.0	117,905	9.0	44,558	3.4	42,471	3.4
Maine	12,487	10.4	12,420	10.2	5,763	4.8	5,708	4.8
New Hampshire	11,270	10.4	11,260	10.2	4,755	4.4	5,239	4.4
Vermont	6,486	11.6	6,016	10.6	2,748	4.9	2,473	4.9
Massachusetts	49,981	8.5	53,370	9.0	17,244	2.9	15,436	2.9
Rhode Island	8,379	8.4	8,235	8.3	3,785	3.8	3,627	3.8
Connecticut	27,456	8.5	26,604	8.2	10,263	3.2	9,988	3.2
Middle Atlantic	314,638	8.4	307,924	8.2	130,828	3.5	123,505	3.5
New York[1]	165,421	9.2	161,834	9.0	64,571	3.6	59,520	3.6
New Jersey	61,052	7.9	60,182	7.8	26,897	3.5	25,644	3.5
Pennsylvania	88,165	7.3	85,908	7.1	39,360	3.3	38,341	3.3
East North Central	343,963	8.2	355,003	8.4	153,086	4.2	154,155[2]	4.2
Ohio	97,334	9.0	98,136	9.0	49,778	4.6	49,273	4.6
Indiana	51,874	9.3	55,119	9.9	—	—	—	—
Illinois	79,100	6.8	83,718	7.2	46,433	4.0	47,034	4.0
Michigan	74,150	8.0	77,558	8.4	39,887	4.3	40,278	4.3
Wisconsin	41,505	8.5	40,472	8.3	16,978	3.5	17,570	3.5
West North Central	155,858	8.8	157,677	8.8	77,487	4.4	75,861	4.2
Minnesota	33,481	7.8	34,325	7.9	14,945	3.5	15,707	3.5
Iowa	25,006	8.8	24,266	8.5	10,761	3.8	9,975	3.8
Missouri	49,867	9.7	51,147	9.9	24,864	4.8	26,330	4.6
North Dakota	4,923	7.4	4,835	7.3	2,371	3.6	2,231	3.6
South Dakota	7,262	10.2	7,100	9.9	2,657	3.7	2,624	3.7
Nebraska	12,349	7.7	12,703	7.9	6,379	4.0	6,354	4.0
Kansas	22,970	9.2	23,301	9.3	15,510	6.2	12,640	5.1
South Atlantic	454,498	10.7	446,779	10.4	218,983	5.2	213,448	5.2
Delaware	5,616	8.5	5,940	8.8	2,972	4.5	2,987	4.5
Maryland	44,064	9.5	47,344	10.1	16,439	3.6	15,635	3.6
District of Columbia	4,947	8.0	4,795	7.9	3,610	5.9	2,398	5.9
Virginia	69,022	11.5	68,868	11.3	26,065	4.3	25,799	4.3
West Virginia	14,400	7.7	13,354	7.2	9,149	4.9	9,379	4.9
North Carolina	51,664	8.0	50,590	7.7	32,367	5.0	32,384	5.0
South Carolina	54,339	15.7	54,335	15.5	14,637	4.2	14,859	4.2
Georgia	73,330	11.6	63,108	9.8	35,709	5.6	30,045	5.6
Florida	137,116	11.1	138,445	10.9	78,035	6.3	79,962	6.3
East South Central	188,658	12.3	181,321	11.8	88,086	5.7	90,583	5.7
Kentucky	49,910	13.4	50,208	13.5	20,456	5.5	20,629	5.5
Tennessee	69,354	14.2	65,005	13.2	31,990	6.5	32,278	6.5
Alabama	44,546	10.9	41,817	10.2	23,411	5.7	24,914	5.7
Mississippi	24,848	9.5	24,291	9.3	12,229	4.7	12,762	4.7
West South Central	276,138	10.3	281,746	10.4	134,464	6.0	133,466[2]	6.0
Arkansas	34,820	14.5	34,612	14.4	16,675	7.0	16,372	7.0
Louisiana	33,870	7.7	38,990	8.9	—	—	—	—
Oklahoma	32,923	10.2	33,112	10.3	23,048	7.1	23,050	7.1
Texas	174,525	10.4	175,032	10.3	94,741	5.6	94,044	5.6
Mountain	240,308	18.0	240,807	17.9	87,751	6.6	83,897	6.6
Montana	6,765	8.4	6,698	8.3	4,074	5.1	4,090	5.1
Idaho	11,213	11.2	13,082	12.9	6,058	6.0	6,043	6.0
Wyoming	4,696	9.8	4,624	9.7	3,307	6.9	3,040	6.9
Colorado	31,536	9.6	31,680	9.6	18,792	5.7	18,709	5.7
New Mexico[3,4]	13,025	8.6	12,746	8.3	7,943	5.3	7,598	5.3
Arizona[1]	35,737	10.2	35,738	10.1	24,940	7.1	23,153	7.1
Utah	16,611	9.8	18,642	10.9	7,824	4.6	8,088	4.6
Nevada	120,725	114.5	117,597	106.3	14,813	14.1	13,176	14.1
Pacific	319,810	8.6	325,059	8.5	186,112	5.0	176,272	5.0
Washington	44,042	9.5	43,684	9.2	26,436	5.7	27,311	5.7
Oregon	22,581	8.2	23,485	8.3	14,891	5.4	15,099	5.4
California	229,983	8.1	234,120	8.1	136,076	4.8	124,889	4.8
Alaska	5,803	11.1	5,786	11.0	3,633	6.9	3,331	6.9
Hawaii	17,401	15.8	17,984	16.2	5,076	4.6	5,642	4.6

(1) Figures for marriages are marriage licenses issued for some counties; (2) Excludes figures for state shown below as not available; (3) Figures for marriages are marriage licenses issued; (4) Figures for divorces include estimates for some counties.
Notes: Data are by State of occurrence, not residence. Figures reflect revisions.

Marriages, Divorces, and Rates in the U.S.
Source: National Center for Health Statistics

Data refer only to events occurring within the United States, including Alaska and Hawaii beginning with 1960. Rates per 1,000 population.

Year	Marriages[1] No.	Rate	Divorces[2] No.	Rate	Year	Marriages[1] No.	Rate	Divorces[2] No.	Rate
1895	620,000	8.9	40,387	0.6	1945	1,612,992	12.2	485,000	[3]3.5
1900	709,000	9.3	55,751	0.7	1950	1,667,231	11.1	385,144	2.6
1905	842,000	10.0	67,976	0.8	1955	1,531,000	9.3	377,000	2.3
1910	948,166	10.3	83,045	0.9	1960	1,523,000	8.5	393,000	2.2
1915	1,007,595	10.0	104,298	1.0	1965	1,800,000	9.3	479,000	2.5
1920	1,274,476	12.0	170,505	1.6	1970	2,158,802	10.6	708,000	3.5
1925	1,188,334	10.3	175,449	1.5	1975	2,152,662	10.0	1,036,000	4.8
1930	1,126,856	9.2	195,961	1.6	1980	2,413,000	10.6	1,182,000	5.2
1935	1,327,000	10.4	218,000	1.7	1985	2,425,000	10.2	1,187,000	5.0
1940	1,595,879	12.1	264,000	2.0	1989	2,404,000	9.7	1,163,000	4.7

(1) Includes estimates and marriage licenses for some states for all years. (2) Includes reported annulments. (3) Divorce rates for 1945 based on population including armed forces overseas.

Median Age at First Marriage, 1890-1989

Source: Bureau of the Census

Year	Men	Women	Year	Men	Women
1890	26.1	22.0	1960	22.8	20.3
1900	25.9	21.9	1965	22.8	20.6
1910	25.1	21.6	1970	23.2	20.8
1920	24.6	21.2	1975	23.5	21.1
1930	24.3	21.3	1980	24.7	22.0
1940	24.3	21.5	1985	25.5	23.3
1950	22.8	20.3	1988	25.9	23.6
1955	22.6	20.2	1989	26.2	23.8

Percent of Population Never Married, 1960-1989

Source: Bureau of the Census

	Women				Men			
	1960	1970*	1980	1989	1960	1970*	1980	1989
Total, 15 years and over	17.3	22.1	22.5	23.0	23.2	28.1	29.6	30.1
Under 40 years	28.1	38.5	38.8	40.6	39.6	47.7	48.8	50.8
40 years and over	7.5	6.2	5.1	5.2	7.6	7.4	5.7	6.2
15-17 years	93.2	97.3	97.0	98.6	98.8	99.4	99.4	99.9
18 years	75.6	82.0	88.0	93.8	94.6	95.1	97.4	97.9
19 years	59.7	68.8	77.6	87.2	87.1	89.9	90.9	96.5
20-24 years	28.4	35.8	50.2	62.5	53.1	54.7	68.8	77.4
20 years	46.0	56.9	66.5	78.8	75.8	78.3	86.0	91.1
21 years	34.6	43.9	59.7	71.1	63.4	66.2	77.2	86.0
22 years	25.6	33.5	48.3	63.7	51.6	52.3	69.9	79.3
23 years	19.4	22.4	41.7	53.4	40.5	42.1	59.1	70.4
24 years	15.7	17.9	33.5	47.8	33.4	33.2	50.0	64.0
25-29 years	10.5	10.5	20.9	29.4	20.8	19.1	33.1	45.9
25 years	13.1	14.0	28.6	42.0	27.9	26.6	44.3	58.9
26 years	11.4	12.2	22.7	32.4	23.5	20.9	36.5	51.4
27 years	10.2	9.1	22.2	28.9	19.8	16.5	31.5	44.4
28 years	9.2	8.9	16.0	23.0	17.5	17.0	26.8	39.4
29 years	8.7	8.0	14.6	21.5	16.0	13.8	24.0	35.6
30-34 years	6.9	6.2	9.5	16.9	11.9	9.4	15.9	25.8
35-39 years	6.1	5.4	6.2	9.9	8.8	7.2	7.8	15.2
40-44 years	6.1	4.9	4.8	6.3	7.3	6.3	7.1	8.3
45-54 years	7.0	4.9	4.7	5.4	7.4	7.5	6.1	6.7
55-64 years	8.0	6.8	4.5	4.4	8.0	7.8	5.3	5.6
65 years and over	8.5	7.7	5.9	5.0	7.7	7.5	4.9	4.7

*Figures for 1970 include persons 14 years of age.

Divorced Persons Per 1,000 Married Persons With Spouse Present, 1960-1988

Source: Bureau of the Census

		Race					Race		
	Total	White	Black	Hispanic[1]		Total	White	Black	Hispanic[1]
Both sexes:					1970	35	32	62	40
1988	133	124	263	137	1960	28	27	45	(NA)
1980	100	92	203	98	Female:				
1970	47	44	83	61	1988	156	146	311	167
1960	35	33	62	(NA)	1980	120	110	258	132
Male:					1970	60	56	104	81
1988	110	102	216	106	1960	42	38	78	(NA)
1980	79	74	149	64					

NA-Not available. (1) Persons of Hispanic origin may be of any race.

Children Involved in Divorces, 1950-1987

Source: Bureau of the Census

Year	Estimated # of children involved	Avg. # of children per decree	Rate per 1,000 children under 18 yrs.	Year	Estimated # of children involved	Avg. # of children per decree	Rate per 1,000 children under 18 yrs.	Year	Estimated # of children involved	Avg. # of children per decree	Rate per 1,000 children under 18 yrs.
1987	1,038,000	0.89	16.3	1974	1,099,000	1.12	16.2	1961	516,000	1.25	7.8
1986	1,064,000	0.90	16.8	1973	1,079,000	1.17	15.7	1960	463,000	1.18	7.2
1985	1,091,000	0.92	17.3	1972	1,021,000	1.20	14.7	1959	468,000	1.18	7.5
1984	1,081,000	0.92	17.2	1971	946,000	1.22	13.6	1958	398,000	1.08	6.5
1983	1,091,000	0.94	17.4	1970	870,000	1.22	12.5	1957	379,000	0.99	6.4
1982	1,108,000	0.94	17.6	1969	840,000	1.31	11.9	1956	361,000	0.95	6.3
1981	1,180,000	0.97	18.7	1968	784,000	1.34	11.1	1955	347,000	0.92	6.3
1980	1,174,000	0.98	17.3	1967	701,000	1.34	9.9	1954	341,000	0.90	6.4
1979	1,181,000	1.00	18.4	1966	669,000	1.34	9.5	1953	330,000	0.85	6.4
1978	1,147,000	1.01	17.7	1965	630,000	1.32	8.9	1952	318,000	0.81	6.2
1977	1,095,000	1.00	16.7	1964	613,000	1.36	8.7	1951	304,000	0.80	6.1
1976	1,117,000	1.03	16.9	1963	562,000	1.31	8.2	1950	299,000	0.78	6.3
1975	1,123,000	1.08	16.7	1962	532,000	1.29	7.9				

Note: Data refer to divorces and annulments in the U.S., involving children under 18 years at age. Beginning in 1960, estimates are made from frequencies based on sample data; for 1950-59, estimates are made from total counts.

Births to Unmarried Women, 1988

Source: National Center for Health Statistics

Age of mother	Number — All races	Number — White	Number — Black	Rate per 1,000 unmarried[1] women in specified group — All races	Rate — White	Rate — Black	Ratio per 1,000 live births — All races	Ratio — White	Ratio — Black
All ages	1,005,299	539,696	426,665	38.6[1]	26.6[1]	88.9[1]	257.1	177.2	634.9
Under 15 years . .	9,907	3,522	6,111	—	—	—	935.7	864.7	988.5
15-19 years . .	312,499	168,641	133,419	36.8	24.8	98.3	653.3	534.6	911.8
15 years.	22,456	10,105	11,702				877.0	785.2	982.2
16 years.	44,101	22,535	20,168	26.5	17.1	74.1	799.7	693.4	969.0
17 years.	69,580	37,861	29,429				725.8	615.3	946.1
18 years.	85,659	47,577	35,100	52.7	36.4	136.1	642.3	529.1	906.9
19 years.	90,703	50,563	37,020				538.7	426.6	845.4
20-24 years	350,905	186,598	151,308	56.7	38.3	138.2	328.7	231.9	686.8
25-29 years	196,365	105,218	82,825	48.1	33.8	99.2	158.5	104.1	493.9
30-34 years	94,874	51,596	38,724	31.7	22.9	58.7	118.1	78.0	413.0
35-39 years	34,408	20,109	12,358	14.9	11.5	25.3	127.7	92.3	379.8
40 years and over	6,341	4,012	1,920	3.2[2]	2.6[2]	5.3[2]	155.5	125.1	370.4

(1) Rates computed by relating total births to unmarried mothers, regardless of age of mother, to unmarried women aged 15-44 years. (2) Rates computed by relating births to unmarried mothers aged 40 years and over to unmarried women aged 40-44 years.
Note: For 42 States and the District of Columbia, marital status of mother is reported on the birth certificate; for 8 States, mother's marital status is inferred.

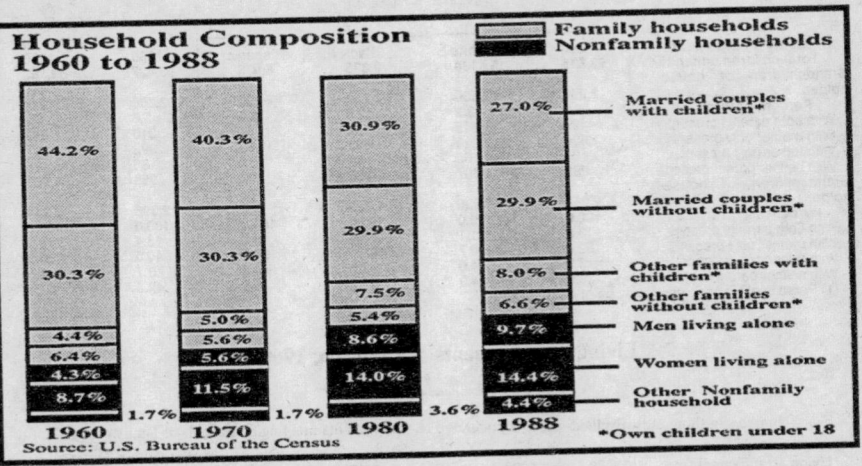

Household Composition 1960 to 1988

Family households
Nonfamily households

	1960	1970	1980	1988	
Married couples with children*	44.2%	40.3%	30.9%	27.0%	
Married couples without children*	30.3%	30.3%	29.9%	29.9%	
Other families with children*	4.4%	5.0%	7.5%	8.0%	
Other families without children*	6.4%	5.6%	5.4%	6.6%	
Men living alone	4.3%	5.6%	8.6%	9.7%	
Women living alone	8.7%	11.5%	14.0%	14.4%	
Other Nonfamily household	1.7%	1.7%	3.6%	4.4%	

Source: U.S. Bureau of the Census   *Own children under 18

Average Family Size, 1940-1989

Source: Bureau of the Census

Year	Size	Year	Size	Year	Size
1940	3.76	1970	3.58	1986	3.21
1950	3.54	1975	3.54	1987	3.19
1955	3.59	1980	3.29	1988	3.17
1960	3.67	1985	3.23	1989	3.16
1965	3.70				

Adults in Unmarried-Couple Households, 1989

Source: Bureau of the Census

(Numbers in thousands)

Male partner	Total	Never married	Married — Separated	Married — Other	Widowed	Divorced
Total.	2,764	1,574	136	6	126	921
Never married.	1,661	1,206	62	3	33	357
Married: Separated.	146	53	33	—	14	46
Other	14	5	1	—	—	8
Widowed.	73	12	1	3	36	21
Divorced.	869	298	39	—	43	489
Percent.	100.0	56.9	4.9	0.2	4.6	33.3
Never married.	60.1	43.6	2.2	0.1	1.2	12.9
Married: Separated.	5.3	1.9	1.2	—	0.5	1.7
Other	0.5	0.2	—	—	—	0.3
Widowed.	2.6	0.4	—	0.1	1.3	0.8
Divorced.	31.4	10.8	1.4	—	1.6	17.7

— Represents zero.

Young Adults Living with Their Parents, 1989

Source: Bureau of the Census

(Numbers in thousands)

Characteristic	Total	18 to 24 years old		Total	25 to 34 years old	
		Men	Women		Men	Women
Total persons	25,629	12,574	13,055	43,238	21,461	21,777
Son/daughter of householder. .	13,449	7,308	6,141	4,858	3,130	1,728
Percent of total	52.5	58.1	47.0	11.2	14.6	7.9
With own children	606	63	543	561	88	473
Son/daughter of house-holder . .	13,449	7,308	6,141	4,858	3,130	1,728
Percent	100.0	100.0	100.0	100.0	100.0	100.0
Never married.	97.3	98.0	96.6	80.5	83.5	74.9
Married, spouse present	1.2	1.0	1.4	3.5	2.7	4.8
Married, spouse absent	0.8	0.6	1.2	6.2	5.0	8.3
Widowed.	—	—	—	0.2	0.1	0.3
Divorced.	0.7	0.5	0.8	9.8	8.7	11.7

— Represents zero.

Children Living with Grandparents, 1970-1989

Source: Bureau of the Census

(Numbers in thousands)

Living arrangement	1989				1980	1970
	Total	White	Black	Hispanic[1]		
Total children under 18	63,637	51,134	9,835	6,973	63,427	69,162
Grandchildren of house-holder.	2,951	1,636	1,232	360	2,306	2,214
Percent of total. . . .	4.6	3.2	12.5	5.2	3.6	3.2
With both parents present	409	345	44	71	310	363
With mother only present .	1,556	829	691	182	922	817
With father only present. .	104	65	31	15	86	78
With neither parent present	882	397	465	92	988	957
Grandchildren of house-holder.	2,951	1,636	1,232	360	2,306	2,214
Percent	100.0	100.0	100.0	100.0	100.0	100.0
With both parents present	13.9	21.1	3.6	19.7	13.4	16.4
With mother only present .	52.7	50.7	56.1	50.6	40.0	36.9
With father only present. .	3.5	4.0	2.5	4.2	3.7	3.5
With neither parent present	29.9	24.3	37.7	25.6	42.8	43.2

(1) Persons of Hispanic origin may be of any race.

Living Arrangements of Children, 1960-1989

Source: Bureau of the Census

(Numbers in thousands. Excludes persons under age 18 who were maintaining households or family groups.)

Living arrangement	1989	1980	1970	1960	% distribution			
					1989	1980	1970	1960
All Races								
Children under 18 years.	63,637	63,427	69,162	63,727	100.0	100.0	100.0	100.0
Living with—								
Two parents	46,549	48,624	58,939	55,877	73.1	76.7	85.2	87.7
One parent	15,493	12,466	8,199	5,829	24.3	19.7	11.9	9.1
Mother only	13,700	11,406	7,452	5,105	21.5	18.0	10.8	8.0
Father only	1,793	1,060	748	724	2.8	1.7	1.1	1.1
Other relatives	1,341	1,949	1,547	1,601	2.1	3.1	2.2	2.5
Nonrelatives only.	254	388	477	420	0.4	0.6	0.7	0.7
Black—[1]								
Children under 18 years.	9,835	9,375	9,422	8,650	100.0	100.0	100.0	100.0
Living with—								
Two parents	3,738	3,956	5,508	5,795	38.0	42.2	58.5	67.0
One parent	5,362	4,297	2,996	1,897	54.5	45.8	31.8	21.9
Mother only	5,023	4,117	2,783	1,723	51.1	43.9	29.5	19.9
Father only	339	180	213	173	3.4	1.9	2.3	2.0
Other relatives	660	999	820	827	6.7	10.7	8.7	9.6
Nonrelatives only.	75	123	97	132	0.8	1.3	1.0	1.5
Hispanic—[2]								
Children under 18 years.	6,973	5,459	4,006[3]	NA	100.0	100.0	100.0	NA
Living with—								
Two parents	4,673	4,116	3,111	NA	67.0	75.4	77.7	NA
One parent	2,129	1,152	NA	NA	30.5	21.1	NA	NA
Mother only	1,940	1,069	NA	NA	27.8	19.6	NA	NA
Father only	189	83	NA	NA	2.7	1.5	NA	NA
Other relatives	142	183	NA	NA	2.0	3.4	NA	NA
Nonrelatives only.	29	8	NA	NA	0.4	0.1	NA	NA

NA = Not available. (1) Black and other races for 1960. (2) Persons of Hispanic origin may be of any race. (3) All persons under 18 years.

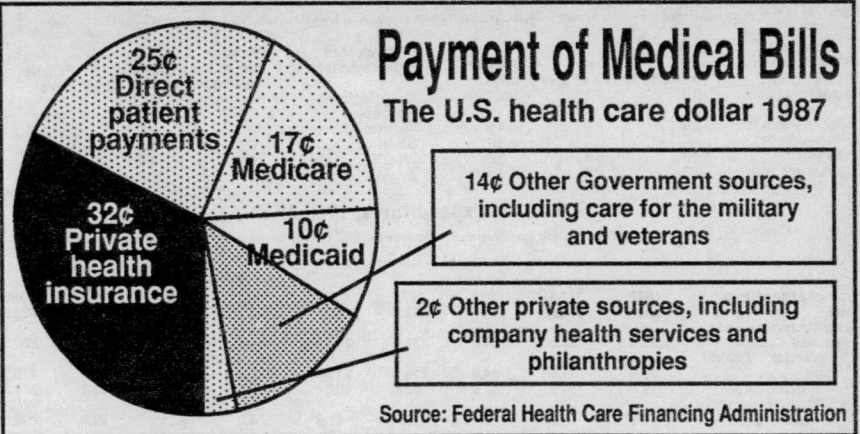

Payment of Medical Bills
The U.S. health care dollar 1987

25¢ Direct patient payments

17¢ Medicare

10¢ Medicaid

32¢ Private health insurance

14¢ Other Government sources, including care for the military and veterans

2¢ Other private sources, including company health services and philanthropies

Source: Federal Health Care Financing Administration

Persons Not Covered by Health Insurance

Source: Bureau of the Census

(Numbers in thousands; monthly average, fourth quarter 1988)

Characteristic	Total	Not covered by health insurance Number	Percent	Characteristic	Total	Not covered by health insurance Number	Percent
All persons.	243,094	31,507	13.0	35-44 years	35,675	3,992	11.2
Age				45-54 years	24,159	2,530	10.5
Less than 16 years .	56,591	8,633	15.3	55-64 years	21,637	2,003	9.3
0-4 years	18,319	3,014	16.5	65 years and over . .	28,782	91	0.3
5-9 years	18,321	2,874	15.7	Race and Hispanic origin			
10-15 years	19,952	2,745	13.8	White.	205,408	24,072	11.7
16-24 years	32,988	7,240	21.9	Black.	29,775	6,028	20.2
25-34 years	43,262	7,017	16.2	Hispanic origin[1]	19,825	5,249	26.5

(1) Persons of Hispanic origin may be of any race.

Inpatient Surgeries

Source: National Center for Health Statistics

(Data are for non-federal short-stay hospitals and exclude newborn infants)

	Number in thousands 1988	1987	Rate per 10,000 population 1988	1987		Number in thousands 1988	1987	Rate per 10,000 population 1988	1987
All surgical procedures.	39,192	26,655	1,605.4	1,061.6	tem	392	398	16.1	16.5
Nervous system	896	563	36.7	23.3	Digestive system	5,257	4,288	214.5	177.4
Endocrine system	111	109	4.5	4.5	Urinary system.	1,706	1,083	69.9	44.8
Eye	547	497	22.4	20.5	Male genital organs . .	633	747	25.9	30.9
Ear	198	176	8.1	7.3	Female genital organs . .	2,501	2,870	102.5	118.8
Nose, mouth, and pharynx	820	930	33.6	38.5	Obstetrical	6,042	5,358	247.5	221.7
Respiratory system	991	745	40.6	30.8	Musculoskeletal system .	3,143	3,313	128.8	137.1
Cardiovascular system . .	3,626	2,978	148.5	123.2	Integumentary system . .	1,475	1,600	60.4	66.2
Hemic and lymphatic sys-									

Chronic Conditions, 1987

Source: National Center for Health Statistics; the most commonly reported chronic conditions among the general population; people with chronic conditions per 1,000 persons by age group.

	Total	Under 18 years	18-44 years	45-64 years	65+ years		Total	Under 18 years	18-44 years	45-64 years	65+ years
Chronic sinusitis .	139.7	61.4	157.5	188.0	173.0	Chronic bronchitis	49.4	54.3	39.0	56.1	64.8
Arthritis	129.9	2.3	53.3	257.1	485.7	Hemorrhoids . . .	45.8	1.3	53.8	78.2	64.5
High blood pres-						Asthma	41.2	49.9	38.7	34.8	41.4
sure	121.5	2.3	64.7	257.8	373.0	Migraine head-					
Deformity/ortho-						ache	38.3	14.2	55.5	45.4	18.4
pedic impairment	111.6	28.8	131.4	150.9	161.1	Dermatitis.	37.5	34.9	42.5	36.1	27.2
Hay fever or aller-						Visual impairment	34.7	9.1	29.2	47.7	90.7
gic rhinitis	93.0	63.4	114.6	99.4	71.4	Varicose veins . .	31.7	—	26.6	56.8	80.2
Hearing impair-						Tinnitus	26.4	1.1	16.0	49.2	83.9
ment	90.8	17.0	48.7	147.6	315.2	Diabetes	25.8	2.2	9.2	54.6	92.4
Heart disease . . .	84.1	23.3	39.8	135.9	295.8						

Average Length of Stay for Inpatients at Short-Stay Hospitals, 1988

Source: National Center for Health Statistics; discharges from non-Federal hospitals, excluding newborn infants. 1988

Selected characteristic	Both sexes	Male	Female		Selected characteristic	Both sexes	Male	Female
	Average length of stay in days					Average length of stay in days		
All patients. . . .	6.5	7.1	6.2		Region			
Age					Northeast.	7.7	8.1	7.4
Under 15 years. .	5.0	5.0	4.9		Midwest.	6.4	6.7	6.2
15-44 years. .	4.7	6.3	4.1		South	6.2	6.8	5.9
45-64 years. . . .	6.8	6.8	6.8		West.	5.8	6.8	5.2
65 years and over	8.9	8.6	9.1					

U.S. Health Expenditures, 1960-1988

Source: Health Care Financing Administration, Office of the Actuary

(amount in billions)

Type of expenditure	1960	1965	1970	1975	1980	1985	1986	1987	1988
Total.	$27.1	$41.6	$74.4	$132.9	$249.1	$420.1	$450.5	$488.8	539.9
Health services and supplies	25.4	38.2	69.1	124.7	237.8	404.7	434.5	471.6	520.5
Personal health care	23.9	35.6	64.9	116.6	218.3	367.2	397.7	434.7	478.3
Hospital care . .	9.3	14.0	27.9	52.4	102.4	167.9	179.3	193.7	211.8
Physicians' services.	5.3	8.2	13.6	23.3	41.9	74.0	82.1	93.0	105.1
Dentists' services.	2.0	2.8	4.7	8.2	14.4	23.3	24.7	27.1	29.4
Other professional services .	0.6	0.9	1.5	3.5	8.7	16.6	18.3	20.2	22.5
Home health care	0.0	0.1	0.1	0.4	1.3	3.8	4.0	4.2	4.4
Drugs and other medical nondurables	4.2	5.9	8.8	13.0	20.1	32.3	35.6	38.6	41.9
Vision products and other medical durables. . .	0.8	1.2	2.0	3.1	5.0	8.4	9.5	9.8	10.8
Nursing home care	1.0	1.7	4.9	9.9	20.0	34.1	36.7	39.7	43.1
Other personal health care . . .	0.7	0.8	1.4	2.7	4.6	6.8	7.6	8.4	9.3
Program administration and net cost of private health insurance.	1.2	1.9	2.8	5.1	12.2	25.2	23.4	22.4	26.3
Government public health activities.	0.4	0.6	1.4	3.0	7.2	12.3	13.5	14.5	15.9
Research and construction.	1.7	3.5	5.3	8.3	11.3	15.4	16.0	17.2	19.4
Research[1]	0.7	1.5	2.0	3.3	5.4	7.8	8.5	9.0	9.9
Construction. . . .	1.0	1.9	3.4	5.0	5.8	7.6	7.4	8.2	9.5

Average annual % change from previous year shown

Type of expenditure	1960	1965	1970	1975	1980	1985	1986	1987	1988
Total.		8.9	12.3	12.3	13.4	11.0	7.2	8.5	10.4
Health services and supplies		8.5	12.6	12.5	13.8	11.2	7.4	8.5	10.4
Personal health care		8.3	12.8	12.4	13.4	11.0	8.3	9.3	10.0
Hospital care . .		8.6	14.7	13.4	14.3	10.4	6.8	8.1	9.3
Physicians' services.		9.2	10.6	11.4	12.5	12.1	10.9	13.3	13.1
Dentists' services.		7.3	10.8	12.1	11.7	10.1	6.4	9.6	8.5
Other professional services .		7.4	11.8	18.3	19.9	13.9	10.0	10.2	11.6
Home health care		9.6	19.7	23.2	27.2	23.3	3.7	4.9	5.9
Drugs and other medical nondurables		6.8	8.4	8.1	9.1	9.9	10.2	8.7	8.5
Vision products and other medical durables. . .		9.0	10.1	8.8	10.1	11.0	13.6	3.4	10.1
Nursing home care		11.6	23.4	15.4	15.0	11.3	7.5	8.2	8.5
Other personal health care . . .		3.5	10.7	14.6	11.0	8.4	11.2	10.5	10.5
Program administration and net cost of private health insurance.		10.5	7.5	12.8	19.3	15.5	-7.2	-4.2	17.7
Government public health activities.		10.8	17.1	17.0	18.9	11.3	9.6	7.8	9.1
Research and construction.		15.2	9.0	9.2	6.4	6.4	3.7	7.8	12.6
Research[1]		17.1	5.1	11.2	10.4	7.4	9.5	4.9	10.1
Construction. . . .		13.9	11.8	8.0	3.3	5.4	-2.4	11.1	15.3

(1) Research and development expenditures of drug companies and other manufacturers and providers of medical equipment and supplies are excluded from "research expenditures," but they are included in the expenditure class in which the product falls.

Average Annual Number of Contacts with Physicians

Source: National Center for Health Statistics; data based on household interviews of civilian noninstitutionalized population, 1985-1987.

Characteristic All family incomes	All ages White	All ages Black	Under 18 years White	Under 18 years Black	18-44 years White	18-44 years Black	45-64 years White	45-64 years Black	65 years and over White	65 years and over Black
					(Number per person per year)					
Total[1]	5.5	4.7	4.5	2.8	4.7	4.5	6.3	7.1	8.8	8.7
Sex										
Male	4.6	3.9	4.5	2.9	3.4	3.3	5.4	6.4	8.3	8.1
Female	6.3	5.4	4.5	2.8	6.0	5.5	7.2	7.7	9.2	9.1
Family income										
Less than $10,000	7.2	5.5	4.4	3.2	6.1	5.5	10.3	9.4	9.6	9.1
$10,000-$19,999	5.6	4.6	4.1	2.5	4.7	4.9	7.2	6.5	8.4	8.9
$20,000-$34,999	5.3	4.3	4.7	2.8	4.7	4.1	6.1	6.9	8.6	8.2
$35,000 or more	5.2	4.6	5.0	3.3	4.7	4.9	5.6	5.5	9.3	7.4
Poverty status										
In poverty	6.1	5.0	3.9	3.1	5.9	5.2	10.7	9.5	9.7	10.3
Not in poverty	5.5	4.7	4.7	2.8	4.7	4.6	6.2	6.5	8.8	8.1
Employment status[2]										
Employed	4.6	4.3	—	—	4.2	4.0	5.1	5.1	7.5	4.8
Unemployed	4.7	4.5	—	—	4.7	3.9	4.8	7.6	4.8	9.8
Not in labor force	8.4	8.4	—	—	6.9	6.4	8.9	10.6	9.0	9.3
Education[2]										
Less than 12 years	6.6	6.5	—	—	4.5	4.2	6.8	7.9	8.6	8.6
12 years	5.6	4.8	—	—	4.6	4.2	6.2	6.4	8.6	8.1
More than 12 years.	5.6	5.6	—	—	4.9	5.1	6.2	6.3	9.2	11.3
Geographic region										
Northeast	5.3	4.9	4.5	2.9	4.2	4.6	6.1	6.5	8.3	11.6
Midwest	5.6	5.5	4.7	3.4	4.9	5.6	6.2	8.7	8.6	8.1
South.	5.3	4.3	4.6	2.6	4.5	4.2	6.2	6.5	8.6	7.9
West	5.9	5.2	4.3	3.5	5.3	4.3	7.0	8.7	10.3	10.6
Place of residence										
MSA	5.6	4.9	4.7	2.9	4.8	4.7	6.5	7.3	8.8	9.0
Central city	5.9	5.1	4.6	3.0	5.0	4.9	7.2	7.6	9.1	9.3
Not central city	5.4	4.4	4.7	2.9	4.7	4.4	6.1	6.7	8.6	7.8
Not MSA	5.2	3.9	4.1	2.4	4.4	3.3	5.7	6.0	8.8	7.7
Marital status[2]										
Married, spouse present . . .	5.6	5.4	—	—	4.7	4.5	5.9	6.1	8.3	7.8
No spouse present[3].	8.0	8.0	—	—	6.1	6.1	8.2	9.1	9.5	9.5
Never married.	4.6	4.2	—	—	4.2	4.0	6.7	6.1	9.2	7.5

(1) Unknowns for any characteristic are included in total. (2) Persons age 18 and over. (3) Includes married, separated, divorced, and widowed.

Physicians by Age, Sex, and Selected Specialties

Source: American Medical Association, Jan. 1, 1988

Total Physicians	Total Physicians* Male 482,490	Total Physicians* Female 86,670	Under 35 yrs. Male 103,735	Under 35 yrs. Female 37,188	35–44 yrs. Male 139,522	35–44 yrs. Female 30,397	45–54 yrs. Male 95,482	45–54 yrs. Female 12,158	55–64 yrs. Male 75,098	55–64 yrs. Female 6,457
Anesthesiology	20,069	4,189	5,654	1,327	6,121	1,454	3,980	877	3,183	377
Cardiovascular Disease	14,361	771	2,876	291	5,513	313	3,221	107	1,773	44
Dermatology	5,705	1,336	830	589	1,995	490	1,466	168	819	58
Diagnostic Radiology	12,382	2,146	3,921	1,121	4,768	772	2,483	180	897	60
Emergency Medicine	11,180	1,745	2,986	765	5,424	722	1,508	177	895	69
Family Practice	37,882	7,062	11,615	3,861	12,947	2,240	5,001	580	5,527	253
Gastroenterology	6,510	358	1,376	154	2,919	160	1,423	32	543	8
General Practice	22,014	2,381	771	261	2,491	698	3,982	571	6,835	467
General Surgery	35,642	2,150	9,707	1,400	8,516	570	7,378	105	6,180	47
Internal Medicine	77,634	17,040	24,216	9,017	25,230	5,560	12,868	1,537	9,450	647
Neurology	7,359	1,304	1,688	502	2,914	529	1,696	183	787	69
Obstetrics/Gynecology	25,644	6,634	4,487	3,345	7,641	2,056	6,290	759	4,808	299
Ophthalmology	14,205	1,376	2,793	643	4,122	479	3,758	142	2,090	72
Orthopedic Surgery	17,886	348	4,373	196	5,408	116	4,509	15	2,477	14
Otolaryngology	7,451	361	1,519	184	2,152	136	2,137	20	964	14
Pathology-Anat./Clin.	12,685	3,527	2,199	1,132	3,594	1,304	3,257	673	2,657	310
Pediatrics	24,199	14,032	6,160	6,149	7,953	4,868	4,847	1,867	3,503	784
Plastic surgery	4,085	271	546	91	1,569	117	1,225	39	520	17
Psychiatry	26,304	7,375	3,812	2,198	7,179	2,424	6,628	1,391	5,587	865
Pulmonary Diseases	5,324	452	1,117	170	2,544	176	1,010	56	405	31
Radiology	7,665	710	362	133	1,388	277	2,773	184	2,184	90
Urological Surgery	9,037	118	1,586	72	2,622	34	2,608	9	1,478	2
Other	5,565	817	381	123	1,135	230	1,267	182	1,473	177
Unspecified	4,282	1,190	2,265	775	708	219	432	106	410	53

*Includes those 65 years and over, those living in U.S. possessions, APO's and FPO's, and those with addresses unknown.

Estimated Cost of Cardiovascular Disease, 1991

According to the American Heart Association, the estimated cost of cardiovascular diseases in 1991 will be $101.2 billion: hospital and nursing home services, $64.7 billion; lost output due to disability, $16.2 billion; physician and nursing services, $14.9 billion; and medications, $5.4 billion. These estimates are an extrapolation from "Health Care Expenditures for Major Diseases in 1980," *Health Care Financing Review*.

Mental Health Facilities

Source: U.S. Institute of Mental Health; Jan. 1987.

	Number of facilities	Inpatient beds		Inpatients		Average daily inpatients (1,000)	Inpatient care episodes[2] (1,000)	Expenditures		Patient care staff[4] (1,000)
		Total (1,000)	Rate[1]	Total (1,000)	Rate[1]			Total (mil. dol.)	Per capita[3] (dol.)	
Total.	4,747	267.6	111.8	237.9	99.4	228.5	2,055	18,459	77	346.5
Mental hospitals										
State and county .	285	119.0	49.7	111.1	46.4	107.1	445	6,326	26	119.0
Private[2].	751	54.7	22.9	47.8	20.0	46.1	305	3,607	15	60.6
General hospitals[3] . .	1,351	45.8	19.1	34.5	14.4	34.4	883	2,878	12	61.1
Veterans Administration	139	26.9	11.2	24.3	10.2	21.2	204	1,338	6	23.6
Free-standing psychiatric outpatient services	773	(x)	(x)	(x)	(x)	(x)	(x)	518	2	9.2
Other[4].	1,448	21.2	8.9	20.2	8.4	19.7	218	3,792	16	73.0

X = not applicable. (1) Rate per 100,000 population. (2) Includes residential treatment centers for emotionally disturbed children. (3) Non-federal hospitals with separate psychiatric services. (4) Includes multiservice mental health facilities with 2 or more settings not elsewhere classified, and freestanding partial care organizations.

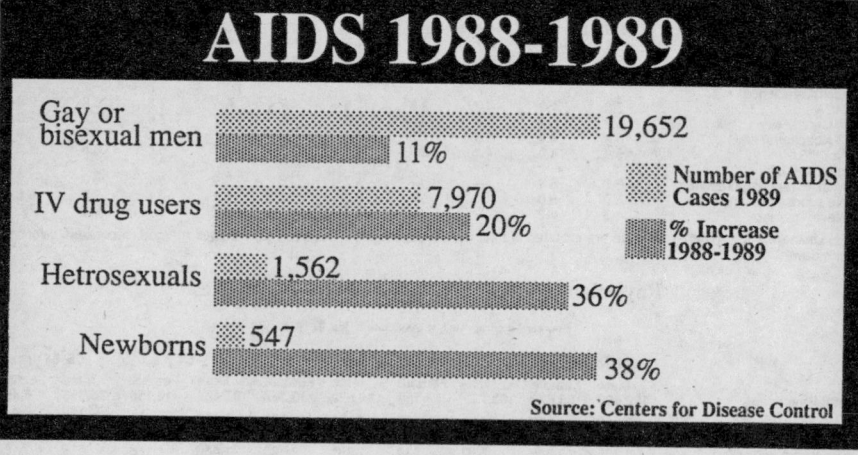

AIDS 1988-1989

Gay or bisexual men — 19,652 — 11%

IV drug users — 7,970 — 20%

Hetrosexuals — 1,562 — 36%

Newborns — 547 — 38%

Number of AIDS Cases 1989

% Increase 1988-1989

Source: Centers for Disease Control

Use of Family Planning Services, 1982 and 1988

Source: National Center for Health Statistics

Age and poverty level income Age	All Races		White		Black	
	1988	1982	1988	1982	1988	1982
			(Number in thousands)			
15-44 years	57,900	54,099	47,077	45,367	7,679	6,985
15-19	9,179	9,521	7,313	7,815	1,409	1,416
20-24	9,413	10,629	7,401	8,855	1,364	1,472
25-29	10,796	10,263	8,672	8,569	1,459	1,335
30-34	10,930	9,381	9,010	7,916	1,406	1,144
35-39	9,583	7,893	7,936	6,697	1,170	884
40-44	7,999	6,412	6,745	5,515	872	734
Poverty level income						
0-149 percent	13,561	13,843	9,052	10,093	3,601	3,338
150 percent or more . . .	44,339	40,256	38,024	35,275	4,078	3,647
Age			(Percent)			
15-44 years	34.5	36.5	34.3	35.8	39.3	43.0
15-19	30.4	30.6	29.2	28.6	40.9	43.4
20-24	59.0	56.2	59.8	54.9	65.5	65.1
25-29	53.0	55.7	54.5	55.9	52.1	56.7
30-34	34.9	33.9	34.8	33.4	38.0	38.3
35-39	17.0	19.4	17.0	19.4	15.6	20.0
40-44	6.0	7.0	5.7	7.0	8.0	7.9
Poverty level income						
0-149 percent	36.2	40.0	35.7	39.2	39.9	43.8
150 percent or more. . . .	34.0	35.3	34.0	34.8	38.8	42.2

AIDS Deaths, 1988 and 1989

Source: National Center for Health Statistics

Sex and age	All races[1] 1989 Number	1989 Rate[2]	1988 Number	1988 Rate[2]	White 1989 Number	1989 Rate[2]	1988 Number	1988 Rate[2]	Black 1989 Number	1989 Rate[2]	1988 Number	1988 Rate[2]
Both sexes												
All ages	21,360	8.6	16,210	6.6	14,730	7.0	10,720	5.2	6,470	21.1	5,300	17.5
Under 15 years	250	0.5	360	0.7	140	0.3	190	0.4	110	1.3	170	2.1
15-24 years	500	1.4	680	1.8	320	1.1	430	1.4	180	3.3	230	4.2
25-34 years	7,400	16.9	5,700	13.1	4,810	13.1	3,470	9.5	2,540	45.6	2,160	39.2
35-44 years	8,620	23.6	6,090	17.3	6,060	19.4	4,100	13.6	2,480	62.2	1,950	51.2
45-54 years	2,990	12.0	2,260	9.4	2,170	10.1	1,660	8.0	800	30.6	580	22.7
55 years and over	1,570	3.0	1,090	2.1	1,220	2.6	870	1.9	340	7.2	200	4.3
Not stated	20	—	10	—	10	—	—	—	10	—	10	—
Age-adjusted rate	—	8.3	—	6.5	—	6.7	—	5.0	—	21.7	—	18.1
Male												
All ages	19,060	15.8	14,300	11.9	13,750	13.5	9,840	9.7	5,140	35.3	4,290	29.9
Under 15 years	110	0.4	200	0.7	70	0.3	120	0.5	40	0.9	80	1.9
15-24 years	420	2.3	570	3.0	270	1.8	370	2.4	150	5.6	180	6.6
25-34 years	6,490	29.6	4,980	22.8	4,450	24.0	3,190	17.3	1,990	75.6	1,720	66.2
34-44 years	7,860	43.6	5,490	31.6	5,790	37.2	3,850	25.6	1,990	109.5	1,600	92.2
45-54 years	2,780	23.0	2,110	18.0	2,090	19.8	1,580	15.4	670	57.3	510	44.5
55 years and over	1,390	6.1	930	4.1	1,070	5.3	730	3.6	300	15.0	190	9.6
Not stated	10	—	10	—	10	—	—	—	—	—	10	—
Age adjusted rate	—	15.0	—	11.5	—	12.6	—	9.3	—	37.7	—	31.9
Female												
All ages	2,300	1.8	1,910	1.5	970	0.9	880	0.8	1,330	8.3	1,010	6.4
Under 15 years	140	0.5	160	0.6	70	0.3	70	0.3	70	1.7	90	2.2
15-24 years	80	0.4	110	0.6	50	0.3	60	0.4	30	1.1	50	1.8
25-34 years	910	4.2	720	3.3	360	2.0	280	1.5	550	18.7	440	15.1
35-44 years	760	4.1	600	3.4	270	1.7	250	1.7	490	22.6	350	16.9
45-54 years	210	1.6	150	1.2	80	0.7	80	0.8	130	9.0	70	5.0
55 years and over	180	0.6	160	0.5	140	0.5	140	0.5	40	1.5	10	0.4
Not stated	10	—	—	—	—	—	—	—	10	—	—	—
Age-adjusted rate	—	1.7	—	1.5	—	0.8	—	0.8	—	8.1	—	6.3

(1) Includes races other than white and black. (2) Figures for age not stated are included in "All ages" but are not distributed among age groups. Notes: AIDS = human immunodificiency virus infection. Data are provisional, estimated from a 10-percent sample of deaths. Rates per 100,000 population in specified group. Figures may differ from those previously published. Due to rounding of estimates, figures may not add to totals.

Contraceptive Use, 1982 and 1988

Source: National Center for Health Statistics

Age, race, and marital status	Number of women (in thousands)	% Using any method	Female sterilization	Male sterilization	Pill	IUD % distribution	Diaphragm	Condom	Other methods
1988									
All women 15-44 yrs.	57,900	60.3	27.5	11.7	30.7	2.0	5.7	14.6	7.7
Age									
15-24	18,592	45.7	3.6	1.3	64.9	0.2	2.7	20.8	6.5
25-34	21,726	66.3	25.0	10.2	32.6	2.1	7.3	13.7	9.1
35-44	17,582	68.3	47.6	20.8	4.3	3.1	6.0	11.2	6.9
Race									
White	47,077	61.8	26.1	13.6	29.8	1.8	6.2	14.9	7.5
Black	7,679	56.7	38.1	0.9	38.0	3.1	1.9	10.3	7.8
Marital status									
Never married	21,058	41.9	6.4	1.8	59.0	1.3	4.9	19.6	7.0
Currently married	29,147	74.3	31.4	17.3	20.4	2.0	6.2	14.3	8.4
Formerly married	7,695	57.6	50.7	3.6	25.3	3.6	5.3	5.9	5.7
1982									
All women 15-44 yrs.	54,099	55.7	23.2	10.9	28.0	7.1	8.1	12.0	10.7
Age									
15-24	20,150	40.8	3.2	2.7	57.6	3.4	9.0	13.5	10.6
25-34	19,644	66.7	22.1	10.1	25.7	9.7	10.3	11.4	10.7
35-44	14,305	61.6	43.5	19.9	3.7	6.9	4.0	11.3	10.8
Race									
White	45,367	56.7	22.1	12.2	26.7	6.9	8.8	12.7	10.7
Black	6,985	52.0	30.0	1.4	38.0	9.1	3.5	6.2	11.7
Marital status									
Never married	19,164	35.3	3.7	1.8	53.0	5.4	13.4	11.6	11.1
Currently married	26,231	69.7	26.9	15.5	19.3	6.9	6.5	14.1	10.8
Formerly married	6,704	55.5	39.2	3.4	28.4	11.5	6.7	1.5	9.2

U.S. Crime Rate Up 1.4% in 1989

Source: 1989 *Uniform Crime Reports*, FBI

The crime rate rose 1.4 percent in 1989, according to the FBI's Uniform Crime Reports. From 1988 to 1989, overall violent crime increased by 5 percent, and property crime increased by 2 percent.

Overall, the number of crimes committed nationwide rose to 14.25 million in 1989.

The rate of murders was up 3.6 percent; rape, up 1.3 percent; robbery, 5.5 percent; aggravated assault 3.6 percent; burglary, down 2.5 percent; larceny, up 1.2 percent; and auto theft, up 8.1 percent.

The FBI urged caution in interpreting the figures.

Crime Rates by Region, Geographic Division, and State, 1989

Source: 1989 *Uniform Crime Reports*, FBI

(Per 100,000)

Area	Total	Violent crime[1]	Property crime[2]	Murder	Rape	Robbery	Aggravated assault	Burglary	Larceny-theft	Motor vehicle theft
United States Total	5,741.0	663.1	5,077.9	8.7	38.1	233.0	383.4	1,276.3	3,171.3	630.4
Northeast	5,072.1	709.6	4,362.4	7.8	28.3	322.7	350.7	1,007.4	2,586.1	768.9
New England	4,854.1	494.8	4,359.3	4.4	28.6	158.8	303.0	1,064.5	2,591.6	703.2
Connecticut	5,270.0	511.8	4,758.2	5.9	27.5	214.8	263.6	1,236.0	2,824.4	697.8
Maine	3,583.6	137.2	3,446.5	3.2	18.7	24.0	91.2	802.8	2,460.5	183.2
Massachusetts	5,136.0	675.0	4,461.0	4.3	31.8	202.6	436.3	1,065.5	2,484.8	910.7
New Hampshire	3,596.2	168.5	3,427.7	3.3	29.5	23.8	111.8	736.9	2,446.9	244.0
Rhode Island	5,224.8	378.0	4,846.9	4.9	26.7	112.4	234.0	1,206.9	2,715.8	924.1
Vermont	4,088.5	132.8	3,955.7	1.9	23.1	18.0	89.8	1,029.1	2,727.7	198.9
Middle Atlantic	5,147.3	783.9	4,363.4	9.0	28.2	379.4	367.2	987.7	2,584.2	791.6
New Jersey	5,269.4	609.0	4,660.4	5.1	31.7	273.3	299.0	976.6	2,764.7	919.2
New York	6,293.2	1,131.2	5,162.1	12.5	29.2	579.3	510.1	1,176.2	3,033.2	952.7
Pennsylvania	3,360.4	378.6	2,981.8	6.3	24.6	149.7	198.0	713.7	1,798.7	469.4
Midwest	4,948.8	528.3	4,420.5	6.6	39.0	177.1	305.6	1,013.0	2,936.4	471.1
East North Central	5,149.5	588.8	4,560.7	7.6	43.6	207.4	330.2	1,040.1	2,992.6	528.0
Illinois	5,639.2	845.9	4,793.3	9.0	35.7	335.7	465.4	1,076.0	3,109.9	607.4
Indiana	4,440.0	406.5	4,033.5	6.3	32.3	101.4	266.5	969.1	2,673.2	391.1
Michigan	5,968.3	709.2	5,259.2	10.7	71.4	222.3	404.7	1,224.8	3,311.7	722.6
Ohio	4,733.2	468.6	4,264.6	6.0	44.7	170.9	247.1	1,018.2	2,811.1	435.3
Wisconsin	4,164.8	222.6	3,942.2	3.6	20.4	75.2	123.4	733.2	2,877.3	331.7
West North Central	4,472.9	384.9	4,088.0	4.3	28.1	105.2	247.3	948.6	2,803.1	336.4
Iowa	4,081.4	266.3	3,815.1	1.9	16.2	39.0	209.2	846.9	2,809.9	158.3
Kansas	4,982.8	400.8	4,582.0	5.5	36.5	99.8	259.1	1,188.7	3,096.0	297.4
Minnesota	4,383.2	288.3	4,094.9	2.5	31.3	94.8	159.6	896.9	2,818.1	379.9
Missouri	5,127.1	632.6	4,494.6	7.9	30.8	195.0	398.9	1,135.8	2,835.2	523.6
Nebraska	4,091.6	279.5	3,812.1	2.5	23.6	52.0	201.4	745.5	2,880.4	186.2
North Dakota	2,560.9	63.2	2,497.7	.6	11.8	9.2	41.5	358.9	2,025.8	113.0
South Dakota	2,685.2	135.5	2,549.7	1.3	32.0	11.7	90.5	474.7	1,966.0	109.0
South	6,205.1	675.0	5,530.1	10.8	40.7	217.1	406.4	1,553.5	3,404.3	572.3
South Atlantic	6,425.0	767.8	5,657.2	11.0	40.7	260.5	455.5	1,566.9	3,536.3	554.1
Delaware	4,865.2	556.5	4,308.8	5.1	84.5	138.8	328.1	902.2	3,015.5	391.1
District of Columbia	10,293.4	2,141.9	8,151.5	71.9	30.8	1,083.1	956.1	1,950.3	4,828.5	1,372.7
Florida	8,804.5	1,109.4	7,695.1	11.1	49.7	404.0	644.6	2,282.8	4,606.6	805.7
Georgia	7,073.1	735.8	6,337.3	12.7	48.9	271.1	403.0	1,712.5	3,971.1	653.7
Maryland	5,562.6	855.4	4,707.2	11.6	38.0	332.1	473.7	1,123.5	2,919.5	664.2
North Carolina	5,253.8	546.4	4,707.4	8.9	29.9	133.5	374.1	1,503.5	2,918.6	285.3
South Carolina	5,619.2	813.7	4,805.6	9.1	46.5	130.2	627.8	1,392.8	3,070.8	342.1
Virginia	4,211.4	312.5	3,898.9	7.9	26.9	106.5	171.3	756.9	2,831.2	310.9
West Virginia	2,362.8	146.7	2,216.2	6.5	18.7	42.7	78.8	625.5	1,432.8	156.8
East South Central	4,084.8	473.2	3,611.6	9.0	35.6	119.0	309.7	1,085.5	2,191.1	334.0
Alabama	4,627.8	590.8	4,037.0	10.2	31.0	133.9	415.7	1,146.8	2,592.8	297.5
Kentucky	3,317.1	356.9	2,960.2	7.9	24.6	76.1	248.3	819.1	1,921.4	219.8
Mississippi	3,515.3	311.2	3,204.1	9.7	38.8	78.3	184.4	1,145.3	1,879.7	179.2
Tennessee	4,513.6	548.9	3,964.7	8.4	46.0	160.4	334.1	1,206.9	2,224.9	532.9
West South Central	7,063.8	642.1	6,421.7	11.5	43.5	203.8	383.3	1,798.7	3,885.7	737.3
Arkansas	4,555.7	473.7	4,082.0	8.4	38.4	110.6	316.3	1,194.4	2,621.9	265.6
Louisiana	6,241.3	781.8	5,459.5	14.9	38.2	237.3	491.4	1,464.7	3,473.5	521.3
Oklahoma	5,502.6	491.5	5,011.1	6.5	37.5	126.2	321.3	1,563.6	2,862.0	585.5
Texas	7,926.9	658.5	7,268.4	11.9	46.8	233.1	376.6	2,014.9	4,365.0	888.5
West	6,550.4	754.2	5,796.2	8.3	42.2	236.0	467.7	1,387.7	3,633.1	775.4
Mountain	6,250.3	472.3	5,778.0	5.3	35.9	100.5	330.5	1,296.8	4,041.9	439.3
Arizona	8,059.7	599.6	7,460.2	6.7	36.2	139.0	417.7	1,667.2	5,106.1	686.9
Colorado	6,039.4	471.4	5,568.0	4.4	36.2	90.0	340.8	1,250.4	3,864.8	452.9
Idaho	3,931.0	254.6	3,676.3	2.6	23.3	15.0	213.8	872.1	2,645.5	158.8
Montana	3,997.5	116.0	3,881.5	2.9	18.0	17.0	78.2	691.7	2,964.3	225.6
Nevada	6,271.7	625.3	5,646.4	8.2	59.6	250.6	306.9	1,404.8	3,662.1	579.6
New Mexico	6,573.8	703.9	5,870.0	8.6	45.9	105.2	544.1	1,711.1	3,809.0	349.9
Utah	5,682.1	258.8	5,423.4	2.6	28.6	52.6	174.9	897.0	4,288.8	237.6
Wyoming	3,889.1	258.3	3,630.7	4.4	28.2	17.1	208.6	631.8	2,861.7	137.3
Pacific	6,656.3	853.8	5,802.6	9.4	44.4	283.8	516.1	1,419.8	3,488.8	894.1
Alaska	4,779.9	497.7	4,282.2	8.0	52.9	67.6	369.3	826.9	3,000.2	455.0
California	6,763.4	977.7	5,785.8	10.9	41.2	331.8	593.8	1,412.3	3,346.5	1,026.9
Hawaii	6,270.4	270.1	6,000.3	4.8	44.6	83.2	137.6	1,343.4	4,260.3	396.6
Oregon	6,161.1	518.6	5,642.5	4.8	46.6	151.8	315.4	1,425.4	3,677.0	540.1
Washington[3]	6,593.8	471.7	6,122.1	4.4	61.7	140.1	265.5	1,545.1	4,119.3	457.6
Puerto Rico[3]	3,277.0	650.9	2,626.1	13.9	15.2	394.0	227.8	1,004.3	1,131.1	490.7

(1) Violent crimes are murder, rape, robbery and aggravated assault; (2) Property crimes are burglary, larceny-theft, and motor vehicle theft. (3) Not included in U.S. totals.

Crime in the U.S., 1980-1989

Source: 1989 *Uniform Crime Reports*, FBI

Population[1]	Crime Index total[2]	Violent crime[3]	Property crime[4]	Murder and non-negligent man-slaughter	Forcible rape	Robbery	Burglary	Larceny theft
			Number of offenses					
1980-225,349,264. . .	13,408,300	1,344,520	12,063,700	23,040	82,990	565,840	3,795,200	7,136,900
1982-231,534,000. . .	12,974,400	1,322,390	11,652,000	21,010	78,770	553,130	3,447,100	7,142,500
1983-233,981,000. . .	12,108,600	1,258,090	10,850,500	19,310	78,920	506,570	3,129,900	6,712,800
1985-238,740,000. . .	12,431,400	1,328,870	11,102,600	18,980	87,670	497,870	3,073,300	6,926,400
1986-241,077,000. . .	13,211,900	1,489,170	11,722,700	20,610	91,460	542,780	3,241,400	7,257,200
1987-243,400,000. . .	13,508,700	1,484,000	12,024,700	20,100	91,110	517,700	3,236,200	7,499,900
1988-245,807,000. . .	13,923,100	1,566,220	12,356,900	20,680	92,490	542,970	3,218,100	7,705,900
1989-248,239,000. . .	14,251,400	1,646,040	12,605,400	21,500	94,500	578,330	3,168,200	7,872,400
			Percent change; number of offenses:					
1989/1988.	+2.4	+5.1	+2.0	+4.0	+2.2	+6.5	-1.6	+2.2
1989/1985.	+14.6	+23.9	+13.5	+13.3	+6.6	+16.2	+3.1	+13.7
1989/1980.	+6.3	+22.4	+4.5	-6.7	+13.9	+2.2	-16.5	+10.3
			Rate per 100,000 inhabitants:					
1980	5,950.0	596.6	5,353.3	10.2	36.8	251.1	1,684.1	3,167.0
1982	5,603.6	571.1	5,032.5	9.1	34.0	238.9	1,488.8	3,084.8
1983	5,175.0	537.7	4,637.4	8.3	33.7	216.5	1,337.7	2,868.9
1985	5,207.1	556.6	4,650.5	7.9	37.1	208.5	1,287.3	2,901.2
1986	5,480.4	617.3	4,862.6	8.6	37.9	225.1	1,344.6	3,010.3
1987	5,550.0	609.7	4,904.3	8.3	37.4	212.7	1,329.6	3,081.3
1988	5,664.2	637.2	5,027.1	8.4	37.6	220.9	1,309.2	3,134.9
1989	5,741.0	663.1	5,077.9	8.7	38.1	233.0	1,276.3	3,171.3
			Percent change; rate per 100,000 inhabitants:					
1989/1988.	+1.4	+4.1	+1.0	+3.6	+1.3	+5.5	-2.5	+1.2
1989/1985.	+10.3	+19.1	+9.2	+10.1	+2.7	+11.8	-.9	+9.3
1989/1970.	-3.5	+11.1	-5.1	-14.7	+3.5	-7.2	-24.2	+.1

(1) Populations are Bureau of the Census provisional estimates as of July 1, except April 1, 1980, preliminary census counts, and are subject to change. (2) Because of rounding, the offenses may not add to totals. (3) Violent crimes are offenses of murder, forcible rape, robbery, and aggravated assault. Property crimes are offenses of burglary, larceny-theft, and motor vehicle theft. Data are not included for the property crime of arson. (4) All rates were calculated on the offenses before rounding.

Law Enforcement Officers

Source: 1989 *Uniform Crime Reports*, FBI

The Nation's law enforcement community employed an average of 2.2 full-time officers for every 1,000 inhabitants as of October 31, 1989. Considering full-time civilians, the overall law enforcement employee rate was 2.9 per 1,000 inhabitants according to 12,218 city, county, and state police agencies. These agencies collectively offered law enforcement service to a population of nearly 230 million, employing 496,353 officers and 180,294 civilians.

The law enforcement employee average for all cities nationwide was 2.7 per 1,000 inhabitants. City law enforcement employee averages ranged from 2.2 per 1,000 inhabitants in those with populations from 10,000 to 99,000 to 3.5 for those with populations of 250,000 or more. Rural and suburban counties averaged full-time law enforcement employee rates of 3.6 and 3.3 per 1,000 population, respectively.

Regionally, the highest law enforcement employee rate was in the Northeast and the South, each with 2.9. The Midwest rate was 2.5 and the West 2.4.

Nationally, males comprised 92 percent of all sworn employees. Ninety-four percent of the officers in rural counties and 92 percent of those in cities were males, while in suburban counties they accounted for 89 percent.

Civilians made up 27 percent of the total U.S. law enforcement employee force. They represented 22 percent of the police employees in cities, 33 percent of those in rural counties, and 34 percent of the suburban law enforcement strength.

Sixty-seven law enforcement officers were feloniously slain in the line of duty, 11 less than in 1988. Another 78 officers were killed due to accidents occurring while performing official duties.

Murder Weapons, 1985-1989

Source: 1989 *Uniform Crime Reports*, FBI

Weapon	1985	1986	1987	1988	1989
Total	17,545	19,257	17,963	17,971	18,954
Total Firearms.	10,296	11,381	10,612	10,895	11,832
Handguns	7,548	8,460	7,847	8,147	9,013
Rifles.	810	788	776	753	865
Shotguns	1,188	1,296	1,101	1,105	1,173
Other guns	24	22	16	15	34
Firearms-not stated	726	815	872	875	747
Cutting or stabbing instruments	3,694	3,957	3,643	3,457	3,458
Blunt objects (clubs, hammers, etc.)	972	1,099	1,045	1,126	1,128
Personal weapons (hands, fists, feet, etc.)[1]	1,180	1,310	1,165	1,095	1,050
Poison	7	14	34	15	11
Explosives	11	16	12	34	16
Fire	243	230	200	255	234
Narcotics	31	23	24	36	17
Drowning	43	49	51	38	60
Strangulation.	311	341	360	331	366
Asphyxiation	115	160	115	73	101
Other weapons or weapons not stated	642	677	702	616	681

(1) Pushing is included in personal weapons.

State and Federal Prison Population; Death Penalty

Source: Prison population: Bureau of Justice Statistics, U.S. Dept. of Justice, Dec. 31, 1989; death penalty: NAACP Legal Defense and Educational Fund; "Executions" and "Death penalty" as of Dec. 31, 1989; "Under sentence of death" as of July, 1989.

The number of prisoners under jurisdiction of Federal or State correction authorities at year end 1989 reached a record 710,054. From 1980 through 1989 there was an increase of about 115% in the prison population. The 1989 increase meant a nationwide need for more than 1,600 new prison bedspaces per week.

	Sentenced to more than 1 yr.		Incarceration rate 1989*	Death penalty		
	Advance 1989	% change 1988-89		Under sentence of death	Executions	Death penalty
Total	679,263	12.5%	274	2,210	NA	—
Federal institutions	47,168	10.4	19.9	5	NA	Yes
State institutions	632,095	12.7	255	2,205	16	36
Northeast	110,181	16.6%	216	141	0	—
Connecticut	6,309	33.6	194	1	0	Yes
Maine	1,432	18.0	116	0	0	No
Massachusetts	7,268	12.6	123	0	0	No
New Hampshire	1,166	14.4	104	0	0	Yes
New Jersey	19,439	14.8	251	25	0	Yes
New York	51,227	15.0	285	0	0	No
Pennsylvania	21,256	18.9	176	115	0	Yes
Rhode Island	1,467	24.4	147	0	0	No
Vermont	617	11.6	108	0	0	No
Midwest	136,221	13.4%	226	348	1	—
Illinois	24,712	17.2	211	120	0	Yes
Indiana	12,220	8.4	218	50	0	Yes
Iowa	3,584	18.1	126	0	0	No
Kansas	5,622	-3.4	223	0	0	No
Michigan	31,746	15.0	342	0	0	No
Minnesota	3,103	10.9	71	0	0	No
Missouri	13,919	14.3	269	73	1	Yes
Nebraska	2,321	12.3	144	13	0	Yes
North Dakota	404	-2.4	61	0	0	No
Ohio	30,538	15.4	279	92	0	Yes
South Dakota	1,277	25.2	178	0	0	Yes
Wisconsin	6,775	7.1	139	0	0	No
South	249,284	9.9%	290	1,285	13	—
Alabama	13,575	9.9	329	93	4	Yes
Arkansas	6,306	14.3	261	31	0	Yes
Delaware	2,337	5.9	344	7	0	Yes
District of Columbia	6,771	2.2	1,129	0	0	No
Florida	39,966	15.2	311	294	2	Yes
Georgia	19,619	8.9	302	102	1	Yes
Kentucky	8,289	16.4	222	28	0	Yes
Louisiana	17,257	6.2	395	39	0	Yes
Maryland	15,378	13.3	325	19	0	Yes
Mississippi	7,770	6.2	294	45	1	Yes
North Carolina	16,695	2.7	252	81	0	Yes
Oklahoma	11,423	9.3	355	98	0	Yes
South Carolina	14,808	14.8	419	46	0	Yes
Tennessee	10,562	—	213	69	0	Yes
Texas	40,789	.9	239	283	4	Yes
Virginia	16,273	16.8	265	40	1	Yes
West Virginia	1,536	5.6	83	0	0	No
West	136,409	14.0%	264	441	2	—
Alaska	1,908	2.5	363	0	0	No
Arizona	12,726	9.9	354	86	0	Yes
California	84,338	14.3	286	247	0	Yes
Colorado	7,318	26.9	220	3	0	Yes
Hawaii	1,606	6.4	143	0	0	No
Idaho	1,850	17.0	181	16	0	Yes
Montana	1,362	7.1	169	10	0	Yes
Nevada	5,387	10.4	473	45	2	Yes
New Mexico	2,861	5.1	186	2	0	Yes
Oregon	6,744	12.6	237	15	0	Yes
Utah	2,355	21.1	137	8	0	Yes
Washington	6,928	19.1	144	7	0	Yes
Wyoming	1,026	8.6	217	2	0	Yes

*The number of prisoners with sentences of more than 1 year per 100,000 resident population.

Arrests for Drug Abuse Violations, 1989

Source: 1989 Uniform Crime Reports, FBI

(Percent distribution)

	United States Total	North-eastern States	Mid-western States	South-ern States	West-ern States		United States Total	North-eastern States	Mid-western States	South-ern States	West-ern States
Total[1]	100.0	100.0	100.0	100.0	100.0	Possession: . . .	67.6	63.1	54.4	70.6	74.2
Sale/manufacture:	32.4	36.9	45.6	29.4	25.8	Heroin or cocaine and their					
Heroin or cocaine and their						derivatives . . .	34.7	37.4	16.8	29.9	43.8
derivatives . . .	19.1	30.0	9.3	17.4	16.6	Marijuana	23.1	21.9	28.5	33.2	14.2
Marijuana	6.2	4.7	10.9	6.1	5.5	Synthetic or man-ufactured drugs	1.4	1.2	1.1	3.1	0.5
Synthetic or man-ufactured drugs	0.7	0.8	0.7	1.4	0.2	Other dangerous nonnarcotic					
Other dangerous nonnarcotic						drugs	8.4	2.6	8.0	4.4	15.7
drugs	6.3	1.3	24.7	4.5	3.5	(1) Because of rounding, percentages may not add to totals.					

Federal Bureau of Investigation

The Federal Bureau of Investigation (FBI) is the principal investigative arm of the U.S. Department of Justice, and is located at 10th Street and Pennsylvania Avenue, Northwest, Washington, D.C. 20535. It investigates all violations of Federal law except those specifically assigned to some other agency by legislative action. The FBI's jurisdiction includes a wide range of responsibilities in the criminal, civil, and security fields. Priority has been assigned to six areas—counterterrorism, drugs, foreign counterintelligence, organized crime, white-collar crime, and violent crime. On Jan. 28, 1982, the Attorney General assigned concurrent jurisdiction for the enforcement of the Controlled Substances Act to the FBI and the Drug Enforcement Administration (DEA).

The FBI also offers cooperative services to duly authorized law enforcement agencies; these services include fingerprint identification, laboratory examination, police training,

and the National Crime Information Center.

The FBI has 56 field offices in the principal cities of the country. (Consult telephone directories for locations and phone numbers.)

An applicant for the position of Special Agent of the FBI must be a citizen of the U.S., at least 23 and under 35 years old, and a graduate of an accredited law school or of an accredited college or university with a major in accounting. In addition, applicants with a four-year degree from an accredited college or university with a major in other academic areas may qualify with three additional years of full-time work experience. Specialized need areas include languages, science, and financial analysis. Those appointed to the Special Agent position must complete an initial training period of 16 weeks at the FBI Academy, Quantico, Virginia.

U.S. Fires, 1988

Source: National Fire Protection Assn., Quincy, Mass.

Fires
- Fires attended by public fire departments increased by 4.6 percent to 2,436,500.
- Fires in outside properties increased 10.3 percent to 1,214,000.
- Residential properties accounted for 74 percent, or 552,500, of all structure fires.
- Fires in structures decreased by 1.7 percent to 745,000.
- The South's fire incident rate was highest, at 11.5 fires per thousand population.

Fire Deaths
- Civilian fire deaths increased by 7.0 percent to 6,215.
- Home fire deaths, which accounted for about 80 percent of all fire fatalities, increased by 8 percent to 4,955.
- The South had the highest rate of civilian fire deaths, at 32.3 per million population, 28 percent higher than the national average.

Fire Injuries
- Civilian injuries increased 9.2 percent to 30,800. This estimate is on the low side, due to under-reporting of civilian injuries to the fire service.
- Residential properties were the site of 73.4 percent, or 22,600, of civilian injuries, while nonresidential structures saw 11.9 percent, or 3,675.
- The Northeast had the highest civilian injury rate, with 140.4 per million population.

Property Damage
- Property losses increased by a significant 16.7 percent to an estimated $8.352 billion. Three large-loss industrial fires were responsible for 5.6 percent, or $464 million, of this increase.
- Structure fires caused $7.188 billion, or 86 percent, of all property damage.
- Residential properties incurred $4.020 billion, or 56 percent, of all structure property loss.
- The South's property loss rate was 24 percent higher than the national average, at $42 per person.

Incendiary and Suspicious Fires
- The number of structure fires that were set deliberately, or are suspected of having been set, was down 5.2 percent to 99,500.
- Incendiary and suspicious fires accounted for 13.4 percent of all structure fires and 22.2 percent of all structure property loss.
- The average loss per incendiary fire was up 5.8 percent to $16,020.
- Incendiary and suspicious structure fires resulted in 740 civilian deaths, an increase of 1.4 percent, and $1.594 billion in property damage, a slight increase of 0.3 percent.
- Incendiary and suspicious vehicle fires increased 3.9 percent to 53,000 and resulted in $151 million in property damage, up 11.9 percent.

Civilian Fire Deaths and Injuries

Structure Fires by Property Use

Source: National Fire Protection Assn., Quincy, Mass.

	Deaths	%	Injuries	%		No. of fires	Property loss (thousands)
Residential (total)	5,065	81.5	22,600	73.4	Public assembly	20,000	$279,000
One-and Two-Family					Educational	10,000	112,000
Dwellings[1]	4,125	66.4	17,125	55.6	Institutional	14,000	23,000
Apartments	830	13.4	4,950	16.1	Residential	552,500	4,020,000
Hotels and Motels	45	0.7	350	1.1	One-/2-family dwellings[1] . .	432,500	3,349,000
Other Residential. . . .	65	1.0	175	0.6	Apartments	106,000	548,000
Non Residential					Hotels, motels.	8,000	700,000
Structures[2]	215	3.5	3,675	11.9	Other residential	6,000	23,000
Highway Vehicles	800	12.9	2,750	8.9	Stores and offices	38,000	754,000
Other Vehicles[3]	65	1.0	200	0.7	Industry, utility, defense[5] . . .	27,000	1,079,000
All Other[4]	70	1.1	1,575	5.1	Storage in structures[6].	50,000	735,000
					Special structures	33,500	168,000
Total	6,215		30,800		Total	745,000	$2,188,000

Fire Losses — Total and Per Capita; 1960 to 1988

Source: 1960, National Board of Fire Underwriters, New York, NY; thereafter, Insurance Information Institute, New York, NY

(Prior to 1962, excludes Alaska and Hawaii. Includes allowance for uninsured and unreported losses but excludes losses to government property and forests. Based on incurred losses.)

Year	Total (mil. dol.)	Per capita[1]	Year	Total (mil. dol.)	Per capita[1]	Year	Total (mil. dol.)	Per capita[1]
1960	1,108	$6.19	1981	5,625	$24.50	1985	7,753	$32.47
1965	1,456	7.51	1982	5,894	25.41	1986	8,488	35.21
1970	2,328	11.41	1983	6,320	26.98	1987	8,634	35.44
1975	3,190	14.81	1984	7,602	32.15	1988	9,626	39.12
1980	5,579	24.55						

(1) Based on Bureau of the Census estimated resident population as of July 1.

Years of Life Expected at Birth

Source: National Center for Health Statistics

Year	Total	Total Male	Female	White Total	White Male	Female	Black and Other Total	Male	Female
1920*	54.1	53.6	54.6	54.9	54.4	55.6	45.3	45.5	45.2
1930	59.7	58.1	61.6	61.4	59.7	63.5	48.1	47.3	49.2
1940	62.9	60.8	65.2	64.2	62.1	66.6	53.1	51.5	54.9
1950	68.2	65.6	71.1	69.1	66.5	72.2	60.8	59.1	62.9
1960	69.7	66.6	73.1	70.6	67.4	74.1	63.6	61.1	66.3
1965	70.2	66.8	73.7	71.0	67.6	74.7	64.1	61.1	67.4
1970	70.8	67.1	74.7	71.7	68.0	75.6	65.3	61.3	69.4
1971	71.1	67.4	75.0	72.0	68.3	75.8	65.6	61.6	69.8
1972	71.2	67.4	75.1	72.0	68.3	75.9	65.7	61.5	70.1
1973	71.4	67.6	75.3	72.2	68.5	76.1	66.1	62.0	70.3
1974	72.0	68.2	75.9	72.8	69.0	76.7	67.1	62.9	71.3
1975	72.6	68.8	76.6	73.4	69.5	77.3	68.0	63.7	72.4
1976	72.9	69.1	76.8	73.6	69.9	77.5	68.4	64.2	72.7
1977	73.3	69.5	77.2	74.0	70.2	77.9	68.9	64.7	73.2
1979	73.9	70.0	77.8	74.6	70.8	78.4	69.8	65.4	74.1
1980	73.7	70.0	77.5	74.4	70.7	78.1	69.5	65.3	73.6
1981	74.2	70.4	77.8	74.8	71.1	78.4	70.3	66.1	74.4
1982	74.5	70.9	78.1	75.1	71.5	78.7	71.0	66.8	75.0
1983	74.6	71.0	78.1	75.2	71.7	78.7	71.1	67.2	74.3
1984	74.7	71.2	78.2	75.3	71.8	78.7	71.3	67.4	75.0
1985	74.7	71.2	78.2	75.3	71.9	78.7	71.2	67.2	75.0
1986	74.8	71.3	78.3	75.4	72.0	78.8	71.2	67.2	75.1
1987	75.0	71.5	78.4	75.6	72.2	78.9	71.3	67.3	75.2
1988ᵖ	74.9	71.4	78.3	75.5	72.1	78.9	71.5	67.4	75.5
1989ᵖ	75.2	71.8	78.5	75.9	72.6	79.1	71.7	67.5	75.7

p = preliminary * Data prior to 1940 for death-registration states only.

Average Height and Weight for Children

Source: *Physicians Handbook*, 1983

Boys Age Years	ft	Height in	cm	Weight lb	kg	Girls Age Years	ft	Height in	cm	Weight lb	kg
(Birth)	1	8	50.8	7½	3.4	(Birth)	1	8	50.8	7½	3.4
½	2	2	66.0	17	7.7	½	2	2	66.0	16	7.2
1	2	5	73.6	21	9.5	1	2	5	73.6	20	9.1
2	2	9	83.8	26	11.8	2	2	9	83.8	25	11.3
3	3	0	91.4	31	14.0	3	3	0	91.4	30	13.6
4	3	3	99.0	34	15.4	4	3	3	99.0	33	15.0
5	3	6	106.6	39	17.7	5	3	5	104.1	38	17.2
6	3	9	114.2	46	20.9	6	3	8	111.7	45	20.4
7	3	11	119.3	51	23.1	7	3	11	119.3	49	22.2
8	4	2	127.0	57	25.9	8	4	2	127.0	56	25.4
9	4	4	132.0	63	28.6	9	4	4	132.0	62	28.1
10	4	6	137.1	69	31.3	10	4	6	137.1	69	31.3
11	4	8	142.2	77	34.9	11	4	8	142.2	77	34.9
12	4	10	147.3	83	37.7	12	4	10	147.3	86	39.0
13	5	0	152.4	92	41.7	13	5	0	152.4	98	45.5
14	5	2	157.5	107	48.5	14	5	2	157.5	107	48.5

This table gives a general picture of American children at specific ages. When used as a standard, the individual variation in children's growth should not be overlooked. In most cases the height-weight relationship is probably a more valid index of weight status than a weight-for-age assessment.

Average Weight of Americans by Height and Age

Source: Society of Actuaries; from the *1979 Build and Blood Pressure Study*
The figures represent weights in ordinary indoor clothing and shoes, and heights with shoes.

Men Height	20-24	25-29	30-39	40-49	50-59	60-69	Women Height	20-24	25-29	30-39	40-49	50-59	60-69
5'2"	130	134	138	140	141	140	4'10"	105	110	113	118	121	123
5'3"	136	140	143	144	145	144	4'11"	110	112	115	121	125	127
5'4"	139	143	147	149	150	149	5'0"	112	114	118	123	127	130
5'5"	143	147	151	154	155	153	5'1"	116	119	121	127	131	133
5'6"	148	152	156	158	159	158	5'2"	120	121	124	129	133	136
5'7"	153	156	160	163	164	163	5'3"	124	125	128	133	137	140
5'8"	157	161	165	167	168	167	5'4"	127	128	131	136	141	143
5'9"	163	166	170	172	173	172	5'5"	130	132	134	139	144	147
5'10"	167	171	174	176	177	176	5'6"	133	134	137	143	147	150
5'11"	171	175	179	181	182	181	5'7"	137	138	141	147	152	155
6'0"	176	181	184	186	187	186	5'8"	141	142	145	150	156	158
6'1"	182	186	190	192	193	191	5'9"	146	148	150	155	159	161
6'2"	187	191	195	197	198	196	5'10"	149	150	153	158	162	163
6'3"	193	197	201	203	204	200	5'11"	155	156	159	162	166	167
6'4"	198	202	206	208	209	207	6'0"	157	159	164	168	171	172

SPORTS IN 1990

Olympic Games Records

The modern Olympic Games, first held in Athens, Greece in 1896, were the result of efforts by Baron Pierre de Coubertin, a French educator, to promote interest in education and culture, also to foster better international understanding through the universal medium of youth's love of athletics.

His source of inspiration for the Olympic Games was the ancient Greek Olympic Games, most notable of the four Panhellenic celebrations. The games were combined patriotic, religious, and athletic festivals held every four years. The first such recorded festival was held in 776 B.C., the date from which the Greeks began to keep their calendar by "Olympiads," or four-year spans between the games.

The first Olympiad is said to have consisted merely of a 200-yard foot race near the small city of Olympia, but the games gained in scope and became demonstrations of national pride. Only Greek citizens — amateurs — were permitted to participate. Winners received laurel, wild olive, and palm wreaths and were accorded many special privileges. Under the Roman emperors, the games deteriorated into professional carnivals and circuses. Emperor Theodosius banned them in 394 A.D.

Baron de Coubertin enlisted 9 nations to send athletes to the first modern Olympics in 1896; now more than 100 nations compete. Winter Olympic Games were started in 1924.

Sites of Olympic Games

1896 Athens	1920 Antwerp	1952 Helsinki	1976 Montreal
1900 Paris	1924 Paris	1956 Melbourne	1980 Moscow
1904 St. Louis	1928 Amsterdam	1960 Rome	1984 Los Angeles
1906 Athens*	1932 Los Angeles	1964 Tokyo	1988 Seoul
1908 London	1936 Berlin	1968 Mexico City	1992 Barcelona
1912 Stockholm	1948 London	1972 Munich	

*Games not recognized by International Olympic Committee. Games 6 (1916), 12 (1940), and 13 (1944) were not celebrated. The 1980 games were boycotted by 62 nations, including the U.S. The 1984 games were boycotted by the USSR and most eastern bloc nations. East and West Germany began competing separately in 1968.

Olympic Games Champions, 1896—1988

(*Indicates Gold Medal-Winning Record)

Track and Field — Men

100-Meter Run

1896	Thomas Burke, United States	12s
1900	Francis W. Jarvis, United States	11.0s
1904	Archie Hahn, United States	11s
1908	Reginald Walker, South Africa	10.8s
1912	Ralph Craig, United States	10.8s
1920	Charles Paddock, United States	10.8s
1924	Harold Abrahams, Great Britain	10.6s
1928	Percy Williams, Canada	10.8s
1932	Eddie Tolan, United States	10.3s
1936	Jesse Owens, United States	10.3s
1948	Harrison Dillard, United States	10.3s
1952	Lindy Remigino, United States	10.4s
1956	Bobby Morrow, United States	10.5s
1960	Armin Hary, Germany	10.2s
1964	Bob Hayes, United States	10.0s
1968	Jim Hines, United States	9.95s
1972	Valery Borzov, USSR	10.14s
1976	Hasely Crawford, Trinidad	10.06s
1980	Allan Wells, Great Britain	10.25s
1984	Carl Lewis, United States	9.99s
1988	Carl Lewis, United States	9.92s*

200-Meter Run

1900	Walter Tewksbury, United States	22.2s
1904	Archie Hahn, United States	21.6s
1908	Robert Kerr, Canada	22.6s
1912	Ralph Craig, United States	21.7s
1920	Allan Woodring, United States	22s
1924	Jackson Scholz, United States	21.6s
1928	Percy Williams, Canada	21.8s
1932	Eddie Tolan, United States	21.2s
1936	Jesse Owens, United States	20.7s
1948	Mel Patton, United States	21.1s
1952	Andrew Stanfield, United States	20.7s
1956	Bobby Morrow, United States	20.6s
1960	Livio Berruti, Italy	20.5s
1964	Henry Carr, United States	20.3s
1968	Tommie Smith, United States	19.83s
1972	Valeri Borzov, USSR	20.00s
1976	Donald Quarrie, Jamaica	20.23s
1980	Pietro Mennea, Italy	20.19s
1984	Carl Lewis, United States	19.80s
1988	Joe DeLoach, United States	19.75s*

400-Meter Run

1896	Thomas Burke, United States	54.2s
1900	Maxey Long, United States	49.4s
1904	Harry Hillman, United States	49.2s
1908	Wyndham Halswelle, Great Britain, walkover	50s
1912	Charles Reidpath, United States	48.2s
1920	Bevil Rudd, South Africa	49.6s
1924	Eric Liddell, Great Britain	47.6s
1928	Ray Barbuti, United States	47.8s
1932	William Carr, United States	46.2s
1936	Archie Williams, United States	46.5s
1948	Arthur Wint, Jamaica, B W I	46.2s
1952	George Rhoden, Jamaica, B W I	45.9s
1956	Charles Jenkins, United States	46.7s
1960	Otis Davis, United States	44.9s
1964	Michael Larrabee, United States	45.1s
1968	Lee Evans, United States	43.8s*
1972	Vincent Matthews, United States	44.66s
1976	Alberto Juantorena, Cuba	44.26s
1980	Viktor Markin, USSR	44.60s
1984	Alonzo Babers, United States	44.27s
1988	Steven Lewis, United States	43.87s

800-Meter Run

1896	Edwin Flack, Australia	2m. 11s
1900	Alfred Tysoe, Great Britain	2m. 1.2s
1904	James Lightbody, United States	1m. 56s
1908	Mel Sheppard, United States	1m. 52.8s
1912	James Meredith, United States	1m. 51.9s
1920	Albert Hill, Great Britain	1m. 53.4s
1924	Douglas Lowe, Great Britain	1m. 52.4s
1928	Douglas Lowe, Great Britain	1m. 51.8s
1932	Thomas Hampson, Great Britain	1m. 49.8s
1936	John Woodruff, United States	1m. 52.9s
1948	Mal Whitfield, United States	1m. 49.2s
1952	Mal Whitfield, United States	1m. 49.2s
1956	Thomas Courtney, United States	1m. 47.7s
1960	Peter Snell, New Zealand	1m. 46.3s
1964	Peter Snell, New Zealand	1m. 45.1s
1968	Ralph Doubell, Australia	1m. 44.3s
1972	Dave Wottle, United States	1m. 45.9s
1976	Alberto Juantorena, Cuba	1m. 43.50s
1980	Steve Ovett, Great Britain	1m. 45.40s
1984	Joaquim Cruz, Brazil	1m. 43.00s*
1988	Paul Ereng, Kenya	1m. 43.45s

1,500-Meter Run

1896	Edwin Flack, Australia	4m. 33.2s
1900	Charles Bennett, Great Britain	4m. 6.2s
1904	James Lightbody, United States	4m. 5.4s
1908	Mel Sheppard, United States	4m. 3.4s
1912	Arnold Jackson, Great Britain	3m. 56.8s
1920	Albert Hill, Great Britain	4m. 1.8s
1924	Paavo Nurmi, Finland	3m. 53.6s
1928	Harry Larva, Finland	3m. 53.2s
1932	Luigi Beccali, Italy	3m. 51.2s
1936	Jack Lovelock, New Zealand	3m. 47.8s
1948	Henri Eriksson, Sweden	3m. 49.8s
1952	Joseph Barthel, Luxemburg	3m. 45.2s
1956	Ron Delany, Ireland	3m. 41.2s
1960	Herb Elliott, Australia	3m. 35.6s
1964	Peter Snell, New Zealand	3m. 38.1s
1968	Kipchoge Keino, Kenya	3m. 34.9s
1972	Pekka Vasala, Finland	3m. 36.3s
1976	John Walker, New Zealand	3m. 39.17s
1980	Sebastian Coe, Great Britain	3m. 38.4s
1984	Sebastian Coe, Great Britain	3m. 32.53s*
1988	Peter Rono, Kenya	3m. 35.96s

3,000-Meter Steeplechase

1920	Percy Hodge, Great Britain	10m. 0.4s
1924	Willie Ritola, Finland	9m. 33.6s
1928	Toivo Loukola, Finland	9m. 21.8s
1932	Volmari Iso-Hollo, Finland	10m. 33.4s
	(About 3,450 mtrs. extra lap by error)	
1936	Volmari Iso-Hollo, Finland	9m. 3.8s
1948	Thore Sjoestrand, Sweden	9m. 4.6s
1952	Horace Ashenfelter, United States	8m. 45.4s
1956	Chris Brasher, Great Britain	8m. 41.2s
1960	Zdzislaw Krzyszkowiak, Poland	8m. 34.2s
1964	Gaston Roelants, Belgium	8m. 30.8s
1968	Amos Biwott, Kenya	8m. 51s
1972	Kipchoge Keino, Kenya	8m. 23.6s
1976	Anders Garderud, Sweden	8m. 08.2s
1980	Bronislaw Malinowski, Poland	8m. 09.7s
1984	Julius Korir, Kenya	8m. 11.8s
1988	Julius Kariuki, Kenya	8m. 05.51s*

5,000-Meter Run

1912	Hannes Kolehmainen, Finland	14m. 36.6s
1920	Joseph Guillemot, France	14m. 55.6s
1924	Paavo Nurmi, Finland	14m. 31.2s
1928	Willie Ritola, Finland	14m. 38s
1932	Lauri Lehtinen, Finland	14m. 30s
1936	Gunnar Hockert, Finland	14m. 22.2s
1948	Gaston Reiff, Belgium	14m. 17.6s
1952	Emil Zatopek, Czechoslovakia	14m. 6.6s
1956	Vladimir Kuts, USSR	13m. 39.6s
1960	Murray Halberg, New Zealand	13m. 43.4s
1964	Bob Schul, United States	13m. 48.8s
1968	Mohamed Gammoudi, Tunisia	14m. 05.0s
1972	Lasse Viren, Finland	13m. 26.4s
1976	Lasse Viren, Finland	13m. 24.76s
1980	Miruts Yifter, Ethiopia	13m. 21.0s
1984	Said Aouita, Morocco	13m. 05.59s*
1988	John Ngugi, Kenya	13m. 11.70s

10,000-Meter Run

1912	Hannes Kolehmainen, Finland	31m. 20.8s
1920	Paavo Nurmi, Finland	31m. 45.8s
1924	Willie Ritola, Finland	30m. 23.2s
1928	Paavo Nurmi, Finland	30m. 18.8s
1932	Janusz Kusocinski, Poland	30m. 11.4s
1936	Ilmari Salminen, Finland	30m. 15.4s
1948	Emil Zatopek, Czechoslovakia	29m. 59.6s
1952	Emil Zatopek, Czechoslovakia	29m. 17.0s
1956	Vladimir Kuts, USSR	28m. 45.6s
1960	Pyotr Bolotnikov, USSR	28m. 32.2s
1964	Billy Mills, United States	28m. 24.4s
1968	Naftali Temu, Kenya	29m. 27.4s
1972	Lasse Viren, Finland	27m. 38.4s
1976	Lasse Viren, Finland	27m. 40.38s
1980	Miruts Yifter, Ethiopia	27m. 42.7s
1984	Alberto Cova, Italy	27m. 47.54
1988	Brahim Boutaib, Morocco	27m. 21.46s*

Marathon

1896	Spiridon Loues, Greece	2h. 58m. 50s
1900	Michel Theato, France	2h. 59m. 45s
1904	Thomas Hicks, United States	3h. 28m. 63s
1908	John J. Hayes, United States	2h. 55m. 18.4s
1912	Kenneth McArthur, South Africa	2h. 36m. 54.8s
1920	Hannes Kolehmainen, Finland	2h. 32m. 35.8s
1924	Albin Stenroos, Finland	2h. 41m. 22.6s
1928	A.B. El Ouafi, France	2h. 32m. 57s
1932	Juan Zabala, Argentina	2h. 31m. 36s
1936	Kijung Son, Japan (Korean)	2h. 29m. 19.2s
1948	Delfo Cabrera, Argentina	2h. 34m. 51.6s
1952	Emil Zatopek, Czechoslovakia	2h. 23m. 03.2s
1956	Alain Mimoun, France	2h. 25m.
1960	Abebe Bikila, Ethiopia	2h. 15m. 16.2s
1964	Abebe Bikila, Ethiopia	2h. 12m. 11.2s
1968	Mamo Wolde, Ethiopia	2h. 20m. 26.4s
1972	Frank Shorter, United States	2h. 12m. 19.8s
1976	Waldemar Cierpinski, E. Germany	2h. 09m. 55s
1980	Waldemar Cierpinski, E. Germany	2h. 11m. 03s
1984	Carlos Lopes, Portugal	2h. 09m. 21 s*
1988	Gelindo Bordin, Italy	2h. 10m. 32s

20-Kilometer Walk

1956	Leonid Spirin, USSR	1h. 31m. 27.4s
1960	Vladimir Golubnichy, USSR	1h. 33m. 7.2s
1964	Kenneth Mathews, Great Britain	1h. 29m. 34.0s
1968	Vladimir Golubnichy, USSR	1h. 33m. 58.4s
1972	Peter Frenkel, E. Germany	1h. 26m. 42.4s
1976	Daniel Bautista, Mexico	1h. 24m. 40.6s
1980	Maurizio Damilano, Italy	1h. 23m. 35.5s
1984	Ernesto Canto, Mexico	1h. 23m. 13.0s
1988	Josef Pribilinec, Czech	1h. 19m. 57.0s*

50-Kilometer Walk

1932	Thomas W. Green, Great Britain	4h. 50m. 10s
1936	Harold Whitlock, Great Britain	4h. 30m. 41.4s
1948	John Ljunggren, Sweden	4h. 41m. 52s
1952	Giuseppe Dordoni, Italy	4h. 28m. 07.8s
1956	Norman Read, New Zealand	4h. 30m. 42.8s
1960	Donald Thompson, Great Britain	4h. 25m. 30s
1964	Abdon Pamich, Italy	4h. 11m. 12.4s
1968	Christoph Hohne, E. Germany	4h. 20m. 13.6s
1972	Bern Kannenberg, W. Germany	3h. 56m. 11.6s
1980	Hartwig Gauter, E. Germany	3h. 49m. 24.0s
1984	Raul Gonzalez, Mexico	3h. 47m. 26.0
1988	Vayachselav Ivanenko, USSR	3h. 38m. 29.0s*

110-Meter Hurdles

1896	Thomas Curtis, United States	17.6s
1900	Alvin Kraenzlein, United States	15.4s
1904	Frederick Schule, United States	16s
1908	Forrest Smithson, United States	15s
1912	Frederick Kelly, United States	15.1s
1920	Earl Thomson, Canada	14.8s
1924	Daniel Kinsey, United States	15s
1928	Sydney Atkinson, South Africa	14.8s
1932	George Saling, United States	14.6s
1936	Forrest Towns, United States	14.2s
1948	William Porter, United States	13.9s
1952	Harrison Dillard, United States	13.7s
1956	Lee Calhoun, United States	13.5s
1960	Lee Calhoun, United States	13.8s
1964	Hayes Jones, United States	13.6s
1968	Willie Davenport, United States	13.3s
1972	Rod Milburn, United States	13.24s
1976	Guy Drut, France	13.30s
1980	Thomas Munkelt, E. Germany	13. 39s
1984	Roger Kingdom, United States	13.20s
1988	Roger Kingdom, United States	12.98*

400-Meter Hurdles

1900	J.W.B. Tewksbury, United States	57.6s
1904	Harry Hillman, United States	53s
1908	Charles Bacon, United States	55s
1920	Frank Loomis, United States	54s
1924	F. Morgan Taylor, United States	52.6s
1928	Lord Burghley, Great Britain	53.4s
1932	Robert Tisdall, Ireland	51.7s
1936	Glenn Hardin, United States	52.4s
1948	Roy Cochran, United States	51.1s
1952	Charles Moore, United States	50.8s
1956	Glenn Davis, United States	50.1s
1960	Glenn Davis, United States	49.3s
1964	Rex Cawley, United States	49.6s
1968	Dave Hemery, Great Britain	48.12s
1972	John Akii-Bua, Uganda	47.82s
1976	Edwin Moses, United States	47.64s
1980	Volker Beck, E. Germany	48.70s
1984	Edwin Moses, United States	47.75s
1988	Andre Phillips, United States	47.19s*

High Jump

1896	Ellery Clark, United States	5ft. 11 1-4 in.
1900	Irving Baxter, United States	6ft. 2 4-5 in.
1904	Samuel Jones, United States	5ft. 11 in.
1908	Harry Porter, United States	6ft. 3 in.
1912	Alma Richards, United States	6ft. 4 in.
1920	Richmond Landon, United States	6ft. 4 in.
1924	Harold Osborn, United States	6ft. 6 in.
1928	Robert W. King, United States	6ft. 4 1-2 in.
1932	Duncan McNaughton, Canada	6ft. 5 5-8 in.
1936	Cornelius Johnson, United States	6ft. 8 in.
1948	John L. Winter, Australia	6ft. 6 in.
1952	Walter Davis, United States	6ft. 8.32 in.
1956	Charles Dumas, United States	6ft. 11 1-2 in.
1960	Robert Shavlakadze, USSR	7ft. 1 in.
1964	Valery Brumel, USSR	7ft. 1 3-4 in.
1968	Dick Fosbury, United States	7ft. 4 1-4 in.
1972	Yuri Tarmak, USSR	7ft. 3 3-4 in.
1976	Jacek Wszola, Poland	7ft. 4 1-2 in.
1980	Gerd Wessig, E. Germany	7ft. 8 3-4 in.
1984	Dietmar Mogenburg, W. Germany	7ft. 8 1-2 in.
1988	Guennadi Avdeenko, USSR	7ft 9 1-2 in.*

Long Jump

1896	Ellery Clark, United States	20ft. 10 in.
1900	Alvin Kraenzlein, United States	23ft. 6 3-4 in.
1904	Myer Prinstein, United States	24ft. 1 in.
1908	Frank Irons, United States	24ft. 6 1-2 in.
1912	Albert Gutterson, United States	24ft. 11 1-4 in.
1920	William Pettersson, Sweden	23ft. 5 1-2 in.
1924	DeHart Hubbard, United States	24ft. 5 in.
1928	Edward B. Hamm, United States	25ft. 4 1-2 in.
1932	Edward Gordon, United States	25ft. 3-4 in.
1936	Jesse Owens, United States	26ft. 5 1-2 in.
1948	William Steele, United States	25ft. 8 in.
1952	Jerome Biffle, United States	24ft. 10 in.
1956	Gregory Bell, United States	25ft. 8 1-4 in.
1960	Ralph Boston, United States	26ft. 7 3-4 in.
1964	Lynn Davies, Great Britain	26ft. 5 3-4 in.
1968	Bob Beamon, United States	29ft. 2 1-2 in.*
1972	Randy Williams, United States	27ft. 1-2 in.
1976	Arnie Robinson, United States	27ft. 4 1-2 in.
1980	Lutz Dombrowski, E. Germany	28ft. 1-4 in.
1984	Carl Lewis, United States	28ft. 1-4 in.
1988	Carl Lewis, United States	28ft. 7 1-4 in.

400-Meter Relay

1912	Great Britain	42.4s
1920	United States	42.2s
1924	United States	41s
1928	United States	41s
1932	United States	40s
1936	United States	39.8s
1948	United States	40.6s
1952	United States	40.1s
1956	United States	39.5s
1960	Germany (U.S. disqualified)	39.5s
1964	United States	39.0s
1968	United States	38.2s
1972	United States	38.19s
1976	United States	38.33s
1980	USSR	38.26s
1984	United States	37.83s*
1988	USSR (U.S. disqualified)	38.19s

1,600-Meter Relay

1908	United States	3m. 29.4s
1912	United States	3m. 16.6s
1920	Great Britain	3m. 22.2s
1924	United States	3m. 16s
1928	United States	3m. 14.2s
1932	United States	3m. 8.2s
1936	Great Britain	3m. 9s
1948	United States	3m. 10.4s
1952	Jamaica, B.W.I.	3m. 03.9s
1956	United States	3m. 04.8s
1960	United States	3m. 02.2s
1964	United States	3m. 00.7s
1968	United States	2m. 56.16s*
1972	Kenya	2m. 59.8s
1976	United States	2m. 58.65s
1980	USSR	3m. 01.1s
1984	United States	2m. 57.91 s
1988	United States	2m. 56.16s*

Pole Vault

1895	William Hoyt, United States	10ft. 10 in.
1900	Irving Baxter, United States	10ft. 10 in.
1904	Charles Dvorak, United States	11ft. 5 3-4 in.
1908	A. C. Gilbert, United States	
	Edward Cook Jr., United States	12ft. 2 in.
1912	Harry Babcock, United States	12ft. 11 1-2 in.
1920	Frank Foss, United States	13ft. 5 in.
1924	Lee Barnes, United States	12ft. 11 1-2 in.
1928	Sabin W. Carr, United States	13ft. 9 1-4 in.
1932	William Miller, United States	14ft. 1 3-4 in.
1936	Earle Meadows, United States	14ft. 3 1-4 in.
1948	Guinn Smith, United States	14ft. 1 1-4 in.
1952	Robert Richards, United States	14ft. 11 in.
1956	Robert Richards, United States	14ft. 11 1-2 in.
1960	Don Bragg, United States	15ft. 5 in.
1964	Fred Hansen, United States	16ft. 8 3-4 in.
1968	Bob Seagren, United States	17ft. 8 1-2 in.
1972	Wolfgang Nordwig, E. Germany	18ft. 1-2 in.
1976	Tadeusz Slusarski, Poland	18ft. 1-2 in.
1980	Wladyslaw Kozakiewicz, Poland	18ft. 11 1-2 in.
1984	Pierre Quinon, France	18ft. 10 1-4 in.
1988	Sergei Bubka, USSR	19ft. 9 1-4 in.*

Hammer Throw

1900	John Flanagan, United States	163ft. 1 in.
1904	John Flanagan, United States	168ft. 1 in.
1908	John Flanagan, United States	170ft. 4 1-4 in.
1912	Matt McGrath, United States	179ft. 7 1-8 in.
1920	Pat Ryan, United States	173ft. 5 5-8 in.
1924	Fred Tootell, United States	174ft. 10 1-8 in.
1928	Patrick O'Callaghan, Ireland	168ft. 7 1-2 in.
1932	Patrick O'Callaghan, Ireland	176ft. 11 1-8 in.
1936	Karl Hein, Germany	185ft. 4 in.
1948	Imre Nemeth, Hungary	183ft. 11 1-2 in.
1952	Jozsef Csermak, Hungary	197ft. 11 9-16 in.
1956	Harold Connolly, United States	207ft. 3 1-2 in.
1960	Vasily Rudenkov, USSR	220ft. 1 5-8 in.
1964	Romuald Klim, USSR	228ft. 9 1-2 in.
1968	Gyula Zsivotsky, Hungary	240ft. 8 in.
1972	Anatoli Bondarchuk, USSR	247ft. 8 in.
1976	Yuri Syedykh, USSR	254ft. 4 in.
1980	Yuri Syedykh, USSR	268ft. 4 1-2 in.
1984	Juha Tiainen, Finland	256ft. 2 in.
1988	Sergei Litinov, USSR	278ft. 2 1-2 in.*

Discus Throw

1896	Robert Garrett, United States	95ft. 7 1-2 in.
1900	Rudolf Bauer, Hungary	118ft. 3 in.
1904	Martin Sheridan, United States	128ft. 10 1-2 in.
1908	Martin Sheridan, United States	134ft. 2 in.
1912	Armas Taipale, Finland	148ft. 3 in.
	Both hands—Armas Taipale, Finland	271ft. 10 1-4 in.
1920	Elmer Niklander, Finland	146ft. 7 in.
1924	Clarence Houser, United States	151ft. 4 in.
1928	Clarence Houser, United States	155ft. 3 in.
1932	John Anderson, United States	162ft. 4 in.
1936	Ken Carpenter, United States	165ft. 7 in.
1948	Adolfo Consolini, Italy	173ft. 2 in.
1952	Sim Iness, United States	180ft. 6.85 in.
1956	Al Oerter, United States	184ft. 10 1-2 in.
1960	Al Oerter, United States	194ft. 2 in.
1964	Al Oerter, United States	200ft. 1 1-2 in.
1968	Al Oerter, United States	212ft. 6 1-2 in.
1972	Ludvik Danek, Czechoslovakia	211ft. 3 in.
1976	Mac Wilkins, United States	221ft. 5.4 in.
1980	Viktor Rashchupkin, USSR	218ft. 8 in.
1984	Rolf Dannenberg, W. Germany	218ft. 6 in.
1988	Jurgen Schult, E. Germany	225ft. 9 1-4 in.*

Triple Jump

1896	James Connolly, United States	44ft. 11 3-4 in.
1900	Myer Prinstein, United States	47ft. 5 3-4 in.
1904	Myer Prinstein, United States	47 ft.
1908	Timothy Ahearne, Great Britain, Ireland	48ft. 11 1-4 in.
1912	Gustaf Lindblom, Sweden	48ft. 5 1-4 in.
1920	Vilho Tuulos, Finland	47ft. 7 in.
1924	Anthony Winter, Australia	50ft. 11 1-4 in.
1928	Mikio Oda, Japan	49ft. 11 in.
1932	Chuhei Nambu, Japan	51ft. 7 in.
1936	Naoto Tajima, Japan	52ft. 6 in.
1948	Arne Ahman, Sweden	50ft. 6 1-4 in.
1952	Adhemar da Silva, Brazil	53ft. 2 3-4 in.
1956	Adhemar da Silva, Brazil	53ft. 7 3-4 in.
1960	Jozef Schmidt, Poland	55ft. 2 in.
1964	Jozef Schmidt, Poland	55ft. 3 1-2 in.

(continued)

1968	Viktor Saneev, USSR	57ft. 3-4 in.
1972	Viktor Saneev, USSR	56ft. 11 in.
1976	Viktor Saneev, USSR	56ft. 8 3-4 in.
1980	Jaak Uudmaa, USSR	56ft. 11 1-4 in.
1984	Al Joyner, United States	56ft. 7 1-2 in.
1988	Hristo Markov, Bulgaria	57ft. 9 1-4 in.*

16-lb. Shot Put

1896	Robert Garrett, United States	36ft. 9 3-4 in.
1900	Richard Sheldon, United States	46ft. 3 1-4 in.
1904	Ralph Rose, United States	48ft. 7 in.
1908	Ralph Rose, United States	46ft. 7 1-2 in.
1912	Pat McDonald, United States	50ft. 4 in.
	Both hands—Ralph Rose, United States	90ft. 5 1-2 in.
1920	Ville Porhola, Finland	48ft. 7 1-4 in.
1924	Clarence Houser, United States	49ft. 2 1-4 in.
1928	John Kuck, United States	52ft. 3-4 in.
1932	Leo Sexton, United States	52ft. 6 in.
1936	Hans Woellke, Germany	53ft. 1 3-4 in.
1948	Wilbur Thompson, United States	56ft. 2 in.
1952	Parry O'Brien, United States	57ft. 1-2 in.
1956	Parry O'Brien, United States	60ft. 11 1-4 in.
1960	William Nieder, United States	64ft. 6 3-4 in.
1964	Dallas Long, United States	66ft. 8 1-2 in.
1968	Randy Matson, United States	67ft. 4 3-4 in.
1972	Wladyslaw Komar, Poland	69ft. 6 in.
1976	Udo Beyer, E. Germany	69ft. 3-4 in.
1980	Vladimir Kiselyov, USSR	70ft. 1-2 in.
1984	Alessandro Andrei, Italy	69ft. 9 in.
1988	Ulf Timmermann, E. Germany	73ft. 8 3-4 in.*

Javelin

1908	Erik Lemming, Sweden	178ft. 7 1-2 in.
	Held in middle—Erik Lemming, Sweden	179ft. 10 1-2 in.
1912	Erik Lemming, Sweden	198ft. 11 1-4 in.
	Both hands, Julius Saaristo, Finland	358ft. 11 7-8 in.
1920	Jonni Myrra, Finland	215ft. 9 3-4 in.
1924	Jonni Myrra, Finland	206ft. 6 3-4 in.
1928	Eric Lundkvist, Sweden	218ft. 6 1-8 in.

1932	Matti Jarvinen, Finland	238ft. 6 in.
1936	Gerhard Stoeck, Germany	235ft. 8 5-16 in.
1948	Kaj Rautavaara, Finland	228ft. 10 1-2 in.
1952	Cy Young, United States	242ft. 0.79 in.
1956	Egil Danielson, Norway	281ft. 2 1-4 in.
1960	Viktor Tsibulenko, USSR	277ft. 8 3-8 in.
1964	Pauli Nevala, Finland	271ft. 2 1-2 in.
1968	Janis Lusis, USSR	295ft. 7 1-4 in.
1972	Klaus Wolfermann, W. Germany	296ft. 10 in.
1976	Miklos Nemeth, Hungary	310ft. 4 in.*
1980	Dainis Kula, USSR	299ft. 2 3-8 in.
1984	Arto Haerkoenen, Finland	284ft. 8 in.
1988	Tapio Korjus, Finland	276ft. 6 in.

Decathlon

1912	Hugo Wieslander, Sweden	7,724.49 pts.(a)
1920	Helge Lovland, Norway	6,804.35 pts.
1924	Harold Osborn, United States	7,710.77 pts.
1928	Paavo Yrjola, Finland	8,053.29 pts.
1932	James Bausch, United States	8,462.23 pts.
1936	Glenn Morris, United States	7,900 pts.
1948	Robert Mathias, United States	7,139 pts.
1952	Robert Mathias, United States	7,887 pts.
1956	Milton Campbell, United States	7,937 pts.
1960	Rafer Johnson, United States	8,392 pts.
1964	Willi Holdorf, Germany	7,887 pts.(c)
1968	Bill Toomey, United States	8,193 pts.
1972	Nikolai Avilov, USSR	8,454 pts.
1976	Bruce Jenner, United States	8,617 pts.
1980	Daley Thompson, Great Britain	8,495 pts.
1984	Daley Thompson, Great Britain	8,798 pts.*(b)
1988	Christian Schenk, E. Germany	8,488 pts.

(a) Jim Thorpe of the U.S. won the 1912 Decathlon with 8,413 pts. but was disqualified and had to return his medals because he had played professional baseball prior to the Olympic games. The medals were restored posthumously in 1982. (b) Scoring change effective Apr., 1985. (c) Former point systems used prior to 1964.

Track and Field—Women

100-Meter Run

1928	Elizabeth Robinson, United States	12.2s
1932	Stella Walsh, Poland	11.9s
1936	Helen Stephens, United States	11.5s
1948	Francina Blankers-Koen, Netherlands	11.9s
1952	Marjorie Jackson, Australia	11.5s
1956	Betty Cuthbert, Australia	11.5s
1960	Wilma Rudolph, United States	11.0s
1964	Wyomia Tyus, United States	11.4s
1968	Wyomia Tyus, United States	11.0s
1972	Renate Stecher, E. Germany	11.07s
1976	Annegret Richter, W. Germany	11.08s
1980	Lyudmila Kondratyeva, USSR	11.6s
1984	Evelyn Ashford, United States	10.97s
1988	Florence Griffith-Joyner, United States	10.54s*

200-Meter Run

1948	Francina Blankers-Koen, Netherlands	24.4s
1952	Marjorie Jackson, Australia	23.7s
1956	Betty Cuthbert, Australia	23.4s
1960	Wilma Rudolph, United States	24.0s
1964	Edith McGuire, United States	23.0s
1968	Irena Szewinska, Poland	22.5s
1972	Renate Stecher, E. Germany	22.40s
1976	Barbel Eckert, E. Germany	22.37s
1980	Barbel Wockel, E. Germany	22.03
1984	Valerie Brisco-Hooks, United States	21.81s
1988	Florence Griffith-Joyner, United States	21.34s*

400-Meter Run

1964	Betty Cuthbert, Australia	52s
1968	Colette Besson, France	52s
1972	Monika Zehrt, E. Germany	51.08s
1976	Irena Szewinska, Poland	49.29s
1980	Marita Koch, E. Germany	48.88s
1984	Valerie Brisco-Hooks, United States	48.83s
1988	Olga Bryzgina, USSR	48.65s*

800-Meter Run

1928	Lina Radke, Germany	2m. 16.8s
1960	Ludmila Shevtsova, USSR	2m. 4.3s
1964	Ann Packer, Great Britain	2m. 1.1s

1968	Madeline Manning, United States	2m. 0.9s
1972	Hildegard Falck, W. Germany	1m. 58.6s
1976	Tatyana Kazankina, USSR	1m. 54.94s
1980	Nadezhda Olizayrenko, USSR	1m. 53.5s*
1984	Doina Melinte, Romania	1m. 57.6s
1988	Sigrun Wodars, E. Germany	1m. 56.10s

1,500-Meter Run

1972	Lyudmila Bragina, USSR	4m. 01.4s
1976	Tatyana Kazankina, USSR	4m. 05.48s
1980	Tatyana Kazankina, USSR	3m. 56.6s
1984	Gabriella Dorio, Italy	4m. 03.25s
1988	Paula Ivan, Romania	3m. 53.96s*

3,000-Meter Run

1984	Maricica Puica, Romania	8:35.96s
1988	Tatyana Samolenko, USSR	8:26.53s*

10,000-Meter Run

1988	Olga Boldarenko, USSR	31m. 44.69s*

400-Meter Relay

1928	Canada	48.4s
1932	United States	46.9s
1936	United States	46.9s
1948	Netherlands	47.5s
1952	United States	45.9s
1956	Australia	44.5s
1960	United States	44.5s
1964	Poland	43.6s
1968	United States	42.8s
1972	West Germany	42.81s
1976	East Germany	42.55s
1980	East Germany	41.60s*
1984	United States	41.65s
1988	United States	41.98s

1,600-Meter Relay

1972	East Germany	3m. 23s
1976	East Germany	3m. 19.23s

1980	USSR.	3m. 20.02s
1984	United States	3m. 18.29s
1988	USSR.	3 m. 15.18s*

80-Meter Hurdles

1932	"Babe" Didrikson, United States	11.7s
1936	Trebisonda Valla, Italy.	11.7s
1948	Francina Blankers-Koen, Netherlands.	11.2s
1952	Shirley Strickland de la Hunty, Australia	10.9s
1956	Shirley Strickland de la Hunty, Australia	10.7s
1960	Irina Press, USSR.	10.8s
1964	Karin Balzer, Germany	10.5s
1968	Maureen Caird, Australia	10.3s*

100-Meter Hurdles

1972	Annelie Ehrhardt, E. Germany	12.59s
1976	Johanna Schaller, E. Germany	12.77s
1980	Vera Komisova, USSR.	12.56s
1984	Benita Brown-Fitzgerald, United States	12.84s
1988	Jordanka Donkova, Bulgaria.	12.38s*

400-Meter Hurdles

1984	Nawal el Moutawakil, Morocco	54.61s
1988	Debra Flintoff-King, Australia	53.17s*

10,000-Meter Run

1988	Olga Boldarenko, USSR.	31m. 44.69s*

Heptathlon

1984	Glynis Nunn, Australia.	6,390 pts.
1988	Jackie Joyner-Kersee, United States	7,215 pts.*

High Jump

1928	Ethel Catherwood, Canada	5ft. 2 1-2 in.
1932	Jean Shiley, United States.	5ft. 5 1-4 in.
1936	Ibolya Csak, Hungary.	5ft. 3 in.
1948	Alice Coachman, United States.	5ft. 6 1-8 in.
1952	Esther Brand, South Africa	5ft. 5 3-4 in.
1956	Mildred L. McDaniel, United States.	5ft. 9 1-4 in.
1960	Iolanda Balas, Romania	6ft. 3-4 in.
1964	Iolanda Balas, Romania	6ft. 2 3-4 in.
1968	Miloslava Reskova, Czechoslovakia	5ft. 11 1-2 in.
1972	Ulrike Meyfarth, W. Germany	6ft. 4 in.
1976	Rosemarie Ackermann, E. Germany	6ft. 3 3-4 in.
1980	Sara Simeoni, Italy	6ft. 5 1-2 in.
1984	Ulrike Meyfarth, W. Germany	6ft. 7 1-2 in.
1988	Louise Ritter, United States.	6ft. 8 in.*

Discus Throw

1928	Helena Konopacka, Poland.	129ft. 11 3-4 in.
1932	Lillian Copeland, United States.	133ft. 2 in.
1936	Gisela Mauermayer, Germany.	156ft. 3 in.
1948	Micheline Ostermeyer, France.	137ft. 6 1-2 in.
1952	Nina Romaschkova, USSR.	168ft. 8 in.

1956	Olga Fikotova, Czechoslovakia.	176ft. 1 in.
1960	Nina Ponomareva, USSR.	180ft. 8 1-4 in.
1964	Tamara Press, USSR	187ft. 10 in.
1968	Lia Manoliu, Romania.	191ft. 2 in.
1972	Faina Melnik, USSR.	218ft. 7 in.
1976	Evelin Schlaak, E. Germany	226ft. 4 in.
1980	Evelin Jahl, E. Germany.	229ft. 6 in.
1984	Ria Stalman, Netherlands.	214ft. 5 in.
1988	Martina Hellmann, E. Germany.	237ft. 2 1-4 in.*

Javelin Throw

1932	"Babe" Didrikson, United States	143ft. 4 in.
1936	Tilly Fleischer, Germany	148ft. 2 3-4 in.
1948	Herma Bauma, Austria	149ft. 6 in.
1952	Dana Zatopkova, Czechoslovakia	165ft. 7 in.
1956	Inese Jaunzeme, USSR.	176ft. 8 in.
1960	Elvira Ozolina, USSR.	183ft. 8 in.
1964	Mihaela Penes, Romania.	198ft. 7 1-2 in.
1968	Angela Nemeth, Hungary.	198ft. 1-2 in.
1972	Ruth Fuchs, E. Germany	209ft. 7 in.
1976	Ruth Fuchs, E. Germany	216ft. 4 in.
1980	Maria Colon, Cuba.	224ft. 5 in.
1984	Tessa Sanderson, Great Britain	228ft. 2 in.
1988	Petra Felke, E. Germany	245ft.*

Shot Put (8lb., 13oz.)

1948	Micheline Ostermeyer, France.	45ft. 1 1-2 in.
1952	Galina Zybina, USSR.	50ft. 1 3-4 in.
1956	Tamara Tishkyevich, USSR.	54ft. 5 in.
1960	Tamara Press, USSR.	56ft. 10 in.
1964	Tamara Press, USSR.	59ft. 6 1-4 in.
1968	Margitta Gummel, E. Germany	64ft. in.
1972	Nadezhda Chizova, USSR.	69ft.
1976	Ivanka Hristova, Bulgaria.	69ft. 5 1-4 in.
1980	Ilona Slupianek, E. Germany.	73ft. 6 1-4 in.*
1984	Claudia Losch, W. Germany.	67ft. 2 1-4 in.
1988	Natalya Lisovskaya, USSR.	72ft 11 1-2 in.

Long Jump

1948	Olga Gyarmati, Hungary.	18ft. 8 1-4 in.
1952	Yvette Williams, New Zealand.	20ft. 5 3-4 in.
1956	Elzbieta Krzeskinska, Poland.	20ft. 9 3-4 in.
1960	Vyera Krepkina, USSR.	20ft. 10 3-4 in.
1964	Mary Rand, Great Britain.	22ft. 2 1-4 in.
1968	Viorica Viscopoleanu, Romania.	22ft. 4 1-2 in.
1972	Heidemarie Rosendahl, W. Germany	22ft. 3 in.
1976	Angela Voigt, E. Germany	22ft. 3-4 in.
1980	Tatyana Kolpakova, USSR.	23ft. 2 in.
1984	Anisoara Stanciu, Romania.	22ft. 10 in.
1988	Jackie Joyner-Kersee, United States.	24ft 3 1-2 in.*

Marathon

1984	Joan Benoit, United States	2h. 24m. 52s*
1988	Rosa Mota, Portugal	2h. 25m. 40s

Swimming—Men

50-Meter Freestyle

1988	Matt Biondi, U.S.	22.14*

100-Meter Freestyle

1896	Alfred Hajos, Hungary	1:22.2
1904	Zoltan de Halmay, Hungary (100 yards)	1:02.8
1908	Charles Daniels, U.S.	1:05.6
1912	Duke P. Kahanamoku, U.S.	1:03.4
1920	Duke P. Kahanamoku, U.S.	1:01.4
1924	John Weissmuller, U.S.	59.0
1928	John Weissmuller, U.S.	58.6
1932	Yasuji Miyazaki, Japan.	58.2
1936	Ferenc Csik, Hungary.	57.6
1948	Wally Ris, U.S.	57.3
1952	Clark Scholes, U.S.	57.4
1956	Jon Henricks, Australia.	55.4
1960	John Devitt, Australia.	55.2
1964	Don Schollander, U.S.	53.4
1968	Mike Wenden, Australia.	52.2
1972	Mark Spitz, U.S.	51.22
1976	Jim Montgomery, U.S.	49.99
1980	Jorg Woithe, E. Germany	50.40
1984	Rowdy Gaines, U.S.	49.80
1988	Matt Biondi, United States.	48.63*

200-Meter Freestyle

1968	Mike Wenden, Australia	1:55.2
1972	Mark Spitz, U.S.	1:52.78
1976	Bruce Furniss, U.S.	1:50.29
1980	Sergei Kopliakov, USSR.	1:49.81
1984	Michael Gross, W. Germany	1:47.44
1988	Duncan Armstrong, Australia.	1:47.25*

400-Meter Freestyle

1904	C. M. Daniels, U.S. (440 yards)	6:16.2
1908	Henry Taylor, Great Britain.	5:36.8
1912	George Hodgson, Canada.	5:24.4
1920	Norman Ross, U.S.	5:26.8
1924	John Weissmuller, U.S.	5:04.2
1928	Albert Zorilla, Argentina	5:01.6
1932	Clarence Crabbe, U.S.	4:48.4
1936	Jack Medica, U.S.	4:44.5
1948	William Smith, U.S.	4:41.0
1952	Jean Boiteux, France.	4:30.7
1956	Murray Rose, Australia.	4:27.3
1960	Murray Rose, Australia.	4:18.3
1964	Don Schollander, U.S.	4:12.2
1968	Mike Burton, U.S.	4:09.0
1972	Brad Cooper, Australia.	4:00.27
1976	Brian Goodell, U.S.	3:51.93

(continued)

1980	Vladimir Salnikov, USSR	3:51.31
1984	George DiCarlo, U.S.	3:51.23
1988	Ewe Dassler, E. Germany	3:46.95*

1,500-Meter Freestyle

1908	Henry Taylor, Great Britain	22:48.4
1912	George Hodgson, Canada	22:00.0
1920	Norman Ross, U.S.	22:23.2
1924	Andrew Charlton, Australia	20:06.6
1928	Arne Borg, Sweden	19:51.8
1932	Kusuo Kitamura, Japan	19:12.4
1936	Noboru Terada, Japan	19:13.7
1948	James McLane, U.S.	19:18.5
1952	Ford Konno, U.S.	18:30.3
1956	Murray Rose, Australia	17:58.9
1960	Jon Konrads, Australia	17:19.6
1964	Robert Windle, Australia	17:01.7
1968	Mike Burton, U.S.	16:38.9
1972	Mike Burton, U.S.	15:52.58
1976	Brian Goodell, U.S.	15:02.40
1980	Vladimir Salnikov, USSR	14:58.27*
1984	Michael O'Brien, U.S.	15:05.20
1988	Vladimir Salnikov, USSR	15:00.40

400-Meter Medley Relay

1960	United States	4:05.4
1964	United States	3:58.4
1968	United States	3:54.9
1972	United States	3:48.16
1976	United States	3:42.22
1980	Australia	3:45.70
1984	United States	3:39.30
1988	United States	3:36.93*

400-Meter Freestyle Relay

1964	United States	3:31.2
1968	United States	3:31.7
1972	United States	3:26.42
1984	United States	3:19.03
1988	United States	3:16.53*

800-Meter Freestyle Relay

1908	Great Britain	10:55.6
1912	Australia	10:11.6
1920	United States	10:04.4
1924	United States	9:53.4
1928	United States	9:36.2
1932	Japan	8:58.4
1936	Japan	8:51.5
1948	United States	8:46.0
1952	United States	8:31.1
1956	Australia	8:23.6
1960	United States	8:10.2
1964	United States	7:52.1
1968	United States	7:52.33
1972	United States	7:35.78
1976	United States	7:23.22
1980	USSR	7:23.50
1984	United States	7:15.69
1988	United States	7:12.51*

100-Meter Backstroke

1904	Walter Brack, Germany (100 yds.)	1:16.8
1908	Arno Bieberstein, Germany	1:24.6
1912	Harry Hebner, U.S.	1:21.2
1920	Warren Kealoha, U.S.	1:15.2
1924	Warren Kealoha, U.S.	1:13.2
1928	George Kojac, U.S.	1:08.2
1932	Masaji Kiyokawa, Japan	1:08.6
1936	Adolph Kiefer, U.S.	1:05.9
1948	Allen Stack, U.S.	1:06.4
1952	Yoshi Oyakawa, U.S.	1:05.4
1956	David Thiele, Australia	1:02.2
1960	David Thiele, Australia	1:01.9
1968	Roland Matthes, E. Germany	58.7
1972	Roland Matthes, E. Germany	56.58
1976	John Naber, U.S.	55.49
1980	Bengt Baron, Sweden	56.33
1984	Rick Carey, U.S.	55.79
1988	Daichi Suzuki, Japan	55.05*

200-Meter Backstroke

1964	Jed Graef, U.S.	2:10.3
1968	Roland Matthes, E. Germany	2:09.6
1972	Roland Matthes, E. Germany	2:02.82
1976	John Naber, U.S.	1:59.19*

1980	Sandor Wladar, Hungary	2:01.93
1984	Rick Carey, U.S.	2:00.23
1988	Igor Polianski, USSR	1:59.37

100-Meter Breaststroke

1968	Don McKenzie, U.S.	1:07.7
1972	Nobutaka Taguchi, Japan	1:04.94
1976	John Hencken, U.S.	1:03.11
1980	Duncan Goodhew, Great Britain	1:03.44
1984	Steve Lundquist, U.S.	1:01.65*
1988	Adrian Moorhouse, Great Britain	1:02.04

200-Meter Breaststroke

1908	Frederick Holman, Great Britain	3:09.2
1912	Walter Bathe, Germany	3:01.8
1920	Haken Malmroth, Sweden	3:04.4
1924	Robert Skelton, U.S.	2:56.6
1928	Yoshiyuki Tsuruta, Japan	2:48.8
1932	Yoshiyuki Tsuruta, Japan	2:45.4
1936	Tetsuo Hamuro, Japan	2:41.5
1948	Joseph Verdeur, U.S.	2:39.3
1952	John Davies, Australia	2:34.4
1956	Masaru Furukawa, Japan	2:34.7
1960	William Mulliken, U.S.	2:37.4
1964	Ian O'Brien, Australia	2:27.8
1968	Felipe Munoz, Mexico	2:28.7
1972	John Hencken, U.S.	2:21.55
1976	David Wilkie, Great Britain	2:15.11
1980	Robertas Zhulpa, USSR	2:15.85
1984	Victor Davis, Canada	2:13.34*
1988	Jozsef Szabo, Hungary	2:13.52

100-Meter Butterfly

1968	Doug Russell, U.S.	55.9
1972	Mark Spitz, U.S.	54.27
1976	Matt Vogel, U.S.	54.35
1980	Par Arvidsson, Sweden	54.92
1984	Michael Gross, W. Germany	53.08
1988	Anthony Nesty, Suriname	53.00*

200-Meter Butterfly

1956	William Yorzyk, U.S.	2:19.3
1960	Michael Troy, U.S.	2:12.8
1964	Kevin J. Berry, Australia	2:06.6
1968	Carl Robie, U.S.	2:08.7
1972	Mark Spitz, U.S.	2:00.70
1976	Mike Bruner, U.S.	1:59.23
1980	Sergei Fesenko, USSR	1:59.76
1984	Jon Sieben, Australia	1:57.04
1988	Michael Gross, W. Germany	1:56.94*

200-Meter Individual Medley

1968	Charles Hickcox, U.S.	2:12.0
1972	Gunnar Larsson, Sweden	2:07.17
1984	Alex Baumann, Canada	2:01.42
1988	Tamas Darnyi, Hungary	2:00.17*

400-Meter Individual Medley

1964	Dick Roth, U.S.	4:45.4
1968	Charles Hickcox, U.S.	4:48.4
1972	Gunnar Larsson, Sweden	4:31.98
1976	Rod Strachan, U.S.	4:23.68
1980	Aleksandr Sidorenko, USSR	4:22.89
1984	Alex Baumann, Canada	4:17.41
1988	Tamas Darnyi, Hungary	4:14.75*

Springboard Diving — Points

1908	Albert Zurner, Germany	85.5
1912	Paul Guenther, Germany	79.23
1920	Louis Kuehn, U.S.	675.40
1924	Albert White, U.S.	97.46
1928	Pete Desjardins, U.S.	185.04
1932	Michael Galitzen, U.S.	161.38
1936	Richard Degener, U.S.	163.57
1948	Bruce Harlan, U.S.	163.64
1952	David Browning, U.S.	205.29
1956	Robert Clotworthy, U.S.	159.56
1960	Gary Tobian, U.S.	170.00
1964	Kenneth Sitzberger, U.S.	159.90
1968	Bernie Wrightson, U.S.	170.15
1972	Vladimir Vasin, USSR	594.09
1976	Phil Boggs, U.S.	619.52
1980	Aleksandr Portnov, USSR	905.02
1984	Greg Louganis, U.S.	754.41
1988	Greg Louganis, U.S.	730.80

	Platform Diving	**Points**
1904	Dr. G.E. Sheldon, U.S.	12.75
1908	Hjalmar Johansson, Sweden	83.75
1912	Erik Adlerz, Sweden	73.94
1920	Clarence Pinkston, U.S.	100.67
1924	Albert White, U.S.	97.46
1928	Pete Desjardins, U.S.	98.74
1932	Harold Smith, U.S.	124.80
1936	Marshall Wayne, U.S.	113.58
1948	Sammy Lee, U.S.	130.05
1952	Sammy Lee, U.S.	156.28
1956	Joaquin Capilla, Mexico	152.44
1960	Robert Webster, U.S.	165.56
1964	Robert Webster, U.S.	148.58
1968	Klaus Dibiasi, Italy	164.18
1972	Klaus Dibiasi, Italy	504.12
1976	Klaus Dibiasi, Italy	600.51
1980	Falk Hoffmann, E. Germany	835.65
1984	Greg Louganis, U.S.	710.91
1988	Greg Louganis, U.S.	638.61

Swimming—Women

50-Meter Freestyle

1988	Kristin Otto, E. Germany	25.49*

100-Meter Freestyle

1912	Fanny Durack, Australia	1:22.2
1920	Ethelda Bleibtrey, U.S.	1:13.6
1924	Ethel Lackie, U.S.	1:12.4
1928	Albina Osipowich, U.S.	1:11.0
1932	Helene Madison, U.S.	1:06.8
1936	Hendrika Mastenbroek, Holland	1:05.9
1948	Greta Andersen, Denmark	1:06.3
1952	Katalin Szoke, Hungary	1:06.8
1956	Dawn Fraser, Australia	1:02.0
1960	Dawn Fraser, Australia	1:01.2
1964	Dawn Fraser, Australia	59.5
1968	Jan Henne, U.S.	1:00.0
1972	Sandra Neilson, U.S.	58.59
1976	Kornelia Ender, E. Germany	55.65
1980	Barbara Krause, E. Germany	54.79*
1984	(tie) Carrie Steinseifer, U.S.	55.92
	Nancy Hogshead, U.S.	55.92
1988	Kristin Otto, E. Germany	54.93

200-Meter Freestyle

1968	Debbie Meyer, U.S.	2:10.5
1972	Shane Gould, Australia	2:03.56
1976	Kornelia Ender, E. Germany	1:59.26
1980	Barbara Krause, E. Germany	1:58.33
1984	Mary Wayte, U.S.	1:59.23
1988	Heike Friedrich, E. Germany	1:57.65*

400-Meter Freestyle

1924	Martha Norelius, U.S.	6:02.2
1928	Martha Norelius, U.S.	5:42.8
1932	Helene Madison, U.S.	5:28.5
1936	Hendrika Mastenbroek, Netherlands	5:26.4
1948	Ann Curtis, U.S.	5:17.8
1952	Valerie Gyenge, Hungary	5:12.1
1956	Lorraine Crapp, Australia	4:54.6
1960	Susan Chris von Saltza, U.S.	4:50.6
1964	Virginia Duenkel, U.S.	4:43.3
1968	Debbie Meyer, U.S.	4:31.8
1972	Shane Gould, Australia	4:19.44
1976	Petra Thuemer E. Germany	4:09.89
1980	Ines Diers, E. Germany	4:08.76
1984	Tiffany Cohen, U.S.	4:07.10
1988	Janet Evans, U.S.	4:03.85*

800-Meter Freestyle

1968	Debbie Meyer, U.S.	9:24.0
1972	Keena Rothhammer, U.S.	8:53.68
1976	Petra Thuemer, E. Germany	8:37.14
1980	Michelle Ford, Australia	8:28.90
1984	Tiffany Cohen, U.S.	8:24.95
1988	Janet Evans, U.S.	8:20.20*

100-Meter Backstroke

1924	Sybil Bauer, U.S.	1:23.2
1928	Marie Braun, Netherlands	1:22.0
1932	Eleanor Holm, U.S.	1:19.4
1936	Dina Senff, Netherlands	1:18.9
1948	Karen Harup, Denmark	1:14.4
1952	Joan Harrison, South Africa	1:14.3
1956	Judy Grinham, Great Britain	1:12.9
1960	Lynn Burke, U.S.	1:09.3
1964	Cathy Ferguson, U.S.	1:07.7
1968	Kaye Hall, U.S.	1:06.2
1972	Melissa Belote, U.S.	1:05.78
1976	Ulrike Richter, E. Germany	1:01.83
1980	Rica Reinisch, E. Germany	1:00.86*
1984	Theresa Andrews, U.S.	1:02.55
1988	Kristin Otto, E. Germany	1:00.89

200-Meter Backstroke

1968	Pokey Watson, U.S.	2:24.8
1972	Melissa Belote, U.S.	2:19.19
1976	Ulrike Richter, E. Germany	2:13.43
1980	Rica Reinisch, E. Germany	2:11.77
1984	Jolanda De Rover, Netherlands	2:12.38
1988	Krisztina Egerszegi, Hungary	2:09.29*

100-Meter Breaststroke

1968	Djurdjica Bjedov, Yugoslavia	1:15.8
1972	Cathy Carr, U.S.	1:13.58
1976	Hannelore Anke, E. Germany	1:11.16
1980	Ute Geweniger, E. Germany	1:10.22
1984	Petra Van Staveren, Netherlands	1:09.88
1988	Tania Dangalakova, Bulgaria	1:07.95*

200-Meter Breaststroke

1924	Lucy Morton, Great Britain	3:33.2
1928	Hilde Schrader, Germany	3:12.6
1932	Clare Dennis, Australia	3:06.3
1936	Hideko Maehata, Japan	3:03.6
1948	Nelly Van Vliet, Netherlands	2:57.2
1952	Eva Szekely, Hungary	2:51.7
1956	Ursula Happe, Germany	2:53.1
1960	Anita Lonsbrough, Great Britain	2:49.5
1964	Galina Prozumenschikova, USSR	2:46.4
1968	Sharon Wichman, U.S.	2:44.4
1972	Beverly Whitfield, Australia	2:41.71
1976	Marina Koshevaia, USSR	2:33.35
1980	Lina Kachushite, USSR	2:29.54
1984	Anne Ottenbrite, Canada	2:30.38
1988	Silke Hoerner, E. Germany	2:26.71*

200-Meter Individual Medley

1968	Claudia Kolb, U.S.	2:24.7
1972	Shane Gould, Australia	2:23.07
1984	Tracy Caulkins, U.S.	2:12.64
1988	Daniela Hunger, E. Germany	2:12.59*

400-Meter Individual Medley

1964	Donna de Varona, U.S.	5:18.7
1968	Claudia Kolb, U.S.	5:08.5
1972	Gail Neall, Australia	5:02.97
1976	Ulrike Tauber, E. Germany	4:42.77
1980	Petra Schneider, E. Germany	4:36.29*
1984	Tracy Caulkins, U.S.	4:39.24
1988	Janet Evans, U.S.	4:37.76

100-Meter Butterfly

1956	Shelley Mann, U.S.	1:11.0
1960	Carolyn Schuler, U.S.	1:09.5
1964	Sharon Stouder, U.S.	1:04.7
1968	Lynn McClements, Australia	1:05.5
1972	Mayumi Aoki, Japan	1:03.34
1976	Kornelia Ender, E. Germany	1:00.13
1980	Caren Metschuck, E. Germany	1:00.42
1984	Mary T. Meagher, U.S.	59.26
1988	Kristin Otto, E. Germany	59.00*

200-Meter Butterfly

1968	Ada Kok, Netherlands	2:24.7
1972	Karen Moe, U.S.	2:15.57
1976	Andrea Pollack, E. Germany	2:11.41
1980	Ines Geissler, E. Germany	2:10.44
1984	Mary T. Meagher, U.S.	2:06.90*
1988	Kathleen Nord, E. Germany	2:09.51

400-Meter Medley Relay

1960	United States	4:41.1
1960	United States	4:33.9
1968	United States	4:28.3

(continued)

1972	United States	4:20.75
1976	East Germany	4:07.95
1980	East Germany	4:06.67
1984	United States	4:08.34
1988	E. Germany	4:03.74*

400-Meter Freestyle Relay

1912	Great Britain	5:52.8
1920	United States	5:11.6
1924	United States	4:58.8
1928	United States	4:47.6
1932	United States	4:38.0
1936	Netherlands	4:36.0
1948	United States	4:29.2
1952	Hungary	4:24.4
1956	Australia	4:17.1
1960	United States	4:08.9
1964	United States	4:03.8
1968	United States	4:02.5
1972	United States	3:55.19
1976	United States	3:44.82
1980	East Germany	3:42.71
1984	United States	3:43.43
1988	E. Germany	3:40.63*

Springboard Diving

		Points
1920	Aileen Riggin, U.S.	539.90
1924	Elizabeth Becker, U.S.	474.50
1928	Helen Meany, U.S.	78.62
1932	Georgia Coleman U.S.	87.52

1936	Marjorie Gestring, U.S.	89.27
1948	Victoria M. Draves, U.S.	108.74
1952	Patricia McCormick, U.S.	147.30
1956	Patricia McCormick, U.S.	142.36
1960	Ingrid Kramer, Germany	155.81
1964	Ingrid Engel-Kramer, Germany	145.00
1968	Sue Gossick, U.S.	150.77
1972	Micki King, U.S.	450.03
1976	Jenni Chandler, U.S.	506.19
1980	Irina Kalinina, USSR	725.91
1984	Sylvie Bernier, Canada	530.70
1988	Gao Min, China	580.23

Platform Diving

		Points
1912	Greta Johansson, Sweden	39.90
1920	Stefani Fryland-Clausen, Denmark	34.60
1924	Caroline Smith, U.S.	33.20
1928	Elizabeth B. Pinkston, U.S.	31.60
1932	Dorothy Poynton, U.S.	40.26
1936	Dorothy Poynton Hill, U.S.	33.93
1948	Victoria M. Draves, U.S.	68.87
1952	Patricia McCormick, U.S.	79.37
1956	Patricia McCormick, U.S.	84.85
1960	Ingrid Kramer, Germany	91.28
1964	Lesley Bush, U.S.	99.80
1968	Milena Duchkova, Czech	109.59
1972	Ulrika Knape, Sweden	390.00
1976	Elena Vaytsekhouskaya, USSR	406.59
1980	Martina Jaschke, E. Germany	596.25
1984	Zhou Jihong, China	435.51
1988	Xu Yanmei, China	445.20

Boxing

Light Flyweight (106 lbs)
1968	Francisco Rodriguez, Venezuela
1972	Gyorgy Gedo, Hungary
1976	Jorge Hernandez, Cuba
1980	Shamil Sabyrov, USSR
1984	Paul Gonzalez, U.S.
1988	Ivailo Hristov, Bulgaria

Flyweight (112½ lbs)
1904	George Finnegan, U.S.
1920	William Di Gennara, U.S.
1924	Fidel LaBarba, U.S.
1928	Antal Kocsis, Hungary
1932	Istvan Enekes, Hungary
1936	Willi Kaiser, Germany
1948	Pascual Perez, Argentina
1952	Nathan Brooks, U.S.
1956	Terence Spinks, Great Britain
1960	Gyula Torok, Hungary
1964	Fernando Atzori, Italy
1968	Ricardo Delgado, Mexico
1972	Georgi Kostadinov, Bulgaria
1976	Leo Randolph, U.S.
1980	Peter Lessov, Bulgaria
1984	Steve McCrory, U.S.
1988	Kim Kwang Sun, S. Korea

Bantamweight (119½ lbs)
1904	Oliver Kirk, U.S.
1908	A Henry Thomas, Great Britain
1920	Clarence Walker, South Africa
1924	William Smith, South Africa
1928	Vittorio Tamagnini, Italy
1932	Horace Gwynne, Canada
1936	Ulderico Sergo, Italy
1948	Tibor Csik, Hungary
1952	Pentti Hamalainen, Finland
1956	Wolfgang Behrendt, E. Germany
1960	Oleg Grigoryev, USSR
1964	Takao Sakurai, Japan
1968	Valery Sokolov, USSR
1972	Orlando Martinez, Cuba
1976	Yong-Jo Gu, N. Korea
1980	Juan Hernandez, Cuba
1984	Maurizio Stecca, Italy
1988	Kennedy McKinney, U.S.

Featherweight (126 lbs)
1904	Oliver Kirk, U.S.
1908	Richard Gunn, Great Britain
1920	Paul Fritsch, France
1924	John Fields, U.S.
1928	Lambertus van Klaveren, Netherlands
1932	Carmelo Robledo, Argentina
1936	Oscar Casanovas, Argentina

1948	Ernesto Formenti, Italy
1952	Jan Zachara, Czech.
1956	Vladimir Safronov, USSR
1960	Francesco Musso, Italy
1964	Stanislav Stephashkin, USSR
1968	Antonin Roldan, Mexico
1972	Boris Kousnetsov, USSR
1976	Angel Herrera, Cuba
1980	Rudi Fink, E. Germany
1984	Meldrick Taylor, U.S.
1988	Giovanni Parisi, Italy

Lightweight (132 lbs)
1904	Harry Spanger, U.S.
1908	Frederick Grace, Great Britain
1920	Samuel Mosberg, U.S.
1924	Hans Nielsen, Denmark
1928	Carlo Orlandi, Italy
1932	Lawrence Stevens, South Africa
1936	Imre Harangi, Hungary
1948	Gerald Dreyer, South Africa
1952	Aureliano Bolognesi, Italy
1956	Richard McTaggart, Great Britain
1960	Kazimierz Pazdzior, Poland
1964	Jozef Grudzien, Poland
1968	Ronald Harris, U.S.
1972	Jan Szczepanski, Poland
1976	Howard Davis, U.S.
1980	Angel Herrera, Cuba
1984	Pernell Whitaker, U.S.
1988	Andreas Zuelow, E. Germany

Light Welterweight (140 lbs)
1952	Charles Adkins, U.S.
1956	Vladimir Yengibaryan, USSR
1960	Bohumil Nemecek, Czech.
1964	Jerzy Kulej, Poland
1968	Jerzy Kulej, Poland
1972	Ray Seales, U.S.
1976	Ray Leonard, U.S.
1980	Patrizio Oliva, Italy
1984	Jerry Page, U.S.
1988	Viatcheslav Janovski, USSR

Welterweight (148 lbs)
1904	Albert Young, U.S.
1920	Albert Schneider, Canada
1924	Jean Delarge, Belgium
1928	Edward Morgan, New Zealand
1932	Edward Flynn, U.S.
1936	Sten Suvio, Finland
1948	Julius Torma, Czech.
1952	Zygmunt Chychia, Poland
1956	Nicolae Linca, Romania
1960	Giovanni Benvenuti, Italy
1964	Marian Kasprzyk, Poland

1968	Manfred Wolke, E. Germany
1972	Emilio Correa, Cuba
1976	Jochen Bachfeld, E. Germany
1980	Andres Aldama, Cuba
1984	Mark Breland, U.S.
1988	Robert Wangila, Kenya

Light Middleweight (156 lbs)
1952	Laszio Papp, Hungary
1956	Laszio Papp, Hungary
1960	Wilbert McClure, U.S.
1964	Boris Lagutin, USSR
1968	Boris Lagutin, USSR
1972	Dieter Kottysch, W. Germany
1976	Jerzy Rybicki, Poland
1980	Armando Martinez, Cuba
1984	Frank Tate, U.S.
1988	Park Si Hun, S. Korea

Middleweight (165½ lbs)
1904	Charles Mayer, U.S.
1908	John Douglas, Great Britain
1920	Harry Mallin, Great Britain
1924	Harry Mallin, Great Britain
1928	Piero Toscani, Italy
1932	Carmen Barth, U.S.
1936	Jean Despeaux, France
1948	Laszio Papp, Hungary
1952	Floyd Patterson, U.S.
1956	Gennady Schatkov, USSR
1960	Edward Crook, U.S.
1964	Valery Popenchenko, USSR
1968	Christopher Finnegan, Great Britain
1972	Vyacheslav Lemechev, USSR
1976	Michael Spinks, U.S.
1980	Jose Gomez, Cuba
1984	Joon-Sup Shin, S. Korea
1988	Henry Maske, E. Germany

Light Heavyweight (179 lbs)
1920	Edward Eagan, U.S.
1924	Harry Mitchell, Great Britain
1928	Victor Avendano, Argentina
1932	David Carstens, South Africa
1936	Roger Michelot, France
1948	George Hunter, South Africa
1952	Norvel Lee, U.S.
1956	James Boyd, U.S.
1960	Cassius Clay, U.S.
1964	Cosimo Pinto, Italy
1968	Dan Poznyak, USSR
1972	Mate Parlov, Yugoslavia
1976	Leon Spinks, U.S.
1980	Slobodan Kacar, Yugoslavia
1984	Anton Josipovic, Yugoslavia

1988 Andrew Maynard, U.S.

Heavyweight (200½ lbs)
1984 Henry Tillman, U.S.
1988 Ray Mercer, U.S.

Super Heavyweight (Unlimited)
(known as heavyweight from 1904-1980)
1904 Samuel Berger, U.S.
1908 Albert Oldham, Great Britain

1920 Ronald Rawson, Great Britain
1924 Otto von Porat, Norway
1928 Arturo Rodriguez Jurado, Argentina
1932 Santiago Lovell, Argentina
1936 Herbert Runge, Germany
1948 Rafael Inglesias, Argentina
1952 H. Edward Sanders, U.S.
1956 T. Peter Rademacher, U.S.

1960 Franco De Piccoli, Italy
1964 Joe Frazier, U.S.
1968 George Foreman, U.S.
1972 Teofilo Stevenson, Cuba
1976 Teofilo Stevenson, Cuba
1980 Teofilo Stevenson, Cuba
1984 Tyrell Biggs, U.S.
1988 Lennox Lewis, Canada

24th Summer Olympics

Seoul, S. Korea, Sept. 17-24, 1988

A record 13,674 athletes gathered in Seoul, South Korea in September for 16 days to compete in the Games of the XXIV Olympiad. The athletes represented 161 nations, 21 more than had participated in any previous Olympics, and competed for 237 gold medals in 26 sports at a cost of $3.1 billion to the South Korean government. The Soviet Union won the most medals, East Germany finished second, and the United States third.

The 1988 games will be remembered mostly for the long-awaited showdown in the 100-meter race between Ben Johnson, the Canadian sprinter and world record holder, and his archrival, Carl Lewis of the United States. Johnson won the race in world record time. Three days later, Johnson was stripped of his gold medal and world record because he had tested positive for the anabolic steroid stanozolol. Two weightlifters from Bulgaria were also stripped of their gold medals for taking drugs. In all, 10 of the athletes tested were disqualified by the International Olympic Committee for using banned substances.

Sports fans in the United States had much to cheer about. Swimmers Matt Biondi won 5 gold medals and Janet Evans won gold in three events. Greg Louganis repeated his 1984 performance by winning the springboard and platform diving events. Florence Griffith-Joyner won the 100 and 200-meter races while her sister-in-law, Jackie Joyner-Kersee was the Heptathlon and long jump champion. The U.S. men won the volleyball gold medal. The biggest disappointment was the defeat of the men's basketball team by the Soviet Union, only the second loss in history for a U.S. Olympic basketball team.

Final Medal Standings

	Gold	Silver	Bronze	Total
USSR	55	31	46	132
East Germany	37	35	30	102
United States	36	31	27	94
West Germany	11	14	15	40
Bulgaria	10	12	13	35
South Korea	12	10	11	33
China	5	11	12	28
Romania	7	11	6	24
Great Britain	5	10	9	24
Hungary	11	6	6	23
France	6	4	6	16
Poland	2	5	9	16
Italy	6	4	4	14
Japan	4	3	7	14
Australia	3	6	5	14
New Zealand	3	2	8	13
Yugoslavia	3	4	5	12
Sweden	0	4	7	11
Canada	3	2	5	10
Kenya	5	2	2	9
Netherlands	2	2	5	9
Czechoslovakia	3	3	2	8
Brazil	1	2	3	6
Norway	2	3	0	5
Denmark	2	1	1	4
Finland	1	1	2	4
Spain	1	1	2	4
Switzerland	0	2	2	4
Morocco	1	0	2	3
Turkey	1	1	0	2
Jamaica	0	2	0	2
Argentina	0	1	1	2
Belgium	0	0	2	2
Mexico	0	0	2	2
Austria	1	0	0	1
Portugal	1	0	0	1
Suriname	1	0	0	1
Chile	0	1	0	1
Costa Rica	0	1	0	1
Indonesia	0	1	0	1
Iran	0	1	0	1
Netherlands Antilles	0	1	0	1
Peru	0	1	0	1
Senegal	0	1	0	1
Virgin Islands	0	1	0	1
Colombia	0	0	1	1
Djibouti	0	0	1	1
Greece	0	0	1	1
Mongolia	0	0	1	1
Pakistan	0	0	1	1
Philippines	0	0	1	1
Thailand	0	0	1	1

Olympic Information

Symbol: Five rings or circles, linked together to represent the sporting friendship of all peoples. The rings also symbolize the 5 continents—Europe, Asia, Africa, Australia, and America. Each ring is a different color—blue, yellow, black, green, and red.

Flag: The symbol of the 5 rings on a plain white background.

Motto: "Citius, Altius, Fortius." Latin meaning "faster, higher, braver," or the modern interpretation "swifter, higher, stronger". The motto was coined by Father Didon, a French educator, in 1895.

Creed: "The most important thing in the Olympic Games is not to win but to take part, just as the most important thing in life is not the triumph but the struggle. The essential thing is not to have conquered but to have fought well."

Oath: An athlete of the host country recites the following at the opening ceremony. "In the name of all competitors I promise that we will take part in these Olympic Games, respecting and abiding by the rules which govern them, in the true spirit of sportsmanship for the glory of sport and the honor of our teams." Both the oath and the creed were composed by Pierre de Coubertin, the founder of the modern Games.

Flame: Symbolizes the continuity between the ancient and modern Games. The modern version of the flame was adopted in 1936. The torch used to kindle the flame is first lit by the sun's rays at Olympia, Greece, and then carried to the site of the Games by relays of runners. Ships and planes are used when necessary.

Other Summer Olympics Gold Medalists in 1988

Archery

Men—Jay Barrs, U.S.
Men's Team—S. Korea.
Women—Kim Soo-Nyung, S. Korea.
Women's Team—S. Korea.

Basketball

Men—1. USSR; 2. Yugoslavia; 3. U.S.
Women—1. U.S.; 2. Yugoslavia; 3. USSR.

Canoeing—Men

K1-500M—Zsolt Gyulay, Hungary.
K2-500M—Ian Ferguson, Paul MacDonald, New Zealand.
K1-1,000M—Greg Barton, U.S.
K2-1,000M—Greg Barton, N. Bellingham, U.S.
K4-1,000M—Hungary.
C1-500M—Olaf Heukrodt, E. Germany.
C2-500M—Victor Reneiski, Nikolai Jouravski, USSR.
C1-1,000M—Ivan Klementiev, USSR.
C2-1,000M—Victor Reneiski, Nikolai Jouravski, USSR.

Canoeing—Women

K1-500M—Vania Guecheva, Bulgaria.
K2-500M—Birgit Schmidt, Anke Nothnagel, E. Germany.
K4-500M—E. Germany.

Cycling

4,000 Individual Pursuit—Gintaoutas Umaras, USSR.
Sprint—Lutz Hesslich, E. Germany.
4,000 Team Pursuit—USSR.
50 Km Points Race—Dan Forst, Denmark.
1K Time Trial— Alexandr Kiritchenko, USSR.
100K Team Time Trial—E. Germany.
Road Race—Olaf Ludwig, E. Germany.
Women's Sprint—Erika Saloumiae, USSR.
Women's Road Race—Monique Knol, Netherlands.

Diving

Women's Platform—Xu Yanmei, China.
Women's Springboard—Gao Min, China.
Men's Springboard—Greg Louganis, U.S.
Men's Platform—Greg Louganis, U.S.

Equestrian

Individual 3-Day Event—Mark Todd, New Zealand.
Team 3-Day Event—W. Germany.
Individual Dressage—Nicole Uphoff, W. Germany.
Team Dressage—W. Germany.
Individual Jumping—Pierre Durand, France.
Team Jumping—W. Germany.

Fencing—Men

Foil Individual—Stefano Cerioni, Italy.
Team Foil—USSR.
Sabre Individual—Jean-Francois Lamour, France.
Team Sabre—Hungary.
Epée Individual—Arnd Schmitt, W. Germany.
Epée Team—France.

Fencing—Women

Foil Individual—Anja Fichtel, W. Germany.
Team Foil—W. Germany.

Field Hockey

Men—1. Great Britain; 2. W. Germany; 3. Netherlands.
Women—1. Australia; 2. S. Korea; 3. Netherlands.

Gymnastics—Men

Team—USSR.
All Around—Vladimir Artemov, USSR.
Floor Exercise—Sergei Kharikov, USSR.
Pommel Horse—Dimitri Bilozerchev, USSR.
Rings—Dimitri Bilozerchev, USSR.
Vault—Lou Yun, China.

Parallel Bars—Vladimir Artemov, USSR.
Horizontal Bar—Vladimir Artemov, USSR.

Gymnastics—Women

Team—USSR.
All-Around—Yelena Shoushunova, USSR.
Vault—Svetlana Boguinskaya, USSR.
Uneven Parallel Bars—Daniela Silivas, Romania.
Balance Beam—Daniela Silivas, Romania.
Floor Exercise—Daniela Silivas, Romania.

Rhythmic Gymnastics

Marina Lobatch, USSR.

Judo

133 Pounds—Kim Jae Yup, S. Korea.
143 Pounds—Lee Kyung-Keun, S. Korea.
156 Pounds—Marc Alexandre, France.
172 Pounds—Waldemar Legien, Poland.
189 Pounds—Peter Seisenbacher, Austria.
209 Pounds—Aurelio Miguel, Brazil.
Over 209 Pounds—Hitoshi Saito, Japan.

Modern Pentathlon

Individual—Janos Martinek, Hungary.
Team—Hungary.

Rowing—Men

Single Sculls—Tomas Lange, E. Germany.
Double Sculls—Netherlands.
Coxless Pairs—Great Britain.
Coxed Pairs—Italy.
Coxed Fours—E. Germany.
Coxless Fours—E. Germany.
Quadruple Sculls—Italy.
Eights—W. Germany.

Rowing—Women

Single Sculls—Jutta Behrendt, E. Germany.
Double Sculls—E. Germany.
Coxless Pairs—Romania.
Coxless Fours—E. Germany.
Quadruple Sculls—E. Germany.
Eights—E. Germany.

Shooting—Men

Smallbore Standard Rifle—Miroslav Varga, Czechoslovakia.
Smallbore Free Rifle—Malcolm Cooper, Great Britain.
Free Pistol—Sorin Babii, Romania.
Air Rifle—Goran Maksimovic, Yugoslavia.
Rapid-Fire Pistol—Afanasi Kouzmine, USSR.
Running Target—Tor Heiestad, Norway.
Air Pistol—Taniou Kiruakov, Bulgaria.

Shooting—Women

Air Rifle—Irina Cilova, USSR.
Sport Pistol—Nino Saloukvadze, USSR.
Air Pistol—Jasna Sekaric, Yugoslavia.
Smallbore Standard Rifle—Silvia Sperber, W. Germany.

Shooting—Mixed

Skeet—Axel Wegner, E. Germany.
Trap—Dmitri Monakov, USSR.

Soccer

Championship—1. USSR; 2. Brazil; 3. W. Germany.

Synchronized Swimming

Solo—Carolyn Waldo, Canada.
Duet—Michelle Cameron, Carolyn Waldo, Canada.

Table Tennis—Men

Singles—Yoo Nam Kyu, S. Korea.

Doubles—Chen Longcan, Wei Qingquang, China.

Table Tennis—Women

Singles—Chen Jing, China.
Doubles—Hyun Jung Hwa, Yang Young Ja, S. Korea.

Team Handball

Men—1. USSR. S. Korea; 3. Yugoslavia.
Women—1. S. Korea. Norway; 3. Yugoslavia.

Tennis—Men

Singles—Miloslav Mecir, Czech.
Doubles—Ken Flach, Robert Seguso, U.S.

Tennis—Women

Singles—Steffi Graf, W. Germany.
Doubles—Pam Shriver, Zina Garrison, U.S.

Volleyball

Men—1. U.S.; 2. USSR; 3. Argentina.
Women—1. USSR; 2. Peru; 3. China.

Water Polo

Championship—1. Yugoslavia; 2. U.S.; 3. USSR.

Weight Lifting

115 Pounds—Sevdalin Marinov, Bulgaria.
123 Pounds—Oxen Mirzoian, USSR.
132 Pounds—Naim Suleymanogulu, Turkey.
149 Pounds—Joachim Kunz, E. Germany.
165 Pounds—Borislav Guidikov, Bulgaria.
182 Pounds—Israil Arsamakov, USSR.
198 Pounds—Anatoli Khrapatyi, USSR.

220 Pounds—Pavel Kouzntsov, USSR.
242 Pounds—Yuri Zakharevitch, USSR.
Over 242 Pounds—Aleksandr Kourlovich, USSR.

Wrestling—Greco-Roman

106 Pounds—Vicenzo Maenza, Italy.
115 Pounds—Jon Ronningen, Norway.
126 Pounds—Andras Sike, Hungary.
137 Pounds—Kamandar Madjidov, USSR.
150 Pounds—Levon Djoulfalakian, USSR.
163 Pounds—Kim Young Nam, S. Korea.
181 Pounds—Mikhail Marniachvili, USSR.
198 Pounds—Atanas Komchev, Bulgaria.
220 Pounds—Andrzej Wronski, Poland.
286 Pounds—Alexander Kareline, USSR.

Wrestling—Freestyle

106 Pounds—Takashi Kobayashi, Japan.
115 Pounds—Mitsuru Sato, Japan.
126 Pounds—Serguei Beloglazov, USSR.
137 Pounds—John Smith, U.S.
150 Pounds—Arsen Fadzaev, USSR.
163 Pounds—Ken Monday, U.S.
181 Pounds—Han Myang-Woo, S. Korea.
198 Pounds—Makharbek Khadartsev, USSR.
220 Pounds—Vasile Puscasu, Romania.
286 Pounds—David Gobedjichvili, USSR.

Yachting

Board Sailing—Bruce Kendall, New Zealand.
Finn—José Luis Doreste, Spain.
Flying Dutchman—Denmark.
Soling—E. Germany.
Star—Great Britain.
Tornado—France.
Men's 470—France.
Women's 470—U.S.

Winter Olympic Games Champions, 1924-1988

Sites of Games

1924 Chamonix, France	1956 Cortina d'Ampezzo, Italy	1976 Innsbruck, Austria
1928 St. Moritz, Switzerland	1960 Squaw Valley, Cal.	1980 Lake Placid, N.Y.
1932 Lake Placid, N.Y.	1964 Innsbruck, Austria	1984 Sarajevo, Yugoslavia
1936 Garmisch-Partenkirchen, Germany	1968 Grenoble, France	1988 Calgary, Alberta
1948 St. Moritz, Switzerland	1972 Sapporo, Japan	1992 Albertville, France (scheduled)
1952 Oslo, Norway		

Bobsledding

4-Man Bob

	(Driver in parentheses)	Time
1924	Switzerland (Eduard Scherrer)	5:45.54
1928	United States (William Fiske) (5-man)	3:20.50
1932	United States (William Fiske)	7:53.68
1936	Switzerland (Pierre Musy)	5:19.85
1948	United States (Francis Tyler)	5:20.10
1952	Germany (Andreas Ostler)	5:07.84
1956	Switzerland (Franz Kapus)	5:10.44
1964	Canada (Victor Emery)	4:14.46
1968	Italy (Eugenio Monti) (2 races)	2:17.39
1972	Switzerland (Jean Wicki)	4:43.07
1976	E. Germany (Meinhard Nehmer)	3:40.43
1980	E. Germany (Meinhard Nehmer)	3:59.92
1984	E. Germany (Wolfgang Hoppe)	3:20.22
1988	Switzerland (Ekkehard Fasser)	3:47.51

2-Man Bob

		Time
1932	United States (Hubert Stevens)	8:14.74
1936	United States (Ivan Brown)	5:29.29
1948	Switzerland (F. Endrich)	5:29.20
1952	Germany (Andreas Ostler)	5:24.54
1956	Italy (Dalla Costa)	5:30.14
1964	Great Britain (Anthony Nash)	4:21.90
1968	Italy (Eugenio Monti)	4:41.54
1972	W. Germany (Wolfgang Zimmerer)	4:57.07
1976	E. Germany (Meinhard Nehmer)	3:44.42
1980	Switzerland (Erich Schaerer)	4:09.36
1984	E.Germany (Wolfgang Hoppe)	3:25.56
1988	USSR (Janis Kipours)	3:54.19

Luge

Men's Singles

		Time
1964	Thomas Koehler, Germany	3:26.77
1968	Manfred Schmid, Austria	2:52.48
1972	Wolfgang Scheidel, E. Germany	3:27.58
1976	Detlef Guenther, E. Germany	3:27.688
1980	Bernhard Glass, E. Germany	2:54.796
1984	Paul Hildgartner, Italy	3:04.258
1988	Jens Mueller, E. Germany	3:05.548

Men's Pairs

		Time
1964	Austria	1:41.62
1968	E. Germany	1:35.85
1972	Italy, E. Germany (tie)	1:28.35
1976	E. Germany	1:25.604
1980	E. Germany	1:19.331
1984	W. Germany	1:23.620
1988	E. Germany	1:31.940

Women's Singles

		Time
1964	Ortun Enderlein, Germany	3:24.67
1968	Erica Lechner, Italy	2:28.66
1972	Anna M. Muller, E. Germany	2:59.18
1976	Margit Schumann, E. Germany	2:50.621
1980	Vera Zozulya, USSR	2:36.537
1984	Steffi Martin, E. Germany	2:46.570
1988	Steffi Walter, E. Germany	3:03.973

Biathlon

10 Kilometers

	Time
1980 Frank Ullrich, E. Germany	32:10.69
1984 Eirik Kvalfoss, Norway	30:53.80
1988 Frank-Peter Roetsch, E. Germany	25:08.10

20 Kilometers

	Time
1960 Klas Lestander, Sweden	1:33:21.6
1964 Vladimir Melanin, USSR	1:20:26.8
1968 Magnar Solberg, Norway	1:13:45.9
1972 Magnar Solberg, Norway	1:15:55.50
1976 Nikolai Kruglov, USSR	1:14:12.26
1980 Anatoly Aljabiev, USSR	1:08:16.31
1984 Peter Angerer, W. Germany	1:11:52.7
1988 Frank-Peter Roetsch, E. Germany	0:56:33.33

30-Kilometer Relay

	Time
1968 USSR, Norway, Sweden	2:13:02.4
1972 USSR, Finland, E. Germany	1:51:44.92
1976 USSR, Finland, E. Germany	1:57:55.64
1980 USSR, E. Germany, W. Germany (30 km.)	1:34:03.27
1984 USSR, Norway, W. Germany	1:38:51.70
1988 USSR, W. Germany, Italy	1:22:30.00

Figure Skating

Men's Singles

1908 Ulrich Salchow, Sweden
1920 Gillis Grafstrom, Sweden
1924 Gillis Grafstrom, Sweden
1928 Gillis Grafstrom, Sweden
1932 Karl Schaefer, Austria
1936 Karl Schaefer, Austria
1948 Richard Button, U.S.
1952 Richard Button, U.S.
1956 Hayes Alan Jenkins, U.S.
1960 David W. Jenkins, U.S.
1964 Manfred Schnelldorfer, Germany
1968 Wolfgang Schwartz, Austria
1972 Ondrej Nepela, Czechoslovakia
1976 John Curry, Great Britain
1980 Robin Cousins, Great Britain
1984 Scott Hamilton, U.S.
1988 Brian Boitano, U.S.

Women's Singles

1908 Madge Syers, Great Britain
1920 Magda Julin-Mauroy, Sweden
1924 Herma von Szabo-Planck, Austria
1928 Sonja Henie, Norway
1932 Sonja Henie, Norway
1936 Sonja Henie, Norway
1948 Barbara Ann Scott, Canada
1952 Jeanette Altwegg, Great Britain
1956 Tenley Albright, U.S.
1960 Carol Heiss, U.S.
1964 Sjoukje Dijkstra, Netherlands
1968 Peggy Fleming, U.S.
1972 Beatrix Schuba, Austria
1976 Dorothy Hamill, U.S.
1980 Anett Poetzsch, E. Germany
1984 Katarina Witt, E. Germany
1988 Katarina Witt, E. Germany

Pairs

1908 Anna Hubler & Heinrich Burger, Germany
1920 Ludovika & Walter Jakobsson, Finland
1924 Helene Engelman & Alfred Berger, Austria
1928 Andree Joly & Pierre Brunet, France
1932 Andree Joly & Pierre Brunet, France
1936 Maxi Herber & Ernst Baier, Germany
1948 Micheline Lannoy & Pierre Baugniet, Belgium
1952 Ria and Paul Falk, Germany
1956 Elisabeth Schwartz & Kurt Oppelt, Austria
1960 Barbara Wagner & Robert Paul, Canada
1964 Ludmila Beloussova & Oleg Protopopov, USSR
1968 Ludmila Beloussova & Oleg Protopopov, USSR
1972 Irina Rodnina & Alexei Ulanov, USSR
1976 Irina Rodnina & Aleksandr Zaitzev, USSR
1980 Irina Rodnina & Aleksandr Zaitzev, USSR
1984 Elena Valova & Oleg Vassiliev, USSR
1988 Ekaterina Gordeeva & Sergei Grinkov, USSR

Ice Dancing

1976 Ludmila Pakhomova & Aleksandr Gorschkov, USSR
1980 Natalya Linichuk & Gennadi Karponosov, USSR
1984 Jayne Torvill & Christopher Dean, Great Britain
1988 Natalia Bestemianova & Andrei Bukin, USSR

Ice Hockey

1920 Canada, U.S., Czechoslovakia
1924 Canada, U.S., Great Britain
1928 Canada, Sweden, Switzerland
1932 Canada, U.S., Germany
1936 Great Britain, Canada, U.S.
1948 Canada, Czechoslovakia, Switzerland
1952 Canada, U.S., Sweden
1956 USSR, U.S., Canada
1960 U.S., Canada, USSR
1964 USSR, Sweden, Czechoslovakia
1968 USSR, Czechoslovakia, Canada
1972 USSR, U.S., Czechoslovakia
1976 USSR, Czechoslovakia, W. Germany
1980 U.S., USSR, Sweden
1984 USSR, Czechoslovakia, Sweden
1988 USSR, Finland, Sweden

Alpine Skiing

Men's Downhill

	Time
1948 Henri Oreiller, France	2:55.0
1952 Zeno Colo, Italy	2:30.8
1956 Anton Sailer, Austria	2:52.2
1960 Jean Vuarnet, France	2:06.0
1964 Egon Zimmermann, Austria	2:18.16
1968 Jean-Claude Killy, France	1:59.85
1972 Bernhard Russi, Switzerland	1:51.43
1976 Franz Klammer, Austria	1:45.73
1980 Leonhard Stock, Austria	1:45.50
1984 Bill Johnson, U.S.	1:45.59
1988 Pirmin Zurbriggen, Switzerland	1:59.63

Men's Super Giant Slalom

	Time
1988 Franck Piccard, France	1:39.66

Men's Giant Slalom

	Time
1952 Stein Eriksen, Norway	2:25.0
1956 Anton Sailer, Austria	3:00.1
1960 Roger Staub, Switzerland	1:48.3
1964 Francois Bonlieu, France	1:46.71
1968 Jean-Claude Killy, France	3:29.28
1972 Gustavo Thoeni, Italy	3:09.62
1976 Heini Hemmi, Switzerland	3:26.97
1980 Ingemar Stenmark, Sweden	2:40.74
1984 Max Julen, Switzerland	2:41.18
1988 Alberto Tomba, Italy	2:06:37

Men's Slalom

	Time
1948 Edi Reinalter, Switzerland	2:10.3
1952 Othmar Schneider, Austria	2:00.0
1956 Anton Sailer, Austria	194.7 pts.
1960 Ernst Hinterseer, Austria	2:08.9
1964 Josef Stiegler, Austria	2:11.13
1968 Jean-Claude Killy, France	1:39.73
1972 Francisco Fernandez Ochoa, Spain	1:49.27
1976 Piero Gros, Italy	2:03.29
1980 Ingemar Stenmark, Sweden	1:44.26
1984 Phil Mahre, U.S.	1:39.41
1988 Alberto Tomba	1:39.47

Men's Combined

	Points
1988 Hubert Strolz, Austria	36.55

Women's Downhill

	Time
1948 Hedi Schlunegger, Switzerland	2:28.3
1952 Trude Jochum-Beiser, Austria	1:47.1
1956 Madeleine Berthod, Switzerland	1:40.7
1960 Heidi Biebl, Germany	1:37.6
1964 Christl Haas, Austria	1:55.39
1968 Olga Pall, Austria	1:40.87
1972 Marie Therese Nadig, Switzerland	1:36.68
1976 Rosi Mittermaier, W. Germany	1:46.16
1980 Annemarie Proell Moser, Austria	1:37.52
1984 Michela Figini, Switzerland	1:13.36
1988 Marina Kiehl, W. Germany	1:25.86

Women's Super Giant Slalom

		Time
1988	Sigrid Wolf, Austria	1:19.03

Women's Giant Slalom

		Time
1952	Andrea Mead Lawrence, U.S.	2:06.8
1956	Ossi Reichert, Germany	1:56.5
1960	Yvonne Ruegg, Switzerland	1:39.9
1964	Marielle Goitschel, France	1:52.24
1968	Nancy Greene, Canada	1:51.97
1972	Marie Therese Nadig, Switzerland	1:29.90
1976	Kathy Kreiner, Canada	1:29.13
1980	Hanni Wenzel, Liechtenstein (2 runs)	2:41.66
1984	Debbie Armstrong, U.S.	2:20.98
1988	Vreni Schneider, Switzerland	2:06.49

Women's Slalom

		Time
1948	Gretchen Fraser, U.S.	1:57.2
1952	Andrea Mead Lawrence, U.S.	2:10.6
1956	Renee Colliard, Switzerland	112.3 pts.
1960	Anne Heggtveigt, Canada	1:49.6
1964	Christine Goitschel, France	1:29.86
1968	Marielle Goitschel, France	1:25.86
1972	Barbara Cochran, U.S.	1:31.24
1976	Rosi Mittermaier, W. Germany	1:30.54
1980	Hanni Wenzel, Liechtenstein	1:25.09
1984	Paoletta Magoni, Italy	1:36.47
1988	Vreni Schneider, Switzerland	1:36.69

Women's Combined

		Points
1988	Anita Wachter, Austria	29.25

Nordic Skiing

Men's Cross-Country Events
15 kilometers (9.3 miles)

		Time
1924	Thorleif Haug, Norway	1:14:31
1928	Johan Grottumsbraaten, Norway	1:37:01
1932	Sven Utterstrom, Sweden	1:23:07
1936	Erik-August Larsson, Sweden	1:14:38
1948	Martin Lundstrom, Sweden	1:13:50
1952	Hallgeir Brenden, Norway	1:01:34
1956	Hallgeir Brenden, Norway	49:39.0
1960	Haakon Brusveen, Norway	51:55.5
1964	Eero Maentyranta, Finland	50:54.1
1968	Harald Groenningen, Norway	47:54.2
1972	Sven-Ake Lundback, Sweden	45:28.24
1976	Nikolai Balukov, USSR	43:58.47
1980	Thomas Wassberg, Sweden	41:57.63
1984	Gunde Svan, Sweden	41:25.6
1988	Mikhail Deviatiarov, USSR	41:18.9

(Note: approx. 18-km. course 1924-1952)

30 kilometers (18.6 miles)

		Time
1956	Veikko Hakulinen, Finland	1:44:06.0
1960	Sixten Jernberg, Sweden	1:51:03.9
1964	Eero Maentyranta, Finland	1:30:50.7
1968	Franco Nones, Italy	1:35:39.2
1972	Vyacheslav Vedenine, USSR	1:36:31.15
1976	Sergei Saveliev, USSR	1:30:29.38
1980	Nikolai Zimyatov, USSR	1:27:02.80
1984	Nikolai Zimyatov, USSR	1:28:56.3
1988	Aleksei Prokourorov, USSR	1:24:26.3

50 kilometers (31.2 miles)

		Time
1924	Thorleif Haug, Norway	3:44:32.0
1928	Per Erik Hedlund, Sweden	4:52:03.0
1932	Veli Saarinen, Finland	4:28:00.0
1936	Elis Wiklund, Sweden	3:30:11.0
1948	Nils Karlsson, Sweden	3:47:48.0
1952	Veikko Hakulinen, Finland	3:33:33.0
1956	Sixten Jernberg, Sweden	2:50:27.0
1960	Kalevi Hamalainen, Finland	2:59:06.3
1964	Sixten Jernberg, Sweden	2:43:52.6
1968	Ole Ellefsaeter, Norway	2:28:45.8
1972	Paal Tyldum, Norway	2:43:14.75
1976	Ivar Formo, Norway	2:37:30.05
1980	Nikolai Zimyatov, USSR	2:27:24.60
1984	Thomas Wassberg, Sweden	2:15:55.8
1988	Gunde Svan, Sweden	2:04:30.9

40-km. Relay

		Time
1936	Finland, Norway, Sweden	2:41:33.0
1948	Sweden, Finland, Norway	2:32:08.0
1952	Finland, Norway, Sweden	2:20:16.0
1956	USSR, Finland, Sweden	2:15:30.0
1960	Finland, Norway, USSR	2:18:45.6
1964	Sweden, Finland, USSR	2:18:34.6

1968	Norway, Sweden, Finland	2:08:33.5
1972	USSR, Norway, Switzerland	2:04:47.94
1976	Finland, Norway, USSR	2:07:59.72
1980	USSR, Norway, Finland	1:57:03.46
1984	Sweden, USSR, Finland	1:55:06.30
1988	Sweden, USSR, Czechoslovakia	1:43:58.60

Combined Cross-Country & Jumping

		Points
1924	Thorleif Haug, Norway	453.800
1928	Johan Grottumsbraaten, Norway	427.800
1932	Johan Grottumsbraaten, Norway	446.000
1936	Oddbjorn Hagen, Norway	430.300
1948	Heikki Hasu, Finland	448.800
1952	Simon Slattvik, Norway	451.621
1956	Sverre Stensersen, Norway	455.000
1960	Georg Thoma, Germany	457.952
1964	Tormod Knutsen, Norway	469.280
1968	Franz Keller, W. Germany	449.040
1972	Ulrich Wehling, E. Germany	413.340
1976	Ulrich Wehling, E. Germany	423.390
1980	Ulrich Wehling, E. Germany	432.200
1984	Tom Sandberg, Norway	422.595
1988	Hippolyt Kempf, Switzerland	235.8

Men's Team Ski Jumping (90 meters)

		Points
1988	Finland, Yugoslavia, Norway	634.400

Ski Jumping (90 meters)

		Points
1924	Jacob Thams, Norway	227.5
1928	Alfred Andersen, Norway	230.5
1932	Birger Ruud, Norway	228.1
1936	Birger Ruud, Norway	232.0
1948	Petter Hugsted, Norway	228.1
1952	Arnfinn Bergmann, Norway	226.0
1956	Antti Hyvarinen, Finland	227.0
1960	Helmut Recknagel, Germany	227.2
1964	Toralf Engan, Norway	230.7
1968	Vladimir Beloussov, USSR	231.3
1972	Wojiech Fortuna, Poland	219.9
1976	Karl Schnabl, Austria	234.8
1980	Jouko Tormanen, Finland	271.0
1984	Matti Nykaenen, Finland	231.2
1988	Matti Nykaenen, Finland	224.0

Men's Team Combined

		Time
1988	W. Germany, Switzerland, Austria	1:20:46.0

Ski Jumping (70 meters)

		Points
1964	Veikko Kankkonen, Finland	229.9
1968	Jiri Raska, Czechoslovakia	216.5
1972	Yukio Kasaya, Japan	244.2
1976	Hans Aschenbach, E. Germany	252.0
1980	Anton Innauer, Austria	266.3
1984	Jens Weissflog, E. Germany	215.2
1988	Matti Nykaenen, Finland	229.1

Women's Events
5 kilometers (approx. 3.1 miles)

		Time
1964	Claudia Boyarskikh, USSR	17:50.5
1968	Toini Gustafsson, Sweden	16:45.2
1972	Galina Koulacova, USSR	17:00.50
1976	Helena Takalo, Finland	15:48.69
1980	Raisa Smetanina, USSR	15:06.92
1984	Marja-Liisa Haemaelainen, Finland	17:04.0
1988	Marjo Matikainen, Finland	15:04.0

10 kilometers

		Time
1952	Lydia Wideman, Finland	41:40.0
1956	Lyubov Kosyreva, USSR	38:11.0
1960	Maria Gusakova, USSR	39:46.6
1964	Claudia Boyarskikh, USSR	40:24.3
1968	Toini Gustafsson, Sweden	36:46.5
1972	Galina Koulacova, USSR	34:17.82
1976	Raisa Smetanina, USSR	30:13.41
1980	Barbara Petzold, E. Germany	30:31.54
1984	Marja-Liisa Haemaelainen, Finland	31:44.2
1988	Vida Ventsene, USSR	30:08.3

20 kilometers

		Time
1984	Marja-Liisa Haemaelainen, Finland	1:01:45.0
1988	Tamara Tikhonova, USSR	55:53.6

20-km. Relay

		Time
1956	Finland, USSR, Sweden (15 km.)	1:09:01.0
1960	Sweden, USSR, Finland (15 km.)	1:04:21.4
1964	USSR, Sweden, Finland (15 km.)	59:20.2
1968	Norway, Sweden, USSR (15 km.)	57:30.0

(continued)

1972 USSR, Finland, Norway (15 km.).	48:46.15
1976 USSR, Finland, E. Germany	1:07:49.75
1980 E. Germany, USSR, Norway	1:02:11.10
1984 Norway, Czechoslovakia, Finland	1:06:49.70
1988 USSR, Norway, Finland	59:51.1

Speed Skating

Men's 500 meters

	Time
1924 Charles Jewtraw, U.S.	0:44.0
1928 Thunberg, Finland & Evensen, Norway (tie)	0:43.4
1932 John A. Shea, U.S.	0:43.4
1936 Ivar Ballangrud, Norway	0:43.4
1948 Finn Helgesen, Norway	0:43.1
1952 Kenneth Henry, U.S.	0:43.2
1956 Evgeniy Grishin, USSR	0:40.2
1960 Evgeniy Grishin, USSR	0:40.2
1964 Terry McDermott, U.S.	0:40.1
1968 Erhard Keller, W. Germany	0:40.3
1972 Erhard Keller, W. Germany	0:39.44
1976 Evgeny Kulikov, USSR	0:39.17
1980 Eric Heiden, U.S.	0:38.03
1984 Sergei Fokichev, USSR	0:38.19
1988 Jens-Uwe Mey, E. Germany	0:36.45

Men's 1,000 meters

	Time
1976 Peter Mueller, U.S.	1:19.32
1980 Eric Heiden, U.S.	1:15.18
1984 Gaetan Boucher, Canada	1:15.80
1988 Nikolai Guiliaev, USSR	1:13.03

Men's 1,500 meters

	Time
1924 Clas Thunberg, Finland	2:20.8
1928 Clas Thunberg, Finland	2:21.1
1932 John A. Shea, U.S.	2:57.5
1936 Charles Mathiesen, Norway	2:19.2
1948 Sverre Farstad, Norway	2:17.6
1952 Hjalmar Andersen, Norway	2:20.4
1956 Grishin, & Mikhailov, both USSR (tie)	2:08.6
1960 Aas, Norway & Grishin, USSR (tie)	2:10.4
1964 Ants Anston, USSR	2:10.3
1968 Cornelis Verkerk, Netherlands	2:03.4
1972 Ard Schenk, Netherlands	2:02.96
1976 Jan Egil Storholt, Norway	1:59.38
1980 Eric Heiden, U.S.	1:55.44
1984 Gaetan Boucher, Canada	1:58.36
1988 Andre Hoffmann, E. Germany	1:52.06

Men's 5,000 meters

	Time
1924 Clas Thunberg, Finland	8:39.0
1928 Ivar Ballangrud, Norway	8:50.5
1932 Irving Jaffee, U.S.	9:40.8
1936 Ivar Ballangrud, Norway	8:19.6
1948 Reidar Liaklev, Norway	8:29.4
1952 Hjalmar Andersen, Norway	8:10.6
1956 Boris Shilkov, USSR	7:48.7
1960 Viktor Kosichkin, USSR	7:51.3
1964 Knut Johannesen, Norway	7:38.4
1968 F. Anton Maier, Norway	7:22.4
1972 Ard Schenk, Netherlands	7:23.61
1976 Sten Stensen, Norway	7:24.48
1980 Eric Heiden, U.S.	7:02.29
1984 Sven Tomas Gustafson, Sweden	7:12:28
1988 Tomas Gustafson, Sweden	6:44:63

Men's 10,000 meters

	Time
1924 Julius Skutnabb, Finland	18:04.8
1928 Event not held, thawing of ice	
1932 Irving Jaffee, U.S.	19:13.6
1936 Ivar Ballangrud, Norway	17:24.3
1948 Ake Seyffarth, Sweden	17:26.3
1952 Hjalmar Andersen, Norway	16:45.8
1956 Sigvard Ericsson, Sweden	16:35.9
1960 Knut Johannesen, Norway	15:46.6
1964 Jonny Nilsson, Sweden	15:50.1
1968 Jonny Hoeglin, Sweden	15:23.6
1972 Ard Schenk, Netherlands	15:01.35
1976 Piet Kleine, Netherlands	14:50.59
1980 Eric Heiden, U.S.	14:28.13
1984 Igor Malkov, USSR	14:39.90
1988 Tomas Gustafson, Sweden	13:48.20

Women's 500 meters

	Time
1960 Helga Haase, Germany	0:45.9
1964 Lydia Skoblikova, USSR	0:45.0
1968 Ludmila Titova, USSR	0:46.1
1972 Anne Henning, U.S.	0:43.33
1976 Sheila Young, U.S.	0:42.76
1980 Karin Enke, E. Germany	0:41.78
1984 Christa Rothenburger, E. Germany	0:41.02
1988 Bonnie Blair, U.S.	0:39.10

Women's 1,000 meters

	Time
1960 Klara Guseva, USSR	1:34.1
1964 Lydia Skoblikova, USSR	1:33.2
1968 Carolina Geijssen, Netherlands	1:32.6
1972 Monika Pflug, W. Germany	1:31.40
1976 Tatiana Averina, USSR	1:28.43
1980 Natalya Petruseva, USSR	1:24.10
1984 Karin Enke, E. Germany	1:21.61
1988 Christa Rothenburger, E. Germany	1:17.65

Women's 1,500 meters

	Time
1960 Lydia Skoblikova, USSR	2:52.2
1964 Lydia Skoblikova, USSR	2:22.6
1968 Kaija Mustonen, Finland	2:22.4
1972 Dianne Holum, U.S.	2:20.85
1976 Galina Stepanskaya, USSR	2:16.58
1980 Anne Borckink, Netherlands	2:10.95
1984 Karin Enke, E. Germany	2:03.42
1988 Yvonne van Gennip, Netherlands	2:00.68

Women's 3,000 meters

	Time
1960 Lydia Skoblikova, USSR	5:14.3
1964 Lydia Skoblikova, USSR	5:14.9
1968 Johanna Schut, Netherlands	4:56.2
1972 Christina Baas-Kaiser, Netherlands	4:52.14
1976 Tatiana Averina, USSR	4:45.19
1980 Bjoerg Eva Jensen, Norway	4:32.13
1984 Andrea Schoene, E. Germany	4:24.79
1988 Yvonne van Gennip, Netherlands	4:11.94

Women's 5,000 meters

	Time
1988 Yvonne van Gennip, Netherlands	7:14:13

Winter Olympic Medal Winners in 1988

Calgary, Alberta, Canada, Feb. 13-28, 1988

	Gold	Silver	Bronze	Total		Gold	Silver	Bronze	Total
Soviet Union	11	9	9	29	United States	2	1	3	6
East Germany	9	10	6	25	Italy	2	1	2	5
Switzerland	5	5	5	15	Norway	0	3	2	5
Austria	3	5	2	10	Canada	0	2	3	5
West Germany	2	4	2	8	Yugoslavia	0	2	1	3
Finland	4	0	3	7	Czechoslovakia	0	1	2	3
The Netherlands	3	2	2	7	France	1	0	1	2
Sweden	4	0	2	6	Japan	0	0	1	1
					Liechtenstein	0	0	1	1

National Hockey League, 1989-90

Final Standings

Wales Conference

Adams Division

	GP	W	L	T	PTS	GF	GA
Boston	80	46	25	9	101	289	232
Buffalo	80	45	27	8	98	286	248
Montreal . . .	80	41	28	11	93	288	234
Hartford	80	38	33	9	85	275	268
Quebec	80	12	61	7	31	240	407

Patrick Division

	GP	W	L	T	PTS	GF	GA
N.Y. Rangers.	80	36	31	13	85	279	267
New Jersey .	80	37	34	9	83	295	288
Washington. .	80	36	38	6	78	284	275
N.Y. Islanders	80	31	38	11	73	281	288
Pittsburgh. . .	80	32	40	8	72	318	359
Philadelphia .	80	30	39	11	71	290	297

Campbell Conference

Norris Division

	GP	W	L	T	PTS	GF	GA
Chicago. . . .	80	41	33	6	88	316	294
St. Louis . . .	80	37	34	9	83	295	279
Toronto	80	38	38	4	80	337	358
Minnesota . .	80	36	40	4	76	284	291
Detroit	80	28	38	14	70	288	323

Smythe Division

	GP	W	L	T	PTS	GF	GA
Calgary	80	42	23	15	99	348	265
Edmonton . . .	80	38	28	14	90	315	283
Winnipeg . . .	80	37	32	11	85	298	290
Los Angeles .	80	34	39	7	75	338	337
Vancouver . .	80	25	41	14	64	245	306

Oilers Win Fifth Stanley Cup Championship

The Edmonton Oilers defeated the Boston Bruins 4 games to 1 to win their 5th Stanley Cup championship in the past 7 years. Goalie Bill Ranford of the Oilers was chosen the most valuable player in the playoffs.

Stanley Cup Playoff Results

Wales Conference

N.Y. Rangers defeated N.Y. Islanders 4-1
Washington defeated New Jersey 4-2
Montreal defeated Buffalo 4-2
Boston defeated Hartford 4-3
Washington defeated N.Y. Rangers 4-1
Boston defeated Montreal 4-1
Boston defeated Washington 4-1

Campbell Conference

St. Louis defeated Toronto 4-1
Los Angeles defeated Calgary 4-2
Chicago defeated Minnesota 4-3
Edmonton defeated Winnipeg 4-3
Edmonton defeated Los Angeles 4-0
Chicago defeated St. Louis 4-3
Edmonton defeated Chicago 4-2

Finals

Edmonton defeated Boston 4-1

Stanley Cup Champions Since 1927

Year	Champion	Coach	Final opponent	Year	Champion	Coach	Final opponent
1927	Ottawa	Dave Gill	Boston	1959	Montreal	Toe Blake	Toronto
1928	N.Y. Rangers	Lester Patrick	Montreal	1960	Montreal	Toe Blake	Toronto
1929	Boston	Cy Denneny	N.Y. Rangers	1961	Chicago	Rudy Pilous	Detroit
1930	Montreal	Cecil Hart	Boston	1962	Toronto	Punch Imlach	Chicago
1931	Montreal	Cecil Hart	Chicago	1963	Toronto	Punch Imlach	Detroit
1932	Toronto	Dick Irvin	N.Y. Rangers	1964	Toronto	Punch Imlach	Detroit
1933	New York	Lester Patrick	Toronto	1965	Montreal	Toe Blake	Chicago
1934	Chicago	Tommy Gorman	Detroit	1966	Montreal	Toe Blake	Detroit
1935	Montreal Maroons	Tommy Gorman	Toronto	1967	Toronto	Punch Imlach	Montreal
1936	Detroit	Jack Adams	Toronto	1968	Montreal	Toe Blake	St. Louis
1937	Detroit	Jack Adams	N.Y. Rangers	1969	Montreal	Claude Ruel	St. Louis
1938	Chicago	Bill Stewart	Toronto	1970	Boston	Harry Sinden	St. Louis
1939	Boston	Art Ross	Toronto	1971	Montreal	Al MacNeil	Chicago
1940	N.Y. Rangers	Frank Boucher	Toronto	1972	Boston	Tom Johnson	N.Y. Rangers
1941	Boston	Cooney Weiland	Detroit	1973	Montreal	Scotty Bowman	Chicago
1942	Toronto	Hap Day	Detroit	1974	Philadelphia	Fred Shero	Boston
1943	Detroit	Jack Adams	Boston	1975	Philadelphia	Fred Shero	Buffalo
1944	Montreal	Dick Irvin	Chicago	1976	Montreal	Scotty Bowman	Philadelphia
1945	Toronto	Hap Day	Detroit	1977	Montreal	Scotty Bowman	Boston
1946	Montreal	Dick Irvin	Boston	1978	Montreal	Scotty Bowman	Boston
1947	Toronto	Hap Day	Montreal	1979	Montreal	Scotty Bowman	N.Y. Rangers
1948	Toronto	Hap Day	Detroit	1980	N.Y. Islanders	Al Arbour	Philadelphia
1949	Toronto	Hap Day	Detroit	1981	N.Y. Islanders	Al Arbour	Minnesota
1950	Detroit	Tommy Ivan	N.Y. Rangers	1982	N.Y. Islanders	Al Arbour	Vancouver
1951	Toronto	Joe Primeau	Montreal	1983	N.Y. Islanders	Al Arbour	Edmonton
1952	Detroit	Tommy Ivan	Montreal	1984	Edmonton	Glen Sather	N.Y. Islanders
1953	Montreal	Dick Irvin	Boston	1985	Edmonton	Glen Sather	Philadelphia
1954	Detroit	Tommy Ivan	Montreal	1986	Montreal	Jean Perron	Calgary
1955	Detroit	Jimmy Skinner	Montreal	1987	Edmonton	Glen Sather	Philadelphia
1956	Montreal	Toe Blake	Detroit	1988	Edmonton	Glen Sather	Boston
1957	Montreal	Toe Blake	Boston	1989	Calgary	Terry Crisp	Montreal
1958	Montreal	Toe Blake	Boston	1990	Edmonton	John Muckler	Boston

Individual Leaders

Points

Wayne Gretzky, Los Angeles, 142; Mark Messier, Edmonton, 129; Steve Yzerman, Detroit, 127; Mario Lemieux, Pittsburgh, 123; Brett Hull, St. Louis, 113.

Goal Scoring

Brett Hull, St. Louis, 72; Steve Yzerman, Detroit, 62; Cam Neely, Boston, 55; Brian Bellows, Minnesota, 55; Pat LaFontaine, N.Y. Islanders, 54.

Assists

Wayne Gretzky, Los Angeles, 102; Mark Messier, Edmonton, 84; Adam Oates, St. Louis, 79; Mario Lemieux, Pittsburgh, 78; Paul Coffey, Pittsburgh, 74.

Power-play goals

Brett Hull, St. Louis, 27; Cam Neely, Boston, 25; Mike Gartner, Minn.-N.Y. Rangers, 21; Brian Bellows, Minnesota, 21; Luc Robitaille, Los Angeles, 20.

Short hand goals

Steve Yzerman, Detroit, 7; Dave McIlwain, Winnipeg, 7; Mark Messier, Edmonton, 6; Craig MacTavish, Edmonton, 6.

Shooting percentage

(minimum 80 shots)

Luc Robitaille, Los Angeles, 24.8; Pat Elynuik, Winnipeg, 24.2; Mike Ridley, Washington, 24.2; Paul MacLean, St. Louis, 24.1; Craig Janney, Boston, 22.9.

Plus/Minus

Paul Cavallini, St. Louis, 38; Stephane Richer, Montreal, 35; Jamie Macoun, Calgary, 34; Shayne Corson, Montreal, 33; Sergei Makarov, Calgary, 33.

Goaltending Leaders

(minimum 25 games)

Goals against average

Patrick Roy, Montreal, 2.53; Mike Liut, Hartford-Wash., 2.53; Rejean Lemelin, Boston, 2.81; Daren Puppa, Buffalo, 2.89; Andy Moog, Boston, 2.89.

Wins

Patrick Roy, Montreal, 31; Daren Puppa, Buffalo, 31; Jon Casey, Minnesota, 31; Andy Moog, Boston, 24; Bill Ranford, Edmonton, 24.

Save percentage

Patrick Roy, Montreal, .912; Mike Liut, Hartford-Wash., .905; Daren Puppa, Buffalo, .903; Clint Malarchuk, Buffalo, .903; Mark Fitzpatrick, N.Y. Islanders, .898.

Shutouts

Mike Liut, Hartford-Wash., 4; Andy Moog, Boston, 3; Mark Fitzpatrick, N.Y. Islanders, 3; Patrick Roy, Montreal, 3; Jon Casey, Minnesota, 3.

Individual Scoring

(40 or more games played)

Boston Bruins

	GP	G	A	Pts	+/−	PIM
Cam Neely	76	55	37	92	10	117
Ray Bourque	76	19	65	84	31	50
Craig Janney	55	24	38	62	3	4
Bob Carpenter	80	25	31	56	3−	97
Bob Sweeney	70	22	24	46	2	93
Dave Poulin	60	15	27	42	16	24
Brian Propp	54	16	24	40	5	41
Dave Christian	78	15	25	40	8−	12
Andy Brickley	43	12	28	40	11	8
John Carter	76	17	22	39	17	26
Greg Hawgood	77	11	27	38	12	76
Glen Wesley	78	9	27	36	6	48
Garry Galley	71	8	27	35	2	75
Randy Burridge	63	17	15	32	9	47
Bob Gould	77	8	17	25	3−	92
Jim Wiemer	61	5	14	19	11	63
Rob Cimetta	47	8	9	17	4	33
Lyndon Byers	43	4	4	8	0	159
Don Sweeney	58	3	5	8	11	58
Allen Pedersen	68	1	2	3	5−	71
Andy Moog	46	0	3	3	0	18
Rejean Lemelin	43	0	0	0	0	32

Buffalo Sabres

	GP	G	A	Pts	+/−	PIM
Pierre Turgeon	80	40	66	106	10	29
Dave Andreychuk	73	40	42	82	6	42
Phil Housley	80	21	60	81	11	32
Christian Ruuttu	75	19	41	60	9	66
Rick Vaive	70	29	19	48	9	74
Doug Bodger	71	12	36	48	0	64
Alexander Mogilny	65	15	28	43	8	16
Mike Foligno	61	15	25	40	13	99
Scott Arniel	79	18	14	32	4	77
Dave Snuggerud	80	14	16	30	8	41
Mike Ramsey	73	4	21	25	21	47
Uwe Krupp	74	3	20	23	15	85
Mike Hartman	60	11	10	21	10−	211
Jay Wells	60	3	17	20	5	129
Benoit Hogue	45	11	7	18	0	79
Grant Ledyard	67	2	13	15	2	37
Dean Kennedy	80	2	12	14	12−	53
Jeff Parker	61	4	5	9	9−	70
Daren Puppa	56	0	4	4	0	4

Calgary Flames

	GP	G	A	Pts	+/−	PIM
Joe Nieuwendyk	79	45	50	95	32	40
Doug Gilmour	78	24	67	91	20	54
Al MacInnis	79	28	62	90	20	82
Sergei Makarov	80	24	62	86	33	55
Gary Suter	76	16	60	76	4	97
Gary Roberts	78	39	33	72	31	222
Joe Mullen	78	36	33	69	6	24
Theo Fleury	80	31	35	66	22	157
Paul Ranheim	80	26	28	54	27	23
Brian MacLellan	65	20	18	38	3−	26
Jamie Macoun	78	8	27	35	34	70
Joel Otto	75	13	20	33	4	116
Jiri Hrdina	64	12	18	30	10	31
Dana Murzyn	78	7	13	20	19	140
Brad McCrimmon	79	4	15	19	18	78
Ric Nattress	49	1	14	15	14	26
Colin Patterson	61	5	3	8	4−	20
Jim Korn	46	2	5	7	0	125
Tim Hunter	67	2	3	5	9−	279
Mike Vernon	47	0	3	3	0	21

Chicago Black Hawks

	GP	G	A	Pts	+/−	PIM
Steve Larmer	80	31	59	90	25	40
Denis Savard	60	27	53	80	8	56
Doug Wilson	70	23	50	73	13	40
Steve Thomas	76	40	30	70	3−	91
Adam Creighton	80	34	36	70	4	224
Jeremy Roenick	78	26	40	66	2	54
Troy Murray	68	17	38	55	2−	86
Dirk Graham	73	22	32	54	1	102
Michel Goulet	65	20	30	50	32−	51
Greg Gilbert	70	12	25	37	27	54
Dave Manson	59	5	23	28	4	301
Jocelyn Lemieux	73	14	13	27	1	108
Keith Brown	67	5	20	25	26	87
Bob Murray	49	5	19	24	3	45
Al Secord	43	14	7	21	5	131
Mike Hudson	49	9	12	21	3−	67
Trent Yawney	70	5	15	20	6−	82
Duane Sutter	72	4	14	18	2−	156
Steve Konroyd	75	3	14	17	6	34
Wayne Presley	49	6	7	13	19−	67
Bob McGill	69	2	10	12	7−	204
Wayne Van Dorp	61	7	4	11	3−	303
Greg Millen	49	0	1	1	0	0
Jacques Cloutier	43	0	0	0	0	8

Detroit Red Wings

	GP	G	A	Pts	+/-	PIM
Steve Yzerman	79	62	65	127	5-	79
Gerard Gallant	69	36	44	80	6-	254
Bernie Federko	73	17	40	57	8-	24
Shawn Burr	76	24	32	56	14	82
John Chabot	69	9	40	49	5	24
Steve Chiasson	67	14	28	42	16-	114
Jimmy Carson	48	21	18	39	7-	8
Joey Kocur	71	16	20	36	5-	268
Dave Barr	62	10	25	35	1	15
Marc Habscheid	62	15	11	26	1	33
Rick Zombo	77	5	20	25	13	95
Daniel Shank	57	11	13	24	1	143
Lee Norwood	64	8	14	22	15	95
Borje Salming	49	2	17	19	20	52
Mike O'Connell	66	4	14	18	11-	22
Kevin McClelland	71	5	6	11	6-	196
Doug Houda	73	2	9	11	6-	127
Robert Picard	44	0	8	8	4-	48
Torrie Robertson	42	1	5	6	3-	112
Glen Hanlon	45	0	3	3	0	24

Edmonton Oilers

	GP	G	A	Pts	+/-	PIM
Mark Messier	79	45	84	129	19	79
Jari Kurri	78	33	60	93	18	48
Glenn Anderson	73	34	38	72	1-	107
Petr Klima	76	30	33	63	9-	72
Esa Tikkanen	79	30	33	63	17	161
Craig Simpson	80	29	32	61	2-	180
Craig MacTavish	80	21	22	43	13	89
Steve Smith	75	7	34	41	6	171
Kevin Lowe	78	7	26	33	18	140
Joe Murphy	71	10	19	29	5	60
Mark Lamb	58	12	16	28	10	42
Martin Gelinas	46	17	8	25	0	30
Randy Gregg	48	4	20	24	24	42
Charlie Huddy	70	1	23	24	13-	56
Adam Graves	76	9	13	22	0	136
Craig Muni	71	5	12	17	22	81
Geoff Smith	74	4	11	15	13	52
Reijo Ruotsalainen	41	3	12	15	5-	20
Jeff Beukeboom	46	1	12	13	5	86
Kelly Buchberger	55	2	6	8	6-	168
Dave Brown	60	0	6	6	3-	145
Bill Ranford	56	0	2	2	0	18

Hartford Whalers

	GP	G	A	Pts	+/-	PIM
Ron Francis	80	32	69	101	13	73
Pat Verbeek	80	44	45	89	1	228
Kevin Dineen	67	25	41	66	7	164
Scott Young	80	24	40	64	24-	47
Ray Ferraro	79	25	29	54	15-	109
Dean Evason	78	18	25	43	7	138
Dave Babych	72	6	37	43	16-	62
Mikael Andersson	50	13	24	37	0	6
Brad Shaw	64	3	32	35	2	40
Todd Krygier	58	18	12	30	4	52
Randy Cunneyworth	71	14	15	29	11-	75
Dave Tippett	66	8	19	27	0	32
Mike Tomlak	70	7	14	21	5	48
Yvon Corriveau	63	13	7	20	2	72
Randy Ladouceur	71	3	12	15	6-	143
Ulf Samuelsson	55	2	11	13	15	167
Adam Burt	63	4	8	12	3	105
Grant Jennings	64	3	6	9	4-	154
Ed Kastelic	67	6	2	8	3-	198
Joel Quenneville	44	1	4	5	9	34
Peter Sidorkiewicz	46	0	1	1	0	4

Los Angeles Kings

	GP	G	A	Pts	+/-	PIM
Wayne Gretzky	73	40	102	142	8	42
Luc Robitaille	80	52	49	101	8	38
Tomas Sandstrom	76	32	39	71	11-	128
John Tonelli	73	31	37	68	8-	62
Steve Duchesne	79	20	42	62	3-	36
Steve Kasper	77	17	28	45	4	27
Mike Krushelnyski	63	16	25	41	7	50
Dave Taylor	58	15	26	41	17	96
Larry Robinson	64	7	32	39	7	34
Robert Kudelski	62	23	13	36	7-	49
Marty McSorley	75	15	21	36	2	322

	GP	G	A	Pts	+/-	PIM
Tony Granato	56	12	24	36	1-	122
Todd Elik	48	10	23	33	4	41
Mikko Makela	65	9	17	26	14-	18
Brian Benning	55	6	19	25	2-	105
Keith Crowder	55	4	13	17	2	93
Mike Allison	55	2	11	13	6-	78
Jay Miller	68	10	2	12	6-	224
Tim Watters	62	1	10	11	23	92
Tom Laidlaw	57	1	8	9	4	42
Barry Beck	52	1	78	3	53	
Kelly Hrudey	52	0	0	0	0	18

Minnesota North Stars

	GP	G	A	Pts	+/-	PIM
Brian Bellows	80	55	44	99	3-	72
Neal Broten	80	23	62	85	16-	45
Dave Gagner	79	40	38	78	1-	54
Mike Modano	80	29	46	75	7-	63
Larry Murphy	77	10	58	68	13-	44
Ulf Dahlen	76	20	22	42	3-	30
Aaron Broten	77	19	17	36	23-	58
Don Barber	44	15	19	34	4	32
Basil McRae	66	9	17	26	5-	351
Shawn Chambers	78	8	18	26	2-	81
Stewart Gavin	80	12	13	25	9	76
Gaetan Duchesne	72	12	8	20	5	33
Perry Berezan	64	3	12	15	4-	31
Ville Siren	53	1	13	14	1	60
Curt Giles	74	1	12	13	3	48
Mark Tinordi	66	3	7	10	0	240
Frantisek Musil	56	2	8	10	0	109
Shane Churla	53	2	3	5	4-	292
Jon Casey	61	0	3	3	0	18

Montreal Canadiens

	GP	G	A	Pts	+/-	PIM
Stephane Richer	75	51	40	91	35	46
Shayne Corson	76	31	44	75	33	144
Russ Courtnall	80	27	32	59	14	27
Guy Carbonneau	68	19	36	55	21	37
Brian Skrudland	59	11	31	42	21	56
Mike McPhee	56	23	18	41	28	47
Mats Naslund	72	21	20	41	3	19
Petr Svoboda	60	5	31	36	20	98
Stephan Lebeau	57	15	20	35	13	11
Chris Chelios	53	9	22	31	20	136
Bobby Smith	53	12	14	26	4-	35
Brent Gilchrist	57	9	15	24	3	28
Mike Keane	74	9	15	24	0	78
Ryan Walter	70	8	16	24	4	59
Matt Schneider	44	7	14	21	2	25
Eric Desjardins	55	3	13	16	1	51
Craig Ludwig	73	1	15	16	24	108
Sylvain Lefebvre	68	3	10	13	18	61
Todd Ewen	44	4	6	10	1-	169
Patrick Roy	54	0	5	5	0	0

New Jersey Devils

	GP	G	A	Pts	+/-	PIM
Kirk Muller	80	30	56	86	1-	74
John MacLean	80	41	38	79	17	80
Patrik Sundstrom	74	27	49	76	15	34
Peter Stastny	74	29	44	73	46-	40
Brendan Shanahan	73	30	42	72	15	137
Bruce Driver	75	7	46	53	6	63
Sylvain Turgeon	72	30	17	47	8-	81
Mark Johnson	63	16	29	45	8-	12
Viacheslav Fetisov	72	8	34	42	9	52
Doug Brown	69	14	20	34	7	16
Janne Ojanen	64	17	13	30	5-	12
Tommy Albelin	68	6	23	29	1-	63
Bob Brooke	73	12	14	26	2-	63
David Maley	67	8	17	25	2-	160
Ken Daneyko	74	6	15	21	0	216
Randy Velischek	62	0	6	6	4	72
Jamie Huscroft	42	2	3	5	2-	144
Sean Burke	52	0	1	1	0	38

New York Islanders

	GP	G	A	Pts	+/-	PIM
Pat LaFontaine	74	54	51	105	13-	38
Brent Sutter	67	33	35	68	9	65
Doug Crossman	80	15	44	59	3	54

(continued)

	GP	G	A	Pts	+/-	PIM
Jeff Norton	60	4	49	53	9-	65
Patrick Flatley	62	17	32	49	10	101
Randy Wood	74	24	24	48	10-	39
Don Maloney	79	16	27	43	6	47
Derek King	46	13	27	40	2	20
Dave Volek	80	17	22	39	2-	41
Hubie McDonough	76	21	15	36	14	36
Alan Kerr	75	15	20	35	1-	129
Gary Nylund	64	4	21	25	8	144
Bryan Trottier	59	13	11	24	11-	29
Brad Lauer	63	6	18	24	5	19
Gerald Diduck	76	3	17	20	2	163
Mick Vukota	76	4	8	12	10	290
Jari Gronstrand	48	3	5	8	1-	29
Ken Baumgartner	65	1	5	6	4-	222
Mark Fitzpatrick	47	0	2	2	0	18

New York Rangers

	GP	G	A	Pts	+/-	PIM
Bernie Nicholls	79	39	73	112	9-	86
Mike Gartner	79	45	41	86	4-	38
John Ogrodnick	80	43	31	74	11	44
Brian Mullen	76	27	41	68	7	42
Darren Turcotte	76	32	34	66	3	32
Kelly Kisio	68	22	44	66	11	105
James Patrick	73	14	43	57	4	50
Brian Leetch	72	11	45	56	18-	26
Troy Mallette	79	13	16	29	8-	305
Carey Wilson	41	9	17	26	4	57
Mark Hardy	54	0	15	15	4	94
Miloslav Horava	45	4	10	14	10	26
Kris King	68	6	7	13	2	286
Mark Janssens	80	5	8	13	26-	161
Jan Erixon	58	4	9	13	17-	8
Randy Moller	60	1	12	13	1-	139
Ron Greschner	55	1	9	10	7-	53
Lindy Ruff	56	3	6	9	10-	177
John Vanbiesbrouck	47	0	2	2	0	24

Philadelphia Flyers

	GP	G	A	Pts	+/-	PIM
Rick Tocchet	75	37	59	96	4	196
Murray Craven	76	25	50	75	2	42
Mike Bullard	70	27	37	64	0	67
Pelle Eklund	70	23	39	62	7	16
Tim Kerr	40	24	24	48	3-	34
Ron Sutter	75	22	26	48	2	104
Ilkka Sinisalo	59	23	23	46	6	26
Gord Murphy	75	14	27	41	7-	95
Ken Linseman	61	11	25	36	5	96
Mark Howe	40	7	21	28	22	24
Keith Acton	69	13	14	27	2-	80
Scott Mellanby	57	6	17	23	4-	77
Kjell Samuelsson	66	5	17	22	20	91
Terry Carkner	63	4	18	22	8-	167
Craig Berube	74	4	14	18	7-	291
Kevin Maguire	66	7	9	16	4-	121
Kerry Huffman	43	1	12	13	3-	34
Tony Horacek	48	5	5	10	6	117
Derrick Smith	55	3	6	9	15-	32
Jeff Chychrun	79	2	7	9	12-	250
Ken Wregget	51	0	2	2	0	12

Pittsburgh Penguins

	GP	G	A	Pts	+/-	PIM
Mario Lemieux	59	45	78	123	18-	78
Paul Coffey	80	29	74	103	25-	95
John Cullen	72	32	60	92	13-	138
Rob Brown	80	33	47	80	10-	102
Kevin Stevens	76	29	41	70	13-	171
Mark Recchi	74	30	37	67	6	44
Tony Tanti	78	28	36	64	10-	72
Phil Bourque	76	22	17	39	7-	108
Bob Errey	78	20	19	39	3	109
Zarley Zalapski	51	6	25	31	14-	37
Barry Pederson	54	6	25	31	13-	39
Troy Loney	67	11	16	27	9-	168
Randy Gilhen	61	5	11	16	8-	54
Jim Johnson	75	3	13	16	20-	154
Randy Hillier	61	3	12	15	11	71
Chris Dahlquist	62	4	10	14	2-	56
Gilbert Delorme	54	3	7	10	3	44
Doug Smith	40	4	5	9	1-	97

	GP	G	A	Pts	+/-	PIM
Gord Dineen	69	1	8	9	6	125
Jim Kyte	56	3	1	4	10-	125
Wendell Young	43	0	4	4	0	8
Alain Chevrier	42	0	3	3	0	8

Quebec Nordiques

	GP	G	A	Pts	+/-	PIM
Joe Sakic	80	39	63	102	40-	27
Michel Petit	63	12	24	36	38-	215
Tony McKegney	62	18	12	30	29-	53
Marc Fortier	59	13	17	30	16-	28
Tony Hrkac	50	9	20	29	4-	10
Mike Hough	43	13	13	26	24-	84
Claude Loiselle	72	11	14	25	27-	104
Paul Gillis	71	8	14	22	24-	234
Jeff Jackson	65	8	12	20	21-	71
Iirvo Jarvi	41	7	13	20	11-	18
Joe Cirella	56	4	14	18	27-	104
Mario Marois	67	3	15	18	45-	104
Lucien Deblois	70	9	8	17	29-	45
Ken McRae	66	7	8	15	38-	191
Bryan Fogarty	45	4	10	14	47-	31
Steven Finn	64	3	9	12	33-	208
Craig Wolanin	50	1	10	11	11-	57
Darin Kimble	44	5	5	10	20-	185
Curtis Leschyshyn	68	2	6	8	41-	44

St. Louis Blues

	GP	G	A	Pts	+/-	PIM
Brett Hull	80	72	41	113	1-	24
Adam Oates	80	23	79	102	9	30
Peter Zezel	73	25	47	72	9-	30
Paul MacLean	78	34	33	67	2	100
Rod Brind'Amour	79	26	35	61	23	46
Sergio Momesso	79	24	32	56	15-	199
Jeff Brown	77	16	38	54	26-	55
Paul Cavallini	80	8	39	47	38	106
Gino Cavallini	80	15	15	30	8-	77
Dave Lowry	78	19	6	25	1	75
Rick Meagher	76	8	17	25	4	47
Steve Tuttle	71	12	10	22	6-	4
Rich Sutter	74	11	9	20	3-	155
Gordie Roberts	75	3	14	17	12-	140
Mike Lalor	78	0	16	16	6-	81
Glen Featherstone	58	0	12	12	1-	145
Harold Snepsts	46	1	4	5	1-	36
Kelly Chase	43	1	3	4	1-	244
Vincent Riendeau	43	0	0	0	0	6

Toronto Maple Leafs

	GP	G	A	Pts	+/-	PIM
Gary Leeman	80	51	44	95	4	63
Vincent Damphousse	80	33	61	94	2	56
Ed Olczyk	79	32	56	88	0	78
Dan Marois	68	39	37	76	1	82
Mark Osborne	78	23	50	73	2	91
Al Iafrate	75	21	42	63	4-	135
Tom Kurvers	71	15	37	52	9-	29
Rob Ramage	80	8	41	49	1-	202
Tom Fergus	54	19	26	45	18-	62
Lou Franceschetti	80	21	15	36	12-	127
Dave Reid	70	9	19	28	8-	9
Gilles Thibaudeau	41	11	15	26	8	30
Dan Daoust	65	7	11	18	1	89
Luke Richardson	67	4	14	18	1-	122
John McIntyre	59	5	12	17	12-	117
Scott Pearson	41	5	10	15	7-	90
Todd Gill	48	1	14	15	8-	92
Brad Marsh	79	1	13	14	14	95
John Kordic	55	9	4	13	8-	252
Brian Curran	72	2	9	11	2-	301
Allan Bester	42	0	2	2	0	4

Vancouver Canucks

	GP	G	A	Pts	+/-	PIM
Dan Quinn	78	25	38	63	17-	49
Paul Reinhart	67	17	40	57	2	30
Trevor Linden	73	21	30	51	17-	43
Greg Adams	65	30	20	50	8-	18
Brian Bradley	67	19	29	48	5	65
Petri Skriko	77	15	33	48	21-	36
Igor Larionov	74	17	27	44	5-	20
Doug Lidster	80	8	28	36	16-	36

	GP	G	A	Pts	+/-	PIM
Vladimir Krutov	61	11	23	34	5-	20
Jyrki Lumme	65	4	26	30	17	49
Jim Sandlak	70	15	8	23	15-	104
Steve Bozek	58	14	9	23	3-	32
Andrew McBain	67	9	14	23	11-	73
Garth Butcher	80	6	14	20	10-	205
Stan Smyl	47	1	15	16	14-	71
Robert Nordmark	44	2	11	13	16-	34
Jim Benning	45	3	9	12	4	26
Kirk McLean	63	0	3	3	0	6
Larry Melnyk	67	0	2	2	27-	91

Washington Capitals

	GP	G	A	Pts	+/-	PIM
Dino Ciccarelli	80	41	38	79	5-	122
Geoff Courtnall	80	35	39	74	27	104
Mike Ridley	74	30	43	73	0	27
Michal Pivonka	77	25	39	64	7-	54
Dale Hunter	80	23	39	62	17	233
Kevin Hatcher	80	13	41	54	4	102
Kelly Miller	80	18	22	40	2-	49
Scott Stevens	56	11	29	40	1	154
Calle Johansson	70	8	31	39	7	25
Stephen Leach	70	18	14	32	10	104
John Tucker	46	10	21	31	8	12
Bob Rouse	70	4	16	20	2-	123
Alan May	77	7	10	17	1-	339
Bob Joyce	47	6	10	16	6-	26

	GP	G	A	Pts	+/-	PIM
Bill Houlder	41	1	11	12	8	28
John Druce	45	8	3	11	3-	52
Rob Murray	41	2	7	9	10-	58
Rod Langway	58	0	8	8	7	39
Don Beaupre	48	0	1	1	0	24

Winnipeg Jets

	GP	G	A	Pts	+/-	PIM
Dale Hawerchuk	79	26	55	81	11-	60
Pat Elynuik	80	32	42	74	2	83
Thomas Steen	53	18	48	66	2	35
Brent Ashton	79	22	34	56	4	37
Fredrik Olausson	77	9	46	55	1-	32
Dave McLlwain	80	25	26	51	1-	60
Paul Fenton	80	32	18	50	2	40
Doug Smail	79	25	24	49	15	63
Greg Paslawski	71	18	30	48	4-	14
Dave Ellett	77	17	29	46	15-	96
Teppo Numminen	79	11	32	43	4-	20
Paul MacDermid	73	13	22	35	5	169
Moe Mantha	73	2	26	28	8	28
Laurie Boschman	66	10	17	27	11-	103
Randy Carlyle	53	3	15	18	8	50
Mark Kumpel	56	8	9	17	5-	21
Phil Sykes	48	9	6	15	8-	26
Peter Taglianetti	49	3	6	9	20	136
Gord Donnelly	55	3	3	6	3	222
Shawn Cronin	61	0	4	4	16-	243

Conn Smythe Trophy (MVP in Playoffs)

Year	Player
1965	Jean Beliveau, Montreal
1966	Roger Crozier, Detroit
1967	Dave Keon, Toronto
1968	Glenn Hall, St. Louis
1969	Serge Savard, Montreal
1970	Bobby Orr, Boston
1971	Ken Dryden, Montreal
1972	Bobby Orr, Boston
1973	Yvan Cournoyer, Montreal
1974	Bernie Parent, Philadelphia
1975	Bernie Parent, Philadelphia
1976	Reg Leach, Philadelphia
1977	Guy Lafleur, Montreal
1978	Larry Robinson, Montreal
1979	Bob Gainey, Montreal
1980	Bryan Trottier, N.Y. Islanders
1981	Butch Goring, N.Y. Islanders
1982	Mike Bossy, N.Y. Islanders
1983	Billy Smith, N.Y. Islanders
1984	Mark Messier, Edmonton
1985	Wayne Gretzky, Edmonton
1986	Patrick Roy, Montreal
1987	Ron Hextall, Philadelphia
1988	Wayne Gretzky, Edmonton
1989	Al MacInnis, Calgary
1990	Bill Ranford, Edmonton

Ross Trophy (Leading Scorer)

Year	Player
1927	Bill Cook, N.Y. Rangers
1928	Howie Morenz, Montreal
1929	Ace Bailey, Toronto
1930	Cooney Weiland, Boston
1931	Howie Morenz, Montreal
1932	Harvey Jackson, Toronto
1933	Bill Cook, N.Y. Rangers
1934	Charlie Conacher, Toronto
1935	Charlie Conacher, Toronto
1936	Dave Schriner, N.Y. Americans
1937	Dave Schriner, N.Y. Americans
1938	Gordie Drillon, Toronto
1939	Toe Blake, Montreal
1940	Milt Schmidt, Boston
1941	Bill Cowley, Boston
1942	Bryan Hextall, N.Y. Rangers
1943	Doug Bentley, Chicago
1944	Herbie Cain, Boston
1945	Elmer Lach, Montreal
1946	Max Bentley, Chicago
1947	Max Bentley, Chicago
1948	Elmer Lach, Montreal
1949	Roy Conacher, Chicago
1950	Ted Lindsay, Detroit
1951	Gordie Howe, Detroit
1952	Gordie Howe, Detroit
1953	Gordie Howe, Detroit
1954	Gordie Howe, Detroit
1955	Bernie Geoffrion, Montreal
1956	Jean Beliveau, Montreal
1957	Gordie Howe, Detroit
1958	Dickie Moore, Montreal
1959	Dickie Moore, Montreal
1960	Bobby Hull, Chicago
1961	Bernie Geoffrion, Montreal
1962	Bobby Hull, Chicago
1963	Gordie Howe, Detroit
1964	Stan Mikita, Chicago
1965	Stan Mikita, Chicago
1966	Bobby Hull, Chicago
1967	Stan Mikita, Chicago
1968	Stan Mikita, Chicago
1969	Phil Esposito, Boston
1970	Bobby Orr, Boston
1971	Phil Esposito, Boston
1972	Phil Esposito, Boston
1973	Phil Esposito, Boston
1974	Phil Esposito, Boston
1975	Bobby Orr, Boston
1976	Guy Lafleur, Montreal
1977	Guy Lafleur, Montreal
1978	Guy Lafleur, Montreal
1979	Bryan Trottier, N.Y. Islanders
1980	Marcel Dionne, Los Angeles
1981	Wayne Gretzky, Edmonton
1982	Wayne Gretzky, Edmonton
1983	Wayne Gretzky, Edmonton
1984	Wayne Gretzky, Edmonton
1985	Wayne Gretzky, Edmonton
1986	Wayne Gretzky, Edmonton
1987	Wayne Gretzky, Edmonton
1988	Mario Lemieux, Pittsburgh
1989	Mario Lemieux, Pittsburgh
1990	Wayne Gretzky, Los Angeles

James Norris Memorial Trophy (Outstanding Defenseman)

Year	Player
1954	Red Kelly, Detroit
1955	Doug Harvey, Montreal
1956	Doug Harvey, Montreal
1957	Doug Harvey, Montreal
1958	Doug Harvey, Montreal
1959	Tom Johnson, Montreal
1960	Doug Harvey, Montreal
1961	Doug Harvey, Montreal
1962	Doug Harvey, N.Y. Rangers
1963	Pierre Pilote, Chicago
1964	Pierre Pilote, Chicago
1965	Pierre Pilote, Chicago
1966	Jacques Laperriere, Montreal
1967	Harry Howell, N.Y. Rangers
1968	Bobby Orr, Boston
1969	Bobby Orr, Boston
1970	Bobby Orr, Boston
1971	Bobby Orr, Boston
1972	Bobby Orr, Boston
1973	Bobby Orr, Boston
1974	Bobby Orr, Boston
1975	Bobby Orr, Boston
1976	Denis Potvin, N.Y. Islanders
1977	Larry Robinson, Montreal
1978	Denis Potvin, N.Y. Islanders
1979	Denis Potvin, N.Y. Islanders
1980	Larry Robinson, Montreal
1981	Randy Carlyle, Pittsburgh
1982	Doug Wilson, Chicago
1983	Rod Langway, Washington
1984	Rod Langway, Washington
1985	Paul Coffey, Edmonton
1986	Paul Coffey, Edmonton
1987	Ray Bourque, Boston
1988	Ray Bourque, Boston
1989	Chris Chelios, Montreal
1990	Ray Bourque, Boston

*Vezina Trophy (Leading Goalie)

1927	George Hainsworth, Montreal	1950	Bill Durnan, Montreal	1972	Esposito, Smith, Chicago
1928	George Hainsworth, Montreal	1951	Al Rollins, Toronto	1973	Ken Dryden, Montreal
1929	George Hainsworth, Montreal	1952	Terry Sawchuk, Detroit	1974	Bernie Parent, Philadelphia;
1930	Tiny Thompson, Boston	1953	Terry Sawchuk, Detroit		Tony Esposito, Chicago
1931	Roy Worters, N.Y. Americans	1954	Harry Lumley, Toronto	1975	Bernie Parent, Philadelphia
1932	Charlie Gardiner, Chicago	1955	Terry Sawchuk, Detroit	1976	Ken Dryden, Montreal
1933	Tiny Thompson, Boston	1956	Jacques Plante, Montreal	1977	Dryden, Larocque, Montreal
1934	Charlie Gardiner, Chicago	1957	Jacques Plante, Montreal	1978	Dryden, Larocque, Montreal
1935	Lorne Chabot, Chicago	1958	Jacques Plante, Montreal	1979	Dryden, Larocque, Montreal
1936	Tiny Thompson, Boston	1959	Jacques Plante, Montreal	1980	Sauve, Edwards, Buffalo
1937	Normie Smith, Detroit	1960	Jacques Plante, Montreal	1981	Sevigny, Larocque, Herron,
1938	Tiny Thompson, Boston	1961	John Bower, Toronto		Montreal
1939	Frank Brimsek, Boston	1962	Jacques Plante, Montreal	1982	Bill Smith, N.Y. Islanders
1940	Dave Kerr, N.Y. Rangers	1963	Glenn Hall, Chicago	1983	Pete Peeters, Boston
1941	Turk Broda, Toronto	1964	Charlie Hodge, Montreal	1984	Tom Barrasso, Buffalo
1942	Frank Brimsek, Boston	1965	Sawchuk, Bower, Toronto	1985	Pelle Lindbergh, Philadelphia
1943	Johnny Mowers, Detroit	1966	Worsley, Hodge, Montreal	1986	John Vanbiesbrouck, N.Y.
1944	Bill Durnan, Montreal	1967	Hall, DeJordy, Chicago		Rangers
1945	Bill Durnan, Montreal	1968	Worsley, Vachon, Montreal	1987	Ron Hextall, Philadelphia
1946	Bill Durnan, Montreal	1969	Hall, Plante, St. Louis	1988	Grant Fuhr, Edmonton
1947	Bill Durnan, Montreal	1970	Tony Esposito, Chicago	1989	Patrick Roy, Montreal
1948	Turk Broda, Toronto	1971	Giacomin, Villemure, N.Y.	1990	Patrick Roy, Montreal
1949	Bill Durnan, Montreal		Rangers		

* Awarded to goalie who played a minimum 25 games for the team which allowed the fewest goals; since 1982, awarded to outstanding goalie.

Calder Memorial Trophy (Rookie of the Year)

1933	Carl Voss, Detroit	1951	Terry Sawchuk, Detroit	1971	Gilbert Perreault, Buffalo
1934	Russ Blinco, Montreal	1952	Bernie Geoffrion, Montreal	1972	Ken Dryden, Montreal
	Maroons	1953	Gump Worsley, N.Y. Rangers	1973	Steve Vickers, N.Y. Rangers
1935	Dave Schriner, N.Y. Americans	1954	Camille Henry, N.Y. Rangers	1974	Denis Potvin, N.Y. Islanders
1936	Mike Karakas, Chicago	1955	Ed Litzenberger, Chicago	1975	Eric Vail, Atlanta
1937	Syl Apps, Toronto	1956	Glenn Hall, Detroit	1976	Bryan Trottier, N.Y. Islanders
1938	Cully Dahlstrom, Chicago	1957	Larry Regan, Boston	1977	Willi Plett, Atlanta
1939	Frank Brimsek, Boston	1958	Frank Mahovlich, Toronto	1978	Mike Bossy, N.Y. Islanders
1940	Kilby Macdonald, N.Y.	1959	Ralph Backstrom, Montreal	1979	Bobby Smith, Minnesota
	Rangers	1960	Bill Hay, Chicago	1980	Ray Bourque, Boston
1941	John Quilty, Montreal	1961	Dave Keon, Toronto	1981	Peter Stastny, Quebec
1942	Grant Warwick, N.Y. Rangers	1962	Bobby Rousseau, Montreal	1982	Dale Hawerchuk, Winnipeg
1943	Gaye Stewart, Toronto	1963	Kent Douglas, Toronto	1983	Steve Larmer, Chicago
1944	Gus Bodnar, Toronto	1964	Jacques Laperriere, Montreal	1984	Tom Barrasso, Buffalo
1945	Frank McCool, Toronto	1965	Roger Crozier, Detroit	1985	Mario Lemieux, Pittsburgh
1946	Edgar Laprade, N.Y. Rangers	1966	Brit Selby, Toronto	1986	Gary Suter, Calgary
1947	Howie Meeker, Toronto	1967	Bobby Orr, Boston	1987	Luc Robitaille, Los Angeles
1948	Jim McFadden, Detroit	1968	Derek Sanderson, Boston	1988	Joe Nieuwendyk, Calgary
1949	Pentti Lund, N.Y. Rangers	1969	Danny Grant, Minnesota	1989	Brian Leetch, N.Y. Rangers
1950	Jack Gelineau, Boston	1970	Tony Esposito, Chicago	1990	Sergei Makarov, Calgary

Lady Byng Memorial Trophy (Most Gentlemanly Player)

1925	Frank Nighbor, Ottawa	1948	Buddy O'Connor, N.Y.	1970	Phil Goyette, St. Louis
1926	Frank Nighbor, Ottawa		Rangers	1971	John Bucyk, Boston
1927	Billy Burch, N.Y. Americans	1949	Bill Quackenbush, Detroit	1972	Jean Ratelle, N.Y. Rangers
1928	Frank Boucher, N.Y. Rangers	1950	Edgar Laprade, N.Y. Rangers	1973	Gil Perreault, Buffalo
1929	Frank Boucher, N.Y. Rangers	1951	Red Kelly, Detroit	1974	John Bucyk, Boston
1930	Frank Boucher, N.Y. Rangers	1952	Sid Smith, Toronto	1975	Marcel Dionne, Detroit
1931	Frank Boucher, N.Y. Rangers	1953	Red Kelly, Detroit	1976	Jean Ratelle, N.Y. R.-Boston
1932	Joe Primeau, Toronto	1954	Red Kelly, Detroit	1977	Marcel Dionne, Los Angeles
1933	Frank Boucher, N.Y. Rangers	1955	Sid Smith, Toronto	1978	Butch Goring, Los Angeles
1934	Frank Boucher, N.Y. Rangers	1956	Earl Reibel, Detroit	1979	Bob MacMillan, Atlanta
1935	Frank Boucher, N.Y. Rangers	1957	Andy Hebenton, N.Y. Rangers	1980	Wayne Gretzky, Edmonton
1936	Doc Romnes, Chicago	1958	Camille Henry, N.Y. Rangers	1981	Butch Goring, N.Y. Islanders
1937	Marty Barry, Detroit	1959	Alex Delvecchio, Detroit	1982	Rick Middleton, Boston
1938	Gordie Drillon, Toronto	1960	Don McKenney, Boston	1983	Mike Bossy, N.Y. Islanders
1939	Clint Smith, N.Y. Rangers	1961	Red Kelly, Toronto	1984	Mike Bossy, N.Y. Islanders
1940	Bobby Bauer, Boston	1962	Dave Keon, Toronto	1985	Jari Kurri, Edmonton
1941	Bobby Bauer, Boston	1963	Dave Keon, Toronto	1986	Mike Bossy, N.Y. Islanders
1942	Syl Apps, Toronto	1964	Ken Wharram, Chicago	1987	Joe Mullen, Calgary
1943	Max Bentley, Chicago	1965	Bobby Hull, Chicago	1988	Mats Naslund, Montreal
1944	Clint Smith, Chicago	1966	Alex Delvecchio, Detroit	1989	Joe Mullen, Calgary
1945	Bill Mosienko, Chicago	1967	Stan Mikita, Chicago	1990	Brett Hull, St. Louis
1946	Toe Blake, Montreal	1968	Stan Mikita, Chicago		
1947	Bobby Bauer, Boston	1969	Alex Delvecchio, Detroit		

Frank J. Selke Trophy (Best Defensive Forward)

1978	Bob Gainey, Montreal	1983	Bobby Clarke, Philadelphia	1988	Guy Carbonneau, Montreal
1979	Bob Gainey, Montreal	1984	Doug Jarvis, Washington	1989	Guy Carbonneau, Montreal
1980	Bob Gainey, Montreal	1985	Craig Ramsay, Buffalo	1990	Rick Meagher, St. Louis
1981	Bob Gainey, Montreal	1986	Troy Murray, Chicago		
1982	Steve Kasper, Boston	1987	Dave Poulin, Philadelphia		

Hart Memorial Trophy (MVP)

1927	Herb Gardiner, Montreal	1948	Buddy O'Connor, N.Y. Rangers	1969	Phil Esposito, Boston
1928	Howie Morenz, Montreal			1970	Bobby Orr, Boston
1929	Roy Worters, N.Y. Americans	1949	Sid Abel, Detroit	1971	Bobby Orr, Boston
1930	Nels Stewart, Montreal Maroons	1950	Chuck Rayner, N.Y. Rangers	1972	Bobby Orr, Boston
		1951	Milt Schmidt, Boston	1973	Bobby Clarke, Philadelphia
1931	Howie Morenz, Montreal	1952	Gordie Howe, Detroit	1974	Phil Esposito, Boston
1932	Howie Morenz, Montreal	1953	Gordie Howe, Detroit	1975	Bobby Clarke, Philadelphia
1933	Eddie Shore, Boston	1954	Al Rollins, Chicago	1976	Bobby Clarke, Philadelphia
1934	Aurel Joliat, Montreal	1955	Ted Kennedy, Toronto	1977	Guy Lafleur, Montreal
1935	Eddie Shore, Boston	1956	Jean Beliveau, Montreal	1978	Guy Lafleur, Montreal
1936	Eddie Shore, Boston	1957	Gordie Howe, Detroit	1979	Bryan Trottier, N.Y. Islanders
1937	Babe Siebert, Montreal	1958	Gordie Howe, Detroit	1980	Wayne Gretzky, Edmonton
1938	Eddie Shore, Boston	1959	Andy Bathgate, N.Y. Rangers	1981	Wayne Gretzky, Edmonton
1939	Toe Blake, Montreal	1960	Gordie Howe, Detroit	1982	Wayne Gretzky, Edmonton
1940	Ebbie Goodfellow, Detroit	1961	Bernie Geoffrion, Montreal	1983	Wayne Gretzky, Edmonton
1941	Bill Cowley, Boston	1962	Jacques Plante, Montreal	1984	Wayne Gretzky, Edmonton
1942	Tom Anderson, N.Y. Americans	1963	Gordie Howe, Detroit	1985	Wayne Gretzky, Edmonton
		1964	Jean Beliveau, Montreal	1986	Wayne Gretzky, Edmonton
1943	Bill Cowley, Boston	1965	Bobby Hull, Chicago	1987	Wayne Gretzky, Edmonton
1944	Babe Pratt, Toronto	1966	Bobby Hull, Chicago	1988	Mario Lemieux, Pittsburgh
1945	Elmer Lach, Montreal	1967	Stan Mikita, Chicago	1989	Wayne Gretzky, Los Angeles
1946	Max Bentley, Chicago	1968	Stan Mikita, Chicago	1990	Mark Messier, Edmonton
1947	Maurice Richard, Montreal				

NHL All Star Team, 1990

First team	Position	Second team
Patrick Roy, Montreal	Goalie	Darren Puppa, Buffalo
Ray Bourque, Boston	Defense	Paul Coffey, Pittsburgh
Al Macinnis, Calgary	Defense	Doug Wilson, Chicago
Mark Messier, Edmonton	Center	Wayne Gretzky, Los Angeles
Brett Hull, St. Louis	Right Wing	Cam Neely, Boston
Luc Robitaille, Los Angeles	Left Wing	Brian Bellows, Minnesota

All-Time NHL Scoring Leaders

At end of 1989-90 season. *Active player.

	Games	G	A	Pts		Games	G	A	Pts
Wayne Gretzky*	847	677	1,302	1,979	Guy Lafleur*	1,067	548	777	1,325
Gordie Howe	1,767	801	1,049	1,850	Alex Delvecchio	1,549	456	825	1,281
Marcel Dionne	1,348	731	1,040	1,771	Jean Ratelle	1,281	491	776	1,267
Phil Esposito	1,282	717	873	1,590	Norm Ullman	1,410	490	739	1,229
Stan Mikita	1,394	541	926	1,467	Jean Beliveau	1,215	507	712	1,219
Bryan Trottier*	1,123	500	853	1,353	Bobby Clarke	1,144	358	852	1,210
John Bucyk	1,540	556	813	1,369	Bobby Hull	1,063	610	560	1,170
Gil Perreault	1,191	512	814	1,326					

NCAA Hockey Champions

1948	Michigan	1959	North Dakota	1970	Cornell	1981	Wisconsin
1949	Boston College	1960	Denver	1971	Boston Univ.	1982	North Dakota
1950	Colorado College	1961	Denver	1972	Boston Univ.	1983	Wisconsin
1951	Michigan	1962	Michigan Tech	1973	Wisconsin	1984	Bowling Green
1952	Michigan	1963	North Dakota	1974	Minnesota	1985	RPI
1953	Michigan	1964	Michigan	1975	Michigan Tech	1986	Michigan State
1954	RPI	1965	Michigan Tech	1976	Minnesota	1987	North Dakota
1955	Michigan	1966	Michigan State	1977	Wisconsin	1988	Lake Superior St.
1956	Michigan	1967	Cornell	1978	Boston Univ.	1989	Harvard
1957	Colorado College	1968	Denver	1979	Minnesota	1990	Wisconsin
1958	Denver	1969	Denver	1980	North Dakota		

Major Indoor Soccer League in 1990

The San Diego Sockers defeated the Baltimore Blast 4 games to 2 to win the Major Indoor Soccer League championship series. It was the 6th title in eight years for the San Diego team. Brian Quinn of the Sockers was voted the most valuable player in the series.

Westminster Kennel Club

Year	Best-in-show	Breed	Owner
1981	Ch. Dhandy Favorite Woodchuck	Pug	Robert Houslohner
1982	Ch. St. Aubrey Dragonora of Elsdon	Pekingese	Anne Snelling
1983	Ch. Kabik's The Challenger	Afghan	Chris & Marguerite Terrell
1984	Ch. Seaward's Blackbeard	Newfoundland	Elinor Ayers
1985	Ch. Braeburn's Close Encounter	Scottish terrier	Sonnie Novick
1986	Ch. Marjetta National Acclaim	Pointer	Mrs. Alan Robson & Michael Zollo
1987	Ch. Covy Tucker Hill's Manhattan	German shepherd	Shirley Braunstein & Jane Firestone
1988	Ch. Great Elms Prince Charming II	Pomeranian	Skip Piazza & Olga Baker
1989	Ch. Royal Tudor's Wild As The Wind	Doberman	Sue & Art Kemp, Richard & Carolyn Vida, Beth Wilhite
1990	Ch. Wendessa Crown Prince	Pekingese	Ed Jenner

IGFA Freshwater & Saltwater All-Tackle World Records

Source: International Game Fish Association. Records confirmed to Jan., 1990

Saltwater Fish

Species	Weight	Where caught	Date	Angler
Albacore	88 lbs. 2 oz.	Pt. Mogan, Canary Islands	Nov. 19, 1977	Siegfried Dickemann
Amberjack, greater	155 lbs. 10 oz.	Bermuda	June 24, 1981	Joseph Dawson
Amberjack, Pacific	104 lbs.	Baja, Mexico	July 4, 1984	Richard Cresswell
Barracuda, great	83 lbs.	Lagos, Nigeria	Jan. 13, 1952	K.J.W. Hackett
Barracuda, Mexican	21 lbs.	Costa Rica	Mar. 27, 1987	E. Greg Kent
Barracuda, slender	17 lbs. 4 oz.	Sitra Channel, Bahrain	Nov. 21, 1985	Roger Cranswick
Bass, barred sand	13 lbs. 3 oz.	Huntington Beach, Cal.	Aug. 29, 1988	Robert Halal
Bass, black sea	9 lbs. 8 oz.	Virginia Beach, Va.	Jan. 9, 1987	Joe Mizelle Jr.
Bass, European	20 lbs. 11 oz.	Stes Maries de la Mer, France	May 6, 1986	Jean Baptiste Bayle
Bass, giant sea	563 lbs. 8 oz.	Anacaba Island, Cal.	Aug. 20, 1968	James D. McAdam Jr.
Bass, striped	78 lbs. 8 oz.	Atlantic City, N.J.	Sept. 21, 1982	Albert McReynolds
Bluefish	31 lbs. 12 oz.	Hatteras Inlet, N.C.	Jan. 30, 1972	James M. Hussey
Bonefish	19 lbs.	Zululand, S. Africa	May 26, 1962	Brian W. Batchelor
Bonito, Atlantic	18 lbs. 14 oz.	Fayal I., Azores	July 8, 1953	D. G. Higgs
Bonito, Pacific	23 lbs. 8 oz.	Victoria, Mahe Seychelles	Feb. 19, 1975	Anne Cochain
Cabezon	18 lbs.	Pt. Townsend, Wash.	Apr. 28, 1988	Mark Mokodean
Cobia	135 lbs. 9 oz.	Shark Bay, Australia	July 9, 1985	Peter W. Goulding
Cod, Atlantic	98 lbs. 12 oz.	Isle of Shoals, N.H.	June 8, 1969	Alphonse Bielevich
Cod, Pacific	30 lbs.	Andrew Bay, Alaska	June 7, 1984	Donald Vaughn
Conger	102 lbs. 8 oz.	Devon, England	July 18, 1983	Raymond E. Street
Dolphin	87 lbs.	Papagallo Gulf, Costa Rica	Sept. 25, 1976	Manual Salazar
Drum, black	113 lbs. 1 oz.	Lewes, Del.	Sept. 15, 1975	Gerald Townsend
Drum, red	94 lbs. 2 oz.	Avon, N.C.	Nov. 7, 1984	David Deuel
Eel, African mottled	36 lbs. 1 oz.	Durban, So. Africa	June 10, 1984	Ferdie van Nooten
Eel, American	4 lb. 7 oz.	Lake Ronkonkoma, N.Y.	Nov. 15, 1986	William C. Cummings
Flounder, southern	20 lb. 9 oz.	Nassau Sound, Fla.	Dec. 23, 1983	Larenza Mungin
Flounder, summer	22 lbs. 7 oz.	Montauk, N.Y.	Sept. 15, 1975	Charles Nappi
Grouper, Warsaw	436 lbs. 12 oz.	Gulf of Mexico, Destin, Fla.	Dec. 22, 1985	Steve Haeusler
Halibut, Atlantic	255 lbs. 4 oz.	Gloucester, Mass.	July 28, 1989	Sonny Manley
Halibut, California	53 lbs. 4 oz.	Santa Rosa Is., Cal.	July 7, 1988	Russell Harmon
Halibut, Pacific	356 lbs. 8 oz.	Juneau, Alaska	Nov. 8, 1986	Gregory Olsen
Jack, crevalle	54 lbs. 7oz.	Pt. Michel, Gabon	Jan. 15, 1982	Thomas Gibson Jr.
Jack, horse-eye	24 lbs. 8 oz.	Miami, Fla.	Dec. 20, 1982	Tito Schnau
Jack, Pacific crevalle	24 lbs.	Baja, Cal., Mex.	Apr. 30, 1987	Sharon Swanson
Jewfish	680 lbs.	Fernandina Beach, Fla.	May 20, 1961	Lynn Joyner
Kawakawa	29 lbs.	Clarion Is., Mexico	Dec. 17, 1986	Ronald Nakamura
Lingcod	64 lbs.	Elfin Cove, Alaska	Aug. 2, 1988	David Bauer
Mackerel, cero	17 lbs. 2 oz.	Islamorada, Fla.	Apr. 5, 1986	G. Michael Mills
Mackerel, king	90 lbs.	Key West, Fla.	Feb. 16, 1976	Norton Thornton
Mackerel, Spanish	13 lbs.	Ocracoke Inlet, N.C.	Nov. 4, 1987	Robert Cranton
Marlin, Atlantic blue	1,282 lbs.	St. Thomas, Virgin Islands	Aug. 6, 1977	Larry Martin
Marlin, black	1,560 lbs.	Cabo Blanco, Peru	Aug. 4, 1953	A. C. Glassell Jr.
Marlin, Pacific blue	1,376 lbs.	Kaaiwa Pt., Hawaii	May. 31, 1982	J.W. deBeaubien
Marlin, striped	494 lbs.	Tutukaka, New Zealand	Jan. 16, 1986	Bill Boniface
Marlin, white	181 lbs. 14 oz.	Vitoria, Brazil	Dec. 8, 1979	Evandro Luiz Caser
Permit	51 lbs. 8 oz.	Lake Worth, Fla.	Apr. 28, 1978	William M. Kenney
Pollack	26 lbs. 7 oz.	Devon, England	Dec. 30, 1984	Robert Perry
Pollock	46 lbs. 7 oz.	Brielle, N.J.	May 26, 1975	John Tomes Holton
Pompano, African	49 lbs.	Stuart, Fla.	Feb. 4, 1977	Lawrence Hofman
Roosterfish	114 lbs.	La Paz, Mexico	June 1, 1960	Abe Sackheim
Runner, blue	7 lbs.	Bimini, Bahamas	July 26, 1989	Linda Schulz
Runner, rainbow	33 lbs. 10 oz.	Clarion Is., Mexico	Mar. 14, 1976	Ralph A. Mikkelsen
Sailfish, Atlantic	128 lbs. 1 oz.	Luanda, Angola	Mar. 27, 1974	Harm Steyn
Sailfish, Pacific	221 lbs.	Santa Cruz Is., Ecuador	Feb. 12, 1947	C. W. Stewart
Seabass, white	83 lbs. 12 oz.	San Felipe, Mexico	Mar. 31, 1953	L.C. Baumgardner
Seatrout, spotted	16 lbs.	Mason's Beach, Va.	May 28, 1977	William Katko
Shark, blue	437 lbs.	Catherine Bay, N.S.W. Australia	Oct. 2, 1976	Peter Hyde
Shark, Greenland	1,708 lbs. 9 oz.	Trondheim, Norway	Oct. 18, 1987	Terje Nordtvedt
Shark, hammerhead	991 lbs.	Sarasota, Fla.	May 30, 1982	Allen Ogle
Shark, man-eater or white	2,664 lbs.	Ceduna, Australia	Apr. 21, 1959	Alfred Dean
Shark, mako	1,115 lbs.	Black R., Mauritius	Nov. 16, 1988	Patrick Guillanton
Shark, porbeagle	465 lbs.	Cornwall, England	July 23, 1976	Jorge Potier
Shark, thresher	802 lbs.	Tutukaka, New Zealand	Feb. 8, 1981	Dianne North
Shark, tiger	1,780 lbs.	Cherry Grove, S.C.	June 14, 1964	Walter Maxwell
Skipjack, black	20 lbs. 5 oz.	Baja, Mexico	Oct. 14, 1983	Roger Torriero
Snapper, cubera	121 lbs. 8 oz.	Cameron, La.	July 5, 1982	Mike Hebert
Snook	53 lbs. 10 oz.	Costa Rica	Oct. 18, 1978	Gilbert Ponzi
Spearfish	90 lbs. 13 oz.	Madeira Island, Portugal	June 2, 1980	Joseph Larkin
Swordfish	1,182 lbs.	Iquique, Chile	May 7, 1953	L. Marron
Tanguigue	99 lbs.	Natal, So. Africa	Mar. 14, 1982	Michael J. Wilkinson
Tarpon	283 lbs.	Lake Maracaibo, Venezuela	Mar. 19, 1956	M. Salazar
Tautog	24 lbs.	Wachapreagee, Va.	Aug. 25, 1987	Gregory Bell
Tope	72 lbs. 12 oz.	Parengarenga Harbor, New Zealand	Dec. 19, 1966	Melanie Feldman
Trevally, bigeye	15 lbs.	Isla Coiba, Panama	Jan. 18, 1984	Sally Timms
Trevally, giant	137 lbs. 9 oz.	McKenzie St. Park, Hawaii	July 13, 1983	Roy Gushiken
Tuna, Atlantic bigeye	375 lbs. 8 oz.	Ocean City, Md.	Aug. 26, 1977	Cecil Browne
Tuna, blackfin	42 lbs.	Bermuda	June 2, 1978	Alan J. Card
		Bermuda	July 18, 1989	Gilbert Pearman

Species	Weight	Where caught	Date	Angler
Tuna, bluefin	1,496 lbs.	Aulds Cove, Nova Scotia	Oct. 26, 1979	Ken Fraser
Tuna, longtail	79 lbs. 2 oz.	Montague Is., N.S.W., Australia	Apr. 12, 1982	Tim Simpson
Tuna, Pacific bigeye	435 lbs.	Cabo Blanco, Peru	Apr. 17, 1957	Dr. Russel Lee
Tuna, skipjack	41 lbs. 14 oz.	Mauritius	Nov. 12, 1985	Edmund Heinzen
Tuna, southern bluefin	348 lbs. 5 oz.	Whakatane, New Zealand	Jan. 16, 1981	Rex Wood
Tuna, yellowfin	388 lbs. 12 oz.	San Benedicto Island, Mexico	Apr. 1, 1977	Curt Wiesenhutter
Tunny, little	35 lbs. 2 oz.	Cap de Garde, Algeria	Dec. 14, 1988	Jean Yves Chatard
Wahoo	149 lbs.	Cay Cay, Bahamas	June 15, 1962	John Pirovano
Weakfish	19 lbs. 2 oz.	Jones Beach Inlet, N.Y.	Oct. 11, 1984	Dennis Rooney
Yellowtail, California	78 lbs.	Alijos Rocks, Mexico	June 27, 1987	Richard Cresswell
Yellowtail, southern	114 lbs. 10 oz.	Tauranga, New Zealand	Feb. 5, 1984	Mike Godfrey

Freshwater Fish

Species	Weight	Where caught	Date	Angler
Barramundi	59 lbs. 12 oz.	Pt. Stuart, Australia	Apr. 7, 1983	Andrew Davern
Bass, largemouth	22 lbs. 4 oz.	Montgomery Lake, Ga.	June 2, 1932	George W. Perry
Bass, peacock	26 lbs. 8 oz.	Matevini R., Colombia	Jan. 26, 1982	Rod Neubert
Bass, redeye	8 lbs. 3 oz.	Flint River, Ga.	Oct. 23, 1977	David A. Hubbard
Bass rock	3 lbs.	York River, Ont.	Aug. 1, 1974	Peter Gulgin
Bass, smallmouth	11 lbs. 15 oz.	Dale Hollow Lake, Ky.	July 9, 1955	David L. Hayes
Bass, Suwannee	3 lbs. 14 oz.	Suwannee River, Fla.	Mar. 2, 1985	Ronnie Everett
Bass, white	6 lbs. 13 oz.	L. Orange, Va.	July 31, 1989	Ronald Sprouse
Bass, whiterock	24 lbs. 3 oz.	Leesville L., Va.	May 12, 1989	David Lambert
Bass, yellow	2 lbs. 4 oz.	Lake Monroe, Ind.	Mar. 27, 1977	Donald L. Stalker
Bluegill	4 lbs. 12 oz.	Ketona Lake, Ala.	Apr. 9, 1950	T.S. Hudson
Bowfin	21 lbs. 8 oz.	Florence, S.C.	Jan. 29, 1980	Robert Harmon
Buffalo, bigmouth	70 lbs. 5 oz.	Bastrop, La.	Apr. 21, 1980	Delbert Sisk
Buffalo, black	55 lbs. 8 oz.	Cherokee L., Tenn.	May 3, 1984	Edward McLain
Buffalo, smallmouth	68 lbs. 8 oz.	L. Hamilton, Ark.	May 16, 1984	Jerry Dolezal
Bullhead, brown	5 lbs. 8 oz.	Veal Pond, Ga.	May 22, 1975	Jimmy Andrews
Bullhead, yellow	4 lbs. 4 oz.	Mormon Lake, Ariz.	May 11, 1984	Emily Williams
Burbot	18 lbs. 4 oz.	Pickford, Mich.	Jan. 31, 1980	Thomas Courtemanche
Carp	75 lbs. 11 oz.	Lac de St. Cassien, France	May 21, 1987	Leo van der Gugten
Catfish, blue	97 lbs.	Missouri River, S.D.	Sept. 16, 1959	E.B. Elliott
Catfish, channel	58 lbs.	Santee-Cooper Res., S.C.	July 7, 1964	W.B. Whaley
Catfish, flathead	91 lbs. 4 oz.	L. Lewisville, Tex.	Mar. 28, 1982	Mike Rogers
Catfish, white	17 lbs. 7 oz.	Success L., Tulare, Cal.	Nov. 15, 1981	Chuck Idell
Char, Arctic	32 lbs. 9 oz.	Tree River, Canada	July 30, 1981	Jeffrey Ward
Crappie, white	5 lbs. 3 oz.	Enid Dam, Miss.	July 31, 1957	Fred L. Bright
Dolly Varden	12 lbs.	Noatak R., Alaska	July 10, 1987	Kenneth Ait
Dorado	51 lbs. 5 oz.	Corrientes, Argentina	Sept. 27, 1984	Armando Giudice
Drum, freshwater	54 lbs. 8 oz.	Nickajack Lake, Tenn.	Apr. 20, 1972	Benny E. Hull
Gar, alligator	279 lbs.	Rio Grande River, Tex.	Dec. 2, 1951	Bill Valverde
Gar, Florida	21 lbs. 3 oz.	Boca Raton, Fla.	June 3, 1981	Jeff Sabol
Gar, longnose	50 lbs. 5 oz.	Trinity River, Tex.	July 30, 1954	Townsend Miller
Gar, shortnose	5 lbs.	Sally Jones L., Oklahoma	Apr. 26, 1985	Buddy Croslin
Gar, spotted	8 lbs. 12 oz.	Tennessee R., Ala.	Aug. 26, 1987	Winston Baker
Grayling, Arctic	5 lbs. 15 oz.	Katseyedie River, N.W.T.	Aug. 16, 1967	Jeanne P. Branson
Inconnu	53 lbs.	Pah R., Alaska	Aug. 20, 1986	Lawrence Hudnall
Kokanee	9 lbs. 6 oz.	Okanagan Lake, Vernon, B.C.	June 18, 1988	Norm Kuhn
Muskellunge	69 lbs. 15 oz.	St. Lawrence River, N.Y.	Sept. 22, 1957	Arthur Lawton
Muskellunge, tiger	51 lbs. 3 oz.	Lac Vieux-Desert, Wis., Mich.	July 16, 1919	John Knobla
Perch, Nile	152 lbs. 1 oz.	Tende Bay, Uganda	June 4, 1989	Kurt Fenster
Perch, white	4 lbs. 12 oz.	Messalonskee Lake, Me.	June 4, 1949	Mrs. Earl Small
Perch, yellow	4 lbs. 3 oz.	Bordentown, N.J.	May, 1865	Dr. C.C. Abbot
Pickerel, chain	9 lbs. 6 oz.	Homerville, Ga.	Feb. 17, 1961	Baxley McQuaig Jr.
Pike, northern	55 lbs. 1 oz.	Lake of Grefeern, W., Germany	Oct. 16, 1986	Lothar Louis
Redhorse, greater	9 lbs. 3 oz.	Salmon R., Pulaski, N.Y.	May 11, 1985	Jason Wilson
Redhorse, silver	11 lbs. 7 oz.	Plum Creek, Wis.	May 29, 1985	Neal Long
Salmon, Atlantic	79 lbs. 2 oz.	Tana River, Norway	1928	Henrik Henriksen
Salmon, chinook	97 lbs. 4 oz.	Kenai R., Alas.	May 17, 1985	Les Anderson
Salmon, chum	32 lbs.	Behm Canal, Alas.	June 7, 1985	Fredrick Thynes
Salmon, coho	33 lbs. 4 oz.	Salmon R., Pulaski, N.Y.	Sept. 27, 1989	Jerry Lifton
Salmon, pink	13 lbs. 9 oz.	Morse, Kenai rivers, Alas.	Aug. 17, 1974	Steven A. Lee
Salmon, sockeye	15 lbs. 3 oz.	Kenai R., Alaska	Aug. 9, 1987	Stan Roach
Sauger	8 lbs. 12 oz.	Lake Sakakawea, N.D.	Oct. 6, 1971	Mike Fischer
Shad, American	11 lbs. 4 oz.	Connecticut R., Mass.	May 19, 1986	Bob Thibodo
Sturgeon, white	468 lbs.	Benicia, Cal.	July 9, 1983	Joey Pallotta 3d
Sunfish, green	2 lbs. 2 oz.	Stockton Lake, Mo.	June 18, 1971	Paul M. Dilley
Sunfish, redbreast	1 lb. 12 oz.	Suwannee R., Fla.	May 29, 1984	Alvin Buchanan
Sunfish, redear	4 lbs. 13 oz.	Marianna, Fla.	Mar. 13, 1986	Joey Floyd
Tigerfish	97 lbs.	Zaire R., Kinshasa, Zaire	July 9, 1988	Raymond Houtmans
Tilapia	6 lbs.	L. Okeechobee, Fla.	June 24, 1989	Joseph M. Tucker
Trout, Apache	2 lb. 10 oz.	Apache Res., Ariz.	June 27, 1989	Mike Shannon
Trout, brook	14 lbs. 8 oz.	Nipigon River, Ont.	July 1916	Dr. W.J. Cook
Trout, brown	35 lbs. 15 oz.	Nahuel Huapi, Argentina	Dec. 16, 1952	Eugenio Cavaglia
Trout, bull	32 lbs.	L. Pend Oreille, Ida.	Oct. 27, 1949	N.L. Higgins
Trout, cutthroat	41 lbs.	Pyramid Lake, Nev.	Dec. 1925	J. Skimmerhorn
Trout, golden	11 lbs.	Cook's Lake, Wyo.	Aug. 5, 1948	Charles S. Reed
Trout, lake	65 lbs.	Great Bear Lake, N.W.T.	Aug. 8, 1970	Larry Daunis
Trout, rainbow	42 lbs. 2 oz.	Bell Island, Alas.	June 22, 1970	David Robert White
Trout, tiger	20 lbs. 13 oz.	Lake Michigan, Wis.	Aug. 12, 1978	Pete Friedland
Walleye	25 lbs.	Old Hickory Lake, Tenn.	Aug. 1, 1960	Mabry Harper
Warmouth	2 lbs. 7 oz.	Yellow R., Holt, Fla.	Oct. 19, 1985	Tony D. Dempsey
Whitefish, lake	14 lbs. 6 oz.	Meaford, Ont.	May 21, 1984	Dennis Laycock
Whitefish, mountain	5 lbs. 6 oz.	Rioh R., Sask.	June 15, 1988	John Beli
Whitefish, river	11 lbs. 2 oz.	Nymoua, Sweden	Dec. 9, 1984	Jorgen Larsson
Whitefish, round	6 lbs.	Putahow R., Manitoba	June 14, 1984	Allen Ristori
Zander	22 lbs. 2 oz.	Trosa, Sweden	June 12, 1986	Harry Lee Tennison

COLLEGE BASKETBALL

Final Regular Season Conference Standings, 1989–90

American South

	Confer-ence W	L	Over-all Record W	L
New Orleans	8	2	19	10
La. Tech	8	2	20	7
Texas-Pan Am.	7	3	21	9
SW Louisiana	4	6	20	9
Arkansas St.	2	8	15	13
Lamar	1	9	7	21

Tournament Champion—New Orleans.

Atlantic Coast

	Confer-ence W	L	Over-all Record W	L
Clemson	10	4	24	8
Duke	9	5	24	8
Georgia Tech	8	6	23	6
North Carolina	8	6	19	12
Virginia	6	8	19	10
N.C. State	6	8	18	12
Maryland	6	8	18	13
Wake Forest	3	11	12	16

Tournament Champion—Georgia Tech.

Atlantic 10

	Confer-ence W	L	Over-all Record W	L
Temple	15	3	20	10
Penn St.	13	5	21	8
West Virginia	11	7	16	12
Rhode Island	11	7	15	13
Rutgers	11	7	16	16
Massachusetts	10	8	17	13
George Washington	6	12	14	17
St. Joseph's	5	13	7	21
Duquesne	5	13	7	22
St. Bonaventure	3	15	8	20

Tournament Champion—Temple.

Big East

	Confer-ence W	L	Over-all Record W	L
Syracuse	12	4	24	5
Connecticut	12	4	27	5
Georgetown	11	5	23	6
St. John's	10	6	23	9
Providence	8	8	17	11
Villanova	8	8	18	14
Seton Hall	5	11	12	16
Pittsburgh	5	11	12	17
Boston College	1	15	8	20

Tournament Champion—Connecticut.

Big Eight

	Confer-ence W	L	Over-all Record W	L
Missouri	12	2	26	5
Kansas	11	3	29	4
Oklahoma	11	3	26	4
Kansas St.	7	7	17	14
Oklahoma St.	6	8	16	13
Iowa St.	4	10	10	18
Nebraska	3	11	10	18
Colorado	2	12	12	17

Tournament Champion—Oklahoma.

Big Sky

	Confer-ence W	L	Over-all Record W	L
Idaho	13	3	25	5
E. Washington	11	5	18	11
Montana	10	6	18	11
Nevada-Reno	9	7	15	13
Montana St.	8	8	17	12
Weber St.	8	8	14	15
Boise St.	7	9	12	15
N. Arizona	3	13	8	20
Idaho St.	3	13	6	21

Tournament Champion—Idaho.

Big South

	Confer-ence W	L	Over-all Record W	L
Coastal Carolina	11	1	23	6
N.C.-Asheville	7	5	18	12
Campbell	7	5	15	13
Winthrop	6	6	19	10
Baptist College	4	8	9	19
Augusta	4	8	8	20
Radford	3	9	7	22

Tournament Champion—Coastal Carolina.

Big Ten

	Confer-ence W	L	Over-all Record W	L
Michigan St.	15	3	26	5
Purdue	13	5	21	7
Michigan	12	6	22	7
Minnesota	11	7	20	8
Illinois	11	7	20	7
Ohio St.	10	8	16	12
Indiana	8	10	18	10
Wisconsin	4	14	14	17
Iowa	4	14	12	16
Northwestern	2	16	9	19

East Coast

	Confer-ence W	L	Over-all Record W	L
Towson St.	8	6	18	12
Lehigh	8	6	18	12
Hofstra	8	6	13	15
Delaware	7	7	16	13
Lafayette	7	7	15	13
Drexel	7	7	13	15
Bucknell	6	8	15	14
Rider	5	9	10	18

Tournament Champion—Towson St.

Big West

	Confer-ence W	L	Over-all Record W	L
New Mexico St.	16	2	26	4
UNLV	16	2	28	5
UC-Santa Barbara	13	5	20	8
Long Beach St.	12	6	22	7
Utah St.	8	10	14	16
Pacific Univ.	7	11	15	14
CS-Fullerton	6	12	13	16
San Jose St.	5	13	8	20
Fresno St.	4	14	10	19
UC-Irvine	3	15	5	23

Tournament Champion—UNLV.

Colonial

	Confer-ence W	L	Over-all Record W	L
James Madison	11	3	20	10
Richmond	10	4	22	9
American Univ.	10	4	20	9
George Mason	10	4	20	12
East Carolina	6	8	13	18
N.C.-Wilmington	3	11	8	20
William & Mary	2	12	6	22

Tournament Champion—Richmond.

North Atlantic

	Confer-ence W	L	Over-all Record W	L
Northeastern	9	3	16	12
Boston Univ.	9	3	17	11
Hartford	8	4	17	10
Maine	6	6	11	16
Vermont	4	8	12	17
Colgate	3	9	7	21
New Hampshire	3	9	5	22

Tournament Champion—Boston Univ.

Northeast

	Confer-ence W	L	Over-all Record W	L
Robert Morris	12	4	22	7
Monmouth	11	5	17	12
Marist	10	6	17	11
St. Francis (Pa.)	10	6	17	11
Mt. St. Mary's	10	6	16	12
FDU	8	8	16	13
Wagner	6	10	11	17
St. Francis (NY)	4	12	9	18
Long Island	1	15	3	23

Tournament Champion—Robert Morris.

Ivy League

	Confer-ence W	L	Over-all Record W	L
Princeton	11	3	20	6
Yale	10	4	19	7
Dartmouth	7	7	12	14
Harvard	7	7	12	14
Penn	7	7	12	14
Brown	7	7	10	16
Cornell	5	9	12	17
Columbia	2	12	4	22

Metro

	Confer-ence W	L	Over-all Record W	L
Louisville	12	2	26	7
Southern Miss	9	5	20	11
Cincinnati	9	5	19	13
Memphis St.	8	6	18	11
Florida St.	6	8	16	15
South Carolina	6	8	14	14
Virginia Tech	5	9	13	18
Tulane	1	13	4	24

Tournament Champion—Louisville.

Metro Atlantic

North

	Confer-ence W	L	Over-all Record W	L
Holy Cross	14	2	24	5
Siena	11	5	16	13
Fordham	10	6	19	12
Canisius	5	11	11	18
Army	5	11	10	19
Niagara	5	11	6	22

South

	Confer-ence W	L	Over-all Record W	L
La Salle	16	0	29	1
Iona	8	8	13	15
St. Peter's	7	9	14	14
Manhattan	7	9	11	17
Fairfield	6	10	10	19
Loyola (Md.)	2	14	4	24

Tournament Champion—La Salle.

Mid-American

	Confer-ence W	L	Over-all Record W	L
Ball St.	13	3	23	6
Kent St.	12	4	21	7
Bowling Green	9	7	18	10
Miami (Ohio)	9	7	14	15
E. Michigan	8	8	19	13
Toledo	7	9	12	16
Cent. Michigan	6	10	13	16
Ohio Univ.	5	11	12	16
W. Michigan	3	13	9	18

Tournament Champion—Ball St.

Mid-Continent

	Confer-ence W	L	Over-all Record W	L
SW Missouri St.	11	1	22	5
Wisconsin-Green Bay	9	3	21	7
N. Iowa	6	6	20	8
Ill.-Chicago	6	6	16	11
W. Illinois	6	6	15	12
E. Illinois	3	9	10	17
Valparaiso	1	11	4	23
Cleveland St.	0	0	15	13

Tournament Champion—Northern Iowa.

Mid-Eastern

	Confer-ence W	L	Over-all Record W	L
Coppin St.	15	1	26	6
Florida A&M	13	3	18	11
Delaware St.	9	7	14	14
S. Carolina St.	8	8	13	16
Bethune-Cookman	8	8	10	18
N. Carolina A&T	6	10	13	16
Howard Univ.	5	11	8	20
Maryland-E. Shore	4	12	10	17
Morgan St.	4	12	8	20

Tournament Champion—Coppin St.

Midwestern

	Confer-ence W	L	Over-all Record W	L
Xavier (Ohio)	12	2	26	4
Dayton	10	4	21	9
St. Louis	9	5	17	11
Marquette	9	5	15	13
Evansville	8	6	17	15
Detroit	3	11	10	18
Loyola (Ill.)	3	11	7	22
Butler	2	12	6	22

Tournament Champion—Dayton.

Southern Missouri Valley

	Conference W	L	Overall W	L
S. Illinois	10	4	26	7
Creighton	9	5	21	11
Illinois St.	9	5	18	12
Tulsa	9	5	17	12
Bradley	6	8	11	20
Wichita St.	6	8	10	19
Drake	5	9	13	18
Indiana St.	2	12	8	20

Tournament Champion—Illinois St.

Ohio Valley

	Conference W	L	Overall W	L
Murray St.	10	2	21	8
Tennessee Tech.	9	3	19	9
Morehead St.	7	5	16	13
E. Kentucky	7	5	13	17
Middle Tennessee	5	7	12	16
Austin Peay	2	10	10	19
Tennessee St.	2	10	7	21

Tournament Champion—Murray St.

Pacific-10

	Conference W	L	Overall W	L
Oregon St.	15	3	22	6
Arizona	15	3	23	6
California	12	6	21	9
UCLA	11	7	20	9
Oregon	10	8	15	13
Stanford	9	9	18	11
Arizona St.	6	12	15	15
USC	6	12	12	16
Washington	5	13	12	17
Washington St.	1	17	6	22

Tournament Champion—Arizona.

Southern

	Conference W	L	Overall W	L
E. Tennessee St.	12	2	27	6
Marshall	9	5	15	13
Appalachian St.	8	6	19	11
Tenn.-Chattanooga	7	7	14	14
VMI	7	7	14	15
Furman	5	9	15	16
Citadel	5	9	12	16
W. Carolina	3	11	10	18

Tournament Champion—E. Tenn. St.

Southeastern

	Conference W	L	Overall W	L
Georgia	13	5	20	8
Alabama	12	6	23	8
LSU	12	6	22	8
Tennessee	10	8	15	13
Kentucky	10	8	14	14
Mississippi	8	10	13	16
Auburn	8	10	13	16
Mississippi St.	7	11	15	13
Vanderbilt	7	11	16	14
Florida	3	15	7	21

Tournament Champion—Alabama.

Southland

	Conference W	L	Overall W	L
NE Louisiana	13	1	21	7
McNeese St.	11	3	14	13
SW Texas St.	9	5	13	15
Sam Houston St.	8	6	10	18
Texas-Arlington	6	8	13	15
NW Louisiana	5	9	10	18
North Texas	3	11	4	25
S.F. Austin	1	13	2	25

Tournament Champion—NE Louisiana.

Southwest

	Conference W	L	Overall W	L
Arkansas	14	2	25	4
Houston	13	3	25	6
Texas	12	4	21	8
Texas Christian	9	7	16	13
Baylor	7	9	16	13
Texas A&M.	7	9	14	17
Rice	5	11	11	17
SMU	5	11	10	18
Texas Tech	0	16	5	22

Tournament Champion—Arkansas.

Southwestern

	Conference W	L	Overall W	L
Southern Univ.	12	2	25	4
Texas So.	10	4	18	11
Alabama St.	7	7	15	13
Mississippi Valley	7	7	11	18
Alcorn St.	6	8	7	22
Prairie View	5	9	9	18
Grambling St.	5	9	9	19
Jackson St.	4	10	9	19

Tournament Champion—Texas So.

Sun Belt

	Conference W	L	Overall W	L
Alabama-Birmingham	12	2	22	8
South Florida	9	5	20	10
Old Dominion	7	7	14	14
W. Kentucky	7	7	13	17
N.C.-Charlotte	6	8	16	14
Jacksonville	5	9	13	16
South Alabama	5	9	11	17
Va. Commonwealth	5	9	11	17

Tournament Champion—South Florida.

Trans America

	Conference W	L	Overall W	L
Centenary	14	2	22	8
Texas-San Antonio	13	3	21	7
Arkansas-Little Rock	12	4	19	9
Georgia Southern	11	5	17	10
Stetson	8	8	14	17
Hardin Simmons	5	11	9	18
Samford	4	12	6	21
Georgia St.	3	13	5	22
Mercer	2	14	7	20

Tournament Champion—Arkansas-Little Rock.

West Coast

	Conference W	L	Overall W	L
Loyola, Marymount	13	1	23	5
Pepperdine	10	4	17	11
San Diego	9	5	16	12
Portland	7	7	11	17
Santa Clara	6	8	9	19
San Francisco	4	10	8	20
St. Mary's	4	10	7	20
Gonzaga	3	11	8	20

Tournament Champion—Loyola
(Tournament not completed)

Western Athletic

	Conference W	L	Overall W	L
Colorado St.	11	5	21	8
BYU	11	5	21	8
Hawaii	10	6	23	9
UTEP	10	6	21	10
New Mexico	9	7	17	12
Utah	7	9	16	14
Wyoming	7	9	15	14
San Diego St.	4	12	13	18
Air Force	3	13	12	20

Tournament Champion—UTEP.

Independents

	W	L
Wright St.	21	7
N. Illinois	17	11
Akron	16	12
Notre Dame	16	12
De Paul	18	14
Miami, Fla.	13	15
Mo.-Kansas City	13	15
S. Utah	13	15
Md. Baltimore Co.	12	16
U.S. International	12	16
Liberty	11	17
Youngstown St.	8	20
Brooklyn	7	21
Central Florida	7	21
Florida International	7	21
Chicago St.	6	22
Central Connecticut	5	22
Nicholls St.	4	23
Davidson	4	24

National Invitation Tournament Champions

Year	Champion	Year	Champion	Year	Champion	Year	Champion
1938	Temple	1952	LaSalle	1966	Brigham Young	1980	Virginia
1939	Long Island Univ.	1953	Seton Hall	1967	Southern Illinois	1981	Tulsa
1940	Colorado	1954	Holy Cross	1968	Dayton	1982	Bradley
1941	Long Island Univ.	1955	Duquesne	1969	Temple	1983	Fresno State
1942	West Virginia	1956	Louisville	1970	Marquette	1984	Michigan
1943	St. John's	1957	Bradley	1971	North Carolina	1985	UCLA
1944	St. John's	1958	Xavier (Ohio)	1972	Maryland	1986	Ohio State
1945	De Paul	1959	St. John's	1973	Virginia Tech	1987	Southern Mississippi
1946	Kentucky	1960	Bradley	1974	Purdue	1988	Connecticut
1947	Utah	1961	Providence	1975	Princeton	1989	St. John's
1948	St. Louis	1962	Dayton	1976	Kentucky	1990	Vanderbilt
1949	San Francisco	1963	Providence	1977	St. Bonaventure		
1950	CCNY	1964	Bradley	1978	Texas		
1951	Brigham Young	1965	St. John's	1979	Indiana		

NCAA Division I Women's Champions

Year	Champion	Coach	Final opponent	Year	Champion	Coach	Final opponent
1982	Louisiana Tech	Sonja Hogg	Cheyney	1987	Tennessee	Pat Head Summitt	Louisiana Tech
1983	USC	Linda Sharp	Louisiana Tech	1988	Louisiana Tech	Leon Barmore	Auburn
1984	USC	Linda Sharp	Tennessee	1989	Tennessee	Pat Head Summitt	Auburn
1985	Old Dominion	Marianne Stanley	Georgia	1990	Stanford	Tara VanDerveer	Auburn
1986	Texas	Jody Conradt	USC				

1990 NCAA Basketball Tournament

EAST

(1) U. Conn. 76
(16) Boston University 52
— U. Conn. 74
(8) Indiana 63
(9) California 65
— California 54
— U. Conn. 71

(5) Clemson 49
(12) BYU 47
— Clemson 79
(4) La Salle 79
(13) So. Miss. 63
— La Salle 75
— Clemson 70

— U. Conn. 78

(6) St. John's 81
(11) Temple 65
— St. John's 72
(3) Duke 81
(14) Richmond 46
— Duke 76
— Duke 90

(7) UCLA 68
(10) UAB 56
— UCLA 71
(2) Kansas 79
(15) Robert Morris 71
— Kansas 70
— UCLA 81

— Duke 79

Duke 97

MIDWEST

(1) Oklahoma 77
(16) Towson State 68
— Oklahoma 77
(8) North Carolina 83
(9) S.W. Missouri State 70
— North Carolina 79
— North Carolina 73

(5) Illinois 86
(12) Dayton 88
— Dayton 84
(4) Arkansas 68
(13) Princeton 64
— Arkansas 86
— Arkansas 96

— Arkansas 88

(6) Xavier 87
(11) Kansas State 79
— Xavier 74
(3) Georgetown 70
(14) Texas So. 52
— Georgetown 71
— Xavier 89

(7) Georgia 88
(10) Texas 100
— Texas 73
(2) Purdue 75
(15) N.E. Louisiana 63
— Purdue 72
— Texas 102

— Texas 85

Arkansas 83

SOUTHEAST

(1) Michigan State 75
(16) Murray State 71
— Michigan State 62
(8) Houston 66
(9) UCSB 70
— UCSB 58
— Michigan State 80

(5) LSU 70
(12) Villanova 63
— LSU 91
(4) Georgia Tech 99
(13) E. Tenn. State 83
— Georgia Tech 94
— Georgia Tech 81

— Georgia Tech 93

(6) Minnesota 64
(11) UTEP 61
— Minnesota 81
(3) Missouri 71
(14) Northern Iowa 74
— Northern Iowa 78
— Minnesota 82

(7) Virginia 75
(10) Notre Dame 67
— Virginia 61
(2) Syracuse 70
(15) Coppin State 48
— Syracuse 63
— Syracuse 75

— Minnesota 91

Georgia Tech 81

WEST

(1) UNLV 102
(16) Ark-Little Rock 72
— UNLV 76
(8) Ohio State 84
(9) Providence 83
— Ohio State 65
— UNLV 69

(5) Oregon State 53
(12) Ball State 54
— Ball State 62
(4) Louisville 78
(13) Idaho 59
— Louisville 60
— Ball State 67

— UNLV 131

(6) New Mexico State 92
(11) Loyola Marymount 111
— Loy. Mary. 149
(3) Michigan 76
(14) Illinois State 70
— Michigan 115
— Loy. Mary. 62

(7) Alabama 71
(10) Colorado State 54
— Alabama 77
(2) Arizona 79
(15) South Florida 67
— Arizona 55
— Alabama 60

— Loy. Mary. 101

UNLV 90

Duke 73
UNLV 103

NCAA Division I Champions

Year	Champion	Coach	Final opponent	Score	Outstanding player	Site
1939	Oregon	Howard Hobson	Ohio St.	46-33	None	Evanston, Ill.
1940	Indiana	Branch McCracken	Kansas	60-42	Marvin Huffman, Indiana	Kansas City, Mo.
1941	Wisconsin	Harold Foster	Washington St.	39-34	John Kotz, Wisconsin	Kansas City, Mo.
1942	Stanford	Everett Dean	Dartmouth	53-38	Howard Dallmar, Stanford	Kansas City, Mo.
1943	Wyoming	Everett Shelton	Georgetown	46-34	Ken Sailors, Wyoming	New York, N.Y.
1944	Utah	Vadal Peterson	Dartmouth	42-40(1)	Arnold Ferrin, Utah	New York, N.Y.
1945	Oklahoma St.(2)	Henry Iba	NYU	49-45	Bob Kurland, Oklahoma St.	New York, N.Y.
1946	Oklahoma St.(2)	Henry Iba	North Carolina	43-40	Bob Kurland, Oklahoma St.	New York, N.Y.
1947	Holy Cross	Alvin Julian	Oklahoma	58-47	George Kaftan, Holy Cross	New York, N.Y.
1948	Kentucky	Adolph Rupp	Baylor	58-42	Alex Groza, Kentucky	New York, N.Y.
1949	Kentucky	Adolph Rupp	Oklahoma St.	46-36	Alex Groza, Kentucky	Seattle, Wash.
1950	CCNY	Nat Holman	Bradley	71-68	Irwin Dambrot, CCNY	New York, N.Y.
1951	Kentucky	Adolph Rupp	Kansas St.	68-58	None	Minneapolis, Minn.
1952	Kansas	Forrest Allen	St. John's	80-63	Clyde Lovellette, Kansas	Seattle, Wash.
1953	Indiana	Branch McCracken	Kansas	69-68	B.H. Born, Kansas	Kansas City, Mo.
1954	La Salle	Kenneth Loeffler	Bradley	92-76	Tom Gola, La Salle	Kansas City, Mo.
1955	San Francisco	Phil Woolpert	LaSalle	77-63	Bill Russell, San Francisco	Kansas City, Mo.
1956	San Francisco	Phil Woolpert	Iowa	83-71	Hal Lear, Temple	Evanston, Ill.
1957	N. Carolina	Frank McGuire	Kansas	54-53(1)	Wilt Chamberlain, Kansas	Kansas City, Mo.
1958	Kentucky	Adolph Rupp	Seattle	84-72	Elgin Baylor, Seattle	Louisville, Ky.
1959	California	Pete Newell	W. Virginia	71-70	Jerry West, W. Virginia	Louisville, Ky.
1960	Ohio St.	Fred Taylor	California	75-55	Jerry Lucas, Ohio St.	San Francisco, Cal.
1961	Cincinnati	Edwin Jucker	Ohio St.	70-65(1)	Jerry Lucas, Ohio St.	Kansas City, Mo.
1962	Cincinnati	Edwin Jucker	Ohio St.	71-59	Paul Hogue, Cincinnati	Louisville, Ky.
1963	Loyola (Ill.)	George Ireland	Cincinnati	60-58(1)	Art Heyman, Duke	Louisville, Ky.
1964	UCLA	John Wooden	Duke	98-83	Walt Hazzard, UCLA	Kansas City, Mo.
1965	UCLA	John Wooden	Michigan	91-80	Bill Bradley, Princeton	Portland, Ore.
1966	Texas-El Paso(3)	Don Haskins	Kentucky	72-65	Jerry Chambers, Utah	College Park, Md.
1967	UCLA	John Wooden	Dayton	79-64	Lew Alcindor, UCLA	Louisville, Ky.
1968	UCLA	John Wooden	N. Carolina	78-55	Lew Alcindor, UCLA	Los Angeles, Cal.
1969	UCLA	John Wooden	Purdue	92-72	Lew Alcindor, UCLA	Louisville, Ky.
1970	UCLA	John Wooden	Jacksonville	80-69	Sidney Wicks, UCLA	College Park, Md.
1971	UCLA	John Wooden	Villanova*	68-62	Howard Porter, Villanova*	Houston, Tex.
1972	UCLA	John Wooden	Florida St.	81-76	Bill Walton, UCLA	Los Angeles, Cal.
1973	UCLA	John Wooden	Memphis St.	87-66	Bill Walton, UCLA	St. Louis, Mo.
1974	N. Carolina St.	Norm Sloan	Marquette	76-64	David Thompson, N.C. St.	Greensboro, N.C.
1975	UCLA	John Wooden	Kentucky	92-85	Richard Washington, UCLA	San Diego, Cal.
1976	Indiana	Bob Knight	Michigan	86-68	Kent Benson, Indiana	Philadelphia, Pa.
1977	Marquette	Al McGuire	N. Carolina	67-59	Butch Lee, Marquette	Atlanta, Ga.
1978	Kentucky	Joe Hall	Duke	94-88	Jack Givens, Kentucky	St. Louis, Mo.
1979	Michigan St.	Jud Heathcote	Indiana St.	75-64	Magic Johnson, Michigan St.	Salt Lake City, Ut.
1980	Louisville	Denny Crum	UCLA*	59-54	Darrell Griffith, Louisville	Indianapolis, Ind.
1981	Indiana	Bob Knight	N. Carolina	63-50	Isiah Thomas, Indiana	Philadelphia, Pa.
1982	N. Carolina	Dean Smith	Georgetown	63-62	James Worthy, No. Carolina	New Orleans, La.
1983	N. Carolina St.	Jim Valvano	Houston	54-52	Akeem Olajuwon, Houston	Albuquerque, N.M.
1984	Georgetown	John Thompson	Houston	84-75	Patrick Ewing, Georgetown	Seattle, Wash.
1985	Villanova	Rollie Massimino	Georgetown	66-64	Ed Pinckney, Villanova	Lexington, Ky.
1986	Louisville	Denny Crum	Duke	72-69	Pervis Ellison, Louisville	Dallas, Tex.
1987	Indiana	Bob Knight	Syracuse	74-73	Keith Smart, Indiana	New Orleans, La.
1988	Kansas	Larry Brown	Oklahoma	83-79	Danny Manning, Kansas	Kansas City, Mo.
1989	Michigan	Steve Fisher	Seton Hall	80-79(1)	Glen Rice, Michigan	Seattle, Wash.
1990	UNLV	Jerry Tarkanian	Duke	103-73	Anderson Hunt, UNLV	Denver, Col.

*Declared ineligible subsequent to the tournament. (1) Overtime. (2) Known as Oklahoma A&M at that time. (3) Known as Texas Western at that time.

NCAA Division I Career Scoring Leaders

Player, team	Seasons	G	FG	FT	Pts.	Avg.
Pete Maravich, Louisiana State	1968-70	83	1387	893	3667	44.2
Austin Carr, Notre Dame	1969-71	74	1017	526	2560	34.6
Oscar Robertson, Cincinnati	1958-60	88	1052	869	2973	33.8
Calvin Murphy, Niagara	1968-70	77	947	654	2548	33.1
Dwight Lamar, SW Louisiana	1972-73	57	768	326	1862	32.7
Frank Selvy, Furman	1952-54	78	922	694	2538	32.5
Rick Mount, Purdue	1968-70	72	910	503	2323	32.3
Darrell Floyd, Furman	1954-56	71	868	545	2281	32.1
Nick Werkman, Seton Hall	1962-64	71	812	649	2273	32.0
Willie Humes, Idaho State	1970-71	48	565	380	1510	31.5
William Averitt, Pepperdine	1972-73	49	615	311	1541	31.4
Elgin Baylor, Col. Idaho, Seattle	55, 57-58	80	956	588	2500	31.3
Elvin Hayes, Houston	1966-68	93	1215	454	2884	31.0
Freeman Williams, Portland State	1975-1978	106	1369	511	3249	30.7
Larry Bird, Indiana State	1977-79	94	1154	542	2850	30.3

John R. Wooden Award

Awarded annually to the nation's outstanding college basketball playing student-athlete by a poll of sports writers and broadcasters.

1977	Marques Johnson, UCLA	1982	Ralph Sampson, Virginia	1987	David Robinson, Navy
1978	Phil Ford, North Carolina	1983	Ralph Sampson, Virginia	1988	Danny Manning, Kansas
1979	Larry Bird, Indiana State	1984	Michael Jordan, North Carolina	1989	Sean Elliott, Arizona
1980	Darrell Griffith, Louisville	1985	Chris Mullin, St. John's	1990	Lionel Simmons, La Salle
1981	Danny Ainge, Brigham Young	1986	Walter Berry, St. John's		

Division I College Basketball Leaders in 1989-1990 Season
(through games of Monday, Mar. 12)

Scoring

	G	Pts	Avg
Bo Kimble, Loyola-Marymount	28	988	35.3
Kevin Bradshaw, U.S. International	28	875	31.3
Dave Jamerson, Ohio	28	874	31.2
Alphonzo Ford, Mississippi	27	808	29.9
Steve Rogers, Alabama St.	28	831	29.7
Hank Gathers, Loyola-Marymount	26	754	29.0
Darryl Brooks, Tennessee St.	24	690	28.8
Chris Jackson, LSU	30	860	28.7
Dennis Scott, Georgia Tech.	30	817	27.2
Mark Stevenson, Duquesne	29	788	27.2

Rebounds

	G	No.	Avg
Anthony Bonner, St. Louis	28	381	13.6
Eric McArthur, UC Santa Barbara	27	359	13.3
Lee Campbell, Southwest Mo. St.	28	355	12.7
Tyrone Hill, Xavier (Ohio)	29	365	12.6
Cedric Ceballos, Cal. St. Fullerton	29	362	12.5
Hakim Shahid, South Florida	30	373	12.4
Derrick Coleman, Syracuse	30	365	12.2
Ron Draper, American	29	352	12.1
Shaquille O'Neal, LSU	30	360	12.0
Steve Stevenson, Prairie View	26	302	11.6

Blocked Shots Per Game

	G	NO	AVG
Kenny Green, Rhode Island	26	124	4.8
Dikembe Mutombo, Georgetown	29	123	4.2
Kevin Roberson, Vermont	30	114	3.8
Lorenzo Williams, Stetson	32	121	3.8
Steve Stevenson, Prairie View	26	97	3.7

Assists

	G	No.	Avg
Todd Lehman, Drexel	28	260	9.3
Aaron Mitchell, Southwestern La.	29	264	9.1
Keith Jennings, East Tenn. St.	33	292	8.8
Kenny Anderson, Georgia Tech.	30	257	8.6
Otis Livingston, Idaho	30	250	8.3
Gary Payton, Oregon St.	28	232	8.3
Lamar Holt, Prairie View	26	213	8.2
Tony Edmond, Texas Christian	29	234	8.1

Field-Goal Percentage

	FG	FGA	Pct.
Stephen Scheffler, Purdue	160	220	72.7
Lee Campbell, Southwest Mo. St.	189	268	70.5
Felton Spencer, Louisville	177	257	68.9
Brian Parker, Cleveland St.	155	236	65.7
Larry Stewart, Coppin St.	226	345	65.5
Brian Hill, Evansville	180	278	64.7
Hakim Shahid, South Florida	196	305	64.3
Larry Johnson, UNLV	260	414	62.8

3-Pt. FG Percentage

	FG	FGA	Pct
Matt Lapin, Princeton	70	128	54.7
Lee Mayberry, Arkansas	58	109	53.2
Mike Iuzzolino, St. Francis (Pa.)	79	153	51.6
Dwight Pernell, Holy Cross	77	150	51.3
Tony Bennett, Wis.-Green Bay	65	129	50.4
Jeff Gueldner, Kansas	66	131	50.4
Steve Hood, James Madison	68	136	50.0
Brett Andricks, Tex.-Pan American	57	114	50.0

NCAA Division I Basketball Statistical Trends

Averages and percentages are for both teams, per game.

Year	Games	FG Made	FG Att.	Pct.	FT Made	FT Att.	Pct.	PF	Pts.
1948	3945	40.6	138.7	29.3	25.3	42.2	59.8	36.9	106.5
1950	3659	43.2	136.8	31.6	28.7	46.5	61.8	39.0	115.1
1952	4009	47.5	140.6*	33.7	31.6	50.5	62.6	44.9*	126.6
1955	3829	51.1	138.6	36.9	43.1*	64.7	66.5	37.9	145.3
1958	4153	51.6	134.2	38.4	33.6	50.5	66.4	36.4	136.8
1960	4295	52.6	132.3	39.8	34.7	51.5	67.4	36.7	139.9
1961	4238	53.3	131.1	40.7	34.7	50.9	68.2	36.4	141.3
1963	4180	53.2	127.6	41.7	32.6	47.8	68.2	36.4	139.0
1965	4520	58.3	135.4	43.1	34.7	50.3	69.0	38.5	151.4
1967	4602	57.7	131.9	43.8	34.4	49.8	69.0	38.3	149.8
1969	4883	58.2	132.8	43.8	34.8	50.8	68.4	37.9	151.2
1971	5232	60.2	135.6	44.4	35.0	51.3	68.1	38.5	155.4*
1973	5582	62.3*	139.2	44.8	26.2	38.3	68.4	38.4	150.9
1975	6147	62.9	136.7	46.0	27.4	39.7	69.0	40.3	153.1
1977	6676	60.7	129.8	46.7	28.4	41.0	69.4	40.2	149.7
1979	7131	59.2	124.1	47.7	29.5	42.2	69.7*	41.1	147.9
1981	7407	55.6	115.9	48.0	29.0	42.0	68.9	40.2	140.2
1983	7957	54.3	114.0	47.7	29.0	42.3	68.5	39.7	138.7
1985	8269	54.5	113.9	47.9	29.3	42.5	68.9	39.3	138.3
1986	8360	54.7	114.6	47.7	29.4	42.5	69.1	39.1	138.7
1987	8580	54.4	117.3	46.6	29.7	43.0	69.1	39.3	145.5
1988	8587	54.8	116.6	47.0	30.2	43.8	68.9	39.4	147.8
1989	8677*	55.7	118.5	47.0	31.1	45.0	69.1	40.2	151.4

*All-time high.

World Almanac All-America Team in 1990

First team	Position	Second team
Alonzo Mourning, Georgetown	Center	Doug Smith, Missouri
Lionel Simmons, LaSalle	Forward	Hank Gathers, Loyola, Marymount
Derrick Coleman, Syracuse	Forward	Larry Johnson, UNLV
Gary Payton, Oregon St.	Guard	Kenny Anderson, Georgia Tech
Chris Jackson, LSU	Guard	Kendall Gill, Illinois
Coach of the Year — Jim Calhoun, Connecticut		Player of the Year — Lionel Simmons

World Almanac All-America Women's Team in 1990

First team	Position	Second team
Venus Lacy, Louisiana Tech	Center	Pauline Jordan, UNLV
Dale Hodges, St. Joseph's (PA.)	Forward	Daedra Charles, Tennessee
Portia Hill, Stephen F. Austin	Forward	Wendy Scholtens, Vanderbilt
Jennifer Azzi, Stanford	Guard	Franthea Price, Iowa
Andrea Stinson, North Carolina St.	Guard	Edna Campbell, Texas
Coach of the Year — Leon Barmore, Louisiana Tech		Player of the Year — Venus Lacy, Louisiana Tech

GTE Academic All-America Basketball Team in 1990

The 1990 GTE Academic All-America University and College basketball teams were chosen by the College Sports Information Directors of America. A player must be a starter or key reserve and carry a minimum cumulative grade average of 3.2 on a 4.0 scale.

University Division	Position	College Division
David Jamerson, Ohio Univ.	Forward	Philip Hutcheson, David Liscomb
Alec Kessler, Georgia	Forward	Dan Nettleton, Wartburg
Andy Toolson, Brigham Young	Forward	Mark Slayman, Ohio Wesleyan
Michael Iuzzolino, St. Francis, Pa.	Guard	S. Juan Mitchell, Monmouth, Ill.
Dean Smith, Maine	Guard	Gary Townsend, Arkansas Tech.

NATIONAL BASKETBALL ASSOCIATION, 1989-90
Final Standing

Eastern Conference

Atlantic Division

Club	W	L	Pct	GB
Philadelphia	53	29	.646	...
Boston	52	30	.634	1
New York	45	37	.549	8
Washington	31	51	.378	22
Miami	18	64	.220	35
New Jersey	17	65	.207	36

Central Division

Club	W	L	Pct	GB
Detroit	59	23	.720	...
Chicago	55	27	.671	4
Milwaukee	44	38	.537	15
Cleveland	42	40	.512	17
Indiana	42	40	.512	17
Atlanta	41	41	.500	18
Orlando	18	64	.220	41

Western Conference

Midwest Division

Club	W	L	Pct	GB
San Antonio	56	26	.683	...
Utah	55	27	.671	1
Dallas	47	35	.573	9
Denver	43	39	.524	13
Houston	41	41	.500	15
Minnesota	22	60	.268	34
Charlotte	19	63	.232	37

Pacific Division

Club	W	L	Pct	GB
Los Angeles Lakers	63	19	.768	...
Portland	59	23	.720	4
Phoenix	54	28	.659	9
Seattle	41	41	.500	22
Golden State	37	45	.451	26
Los Angeles Clippers	30	52	.366	33
Sacramento	23	59	.280	40

NBA Playoff Results

Eastern Division

Detroit defeated Indiana 3 games to 0
Chicago defeated Milwaukee 3 games to 1
New York defeated Boston 3 games to 2
Philadelphia defeated Cleveland 3 games to 2
Detroit defeated New York 4 games to 1
Chicago defeated Philadelphia 4 games to 1
Detroit defeated Chicago 4 games to 3

Western Division

Portland defeated Dallas 3 games to 0
San Antonio defeated Denver 3 games to 0
L.A. Lakers defeated Houston 3 games to 1
Phoenix defeated Utah 3 games to 2
Phoenix defeated L.A. Lakers 4 games to 1
Portland defeated San Antonio 4 games to 3
Portland defeated Phoenix 4 games to 2

Championship

Detroit defeated Portland 4 games to 1

Pistons Repeat as Champions by Defeating Trail Blazers

The Detroit Pistons won their second consecutive National Basketball Association championship by defeating the Portland Trail Blazers 4 games to 1. Isiah Thomas of the Pistons was named the most valuable player of the finals.

Portland Trail Blazers

	FG M-A	FT M-A	Reb	Ast	Avg
Drexler	51-94	28-37	39	31	26.4
Kersey	35-74	25-32	35	6	19.0
Porter	24-61	40-45	13	42	19.0
Duckworth	34-65	10-15	28	0	15.6
Williams	20-43	16-25	45	9	11.2
Robinson	8-32	3-6	12	4	3.8
Young	6-15	1-3	7	8	3.0
Petrovic	5-14	0-0	1	2	2.5
Cooper	4-12	1-4	20	1	1.8
Bryant	0-0	1-2	2	0	0.5
Totals	187-410	125-169	202	103	102.0

Detroit Pistons

	FG M-A	FT M-A	Reb	Ast	Avg
Thomas	52-96	23-31	26	35	27.6
Dumars	34-82	33-37	14	28	20.6
Edwards	29-65	14-25	19	4	14.4
Laimbeer	24-54	10-10	67	12	13.2
Johnson	25-46	11-14	10	6	12.2
Aguirre	15-45	14-21	18	4	9.6
Salley	12-32	9-13	32	2	6.6
Rodman	4-9	1-4	22	3	2.3
Greenwood	1-3	1-2	9	0	1.0
Henderson	1-1	0-0	0	0	1.0
Hastings	0-1	0-0	0	0	0.0
Totals	197-434	116-157	217	94	107.0

NBA Champions 1947-1990

Year	Eastern Conference (Regular season)	Western Conference (Regular season)	Winner (Playoffs)	Coach (Playoffs)	Runner-up (Playoffs)
1947	Washington	Chicago	Philadelphia	Ed Gottlieb	Chicago
1948	Philadelphia	St. Louis	Baltimore	Buddy Jeannette	Philadelphia
1949	Washington	Rochester	Minneapolis	John Kundla	Washington
1950	Syracuse	Minneapolis	Minneapolis	John Kundla	Syracuse
1951	Philadelphia	Minneapolis	Rochester	Lester Harrison	New York
1952	Syracuse	Rochester	Minneapolis	John Kundla	New York
1953	New York	Minneapolis	Minneapolis	John Kundla	New York
1954	New York	Minneapolis	Minneapolis	John Kundla	Syracuse
1955	Syracuse	Ft. Wayne	Syracuse	Al Cervi	Ft. Wayne
1956	Philadelphia	Ft. Wayne	Philadelphia	George Senesky	Ft. Wayne
1957	Boston	St. Louis	Boston	Red Auerbach	St. Louis
1958	Boston	St. Louis	St. Louis	Alex Hannum	Boston
1959	Boston	St. Louis	Boston	Red Auerbach	Minneapolis
1960	Boston	St. Louis	Boston	Red Auerbach	St. Louis
1961	Boston	St. Louis	Boston	Red Auerbach	St. Louis
1962	Boston	Los Angeles	Boston	Red Auerbach	Los Angeles
1963	Boston	Los Angeles	Boston	Red Auerbach	Los Angeles
1964	Boston	San Francisco	Boston	Red Auerbach	San Francisco
1965	Boston	Los Angeles	Boston	Red Auerbach	Los Angeles
1966	Philadelphia	Los Angeles	Boston	Red Auerbach	Los Angeles
1967	Philadelphia	San Francisco	Philadelphia	Alex Hannum	San Francisco
1968	Philadelphia	St. Louis	Boston	Bill Russell	Los Angeles
1969	Baltimore	Los Angeles	Boston	Bill Russell	Los Angeles
1970	New York	Atlanta	New York	Red Holzman	Los Angeles

Year	Atlantic	Central	Midwest	Pacific	Winner	Coach	Runner-up
1971	New York	Baltimore	Milwaukee	Los Angeles	Milwaukee	Larry Costello	Baltimore
1972	Boston	Baltimore	Milwaukee	Los Angeles	Los Angeles	Bill Sharman	New York
1973	Boston	Baltimore	Milwaukee	Los Angeles	New York	Red Holzman	Los Angeles
1974	Boston	Capital	Milwaukee	Los Angeles	Boston	Tom Heinsohn	Milwaukee
1975	Boston	Washington	Chicago	Golden State	Golden State	Al Attles	Washington
1976	Boston	Cleveland	Milwaukee	Golden State	Boston	Tom Heinsohn	Phoenix
1977	Philadelphia	Houston	Denver	Los Angeles	Portland	Jack Ramsay	Philadelphia
1978	Philadelphia	San Antonio	Denver	Portland	Washington	Dick Motta	Seattle
1979	Washington	San Antonio	Kansas City	Seattle	Seattle	Len Wilkens	Washington
1980	Boston	Atlanta	Milwaukee	Los Angeles	Los Angeles	Paul Westhead	Philadelphia
1981	Boston	Milwaukee	San Antonio	Phoenix	Boston	Bill Fitch	Houston
1982	Boston	Milwaukee	San Antonio	Los Angeles	Los Angeles	Pat Riley	Philadelphia
1983	Philadelphia	Milwaukee	San Antonio	Los Angeles	Philadelphia	Billy Cunningham	Los Angeles
1984	Boston	Milwaukee	Utah	Los Angeles	Boston	K.C. Jones	Los Angeles
1985	Boston	Milwaukee	Denver	L.A. Lakers	L.A. Lakers	Pat Riley	Boston
1986	Boston	Milwaukee	Houston	L.A. Lakers	Boston	K.C. Jones	Houston
1987	Boston	Atlanta	Dallas	L.A. Lakers	L.A. Lakers	Pat Riley	Boston
1988	Boston	Detroit	Denver	L.A. Lakers	L.A. Lakers	Pat Riley	Detroit
1989	New York	Detroit	Utah	L.A. Lakers	Detroit	Chuck Daly	L.A. Lakers
1990	Philadelphia	Detroit	San Antonio	L.A. Lakers	Detroit	Chuck Daly	Portland

NBA Most Valuable Player

Year	Player
1956	Bob Pettit, St. Louis
1957	Bob Cousy, Boston
1958	Bill Russell, Boston
1959	Bob Pettit, St. Louis
1960	Wilt Chamberlain, Philadelphia
1961	Bill Russell, Boston
1962	Bill Russell, Boston
1963	Bill Russell, Boston
1964	Oscar Robertson, Cincinnati
1965	Bill Russell, Boston
1966	Wilt Chamberlain, Philadelphia
1967	Wilt Chamberlain, Philadelphia
1968	Wilt Chamberlain, Philadelphia
1969	Wes Unseld, Baltimore
1970	Willis Reed, New York
1971	Lew Alcindor, Milwaukee
1972	Kareem Abdul-Jabbar (Alcindor), Milwaukee
1973	Dave Cowens, Boston
1974	Kareem Abdul-Jabbar, Milwaukee
1975	Bob McAdoo, Buffalo
1976	Kareem Abdul-Jabbar, Los Angeles
1977	Kareem Abdul-Jabbar, Los Angeles
1978	Bill Walton, Portland
1979	Moses Malone, Houston
1980	Kareem Abdul-Jabbar, Los Angeles
1981	Julius Erving, Philadelphia
1982	Moses Malone, Houston
1983	Moses Malone, Philadelphia
1984	Larry Bird, Boston
1985	Larry Bird, Boston
1986	Larry Bird, Boston
1987	Magic Johnson, L.A. Lakers
1988	Michael Jordan, Chicago
1989	Magic Johnson, L.A. Lakers
1990	Magic Johnson, L.A. Lakers

1989-1990 NBA Individual Highs

Minutes played, season — 3238, McCray, Sacramento.

Points, game — 69, Jordan, Chicago vs. Cleveland, 3/28 (OT).

Field goals made, game — 23, Jordan, Chicago at Cleveland, 3/28 (OT).

Field goal attempts, game — 43, Jordan, Chicago vs. Orlando, 2/14 (OT).

3-pt. field goals made, game — 9, Ellis, Seattle vs. L.A. Clippers, 4/20.

Free throws made, game — 23, K. Johnson, Phoenix vs. Utah, 4/9 (OT).

Rebounds, game — 27, Donaldson, Dallas vs. Portland, 12/29 (3 OT).

Offensive rebounds, game — 16, Cummings, San Antonio vs. Golden St., 2/28 (OT).

Defensive rebounds, game — 22, Donaldson, Dallas vs. Portland, 12/29 (3 OT); Olajuwon, Houston vs. Detroit 2/27 (OT).

Offensive rebounds, season — 364, Malone, Atlanta.

Defensive rebounds, season — 850, Olajuwon, Houston.

Assists, game — 27, Stockton, Utah at New York, 12/19.

Blocked shots, game — 13, Bol, Golden St. vs. New Jersey, 2/2.

Personal fouls, season — 328, Smits, Indiana.

Statistical Leaders, 1989-1990

Scoring

	G	FG	Pts	Avg
Jordan, Chicago	82	1034	2753	33.6
Malone, Utah	82	914	2540	31.0
Ewing, New York	82	922	2347	28.6
Chambers, Phoenix	81	810	2201	27.2
Wilkins, Atlanta	80	810	2138	26.7
Barkley, Philadelphia	79	706	1989	25.2
Mullin, Golden St.	78	682	1956	25.1
Miller, Indiana	82	661	2016	24.6
Olajuwon, Houston	82	806	1995	24.3
Robinson, San Antonio	82	690	1993	24.3
Bird, Boston	75	718	1820	24.3
Malone, Washington	75	781	1820	24.3
Drexler, Portland	73	670	1703	23.3
Campbell, Minnesota	82	723	1903	23.2
K. Johnson, Phoenix	74	578	1665	22.5
Cummings, San Antonio	81	728	1818	22.4
King, Washington	82	711	1837	22.4
Johnson, L.A. Lakers	79	546	1765	22.3
Tisdale, Sacramento	79	726	1758	22.3
Richmond, Golden St.	78	640	1720	22.1

Rebounds Per Game

	G	Def	Tot	Avg
Olajuwon, Houston	82	850	1149	14.0
Robinson, San Antonio	82	680	983	12.0
Barkley, Philadelphia	79	548	909	11.5
Malone, Utah	82	679	911	11.1
Ewing, New York	82	658	893	10.9
Seikaly, Miami	74	513	766	10.4
Parish, Boston	79	537	796	10.1
Malone, Atlanta	81	448	812	10.0
Cage, Seattle	82	515	821	10.0
Williams, Portland	82	550	800	9.8

Field Goal Percentage

	FG	FGA	Pct
West, Phoenix	331	530	.625
Barkley, Philadelphia	706	1177	.600
Parish, Boston	505	871	.580
Malone, Utah	914	1627	.562
Woolridge, L.A. Lakers	306	550	.556
Ewing, New York	922	1673	.551
McHale, Boston	648	1181	.549
Thorpe, Houston	547	998	.548
Worthy, L.A. Lakers	711	1298	.548
Williams, Portland	413	754	.548

Free Throw Percentage

	FT	FTA	Pct
Bird, Boston	319	343	.930
E. Johnson, Phoenix	188	205	.917
Davis, Denver	207	227	.912
Dumars, Detroit	297	330	.900
McHale, Boston	393	440	.893
Porter, Portland	421	472	.892
Johnson, L.A. Lakers	567	637	.890
Mullin, Golden St.	505	568	.889
Hawkins, Philadelphia	387	436	.888
Price, Cleveland	300	338	.888

Assists Per Game

	G	Ast	Avg
Stockton, Utah	78	1134	14.5
Johnson, L.A. Lakers	79	907	11.5
K. Johnson, Phoenix	74	846	11.4
Bogues, Charlotte	81	867	10.7
Grant, L.A. Lakers	44	442	10.0
Thomas, Detroit	81	765	9.4
Price, Cleveland	73	666	9.1
Porter, Portland	80	726	9.1
Hardaway, Golden St.	79	689	8.7
Walker, Washington	81	652	8.0

3-Point Field Goal Percentage

	FG	FGA	Pct
Kerr, Cleveland	73	144	.507
Hodges, Chicago	87	181	.481
Petrovic, Portland	34	74	.459
Sundvold, Miami	44	100	.440
Scott, L.A. Lakers	93	220	.423
Hawkins, Philadelphia	84	200	.420
Ehlo, Cleveland	104	248	.419
Stockton, Utah	47	113	.416
Miller, Indiana	150	362	.414
Lever, Denver	36	87	.414

Steals Per Game

	G	Stl	Avg
Jordan, Chicago	82	227	2.77
Stockton, Utah	78	207	2.65
Pippen, Chicago	82	211	2.57
Robertson, Milwaukee	81	207	2.56
Harper, Dallas	82	187	2.28
Corbin, Minnesota	82	175	2.13
Lever, Denver	79	168	2.13
Olajuwon, Houston	82	174	2.12
Conner, New Jersey	82	172	2.10
Hardaway, Golden St.	79	165	2.09

Blocked Shots Per Game

	G	Blk	Avg
Olajuwon, Houston	82	376	4.59
Ewing, New York	82	327	3.99
Robinson, San Antonio	82	319	3.80
Bol, Golden St.	75	238	3.17
Benjamin, L.A. Clippers	71	187	2.63
Eaton, Utah	82	201	2.45
Jones, Washington	81	197	2.43
West, Phoenix	82	184	2.24
Smits, Indiana	82	169	2.06
J. Williams, Cleveland	82	167	2.04

NBA All League Team in 1990

First team	Position	Second team
Karl Malone, Utah	Forward	Tom Chambers, Phoenix
Charles Barkley, Philadelphia	Forward	Larry Bird, Boston
Patrick Ewing, New York	Center	Akeem Olajuwon, Houston
Magic Johnson, L.A. Lakers	Guard	John Stockton, Utah
Michael Jordan, Chicago	Guard	Kevin Johnson, Phoenix

NBA All-Defensive Team in 1990

First team	Position	Second team
Dennis Rodman, Detroit	Forward	Kevin McHale, Boston
Buck Williams, Portland	Forward	Rick Mahorn, Philadelphia
Akeem Olajuwon, Houston	Center	David Robinson, San Antonio
Michael Jordan, Chicago	Guard	Alvin Robertson, Milwaukee
Joe Dumars, Detroit	Guard	Derek Harper, Dallas

Individual Statistics, 1989-1990

(Over 600 Minutes Played)

Atlanta Hawks

	Min per game	FG%	FT%	RBs per game	Ast per game	Pts	Pts per game
Wilkins	36.1	.484	.807	6.5	2.5	2138	26.7
Malone	33.8	.480	.781	10.0	1.6	1528	18.9
Rivers	31.8	.454	.812	4.2	5.5	598	12.5
Willis	28.1	.519	.683	8.0	0.7	1006	12.4
Smith	30.6	.466	.821	2.0	5.6	943	11.9
Battle	24.6	.506	.756	1.7	2.6	654	10.9
Webb	26.6	.477	.871	2.5	5.8	751	9.2
Long	21.5	.453	.836	1.7	1.8	404	8.4
Carr	18.3	.516	.775	3.4	1.2	335	7.6
Levingston	22.7	.509	.680	4.3	1.1	516	6.9
Volkov	13.0	.482	.583	1.7	1.2	357	5.0
Koncak	18.1	.614	.532	4.2	2.3	198	3.7

Dallas Mavericks

	Min per game	FG%	FT%	Rbs per game	Ast per game	Pts	Pts per game
Blackman	36.7	.498	.844	3.5	3.6	1552	19.4
Harper	36.7	.488	.794	3.0	7.4	1473	18.0
Tarpley	36.6	.451	.756	13.1	1.5	758	16.8
Perkins	35.1	.493	.778	7.5	2.3	1206	15.9
Dantley	28.9	.477	.787	3.8	1.8	662	14.7
Donaldson	31.0	.539	.700	8.6	0.8	665	9.1
H. Williams	27.1	.444	.679	4.8	1.5	700	8.6
Davis	17.7	.490	.770	1.3	3.3	470	6.4
Wennington	13.6	.449	.800	3.3	0.7	270	4.5
White	12.9	.369	.562	3.1	0.4	237	3.0
Jones	9.8	.371	.681	1.2	0.4	195	3.0

Boston Celtics

	Min per game	FG%	FT%	RBs per game	Ast per game	Pts	Pts per game
Bird	39.3	.473	.930	9.5	7.5	1820	24.3
McHale	33.2	.549	.893	8.3	2.1	1712	20.9
Lewis	31.9	.496	.808	4.4	2.8	1340	17.0
Parish	30.3	.580	.747	10.1	1.3	1243	15.7
Johnson	27.1	.434	.843	2.7	6.5	531	7.1
Paxson	17.8	.453	.811	1.1	1.9	460	6.4
Kleine	16.9	.480	.830	4.4	0.6	435	5.4
Gamble	13.9	.455	.794	1.6	1.7	362	5.1
M. Smith	9.5	.476	.828	1.5	1.2	327	5.0
Pinckney	14.1	.542	.773	2.9	0.9	362	4.7
Bagley	20.3	.459	.744	1.6	5.5	230	4.3

Denver Nuggets

	Min per game	FG%	FT%	RBs per game	Ast per game	Pts	Pts per game
Lever	35.8	.443	.804	9.3	6.5	1443	18.3
English	27.6	.491	.880	0.3	2.8	1433	17.9
Davis	23.7	.481	.912	2.6	2.2	1207	17.5
Adams	34.1	.402	.850	2.8	6.3	1221	15.5
Rasmussen	24.6	.497	.828	7.3	1.0	1001	12.4
Schayes	22.5	.494	.852	6.5	1.2	551	10.4
Carroll	22.6	.411	.774	5.8	1.3	761	10.0
Lichti	16.8	.486	.747	1.9	1.5	630	8.0
Hanzlik	19.8	.452	.743	2.6	2.3	500	6.2
Kempton	14.9	.490	.675	3.1	1.7	383	5.4
Lane	14.3	.469	.367	5.4	0.1	334	5.0
Hughes	14.9	.411	.676	1.2	1.9	209	3.5
Dunn	10.1	.454	.667	2.1	0.7	114	1.8

Charlotte Hornets

	Min per game	FG%	FT%	RBs per game	Ast per game	Pts	Pts per game
Chapman	32.6	.408	.750	3.3	2.4	945	17.5
Gilliam	31.9	.515	.723	7.9	1.3	1271	16.7
Curry	27.8	.466	.923	2.5	2.4	1070	16.0
Tripucka	30.4	.430	.883	4.1	2.8	1232	15.6
J.R. Reid	33.6	.440	.664	8.4	1.2	908	11.1
Bogues	33.9	.491	.791	2.6	10.7	763	9.4
Keys	20.2	.432	.721	3.2	1.1	701	8.8
Gattison	14.9	.550	.682	3.1	0.6	372	5.9
R. Reid	16.7	.391	.628	2.1	1.3	414	5.8
Anderson	11.2	.417	.783	2.4	1.0	231	4.3

Detroit Pistons

	Min per game	FG%	FT%	RBs per game	Ast per game	Pts	Pts per game
Thomas	37.0	.438	.775	3.8	9.4	1492	18.4
Dumars	34.4	.480	.900	2.8	4.9	1335	17.8
Edwards	27.8	.498	.749	4.2	0.8	1189	14.5
Aguirre	25.7	.488	.756	3.9	1.9	1099	14.1
Laimbeer	33.0	.484	.854	9.6	2.1	981	12.1
Johnson	24.0	.431	.668	3.1	3.1	804	9.8
Rodman	30.0	.581	.654	9.7	0.9	719	8.8
Salley	23.3	.512	.713	5.4	0.8	593	7.2

Chicago Bulls

	Min per game	FG%	FT%	RBs per game	Ast per game	Pts	Pts per game
Jordan	39.0	.526	.848	6.9	6.3	2753	33.6
Pippen	38.3	.489	.675	6.7	5.4	1351	16.5
Grant	34.4	.523	.699	7.9	2.8	1071	13.4
Cartwright	30.4	.488	.811	6.5	2.0	811	11.4
Paxson	28.6	.516	.824	1.5	6.4	819	10.0
King	21.7	.504	.727	4.7	1.1	728	8.9
Hodges	16.7	.438	.909	0.8	1.7	407	6.5
Armstrong	15.9	.485	.885	1.3	2.5	452	5.6
Perdue	11.5	.414	.692	2.8	0.6	294	3.8

Golden State Warriors

	Min per game	FG%	FT%	RBs per game	Ast per game	Pts	Pts per game
Mullin	36.3	.536	.889	0.2	4.1	1956	25.1
Richmond	35.9	.497	.866	4.6	2.9	1720	22.1
Teagle	29.0	.480	.830	4.5	1.9	1323	16.1
Hardaway	33.7	.471	.764	3.9	8.7	1162	14.7
Marciulionis	22.6	.519	.787	2.9	1.6	905	12.1
Higgins	24.3	.481	.821	5.1	1.6	909	11.1
Tolbert	19.2	.493	.726	5.2	0.8	616	8.8
Garland	17.5	.375	.841	2.2	3.1	270	5.3
Bol	17.5	.510		3.7	0.5	146	1.9

Cleveland Cavaliers

	Min per game	FG%	FT%	RBs per game	Ast per game	Pts	Pts per game
Price	37.1	.459	.888	3.4	9.1	1430	19.6
J. Williams	33.9	.493	.739	8.1	2.0	1381	16.8
Daugherty	35.1	.479	.704	9.1	3.2	690	16.8
Nance	33.3	.511	.778	8.3	2.6	1011	16.3
Ehlo	35.7	.464	.681	5.4	4.6	1102	13.6
Keys	18.6	.421	.744	2.9	0.8	365	7.6
Brown	17.9	.470	.762	3.1	0.7	545	7.3
Kerr	21.3	.444	.863	1.3	3.2	520	6.7
Bennett	18.0	.479	.667	3.4	1.0	338	6.1
Rollins	14.0	.456	.688	3.2	0.5	125	2.6

Houston Rockets

	Min per game	FG%	FT%	RBs per game	Ast per game	Pts	Pts per game
Olajuwon	38.1	.501	.713	14.0	2.9	1995	24.3
Thorpe	36.0	.548	.688	9.0	3.2	1401	17.1
Wiggins	28.1	.488	.810	4.3	1.6	1024	15.5
Johnson	34.5	.495	.759	4.6	3.1	1215	14.8
Floyd	32.1	.451	.806	2.4	7.3	1000	12.2
Maxwell	25.1	.439	.645	2.9	3.7	714	9.0
Woodson	15.9	.395	.721	1.4	1.1	394	6.5
Lucas	19.1	.375	.764	1.8	4.9	286	5.8
Bowie	13.9	.406	.741	1.8	1.5	284	4.3
Smith	17.6	.474	.364	6.1	0.9	222	3.0

Indiana Pacers

	Min per game	FG%	FT%	RBs per game	Ast per game	Pts	Pts per game
Miller	38.9	.514	.868	3.6	3.8	2016	24.6
Person	35.2	.487	.781	5.8	3.0	1515	19.7
Schrempf	33.0	.516	.820	7.9	3.2	1267	16.2
Smits	29.3	.533	.811	6.2	1.7	1271	15.5
Fleming	35.1	.508	.782	3.9	7.4	1176	14.3
Thompson	25.9	.473	.799	7.7	1.3	554	6.8
Sanders	18.7	.470	.733	2.8	1.1	510	6.2
Green	13.4	.433	.843	0.8	2.6	244	3.5

Los Angeles Clippers

	Min per game	FG%	FT%	RBs per game	Ast per game	Pts	Pts per game
Harper	39.1	.473	.788	5.9	5.2	798	22.8
Smith	35.0	.520	.794	6.7	1.5	1645	21.1
Manning	32.0	.533	.741	5.9	2.6	1154	16.3
Norman	33.3	.510	.632	6.7	2.3	1128	16.1
Benjamin	32.6	.526	.732	9.3	2.2	959	13.5
Grant	34.8	.466	.779	4.4	10.0	575	13.1
Garland	22.3	.401	.836	2.7	3.8	574	7.3
Garrick	23.6	.494	.772	2.2	4.0	508	7.0
Martin	19.6	.411	.705	2.3	0.6	433	6.3
Wolf	17.2	.395	.775	3.0	0.8	370	4.8
Rivers	13.9	.406	.756	1.7	3.0	219	4.2

Los Angeles Lakers

	Min per game	FG%	FT%	RBs per game	Ast per game	Pts	Pts per game
Johnson	37.2	.480	.890	6.6	11.5	1765	22.3
Worthy	37.0	.548	.782	6.0	3.6	1685	21.1
Scott	33.7	.470	.766	3.1	3.6	1197	15.5
Green	33.0	.478	.751	8.7	1.1	1061	12.9
Wooldridge	22.9	.556	.733	3.0	1.5	788	12.7
Thompson	26.9	.500	.706	6.8	0.6	706	10.1
Divac	19.6	.499	.708	6.2	0.9	701	8.5
Cooper	23.1	.387	.883	2.8	2.7	515	6.4
Drew	16.7	.444	.767	1.2	2.7	418	5.2

Miami Heat

	Min per game	FG%	FT%	RBs per game	Ast per game	Pts	Pts per game
Seikaly	32.6	.502	.594	10.4	1.1	1228	16.6
Douglas	30.5	.494	.687	2.5	7.6	1155	14.3
Rice	30.0	.439	.734	4.6	1.8	1048	13.6
Edwards	28.3	.412	.760	3.6	3.2	938	12.0
Thompson	27.1	.516	.622	7.0	2.1	867	11.0
Frank	22.9	.458	.765	5.0	1.1	735	9.5
Long	23.0	.483	.714	5.0	1.2	686	8.5
Sundvold	13.8	.408	.846	1.1	1.6	384	6.1
Sparrow	21.4	.412	.766	1.7	3.6	487	5.9
Davis	14.0	.466	.621	3.6	0.4	298	4.7

Milwaukee Bucks

	Min per game	FG%	FT%	RBs per game	Ast per game	Pts	Pts per game
Pierce	30.0	.510	.839	2.8	2.3	1359	23.0
Humphries	34.8	.494	.786	3.3	5.8	1237	15.3
Robertson	32.1	.503	.741	6.9	5.5	1153	14.2
Sikma	31.7	.416	.885	6.9	3.2	986	13.9
Pressey	24.6	.472	.758	3.0	4.3	628	11.0
Roberts	27.3	.495	.783	3.8	1.8	857	10.5
Lohaus	24.3	.460	.728	5.0	2.1	732	9.2
Anderson	21.5	.507	.535	6.2	0.4	529	8.8
Grayer	20.1	.460	.651	3.1	1.5	548	7.7
Brown	10.4	.427	.679	1.2	0.7	219	3.6

Minnesota Timberwolves

	Min per game	FG%	FT%	RBs per game	Ast per game	Pts	Pts per game
Campbell	38.6	.457	.787	5.5	2.6	1903	23.2
Corbin	36.7	.481	.770	7.4	2.6	1203	14.7
Mitchell	30.2	.446	.768	5.8	1.1	1012	12.7
Richardson	31.5	.461	.589	2.6	6.8	938	11.4
Breuer	23.2	.428	.653	5.1	1.2	722	8.9

	Min per game	FG%	FT%	RBs per game	Ast per game	Pts	Pts per game
Murphy	30.4	.471	.709	6.9	1.3	680	8.3
Roth	14.9	.379	.746	1.6	1.6	486	6.8
Royal	11.3	.459	.777	2.1	0.7	387	5.9
Sellers	11.9	.406	.795	1.5	0.6	264	4.5
Lowe	21.8	.319	.722	2.0	4.2	187	2.3

New Jersey Nets

	Min per game	FG%	FT%	RBs per game	Ast per game	Pts	Pts per game
Hopson	32.3	.434	.792	3.5	1.9	1251	15.8
Hinson	31.7	.507	.869	6.8	0.9	376	15.0
Morris	30.6	.422	.722	5.3	1.8	1187	14.8
Bowie	32.5	.416	.776	10.1	1.3	998	14.7
Short	27.0	.455	.835	3.0	1.8	1072	13.1
Blaylock	25.3	.371	.778	2.8	4.2	505	10.1
Shackleford	22.2	.462	.687	6.8	0.8	573	8.2
Conner	28.7	.414	.804	3.2	4.7	648	7.9
Dudley	16.1	.411	.319	6.6	0.6	350	5.5
Haley	16.2	.398	.680	4.5	0.4	361	5.4
Myers	14.4	.396	.660	1.8	2.6	244	4.7

New York Knickerbockers

	Min per game	FG%	FT%	RBs per game	Ast per game	Pts	Pts per game
Ewing	38.6	.551	.775	10.9	2.2	2347	28.6
Oakley	36.0	.524	.761	11.9	2.4	889	14.6
G. Wilkins	31.8	.457	.803	4.5	4.0	1191	14.5
Newman	28.5	.476	.799	2.4	2.3	1032	12.9
Jackson	29.6	.437	.727	3.9	7.4	809	9.9
Cheeks	31.1	.504	.847	3.0	5.6	789	9.7
Tucker	21.3	.417	.767	2.1	2.1	667	8.2
Walker	23.5	.531	.723	5.0	0.7	535	7.9
E. Wilkins	12.3	.455	.605	3.4	0.2	371	4.7

Orlando Magic

	Min per game	FG%	FT%	RBs per game	Ast per game	Pts	Pts per game
Catledge	33.3	.477	.702	7.6	1.0	1435	19.4
Theus	30.9	.439	.853	2.9	5.4	1438	18.9
Smith	25.3	.492	.761	4.6	2.3	875	13.5
Reynolds	27.1	.417	.742	4.8	2.7	858	12.8
Anderson	22.0	.494	.705	3.9	1.5	931	11.5
Vincent	26.3	.457	.879	3.1	5.6	705	11.2
Green	25.5	.468	.651	8.1	1.4	761	10.4
Ansley	17.0	.497	.722	5.0	0.6	626	8.7
Skiles	20.9	.409	.874	2.3	4.8	536	7.7
Wiley	16.0	.442	.737	0.8	2.9	229	5.7
Turner	18.4	.429	.778	3.8	0.9	308	5.1
Acres	21.1	.484	.692	5.4	0.8	362	4.5

Philadelphia 76ers

	Min per game	FG%	FT%	RBs per game	Ast per game	Pts	Pts per game
Barkley	39.1	.600	.749	11.5	3.9	1989	25.2
Hawkins	34.8	.460	.888	3.7	3.2	1515	18.5
Dawkins	35.4	.489	.861	3.0	7.4	1162	14.3
Gminski	32.8	.457	.821	8.5	1.6	1112	13.7
Anderson	26.8	.451	.838	3.8	1.8	926	11.9
Mahorn	30.3	.497	.715	7.6	1.3	811	10.8
Smith	18.7	.508	.699	2.3	1.5	668	8.9
Brooks	13.5	.431	.877	0.6	2.9	319	4.4

Phoenix Suns

	Min per game	FG%	FT%	RBs per game	Ast per game	Pts	Pts per game
Chambers	37.6	.501	.861	7.0	2.3	2201	27.2
Johnson	37.6	.499	.838	3.6	11.4	1665	22.5
Hornacek	34.0	.536	.856	4.7	5.0	1179	17.6
E. Johnson	28.3	.453	.917	3.8	1.7	1080	16.9
Majerle	30.7	.424	.762	5.9	2.6	809	11.1
West	29.3	.625	.691	8.9	0.5	861	10.5
Rambis	25.7	.509	.646	7.1	1.8	462	6.2
Perry	10.2	.513	.589	2.5	0.3	254	4.2
Battle	12.3	.547	.671	2.1	0.6	242	4.1
Lang	13.7	.557	.653	3.7	0.3	258	3.5
Grant	10.1	.384	.661	0.9	2.5	208	3.1

Portland Trail Blazers

	Min per game	FG%	FT%	RBs per game	Ast per game	Pts	Pts per game
Drexler	36.8	.494	.774	6.9	5.9	1703	23.3
Porter	34.8	.462	.892	3.4	9.1	1406	17.6
Duckworth	30.0	.478	.740	0.2	1.1	1327	16.2
Kersey	34.7	.478	.690	8.4	2.3	1310	16.0
Williams	34.2	.548	.706	9.8	1.4	1114	13.6
Robinson	19.1	.397	.550	3.8	0.9	746	9.1
Petrovic	12.6	.485	.844	1.4	1.5	583	7.6
Young	17.0	.421	.813	1.5	2.8	383	4.7
Cooper	14.9	.454	.641	4.3	0.6	301	3.8

Seattle SuperSonics

	Min per game	FG%	FT%	RBs per game	Ast per game	Pts	Pts per game
Ellis	37.0	.497	.818	4.3	2.0	1293	23.5
McDaniel	35.2	.496	.733	6.5	2.5	1471	21.3
McKey	34.4	.493	.782	6.1	2.3	1254	15.7
Threatt	22.8	.506	.828	1.8	3.3	744	11.4
Cage	31.6	.504	.698	10.0	0.9	798	9.7
Barros	20.1	.405	.809	1.6	2.5	782	9.7
Kemp	13.8	.479	.736	4.3	0.3	525	6.5
McMillan	28.5	.473	.641	4.9	7.3	523	6.4
Polynice	13.7	.540	.475	3.8	0.2	360	4.6

Sacramento Kings

	Min per game	FG%	FT%	RBs per game	Ast per game	Pts	Pts per game
Tisdale	37.2	.525	.783	7.5	1.4	1758	22.3
Ainge	36.4	.438	.831	4.3	6.0	1342	17.9
McCray	39.5	.515	.784	8.2	4.6	1358	16.6
Smith	38.0	.461	.809	2.6	6.6	688	15.0
Carr	22.4	.494	.795	4.2	1.5	949	12.3
Del Negro	24.4	.462	.871	2.6	3.3	739	9.7
Pressley	22.3	.424	.780	4.3	2.1	636	8.8
Ellison	25.5	.442	.628	5.8	1.9	271	8.0
Toney	15.1	.348	.807	0.9	2.7	264	4.1
Allen	11.8	.444	.535	2.2	0.4	235	3.7
Kite	21.3	.432	.500	5.3	1.1	230	3.2

Utah Jazz

	Min per game	FG%	FT%	RBs per game	Ast per game	Pts	Pts per game
Malone	38.1	.562	.762	11.1	2.8	2540	31.0
Stockton	37.3	.514	.819	2.6	14.5	1345	17.2
Bailey	31.5	.481	.779	5.0	1.7	1162	14.2
Griffith	17.6	.464	.654	2.0	0.8	733	8.9
Edwards	23.0	.507	.719	3.1	1.8	727	8.9
Hansen	26.8	.467	.516	2.8	1.8	617	7.6
Eaton	27.8	.527	.669	7.3	0.5	395	4.8
Leckner	9.9	.563	.743	2.5	0.2	331	4.3
Rudd	11.0	.429	.660	0.7	2.3	273	3.5

San Antonio Spurs

	Min per game	FG%	FT%	RBs per game	Ast per game	Pts	Pts per game
Robinson	36.6	.531	.732	12.0	2.0	1993	24.3
Cummings	34.8	.475	.780	8.4	2.7	1818	22.4
Anderson	34.0	.492	.748	4.5	4.4	1288	15.7
Strickland	26.1	.454	.626	3.2	5.7	868	10.6
Elliott	25.1	.481	.866	3.7	1.9	810	10.0
Maxwell	22.8	.435	.621	2.9	3.0	340	6.9
Williams	15.8	.388	.765	1.8	1.1	320	6.8
Wingate	23.8	.488	.777	2.5	2.7	527	6.8
Brickowski	18.4	.545	.674	4.2	1.3	517	6.6
Jones	12.3	.465	.704	3.2	0.3	173	2.4

Washington Bullets

	Min per game	FG%	FT%	RBs per game	Ast per game	Pts	Pts per game
Malone	34.2	.491	.877	2.7	3.2	1820	24.3
King	32.8	.487	.803	4.9	4.6	1837	22.4
Williams	35.1	.474	.774	7.6	4.7	327	18.2
Eackles	21.7	.439	.750	2.2	2.3	1055	13.5
Alarie	23.1	.473	.812	4.6	1.7	860	10.5
Walker	35.6	.454	.687	8.8	8.0	772	9.8
Grant	22.8	.473	.701	4.2	1.6	664	8.2
Hammonds	13.2	.437	.643	2.1	0.8	321	5.3
Colter	13.4	.478	.831	2.4	0.7	361	4.9
Turpin	13.9	.526	.789	3.7	0.5	276	4.7
Jones	27.7	.508	.648	6.2	1.7	256	3.2

All-Time NBA Statistical Leaders

(at the start of the 1989-90 season. *Includes 1989-90 season.)

Scoring Average
(400 games or 10,000 Points Minimum)

	G	Pts.	Avg
*Michael Jordan	427	14,016	32.8
Wilt Chamberlain	1,045	31,419	30.1
Elgin Baylor	846	23,149	27.4
Jerry West	932	25,192	27.0
Bob Pettit	792	20,880	26.4
George Gervin	791	20,708	26.2
*Dominique Wilkins	639	16,695	26.1
Oscar Robertson	1,040	26,710	25.7
*Larry Bird	792	19,719	24.8
*Adrian Dantley	945	23,120	24.4

Field Goal Percentage
(2,000 FGM Minimum)

	FGA	FGM	Pct.
Artis Gilmore	9,570	5,732	.599
James Donaldson	4,015	2,356	.587
Charles Barkley	5,252	3,032	.577
Steve Johnson	4,810	2,759	.574
Darryl Dawkins	6,060	3,468	.572
Kevin McHale	8,958	5,057	.565
Jeff Ruland	3,685	2,080	.564
Kareem Abdul-Jabbar	28,307	15,837	.559
Larry Nance	7,329	4,081	.557
James Worthy	7,464	4,151	.556

Free Throw Percentage
(1,200 FTM Minimum)

	FTA	FTM	Pct.
Rick Barry	4,243	3,818	.900
*Larry Bird	4,088	3,675	.898
Calvin Murphy	3,864	3,445	.892
*Ricky Pierce	1,864	1,661	.891
Bill Sharman	3,357	3,143	.884
*Kiki Vandeweghe	2,960	2,579	.871
Mike Newlin	3,456	3,005	.870
*Jeff Malone	2,231	1,939	.869
John Long	1,996	1,719	.861

Points

	Pts.
Kareem Abdul-Jabbar	38,387
Wilt Chamberlain	31,419
Elvin Hayes	27,313
Oscar Robertson	26,710
John Havlicek	26,395
Jerry West	25,192
*Moses Malone	24,868
*Alex English	24,850
Elgin Baylor	23,149

Games Played

Kareem Abdul-Jabbar	1,560
Elvin Hayes	1,303
John Havlicek	1,270
Paul Silas	1,254
Hal Greer	1,122
Len Wilkens	1,077
Dolph Schayes	1,059
Johnny Green	1,057
Don Nelson	1,053

Assists

Oscar Robertson	9,887
*Magic Johnson	8,932
Len Wilkens	7,211
*Isiah Thomas	6,985
Bob Cousy	6,955
Guy Rodgers	6,917
Nate Archibald	6,476
*John Lucas	6,454
Norm Nixon	6,386

Field Goals Made

Kareem Abdul-Jabbar	15,837
Wilt Chamberlain	12,681
Elvin Hayes	10,976
John Havlicek	10,513
*Alex English	10,337
Oscar Robertson	9,508
Jerry West	9,016
Elgin Baylor	8,693
*Moses Malone	8,587

Rebounds

Wilt Chamberlain	23,924
Bill Russell	21,620
Kareem Abdul-Jabbar	17,440
Elvin Hayes	16,279
*Moses Malone	14,483
Nate Thurmond	14,464
Walt Bellamy	14,241
Wes Unseld	13,769
Jerry Lucas	12,942

NBA Scoring Leaders

Year	Scoring champion	Pts	Avg	Year	Scoring champion	Pts	Avg
1947	Joe Fulks, Philadelphia	1,389	23.2	1970	Jerry West, Los Angeles	2,309	31.2
1948	Max Zaslofsky, Chicago	1,007	21.0	1971	Lew Alcindor, Milwaukee	2,596	31.7
1949	George Mikan, Minneapolis	1,698	28.3	1972	Kareem Abdul-Jabbar (Alcindor), Milwau-		
1950	George Mikan, Minneapolis	1,865	27.4		kee	2,822	34.8
1951	George Mikan, Minneapolis	1,932	28.4	1973	Nate Archibald, Kansas City-Omaha	2,719	34.0
1952	Paul Arizin, Philadelphia	1,674	25.4	1974	Bob McAdoo, Buffalo	2,261	30.6
1953	Neil Johnston, Philadelphia	1,564	22.3	1975	Bob McAdoo, Buffalo	2,831	34.5
1954	Neil Johnston, Philadelphia	1,759	24.4	1976	Bob McAdoo, Buffalo	2,427	31.1
1955	Neil Johnston, Philadelphia	1,631	22.7	1977	Pete Maravich, New Orleans	2,273	31.1
1956	Bob Pettit, St. Louis	1,849	25.7	1978	George Gervin, San Antonio	2,232	27.2
1957	Paul Arizin, Philadelphia	1,817	25.6	1979	George Gervin, San Antonio	2,365	29.6
1958	George Yardley, Detroit	2,001	27.8	1980	George Gervin, San Antonio	2,585	33.1
1959	Bob Pettit, St. Louis	2,105	29.2	1981	Adrian Dantley, Utah	2,452	30.7
1960	Wilt Chamberlain, Philadelphia	2,707	37.9	1982	George Gervin, San Antonio	2,551	32.3
1961	Wilt Chamberlain, Philadelphia	3,033	38.4	1983	Alex English, Denver	2,326	28.4
1962	Wilt Chamberlain, Philadelphia	4,029	50.4	1984	Adrian Dantley, Utah	2,418	30.6
1963	Wilt Chamberlain, San Francisco	3,586	44.8	1985	Bernard King, New York	1,809	32.9
1964	Wilt Chamberlain, San Francisco	2,948	36.5	1986	Dominique Wilkins, Atlanta	2,366	30.3
1965	Wilt Chamberlain, San Fran., Phila.	2,534	34.7	1987	Michael Jordan, Chicago	3,041	37.1
1966	Wilt Chamberlain, Philadelphia	2,649	33.5	1988	Michael Jordan, Chicago	2,868	35.0
1967	Rick Barry, San Francisco	2,775	35.6	1989	Michael Jordan, Chicago	2,633	32.5
1968	Dave Bing, Detroit	2,142	27.1	1990	Michael Jordan, Chicago	2,753	33.6
1969	Elvin Hayes, San Diego	2,327	28.4				

NBA Rookie of the Year

Year	Player	Year	Player	Year	Player
1953	Don Meineke, Ft. Wayne	1966	Rick Barry, San Francisco	1978	Walter Davis, Phoenix
1954	Ray Felix, Baltimore	1967	Dave Bing, Detroit	1979	Phil Ford, Kansas City
1955	Bob Pettit, Milwaukee	1968	Earl Monroe, Baltimore	1980	Larry Bird, Boston
1956	Maurice Stokes, Rochester	1969	Wes Unseld, Baltimore	1981	Darrell Griffith, Utah
1957	Tom Heinsohn, Boston	1970	Lew Alcindor, Milwaukee	1982	Buck Williams, New Jersey
1958	Woody Sauldsberry, Philadelphia	1971	Dave Cowens, Boston;	1983	Terry Cummings, San Diego
1959	Elgin Baylor, Minneapolis		Geoff Petrie, Portland (tie)	1984	Ralph Sampson, Houston
1960	Wilt Chamberlain, Philadelphia	1972	Sidney Wicks, Portland	1985	Michael Jordan, Chicago
1961	Oscar Robertson, Cincinnati	1973	Bob McAdoo, Buffalo	1986	Patrick Ewing, New York
1962	Walt Bellamy, Chicago	1974	Ernie DiGregorio, Buffalo	1987	Chuck Person, Indiana
1963	Terry Dischinger, Chicago	1975	Keith Wilkes, Golden State	1988	Mark Jackson, New York
1964	Jerry Lucas, Cincinnati	1976	Alvan Adams, Phoenix	1989	Mitch Richmond, Golden State
1965	Willis Reed, New York	1977	Adrian Dantley, Buffalo	1990	David Robinson, San Antonio

Individuals in The Basketball Hall of Fame

Springfield, Mass.

Arizin, Paul
Barlow, Thomas
Barry, Rick
Baylor, Elgin
Beckman, John
Bing, Dave
Borgmann, Bennie
Bradley, Bill
Brennan, Joseph
Cervi, Al
Chamberlain, Wilt
Cooper, Charles
Cousy, Bob
Cunningham, Billy
Davies, Bob
DeBernardi, Forrest
DeBusschere, Dave
Dehnert, Dutch
Endacott, Paul
Foster, Bud
Frazier, Walt
Friedman, Max
Fulks, Joe
Gale, Lauren
Gates, Pop
Gola, Tom
Greer, Hal
Gruenig, Ace
Hagan, Cliff
Hanson, Victor
Havlicek, John
Hayes, Elvin
Heinsohn, Tom
Holman, Nat

Houbregs, Bob
Hyatt, Chuck
Johnson, William
Johnston, Neil
Jones, K.C.
Jones, Sam
Krause, Moose
Kurland, Bob
Lapchick, Joe
Lovellette, Clyde
Lucas, Jerry
Luisetti, Hank
Macauley, Ed
Maravich, Pete
Martin, Slater
McCracken, Branch
McCracken, Jack
McDermott, Bobby
Mikan, George
Monroe, Earl
Murphy, Stretch
Page, Pat
Pettit, Bob
Phillip, Andy
Pollard, Jim
Ramsey, Frank
Reed, Willis
Robertson, Oscar
Roosma, John S.
Russell, Honey
Russell, Bill
Schayes, Adolph
Schmidt, Ernest
Schommer, John
Sedran, Barney

Sharman, Bill
Steinmetz, Christian
Thompson, Cat
Thurmond, Nate
Twyman, Jack
Unseld, Wes
Vandivier, Fuzzy
Wachter, Edward
Wanzer, Bobby
West, Jerry
Wilkins, Lenny
Wooden, John

Coaches
Auerbach, Red
Barry, Sam
Blood, Ernest
Cann, Howard
Carlson, Dr. H. C.
Carnevale, Ben
Case, Everett
Dean, Everett
Diddle, Edgar
Drake, Bruce
Gaines, Clarence
Gardner, Jack
Gill, Slats
Hickey, Edgar
Hobson, Howard
Holzman, Red
Iba, Hank
Julian, Alvin
Keaney, Frank
Keogan, George
Lambert, Ward
Litwack, Harry

Loeffler, Kenneth
Lonborg, Dutch
McCutchan, Arad
McGuire, Frank
McLendon, John
Meyer, Ray
Meanwell, Dr. W.E.
Miller, Ralph
Newell, Pete
Rupp, Adolph
Sachs, Leonard
Shelton, Everett
Smith, Dean
Taylor, Fred
Teague, Bertha
Wade, Margaret
Watts, Stan
Wooden, John

Referees
Enright, James
Hepbron, George
Hoyt, George
Kennedy, Matthew
Leith, Lloyd
Mihalik, Red
Nucatola, John
Quigley, Ernest
Shirley, J. Dallas
Tobey, David
Walsh, David

Contributors
Abbott, Senda B.
Allen, Phog
Bee, Clair
Brown, Walter

Bunn, John
Douglas, Bob
Duer, Al O.
Fagan, Cliff
Fisher, Harry
Gottlieb, Edward
Gulick, Dr. L. H.
Harrison, Lester
Hepp, Dr. Ferenc
Hickox, Edward
Hinkle, Tony
Irish, Ned
Jones, R. W.
Kennedy, Walter
Liston, Emil
Mokray, Bill
Morgan, Ralph
Morgenweck, Frank
Naismith, Dr. James
O'Brien, John
Olsen, Harold
Podoloff, Maurice
Porter, H. V.
Reis, William
Ripley, Elmer
St. John, Lynn
Saperstein, Abe
Schabinger, Arthur
Stagg, Amos Alonzo
Steitz, Edward
Taylor, Chuck
Tower, Oswald
Trester, Arthur
Wells, Clifford
Wilke, Lou

MVP in Playoffs

1969	Jerry West, Los Angeles	1977	Bill Walton, Portland	1985	Kareem Abdul-Jabbar, L.A. Lakers
1970	Willis Reed, New York	1978	Wes Unseld, Washington		
1971	Lew Alcindor, Milwaukee	1979	Dennis Johnson, Seattle	1986	Larry Bird, Boston
1972	Wilt Chamberlain, Los Angeles	1980	Magic Johnson, Los Angeles	1987	Magic Johnson, L.A. Lakers
1973	Willis Reed, New York	1981	Cedric Maxwell, Boston	1988	James Worthy, L.A. Lakers
1974	John Havlicek, Boston	1982	Magic Johnson, Los Angeles	1989	Joe Dumars, Detroit
1975	Rick Barry, Golden State	1983	Moses Malone, Philadelphia	1990	Isiah Thomas, Detroit
1976	Jo Jo White, Boston	1984	Larry Bird, Boston		

1990 NBA Player Draft

The following are the first round picks of the National Basketball Association.

New Jersey—Derrick Coleman, Syracuse
Seattle—Gary Payton, Oregon State
Denver—Chris Jackson, LSU
Orlando—Dennis Scott, Georgia Tech
Charlotte—Kendall Gill, Illinois
Minnesota—Felton Spencer, Louisville
Sacramento—Lionel Simmons, La Salle
L.A. Clippers—Bo Kimball, Loyola Marymount
Miami—Willie Burton, Minnesota
Atlanta—Rumeal Robinson, Michigan
Golden State—Tyrone Hill, Xavier
Houston—Alec Kessler,[1] Georgia
L.A. Clippers—Lon Vaught, Michigan
Sacramento—Travis Mays, Texas

Miami—Dave Jamerson,[2] Ohio Univ.
Milwaukee—Terry Mills,[3] Michigan
New York—Jerrod Mustaf, Maryland
Sacramento—Duane Causwell, Temple
Boston—Dee Brown, Jacksonville
Minnesota—Gerald Glass, Mississippi
Phoenix—Jayson Williams, St. John's
New Jersey—Tate George, Connecticut
Sacramento—Anthony Bonner, St. Louis
San Antonio—Dwayne Schintzius, Florida
Portland—Alaa Abdelnaby, Duke
Detroit—Lance Blanks, Texas
L.A. Lakers—Elden Campbell, Clemson

(1) Traded to Miami; (2) Traded to Houston; (3) Traded to Denver.

First Round NBA Draft Picks, 1966-90

Year	Team	Player, college	Year	Team	Player, college
1966	New York	Cazzie Russell, Michigan	1979	L.A. Lakers	Magic Johnson, Michigan St.
1967	Detroit	Jimmy Walker, Providence	1980	Golden State	Joe Barry Carroll, Purdue
1968	Houston	Elvin Hayes, Houston	1981	Dallas	Mark Aguirre, DePaul
1969	Milwaukee	Lew Alcindor, UCLA*	1982	L.A. Lakers	James Worthy, N. Carolina
1970	Detroit	Bob Lanier, St. Bonaventure	1983	Houston	Ralph Sampson, Virginia
1971	Cleveland	Austin Carr, Notre Dame	1984	Houston	Akeem Olajuwon, Houston
1972	Portland	LaRue Martin, Loyola-Chicago	1985	New York	Patrick Ewing, Georgetown
1973	Philadelphia	Doug Collins, Illinois St.	1986	Cleveland	Brad Daugherty, N. Carolina
1974	Portland	Bill Walton, UCLA	1987	San Antonio	David Robinson, Navy
1975	Atlanta	David Thompson,[1] N.C. State	1988	L.A. Clippers	Danny Manning, Kansas
1976	Houston	John Lucas, Maryland	1989	Sacramento	Pervis Ellison, Louisville
1977	Milwaukee	Kent Benson, Indiana	1990	New Jersey	Derrick Coleman, Syracuse
1978	Portland	Mychal Thompson, Minnesota			

*Later Kareem Abdul-Jabbar. (1) Signed with Denver of ABA.

Professional Sports Arenas

The seating capacity of sports arenas can vary depending on the event being presented. The figures below are the normal seating capacity for basketball. (*) indicates hockey seating capacity. Domed stadiums can dramatically increase seating capacity for special occasions.

Name, location	Capacity	Name, location	Capacity
ARCO Arena, Sacramento	17,014	Miami Arena	15,008
Arizona Veteran's Memorial Coliseum, Phoenix	14,487	Montreal Forum	*16,074
Boston Garden	14,890-*14,451	Nassau Veterans Memorial Coliseum, Uniondale, N.Y.	*16,267
Bradley Center, Milwaukee	18,633	Northlands Coliseum, Edmonton	*17,502(a)
Buffalo Memorial Auditorium	17,900-*16,433(a)	Oakland Coliseum Arena	15,025
Capital Centre, Landover, Md.	18,756-*18,130	Olympic Saddledome, Calgary, Alta.	*16,798
Charlotte Coliseum	23,388	The Omni, Atlanta	16,371
Chicago Stadium	17,339-*17,317	Orlando Arena, Orlando, Fla.	15,500
The Coliseum, Richfield Township, Oh.	20,273	Pacific Coliseum, Vancouver, B.C.	*16,553
Great Western Forum	17,505-*16,005	Palace, Auburn Hills, Mich.	21,454
Hartford Civic Center	*15,200	Pittsburgh Civic Arena	*16,033
HemisFair Arena, San Antonio	15,861	Portland Memorial Coliseum	12,880
Joe Louis Sports Arena, Detroit	*19,275	Quebec Coliseum	*15,434
Los Angeles Memorial Sports Arena	15,310	Reunion Arena, Dallas	17,007
Madison Square Garden, New York	18,212-*17,500	St. Louis Arena	17,666
Maple Leaf Gardens, Toronto	*16,382(a)	Salt Palace, Salt Lake City	12,616-*10,594
Market Square Arena, Indianapolis	16,912-*15,822	Seattle Coliseum	14,250
McNichols Sports Arena, Denver	17,022-*16,399	Spectrum, Philadelphia	18,168-*17,211
Meadowlands Arena, E. Rutherford, N.J.	20,039-*19,040	The Summit, Houston	16,279
Metrodome, Minneapolis	25,810	Winnipeg Arena	*15,401
Met. Sports Center, Bloomington, Minn.	*15,449		

(a) includes standees

Figure Skating Champions

	U.S. Champions			World Champions	
Men	Women	Year	Men	Women	
Dick Button	Tenley Albright	1952	Dick Button, U.S.	Jacqueline du Bief, France
Hayes Jenkins	Tenley Albright	1953	Hayes Jenkins, U.S.	Tenley Albright, U.S.
Hayes Jenkins	Tenley Albright	1954	Hayes Jenkins, U.S.	Gundi Busch, W. Germany
Hayes Jenkins	Tenley Albright	1955	Hayes Jenkins, U.S.	Tenley Albright, U.S.
Hayes Jenkins	Tenley Albright	1956	Hayes Jenkins, U.S.	Carol Heiss, U.S.
Dave Jenkins	Carol Heiss	1957	Dave Jenkins, U.S.	Carol Heiss, U.S.
Dave Jenkins	Carol Heiss	1958	Dave Jenkins, U.S.	Carol Heiss, U.S.
Dave Jenkins	Carol Heiss	1959	Dave Jenkins, U.S.	Carol Heiss, U.S.
Dave Jenkins	Carol Heiss	1960	Alain Giletti, France	Carol Heiss, U.S.
Bradley Lord	Laurence Owen	1961	none	none
Monty Hoyt	Barbara Roles Pursley	1962	Don Jackson, Canada	Sjoukje Dijkstra, Neth.
Tommy Litz	Lorraine Hanlon	1963	Don McPherson, Canada	Sjoukje Dijkstra, Neth.
Scott Allen	Peggy Fleming	1964	Manfred Schnelldorfer, W. Germany	Sjoukje Dijkstra, Neth.
Gary Visconti	Peggy Fleming	1965	Alain Calmat, France	Petra Burka, Canada
Scott Allen	Peggy Fleming	1966	Emmerich Danzer, Austria	Peggy Fleming, U.S.
Gary Visconti	Peggy Fleming	1967	Emmerich Danzer, Austria	Peggy Fleming, U.S.
Tim Wood	Peggy Fleming	1968	Emmerich Danzer, Austria	Peggy Fleming, U.S.
Tim Wood	Janet Lynn	1969	Tim Wood, U.S.	Gabriele Seyfert, E. Germany
Tim Wood	Janet Lynn	1970	Tim Wood, U.S.	Gabriele Seyfert, E. Germany
John Misha Petkevich	Janet Lynn	1971	Ondrej Nepela, Czech.	Beatrix Schuba, Austria
Ken Shelley	Janet Lynn	1972	Ondrej Nepela, Czech.	Beatrix Schuba, Austria
Gordon McKellen Jr.	Janet Lynn	1973	Ondrej Nepela, Czech.	Karen Magnussen, Canada
Gordon McKellen Jr.	Dorothy Hamill	1974	Jan Hoffmann, E. Germany	Christine Errath, E. Germany
Gordon McKellen Jr.	Dorothy Hamill	1975	Sergei Volkov, USSR	Dianne de Leeuw, Neth.-U.S.
Terry Kubicka	Dorothy Hamill	1976	John Curry, Gt. Britain	Dorothy Hamill, U.S.
Charles Tickner	Linda Fratianne	1977	Vladimir Kovalev, USSR	Linda Fratianne, U.S.
Charles Tickner	Linda Fratianne	1978	Charles Tickner, U.S.	Anett Potzsch, E. Germany
Charles Tickner	Linda Fratianne	1979	Vladimir Kovalev, USSR	Linda Fratianne, U.S.
Charles Tickner	Linda Fratianne	1980	Jan Hoffmann, E. Germany	Anett Potzsch, E. Germany
Scott Hamilton	Elaine Zayak	1981	Scott Hamilton, U.S.	Denise Biellmann, Switzerland
Scott Hamilton	Rosalynn Sumners	1982	Scott Hamilton, U.S.	Elaine Zayak, U.S.
Scott Hamilton	Rosalynn Sumners	1983	Scott Hamilton, U.S.	Rosalynn Sumners, U.S.
Scott Hamilton	Rosalynn Sumners	1984	Scott Hamilton, U.S.	Katarina Witt, E. Germany
Brian Boitano	Tiffany Chin	1985	Aleksandr Fadeev, USSR	Katarina Witt, E. Germany
Brian Boitano	Debi Thomas	1986	Brian Boitano, U.S.	Debi Thomas, U.S.
Brian Boitano	Jill Trenary	1987	Brian Orser, Canada	Katarina Witt, E. Germany
Brian Boitano	Debi Thomas	1988	Brian Boitano, U.S.	Katarina Witt, E. Germany
Christopher Bowman	Jill Trenary	1989	Kurt Browning, Canada	Midori Ito, Japan
Todd Eldredge	Jill Trenary	1990	Kurt Browning, Canada	Jill Trenary, U.S.

U.S. Pairs and Dancing Champions in 1990

Kristi Yamaguchi and Rudi Galindo won the 1990 U.S. pairs figure skating championship in Salt Lake City, Ut. Susan Wynne and Joseph Druar triumphed in ice dancing.

Curling Champions

Source: North American Curling News

World Champions

Year	Country, skip	Year	Country, skip	Year	Country, skip
1976	United States, Bruce Roberts	1981	Switzerland, Jurg Tanner	1986	Canada, Ed Luckowich
1977	Sweden, Ragnar Kamp	1982	Canada, Al Hackner	1987	Canada, Russ Howard
1978	United States, Bob Nichols	1983	Canada, Ed Werenich	1988	Norway, Eigil Ramsfjell
1979	Norway, Kristian Soerum	1984	Norway, Eigil Ramsfjell	1989	Canada, Pat Ryan
1980	Canada, Rich Folk	1985	Canada, Al Hackner	1990	Canada, Ed Werenich

U.S. Men's Champions

Year	State, skip	Year	State, skip	Year	State, skip
1976	Minnesota, Bruce Roberts	1981	Wisconsin, Somerville-Nichols	1986	Wisconsin, Steve Brown
1977	Minnesota, Bruce Roberts	1982	Wisconsin, Steve Brown	1987	Washington, Jim Vukich
1978	Wisconsin, Bob Nichols	1983	Colorado, Don Cooper	1988	Washington, Doug Jones
1979	Minnesota, Scotty Baird	1984	Minnesota, Bruce Roberts	1989	Washington, Jim Vukich
1980	Minnesota, Paul Pustover	1985	Illinois, Tim Wright	1990	Washington, Doug Jones

U.S. Ladies Champions

Year	State, skip	Year	State, skip	Year	State, skip
1979	Washington, Nancy Langley	1983	Washington, Nancy Langley	1987	Washington, Sharon Good
1980	Washington, Sharon Kozai	1984	Minnesota, Amy Hatten	1988	Washington, Nancy Langey
1981	Washington, Nancy Langley	1985	Alaska, Bev Birklid	1989	North Dakota, Jan Lagasse
1982	Illinois, Ruth Schwenker	1986	Minnesota, Gerri Tilden	1990	Colorado, Bev Behnke

THOROUGHBRED RACING

Triple Crown Winners

Since 1920, colts have carried 126 lbs. in triple crown events; fillies 121 lbs.

(Kentucky Derby, Preakness, and Belmont Stakes)

Year	Horse	Jockey	Trainer	Year	Horse	Jockey	Trainer
1919	Sir Barton	J. Loftus	H. G. Bedwell	1946	Assault	Mehrtens	M. Hirsch
1930	Gallant Fox	E. Sande	J. Fitzsimmons	1948	Citation	E. Arcaro	H.A. Jones
1935	Omaha	W. Sanders	J. Fitzsimmons	1973	Secretariat	R. Turcotte	L. Laurin
1937	War Admiral	C. Kurtsinger	G. Conway	1977	Seattle Slew	J. Cruguet	W.H. Turner Jr.
1941	Whirlaway	E. Arcaro	B.A. Jones	1978	Affirmed	S. Cauthen	L.S. Barrera
1943	Count Fleet	J. Longden	G.D. Cameron				

Kentucky Derby

Churchill Downs, Louisville, Ky.; inaugurated 1875; distance 1-1/4 miles; 1-1/2 miles until 1896. 3-year olds.
Best time: 1:59.2, Secretariat, 1973

Year	Winner	Jockey	Year	Winner	Jockey	Year	Winner	Jockey
1875	Aristides	O. Lewis	1914	Old Rosebud	J. McCabe	1953	Dark Star	H. Moreno
1876	Vagrant	R. Swim	1915	Regret*	J. Notter	1954	Determine	R. York
1877	Baden Baden	W. Walker	1916	George Smith	J. Loftus	1955	Swaps	W. Shoemaker
1878	Day Star	J. Carter	1917	Omar Khayyam	C. Borel	1956	Needles	D. Erb
1879	Lord Murphy	C. Schauer	1918	Exterminator	W. Knapp	1957	Iron Liege	W. Hartack
1880	Fonso	G. Lewis	1919	Sir Barton	J. Loftus	1958	Tim Tam	I. Valenzuela
1881	Hindoo	J. McLaughlin	1920	Paul Jones	T. Rice	1959	Tomy Lee	W. Shoemaker
1882	Apollo	B. Hurd	1921	Behave Yourself	C. Thompson	1960	Venetian Way	W. Hartack
1883	Leonatus	W. Donohue	1922	Morvich	A. Johnson	1961	Carry Back	J. Sellers
1884	Buchanan	I. Murphy	1923	Zev	E. Sande	1962	Decidedly	W. Hartack
1885	Joe Cotton	E. Henderson	1924	Black Gold	J. D. Mooney	1963	Chateaugay	B. Baeza
1886	Ben Ali	P. Duffy	1925	Flying Ebony	E. Sande	1964	Northern Dancer	W. Hartack
1887	Montrose	I. Lewis	1926	Bubbling Over	A. Johnson	1965	Lucky Debonair	W. Shoemaker
1888	Macbeth II	G. Covington	1927	Whiskery	L. McAtee	1966	Kauai King	D. Brumfield
1889	Spokane	T. Kiley	1928	Reigh Count	C. Lang	1967	Proud Clarion	R. Ussery
1890	Riley	I. Murphy	1929	Clyde Van Dusen	L. McAtee	1968	Dancer's Image (a)	R. Ussery
1891	Kingman	I. Murphy	1930	Gallant Fox	E. Sande	1969	Majestic Prince	W. Hartack
1892	Azra	A. Clayton	1931	Twenty Grand	C. Kurtsinger	1970	Dust Commander	M. Manganello
1893	Lookout	E. Kunze	1932	Burgoo King	E. James	1971	Canonero II	G. Avila
1894	Chant	F. Goodale	1933	Brokers Tip	D. Meade	1972	Riva Ridge	R. Turcotte
1895	Halma	J. Perkins	1934	Cavalcade	M. Garner	1973	Secretariat	R. Turcotte
1896	Ben Brush	W. Simms	1935	Omaha	W. Saunders	1974	Cannonade	A. Cordero
1897	Typhoon II	F. Garner	1936	Bold Venture	I. Hanford	1975	Foolish Pleasure	J. Vasquez
1898	Plaudit	W. Simms	1937	War Admiral	C. Kurtsinger	1976	Bold Forbes	A. Cordero
1899	Manuel	F. Taral	1938	Lawrin	E. Arcaro	1977	Seattle Slew	J. Cruguet
1900	Lieut. Gibson	J. Boland	1939	Johnstown	J. Stout	1978	Affirmed	S. Cauthen
1901	His Eminence	J. Winkfield	1940	Gallahadion	C. Bierman	1979	Spectacular Bid	R. Franklin
1902	Alan-a-Dale	J. Winkfield	1941	Whirlaway	E. Arcaro	1980	Genuine Risk*	J. Vasquez
1903	Judge Himes	H. Booker	1942	Shut Out	W. D. Wright	1981	Pleasant Colony	J. Velasquez
1904	Elwood	F. Prior	1943	Count Fleet	J. Longden	1982	Gato del Sol	E. Delahoussaye
1905	Agile	J. Martin	1944	Pensive	C. McCreary	1983	Sunny's Halo	E. Delahoussaye
1906	Sir Huon	R. Troxler	1945	Hoop, Jr.	E. Arcaro	1984	Swale	L. Pincay
1907	Pink Star	A. Minder	1946	Assault	E. Arcaro	1985	Spend a Buck	A. Cordero
1908	Stone Street	A. Pickens	1947	Jet Pilot	E. Guerin	1986	Ferdinand	W. Shoemaker
1909	Wintergreen	V. Powers	1948	Citation	E. Arcaro	1987	Alysheba	C. McCarron
1910	Donau	F. Herbert	1949	Ponder	S. Brooks	1988	Winning Colors*	G. Stevens
1911	Meridian	G. Archibald	1950	Middleground	W. Boland	1989	Sunday Silence	P. Valenzuela
1912	Worth	C.H. Shilling	1951	Count Turf	C. McCreary	1990	Unbridled	C. Perret
1913	Donerail	R. Goose	1952	Hill Gail	E. Arcaro			

(a) Dancer's Image was disqualified from purse money after tests disclosed that he had run with a pain-killing drug, phenylbutazone, in his system. All wagers were paid on Dancer's Image. Forward Pass was awarded first place money.
   The Kentucky Derby has been won five times by two jockeys, Eddie Arcaro, 1938, 1941, 1945, 1948 and 1952; and Bill Hartack, 1957, 1960, 1962, 1964 and 1969; four times by Willie Shoemaker, 1955, 1959, 1965, and 1986; and three times by each of three jockeys, Isaac Murphy, 1884, 1890, and 1891; Earle Sande, 1923, 1925 and 1930; and Angel Cordero in 1974, 1976 and 1985. *Regret, Genuine Risk and Winning Colors are the only fillies to win the Derby.

Preakness

Pimlico, Baltimore, Md.; inaugurated 1873; 1 3-16 miles, 3 yr. olds. Best time: 1:53.2, Tank's Prospect, 1985

Year	Winner	Jockey	Year	Winner	Jockey	Year	Winner	Jockey
1873	Survivor	G. Barbee	1885	Tecumseh	J. McLaughlin	1900	Hindus	H. Spencer
1874	Culpepper	M. Donohue	1886	The Bard	S. H. Fisher	1901	The Parader	F. Landry
1875	Tom Ochiltree	L. Hughes	1887	Dunboyne	W. Donohue	1902	Old England	L. Jackson
1876	Shirley	G. Barbee	1888	Refund	F. Littlefield	1903	Flocarline	W. Gannon
1877	Cloverbrook	C. Holloway	1889	Buddhist	G. Anderson	1904	Bryn Mawr	E. Hildebrand
1878	Duke of Magenta	C. Holloway	1890	Montague	W. Martin	1905	Cairngorm	W. Davis
1879	Harold	L. Hughes	1894	Assignee	F. Taral	1906	Whimsical	W. Miller
1880	Grenada	L. Hughes	1895	Belmar	F. Taral	1907	Don Enrique	G. Mountain
1881	Saunterer	W. Costello	1896	Margrave	H. Griffin	1908	Royal Tourist	E. Dugan
1882	Vanguard	W. Costello	1897	Paul Kauvar	C. Thorpe	1909	Effendi	W. Doyle
1883	Jacobus	G. Barbee	1898	Sly Fox	W. Simms	1910	Layminster	R. Estep
1884	Knight of Ellerslie	S. H. Fisher	1899	Half Time	R. Clawson	1911	Watervale	E. Dugan

Year	Winner	Jockey	Year	Winner	Jockey	Year	Winner	Jockey
1912	Colonel Holloway	C. Turner	1938	Dauber	M. Peters	1965	Tom Rolfe	R. Turcotte
1913	Buskin	J. Butwell	1939	Challedon	G. Seabo	1966	Kauai King	D. Brumfield
1914	Holiday	A. Schuttinger	1940	Bimelech	F.A. Smith	1967	Damascus	W. Shoemaker
1915	Rhine Maiden	D. Hoffman	1941	Whirlaway	E. Arcaro	1968	Forward Pass	I. Valenzuela
1916	Damrosch	L. McAtee	1942	Alsab	B. James	1969	Majestic Prince	W. Hartack
1917	Kalitan	E. Haynes	1943	Count Fleet	J. Longden	1970	Personality	E. Belmonte
1918	War Cloud	J. Loftus	1944	Pensive	C. McCreary	1971	Canonero II	G. Avila
	Jack Hare Jr.	C. Peak	1945	Polynesian	W.D. Wright	1972	Bee Bee Bee	E. Nelson
1919	Sir Barton	J. Loftus	1946	Assault	W. Mehrtens	1973	Secretariat	R. Turcotte
1920	Man o' War	C. Kummer	1947	Faultless	D. Dodson	1974	Little Current	M. Rivera
1921	Broomspun	F. Coltiletti	1948	Citation	E. Arcaro	1975	Master Derby	D. McHargue
1922	Pillory	L. Morris	1949	Capot	T. Atkinson	1976	Elocutionist	J. Lively
1923	Vigil	B. Marinelli	1950	Hill Prince	E. Arcaro	1977	Seattle Slew	J. Cruguet
1924	Nellie Morse	J. Merimee	1951	Bold	E. Arcaro	1978	Affirmed	S. Cauthen
1925	Coventry	C. Kummer	1952	Blue Man	C. McCreary	1979	Spectacular Bid	R. Franklin
1926	Display	J. Maiben	1953	Native Dancer	E. Guerin	1980	Codex	A. Cordero
1927	Bostonian	A. Abel	1954	Hasty Road	J. Adams	1981	Pleasant Colony	J. Velasquez
1928	Victorian	R. Workman	1955	Nashua	E. Arcaro	1982	Aloma's Ruler	J. Kaenel
1929	Dr. Freeland	L. Schaefer	1956	Fabius	W. Hartack	1983	Deputed Testamony	D. Miller
1930	Gallant Fox	E. Sande	1957	Bold Ruler	E. Arcaro	1984	Gate Dancer	A. Cordero
1931	Mate	G. Ellis	1958	Tim Tam	I. Valenzuela	1985	Tank's Prospect	P. Day
1932	Burgoo King	E. James	1959	Royal Orbit	W. Harmatz	1986	Snow Chief	A. Solis
1933	Head Play	C. Kurtsinger	1960	Bally Ache	R. Ussery	1987	Alysheba	C. McCarron
1934	High Quest	R. Jones	1961	Carry Back	J. Sellers	1988	Risen Star	E. Delahoussaye
1935	Omaha	W. Saunders	1962	Greek Money	J.L. Rotz	1989	Sunday Silence	P. Valenzuela
1936	Bold Venture	G. Woolf	1963	Candy Spots	W. Shoemaker	1990	Summer Squall	P. Day
1937	War Admiral	C. Kurtsinger	1964	Northern Dancer	W. Hartack			

Belmont Stakes

Elmont, N.Y.; inaugurated 1867; 1 1/2 miles, 3 year olds. Fastest time: 2:24, Secretariat

Year	Winner	Jockey	Year	Winner	Jockey	Year	Winner	Jockey
1867	Ruthless	J. Gilpatrick	1908	Colin	J. Notter	1951	Counterpoint	D. Gorman
1868	General Duke	R. Swim	1909	Joe Madden	E. Dugan	1952	One Count	E. Arcaro
1869	Fenian	C. Miller	1910	Sweep	J. Butwell	1953	Native Dancer	E. Guerin
1870	Kingfisher	W. Dick	1913	Prince Eugene	R. Troxler	1954	High Gun	E. Guerin
1871	Harry Bassett	W. Miller	1914	Luke McLuke	M. Buxton	1955	Nashua	E. Arcaro
1872	Joe Daniels	J. Rowe	1915	The Finn	G. Byrne	1956	Needles	D. Erb
1873	Springbok	J. Rowe	1916	Friar Rock	E. Haynes	1957	Gallant Man	W. Shoemaker
1874	Saxon	G. Barbee	1917	Hourless	J. Butwell	1958	Cavan	P. Anderson
1875	Calvin	R. Swim	1918	Johren	F. Robinson	1959	Sword Dancer	W. Shoemaker
1876	Algerine	W. Donohue	1919	Sir Barton	J. Loftus	1960	Celtic Ash	W. Hartack
1877	Cloverbrook	C. Holloway	1920	Man o' War	C. Kummer	1961	Sherluck	B. Baeza
1878	Duke of Magenta	L. Hughes	1921	Grey Lag	E. Sande	1962	Jaipur	W. Shoemaker
1879	Spendthrift	S. Evans	1922	Pillory	C.H. Miller	1963	Chateaugay	B. Baeza
1880	Grenada	L. Hughes	1923	Zev	E. Sande	1964	Quadrangle	M. Ycaza
1881	Saunterer	T. Costello	1924	Mad Play	E. Sande	1965	Hail to All	J. Sellers
1882	Forester	J. McLaughlin	1925	American Flag	A. Johnson	1966	Amberoid	W. Boland
1883	George Kinney	J. McLaughlin	1926	Crusader	A. Johnson	1967	Damascus	W. Shoemaker
1884	Panique	J. McLaughlin	1927	Chance Shot	E. Sande	1968	Stage Door Johnny	H. Gustines
1885	Tyrant	P. Duffy	1928	Vito	C. Kummer	1969	Arts and Letters	B. Baeza
1886	Inspector B.	J. McLaughlin	1929	Blue Larkspur	M. Garner	1970	High Echelon	J.L. Rotz
1887	Hanover	J. McLaughlin	1930	Gallant Fox	E. Sande	1971	Pass Catcher	W. Blum
1888	Sir Dixon	J. McLaughlin	1931	Twenty Grand	C. Kurtsinger	1972	Riva Ridge	R. Turcotte
1889	Eric	W. Hayward	1932	Faireno	T. Malley	1973	Secretariat	R. Turcotte
1890	Burlington	S. Barnes	1933	Hurryoff	M. Garner	1974	Little Current	M. Rivera
1891	Foxford	E. Garrison	1934	Peace Chance	W.D. Wright	1975	Avatar	W. Shoemaker
1892	Patron	W. Hayward	1935	Omaha	W. Saunders	1976	Bold Forbes	A. Cordero
1893	Comanche	W. Simms	1936	Granville	J. Stout	1977	Seattle Slew	J. Cruguet
1894	Henry of Navarre	W. Simms	1937	War Admiral	C. Kurtsinger	1978	Affirmed	S. Cauthen
1895	Belmar	F. Taral	1938	Pasteurized	J. Stout	1979	Coastal	R. Hernandez
1896	Hastings	H. Griffin	1939	Johnstown	J. Stout	1980	Temperence Hill	E. Maple
1897	Scottish Chieftain	J. Scherrer	1940	Bimelech	F.A. Smith	1981	Summing	G. Martens
1898	Bowling Brook	F. Littlefield	1941	Whirlaway	E. Arcaro	1982	Conquistador Cielo	L. Pincay
1899	Jean Bereaud	R.R. Clawson	1942	Shut Out	E. Arcaro	1983	Caveat	L. Pincay
1900	Ildrim	N. Turner	1943	Count Fleet	J. Longden	1984	Swale	L. Pincay
1901	Commando	H. Spencer	1944	Bounding Home	G.L. Smith	1985	Creme Fraiche	E. Maple
1902	Masterman	J. Bullman	1945	Pavot	E. Arcaro	1986	Danzig Connection	C. McCarron
1903	Africander	J. Bullman	1946	Assault	W. Mehrtens	1987	Bet Twice	C. Perret
1904	Delhi	G. Odom	1947	Phalanx	R. Donoso	1988	Risen Star	E. Delahoussaye
1905	Tanya	E. Hildebrand	1948	Citation	E. Arcaro	1989	Easy Goer	P. Day
1906	Burgomaster	L. Lyne	1949	Capot	T. Atkinson	1990	Go and Go	M. Kinane
1907	Peter Pan	G. Mountain	1950	Middleground	W. Boland			

Eclipse Awards in 1989

Sponsored by the Thoroughbred Racing Assn., Daily Racing Form, and the National Turf Writers Assn.

Horse of the Year—Sunday Silence
Best 2-year-old colt—Rhythm
Best 2-year-old filly—Go For Wand
Best 3-year-old colt—Sunday Silence
Best 3-year-old filly—Open Mind
Best colt, horse, or gelding (4-year-olds & up)—Blushing John
Best filly or mare (4-year-olds & up)—Bayakoa
Best male turf horse—Steinlen

Best turf filly or mare—Brown Bess
Best sprinter—Safely Kept
Best steeplechase horse—Highland Bud
Best trainer—Charlie Whittingham
Best jockey—Kent Desormeaux
Best apprentice jockey—Mike Luzzi
Best breeder—North Ridge Farm

Annual Leading Money-Winning Horses

Year	Horse	Amount	Year	Horse	Amount	Year	Horse	Amount
1948	Citation	$709,470	1962	Never Bend	$402,969	1976	Forego	$491,701
1949	Ponder	321,825	1963	Candy Spots	604,481	1977	Seattle Slew	641,370
1950	Noor	346,940	1964	Gun Bow	580,100	1978	Affirmed	901,541
1951	Counterpoint	250,525	1965	Buckpasser	568,096	1979	Spectacular Bid	1,279,334
1952	Crafty Admiral	277,255	1966	Buckpasser	669,078	1980	Temperence Hill	1,130,452
1953	Native Dancer	513,425	1967	Damascus	817,941	1981	John Henry	1,148,800
1954	Determine	328,700	1968	Forward Pass	546,674	1982	Perrault	1,197,400
1955	Nashua	752,550	1969	Arts and Letters	555,604	1983	All Along	2,138,963
1956	Needles	440,850	1970	Personality	444,049	1984	Slew O'Gold	2,627,944
1957	Round Table	600,383	1971	Riva Ridge	503,263	1985	Spend a Buck	3,552,704
1958	Round Table	662,780	1972	Droll Roll	471,633	1986	Snow Chief	1,875,200
1959	Sword Dancer	537,004	1973	Secretariat	860,404	1987	Alysheba	2,511,156
1960	Bally Ache	455,045	1974	Chris Evert	551,063	1988	Alysheba	3,808,600
1961	Carry Back	565,349	1975	Foolish Pleasure	716,278	1989	Sunday Silence	4,578,454

Annual Leading Jockey—Money Won

Year	Jockey	Amount	Year	Jockey	Amount	Year	Jockey	Amount
1957	Bill Hartack	$3,060,501	1968	Braulio Baeza	$2,835,108	1979	Laffit Pincay Jr.	$8,193,535
1958	Willie Shoemaker	2,961,693	1969	Jorge Velasquez	2,542,315	1980	Chris McCarron	7,663,300
1959	Willie Shoemaker	2,843,133	1970	Laffit Pincay Jr.	2,626,526	1981	Chris McCarron	8,397,604
1960	Willie Shoemaker	2,123,961	1971	Laffit Pincay Jr.	3,784,377	1982	Angel Cordero Jr.	9,483,590
1961	Willie Shoemaker	2,690,819	1972	Laffit Pincay Jr.	3,225,827	1983	Angel Cordero Jr.	10,116,697
1962	Willie Shoemaker	2,916,844	1973	Laffit Pincay Jr.	4,093,492	1984	Chris McCarron	12,045,813
1963	Willie Shoemaker	2,526,925	1974	Laffit Pincay Jr.	4,251,060	1985	Laffit Pincay Jr.	13,353,299
1964	Willie Shoemaker	2,649,553	1975	Braulio Baeza	3,695,198	1986	Jose Santos	11,329,297
1965	Braulio Baeza	2,582,702	1976	Angel Cordero Jr.	4,709,500	1987	Jose Santos	12,375,433
1966	Braulio Baeza	2,951,022	1977	Steve Cauthen	6,151,750	1988	Jose Santos	14,877,298
1967	Braulio Baeza	3,088,888	1978	Darrel McHargue	6,029,885	1989	Jose Santos	13,838,389

Table Tennis in 1990
U.S. National Closed

Berkeley, Cal., Jan. 10-14, 1990

Men's Singles — Sean O'Neill.
Women's Singles — In Sook Bhushan.
Men's Doubles — Jim & Scott Butler.

Women's Doubles — In Sook Bhushan & Diana Gee.
Mixed Doubles — Brian Masters & In Sook Bhushan.

U.S. National Open

Baltimore, Md., June 12-18, 1990

Men's Singles — Jan-Ove Waldner, Sweden.
Women's Singles — Ding Yaping, China.
Men's Doubles — Ilija Lupulesku & Zoran Primorac, Yugoslavia.

Women's Doubles — Gao Jun & Liu Wei, China.
Mixed Doubles — Chen Zhibin & Gao Jun, China.
Men's Team — China.
Women's Team — China.

Professional Sports Directory

Baseball

Commissioner's Office
350 Park Ave.
New York, NY 10022

National League

National League Office
350 Park Ave.
New York, NY 10022

Atlanta Braves
PO Box 4064
Atlanta, GA 30302

Chicago Cubs
Wrigley Field
Chicago, IL 60613

Cincinnati Reds
100 Riverfront Stadium
Cincinnati, OH 45202

Houston Astros
Astrodome
Houston, TX 77001

Los Angeles Dodgers
Dodger Stadium
Los Angeles, CA 90012

Montreal Expos
PO Box 500, Station M
Montreal, Que. H1V 3P2

New York Mets
Shea Stadium
Flushing, NY 11368

Philadelphia Phillies
PO Box 7575
Philadelphia, PA 19101

Pittsburgh Pirates
Three Rivers Stadium
Pittsburgh, PA 15212

St. Louis Cardinals
Busch Stadium
St. Louis, MO 63102

San Diego Padres
PO Box 2000
San Diego, CA 92120

San Francisco Giants
Candlestick Park
San Francisco, CA 94124

American League

American League Office
350 Park Ave.
New York, NY 10022

Baltimore Orioles
Memorial Stadium
Baltimore, MD 21218

Boston Red Sox
24 Yawkey Way
Boston, MA 02215

California Angels
Anaheim Stadium
Anaheim, CA 92806

Chicago White Sox
324 W. 35th St.
Chicago, IL 60616

Cleveland Indians
Cleveland Stadium
Cleveland, OH 44114

Detroit Tigers
Tiger Stadium
Detroit, MI 48216

Kansas City Royals
P.O. Box 419969
Kansas City, MO 64141

Milwaukee Brewers
Milwaukee County Stadium
Milwaukee, WI 53214

Minnesota Twins
501 Chicago Ave. South
Minneapolis, MN 55415

New York Yankees
Yankee Stadium
Bronx, NY 10451

Oakland A's
Oakland Coliseum
Oakland, CA 94621

Seattle Mariners
P.O. Box 4100
Seattle, WA 98104

Texas Rangers
1250 Copeland Rd.
Arlington, TX 76004

Toronto Blue Jays
300 The Esplanade West
Toronto, Ont. M5V 3B3

National Football League

League Office
410 Park Avenue
New York, NY 10022

Atlanta Falcons
Suwanee Road
Suwanee, GA 30174

Buffalo Bills
1 Bills Drive
Orchard Park, NY 14127

Chicago Bears
250 N. Washington Rd.
Lake Forest, IL 60045

Cincinnati Bengals
200 Riverfront Stadium
Cincinnati, OH 45202

Cleveland Browns
Cleveland Stadium
Cleveland, OH 44114

Dallas Cowboys
One Cowboys Pkwy.
Irving, TX 75063

Denver Broncos
5700 Logan St.
Denver, CO 80216

Detroit Lions
1200 Featherstone Rd.
Pontiac, MI 48057

Green Bay Packers
1265 Lombardi Ave.
Green Bay, WI 54303

Houston Oilers
P.O. Box 1516
Houston, TX 77251

Indianapolis Colts
P.O. Box 53500
Indianapolis, IN 46253

Kansas City Chiefs
1 Arrowhead Drive
Kansas City, MO 64129

Los Angeles Raiders
332 Center St.
El Segundo, CA 90245

Los Angeles Rams
2327 W. Lincoln Ave.
Anaheim, CA 92801

Miami Dolphins
2269 NW 199 St.
Miami, FL 33056

Minnesota Vikings
9520 Viking Dr.
Eden Prairie, MN 55344

New England Patriots
Sullivan Stadium
Foxboro, MA 02035

New Orleans Saints
6928 Saints Dr.
Metairie, LA 70003

New York Giants
Giants Stadium
E. Rutherford, NJ 07073

New York Jets
598 Madison Ave.
New York, NY 10022

Philadelphia Eagles
Veterans Stadium
Philadelphia, PA 19148

Phoenix Cardinals
51 W 3d St.
Tempe, AZ 85281

Pittsburgh Steelers
Three Rivers Stadium
Pittsburgh, PA 15212

San Diego Chargers
P.O. Box 20666
San Diego, CA 92120

San Francisco 49ers
4949 Centennial Blvd.
Santa Clara, CA 95054

Seattle Seahawks
11220 NE 53d St.
Kirkland, WA 98033

Tampa Bay Buccaneers
1 Buccaneer Place
Tampa, FL 33607

Washington Redskins
PO Box 17247
Dulles Intl. Airport
Washington, DC 20041

National Basketball Association

League Office
645 5th Ave.
New York, NY 10022

Atlanta Hawks
1 CNN Center
Atlanta, GA 30303

Boston Celtics
Boston Garden
Boston, MA 02114

Charlotte Hornets
2 First Union Center
Charlotte, NC 28282

Chicago Bulls
980 North Michigan Ave.
Chicago, IL 60611

Cleveland Cavaliers
2923 Statesboro Rd.
Richfield, OH 44286

Dallas Mavericks
777 Sports St.
Dallas, TX 75207

Denver Nuggets
1635 Clay St.
Denver, CO 80204

Detroit Pistons
1 Championship Dr.
Auburn Hills, MI 48057

Golden State Warriors
Oakland Coliseum
Oakland, CA 94621

Houston Rockets
The Summit
Houston, TX 77046

Indiana Pacers
300 E. Market St.
Indianapolis, IN 46204

Los Angeles Clippers
3939 S. Figueroa
Los Angeles, CA 90037

Los Angeles Lakers
PO Box 10
Inglewood, CA 90306

Miami Heat
Miami Arena
Miami, FL 33136

Milwaukee Bucks
1001 N. 4th St.
Milwaukee, WI 53203

Minnesota Timberwolves
730 Hennepin Ave.
Minneapolis, MN 55403

New Jersey Nets
Meadowlands Arena
E. Rutherford, NJ 07073

New York Knickerbockers
4 Pennsylvania Plaza
New York, NY 10001

Orlando Magic
1 Magic Place
Orlando, FL 32801

Philadelphia 76ers
PO Box 25040
Philadelphia, PA 19147

Phoenix Suns
2910 N. Central Ave.
Phoenix, AZ 85012

Portland Trail Blazers
700 NE Multnomah St.
Portland, OR 97232

Sacramento Kings
One Sports Pkwy.
Sacramento, CA 95834

San Antonio Spurs
600 E. Market St.
San Antonio, TX 78205

Seattle SuperSonics
190 Queen Ann Ave. N.
Seattle, WA 98109

Utah Jazz
5 Triad Center
Salt Lake City, UT 84180

Washington Bullets
1 Harry S. Truman Dr.
Landover, MD 20785

National Hockey League

League Headquarters
Sun Life Bldg.
Montreal, Quebec H3B 2W2

Boston Bruins
150 Causeway St.
Boston, MA 02114

Buffalo Sabres
Memorial Auditorium
Buffalo, NY 14202

Calgary Flames
P.O. Box 1540
Calgary, Alta. T2P 3B9

Chicago Black Hawks
1800 W. Madison St.
Chicago, IL 60612

Detroit Red Wings
600 Civic Center Drive
Detroit, MI 48226

Edmonton Oilers
Northlands Coliseum
Edmonton, Alta. T5B 4M9

Hartford Whalers
One Civic Center Plaza
Hartford, CT 06103

Los Angeles Kings
39 W. Manchester Blvd.
Inglewood, CA 90306

Minnesota North Stars
7901 Cedar Ave. S.
Bloomington, MN 55420

Montreal Canadiens
2313 St. Catherine St., West
Montreal, Quebec H3H 1N2

New Jersey Devils
Meadowlands Arena
E. Rutherford, NJ 07073

New York Islanders
Nassau Coliseum
Uniondale, NY 11553

New York Rangers
4 Pennsylvania Plaza
New York, NY 10001

Philadelphia Flyers
Pattison Place
Philadelphia, PA 19148

Pittsburgh Penguins
Civic Arena
Pittsburgh, PA 15219

Quebec Nordiques
2205 Ave. du Colisee
Quebec, Que. G1L 4W7

St. Louis Blues
5700 Oakland Ave.
St. Louis, MO 63110

Toronto Maple Leafs
60 Carlton St.
Toronto, Ont. M5B 1L1

Vancouver Canucks
100 North Renfrew St.
Vancouver, B.C. V5K 3N7

Washington Capitals
Capital Centre
Landover, MD 20785

Winnipeg Jets
15-1430 Maroons Road
Winnipeg, Man. R3G 0L5

COLLEGE FOOTBALL

Annual Results of Major Bowl Games

(Note: Dates indicate the year that the game was played.)

Rose Bowl, Pasadena

1902 Michigan 49, Stanford 0
1916 Wash. State 14, Brown 0
1917 Oregon 14, Pennsylvania 0
1918-19   Service teams
1920 Harvard 7, Oregon 6
1921 California 28, Ohio State 0
1922 Wash. & Jeff. 0, California 0
1923 So. California 14, Penn State 3
1924 Navy 14, Washington 14
1925 Notre Dame 27, Stanford 10
1926 Alabama 20, Washington 19
1927 Alabama 7, Stanford 7
1928 Stanford 7, Pittsburgh 6
1929 Georgia Tech 8, California 7
1930 So. California 47, Pittsburgh 14
1931 Alabama 24, Wash. State 0
1932 So. California 21, Tulane 12
1933 So. California 35, Pittsburgh 0
1934 Columbia 7, Stanford 0
1935 Alabama 29, Stanford 13
1936 Stanford 7, So. Methodist 0
1937 Pittsburgh 21, Washington 0
1938 California 13, Alabama 0
1939 So. California 7, Duke 3
1940 So. California 14, Tennessee 0
1941 Stanford 21, Nebraska 13

1942 Oregon St. 20, Duke 16
    (at Durham)
1943 Georgia 9, UCLA 0
1944 So. California 29, Washington 0
1945 So. California 25, Tennessee 0
1946 Alabama 34, So. California 14
1947 Illinois 45, UCLA 14
1948 Michigan 49, So. California 0
1949 Northwestern 20, California 14
1950 Ohio State 17, California 14
1951 Michigan 14, California 6
1952 Illinois 40, Stanford 7
1953 So. California 7, Wisconsin 0
1954 Mich. State 28, UCLA 20
1955 Ohio State 20, So. California 7
1956 Mich. State 17, UCLA 14
1957 Iowa 35, Oregon St. 19
1958 Ohio State 10, Oregon 7
1959 Iowa 38, California 12
1960 Washington 44, Wisconsin 8
1961 Washington 17, Minnesota 7
1962 Minnesota 21, UCLA 3
1963 So. California 42, Wisconsin 37
1964 Illinois 17, Washington 7
1965 Michigan 34, Oregon St. 7

1966 UCLA 14, Mich. State 12
1967 Purdue 14, So. California 13
1968 Southern Cal. 14, Indiana 3
1969 Ohio State 27, Southern Cal 16
1970 Southern Cal 10, Michigan 3
1971 Stanford 27, Ohio State 17
1972 Stanford 13, Michigan 12
1973 So. California 42, Ohio State 17
1974 Ohio State 42, So. California 21
1975 So. California 18, Ohio State 17
1976 UCLA 23, Ohio State 10
1977 So. California 14, Michigan 6
1978 Washington 27, Michigan 20
1979 So. California 17, Michigan 10
1980 So. California 17, Ohio State 16
1981 Michigan 23, Washington 6
1982 Washington 28, Iowa 0
1983 UCLA 24, Michigan 14
1984 UCLA 45, Illinois 9
1985 So. California 20, Ohio State 17
1986 UCLA 45, Iowa 28
1987 Arizona St. 22, Michigan 15
1988 Mich. State 20, Southern Cal. 17
1989 Mich State 22, Southern Cal. 14
1990 Southern Cal. 17, Michigan 10

Orange Bowl, Miami

1935 Bucknell 26, Miami (Fla.) 0
1936 Catholic U. 20, Mississippi 19
1937 Duquesne 13, Miss. State 12
1938 Auburn 6, Mich. State 0
1939 Tennessee 17, Oklahoma 0
1940 Georgia Tech 21, Missouri 7
1941 Miss. State 14, Georgetown 7
1942 Georgia 40, TCU 26
1943 Alabama 37, Boston Col. 21
1944 LSU 19, Texas A&M 14
1945 Tulsa 26, Georgia Tech 12
1946 Miami (Fla.) 13, Holy Cross 6
1947 Rice 8, Tennessee 0
1948 Georgia Tech 20, Kansas 14
1949 Texas 41, Georgia 28
1950 Santa Clara 21, Kentucky 13
1951 Clemson 15, Miami (Fla.) 14
1952 Georgia Tech 17, Baylor 14
1953 Alabama 61, Syracuse 6

1954 Oklahoma 7, Maryland 0
1955 Duke 34, Nebraska 7
1956 Oklahoma 20, Maryland 6
1957 Colorado 27, Clemson 21
1958 Oklahoma 48, Duke 21
1959 Oklahoma 21, Syracuse 6
1960 Georgia 14, Missouri 0
1961 Missouri 21, Navy 14
1962 LSU 25, Colorado 7
1963 Alabama 17, Oklahoma 0
1964 Nebraska 13, Auburn 7
1965 Texas 21, Alabama 17
1966 Alabama 39, Nebraska 28
1967 Florida 27, Georgia Tech 12
1968 Oklahoma 26, Tennessee 24
1969 Penn State 15, Kansas 14
1970 Penn State 10, Missouri 3
1971 Nebraska 17, Louisiana St. 12
1972 Nebraska 38, Alabama 6

1973 Nebraska 40, Notre Dame 6
1974 Penn State 16, Louisiana St. 9
1975 Notre Dame 13, Alabama 11
1976 Oklahoma 14, Michigan 6
1977 Ohio State 27, Colorado 10
1978 Arkansas 31, Oklahoma 6
1979 Oklahoma 31, Nebraska 24
1980 Oklahoma 24, Florida St. 7
1981 Oklahoma 18, Florida St. 17
1982 Clemson 22, Nebraska 15
1983 Nebraska 21, Louisiana St. 20
1984 Miami (Fla.) 31, Nebraska 30
1985 Washington 28, Oklahoma 17
1986 Oklahoma 25, Penn State 10
1987 Oklahoma 42, Arkansas 8
1988 Miami (Fla.) 20, Oklahoma 14
1989 Miami (Fla.) 23, Nebraska 3
1990 Notre Dame 21, Colorado 6

Sugar Bowl, New Orleans

1935 Tulane 20, Temple 14
1936 TCU 3, LSU 2
1937 Santa Clara 21, LSU 14
1938 Santa Clara 6, LSU 0
1939 TCU 15, Carnegie Tech 7
1940 Texas A&M 14, Tulane 13
1941 Boston Col. 19, Tennessee 13
1942 Fordham 2, Missouri 0
1943 Tennessee 14, Tulsa 7
1944 Georgia Tech 20, Tulsa 18
1945 Duke 29, Alabama 26
1946 Oklahoma A&M 33, St. Mary's 13
1947 Georgia 20, No. Carolina 10
1948 Texas 27, Alabama 7
1949 Oklahoma 14, No. Carolina 6
1950 Oklahoma 35, LSU 0
1951 Kentucky 13, Oklahoma 7
1952 Maryland 28, Tennessee 13
1953 Georgia Tech. 24, Mississippi 7

1954 Georgia Tech 42, West Virginia 19
1955 Navy 21, Mississippi 0
1956 Georgia Tech 7, Pittsburgh 0
1957 Baylor 13, Tennessee 7
1958 Mississippi 39, Texas 7
1959 LSU 7, Clemson 0
1960 Mississippi 21, LSU 0
1961 Mississippi 14, Rice 6
1962 Alabama 10, Arkansas 3
1963 Mississippi 17, Arkansas 13
1964 Alabama 12, Mississippi 7
1965 LSU 13, Syracuse 10
1966 Missouri 20, Florida 18
1967 Alabama 34, Nebraska 7
1968 LSU 20, Wyoming 13
1969 Arkansas 16, Georgia 2
1970 Mississippi 27, Arkansas 22
1971 Tennessee 34, Air Force 13
1972 Oklahoma 40, Auburn 22

*1972 (Dec.) Okla. 14, Penn State 0
1973 Notre Dame 24, Alabama 23
1974 Nebraska 13, Florida 10
1975 Alabama 13, Penn State 6
1977 (Jan.) Pittsburgh 27, Georgia 3
1978 Alabama 35, Ohio State 6
1979 Alabama 14, Penn State 7
1980 Alabama 24, Arkansas 9
1981 Georgia 17, Notre Dame 10
1982 Pittsburgh 24, Georgia 20
1983 Penn State 27, Georgia 23
1984 Auburn 9, Michigan 7
1985 Nebraska 28, Louisiana St. 10
1986 Tennessee 35, Miami (Fla.) 7
1987 Nebraska 30, Louisiana St. 15
1988 Syracuse 16, Auburn 16
1989 Florida St. 13, Auburn 7
1990 Miami 33, Alabama 25
*Penn St. awarded game by forfeit

Fiesta Bowl, Tempe

1971 Arizona St. 45, Florida St. 38
1972 Arizona St. 49, Missouri 35
1973 Arizona St. 28, Pittsburgh 7
1974 Okla. St. 16, Brigham Young 6
1975 Arizona St. 17, Nebraska 14
1976 Oklahoma 41, Wyoming 7
1977 Penn St. 42, Arizona St. 30

1978 UCLA 10, Arkansas 10
1979 Pittsburgh 16, Arizona 10
1980 Penn St. 31, Ohio St. 19
1982 (Jan.) Penn St. 26, USC 10
1983 Arizona St. 32, Oklahoma 21
1984 Ohio State 28, Pittsburgh 23

1985 UCLA 39, Miami 37
1986 Michigan 27, Nebraska 23
1987 Penn St. 14, Miami (Fla.) 10
1988 Florida St. 31, Nebraska 28
1989 Notre Dame 34, W. Virginia 21
1990 Florida St. 41, Nebraska 17

Hall of Fame Bowl, Tampa

1986 (Dec.) Boston Coll. 27, Georgia 24
1988 (Jan.) Michigan 28, Alabama 24

1989 Syracuse 23, LSU 10

1990 Auburn 31, Ohio St. 14

Cotton Bowl, Dallas

1937 TCU 16, Marquette 6
1938 Rice 28, Colorado 14
1939 St. Mary's 20, Texas Tech 13
1940 Clemson 6, Boston Col. 3
1941 Texas A&M 13, Fordham 12
1942 Alabama 29, Texas A&M 21
1943 Texas 14, Georgia Tech 7
1944 Randolph Field 7, Texas 7
1945 Oklahoma A&M 34, TCU 0
1946 Texas 40, Missouri 27
1947 Arkansas 0, LSU 0
1948 So. Methodist 13, Penn State 13
1949 So. Methodist 21, Oregon 13
1950 Rice 27, No. Carolina 13
1951 Tennessee 20, Texas 14
1952 Kentucky 20, TCU 7
1953 Texas 16, Tennessee 0
1954 Rice 28, Alabama 6

1955 Georgia Tech 14, Arkansas 6
1956 Mississippi 14, TCU 13
1957 TCU 28, Syracuse 27
1958 Navy 20, Rice 7
1959 TCU 0, Air Force 0
1960 Syracuse 23, Texas 14
1961 Duke 7, Arkansas 6
1962 Texas 12, Mississippi 7
1963 LSU 13, Texas 0
1964 Texas 28, Navy 6
1965 Arkansas 10, Nebraska 7
1966 LSU 14, Arkansas 7
1967 Georgia 24, So. Methodist 9
1968 Texas A&M 20, Alabama 16
1969 Texas 36, Tennessee 13
1970 Texas 21, Notre Dame 17
1971 Notre Dame 24, Texas 11
1972 Penn State 30, Texas 6

1973 Texas 17, Alabama 13
1974 Nebraska 19, Texas 3
1975 Penn State 41, Baylor 20
1976 Arkansas 31, Georgia 10
1977 Houston 30, Maryland 21
1978 Notre Dame 38, Texas 10
1979 Notre Dame 35, Houston 34
1980 Houston 17, Nebraska 14
1981 Alabama 30, Baylor 2
1982 Texas 14, Alabama 12
1983 SMU 7, Pittsburgh 3
1984 Georgia 10, Texas 9
1985 Boston Coll. 45, Houston 28
1986 Texas A&M 36, Auburn 16
1987 Ohio St. 28, Texas A&M 12
1988 Texas A&M 35, Notre Dame 10
1989 UCLA 17, Arkansas 3
1990 Tennessee 31, Arkansas 27

John Hancock Bowl, El Paso (Sun Bowl until 1989)

1936 Hardin Simmons 14, New Mex. St. 14
1937 Hardin-Simmons 34, Texas Mines 6
1938 West Virginia 7, Texas Tech 6
1939 Utah 26, New Mexico 0
1940 Catholic U. 0, Arizona St. 0
1941 Western Reserve 26, Arizona St. 13
1942 Tulsa 6, Texas Tech 0
1943 2d Air Force 13, Hardin-Simmons 7
1944 Southwestern (Tex.) 7, New Mexico 0
1945 Southwestern (Tex.) 35, U. of Mex. 0
1946 New Mexico 34, Denver 24
1947 Cincinnati 18, Virginia Tech 6
1948 Miami (O.) 13, Texas Tech 12
1949 West Virginia 21, Texas Mines 12
1950 Texas Western 33, Georgetown 20
1951 West Texas St. 14, Cincinnati 13
1952 Texas Tech 25, Col. Pacific 14

1953 Col. Pacific 26, Miss. Southern 7
1954 Texas Western 37, Miss. Southern 14
1955 Texas Western 47, Florida St. 20
1956 Wyoming 21, Texas Tech 14
1957 Geo. Washington 13, Tex. Western 0
1958 Louisville 34, Drake 20
1959 Wyoming 14, Hardin-Simmons 6
1960 New Mexico St. 28, No. Texas St. 8
1961 New Mexico St. 20, Utah State 13
1962 Villanova 17, Wichita 9
1963 West Texas St. 15, Ohio U. 14
1964 Oregon 21, So. Methodist 14
1965 Georgia 7, Texas Tech 0
1966 Texas Western 13, TCU 12
1967 Wyoming 28, Florida St. 20
1968 UTex El Paso 14, Mississippi 7
1969 Auburn 34, Arizona 10
1969 (Dec.) Nebraska 45, Georgia 6

1970 Georgia Tech. 17, Texas Tech. 9
1971 LSU 33, Iowa State 15
1972 North Carolina 32, Texas Tech 28
1973 Missouri 34, Auburn 17
1974 Mississippi St. 26, No. Carolina 24
1975 Pittsburgh 33, Kansas 19
1977 (Jan.) Texas A&M 37, Florida 14
1977 (Dec.) Stanford 24, Louisiana St. 14
1978 Texas 42, Maryland 0
1979 Washington 14, Texas 7
1980 Nebraska 31, Mississippi St. 17
1981 Oklahoma 40, Houston 14
1982 North Carolina 26, Texas 10
1983 Alabama 28, SMU 7
1984 Maryland 28, Tennessee 27
1985 Georgia 13, Arizona 13
1986 Alabama 28, Washington 6
1987 Oklahoma St. 35, West Virginia 33
1988 Alabama 29, Army 28
1989 Pittsburgh 31, Texas A&M 28

Gator Bowl, Jacksonville

1946 Wake Forest 26, So. Carolina 14
1947 Oklahoma 34, N.C. State 13
1948 Maryland 20, Georgia 20
1949 Clemson 24, Missouri 23
1950 Maryland 20, Missouri 7
1951 Wyoming 20, Wash. & Lee 7
1952 Miami (Fla.) 14, Clemson 0
1953 Florida 14, Tulsa 13
1954 Texas Tech 35, Auburn 13
1955 Auburn 33, Baylor 13
1956 Vanderbilt 25, Auburn 13
1957 Georgia Tech 21, Pittsburgh 14
1958 Tennessee 3, Texas A&M 0
1959 Mississippi 7, Florida 3
1960 Arkansas 14, Georgia Tech 7

1961 Florida 13, Baylor 12
1962 Penn State 30, Georgia Tech 15
1963 Florida 17, Penn State 7
1964 No. Carolina 35, Air Force 0
1965 Florida St. 36, Oklahoma 19
1966 Georgia Tech 31, Texas Tech 21
1967 Tennessee 18, Syracuse 12
1968 Penn State 17, Florida St. 17
1969 Missouri 35, Alabama 10
1969 (Dec.) Florida 14, Tenn. 13
1971 (Jan.) Auburn 35, Mississippi 28
1972 Georgia 7, N. Carolina 3
1973 Auburn 24, Colorado 3
1973 (Dec.) Tex. Tech. 28, Tenn. 19
1974 Auburn 27, Texas 3

1975 Maryland 13, Florida 0
1976 Notre Dame 20, Penn State 9
1977 Pittsburgh 34, Clemson 3
1978 Clemson 17, Ohio State 15
1979 No. Carolina 17, Michigan 15
1980 Pittsburgh 37, So. Carolina 9
1981 No. Carolina 31, Arkansas 27
1982 Florida St. 31, West Va. 12
1983 Florida 14, Iowa 6
1984 Oklahoma St. 21, So. Carolina 14
1985 Florida St. 34, Oklahoma St. 23
1986 Clemson 27, Stanford 21
1987 LSU 30, So. Carolina 13
1989 (Jan.) Georgia 34, Michigan St. 27
1989 (Dec.) Clemson 27, W. Va. 7

Liberty Bowl, Memphis

1970 Tulane 17, Colorado 3
1971 Tennessee 14, Arkansas 13
1972 Georgia Tech 31, Iowa State 30
1973 No. Carolina St. 31, Kansas 18
1974 Tennessee 7, Maryland 3
1975 USC 20, Texas A&M 0
1976 Alabama 36, UCLA 6
1977 Nebraska 21, N. Carolina 17
1978 Missouri 20, Louisiana St. 15
1979 Penn St. 9, Tulane 6

1980 Purdue 28, Missouri 25
1981 Ohio State 31, Navy 28
1982 Alabama 21, Illinois 15
1983 Notre Dame 19, Boston Coll. 18
1984 Auburn 21, Arkansas 15
1985 Baylor 21, Louisiana St. 7
1986 Tennessee 21, Minnesota 14
1987 Georgia 20, Arkansas 17
1988 Indiana 34, S. Carolina 10
1989 Mississippi 42, Air Force 29

Freedom Bowl, Anaheim

1984 Iowa 55, Texas 17
1985 Washington 20, Colorado 17

1986 UCLA 31, Brigham Young 10
1987 Arizona St. 33, Air Force 28

1988 Brigham Young 20, Colorado 17
1989 Washington 34, Florida 7

Copper Bowl, Tucson

1989 Arizona 17, N.C. St. 10

Independence Bowl, Shreveport

1976 McNeese St. 20, Tulsa 16
1977 Louisiana 24, Louisville 14
1978 E. Carolina 35, La. Tech 13
1979 Syracuse 31, McNeese St. 7
1980 So. Miss. 16, McNeese St. 14

1981 Texas A&M 33, Oklahoma St. 16
1982 Wisconsin 14, Kansas St. 3
1983 Air Force 9, Mississippi 3
1984 Air Force 23, Virginia Tech 7
1985 Minnesota 20, Clemson 13

1986 Mississippi 20, Texas Tech 17
1987 Washington 24, Tulane 12
1988 S. Mississippi 38, UTEP 18
1989 Oregon 27, Tulsa 24

1947 Catawba 31, Maryville 6
1948 Catawba 7, Marshall 0
1949 Murray State 21, Sul Ross St. 21
1950 St. Vincent 7, Emory & Henry 6
1951 Morris Harvey 35, Emory & Henry 14
1952 Stetson 35, Arkansas St. 20
1953 East Texas St. 33, Tenn. Tech 0
1954 East Texas St. 7, Arkansas St. 7
1955 Neb.-Omaha 7, Eastern Kentucky 6
1956 Juniata 6, Missouri Valley 6
1957 West Texas St. 20, So. Miss. 13
1958 East Texas St. 10, So. Miss. 9
1958 (Dec.) East Texas St. 26, Missouri Valley 7

Citrus Bowl, Orlando

1960 (Jan.) Middle Tenn. 21, Presbyterian 12
1960 (Dec.) Citadel 27, Tenn. Tech 0
1961 Lamar 21, Middle Tennessee 14
1962 Houston 49, Miami (O.) 21
1963 Western Ky. 27, Coast Guard 0
1964 E. Carolina 14, Massachusetts 13
1965 East Carolina 31, Maine 0
1966 Morgan State 14, West Chester 6
1967 Tenn.-Martin 25, West Chester 8
1968 Richmond 49, Ohio U. 42
1969 Toledo 56, Davidson 33
1970 Toledo 40, William & Mary 12
1971 Toledo 28, Richmond 3
1972 Tampa 21, Kent State 18
1973 Miami (O.) 16, Florida 7

1974 Miami (O.) 21, Georgia 10
1975 Miami (O.) 20, South Carolina 7
1976 Okla. St. 49, Brigham Young 21
1977 Florida St. 40, Texas Tech 17
1978 N.C. State 30, Pittsburgh 17
1979 LSU 34, Wake Forest 10
1980 Florida 35, Maryland 20
1981 Missouri 19, Southern Miss. 17
1982 Auburn 33, Boston College 26
1983 Tennessee 30, Maryland 23
1984 Georgia 17, Florida St. 17
1985 Ohio St. 10, Brigham Young 7
1987 (Jan.) Auburn 16, USC 7
1988 Clemson 35, Penn St. 10
1989 Clemson 13, Oklahoma 6
1990 Illinois 31, Virginia 21

1968 LSU 31, Florida St. 27
1969 West Virginia 14, S. Carolina 3
1970 Arizona St. 48, N. Carolina 26
1971 Mississippi 41, Georgia Tech. 18
1972 N. Carolina St. 49, W. Va. 13
1973 Georgia 17, Maryland 16
1974 Vanderbilt 6, Texas Tech. 6
1975 W. Virginia 13, No. Carolina St. 10

Peach Bowl, Atlanta

1976 Kentucky 21, North Carolina 0
1977 N. Carolina 24, Iowa St. 14
1978 Purdue 41, Georgia Tech. 21
1979 Baylor 24, Clemson 18
1981 (Jan.) Miami 20, Virginia Tech. 10
1981 (Dec.) West Virginia 26, Florida 6
1982 Iowa 28, Tennessee 22

1983 Florida St. 28, North Carolina 3
1984 Virginia 27, Purdue 22
1985 Army 31, Illinois 29
1986 Va. Tech 25, N.C. State 24
1988 (Jan.) Tennessee 28, Indiana 22
1988 (Dec.) N.C. State 28, Iowa 23
1989 Syracuse 19, Georgia 18

1977 Maryland 17, Minnesota 7
1978 Texas A&M 28, Iowa St. 12
1979 Missouri 24, So. Carolina 14
1980 Arkansas 34, Tulane 15
1981 Mississippi St. 10, Kansas 0

All-American Bowl, Birmingham

1982 Air Force 36, Vanderbilt 28
1983 W. Virginia 20, Kentucky 16
1984 Kentucky 20, Wisconsin 19
1985 Georgia Tech 17, Michigan St. 14

1986 Florida St. 27, Indiana 13
1987 Virginia 22, Brigham Young 16
1988 Florida 14, Illinois 10
1989 Texas Tech 49, Duke 21

1978 Navy 23, Brigham Young 16
1979 Indiana 38, Brigham Young 37
1980 Brigham Young 46, SMU 45
1981 Brigham Young 38, Wash. St. 36

Holiday Bowl, San Diego

1982 Ohio State 47, Brigham Young 17
1983 Brigham Young 21, Missouri 17
1984 Brigham Young 24, Michigan 17
1985 Arkansas 18, Arizona St. 17

1986 Iowa 39, San Diego St. 38
1987 Iowa 20, Wyoming 19
1988 Oklahoma St. 62, Wyoming 14
1989 Penn St. 50, Brigham Young 39

1982 Washington 21, Maryland 20
1983 Penn State 13, Washington 10
1984 SMU 27, Notre Dame 20

Aloha Bowl, Honolulu

1985 Alabama 24, USC 3
1986 Arizona 30, North Carolina 21
1987 UCLA 20, Florida 16

1988 Washington St. 24, Houston 22
1989 Michigan St. 33, Hawaii 13

1981 Toledo 27, San Jose St. 25
1982 Fresno St. 29, Bowling Green 28
1983 N. Illinois 20, Cal. State Fullerton 13

California Bowl, Fresno

1984 Nevada-Las Vegas 30, Toledo 13
1985 Fresno St. 51, Bowling Green 7
1986 San Jose St. 37, Miami (Oh.) 7

1987 E. Michigan 30, San Jose St. 27
1988 Fresno St. 35, W. Michigan 30
1989 Fresno St. 27, Ball St. 6

College Division I Football Teams

Team	Nickname	Team colors	Conference	Coach	1989 record (W-L-T)
Air Force	Falcons	Blue & silver	Western Athletic	Fisher De Berry	8-4-1
Akron	Zips	Blue & Gold	Independent	Gerry Faust	6-4-1
Alabama	Crimson Tide	Crimson & white	Southeastern	Gene Stallings	10-2-0
Alabama State	Hornets	Black & gold	Southwestern	Houston Markham	5-5-1
Alcorn State	Braves	Purple & gold	Southwestern	Theo Danzy	7-3-0
Appalachian State	Mountaineers	Black & gold	Southern	Jerry Moore	9-3-0
Arizona	Wildcats	Red & blue	Pacific Ten	Dick Tomey	8-4-0
Arizona State	Sun Devils	Maroon & gold	Pacific Ten	Larry Marmie	6-4-1
Arkansas	Razorbacks	Cardinal & white	Southwest	Jack Crowe	10-2-0
Arkansas State	Indians	Scarlet & black	Independent	Al Kincaid	5-6-0
Army	Cadets	Black, gold, gray	Independent	Jim Young	6-5-0
Auburn	Tigers	Orange & blue	Southeastern	Pat Dye	10-2-0
Austin Peay State	Governors	Red & white	Ohio Valley	John Palermo	0-11-0
Ball State	Cardinals	Cardinal & white	Mid-American	Paul Schudel	7-3-2
Baylor	Bears	Green & gold	Southwest	Grant Teaff	5-6-0
Bethune-Cookman	Wildcats	Maroon & gold	Mid-Eastern	Larry Little	4-6-0
Boise State	Broncos	Orange & Blue	Big Sky	Skip Hall	6-5-0
Boston College	Eagles	Maroon & gold	Independent	Jack Bicknell	2-9-0
Boston Univ.	Terriers	Scarlet & white	Yankee	Dan Allen	4-7-0
Bowling Green	Falcons	Orange & brown	Mid-American	Moe Ankney	5-6-0
Brigham Young	Cougars	Royal blue & white	Western Athletic	LaVell Edwards	10-3-0
Brown	Bears	Brown, cardinal, white	Ivy	Mickey Kwiatkowski	2-8-0
Bucknell	Bisons	Orange & blue	Patriot	Lou Maranzana	5-5-0
California	Golden Bears	Blue & gold	Pacific Ten	Bruce Snyder	4-7-0
Central Florida	Knights	Black & gold	Independent	Gene McDowell	7-3-0
Central Michigan	Chippewas	Maroon & gold	Mid-American	Herb Deromedi	5-5-1
Cincinnati	Bearcats	Red & black	Independent	Tim Murphy	1-9-1

Team	Nickname	Team colors	Conference	Coach	1989 record (W-L-T)
Citadel	Bulldogs	Blue & white	Southern	Charles Taaffe	5-5-1
Clemson	Tigers	Purple & orange	Atlantic Coast	Ken Hatfield	10-2-0
Colgate	Red Raiders	Maroon	Patriot	Mike Foley	4-7-0
Colorado State	Rams	Green & gold	Western Athletic	Earle Bruce	5-5-1
Colorado	Buffaloes	Silver, gold & blue	Big Eight	Bill McCartney	11-1-0
Columbia	Lions	Blue & white	Ivy	Ray Tellier	1-9-0
Connecticut	Huskies	Blue & white	Yankee	Tom Jackson	8-3-0
Cornell	Big Red	Carnelian & white	Ivy	Jim Hofher	4-6-0
Dartmouth	Big Green	Dartmouth green & white	Ivy	Buddy Teevens	5-5-0
Davidson	Wildcats	Red & black	Independent	Dave Fagg	2-8-0
Delaware	Fightin' Blue Hens	Blue & gold	Yankee	Harold Raymond	7-4-0
Delaware State	Hornets	Red & blue	Mid-Eastern	William Collick	7-4-0
Duke	Blue Devils	Royal blue & white	Atlantic Coast	Barry Wilson	8-4-0
East Carolina	Pirates	Purple & gold	Independent	Bill Lewis	5-5-1
East Tennessee St.	Buccaneers	Blue & gold	Southern	Don Riley	4-7-0
Eastern Illinois	Panthers	Blue & Gray	Gateway	Bob Spoo	9-4-0
Eastern Kentucky	Colonels	Maroon & white	Ohio Valley	Roy Kidd	9-3-0
Eastern Michigan	Hurons	Green & white	Mid-American	Jim Harkema	7-3-1
Eastern Washington	Eagles	Red & white	Big Sky	Dick Zornes	4-6-0
Florida	Gators	Orange & blue	Southeastern	Steve Spurrier	7-5-0
Florida A&M	Rattlers	Orange & green	Mid-Eastern	Ken Riley	6-5-0
Florida State	Seminoles	Garnet & gold	Independent	Bobby Bowden	10-2-0
Fordham	Rams	Maroon & white	Patriot	Larry Glueck	2-6-0
Fresno State	Bulldogs	Cardinal & blue	Big West	Jim Sweeney	11-1-0
Fullerton, Cal State	Titans	Blue, orange, white	Big West	Gene Murphy	6-4-1
Furman	Paladins	Purple & white	Southern	Jimmy Satterfield	12-2-0
Georgia	Bulldogs	Red & black	Southeastern	Ray Goff	6-6-0
Georgia Southern	Eagles	Blue & white	Independent	Tom Stowers	15-0-0
Georgia Tech	Yellow Jackets	Old gold & white	Atlantic Coast	Bobby Ross	7-4-0
Grambling	Tigers	Black & gold	Southwestern	Eddie Robinson	9-3-0
Harvard	Crimson	Crimson	Ivy	Joe Restic	5-5-0
Hawaii	Rainbow Warriors	Green & white	Western Athletic	Bob Wagner	9-3-1
Holy Cross	Crusaders	Royal purple	Patriot	Mike Duffner	10-1-0
Houston	Cougars	Scarlet & white	Southwest	John Jenkins	9-2-0
Howard	Bison	Blue & white	Mid-Eastern	Steve Wilson	8-3-0
Idaho	Vandals	Silver & gold	Big Sky	John L. Smith	9-3-0
Idaho State	Bengals	Orange & black	Big Sky	Garth Hall	3-7-0
Illinois	Fighting Illini	Orange & blue	Big Ten	John Mackovic	10-2-0
Illinois State	Redbirds	Red & white	Gateway	Jim Heacock	5-6-0
Indiana	Fightin' Hoosiers	Cream & crimson	Big Ten	Bill Mallory	5-6-0
Indiana State	Sycamores	Blue & white	Gateway	Dennis Raetz	4-7-0
Iowa	Hawkeyes	Old gold & black	Big Ten	Hayden Fry	5-6-0
Iowa State	Cyclones	Cardinal & gold	Big Eight	Jim Walden	6-5-0
Jackson State	Tigers	Blue & white	Southwestern	W.C. Gorden	8-4-0
James Madison	Dukes	Purple & gold	Independent	Joe Purzycki	5-4-1
Kansas	Jayhawks	Crimson & blue	Big Eight	Glen Mason	4-7-0
Kansas State	Wildcats	Purple & white	Big Eight	Bill Snyder	1-10-0
Kent State	Golden Flashes	Blue & gold	Mid-American	Dick Crum	0-11-0
Kentucky	Wildcats	Blue & white	Southeastern	Bill Curry	6-5-0
Lafayette	Leopards	Maroon & white	Patriot	Bill Russo	5-5-0
Lehigh	Engineers	Brown & white	Patriot	Hank Small	5-6-0
Liberty	Flames	Red, White, Blue	Independent	Sam Rutigliano	7-3-0
Long Beach State	Forty-Niners	Brown & gold	Big West	George Allen	4-8-0
Louisiana State	Fighting Tigers	Purple & gold	Southeastern	Mike Archer	4-7-0
Louisiana Tech	Bulldogs	Red & blue	Independent	Joe Raymond Peace	5-4-1
Louisville	Cardinals	Red, black, white	Independent	Howard Schnellenberger	6-5-0
Maine	Black Bears	Blue & white	Yankee	Kirk Ferentz	9-3-0
Marshall	Thundering Herd	Green & white	Southern	Jim Donnan	6-5-0
Maryland	Terps	Red, white, black & gold	Atlantic Coast	Joe Krivak	3-7-1
Massachusetts	Minutemen	Maroon & white	Yankee	Jim Reid	5-5-1
McNeese State	Cowboys	Blue & gold	Southland	Bobby Keasler	5-6-0
Memphis State	Tigers	Blue & gray	Independent	Chuck Stobart	2-9-0
Miami (Fla.)	Hurricanes	Orange, green, white	Independent	Dennis Erickson	11-1-0
Miami (Ohio)	Redskins	Red & white	Mid-American	Randy Walker	2-8-1
Michigan	Wolverines	Maize & blue	Big Ten	Gray Moeller	10-2-0
Michigan State	Spartans	Green & white	Big Ten	George Perles	8-4-0
Middle Tennessee St.	Blue Raiders	Blue & white	Ohio Valley	Boots Donnelly	9-4-0
Minnesota	Golden Gophers	Maroon & gold	Big Ten	John Gutekunst	6-5-0
Mississippi	Rebels	Red & blue	Southeastern	Billy Brewer	8-4-0
Mississippi State	Bulldogs	Maroon & white	Southeastern	Rocky Felker	5-6-0
Miss. Valley	Delta Devils	Green & white	Southwestern	Larry Dorsey	1-9-0
Missouri	Tigers	Old gold & black	Big Eight	Bob Stull	2-9-0
Montana	Grizzlies	Copper, silver, gold	Big Sky	Don Read	11-3-0
Montana State	Bobcats	Blue & gold	Big Sky	Earle Solomonson	4-7-0
Morehead State	Eagles	Blue & gold	Ohio Valley	Cole Proctor	5-6-0
Morgan State	Bears	Blue & orange	Mid-Eastern	Ed Wynch	4-6-1
Murray State	Racers	Blue & gold	Ohio Valley	Mike Mahoney	6-4-1
Navy	Midshipmen	Navy blue & gold	Independent	George Chaump	3-8-0
Nebraska	Cornhuskers	Scarlet & cream	Big Eight	Tom Osborne	10-2-0
Nevada-Las Vegas	Rebels	Scarlet & gray	Big West	Jim Strong	4-7-0
Nevada-Reno	Wolf Pack	Silver & blue	Big Sky	Chris Ault	7-4-0
New Hampshire	Wildcats	Blue & white	Yankee	Bill Bowes	7-3-0
New Mexico	Lobos	Cherry & silver	Western Athletic	Mike Sheppard	2-10-0

Team	Nickname	Team colors	Conference	Coach	1989 record (W-L-T)
New Mexico State	Aggies	Crimson & white	Big West	Jim Hess	0-11-0
Nicholls St.	Colonels	Red & grey	Independent	Phil Greco	5-6-0
North Carolina	Tar Heels	Blue & white	Atlantic Coast	Mack Brown	1-10-0
North Carolina A & T.	Aggies	Blue & gold	Mid-Eastern	Bill Hayes	5-6-0
North Carolina State	Wolfpack	Red & white	Atlantic Coast	Dick Sheridan	7-5-0
North Texas	Mean Green, Eagles	Green & white	Southland	Corky Nelson	5-6-0
Northeast Louisiana	Indians	Maroon & gold	Southland	Dave Roberts	4-6-1
Northeastern	Huskies	Red & black	Independent	Paul Pawlak	3-7-0
Northern Arizona	Lumberjacks	Blue & gold	Big Sky	Steve Axman	3-8-0
Northern Illinois	Huskies	Cardinal & black	Independent	Jerry Pettibone	9-2-0
Northern Iowa	Panthers	Purple & Old Gold	Gateway	Terry Allen	8-3-0
Northwestern	Wildcats	Purple & white	Big Ten	Francis Peay	0-11-0
Northwestern State	Demons	Purple & White	Southland	Sam Goodwin	4-5-2
Notre Dame	Fighting Irish	Gold & blue	Independent	Lou Holtz	12-1-0
Ohio State	Buckeyes	Scarlet & gray	Big Ten	John Cooper	8-4-0
Ohio Univ	Bobcats	Green & white	Mid-American	Tom Lichtenberg	1-9-1
Oklahoma	Sooners	Crimson & cream	Big Eight	Gary Gibbs	7-4-0
Oklahoma State	Cowboys	Orange & black	Big Eight	Pat Jones	4-7-0
Oregon	Ducks	Green & Yellow	Pacific Ten	Rich Brooks	8-4-0
Oregon State	Beavers	Orange & black	Pacific Ten	Dave Kragthrope	4-7-1
Pacific	Tigers	Orange & black	Big West	Walt Harris	2-10-0
Penn State	Nittany Lions	Blue & white	Independent	Joe Paterno	8-3-1
Pennsylvania	Red & Blue, Quakers	Red & blue	Ivy	Gary Steele	4-6-0
Pittsburgh	Panthers	Gold & blue	Independent	Paul Hackett	8-3-1
Princeton	Tigers	Orange & black	Ivy	Steve Tosches	7-2-1
Purdue	Boilermakers	Old gold & black	Big Ten	Fred Akers	3-8-0
Rhode Island	Rams	Blue & white	Yankee	Bob Griffin	3-8-0
Rice	Owls	Blue & gray	Southwest	Fred Goldsmith	2-8-1
Richmond	Spiders	Red & blue	Yankee	Jim Marshall	1-10-0
Rutgers	Scarlet Knights	Scarlet	Independent	Doug Graber	2-7-2
Sam Houston State	Bear Kats	Orange & white	Southland	Ron Randleman	3-8-0
Samford	Bulldogs	Crimson & Blue	Independent	Terry Bowden	4-7-0
San Diego State	Aztecs	Scarlet & black	Western Athletic	Al Luginbill	6-5-1
San Jose State	Spartans	Gold & white	Big West	Terry Shea	6-5-0
South Carolina	Fighting Gamecocks	Garnet & black	Independent	Sparky Woods	6-4-1
South Carolina State	Bulldogs	Garnet & blue	Mid-Eastern	Willie Jeffries	5-6-0
Southern-Baton Rouge	Jaguars	Blue & gold	Southwestern	Gerald Kimble	6-4-1
Southern California	Trojans	Cardinal & gold	Pacific Ten	Larry Smith	9-2-1
Southern Illinois	Salukis	Maroon & white	Gateway	Bob Smith	2-9-0
Southern Methodist	Mustangs	Red & blue	Southwest	Forrest Gregg	2-9-0
Southern Mississippi	Golden Eagles	Black & gold	Independent	Curley Hallman	5-6-0
SW Missouri St.	Bears	Maroon & white	Gateway	Jesse Branch	10-3-0
SW Texas St.	Bobcats	Maroon & gold	Southland	Dennis Franchione	5-6-0
Southwestern La.	Ragin' Cajuns	Vermillion & white	Independent	Nelson Stokley	7-4-0
Stanford	Cardinal	Cardinal & white	Pacific Ten	Dennis Green	3-8-0
Stephen F. Austin St.	Lumberjacks	Purple & white	Southland	Lynn Graves	12-2-1
Syracuse	Orangemen	Orange	Independent	Dick MacPherson	8-4-0
Temple	Owls	Cherry & white	Independent	Jerry Berndt	1-10-0
Tennessee	Volunteers	Orange & white	Southeastern	John Majors	11-1-0
Tenn.-Chattanooga.	Moccasins	Navy blue & gold	Southern	Buddy Nix	3-7-1
Tennessee State	Tigers	Blue & white	Ohio Valley	Joe Gilliam Sr.	5-5-1
Tennessee Tech	Golden Eagles	Purple & gold	Ohio Valley	Jim Ragland	4-6-0
Texas	Longhorns	Orange & white	Southwest	David McWilliams	5-6-0
Texas-El Paso	Miners	Orange, white, blue	Western Athletic	David Lee	2-10-0
Texas A & M	Aggies	Maroon & white	Southwest	R.C. Slocum	8-4-0
Texas Christian	Horned Frogs	Purple & white	Southwest	Jim Wacker	4-7-0
Texas Southern	Tigers	Maroon & gray	Southwestern	Walter Highsmith	3-7-1
Texas Tech	Red Raiders	Scarlet & black	Southwest	Spike Dykes	9-3-0
Toledo	Rockets	Blue & gold	Mid-American	Nick Saban	6-5-0
Towson St.	Tigers	Gold & white	Independent	Phil Albert	2-8-0
Tulane	Green Wave	Olive green & sky blue	Independent	Greg Davis	4-8-0
Tulsa	Golden Hurricane	Blue & gold	Independent	Dave Rader	6-6-0
UCLA	Bruins	Navy blue & gold	Pacific Ten	Terry Donahue	3-7-1
Utah State	Aggies	Navy blue & white	Big West	Chuck Shelton	4-7-0
Utah	Utes	Crimson & white	Western Athletic	Ron McBride	4-8-0
Vanderbilt	Commodores	Black & gold	Southeastern	Watson Brown	1-10-0
Villanova	Wildcats	Blue & white	Yankee	Andy Talley	8-4-0
Virginia	Cavaliers	Orange & blue	Atlantic Coast	George Welsh	10-3-0
VMI	Keydets	Red, white & yellow	Southern	Jim Shuck	2-8-1
Virginia Tech	Gobblers, Hokies	Orange & maroon	Independent	Frank Beamer	6-4-1
Wake Forest	Demon Deacons	Old gold & black	Atlantic Coast	Bill Dooley	2-8-1
Washington	Huskies	Purple & gold	Pacific Ten	Don James	8-4-0
Washington State	Cougars	Crimson & gray	Pacific Ten	Mike Price	6-5-0
Weber State	Wildcats	Purple & white	Big Sky	Dave Arsianian	3-8-0
West Virginia	Mountaineers	Old gold & blue	Independent	Don Nehlen	8-3-1
Western Carolina	Catamounts	Purple & gold	Southern	Steve Hodgin	3-7-1
Western Illinois	Leathernecks	Purple & Gold	Gateway	Randy Ball	4-7-0
Western Kentucky	Hilltoppers	Red & white	Independent	Jack Harbaugh	6-5-0
Western Michigan	Broncos	Brown & gold	Mid-American	Al Molde	5-6-0
William & Mary	Tribe	Green & gold	Independent	Jimmye Laycock	8-3-1
Wisconsin	Badgers	Cardinal & white	Big Ten	Barry Alvarez	2-9-0
Wyoming	Cowboys	Brown & yellow	Western Athletic	Paul Roach	5-6-0
Yale	Bulldogs, Elis	Yale blue & white	Ivy	Carmen Cozza	8-2-0
Youngstown St.	Penguins	Scarlet & white	Independent	Jim Tressel	9-4-0

College Football Conference Champions

Atlantic Coast	Ivy League	Big Eight	Big Ten
1975 Maryland	1975 Harvard	1975 Oklahoma, Nebraska	19754 Ohio State
1976 Maryland	1976 Yale, Brown	1976 Oklahoma, Colorado,	1976 Michigan, Ohio State
1977 North Carolina	1977 Yale	Oklahoma State	1977 Michigan, Ohio State
1978 Clemson	1978 Dartmouth	1977 Oklahoma	1978 Michigan St., Michigan
1979 No. Carolina St.	1979 Yale	1978 Nebraska, Oklahoma	1979 Ohio State
1980 North Carolina	1980 Yale	1979 Oklahoma	1980 Michigan
1981 Clemson	1981 Yale, Dartmouth	1980 Oklahoma	1981 Iowa, Ohio State
1982 Clemson	1982 Harvard, Dartmouth, Penn	1981 Nebraska	1982 Michigan
1983 Maryland	1983 Harvard, Penn	1982 Nebraska	1983 Illinois
1984 Maryland	1984 Penn	1983 Nebraska	1984 Ohio State
1985 Maryland	1985 Penn	1984 Nebraska, Oklahoma	1985 Iowa
1986 Clemson	1986 Penn	1985 Oklahoma	1986 Michigan, Ohio State
1987 Clemson	1987 Harvard	1986 Oklahoma	1987 Michigan St.
1988 Clemson	1988 Penn, Cornell	1987 Oklahoma	1988 Michigan
1989 Virginia, Duke	1989 Yale, Princeton	1988 Nebraska	1989 Michigan
		1989 Colorado	

Mid-America	Southern	Southeastern	Southwest
1975 Miami	1975 Richmond	1975 Alabama	1975 Texas A&M, Texas, Arkansas
1976 Ball State	1976 East Carolina	1976 Georgia	1976 Houston
1977 Miami	1977 Tenn.-Chattanooga	1977 Alabama	1977 Texas
1978 Ball State	1978 Tenn.-Chattanooga, Furman	1978 Alabama	1978 Houston
1979 Central Michigan	1979 Tenn.-Chattanooga	1979 Alabama	1979 Houston, Arkansas
1980 Central Michigan	1980 Furman	1980 Georgia	1980 Baylor
1981 Toledo	1981 Furman	1981 Georgia, Alabama	1981 SMU
1982 Bowling Green	1982 Furman	1982 Georgia	1982 SMU
1983 Northern Illinois	1983 Furman	1983 Auburn	1983 Texas
1984 Toledo	1984 Tenn.-Chattanooga	1984 Florida (title vacated)	1984 SMU, Texas
1985 Bowling Green	1985 Furman	1985 Tennessee	1985 Texas A&M
1986 Miami	1986 Appalachian St.	1986 LSU	1986 Texas A&M
1987 E. Michigan	1987 Appalachian St.	1987 Auburn	1987 Texas A&M
1988 W. Michigan	1988 Marshall, Furman	1988 Auburn, LSU	1988 Arkansas
1989 Ball State	1989 Furman	1989 Alabama, Tennessee	1989 Arkansas

Pacific Ten	Western Athletic	Big West
1975 UCLA, Cal.	1975 Arizona State	1975 San Jose St.
1976 USC	1976 Wyoming, Brigham Young	1976 San Diego State
1977 Washington	1977 Brigham Young, Arizona St.	1977 Fresno State
1978 USC	1978 Brigham Young	1978 Utah St., San Jose St.
1979 USC	1979 Brigham Young	1979 San Jose St.
1980 Washington	1980 Brigham Young	1980 Long Beach State
1981 Washington	1981 Brigham Young	1981 San Jose State
1982 UCLA	1982 Brigham Young	1982 Fresno State
1983 UCLA	1983 Brigham Young	1983 Cal State-Fullerton
1984 USC	1984 Brigham Young	1984 Nevada-Las Vegas
1985 UCLA	1985 Brigham Young, Air Force	1985 Fresno State
1986 Arizona State	1986 San Diego State	1986 San Jose State
1987 UCLA, USC	1987 Wyoming	1987 San Jose State
1988 USC	1988 Wyoming	1988 Fresno State
1989 USC	1989 Brigham Young	1989 Fresno State

Outland Award

Honoring the outstanding interior lineman selected by the Football Writers' Association of America.

1946 George Connor, Notre Dame, T	1961 Merlin Olsen, Utah State, T	1976 Ross Browner, Notre Dame, DE
1947 Joe Steffy, Army, G	1962 Bobby Bell, Minnesota, T	1977 Brad Shearer, Texas, DT
1948 Bill Fischer, Notre Dame, G	1963 Scott Appleton, Texas, T	1978 Greg Roberts, Oklahoma, G
1949 Ed Bagdon, Michigan St., G	1964 Steve Delong, Tennessee, T	1979 Jim Ritcher, No. Carolina St., C
1950 Bob Gain, Kentucky, T	1965 Tommy Nobis, Texas, G	1980 Mark May, Pittsburgh, OT
1951 Jim Weatherall, Oklahoma, T	1966 Loyd Phillips, Arkansas, T	1981 Dave Rimington, Nebraska, C
1952 Dick Modzelewski, Maryland, T	1967 Ron Yary, Southern Cal, T	1982 Dave Rimington, Nebraska, C
1953 J. D. Roberts, Oklahoma, G	1968 Bill Stanfill, Georgia, T	1983 Dean Steinkuhler, Nebraska, G
1954 Bill Brooks, Arkansas, G	1969 Mike Reid, Penn State, DT	1984 Bruce Smith, Virginia Tech, DT
1955 Calvin Jones, Iowa, G	1970 Jim Stillwagon, Ohio State, LB	1985 Mike Ruth, Boston College, DT
1956 Jim Parker, Ohio State, G	1971 Larry Jacobson, Nebraska, DT	1986 Jason Buck, BYU, DT
1957 Alex Karras, Iowa, T	1972 Rich Glover, Nebraska, MG	1987 Chad Hennings, Air Force, DT
1958 Zeke Smith, Auburn, G	1973 John Hicks, Ohio State, G	1988 Tracy Rocker, Auburn, DT
1959 Mike McGee, Duke, T	1974 Randy White, Maryland, DE	1989 Mohammed Elewonibi, BYU, G
1960 Tom Brown, Minnesota, G	1975 Lee Roy Selmon, Oklahoma, DT	

All-Time Division I-A Coaching Victories

Paul "Bear" Bryant 323	Vince Dooley 201	Carl Snavely 180
Amos Alonzo Stagg 314	Dana Bible 198	Gil Dobie 180
Glenn "Pop" Warner 313	Dan McGugin 197	Jerry Claiborne 179
Woody Hayes 238	Fielding Yost 196	Ben Schwartzwalder 178
Bo Schembechler 234	Bobby Bowden 195	Ralph Jordan 176
Joe Paterno 220	Howard Jones 194	Frank Kush 176
Jess Neely 207	John Vaught 190	Lynn "Pappy" Waldorf 174
Warren Woodson 203	John Heisman 185	Bob Neyland 173
Eddie Anderson 201	Darrell Royal 184	

Eddie Robinson of Grambling State Univ. holds the record for most college football victories with 358 at the start of the 1990 season.

National College Football Champions

The NCAA recognizes as unofficial national champion the team selected each year by the AP (poll of writers) and the UPI (poll of coaches). When the polls disagree both teams are listed. The AP poll originated in 1936 and the UPI poll in 1950.

1936	Minnesota	1950	Oklahoma	1964	Alabama	1978	Alabama, So. Cal.
1937	Pittsburgh	1951	Tennessee	1965	Alabama, Mich. State	1979	Alabama
1938	Texas Christian	1952	Michigan State	1966	Notre Dame	1980	Georgia
1939	Texas A&M	1953	Maryland	1967	Southern Cal.	1981	Clemson
1940	Minnesota	1954	Ohio State, UCLA	1968	Ohio State	1982	Penn State
1941	Minnesota	1955	Oklahoma	1969	Texas	1983	Miami (Fla.)
1942	Ohio State	1956	Oklahoma	1970	Nebraska, Texas	1984	Brigham Young
1943	Notre Dame	1957	Auburn, Ohio State	1971	Nebraska,	1985	Oklahoma
1944	Army	1958	Louisiana State	1972	Southern Cal.	1986	Penn State
1945	Army	1959	Syracuse	1973	Notre Dame, Alabama	1987	Miami (Fla.)
1946	Notre Dame	1960	Minnesota	1974	Oklahoma, So. Cal.	1988	Notre Dame
1947	Notre Dame	1961	Alabama	1975	Oklahoma	1989	Miami (Fla.)
1948	Michigan	1962	Southern Cal.	1976	Pittsburgh		
1949	Notre Dame	1963	Texas	1977	Notre Dame		

College Football Coach of the Year

(Selected by the American Football Coaches Assn. & the Football Writers Assn. of America)

AFCA		FWAA	AFCA
1935	Lynn Waldorf, Northwestern	1957 Woody Hayes, Ohio St.	Woody Hayes, Ohio St.
1936	Dick Harlow, Harvard	1958 Paul Dietzel, LSU	Paul Dietzel, LSU
1937	Edward Mylin, Lafayette	1959 Ben Schwartzwalder, Syracuse	Ben Schwartzwalder, Syracuse
1938	Bill Kern, Carnegie Tech	1960 Murray Warmath, Minnesota	Murray Warmath, Minnesota
1939	Eddie Anderson, Iowa	1961 Darrell Royal, Texas	Paul "Bear" Bryant, Alabama
1940	Clark Shaughnessy, Stanford	1962 John McKay, USC	John McKay, USC
1941	Frank Leahy, Notre Dame	1963 Darrell Royal, Texas	Darrell Royal, Texas
1942	Bill Alexander, Georgia Tech	1964 Ara Parseghian, Notre Dame	Frank Broyles, Arkansas; Ara Parseghian, Notre Dame
1943	Amos Alonzo Stagg, Pacific	1965 Duffy Daugherty, Michigan St.	Tommy Prothro, UCLA
1944	Carroll Widdoes, Ohio St.	1966 Tom Cahill, Army	Tom Cahill, Army
1945	Bo McMillin, Indiana	1967 John Pont, Indiana	John Pont, Indiana
1946	Earl "Red" Blaik, Army	1968 Woody Hayes, Ohio St.	Joe Paterno, Penn St.
1947	Fritz Crisler, Michigan	1969 Bo Schembechler, Michigan	Bo Schembechler, Michigan
1948	Bennie Oosterbaan, Michigan	1970 Alex Agase, Northwestern	Charles McClendon, LSU; Darrell Royal, Texas
1949	Bud Wilkinson, Oklahoma	1971 Bob Devaney, Nebraska	Paul "Bear" Bryant, Alabama
1950	Charlie Caldwell, Princeton	1972 John McKay, USC	John McKay, USC
1951	Chuck Taylor, Stanford	1973 Johnny Majors, Pittsburgh	Paul "Bear" Bryant, Alabama
1952	Biggie Munn, Michigan St.	1974 Grant Teaff, Baylor	Grant Teaff, Baylor
1953	Jim Tatum, Maryland	1975 Woody Hayes, Ohio St.	Frank Kush, Arizona St.
1954	Henry "Red" Sanders, UCLA	1976 Johnny Majors, Pittsburgh	Johnny Majors, Pittsburgh
1955	Duffy Daugherty, Michigan St.	1977 Lou Holtz, Arkansas	Don James, Washington
1956	Bowden Wyatt, Tennessee	1978 Joe Paterno, Penn St.	Joe Paterno, Penn St.
		1979 Earle Bruce, Ohio St.	Earle Bruce, Ohio St.
		1980 Vince Dooley, Georgia	Vince Dooley, Georgia
		1981 Danny Ford, Clemson	Danny Ford, Clemson
		1982 Joe Paterno, Penn St.	Joe Paterno, Penn St.
		1983 Howard Schnellenberger, Miami (Fla.)	Ken Hatfield, Air Force
		1984 LaVell Edwards, Brigham Young	LaVell Edwards, Brigham Young
		1985 Fisher De Berry, Air Force	Fisher De Berry, Air Force
		1986 Joe Paterno, Penn St.	Joe Paterno, Penn St.
		1987 Dick MacPherson, Syracuse	Dick MacPherson, Syracuse
		1988 Lou Holtz, Notre Dame	Don Nehlen, W. Virginia
		1989 Bill McCartney, Colorado	Bill McCartney, Colorado

Longest Division I-A Winning Streaks

Wins	Team	Years	Ended by	Score
47	Oklahoma	1953-57	Notre Dame	7-0
39	Washington	1908-14	Oregon State	0-0
37	Yale	1890-93	Princeton	6-0
37	Yale	1887-89	Princeton	10-0
35	Toledo	1969-71	Tampa	21-0
34	Pennsylvania	1894-96	Lafayette	6-4
31	Oklahoma	1948-50	Kentucky	13-7
31	Pittsburgh	1914-18	Cleveland Naval Reserve	10-9
31	Pennsylvania	1896-98	Harvard	10-0
30	Texas	1968-70	Notre Dame	24-11
29	Michigan	1901-03	Minnesota	6-6
28	Alabama	1978-80	Mississippi State	6-3
28	Oklahoma	1973-75	Kansas	23-3
28	Michigan State	1950-53	Purdue	6-0
27	Nebraska	1901-04	Colorado	6-0
26	Cornell	1921-24	Williams	14-7
26	Michigan	1903-05	Chicago	2-0
26	Michigan	1946-49	Army	21-7
25	Army	1944-46	Notre Dame	0-0
25	Southern Cal	1931-33	Oregon State	0-0
25	Brigham Young	1983-85	UCLA	27-24

Heisman Trophy Winners

Awarded annually to the nation's outstanding college football player.

1935	Jay Berwanger, Chicago, HB	1954	Alan Ameche, Wisconsin, FB	1972	Johnny Rodgers, Nebraska, RB-R
1936	Larry Kelley, Yale, E	1955	Howard Cassady, Ohio St., HB	1973	John Cappelletti, Penn State, RB
1937	Clinton Frank, Yale, HB	1956	Paul Hornung, Notre Dame, QB	1974	Archie Griffin, Ohio State, RB
1938	David O'Brien, Tex. Christian, QB	1957	John Crow, Texas A & M, HB	1975	Archie Griffin, Ohio State, RB
1939	Nile Kinnick, Iowa, HB	1958	Pete Dawkins, Army, HB	1976	Tony Dorsett, Pittsburgh, RB
1940	Tom Harmon, Michigan, HB	1959	Billy Cannon, La. State, HB	1977	Earl Campbell, Texas, RB
1941	Bruce Smith, Minnesota, HB	1960	Joe Bellino, Navy, HB	1978	Billy Sims, Oklahoma, RB
1942	Frank Sinkwich, Georgia, HB	1961	Ernest Davis, Syracuse, HB	1979	Charles White, USC, RB
1943	Angelo Bertelli, Notre Dame, QB	1962	Terry Baker, Oregon State, QB	1980	George Rogers, So. Carolina, RB
1944	Leslie Horvath, Ohio State, QB	1963	Roger Staubach, Navy, QB	1981	Marcus Allen, USC, RB
1945	Felix Blanchard, Army, FB	1964	John Huarte, Notre Dame, QB	1982	Herschel Walker, Georgia, RB
1946	Glenn Davis, Army, HB	1965	Mike Garrett, USC, HB	1983	Mike Rozier, Nebraska, RB
1947	John Lujack, Notre Dame, QB	1966	Steve Spurrier, Florida, QB	1984	Doug Flutie, Boston College, QB
1948	Doak Walker, SMU, HB	1967	Gary Beban, UCLA, QB	1985	Bo Jackson, Auburn, RB
1949	Leon Hart, Notre Dame, E	1968	O. J. Simpson, USC, RB	1986	Vinny Testaverde, Miami, QB
1950	Vic Janowicz, Ohio State, HB	1969	Steve Owens, Oklahoma, RB	1987	Tim Brown, Notre Dame, WR
1951	Richard Kazmaier, Princeton, HB	1970	Jim Plunkett, Stanford, QB	1988	Barry Sanders, Oklahoma St., RB
1952	Billy Vessels, Oklahoma, HB	1971	Pat Sullivan, Auburn, QB	1989	Andre Ware, Houston, QB
1953	John Lattner, Notre Dame, HB				

Vince Lombardi Award

Honoring the outstanding lineman, sponsored by the Rotary Club of Houston

1970	Jim Stillwagon, Ohio State, MG	1977	Ross Browner, Notre Dame, DE	1984	Tony Degrate, Texas, DT
1971	Walt Patulski, Notre Dame, DE	1978	Bruce Clark, Penn State, DT	1985	Tony Casillas, Oklahoma, NG
1972	Rich Glover, Nebraska, MG	1979	Brad Budde, USC, G	1986	Cornelius Bennett, Alabama, DE
1973	John Hicks, Ohio State, OT	1980	Hugh Green, Pittsburgh, DE	1987	Chris Spielman, Ohio State, LB
1974	Randy White, Maryland, DT	1981	Kenneth Sims, Texas, DT	1988	Tracy Rocker, Auburn, DT
1975	Lee Roy Selmon, Oklahoma, DT	1982	Dave Rimington, Nebraska, C	1989	Percy Snow, Michigan St., LB
1976	Wilson Whitley, Houston, DT	1983	Dean Steinkuhler, Nebraska, G		

All-Time Division I-A Percentage Leaders

(Classified as Division I-A for the last 10 years; record includes bowl games; ties computed as half won and half lost)

	Years	Won	Lost	Tied	Pct.	Bowl Games W	L	T
Notre Dame	101	683	203	40	.759	10	5	0
Michigan	110	703	233	33	.743	9	12	0
Alabama	95	651	228	43	.729	23	16	3
Oklahoma	95	628	227	50	.722	18	10	1
Texas	97	661	255	31	.714	16	15	2
USC	97	605	232	50	.710	22	11	0
Ohio St.	100	626	253	50	.701	11	11	0
Penn St.	103	637	279	41	.687	16	8	2
Nebraska	100	635	281	39	.685	14	14	0
Tennessee	93	600	266	50	.682	16	14	0
Central Michigan	89	456	239	31	.649	3	0	0
Louisiana St.	96	556	298	46	.643	11	16	1
Army	100	567	304	50	.643	2	1	0
Arizona St.	77	422	233	24	.639	9	5	1
Miami (Ohio)	101	525	288	39	.639	5	2	0
Georgia	96	561	315	53	.632	13	13	3
Washington	100	524	301	49	.628	10	7	1
Auburn	97	529	321	44	.616	11	9	2
Minnesota	106	541	329	43	.616	2	3	0
Michigan St.	93	499	305	42	.615	4	5	0
Florida St.	43	272	170	16	.611	10	7	2
Arkansas	96	533	335	38	.609	9	14	3
Pittsburgh	100	551	354	41	.604	8	10	0
UCLA	71	409	262	37	.604	9	7	1

Canadian Football League Championships

Winners of Eastern and Western divisions meet in championship game for Grey Cup (donated by Governor-General Earl Grey in 1909). Canadian football features 3 downs, 110-yard field, and each team can have 12 players on field at one time.

1956	Edmonton Eskimos 50, Montreal Alouettes 27	1973	Ottawa Rough Riders 22, Edmonton Eskimos 18
1957	Hamilton Tiger-Cats 32, Winnipeg Blue Bombers 7	1974	Montreal Alouettes 20, Edmonton Eskimos 7
1958	Winnipeg Blue Bombers 35, Hamilton Tiger-Cats 28	1975	Edmonton Eskimos 9, Montreal Alouettes 8
1959	Winnipeg Blue Bombers 21, Hamilton Tiger-Cats 7	1976	Ottawa Rough Riders 23, Saskatchewan Roughriders 20
1960	Ottawa Rough Riders 16, Edmonton Eskimos 6	1977	Montreal Alouettes 41, Edmonton Eskimos 6
1961	Winnipeg Blue Bombers 21, Hamilton Tiger-Cats 14	1978	Edmonton Eskimos 20, Montreal Alouettes 13
1962	Winnipeg Blue Bombers 28, Hamilton Tiger-Cats 27	1979	Edmonton Eskimos 17, Montreal Alouettes 9
1963	Hamilton Tiger-Cats 21, British Columbia Lions 10	1980	Edmonton Eskimos 48, Hamilton Tiger-Cats 10
1964	British Columbia Lions 34, Hamilton Tiger-Cats 24	1981	Edmonton Eskimos 26, Ottawa Rough Riders 23
1965	Hamilton Tiger-Cats 22, Winnipeg Blue Bombers 16	1982	Edmonton Eskimos 32, Toronto Argonauts 16
1966	Saskatchewan Roughriders 29, Ottawa Rough Riders 14	1983	Toronto Argonauts 18, B.C. Lions 17
1967	Hamilton Tiger-Cats 24, Saskatchewan Roughriders 1	1984	Winnipeg Blue Bombers 47, Hamilton Tiger-Cats 17
1968	Ottawa Rough Riders 24, Calgary Stampeders 21	1985	B.C. Lions 37, Hamilton Tiger-Cats 24
1969	Ottawa Rough Riders 29, Saskatchewan Roughriders 11	1986	Hamilton Tiger-Cats 39, Edmonton Eskimos 15
1970	Montreal Alouettes 23, Calgary Stampeders 10	1987	Edmonton Eskimos 38, Toronto Argonauts 36
1971	Calgary Stampeders 14, Toronto Argonauts 11	1988	Winnipeg Blue Bombers 22, B.C. Lions 21
1972	Hamilton Tiger-Cats 13, Saskatchewan Roughriders 10	1989	Saskatchewan Roughriders 43, Hamilton Tiger-Cats 40

NATIONAL FOOTBALL LEAGUE

Final 1989 Standings

National Conference

Eastern Division

	W	L	T	Pct	Pts	Opp
New York Giants	12	4	0	.750	348	252
Philadelphia	11	5	0	.688	342	274
Washington	10	6	0	.625	386	308
Phoenix	5	11	0	.313	258	377
Dallas	1	15	0	.063	204	393

Central Division

	W	L	T	Pct	Pts	Opp
Minnesota	10	6	0	.625	351	275
Green Bay	10	6	0	.625	362	356
Detroit	7	9	0	.438	312	364
Chicago	6	10	0	.375	358	377
Tampa Bay	5	11	0	.313	320	419

Western Division

	W	L	T	Pct	Pts	Opp
San Francisco	14	2	0	.875	442	253
Los Angeles Rams	11	5	0	.688	426	344
New Orleans	9	7	0	.563	386	301
Atlanta	3	13	0	.188	279	437

American Conference

Eastern Division

	W	L	T	Pct	Pts	Opp
Buffalo	9	7	0	.563	409	317
Indianapolis	8	8	0	.500	298	301
Miami	8	8	0	.500	331	379
New England	5	11	0	.313	297	391
New York Jets	4	12	0	.250	253	411

Central Division

	W	L	T	Pct	Pts	Opp
Cleveland	9	6	1	.594	334	254
Houston	9	7	0	.563	365	412
Pittsburgh	9	7	0	.563	265	326
Cincinnati	8	8	0	.500	404	285

Western Division

	W	L	T	Pct	Pts	Opp
Denver	11	5	0	.688	362	226
Kansas City	8	7	1	.531	318	286
Los Angeles Raiders	8	8	0	.500	315	297
Seattle	7	9	0	.438	241	327
San Diego	6	10	0	.375	266	290

NFC Playoffs—L.A. Rams 21, Philadelphia 7; L.A. Rams 19, N.Y. Giants 13; San Francisco 41, Minnesota 13; San Francisco 30, L.A. Rams 3

AFC Playoffs—Pittsburgh 26, Houston 23; Denver 24, Pittsburgh 23; Cleveland 34, Buffalo 30; Denver 37, Cleveland 21.

49ers Crush Broncos in Super Bowl

The San Francisco 49ers easily defeated the Denver Broncos, 55-10, to win Super Bowl XXIV. It was a record-tying 4th Super Bowl victory for the 49ers. Joe Montana, quarterback of the 49ers, was chosen the game's most valuable player for a record 3rd time.

Score by Quarters

San Francisco	13	14	14	14—55
Denver	3	0	7	0—10

Scoring

San Francisco—Rice 20 yd. pass from Montana (Cofer kick)
Denver—Treadwill 42 yd. field goal
San Francisco—Jones 7 yd. pass from Montana
San Francisco—Rathman 1 yd. run (Cofer kick)
San Francisco—Rice 38 yd. pass from Montana (Cofer kick)
San Francisco—Rice 28 yd. pass from Montana (Cofer kick)
San Francisco—Taylor 35 yd. pass from Montana (Cofer kick)
Denver—Elway 3 yd. run (Treadwell kick)
San Francisco—Rathman 3 yd. run (Cofer kick)
San Francisco—Craig 1 yd. run (Cofer kick)

Individual Statistics

Rushing — San Francisco, Craig 20-69, Rathman 11-38, Montana 2-15, Flagler 6-14, Young 4-6, Sydney 1-2. Denver, Humphrey 12-61, Elway 4-8, Winder 1-(minus 5).

Passing — San Francisco, Montana 22-29-0-297, Young 2-3-0-20. Denver, Elway 10-26-2-108, Kubiak 1-3-0-28.

Receiving — San Francisco, Rice 7-148, Craig 5-34, Rathman 4-43, Taylor 3-49, Sherrard 1-13, Walls 1-9, Jones 1-7, Williams 1-7, Sydney 1-7. Denver, Humphrey 3-38, Sewell 2-22, Johnson 2-21, Nattiel 1-28, Bratton 1-1 Winder 1-7, Kay 1-6.

Team Statistics

	San Francisco	Denver
First downs	28	12
Total net yards	461	167
Total plays	77	52
Avg gain	6.0	3.2
Rushing yards	144	64
Passing yards	317	103
Yards per pass	9.6	2.9
Punts-average	4-40	6-39
Penalties-yards	4-38	0-0
Fumbles-lost	0-0	3-2
Time of possession	39:31	20:29

Super Bowl

Year	Winner	Loser	Winning coach	Site
1967	Green Bay Packers, 35	Kansas City Chiefs, 10	Vince Lombardi	Los Angeles Coliseum
1968	Green Bay Packers, 33	Oakland Raiders, 14	Vince Lombardi	Orange Bowl, Miami
1969	New York Jets, 16	Baltimore Colts, 7	Weeb Ewbank	Orange Bowl, Miami
1970	Kansas City Chiefs, 23	Minnesota Vikings, 7	Hank Stram	Tulane Stadium, New Orleans
1971	Baltimore Colts, 16	Dallas Cowboys, 13	Don McCafferty	Orange Bowl, Miami
1972	Dallas Cowboys, 24	Miami Dolphins, 3	Tom Landry	Tulane Stadium, New Orleans
1973	Miami Dolphins, 14	Washington Redskins, 7	Don Shula	Los Angeles Coliseum
1974	Miami Dolphins, 24	Minnesota Vikings, 7	Don Shula	Rice Stadium, Houston
1975	Pittsburgh Steelers, 16	Minnesota Vikings, 6	Chuck Noll	Tulane Stadium, New Orleans
1976	Pittsburgh Steelers, 21	Dallas Cowboys, 17	Chuck Noll	Orange Bowl, Miami
1977	Oakland Raiders, 32	Minnesota Vikings, 14	John Madden	Rose Bowl, Pasadena
1978	Dallas Cowboys, 27	Denver Broncos, 10	Tom Landry	Superdome, New Orleans
1979	Pittsburgh Steelers, 35	Dallas Cowboys, 31	Chuck Noll	Orange Bowl, Miami
1980	Pittsburgh Steelers, 31	Los Angeles Rams, 19	Chuck Noll	Rose Bowl, Pasadena
1981	Oakland Raiders, 27	Philadelphia Eagles, 10	Tom Flores	Superdome, New Orleans
1982	San Francisco 49ers, 26	Cincinnati Bengals, 21	Bill Walsh	Silverdome, Pontiac, Mich.
1983	Washington Redskins, 27	Miami Dolphins, 17	Joe Gibbs	Rose Bowl, Pasadena
1984	Los Angeles Raiders, 38	Washington Redskins, 9	Tom Flores	Tampa Stadium
1985	San Francisco 49ers, 38	Miami Dolphins, 16	Bill Walsh	Stanford Stadium, Palo Alto, Cal.
1986	Chicago Bears, 46	New England Patriots, 10	Mike Ditka	Superdome, New Orleans
1987	New York Giants, 39	Denver Broncos, 20	Bill Parcells	Rose Bowl, Pasadena
1988	Washington Redskins, 42	Denver Broncos, 10	Joe Gibbs	San Diego Stadium
1989	San Francisco 49ers, 20	Cincinnati Bengals, 16	Bill Walsh	Joe Robbie Stadium, Miami
1990	San Francisco 49ers, 55	Denver Broncos, 10	George Siefert	Superdome, New Orleans

National Football League Champions

Year	East Winner (W-L-T)	West Winner (W-L-T)	Playoff
1933	New York Giants (11-3-0)	Chicago Bears (10-2-1)	Chicago Bears 23, New York 21
1934	New York Giants (8-5-0)	Chicago Bears (13-0-0)	New York 30, Chicago Bears 13
1935	New York Giants (9-3-0)	Detroit Lions (7-3-2)	Detroit 26, New York 7
1936	Boston Redskins (7-5-0)	Green Bay Packers (10-1-1)	Green Bay 21, Boston 6
1937	Washington Redskins (8-3-0)	Chicago Bears (9-1-1)	Washington 28, Chicago Bears 21
1938	New York Giants (8-2-1)	Green Bay Packers (8-3-0)	New York 23, Green Bay 17
1939	New York Giants (9-1-1)	Green Bay Packers (9-2-0)	Green Bay 27, New York 0
1940	Washington Redskins (9-2-0)	Chicago Bears (8-3-0)	Chicago Bears 73, Washington 0
1941	New York Giants (8-3-0)	Chicago Bears (10-1-1)(a)	Chicago Bears 37, New York 9
1942	Wash. Redskins (10-1-1)	Chicago Bears (11-0-0)	Washington 14, Chicago Bears 6
1943	Wash. Redskins (6-3-1)(a)	Chicago Bears (8-1-1)	Chicago Bears, 41, Washington 21
1944	New York Giants (8-1-1)	Green Bay Packers (8-2-0)	Green Bay 14, New York 7
1945	Wash. Redskins (8-2-0)	Cleveland Rams (9-1-0)	Cleveland 15, Washington 14
1946	New York Giants (7-3-1)	Chicago Bears (8-2-1)	Chicago Bears 24, New York 14
1947	Philadelphia Eagles (8-4-0)(a)	Chicago Cardinals (9-3-0)	Chicago Cardinals 28, Philadelphia 21
1948	Philadelphia Eagles (9-2-1)	Chicago Cardinals (11-1-0)	Philadelphia 7, Chicago Cardinals 0
1949	Philadelphia Eagles (11-1-0)	Los Angeles Rams (8-2-2)	Philadelphia 14, Los Angeles 0
1950	Cleveland Browns (10-2-0)(a)	Los Angeles Rams (9-3-0)(a)	Cleveland 30, Los Angeles 28
1951	Cleveland Browns (11-1-0)	Los Angeles Rams (8-4-0)	Los Angeles 24, Cleveland 17
1952	Cleveland Browns (8-4-0)	Detroit Lions (9-3-0)(a)	Detroit 17, Cleveland 7
1953	Cleveland Browns (11-1-0)	Detroit Lions (10-2-0)	Detroit 17, Cleveland 16
1954	Cleveland Browns (9-3-0)	Detroit Lions (9-2-1)	Cleveland 56, Detroit 10
1955	Cleveland Browns (9-2-1)	Los Angeles Rams (8-3-1)	Cleveland 38, Los Angeles 14
1956	New York Giants (8-3-1)	Chicago Bears (9-2-1)	New York 47, Chicago Bears 7
1957	Cleveland Browns (9-2-1)	Detroit Lions (8-4-0)(a)	Detroit 59, Cleveland 14
1958	New York Giants (9-3-0)(a)	Baltimore Colts (9-3-0)	Baltimore 23, New York 17(b)
1959	New York Giants (10-2-0)	Baltimore Colts (9-3-0)	Baltimore 31, New York 16
1960	Philadelphia Eagles (10-2-0)	Green Bay Packers (8-4-0)	Philadelphia 17, Green Bay 13
1961	New York Giants (10-3-1)	Green Bay Packers (11-3-0)	Green Bay 37, New York 0
1962	New York Giants (12-2-0)	Green Bay Packers (13-1-0)	Green Bay 16, New York 7
1963	New York Giants (11-3-0)	Chicago Bears (11-1-2)	Chicago 14, New York 10
1964	Cleveland Browns (10-3-1)	Baltimore Colts (12-2-0)	Cleveland 27, Baltimore 0
1965	Cleveland Browns (11-3-0)	Green Bay Packers (10-3-1)(a)	Green Bay 23, Cleveland 12
1966	Dallas Cowboys (10-3-1)	Green Bay Packers (12-2-0)	Green Bay 34, Dallas 27

(a) Won divisional playoff. (b) Won at 8:15 sudden death overtime period.

Year	Conference	Division	Winner (W-L-T)	Playoff
1967	East	Century	Cleveland (9-5-0)	Dallas 52, Cleveland 14
		Capitol	Dallas (9-5-0)	
	West	Central	Green Bay (9-4-1)	Green Bay 28, Los Angeles 7
		Coastal	Los Angeles (11-1-2)(a)	Green Bay 21, Dallas 17
1968	East	Century	Cleveland (10-4-0)	Cleveland 31, Dallas 20
		Capitol	Dallas (12-2-0)	
	West	Central	Minnesota (8-6-0)	Baltimore 24, Minnesota 14
		Coastal	Baltimore (13-1-0)	Baltimore 34, Cleveland 0
1969	East	Century	Cleveland (10-3-1)	Cleveland 38, Dallas 14
		Capitol	Dallas (11-2-1)	
	West	Central	Minnesota (12-2-0)	Minnesota 23, Los Angeles 20
		Coastal	Los Angeles (11-3-0)	Minnesota 27, Cleveland 7
1970	American	Eastern	Baltimore (11-2-1)	Baltimore 17, Cincinnati 0
		Central	Cincinnati (8-6-0)	Oakland 21, Miami 14
		Western	Oakland (8-4-2)	Baltimore 27, Oakland 17
	National	Eastern	Dallas (10-4-0)	Dallas 5, Detroit 0
		Central	Minnesota (12-2-0)	San Francisco 17, Minnesota 14
		Western	San Francisco (10-3-1)	Dallas 17, San Francisco 10
1971	American	Eastern	Miami (10-3-1)	Miami 27, Kansas City 24
		Central	Cleveland (9-5-0)	Baltimore 20, Cleveland 3
		Western	Kansas City (10-3-1)	Miami 21, Baltimore 0
	National	Eastern	Dallas (11-3-0)	Dallas 20, Minnesota 12
		Central	Minnesota (11-3-0)	San Francisco 24, Washington 20
		Western	San Francisco (9-5-0)	Dallas 14, San Francisco 3
1972	American	Eastern	Miami (14-0-0)	Miami 20, Cleveland 14
		Central	Pittsburgh (11-3-0)	Pittsburgh 13, Oakland 7
		Western	Oakland (10-3-1)	Miami 21, Pittsburgh 17
	National	Eastern	Washington (11-3-0)	Washington 16, Green Bay 3
		Central	Green Bay (10-4-0)	Dallas 30, San Francisco 28
		Western	San Francisco (8-5-1)	Washington 26, Dallas 3
1973	American	Eastern	Miami (12-2-0)	Miami 34, Cincinnati 16
		Central	Cincinnati (10-4-0)	Oakland 33, Pittsburgh 14
		Western	Oakland (9-4-1)	Miami 27, Oakland 10
	National	Eastern	Dallas (10-4-0)	Dallas 27, Los Angeles 16
		Central	Minnesota (12-2-0)	Minnesota 27, Washington 20
		Western	Los Angeles (12-2-0)	Minnesota 27, Dallas 10
1974	American	Eastern	Miami (11-3-0)	Oakland 28, Miami 26
		Central	Pittsburgh (10-3-1)	Pittsburgh 32, Buffalo 14
		Western	Oakland (12-2-0)	Pittsburgh 24, Oakland 13
	National	Eastern	St. Louis (10-4-0)	Minnesota 30, St. Louis 14
		Central	Minnesota (10-4-0)	Los Angeles 19, Washington 10
		Western	Los Angeles (10-4-0)	Minnesota 14, Los Angeles 10
1975	American	Eastern	Baltimore (10-4-0)	Pittsburgh 28, Baltimore 10
		Central	Pittsburgh (12-2-0)	Oakland 31, Cincinnati 28
		Western	Oakland (11-3-0)	Pittsburgh 16, Oakland 10

(continued)

Year	East Winner (W-L-T)		West Winner (W-L-T)	Playoff
	National	Eastern	St. Louis (11-3-0)	Dallas 17, Minnesota 14
		Central	Minnesota (12-2-0)	Los Angeles 35, St. Louis 23
		Western	Los Angeles (12-2-0)	Dallas 37, Los Angeles 7
1976	American	Eastern	Baltimore (11-3-0)	Pittsburgh 40, Baltimore 14
		Central	Pittsburgh (10-4-0)	Oakland 24, New England 21
		Western	Oakland (13-1-0)	Oakland 24, Pittsburgh 7
	National	Eastern	Dallas (11-3-0)	Minnesota 35, Washington 20
		Central	Minnesota (11-2-1)	Los Angeles 14, Dallas 12
		Western	Los Angeles (10-3-1)	Minnesota 24, Los Angeles 13
1977	American	Eastern	Baltimore (10-4-0)	Oakland 37, Baltimore 31
		Central	Pittsburgh (9-5-0)	Denver 34, Pittsburgh 21
		Western	Denver (12-2-0)	Dallas 37, Chicago 7
	National	Eastern	Dallas (12-2-0)	Minnesota 14, Los Angeles 7
		Central	Minnesota (9-5-0)	Denver 20, Oakland 17
		Western	Los Angeles (10-4-0)	Dallas 23, Minnesota 6
1978	American	Eastern	New England (11-5-0)	Pittsburgh 33, Denver 10
		Central	Pittsburgh (14-2-0)	Houston 31, New England 14
		Western	Denver (10-6-0)	Pittsburgh 34, Houston 5
	National	Eastern	Dallas (12-4-0)	Dallas 27, Atlanta 20
		Central	Minnesota (8-7-1)	Los Angeles 34, Minnesota 10
		Western	Los Angeles (12-4-0)	Dallas 28, Los Angeles 0
1979	American	Eastern	Miami (10-6-0)	Houston 17, San Diego 14
		Central	Pittsburgh (12-4-0)	Pittsburgh 34, Miami 14
		Western	San Diego (12-4-0)	Pittsburgh 27, Houston 13
	National	Eastern	Dallas (11-5-0)	Tampa Bay 24, Philadelphia 17
		Central	Tampa Bay (10-6-0)	Los Angeles 21, Dallas 19
		Western	Los Angeles (9-7-0)	Los Angeles 9, Tampa Bay 0
1980	American	Eastern	Buffalo (11-5-0)	San Diego 20, Buffalo 14
		Central	Cleveland (11-5-0)	Oakland 14, Cleveland 12
		Western	San Diego (11-5-0)	Oakland 34, San Diego 27
	National	Eastern	Philadelphia (12-4-0)	Philadelphia 31, Minnesota 16
		Central	Minnesota (9-7-0)	Dallas 30, Atlanta 27
		Western	Atlanta (12-4-0)	Philadelphia 20, Dallas 7
1981	American	Eastern	Miami (11-4-1)	San Diego 41, Miami 38
		Central	Cincinnati (12-4-0)	Cincinnati 28, Buffalo 21
		Western	San Diego (10-6-0)	Cincinnati 27, San Diego 7
	National	Eastern	Dallas (12-4-0)	Dallas 38, Tampa Bay 0
		Central	Tampa Bay (9-7-0)	San Francisco 38, N.Y. Giants 24
		Western	San Francisco (13-3-0)	San Francisco 28, Dallas 27
1982	American		L.A. Raiders (8-1-0)	
	National		Washington (8-1-0)	Strike-shortened season

AFC playoffs—Miami 28, New England 13; L.A. Raiders 27, Cleveland 10; N.Y. Jets 44, Cincinnati 17; San Diego 31, Pittsburgh 28; N.Y. Jets 17, L.A. Raiders 14; Miami 34, San Diego 13; Miami 14, N.Y. Jets 0. **NFC playoffs**—Washington 31, Detroit 7; Green Bay 41, St. Louis 16; Dallas 30, Tampa Bay 17; Minnesota 30, Atlanta 24; Washington 21, Minnesota 7; Dallas 37, Green Bay 26; Washington 31, Dallas 17.

Year	East Winner (W-L-T)		West Winner (W-L-T)	Playoff
1983	American	Eastern	Miami (12-4-0)	Seattle 27, Miami 20
		Central	Pittsburgh (10-6-0)	L.A. Raiders 38, Pittsburgh 10
		Western	L.A. Raiders (12-4-0)	L.A. Raiders 30, Seattle 14
	National	Eastern	Washington (14-2-0)	Washington 51, L.A. Rams 7
		Central	Detroit (9-7-0)	San Francisco 24, Detroit 23
		Western	San Francisco (10-6-0)	Washington 24, San Francisco 21
1984	American	Eastern	Miami (14-2-0)	Miami 31, Seattle 10
		Central	Pittsburgh (9-7-0)	Pittsburgh 24, Denver 17
		Western	Denver (13-3-0)	Miami 45, Pittsburgh 28
	National	Eastern	Washington (11-5-0)	Chicago 23, Washington 19
		Central	Chicago (10-6-0)	San Francisco 21, N.Y. Giants 10
		Western	San Francisco (15-1-0)	San Francisco 23, Chicago 0
1985	American	Eastern	Miami (12-4-0)	New England 27, L.A. Raiders 20
		Central	Cleveland (8-8-0)	Miami 24, Cleveland 21
		Western	L.A. Raiders (12-4-0)	New England 31, Miami 14
	National	Eastern	Dallas (10-6-0)	Chicago 21, N.Y. Giants 0
		Central	Chicago (15-1-0)	L.A. Rams 20, Dallas 0
		Western	L.A. Rams (11-5-0)	Chicago 24, L.A. Rams 0
1986	American	Eastern	New England (11-5-0)	Denver 22, New England 17
		Central	Cleveland (12-4-0)	Cleveland 23, N.Y. Jets 20
		Western	Denver (11-5-0)	Denver 23, Cleveland 20
	National	Eastern	N.Y. Giants (14-2-0)	N.Y. Giants 49, San Francisco 3
		Central	Chicago (14-2-0)	Washington 27, Chicago 13
		Western	San Francisco (10-5-1)	N.Y. Giants 17, Washington 0
1987	American	Eastern	Indianapolis (9-6-0)	Cleveland 38, Indianapolis 21
		Central	Cleveland (10-5-0)	Denver 34, Houston 10
		Western	Denver (10-4-1)	Denver 38, Cleveland 33
	National	Eastern	Washington (11-4-0)	Washington 21, Chicago 7
		Central	Chicago (11-4-0)	Minnesota 36, San Francisco 24
		Western	San Francisco (13-2-0)	Washington 17, Minnesota 10
1988	American	Eastern	Buffalo (12-4-0)	Buffalo 17, Houston 10
		Central	Cincinnati (12-4-0)	Cincinnati 21, Seattle 13
		Western	Seattle (9-7-0)	Cincinnati 21, Buffalo 10
	National	Eastern	Philadelphia (10-6-0)	Chicago 20, Philadelphia 12
		Central	Chicago (12-4-0)	San Francisco 34, Minnesota 9
		Western	San Francisco (10-6-0)	San Francisco 28, Chicago 3
1989	American	Eastern	Buffalo (9-7-0)	Cleveland 34, Buffalo 30
		Central	Cleveland (9-6-1)	Denver 24, Pittsburgh 23
		Western	Denver (11-5-0)	Denver 37, Cleveland 21
	National	Eastern	N.Y. Giants (12-4-0)	San Francisco 41, Minnesota 13
		Central	Minnesota (10-6-0)	L.A. Rams 19, N.Y. Giants 13
		Western	San Francisco (14-2-0)	San Francisco 30, L.A. Rams 3

World Almanac/NEA Bert Bell Memorial Trophy Winners

The World Almanac/NEA Bert Bell Memorial Trophy, named after the former NFL commissioner, is awarded annually to the outstanding NFL rookie as chosen by a panel of sports experts.

1964	Charlie Taylor, Washington, WR		1976	AFC: Mike Haynes, New England, CB
1965	Gale Sayers, Chicago, RB			NFC: Sammy White, Minnesota, WR
1966	Tommy Nobis, Atlanta, LB		1977	Tony Dorsett, Dallas, RB
1967	Mel Farr, Detroit, RB		1978	Earl Campbell, Houston, RB
1968	Earl McCullouch, Detroit, WR		1979	Ottis Anderson, St. Louis, RB
1969	Calvin Hill, Dallas, RB		1980	Billy Sims, Detroit, RB
1970	Raymond Chester, Oakland, TE		1981	Lawrence Taylor, N.Y. Giants, LB
1971	AFC: Jim Plunkett, New England, QB		1982	Marcus Allen, L.A. Raiders, RB
	NFC: John Brockington, Green Bay, RB		1983	Eric Dickerson, L.A. Rams, RB
1972	AFC: Franco Harris, Pittsburgh, RB		1984	Louis Lipps, Pittsburgh, WR
	NFC: Willie Buchanon, Green Bay, DB		1985	Eddie Brown, Cincinnati, WR
1973	AFC: Boobie Clark, Cincinnati, RB		1986	Rueben Mayes, New Orleans, RB
	NFC: Chuck Foreman, Minnesota, RB		1987	Bo Jackson, L.A. Raiders, RB
1974	Don Woods, San Diego, RB		1988	John Stephens, New England, RB
1975	AFC: Robert Brazile, Houston, LB		1989	Barry Sanders, Detroit, RB
	NFC: Steve Bartkowski, Atlanta, QB			

World Almanac/NEA George Halas Trophy Winners

The World Almanac/NEA Halas Trophy, named after football coach George Halas, is awarded annually to the outstanding defensive player in the NFL as chosen by a panel of sports experts.

1966	Larry Wilson, St. Louis	1975	Curley Culp, Houston	1983	Jack Lambert, Pittsburgh
1967	Deacon Jones, Los Angeles	1976	Jerry Sherk, Cleveland	1984	Mike Haynes, L.A. Raiders
1968	Deacon Jones, Los Angeles	1977	Harvey Martin, Dallas	1985	Howie Long, L.A. Raiders
1969	Dick Butkus, Chicago	1978	Randy Gradishar, Denver		Andre Tippett, New England
1970	Dick Butkus, Chicago	1979	Lee Roy Selmon, Tampa Bay	1986	Lawrence Taylor, N.Y. Giants
1971	Carl Eller, Minnesota	1980	Lester Hayes, Oakland	1987	Reggie White, Philadelphia
1972	Joe Greene, Pittsburgh	1981	Joe Klecko, N.Y. Jets	1988	Mike Singletary, Chicago
1973	Alan Page, Minnesota	1982	Mark Gastineau, N.Y. Jets	1989	Tim Harris, Green Bay
1974	Joe Greene, Pittsburgh				

World Almanac/NEA Jim Thorpe Trophy Winners

The World Almanac/NEA Jim Thorpe Trophy goes to the most valuable player as chosen by the NFL Players Association in 1989.

1955	Harlon Hill, Chicago Bears		1973	O.J. Simpson, Buffalo Bills
1956	Frank Gifford, N.Y. Giants		1974	Ken Stabler, Oakland Raiders
1957	John Unitas, Baltimore Colts		1975	Fran Tarkenton, Minnesota Vikings
1958	Jim Brown, Cleveland Browns		1976	Bert Jones, Baltimore Colts
1959	Charley Conerly, N.Y. Giants		1977	Walter Payton, Chicago Bears
1960	Norm Van Brocklin, Philadelphia Eagles		1978	Earl Campbell, Houston Oilers
1961	Y.A. Tittle, N.Y. Giants		1979	Earl Campbell, Houston Oilers
1962	Jim Taylor, Green Bay Packers		1980	Earl Campbell, Houston Oilers
1963	Jim Brown, Cleveland Browns; Y.A. Tittle, N.Y. Giants		1981	Ken Anderson, Cincinnati Bengals
1964	Lenny Moore, Baltimore Colts		1982	Dan Fouts, San Diego Chargers
1965	Jim Brown, Cleveland Browns		1983	Joe Theismann, Washington Redskins
1966	Bart Starr, Green Bay Packers		1984	Dan Marino, Miami Dolphins
1967	John Unitas, Baltimore Colts		1985	Walter Payton, Chicago Bears
1968	Earl Morrall, Baltimore Colts		1986	Phil Simms, N.Y. Giants
1969	Roman Gabriel, Los Angeles Rams		1987	Jerry Rice, San Francisco
1970	John Brodie, San Francisco 49ers		1988	Roger Craig, San Francisco
1971	Bob Griese, Miami Dolphins		1989	Joe Montana, San Francisco
1972	Larry Brown, Washington Redskins			

Super Bowl MVPs

1967	Bart Starr, Green Bay	1975	Franco Harris, Pittsburgh	1983	John Riggins, Washington
1968	Bart Starr, Green Bay	1976	Lynn Swann, Pittsburgh	1984	Marcus Allen, L.A. Raiders
1969	Joe Namath, N.Y. Jets	1977	Fred Biletnikoff, Oakland	1985	Joe Montana, San Francisco
1970	Len Dawson, Kansas City	1978	Randy White, Harvey Martin, Dallas	1986	Richard Dent, Chicago
1971	Chuck Howley, Dallas	1979	Terry Bradshaw, Pittsburgh	1987	Phil Simms, N.Y. Giants
1972	Roger Staubach, Dallas	1980	Terry Bradshaw, Pittsburgh	1988	Doug Williams, Washington
1973	Jake Scott, Miami	1981	Jim Plunkett, Oakland	1989	Jerry Rice, San Francisco
1974	Larry Csonka, Miami	1982	Joe Montana, San Francisco	1990	Joe Montana, San Francisco

American Football League

Year	Eastern Division	Western Division	Playoff
1960	Houston Oilers (10-4-0)	L. A. Chargers (10-4-0)	Houston 24, Los Angeles 16
1961	Houston Oilers (10-3-1)	San Diego Chargers (12-2-0)	Houston 10, San Diego 3
1962	Houston Oilers (11-3-0)	Dallas Texans (11-3-0)	Dallas 20, Houston 17(b)
1963	Boston Patriots (8-6-1)(a)	San Diego Chargers (11-3-0)	San Diego 51, Boston 10
1964	Buffalo Bills (12-2-0)	San Diego Chargers (8-5-1)	Buffalo 20, San Diego 7
1965	Buffalo Bills (10-3-1)	San Diego Chargers (9-2-3)	Buffalo 23, San Diego 0
1966	Buffalo Bills (9-4-1)	Kansas City Chiefs (11-2-1)	Kansas City 31, Buffalo 7
1967	Houston Oilers (9-4-1)	Oakland Raiders (13-1-0)	Oakland 40, Houston 7
1968	New York Jets (11-3-0)	Oakland Raiders (12-2-0)(a)	New York 27, Oakland 23
1969	New York Jets (10-4-0)	Oakland Raiders (12-1-1)	Kansas City 17, Oakland 7(c)

(a) won divisional playoff (b) won at 2:45 of second overtime. (c) Kansas City defeated Jets to make playoffs.

National Football Conference Leaders

(National Football League, 1960-69)

Passing

Player, team	Atts	Com	YG	TD	Year
Milt Plum, Cleveland	250	151	2,297	21	1960
Milt Plum, Cleveland	302	177	2,416	18	1961
Bart Starr, Green Bay	285	178	2,438	12	1962
Y.A. Tittle, N.Y. Giants	367	221	3,145	36	1963
Bart Starr, Green Bay	272	163	2,144	15	1964
Rudy Bukich, Chicago	312	176	2,641	20	1965
Bart Starr, Green Bay	251	156	2,257	14	1966
Sonny Jurgensen, Washington	508	288	3,747	31	1967
Earl Morrall, Baltimore	317	182	2,909	26	1968
Sonny Jurgensen, Washington	442	274	3,102	22	1969
John Brodie, San Francisco	378	223	2,941	24	1970
Roger Staubach, Dallas	211	126	1,882	15	1971
Norm Snead, N.Y. Giants	325	196	2,307	17	1972
Roger Staubach, Dallas	286	179	2,428	23	1973
Sonny Jurgensen, Washington	167	107	1,185	11	1974
Fran Tarkenton, Minnesota	425	273	2,994	25	1975
James Harris, Los Angeles	158	91	1,460	8	1976
Roger Staubach, Dallas	361	210	2,620	18	1977
Roger Staubach, Dallas	413	231	3,190	25	1978
Roger Staubach, Dallas	461	267	3,586	27	1979
Ron Jaworski, Philadelphia	451	257	3,529	27	1980
Joe Montana, San Francisco	488	311	3,565	19	1981
Joe Thiesmann, Washington	252	161	2,033	13	1982
Steve Bartkowski, Atlanta	423	274	3,167	22	1983
Joe Montana, San Francisco	432	279	3,630	28	1984
Joe Montana, San Francisco	494	303	3,653	27	1985
Tommy Kramer, Minnesota	372	208	3,000	24	1986
Joe Montana, San Francisco	398	266	3,054	31	1987
Wade Wilson, Minnesota	332	204	2,746	15	1988
Joe Montana, San Francisco	386	271	3,521	26	1989

Pass-Receiving

Player, team	Ct	YG	TD	Year
Raymond Berry, Baltimore	74	1,298	10	1960
Jim Phillips, L.A. Rams	78	1,092	5	1961
Bobby Mitchell, Washington	72	1,384	11	1962
Bobby Joe Conrad, St. Louis	73	967	10	1963
Johnny Morris, Chicago	93	1,200	10	1964
Dave Parks, San Francisco	80	1,344	12	1965
Charley Taylor, Washington	72	1,119	12	1966
Charley Taylor, Washington	70	990	9	1967
Clifton McNeil, San Francisco	71	994	7	1968
Dan Abramowicz, New Orleans	73	1,015	7	1969
Dick Gordon, Chicago	71	1,026	13	1970
Bob Tucker, Giants	59	791	4	1971
Harold Jackson, Philadelphia	62	1,048	4	1972
Harold Carmichael, Philadelphia	67	1,116	9	1973
Charles Young, Philadelphia	63	696	3	1974
Chuck Foreman, Minnesota	73	691	9	1975
Drew Pearson, Dallas	58	806	6	1976
Ahmad Rashad, Minnesota	51	681	2	1977
Rickey Young, Minnesota	88	704	5	1978
Ahmad Rashad, Minnesota	80	1,156	9	1979
Earl Cooper, San Francisco	83	567	4	1980
Dwight Clark, San Francisco	85	1,105	4	1981
Dwight Clark, San Francisco	60	913	5	1982
Roy Green, St. Louis	78	1,227	14	1983
Charlie Brown, Washington	78	1,225	8	
Earnest Gray, N.Y. Giants	78	1,139	5	
Art Monk, Washington	106	1,372	7	1984
Roger Craig, San Francisco	92	1,016	6	1985
Jerry Rice, San Francisco	86	1,570	15	1986
J.T. Smith, St. Louis	91	1,117	8	1987
Henry Ellard, L.A. Rams	86	1,414	10	1988
Sterling Sharpe, Green Bay	90	1,423	12	1989

Scoring

Player, team	TD	PAT	FG	Pts	Year
Paul Hornung, Green Bay	15	41	15	176	1960
Paul Hornung, Green Bay	10	41	15	146	1961
Jim Taylor, Green Bay	19	0	0	114	1962
Don Chandler, N.Y. Giants	0	52	18	106	1963
Lenny Moore, Baltimore	20	0	0	120	1964
Gale Sayers, Chicago	22	0	0	132	1965
Bruce Gossett, L.A. Rams	0	29	28	113	1966
Jim Bakken, St. Louis	0	36	27	117	1967
Leroy Kelly, Cleveland	20	0	0	120	1968
Fred Cox, Minnesota	0	43	26	121	1969
Fred Cox, Minnesota	0	35	30	125	1970
Curt Knight, Washington	0	27	29	114	1971
Chester Marcol, Green Bay	0	29	33	128	1972
David Ray, Los Angeles	0	40	30	130	1973
Chester Marcol, Green Bay	0	19	25	94	1974
Chuck Foreman, Minnesota	22	0	0	132	1975
Mark Moseley, Washington	0	31	22	97	1976
Walter Payton, Chicago	16	0	0	96	1977
Frank Corrall, Los Angeles	0	31	29	118	1978
Mark Moseley, Washington	0	39	25	114	1979
Ed Murray, Detroit	0	35	27	116	1980
Ed Murray, Detroit	0	46	25	121	1981
Wendell Tyler, L.A. Rams	13	0	0	78	1982
Mark Moseley, Washington	0	62	33	161	1983
Ray Wersching, San Francisco	0	56	25	131	1984
Kevin Butler, Chicago	0	51	31	144	1985
Kevin Butler, Chicago	0	36	28	120	1986
Jerry Rice, San Francisco	23	0	0	138	1987
Mike Cofer, San Francisco	0	40	27	121	1988
Mike Cofer, San Francisco	0	49	29	136	1989

Rushing

Player, team	Yds	Atts	TD
Jim Brown, Cleveland	1,257	215	9
Jim Brown, Cleveland	1,408	305	8
Jim Taylor, Green Bay	1,474	272	19
Jim Brown, Cleveland	1,863	291	12
Jim Brown, Cleveland	1,446	280	7
Jim Brown, Cleveland	1,544	289	17
Gale Sayers, Chicago	1,231	229	8
Leroy Kelly, Cleveland	1,205	235	11
Leroy Kelly, Cleveland	1,239	248	16
Gale Sayers, Chicago	1,032	236	8
Larry Brown, Washington	1,125	237	5
John Brockington, Green Bay	1,105	216	4
Larry Brown, Washington	1,216	285	8
John Brockington, Green Bay	1,144	265	3
Lawrence McCutcheon, Los Angeles	1,109	236	3
Jim Otis, St. Louis	1,076	269	5
Walter Payton, Chicago	1,390	311	13
Walter Payton, Chicago	1,852	339	14
Walter Payton, Chicago	1,395	333	11
Walter Payton, Chicago	1,610	369	14
Walter Payton, Chicago	1,460	317	6
George Rogers, New Orleans	1,674	378	13
Tony Dorsett, Dallas	745	177	5
Eric Dickerson, L.A. Rams	1,808	390	18
Eric Dickerson, L.A. Rams	2,105	379	14
Gerald Riggs, Atlanta	1,719	397	10
Eric Dickerson, L.A. Rams	1,821	404	11
Charles White, L.A. Rams	1,374	324	11
Herschel Walker, Dallas	1,514	361	5
Barry Sanders, Detroit	1,470	280	14

American Football Conference Leaders

(American Football League, 1960-1969)

Passing

Player, team	Atts	Com	YG	TD	Year
Jack Kemp, Los Angeles	406	211	3,018	20	1960
George Blanda, Houston	362	187	3,330	36	1961
Len Dawson, Dallas	310	189	2,759	29	1962
Tobin Rote, Kansas City	286	170	2,510	20	1963
Len Dawson, Kansas City	354	199	2,879	30	1964
John Hadl, San Diego	348	174	2,798	20	1965
Len Dawson, Kansas City	284	159	2,527	26	1966
Daryle Lamonica, Oakland	425	220	3,228	30	1967
Len Dawson, Kansas City	224	131	2,109	17	1968
Greg Cook, Cincinnati	197	106	1,854	15	1969
Daryle Lamonica, Oakland	356	179	2,516	22	1970

Pass-Receiving

Player, team	Ct	YG	TD	Year
Lionel Taylor, Denver	92	1,235	12	1960
Lionel Taylor, Denver	100	1,176	4	1961
Lionel Taylor, Denver	77	908	4	1962
Lionel Taylor, Denver	78	1,101	10	1963
Charley Hennigan, Houston	101	1,546	8	1964
Lionel Taylor, Denver	85	1,131	6	1965
Lance Alworth, San Diego	73	1,383	13	1966
George Sauer, N.Y. Jets	75	1,189	6	1967
Lance Alworth, San Diego	68	1,312	10	1968
Lance Alworth, San Diego	64	1,003	4	1969
Marlin Briscoe, Buffalo	57	1,036	8	1970

Passing

Player, team	Atts	Com	YG	TD	Year
Bob Griese, Miami	263	145	2,089	19	1971
Earl Morrall, Miami	150	83	1,360	11	1972
Ken Stabler, Oakland	260	163	1,997	14	1973
Ken Anderson, Cincinnati	328	213	2,667	18	1974
Ken Anderson, Cincinnati	377	228	3,169	21	1975
Ken Stabler, Oakland	291	194	2,737	27	1976
Bob Griese, Miami	307	180	2,252	22	1977
Terry Bradshaw, Pittsburgh	368	207	2,915	28	1978
Dan Fouts, San Diego	530	332	4,082	24	1979
Brian Sipe, Cleveland	554	337	4,132	30	1980
Ken Anderson, Cincinnati	479	300	3,754	29	1981
Ken Anderson, Cincinnati	309	218	2,495	12	1982
Dan Marino, Miami	296	173	2,210	20	1983
Dan Marino, Miami	564	362	5,084	48	1984
Ken O'Brien, N.Y. Jets	488	297	3,888	25	1985
Dan Marino, Miami	623	378	4,746	44	1986
Bernie Kosar, Cleveland	389	241	3,033	22	1987
Boomer Esiason, Cincinnati	388	223	3,572	28	1988
Boomer Esiason, Cincinnati	455	258	3,525	28	1989

Pass-Receiving

Year	Player, team	Ct	YG	TD
1971	Fred Biletnikoff, Oakland	61	929	9
1972	Fred Biletnikoff, Oakland	58	802	7
1973	Fred Willis, Houston	57	371	1
1974	Lydell Mitchell, Baltimore	72	544	2
1975	Reggie Rucker, Cleveland	60	770	3
	Lydell Mitchell, Baltimore	60	554	4
1976	MacArthur Lane, Kansas City	66	686	1
1977	Lydell Mitchell, Baltimore	71	620	4
1978	Steve Largent, Seattle	71	1,168	8
1979	Joe Washington, Baltimore	82	750	3
1980	Kellen Winslow, San Diego	89	1,290	9
1981	Kellen Winslow, San Diego	88	1,075	10
1982	Kellen Winslow, San Diego	54	721	6
1983	Todd Christensen, L.A. Raiders	92	1,247	12
1984	Ozzie Newsome, Cleveland	89	1,001	5
1985	Lionel James, San Diego	86	1,027	6
1986	Todd Christensen, L.A. Raiders	95	1,153	8
1987	Al Toon, N.Y. Jets	68	976	5
1988	Al Toon, N.Y. Jets	93	1,067	5
1989	Andre Reed, Buffalo	88	1,312	9

Scoring

Player, team	TD	PAT	FG	Pts	Year
Gene Mingo, Denver	6	33	18	123	1960
Gino Cappelletti, Boston	8	48	17	147	1961
Gene Mingo, Denver	4	32	27	137	1962
Gino Cappelletti, Boston	2	35	22	113	1963
Gino Cappelletti, Boston	7	36	25	155	1964
Gino Cappelletti, Boston	9	27	17	132	1965
Gino Cappelletti, Boston	6	35	16	119	1966
George Blanda, Oakland	0	56	20	116	1967
Jim Turner, N.Y. Jets	0	43	34	145	1968
Jim Turner, N.Y. Jets	0	33	32	129	1969
Jan Stenerud, Kansas City	0	26	30	116	1970
Garo Yepremian, Miami	0	33	28	117	1971
Bobby Howfield, N.Y. Jets	0	40	27	121	1972
Roy Gerela, Pittsburgh	0	36	29	123	1973
Roy Gerela, Pittsburgh	0	33	20	93	1974
O.J. Simpson, Buffalo	23	0	0	138	1975
Toni Linhart, Baltimore	0	49	20	109	1976
Errol Mann, Oakland	0	39	20	99	1977
Pat Leahy, N.Y. Jets	0	41	22	107	1978
John Smith, New England	0	46	23	115	1979
John Smith, New England	0	51	26	129	1980
Jim Breech, Cincinnati	0	49	22	115	1981
Marcus Allen, L.A. Raiders	14	0	0	84	1982
Gary Anderson, Pittsburgh	0	38	27	119	1983
Gary Anderson, Pittsburgh	0	45	24	117	1984
Gary Anderson, Pittsburgh	0	40	33	139	1985
Tony Franklin, New England	0	44	32	140	1986
Jim Breech, Cincinnati	0	25	24	97	1987
Scott Norwood, Buffalo	0	33	32	129	1988
David Treadwell	0	39	27	120	1989

*1,011 AFC yards led conference.

Rushing

Year	Player, team	Yds	Atts	TD
1960	Abner Haynes, Dallas	875	156	9
1961	Billy Cannon, Houston	948	200	6
1962	Cookie Gilchrist, Buffalo	1,096	214	13
1963	Clem Daniels, Oakland	1,099	215	3
1964	Cookie Gilchrist, Buffalo	981	230	6
1965	Paul Lowe, San Diego	1,121	222	7
1966	Jim Nance, Boston	1,458	299	11
1967	Jim Nance, Boston	1,216	269	7
1968	Paul Robinson, Cincinnati	1,023	238	8
1969	Dick Post, San Diego	873	182	6
1970	Floyd Little, Denver	901	209	3
1971	Floyd Little, Denver	1,133	284	6
1972	O.J. Simpson, Buffalo	1,251	292	6
1973	O.J. Simpson, Buffalo	2,003	332	12
1974	Otis Armstrong, Denver	1,407	263	9
1975	O.J. Simpson, Buffalo	1,817	329	16
1976	Mark van Eeghen, Oakland	1,273	324	7
1977	O.J. Simpson, Buffalo	1,503	290	8
1978	Earl Campbell, Houston	1,450	302	13
1979	Earl Campbell, Houston	1,697	368	19
1980	Earl Campbell, Houston	1,934	373	13
1981	Earl Campbell, Houston	1,376	361	10
1982	Freeman McNeil, N.Y. Jets	786	151	6
1983	Curt Warner, Seattle	1,446	335	13
1984	Earnest Jackson, San Diego	1,179	296	8
1985	Marcus Allen, L.A. Raiders	1,759	380	11
1986	Curt Warner, Seattle	1,481	319	13
1987	Eric Dickerson, L.A. Rams, Indianapolis	1,288*	283	6
1988	Eric Dickerson, Indianapolis	1,659	388	14
1989	Christian Okoye, Kansas City	1,480	370	12

World Almanac/NEA All-Pro Team in 1989

Chosen by a panel of sports experts representing the World Almanac, its co-sponsoring newspapers, and its publisher, Newspaper Enterprise Assn.

First team	Offense	Second team
Jerry Rice, San Francisco	Wide receiver	Andre Reed, Buffalo
Sterling Sharpe, Green Bay	Wide receiver	Mark Carrier, Tampa Bay
Rodney Holman, Cincinnati	Tight end	Steve Jordan, Minnesota
Anthony Munoz, Cincinnati	Tackle	Lomas Brown, Detroit
Jackie Slater, L.A. Rams	Tackle	Chris Hinton, Indianapolis
Rich Moran, Green Bay	Guard	Bruce Matthews Houston
Mike Munchak, Houston	Guard	Tom Newberry, L.A. Rams
Jay Hilgenberg, Chicago	Center	Keith Loudermilk, Minnesota
Joe Montana, San Francisco	Quarterback	Jim Everett, L.A. Rams
Christian Okoye, Kansas City	Running back	Barry Sanders, Detroit
Thurman Thomas, Buffalo	Running back	Dalton Hilliard, New Orleans
Mike Cofer, San Francisco	Placekicker	Mike Lansford, L.A. Rams

First team	Defense	Second team
Reggie White, Philadelphia	End	Bruce Smith, Buffalo
Chris Doleman, Minnesota	End	Howie Long, L.A. Raiders
Michael Dean Perry, Cleveland	Nose tackle	Jerry Ball, Detroit
Keith Millard, Minnesota	Tackle	Jerome Brown, Philadelphia
Vaughn Johnson, New Orleans	Inside linebacker	Billy Ray Smith, San Diego
Karl Mecklenburg, Denver	Inside linebacker	Michael Walter, San Francisco
Tim Harris, Green Bay	Outside Linebacker	Pat Swilling, New Orleans
Kevin Greene, L.A. Rams	Outside linebacker	Lawrence Taylor, N.Y. Giants
Albert Lewis, Kansas City	Cornerback	Eric Allen, Philadelphia
Mark Collins, N.Y. Giants	Cornerback	Frank Minnifield, Cleveland
Joey Browner, Minnesota	Safety	Erik McMillan, N.Y. Jets
Tim McDonald, Phoenix	Safety	David Fulcher, Cincinnati
Greg Montgomery, Houston	Punter	Reggie Roby, Miami

1989 NFL Individual Leaders

National Football Conference

Passing

	Att	Comp	Pct comp	Yards	Avg gain	TD	Pct TD	Long	Int	Rating points
Joe Montana, San Francisco...	386	271	70.2	3521	9.12	26	6.7	95	8	112.4
Jim Everett, L.A. Rams......	518	304	58.7	4310	8.32	29	5.6	78	17	90.6
Mark Rypien, Washington......	476	280	58.8	3768	7.92	22	4.6	80	13	88.1
Bobby Hebert, New Orleans...	353	222	62.9	2686	7.61	15	4.2	54	15	82.7
Don Majkowski, Green Bay....	599	353	58.9	4318	7.21	27	4.5	79	20	82.3
Phil Simms, N.Y. Giants.....	405	228	56.3	3061	7.56	14	3.5	62	14	77.6
Chris Miller, Atlanta.......	526	280	53.2	3459	6.58	16	3.0	72	10	76.1
Randall Cunningham, Philadelphia	532	290	54.5	3400	6.39	21	3.9	66	15	75.5
Wade Wilson, Minnesota.....	362	194	53.6	2543	7.02	9	2.5	50	12	70.5
Gary Hogeboom, Phoenix....	364	204	56.0	2591	7.12	14	3.8	59	19	69.5

Rushing

	Att	Yds	Avg	TD
Barry Sanders, Detroit........	280	1470	5.3	14
Neal Anderson, Chicago......	274	1275	4.7	11
Dalton Hilliard, New Orleans....	344	1262	3.7	13
Greg Bell, L.A. Rams........	272	1137	4.2	15
Roger Craig, San Francisco....	271	1054	3.9	6
Ottis Anderson, N.Y. Giants....	325	1023	3.1	14
Herschel Walker, Dall.-Minn....	250	915	3.7	7
Gerald Riggs, Washington......	201	834	4.1	4
Brent Fullwood, Green Bay.....	204	821	4.0	5
John Settle, Atlanta.........	179	689	3.8	3

Pass Receiving

	No	Yds	Avg	TD
Sterling Sharpe, Green Bay.....	90	1423	15.8	12
Mark Carrier, Tampa Bay......	86	1422	16.5	9
Art Monk, Washington........	86	1186	13.8	8
Jerry Rice, San Francisco.....	82	1483	18.1	17
Ricky Sanders, Washington.....	80	1138	14.2	4
Gary Clark, Washington.......	79	1229	15.6	9
Tom Rathman, San Francisco....	73	616	8.4	1
Henry Ellard, L.A. Rams.......	70	1382	19.7	8
Richard Johnson, Detroit......	70	1091	15.6	8
Eric Martin, New Orleans.....	68	1090	16.0	8

Scoring-Touchdowns

	TD	Rush	Pass	Pts
Dalton Hilliard, New Orleans....	18	13	5	108
Jerry Rice, San Francisco......	17	0	17	102
Neal Anderson, Chicago......	15	11	4	90
Greg Bell, L.A. Rams........	15	15	0	90
Ottis Anderson, N.Y. Giants....	14	14	0	84
Barry Sanders, Detroit.......	14	14	0	84
*Sterling Sharpe, Green Bay....	13	0	12	78
Cris Carter, Philadelphia.......	11	0	11	66
John Taylor, San Francisco....	10	0	10	60
*Herschel Walker, Dall.-Minn....	10	7	2	60
* One TD via return.				

Scoring-Kicking

	XP	XPA	FG	FGA	Pts
Mike Cofer, San Francisco..	49	51	29	36	136
Chris Lohmiller, Washington..	41	41	29	40	128
Rich Karlis, Minnesota.....	27	28	31	39	120
Mike Lansford, L.A. Rams....	51	51	23	30	120
Chris Jacke, Green Bay.....	42	42	22	28	108
Morten Andersen, N.O.....	44	45	20	29	104
Donald Igwebuike, Tampa Bay	33	35	22	28	99
Eddie Murray, Detroit.....	36	36	20	21	96

	XP	XPA	FG	FGA	Pts
Greg Davis, N.E.-Atlanta....	25	28	23	34	94
Kevin Butler, Chicago.....	43	45	15	19	88

Interceptions

	No	Yds	Long	TD
Eric Allen, Philadelphia........	8	38	18	0
Tim McDonald, Phoenix......	7	170	53	1
Jerry Holmes, Detroit........	6	77	36	1
Harry Hamilton, Tampa Bay....	6	70	30	0
Dave Waymer, New Orleans....	6	66	42	0
Jerry Gray, L.A. Rams........	6	48	27	1

Kickoff Returns

	No	Yds	Avg	TD
Mel Gray, Detroit..........	24	640	26.7	0
James Dixon, Dallas........	47	1181	25.1	1
Joe Howard, Washington.....	21	522	24.9	1
Dennis Gentry, Chicago.....	28	667	23.8	0
Dave Meggett, N.Y. Giants....	27	577	21.4	0
Thomas Sanders, Chicago....	23	491	21.3	1
A.J. Johnson, Washington....	24	504	21.0	0
Deion Sanders, Atlanta.....	35	725	20.7	0
Ron Brown, L.A. Rams.......	47	968	20.6	0
Vai Sikahema, Phoenix.......	43	874	20.3	0

Punt Returns

	No	Yds	Avg	TD
Walter Stanley, Detroit........	36	496	13.8	0
Dave Meggett, N.Y. Giants....	46	582	12.7	1
Vai Sikahema, Phoenix.......	37	433	11.7	0
John Taylor, San Francisco....	36	417	11.6	0
Willie Drewrey, Tampa Bay....	20	220	11.0	0
Deion Sanders, Atlanta......	28	307	11.0	1
Leo Lewis, Minnesota........	44	446	10.1	0
Joe Howard, Washington.....	21	200	9.5	0
Darryl Henley, L.A. Rams.....	29	273	9.4	0
Gizmo Williams, Philadelphia....	30	267	8.9	0

Punters

	No	Yds	Avg	Long
Rich Camarillo, Phoenix.......	76	3298	43.4	58
Jim Arnold, Detroit.........	82	3538	43.1	64
Sean Landeta, N.Y. Giants....	70	3019	43.1	71
Ralf Mojsiejenko, Washington..	62	2663	43.0	74
Scott Fulhage, Atlanta.......	84	3472	41.3	65
Mike Saxon, Dallas.........	79	3233	40.9	56
Don Bracken, Green Bay.....	66	2682	40.6	63
Barry Helton, San Francisco..	55	2226	40.5	56
Bucky Scribner, Minnesota....	72	2864	39.8	55
Tommy Barnhardt, New Orleans..	55	2179	39.6	56

Sacks

	No		No		No
Doleman, Chris, Minnesota..	21	Swilling, Pat, New Orleans...	16½	Jeffcoat, Jim, Dallas..........	12
Harris, Tim, Green Bay.....	19½	Simmons, Clyde, Philadelphia..	15½	Noga, Al, Minnesota........	11½
Millard, Keith, Minnesota....	18	Taylor, Lawrence, N.Y. Giants..	15	White, Reggie, Philadelphia..	11
Greene, Kevin, L.A. Rams...	16½				

American Football Conference

Passing

	Att	Comp	Pct comp	Yards	Avg gain	TD	Pct TD	Long	Int	Rating points
Boomer Esiason, Cincinnati . .	455	258	56.7	3525	7.75	28	6.2	74	11	92.1
Warren Moon, Houston	464	280	60.3	3631	7.83	23	5.0	55	14	88.9
Jim Kelly, Buffalo	391	228	58.3	3130	8.01	25	6.4	78	18	86.2
Bernie Kosar, Cleveland . . .	513	303	59.1	3533	6.89	18	3.5	97	14	80.3
Dan Marino, Miami	550	308	56.0	3997	7.27	24	4.4	78	22	76.9
Steve DeBerg, Kansas City . .	324	196	60.5	2529	7.81	11	3.4	50	16	75.8
Dave Krieg, Seattle	499	286	57.3	3309	6.63	21	4.2	60	20	74.8
Ken O'Brien, N.Y. Jets	477	288	60.4	3346	7.01	12	2.5	57	18	74.3
John Elway, Denver	416	223	53.6	3051	7.33	18	4.3	69	18	73.7
Jim McMahon, San Diego . . .	318	176	55.3	2132	6.70	10	3.1	69	10	73.5

Rushing

	Att	Yds	Avg	TD
Christian Okoye, Kansas City	370	1480	4.0	12
Eric Dickerson, Indianapolis	314	1311	4.2	7
Thurman Thomas, Buffalo	298	1244	4.2	6
James Brooks, Cincinnati	221	1239	5.6	7
Bobby Humphrey, Denver	294	1151	3.9	7
Bo Jackson, L.A. Raiders	173	950	5.5	4
John Stephens, New England	244	833	3.4	7
Tim Worley, Pittsburgh.	195	770	3.9	5
Johnny Hector, N.Y. Jets	177	702	4.0	3
Marion Butts, San Diego	170	683	4.0	9

Pass Receiving

	No	Yds	Avg	TD
Andre Reed, Buffalo	88	1312	14.9	9
Brian Blades, Seattle.	77	1063	13.8	5
Vance Johnson, Denver	76	1095	14.4	7
John L. Williams, Seattle	76	657	8.6	6
Anthony Miller, San Diego	75	1252	16.7	10
Drew Hill, Drew, Houston	66	938	14.2	8
Webster Slaughter, Cleveland . . .	65	1236	19.0	6
Tim McGee, Cincinnati	65	1211	18.6	8
Mark Clayton, Miami	64	1011	15.8	9
Bill Brooks, Indianapolis	63	919	14.6	4

Scoring-Touchdowns

	TD	Rush	Pass	Pts
Christian Okoye, Kansas City	12	12	0	72
Thurman Thomas, Buffalo	12	6	6	72
*Anthony Miller, San Diego	11	0	10	66
Eric Metcalf, Cleveland	10	6	4	60
James Brooks, Cincinnati	9	7	2	54
Marion Butts, San Diego	9	9	0	54
Mark Clayton, Miami	9	0	9	54
Mervyn Fernandez, L.A. Raiders . .	9	0	9	54
Rodney Holman, Cincinnati	9	0	9	54
Andre Reed, Buffalo	9	0	9	54
* One TD via return.				

Scoring-Kicking

	XP	XPA	FG	FGA	Pts
David Treadwell, Denver	39	40	27	33	120
Scott Norwood, Buffalo	46	47	23	30	115
Tony Zendejas, Houston.	40	40	25	37	115
Nick Lowery, Kansas City . . .	34	35	24	33	106
Jeff Jaeger, L.A. Raiders . . .	34	34	23	34	103
Pete Stoyanovich, Miami . . .	38	39	19	26	95

Dean Biasucci, Indianapolis . .	31	32	21	27	94
Gary Anderson, Pittsburgh. . . .	28	28	21	30	91
Matt Bahr, Cleveland.	40	40	16	24	88
Chris Bahr, San Diego	29	30	17	25	80

Interceptions

	No	Yds	Long	TD
Felix Wright, Cleveland	9	91	27	1
David Fulcher, Cincinnati	8	87	22	0
Keith Taylor, Indianapolis	7	225	80	1
Gill Byrd, San Diego	7	38	22	0
Erik McMillan, N.Y. Jets	6	180	92	1
Tyrone Braxton, Denver	6	103	34	1

Kickoff Returns

	No	Yds	Avg	TD
Rod Woodson, Pittsburgh	36	982	27.3	1
Marc Logan, Miami.	24	613	25.5	1
Anthony Miller, San Diego.	21	533	25.4	1
Sammy Martin, New England	24	584	24.3	0
James Jefferson, Seattle	22	511	23.2	1
Eric Metcalf, Cleveland	31	718	23.2	0
Stanford Jennings, Cincinnati . . .	26	525	20.2	0
Ken Bell, Denver	30	602	20.1	0
Stefon Adams, L.A. Raiders	22	425	19.3	0
JoJo Townsell, N.Y. Jets	34	653	19.2	0

Punt Returns

	No	Yds	Avg	TD
Clarence Verdin, Indianapolis	23	296	12.9	1
Gerald McNeil, Cleveland	49	496	10.1	0
JoJo Townsell, N.Y. Jets	33	299	9.1	0
Mickey Sutton, G.B.-Buffalo	31	273	8.8	0
Rod Woodson, Pittsburgh	29	207	7.1	0
Ken Bell, Denver	21	143	6.8	0

Punters

	No	Yds	Avg	Long
Greg Montgomery, Houston.	56	2422	43.3	63
Rohn Stark, Indianapolis.	79	3392	42.9	64
Reggie Roby, Miami	58	2458	42.4	58
Harry Newsome, Pittsburgh.	82	3368	41.1	57
Jeff Gossett, L.A. Raiders	67	2711	40.5	60
Mike Horan, Denver	77	3111	40.4	63
Kelly Goodburn, Kansas City	67	2688	40.1	54
Hank Ilesic, San Diego	76	3049	40.1	64
Lee Johnson, Cincinnati	61	2446	40.1	62
Ruben Rodriguez, Seattle	75	2995	39.9	59

Sacks

	No		No.		No
Williams, Lee, San Diego . . .	14	Porter, Rufus, Seattle	10½	Grossman, Burt, San Diego . .	10
Smith, Bruce, Buffalo	13	Townsend, Greg, L.A. Raiders	10½	Hand, Jon, Indianapolis	10
O'Neal, Leslie, San Diego . . .	12½	Cross, Jeff, Miami	10	Thomas, Derrick, Kansas City.	10
Fletcher, Simon, Denver	12				

All-Time Professional Football Records

NFL, AFL, and All-American Football Conference

(at start of 1990 season)

Leading Lifetime Rushers

Player	League	Yrs	Att	Yards	Avg	Player	League	Yrs	Att	Yards	Avg
Walter Payton	NFL	13	3,838	16,726	4.4	Jim Taylor	NFL	10	1,941	8,597	4.4
Tony Dorsett	NFL	12	2,936	12,739	4.3	Larry Csonka	AFL-NFL	11	1,891	8,081	4.3
Jim Brown	NFL	9	2,359	12,312	5.2	Gerald Riggs	NFL	8	1,788	7,465	4.2
Franco Harris	NFL	13	2,949	12,120	4.1	Mike Pruitt	NFL	11	1,844	7,378	4.0
John Riggins	NFL	14	2,916	11,352	3.9	Marcus Allen	NFL	8	1,781	7,275	4.1
O.J. Simpson	AFL-NFL	11	2,404	11,236	4.7	Leroy Kelly	NFL	10	1,727	7,274	4.2
Eric Dickerson	NFL	6	2,136	9,915	4.6	George Rogers	NFL	7	1,692	7,176	4.2
Joe Perry	AAFC-NFL	16	1,929	9,723	5.0	Freeman McNeil	NFL	9	1,605	7,146	4.5
Earl Campbell	NFL	8	2,187	9,407	4.3	John Henry Johnson	NFL-AFL	13	1,571	6,803	4.3
O.J. Anderson	NFL	11	2,274	9,317	4.1	Wilbert Montgomery	NFL	9	1,540	6,789	4.4

Most Yards Gained, Season — 2,105, Eric Dickerson, Los Angeles Rams, 1984.
Most Yards Gained, Game — 275, Walter Payton, Chicago Bears vs. Minnesota Vikings, Nov. 20, 1977.
Most Games, 100 Yards or more, Season — 12, Eric Dickerson, Los Angeles Rams, 1984.
Most Games, 100 Yards or more, Career — 77, Walter Payton, Chicago Bears, 1975-87.
Most Touchdowns Rushing, Career — 110, Walter Payton, Chicago Bears, 1975-1987.
Most Touchdowns Rushing, Season — 24, John Riggins, Washington Redskins, 1983.
Most Touchdowns Rushing, Game — 6, Ernie Nevers, Chicago Cardinals vs. Chicago Bears, Nov. 8, 1929.
Most Rushing Attempts, Season — 407, James Wilder, Tampa Bay Buccaneers, 1984.
Most Rushing Attempts, Game — 45, Jamie Morris, Washington Redskins vs. Cincinnati Bengals, Dec. 17, 1988.
Longest run from Scrimmage — 99 yds., Tony Dorsett, Dallas vs. Minnesota, Jan. 3, 1983 (scored touchdown).

Leading Lifetime Passers

(Minimum 1,500 attempts)

Player	League	Yrs	Att	Comp	Yds	Pts*	Player	League	Yrs	Att	Comp	Yds	Pts*
Joe Montana	NFL	11	4,059	2,593	31,054	94.0	Len Dawson	NFL-AFL	19	3,741	2,136	28,711	82.6
Dan Marino	NFL	7	3,650	2,174	27,853	89.3	Ken Anderson	NFL	16	4,475	2,654	32,838	81.9
Otto Graham	AAFC-NFL	10	2,626	1,464	23,584	86.6	Danny White	NFL	13	2,950	1,761	21,959	81.7
Boomer Esiason	NFL	6	2,285	1,296	18,350	87.3	Bart Starr	NFL	16	3,149	1,808	24,718	80.5
Dave Krieg	NFL	10	2,843	1,644	20,858	83.7	Fran Tarkenton	NFL	18	6,467	3,686	47,003	80.4
Roger Staubach	NFL	11	2,958	1,685	22,700	83.4	Tony Eason	NFL	7	1,536	898	10,987	80.3
Bernie Kosar	NFL	5	1,940	1,134	13,888	83.4	Dan Fouts	NFL	15	5,604	3,294	43,040	80.2
Ken O'Brien	NFL	6	2,467	1,471	17,589	83.0	Jim McMahon	NFL	8	1,831	1,050	13,335	79.2
Jim Kelly	NFL	4	1,742	1,032	12,901	82.7	Johnny Unitas	NFL	18	5,186	2,830	40,239	78.2
Neil Lomax	NFL	8	3,153	1,817	22,771	82.7	Bert Jones	NFL	10	2,551	1,430	18,190	78.2
Sonny Jurgensen	NFL	18	4,262	2,433	32,224	82.6							

*Rating points based on performances in the following categories: Percentage of completions, percentage of touchdown passes, percentage of interceptions, and average gain per pass attempt.

Most Yards Gained, Season — 5,084, Dan Marino, Miami Dolphins, 1984.
Most Yards Gained, Game — 554, Norm Van Brocklin, Los Angeles Rams vs. New York Yankees, Sept. 18, 1951 (27 completions in 41 attempts).
Most Touchdowns Passing, Career — 342, Fran Tarkenton, Minnesota Vikings, 1961-66; N.Y. Giants, 1967-71; Vikings, 1972-78.
Most Touchdown Passing, Season — 48, Dan Marino, Miami Dolphins, 1984.
Most Touchdown Passing, Game — 7, Sid Luckman, Chicago Bears vs. New York Giants, Nov. 14, 1943; Adrian Burk, Philadelphia Eagles vs. Washington Redskins, Oct. 17, 1954; George Blanda, Houston Oilers vs. New York Titans, Nov. 19, 1961; Y.A. Tittle, New York Giants vs. Washington Redskins, Oct. 28, 1962; Joe Kapp, Minnesota Vikings vs. Baltimore Colts, Sept. 28, 1969.
Most Passing Attempts, Season — 623, Dan Marino, Miami Dolphins, 1986.
Most Passing Attempts, Game — 68, George Blanda, Houston Oilers vs. Buffalo Bills, Nov. 1, 1964 (37 completions).
Most Passes Completed, Season — 378, Dan Marino, Miami Dolphins, 1986.
Most Passes Completed, Game — 42, Richard Todd, N.Y. Jets vs. San Francisco 49ers, Sept. 21, 1980.
Most Consecutive Passes Completed — 22, Joe Montana, S. F. vs. Cleveland, (5), Nov. 29, & Green Bay (17), Dec. 6, 1987.
Most Consecutive Games, Touchdown Passes — 47, John Unitas, Baltimore Colts, 1956-1960.

Leading Lifetime Receivers

Player	League	Yrs	No	Yds	Avg	Player	League	Yrs	No	Yds	Avg
Steve Largent	NFL	14	819	13,089	16.0	Harold Jackson	NFL	16	579	10,372	17.9
Charlie Joiner	NFL	18	750	12,146	16.2	Lionel Taylor	AFL	10	567	7,195	12.7
Art Monk	NFL	10	662	9,165	13.8	Wes Chandler	NFL	11	559	8,966	16.0
Charley Taylor	NFL	13	649	9,110	14.0	Lance Alworth	AFL-NFL	11	542	10,266	18.9
Ozzie Newsome	NFL	12	639	7,740	12.1	Kellen Winslow	NFL	9	541	6,741	12.5
Don Maynard	AFL-NFL	15	633	11,834	18.7	John Stallworth	NFL	14	537	8,723	16.2
Raymond Berry	NFL	13	631	9,275	14.7	Stanley Morgan	NFL	13	534	10,352	19.4
James Lofton	NFL	12	607	11,251	18.5	J.T. Smith	NFL	12	526	6,749	12.8
Harold Carmichael	NFL	14	590	8,985	15.2	Bobby Mitchell	NFL	11	521	7,954	15.3
Fred Biletnikoff	AFL-NFL	14	589	8,974	15.2	Nat Moore	NFL	13	510	7,546	14.8

Most Yards Gained, Season — 1,746, Charley Hennigan, Houston Oilers, 1961.
Most Yards Gained, Game — 336, Willie Anderson, L.A. Rams vs. New Orleans, Nov. 26, 1989.
Most Pass Receptions, Season — 106, Art Monk, Washington Redskins, 1984.
Most Pass Receptions, Game — 18, Tom Fears, Los Angeles Rams vs. Green Bay Packers, Dec. 3, 1950 (189 yards).
Most Consecutive Games, Pass Receptions — 177, Steve Largent, Seattle Seahawks, 1976-1989.
Most Touchdown Passes, Career — 100, Steve Largent, Seattle Seahawks, 1976-1989.
Most Touchdown Passes, Season — 22, Jerry Rice, San Francisco 49ers, 1987.
Most Touchdown Passes, Game — 5, Bob Shaw, Chicago Cardinals vs. Baltimore Colts, Oct. 2, 1950; Kellen Winslow, San Diego vs. Oakland, Nov. 22, 1981.

Leading Lifetime Scorers

Player	League	Yrs	TD	PAT	FG	Total	Player	League	Yrs	TD	PAT	FG	Total
George Blanda	NFL-AFL	26	9	943	335	2,002	Don Cockroft	NFL	13	0	432	216	1,080
Jan Stenerud	AFL-NFL	19	0	580	373	1,699	Garo Yepremian	AFL-NFL	14	0	444	210	1,074
Lou Groza	AAFC-NFL	21	1	810	264	1,608	Bruce Gossett	NFL	11	0	374	219	1,031
Jim Turner	AFL-NFL	16	1	521	304	1,439	Nick Lowery	NFL	11	0	338	225	1,013
Mark Moseley	NFL	16	0	482	300	1,382	Sam Baker	NFL	15	2	428	179	977
Jim Bakken	NFL	17	0	534	282	1,380	Jim Breech	NFL	11	0	418	184	970
Fred Cox	NFL	15	0	519	282	1,365	Rafael Septien	NFL	10	0	420	180	960
Pat Leahy	NFL	16	0	496	255	1,261	Lou Michaels	NFL	13	1	386	187	955*
Chris Bahr	NFL	14	0	490	241	1,213	Eddie Murray		10	0	307	212	943
Gino Cappelletti	AFL	11	42	350	176	1,130	*Includes safety.						
Ray Wersching	NFL	15	0	456	222	1,122							

Most Points, Season — 176, Paul Hornung, Green Bay Packers, 1960 (15 TD's, 41 PAT's, 15 FG's).
Most Points, Game — 40, Ernie Nevers, Chicago Cardinals vs. Chicago Bears, Nov. 28, 1929 (6 TD's, 4 PAT's).
Most Touchdowns, Season — 24, John Riggins, Washington Redskins, 1984 (24 rushing).
Most Touchdowns, Game — 6, Ernie Nevers, Chicago Cardinals vs. Chicago Bears, Nov. 28, 1929 (6 rushing); Dub Jones, Cleveland Browns vs. Chicago Bears, Nov. 25, 1951 (4 rushing, 2 pass receptions); Gale Sayers, Chicago Bears vs. San Francisco 49ers, Dec. 12, 1965 (4 rushing, 1 pass reception, 1 punt return).
Most Points After Touchdown, Season — 66, Uwe von Schamann, Miami Dolphins, 1984.
Most Consecutive Points After Touchdown — 234, Tommy Davis, San Francisco 49ers, 1959-1969.
Most Field Goals, Game — 7, Jim Bakken, St. Louis Cardinals vs. Pittsburgh Steelers, Sept. 24, 1967; Rich Karlis, Minn. Vikings vs. L.A. Rams, Nov. 5, 1989.
Most Field Goals, Season — 35, Ali Haji-Sheikh, N.Y. Giants, 1983.
Most Field Goals Attempted, Season — 49, Bruce Gossett, Los Angeles Rams, 1966; Curt Knight, Washington Redskins, 1971.
Most Field Goals Attempted, Game — 9, Jim Bakken, St. Louis Cardinals vs. Pittsburgh Steelers, Sept. 24, 1967 (7 successful).
Most Consecutive Field Goals — 24, Kevin Butler, Chicago Bears, 1988-1989.
Most Consecutive Games, Field Goal — 31, Fred Cox, Minnesota Vikings, 1968-1970.
Longest Field Goal — 63 yds., Tom Dempsey, New Orleans Saints vs. Detroit Lions, Nov. 8, 1970.
Highest Field Goal Completion Percentage, Season (20 attempts) — 95.24 Mark Moseley, Washington Redskins, 1982; Eddie Murray, Detroit Lions, 1988 & 1989 (20 FG's in 21 attempts).

Pass Interceptions

Most Passes Had Intercepted, Game — 8, Jim Hardy, Chicago Cardinals vs. Philadelphia Eagles, Sept. 24, 1950 (39 attempts)
Most Passes Had Intercepted, Season — 42, George Blanda, Houston Oilers, 1962 (418 attempts).
Most Passes Had Intercepted, Career — 277, George Blanda, Chicago Bears, 1949-1958; Houston Oilers, 1960-1966; Oakland Raiders, 1967-1975 (4,000 attempts).
Most Consecutive Passes Attempted Without Interception — 294, Bart Starr, Green Bay Packers, 1964-1965.
Most Interceptions By, Season — 14, Dick Lane, Los Angeles Rams, 1952.
Most Interceptions By, Career — 81, Paul Krause, Washington Redskins, 1964-67; Minnesota Vikings, 1968-79.
Most Consecutive Games, Passes Intercepted By — 8, Tom Morrow, Oakland Raiders, 1962 (4), 1963 (4).

Punting

Most Punts, Game — 15, John Teltschick, Philadelphia Eagles vs. N.Y. Giants, Dec. 6, 1987.
Most Punts, Career — 1,154, Dave Jennings, N.Y. Giants, 1974-1984; N.Y. Jets, 1985-1987.
Most Punts, Season — 114, Bob Parsons, Chicago Bears, 1981.
Highest Punting Average, Season (20 punts) — 51.40, Sam Baugh, Washington Redskins, 1940 (35 punts).
Longest Punt — 98 yds., Steve O'Neal, New York Jets vs. Denver Broncos, Sept. 21, 1969.

Kickoff Returns

Most Yardage Returning Kickoffs, Career — 6,922, Ron Smith, Chicago Bears, 1965; Atlanta Falcons, 1966-67; Los Angeles Rams, 1968-69; Chicago Bears, 1970-72; San Diego Chargers, 1973; Oakland Raiders, 1974.
Most Yardage Returning Kickoffs, Season — 1,345, Buster Rhymes, Minnesota Vikings, 1985.
Most Yardage Returning Kickoffs, Game — 294, Wally Triplett, Detroit Lions vs. Los Angeles Rams, Oct. 29, 1950 (4 returns).
Most Touchdowns Scored via Kickoff Returns, Career — 6, Ollie Matson, Chicago Cardinals, 1952 (2), 1954, 1956, 1958 (2); Gale Sayers, Chicago Bears, 1965, 1966 (2), 1967 (3); Travis Williams, Green Bay Packers, 1967 (4), 1969; Los Angeles Rams, 1971.
Most Touchdowns Scored via Kickoff Returns, Game — 2, Tim Brown, Philadelphia Eagles vs. Dallas Cowboys, Nov. 6, 1966; Travis Williams, Green Bay Packers vs. Cleveland Browns, Nov. 12, 1967; Ron Brown, Los Angeles Rams vs. Green Bay Packers, Nov. 24, 1985.
Most Kickoff Returns, Career — 275, Ron Smith, Chicago Bears, 1965; Atlanta Falcons, 1966-67; Los Angeles Rams, 1968-69; Chicago Bears, 1970-72; San Diego Chargers, 1973; Oakland Raiders, 1974.
Most Kickoff Returns, Season — 60, Drew Hill, Los Angeles Rams, 1981.
Longest Kickoff Return — 106 yds., Al Carmichael, Green Bay Packers vs. Chicago Bears, October 7, 1956; Noland Smith, Kansas City vs. Denver, Dec. 17, 1967; Roy Green, St. Louis Cardinals vs. Dallas Cowboys, Oct. 21, 1979 (all scored TD).

Punt Returns

Most Yardage Returning Punts, Career — 3,317, Billy Johnson, Houston, 1974-80, Atlanta, 1982-87, Washington, 1988.
Most Yardage Returning Punts, Season — 692, Fulton Walker, Miami-L.A. Raiders, 1985.
Most Yardage Returning Punts, Game — 207, Leroy Irvin, Los Angeles Rams vs. Atlanta Falcons, Oct. 11, 1981.
Most Touchdowns Scored via Punt Returns, Career — 8, Jack Christiansen, Detroit Lions, 1951-1958; Rick Upchurch, Denver Broncos, 1975-83.
Most Punt Returns, Career — 282, Billy Johnson, Houston Oilers, 1974-1980; Atlanta Falcons, 1982-1987; Washington, 1988.
Most Punt Returns, Season — 70, Danny Reece, Tampa Bay Buccaneers, 1979.

Miscellaneous Records

Most Fumbles, Season — 18, Dave Krieg, Seattle Seahawks, 1989.
Most Fumbles, Game — 7, Len Dawson, Kansas City Chiefs vs. San Diego Chargers, Nov. 15, 1964.
Most Sacks, Career — 104, Lawrence Taylor, N.Y. Giants, 1982-89.
Most Sacks, Season — 22, Mark Gastineau, N.Y. Jets, 1984.
Most Seasons, Active Player — 26, George Blanda, Chicago Bears, 1949-1958; Houston Oilers, 1960-1966 and Oakland, 67-75.
Most Consecutive Games Played, Career — 282, Jim Marshall, Cleveland Browns, 1960; Minnesota Vikings, 1961-1979.

Number One NFL Draft Choices, 1936-90

Year	Team	Player, Pos., College	Year	Team	Player, Pos., College
1936	Philadelphia	Jay Berwanger, HB, Chicago	1964	San Francisco	Dave Parks, E, Texas Tech
1937	Philadelphia	Sam Francis, FB, Nebraska	1965	N.Y. Giants	Tucker Frederickson, HB, Auburn
1938	Cleve.Rams	Corbett Davis, FB, Indiana	1966	Atlanta	Tommy Nobis, LB, Texas
1939	Chi.Cards	Ki Aldrich, C, TCU	1967	Baltimore	Bubba Smith, DT, Michigan St.
1940	Chi.Cards	George Cafego, HB, Tennessee	1968	Minnesota	Ron Yary, T, USC
1941	Chi.Bears	Tom Harmon, HB, Michigan	1969	Buffalo	O.J. Simpson, RB, USC
1942	Pittsburgh	Bill Dudley, HB, Virginia	1970	Pittsburgh	Terry Bradshaw, QB, La.Tech
1943	Detroit	Frank Sinkwich, HB, Georgia	1971	New England	Jim Plunkett, QB, Stanford
1944	Boston Yanks	Angelo Bertelli, QB, Notre Dame	1972	Buffalo	Walt Patulski, DE, Notre Dame
1945	Chi.Cards	Charley Trippi, HB, Georgia	1973	Houston	John Matuszak, DE, Tampa
1946	Boston Yanks	Frank Dancewicz, QB, Notre Dame	1974	Dallas	Ed "Too Tall" Jones, Tenn.St.
1947	Chi.Bears	Bob Fenimore, HB, Okla. A&M	1975	Atlanta	Steve Bartkowski, QB, Cal.
1948	Washington	Harry Gilmer, QB, Alabama	1976	Tampa Bay	Lee Roy Selmon, DE, Oklahoma
1949	Philadelphia	Chuck Bednarik, C, Penn	1977	Tampa Bay	Ricky Bell, RB, USC
1950	Detroit	Leon Hart, E, Notre Dame	1978	Houston	Earl Campbell, RB, Texas
1951	N.Y. Giants	Kyle Rote, HB, SMU	1979	Buffalo	Tom Cousineau, LB, Ohio St.
1952	L.A. Rams	Bill Wade, QB, Vanderbilt	1980	Detroit	Billy Sims, RB, Oklahoma
1953	San Francisco	Harry Babcock, E, Georgia	1981	New Orleans	George Rogers, RB, S.Carolina
1954	Cleveland	Bobby Garrett, QB, Stanford	1982	New England	Kenneth Sims, DT, Texas
1955	Baltimore	George Shaw, QB, Oregon	1983	Baltimore	John Elway, QB, Stanford
1956	Pittsburgh	Gary Glick, DB, Col. A&M	1984	New England	Irving Fryar, WR, Nebraska
1957	Green Bay	Paul Hornung, HB, Notre Dame	1985	Buffalo	Bruce Smith, DE, Va.Tech
1958	Chi.Cards	King Hill, QB, Rice	1986	Tampa Bay	Bo Jackson, RB, Auburn
1959	Green Bay	Randy Duncan, QB, Iowa	1987	Tampa Bay	Vinny Testaverde, QB, Miami, (Fla.)
1960	L.A. Rams	Billy Cannon, HB, LSU	1988	Atlanta	Aundray Bruce, LB, Auburn
1961	Minnesota	Tommy Mason, HB, Tulane	1989	Dallas	Troy Aikman, QB, UCLA
1962	Washington	Ernie Davis, HB, Syracuse	1990	Indianapolis	Jeff George, QB, Illinois
1963	L.A. Rams	Terry Baker, QB, Oregon St.			

First-Round Selections in the 1990 NFL Draft

Team	Player	Pos.	College	Team	Player	Pos.	College
1—Colts	*Jeff George	QB	Illinois	14—Saints	Renaldo Turnbull	DE	West Virginia
2—Jets	Blair Thomas	RB	Penn State	15—Oilers	*Lamar Lathon	LB	Houston
3—Seahawks	Cortez Kennedy	DT	Miami	16—Bills	J.D. Williams	DB	Fresno St.
4—Buccaneers	*Keith McCants	LB	Alabama	17—Cowboys	*Emmitt Smith	RB	Florida
5—Chargers	*Junior Seau	LB	USC	18—Packers	Tony Bennett	LB	Mississippi
6—Bears	*Mark Carrier	DB	USC	19—Packers	Darrell Thompson	RB	Minnesota
7—Lions	*Andre Ware	QB	Houston	20—Falcons	Steve Broussard	RB	Washington St.
8—Patriots	Chris Singleton	LB	Arizona	21—Steelers	Eric Green	TE	Liberty
9—Dolphins	Richmond Webb	OT	Texas A&M	22—Eagles	Ben Smith	DB	Georgia
10—Patriots	Ray Agnew	DT	N.C. State	23—Rams	Bern Brostek	C	Washington
11—Raiders	Anthony Smith	DL	Arizona	24—Giants	*Rodney Hampton	RB	Georgia
12—Bengals	James Francis	LB	Baylor	25—49ers	Dexter Carter	RB	Florida St.
13—Chiefs	Percy Snow	LB	Michigan St.	*Juniors who gave up final year of college eligibility			

Pro Football Hall of Fame, Canton, Ohio

Herb Adderley
Lance Alworth
Doug Atkins
Morris (Red) Badgro
Cliff Battles
Sammy Baugh
Chuck Bednarik
Bert Bell
Bobby Bell
Raymond Berry
Charles Bidwell
Fred Biletnikoff
George Blanda
Mel Blount
Terry Bradshaw
Jim Brown
Paul Brown
Roosevelt Brown
Willie Brown
Buck Buchanan
Dick Butkus
Tony Canadeo
Joe Carr
Guy Chamberlin
Jack Christiansen
Dutch Clark
George Connor
Jim Conzelman
Larry Csonka
Willie Davis
Len Dawson

Mike Ditka
Art Donovan
Paddy Driscoll
Bill Dudley
Turk Edwards
Weeb Ewbank
Tom Fears
Ray Flaherty
Len Ford
Dr. Daniel Fortmann
Frank Gatski
Bill George
Frank Gifford
Sid Gillman
Otto Graham
Red Grange
Joe Greene
Forrest Gregg
Bob Griese
Lou Groza
Joe Guyon
George Halas
Jack Ham
Franco Harris
Ed Healey
Mel Hein
Ted Hendricks
Pete Henry
Arnold Herber
Bill Hewitt
Clarke Hinkle

Elroy (Crazy Legs) Hirsch
Paul Hornung
Ken Houston
Cal Hubbard
Sam Huff
Lamar Hunt
Don Hutson
John Henry Johnson
Deacon Jones
Sonny Jurgensen
Walt Kiesling
Frank (Bruiser) Kinard
Curly Lambeau
Jack Lambert
Tom Landry
Dick (Night Train) Lane
Jim Langer
Willie Lanier
Yale Lary
Dante Lavelli
Bobby Layne
Tuffy Leemans
Bob Lilly
Vince Lombardi
Sid Luckman
Link Lyman
Tim Mara
Gino Marchetti
George Marshall
Ollie Matson
Don Maynard

George McAfee
Mike McCormack
Hugh McElhenny
John (Blood) McNally
Mike Michalske
Wayne Millner
Bobby Mitchell
Ron Mix
Lenny Moore
Marion Motley
George Musso
Bronko Nagurski
Joe Namath
Greasy Neale
Ernie Nevers
Ray Nitschke
Leo Nomellini
Merlin Olsen
Jim Otto
Steve Owen
Alan Page
Clarence (Ace) Parker
Jim Parker
Joe Perry
Pete Pihos
Hugh (Shorty) Ray
Dan Reeves
Jim Ringo
Andy Robustelli
Art Rooney
Pete Rozelle

Bob St. Clair
Gale Sayers
Joe Schmidt
Art Shell
O.J. Simpson
Bart Starr
Roger Staubach
Ernie Stautner
Ken Strong
Joe Stydahar
Fran Tarkenton
Charlie Taylor
Jim Taylor
Jim Thorpe
Y.A. Tittle
George Trafton
Charlie Trippi
Emlen Tunnell
Clyde (Bulldog) Turner
Johnny Unitas
Gene Upshaw
Norm Van Brocklin
Steve Van Buren
Doak Walker
Paul Warfield
Bob Waterfield
Arnie Weinmeister
Bill Willis
Larry Wilson
Alex Wojciechowicz
Willie Wood

NFL Stadiums

Name, location	Capacity	Name, location	Capacity
Anaheim Stadium, Anaheim, Cal.	69,007	Mile High Stadium, Denver, Col.	76,273
Arrowhead Stadium, Kansas City, Mo.	78,067	Milwaukee County Stadium.	56,051
Astrodome, Houston, Tex.	61,000	Pontiac Silverdome, Mich..	80,500
Atlanta-Fulton County Stadium.	59,673	Rich Stadium, Buffalo, N.Y.	80,290
Candlestick Park, San Francisco, Cal..	64,252	Riverfront Stadium, Cincinnati, Oh..	59,754
Cleveland Stadium.	80,098	Joe Robbie Stadium, Miami, Fla.	75,000
Giants Stadium, E. Rutherford, N.J.	76,891	San Diego Jack Murphy Stadium, San Diego.	60,750
Hoosier Dome, Indianapolis, Ind.	60,127	Soldier Field, Chicago, Ill.	66,949
Robert F. Kennedy Stadium, Wash., D.C.	55,750	Sullivan Stadium, Foxboro, Mass.	60,794
Kingdome, Seattle, Wash.	64,984	Sun Devil Stadium, Tempe, Ariz.	72,000
Lambeau Field, Green Bay, Wis.	57,063	Tampa Stadium, Tampa, Fla.	74,314
Los Angeles Memorial Coliseum.	92,488	Texas Stadium, Irving, Tex.	63,855
Louisiana Superdome, New Orleans.	69,573	Three Rivers Stadium, Pittsburgh, Pa..	59,000
Metrodome, Minneapolis	63,000	Veterans Stadium, Philadelphia, Pa..	65,356

BOWLING

PBA Leading Money Winners

Total winnings are from PBA, ABC Masters, and BPAA All-Star tournaments only, and do not include numerous other tournaments or earnings from special television shows and matches.

Year	Bowler	Amount	Year	Bowler	Amount	Year	Bowler	Amount
1962	Don Carter	$49,972	1972	Don Johnson	$56,648	1981	Earl Anthony	$164,735
1963	Dick Weber	46,333	1973	Don McCune	69,000	1982	Earl Anthony	134,760
1964	Bob Strampe.	33,592	1974	Earl Anthony	99,585	1983	Earl Anthony	135,605
1965	Dick Weber.	47,674	1975	Earl Anthony	107,585	1984	Mark Roth	158,712
1966	Wayne Zahn	54,720	1976	Earl Anthony	110,833	1985	Mike Aulby	201,200
1967	Dave Davis	54,165	1977	Mark Roth	105,583	1986	Walter Ray Williams Jr.	145,550
1968	Jim Stefanich	67,377	1978	Mark Roth	134,500	1987	Pete Weber	175,491
1969	Billy Hardwick	64,160	1979	Mark Roth	124,517	1988	Brian Voss	225,485
1970	Mike McGrath	52,049	1980	Wayne Webb	116,700	1989	Mike Aulby	298,237
1971	Johnny Petraglia	85,065						

Leading PBA Averages by Year

Year	Bowler	Average	Year	Bowler	Average	Year	Bowler	Average
1962	Don Carter	212.844	1972	Don Johnson	215.290	1981	Mark Roth	216.699
1963	Billy Hardwick.	210.346	1973	Earl Anthony	215.799	1982	Marshall Holman	212.844
1964	Ray Bluth	210.512	1974	Earl Anthony	219.394	1983	Earl Anthony	216.645
1965	Dick Weber	211.895	1975	Earl Anthony	219.060	1984	Marshall Holman	213.911
1966	Wayne Zahn	208.663	1976	Mark Roth	215.970	1985	Mark Baker	213.718
1967	Wayne Zahn	212.342	1977	Mark Roth	218.174	1986	John Gant	214.378
1968	Jim Stefanich	211.895	1978	Mark Roth	219.834	1987	Marshall Holman	216.801
1969	Bill Hardwick	212.957	1979	Mark Roth	221.662	1988	Mark Roth	218.036
1970	Nelson Burton Jr.	214.908	1980	Earl Anthony	218.535	1989	Pete Weber	215.432
1971	Don Johnson	213.977						

Firestone Tournament of Champions

Year	Winner	Year	Winner	Year	Winner	Year	Winner
1965	Billy Hardwick	1972	Mike Durbin	1979	George Pappas	1986	Marshall Holman
1966	Wayne Zahn	1973	Jim Godman	1980	Wayne Webb	1987	Pete Weber
1967	Jim Stefanich	1974	Earl Anthony	1981	Steve Cook	1988	Mark Williams
1968	Dave Davis	1975	Dave Davis	1982	Mike Durbin	1989	Del Ballard Jr.
1969	Jim Godman	1976	Marshall Holman	1983	Joe Berardi	1990	Dave Ferraro
1970	Don Johnson	1977	Mike Berlin	1984	Mike Durbin		
1971	Johnny Petraglia	1978	Earl Anthony	1985	Mark Williams		

PBA Hall of Fame

Performance

Bill Allen	Jim Godman	Mark Roth
Glenn Allison	Johnny Guenther	Jim St. John
Earl Anthony	Billy Hardwick	Carmen Salvino
Barry Asher	Tommy Hudson	Bob Strampe
Ray Bluth	Don Johnson	Harry Smith
Nelson Burton Jr.	Joe Joseph	Dave Soutar
Don Carter	Larry Laub	Jim Stefanich
Dave Davis	Mike McGrath	Dick Weber
Gary Dickinson	George Pappas	Billy Welu
Mike Durbin	Johnny Petraglia	Wayne Zahn
Buzz Fazio	Dick Ritger	

Meritorious service

John Archibald	Ted Hoffman Jr.
Eddie Elias	John Jowdy
Frank Esposito	Joe Kelley
Dick Evans	Steve Nagy
Raymond Firestone	Chuck Pezzano
E. A. "Bud" Fisher	Joe Richards
Lou Frantz	Chris Schenkel
Harry Golden	Lorraine Stilzlein

American Bowling Congress Championships in 1990

Regular Division

Individual—Bob Hochrein, Dubuque, Ia., 791.
All Events—Mike Neumann, Tonawanda, N.Y., 2,168.
Doubles—Mike Neumann & Bob Ujvari, Tonawanda, N.Y., 1,448.

Team—Brunswick Rhinos No. 1, Tonawanda, N.Y. & State Farm Agency, Detroit, Mich., 3,201.

Booster Division

Team—Pro World Pro Shop, Milwaukee, Wis., 2,934.

All-Time Records for League and Tournament Play

Type of record	Holder of record	Year	Score	Competition
High team total	Budweiser Beer, St. Louis	1958	3,858	League
High team game	Soutarls Pro Shop, Kansas City, Mo	1990	1,384	League
High doubles total	Thomas Jordan & Ken Yonker Jr, Paterson, N.J.	1989	1,655	League
High doubles game	John Cotta and Steve Larson, Manteca, Cal.	1981	600	Tournament
	Jeff Mraz & Dave Roney, Canton, Oh.	1987	600	Tournament
	William Gruner & Dave Conway, Sacramento, Cal.	1990	600	League
High individual total	Thomas Jordan, Paterson, N.J.	1989	899	League
High all events score	Paul Andrews, East Moline, Ill.	1981	2,415	Tournament

Masters Bowling Tournament Champions

Year	Winner	Year	Winner	Year	Winner
1980	Neil Burton, St. Louis, Mo.	1984	Earl Anthony, Dublin, Cal.	1988	Del Ballard Jr., Richardson, Tex.
1981	Randy Lightfoot, St. Charles, Mo.	1985	Steve Wunderlich, St. Louis, Mo.	1989	Mike Aulby, Indianapolis, Ind.
1982	Joe Berardi, Brooklyn, N.Y.	1986	Mark Fahy, Chicago, Ill.	1990	Chris Warren, Dallas, Tex.
1983	Mike Lastowski, Havre de Grace, Md.	1987	Rick Steelsmith, Wichita, Kan.		

Bowlers with 15 or More Sanctioned 300 Games

Bob Learn Jr, Erie, Pa.	39	Dave Heller, Highland Falls, N.Y. . . .	21	Dave Williams, Sebastopal, Cal.	17
Jim Johnson Jr., Wilmington, Del. . . .	33	Mark Stibora, Cleveland, Oh.	20	Don Johnson, Las Vegas, Nev.	16
John Wilcox Jr., Shavertown, Pa. . . .	32	Mitch Jabczenski, Detroit, Mich.	20	Byron Russell, Tulsa, Okla.	16
Ron Woolet, Louisville, Ky.	30	Dave Soutar, Kansas City, Mo.	19	Dave Davis, Tinton Falls, N.J.	15
Elvin Mesger, Sullivan, Mo.	27	Steve Carson, Oklahoma City, Okla .	19	Ronnie Graham, Louisville, Ky.	15
Tony Torrice, Wolcott, Conn.	23	Dick Weber, St. Louis, Mo.	18	Don McCune, Munster, Ind.	15
Teata Semiz, Fairfield, N.J.	22	George Billick, Old Forge, Pa.	17	Bob Hart, Columbus, Oh.	15

Women's International Bowling Congress Champions in 1990

All Events—Carol Norman, Ardmore, Okla.
Singles—(Tie) Dana Miller-Mackie, Sydney, Aust. & Paula Carter, Miami, Fla.

Doubles—Margi Melvin & Ann Meconnahey, Newark, Bear, Del.
Team—R.A.T.'s, Team, Lakeland, Fla.

Most Sanctioned 300 Games

Jeanne Maiden, Solon, Oh. 16	Aleta Sill, Dearborn, Mich. 9	Linda Kelly, Huber Hts., Oh. 6
Vicki Fischel, Westminster, Cal. 10	Donna Adamek, Victorville, Cal. 8	Carol Norman, Ardmore, Okla. 6
Betty Morris, Stockton, Cal. 9	Robin Romeo, Van Nuys, Cal. 8	Cheryl Daniels, Detroit, Mich. 6
Cindy Coburn-Carroll, Buffalo, N.Y. 9	Toni Gillard, Beverly, Oh. 6	
Tish Johnson, Panorama City, Cal. 9	Ann Marie Pike, Cypress, Cal. 6	

James E. Sullivan Memorial Trophy Winners

The James E. Sullivan Memorial Trophy, named after the former president of the AAU and inaugurated in 1930, is awarded annually by the AAU to the athlete who "by his or her performance, example and influence as an amateur, has done the most during the year to advance the cause of sportsmanship."

Year	Winner	Sport	Year	Winner	Sport	Year	Winner	Sport
1930	Bobby Jones	Golf	1951	Rev. Robert Richards	Track	1972	Frank Shorter	Track
1931	Barney Berlinger . . .	Track	1952	Horace Ashenfelter .	Track	1973	Bill Walton	Basketball
1932	Jim Bausch	Track	1953	Dr. Sammy Lee . . .	Diving	1974	Rick Wohlhuter	Track
1933	Glenn Cunningham. .	Track	1954	Mal Whitfield	Track	1975	Tim Shaw	Swimming
1934	Bill Bonthron	Track	1955	Harrison Dillard . . .	Track	1976	Bruce Jenner	Track
1935	Lawson Little	Golf	1956	Patricia McCormick .	Diving	1977	John Naber	Swimming
1936	Glenn Morris	Track	1957	Bobby Joe Morrow .	Track	1978	Tracy Caulkins	Swimming
1937	Don Budge	Tennis	1958	Glenn Davis	Track	1979	Kurt Thomas	Gymnastics
1938	Don Lash	Track	1959	Parry O'Brien	Track	1980	Eric Heiden	Speed Skating
1939	Joe Burk.	Rowing	1960	Rafer Johnson. . . .	Track	1981	Carl Lewis.	Track
1940	Greg Rice	Track	1961	Wilma Rudolph Ward	Track	1982	Mary Decker	Track
1941	Leslie MacMitchell . .	Track	1962	James Beatty	Track	1983	Edwin Moses	Track
1942	Cornelius Warmerdam	Track	1963	John Pennel	Track	1984	Greg Louganis	Diving
1943	Gilbert Dodds	Track	1964	Don Schollander . .	Swimming	1985	Joan Benoit Samuel-	
1944	Ann Curtis.	Swimming	1965	Bill Bradley.	Basketball		son	Marathon
1945	Doc Blanchard	Football	1966	Jim Ryun	Track	1986	Jackie Joyner-Kersee	Track
1946	Arnold Tucker.	Football	1967	Randy Matson	Track	1987	Jim Abbott.	Baseball
1947	John Kelly Jr.	Rowing	1968	Debbie Meyer	Swimming	1988	Florence Griffith	
1948	Robert Mathias . . .	Track	1969	Bill Toomey	Track		Joyner.	Track
1949	Dick Button.	Skating	1970	John Kinsella.	Swimming	1989	Janet Evans	Swimming
1950	Fred Wilt	Track	1971	Mark Spitz	Swimming			

Iditarod Trail Sled Dog Race in 1990

Susan Butcher won the 1990 Iditarod Trail Sled Dog Race by completing the 1,158-mile race from Anchorage to Nome, Alaska in a record 11 days 1 hour 53 minutes 23 seconds. It was the fourth time in the past 5 years that Butcher has won the race. The victory was worth $50,000, plus $25,000 from one of her sponsors. Joe Runyan, the 1989 champion, finished second.

The America's Cup

The United States yacht *Stars & Stripes* defeated the New Zealand yacht *New Zealand* in 2 consecutive races to win the best-of-three series in the waters off San Diego, Cal. *Stars & Stripes* was skippered by Dennis Connor, as it had been when the Cup was recaptured from Australia in 1987.

The New Zealand syndicate, however, went to court to have the result of the races invalidated, claiming that the Americans did not live up to the America's Cup Deed of Gift which, they claim, says that the competing boats must be similar. The Americans used a catamaran, the New Zealanders a monohulled ship. On Mar. 28, 1989, a New York State Supreme Court justice ruled that the San Diego Yacht Club had beaten its challenger unfairly and must forfeit the America's Cup to New Zealand. On Sept. 19, a New York appeals court overturned the ruling, and the N.Y. State Court of Appeals upheld that decision, Apr. 26, 1990. The next America's Cup competition is scheduled for May 1992 in San Diego.

Competition for the America's Cup grew out of the first contest to establish a world yachting championship, one of the carnival features of the London Exposition of 1851. The race, open to all classes of yachts from all over the world, covered a 60-mile course around the Isle of Wight; the prize was a cup worth about $500, donated by the Royal Yacht Squadron of England, known as the "America's Cup" because it was first won by the United States yacht *America*. Successive efforts of British and Australian yachtsmen had failed to win the famous trophy until 1983 when the Australian yacht *Australia II* defeated the U.S. entry *Liberty*.

Winners of the America's Cup

1851	America		1930	Enterprise defeated Shamrock V, England, (4-0)
1870	Magic defeated Cambria, England, (1-0)		1934	Rainbow defeated Endeavour, England, (4-2)
1871	Columbia (first three races) and Sappho (last two		1937	Ranger defeated Endeavour II, England, (4-0)
	races) defeated Livonia, England, (4-1)		1958	Columbia defeated Sceptre, England, (4-0)
1876	Madeline defeated Countess of Dufferin, Canada, (2-0)		1962	Weatherly defeated Gretel, Australia, (4-1)
1881	Mischief defeated Atalanta, Canada, (2-0)		1964	Constellation defeated Sovereign, England, (4-0)
1885	Puritan defeated Genesta, England, (2-0)		1967	Intrepid defeated Dame Pattie, Australia, (4-0)
1886	Mayflower defeated Galatea, England, (2-0)		1970	Intrepid defeated Gretel II, Australia, (4-1)
1887	Volunteer defeated Thistle, Scotland, (2-0)		1974	Courageous defeated Southern Cross, Australia, (4-0)
1893	Vigilant defeated Valkyrie II, England, (3-0)		1977	Courageous defeated Australia, Australia, (4-0)
1895	Defender defeated Valkyrie III, England, (3-0)		1980	Freedom defeated Australia, Australia, (4-1)
1899	Columbia defeated Shamrock, England, (3-0)		1983	Australia II, Australia defeated Liberty, (4-3)
1901	Columbia defeated Shamrock II, England, (3-0)		1987	Stars & Stripes defeated Kookaburra III, Australia, (4-0)
1903	Reliance defeated Shamrock III, England, (3-0)		1988	Stars & Stripes defeated New Zealand, New Zealand,
1920	Resolute defeated Shamrock IV, England, (3-2)			(2-0)

Pro Rodeo Championship Standings in 1989

Event	Winner	Money won	Event	Winner	Money won
All Around	Ty Murray, Odessa, Tex.	$134,806	Steer Roping	Guy Allen, Lovington, N.M.	$44,386
Saddle Bronc	Clint Johnson, Spearfish, S.D.	89,687	Team Roping	Jake Barnes, Bloomfield, N.M. &	
Bareback	Marvin Garrett, Gillette, Wyo.	105,931		Clay O'Brien Cooper, Gilbert, Ariz.	90,455
Bull Riding	Richard Hedeman, Bowie, Tex.	122,765	Women's Barrel		
Calf Roping	Rabe Rabon, San Antonio, Fla.	89,301	Racing	Charmayne James Rodman, Galt,	
Steer Wrestling	John W. Jones Jr., Morro Bay, Cal.	94,304		Cal.	96,651

Pro Rodeo Cowboy All Around Champions

Year	Winner	Money won	Year	Winner	Money won
1968	Larry Mahan, Salem, Ore.	$49,129	1979	Tom Ferguson, Miami, Okla.	$96,272
1969	Larry Mahan, Brooks, Ore.	57,726	1980	Paul Tierney, Rapid City, S.D.	105,568
1970	Larry Mahan, Brooks, Ore.	41,493	1981	Jimmie Cooper, Monument, N.M.	105,862
1971	Phil Lyne, George West, Tex.	49,245	1982	Chris Lybbert, Coyote, Cal.	123,709
1972	Phil Lyne, George West, Tex.	60,852	1983	Roy Cooper, Durant, Okla.	153,391
1973	Larry Mahan, Dallas, Tex.	64,447	1984	Dee Pickett, Caldwell, Ida.	122,618
1974	Tom Ferguson, Miami, Okla.	66,929	1985	Lewis Feild, Elk Ridge, Ut.	130,347
1975	Leo Camarillo, Oakdale, Cal.	50,300	1986	Lewis Feild, Elk Ridge, Ut.	166,042
	Tom Ferguson, Miami, Okla.	50,300	1988	Lewis Feild, Elk Ridge, Ut.	144,335
1976	Tom Ferguson, Miami, Okla.	87,908	1988	Dave Appleton, Arlington, Tex.	121,546
1977	Tom Ferguson, Miami, Okla.	76,730	1989	Ty Murray, Odessa, Tex.	134,806
1978	Tom Ferguson, Miami, Okla.	103,734			

U.S. Long Course Swimming Championships in 1990

Austin, Tex., Aug. 1-4, 1990

Men

50M Freestyle—Tom Jager. Time—0:22.26.
100M Freestyle—Shaun Jordan. Time—0:49.68.
200M Freestyle—Troy Dalbey. Time—1:48.69.
400M Freestyle—Dan Jorgensen.Time—3:49.80.
800M Freestyle—Dan Jorgensen. Time—7:59.97.
100M Breaststroke—Eric Wunderlich. Time—1:01.89.
200M Breaststroke—Mike Barrowman. Time—2:11.55.
100M Butterfly—Mark Henderson. Time—0:53.92.
200M Butterfly—Melvin Stewart. Time—1:57.43.
100M Backstroke—Jeff Rouse. Time—0:54.86.
200M Backstroke—Jeff Rouse. Time—2:00.13.
400M Individual Medley—Eric Namesnik. Time—4:15.57.

Women

100M Freestyle—Nicole Haislett. Time—0:55.84.
200M Freestyle—Janet Evans. Time—2:00.27.
400M Freestyle—Janet Evans. Time—4:08.67.
800M Freestyle—Janet Evans. Time—8:24.32.
1,500M Freestyle—Julie Kole. Time—16:38.56.
100M Breaststroke—Toni DeSilva. Time—1:10.09.
200M Breaststroke—Mary Blanchard. Time—2:32.45.
100M Backstroke—Jodi Wilson. Time—1:05.52.
100M Butterfly—Chrissy Ahmann-Leighton. Time—1:00.47.
200M Individual Medley—Summer Sanders. Time—2:14.36.
400M Individual Medley—Erika Hansen. Time—4:40.84.

World Swimming Records

As of Sept., 1990

Men's Records

Freestyle

Distance	Time	Holder	Country	Where made	Date
50 Meters	0:21.81	Tom Jager	U.S.	Nashville	Mar. 1990
100 Meters	0:48.42	Matt Biondi	U.S.	Austin, Tex.	Aug. 10, 1988
200 Meters	1:46.69	Giorgio Lamberti	Italy	Bonn	Aug. 15, 1989
400 Meters	3:46.95	Ewe Dassler	E. Germany	Seoul	Sept. 23, 1988
800 Meters	7:50.64	Vladimir Salnikov	USSR	Moscow	July 4, 1986
1,500 Meters	14:54.76	Vladimir Salnikov	USSR	Moscow	Feb. 22, 1983

Breaststroke

100 Meters	1:01.49	Adrian Moorhouse	Gt. Britain	Bonn	Aug. 15, 1989
200 Meters	2:11.53	Mike Barrowman	U.S.	Seattle	July, 1990

Butterfly

100 Meters	0:52.84	Pablo Morales	U.S.	Orlando, Fla.	June 23, 1986
200 Meters	1:56.24	Michael Gross	W. Germany	Bonn	June 27, 1986

Backstroke

100 Meters	0:54.51	David Berkoff	U.S.	Seoul	Sept. 24, 1988
200 Meters	1:58.14	Igor Polianskiy	USSR	Erfurt, E. Germany	Mar. 3, 1985

Individual Medley

200 Meters	2:00.11	Dave Wharton	U.S.	Tokyo	Aug. 20, 1989
400 Meters	4:15.42	Tamas Darnyi	Hungary	Seoul	Sept. 21, 1988

Freestyle Relays

400 M. (4×100)	3:16.53	Jacobs, Dalbey, Jager, Biondi	U.S.	Seoul	Sept. 23, 1988
800 M. (4×200)	7:12.51	Dalbey, Cetlinsky, Gjertsen, Biondi	U.S.	Seoul	Sept. 21, 1988

Medley Relays

400 M. (4×100)	3:36.93	Berkoff, Schroeder, Jacobs, Biondi	U.S.	Seoul	Sept. 25, 1988

Women's Records

Freestyle

Distance	Time	Holder	Country	Where made	Date
50 Meters	0:24.98	Yang Wenyi	China	China	Apr. 11, 1988
100 Meters	0:54.73	Kristin Otto	E. Germany	Madrid	Aug. 19, 1986
200 Meters	1:57.55	Heike Friedrich	E. Germany	Berlin	June 18, 1986
400 Meters	4:03.85	Janet Evans	U.S.	Seoul	Sept. 22, 1988
800 Meters	8:16.22	Janet Evans	U.S.	Tokyo	Aug. 20, 1989
1,500 Meters	15:52.10	Janet Evans	U.S.	Orlando, Fla.	Mar. 26, 1988

Breaststroke

100 Meters	1:07.91	Silke Hoerner	E. Germany	Strasbourg, France	Aug. 21, 1987
200 Meters	2:26.71	Silke Hoerner	E. Germany	Seoul	Sept. 21, 1988

Butterfly

100 Meters	0:57.93	Mary T. Meagher	U.S.	Brown Deer, Wis.	Aug. 16, 1981
200 Meters	2:05.96	Mary T. Meagher	U.S.	Brown Deer, Wis.	Aug. 13, 1981

Backstroke

100 Meters	1:00.59	Ina Kleber	E. Germany	Moscow	Aug. 24, 1984
200 Meters	2:08.60	Betsy Mitchell	U.S.	Orlando, Fla.	June 27, 1986

Individual Medley

200 Meters	2:11.73	Uta Geweniger	E. Germany	Berlin	July 4, 1981
400 Meters	4:36.10	Petra Schneider	E. Germany	Ecuador	Aug. 1, 1982

Freestyle Relays

400 M. (4×100)	3:40.57	(Otto, Stellmach, Friedrich, Schulze)	E. Germany	Madrid	Aug. 19, 1986
800 M. (4×200)	7:55.47	Stellmach, Strauss, Mohring, Friedrich)	E. Germany	Strasbourg, France	Aug. 18, 1987

Medley Relays

400 M. (4×100)	4:03.69	National Team (Kleber, Gerasch, Geissler, Meineke)	E. Germany	Moscow	Aug. 24, 1984

TRACK AND FIELD

World Track and Field Records

As of Sept. 1990

*Indicates pending record; some new records await confirmation. The International Amateur Athletic Federation, the world body of track and field, recognizes only records in metric distances except for the mile.

Men's Records

Running

Event	Record	Holder	Country	Date	Where made
100 meters	9.92 s.	Carl Lewis	U.S.	Sept. 23, 1988	Seoul
200 meters	19.72 s.	Pietro Mennea	Italy	Sept. 17, 1979	Mexico City
400 meters	43.29 s.	Butch Reynolds	U.S.	Aug. 16, 1988	Zurich
800 meters	1 m., 41.73 s.	Sebastian Coe	Gr. Britain	June 10, 1981	Florence, Italy
1,000 meters	2 m., 12.18 s.	Sebastian Coe	Gr. Britain	July 11, 1981	Oslo
1,500 meters	3 m., 29.46 s.	Said Aouita	Morocco	Aug. 23, 1985	W. Berlin
1 mile	3 m., 46.32 s.	Steve Cram	Gr. Britain	July 27, 1985	Oslo
2,000 meters	4 m., 50.81 s.	Said Aouita	Morocco	July 16, 1987	Paris
3,000 meters	7 m., 29.45 s.	Said Aouita	Morocco	Aug. 20, 1989	Cologne
5,000 meters	12 m., 58.39 s.	Said Aouita	Morocco	July 22, 1987	Rome
10,000 meters	27 m., 08.23 s.	Arturo Barrios	Mexico	Aug. 18, 1989	W. Berlin
20,000 meters	57 m., 24.2 s.	Jos Hermens	Netherlands	May 1, 1976	Netherlands
25,000 meters	1 hr., 13 m., 55.8 s.	Toshihiko Seko	Japan	Mar. 22, 1981	New Zealand
30,000 meters	1 hr., 29 m., 18.8 s.	Toshihiko Seko	Japan	Mar. 22, 1981	New Zealand
3,000 meter stpl	8 m., 05.35 s.	Peter Koech	Kenya	July 3, 1989	Stockholm
Marathon	2 hr., 6 m., 50 s.	Belayneh Densimo	Ethiopia	Apr. 17, 1988	Rotterdam

Hurdles

110 meters	12.92 s.	Roger Kingdom	U.S.	Aug. 16, 1989	Zurich
400 meters	47.02 s.	Edwin Moses	U.S.	Aug. 31, 1983	Koblenz, W. Ger.

Relay Races

400 mtrs.	37.83 s.	(Graddy, Brown, Smith, Lewis)	U.S.	Aug. 11, 1984	Los Angeles
800 mtrs. (4×200)	1 m., 19.38 s.	(Lewis, Everett, Burrell, Heard)	U.S.	Aug. 23, 1989	W. Germany
1,600 mtrs. (4×400)	2 m., 56.16 s.	(Matthews, Freeman, James, Evans)	U.S.	Oct. 20, 1968	Mexico City
		(Everett, Lewis, Robinzine, Reynolds)	U.S.	Oct 1, 1988	Seoul
3,200 mtrs. (4×800)	7 m., 03.89 s.	National team	Gr. Britain	Aug. 30, 1982	London

Field Events

High jump	8 ft.	Javier Sotomayor	Cuba	July 29, 1989	Puerto Rico
Long jump	29 ft., 2½ in.	Bob Beamon	U.S.	Oct. 18, 1968	Mexico City
Triple jump	58 ft., 11½ in.	Willie Banks	U.S.	June 16, 1985	Indianapolis
Pole vault	19 ft., 10½ in.	Sergei Bubka	USSR	July 10, 1988	Nice, France
16 lb. shot put	*75 ft., 10¼ in.	Randy Barnes	U.S.	May, 1990	Los Angeles
Discus	243 ft.	Juergen Schult	E. Germany	June 6, 1986	E. Germany
Javelin	*298 ft. 6 in.	Steve Backley	Gr. Britain	July, 1990	London
16 lb. hammer	284 ft., 7 in.	Yuri Sedykh	USSR	Aug. 30, 1986	Stuttgart
Decathlon	8,647 pts.	Daley Thompson	Gr. Britain	Aug. 8-9, 1984	Los Angeles

Walking

30 km.	2 h., 7 min., 59.8 s.	Jose Martin	Spain	Aug. 4, 1979	Barcelona
50 km.	3 hr., 41 m., 38.4 s.	Raul Gonzales	Mexico	May 25, 1979	Norway

Women's Records

Running

100 meters	10.49 s.	Florence Griffith Joyner	U.S.	July 16, 1988	Indianapolis
200 meters	21.34 s.	Florence Griffith Joyner	U.S.	Sept. 29, 1988	Seoul
400 meters	47.60 s.	Marita Koch	E. Germany	Oct. 6, 1985	Canberra
800 meters	1 m., 53.28 s.	Jarmila Kratochvilova	Czech.	July 26, 1983	Munich
1,500 meters	3 m., 52.47 s.	Tatyana Kazankina	USSR	Aug. 13, 1980	Zurich
1 mile	4 m., 15.61 s.	Paula Ivan	Romania	July 10, 1989	Nice
2,000 meters	5 m., 28.69 s.	Maricica Puica	Romania	July 11, 1986	London
3,000 meters	8 m., 22.62 s.	Tatyana Kazankina	USSR	Aug. 26, 1984	Leningrad
5,000 meters	14 m., 37.33 s.	Ingrid Kristiansen	Norway	Aug. 5, 1986	Stockholm
10,000 meters	30 m., 13.74 s.	Ingrid Kristiansen	Norway	July 5, 1986	Oslo
Marathon	2 h., 21 m., 06 s.	Ingrid Kristiansen	Norway	Apr. 21, 1985	London

Hurdles

100 meters	12.21 s.	Yordanka Donkova	Bulgaria	Aug. 21, 1988	Bulgaria
400 meters	52.94 s.	Marina Stepanova	USSR	Sept. 17, 1986	USSR

Field Events

High jump	6 ft., 10¼ in.	Stefka Kostadinova	Bulgaria	Aug. 30, 1987	Rome
Shot put	74 ft., 3 in.	Natalya Lisouskaya	USSR	June 7, 1987	Moscow
Long jump	24 ft., 8¼ in.	Galina Chistyakova	USSR	June 11, 1988	Leningrad
Triple Jump	47 ft., 7¾ in.	Galina Chistyakova	USSR	July 3, 1989	Moscow

(continued)

Event	Record	Holder	Country	Date	Where made
Discus	252 ft.	Gabriele Reinsch	E. Germany	July 9, 1988	E. Germany
Javelin	262 ft., 5 in.	Petra Felke	E. Germany	Sept. 9, 1988	Potsdam
Heptathlon	7,291 pts.	Jackie Joyner-Kersee	U.S.	Sept. 23-24, 1988	Seoul

Relay Races

400 mtrs. (4×100)	41.37 s.	National team	E. Germany	Oct. 6, 1985	Canberra
800 mtrs. (4×200)	1 m., 28.15 s.	National team	E. Germany	Aug. 9, 1980	E. Germany
1,600 mtrs. (4×400)	3 m., 15.18 s.	National team	USSR	Oct. 1, 1988	Seoul
3,200 mtrs. (4×800)	7 m., 50.17 s.	National team	USSR	Aug. 5, 1984	Moscow

World Record for the One-Mile Run

The following shows how the world record for the one-mile run has been lowered since Roger Bannister broke the 4-minute barrier in 1954

3:59.4 — 3:58 — 3:57.2 — 3:54.5 — 3:54.4 — 3:54.1 — 3:53.6 — 3:51.3 — 3:51.1 — 3:51 — 3:49.4 — 3:49 — 3:48.8 — 3:48.53 — 3:48.4 — 3:47.33 — 3:46.32

Roger Bannister (1954)	Derek Ibbotson (1957)	Peter Snell (1962)	Michel Jazy (1965)	Jim Ryun (1967)	John Walker (1975)	Steve Ovett (1980)	Steve Ovett (1981)	Steve Cram (1985)
John Landy (1954)	Herb Elliot (1958)	Peter Snell (1964)	Jim Ryun (1966)	Filbert Bayi (1975)	Sebastian Coe (1979)	Sebastian Coe (1981)	Sebastian Coe (1981)	

World Track and Field Indoor Records

As of Sept., 1990

The International Amateur Athletic Federation began recognizing world indoor track & field records as official on January 1, 1987. Prior to that, there were only unofficial world indoor bests. World indoor bests set prior to January 1, 1987 are subject to approval as world records providing they meet the prescribed IAAF world records criteria, including drug testing. To be accepted as a world indoor record, a performance must meet the same criteria as a world record outdoors except that a track performance can't be set on an indoor track larger than 200 meters. *Record pending.

Men

Event	Record	Holder	Country	Date	Where made
60 meters	6.50	Lee McRae	U.S.	Mar. 7, 1987	Indianapolis
200 meters	20.36	Bruno Marie-Rose	France	Feb. 22, 1987	Lievin
400 meters	*45.04	Danny Everett	U.S.	Feb. 4, 1990	W. Germany
800 meters	1:44.84	Paul Ereng	Kenya	Mar., 1989	Budapest
1,000 meters	2:16.62	Rob Druppers	Netherlands	Feb. 20, 1988	The Hague
1,500 meters	*3:34.21	Peter Elliott	Gr. Britain	Feb. 28, 1990	Seville, Spain
1 Mile	3:49.78	Eamonn Coghlan	Ireland	Feb. 27, 1983	E. Rutherford
3,000 meters	7:39.2	Emiel Puttemans	Belgium	Feb. 18, 1973	New York
5,000 meters	13:20.4	Suleiman Nyambui	Tanzania	Feb. 6, 1981	New York
50-meter hurdles	6.25	Mark McKoy	Canada	Mar. 5, 1986	Kobe
60-meter hurdles	7.36	Roger Kingdom	U.S.	Mar. 9, 1989	Athens
High Jump	7 ft. 11½ in.	Javier Sotomayor	Cuba	Mar., 1989	San Juan
Pole Vault	*19 ft. 10¼ in.	Sergey Bubka	USSR	Mar. 17, 1990	USSR
Long Jump	28 ft. 10¼ in.	Carl Lewis	U.S.	Feb. 27, 1984	New York
Triple Jump	58 ft. 3¼ in.	Mike Conley	U.S.	Feb. 27, 1987	New York
Shot Put	74 ft. 4¼ in.	Randy Barnes	U.S.	Jan., 1989	Los Angeles

Women

Event	Record	Holder	Country	Date	Where made
60 meters	7.00	Nellie Cooman-Fiere	Holland	Feb. 23, 1986	Madrid
200 meters	22.27	Heike Drechsler	E. Germany	Mar. 7, 1987	Indianapolis
400 meters	49.59	Jarmila Kratochvilova	Czechoslovakia	Mar. 7, 1982	Milan
500 meters	1:07.67	Olga Nazarova	USSR	Jan. 10, 1988	Moscow
800 meters	1:56.40	Christine Wachtel	E. Germany	Feb. 13, 1988	Vienna
1,000 meters	2:34.8	Brigitte Kraus	W. Germany	Feb. 19, 1978	Dortmund
1,500 meters	4:00.8	Mary Decker-Slaney	U.S.	Feb. 8, 1980	New York
1 Mile	*4:17.13	Doina Melinte	Romania	Feb. 9, 1990	E. Rutherford
3,000 meters	8:33.82	Elly Van Hulst	Netherlands	Mar., 1989	Budapest
5,000 meters	15:25.02	Brenda Webb	U.S.	Jan. 30, 1988	Gainesville
55-meter hurdles	7:37	Cornelia Oschkenat	E. Germany	Feb., 1987	New York
		Jackie Joyner-Kersee	U.S.	Feb., 1989	New York
60-meter hurdles	*7.69	Lyudmila Narozhi-Lenko	USSR	Feb., 1990	USSR
High Jump	6 ft. 9 in.	Stefka Kostadinova	Bulgaria	Feb. 20, 1988	Piraeus, Greece
Long Jump	24 ft. 2¼ in.	Heike Drechsler	E. Germany	Feb. 13, 1988	Vienna
Shot Put	73 ft. 10 in.	Helena Fibingerova	Czechoslovakia	Feb. 19, 1977	Jablonec

National Track & Field Hall of Fame

Indianapolis, Ind.

Jesse Abramson	Harrison Dillard	Jim Hines	Michael Murphy	Andy Stanfield
Dave Albritton	Ken Doherty	Bud Houser	Lon Myers	Les Steers
Horace Ashenfelter	Charles Dumas	DeHart Hubbard	Cordner Nelson	Helen Stephens
Andy Bakjian	Bill Easton	Edward Hurt	Parry O'Brien	James Sullivan
Weems Baskin	James (Jumbo) Elliott	Wilbur Hutsell	Al Oerter	Ed Temple
James Bausch	Lee Evans	Neil Jackson	Harold Osborn	Dink Templeton
Bob Beamon	Barney Ewell	Bruce Jenner	Jesse Owens	John Thomas
Percy Beard	Ray Ewry	Rafer Johnson	Charlie Paddock	Earl Thomson
Jim Beatty	Mae Faggs (Starr)	Hayes Jones	Mel Patton	Jim Thorpe
Greg Bell	Barbara Ferrell	Thomas Jones	Eulace Peacock	Eddie Tolan
Dee Boeckman	Dan Ferris	Payton Jordan	Steve Prefontaine	Bill Toomey
Tom Botts	John Flanagan	John Kelley	Joie Ray	Forrest Towns
Ralph Boston	Dick Fosbury	Abel Kiviat	Greg Rice	Wyomia Tyus
Bill Bowerman	Bob Giegengack	Alvin Kraenzlein	Bob Richards	LeRoy Walker
Avery Brundage	Fortune Gordien	Ron Laird	Betty Robinson (Schwartz)	Stella Walsh
Jim Bush	John Griffith	Clyde Littlefield	Ralph Rose	Cornelius Warmerdam
Lee Calhoun	Archie Hahn	Bob Mathias	Wilma Rudolph	Martha Watson
Milt Campbell	Evelyne Hall	Randy Matson	Jim Ryun	Willye White
Alice Coachman (Davis)	Brutus Hamilton	Mildred McDaniel	Jackson Scholz	Mal Whitfield
Harold Connolly	Glenn Hardin	Edith McGuire (DuVall)	Bob Seagren	Fred Wilt
Tom Courtney	Ted Haydon	Ted Meredith	Mel Sheppard	Lloyd "Bud" Winter
Dean Cromwell	Billy Hayes	Ralph Metcalfe	Martin Sheridan	Rick Wohlhuter
Glenn Cunningham	Bob Hayes	Billy Mills	Frank Shorter	John Woodruff
William Curtis	Ward Haylett	Madeline Manning-Mims	Dave Sime	Dave Wottle
Willie Davenport	Bud Held	Jack Moakley	Robert Simpson	Frank Wykoff
Glenn Davis	Doris Brown Heritage	Tom Moore	Tommie Smith	Joe Yancey
Harold Davis	Ralph Higgins	Bobby Morrow	Larry Snyder	George Young
Mildred (Babe) Didrikson	Harry Hillman			

NCAA Outdoor Championships

Provo, Ut., June 1-3, 1990

Men

100 Meters—Leroy Burrell, Houston. **Time**—0:09.94.
200 Meters—Michael Johnson, Baylor. **Time**—0:20.31.
400 Meters—Steve Lewis, UCLA. **Time**—0:45.19.
800 Meters—Mark Everett, Florida. **Time**—1:44.70.
1,500 Meters—Bob Kennedy, Indiana. **Time**—3:40.42.
5,000 Meters—John Traufmann, Georgetown. **Time**—14:07.47.
110-Meter Hurdles—Chris Lancaster, Indiana St. **Time**—0:13.45.
400-Meter Hurdles—McClinton Neal, Texas-Ari. **Time**—0:49.23.
High Jump—Charles Austin, SW Texas St. 7 ft. 7¾ in.
Long Jump—Llewellyn Starks, LSU. 26 ft. 5¾ in.
Triple Jump—Edrick Floreal, Arkansas. 56 ft. 6½ in.
Shot Put—Shane Collins, Arizona St. 66 ft. 3¼ in.
Hammer Throw—Scott McGee, Oregon. 217 ft. 8 in.
Pole Vault—Istvan Bagyula, George Mason. 18 ft. 4½ in.
Decathlon—Drew Fucci, SW Texas St. 7,779 pts.
Team champion—LSU.

Women

100 Meters—Esther Jones, LSU. **Time**—0:11.14.
200 Meters—Esther Jones. **Time**—0:22.49.
400 Meters—Maicel Malone, Arizona St. **Time**—0:51.25.
800 Meters—Suzy Favor, Wisconsin. **Time**—1:59.11.
1,500 Meters—Suzy Favor. **Time**—4:08.26.
3,000 Meters—Sonia O'Sullivan, Villanova. **Time**—8:56.27.
5,000 Meters—Valerie McGovern, Kentucky. **Time**—15:45.72.
100-Meter Hurdles—Lynda Tolbert, Arizona St. **Time**—0:12.84.
400-Meter Hurdles—Janeene Vickers, UCLA. **Time**—0:55.40.
High Jump—Angie Bradburn, Texas. 6 ft. 2¾ in.
Long Jump—Sheila Hudson, California. 22 ft. 1 in.
Triple Jump—Sheila Hudson. 46 ft. ¾ in.
Shot Put—Tracie Millett, UCLA. 53 ft. 7 in.
Discus—Tracie Millett. 183 ft. 9 in.
Team champion—LSU.

USA/Mobil Outdoor Championships

Norwalk, Cal., June 15-17, 1990

Men

100 Meters—Carl Lewis. **Time**—0:10.05.
200 Meters—Michael Johnson. **Time**—0:19.90.
400 Meters—Steve Lewis. **Time**—0:44.75.
800 Meters—Mark Everett. **Time**—1:45.01.
1,500 Meters—Joe Falcon. **Time**—3:37.49.
5,000 Meters—Doug Padilla. **Time**—13:41.85.
110-Meter Hurdles—Roger Kingdom. **Time**—0:13.22.
400-Meter Hurdles—David Patrick. **Time**—0:48.79.
High Jump—Hollis Conway. 7 ft. 8¾ in.
Pole Vault—Earl Bell. 18 ft. 10 in.
Long Jump—Mike Powell. 27 ft. ½ in.
Triple Jump—Kenny Harrison. 56 ft. 3¼ in.
Discus—Kami Keshmiri. 204 ft. 5 in.
Hammer—Ken Flax. 249 ft. 6 in.
Javelin—Vince Lobosky. 261 ft. 3 in.
Shot Put—Jim Doehring. 69 ft. 6¾ in.
Decathlon—Dave Johnson. 8,600 pts.

Women

100 Meters—Michelle Finn. **Time**—0:11.20.
200 Meters—Grace Jackson. **Time**—0:22.48.
400 Meters—Maicel Malone. **Time**—0:51.23.
800 Meters—Meredith Rainey. **Time**—2:00.70.
1,500 Meters—Suzy Favor. **Time**—4:13.47.
3,000 Meters—Lynn Jennings. **Time**—8:51.97.
5,000-Meters—Patti Sue Plumer. **Time**—15:45.67.
100-Meter Hurdles—LaVonna Martin. **Time**—0:12.90.
400-Meter Hurdles—Janeene Vickers. **Time**—0:54.80.
Long Jump—Jackie Joyner-Kersee. 23 ft. 2¾ in.
Shot Put—Connie Price. 60 ft. 10¾ in.
Javelin—Karin Smith. 206 ft. 3 in.
Discus—Connie Price. 191 ft. 6 in.
High Jump—Yolanda Henry. 6 ft. 5 in.
Triple Jump—Sheila Hudson. 46 ft. 2 in.
Heptathlon—Cindy Greiner. 6,262 pts.

Boxing Champions by Classes

As of Sept. 15, 1990 the only generally accepted title holders were in the heavyweight and lightweight division. There are numerous governing bodies in boxing including the World Boxing Council, the World Boxing Assn., the International Boxing Federation, the United States Boxing Assn., the North American Boxing Federation, and the European Boxing Union. Other organizations are recognized by TV networks and the print media. All the governing bodies have their own champions and assorted boxing divisions. The following are the recognized champions in the principal divisions of the World Boxing Association, the World Boxing Council, and the International Boxing Federation.

Class, Weight Limit	WBA	WBC	IBF
Heavyweight	Buster Douglas, U.S.	Buster Douglas, U.S.	Buster Douglas, U.S.
Cruiserweight (195 lbs.) . . .	Robert Daniels, U.S.	Massimiliano Duran, Italy	Jeff Lampkin, U.S.
Light Heavyweight (175 lbs.) . . .	Virgil Hill, U.S.	Dennis Andries, Gt. Britain	Charles Williams, U.S.
Middleweight (160 lbs.)	Mike McCallum, U.S.	vacant	Michael Nunn, U.S.
Jr. Middleweight (154 lbs.)	Julian Jackson, Virgin Islands	Terry Norris, U.S.	Gianfranco Rosi, Italy
Welterweight (147 lbs.)	Aaron Davis, U.S.	Maurice Blocker, U.S.	Simon Brown, U.S.
Jr. Welterweight (140 lbs.)	Juan Coggi, Argentina	Julio Cesar Chavez, Mexico	Julio Cesar Chavez, Mexico
Lightweight (135 lbs.)	Pernell Whitaker, U.S.	Pernell Whitaker, U.S.	Pernell Whitaker, U.S.
Jr. Lightweight (130 lbs.)	Brian Mitchell, So. Africa	Vacant	Tony Lopez, U.S.
Featherweight (126 lbs.)	Antonio Esparragoza, Venezuela	Marcos Villasana, Mexico	Jorge Paez, Mexico
Jr. Featherweight (122 lbs.) . . .	Vacant	Paul Banke, U.S.	Welcome Ncita, S. Africa
Bantamweight (118 lbs.)	Luisito Espinosa, Philippines	Raul Perez, Mexico	Orlando Canizales, U.S.
Flyweight (112 lbs.)	Yukihito Tamakuma, Japan	Sot Chitalada, Thailand	Dave McAuley, Ireland

Ring Champions by Years

*Abandoned title

Heavyweights

1882-1892	John L. Sullivan (a)
1892-1897	James J. Corbett (b)
1897-1899	Robert Fitzsimmons
1899-1905	James J. Jeffries (c)
1905-1906	Marvin Hart
1906-1908	Tommy Burns
1908-1915	Jack Johnson
1915-1919	Jess Willard
1919-1926	Jack Dempsey
1926-1928	Gene Tunney*
1928-1930	vacant
1930-1932	Max Schmeling
1932-1933	Jack Sharkey
1933-1934	Primo Carnera
1934-1935	Max Baer
1935-1937	James J. Braddock
1937-1949	Joe Louis*
1949-1951	Ezzard Charles
1951-1952	Joe Walcott
1952-1956	Rocky Marciano*
1956-1959	Floyd Patterson
1959-1960	Ingemar Johansson
1960-1962	Floyd Patterson
1962-1964	Sonny Liston
1964-1967	Cassius Clay* (Muhammad Ali) (d)
1970-1973	Joe Frazier
1973-1974	George Foreman
1974-1978	Muhammad Ali
1978-1979	Leon Spinks (e), Muhammad Ali*
1978	Ken Norton (WBC), Larry Holmes (WBC) (f)
1979	John Tate (WBA)
1980	Mike Weaver (WBA)
1982	Michael Dokes (WBA)
1983	Gerrie Coetzee (WBA)
1984	Tim Witherspoon (WBC); Pinklon Thomas (WBC); Greg Page (WBA)
1985	Tony Tubbs (WBA); Michael Spinks (IBF)
1986	Tim Witherspoon (WBA); Trevor Berbick (WBC); Mike Tyson (WBC); James (Bonecrusher) Smith (WBA).
1987	Mike Tyson (WBA).
1990	James "Buster" Douglas (WBA, WBC, IBF)

(a) London Prize Ring (bare knuckle champion).
(b) First Marquis of Queensberry champion.
(c) Jeffries abandoned the title (1905) and designated Marvin Hart and Jack Root as logical contenders and agreed to referee a fight between them, the winner to be declared champion. Hart defeated Root in 12 rounds (1905) and in turn was defeated by Tommy Burns (1906) who immediately laid claim to the title. Jack Johnson defeated Burns (1908) and was recognized as champion. He clinched the title by defeating Jeffries in an attempted comeback (1910).
(d) Title declared vacant by the WBA and other groups in 1967 after Clay's refusal to fulfill his military obligation. Joe Frazier was recognized as champion by 6 states, Mexico, and So.

America. Jimmy Ellis was declared champion by the WBA. Frazier KOd Ellis, Feb. 16, 1970.
(e) After Spinks defeated Ali, the WBC recognized Ken Norton as champion. Norton subsequently lost his title to Larry Holmes.
(f) Holmes was stripped of his WBC title in 1984. He was the IBF champion when he lost to Michael Spinks.

Light Heavyweights

1903	Jack Root, George Gardner
1903-1905	Bob Fitzsimmons
1905-1912	Philadelphia Jack O'Brien*
1912-1916	Jack Dillon
1916-1920	Battling Levinsky
1920-1922	George Carpentier
1922-1923	Battling Siki
1923-1925	Mike McTigue
1925-1926	Paul Berlenbach
1926-1927	Jack Delaney*
1927-1929	Tommy Loughran*
1930-1934	Maxey Rosenbloom
1934-1935	Bob Olin
1935-1939	John Henry Lewis*
1939	Melio Bettina
1939-1941	Billy Conn*
1941	Anton Christoforidis (won NBA title)
1941-1948	Gus Lesnevich, Freddie Mills
1948-1950	Freddie Mills
1950-1952	Joey Maxim
1952-1960	Archie Moore
1961-1962	vacant
1962-1963	Harold Johnson
1963-1965	Willie Pastrano
1965-1966	Jose Torres
1966-1968	Dick Tiger
1968-1974	Bob Foster*, John Conteh (WBA)
1975-1977	John Conteh (WBC), Miguel Cuello (WBC), Victor Galindez (WBA)
1978	Mike Rossman (WBA), Mate Parlov (WBC), Marvin Johnson (WBC)
1979	Victor Galindez (WBA), Matthew Saad Muhammad (WBC)
1980	Eddie Mustava Muhammad (WBA)
1981	Michael Spinks (WBA), Dwight Braxton (WBC)
1983	Michael Spinks
1986	Marvin Johnson (WBA); Dennis Andries (WBC)
1987	Thomas Hearns (WBC); Leslie Stewart (WBA); Virgil Hill (WBA); Don Lalonde (WBC).
1988	Ray Leonard* (WBC)
1989	Jeff Harding (WBC)
1990	Dennis Andries (WBC)

Middleweights

1884-1891	Jack "Nonpareil" Dempsey
1891-1897	Bob Fitzsimmons*
1897-1907	Tommy Ryan*
1907-1908	Stanley Ketchel, Billy Papke
1908-1910	Stanley Ketchel
1911-1913	vacant

1913	Frank Klaus, George Chip
1914-1917	Al McCoy
1917-1920	Mike O'Dowd
1920-1923	Johnny Wilson
1923-1926	Harry Greb
1926-1931	Tiger Flowers, Mickey Walker
1931-1932	Gorilla Jones (NBA)
1932-1937	Marcel Thil
1938	Al Hostak (NBA), Solly Krieger (NBA)
1939-1940	Al Hostak (NBA)
1941-1947	Tony Zale
1947-1948	Rocky Graziano
1948	Tony Zale, Marcel Cerdan
1949-1951	Jake LaMotta
1951	Ray Robinson, Randy Turpin, Ray Robinson*
1953-1955	Carl (Bobo) Olson
1955-1957	Ray Robinson
1957	Gene Fullmer, Ray Robinson, Carmen Basilio
1958	Ray Robinson
1959	Gene Fullmer (NBA); Ray Robinson (N.Y.)
1960	Gene Fullmer (NBA); Paul Pender (New York and Mass.)
1961	Gene Fullmer (NBA); Terry Downes (New York, Mass., Europe)
1962	Gene Fullmer, Dick Tiger (NBA), Paul Pender (New York and Mass.)*
1963	Dick Tiger (universal).
1963-1965	Joey Giardello
1965-1966	Dick Tiger
1966-1967	Emile Griffith
1967	Nino Benvenuti
1967-1968	Emile Griffith
1968-1970	Nino Benvenuti
1970-1977	Carlos Monzon*
1977-1978	Rodrigo Valdez
1978-1979	Hugo Corro
1979-1980	Vito Antuofermo
1980	Alan Minter, Marvin Hagler
1987	Ray Leonard* (WBC); Thomas Hearns (WBC); Sumbu Kalambay (WBA).
1988	Iran Barkley (WBC)
1989	Mike McCallum (WBA); Roberto Duran (WBC)

Welterweights

1892-1894	Mysterious Billy Smith
1894-1896	Tommy Ryan
1896	Kid McCoy*
1900	Rube Ferns, Matty Matthews
1901	Rube Ferns
1901-1904	Joe Walcott
1904-1906	Dixie Kid, Joe Walcott, Honey Mellody
1907-1911	Mike Sullivan
1911-1915	vacant
1915-1919	Ted Lewis
1919-1922	Jack Britton
1922-1926	Mickey Walker
1926	Pete Latzo
1927-1929	Joe Dundee
1929	Jackie Fields
1930	Jack Thompson, Tommy Freeman
1931	Freeman, Thompson, Lou Brouillard
1932	Jackie Fields
1933	Young Corbett, Jimmy McLarnin
1934	Barney Ross, Jimmy McLarnin
1935-1938	Barney Ross
1938-1940	Henry Armstrong
1940-1941	Fritzie Zivic
1941-1946	Fred Cochrane
1946-1946	Marty Servo*; Ray Robinson (a)
1946-1950	Ray Robinson*
1951	Johnny Bratton (NBA)
1951-1954	Kid Gavilan
1954-1955	Johnny Saxton
1955	Tony De Marco, Carmen Basilio
1956	Carmen Basilio, Johnny Saxton, Basilio
1957	Carmen Basilio*
1958-1960	Virgil Akins, Don Jordan
1960	Benny Paret
1961	Emile Griffith, Benny Paret
1962	Emile Griffith
1963	Luis Rodriguez, Emile Griffith
1964-1966	Emile Griffith*
1966-1969	Curtis Cokes
1969-1970	Jose Napoles, Billy Backus
1971-1975	Jose Napoles
1975-1976	John Stracey (WBC), Angel Espada (WBA)
1976-1979	Carlos Palomino (WBC), Jose Cuevas (WBA)
1979	Wilfredo Benitez (WBC), Sugar Ray Leonard (WBC)

1980	Roberto Duran (WBC), Thomas Hearns (WBA), Sugar Ray Leonard (WBC)
1981-1982	Sugar Ray Leonard*
1983	Donald Curry (WBA); Milton McCrory (WBC)
1985	Donald Curry
1986	Lloyd Honeyghan (WBC)
1987	Mark Breland (WBA); Marlon Starling (WBA); Jorge Vaca (WBC).
1988	Tomas Molinares (WBA); Lloyd Honeyghan (WBC).
1989	Marlon Starling (WBC); Mark Breland (WBA)
1990	Maurice Blocker (WBC); Aaron Davis (WBA)

(a) Robinson gained the title by defeating Tommy Bell in an elimination agreed to by the NY Commission and the NBA. Both claimed Robinson waived his title when he won the middleweight crown from LaMotta in 1951.

Lightweights

1896-1899	Kid Lavigne
1899-1902	Frank Erne
1902-1908	Joe Gans
1908-1910	Battling Nelson
1910-1912	Ad Wolgast
1912-1914	Willie Ritchie
1914-1917	Freddie Welsh
1917-1925	Benny Leonard*
1925	Jimmy Goodrich, Rocky Kansas
1926-1930	Sammy Mandell
1930	Al Singer, Tony Canzoneri
1930-1933	Tony Canzoneri
1933-1935	Barney Ross*
1935-1936	Tony Canzoneri
1936-1938	Lou Ambers
1938	Henry Armstrong
1939	Lou Ambers
1940	Lew Jenkins
1941-1943	Sammy Angott
1944	S. Angott (NBA), J. Zurita (NBA)
1945-1951	Ike Williams (NBA: later universal)
1951-1952	James Carter
1952	Lauro Salas, James Carter
1953-1954	James Carter
1954	Paddy De Marco; James Carter
1955	James Carter; Bud Smith
1956	Bud Smith, Joe Brown
1956-1962	Joe Brown
1962-1965	Carlos Ortiz
1965	Ismael Laguna
1965-1968	Carlos Ortiz
1968-1969	Teo Cruz
1969-1970	Mando Ramos
1970	Ismael Laguna, Ken Buchanan (WBA)
1971	Mando Ramos (WBC), Pedro Carrasco (WBC)
1972-1979	Roberto Duran* (WBA)
1972	Pedro Carrasco, Mando Ramos, Chango Carmona, Rodolfo Gonzalez (all WBC)
1974-1976	Guts Ishimatsu (WBC)
1976-1977	Esteban De Jesus (WBC)
1979	Jim Watt (WBC), Ernesto Espana (WBA)
1980	Hilmer Kenty (WBA)
1981	Alexis Arguello (WBC), Sean O'Grady (WBA), Arturo Frias (WBA)
1982-1984	Ray Mancini (WBA)
1983	Edwin Rosario (WBC)
1984	Livingstone Bramble (WBA); Jose Luis Ramirez (WBC)
1985	Hector (Macho) Camacho (WBC)
1986	Edwin Rosario (WBA); Jose Luis Ramirez (WBC).
1987	Julio Cesar Chavez (WBA).
1989	Edwin Rosario (WBA); Pernell Whitaker (WBC).
1990	Juan Nazario (WBA); Pernell Whitaker (WBA)

Featherweights

1892-1900	George Dixon (disputed)
1900-1901	Terry McGovern, Young Corbett*
1901-1912	Abe Attell
1912-1923	Johnny Kilbane
1923	Eugene Criqui, Johnny Dundee
1923-1925	Johnny Dundee*
1925-1927	Kid Kaplan*
1927-1928	Benny Bass, Tony Canzoneri
1928-1929	Andre Routis
1929-1932	Battling Battalino*
1932-1934	Tommy Paul (NBA)
1933-1936	Freddie Miller
1936-1937	Petey Sarron

1937-1938	Henry Armstrong*
1938-1940	Joey Archibald (b)
1940-41	Harry Jeffra
1942-1948	Willie Pep
1948-1949	Sandy Saddler
1949-1950	Willie Pep
1950-1957	Sandy Saddler*
1957-1959	Hogan (Kid) Bassey
1959-1963	Davey Moore
1963-1964	Sugar Ramos
1964-1967	Vicente Saldivar*
1968-1971	Paul Rojas (WBA), Sho Saijo (WBA)
1971	Antonio Gomez (WBA), Kuniaki Shibada (WBC)
1972	Ernesto Marcel* (WBA), Clemente Sanchez* (WBC), Jose Legra (WBC)
1973	Eder Jofre (WBC)
1974	Ruben Olivares (WBA), Alexis Arguello (WBA), Bobby Chacon (WBC)
1975	Ruben Olivares (WBC), David Kotey (WBC)

1976	Danny Lopez (WBC)
1977	Rafael Ortega (WBA)
1978	Cecilio Lastra (WBA), Eusebio Pedrosa (WBA)
1980	Salvador Sanchez (WBC)
1982	Juan LaPorte (WBC)
1984	Wilfredo Gomez (WBC); Azumah Nelson (WBC)
1985	Barry McGuigan (WBA)
1986	Steve Cruz (WBA)
1987	Antonio Esparragoza (WBA)
1988	Jeff Fenech (WBC)
1990	Marcos Villasana (WBC)

(b) After Petey Scalzo knocked out Archibald in an overweight match and was refused a title bout, the NBA named Scalzo champion. The NBA title succession: Scalzo, 1938-1941; Richard Lemos, 1941; Jackie Wilson, 1941-1943; Jackie Callura, 1943; Phil Terranova, 1943-1944; Sal Bartolo, 1944-1946.

History of Heavyweight Championship Bouts

*Title Changed Hands

1889—July 8—John L. Sullivan def. Jake Kilrain, 75, Richburg, Miss. Last championship bare knuckles bout.

*1892—Sept. 7—James J. Corbett def. John L. Sullivan, 21, New Orleans. Big gloves used for first time.

1894—Jan. 25—James J. Corbett KOd Charley Mitchell, 3, Jacksonville, Fla.

*1897—Bob Fitzsimmons def. James J. Corbett, 14, Carson City, Nev.

1899—June 9—James J. Jeffries def. Bob Fitzsimmons, 11, Coney Island, N.Y.

1899—Nov. 3—James J. Jeffries def. Tom Sharkey, 25, Coney Island, N.Y.

1900—May 11—James J. Jeffries KOd James J. Corbett, 23, Coney Island, N.Y.

1901—Nov. 15—James J. Jeffries KOd Gus Ruhlin, 5, San Francisco.

1902—July 25—James J. Jeffries KOd Bob Fitzsimmons, 8, San Francisco.

1903—Aug. 14—James J. Jeffries KOd James J. Corbett, 10, San Francisco.

1904—Aug. 26—James J. Jeffries KOd Jack Monroe, 2, San Francisco.

*1905—James J. Jeffries retired, July 3—Marvin Hart KOd Jack Root, 12, Reno. Jeffries refereed and presented the title to the victor. Jack O'Brien also claimed the title.

*1906—Feb. 23—Tommy Burns def. Marvin Hart, 20, Los Angeles.

1906—Nov. 28—Philadelphia Jack O'Brien and Tommy Burns, 20, draw, Los Angeles.

1907—May 8—Tommy Burns def. Jack O'Brien, 20, Los Angeles.

1907—July 4—Tommy Burns KOd Bill Squires, 1, Colma, Cal.

1907—Dec. 2—Tommy Burns KOd Gunner Moir, 10, London.

1908—Feb. 10—Tommy Burns KOd Jack Palmer, 4, London.

1908—March 17—Tommy Burns KOd Jem Roche, 1, Dublin.

1908—April 18—Tommy Burns KOd Jewey Smith, 5, Paris.

1908—June 13—Tommy Burns KOd Bill Squires, 8, Paris.

1908—Aug. 24—Tommy Burns KOd Bill Squires, 13, Sydney, New South Wales.

1908—Sept. 2—Tommy Burns KOd Bill Lang, 2, Melbourne, Australia.

*1908—Dec. 26—Jack Johnson KOd Tommy Burns, 14, Sydney, Australia. Police halted contest.

1909—May 19—Jack Johnson and Jack O'Brien, 6, draw, Philadelphia.

1909—June 30—Jack Johnson and Tony Ross, 6, draw, Pittsburgh.

1909—Sept. 9—Jack Johnson and Al Kaufman, 10, draw, San Francisco.

1909—Oct. 16—Jack Johnson KOd Stanley Ketchel, 12, Colma, Cal.

1910—July 4—Jack Johnson KOd Jim Jeffries, 15, Reno, Nev. Jeffries came back from retirement.

1912—July 4—Jack Johnson def. Jim Flynn, 9, Las Vegas, N.M. Contest stopped by police.

1913—Nov. 28—Jack Johnson KOd Andre Spaul, 2, Paris.

1913—Dec. 9—Jack Johnson and Jim Johnson, 10, draw, Paris. Bout called a draw when Jack Johnson declared he had broken his arm.

1914—June 27—Jack Johnson def. Frank Moran, 20, Paris.

*1915—April 5—Jess Willard KOd Jack Johnson, 26, Havana, Cuba.

1916—March 25—Jess Willard and Frank Moran, 10, draw, New York.

*1919—July 4—Jack Dempsey KOd Jess Willard, Toledo, Oh. Willard failed to answer bell for 4th round.

1920—Sept. 6—Jack Dempsey KOd Billy Miske, 3, Benton Harbor, Mich.

1920—Dec. 14—Jack Dempsey KOd Bill Brennan, 12, New York.

1921—July 2—Jack Dempsey KOd George Carpentier, 4, Boyle's Thirty Acres, Jersey City, N.J. Carpentier had held the so-called white heavyweight title since July 16, 1914, in a series established in 1913, after Jack Johnson's exile in Europe late in 1912.

1923—July 4—Jack Dempsey def. Tom Gibbons, 15, Shelby, Mont.

1923—Sept. 14—Jack Dempsey KOd Luis Firpo, 2, New York.

*1926—Sept. 23—Gene Tunney def. Jack Dempsey, 10, Philadelphia. ·

1927—Sept. 22—Gene Tunney def. Jack Dempsey, 10, Chicago.

1928—July 26—Gene Tunney KOd Tom Heeney, 11, New York; soon afterward he announced his retirement.

*1930—June 12—Max Schmeling def. Jack Sharkey, 4, New York. Sharkey fouled Schmeling in a bout which was generally considered to have resulted in the election of a successor to Gene Tunney, New York.

1931—July 3—Max Schmeling KOd Young Stribling, 15, Cleveland.

*1932—June 21—Jack Sharkey def. Max Schmeling, 15, New York.

*1933—June 29—Primo Carnera KOd Jack Sharkey, 6, New York.

1933—Oct. 22—Primo Carnera def. Paulino Uzcudun, 15, Rome.

1934—March 1—Primo Carnera def. Tommy Loughran, 15, Miami.

*1934—June 14—Max Baer KOd Primo Carnera, 11, New York.

*1935—June 13—James J. Braddock def. Max Baer, 15, New York.

*1937—June 22—Joe Louis KOd James J. Braddock, 8, Chicago.

1937—Aug. 30—Joe Louis def. Tommy Farr, 15, New York.

1938—Feb. 23—Joe Louis KOd Nathan Mann, 3, New York.

1938—April 1—Joe Louis KOd Harry Thomas, 5, New York.

1938—June 22—Joe Louis KOd Max Schmeling, 1, New York.

1939—Jan. 25—Joe Louis KOd John H. Lewis, 1, New York.

1939—April 17—Joe Louis KOd Jack Roper, 1, Los Angeles.

1939—June 28—Joe Louis KOd Tony Galento, 4, New York.

1939—Sept. 20—Joe Louis KOd Bob Pastor, 11, Detroit.

1940—February 9—Joe Louis def. Arturo Godoy, 15, New York.

1940—March 29—Joe Louis KOd Johnny Paycheck, 2, New York.

1940—June 20—Joe Louis KOd Arturo Godoy, 8, New York.

1940—Dec. 16—Joe Louis KOd Al McCoy, 6, Boston.

1941—Jan. 31—Joe Louis KOd Red Burman, 5, New York.

1941—Feb. 17—Joe Louis KOd Gus Dorzaio, 2, Philadelphia.

1941—March 21—Joe Louis KOd Abe Simon, 13, Detroit.

1941—April 8—Joe Louis KOd Tony Musto, 9, St. Louis.

1941—May 23—Joe Louis def. Buddy Baer, 7, Washington, D.C., on a disqualification.
1941—June 18—Joe Louis KOd Billy Conn, 13, New York.
1941—Sept. 29—Joe Louis KOd Lou Nova, 6, New York.
1942—Jan. 9—Joe Louis KOd Buddy Baer, 1, New York.
1942—March 27—Joe Louis KOd Abe Simon, 6, New York.
1946—June 19—Joe Louis KOd Billy Conn, 8, New York.
1946—Sept. 18—Joe Louis KOd Tami Mauriello, 1, New York.
1947—Dec. 5—Joe Louis def. Joe Walcott, 15, New York.
1948—June 25—Joe Louis KOd Joe Walcott, 11, New York.
*1949—June 22—Following Joe Louis' retirement Ezzard Charles def. Joe Walcott, 15, Chicago, NBA recognition only.
1949—Aug. 10—Ezzard Charles KOd Gus Lesnevich, 7, New York.
1949—Oct. 14—Ezzard Charles KOd Pat Valentino, 8, San Francisco; clinched American title.
1950—Aug. 15—Ezzard Charles KOd Freddy Beshore, 14, Buffalo.
1950—Sept. 27—Ezzard Charles def. Joe Louis in latter's attempted comeback, 15, New York; universal recognition.
1950—Dec. 5—Ezzard Charles KOd Nick Barone, 11, Cincinnati.
1951—Jan. 12—Ezzard Charles KOd Lee Oma, 10, New York.
1951—March 7—Ezzard Charles def. Joe Walcott, 15, Detroit.
1951—May 30—Ezzard Charles def. Joey Maxim, light heavyweight champion, 15, Chicago.
*1951—July 18—Joe Walcott KOd Ezzard Charles, 7, Pittsburgh.
1952—June 5—Joe Walcott def. Ezzard Charles, 15, Philadelphia.
*1952—Sept. 23—Rocky Marciano KOd Joe Walcott, 13, Philadelphia.
1953—May 15—Rocky Marciano KOd Joe Walcott, 1, Chicago.
1953—Sept. 24—Rocky Marciano KOd Roland LaStarza, 11, New York.
1954—June 17—Rocky Marciano def. Ezzard Charles, 15, New York.
1954—Sept. 17—Rocky Marciano KOd Ezzard Charles, 8, New York.
1955—May 16—Rocky Marciano KOd Don Cockell, 9, San Francisco.
1955—Sept. 21—Rocky Marciano KOd Archie Moore, 9, New York. Marciano retired undefeated, Apr. 27, 1956.
*1956—Nov. 30—Floyd Patterson KOd Archie Moore, 5, Chicago.
1957—July 29—Floyd Patterson KOd Hurricane Jackson, 10, New York.
1957—Aug. 22—Floyd Patterson KOd Pete Rademacher, 6, Seattle.
1958—Aug. 18—Floyd Patterson KOd Roy Harris, 12, Los Angeles.
1959—May 1—Floyd Patterson KOd Brian London, 11, Indianapolis.
*1959—June 26—Ingemar Johansson KOd Floyd Patterson, 3, New York.
*1960—June 20—Floyd Patterson KOd Ingemar Johansson, 5, New York. First heavyweight in boxing history to regain title.
1961—Mar. 13—Floyd Patterson KOd Ingemar Johansson, 6, Miami Beach.
1961—Dec. 4—Floyd Patterson KOd Tom McNeeley, 4, Toronto.
*1962—Sept. 25—Sonny Liston KOd Floyd Patterson, 1, Chicago.
1963—July 22—Sonny Liston KOd Floyd Patterson, 1, Las Vegas.
*1964—Feb. 25—Cassius Clay KOd Sonny Liston, 7, Miami Beach.
1965—May 25—Cassius Clay KOd Sonny Liston, 1, Lewiston, Maine.
1965—Nov. 11—Cassius Clay KOd Floyd Patterson, 12, Las Vegas.
1966—Mar. 29—Cassius Clay def. George Chuvalo, 15, Toronto.
1966—May 21—Cassius Clay KOd Henry Cooper, 6, London.
1966—Aug. 6—Cassius Clay KOd Brian London, 3, London.

1966—Sept. 10—Cassius Clay KOd Karl Mildenberger, 12, Frankfurt, Germany.
1966—Nov. 14—Cassius Clay KOd Cleveland Williams, 3, Houston.
1967—Feb. 6—Cassius Clay def. Ernie Terrell, 15, Houston.
1967—Mar. 22—Cassius Clay KOd Zora Folley, 7, New York. Clay was stripped of his title by the WBA and others for refusing military service.
*1970—Feb. 16—Joe Frazier KOd Jimmy Ellis, 5, New York.
1970—Nov. 18—Joe Frazier KOd Bob Foster, 2, Detroit.
1971—Mar. 8—Joe Frazier def. Cassius Clay (Muhammad Ali), 15, New York.
1972—Jan. 15—Joe Frazier KOd Terry Daniels, 4, New Orleans.
1972—May 25—Joe Frazier KOd Ron Stander, 5, Omaha.
*1973—Jan. 22—George Foreman KOd Joe Frazier, 2, Kingston, Jamaica.
1973—Sept. 1—George Foreman KOd Joe Roman, 1, Tokyo.
1974—Mar. 3—George Foreman KOd Ken Norton, 2, Caracas.
*1974—Oct. 30—Muhammad Ali KOd George Foreman, 8, Zaire.
1975—Mar. 24—Muhammad Ali KOd Chuck Wepner, 15, Cleveland.
1975—May 16—Muhammad Ali KOd Ron Lyle, 11, Las Vegas.
1975—June 30—Muhammad Ali def. Joe Bugner, 15, Malaysia.
1975—Oct. 1—Muhammad Ali KOd Joe Frazier, 14, Manila.
1976—Feb. 20—Muhammad Ali KOd Jean-Pierre Coopman, 5, San Juan.
1976—Apr. 30—Muhammad Ali def. Jimmy Young, 15, Landover, Md.
1976—May 25—Muhammad Ali KOd Richard Dunn, 5, Munich.
1976—Sept. 28—Muhammad Ali def. Ken Norton, 15, New York.
1977—May 16—Muhammad Ali def. Alfredo Evangelista, 15, Landover, Md.
1977—Sept. 29—Muhammad Ali def. Earnie Shavers, 15, New York.
*1978—Feb. 15—Leon Spinks def. Muhammad Ali, 15, Las Vegas.
*1978—Sept. 15—Muhammad Ali def. Leon Spinks, 15, New Orleans. Ali retired in 1979.

(Bouts when title changed hands only)

*1978—June 9—(WBC) Larry Holmes def. Ken Norton, 15, Las Vegas.
*1980—Mar. 31—(WBA) Mike Weaver KOd John Tate, 15, Knoxville.
*1982—Dec. 10—(WBA) Michael Dokes KOd Mike Weaver, 1, Las Vegas.
*1983—Sept. 23—(WBA) Gerrie Coetzee KOd Michael Dokes, 10, Richfield, Oh.
1984—Mar. 10—(WBC) Tim Witherspoon def. Greg Page, 12, Las Vegas, Nev.
1984—Aug. 31—(WBC) Pinklon Thomas def. Tim Witherspoon, 12, Las Vegas, Nev.
1984—Dec. 2—(WBA) Greg Page KOd Gerrie Coetzee, 8, Sun City, Bophuthatswana
1985—Apr. 29—(WBA) Tony Tubbs def. Greg Page, 15, Buffalo, N.Y.
1985—Sept. 21—(IBF) Michael Spinks def. Larry Holmes, 15, Las Vegas, Nev.
1986—Jan. 17—(WBA) Tim Witherspoon def. Tony Tubbs, 15, Atlanta, Ga.
1986—Mar. 23—(WBC) Trevor Berbick def. Pinklon Thomas, 12, Miami, Fla.
1986—Nov. 22—(WBC) Mike Tyson KOd Trevor Berbick, 2, Las Vegas.
1986—Dec. 12—(WBA) James (Bonecrusher) Smith KOd Tim Witherspoon, 1, New York.
*(1987—Mar. 7—(WBA) Mike Tyson def. James (Bonecrusher) Smith, 12, Las Vegas.
1990—Feb. 11—(WBA, WBC, IBF) James "Buster" Douglas KOd Mike Tyson, 10, Tokyo.

NCAA Wrestling Champions

Year	Champion	Year	Champion	Year	Champion	Year	Champion	Year	Champion
1964	Oklahoma State	1970	Iowa State	1976	Iowa	1981	Iowa	1986	Iowa
1965	Iowa State	1971	Oklahoma State	1977	Iowa State	1982	Iowa	1987	Iowa State
1966	Oklahoma State	1972	Iowa State	1978	Iowa	1983	Iowa	1988	Arizona State
1967	Michigan State	1973	Iowa State	1979	Iowa	1984	Iowa	1989	Oklahoma State
1968	Oklahoma State	1974	Oklahoma	1980	Iowa	1985	Iowa	1990	Oklahoma State
1969	Iowa State	1975	Iowa						

Tennis

U.S. Open Champions

Men's Singles

Year	Champion	Final opponent	Year	Champion	Final opponent
1910	William Larned	T. C. Bundy	1951	Frank Sedgman	E. Victor Seixas Jr.
1911	William Larned	Maurice McLoughlin	1952	Frank Sedgman	Gardnar Mulloy
1912	Maurice McLoughlin	Wallace Johnson	1953	Tony Trabert	E. Victor Seixas Jr.
1913	Maurice McLoughlin	Richard Williams	1954	E. Victor Seixas Jr.	Rex Hartwig
1914	Richard Williams	Maurice McLoughlin	1955	Tony Trabert	Ken Rosewall
1915	William Johnston	Maurice McLoughlin	1956	Ken Rosewall	Lewis Hoad
1916	Richard Williams	William Johnston	1957	Malcolm Anderson	Ashley Cooper
1917	Richard Murray	N. W. Niles	1958	Ashley Cooper	Malcolm Anderson
1918	Richard Murray	Bill Tilden	1959	Neale A. Fraser	Alejandro Olmedo
1919	William Johnston	Bill Tilden	1960	Neale A. Fraser	Rod Laver
1920	Bill Tilden	William Johnston	1961	Roy Emerson	Rod Laver
1921	Bill Tilden	Wallace Johnson	1962	Rod Laver	Roy Emerson
1922	Bill Tilden	William Johnston	1963	Rafael Osuna	F. A. Froehling 3d
1923	Bill Tilden	William Johnston	1964	Roy Emerson	Fred Stolle
1924	Bill Tilden	William Johnston	1965	Manuel Santana	Cliff Drysdale
1925	Bill Tilden	William Johnston	1966	Fred Stolle	John Newcombe
1926	Rene Lacoste	Jean Borotra	1967	John Newcombe	Clark Graebner
1927	Rene Lacoste	Bill Tilden	1968	Arthur Ashe	Tom Okker
1928	Henri Cochet	Francis Hunter	1969	Rod Laver	Tony Roche
1929	Bill Tilden	Francis Hunter	1970	Ken Rosewall	Tony Roche
1930	John Doeg	Francis Shields	1971	Stan Smith	Jan Kodes
1931	H. Ellsworth Vines	George Lott	1972	Ilie Nastase	Arthur Ashe
1932	H. Ellsworth Vines	Henri Cochet	1973	John Newcombe	Jan Kodes
1933	Fred Perry	John Crawford	1974	Jimmy Connors	Ken Rosewall
1934	Fred Perry	Wilmer Allison	1975	Manuel Orantes	Jimmy Connors
1935	Wilmer Allison	Sidney Wood	1976	Jimmy Connors	Bjorn Borg
1936	Fred Perry	Don Budge	1977	Guillermo Vilas	Jimmy Connors
1937	Don Budge	Baron G. von Cramm	1978	Jimmy Connors	Bjorn Borg
1938	Don Budge	C. Gene Mako	1979	John McEnroe	Vitas Gerulaitis
1939	Robert Riggs	S. Welby Van Horn	1980	John McEnroe	Bjorn Borg
1940	Don McNeill	Robert Riggs	1981	John McEnroe	Bjorn Borg
1941	Robert Riggs	F. L. Kovacs	1982	Jimmy Connors	Ivan Lendl
1942	F. R. Schroeder Jr.	Frank Parker	1983	Jimmy Connors	Ivan Lendl
1943	Joseph Hunt	Jack Kramer	1984	John McEnroe	Ivan Lendl
1944	Frank Parker	William Talbert	1985	Ivan Lendl	John McEnroe
1945	Frank Parker	William Talbert	1986	Ivan Lendl	Miloslav Mecir
1946	Jack Kramer	Thomas Brown Jr.	1987	Ivan Lendl	Mats Wilander
1947	Jack Kramer	Frank Parker	1988	Mats Wilander	Ivan Lendl
1948	Pancho Gonzales	Eric Sturgess	1989	Boris Becker	Ivan Lendl
1949	Pancho Gonzales	F. R. Schroeder Jr.	1990	Pete Sampras	Andre Agassi
1950	Arthur Larsen	Herbert Flam			

Women's Singles

Year	Champion	Final opponent	Year	Champion	Final opponent
1926	Molla B. Mallory	Elizabeth Ryan	1959	Maria Bueno	Christine Truman
1927	Helen Wills	Betty Nuthall	1960	Darlene Hard	Maria Bueno
1928	Helen Wills	Helen Jacobs	1961	Darlene Hard	Ann Haydon
1929	Helen Wills	M. Watson	1962	Margaret Smith	Darlene Hard
1930	Betty Nuthall	L. A. Harper	1963	Maria Bueno	Margaret Smith
1931	Helen Wills Moody	E. B. Whittingstall	1964	Maria Bueno	Carole Graebner
1932	Helen Jacobs	Carolin A. Babcock	1965	Margaret Smith	Billie Jean Moffitt
1933	Helen Jacobs	Helen Wills Moody	1966	Maria Bueno	Nancy Richey
1934	Helen Jacobs	Sarah H. Palfrey	1967	Billie Jean King	Ann Haydon Jones
1935	Helen Jacobs	Sarah P. Fabyan	1968	Virginia Wade	Billie Jean King
1936	Alice Marble	Helen Jacobs	1969	Margaret Court	Nancy Richey
1937	Anita Lizana	Jadwiga Jedrzejowska	1970	Margaret Court	Rosemary Casals
1938	Alice Marble	Nancye Wynne	1971	Billie Jean King	Rosemary Casals
1939	Alice Marble	Helen Jacobs	1972	Billie Jean King	Kerry Melville
1940	Alice Marble	Helen Jacobs	1973	Margaret Court	Evonne Goolagong
1941	Sarah Palfrey Cooke	Pauline Betz	1974	Billie Jean King	Evonne Goolagong
1942	Pauline Betz	Louise Brough	1975	Chris Evert	Evonne Goolagong
1943	Pauline Betz	Louise Brough	1976	Chris Evert	Evonne Goolagong
1944	Pauline Betz	Margaret Osborne	1977	Chris Evert	Wendy Turnbull
1945	Sarah P. Cooke	Pauline Betz	1978	Chris Evert	Pam Shriver
1946	Pauline Betz	Doris Hart	1979	Tracy Austin	Chris Evert Lloyd
1947	Louise Brough	Margaret Osborne	1980	Chris Evert Lloyd	Hana Mandlikova
1948	Margaret Osborne duPont	Louise Brough	1981	Tracy Austin	Martina Navratilova
1949	Margaret Osborne duPont	Doris Hart	1982	Chris Evert Lloyd	Hana Mandlikova
1950	Margaret Osborne duPont	Doris Hart	1983	Martina Navratilova	Chris Evert Lloyd
1951	Maureen Connolly	Shirley Fry	1984	Martina Navratilova	Chris Evert Lloyd
1952	Maureen Connolly	Doris Hart	1985	Hana Mandlikova	Martina Navratilova
1953	Maureen Connolly	Doris Hart	1986	Martina Navratilova	Helena Sukova
1954	Doris Hart	Louise Brough	1987	Martina Navratilova	Steffi Graf
1955	Doris Hart	Patricia Ward	1988	Steffi Graf	Gabriela Sabatini
1956	Shirley Fry	Althea Gibson	1989	Steffi Graf	Martina Navratilova
1957	Althea Gibson	Louise Brough	1990	Gabriela Sabatini	Steffi Graf
1958	Althea Gibson	Darlene Hard			

Men's Doubles

Year	Champions	Year	Champions
1945	Gardnar Mulloy—William Talbert	1968	Robert Lutz—Stan Smith
1946	Gardnar Mulloy—William Talbert	1969	Fred Stolle—Ken Rosewall
1947	Jack Kramer—Frederick Schroeder Jr.	1970	Pierre Barthes—Nicki Pilic
1948	Gardnar Mulloy—William Talbert	1971	John Newcombe—Roger Taylor
1949	John Bromwich—William Sidwell	1972	Cliff Drysdale—Roger Taylor
1950	John Bromwich—Frank Sedgman	1973	John Newcombe—Owen Davidson
1951	Frank Sedgman—Kenneth McGregor	1974	Bob Lutz—Stan Smith
1952	Mervyn Rose—E. Victor Seixas Jr.	1975	Jimmy Connors—Ilie Nastase
1953	Rex Hartwig—Mervyn Rose	1976	Marty Riessen—Tom Okker
1954	E. Victor Seixas Jr.—Tony Trabert	1977	Bob Hewitt—Frew McMillan
1955	Kosei Kamo—Atsushi Miyagi	1978	Stan Smith—Bob Lutz
1956	Lewis Hoad—Ken Rosewall	1979	John McEnroe—Peter Fleming
1957	Ashley Cooper—Neale Fraser	1980	Bob Lutz—Stan Smith
1958	Hamilton Richardson—Alejandro Olmedo	1981	John McEnroe—Peter Fleming
1959	Neale A. Fraser—Roy Emerson	1982	Kevin Curren—Steve Denton
1960	Neale A. Fraser—Roy Emerson	1983	John McEnroe—Peter Fleming
1961	Dennis Ralston—Chuck McKinley	1984	Tomas Smid—John Fitzgerald
1962	Rafael Osuna—Antonio Palafox	1985	Ken Flach—Robert Seguso
1963	Dennis Ralston—Chuck McKinley	1986	Andres Gomez—Slobodan Zivojinovic
1964	Dennis Ralston—Chuck McKinley	1987	Stefan Edberg—Anders Jarryd
1965	Roy Emerson—Fred Stolle	1988	Sergio Casal—Emilio Sanchez
1966	Roy Emerson—Fred Stolle	1989	John McEnroe—Mark Woodforde
1967	John Newcombe—Tony Roche	1990	Pieter Aldrich—Danie Visser

Women's Doubles

Year	Champions	Year	Champions
1945	A. Louise Brough—Margaret Osborne	1968	Maria Bueno—Margaret S. Court
1946	A. Louise Brough—Margaret Osborne	1969	Francoise Durr—Darlene Hard
1947	A. Louise Brough—Margaret Osborne	1970	M. S. Court—Judy Tegart Dalton
1948	A. Louise Brough—Mrs. M. O. du Pont	1971	Rosemary Casals—Judy Tegart Dalton
1949	A. Louise Brough—Mrs. M. O. du Pont	1972	Francoise Durr—Betty Stove
1950	A. Louise Brough—Mrs. M. O. du Pont	1973	Margaret S. Court—Virginia Wade
1951	Doris Hart—Shirley Fry	1974	Billie Jean King—Rosemary Casals
1952	Doris Hart—Shirley Fry	1975	Margaret Court—Virginia Wade
1953	Doris Hart—Shirley Fry	1976	Linky Boshoff—Ilana Kloss
1954	Doris Hart—Shirley Fry	1977	Betty Stove—Martina Navratilova
1955	A. Louise Brough—Mrs. M. O. du Pont	1978	Martina Navratilova—Billie Jean King
1956	A. Louise Brough—Mrs. M. O. du Pont	1979	Betty Stove—Wendy Turnbull
1957	A. Louise Brough—Mrs. M. O. du Pont	1980	Billie Jean King—Martina Navratilova
1958	Darlene Hard—Jeanne Arth	1981	Anne Smith—Kathy Jordan
1959	Darlene Hard—Jeanne Arth	1982	Rosemary Casals—Wendy Turnbull
1960	Darlene Hard—Maria Bueno	1983	Martina Navratilova—Pam Shriver
1961	Darlene Hard—Lesley Turner	1984	Martina Navratilova—Pam Shriver
1962	Maria Bueno—Darlene Hard	1985	Claudia Kohde-Kilsch—Helena Sukova
1963	Margaret Smith—Robyn Ebbern	1986	Martina Navratilova—Pam Shriver
1964	Billie Jean Moffitt—Karen Susman	1987	Martina Navratilova—Pam Shriver
1965	Carole C. Graebner—Nancy Richey	1988	Gigi Fernandez—Robin White
1966	Maria Bueno—Nancy Richey	1989	Martina Navratilova—Hana Mandlikova
1967	Rosemary Casals—Billie Jean King	1990	Gigi Fernandez—Martina Navratilova

Davis Cup Challenge Round

Year	Result	Year	Result	Year	Result
1900	United States 5, British Isles 0	1931	France 3, Great Britain 2	1963	United States 3, Australia 2
1901	(not played)	1932	France 3, United States 2	1964	Australia 3, United States 2
1902	United States 3, British Isles 2	1933	Great Britain 3, France 2	1965	Australia 4, Spain 1
1903	British Isles 4, United States 1	1934	Great Britain 4, United States 1	1966	Australia 4, India 1
1904	British Isles 5, Belgium 0	1935	Great Britain 5, United States 0	1967	Australia 4, Spain 1
1905	British Isles 5, United States 0	1936	Great Britain 3, Australia 2	1968	United States 4, Australia 1
1906	British Isles 5, United States 0	1937	United States 4, Great Britain 1	1969	United States 5, Romania 0
1907	Australia 3, British Isles 2	1938	United States 3, Australia 2	1970	United States 5, W. Germany 0
1908	Australasia 3, United States 2	1939	Australia 3, United States 2	1971	United States 3, Romania 2
1909	Australasia 5, United States 0	1940-45	(not played)	1972	United States 3, Romania 2
1910	(not played)	1946	United States 5, Australia 0	1973	Australia 5, United States 0
1911	Australasia 5, United States 0	1947	United States 4, Australia 1	1974	South Africa (default by India)
1912	British Isles 3, Australasia 2	1948	United States 5, Australia 0	1975	Sweden 3, Czech. 2
1913	United States 3, British Isles 2	1949	United States 4, Australia 1	1976	Italy 4, Chile 1
1914	Australasia 3, United States 2	1950	Australia 4, United States 1	1977	Australia 3, Italy 1
1915-18	(not played)	1951	Australia 3, United States 2	1978	United States 4, Great Britain 1
1919	Australasia 4, British Isles 1	1952	Australia 4, United States 1	1979	United States 5, Italy 0
1920	United States 5, Australasia 0	1953	Australia 3, United States 2	1980	Czechoslovakia 4, Italy 1
1921	United States 5, Japan 0	1954	United States 3, Australia 2	1981	United States 3, Argentina 1
1922	United States 4, Australasia 1	1955	Australia 5, United States 0	1982	United States 3, France, 0
1923	United States 4, Australasia 1	1956	Australia 5, United States 0	1983	Australia 3, Sweden 2
1924	United States 5, Australasia 0	1957	Australia 3, United States 2	1984	Sweden 3, United States 0
1925	United States 5, France 0	1958	United States 3, Australia 2	1985	Sweden 3, W. Germany 2
1926	United States 4, France 1	1959	Australia 3, United States 2	1986	Australia 3, Sweden 2
1927	France 3, United States 2	1960	Australia 4, Italy 1	1987	Sweden 5, India 0
1928	France 4, United States 1	1961	Australia 5, Italy 0	1988	W. Germany 4, Sweden 1
1929	France 3, United States 2	1962	Australia 5, Mexico 0	1989	W. Germany 3, Sweden 2
1930	France 4, United States 1				

All-England Champions, Wimbledon

Men's Singles

Year	Champion	Final opponent	Year	Champion	Final opponent
1933	Jack Crawford	Ellsworth Vines	1965	Roy Emerson	Fred Stolle
1934	Fred Perry	Jack Crawford	1966	Manuel Santana	Dennis Ralston
1935	Fred Perry	Gottfried von Cramm	1967	John Newcombe	Wilhelm Bungert
1936	Fred Perry	Gottfried von Cramm	1968	Rod Laver	Tony Roche
1937	Donald Budge	Gottfried von Cramm	1969	Rod Laver	John Newcombe
1938	Donald Budge	Wilfred Austin	1970	John Newcombe	Ken Rosewall
1939	Bobby Riggs	Elwood Cooke	1971	John Newcombe	Stan Smith
1940-45	not held		1972	Stan Smith	Ilie Nastase
1946	Yvon Petra	Geoff E. Brown	1973	Jan Kodes	Alex Metreveli
1947	Jack Kramer	Tom P. Brown	1974	Jimmy Connors	Ken Rosewall
1948	Bob Falkenburg	John Bromwich	1975	Arthur Ashe	Jimmy Connors
1949	Ted Schroeder	Jaroslav Drobny	1976	Bjorn Borg	Ilie Nastase
1950	Budge Patty	Frank Sedgman	1977	Bjorn Borg	Jimmy Connors
1951	Dick Savitt	Ken McGregor	1978	Bjorn Borg	Jimmy Connors
1952	Frank Sedgman	Jaroslav Drobny	1979	Bjorn Borg	Roscoe Tanner
1953	Vic Seixas	Kurt Nielsen	1980	Bjorn Borg	John McEnroe
1954	Jaroslav Drobny	Ken Rosewall	1981	John McEnroe	Bjorn Borg
1955	Tony Trabert	Kurt Nielsen	1982	Jimmy Connors	John McEnroe
1956	Lew Hoad	Ken Rosewall	1983	John McEnroe	Chris Lewis
1957	Lew Hoad	Ashley Cooper	1984	John McEnroe	Jimmy Connors
1958	Ashley Cooper	Neale Fraser	1985	Boris Becker	Kevin Curren
1959	Alex Olmedo	Rod Laver	1986	Boris Becker	Ivan Lendl
1960	Neale Fraser	Rod Laver	1987	Pat Cash	Ivan Lendl
1961	Rod Laver	Chuck McKinley	1988	Stefan Edberg	Boris Becker
1962	Rod Laver	Martin Mulligan	1989	Boris Becker	Stefan Edberg
1963	Chuck McKinley	Fred Stolle	1990	Stefan Edberg	Boris Becker
1964	Roy Emerson	Fred Stolle			

Women's Singles

Year	Champion	Year	Champion	Year	Champion	Year	Champion
1946	Pauline Betz	1958	Althea Gibson	1969	Ann Haydon-Jones	1980	Evonne Goolagong
1947	Margaret Osborne	1959	Maria Bueno	1970	Margaret Court	1981	Chris Evert Lloyd
1948	Louise Brough	1960	Maria Bueno	1971	Evonne Goolagong	1982	Martina Navratilova
1949	Louise Brough	1961	Angela Mortimer	1972	Billie Jean King	1983	Martina Navratilova
1950	Louise Brough	1962	Karen Hantze-Susman	1973	Billie Jean King	1984	Martina Navratilova
1951	Doris Hart	1963	Margaret Smith	1974	Chris Evert	1985	Martina Navratilova
1952	Maureen Connolly	1964	Maria Bueno	1975	Billie Jean King	1986	Martina Navratilova
1953	Maureen Connolly	1965	Margaret Smith	1976	Chris Evert	1987	Martina Navratilova
1954	Maureen Connolly	1966	Billie Jean King	1977	Virginia Wade	1988	Steffi Graf
1955	Louise Brough	1967	Billie Jean King	1978	Martina Navratilova	1989	Steffi Graf
1956	Shirley Fry	1968	Billie Jean King	1979	Martina Navratilova	1990	Martina Navratilova
1957	Althea Gibson						

French Open Champions

Year	Men	Women	Year	Men	Women
1969	Rod Laver	Margaret Smith Court	1980	Bjorn Borg	Chris Evert Lloyd
1970	Jan Kodes	Margaret Smith Court	1981	Bjorn Borg	Hana Mandlikova
1971	Jan Kodes	Evonne Goolagong	1982	Mats Wilander	Martina Navratilova
1972	Andres Gimeno	Billie Jean King	1983	Yannick Noah	Chris Evert Lloyd
1973	Ilie Nastase	Margaret Court	1984	Ivan Lendl	Martina Navratilova
1974	Bjorn Borg	Chris Evert	1985	Mats Wilander	Chris Evert Lloyd
1975	Bjorn Borg	Chris Evert	1986	Ivan Lendl	Chris Evert Lloyd
1976	Adriano Panatta	Sue Barker	1987	Ivan Lendl	Steffi Graf
1977	Guillermo Vilas	Mima Jausovec	1988	Mats Wilander	Steffi Graf
1978	Bjorn Borg	Virginia Ruzici	1989	Michael Chang	Arantxa Sanchez
1979	Bjorn Borg	Chris Evert Lloyd	1990	Andres Gomez	Monica Seles

The World Cup

The World Cup, emblematic of International soccer supremacy, was won by West Germany on July 8, 1990, with a 1-0 victory over defending champion Argentina on a penalty shot in the 84th minute. It was the lowest-scoring final in the 60 years of World Cup play. It was the 3d World Cup title for West Germany, equaling Brazil and Italy. Winners and sites of previous World Cup play follow:

Year	Winner	Final opponent	Site	Year	Winner	Final opponent	Site
1930	Uruguay	Argentina	Uruguay	1966	England	W. Germany	England
1934	Italy	Czechoslovakia	Italy	1970	Brazil	Italy	Mexico
1938	Italy	Hungary	France	1974	W. Germany	Netherlands	W. Germany
1950	Uruguay	Brazil	Brazil	1978	Argentina	Netherlands	Argentina
1954	W. Germany	Hungary	Switzerland	1982	Italy	W. Germany	Spain
1958	Brazil	Sweden	Sweden	1986	Argentina	W. Germany	Mexico
1962	Brazil	Czechoslovakia	Chile	1990	W. Germany	Argentina	Italy

Tour de France in 1990

Greg LeMond of the United States won the 77th Tour de France, the world's most prestigious bicycle race, for the second consecutive year. His margin of victory was 2 minutes 16 seconds, and he completed the 21-day, about 2,000 mile race in a total time of 90 hours 43 minutes 20 seconds. Claudio Chiappucci of Italy finished second.

Notable Sports Personalities

Henry Aaron, b. 1934: Milwaukee-Atlanta outfielder hit record 755 home runs; led NL 4 times.

Kareem Abdul-Jabbar, b. 1947: Milwaukee, L.A. Lakers center; MVP 6 times; leading scorer twice; playoff MVP, 1971, 1985; all-time leading NBA scorer.

Grover Cleveland Alexander, (1887-1950): pitcher won 374 NL games; pitched 16 shutouts, 1916.

Muhammad Ali, b. 1942: 3-time heavyweight champion.

Ken Anderson, b. 1949: Cinn. Bengals quarterback led AFC in passing 4 times.

Mario Andretti, b. 1940; won Indy 500, 1969; Grand Prix champ, 1978.

Eddie Arcaro, b. 1916: jockey rode 4,779 winners including the Kentucky Derby 5 times; the Preakness and Belmont Stakes 6 times each.

Henry Armstrong, b. 1912: boxer held feather-, welter-, lightweight titles simultaneously, 1937-38.

Arthur Ashe, b. 1943: U.S. singles champ, 1968, Wimbledon champ, 1975.

Red Auerbach, b. 1917: coached Boston Celtics to 9 NBA championships.

Ernie Banks, b. 1931: Chicago Cubs slugger hit 512 NL homers; twice MVP.

Roger Bannister, b. 1929: Briton ran first sub 4-minute mile, May 6, 1954.

Rick Barry, b. 1944: NBA scoring leader, 1967; ABA, 1969.

Sammy Baugh, b. 1914: Washington Redskins quarterback held numerous records upon retirement after 16 pro seasons.

Elgin Baylor, b. 1934: L.A. Lakers forward; 1st team all-star 10 times.

Bob Beamon, b. 1946: long jumper won 1968 Olympic gold medal with record 29 ft. 2½ in.

Jean Beliveau, b. 1931: Montreal Canadiens center scored 507 goals; twice MVP.

Johnny Bench, b. 1947: Cincinnati Reds catcher; MVP twice; led league in home runs twice, RBIs 3 times.

Patty Berg, b. 1918: won over 80 golf tournaments; AP Woman Athlete-of-the-Year 3 times.

Yogi Berra, b. 1925: N.Y. Yankees catcher; MVP 3 times; played in 14 World Series.

Raymond Berry, b. 1933: Baltimore Colts receiver caught 631 passes.

Matt Biondi, b. 1965: swimmer won 5 gold medals at 1988 Olympics.

Larry Bird, b. 1956: Boston Celtics forward; chosen MVP 1984-86, playoff MVP, 1984, 1986.

George Blanda, b. 1927: quarterback, kicker; 26 years as active player, scoring record 2,002 points.

Wade Boggs, b. 1958: AL Batting champ, 1983, 1985-88.

Bjorn Borg, b. 1956: led Sweden to first Davis Cup, 1975; Wimbledon champion, 5 times.

Mike Bossy, b.1957; N.Y. Islanders right wing scored over 50 goals 8 times.

Terry Bradshaw, b. 1948; Pittsburgh Steelers quarterback led team to 4 Super Bowl titles.

George Brett, b. 1953: Kansas City Royals 3d baseman led AL in batting, 1976, 1980; MVP, 1980.

Lou Brock, b. 1939: St. Louis Cardinals outfielder stole record 118 bases, 1974; record 938 career; led NL 8 times.

Jimmy Brown, b. 1936: Cleveland Browns fullback ran for 12,312 career yards; MVP 3 times.

Paul "Bear" Bryant, (1913-1983), college football coach with 323 victories.

Maria Bueno, b. 1939: U.S. singles champ 4 times; Wimbledon champ 3 times.

Dick Butkus, b. 1942: Chicago Bears linebacker twice chosen best NFL defensive player.

Dick Button, b. 1929: figure skater won 1948, 1952 Olympic gold medals; world titlist, 1948-52.

Walter Camp, (1859-1925): Yale football player, coach, athletic director; established many rules; promoted All-America designations.

Roy Campanella, b. 1921: Brooklyn Dodgers catcher; MVP 3 times.

Earl Campbell, b. 1955: NFL running back; NFL MVP 1978-1980.

Jose Canseco, b. 1964: Oakland A's outfielder; AL MVP 1988.

Rod Carew, b. 1945: AL infielder won 7 batting titles; MVP, 1977.

Steve Carlton, b. 1944: NL pitcher won 20 games 5 times, Cy Young award 4 times.

Billy Casper, b. 1931: PGA Player-of-the-Year 3 times; U.S. Open champ twice.

Wilt Chamberlain, b. 1936: center was NBA leading scorer 7 times; MVP 4 times.

Bobby Clarke, b. 1949: Philadelphia Flyers center led team to 2 Stanley Cup championships: MVP 3 times.

Roberto Clemente, (1934-1972): Pittsburgh Pirates outfielder won 4 batting titles; MVP, 1966.

Ty Cobb, (1886-1961): Detroit Tigers outfielder had record .367 lifetime batting average, 12 batting titles.

Sebastian Coe, b. 1956: Briton won Olympic 1,500-meter run, 1980, 1984.

Nadia Comaneci, b. 1961: Romanian gymnast won 3 gold medals, achieved 7 perfect scores, 1976 Olympics.

Maureen Connolly, (1934-1969): won tennis "grand slam," 1953; AP Woman-Athlete-of-the-Year 3 times.

Jimmy Connors, b. 1952: U.S. singles champ 5 times; Wimbledon champ twice.

James J. Corbett, (1866-1933): heavyweight champion, 1892-97; credited with being the first "scientific" boxer.

Angel Cordero, b. 1942: jockey won over 6,000 races; leading money winner, 1976, 1982-83.

Margaret Smith Court, b. 1942: Australian won U.S. singles championship 5 times; Wimbledon champ 3 times.

Bob Cousy, b. 1928: Boston Celtics guard led team to 6 NBA championships; MVP, 1957.

Andre Dawson, b. 1954: slugger led NL in home runs, MVP, 1987.

Dizzy Dean, (1911-1974): colorful pitcher for St. Louis Cardinals "Gashouse Gang" in the 30s; MVP, 1934.

Jack Dempsey, (1895-1983); heavyweight champion, 1919-26.

Eric Dickerson, b. 1960: running back ran for NFL record 2,105 yds., 1984; led NFC 3 times, AFC twice.

Joe DiMaggio, b. 1914: N.Y. Yankees outfielder hit safely in record 56 consecutive games, 1941; MVP 3 times.

Leo Durocher, b. 1906: manager won 3 NL pennants.

Gertrude Ederle, b. 1906: first woman to swim English Channel, broke existing men's record, 1926.

Julius Erving, b. 1950: MVP and leading scorer in ABA 3 times; NBA MVP, 1981.

Phil Esposito, b. 1942: NHL scoring leader 5 times.

Chris Evert, b. 1954: U.S. singles champ 6 times, Wimbledon champ 3 times.

Patrick Ewing, b. 1962: center led Georgetown Univ. to 1984 NCAA championship.

Ray Ewry, (1873-1937): track and field star won 8 gold medals, 1900, 1904, and 1908 Olympics.

Juan Fangio, b. 1911: World Grand Prix champion 5 times.

Bob Feller, b. 1918: Cleveland Indians pitcher won 266 games; pitched 3 no-hitters, 12 one-hitters.

Peggy Fleming, b. 1948: world figure skating champion, 1966-68; gold medalist 1968 Olympics.

Whitey Ford, b. 1928: N.Y. Yankees pitcher won record 10 World Series games.

Dick Fosbury, b. 1947: high jumper won 1968 Olympic gold medal; developed the "Fosbury Flop."

Jimmie Foxx, (1907-1967): Red Sox, Athletics slugger; MVP 3 times; triple crown, 1933.

A.J. Foyt, b. 1935: won Indy 500 4 times; U.S. Auto Club champ 7 times.

Joe Frazier, b. 1944: heavyweight champion, 1970-73.

Lou Gehrig, (1903-1941): N.Y. Yankees 1st baseman played record 2,130 consecutive games; MVP, 1936.

George Gervin, b. 1952: leading NBA scorer, 1978-80, 1982.

Althea Gibson, b. 1927: twice U.S. and Wimbledon singles champ.

Bob Gibson, b. 1935: St. Louis Cardinals pitcher won Cy Young award twice; struck out 3,117 batters.

Frank Gifford, b. 1930: N.Y. Giants back; MVP, 1956.

Dwight Gooden, b. 1964: N.Y. Mets pitcher was NL Rookie of Year, 1984; Cy Young award, 1985.

Steffi Graf, b. 1969: W. German won tennis "grand slam," 1988; U.S. champ 1988, 1989.

Otto Graham, b. 1921: Cleveland Browns quarterback; all-pro 4 times.

Red Grange, b 1903: All-America at Univ. of Illinois 1923-25; played for Chicago Bears, 1925-35.

Joe Greene, b. 1946: Pittsburgh Steelers lineman; twice NFL outstanding defensive player.

Wayne Gretzky, b. 1961: Edmonton Oilers center scored record 92 goals, 212 pts., 1982; MVP, 1980-87, 1989.

Florence Griffith Joyner, b. 1959: sprinter won 3 gold medals at 1988 Olympics.

Lefty Grove, (1900-1975): pitcher won 300 AL games; 20-game winner 8 times.

Tony Gwynn, b. 1960: NL batting champ, 1984, 1987-1989.

Walter Hagen, (1892-1969): won PGA championship 5 times. British Open 4 times.

George Halas, (1895-1983): founder-coach of Chicago Bears; won 5 NFL championships.

Bill Hartack, b. 1932: jockey rode 5 Kentucky Derby winners.

John Havlicek, b. 1940: Boston Celtics forward scored over 26,000 NBA points.

Eric Heiden, b. 1958: speed skater won 5 1980 Olympic gold medals.

Rickey Henderson, b. 1958: AL outfielder stole record 130 bases, 1982.

Sonja Henie, (1912-1969): world champion figure skater, 1927-36; Olympic gold medalist, 1928, 1932, 1936.

Ben Hogan, b. 1912: won 4 U.S. Open championships, 2 PGA, 2 Masters.

Rogers Hornsby, (1896-1963): NL 2d baseman batted record .424 in 1924; twice won triple crown; batting leader, 1920-25.

Paul Hornung, b. 1935: Green Bay Packers runner-placekicker scored record 176 points, 1960.

Gordie Howe, b. 1928: hockey forward; NHL MVP 6 times.

Carl Hubbell, (1903-1988): N.Y. Giants pitcher; 20-game winner 5 consecutive years, 1933-37.

Bobby Hull, b. 1939: NHL all-star 10 times.

Catfish Hunter b. 1946: pitched perfect game, 1968; 20-game winner 5 times.

Don Hutson, b. 1913: Green Bay Packers receiver caught 99 NFL touchdown passes.

Reggie Jackson, b. 1946: slugger led AL in home runs 4 times; MVP, 1973; hit 5 World Series home runs, 1977.

Jack Johnson, (1878-1946): heavyweight champion, 1910-15.

Magic Johnson, b. 1959: NBA MVP 1987, 1989, 1990. Playoff MVP 1980, 1982, 1987.

Walter Johnson, (1887-1946): Washington Senators pitcher won 413 games.

Bobby Jones, (1902-1971); won "grand slam of golf" 1930; U.S. Amateur champ 5 times, U.S. Open champ 4 times.

Deacon Jones, b. 1938: L.A. Rams lineman; twice NFL outstanding defensive player.

Michael Jordan, b. 1963: NBA leading scorer, 1987-90; MVP, 1988.

Sonny Jurgensen, b. 1934: quarterback named all-pro 5 times.

Duke Kahanamoku, (1890-1968): swimmer won 1912, 1920 Olympic gold medals in 100-meter freestyle.

Harmon Killebrew, b. 1936: Minnesota Twins slugger led AL in home runs 6 times.

Jean Claude Killy, b. 1943: French skier won 3 1968 Olympic gold medals.

Ralph Kiner, b. 1922: Pittsburgh Pirates slugger led NL in home runs 7 consecutive years, 1946-52.

Billie Jean King, b. 1943: U.S. singles champ 4 times; Wimbledon champ 6 times.

Bob Knight, b. 1940: Indiana U. basketball coach lead team to NCAA championships 1976, 1981, 1987.

Olga Korbut, b. 1955: Soviet gymnast won 3 1972 Olympic gold medals.

Sandy Koufax, b. 1935: Dodgers pitcher won Cy Young award 3 times; lowest ERA in NL, 1962-66; pitched 4 no-hitters, one a perfect game.

Guy Lafleur, b. 1951: forward led NHL in scoring 3 times; MVP, 1977, 1978.

Tom Landry, b. 1924: Dallas Cowboys head coach 1960-88.

Rod Laver, b. 1938: Australian won tennis "grand slam," 1962, 1969; Wimbledon champ 4 times.

Mario Lemieux, b. 1965: NHL leading scorer, 1988-1989; MVP, 1988.

Ivan Lendl, b. 1960: U.S. singles champ, 1985-87.

Sugar Ray Leonard, b. 1956: former world welterweight champ.

Carl Lewis, b. 1961: track and field star won 4 1984 Olympic gold medals.

Vince Lombardi, (1913-1970): Green Bay Packers coach led, team to 5 NFL championships and 2 Super Bowl victories.

Joe Louis, (1914-1981): 1914: heavyweight champion, 1937-49.

Sid Luckman, b. 1916: Chicago Bears quarterback led team to 4 NFL championships; MVP, 1943.

Connie Mack, (1862-1956): Philadelphia Athletics manager, 1901-50; won 9 pennants, 3 championships.

Bill Madlock, b. 1951: NL batting leader 4 times.

Moses Malone, b. 1955: NBA center was MVP 1979, 1982, 1983.

Mickey Mantle, b. 1931: N.Y. Yankees outfielder; triple crown, 1956; 18 World Series home runs.

Pete Maravich (1948-1988): guard scored NCAA record 44.2 ppg during collegiate career; led NBA in scoring, 1977.

Rocky Marciano, (1923-1969): heavyweight champion, 1952-56; retired undefeated.

Dan Marino, b. 1961: Miami Dolphins quarterback passed for NFL record 5,084 yds, 1984.

Roger Maris, (1934-1985): N.Y. Yankees outfielder hit record 61 home runs, 1961; MVP, 1960 and 1961.

Eddie Mathews, b. 1931: Milwaukee-Atlanta 3d baseman hit 512 career home runs.

Christy Mathewson, (1880-1925): N.Y. Giants pitcher won 373 games.

Bob Mathias, b. 1930: decathlon gold medalist, 1948, 1952.

Don Mattingly, b. 1961: N.Y. Yankees 1st baseman won 1984 AL batting title; MVP, 1985.

Willie Mays, b. 1931: N.Y.-S.F. Giants center fielder hit 660 home runs; twice MVP.

Willie McCovey, b. 1938: S.F. Giants slugger hit 521 home runs; led NL 3 times.

John McEnroe, b. 1959: U.S. singles champ, 1979-81, 1984; Wimbledon champ, 1981, 1983-84.

John McGraw, (1873-1934): N.Y. Giants manager led team to 10 pennants, 3 championships.

Mark Messier, b. 1960: Edmonton Oilers Center chosen NHL MVP, 1990; Conn Smythe Trophy, 1984.

George Mikan, b. 1924: Minneapolis Lakers center selected in a 1950 AP poll as the greatest basketball player of the first half of the 20th century.

Stan Mikita, b. 1940: Chicago Black Hawks center led NHL in scoring 4 times; MVP twice.

Joe Montana, b. 1956: S.F. 49ers QB was Super Bowl MVP, 1982, 1985, 1990.

Archie Moore, b. 1913: world light-heavyweight champion, 1952-62.

Howie Morenz, (1902-1937): Montreal Canadiens forward chosen in a 1950 Canadian press poll as the outstanding hockey player of the first half of the 20th century.

Joe Morgan, b. 1943: National League MVP, 1975, 1976.

Thurman Munson, (1947-1979): N.Y. Yankees catcher; MVP, 1976.

Dale Murphy, b. 1956: outfielder chosen NL MVP 1982, 1983.

Stan Musial, b. 1920: St. Louis Cardinals star won 7 NL batting titles; MVP 3 times.

Bronko Nagurski, (1908-1990): Chicago Bears fullback and tackle; gained over 4,000 yds. rushing.

Joe Namath, b. 1943: quarterback led N.Y. Jets to 1969 Super Bowl title.

Martina Navratilova, b. 1956: Wimbledon champ 8 times, U.S. champ 1983-1984; 1986-87.

Byron Nelson, b. 1912: won 11 consecutive golf tournaments in 1945; twice Masters and PGA titlist.

Ernie Nevers, (1903-1976): Stanford star selected the best college fullback to play between 1919-1969.

John Newcombe, b. 1943: Australian twice U.S. singles champ; Wimbledon titlist 3 times.

Jack Nicklaus, b. 1940: PGA Player-of-the-Year, 1967, 1972; leading money winner 8 times; won Masters 6 times.

Chuck Noll, b. 1931: Pittsburgh Steelers coach led team to 4 Super Bowl titles.

Paavo Nurmi, (1897-1973): Finnish distance runner won 6 Olympic gold medals, 1920, 1924, 1928.

Al Oerter, b. 1936: discus thrower won gold medal at 4 consecutive Olympics, 1956-68.

Bobby Orr, b. 1948: Boston Bruins defenseman; Norris Trophy 8 times; led NHL in scoring twice, assists 5 times.

Mel Ott, (1909-1958): N.Y. Giants outfielder hit 511 home runs; led NL 6 times.

Jesse Owens, (1913-1980): track and field star won 4 1936 Olympic gold medals.

Satchel Paige, (1906-1982): pitcher starred in Negro leagues, 1924-48; entered major leagues at age 42.

Arnold Palmer, b. 1929: golf's first $1 million winner; won 4 Masters, 2 British Opens.

Jim Palmer, b. 1945: Baltimore Orioles pitcher; Cy Young award 3 times; 20-game winner 7 times.

Floyd Patterson, b. 1935: twice heavyweight champion.

Walter Payton, b. 1954: Chicago Bears running back has most rushing yards in NFL history; leading NFC rusher, 1976-80.

Pele, b. 1940: Brazilian soccer star scored 1,281 goals during 22-year career.

Bob Pettit, b. 1932: first NBA player to score 20,000 points; twice NBA scoring leader.

Richard Petty, b. 1937: NASCAR national champ 7 times; 7-times Daytona 500 winner.

Laffit Pincay Jr., b. 1946: leading money-winning jockey, 1970-74, 1979.

Jacques Plante, (1929-1986): goalie, 7 Vezina trophies; first goalie to wear a mask in a game.

Kirby Puckett, b. 1961: Minn. Twins outfielder won AL Batting Title, 1989; led AI in hits, 1987-89.

Willis Reed, b. 1942: N.Y. Knicks center; MVP, 1970; playoff MVP, 1970, 1973.

Jerry Rice, b. 1962: S.F. 49ers receiver chosen 1989 Super Bowl MVP.

Jim Rice, b. 1953: Boston Red Sox outfielder led AL in home runs, 1977-78, 1983; MVP 1978.

Maurice Richard, b. 1921: Montreal Canadiens forward scored 544 regular season goals, 82 playoff goals.

Branch Rickey, (1881-1965): executive instrumental in breaking baseball's color barrier, 1947; initiated farm system, 1919.

Oscar Robertson, b. 1938: guard averaged career 25.7 points per game; record 9,887 career assists; MVP, 1964.

Brooks Robinson, b. 1937: Baltimore Orioles 3d baseman played in 4 World Series; MVP, 1964.

Frank Robinson, b. 1935: slugger MVP in both NL and AL; triple crown winner, 1966; first black manager in majors.

Jackie Robinson, (1919-1972): broke baseball's color barrier with Brooklyn Dodgers, 1947; MVP, 1949.

Larry Robinson, b. 1951: NHL defenseman won Norris trophy, 1977, 1980.

Sugar Ray Robinson, (1920-1989): middleweight champion 5 times, welterweight champion.

Knute Rockne, (1888-1931): Notre Dame football coach, 1918-31; revolutionized game by stressing forward pass.

Pete Rose, b. 1941: won 3 NL batting titles; hit safely in 44 consecutive games, 1978; has most major league hits.

Wilma Rudolph, b. 1940: sprinter won 3 1960 Olympic gold medals.

Bill Russell, b. 1934: Boston Celtics center led team to 11 NBA titles; MVP 5 times; first black coach of major pro sports team.

Babe Ruth, (1895-1948): N.Y. Yankees outfielder hit 60 home runs, 1927; 714 lifetime; led AL 11 times.

Johnny Rutherford, b. 1938: auto racer won Indy 500 3 times.

Nolan Ryan, b. 1947: pitcher struck out record 383 batters, 1973; first to strike out 5,000 batters; pitched record 6 no-hitters; won 300th game, 1990.

Bret Saberhagen, b. 1964: K.C. Royals pitcher won Cy Young award, 1985, 1989; WS MVP, 1985.

Gene Sarazen, b. 1902: won PGA championship 3 times, U.S. Open twice; developer of sand wedge.

Gale Sayers, b. 1943: Chicago Bears back twice led NFC in rushing.

Mike Schmidt, b. 1949: Phillies 3d baseman led NL in home runs, 1974-76, 1980-81, 1983-84, 1986; NL MVP, 1980, 1981, 1986.

Tom Seaver, b. 1944: pitcher won NL Cy Young award 3 times, won 311 major league games.

Bill Shoemaker, b. 1931: jockey rode 3 Kentucky Derby and 5 Belmont Stakes winners; leading career money winner.

Eddie Shore, (1902-1985): Boston Bruins defenseman; MVP 4 times, first-team all-star 7 times.

Al Simmons, (1902-1956): AL outfielder had lifetime .334 batting average.

O.J. Simpson, b. 1947: running back rushed for 2,003 yds., 1973; AFC leading rusher 4 times.

George Sisler, (1893-1973): St. Louis Browns 1st baseman had record 257 hits, 1920; batted .340 lifetime.

Billy Smith, b. 1950: N.Y. Islanders goalie led team to 4 Stanley Cup championships.

Sam Snead, b. 1912: PGA and Masters champ 3 times each.

Warren Spahn, b. 1921: pitcher won 363 NL games; 20-game winner 13 times; Cy Young award, 1957.

Tris Speaker, (1885-1958): AL outfielder batted .344 over 22 seasons; hit record 793 career doubles.

Mark Spitz, b. 1950: swimmer won 7 1972 Olympic gold medals.

Amos Alonzo Stagg, (1862-1965): coached Univ. of Chicago football team for 41 years, including 5 undefeated seasons; introduced huddle, man-in-motion, and end-around play.

Willie Stargell, b. 1941: Pittsburgh Pirate slugger chosen NL, World Series MVP, 1979.

Bart Starr, b. 1934: Green Bay Packers quarterback led team to 5 NFL titles and 2 Super Bowl victories.

Roger Staubach, b. 1942: Dallas Cowboys quarterback; leading NFC passer 5 times.

Casey Stengel, (1890-1975): managed Yankees to 10 pennants, 7 championships, 1949-60.

Jackie Stewart, b. 1939: Scot auto racer retired with 27 Grand Prix victories.

John L. Sullivan, (1858-1918): last bareknuckle heavyweight champion, 1882-1892.

Fran Tarkenton, b. 1940: quarterback holds career passing records for touchdowns, completions, yardage.

Gustavo Thoeni, b. 1951: Italian 4-time world alpine ski champ.

Jim Thorpe, (1888-1953): football All-America, 1911, 1912; won pentathlon and decathlon, 1912 Olympics.

Bill Tilden, (1893-1953): U.S. singles champ 7 times; played on 11 Davis Cup teams.

Y.A. Tittle, b. 1926: N.Y. Giants quarterback; MVP, 1961, 1963.

Lee Trevino, b. 1939: won the U.S. and British Open championships twice.

Bryan Trottier, b. 1956: center led N.Y. Islanders to 4 consecutive Stanley Cup championships, 1980-83.

Mike Tyson, b. 1966: world heavyweight champion, 1987-90.

Wyomia Tyus, b. 1945: sprinter won 1964, 1968 Olympic 100-meter dash.

Johnny Unitas, b. 1933: Baltimore Colts quarterback passed for over 40,000 yds.; MVP, 1957, 1967.

Al Unser, b. 1939: Indy 500 winner, 4 times.

Bobby Unser, b. 1934: Indy 500 winner 3 times.

Fernando Valenzuela, b. 1960: L.A. Dodgers pitcher won Cy Young award, 1981.

Norm Van Brocklin, (1926-1983): quarterback passed for game record 554 yds., 1951; MVP, 1960.

Honus Wagner, (1874-1955): Pittsburgh Pirates shortstop won 8 NL batting titles.

Tom Watson, b. 1949: golfer won British Open 5 times.

Johnny Weissmuller, (1903-1984): swimmer won 52 national championships, 5 Olympic gold medals; set 67 world records.

Jerry West, b. 1938: L.A. Lakers guard had career average 27 points per game; first team all-star 10 times.

Kathy Whitworth, b. 1939: women's golf leading money winner 8 times; first woman to earn over $300,000.

Ted Williams, b. 1918: Boston Red Sox outfielder won 6 batting titles; last major leaguer to hit over .400: .406 in 1941: .344 lifetime batting average.

John Wooden, b. 1910: coached UCLA basketball team to 10 national championships.

Mickey Wright, b. 1935: won LPGA championship 4 times, Vare Trophy 5 times; twice AP Woman-Athlete-of-the-Year.

Carl Yastrzemski, b. 1939: Boston Red Sox slugger won 3 batting titles, triple crown, 1967.

Cy Young, (1867-1955): pitcher won record 511 major league games.

Babe Didrikson Zaharias, (1914-1956): track star won 2 1932 Olympic gold medals; won numerous golf tournaments.

Goodwill Games of 1990

The second edition of the Goodwill Games was contested in Seattle, Wash. from July 21 through August 5. The USSR won the most gold medals.

Final Medal Standings

Country	Gold	Silver	Bronze	Total	Country	Gold	Silver	Bronze	Total
USSR	66	68	54	188	Jamaica	1	1	2	4
U.S.	60	53	48	161	Great Britain	0	2	2	4
East Germany	11	8	24	43	Yugoslavia	2	1	0	3
Bulgaria	8	7	9	24	Denmark	1	1	1	3
China	6	7	3	16	Turkey	0	2	1	3
West Germany	4	3	8	15	Mongolia	1	1	0	2
Japan	2	3	10	15	Ethiopia	0	2	0	2
Cuba	6	4	3	13	New Zealand	0	2	0	2
Canada	4	1	6	11	Kenya	0	1	1	2
Romania	2	4	2	8	Czechoslovakia	1	0	0	1
Spain	3	2	2	7	Mexico	1	0	0	1
South Korea	3	2	2	7	Morocco	1	0	0	1
Hungary	1	1	5	7	Suriname	1	0	0	1
Netherlands	1	1	5	7	Bahamas	0	1	0	1
Australia	0	4	3	7	France	0	0	1	1
Brazil	0	1	6	7	Ireland	0	0	1	1
Poland	4	1	0	5	Sweden	0	0	1	1
Italy	2	2	1	5	Virgin Islands	0	0	1	1

GOLF

United States Open

Year	Winner	Year	Winner	Year	Winner	Year	Winner
1903	Willie Anderson	1925	Willie MacFarlane	1949	Cary Middlecoff	1970	Tony Jacklin
1904	Willie Anderson	1926	Bobby Jones*	1950	Ben Hogan	1971	Lee Trevino
1905	Willie Anderson	1927	Tommy Armour	1951	Ben Hogan	1972	Jack Nicklaus
1906	Alex Smith	1928	John Farrell	1952	Julius Boros	1973	Johnny Miller
1907	Alex Ross	1929	Bobby Jones*	1953	Ben Hogan	1974	Hale Irwin
1908	Fred McLeod	1930	Bobby Jones*	1954	Ed Furgol	1975	Lou Graham
1909	George Sargent	1931	Wm. Burke	1955	Jack Fleck	1976	Jerry Pate
1910	Alex Smith	1932	Gene Sarazen	1956	Cary Middlecoff	1977	Hubert Green
1911	John McDermott	1933	John Goodman*	1957	Dick Mayer	1978	Andy North
1912	John McDermott	1934	Olin Dutra	1958	Tommy Bolt	1979	Hale Irwin
1913	Francis Ouimet*	1935	Sam Parks Jr.	1959	Billy Casper	1980	Jack Nicklaus
1914	Walter Hagen	1936	Tony Manero	1960	Arnold Palmer	1981	David Graham
1915	Jerome Travers*	1937	Ralph Guldahl	1961	Gene Littler	1982	Tom Watson
1916	Chick Evans*	1938	Ralph Guldahl	1962	Jack Nicklaus	1983	Larry Nelson
1917-18	(Not played)	1939	Byron Nelson	1963	Julius Boros	1984	Fuzzy Zoeller
1919	Walter Hagen	1940	Lawson Little	1964	Ken Venturi	1985	Andy North
1920	Edward Ray	1941	Craig Wood	1965	Gary Player	1986	Ray Floyd
1921	Jim Barnes	1942-45	(Not played)	1966	Billy Casper	1987	Scott Simpson
1922	Gene Sarazen	1946	Lloyd Mangrum	1967	Jack Nicklaus	1988	Curtis Strange
1923	Bobby Jones*	1947	L. Worsham	1968	Lee Trevino	1989	Curtis Strange
1924	Cyril Walker	1948	Ben Hogan	1969	Orville Moody	1990	Hale Irwin
*Amateur						*Amateur	

Professional Golfer's Association Championships

Year	Winner	Year	Winner	Year	Winner	Year	Winner
1922	Gene Sarazen	1939	Henry Picard	1957	Lionel Hebert	1974	Lee Trevino
1923	Gene Sarazen	1940	Byron Nelson	1958	Dow Finsterwald	1975	Jack Nicklaus
1924	Walter Hagen	1941	Victor Ghezzi	1959	Bob Rosburg	1976	Dave Stockton
1925	Walter Hagen	1942	Sam Snead	1960	Jay Hebert	1977	Lanny Wadkins
1926	Walter Hagen	1944	Bob Hamilton	1961	Jerry Barber	1978	John Mahaffey
1927	Walter Hagen	1945	Byron Nelson	1962	Gary Player	1979	David Graham
1928	Leo Diegel	1946	Ben Hogan	1963	Jack Nicklaus	1980	Jack Nicklaus
1929	Leo Diegel	1947	Jim Ferrier	1964	Bob Nichols	1981	Larry Nelson
1930	Tommy Armour	1948	Ben Hogan	1965	Dave Marr	1982	Ray Floyd
1931	Tom Creavy	1949	Sam Snead	1966	Al Geiberger	1983	Hal Sutton
1932	Olin Dutra	1950	Chandler Harper	1967	Don January	1984	Lee Trevino
1933	Gene Sarazen	1951	Sam Snead	1968	Julius Boros	1985	Hubert Green
1934	Paul Runyan	1952	James Turnesa	1969	Ray Floyd	1986	Bob Tway
1935	Johnny Revolta	1953	Walter Burkemo	1970	Dave Stockton	1987	Larry Nelson
1936	Denny Shute	1954	Melvin Harbert	1971	Jack Nicklaus	1988	Jeff Sluman
1937	Denny Shute	1955	Doug Ford	1972	Gary Player	1989	Payne Stewart
1938	Paul Runyan	1956	Jack Burke	1973	Jack Nicklaus	1990	Wayne Grady

Masters Golf Tournament Champions

Year	Winner	Year	Winner	Year	Winner	Year	Winner
1934	Horton Smith	1950	Jimmy Demaret	1964	Arnold Palmer	1978	Gary Player
1935	Gene Sarazen	1951	Ben Hogan	1965	Jack Nicklaus	1979	Fuzzy Zoeller
1936	Horton Smith	1952	Sam Snead	1966	Jack Nicklaus	1980	Severiano Ballesteros
1937	Byron Nelson	1953	Ben Hogan	1967	Gay Brewer Jr.	1981	Tom Watson
1938	Henry Picard	1954	Sam Snead	1968	Bob Goalby	1982	Craig Stadler
1939	Ralph Guldahl	1955	Cary Middlecoff	1969	George Archer	1983	Severiano Ballesteros
1940	Jimmy Demaret	1956	Jack Burke	1970	Billy Casper	1984	Ben Crenshaw
1941	Craig Wood	1957	Doug Ford	1971	Charles Coody	1985	Bernhard Langer
1942	Byron Nelson	1958	Arnold Palmer	1972	Jack Nicklaus	1986	Jack Nicklaus
1943-1945	(Not played)	1959	Art Wall Jr.	1973	Tommy Aaron	1987	Larry Mize
1946	Herman Keiser	1960	Arnold Palmer	1974	Gary Player	1988	Sandy Lyle
1947	Jimmy Demaret	1961	Gary Player	1975	Jack Nicklaus	1989	Nick Faldo
1948	Claude Harmon	1962	Arnold Palmer	1976	Ray Floyd	1990	Nick Faldo
1949	Sam Snead	1963	Jack Nicklaus	1977	Tom Watson		

British Open Golf Champions

Year	Winner	Year	Winner	Year	Winner	Year	Winner
1930	Bobby Jones	1949	Bobby Locke	1963	Bob Charles	1977	Tom Watson
1931	Tommy Armour	1950	Bobby Locke	1964	Tony Lema	1978	Jack Nicklaus
1932	Gene Sarazen	1951	Max Faulkner	1965	Peter Thomson	1979	Seve Ballesteros
1933	Denny Shute	1952	Bobby Locke	1966	Jack Nicklaus	1980	Tom Watson
1934	Henry Cotton	1953	Ben Hogan	1967	Roberto de Vicenzo	1981	Bill Rogers
1935	Alf Perry	1954	Peter Thomson	1968	Gary Player	1982	Tom Watson
1936	Alf Padgham	1955	Peter Thomson	1969	Tony Jacklin	1983	Tom Watson
1937	T.H. Cotton	1956	Peter Thomson	1970	Jack Nicklaus	1984	Seve Ballesteros
1938	R.A. Whitcombe	1957	Bobby Locke	1971	Lee Trevino	1985	Sandy Lyle
1939	Richard Burton	1958	Peter Thomson	1972	Lee Trevino	1986	Greg Norman
1940-45	(Not played)	1959	Gary Player	1973	Tom Weiskopf	1987	Nick Faldo
1946	Sam Snead	1960	Kel Nagle	1974	Gary Player	1988	Seve Ballesteros
1947	Fred Daly	1961	Arnold Palmer	1975	Tom Watson	1989	Mark Calcavecchia
1948	Henry Cotton	1962	Arnold Palmer	1976	Johnny Miller	1990	Nick Faldo

Professional Golf Tournaments in 1990

Date	Event	Winner	Score	Prize
Jan. 7	Tournament of Champions, Carlsbad, Cal.	Paul Azinger	272	$135,000
Jan. 14	Tucson Open, Ariz.	Robert Gamez	270	162,000
Jan. 21	Bob Hope Chrysler Classic, LaQuinta, Cal.	Peter Jacobsen	339	180,000
Jan. 28	Phoenix Open, Ariz.	Tommy Armour 3d	267	162,000
Feb. 4	A.T.&T. National Pro-Am, Pebble Beach, Cal.	Mark O'Meara	281	180,000
Feb. 11	Hawaiian Open, Honolulu	David Ishii	279	180,000
Feb. 25	Los Angeles Open	Fred Couples	266	180,000
Feb. 18	Shearson Lehman Hutton Open, La Jolla, Cal.	Dan Forsman	275	162,000
Mar. 4	Doral Ryder Open, Miami, Fla.	Greg Norman	*273	252,000
Mar. 18	Tournament Players Championship, Ponte Vedra, Fla.	Jodie Mudd	278	270,000
Mar. 25	Nestle Invitational, Orlando, Fla.	Robert Gamez	274	162,000
Apr. 8	Masters Tournament, Augusta, Ga.	Nick Faldo	*278	225,000
Apr. 16	Heritage Classic, Hilton Head, S.C.	Payne Stewart	*276	180,000
Apr. 22	Greater Greensboro Open, N.C.	Steve Elkington	282	225,000
Apr. 29	USF&G Classic, New Orleans	David Frost	276	180,000
May 6	Byron Nelson Classic, Irving, Tex.	Payne Stewart	202	180,000
May 13	Memorial Tournament, Dublin, Oh.	Greg Norman	216	180,000
May 20	Colonial National Tournament, Ft. Worth, Tex.	Ben Crenshaw	272	180,000
May 28	Atlanta Classic, Ga.	Wayne Levi	275	180,000
June 3	Kemper Open, Potomac, Md.	Gil Morgan	274	180,000
June 10	Western Open, Oak Brook, Ill.	Wayne Levi	275	180,000
June 18	U.S. Open, Medinah, Ill.	Hale Irwin	*280	220,000
June 24	Buick Classic, Harrison, N.Y.	Hale Irwin	269	180,000
July 1	Greater Hartford Open, Conn.	Wayne Levi	267	180,000
July 8	Anheuser-Busch Classic, Williamsburg, Va.	Lanny Wadkins	266	180,000
July 15	Bank of Boston Classic, Sutton, Mass.	Morris Hatalsky	275	162,000
July 30	Buick Open, Grand Blanc, Mich.	Chip Beck	272	180,000
Aug. 5	St. Jude Classic, Memphis, Tenn.	Tom Kite	*269	180,000
Aug. 12	PGA Championship, Shoal Creek, Ala.	Wayne Grady	282	225,000
Aug. 20	The International, Castle Rock, Col.	Davis Love 3d	+14 pts.	180,000
Aug. 26	World Series of Golf, Akron, Oh.	Jose-Maria Olazabal	262	198,000
Sept. 2	Greater Milwaukee Open	Jim Gallagher	*271	162,000
Sept. 9	Hardee's Classic, Coal Valley, Ill.	Joey Sindelar	*268	180,000
Sept. 16	Canadian Open, Oakville, Ont.	Wayne Levi	278	180,000
Sept. 23	B.C. Open, Endicott, N.Y.	Nolan Henke	268	126,000
Sept. 30	Southern Open, Columbus, Ga.	Kenny Knox	*265	108,000
Oct. 7	Texas Open, San Antonio	Mark O'Meara	261	144,000

Women

Date	Event	Winner	Score	Prize
Jan. 21	Jamaica Classic, Montego, Jamaica	Patty Sheehan	212	$75,000
Feb. 18	Inverrary Classic, Lauderhill, Fla.	Jane Crafter	209	60,000
Feb. 25	Hawaiian Open, Honolulu	Beth Daniel	210	52,000
Mar. 4	Kemper Open, Wailea, Ha.	Beth Daniel	283	75,000
Mar. 18	Tucson Open, Tucson, Ariz.	Colleen Walker	276	45,000
Mar. 26	Turquoise Classic, Phoenix, Ariz.	Pat Bradley	280	75,000
Apr. 1	Dinah Shore Invitational, Rancho Mirage, Cal.	Betsy King	283	90,000
Apr. 8	Red Robin Classic, Poway, Cal.	Kris Monaghan	276	45,000
May 6	Sara Lee Classic, Nashville, Tenn.	Ayako Okamoto	210	63,000
May 13	Crestar Classic, Chesapeake, Va.	Dottie Mochrie	200	52,000
May 27	Corning Classic, Corning, N.Y.	Pat Bradley	274	52,000
June 3	Lady Keystone Open, Hershey, Pa.	Cathy Gerring	208	45,000
June 10	McDonald's Championship, Wilmington, Del.	Patty Sheehan	275	97,000
June 24	Rochester International, N.Y.	Patty Sheehan	278	60,000
July 1	Du Maurier Classic, Kitchener, Ont.	Cathy Johnson	276	90,000
July 8	Jamie Farr Toledo Classic, Oh.	Tina Purtzin	205	48,000
July 15	U.S. Women's Open, Duluth, Ga.	Betsy King	284	85,000
Aug. 5	Boston Five Classic, Danvers, Mass.	Barb Mucha	277	52,000
Aug. 12	Stratton Classic, Vt.	Cathy Gerring	*281	67,000
Aug. 20	Big Apple Classic, New Rochelle, N.Y.	Betsy King	273	60,000
Aug. 26	Northgate Classic, Brooklyn Park, Minn.	Beth Daniel	203	52,000
Sept. 9	Cellular One-Ping Championship, Portland, Ore.	Patty Sheehan	208	52,000
Sept. 16	Safeco Classic, Kent, Wash.	Patty Sheehan	270	45,000
Sept. 23	MBS Calssic, Buena Park, Cal.	Nancy Lopez	*281	48,000
Oct. 7	Centel Classic, Tallahassee, Fla.	Beth Daniel	271	150,000

*Won playoff.

U.S. Women's Open Golf Champions

Year	Winner	Year	Winner	Year	Winner	Year	Winner
1948	"Babe" Zaharias	1959	Mickey Wright	1970	Donna Caponi	1981	Pat Bradley
1949	Louise Suggs	1960	Betsy Rawls	1971	JoAnne Carner	1982	Janet Alex
1950	"Babe" Zaharias	1961	Mickey Wright	1972	Susie Maxwell Berning	1983	Jan Stephenson
1951	Betsy Rawls	1962	Murle Lindstrom	1973	Susie Maxwell Berning	1984	Hollis Stacy
1952	Louise Suggs	1963	Mary Mills	1974	Sandra Haynie	1985	Kathy Baker
1953	Betsy Rawls	1964	Mickey Wright	1975	Sandra Palmer	1986	Jane Geddes
1954	"Babe" Zaharias	1965	Carol Mann	1976	JoAnne Carner	1987	Laura Davies
1955	Fay Crocker	1966	Sandra Spuzich	1977	Hollis Stacy	1988	Liselotte Neumann
1956	Mrs. K. Cornelius	1967	Catherine Lacoste*	1978	Hollis Stacy	1989	Betsy King
1957	Betsy Rawls	1968	Susie Maxwell Berning	1979	Jerilyn Britz	1990	Betsy King
1958	Mickey Wright	1969	Donna Caponi	1980	Amy Alcott		

*Amateur

PGA Leading Money Winners

Year	Player	Dollars	Year	Player	Dollars	Year	Player	Dollars
1946	Ben Hogan	$42,556	1961	Gary Player	$64,540	1976	Jack Nicklaus	$266,438
1947	Jimmy Demaret	27,936	1962	Arnold Palmer	81,448	1977	Tom Watson	310,653
1948	Ben Hogan	36,812	1963	Arnold Palmer	128,230	1978	Tom Watson	362,429
1949	Sam Snead	31,593	1964	Jack Nicklaus	113,284	1979	Tom Watson	462,636
1950	Sam Snead	35,758	1965	Jack Nicklaus	140,752	1980	Tom Watson	530,808
1951	Lloyd Mangrum	26,088	1966	Billy Casper	121,944	1981	Tom Kite	375,699
1952	Julius Boros	37,032	1967	Jack Nicklaus	188,988	1982	Craig Stadler	446,462
1953	Lew Worsham	34,002	1968	Billy Casper	205,168	1983	Hal Sutton	426,668
1954	Bob Toski	65,819	1969	Frank Beard	175,223	1984	Tom Watson	476,260
1955	Julius Boros	65,121	1970	Lee Trevino	157,037	1985	Curtis Strange	542,321
1956	Ted Kroll	72,835	1971	Jack Nicklaus	244,490	1986	Greg Norman	653,296
1957	Dick Mayer	65,835	1972	Jack Nicklaus	320,542	1987	Curtis Strange	925,941
1958	Arnold Palmer	42,407	1973	Jack Nicklaus	308,362	1988	Curtis Strange	1,147,644
1959	Art Wall Jr.	53,167	1974	Johnny Miller	353,201	1989	Tom Kite	1,395,278
1960	Arnold Palmer	75,262	1975	Jack Nicklaus	323,149			

LPGA Leading Money Winners

Year	Winner	Dollars	Year	Winner	Dollars	Year	Winner	Dollars
1954	Patty Berg	$16,011	1966	Kathy Whitworth	$33,517	1978	Nancy Lopez	$189,813
1955	Patty Berg	16,492	1967	Kathy Whitworth	32,937	1979	Nancy Lopez	215,987
1956	Marlene Hagge	20,235	1968	Kathy Whitworth	48,379	1980	Beth Daniel	231,000
1957	Patty Berg	16,272	1969	Carol Mann	49,152	1981	Beth Daniel	206,977
1958	Beverly Hanson	12,629	1970	Kathy Whitworth	30,235	1982	JoAnne Carner	310,399
1959	Betsy Rawls	26,774	1971	Kathy Whitworth	41,181	1983	JoAnne Carner	291,404
1960	Louise Suggs	16,892	1972	Kathy Whitworth	65,063	1984	Betsy King	266,771
1961	Mickey Wright	22,236	1973	Kathy Whitworth	82,854	1985	Nancy Lopez	416,472
1962	Mickey Wright	21,641	1974	JoAnne Carner	87,094	1986	Pat Bradley	492,021
1963	Mickey Wright	31,269	1975	Sandra Palmer	94,805	1987	Ayako Okamoto	466,034
1964	Mickey Wright	29,800	1976	Judy Rankin	150,734	1988	Sherri Turner	347,255
1965	Kathy Whitworth	28,658	1977	Judy Rankin	122,890	1989	Betsy King	654,132

Lacrosse Champions in 1990

World Championship—Perth, Australia, July 15: U.S. 19, Canada 15.

U.S. Club Lacrosse Association Championship—Baltimore, Md., June 8: Mt. Washington Club (Baltimore) 13, N.Y. A.C. 7.

NCAA Division I Championship—Piscataway, N.J., May 28: Syracuse 21, Loyola (Baltimore) 9.

NCAA Division III Championship—Geneva, N.Y., May 19: Hobart College 18, Washington College 6.

USILA All-Star Game—Baltimore, Md., June 9: North 18, South 16.

National Junior College Championship—Herkimer, N.Y., May 12: Nassau C.C. 16, Essex C.C. 9.

NCAA Women's Lacrosse Championship, Division I—Princeton, N.J., May 20: Harvard 8, Maryland 7.

USILA Division I All America Team

Attack: Greg Burns, Syracuse; Tom Marechek, Syracuse; Jim Blanding, Loyola.

Midfield: Jon Reese, Yale; Gary Gait, Syracuse; Paul Gait, Syracuse; Greg Rinaldi, Rutgers.

Defense: Bryan Martin, Yale; Pat McCabe, Syracuse; Joe Breschi, North Carolina.

Goal: Tom Guido, Yale.

Coach of the Year: Mike Waldvogel, Yale.

Note: 4 midfielders selected for the 3 midfield positions.

USILA Division III All America Team

Attack: William Miller, Hobart; Tim Hormes, Washington; Lance Savage, Hobart.

Midfield: Michael DeMaria, Hobart; Matthew Kerwick, Hobart; Bob Martino, Washington; Ken Knapp, Ohio Wesleyan.

Defense: Mike Warnes, Ohio Wesleyan; Peter Bennett, Hobart; Brad Edwards, Gettysburg.

Goal: Dave Slomkowski, Washington.

Coach of the Year: Al Brown, Alfred.

Note: 4 midfielders selected for the 3 midfield positions.

NCAA Division I Champions

Year	Champion	Year	Champion	Year	Champion	Year	Champion
1971	Cornell	1976	Cornell	1981	North Carolina	1986	North Carolina
1972	Virginia	1977	Cornell	1982	North Carolina	1987	Johns Hopkins
1973	Maryland	1978	Johns Hopkins	1983	Syracuse	1988	Syracuse
1974	Johns Hopkins	1979	Johns Hopkins	1984	Johns Hopkins	1989	Syracuse
1975	Maryland	1980	Johns Hopkins	1985	Johns Hopkins	1990	Syracuse

American Power Boat Assn. Gold Cup Champions

Year	Boat	Driver	Year	Boat	Driver
1973	Miss Budweiser	Dean Chenoweth	1982	Atlas Van Lines	Chip Hanauer
1974	Pay 'N Pak	George Henley	1983	Atlas Van Lines	Chip Hanauer
1975	Pay 'N Pak	George Henley	1984	Atlas Van Lines	Chip Hanauer
1976	Miss U.S.	Tom D'Eath	1985	Miller American	Chip Hanauer
1977	Atlas Van Lines	Bill Muncey	1986	Miller American	Chip Hanauer
1978	Atlas Van Lines	Bill Muncey	1987	Miller American	Chip Hanauer
1979	Atlas Van Lines	Bill Muncey	1988	Miller American	Chip Hanauer
1980	Miss Budweiser	Dean Chenoweth	1989	Miss Budweiser	Tom D'Eath
1981	Miss Budweiser	Dean Chenoweth	1990	Miss Budweiser	Tom D'Eath

Rifle and Pistol Individual Championships in 1990

Source: National Rifle Association of America

National Outdoor Rifle and Pistol Championships

Pistol — James R. Lenardson, Toledo, Oh., 1764-90X.
Civilian Pistol — Allen B. Fulford, Vienna, Ga., 1759-82X.
Woman Pistol — Roxane Conrad, Quantico, Va., 1733-74X.
Collegiate Pistol — Keith Hanzel, Falls Church, Va., 1708-54X.
Smallbore Rifle Prone — T.R. Bishop, Lenoir, N.C., 6388-483X.
Civilian Smallbore Rifle Prone — T.R. Bishop, 6388-483X.
Woman Smallbore Rifle Prone — Edie Reynolds, Raleigh, N.C., 6385-467X.
Collegiate Smallbore Rifle Prone — Erin Gestl, Bethlehem, Pa., 6382-486X.
Smallbore Rifle 3-Position — James Meredith, Columbus, Ga., 2261.

Civilian Smallbore 3-Position — Lones Wigger, Colorado Springs, Col., 2259.
Woman Smallbore 3-Position — Rhonda Barush, Columbus, Ga., 2229.
Collegiate Smallbore 3-Position — Erin Gestl, 2231.
Highpower Rifle — G. David Tubb, Canadian, Tex., 2380-108X.
Woman Highpower Rifle — Nancy Gallagher-Tompkins, Long Beach, Cal., 2354-86X.
Civilian Highpower Rifle — G. David Tubb, 2380-108X.

U.S. NRA International Shooting Championship

Smallbore Free Rifle Prone — Bill Meek, Riverside, Cal., 1296.5.
Smallbore Free Rifle Position — Bob Foth, Colorado Springs, Col., 2424.6.
Men's Air Rifle — Bob Foth, 1284.9.
Women's Air Rifle — Launi Meili, Cheney, Wash., 881.9.
Women's Smallbore Rifle Prone — Deena Wigger, Colorado Springs, Col., 1176.
Women's Standard Rifle 3-Position — Deena Wigger, 1265.1.
Free Pistol — Erich Buljung, Columbus, Ga., 1219.
Rapid Fire Pistol — John McNally, Columbus, Ga., 1453.
Center Fire Pistol — Eduardo Suarez, Ft. Benning, Ga., 1163.
Standard Pistol — John McNally, 1146.

Men's Air Pistol — Don Nygord, LaCrescenta, Cal., 1246.3.
Women's Air Pistol — Connie Petracek, Nashville, Tenn., 847.7.
Women's Sport Pistol — Bettie Blocksome, Hartselle, Ala., 1246.
International Trap — George Haas, III, Ontario, Cal., 414.
Women's International Trap — Denise Morrison, Columbus, Ga., 292.
International Skeet — Michael Schmidt Jr., St. Paul, Minn., 415.
Women's International Skeet —Connie Fluker, Deer Park, Tex., 299.

National Indoor Rifle & Pistol Championships

Smallbore Rifle 4-Position — Thomas A. Tamas, Columbus, Ga., 800.
Smallbore Rifle NRA 3-Position — Karen E. Monez, Colorado Springs, Col., 1191.
Smallbore Rifle International — Thomas A. Tamas, 1175.
Woman Smallbore Rifle 4-Position — Karen E. Monez, 799.
Woman Smallbore Rifle NRA 3-Position — Karen Monez, 1191.
Woman International Smallbore Rifle — Debbie L. Sinclair, Tigard, Ore., 1161.
Air Rifle — Robert J. Foth, Colorado Springs, Col., 587.
Woman Air Rifle — Rhonda Barush, Columbus, Ga., 581.

Conventional Pistol — Charles E. Baxter, Argyle, Tex., 889.
Woman Conventional Pistol — Marcia A. Yarow, Marlborough, Mass., 851.
International Free Pistol — Jimmie W. McCoy, Columbus, Ga., 559.
International Standard Pistol — James V. Marsh, Annapolis, Md., 571.
Woman International Standard Pistol — Patricia Ann Zidek, Hopewell Jct., N.Y., 536.
Air Pistol — Donald C. Nygord, LaCrescenta, Cal., 584
Woman Air Pistol — Michele D. Oberholz, Virginia Beach, Va., 550.

Skiing

World Cup Alpine Champions

Men

1967	Jean Claude Killy, France	1975	Gustavo Thoeni, Italy	1983	Phil Mahre, U.S.
1968	Jean Claude Killy, France	1976	Ingemar Stenmark, Sweden	1984	Pirmin Zurbriggen, Switzerland
1969	Karl Schranz, Austria	1977	Ingemar Stenmark, Sweden	1985	Marc Girardelli, Luxembourg
1970	Karl Schranz, Austria	1978	Ingemar Stenmark, Sweden	1986	Marc Girardelli, Luxembourg
1971	Gustavo Thoeni, Italy	1979	Peter Luescher, Switzerland	1987	Pirmin Zurbriggen, Switzerland
1972	Gustavo Thoeni, Italy	1980	Andreas Wenzel, Liechtenstein	1988	Pirmin Zurbriggen, Switzerland
1973	Gustavo Thoeni, Italy	1981	Phil Mahre, U.S.	1989	Marc Girardelli, Luxembourg
1974	Piero Gros, Italy	1982	Phil Mahre, U.S.	1990	Pirmin Zurbriggen, Switzerland

Women

1967	Nancy Greene, Canada	1975	Annemarie Proell, Austria	1983	Tamara McKinney, U.S.
1968	Nancy Greene, Canada	1976	Rose Mittermaier, W. Germany	1984	Erika Hess, Switzerland
1969	Gertrud Gabl, Austria	1977	Lise-Marie Morerod, Switzerland	1985	Michela Figini, Switzerland
1970	Michele Jacot, France	1978	Hanni Wenzel, Liechtenstein	1986	Maria Walliser, Switzerland
1971	Annemarie Proell, Austria	1979	Annemarie Proell Moser, Austria	1987	Maria Walliser, Switzerland
1972	Annemarie Proell, Austria	1980	Hanni Wenzel, Liechtenstein	1988	Michela Figini, Switzerland
1973	Annemarie Proell, Austria	1981	Marie-Theres Nadig, Switzerland	1989	Vreni Schneider, Switzerland
1974	Annemarie Proell, Austria	1982	Erika Hess, Switzerland	1990	Petra Kronberger, Austria

U.S. Alpine Championships in 1990

Crested Butte, Col.

Men

Downhill—Skip Merrick
Slalom—Felix McGrath
Giant Slalom—Tommy Moe
Super Giant Slalom—A.J. Kitt
Combined—Kyle Wieche

Women

Downhill—Lucie Laroche
Slalom—Monique Pelletier
Giant Slalom—Kristi Terzian
Super Giant Slalom—Krista Schmidinger
Combined—Julie Parisien

Auto Racing

Indianapolis 500 Winners

Year	Winner, Car	MPH	Year	Winner, Car	MPH
1911	Ray Harroun, Marmon Wasp	74.59	1953	Bill Vukovich, Fuel Injection	128.740
1912	Joe Dawson, National	78.72	1954	Bill Vukovich, Fuel Injection	130.840
1913	Jules Goux, Peugeot	75.933	1955	Bob Sweikert, John Zink Special	128.209
1914	Rene Thomas, Delage	82.47	1956	Pat Flaherty, John Zink Special	128.490
1915	Ralph DePalma, Mercedes	89.84	1957	Sam Hanks, Belond Exhaust	135.601
1916	Dario Resta, Peugeot	84.00	1958	Jimmy Bryan, Belond A.P.	133.791
1917-18	race not held		1959	Rodger Ward, Leader Card Special	135.857
1919	Howdy Wilcox, Peugeot	88.05	1960	Jim Rathmann, Ken Paul Special	138.767
1920	Gaston Chevrolet, Monroe	88.16	1961	A.J. Foyt, Bowes Seal Fast	139.130
1921	Tommy Milton, Frontenac	89.62	1962	Rodger Ward, Leader Card Special	140.293
1922	Jimmy Murphy, Murphy Special	94.48	1963	Parnelli Jones, Agajanian Special	143.137
1923	Tommy Milton, H.C.S.	90.95	1964	A.J. Foyt, Sheraton-Thompson Special	147.350
1924	L.L. Corum-Joe Boyer, Duesenberg	98.23	1965	Jim Clark, Lotus-Ford	150.686
1925	Pete DePaolo, Duesenberg	101.13	1966	Graham Hill, American Red Ball	144.317
1926	Frank Lockhart, Miller	95.904	1967	A.J. Foyt, Sheraton-Thompson Special	151.207
1927	George Souders, Duesenberg	97.545	1968	Bobby Unser, Rislone Special	152.882
1928	Louis Meyer, Miller	99.482	1969	Mario Andretti, STP Oil Treatment Special	156.867
1929	Ray Keech, Simplex	97.585	1970	Al Unser, Johnny Lightning Special	155.749
1930	Billy Arnold, Miller-Hartz	100.448	1971	Al Unser, Johnny Lightning Special	157.735
1931	Louis Schneider, Bowes Seal Fast	96.629	1972	Mark Donohue, Sunoco McLaren	162.962
1932	Fred Frame, Miller-Hartz	104.144	1973	Gordon Johncock, STP Double Oil Filter	159.036
1933	Louis Meyer, Tydol	104.162	1974	Johnny Rutherford, McLaren	158.589
1934	Bill Cummings, Boyle Products	104.863	1975	Bobby Unser, Jorgenson Eagle	149.213
1935	Kelly Petillo, Gilmore Speedway	106.240	1976	Johnny Rutherford, Hygain McLaren	148.725
1936	Louis Meyer, Ring Free	109.069	1977	A.J. Foyt, Gilmore Coyote-Ford	161.331
1937	Wilbur Shaw, Shaw-Gilmore	113.580	1978	Al Unser, Lola Cosworth	161.363
1938	Floyd Roberts, Burd Piston Ring	117.200	1979	Rick Mears, Penske-Cosworth	158.899
1939	Wilbur Shaw, Boyle	115.035	1980	Johnny Rutherford, Chaparral-Cosworth	142.862
1940	Wilbur Shaw, Boyle	114.277	1981	Bobby Unser, Penske-Cosworth	139.085
1941	Floyd Davis-Mauri Rose, Knock-Out-Hose Clip	115.117	1982	Gordon Johncock, Wildcat-Cosworth	162.026
1942-45	race not held		1983	Tom Sneva, March-Cosworth	162.117
1946	George Robson, Thorne Engineering	114.820	1984	Rick Mears, March-Cosworth	163.621
1947	Mauri Rose, Blue Crown Special	116.338	1985	Danny Sullivan, March-Cosworth	152.982
1948	Mauri Rose, Blue Crown Special	119.814	1986	Bobby Rahal, March-Cosworth	170.722
1949	Bill Holland, Blue Crown Special	121.327	1987	Al Unser, March-Cosworth	162.175
1950	Johnny Parsons, Wynn Kurtis Kraft	124.002	1988	Rick Mears, Penske-Chevy V8	144.809
1951	Lee Wallard, Belanger	126.224	1989	Emerson Fittipaldi, Penske PC 18-Chevy	167.581
1952	Troy Ruttman, Agajanian	128.922	1990	Arie Luyendyk, Lola-Chevy	185.984

The race was less than 500 miles in the following years: 1916 (300 mi.), 1926 (400 mi.), 1950 (345 mi.), 1973 (332.5 mi.), 1975 (435 mi.), 1976 (255 mi.). Race record—185,984 MPH, Arie Luyendyk, 1990.

Notable One-Mile Speed Records

Date	Driver	Car	MPH	Date	Driver	Car	MPH
1/26/06	Marriott	Stanley (Steam)	127.659	9/ 3/35	Campbell	Bluebird Special	301.13
3/16/10	Oldfield	Benz	131.724	11/19/37	Eyston	Thunderbolt 1	311.42
4/23/11	Burman	Benz	141.732	9/16/38	Eyston	Thunderbolt 1	357.5
2/12/19	DePalma	Packard	149.875	8/23/39	Cobb	Railton	368.9
4/27/20	Milton	Dusenberg	155.046	9/16/47	Cobb	Railton-Mobil	394.2
4/28/26	Parry-Thomas	Thomas Spl.	170.624	8/ 5/63	Breedlove	Spirit of America	407.45
3/29/27	Seagrave	Sunbeam	203.790	10/27/64	Arfons	Green Monster	536.71
4/22/28	Keech	White Triplex	207.552	11/15/65	Breedlove	Spirit of America	600.601
3/11/29	Seagrave	Irving-Napier	231.446	10/23/70	Gabelich	Blue Flame	622.407
2/ 5/31	Campbell	Napier-Campbell	246.086	10/9/79	Barrett	Budweiser Rocket	638.637*
2/24/32	Campbell	Napier-Campbell	253.96	10/4/83	Noble	Thrust 2	633.6
2/22/33	Campbell	Napier-Campbell	272.109	*not recognized as official by sanctioning bodies.			

CART Champions

(U.S. Auto Club Champions prior to 1979)

Year	Driver	Year	Driver	Year	Driver	Year	Driver
1960	A. J. Foyt	1968	Bobby Unser	1976	Gordon Johncock	1983	Al Unser
1961	A. J. Foyt	1969	Mario Andretti	1977	Tom Sneva	1984	Mario Andretti
1962	Rodger Ward	1970	Al Unser	1978	Tom Sneva	1985	Al Unser
1963	A. J. Foyt	1971	Joe Leonard	1979	Rick Mears	1986	Bobby Rahal
1964	A. J. Foyt	1972	Joe Leonard	1980	Johnny Rutherford	1987	Bobby Rahal
1965	Mario Andretti	1973	Roger McCluskey	1981	Rick Mears	1988	Danny Sullivan
1966	Mario Andretti	1974	Bobby Unser	1982	Rick Mears	1989	Emerson Fittipaldi
1967	A. J. Foyt	1975	A. J. Foyt				

Le Mans 24-Hour Race in 1990

Martin Brundle of the U.K., Price Cobb of the U.S., and John Nielson of Denmark drove their Jaguar XJR 12 to victory in the 1990 Le Mans 24-hour race.

NASCAR Racing in 1990

Winston Cup Races

Date	Race, site	Winner	Car	Average MPH
Feb. 18	Daytona 500, Daytona Beach, Fla.	Derrike Cope	Chevrolet	165.761
Feb. 25	Pontiac Excitement 400, Richmond, Va.	Mark Martin	Ford	92.158
Mar. 4	Goodwrench 500, Rockingham, N.C.	Kyle Petty	Pontiac	122.864
Mar. 18	Motorcraft 500, Atlanta, Ga.	Dale Earnhardt	Chevrolet	156.849
Apr. 1	Transouth 500, Darlington, S.C.	Dale Earnhardt	Chevrolet	124.073
Apr. 8	Valleydale Meats 500, Bristol, Tenn.	Davey Allison	Ford	87.258
Apr. 22	First Union 400, N. Wilkesboro, N.C.	Brett Bodine	Buick	83.908
Apr. 29	Hanes Activewear 500, Martinsville, Va.	Geoff Bodine	Ford	77.423
May 6	Winston 500, Talladega, Ala.	Dale Earnhardt	Chevrolet	159.571
May 27	Coca Cola 600, Charlotte, N.C.	Rusty Wallace	Pontiac	137.650
June 3	Budweiser 500, Dover, Del.	Derrike Cope	Chevrolet	123.960
June 10	Banquet Frozen Foods 300, Sonoma, Cal.	Rusty Wallace	Pontiac	69.245
June 17	Miller Genuine Draft 500, Pocono, Pa.	Harry Gant	Oldsmobile	120.600
June 24	Miller Genuine Draft 400, Brooklyn, Mich.	Dale Earnhardt	Chevrolet	150.219
July 7	Pepsi 400, Daytona Beach, Fla.	Dale Earnhardt	Chevrolet	160.894
July 22	AC Spark Plug 500, Pocono, Pa.	Geoff Bodine	Ford	124.070
Aug. 12	Watkins Glen International, N.Y.	Ricky Rudd	Chevrolet	92.452
Aug. 19	Champion Spark Plug 400, Brooklyn, Mich.	Mark Martin	Ford	138.822
Aug. 25	Busch 500, Bristol, Tenn.	Ernie Irvan	Chevrolet	91.782
Sept. 2	Southern 500, Darlington, S.C.	Dale Earnhardt	Chevrolet	123.141
Sept. 9	Miller Genuine Draft 400, Richmond, Va.	Dale Earnhardt	Chevrolet	95.567
Sept. 16	Delaware 500, Dover, Del.	Bill Elliott	Ford	125.945
Sept. 23	Goody's 500, Martinsville, Va.	Geoff Bodine	Ford	76.386

Winston Cup Champions (NASCAR)

Year	Driver	Year	Driver	Year	Driver	Year	Driver
1949	Red Byron	1960	Rex White	1970	Bobby Isaac	1980	Dale Earnhardt
1950	Bill Rexford	1961	Ned Jarrett	1971	Richard Petty	1981	Darrell Waltrip
1951	Herb Thomas	1962	Joe Weatherly	1972	Richard Petty	1982	Darrell Waltrip
1952	Tim Flock	1963	Joe Weatherly	1973	Benny Parson	1983	Bobby Allison
1953	Herb Thomas	1964	Richard Petty	1974	Richard Petty	1984	Terry Labonte
1954	Lee Petty	1965	Ned Jarrett	1975	Richard Petty	1985	Darrell Waltrip
1955	Tim Flock	1966	David Pearson	1976	Cale Yarborough	1986	Dale Earnhardt
1956	Buck Baker	1967	Richard Petty	1977	Cale Yarborough	1987	Dale Earnhardt
1957	Buck Baker	1968	David Pearson	1978	Cale Yarborough	1988	Bill Elliott
1958	Lee Petty	1969	David Pearson	1979	Richard Petty	1989	Rusty Wallace
1959	Lee Petty						

Daytona 500 Winners

Year	Driver, car	Avg. MPH	Year	Driver, car	Avg. MPH
1959	Lee Petty, Oldsmobile	135.521	1975	Benny Parsons, Chevrolet	153.649
1960	Junior Johnson, Chevrolet	124.740	1976	David Pearson, Mercury	152.181
1961	Marvin Panch, Pontiac	149.601	1977	Cale Yarborough, Chevrolet	153.218
1962	Fireball Roberts, Pontiac	152.529	1978	Bobby Allison, Ford	159.730
1963	Tiny Lund, Ford	151.566	1979	Richard Petty, Oldsmobile	143.977
1964	Richard Petty, Plymouth	154.334	1980	Buddy Baker, Oldsmobile	177.602
1965	Fred Lorenzen, Ford (a)	141.539	1981	Richard Petty, Buick	169.651
1966	Richard Petty, Plymouth (b)	160.627	1982	Bobby Allison, Buick	153.991
1967	Mario Andretti, Ford	146.926	1983	Cale Yarborough, Pontiac	155.979
1968	Cale Yarborough, Mercury	143.251	1984	Cale Yarborough, Chevrolet	150.994
1969	Lee Roy Yarborough, Ford	160.875	1985	Bill Elliott, Ford	172.265
1970	Pete Hamilton, Plymouth	149.601	1986	Geoff Bodine, Chevrolet	148.124
1971	Richard Petty, Plymouth	144.456	1987	Bill Elliott, Ford	176.263
1972	A. J. Foyt, Mercury	161.550	1988	Bobby Allison, Buick	137,531
1973	Richard Petty, Dodge	157.205	1989	Darrell Waltrip, Chevrolet	148.466
1974	Richard Petty, Dodge (c)	140.894	1990	Derrike Cope, Chevrolet	165.761

(a) 322.5 miles. (b) 495 miles. (c) 450 miles.

World Grand Prix Champions

Year	Driver	Year	Driver	Year	Driver
1951	Jan Fangio, Argentina	1964	John Surtees, England	1977	Niki Lauda, Austria
1952	Alberto Ascari, Italy	1965	Jim Clark, Scotland	1978	Mario Andretti, U.S.
1953	Alberto Ascari, Italy	1966	Jack Brabham, Australia	1979	Jody Scheckter, So. Africa
1954	Juan Fangio, Argentina	1967	Denis Hulme, New Zealand	1980	Alan Jones, Australia
1955	Juan Fangio, Argentina	1968	Graham Hill, England	1981	Nelson Piquet, Brazil
1956	Juan Fangio, Argentina	1969	Jackie Stewart, Scotland	1982	Keke Rosberg, Finland
1957	Juan Fangio, Argentina	1970	Jochen Rindt, Austria	1983	Nelson Piquet, Brazil
1958	Mike Hawthorne, England	1971	Jackie Stewart, Scotland	1984	Niki Lauda, Austria
1959	Jack Brabham, Australia	1972	Emerson Fittipaldi, Brazil	1985	Alain Prost, France
1960	Jack Brabham, Australia	1973	Jackie Stewart, Scotland	1986	Alain Prost, France
1961	Phil Hill, United States	1974	Emerson Fittipaldi, Brazil	1987	Nelson Piquet, Brazil
1962	Graham Hill, England	1975	Niki Lauda, Austria	1988	Ayrton Senna, Brazil
1963	Jim Clark, Scotland	1976	James Hunt, England	1989	Alain Prost, France

Grand Prix for Formula 1 Cars in 1990

Grand Prix	Winner, car	Grand Prix	Winner, car
Belgian	Ayrton Senna, McLaren-Honda	Italian	Ayrton Senna, McLaren-Honda
Brazilian	Alain Prost, Ferrari	Mexico	Alain Prost, Ferrari
British	Alain Prost, Ferrari	Monaco	Ayrton Senna, McLaren-Honda
Canadian	Ayrton Senna, McLaren-Honda	San Marino	Riccardo Patrese, Williams-Renault
French	Alain Prost, Ferrari	Spanish	Alain Prost, Ferrari
German	Ayrton Senna, McLaren-Honda	United States	Ayrton Senna, McLaren-Honda
Hungarian	Thierry Boutsen, Williams-Renault		

Chess

Source: U.S. Chess Federation

Chess dates back to antiquity, its exact origin unknown. The best players of their time, regarded by later generations as world champions, were Francois Philidor, Alexandre Deschappelles, Louis de la Bourdonnais, all France; Howard Staunton, England; Adolph Anderssen, Germany and Paul Morphy, U.S. In 1866 Wilhelm Steinitz defeated Adolph Anderssen and claimed the world champion title. Official world champions since the title was first used follow:

1866-1894 Wilhelm Steinitz, Austria	1948-1957 Mikhail Botvinnik, USSR	1969-1972 Boris Spassky, USSR
1894-1921 Emanuel Lasker, Germany	1957-1958 Vassily Smyslov, USSR	1972-1975 Bobby Fischer, U.S. (a)
1921-1927 Jose R. Capablanca, Cuba	1958-1959 Mikhail Botvinnik, USSR	1975-1985 Anatoly Karpov, USSR
1927-1935 Alexander A. Alekhine, France	1960-1961 Mikhail Tal, USSR	1985 Gary Kasparov, USSR
1935-1937 Max Euwe, Netherlands	1961-1963 Mikhail Botvinnik, USSR	
1937-1946 Alexander A. Alekhine, France	1963-1969 Tigran Petrosian, USSR	

(a) Defaulted championship after refusal to accept International Chess Federation rules for a championship match, April 1975.

United States Champions

Unofficial champions	1895-1897 Jackson Showalter	1968-1969 Larry Evans	1983	(tie) Walter Browne
1857-1871 Paul Morphy	1897-1906 Harry Pillsbury	1969-1972 Samuel Reshevsky		Larry Christiansen
1871-1876 George Mackenzie	1906-1909 vacant	1972-1973 Robert Byrne		Roman
1876-1880 James Mason	1909-1936 Frank Marshall	1973-1974 Lubomir Kavalek,		Dzindzichashvili
1880-1889 George Mackenzie	1936-1944 Samuel Reshevsky	John Grefe	1984-1985 Lev Alburt
1889-1890 S. Lipschutz	1944-1946 Arnold Denker	1974-1977 Walter Browne	1986 Yasser Seirawan
1890 Jackson Showalter	1946-1948 Samuel Reshevsky	1978-1980 Lubomir Kavalek	1987 (tie) Joel Benjamin
1890-1891 Max Judd	1948-1951 Herman Steiner	1980-1981 (tie) Larry Evans,	Nick DeFirmian
Official champions	1951-1954 Larry Evans	Larry Christiansen,	1988 Michael Wilder
1891-1892 Jackson Showalter	1954-1957 Arthur Bisguier	Walter Browne	1989 (tie) Stuart Rachels,
1892-1894 S. Lipschutz	1957-1961 Bobby Fischer	1981-1983 (tie) Walter Browne,	Yasser Seirawan,
1894 Jackson Showalter	1961-1962 Larry Evans	Yasser Seirawan	Roman Dzindzicha-
1894-1895 Albert Hodges	1962-1968 Bobby Fischer		shvili

U.S. Outdoor Diving Championships in 1990

Dallas, Tex., Aug. 16-18, 1990

Men	**Women**
One Meter—Pat Evans.	**One Meter**—Krista Wilson.
Three Meter—Kent Ferguson.	**Three Meter**—Wendy Lucero.
Platform—Matt Scoggin.	**Platform**—Wendy Lian Williams.

U.S. Gymnastics Championships in 1990

Denver, Col., July 15-18, 1990

Men	**Women**
Floor exercise—Bob Stelter.	**Vault**—Brandy Johnson.
Pommel horse—Patrick Kirksey.	**Uneven bars**—Sandy Woolsey.
Still rings—Scott Keswick.	**Balance beam**—Elizabeth Okino.
Vault—Lance Ringnald.	**Floor exercise**—Brandy Johnson.
Parallel bars—(Tie) Lance Ringnald, Trent Dimas.	**All Around**—Kim Zmeskal.
Horizontal Bars—(Tie) Lance Ringnald, Trent Dimas.	
All Around—Lance Ringnald.	

Harness Racing

Harness Horse of the Year

(Chosen by the U.S. Trotting Assn. and the U.S. Harness Writers Assn.)

1950	Proximity	1960	Adios Butler	1970	Fresh Yankee	1980	Niatross
1951	Pronto Don	1961	Adios Butler	1971	Albatross	1981	Fan Hanover
1952	Good Time	1962	Su Mac Lad	1972	Albatross	1982	Cam Fella
1953	Hi Lo's Forbes	1963	Speedy Scot	1973	Sir Dalrae	1983	Cam Fella
1954	Stenographer	1964	Bret Hanover	1974	Delmonica Hanover	1984	Fancy Crown
1955	Scott Frost	1965	Bret Hanover	1975	Savior	1985	Nihilator
1956	Scott Frost	1966	Bret Hanover	1976	Keystone Ore	1986	Forrest Skipper
1957	Torpid	1967	Nevele Pride	1977	Green Speed	1987	Mack Lobell
1958	Emily's Pride	1968	Nevele Pride	1978	Abercrombie	1988	Mack Lobell
1959	Bye Bye Byrd	1969	Nevele Pride	1979	Niatross	1989	Matt's Scooter

The Hambletonian (3-year-old trotters)

Year	Winner	Driver	Year	Winner	Driver
1965	Egyptian Candor	Del Cameron	1978	Speedy Somolli	Howard Beissinger
1966	Kerry Way	Frank Ervin	1979	Legend Hanover	George Sholty
1967	Speedy Streak	Del Cameron	1980	Burgomeister	Bill Haughton
1968	Nevele Pride	Stanley Dancer	1981	Shiaway St. Pat	Ray Remmen
1969	Lindy's Pride	Howard Beissinger	1982	Speed Bowl	Tommy Haughton
1970	Timothy T	John Simpson Sr.	1983	Duenna	Stanley Dancer
1971	Speedy Crown	Howard Beissinger	1984	Historic Freight	Ben Webster
1972	Super Bowl	Stanley Dancer	1985	Prakas	Bill O'Donnell
1973	Flirth	Ralph Baldwin	1986	Nuclear Kosmos	Ulf Thoresen
1974	Christopher T	Bill Haughton	1987	Mack Lobell	John Campbell
1975	Bonefish	Stanley Dancer	1988	Armbro Goal	John Campbell
1976	Steve Lobell	Bill Haughton	1989	Park Avenue Joe	Ron Waples
1977	Green Speed	Bill Haughton	1990	Harmonious	John Campbell

Leading Drivers

Races Won

Year	Driver		Year	Driver		Year	Driver		Year	Driver	
1967	Bob Farrington .	277	1973	Herve Filion. . .	445	1979	Ron Waples . . .	443	1984	Michel Lachance	466
1968	Herve Filion. . .	407	1974	Herve Filion. . .	637	1980	Herve Filion. . .	474	1985	Michel Lachance	592
1969	Herve Filion. . .	394	1975	Daryl Buse . . .	360	1981	Eddie Davis. . .	404	1986	Michel Lachance	770
1970	Herve Filion. . .	486	1976	Herve Filion. . .	445		Herve Filion. . .	404	1987	Michel Lachance	715
1971	Herve Filion. . .	543	1977	Herve Filion. . .	441	1982	Herve Filion. . .	495	1988	Herve Filion. . .	798
1972	Herve Filion. . .	605	1978	Herve Filion. . .	423	1983	Eddie Davis. . .	470	1989	Herve Filion. . .	806

Money Won

Year	Driver	Amount	Year	Driver	Amount	Year	Driver	Amount
1966	Stanley Dancer. . .	$1,218,403	1974	Herve Filion.	$3,474,315	1982	Bill O'Donnell. . . .	$5,755,067
1967	Bill Haughton	1,305,773	1975	Carmine Abbatiello	2,275,093	1983	John Campbell . . .	6,104,082
1968	Bill Haughton	1,654,172	1976	Herve Filion.	2,241,045	1984	Bill O'Donnell. . . .	9,059,184
1969	Del Insko	1,635,463	1977	Herve Filion.	2,551,058	1985	Bill O'Donnell. . . .	10,207,372
1970	Herve Filion.	1,647,837	1978	Carmine Abbatiello	3,344,457	1986	John Campbell . . .	9,515,055
1971	Herve Filion.	1,915,945	1979	John Campbell . . .	3,308,984	1987	John Campbell . . .	10,186,495
1972	Herve Filion.	2,473,265	1980	John Campbell . . .	3,732,306	1988	John Campbell . . .	11,148,565
1973	Herve Filion.	2,233,302	1981	Bill O'Donnell. . . .	4,065,608	1989	John Campbell . . .	9,738,450

Notable Sports Records

(Nov. 1989-Oct. 1990)

Baseball

—Rickey Henderson stole his 893d base to set a new American League record.

—Ryne Sandberg set a major league record for 2nd basemen by handling 480 consecutive chances without an error.

—Cal Ripkin set an American League record by playing in his 73rd consecutive errorless game at shortstop.

—Dave Stieb pitched the season's 9th no-hit-game to set a new modern record for most no-hitters in a season. Others pitching no hitters in 1990 were Mark Langston/Mike Witt, California; Nolan Ryan, Texas; Randy Johnson, Seattle; Dave Stewart, Oakland; Fernando Valenzuela, Los Angeles; Andy Hawkins, N.Y. Yankees; Melido Perez, Chicago White Sox; and Terry Mulholland, Philadelphia.

—Carlton Fisk hit his 328th home run as a catcher to set a major league record.

—Andre Dawson entered the record books when he was walked 5 times intentionally in a game against the Cincinnati Reds.

—The Toronto Blue Jays set a major league attendance record of 3,885,284.

—The Boston Red Sox became the first major league team to hit into 2 triple plays in a game.

—Gary Carter set a record when he caught his 1,862 major league game.

—Ken Griffey Jr. and Ken Griffey Sr. of the Seattle Mariners became the first father and son to play on the same major league team.

—Bobby Thigpen set a major league record by recording 57 saves in a season.

—George Brett became the first major leaguer to win a batting championship in 3 separate decades.

—Willie McGee became the first major leaguer to win a batting title in one league while playing in another.

—Barry Bonds became the first major leaguer to drive in 100 runs, hit 30 home runs, and steal 50 bases while batting .300.

—Billy Hatcher of the Cincinnati Reds set a World Series record with 7 consecutive hits.

Basketball

—The Boston Celtics scored an NBA playoff record 157 points in the 2nd game of the series against the N.Y. Knicks.

—John Stockton set a new NBA record with 1,134 assists in a season.

—The Boston Celtics set an NBA record by making 83.29% of their free throws.

—Dale Ellis set a single-game NBA record with nine 3-point field goals.

—The Minnesota Timberwolves set an NBA record with total attendance of 1,072,572 for the season.

—UNLV defeated Duke 103-73 to record the largest margin of victory in the NCAA championship game.

—Oklahoma Univ. scored an NCAA record 97 points in the first half in a game against U.S. International; in the same game, they set an NCAA record for shots taken, 147.

Football

—Joe Montana set the following career Super Bowl records: completions, 83; attempts, 122; completion percentage, 68.0; touchdown passes, 11; yards passing, 1,142. His five touchdown passes established a new single-game mark.

—Jerry Rice set Super Bowl game (3) and career (4) touchdown reception records.

—Roger Craig caught a Super Bowl career record 20 passes.

—Steve Largent retired with the following NFL records: touchdown receptions, 100; consecutive games with a reception, 177; most career receptions, 819; and most reception yardage, 13,189.

—Willie Anderson of the L.A. Rams set an NFL single-game record for receiving yardage with 336 yards on 15 receptions in a game against the New Orleans Saints.

Others

—Jari Kurri scored his 90th goal to set a new NHL career playoff record.

—Jockey Kent Desormeaux rode 597 winners in 1989 for a new record.

—Arie Luyendyk won the Indianapolis 500 auto race with a record 185.984 mph.

—Al Unser Jr. drove the fastest 500-mile Indy-car race with a record 189.727 mph.

BASEBALL
Major League Pennant Winners, 1901–1990

National League | ### American League

Year	Winner	Won	Lost	Pct	Manager	Year	Winner	Won	Lost	Pct	Manager
1901	Pittsburgh	90	49	.647	Clarke	1901	Chicago	83	53	.610	Griffith
1902	Pittsburgh	103	36	.741	Clarke	1902	Philadelphia	83	53	.610	Mack
1903	Pittsburgh	91	49	.650	Clarke	1903	Boston	91	47	.659	Collins
1904	New York	106	47	.693	McGraw	1904	Boston	95	59	.617	Collins
1905	New York	105	48	.686	McGraw	1905	Philadelphia	92	56	.622	Mack
1906	Chicago	116	36	.763	Chance	1906	Chicago	93	58	.616	Jones
1907	Chicago	107	45	.704	Chance	1907	Detroit	92	58	.613	Jennings
1908	Chicago	99	55	.643	Chance	1908	Detroit	90	63	.588	Jennings
1909	Pittsburgh	110	42	.724	Clarke	1909	Detroit	98	54	.645	Jennings
1910	Chicago	104	50	.675	Chance	1910	Philadelphia	102	48	.680	Mack
1911	New York	99	54	.647	McGraw	1911	Philadelphia	101	50	.669	Mack
1912	New York	103	48	.682	McGraw	1912	Boston	105	47	.691	Stahl
1913	New York	101	51	.664	McGraw	1913	Philadelphia	96	57	.627	Mack
1914	Boston	94	59	.614	Stallings	1914	Philadelphia	99	53	.651	Mack
1915	Philadelphia	90	62	.592	Moran	1915	Boston	101	50	.669	Carrigan
1916	Brooklyn	94	60	.610	Robinson	1916	Boston	91	63	.591	Carrigan
1917	New York	98	56	.636	McGraw	1917	Chicago	100	54	.649	Rowland
1918	Chicago	84	45	.651	Mitchell	1918	Boston	75	51	.595	Barrow
1919	Cincinnati	96	44	.686	Moran	1919	Chicago	88	52	.629	Gleason
1920	Brooklyn	93	60	.604	Robinson	1920	Cleveland	98	56	.636	Speaker
1921	New York	94	56	.614	McGraw	1921	New York	98	55	.641	Huggins
1922	New York	93	61	.604	McGraw	1922	New York	94	60	.610	Huggins
1923	New York	95	58	.621	McGraw	1923	New York	98	54	.645	Huggins
1924	New York	93	60	.608	McGraw	1924	Washington	92	62	.597	Harris
1925	Pittsburgh	95	58	.621	McKechnie	1925	Washington	96	55	.636	Harris
1926	St. Louis	89	65	.578	Hornsby	1926	New York	91	63	.591	Huggins
1927	Pittsburgh	94	60	.610	Bush	1927	New York	110	44	.714	Huggins
1928	St. Louis	95	59	.617	McKechnie	1928	New York	101	53	.656	Huggins
1929	Chicago	98	54	.645	McCarthy	1929	Philadelphia	104	46	.693	Mack
1930	St. Louis	92	62	.597	Street	1930	Philadelphia	102	52	.662	Mack
1931	St. Louis	101	53	.656	Street	1931	Philadelphia	107	45	.704	Mack
1932	Chicago	90	64	.584	Grimm	1932	New York	107	47	.695	McCarthy
1933	New York	91	61	.599	Terry	1933	Washington	99	53	.651	Cronin
1934	St. Louis	95	58	.621	Frisch	1934	Detroit	101	53	.656	Cochrane
1935	Chicago	100	54	.649	Grimm	1935	Detroit	93	58	.616	Cochrane
1936	New York	91	62	.597	Terry	1936	New York	102	51	.667	McCarthy
1937	New York	95	57	.625	Terry	1937	New York	102	52	.662	McCarthy
1938	Chicago	89	63	.586	Hartnett	1938	New York	99	53	.651	McCarthy
1939	Cincinnati	97	57	.630	McKechnie	1939	New York	106	45	.702	McCarthy
1940	Cincinnati	100	53	.654	McKechnie	1940	Detroit	90	64	.584	Baker
1941	Brooklyn	100	54	.649	Durocher	1941	New York	101	53	.656	McCarthy
1942	St. Louis	106	48	.688	Southworth	1942	New York	103	51	.669	McCarthy
1943	St. Louis	105	49	.682	Southworth	1943	New York	98	56	.636	McCarthy
1944	St. Louis	105	49	.682	Southworth	1944	St. Louis	89	65	.578	Sewell
1945	Chicago	98	56	.636	Grimm	1945	Detroit	88	65	.575	O'Neill
1946	St. Louis	98	58	.628	Dyer	1946	Boston	104	50	.675	Cronin
1947	Brooklyn	94	60	.610	Shotton	1947	New York	97	57	.630	Harris
1948	Boston	91	62	.595	Southworth	1948	Cleveland	97	58	.626	Boudreau
1949	Brooklyn	97	57	.630	Shotton	1949	New York	97	57	.630	Stengel
1950	Philadelphia	91	63	.591	Sawyer	1950	New York	98	56	.636	Stengel
1951	New York	98	59	.624	Durocher	1951	New York	98	56	.636	Stengel
1952	Brooklyn	96	57	.627	Dressen	1952	New York	95	59	.617	Stengel
1953	Brooklyn	105	49	.682	Dressen	1953	New York	99	52	.656	Stengel
1954	New York	97	57	.630	Durocher	1954	Cleveland	111	43	.721	Lopez
1955	Brooklyn	98	55	.641	Alston	1955	New York	96	58	.623	Stengel
1956	Brooklyn	93	61	.604	Alston	1956	New York	97	57	.630	Stengel
1957	Milwaukee	95	59	.617	Haney	1957	New York	98	56	.636	Stengel
1958	Milwaukee	92	62	.597	Haney	1958	New York	92	62	.597	Stengel
1959	Los Angeles	88	68	.564	Alston	1959	Chicago	94	60	.610	Lopez
1960	Pittsburgh	95	59	.617	Murtaugh	1960	New York	97	57	.630	Stengel
1961	Cincinnati	93	61	.604	Hutchinson	1961	New York	109	53	.673	Houk
1962	San Francisco	103	62	.624	Dark	1962	New York	96	66	.593	Houk
1963	Los Angeles	99	63	.611	Alston	1963	New York	104	57	.646	Houk
1964	St. Louis	93	69	.574	Keane	1964	New York	99	63	.611	Berra
1965	Los Angeles	97	65	.599	Alston	1965	Minnesota	102	60	.630	Mele
1966	Los Angeles	95	67	.586	Alston	1966	Baltimore	97	63	.606	Bauer
1967	St. Louis	101	60	.627	Schoendienst	1967	Boston	92	70	.568	Williams
1968	St. Louis	97	65	.599	Schoendienst	1968	Detroit	103	59	.636	Smith

National League

Year	Winner	East W	L	Pct	Manager	Winner	West W	L	Pct	Manager	Playoff winner
1969	N.Y. Mets	100	62	.617	Hodges	Atlanta	93	69	.574	Harris	New York
1970	Pittsburgh	89	73	.549	Murtaugh	Cincinnati	102	60	.630	Anderson	Cincinnati
1971	Pittsburgh	97	65	.599	Murtaugh	San Francisco	90	72	.556	Fox	Pittsburgh
1972	Pittsburgh	96	59	.619	Virdon	Cincinnati	95	59	.617	Anderson	Cincinnati
1973	N.Y. Mets	82	79	.509	Berra	Cincinnati	99	63	.611	Anderson	New York
1974	Pittsburgh	88	74	.543	Murtaugh	Los Angeles	102	60	.630	Alston	Los Angeles
1975	Pittsburgh	92	69	.571	Murtaugh	Cincinnati	108	54	.667	Anderson	Cincinnati
1976	Philadelphia	101	61	.623	Ozark	Cincinnati	102	60	.630	Anderson	Cincinnati

Year	Winner	**East** W	L	Pct	Manager	Winner	**West** W	L	Pct	Manager	**Playoff** winner
1977	Philadelphia .	101	61	.623	Ozark	Los Angeles . . .	98	64	.605	Lasorda	Los Angeles
1978	Philadelphia .	90	72	.556	Ozark	Los Angeles . . .	95	67	.586	Lasorda	Los Angeles
1979	Pittsburgh. . .	98	64	.605	Tanner	Cincinnati.	90	71	.559	McNamara	Pittsburgh
1980	Philadelphia .	91	71	.562	Green	Houston	93	70	.571	Virdon	Philadelphia
1981(a)	Philadelphia .	34	21	.618	Green	Los Angeles . . .	36	21	.632	Lasorda	(c)
1981(b)	Montreal . . .	30	23	.566	Williams, Fanning	Houston	33	20	.623	Virdon	Los Angeles
1982	St. Louis . . .	92	70	.568	Herzog	Atlanta	89	73	.549	Torre	St. Louis
1983	Philadelphia .	90	72	.556	Corrales, Owens	Los Angeles . . .	91	71	.562	Lasorda	Philadelphia
1984	Chicago. . . .	96	65	.596	Frey	San Diego	92	70	.568	Williams	San Diego
1985	St. Louis . . .	101	61	.623	Herzog	Los Angeles . . .	95	67	.586	Lasorda	St. Louis
1986	N.Y. Mets. . .	108	54	.667	Johnson	Houston	96	66	.593	Lanier	New York
1987	St. Louis . . .	95	67	.586	Herzog	San Francisco. .	90	72	.556	Craig	St. Louis
1988	N.Y. Mets. . .	100	60	.625	Johnson	Los Angeles . . .	94	67	.584	Lasorda	Los Angeles
1989	Chicago. . . .	93	69	.571	Zimmer	San Francisco . .	92	70	.568	Craig	San Francisco
1990	Pittsburgh. . .	95	67	.586	Leyland	Cincinnati.	91	71	.562	Piniella	Cincinnati

American League

Year	Winner	**East** W	L	Pct	Manager	Winner	**West** W	L	Pct	Manager	**Playoff** winner
1969	Baltimore . . .	109	53	.673	Weaver	Minnesota	97	65	.599	Martin	Baltimore
1970	Baltimore . . .	108	54	.667	Weaver	Minnesota	98	64	.605	Rigney	Baltimore
1971	Baltimore . . .	101	57	.639	Weaver	Oakland	101	60	.627	Williams	Baltimore
1972	Detroit.	86	70	.551	Martin	Oakland	93	62	.600	Williams	Oakland
1973	Baltimore . . .	97	65	.599	Weaver	Oakland	94	68	.580	Williams	Oakland
1974	Baltimore . . .	91	71	.562	Weaver	Oakland	90	72	.556	Dark	Oakland
1975	Boston.	95	65	.594	Johnson	Oakland	98	64	.605	Dark	Boston
1976	New York . . .	97	62	.610	Martin	Kansas City . . .	90	72	.556	Herzog	New York
1977	New York . . .	100	62	.617	Martin	Kansas City . . .	102	60	.630	Herzog	New York
1978	New York . . .	100	63	.613	Martin, Lemon	Kansas City . . .	92	70	.568	Herzog	New York
1979	Baltimore . . .	102	57	.642	Weaver	California	88	74	.543	Fregosi	Baltimore
1980	New York . . .	103	59	.636	Howser	Kansas City . . .	97	65	.599	Frey	Kansas City
1981(a)	New York . . .	34	22	.607	Michael	Oakland	37	23	.617	Martin	(d)
1981(b)	Milwaukee . .	31	22	.585	Rodgers	Kansas City . . .	30	23	.566	Frey, Howser	New York
1982	Milwaukee . .	95	67	.586	Rodgers, Kuenn	California	93	69	.574	Mauch	Milwaukee
1983	Baltimore . . .	98	64	.605	Altobelli	Chicago	99	63	.611	LaRussa	Baltimore
1984	Detroit.	104	58	.642	Anderson	Kansas City . . .	84	78	.519	Howser	Detroit
1985	Toronto	99	62	.615	Cox	Kansas City . . .	91	71	.562	Howser	Kansas City
1986	Boston.	95	66	.590	McNamara	California	92	70	.568	Mauch	Boston
1987	Detroit.	98	64	.605	Anderson	Minnesota	85	77	.525	Kelly	Minnesota
1988	Boston.	89	73	.549	McNamara, Morgan	Oakland	104	58	.642	LaRussa	Oakland
1989	Toronto	89	73	.549	Williams,Gaston	Oakland	99	63	.611	LaRussa	Oakland
1990	Boston.	88	74	.543	Morgan	Oakland	103	59	.636	LaRussa	Oakland

(a) First half; (b) Second half; (c) Montreal and L.A. won the divisional playoffs; (d) N.Y. and Oakland won the divisional playoffs.

Baseball Stadiums

National League

Team		Surface	**Home run distances (ft.)** LF	Center	RF	**Seating** capacity
Atlanta Braves.	Atlanta-Fulton County Stadium	Natural grass	330	402	330	52,003
Chicago Cubs	Wrigley Field.	Natural grass	355	400	353	39,600
Cincinnati Reds	Riverfront Stadium	Artificial	330	404	330	52,392
Houston Astros	Astrodome	Artificial	330	400	330	45,000
Los Angeles Dodgers	Dodger Stadium	Natural grass	330	395	330	56,000
Montreal Expos	Olympic Stadium	Artificial	325	404	325	59,149
New York Mets	Shea Stadium	Natural grass	338	410	338	55,300
Philadelphia Phillies	Veterans Stadium.	Artificial	330	408	330	64,538
Pittsburgh Pirates	Three Rivers Stadium.	Artificial	335	400	335	58,727
St. Louis Cardinals	Busch Stadium	Artificial	330	414	330	54,224
San Diego Padres	Jack Murphy Stadium	Natural grass	327	405	327	58,433
San Francisco Giants	Candlestick Park	Natural grass	335	400	330	58,000

American League

Team		Surface	LF	Center	RF	Seating capacity
Baltimore Orioles	Memorial Stadium.	Natural grass	309	405	309	54,017
Boston Red Sox	Fenway Park	Natural grass	315	420	302	34,182
California Angels	Anaheim Stadium	Natural grass	333	404	333	64,593
Chicago White Sox	Comiskey Park[1].	Natural grass	—	—	—	43,500
Cleveland Indians	Cleveland Stadium	Natural grass	320	400	320	74,483
Detroit Tigers	Tiger Stadium	Natural grass	340	440	325	52,416
Kansas City Royals	Royals Stadium	Artificial	330	410	330	40,625
Milwaukee Brewers	Milwaukee County Stadium	Natural grass	315	402	315	53,192
Minnesota Twins.	Hubert H. Humphrey Metrodome	Artificial	343	408	327	55,883
New York Yankees	Yankee Stadium	Natural grass	318	408	314	57,545
Oakland A's	Oakland Coliseum	Natural grass	330	400	330	49,219
Seattle Mariners	Kingdome	Artificial	316	410	316	58,150
Texas Rangers	Arlington Stadium	Natural grass	330	400	330	43,508
Toronto Blue Jays	Skydome	Artificial	330	400	330	53,000

(1) New Comiskey Park will open in 1991.

Home Run Leaders

National League

Year	Player, Club	HR
1901	Sam Crawford, Cincinnati	16
1902	Thomas Leach, Pittsburgh	6
1903	James Sheckard, Brooklyn	9
1904	Harry Lumley, Brooklyn	9
1905	Fred Odwell, Cincinnati	9
1906	Timothy Jordan, Brooklyn	12
1907	David Brain, Boston	10
1908	Timothy Jordan, Brooklyn	12
1909	Red Murray, New York	7
1910	Fred Beck, Bos., Frank Schulte, Chi.	10
1911	Frank Schulte, Chicago	21
1912	Henry Zimmerman, Chicago	14
1913	Gavvy Cravath, Philadelphia	19
1914	Gavvy Cravath, Philadelphia	19
1915	Gavvy Cravath, Philadelphia	24
1916	Dave Robertson, N.Y., Fred (Cy) Williams, Chi.	12
1917	Dave Robertson, N.Y., Gavvy Cravath, Phil.	12
1918	Gavvy Cravath, Philadelphia	8
1919	Gavvy Cravath, Philadelphia	12
1920	Cy Williams, Philadelphia	15
1921	George Kelly, New York	23
1922	Rogers Hornsby, St. Louis	42
1923	Cy Williams, Philadelphia	41
1924	Jacques Fournier, Brooklyn	27
1925	Rogers Hornsby, St. Louis	39
1926	Hack Wilson, Chicago	21
1927	Hack Wilson, Chicago; Cy Williams, Philadelphia	30
1928	Hack Wilson, Chicago; Jim Bottomley, St. Louis	31
1929	Chuck Klein, Philadelphia	43
1930	Hack Wilson, Chicago	56
1931	Chuck Klein, Philadelphia	31
1932	Chuck Klein, Philadelphia, Mel Ott, New York	38
1933	Chuck Klein, Philadelphia	28
1934	Rip Collins, St. Louis; Mel Ott, New York	35
1935	Walter Berger, Boston	34
1936	Mel Ott, New York	33
1937	Mel Ott, New York; Joe Medwick, St. Louis	31
1938	Mel Ott, New York	36
1939	John Mize, St. Louis	28
1940	John Mize, St. Louis	43
1941	Dolph Camilli, Brooklyn	34
1942	Mel Ott, New York	30
1943	Bill Nicholson, Chicago	29
1944	Bill Nicholson, Chicago	33
1945	Tommy Holmes, Boston	28
1946	Ralph Kiner, Pittsburgh	23
1947	Ralph Kiner, Pittsburgh; John Mize, New York	51
1948	Ralph Kiner, Pittsburgh; John Mize, New York	40
1949	Ralph Kiner, Pittsburgh	54
1950	Ralph Kiner, Pittsburgh	47
1951	Ralph Kiner, Pittsburgh	42
1952	Ralph Kiner, Pittsburgh; Hank Sauer, Chicago	37
1953	Ed Mathews, Milwaukee	47
1954	Ted Kluszewski, Cincinnati	49
1955	Willie Mays, New York	51
1956	Duke Snider, Brooklyn	43
1957	Hank Aaron, Milwaukee	44
1958	Ernie Banks, Chicago	47
1959	Ed Mathews, Milwaukee	46
1960	Ernie Banks, Chicago	41
1961	Orlando Cepeda, San Francisco	46
1962	Willie Mays, San Francisco	49
1963	Hank Aaron, Milwaukee, Willie McCovey, S.F.	44
1964	Willie Mays, San Francisco	47
1965	Willie Mays, San Francisco	52
1966	Hank Aaron, Atlanta	44
1967	Hank Aaron, Atlanta	39
1968	Willie McCovey, San Francisco	36
1969	Willie McCovey, San Francisco	45
1970	Johnny Bench, Cincinnati	45
1971	Willie Stargell, Pittsburgh	48
1972	Johnny Bench, Cincinnati	40
1973	Willie Stargell, Pittsburgh	44
1974	Mike Schmidt, Philadelphia	36
1975	Mike Schmidt, Philadelphia	38
1976	Mike Schmidt, Philadelphia	38
1977	George Foster, Cincinnati	52
1978	George Foster, Cincinnati	40
1979	Dave Kingman, Chicago	48
1980	Mike Schmidt, Philadelphia	48
1981	Mike Schmidt, Philadelphia	31
1982	Dave Kingman, New York	37
1983	Mike Schmidt, Philadelphia	40

American League

Year	Player, Club	HR
1901	Napoleon Lajoie, Philadelphia	14
1902	Socks Seybold, Philadelphia	16
1903	Buck Freeman, Boston	13
1904	Harry Davis, Philadelphia	10
1905	Harry Davis, Philadelphia	8
1906	Harry Davis, Philadelphia	12
1907	Harry Davis, Philadelphia	8
1908	Sam Crawford, Detroit	7
1909	Ty Cobb, Detroit	9
1910	Jake Stahl, Boston	10
1911	J. Franklin Baker, Philadelphia	11
1912	J. Franklin Baker, Philadelphia, Tris Speaker, Boston	10
1913	J. Franklin, Baker, Philadelphia	12
1914	J. Franklin, Baker, Philadelphia	9
1915	Robert Roth, Chicago-Cleveland	7
1916	Wally Pipp, New York	12
1917	Wally Pipp, New York	9
1918	Babe Ruth, Bos., Tilly Walker, Phil.	11
1919	Babe Ruth, Boston	29
1920	Babe Ruth, New York	54
1921	Babe Ruth, New York	59
1922	Ken Williams, St. Louis	39
1923	Babe Ruth, New York	41
1924	Babe Ruth, New York	46
1925	Bob Meusel, New York	33
1926	Babe Ruth, New York	47
1927	Babe Ruth, New York	60
1928	Babe Ruth, New York	54
1929	Babe Ruth, New York	46
1930	Babe Ruth, New York	49
1931	Babe Ruth, Lou Gehrig, New York	46
1932	Jimmie Foxx, Philadelphia	58
1933	Jimmie Foxx, Philadelphia	48
1934	Lou Gehrig, New York	49
1935	Jimmie Foxx, Philadelphia, Hank Greenberg, Detroit	36
1936	Lou Gehrig, New York	49
1937	Joe DiMaggio, New York	46
1938	Hank Greenberg, Detroit	58
1939	Jimmie Foxx, Boston	35
1940	Hank Greenberg, Detroit	41
1941	Ted Williams, Boston	37
1942	Ted Williams, Boston	36
1943	Rudy York, Detroit	34
1944	Nick Etten, New York	22
1945	Vern Stephens, St. Louis	24
1946	Hank Greenberg, Detroit	44
1947	Ted Williams, Boston	32
1948	Joe DiMaggio, New York	39
1949	Ted Williams, Boston	43
1950	Al Rosen, Cleveland	37
1951	Gus Zernial, Chicago-Philadelphia	33
1952	Larry Doby, Cleveland	32
1953	Al Rosen, Cleveland	43
1954	Larry Doby, Cleveland	32
1955	Mickey Mantle, New York	37
1956	Mickey Mantle, New York	52
1957	Roy Sievers, Washington	42
1958	Mickey Mantle, New York	42
1959	Rocky Colavito, Cleve., Harmon Killebrew, Wash.	42
1960	Mickey Mantle, New York	40
1961	Roger Maris, New York	61
1962	Harmon Killebrew, Minnesota	48
1963	Harmon Killebrew, Minnesota	45
1964	Harmon Killebrew, Minnesota	49
1965	Tony Conigliaro, Boston	32
1966	Frank Robinson, Baltimore	49
1967	Carl Yastrzemski, Boston, Harmon Killebrew, Minn.	44
1968	Frank Howard, Washington	44
1969	Harmon Killebrew, Minnesota	49
1970	Frank Howard, Washington	44
1971	Bill Melton, Chicago	33
1972	Dick Allen, Chicago	37
1973	Reggie Jackson, Oakland	32
1974	Dick Allen, Chicago	32
1975	George Scott, Milwaukee; Reggie Jackson, Oakland	36
1976	Graig Nettles, New York	32
1977	Jim Rice, Boston	39
1978	Jim Rice, Boston	46
1979	Gorman Thomas, Milwaukee	45
1980	Reggie Jackson, New York; Ben Oglivie, Milwaukee	41
1981	Bobby Grich, California; Tony Armas, Oakland; Dwight Evans, Boston; Eddie Murray, Baltimore	22
1982	Gorman Thomas, Milwaukee; Reggie Jackson, Cal.	39
1983	Jim Rice, Boston	39

Year	Player, Club	HR	Year	Player, Club	HR
1984	Mike Schmidt, Phil.; Dale Murphy, Atlanta	36	1984	Tony Armas, Boston	43
1985	Dale Murphy, Atlanta	37	1985	Darrell Evans, Detroit	40
1986	Mike Schmidt, Philadelphia	37	1986	Jesse Barfield, Toronto	40
1987	Andre Dawson, Chicago	49	1987	Mark McGwire, Oakland	49
1988	Darryl Strawberry, New York	39	1988	Jose Canseco, Oakland	42
1989	Kevin Mitchell, San Francisco	47	1989	Fred McGriff, Toronto	36
1990	Ryne Sandberg, Chicago	40	1990	Cecil Fielder, Detroit	51

Runs Batted In Leaders

	National League			American League	
Year	Player, Club	RBI	Year	Player, Club	RBI
1907	Honus Wagner, Pittsburgh	91	1907	Ty Cobb, Detroit	116
1908	Honus Wager, Pittsburgh	106	1908	Ty Cobb, Detroit	101
1909	Honus Wagner, Pittsburgh	102	1909	Ty Cobb, Detroit	115
1910	Sherwood Magee, Philadelphia	116	1910	Sam Crawford, Detroit	115
1911	Frank Schulte, Chicago	121	1911	Ty Cobb, Detroit	144
1912	Henry Zimmerman, Chicago	98	1912	J. Franklin Baker, Philadelphia	133
1913	Gavvy Cravath, Philadelphia	118	1913	J. Franklin Baker, Philadelphia	126
1914	Sherwood Magee, Philadelphia	101	1914	Sam Crawford, Detroit	112
1915	Gavvy Cravath, Philadelphia	118	1915	Sam Crawford, Detroit	116
1916	Hal Chase, Cincinnati	94	1916	Wally Pipp, New York	99
1917	Henry Zimmerman, New York	100	1917	Robert Veach, Detroit	115
1918	Frederick Merkle, Chicago	71	1918	George Burns, Phila., Robert Veach, Detroit	74
1919	Hi Myers, Boston	72	1919	Babe Ruth, Boston	112
1920	George Kelly, N.Y., Rogers Hornsby, St. Louis	94	1920	Babe Ruth, New York	137
1921	Rogers Hornsby, St. Louis	126	1921	Babe Ruth, New York	171
1922	Rogers Hornsby, St. Louis	152	1922	Ken Williams, St. Louis	155
1923	Emil Meusel, New York	125	1923	Babe Ruth, New York	131
1924	George Kelly, New York	136	1924	Goose Goslin, Washington	129
1925	Rogers Hornsby, St. Louis	143	1925	Bob Meusel, New York	138
1926	Jim Bottomley, St. Louis	120	1926	Babe Ruth, New York	145
1927	Paul Waner, Pittsburgh	131	1927	Lou Gehrig, New York	175
1928	Jim Bottomley, St. Louis	136	1928	Babe Ruth, N.Y., Lou Gehrig, N.Y.	142
1929	Hack Wilson, Chicago	159	1929	Al Simmons, Philadelphia	157
1930	Hack Wilson, Chicago	190	1930	Lou Gehrig, New York	174
1931	Chuck Klein, Philadelphia	121	1931	Lou Gehrig, New York	184
1932	Don Hurst, Philadelphia	143	1932	Jimmie Foxx, Philadelphia	169
1933	Chuck Klein, Philadelphia	120	1933	Jimmie Foxx, Philadelphia	163
1934	Mel Ott, New York	135	1934	Lou Gehrig, New York	165
1935	Walter Berger, Boston	130	1935	Hank Greenberg, Detroit	170
1936	Joe Medwick, St. Louis	138	1936	Hal Trosky, Cleveland	162
1937	Joe Medwick, St. Louis	154	1937	Hank Greenberg, Detroit	183
1938	Joe Medwick, St. Louis	122	1938	Jimmie Foxx, Boston	175
1939	Frank McCormick, Cincinnati	128	1939	Ted Williams, Boston	145
1940	John Mize, St. Louis	137	1940	Hank Greenberg, Detroit	150
1941	Adolph Camilli, Brooklyn	120	1941	Joe DiMaggio, New York	125
1942	John Mize, New York	110	1942	Ted Williams, Boston	137
1943	Bill Nicholson, Chicago	128	1943	Rudy York, Detroit	118
1944	Bill Nicholson, Chicago	122	1944	Vern Stephens, St. Louis	109
1945	Dixie Walker, Brooklyn	124	1945	Nick Etten, New York	111
1946	Enos Slaughter, St. Louis	130	1946	Hank Greenberg, Detroit	127
1947	John Mize, New York	138	1947	Ted Williams, Boston	114
1948	Stan Musial, St. Louis	131	1948	Joe DiMaggio, New York	155
1949	Ralph Kiner, Pittsburgh	127	1949	Ted Williams, Bos., Vern Stephens, Bos.	159
1950	Del Ennis, Philadelphia	126	1950	Walt Dropo, Bos., Vern Stephens, Bos.	144
1951	Monte Irvin, New York	121	1951	Gus Zernial, Chicago-Philadelphia	129
1952	Hank Sauer, Chicago	121	1952	Al Rosen, Cleveland	105
1953	Roy Campanella, Brooklyn	142	1953	Al Rosen, Cleveland	145
1954	Ted Kluszewski, Cincinnati	141	1954	Larry Doby, Cleveland	126
1955	Duke Snider, Brooklyn	136	1955	Ray Boone, Detroit, Jackie Jensen, Boston	116
1956	Stan Musial, St. Louis	109	1956	Mickey Mantle, New York	130
1957	Hank Aaron, Milwaukee	132	1957	Roy Sievers, Washington	114
1958	Ernie Banks, Chicago	129	1958	Jackie Jensen, Boston	122
1959	Ernie Banks, Chicago	143	1959	Jackie Jensen, Boston	112
1960	Hank Aaron, Milwaukee	126	1960	Roger Maris, New York	112
1961	Orlando Cepeda, San Francisco	142	1961	Roger Maris, New York	142
1962	Tommy Davis, Los Angeles	153	1962	Harmon Killebrew, Minnesota	126
1963	Hank Aaron, Milwaukee	130	1963	Dick Stuart, Boston	118
1964	Ken Boyer, St. Louis	119	1964	Brooks Robinson, Baltimore	118
1965	Deron Johnson, Cincinnati	130	1965	Rocky Colavito, Cleveland	108
1966	Hank Aaron, Atlanta	127	1966	Frank Robinson, Baltimore	122
1967	Orlando Cepeda, St. Louis	111	1967	Carl Yastrzemski, Boston	121
1968	Willie McCovey, San Francisco	105	1968	Ken Harrelson, Boston	109
1969	Willie McCovey, San Francisco	126	1969	Harmon Killebrew, Minnesota	140
1970	Johnny Bench, Cincinnati	148	1970	Frank Howard, Washington	126
1971	Joe Torre, St. Louis	137	1971	Harmon Killebrew, Minnesota	119
1972	Johnny Bench, Cincinnati	125	1972	Dick Allen, Chicago	113
1973	Willie Stargell, Pittsburgh	119	1973	Reggie Jackson, Oakland	117
1974	Johnny Bench, Cincinnati	129	1974	Jeff Burroughs, Texas	118
1975	Greg Luzinski, Philadelphia	120	1975	George Scott, Milwaukee	109
1976	George Foster, Cincinnati	121	1976	Lee May, Baltimore	109
1977	George Foster, Cincinnati	149	1977	Larry Hisle, Minnesota	119
1978	George Foster, Cincinnati	120	1978	Jim Rice, Boston	139
1979	Dave Winfield, San Diego	118	1979	Don Baylor, California	139
1980	Mike Schmidt, Philadelphia	121	1980	Cecil Cooper, Milwaukee	122
1981	Mike Schmidt, Philadelphia	91	1981	Eddie Murray, Baltimore	78

Year	Player, Club	RBI	Year	Player, Club	RBI
1982	Dale Murphy, Atlanta; Al Oliver, Montreal	109	1982	Hal McRae, Kansas City	133
1983	Dale Murphy, Atlanta	121	1983	Cecil Cooper, Milwaukee; Jim Rice, Boston	126
1984	Mike Schmidt, Phil.; Gary Carter, Montreal	106	1984	Tony Armas, Boston	123
1985	Dave Parker, Cincinnati	125	1985	Don Mattingly, New York	145
1986	Mike Schmidt, Philadelphia	119	1986	Joe Carter, Cleveland	121
1987	Andre Dawson, Chicago	137	1987	George Bell, Toronto	134
1988	Will Clark, San Francisco	109	1988	Jose Canseco, Oakland	124
1989	Kevin Mitchell, San Francisco	125	1989	Ruben Sierra, Texas	119
1990	Matt Williams, San Francisco	122	1990	Cecil Fielder, Detroit	132

Batting Champions

	National League				American League		
Year	Player	Club	Pct.	Year	Player	Club	Pct.
1901	Jesse C. Burkett	St. Louis	.382	1901	Napoleon Lajoie	Philadelphia	.422
1902	Clarence Beaumont	Pittsburgh	.357	1902	Ed Delahanty	Washington	.376
1903	Honus Wagner	Pittsburgh	.355	1902	Napoleon Lajoie	Cleveland	.355
1904	Honus Wagner	Pittsburgh	.349	1904	Napoleon Lajoie	Cleveland	.381
1905	James Seymour	Cincinnati	.377	1905	Elmer Flick	Cleveland	.308
1906	Honus Wagner	Pittsburgh	.339	1906	George Stone	St. Louis	.358
1907	Honus Wagner	Pittsburgh	.350	1907	Ty Cobb	Detroit	.350
1908	Honus Wagner	Pittsburgh	.354	1908	Ty Cobb	Detroit	.324
1909	Honus Wagner	Pittsburgh	.339	1909	Ty Cobb	Detroit	.377
1910	Sherwood Magee	Philadelphia	.331	1910	Ty Cobb	Detroit	.385
1911	Honus Wagner	Pittsburgh	.334	1911	Ty Cobb	Detroit	.420
1912	Henry Zimmerman	Chicago	.372	1912	Ty Cobb	Detroit	.410
1913	Jacob Daubert	Brooklyn	.350	1913	Ty Cobb	Detroit	.390
1914	Jacob Daubert	Brooklyn	.329	1914	Ty Cobb	Detroit	.368
1915	Larry Doyle	New York	.320	1915	Ty Cobb	Detroit	.369
1916	Hal Chase	Cincinnati	.339	1916	Tris Speaker	Cleveland	.386
1917	Edd Roush	Cincinnati	.341	1917	Ty Cobb	Detroit	.383
1918	Zach Wheat	Brooklyn	.335	1918	Ty Cobb	Detroit	.382
1919	Edd Roush	Cincinnati	.321	1919	Ty Cobb	Detroit	.384
1920	Rogers Hornsby	St. Louis	.370	1920	George Sisler	St. Louis	.407
1921	Rogers Hornsby	St. Louis	.397	1921	Harry Heilmann	Detroit	.394
1922	Rogers Hornsby	St. Louis	.401	1922	George Sisler	St. Louis	.420
1923	Rogers Hornsby	St. Louis	.384	1923	Harry Heilmann	Detroit	.403
1924	Rogers Hornsby	St. Louis	.424	1924	Babe Ruth	New York	.378
1925	Rogers Hornsby	St. Louis	.403	1925	Harry Heilmann	Detroit	.393
1926	Eugene Hargrave	Cincinnati	.353	1926	Henry Manush	Detroit	.378
1927	Paul Waner	Pittsburgh	.380	1927	Harry Heilmann	Detroit	.398
1928	Rogers Hornsby	Boston	.387	1928	Goose Goslin	Washington	.379
1929	Lefty O'Doul	Philadelphia	.398	1929	Lew Fonseca	Cleveland	.369
1930	Bill Terry	New York	.401	1930	Al Simmons	Philadelphia	.381
1931	Chick Hafey	St. Louis	.349	1931	Al Simmons	Philadelphia	.390
1932	Lefty O'Doul	Brooklyn	.368	1932	Dale Alexander	Detroit-Boston	.367
1933	Chuck Klein	Philadelphia	.368	1933	Jimmie Foxx	Philadelphia	.356
1934	Paul Waner	Pittsburgh	.362	1934	Lou Gehrig	New York	.363
1935	Arky Vaughan	Pittsburgh	.385	1935	Buddy Myer	Washington	.349
1936	Paul Waner	Pittsburgh	.373	1936	Luke Appling	Chicago	.388
1937	Joe Medwick	St. Louis	.374	1937	Charlie Gehringer	Detroit	.371
1938	Ernie Lombardi	Cincinnati	.342	1938	Jimmie Foxx	Boston	.349
1939	John Mize	St. Louis	.349	1939	Joe DiMaggio	New York	.381
1940	Debs Garms	Pittsburgh	.355	1940	Joe DiMaggio	New York	.352
1941	Pete Reiser	Brooklyn	.343	1941	Ted Williams	Boston	.406
1942	Ernie Lombardi	Boston	.330	1942	Ted Williams	Boston	.356
1943	Stan Musial	St. Louis	.357	1943	Luke Appling	Chicago	.328
1944	Dixie Walker	Brooklyn	.357	1944	Lou Boudreau	Cleveland	.327
1945	Phil Cavarretta	Chicago	.355	1945	George Stirnweiss	New York	.309
1946	Stan Musial	St. Louis	.365	1946	Mickey Vernon	Washington	.353
1947	Harry Walker	Philadelphia	.363	1947	Ted Williams	Boston	.343
1948	Stan Musial	St. Louis	.376	1948	Ted Williams	Boston	.369
1949	Jackie Robinson	Brooklyn	.342	1949	George Kell	Detroit	.343
1950	Stan Musial	St. Louis	.346	1950	Billy Goodman	Boston	.354
1951	Stan Musial	St. Louis	.355	1951	Ferris Fain	Philadelphia	.344
1952	Stan Musial	St. Louis	.336	1952	Ferris Fain	Philadelphia	.327
1953	Carl Furillo	Brooklyn	.344	1953	Mickey Vernon	Washington	.337
1954	Willie Mays	New York	.345	1954	Roberto Avila	Cleveland	.341
1955	Richie Ashburn	Philadelphia	.338	1955	Al Kaline	Detroit	.340
1956	Hank Aaron	Milwaukee	.328	1956	Mickey Mantle	New York	.353
1957	Stan Musial	St. Louis	.351	1957	Ted Williams	Boston	.388
1958	Richie Ashburn	Philadelphia	.350	1958	Ted Williams	Boston	.328
1959	Hank Aaron	Milwaukee	.355	1959	Harvey Kuenn	Detroit	.353
1960	Dick Groat	Pittsburgh	.325	1960	Pete Runnels	Boston	.320
1961	Roberto Clemente	Pittsburgh	.351	1961	Norm Cash	Detroit	.361
1962	Tommy Davis	Los Angeles	.346	1962	Pete Runnels	Boston	.326
1963	Tommy Davis	Los Angeles	.326	1963	Carl Yastrzemski	Boston	.321
1964	Roberto Clemente	Pittsburgh	.339	1964	Tony Oliva	Minnesota	.323
1965	Roberto Clemente	Pittsburgh	.329	1965	Tony Oliva	Minnesota	.321
1966	Matty Alou	Pittsburgh	.342	1966	Frank Robinson	Baltimore	.316
1967	Roberto Clemente	Pittsburgh	.357	1967	Carl Yastrzemski	Boston	.326
1968	Pete Rose	Cincinnati	.335	1968	Carl Yastrzemski	Boston	.301
1969	Pete Rose	Cincinnati	.348	1969	Rod Carew	Minnesota	.332
1970	Rico Carty	Atlanta	.366	1970	Alex Johnson	California	.328
1971	Joe Torre	St. Louis	.363	1971	Tony Oliva	Minnesota	.337
1972	Billy Williams	Chicago	.333	1972	Rod Carew	Minnesota	.318
1973	Pete Rose	Cincinnati	.338	1973	Rod Carew	Minnesota	.350
1974	Ralph Garr	Atlanta	.353	1974	Rod Carew	Minnesota	.364

Year	Player	Club	Pct.	Year	Player	Club	Pct.
1975	Bill Madlock	Chicago	.354	1975	Rod Carew	Minnesota	.359
1976	Bill Madlock	Chicago	.339	1976	George Brett	Kansas City	.333
1977	Dave Parker	Pittsburgh	.338	1977	Rod Carew	Minnesota	.388
1978	Dave Parker	Pittsburgh	.334	1978	Rod Carew	Minnesota	.333
1979	Keith Hernandez	St. Louis	.344	1979	Fred Lynn	Boston	.333
1980	Bill Buckner	Chicago	.324	1980	George Brett	Kansas City	.390
1981	Bill Madlock	Pittsburgh	.341	1981	Carney Lansford	Boston	.336
1982	Al Oliver	Montreal	.331	1982	Willie Wilson	Kansas City	.332
1983	Bill Madlock	Pittsburgh	.323	1983	Wade Boggs	Boston	.361
1984	Tony Gwynn	San Diego	.351	1984	Don Mattingly	New York	.343
1985	Willie McGee	St. Louis	.353	1985	Wade Boggs	Boston	.368
1986	Tim Raines	Montreal	.334	1986	Wade Boggs	Boston	.357
1987	Tony Gwynn	San Diego	.369	1987	Wade Boggs	Boston	.363
1988	Tony Gwynn	San Diego	.313	1988	Wade Boggs	Boston	.366
1989	Tony Gwynn	San Diego	.336	1989	Kirby Puckett	Minnesota	.339
1990	Willie McGee	St. Louis	.335	1990	George Brett	Kansas City	.329

Earned-Run Average Leaders

National League

Year	Player, club	G	IP	ERA
1972	Steve Carlton, Philadelphia	41	346	1.98
1973	Tom Seaver, New York	36	290	2.07
1974	Buzz Capra, Atlanta	39	217	2.28
1975	Randy Jones, San Diego	37	285	2.24
1976	John Denny, St. Louis	30	207	2.52
1977	John Candelaria, Pittsburgh	33	231	2.34
1978	Craig Swan, New York	29	207	2.43
1979	J. R. Richard, Houston	38	292	2.71
1980	Don Sutton, Los Angeles	32	212	2.21
1981	Nolan Ryan, Houston	21	149	1.69
1982	Steve Rogers, Montreal	35	277	2.40
1983	Atlee Hammaker, San Fran.	23	172	2.25
1984	Alejandro Pena, Los Angeles	28	199	2.48
1985	Dwight Gooden, New York	35	276	1.53
1986	Mike Scott, Houston	37	275	2.22
1987	Nolan Ryan, Houston	34	211	2.76
1988	Joe Magrane, St. Louis	24	165	2.18
1989	Scott Garrelts, San Francisco	30	193	2.28
1990	Danny Darwin, Houston	48	162	2.21

American League

Year	Player, club	G	IP	ERA
1972	Luis Tiant, Boston	43	179	1.91
1973	Jim Palmer, Baltimore	38	296	2.40
1974	Catfish Hunter, Oakland	41	318	2.49
1975	Jim Palmer, Baltimore	39	323	2.09
1976	Mark Fidrych, Detroit	31	250	2.34
1977	Frank Tanana, California	31	241	2.54
1978	Ron Guidry, New York	35	274	1.74
1979	Ron Guidry, New York	33	236	2.78
1980	Rudy May, New York	41	175	2.47
1981	Steve McCatty, Oakland	22	186	2.32
1982	Rick Sutcliffe, Cleveland	34	216	2.96
1983	Rick Honeycutt, Texas	25	174	2.42
1984	Mike Boddicker, Baltimore	34	261	2.79
1986	Dave Stieb, Toronto	36	265	2.48
1986	Roger Clemens, Boston	33	254	2.48
1987	Jimmy Key, Toronto	36	261	2.76
1988	Allan Anderson, Minnesota	30	202	2.45
1989	Bret Saberhagen, Kansas City	36	262	2.16
1990	Roger Clemens, Boston	31	228	1.93

ERA is computed by multiplying earned runs allowed by 9, then dividing by innings pitched.

Major League Leaders in 1990

National League

Batting

McGee, St. Louis, .335; Murray, Los Angeles, .330; Magadan, New York, .328; Dykstra, Philadelphia, .325; Dawson, Chicago, .310.

Home Runs

Sandberg, Chicago, 40; Strawberry, New York, 37; Mitchell, San Francisco, 35; Bonds, Pittsburgh, 33; Williams, San Francisco, 33.

Runs Batted In

Williams, San Francisco, 122; Bonilla, Pittsburgh, 120; Carter, San Diego, 115; Bonds, Pittsburgh, 114; Strawberry, New York, 108.

Hits

Butler, San Francisco, 192; Dykstra, Philadelphia, 192; Sandberg, Chicago, 188; Larkin, Cincinnati, 185; Wallach, Montreal, 185.

Stolen Bases

Coleman, St. Louis, 77; Yelding, Houston, 64; Bonds, Pittsburgh, 52; Butler, San Francisco, 51; Nixon, Montreal, 50.

On-Base Pct.

Dykstra, Philadelphia, .418; Magadan, New York, .417; Murray, Los Angeles, .414; Bonds, Pittsburgh, .406; Butler, San Francisco, .397.

Doubles

Jefferies, New York, 40; Bonilla, Pittsburgh, 39; Sabo, Cincinnati, 38; Johnson, New York, 37; Wallach, Montreal, 37.

Triples

Duncan, Cincinnati, 11; Gwynn, San Diego, 10; Butler, San Francisco, 9; Coleman, St. Louis, 9; L. Smith, Atlanta, 9.

Earned-Run Average

Darwin, Houston, 2.21; Smith, Pittsburgh, 2.55; Whitson, San Diego, 2.60; Viola, New York, 2.63; Rijo, Cincinnati, 2.70.

Saves

Franco, New York, 33; Myers, Cincinnati, 31; L. Smith, St. Louis, 27; Lefferts, San Diego, 23; Smith, Houston, 23.

Strikeouts

Cone, New York, 233; Gooden, New York, 223; Martinez, Los Angeles, 223; Viola, New York, 182; Fernandez, New York, 181.

American League

Batting

Brett, Kansas City, .329; R. Henderson, Oakland, .325; Palmeiro, Texas, .319; Trammell, Detroit, .304; Boggs, Boston, .302; E. Martinez, Seattle, .302.

Home Runs

Fielder, Detroit, 51; McGwire, Oakland, 39; Canseco, Oakland, 37; McGriff, Toronto, 35; Gruber, Toronto, 31.

Runs Batted In

Fielder, Detroit, 132; Gruber, Toronto, 118; McGwire, Oakland, 108; Canseco, Oakland, 101; Sierra, Texas, 96.

Hits

Palmeiro, Texas, 191; Boggs, Boston, 187; Kelly, New York, 183; Greenwell, Boston, 181; Brett, Kansas City, 179.

Stolen Bases

R. Henderson, Oakland, 65; Sax, New York, 43; Kelly, New York, 42; Cole, Cleveland, 40; Pettis, Texas, 38.

On-Base Pct.

R. Henderson, Oakland, .439; McGriff, Toronto, .400; E. Martinez, Seattle, .397; Brett, Kansas City, .387; Davis, Seattle, .387.

Doubles

Brett, Kansas City, 45; J. Reed, Boston, 45; Boggs, Boston, 44; Calderon, Chicago, 44; Harper, Minnesota, 42.

Triples

Fernandez, Toronto, 17; Sosa, Chicago, 10; Johnson, Chicago, 9; Liriano, Tor., Minn., 9; Polonia, N.Y., Cal., 9.

Earned-Run Average

Clemens, Boston, 1.93; Finley, California, 2.40; Stewart, Oakland, 2.56; Appier, Kansas City, 2.76; Stieb, Toronto, 2.95.

Saves

Thigpen, Chicago, 57; Eckersley, Oakland, 48; Jones, Cleveland, 43; Olson, Baltimore, 37; Righetti, New York, 36.

Strikeouts

Ryan, Texas, 232; Witt, Texas, 221; Hanson, Seattle, 211; Clemens, Boston, 209; Langston, California, 195.

National League Records in 1990

Final standings

Eastern Division

	W	L	Pct	GB	Home	Away	vs West	One Run	After 7 Lead	After 7 Trail	Runs Avg	Runs vs.
Pittsburgh	95	67	.586	—	49-32	46-35	45-26	28-20	75-4	6-56	4.5	3.8
New York	91	71	.562	4	52-29	39-42	40-32	24-28	74-4	9-57	4.8	3.8
Montreal	85	77	.525	10	47-34	38-43	36-36	29-30	67-7	9-57	4.1	3.7
Philadelphia . . .	77	85	.475	18	41-40	36-45	39-33	27-26	57-5	10-66	4.0	4.5
Chicago	77	85	.475	18	39-42	38-43	34-40	25-29	57-10	6-68	4.3	4.8
St. Louis	70	92	.432	25	34-47	36-45	31-41	21-25	61-9	4-71	3.7	4.3

Western Division

	W	L	Pct	GB	Home	Away	vs East	One Run	After 7 Lead	After 7 Trail	Runs Avg	Runs vs.
Cincinnati. . . .	91	71	.562	—	46-35	45-36	45-27	20-18	75-5	4-56	4.3	3.7
Los Angeles . . .	86	76	.531	5	47-34	39-42	39-32	26-16	69-5	10-63	4.5	4.2
San Francisco . .	85	77	.525	6	49-32	36-45	34-40	24-22	67-9	7-56	4.4	4.4
Houston	75	87	.463	16	49-32	26-55	32-40	24-23	50-8	7-63	3.5	4.0
San Diego	75	87	.463	16	37-44	38-43	26-46	19-26	57-8	6-66	4.2	4.2
Atlanta	65	97	.401	26	37-44	28-53	33-38	19-20	52-10	7-77	4.2	5.1

National League Championship Series

Pittsburgh 4, Cincinnati 3
Cincinnati 2, Pittsburgh 1

Cincinnati 6, Pittsburgh 3
Cincinnati 5, Pittsburgh 2

Pittsburgh 3, Cincinnati 2
Cincinnati 2, Pittsburgh 1

Team Batting

	Avg.	AB	R	H	HR	RBI
Cincinnati.	.265	5525	693	1466	125	644
Chicago.	.263	5600	690	1474	136	649
San Francisco	.262	5573	719	1459	152	681
Los Angeles	.262	5491	728	1436	129	669
Pittsburgh.	.259	5388	733	1395	138	693
San Diego	.257	5554	673	1429	123	628
New York	.256	5504	775	1410	172	734
St. Louis	.256	5462	599	1398	73	554
Philadelphia	.255	5535	646	1410	103	619
Atlanta	.250	5504	682	1376	162	636
Montreal	.250	5453	662	1363	114	607
Houston	.242	5379	573	1301	94	536

Team Pitching

	ERA	IP	H	BB	SO	Sv
Montreal	3.37	1473	1349	510	991	50
Cincinnati.	3.39	1456	1338	543	1029	50
Pittsburgh.	3.40	1447	1367	413	848	43
New York	3.43	1440	1339	444	1217	41
Houston	3.61	1450	1396	496	854	37
San Diego	3.68	1461	1437	507	928	35
Los Angeles	3.72	1442	1364	478	1021	29
St. Louis	3.87	1443	1432	475	833	39
Philadelphia	4.07	1449	1381	651	840	35
San Francisco	4.08	1446	1477	553	788	45
Chicago.	4.34	1442	1510	572	877	42
Atlanta	4.58	1429	1527	579	938	30

Individual Batting (at least 135 at-bats); Individual Pitching (at least 50 innings)

*Left-handed batter, pitcher; **Switch hitter

Atlanta Braves

Batting	Avg	AB	R	H	HR	RBI
L. Smith	.305	466	72	142	9	42
Gant	.303	575	107	174	32	84
Treadway*	.283	474	56	134	11	59
Justice*	.282	439	76	124	28	78
Cabrera	.277	137	14	38	7	25
Blauser	.269	386	46	104	8	39
Gregg*	.264	239	18	63	5	32
Olson	.262	298	36	78	7	36
McDowell*	.243	305	47	74	7	25
Presley	.242	541	59	131	19	72
Lemke**	.226	239	22	54	0	21
Thomas	.219	278	26	61	5	30
Whitt*	.172	180	14	31	2	10

Pitching	W	L	ERA	IP	BB	SO	Sv
Leibrandt*	9	11	3.16	162.1	35	76	0
Smoltz	14	11	3.85	231.1	90	170	0
Castillo*	5	1	4.23	76.2	20	64	1
Glavine*	10	12	4.28	214.1	78	129	0
Parrett	5	10	4.64	108.2	55	86	2
Grant	2	3	4.73	91.1	37	69	3
P. Smith	5	6	4.79	77.0	24	56	-0
Avery*	3	11	5.64	99.0	45	75	0
Clary	1	10	5.67	101.2	39	44	0
Luecken	1	4	5.77	53.0	30	35	1

Chicago Cubs

Batting	Avg	AB	R	H	HR	RBI
Dawson	.310	529	72	164	27	100
Grace*	.309	589	72	182	9	82
Sandberg	.306	615	116	188	40	100
Clark*	.275	171	22	47	5	20
Girardi	.270	419	36	113	1	38
Ramos	.265	226	22	60	2	17
Walton	.263	392	63	103	2	21
Dunston	.262	545	73	143	17	66
D. Smith*	.262	290	34	76	6	27
Salazar	.254	410	44	104	12	47
Dascenzo**	.253	241	27	61	1	26
Wilkerson**	.220	186	21	41	0	16
Wynne*	.204	186	21	38	4	19

Pitching	W	L	ERA	IP	BB	SO	Sv
Assenmacher* . .	7	2	2.80	103.0	36	95	10
Harkey	12	6	3.26	173.2	59	94	0
Maddux	15	15	3.46	237.0	71	144	0
Williams*	1	8	3.93	66.1	50	55	16
Long	6	1	4.37	55.2	21	32	5
Lancaster	9	5	4.62	109.0	40	65	6
Wilson*	4	9	4.79	139.0	43	95	1
Pico	4	4	4.79	92.0	37	37	2
Bielecki	8	11	4.93	168.0	70	103	1
Nunez	4	7	6.53	60.2	34	40	0

Cincinnati Reds

Batting	Avg	AB	R	H	HR	RBI
Morris*	.340	309	50	105	7	36
Duncan	.306	435	67	133	10	55
Larkin	.301	614	85	185	7	67
Doran**	.300	403	59	121	7	37
Oester**	.299	154	10	46	0	13
Braggs	.299	201	22	60	6	28
Hatcher	.276	504	68	139	5	25
O'Neill*	.270	503	59	136	16	78
Sabo	.270	567	95	153	25	71
Davis	.260	453	84	118	24	86
Winningham*	.256	160	20	41	3	17
Benzinger**	.253	376	35	95	5	46
Reed*	.251	175	12	44	3	16
Quinones**	.241	145	10	35	2	17
Oliver	.231	364	34	84	8	52

Pitching	W	L	ERA	IP	BB	SO	Sv
Dibble	8	3	1.74	98.0	34	136	11
Myers*	4	6	2.08	86.2	38	98	31
Rijo	14	8	2.70	197.0	78	152	0
Charlton*	12	9	2.74	154.1	70	117	2
Armstrong	12	9	3.42	166.0	59	110	0
Layana	5	3	3.49	80.0	44	53	2
Jackson*	6	6	3.61	117.1	40	76	0
Browning*	15	9	3.80	227.2	52	99	0
Birtsas*	1	3	3.86	51.1	24	41	0
Mahler	7	6	4.28	134.2	39	68	4
Scudder	5	5	4.90	71.2	30	42	0

Montreal Expos

Batting	Avg	AB	R	H	HR	RBI
Wallach	.296	626	69	185	21	98
DeShields*	.289	499	69	144	4	45
Raines**	.287	457	65	131	9	62
Da. Martinez*	.279	391	60	109	11	39
Noboa	.266	158	15	42	0	14
Grissom	.257	288	42	74	3	29
Galarraga	.256	579	65	148	20	87
Nixon**	.251	231	46	58	1	20
Fitzgerald	.243	313	36	76	9	41
Aldrete*	.242	161	22	39	1	18
Walker*	.241	419	59	101	19	51
Owen**	.234	453	55	106	5	35
Foley*	.213	164	11	35	0	12
Santovenia	.190	163	13	31	6	28

Pitching	W	L	ERA	IP	BB	SO	Sv
Frey*	8	2	2.10	55.2	29	29	9
Burke	3	3	2.52	75.0	21	47	20
Ruskin*	3	2	2.75	75.1	38	57	2
Nabholz*	6	2	2.83	70.0	32	53	0
Boyd	10	6	2.93	190.2	52	113	0
De. Martinez	10	11	2.95	226.0	49	156	0
Sampen	12	7	2.99	90.1	33	69	2
Mohorcic	1	2	3.23	53.0	18	29	2
Gardner	7	9	3.42	152.2	61	135	0
Gross	9	12	4.57	163.1	65	111	0
Hall*	4	7	5.09	58.1	29	40	3

Houston Astros

Batting	Avg	AB	R	H	HR	RBI
Candaele**	.286	262	30	75	3	22
Biggio	.276	555	53	153	4	42
Stubbs*	.261	448	59	117	23	71
Ramirez	.261	445	44	116	2	37
Yelding	.254	511	69	130	1	28
Davis	.251	327	44	82	22	64
Wilson	.245	368	42	90	10	55
Caminiti**	.242	541	52	131	4	51
Oberkfell*	.207	150	10	31	1	12
Anthony*	.192	239	26	46	10	29
Young**	.175	154	15	27	1	4

Pitching	W	L	ERA	IP	BB	SO	Sv
Andersen	5	2	1.95	73.2	24	68	6
Darwin	11	4	2.21	162.2	31	109	2
Smith	6	6	2.39	60.1	20	50	23
Portugal	11	10	3.62	196.2	67	136	0
Deshaies*	7	12	3.78	209.1	84	119	0
Scott	9	13	3.81	205.2	66	121	0
Gullickson	10	14	3.82	193.1	61	73	0
Agosto*	9	8	4.29	92.1	39	50	4
Hernandez	2	1	4.62	62.1	24	24	0
Clancy	2	8	6.51	76.0	33	44	1

New York Mets

Batting	Avg	AB	R	H	HR	RBI
Magadan*	.328	451	74	148	6	72
Sasser*	.307	270	31	83	6	41
Jefferies*	.283	604	96	171	15	68
Strawberry*	.277	542	92	150	37	108
Boston*	.273	366	65	100	12	45
McReynolds	.269	521	75	140	24	82
Herr**	.261	547	48	143	5	60
Miller	.258	233	42	60	1	12
Carreon	.250	188	30	47	10	26
Teufel	.246	175	28	43	10	24
Johnson**	.244	590	89	144	23	90
Marshall	.239	163	24	39	6	27
Elster	.207	314	36	65	9	45

Pitching	W	L	ERA	IP	BB	SO	Sv
Schatzeder*	1	3	2.20	69.2	23	39	0
Franco*	5	3	2.53	67.2	21	56	33
Viola*	20	12	2.67	249.2	60	182	0
Pena	3	3	3.20	76.0	22	76	5
Cone	14	10	3.23	211.2	65	233	0
Whitehurst	1	0	3.29	65.2	9	46	2
Fernandez*	9	14	3.46	179.1	67	181	0
Ojeda*	7	6	3.66	118.0	40	62	0
Gooden	19	7	3.83	232.2	70	223	0
Darling	7	9	4.50	126.0	44	99	0

Los Angeles Dodgers

Batting	Avg	AB	R	H	HR	RBI
Murray**	.330	558	96	184	26	95
Javier**	.304	276	56	84	3	24
Harris*	.304	431	61	131	2	29
Sharperson	.297	357	42	106	3	36
Daniels*	.296	450	81	133	27	94
Gwynn*	.284	141	19	40	5	22
Brooks	.266	568	74	151	20	91
Scioscia*	.264	435	46	115	12	66
Gibson*	.260	315	59	82	8	38
Samuel	.242	492	62	119	13	52
Griffin**	.210	461	38	97	1	35

Pitching	W	L	ERA	IP	BB	SO	Sv
Howell	5	5	2.18	66.0	20	59	16
Crews	4	5	2.77	107.1	24	76	5
Gott	3	5	2.90	62.0	34	44	3
Martinez	20	6	2.92	234.1	67	223	0
Hartley	6	3	2.95	79.1	30	76	1
Neidlinger	5	3	3.28	74.0	15	46	0
Morgan	11	15	3.75	211.0	60	106	0
Cook*	9	4	3.92	156.0	56	64	1
Belcher	9	9	4.00	153.0	48	102	0
Valenzuela*	13	13	4.59	204.0	77	115	0

Philadelphia Phillies

Batting	Avg	AB	R	H	HR	RBI
Dykstra*	.325	590	106	192	9	60
Kruk*	.291	443	52	129	7	67
Daulton*	.268	459	62	123	12	57
V. Hayes*	.261	467	70	122	17	73
C. Hayes	.258	561	56	145	10	57
Thon	.255	552	54	141	8	48
Murphy	.245	563	60	138	24	83
Ready	.244	217	26	53	1	26
Jordan	.241	324	32	78	5	44

Pitching	W	L	ERA	IP	BB	SO	Sv
Grimsley	3	2	3.30	57.1	43	41	0
Mulholland*	9	10	3.34	180.2	42	75	0
Boever	3	6	3.36	88.1	51	75	14
DeJesus	7	8	3.74	130.0	73	87	0
Akerfelds	5	2	3.77	93.0	54	42	3
McDowell	6	8	3.86	86.1	35	39	22
Combs*	10	10	4.07	183.1	86	108	0
Carman*	6	2	4.15	86.2	38	58	1
Howell	8	7	4.64	106.2	49	70	0
Greene	3	3	5.08	51.1	26	21	0
Ruffin*	6	13	5.38	149.0	62	79	0

Pittsburgh Pirates

Batting	Avg	AB	R	H	HR	RBI
Bonds*	.301	519	104	156	33	114
Slaught	.300	230	27	69	4	29
Backman**	.292	315	62	92	2	28
Reynolds**	.288	215	25	62	0	19
Van Slyke*	.284	493	67	140	17	77
Bonilla**	.280	625	112	175	32	120
Bream*	.270	389	39	105	15	67
Lind	.261	514	46	134	1	48
LaVilliere*	.258	279	27	72	3	31
Bell	.254	583	93	148	7	52
Redus	.247	227	32	56	6	23
King	.245	371	46	91	14	53
Martinez	.240	217	26	52	10	35

Pitching	W	L	ERA	IP	BB	SO	Sv
Landrum	7	3	2.13	71.2	21	39	13
Tomlin*	4	4	2.55	77.2	12	42	0
Smith*	12	9	2.55	215.1	50	130	0
Drabek	22	6	2.76	231.1	56	131	0
Patterson*	8	5	2.95	94.2	21	70	5
Kipper*	5	2	3.02	62.2	26	35	3
Heaton*	12	9	3.45	146.0	38	68	0
Belinda	3	4	3.55	58.1	29	55	8
Power	1	3	3.66	51.2	17	42	7
Walk	7	5	3.75	129.2	36	73	1
Reed	2	3	4.36	53.2	12	27	1
Smiley*	9	10	4.64	149.1	36	86	0
Terrell	2	7	5.88	82.2	33	34	0

San Diego Padres

Batting	Avg	AB	R	H	HR	RBI
Roberts**	.309	556	104	172	9	44
Gwynn*	.309	573	79	177	4	72
Alomar**	.287	586	80	168	6	60
Santiago	.270	344	42	93	11	53
Ja. Clark	.266	334	59	89	25	62
Pagliarulo*	.254	398	29	101	7	38
Templeton**	.248	505	45	125	9	59
Abner	.245	184	17	45	1	15
Lynn*	.240	196	18	47	6	23
Carter	.232	634	79	147	24	115
Parent	.222	189	13	42	3	16
Stephenson*	.209	182	26	38	4	19

Pitching	W	L	ERA	IP	BB	SO	Sv
Harris	8	8	2.30	117.1	49	97	9
Lefferts*	7	5	2.52	78.2	22	60	23
Whitson	14	9	2.60	228.2	47	127	0
Hurst*	11	9	3.14	223.2	63	162	0
Benes	10	11	3.60	192.1	69	140	0
Hammaker*	4	9	4.36	86.2	27	44	0
Schiraldi	3	8	4.41	104.0	60	74	1
Rasmussen*	11	15	4.51	187.2	62	86	0
Lilliquist*	5	11	5.31	122.0	42	63	0
Show*	6	8	5.76	106.1	41	55	1

St. Louis Cardinals

Batting	Avg	AB	R	H	HR	RBI
McGee**	.335	501	76	168	3	62
Coleman**	.292	497	73	145	6	39
Hudler	.282	220	31	62	7	22
Guerrero	.281	498	42	140	13	80
Pagnozzi	.277	220	20	61	2	23
O. Smith**	.254	512	61	130	1	50
Oquendo**	.252	469	38	118	1	37
Zeile	.244	495	62	121	15	57
Pendleton**	.230	447	46	103	6	58
Thompson*	.218	418	42	91	6	30

Pitching	W	L	ERA	IP	BB	SO	Sv
L. Smith	3	4	2.10	68.2	20	70	27
Tudor*	12	4	2.40	146.1	30	63	0
Niedenfuer	0	6	3.46	65.0	25	32	2
Tewksbury	10	9	3.47	145.1	15	50	1
Dayley*	4	4	3.56	73.1	30	51	2
Magrane*	10	17	3.59	203.1	59	100	0
B. Smith	9	8	4.27	141.1	30	78	0
DeLeon	7	19	4.43	182.2	86	164	0
DiPino*	5	2	4.56	81.0	31	49	3
Terry	2	6	4.75	72.0	27	35	2
Matthews	0	5	5.33	50.2	30	18	0
Hill	5	6	5.49	78.2	33	58	0

San Francisco Giants

Batting	Avg	AB	R	H	HR	RBI
Butler*	.309	622	108	192	3	44
Clark*	.295	600	91	177	19	95
Kingery*	.295	207	24	61	0	24
Leach	.293	174	24	51	2	16
Mitchell	.290	524	90	152	35	93
Kennedy*	.277	303	25	84	2	26
Williams	.277	617	87	171	33	122
Carter	.254	244	24	62	9	27
Bass**	.252	214	25	54	7	32
Uribe**	.248	415	35	103	1	24
Litton	.245	204	17	50	1	24
Thompson	.245	498	67	122	15	56
Riles*	.200	155	22	31	8	21

Pitching	W	L	ERA	IP	BB	SO	Sv
Brantley	5	3	1.56	86.2	33	61	19
Oliveras	2	2	2.77	55.1	21	41	2
Thurmond*	2	3	3.34	56.2	18	24	4
Downs	3	2	3.43	63.0	20	31	0
Burkett	14	7	3.79	204.0	61	118	1
Reuschel	3	6	3.93	87.0	31	49	1
LaCoss	6	4	3.94	77.2	39	39	0
Wilson*	8	7	4.00	110.1	49	66	0
Garrelts	12	11	4.15	182.0	70	80	0
Bedrosian	9	9	4.20	79.1	44	43	17
Robinson	10	7	4.57	157.2	41	78	0

Cy Young Award Winners

Year	Player, club	Year	Player, club	Year	Player, club
1956	Don Newcombe, Dodgers	1971	(NL) Ferguson Jenkins, Cubs	1981	(NL) Fernando Valenzuela, Dodgers
1957	Warren Spahn, Braves		(AL) Vida Blue, A's		(AL) Rollie Fingers, Brewers
1958	Bob Turley, Yankees	1972	(NL) Steve Carlton, Phillies	1982	(NL) Steve Carlton, Phillies
1959	Early Wynn, White Sox		(AL) Gaylord Perry, Indians		(AL) Pete Vuckovich, Brewers
1960	Vernon Law, Pirates	1973	(NL) Tom Seaver, Mets	1983	(NL) John Denny, Phillies
1961	Whitey Ford, Yankees		(AL) Jim Palmer, Orioles		(AL) LaMarr Hoyt, White Sox
1962	Don Drysdale, Dodgers	1974	(NL) Mike Marshall, Dodgers	1984	(NL) Rick Sutcliffe, Cubs
1963	Sandy Koufax, Dodgers		(AL) Jim (Catfish) Hunter, A's		(AL) Willie Hernandez, Tigers
1964	Dean Chance, Angels	1975	(NL) Tom Seaver, Mets	1985	(NL) Dwight Gooden, Mets
1965	Sandy Koufax, Dodgers		(AL) Jim Palmer, Orioles		(AL) Bret Saberhagen, Royals
1966	Sandy Koufax, Dodgers	1976	(NL) Randy Jones, Padres	1986	(NL) Mike Scott, Astros
1967	(NL) Mike McCormick, Giants		(AL) Jim Palmer, Orioles		(AL) Roger Clemens, Red Sox
	(AL) Jim Lonborg, Red Sox	1977	(NL) Steve Carlton, Phillies	1987	(NL) Steve Bedrosian, Phillies
1968	(NL) Bob Gibson, Cardinals		(AL) Sparky Lyle, Yankees		(AL) Roger Clemens, Red Sox
	(AL) Dennis McLain, Tigers	1978	(NL) Gaylord Perry, Padres	1988	(NL) Orel Hershiser, Dodgers
1969	(NL) Tom Seaver, Mets		(AL) Ron Guidry, Yankees		(AL) Frank Viola, Twins
	(AL) (tie) Dennis McLain, Tigers	1979	(NL) Bruce Sutter, Cubs	1989	(NL) Mark Davis, Padres
	Mike Cuellar, Orioles		(AL) Mike Flanagan, Orioles		(AL) Bret Saberhagan, Royals
1970	(NL) Bob Gibson, Cardinals	1980	(NL) Steve Carlton, Phillies		
	(AL) Jim Perry, Twins		(AL) Steve Stone, Orioles		

National Baseball Hall of Fame and Museum

Cooperstown, N.Y.

Aaron, Hank
Alexander, Grover Cleveland
Alston, Walt
Anson, Cap
Aparicio, Luis
Appling, Luke
Averill, Earl
Baker, Home Run
Bancroft, Dave
Banks, Ernie
Barlick, Al
Barrow, Edward G.
Beckley, Jake
Bell, Cool Papa
Bench, Johnny
Bender, Chief
Berra, Yogi
Bottomley, Jim
Boudreau, Lou
Bresnahan, Roger
Brock, Lou
Brouthers, Dan
Brown (Three Finger), Mordecai
Bulkeley, Morgan C.
Burkett, Jesse C.
Campanella, Roy
Carey, Max
Cartwright, Alexander
Chadwick, Henry
Chance, Frank
Chandler, Happy
Charleston, Oscar
Chesbro, John
Clarke, Fred
Clarkson, John
Clemente, Roberto
Cobb, Ty
Cochrane, Mickey
Collins, Eddie
Collins, James
Combs, Earle
Comiskey, Charles A.

Conlan, Jocko
Connolly, Thomas H.
Connor, Roger
Coveleski, Stan
Crawford, Sam
Cronin, Joe
Cummings, Candy
Cuyler, Kiki
Dandridge, Ray
Dean, Dizzy
Delahanty, Ed
Dickey, Bill
DiHigo, Martin
DiMaggio, Joe
Doerr, Bobby
Drysdale, Don
Duffy, Hugh
Evans, Billy
Evers, John
Ewing, Buck
Faber, Urban
Feller, Bob
Ferrell, Rick
Flick, Elmer H.
Ford, Whitey
Foster, Andrew
Foxx, Jimmie
Frick, Ford
Frisch, Frank
Galvin, Pud
Gehrig, Lou
Gehringer, Charles
Gibson, Bob
Gibson, Josh
Giles, Warren
Gomez, Lefty
Goslin, Goose
Greenberg, Hank
Griffith, Clark
Grimes, Burleigh
Grove, Lefty
Hafey, Chick

Haines, Jesee
Hamilton, Bill
Harridge, Will
Harris, Bucky
Hartnett, Gabby
Heilmann, Harry
Herman, Billy
Hooper, Harry
Hornsby, Rogers
Hoyt, Waite
Hubbard, Cal
Hubbell, Carl
Huggins, Miller
Hunter, Catfish
Irvin, Monte
Jackson, Travis
Jennings, Hugh
Johnson, Byron
Johnson, William (Judy)
Johnson, Walter
Joss, Addie
Kaline, Al
Keefe, Timothy
Keeler, William
Kell, George
Kelley, Joe
Kelly, George
Kelly, King
Killebrew, Harmon
Kiner, Ralph
Klein, Chuck
Klem, Bill
Koufax, Sandy
Lajoie, Napoleon
Landis, Kenesaw M.
Lemon, Bob
Leonard, Buck
Lindstrom, Fred
Lloyd, Pop
Lombardi, Ernie
Lopez, Al
Lyons, Ted

Mack, Connie
MacPhail, Larry
Mantle, Mickey
Manush, Henry
Maranville, Rabbit
Marichal, Juan
Marquard, Rube
Mathews, Eddie
Mathewson, Christy
Mays, Willie
McCarthy, Joe
McCarthy, Thomas
McCovey, Willie
McGinnity, Joe
McGraw, John
McKechnie, Bill
Medwick, Joe
Mize, Johnny
Morgan, Joe
Musial, Stan
Nichols, Kid
O'Rourke, James
Ott, Mel
Paige, Satchel
Palmer, Jim
Pennock, Herb
Plank, Ed
Radbourn, Charlie
Reese, Pee Wee
Rice, Sam
Rickey, Branch
Rixey, Eppa
Roberts, Robin
Robinson, Brooks
Robinson, Frank
Robinson, Jackie
Robinson, Wilbert
Roush, Edd
Ruffing, Red
Rusie, Amos
Ruth, Babe
Schalk, Ray

Schoendienst, Red
Sewell, Joe
Simmons, Al
Sisler, George
Slaughter, Enos
Snider, Duke
Spahn, Warren
Spalding, Albert
Speaker, Tris
Stargell, Willie
Stengel, Casey
Terry, Bill
Thompson, Sam
Tinker, Joe
Traynor, Pie
Vance, Dazzy
Vaughan, Arky
Waddell, Rube
Wagner, Honus
Wallace, Roderick
Walsh, Ed.
Waner, Lloyd
Waner, Paul
Ward, John
Weiss, George
Welch, Mickey
Wheat, Zach
Wilhelm, Hoyt
Williams, Billy
Williams, Ted
Wilson, Hack
Wright, George
Wright, Harry
Wynn, Early
Yastrzemski, Carl
Yawkey, Tom
Young, Cy
Youngs, Ross

All-Star Baseball Games, 1933-1990

Year	Winner	Score	Location	Year	Winner	Score	Location
1933	American	4-2	Chicago	1962	National (3)	3-1	Washington
1934	American	9-7	New York	1962	American	9-4	Chicago
1935	American	4-1	Cleveland	1963	National	5-3	Cleveland
1936	National	4-3	Boston	1964	National	7-4	New York
1937	American	8-3	Washington	1965	National	6-5	Minnesota
1938	National	4-1	Cincinnati	1966	National (3)	2-1	St. Louis
1939	American	3-1	New York	1967	National (4)	2-1	Anaheim
1940	National	4-0	St. Louis	1968*	National	1-0	Houston
1941	American	7-5	Detroit	1969	National	9-3	Washington
1942	American	3-1	New York	1970*	National (2)	5-4	Cincinnati
1943*	American	5-3	Philadelphia	1971*	American	6-4	Detroit
1944*	National	7-1	Pittsburgh	1972*	National	4-3	Atlanta
1945	(not played)			1973*	National	7-1	Kansas City
1946	American	12-0	Boston	1974*	National	7-2	Pittsburgh
1947	American	2-1	Chicago	1975*	National	6-3	Milwaukee
1948	American	5-2	St. Louis	1976*	National	7-1	Philadelphia
1949	American	11-7	New York	1977*	National	7-5	New York
1950	National (1)	4-3	Chicago	1978*	National	7-3	San Diego
1951	National	8-3	Detroit	1979*	National	7-6	Seattle
1952	National	3-2	Philadelphia	1980*	National	4-2	Los Angeles
1953	National	5-1	Cincinnati	1981*	National	5-4	Cleveland
1954	American	11-9	Cleveland	1982*	National	4-1	Montreal
1955	National (2)	6-5	Milwaukee	1983*	American	13-3	Chicago
1956	National	7-3	Washington	1984*	National	3-1	San Francisco
1957	American	6-5	St. Louis	1985*	National	6-1	Minneapolis
1958	American	4-3	Baltimore	1986*	American	3-2	Houston
1959	National	5-4	Pittsburgh	1987*	National (5)	2-0	Oakland
1959	American	5-3	Los Angeles	1988*	American	2-1	Cincinnati
1960	National	5-3	Kansas City	1989*	American	5-3	Anaheim
1960	National	6-0	New York	1990*	American	2-0	Chicago
1961	National (3)	5-4	San Francisco				
1961	Called-rain	1-1	Boston				

(1) 14 innings, (2) 12 innings, (3) 10 innings, (4) 15 innings (5) 13 innings. *Night game.

American League Records in 1990

Final Standings

Eastern Division

	W	L	Pct	GB	Home	Away	vs West	One Run	After 7 Lead	After 7 Trail	Runs Avg	Runs vs.
Boston	88	74	.543	—	51-30	37-44	37-47	31-22	65-7	7-55	4.3	4.1
Toronto.	86	76	.531	2	44-37	42-39	42-41	23-27	75-1	5-63	4.7	4.1
Detroit.	79	83	.488	9	39-42	40-41	43-40	22-22	69-6	3-69	4.6	4.6
Cleveland	77	85	.475	11	41-40	36-45	43-41	16-24	63-3	6-75	4.5	4.5
Baltimore.	76	85	.472	11½	40-40	36-45	42-41	22-26	55-8	7-68	4.2	4.3
Milwaukee	74	88	.457	14	39-42	35-46	31-52	17-23	63-8	5-71	4.5	4.7
New York	67	95	.414	21	37-44	30-51	30-54	23-29	52-6	5-80	3.7	4.6

Western Division

	W	L	Pct	GB	Home	Away	vs East	One Run	After 7 Lead	After 7 Trail	Runs Avg	Runs vs.
Oakland	103	59	.636	—	51-30	52-29	56-27	24-17	84-2	7-52	4.5	3.6
Chicago	94	68	.580	9	49-31	45-37	46-37	30-22	80-7	5-51	4.2	3.9
Texas.	83	79	.512	20	47-35	36-44	45-38	37-21	65-5	7-64	4.2	4.3
California	80	82	.494	23	42-39	38-43	42-42	23-21	62-3	5-69	4.3	4.4
Seattle	77	85	.475	26	38-43	39-42	40-44	20-27	63-6	6-64	3.9	4.2
Kansas City . . .	75	86	.466	27½	45-36	30-50	41-40	26-26	66-8	3-70	4.4	4.4
Minnesota	74	88	.457	29	41-40	33-48	42-41	21-20	62-4	2-76	4.1	4.4

American League Championship Series

Oakland 9, Boston 1   Oakland 4, Boston 1
Oakland 4, Boston 1   Oakland 3, Boston 1

Team Batting

	Avg.	AB	R	H	HR	RBI
Boston	.272	5516	699	1502	106	660
Cleveland	.267	5485	732	1465	110	675
Kansas City . . .	.267	5488	707	1465	100	660
Minnesota	.265	5499	666	1458	100	625
Toronto	.265	5589	767	1479	167	729
California	.260	5570	690	1448	147	646
Seattle	.259	5474	640	1419	107	610
Texas	.259	5469	676	1416	110	641
Detroit	.259	5479	750	1418	172	714
Chicago	.258	5402	682	1393	106	637
Milwaukee	.256	5503	732	1408	128	680
Oakland	.254	5433	733	1379	164	693
Baltimore	.245	5410	669	1328	132	623
New York	.241	5483	603	1322	147	561

Team Pitching

	ERA	IP	H	BB	SO	Sv
Oakland	3.18	1456	1287	494	831	64
Chicago	3.61	1449	1313	548	914	68
Seattle	3.69	1443	1319	606	1064	41
Boston	3.72	1442	1439	519	997	44
California	3.79	1454	1482	544	944	42
Texas	3.83	1444	1343	623	997	36
Toronto	3.84	1454	1434	445	892	48
Kansas City . . .	3.93	1420	1449	560	1006	33
Baltimore	4.04	1435	1445	537	776	43
Milwaukee	4.08	1445	1558	469	771	42
Minnesota	4.12	1435	1509	489	872	43
New York	4.21	1444	1430	618	909	41
Cleveland	4.26	1427	1491	518	860	47
Detroit	4.39	1430	1401	661	856	44

Individual Batting (at least 115 at-bats); Individual Pitching (at least 50 innings)

*Left-handed batter, pitcher; **Switch hitter

Baltimore Orioles

Batting	Avg	AB	R	H	HR	RBI
B. Ripken	.291	406	48	118	3	38
Orsulak*	.269	413	49	111	11	57
Milligan	.265	362	64	96	20	60
Finley*	.256	464	46	119	3	37
Hulett	.255	153	16	39	3	16
C. Ripken	.250	600	78	150	21	84
Horn*	.248	246	30	61	14	45
Melvin	.243	301	30	73	5	37
Devereaux	.240	367	48	88	12	49
Anderson*	.231	234	24	54	3	24
Kittle	.231	338	33	78	18	46
Worthington	.226	425	46	96	8	44
Tettleton**	.223	444	68	99	15	51

Pitching	W	L	ERA	IP	BB	SO	Sv
Williamson	8	2	2.21	85.1	28	60	1
Olson	6	5	2.42	74.1	31	74	37
McDonald	8	5	2.43	118.2	35	65	0
Price*	3	4	3.58	65.1	24	54	0
Johnson	13	9	4.10	180.0	43	68	0
Harnisch	11	11	4.34	188.2	86	122	0
Milacki	5	8	4.46	135.1	61	60	0
Holton	2	3	4.50	58.0	21	27	0
Mitchell	6	6	4.64	114.1	48	43	0
Ballard*	2	11	4.93	133.1	42	50	0

Boston Red Sox

Batting	Avg	AB	R	H	HR	RBI
Boggs*	.302	619	89	187	6	63
Greenwell*	.297	610	71	181	14	73
Burks	.296	588	89	174	21	89
Jo. Reed	.289	598	70	173	5	51
Quintana	.287	512	56	147	7	67
Romine	.272	136	21	37	2	14
Brunansky	.267	461	61	123	15	71
Pena	.263	491	62	129	7	56
Evans	.249	445	66	111	13	63
Barrett	.226	159	15	36	0	13
Rivera	.225	346	38	78	7	45

Pitching	W	L	ERA	IP	BB	SO	Sv
Clemens	21	6	1.93	228.1	54	209	0
Reardon	5	3	3.16	51.1	19	33	21
Boddicker	17	8	3.36	228.0	69	143	0
Bolton	10	5	3.38	119.2	47	65	0
Kiecker	8	9	3.97	152.0	54	93	0
Harris	13	9	4.00	184.1	77	117	0
Gray	2	4	4.44	50.2	15	50	9
Lamp	3	5	4.68	105.2	30	49	0
Je. Reed	2	2	4.82	52.1	19	19	2
Gardner	3	7	4.89	77.1	35	58	0
Murphy*	0	6	6.32	57.0	32	54	7

California Angels

Batting	Avg	AB	R	H	HR	RBI
Polonia*	.335	403	52	135	2	35
Anderson	.308	143	16	44	1	5
Ray**	.277	404	47	112	5	43
Downing	.273	330	47	90	14	51
Parrish	.268	470	54	126	24	70
Joyner*	.268	310	35	83	8	41
Schu	.268	157	19	42	6	14
Winfield	.267	475	70	127	21	78
Davis**	.265	412	58	109	12	58
Hill**	.264	352	36	93	3	32
Venable*	.259	189	26	49	4	21
Bichette	.255	349	40	89	15	53
Schofield	.255	310	41	79	1	18
Howell*	.228	316	35	72	8	33
White**	.217	443	57	96	11	44
Stevens	.214	248	228	53	7	32

Pitching	W	L	ERA	IP	BB	SO	Sv
Finley*	18	9	2.40	236.0	81	177	0
Fraser	5	4	3.08	76.0	24	32	2
Eichhorn	2	5	3.08	84.2	23	69	13
Harvey	4	4	3.22	64.1	35	82	25
McCaskill	12	11	3.25	174.1	72	78	0
Fetters	1	1	4.12	67.2	20	35	1
Langston*	10	17	4.40	223.0	104	195	0
Abbott*	10	14	4.51	211.2	72	105	0
Blyleven	8	7	5.24	134.0	25	69	0

Chicago White Sox

Batting	Avg	AB	R	H	HR	RBI
Thomas	.330	191	39	63	7	31
Fisk	.285	452	65	129	18	65
Johnson*	.285	541	76	154	1	51
Guillen*	.279	516	61	144	1	58
Pasqua*	.274	325	43	89	13	58
Calderon	.273	607	85	166	14	74
Bradley	.256	422	59	108	4	31
Ventura*	.249	493	48	123	5	54
Karkovice	.246	183	30	45	6	20
Fletcher	.242	509	54	123	4	56
Sosa	.233	532	72	124	15	70
Martinez	.224	272	18	61	4	24
Lyons*	.192	146	22	28	1	11

Pitching	W	L	ERA	IP	BB	SO	Sv
Thigpen	4	6	1.83	88.2	32	70	57
Jones	11	4	2.31	74.0	33	45	1
Hibbard*	14	9	3.16	211.0	55	92	0
Edwards*	5	3	3.22	95.0	41	63	2
King	12	4	3.28	151.0	40	70	0
Pall	3	5	3.32	76.0	24	39	2
Patterson*	2	1	3.39	66.1	34	40	2
Fernandez	5	5	3.80	87.2	34	61	0
McDowell	14	9	3.82	205.0	77	165	0
Peterson	2	5	4.55	85.0	26	29	0
Perez	13	14	4.61	197.0	86	161	0
Radinsky*	6	1	4.82	52.1	36	46	4

Cleveland Indians

Batting	Avg	AB	R	H	HR	RBI
Cole*	.300	227	43	68	0	13
C. James	.299	528	62	158	12	70
Jacoby	.293	553	77	162	14	75
Alomar	.290	445	60	129	9	66
D. James*	.274	248	28	68	1	22
Maldonado	.273	590	76	161	22	95
Browne**	.267	513	92	137	6	50
Brookens	.266	154	18	41	1	20
Baerga**	.260	312	46	81	7	47
Fermin	.256	414	47	106	1	40
Skinner	.252	139	16	35	2	16
Webster**	.252	437	58	110	12	55
Snyder	.233	438	46	102	14	55

Pitching	W	L	ERA	IP	BB	SO	Sv
Jones	5	5	2.56	84.1	22	55	43
Olin	4	4	3.41	92.1	26	64	1
Candiotti	15	11	3.65	202.0	55	128	0
Orosco*	5	4	3.90	64.2	38	55	2
Farrell	4	5	4.28	96.2	33	44	0
Swindell*	12	9	4.40	214.2	47	135	0
S. Valdez	6	6	4.75	102.1	35	63	0
Walker	2	6	4.88	75.2	42	34	0

Detroit Tigers

Batting	Avg	AB	R	H	HR	RBI
Trammell	.304	559	71	170	14	89
Fryman	.297	232	32	69	9	27
Bergman*	.278	205	21	57	2	26
Fielder	.277	573	104	159	51	132
Heath	.270	370	46	100	7	38
Sheets*	.261	360	40	94	10	52
Lemon	.258	322	39	83	5	32
Ward	.256	309	32	79	9	46
Phillips**	.251	573	97	144	8	55
Moseby*	.248	431	64	107	14	51
Shelby**	.248	222	22	55	4	20
Whitaker*	.237	472	75	112	18	60
Salas*	.232	164	18	38	9	24
Coles	.209	215	22	45	3	20

Pitching	W	L	ERA	IP	BB	SO	Sv
Nunez	3	1	2.24	80.1	37	66	6
Gleaton*	1	3	2.94	82.2	25	56	13
Gibson*	5	4	3.05	97.1	44	56	3
Henneman	8	6	3.05	94.1	33	50	22
Parker	3	3	3.58	73.0	32	40	0
Petry	10	9	4.45	149.2	77	73	0
Morris	15	18	4.51	249.2	97	162	0
Terrell	6	4	4.54	75.1	24	30	0
Searcy*	2	7	4.66	75.1	51	66	0
DuBois*	3	5	5.09	58.1	22	34	0
Tanana*	9	8	5.31	176.1	66	114	1
Robinson	10	9	5.96	145.0	88	76	0

Kansas City Royals

Batting	Avg	AB	R	H	HR	RBI
Brett*	.329	544	82	179	14	87
Wilson**	.290	307	49	89	2	42
McRae**	.286	168	21	48	2	23
Eisenreich*	.280	496	61	139	5	51
Seitzer	.275	622	91	171	6	38
Tabler	.272	195	12	53	1	19
Jackson	.272	405	74	110	28	78
Tartabull	.268	313	41	84	15	60
MacFarlane	.255	400	37	102	6	58
Perry*	.254	465	57	118	8	57
Stillwell**	.249	506	60	126	3	51
Pecota	.242	240	43	58	5	20
White	.216	241	20	52	2	21

Pitching	W	L	ERA	IP	BB	SO	Sv
Farr	13	7	1.98	127.0	48	94	1
Montgomery	6	5	2.39	94.1	34	94	24
Appier	12	8	2.76	185.2	54	127	0
McGaffigan	4	3	3.09	78.2	28	49	1
Aquino	4	1	3.16	68.1	27	28	0
Saberhagen	5	9	3.27	135.0	28	87	0
Gordon	12	11	3.73	195.1	99	175	0
Crawford	5	4	4.16	80.0	23	54	1
Gubicza	4	7	4.50	94.0	38	71	0
S. Davis	7	10	4.74	112.0	35	62	0
M. Davis*	2	7	5.11	68.2	52	73	6

Milwaukee Brewers

Batting	Avg	AB	R	H	HR	RBI
Hamilton*	.295	156	27	46	1	18
Sheffield	.294	487	67	143	10	67
Parker*	.289	610	71	176	21	92
Molitor	.285	418	64	119	12	45
Surhoff*	.276	474	55	131	6	59
Felder**	.274	237	38	65	3	27
Diaz	.271	218	27	59	0	14
Gantner*	.263	323	36	85	0	25
Brock*	.248	367	42	91	7	50
Yount	.247	587	98	145	17	77
Spiers*	.242	363	44	88	2	36
Vaughn	.220	382	51	84	17	61
Deer	.209	440	57	92	27	69

Pitching	W	L	ERA	IP	BB	SO	Sv
Robinson	12	5	2.91	148.1	37	57	0
Crim	3	5	3.47	85.2	23	39	11
Higuera*	11	10	3.76	170.0	50	129	0
Mirabella	4	2	3.97	59.0	27	28	0
Krueger*	6	8	3.98	129.0	54	64	0
Bosio	4	9	4.00	132.2	38	76	0
Knudson	10	9	4.12	168.1	40	56	0
Plesac*	3	7	4.43	69.0	31	65	24
Edens	4	5	4.45	89.0	33	40	2
Navarro	8	7	4.46	149.1	41	75	1

Minnesota Twins

Batting

Batting	Avg	AB	R	H	HR	RBI
Ortiz	.335	170	18	57	0	18
Mack	.326	313	50	102	8	44
Puckett	.298	551	82	164	12	80
Harper	.294	479	61	141	6	54
Hrbek*	.287	492	61	141	22	79
Gladden	.275	534	64	147	5	40
Larkin**	.269	401	46	108	5	42
Bush*	.243	181	17	44	6	18
Newman**	.242	388	43	94	0	30
Manrique	.237	228	22	54	5	29
Gagne	.235	388	38	91	7	38
Liriano**	.234	355	46	83	1	28
Gaetti	.229	577	61	132	16	85
Moses**	.221	172	26	38	1	14

Pitching

Pitching	W	L	ERA	IP	BB	SO	Sv
Aguilera	5	3	2.76	65.1	19	61	32
Erickson	8	4	2.87	113.0	51	53	0
Leach	2	5	3.20	81.2	21	46	2
Berenguer	8	5	3.41	100.1	58	77	0
Guthrie*	7	9	3.79	144.2	39	101	0
Tapani	12	8	4.07	159.1	29	101	0
Drummond	3	5	4.35	91.0	36	49	1
Anderson*	7	18	4.53	188.2	39	82	0
Smith	5	10	4.81	153.1	47	67	0
West*	7	9	5.10	146.1	78	92	0

New York Yankees

Batting

Batting	Avg	AB	R	H	HR	RBI
Cerone	.302	139	12	42	2	11
Kelly	.285	641	85	183	15	61
Sax	.260	615	70	160	4	42
Hall*	.258	360	41	93	12	46
Leyritz	.257	303	28	78	5	25
Mattingly*	.256	394	40	101	5	42
Maas*	.252	254	42	64	21	41
Nokes*	.248	351	33	87	11	40
Azocar*	.248	214	18	53	5	19
Barfield	.246	476	69	117	25	78
Espinoza	.224	438	31	98	2	20
Geren	.213	277	21	59	8	31
Valarde	.210	229	21	48	5	19
Balboni	.192	266	24	51	17	34
Blowers	.188	144	16	27	5	21

Pitching

Pitching	W	L	ERA	IP	BB	SO	Sv
Plunk	6	3	2.72	72.2	43	67	0
Guetterman*	11	7	3.39	93.0	26	48	2
Robinson	3	6	3.45	88.2	34	43	0
Righetti*	1	1	3.57	53.0	26	43	36
Witt	5	9	4.00	117.0	47	74	1
LaPoint*	7	10	4.11	157.2	57	67	0
Leary	9	19	4.11	208.0	78	138	0
Cadaret*	5	4	4.15	121.1	64	80	3
Cary*	6	12	4.19	156.2	55	134	0
Hawkins	5	12	5.37	157.2	82	74	0
Jones	1	2	6.30	50.0	23	25	0

Oakland A's

Batting

Batting	Avg	AB	R	H	HR	RBI
R. Henderson	.325	489	119	159	28	61
Baines*	.284	415	52	118	16	65
J. Canseco	.274	481	83	132	37	101
D. Henderson	.271	450	65	122	20	63
Lansford	.268	507	58	136	3	50
Weiss**	.265	445	50	118	2	35
Jose**	.264	341	42	90	8	39
Randolph	.257	292	37	75	1	21
Steinbach	.251	379	32	95	9	57
McGwire	.235	523	87	123	39	108
Hassey*	.213	254	18	54	5	22
Gallego	.206	389	36	80	3	34
Jennings*	.192	156	19	30	2	14
Blankenship	.191	136	18	26	0	10

Pitching

Pitching	W	L	ERA	IP	BB	SO	Sv
Eckersley	4	2	0.61	73.1	4	73	48
Nelson	3	3	1.57	74.2	17	38	5
Stewart	22	11	2.56	267.0	83	166	0
Honeycutt*	2	2	2.70	63.1	22	38	7
Welch	27	6	2.95	238.0	77	127	0
Burns	3	3	2.97	78.2	32	43	3
Sanderson	17	11	3.88	206.1	66	128	0
Moore	13	15	4.65	199.1	84	73	0
Young*	9	6	4.85	124.1	53	56	0

Seattle Mariners

Batting

Batting	Avg	AB	R	H	HR	RBI
E. Martinez	.302	487	71	147	11	49
Griffey Jr.*	.300	597	91	179	22	80
Davis*	.283	494	63	140	17	68
Buhner	.276	163	16	45	7	33
Jones	.260	204	23	53	6	24
Cotto	.259	355	40	92	4	33
Reynolds**	.252	642	100	162	5	55
Leonard	.251	478	39	120	10	75
Vizquel**	.247	255	19	63	2	18
Briley*	.246	337	40	83	5	29
Brumley**	.224	147	19	33	0	7
O'Brien*	.224	366	32	82	5	27
Bradley*	.223	233	11	52	1	28
Valle	.214	308	37	66	7	33

Pitching

Pitching	W	L	ERA	IP	BB	SO	Sv
Schooler	1	4	2.25	56.0	16	45	30
Swift	6	4	2.39	128.0	21	42	6
Comstock	7	4	2.89	56.0	26	50	2
Hanson	18	9	3.24	236.0	68	211	0
Young*	8	18	3.51	225.1	107	176	0
Johnson*	14	11	3.65	219.2	120	194	0
Holman	11	11	4.03	189.2	66	121	0
Jackson	5	7	4.54	77.1	44	69	3

Texas Rangers

Batting

Batting	Avg	AB	R	H	HR	RBI
Palmeiro*	.319	598	72	191	14	89
Daugherty**	.300	310	36	93	6	47
Franco	.296	582	96	172	11	69
Sierra**	.280	608	70	170	16	96
Petralli*	.255	325	28	83	0	21
Stanley	.249	189	21	47	2	19
Huson*	.240	396	57	95	0	28
Pettis**	.239	423	66	101	3	31
Incaviglia	.233	529	59	123	24	85
Buechele	.215	251	30	54	7	30
Coolbaugh	.200	180	21	36	2	13
Kunkel	.170	200	17	34	3	17

Pitching

Pitching	W	L	ERA	IP	BB	SO	Sv
Arnsberg	6	1	2.15	62.2	33	44	5
Rogers*	10	6	3.13	97.2	42	74	15
Witt	17	10	3.36	222.0	110	221	0
Ryan	13	9	3.44	204.0	74	232	0
Brown	12	10	3.60	180.0	60	88	0
Hough	12	12	4.07	218.2	119	114	0
Jeffcoat*	5	6	4.47	110.2	28	58	5
Moyer*	2	6	4.66	102.1	39	58	0

Toronto Blue Jays

Batting

Batting	Avg	AB	R	H	HR	RBI
McGriff*	.300	557	91	167	35	88
Borders	.286	346	36	99	15	49
Fernandez**	.276	635	84	175	4	66
Gruber	.274	592	92	162	31	118
Olerud*	.265	358	43	95	14	48
Wilson**	.265	588	81	156	3	51
Bell	.265	562	67	149	21	86
Felix**	.263	463	73	122	15	65
Lee**	.243	391	45	95	6	41
Myers*	.236	250	33	59	5	22
Hill	.231	260	47	60	12	32
Williams	.161	155	23	25	0	13

Pitching

Pitching	W	L	ERA	IP	BB	SO	Sv
Henke	2	4	2.17	74.2	19	75	32
Stieb	18	6	2.93	208.2	64	125	0
Wells*	11	6	3.14	189.0	45	115	3
Ward	2	8	3.45	127.2	42	112	11
Black*	13	11	3.57	206.2	61	106	0
Acker	4	4	3.83	91.2	30	54	1
Candelaria*	7	6	3.95	79.2	20	63	5
Blair	3	5	4.06	68.2	28	43	0
Key*	13	7	4.25	154.2	22	88	0
Stottlemyre	13	17	4.34	203.0	69	115	0
Wills	6	4	4.73	99.0	38	72	0
Cerutti	9	9	4.76	140.0	49	49	0

Most Valuable Player
Baseball Writers' Association
National League

Year	Player, team	Year	Player, team	Year	Player, team
1931	Frank Frisch, St. Louis	1951	Roy Campanella, Brooklyn	1971	Joe Torre, St. Louis
1932	Charles Klein, Philadelpha	1952	Hank Sauer, Chicago	1972	Johnny Bench, Cincinnati
1933	Carl Hubbell, New York	1953	Roy Campanella, Brooklyn	1973	Pete Rose, Cincinnati
1934	Dizzy Dean, St. Louis	1954	Willie Mays, New York	1974	Steve Garvey, Los Angeles
1935	Gabby Hartnett, Chicago	1955	Roy Campanella, Brooklyn	1975	Joe Morgan, Cincinnati
1936	Carl Hubbell, New York	1956	Don Newcombe, Brooklyn	1976	Joe Morgan, Cincinnati
1937	Joe Medwick, St. Louis	1957	Henry Aaron, Milwaukee	1977	George Foster, Cincinnati
1938	Ernie Lombardi, Cincinnati	1958	Ernie Banks, Chicago	1978	Dave Parker, Pittsburgh
1939	Bucky Walters, Cincinnati	1959	Ernie Banks, Chicago	1979	(tie) Willie Stargell, Pittsburgh
1940	Frank McCormick, Cincinnati	1960	Dick Groat, Pittsburgh		Keith Hernandez, St. Louis
1941	Dolph Camilli, Brooklyn	1961	Frank Robinson, Cincinnati	1980	Mike Schmidt, Philadelphia
1942	Mort Cooper, St. Louis	1962	Maury Wills, Los Angeles	1981	Mike Schmidt, Philadelphia
1943	Stan Musial, St. Louis	1963	Sandy Koufax, Los Angeles	1982	Dale Murphy, Atlanta
1944	Martin Marion, St. Louis	1964	Ken Boyer, St. Louis	1983	Dale Murphy, Atlanta
1945	Phil Cavarretta, Chicago	1965	Willie Mays, San Francisco	1984	Ryne Sandberg, Chicago
1946	Stan Musial, St. Louis	1966	Roberto Clemente, Pittsburgh	1985	Willie McGee, St. Louis
1947	Bob Elliott, Boston	1967	Orlando Cepeda, St. Louis	1986	Mike Schmidt, Philadelphia
1948	Stan Musial, St. Louis	1968	Bob Gibson, St. Louis	1987	Andre Dawson, Chicago
1949	Jackie Robinson, Brooklyn	1969	Willie McCovey, San Francisco	1988	Kirk Gibson, Los Angeles
1950	Jim Konstanty, Philadelphia	1970	Johnny Bench, Cincinnati	1989	Kevin Mitchell, San Francisco

American League

Year	Player, team	Year	Player, team	Year	Player, team
1931	Lefty Grove, Philadelphia	1951	Yogi Berra, New York	1971	Vida Blue, Oakland
1932	Jimmy Foxx, Philadelphia	1952	Bobby Shantz, Philadelphia	1972	Dick Allen, Chicago
1933	Jimmy Foxx, Philadelphia	1953	Al Rosen, Cleveland	1973	Reggie Jackson, Oakland
1934	Mickey Cochrane, Detroit	1954	Yogi Berra, New York	1974	Jeff Burroughs, Texas
1935	Henry Greenberg, Detroit	1955	Yogi Berra, New York	1975	Fred Lynn, Boston
1936	Lou Gehrig, New York	1956	Mickey Mantle, New York	1976	Thurman Munson, New York
1937	Charley Gehringer, Detroit	1957	Mickey Mantle, New York	1977	Rod Carew, Minnesota
1938	Jimmy Foxx, Boston	1958	Jackie Jensen, Boston	1978	Jim Rice, Boston
1939	Joe DiMaggio, New York	1959	Nellie Fox, Chicago	1979	Don Baylor, California
1940	Hank Greenberg, Detroit	1960	Roger Maris, New York	1980	George Brett, Kansas City
1941	Joe DiMaggio, New York	1961	Roger Maris, New York	1981	Rollie Fingers, Milwaukee
1942	Joe Gordon, New York	1962	Mickey Mantle, New York	1982	Robin Yount, Milwaukee
1943	Spurgeon Chandler, New York	1963	Elston Howard, New York	1983	Cal Ripken Jr., Baltimore
1944	Hal Newhouser, Detroit	1964	Brooks Robinson, Baltimore	1984	Willie Hernandez, Detroit
1945	Hal Newhouser, Detroit	1965	Zoilo Versalles, Minnesota	1985	Don Mattingly, New York
1946	Ted Williams, Boston	1966	Frank Robinson, Baltimore	1986	Roger Clemens, Boston
1947	Joe DiMaggio, New York	1967	Carl Yastrzemski, Boston	1987	George Bell, Toronto
1948	Lou Boudreau, Cleveland	1968	Denny McLain, Detroit	1988	Jose Canseco, Oakland
1949	Ted Williams, Boston	1969	Harmon Killebrew, Minnesota	1989	Robin Yount, Milwaukee
1950	Phil Rizzuto, New York	1970	John (Boog) Powell, Baltimore		

Rookie of the Year
Baseball Writers' Association

1947—Combined selection—Jackie Robinson, Brooklyn, 1b
1948—Combined selection—Alvin Dark, Boston, N.L. ss

National League

Year	Player, team	Year	Player, team	Year	Player, team
1949	Don Newcombe, Brooklyn, p	1964	Richie Allen, Philadelphia, 3b	1977	Andre Dawson, Montreal, of
1950	Sam Jethroe, Boston, of	1965	Jim Lefebvre, Los Angeles, 2b	1978	Bob Horner, Atlanta, 3b
1951	Willie Mays, New York, of	1966	Tommy Helms, Cincinnati, 2b	1979	Rick Sutcliffe, Los Angeles, p
1952	Joe Black, Brooklyn, p	1967	Tom Seaver, New York, p	1980	Steve Howe, Los Angeles, p
1953	Jim Gilliam, Brooklyn, 2b	1968	Johnny Bench, Cincinnati c	1981	Fernando Valenzuela, Los Angeles, p
1954	Wally Moon, St. Louis, of	1969	Ted Sizemore, Los Angeles, 2b		
1955	Bill Virdon, St. Louis, of	1970	Carl Morton, Montreal, p	1982	Steve Sax, Los Angeles, 2b
1956	Frank Robinson, Cincinnati, of	1971	Earl Williams, Atlanta, c	1983	Darryl Strawberry, New York, of
1957	Jack Sanford, Philadelphia, p	1972	Jon Matlack, New York, p	1984	Dwight Gooden, New York, p
1958	Orlando Cepeda, S.F., 1b	1973	Gary Matthews, S.F., of	1985	Vince Coleman, St. Louis, of
1959	Willie McCovey, S.F., 1b	1974	Bake McBride, St. Louis, of	1986	Todd Worrell, St. Louis, p
1960	Frank Howard, Los Angeles, of	1975	John Montefusco, S.F., p	1987	Benito Santiago, San Diego, c
1961	Billy Williams, Chicago, of	1976	(tie) Butch Metzger, San Diego, p	1988	Chris Sabo, Cincinnati, 3b
1962	Ken Hubbs, Chicago, 2b		Pat Zachry, Cincinnati, p	1989	Jerome Walton, Chicago, of
1963	Pete Rose, Cincinnati, 2b				

American League

Year	Player, team	Year	Player, team	Year	Player, team
1949	Roy Sievers, St. Louis, of	1963	Gary Peters, Chicago, p	1977	Eddie Murray, Baltimore, dh
1950	Walt Dropo, Boston, 1b	1964	Tony Oliva, Minnesota, of	1978	Lou Whitaker, Detroit, 2b
1951	Gil McDougald, New York, 3b	1965	Curt Blefary, Baltimore, of	1979	(tie) John Castino, Minnesota, 3b
1952	Harry Byrd, Philadelphia, p	1966	Tommie Agee, Chicago, of		Alfredo Griffin, Toronto, ss
1953	Harvey Kuenn, Detroit, ss	1967	Rod Carew, Minnesota, 2b	1980	Joe Charboneau, Cleveland, of
1954	Bob Grim, New York, p	1968	Stan Bahnsen, New York, p	1981	Dave Righetti, New York, p
1955	Herb Score, Cleveland, p	1969	Lou Piniella, Kansas City, of	1982	Cal Ripken Jr., Baltimore, ss, 3b
1956	Luis Aparicio, Chicago, ss	1970	Thurman Munson, New York, c	1983	Ron Kittle, Chicago, of
1957	Tony Kubek, New York, if-of	1971	Chris Chambliss, Cleveland, 1b	1984	Alvin Davis, Seattle, 1B
1958	Albie Pearson, Washington, of	1972	Carlton Fisk, Boston, c	1985	Ozzie Guillen, Chicago, ss
1959	Bob Allison, Washington, of	1973	Al Bumbry, Baltimore, of	1986	Jose Canseco, Oakland, of
1960	Ron Hansen, Baltimore, ss	1974	Mike Hargrove, Texas, 1b	1987	Mark McGwire, Oakland, 1b
1961	Don Schwall, Boston, p	1975	Fred Lynn, Boston, of	1988	Walt Weiss, Oakland, ss
1962	Tom Tresh, New York, if-of	1976	Mark Fidrych, Detroit, p	1989	Gregg Olson, Baltimore, p

1990 World Series Composite Box Score

Oakland Athletics

	g	ab	r	h	2b	3b	hr	rbi	so	bb	avg	po	a	e	pct
Doug Jennings ph	1	1	0	1	0	0	0	0	0	0	1.000	0	0	0	.000
Rickey Henderson lf	4	15	2	5	2	0	1	1	4	3	.333	12	1	0	1.000
Ron Hassey c	3	6	0	2	0	0	0	1	0	0	.333	2	0	1	.667
Carney Lansford 3b	4	15	0	4	0	0	0	1	0	1	.267	1	14	0	1.000
Willie Randolph 2b	4	15	0	4	0	0	0	0	0	1	.267	14	12	0	1.000
Dave Henderson cf	4	13	2	3	1	0	0	0	3	1	.231	7	0	0	1.000
Mark McGwire 1b	4	14	1	3	0	0	0	0	4	2	.214	42	1	2	.956
Willie McGee cf	4	10	1	2	1	0	0	0	2	0	.200	5	0	0	1.000
Harold Baines dh	3	7	1	1	0	0	1	2	2	1	.143	0	0	0	.000
Terry Steinbach c	3	8	0	1	0	0	0	0	1	0	.125	8	1	0	1.000
Mike Gallego ss	4	11	0	1	0	0	0	1	3	1	.091	7	10	1	.944
Jose Canseco rf	4	12	1	1	0	0	2	3	3	2	.083	4	0	1	1.000
Jamie Quirk c	1	3	0	0	0	0	0	0	2	0	.000	2	2	0	1.000
Bob Welch p	1	3	0	0	0	0	0	0	2	0	.000	0	2	0	1.000
Dave Stewart p	2	1	0	0	0	0	0	0	1	0	.000	0	2	0	1.000
Lance Blankenship ph	1	1	0	0	0	0	0	0	1	0	.000	2	1	1	.750
Mike Bordick ss	3	0	0	0	0	0	0	0	0	0	.000	0	0	0	.000
Todd Burns p	2	0	0	0	0	0	0	0	0	0	.000	0	1	0	1.000
Dennis Eckersley p	2	0	0	0	0	0	0	0	0	0	.000	0	0	0	.000
Gene Nelson p	2	0	0	0	0	0	0	0	0	0	.000	0	0	0	.000
Scott Sanderson p	2	0	0	0	0	0	0	0	0	0	.000	0	0	0	.000
Rick Honeycutt p	1	0	0	0	0	0	0	0	0	0	.000	0	0	0	.000
Joe Klink p	1	0	0	0	0	0	0	0	0	0	.000	0	0	0	.000
Mike Moore p	1	0	0	0	0	0	0	0	0	0	.000	0	0	0	.000
Curt Young p	1	0	0	0	0	0	0	0	0	0	.000	0	0	0	.000
Totals	4	135	8	28	4	0	3	8	28	12	.207	106	46	5	.968

Cincinnati Reds

	g	ab	r	h	2b	3b	hr	rbi	so	bb	avg	po	a	e	pct
Billy Bates ph	1	1	1	1	0	0	0	0	0	0	1.000	0	0	0	.000
Ron Oester ph	1	1	0	1	0	0	0	0	0	0	1.000	0	0	0	.000
Billy Hatcher cf	4	12	6	9	4	1	0	1	0	2	.750	0	0	0	.000
Chris Sabo 3b	4	16	2	9	1	0	2	5	2	2	.563	11	14	0	1.000
Herm Winningham cf	2	4	1	2	1	0	0	2	2	2	.500	3	0	0	1.000
Barry Larkin ss	4	17	3	6	1	1	0	1	0	2	.353	1	14	0	1.000
Joe Oliver c	4	18	2	6	3	0	0	2	1	0	.333	28	0	3	.903
Jose Rijo p	2	3	0	1	0	0	0	0	0	0	.333	0	2	0	1.000
Eric Davis lf	4	14	3	4	0	0	1	5	0	0	.286	4	0	0	1.000
Todd Benzinger 1b	4	11	1	2	0	0	0	0	0	0	.182	23	0	0	1.000
Mariano Duncan 2b	4	14	1	2	1	0	0	1	2	2	.143	9	9	0	1.000
Paul O'Neill rf	4	12	2	1	0	0	0	1	2	2	.083	9	1	0	1.000
Hal Morris 1b	4	14	0	1	0	0	0	0	2	5	.071	11	0	0	1.000
Glenn Braggs lf	2	4	0	0	0	0	0	2	1	1	.000	18	1	0	1.000
Danny Jackson p	1	1	0	0	0	0	0	0	0	1	.000	0	0	0	.000
Rob Dibble p	3	0	0	0	0	0	0	0	1	0	.000	0	1	1	.500
Randy Myers p	3	0	0	0	0	0	0	0	0	0	.000	1	3	0	1.000
Jack Armstrong p	1	0	0	0	0	0	0	0	0	0	.000	0	0	0	.000
Tom Browning p	1	0	0	0	0	0	0	0	0	0	.000	0	0	0	.000
Norm Charlton p	1	0	0	0	0	0	0	0	0	0	.000	0	0	0	.000
Scott Scudder p	1	0	0	0	0	0	0	0	0	0	.000	0	0	0	.000
Totals	4	142	22	45	9	2	3	22	9	15	.317	111	41	4	.974

Pitching Summary

Oakland Athletics

	g	cg	ip	h	r	bb	so	hb	wp	w	l	sv	pct	er	era
Gene Nelson	2	0	5	3	0	2	0	0	0	0	0	0	.000	0	0.00
Rick Honeycutt	1	0	1⅔	2	0	1	0	0	0	0	0	0	.000	0	0.00
Curt Young	1	0	1	1	0	0	0	0	0	0	0	0	.000	0	0.00
Joe Klink	1	0	0	0	0	1	0	0	0	0	0	0	.000	0	0.00
Dave Stewart	2	1	13	10	6	6	5	1	0	0	2	0	.000	5	3.46
Bob Welch	1	0	7⅓	9	4	2	2	0	0	0	2	0	.000	4	4.91
Mike Moore	1	0	2⅔	8	6	0	0	0	0	0	1	0	.000	2	6.75
Dennis Eckersley	2	0	1⅓	3	1	0	1	0	0	0	1	0	.000	1	6.75
Scott Sanderson	2	0	1⅔	4	2	1	0	0	1	0	0	0	.000	2	10.80
Todd Burns	2	0	1⅔	5	3	2	0	0	1	0	0	0	.000	3	16.20
Totals	4	1	35⅓	45	22	15	9	1	2	0	4	0	.000	17	4.33

Cincinnati Reds

	g	cg	ip	h	r	bb	so	hb	wp	w	l	sv	pct	er	era
Rob Dibble	3	0	4⅔	3	0	1	4	0	1	1	0	0	1.000	0	0.00
Randy Myers	3	0	3	2	0	0	3	0	0	0	0	1	.000	0	0.00
Jack Armstrong	1	0	3	1	0	3	3	0	0	0	0	0	.000	0	0.00
Scott Scudder	1	0	1⅓	0	0	2	2	0	0	0	0	0	.000	0	0.00
Norm Charlton	1	0	1	1	0	0	0	0	0	0	0	0	.000	0	0.00
Jose Rijo	2	0	15⅓	9	1	5	14	0	0	2	0	0	1.000	1	0.59
Tom Browning	1	0	6	6	3	2	2	0	0	1	0	0	1.000	3	4.50
Danny Jackson	1	0	2⅔	6	4	2	0	0	0	0	0	0	1.000	3	10.13
Totals	4	0	37	28	8	12	28	0	1	4	0	0	1.000	7	1.70

Composite Score By Innings

Oakland	2	2	4	0	0	0	0	0	0	0	—		8
Cincinnati	4	1	9	1	3	0	0	3	0	1	—		22

1990 World Series

First Game

Oakland	ab	r	h	bi	Cincinnati	ab	r	h	bi
R. Henderson, lf	5	0	3	0	Larkin, ss	4	1	0	0
McGee, cf	5	0	1	0	Hatcher, cf	3	3	3	1
Canseco, rf	2	0	0	0	O'Neill, rf	2	1	0	1
McGwire, 1b	3	0	0	0	Davis, lf	4	2	2	3
Lansford, 3b	4	0	2	0	Morris, 1b	4	0	1	0
Steinbach, c	4	0	1	0	Sabo, 3b	3	0	1	2
Randolph, 2b	4	0	1	0	Oliver, c	4	0	1	0
Gallego, ss	4	0	0	0	Duncan, 2b	3	0	1	0
Stewart, p	1	0	0	0	Rijo, p	3	0	1	0
Jennings, ph	1	0	1	0	Dibble, p	0	0	0	0
Burns, p	0	0	0	0	Benzinger, ph	1	0	0	0
Nelson, p	0	0	0	0	Myers, p	0	0	0	0
Hassey, ph	1	0	0	0					
Sanderson, p	0	0	0	0					
Eckersley, p	0	0	0	0					
D.Henderson, ph	1	0	0	0					
Totals	**35**	**0**	**9**	**0**	**Totals**	**31**	**7**	**10**	**7**

```
Oakland . . . . . . . . . .   0 0 0   0 0 0   0 0 0—0
Cincinnati . . . . . . . . .  2 0 2   0 3 0   0 x—7
```

Oakland	ip	h	r	er	bb	so
Stewart L, 0-1	4	3	4	4	4	3
Burns	⅔	4	3	3	1	0
Nelson	1⅓	2	0	0	1	0
Sanderson	1	1	0	0	0	0
Eckersley	1	0	0	0	0	1
Cincinnati						
Rijo W, 1-0	7	7	0	0	2	5
Dibble	1	1	0	0	1	0
Myers	1	1	0	0	0	2

E - Gallego. DP - Oakland 2, Cincinnati 1. LOB - Oakland 11, Cincinnati 6. 2B - R. Henderson 2, Hatcher 2. HR - Davis (1). SB - McGee (1), Lansford (1).

How runs were scored—Two in Reds first: Hatcher walked. Davis hit a home run.

Two in Reds third: Larkin walked. Hatcher doubled scoring Larkin. O'Neill grounded out scoring Hatcher.

Three in Reds fifth: Larkin walked. Hatcher doubled. O'Neill walked. Davis singled scoring Hatcher. Morris grounded out advancing the runners. Sabo singled scoring O'Neill and Davis.

Third Game

Cincinnati	ab	r	h	bi	Oakland	ab	r	h	bi
Larkin, ss	5	0	2	1	R. Henderson, lf	3	1	1	1
Hatcher, cf	5	1	2	0	Lansford, 3b	3	0	0	0
O'Neill, rf	3	1	1	0	Canseco, rf	4	0	0	0
Davis, lf	5	1	2	1	D.Henderson, cf	4	1	1	0
Morris, dh	4	0	0	1	Baines, dh	4	1	1	2
Sabo, 3b	4	2	2	3	McGwire, 1b	4	0	1	0
Benzinger, 1b	5	1	2	0	Steinbach, c	4	0	0	0
Oliver, c	5	1	2	1	Randolph, 2b	4	0	3	0
Duncan, 2b	4	1	1	1	Gallego, ss	2	0	0	0
					McGee, ph	1	0	0	0
					Bordick, ss	0	0	0	0
					Blankenship, ph	1	0	0	0
Totals	**40**	**8**	**14**	**8**	**Totals**	**34**	**3**	**7**	**3**

```
Cincinnati . . . . . . . . .  0 1 7   0 0 0   0 0 0—8
Oakland . . . . . . . . . .   0 2 1   0 0 0   0 0 0—3
```

Cincinnati	ip	h	r	er	bb	so
Browning W,1-0	6	6	3	3	2	2
Dibble	1⅔	0	0	0	0	2
Myers	1⅓	1	0	0	0	1
Oakland						
Moore L, 0-1	2⅔	8	6	2	0	1
Sanderson	⅔	3	2	2	1	0
Klink	0	1	0	0	0	0
Nelson	3⅔	1	0	0	1	0
Burns	1	1	0	0	0	0
Young	1	0	0	0	0	1

E - McGwire, Oliver. DP - Oakland 2. LOB - Cincinnati 9, Oakland 6. 2B - D. Henderson, Oliver. 3B - Larkin. HR - Sabo 2 (2), Baines (1), R. Henderson (1). SB - Duncan (1), O'Neill (1), R. Henderson (2), Randolph (1).

How runs were scored—One in Reds second: Sabo hit a home run. Two in Athletics second: D. Henderson doubled. Baines hit a home run scoring D. Henderson.

Seven in Reds third: Hatcher singled. O'Neill was safe on an error. Davis singled scoring Hatcher. Morris grounded out scoring O'Neill. Sabo hit a home run scoring Davis. Benzinger singled. Oliver doubled scoring Benzinger. Duncan singled scoring Oliver. Larkin tripled scoring Duncan.

One in Athletics third: R. Henderson hit a home run.

Second Game

Oakland	ab	r	h	bi	Cincinnati	ab	r	h	bi
R. Henderson, lf	4	1	1	0	Larkin, ss	5	1	3	0
Lansford, 3b	4	0	1	0	Hatcher, cf	4	2	4	1
Canseco, rf	5	1	1	2	O'Neill, rf	4	0	0	0
McGwire, 1b	4	1	2	0	Davis, lf	5	0	0	1
D.Henderson, cf	4	1	2	0	Morris, 1b	3	0	0	0
Steinbach, c	0	0	0	0	Braggs, ph	1	0	0	0
Randolph, 2b	4	0	0	0	Dibble, p	0	0	0	0
Hassey, c	4	0	2	1	Bates, ph	1	1	1	0
Bordick, pr-ss	0	0	0	0	Sabo, 3b	5	0	3	0
Gallego, ss	4	0	1	1	Oliver, c	5	1	2	1
Baines, ph	1	0	0	0	Duncan, 2b	3	0	0	0
Eckersley, p	0	0	0	0	Jackson, p	1	0	0	0
Welch, p	3	0	0	0	Scudder, p	0	0	0	0
Honeycutt, p	0	0	0	0	Oester, ph	1	0	1	1
McGee, cf	0	0	0	0	Armstrong, p	0	0	0	0
					Winningham, ph	1	0	0	0
					Charlton, p	0	0	0	0
					Benzinger, 1b	1	0	0	0
Totals	**37**	**4**	**10**	**4**	**Totals**	**40**	**5**	**14**	**5**

```
Oakland . . . . . . . . . .   1 0 3   0 0 0   0 0 0—4
Cincinnati . . . . . . . . .  2 0 0   1 0 0   0 1 0   1—5
```

Oakland	ip	h	r	er	bb	so
Welch	7⅓	9	4	4	2	2
Honeycutt	1⅔	2	0	0	1	0
Eckersley L, 0-1	⅓	3	1	0	0	0
Cincinnati						
Jackson	2⅔	6	4	3	2	0
Scudder	1⅓	0	0	0	2	2
Armstrong	3	1	0	0	0	3
Charlton	1	1	0	0	0	0
Dibble W, 1-0	2	2	0	0	0	2

E - Jackson, Oliver, Hassey, McGwire. DP - Cincinnati 1. LOB - Oakland 10, Cincinnati 10. 2B - Larkin, Hatcher 2, Oliver. 3B - Hatcher. HR - Canseco (1). SB - R. Henderson (1). S - Lansford, Welch. SF - Hassey.

How runs were scored—One in Athletics first: R. Henderson singled, stole second, and went to third on a ground out. Canseco grounded out scoring R. Henderson.

Two in Reds first: Larkin doubled. Hatcher doubled scoring Larkin. Davis grounded out scoring Hatcher.

Three in Athletics third: Canseco hit a home run. McGwire singled. D. Henderson and Randolph walked. Hassey hit a sacrifice fly scoring McGwire. Gallego singled scoring D. Henderson.

One in Reds fourth: Oliver doubled. Oester singled scoring Oliver.

One in Reds eighth: Hatcher tripled. Braggs grounded out scoring Hatcher.

One in Reds tenth: Bates and Sabo singled. Oliver singled scoring Bates.

Fourth Game

Cincinnati	ab	r	h	bi	Oakland	ab	r	h	bi
Larkin, ss	3	1	1	0	R. Henderson, lf	3	0	0	0
Hatcher, cf	0	0	0	0	McGee, rf	4	1	1	0
Winningham, cf	3	1	2	0	D.Henderson, cf	4	0	0	0
O'Neill, rf	3	0	0	1	Baines, dh	2	0	0	0
Davis, lf	0	0	0	0	J. Canseco, ph	1	0	0	0
Braggs, ph-lf	3	0	0	1	Lansford, 3b	4	0	1	1
Morris, dh	3	0	0	1	Quirk, c	3	0	0	0
Sabo, 3b	4	0	3	0	McGwire, 1b	3	0	0	0
Benzinger, 1b	4	0	0	0	Randolph, 2b	3	0	0	0
Oliver, c	4	0	1	0	Gallego, ss	2	0	0	0
Duncan, 2b	4	0	0	0	Hassey, ph	1	0	0	0
					Bordick, ss	0	0	0	0
Totals	**31**	**2**	**7**	**4**	**Totals**	**29**	**1**	**2**	**1**

```
Cincinnati . . . . . . . . .  0 0 0   0 0 0   0 2 0—2
Oakland . . . . . . . . . .   1 0 0   0 0 0   0 0 0—1
```

Cincinnati	ip	h	r	er	bb	so
Rijo W,2-0	8⅓	2	1	1	3	9
Myers S,1	⅔	0	0	0	0	0
Oakland						
Stewart L,0-2	9	7	2	1	2	2

E - Oliver, Stewart. DP - Oakland 1. LOB - Cincinnati 7, Oakland 4. 2B - McGee, Baines, Sabo. SB - Gallego (1), R. Henderson (3). S - O'Neill. SF - Morris.

How runs were scored—One in Athletics first: McGee doubled. Lansford singled scoring McGee.

Two in Reds eighth: Larkin and Winningham singled. O'Neill was safe on an error. Braggs grounded out scoring Larkin. Morris hit a sacrifice fly scoring Winningham.

World Series Results, 1903-1990

1903 Boston AL 5, Pittsburgh NL 3
1904 No series
1905 New York NL 4, Philadelphia AL 1
1906 Chicago AL 4, Chicago NL 2
1907 Chicago NL 4, Detroit AL 0, 1 tie
1908 Chicago NL 4, Detroit AL 1
1909 Pittsburgh NL 4, Detroit AL 3
1910 Philadelphia AL 4, Chicago NL 1
1911 Philadelphia AL 4, New York NL 2
1912 Boston AL 4, New York NL 3, 1 tie
1913 Philadelphia AL 4, New York NL 1
1914 Boston NL 4, Philadelphia AL 0
1915 Boston AL 4, Philadelphia NL 1
1916 Boston AL 4, Brooklyn NL 1
1917 Chicago AL 4, New York NL 2
1918 Boston AL 4, Chicago NL 2
1919 Cincinnati NL 5, Chicago AL 3
1920 Cleveland AL 5, Brooklyn NL 2
1921 New York NL 5, New York AL 3
1922 New York NL 4, New York AL 0, 1 tie
1923 New York AL 4, New York NL 2
1924 Washington AL 4, New York NL 3
1925 Pittsburgh NL 4, Washington AL 3
1926 St. Louis NL 4, New York AL 3
1927 New York AL 4, Pittsburgh NL 0
1928 New York AL 4, St. Louis NL 0
1929 Philadelphia AL 4, Chicago NL 1
1930 Philadelphia AL 4, St. Louis NL 2
1931 St. Louis NL 4, Philadelphia AL 3
1932 New York AL 4, Chicago NL 0
1933 New York NL 4, Washington AL 1

1934 St. Louis NL 4, Detroit AL 3
1935 Detroit AL 4, Chicago NL 2
1936 New York AL 4, New York NL 2
1937 New York AL 4, New York NL 1
1938 New York AL 4, Chicago NL 0
1939 New York AL 4, Cincinnati NL 0
1940 Cincinnati NL 4, Detroit AL 3
1941 New York AL 4, Brooklyn NL 1
1942 St. Louis NL 4, New York AL 1
1943 New York AL 4, St. Louis NL 1
1944 St. Louis NL 4, St. Louis AL 2
1945 Detroit AL 4, Chicago NL 3
1946 St. Louis NL 4, Boston AL 3
1947 New York AL 4, Brooklyn NL 3
1948 Cleveland AL 4, Boston NL 2
1949 New York AL 4, Brooklyn NL 1
1950 New York AL 4, Philadelphia NL 0
1951 New York AL 4, New York NL 2
1952 New York AL 4, Brooklyn NL 3
1953 New York AL 4, Brooklyn NL 2
1954 New York NL 4, Cleveland AL 0
1955 Brooklyn NL 4, New York AL 3
1956 New York AL 4, Brooklyn NL 3
1957 Milwaukee NL 4, New York AL 3
1958 New York AL 4, Milwaukee NL 3
1959 Los Angeles NL 4, Chicago AL 2
1960 Pittsburgh NL 4, New York AL 3
1961 New York AL 4, Cincinnati NL 1
1962 New York AL 4, San Francisco NL 3

1963 Los Angeles NL 4, New York AL 0
1964 St. Louis NL 4, New York AL 3
1965 Los Angeles NL 4, Minnesota AL 3
1966 Baltimore AL 4, Los Angeles NL 0
1967 St. Louis NL 4, Boston AL 3
1968 Detroit AL 4, St. Louis NL 3
1969 New York NL 4, Baltimore AL 1
1970 Baltimore AL 4, Cincinnati NL 1
1971 Pittsburgh NL 4, Baltimore AL 3
1972 Oakland AL 4, Cincinnati NL 3
1973 Oakland AL 4, New York NL 3
1974 Oakland AL 4, Los Angeles NL 1
1975 Cincinnati NL 4, Boston AL 3
1976 Cincinnati NL 4, New York AL 0
1977 New York AL 4, Los Angeles NL 2
1978 New York AL 4, Los Angeles NL 2
1979 Pittsburgh NL 4, Baltimore AL 3
1980 Philadelphia NL 4, Kansas City AL 2
1981 Los Angeles NL 4, New York AL 2
1982 St. Louis NL 4, Milwaukee AL 3
1983 Baltimore AL 4, Philadelphia NL 1
1984 Detroit AL 4, San Diego NL 1
1985 Kansas City AL 4, St. Louis NL 3
1986 New York NL 4, Boston AL 3
1987 Minnesota AL 4, St. Louis NL 3
1988 Los Angeles NL 4, Oakland AL 1
1989 Oakland AL 4, San Francisco NL 0
1990 Cincinnati NL 4, Oakland AL 0

World Series MVPs

1955 Johnny Podres, Brooklyn (NL)
1956 Don Larsen, New York (AL)
1957 Lew Burdette, Milwaukee (NL)
1958 Bob Turley, New York (AL)
1959 Larry Sherry, Los Angeles (NL)
1960 Bobby Richardson, New York (AL)
1961 Whitey Ford, New York (AL)
1962 Ralph Terry, New York (AL)
1963 Sandy Koufax, Los Angeles (NL)
1964 Bob Gibson, St. Louis (NL)
1965 Sandy Koufax, Los Angeles (NL)
1966 Frank Robinson, Baltimore (AL)
1967 Bob Gibson, St. Louis (NL)
1968 Mickey Lolich, Detroit (AL)

1969 Donn Clendenon, New York (NL)
1970 Brooks Robinson, Baltimore (AL)
1971 Roberto Clemente, Pittsburgh (NL)
1972 Gene Tenace, Oakland (AL)
1973 Reggie Jackson, Oakland (AL)
1974 Rollie Fingers, Oakland (AL)
1975 Pete Rose, Cincinnati (NL)
1976 Johnny Bench, Cincinnati (NL)
1977 Reggie Jackson, New York (AL)
1978 Bucky Dent, New York (AL)
1979 Willie Stargell, Pittsburgh (NL)
1980 Mike Schmidt, Philadelphia (NL)

1981 Ron Cey, Pedro Guerrero, Steve Yeager, Los Angeles (NL)
1982 Darrell Porter, St. Louis (NL)
1983 Rick Dempsey, Baltimore (AL)
1984 Alan Trammell, Detroit (AL)
1985 Bret Saberhagen, Kansas City (AL)
1986 Ray Knight, New York (NL)
1987 Frank Viola, Minnesota (AL)
1988 Orel Hershiser, Los Angeles (NL)
1989 Dave Stewart, Oakland (AL)
1990 Jose Rijo, Cincinnati (NL)

All-Time Major League Leaders

(Includes 1990 season)

Games		At Bats		Runs Batted In		Stolen Bases Since 1898	
Pete Rose	3562	Pete Rose	14,043	Hank Aaron	2297		
Carl Yastrzemski	3308	Hank Aaron	12,364	Babe Ruth	2204	Lou Brock	938
Hank Aaron	3298	Carl Yastrzemski	11,988	Lou Gehrig	1990	Rickey Henderson	936
Ty Cobb	3033	Ty Cobb	11,429	Ty Cobb	1961	Ty Cobb	892
Stan Musial	3026	Stan Musial	10,972	Stan Musial	1951	Eddie Collins	742
Willie Mays	2992	Willie Mays	10,881	Jimmie Foxx	1922	Max Carey	738
Rusty Staub	2951	Brooks Robinson	10,654	Willie Mays	1903	Honus Wagner	703
Brooks Robinson	2896	Honus Wagner	10,427	Mel Ott	1860	Joe Morgan	689
Al Kaline	2834	Lou Brock	10,332	Carl Yastrzemski	1844	Bert Campaneris	649
Eddie Collins	2826	Luis Aparicio	10,230	Ted Williams	1839	Tim Raines	634
						Maury Wills	586

Runs		Hits		Strikeouts		Shutouts	
Ty Cobb	2245	Pete Rose	4256	Nolan Ryan	5258	Walter Johnson	110
Hank Aaron	2174	Ty Cobb	4191	Steve Carlton	4136	Grover C. Alexander	90
Babe Ruth	2174	Hank Aaron	3771	Tom Seaver	3640	Christy Mathewson	83
Pete Rose	2165	Stan Musial	3630	Bert Blyleven	3631	Cy Young	77
Willie Mays	2062	Tris Speaker	3515	Don Sutton	3574	Eddie Plank	69
Stan Musial	1949	Honus Wagner	3430	Gaylord Perry	3534	Warren Spahn	63
Lou Gehrig	1888	Carl Yastrzemski	3419	Walter Johnson	3508	Mordecai Brown	63
Tris Speaker	1881	Eddie Collins	3309	Phil Niekro	3340	Tom Seaver	61
Mel Ott	1859	Willie Mays	3283	Ferguson Jenkins	3192	Bert Blyleven	60
Frank Robinson	1829	Nap Lajoie	3252	Bob Gibson	3117	Nolan Ryan	59

Fielder Hits 51 Home Runs

Cecil Fielder of the Detroit Tigers became the 11th major league player to hit 50-or-more home runs in a season.

Roger Maris, 1961	61	Hack Wilson, 1930	56	Mickey Mantle, 1956	52	Johnny Mize, 1947	51
Babe Ruth, 1927	60	Babe Ruth, 1920	54	Willie Mays, 1965	52	Willie Mays, 1955	51
Babe Ruth, 1921	59	Babe Ruth, 1928	54	George Foster, 1977	52	Cecil Fielder, 1990	51
Jimmie Foxx, 1932	58	Ralph Kiner, 1949	54	Ralph Kiner, 1947	51	Jimmie Foxx, 1938	50
Hank Greenberg, 1938	58	Mickey Mantle, 1961	54				

The Sporting News Gold Glove Awards in 1989

National League

Andres Galarraga, Montreal, first base.
Ryne Sandberg, Chicago, second base.
Terry Pendleton, St. Louis, third base.
Ozzie Smith, St. Louis, shortstop.
Tony Gwynn, San Diego, outfield.
Andy Van Slyke, Pittsburgh, outfield.
Eric Davis, Cincinnati, outfield.
Benito Santaigo, San Diego, catcher.
Ron Darling, N.Y. Mets, pitcher.

American League

Don Mattingly, New York, first base.
Harold Reynolds, Seattle, second base.
Gary Gaetti, Minnesota, third base.
Tony Fernandez, Toronto, shortstop.
Gary Pettis, Detroit, outfield.
Kirby Puckett, Minnesota, outfield.
Devon White, California, outfield.
Bob Boone, California, catcher.
Bret Saberhagen, Kansas City, pitcher.

The following are the players at each position who have won the most Gold Gloves since the award was instituted in 1957.

First base:	Keith Hernandez... 11	Shortstop:	Ozzie Smith..... 10			Dwight Evans..... 8
	George Scott..... 8		Luis Aparicio..... 9			Garry Maddox.... 8
Second base:	Bill Mazeroski.... 8	Outfield:	Roberto Clemente.. 12	Catcher:	Johnny Bench.... 10
	Frank White..... 8		Willie Mays...... 12		Bob Boone...... 7
Third base:	Brooks Robinson... 16		Al Kaline....... 10	Pitcher:	Jim Kaat....... 16
	Mike Schmidt..... 10		Paul Blair....... 8		Bob Gibson...... 9

All-Time Home Run Leaders

Player	HR	Player	HR	Player	HR	Player	HR
Hank Aaron.....	755	Lou Gehrig......	493	Carlton Fisk.....	354	Tony Perez.....	379
Babe Ruth......	714	Stan Musial.....	475	Dick Allen.....	351	Eddie Murray....	379
Willie Mays.....	660	Willie Stargell....	475	George Foster....	348	Dwight Evans....	379
Frank Robinson...	586	Carl Yastrzemski..	452	Andre Dawson...	346	Dave Winfield....	378
Harmon Killebrew..	573	Dave Kingman....	442	Ron Santo......	342	Dale Murphy.....	378
Reggie Jackson...	563	Billy Williams....	426	John (Boog) Powell.	339	Norm Cash.....	377
Mike Schmidt....	548	Darrell Evans....	414	Don Baylor.....	338	Rocky Colavito...	374
Mickey Mantle....	536	Duke Snider.....	407	Joe Adcock.....	336	Gil Hodges.....	370
Jimmy Foxx.....	534	Al Kaline.......	399	Bobby Bonds....	332	Ralph Kiner.....	369
Ted Williams....	521	Graig Nettles....	390	Hank Greenberg...	331	Joe DiMaggio....	361
Willie McCovey...	521	Johnny Bench....	389	Dave Parker.....	328	John Mize......	359
Ed Mathews.....	512	Frank Howard....	382	Willie Horton....	325	Yogi Berra......	358
Ernie Banks.....	512	Jim Rice.......	382	Robin Yount.....	325	Lee May.......	354
Mel Ott........	511	Orlando Cepeda..	379				

Pitchers with 300 Major League Wins

Cy Young	511	Warren Spahn	363	Steve Carlton	329	Phil Niekro	318	Old Hoss Radbourn	308
Walter Johnson	416	Pud Galvin	361	Eddie Plank	327	Gaylord Perry	314	Nolan Ryan	302
Christy Mathewson	373	Kid Nichols	360	John Clarkson	326	Tom Seaver	311	Lefty Grove	300
Grover Alexander	373	Tim Keefe	344	Don Sutton	324	Mickey Welch	311	Early Wynn	300

World Almanac All-Major League Baseball Team in 1990

The team was chosen by a panel of sports experts on behalf of the World Almanac.

Position	Player, team	Position	Player, team
First base	Cecil Fielder, Detroit Tigers	Catcher	Tony Pena, Boston Red Sox
Second base	Ryne Sandberg, Chicago Cubs	Right-hand pitcher	Bob Welch, Oakland A's
Third base	Kelly Gruber, Toronto Blue Jays	Left-hand pitcher	Chuck Finley, California Angels
Shortstop	Barry Larkin, Cincinnati Reds	Relief pitcher	Bobby Thigpen, Chicago White Sox
Outfield	Barry Bonds, Pittsburgh Pirates	Rookie of the Year	Dave Justice, Atlanta Braves
Outfield	Rickey Henderson, Oakland A's	Player of the Year	Rickey Henderson, Oakland A's
Outfield	Darryl Strawberry, N.Y. Mets	Manager of the Year	Jeff Torborg, Chicago White Sox

NCAA Baseball Champions

1947	California	1958	USC	1969	Arizona St.	1980	Arizona
1948	USC	1959	Oklahoma St.	1970	USC	1981	Arizona St.
1949	Texas	1960	Minnesota	1971	USC	1982	Miami, Fla.
1950	Texas	1961	USC	1972	USC	1983	Texas
1951	Oklahoma	1962	Michigan	1973	USC	1984	Cal. St.-Fullerton
1952	Holy Cross	1963	USC	1974	USC	1985	Miami, Fla.
1953	Michigan	1964	Minnesota	1975	Texas	1986	Arizona
1954	Missouri	1965	Arizona St.	1976	Arizona	1987	Stanford
1955	Wake Forest	1966	Ohio St.	1977	Arizona St.	1988	Stanford
1956	Minnesota	1967	Arizona St.	1978	USC	1989	Wichita St.
1957	California	1968	USC	1979	Cal. St.-Fullerton	1990	Georgia

Little League World Series in 1990

The team from Taiwan won the 1990 Little League World Series by defeating the team from Shippensburg, Pa. 9-0 at Williamsport, Pa. It was the 14th Little League World Series title in 17 appearances for the Taiwan team.

1989 World Series

Because of the major earthquake which struck the San Francisco Bay area just minutes before the start of the 3rd game of the 1989 World Series on Oct. 17, and the resulting delay, *The World Almanac, 1990* was unable to include coverage of the conclusion of the series. The following is the composite box score and summary of each game.

Composite Box Score

Oakland Athletics

Batting*	Avg	AB	R	H	HR	RBI	SB
Lance Blankenship ...	.500	2	1	1	0	0	0
Rickey Henderson ...	.474	19	4	9	1	3	3
Carney Lansford ...	.438	16	5	7	1	4	0
Jose Canseco ...	.357	14	5	5	1	3	1
Mike Moore ...	.333	3	1	1	0	2	0
Dave Henderson ...	.308	13	6	4	2	4	0
Mark McGwire ...	.294	17	0	5	0	1	0
Terry Steinbach ...	.250	16	3	4	1	7	0
Tony Phillips ...	.235	17	2	4	1	3	0
Dave Parker ...	.222	9	2	2	1	2	0
Walt Weiss ...	.133	15	3	2	1	1	0
Dave Stewart ...	.000	3	0	0	0	0	0
Mike Gallego ...	.000	1	0	0	0	0	0
Ken Phelps ...	.000	1	0	0	0	0	0
Totals ...	.301	146	32	44	9	30	4

Pitching	W-L	ERA	IP	H	BB	SO
Dennis Eckersley ...	0-0	0.00	1.2	0	0	0
Todd Burns ...	0-0	0.00	1.2	1	0	0
Dave Stewart ...	2-0	1.69	16.0	10	2	14
Mike Moore ...	2-0	2.08	13.0	9	3	10
Rick Honeycutt ...	0-0	6.75	2.2	4	0	2
Gene Nelson ...	0-0	54.00	1.0	4	2	1
Totals ...	4-0	3.50	36.0	28	8	27

*At least one official at bat.

San Francisco Giants

Batting*	Avg	AB	R	H	HR	RBI	SB
Kirt Manwaring ...	1.000	1	1	1	0	0	0
Greg Litton ...	.500	6	1	3	1	3	0
Bill Bathe ...	.500	2	1	1	1	3	0
Ken Oberkfell ...	.333	6	1	2	0	0	0
Kevin Mitchell ...	.294	17	2	5	1	2	0
Brett Butler ...	.286	14	1	4	0	1	2
Will Clark ...	.250	16	2	4	0	0	0
Donell Nixon ...	.200	5	1	1	0	0	0
Jose Uribe ...	.200	5	1	1	0	0	0
Terry Kennedy ...	.167	12	1	2	0	2	0
Matt Williams ...	.125	16	1	2	1	1	0
Robby Thompson ...	.091	11	0	1	0	2	0
Candy Maldonado ...	.091	11	1	1	0	0	0
Scott Garrelts ...	.000	1	0	0	0	0	0
Mike LaCoss ...	.000	1	0	0	0	0	0
Pat Sheridan ...	.000	2	0	0	0	0	0
Ernest Riles ...	.000	6	0	0	0	0	0
Totals ...	.209	134	14	28	4	14	2

Pitching	W-L	ERA	IP	H	BB	SO
Steve Bedrosian ...	0-0	0.00	2.2	0	2	2
Craig Lefferts ...	0-0	3.38	2.2	2	2	1
Jeff Brantley ...	0-0	4.15	4.1	5	3	1
Mike LaCoss ...	0-0	6.23	3.1	4	3	2
Kelly Downs ...	0-0	7.71	4.2	3	2	4
Scott Garrelts ...	0-2	9.82	7.1	13	1	8
Rick Reuschel ...	0-1	11.25	4.0	5	4	2
Atlee Hammaker ...	0-0	15.43	2.1	8	0	2
Don Robinson ...	0-1	21.60	1.2	4	1	0
Totals ...	0-4	8.21	34.0	44	18	22

Game 1

San Francisco ...... 0 0 0 0 0 0 0 0 0—0 5 1
Oakland .... 0 3 1 1 0 0 0 0 x—5 11 1
Win — Stewart; Loss — Garrelts, HR: Parker (1), Weiss (1)
RBI: R. Henderson, Parker, Phillips, Weiss.

Game 2

San Francisco ...... 0 0 1 0 0 0 0 0 0—1 4 0
Oakland .... 1 0 0 4 0 0 0 0 x—5 7 0
Win — Moore, Loss — Reuschel, HR: Steinbach (1), RBI: Thompson, Steinbach 3, Lansford, Parker. SB: Butler 2, R. Henderson.

Game 3

(Delayed 10 days following earthquake.)

Oakland .... 2 0 0 2 4 1 0 4 0—13 14 0
San Francisco ...... 0 1 0 2 0 0 0 4—7 10 3
Win — Stewart, Loss — Garrelts, HR: D. Henderson 2 (2), Phillips (1), Canseco (1), Lansford (1), Williams (1), Bathe (1). RBI: D. Henderson 4 Steinbach, Phillips, Bathe 3, Kennedy 2, Litton, Williams. SB: R. Henderson 2 (3).

Game 4

Oakland .... 1 3 0 0 3 1 0 1 0—9 12 0
San Francisco ...... 0 0 0 0 2 4 0 0—6 9 0
Win — Moore, Loss — Robinson, Save — Eckersley, HR: R. Henderson (1), Mitchell (1), Litton (1). RBI: Steinbach 3, R. Henderson 3, D. Henderson 2, Moore 2, Lansford, Phillips, Mitchell 2, Litton 2, Butler, Thompson. SB: Canseco (1).

Major League Perfect Games Since 1900

Year	Player	Clubs	Score	Year	Player	Clubs	Score
1904	Cy Young	Boston vs. Phil. (AL)	3-0	1964	Jim Bunning	Phil. vs. N.Y. Mets (NL) ...	6-0
1908	Addie Joss	Cleveland vs. Chicago (AL) .	1-0	1965	Sandy Koufax ...	Los Angeles vs. Chic. (NL) .	1-0
1917	Ernie Shore (a) ...	Boston vs. Wash. (AL)	4-0	1968	Jim Hunter	Oakland vs. Minn. (AL)	4-0
1922	Charles Robertson	Chicago vs. Detroit (AL) ..	2-0	1981	Len Barker	Cleveland vs. Toronto (AL) .	3-0
1956	Don Larsen (b) ..	N.Y. Yankees vs. Brooklyn .	2-0	1984	Mike Witt	California vs. Texas (AL) ...	1-0
1959	Harvey Haddix (c)	Pitts. vs. Milwaukee (NL) ..	0-1	1988	Tom Browning	Cincinnati vs. L.A. (NL). ...	1-0

(a) Babe Ruth, the starting pitcher, was ejected from the game after walking the first batter. Shore replaced him and the base-runner was out stealing. Shore retired the next 26 batters. (b) World Series. (c) Pitched 12 perfect innings, lost in 13th on an error, sacrifice bunt, walk, and double.

Ten Most Dramatic Sports Events, Nov. 1989—Oct. 1990

Selected by The World Almanac Sports Staff

—In one of the biggest upsets in boxing history, James (Buster) Douglas knocked out Mike Tyson in the 10th round in Tokyo to win the world heavyweight championship.

—The Cincinnati Reds shocked the baseball world by defeating the defending champion Oakland Athletics in 4 straight games.

—West Germany scored a 1-0 victory over Argentina to win the World Cup soccer competition. The game was watched by a worldwide TV audience estimated at one billion viewers.

—Nolan Ryan of the Texas Rangers won his 300th major league game. The 43-year-old righthander became the 20th pitcher to record 300 victories.

—Pete Sampras became the youngest man to win the U.S. Open singles championship. The 19 year old defeated Andre Agassi in the finals.

—The Miami Hurricanes beat Alabama in the Sugar Bowl 33-25 to clinch the national championship, as top-ranked Colorado lost to Notre Dame in the Orange Bowl.

—Arie Luyendyk of the Netherlands, who had not won an Indy car race in 75 tries, won the Indianapolis 500 with a record 185.984 mph.

—UNLV defeated Duke 103-73 to win the NCAA basketball championship. It was the first national championship for the Runnin' Rebels whose margin of victory was the largest in the history of the championship game.

—Cecil Fielder became the 11th major league player to hit 50 home runs in a season. He was the first since George Foster accomplished the feat in 1977.

—Nick Faldo of England won a sudden-death playoff against Ray Floyd to win the Masters golf championship for the 2nd consecutive year. Faldo became only the second golfer to win consecutive Masters.

Deaths, Oct. 20, 1989—Oct. 31, 1990

A

Abernathy, Rev. Ralph David, 64; civil rights leader who was closely associated with Rev. Dr. Martin Luther King Jr.; Atlanta, Apr. 17.

Ailey, Alvin, 58; choreographer, dancer, and director who played a major role in establishing black modern dance; New York, Dec. 1.

B

Bailey, Pearl, 72; singer and entertainer for some 6 decades; Philadelphia, Aug. 17.

Ballard, Harold, 86; owner of the Toronto Maple Leafs of the NHL; Toronto, Apr. 11.

Bari, Lynn, 75; actress who appeared in some 50 films in the 1930s and 1940s; Goleta, Cal., Nov. 20.

Baum, Kurt, 81; tenor who starred at the Metropolitan Opera in the 1940s and 1950s; New York, Dec. 27.

Bavier, Frances, 86; actress best known as Aunt Bee on TVs "The Andy Griffith Show;" Siler City, N.C., Dec. 6.

Beck, C.C., 79; comic book artist who created the "Captain Marvel" character in 1940; Gainesville, Fla., Nov. 22.

Beckett, Samuel, 83; Irish writer who was a major figure in 20th century drama and fiction; won 1969 Nobel Prize in Literature; Paris, Dec. 22.

Bernstein, Leonard, 72; a leading orchestral conductor of the 20th century; composer of musicals, "West Side Story"; New York, Oct. 14.

Bettelheim, Bruno, 86; psychoanalyst who pioneered in treating childhood mental disturbances; Silver Springs, Md., Mar. 13.

Blaize, Herbert, 71; prime minister of Grenada since 1983; Grenada, Dec. 19.

Blakey, Art, 71; jazz drummer and band leader; New York, Oct. 16.

Boggs, Phil, 40; diver who won the 1976 Olympic gold medal in springboard diving; Miami, July 4.

Bridges, Harry, 88; labor leader who organized the West Coast longshoremen's union in the 1930s; San Francisco, Mar. 30.

Broyard, Anatole, 70; book critic and editor for the N.Y. Times, 1971-89; Boston, Oct. 11.

Bunshaft, Gordon, 81; architect famed for modernist skyscrapers, museums, and libraries; New York, Aug. 6.

Burrud, Bill, 65; producer and narrator of TV nature shows and travelogues; Sunset Beach, Cal., July 12.

C

Capucine, 57; French-born actress who was popular in films in the 1960s; Lausanne, Switzerland, Mar. 17.

Carvel, Tom, 84; founder of and spokesman for the soft ice cream chain; Pine Plains, N.Y., Oct. 21.

Casiraghi, Stefano, 30; husband of Princess Caroline of Monaco; off St-Jean-Cap-Ferrat, France, Oct. 3.

Ceausescu, Nicolae, 71; absolute ruler of Romania for 24 years; Bucharest, Dec. 25.

Childs, Marquis W., 87; journalist, columnist, and author who won the Pulitzer Prize for commentary in 1970; San Francisco, June 30.

Christy, June, 64; jazz singer popular in the 1940s and 1950s; Los Angeles, June 21.

Clifton, Nat "Sweetwater," 65; basketball star for the Harlem Globetrotters and, in the 1950s, the N.Y. Knicks; Chicago, Aug. 31.

Conigliaro, Tony, 45; major league outfielder mostly with the Red Sox; Boston, Feb. 24.

Cugat, Xavier, 90; bandleader who introduced many Latin American Rhythms in the U.S.; popularized the rumba; Barcelona, Spain, Oct. 27.

Cullen, Bill, 70; host and panelist on numerous TV game shows for over 30 years; Los Angeles, July 7.

D

Davies, Bobby, 70; basketball hall of fame player and coach; Hilton Head, S.C., Apr. 22.

Davis Jr., Sammy, 64; singer, dancer, and actor who was a leading entertainer for almost 6 decades; Los Angeles, May 16.

Davis, Walter, 57; jazz pianist; New York, June 2.

Davis, Victor, 25; Canadian swimmer who won a 1984 Olympic gold medal in the 200-meter breaststroke; nr. Montreal, Nov. 13.

Davison, Wild Bill, 83; jazz cornetist; Santa Barbara, Cal., Nov. 14.

Day, Clarence "Hap", 88; hockey coach who led the Toronto Maple Leafs to 5 Stanley Cup championships; St. Thomas, Ontario, Feb. 17.

Dexter, John, 64; British theater and opera director; London, Mar. 23.

Doe, Samuel K., 38; president of Liberia; Liberia, Sept. 10.

Donatelli, Augie, 76; major league baseball umpire for 24 years; St. Petersburg, Fla., May 24.

Duarte, Jose Napoleon, 64; former president of El Salvador; San Salvador, Feb. 23.

Duff, Howard, 76; character actor in radio, TV, and films for some 40 years; Santa Barbara, Cal., July 9.

Dunne, Irene, 91; actress and singer who starred in films in the 1930s and 1940s; Los Angeles, Sept. 4.

E

Edwards, Douglas, 73; broadcast journalist for 56 years; first TV anchorman; Sarasota, Fla., Oct. 13.

Enriquez, Rene, 58; actor best known for his role in the "Hill Street Blues" TV series; Tarzana, Cal., Mar. 23.

Evans, Ronald, E., 56; astronaut who piloted the Apollo 17 mission in 1972; Scottsdale, Ariz., Apr. 7.

F

Fain, Sammy, 87; songwriter who wrote numerous popular songs; won 2 Oscars; Los Angeles, Dec. 6.

Farrell, Charles, 88; actor who starred in silent films and early TV, "My Little Margie"; Palm Springs, Cal., May 6.

Fogerty, Tom, 48; rhythm guitarist and co-founder of Creedence Clearwater Revival band; Scottsdale, Ariz., Sept. 6

Forbes, Malcolm, 70; publisher of *Forbes* magazine; Far Hills, N.J., Feb. 24.

Franchi, Sergio, 57; tenor who was popular in recordings and nightclubs; Stonington, Conn., May 1.

G

Garbo, Greta, 84; Swedish-born actress who was a leading film star of the 1930s; New York, Apr. 15.

Gardner, Ava, 67; actress who was a Hollywood leading lady in the 1940s and 1950s; London, Jan. 25.

Gathers, Hank, 23; basketball All-America at Loyola-Marymount; Los Angeles, Mar. 4.

Gilford, Jack, 81; actor and comedian who appeared in films, TV, and the theater; New York, June 4.

Goddard, Paulette, 84; actress who starred in numerous 1930s and 1940s films; Ronco, Switzerland, Apr. 23.

Goldberg, Arthur, 81; former associate justice of the U.S. Supreme Court; later U.S. rep. to the UN; Washington, D.C., Jan. 19.

Goldfarb, David, 71; Soviet-Jewish geneticist who won 7-year battle to emigrate in 1986; Washington, D.C., Feb. 24.

Gordon, Dexter, 67; jazz tenor saxophonist who starred in the 1986 film "Round Midnight"; Philadelphia, Apr. 25

Goulding, Ray, 68; satirist who was part of the Bob and Ray comedy team since the 1950s; Manhasset, N.Y., Mar. 24.

Graziano, Rocky, 71; middleweight boxing champion in the 1940s; New York, May 22.

H

Hale Jr., Alan, 71; actor best known as the Skipper on TVs "Gilligan's Island"; Los Angeles, Jan. 2.

Halston, 57; designer who personified U.S. fashion in the 1970s; San Francisco, Mar. 26.

Hamer, Rusty, 42; former child actor who appeared in the "Make Room for Daddy" TV series, 1953-64; De Ridder, La., Jan. 18.

Harmon, Tom, 70; football broadcaster and star at the Univ. of Michigan; won 1940 Heisman Trophy; Los Angeles, Mar. 15.

Harrison, Rex, 82; British stage and film actor best known for his portrayal of Prof. Henry Higgins in "My Fair Lady"; New York, June 1.

Harvey, Doug, 65; NHL defenseman who won the Norris Trophy 7 times; Montreal, Dec. 26.

Haynsworth Jr., Clement, 77; federal judge whose 1969 nomination to the Supreme Court was rejected by the U.S. Senate; Greenville, S.C., Nov. 22.

Henson, Jim, 53; puppeteer who created the Muppets; New York, May 16.

Horowitz, Vladimir, 85; pianist who was a classical music virtuoso for some 60 years; New York, Nov. 5.

I

Ibarruri, Dolores, "La Pasionaria", 93; legendary orator of the Spanish Civil War; Madrid, Nov. 12.

Ireland, Jill, 54; British-born actress who chronicled her long battle against cancer; Malibu, Cal., May 18.

J

Jackson, Larry, 59; pitcher who won 194 major league games; Boise, Ida., Aug. 28.

K

Keller, Charlie, 73; outfielder for the N.Y. Yankees in the 1940s; Frederick, Md., May 23.

Kennedy, Arthur, 75; actor who starred in the theater and some 70 films; Branford, Conn., Jan. 5.

Klein, Gene, 69; former owner of the San Diego Chargers and thoroughbred race horses; La Jolla, Cal., Mar. 12.

Kreisky, Bruno, 79; chancellor of Austria, 1970-83; Vienna, July 29.

L

Lanson, Snooky, 76; singer on the TV show, "Your Hit Parade", 1950-57; Nashville, July 2.

Lasky, Victor, 72; columnist and author famed for outspoken anti-communist views; Washington, D.C., Feb. 22.

Lausche, Frank, 94; Ohio political leader who served as governor for 5 terms and U.S. senator for 2 terms; Cleveland, Apr. 21.

Lavagetto, Cookie, 77; major league baseball player, manager, and coach; Orinda, Cal., Aug. 10.

Le Duc Tho, 79; Vietnamese diplomat who shared 1973 Nobel Peace Prize; Hanoi, Oct. 13.

LeMay, Gen. Curtis, 83; former Air Force chief of staff who was a leading advocate of strategic air power; March AFB, Cal., Oct. 1.

M

Mangano, Silvana, 59; Italian film actress, *Bitter Rice;* Madrid, Dec. 16.

Martin, Billy, 61; baseball player and manager (5 times with N.Y. Yankees); nr. Binghamton, N.Y., Dec. 25.

Matsunaga, Spark M., 73; U.S. senator from Hawaii since 1977; Toronto, Apr. 15.

McCrea, Joel, 84; actor who starred in some 80 films, mostly westerns; Woodland Hills, Cal., Oct. 20.

Menninger, Karl, 96; one of the foremost practitioners and advocates of psychiatry in the U.S.; Topeka, Kan., July 18.

Merrill, Gary, 74; actor who appeared in some 40 films; Falmouth, Me., Mar. 5.

Moravia, Alberto, 82; Italian novelist; Rome, Sept. 26.

Morial, Ernest, 60; mayor of New Orleans, 1978-86; New Orleans, Dec. 24.

Moses, Wally, 80; baseball player and coach who had 2,138 major league hits; Vidalia, Ga., Oct. 10.

Mumford, Lewis, 94; social critic, philosopher, and city planner; Amenia, N.Y., Jan. 26.

Mydland, Brent, 37; keyboardist for the Grateful Dead rock band since 1979; Lafayette, Cal., July 26.

N

Nagurski, Bronko, 81; star running back and tackle for the Chicago Bears in the 1920s and 1930s; International Falls, Minn., Jan. 7.

Noyce, Robert N., 62; an inventor of the microchip, which revolutionized the electronics industry; Austin, Tex., June 3.

O

O'Brien, Lawrence, 73; Democratic Party strategist who was closely associated with JFK; National Basketball Assn. commissioner 1975-1984; New York, Sept. 28.

P

Paley, William S., 89; broadcasting pioneer who built the CBS communications empire; New York, Oct. 26.

Pan, Hermes, 79; choreographer who, with Fred Astaire, created classic dances for films; Beverly Hills, Cal., Sept. 19.

Payne, John, 77; actor who was a leading man in 1940s and 1950s films; Malibu, Cal., Dec. 6.

Percy, Walker, 74; novelist who won the 1961 National Book Award for *The Moviegoer;* Covington, La., May 10

Peter, Laurence J., 70; author whose *The Peter Principle* satirized the business world; Palos Verdes Estates, Cal., Jan. 12.

Powell, Michael, 84; British film director, *The Red Shoes;* Gloucestershire, England, Feb. 19.

Q

Quayle, Anthony, 76; British actor and director; London, Oct. 20.

R

Rappaport, David, 38; English-born character actor who appeared often on TV; Los Angeles, May 2.

Ray, Johnnie, 63; singer who was popular in the 1950s, "Cry"; Los Angeles, Feb. 24.

Reischauer, Edwin, 79; diplomat and scholar who specialized in East Asian affairs; La Jolla, Cal., Sept. 1.

Rhodes, Erik, 84; actor best remembered for playing continental gigolos in Astaire-Rogers musicals of the 1930s; Oklahoma City, Feb. 17.

Robbie, Joe, 73; owner of the NFL Miami Dolphins; Miami, Jan. 7.

Roosevelt, Elliott, 80; son of FDR; mystery writer; Scottsdale, Ariz., Oct. 27.

Rose, David, 80; Hollywood film and TV composer who won 5 Grammy awards and 4 Emmy awards; Burbank, Cal., Aug. 23.

S

St. Jacques, Raymond, 60; actor who appeared in numerous TV dramas and films; Los Angeles, Aug. 27.

Sakharov, Andrei, 68; Soviet physicist who won the 1975 Nobel Peace Prize; symbol of Soviet dissidence; Moscow, Dec. 14.

Salmi, Albert, 62; actor appeared in films, TV, and the theater; Spokane, Wash., found Apr. 23.

Shannon, Del, 50; singer and songwriter who was popular in the 1960s, "Runaway"; Santa Clara, Cal., Feb. 9.

Skinner, B.F., 86; psychologist who championed behaviorism; Cambridge, Mass., Aug. 18.

Smith, Stephen, 62; political strategist and brother-in-law of the Kennedys; New York, Aug. 19.

Smith, William French, 73; U.S. Attorney General, 1981-85; Los Angeles, Oct. 29.

Snyder, Mitch, 46; advocate for the homeless; Washington, D.C., found July 5.

Spewack, Bella, 91; co-author, with husband, Samuel, of several wacky Broadway comedies in the 1930s; New York, Apr. 27.

Stanwyck, Barbara, 82; actress who was a major film star of the 1930s and 1940s; starred on TV in the 1960s, in "The Big Valley"; Santa Monica, Cal., Jan. 20.

Steber, Eleanor, 76; soprano who starred at the Metropolitan Opera in the 1940s and 1950s; Langhorne, Pa., Oct. 3.

Stoneham, Horace, 86; owner of the New York-San Francisco Giants baseball team, 1936-76; Scottsdale, Ariz., Jan. 7.

T

Tayback, Vic, 60; actor best known as Mel on the "Alice" TV series; Glendale, Cal., May 25.

Taylor, A.J.P., 84; British historian; London, Sept. 7.

Terry-Thomas, 78; British comedian and actor; Surrey, England, Jan. 8.

Tibbs, Casey, 60; rodeo rider who won 9 world championships; Ramona, Cal., Jan. 28.

V

Van Cleef, Lee, 64; actor who played a villain in numerous "spaghetti westerns"; Oxnard, Cal., Dec. 16.

Van Heusen, Jimmy, 77; songwriter who was one of Hollywood's most successful composers in the 1940s and 1950s; Rancho Mirage, Cal., Feb. 7.

Vaughan, Sarah, 66; leading jazz singer for nearly 50 years; Hidden Hills, Cal., Apr. 3.

Vaughan, Stevie Ray, 35; blues guitarist; East Troy, Wis., Aug. 27.

W

Wallace, Irving, 74; writer who was one of the most widely-read authors of the 20th century; Los Angeles, June 29.

Wang, An, 70; inventor and founder of computer company; Boston, Mar. 24.

White, Patrick, 78; Australian novelist who won the 1973 Nobel Prize in Literature; nr. Sydney, Sept. 30.

White, Ryan, 18; AIDS victim who led fight for greater understanding and compassion for those with the disease; Indianapolis, Apr. 8.

Off-Beat News Stories of 1990

And leave the driving to us — When Charles Boyer, the driver of a Greyhound bus, heard a passenger shout that there was a bomb in the bathroom, he slammed on the brakes and waved down a state trooper. The police closed Interstate 95's southbound lanes for about 2 hours, stalling traffic for 15 miles. After questioning passengers, the police began to suspect that a mistake had been made. The mistake turned out to involve a homeless man who was trying to avoid the $8 price of a ticket from Philadelphia to Baltimore by hiding in the bathroom. The passenger who spotted him had called to the driver, "There's a *bum* in the bathroom."

How Sweet It Is — Half a million gallons of ooze ran through the streets of Loveland, Colo. for over half a mile, forcing the closing of a kindergarten and blocking access to several businesses. Officials took precautions against what they thought was a potentially dan-

gerous chemical before the spill was identified as molasses. The molasses, used as an animal-feed supplement to barley or other grains had been stored in a 3-story tank which had ruptured. Even before the molasses spill, the town was nicknamed Sweetheart City, and postmarked special Valentine's Day greetings on thousands of envelopes each year.

Horseplay — Jockey Sylvester Carmouche was banned from racing in Louisiana for 10 years after a state racing commission found him guilty of cheating, by hiding in the fog, to win a race at Delta Downs in Lafayette. Carmouche was accused of hiding in a dense fog aboard 23-1 long shot Landing Officer. When the field came back around the turn in the mile race, he joined the other horses and won the race by 24 lengths. Track veterinarian James Broussard testified that after the race the horse wasn't breathing heavily and the the horse's leg wrappings were clean. "In my opinion, Landing Officer did not appear to have participated in a mile race," he said.

Mr. Ed (gar Hoover) — An FBI undercover horse had more success: he won at least one race and placed in about half of his outings. The FBI bought the horse for use in an investigation of race-fixing at Finger Lakes Race Track in New York. The horse did not uncover any wrongdoing, but he did earn about $1,000 a month in purse money, enough to offset the cost of upkeep. The animal, whose name was kept secret to protect the identities of those involved in the scheme, later was sold to a private owner and continued racing. A spokesman said, "We wish him well. He served as a real good representative of the bureau."

Who's on first — Steve Lyons of the Chicago White Sox was safe on a close play at first base in a game against the Detroit Tigers. While an argument ensued, Lyons calmly pulled his pants down to his knees and began dusting the dirt from his legs, which were clad only in shorts and an athletic supporter. When the crowd of 15,000 roared, Lyons quickly pulled up his pants and tried to regain his composure, "I just forgot where I was," he said.

Take me out to the crowd — In Toronto, Blue Jays fans were treated to a rare sight at a baseball park when they saw a naked man and a towel-clad woman in an intimate interlude at the Sky-Dome Hotel. The lights were off in the $800-a-day room overlooking the diamond, but the ballpark lights revealed more than the Blue Jays-Seattle Mariners game. Blue Jays president Paul Beeston said, "I never suspected in my wildest dreams that someone would be doing it right in front of the window."

Losing streak — In Zimbabwe, 4 soccer players were banned for life after they urinated on the field as part of a witchcraft rite that they had hoped would change their losing ways. Soccer official Nelson Chirwa said, "I would like to advise all football teams that next time they should go to a better witch doctor rather than indulge in such disgusting acts."

Cover-up — Playboy Enterprises, whose stock certificates have been graced with the nude image of the February 1971 Playmate since the company went public in 1971, announced that it would replace the nude model with a clothed one. The company pointed out that it had 14,000 single-share stockholders, many of whom had bought the one share just to get the racy certificate. Since it was costing the company $100,000 annually to service the accounts of those shareholders, Playboy hoped to reduce that expense by issuing a certificate less likely to encourage novelty purchases.

Bus(ted) — The police arrested Darius McCollum for stealing a New York City bus and taking it for a joy ride. McCollum then confessed to taking 13 of the 22 buses that had been stolen from the New York City Transit Authority in the previous 12 months. Police described McCollum, who was wearing a bus driver's uniform when he was seized driving the stolen bus, as a "bus buff" familiar with bus jargon and operations. The officers said that he had apparently stolen the buses "for the fun of it and usually parked them near depots, so they could be recovered."

Do as I say, not as I do — Although the Sierra Club has been promoting recycling, officials said they didn't use recycled paper in their lushly illustrated nature calendars because photographs don't reproduce well on it. Two Denver-area club managers called that stance hypocritical and stopped selling the annual fund-raising calendars. One official warned that a "real revolt" was possible among members statewide.

Cardboard cops — A food store chain in Dallas, Tex. installed three 6-foot-tall cardboard-cutouts of police officers as psychological deterents to shoplifting. In London, where this idea originated, police reported a decline in thefts after stores were equipped with cardboard bobbies. A police spokesman said that the photos "Make it appear that wherever you move, they are looking at you."

Commemorative Commission day — Momentum has been building in Congress to turn over the job of selecting commemorative days, weeks, months, etc. to a commemorative commission. An astonishing 38 percent of all laws passed last year celebrated a day, week, month, or decade, adding up to about 250 commemorative bills each session. Americans celebrated National Prune Day, Tap Dance Day, Dairy Goat Awareness Week, and National Family Bread Baking Month.

Bo knows quick exits — Bo Kidd, a forward for the John Marshall High School basketball team, picked up 10 fouls in a day while playing in varsity and junior varsity games. Kidd fouled out in just one quarter in the JV game and had 5 fouls in 2 quarters of the varsity game. Asked about his quick exits, Kidd said, "I have a short temper and get mad easily."

Get along, little doggie — The Ten Ring Gun Club of Nucla, Colo. organized a prairie dog shooting contest to thin out the prairie dog herd. They also hoped that the contest would serve as a tourist attraction and invited hunting enthusiasts and visitors to the depressed town for the event, where they estimated about 500 prairie dogs would perish. When animal rights advocates learned about the contest they enlisted Governor Roy Romer to oppose the event. The governor called the hunt a cruel spectacle and not a proper method of exterminating rodents. The gun club held an open meeting to decide the fate of the contest, and only 3 of 318 people voted against the plan. The area was so desperate for jobs that they previously had tried unsuccessfully to lure a low-level radioactive waste dump to the area. One resident said, "Nucla needs something to bring it back to life. I don't care if it's a prairie dog shoot or a yuppie shoot."

Lawn and order — Dr. Brian McCandless kept the 3 acres of lawn around his 19th-century home trim by employing a flock of sheep. "They're quieter than lawn mowers and more pastoral, picturesque," he claimed. But his Cohoes, N.Y. neighbors said that the sheep had no place in an urban setting. "They are disgusting," one neighbor complained, "and when it's hot, the odor is unbelievable." The sheep also meandered off Dr. McCandless's property. Mayor Robert Signoracci reported, "I've had about 50 calls about sheep running and doing their thing on people's lawns." As a result, the city's animal-control ordinance was rewritten to fine homeowners whose barnyard animals ran loose.

The hole story — Manholes disappeared from the streets of Sacramento, Cal. The Public works department announced a contest to find a gender-neutral name for the places in the street where workers go to make underground repairs. Some suggestions included "sewer viewer," "peopleholes," "peepholes," "sewer hole," and "utility access hole." It was finally decided that "maintenance hole" would do. It was also noted that with the new name, officials would not have to change the "MH" abbreviation already in use on city utility maps.

QUICK REFERENCE INDEX

For complete Index, see pp. 3-31